TheStreet Ratings'
Guide to Stock Mutual Funds

TheStreet Ratings'
Guide to Stock Mutual Funds

A Quarterly Compilation of Investment Ratings
and Analyses Covering Equity and Balanced Mutual Funds

Spring 2017

GREY HOUSE PUBLISHING

TheStreet, Inc.
14 Wall Street, 15th Floor
New York, NY 10005
800-706-2501

TheStreet Ratings

Grey House
Publishing

4919 Route 22
PO Box 56
Amenia, NY 12501-0056

Edition No. 75, Spring 2017

ISBN: 978-1-68217-435-7
ISSN: 2158-6144

Contents

Terms and Conditions

This Document is prepared strictly for the confidential use of our customer(s). It has been provided to you at your specific request. It is not directed to, or intended for distribution to or use by, any person or entity who is a citizen or resident of or located in any locality, state, country or other jurisdiction where such distribution, publication, availability or use would be contrary to law or regulation or which would subject TheStreet or its affiliates to any registration or licensing requirement within such jurisdiction.

No part of the analysts' compensation was, is, or will be, directly or indirectly, related to the specific recommendations or views expressed in this research report.

This Document is not intended for the direct or indirect solicitation of business. TheStreet, Inc. and its affiliates disclaims any and all liability to any person or entity for any loss or damage caused, in whole or in part, by any error (negligent or otherwise) or other circumstances involved in, resulting from or relating to the procurement, compilation, analysis, interpretation, editing, transcribing, publishing and/or dissemination or transmittal of any information contained herein.

TheStreet has not taken any steps to ensure that the securities or investment vehicle referred to in this report are suitable for any particular investor. The investment or services contained or referred to in this report may not be suitable for you and it is recommended that you consult an independent investment advisor if you are in doubt about such investments or investment services. Nothing in this report constitutes investment, legal, accounting or tax advice or a representation that any investment or strategy is suitable or appropriate to your individual circumstances or otherwise constitutes a personal recommendation to you.

The ratings and other opinions contained in this Document must be construed solely as statements of opinion from TheStreet, Inc., and not statements of fact. Each rating or opinion must be weighed solely as a factor in your choice of an institution and should not be construed as a recommendation to buy, sell or otherwise act with respect to the particular product or company involved.

Past performance should not be taken as an indication or guarantee of future performance, and no representation or warranty, expressed or implied, is made regarding future performance. Information, opinions and estimates contained in this report reflect a judgment at its original date of publication and are subject to change without notice. TheStreet offers a notification service for rating changes on companies you specify. For more information call 1-800-706-2501 or visit www.thestreet.com/ratings. The price, value and income from any of the securities or financial instruments mentioned in this report can fall as well as rise.

This Document and the information contained herein is copyrighted by TheStreet, Inc. Any copying, displaying, selling, distributing or otherwise delivering of this information or any part of this Document to any other person, without the express written consent of TheStreet, Inc. except by a reviewer or editor who may quote brief passages in connection with a review or a news story, is prohibited.

Welcome to TheStreet Ratings
Guide to Stock Mutual Funds

With the growing popularity of mutual fund investing, consumers need a reliable source to help them track and evaluate the performance of their mutual fund holdings. Plus, they need a way of identifying and monitoring other funds as potential new investments. Unfortunately, the hundreds of performance and risk measures available – multiplied by the vast number of mutual fund investments on the market today – can make this a daunting task for even the most sophisticated investor.

TheStreet Investment Ratings simplify the evaluation process. We condense all of the available mutual fund data into a single composite opinion of each fund's risk-adjusted performance. This allows you to instantly identify those funds that have historically done well and those that have underperformed the market. While there is no guarantee of future performance, TheStreet Investment Ratings provide a solid framework for making informed investment decisions.

TheStreet Ratings' Mission Statement

TheStreet Ratings' mission is to empower consumers, professionals, and institutions with high quality advisory information for selecting or monitoring financial investments.

In doing so, TheStreet Ratings will adhere to the highest ethical standards by maintaining our independent, unbiased outlook and approach to advising our customers.

Why rely on TheStreet Ratings?

Our mission is to provide fair, objective information to help professionals and consumers alike make educated purchasing decisions.

At TheStreet Ratings, objectivity and total independence are never compromised. We never take a penny from rated companies for issuing our ratings, and we publish them without regard for the companies' preferences. TheStreet's ratings are more frequently reviewed and updated than any other ratings, so you can be sure that the information you receive is accurate and current.

Our rating scale, from A to E, is easy to understand as follows:

	Rating	Description
Top 10% of stock mutual funds	A	Excellent
Next 20% of stock mutual funds	B	Good
Middle 40% of stock mutual funds	C	Fair
Next 20% of stock mutual funds	D	Weak
Bottom 10% of stock mutual funds	E	Very Weak

In addition, a plus or minus sign designates that a fund is in the top third or bottom third of funds with the same letter grade.

Thank you for your trust and purchase of this Guide. If you have any comments, or wish to review other products from TheStreet Ratings, please call 1-800-706-2501 or visit www.thestreetratings.com. We look forward to hearing from you.

How to Use This Guide

The purpose of the *Guide to Stock Mutual Funds* is to provide investors with a reliable source of investment ratings and analyses on a timely basis. We realize that past performance is an important factor to consider when making the decision to purchase shares in a mutual fund. The ratings and analyses in this Guide can make that evaluation easier when you are considering:

- growth funds
- index funds
- balanced funds
- sector or international funds

However, this Guide does not include pure bond funds and money market funds since they are not comparable investments to funds invested exclusively or partially in equities. For information on bond and money market funds, refer to *TheStreet Ratings Guide to Bond and Money Market Mutual Funds*. The rating for a particular fund indicates our opinion regarding that fund's past risk-adjusted performance.

When evaluating a specific mutual fund, we recommend you follow these steps:

Step 1   **Confirm the fund name and ticker symbol.** To ensure you evaluate the correct mutual fund, verify the fund's exact name and ticker symbol as it was given to you in its prospectus or appears on your account statement. Many funds have similar names, so you want to make sure the fund you look up is really the one you are interested in evaluating.

Step 2   **Check the fund's Investment Rating.** Turn to Section I, the Index of Stock Mutual Funds, and locate the fund you are evaluating. This section contains all stock mutual funds analyzed by TheStreet Ratings including those that did not receive an Investment Rating. All funds are listed in alphabetical order by the name of the fund with the ticker symbol following the name for additional verification. Once you have located your specific fund, the first column after the ticker symbol shows its Investment Rating and corresponding percentile. Turn to *About TheStreet Investment Ratings* on page 7 for information about what this rating means.

Step 3   **Analyze the supporting data.** Following TheStreet Investment Rating are some of the various measures we have used in rating the fund. Refer to the Section I introduction (beginning on page 15) to see what each of these factors measures. In most cases, lower rated funds will have a low performance rating and/or a low risk rating (i.e., high volatility). Bear in mind, however, that TheStreet Investment Rating is the result of a complex computer-generated analysis which cannot be reproduced using only the data provided here.

When looking to identify a mutual fund that achieves your specific investing goals, we recommend the following:

Step 4   **Take our Investor Profile Quiz.** Turn to the Appendix and take our Investor Profile Quiz to help determine your level of risk tolerance. After you have scored yourself, the last page of the quiz will refer you to the risk category in Section VII (Top-Rated Stock Mutual Funds by Risk Category) that is best for you. There you can choose a fund that has historically provided top notch returns while keeping the risk at a level that is suited to your investment style.

Step 5   **View the 100 top performing funds.** If your priority is to achieve the highest return, regardless of the amount of risk, turn to Section V which lists the top 100 stock mutual funds with the best financial performance. Keep in mind that past performance alone is not always a true indicator of the future since these funds have already experienced a run up in price and could be due for a correction.

Step 6   **View the 100 funds with the lowest risk.** On the other hand, if capital preservation is your top priority, turn to Section VI which lists the top 100 stock mutual funds with the lowest risk. These funds will have lower performance ratings than most other funds, but can provide a safe harbor for your savings.

Step 7   **View the top-rated funds by fund type.** If you are looking to invest in a particular type of mutual fund (e.g., aggressive growth or a balanced fund), turn to Section VIII, Top-Rated Stock Mutual Funds by Fund Type. There you will find the top 100 stock mutual funds with the highest performance rating in each category. Please be careful to also consider the risk component when selecting a fund from one of these lists.

Step 8   **Refer back to Section I.** Once you have identified a particular fund that interests you, refer back to Section I, the Index of Stock Mutual Funds, for a more thorough analysis.

Always remember:

Step 9   **Read our warnings and cautions.** In order to use TheStreet Investment Ratings most effectively, we strongly recommend you consult the Important Warnings and Cautions listed on page 11. These are more than just "standard disclaimers." They are very important factors you should be aware of before using this Guide.

Step 10   **Stay up to date.** Periodically review the latest TheStreet Investment Ratings for the funds that you own to make sure they are still in line with your investment goals and level of risk tolerance. For information on how to acquire follow-up reports on a particular mutual fund, call 1-800-706-2501 or visit www.thestreetratings.com.

Data Source: Thomson Wealth Management
1455 Research Boulevard
Rockville, MD 20850

Date of data analyzed: Feb 28, 2017

About TheStreet Investment Ratings

TheStreet Investment Ratings represent a completely independent, unbiased opinion of a mutual fund's historical risk-adjusted performance. Each fund's rating is based on two primary components:

Primary Component #1   A fund's **Performance Rating** is based on its total return to shareholders over the last trailing three years, including share price appreciation and distributions to shareholders. This total return figure is stated net of the expenses and fees charged by the fund, and we also make additional adjustments for any front-end or deferred sales loads.

This adjusted return is then weighted to give more recent performance a slightly greater emphasis. Thus, two mutual funds may have provided identical returns to their shareholders over the last three years, but the one with the better performance in the last 12 months will receive a slightly higher performance rating.

Primary Component #2   The **Risk Rating** is based on the level of volatility in the fund's monthly returns, also over the last trailing three years. We use several statistical measures – standard deviation, semi-deviation and a drawdown factor – as our barometer of volatility. Funds with more volatility relative to other mutual funds are considered riskier, and thus receive a lower risk rating. By contrast, funds with a very stable returns are considered less risky and receive a higher risk rating.

Note that none of the mutual funds listed in this publication have received a risk rating in the A (Excellent) range. This is because all stock investments, by their very nature, involve at least some degree of risk.

The two ratings have totally independent meanings. Rarely will you ever find a mutual fund that has both a very high Performance Rating plus, at the same time, a very high Risk Rating. Therefore, the funds that receive the highest overall Investment Ratings are those that combine the ideal combination of both primary components. There is always a tradeoff between risk and reward. That is why we suggest you assess your own personal risk tolerance using the quiz in the Appendix section as a part of your decision-making process.

TheStreet Investment Ratings employ a ranking system to evaluate both safety and performance. Based on these measures, funds are divided into percentiles, and an individual performance rating and a risk rating are assigned to each fund. Then these measures are combined to derive a fund's composite percentile ranking. Finally, TheStreet Investment Ratings are assigned to their corresponding percentile rankings as shown on page 3.

How Our Ratings Differ From Those of Other Services

Balanced approach: TheStreet Investment Ratings are designed to meet the needs of aggressive *as well as* conservative investors. We realize that your investment goals can be different from those of other investors based upon your age, income, and tolerance for risk. Therefore, our ratings balance a fund's performance against the amount of risk it poses to identify those funds that have achieved the optimum mix of both factors. Some of these top funds have achieved excellent returns with only average risk. Others have achieved average returns with only moderate risk. Whatever your personal preferences, we can help you identify a top notch fund that meets your investing style.

Other Investment rating firms give a far greater weight to performance and insufficient consideration to risk. In effect, they are betting too heavily on a continuing bull market and not giving enough consideration to the risk of a decline. While performance is obviously a very important factor to consider, we believe that the riskiness of a fund is also very important. Therefore, we weigh these two components more equally when assigning TheStreet Investment Ratings.

But we don't stop there. We also assign a separate performance rating and risk rating to each fund so you can focus on the component that is most important to you. In fact, Sections V, VI, and VII are designed specifically to help you select the best stock mutual funds based on these two factors. No other source gives you the cream of the crop in this manner.

Easy to use: Unlike those of other services, TheStreet Investment Ratings are extremely intuitive and easy to use. Our rating scale (A to E) is easily understood by members of the general public based on their familiarity with school grades. So, there are no stars to count and no numbering systems to interpret.

More funds: *TheStreet Ratings Guide to Stock Mutual Funds* tracks more mutual funds than any other publication – with updates that come out more frequently than those of other rating agencies. We've included more than 15,000 funds in this edition, all of which are updated every three months. Compare that to other investment rating agencies, such as Morningstar, where coverage stops after the top 1,500 funds and it takes five months for a fund to cycle through their publication's update process.

Recency: Recognizing that every fund's performance is going to have its peaks and valleys, superior long-term performance is a major consideration in TheStreet Investment Ratings. Even so, we do not give a fund a top rating solely because it did well 10 or 15 years ago. Times change and the top performing funds in the current economic environment are often very different from those of a decade ago. Thus, our ratings are designed to keep you abreast of the best funds available *today* and in the *near future,* not the distant past.

No bias toward load funds: In keeping with our conservative, consumer-oriented nature, we adjust the performance for so-called "load" funds differently from other rating agencies. We spread the impact to you of front-end loads and back-end loads (a.k.a. deferred sales charges) over a much shorter period in our evaluation of a fund. Thus our performance rating, as well as the overall TheStreet Investment Rating, more fully reflects the actual returns the typical investor experiences when placing money in a load fund.

What Our Ratings Mean

A   **Excellent**. The mutual fund has an excellent track record for maximizing performance while minimizing risk, thus delivering the best possible combination of total return on investment and reduced volatility. It has made the most of the recent economic environment to maximize risk-adjusted returns compared to other mutual funds. While past performance is just an indication – not a guarantee – we believe this fund is among the most likely to deliver superior performance relative to risk in the future.

B   **Good.** The mutual fund has a good track record for balancing performance with risk. Compared to other mutual funds, it has achieved above-average returns given the level of risk in its underlying investments. While the risk-adjusted performance of any mutual fund is subject to change, we believe that this fund has proven to be a good investment in the recent past.

C   **Fair.** In the trade-off between performance and risk, the mutual fund has a track record which is about average. It is neither significantly better nor significantly worse than most other mutual funds. With some funds in this category, the total return may be better than average, but this can be misleading since the higher return was achieved with higher than average risk. With other funds, the risk may be lower than average, but the returns are also lower. In short, based on recent history, there is no particular advantage to investing in this fund.

D   **Weak.** The mutual fund has underperformed the universe of other funds given the level of risk in its underlying investments, resulting in a weak risk-adjusted performance. Thus, its investment strategy and/or management has not been attuned to capitalize on the recent economic environment. While the risk-adjusted performance of any mutual fund is subject to change, we believe that this fund has proven to be a bad investment over the recent past.

E   **Very Weak.** The mutual fund has significantly underperformed most other funds given the level of risk in its underlying investments, resulting in a very weak risk-adjusted performance. Thus, its investment strategy and/or management has done just the opposite of what was needed to maximize returns in the recent economic environment. While the risk-adjusted performance of any mutual fund is subject to change, we believe this fund has proven to be a very bad investment in the recent past.

+   **The plus sign** is an indication that the fund is in the top third of its letter grade.

-   **The minus sign** is an indication that the fund is in the bottom third of its letter grade.

U   **Unrated.** The mutual fund is unrated because it is too new to make a reliable assessment of its risk-adjusted performance. Typically, a fund must be established for at least three years before it is eligible to receive a TheStreet Investment Rating.

Important Warnings and Cautions

1. **A rating alone cannot tell the whole story.** Please read the explanatory information contained here, in the section introductions and in the appendix. It is provided in order to give you an understanding of our rating methodology as well as to paint a more complete picture of a mutual fund's strengths and weaknesses.

2. **Investment ratings shown in this Guide were current as of the publication date.** In the meantime, the rating may have been updated based on more recent data. TheStreet Ratings offers a notification service for ratings changes on companies that you specify. For more information call 1-800-706-2501 or visit www.thestreet.com/ratings.

3. **When deciding to buy or sell shares in a specific mutual fund, your decision must be based on a wide variety of factors in addition to TheStreet Investment Rating.** These include any charges you may incur from switching funds, to what degree it meets your long-term planning needs, and what other choices are available to you.

4. **TheStreet Investment Ratings represent our opinion of a mutual fund's past risk-adjusted performance.** As such, a high rating means we feel that the mutual fund has performed very well for its shareholders compared to other stock mutual funds. A high rating is not a guarantee that a fund will continue to perform well, nor is a low rating a prediction of continued weak performance. TheStreet Investment Ratings are not deemed to be a recommendation concerning the purchase or sale of any mutual fund.

5. **A mutual fund's individual performance is not the only factor in determining its rating.** Since TheStreet Investment Ratings are based on performance relative to other funds, it is possible for a fund's rating to be upgraded or downgraded based strictly on the improved or deteriorated performance of other funds.

6. **All funds that have the same TheStreet Investment Rating should be considered to be essentially equal from a risk/reward perspective.** This is true regardless of any differences in the underlying numbers which might appear to indicate greater strengths.

7. **Our rating standards are more consumer-oriented than those used by other rating agencies.** We make more conservative assumptions about the amortization of loads and other fees as we attempt to identify those funds that have historically provided superior returns with only little or moderate risk.

8. **We are an independent rating agency and do not depend on the cooperation of the managers operating the mutual funds we rate.** Our data are derived, for the most part, from price quotes obtained and documented on the open market. This is supplemented by information collected from the mutual fund prospectuses and regulatory filings. Although we seek to maintain an open line of communication with the mutual fund managers, we do not grant them the right to stop or influence publication of the ratings. This policy stems from the fact that this Guide is designed for the information of the consumer.

9. **This Guide does not cover bond and money market funds.** Because bond and money market funds represent a whole separate class of investments with unique risk profiles and performance expectations, they are excluded from this publication.

Section I

Index of
Stock Mutual Funds

An analysis of all rated and selected unrated

Equity Mutual Funds.

Funds are listed in alphabetical order.

Section I Contents

<u>*Left Pages*</u>

1. Fund Type   The mutual fund's peer category based on an analysis of its investment portfolio.

AG	Aggressive Growth	HL	Health
AA	Asset Allocation	IN	Income
BA	Balanced	IX	Index
CV	Convertible	MC	Mid Cap
EM	Emerging Market	OT	Other
EN	Energy/Natural Resources	PM	Precious Metals
FS	Financial Services	RE	Real Estate
FO	Foreign	SC	Small Cap
GL	Global	TC	Technology
GR	Growth	UT	Utilities
GI	Growth and Income		

A blank fund type means that the mutual fund has not yet been categorized.

2. Fund Name   The name of the mutual fund as stated in its prospectus, which can sometimes differ slightly from the name that the company uses for advertising. If you cannot find the particular mutual fund you are interested in, or if you have any doubts regarding the precise name, verify the information with your broker or on your account statement. Also, use the fund's ticker symbol for confirmation. (See column 3.)

3. Ticker Symbol   The unique alphabetic symbol used for identifying and trading a specific mutual fund. No two funds can have the same ticker symbol, and the ticker symbol for mutual funds always ends with an "X".

A handful of funds currently show no associated ticker symbol. This means that the fund is either small or new since the NASD only assigns a ticker symbol to funds with at least $25 million in assets or 1,000 shareholders.

4. Overall Investment Rating   Our overall rating is measured on a scale from A to E based on each fund's risk-adjusted performance. Please see page 10 for specific descriptions of each letter grade. Also, refer to page 7 for information on how our ratings are derived. Most important, when using this rating, please be sure to consider the warnings beginning on page 11 regarding the ratings' limitations and the underlying assumptions.

5. Phone   The telephone number of the company managing the fund. Call this number to receive a prospectus or other information about the fund.

6. **Performance Rating/Points**   A letter grade rating based solely on the mutual fund's financial performance over the trailing three years, without any consideration for the amount of risk the fund poses. Like the overall Investment Rating, the Performance Rating is measured on a scale from A to E for ease of interpretation. The points score indicates where the Performance Rating falls on a scale of 0 to 10.

7. **3-Month Total Return**   The total return the fund has provided to investors over the preceding three months. This total return figure is computed based on the fund's dividends, capital gains, and any other distributions to holders, as well as its share price appreciation/depreciation during the period, net of the expenses and fees it imposes on its shareholders. Although the total return figure does not reflect an adjustment for any loads the fund may carry, such adjustments have been made in deriving TheStreet Investment Ratings. The 3-Month Total Return shown here is not annualized.

8. **6-Month Total Return**   The total return the fund has provided investors over the preceding six months, not annualized.

9. **1-Year Total Return**   The total return the fund has provided investors over the preceding twelve months.

10. **1-Year Total Return Percentile**   The fund's percentile rank based on its one-year performance compared to that of all other equity funds in existence for at least one year. A score of 99 is the best possible, indicating that the fund outperformed 99% of the other mutual funds. Zero is the worst possible percentile score.

11. **3-Year Total Return**   The total annual return the fund has provided investors over the preceding three years.

12. **3-Year Total Return Percentile**   The fund's percentile rank based on its three-year performance compared to that of all other equity funds in existence for at least three years. A score of 99 is the best possible, indicating that the fund outperformed 99% of the other mutual funds. Zero is the worst possible percentile score.

13. **5-Year Total Return**   The total annual return the fund has provided investors over the preceding five years.

14. **5-Year Total Return Percentile**   The fund's percentile rank based on its five-year performance compared to that of all other equity funds in existence for at least five years. A score of 99 is the best possible, indicating that the fund outperformed 99% of the other mutual funds. Zero is the worst possible percentile score.

15. Dividend Yield

Distributions provided to fund investors over the preceding 12 months, expressed as a percent of the fund's current share price. Dividend distributions are based on a fund's need to pass earnings from both dividends and gains on the sale of investments along to shareholders. Thus, these dividend distributions are included as a part of the fund's total return.

Keep in mind that a higher dividend yield means more current income, as opposed to capital appreciation, which in turn means a higher tax liability in the year of the distribution.

16. Expense Ratio

The expense ratio is taken directly from each fund's annual report with no further calculation. It indicates the percentage of the fund's assets that are deducted each fiscal year to cover its expenses, although for practical purposes, it is actually accrued daily. Typical fund expenses include 12b-1 fees, management fees, administrative fees, operating costs, and all other asset-based costs incurred by the fund. Brokerage costs incurred by the fund to buy or sell shares of the underlying stocks, as well as any sales loads levied on investors, are not included in the expense ratio.

If a mutual fund's net assets are small, its expense ratio can be quite high because the fund must cover its expenses from a smaller asset base. Conversely, as the net assets of the fund grow, the expense percentage should ideally diminish since the expenses are being spread across a larger asset base.

Funds with higher expense ratios are generally less attractive since the expense ratio represents a hurdle that must be met before the investment becomes profitable to its shareholders. Since a fund's expenses affect its total return though, they are already factored into its Investment Rating.

Right Pages

1. Risk Rating/Points

A letter grade rating based solely on the mutual fund's risk as determined by its monthly performance volatility over the trailing three years. The risk rating does not take into consideration the overall financial performance the fund has achieved or the total return it has provided to its shareholders. Like the overall Investment Rating, the Risk Rating is measured on a scale from A to E for ease of interpretation. The points score indicates where the Risk Rating falls on a scale of 0 to 10.

2. Standard Deviation

A statistical measure of the amount of volatility in a fund's monthly performance over the last trailing 36 months. In absolute terms, standard deviation provides a historical measure of a fund's deviation from its mean, or average, monthly total return over the period. A high standard deviation indicates a high degree of volatility in the past, which usually means you should expect to see a high degree of volatility in the future as well. This translates into higher risk since a large negative swing could easily become a sizable loss in the event you need to liquidate your shares.

3.   Beta

The level of correlation between the fund's monthly performance over the last trailing 36 months and the performance of its investment category as a whole.

A beta of 1.00 means that the fund's returns have matched those of the index one for one during the stock market's ups and downs. A beta of 1.10 means that on average the fund has outperformed the index by 10% during rising markets and underperformed it by 10% during falling markets. Conversely, a beta of 0.85 means that the fund has typically perfomed 15% worse than the overall market during up markets and 15% better during down markets.

4.   Net Asset Value (NAV)

The fund's share price as of the date indicated. A fund's NAV is computed by dividing the value of the fund's asset holdings, less accrued fees and expenses, by the number of its shares outstanding.

5.   Net Assets

The total value (stated in millions of dollars) of all of the fund's asset holdings including stocks, bonds, cash, and other financial instruments, less accrued expenses and fees.

Larger funds have the advantage of being able to spread their expenses over a greater asset base so that the effect per share is lessened. On the other hand, if a fund becomes too large, it can be more difficult for the fund manager to buy and sell investments for the benefit of shareholders.

6.   Cash %

The percentage of the fund's assets held in cash or money market funds as of the last reporting period. Investments in this area will tend to hamper the fund's returns while adding to its stability during market swings.

7.   Stocks %

The percentage of the fund's assets held in common or preferred stocks as of the last reporting period. Since stocks are inherently riskier investments than the other categories, it is common for funds invested primarily or exclusively in stocks to receive a lower risk rating.

8.   Bonds %

The percentage of the fund's assets held in bonds as of the last reporting period. This category includes corporate bonds, municipal bonds, and government bonds such as T-bills and T-bonds.

9.   Other %

The percentage of the fund's assets invested as of the last reporting period in other types of financial instruments such as convertible securities, options, and warrants.

10.	**Portfolio Turnover Ratio**	The average annual portion of the fund's holdings that have been moved from one specific investment to another over the past three years. This indicates the amount of buying and selling the fund manager engages in. A portfolio turnover ratio of 100% signifies that on average, the entire value of the fund's assets is turned over once during the course of a year.
		A high portfolio turnover ratio has implications for shareholders since the fund is required to pass all realized earnings along to shareholders each year. Thus a high portfolio turnover ratio will result in higher annual distributions for shareholders, effectively increasing their annual taxable income. In contrast, a low turnover ratio means a higher level of unrealized gains that will not be taxable until you sell your shares in the fund.
11.	**Last Bull Market Return**	The fund's performance during the most recent stock bull market. Use this field in combination with the Last Bear Market Return (next column) to assess how well the fund anticipates and reacts to changing market conditions.
		Keep in mind that lower risk funds tend to under-perform higher risk funds during a bull market due to the risk/reward tradeoff.
12.	**Last Bear Market Return**	The fund's performance during the most recent stock bear market. Use this field in combination with the Last Bull Market Return (previous column) to assess how well the fund anticipates and reacts to changing market conditions.
		Keep in mind that lower risk funds tend to fare better than higher risk funds during a bear market although they may still record a net loss.
13.	**Manager Quality Percentile**	The manager quality percentile is based on a ranking of the fund's alpha, a statistical measure representing the difference between a fund's actual returns and its expected performance given its level of risk. Fund managers who have been able to exceed the fund's statistically expected performance receive a high percentile rank with 99 representing the highest possible score. At the other end of the spectrum, fund managers who have actually detracted from the fund's expected performance receive a low percentile rank with 0 representing the lowest possible score.
14.	**Manager Tenure**	The number of years the current manager has been managing the fund. Since fund managers who deliver substandard returns are usually replaced, a long tenure is usually a good sign that shareholders are satisfied that the fund is achieving its stated objectives.
15.	**Initial Purchase Minimum**	The minimum investment amount, stated in dollars, that the fund management company requires in order for you to initially purchase shares in the fund. In theory, funds with high purchase minimums are able to keep expenses down because they have fewer accounts to administer. Don't be misled, however, by the misconception that a fund with a high purchase minimum will deliver superior results simply because it is designed for "high rollers."

16. Additional Purchase Minimum

The minimum subsequent fund purchase, stated in dollars, that you can make once you have opened an existing account. This minimum may be lowered or waived if you participate in an electronic transfer plan where shares of the fund are automatically purchased at regularly scheduled intervals.

17. Front End Load

A fee charged on all new investments in the fund, stated as a percentage of the initial investment. Thus a fund with a 4% front-end load means that only 96% of your initial investment is working for you while the other 4% is immediately sacrificed to the fund company. It is generally best to avoid funds that charge a front-end load since there is usually a comparable no-load fund available to serve as an alternative.

While a fund's total return does not reflect the expense to shareholders of a front end load, we have factored this fee into our evaluation when deriving its TheStreet Investment Rating.

18. Back End Load

Also known as a deferred sales charge, this fee is levied when you sell the fund, and is stated as a percentage of your total sales price. For instance, investing in a fund with a 5% back-end load means that you will only receive 95% of your total investment when you sell the fund. The remaining 5% goes to the fund company. As with front-end loads, it is generally best to avoid funds that charge a back-end load since there is usually a comparable no-load fund available to serve as an alternative.

While a fund's total return does not reflect the expense to shareholders of a back-end load, we have factored this fee into our evaluation when deriving its TheStreet Investment Rating.

I. Index of Stock Mutual Funds

Fund Type	Fund Name	Ticker Symbol	Overall Investment Rating	Phone	Performance Rating/Pts	3 Mo	6 Mo	1Yr / Pct	3Yr / Pct	5Yr / Pct	Dividend Yield	Expense Ratio
BA	1290 DoubleLine Dynamic Alloc I	TNVDX	U	(888) 310-0416	U /	4.43	3.84	--	--	--	0.00	1.63
FS	1290 Unconstrained Bond Managers I	TNUIX	U	(888) 310-0416	U /	1.40	2.17	6.10 / 5	--	--	2.85	1.36
GR	13D Activist A	DDDAX	C+	(877) 413-3228	B- / 7.2	6.68	12.74	33.69 /92	6.53 /69	14.47 /95	0.00	1.75
GR	13D Activist C	DDDCX	B-	(877) 413-3228	B / 7.6	6.46	12.34	32.73 /91	5.73 /62	--	0.00	2.50
GR	13D Activist I	DDDIX	B	(877) 413-3228	B+ / 8.4	6.75	12.93	34.06 /93	6.80 /70	14.77 /96	0.00	1.50
GL	1789 Growth and Income A	PSEAX	C-	(888) 202-1388	D+ / 2.5	4.34	2.59	12.76 /21	4.45 /48	--	0.97	1.32
GL	1789 Growth and Income C	PSECX	C-	(888) 202-1388	D+ / 2.8	4.06	2.21	11.86 /17	3.66 /39	6.41 /31	0.30	2.07
GL	1789 Growth and Income P	PSEPX	C	(888) 202-1388	C- / 3.5	4.38	2.71	12.99 /22	4.70 /51	--	1.24	1.07
FS	1919 Financial Services A	SBFAX	A+	(844) 828-1919	A+ / 9.9	9.48	23.51	44.51 /98	14.96 /99	18.45 /99	0.24	1.45
FS	1919 Financial Services C	SFSLX	A+	(844) 828-1919	A+ / 9.9	9.31	23.06	43.53 /98	14.18 /99	17.64 /98	0.00	2.22
FS	1919 Financial Services I	LMRIX	A+	(844) 828-1919	A+ / 9.9	9.53	23.69	45.04 /98	15.42 /99	18.89 /99	0.55	1.20
GI	1919 Socially Responsive Balanced A	SSIAX	D+	(844) 828-1919	C- / 3.4	5.82	5.24	14.34 /27	4.93 /53	7.32 /37	0.59	1.21
GI	● 1919 Socially Responsive Balanced B	SESIX	D+	(844) 828-1919	C- / 3.6	5.49	4.50	12.93 /21	3.91 /42	6.22 /30	0.02	1.83
GI	1919 Socially Responsive Balanced	SESLX	C-	(844) 828-1919	C- / 3.9	5.62	4.96	13.52 /24	4.18 /45	6.56 /32	0.01	2.01
GI	1919 Socially Responsive Balanced I	LMRNX	C-	(844) 828-1919	C / 4.7	5.84	5.44	14.63 /28	5.19 /56	7.61 /39	0.90	1.06
GR	361 Domestic Long Short Equity Y	ADMWX	U	(888) 736-1227	U /	3.25	1.01	--	--	--	0.00	2.42
GL	361 Global Counter-Trend Fund I	AGFZX	C	(888) 736-1227	D+ / 2.5	1.91	4.79	9.54 /11	3.32 /35	--	0.00	2.47
GL	361 Global Counter-Trend Fund Inv	AGFQX	C	(888) 736-1227	D+ / 2.4	1.93	4.73	9.29 /10	3.11 /33	--	0.00	2.72
GL	361 Global Long Short Equity I	AGAZX	U	(888) 736-1227	U /	5.44	5.15	6.52 / 5	--	--	0.66	3.20
GL	361 Global Long Short Equity Inv	AGAQX	U	(888) 736-1227	U /	5.42	5.03	6.21 / 5	--	--	0.29	3.43
GL	361 Global Long Short Equity Y	AGAWX	B+	(888) 736-1227	C / 5.0	5.52	5.33	6.70 / 5	7.86 /78	--	0.75	3.10
GL	361 Managed Futures Strategy I	AMFZX	D+	(888) 736-1227	E / 0.5	-2.22	-2.73	-0.99 / 1	-0.19 /13	3.55 /13	0.00	1.87
GL	361 Managed Futures Strategy Inv	AMFQX	D+	(888) 736-1227	E / 0.4	-2.33	-2.85	-1.27 / 1	-0.43 /12	3.29 /12	0.00	2.12
IN	AAM Bahl and Gaynor Income Gro A	AFNAX	B-	(888) 966-9661	C+ / 6.6	7.12	6.60	19.93 /52	9.24 /88	--	1.50	1.28
IN	AAM Bahl and Gaynor Income Gro C	AFYCX	B-	(888) 966-9661	C+ / 6.9	6.90	6.19	18.93 /47	8.39 /82	--	0.97	2.03
IN	AAM Bahl and Gaynor Income Gro I	AFNIX	A-	(888) 966-9661	B / 7.8	7.24	6.79	20.23 /53	9.59 /91	--	1.80	1.03
GR	Aasgard Dividend Gr Sm & MC No	AADGX	U	(888) 263-6443	U /	4.95	8.12	--	--	--	0.00	2.02
AA	AB All Market Income Adv	MRKYX	U	(800) 221-5672	U /	5.13	4.22	16.83 /38	--	--	6.56	3.40
AA	AB All Mkt Real Return Z	AMTZX	D-	(800) 221-5672	E / 0.3	3.92	6.48	23.87 /69	-6.38 / 2	-3.86 / 2	2.68	0.96
BA	AB Bal Wealth Strat A	ABWAX	C-	(800) 221-5672	D+ / 2.7	4.85	4.25	14.23 /27	3.51 /37	5.82 /27	2.97	1.30
BA	AB Bal Wealth Strat Adv	ABWYX	C	(800) 221-5672	C- / 3.6	4.94	4.49	14.52 /28	3.78 /40	6.13 /29	3.34	1.05
BA	● AB Bal Wealth Strat B	ABWBX	C	(800) 221-5672	D+ / 2.9	4.64	3.88	13.35 /23	2.74 /29	5.04 /21	1.54	2.06
BA	AB Bal Wealth Strat C	ABWCX	C-	(800) 221-5672	D+ / 2.9	4.67	3.90	13.35 /23	2.74 /29	5.05 /22	2.33	2.05
BA	AB Bal Wealth Strat I	ABWIX	C	(800) 221-5672	C- / 3.6	4.86	4.41	14.46 /28	3.74 /40	6.10 /29	3.33	1.07
BA	AB Bal Wealth Strat K	ABWKX	C	(800) 221-5672	C- / 3.4	4.86	4.26	14.19 /26	3.41 /36	5.74 /27	2.96	1.39
BA	AB Bal Wealth Strat R	ABWRX	C	(800) 221-5672	C- / 3.1	4.78	4.10	13.76 /24	3.10 /33	5.43 /24	2.66	1.71
GR	AB Concentrated Growth A	WPASX	B	(800) 221-5672	B- / 7.5	7.26	8.76	22.19 /63	9.08 /87	--	0.00	1.27
GR	AB Concentrated Growth Adv	WPSGX	B+	(800) 221-5672	B+ / 8.5	7.36	8.92	22.48 /64	9.34 /89	12.50 /79	0.00	1.01
GR	AB Concentrated Growth C	WPCSX	B	(800) 221-5672	B / 7.7	7.09	8.38	21.26 /59	8.28 /81	--	0.00	2.01
GR	AB Concentrated Growth I	WPSIX	B+	(800) 221-5672	B+ / 8.5	7.35	8.95	22.54 /65	9.39 /89	--	0.00	0.98
GR	AB Concentrated Growth K	WPSKX	B+	(800) 221-5672	B+ / 8.3	7.30	8.79	22.23 /63	9.09 /87	--	0.00	1.24
GR	AB Concentrated Growth R	WPRSX	B+	(800) 221-5672	B / 8.1	7.21	8.67	21.90 /62	8.81 /85	--	0.00	1.50
GR	AB Concentrated Growth Z	WPSZX	B+	(800) 221-5672	B+ / 8.5	7.35	8.95	22.56 /65	9.36 /89	12.52 /79	0.00	0.96
FO	AB Concentrated Intl Growth Adv	CIGYX	U	(800) 221-5672	U /	7.49	2.05	12.31 /19	--	--	0.77	17.53
AA	AB Consv Wealth Strat A	ABPAX	C-	(800) 221-5672	D- / 1.5	2.87	2.03	7.69 / 7	2.47 /27	3.47 /13	2.37	1.25
AA	AB Consv Wealth Strat Adv	ABPYX	C	(800) 221-5672	D / 2.0	2.93	2.10	7.91 / 7	2.71 /29	3.75 /14	2.71	1.00
AA	● AB Consv Wealth Strat B	ABPBX	C	(800) 221-5672	D / 1.6	2.64	1.55	6.79 / 6	1.69 /22	2.71 /10	0.00	2.00
AA	AB Consv Wealth Strat C	ABPCX	C-	(800) 221-5672	D / 1.6	2.70	1.61	6.88 / 6	1.70 /22	2.72 /10	1.66	2.00
AA	AB Consv Wealth Strat I	APWIX	C	(800) 221-5672	D / 2.0	2.95	2.12	7.94 / 7	2.68 /29	3.72 /14	2.72	1.02
AA	AB Consv Wealth Strat K	APWKX	C	(800) 221-5672	D / 1.8	2.82	1.90	7.56 / 7	2.36 /26	3.40 /12	2.35	1.34
AA	AB Consv Wealth Strat R	APPRX	C	(800) 221-5672	D / 1.7	2.70	1.70	7.16 / 6	2.04 /24	3.07 /11	2.07	1.65
GR	AB Core Opportunities A	ADGAX	B	(800) 221-5672	B / 7.8	6.71	9.70	19.87 /51	10.10 /94	13.62 /90	0.10	1.23

● Denotes fund is closed to new investors
* Denotes fund is included in Section II

RISK	3 Year		NET ASSETS		ASSET				Portfolio	BULL / BEAR		FUND MANAGER		MINIMUMS		LOADS	
Risk Rating/Pts	Standard Deviation	Beta	NAV As of 2/28/17	Total $(Mil)	Cash %	Stocks %	Bonds %	Other %	Turnover Ratio	Last Bull Market Return	Last Bear Market Return	Manager Quality Pct	Manager Tenure (Years)	Initial Purch. $	Additional Purch. $	Front End Load	Back End Load
U /	N/A	N/A	10.81	55	6	21	71	2	56	N/A	N/A	N/A	1	1,000,000	0	0.0	0.0
U /	N/A	N/A	9.93	70	0	0	100	0	152	N/A	N/A	N/A	N/A	1,000,000	0	0.0	0.0
C /5.1	14.0	1.13	18.85	47	9	90	0	1	119	N/A	N/A	15	6	2,500	500	5.8	2.0
C /5.1	13.9	1.13	18.94	24	9	90	0	1	119	N/A	N/A	10	6	2,500	500	0.0	2.0
C /5.2	13.9	1.12	19.13	193	9	90	0	1	119	N/A	N/A	17	6	1,000,000	0	0.0	2.0
B- /7.1	8.5	0.57	12.63	2	2	78	18	2	5	N/A	N/A	94	6	2,000	100	5.3	1.0
B- /7.2	8.5	0.57	12.59	9	2	78	18	2	5	60.6	-15.7	92	6	2,000	100	0.0	1.0
B- /7.1	8.5	0.57	12.66	2	2	78	18	2	5	N/A	N/A	95	6	2,000	100	0.0	1.0
C+ /6.1	14.1	1.00	24.53	104	1	95	2	2	20	185.7	-18.7	87	3	1,000	50	5.8	0.0
C+ /6.1	14.1	1.00	22.82	42	1	95	2	2	20	175.1	-19.0	84	3	1,000	50	0.0	0.0
C+ /6.1	14.1	1.00	24.75	53	1	95	2	2	20	191.4	-18.6	89	3	1,000,000	0	0.0	0.0
C+ /5.7	7.1	0.68	17.06	100	0	69	29	2	26	63.6	-10.9	47	11	1,000	50	5.8	0.0
C+ /5.6	7.1	0.68	16.66	1	0	69	29	2	26	54.7	-11.3	34	11	1,000	50	0.0	0.0
C+ /5.7	7.2	0.68	17.23	12	0	69	29	2	26	57.5	-11.1	36	11	1,000	50	0.0	0.0
C+ /5.7	7.1	0.68	17.04	7	0	69	29	2	26	66.0	-10.7	51	11	1,000,000	0	0.0	0.0
U /	N/A	N/A	10.14	28	0	0	0	100	123	N/A	N/A	N/A	1	1,000,000	0	0.0	0.0
B /8.6	8.4	0.06	10.85	37	0	0	0	100	0	N/A	N/A	91	3	100,000	0	0.0	0.0
B /8.7	8.3	0.06	10.77	18	0	0	0	100	0	N/A	N/A	90	3	2,500	0	0.0	0.0
U /	N/A	N/A	11.35	384	0	0	0	100	229	N/A	N/A	N/A	3	2,500	0	0.0	0.0
U /	N/A	N/A	11.33	85	0	0	0	100	229	N/A	N/A	N/A	3	2,500	0	0.0	0.0
B /8.9	7.5	0.25	11.37	35	0	0	0	100	229	N/A	N/A	98	3	1,000,000	0	0.0	0.0
B /8.3	6.2	0.13	11.03	365	0	0	0	100	17	N/A	N/A	63	6	100,000	0	0.0	0.0
B /8.3	6.2	0.13	10.89	128	0	0	0	100	17	N/A	N/A	60	6	2,500	0	0.0	0.0
B- /7.0	9.4	0.86	15.00	60	1	98	0	1	27	N/A	N/A	75	5	2,500	500	5.5	2.0
B- /7.0	9.4	0.86	14.89	63	1	98	0	1	27	N/A	N/A	67	5	2,500	500	0.0	2.0
B- /7.0	9.4	0.86	15.04	310	1	98	0	1	27	N/A	N/A	77	5	25,000	5,000	0.0	2.0
U /	N/A	N/A	11.71	29	0	0	0	100	0	N/A	N/A	N/A	1	2,500	500	0.0	0.0
U /	N/A	N/A	10.11	34	5	54	39	2	88	N/A	N/A	N/A	3	0	0	0.0	0.0
C+ /5.9	13.6	1.23	8.42	9	4	64	31	1	119	-4.4	-21.3	0	2	0	0	0.0	0.0
B- /7.5	6.9	1.05	13.99	655	10	52	36	2	14	52.2	-14.7	22	14	2,500	50	4.3	0.0
B- /7.4	6.8	1.05	14.07	86	10	52	36	2	14	54.5	-14.6	25	14	0	0	0.0	0.0
B- /7.6	6.8	1.04	14.07	12	10	52	36	2	14	46.2	-14.9	16	14	2,500	50	0.0	0.0
B- /7.5	6.8	1.05	13.88	185	10	52	36	2	14	46.4	-15.0	16	14	2,500	50	0.0	0.0
B- /7.5	6.8	1.04	14.02	12	10	52	36	2	14	54.4	-14.6	25	14	0	0	0.0	0.0
B- /7.5	6.8	1.05	13.96	23	10	52	36	2	14	51.7	-14.8	21	14	0	0	0.0	0.0
B- /7.5	6.8	1.05	13.95	7	10	52	36	2	14	49.2	-14.9	19	14	0	0	0.0	0.0
C+ /5.9	11.9	1.06	30.34	24	1	98	0	1	44	N/A	N/A	49	4	2,500	50	4.3	0.0
C+ /5.6	11.9	1.06	30.56	266	1	98	0	1	44	124.0	-11.4	52	4	0	0	0.0	0.0
C+ /5.9	11.9	1.05	29.66	19	1	98	0	1	44	N/A	N/A	39	4	2,500	50	0.0	0.0
C+ /6.0	11.9	1.06	30.60	N/A	1	98	0	1	44	N/A	N/A	53	4	0	0	0.0	0.0
C+ /5.9	11.9	1.06	30.35	N/A	1	98	0	1	44	N/A	N/A	49	4	0	0	0.0	0.0
C+ /5.9	11.9	1.06	30.11	N/A	1	98	0	1	44	N/A	N/A	45	4	0	0	0.0	0.0
C+ /5.9	11.9	1.06	30.58	55	1	98	0	1	44	124.2	-11.4	52	4	0	0	0.0	0.0
U /	N/A	N/A	9.20	30	0	96	2	2	42	N/A	N/A	N/A	2	0	0	0.0	0.0
B /8.8	3.8	0.58	12.32	169	1	29	69	1	5	27.8	-7.1	51	N/A	2,500	50	4.3	0.0
B /8.8	3.8	0.57	12.37	9	1	29	69	1	5	29.7	-6.9	55	N/A	0	0	0.0	0.0
B /8.9	3.8	0.58	12.42	2	1	29	69	1	5	22.7	-7.3	40	N/A	2,500	50	0.0	0.0
B /8.9	3.8	0.59	12.16	67	1	29	69	1	5	22.8	-7.3	40	N/A	2,500	50	0.0	0.0
B /8.8	3.8	0.58	12.34	1	1	29	69	1	5	29.5	-7.0	54	N/A	0	0	0.0	0.0
B /8.8	3.8	0.58	12.29	7	1	29	69	1	5	27.3	-7.1	49	N/A	0	0	0.0	0.0
B /8.9	3.8	0.58	12.31	5	1	29	69	1	5	25.1	-7.3	45	N/A	0	0	0.0	0.0
C /5.5	9.0	0.83	19.40	149	3	81	15	1	96	134.1	-16.2	82	18	2,500	50	4.3	0.0

Data as of February 28, 2017

					PERFORMANCE							
	99 Pct = Best 0 Pct = Worst				Perfor-	Total Return % through 2/28/17			Annualized		Incl. in Returns	
Fund Type	Fund Name	Ticker Symbol	Overall Investment Rating	Phone	mance Rating/Pts	3 Mo	6 Mo	1Yr / Pct	3Yr / Pct	5Yr / Pct	Dividend Yield	Expense Ratio
GR	AB Core Opportunities Adv	ADGYX	B+	(800) 221-5672	B+ / 8.8	6.75	9.85	20.20 /53	10.41 /95	13.96 /93	0.23	0.98
GR	● AB Core Opportunities B	ADGBX	B	(800) 221-5672	B+ / 8.4	6.60	9.64	19.67 /50	9.86 /93	13.33 /87	0.00	2.01
GR	AB Core Opportunities C	ADGCX	B	(800) 221-5672	B / 8.0	6.48	9.25	18.92 /47	9.30 /89	12.82 /82	0.00	1.99
GR	AB Core Opportunities I	ADGIX	B+	(800) 221-5672	B+ / 8.8	6.76	9.83	20.20 /53	10.42 /95	13.98 /93	0.25	0.92
GR	AB Core Opportunities K	ADGKX	B+	(800) 221-5672	B+ / 8.6	6.66	9.69	19.85 /51	10.13 /94	13.68 /90	0.07	1.27
GR	AB Core Opportunities R	ADGRX	B+	(800) 221-5672	B+ / 8.4	6.60	9.56	19.57 /50	9.86 /93	13.37 /87	0.00	1.54
GR	AB Core Opportunities Z	ADGZX	A+	(800) 221-5672	B+ / 8.8	6.77	9.84	20.27 /53	10.44 /96	13.87 /92	0.27	0.85
MC	AB Discovery Gro A	CHCLX	D	(800) 221-5672	C- / 4.2	5.99	8.94	26.08 /76	2.63 /28	9.80 /57	0.00	0.99
MC	AB Discovery Gro Adv	CHCYX	D+	(800) 221-5672	C / 5.4	6.19	9.10	26.43 /78	2.87 /30	10.05 /59	0.00	0.77
MC	● AB Discovery Gro B	CHCBX	D-	(800) 221-5672	C / 4.4	5.77	8.73	25.10 /74	1.75 /22	8.85 /49	0.00	1.81
MC	AB Discovery Gro C	CHCCX	D-	(800) 221-5672	C / 4.4	5.90	8.65	25.10 /74	1.79 /23	8.91 /50	0.00	1.77
MC	AB Discovery Gro I	CHCIX	D+	(800) 221-5672	C / 5.3	6.03	9.08	26.28 /77	2.86 /30	10.07 /59	0.00	0.76
MC	AB Discovery Gro K	CHCKX	D+	(800) 221-5672	C / 5.0	6.03	9.01	25.95 /76	2.50 /27	9.68 /56	0.00	1.10
MC	AB Discovery Gro R	CHCRX	D	(800) 221-5672	C / 4.7	5.94	8.78	25.46 /75	2.18 /25	9.33 /53	0.00	1.39
MC	AB Discovery Gro Z	CHCZX	C-	(800) 221-5672	C / 5.4	6.13	9.18	26.38 /77	2.91 /31	9.98 /58	0.00	0.68
SC	AB Discovery Value A	ABASX	B-	(800) 221-5672	B+ / 8.6	2.97	13.26	33.59 /92	8.72 /85	13.71 /91	0.16	1.15
SC	AB Discovery Value Adv	ABYSX	B	(800) 221-5672	A / 9.4	3.03	13.41	33.94 /93	9.03 /87	14.05 /93	0.37	0.90
SC	● AB Discovery Value B	ABBSX	B	(800) 221-5672	A- / 9.1	2.94	13.20	33.49 /92	8.63 /84	13.63 /90	0.01	1.92
SC	AB Discovery Value C	ABCSX	B-	(800) 221-5672	B+ / 8.8	2.81	12.81	32.61 /91	7.96 /79	12.90 /83	0.00	1.90
SC	AB Discovery Value I	ABSIX	B	(800) 221-5672	A / 9.4	3.04	13.40	33.96 /93	9.06 /87	14.08 /94	0.40	0.88
SC	AB Discovery Value K	ABSKX	B	(800) 221-5672	A- / 9.2	2.96	13.18	33.49 /92	8.68 /84	13.69 /91	0.12	1.23
SC	AB Discovery Value R	ABSRX	B	(800) 221-5672	A- / 9.0	2.87	12.97	33.02 /92	8.34 /82	13.33 /87	0.00	1.54
SC	AB Discovery Value Z	ABSZX	A	(800) 221-5672	A / 9.4	3.07	13.44	34.03 /93	9.14 /88	14.00 /93	0.46	0.81
EM	AB Emerging Markets Multi Asset A	ABAEX	C-	(800) 221-5672	C- / 3.9	8.26	3.63	19.49 /49	4.01 /43	0.31 / 5	3.88	2.71
EM	AB Emerging Markets Multi Asset	ABYEX	C	(800) 221-5672	C / 5.0	8.35	3.76	19.84 /51	4.31 /46	0.59 / 5	4.24	2.43
EM	AB Emerging Markets Multi Asset C	ABCEX	C-	(800) 221-5672	C- / 4.1	8.06	3.26	18.61 /45	3.25 /34	-0.42 / 4	3.43	3.49
EM	AB Emerging Markets Multi Asset I	ABIEX	C	(800) 221-5672	C / 5.0	8.32	3.72	19.80 /51	4.31 /46	0.60 / 5	4.35	2.33
EM	AB Emerging Markets Multi Asset K	ABKEX	C	(800) 221-5672	C / 4.8	8.22	3.63	19.51 /49	4.02 /43	0.35 / 5	4.01	2.70
EM	AB Emerging Markets Multi Asset R	ABREX	C	(800) 221-5672	C / 4.6	8.22	3.51	19.27 /48	3.78 /40	0.11 / 5	3.84	3.16
UT	AB Equity Income A	AUIAX	C+	(800) 221-5672	C+ / 6.5	7.28	8.72	20.66 /56	7.35 /74	10.75 /64	2.59	0.98
UT	AB Equity Income Adv	AUIYX	B	(800) 221-5672	B- / 7.4	7.34	8.83	20.95 /57	7.65 /76	11.07 /66	2.92	0.73
UT	● AB Equity Income B	AUIBX	C+	(800) 221-5672	C+ / 6.7	7.06	8.31	19.77 /51	6.55 /69	9.93 /58	1.97	1.75
UT	AB Equity Income C	AUICX	C+	(800) 221-5672	C+ / 6.7	7.05	8.30	19.75 /51	6.58 /69	9.96 /58	2.06	1.73
UT	AB Equity Income I	AUIIX	B	(800) 221-5672	B- / 7.4	7.33	8.81	20.92 /57	7.63 /76	11.06 /66	2.95	0.74
UT	AB Equity Income K	AUIKX	B	(800) 221-5672	B- / 7.2	7.28	8.66	20.58 /55	7.30 /74	10.71 /63	2.64	1.07
UT	AB Equity Income R	AUIRX	C+	(800) 221-5672	C+ / 6.9	7.19	8.49	20.21 /53	6.97 /72	10.37 /61	2.39	1.38
IN	AB Equity Income Z	AUIZX	A-	(800) 221-5672	B- / 7.5	7.37	8.87	21.09 /58	7.74 /77	11.03 /66	3.04	0.64
RE	AB Glbl Real Est Inv A	AREAX	D+	(800) 221-5672	D+ / 2.7	5.98	-3.18	10.77 /14	5.59 /60	8.05 /43	3.52	1.29
RE	AB Glbl Real Est Inv Adv	ARSYX	C-	(800) 221-5672	C- / 3.7	5.94	-3.09	11.02 /14	5.85 /63	8.33 /45	3.99	1.04
RE	● AB Glbl Real Est Inv B	AREBX	C-	(800) 221-5672	D+ / 2.9	5.69	-3.63	9.86 /11	4.75 /51	7.19 /36	2.86	2.09
RE	AB Glbl Real Est Inv C	ARECX	C-	(800) 221-5672	D+ / 2.9	5.66	-3.62	9.92 /11	4.80 /52	7.25 /36	2.98	2.05
RE	AB Glbl Real Est Inv I	AEEIX	C-	(800) 221-5672	C- / 3.8	6.02	-3.04	11.19 /15	5.94 /64	8.44 /46	4.03	0.99
RE	AB Glbl Real Est Inv K	ARRKX	C-	(800) 221-5672	C- / 3.5	5.94	-3.23	10.75 /14	5.59 /60	8.06 /43	3.69	1.30
RE	AB Glbl Real Est Inv R	ARRRX	C-	(800) 221-5672	C- / 3.2	5.89	-3.38	10.39 /13	5.26 /57	7.74 /40	3.41	1.62
GL	AB Global Core Equity Adv	GCEYX	U	(800) 221-5672	U /	8.10	6.64	21.53 /60	--	--	0.94	1.08
BA	AB Global Risk Alloc A	CABNX	C-	(800) 221-5672	D+ / 2.9	4.58	3.99	15.17 /31	3.77 /40	4.23 /16	5.14	1.27
BA	AB Global Risk Alloc Adv	CBSYX	C	(800) 221-5672	C- / 3.8	4.68	4.09	15.49 /32	4.04 /43	4.52 /18	5.58	1.02
BA	● AB Global Risk Alloc B	CABBX	C-	(800) 221-5672	C- / 3.1	4.36	3.63	14.36 /27	2.97 /31	3.44 /13	4.98	2.05
BA	AB Global Risk Alloc C	CBACX	C-	(800) 221-5672	C- / 3.1	4.36	3.57	14.32 /27	3.00 /32	3.46 /13	5.12	2.02
BA	AB Global Risk Alloc I	CABIX	C	(800) 221-5672	C- / 4.0	4.68	4.22	15.65 /33	4.21 /45	4.68 /19	5.78	0.91
BA	AB Global Risk Alloc K	CBSKX	C	(800) 221-5672	C- / 3.6	4.63	3.97	15.18 /31	3.75 /40	4.23 /16	5.29	1.30
BA	AB Global Risk Alloc R	CBSRX	C-	(800) 221-5672	C- / 3.4	4.56	3.83	14.81 /29	3.43 /36	3.91 /15	4.85	1.61

Risk Rating/Pts	Standard Deviation	Beta	NAV As of 2/28/17	Total $(Mil)	Cash %	Stocks %	Bonds %	Other %	Portfolio Turnover Ratio	Last Bull Market Return	Last Bear Market Return	Manager Quality Pct	Manager Tenure (Years)	Initial Purch. $	Additional Purch. $	Front End Load	Back End Load
C+ / 5.6	9.0	0.82	19.86	49	3	81	15	1	96	137.8	-16.1	84	18	0	0	0.0	0.0
C / 5.2	9.0	0.82	17.57	2	3	81	15	1	96	130.9	-16.3	81	18	2,500	50	0.0	0.0
C / 5.1	9.0	0.82	16.73	36	3	81	15	1	96	125.2	-16.5	78	18	2,500	50	0.0	0.0
C+ / 5.6	9.0	0.82	20.06	2	3	81	15	1	96	137.9	-16.1	84	18	0	0	0.0	0.0
C / 5.5	9.0	0.82	19.56	4	3	81	15	1	96	134.7	-16.2	83	18	0	0	0.0	0.0
C / 5.4	9.0	0.83	18.87	5	3	81	15	1	96	131.4	-16.2	81	18	0	0	0.0	0.0
B- / 7.3	9.0	0.83	20.08	1	3	81	15	1	96	136.7	-16.2	84	18	0	0	0.0	0.0
C- / 3.5	15.6	1.17	9.38	569	0	98	0	2	67	106.9	-22.6	4	9	2,500	50	4.3	0.0
C- / 3.6	15.6	1.17	9.95	950	0	98	0	2	67	109.5	-22.5	4	9	0	0	0.0	0.0
D+ / 2.8	15.5	1.16	6.23	1	0	98	0	2	67	97.4	-22.7	3	9	2,500	50	0.0	0.0
D+ / 2.8	15.6	1.17	6.28	47	0	98	0	2	67	98.2	-22.8	3	9	2,500	50	0.0	0.0
C- / 3.6	15.6	1.17	9.85	150	0	98	0	2	67	109.9	-22.5	4	9	0	0	0.0	0.0
C- / 3.5	15.6	1.16	9.32	16	0	98	0	2	67	105.7	-22.5	3	9	0	0	0.0	0.0
C- / 3.4	15.6	1.17	8.92	22	0	98	0	2	67	102.2	-22.7	3	9	0	0	0.0	0.0
C / 4.7	15.6	1.17	9.87	134	0	98	0	2	67	108.6	-22.6	4	9	0	0	0.0	0.0
C / 4.3	14.2	0.85	22.01	522	0	99	0	1	47	140.8	-26.6	89	N/A	2,500	50	4.3	0.0
C / 4.3	14.2	0.85	22.49	1,301	0	99	0	1	47	144.7	-26.5	90	N/A	0	0	0.0	0.0
C- / 4.2	14.2	0.85	20.72	3	0	99	0	1	47	139.7	-26.7	89	N/A	2,500	50	0.0	0.0
C- / 4.0	14.2	0.85	19.68	143	0	99	0	1	47	131.7	-26.8	86	N/A	2,500	50	0.0	0.0
C- / 4.2	14.2	0.85	21.86	258	0	99	0	1	47	145.0	-26.5	90	N/A	0	0	0.0	0.0
C / 4.3	14.2	0.85	21.71	66	0	99	0	1	47	140.7	-26.6	89	N/A	0	0	0.0	0.0
C / 4.3	14.2	0.84	21.46	100	0	99	0	1	47	136.6	-26.7	88	N/A	0	0	0.0	0.0
C+ / 6.0	14.2	0.85	21.83	303	0	99	0	1	47	143.8	-26.6	91	N/A	0	0	0.0	0.0
C+ / 6.0	11.4	0.66	9.09	5	10	47	41	2	108	21.7	N/A	89	6	2,500	50	4.3	0.0
C+ / 6.0	11.4	0.67	9.11	30	10	47	41	2	108	23.6	N/A	90	6	0	0	0.0	0.0
C+ / 6.1	11.4	0.66	9.06	N/A	10	47	41	2	108	17.1	N/A	86	6	2,500	50	0.0	0.0
C+ / 6.0	11.5	0.67	9.05	17	10	47	41	2	108	23.6	N/A	90	6	0	0	0.0	0.0
C+ / 6.0	11.4	0.66	9.05	N/A	10	47	41	2	108	21.9	N/A	89	6	0	0	0.0	0.0
C+ / 6.0	11.4	0.67	9.06	N/A	10	47	41	2	108	20.3	N/A	88	6	0	0	0.0	0.0
C+ / 6.2	10.1	0.14	27.71	330	0	99	0	1	117	99.4	-16.1	95	7	2,500	50	4.3	0.0
C+ / 6.2	10.1	0.14	27.96	245	0	99	0	1	117	102.5	-16.0	96	7	0	0	0.0	0.0
C+ / 6.2	10.1	0.14	27.34	2	0	99	0	1	117	91.6	-16.3	94	7	2,500	50	0.0	0.0
C+ / 6.2	10.1	0.14	27.33	129	0	99	0	1	117	91.8	-16.4	94	7	2,500	50	0.0	0.0
C+ / 6.2	10.1	0.14	27.65	1	0	99	0	1	117	102.6	-16.0	96	7	0	0	0.0	0.0
C+ / 6.2	10.1	0.14	27.70	5	0	99	0	1	117	99.0	-16.1	95	7	0	0	0.0	0.0
C+ / 6.2	10.1	0.14	27.56	17	0	99	0	1	117	95.8	-16.2	95	7	0	0	0.0	0.0
B- / 7.2	10.1	0.95	27.65	2	0	99	0	1	117	101.9	-16.1	47	7	0	0	0.0	0.0
C+ / 6.5	11.2	0.76	14.17	73	12	87	0	1	73	78.6	-22.0	39	5	2,500	50	4.3	0.0
C+ / 6.5	11.2	0.76	14.03	32	12	87	0	1	73	81.3	-22.0	43	5	0	0	0.0	0.0
C+ / 6.5	11.2	0.77	14.00	1	12	87	0	1	73	71.2	-22.3	29	5	2,500	50	0.0	0.0
C+ / 6.5	11.2	0.76	13.99	21	12	87	0	1	73	71.7	-22.3	30	5	2,500	50	0.0	0.0
C+ / 6.5	11.2	0.77	14.12	5	12	87	0	1	73	82.1	-21.9	44	5	0	0	0.0	0.0
C+ / 6.5	11.2	0.76	14.06	10	12	87	0	1	73	78.8	-22.0	39	5	0	0	0.0	0.0
C+ / 6.5	11.2	0.76	14.00	9	12	87	0	1	73	75.9	-22.2	35	5	0	0	0.0	0.0
U /	N/A	N/A	10.95	237	0	99	0	1	51	N/A	N/A	N/A	3	0	0	0.0	0.0
B- / 7.0	6.6	0.82	15.62	229	8	27	64	1	250	44.6	-10.3	45	5	2,500	50	4.3	0.0
B- / 7.0	6.6	0.81	15.74	14	8	27	64	1	250	46.8	-10.2	49	5	0	0	0.0	0.0
C+ / 6.9	6.6	0.82	14.19	3	8	27	64	1	250	38.8	-10.5	34	5	2,500	50	0.0	0.0
C+ / 6.9	6.6	0.82	14.22	40	8	27	64	1	250	39.0	-10.5	35	5	2,500	50	0.0	0.0
B- / 7.0	6.5	0.81	15.72	2	8	27	64	1	250	48.0	-10.1	52	5	0	0	0.0	0.0
B- / 7.0	6.6	0.82	15.59	2	8	27	64	1	250	44.6	-10.2	45	5	0	0	0.0	0.0
B- / 7.0	6.6	0.81	15.51	3	8	27	64	1	250	42.2	-10.4	40	5	0	0	0.0	0.0

Fund Type	Fund Name	Ticker Symbol	Overall Investment Rating	Phone	PERFORMANCE Performance Rating/Pts	Total Return % through 2/28/17 3 Mo	6 Mo	1Yr / Pct	Annualized 3Yr / Pct	5Yr / Pct	Incl. in Returns Dividend Yield	Expense Ratio
GR	AB Growth Fund A	AGRFX	B-	(800) 221-5672	B- / 7.4	8.82	7.11	18.14 /43	9.79 /92	13.06 /84	0.00	1.28
GR	AB Growth Fund Adv	AGRYX	B+	(800) 221-5672	B+ / 8.4	8.90	7.24	18.44 /45	10.07 /94	13.38 /88	0.00	1.03
GR	● AB Growth Fund B	AGBBX	C+	(800) 221-5672	B / 7.6	8.64	6.70	17.23 /39	8.90 /86	12.17 /76	0.00	2.08
GR	AB Growth Fund C	AGRCX	C+	(800) 221-5672	B / 7.6	8.62	6.71	17.24 /39	8.95 /86	12.23 /76	0.00	2.03
GR	AB Growth Fund I	AGFIX	B+	(800) 221-5672	B+ / 8.5	8.95	7.33	18.58 /45	10.19 /94	13.53 /89	0.00	0.94
GR	AB Growth Fund K	AGFKX	B	(800) 221-5672	B / 8.2	8.83	7.11	18.15 /44	9.81 /92	13.15 /85	0.00	1.26
GR	AB Growth Fund R	AGFRX	B	(800) 221-5672	B / 7.9	8.74	6.95	17.77 /42	9.46 /90	12.78 /82	0.00	1.59
RE	AB Inst Global RealEst II	ARIIX	C	(800) 221-5672	C- / 4.1	6.21	-2.80	11.58 /16	6.31 /67	8.75 /48	5.00	0.68
FO	AB International Port A	AIZAX	D-	(800) 221-5672	E+ / 0.8	6.42	2.02	12.49 /20	-0.31 /12	3.61 /13	1.68	2.11
FO	● AB International Port B	AIZBX	D-	(800) 221-5672	E+ / 0.9	6.22	1.61	11.65 /17	-1.03 / 9	2.79 /10	0.67	2.82
FO	AB International Port C	AIZCX	D-	(800) 221-5672	E+ / 0.9	6.24	1.65	11.68 /17	-1.03 / 9	2.95 /11	0.88	2.85
FO	AB International Port Z	AIZZX	U		U /	6.47	2.15	12.78 /21	--	--	2.00	N/A
FO	AB International Sm Cp Adv	IRCYX	U	(800) 221-5672	U /	8.11	4.04	17.52 /41	--	--	1.45	N/A
FO	AB International Sm Cp Z	IRCZX	U	(800) 221-5672	U /	8.11	4.05	17.52 /41	--	--	1.45	1.14
FO	AB International Strategic Eqty Adv	STEYX	U	(800) 221-5672	U /	6.96	6.02	16.27 /35	--	--	1.33	N/A
FO	AB International Strategic Eqty Z	STEZX	U	(800) 221-5672	U /	6.94	6.01	16.24 /35	--	--	1.33	1.05
FO	AB International Value A	ABIAX	D-	(800) 221-5672	D- / 1.0	7.98	5.41	15.01 /30	-0.42 /12	4.17 /16	0.15	1.40
FO	AB International Value Adv	ABIYX	D	(800) 221-5672	D- / 1.5	8.07	5.56	15.35 /31	-0.15 /13	4.46 /18	0.32	1.14
FO	● AB International Value B	ABIBX	D-	(800) 221-5672	D- / 1.1	7.76	5.07	14.18 /26	-1.17 / 9	3.38 /12	0.00	2.23
FO	AB International Value C	ABICX	D-	(800) 221-5672	D- / 1.1	7.78	4.97	14.09 /26	-1.16 / 9	3.40 /12	0.00	2.15
FO	AB International Value I	AIVIX	D	(800) 221-5672	D+ / 2.4	8.13	5.65	15.69 /33	0.07 /14	4.70 /19	0.52	0.93
FO	AB International Value K	AIVKX	D	(800) 221-5672	D- / 1.4	8.02	5.45	15.18 /31	-0.36 /12	4.26 /17	0.25	1.38
FO	AB International Value R	AIVRX	D	(800) 221-5672	D- / 1.3	7.91	5.24	14.81 /29	-0.67 /11	3.92 /15	0.04	1.69
FO	AB Intl Growth A	AWPAX	E+	(800) 221-5672	E / 0.5	6.43	-1.73	11.47 /16	-1.43 / 8	2.29 / 9	0.69	1.35
FO	AB Intl Growth Adv	AWPYX	D-	(800) 221-5672	E+ / 0.8	6.50	-1.65	11.69 /17	-1.17 / 9	2.57 / 9	0.93	1.10
FO	● AB Intl Growth B	AWPBX	E+	(800) 221-5672	E / 0.5	6.19	-2.18	10.49 /13	-2.22 / 6	1.50 / 7	0.00	2.18
FO	AB Intl Growth C	AWPCX	E+	(800) 221-5672	E+ / 0.6	6.23	-2.10	10.60 /13	-2.17 / 6	1.54 / 7	0.00	2.11
FO	AB Intl Growth I	AWPIX	D-	(800) 221-5672	E+ / 0.9	6.53	-1.54	11.81 /17	-1.02 / 9	2.74 /10	1.17	0.95
FO	AB Intl Growth K	AWPKX	D-	(800) 221-5672	E+ / 0.8	6.45	-1.68	11.44 /16	-1.40 / 8	2.34 / 9	0.78	1.36
FO	AB Intl Growth R	AWPRX	D-	(800) 221-5672	E+ / 0.7	6.33	-1.88	11.05 /15	-1.72 / 7	2.02 / 8	0.38	1.67
GR	AB Lg Cap Growth A	APGAX	B	(800) 221-5672	B+ / 8.3	8.92	7.53	19.31 /49	11.18 /97	14.92 /97	0.00	1.01
GR	AB Lg Cap Growth Adv	APGYX	B+	(800) 221-5672	A- / 9.2	9.01	7.67	19.61 /50	11.46 /98	15.20 /97	0.12	0.77
GR	● AB Lg Cap Growth B	APGBX	B-	(800) 221-5672	B+ / 8.5	8.73	7.21	18.43 /45	10.29 /95	13.98 /93	0.00	1.81
GR	AB Lg Cap Growth C	APGCX	B-	(800) 221-5672	B+ / 8.5	8.72	7.12	18.43 /45	10.35 /95	14.05 /93	0.00	1.77
GR	AB Lg Cap Growth I	ALLIX	B+	(800) 221-5672	A- / 9.2	8.99	7.67	19.67 /50	11.53 /98	15.30 /97	0.13	0.67
GR	AB Lg Cap Growth K	ALCKX	B+	(800) 221-5672	A- / 9.0	8.92	7.50	19.28 /48	11.14 /97	14.89 /97	0.00	1.06
GR	AB Lg Cap Growth R	ABPRX	B	(800) 221-5672	B+ / 8.8	8.81	7.32	18.87 /46	10.80 /97	14.54 /96	0.00	1.37
GR	AB Lg Cap Growth Z	APGZX	A+	(800) 221-5672	A- / 9.1	9.02	7.70	19.74 /51	11.40 /98	15.05 /97	0.16	0.64
GR	AB Long Short Multi Manager Adv	LSYMX	U	(800) 221-5672	U /	2.42	6.15	7.35 / 6	--	--	0.00	6.03
GL	AB Multi-Manager Alt Strat Adv	ALTYX	U	(800) 221-5672	U /	2.88	3.71	6.72 / 5	--	--	0.94	3.32
GL	AB Multi-Manager Alt Strat Z	ALTZX	U	(800) 221-5672	U /	2.88	3.71	6.73 / 5	--	--	0.94	3.18
GI	AB Multi-Manager Sel 2015 K	TDCKX	U	(800) 221-5672	U /	4.50	3.79	13.05 /22	--	--	1.96	1.97
GI	AB Multi-Manager Sel 2020 K	TDDKX	U	(800) 221-5672	U /	5.00	4.59	14.41 /27	--	--	1.81	1.65
GI	AB Multi-Manager Sel 2025 K	TDGKX	U	(800) 221-5672	U /	5.58	5.38	16.12 /35	--	--	1.74	1.54
GI	AB Multi-Manager Sel 2030 K	TDHKX	U	(800) 221-5672	U /	5.94	6.14	17.65 /41	--	--	1.59	1.68
GI	AB Multi-Manager Sel 2035 K	TDMKX	U	(800) 221-5672	U /	6.37	6.88	19.01 /47	--	--	1.33	1.79
GI	AB Multi-Manager Sel 2040 K	TDJKX	U	(800) 221-5672	U /	6.47	6.99	19.58 /50	--	--	1.19	1.93
GI	AB Multi-Manager Sel 2045 K	TDNKX	U	(800) 221-5672	U /	6.48	7.20	20.03 /52	--	--	1.16	2.22
GI	AB Relative Value A	CABDX	B+	(800) 221-5672	B- / 7.2	5.83	10.38	21.25 /58	8.64 /84	12.76 /82	1.61	0.95
GI	AB Relative Value Advisor	CBBYX	A-	(800) 221-5672	B / 8.1	5.89	10.60	21.40 /59	8.88 /86	13.12 /85	1.92	0.66
GI	● AB Relative Value B	CBBDX	B+	(800) 221-5672	B- / 7.4	5.74	9.92	20.28 /54	7.86 /78	11.98 /74	0.77	1.73
GI	AB Relative Value C	CBBCX	B+	(800) 221-5672	B- / 7.3	5.61	9.80	20.19 /53	7.80 /77	11.95 /74	0.96	1.70

● Denotes fund is closed to new investors
* Denotes fund is included in Section II

www.thestreetratings.com

RISK			NET ASSETS		ASSET				Portfolio	BULL / BEAR		FUND MANAGER		MINIMUMS		LOADS	
	3 Year		NAV							Last Bull	Last Bear	Manager	Manager	Initial	Additional	Front	Back
Risk Rating/Pts	Standard Deviation	Beta	As of 2/28/17	Total $(Mil)	Cash %	Stocks %	Bonds %	Other %	Turnover Ratio	Market Return	Market Return	Quality Pct	Tenure (Years)	Purch. $	Purch. $	End Load	End Load
C /5.3	11.0	0.95	65.41	589	0	98	0	2	47	129.1	-17.1	71	9	2,500	50	4.3	0.0
C /5.4	11.0	0.95	70.40	25	0	98	0	2	47	132.6	-17.0	73	9	0	0	0.0	0.0
C /4.4	11.0	0.95	37.60	12	0	98	0	2	47	119.4	-17.4	61	9	2,500	50	0.0	0.0
C /4.4	11.0	0.95	38.06	70	0	98	0	2	47	120.1	-17.3	61	9	2,500	50	0.0	0.0
C /5.4	11.0	0.95	70.01	12	0	98	0	2	47	134.3	-16.9	74	9	0	0	0.0	0.0
C /5.3	11.0	0.95	66.95	2	0	98	0	2	47	130.2	-17.0	71	9	0	0	0.0	0.0
C /5.3	11.0	0.95	64.19	2	0	98	0	2	47	126.2	-17.1	67	9	0	0	0.0	0.0
C+ /6.7	11.2	0.76	10.60	333	12	86	0	2	71	85.1	-21.4	49	5	2,000,000	0	0.0	0.0
C+ /6.2	11.0	0.86	15.29	3	2	97	0	1	77	37.6	-25.8	72	N/A	2,500	50	4.3	0.0
C+ /6.4	11.0	0.86	15.60	N/A	2	97	0	1	77	31.8	-26.0	63	N/A	2,500	50	0.0	0.0
C+ /6.3	11.0	0.86	15.36	1	2	97	0	1	77	32.8	-26.0	63	N/A	2,500	50	0.0	0.0
U /	N/A	N/A	15.29	162	2	97	0	1	77	N/A	N/A	N/A	6	0	0	0.0	0.0
U /	N/A	N/A	10.78	435	1	96	2	1	51	N/A	N/A	N/A	2	5,000	0	0.0	0.0
U /	N/A	N/A	10.78	270	1	96	2	1	51	N/A	N/A	N/A	2	0	0	0.0	0.0
U /	N/A	N/A	10.77	897	0	0	0	100	79	N/A	N/A	N/A	2	10,000	0	0.0	0.0
U /	N/A	N/A	10.78	437	0	0	0	100	79	N/A	N/A	N/A	2	0	0	0.0	0.0
C+ /6.0	12.3	0.95	12.86	132	0	98	0	2	71	44.5	-27.9	71	5	2,500	50	4.3	0.0
C+ /6.0	12.3	0.95	13.14	62	0	98	0	2	71	46.7	-27.9	74	5	0	0	0.0	0.0
C+ /6.2	12.3	0.95	12.64	1	0	98	0	2	71	38.7	-28.2	62	5	2,500	50	0.0	0.0
C+ /6.1	12.3	0.95	12.47	42	0	98	0	2	71	38.9	-28.2	62	5	2,500	50	0.0	0.0
C+ /6.0	12.3	0.95	12.84	3	0	98	0	2	71	48.4	-27.7	76	5	0	0	0.0	0.0
C+ /6.0	12.3	0.95	12.82	12	0	98	0	2	71	45.1	-27.9	72	5	0	0	0.0	0.0
C+ /6.0	12.3	0.96	12.75	16	0	98	0	2	71	42.5	-27.9	68	5	0	0	0.0	0.0
C /5.5	12.8	0.93	15.64	198	2	97	0	1	45	35.3	-27.0	58	6	2,500	50	4.3	0.0
C+ /5.6	12.7	0.92	15.90	36	2	97	0	1	45	37.4	-27.0	62	6	0	0	0.0	0.0
C /5.5	12.7	0.93	13.90	1	2	97	0	1	45	29.6	-27.2	47	6	2,500	50	0.0	0.0
C /5.5	12.8	0.93	13.98	34	2	97	0	1	45	30.0	-27.3	48	6	2,500	50	0.0	0.0
C+ /5.6	12.7	0.92	15.80	2	2	97	0	1	45	38.7	-26.9	64	6	0	0	0.0	0.0
C+ /5.6	12.7	0.92	15.57	5	2	97	0	1	45	35.7	-27.0	59	6	0	0	0.0	0.0
C /5.5	12.7	0.92	15.45	12	2	97	0	1	45	33.4	-27.1	54	6	0	0	0.0	0.0
C /4.9	10.4	0.90	41.04	1,703	1	93	5	1	59	149.5	-18.6	84	5	2,500	50	4.3	0.0
C /5.1	10.4	0.90	44.34	1,433	1	93	5	1	59	152.7	-18.5	85	5	0	0	0.0	0.0
C- /4.1	10.4	0.90	31.27	23	1	93	5	1	59	138.6	-18.9	79	5	2,500	50	0.0	0.0
C- /4.2	10.4	0.90	31.65	428	1	93	5	1	59	139.3	-18.9	79	5	2,500	50	0.0	0.0
C /5.1	10.5	0.90	44.11	177	1	93	5	1	59	154.1	-18.5	85	5	0	0	0.0	0.0
C /5.0	10.5	0.90	41.77	79	1	93	5	1	59	149.4	-18.6	84	5	0	0	0.0	0.0
C /4.8	10.4	0.90	39.64	47	1	93	5	1	59	145.2	-18.7	82	5	0	0	0.0	0.0
C+ /6.5	10.4	0.90	44.13	241	1	93	5	1	59	151.0	-18.6	85	5	0	0	0.0	0.0
U /	N/A	N/A	10.37	32	0	0	0	100	146	N/A	N/A	N/A	3	0	0	0.0	0.0
U /	N/A	N/A	10.19	44	0	0	0	100	189	N/A	N/A	N/A	N/A	0	0	0.0	0.0
U /	N/A	N/A	10.18	318	0	0	0	100	189	N/A	N/A	N/A	N/A	0	0	0.0	0.0
U /	N/A	N/A	10.38	38	14	39	46	1	83	N/A	N/A	N/A	3	0	0	0.0	0.0
U /	N/A	N/A	10.47	76	6	49	43	2	81	N/A	N/A	N/A	3	0	0	0.0	0.0
U /	N/A	N/A	10.55	111	17	53	29	1	75	N/A	N/A	N/A	3	0	0	0.0	0.0
U /	N/A	N/A	10.69	77	5	68	26	1	72	N/A	N/A	N/A	3	0	0	0.0	0.0
U /	N/A	N/A	10.77	68	15	69	15	1	74	N/A	N/A	N/A	3	0	0	0.0	0.0
U /	N/A	N/A	10.76	48	13	75	10	2	69	N/A	N/A	N/A	3	0	0	0.0	0.0
U /	N/A	N/A	10.83	39	11	78	9	2	67	N/A	N/A	N/A	3	0	0	0.0	0.0
C+ /6.9	9.7	0.90	5.76	1,249	0	91	8	1	72	127.2	-16.1	64	13	2,500	50	4.3	0.0
C+ /6.9	9.7	0.90	5.80	123	0	91	8	1	72	130.1	-15.8	67	13	0	0	0.0	0.0
B- /7.1	9.7	0.90	5.78	18	0	91	8	1	72	117.7	-16.2	55	13	2,500	50	0.0	0.0
B- /7.0	9.7	0.90	5.74	206	0	91	8	1	72	118.2	-16.4	54	13	2,500	50	0.0	0.0

Fund Type	Fund Name	Ticker Symbol	Overall Investment Rating	Phone	Performance Rating/Pts	3 Mo	6 Mo	1Yr / Pct	3Yr / Pct	5Yr / Pct	Dividend Yield	Expense Ratio
	99 Pct = Best							Total Return % through 2/28/17			Incl. in Returns	
	0 Pct = Worst								Annualized			
GI	AB Relative Value I	CBBIX	A	(800) 221-5672	B / 8.2	6.06	10.55	21.47 /60	9.00 /87	13.15 /85	1.95	0.68
GI	AB Relative Value K	CBBKX	A-	(800) 221-5672	B / 7.9	5.92	10.32	21.02 /57	8.66 /84	12.83 /82	1.73	1.01
GI	AB Relative Value R	CBBRX	A-	(800) 221-5672	B / 7.7	5.88	10.32	20.89 /57	8.37 /82	12.53 /79	1.49	1.31
GI	AB Relative Value Z	CBBZX	A+	(800) 221-5672	B / 8.1	5.92	10.40	21.31 /59	8.93 /86	13.01 /84	1.81	0.59
GR	AB Select US Eq A	AUUAX	B	(800) 221-5672	B- / 7.2	7.07	8.55	20.41 /54	8.87 /86	12.98 /83	0.00	1.45
GR	AB Select US Eq Adv	AUUYX	B+	(800) 221-5672	B / 8.1	7.13	8.67	20.69 /56	9.14 /88	13.29 /87	0.54	1.20
GR	AB Select US Eq C	AUUCX	B	(800) 221-5672	B- / 7.3	6.85	8.16	19.53 /50	8.08 /79	12.17 /76	0.00	2.20
GR	AB Select US Eq I	AUUIX	B+	(800) 221-5672	B / 8.1	7.13	8.68	20.73 /56	9.14 /88	13.26 /86	0.54	1.18
GR	AB Select US Eq K	AUUKX	B+	(800) 221-5672	B / 7.8	7.03	8.52	20.34 /54	8.77 /85	12.92 /83	0.20	1.60
GR	AB Select US Eq R	AUURX	B	(800) 221-5672	B / 7.7	6.89	8.39	20.01 /52	8.58 /84	12.67 /81	0.10	1.72
GR	AB Select US LS A	ASLAX	C-	(800) 221-5672	D / 1.9	3.43	3.69	10.33 /12	2.74 /29	--	0.00	2.16
GR	AB Select US LS Adv	ASYLX	C	(800) 221-5672	D+ / 2.6	3.47	3.83	10.60 /13	2.97 /31	--	0.00	1.91
GR	AB Select US LS C	ASCLX	C-	(800) 221-5672	D / 2.0	3.18	3.36	9.46 /10	1.98 /24	--	0.00	2.91
GR	AB Select US LS I	ASILX	C	(800) 221-5672	D+ / 2.6	3.56	3.91	10.68 /13	3.06 /32	--	0.00	1.87
GR	AB Select US LS K	ASLKX	C-	(800) 221-5672	D+ / 2.4	3.42	3.69	10.32 /12	2.77 /30	--	0.00	2.14
GR	AB Select US LS R	ASRLX	C-	(800) 221-5672	D+ / 2.3	3.28	3.55	10.04 /12	2.50 /27	--	0.00	2.45
SC	● AB Sm Cap Growth A	QUASX	D-	(800) 221-5672	C / 4.5	6.78	11.36	32.84 /91	1.03 /18	10.24 /60	0.00	1.28
SC	● AB Sm Cap Growth Adv	QUAYX	D	(800) 221-5672	C+ / 5.7	6.83	11.48	33.14 /92	1.28 /20	10.53 /62	0.00	1.02
SC	● AB Sm Cap Growth B	QUABX	E+	(800) 221-5672	C / 4.7	6.56	11.09	31.81 /90	0.20 /14	9.35 /53	0.00	2.08
SC	● AB Sm Cap Growth C	QUACX	E+	(800) 221-5672	C / 4.8	6.58	10.95	31.81 /90	0.26 /15	9.42 /54	0.00	2.03
SC	● AB Sm Cap Growth I	QUAIX	D	(800) 221-5672	C+ / 5.7	6.84	11.50	33.24 /92	1.36 /20	10.62 /63	0.00	0.92
SC	● AB Sm Cap Growth K	QUAKX	D-	(800) 221-5672	C / 5.5	6.80	11.38	32.92 /91	1.05 /18	10.29 /60	0.00	1.23
SC	● AB Sm Cap Growth R	QUARX	D-	(800) 221-5672	C / 5.2	6.69	11.20	32.49 /91	0.72 /17	9.93 /58	0.00	1.56
SC	AB Sm Cap Growth Z	QUAZX	U	(800) 221-5672	U /	6.85	11.56	33.39 /92	--	--	0.00	0.85
SC	AB Sm Cap Value A	SCAVX	U	(800) 221-5672	U /	3.00	14.40	36.15 /95	--	--	0.00	1.89
SC	AB Sm Cap Value Adv	SCYVX	U	(800) 221-5672	U /	3.07	14.51	36.45 /95	--	--	0.00	1.64
GR	AB Small Cap Core Adv	SCRYX	U	(800) 221-5672	U /	3.06	13.30	29.40 /85	--	--	0.25	N/A
GR	AB Small Cap Core Z	SCRZX	U	(800) 221-5672	U /	3.00	13.23	29.32 /85	--	--	0.28	0.90
TC	AB Sustainable Global Thematic A	ALTFX	C-	(800) 221-5672	C / 5.1	8.30	4.45	24.69 /72	4.71 /51	7.33 /37	3.56	1.45
TC	AB Sustainable Global Thematic Adv	ATEYX	C+	(800) 221-5672	C+ / 6.2	8.36	4.59	25.00 /73	4.99 /54	7.63 /39	3.83	1.20
TC	● AB Sustainable Global Thematic B	ATEBX	C	(800) 221-5672	C / 5.3	8.09	4.16	23.71 /69	3.86 /41	6.47 /31	3.54	2.28
TC	AB Sustainable Global Thematic C	ATECX	C	(800) 221-5672	C / 5.3	8.09	4.05	23.74 /69	3.92 /42	6.53 /32	3.77	2.21
TC	AB Sustainable Global Thematic I	AGTIX	C+	(800) 221-5672	C+ / 6.4	8.43	4.71	25.32 /74	5.24 /57	7.91 /41	4.00	0.94
TC	AB Sustainable Global Thematic K	ATEKX	C+	(800) 221-5672	C+ / 6.1	8.33	4.51	24.84 /73	4.86 /53	7.52 /38	3.81	1.31
TC	AB Sustainable Global Thematic R	ATERX	C	(800) 221-5672	C+ / 5.8	8.24	4.36	24.45 /71	4.54 /49	7.19 /36	3.60	1.61
AA	AB Tax-Mgd Bal Wealth Strat A	AGIAX	C-	(800) 221-5672	D / 1.6	4.12	2.07	7.87 / 7	2.50 /27	4.10 /16	1.33	1.36
AA	AB Tax-Mgd Bal Wealth Strat Adv	AGIYX	C-	(800) 221-5672	D / 2.2	4.17	2.20	8.08 / 8	2.76 /30	4.38 /17	1.66	1.11
AA	● AB Tax-Mgd Bal Wealth Strat B	AGIBX	C-	(800) 221-5672	D / 1.7	3.89	1.62	7.02 / 6	1.71 /22	3.32 /12	0.00	2.11
AA	AB Tax-Mgd Bal Wealth Strat C	AGICX	C-	(800) 221-5672	D / 1.7	3.89	1.68	6.95 / 6	1.72 /22	3.34 /12	0.57	2.11
FO	AB Tax-Mgd Intl Port A	ABXAX	D-	(800) 221-5672	E+ / 0.8	6.23	1.80	12.26 /19	-0.33 /12	3.67 /14	1.72	1.59
FO	● AB Tax-Mgd Intl Port B	ABXBX	D-	(800) 221-5672	E+ / 0.9	6.02	1.44	11.44 /16	-1.06 / 9	2.90 /10	1.01	2.35
FO	AB Tax-Mgd Intl Port C	ABXCX	D-	(800) 221-5672	E+ / 0.9	6.05	1.49	11.45 /16	-1.06 / 9	2.92 /10	0.92	2.34
FO	AB Tax-Mgd Intl Port Z	ABXZX	U		U /	6.34	1.98	12.52 /20	--	--	2.03	N/A
GR	AB Tax-Mgd Wlth App Strat A	ATWAX	C-	(800) 221-5672	C- / 4.1	6.73	6.38	18.39 /45	4.35 /47	8.20 /44	1.76	1.25
GR	AB Tax-Mgd Wlth App Strat Adv	ATWYX	C	(800) 221-5672	C / 5.1	6.77	6.48	18.63 /46	4.60 /50	8.48 /46	2.08	1.00
GR	● AB Tax-Mgd Wlth App Strat B	ATWBX	C-	(800) 221-5672	C / 4.3	6.52	5.94	17.53 /41	3.57 /38	7.40 /37	0.90	2.01
GR	AB Tax-Mgd Wlth App Strat C	ATWCX	C-	(800) 221-5672	C / 4.3	6.53	5.95	17.53 /41	3.57 /38	7.41 /37	1.13	2.00
IN	AB Value A	ABVAX	C+	(800) 221-5672	C+ / 5.8	5.54	10.98	22.32 /64	5.75 /62	11.13 /67	1.02	0.98
IN	AB Value Adv	ABVYX	C+	(800) 221-5672	C+ / 6.8	5.65	11.09	22.62 /65	6.03 /64	11.46 /69	1.31	0.73
IN	● AB Value B	ABVBX	C+	(800) 221-5672	C+ / 6.6	5.56	10.98	22.37 /64	5.71 /62	11.09 /67	0.96	1.78
IN	AB Value C	ABVCX	C+	(800) 221-5672	C+ / 6.0	5.41	10.55	21.41 /59	4.99 /54	10.35 /61	0.38	1.73
IN	AB Value I	ABVIX	C+	(800) 221-5672	C+ / 6.9	5.60	11.08	22.61 /65	6.09 /65	11.52 /70	1.36	0.69

● Denotes fund is closed to new investors
∗ Denotes fund is included in Section II

RISK Risk Rating/Pts	3 Year Standard Deviation	3 Year Beta	NET ASSETS NAV As of 2/28/17	NET ASSETS Total $(Mil)	ASSET Cash %	ASSET Stocks %	ASSET Bonds %	ASSET Other %	Portfolio Turnover Ratio	BULL/BEAR Last Bull Market Return	BULL/BEAR Last Bear Market Return	FUND MANAGER Manager Quality Pct	FUND MANAGER Manager Tenure (Years)	MINIMUMS Initial Purch. $	MINIMUMS Additional Purch. $	LOADS Front End Load	LOADS Back End Load
C+ / 6.9	9.6	0.90	5.85	26	0	91	8	1	72	131.2	-15.9	69	13	0	0	0.0	0.0
C+ / 6.9	9.6	0.90	5.71	8	0	91	8	1	72	127.2	-15.9	64	13	0	0	0.0	0.0
C+ / 6.9	9.6	0.90	5.67	10	0	91	8	1	72	123.7	-16.0	61	13	0	0	0.0	0.0
B- / 7.5	9.6	0.90	5.85	68	0	91	8	1	72	129.7	-16.1	68	13	0	0	0.0	0.0
C+ / 6.0	9.9	0.92	15.96	13	3	96	0	1	269	N/A	N/A	64	6	2,500	50	4.3	0.0
C+ / 6.0	9.9	0.93	15.93	249	3	96	0	1	269	N/A	N/A	67	6	0	0	0.0	0.0
C+ / 5.9	9.9	0.92	15.35	12	3	96	0	1	269	N/A	N/A	55	6	2,500	50	0.0	0.0
C+ / 5.9	9.9	0.92	15.79	18	3	96	0	1	269	N/A	N/A	67	6	0	0	0.0	0.0
C+ / 6.0	9.9	0.92	15.76	3	3	96	0	1	269	N/A	N/A	63	6	0	0	0.0	0.0
C+ / 6.0	9.9	0.92	15.66	N/A	3	96	0	1	269	N/A	N/A	61	6	0	0	0.0	0.0
B- / 7.9	5.9	0.54	12.07	138	38	61	0	1	519	N/A	N/A	36	5	2,500	50	4.3	0.0
B / 8.0	5.9	0.54	12.21	709	38	61	0	1	519	N/A	N/A	40	5	0	0	0.0	0.0
B- / 7.8	5.9	0.54	11.69	122	38	61	0	1	519	N/A	N/A	28	5	2,500	50	0.0	0.0
B / 8.0	5.9	0.54	12.23	12	38	61	0	1	519	N/A	N/A	40	5	0	0	0.0	0.0
B- / 7.9	6.0	0.55	12.08	N/A	38	61	0	1	519	N/A	N/A	36	5	0	0	0.0	0.0
B- / 7.9	5.9	0.54	11.95	N/A	38	61	0	1	519	N/A	N/A	33	5	0	0	0.0	0.0
D / 1.7	18.5	1.07	44.97	365	0	99	0	1	70	115.5	-24.4	8	13	2,500	50	4.3	0.0
D / 1.8	18.5	1.07	48.43	268	0	99	0	1	70	118.5	-24.3	9	13	0	0	0.0	0.0
D- / 1.0	18.5	1.07	30.84	2	0	99	0	1	70	106.1	-24.6	6	13	2,500	50	0.0	0.0
D- / 1.0	18.5	1.07	31.21	38	0	99	0	1	70	106.9	-24.6	6	13	2,500	50	0.0	0.0
D / 1.8	18.5	1.07	48.24	302	0	99	0	1	70	119.6	-24.2	10	13	0	0	0.0	0.0
D / 1.7	18.5	1.07	45.98	43	0	99	0	1	70	116.0	-24.3	8	13	0	0	0.0	0.0
D / 1.6	18.5	1.07	43.95	36	0	99	0	1	70	112.2	-24.4	7	13	0	0	0.0	0.0
U /	N/A	N/A	48.32	69	0	99	0	1	70	N/A	N/A	N/A	17	0	0	0.0	0.0
U /	N/A	N/A	12.96	163	0	0	0	100	43	N/A	N/A	N/A	3	2,500	50	4.3	0.0
U /	N/A	N/A	13.03	33	0	0	0	100	43	N/A	N/A	N/A	3	0	0	0.0	0.0
U /	N/A	N/A	11.72	665	0	0	0	100	88	N/A	N/A	N/A	2	5,000	0	0.0	0.0
U /	N/A	N/A	11.71	141	0	0	0	100	88	N/A	N/A	N/A	2	0	0	0.0	0.0
C / 5.3	13.6	1.11	93.36	497	1	96	2	1	40	71.2	-29.9	6	4	2,500	50	4.3	0.0
C / 5.3	13.6	1.11	98.54	81	1	96	2	1	40	73.8	-29.8	7	4	0	0	0.0	0.0
C / 5.3	13.6	1.11	77.39	10	1	96	2	1	40	63.9	-30.1	5	4	2,500	50	0.0	0.0
C / 5.3	13.6	1.11	77.85	63	1	96	2	1	40	64.5	-30.1	5	4	2,500	50	0.0	0.0
C / 5.3	13.6	1.11	98.68	1	1	96	2	1	40	76.4	-29.7	8	4	0	0	0.0	0.0
C / 5.3	13.6	1.11	95.35	10	1	96	2	1	40	73.0	-29.8	7	4	0	0	0.0	0.0
C / 5.3	13.6	1.11	92.45	3	1	96	2	1	40	70.1	-29.9	6	4	0	0	0.0	0.0
B / 8.3	4.4	0.66	13.21	69	7	35	56	2	25	35.8	-9.1	43	25	2,500	50	4.3	0.0
B / 8.2	4.4	0.66	13.23	40	7	35	56	2	25	37.8	-8.9	46	25	0	0	0.0	0.0
B / 8.4	4.5	0.67	13.41	1	7	35	56	2	25	30.6	-9.4	32	25	2,500	50	0.0	0.0
B / 8.3	4.4	0.66	13.26	24	7	35	56	2	25	30.6	-9.4	33	25	2,500	50	0.0	0.0
C+ / 6.2	11.0	0.86	15.34	2	2	97	0	1	69	37.9	-25.8	72	6	2,500	50	4.3	0.0
C+ / 6.3	11.0	0.86	15.54	N/A	2	97	0	1	69	32.4	-26.1	63	6	2,500	50	0.0	0.0
C+ / 6.3	11.0	0.86	15.41	N/A	2	97	0	1	69	32.6	-26.1	63	6	2,500	50	0.0	0.0
U /	N/A	N/A	15.35	340	2	97	0	1	69	N/A	N/A	N/A	6	0	0	0.0	0.0
C+ / 5.7	9.8	0.91	15.59	32	6	84	8	2	47	79.3	-21.7	15	24	2,500	50	4.3	0.0
C+ / 5.7	9.8	0.91	15.63	644	6	84	8	2	47	82.0	-21.6	17	24	0	0	0.0	0.0
C+ / 5.8	9.8	0.91	15.50	1	6	84	8	2	47	72.2	-21.9	11	24	2,500	50	0.0	0.0
C+ / 5.8	9.8	0.91	15.37	14	6	84	8	2	47	72.5	-21.9	11	24	2,500	50	0.0	0.0
C+ / 6.4	12.0	1.09	14.92	51	0	99	0	1	91	106.8	-21.4	12	8	2,500	50	4.3	0.0
C+ / 6.4	12.0	1.09	14.92	334	0	99	0	1	91	110.1	-21.2	14	8	0	0	0.0	0.0
C+ / 6.4	12.0	1.09	14.99	1	0	99	0	1	91	106.3	-21.4	12	8	2,500	50	0.0	0.0
C+ / 6.4	12.0	1.09	14.90	15	0	99	0	1	91	99.1	-21.6	8	8	2,500	50	0.0	0.0
C+ / 6.4	12.0	1.09	14.79	3	0	99	0	1	91	110.7	-21.2	14	8	0	0	0.0	0.0

Fund Type	Fund Name	Ticker Symbol	Overall Investment Rating	Phone	PERFORMANCE Performance Rating/Pts	Total Return % through 2/28/17 3 Mo	6 Mo	1Yr / Pct	Annualized 3Yr / Pct	5Yr / Pct	Incl. in Returns Dividend Yield	Expense Ratio
	99 Pct = Best											
	0 Pct = Worst											
IN	AB Value K	ABVKX	C+	(800) 221-5672	C+ / 6.6	5.57	10.87	22.21 /63	5.65 /61	11.07 /66	1.01	1.11
IN	AB Value R	ABVRX	C+	(800) 221-5672	C+ / 6.3	5.48	10.72	21.85 /61	5.34 /58	10.74 /64	0.63	1.41
GR	AB Wealth Appreciation Strat A	AWAAX	C-	(800) 221-5672	C- / 3.7	6.19	6.47	18.69 /46	3.72 /39	7.31 /37	2.94	1.43
GR	AB Wealth Appreciation Strat Adv	AWAYX	C	(800) 221-5672	C / 4.8	6.27	6.62	19.05 /47	4.00 /43	7.60 /39	3.32	1.18
GR	● AB Wealth Appreciation Strat B	AWABX	C-	(800) 221-5672	C- / 3.9	5.99	6.06	17.78 /42	2.94 /31	6.52 /32	1.87	2.18
GR	AB Wealth Appreciation Strat C	AWACX	C-	(800) 221-5672	C- / 3.9	5.94	6.01	17.83 /42	2.94 /31	6.51 /32	2.30	2.18
GR	AB Wealth Appreciation Strat I	AWAIX	C	(800) 221-5672	C / 4.7	6.23	6.51	18.94 /47	3.92 /42	7.54 /39	3.28	1.23
GR	AB Wealth Appreciation Strat K	AWAKX	C	(800) 221-5672	C / 4.4	6.17	6.38	18.58 /45	3.60 /38	7.20 /36	2.96	1.54
GR	AB Wealth Appreciation Strat R	AWARX	C-	(800) 221-5672	C- / 4.2	6.11	6.26	18.20 /44	3.26 /34	6.88 /34	2.65	1.87
GL	Abbey Capital Futures Strategy I	ABYIX	U	(844) 261-6484	U /	1.83	-1.10	-7.31 / 0	--	--	0.00	2.17
FO	Aberdeen Asia-Pac X-Japan Eq Inst	AAPIX	C-	(866) 667-9231	C / 5.0	9.06	5.32	28.99 /84	1.78 /23	2.27 / 9	0.00	1.27
FO	Aberdeen Asia-Pac X-Japan Eq IS	AAPEX	C-	(866) 667-9231	C / 4.9	8.96	5.23	29.02 /84	1.76 /22	2.23 / 9	0.00	1.30
FO	Aberdeen Asia-Pacific X-Japan Eq A	APJAX	D	(866) 667-9231	C- / 3.6	8.99	5.15	28.86 /84	1.57 /21	2.05 / 8	0.00	1.51
FO	Aberdeen Asia-Pacific X-Japan Eq C	APJCX	D+	(866) 667-9231	C- / 4.2	8.89	4.81	27.93 /81	0.88 /18	1.33 / 7	0.00	2.27
FO	Aberdeen Asia-Pacific X-Japan Eq R	APJRX	D+	(866) 667-9231	C / 4.6	8.93	5.07	28.57 /83	1.33 /20	1.78 / 8	0.00	1.73
FO	Aberdeen China Oppty A	GOPAX	D	(866) 667-9231	D+ / 2.6	5.05	5.80	22.38 /64	1.69 /22	-0.51 / 4	0.97	2.50
FO	Aberdeen China Oppty C	GOPCX	D	(866) 667-9231	C- / 3.1	4.92	5.41	21.63 /60	0.98 /18	-1.22 / 3	0.00	3.24
FO	Aberdeen China Oppty Inst	GOPIX	D+	(866) 667-9231	C- / 3.8	5.21	5.96	22.90 /66	1.97 /24	-0.24 / 4	1.29	2.21
FO	Aberdeen China Oppty Inst Svc	GOPSX	D+	(866) 667-9231	C- / 3.8	5.17	5.92	22.58 /65	1.92 /23	-0.28 / 4	1.20	2.24
FO	Aberdeen China Oppty R	GOPRX	D+	(866) 667-9231	C- / 3.3	5.01	5.66	22.15 /63	1.33 /20	-0.87 / 4	0.78	2.78
AA	Aberdeen Diversified Alt A	GASAX	C-	(866) 667-9231	E+ / 0.6	1.75	1.29	4.27 / 3	0.35 /15	3.52 /13	0.31	2.33
AA	Aberdeen Diversified Alt C	GAMCX	C-	(866) 667-9231	E+ / 0.7	1.67	1.00	3.75 / 3	-0.29 /12	2.82 /10	0.09	3.05
AA	Aberdeen Diversified Alt Inst	GASIX	C-	(866) 667-9231	D- / 1.1	1.91	1.53	4.68 / 4	0.67 /16	3.85 /14	0.60	2.03
AA	Aberdeen Diversified Alt R	GASRX	C-	(866) 667-9231	E+ / 0.9	1.66	1.18	4.02 / 3	0.07 /14	3.18 /11	0.22	2.58
AA	Aberdeen Diversified Inc A	GMAAX	D+	(866) 667-9231	D / 2.2	4.57	3.05	13.43 /23	3.44 /36	4.69 /19	2.78	1.77
AA	Aberdeen Diversified Inc C	GMACX	C-	(866) 667-9231	D+ / 2.6	4.45	2.70	12.71 /21	2.72 /29	3.95 /15	2.29	2.52
AA	Aberdeen Diversified Inc Inst	GMAIX	C-	(866) 667-9231	C- / 3.4	4.64	3.20	13.85 /25	3.76 /40	5.00 /21	3.22	1.50
AA	Aberdeen Diversified Inc R	GMRRX	C-	(866) 667-9231	D+ / 2.9	4.52	2.82	13.15 /22	3.04 /32	4.26 /17	2.69	2.08
AA	Aberdeen Dynamic Alloc A	GMMAX	C-	(866) 667-9231	D / 1.8	4.27	2.50	11.31 /15	2.84 /30	5.04 /21	1.81	1.83
AA	Aberdeen Dynamic Alloc C	GMMCX	C-	(866) 667-9231	D / 2.1	4.05	2.20	10.63 /13	2.12 /25	4.28 /17	1.29	2.59
AA	Aberdeen Dynamic Alloc Inst	GMMIX	C	(866) 667-9231	D+ / 2.8	4.41	2.80	11.78 /17	3.16 /33	5.37 /24	2.07	1.64
AA	Aberdeen Dynamic Alloc R	GAGRX	C-	(866) 667-9231	D+ / 2.3	4.21	2.40	11.00 /14	2.43 /27	4.66 /19	1.59	2.14
EM	● Aberdeen Emerging Markets A	GEGAX	D-	(866) 667-9231	D+ / 2.6	7.98	1.21	24.56 /72	1.50 /21	0.08 / 4	0.78	1.49
EM	● Aberdeen Emerging Markets C	GEGCX	D	(866) 667-9231	C- / 3.1	7.84	0.92	23.85 /69	0.85 /17	-0.57 / 4	0.21	2.24
EM	● Aberdeen Emerging Markets Inst	ABEMX	D	(866) 667-9231	C- / 3.9	8.09	1.41	25.07 /73	1.84 /23	0.43 / 5	1.15	1.13
EM	● Aberdeen Emerging Markets Inst Svc	AEMSX	D	(866) 667-9231	C- / 3.8	8.10	1.33	24.90 /73	1.64 /22	0.20 / 5	1.01	1.24
EM	● Aberdeen Emerging Markets R	GEMRX	D	(866) 667-9231	C- / 3.4	7.89	1.07	24.35 /71	1.15 /19	-0.23 / 4	0.70	1.74
GR	Aberdeen Equity Long-Short A	MLSAX	E+	(866) 667-9231	D- / 1.3	2.13	3.06	8.70 / 9	1.98 /24	2.56 / 9	0.00	3.11
GR	Aberdeen Equity Long-Short C	MLSCX	E-	(866) 667-9231	D- / 1.5	1.77	2.59	7.82 / 7	1.24 /19	1.83 / 8	0.00	3.89
GR	Aberdeen Equity Long-Short Inst	GGUIX	D-	(866) 667-9231	D / 1.9	2.05	3.16	8.95 / 9	2.27 /26	2.88 /10	0.00	2.83
GR	Aberdeen Equity Long-Short Inst Svc	AELSX	E+	(866) 667-9231	D / 1.8	2.08	2.99	8.75 / 9	2.04 /24	2.63 /10	0.00	2.89
GR	Aberdeen Equity Long-Short R	GLSRX	E+	(866) 667-9231	D / 1.6	1.91	2.77	8.24 / 8	1.56 /21	2.12 / 8	0.00	3.39
GL	Aberdeen Global Equity A	GLLAX	D-	(866) 667-9231	D- / 1.0	7.63	3.70	18.69 /46	-0.21 /13	3.59 /13	0.66	1.58
GL	Aberdeen Global Equity C	GLLCX	D-	(866) 667-9231	D- / 1.3	7.42	3.35	17.82 /42	-0.85 /10	2.91 /10	0.45	2.36
GL	Aberdeen Global Equity Inst	GWLIX	D	(866) 667-9231	D+ / 2.5	7.73	3.89	19.07 /47	0.14 /14	3.74 /14	1.02	1.23
GL	Aberdeen Global Equity IS	GLLSX	D	(866) 667-9231	D+ / 2.5	7.65	3.86	19.06 /47	0.12 /14	3.97 /15	1.02	1.28
GL	Aberdeen Global Equity R	GWLRX	D-	(866) 667-9231	D- / 1.4	7.47	3.56	18.32 /44	-0.55 /11	3.30 /12	0.77	1.86
GL	Aberdeen International Sm Cap A	WVCCX	D-	(866) 667-9231	D+ / 2.3	5.45	1.12	16.76 /37	3.00 /32	6.79 /33	0.50	1.81
GL	Aberdeen International Sm Cap C	CPVCX	D-	(866) 667-9231	D+ / 2.7	5.29	0.81	16.00 /34	2.28 /26	6.06 /29	0.00	2.63
GL	Aberdeen International Sm Cap Inst	ABNIX	D	(866) 667-9231	C- / 3.4	5.56	1.31	17.16 /39	3.32 /35	7.13 /35	0.82	1.56
GL	Aberdeen International Sm Cap IS	AGISX	D	(866) 667-9231	C- / 3.3	5.54	1.21	17.00 /38	3.09 /33	6.89 /34	0.18	1.63
GL	Aberdeen International Sm Cap R	WPVAX	D	(866) 667-9231	C- / 3.0	5.36	0.95	16.40 /36	2.67 /29	6.50 /31	0.42	2.13

● Denotes fund is closed to new investors
* Denotes fund is included in Section II

www.thestreetratings.com

RISK Rating/Pts	3 Year Standard Deviation	Beta	NAV As of 2/28/17	Total $(Mil)	Cash %	Stocks %	Bonds %	Other %	Portfolio Turnover Ratio	Last Bull Market Return	Last Bear Market Return	Manager Quality Pct	Manager Tenure (Years)	Initial Purch. $	Additional Purch. $	Front End Load	Back End Load
C+ / 6.4	12.0	1.09	14.66	12	0	99	0	1	91	106.1	-21.4	11	8	0	0	0.0	0.0
C+ / 6.4	12.0	1.09	14.82	1	0	99	0	1	91	102.9	-21.5	10	8	0	0	0.0	0.0
C+ / 6.3	9.7	0.90	15.15	353	7	82	9	2	9	72.8	-22.7	12	14	2,500	50	4.3	0.0
C+ / 6.2	9.8	0.90	15.11	857	7	82	9	2	9	75.3	-22.6	14	14	0	0	0.0	0.0
C+ / 6.4	9.7	0.90	15.29	9	7	82	9	2	9	66.0	-23.0	8	14	2,500	50	0.0	0.0
C+ / 6.3	9.8	0.90	15.09	92	7	82	9	2	9	66.1	-23.0	8	14	2,500	50	0.0	0.0
C+ / 6.2	9.7	0.90	15.08	2	7	82	9	2	9	75.1	-22.7	13	14	0	0	0.0	0.0
C+ / 6.3	9.7	0.90	15.06	13	7	82	9	2	9	71.9	-22.7	11	14	0	0	0.0	0.0
C+ / 6.3	9.7	0.90	15.06	4	7	82	9	2	9	69.1	-22.8	9	14	0	0	0.0	0.0
U /	N/A	N/A	11.67	808	0	0	0	100	0	N/A	N/A	N/A	3	1,000,000	1,000	0.0	0.0
C / 4.6	14.9	0.97	11.08	9	1	98	0	1	40	33.1	-19.1	86	22	1,000,000	0	0.0	0.0
C / 4.6	14.8	0.97	11.07	2	1	98	0	1	40	33.0	-19.2	86	22	1,000,000	0	0.0	0.0
C / 4.6	14.8	0.97	11.03	1	1	98	0	1	40	N/A	N/A	85	22	1,000	50	5.8	0.0
C / 4.6	14.9	0.98	10.90	N/A	1	98	0	1	40	N/A	N/A	81	22	1,000	50	0.0	0.0
C / 4.6	14.8	0.97	10.98	N/A	1	98	0	1	40	N/A	N/A	84	22	0	0	0.0	0.0
C / 5.1	14.6	0.92	19.00	7	2	97	0	1	16	18.1	-20.1	85	8	1,000	50	5.8	0.0
C / 5.1	14.6	0.92	18.33	3	2	97	0	1	16	13.6	-20.3	82	8	1,000	50	0.0	0.0
C / 5.1	14.7	0.91	19.10	1	2	97	0	1	16	19.8	-20.0	87	8	1,000,000	0	0.0	0.0
C / 5.1	14.6	0.91	19.08	1	2	97	0	1	16	19.6	-20.0	86	8	1,000,000	0	0.0	0.0
C / 5.1	14.7	0.92	18.70	2	2	97	0	1	16	15.9	-20.2	84	8	0	0	0.0	0.0
B+ / 9.1	3.5	0.50	12.72	13	38	26	34	2	36	36.6	-17.9	30	N/A	1,000	50	5.8	0.0
B+ / 9.1	3.5	0.50	12.19	9	38	26	34	2	36	31.6	-18.2	24	N/A	1,000	50	0.0	0.0
B+ / 9.1	3.5	0.50	12.85	23	38	26	34	2	36	38.8	-17.9	34	N/A	1,000,000	0	0.0	0.0
B+ / 9.1	3.4	0.50	12.59	2	38	26	34	2	36	34.1	-18.0	28	N/A	0	0	0.0	0.0
B- / 7.1	5.6	0.81	12.05	5	4	40	54	2	21	40.2	-12.1	41	11	1,000	50	5.8	0.0
B- / 7.1	5.6	0.81	11.78	12	4	40	54	2	21	35.1	-12.5	32	11	1,000	50	0.0	0.0
B- / 7.1	5.6	0.81	12.05	1	4	40	54	2	21	42.6	-12.1	45	11	1,000,000	0	0.0	0.0
B- / 7.0	5.7	0.82	11.92	N/A	4	40	54	2	21	37.1	-12.3	35	11	0	0	0.0	0.0
B / 8.1	6.5	0.96	13.12	7	8	47	44	1	40	45.5	-15.0	22	2	1,000	50	5.8	0.0
B / 8.1	6.5	0.97	12.84	9	8	47	44	1	40	39.9	-15.2	16	2	1,000	50	0.0	0.0
B / 8.1	6.5	0.96	13.10	1	8	47	44	1	40	48.0	-14.9	25	2	1,000,000	0	0.0	0.0
B / 8.1	6.5	0.96	13.04	1	8	47	44	1	40	42.7	-15.0	19	2	0	0	0.0	0.0
C / 4.3	15.5	0.90	13.43	177	1	98	0	1	9	22.0	-18.2	73	10	1,000	50	5.8	0.0
C- / 4.2	15.5	0.90	13.32	24	1	98	0	1	9	17.7	-18.4	66	10	1,000	50	0.0	0.0
C- / 4.2	15.5	0.90	13.45	7,466	1	98	0	1	9	24.3	-18.1	76	10	1,000,000	0	0.0	0.0
C- / 4.2	15.5	0.90	13.44	299	1	98	0	1	9	22.8	-18.3	74	10	1,000,000	0	0.0	0.0
C- / 4.2	15.5	0.90	13.34	55	1	98	0	1	9	20.0	-18.2	69	10	0	0	0.0	0.0
C- / 4.1	5.8	0.51	8.05	10	60	39	0	1	36	23.4	-9.1	32	18	1,000	50	5.8	0.0
D- / 1.5	5.8	0.50	4.00	3	60	39	0	1	36	18.8	-9.4	25	18	1,000	50	0.0	0.0
C / 4.3	5.8	0.50	8.43	36	60	39	0	1	36	25.5	-9.0	36	18	1,000,000	0	0.0	0.0
C- / 4.2	5.8	0.50	8.25	1	60	39	0	1	36	23.9	-9.0	33	18	1,000,000	0	0.0	0.0
C- / 3.7	5.8	0.50	7.46	3	60	39	0	1	36	20.7	-9.1	28	18	0	0	0.0	0.0
C+ / 5.7	11.1	0.77	12.96	57	1	98	0	1	22	40.3	-17.6	73	8	1,000	50	5.8	0.0
C+ / 5.7	11.1	0.77	12.23	3	1	98	0	1	22	35.3	-17.8	65	8	1,000	50	0.0	0.0
C+ / 5.7	11.1	0.77	12.98	38	1	98	0	1	22	41.4	-17.5	76	8	1,000,000	0	0.0	0.0
C+ / 5.8	11.1	0.77	13.12	1	1	98	0	1	22	43.0	-17.6	76	8	1,000,000	0	0.0	0.0
C+ / 5.7	11.1	0.77	12.44	3	1	98	0	1	22	38.2	-17.6	69	8	0	0	0.0	0.0
C / 4.6	11.0	0.76	26.11	49	4	95	0	1	36	61.6	-16.4	91	8	1,000	50	5.8	0.0
C / 4.4	11.0	0.76	24.08	1	4	95	0	1	36	55.7	-16.6	88	8	1,000	50	0.0	0.0
C / 4.6	11.0	0.76	26.13	19	4	95	0	1	36	64.4	-16.2	92	8	1,000,000	0	0.0	0.0
C / 4.6	11.0	0.76	26.26	N/A	4	95	0	1	36	62.5	-16.2	91	8	1,000,000	0	0.0	0.0
C / 4.5	11.0	0.76	24.90	1	4	95	0	1	36	59.2	-16.5	89	8	0	0	0.0	0.0

Fund Type	Fund Name	Ticker Symbol	Overall Investment Rating	Phone	Performance Rating/Pts	3 Mo	6 Mo	1Yr / Pct	3Yr / Pct	5Yr / Pct	Dividend Yield	Expense Ratio
	99 Pct = Best / 0 Pct = Worst							Total Return % through 2/28/17	Annualized		Incl. in Returns	
FO	Aberdeen Intl Equity A	GIGAX	E+	(866) 667-9231	E / 0.4	7.15	2.00	18.12 /43	-2.87 / 5	1.29 / 7	1.21	1.38
FO	Aberdeen Intl Equity C	GIGCX	E+	(866) 667-9231	E+ / 0.6	6.95	1.64	17.24 /39	-3.55 / 4	0.59 / 5	0.61	2.13
FO	Aberdeen Intl Equity Inst	GIGIX	E+	(866) 667-9231	E+ / 0.8	7.30	2.27	18.59 /45	-2.55 / 5	1.62 / 7	1.70	1.02
FO	Aberdeen Intl Equity Inst Svc	GIGSX	E+	(866) 667-9231	E+ / 0.8	7.24	2.19	18.46 /45	-2.68 / 5	1.49 / 7	1.62	1.13
FO	Aberdeen Intl Equity R	GIRRX	E+	(866) 667-9231	E+ / 0.7	7.12	1.90	17.89 /42	-3.14 / 4	1.02 / 6	1.09	1.63
FO	Aberdeen Select Intl Equity A	BJBIX	E+	(866) 667-9231	D / 1.7	13.33	8.01	24.54 /72	-1.69 / 7	1.68 / 7	0.92	1.28
FO	Aberdeen Select Intl Equity I	JIEIX	E+	(866) 667-9231	D / 1.8	13.40	8.16	24.81 /73	-1.44 / 8	1.94 / 8	1.16	1.03
FO	Aberdeen Select Intl Equity II A	JETAX	E+	(866) 667-9231	D- / 1.3	11.01	5.87	21.39 /59	-2.12 / 6	1.60 / 7	1.51	1.38
FO	Aberdeen Select Intl Equity II I	JETIX	E+	(866) 667-9231	D- / 1.4	11.00	5.98	21.64 /60	-1.83 / 7	1.88 / 8	1.79	1.13
GR	Aberdeen US Multi Cap Equity A	GXXAX	C	(866) 667-9231	C+ / 5.7	6.30	7.06	22.93 /66	6.48 /68	9.94 /58	0.11	1.25
GR	Aberdeen US Multi Cap Equity C	GXXCX	C+	(866) 667-9231	C+ / 6.2	6.04	6.60	22.03 /62	5.72 /62	9.17 /52	0.00	2.09
GR	Aberdeen US Multi Cap Equity Inst	GGLIX	B-	(866) 667-9231	B- / 7.0	6.35	7.15	23.21 /67	6.78 /70	10.27 /60	0.30	1.00
GR	Aberdeen US Multi Cap Equity IS	GXXIX	C+	(866) 667-9231	C+ / 6.9	6.30	7.10	23.08 /67	6.68 /70	10.18 /60	0.25	1.08
GR	Aberdeen US Multi Cap Equity R	GGLRX	C+	(866) 667-9231	C+ / 6.5	6.16	6.86	22.36 /64	6.17 /66	9.66 /56	0.00	1.61
SC	Aberdeen US Small Cap Eq A	GSXAX	A+	(866) 667-9231	A- / 9.0	3.51	8.73	26.01 /76	12.62 /98	15.91 /98	0.00	1.48
SC	Aberdeen US Small Cap Eq C	GSXCX	A+	(866) 667-9231	A / 9.3	3.32	8.34	25.12 /74	11.84 /98	15.10 /97	0.00	2.23
SC	Aberdeen US Small Cap Eq Inst	GSCIX	A+	(866) 667-9231	A+ / 9.7	3.61	8.92	26.36 /77	12.98 /99	16.28 /98	0.00	1.22
SC	Aberdeen US Small Cap Eq R	GNSRX	A+	(866) 667-9231	A / 9.5	3.44	8.65	25.68 /75	12.35 /98	15.63 /98	0.00	1.75
SC	Aberdeen US Small Cap Eqty Inst	GSXIX	A+	(866) 667-9231	A+ / 9.7	3.61	8.92	26.38 /77	12.96 /99	16.24 /98	0.00	1.19
IX	Absolute Credit Opportunities Inst	AOFOX	D	(800) 754-8757	D- / 1.0	0.51	0.20	1.56 / 2	1.63 /22	-0.26 / 4	1.67	2.62
GR	Absolute Strategies Inst	ASFIX	D-	(800) 754-8757	E / 0.5	-1.98	-2.64	-3.65 / 1	0.22 /14	0.08 / 4	0.00	2.68
GR	Absolute Strategies R	ASFAX	D-	(800) 754-8757	E / 0.4	-2.15	-2.92	-4.14 / 1	-0.33 /12	-0.41 / 4	0.00	3.26
FO	AC ONE China Fund Institutional	ACOIX	E+	(888) 964-0788	D / 2.1	3.20	1.42	22.01 /62	0.48 /16	--	0.15	3.79
EM	● Acadian Emerging Markets Inv	AEMGX	C	(866) 777-7818	C+ / 6.9	12.52	9.81	35.53 /94	2.79 /30	0.64 / 6	1.81	1.44
GR	ACM Dynamic Opportunity A	ADOAX	U		U /	4.01	2.26	5.04 / 4	--	--	0.00	2.49
GL	ACR Multi-Strategy Qual Ret MQR I	MQRIX	U	(855) 955-9552	U /	2.82	3.32	10.63 /13	--	--	0.00	3.40
FO	Acuitas International Sm Cap Inst	AISCX	U		U /	6.78	5.63	17.42 /40	--	--	2.00	2.16
SC	Acuitas US Microcap Inst	AFMCX	U		U /	-0.25	8.76	26.47 /78	--	--	0.00	2.06
GL	Adalta International Fund	BMGEX	D+	(800) 943-6786	C- / 3.2	8.47	6.10	17.00 /38	1.95 /24	3.52 /13	1.08	2.14
SC	Adirondack Small Cap	ADKSX	C	(888) 686-2729	C+ / 5.9	2.75	10.69	26.46 /78	4.21 /45	11.69 /71	0.00	1.25
SC	Adv Inn Cir Champlain Sm Comp Adv	CIPSX	A-	(866) 777-7818	A+ / 9.8	4.55	12.81	45.75 /99	11.30 /97	13.71 /91	0.00	1.34
SC	Adv Inn Cir Champlain Sm Comp Inst	CIPNX	U	(866) 777-7818	U /	4.60	12.97	--	--	--	0.00	1.09
IN	Adv Inn Cir FMC Select Fd	FMSLX	D+	(866) 777-7818	D+ / 2.9	6.63	0.86	9.69 /11	3.82 /41	8.69 /48	0.57	0.98
SC	Adv Inn Cir ICM Sm Co I	ICSCX	C+	(866) 777-7818	A+ / 9.7	3.96	15.38	37.19 /96	9.41 /90	13.58 /90	0.26	0.94
FO	Adv Inn Cir McKee Intl Eqty I	MKIEX	D-	(866) 777-7818	D- / 1.5	7.33	6.51	18.73 /46	-0.48 /11	4.25 /17	1.58	0.99
GR	Adv Inn Cir Reaves Util and EI I	RSRFX	B-	(866) 777-7818	B- / 7.3	6.10	5.36	22.31 /64	8.02 /79	10.38 /61	2.24	1.31
GR	Adv Inn Cir TS&W Eq Port Inst	TSWEX	C+	(866) 777-7818	C+ / 6.6	6.57	7.37	19.76 /51	7.10 /73	10.75 /64	0.42	1.54
GR	Adv Series Tr-Capital Adv Growth	CIAOX	B	(866) 777-7818	B / 7.7	7.12	7.84	23.27 /67	7.95 /79	11.06 /66	0.21	1.51
BA	Advantus Dynamic Managed Vol Inst	VVMIX	U	(800) 665-6005	U /	6.70	7.18	16.19 /35	--	--	1.68	1.60
GR	Advantus Managed Volatility Eq Inst	VMEIX	U	(800) 665-6005	U /	6.26	2.76	8.37 / 8	--	--	1.99	1.84
IN	Advantus Strat Dividend Inc Instl	VSDIX	C+	(800) 665-6005	C+ / 6.2	7.74	0.63	17.57 /41	7.46 /75	--	2.39	1.10
GR	AdvisorOne CLS Glbl Agg Eq N	CLACX	B	(866) 811-0225	B- / 7.2	8.14	10.38	27.63 /81	5.25 /57	9.42 /54	1.31	1.93
GR	AdvisorOne CLS Glbl Dvsfd Eq N	CLSAX	C+	(866) 811-0225	C / 5.3	7.42	7.29	21.74 /61	3.83 /41	7.48 /38	2.80	1.45
GI	AdvisorOne CLS Global Growth N	CLBLX	C	(866) 811-0225	C- / 3.9	5.83	5.06	17.24 /39	3.31 /35	6.55 /32	2.43	1.55
GR	AdvisorOne CLS Growth and Income	CLERX	C	(866) 811-0225	D+ / 2.7	4.34	3.09	12.49 /20	2.75 /30	4.78 /20	1.86	1.56
GI	AdvisorOne CLS International Eqty N	CLHAX	E	(866) 811-0225	C- / 3.1	6.67	4.89	15.63 /33	2.12 /25	4.58 /19	1.52	2.66
GR	AdvisorOne CLS Shelter N	CLSHX	C+	(866) 811-0225	C+ / 6.8	7.08	8.84	20.30 /54	6.48 /68	8.24 /44	0.86	1.42
GL	AdvisorOne Horizon Active RA N	ARANX	U	(866) 811-0225	U /	6.45	5.63	15.23 /31	--	--	0.82	1.72
GR	Advisory Research All Cap Value	ADVGX	C+	(888) 665-1414	B / 8.1	7.47	12.04	28.57 /83	7.44 /75	10.96 /65	0.62	1.24
MC	Advisory Research Emerging Mkts	ADVMX	C-	(888) 665-1414	C- / 3.4	7.65	3.29	24.83 /73	1.44 /21	--	2.04	1.95
GL	Advisory Research Global Val	ADVWX	D+	(888) 665-1414	C / 4.3	6.14	8.30	22.27 /63	2.91 /31	7.63 /39	1.10	2.07
FO	Advisory Research Intl All Cap Val	ADVEX	E+	(888) 665-1414	E+ / 0.9	6.28	5.38	14.85 /29	-1.41 / 8	5.11 /22	2.77	16.04

● Denotes fund is closed to new investors

✻ Denotes fund is included in Section II

Risk Rating/Pts	3 Year Standard Deviation	Beta	NAV As of 2/28/17	Total $(Mil)	Cash %	Stocks %	Bonds %	Other %	Portfolio Turnover Ratio	Last Bull Market Return	Last Bear Market Return	Manager Quality Pct	Manager Tenure (Years)	Initial Purch. $	Additional Purch. $	Front End Load	Back End Load
C /4.8	12.6	0.89	12.98	44	2	97	0	1	28	23.4	-18.3	37	8	1,000	50	5.8	0.0
C /4.8	12.7	0.90	12.22	14	2	97	0	1	28	18.8	-18.6	29	8	1,000	50	0.0	0.0
C /4.8	12.6	0.89	13.29	304	2	97	0	1	28	25.6	-18.2	42	8	1,000,000	0	0.0	0.0
C /4.8	12.6	0.90	13.24	98	2	97	0	1	28	24.6	-18.2	40	8	1,000,000	0	0.0	0.0
C /4.8	12.7	0.90	12.40	7	2	97	0	1	28	21.6	-18.4	34	8	0	0	0.0	0.0
C- /4.1	13.5	0.94	24.16	179	3	96	0	1	23	22.9	-28.4	55	4	1,000	50	0.0	0.0
C- /4.1	13.5	0.94	24.74	33	3	96	0	1	23	24.7	-28.3	58	4	1,000,000	0	0.0	0.0
C- /4.2	13.0	0.91	10.34	50	1	98	0	1	23	23.8	-28.0	48	4	1,000	50	0.0	0.0
C- /4.1	13.0	0.91	10.33	43	1	98	0	1	23	25.7	-28.0	53	4	1,000,000	0	0.0	0.0
C /5.5	10.5	0.97	12.00	238	1	98	0	1	63	96.4	-20.2	28	17	1,000	50	5.8	0.0
C /5.3	10.6	0.98	10.65	6	1	98	0	1	63	88.8	-20.3	21	17	1,000	50	0.0	0.0
C /5.5	10.5	0.97	12.68	7	1	98	0	1	63	99.4	-20.1	32	17	1,000,000	0	0.0	0.0
C /5.5	10.5	0.97	12.66	108	1	98	0	1	63	N/A	N/A	30	17	1,000,000	0	0.0	0.0
C /5.4	10.5	0.97	11.33	N/A	1	98	0	1	63	93.6	-20.2	25	17	0	0	0.0	0.0
B- /7.0	12.4	0.74	32.75	361	0	99	0	1	32	172.5	-27.7	98	9	1,000	50	5.8	0.0
B- /7.0	12.4	0.74	28.59	104	0	99	0	1	32	162.3	-27.8	97	9	1,000	50	0.0	0.0
B- /7.0	12.4	0.74	34.42	1,288	0	99	0	1	32	177.1	-27.5	98	9	1,000,000	0	0.0	0.0
B- /7.0	12.4	0.74	30.39	19	0	99	0	1	32	168.9	-27.7	98	9	0	0	0.0	0.0
B- /7.0	12.4	0.74	34.45	62	0	99	0	1	32	176.7	-27.5	98	9	1,000,000	0	0.0	0.0
C+ /6.9	2.3	-0.06	9.80	13	17	0	50	33	83	1.3	-4.6	87	9	1,000,000	0	0.0	0.0
C+ /6.6	4.5	-0.35	8.88	537	42	12	24	22	70	0.2	1.9	92	12	1,000,000	0	0.0	0.0
C+ /6.4	4.4	-0.35	8.61	24	42	12	24	22	70	-2.4	1.8	90	12	250,000	100	0.0	0.0
C- /3.6	19.8	0.99	12.90	11	0	97	1	2	18	N/A	N/A	79	5	25,000	500	0.0	2.0
C- /4.2	15.8	0.96	18.32	838	0	0	0	100	32	26.8	-26.0	82	23	2,500	1,000	0.0	2.0
U /	N/A	N/A	15.83	31	73	26	0	1	652	N/A	N/A	N/A	2	2,000	500	5.8	1.0
U /	N/A	N/A	10.46	57	33	39	26	2	5	N/A	N/A	N/A	3	10,000	100	0.0	2.0
U /	N/A	N/A	9.58	44	1	95	2	2	104	N/A	N/A	N/A	3	100,000	0	0.0	1.0
U /	N/A	N/A	11.93	85	0	96	2	2	52	N/A	N/A	N/A	3	100,000	0	0.0	1.0
C+ /5.6	10.4	0.68	16.78	18	14	85	0	1	38	41.7	-21.6	86	N/A	2,500	1,000	0.0	2.0
C /5.0	14.2	0.84	22.38	287	3	96	0	1	32	110.1	-21.9	55	12	3,000	50	0.0	0.0
C /4.8	14.7	0.89	20.17	749	3	96	0	1	27	130.1	-19.0	95	13	10,000	0	0.0	0.0
U /	N/A	N/A	20.20	524	3	96	0	1	27	N/A	N/A	N/A	13	1,000,000	0	0.0	0.0
C+ /5.9	9.4	0.83	27.80	252	0	99	0	1	32	80.1	-16.9	18	7	10,000	1,000	0.0	0.0
D+ /2.7	15.0	0.91	31.60	713	0	96	3	1	32	144.8	-25.0	90	18	2,500,000	1,000	0.0	0.0
C+ /5.6	12.4	1.00	11.81	163	4	95	0	1	7	47.3	-25.9	71	17	2,500	100	0.0	1.0
C /5.4	9.5	0.56	10.22	48	2	96	1	1	84	87.6	-10.0	86	13	1,000,000	0	0.0	0.0
C /5.3	10.1	0.94	12.93	42	2	91	5	2	66	102.8	-20.9	39	2	2,500	100	0.0	1.0
C+ /5.6	11.3	1.05	25.51	49	7	80	12	1	44	100.7	-12.8	35	16	5,000	250	0.0	0.0
U /	N/A	N/A	11.48	33	5	46	48	1	36	N/A	N/A	N/A	2	100,000	1,000	0.0	0.0
U /	N/A	N/A	11.02	40	0	0	0	100	15	N/A	N/A	N/A	2	100,000	1,000	0.0	0.0
C+ /6.4	10.9	0.61	11.22	86	15	73	10	2	82	N/A	N/A	81	5	100,000	1,000	0.0	0.0
C+ /5.8	11.5	1.05	14.02	105	4	94	1	1	35	95.4	-23.4	12	8	2,500	250	0.0	0.0
C+ /6.2	10.5	0.95	17.47	436	0	98	0	2	58	76.5	-22.4	10	4	2,500	250	0.0	0.0
B- /7.1	8.5	0.78	11.17	237	3	81	14	2	88	62.7	-17.7	18	4	2,500	250	0.0	0.0
B /8.5	5.7	0.47	10.99	339	0	44	55	1	56	44.0	-11.7	46	4	2,500	250	0.0	0.0
D- /1.2	10.1	0.73	4.30	20	1	98	0	1	230	43.9	-13.7	13	3	2,500	250	0.0	0.0
C+ /6.3	9.5	0.89	12.95	121	1	98	0	1	346	47.9	-14.7	39	N/A	2,500	250	0.0	0.0
U /	N/A	N/A	20.37	321	0	0	0	100	541	N/A	N/A	N/A	3	2,500	250	0.0	0.0
C- /3.6	10.2	0.94	13.74	20	3	96	0	1	56	98.6	-16.9	44	15	2,500	500	0.0	2.0
C+ /6.7	14.4	0.67	9.49	31	7	92	0	1	32	N/A	N/A	17	4	2,500	500	0.0	2.0
C /4.9	10.7	0.75	12.09	13	2	97	0	1	71	72.8	-23.2	90	8	2,500	500	0.0	2.0
C /4.4	12.0	0.90	8.45	N/A	2	97	0	1	49	44.2	N/A	58	7	2,500	500	0.0	2.0

| | | | | | PERFORMANCE | | | | | | | |
Fund Type	Fund Name	Ticker Symbol	Overall Investment Rating	Phone	Perfor-mance Rating/Pts	3 Mo	6 Mo	1Yr / Pct	3Yr / Pct	5Yr / Pct	Dividend Yield	Expense Ratio
FO	Advisory Research Intl SC Val I	ADVLX	C	(888) 665-1414	C- / 3.1	6.40	7.56	19.97 /52	1.33 /20	--	1.24	1.21
FO	Advisory Research Intl SC Val Inv	ADVIX	D+	(888) 665-1414	C- / 3.1	6.26	7.52	19.93 /52	1.31 /20	7.61 /39	1.20	1.25
EN	Advisory Research MLP & Engy Inc A	INFRX	E-		D / 2.1	3.20	7.83	53.52 /99	-1.69 / 7	3.05 /11	6.60	1.40
EN	Advisory Research MLP & Engy Inc C	INFFX	E		D+ / 2.3	2.99	7.38	52.35 /99	-2.46 / 6	--	6.23	2.15
EN	Advisory Research MLP & Engy Inc I	INFIX	E		C- / 3.0	3.21	7.84	53.81 /99	-1.47 / 8	3.94 /15	7.26	1.15
EN	Advisory Research MLP & Engy Infra	MLPPX	E		D+ / 2.5	3.20	7.92	55.01 /99	-2.54 / 5	3.39 /12	7.44	1.00
SC	Advisory Research Small Co Opptys	ADVSX	B+	(888) 665-1414	B / 7.7	3.79	10.28	30.66 /87	7.28 /74	--	0.55	4.31
SC	Aegis Value A	AVFAX	E	(800) 528-3780	C- / 3.7	7.43	8.19	63.76 /99	-1.67 / 7	--	1.31	1.78
SC	Aegis Value I	AVALX	E+	(800) 528-3780	C / 4.7	7.50	8.32	64.01 /99	-1.46 / 8	8.06 /43	1.46	1.53
FO	AI International A	IIESX	E+	(866) 410-2006	E / 0.5	5.85	2.47	15.11 /30	-2.04 / 7	3.51 /13	1.79	1.79
EM	AI International Institutional	IMSSX	E+	(866) 410-2006	D- / 1.0	5.97	2.77	15.67 /33	-1.58 / 8	4.01 /15	2.29	1.29
BA	AIG Active Allocation A	FBAAX	C	(800) 858-8850	C- / 3.0	4.37	4.89	16.03 /34	4.18 /45	6.51 /32	1.39	1.73
BA	AIG Active Allocation B	FBABX	C+	(800) 858-8850	C- / 3.5	4.20	4.47	15.26 /31	3.47 /37	5.79 /27	0.86	2.49
BA	AIG Active Allocation C	FBACX	C+	(800) 858-8850	C- / 3.5	4.26	4.54	15.40 /32	3.53 /37	5.83 /27	0.89	2.37
BA	AIG Active Allocation I		C+	(800) 858-8850	C- / 4.0	4.35	4.79	16.05 /34	4.14 /44	6.48 /31	1.45	3.21
GI	AIG Commodity Strat A	SUNAX	U	(800) 858-8850	U /	1.66	5.92	15.96 /34	--	--	0.00	2.55
* GI	AIG Foc Dividend Strategy A	FDSAX	C+	(800) 858-8850	C+ / 6.7	3.50	6.89	19.31 /49	9.64 /91	14.10 /94	2.66	1.06
GI	AIG Foc Dividend Strategy B	FDSBX	B	(800) 858-8850	B- / 7.1	3.33	6.57	18.51 /45	8.94 /86	13.36 /87	2.25	1.71
GI	AIG Foc Dividend Strategy C	FDSTX	B	(800) 858-8850	B- / 7.1	3.34	6.52	18.56 /45	8.91 /86	13.37 /87	2.27	1.71
GI	AIG Foc Dividend Strategy W	FDSWX	B+	(800) 858-8850	B / 7.8	3.60	7.06	19.56 /50	9.86 /93	14.29 /95	3.01	0.86
GR	AIG Focused Alpha LCF A	SFLAX	C+	(800) 858-8850	C+ / 6.5	7.58	11.25	22.10 /63	6.94 /71	12.93 /83	0.00	1.66
GR	AIG Focused Alpha LCF C	SFLCX	C+	(800) 858-8850	B- / 7.0	7.44	10.91	21.32 /59	6.26 /66	12.23 /76	0.00	2.31
GR	AIG Focused Alpha LCF W	SFLWX	B-	(800) 858-8850	B- / 7.5	7.62	11.31	22.26 /63	7.09 /73	13.12 /85	0.00	1.54
GR	AIG Focused Multi-Cap Growth A	FOCAX	D	(800) 858-8850	C- / 3.9	8.35	4.86	15.47 /32	5.21 /56	11.10 /67	0.00	1.67
GR	AIG Focused Multi-Cap Growth C	FOCCX	D+	(800) 858-8850	C / 4.5	8.19	4.52	14.72 /29	4.51 /49	10.38 /61	0.00	2.33
GR	AIG Focused Multi-Cap Growth W	FOCWX	C-	(800) 858-8850	C / 5.3	8.43	5.01	15.73 /33	5.41 /59	11.30 /68	0.00	1.47
GL	AIG Global Trends A	GTFAX	D+	(800) 858-8850	E / 0.5	3.33	1.64	4.40 / 3	-0.19 /13	-0.29 / 4	0.00	2.44
GL	AIG Global Trends C	GTFCX	D+	(800) 858-8850	E+ / 0.6	3.20	1.29	3.71 / 3	-0.83 /10	-0.94 / 3	0.00	3.17
AA	AIG Income Explorer A	IEAAX	C-	(800) 858-8850	C- / 4.0	6.80	4.48	20.88 /57	4.53 /49	--	3.96	2.69
AA	AIG Income Explorer C	IEACX	C-	(800) 858-8850	C / 4.6	6.57	4.16	20.07 /52	3.85 /41	--	3.61	3.67
AA	AIG Income Explorer W	IEAWX	C	(800) 858-8850	C / 5.4	6.85	4.59	21.11 /58	4.74 /51	--	4.38	5.01
FO	AIG Intl Dividend Strat A	SIEAX	E	(800) 858-8850	E- / 0.2	7.72	3.45	20.17 /53	-5.98 / 2	-3.07 / 2	2.43	1.88
FO	AIG Intl Dividend Strat C	SIETX	E	(800) 858-8850	E / 0.3	7.55	3.12	19.32 /49	-6.61 / 2	-3.70 / 2	2.24	2.55
FO	● AIG Intl Dividend Strat I	NAOIX	E	(800) 858-8850	E / 0.3	7.77	3.45	20.31 /54	-5.86 / 2	-2.94 / 2	2.62	1.71
FO	AIG Japan A	SAESX	C+	(800) 858-8850	C+ / 6.4	10.08	10.24	26.81 /79	5.48 /59	7.45 /38	0.48	2.14
FO	AIG Japan C	SAJCX	C+	(800) 858-8850	C+ / 6.9	9.90	9.90	26.11 /77	4.81 /52	6.77 /33	0.03	3.05
GR	AIG Multi-Asset Allocation A	FASAX	C	(800) 858-8850	C- / 3.4	4.18	5.91	18.27 /44	4.36 /47	6.40 /31	1.14	1.76
GR	AIG Multi-Asset Allocation B	FMABX	C+	(800) 858-8850	C- / 3.9	3.94	5.48	17.45 /40	3.61 /38	5.67 /26	0.50	2.44
GR	AIG Multi-Asset Allocation C	FMATX	C+	(800) 858-8850	C- / 4.0	4.02	5.57	17.48 /41	3.67 /39	5.73 /27	0.58	2.40
GR	AIG Multi-Asset Allocation I		C+	(800) 858-8850	C / 4.4	4.13	5.80	18.14 /43	4.28 /46	6.34 /31	1.17	3.30
IN	AIG Select Dividend Growth A	SDVAX	U	(800) 858-8850	U /	1.55	7.52	24.81 /73	--	--	1.55	1.59
SC	AIG Small Cap A	SASAX	B	(800) 858-8850	B+ / 8.5	4.90	12.57	37.71 /96	7.93 /78	--	0.00	2.05
SC	AIG Small Cap C	SASCX	B+	(800) 858-8850	A- / 9.0	4.70	12.17	36.83 /96	7.22 /73	--	0.00	6.69
SC	AIG Small Cap W	SASWX	B+	(800) 858-8850	A / 9.4	4.93	12.63	37.92 /96	8.13 /80	--	0.00	15.38
GR	AIG Strategic Value Fund A	SFVAX	B-	(800) 858-8850	C+ / 6.6	5.96	9.52	20.58 /55	8.19 /80	12.05 /75	1.20	1.43
GR	AIG Strategic Value Fund C	SFVTX	B+	(800) 858-8850	B- / 7.1	5.73	9.19	19.80 /51	7.48 /75	11.31 /68	0.74	2.09
GR	Akre Focus Inst	AKRIX	B	(877) 862-9556	B- / 7.0	5.29	5.75	20.15 /53	8.45 /82	14.26 /94	0.00	1.06
GR	Akre Focus Retail	AKREX	C+	(877) 862-9556	C+ / 6.8	5.22	5.60	19.80 /51	8.16 /80	13.95 /93	0.00	1.34
GR	Akre Focus Supra Institutional	AKRSX	U	(877) 862-9556	U /	5.33	5.78	20.29 /54	--	--	0.00	1.00
IN	Al Frank Dividend Value Adv	VALEX	C+	(888) 263-6443	C+ / 6.9	8.15	11.77	25.50 /75	5.53 /60	11.10 /67	1.43	1.73
IN	Al Frank Dividend Value Inv	VALDX	C+	(888) 263-6443	C+ / 6.7	8.09	11.60	25.12 /74	5.24 /57	10.82 /64	1.19	1.98
GR	Al Frank Fund Adv	VALAX	C+	(888) 263-6443	B / 7.7	7.19	13.95	29.21 /85	6.13 /65	11.82 /73	1.40	1.32

● Denotes fund is closed to new investors
* Denotes fund is included in Section II

www.thestreetratings.com

RISK			NET ASSETS		ASSET				Portfolio Turnover Ratio	BULL / BEAR		FUND MANAGER		MINIMUMS		LOADS	
Risk Rating/Pts	3 Year Standard Deviation	Beta	NAV As of 2/28/17	Total $(Mil)	Cash %	Stocks %	Bonds %	Other %		Last Bull Market Return	Last Bear Market Return	Manager Quality Pct	Manager Tenure (Years)	Initial Purch. $	Additional Purch. $	Front End Load	Back End Load
B- /7.4	10.8	0.78	11.70	44	6	93	0	1	38	N/A	N/A	83	8	500,000	500	0.0	2.0
C /5.4	10.7	0.78	11.69	16	6	93	0	1	38	59.6	-20.2	83	8	2,500	500	0.0	2.0
D- /1.4	21.6	0.86	10.01	59	38	31	29	2	37	36.1	N/A	90	7	2,500	500	5.5	2.0
D- /1.4	21.6	0.86	10.04	92	38	31	29	2	37	N/A	N/A	86	7	2,500	500	0.0	2.0
D- /1.4	21.6	0.86	9.83	800	38	31	29	2	37	43.1	-11.9	91	7	1,000,000	100,000	0.0	2.0
D- /1.2	22.4	0.88	9.63	444	38	34	27	1	29	41.4	-10.9	87	7	5,000,000	500	0.0	2.0
C+ /6.2	12.7	0.75	12.03	7	9	90	0	1	123	N/A	N/A	86	4	2,500	500	0.0	2.0
E+ /0.8	28.8	0.73	16.60	5	5	94	0	1	140	N/A	N/A	7	19	2,000	250	3.8	0.0
E+ /0.9	28.8	0.73	16.69	136	5	94	0	1	140	82.2	-23.7	7	19	1,000,000	250	0.0	0.0
C /4.8	12.1	0.96	10.70	N/A	29	68	1	2	116	36.3	-20.9	50	3	5,000	250	5.8	0.0
C /4.9	12.1	0.51	10.98	34	29	68	1	2	116	39.9	-20.8	41	3	3,000,000	5,000	0.0	0.0
B /8.0	7.4	1.14	16.36	83	8	54	37	1	29	52.0	-10.0	22	15	500	100	5.8	0.0
B /8.0	7.4	1.14	16.20	14	8	54	37	1	29	46.6	-10.3	16	15	500	100	0.0	0.0
B /8.0	7.4	1.14	16.27	53	8	54	37	1	29	46.8	-10.2	17	15	500	100	0.0	0.0
B /8.0	7.4	1.15	16.39	1	8	54	37	1	29	51.8	-10.0	21	15	0	0	0.0	0.0
U /	N/A	N/A	7.34	36	59	1	39	1	50	N/A	N/A	N/A	2	500	100	5.8	0.0
C+ /6.2	9.9	0.86	17.81	5,128	0	98	0	2	60	129.5	-8.9	78	4	500	100	5.8	0.0
C+ /6.2	9.9	0.86	17.67	411	0	98	0	2	60	121.7	-9.2	72	4	500	100	0.0	0.0
C+ /6.1	9.9	0.86	17.65	3,844	0	98	0	2	60	121.5	-9.1	72	4	500	100	0.0	0.0
C+ /6.1	9.9	0.86	17.81	4,239	0	98	0	2	60	131.4	-8.9	79	4	50,000	0	0.0	0.0
C /5.3	10.6	0.91	26.69	449	0	99	0	1	38	125.0	-21.7	41	5	500	100	5.8	0.0
C /5.2	10.6	0.91	25.72	114	0	99	0	1	38	N/A	N/A	33	5	500	100	0.0	0.0
C /5.3	10.6	0.91	26.97	10	0	99	0	1	38	127.0	-21.7	43	5	50,000	0	0.0	0.0
C /4.4	10.1	0.79	25.26	378	5	94	0	1	29	101.2	-20.0	36	5	500	100	5.8	0.0
C /4.3	10.2	0.79	24.28	82	5	94	0	1	29	N/A	N/A	28	5	500	100	0.0	0.0
C /4.4	10.1	0.79	25.55	27	5	94	0	1	29	103.5	-20.0	38	5	50,000	0	0.0	0.0
B /8.7	4.5	0.37	13.05	32	77	0	22	1	0	3.3	N/A	49	N/A	500	100	5.8	0.0
B /8.6	4.5	0.37	12.59	4	77	0	22	1	0	-0.2	N/A	40	N/A	500	100	0.0	0.0
C+ /5.9	7.9	1.01	15.05	25	0	49	49	2	54	N/A	N/A	36	4	500	100	5.8	0.0
C+ /5.9	7.9	1.01	15.02	4	0	49	49	2	54	N/A	N/A	28	4	500	100	0.0	0.0
C+ /5.9	7.9	1.01	15.05	1	0	49	49	2	54	N/A	N/A	39	4	50,000	0	0.0	0.0
C- /3.4	16.0	1.07	8.77	66	0	99	0	1	248	-0.9	-25.3	9	5	500	100	5.8	0.0
C- /3.4	16.0	1.06	7.96	14	0	99	0	1	248	-4.3	-25.7	6	5	500	100	0.0	0.0
C- /3.4	16.0	1.07	8.87	N/A	0	99	0	1	248	-0.2	-25.4	10	5	0	0	0.0	0.0
C /5.2	14.2	0.91	7.72	25	1	98	0	1	151	N/A	N/A	96	5	500	100	5.8	0.0
C /5.1	14.2	0.91	7.35	5	1	98	0	1	151	N/A	N/A	95	5	500	100	0.0	0.0
B- /7.9	7.9	0.74	17.02	159	9	61	28	2	18	43.7	-9.6	31	15	500	100	5.8	0.0
/8.0	7.9	0.74	16.99	21	9	61	28	2	18	38.4	-9.8	24	15	500	100	0.0	0.0
/7.9	7.9	0.74	16.98	95	9	61	28	2	18	38.8	-9.8	25	15	500	100	0.0	0.0
/7.9	7.9	0.74	17.01	N/A	9	61	28	2	18	43.3	N/A	31	15	0	0	0.0	0.0
U /	N/A	N/A	16.12	43	0	99	0	1	69	N/A	N/A	N/A	3	500	100	5.8	0.0
/4.9	15.8	0.99	17.79	48	1	98	0	1	67	N/A	N/A	81	3	500	100	5.8	0.0
/4.9	15.8	0.99	17.40	1	1	98	0	1	67	N/A	N/A	76	3	500	100	0.0	0.0
/4.9	15.8	0.99	17.90	2	1	98	0	1	67	N/A	N/A	82	3	50,000	0	0.0	0.0
B- /7.4	10.1	0.94	28.63	193	0	99	0	1	56	115.4	-19.3	53	4	500	100	5.8	0.0
B- /7.4	10.1	0.94	26.54	56	0	99	0	1	56	107.8	-19.6	44	4	500	100	0.0	0.0
C+ /6.5	10.7	0.94	26.77	1,837	3	89	6	2	13	139.2	-5.9	57	8	250,000	25,000	0.0	1.0
C+ /6.5	10.7	0.94	26.32	3,575	3	89	6	2	13	135.6	-6.0	53	8	2,000	250	0.0	1.0
U /	N/A	N/A	26.80	390	3	89	6	2	13	N/A	N/A	N/A	8	300,000,000	0	0.0	1.0
/4.7	11.2	1.02	13.49	1	1	95	3	1	15	110.2	-20.9	16	13	100,000	100	0.0	2.0
/4.7	11.2	1.02	13.57	15	1	95	3	1	15	107.3	-21.0	14	13	1,000	100	0.0	2.0
/4.5	12.3	1.10	24.57	3	0	96	2	2	12	117.3	-22.5	14	19	100,000	100	0.0	2.0

					PERFORMANCE							
	99 Pct = Best 0 Pct = Worst		Overall		Perfor-	Total Return % through 2/28/17					Incl. in Returns	
		Ticker	Investment		mance				Annualized		Dividend	Expense
Fund Type	Fund Name	Symbol	Rating	Phone	Rating/Pts	3 Mo	6 Mo	1Yr / Pct	3Yr / Pct	5Yr / Pct	Yield	Ratio
GR	Al Frank Fund Inv	VALUX	C+	(888) 263-6443	B- / 7.5	7.13	13.80	28.90 /84	5.97 /64	11.61 /71	1.17	1.58
BA	Alger Balanced I2	ABLOX	B	(800) 254-3796	C+ / 6.8	6.38	7.28	17.14 /39	7.80 /77	7.67 /39	1.84	0.92
GR	Alger Capital Apprec I2	ALVOX	C+	(800) 254-3796	B / 8.1	9.68	8.43	20.57 /55	8.62 /84	13.36 /87	0.17	0.93
GR	Alger Capital Apprec S		C+	(800) 254-3796	B / 7.9	9.61	8.29	20.26 /53	8.33 /81	13.04 /84	0.00	1.20
GR	Alger Capital Appreciation A	ACAAX	C+	(800) 254-3796	B- / 7.1	9.80	8.50	20.52 /55	8.45 /82	13.09 /85	0.00	1.23
GR	Alger Capital Appreciation B	ACAPX	C	(800) 254-3796	B- / 7.4	9.63	8.04	19.51 /49	7.58 /76	12.19 /76	0.00	2.01
GR	Alger Capital Appreciation C	ALCCX	C	(800) 254-3796	B- / 7.4	9.64	8.06	19.63 /50	7.64 /76	12.23 /76	0.00	1.99
GR	Alger Capital Appreciation Focus A	ALAFX	B	(800) 254-3796	B- / 7.5	9.71	9.16	20.78 /56	9.18 /88	--	0.00	1.32
GR	Alger Capital Appreciation Focus C	ALCFX	B+	(800) 254-3796	B / 7.9	9.48	8.74	19.88 /51	8.37 /82	--	0.00	2.09
GR	Alger Capital Appreciation Focus I	ALGRX	A-	(800) 254-3796	B+ / 8.5	9.70	9.16	20.77 /56	9.27 /89	12.35 /78	0.00	1.33
GR	Alger Capital Appreciation Focus Z	ALZFX	A-	(800) 254-3796	B+ / 8.7	9.81	9.32	21.05 /58	9.58 /91	--	0.00	1.34
GR	Alger Capital Appreciation Fund Z	ACAZX	B-	(800) 254-3796	B / 8.2	9.90	8.69	20.93 /57	8.80 /85	13.46 /88	0.00	0.90
GR	Alger Capital Appreciation Inst I	ALARX	B-	(800) 254-3796	B / 8.1	9.82	8.51	20.53 /55	8.55 /83	13.18 /86	0.00	1.12
GR	Alger Capital Appreciation Inst R	ACARX	C+	(800) 254-3796	B / 7.7	9.69	8.25	19.97 /52	8.02 /79	12.63 /80	0.00	1.61
GL	Alger Dynamic Opportunities A	SPEDX	D+	(800) 254-3796	D+ / 2.4	5.93	6.82	11.90 /18	3.06 /32	6.11 /29	0.00	2.20
GL	Alger Dynamic Opportunities C	ADOCX	C-	(800) 254-3796	D+ / 2.7	5.70	6.35	11.05 /15	2.27 /26	5.31 /23	0.00	2.98
GL	Alger Dynamic Opportunities Fund Z	ADOZX	C-	(800) 254-3796	C- / 3.5	5.99	6.95	12.24 /19	3.37 /35	6.39 /31	0.00	1.93
EM	Alger Emerging Markets A	AAEMX	D-	(800) 254-3796	D- / 1.4	8.05	2.55	25.13 /74	-0.11 /13	1.24 / 7	0.00	2.51
EM	Alger Emerging Markets C	ACEMX	D-	(800) 254-3796	D / 1.6	7.88	2.18	24.13 /70	-0.88 /10	0.46 / 5	0.00	3.31
EM	Alger Emerging Markets I	AIEMX	D-	(800) 254-3796	D / 1.9	7.98	2.56	25.00 /73	-0.13 /13	1.21 / 6	0.00	2.44
EM	Alger Emerging Markets Z	AZEMX	D+	(800) 254-3796	C- / 3.2	8.02	2.65	25.37 /74	0.25 /14	--	0.00	2.35
FO	Alger Global Growth A	CHUSX	D+	(800) 254-3796	D+ / 2.4	5.25	5.60	16.00 /34	2.58 /28	6.01 /28	0.91	2.03
FO	Alger Global Growth C	CHUCX	D+	(800) 254-3796	D+ / 2.8	5.02	5.18	15.07 /30	1.82 /23	5.21 /23	0.30	2.80
GL	Alger Global Growth I	AFGIX	C-	(800) 254-3796	C- / 3.5	5.30	5.66	16.21 /35	2.82 /30	--	4.91	2.02
GL	Alger Global Growth Z	AFGZX	C-	(800) 254-3796	C- / 3.7	5.28	5.78	16.43 /36	3.07 /32	--	1.11	2.20
GI	Alger Growth & Income I2	AIGOX	A+	(800) 254-3796	A- / 9.1	8.55	11.23	23.61 /69	9.90 /93	12.60 /80	1.64	0.94
BA	Alger Growth and Income A	ALBAX	A	(800) 254-3796	B / 8.2	8.41	11.00	23.42 /68	9.82 /92	12.34 /77	1.37	1.15
BA	Alger Growth and Income C	ALBCX	A	(800) 254-3796	B+ / 8.6	8.24	10.62	22.55 /65	9.00 /87	11.49 /70	0.81	1.90
GI	Alger Growth and Income Z	AGIZX	A+	(800) 254-3796	A- / 9.2	8.50	11.19	23.79 /69	10.10 /94	--	1.67	0.91
HL	Alger Health Sciences Fund A	AHSAX	C	(800) 254-3796	A+ / 9.9	29.45	25.15	37.94 /96	8.87 /86	14.82 /96	0.00	1.31
HL	Alger Health Sciences Fund C	AHSCX	C-	(800) 254-3796	A+ / 9.9	29.21	24.66	36.86 /96	8.04 /79	13.94 /93	0.00	2.08
GR	Alger International Growth A	ALGAX	D-	(800) 254-3796	E / 0.4	4.20	0.95	9.00 / 9	-1.11 / 9	3.07 /11	1.57	1.32
GR	Alger International Growth B	AFGPX	D-	(800) 254-3796	E+ / 0.6	4.01	0.55	8.25 / 8	-1.81 / 7	2.35 / 9	1.22	2.04
GR	Alger International Growth C	ALGCX	D-	(800) 254-3796	E+ / 0.6	4.05	0.58	8.22 / 8	-1.85 / 7	2.27 / 9	1.04	2.09
FO	Alger International Growth Fund I	AIGIX	D-	(800) 254-3796	E+ / 0.8	4.25	1.07	9.31 /10	-0.90 /10	--	1.85	1.30
GR	Alger International Growth Z	ALCZX	D-	(800) 254-3796	E+ / 0.9	4.27	1.20	9.58 /11	-0.66 /11	3.52 /13	2.10	1.03
GR	Alger LargeCap Growth I2	AAGOX	D+	(800) 254-3796	C+ / 5.8	8.53	8.10	18.59 /45	5.03 /54	10.23 /60	0.00	0.86
GR	Alger LargeCap Growth S		D	(800) 254-3796	C / 5.5	8.43	7.89	18.12 /43	4.63 /50	9.81 /57	0.00	1.21
GR	Alger Mid Cap Focus A	SPEAX	E+	(800) 254-3796	D- / 1.4	5.53	4.44	12.94 /21	0.36 /15	8.42 /46	0.00	2.48
GR	Alger Mid Cap Focus C	AACYX	E+	(800) 254-3796	D- / 1.2	5.24	3.91	12.05 /18	-0.30 /12	7.72 /40	0.00	3.41
GR	Alger Mid Cap Focus I	AAIYX	D-	(800) 254-3796	D / 1.9	5.45	4.37	12.99 /22	0.35 /15	8.42 /46	0.00	2.50
MC	Alger Mid Cap Growth Fund A	AMGAX	C-	(800) 254-3796	C / 4.9	10.78	9.84	22.60 /65	3.57 /38	10.03 /59	0.00	1.32
MC	Alger Mid Cap Growth Fund B	AMCGX	C-	(800) 254-3796	C / 5.4	10.64	9.47	21.72 /61	2.86 /30	9.26 /53	0.00	2.02
MC	Alger Mid Cap Growth Fund C	AMGCX	C-	(800) 254-3796	C / 5.2	10.51	9.34	21.55 /60	2.70 /29	9.12 /52	0.00	2.12
MC	Alger Mid Cap Growth I2	AMGOX	C	(800) 254-3796	C+ / 6.2	10.71	9.97	23.05 /67	3.79 /40	10.28 /60	0.00	0.96
MC	Alger Mid Cap Growth Inst I	ALMRX	C+	(800) 254-3796	C+ / 6.9	11.57	10.82	24.14 /70	4.59 /50	10.86 /65	0.00	1.20
MC	Alger Mid Cap Growth Inst R	AGIRX	C	(800) 254-3796	C+ / 6.5	11.45	10.53	23.41 /68	4.02 /43	10.28 /60	0.00	1.74
MC	Alger Mid Cap Growth S		C	(800) 254-3796	C+ / 5.8	10.54	9.77	22.46 /64	3.38 /36	9.84 /57	0.00	1.34
GR	Alger Responsible Investing A	SPEGX	C	(800) 254-3796	C / 5.0	8.50	8.50	18.00 /43	5.48 /59	10.60 /63	0.00	1.29
GR	Alger Responsible Investing C	AGFCX	C+	(800) 254-3796	C / 5.4	8.26	8.14	17.13 /39	4.67 /50	9.73 /56	0.00	2.07
GR	Alger Responsible Investing I	AGIFX	C+	(800) 254-3796	C+ / 6.1	8.51	8.51	18.03 /43	5.49 /59	10.62 /63	0.00	1.27
GR	Alger Small Cap Focus A	AOFAX	D+	(800) 254-3796	C+ / 5.7	3.90	6.83	33.09 /92	4.64 /50	10.72 /64	0.00	1.82

● Denotes fund is closed to new investors

* Denotes fund is included in Section II

RISK	3 Year		NET ASSETS		ASSET				Portfolio	BULL / BEAR		FUND MANAGER		MINIMUMS		LOADS	
Risk Rating/Pts	Standard Deviation	Beta	NAV As of 2/28/17	Total $(Mil)	Cash %	Stocks %	Bonds %	Other %	Portfolio Turnover Ratio	Last Bull Market Return	Last Bear Market Return	Manager Quality Pct	Manager Tenure (Years)	Initial Purch. $	Additional Purch. $	Front End Load	Back End Load
C /4.5	12.3	1.10	24.53	71	0	96	2	2	12	115.1	-22.6	13	19	1,000	100	0.0	2.0
B /8.3	6.7	1.07	16.01	74	5	66	27	2	10	62.8	-9.3	72	6	0	0	0.0	0.0
C- /3.9	12.0	1.05	73.26	517	3	96	0	1	142	133.0	-18.6	44	13	0	0	0.0	0.0
C- /3.8	12.0	1.05	70.38	43	3	96	0	1	142	N/A	N/A	40	13	0	0	0.0	0.0
C /4.4	12.1	1.06	21.91	1,403	2	96	0	2	104	129.5	-18.8	41	13	1,000	50	5.3	0.0
C- /3.9	12.1	1.05	17.71	16	2	96	0	2	104	119.7	-19.1	30	13	1,000	50	0.0	0.0
C- /3.9	12.2	1.06	17.80	304	2	96	0	2	104	120.3	-19.1	31	13	1,000	50	0.0	0.0
C+ /6.0	12.2	1.05	26.45	19	6	93	0	1	127	N/A	N/A	51	5	1,000	50	5.3	0.0
C+ /6.0	12.2	1.04	25.63	16	6	93	0	1	127	N/A	N/A	41	5	1,000	50	0.0	0.0
C+ /6.1	12.2	1.05	26.57	21	6	93	0	1	127	118.4	-16.8	53	5	0	0	0.0	0.0
C+ /6.1	12.2	1.04	26.86	27	6	93	0	1	127	N/A	N/A	57	5	500,000	0	0.0	0.0
C /4.5	12.2	1.06	22.36	830	2	96	0	2	104	133.6	-18.7	45	13	500,000	0	0.0	0.0
C /4.9	12.0	1.05	28.85	2,448	3	96	0	1	95	131.1	-19.0	43	12	0	0	0.0	0.0
C /4.6	12.1	1.05	26.16	614	3	96	0	1	95	125.1	-19.1	36	12	0	0	0.0	0.0
C+ /6.9	8.1	0.47	12.66	26	13	51	34	2	147	47.3	-14.8	90	8	1,000	50	5.3	0.0
C+ /6.8	8.1	0.47	12.02	6	13	51	34	2	147	41.4	-15.0	87	8	1,000	50	0.0	0.0
C+ /6.9	8.1	0.47	12.89	46	13	51	34	2	147	49.6	-14.7	91	8	500,000	0	0.0	0.0
C /5.1	14.9	0.87	9.26	6	4	95	0	1	66	27.5	-27.7	54	7	1,000	50	5.3	0.0
C /5.0	14.9	0.86	8.90	3	4	95	0	1	66	22.3	-27.9	43	7	1,000	50	0.0	0.0
C /5.1	15.0	0.87	9.20	14	4	95	0	1	66	27.2	-27.7	54	7	0	0	0.0	0.0
C+ /5.8	14.9	0.87	9.29	18	4	95	0	1	66	N/A	N/A	59	7	500,000	0	0.0	0.0
C+ /6.5	10.6	0.72	21.58	20	4	95	0	1	138	63.9	-29.4	89	14	1,000	50	5.3	0.0
C+ /6.4	10.6	0.72	20.50	5	4	95	0	1	138	57.3	-29.6	86	14	1,000	50	0.0	0.0
C+ /6.4	10.6	0.72	20.92	N/A	4	95	0	1	138	N/A	N/A	90	14	0	0	0.0	0.0
C+ /6.5	10.6	0.72	21.94	4	4	95	0	1	138	N/A	N/A	91	14	500,000	0	0.0	0.0
B- /7.4	9.9	0.95	18.63	37	6	93	0	1	17	118.7	-14.0	72	14	0	0	0.0	0.0
C+ /6.9	9.8	1.52	36.56	71	6	93	0	1	5	115.0	-12.9	54	6	1,000	50	5.3	0.0
C+ /6.9	9.8	1.52	36.07	23	6	93	0	1	5	106.5	-13.2	44	6	1,000	50	0.0	0.0
C+ /6.9	9.8	0.94	36.60	16	6	93	0	1	5	N/A	N/A	74	6	500,000	0	0.0	0.0
E+ /0.6	21.4	1.26	21.45	80	0	99	0	1	93	129.8	-12.9	21	12	1,000	50	5.3	0.0
E- /0.2	21.4	1.26	17.34	33	0	99	0	1	93	120.4	-13.2	15	12	1,000	50	0.0	0.0
C+ /6.2	11.1	0.84	14.65	104	3	96	0	1	135	42.6	-16.7	2	4	1,000	50	5.3	0.0
C+ /6.2	11.0	0.84	12.85	24	3	96	0	1	135	37.1	-16.9	2	4	1,000	50	0.0	0.0
C+ /6.1	11.0	0.84	12.55	14	3	96	0	1	135	36.4	-16.9	2	4	1,000	50	0.0	0.0
C+ /6.2	11.1	0.83	14.61	7	3	96	0	1	135	N/A	N/A	65	4	0	0	0.0	0.0
C+ /6.2	11.1	0.84	14.77	20	3	96	0	1	135	45.8	-16.6	3	4	500,000	0	0.0	0.0
D+ /2.6	13.7	1.14	57.23	252	1	98	0	1	239	99.4	-16.7	6	16	0	0	0.0	0.0
D+ /2.6	13.7	1.14	56.09	5	1	98	0	1	239	N/A	N/A	5	16	0	0	0.0	0.0
C /4.6	13.9	1.18	12.22	7	11	88	0	1	112	88.1	-21.5	1	2	1,000	50	5.3	0.0
C /4.5	13.9	1.18	11.44	N/A	11	88	0	1	112	81.8	-21.8	1	2	1,000	50	0.0	0.0
C /4.6	13.9	1.18	12.18	2	11	88	0	1	112	88.2	-21.6	1	2	0	0	0.0	0.0
C /5.0	13.7	0.98	11.61	125	9	90	0	1	99	104.0	-27.4	11	7	1,000	50	5.3	0.0
C /4.9	13.6	0.98	9.36	19	9	90	0	1	99	96.2	-27.6	8	7	1,000	50	0.0	0.0
C /4.9	13.6	0.98	9.25	19	9	90	0	1	99	94.7	-27.6	7	7	1,000	50	0.0	0.0
C /4.8	13.7	0.99	21.51	125	4	95	0	1	117	105.5	-27.3	12	7	0	0	0.0	0.0
C /4.8	13.8	0.99	24.79	83	4	95	0	1	96	110.3	-27.1	18	7	0	0	0.0	0.0
C /4.7	13.8	1.00	22.88	14	4	95	0	1	96	104.3	-27.2	13	7	0	0	0.0	0.0
C /4.8	13.7	0.99	20.45	4	4	95	0	1	117	N/A	N/A	10	7	0	0	0.0	0.0
C+ /6.4	11.0	1.01	9.71	32	1	98	0	1	20	99.6	-17.4	16	11	1,000	50	5.3	0.0
C+ /6.3	11.0	1.01	9.05	6	1	98	0	1	20	91.1	-17.5	11	11	1,000	50	0.0	0.0
C+ /6.4	11.0	1.01	9.70	12	1	98	0	1	20	99.8	-17.4	16	11	0	0	0.0	0.0
C- /3.5	16.3	1.18	12.51	39	8	91	0	1	76	111.4	-26.8	5	2	1,000	50	5.3	0.0

Fund Type	Fund Name	Ticker Symbol	Overall Investment Rating	Phone	Performance Rating/Pts	3 Mo	6 Mo	1Yr / Pct	3Yr / Pct	5Yr / Pct	Dividend Yield	Expense Ratio
GR	Alger Small Cap Focus C	AOFCX	C-	(800) 254-3796	C+ / 6.1	3.71	6.51	32.03 /90	3.95 /42	9.99 /58	0.00	2.53
GR	Alger Small Cap Focus I	AOFIX	C-	(800) 254-3796	C+ / 6.8	3.89	6.83	32.99 /92	4.80 /52	10.93 /65	0.00	1.56
GR	Alger Small Cap Focus Z	AGOZX	C	(800) 254-3796	C+ / 6.9	3.94	7.04	33.30 /92	5.09 /55	11.23 /68	0.00	1.56
SC	Alger Small Cap Growth Fund A	ALSAX	E	(800) 254-3796	C- / 4.2	7.08	10.06	30.46 /87	1.51 /21	7.94 /42	0.00	1.35
SC	Alger Small Cap Growth Fund B	ALSCX	E	(800) 254-3796	C / 4.6	6.85	9.64	29.38 /85	0.71 /17	7.09 /35	0.00	2.16
SC	Alger Small Cap Growth Fund C	AGSCX	E	(800) 254-3796	C / 4.6	6.85	9.73	29.58 /85	0.72 /17	7.07 /35	0.00	2.16
SC	Alger Small Cap Growth Fund Z	ASCZX	D-	(800) 254-3796	C+ / 5.7	7.24	10.17	31.05 /88	1.90 /23	8.34 /45	0.00	1.04
SC	Alger Small Cap Growth Inst I	ALSRX	D-	(800) 254-3796	C+ / 6.4	8.21	11.90	32.82 /91	2.15 /25	8.48 /46	0.00	1.25
SC	Alger Small Cap Growth Inst R	ASIRX	E+	(800) 254-3796	C+ / 5.9	8.01	11.59	32.06 /90	1.63 /22	7.93 /41	0.00	1.74
SC	Alger Small Cap Growth Inst Z2	AISZX	U	(800) 254-3796	U /	8.26	12.09	--	--	--	0.00	N/A
SC	Alger SmallCap Growth I2	AASOX	E+	(800) 254-3796	C+ / 5.8	7.37	10.79	31.21 /89	2.01 /24	8.45 /46	0.00	0.96
MC	Alger SMid Cap Growth Fund A	ALMAX	E-	(800) 254-3796	C- / 3.6	5.39	7.00	24.95 /73	2.71 /29	8.71 /48	0.00	1.30
MC	Alger SMid Cap Growth Fund C	ALMCX	E	(800) 254-3796	C- / 4.0	5.17	6.50	23.82 /69	1.88 /23	7.84 /41	0.00	2.07
MC	Alger SMid Cap Growth Fund I	ASIMX	E	(800) 254-3796	C / 4.8	5.48	7.15	25.14 /74	2.74 /29	8.73 /48	0.00	1.31
MC	Alger SMid Cap Growth Fund Z	ASMZX	E	(800) 254-3796	C / 5.0	5.46	7.10	25.31 /74	3.07 /32	9.07 /51	0.00	0.99
MC	Alger SMidCap Growth I2	AAMOX	E	(800) 254-3796	C / 4.6	4.43	6.32	22.60 /65	3.34 /35	12.84 /82	0.00	1.16
GR	Alger Spectra A	SPECX	C+	(800) 254-3796	B- / 7.1	9.82	8.35	20.37 /54	8.49 /83	13.20 /86	0.00	1.34
GR	Alger Spectra C	ASPCX	C+	(800) 254-3796	B- / 7.4	9.63	7.92	19.47 /49	7.66 /76	12.35 /78	0.00	2.11
GR	Alger Spectra Fund Z	ASPZX	B-	(800) 254-3796	B / 8.2	9.95	8.56	20.76 /56	8.82 /86	13.56 /89	0.00	1.19
GR	Alger Spectra I	ASPIX	B-	(800) 254-3796	B / 8.0	9.86	8.39	20.38 /54	8.49 /83	13.23 /86	0.00	1.35
IN	All Terrain Opportunity Inst	TERIX	U	(877) 743-7820	U /	3.28	3.04	6.96 / 6	--	--	1.83	3.35
GL	AllianzGI Best Styles Glbl Eq A	ALLGX	C+	(800) 988-8380	C / 5.1	8.50	8.44	20.00 /52	5.27 /57	--	0.00	1.22
GL	AllianzGI Best Styles Glbl Eq Inst	ALLHX	B-	(800) 988-8380	C+ / 6.5	8.59	8.73	20.45 /55	5.58 /60	--	1.59	0.68
GL	AllianzGI Best Styles Glbl Eq R6	AGERX	B-	(800) 988-8380	C+ / 6.5	8.63	8.77	20.58 /55	5.67 /61	--	1.67	0.70
FO	AllianzGI Best Styles Intl Eq R6	ASESX	U	(800) 988-8380	U /	7.83	6.68	16.02 /34	--	--	9.78	1.44
GR	AllianzGI Best Styles US Eq R6	ALSEX	U	(800) 988-8380	U /	7.66	10.22	22.62 /65	--	--	1.40	0.61
CV	● AllianzGI Convertible A	ANZAX	D	(800) 988-8380	D+ / 2.3	4.67	5.10	16.82 /38	2.43 /27	7.93 /41	2.26	0.98
CV	● AllianzGI Convertible Admn	ANNAX	D+	(800) 988-8380	C- / 3.3	4.72	5.16	16.95 /38	2.54 /28	8.02 /42	2.52	0.89
CV	● AllianzGI Convertible C	ANZCX	D	(800) 988-8380	D+ / 2.7	4.47	4.74	15.98 /34	1.70 /22	7.15 /36	1.68	1.71
CV	● AllianzGI Convertible Inst	ANNPX	D+	(800) 988-8380	C- / 3.5	4.77	5.32	17.23 /39	2.78 /30	8.28 /44	2.76	0.66
CV	● AllianzGI Convertible P	ANCMX	D+	(800) 988-8380	C- / 3.4	4.77	5.25	17.12 /39	2.71 /29	8.19 /44	2.67	0.69
CV	● AllianzGI Convertible R	ANZRX	D	(800) 988-8380	D+ / 2.9	4.57	4.88	16.30 /35	2.04 /24	7.50 /38	1.95	1.36
EM	AllianzGI Emerging Markets Opp A	AOTAX	D+	(800) 988-8380	C- / 3.3	9.20	7.10	25.11 /74	1.25 /20	0.83 / 6	1.52	1.61
EM	AllianzGI Emerging Markets Opp C	AOTCX	D+	(800) 988-8380	C- / 3.7	8.97	6.63	24.17 /70	0.49 /16	0.08 / 5	0.47	2.36
EM	AllianzGI Emerging Markets Opp Inst	AOTIX	C-	(800) 988-8380	C / 4.7	9.28	7.25	25.50 /75	1.60 /22	1.18 / 6	1.73	1.26
EM	AllianzGI Emerging Markets Opp P	AEMPX	C-	(800) 988-8380	C / 4.6	9.29	7.20	25.43 /75	1.51 /21	1.09 / 6	1.81	1.36
EM	AllianzGI Emerging Mkts Cons Inst	AERIX	U	(800) 988-8380	U /	9.93	4.50	25.32 /74	--	--	1.11	2.97
GR	AllianzGI Focused Growth A	PGWAX	C	(800) 988-8380	C / 5.4	7.19	4.61	17.29 /40	7.44 /75	13.59 /90	0.00	1.11
GR	AllianzGI Focused Growth Admn	PGFAX	C+	(800) 988-8380	C+ / 6.6	7.23	4.67	17.43 /40	7.55 /76	13.71 /91	0.00	1.01
GR	AllianzGI Focused Growth C	PGWCX	C	(800) 988-8380	C+ / 5.9	7.02	4.24	16.44 /36	6.65 /69	12.75 /81	0.00	1.86
GR	AllianzGI Focused Growth Inst	PGFIX	C+	(800) 988-8380	C+ / 6.8	7.30	4.82	17.73 /42	7.82 /78	13.99 /93	0.00	0.76
GR	AllianzGI Focused Growth P	AOGPX	C+	(800) 988-8380	C+ / 6.7	7.28	4.75	17.60 /41	7.71 /77	13.87 /92	0.00	0.86
GR	AllianzGI Focused Growth R	PPGRX	C+	(800) 988-8380	C+ / 6.3	7.15	4.50	17.02 /38	7.17 /73	13.31 /87	0.00	1.36
GL	AllianzGI Glbl Fndmtl Strat A	AZDAX	D+	(800) 988-8380	D- / 1.3	4.22	0.71	8.83 / 9	2.15 /25	--	2.11	2.30
GL	AllianzGI Glbl Fndmtl Strat C	AZDCX	D+	(800) 988-8380	D / 1.6	4.04	0.34	8.03 / 7	1.36 /20	--	1.93	2.82
GL	AllianzGI Glbl Fndmtl Strat Inst	AZDIX	C-	(800) 988-8380	D / 2.0	4.29	0.81	9.09 /10	2.38 /27	--	2.32	1.81
GL	AllianzGI Glbl Fndmtl Strat P	AZDPX	C-	(800) 988-8380	D / 2.0	4.29	0.74	9.02 / 9	2.27 /26	--	2.44	1.83
AA	AllianzGI Global Allocation A	PALAX	C-	(800) 988-8380	D / 1.7	5.90	3.25	10.39 /13	2.19 /25	4.74 /20	1.46	1.56
AA	AllianzGI Global Allocation Admn	AGAMX	C	(800) 988-8380	D+ / 2.4	6.00	3.42	10.59 /13	2.22 /25	4.75 /20	1.83	1.51
AA	AllianzGI Global Allocation C	PALCX	C-	(800) 988-8380	D / 2.0	5.74	2.94	9.58 /11	1.43 /21	3.98 /15	0.84	2.33
AA	AllianzGI Global Allocation Inst	PALLX	C	(800) 988-8380	D+ / 2.5	5.96	3.40	10.68 /13	2.43 /27	5.00 /21	2.23	1.35
AA	AllianzGI Global Allocation P	AGAPX	C	(800) 988-8380	D+ / 2.5	5.95	3.43	10.75 /14	2.46 /27	5.00 /21	2.38	1.26

● Denotes fund is closed to new investors
* Denotes fund is included in Section II

www.thestreetratings.com

Risk Rating/Pts	3 Year Standard Deviation	Beta	NAV As of 2/28/17	Total $(Mil)	Cash %	Stocks %	Bonds %	Other %	Portfolio Turnover Ratio	Last Bull Market Return	Last Bear Market Return	Manager Quality Pct	Manager Tenure (Years)	Initial Purch. $	Additional Purch. $	Front End Load	Back End Load
C- /3.4	16.3	1.17	11.46	28	8	91	0	1	76	103.9	-27.1	4	2	1,000	50	0.0	0.0
C- /3.6	16.3	1.18	12.82	74	8	91	0	1	76	113.6	-26.8	5	2	0	0	0.0	0.0
C- /3.6	16.3	1.18	12.93	150	8	91	0	1	76	116.7	-26.7	6	2	500,000	0	0.0	0.0
E+ /0.6	16.8	1.00	7.11	93	1	98	0	1	55	89.2	-27.1	14	2	1,000	50	5.3	0.0
E- /0.2	16.8	1.00	5.46	5	1	98	0	1	55	82.7	-27.2	9	2	1,000	50	0.0	0.0
E- /0.1	16.9	1.01	5.30	9	1	98	0	1	55	79.7	-27.2	9	2	1,000	50	0.0	0.0
E+ /0.6	16.8	1.00	7.26	22	1	98	0	1	55	91.6	-26.9	17	2	500,000	0	0.0	0.0
E- /0.0	16.9	1.01	17.40	120	1	98	0	1	55	92.5	-26.6	18	16	0	0	0.0	0.0
E- /0.0	16.9	1.01	14.83	13	1	98	0	1	55	87.4	-26.7	14	16	0	0	0.0	0.0
U /	N/A	N/A	17.43	54	1	98	0	1	55	N/A	N/A	N/A	16	500,000	0	0.0	0.0
E- /0.1	16.6	0.99	20.08	190	7	92	0	1	125	91.8	-26.7	18	2	0	0	0.0	0.0
E- /0.0	15.2	1.12	10.63	72	0	100	0	0	164	94.9	-26.1	4	1	1,000	50	5.3	0.0
E- /0.0	15.1	1.12	8.00	30	0	100	0	0	164	86.7	-26.3	3	1	1,000	50	0.0	0.0
E- /0.0	15.1	1.12	10.86	18	0	100	0	0	164	95.1	-26.0	4	1	0	0	0.0	0.0
E- /0.0	15.2	1.12	11.09	36	0	100	0	0	164	98.5	-26.0	5	1	500,000	0	0.0	0.0
E- /0.0	14.3	1.04	1.95	4	1	98	0	1	121	135.1	-26.0	8	1	0	0	0.0	0.0
C /4.6	12.2	1.05	18.19	1,604	2	97	0	1	109	130.7	-18.8	42	13	1,000	50	5.3	0.0
C /4.4	12.2	1.05	16.93	766	2	97	0	1	109	121.4	-19.1	32	13	1,000	50	0.0	0.0
C /4.6	12.2	1.05	18.54	2,080	2	97	0	1	109	134.4	-18.7	46	13	500,000	0	0.0	0.0
C /4.6	12.2	1.05	18.36	790	2	97	0	1	109	130.9	-18.8	42	13	0	0	0.0	0.0
U /	N/A	N/A	24.88	33	0	0	0	100	206	N/A	N/A	N/A	3	2,500	100	5.8	1.0
B- /7.4	10.6	0.78	16.77	1	1	98	0	1	70	N/A	N/A	96	4	1,000	50	5.5	0.0
B- /7.4	10.6	0.78	16.60	2	1	98	0	1	70	N/A	N/A	96	4	1,000,000	0	0.0	0.0
B- /7.4	10.6	0.78	16.70	711	1	98	0	1	70	N/A	N/A	96	4	0	0	0.0	0.0
U /	N/A	N/A	13.57	32	3	96	0	1	103	N/A	N/A	N/A	3	0	0	0.0	0.0
U /	N/A	N/A	16.87	120	3	96	0	1	64	N/A	N/A	N/A	4	0	0	0.0	0.0
C /5.3	9.0	1.02	31.96	234	7	8	0	85	101	72.5	-17.1	40	23	1,000	50	5.5	0.0
C /5.2	9.0	1.02	31.91	1	7	8	0	85	101	73.3	-17.1	42	23	1,000,000	0	0.0	0.0
C /5.3	9.0	1.02	32.11	56	7	8	0	85	101	65.8	-17.4	31	23	1,000	50	0.0	0.0
C /5.2	9.0	1.02	31.72	997	7	8	0	85	101	75.6	-17.0	45	23	1,000,000	0	0.0	0.0
C /5.2	8.9	1.02	31.80	85	7	8	0	85	101	74.8	-17.1	44	23	1,000,000	0	0.0	0.0
C /5.3	9.0	1.02	31.90	1	7	8	0	85	101	69.0	-17.3	35	23	0	0	0.0	0.0
C /5.5	14.0	0.83	24.63	144	3	96	0	1	85	24.9	-29.1	72	10	1,000	50	5.5	0.0
C+ /5.6	14.0	0.83	24.26	11	3	96	0	1	85	20.0	-29.3	63	10	1,000	50	0.0	0.0
C /5.5	14.0	0.83	24.81	70	3	96	0	1	85	27.3	-29.0	75	10	1,000,000	0	0.0	0.0
C /5.5	14.0	0.83	24.22	25	3	96	0	1	85	26.6	-29.0	74	10	1,000,000	0	0.0	0.0
U /	N/A	N/A	13.79	39	4	95	0	1	91	N/A	N/A	N/A	3	1,000,000	0	0.0	0.0
C /5.4	11.6	1.00	43.54	365	0	99	0	1	55	130.8	-16.8	35	5	1,000	50	5.5	0.0
C /5.3	11.6	1.00	37.83	10	0	99	0	1	55	132.1	-16.8	36	5	1,000,000	0	0.0	0.0
C /4.9	11.6	1.00	30.68	231	0	99	0	1	55	121.7	-17.1	27	5	1,000	50	0.0	0.0
C /5.3	11.6	1.00	40.14	201	0	99	0	1	55	135.3	-16.7	40	5	1,000,000	0	0.0	0.0
C /5.1	11.6	1.00	33.91	56	0	99	0	1	55	133.9	-16.7	39	5	1,000,000	0	0.0	0.0
C /5.1	11.6	1.00	33.61	21	0	99	0	1	55	127.7	-16.9	32	5	0	0	0.0	0.0
B- /7.5	5.5	0.40	14.70	N/A	8	34	56	2	37	N/A	N/A	87	4	1,000	50	5.5	0.0
B- /7.7	5.6	0.40	14.72	N/A	8	34	56	2	37	N/A	N/A	83	4	1,000	50	0.0	0.0
B- /7.6	5.6	0.40	14.85	16	8	34	56	2	37	N/A	N/A	88	4	1,000,000	0	0.0	0.0
B- /7.6	5.6	0.40	14.80	N/A	8	34	56	2	37	N/A	N/A	87	4	1,000,000	0	0.0	0.0
B /8.0	6.3	0.93	11.45	45	41	51	7	1	57	43.5	-15.4	19	15	1,000	50	5.5	0.0
B /8.1	6.3	0.92	11.73	N/A	41	51	7	1	57	43.8	-15.5	19	15	1,000,000	0	0.0	0.0
B /8.0	6.3	0.93	11.58	41	41	51	7	1	57	38.1	-15.8	13	15	1,000	50	0.0	0.0
B /8.0	6.2	0.92	11.28	70	41	51	7	1	57	45.7	-15.4	21	15	1,000,000	0	0.0	0.0
B /8.0	6.2	0.92	11.40	2	41	51	7	1	57	45.6	-15.4	21	15	1,000,000	0	0.0	0.0

Fund Type	Fund Name	Ticker Symbol	Overall Investment Rating	Phone	Performance Rating/Pts	3 Mo	6 Mo	1Yr / Pct	Annualized 3Yr / Pct	Annualized 5Yr / Pct	Dividend Yield	Expense Ratio
AA	AllianzGI Global Allocation R	AGARX	C-	(800) 988-8380	D+ / 2.3	5.83	3.17	10.20 /12	2.01 /24	4.55 /18	1.76	1.76
GL	AllianzGI Global Allocation R6	AGASX	U	(800) 988-8380	U /	5.94	3.39	10.75 /14	--	--	2.45	1.26
AA	AllianzGI Global Dynamic Alloc A	ASGAX	D	(800) 988-8380	D- / 1.3	5.25	3.01	9.66 /11	1.07 /19	4.64 /19	0.00	1.78
AA	AllianzGI Global Dynamic Alloc Adm	AGFAX	D	(800) 988-8380	D / 1.8	5.19	3.00	9.65 /11	1.07 /19	4.65 /19	0.00	1.94
AA	AllianzGI Global Dynamic Alloc C	ASACX	D	(800) 988-8380	D- / 1.5	5.06	2.61	8.83 / 9	0.29 /15	3.83 /14	0.00	2.74
AA	AllianzGI Global Dynamic Alloc Inst	AGAIX	D	(800) 988-8380	D+ / 1.9	5.25	3.12	9.96 /12	1.31 /20	4.91 /21	0.06	1.50
AA	AllianzGI Global Dynamic Alloc P	AGSPX	D	(800) 988-8380	D / 1.9	5.22	3.10	9.87 /11	1.21 /19	4.80 /20	0.55	1.52
AA	AllianzGI Global Dynamic Alloc R	ASFRX	D	(800) 988-8380	D / 1.7	5.11	2.86	9.41 /10	0.81 /17	4.38 /17	0.00	2.30
GL	AllianzGI Global Dynamic Alloc R6	ADYFX	U	(800) 988-8380	U /	5.28	3.21	10.11 /12	--	--	0.46	1.41
EN	AllianzGI Global Natural Res A	ARMAX	E-	(800) 988-8380	E- / 0.2	-4.98	2.26	26.97 /79	-6.17 / 2	-1.07 / 3	0.80	1.44
EN	AllianzGI Global Natural Res C	ARMCX	E-	(800) 988-8380	E- / 0.2	-5.21	1.77	25.88 /76	-6.90 / 2	-1.83 / 3	0.03	2.19
EN	AllianzGI Global Natural Res Inst	RGLIX	E-	(800) 988-8380	E / 0.3	-4.94	2.39	27.28 /80	-5.87 / 2	-0.73 / 4	0.82	1.09
EN	AllianzGI Global Natural Res P	APGPX	E-	(800) 988-8380	E / 0.3	-4.91	2.35	27.29 /80	-5.93 / 2	-0.82 / 4	0.97	1.19
GL	AllianzGI Global Small Cap A	RGSAX	D-	(800) 988-8380	D / 1.7	4.54	3.71	16.78 /37	0.99 /18	9.40 /54	0.00	1.61
GL	AllianzGI Global Small Cap C	RGSCX	D	(800) 988-8380	D / 2.0	4.35	3.32	15.93 /34	0.24 /14	8.59 /47	0.00	2.36
GL	AllianzGI Global Small Cap Inst	DGSCX	D	(800) 988-8380	D+ / 2.6	4.63	3.89	17.20 /39	1.35 /20	9.79 /57	0.00	1.26
GL	AllianzGI Global Small Cap P	ARSPX	D	(800) 988-8380	D+ / 2.5	4.59	3.83	17.07 /39	1.25 /20	9.68 /56	0.00	1.36
GL	AllianzGI Global Water A	AWTAX	D+	(800) 988-8380	D- / 1.3	3.72	-2.50	12.21 /19	1.84 /23	8.00 /42	0.32	1.44
GL	AllianzGI Global Water C	AWTCX	D+	(800) 988-8380	D- / 1.5	3.57	-2.88	11.40 /16	1.07 /19	7.18 /36	0.00	2.23
GL	AllianzGI Global Water Inst	AWTIX	D+	(800) 988-8380	D / 2.0	3.86	-2.34	12.55 /20	2.16 /25	8.35 /45	0.80	1.17
GL	AllianzGI Global Water P	AWTPX	D+	(800) 988-8380	D / 1.9	3.80	-2.39	12.43 /19	2.10 /25	8.24 /44	0.57	1.16
HL	AllianzGI Health Sciences A	RAGHX	D+	(800) 988-8380	C+ / 6.1	9.26	4.81	16.52 /36	8.29 /81	15.09 /97	0.00	1.47
HL	AllianzGI Health Sciences C	RCGHX	D	(800) 988-8380	C+ / 6.5	9.09	4.44	15.67 /33	7.48 /75	14.24 /94	0.00	2.22
GI	AllianzGI Income and Growth A	AZNAX	C-	(800) 988-8380	C- / 4.0	5.78	6.67	19.81 /51	4.52 /49	7.62 /39	2.88	1.29
GI	AllianzGI Income and Growth C	AZNCX	C	(800) 988-8380	C / 4.5	5.62	6.29	18.92 /47	3.75 /40	6.81 /33	2.68	2.04
GI	AllianzGI Income and Growth Inst	AZNIX	C+	(800) 988-8380	C / 5.5	5.89	6.89	20.21 /53	4.88 /53	7.99 /42	3.22	0.94
GI	AllianzGI Income and Growth P	AIGPX	C+	(800) 988-8380	C / 5.4	5.91	6.88	20.17 /53	4.78 /52	7.88 /41	3.17	1.04
GI	AllianzGI Income and Growth R	AIGRX	C	(800) 988-8380	C / 4.9	5.72	6.52	19.56 /50	4.24 /46	7.34 /37	2.85	1.54
FO	AllianzGI International Growth Inst	GLIIX	U	(800) 988-8380	U /	7.22	-1.67	14.34 /27	--	--	0.11	5.71
FO	AllianzGI International Sm Cp A	AOPAX	D-	(800) 988-8380	E+ / 0.9	6.07	0.91	7.94 / 7	0.09 /14	7.37 /37	0.89	1.63
FO	AllianzGI International Sm Cp C	AOPCX	E+	(800) 988-8380	E+ / 0.8	5.89	0.53	7.13 / 6	-0.65 /11	6.57 /32	0.75	2.42
FO	AllianzGI International Sm Cp Inst	ALOIX	D-	(800) 988-8380	D- / 1.4	6.16	1.03	8.18 / 8	0.33 /15	7.62 /39	0.99	1.39
FO	AllianzGI International Sm Cp P	ALOPX	D-	(800) 988-8380	D- / 1.4	6.12	0.97	8.09 / 8	0.25 /14	7.54 /39	1.02	1.37
FO	AllianzGI International Sm Cp R	ALORX	D-	(800) 988-8380	D- / 1.0	6.05	0.78	7.66 / 7	-0.15 /13	7.11 /35	0.96	2.09
SC	AllianzGI Micro Cap A	GMCAX	D-	(800) 988-8380	C / 4.5	3.14	7.79	31.23 /89	3.18 /33	12.52 /79	0.00	2.07
SC	AllianzGI Micro Cap Inst	AMCIX	D+	(800) 988-8380	C+ / 5.7	3.19	7.86	31.39 /89	3.27 /34	12.70 /81	0.00	1.80
SC	AllianzGI Micro Cap P	AAMPX	D+	(800) 988-8380	C+ / 5.7	3.13	7.82	31.26 /89	3.28 /34	12.65 /80	0.00	1.80
MC	AllianzGI Mid-Cap A	RMDAX	C-	(800) 988-8380	C+ / 6.5	6.89	7.48	27.28 /80	6.53 /69	10.73 /64	0.00	1.13
MC	AllianzGI Mid-Cap Administrative	DRMAX	C	(800) 988-8380	B- / 7.5	7.13	7.70	27.34 /80	6.63 /69	10.87 /65	0.00	1.03
MC	AllianzGI Mid-Cap C	RMDCX	C-	(800) 988-8380	C+ / 6.9	7.00	7.34	26.38 /77	5.83 /63	9.89 /57	0.00	1.88
MC	AllianzGI Mid-Cap Institutional	DRMCX	C+	(800) 988-8380	B / 7.7	7.19	7.73	27.49 /80	6.94 /71	11.14 /67	0.00	0.78
MC	AllianzGI Mid-Cap P	ARMPX	C+	(800) 988-8380	B / 7.6	6.96	7.77	27.65 /81	6.88 /71	11.05 /66	0.00	0.88
MC	AllianzGI Mid-Cap R	PRMRX	C	(800) 988-8380	B- / 7.3	6.97	7.57	27.23 /80	6.39 /67	10.53 /62	0.00	1.38
AA	AllianzGI Multi Asset RI Ret A	ALRAX	E+	(800) 988-8380	E / 0.3	1.16	0.86	13.65 /24	-3.40 / 4	--	1.65	5.76
AA	AllianzGI Multi Asset RI Ret C	ALLCX	E+	(800) 988-8380	E / 0.3	0.97	0.44	12.90 /21	-4.12 / 3	--	0.36	6.33
AA	AllianzGI Multi Asset RI Ret Inst	ALRNX	E+	(800) 988-8380	E / 0.4	1.19	0.96	14.04 /26	-3.17 / 4	--	1.32	5.34
AA	AllianzGI Multi Asset RI Ret P	ALRPX	E+	(800) 988-8380	E / 0.4	1.19	0.96	13.89 /25	-3.25 / 4	--	1.24	5.42
IN	AllianzGI NFJ Dividend Value A	PNEAX	C+	(800) 988-8380	C+ / 6.3	6.10	11.62	24.73 /72	6.15 /66	10.11 /59	1.99	1.08
IN	AllianzGI NFJ Dividend Value Admn	ANDAX	B+	(800) 988-8380	B- / 7.3	6.12	11.67	24.84 /73	6.26 /66	10.22 /60	2.17	0.98
IN	AllianzGI NFJ Dividend Value C	PNECX	C+	(800) 988-8380	C+ / 6.7	5.93	11.26	23.87 /69	5.37 /58	9.29 /53	1.43	1.83
IN	AllianzGI NFJ Dividend Value Inst	NFJEX	B+	(800) 988-8380	B- / 7.5	6.21	11.81	25.24 /74	6.53 /69	10.52 /62	2.40	0.73
IN	AllianzGI NFJ Dividend Value P	ADJPX	B+	(800) 988-8380	B- / 7.4	6.13	11.75	25.02 /73	6.43 /68	10.39 /61	2.31	0.83

Notes at top of table:
99 Pct = Best
0 Pct = Worst

• Denotes fund is closed to new investors
* Denotes fund is included in Section II

www.thestreetratings.com

Risk Rating/Pts	3 Year Standard Deviation	Beta	NAV As of 2/28/17	Total $(Mil)	Cash %	Stocks %	Bonds %	Other %	Portfolio Turnover Ratio	Last Bull Market Return	Last Bear Market Return	Manager Quality Pct	Manager Tenure (Years)	Initial Purch. $	Additional Purch. $	Front End Load	Back End Load
B /8.0	6.2	0.92	11.34	N/A	41	51	7	1	57	42.2	-15.6	18	15	0	0	0.0	0.0
U /	N/A	N/A	11.25	295	41	51	7	1	57	N/A	N/A	N/A	8	0	0	0.0	0.0
C+ /6.4	6.2	0.90	18.84	5	33	38	27	2	79	49.3	-20.7	12	2	1,000	50	5.5	0.0
C+ /6.4	6.2	0.90	18.86	N/A	33	38	27	2	79	49.4	-20.7	12	2	1,000,000	0	0.0	0.0
C+ /6.5	6.2	0.90	18.49	1	33	38	27	2	79	43.3	-21.0	8	2	1,000	50	0.0	0.0
C+ /6.3	6.2	0.91	18.89	34	33	38	27	2	79	51.5	-20.6	13	2	1,000,000	0	0.0	0.0
C+ /6.4	6.2	0.90	18.78	11	33	38	27	2	79	50.7	-20.7	13	2	1,000,000	0	0.0	0.0
C+ /6.4	6.2	0.90	18.72	N/A	33	38	27	2	79	47.4	-20.8	10	2	0	0	0.0	0.0
U /	N/A	N/A	18.84	200	33	38	27	2	79	N/A	N/A	N/A	2	0	0	0.0	0.0
D /1.7	19.4	0.92	15.58	14	0	100	0	0	177	19.0	-31.0	56	13	1,000	50	5.5	0.0
D /1.6	19.4	0.92	14.66	4	0	100	0	0	177	14.1	-31.3	44	13	1,000	50	0.0	0.0
D /1.7	19.4	0.92	15.95	12	0	100	0	0	177	21.2	-30.9	60	13	1,000,000	0	0.0	0.0
D /1.6	19.4	0.92	15.79	5	0	100	0	0	177	20.6	-31.0	59	13	1,000,000	0	0.0	0.0
C /5.5	11.9	0.74	44.48	60	2	97	0	1	87	94.4	-23.8	81	7	1,000	50	5.5	0.0
C /5.5	11.9	0.74	39.80	21	2	97	0	1	87	86.7	-24.0	76	7	1,000	50	0.0	0.0
C+ /5.6	12.0	0.74	47.23	115	2	97	0	1	87	98.1	-23.6	83	7	1,000,000	0	0.0	0.0
C+ /5.6	12.0	0.74	46.90	20	2	97	0	1	87	97.1	-23.7	83	7	1,000,000	0	0.0	0.0
B- /7.2	10.4	0.64	13.70	188	5	94	0	1	55	74.0	-19.8	86	9	1,000	50	5.5	0.0
B- /7.2	10.4	0.63	13.17	85	5	94	0	1	55	67.0	-20.2	82	9	1,000	50	0.0	0.0
B- /7.2	10.4	0.63	13.53	87	5	94	0	1	55	76.9	-19.8	87	9	1,000,000	0	0.0	0.0
B- /7.2	10.4	0.64	13.75	170	5	94	0	1	55	76.1	-19.8	87	9	1,000,000	0	0.0	0.0
D+ /2.5	15.4	1.04	29.62	151	6	93	0	1	113	138.0	-15.0	40	12	1,000	50	5.5	0.0
D /1.8	15.4	1.04	23.77	12	6	93	0	1	113	128.6	-15.2	31	12	1,000	50	0.0	0.0
C+ /6.4	7.6	0.70	11.33	1,111	2	40	32	26	94	67.8	-14.4	38	10	1,000	50	5.5	0.0
C+ /6.2	7.7	0.71	10.56	1,118	2	40	32	26	94	61.0	-14.6	28	10	1,000	50	0.0	0.0
C+ /6.5	7.7	0.71	11.66	222	2	40	32	26	94	70.9	-14.3	42	10	1,000,000	0	0.0	0.0
C+ /6.4	7.7	0.71	11.57	638	2	40	32	26	94	70.1	-14.3	41	10	1,000,000	0	0.0	0.0
C+ /6.4	7.7	0.71	11.33	3	2	40	32	26	94	65.4	-14.4	34	10	0	0	0.0	0.0
U /	N/A	N/A	15.99	28	0	100	0	0	20	N/A	N/A	N/A	2	1,000,000	0	0.0	0.0
C /5.3	11.2	0.78	33.46	8	2	97	0	1	76	65.1	-24.5	75	5	1,000	50	5.5	0.0
C /5.2	11.2	0.78	32.66	2	2	97	0	1	76	58.5	-24.8	68	5	1,000	50	0.0	0.0
C /5.5	11.2	0.78	34.77	24	2	97	0	1	76	67.3	-24.4	77	5	1,000,000	0	0.0	0.0
C /5.4	11.2	0.78	33.54	40	2	97	0	1	76	66.6	-24.4	77	5	1,000,000	0	0.0	0.0
C /5.3	11.2	0.78	32.94	N/A	2	97	0	1	76	62.9	-24.6	73	5	0	0	0.0	0.0
D+ /2.8	19.8	1.19	13.89	3	2	97	0	1	39	143.3	-35.5	17	10	1,000	50	5.5	0.0
D+ /2.8	19.8	1.19	14.04	31	2	97	0	1	39	145.4	-35.4	17	10	1,000,000	0	0.0	0.0
D+ /2.8	19.8	1.19	13.96	1	2	97	0	1	39	144.6	-35.5	18	10	1,000,000	0	0.0	0.0
C- /3.8	13.1	0.97	3.58	89	1	98	0	1	73	109.7	-22.7	39	12	1,000	50	5.5	0.0
C- /3.9	13.1	0.97	3.76	1	1	98	0	1	73	111.1	-22.9	41	12	1,000,000	0	0.0	0.0
C- /3.4	13.0	0.97	3.06	167	1	98	0	1	73	101.5	-22.9	32	12	1,000	50	0.0	0.0
C- /4.0	13.0	0.96	4.02	24	1	98	0	1	73	114.2	-22.7	46	12	1,000,000	0	0.0	0.0
C- /4.0	13.1	0.97	4.00	5	1	98	0	1	73	113.3	-22.7	44	12	1,000,000	0	0.0	0.0
C- /3.7	13.2	0.98	3.54	2	1	98	0	1	73	107.8	-22.9	36	12	0	0	0.0	0.0
C /5.3	9.2	0.90	13.29	1	0	49	50	1	60	N/A	N/A	2	5	1,000	50	5.5	0.0
C /5.4	9.2	0.91	13.33	N/A	0	49	50	1	60	N/A	N/A	2	5	1,000	50	0.0	0.0
C /5.4	9.2	0.90	13.47	3	0	49	50	1	60	N/A	N/A	2	5	1,000,000	0	0.0	0.0
C /5.3	9.2	0.90	13.44	N/A	0	49	50	1	60	N/A	N/A	2	5	1,000,000	0	0.0	0.0
C+ /6.7	11.0	0.99	17.29	662	2	97	0	1	42	98.3	-16.8	24	17	1,000	50	5.5	0.0
C+ /6.7	10.9	0.99	17.50	372	2	97	0	1	42	99.2	-16.7	25	17	1,000,000	0	0.0	0.0
C+ /6.7	11.0	0.99	17.41	338	2	97	0	1	42	90.3	-17.0	17	17	1,000	50	0.0	0.0
C+ /6.7	11.0	0.99	17.40	1,732	2	97	0	1	42	102.0	-16.6	26	17	1,000,000	0	0.0	0.0
C+ /6.7	11.0	0.99	17.40	681	2	97	0	1	42	101.0	-16.7	26	17	1,000,000	0	0.0	0.0

					PERFORMANCE						Incl. in Returns	
	99 Pct = Best						Total Return % through 2/28/17					
	0 Pct = Worst		Overall		Perfor-				Annualized		Dividend	Expense
Fund		Ticker	Investment		mance				3Yr / Pct	5Yr / Pct		
Type	Fund Name	Symbol	Rating	Phone	Rating/Pts	3 Mo	6 Mo	1Yr / Pct			Yield	Ratio
IN	AllianzGI NFJ Dividend Value R	PNERX	B+	(800) 988-8380	B- / 7.0	6.06	11.52	24.52 /72	5.90 /63	9.84 /57	1.89	1.33
IN	AllianzGI NFJ Dividend Value R6	ANDVX	B+	(800) 988-8380	B- / 7.5	6.17	11.86	25.28 /74	6.56 /69	10.54 /62	2.46	0.68
EM	AllianzGI NFJ Emerg Mkts Value A	AZMAX	C	(800) 988-8380	C+ / 5.7	8.97	6.37	33.25 /92	3.67 /39	--	2.55	6.40
EM	AllianzGI NFJ Emerg Mkts Value C	AZMCX	C	(800) 988-8380	C+ / 6.1	8.78	5.96	32.25 /90	2.89 /31	--	1.27	7.24
EM	AllianzGI NFJ Emerg Mkts Value Inst	AZMIX	C+	(800) 988-8380	C+ / 6.9	9.16	6.58	33.61 /92	3.94 /42	--	2.20	5.78
EM	AllianzGI NFJ Emerg Mkts Value P	AZMPX	C+	(800) 988-8380	C+ / 6.9	9.11	6.56	33.54 /92	3.88 /41	--	3.61	5.72
GL	AllianzGI NFJ Global Div Val A	ANUAX	D-	(800) 988-8380	D+ / 2.6	8.12	8.47	18.33 /44	1.43 /21	4.88 /20	2.42	1.72
GL	AllianzGI NFJ Global Div Val C	ANUCX	D-	(800) 988-8380	C- / 3.0	7.90	7.98	17.40 /40	0.62 /16	4.05 /15	2.17	2.56
GL	AllianzGI NFJ Global Div Val Inst	ANUIX	D	(800) 988-8380	C- / 3.8	8.29	8.59	18.65 /46	1.68 /22	5.15 /22	2.93	1.40
GL	AllianzGI NFJ Global Div Val P	ANUPX	D	(800) 988-8380	C- / 3.7	8.17	8.51	18.53 /45	1.57 /21	5.05 /22	2.71	1.44
FO	AllianzGI NFJ Internatl Value A	AFJAX	E	(800) 988-8380	E- / 0.1	6.50	2.33	8.50 / 8	-7.22 / 1	-1.33 / 3	2.48	1.33
FO	AllianzGI NFJ Internatl Value Admn	AIVAX	E	(800) 988-8380	E- / 0.1	6.52	2.30	8.52 / 8	-7.14 / 1	-1.23 / 3	2.71	1.23
FO	AllianzGI NFJ Internatl Value C	AFJCX	E	(800) 988-8380	E- / 0.1	6.27	1.85	7.61 / 7	-7.93 / 1	-2.08 / 3	2.09	2.08
FO	AllianzGI NFJ Internatl Value Inst	ANJIX	E	(800) 988-8380	E- / 0.1	6.60	2.48	8.85 / 9	-6.90 / 2	-0.98 / 3	2.90	0.98
FO	AllianzGI NFJ Internatl Value P	AFVPX	E	(800) 988-8380	E- / 0.1	6.56	2.36	8.71 / 9	-7.01 / 1	-1.09 / 3	2.83	1.08
FO	AllianzGI NFJ Internatl Value R	ANJRX	E	(800) 988-8380	E- / 0.1	6.45	2.17	8.18 / 8	-7.46 / 1	-1.58 / 3	2.45	1.58
FO	AllianzGI NFJ Internatl Value R6	ANAVX	E	(800) 988-8380	E- / 0.2	6.59	2.49	8.89 / 9	-6.86 / 2	-0.96 / 3	3.05	0.93
FO	AllianzGI NFJ Intl Sm Cap Val A	AJVAX	E+	(800) 988-8380	E+ / 0.7	5.95	0.66	10.59 /13	-0.10 /13	--	3.04	2.54
FO	AllianzGI NFJ Intl Sm Cap Val C	AJVCX	E+	(800) 988-8380	E+ / 0.9	5.71	0.29	9.80 /11	-0.83 /10	--	5.85	3.30
FO	AllianzGI NFJ Intl Sm Cap Val Inst	AJVIX	D-	(800) 988-8380	D- / 1.5	5.95	0.80	10.92 /14	0.16 /14	--	5.76	2.21
FO	AllianzGI NFJ Intl Sm Cap Val P	AJVPX	D-	(800) 988-8380	D- / 1.5	5.91	0.72	10.77 /14	0.03 /13	--	7.47	3.37
FO	AllianzGI NFJ Intl Value II A	NFJAX	E+	(800) 988-8380	E- / 0.2	5.38	1.41	9.00 / 9	-3.21 / 4	2.27 / 9	2.52	1.76
FO	AllianzGI NFJ Intl Value II C	NFJCX	D-	(800) 988-8380	E / 0.3	5.11	0.97	8.13 / 8	-3.96 / 3	1.49 / 7	2.12	2.49
FO	AllianzGI NFJ Intl Value II Inst	NFJIX	D-	(800) 988-8380	E / 0.4	5.43	1.48	9.25 /10	-3.00 / 4	2.53 / 9	2.91	1.40
FO	AllianzGI NFJ Intl Value II P	NFJPX	D-	(800) 988-8380	E / 0.4	5.43	1.49	9.15 /10	-3.04 / 4	2.46 / 9	1.95	1.42
GR	AllianzGI NFJ Large Cap Value A	PNBAX	A-	(800) 988-8380	B / 7.7	6.86	13.44	27.29 /80	7.85 /78	11.73 /72	1.50	1.11
GR	AllianzGI NFJ Large Cap Value Admn	ALNFX	A+	(800) 988-8380	B+ / 8.7	6.91	13.48	27.45 /80	7.96 /79	11.84 /73	1.67	1.01
GR	AllianzGI NFJ Large Cap Value C	PNBCX	A-	(800) 988-8380	B / 8.0	6.69	12.99	26.34 /77	7.05 /72	10.90 /65	0.69	1.86
GR	AllianzGI NFJ Large Cap Value Inst	ANVIX	A+	(800) 988-8380	B+ / 8.9	6.99	13.64	27.77 /81	8.25 /81	12.13 /75	2.04	0.76
GR	AllianzGI NFJ Large Cap Value P	ALCPX	A+	(800) 988-8380	B+ / 8.8	6.95	13.59	27.63 /81	8.13 /80	12.02 /74	1.97	0.86
GR	AllianzGI NFJ Large Cap Value R	ANLRX	A	(800) 988-8380	B+ / 8.4	6.81	13.31	27.00 /79	7.59 /76	11.46 /70	1.26	1.36
GL	AllianzGI NFJ Mid-Cap Value A	PQNAX	A+	(800) 988-8380	A- / 9.1	9.41	15.00	31.95 /90	9.11 /87	12.42 /78	1.09	1.30
GL	AllianzGI NFJ Mid-Cap Value Admn	PRAAX	A+	(800) 988-8380	A+ / 9.6	9.46	15.06	32.09 /90	9.23 /88	12.53 /79	1.17	1.20
GL	AllianzGI NFJ Mid-Cap Value C	PQNCX	A+	(800) 988-8380	A / 9.4	9.22	14.55	31.02 /88	8.30 /81	11.58 /71	0.80	2.05
GL	AllianzGI NFJ Mid-Cap Value Inst	PRNIX	A+	(800) 988-8380	A+ / 9.7	9.53	15.20	32.43 /91	9.50 /90	12.82 /82	1.31	0.95
GL	AllianzGI NFJ Mid-Cap Value P	ANRPX	A+	(800) 988-8380	A+ / 9.7	9.50	15.14	32.31 /90	9.39 /89	12.71 /81	1.78	1.05
GL	AllianzGI NFJ Mid-Cap Value R	PRNRX	A+	(800) 988-8380	A+ / 9.6	9.38	14.89	31.68 /89	8.86 /86	12.15 /76	0.90	1.55
SC	● AllianzGI NFJ Small Cap Value A	PCVAX	D+	(800) 988-8380	C+ / 6.8	5.44	14.48	31.73 /89	5.30 /58	9.62 /55	1.24	1.23
SC	● AllianzGI NFJ Small Cap Value Admn	PVADX	C-	(800) 988-8380	B / 7.9	5.49	14.50	31.99 /90	5.46 /59	9.79 /57	1.48	1.13
SC	● AllianzGI NFJ Small Cap Value C	PCVCX	D+	(800) 988-8380	B- / 7.2	5.24	14.03	30.77 /88	4.51 /49	8.80 /49	0.84	1.98
SC	● AllianzGI NFJ Small Cap Value Inst	PSVIX	C-	(800) 988-8380	B / 8.0	5.52	14.64	32.22 /90	5.71 /62	10.05 /59	1.52	0.88
SC	● AllianzGI NFJ Small Cap Value P	ASVPX	C-	(800) 988-8380	B / 7.9	5.53	14.60	32.09 /90	5.56 /60	9.90 /58	1.43	0.98
SC	● AllianzGI NFJ Small Cap Value R	PNVRX	C-	(800) 988-8380	B / 7.6	5.40	14.32	31.46 /89	5.03 /54	9.35 /53	1.00	1.48
SC	AllianzGI NFJ Small Cap Value R6	ANFVX	C-	(800) 988-8380	B / 8.1	5.56	14.66	32.28 /90	5.76 /62	10.09 /59	1.62	0.83
GI	AllianzGI Retirement 2020 A	AGLAX	C-	(800) 988-8380	D / 1.9	4.42	2.77	12.25 /19	2.76 /30	3.76 /14	2.30	1.26
GI	AllianzGI Retirement 2020 Admn	AGLMX	C	(800) 988-8380	D+ / 2.7	4.43	2.84	12.28 /19	2.81 /30	3.79 /14	2.24	1.11
GI	AllianzGI Retirement 2020 C	ABSCX	C-	(800) 988-8380	D / 2.2	4.25	2.38	11.41 /16	2.01 /24	2.97 /11	2.00	2.01
GI	AllianzGI Retirement 2020 P	AGLPX	C	(800) 988-8380	D+ / 2.8	4.47	2.90	12.60 /20	3.07 /32	4.07 /16	2.87	0.86
GI	AllianzGI Retirement 2020 R	AGLRX	C-	(800) 988-8380	D+ / 2.4	4.30	2.56	11.87 /17	2.41 /27	3.39 /12	1.97	1.51
GI	AllianzGI Retirement 2020 R6	AGNIX	C	(800) 988-8380	D+ / 2.9	4.48	2.91	12.65 /20	3.16 /33	4.16 /16	2.93	0.76
GL	AllianzGI Retirement 2025 A	GVSAX	C-	(800) 988-8380	D+ / 2.4	5.11	3.98	14.37 /27	3.27 /34	4.19 /16	1.73	1.29
GL	AllianzGI Retirement 2025 Admn	GVDAX	C	(800) 988-8380	C- / 3.3	5.13	4.01	14.38 /27	3.30 /35	4.22 /16	2.09	1.14

● Denotes fund is closed to new investors
∗ Denotes fund is included in Section II

42

Risk Rating/Pts	3 Year Standard Deviation	Beta	NAV As of 2/28/17	Total $(Mil)	Cash %	Stocks %	Bonds %	Other %	Portfolio Turnover Ratio	Last Bull Market Return	Last Bear Market Return	Manager Quality Pct	Manager Tenure (Years)	Initial Purch. $	Additional Purch. $	Front End Load	Back End Load
C+ / 6.7	11.0	0.99	17.24	147	2	97	0	1	42	95.5	-16.8	21	17	0	0	0.0	0.0
C+ / 6.7	11.0	0.99	17.37	117	2	97	0	1	42	102.2	-16.6	27	17	0	0	0.0	0.0
C / 5.0	15.5	0.94	14.79	4	6	93	0	1	104	N/A	N/A	86	5	1,000	50	5.5	0.0
C / 5.0	15.5	0.94	14.87	N/A	6	93	0	1	104	N/A	N/A	82	5	1,000	50	0.0	0.0
C / 5.0	15.5	0.94	15.04	5	6	93	0	1	104	N/A	N/A	87	5	1,000,000	0	0.0	0.0
C / 4.9	15.5	0.94	14.69	12	6	93	0	1	104	N/A	N/A	87	5	1,000,000	0	0.0	0.0
C- / 4.1	11.0	0.81	16.64	4	0	98	0	2	52	56.6	-20.9	84	8	1,000	50	5.5	0.0
C- / 3.9	11.0	0.81	16.11	5	0	98	0	2	52	50.0	-21.2	79	8	1,000	50	0.0	0.0
C- / 3.9	11.0	0.81	16.39	13	0	98	0	2	52	58.8	-20.8	85	8	1,000,000	0	0.0	0.0
C- / 3.9	11.0	0.81	16.55	1	0	98	0	2	52	58.0	-20.9	85	8	1,000,000	0	0.0	0.0
C / 4.6	13.2	1.03	17.05	154	0	99	0	1	50	13.7	-23.1	5	14	1,000	50	5.5	0.0
C / 4.6	13.2	1.02	17.10	6	0	99	0	1	50	14.2	-23.0	5	14	1,000,000	0	0.0	0.0
C / 4.6	13.2	1.03	16.77	60	0	99	0	1	50	9.0	-23.3	4	14	1,000	50	0.0	0.0
C / 4.6	13.2	1.02	17.16	102	0	99	0	1	50	15.8	-23.0	6	14	1,000,000	0	0.0	0.0
C / 4.6	13.2	1.02	17.13	139	0	99	0	1	50	15.1	-23.0	5	14	1,000,000	0	0.0	0.0
C / 4.6	13.2	1.02	17.06	13	0	99	0	1	50	12.1	-23.2	4	14	0	0	0.0	0.0
C / 4.6	13.2	1.03	17.12	44	0	99	0	1	50	16.0	-23.0	6	14	0	0	0.0	0.0
C / 5.1	12.3	0.91	17.35	1	7	92	0	1	95	N/A	N/A	74	5	1,000	50	5.5	0.0
C / 5.0	12.3	0.91	16.58	1	7	92	0	1	95	N/A	N/A	66	5	1,000	50	0.0	0.0
C / 5.2	12.3	0.91	17.40	1	7	92	0	1	95	N/A	N/A	76	5	1,000,000	0	0.0	0.0
C / 4.9	12.3	0.91	16.77	N/A	7	92	0	1	95	N/A	N/A	75	5	1,000,000	0	0.0	0.0
C+ / 5.8	11.8	0.92	15.60	N/A	5	94	0	1	48	N/A	N/A	33	6	1,000	50	5.5	0.0
C+ / 5.9	11.8	0.92	15.53	N/A	5	94	0	1	48	N/A	N/A	25	6	1,000	50	0.0	0.0
C+ / 5.8	11.8	0.92	15.65	31	5	94	0	1	48	N/A	N/A	36	6	1,000,000	0	0.0	0.0
C+ / 5.9	11.8	0.92	15.75	N/A	5	94	0	1	48	N/A	N/A	35	6	1,000,000	0	0.0	0.0
C+ / 6.9	11.1	1.02	23.53	147	0	99	0	1	51	109.8	-16.8	38	17	1,000	50	5.5	0.0
C+ / 6.9	11.1	1.02	23.85	1	0	99	0	1	51	111.0	-16.7	39	17	1,000,000	0	0.0	0.0
C+ / 6.9	11.1	1.02	23.75	82	0	99	0	1	51	101.5	-17.0	29	17	1,000	50	0.0	0.0
C+ / 6.9	11.1	1.02	23.44	146	0	99	0	1	51	113.9	-16.6	43	17	1,000,000	0	0.0	0.0
C+ / 6.9	11.1	1.02	23.76	16	0	99	0	1	51	112.8	-16.7	42	17	1,000,000	0	0.0	0.0
C+ / 6.9	11.1	1.02	23.75	8	0	99	0	1	51	107.1	-16.9	35	17	0	0	0.0	0.0
C+ / 6.7	11.4	0.71	28.91	401	7	92	0	1	50	119.6	-19.9	99	8	1,000	50	5.5	0.0
C+ / 6.7	11.4	0.71	29.77	5	7	92	0	1	50	120.9	-19.8	99	8	1,000,000	0	0.0	0.0
C+ / 6.6	11.4	0.71	24.20	189	7	92	0	1	50	111.1	-20.2	99	8	1,000	50	0.0	0.0
C+ / 6.7	11.4	0.71	30.72	37	7	92	0	1	50	123.9	-19.8	99	8	1,000,000	0	0.0	0.0
C+ / 6.5	11.4	0.71	23.93	23	7	92	0	1	50	122.8	-19.8	99	8	1,000,000	0	0.0	0.0
C+ / 6.6	11.4	0.71	25.25	6	7	92	0	1	50	116.8	-20.0	99	8	0	0	0.0	0.0
D / 1.7	12.9	0.76	24.19	965	11	88	0	1	48	91.4	-18.5	74	26	1,000	50	5.5	0.0
D / 1.7	12.9	0.76	24.12	456	11	88	0	1	48	93.1	-18.4	75	26	1,000,000	0	0.0	0.0
D / 1.6	12.9	0.76	22.04	176	11	88	0	1	48	83.8	-18.8	66	26	1,000	50	0.0	0.0
/ 1.9	12.9	0.76	26.60	1,366	11	88	0	1	48	95.6	-18.4	77	26	1,000,000	0	0.0	0.0
/ 1.9	12.9	0.76	26.48	63	11	88	0	1	48	94.0	-18.4	76	26	1,000,000	0	0.0	0.0
/ 1.8	12.9	0.76	25.48	62	11	88	0	1	48	88.9	-18.6	72	26	0	0	0.0	0.0
D / 1.8	12.9	0.76	26.52	522	11	88	0	1	48	95.9	-18.4	78	26	0	0	0.0	0.0
/ 7.9	5.0	0.41	19.12	13	18	25	55	2	106	33.2	-9.3	56	9	1,000	50	5.5	0.0
B- / 7.9	5.0	0.40	19.25	1	18	25	55	2	106	33.4	-9.3	57	9	1,000,000	0	0.0	0.0
/ 8.0	5.0	0.40	19.06	N/A	18	25	55	2	106	27.8	-9.6	46	9	1,000	50	0.0	0.0
B- / 7.8	5.0	0.41	19.27	26	18	25	55	2	106	35.4	-9.3	60	9	1,000,000	0	0.0	0.0
B- / 7.9	5.0	0.41	19.20	N/A	18	25	55	2	106	30.7	-9.4	51	9	0	0	0.0	0.0
B- / 7.8	5.0	0.41	19.29	15	18	25	55	2	106	36.0	-9.2	61	9	0	0	0.0	0.0
B- / 7.9	5.5	0.41	17.17	7	18	31	49	2	115	N/A	N/A	91	6	1,000	50	5.5	0.0
B- / 7.9	5.5	0.41	17.17	1	18	31	49	2	115	N/A	N/A	91	6	1,000,000	0	0.0	0.0

	99 Pct = Best 0 Pct = Worst				PERFORMANCE						Incl. in Returns	
			Overall		Perfor-	Total Return % through 2/28/17			Annualized		Dividend	Expense
Fund Type	Fund Name	Ticker Symbol	Investment Rating	Phone	mance Rating/Pts	3 Mo	6 Mo	1Yr / Pct	3Yr / Pct	5Yr / Pct	Yield	Ratio
GL	AllianzGI Retirement 2025 P	GVSPX	C	(800) 988-8380	C- / 3.5	5.19	4.13	14.70 /28	3.57 /38	4.51 /18	2.67	0.89
GL	AllianzGI Retirement 2025 R	GVSRX	C	(800) 988-8380	C- / 3.0	4.98	3.73	13.90 /25	2.89 /31	3.81 /14	2.11	1.54
GL	AllianzGI Retirement 2025 R6	GVSIX	C+	(800) 988-8380	C- / 3.6	5.26	4.20	14.84 /29	3.70 /39	4.60 /19	2.74	0.79
GR	AllianzGI Retirement 2030 A	ABLAX	C-	(800) 988-8380	D+ / 2.8	5.92	5.23	16.15 /35	3.27 /34	4.69 /19	1.62	1.24
GR	AllianzGI Retirement 2030 Admn	ABAMX	C	(800) 988-8380	C- / 3.8	5.93	5.20	16.18 /35	3.32 /35	4.73 /19	1.95	1.09
GR	AllianzGI Retirement 2030 C	ABLCX	C	(800) 988-8380	C- / 3.2	5.72	4.76	15.21 /31	2.48 /27	3.89 /15	1.39	1.99
GR	AllianzGI Retirement 2030 P	ABLPX	C+	(800) 988-8380	C- / 4.0	5.98	5.35	16.43 /36	3.58 /38	5.00 /21	2.34	0.84
GR	AllianzGI Retirement 2030 R	ABLRX	C	(800) 988-8380	C- / 3.4	5.80	4.96	15.66 /33	2.90 /31	4.32 /17	1.79	1.49
GR	AllianzGI Retirement 2030 R6	ABLIX	C+	(800) 988-8380	C- / 4.1	5.99	5.37	16.54 /36	3.67 /39	5.09 /22	2.40	0.74
GL	AllianzGI Retirement 2035 A	GVRAX	C	(800) 988-8380	C- / 3.3	6.62	6.50	18.13 /43	3.56 /38	5.31 /23	1.77	1.16
GL	AllianzGI Retirement 2035 Admn	GVLAX	C+	(800) 988-8380	C / 4.5	6.66	6.60	18.19 /44	3.62 /38	5.37 /24	2.09	1.01
GL	AllianzGI Retirement 2035 P	GVPAX	C+	(800) 988-8380	C / 4.7	6.72	6.72	18.51 /45	3.89 /41	5.64 /26	2.37	0.76
GL	AllianzGI Retirement 2035 R	GVRRX	C+	(800) 988-8380	C- / 4.1	6.54	6.29	17.65 /41	3.19 /34	4.95 /21	1.78	1.41
GL	AllianzGI Retirement 2035 R6	GVLIX	C+	(800) 988-8380	C / 4.8	6.71	6.71	18.54 /45	3.98 /43	5.73 /27	2.48	0.66
GR	AllianzGI Retirement 2040 A	AVSAX	C	(800) 988-8380	C- / 3.8	7.12	7.28	19.87 /51	3.68 /39	5.67 /26	1.62	1.11
GR	AllianzGI Retirement 2040 Admn	AVAMX	C+	(800) 988-8380	C / 4.9	7.17	7.33	19.96 /52	3.72 /39	5.71 /26	2.04	0.96
GR	AllianzGI Retirement 2040 C	AVSCX	C	(800) 988-8380	C- / 4.2	6.92	6.86	18.98 /47	2.92 /31	4.88 /20	1.35	1.86
GR	AllianzGI Retirement 2040 P	AVSPX	C+	(800) 988-8380	C / 5.2	7.20	7.47	20.28 /54	4.02 /43	6.00 /28	2.42	0.71
GR	AllianzGI Retirement 2040 R	AVSRX	C+	(800) 988-8380	C / 4.6	7.01	7.06	19.46 /49	3.32 /35	5.31 /23	1.90	1.36
GR	AllianzGI Retirement 2040 R6	AVTIX	C+	(800) 988-8380	C / 5.2	7.23	7.49	20.35 /54	4.11 /44	6.08 /29	2.50	0.61
GL	AllianzGI Retirement 2045 A	GBVAX	C	(800) 988-8380	C- / 4.2	7.37	7.79	21.40 /59	3.91 /42	6.03 /28	1.71	1.08
GL	AllianzGI Retirement 2045 Admn	GBMAX	C+	(800) 988-8380	C / 5.4	7.37	7.79	21.45 /59	3.96 /42	6.06 /29	2.38	0.93
GL	AllianzGI Retirement 2045 P	GBVPX	C+	(800) 988-8380	C+ / 5.6	7.46	7.94	21.77 /61	4.25 /46	6.36 /31	2.49	0.68
GL	AllianzGI Retirement 2045 R	GBVRX	C+	(800) 988-8380	C / 5.0	7.23	7.53	20.96 /57	3.55 /38	5.66 /26	1.96	1.33
GL	AllianzGI Retirement 2045 R6	GBVIX	C+	(800) 988-8380	C+ / 5.7	7.51	7.98	21.92 /62	4.38 /47	6.47 /31	2.59	0.58
GR	AllianzGI Retirement 2050 A	ASNAX	C	(800) 988-8380	C- / 4.2	7.48	7.86	21.78 /61	3.83 /41	6.07 /29	1.98	1.07
GR	AllianzGI Retirement 2050 Admn	ANAMX	C+	(800) 988-8380	C / 5.4	7.50	7.87	21.85 /61	3.88 /41	6.11 /29	2.31	0.92
GR	AllianzGI Retirement 2050 C	ASNCX	C	(800) 988-8380	C / 4.7	7.29	7.51	20.91 /57	3.07 /32	5.26 /23	1.65	1.82
GR	AllianzGI Retirement 2050 P	ASNPX	C+	(800) 988-8380	C+ / 5.6	7.54	8.02	22.15 /63	4.16 /45	6.39 /31	2.56	0.67
GR	AllianzGI Retirement 2050 R	ASNRX	C+	(800) 988-8380	C / 5.0	7.29	7.61	21.30 /59	3.46 /36	5.70 /26	2.03	1.32
GR	AllianzGI Retirement 2050 R6	ASNIX	C+	(800) 988-8380	C+ / 5.7	7.62	8.10	22.30 /64	4.26 /46	6.50 /31	2.64	0.57
GL	AllianzGI Retirement 2055 A	GLIAX	C	(800) 988-8380	C- / 4.1	7.38	7.76	21.28 /59	3.76 /40	6.05 /29	1.72	1.07
GL	AllianzGI Retirement 2055 Admn	GLRAX	C+	(800) 988-8380	C / 5.3	7.43	7.81	21.38 /59	3.80 /40	6.10 /29	1.93	0.92
GL	AllianzGI Retirement 2055 P	GLIPX	C+	(800) 988-8380	C / 5.5	7.49	7.92	21.73 /61	4.09 /44	6.40 /31	2.17	0.67
GL	AllianzGI Retirement 2055 R	GLLRX	C	(800) 988-8380	C / 4.9	7.29	7.55	20.88 /57	3.41 /36	5.69 /26	1.66	1.32
GL	AllianzGI Retirement 2055 R6	GBLIX	C+	(800) 988-8380	C+ / 5.6	7.52	7.95	21.79 /61	4.18 /45	6.48 /31	2.22	0.57
GI	AllianzGI Retirement Income A	AGRAX	C-	(800) 988-8380	D / 2.2	4.38	2.49	13.30 /23	3.39 /36	3.93 /15	3.51	1.20
GI	AllianzGI Retirement Income Admn	ARAMX	C-	(800) 988-8380	D+ / 2.7	4.37	2.49	12.22 /19	3.08 /33	3.76 /14	3.27	1.05
GI	AllianzGI Retirement Income C	ARTCX	C-	(800) 988-8380	D+ / 2.5	4.15	2.07	12.40 /19	2.62 /28	3.15 /11	2.45	1.95
GI	AllianzGI Retirement Income P	AGRPX	C-	(800) 988-8380	C- / 3.2	4.41	2.59	13.63 /24	3.70 /39	4.26 /17	4.09	0.80
GI	AllianzGI Retirement Income R	ASRRX	C-	(800) 988-8380	D+ / 2.8	4.30	2.31	12.94 /21	3.05 /32	3.58 /13	3.16	1.45
GI	AllianzGI Retirement Income R6	AVRIX	C-	(800) 988-8380	C- / 3.3	4.45	2.67	13.76 /24	3.80 /40	4.35 /17	4.28	0.70
SC	AllianzGI Small Cap Blend A	AZBAX	C+	(800) 988-8380	C+ / 6.4	4.99	11.74	28.55 /83	5.77 /62	--	0.00	1.31
SC	AllianzGI Small Cap Blend C	AZBCX	C+	(800) 988-8380	C+ / 6.8	4.81	11.34	27.63 /81	4.98 /54	--	0.00	2.06
SC	AllianzGI Small Cap Blend Inst	AZBIX	B-	(800) 988-8380	B / 7.6	5.16	11.99	29.11 /84	6.15 /66	--	0.00	0.96
SC	AllianzGI Small Cap Blend P	AZBPX	B-	(800) 988-8380	B- / 7.5	5.08	11.86	28.87 /84	6.03 /64	--	0.00	1.06
IN	AllianzGI Structured Return A	AZIAX	C-	(800) 988-8380	D / 1.7	0.89	2.56	5.30 / 4	4.53 /49	--	0.38	1.29
IN	AllianzGI Structured Return C	AZICX	C	(800) 988-8380	D / 2.0	0.70	2.15	4.54 / 4	3.77 /40	--	0.00	2.09
IN	AllianzGI Structured Return Inst	AZIIX	C	(800) 988-8380	D+ / 2.5	0.87	2.59	5.52 / 4	4.78 /52	--	0.38	1.00
IN	AllianzGI Structured Return P	AZIPX	C	(800) 988-8380	D+ / 2.5	0.88	2.60	5.48 / 4	4.71 /51	--	0.75	1.06
TC	AllianzGI Technology A	RAGTX	C	(800) 988-8380	B+ / 8.4	11.18	10.74	27.88 /81	8.75 /85	14.41 /95	0.00	1.67
TC	AllianzGI Technology Administrative	DGTAX	C+	(800) 988-8380	A / 9.3	11.22	10.81	28.01 /82	8.86 /86	14.55 /96	0.00	1.57

● Denotes fund is closed to new investors
★ Denotes fund is included in Section II

www.thestreetratings.com

RISK Risk Rating/Pts	3 Year Standard Deviation	Beta	NAV As of 2/28/17	Total $(Mil)	Cash %	Stocks %	Bonds %	Other %	Portfolio Turnover Ratio	Last Bull Market Return	Last Bear Market Return	Manager Quality Pct	Manager Tenure (Years)	Initial Purch. $	Additional Purch. $	Front End Load	Back End Load
B- / 7.8	5.5	0.41	17.14	36	18	31	49	2	115	N/A	N/A	92	6	1,000,000	0	0.0	0.0
B- / 7.9	5.5	0.41	17.03	N/A	18	31	49	2	115	N/A	N/A	90	6	0	0	0.0	0.0
B- / 7.8	5.5	0.41	17.16	18	18	31	49	2	115	N/A	N/A	92	6	0	0	0.0	0.0
B- / 7.6	6.2	0.54	20.60	8	16	40	43	1	105	42.6	-13.9	44	9	1,000	50	5.5	0.0
B- / 7.5	6.2	0.54	20.76	1	16	40	43	1	105	43.0	-13.9	44	9	1,000,000	0	0.0	0.0
B- / 7.6	6.3	0.55	20.41	1	16	40	43	1	105	36.8	-14.1	33	9	1,000	50	0.0	0.0
B- / 7.5	6.2	0.54	20.79	36	16	40	43	1	105	44.9	-13.8	48	9	1,000,000	0	0.0	0.0
B- / 7.6	6.2	0.54	20.52	N/A	16	40	43	1	105	39.9	-14.0	39	9	0	0	0.0	0.0
B- / 7.5	6.2	0.54	20.83	20	16	40	43	1	105	45.7	-13.8	49	9	0	0	0.0	0.0
B- / 7.6	7.0	0.53	18.26	9	14	50	35	1	97	N/A	N/A	92	6	1,000	50	5.5	0.0
B- / 7.6	7.0	0.53	18.31	1	14	50	35	1	97	N/A	N/A	92	6	1,000,000	0	0.0	0.0
B- / 7.5	7.0	0.53	18.33	31	14	50	35	1	97	N/A	N/A	93	6	1,000,000	0	0.0	0.0
B- / 7.6	7.0	0.53	18.18	1	14	50	35	1	97	N/A	N/A	91	6	0	0	0.0	0.0
B- / 7.5	7.0	0.53	18.35	11	14	50	35	1	97	N/A	N/A	93	6	0	0	0.0	0.0
B- / 7.0	8.0	0.71	21.08	4	13	62	23	2	101	53.7	-19.3	27	9	1,000	50	5.5	0.0
B- / 7.0	8.0	0.71	21.07	N/A	13	62	23	2	101	54.0	-19.2	28	9	1,000,000	0	0.0	0.0
B- / 7.1	8.0	0.71	20.93	N/A	13	62	23	2	101	47.6	-19.5	20	9	1,000	50	0.0	0.0
C+ / 6.9	8.0	0.71	21.15	23	13	62	23	2	101	56.4	-19.2	31	9	1,000,000	0	0.0	0.0
B- / 7.0	8.0	0.71	20.85	N/A	13	62	23	2	101	50.9	-19.3	24	9	0	0	0.0	0.0
C+ / 6.9	8.0	0.71	21.19	19	13	62	23	2	101	57.1	-19.1	32	9	0	0	0.0	0.0
C+ / 6.9	8.6	0.65	18.40	4	11	70	18	1	103	N/A	N/A	93	6	1,000	50	5.5	0.0
C+ / 6.9	8.6	0.65	18.32	1	11	70	18	1	103	N/A	N/A	93	6	1,000,000	0	0.0	0.0
C+ / 6.9	8.6	0.65	18.42	14	11	70	18	1	103	N/A	N/A	94	6	1,000,000	0	0.0	0.0
C+ / 6.9	8.6	0.65	18.23	N/A	11	70	18	1	103	N/A	N/A	92	6	0	0	0.0	0.0
C+ / 6.9	8.6	0.65	18.47	10	11	70	18	1	103	N/A	N/A	94	6	0	0	0.0	0.0
C+ / 6.4	9.0	0.80	20.48	3	11	71	16	2	89	58.8	-20.5	20	9	1,000	50	5.5	0.0
C+ / 6.4	8.9	0.80	20.54	1	11	71	16	2	89	59.2	-20.5	21	9	1,000,000	0	0.0	0.0
C+ / 6.4	8.9	0.80	20.20	N/A	11	71	16	2	89	52.4	-20.8	15	9	1,000	50	0.0	0.0
C+ / 6.3	8.9	0.80	20.62	12	11	71	16	2	89	61.4	-20.4	24	9	1,000,000	0	0.0	0.0
C+ / 6.4	8.9	0.80	20.34	N/A	11	71	16	2	89	55.8	-20.7	18	9	0	0	0.0	0.0
C+ / 6.3	8.9	0.80	20.70	13	11	71	16	2	89	62.3	-20.5	24	9	0	0	0.0	0.0
C+ / 6.4	9.0	0.68	17.64	2	11	71	17	1	92	N/A	N/A	93	6	1,000	50	5.5	0.0
C+ / 6.4	9.0	0.68	17.67	N/A	11	71	17	1	92	N/A	N/A	93	6	1,000,000	0	0.0	0.0
C+ / 6.4	9.0	0.68	17.76	5	11	71	17	1	92	N/A	N/A	94	6	1,000,000	0	0.0	0.0
C+ / 6.4	9.0	0.68	17.54	N/A	11	71	17	1	92	N/A	N/A	92	6	0	0	0.0	0.0
C+ / 6.4	9.0	0.68	17.82	4	11	71	17	1	92	N/A	N/A	94	6	0	0	0.0	0.0
B- / 7.2	4.8	0.37	18.33	10	14	21	63	2	116	32.3	-6.4	69	9	1,000	50	5.5	0.0
B- / 7.3	4.8	0.36	18.61	2	14	21	63	2	116	31.2	-6.4	66	9	1,000,000	0	0.0	0.0
B- / 7.3	4.8	0.37	18.30	3	14	21	63	2	116	26.9	-6.7	59	9	1,000	50	0.0	0.0
B- / 7.2	4.8	0.37	18.51	17	14	21	63	2	116	34.5	-6.3	72	9	1,000,000	0	0.0	0.0
B- / 7.3	4.8	0.37	19.02	N/A	14	21	63	2	116	29.9	-6.6	65	9	0	0	0.0	0.0
B- / 7.1	4.8	0.37	18.07	21	14	21	63	2	116	35.1	-6.3	73	9	0	0	0.0	0.0
C / 5.2	13.5	0.84	19.47	35	3	96	0	1	139	N/A	N/A	74	4	1,000	50	5.5	0.0
C / 5.2	13.5	0.84	19.10	38	3	96	0	1	139	N/A	N/A	65	4	1,000	50	0.0	0.0
C / 5.2	13.5	0.84	19.67	3	3	96	0	1	139	N/A	N/A	76	4	1,000,000	0	0.0	0.0
C / 5.2	13.5	0.84	19.57	3	3	96	0	1	139	N/A	N/A	75	4	1,000,000	0	0.0	0.0
B / 8.6	3.0	0.17	15.73	122	16	83	0	1	500	N/A	N/A	89	5	1,000	50	5.5	0.0
B / 8.6	3.0	0.17	15.28	15	16	83	0	1	500	N/A	N/A	86	5	1,000	50	0.0	0.0
B / 8.6	3.0	0.17	15.85	129	16	83	0	1	500	N/A	N/A	90	5	1,000,000	0	0.0	0.0
B / 8.6	3.0	0.17	15.70	61	16	83	0	1	500	N/A	N/A	89	5	1,000,000	0	0.0	0.0
D+ / 2.5	14.8	1.20	54.77	416	7	92	0	1	171	124.8	-22.2	26	22	1,000	50	5.5	0.0
D+ / 2.6	14.9	1.20	57.40	72	7	92	0	1	171	126.2	-22.2	27	22	1,000,000	0	0.0	0.0

Fund Type	Fund Name	Ticker Symbol	Overall Investment Rating	Phone	Performance Rating/Pts	3 Mo	6 Mo	1Yr / Pct	3Yr / Pct	5Yr / Pct	Dividend Yield	Expense Ratio
TC	AllianzGI Technology C	RCGTX	C	(800) 988-8380	B+ / 8.8	10.99	10.35	26.92 /79	7.95 /79	13.56 /89	0.00	2.42
TC	AllianzGI Technology Institutional	DRGTX	C+	(800) 988-8380	A / 9.4	11.27	10.94	28.31 /82	9.13 /88	14.83 /97	0.00	1.32
TC	AllianzGI Technology P	ARTPX	C+	(800) 988-8380	A / 9.4	11.25	10.88	28.19 /82	9.02 /87	14.72 /96	0.00	1.42
SC	AllianzGI Ultra Micro Cap A	GUCAX	E	(800) 988-8380	D- / 1.2	3.64	9.17	23.85 /69	-0.70 /10	11.71 /72	0.00	2.08
SC	AllianzGI Ultra Micro Cap Inst	AUMIX	E	(800) 988-8380	D / 1.8	3.73	9.29	24.31 /71	-0.47 /11	11.97 /74	0.00	1.79
SC	AllianzGI Ultra Micro Cap P	AAUPX	E	(800) 988-8380	D / 1.8	3.74	9.26	24.24 /71	-0.42 /12	11.99 /74	0.00	1.81
IX	AllianzGI US Equity Hedged A	AZUAX	C-	(800) 988-8380	C- / 3.0	5.25	6.49	13.78 /24	4.08 /44	--	1.30	2.38
IX	AllianzGI US Equity Hedged C	AZUCX	C-	(800) 988-8380	C- / 3.4	5.08	6.03	12.96 /21	3.31 /35	--	0.96	3.00
IX	AllianzGI US Equity Hedged Inst	AZUIX	C	(800) 988-8380	C- / 4.2	5.31	6.54	14.04 /26	4.34 /47	--	1.16	2.05
IX	AllianzGI US Equity Hedged P	AZUPX	C	(800) 988-8380	C- / 4.1	5.33	6.50	13.95 /25	4.21 /45	--	2.38	1.98
SC	AllianzGI US Small-Cap Growth A	AEGAX	E-	(800) 988-8380	E+ / 0.9	4.16	5.84	22.67 /65	-1.42 / 8	7.20 /36	0.00	1.75
SC	AllianzGI US Small-Cap Growth C	AEGCX	E-	(800) 988-8380	D- / 1.0	3.89	5.34	21.51 /60	-2.26 / 6	6.35 /31	0.00	2.59
SC	AllianzGI US Small-Cap Growth Inst	AEMIX	E-	(800) 988-8380	D- / 1.4	4.22	5.94	22.98 /67	-1.21 / 9	7.50 /38	0.00	1.53
SC	AllianzGI US Small-Cap Growth P	AEGPX	E-	(800) 988-8380	D- / 1.4	4.09	5.82	22.76 /66	-1.32 / 8	7.39 /37	0.00	1.55
SC	AllianzGI US Small-Cap Growth R	AEGRX	E-	(800) 988-8380	D- / 1.2	3.98	5.61	22.28 /63	-1.71 / 7	6.94 /34	0.00	2.03
GL	Alpha Risk Hedged Div Eqty Adv	CANOX	C-	(877) 773-3863	E+ / 0.6	1.29	2.27	2.38 / 2	-0.84 /10	--	0.00	4.30
GL	Alpha Risk Hedged Div Eqty Inst	CANTX	C	(877) 773-3863	D- / 1.0	1.66	2.94	3.60 / 3	0.20 /14	--	0.00	3.30
GR	AlphaCentric Hedged Market Oppty I	HMXIX	B	(844) 223-8637	C- / 3.6	1.03	2.66	6.29 / 5	6.55 /69	10.49 /62	0.00	N/A
GL	● AlphaCore Absolute Institutional	GDAMX	D-	(855) 447-2532	C- / 3.2	1.59	1.06	13.18 /22	4.89 /53	8.45 /46	1.21	1.57
GR	AlphaMark Large Cap Growth Fund	AMLCX	C	(866) 420-3350	B- / 7.3	5.82	8.62	24.22 /71	7.56 /76	12.45 /79	0.01	1.98
SC	AlphaOne Small Cap Opps I	AOMCX	B+	(855) 425-7426	A / 9.5	2.48	15.70	34.31 /93	10.10 /94	13.95 /93	0.00	1.29
SC	AlphaOne Small Cap Opps Inv	AOMAX	B+	(855) 425-7426	A / 9.5	2.43	15.54	33.85 /93	9.87 /93	13.68 /90	0.00	1.54
GL	Alpine Dynamic Dividend A	ADAVX	C	(888) 785-5578	C+ / 5.6	8.16	9.02	23.71 /69	5.64 /61	7.19 /36	5.79	1.52
IN	Alpine Dynamic Dividend Inst	ADVDX	C+	(888) 785-5578	C+ / 6.9	8.53	9.45	24.00 /70	5.90 /63	7.45 /38	6.35	1.27
RE	Alpine Emg Mkts Real Estate A	AEAMX	E+	(888) 785-5578	D- / 1.4	9.47	-2.93	17.92 /42	0.42 /15	-0.85 / 4	1.70	3.22
RE	Alpine Emg Mkts Real Estate Inst	AEMEX	D-	(888) 785-5578	D / 2.2	9.48	-2.83	18.20 /44	0.68 /17	-0.60 / 4	2.08	2.97
FS	Alpine Financial Services A	ADAFX	A+	(888) 785-5578	A+ / 9.9	11.79	28.14	55.39 /99	9.82 /92	17.09 /98	0.02	2.32
FS	Alpine Financial Services Inst	ADFSX	A+	(888) 785-5578	A+ / 9.9	11.87	28.28	55.88 /99	10.12 /94	17.39 /98	0.28	2.07
OT	Alpine Global Infrastructure Fd A	AIAFX	D+	(888) 785-5578	C- / 3.4	9.16	5.76	21.72 /61	2.83 /30	8.09 /43	3.65	1.53
GL	Alpine Global Infrastructure Inst	AIFRX	C-	(888) 785-5578	C / 4.7	9.22	5.88	21.98 /62	3.08 /33	8.36 /45	4.10	1.28
RE	Alpine Intl Real Estate A	EGALX	E	(888) 785-5578	E / 0.3	7.07	-2.67	9.09 /10	-2.50 / 5	-0.58 / 4	0.00	1.70
RE	Alpine Intl Real Estate Inst	EGLRX	E+	(888) 785-5578	E / 0.5	7.18	-2.56	9.43 /10	-2.23 / 6	-0.31 / 4	0.14	1.45
RE	Alpine Realty Inc and Growth A	AIAGX	B-	(888) 785-5578	B / 7.6	9.18	0.42	19.75 /51	11.73 /98	11.61 /71	2.80	1.61
RE	Alpine Realty Inc and Growth Inst	AIGYX	B	(888) 785-5578	B+ / 8.7	9.20	0.48	19.98 /52	11.98 /98	11.87 /73	3.17	1.36
GL	Alpine Rising Dividend A	AAADX	B-	(888) 785-5578	C+ / 6.7	7.64	10.23	24.38 /71	7.36 /74	11.03 /66	2.93	2.19
GL	Alpine Rising Dividend Inst	AADDX	A-	(888) 785-5578	B / 7.8	7.67	10.33	24.58 /72	7.60 /76	11.28 /68	3.31	1.94
GR	Alpine Small Cap A	ADIAX	C	(888) 785-5578	C+ / 6.1	6.58	12.22	36.48 /95	3.38 /36	8.43 /46	0.00	2.15
GR	Alpine Small Cap Institutional	ADINX	C+	(888) 785-5578	B- / 7.2	6.67	12.38	36.82 /96	3.67 /39	8.72 /48	0.00	1.90
OT	ALPS CoreComm Mgt CompComm	JCRAX	E	(866) 759-5679	E- / 0.1	2.20	6.34	20.47 /55	-10.36 / 1	-8.36 / 1	0.05	1.47
OT	ALPS CoreComm Mgt CompComm	JCRCX	E	(866) 759-5679	E- / 0.1	2.08	6.04	19.84 /51	-10.90 / 1	-8.94 / 1	0.00	2.07
OT	ALPS CoreComm Mgt CompComm	JCRIX	E	(866) 759-5679	E- / 0.1	2.38	6.67	20.85 /57	-10.08 / 1	-8.10 / 1	0.10	1.17
EN	ALPS/Alerian MLP Infra Idx A	ALERX	E-	(866) 759-5679	D- / 1.3	9.75	9.49	42.31 /98	-3.73 / 3	--	6.71	1.78
EN	ALPS/Alerian MLP Infra Idx C	ALRCX	E-	(866) 759-5679	D / 1.7	9.60	9.33	41.67 /98	-4.02 / 3	--	7.22	2.38
EN	ALPS/Alerian MLP Infra Idx I	ALRIX	E-	(866) 759-5679	D / 1.9	9.93	9.67	42.64 /98	-3.47 / 4	--	7.02	1.38
FO	ALPS/Kotak India Growth A	INDAX	B-	(866) 759-5679	A+ / 9.9	10.37	3.04	39.20 /97	18.45 /99	11.17 /67	0.00	3.51
FO	ALPS/Kotak India Growth C	INFCX	B-	(866) 759-5679	A+ / 9.9	10.23	2.81	38.36 /97	17.68 /99	10.46 /62	0.00	4.11
FO	ALPS/Kotak India Growth I	INDIX	B-	(866) 759-5679	A+ / 9.9	10.42	3.23	39.57 /97	18.88 /99	11.55 /70	0.00	3.10
FS	ALPS/Red Rocks Listed Priv Eq A	LPEFX	C-	(866) 759-5679	C / 4.3	8.12	11.46	24.86 /73	3.11 /33	12.39 /78	1.39	2.03
FS	ALPS/Red Rocks Listed Priv Eq C	LPFCX	C-	(866) 759-5679	C / 4.7	7.73	11.02	23.82 /69	2.35 /26	11.62 /71	1.47	2.53
FS	ALPS/Red Rocks Listed Priv Eq I	LPEIX	C	(866) 759-5679	C+ / 5.7	8.09	11.56	25.20 /74	3.43 /36	12.72 /81	1.53	1.73
FS	ALPS/Red Rocks Listed Priv Eq R	LPERX	C	(866) 759-5679	C / 5.2	7.91	11.34	24.36 /71	2.96 /31	12.35 /78	1.72	2.17
GI	ALPS/WMC Research Value A	AMWYX	D+	(866) 759-5679	B / 7.6	7.10	10.10	28.03 /82	8.10 /80	13.11 /85	0.14	1.49

● Denotes fund is closed to new investors
∗ Denotes fund is included in Section II

RISK			NET ASSETS		ASSET				Portfolio Turnover Ratio	BULL / BEAR		FUND MANAGER		MINIMUMS		LOADS	
	3 Year		NAV							Last Bull	Last Bear	Manager	Manager	Initial	Additional	Front	Back
Risk Rating/Pts	Standard Deviation	Beta	As of 2/28/17	Total $(Mil)	Cash %	Stocks %	Bonds %	Other %		Market Return	Market Return	Quality Pct	Tenure (Years)	Purch. $	Purch. $	End Load	End Load
D /1.7	14.9	1.20	44.63	116	7	92	0	1	171	115.8	-22.4	19	22	1,000	50	0.0	0.0
D+ /2.8	14.9	1.20	60.21	582	7	92	0	1	171	129.2	-22.1	30	22	1,000,000	0	0.0	0.0
D+ /2.7	14.9	1.20	59.41	45	7	92	0	1	171	128.0	-22.1	29	22	1,000,000	0	0.0	0.0
D+ /2.6	18.5	1.12	21.11	16	1	98	0	1	32	131.5	-29.5	4	9	1,000	50	5.5	0.0
D+ /2.6	18.5	1.12	21.43	21	1	98	0	1	32	134.7	-29.4	4	9	1,000,000	0	0.0	0.0
D+ /2.6	18.5	1.12	21.38	6	1	98	0	1	32	134.4	-29.4	4	9	1,000,000	0	0.0	0.0
B- /7.1	6.2	0.58	17.04	1	7	92	0	1	6	N/A	N/A	50	5	1,000	50	5.5	0.0
C+ /6.9	6.3	0.58	16.41	N/A	7	92	0	1	6	N/A	N/A	39	5	1,000	50	0.0	0.0
B- /7.0	6.2	0.58	17.13	4	7	92	0	1	6	N/A	N/A	53	5	1,000,000	0	0.0	0.0
B- /7.0	6.2	0.58	16.85	N/A	7	92	0	1	6	N/A	N/A	52	5	1,000,000	0	0.0	0.0
D- /1.4	17.0	1.04	11.64	1	1	98	0	1	120	88.0	-30.4	3	10	1,000	50	5.5	0.0
D- /1.2	17.0	1.04	10.83	1	1	98	0	1	120	80.0	-30.6	3	10	1,000	50	0.0	0.0
D- /1.5	17.0	1.04	11.97	15	1	98	0	1	120	90.7	-30.3	4	10	1,000,000	0	0.0	0.0
D- /1.5	17.0	1.04	11.86	1	1	98	0	1	120	89.7	-30.3	3	10	1,000,000	0	0.0	0.0
D- /1.3	17.0	1.04	11.39	N/A	1	98	0	1	120	85.4	-30.5	3	10	0	0	0.0	0.0
B+ /9.2	4.0	0.26	9.45	2	12	57	30	1	270	N/A	N/A	46	N/A	250	50	0.0	0.0
B+ /9.6	3.9	0.26	9.79	2	12	57	30	1	270	N/A	N/A	61	N/A	250	50	0.0	0.0
B+ /9.9	4.7	0.12	18.46	8	0	0	0	100	0	83.4	N/A	95	1	2,500	100	0.0	0.0
C- /3.1	11.3	0.78	9.56	14	0	0	0	100	338	69.5	N/A	95	6	0	0	0.0	1.0
C- /3.5	11.3	1.01	14.09	24	0	99	0	1	59	119.8	-19.9	35	9	1,000	100	0.0	1.5
C /4.5	15.9	0.93	13.11	152	4	95	0	1	27	127.7	-20.7	92	6	250,000	10,000	0.0	2.0
C /4.5	15.8	0.92	12.93	1	4	95	0	1	27	124.8	-20.8	91	6	2,500	100	0.0	2.0
C+ /5.8	11.0	0.81	3.78	4	3	96	0	1	88	N/A	N/A	96	6	2,500	0	5.5	1.0
C+ /5.8	11.1	1.02	3.78	154	3	96	0	1	88	69.8	-29.1	18	6	1,000,000	0	0.0	1.0
C- /4.1	19.0	0.56	14.37	N/A	5	94	0	1	67	N/A	N/A	12	9	2,500	0	5.5	1.0
C- /4.0	19.0	0.55	14.36	4	5	94	0	1	67	24.4	-27.9	13	9	1,000,000	0	0.0	1.0
C+ /5.7	16.0	1.11	17.14	3	10	89	0	1	93	N/A	N/A	27	2	2,500	0	5.5	1.0
C+ /5.7	16.0	1.11	17.24	18	10	89	0	1	93	164.2	-28.2	30	2	1,000,000	0	0.0	1.0
C /5.3	11.4	0.83	18.52	16	7	92	0	1	58	N/A	N/A	11	9	2,500	0	5.5	1.0
C /5.3	11.4	0.79	18.55	140	7	92	0	1	58	79.1	-20.7	91	9	1,000,000	0	0.0	1.0
C /5.0	13.7	0.48	19.69	N/A	7	92	0	1	33	N/A	N/A	4	28	2,500	0	5.5	1.0
C /5.0	13.7	0.48	19.81	106	7	92	0	1	33	19.1	-31.6	5	28	1,000,000	0	0.0	1.0
C /4.9	15.1	1.10	23.17	3	0	100	0	0	15	N/A	N/A	69	18	2,500	0	5.5	1.0
C /4.9	15.1	1.10	23.20	112	0	100	0	0	15	114.6	-18.0	71	18	1,000,000	0	0.0	1.0
B- /7.1	11.3	0.74	16.52	1	4	95	0	1	93	N/A	N/A	98	7	2,500	0	5.5	1.0
B- /7.1	11.3	0.74	16.52	95	4	95	0	1	93	105.8	-17.5	98	7	1,000,000	0	0.0	1.0
C /4.9	16.6	1.11	17.81	1	4	95	0	1	85	N/A	N/A	4	3	2,500	0	5.5	1.0
C /4.9	16.6	1.11	18.06	14	4	95	0	1	85	91.7	-21.2	4	3	1,000,000	0	0.0	1.0
C- /3.6	14.5	0.58	7.61	47	3	33	63	1	50	-25.6	-22.5	0	7	2,500	0	5.5	2.0
C- /3.6	14.6	0.58	7.37	9	3	33	63	1	50	-28.1	-22.6	0	7	2,500	0	0.0	2.0
C- /3.6	14.6	0.58	7.63	543	3	33	63	1	50	-24.4	-22.3	0	7	1,000,000	0	0.0	2.0
D- /1.4	20.4	0.68	7.63	12	100	0	0	0	63	N/A	N/A	71	5	2,500	0	5.5	0.0
D- /1.4	20.4	0.67	7.51	10	100	0	0	0	63	N/A	N/A	67	5	2,500	0	0.0	0.0
D- /1.4	20.4	0.68	7.72	25	100	0	0	0	63	N/A	N/A	74	5	1,000,000	0	0.0	0.0
D+ /2.7	19.5	0.72	12.26	6	1	98	0	1	23	82.5	-20.6	99	6	2,500	0	5.5	2.0
D+ /2.6	19.5	0.72	11.77	2	1	98	0	1	23	76.5	-20.9	99	6	2,500	0	0.0	2.0
D+ /2.8	19.5	0.72	12.53	13	1	98	0	1	23	86.1	-20.6	99	6	1,000,000	0	0.0	2.0
C /5.5	11.8	0.64	6.75	54	8	91	0	1	30	107.5	-30.8	19	10	2,500	0	5.5	2.0
C /5.4	11.7	0.64	6.45	15	8	91	0	1	30	99.7	-31.0	14	10	2,500	0	0.0	2.0
C+ /5.6	11.8	0.64	6.85	151	8	91	0	1	30	111.1	-30.8	22	10	1,000,000	0	0.0	2.0
C /5.4	11.7	0.64	5.85	3	8	91	0	1	30	106.9	-30.9	18	10	0	0	0.0	2.0
D- /1.5	11.4	1.07	9.15	55	0	98	0	2	78	124.3	-20.5	35	2	2,500	0	5.5	0.0

Data as of February 28, 2017

Fund Type	Fund Name	Ticker Symbol	Overall Investment Rating	Phone	PERFORMANCE Perfor-mance Rating/Pts	3 Mo	6 Mo	1Yr / Pct	Annualized 3Yr / Pct	5Yr / Pct	Incl. in Returns Dividend Yield	Expense Ratio
	99 Pct = Best											
	0 Pct = Worst											
GI	ALPS/WMC Research Value C	AMWCX	D+	(866) 759-5679	B / 7.9	6.89	9.60	26.95 /79	7.30 /74	12.28 /77	0.03	2.24
GI	ALPS/WMC Research Value I	AMWIX	C-	(866) 759-5679	B+ / 8.7	7.09	10.15	28.29 /82	8.35 /82	13.37 /88	0.18	1.24
GL	Altegris Futures Evolution Strat C	EVOCX	D	(877) 772-5838	D+ / 2.7	2.51	-3.68	-7.52 / 0	7.83 /78	3.98 /15	6.41	2.72
IN	Altegris Macro Strategy A	MCRAX	D-	(877) 772-5838	E / 0.5	0.24	2.54	0.38 / 1	0.91 /18	-2.84 / 2	1.58	2.50
IN	Altegris Macro Strategy C	MCRCX	D-	(877) 772-5838	E+ / 0.6	0.10	2.35	-0.34 / 1	0.18 /14	-3.56 / 2	0.10	3.25
IN	Altegris Macro Strategy I	MCRIX	D-	(877) 772-5838	E+ / 0.9	0.33	2.75	0.61 / 2	1.17 /19	-2.59 / 2	2.18	2.23
IN	Altegris Macro Strategy N	MCRNX	D-	(877) 772-5838	E+ / 0.8	0.18	2.63	0.32 / 1	0.93 /18	-2.85 / 2	1.91	2.51
IN	Altegris Managed Futures Strategy A	MFTAX	D+	(877) 772-5838	D- / 1.0	3.48	-2.64	-3.96 / 1	4.32 /46	1.07 / 6	7.19	1.98
IN	Altegris Managed Futures Strategy C	MFTCX	D+	(877) 772-5838	D- / 1.2	3.20	-3.02	-4.79 / 1	3.55 /38	0.31 / 5	7.01	2.73
IN	Altegris Managed Futures Strategy I	MFTIX	D+	(877) 772-5838	D / 1.6	3.58	-2.47	-3.77 / 1	4.60 /50	1.33 / 7	7.80	1.73
GL	Altegris Managed Futures Strategy O	MFTOX	D+	(877) 772-5838	D- / 1.5	3.51	-2.62	-3.94 / 1	4.36 /47	—	7.54	1.97
GL	Altegris Multi Strat Alternative A	MULAX	D	(877) 772-5838	E / 0.3	1.97	-0.57	-0.57 / 1	-0.12 /13	—	2.96	3.50
GL	Altegris Multi Strat Alternative I	MULIX	D+	(877) 772-5838	E+ / 0.6	2.05	-0.27	-0.16 / 1	0.18 /14	—	3.44	3.25
GL	Altegris Multi Strat Alternative N	MULNX	D+	(877) 772-5838	E+ / 0.6	1.96	-0.46	-0.46 / 1	-0.01 /13	—	3.25	3.50
RE	Altegris/AACA Opportunistic RE A	RAAAX	A-	(877) 772-5838	A+ / 9.6	11.28	7.54	30.17 /87	12.92 /99	—	0.22	3.35
RE	Altegris/AACA Opportunistic RE I	RAAIX	A	(877) 772-5838	A+ / 9.8	11.35	7.68	30.40 /87	13.17 /99	—	0.35	3.10
RE	Altegris/AACA Opportunistic RE N	RAANX	A	(877) 772-5838	A+ / 9.8	11.29	7.55	30.20 /87	12.86 /99	—	0.23	3.35
FS	Altrius Enhanced Income I	KEUIX	U	(844) 524-9366	U /	3.30	3.79	13.79 /24	--	—	3.78	2.02
SC	Am Beacon Stephens Small Cap Gro	SPWAX	E+	(800) 658-5811	D+ / 2.4	2.64	5.34	28.09 /82	0.69 /17	8.65 /48	0.00	1.49
SC	Am Beacon Stephens Small Cap Gro	SPWCX	E	(800) 658-5811	D / 1.9	2.47	4.93	27.13 /79	-0.08 /13	7.84 /41	0.00	2.27
SC	Am Beacon Stephens Small Cap Gro	SPWYX	D-	(800) 658-5811	C- / 3.6	2.71	5.50	28.44 /83	1.00 /18	9.05 /51	0.00	1.15
EM	Amana Developing World Inst	AMIDX	E+	(800) 732-6262	E / 0.3	4.36	-5.64	7.47 / 6	-3.08 / 4	-2.25 / 3	0.72	1.20
EM	Amana Developing World Investor	AMDWX	E+	(800) 732-6262	E / 0.3	4.44	-5.62	7.21 / 6	-3.33 / 4	-2.44 / 2	0.27	1.51
GR	Amana Growth Institutional	AMIGX	B+	(800) 732-6262	B+ / 8.3	10.07	7.77	21.49 /60	8.83 /86	10.83 /64	0.74	0.85
GR	Amana Growth Investor	AMAGX	B	(800) 732-6262	B / 8.1	10.04	7.70	21.25 /58	8.59 /84	10.66 /63	0.62	1.09
IN	Amana Income Institutional	AMINX	C+	(800) 732-6262	C+ / 6.5	6.89	4.92	18.58 /45	7.09 /73	10.96 /65	1.68	0.90
IN	Amana Income Investor	AMANX	C+	(800) 732-6262	C+ / 6.3	6.86	4.81	18.30 /44	6.82 /71	10.77 /64	1.29	1.15
GR	Amer Beacon Bridgeway LC Gro Inst	BRLGX	A+	(800) 658-5811	B+ / 8.9	7.64	10.27	20.26 /53	10.38 /95	14.67 /96	0.61	1.00
GR	Amer Beacon Bridgeway LC Val A	BWLAX	A	(800) 658-5811	B / 8.0	4.68	10.65	24.77 /72	10.17 /94	15.02 /97	0.88	1.12
GR	Amer Beacon Bridgeway LC Val C	BWLCX	A	(800) 658-5811	B+ / 8.4	4.49	10.24	23.84 /69	9.34 /89	14.21 /94	0.31	1.87
GR	Amer Beacon Bridgeway LC Val Inst	BRLVX	A+	(800) 658-5811	A- / 9.2	4.78	10.85	25.20 /74	10.56 /96	15.51 /98	1.29	0.79
GR	Amer Beacon Bridgeway LC Val Inv	BWLIX	A+	(800) 658-5811	A- / 9.0	4.70	10.64	24.79 /73	10.22 /94	15.14 /97	1.00	1.09
GR	Amer Beacon Bridgeway LC Val Y	BWLYX	A+	(800) 658-5811	A- / 9.2	4.81	10.85	25.19 /74	10.54 /96	15.44 /98	1.23	0.81
GL	AmericaFirst Defensive Growth A	DGQAX	E	(877) 217-8363	E- / 0.2	4.77	-4.45	-9.16 / 0	-0.68 /11	4.85 /20	0.00	2.88
GL	AmericaFirst Defensive Growth I	DGQIX	E+	(877) 217-8363	E / 0.4	4.94	-4.24	-8.68 / 0	0.31 /15	5.70 /26	0.00	2.62
GL	AmericaFirst Defensive Growth U	DGQUX	E	(877) 217-8363	E- / 0.2	4.73	-4.69	-9.62 / 0	-1.20 / 9	4.31 /17	0.00	3.63
GI	AmericaFirst Income A	AFPAX	D	(877) 217-8363	D- / 1.1	6.40	9.34	18.13 /43	-0.53 /11	2.53 / 9	5.72	2.73
GI	AmericaFirst Income I	AFPIX	C-	(877) 217-8363	D+ / 2.8	6.43	9.55	19.01 /47	0.16 /14	3.18 /11	6.10	2.37
GI	AmericaFirst Income U	AFPUX	D	(877) 217-8363	D- / 1.1	6.28	9.02	17.58 /41	-1.01 / 9	2.06 / 8	5.29	3.42
GI	AmericaFirst Quantitative Strgy A	AFIAX	D-	(877) 217-8363	E / 0.3	4.78	2.70	7.45 / 6	-2.24 / 6	4.81 /20	3.16	1.98
GI	AmericaFirst Quantitative Strgy C	AFISX	D-	(877) 217-8363	E / 0.3	4.48	2.22	6.54 / 5	-2.98 / 5	4.03 /15	1.17	2.74
IN	AmericaFirst Seasonal Rotation A	STQAX	C	(877) 217-8363	C / 4.8	6.39	11.96	27.73 /81	3.09 /33	—	0.00	3.01
IN	AmericaFirst Seasonal Rotation I	STQIX	C+	(877) 217-8363	C+ / 6.3	6.55	12.22	28.41 /83	3.60 /38	—	0.00	2.68
IN	AmericaFirst Seasonal Rotation U	STQUX	C	(877) 217-8363	C / 4.8	6.27	11.69	27.05 /79	2.56 /28	—	0.00	3.77
IN	AmericaFirst Tactical Alpha A	ABRFX	D+	(877) 217-8363	D- / 1.3	2.95	4.98	10.39 /13	1.32 /20	3.81 /14	0.00	3.21
IN	AmericaFirst Tactical Alpha I	ABRWX	C-	(877) 217-8363	D+ / 2.4	3.14	5.35	11.89 /18	2.40 /27	4.70 /19	0.00	2.97
IN	AmericaFirst Tactical Alpha U	ABRUX	D+	(877) 217-8363	D- / 1.3	2.78	4.78	9.84 /11	0.80 /17	3.31 /12	0.00	3.96
EM	American Beacon Acadian EM MV A	ACDAX	E+	(800) 658-5811	E+ / 0.6	6.35	0.43	15.63 /33	-0.73 /10	—	1.40	2.11
EM	American Beacon Acadian EM MV C	ACDCX	E+	(800) 658-5811	E+ / 0.7	6.19	0.06	14.79 /29	-1.45 / 8	—	0.66	2.88
EM	American Beacon Acadian EM MV	ACDIX	D-	(800) 658-5811	D- / 1.1	6.40	0.61	16.16 /35	-0.32 /12	—	1.75	1.69
EM	American Beacon Acadian EM MV	ACDPX	D-	(800) 658-5811	D- / 1.0	6.28	0.45	15.69 /33	-0.66 /11	—	1.51	1.99
EM	American Beacon Acadian EM MV Y	ACDYX	D-	(800) 658-5811	D- / 1.1	6.42	0.61	15.94 /34	-0.40 /12	—	1.76	1.78

● Denotes fund is closed to new investors
* Denotes fund is included in Section II

48

Risk Rating/Pts	Standard Deviation (3 Year)	Beta	NAV As of 2/28/17	Total $(Mil)	Cash %	Stocks %	Bonds %	Other %	Portfolio Turnover Ratio	Last Bull Market Return	Last Bear Market Return	Manager Quality Pct	Manager Tenure (Years)	Initial Purch. $	Additional Purch. $	Front End Load	Back End Load
D- /1.3	11.4	1.07	8.79	1	0	98	0	2	78	115.6	-20.8	26	2	2,500	0	0.0	0.0
D /1.6	11.4	1.07	9.37	45	0	98	0	2	78	127.3	-20.4	37	2	1,000,000	0	0.0	0.0
C+ /5.6	12.2	-0.15	9.68	35	32	0	67	1	59	N/A	N/A	98	6	5,000	250	0.0	1.0
C+ /6.3	6.9	-0.03	7.01	2	37	0	62	1	747	-16.4	N/A	82	6	2,500	250	5.8	1.0
C+ /6.2	6.8	-0.03	6.83	1	37	0	62	1	747	N/A	N/A	77	6	5,000	250	0.0	1.0
C+ /6.4	6.8	-0.03	7.09	4	37	0	62	1	747	-15.2	N/A	83	6	1,000,000	250	0.0	1.0
C+ /6.3	6.8	-0.03	6.99	20	37	0	62	1	747	-16.4	N/A	82	6	2,500	250	0.0	1.0
B- /7.5	8.9	-0.04	8.56	86	25	0	74	1	231	1.6	-4.2	94	7	2,500	250	5.8	1.0
B- /7.5	8.9	-0.04	8.27	14	25	0	74	1	231	-2.5	-4.5	93	7	5,000	250	0.0	1.0
B- /7.5	8.9	-0.04	8.67	71	25	0	74	1	231	3.1	-4.1	95	7	1,000,000	250	0.0	1.0
B- /7.5	8.9	-0.13	8.56	1	25	0	74	1	231	N/A	N/A	94	7	2,500	250	0.0	1.0
B- /7.9	4.1	0.15	8.89	1	36	18	37	9	19	N/A	N/A	72	3	2,500	250	5.8	1.0
B- /7.9	4.1	0.14	8.91	4	36	18	37	9	19	N/A	N/A	75	3	1,000,000	2,500	0.0	1.0
B /8.0	4.1	0.15	8.91	24	36	18	37	9	19	N/A	N/A	73	3	2,500	250	0.0	1.0
C /5.2	12.1	0.77	14.01	6	1	98	0	1	70	N/A	N/A	93	N/A	2,500	250	5.8	1.0
C /5.2	12.1	0.77	14.03	130	1	98	0	1	70	N/A	N/A	94	N/A	1,000,000	250	0.0	1.0
C /5.2	12.1	0.77	14.00	10	1	98	0	1	70	N/A	N/A	93	N/A	2,500	250	0.0	1.0
U /	N/A	N/A	10.76	46	0	0	0	100	0	N/A	N/A	N/A	2	10,000	1,000	0.0	2.0
D+ /2.9	16.0	0.95	15.82	7	0	99	0	1	25	N/A	N/A	11	12	2,500	50	0.0	0.0
D+ /2.7	16.0	0.95	15.18	1	0	99	0	1	25	N/A	N/A	7	12	1,000	50	5.8	0.0
C- /3.0	16.0	0.95	16.93	81	0	99	0	1	25	93.9	-21.9	13	12	100,000	50	0.0	0.0
C /5.5	10.4	0.57	9.29	12	8	91	0	1	33	-1.7	-12.3	22	5	100,000	25	0.0	0.0
C /5.5	10.5	0.57	9.28	13	8	91	0	1	33	-2.7	-12.3	20	5	250	25	0.0	0.0
C /5.5	11.0	1.01	32.53	411	2	97	0	1	0	99.2	-15.6	52	23	100,000	25	0.0	0.0
C /5.5	11.0	1.01	32.46	1,089	2	97	0	1	0	97.7	-15.6	49	23	250	25	0.0	0.0
C+ /6.4	10.2	0.94	46.95	361	1	98	0	1	0	95.5	-15.5	39	27	100,000	25	0.0	0.0
C+ /6.4	10.2	0.94	47.07	968	1	98	0	1	0	93.8	-15.5	36	27	250	25	0.0	0.0
B- /7.5	10.8	0.95	25.98	141	0	0	0	100	100	147.0	-20.0	76	14	250,000	50	0.0	0.0
B- /7.0	10.4	0.95	26.71	156	6	93	0	1	43	N/A	N/A	74	14	2,500	50	5.8	0.0
B- /7.0	10.4	0.95	26.11	105	6	93	0	1	43	N/A	N/A	66	14	1,000	50	0.0	0.0
B- /7.0	10.4	0.95	26.99	1,279	6	93	0	1	43	148.5	-18.4	77	14	250,000	50	0.0	0.0
B- /7.0	10.4	0.95	26.83	1,630	6	93	0	1	43	N/A	N/A	75	14	2,500	50	0.0	0.0
B- /7.0	10.4	0.95	26.93	1,084	6	93	0	1	43	N/A	N/A	77	14	100,000	50	0.0	0.0
C /4.9	9.2	0.34	10.30	16	1	98	0	1	118	43.6	N/A	66	6	1,000	50	5.0	1.0
C /5.0	9.2	0.34	10.83	16	1	98	0	1	118	50.2	N/A	76	6	1,000,000	50	0.0	1.0
C /4.7	9.2	0.34	9.95	7	1	98	0	1	118	39.6	N/A	59	6	1,000	50	2.5	1.0
C+ /6.5	8.6	0.65	7.43	7	8	61	29	2	349	26.0	-16.3	5	7	1,000	50	4.0	1.0
C+ /6.6	8.6	0.65	7.54	3	8	61	29	2	349	30.2	-16.0	7	7	1,000,000	50	0.0	1.0
C+ /6.5	8.7	0.66	7.44	5	8	61	29	2	349	22.8	-16.4	4	7	1,000	50	2.0	1.0
C+ /6.2	8.2	0.63	5.53	8	10	72	17	1	418	42.1	-12.7	3	10	1,000	50	4.0	1.0
C+ /6.3	8.3	0.63	5.59	8	10	72	17	1	418	36.4	-13.0	3	10	1,000	50	1.0	1.0
C+ /6.0	12.9	0.76	11.33	3	3	96	0	1	445	N/A	N/A	17	4	1,000	50	5.0	1.0
C+ /6.0	12.9	0.77	11.39	4	3	96	0	1	445	N/A	N/A	21	4	1,000,000	50	0.0	1.0
C+ /6.0	13.0	0.76	11.18	2	3	96	0	1	445	N/A	N/A	13	4	1,000	50	2.5	1.0
B- /7.9	9.6	0.54	12.22	5	35	37	26	2	333	40.7	-19.8	21	7	1,000	50	5.0	1.0
B /8.0	9.7	0.55	12.80	1	35	37	26	2	333	46.9	-19.6	32	7	1,000,000	50	0.0	1.0
B- /7.8	9.6	0.54	11.83	4	35	37	26	2	333	37.0	-20.0	17	7	1,000	50	2.5	1.0
C /5.3	12.5	0.75	9.40	1	4	95	0	1	35	N/A	N/A	48	N/A	2,500	50	5.8	2.0
C /5.3	12.6	0.75	9.29	1	4	95	0	1	35	N/A	N/A	37	N/A	1,000	50	0.0	2.0
C /5.3	12.6	0.75	9.44	54	4	95	0	1	35	N/A	N/A	54	N/A	250,000	50	0.0	2.0
C /5.3	12.6	0.75	9.38	4	4	95	0	1	35	N/A	N/A	49	N/A	2,500	50	0.0	2.0
C /5.3	12.6	0.75	9.41	24	4	95	0	1	35	N/A	N/A	52	N/A	100,000	50	0.0	2.0

Fund Type	Fund Name	Ticker Symbol	Overall Investment Rating	Phone	Performance Rating/Pts	3 Mo	6 Mo	1Yr / Pct	3Yr / Pct	5Yr / Pct	Dividend Yield	Expense Ratio
					PERFORMANCE			Total Return % through 2/28/17	Annualized		Incl. in Returns	
GL	American Beacon AHL Mg Fut Str	AHLIX	U	(800) 658-5811	U /	2.43	0.38	-6.07 / 0	--	--	0.00	2.26
GL	American Beacon AHL Mg Fut Str Inv	AHLPX	U	(800) 658-5811	U /	2.36	0.19	-6.37 / 0	--	--	0.00	2.41
GL	American Beacon AHL Mg Fut Str Y	AHLYX	U	(800) 658-5811	U /	2.34	0.19	-6.17 / 0	--	--	0.00	2.29
BA	American Beacon Balanced A	ABFAX	C+	(800) 658-5811	C / 4.4	3.94	7.72	19.53 /50	5.62 /61	8.76 /48	1.55	0.98
BA	American Beacon Balanced Adv	ABLSX	B-	(800) 658-5811	C+ / 5.6	3.90	7.66	19.40 /49	5.54 /60	8.71 /48	1.44	1.07
BA	American Beacon Balanced C	ABCCX	C+	(800) 658-5811	C / 5.0	3.71	7.33	18.61 /45	4.83 /52	7.95 /42	0.94	1.73
BA	American Beacon Balanced Inst	AADBX	B-	(800) 658-5811	C+ / 6.1	4.07	7.97	20.06 /52	6.09 /65	9.25 /53	1.82	0.59
BA	American Beacon Balanced Inv	AABPX	B-	(800) 658-5811	C+ / 5.7	3.96	7.76	19.58 /50	5.69 /61	8.87 /49	1.71	0.92
BA	American Beacon Balanced Y	ACBYX	B-	(800) 658-5811	C+ / 6.1	4.29	8.17	20.12 /53	6.05 /65	9.18 /52	1.69	0.67
EM	American Beacon Glb Ev FM Inc A	AGUAX	C-	(800) 658-5811	C- / 3.1	4.74	4.95	17.94 /43	4.32 /46	--	7.30	1.56
EM	American Beacon Glb Ev FM Inc C	AGECX	C-	(800) 658-5811	C- / 3.3	4.58	4.65	17.17 /39	3.37 /35	--	7.13	2.32
EM	American Beacon Glb Ev FM Inc Inst	AGEIX	C	(800) 658-5811	C / 4.3	4.82	5.14	18.33 /44	4.68 /51	--	7.99	1.16
EM	American Beacon Glb Ev FM Inc Inv	AGEPX	C	(800) 658-5811	C- / 4.0	4.77	4.99	17.98 /43	4.36 /47	--	7.70	1.54
EM	American Beacon Glb Ev FM Inc Y	AGEYX	C	(800) 658-5811	C / 4.3	4.81	5.10	18.23 /44	4.63 /50	--	7.92	1.26
GL	American Beacon GLG Tot Rtn Ultra	GLGUX	U	(800) 658-5811	U /	4.21	5.37	--	--	--	0.00	N/A
GR	American Beacon Holland LC Gr A	LHGAX	C-	(800) 658-5811	C / 5.4	7.95	6.77	18.75 /46	6.66 /69	10.60 /63	0.00	1.30
GR	American Beacon Holland LC Gr C	LHGCX	C	(800) 658-5811	C+ / 6.0	7.79	6.42	17.93 /42	5.88 /63	--	0.00	2.06
GR	American Beacon Holland LC Gr Inst	LHGIX	C+	(800) 658-5811	C+ / 6.9	8.04	6.98	19.23 /48	7.10 /73	11.09 /67	0.00	0.90
GI	American Beacon Holland LC Gr Inv	LHGFX	C	(800) 658-5811	C+ / 6.6	8.00	6.83	18.86 /46	6.74 /70	10.70 /63	0.00	1.25
GR	American Beacon Holland LC Gr Y	LHGYX	C+	(800) 658-5811	C+ / 6.8	8.05	6.94	19.12 /48	6.95 /72	--	0.00	1.09
FO	American Beacon Intl Eq A	AIEAX	E+	(800) 658-5811	E / 0.4	5.73	3.66	13.73 /24	-2.67 / 5	4.73 /19	2.05	1.12
FO	American Beacon Intl Eq Adv	AAISX	E+	(800) 658-5811	E+ / 0.6	5.76	3.62	13.71 /24	-2.73 / 5	4.70 /19	1.89	1.20
FO	American Beacon Intl Eq C	AILCX	E+	(800) 658-5811	E / 0.5	5.57	3.26	12.87 /21	-3.41 / 4	3.96 /15	1.93	1.87
FO	American Beacon Intl Eq Inst	AAIEX	D-	(800) 658-5811	E+ / 0.7	5.84	3.85	14.19 /26	-2.29 / 6	5.21 /23	2.43	0.74
FO	American Beacon Intl Eq Inv	AAIPX	D-	(800) 658-5811	E+ / 0.7	5.77	3.70	13.77 /24	-2.62 / 5	4.85 /20	2.11	1.07
FO	American Beacon Intl Eq Y	ABEYX	D-	(800) 658-5811	E+ / 0.7	5.85	3.81	14.09 /26	-2.36 / 6	5.11 /22	2.28	0.81
GR	American Beacon Ionic Str Arb Inst	IONIX	U	(800) 658-5811	U /	0.15	1.06	1.36 / 2	--	--	4.67	2.70
GR	American Beacon Ionic Str Arb Y	IONYX	U	(800) 658-5811	U /	0.13	1.05	1.25 / 2	--	--	4.67	2.65
GR	American Beacon Lg Cap Val A	ALVAX	C+	(800) 658-5811	B- / 7.2	5.73	12.54	29.66 /86	7.05 /72	12.22 /76	1.84	0.98
GR	American Beacon Lg Cap Val C	ALVCX	C+	(800) 658-5811	B / 7.7	5.51	12.07	28.62 /83	6.24 /66	11.35 /69	1.06	1.74
GR	American Beacon Lg Cap Val Inst	AADEX	B	(800) 658-5811	B+ / 8.6	5.82	12.74	30.16 /87	7.48 /75	12.72 /81	2.08	0.59
GR	American Beacon Lg Cap Val	AAGPX	B-	(800) 658-5811	B+ / 8.3	5.72	12.54	29.72 /86	7.12 /73	12.33 /77	1.90	0.94
GR	American Beacon Lg Cap Val Svc	AVASX	B-	(800) 658-5811	B / 8.2	5.66	12.44	29.48 /85	6.96 /72	12.16 /76	1.76	1.08
GR	American Beacon Lg Cap Val Y	ABLYX	B	(800) 658-5811	B+ / 8.5	5.82	12.70	30.07 /87	7.40 /75	12.64 /80	2.03	0.68
IN	American Beacon London Co I Eq A	ABCAX	A-	(800) 658-5811	B- / 7.3	7.30	6.99	19.52 /49	10.09 /94	--	1.51	1.14
IN	American Beacon London Co I Eq C	ABECX	A	(800) 658-5811	B / 7.8	7.14	6.63	18.72 /46	9.29 /89	--	0.95	1.88
IN	American Beacon London Co I Eq	ABCIX	A+	(800) 658-5811	B+ / 8.6	7.40	7.21	20.00 /52	10.52 /96	--	1.92	0.78
IN	American Beacon London Co I Eq Inv	ABCVX	A+	(800) 658-5811	B+ / 8.4	7.34	7.12	19.62 /50	10.20 /94	--	1.65	1.07
IN	American Beacon London Co I Eq Y	ABCYX	A+	(800) 658-5811	B+ / 8.6	7.34	7.19	19.86 /51	10.45 /96	--	1.87	0.83
MC	American Beacon MidCap Val A	ABMAX	B+	(800) 658-5811	B+ / 8.7	7.14	15.35	33.72 /92	8.08 /80	13.62 /90	0.99	1.26
MC	American Beacon MidCap Val C	AMCCX	B+	(800) 658-5811	A- / 9.0	6.96	14.85	32.66 /91	7.26 /74	12.77 /82	0.45	2.02
MC	American Beacon MidCap Val F	AMCSX	A-	(800) 658-5811	A / 9.4	7.12	15.25	33.50 /92	7.94 /78	13.53 /89	0.91	1.38
MC	American Beacon MidCap Val Inst	AACIX	A-	(800) 658-5811	A+ / 9.6	7.28	15.54	34.21 /93	8.51 /83	14.13 /94	1.37	0.95
MC	American Beacon MidCap Val	AMPAX	A-	(800) 658-5811	A / 9.5	7.17	15.43	33.90 /93	8.27 /81	13.86 /92	1.14	0.86
MC	American Beacon MidCap Val Y	ACMYX	A-	(800) 658-5811	A / 9.5	7.26	15.51	34.12 /93	8.44 /82	14.05 /93	1.31	1.10
GL	American Beacon SGA Global Gro A	SGAAX	C	(800) 658-5811	C / 5.2	7.53	0.67	21.59 /60	7.01 /72	--	0.00	3.06
GL	American Beacon SGA Global Gro C	SGACX	C	(800) 658-5811	C+ / 5.8	7.30	0.29	20.69 /56	6.20 /66	--	0.00	3.77
GL	American Beacon SGA Global Gro	SGAGX	C+	(800) 658-5811	C+ / 6.7	7.70	0.91	22.12 /63	7.46 /75	8.89 /50	0.00	2.63
GL	American Beacon SGA Global Gro	SGAPX	C+	(800) 658-5811	C+ / 6.4	7.59	0.67	21.65 /60	7.03 /72	--	0.00	3.09
GL	American Beacon SGA Global Gro Y	SGAYX	C+	(800) 658-5811	C+ / 6.7	7.66	0.85	21.94 /62	7.35 /74	--	0.00	2.73
SC	American Beacon Sm Cap Val A	ABSAX	B	(800) 658-5811	B+ / 8.6	4.50	15.85	35.56 /95	8.08 /80	13.06 /84	0.45	1.23
SC	American Beacon Sm Cap Val Adv	AASSX	B+	(800) 658-5811	A / 9.4	4.48	15.78	35.39 /94	7.98 /79	13.00 /84	0.39	1.32

99 Pct = Best
0 Pct = Worst

● Denotes fund is closed to new investors

* Denotes fund is included in Section II

www.thestreetratings.com

Risk Rating/Pts	3 Year Standard Deviation	Beta	NAV As of 2/28/17	Total $(Mil)	Cash %	Stocks %	Bonds %	Other %	Portfolio Turnover Ratio	Last Bull Market Return	Last Bear Market Return	Manager Quality Pct	Manager Tenure (Years)	Initial Purch. $	Additional Purch. $	Front End Load	Back End Load
U /	N/A	N/A	10.53	375	0	0	0	100	0	N/A	N/A	N/A	3	250,000	50	0.0	0.0
U /	N/A	N/A	10.43	30	0	0	0	100	0	N/A	N/A	N/A	3	2,500	50	0.0	0.0
U /	N/A	N/A	10.49	66	0	0	0	100	0	N/A	N/A	N/A	3	100,000	50	0.0	0.0
B- /7.1	7.5	1.09	14.83	26	6	57	35	2	16	76.8	-11.2	42	30	2,500	50	5.8	0.0
B- /7.2	7.5	1.09	15.67	11	6	57	35	2	16	76.3	-11.2	41	30	2,500	50	0.0	0.0
B- /7.1	7.5	1.10	14.97	43	6	57	35	2	16	69.8	-11.5	32	30	1,000	50	0.0	0.0
B- /7.3	7.5	1.09	16.55	498	6	57	35	2	16	81.3	-11.1	48	30	250,000	50	0.0	0.0
B- /7.1	7.5	1.09	14.85	146	6	57	35	2	16	77.9	-11.2	43	30	2,500	50	0.0	0.0
B- /7.3	7.5	1.09	16.63	69	6	57	35	2	16	80.4	-11.0	48	30	100,000	50	0.0	0.0
C+ /6.7	5.9	0.28	9.18	5	3	0	96	1	68	N/A	N/A	92	3	2,500	50	4.8	2.0
C+ /6.7	5.8	0.28	9.16	2	3	0	96	1	68	N/A	N/A	89	3	1,000	50	0.0	2.0
C+ /6.7	5.8	0.28	9.18	15	3	0	96	1	68	N/A	N/A	93	3	250,000	50	0.0	2.0
C+ /6.7	5.9	0.28	9.18	24	3	0	96	1	68	N/A	N/A	93	3	2,500	50	0.0	2.0
C+ /6.7	5.9	0.28	9.19	27	3	0	96	1	68	N/A	N/A	93	3	100,000	50	0.0	2.0
U /	N/A	N/A	10.77	67	0	0	0	100	0	N/A	N/A	N/A	1	500,000,000	50	0.0	0.0
C /4.6	12.0	1.09	25.68	2	2	97	0	1	24	100.8	-14.3	18	5	2,500	50	5.8	0.0
C /4.5	12.0	1.09	24.52	N/A	2	97	0	1	24	N/A	N/A	13	5	1,000	50	0.0	0.0
C /4.7	11.9	1.09	26.50	14	2	97	0	1	24	105.5	-14.2	22	5	250,000	50	0.0	0.0
C /4.7	12.0	1.09	25.93	73	2	97	0	1	24	101.8	-14.3	19	5	2,500	50	0.0	0.0
C /4.7	11.9	1.09	26.32	1	2	97	0	1	24	N/A	N/A	21	5	100,000	50	0.0	0.0
C /5.5	11.6	0.93	17.63	22	5	94	0	1	25	47.1	-25.2	40	18	2,500	50	5.8	0.0
C /5.5	11.6	0.93	18.08	23	5	94	0	1	25	46.8	-25.2	39	18	2,500	50	0.0	0.0
C /5.5	11.6	0.93	17.12	6	5	94	0	1	25	41.3	-25.5	31	18	1,000	50	0.0	0.0
C /5.5	11.6	0.93	17.80	1,445	5	94	0	1	25	50.8	-25.1	46	18	250,000	50	0.0	0.0
C /5.5	11.6	0.93	17.66	324	5	94	0	1	25	47.9	-25.2	41	18	2,500	50	0.0	0.0
C /5.5	11.6	0.93	18.46	855	5	94	0	1	25	50.1	-25.1	45	18	100,000	50	0.0	0.0
U /	N/A	N/A	9.03	71	0	0	0	100	159	N/A	N/A	N/A	2	250,000	50	0.0	0.0
U /	N/A	N/A	9.03	61	0	0	0	100	159	N/A	N/A	N/A	2	100,000	50	0.0	0.0
C /4.4	12.2	1.11	26.51	45	4	95	0	1	25	120.2	-19.7	20	30	2,500	50	5.8	0.0
C /4.5	12.3	1.11	26.32	9	4	95	0	1	25	111.3	-19.9	14	30	1,000	50	0.0	0.0
C /4.6	12.3	1.11	28.64	5,199	4	95	0	1	25	125.7	-19.5	24	30	250,000	50	0.0	0.0
C /4.5	12.3	1.11	26.79	2,192	4	95	0	1	25	121.6	-19.7	20	30	2,500	50	0.0	0.0
C /4.5	12.3	1.11	26.46	107	4	95	0	1	25	119.9	-19.7	19	30	2,500	50	0.0	0.0
C /4.6	12.3	1.11	28.47	351	4	95	0	1	25	124.8	-19.6	23	30	100,000	50	0.0	0.0
B- /7.4	9.6	0.88	15.93	97	4	94	0	2	20	N/A	N/A	79	5	2,500	50	5.8	0.0
B- /7.4	9.6	0.88	15.83	181	4	94	0	2	20	N/A	N/A	74	5	1,000	50	0.0	0.0
B- /7.4	9.6	0.88	16.08	214	4	94	0	2	20	N/A	N/A	82	5	250,000	50	0.0	0.0
B- /7.4	9.6	0.88	16.03	36	4	94	0	2	20	N/A	N/A	80	5	2,500	50	0.0	0.0
B- /7.4	9.6	0.88	16.00	666	4	94	0	2	20	N/A	N/A	81	5	100,000	50	0.0	0.0
C /5.3	13.2	1.04	15.78	21	6	93	0	1	27	139.6	-22.3	51	13	2,500	50	5.8	0.0
C /5.3	13.2	1.05	15.33	7	6	93	0	1	27	130.0	-22.5	40	13	1,000	50	0.0	0.0
C /5.3	13.2	1.05	15.79	7	6	93	0	1	27	138.5	-22.2	49	13	2,500	50	0.0	0.0
C /5.3	13.3	1.05	16.13	229	6	93	0	1	27	145.4	-22.1	56	13	250,000	50	0.0	0.0
C /5.3	13.3	1.05	16.29	276	6	93	0	1	27	142.4	-22.2	53	13	2,500	50	0.0	0.0
C /5.3	13.2	1.05	16.01	84	6	93	0	1	27	144.6	-22.2	55	13	100,000	50	0.0	0.0
C+ /5.6	12.7	0.90	15.50	1	6	93	0	1	39	N/A	N/A	98	7	2,500	50	5.8	0.0
C+ /5.6	12.7	0.91	15.08	1	6	93	0	1	39	N/A	N/A	97	7	1,000	50	0.0	0.0
C+ /5.8	12.7	0.90	15.74	8	6	93	0	1	39	86.9	-14.2	98	7	250,000	50	0.0	0.0
C+ /5.6	12.7	0.90	15.52	12	6	93	0	1	39	N/A	N/A	98	7	2,500	50	0.0	0.0
C+ /5.6	12.7	0.90	15.68	2	6	93	0	1	39	N/A	N/A	98	7	100,000	50	0.0	0.0
C /4.5	14.8	0.91	26.66	69	3	96	0	1	53	140.9	-26.6	85	19	2,500	50	5.8	0.0
C /4.6	14.8	0.91	26.77	113	3	96	0	1	53	140.5	-26.5	84	19	2,500	50	0.0	0.0

Fund Type	Fund Name	Ticker Symbol	Overall Investment Rating	Phone	PERFORMANCE						Incl. in Returns	
	99 Pct = Best / 0 Pct = Worst				Perfor-mance Rating/Pts	Total Return % through 2/28/17			Annualized		Dividend Yield	Expense Ratio
						3 Mo	6 Mo	1Yr / Pct	3Yr / Pct	5Yr / Pct		
SC	American Beacon Sm Cap Val C	ASVCX	B	(800) 658-5811	A- / 9.0	4.33	15.39	34.60 /94	7.26 /74	12.21 /76	0.00	1.99
SC	American Beacon Sm Cap Val Inst	AVFIX	B+	(800) 658-5811	A / 9.5	4.59	16.02	36.08 /95	8.51 /83	13.56 /89	0.79	0.82
SC	American Beacon Sm Cap Val Inv	AVPAX	B+	(800) 658-5811	A / 9.4	4.53	15.88	35.63 /95	8.16 /80	13.17 /86	0.53	1.16
SC	American Beacon Sm Cap Val Y	ABSYX	B+	(800) 658-5811	A / 9.5	4.58	15.98	36.01 /95	8.42 /82	13.46 /88	0.74	0.91
MC	American Beacon Stephens MC Gr A	SMFAX	D+	(800) 658-5811	C / 5.3	7.78	9.40	28.19 /82	3.98 /43	9.69 /56	0.00	1.40
MC	American Beacon Stephens MC Gr C	SMFCX	C-	(800) 658-5811	C+ / 5.8	7.57	8.92	27.22 /80	3.18 /33	8.87 /49	0.00	2.15
MC	American Beacon Stephens MC Gr	SFMIX	C	(800) 658-5811	C+ / 6.9	8.17	9.87	29.06 /84	4.51 /49	10.21 /60	0.00	1.02
MC	American Beacon Stephens MC Gr	STMGX	C-	(800) 658-5811	C+ / 6.5	7.63	9.25	28.12 /82	3.97 /43	9.72 /56	0.00	1.36
MC	American Beacon Stephens MC Gr Y	SMFYX	C	(800) 658-5811	C+ / 6.7	7.80	9.50	28.55 /83	4.29 /46	10.06 /59	0.00	1.10
SC	American Beacon Stephens SC Gr	STSIX	D-	(800) 658-5811	C- / 3.7	2.70	5.48	28.48 /83	1.09 /19	9.13 /52	0.00	1.09
SC	American Beacon Stephens SC Gr	STSGX	D-	(800) 658-5811	C- / 3.5	2.68	5.37	28.29 /82	0.79 /17	8.84 /49	0.00	1.41
SC	American Beacon Zebra Sm Cap Eq	AZSAX	B	(800) 658-5811	B+ / 8.3	4.46	13.68	31.44 /89	8.85 /86	13.18 /86	1.04	1.91
SC	American Beacon Zebra Sm Cap Eq	AZSCX	B+	(800) 658-5811	B+ / 8.8	4.28	13.30	30.46 /87	8.02 /79	12.32 /77	0.66	2.66
SC	American Beacon Zebra Sm Cap Eq	AZSIX	A-	(800) 658-5811	A / 9.4	4.59	13.95	31.96 /90	9.27 /89	13.67 /90	1.10	1.54
SC	American Beacon Zebra Sm Cap Eq	AZSPX	B+	(800) 658-5811	A- / 9.2	4.47	13.69	31.46 /89	8.86 /86	13.25 /86	1.11	1.75
SC	American Beacon Zebra Sm Cap Eq	AZSYX	A-	(800) 658-5811	A / 9.4	4.55	13.82	31.83 /90	9.16 /88	13.57 /89	1.09	1.59
GR	American Century Adaptive AC Adv	ACMFX	B	(800) 345-6488	B- / 7.1	5.12	6.89	22.36 /64	7.66 /76	12.46 /79	0.72	1.41
GR	American Century Adaptive AC Inst	ACMHX	B+	(800) 345-6488	B- / 7.5	5.29	7.13	22.92 /66	8.16 /80	12.97 /83	1.14	0.96
GR	American Century Adaptive AC Inv	ACMNX	B+	(800) 345-6488	B- / 7.3	5.23	7.03	22.71 /65	7.94 /78	12.75 /81	0.96	1.16
GR	American Century Adaptive AC R	ACMEX	B	(800) 345-6488	B- / 7.0	5.09	6.75	22.13 /63	7.41 /75	12.18 /76	0.47	1.66
GR	American Century Adaptive Eqty Inst	AVDIX	B+	(800) 345-6488	B+ / 8.9	7.96	10.47	26.87 /79	9.60 /91	13.89 /92	1.09	1.06
GR	American Century Adaptive Eqty Inv	AMVIX	B+	(800) 345-6488	B+ / 8.8	8.03	10.39	26.63 /78	9.37 /89	13.68 /90	0.92	1.26
SC	American Century All Cap Gro A	ACAQX	C-	(800) 345-6488	C+ / 5.8	7.32	6.00	19.38 /49	7.44 /75	10.74 /64	0.00	1.25
SC	American Century All Cap Gro C	ACAHX	C	(800) 345-6488	C+ / 6.3	7.10	5.62	18.51 /45	6.64 /69	9.91 /58	0.00	2.00
SC	American Century All Cap Gro Inst	ACAJX	C+	(800) 345-6488	B- / 7.2	7.45	6.23	19.93 /52	7.93 /78	11.23 /68	0.00	0.80
SC	American Century All Cap Gro Inv	TWGTX	C+	(800) 345-6488	B- / 7.0	7.37	6.14	19.70 /50	7.71 /77	11.02 /66	0.00	1.00
SC	American Century All Cap Gro R	ACAWX	C	(800) 345-6488	C+ / 6.7	7.23	5.86	19.09 /48	7.18 /73	10.46 /62	0.00	1.50
GR	American Century Alt Eq MN A	ALIAX	C-	(800) 345-6488	E- / 0.2	-1.28	-0.09	-3.05 / 1	-0.64 /11	0.55 / 5	0.00	3.18
GR	American Century Alt Eq MN C	ALICX	C-	(800) 345-6488	E / 0.3	-1.48	-0.40	-3.76 / 1	-1.40 / 8	-0.22 / 4	0.00	3.93
GR	American Century Alt Eq MN Inst	ALISX	C-	(800) 345-6488	E / 0.5	-1.23	0.09	-2.68 / 1	-0.24 /12	0.97 / 6	0.00	2.73
GR	American Century Alt Eq MN Inv	ALHIX	C-	(800) 345-6488	E / 0.4	-1.25	0.00	-2.81 / 1	-0.42 /12	0.78 / 6	0.00	2.93
GR	American Century Alt Eq MN R	ALIRX	C-	(800) 345-6488	E / 0.4	-1.41	-0.28	-3.31 / 1	-0.93 /10	0.27 / 5	0.00	3.43
GI	American Century Alt Inc A	ALNAX	U	(800) 345-6488	U /	2.53	2.94	12.17 /19	--	--	4.07	2.32
GI	American Century Alt Inc Inv	ALNNX	U	(800) 345-6488	U /	2.61	2.96	12.33 /19	--	--	4.57	2.07
GR	American Century Alt MN Val A	ACVQX	C	(800) 345-6488	D- / 1.1	1.08	1.08	2.33 / 2	3.15 /33	2.73 /10	0.00	4.34
GR	American Century Alt MN Val C	ACVHX	C	(800) 345-6488	D- / 1.3	0.83	0.63	1.42 / 2	2.36 /26	1.95 / 8	0.00	5.09
GR	American Century Alt MN Val Inst	ACVKX	C+	(800) 345-6488	D / 1.8	1.15	1.34	2.75 / 2	3.61 /38	3.20 /12	0.00	3.89
GR	American Century Alt MN Val Inv	ACVVX	C+	(800) 345-6488	D / 1.7	1.07	1.16	2.49 / 2	3.38 /36	2.97 /11	0.00	4.09
GR	American Century Alt MN Val R	ACVWX	C+	(800) 345-6488	D- / 1.5	1.00	0.91	2.07 / 2	2.91 /31	2.47 / 9	0.00	4.59
BA	American Century Balanced Inst	ABINX	C+	(800) 345-6488	C / 4.8	4.97	4.48	14.62 /28	5.65 /61	8.05 /43	1.60	0.70
BA	American Century Balanced Inv	TWBIX	C+	(800) 345-6488	C / 4.6	4.92	4.37	14.40 /27	5.44 /59	7.84 /41	1.41	0.90
GI	American Century Capital Val A	ACCVX	B+	(800) 345-6488	B+ / 8.4	7.20	11.69	28.87 /84	9.25 /88	12.99 /84	1.15	1.35
GI	American Century Capital Val Inst	ACPIX	A-	(800) 345-6488	A / 9.4	7.31	11.89	29.31 /85	9.71 /92	13.47 /89	1.65	0.90
GI	American Century Capital Val Inv	ACTIX	A-	(800) 345-6488	A / 9.4	7.22	11.81	29.11 /84	9.51 /90	13.23 /86	1.46	1.10
GR	American Century Core Eq Plus A	ACPQX	C	(800) 345-6488	C+ / 6.2	6.78	9.02	20.44 /55	7.36 /74	12.26 /77	0.55	2.14
GR	American Century Core Eq Plus C	ACPHX	C	(800) 345-6488	C+ / 6.6	6.61	8.55	19.52 /49	6.55 /69	11.41 /69	0.29	2.89
GR	American Century Core Eq Plus Inst	ACPKX	C+	(800) 345-6488	B- / 7.5	6.99	9.32	20.99 /57	7.86 /78	12.77 /82	0.76	1.69
GR	American Century Core Eq Plus Inv	ACPVX	C+	(800) 345-6488	B- / 7.3	6.84	9.16	20.71 /56	7.63 /76	12.54 /79	0.68	1.89
GR	American Century Core Eq Plus R	ACPWX	C+	(800) 345-6488	B- / 7.0	6.81	8.89	20.19 /53	7.10 /73	11.98 /74	0.49	2.39
GR	American Century Discpl Gr A	ADCVX	C+	(800) 345-6488	C+ / 6.8	8.07	8.97	21.97 /62	7.91 /78	11.83 /73	0.46	1.28
GR	American Century Discpl Gr C	ADCCX	B	(800) 345-6488	B- / 7.2	7.90	8.54	21.09 /58	7.11 /73	11.00 /66	0.19	2.03
GR	American Century Discpl Gr Inst	ADCIX	B+	(800) 345-6488	B / 8.1	8.22	9.22	22.60 /65	8.41 /82	12.33 /77	0.76	0.83

● Denotes fund is closed to new investors

* Denotes fund is included in Section II

www.thestreetratings.com

RISK	3 Year		NET ASSETS		ASSET					BULL / BEAR		FUND MANAGER		MINIMUMS		LOADS	
Risk Rating/Pts	Standard Deviation	Beta	NAV As of 2/28/17	Total $(Mil)	Cash %	Stocks %	Bonds %	Other %	Portfolio Turnover Ratio	Last Bull Market Return	Last Bear Market Return	Manager Quality Pct	Manager Tenure (Years)	Initial Purch. $	Additional Purch. $	Front End Load	Back End Load
C /4.5	14.8	0.91	25.83	16	3	96	0	1	53	131.2	-26.8	80	19	1,000	50	0.0	0.0
C /4.6	14.8	0.91	28.03	5,773	3	96	0	1	53	147.0	-26.4	86	19	250,000	50	0.0	0.0
C /4.6	14.8	0.91	27.09	699	3	96	0	1	53	142.5	-26.5	85	19	2,500	50	0.0	0.0
C /4.6	14.8	0.91	27.69	392	3	96	0	1	53	145.9	-26.4	86	19	100,000	50	0.0	0.0
C- /3.8	13.6	1.00	16.99	15	1	98	0	1	19	N/A	N/A	13	13	2,500	50	5.8	0.0
C- /3.7	13.6	1.00	16.27	2	1	98	0	1	19	N/A	N/A	9	13	1,000	50	0.0	0.0
C- /3.9	13.6	1.00	19.77	55	1	98	0	1	19	102.0	-16.9	17	13	250,000	50	0.0	0.0
C- /3.8	13.6	1.00	17.04	14	1	98	0	1	19	97.4	-17.1	13	13	2,500	50	0.0	0.0
C- /3.9	13.6	1.00	19.69	3	1	98	0	1	19	N/A	N/A	15	13	100,000	50	0.0	0.0
C- /3.0	16.0	0.95	17.00	476	0	99	0	1	25	94.6	-21.8	13	12	250,000	50	0.0	0.0
D+ /2.9	16.0	0.95	15.96	51	0	99	0	1	25	91.9	-21.9	11	12	2,500	50	0.0	0.0
C /5.3	14.5	0.87	15.81	6	4	95	0	1	50	133.0	-20.7	89	7	2,500	50	5.8	0.0
C /5.2	14.5	0.87	15.23	2	4	95	0	1	50	123.7	-21.0	86	7	1,000	50	0.0	0.0
C /5.3	14.5	0.87	15.86	2	4	95	0	1	50	138.9	-20.6	90	7	250,000	50	0.0	0.0
C /5.3	14.4	0.87	15.80	10	4	95	0	1	50	133.9	-20.7	89	7	2,500	50	0.0	0.0
C /5.3	14.5	0.87	15.99	17	4	95	0	1	50	137.6	-20.6	90	7	100,000	50	0.0	0.0
C+ /6.5	11.0	1.01	19.63	8	3	96	0	1	126	108.0	-12.5	37	10	2,500	50	0.0	0.0
C+ /6.5	11.0	1.01	19.95	10	3	96	0	1	126	113.1	-12.3	44	10	5,000,000	50	0.0	0.0
C+ /6.5	11.0	1.01	19.82	75	3	96	0	1	126	110.8	-12.3	40	10	2,500	50	0.0	0.0
C+ /6.5	11.0	1.01	19.41	4	3	96	0	1	126	105.2	-12.5	34	10	2,500	50	0.0	0.0
C /5.5	11.5	1.08	11.24	3	0	0	0	100	116	129.0	-13.7	53	9	5,000,000	50	0.0	2.0
C /5.5	11.5	1.08	11.00	96	0	0	0	100	116	126.9	-13.9	50	9	2,500	50	0.0	2.0
C /4.4	11.6	0.58	30.23	12	0	99	0	1	49	104.3	-18.0	91	16	2,500	50	5.8	0.0
C- /4.2	11.6	0.58	28.69	5	0	99	0	1	49	96.2	-18.3	88	16	2,500	50	0.0	0.0
C /4.5	11.6	0.58	31.17	N/A	0	99	0	1	49	109.3	-17.9	93	16	5,000,000	50	0.0	0.0
C /4.4	11.6	0.58	30.76	1,022	0	99	0	1	49	107.1	-17.9	92	16	2,500	50	0.0	0.0
C /4.3	11.6	0.58	29.71	15	0	99	0	1	49	101.6	-18.1	90	16	2,500	50	0.0	0.0
B+ /9.9	2.5	-0.06	10.79	10	99	0	0	1	235	6.0	0.7	72	12	2,500	50	5.8	0.0
B+ /9.9	2.5	-0.05	9.98	7	99	0	0	1	235	1.7	0.4	62	12	2,500	50	0.0	0.0
B+ /9.9	2.5	-0.06	11.27	16	99	0	0	1	235	8.5	0.9	76	12	5,000,000	0	0.0	0.0
B+ /9.9	2.5	-0.06	11.05	89	99	0	0	1	235	7.4	0.8	74	12	2,500	50	0.0	0.0
B+ /9.9	2.5	-0.05	10.51	4	99	0	0	1	235	4.5	0.6	68	12	2,500	50	0.0	0.0
U /	N/A	N/A	9.69	38	0	0	0	100	98	N/A	N/A	N/A	2	2,500	50	5.8	0.0
U /	N/A	N/A	9.69	110	0	0	0	100	98	N/A	N/A	N/A	2	2,500	50	0.0	0.0
B+ /9.9	1.9	-0.04	10.49	109	99	0	0	1	679	N/A	N/A	91	6	2,500	50	5.8	0.0
B+ /9.9	1.9	-0.04	10.04	36	99	0	0	1	679	N/A	N/A	89	6	2,500	50	0.0	0.0
B+ /9.9	1.9	-0.04	10.76	177	99	0	0	1	679	N/A	N/A	93	6	5,000,000	50	0.0	0.0
B+ /9.9	1.9	-0.04	10.63	409	99	0	0	1	679	N/A	N/A	92	6	2,500	50	0.0	0.0
B+ /9.9	1.9	-0.03	10.34	N/A	99	0	0	1	679	N/A	N/A	91	6	2,500	50	0.0	0.0
B- /7.0	6.4	1.02	18.19	60	0	58	41	1	104	69.5	-8.1	50	12	5,000,000	50	0.0	0.0
B- /7.0	6.4	1.02	18.18	797	0	58	41	1	104	67.7	-8.2	47	12	2,500	50	0.0	0.0
C /5.4	11.4	1.06	9.12	5	0	99	0	1	45	124.5	-17.5	51	17	2,500	50	5.8	0.0
C /5.4	11.4	1.05	9.16	2	0	99	0	1	45	129.9	-17.4	57	17	5,000,000	50	0.0	0.0
C /5.4	11.4	1.05	9.14	151	0	99	0	1	45	127.1	-17.4	55	17	2,500	50	0.0	0.0
C /4.7	10.0	0.94	14.02	1	1	98	0	1	107	N/A	N/A	43	6	2,500	50	5.8	0.0
C /4.6	10.0	0.94	13.71	N/A	1	98	0	1	107	N/A	N/A	32	6	2,500	50	0.0	0.0
C /4.6	9.9	0.94	14.08	1	1	98	0	1	107	N/A	N/A	50	6	5,000,000	0	0.0	0.0
C /4.7	10.0	0.94	14.06	178	1	98	0	1	107	N/A	N/A	46	6	2,500	50	0.0	0.0
C /4.7	10.0	0.94	13.96	N/A	1	98	0	1	107	N/A	N/A	39	6	2,500	50	0.0	0.0
C+ /6.2	10.6	1.00	21.02	114	0	99	0	1	113	119.1	-16.4	41	12	2,500	50	5.8	0.0
C+ /6.1	10.7	1.00	20.08	46	0	99	0	1	113	110.5	-16.7	31	12	2,500	50	0.0	0.0
C+ /6.2	10.7	1.00	21.22	232	0	99	0	1	113	124.5	-16.3	48	12	5,000,000	0	0.0	0.0

Fund Type	Fund Name	Ticker Symbol	Overall Investment Rating	Phone	Performance Rating/Pts	Total Return % through 2/28/17			Annualized		Incl. in Returns	
	99 Pct = Best / 0 Pct = Worst					3 Mo	6 Mo	1Yr / Pct	3Yr / Pct	5Yr / Pct	Dividend Yield	Expense Ratio
GR	American Century Discpl Gr Inv	ADSIX	B+	(800) 345-6488	B / 7.9	8.19	9.08	22.30 /64	8.19 /80	12.11 /75	0.58	1.03
GR	American Century Discpl Gr R	ADRRX	B+	(800) 345-6488	B / 7.6	8.02	8.81	21.69 /61	7.65 /76	11.54 /70	0.39	1.53
GR	American Century Disp Gr Plus A	ACDQX	C+	(800) 345-6488	C+ / 6.5	6.11	7.05	18.27 /44	8.87 /86	12.57 /80	0.00	2.16
GR	American Century Disp Gr Plus C	ACDHX	C+	(800) 345-6488	C+ / 6.9	5.91	6.62	17.42 /40	8.05 /79	11.73 /72	0.00	2.91
GR	American Century Disp Gr Plus Inst	ACDKX	B+	(800) 345-6488	B / 7.7	6.25	7.25	18.76 /46	9.35 /89	13.06 /84	0.24	1.71
GR	American Century Disp Gr Plus Inv	ACDJX	B+	(800) 345-6488	B / 7.6	6.16	7.16	18.60 /45	9.13 /88	12.86 /82	0.04	1.91
GR	American Century Disp Gr Plus R	ACDWX	B	(800) 345-6488	B- / 7.2	5.99	6.88	17.97 /43	8.58 /84	12.29 /77	0.00	2.41
EM	American Century Emerg Mkts Val A	AEVLX	E	(800) 345-6488	E+ / 0.8	8.56	6.39	28.94 /84	-2.91 / 5	--	0.97	1.84
EM	American Century Emerg Mkts Val C	AEVTX	E	(800) 345-6488	D- / 1.0	8.36	6.03	27.85 /81	-3.65 / 4	--	0.33	2.59
EM	American Century Emerg Mkts Val	AEVNX	E+	(800) 345-6488	D- / 1.5	8.74	6.72	29.47 /85	-2.47 / 6	--	1.44	1.39
EM	American Century Emerg Mkts Val	AEVVX	E+	(800) 345-6488	D- / 1.4	8.67	6.65	29.21 /85	-2.66 / 5	--	1.25	1.59
EM	American Century Emerg Mkts Val R	AEVRX	E+	(800) 345-6488	D- / 1.2	8.45	6.27	28.45 /83	-3.16 / 4	--	0.79	2.09
EM	American Century Emerging Mkt A	AEMMX	D	(800) 345-6488	C- / 3.1	7.38	2.66	24.75 /72	2.26 /26	2.22 / 9	0.00	1.94
EM	American Century Emerging Mkt C	ACECX	D+	(800) 345-6488	C- / 3.5	7.21	2.25	23.75 /69	1.50 /21	1.47 / 7	0.00	2.69
EM	American Century Emerging Mkt Inst	AMKIX	D+	(800) 345-6488	C- / 4.1	7.51	2.83	25.25 /74	2.67 /29	2.64 /10	0.28	1.49
EM	American Century Emerging Mkt Inv	TWMIX	D+	(800) 345-6488	C- / 4.0	7.47	2.79	24.97 /73	2.51 /28	2.47 / 9	0.11	1.69
EM	American Century Emerging Mkt R	AEMRX	D+	(800) 345-6488	C- / 3.5	7.32	2.52	24.34 /71	1.97 /24	1.94 / 8	0.00	2.19
EM	American Century Emerging Mkt R6	AEDMX	C-	(800) 345-6488	C- / 4.2	7.49	2.93	25.37 /74	2.86 /30	--	0.40	1.34
GR	American Century Equity Growth A	BEQAX	C+	(800) 345-6488	C+ / 6.7	7.48	9.02	23.57 /68	7.59 /76	11.91 /73	0.99	0.92
GR	American Century Equity Growth C	AEYCX	C+	(800) 345-6488	B- / 7.1	7.29	8.60	22.61 /65	6.77 /70	11.07 /66	0.37	1.67
GR	American Century Equity Growth Inst	AMEIX	B	(800) 345-6488	B / 8.0	7.59	9.22	24.11 /70	8.05 /79	12.41 /78	1.45	0.47
GR	American Century Equity Growth Inv	BEQGX	B-	(800) 345-6488	B / 7.9	7.54	9.12	23.84 /69	7.84 /78	12.19 /76	1.27	0.67
GR	American Century Equity Growth R	AEYRX	C+	(800) 345-6488	B- / 7.5	7.36	8.84	23.21 /67	7.30 /74	11.62 /71	0.82	1.17
IN	● American Century Equity Income A	TWEAX	B+	(800) 345-6488	B+ / 8.4	6.68	7.54	23.45 /68	11.35 /97	12.20 /76	1.47	1.19
IN	● American Century Equity Income C	AEYIX	A-	(800) 345-6488	B+ / 8.8	6.46	7.12	22.55 /65	10.53 /96	11.35 /69	0.87	1.94
IN	● American Century Equity Income Inst	ACIIX	A+	(800) 345-6488	A / 9.5	6.80	7.78	23.97 /70	11.84 /98	12.69 /81	1.96	0.74
IN	● American Century Equity Income Inv	TWEIX	A	(800) 345-6488	A / 9.4	6.63	7.56	23.75 /69	11.63 /98	12.48 /79	1.78	0.94
IN	● American Century Equity Income R	AEURX	A	(800) 345-6488	A- / 9.1	6.63	7.42	23.23 /67	11.07 /97	11.93 /74	1.33	1.44
IN	● American Century Equity Income R6	AEUDX	A+	(800) 345-6488	A / 9.5	6.84	7.86	24.28 /71	12.04 /98	--	2.09	0.59
GR	American Century Focus Dyn Gr Adv	ACFDX	C+	(800) 345-6488	C+ / 6.8	8.05	5.45	23.37 /68	6.31 /67	11.13 /67	0.82	1.36
GR	American Century Focus Dyn Gr Inst	ACFSX	C+	(800) 345-6488	B- / 7.1	8.20	5.75	23.92 /70	6.80 /70	11.64 /71	1.24	0.91
GR	American Century Focus Dyn Gr Inv	ACFOX	C+	(800) 345-6488	C+ / 6.9	8.14	5.55	23.69 /69	6.58 /69	11.39 /69	1.05	1.11
GR	American Century Focus Dyn Gr R	ACFCX	C+	(800) 345-6488	C+ / 6.6	8.03	5.34	23.05 /67	6.06 /65	10.86 /65	0.59	1.61
RE	American Century Gl Real Estate A	ARYMX	D	(800) 345-6488	D / 1.7	5.87	-4.81	9.25 /10	4.19 /45	7.35 /37	3.83	1.46
RE	American Century Gl Real Estate C	ARYTX	D	(800) 345-6488	D / 2.0	5.74	-5.21	8.43 / 8	3.40 /36	6.54 /32	3.32	1.71
RE	American Century Gl Real Estate Ins	ARYNX	D+	(800) 345-6488	D+ / 2.8	5.97	-4.61	9.76 /11	4.63 /50	7.84 /41	4.52	1.01
RE	American Century Gl Real Estate Inv	ARYVX	D+	(800) 345-6488	D+ / 2.6	6.04	-4.64	9.53 /11	4.45 /48	7.62 /39	4.32	1.21
RE	American Century Gl Real Estate R	ARYWX	D+	(800) 345-6488	D+ / 2.3	5.79	-4.97	8.97 / 9	3.92 /42	7.09 /35	3.82	1.71
RE	American Century Gl Real Estate R6	ARYDX	D+	(800) 345-6488	D+ / 2.9	6.13	-4.54	9.93 /11	4.79 /52	--	4.67	0.86
GL	American Century Global Alloc A	AGAEX	D	(800) 345-6488	E / 0.5	4.09	0.88	10.57 /13	-0.73 /10	2.07 / 8	0.72	2.48
GL	American Century Global Alloc C	AGAGX	D	(800) 345-6488	E+ / 0.7	3.95	0.52	9.80 /11	-1.48 / 8	1.31 / 7	0.03	3.23
GL	American Century Global Alloc Inst	AGANX	D+	(800) 345-6488	D- / 1.0	4.23	1.14	11.02 /14	-0.30 /12	2.54 / 9	1.20	2.03
GL	American Century Global Alloc Inv	AGAVX	D	(800) 345-6488	D- / 1.0	4.23	1.04	10.93 /14	-0.47 /11	2.34 / 9	1.01	2.23
GL	American Century Global Alloc R	AGAFX	D	(800) 345-6488	E+ / 0.8	4.04	0.73	10.31 /12	-0.98 / 9	1.81 / 8	0.52	2.73
PM	American Century Global Gold A	ACGGX	E-	(800) 345-6488	E / 0.5	11.35	-9.72	23.93 /70	-2.53 / 5	-14.15 / 0	8.95	0.93
PM	American Century Global Gold C	AGYCX	E-	(800) 345-6488	E+ / 0.6	11.18	-10.10	22.97 /66	-3.25 / 4	-14.80 / 0	9.11	1.68
PM	American Century Global Gold I	AGGNX	E-	(800) 345-6488	E+ / 0.9	11.45	-9.54	24.48 /72	-2.09 / 6	-13.77 / 0	9.68	0.48
PM	American Century Global Gold Inv	BGEIX	E-	(800) 345-6488	E+ / 0.9	11.57	-9.60	24.27 /71	-2.27 / 6	-13.93 / 0	9.56	0.68
PM	American Century Global Gold R	AGGWX	E-	(800) 345-6488	E+ / 0.7	11.28	-9.83	23.65 /69	-2.78 / 5	-14.36 / 0	9.32	1.18
GL	American Century Global Growth A	AGGRX	D-	(800) 345-6488	D+ / 2.3	6.96	4.11	16.43 /36	2.22 /25	8.06 /43	0.00	1.33
GL	American Century Global Growth C	AGLCX	D-	(800) 345-6488	D+ / 2.7	6.76	3.68	15.59 /32	1.47 /21	7.27 /36	0.00	2.08
GL	American Century Global Growth Inst	AGGIX	D	(800) 345-6488	C- / 3.2	7.06	4.31	16.93 /38	2.67 /29	8.56 /47	0.00	0.88

● Denotes fund is closed to new investors
* Denotes fund is included in Section II

54

RISK Risk Rating/Pts	3 Year Standard Deviation	Beta	NET ASSETS NAV As of 2/28/17	Total $(Mil)	ASSET Cash %	Stocks %	Bonds %	Other %	Portfolio Turnover Ratio	BULL/BEAR Last Bull Market Return	Last Bear Market Return	FUND MANAGER Manager Quality Pct	Manager Tenure (Years)	MINIMUMS Initial Purch. $	Additional Purch. $	LOADS Front End Load	Back End Load
C+ / 6.2	10.7	1.00	21.15	399	0	99	0	1	113	122.0	-16.3	45	12	2,500	50	0.0	0.0
C+ / 6.2	10.7	1.00	20.74	11	0	99	0	1	113	116.1	-16.5	38	12	2,500	50	0.0	0.0
C+ / 6.5	10.9	0.99	18.06	4	0	100	0	0	121	N/A	N/A	55	6	2,500	50	5.8	0.0
C+ / 6.4	10.9	0.99	17.39	2	0	100	0	0	121	N/A	N/A	44	6	2,500	50	0.0	0.0
C+ / 6.5	10.9	0.99	18.22	N/A	0	100	0	0	121	N/A	N/A	61	6	5,000,000	0	0.0	0.0
C+ / 6.5	10.9	0.99	18.22	32	0	100	0	0	121	N/A	N/A	58	6	2,500	50	0.0	0.0
C+ / 6.5	10.9	0.99	17.86	N/A	0	100	0	0	121	N/A	N/A	51	6	2,500	50	0.0	0.0
C- / 4.1	17.4	1.05	7.88	3	2	97	0	1	78	N/A	N/A	17	4	2,500	50	5.8	0.0
C- / 4.1	17.3	1.05	7.86	N/A	2	97	0	1	78	N/A	N/A	12	4	2,500	50	0.0	0.0
C- / 4.1	17.4	1.06	7.89	2	2	97	0	1	78	N/A	N/A	21	4	5,000,000	0	0.0	0.0
C- / 4.1	17.4	1.05	7.89	5	2	97	0	1	78	N/A	N/A	19	4	2,500	50	0.0	0.0
C- / 4.1	17.4	1.05	7.87	N/A	2	97	0	1	78	N/A	N/A	15	4	2,500	50	0.0	0.0
C / 5.1	14.6	0.87	8.87	35	2	96	1	1	59	37.0	-30.3	79	11	2,500	50	5.8	0.0
C / 5.1	14.6	0.87	8.18	7	2	96	1	1	59	31.6	-30.5	74	11	2,500	50	0.0	0.0
C / 5.1	14.6	0.87	9.45	40	2	96	1	1	59	40.2	-30.1	82	11	5,000,000	50	0.0	2.0
C / 5.1	14.6	0.87	9.21	532	2	96	1	1	59	38.8	-30.1	81	11	2,500	50	0.0	2.0
C / 5.1	14.6	0.87	8.94	3	2	96	1	1	59	35.2	-30.4	77	11	2,500	50	0.0	2.0
C / 5.2	14.6	0.87	9.47	38	2	96	1	1	59	N/A	N/A	83	11	0	0	0.0	2.0
C / 5.0	10.6	1.02	31.04	139	0	98	0	2	91	117.3	-15.8	35	12	2,500	50	5.8	0.0
C / 5.0	10.6	1.01	30.75	12	0	98	0	2	91	108.7	-16.1	27	12	2,500	50	0.0	0.0
C / 5.0	10.6	1.02	31.11	465	0	98	0	2	91	122.6	-15.7	41	12	5,000,000	0	0.0	0.0
C / 5.0	10.6	1.01	31.08	2,610	0	98	0	2	91	120.2	-15.8	38	12	2,500	50	0.0	0.0
C / 5.0	10.6	1.01	31.04	32	0	98	0	2	91	114.3	-15.9	32	12	2,500	50	0.0	0.0
C+ / 6.1	7.6	0.67	9.17	2,237	6	83	5	6	88	104.7	-12.3	93	23	2,500	50	5.8	0.0
C+ / 6.2	7.5	0.67	9.16	719	6	83	5	6	88	96.3	-12.5	91	23	2,500	50	0.0	0.0
C+ / 6.1	7.5	0.67	9.18	1,543	6	83	5	6	88	109.4	-12.0	94	23	5,000,000	50	0.0	0.0
C+ / 6.1	7.6	0.67	9.17	7,320	6	83	5	6	88	107.4	-12.2	94	23	2,500	50	0.0	0.0
C+ / 6.2	7.6	0.67	9.14	116	6	83	5	6	88	101.9	-12.3	93	23	2,500	50	0.0	0.0
C+ / 6.1	7.5	0.67	9.19	464	6	83	5	6	88	N/A	N/A	95	23	0	0	0.0	0.0
C / 5.2	11.7	1.03	17.77	N/A	0	99	0	1	250	100.0	-13.6	21	1	2,500	50	0.0	0.0
C / 5.1	11.7	1.03	17.93	N/A	0	99	0	1	250	105.0	-13.5	26	1	5,000,000	50	0.0	0.0
C / 5.2	11.7	1.03	17.87	12	0	99	0	1	250	102.6	-13.5	24	1	2,500	50	0.0	0.0
C / 5.2	11.7	1.03	17.67	N/A	0	99	0	1	250	97.4	-13.8	19	1	2,500	50	0.0	0.0
C+ / 6.3	11.7	0.81	11.14	15	12	87	0	1	250	68.2	-17.3	19	6	2,500	50	5.8	0.0
C+ / 6.3	11.7	0.81	11.14	7	12	87	0	1	250	61.6	-17.6	13	6	2,500	50	0.0	0.0
C+ / 6.2	11.7	0.81	11.13	3	12	87	0	1	250	72.3	-17.1	23	6	5,000,000	50	0.0	0.0
C+ / 6.2	11.7	0.81	11.14	54	12	87	0	1	250	70.6	-17.2	21	6	2,500	50	0.0	0.0
C+ / 6.3	11.7	0.81	11.15	N/A	12	87	0	1	250	66.0	-17.4	17	6	2,500	50	0.0	0.0
C+ / 6.2	11.7	0.81	11.13	8	12	87	0	1	250	N/A	N/A	25	6	0	0	0.0	0.0
B- / 7.4	6.9	0.99	10.40	4	24	46	29	1	40	N/A	N/A	13	5	2,500	50	5.8	0.0
B- / 7.5	6.9	0.99	10.34	5	24	46	29	1	40	N/A	N/A	9	5	2,500	50	0.0	0.0
B- / 7.4	6.9	0.99	10.44	1	24	46	29	1	40	N/A	N/A	16	5	5,000,000	50	0.0	0.0
B- / 7.4	6.9	0.99	10.43	5	24	46	29	1	40	N/A	N/A	15	5	2,500	50	0.0	0.0
B- / 7.4	6.9	0.98	10.38	N/A	24	46	29	1	40	N/A	N/A	12	5	2,500	50	0.0	0.0
E- / 0.0	45.7	2.52	8.59	10	0	99	0	1	11	-52.1	-15.0	87	12	2,500	50	5.8	0.0
E- / 0.0	45.7	2.51	8.28	2	0	99	0	1	11	-54.0	-15.3	84	12	2,500	50	0.0	0.0
E- / 0.0	45.6	2.51	8.80	13	0	99	0	1	11	-51.0	-14.9	89	12	5,000,000	0	0.0	1.0
E- / 0.0	45.6	2.52	8.74	381	0	99	0	1	11	-51.5	-14.9	88	12	2,500	50	0.0	1.0
E- / 0.0	45.7	2.52	8.53	5	0	99	0	1	11	-52.8	-15.1	86	12	2,500	50	0.0	1.0
C / 4.4	11.6	0.85	11.25	35	0	99	0	1	57	78.7	-20.6	88	16	2,500	50	5.8	0.0
C- / 4.2	11.5	0.85	9.99	6	0	99	0	1	57	71.6	-20.9	84	16	2,500	50	0.0	0.0
C / 4.5	11.5	0.85	11.72	41	0	99	0	1	57	83.3	-20.6	89	16	5,000,000	50	0.0	2.0

	99 Pct = Best / 0 Pct = Worst				PERFORMANCE							
						Total Return % through 2/28/17					Incl. in Returns	
									Annualized			
Fund Type	Fund Name	Ticker Symbol	Overall Investment Rating	Phone	Perfor-mance Rating/Pts	3 Mo	6 Mo	1Yr / Pct	3Yr / Pct	5Yr / Pct	Dividend Yield	Expense Ratio
GL	American Century Global Growth Inv	TWGGX	D	(800) 345-6488	C- / 3.1	6.98	4.19	16.79 /38	2.47 /27	8.34 /45	0.00	1.08
GL	American Century Global Growth R	AGORX	D-	(800) 345-6488	D+ / 2.7	6.85	3.97	16.17 /35	1.97 /24	7.81 /41	0.00	1.58
GL	American Century Global Growth R6	AGGDX	D	(800) 345-6488	C- / 3.3	7.03	4.39	17.10 /39	2.81 /30	--	0.00	0.73
GR	American Century Growth A	TCRAX	C	(800) 345-6488	C+ / 6.9	8.93	8.51	20.80 /56	8.43 /82	11.29 /68	0.30	1.22
GR	American Century Growth C	TWRCX	C	(800) 345-6488	B- / 7.4	8.74	8.11	19.91 /51	7.63 /76	10.45 /62	0.00	1.97
GR	American Century Growth Inst	TWGIX	C+	(800) 345-6488	B+ / 8.3	9.07	8.74	21.34 /59	8.92 /86	11.79 /72	0.72	0.77
GR	American Century Growth Inv	TWCGX	C+	(800) 345-6488	B / 8.1	9.00	8.62	21.11 /58	8.71 /85	11.56 /70	0.54	0.97
GR	American Century Growth R	AGWRX	C	(800) 345-6488	B / 7.8	8.89	8.38	20.52 /55	8.17 /80	11.01 /66	0.08	1.47
GR	American Century Growth R6	AGRDX	C+	(800) 345-6488	B+ / 8.4	9.13	8.83	21.54 /60	9.09 /87	--	0.86	0.62
MC	American Century Heritage A	ATHAX	D-	(800) 345-6488	C- / 3.6	5.65	4.09	20.22 /53	4.43 /48	9.62 /55	0.00	1.25
MC	American Century Heritage C	AHGCX	D-	(800) 345-6488	C- / 4.2	5.53	3.75	19.37 /49	3.66 /39	8.81 /49	0.00	2.00
MC	American Century Heritage Inst	ATHIX	D	(800) 345-6488	C / 5.2	5.80	4.36	20.78 /56	4.90 /53	10.11 /59	0.00	0.80
MC	American Century Heritage Inv	TWHIX	D	(800) 345-6488	C / 5.1	5.72	4.21	20.54 /55	4.68 /51	9.89 /57	0.00	1.00
MC	American Century Heritage R	ATHWX	D	(800) 345-6488	C / 4.6	5.57	3.97	19.92 /52	4.16 /45	9.34 /53	0.00	1.50
GR	American Century Heritage R6	ATHDX	D+	(800) 345-6488	C / 5.4	5.85	4.42	20.98 /57	5.07 /55	10.16 /59	0.00	0.65
GI	American Century Inc and Gr A	AMADX	C+	(800) 345-6488	C+ / 6.9	7.00	8.61	24.47 /72	8.04 /79	12.33 /77	1.78	0.93
GI	American Century Inc and Gr C	ACGCX	B	(800) 345-6488	B- / 7.4	6.80	8.23	23.57 /68	7.23 /73	11.49 /70	1.21	1.68
GI	American Century Inc and Gr Inst	AMGIX	B+	(800) 345-6488	B+ / 8.3	7.12	8.87	25.02 /73	8.52 /83	12.83 /82	2.29	0.48
GI	American Century Inc and Gr Inv	BIGRX	B+	(800) 345-6488	B / 8.1	7.07	8.77	24.77 /72	8.31 /81	12.61 /80	2.11	0.68
GI	American Century Inc and Gr R	AICRX	B	(800) 345-6488	B / 7.7	6.89	8.46	24.14 /70	7.76 /77	12.05 /75	1.66	1.18
FO	American Century Intl Core Eq A	ACIQX	D-	(800) 345-6488	E / 0.5	8.14	6.36	13.54 /24	-1.99 / 7	5.36 /24	2.21	1.43
FO	American Century Intl Core Eq C	ACIKX	D-	(800) 345-6488	E+ / 0.7	7.91	5.98	12.74 /21	-2.74 / 5	4.56 /18	1.62	2.18
FO	American Century Intl Core Eq Inst	ACIUX	D-	(800) 345-6488	E+ / 0.9	8.21	6.57	14.06 /26	-1.58 / 8	5.80 /27	2.78	0.98
FO	American Century Intl Core Eq Inv	ACIMX	D-	(800) 345-6488	E+ / 0.8	8.14	6.50	13.85 /25	-1.78 / 7	5.60 /25	2.59	1.18
FO	American Century Intl Core Eq R	ACIRX	D-	(800) 345-6488	E+ / 0.7	8.03	6.24	13.30 /23	-2.24 / 6	5.08 /22	2.11	1.68
FO	American Century Intl Disc A	ACIDX	E+	(800) 345-6488	E / 0.4	6.93	3.10	10.93 /14	-2.00 / 7	6.52 /32	0.27	1.87
FO	American Century Intl Disc C	TWECX	E+	(800) 345-6488	E / 0.5	6.77	2.72	10.07 /12	-2.74 / 5	5.72 /26	0.00	2.62
FO	American Century Intl Disc Inst	TIDIX	D-	(800) 345-6488	E+ / 0.7	7.07	3.29	11.42 /16	-1.56 / 8	6.99 /34	0.69	1.42
FO	American Century Intl Disc Inv	TWEGX	E+	(800) 345-6488	E+ / 0.7	7.08	3.25	11.25 /15	-1.75 / 7	6.80 /33	0.51	1.62
FO	American Century Intl Disc R	TWERX	E+	(800) 345-6488	E / 0.5	6.84	2.97	10.68 /13	-2.24 / 6	6.25 /30	0.05	2.12
FO	American Century Intl Gr A	TWGAX	E	(800) 345-6488	E- / 0.2	5.24	0.69	8.08 / 8	-3.14 / 4	4.37 /17	0.21	1.49
FO	American Century Intl Gr C	AIWCX	E	(800) 345-6488	E / 0.3	5.03	0.28	7.32 / 6	-3.86 / 3	3.59 /13	0.00	2.24
FO	American Century Intl Gr Inst	TGRIX	E	(800) 345-6488	E / 0.4	5.39	0.88	8.59 / 9	-2.69 / 5	4.83 /20	0.66	1.04
FO	American Century Intl Gr Inv	TWIEX	E	(800) 345-6488	E / 0.3	5.34	0.76	8.42 / 8	-2.91 / 5	4.63 /19	0.47	1.17
FO	American Century Intl Gr R	ATGRX	E	(800) 345-6488	E / 0.3	5.13	0.45	7.85 / 7	-3.38 / 4	4.09 /16	0.00	1.74
FO	American Century Intl Gr R6	ATGDX	E	(800) 345-6488	E / 0.4	5.35	0.94	8.76 / 9	-2.55 / 5	--	0.81	0.89
FO	American Century Intl Opps A	AIVOX	D-	(800) 345-6488	D- / 1.3	7.47	2.26	12.97 /22	0.03 /13	8.33 /45	0.00	1.96
FO	American Century Intl Opps C	AIOCX	D-	(800) 345-6488	D- / 1.1	7.31	1.85	12.23 /19	-0.70 /10	7.55 /39	0.00	2.71
FO	American Century Intl Opps Inst	ACIOX	D-	(800) 345-6488	D / 1.8	7.60	2.58	13.56 /24	0.48 /16	8.78 /49	0.22	1.51
FO	American Century Intl Opps Inv	AIOIX	D-	(800) 345-6488	D / 1.7	7.58	2.51	13.46 /23	0.31 /15	8.63 /47	0.04	1.71
FO	American Century Intl Opps R	AIORX	D-	(800) 345-6488	D- / 1.1	7.41	2.16	12.80 /21	-0.19 /13	8.07 /43	0.00	2.21
FO	American Century Intl Value A	MEQAX	E+	(800) 345-6488	E / 0.5	6.66	7.83	17.44 /40	-2.85 / 5	4.08 /16	0.39	1.57
FO	American Century Intl Value C	ACCOX	E+	(800) 345-6488	E+ / 0.7	6.41	7.44	16.59 /37	-3.54 / 4	3.29 /12	0.00	2.32
FO	American Century Intl Value Inst	ACVUX	E+	(800) 345-6488	E+ / 0.8	6.74	8.05	18.05 /43	-2.37 / 6	4.58 /19	0.85	1.12
FO	American Century Intl Value Inv	ACEVX	E+	(800) 345-6488	E+ / 0.8	6.67	7.98	17.81 /42	-2.57 / 5	4.33 /17	0.66	1.32
FO	American Century Intl Value R	ACVRX	E+	(800) 345-6488	E+ / 0.6	6.58	7.60	17.08 /39	-3.08 / 4	3.83 /14	0.18	1.82
FO	American Century Intl Value R6	ACVDX	E+	(800) 345-6488	E+ / 0.9	6.75	8.07	18.23 /44	-2.26 / 6	--	1.00	0.97
GR	American Century Lrge Comp Val A	ALPAX	A-	(800) 345-6488	B / 8.1	6.89	10.74	28.12 /82	9.17 /88	12.95 /83	1.40	1.09
GR	American Century Lrge Comp Val C	ALPCX	A	(800) 345-6488	B+ / 8.6	6.79	10.31	27.19 /80	8.39 /82	12.10 /75	0.81	1.84
GR	American Century Lrge Comp Val Inst	ALVSX	A+	(800) 345-6488	A / 9.3	7.02	10.87	28.66 /83	9.66 /91	13.44 /88	1.89	0.64
GR	American Century Lrge Comp Val Inv	ALVIX	A+	(800) 345-6488	A- / 9.2	6.96	10.87	28.41 /83	9.48 /90	13.25 /86	1.71	0.84
GR	American Century Lrge Comp Val R	ALVRX	A+	(800) 345-6488	B+ / 8.9	6.82	10.47	27.80 /81	8.90 /86	12.67 /81	1.26	1.34

● Denotes fund is closed to new investors

* Denotes fund is included in Section II

| RISK | 3 Year | | NET ASSETS | | ASSET | | | | Portfolio Turnover Ratio | BULL / BEAR | | FUND MANAGER | | MINIMUMS | | LOADS | |
Risk Rating/Pts	Standard Deviation	Beta	NAV As of 2/28/17	Total $(Mil)	Cash %	Stocks %	Bonds %	Other %		Last Bull Market Return	Last Bear Market Return	Manager Quality Pct	Manager Tenure (Years)	Initial Purch. $	Additional Purch. $	Front End Load	Back End Load
C /4.5	11.6	0.85	11.53	389	0	99	0	1	57	81.2	-20.6	89	16	2,500	50	0.0	2.0
C /4.4	11.5	0.85	11.12	8	0	99	0	1	57	76.4	-20.8	87	16	2,500	50	0.0	2.0
C /4.5	11.6	0.85	11.76	18	0	99	0	1	57	N/A	N/A	90	16	0	0	0.0	2.0
C- /3.7	11.2	1.03	29.34	145	1	98	0	1	36	111.1	-17.3	44	20	2,500	50	5.8	0.0
C- /3.5	11.2	1.03	28.39	10	1	98	0	1	36	102.7	-17.6	34	20	2,500	50	0.0	0.0
C- /3.7	11.2	1.03	30.62	1,107	1	98	0	1	36	116.2	-17.2	51	20	5,000,000	50	0.0	0.0
C- /3.7	11.2	1.03	30.15	5,394	1	98	0	1	36	113.9	-17.2	48	20	2,500	50	0.0	0.0
C- /3.6	11.2	1.03	28.83	98	1	98	0	1	36	108.2	-17.4	41	20	2,500	50	0.0	0.0
C- /3.7	11.2	1.03	30.60	803	1	98	0	1	36	N/A	N/A	53	20	0	0	0.0	0.0
D+ /2.8	12.3	0.93	20.04	543	1	98	0	1	62	95.5	-21.5	21	14	2,500	50	5.8	0.0
D /2.2	12.3	0.93	16.64	99	1	98	0	1	62	87.9	-21.7	15	14	2,500	50	0.0	0.0
C- /3.1	12.3	0.93	22.64	144	1	98	0	1	62	100.4	-21.3	26	14	5,000,000	50	0.0	0.0
C- /3.0	12.3	0.93	21.46	3,991	1	98	0	1	62	98.2	-21.4	24	14	2,500	50	0.0	0.0
D+ /2.8	12.3	0.93	20.13	42	1	98	0	1	62	92.9	-21.5	19	14	2,500	50	0.0	0.0
C- /3.2	12.3	1.04	22.79	140	1	98	0	1	62	100.7	-21.4	11	14	0	0	0.0	0.0
C+ /5.8	10.5	1.00	37.64	216	0	98	0	2	79	118.7	-16.2	43	7	2,500	50	5.8	0.0
C+ /5.8	10.5	1.00	37.54	8	0	98	0	2	79	110.0	-16.4	33	7	2,500	50	0.0	0.0
C+ /5.8	10.5	1.00	37.75	176	0	98	0	2	79	124.0	-16.0	49	7	5,000,000	0	0.0	0.0
C+ /5.8	10.5	1.00	37.70	1,711	0	98	0	2	79	121.6	-16.1	47	7	2,500	50	0.0	0.0
C+ /5.8	10.5	1.00	37.66	27	0	98	0	2	79	115.7	-16.2	39	7	2,500	50	0.0	0.0
C+ /5.7	11.6	0.92	8.20	5	2	97	0	1	117	47.7	-23.9	50	10	2,500	50	5.8	0.0
C+ /5.7	11.6	0.92	8.17	1	2	97	0	1	117	41.8	-24.2	39	10	2,500	50	0.0	0.0
C+ /5.6	11.5	0.91	8.20	1	2	97	0	1	117	51.3	-23.8	56	10	5,000,000	0	0.0	2.0
C+ /5.7	11.5	0.91	8.19	18	2	97	0	1	117	49.6	-23.9	53	10	2,500	50	0.0	2.0
C+ /5.7	11.6	0.92	8.18	1	2	97	0	1	117	45.7	-24.0	47	10	2,500	50	0.0	2.0
C /5.4	12.4	0.83	12.65	5	1	98	0	1	139	59.6	-29.3	50	23	10,000	50	5.8	0.0
C /5.3	12.4	0.83	12.46	1	1	98	0	1	139	53.1	-29.5	39	23	10,000	50	0.0	0.0
C /5.5	12.3	0.83	13.17	20	1	98	0	1	139	63.5	-29.2	56	23	5,000,000	50	0.0	2.0
C /5.5	12.3	0.83	13.01	427	1	98	0	1	139	61.8	-29.3	53	23	10,000	50	0.0	2.0
C /5.4	12.4	0.83	12.81	N/A	1	98	0	1	139	57.4	-29.3	46	23	10,000	50	0.0	2.0
C /4.5	11.3	0.87	11.16	110	0	98	0	2	70	44.5	-24.4	34	15	2,500	50	5.8	0.0
C /4.5	11.3	0.87	10.85	6	0	98	0	2	70	38.8	-24.7	26	15	2,500	50	0.0	0.0
C /4.5	11.4	0.87	11.00	61	0	98	0	2	70	48.1	-24.3	40	15	5,000,000	50	0.0	2.0
C /4.5	11.4	0.87	11.07	1,253	0	98	0	2	70	46.4	-24.3	37	15	2,500	50	0.0	2.0
C /4.6	11.4	0.87	11.27	3	0	98	0	2	70	42.5	-24.5	31	15	2,500	50	0.0	2.0
C /4.5	11.3	0.87	11.00	38	0	98	0	2	70	N/A	N/A	42	15	0	0	0.0	2.0
C /5.4	11.8	0.73	9.06	15	0	99	0	1	130	78.2	-25.8	75	16	10,000	50	5.8	0.0
C /5.4	11.9	0.73	8.81	2	0	99	0	1	130	71.5	-26.2	67	16	10,000	50	0.0	0.0
C /5.4	11.8	0.73	9.21	7	0	99	0	1	130	82.6	-25.8	78	16	5,000,000	50	0.0	2.0
C /5.4	11.9	0.73	9.13	110	0	99	0	1	130	81.0	-25.8	77	16	10,000	50	0.0	2.0
C /5.4	11.9	0.72	8.99	1	0	99	0	1	130	75.9	-25.9	73	16	10,000	50	0.0	2.0
C /5.1	12.3	0.97	7.87	11	2	96	0	2	76	41.9	-23.2	38	6	2,500	50	5.8	0.0
C /5.2	12.2	0.97	7.80	4	2	96	0	2	76	36.3	-23.4	29	6	2,500	50	0.0	0.0
C /5.1	12.3	0.97	7.84	8	2	96	0	2	76	45.7	-23.1	45	6	5,000,000	50	0.0	2.0
C /5.1	12.2	0.97	7.84	15	2	96	0	2	76	43.9	-23.1	42	6	2,500	50	0.0	2.0
C /5.1	12.2	0.97	7.83	1	2	96	0	2	76	40.1	-23.3	35	6	2,500	50	0.0	2.0
C /5.1	12.3	0.97	7.84	51	2	96	0	2	76	N/A	N/A	47	6	0	0	0.0	2.0
C+ /6.7	11.4	1.05	10.16	58	2	97	0	1	56	124.2	-17.2	51	13	2,500	50	5.8	0.0
C+ /6.7	11.5	1.06	10.15	9	2	97	0	1	56	115.4	-17.5	39	13	2,500	50	0.0	0.0
C+ /6.7	11.4	1.05	10.17	40	2	97	0	1	56	129.7	-17.1	56	13	5,000,000	50	0.0	0.0
C+ /6.7	11.4	1.05	10.17	630	2	97	0	1	56	127.3	-17.2	54	13	2,500	50	0.0	0.0
C+ /6.7	11.4	1.06	10.16	6	2	97	0	1	56	121.2	-17.4	46	13	2,500	50	0.0	0.0

Fund Type	Fund Name	Ticker Symbol	Overall Investment Rating	Phone	Performance Rating/Pts	3 Mo	6 Mo	1Yr / Pct	3Yr / Pct (Annualized)	5Yr / Pct (Annualized)	Dividend Yield	Expense Ratio
GI	American Century Lrge Comp Val R6	ALVDX	A+	(800) 345-6488	A / 9.4	7.06	11.07	28.98 /84	9.86 /93	--	2.02	0.49
MC	● American Century Mid Cap Val A	ACLAX	A-	(800) 345-6488	A+ / 9.6	5.17	11.49	30.92 /88	12.53 /98	15.18 /97	0.93	1.26
MC	● American Century Mid Cap Val C	ACCLX	A-	(800) 345-6488	A+ / 9.7	4.99	11.09	30.03 /86	11.70 /98	14.31 /95	0.40	2.01
MC	● American Century Mid Cap Val Inst	AVUAX	A	(800) 345-6488	A+ / 9.8	5.28	11.79	31.50 /89	13.04 /99	15.70 /98	1.39	0.81
MC	● American Century Mid Cap Val Inv	ACMVX	A	(800) 345-6488	A+ / 9.8	5.29	11.68	31.26 /89	12.82 /99	15.46 /98	1.21	1.01
MC	● American Century Mid Cap Val R	AMVRX	A-	(800) 345-6488	A+ / 9.7	5.11	11.38	30.61 /87	12.25 /98	14.89 /97	0.77	1.51
MC	● American Century Mid Cap Val R6	AMDVX	A	(800) 345-6488	A+ / 9.8	5.33	11.81	31.70 /89	13.21 /99	--	1.52	0.66
GL	American Century Mlti Asst Inc Inv	AMJVX	U	(800) 345-6488	U /	5.23	3.36	15.53 /32	--	--	4.69	1.26
SC	American Century New Opps A	TWNAX	D	(800) 345-6488	C / 5.5	6.46	8.65	28.29 /82	4.70 /51	10.69 /63	0.00	1.75
SC	American Century New Opps C	TWNCX	D+	(800) 345-6488	C+ / 6.1	6.34	8.34	27.43 /80	3.93 /42	9.87 /57	0.00	2.50
SC	American Century New Opps Inst	TWNIX	C-	(800) 345-6488	C+ / 6.6	6.61	8.93	28.84 /84	5.17 /56	11.21 /68	0.00	1.30
SC	American Century New Opps Inv	TWNOX	C-	(800) 345-6488	C+ / 6.5	6.52	8.88	28.69 /83	4.98 /54	10.99 /66	0.00	1.50
SC	American Century New Opps R	TWNRX	D+	(800) 345-6488	C+ / 6.1	6.39	8.52	27.97 /82	4.46 /48	10.43 /61	0.00	2.00
GR	American Century NT Core Eq Inst	ACNKX	A	(800) 345-6488	B- / 7.4	6.86	9.20	20.86 /57	7.74 /77	12.68 /81	0.78	1.68
GR	American Century NT Disc Gro Inst	ANDGX	U	(800) 345-6488	U /	8.12	9.09	22.41 /64	--	--	0.67	0.82
GR	American Century NT Disc Gro Inv	ANTDX	U	(800) 345-6488	U /	8.01	8.98	22.19 /63	--	--	0.49	1.02
EM	American Century NT Emg Market	ACLKX	C-	(800) 345-6488	C / 4.3	7.40	2.61	25.06 /73	2.48 /27	2.37 / 9	0.75	1.49
EM	American Century NT Emg Market R6	ACKDX	C-	(800) 345-6488	C / 4.5	7.36	2.67	25.13 /74	2.65 /29	--	0.89	1.34
GR	American Century NT Equity Gr Inst	ACLEX	B	(800) 345-6488	B / 7.9	7.54	9.16	23.92 /70	7.92 /78	12.33 /77	1.23	0.47
RE	American Century NT Gl Rl Est Inst	ANRHX	U	(800) 345-6488	U /	5.95	-4.62	9.69 /11	--	--	4.27	1.00
RE	American Century NT Gl Rl Est Inv	ANREX	U	(800) 345-6488	U /	5.86	-4.72	9.47 /10	--	--	4.07	1.20
RE	American Century NT Gl Rl Est R6	ANRDX	U	(800) 345-6488	U /	6.00	-4.57	9.85 /11	--	--	4.42	0.85
GR	American Century NT Growth Inst	ACLTX	B-	(800) 345-6488	B / 8.1	8.87	8.51	21.11 /58	8.67 /84	11.70 /72	0.72	0.77
GR	American Century NT Growth R6	ACDTX	B-	(800) 345-6488	B / 8.2	8.90	8.61	21.24 /58	8.85 /86	--	0.86	0.62
GR	American Century NT Heritage Inst	ACLWX	C-	(800) 345-6488	C / 5.2	5.82	4.34	20.78 /56	4.89 /53	10.06 /59	0.00	0.80
MC	American Century NT Heritage R6	ACDUX	C-	(800) 345-6488	C / 5.4	5.86	4.48	20.96 /57	5.03 /54	--	0.00	0.65
FO	American Century NT Intl Gr Inst	ACLNX	E+	(800) 345-6488	E / 0.4	5.24	0.93	8.28 / 8	-2.76 / 5	4.71 /19	0.89	0.98
FO	American Century NT Intl Gr R6	ACDNX	E+	(800) 345-6488	E / 0.5	5.18	0.88	8.33 / 8	-2.62 / 5	--	1.04	0.83
FO	American Century NT Intl Value Inst	ANTYX	U	(800) 345-6488	U /	7.05	8.54	18.12 /43	--	--	3.16	1.11
FO	American Century NT Intl Value Inv	ANTVX	U	(800) 345-6488	U /	7.08	8.45	17.88 /42	--	--	2.96	1.31
FO	American Century NT Intl Value R6	ANTWX	U	(800) 345-6488	U /	7.09	8.57	18.30 /44	--	--	3.31	0.96
FO	American Century NT Itl SM Cap Inst	ANTMX	U	(800) 345-6488	U /	6.35	3.01	11.18 /15	--	--	0.16	1.27
FO	American Century NT Itl SM Cap Inv	ANTSX	U	(800) 345-6488	U /	6.28	2.94	11.11 /15	--	--	0.00	1.47
GR	American Century NT Lrg Co Val Inst	ACLLX	B+	(800) 345-6488	A- / 9.1	6.94	10.90	28.53 /83	9.21 /88	13.14 /85	1.84	0.64
GI	American Century NT Lrg Co Val R6	ACDLX	B+	(800) 345-6488	A- / 9.2	7.07	10.98	28.82 /84	9.40 /90	--	1.97	0.49
MC	American Century NT Md Cp Val Inst	ACLMX	A	(800) 345-6488	A+ / 9.8	5.26	11.71	31.72 /89	13.10 /99	15.74 /98	1.45	0.81
MC	American Century NT Md Cp Val R6	ACDSX	A	(800) 345-6488	A+ / 9.8	5.31	11.80	31.92 /90	13.27 /99	--	1.58	0.66
SC	American Century NT Sm Comp Inst	ACLOX	C+	(800) 345-6488	B / 7.8	5.29	11.86	29.14 /84	6.46 /68	12.68 /81	0.56	0.67
AA	American Century One Chc Agg Inv	AOGIX	C	(800) 345-6488	C / 5.2	5.86	5.51	18.28 /44	5.18 /56	8.59 /47	1.37	1.01
AA	American Century One Chc Conv Inv	AOCIX	C	(800) 345-6488	C- / 3.0	3.69	2.40	11.13 /15	3.93 /42	5.75 /27	1.44	0.81
AA	American Century One Chc Mod Inv	AOMIX	C+	(800) 345-6488	C- / 4.2	4.96	4.32	15.25 /31	4.63 /50	7.36 /37	1.24	0.91
AA	American Century One Chc VryAgg	AOVIX	C	(800) 345-6488	C+ / 6.4	6.84	7.18	21.66 /60	5.81 /63	9.89 /57	0.87	1.07
AA	American Century One Chc VryCon	AONIX	C	(800) 345-6488	D / 2.2	2.53	1.17	8.16 / 8	3.40 /36	3.98 /15	1.34	0.70
GI	American Century OneChoice 2020 A	ARBMX	C-	(800) 345-6488	D / 2.1	3.77	2.99	11.67 /17	3.81 /41	5.99 /28	0.98	1.07
GI	American Century OneChoice 2020 C	ARNCX	C	(800) 345-6488	D+ / 2.5	3.59	2.64	10.90 /14	3.04 /32	5.21 /23	0.29	1.82
GI	American Century OneChoice 2020 I	ARBSX	C+	(800) 345-6488	C- / 3.4	3.89	3.20	12.26 /19	4.28 /46	6.46 /31	1.48	0.62
GI	American Century OneChoice 2020	ARBVX	C	(800) 345-6488	C- / 3.2	3.85	3.08	11.94 /18	4.07 /44	6.25 /30	1.28	0.82
GI	American Century OneChoice 2020 R	ARBRX	C	(800) 345-6488	D+ / 2.9	3.69	2.82	11.49 /16	3.55 /38	5.74 /27	0.79	1.32
GI	American Century OneChoice 2020	ARBDX	C+	(800) 345-6488	C- / 3.4	3.84	3.18	12.32 /19	4.39 /47	--	1.33	0.55
BA	American Century OneChoice 2025 A	ARWAX	C-	(800) 345-6488	D+ / 2.4	4.10	3.29	12.74 /21	4.08 /44	6.45 /31	0.94	1.10
BA	American Century OneChoice 2025 C	ARWCX	C	(800) 345-6488	D+ / 2.8	3.91	2.95	11.96 /18	3.31 /35	5.66 /26	0.26	1.85
BA	American Century OneChoice 2025 I	ARWFX	C+	(800) 345-6488	C- / 3.7	4.20	3.53	13.25 /23	4.55 /49	6.94 /34	1.43	0.65

99 Pct = Best
0 Pct = Worst

RISK Risk Rating/Pts	3 Year Standard Deviation	Beta	NET ASSETS NAV As of 2/28/17	Total $(Mil)	ASSET Cash %	Stocks %	Bonds %	Other %	Portfolio Turnover Ratio	BULL / BEAR Last Bull Market Return	Last Bear Market Return	FUND MANAGER Manager Quality Pct	Manager Tenure (Years)	MINIMUMS Initial Purch. $	Additional Purch. $	LOADS Front End Load	Back End Load
C+ / 6.7	11.4	1.05	10.18	130	2	97	0	1	56	N/A	N/A	59	13	0	0	0.0	0.0
C / 5.2	10.1	0.81	17.83	1,580	1	97	0	2	66	143.8	-17.3	94	13	2,500	50	5.8	0.0
C / 5.2	10.1	0.81	17.67	164	1	97	0	2	66	134.0	-17.4	92	13	2,500	50	0.0	0.0
C / 5.2	10.1	0.81	17.88	1,563	1	97	0	2	66	149.8	-17.1	95	13	5,000,000	50	0.0	0.0
C / 5.2	10.1	0.81	17.87	4,309	1	97	0	2	66	147.1	-17.2	95	13	2,500	50	0.0	0.0
C / 5.2	10.1	0.81	17.78	156	1	97	0	2	66	140.3	-17.2	94	13	2,500	50	0.0	0.0
C / 5.2	10.1	0.81	17.88	1,282	1	97	0	2	66	N/A	N/A	95	13	0	0	0.0	0.0
U /	N/A	N/A	10.01	45	0	0	0	100	195	N/A	N/A	N/A	3	2,500	50	0.0	0.0
D+ / 2.8	15.0	0.89	10.62	7	3	96	0	1	100	114.8	-27.7	57	11	2,500	50	5.8	0.0
D+ / 2.7	15.0	0.89	9.96	N/A	3	96	0	1	100	106.2	-27.8	47	11	2,500	50	0.0	0.0
D+ / 2.9	15.1	0.89	11.04	N/A	3	96	0	1	100	120.0	-27.5	62	11	5,000,000	50	0.0	2.0
D+ / 2.9	15.1	0.89	10.86	181	3	96	0	1	100	117.8	-27.6	60	11	2,500	50	0.0	2.0
D+ / 2.8	15.0	0.89	10.40	N/A	3	96	0	1	100	112.2	-27.8	54	11	2,500	50	0.0	2.0
B / 8.0	9.9	0.94	14.96	585	0	0	0	100	109	N/A	N/A	48	6	0	0	0.0	0.0
U /	N/A	N/A	10.90	445	0	98	0	2	118	N/A	N/A	N/A	2	0	0	0.0	0.0
U /	N/A	N/A	10.89	104	0	98	0	2	118	N/A	N/A	N/A	2	0	0	0.0	0.0
C / 5.1	14.7	0.88	10.94	413	0	99	0	1	75	37.7	-29.9	81	11	0	0	0.0	0.0
C / 5.1	14.7	0.88	10.93	46	0	99	0	1	75	N/A	N/A	82	11	0	0	0.0	0.0
C / 5.3	10.6	1.01	12.76	1,732	0	98	0	2	94	120.8	-15.4	40	11	0	0	0.0	0.0
U /	N/A	N/A	9.24	276	11	88	0	1	264	N/A	N/A	N/A	2	0	0	0.0	0.0
U /	N/A	N/A	9.24	114	11	88	0	1	264	N/A	N/A	N/A	2	0	0	0.0	0.0
U /	N/A	N/A	9.24	31	11	88	0	1	264	N/A	N/A	N/A	2	0	0	0.0	0.0
C / 4.6	11.2	1.03	15.79	1,174	0	99	0	1	60	114.2	-16.9	47	11	0	0	0.0	0.0
C / 4.6	11.2	1.03	15.77	130	0	99	0	1	60	N/A	N/A	50	11	0	0	0.0	0.0
C / 4.4	12.3	1.04	13.03	696	0	99	0	1	73	97.5	-21.7	10	11	0	0	0.0	0.0
C / 4.4	12.3	0.93	13.11	78	0	99	0	1	73	N/A	N/A	27	11	0	0	0.0	0.0
C / 5.1	11.2	0.85	10.02	885	2	97	0	1	69	47.0	-24.4	39	9	0	0	0.0	0.0
C / 5.1	11.2	0.86	10.01	100	2	97	0	1	69	N/A	N/A	41	9	0	0	0.0	0.0
U /	N/A	N/A	9.07	606	1	96	1	2	81	N/A	N/A	N/A	2	0	0	0.0	0.0
U /	N/A	N/A	9.07	217	1	96	1	2	81	N/A	N/A	N/A	2	0	0	0.0	0.0
U /	N/A	N/A	9.07	70	1	96	1	2	81	N/A	N/A	N/A	2	0	0	0.0	0.0
U /	N/A	N/A	10.50	146	1	98	0	1	138	N/A	N/A	N/A	2	0	0	0.0	0.0
U /	N/A	N/A	10.50	67	1	98	0	1	138	N/A	N/A	N/A	2	0	0	0.0	0.0
C / 5.1	11.5	1.06	12.01	1,712	0	98	0	2	61	126.6	-17.3	49	11	0	0	0.0	0.0
C / 5.1	11.6	1.06	12.02	192	0	98	0	2	61	N/A	N/A	52	11	0	0	0.0	0.0
C / 5.4	10.1	0.81	13.87	937	1	97	0	2	67	150.1	-16.9	95	11	0	0	0.0	0.0
C / 5.3	10.1	0.81	13.87	105	1	97	0	2	67	N/A	N/A	95	11	0	0	0.0	0.0
C- / 3.8	15.2	0.95	10.14	426	0	99	0	1	107	130.7	-22.8	73	11	0	0	0.0	0.0
C+ / 6.0	8.7	1.35	15.36	1,154	1	79	19	1	12	78.8	-15.8	18	N/A	2,500	50	0.0	0.0
B / 8.2	5.3	0.83	13.16	1,163	0	46	53	1	19	46.7	-7.0	46	N/A	2,500	50	0.0	0.0
B- / 7.4	7.1	1.11	14.73	1,731	0	65	33	2	11	64.2	-12.0	29	N/A	2,500	50	0.0	0.0
C / 4.7	10.4	1.60	16.27	264	3	96	0	1	11	94.1	-19.2	10	N/A	2,500	50	0.0	0.0
B+ / 9.1	3.6	0.53	11.91	430	0	26	73	1	24	30.0	-2.8	68	13	2,500	50	0.0	0.0
B / 8.1	5.5	0.51	11.96	347	0	47	52	1	17	50.9	-9.3	55	9	2,500	50	5.8	0.0
B / 8.2	5.5	0.52	11.99	8	0	47	52	1	17	45.0	-9.6	45	9	2,500	50	0.0	0.0
B / 8.0	5.5	0.51	11.97	753	0	47	52	1	17	54.7	-9.2	61	9	5,000,000	0	0.0	0.0
B / 8.1	5.5	0.51	11.97	719	0	47	52	1	17	53.0	-9.3	59	9	2,500	50	0.0	0.0
B / 8.2	5.6	0.52	11.96	149	0	47	52	1	17	49.0	-9.5	51	9	2,500	50	0.0	0.0
B / 8.5	5.5	0.51	10.98	248	0	47	52	1	17	N/A	N/A	62	9	0	0	0.0	0.0
B- / 7.8	6.0	0.94	14.11	515	0	52	47	1	12	55.8	-10.6	37	13	2,500	50	5.8	0.0
B / 8.0	6.0	0.95	14.13	8	0	52	47	1	12	49.6	-10.9	27	13	2,500	50	0.0	0.0
B- / 7.7	6.0	0.95	14.11	937	0	52	47	1	12	59.5	-10.4	42	13	5,000,000	0	0.0	0.0

Fund Type	Fund Name	Ticker Symbol	Overall Investment Rating	Phone	PERFORMANCE						Incl. in Returns	
	99 Pct = Best / 0 Pct = Worst				Perfor-mance Rating/Pts	Total Return % through 2/28/17			Annualized		Dividend Yield	Expense Ratio
						3 Mo	6 Mo	1Yr / Pct	3Yr / Pct	5Yr / Pct		
BA	American Century OneChoice 2025	ARWIX	C	(800) 345-6488	C- / 3.6	4.14	3.40	13.02 /22	4.34 /47	6.72 /33	1.24	0.85
BA	American Century OneChoice 2025 R	ARWRX	C	(800) 345-6488	C- / 3.2	3.99	3.18	12.46 /20	3.82 /41	6.19 /30	0.75	1.35
BA	American Century OneChoice 2025	ARWDX	C+	(800) 345-6488	C- / 3.8	4.23	3.57	13.39 /23	4.68 /51	—	1.32	0.58
AA	American Century OneChoice 2030 A	ARCMX	C-	(800) 345-6488	D+ / 2.7	4.37	3.77	13.74 /24	4.37 /47	6.99 /34	0.87	1.12
GI	American Century OneChoice 2030 C	ARWOX	C	(800) 345-6488	C- / 3.1	4.18	3.40	12.95 /21	3.57 /38	6.18 /30	0.18	1.87
AA	American Century OneChoice 2030 I	ARCSX	C+	(800) 345-6488	C- / 4.1	4.58	4.06	14.33 /27	4.84 /52	7.49 /38	1.36	0.67
AA	American Century OneChoice 2030	ARCVX	C+	(800) 345-6488	C- / 4.0	4.45	3.93	14.10 /26	4.63 /50	7.27 /36	1.16	0.87
AA	American Century OneChoice 2030 R	ARCRX	C	(800) 345-6488	C- / 3.6	4.37	3.68	13.54 /24	4.13 /44	6.74 /33	0.67	1.37
GI	American Century OneChoice 2030	ARCUX	C+	(800) 345-6488	C- / 4.2	4.58	4.01	14.38 /27	4.99 /54	—	1.37	0.60
GI	American Century OneChoice 2035 A	ARYAX	C-	(800) 345-6488	C- / 3.1	4.74	4.39	14.90 /29	4.69 /51	7.60 /39	0.88	1.15
GI	American Century OneChoice 2035 C	ARLCX	C	(800) 345-6488	C- / 3.6	4.58	4.02	14.11 /26	3.89 /42	6.78 /33	0.20	1.90
GI	American Century OneChoice 2035 I	ARLIX	C+	(800) 345-6488	C / 4.6	4.93	4.65	15.48 /32	5.16 /56	8.08 /43	1.37	0.70
GI	American Century OneChoice 2035	ARYIX	C+	(800) 345-6488	C / 4.4	4.79	4.51	15.19 /31	4.93 /53	7.85 /41	1.18	0.90
GI	American Century OneChoice 2035 R	ARYRX	C	(800) 345-6488	C- / 4.0	4.69	4.27	14.70 /28	4.43 /48	7.33 /37	0.69	1.40
GI	American Century OneChoice 2035	ARLDX	B-	(800) 345-6488	C / 4.7	4.88	4.60	15.55 /32	5.29 /57	—	1.37	0.63
GI	American Century OneChoice 2040 A	ARDMX	C	(800) 345-6488	C- / 3.5	5.04	4.87	16.13 /35	4.97 /54	8.14 /43	0.84	1.18
GI	American Century OneChoice 2040 C	ARNOX	C	(800) 345-6488	C- / 4.0	4.92	4.50	15.35 /31	4.20 /45	7.33 /37	0.16	1.93
GI	American Century OneChoice 2040 I	ARDSX	C+	(800) 345-6488	C / 5.1	5.26	5.09	16.75 /37	5.45 /59	8.62 /47	1.33	0.73
GI	American Century OneChoice 2040	ARDVX	C+	(800) 345-6488	C / 4.9	5.13	5.05	16.51 /36	5.26 /57	8.40 /45	1.13	0.93
GI	American Century OneChoice 2040 R	ARDRX	C+	(800) 345-6488	C / 4.4	5.11	4.78	15.94 /34	4.74 /51	7.88 /41	0.65	1.43
GI	American Century OneChoice 2040	ARDUX	B-	(800) 345-6488	C / 5.2	5.25	5.16	16.79 /38	5.61 /61	—	1.38	0.65
GI	American Century OneChoice 2045 A	AROAX	C	(800) 345-6488	C- / 3.9	5.51	5.38	17.47 /40	5.31 /58	8.60 /47	0.84	1.22
GI	American Century OneChoice 2045 C	AROCX	C	(800) 345-6488	C / 4.5	5.32	4.98	16.63 /37	4.54 /49	7.80 /41	0.17	1.97
GI	American Century OneChoice 2045 I	AOOIX	C+	(800) 345-6488	C / 5.5	5.64	5.64	18.05 /43	5.80 /62	9.10 /51	1.33	0.77
GI	American Century OneChoice 2045	AROIX	C+	(800) 345-6488	C / 5.3	5.57	5.50	17.75 /42	5.57 /60	8.87 /49	1.14	0.97
GI	American Century OneChoice 2045 R	ARORX	C+	(800) 345-6488	C / 4.9	5.45	5.24	17.25 /39	5.06 /55	8.34 /45	0.65	1.47
GI	American Century OneChoice 2045	ARDOX	B-	(800) 345-6488	C+ / 5.6	5.62	5.62	18.16 /44	5.93 /64	—	1.38	0.68
GI	American Century OneChoice 2050 A	ARFMX	C	(800) 345-6488	C- / 4.2	5.77	5.69	18.27 /44	5.45 /59	8.80 /49	0.75	1.24
GI	American Century OneChoice 2050 C	ARFDX	C+	(800) 345-6488	C / 4.8	5.64	5.30	17.44 /40	4.69 /51	8.00 /42	0.06	1.99
GI	American Century OneChoice 2050 I	ARFSX	C+	(800) 345-6488	C+ / 5.8	5.90	5.90	18.77 /46	5.95 /64	9.30 /53	1.22	0.79
GI	American Century OneChoice 2050	ARFVX	C+	(800) 345-6488	C+ / 5.6	5.86	5.86	18.55 /45	5.74 /62	9.09 /51	1.03	0.99
GI	American Century OneChoice 2050 R	ARFWX	C+	(800) 345-6488	C / 5.2	5.75	5.58	18.06 /43	5.20 /56	8.54 /47	0.55	1.49
GI	American Century OneChoice 2050	ARFEX	B-	(800) 345-6488	C+ / 5.9	5.94	6.03	19.01 /47	6.07 /65	—	1.39	0.70
AA	American Century OneChoice 2055 A	AREMX	C	(800) 345-6488	C / 4.4	5.92	5.92	18.90 /47	5.62 /61	9.02 /51	0.79	1.24
AA	American Century OneChoice 2055 C	AREFX	C+	(800) 345-6488	C / 5.0	5.76	5.52	18.00 /43	4.85 /52	8.21 /44	0.11	1.99
AA	American Century OneChoice 2055 I	ARENX	C+	(800) 345-6488	C+ / 6.1	6.07	6.23	19.51 /49	6.12 /65	9.52 /55	1.27	0.79
AA	American Century OneChoice 2055	AREVX	C+	(800) 345-6488	C+ / 5.9	6.02	6.10	19.27 /48	5.90 /63	9.30 /53	1.07	0.99
AA	American Century OneChoice 2055 R	AREOX	C+	(800) 345-6488	C / 5.4	5.81	5.81	18.58 /45	5.37 /58	8.75 /48	0.59	1.49
GI	American Century OneChoice 2055	AREUX	B-	(800) 345-6488	C+ / 6.2	6.04	6.23	19.57 /50	6.25 /66	—	1.33	0.71
GI	American Century OneChoice InRe A	ARTAX	C-	(800) 345-6488	D / 2.0	3.54	2.78	11.00 /14	3.59 /38	5.50 /25	0.96	1.04
GI	American Century OneChoice InRe C	ATTCX	C	(800) 345-6488	D+ / 2.3	3.43	2.45	10.29 /12	2.82 /30	4.73 /20	0.38	1.79
GI	American Century OneChoice InRe I	ATTIX	C+	(800) 345-6488	C- / 3.2	3.74	3.02	11.59 /16	4.06 /44	5.98 /28	1.45	0.59
GI	American Century OneChoice InRe	ARTOX	C+	(800) 345-6488	C- / 3.0	3.61	2.92	11.28 /15	3.85 /41	5.77 /27	1.26	0.79
GI	American Century OneChoice InRe R	ARSRX	C	(800) 345-6488	D+ / 2.6	3.48	2.66	10.75 /14	3.31 /35	5.23 /23	0.78	1.29
AA	American Century OneChoice InRe	ARDTX	C+	(800) 345-6488	C- / 3.2	3.77	3.08	11.70 /17	4.20 /45	—	1.50	0.53
RE	American Century Real Estate A	AREEX	C-	(800) 345-6488	C / 5.2	6.74	-3.53	13.43 /23	9.80 /92	10.19 /60	1.89	1.39
RE	American Century Real Estate C	ARYCX	C	(800) 345-6488	C+ / 5.8	6.53	-3.89	12.57 /20	8.98 /87	9.36 /53	1.37	2.14
RE	American Century Real Estate Inst	REAIX	C+	(800) 345-6488	C+ / 6.8	6.85	-3.33	13.94 /25	10.29 /95	10.68 /63	2.42	0.94
RE	American Century Real Estate Inv	REACX	C	(800) 345-6488	C+ / 6.6	6.77	-3.41	13.71 /24	10.07 /94	10.46 /62	2.23	1.14
RE	American Century Real Estate R	AREWX	C	(800) 345-6488	C+ / 6.2	6.70	-3.65	13.13 /22	9.53 /90	9.91 /58	1.76	1.64
RE	American Century Real Estate R6	AREDX	C+	(800) 345-6488	C+ / 6.9	6.86	-3.26	14.07 /26	10.45 /96	—	2.57	0.79
GR	American Century Select A	TWCAX	B	(800) 345-6488	B / 7.7	8.15	9.62	21.80 /61	9.72 /92	11.79 /72	0.10	1.24

● Denotes fund is closed to new investors
* Denotes fund is included in Section II

RISK Rating/Pts	3 Year Standard Deviation	Beta	NAV As of 2/28/17	Total $(Mil)	Cash %	Stocks %	Bonds %	Other %	Portfolio Turnover Ratio	Last Bull Market Return	Last Bear Market Return	Manager Quality Pct	Manager Tenure (Years)	Initial Purch. $	Additional Purch. $	Front End Load	Back End Load
B- /7.8	6.0	0.95	14.11	1,191	0	52	47	1	12	57.8	-10.5	39	13	2,500	50	0.0	0.0
B- /7.9	6.0	0.94	14.10	222	0	52	47	1	12	53.6	-10.7	34	13	2,500	50	0.0	0.0
B /8.5	6.0	0.94	11.19	317	0	52	47	1	12	N/A	N/A	45	11	0	0	0.0	0.0
B- /7.7	6.6	1.03	12.18	414	0	57	42	1	11	61.3	-12.0	32	9	2,500	50	5.8	0.0
B- /7.8	6.6	0.61	12.21	6	0	57	42	1	11	54.8	-12.2	38	N/A	2,500	50	0.0	0.0
B- /7.6	6.5	1.03	12.20	831	0	57	42	1	11	65.3	-11.7	38	9	5,000,000	0	0.0	0.0
B- /7.7	6.5	1.02	12.20	737	0	57	42	1	11	63.4	-11.9	36	9	2,500	50	0.0	0.0
B- /7.8	6.5	1.03	12.19	175	0	57	42	1	11	59.2	-12.0	30	9	2,500	50	0.0	0.0
B /8.2	6.5	0.61	11.27	294	0	57	42	1	11	N/A	N/A	57	9	0	0	0.0	0.0
B- /7.3	7.1	0.67	15.14	442	0	63	35	2	11	67.6	-13.3	46	13	2,500	50	5.8	0.0
B- /7.4	7.2	0.67	15.15	6	0	63	35	2	11	60.9	-13.5	35	13	2,500	50	0.0	0.0
B- /7.2	7.1	0.67	15.16	779	0	63	35	2	11	71.8	-13.1	52	13	5,000,000	0	0.0	0.0
B- /7.3	7.1	0.67	15.14	926	0	63	35	2	11	69.8	-13.2	49	13	2,500	50	0.0	0.0
B- /7.4	7.1	0.67	15.14	210	0	63	35	2	11	65.4	-13.4	42	13	2,500	50	0.0	0.0
B /8.0	7.2	0.67	11.39	235	0	63	35	2	11	N/A	N/A	53	11	0	0	0.0	0.0
B- /7.2	7.8	0.73	12.66	294	0	70	29	1	15	73.8	-14.6	41	9	2,500	50	5.8	0.0
B- /7.3	7.7	0.72	12.67	4	0	70	29	1	15	66.9	-14.9	32	9	2,500	50	0.0	0.0
B- /7.1	7.7	0.72	12.67	631	0	70	29	1	15	78.1	-14.4	48	9	5,000,000	0	0.0	0.0
B- /7.2	7.7	0.73	12.67	543	0	70	29	1	15	76.1	-14.5	45	9	2,500	50	0.0	0.0
B- /7.2	7.7	0.73	12.66	131	0	70	29	1	15	71.5	-14.7	38	9	2,500	50	0.0	0.0
B- /7.7	7.7	0.72	11.48	199	0	70	29	1	15	N/A	N/A	50	9	0	0	0.0	0.0
C+ /6.8	8.3	0.78	15.78	298	1	75	23	1	9	78.8	-15.4	37	N/A	2,500	50	5.8	0.0
C+ /6.9	8.3	0.78	15.81	3	1	75	23	1	9	71.7	-15.7	29	N/A	2,500	50	0.0	0.0
C+ /6.7	8.3	0.78	15.81	602	1	75	23	1	9	83.3	-15.3	44	N/A	5,000,000	0	0.0	0.0
C+ /6.7	8.3	0.78	15.79	640	1	75	23	1	9	81.3	-15.4	41	N/A	2,500	50	0.0	0.0
C+ /6.8	8.3	0.78	15.79	141	1	75	23	1	9	76.5	-15.6	35	N/A	2,500	50	0.0	0.0
B- /7.3	8.4	0.79	11.57	158	1	75	23	1	9	N/A	N/A	45	11	0	0	0.0	0.0
C+ /6.8	8.6	0.81	12.75	176	0	80	19	1	7	81.3	-16.0	36	9	2,500	50	5.8	0.0
C+ /6.9	8.6	0.81	12.78	2	0	80	19	1	7	74.2	-16.3	27	9	2,500	50	0.0	0.0
C+ /6.7	8.6	0.81	12.77	383	0	80	19	1	7	85.8	-15.9	42	9	5,000,000	0	0.0	0.0
C+ /6.7	8.6	0.81	12.76	324	0	80	19	1	7	83.9	-16.0	40	9	2,500	50	0.0	0.0
C+ /6.8	8.6	0.81	12.76	77	0	80	19	1	7	79.1	-16.2	33	9	2,500	50	0.0	0.0
B- /7.1	8.7	0.81	11.57	107	0	80	19	1	7	N/A	N/A	43	9	0	0	0.0	0.0
C+ /6.9	8.9	1.38	13.56	80	0	83	16	1	14	83.5	-16.2	19	6	2,500	50	5.8	0.0
B- /7.0	8.9	1.38	13.56	1	0	83	16	1	14	76.3	-16.4	13	6	2,500	50	0.0	0.0
C+ /6.8	8.9	1.39	13.58	198	0	83	16	1	14	88.1	-16.0	23	6	5,000,000	0	0.0	0.0
C+ /6.9	8.9	1.38	13.58	126	0	83	16	1	14	86.2	-16.1	21	6	2,500	50	0.0	0.0
C+ /6.9	8.9	1.39	13.57	43	0	83	16	1	14	81.2	-16.3	17	6	2,500	50	0.0	0.0
B- /7.0	8.9	0.84	11.82	59	0	83	16	1	14	N/A	N/A	42	6	0	0	0.0	0.0
B /8.5	5.1	0.47	12.79	315	1	44	54	1	22	45.2	-7.3	58	N/A	2,500	50	5.8	0.0
B /8.5	5.1	0.47	12.75	9	1	44	54	1	22	39.6	-7.6	47	N/A	2,500	50	0.0	0.0
B /8.5	5.1	0.47	12.80	495	1	44	54	1	22	48.8	-7.1	64	N/A	5,000,000	0	0.0	0.0
B /8.5	5.1	0.48	12.79	840	1	44	54	1	22	47.3	-7.3	61	N/A	2,500	50	0.0	0.0
B /8.5	5.1	0.47	12.77	188	1	44	54	1	22	43.3	-7.4	54	N/A	2,500	50	0.0	0.0
B /8.7	5.1	0.81	10.70	175	1	44	54	1	22	N/A	N/A	52	11	0	0	0.0	0.0
C /4.8	14.6	1.06	28.88	141	1	98	0	1	149	97.6	-14.8	51	9	2,500	50	5.8	0.0
C /4.7	14.6	1.06	28.33	14	1	98	0	1	149	89.7	-15.1	40	9	2,500	50	0.0	0.0
C /4.7	14.6	1.06	28.96	173	1	98	0	1	149	102.4	-14.6	57	9	5,000,000	50	0.0	0.0
C /4.7	14.6	1.06	28.88	872	1	98	0	1	149	100.3	-14.7	55	9	2,500	50	0.0	0.0
C /4.7	14.6	1.06	28.73	14	1	98	0	1	149	94.9	-14.9	47	9	2,500	50	0.0	0.0
C /4.7	14.6	1.06	28.95	169	1	98	0	1	149	N/A	N/A	59	9	0	0	0.0	0.0
C+ /5.7	11.0	1.00	60.86	41	0	99	0	1	16	118.4	-15.9	65	16	2,500	50	5.8	0.0

			99 Pct = Best / 0 Pct = Worst	Overall Investment Rating		PERFORMANCE							Incl. in Returns	

99 Pct = Best / 0 Pct = Worst

Fund Type	Fund Name	Ticker Symbol	Overall Investment Rating	Phone	Perfor-mance Rating/Pts	3 Mo	6 Mo	1Yr / Pct	3Yr / Pct	5Yr / Pct	Dividend Yield	Expense Ratio
GR	American Century Select C	ACSLX	B+	(800) 345-6488	B / 8.1	7.95	9.22	20.88 /57	8.91 /86	10.96 /65	0.00	1.99
GR	American Century Select Inst	TWSIX	A-	(800) 345-6488	A- / 9.0	8.28	9.86	22.35 /64	10.22 /94	12.31 /77	0.53	0.79
GR	American Century Select Inv	TWCIX	A-	(800) 345-6488	B+ / 8.9	8.21	9.74	22.09 /63	9.99 /93	12.07 /75	0.34	0.99
GR	American Century Select R	ASERX	B+	(800) 345-6488	B+ / 8.5	8.10	9.47	21.50 /60	9.45 /90	11.52 /70	0.00	1.49
GI	American Century Select R6	ASDEX	A-	(800) 345-6488	A- / 9.1	8.32	9.94	22.53 /65	10.38 /95	12.35 /78	0.67	0.64
SC	● American Century Sm Cap Val A	ACSCX	B	(800) 345-6488	A+ / 9.7	7.78	16.34	41.50 /98	9.47 /90	13.57 /89	0.36	1.51
SC	● American Century Sm Cap Val C	ASVNX	B	(800) 345-6488	A+ / 9.7	7.66	16.02	40.58 /97	8.65 /84	12.72 /81	0.08	2.26
SC	● American Century Sm Cap Val Inst	ACVIX	B	(800) 345-6488	A+ / 9.8	7.88	16.70	42.18 /98	9.95 /93	14.08 /94	0.73	1.06
SC	● American Century Sm Cap Val Inv	ASVIX	B	(800) 345-6488	A+ / 9.8	7.77	16.46	41.77 /98	9.73 /92	13.85 /92	0.57	1.26
SC	● American Century Sm Cap Val R	ASVRX	B	(800) 345-6488	A+ / 9.8	7.80	16.22	41.23 /98	9.23 /88	13.30 /87	0.27	1.76
SC	● American Century Sm Cap Val R6	ASVDX	B	(800) 345-6488	A+ / 9.8	7.93	16.65	42.39 /98	10.16 /94	--	0.86	0.91
SC	American Century Small Cap Gro A	ANOAX	C-	(800) 345-6488	C+ / 5.9	5.36	9.89	33.49 /92	4.23 /46	10.94 /65	0.00	1.65
SC	American Century Small Cap Gro C	ANOCX	C-	(800) 345-6488	C+ / 6.4	5.07	9.52	32.48 /91	3.44 /36	10.10 /59	0.00	2.40
SC	American Century Small Cap Gro Inst	ANONX	C	(800) 345-6488	B- / 7.0	5.46	10.19	34.12 /93	4.69 /51	11.43 /69	0.00	1.20
SC	American Century Small Cap Gro Inv	ANOIX	C-	(800) 345-6488	C+ / 6.8	5.35	10.00	33.81 /93	4.47 /48	11.19 /67	0.00	1.40
SC	American Century Small Cap Gro R	ANORX	C-	(800) 345-6488	C+ / 6.4	5.23	9.75	33.05 /92	3.96 /42	10.65 /63	0.00	1.90
GR	American Century Small Cap Gro R6	ANODX	C	(800) 345-6488	B- / 7.1	5.51	10.29	34.36 /93	4.85 /52	--	0.00	1.05
SC	American Century Small Company A	ASQAX	C+	(800) 345-6488	C+ / 6.4	5.37	11.74	28.59 /83	5.84 /63	12.17 /76	0.13	1.13
SC	American Century Small Company C	ASQCX	C+	(800) 345-6488	C+ / 6.9	5.20	11.33	27.59 /81	5.04 /55	11.34 /68	0.00	1.88
SC	American Century Small Company	ASCQX	B	(800) 345-6488	B / 7.7	5.51	11.92	29.14 /84	6.29 /67	12.67 /81	0.55	0.68
SC	American Century Small Company	ASQIX	B-	(800) 345-6488	B / 7.6	5.48	11.83	28.92 /84	6.09 /65	12.46 /79	0.36	0.88
SC	American Century Small Company R	ASCRX	B-	(800) 345-6488	B- / 7.2	5.37	11.61	28.32 /82	5.57 /60	11.89 /73	0.00	1.38
AA	American Century Str Alloc:Agg A	ACVAX	D+	(800) 345-6488	C- / 3.7	5.79	5.26	18.15 /44	4.72 /51	7.97 /42	1.01	1.40
AA	American Century Str Alloc:Agg C	ASTAX	C-	(800) 345-6488	C- / 4.2	5.53	4.84	17.18 /39	3.91 /42	7.15 /36	0.35	2.15
AA	American Century Str Alloc:Agg Inst	AAAIX	C	(800) 345-6488	C / 5.2	5.95	5.40	18.46 /45	5.17 /56	8.45 /46	1.52	0.95
AA	American Century Str Alloc:Agg Inv	TWSAX	C	(800) 345-6488	C / 5.1	5.83	5.43	18.43 /45	4.98 /54	8.23 /44	1.32	1.15
AA	American Century Str Alloc:Agg R	AAARX	C-	(800) 345-6488	C / 4.6	5.67	5.13	17.71 /42	4.43 /48	7.69 /40	0.83	1.65
GI	American Century Str Alloc:Agg R6	AAAUX	C	(800) 345-6488	C / 5.4	5.98	5.57	18.85 /46	5.35 /58	--	1.67	0.80
GI	American Century Str Alloc:Con A	ACCAX	C-	(800) 345-6488	D / 1.8	3.41	2.09	10.26 /12	3.35 /35	5.10 /22	0.81	1.25
GI	American Century Str Alloc:Con C	AACCX	C-	(800) 345-6488	D / 2.1	3.42	1.77	9.55 /11	2.58 /28	4.32 /17	0.31	2.00
GI	American Century Str Alloc:Con Inst	ACCIX	C	(800) 345-6488	D+ / 2.9	3.53	2.33	10.95 /14	3.80 /40	5.55 /25	1.30	0.80
GI	American Century Str Alloc:Con Inv	TWSCX	C-	(800) 345-6488	D+ / 2.7	3.66	2.22	10.72 /14	3.60 /38	5.38 /24	1.10	1.00
GI	American Century Str Alloc:Con R	AACRX	C-	(800) 345-6488	D+ / 2.4	3.34	1.96	10.00 /12	3.07 /32	4.82 /20	0.62	1.50
AA	American Century Str Alloc:Con R6	AACDX	C	(800) 345-6488	C- / 3.0	3.58	2.41	10.90 /14	3.95 /42	--	1.44	0.65
AA	American Century Str Alloc:Mod A	ACOAX	D+	(800) 345-6488	D+ / 2.8	4.80	4.04	14.95 /30	4.19 /45	6.80 /33	0.63	1.32
AA	American Century Str Alloc:Mod C	ASTCX	C-	(800) 345-6488	C- / 3.3	4.62	3.68	14.14 /26	3.37 /35	5.98 /28	0.19	2.07
AA	American Century Str Alloc:Mod Inst	ASAMX	C	(800) 345-6488	C- / 4.2	4.92	4.27	15.42 /32	4.64 /50	7.28 /36	1.09	0.87
AA	American Century Str Alloc:Mod Inv	TWSMX	C-	(800) 345-6488	C- / 4.0	4.87	4.01	15.02 /30	4.37 /47	7.03 /35	0.90	1.07
AA	American Century Str Alloc:Mod R	ASMRX	C-	(800) 345-6488	C- / 3.6	4.75	3.92	14.73 /29	3.90 /42	6.50 /31	0.43	1.57
BA	American Century Str Alloc:Mod R6	ASMDX	C	(800) 345-6488	C / 4.3	4.97	4.21	15.61 /32	4.75 /51	--	1.23	0.72
IN	American Century Sustain Eqty A	AFDAX	B-	(800) 345-6488	C+ / 6.7	6.75	8.73	21.20 /58	8.23 /81	11.97 /74	0.83	1.24
IN	American Century Sustain Eqty C	AFDCX	B+	(800) 345-6488	B- / 7.1	6.51	8.28	20.31 /54	7.42 /75	11.12 /67	0.15	1.99
IN	American Century Sustain Eqty Inst	AFEIX	A-	(800) 345-6488	B / 8.0	6.83	8.94	21.72 /61	8.71 /85	12.46 /79	1.32	0.79
IN	American Century Sustain Eqty Inv	AFDIX	A-	(800) 345-6488	B / 7.8	6.77	8.79	21.46 /60	8.51 /83	12.24 /76	1.13	0.99
IN	American Century Sustain Eqty R	AFDRX	B+	(800) 345-6488	B- / 7.5	6.65	8.59	20.87 /57	7.98 /79	11.68 /71	0.64	1.49
GR	American Century Ultra A	TWUAX	B-	(800) 345-6488	B- / 7.1	8.86	8.80	21.95 /62	8.55 /83	12.71 /81	0.03	1.23
GR	American Century Ultra C	TWCCX	B-	(800) 345-6488	B / 7.6	8.64	8.39	21.02 /57	7.74 /77	11.88 /73	0.00	1.98
GR	American Century Ultra Inst	TWUIX	B+	(800) 345-6488	B+ / 8.5	8.95	9.01	22.44 /64	9.03 /87	13.22 /86	0.44	0.78
GR	American Century Ultra Inv	TWCUX	B	(800) 345-6488	B+ / 8.3	8.90	8.93	22.21 /63	8.82 /86	12.99 /84	0.26	0.98
GR	American Century Ultra R	AULRX	B	(800) 345-6488	B / 7.9	8.77	8.65	21.62 /60	8.27 /81	12.43 /78	0.00	1.48
GR	American Century Ultra R6	AULDX	B+	(800) 345-6488	B+ / 8.6	9.00	9.12	22.67 /65	9.19 /88	--	0.57	0.63
UT	American Century Utilities Inv	BULIX	A	(800) 345-6488	B+ / 8.5	7.73	6.27	16.25 /35	11.16 /97	12.11 /75	2.79	0.68

● Denotes fund is closed to new investors
* Denotes fund is included in Section II

www.thestreetratings.com

RISK			NET ASSETS		ASSET				Portfolio Turnover Ratio	BULL / BEAR		FUND MANAGER		MINIMUMS		LOADS	
	3 Year		NAV							Last Bull	Last Bear	Manager	Manager	Initial	Additional	Front	Back
Risk Rating/Pts	Standard Deviation	Beta	As of 2/28/17	Total $(Mil)	Cash %	Stocks %	Bonds %	Other %		Market Return	Market Return	Quality Pct	Tenure (Years)	Purch. $	Purch. $	End Load	End Load
C+ / 5.6	11.0	1.00	55.67	4	0	99	0	1	16	109.7	-16.1	55	16	2,500	50	0.0	0.0
C+ / 5.7	11.0	1.00	62.97	30	0	99	0	1	16	123.8	-15.7	70	16	5,000,000	50	0.0	0.0
C+ / 5.7	11.0	1.00	62.03	2,452	0	99	0	1	16	121.3	-15.8	68	16	2,500	50	0.0	0.0
C+ / 5.7	11.0	1.00	60.62	3	0	99	0	1	16	115.4	-15.9	61	16	2,500	50	0.0	0.0
C+ / 5.7	11.0	1.00	62.93	9	0	99	0	1	16	124.1	-15.8	72	16	0	0	0.0	0.0
C- / 3.5	15.4	0.94	9.25	142	2	96	0	2	95	134.3	-23.6	89	9	2,500	50	5.8	0.0
C- / 3.4	15.3	0.94	8.97	1	2	96	0	2	95	125.0	-23.8	86	9	2,500	50	0.0	0.0
C- / 3.5	15.3	0.93	9.41	476	2	96	0	2	95	140.1	-23.5	91	9	5,000,000	50	0.0	0.0
C- / 3.5	15.4	0.94	9.33	781	2	96	0	2	95	137.5	-23.6	90	9	2,500	50	0.0	0.0
C- / 3.5	15.3	0.94	9.23	3	2	96	0	2	95	131.3	-23.7	88	9	2,500	50	0.0	0.0
C- / 3.5	15.3	0.94	9.41	150	2	96	0	2	95	N/A	N/A	92	9	0	0	0.0	0.0
C- / 3.6	16.9	1.01	14.55	91	3	95	0	2	130	117.5	-28.8	40	11	2,500	50	5.8	0.0
C- / 3.6	16.9	1.01	13.46	10	3	95	0	2	130	109.0	-29.1	30	11	2,500	50	0.0	0.0
C- / 3.7	16.9	1.01	15.25	296	3	95	0	2	130	122.9	-28.7	46	11	5,000,000	50	0.0	2.0
C- / 3.6	17.0	1.01	14.96	153	3	95	0	2	130	120.5	-28.7	43	11	2,500	50	0.0	2.0
C- / 3.6	16.9	1.00	14.29	3	3	95	0	2	130	114.7	-28.9	36	11	2,500	50	0.0	2.0
C- / 3.7	16.9	1.21	15.33	27	3	95	0	2	130	N/A	N/A	4	11	0	0	0.0	2.0
C / 5.4	15.3	0.95	14.56	37	0	99	0	1	93	125.1	-23.2	66	12	2,500	50	5.8	0.0
C / 5.3	15.3	0.95	14.15	2	0	99	0	1	93	116.1	-23.3	56	12	2,500	50	0.0	0.0
C / 5.4	15.3	0.95	14.93	22	0	99	0	1	93	130.5	-22.9	71	12	5,000,000	0	0.0	0.0
C / 5.4	15.3	0.95	14.87	621	0	99	0	1	93	127.8	-23.0	69	12	2,500	50	0.0	0.0
C / 5.4	15.3	0.95	14.32	17	0	99	0	1	93	121.9	-23.1	62	12	2,500	50	0.0	0.0
C+ / 5.6	8.8	1.36	8.08	247	18	64	17	1	82	73.3	-16.0	14	8	2,500	50	5.8	0.0
C+ / 5.6	8.8	1.35	7.91	69	18	64	17	1	82	66.5	-16.3	9	8	2,500	50	0.0	0.0
C / 5.5	8.7	1.35	7.97	122	18	64	17	1	82	77.7	-15.9	18	8	5,000,000	50	0.0	0.0
C / 5.5	8.8	1.35	8.02	448	18	64	17	1	82	75.7	-15.9	16	8	2,500	50	0.0	0.0
C+ / 5.6	8.7	1.34	8.07	25	18	64	17	1	82	70.9	-16.0	13	8	2,500	50	0.0	0.0
C / 5.4	8.8	0.81	7.96	61	18	64	17	1	82	N/A	N/A	34	8	0	0	0.0	0.0
B- / 7.7	5.2	0.47	5.69	137	17	36	45	2	87	41.8	-7.2	56	8	2,500	50	5.8	0.0
B- / 7.6	5.2	0.46	5.62	36	17	36	45	2	87	36.1	-7.3	46	8	2,500	50	0.0	0.0
B- / 7.7	5.2	0.47	5.70	47	17	36	45	2	87	45.1	-6.8	61	8	5,000,000	50	0.0	0.0
B- / 7.7	5.2	0.47	5.70	247	17	36	45	2	87	43.9	-7.1	58	8	2,500	50	0.0	0.0
B- / 7.7	5.2	0.47	5.68	16	17	36	45	2	87	39.9	-7.1	52	8	2,500	50	0.0	0.0
B- / 7.7	5.1	0.80	5.70	50	17	36	45	2	87	N/A	N/A	50	8	0	0	0.0	0.0
C+ / 6.4	7.1	1.11	6.87	454	15	52	31	2	82	59.4	-12.0	24	8	2,500	50	5.8	0.0
C+ / 6.4	7.2	1.11	6.81	106	15	52	31	2	82	53.0	-12.3	17	8	2,500	50	0.0	0.0
C+ / 6.4	7.2	1.12	6.89	194	15	52	31	2	82	63.5	-12.0	28	8	5,000,000	50	0.0	0.0
C+ / 6.4	7.1	1.11	6.88	568	15	52	31	2	82	61.5	-12.1	26	8	2,500	50	0.0	0.0
C+ / 6.4	7.2	1.12	6.84	56	15	52	31	2	82	57.4	-12.3	21	8	2,500	50	0.0	0.0
C+ / 6.4	7.2	1.12	6.88	106	15	52	31	2	82	N/A	N/A	29	8	0	0	0.0	0.0
B- / 7.0	10.4	0.99	23.78	98	0	99	0	1	71	116.8	-16.2	47	9	2,500	50	5.8	0.0
B- / 7.0	10.4	0.99	23.46	20	0	99	0	1	71	108.1	-16.4	36	9	2,500	50	0.0	0.0
B- / 7.0	10.3	0.98	23.86	6	0	99	0	1	71	121.9	-16.0	54	9	5,000,000	50	0.0	0.0
B- / 7.0	10.4	0.99	23.82	91	0	99	0	1	71	119.7	-16.1	51	9	2,500	50	0.0	0.0
B- / 7.0	10.4	0.99	23.69	4	0	99	0	1	71	113.7	-16.3	44	9	2,500	50	0.0	0.0
C / 5.3	11.8	1.06	36.24	62	0	99	0	1	18	123.7	-15.7	41	9	2,500	50	5.8	0.0
C / 5.2	11.8	1.06	31.45	3	0	99	0	1	18	114.7	-15.9	31	9	2,500	50	0.0	0.0
C / 5.4	11.8	1.06	38.86	203	0	99	0	1	18	129.1	-15.5	47	9	5,000,000	50	0.0	0.0
C / 5.4	11.8	1.06	37.69	8,343	0	99	0	1	18	126.7	-15.6	45	9	2,500	50	0.0	0.0
C / 5.3	11.8	1.06	35.48	10	0	99	0	1	18	120.6	-15.7	37	9	2,500	50	0.0	0.0
C / 5.3	11.8	1.06	38.85	111	0	99	0	1	18	N/A	N/A	49	9	0	0	0.0	0.0
C+ / 6.9	11.3	0.69	18.72	585	1	98	0	1	36	87.2	-4.7	82	7	2,500	50	0.0	0.0

Fund Type	Fund Name	Ticker Symbol	Overall Investment Rating	Phone	Performance Rating/Pts	3 Mo	6 Mo	1Yr / Pct	3Yr / Pct	5Yr / Pct	Dividend Yield	Expense Ratio
GI	American Century Value A	TWADX	B+	(800) 345-6488	B+ / 8.4	5.17	10.45	29.20 /85	9.88 /93	13.14 /85	1.17	1.23
GI	American Century Value C	ACLCX	A-	(800) 345-6488	B+ / 8.8	5.02	10.18	28.25 /82	9.03 /87	12.29 /77	0.57	1.98
GI	American Century Value Inst	AVLIX	A	(800) 345-6488	A / 9.5	5.28	10.80	29.85 /86	10.38 /95	13.63 /90	1.63	0.78
GI	American Century Value Inv	TWVLX	A	(800) 345-6488	A / 9.4	5.23	10.71	29.67 /86	10.14 /94	13.40 /88	1.46	0.98
GI	American Century Value R	AVURX	A-	(800) 345-6488	A- / 9.1	5.09	10.30	28.88 /84	9.60 /91	12.86 /82	1.01	1.48
GI	American Century Value R6	AVUDX	A	(800) 345-6488	A / 9.5	5.32	10.89	30.04 /86	10.50 /96	13.70 /91	1.77	0.63
BA	American Century VP Balanced I	AVBIX	C+	(800) 345-6488	C / 4.6	4.83	4.28	14.28 /27	5.51 /60	7.90 /41	1.45	0.91
GI	American Century VP Inc & Growth I	AVGIX	B+	(800) 345-6488	B / 8.1	7.02	8.64	24.76 /72	8.28 /81	12.62 /80	2.10	0.70
GI	American Century VP Inc & Growth II	AVPGX	B+	(800) 345-6488	B / 7.9	6.95	8.50	24.45 /71	8.01 /79	12.34 /77	1.88	0.95
GL	American Century VP Intl I	AVIIX	E+	(800) 345-6488	E / 0.4	5.31	0.73	8.78 / 9	-2.75 / 5	4.48 /18	1.03	1.33
GL	American Century VP Intl II	ANVPX	E+	(800) 345-6488	E / 0.4	5.21	0.62	8.51 / 8	-2.91 / 5	4.33 /17	0.88	1.48
GR	American Century VP Large Co Val I	AVVIX	A+	(800) 345-6488	A- / 9.2	6.95	10.82	28.47 /83	9.40 /90	13.21 /86	1.83	0.91
MC	American Century VP Mid Cap Val I	AVIPX	A+	(800) 345-6488	A+ / 9.8	5.29	11.72	31.37 /89	12.94 /99	15.54 /98	1.44	1.01
MC	American Century VP Mid Cap Val II	AVMTX	A+	(800) 345-6488	A+ / 9.8	5.20	11.63	31.15 /88	12.76 /99	15.36 /97	1.32	1.16
GR	American Century VP Ultra I	AVPUX	B+	(800) 345-6488	B+ / 8.4	8.94	9.01	22.39 /64	8.93 /86	13.03 /84	0.30	1.01
GR	American Century VP Ultra II	AVPSX	B+	(800) 345-6488	B+ / 8.3	8.87	8.95	22.18 /63	8.78 /85	12.86 /82	0.17	1.16
GI	American Century VP Value I	AVPIX	A+	(800) 345-6488	A / 9.5	5.27	10.70	29.85 /86	10.45 /96	13.74 /91	1.53	0.97
GI	American Century VP Value II	AVPVX	A+	(800) 345-6488	A / 9.4	5.22	10.72	29.78 /86	10.28 /95	13.56 /89	1.39	1.12
GI	American Fds Ins S BlCp IncGr 1A		A+	(800) 421-0180	A+ / 9.6	6.42	10.16	26.63 /78	11.34 /97	14.44 /95	1.92	0.66
GI	American Fds Ins S BlCp IncGr 4		A+	(800) 421-0180	A / 9.4	6.27	9.88	26.03 /76	10.79 /97	13.61 /90	1.71	0.91
GR	American Funds AMCAP 529A	CAFAX	C+	(800) 421-0180	C+ / 6.4	6.58	8.17	22.31 /64	7.60 /76	13.24 /86	0.32	0.77
GR	● American Funds AMCAP 529B	CAFBX	C+	(800) 421-0180	C+ / 6.8	6.35	7.75	21.32 /59	6.75 /70	12.35 /78	0.00	1.55
GR	American Funds AMCAP 529C	CAFCX	C+	(800) 421-0180	C+ / 6.8	6.38	7.78	21.39 /59	6.77 /70	12.36 /78	0.00	1.55
GR	American Funds AMCAP 529E	CAFEX	B-	(800) 421-0180	B- / 7.2	6.52	8.06	22.01 /62	7.34 /74	12.97 /83	0.15	1.00
GR	American Funds AMCAP 529F1	CAFFX	B	(800) 421-0180	B- / 7.5	6.60	8.29	22.53 /65	7.82 /78	13.47 /89	0.53	0.56
* GR	American Funds AMCAP A	AMCPX	C+	(800) 421-0180	C+ / 6.5	6.59	8.20	22.38 /64	7.69 /77	13.34 /87	0.38	0.67
GR	● American Funds AMCAP B	AMPBX	C+	(800) 421-0180	C+ / 6.9	6.37	7.80	21.46 /60	6.88 /71	12.47 /79	0.00	1.43
GR	American Funds AMCAP C	AMPCX	C+	(800) 421-0180	C+ / 6.9	6.38	7.78	21.43 /59	6.82 /71	12.43 /78	0.00	1.48
GR	American Funds AMCAP F1	AMPFX	B-	(800) 421-0180	B- / 7.4	6.56	8.18	22.31 /64	7.63 /76	13.29 /87	0.33	0.73
GR	American Funds AMCAP F2	AMCFX	B	(800) 421-0180	B / 7.6	6.67	8.35	22.66 /65	7.92 /78	13.59 /90	0.61	0.47
GR	American Funds AMCAP F3	FMACX	B	(800) 421-0180	B- / 7.5	6.62	8.23	22.43 /64	7.70 /77	13.35 /87	0.40	0.38
GR	American Funds AMCAP R1	RAFAX	C+	(800) 421-0180	C+ / 6.9	6.42	7.83	21.49 /60	6.85 /71	12.48 /79	0.00	1.47
GR	American Funds AMCAP R2	RAFBX	C+	(800) 421-0180	C+ / 6.9	6.42	7.83	21.45 /59	6.87 /71	12.49 /79	0.00	1.48
GR	American Funds AMCAP R2E	RAEBX	B	(800) 421-0180	B- / 7.1	6.46	7.96	21.86 /61	7.30 /74	12.81 /82	0.32	1.19
GR	American Funds AMCAP R3	RAFCX	B-	(800) 421-0180	B- / 7.2	6.49	8.02	21.99 /62	7.34 /74	12.97 /83	0.12	1.02
GR	American Funds AMCAP R4	RAFEX	B-	(800) 421-0180	B- / 7.4	6.58	8.17	22.33 /64	7.66 /76	13.31 /87	0.39	0.71
GR	American Funds AMCAP R5	RAFFX	B	(800) 421-0180	B / 7.7	6.67	8.37	22.74 /66	7.98 /79	13.65 /90	0.64	0.42
GR	American Funds AMCAP R5E	RAEFX	B	(800) 421-0180	B- / 7.5	6.65	8.30	22.54 /65	7.75 /77	13.38 /88	0.50	0.57
GR	American Funds AMCAP R6	RAFGX	B	(800) 421-0180	B / 7.7	6.66	8.37	22.76 /66	8.03 /79	13.71 /91	0.69	0.37
BA	American Funds Amer Balncd Fd	CLBAX	B-	(800) 421-0180	C / 4.9	5.08	5.79	15.70 /33	7.39 /75	10.17 /60	1.50	0.67
BA	● American Funds Amer Balncd Fd	CLBBX	B	(800) 421-0180	C / 5.4	4.88	5.35	14.73 /29	6.53 /69	9.30 /53	0.61	1.46
BA	American Funds Amer Balncd Fd	CLBCX	B-	(800) 421-0180	C / 5.5	4.89	5.39	14.80 /29	6.56 /69	9.32 /53	0.88	1.44
BA	American Funds Amer Balncd Fd	CLBEX	B-	(800) 421-0180	C+ / 5.9	5.03	5.67	15.40 /32	7.12 /73	9.89 /57	1.38	0.91
BA	American Funds Amer Balncd Fd	CLBFX	B-	(800) 421-0180	C+ / 6.3	5.15	5.91	15.93 /34	7.62 /76	10.41 /61	1.81	0.44
* BA	American Funds Amer Balncd Fd A	ABALX	B-	(800) 421-0180	C / 5.0	5.09	5.82	15.77 /33	7.48 /75	10.26 /60	1.57	0.59
BA	● American Funds Amer Balncd Fd B	BALBX	B-	(800) 421-0180	C / 5.5	4.92	5.43	14.89 /29	6.67 /70	9.43 /54	0.75	1.35
BA	American Funds Amer Balncd Fd C	BALCX	B-	(800) 421-0180	C / 5.5	4.92	5.44	14.85 /29	6.64 /69	9.39 /54	0.96	1.38
BA	American Funds Amer Balncd Fd F1	BALFX	B-	(800) 421-0180	C+ / 6.2	5.08	5.75	15.66 /33	7.41 /75	10.20 /60	1.61	0.66
BA	American Funds Amer Balncd Fd F2	AMBFX	B-	(800) 421-0180	C+ / 6.4	5.15	5.93	15.97 /34	7.68 /77	10.48 /62	1.86	0.39
BA	American Funds Amer Balncd Fd F3	AFMBX	B-	(800) 421-0180	C+ / 6.2	5.09	5.82	15.77 /33	7.48 /75	10.26 /60	1.67	0.29
BA	American Funds Amer Balncd Fd R1	RLBAX	B-	(800) 421-0180	C / 5.5	4.89	5.40	14.81 /29	6.63 /69	9.40 /54	0.95	1.38
BA	American Funds Amer Balncd Fd R2	RLBBX	B-	(800) 421-0180	C / 5.5	4.88	5.40	14.85 /29	6.67 /70	9.44 /54	0.96	1.37

● Denotes fund is closed to new investors
* Denotes fund is included in Section II

www.thestreetratings.com

RISK Risk Rating/Pts	3 Year Standard Deviation	Beta	NAV As of 2/28/17	Total $(Mil)	Cash %	Stocks %	Bonds %	Other %	Portfolio Turnover Ratio	Last Bull Market Return	Last Bear Market Return	Manager Quality Pct	Manager Tenure (Years)	Initial Purch. $	Additional Purch. $	Front End Load	Back End Load
C+ / 5.8	10.4	0.94	9.10	159	1	96	1	2	48	123.4	-16.9	73	24	2,500	50	5.8	0.0
C+ / 5.8	10.3	0.94	8.96	35	1	96	1	2	48	114.3	-17.0	64	24	2,500	50	0.0	0.0
C+ / 5.8	10.4	0.95	9.13	526	1	96	1	2	48	128.9	-16.6	76	24	5,000,000	50	0.0	0.0
C+ / 5.8	10.3	0.93	9.11	2,441	1	96	1	2	48	126.1	-16.6	75	24	2,500	50	0.0	0.0
C+ / 5.8	10.3	0.94	9.10	115	1	96	1	2	48	120.1	-16.8	70	24	2,500	50	0.0	0.0
C+ / 5.8	10.3	0.94	9.13	167	1	96	1	2	48	129.0	-16.6	77	24	0	0	0.0	0.0
C+ / 6.9	6.5	1.03	7.23	124	0	58	41	1	95	68.0	-8.1	47	26	0	0	0.0	0.0
C+ / 6.0	10.6	1.00	9.84	369	0	99	0	1	88	122.2	-16.1	46	7	0	0	0.0	0.0
C+ / 6.0	10.6	1.00	9.84	25	0	99	0	1	88	118.9	-16.1	42	7	0	0	0.0	0.0
C+ / 5.7	11.4	1.58	9.72	161	0	99	0	1	59	45.7	-24.7	2	20	0	0	0.0	0.0
C+ / 5.7	11.4	1.58	9.70	40	0	99	0	1	59	44.5	-24.7	2	20	0	0	0.0	0.0
C+ / 6.6	11.5	1.06	15.96	11	0	99	0	1	63	126.1	-17.2	52	13	0	0	0.0	0.0
C+ / 6.7	10.1	0.81	21.91	406	2	97	0	1	65	147.7	-17.1	95	13	0	0	0.0	0.0
C+ / 6.7	10.1	0.81	21.92	872	2	97	0	1	65	145.6	-17.1	95	13	0	0	0.0	0.0
C / 5.4	11.8	1.06	16.70	42	0	99	0	1	35	127.2	-15.6	46	9	0	0	0.0	0.0
C / 5.4	11.8	1.06	16.44	148	0	99	0	1	35	125.4	-15.7	44	9	0	0	0.0	0.0
B- / 7.1	10.3	0.94	10.81	484	2	97	0	1	47	129.9	-16.6	77	21	0	0	0.0	0.0
B- / 7.1	10.3	0.94	10.82	505	2	97	0	1	47	127.9	-16.7	76	21	0	0	0.0	0.0
B / 8.4	10.4	0.95	14.14	N/A	0	0	0	100	26	136.0	-16.0	82	10	0	0	0.0	0.0
B / 8.0	10.4	0.95	13.98	145	0	0	0	100	26	127.4	-16.1	79	10	0	0	0.0	0.0
C / 5.5	10.3	0.96	28.54	1,528	0	83	16	1	31	126.0	-15.8	44	21	250	50	5.8	0.0
C / 5.3	10.3	0.96	25.85	1	0	83	16	1	31	116.5	-16.1	33	21	250	50	0.0	0.0
C / 5.3	10.3	0.96	25.89	345	0	83	16	1	31	116.6	-16.1	33	21	250	50	0.0	0.0
C / 5.4	10.3	0.96	27.87	73	0	83	16	1	31	123.2	-15.9	40	21	250	50	0.0	0.0
C / 5.5	10.3	0.96	28.73	95	0	83	16	1	31	128.6	-15.7	47	21	250	50	0.0	0.0
C / 5.5	10.4	0.96	28.82	27,276	0	83	16	1	31	127.2	-15.8	45	21	250	50	5.8	0.0
C / 5.3	10.3	0.96	26.10	9	0	83	16	1	31	117.9	-16.0	34	21	250	50	0.0	0.0
C / 5.3	10.3	0.96	25.74	1,503	0	83	16	1	31	117.4	-16.0	34	21	250	50	0.0	0.0
C / 5.5	10.4	0.96	28.58	2,303	0	83	16	1	31	126.6	-15.8	44	21	250	50	0.0	0.0
C / 5.5	10.3	0.96	28.98	6,243	0	83	16	1	31	129.8	-15.7	48	21	250	50	0.0	0.0
C+ / 5.6	10.4	0.96	28.83	3	0	83	16	1	31	127.2	-15.8	45	21	250	50	0.0	0.0
C / 5.3	10.3	0.96	26.41	103	0	83	16	1	31	117.8	-16.1	34	21	250	50	0.0	0.0
C / 5.3	10.4	0.96	26.40	590	0	83	16	1	31	118.0	-16.0	34	21	250	50	0.0	0.0
C+ / 6.5	10.4	0.96	28.61	22	0	83	16	1	31	121.3	-16.0	39	21	250	50	0.0	0.0
C / 5.4	10.4	0.96	28.01	1,233	0	83	16	1	31	123.1	-15.9	40	21	250	50	0.0	0.0
C / 5.5	10.3	0.96	28.58	1,243	0	83	16	1	31	126.8	-15.8	44	21	250	50	0.0	0.0
C / 5.5	10.3	0.96	29.16	1,339	0	83	16	1	31	130.6	-15.7	49	21	250	50	0.0	0.0
C+ / 5.6	10.3	0.96	28.84	N/A	0	83	16	1	31	127.5	-15.8	45	21	250	50	0.0	0.0
C / 5.5	10.4	0.96	29.09	9,613	0	83	16	1	31	131.1	-15.6	49	21	250	50	0.0	0.0
B- / 7.6	6.8	1.06	25.75	3,248	0	55	44	1	82	86.6	-10.0	68	18	250	50	5.8	0.0
B- / 7.7	6.7	1.06	25.85	4	0	55	44	1	82	78.8	-10.3	57	18	250	50	0.0	0.0
B- / 7.7	6.8	1.06	25.70	1,012	0	55	44	1	82	78.9	-10.3	58	18	250	50	0.0	0.0
B- / 7.6	6.7	1.06	25.72	158	0	55	44	1	82	84.2	-10.1	65	18	250	50	0.0	0.0
B- / 7.6	6.7	1.06	25.74	146	0	55	44	1	82	88.9	-9.9	70	18	250	50	0.0	0.0
B- / 7.6	6.7	1.06	25.79	57,703	0	55	44	1	82	87.5	-10.0	69	18	250	50	5.8	0.0
B- / 7.7	6.7	1.06	25.79	35	0	55	44	1	82	80.0	-10.3	60	18	250	50	0.0	0.0
B- / 7.7	6.7	1.06	25.61	8,096	0	55	44	1	82	79.6	-10.2	59	18	250	50	0.0	0.0
B- / 7.6	6.7	1.06	25.76	4,358	0	55	44	1	82	86.9	-10.0	68	18	250	50	0.0	0.0
B- / 7.6	6.8	1.06	25.78	6,573	0	55	44	1	82	89.6	-9.9	71	18	250	50	0.0	0.0
B- / 7.5	6.7	1.06	25.79	23	0	55	44	1	82	87.5	-10.0	69	18	250	50	0.0	0.0
B- / 7.6	6.7	1.06	25.58	148	0	55	44	1	82	79.7	-10.3	59	18	250	50	0.0	0.0
B- / 7.6	6.7	1.06	25.60	1,261	0	55	44	1	82	80.0	-10.3	59	18	250	50	0.0	0.0

Fund Type	Fund Name	Ticker Symbol	Overall Investment Rating	Phone	Performance Rating/Pts	3 Mo	6 Mo	1Yr / Pct	3Yr / Pct	5Yr / Pct	Dividend Yield	Expense Ratio
	99 Pct = Best				PERFORMANCE			Total Return % through 2/28/17	Annualized		Incl. in Returns	
BA	American Funds Amer Balncd Fd R3	RLBCX	B-	(800) 421-0180	C+ / 5.9	5.04	5.67	15.37 /31	7.11 /73	9.89 /57	1.36	0.93
BA	American Funds Amer Balncd Fd R4	RLBEX	B-	(800) 421-0180	C+ / 6.2	5.10	5.81	15.71 /33	7.43 /75	10.22 /60	1.63	0.64
BA	American Funds Amer Balncd Fd R5	RLBFX	B-	(800) 421-0180	C+ / 6.4	5.15	5.94	16.04 /34	7.75 /77	10.54 /62	1.90	0.34
BA	American Funds Amer Balncd Fd	RLEFX	B-	(800) 421-0180	C+ / 6.3	5.16	5.90	15.86 /34	7.51 /75	10.28 /60	1.77	0.42
BA	American Funds Amer Balncd Fd R6	RLBGX	B-	(800) 421-0180	C+ / 6.5	5.21	6.02	16.11 /35	7.81 /78	10.60 /63	1.95	0.29
BA	American Funds Amer Balncd R2E	RAMHX	B	(800) 421-0180	C+ / 5.9	4.95	5.54	15.16 /31	7.15 /73	9.79 /57	1.25	1.08
GI	American Funds Amer Mutual Fd	CMLAX	B+	(800) 421-0180	B- / 7.2	6.79	7.86	22.76 /66	9.16 /88	12.19 /76	1.76	0.69
GI	● American Funds Amer Mutual Fd	CMLBX	B+	(800) 421-0180	B / 7.6	6.60	7.48	21.84 /61	8.31 /81	11.32 /68	0.91	1.48
GI	American Funds Amer Mutual Fd	CMLCX	B+	(800) 421-0180	B / 7.6	6.60	7.47	21.85 /61	8.32 /81	11.33 /68	1.19	1.46
GI	American Funds Amer Mutual Fd	CMLEX	B+	(800) 421-0180	B / 8.0	6.76	7.77	22.50 /64	8.90 /86	11.92 /74	1.66	0.93
GI	American Funds Amer Mutual Fd	CMLFX	A-	(800) 421-0180	B+ / 8.4	6.87	8.00	23.06 /67	9.41 /90	12.45 /79	2.07	0.46
* GI	American Funds Amer Mutual Fd A	AMRMX	B+	(800) 421-0180	B- / 7.3	6.82	7.92	22.88 /66	9.26 /89	12.31 /77	1.84	0.59
GI	● American Funds Amer Mutual Fd B	AMFBX	B+	(800) 421-0180	B / 7.7	6.62	7.52	21.94 /62	8.43 /82	11.45 /69	1.07	1.36
GI	American Funds Amer Mutual Fd C	AMFCX	B+	(800) 421-0180	B / 7.7	6.63	7.52	21.93 /62	8.41 /82	11.41 /69	1.26	1.39
GI	American Funds Amer Mutual Fd F1	AMFFX	A-	(800) 421-0180	B / 8.2	6.81	7.88	22.79 /66	9.18 /88	12.22 /76	1.88	0.67
GI	American Funds Amer Mutual Fd F2	AMRFX	A-	(800) 421-0180	B+ / 8.4	6.87	8.02	23.11 /67	9.46 /90	12.50 /79	2.11	0.42
GI	American Funds Amer Mutual Fd F3	AFMFX	B+	(800) 421-0180	B+ / 8.3	6.85	7.94	22.91 /66	9.27 /89	12.31 /77	1.94	0.30
GI	American Funds Amer Mutual Fd R1	RMFAX	B+	(800) 421-0180	B / 7.7	6.62	7.49	21.87 /61	8.37 /82	11.38 /69	1.22	1.43
GI	American Funds Amer Mutual Fd R2	RMFBX	B+	(800) 421-0180	B / 7.7	6.61	7.49	21.89 /62	8.39 /82	11.41 /69	1.24	1.41
GI	American Funds Amer Mutual Fd	RMEBX	A	(800) 421-0180	B / 8.0	6.69	7.66	22.29 /64	8.82 /86	11.76 /72	1.55	1.09
GI	American Funds Amer Mutual Fd R3	RMFCX	B+	(800) 421-0180	B / 8.0	6.73	7.73	22.43 /64	8.87 /86	11.90 /73	1.63	0.97
GI	American Funds Amer Mutual Fd R4	RMFEX	A-	(800) 421-0180	B / 8.2	6.84	7.92	22.82 /66	9.20 /88	12.24 /76	1.90	0.67
GI	American Funds Amer Mutual Fd R5	RMFFX	A-	(800) 421-0180	B+ / 8.5	6.89	8.05	23.18 /67	9.52 /90	12.58 /80	2.17	0.36
GI	American Funds Amer Mutual Fd	RMFHX	B+	(800) 421-0180	B+ / 8.3	6.86	7.98	23.00 /67	9.31 /89	12.34 /77	2.03	0.52
GI	American Funds Amer Mutual Fd R6	RMFGX	A	(800) 421-0180	B+ / 8.5	6.93	8.10	23.26 /67	9.58 /91	12.64 /80	2.21	0.30
BA	American Funds Balanced 529A	CBAAX	C	(800) 421-0180	C- / 3.2	5.15	3.84	14.03 /25	5.15 /56	---	1.41	0.80
BA	American Funds Balanced 529B	CBBBX	C+	(800) 421-0180	C- / 3.7	4.93	3.48	13.09 /22	4.32 /47	---	0.42	1.61
BA	American Funds Balanced 529C	CBPCX	C+	(800) 421-0180	C- / 3.7	4.87	3.43	13.15 /22	4.33 /47	---	0.77	1.59
BA	American Funds Balanced 529E	CBAEX	C+	(800) 421-0180	C- / 4.1	5.10	3.80	13.80 /25	4.90 /53	---	1.28	1.04
BA	American Funds Balanced 529F1	CBAFX	B-	(800) 421-0180	C / 4.5	5.14	3.96	14.26 /27	5.37 /58	---	1.70	0.58
BA	American Funds Balanced A	BLPAX	C+	(800) 421-0180	C- / 3.3	5.10	3.89	14.11 /26	5.22 /57	---	1.47	0.73
BA	American Funds Balanced B	BLPBX	C+	(800) 421-0180	C- / 3.7	4.94	3.45	13.17 /22	4.38 /47	---	0.54	1.52
BA	American Funds Balanced C	BLPCX	C+	(800) 421-0180	C- / 3.7	4.97	3.56	13.27 /23	4.42 /48	---	0.86	1.50
BA	American Funds Balanced F1	BLPFX	B-	(800) 421-0180	C / 4.3	5.15	3.84	14.06 /26	5.19 /56	---	1.52	0.77
BA	American Funds Balanced F2	BLPEX	B-	(800) 421-0180	C / 4.6	5.16	4.00	14.34 /27	5.45 /59	---	1.77	0.51
BA	American Funds Balanced F3	BLPDX	C	(800) 421-0180	C / 4.4	5.18	3.97	14.19 /26	5.24 /57	---	1.56	0.40
BA	American Funds Balanced R1	RBAAX	C+	(800) 421-0180	C- / 3.7	4.90	3.47	13.22 /22	4.41 /47	---	0.84	1.51
BA	American Funds Balanced R2	RBABX	C+	(800) 421-0180	C- / 3.7	4.97	3.57	13.26 /23	4.41 /47	---	0.87	1.52
BA	American Funds Balanced R2E	RBBEX	C+	(800) 421-0180	C- / 4.1	5.01	3.67	13.50 /23	4.94 /53	---	1.18	1.20
BA	American Funds Balanced R3	RBACX	C+	(800) 421-0180	C- / 4.1	5.09	3.72	13.69 /24	4.86 /53	---	1.27	1.07
BA	American Funds Balanced R4	RBAEX	B-	(800) 421-0180	C / 4.4	5.11	3.88	14.09 /26	5.21 /56	---	1.55	0.76
BA	American Funds Balanced R5	RBAFX	B-	(800) 421-0180	C / 4.6	5.25	4.02	14.38 /27	5.52 /60	---	1.81	0.46
BA	American Funds Balanced R5E	RGPFX	C	(800) 421-0180	C / 4.5	5.15	3.96	14.23 /27	5.28 /57	---	1.59	0.63
BA	American Funds Balanced R6	RBAGX	B-	(800) 421-0180	C / 4.7	5.26	4.05	14.43 /27	5.57 /60	---	1.86	0.40
* IN	American Funds Cap Inc Builder A	CAIBX	C-	(800) 421-0180	D+ / 2.6	5.87	2.58	12.50 /20	4.26 /46	7.12 /35	3.21	0.60
IN	● American Funds Cap Inc Builder B	CIBBX	C-	(800) 421-0180	C- / 3.0	5.66	2.18	11.64 /17	3.47 /37	6.31 /30	2.38	1.36
IN	American Funds Cap Inc Builder C	CIBCX	C-	(800) 421-0180	C- / 3.0	5.68	2.20	11.62 /16	3.43 /36	6.26 /30	2.62	1.40
IN	American Funds Cap Inc Builder F1	CIBFX	C	(800) 421-0180	C- / 3.5	5.86	2.55	12.41 /19	4.19 /45	7.05 /35	3.34	0.67
IN	American Funds Cap Inc Builder F2	CAIFX	C	(800) 421-0180	C- / 3.7	5.93	2.69	12.72 /21	4.46 /48	7.33 /37	3.60	0.40
GR	American Funds Cap Inc Builder F3	CFIHX	C-	(800) 421-0180	C- / 3.6	5.91	2.61	12.54 /20	4.27 /46	7.12 /35	3.40	0.30
IN	American Funds Cap Inc Builder R1	RIRAX	C-	(800) 421-0180	C- / 3.0	5.68	2.18	11.61 /16	3.43 /36	6.27 /30	2.63	1.40
IN	American Funds Cap Inc Builder R2	RIRBX	C-	(800) 421-0180	C- / 3.0	5.66	2.17	11.60 /16	3.44 /36	6.28 /30	2.64	1.40

● Denotes fund is closed to new investors
* Denotes fund is included in Section II

RISK			NET ASSETS		ASSET					BULL / BEAR		FUND MANAGER		MINIMUMS		LOADS	
	3 Year		NAV						Portfolio	Last Bull	Last Bear	Manager	Manager	Initial	Additional	Front	Back
Risk	Standard		As of	Total	Cash	Stocks	Bonds	Other	Turnover	Market	Market	Quality	Tenure	Purch.	Purch.	End	End
Rating/Pts	Deviation	Beta	2/28/17	$(Mil)	%	%	%	%	Ratio	Return	Return	Pct	(Years)	$	$	Load	Load
B- /7.6	6.8	1.06	25.65	3,457	0	55	44	1	82	84.1	-10.1	64	18	250	50	0.0	0.0
B- /7.6	6.7	1.06	25.74	6,209	0	55	44	1	82	87.1	-10.0	68	18	250	50	0.0	0.0
B- /7.6	6.7	1.06	25.82	2,057	0	55	44	1	82	90.2	-9.9	72	18	250	50	0.0	0.0
B- /7.5	6.7	1.06	25.77	3	0	55	44	1	82	87.7	-10.0	69	18	250	50	0.0	0.0
B- /7.6	6.7	1.05	25.81	12,220	0	55	44	1	82	90.7	-9.9	73	18	250	50	0.0	0.0
B /8.2	6.7	1.05	25.69	22	0	55	44	1	82	83.1	-10.2	65	18	250	50	0.0	0.0
C+ /6.5	9.2	0.87	38.51	836	0	88	10	2	18	107.8	-12.7	74	11	250	50	5.8	0.0
C+ /6.5	9.2	0.87	38.54	1	0	88	10	2	18	99.2	-13.0	64	11	250	50	0.0	0.0
C+ /6.5	9.2	0.87	38.27	195	0	88	10	2	18	99.2	-13.0	65	11	250	50	0.0	0.0
C+ /6.5	9.2	0.87	38.36	40	0	88	10	2	18	105.0	-12.8	71	11	250	50	0.0	0.0
C+ /6.5	9.2	0.87	38.58	67	0	88	10	2	18	110.3	-12.7	75	11	250	50	0.0	0.0
C+ /6.5	9.2	0.87	38.60	25,000	0	88	10	2	18	108.9	-12.7	74	11	250	50	5.8	0.0
C+ /6.5	9.2	0.87	38.37	6	0	88	10	2	18	100.4	-13.0	66	11	250	50	0.0	0.0
C+ /6.5	9.2	0.87	38.05	1,247	0	88	10	2	18	100.1	-13.0	65	11	250	50	0.0	0.0
C+ /6.5	9.2	0.87	38.44	1,481	0	88	10	2	18	108.2	-12.7	74	11	250	50	0.0	0.0
C+ /6.5	9.2	0.87	38.60	3,947	0	88	10	2	18	111.0	-12.6	75	11	250	50	0.0	0.0
C+ /5.9	9.2	0.87	38.61	10	0	88	10	2	18	108.9	-12.7	74	11	250	50	0.0	0.0
C+ /6.5	9.3	0.87	38.18	71	0	88	10	2	18	99.8	-13.0	65	11	250	50	0.0	0.0
C+ /6.5	9.2	0.87	38.14	265	0	88	10	2	18	100.0	-13.0	65	11	250	50	0.0	0.0
B- /7.3	9.3	0.87	38.47	9	0	88	10	2	18	103.3	-12.9	70	11	250	50	0.0	0.0
C+ /6.5	9.2	0.87	38.30	657	0	88	10	2	18	104.9	-12.8	71	11	250	50	0.0	0.0
C+ /6.5	9.3	0.87	38.48	694	0	88	10	2	18	108.3	-12.7	74	11	250	50	0.0	0.0
C+ /6.5	9.2	0.87	38.61	322	0	88	10	2	18	111.7	-12.6	76	11	250	50	0.0	0.0
C+ /5.9	9.2	0.87	38.59	N/A	0	88	10	2	18	109.1	-12.7	75	11	250	50	0.0	0.0
C+ /6.5	9.3	0.87	38.63	8,488	0	88	10	2	18	112.3	-12.6	76	11	250	50	0.0	0.0
B /8.2	6.7	1.04	13.67	232	0	59	40	1	13	N/A	N/A	41	5	250	50	5.8	0.0
B /8.2	6.7	1.04	13.70	N/A	0	59	40	1	13	N/A	N/A	31	5	250	50	0.0	0.0
B /8.2	6.7	1.04	13.60	109	0	59	40	1	13	N/A	N/A	31	5	250	50	0.0	0.0
B /8.2	6.7	1.04	13.65	10	0	59	40	1	13	N/A	N/A	37	5	250	50	0.0	0.0
B /8.2	6.7	1.04	13.68	26	0	59	40	1	13	N/A	N/A	44	5	250	50	0.0	0.0
B /8.2	6.7	1.04	13.67	3,416	0	59	40	1	13	N/A	N/A	42	5	250	50	5.8	0.0
B /8.2	6.7	1.04	13.68	1	0	59	40	1	13	N/A	N/A	31	5	250	50	0.0	0.0
B /8.2	6.7	1.04	13.59	914	0	59	40	1	13	N/A	N/A	32	5	250	50	0.0	0.0
B /8.2	6.7	1.04	13.67	132	0	59	40	1	13	N/A	N/A	41	5	250	50	0.0	0.0
B /8.2	6.7	1.04	13.69	267	0	59	40	1	13	N/A	N/A	45	5	250	50	0.0	0.0
C+ /6.7	6.7	1.04	13.68	N/A	0	59	40	1	0	N/A	N/A	42	5	250	50	0.0	0.0
B /8.2	6.7	1.05	13.61	11	0	59	40	1	13	N/A	N/A	31	5	250	50	0.0	0.0
B /8.2	6.7	1.04	13.60	81	0	59	40	1	13	N/A	N/A	32	5	250	50	0.0	0.0
/7.6	6.7	1.04	13.64	6	0	59	40	1	13	N/A	N/A	38	5	250	50	0.0	0.0
B /8.2	6.6	1.03	13.64	86	0	59	40	1	13	N/A	N/A	38	5	250	50	0.0	0.0
B /8.2	6.7	1.04	13.67	68	0	59	40	1	13	N/A	N/A	42	5	250	50	0.0	0.0
B /8.2	6.7	1.04	13.70	13	0	59	40	1	13	N/A	N/A	46	5	250	50	0.0	0.0
C+ /6.8	6.7	1.04	13.68	2	0	59	40	1	13	N/A	N/A	43	5	250	50	0.0	0.0
B /8.2	6.7	1.04	13.70	172	0	59	40	1	13	N/A	N/A	47	5	250	50	0.0	0.0
/7.0	7.8	0.64	59.66	69,953	1	78	19	2	47	56.6	-10.0	44	17	250	50	5.8	0.0
/7.0	7.8	0.64	59.98	28	1	78	19	2	47	50.3	-10.3	34	17	250	50	0.0	0.0
/7.0	7.8	0.64	59.66	5,574	1	78	19	2	47	50.0	-10.3	33	17	250	50	0.0	0.0
/7.0	7.8	0.64	59.65	4,528	1	78	19	2	47	56.1	-10.0	43	17	250	50	0.0	0.0
/7.0	7.8	0.64	59.64	8,887	1	78	19	2	47	58.3	-9.9	47	17	250	50	0.0	0.0
C+ /6.1	7.8	0.64	59.68	6	1	78	19	2	47	56.7	-10.0	44	17	250	50	0.0	0.0
/7.0	7.8	0.64	59.61	130	1	78	19	2	47	50.0	-10.3	33	17	250	50	0.0	0.0
/7.0	7.8	0.64	59.60	623	1	78	19	2	47	50.2	-10.3	33	17	250	50	0.0	0.0

Fund Type	Fund Name	Ticker Symbol	Overall Investment Rating	Phone	Performance Rating/Pts	3 Mo	6 Mo	1Yr / Pct	3Yr / Pct	5Yr / Pct	Dividend Yield	Expense Ratio
AA	American Funds Cap Inc Builder R2E	RCEEX	C-	(800) 421-0180	C- / 3.2	5.74	2.34	11.95 /18	3.79 /40	6.57 /32	3.00	1.11
IN	American Funds Cap Inc Builder R3	RIRCX	C-	(800) 421-0180	C- / 3.3	5.79	2.41	12.11 /18	3.89 /42	6.73 /33	3.07	0.96
IN	American Funds Cap Inc Builder R4	RIREX	C	(800) 421-0180	C- / 3.5	5.87	2.56	12.45 /20	4.21 /45	7.07 /35	3.37	0.65
IN	American Funds Cap Inc Builder R5	RIRFX	C	(800) 421-0180	C- / 3.8	5.94	2.73	12.79 /21	4.51 /49	7.39 /37	3.64	0.37
AA	American Funds Cap Inc Builder R5E	RIRHX	C-	(800) 421-0180	C- / 3.6	5.89	2.64	12.59 /20	4.30 /46	7.14 /35	3.54	0.53
IN	American Funds Cap Inc Builder R6	RIRGX	C	(800) 421-0180	C- / 3.8	5.95	2.74	12.84 /21	4.57 /49	7.44 /38	3.70	0.30
IN	American Funds Cap Inc Buildr 529A	CIRAX	C-	(800) 421-0180	D+ / 2.5	5.86	2.56	12.42 /19	4.17 /45	7.02 /35	3.14	0.69
IN	● American Funds Cap Inc Buildr 529B	CIRBX	C-	(800) 421-0180	D+ / 2.9	5.64	2.14	11.51 /16	3.34 /35	6.17 /30	2.28	1.49
IN	American Funds Cap Inc Buildr 529C	CIRCX	C-	(800) 421-0180	D+ / 2.9	5.66	2.16	11.56 /16	3.36 /35	6.19 /30	2.58	1.46
IN	American Funds Cap Inc Buildr 529E	CIREX	C-	(800) 421-0180	C- / 3.3	5.80	2.44	12.16 /18	3.92 /42	6.77 /33	3.11	0.92
IN	American Funds Cap Inc Buildr	CIRFX	C	(800) 421-0180	C- / 3.7	5.90	2.67	12.67 /20	4.40 /47	7.25 /36	3.55	0.46
GL	American Funds Cap Wld Gr&Inc	CWIAX	C-	(800) 421-0180	C- / 3.7	7.29	5.80	19.91 /51	3.82 /41	8.97 /50	2.07	0.86
GL	● American Funds Cap Wld Gr&Inc	CWIBX	C-	(800) 421-0180	C- / 4.1	7.08	5.39	18.95 /47	3.00 /32	8.10 /43	1.25	1.65
GL	American Funds Cap Wld Gr&Inc	CWICX	C-	(800) 421-0180	C- / 4.1	7.11	5.43	19.00 /47	3.02 /32	8.12 /43	1.48	1.64
GL	American Funds Cap Wld Gr&Inc	CWIEX	C	(800) 421-0180	C / 4.6	7.24	5.71	19.64 /50	3.58 /38	8.72 /48	1.99	1.09
GL	American Funds Cap Wld Gr&Inc	CWIFX	C	(800) 421-0180	C / 5.0	7.37	5.94	20.18 /53	4.05 /43	9.21 /52	2.40	0.64
* GL	American Funds Cap Wld Gr&Inc A	CWGIX	C-	(800) 421-0180	C- / 3.7	7.33	5.86	19.98 /52	3.91 /42	9.05 /51	2.13	0.77
GL	● American Funds Cap Wld Gr&Inc B	CWGBX	C-	(800) 421-0180	C- / 4.2	7.10	5.45	19.05 /47	3.12 /33	8.23 /44	1.29	1.52
GL	American Funds Cap Wld Gr&Inc C	CWGCX	C-	(800) 421-0180	C- / 4.2	7.12	5.44	19.05 /47	3.09 /33	8.19 /44	1.52	1.57
GL	American Funds Cap Wld Gr&Inc F1	CWGFX	C	(800) 421-0180	C / 4.9	7.31	5.83	19.97 /52	3.87 /41	9.03 /51	2.21	0.81
GL	American Funds Cap Wld Gr&Inc F2	WGIFX	C	(800) 421-0180	C / 5.1	7.40	6.00	20.29 /54	4.15 /45	9.33 /53	2.48	0.54
GL	American Funds Cap Wld Gr&Inc F3	FWGIX	C	(800) 421-0180	C / 4.9	7.37	5.91	20.04 /52	3.92 /42	9.06 /51	2.25	0.45
GL	American Funds Cap Wld Gr&Inc R1	RWIAX	C-	(800) 421-0180	C- / 4.2	7.11	5.44	19.08 /48	3.11 /33	8.23 /44	1.57	1.54
GL	American Funds Cap Wld Gr&Inc R2	RWIBX	C-	(800) 421-0180	C- / 4.2	7.11	5.45	19.09 /48	3.13 /33	8.25 /44	1.58	1.54
GL	American Funds Cap Wld Gr&Inc	RWBEX	C+	(800) 421-0180	C / 4.5	7.19	5.61	19.46 /49	3.47 /37	8.51 /46	1.92	1.21
GL	American Funds Cap Wld Gr&Inc R3	RWICX	C	(800) 421-0180	C / 4.6	7.25	5.69	19.61 /50	3.58 /38	8.73 /48	1.98	1.09
GL	American Funds Cap Wld Gr&Inc R4	RWIEX	C	(800) 421-0180	C / 4.9	7.32	5.85	19.96 /52	3.89 /42	9.05 /51	2.25	0.79
GL	American Funds Cap Wld Gr&Inc R5	RWIFX	C	(800) 421-0180	C / 5.2	7.41	6.02	20.35 /54	4.21 /45	9.38 /54	2.52	0.49
GL	American Funds Cap Wld Gr&Inc	RWIHX	C	(800) 421-0180	C / 5.0	7.34	5.91	20.12 /53	3.96 /42	9.09 /51	2.41	0.64
GL	American Funds Cap Wld Gr&Inc R6	RWIGX	C	(800) 421-0180	C / 5.2	7.39	6.02	20.39 /54	4.25 /46	9.43 /54	2.57	0.45
AA	American Funds College 2018 529A	CNEAX	C	(800) 421-0180	D- / 1.0	0.75	0.01	1.88 / 2	2.63 /28	--	1.43	0.75
AA	American Funds College 2018 529B	CNEBX	C	(800) 421-0180	D- / 1.1	0.54	-0.38	1.10 / 2	1.88 /23	--	0.00	1.52
AA	American Funds College 2018 529C	CNECX	C	(800) 421-0180	D- / 1.1	0.52	-0.41	1.09 / 2	1.87 /23	--	0.81	1.51
AA	American Funds College 2018 529E	CNEEX	C	(800) 421-0180	D- / 1.3	0.64	-0.19	1.58 / 2	2.38 /27	--	1.30	0.98
AA	American Funds College 2018 529F1	CNEFX	C	(800) 421-0180	D- / 1.4	0.80	0.15	2.11 / 2	2.88 /31	--	1.72	0.51
AA	American Funds College 2021 529A	CTOAX	C	(800) 421-0180	D- / 1.4	1.79	0.81	5.43 / 4	3.17 /33	--	1.64	0.72
AA	American Funds College 2021 529B	CTOBX	C	(800) 421-0180	D- / 1.5	1.66	0.49	4.64 / 4	2.39 /27	--	0.00	1.50
AA	American Funds College 2021 529C	CTOCX	C	(800) 421-0180	D- / 1.5	1.59	0.42	4.69 / 4	2.36 /26	--	1.07	1.49
AA	American Funds College 2021 529E	CTOEX	C	(800) 421-0180	D / 1.7	1.77	0.70	5.24 / 4	2.90 /31	--	1.52	0.96
AA	American Funds College 2021 529F1	CTOFX	C+	(800) 421-0180	D / 1.9	1.82	0.93	5.64 / 4	3.37 /35	--	1.91	0.49
AA	American Funds College 2024 529A	CFTAX	C+	(800) 421-0180	D / 2.0	3.10	2.31	9.39 /10	3.78 /40	--	1.62	0.73
AA	American Funds College 2024 529B	CCFBX	C+	(800) 421-0180	D / 2.2	2.90	1.93	8.53 / 8	2.95 /31	--	0.00	1.52
AA	American Funds College 2024 529C	CTFCX	C+	(800) 421-0180	D / 2.2	2.98	2.00	8.56 / 8	2.97 /31	--	1.05	1.51
AA	American Funds College 2024 529E	CTFEX	C+	(800) 421-0180	D+ / 2.5	3.16	2.28	9.20 /10	3.53 /37	--	1.49	0.98
AA	American Funds College 2024 529F1	CTFFX	C+	(800) 421-0180	D+ / 2.8	3.20	2.50	9.68 /11	3.99 /43	--	1.88	0.51
GI	American Funds College 2027 529A	CSTAX	C+	(800) 421-0180	D+ / 2.5	3.91	3.06	12.11 /18	4.02 /43	--	1.47	0.78
GI	American Funds College 2027 529B	CTSBX	C+	(800) 421-0180	D+ / 2.6	3.71	2.69	11.17 /15	3.20 /34	--	0.00	1.58
GI	American Funds College 2027 529C	CTSCX	C+	(800) 421-0180	D+ / 2.6	3.75	2.63	11.18 /15	3.19 /34	--	0.88	1.58
GI	American Funds College 2027 529E	CTSEX	C+	(800) 421-0180	C- / 3.1	3.96	3.02	11.83 /17	3.76 /40	--	1.33	1.04
GI	American Funds College 2027 529F1	CTSFX	B-	(800) 421-0180	C- / 3.4	4.00	3.16	12.28 /19	4.24 /46	--	1.71	0.57
GI	American Funds College 2030 529A	CTHAX	C	(800) 421-0180	C- / 3.1	4.75	4.09	14.72 /29	4.32 /47	--	1.45	0.79
GI	American Funds College 2030 529B	CTHBX	C	(800) 421-0180	C- / 3.3	4.58	3.67	13.89 /25	3.50 /37	--	0.00	1.60

Risk Rating/Pts	3 Year Standard Deviation	Beta	NAV As of 2/28/17	Total $(Mil)	Cash %	Stocks %	Bonds %	Other %	Portfolio Turnover Ratio	Last Bull Market Return	Last Bear Market Return	Manager Quality Pct	Manager Tenure (Years)	Initial Purch. $	Additional Purch. $	Front End Load	Back End Load
B- / 7.0	7.8	1.12	59.44	17	1	78	19	2	47	52.3	-10.2	20	17	250	50	0.0	0.0
B- / 7.0	7.8	0.64	59.63	1,013	1	78	19	2	47	53.7	-10.1	39	17	250	50	0.0	0.0
B- / 7.0	7.8	0.64	59.64	785	1	78	19	2	47	56.2	-10.0	43	17	250	50	0.0	0.0
B- / 7.0	7.8	0.64	59.70	228	1	78	19	2	47	58.8	-9.9	47	17	250	50	0.0	0.0
C+ / 5.9	7.8	1.13	59.60	9	1	78	19	2	47	56.8	-10.0	24	17	250	50	0.0	0.0
B- / 7.0	7.8	0.64	59.68	7,567	1	78	19	2	47	59.2	-9.9	48	17	250	50	0.0	0.0
B- / 7.0	7.8	0.63	59.64	2,209	1	78	19	2	47	55.9	-10.0	43	17	250	50	5.8	0.0
B- / 7.0	7.8	0.63	59.93	2	1	78	19	2	47	49.3	-10.3	32	17	250	50	0.0	0.0
B- / 7.0	7.8	0.64	59.58	673	1	78	19	2	47	49.5	-10.3	33	17	250	50	0.0	0.0
B- / 7.0	7.8	0.64	59.63	91	1	78	19	2	47	53.9	-10.1	39	17	250	50	0.0	0.0
B- / 7.0	7.8	0.64	59.66	83	1	78	19	2	47	57.7	-9.9	46	17	250	50	0.0	0.0
C+ / 6.2	10.1	0.78	46.09	3,031	0	92	6	2	35	80.8	-20.8	93	24	250	50	5.8	0.0
C+ / 6.2	10.1	0.78	46.11	4	0	92	6	2	35	73.3	-21.1	91	24	250	50	0.0	0.0
C+ / 6.2	10.1	0.78	45.86	687	0	92	6	2	35	73.4	-21.1	91	24	250	50	0.0	0.0
C+ / 6.2	10.1	0.78	46.02	123	0	92	6	2	35	78.6	-20.9	92	24	250	50	0.0	0.0
C+ / 6.2	10.1	0.78	46.14	126	0	92	6	2	35	83.0	-20.7	94	24	250	50	0.0	0.0
C+ / 6.2	10.1	0.78	46.24	52,380	0	92	6	2	35	81.7	-20.8	93	24	250	50	5.8	0.0
C+ / 6.2	10.1	0.78	46.15	30	0	92	6	2	35	74.3	-21.0	91	24	250	50	0.0	0.0
C+ / 6.2	10.1	0.78	45.72	2,872	0	92	6	2	35	74.0	-21.0	91	24	250	50	0.0	0.0
C+ / 6.2	10.1	0.78	46.15	3,503	0	92	6	2	35	81.4	-20.8	93	24	250	50	0.0	0.0
C+ / 6.2	10.1	0.78	46.22	6,519	0	92	6	2	35	84.2	-20.7	94	24	250	50	0.0	0.0
C+ / 5.7	10.1	0.78	46.26	4	0	92	6	2	35	81.7	-20.8	93	24	250	50	0.0	0.0
C+ / 6.2	10.1	0.78	45.78	228	0	92	6	2	35	74.3	-21.0	91	24	250	50	0.0	0.0
C+ / 6.2	10.1	0.78	45.66	930	0	92	6	2	35	74.6	-21.0	91	24	250	50	0.0	0.0
B- / 7.0	10.1	0.78	46.08	28	0	92	6	2	35	76.7	-21.0	92	24	250	50	0.0	0.0
C+ / 6.2	10.1	0.78	45.93	1,960	0	92	6	2	35	78.7	-20.9	92	24	250	50	0.0	0.0
C+ / 6.2	10.1	0.78	46.13	1,774	0	92	6	2	35	81.6	-20.8	93	24	250	50	0.0	0.0
C+ / 6.2	10.1	0.78	46.27	1,171	0	92	6	2	35	84.6	-20.7	94	24	250	50	0.0	0.0
C+ / 5.7	10.1	0.78	46.19	10	0	92	6	2	35	81.9	-20.8	93	24	250	50	0.0	0.0
C+ / 6.2	10.1	0.78	46.26	10,065	0	92	6	2	35	85.1	-20.7	94	24	250	50	0.0	0.0
B+ / 9.6	2.2	0.14	10.70	625	0	4	95	1	8	N/A	N/A	84	5	250	50	4.3	0.0
B+ / 9.6	2.2	0.13	10.78	N/A	0	4	95	1	8	N/A	N/A	80	5	250	50	0.0	0.0
B+ / 9.6	2.2	0.14	10.60	273	0	4	95	1	8	N/A	N/A	79	5	250	50	0.0	0.0
B+ / 9.6	2.2	0.13	10.66	41	0	4	95	1	8	N/A	N/A	83	5	250	50	0.0	0.0
B+ / 9.6	2.2	0.14	10.72	78	0	4	95	1	8	N/A	N/A	85	5	250	50	0.0	0.0
B+ / 9.6	3.3	0.45	11.15	811	0	23	76	1	5	N/A	N/A	72	5	250	50	4.3	0.0
B+ / 9.6	3.3	0.45	11.26	N/A	0	23	76	1	5	N/A	N/A	63	5	250	50	0.0	0.0
B+ / 9.6	3.3	0.45	11.04	273	0	23	76	1	5	N/A	N/A	62	5	250	50	0.0	0.0
B+ / 9.6	3.2	0.44	11.12	42	0	23	76	1	5	N/A	N/A	69	5	250	50	0.0	0.0
B+ / 9.6	3.3	0.45	11.17	90	0	23	76	1	5	N/A	N/A	N/A	5	250	50	0.0	0.0
B+ / 9.6	4.7	0.71	11.60	772	0	39	60	1	10	N/A	N/A	56	5	250	50	4.3	0.0
B+ / 9.6	4.6	0.70	11.71	N/A	0	39	60	1	10	N/A	N/A	46	5	250	50	0.0	0.0
B+ / 9.6	4.7	0.70	11.48	198	0	39	60	1	10	N/A	N/A	45	5	250	50	0.0	0.0
B+ / 9.6	4.6	0.70	11.57	36	0	39	60	1	10	N/A	N/A	53	5	250	50	0.0	0.0
B+ / 9.6	4.7	0.71	11.63	68	0	39	60	1	10	N/A	N/A	59	5	250	50	0.0	0.0
B+ / 9.1	5.9	0.53	12.11	618	0	52	47	1	9	N/A	N/A	56	5	250	50	4.3	0.0
B+ / 9.1	5.9	0.52	12.19	N/A	0	52	47	1	9	N/A	N/A	46	5	250	50	0.0	0.0
B+ / 9.1	5.9	0.52	11.98	143	0	52	47	1	9	N/A	N/A	46	5	250	50	0.0	0.0
B+ / 9.1	5.9	0.52	12.05	23	0	52	47	1	9	N/A	N/A	53	5	250	50	0.0	0.0
B+ / 9.1	5.9	0.52	12.15	52	0	52	47	1	9	N/A	N/A	60	5	250	50	0.0	0.0
B / 8.1	7.3	0.66	12.71	744	0	65	34	1	4	N/A	N/A	42	5	250	50	4.3	0.0
B / 8.0	7.3	0.65	12.83	N/A	0	65	34	1	4	N/A	N/A	32	5	250	50	0.0	0.0

Fund Type	Fund Name	Ticker Symbol	Overall Investment Rating	Phone	Perfor-mance Rating/Pts	3 Mo	6 Mo	1Yr / Pct	3Yr / Pct	5Yr / Pct	Dividend Yield	Expense Ratio
	99 Pct = Best 0 Pct = Worst							Total Return % through 2/28/17 (Annualized)			Incl. in Returns	
GI	American Funds College 2030 529C	CTYCX	C	(800) 421-0180	C- / 3.3	4.65	3.73	13.90 /25	3.48 /37	--	0.84	1.60
GI	American Funds College 2030 529E	CTHEX	C+	(800) 421-0180	C- / 3.7	4.78	3.96	14.53 /28	4.02 /43	--	1.30	1.06
GI	American Funds College 2030 529F1	CTHFX	C+	(800) 421-0180	C- / 4.1	4.84	4.18	15.08 /30	4.51 /49	--	1.68	0.59
GI	American Funds College 2033 529A	CTLAX	U	(800) 421-0180	U /	5.78	5.47	18.13 /43	--	--	1.26	0.80
GI	American Funds College 2033 529C	CTLCX	U	(800) 421-0180	U /	5.52	4.89	17.06 /39	--	--	0.76	1.63
EM	American Funds Dev Wld G and I	CDWAX	D	(800) 421-0180	D- / 1.0	7.68	4.17	22.55 /65	-0.96 / 9	--	1.70	1.44
EM	American Funds DevWld G and I	CDWBX	D	(800) 421-0180	D- / 1.3	7.62	4.00	22.00 /62	-1.58 / 8	--	1.27	2.24
EM	American Funds DevWld G and I	CDWCX	D	(800) 421-0180	D- / 1.2	7.49	3.67	21.42 /59	-1.77 / 7	--	1.08	2.20
EM	American Funds DevWld G and I	CDWEX	D	(800) 421-0180	D- / 1.4	7.63	4.09	22.20 /63	-1.16 / 9	--	1.64	1.55
EM	American Funds DevWld G and I	CDWFX	D	(800) 421-0180	D / 1.6	7.72	4.28	22.62 /65	-0.79 /10	--	1.98	1.18
EM	American Funds DevWld G and I A	DWGAX	D	(800) 421-0180	D- / 1.0	7.77	4.27	22.49 /64	-0.95 /10	--	1.77	1.39
EM	American Funds DevWld G and I B	DWGBX	D	(800) 421-0180	D- / 1.2	7.51	3.79	21.55 /60	-1.68 / 7	--	0.94	2.11
EM	American Funds DevWld G and I C	DWGCX	D	(800) 421-0180	D- / 1.2	7.48	3.79	21.57 /60	-1.70 / 7	--	1.10	2.13
EM	American Funds DevWld G and I F1	DWGFX	D	(800) 421-0180	D / 1.6	7.79	4.21	22.60 /65	-0.89 /10	--	1.86	1.29
EM	American Funds DevWld G and I F2	DWGHX	D	(800) 421-0180	D / 1.6	7.75	4.34	22.92 /66	-0.65 /11	--	2.11	1.03
EM	American Funds DevWld G and I F3	FDWGX	D-	(800) 421-0180	D / 1.6	7.88	4.37	22.61 /65	-0.91 /10	--	1.87	0.92
EM	American Funds DevWld G and I R1	RDWAX	D	(800) 421-0180	D- / 1.2	7.50	3.81	21.60 /60	-1.64 / 8	--	1.15	2.05
EM	American Funds DevWld G and I R2	RDWBX	D	(800) 421-0180	D- / 1.2	7.53	3.77	21.64 /60	-1.73 / 7	--	1.14	2.02
EM	American Funds DevWld G and I R2E	RDEGX	D	(800) 421-0180	D- / 1.4	7.55	4.07	22.18 /63	-1.12 / 9	--	1.60	1.88
EM	American Funds DevWld G and I R3	RDWCX	D	(800) 421-0180	D- / 1.4	7.74	4.08	22.30 /64	-1.17 / 9	--	1.60	1.58
EM	American Funds DevWld G and I R4	RDWEX	D	(800) 421-0180	D- / 1.5	7.69	4.22	22.51 /65	-0.88 /10	--	1.90	1.29
EM	American Funds DevWld G and I R5	RDWFX	D	(800) 421-0180	D / 1.7	7.77	4.38	22.85 /66	-0.60 /11	--	2.17	0.98
EM	American Funds DevWld G and I R5E	RDWHX	D-	(800) 421-0180	D / 1.6	7.85	4.41	22.83 /66	-0.86 /10	--	2.02	1.14
EM	American Funds DevWld G and I R6	RDWGX	D	(800) 421-0180	D / 1.7	7.78	4.41	22.91 /66	-0.55 /11	--	2.22	0.92
FO	American Funds EuroPacific Gr 529A	CEUAX	D-	(800) 421-0180	D- / 1.5	6.05	2.30	16.54 /36	0.34 /15	5.47 /25	1.10	0.90
FO	● American Funds EuroPacific Gr 529B	CEUBX	D-	(800) 421-0180	D- / 1.2	5.82	1.85	15.60 /32	-0.47 /11	4.62 /19	0.00	1.70
FO	American Funds EuroPacific Gr 529C	CEUCX	D-	(800) 421-0180	D- / 1.2	5.86	1.90	15.65 /33	-0.44 /12	4.65 /19	0.42	1.68
FO	American Funds EuroPacific Gr 529E	CEUEX	D	(800) 421-0180	D / 2.0	5.99	2.18	16.28 /35	0.10 /14	5.21 /23	0.95	1.14
FO	American Funds EuroPacific Gr	CEUFX	D	(800) 421-0180	D / 2.2	6.10	2.40	16.79 /38	0.56 /16	5.69 /26	1.38	0.69
* FO	American Funds EuroPacific Gr A	AEPGX	D-	(800) 421-0180	D- / 1.5	6.08	2.34	16.62 /37	0.41 /15	5.53 /25	1.11	0.83
FO	● American Funds EuroPacific Gr B	AEGBX	D-	(800) 421-0180	D- / 1.3	5.87	1.93	15.72 /33	-0.34 /12	4.75 /20	0.00	1.57
FO	American Funds EuroPacific Gr C	AEPCX	D-	(800) 421-0180	D- / 1.3	5.86	1.92	15.71 /33	-0.38 /12	4.71 /19	0.34	1.62
FO	American Funds EuroPacific Gr F1	AEGFX	D	(800) 421-0180	D / 2.1	6.06	2.31	16.58 /37	0.38 /15	5.51 /25	1.14	0.86
FO	American Funds EuroPacific Gr F2	AEPFX	D	(800) 421-0180	D+ / 2.3	6.15	2.45	16.90 /38	0.65 /16	5.80 /27	1.46	0.60
FO	American Funds EuroPacific Gr F3	FEUPX	D	(800) 421-0180	D / 2.2	6.10	2.36	16.64 /37	0.41 /15	5.54 /25	1.18	0.51
FO	American Funds EuroPacific Gr R1	RERAX	D-	(800) 421-0180	D- / 1.3	5.88	1.95	15.75 /33	-0.36 /12	4.73 /20	0.52	1.61
FO	American Funds EuroPacific Gr R2	RERBX	D-	(800) 421-0180	D- / 1.3	5.88	1.93	15.73 /33	-0.34 /12	4.75 /20	0.48	1.59
FO	American Funds EuroPacific Gr R2E	REEBX	U	(800) 421-0180	U /	5.94	2.10	16.15 /35	--	5.02 /21	1.10	1.31
FO	American Funds EuroPacific Gr R3	RERCX	D	(800) 421-0180	D / 2.0	5.99	2.18	16.26 /35	0.11 /14	5.22 /23	0.90	1.14
FO	American Funds EuroPacific Gr R4	REREX	D	(800) 421-0180	D / 2.2	6.07	2.33	16.60 /37	0.40 /15	5.53 /25	1.21	0.85
FO	American Funds EuroPacific Gr R5	RERFX	D	(800) 421-0180	D+ / 2.3	6.16	2.49	16.99 /38	0.71 /17	5.85 /27	1.50	0.54
FO	American Funds EuroPacific Gr R5E	RERHX	D	(800) 421-0180	D / 2.2	6.13	2.43	16.79 /38	0.48 /16	5.58 /25	1.56	0.70
FO	American Funds EuroPacific Gr R6	RERGX	D	(800) 421-0180	D+ / 2.3	6.17	2.50	17.04 /38	0.75 /17	5.90 /28	1.55	0.50
GI	American Funds Fundamntl Invs	CFNAX	B+	(800) 421-0180	B+ / 8.4	7.31	10.75	26.29 /77	10.02 /93	13.46 /88	1.32	0.69
GI	● American Funds Fundamntl Invs	CFNBX	A-	(800) 421-0180	B+ / 8.8	7.07	10.27	25.26 /74	9.15 /88	12.56 /80	0.51	1.50
GI	American Funds Fundamntl Invs	CFNCX	A-	(800) 421-0180	B+ / 8.8	7.10	10.32	25.31 /74	9.17 /88	12.57 /80	0.71	1.47
GI	American Funds Fundamntl Invs	CFNEX	A	(800) 421-0180	A- / 9.1	7.25	10.61	26.01 /76	9.76 /92	13.19 /86	1.19	0.93
GI	American Funds Fundamntl Invs	CFNFX	A	(800) 421-0180	A / 9.4	7.37	10.86	26.55 /78	10.27 /95	13.71 /91	1.59	0.48
* GI	American Funds Fundamntl Invs A	ANCFX	B+	(800) 421-0180	B+ / 8.5	7.33	10.77	26.37 /77	10.12 /94	13.56 /89	1.38	0.61
GI	● American Funds Fundamntl Invs B	AFIBX	A-	(800) 421-0180	B+ / 8.9	7.12	10.35	25.41 /75	9.29 /89	12.70 /81	0.58	1.38
GI	American Funds Fundamntl Invs C	AFICX	A-	(800) 421-0180	B+ / 8.8	7.13	10.36	25.40 /74	9.25 /88	12.66 /80	0.76	1.41
GI	American Funds Fundamntl Invs F1	AFIFX	A	(800) 421-0180	A / 9.3	7.30	10.75	26.29 /77	10.05 /94	13.50 /89	1.41	0.68

● Denotes fund is closed to new investors
* Denotes fund is included in Section II

www.thestreetratings.com

| RISK | 3 Year | | NET ASSETS | | ASSET | | | | | BULL / BEAR | | FUND MANAGER | | MINIMUMS | | LOADS | |
Risk Rating/Pts	Standard Deviation	Beta	NAV As of 2/28/17	Total $(Mil)	Cash %	Stocks %	Bonds %	Other %	Portfolio Turnover Ratio	Last Bull Market Return	Last Bear Market Return	Manager Quality Pct	Manager Tenure (Years)	Initial Purch. $	Additional Purch. $	Front End Load	Back End Load
B /8.0	7.3	0.66	12.57	149	0	65	34	1	4	N/A	N/A	31	5	250	50	0.0	0.0
B /8.1	7.3	0.66	12.66	26	0	65	34	1	4	N/A	N/A	37	5	250	50	0.0	0.0
B /8.2	7.3	0.66	12.75	51	0	65	34	1	4	N/A	N/A	45	5	250	50	0.0	0.0
U /	N/A	N/A	10.49	248	0	81	17	2	0	N/A	N/A	N/A	N/A	250	50	4.3	0.0
U /	N/A	N/A	10.42	39	0	81	17	2	0	N/A	N/A	N/A	N/A	250	50	0.0	0.0
C+ /6.6	13.5	0.80	9.65	30	5	89	5	1	25	N/A	N/A	43	3	250	50	5.8	0.0
C+ /6.6	13.5	0.80	9.65	N/A	5	89	5	1	25	N/A	N/A	35	3	250	50	0.0	0.0
C+ /6.6	13.4	0.80	9.60	5	5	89	5	1	25	N/A	N/A	32	3	250	50	0.0	0.0
C+ /6.6	13.4	0.80	9.64	1	5	89	5	1	25	N/A	N/A	40	3	250	50	0.0	0.0
C+ /6.6	13.5	0.80	9.65	2	5	89	5	1	25	N/A	N/A	46	3	250	50	0.0	0.0
C+ /6.6	13.4	0.80	9.65	1,391	5	89	5	1	25	N/A	N/A	44	3	250	50	5.8	0.0
C+ /6.6	13.4	0.80	9.65	N/A	5	89	5	1	25	N/A	N/A	34	3	250	50	0.0	0.0
C+ /6.6	13.4	0.80	9.61	114	5	89	5	1	25	N/A	N/A	33	3	250	50	0.0	0.0
C+ /6.6	13.5	0.80	9.66	92	5	89	5	1	25	N/A	N/A	44	3	250	50	0.0	0.0
C+ /6.6	13.4	0.80	9.66	790	5	89	5	1	25	N/A	N/A	48	3	250	50	0.0	0.0
C /5.0	13.4	0.80	9.66	N/A	5	89	5	1	25	N/A	N/A	44	3	250	50	0.0	0.0
C+ /6.6	13.4	0.80	9.62	1	5	89	5	1	25	N/A	N/A	34	3	250	50	0.0	0.0
C+ /6.6	13.5	0.80	9.60	9	5	89	5	1	25	N/A	N/A	33	3	250	50	0.0	0.0
C+ /6.6	13.4	0.80	9.63	N/A	5	89	5	1	25	N/A	N/A	41	3	250	50	0.0	0.0
C+ /6.6	13.5	0.80	9.64	8	5	89	5	1	25	N/A	N/A	40	3	250	50	0.0	0.0
C+ /6.6	13.4	0.80	9.65	7	5	89	5	1	25	N/A	N/A	45	3	250	50	0.0	0.0
C+ /6.6	13.4	0.80	9.66	4	5	89	5	1	25	N/A	N/A	49	3	250	50	0.0	0.0
C /5.0	13.4	0.80	9.65	N/A	5	89	5	1	25	N/A	N/A	45	3	250	50	0.0	0.0
C+ /6.6	13.4	0.80	9.66	29	5	89	5	1	25	N/A	N/A	49	3	250	50	0.0	0.0
C+ /5.6	10.7	0.83	47.12	1,133	0	94	5	1	30	53.2	-24.1	77	11	250	50	5.8	0.0
C+ /5.7	10.7	0.83	47.29	1	0	94	5	1	30	46.7	-24.3	70	11	250	50	0.0	0.0
C+ /5.6	10.7	0.83	46.16	333	0	94	5	1	30	46.9	-24.3	70	11	250	50	0.0	0.0
C+ /5.6	10.7	0.83	46.73	58	0	94	5	1	30	51.2	-24.2	75	11	250	50	0.0	0.0
C /5.5	10.7	0.83	47.09	99	0	94	5	1	30	55.0	-24.0	79	11	250	50	0.0	0.0
C+ /5.6	10.7	0.83	47.64	25,180	0	94	5	1	30	53.7	-24.0	78	11	250	50	5.8	0.0
C+ /5.7	10.7	0.83	48.14	7	0	94	5	1	30	47.6	-24.3	72	11	250	50	0.0	0.0
C+ /5.6	10.7	0.83	46.60	1,229	0	94	5	1	30	47.4	-24.3	71	11	250	50	0.0	0.0
C+ /5.6	10.7	0.83	47.42	4,099	0	94	5	1	30	53.5	-24.1	78	11	250	50	0.0	0.0
C /5.5	10.7	0.83	47.51	22,583	0	94	5	1	30	55.8	-24.0	79	11	250	50	0.0	0.0
C /5.5	10.7	0.83	47.65	N/A	0	94	5	1	30	53.7	-24.0	78	11	250	50	0.0	0.0
C+ /5.6	10.7	0.83	45.92	243	0	94	5	1	30	47.5	-24.3	71	11	250	50	0.0	0.0
C+ /5.6	10.7	0.83	46.29	751	0	94	5	1	30	47.6	-24.3	72	11	250	50	0.0	0.0
U /	10.7	0.83	46.97	184	0	94	5	1	30	49.6	-24.2	N/A	11	250	50	0.0	0.0
C+ /5.6	10.7	0.83	46.70	4,448	0	94	5	1	30	51.3	-24.1	76	11	250	50	0.0	0.0
C+ /5.6	10.7	0.83	46.72	9,781	0	94	5	1	30	53.7	-24.1	78	11	250	50	0.0	0.0
C /5.5	10.7	0.83	47.55	8,452	0	94	5	1	30	56.2	-23.9	80	11	250	50	0.0	0.0
C /5.5	10.7	0.83	47.36	8	0	94	5	1	30	54.0	-24.0	78	11	250	50	0.0	0.0
C /5.5	10.7	0.83	47.59	48,893	0	94	5	1	30	56.6	-23.9	80	11	250	50	0.0	0.0
C+ /6.1	10.5	1.00	57.52	2,120	0	95	4	1	27	128.8	-19.7	68	24	250	50	5.8	0.0
C+ /6.1	10.5	1.00	57.66	2	0	95	4	1	27	119.1	-20.0	57	24	250	50	0.0	0.0
C+ /6.1	10.5	1.00	57.38	502	0	95	4	1	27	119.3	-20.0	58	24	250	50	0.0	0.0
C+ /6.1	10.5	1.00	57.45	84	0	95	4	1	27	125.9	-19.8	65	24	250	50	0.0	0.0
C+ /6.1	10.5	1.00	57.50	109	0	95	4	1	27	131.5	-19.6	70	24	250	50	0.0	0.0
C+ /6.1	10.5	1.00	57.60	49,539	0	95	4	1	27	129.9	-19.7	69	24	250	50	5.8	0.0
C+ /6.1	10.5	1.00	57.57	20	0	95	4	1	27	120.6	-19.9	59	24	250	50	0.0	0.0
C+ /6.1	10.5	1.00	57.25	2,503	0	95	4	1	27	120.2	-20.0	59	24	250	50	0.0	0.0
C+ /6.1	10.5	1.00	57.56	2,788	0	95	4	1	27	129.2	-19.7	68	24	250	50	0.0	0.0

Fund Type	Fund Name	Ticker Symbol	Overall Investment Rating	Phone	Performance Rating/Pts	3 Mo	6 Mo	1Yr / Pct	3Yr / Pct	5Yr / Pct	Dividend Yield	Expense Ratio
GI	American Funds Fundamntl Invs F2	FINFX	A	(800) 421-0180	A / 9.4	7.39	10.88	26.63 / 78	10.34 / 95	13.80 / 92	1.64	0.41
GL	American Funds Fundamntl Invs F3	FUNFX	A-	(800) 421-0180	A / 9.3	7.37	10.81	26.42 / 78	10.13 / 94	13.57 / 89	1.46	0.32
GI	American Funds Fundamntl Invs R1	RFNAX	A-	(800) 421-0180	B+ / 8.8	7.13	10.33	25.38 / 74	9.25 / 88	12.67 / 81	0.76	1.41
GI	American Funds Fundamntl Invs R2	RFNBX	A-	(800) 421-0180	B+ / 8.8	7.11	10.34	25.39 / 74	9.28 / 89	12.70 / 81	0.78	1.39
GL	American Funds Fundamntl Invs R2E	RFEBX	A+	(800) 421-0180	A- / 9.1	7.19	10.51	25.78 / 75	9.72 / 92	13.04 / 84	1.12	1.10
GI	American Funds Fundamntl Invs R3	RFNCX	A	(800) 421-0180	A- / 9.1	7.23	10.59	25.95 / 76	9.74 / 92	13.18 / 86	1.16	0.96
GI	American Funds Fundamntl Invs R4	RFNEX	A	(800) 421-0180	A / 9.3	7.32	10.75	26.33 / 77	10.07 / 94	13.52 / 89	1.43	0.66
GI	American Funds Fundamntl Invs R5	RFNFX	A	(800) 421-0180	A / 9.4	7.40	10.93	26.72 / 78	10.40 / 95	13.86 / 92	1.69	0.35
GL	American Funds Fundamntl Invs R5E	RFNHX	A-	(800) 421-0180	A / 9.3	7.36	10.85	26.50 / 78	10.17 / 94	13.59 / 90	1.59	0.57
GI	American Funds Fundamntl Invs R6	RFNGX	A	(800) 421-0180	A / 9.4	7.41	10.96	26.79 / 79	10.45 / 96	13.92 / 93	1.73	0.31
FO	American Funds Glbl Balanced 529A	CBFAX	D+	(800) 421-0180	D / 1.6	4.56	1.24	12.13 / 18	2.20 / 25	6.29 / 30	1.76	0.93
FO	● American Funds Glbl Balanced 529B	CBFBX	C-	(800) 421-0180	D / 1.8	4.38	0.85	11.23 / 15	1.37 / 20	5.43 / 24	0.89	1.75
FO	American Funds Glbl Balanced 529C	CBFCX	C-	(800) 421-0180	D / 1.8	4.37	0.88	11.28 / 15	1.39 / 20	5.44 / 24	1.12	1.72
FO	American Funds Glbl Balanced 529E	CBFEX	C-	(800) 421-0180	D / 2.1	4.54	1.16	11.89 / 18	1.95 / 24	6.03 / 28	1.65	1.16
FO	American Funds Glbl Balanced	CBFFX	C-	(800) 421-0180	D+ / 2.4	4.61	1.35	12.36 / 19	2.40 / 27	6.50 / 31	2.08	0.72
FO	American Funds Glbl Balanced A	GBLAX	D+	(800) 421-0180	D / 1.6	4.61	1.30	12.20 / 19	2.27 / 26	6.36 / 31	1.83	0.85
FO	● American Funds Glbl Balanced B	GBLBX	C-	(800) 421-0180	D / 1.9	4.38	0.91	11.34 / 16	1.49 / 21	5.56 / 25	0.96	1.62
FO	American Funds Glbl Balanced C	GBLCX	C-	(800) 421-0180	D / 1.9	4.38	0.90	11.32 / 16	1.45 / 21	5.51 / 25	1.17	1.65
FO	American Funds Glbl Balanced F1	GBLEX	C-	(800) 421-0180	D+ / 2.3	4.58	1.27	12.16 / 18	2.22 / 25	6.31 / 30	1.88	0.91
FO	American Funds Glbl Balanced F2	GBLFX	C-	(800) 421-0180	D+ / 2.4	4.66	1.38	12.43 / 19	2.48 / 27	6.59 / 32	2.14	0.65
GL	American Funds Glbl Balanced F3	GFBLX	C-	(800) 421-0180	D+ / 2.3	4.64	1.33	12.23 / 19	2.28 / 26	6.37 / 31	1.94	0.54
FO	American Funds Glbl Balanced R1	RGBLX	C-	(800) 421-0180	D / 1.9	4.40	0.91	11.41 / 16	1.57 / 21	5.72 / 26	1.22	1.64
FO	American Funds Glbl Balanced R2	RGBBX	C-	(800) 421-0180	D / 1.9	4.43	0.93	11.37 / 16	1.48 / 21	5.56 / 25	1.21	1.64
GL	American Funds Glbl Balanced R2E	RGGHX	C-	(800) 421-0180	D / 2.1	4.49	1.08	11.70 / 17	2.00 / 24	5.93 / 28	1.56	1.45
FO	American Funds Glbl Balanced R3	RGBCX	C-	(800) 421-0180	D / 2.1	4.51	1.11	11.87 / 17	1.94 / 24	6.03 / 28	1.63	1.20
FO	American Funds Glbl Balanced R4	RGBEX	C-	(800) 421-0180	D+ / 2.3	4.57	1.26	12.16 / 18	2.25 / 26	6.35 / 31	1.91	0.90
FO	American Funds Glbl Balanced R5	RGBFX	C-	(800) 421-0180	D+ / 2.5	4.68	1.44	12.51 / 20	2.54 / 28	6.65 / 32	2.19	0.60
GL	American Funds Glbl Balanced R5E	RGBHX	C-	(800) 421-0180	D+ / 2.4	4.67	1.39	12.36 / 19	2.33 / 26	6.40 / 31	2.04	0.76
FO	American Funds Glbl Balanced R6	RGBGX	C-	(800) 421-0180	D+ / 2.5	4.65	1.43	12.58 / 20	2.59 / 28	6.70 / 33	2.24	0.54
GL	American Funds Global Growth 529A	CPGAX	C-	(800) 421-0180	C- / 3.7	7.84	5.82	20.03 / 52	3.73 / 40	---	0.87	0.88
GL	American Funds Global Growth 529B	CGGBX	C-	(800) 421-0180	C- / 4.1	7.56	5.38	19.02 / 47	2.85 / 30	---	0.00	1.72
GL	American Funds Global Growth 529C	CPGCX	C-	(800) 421-0180	C- / 4.1	7.58	5.39	19.13 / 48	2.88 / 31	---	0.04	1.70
GL	American Funds Global Growth 529E	CGGEX	C-	(800) 421-0180	C / 4.7	7.81	5.79	19.80 / 51	3.45 / 36	---	0.69	1.16
GL	American Funds Global Growth	CGGFX	C	(800) 421-0180	C / 5.1	7.93	5.99	20.37 / 54	3.93 / 42	---	1.09	0.70
GL	American Funds Global Growth A	PGGAX	C-	(800) 421-0180	C- / 3.8	7.87	5.93	20.15 / 53	3.80 / 40	---	0.91	0.82
GL	American Funds Global Growth B	PGGBX	C-	(800) 421-0180	C- / 4.2	7.61	5.44	19.23 / 48	2.95 / 31	---	0.00	1.64
GL	American Funds Global Growth C	GGPCX	C-	(800) 421-0180	C- / 4.2	7.61	5.49	19.23 / 48	2.96 / 31	---	0.26	1.62
GL	American Funds Global Growth F1	PGGFX	C	(800) 421-0180	C / 4.9	7.85	5.91	20.12 / 53	3.72 / 39	---	0.89	0.89
GL	American Funds Global Growth F2	PGWFX	C	(800) 421-0180	C / 5.1	7.92	5.99	20.43 / 54	4.01 / 43	---	1.16	0.62
GL	American Funds Global Growth F3	PGXFX	C	(800) 421-0180	C / 4.9	7.87	5.93	20.15 / 53	3.80 / 40	---	0.96	0.52
GL	American Funds Global Growth R1	RGGAX	C-	(800) 421-0180	C- / 4.2	7.66	5.54	19.26 / 48	2.96 / 31	---	0.00	1.63
GL	American Funds Global Growth R2	RGGBX	C-	(800) 421-0180	C- / 4.2	7.72	5.53	19.29 / 48	2.95 / 31	---	0.34	1.64
GL	American Funds Global Growth R2E	REBGX	C+	(800) 421-0180	C / 4.8	7.75	5.73	20.03 / 52	3.68 / 39	---	1.10	1.35
GL	American Funds Global Growth R3	RGLCX	C-	(800) 421-0180	C / 4.6	7.74	5.72	19.72 / 51	3.43 / 36	---	0.69	1.19
GL	American Funds Global Growth R4	RGGEX	C	(800) 421-0180	C / 4.9	7.89	5.87	20.19 / 53	3.75 / 40	---	0.97	0.88
GL	American Funds Global Growth R5	RGGFX	C	(800) 421-0180	C / 5.2	7.94	6.08	20.48 / 55	4.05 / 43	---	1.19	0.58
GL	American Funds Global Growth R5E	RGTFX	C	(800) 421-0180	C / 5.0	7.89	6.02	20.28 / 54	3.86 / 41	---	1.03	0.74
GL	American Funds Global Growth R6	RGGGX	C	(800) 421-0180	C / 5.2	7.89	6.04	20.49 / 55	4.10 / 44	---	1.23	0.52
GR	American Funds Gr Fnd of Amer	CGFAX	B-	(800) 421-0180	B / 7.9	7.60	10.20	26.73 / 78	8.94 / 86	13.93 / 93	0.44	0.74
GR	● American Funds Gr Fnd of Amer	CGFBX	B-	(800) 421-0180	B / 8.2	7.39	9.78	25.71 / 75	8.08 / 80	13.03 / 84	0.00	1.54
GR	American Funds Gr Fnd of Amer	CGFCX	B-	(800) 421-0180	B+ / 8.3	7.42	9.78	25.77 / 75	8.10 / 80	13.04 / 84	0.00	1.52
GR	American Funds Gr Fnd of Amer	CGFEX	B	(800) 421-0180	B+ / 8.7	7.55	10.07	26.44 / 78	8.68 / 84	13.65 / 90	0.26	0.98

99 Pct = Best
0 Pct = Worst

● Denotes fund is closed to new investors
* Denotes fund is included in Section II

72

Risk Rating/Pts	3 Year Standard Deviation	Beta	NAV As of 2/28/17	Total $(Mil)	Cash %	Stocks %	Bonds %	Other %	Portfolio Turnover Ratio	Last Bull Market Return	Last Bear Market Return	Manager Quality Pct	Manager Tenure (Years)	Initial Purch. $	Additional Purch. $	Front End Load	Back End Load
C+ / 6.0	10.5	1.00	57.60	9,404	0	95	4	1	27	132.5	-19.6	71	24	250	50	0.0	0.0
C+ / 5.6	10.5	0.74	57.62	10	0	95	4	1	27	129.9	-19.7	99	24	250	50	0.0	0.0
C+ / 6.1	10.5	1.00	57.25	150	0	95	4	1	27	120.3	-19.9	59	24	250	50	0.0	0.0
C+ / 6.1	10.5	1.00	57.23	771	0	95	4	1	27	120.6	-19.9	59	24	250	50	0.0	0.0
C+ / 6.7	10.5	0.73	57.34	26	0	95	4	1	27	124.0	-19.9	99	24	250	50	0.0	0.0
C+ / 6.1	10.5	1.00	57.43	2,269	0	95	4	1	27	125.7	-19.8	64	24	250	50	0.0	0.0
C+ / 6.1	10.5	1.00	57.48	2,432	0	95	4	1	27	129.4	-19.7	68	24	250	50	0.0	0.0
C+ / 6.1	10.5	1.00	57.66	1,907	0	95	4	1	27	133.2	-19.6	72	24	250	50	0.0	0.0
C+ / 5.6	10.5	0.74	57.55	11	0	95	4	1	27	130.2	-19.7	99	24	250	50	0.0	0.0
C+ / 6.0	10.5	1.00	57.64	9,712	0	95	4	1	27	133.8	-19.6	72	24	250	50	0.0	0.0
B- / 7.5	7.0	0.51	30.32	213	0	55	44	1	59	52.4	-12.2	87	N/A	250	50	5.8	0.0
B- / 7.5	7.0	0.51	30.38	N/A	0	55	44	1	59	45.8	-12.5	83	N/A	250	50	0.0	0.0
B- / 7.5	7.0	0.51	30.19	78	0	55	44	1	59	46.0	-12.5	83	N/A	250	50	0.0	0.0
B- / 7.5	7.0	0.51	30.29	13	0	55	44	1	59	50.4	-12.3	86	N/A	250	50	0.0	0.0
B- / 7.4	7.0	0.51	30.34	18	0	55	44	1	59	54.0	-12.1	88	N/A	250	50	0.0	0.0
B- / 7.5	7.0	0.51	30.34	4,574	0	55	44	1	59	53.0	-12.2	87	N/A	250	50	5.8	0.0
B- / 7.5	7.0	0.51	30.40	1	0	55	44	1	59	46.8	-12.5	84	N/A	250	50	0.0	0.0
B- / 7.5	7.0	0.51	30.24	607	0	55	44	1	59	46.5	-12.5	84	N/A	250	50	0.0	0.0
B- / 7.5	7.0	0.51	30.35	173	0	55	44	1	59	52.7	-12.2	87	N/A	250	50	0.0	0.0
B- / 7.4	7.0	0.51	30.36	858	0	55	44	1	59	54.8	-12.1	88	N/A	250	50	0.0	0.0
B- / 7.0	7.0	1.03	30.35	N/A	0	55	44	1	59	53.1	-12.2	42	N/A	250	50	0.0	0.0
B- / 7.5	7.0	0.51	30.26	6	0	55	44	1	59	48.0	-12.5	84	N/A	250	50	0.0	0.0
B- / 7.5	7.0	0.51	30.22	44	0	55	44	1	59	46.9	-12.4	84	N/A	250	50	0.0	0.0
B- / 7.6	7.0	1.03	30.30	N/A	0	55	44	1	59	49.5	-12.4	38	N/A	250	50	0.0	0.0
B- / 7.5	7.0	0.51	30.28	52	0	55	44	1	59	50.4	-12.3	86	N/A	250	50	0.0	0.0
B- / 7.5	7.0	0.51	30.34	30	0	55	44	1	59	52.9	-12.2	87	N/A	250	50	0.0	0.0
B- / 7.4	7.0	0.51	30.39	13	0	55	44	1	59	55.3	-12.1	88	N/A	250	50	0.0	0.0
B- / 7.0	7.0	1.03	30.34	N/A	0	55	44	1	59	53.3	-12.2	43	N/A	250	50	0.0	0.0
B- / 7.4	7.0	0.51	30.37	4,655	0	55	44	1	59	55.6	-12.1	89	N/A	250	50	0.0	0.0
C+ / 5.8	10.4	0.80	14.74	163	1	87	11	1	2	N/A	N/A	93	5	250	50	5.8	0.0
C+ / 5.9	10.5	0.80	14.69	N/A	1	87	11	1	2	N/A	N/A	90	5	250	50	0.0	0.0
C+ / 5.8	10.5	0.80	14.59	56	1	87	11	1	2	N/A	N/A	90	5	250	50	0.0	0.0
C+ / 5.8	10.5	0.80	14.69	6	1	87	11	1	2	N/A	N/A	92	5	250	50	0.0	0.0
C+ / 5.8	10.5	0.81	14.78	12	1	87	11	1	2	N/A	N/A	93	5	250	50	0.0	0.0
C+ / 5.8	10.4	0.80	14.76	1,134	1	87	11	1	2	N/A	N/A	93	5	250	50	5.8	0.0
C+ / 5.9	10.5	0.80	14.74	N/A	1	87	11	1	2	N/A	N/A	90	5	250	50	0.0	0.0
C+ / 5.8	10.5	0.80	14.58	237	1	87	11	1	2	N/A	N/A	90	5	250	50	0.0	0.0
C+ / 5.8	10.5	0.80	14.78	39	1	87	11	1	2	N/A	N/A	93	5	250	50	0.0	0.0
C+ / 5.8	10.5	0.80	14.80	124	1	87	11	1	2	N/A	N/A	93	5	250	50	0.0	0.0
C+ / 5.7	10.4	0.80	14.76	N/A	1	87	11	1	2	N/A	N/A	93	5	250	50	0.0	0.0
C+ / 5.8	10.5	0.80	14.66	3	1	87	11	1	2	N/A	N/A	90	5	250	50	0.0	0.0
C+ / 5.8	10.5	0.81	14.55	52	1	87	11	1	2	N/A	N/A	90	5	250	50	0.0	0.0
C+ / 6.6	10.5	0.80	14.70	1	1	87	11	1	2	N/A	N/A	93	5	250	50	0.0	0.0
C+ / 5.8	10.5	0.80	14.68	25	1	87	11	1	2	N/A	N/A	92	5	250	50	0.0	0.0
C+ / 5.8	10.5	0.81	14.74	13	1	87	11	1	2	N/A	N/A	93	5	250	50	0.0	0.0
C+ / 5.8	10.5	0.80	14.86	6	1	87	11	1	2	N/A	N/A	94	5	250	50	0.0	0.0
C+ / 5.7	10.5	0.80	14.73	N/A	1	87	11	1	2	N/A	N/A	93	5	250	50	0.0	0.0
C+ / 5.8	10.4	0.80	14.88	36	1	87	11	1	2	N/A	N/A	94	5	250	50	0.0	0.0
C / 4.7	11.1	1.00	44.57	6,813	0	92	6	2	31	133.1	-19.0	54	19	250	50	5.8	0.0
C / 4.6	11.1	1.00	42.29	8	0	92	6	2	31	123.2	-19.3	43	19	250	50	0.0	0.0
C / 4.6	11.1	1.00	42.16	1,566	0	92	6	2	31	123.4	-19.3	44	19	250	50	0.0	0.0
C / 4.7	11.1	1.00	44.15	292	0	92	6	2	31	130.0	-19.1	51	19	250	50	0.0	0.0

Fund Type	Fund Name	Ticker Symbol	Overall Investment Rating	Phone	Performance Rating/Pts	3 Mo	6 Mo	1Yr / Pct	3Yr / Pct	5Yr / Pct	Dividend Yield	Expense Ratio
GR	American Funds Gr Fnd of Amer	CGFFX	B	(800) 421-0180	A- / 9.0	7.68	10.33	27.00 /79	9.18 /88	14.17 /94	0.68	0.52
*GR	American Funds Gr Fnd of Amer A	AGTHX	B-	(800) 421-0180	B / 7.9	7.62	10.24	26.82 /79	9.03 /87	14.01 /93	0.50	0.66
GR	● American Funds Gr Fnd of Amer B	AGRBX	B	(800) 421-0180	B+ / 8.3	7.40	9.79	25.83 /76	8.20 /80	13.15 /85	0.00	1.42
GR	American Funds Gr Fnd of Amer C	GFACX	B-	(800) 421-0180	B+ / 8.3	7.42	9.82	25.84 /76	8.17 /80	13.11 /85	0.00	1.46
GR	American Funds Gr Fnd of Amer F1	GFAFX	B	(800) 421-0180	B+ / 8.9	7.59	10.21	26.76 /78	8.98 /87	13.98 /93	0.48	0.71
GR	American Funds Gr Fnd of Amer F2	GFFFX	B+	(800) 421-0180	A- / 9.0	7.69	10.36	27.10 /79	9.27 /89	14.28 /95	0.74	0.44
GR	American Funds Gr Fnd of Amer F3	GAFFX	B+	(800) 421-0180	B+ / 8.9	7.67	10.29	26.87 /79	9.04 /87	14.02 /93	0.53	0.33
GR	American Funds Gr Fnd of Amer R1	RGAAX	B	(800) 421-0180	B+ / 8.3	7.42	9.81	25.84 /76	8.18 /80	13.14 /85	0.00	1.43
GR	American Funds Gr Fnd of Amer R2	RGABX	B	(800) 421-0180	B+ / 8.3	7.42	9.80	25.86 /76	8.23 /81	13.20 /86	0.00	1.42
GR	American Funds Gr Fnd of Amer R2E	RGEBX	A-	(800) 421-0180	B+ / 8.6	7.52	10.00	26.23 /77	8.62 /84	13.48 /89	0.37	1.13
GR	American Funds Gr Fnd of Amer R3	RGACX	B	(800) 421-0180	B+ / 8.7	7.55	10.07	26.42 /78	8.68 /84	13.66 /90	0.22	0.98
GR	American Funds Gr Fnd of Amer R4	RGAEX	B	(800) 421-0180	B+ / 8.9	7.63	10.22	26.77 /79	9.00 /87	14.00 /93	0.52	0.68
GR	American Funds Gr Fnd of Amer R5	RGAFX	B+	(800) 421-0180	A- / 9.1	7.70	10.37	27.15 /80	9.32 /89	14.34 /95	0.76	0.39
GR	American Funds Gr Fnd of Amer R5E	RGAHX	B+	(800) 421-0180	A- / 9.0	7.67	10.33	26.97 /79	9.08 /87	14.05 /93	0.86	0.56
GR	American Funds Gr Fnd of Amer R6	RGAGX	B+	(800) 421-0180	A- / 9.1	7.71	10.41	27.23 /80	9.37 /89	14.39 /95	0.82	0.33
FO	American Funds Gro and Inc 4		U	(800) 421-0180	U /	4.89	3.75	14.79 /29	--	--	0.66	1.10
GL	American Funds Growth 529A	CGPAX	C	(800) 421-0180	C / 5.5	6.81	7.29	22.52 /65	6.04 /64	--	0.83	0.84
GL	American Funds Growth 529B	CGPBX	C+	(800) 421-0180	C+ / 5.9	6.50	6.79	21.45 /59	5.14 /56	--	0.00	1.67
GL	American Funds Growth 529C	CGPCX	C+	(800) 421-0180	C+ / 5.9	6.48	6.77	21.45 /59	5.16 /56	--	0.27	1.65
GL	American Funds Growth 529E	CGPEX	C+	(800) 421-0180	C+ / 6.4	6.66	7.08	22.19 /63	5.74 /62	--	0.65	1.10
GL	American Funds Growth 529F1	CGPFX	C+	(800) 421-0180	C+ / 6.7	6.76	7.32	22.75 /66	6.23 /66	--	1.04	0.64
GL	American Funds Growth A	GWPAX	C	(800) 421-0180	C / 5.5	6.79	7.27	22.57 /65	6.09 /65	--	0.87	0.76
GL	American Funds Growth and Inc	CGNAX	C+	(800) 421-0180	C- / 4.0	6.06	4.99	17.46 /40	5.47 /59	--	1.64	0.80
GL	American Funds Growth and Inc	CGNBX	C+	(800) 421-0180	C / 4.5	5.87	4.55	16.58 /37	4.62 /50	--	0.73	1.59
GL	American Funds Growth and Inc	CGNCX	C+	(800) 421-0180	C / 4.6	5.93	4.58	16.59 /37	4.64 /50	--	1.04	1.57
GL	American Funds Growth and Inc	CGNEX	C+	(800) 421-0180	C / 5.0	5.99	4.87	17.24 /39	5.20 /56	--	1.53	1.03
GL	American Funds Growth and Inc	CGNFX	B-	(800) 421-0180	C / 5.4	6.12	5.03	17.71 /42	5.66 /61	--	1.95	0.57
GL	American Funds Growth and Inc A	GAIOX	C+	(800) 421-0180	C- / 4.1	6.07	4.95	17.56 /41	5.53 /60	--	1.72	0.71
GL	American Funds Growth and Inc B	GAIBX	C+	(800) 421-0180	C / 4.6	5.85	4.53	16.58 /37	4.68 /51	--	0.80	1.51
GL	American Funds Growth and Inc C	GAITX	C+	(800) 421-0180	C / 4.6	5.87	4.63	16.70 /37	4.73 /51	--	1.12	1.49
GL	American Funds Growth and Inc F1	GAIFX	B-	(800) 421-0180	C / 5.2	6.06	4.92	17.51 /41	5.47 /59	--	1.78	0.76
GL	American Funds Growth and Inc F2	GAIEX	B-	(800) 421-0180	C / 5.5	6.13	5.06	17.78 /42	5.76 /62	--	2.01	0.50
GI	American Funds Growth and Inc F3	GAIHX	C+	(800) 421-0180	C / 5.3	6.15	5.03	17.64 /41	5.56 /60	--	1.82	0.39
GL	American Funds Growth and Inc R1	RGNAX	C+	(800) 421-0180	C / 4.6	5.85	4.50	16.60 /37	4.68 /51	--	1.06	1.50
GL	American Funds Growth and Inc R2	RGNBX	C+	(800) 421-0180	C / 4.6	5.88	4.57	16.64 /37	4.69 /51	--	1.14	1.51
GI	American Funds Growth and Inc R2E	RBEGX	B-	(800) 421-0180	C / 5.0	5.95	4.73	16.92 /38	5.25 /57	--	1.43	1.19
GL	American Funds Growth and Inc R3	RAICX	C+	(800) 421-0180	C / 5.0	5.99	4.79	17.16 /39	5.17 /56	--	1.53	1.06
GL	American Funds Growth and Inc R4	RGNEX	B-	(800) 421-0180	C / 5.3	6.07	5.02	17.54 /41	5.50 /59	--	1.80	0.75
GL	American Funds Growth and Inc R5	RGNFX	B-	(800) 421-0180	C / 5.5	6.13	5.16	17.89 /42	5.80 /62	--	2.05	0.45
GI	American Funds Growth and Inc R5E	RGQFX	C+	(800) 421-0180	C / 5.4	6.19	5.10	17.76 /42	5.59 /60	--	1.90	0.61
GL	American Funds Growth and Inc R6	RGNGX	B-	(800) 421-0180	C+ / 5.6	6.16	5.20	17.97 /43	5.86 /63	--	2.10	0.39
GL	American Funds Growth B	GWPBX	C+	(800) 421-0180	C+ / 6.0	6.55	6.84	21.55 /60	5.24 /57	--	0.00	1.58
GL	American Funds Growth C	GWPCX	C+	(800) 421-0180	C+ / 6.0	6.53	6.81	21.59 /60	5.25 /57	--	0.25	1.56
GL	American Funds Growth F1	GWPFX	C+	(800) 421-0180	C+ / 6.6	6.72	7.20	22.50 /64	6.02 /64	--	0.86	0.83
GL	American Funds Growth F2	GWPEX	C+	(800) 421-0180	C+ / 6.8	6.82	7.38	22.79 /66	6.29 /67	--	1.09	0.57
FO	American Funds Growth F3	GWPDX	C+	(800) 421-0180	C+ / 6.7	6.86	7.34	22.64 /65	6.11 /65	--	0.93	0.46
GL	American Funds Growth R1	RGWAX	C+	(800) 421-0180	C+ / 6.0	6.54	6.82	21.62 /60	5.25 /57	--	0.16	1.57
GL	American Funds Growth R2	RGWBX	C+	(800) 421-0180	C+ / 5.9	6.53	6.81	21.58 /60	5.22 /57	--	0.31	1.58
FO	American Funds Growth R2E	RBGEX	C+	(800) 421-0180	C+ / 6.3	6.65	7.00	21.93 /62	5.74 /62	--	0.76	1.25
GL	American Funds Growth R3	RGPCX	C+	(800) 421-0180	C+ / 6.4	6.68	7.10	22.20 /63	5.72 /62	--	0.68	1.13
GL	American Funds Growth R4	RGWEX	C+	(800) 421-0180	C+ / 6.6	6.70	7.18	22.48 /64	6.05 /65	--	0.90	0.82
GL	American Funds Growth R5	RGWFX	C+	(800) 421-0180	C+ / 6.8	6.86	7.41	22.94 /66	6.37 /67	--	1.15	0.52

● Denotes fund is closed to new investors
* Denotes fund is included in Section II

www.thestreetratings.com

RISK Risk Rating/Pts	3 Year Standard Deviation	Beta	NET ASSETS NAV As of 2/28/17	Total $(Mil)	ASSET Cash %	Stocks %	Bonds %	Other %	Portfolio Turnover Ratio	BULL / BEAR Last Bull Market Return	Last Bear Market Return	FUND MANAGER Manager Quality Pct	Manager Tenure (Years)	MINIMUMS Initial Purch. $	Additional Purch. $	LOADS Front End Load	Back End Load
C /4.7	11.1	1.00	44.48	265	0	92	6	2	31	135.7	-19.0	57	19	250	50	0.0	0.0
C /4.7	11.1	1.00	44.99	78,315	0	92	6	2	31	134.0	-19.0	56	19	250	50	5.8	0.0
C /4.7	11.1	1.00	42.57	51	0	92	6	2	31	124.6	-19.3	45	19	250	50	0.0	0.0
C /4.6	11.1	1.00	42.02	4,877	0	92	6	2	31	124.2	-19.3	45	19	250	50	0.0	0.0
C /4.7	11.1	1.00	44.70	8,800	0	92	6	2	31	133.6	-19.0	55	19	250	50	0.0	0.0
C /4.7	11.1	1.00	44.91	15,014	0	92	6	2	31	137.1	-18.9	59	19	250	50	0.0	0.0
C /5.4	11.1	1.00	45.01	12	0	92	6	2	31	134.1	-19.0	56	19	250	50	0.0	0.0
C /4.7	11.1	1.00	42.61	431	0	92	6	2	31	124.6	-19.3	45	19	250	50	0.0	0.0
C /4.7	11.1	1.00	43.01	2,174	0	92	6	2	31	125.1	-19.2	45	19	250	50	0.0	0.0
C+ /6.1	11.1	1.00	44.36	72	0	92	6	2	31	128.0	-19.2	50	19	250	50	0.0	0.0
C /4.7	11.1	1.00	44.20	6,482	0	92	6	2	31	130.2	-19.1	51	19	250	50	0.0	0.0
C /4.7	11.1	1.00	44.61	8,051	0	92	6	2	31	133.8	-19.0	55	19	250	50	0.0	0.0
C /4.7	11.1	1.00	44.96	3,616	0	92	6	2	31	137.7	-18.9	59	19	250	50	0.0	0.0
C /5.4	11.1	1.00	44.72	29	0	92	6	2	31	134.4	-19.0	56	19	250	50	0.0	0.0
C /4.6	11.1	1.00	45.02	18,293	0	92	6	2	31	138.3	-18.9	60	19	250	50	0.0	0.0
U /	N/A	N/A	10.53	77	0	0	0	100	10	N/A	N/A	N/A	N/A	0	0	0.0	0.0
C+ /5.8	10.2	0.76	15.81	437	0	90	9	1	0	N/A	N/A	97	5	250	50	5.8	0.0
C+ /5.8	10.2	0.76	15.66	N/A	0	90	9	1	0	N/A	N/A	96	5	250	50	0.0	0.0
C+ /5.8	10.3	0.76	15.59	151	0	90	9	1	0	N/A	N/A	96	5	250	50	0.0	0.0
C+ /5.8	10.3	0.76	15.72	20	0	90	9	1	0	N/A	N/A	96	5	250	50	0.0	0.0
C+ /5.7	10.3	0.76	15.85	37	0	90	9	1	0	N/A	N/A	97	5	250	50	0.0	0.0
C+ /5.8	10.2	0.76	15.82	2,777	0	90	9	1	0	N/A	N/A	97	5	250	50	5.8	0.0
B- /7.4	8.2	0.61	13.78	369	0	74	24	2	0	N/A	N/A	96	N/A	250	50	5.8	0.0
B- /7.5	8.2	0.61	13.80	N/A	0	74	24	2	0	N/A	N/A	95	N/A	250	50	0.0	0.0
B- /7.4	8.2	0.61	13.71	143	0	74	24	2	0	N/A	N/A	95	N/A	250	50	0.0	0.0
B- /7.4	8.2	0.61	13.75	18	0	74	24	2	0	N/A	N/A	96	N/A	250	50	0.0	0.0
B- /7.4	8.2	0.61	13.79	29	0	74	24	2	0	N/A	N/A	96	N/A	250	50	0.0	0.0
B- /7.4	8.2	0.61	13.78	4,235	0	74	24	2	0	N/A	N/A	96	N/A	250	50	5.8	0.0
B- /7.4	8.2	0.61	13.79	1	0	74	24	2	0	N/A	N/A	95	N/A	250	50	0.0	0.0
B- /7.4	8.2	0.61	13.70	1,001	0	74	24	2	0	N/A	N/A	95	N/A	250	50	0.0	0.0
B- /7.4	8.2	0.61	13.78	129	0	74	24	2	0	N/A	N/A	96	N/A	250	50	0.0	0.0
B- /7.4	8.2	0.61	13.80	263	0	74	24	2	0	N/A	N/A	96	N/A	250	50	0.0	0.0
C+ /6.6	8.2	0.74	13.79	N/A	0	74	24	2	0	N/A	N/A	46	N/A	250	50	0.0	0.0
B- /7.4	8.2	0.61	13.72	6	0	74	24	2	0	N/A	N/A	95	N/A	250	50	0.0	0.0
B- /7.4	8.2	0.61	13.69	103	0	74	24	2	0	N/A	N/A	95	N/A	250	50	0.0	0.0
B- /7.7	8.2	0.74	13.75	5	0	74	24	2	0	N/A	N/A	42	N/A	250	50	0.0	0.0
B- /7.4	8.2	0.61	13.74	68	0	74	24	2	0	N/A	N/A	96	N/A	250	50	0.0	0.0
B- /7.4	8.2	0.61	13.78	62	0	74	24	2	0	N/A	N/A	96	N/A	250	50	0.0	0.0
B- /7.4	8.2	0.61	13.83	10	0	74	24	2	0	N/A	N/A	96	N/A	250	50	0.0	0.0
C+ /6.6	8.2	0.75	13.78	N/A	0	74	24	2	0	N/A	N/A	47	N/A	250	50	0.0	0.0
B- /7.4	8.2	0.61	13.81	62	0	74	24	2	0	N/A	N/A	97	N/A	250	50	0.0	0.0
C+ /5.8	10.3	0.76	15.71	1	0	90	9	1	0	N/A	N/A	96	5	250	50	0.0	0.0
C+ /5.8	10.3	0.76	15.60	652	0	90	9	1	0	N/A	N/A	96	5	250	50	0.0	0.0
C+ /5.8	10.2	0.76	15.81	70	0	90	9	1	0	N/A	N/A	97	5	250	50	0.0	0.0
C+ /5.7	10.3	0.76	15.87	205	0	90	9	1	0	N/A	N/A	97	5	250	50	0.0	0.0
C+ /5.7	10.2	0.76	15.83	N/A	0	90	9	1	0	N/A	N/A	97	5	250	50	0.0	0.0
C+ /5.8	10.3	0.76	15.68	7	0	90	9	1	0	N/A	N/A	96	5	250	50	0.0	0.0
C+ /5.8	10.3	0.76	15.60	111	0	90	9	1	0	N/A	N/A	96	5	250	50	0.0	0.0
C+ /6.7	10.2	0.76	15.68	5	0	90	9	1	0	N/A	N/A	96	5	250	50	0.0	0.0
C+ /5.8	10.3	0.76	15.74	67	0	90	9	1	0	N/A	N/A	96	5	250	50	0.0	0.0
C+ /5.7	10.3	0.76	15.79	36	0	90	9	1	0	N/A	N/A	97	5	250	50	0.0	0.0
C+ /5.7	10.3	0.76	15.93	16	0	90	9	1	0	N/A	N/A	97	5	250	50	0.0	0.0

					PERFORMANCE						Incl. in Returns	
						Total Return % through 2/28/17						
99 Pct = Best									Annualized			
0 Pct = Worst			Ticker	Overall Investment		Perfor-mance						Dividend	Expense
Fund Type	Fund Name	Symbol	Rating	Phone	Rating/Pts	3 Mo	6 Mo	1Yr / Pct	3Yr / Pct	5Yr / Pct	Yield	Ratio
FO	American Funds Growth R5E	RGSFX	C+	(800) 421-0180	C+ / 6.7	6.79	7.34	22.68 /65	6.13 /65	--	0.97	0.69
GL	American Funds Growth R6	RGWGX	C+	(800) 421-0180	C+ / 6.8	6.83	7.39	22.95 /66	6.40 /67	--	1.17	0.47
IN	American Funds Inc Fnd of Amr 529A	CIMAX	C+	(800) 421-0180	C / 4.3	5.26	5.22	17.06 /39	6.18 /66	9.09 /51	2.75	0.66
IN	● American Funds Inc Fnd of Amr 529B	CIMBX	C+	(800) 421-0180	C / 4.9	5.06	4.86	16.14 /35	5.37 /58	8.23 /44	1.94	1.45
IN	American Funds Inc Fnd of Amr 529C	CIMCX	C+	(800) 421-0180	C / 4.9	5.08	4.89	16.19 /35	5.38 /58	8.25 /44	2.20	1.43
IN	American Funds Inc Fnd of Amr 529E	CIMEX	B-	(800) 421-0180	C / 5.3	5.21	5.12	16.79 /38	5.93 /64	8.82 /49	2.70	0.89
IN	American Funds Inc Fnd of Amr	CIMFX	B-	(800) 421-0180	C+ / 5.8	5.37	5.40	17.38 /40	6.43 /68	9.33 /53	3.13	0.43
* IN	American Funds Inc Fnd of Amr A	AMECX	C+	(800) 421-0180	C / 4.4	5.31	5.30	17.18 /39	6.29 /67	9.20 /52	2.82	0.56
IN	● American Funds Inc Fnd of Amr B	IFABX	C+	(800) 421-0180	C / 5.0	5.10	4.88	16.27 /35	5.49 /59	8.37 /45	2.09	1.31
IN	American Funds Inc Fnd of Amr C	IFACX	C+	(800) 421-0180	C / 4.9	5.13	4.90	16.26 /35	5.45 /59	8.33 /45	2.28	1.36
IN	American Funds Inc Fnd of Amr F1	IFAFX	B-	(800) 421-0180	C+ / 5.6	5.26	5.22	17.01 /38	6.20 /66	9.10 /51	2.91	0.65
IN	American Funds Inc Fnd of Amr F2	AMEFX	B-	(800) 421-0180	C+ / 5.8	5.36	5.40	17.40 /40	6.48 /68	9.38 /54	3.16	0.39
AA	American Funds Inc Fnd of Amr F3	FIFAX	C+	(800) 421-0180	C+ / 5.7	5.31	5.30	17.18 /39	6.29 /67	9.20 /52	2.99	0.28
IN	American Funds Inc Fnd of Amr R1	RIDAX	C+	(800) 421-0180	C / 4.9	5.09	4.86	16.18 /35	5.41 /59	8.30 /45	2.24	1.37
IN	American Funds Inc Fnd of Amr R2	RIDBX	C+	(800) 421-0180	C / 4.9	5.11	4.89	16.22 /35	5.44 /59	8.33 /45	2.26	1.36
AA	American Funds Inc Fnd of Amr R2E	RIEBX	B-	(800) 421-0180	C / 5.2	5.16	5.02	16.54 /36	5.83 /63	8.65 /48	2.58	1.09
IN	American Funds Inc Fnd of Amr R3	RIDCX	B-	(800) 421-0180	C / 5.3	5.25	5.13	16.77 /37	5.90 /63	8.79 /49	2.66	0.92
IN	American Funds Inc Fnd of Amr R4	RIDEX	B-	(800) 421-0180	C+ / 5.6	5.31	5.28	17.07 /39	6.21 /66	9.11 /52	2.93	0.62
IN	American Funds Inc Fnd of Amr R5	RIDFX	B-	(800) 421-0180	C+ / 5.8	5.33	5.38	17.39 /40	6.53 /69	9.44 /54	3.21	0.33
AA	American Funds Inc Fnd of Amr R5E	RIDHX	C+	(800) 421-0180	C+ / 5.7	5.32	5.33	17.25 /39	6.32 /67	9.21 /52	3.04	0.49
IN	American Funds Inc Fnd of Amr R6	RIDGX	B-	(800) 421-0180	C+ / 5.9	5.38	5.45	17.49 /41	6.60 /69	9.51 /55	3.25	0.28
GL	American Funds Income 529A	CIPAX	C	(800) 421-0180	C- / 3.2	4.93	4.17	14.81 /29	5.01 /54	--	2.82	0.73
GL	American Funds Income 529B	CIPBX	C+	(800) 421-0180	C- / 3.7	4.76	3.87	13.98 /25	4.23 /46	--	1.95	1.50
GL	American Funds Income 529C	CIPCX	C+	(800) 421-0180	C- / 3.7	4.73	3.78	13.93 /25	4.22 /45	--	2.28	1.50
GL	American Funds Income 529E	CIPEX	C+	(800) 421-0180	C- / 4.2	4.87	4.05	14.55 /28	4.78 /52	--	2.76	0.96
GL	American Funds Income 529F1	CIPFX	C+	(800) 421-0180	C / 4.6	4.99	4.30	15.05 /30	5.26 /57	--	3.20	0.50
GL	American Funds Income A	INPAX	C	(800) 421-0180	C- / 3.3	4.95	4.21	14.90 /29	5.11 /55	--	2.88	0.65
GL	American Funds Income B	INPBX	C+	(800) 421-0180	C- / 3.8	4.70	3.82	14.05 /26	4.28 /46	--	2.01	1.44
GL	American Funds Income C	INPCX	C+	(800) 421-0180	C- / 3.8	4.75	3.91	14.12 /26	4.33 /47	--	2.35	1.42
GL	American Funds Income F1	INPFX	C+	(800) 421-0180	C / 4.4	4.93	4.18	14.93 /30	5.09 /55	--	3.01	0.69
GL	American Funds Income F2	INPEX	B-	(800) 421-0180	C / 4.7	5.01	4.33	15.12 /30	5.36 /58	--	3.26	0.43
AA	American Funds Income F3	INPDX	C+	(800) 421-0180	C / 4.5	5.03	4.30	14.99 /30	5.13 /56	--	3.06	0.32
GL	American Funds Income R1	RNCAX	C+	(800) 421-0180	C- / 3.8	4.75	3.82	14.10 /26	4.30 /46	--	2.34	1.43
GL	American Funds Income R2	RINBX	C+	(800) 421-0180	C- / 3.8	4.76	3.93	14.11 /26	4.30 /46	--	2.35	1.45
AA	American Funds Income R2E	RNBEX	B-	(800) 421-0180	C / 4.3	4.87	4.05	14.79 /29	5.03 /54	--	3.04	1.13
GL	American Funds Income R3	RNCCX	C+	(800) 421-0180	C- / 4.2	4.87	4.07	14.57 /28	4.75 /51	--	2.77	0.99
GL	American Funds Income R4	RINEX	C+	(800) 421-0180	C / 4.5	4.95	4.30	14.97 /30	5.12 /55	--	3.03	0.68
GL	American Funds Income R5	RINFX	B-	(800) 421-0180	C / 4.7	5.03	4.36	15.26 /31	5.39 /58	--	3.30	0.38
AA	American Funds Income R5E	RGOFX	C+	(800) 421-0180	C / 4.5	5.02	4.35	15.08 /30	5.19 /56	--	3.21	0.55
GL	American Funds Income R6	RINGX	B-	(800) 421-0180	C / 4.8	5.04	4.48	15.32 /31	5.45 /59	--	3.35	0.33
GL	American Funds Ins Ser Ast Alloc 4		B	(800) 421-0180	C+ / 6.2	5.47	6.76	18.26 /44	6.56 /69	9.70 /56	1.29	0.79
IN	American Funds Ins Ser Cap InBld 1		U	(800) 421-0180	U /	4.98	1.27	9.69 /11	--	--	3.38	0.56
IN	American Funds Ins Ser Cap InBld 4		U	(800) 421-0180	U /	4.75	0.92	9.07 /10	--	--	2.92	1.05
FO	American Funds Ins Ser Gl Gr&Inc		B+	(800) 421-0180	C / 5.4	6.58	5.53	19.29 /48	5.15 /56	9.67 /56	1.96	0.89
FO	American Funds Ins Ser Gl Gr&Inc 4		B	(800) 421-0180	C / 5.0	6.40	5.26	18.68 /46	4.63 /50	8.75 /48	1.71	1.14
GL	American Funds Ins Ser Glb Bal 1A		C+	(800) 421-0180	C- / 3.0	4.97	2.67	12.83 /21	3.25 /34	5.86 /27	1.45	0.97
GL	American Funds Ins Ser Glb Bal 4		C	(800) 421-0180	D+ / 2.7	4.83	2.43	12.22 /19	2.92 /31	5.61 /26	1.22	1.22
FO	American Funds Ins Ser Glb Gro 4		C+	(800) 421-0180	C / 4.9	6.50	3.67	18.53 /45	4.80 /52	10.16 /59	0.63	1.05
FO	American Funds Ins Ser Glb SmCap		C	(800) 421-0180	C- / 3.4	5.91	4.83	20.90 /57	1.58 /21	8.52 /46	0.41	0.98
FO	American Funds Ins Ser Glb SmCap		C-	(800) 421-0180	C- / 3.0	5.75	4.55	20.32 /54	1.07 /19	7.96 /42	0.08	1.23
GI	American Funds Ins Ser Gr & Inc 1A		A+	(800) 421-0180	A- / 9.0	7.36	10.39	26.21 /77	9.33 /89	14.13 /94	1.43	N/A
GI	American Funds Ins Ser Gr & Inc 4		A+	(800) 421-0180	B+ / 8.6	7.25	10.12	25.59 /75	8.79 /85	13.30 /87	1.07	0.79

● Denotes fund is closed to new investors

* Denotes fund is included in Section II

www.thestreetratings.com

RISK	3 Year		NET ASSETS		ASSET				Portfolio Turnover Ratio	BULL / BEAR		FUND MANAGER		MINIMUMS		LOADS	
Risk Rating/Pts	Standard Deviation	Beta	NAV As of 2/28/17	Total $(Mil)	Cash %	Stocks %	Bonds %	Other %		Last Bull Market Return	Last Bear Market Return	Manager Quality Pct	Manager Tenure (Years)	Initial Purch. $	Additional Purch. $	Front End Load	Back End Load
C+ / 5.7	10.2	0.76	15.79	N/A	0	90	9	1	0	N/A	N/A	97	5	250	50	0.0	0.0
C+ / 5.7	10.3	0.76	15.89	48	0	90	9	1	0	N/A	N/A	97	5	250	50	0.0	0.0
B- / 7.4	7.3	0.67	22.38	1,572	1	68	29	2	52	74.7	-10.1	65	25	250	50	5.8	0.0
B- / 7.4	7.3	0.67	22.40	1	1	68	29	2	52	67.4	-10.4	55	25	250	50	0.0	0.0
B- / 7.4	7.3	0.67	22.28	463	1	68	29	2	52	67.5	-10.4	55	25	250	50	0.0	0.0
B- / 7.4	7.3	0.67	22.31	68	1	68	29	2	52	72.3	-10.2	62	25	250	50	0.0	0.0
B- / 7.4	7.3	0.66	22.39	66	1	68	29	2	52	76.8	-10.0	68	25	250	50	0.0	0.0
B- / 7.4	7.3	0.67	22.43	76,004	1	68	29	2	52	75.5	-10.1	66	25	250	50	5.8	0.0
B- / 7.4	7.3	0.67	22.32	24	1	68	29	2	52	68.5	-10.4	56	25	250	50	0.0	0.0
B- / 7.4	7.3	0.67	22.14	5,882	1	68	29	2	52	68.1	-10.3	56	25	250	50	0.0	0.0
B- / 7.4	7.3	0.66	22.37	4,673	1	68	29	2	52	74.8	-10.1	65	25	250	50	0.0	0.0
B- / 7.4	7.3	0.67	22.42	7,148	1	68	29	2	52	77.2	-10.0	68	25	250	50	0.0	0.0
C+ / 6.7	7.3	1.13	22.43	13	1	68	29	2	52	75.5	-10.1	47	25	250	50	0.0	0.0
B- / 7.4	7.3	0.67	22.27	130	1	68	29	2	52	67.9	-10.4	55	25	250	50	0.0	0.0
B- / 7.4	7.3	0.66	22.17	559	1	68	29	2	52	68.1	-10.4	56	25	250	50	0.0	0.0
B- / 7.4	7.3	1.13	22.37	15	1	68	29	2	52	70.8	-10.3	41	25	250	50	0.0	0.0
B- / 7.4	7.3	0.67	22.34	1,209	1	68	29	2	52	72.1	-10.2	61	25	250	50	0.0	0.0
B- / 7.4	7.3	0.66	22.39	1,230	1	68	29	2	52	74.9	-10.1	65	25	250	50	0.0	0.0
B- / 7.4	7.3	0.66	22.43	577	1	68	29	2	52	77.8	-10.0	69	25	250	50	0.0	0.0
C+ / 6.7	7.3	1.13	22.42	N/A	1	68	29	2	52	75.7	-10.1	47	25	250	50	0.0	0.0
B- / 7.4	7.3	0.67	22.45	5,553	1	68	29	2	52	78.3	-10.0	70	25	250	50	0.0	0.0
B- / 7.9	5.9	0.40	12.16	87	0	46	53	1	8	N/A	N/A	95	5	250	50	5.8	0.0
B- / 7.9	5.9	0.40	12.19	N/A	0	46	53	1	8	N/A	N/A	94	5	250	50	0.0	0.0
B- / 7.9	5.9	0.41	12.10	49	0	46	53	1	8	N/A	N/A	94	5	250	50	0.0	0.0
B- / 7.9	5.9	0.40	12.15	6	0	46	53	1	8	N/A	N/A	95	5	250	50	0.0	0.0
B- / 7.9	5.9	0.41	12.17	9	0	46	53	1	8	N/A	N/A	96	5	250	50	0.0	0.0
B- / 7.9	5.9	0.41	12.16	2,893	0	46	53	1	8	N/A	N/A	95	5	250	50	5.8	0.0
B- / 7.9	5.9	0.40	12.18	N/A	0	46	53	1	8	N/A	N/A	94	5	250	50	0.0	0.0
B- / 7.9	5.9	0.40	12.10	662	0	46	53	1	8	N/A	N/A	94	5	250	50	0.0	0.0
B- / 7.9	5.9	0.40	12.17	86	0	46	53	1	8	N/A	N/A	95	5	250	50	0.0	0.0
B- / 7.9	5.9	0.40	12.18	201	0	46	53	1	8	N/A	N/A	96	5	250	50	0.0	0.0
B- / 7.4	5.9	0.90	12.17	N/A	0	46	53	1	8	N/A	N/A	55	5	250	50	0.0	0.0
B- / 7.9	5.9	0.40	12.11	2	0	46	53	1	8	N/A	N/A	94	5	250	50	0.0	0.0
B- / 7.9	5.9	0.40	12.11	29	0	46	53	1	8	N/A	N/A	94	5	250	50	0.0	0.0
B / 8.4	5.9	0.89	12.15	N/A	0	46	53	1	8	N/A	N/A	54	5	250	50	0.0	0.0
B- / 7.9	5.9	0.40	12.14	28	0	46	53	1	8	N/A	N/A	95	5	250	50	0.0	0.0
B- / 7.9	5.9	0.40	12.17	33	0	46	53	1	8	N/A	N/A	95	5	250	50	0.0	0.0
B- / 7.9	5.9	0.40	12.19	5	0	46	53	1	8	N/A	N/A	96	5	250	50	0.0	0.0
B- / 7.4	5.9	0.90	12.16	N/A	0	46	53	1	8	N/A	N/A	56	5	250	50	0.0	0.0
B- / 7.9	5.9	0.40	12.19	27	0	46	53	1	8	N/A	N/A	96	5	250	50	0.0	0.0
B / 8.9	7.6	1.13	22.42	2,957	0	0	0	100	76	87.3	-13.4	82	N/A	0	0	0.0	0.0
U /	N/A	N/A	9.76	156	0	79	19	2	128	N/A	N/A	N/A	3	0	0	0.0	0.0
U /	N/A	N/A	9.73	256	0	79	19	2	128	N/A	N/A	N/A	3	0	0	0.0	0.0
B / 8.7	9.2	0.70	13.65	N/A	0	0	0	100	37	86.3	-18.2	96	8	0	0	0.0	0.0
B / 8.4	9.2	0.70	13.50	16	0	0	0	100	37	78.5	-18.2	95	8	0	0	0.0	0.0
B / 8.8	7.0	1.05	11.57	N/A	0	0	0	100	76	46.0	N/A	54	6	0	0	0.0	0.0
B / 8.5	6.9	1.05	11.48	11	0	0	0	100	76	44.1	N/A	50	6	0	0	0.0	0.0
B- / 7.6	11.6	0.87	25.27	99	0	0	0	100	29	94.5	-21.8	95	N/A	0	0	0.0	0.0
B- / 7.6	13.4	0.78	21.51	N/A	0	0	0	100	36	77.8	-25.9	85	19	0	0	0.0	0.0
B- / 7.0	13.4	0.78	21.14	46	0	0	0	100	36	73.1	-26.0	82	19	0	0	0.0	0.0
B / 8.3	10.5	0.99	47.15	N/A	0	0	0	100	25	133.0	-17.0	61	8	0	0	0.0	0.0
B- / 7.8	10.5	0.99	46.39	516	0	0	0	100	25	124.5	-17.1	54	8	0	0	0.0	0.0

Fund Type	Fund Name	Ticker Symbol	Overall Investment Rating	Phone	Performance Rating/Pts	3 Mo	6 Mo	1Yr / Pct	3Yr / Pct	5Yr / Pct	Dividend Yield	Expense Ratio
								Total Return % through 2/28/17	Annualized		Incl. in Returns	
GR	American Funds Ins Ser Growth 1A		A+	(800) 421-0180	A+ / 9.6	8.29	11.27	29.02 /84	10.28 /95	13.68 /90	0.86	N/A
GR	American Funds Ins Ser Growth 4		A+	(800) 421-0180	A / 9.4	8.16	10.99	28.38 /82	9.72 /92	13.02 /84	0.48	0.85
FO	American Funds Ins Ser Int G&I 4		D+	(800) 421-0180	E+ / 0.8	6.89	1.61	12.98 /22	-1.82 / 7	3.53 /13	2.34	1.18
FO	American Funds Ins Ser Intl 4		C-	(800) 421-0180	D+ / 2.6	5.88	3.67	20.05 /52	0.53 /16	5.03 /21	1.10	1.04
EM	American Funds Ins Ser New Wrld 1A		C	(800) 421-0180	C- / 3.0	7.11	3.96	21.67 /61	0.57 /16	3.54 /13	0.97	1.04
EM	American Funds Ins Ser New Wrld 4		C-	(800) 421-0180	D+ / 2.6	7.04	3.74	21.16 /58	0.09 /14	2.87 /10	0.59	1.29
FO	American Funds Intl Gr & Inc 529A	CGIAX	E+	(800) 421-0180	E / 0.5	5.97	3.08	14.85 /29	-2.13 / 6	4.22 /16	2.07	1.00
FO	● American Funds Intl Gr & Inc 529B	CGIBX	E+	(800) 421-0180	E+ / 0.6	5.74	2.65	13.96 /25	-2.92 / 5	3.37 /12	1.13	1.81
FO	American Funds Intl Gr & Inc 529C	CIICX	E+	(800) 421-0180	E+ / 0.6	5.76	2.69	13.97 /25	-2.90 / 5	3.39 /12	1.44	1.79
FO	American Funds Intl Gr & Inc 529E	CGIEX	E+	(800) 421-0180	E+ / 0.7	5.88	2.98	14.61 /28	-2.35 / 6	3.97 /15	1.98	1.22
FO	American Funds Intl Gr & Inc 529F1	CGIFX	E+	(800) 421-0180	E+ / 0.9	6.02	3.18	15.10 /30	-1.92 / 7	4.43 /18	2.39	0.79
FO	American Funds Intl Gr & Inc A	IGAAX	E+	(800) 421-0180	E / 0.5	5.98	3.10	14.94 /30	-2.06 / 6	4.29 /17	2.12	0.91
FO	● American Funds Intl Gr & Inc B	IGIBX	E+	(800) 421-0180	E+ / 0.6	5.76	2.71	14.05 /26	-2.80 / 5	3.51 /13	1.35	1.68
FO	American Funds Intl Gr & Inc C	IGICX	E+	(800) 421-0180	E+ / 0.6	5.78	2.73	14.04 /26	-2.83 / 5	3.46 /13	1.48	1.72
FO	American Funds Intl Gr & Inc F1	IGIFX	E+	(800) 421-0180	E+ / 0.8	5.97	3.07	14.89 /29	-2.11 / 6	4.25 /17	2.09	0.96
FO	American Funds Intl Gr & Inc F2	IGFFX	E+	(800) 421-0180	E+ / 0.9	6.04	3.22	15.20 /31	-1.84 / 7	4.52 /18	2.47	0.70
FO	American Funds Intl Gr & Inc F3	IGAIX	D-	(800) 421-0180	E+ / 0.8	6.01	3.13	14.98 /30	-2.05 / 6	4.30 /17	2.25	0.60
FO	American Funds Intl Gr & Inc R1	RIGAX	E+	(800) 421-0180	E+ / 0.6	5.77	2.74	14.12 /26	-2.70 / 5	3.76 /14	1.58	1.68
FO	American Funds Intl Gr & Inc R2	RIGBX	E+	(800) 421-0180	E+ / 0.6	5.78	2.71	14.06 /26	-2.87 / 5	3.43 /13	1.50	1.69
FO	American Funds Intl Gr & Inc R2E	RIIEX	D	(800) 421-0180	E+ / 0.7	5.83	2.88	14.39 /27	-2.36 / 6	3.85 /14	1.88	1.43
FO	American Funds Intl Gr & Inc R3	RGICX	E+	(800) 421-0180	E+ / 0.7	5.92	2.95	14.58 /28	-2.39 / 6	3.94 /15	1.95	1.24
FO	American Funds Intl Gr & Inc R4	RIGEX	E+	(800) 421-0180	E+ / 0.8	5.99	3.11	14.95 /30	-2.07 / 6	4.28 /17	2.25	0.93
FO	American Funds Intl Gr & Inc R5	RIGFX	E+	(800) 421-0180	E+ / 0.9	6.07	3.24	15.27 /31	-1.78 / 7	4.58 /19	2.52	0.63
FO	American Funds Intl Gr & Inc R5E	RIGIX	D-	(800) 421-0180	E+ / 0.8	6.02	3.21	15.10 /30	-2.00 / 7	4.33 /17	2.37	0.80
FO	American Funds Intl Gr & Inc R6	RIGGX	E+	(800) 421-0180	E+ / 0.9	6.07	3.32	15.37 /31	-1.73 / 7	4.64 /19	2.58	0.58
GI	American Funds Inv Co of Amer 529A	CICAX	B-	(800) 421-0180	B / 7.6	6.50	8.90	24.85 /73	9.29 /89	13.26 /86	1.57	0.68
GI	● American Funds Inv Co of Amer 529B	CICBX	B	(800) 421-0180	B / 8.0	6.29	8.47	23.83 /69	8.42 /82	12.37 /78	0.72	1.48
GI	American Funds Inv Co of Amer	CICCX	B	(800) 421-0180	B / 8.0	6.33	8.52	23.91 /69	8.45 /82	12.39 /78	0.98	1.45
GI	American Funds Inv Co of Amer 529E	CICEX	B+	(800) 421-0180	B+ / 8.4	6.44	8.78	24.54 /72	9.02 /87	12.98 /83	1.45	0.92
GI	American Funds Inv Co of Amer	CICFX	B+	(800) 421-0180	B+ / 8.8	6.57	9.04	25.11 /74	9.52 /90	13.51 /89	1.86	0.46
* GI	American Funds Inv Co of Amer A	AIVSX	B-	(800) 421-0180	B / 7.7	6.54	8.96	24.97 /73	9.40 /90	13.38 /88	1.64	0.59
GI	● American Funds Inv Co of Amer B	AICBX	B	(800) 421-0180	B / 8.0	6.31	8.52	23.97 /70	8.55 /83	12.51 /79	0.86	1.36
GI	American Funds Inv Co of Amer C	AICCX	B	(800) 421-0180	B / 8.0	6.34	8.53	23.94 /70	8.51 /83	12.47 /79	1.04	1.39
GI	American Funds Inv Co of Amer F1	AICFX	B+	(800) 421-0180	B+ / 8.6	6.54	8.93	24.84 /73	9.30 /89	13.29 /87	1.66	0.69
GI	American Funds Inv Co of Amer F2	ICAFX	B+	(800) 421-0180	B+ / 8.8	6.56	9.03	25.17 /74	9.59 /91	13.59 /90	1.91	0.41
GI	American Funds Inv Co of Amer F3	FFICX	B+	(800) 421-0180	B+ / 8.7	6.57	8.99	25.00 /73	9.41 /90	13.39 /88	1.74	0.31
GI	American Funds Inv Co of Amer R1	RICAX	B	(800) 421-0180	B / 8.0	6.33	8.50	23.95 /70	8.51 /83	12.47 /79	1.03	1.40
GI	American Funds Inv Co of Amer R2	RICBX	B	(800) 421-0180	B / 8.0	6.31	8.52	23.96 /70	8.53 /83	12.49 /79	1.03	1.39
GI	American Funds Inv Co of Amer R2E	RIBEX	A	(800) 421-0180	B+ / 8.3	6.41	8.69	24.35 /71	8.94 /86	12.81 /82	1.37	1.09
GI	American Funds Inv Co of Amer R3	RICCX	B	(800) 421-0180	B+ / 8.4	6.45	8.77	24.52 /72	8.99 /87	12.97 /83	1.42	0.95
GI	American Funds Inv Co of Amer R4	RICEX	B+	(800) 421-0180	B+ / 8.6	6.53	8.94	24.87 /73	9.33 /89	13.32 /87	1.71	0.64
GI	American Funds Inv Co of Amer R5	RICFX	B+	(800) 421-0180	B+ / 8.8	6.62	9.10	25.28 /74	9.65 /91	13.66 /90	1.94	0.35
GI	American Funds Inv Co of Amer R5E	RICHX	B+	(800) 421-0180	B+ / 8.7	6.57	9.01	25.08 /73	9.44 /90	13.41 /88	1.84	0.43
GI	American Funds Inv Co of Amer R6	RICGX	B+	(800) 421-0180	B+ / 8.9	6.62	9.12	25.33 /74	9.71 /92	13.72 /91	2.00	0.30
AA	American Funds Mgd Risk Asst All P1		C+	(800) 421-0180	C / 4.6	5.13	6.38	15.47 /32	4.83 /52	--	1.49	0.71
AA	American Funds Mgd Risk Asst All P2		C+	(800) 421-0180	C / 4.4	5.06	6.22	15.16 /31	4.56 /49	--	1.23	0.96
GL	American Funds Mgd Risk Gl Alloc		U	(800) 421-0180	U /	4.63	2.21	8.60 / 9	--	--	0.00	1.33
FO	American Funds Mgd Risk Growth P2		U	(800) 421-0180	U /	5.07	5.51	13.35 /23	--	--	0.03	1.16
GI	American Funds Mngd Risk BCIG P1		B	(800) 421-0180	C+ / 6.2	5.96	9.18	17.89 /42	6.09 /65	--	1.68	0.93
GI	American Funds Mngd Risk BCIG P2		B	(800) 421-0180	C+ / 5.8	5.92	8.96	17.42 /40	5.69 /61	--	1.49	1.18
GI	American Funds Mngd Risk Gl P1		B	(800) 421-0180	C / 4.9	6.82	9.20	16.92 /38	3.97 /43	--	1.32	0.81
GI	American Funds Mngd Risk Gl P2		B-	(800) 421-0180	C / 4.6	6.83	9.12	16.71 /37	3.63 /38	--	1.10	1.06

Risk Rating/Pts	Standard Deviation	Beta	NAV As of 2/28/17	Total $(Mil)	Cash %	Stocks %	Bonds %	Other %	Portfolio Turnover Ratio	Last Bull Market Return	Last Bear Market Return	Manager Quality Pct	Manager Tenure (Years)	Initial Purch. $	Additional Purch. $	Front End Load	Back End Load
B /8.1	11.3	1.03	72.33	N/A	0	0	0	100	20	130.0	-19.2	67	14	0	0	0.0	0.0
B- /7.6	11.3	1.03	71.32	484	0	0	0	100	20	123.2	-19.3	61	14	0	0	0.0	0.0
B- /7.8	10.4	0.81	15.08	39	0	0	0	100	35	39.9	-20.6	52	N/A	0	0	0.0	0.0
B- /7.6	11.5	0.88	17.67	71	0	0	0	100	37	50.7	-25.3	79	N/A	0	0	0.0	0.0
B /8.0	11.6	0.63	21.00	N/A	0	0	0	100	39	39.8	-21.7	68	18	0	0	0.0	0.0
B- /7.5	11.6	0.64	20.77	256	0	0	0	100	39	35.2	-21.8	61	18	0	0	0.0	0.0
C /5.1	10.5	0.81	29.58	123	4	84	10	2	37	39.6	-20.1	48	9	250	50	5.8	0.0
C /5.2	10.5	0.82	29.65	N/A	4	84	10	2	37	33.5	-20.4	36	9	250	50	0.0	0.0
C /5.2	10.5	0.82	29.40	29	4	84	10	2	37	33.7	-20.4	37	9	250	50	0.0	0.0
C /5.1	10.5	0.81	29.57	4	4	84	10	2	37	37.8	-20.2	45	9	250	50	0.0	0.0
C /5.1	10.5	0.82	29.63	13	4	84	10	2	37	41.1	-20.0	51	9	250	50	0.0	0.0
C /5.1	10.5	0.82	29.62	4,353	4	84	10	2	37	40.1	-20.1	49	9	250	50	5.8	0.0
C /5.2	10.5	0.82	29.64	1	4	84	10	2	37	34.5	-20.4	38	9	250	50	0.0	0.0
C /5.2	10.5	0.82	29.51	246	4	84	10	2	37	34.2	-20.4	37	9	250	50	0.0	0.0
C /5.1	10.5	0.82	29.64	348	4	84	10	2	37	39.8	-20.1	48	9	250	50	0.0	0.0
C /5.1	10.4	0.81	29.64	3,600	4	84	10	2	37	41.8	-20.0	52	9	250	50	0.0	0.0
C+ /5.7	10.5	0.82	29.63	8	4	84	10	2	37	40.2	-20.1	49	9	250	50	0.0	0.0
C /5.1	10.4	0.81	29.51	8	4	84	10	2	37	36.3	-20.3	39	9	250	50	0.0	0.0
C /5.2	10.5	0.82	29.44	49	4	84	10	2	37	34.0	-20.3	37	9	250	50	0.0	0.0
C+ /6.9	10.4	0.82	29.50	1	4	84	10	2	37	36.8	-20.3	45	9	250	50	0.0	0.0
C /5.1	10.5	0.82	29.55	62	4	84	10	2	37	37.5	-20.2	44	9	250	50	0.0	0.0
C /5.1	10.5	0.82	29.60	80	4	84	10	2	37	40.1	-20.1	49	9	250	50	0.0	0.0
C /5.1	10.5	0.82	29.78	30	4	84	10	2	37	42.3	-20.0	53	9	250	50	0.0	0.0
C+ /5.7	10.5	0.82	29.61	N/A	4	84	10	2	37	40.4	-20.1	50	9	250	50	0.0	0.0
C /5.1	10.5	0.82	29.64	2,196	4	84	10	2	37	42.7	-20.0	54	9	250	50	0.0	0.0
C /5.3	10.3	0.96	38.00	2,469	0	90	9	1	30	123.9	-17.3	64	25	250	50	5.8	0.0
C /5.3	10.3	0.96	38.06	3	0	90	9	1	30	114.4	-17.5	54	25	250	50	0.0	0.0
C /5.3	10.3	0.96	37.83	527	0	90	9	1	30	114.7	-17.6	54	25	250	50	0.0	0.0
C /5.3	10.3	0.96	37.87	88	0	90	9	1	30	120.9	-17.4	61	25	250	50	0.0	0.0
C /5.3	10.3	0.96	37.97	74	0	90	9	1	30	126.6	-17.2	67	25	250	50	0.0	0.0
C /5.3	10.3	0.96	38.09	60,667	0	90	9	1	30	125.1	-17.2	65	25	250	50	5.8	0.0
C /5.3	10.3	0.96	38.02	22	0	90	9	1	30	116.0	-17.5	56	25	250	50	0.0	0.0
C /5.3	10.3	0.96	37.68	1,773	0	90	9	1	30	115.5	-17.5	55	25	250	50	0.0	0.0
C /5.3	10.3	0.96	38.00	2,072	0	90	9	1	30	124.2	-17.3	65	25	250	50	0.0	0.0
C /5.3	10.3	0.96	38.08	5,014	0	90	9	1	30	127.5	-17.2	68	25	250	50	0.0	0.0
C+ /5.6	10.3	0.96	38.10	2	0	90	9	1	30	125.2	-17.2	66	25	250	50	0.0	0.0
C /5.3	10.3	0.96	37.76	88	0	90	9	1	30	115.5	-17.5	55	25	250	50	0.0	0.0
C /5.3	10.3	0.96	37.81	677	0	90	9	1	30	115.7	-17.5	55	25	250	50	0.0	0.0
C+ /6.9	10.3	0.96	37.98	20	0	90	9	1	30	119.0	-17.5	60	25	250	50	0.0	0.0
C /5.3	10.3	0.96	37.94	1,004	0	90	9	1	30	120.7	-17.4	61	25	250	50	0.0	0.0
C /5.3	10.3	0.96	37.99	1,600	0	90	9	1	30	124.5	-17.3	65	25	250	50	0.0	0.0
C /5.3	10.3	0.96	38.10	279	0	90	9	1	30	128.1	-17.1	68	25	250	50	0.0	0.0
C+ /5.6	10.3	0.96	38.07	3	0	90	9	1	30	125.4	-17.2	66	25	250	50	0.0	0.0
C /5.3	10.3	0.96	38.10	7,671	0	90	9	1	30	128.8	-17.1	69	25	250	50	0.0	0.0
B- /7.8	6.6	1.02	12.54	81	0	0	0	100	3	N/A	N/A	39	5	0	0	0.0	0.0
B- /7.6	6.6	1.01	12.53	155	0	0	0	100	3	N/A	N/A	36	5	0	0	0.0	0.0
U /	N/A	N/A	9.72	139	0	0	0	100	15	N/A	N/A	N/A	2	0	0	0.0	0.0
U /	N/A	N/A	10.21	562	0	0	0	100	4	N/A	N/A	N/A	N/A	0	0	0.0	0.0
B /8.1	7.4	0.61	12.16	N/A	8	87	3	2	20	N/A	N/A	71	N/A	0	0	0.0	0.0
B /8.0	7.3	0.61	12.09	19	8	87	3	2	20	N/A	N/A	66	N/A	0	0	0.0	0.0
B /8.3	7.7	0.70	11.70	N/A	0	0	0	100	11	N/A	N/A	32	N/A	0	0	0.0	0.0
B /8.2	7.8	0.70	11.66	9	0	0	0	100	11	N/A	N/A	28	N/A	0	0	0.0	0.0

Fund Type	Fund Name	Ticker Symbol	Overall Investment Rating	Phone	PERFORMANCE Perfor-mance Rating/Pts	3 Mo	6 Mo	1Yr / Pct	Annualized 3Yr / Pct	5Yr / Pct	Incl. in Returns Dividend Yield	Expense Ratio
GR	American Funds Mngd Risk Gro P1		B	(800) 421-0180	C / 5.1	7.71	9.67	17.56 /41	3.92 /42	--	0.43	0.86
GR	American Funds Mngd Risk Gro P2		B	(800) 421-0180	C / 4.8	7.76	9.52	17.34 /40	3.58 /38	--	0.18	1.11
FO	American Funds Mngd Risk Intl P1		D	(800) 421-0180	E / 0.5	4.23	2.52	7.55 / 7	-2.61 / 5	--	1.22	1.06
FO	American Funds Mngd Risk Intl P2		D	(800) 421-0180	E / 0.4	4.15	2.31	7.11 / 6	-3.02 / 4	--	0.90	1.30
FO	American Funds MR Gro and Inc P2		U	(800) 421-0180	U /	5.07	3.99	10.35 /12	--	--	0.26	1.22
GR	American Funds New Economy 529A	CNGAX	C-	(800) 421-0180	C / 4.9	8.59	8.59	21.80 /61	4.74 /51	13.38 /88	0.18	0.86
GR	● American Funds New Economy 529B	CNGBX	C-	(800) 421-0180	C / 5.4	8.39	8.16	20.86 /57	3.90 /42	12.48 /79	0.00	1.66
GR	American Funds New Economy 529C	CNGCX	C-	(800) 421-0180	C / 5.4	8.40	8.18	20.87 /57	3.91 /42	12.48 /79	0.00	1.66
GR	American Funds New Economy 529E	CNGEX	C	(800) 421-0180	C+ / 5.9	8.55	8.49	21.54 /60	4.48 /48	13.10 /85	0.00	1.11
GR	American Funds New Economy	CNGFX	C	(800) 421-0180	C+ / 6.3	8.64	8.70	22.07 /63	4.96 /54	13.61 /90	0.39	0.66
* GR	American Funds New Economy A	ANEFX	C-	(800) 421-0180	C / 5.0	8.60	8.63	21.90 /62	4.82 /52	13.46 /88	0.23	0.78
GR	● American Funds New Economy B	ANFBX	C-	(800) 421-0180	C / 5.5	8.41	8.22	20.96 /57	4.02 /43	12.59 /80	0.00	1.54
GR	American Funds New Economy C	ANFCX	C-	(800) 421-0180	C / 5.5	8.39	8.20	20.91 /57	3.98 /43	12.56 /80	0.00	1.59
GR	American Funds New Economy F1	ANFFX	C	(800) 421-0180	C+ / 6.2	8.63	8.63	21.86 /61	4.78 /52	13.43 /88	0.15	0.83
GR	American Funds New Economy F2	NEFFX	C	(800) 421-0180	C+ / 6.4	8.67	8.76	22.19 /63	5.06 /55	13.74 /91	0.49	0.57
GR	American Funds New Economy F3	FNEFX	C	(800) 421-0180	C+ / 6.2	8.63	8.66	21.93 /62	4.83 /52	13.47 /89	0.24	0.47
GR	American Funds New Economy R1	RNGAX	C-	(800) 421-0180	C / 5.5	8.42	8.23	20.98 /57	4.02 /43	12.61 /80	0.00	1.56
GR	American Funds New Economy R2	RNGBX	C-	(800) 421-0180	C / 5.5	8.43	8.21	20.97 /57	4.01 /43	12.61 /80	0.00	1.57
GR	American Funds New Economy R2E	RNNEX	C+	(800) 421-0180	C+ / 5.9	8.49	8.37	21.32 /59	4.56 /49	13.01 /84	0.18	1.30
GR	American Funds New Economy R3	RNGCX	C	(800) 421-0180	C+ / 5.9	8.53	8.47	21.49 /60	4.48 /48	13.10 /85	0.00	1.12
GR	American Funds New Economy R4	RNGEX	C	(800) 421-0180	C+ / 6.2	8.63	8.63	21.88 /62	4.80 /52	13.46 /88	0.22	0.81
GR	American Funds New Economy R5	RNGFX	C	(800) 421-0180	C+ / 6.5	8.68	8.80	22.26 /63	5.12 /55	13.79 /92	0.51	0.50
GR	American Funds New Economy R5E	RNGHX	C	(800) 421-0180	C+ / 6.3	8.65	8.71	22.03 /62	4.88 /53	13.50 /89	0.38	0.67
GR	American Funds New Economy R6	RNGGX	C	(800) 421-0180	C+ / 6.5	8.71	8.80	22.30 /64	5.17 /56	13.86 /92	0.60	0.46
GL	American Funds New Perspectve	CNPAX	C-	(800) 421-0180	C / 4.4	7.86	5.86	18.89 /47	5.19 /56	10.15 /59	0.65	0.86
GL	● American Funds New Perspectve	CNPBX	C	(800) 421-0180	C / 4.9	7.62	5.40	17.92 /42	4.35 /47	9.27 /53	0.00	1.66
GL	American Funds New Perspectve	CNPCX	C	(800) 421-0180	C / 4.9	7.64	5.46	17.99 /43	4.38 /47	9.30 /53	0.00	1.63
GL	American Funds New Perspectve	CNPEX	C	(800) 421-0180	C / 5.4	7.77	5.72	18.60 /45	4.93 /53	9.88 /57	0.47	1.09
GL	American Funds New Perspectve	CNPFX	C	(800) 421-0180	C+ / 5.8	7.89	5.98	19.15 /48	5.42 /59	10.38 /61	0.91	0.63
* GL	American Funds New Perspectve A	ANWPX	C-	(800) 421-0180	C / 4.5	7.88	5.90	18.99 /47	5.28 /57	10.24 /60	0.70	0.77
GL	● American Funds New Perspectve B	NPFBX	C	(800) 421-0180	C / 5.0	7.63	5.48	18.04 /43	4.48 /48	9.41 /54	0.00	1.53
GL	American Funds New Perspectve C	NPFCX	C	(800) 421-0180	C / 5.0	7.65	5.45	18.02 /43	4.44 /48	9.37 /54	0.00	1.57
GL	American Funds New Perspectve F1	NPFFX	C	(800) 421-0180	C+ / 5.6	7.83	5.84	18.88 /46	5.21 /56	10.18 /60	0.70	0.55
GL	American Funds New Perspectve F2	ANWFX	C	(800) 421-0180	C+ / 5.9	7.93	6.01	19.24 /48	5.50 /59	10.49 /62	0.99	0.55
GL	American Funds New Perspectve F3	FNPFX	C	(800) 421-0180	C+ / 5.7	7.91	5.93	19.03 /47	5.29 /57	10.25 /60	0.75	0.45
GL	American Funds New Perspectve R1	RNPAX	C	(800) 421-0180	C / 5.0	7.66	5.47	18.04 /43	4.44 /48	9.38 /54	0.00	1.56
GL	American Funds New Perspectve R2	RNPBX	C	(800) 421-0180	C / 5.0	7.63	5.46	18.05 /43	4.46 /48	9.40 /54	0.01	1.55
GL	American Funds New Perspectve	RPEBX	C+	(800) 421-0180	C / 5.4	7.74	5.62	18.40 /45	4.94 /53	9.76 /57	0.73	1.24
GL	American Funds New Perspectve R3	RNPCX	C	(800) 421-0180	C / 5.4	7.78	5.70	18.59 /45	4.92 /53	9.87 /57	0.44	1.11
GL	American Funds New Perspectve R4	RNPEX	C	(800) 421-0180	C+ / 5.7	7.86	5.86	18.96 /47	5.24 /57	10.21 /60	0.73	0.81
GL	American Funds New Perspectve R5	RNPFX	C+	(800) 421-0180	C+ / 5.9	7.94	6.05	19.30 /49	5.56 /60	10.54 /62	1.00	0.50
GL	American Funds New Perspectve	RNPHX	C	(800) 421-0180	C+ / 5.7	7.87	5.89	19.03 /47	5.29 /57	10.25 /60	0.85	0.71
GL	American Funds New Perspectve R6	RNPGX	C+	(800) 421-0180	C+ / 6.0	7.96	6.07	19.37 /49	5.61 /61	10.60 /63	1.05	0.45
GL	American Funds New World 529A	CNWAX	D-	(800) 421-0180	D / 1.8	7.80	3.16	20.17 /53	0.14 /14	3.23 /12	0.78	1.13
GL	● American Funds New World 529B	CNWBX	D-	(800) 421-0180	D- / 1.4	7.63	2.77	19.26 /48	-0.66 /11	2.40 / 9	0.00	1.97
GL	American Funds New World 529C	CNWCX	D-	(800) 421-0180	D- / 1.4	7.60	2.76	19.23 /48	-0.65 /11	2.41 / 9	0.11	1.92
GL	American Funds New World 529E	CNWEX	D-	(800) 421-0180	D / 1.6	7.76	3.05	19.93 /52	-0.08 /13	3.00 /11	0.64	1.34
GL	American Funds New World 529F1	CNWFX	D	(800) 421-0180	D+ / 2.7	7.85	3.26	20.42 /54	0.34 /15	3.44 /13	1.04	0.93
* GL	American Funds New World A	NEWFX	D-	(800) 421-0180	D / 1.8	7.82	3.16	20.23 /53	0.20 /14	3.29 /12	0.81	1.07
GL	● American Funds New World B	NEWBX	D-	(800) 421-0180	D- / 1.4	7.62	2.79	19.30 /49	-0.57 /11	2.51 / 9	0.00	1.87
GL	American Funds New World C	NEWCX	D-	(800) 421-0180	D- / 1.4	7.61	2.76	19.28 /48	-0.60 /11	2.47 / 9	0.10	1.88
GL	American Funds New World F1	NWFFX	D	(800) 421-0180	D+ / 2.6	7.81	3.19	20.27 /53	0.22 /14	3.32 /12	0.87	1.03

● Denotes fund is closed to new investors
* Denotes fund is included in Section II

www.thestreetratings.com

Risk Rating/Pts	3 Year Standard Deviation	Beta	NAV As of 2/28/17	Total $(Mil)	Cash %	Stocks %	Bonds %	Other %	Portfolio Turnover Ratio	Last Bull Market Return	Last Bear Market Return	Manager Quality Pct	Manager Tenure (Years)	Initial Purch. $	Additional Purch. $	Front End Load	Back End Load
B /8.3	7.9	0.67	11.46	N/A	0	0	0	100	16	N/A	N/A	35	1	0	0	0.0	0.0
B /8.2	8.0	0.68	11.39	11	0	0	0	100	16	N/A	N/A	30	1	0	0	0.0	0.0
B- /7.1	7.5	0.53	9.36	N/A	7	83	9	1	15	N/A	N/A	40	N/A	0	0	0.0	0.0
B- /7.0	7.5	0.53	9.29	7	7	83	9	1	15	N/A	N/A	34	N/A	0	0	0.0	0.0
U /	N/A	N/A	10.07	561	0	0	0	100	4	N/A	N/A	N/A	N/A	0	0	0.0	0.0
C /4.7	12.1	0.99	38.61	449	0	90	9	1	25	127.7	-18.7	12	26	250	50	5.8	0.0
C /4.7	12.1	0.99	36.09	N/A	0	90	9	1	25	117.9	-19.0	8	26	250	50	0.0	0.0
C /4.7	12.0	0.99	36.03	120	0	90	9	1	25	118.1	-19.0	8	26	250	50	0.0	0.0
C /4.7	12.0	0.99	38.13	23	0	90	9	1	25	124.6	-18.8	11	26	250	50	0.0	0.0
C /4.7	12.1	0.99	38.55	36	0	90	9	1	25	130.2	-18.6	14	26	250	50	0.0	0.0
C /4.7	12.1	0.99	38.96	10,198	0	90	9	1	25	128.6	-18.7	13	26	250	50	5.8	0.0
C /4.7	12.1	0.99	36.13	2	0	90	9	1	25	119.3	-18.9	9	26	250	50	0.0	0.0
C /4.7	12.1	0.99	35.56	473	0	90	9	1	25	118.8	-18.9	8	26	250	50	0.0	0.0
C /4.7	12.0	0.99	39.07	314	0	90	9	1	25	128.3	-18.7	13	26	250	50	0.0	0.0
C /4.7	12.1	0.99	38.90	854	0	90	9	1	25	131.6	-18.6	14	26	250	50	0.0	0.0
C /5.1	12.1	0.99	38.97	N/A	0	90	9	1	25	128.6	-18.7	13	26	250	50	0.0	0.0
C /4.7	12.0	0.99	36.61	48	0	90	9	1	25	119.4	-18.9	9	26	250	50	0.0	0.0
C /4.7	12.0	0.99	36.81	169	0	90	9	1	25	119.4	-19.0	9	26	250	50	0.0	0.0
C+ /5.8	12.1	0.99	38.53	4	0	90	9	1	25	123.5	-18.9	11	26	250	50	0.0	0.0
C /4.7	12.1	0.99	38.20	293	0	90	9	1	25	124.7	-18.8	11	26	250	50	0.0	0.0
C /4.7	12.1	0.99	38.62	374	0	90	9	1	25	128.5	-18.7	13	26	250	50	0.0	0.0
C /4.7	12.1	0.99	39.13	112	0	90	9	1	25	132.2	-18.6	15	26	250	50	0.0	0.0
C /5.1	12.1	0.99	38.81	N/A	0	90	9	1	25	128.9	-18.7	13	26	250	50	0.0	0.0
C /4.7	12.1	0.99	39.00	2,160	0	90	9	1	25	132.9	-18.6	15	26	250	50	0.0	0.0
C /5.5	10.6	0.81	37.39	1,673	0	92	6	2	22	92.0	-19.8	96	13	250	50	5.8	0.0
C+ /5.6	10.6	0.81	36.78	1	0	92	6	2	22	83.9	-20.0	94	13	250	50	0.0	0.0
C+ /5.6	10.6	0.81	36.41	356	0	92	6	2	22	84.0	-20.0	94	13	250	50	0.0	0.0
C+ /5.6	10.6	0.81	37.03	76	0	92	6	2	22	89.4	-19.9	95	13	250	50	0.0	0.0
C /5.5	10.6	0.81	37.30	83	0	92	6	2	22	94.2	-19.7	96	13	250	50	0.0	0.0
C /5.5	10.6	0.81	37.80	36,773	0	92	6	2	22	92.9	-19.7	96	13	250	50	5.8	0.0
C+ /5.6	10.6	0.81	37.29	10	0	92	6	2	22	85.0	-20.0	94	13	250	50	0.0	0.0
C+ /5.6	10.5	0.81	36.48	1,337	0	92	6	2	22	84.7	-20.0	94	13	250	50	0.0	0.0
C /5.5	10.6	0.81	37.57	1,553	0	92	6	2	22	92.3	-19.8	96	13	250	50	0.0	0.0
C /5.5	10.6	0.81	37.70	5,185	0	92	6	2	22	95.3	-19.7	96	13	250	50	0.0	0.0
C+ /5.6	10.6	0.81	37.81	N/A	0	92	6	2	22	92.9	-19.7	96	13	250	50	0.0	0.0
C+ /5.6	10.6	0.81	36.19	82	0	92	6	2	22	84.8	-20.0	94	13	250	50	0.0	0.0
C+ /5.6	10.6	0.81	36.52	522	0	92	6	2	22	85.0	-20.0	94	13	250	50	0.0	0.0
C+ /6.5	10.6	0.81	37.31	36	0	92	6	2	22	88.2	-20.0	95	13	250	50	0.0	0.0
C+ /5.6	10.6	0.81	36.99	1,585	0	92	6	2	22	89.4	-19.9	95	13	250	50	0.0	0.0
C /5.5	10.6	0.81	37.31	1,832	0	92	6	2	22	92.6	-19.8	96	13	250	50	0.0	0.0
C /5.5	10.6	0.81	37.77	1,508	0	92	6	2	22	95.8	-19.7	96	13	250	50	0.0	0.0
C+ /5.6	10.6	0.81	37.64	1	0	92	6	2	22	93.0	-19.7	96	13	250	50	0.0	0.0
C /5.5	10.6	0.81	37.82	10,569	0	92	6	2	22	96.2	-19.6	96	13	250	50	0.0	0.0
C /5.0	11.3	0.83	54.69	726	2	83	14	1	30	38.4	-22.0	76	18	250	50	5.8	0.0
C /5.0	11.3	0.83	53.88	1	2	83	14	1	30	32.5	-22.2	68	18	250	50	0.0	0.0
C /5.0	11.3	0.83	53.34	149	2	83	14	1	30	32.6	-22.2	68	18	250	50	0.0	0.0
C /5.0	11.3	0.83	54.31	34	2	83	14	1	30	36.7	-22.0	74	18	250	50	0.0	0.0
C /4.9	11.3	0.83	54.66	47	2	83	14	1	30	39.9	-21.9	77	18	250	50	0.0	0.0
C /5.0	11.3	0.83	55.14	11,055	2	83	14	1	30	38.9	-21.9	76	18	250	50	5.8	0.0
C /5.0	11.3	0.82	54.53	5	2	83	14	1	30	33.2	-22.2	69	18	250	50	0.0	0.0
C /5.0	11.3	0.83	53.31	749	2	83	14	1	30	33.0	-22.2	69	18	250	50	0.0	0.0
C /5.0	11.3	0.83	54.77	1,188	2	83	14	1	30	39.1	-21.9	76	18	250	50	0.0	0.0

				99 Pct = Best / 0 Pct = Worst		PERFORMANCE							
Fund Type	Fund Name	Ticker Symbol	Overall Investment Rating	Phone		Perfor-mance Rating/Pts	Total Return % through 2/28/17			Annualized		Incl. in Returns	
							3 Mo	6 Mo	1Yr / Pct	3Yr / Pct	5Yr / Pct	Dividend Yield	Expense Ratio
GL	American Funds New World F2	NFFFX	D	(800) 421-0180		D+ / 2.9	7.90	3.34	20.60 /55	0.50 /16	3.60 /13	1.19	0.76
EM	American Funds New World F3	FNWFX	D	(800) 421-0180		D+ / 2.7	7.87	3.22	20.30 /54	0.22 /14	3.31 /12	0.86	0.66
GL	American Funds New World R1	RNWAX	D-	(800) 421-0180		D- / 1.4	7.60	2.77	19.33 /49	-0.56 /11	2.52 / 9	0.16	1.83
GL	American Funds New World R2	RNWBX	D-	(800) 421-0180		D- / 1.5	7.63	2.82	19.40 /49	-0.53 /11	2.54 / 9	0.24	1.79
EM	American Funds New World R2E	RNEBX	D	(800) 421-0180		D / 1.6	7.72	2.97	19.79 /51	-0.17 /13	2.81 /10	0.90	1.45
GL	American Funds New World R3	RNWCX	D-	(800) 421-0180		D / 1.6	7.74	3.03	19.93 /52	-0.08 /13	3.01 /11	0.69	1.34
GL	American Funds New World R4	RNWEX	D	(800) 421-0180		D+ / 2.7	7.84	3.21	20.32 /54	0.25 /14	3.35 /12	1.00	1.01
GL	American Funds New World R5	RNWFX	D	(800) 421-0180		D+ / 2.9	7.91	3.35	20.69 /56	0.56 /16	3.66 /14	1.20	0.71
EM	American Funds New World R5E	RNWHX	D	(800) 421-0180		D+ / 2.7	7.88	3.24	20.39 /54	0.27 /15	3.34 /12	1.30	0.91
GL	American Funds New World R6	RNWGX	D	(800) 421-0180		D+ / 2.9	7.93	3.37	20.72 /56	0.60 /16	3.71 /14	1.28	0.65
GI	American Funds Ret Inc Cons A	NAARX	U	(800) 421-0180		U /	3.51	1.82	9.00 / 9	--	--	1.90	0.83
GI	American Funds Ret Inc Cons C	NGCRX	U	(800) 421-0180		U /	3.34	1.50	8.22 / 8	--	--	1.49	1.53
GI	American Funds Ret Inc Enhanced A	NDARX	U	(800) 421-0180		U /	5.17	4.02	14.48 /28	--	--	2.27	0.80
GI	American Funds Ret Inc Enhanced C	NDCRX	U	(800) 421-0180		U /	5.01	3.60	13.73 /24	--	--	1.84	1.50
GI	American Funds Ret Inc Enhanced	FGFWX	U	(800) 421-0180		U /	5.23	4.12	14.81 /29	--	--	2.59	0.56
GI	American Funds Ret Inc Moderate A	NBARX	U	(800) 421-0180		U /	4.38	3.08	11.90 /18	--	--	2.12	0.77
GI	American Funds Ret Inc Moderate C	NBCRX	U	(800) 421-0180		U /	4.11	2.66	10.99 /14	--	--	1.71	1.47
SC	American Funds SMALLCAP World	CSPAX	D+	(800) 421-0180		C / 4.6	7.05	6.42	24.77 /72	4.22 /45	9.99 /58	0.25	1.17
SC	● American Funds SMALLCAP World	CSPBX	D+	(800) 421-0180		C / 5.0	6.80	5.97	23.71 /69	3.37 /35	9.10 /51	0.00	1.99
SC	American Funds SMALLCAP World	CSPCX	D+	(800) 421-0180		C / 5.1	6.84	6.03	23.78 /69	3.41 /36	9.12 /52	0.00	1.96
SC	American Funds SMALLCAP World	CSPEX	C-	(800) 421-0180		C+ / 5.6	6.98	6.31	24.48 /72	3.99 /43	9.73 /56	0.09	1.38
SC	American Funds SMALLCAP World	CSPFX	C-	(800) 421-0180		C+ / 6.0	7.12	6.54	25.03 /73	4.44 /48	10.22 /60	0.47	0.96
* SC	American Funds SMALLCAP World A	SMCWX	D+	(800) 421-0180		C / 4.6	7.04	6.46	24.81 /73	4.29 /46	10.06 /59	0.31	1.10
SC	● American Funds SMALLCAP World B	SCWBX	D+	(800) 421-0180		C / 5.1	6.83	6.02	23.85 /69	3.49 /37	9.22 /52	0.00	1.87
SC	American Funds SMALLCAP World C	SCWCX	D+	(800) 421-0180		C / 5.1	6.84	6.04	23.82 /69	3.46 /37	9.18 /52	0.00	1.90
SC	American Funds SMALLCAP World	SCWFX	C-	(800) 421-0180		C+ / 5.8	7.04	6.45	24.81 /73	4.28 /46	10.06 /59	0.31	1.11
SC	American Funds SMALLCAP World	SMCFX	C-	(800) 421-0180		C+ / 6.1	7.13	6.61	25.17 /74	4.58 /50	10.37 /61	0.59	0.82
GL	American Funds SMALLCAP World	SFCWX	C	(800) 421-0180		C+ / 5.9	7.09	6.51	24.87 /73	4.31 /46	10.07 /59	0.32	0.71
SC	American Funds SMALLCAP World	RSLAX	D+	(800) 421-0180		C / 5.2	6.86	6.05	23.88 /69	3.52 /37	9.25 /53	0.00	1.85
SC	American Funds SMALLCAP World	RSLBX	C-	(800) 421-0180		C / 5.2	6.86	6.05	23.91 /69	3.52 /37	9.25 /53	0.00	1.84
GL	American Funds SMALLCAP World	RSEBX	C+	(800) 421-0180		C / 5.5	6.95	6.23	24.33 /71	4.00 /43	9.61 /55	0.14	1.51
SC	American Funds SMALLCAP World	RSLCX	C-	(800) 421-0180		C+ / 5.6	6.98	6.31	24.49 /72	3.99 /43	9.74 /56	0.08	1.39
SC	American Funds SMALLCAP World	RSLEX	C-	(800) 421-0180		C+ / 5.8	7.05	6.47	24.85 /73	4.32 /47	10.10 /59	0.35	1.07
SC	American Funds SMALLCAP World	RSLFX	C	(800) 421-0180		C+ / 6.1	7.13	6.64	25.25 /74	4.64 /50	10.44 /62	0.59	0.77
GL	American Funds SMALLCAP World	RSLDX	C	(800) 421-0180		C+ / 5.9	7.12	6.54	25.01 /73	4.37 /47	10.11 /59	0.71	0.98
SC	American Funds SMALLCAP World	RLLGX	C	(800) 421-0180		C+ / 6.2	7.16	6.66	25.31 /74	4.69 /51	10.49 /62	0.67	0.71
AA	American Funds Tax Adv Income A	TAIAX	C+	(800) 421-0180		C- / 3.2	4.45	2.27	11.03 /15	5.58 /60	--	2.44	0.78
AA	American Funds Tax Adv Income B	TXABX	B-	(800) 421-0180		C- / 3.4	4.38	1.99	10.36 /12	4.89 /53	--	1.57	1.48
AA	American Funds Tax Adv Income C	TAICX	B-	(800) 421-0180		C- / 3.4	4.25	1.90	10.26 /12	4.84 /52	--	1.89	1.49
AA	American Funds Tax Adv Income F1	TAIFX	B	(800) 421-0180		C- / 4.0	4.45	2.27	11.06 /15	5.64 /61	--	2.56	0.76
AA	American Funds Tax Adv Income F2	TXIFX	B	(800) 421-0180		C- / 4.2	4.59	2.48	11.40 /16	5.89 /63	--	2.78	0.50
AA	American Funds Tax Adv Income F3	TYIFX	C+	(800) 421-0180		C- / 4.0	4.53	2.35	11.12 /15	5.61 /61	--	2.53	0.39
AA	American Funds Tgt Dte Ret 2010 A	AAATX	C	(800) 421-0180		D+ / 2.4	3.86	3.06	11.41 /16	4.44 /48	6.48 /31	1.58	0.71
AA	American Funds Tgt Dte Ret 2010 B	BBATX	C+	(800) 421-0180		C- / 3.0	3.75	2.95	10.94 /14	3.82 /41	5.78 /27	0.00	1.50
AA	American Funds Tgt Dte Ret 2010 C	CCATX	C+	(800) 421-0180		D+ / 2.8	3.62	2.61	10.46 /13	3.63 /38	5.67 /26	1.13	1.46
AA	American Funds Tgt Dte Ret 2010 F1	FAATX	B-	(800) 421-0180		C- / 3.3	3.83	3.03	11.39 /16	4.44 /48	6.37 /31	1.83	0.71
AA	American Funds Tgt Dte Ret 2010 F2	FBATX	B-	(800) 421-0180		C- / 3.5	3.87	3.07	11.64 /17	4.68 /51	6.63 /32	1.97	0.45
AA	American Funds Tgt Dte Ret 2010 F3	DJTFX	C+	(800) 421-0180		C- / 3.3	3.76	2.96	11.30 /15	4.41 /48	6.46 /31	1.68	N/A
AA	American Funds Tgt Dte Ret 2010 R1	RAATX	C	(800) 421-0180		D+ / 2.8	3.70	2.69	10.52 /13	3.62 /38	5.64 /26	0.84	1.50
AA	American Funds Tgt Dte Ret 2010 R2	RBATX	C	(800) 421-0180		D+ / 2.8	3.56	2.66	10.53 /13	3.68 /39	5.74 /27	0.99	1.45
AA	American Funds Tgt Dte Ret 2010	RBEAX	C+	(800) 421-0180		C- / 3.1	3.67	2.77	10.83 /14	4.11 /44	6.02 /28	1.57	1.14
AA	American Funds Tgt Dte Ret 2010 R3	RCATX	C	(800) 421-0180		C- / 3.1	3.72	2.82	10.97 /14	4.06 /44	6.13 /29	1.44	1.03

● Denotes fund is closed to new investors

* Denotes fund is included in Section II

RISK			NET ASSETS		ASSET				Portfolio Turnover Ratio	BULL / BEAR		FUND MANAGER		MINIMUMS		LOADS	
	3 Year		NAV As of 2/28/17	Total $(Mil)	Cash %	Stocks %	Bonds %	Other %		Last Bull Market Return	Last Bear Market Return	Manager Quality Pct	Manager Tenure (Years)	Initial Purch. $	Additional Purch. $	Front End Load	Back End Load
Risk Rating/Pts	Standard Deviation	Beta															
C /4.9	11.3	0.82	55.02	7,252	2	83	14	1	30	41.1	-21.9	78	18	250	50	0.0	0.0
C /5.5	11.3	0.63	55.17	10	2	83	14	1	30	38.9	-21.9	63	18	250	50	0.0	0.0
C /5.0	11.3	0.83	53.46	27	2	83	14	1	30	33.3	-22.2	69	18	250	50	0.0	0.0
C /5.0	11.3	0.83	53.45	309	2	83	14	1	30	33.5	-22.2	69	18	250	50	0.0	0.0
C+ /6.5	11.3	0.63	54.62	11	2	83	14	1	30	35.3	-22.1	58	18	250	50	0.0	0.0
C /5.0	11.3	0.83	54.38	548	2	83	14	1	30	36.8	-22.0	74	18	250	50	0.0	0.0
C /4.9	11.3	0.83	54.85	607	2	83	14	1	30	39.3	-21.9	77	18	250	50	0.0	0.0
C /4.9	11.3	0.83	55.27	313	2	83	14	1	30	41.6	-21.8	79	18	250	50	0.0	0.0
C /5.5	11.3	0.63	54.74	N/A	2	83	14	1	30	39.1	-21.9	64	18	250	50	0.0	0.0
C /4.9	11.3	0.82	55.13	3,116	2	83	14	1	30	41.9	-21.8	79	18	250	50	0.0	0.0
U /	N/A	N/A	10.62	174	0	0	0	100	0	N/A	N/A	N/A	2	250	50	5.8	0.0
U /	N/A	N/A	10.58	42	0	0	0	100	0	N/A	N/A	N/A	2	250	50	0.0	0.0
U /	N/A	N/A	10.99	290	0	0	0	100	3	N/A	N/A	N/A	2	250	50	5.8	0.0
U /	N/A	N/A	10.95	41	0	0	0	100	3	N/A	N/A	N/A	2	250	50	0.0	0.0
U /	N/A	N/A	11.00	39	0	0	0	100	3	N/A	N/A	N/A	2	250	50	0.0	0.0
U /	N/A	N/A	10.81	322	0	0	0	100	0	N/A	N/A	N/A	2	250	50	5.8	0.0
U /	N/A	N/A	10.76	49	0	0	0	100	0	N/A	N/A	N/A	2	250	50	0.0	0.0
C /4.3	12.2	0.65	48.57	1,068	1	90	8	1	29	96.0	-24.4	71	26	250	50	5.8	0.0
C- /4.1	12.1	0.65	44.76	1	1	90	8	1	29	87.6	-24.7	61	26	250	50	0.0	0.0
C- /4.1	12.2	0.65	44.51	289	1	90	8	1	29	87.8	-24.7	62	26	250	50	0.0	0.0
C /4.3	12.2	0.65	47.36	54	1	90	8	1	29	93.6	-24.5	69	26	250	50	0.0	0.0
C /4.4	12.2	0.65	49.02	97	1	90	8	1	29	98.3	-24.4	74	26	250	50	0.0	0.0
C /4.3	12.2	0.65	49.07	19,106	1	90	8	1	29	96.7	-24.4	72	26	250	50	5.8	0.0
C- /4.1	12.1	0.65	44.40	7	1	90	8	1	29	88.7	-24.7	63	26	250	50	0.0	0.0
C- /4.1	12.1	0.65	43.71	797	1	90	8	1	29	88.4	-24.7	62	26	250	50	0.0	0.0
C /4.3	12.2	0.65	48.55	734	1	90	8	1	29	96.8	-24.4	72	26	250	50	0.0	0.0
C /4.4	12.2	0.65	49.57	2,733	1	90	8	1	29	99.8	-24.4	75	26	250	50	0.0	0.0
C /5.3	12.2	0.78	49.09	1	1	90	8	1	29	96.8	-24.4	94	26	250	50	0.0	0.0
C- /4.1	12.1	0.65	45.03	31	1	90	8	1	29	89.0	-24.7	63	26	250	50	0.0	0.0
C- /4.1	12.1	0.65	45.04	603	1	90	8	1	29	89.1	-24.7	63	26	250	50	0.0	0.0
C+ /6.0	12.2	0.78	48.90	9	1	90	8	1	29	92.2	-24.6	93	26	250	50	0.0	0.0
C /4.3	12.2	0.65	47.28	782	1	90	8	1	29	93.6	-24.5	69	26	250	50	0.0	0.0
C /4.3	12.2	0.65	48.70	767	1	90	8	1	29	97.1	-24.4	72	26	250	50	0.0	0.0
C /4.4	12.2	0.65	50.21	371	1	90	8	1	29	100.4	-24.3	75	26	250	50	0.0	0.0
C /5.3	12.2	0.78	48.97	10	1	90	8	1	29	97.1	-24.4	94	26	250	50	0.0	0.0
C /4.4	12.1	0.65	49.68	3,999	1	90	8	1	29	100.9	-24.3	75	26	250	50	0.0	0.0
B+ /9.1	5.0	0.76	12.79	980	0	47	52	1	1	N/A	N/A	73	5	250	50	3.8	0.0
B+ /9.2	5.0	0.76	12.85	N/A	0	47	52	1	1	N/A	N/A	65	5	250	50	0.0	0.0
B+ /9.1	5.0	0.76	12.71	169	0	47	52	1	1	N/A	N/A	64	5	250	50	0.0	0.0
B+ /9.1	5.0	0.76	12.79	61	0	47	52	1	1	N/A	N/A	73	5	250	50	0.0	0.0
B+ /9.1	5.0	0.77	12.81	72	0	47	52	1	1	N/A	N/A	75	5	250	50	0.0	0.0
B /8.1	5.0	0.76	12.80	N/A	0	47	52	1	0	N/A	N/A	73	5	250	50	0.0	0.0
B /8.2	5.1	0.77	10.45	579	0	42	57	1	14	50.6	-6.9	58	10	250	50	5.8	0.0
B+ /9.2	5.2	0.78	10.62	N/A	0	42	57	1	14	45.2	-7.2	49	10	250	50	0.0	0.0
B+ /9.2	5.0	0.76	10.32	24	0	42	57	1	14	44.5	-7.2	49	10	250	50	0.0	0.0
B+ /9.2	5.1	0.77	10.41	6	0	42	57	1	14	49.6	-7.0	58	10	250	50	0.0	0.0
B+ /9.2	5.1	0.77	10.43	5	0	42	57	1	14	51.6	-6.9	61	10	250	50	0.0	0.0
B /8.2	5.1	0.77	10.44	N/A	0	42	57	1	14	50.5	-6.9	58	10	250	50	0.0	0.0
B /8.4	5.1	0.76	10.40	5	0	42	57	1	14	44.4	-7.2	48	10	250	50	0.0	0.0
B /8.3	5.1	0.77	10.32	130	0	42	57	1	14	45.0	-7.3	48	10	250	50	0.0	0.0
B+ /9.2	5.1	0.77	10.33	21	0	42	57	1	14	47.0	-7.1	54	10	250	50	0.0	0.0
B /8.3	5.1	0.78	10.38	286	0	42	57	1	14	47.9	-7.0	53	10	250	50	0.0	0.0

Fund Type	Fund Name	Ticker Symbol	Overall Investment Rating	Phone	Performance Rating/Pts	3 Mo	6 Mo	1Yr / Pct	3Yr / Pct	5Yr / Pct	Dividend Yield	Expense Ratio
	99 Pct = Best 0 Pct = Worst				**PERFORMANCE** Total Return % through 2/28/17 — Annualized						Incl. in Returns	
AA	American Funds Tgt Dte Ret 2010 R4	RDATX	C+	(800) 421-0180	C- / 3.3	3.79	2.99	11.34 /16	4.42 /48	6.47 /31	1.71	0.71
AA	American Funds Tgt Dte Ret 2010 R5	REATX	C+	(800) 421-0180	C- / 3.6	3.96	3.17	11.69 /17	4.74 /51	6.80 /33	1.98	0.41
AA	American Funds Tgt Dte Ret 2010	RHATX	C+	(800) 421-0180	C- / 3.4	3.94	3.14	11.62 /16	4.53 /49	6.53 /32	1.93	0.50
AA	American Funds Tgt Dte Ret 2010 R6	RFTTX	C+	(800) 421-0180	C- / 3.6	3.91	3.22	11.77 /17	4.80 /52	6.84 /34	2.02	0.35
AA	American Funds Tgt Dte Ret 2015 A	AABTX	C	(800) 421-0180	D+ / 2.5	3.96	3.30	11.92 /18	4.56 /49	7.16 /36	1.51	0.70
AA	American Funds Tgt Dte Ret 2015 B	BBBTX	C+	(800) 421-0180	C- / 3.1	3.95	3.10	11.34 /16	3.97 /43	6.47 /31	0.00	1.47
AA	American Funds Tgt Dte Ret 2015 C	CCBTX	C+	(800) 421-0180	C- / 3.0	3.84	2.88	11.05 /15	3.78 /40	6.35 /31	1.01	1.46
AA	American Funds Tgt Dte Ret 2015 F1	FAKTX	B-	(800) 421-0180	C- / 3.5	4.02	3.26	11.92 /18	4.55 /49	7.04 /35	1.75	0.71
AA	American Funds Tgt Dte Ret 2015 F2	FBBTX	B-	(800) 421-0180	C- / 3.7	4.04	3.38	12.23 /19	4.82 /52	7.32 /37	1.87	0.44
AA	American Funds Tgt Dte Ret 2015 F3	FDBTX	C+	(800) 421-0180	C- / 3.6	4.05	3.39	12.02 /18	4.59 /50	7.17 /36	1.60	N/A
AA	American Funds Tgt Dte Ret 2015 R1	RAJTX	C	(800) 421-0180	D+ / 2.9	3.78	2.82	11.02 /14	3.75 /40	6.33 /30	0.86	1.49
AA	American Funds Tgt Dte Ret 2015 R2	RBJTX	C	(800) 421-0180	C- / 3.0	3.78	2.83	11.02 /14	3.82 /41	6.40 /31	0.86	1.45
AA	American Funds Tgt Dte Ret 2015	RBEJX	C+	(800) 421-0180	C- / 3.2	3.83	3.07	11.44 /16	4.23 /46	6.69 /33	1.55	1.14
AA	American Funds Tgt Dte Ret 2015 R3	RCJTX	C+	(800) 421-0180	C- / 3.3	3.86	3.10	11.57 /16	4.23 /46	6.81 /33	1.32	1.03
AA	American Funds Tgt Dte Ret 2015 R4	RDBTX	C+	(800) 421-0180	C- / 3.5	3.97	3.22	11.85 /17	4.55 /49	7.14 /35	1.62	0.71
AA	American Funds Tgt Dte Ret 2015 R5	REJTX	C+	(800) 421-0180	C- / 3.7	4.05	3.39	12.29 /19	4.87 /53	7.48 /38	1.89	0.40
AA	American Funds Tgt Dte Ret 2015	RHBTX	C+	(800) 421-0180	C- / 3.6	4.04	3.37	12.13 /18	4.65 /50	7.21 /36	1.85	0.49
AA	American Funds Tgt Dte Ret 2015 R6	RFJTX	C+	(800) 421-0180	C- / 3.8	4.11	3.45	12.27 /19	4.94 /53	7.53 /38	1.93	0.35
AA	American Funds Tgt Dte Ret 2020 A	AACTX	C	(800) 421-0180	D+ / 2.8	4.22	3.60	12.81 /21	4.83 /52	7.96 /42	1.20	0.72
AA	American Funds Tgt Dte Ret 2020 B	BBCTX	C+	(800) 421-0180	C- / 3.2	4.02	3.22	11.84 /17	4.02 /43	7.13 /35	0.00	1.48
AA	American Funds Tgt Dte Ret 2020 C	CCCTX	C+	(800) 421-0180	C- / 3.3	4.16	3.26	11.95 /18	4.05 /43	7.15 /36	0.75	1.47
AA	American Funds Tgt Dte Ret 2020 F1	FAOTX	B-	(800) 421-0180	C- / 3.8	4.28	3.65	12.70 /20	4.81 /52	7.83 /41	1.39	0.73
AA	American Funds Tgt Dte Ret 2020 F2	FBCTX	B	(800) 421-0180	C- / 4.1	4.34	3.80	13.14 /22	5.10 /55	8.13 /43	1.54	0.46
AA	American Funds Tgt Dte Ret 2020 F3	FCCTX	C+	(800) 421-0180	C- / 3.9	4.31	3.69	12.91 /21	4.86 /53	7.98 /42	1.27	N/A
AA	American Funds Tgt Dte Ret 2020 R1	RACTX	C+	(800) 421-0180	C- / 3.2	4.00	3.19	11.89 /18	3.99 /43	7.11 /35	0.52	1.51
AA	American Funds Tgt Dte Ret 2020 R2	RBCTX	C+	(800) 421-0180	C- / 3.3	4.08	3.27	11.90 /18	4.09 /44	7.19 /36	0.58	1.47
AA	American Funds Tgt Dte Ret 2020	RBEHX	B-	(800) 421-0180	C- / 3.5	4.18	3.38	12.24 /19	4.47 /48	7.47 /38	1.21	1.15
AA	American Funds Tgt Dte Ret 2020 R3	RCCTX	C+	(800) 421-0180	C- / 3.6	4.15	3.52	12.40 /19	4.51 /49	7.60 /39	1.01	1.04
AA	American Funds Tgt Dte Ret 2020 R4	RDCTX	C+	(800) 421-0180	C- / 3.8	4.26	3.64	12.76 /21	4.84 /52	7.95 /42	1.30	0.73
AA	American Funds Tgt Dte Ret 2020 R5	RECTX	C+	(800) 421-0180	C- / 4.1	4.32	3.80	13.06 /22	5.14 /56	8.28 /44	1.55	0.42
AA	American Funds Tgt Dte Ret 2020	RHCTX	C+	(800) 421-0180	C- / 4.0	4.31	3.78	13.03 /22	4.92 /53	8.02 /42	1.52	0.51
AA	American Funds Tgt Dte Ret 2020 R6	RRCTX	C+	(800) 421-0180	C- / 4.1	4.38	3.85	13.14 /22	5.19 /56	8.33 /45	1.59	0.37
AA	American Funds Tgt Dte Ret 2025 A	AADTX	C	(800) 421-0180	C- / 3.2	4.80	4.37	14.54 /28	5.04 /55	9.15 /52	1.07	0.74
AA	American Funds Tgt Dte Ret 2025 B	BBDTX	C	(800) 421-0180	C- / 3.7	4.52	3.92	13.63 /24	4.21 /45	8.30 /45	0.00	1.51
AA	American Funds Tgt Dte Ret 2025 C	CCDTX	C	(800) 421-0180	C- / 3.7	4.56	3.96	13.74 /24	4.22 /45	8.31 /45	0.63	1.49
AA	American Funds Tgt Dte Ret 2025 F1	FAPTX	C+	(800) 421-0180	C / 4.3	4.82	4.39	14.61 /28	5.01 /54	9.02 /51	1.30	0.74
AA	American Funds Tgt Dte Ret 2025 F2	FBDTX	B-	(800) 421-0180	C / 4.6	4.91	4.56	14.96 /30	5.29 /57	9.31 /53	1.40	0.48
AA	American Funds Tgt Dte Ret 2025 F3	FDDTX	C	(800) 421-0180	C / 4.3	4.80	4.37	14.54 /28	5.04 /55	9.15 /52	1.14	N/A
AA	American Funds Tgt Dte Ret 2025 R1	RADTX	C+	(800) 421-0180	C- / 3.7	4.60	3.91	13.70 /24	4.21 /45	8.30 /45	0.43	1.53
AA	American Funds Tgt Dte Ret 2025 R2	RBDTX	C+	(800) 421-0180	C- / 3.7	4.60	3.99	13.73 /24	4.29 /46	8.39 /45	0.49	1.48
AA	American Funds Tgt Dte Ret 2025	RBEDX	C+	(800) 421-0180	C- / 4.0	4.69	4.18	14.11 /26	4.69 /51	8.66 /48	1.09	1.18
AA	American Funds Tgt Dte Ret 2025 R3	RCDTX	C+	(800) 421-0180	C- / 4.1	4.74	4.22	14.28 /27	4.69 /51	8.79 /49	0.89	1.06
AA	American Funds Tgt Dte Ret 2025 R4	RDDTX	C+	(800) 421-0180	C / 4.3	4.75	4.33	14.51 /28	5.01 /54	9.12 /52	1.17	0.75
AA	American Funds Tgt Dte Ret 2025 R5	REDTX	C+	(800) 421-0180	C / 4.6	4.89	4.55	14.96 /30	5.35 /58	9.48 /54	1.41	0.44
AA	American Funds Tgt Dte Ret 2025	RHDTX	C	(800) 421-0180	C / 4.4	4.80	4.45	14.75 /29	5.12 /55	9.20 /52	1.37	0.53
AA	American Funds Tgt Dte Ret 2025 R6	RFDTX	C+	(800) 421-0180	C / 4.6	4.86	4.52	14.95 /30	5.38 /58	9.51 /55	1.45	0.39
AA	American Funds Tgt Dte Ret 2030 A	AAETX	C	(800) 421-0180	C- / 4.1	5.63	5.46	17.46 /40	5.61 /61	9.90 /58	0.98	0.74
AA	American Funds Tgt Dte Ret 2030 B	BBETX	C+	(800) 421-0180	C / 4.6	5.42	5.00	16.47 /36	4.80 /52	9.06 /51	0.00	1.52
AA	American Funds Tgt Dte Ret 2030 C	CCETX	C+	(800) 421-0180	C / 4.6	5.46	5.04	16.57 /37	4.80 /52	9.06 /51	0.52	1.51
AA	American Funds Tgt Dte Ret 2030 F1	FAETX	B	(800) 421-0180	C / 5.3	5.59	5.42	17.36 /40	5.58 /60	9.76 /57	1.21	0.76
AA	American Funds Tgt Dte Ret 2030 F2	FBETX	B-	(800) 421-0180	C / 5.5	5.66	5.58	17.67 /41	5.86 /63	10.05 /59	1.29	0.50
AA	American Funds Tgt Dte Ret 2030 F3	FCETX	C+	(800) 421-0180	C / 5.3	5.63	5.46	17.46 /40	5.61 /61	9.90 /58	1.04	N/A

RISK			NET ASSETS		ASSET				Portfolio	BULL / BEAR		FUND MANAGER		MINIMUMS		LOADS	
	3 Year		NAV							Last Bull	Last Bear	Manager	Manager	Initial	Additional	Front	Back
Risk Rating/Pts	Standard Deviation	Beta	As of 2/28/17	Total $(Mil)	Cash %	Stocks %	Bonds %	Other %	Turnover Ratio	Market Return	Market Return	Quality Pct	Tenure (Years)	Purch. $	Purch. $	End Load	End Load
B /8.2	5.1	0.77	10.43	322	0	42	57	1	14	50.6	-6.9	58	10	250	50	0.0	0.0
B /8.2	5.1	0.77	10.50	137	0	42	57	1	14	53.1	-6.7	62	10	250	50	0.0	0.0
B /8.2	5.1	0.78	10.41	39	0	42	57	1	14	51.0	-6.9	59	10	250	50	0.0	0.0
B /8.2	5.1	0.78	10.47	719	0	42	57	1	14	53.5	-6.8	62	10	250	50	0.0	0.0
B /8.2	5.2	0.81	11.06	981	0	44	55	1	8	57.4	-9.0	57	10	250	50	5.8	0.0
B+ /9.2	5.3	0.81	11.13	N/A	0	44	55	1	8	51.9	-9.3	49	10	250	50	0.0	0.0
B+ /9.2	5.2	0.80	10.93	43	0	44	55	1	8	51.1	-9.3	47	10	250	50	0.0	0.0
B+ /9.1	5.3	0.81	11.00	13	0	44	55	1	8	56.3	-9.1	56	10	250	50	0.0	0.0
B+ /9.2	5.3	0.81	11.05	15	0	44	55	1	8	58.6	-9.0	60	10	250	50	0.0	0.0
B /8.1	5.3	0.81	11.07	N/A	0	44	55	1	8	57.5	-9.0	57	10	250	50	0.0	0.0
B /8.3	5.2	0.80	10.89	11	0	44	55	1	8	50.9	-9.3	46	10	250	50	0.0	0.0
B /8.3	5.3	0.81	10.90	317	0	44	55	1	8	51.6	-9.3	47	10	250	50	0.0	0.0
B+ /9.2	5.2	0.80	10.93	37	0	44	55	1	8	53.6	-9.2	53	10	250	50	0.0	0.0
B /8.2	5.3	0.80	10.98	530	0	44	55	1	8	54.9	-9.2	53	10	250	50	0.0	0.0
B /8.2	5.2	0.80	11.04	455	0	44	55	1	8	57.5	-9.1	57	10	250	50	0.0	0.0
B /8.1	5.3	0.81	11.12	206	0	44	55	1	8	60.0	-8.9	60	10	250	50	0.0	0.0
B /8.1	5.2	0.80	11.02	37	0	44	55	1	8	57.8	-9.0	58	10	250	50	0.0	0.0
B /8.1	5.2	0.80	11.08	1,056	0	44	55	1	8	60.5	-9.0	62	10	250	50	0.0	0.0
B /8.4	5.8	0.91	11.83	1,786	0	50	49	1	5	66.1	-11.3	50	10	250	50	5.8	0.0
B+ /9.1	5.8	0.90	11.85	N/A	0	50	49	1	5	59.3	-11.6	39	10	250	50	0.0	0.0
B+ /9.1	5.8	0.90	11.68	99	0	50	49	1	5	59.4	-11.6	40	10	250	50	0.0	0.0
B+ /9.0	5.8	0.91	11.77	25	0	50	49	1	5	64.9	-11.4	50	10	250	50	0.0	0.0
B+ /9.0	5.9	0.91	11.82	29	0	50	49	1	5	67.4	-11.3	53	10	250	50	0.0	0.0
B- /7.9	5.9	0.91	11.84	N/A	0	50	49	1	5	66.2	-11.3	50	10	250	50	0.0	0.0
B /8.5	5.8	0.91	11.68	19	0	50	49	1	5	59.1	-11.5	38	10	250	50	0.0	0.0
B /8.5	5.9	0.91	11.65	756	0	50	49	1	5	60.0	-11.6	40	10	250	50	0.0	0.0
B+ /9.0	5.9	0.91	11.70	60	0	50	49	1	5	61.9	-11.5	45	10	250	50	0.0	0.0
B /8.4	5.9	0.91	11.74	1,253	0	50	49	1	5	63.3	-11.4	46	10	250	50	0.0	0.0
B /8.4	5.8	0.91	11.81	1,325	0	50	49	1	5	66.0	-11.3	50	10	250	50	0.0	0.0
B /8.3	5.8	0.91	11.90	569	0	50	49	1	5	68.8	-11.1	54	10	250	50	0.0	0.0
B- /7.9	5.9	0.91	11.79	119	0	50	49	1	5	66.5	-11.3	51	10	250	50	0.0	0.0
B /8.3	5.9	0.91	11.87	3,039	0	50	49	1	5	69.3	-11.2	54	10	250	50	0.0	0.0
B- /7.8	6.8	1.06	12.43	1,878	0	59	40	1	5	79.8	-14.4	38	10	250	50	5.8	0.0
B- /7.6	6.7	1.05	12.41	N/A	0	59	40	1	5	72.3	-14.7	29	10	250	50	0.0	0.0
B- /7.7	6.8	1.06	12.25	112	0	59	40	1	5	72.4	-14.7	28	10	250	50	0.0	0.0
B- /7.9	6.8	1.06	12.36	28	0	59	40	1	5	78.5	-14.5	37	10	250	50	0.0	0.0
B /8.0	6.8	1.06	12.42	37	0	59	40	1	5	81.1	-14.4	41	10	250	50	0.0	0.0
C+ /6.7	6.8	1.06	12.43	N/A	0	59	40	1	5	79.8	-14.4	38	10	250	50	0.0	0.0
B- /7.9	6.8	1.06	12.26	21	0	59	40	1	5	72.5	-14.8	28	10	250	50	0.0	0.0
B- /7.9	6.8	1.06	12.21	990	0	59	40	1	5	73.1	-14.7	29	10	250	50	0.0	0.0
B- /7.8	6.8	1.05	12.30	85	0	59	40	1	5	75.3	-14.7	34	10	250	50	0.0	0.0
B- /7.9	6.8	1.05	12.32	1,393	0	59	40	1	5	76.6	-14.6	34	10	250	50	0.0	0.0
B- /7.8	6.8	1.06	12.40	1,383	0	59	40	1	5	79.8	-14.5	37	10	250	50	0.0	0.0
B- /7.8	6.8	1.06	12.51	690	0	59	40	1	5	82.9	-14.5	42	10	250	50	0.0	0.0
C+ /6.7	6.8	1.06	12.39	111	0	59	40	1	5	80.2	-14.4	39	10	250	50	0.0	0.0
B- /7.8	6.7	1.05	12.47	3,055	0	59	40	1	5	83.3	-14.4	43	10	250	50	0.0	0.0
B- /7.2	8.1	1.26	13.08	1,703	0	71	28	1	3	87.9	-15.8	27	5	250	50	5.8	0.0
B- /7.6	8.0	1.24	13.03	N/A	0	71	28	1	3	80.3	-16.1	21	5	250	50	0.0	0.0
B- /7.6	8.1	1.25	12.90	95	0	71	28	1	3	80.3	-16.1	20	5	250	50	0.0	0.0
B- /7.7	8.0	1.25	13.00	30	0	71	28	1	3	86.5	-15.9	28	5	250	50	0.0	0.0
B- /7.7	8.0	1.25	13.07	24	0	71	28	1	3	89.3	-15.8	31	5	250	50	0.0	0.0
C+ /6.5	8.1	1.26	13.08	N/A	0	71	28	1	3	87.9	-15.8	27	5	250	50	0.0	0.0

I. Index of Stock Mutual Funds

Fund Type	Fund Name	Ticker Symbol	Overall Investment Rating	Phone	Performance Rating/Pts	3 Mo	6 Mo	1Yr / Pct	3Yr / Pct	5Yr / Pct	Dividend Yield	Expense Ratio
AA	American Funds Tgt Dte Ret 2030 R1	RAETX	C+	(800) 421-0180	C / 4.6	5.45	5.03	16.47 /36	4.76 /52	9.05 /51	0.29	1.55
AA	American Funds Tgt Dte Ret 2030 R2	RBETX	C+	(800) 421-0180	C / 4.7	5.43	5.09	16.59 /37	4.87 /53	9.12 /52	0.40	1.50
AA	American Funds Tgt Dte Ret 2030	RBEEX	B-	(800) 421-0180	C / 5.0	5.48	5.15	16.92 /38	5.21 /56	9.38 /54	0.94	1.19
AA	American Funds Tgt Dte Ret 2030 R3	RCETX	C+	(800) 421-0180	C / 5.1	5.55	5.30	17.09 /39	5.29 /57	9.54 /55	0.78	1.08
AA	American Funds Tgt Dte Ret 2030 R4	RDETX	B-	(800) 421-0180	C / 5.3	5.58	5.42	17.42 /40	5.58 /60	9.89 /57	1.06	0.77
AA	American Funds Tgt Dte Ret 2030 R5	REETX	B-	(800) 421-0180	C+ / 5.6	5.71	5.63	17.85 /42	5.94 /64	10.23 /60	1.30	0.46
AA	American Funds Tgt Dte Ret 2030	RHETX	C+	(800) 421-0180	C / 5.4	5.63	5.55	17.67 /41	5.69 /61	9.95 /58	1.26	0.55
AA	American Funds Tgt Dte Ret 2030 R6	RFETX	B-	(800) 421-0180	C+ / 5.6	5.69	5.61	17.86 /42	5.97 /64	10.27 /60	1.34	0.41
AA	American Funds Tgt Dte Ret 2035 A	AAFTX	C+	(800) 421-0180	C / 4.7	6.24	6.15	19.29 /48	5.92 /63	10.17 /60	0.91	0.75
AA	American Funds Tgt Dte Ret 2035 B	BBFTX	B-	(800) 421-0180	C / 5.2	6.02	5.77	18.39 /45	5.11 /55	9.32 /53	0.00	1.54
AA	American Funds Tgt Dte Ret 2035 C	CCFTX	B-	(800) 421-0180	C / 5.2	6.05	5.80	18.38 /45	5.12 /55	9.33 /53	0.43	1.52
AA	American Funds Tgt Dte Ret 2035 F1	FAQTX	B-	(800) 421-0180	C+ / 5.9	6.22	6.14	19.20 /48	5.88 /63	10.03 /59	1.16	0.78
AA	American Funds Tgt Dte Ret 2035 F2	FBFTX	B-	(800) 421-0180	C+ / 6.1	6.26	6.26	19.50 /49	6.15 /66	10.31 /61	1.21	0.51
AA	American Funds Tgt Dte Ret 2035 F3	FDFTX	C+	(800) 421-0180	C+ / 5.9	6.24	6.15	19.29 /48	5.92 /63	10.17 /60	0.97	N/A
AA	American Funds Tgt Dte Ret 2035 R1	RAFTX	C+	(800) 421-0180	C / 5.2	6.01	5.75	18.34 /44	5.10 /55	9.31 /53	0.21	1.55
AA	American Funds Tgt Dte Ret 2035 R2	RBFTX	C+	(800) 421-0180	C / 5.3	6.05	5.80	18.35 /44	5.17 /56	9.39 /54	0.33	1.51
AA	American Funds Tgt Dte Ret 2035	RBEFX	B-	(800) 421-0180	C+ / 5.6	6.10	5.94	18.77 /46	5.55 /60	9.66 /56	0.87	1.21
AA	American Funds Tgt Dte Ret 2035 R3	RCFTX	C+	(800) 421-0180	C+ / 5.7	6.19	6.02	18.87 /46	5.58 /60	9.80 /57	0.73	1.09
AA	American Funds Tgt Dte Ret 2035 R4	RDFTX	C+	(800) 421-0180	C+ / 5.9	6.27	6.19	19.25 /48	5.92 /63	10.16 /59	0.98	0.78
AA	American Funds Tgt Dte Ret 2035 R5	REFTX	C+	(800) 421-0180	C+ / 6.2	6.23	6.31	19.57 /50	6.21 /66	10.47 /62	1.21	0.47
AA	American Funds Tgt Dte Ret 2035	RHFTX	C+	(800) 421-0180	C+ / 6.0	6.24	6.24	19.50 /49	6.00 /64	10.22 /60	1.17	0.56
AA	American Funds Tgt Dte Ret 2035 R6	RFFTX	C+	(800) 421-0180	C+ / 6.2	6.29	6.37	19.68 /50	6.28 /67	10.53 /62	1.25	0.42
AA	American Funds Tgt Dte Ret 2040 A	AAGTX	C+	(800) 421-0180	C / 4.9	6.42	6.42	19.97 /52	6.01 /64	10.33 /61	0.88	0.76
AA	American Funds Tgt Dte Ret 2040 B	BBGTX	B-	(800) 421-0180	C / 5.5	6.22	6.06	18.97 /47	5.22 /57	9.50 /55	0.00	1.55
AA	American Funds Tgt Dte Ret 2040 C	CCGTX	B-	(800) 421-0180	C / 5.4	6.19	6.03	18.92 /47	5.19 /56	9.48 /54	0.43	1.53
AA	American Funds Tgt Dte Ret 2040 F1	FAUTX	B-	(800) 421-0180	C+ / 6.1	6.37	6.37	19.84 /51	5.98 /64	10.19 /60	1.09	0.78
AA	American Funds Tgt Dte Ret 2040 F2	FBGTX	B-	(800) 421-0180	C+ / 6.3	6.44	6.52	20.16 /53	6.22 /66	10.48 /62	1.16	0.52
AA	American Funds Tgt Dte Ret 2040 F3	FCGTX	C+	(800) 421-0180	C+ / 6.2	6.50	6.50	20.06 /52	6.04 /64	10.35 /61	0.93	N/A
AA	American Funds Tgt Dte Ret 2040 R1	RAKTX	C+	(800) 421-0180	C / 5.4	6.24	6.07	18.95 /47	5.17 /56	9.45 /54	0.16	1.57
AA	American Funds Tgt Dte Ret 2040 R2	RBKTX	C+	(800) 421-0180	C / 5.5	6.24	6.07	19.07 /47	5.25 /57	9.54 /55	0.30	1.52
AA	American Funds Tgt Dte Ret 2040	RBEKX	B-	(800) 421-0180	C+ / 5.8	6.32	6.24	19.39 /49	5.66 /61	9.83 /57	0.78	1.22
AA	American Funds Tgt Dte Ret 2040 R3	RCKTX	C+	(800) 421-0180	C+ / 5.8	6.27	6.27	19.53 /50	5.64 /61	9.95 /58	0.68	1.11
AA	American Funds Tgt Dte Ret 2040 R4	RDGTX	C+	(800) 421-0180	C+ / 6.1	6.37	6.45	19.93 /52	5.98 /64	10.30 /61	0.94	0.79
AA	American Funds Tgt Dte Ret 2040 R5	REGTX	C+	(800) 421-0180	C+ / 6.4	6.41	6.57	20.23 /53	6.30 /67	10.63 /63	1.17	0.48
AA	American Funds Tgt Dte Ret 2040	RHGTX	C+	(800) 421-0180	C+ / 6.2	6.42	6.50	20.08 /52	6.09 /65	10.38 /61	1.13	0.57
AA	American Funds Tgt Dte Ret 2040 R6	RFGTX	C+	(800) 421-0180	C+ / 6.4	6.47	6.63	20.34 /54	6.37 /67	10.68 /63	1.21	0.43
AA	American Funds Tgt Dte Ret 2045 A	AAHTX	C+	(800) 421-0180	C / 5.1	6.46	6.70	20.35 /54	6.13 /65	10.41 /61	0.83	0.75
AA	American Funds Tgt Dte Ret 2045 B	BBHTX	B-	(800) 421-0180	C+ / 5.7	6.31	6.31	19.45 /49	5.38 /58	9.59 /55	0.00	1.56
AA	American Funds Tgt Dte Ret 2045 C	CCHTX	B-	(800) 421-0180	C+ / 5.6	6.30	6.22	19.43 /49	5.31 /58	9.54 /55	0.37	1.53
AA	American Funds Tgt Dte Ret 2045 F1	FATTX	B-	(800) 421-0180	C+ / 6.3	6.48	6.64	20.32 /54	6.09 /65	10.26 /60	1.02	0.78
AA	American Funds Tgt Dte Ret 2045 F2	FBHTX	B-	(800) 421-0180	C+ / 6.5	6.53	6.86	20.61 /55	6.36 /67	10.56 /62	1.10	0.52
AA	American Funds Tgt Dte Ret 2045 F3	FCHTX	C+	(800) 421-0180	C+ / 6.3	6.46	6.70	20.35 /54	6.13 /65	10.41 /61	0.88	N/A
AA	American Funds Tgt Dte Ret 2045 R1	RAHTX	C+	(800) 421-0180	C+ / 5.6	6.29	6.29	19.38 /49	5.29 /57	9.53 /55	0.06	1.57
AA	American Funds Tgt Dte Ret 2045 R2	RBHTX	C+	(800) 421-0180	C+ / 5.6	6.29	6.29	19.42 /49	5.36 /58	9.61 /55	0.26	1.53
AA	American Funds Tgt Dte Ret 2045	RBHHX	B-	(800) 421-0180	C+ / 6.0	6.34	6.42	19.86 /51	5.79 /62	9.92 /58	0.73	1.22
AA	American Funds Tgt Dte Ret 2045 R3	RCHTX	C+	(800) 421-0180	C+ / 6.0	6.40	6.48	19.96 /52	5.77 /62	10.03 /59	0.63	1.11
AA	American Funds Tgt Dte Ret 2045 R4	RDHTX	C+	(800) 421-0180	C+ / 6.3	6.47	6.64	20.31 /54	6.11 /65	10.37 /61	0.88	0.79
AA	American Funds Tgt Dte Ret 2045 R5	REHTX	C+	(800) 421-0180	C+ / 6.5	6.51	6.83	20.68 /56	6.43 /68	10.71 /63	1.11	0.49
AA	American Funds Tgt Dte Ret 2045	RHHTX	C+	(800) 421-0180	C+ / 6.4	6.53	6.77	20.57 /55	6.21 /66	10.46 /62	1.08	0.58
AA	American Funds Tgt Dte Ret 2045 R6	RFHTX	C+	(800) 421-0180	C+ / 6.5	6.49	6.81	20.71 /56	6.46 /68	10.75 /64	1.15	0.43
AA	American Funds Tgt Dte Ret 2050 A	AALTX	C+	(800) 421-0180	C / 5.1	6.48	6.72	20.52 /55	6.15 /66	10.41 /61	0.80	0.76
AA	American Funds Tgt Dte Ret 2050 B	BBITX	B-	(800) 421-0180	C+ / 5.9	6.46	6.63	19.99 /52	5.61 /61	9.72 /56	0.03	1.55

● Denotes fund is closed to new investors
∗ Denotes fund is included in Section II

Risk Rating/Pts	3 Year Standard Deviation	Beta	NAV As of 2/28/17	Total $(Mil)	Cash %	Stocks %	Bonds %	Other %	Portfolio Turnover Ratio	Last Bull Market Return	Last Bear Market Return	Manager Quality Pct	Manager Tenure (Years)	Initial Purch. $	Additional Purch. $	Front End Load	Back End Load
B- / 7.3	8.0	1.25	12.92	28	0	71	28	1	3	80.0	-16.0	20	5	250	50	0.0	0.0
B- / 7.3	8.0	1.25	12.85	995	0	71	28	1	3	80.8	-16.0	21	5	250	50	0.0	0.0
B- / 7.6	8.0	1.25	12.94	70	0	71	28	1	3	83.0	-16.1	24	5	250	50	0.0	0.0
B- / 7.2	8.0	1.25	12.97	1,445	0	71	28	1	3	84.7	-15.9	25	5	250	50	0.0	0.0
B- / 7.2	8.1	1.25	13.05	1,483	0	71	28	1	3	87.7	-15.7	27	5	250	50	0.0	0.0
B- / 7.2	8.0	1.25	13.17	697	0	71	28	1	3	91.0	-15.7	31	5	250	50	0.0	0.0
C+ / 6.5	8.1	1.26	13.04	121	0	71	28	1	3	88.4	-15.8	28	5	250	50	0.0	0.0
B- / 7.2	8.0	1.25	13.12	3,701	0	71	28	1	3	91.3	-15.6	32	5	250	50	0.0	0.0
C+ / 6.8	8.7	1.35	13.23	1,283	0	79	20	1	3	90.6	-16.2	24	10	250	50	5.8	0.0
B- / 7.2	8.7	1.35	13.17	N/A	0	79	20	1	3	82.8	-16.5	17	10	250	50	0.0	0.0
B- / 7.2	8.7	1.35	13.05	75	0	79	20	1	3	82.8	-16.5	17	10	250	50	0.0	0.0
B- / 7.3	8.7	1.35	13.17	23	0	79	20	1	3	89.1	-16.3	23	10	250	50	0.0	0.0
B- / 7.3	8.7	1.35	13.22	11	0	79	20	1	3	91.8	-16.2	26	10	250	50	0.0	0.0
C+ / 6.2	8.7	1.35	13.23	N/A	0	79	20	1	3	90.6	-16.2	24	10	250	50	0.0	0.0
C+ / 6.8	8.7	1.35	12.97	17	0	79	20	1	3	82.5	-16.4	17	10	250	50	0.0	0.0
C+ / 6.8	8.7	1.35	12.99	860	0	79	20	1	3	83.3	-16.4	18	10	250	50	0.0	0.0
B- / 7.3	8.7	1.35	13.08	63	0	79	20	1	3	85.8	-16.4	21	10	250	50	0.0	0.0
C+ / 6.8	8.7	1.35	13.11	1,083	0	79	20	1	3	87.2	-16.3	21	10	250	50	0.0	0.0
C+ / 6.8	8.7	1.35	13.20	1,072	0	79	20	1	3	90.3	-16.1	24	10	250	50	0.0	0.0
C+ / 6.8	8.7	1.35	13.31	575	0	79	20	1	3	93.4	-16.0	26	10	250	50	0.0	0.0
C+ / 6.2	8.7	1.35	13.19	89	0	79	20	1	3	91.0	-16.2	25	10	250	50	0.0	0.0
C+ / 6.7	8.7	1.34	13.27	2,578	0	79	20	1	3	93.9	-16.0	28	10	250	50	0.0	0.0
C+ / 6.7	8.9	1.38	13.47	1,111	0	81	18	1	2	92.3	-16.5	23	10	250	50	5.8	0.0
B- / 7.1	8.9	1.37	13.43	N/A	0	81	18	1	2	84.6	-16.8	16	10	250	50	0.0	0.0
B- / 7.1	8.9	1.38	13.28	58	0	81	18	1	2	84.4	-16.8	16	10	250	50	0.0	0.0
B- / 7.2	8.9	1.38	13.41	13	0	81	18	1	2	90.9	-16.6	22	10	250	50	0.0	0.0
B- / 7.2	8.9	1.38	13.46	7	0	81	18	1	2	93.6	-16.5	25	10	250	50	0.0	0.0
C+ / 6.1	8.9	1.38	13.48	N/A	0	81	18	1	2	92.5	-16.5	23	10	250	50	0.0	0.0
C+ / 6.8	8.9	1.38	13.25	17	0	81	18	1	2	84.4	-16.8	16	10	250	50	0.0	0.0
C+ / 6.7	8.9	1.38	13.22	697	0	81	18	1	2	85.1	-16.7	16	10	250	50	0.0	0.0
B- / 7.2	8.9	1.38	13.33	50	0	81	18	1	2	87.5	-16.7	19	10	250	50	0.0	0.0
C+ / 6.7	8.9	1.38	13.35	906	0	81	18	1	2	88.9	-16.6	19	10	250	50	0.0	0.0
C+ / 6.7	8.9	1.38	13.44	970	0	81	18	1	2	92.3	-16.5	22	10	250	50	0.0	0.0
C+ / 6.7	8.9	1.37	13.56	487	0	81	18	1	2	95.3	-16.4	26	10	250	50	0.0	0.0
C+ / 6.1	8.9	1.38	13.43	85	0	81	18	1	2	92.8	-16.5	24	10	250	50	0.0	0.0
C+ / 6.7	8.9	1.38	13.52	2,468	0	81	18	1	2	95.8	-16.3	26	10	250	50	0.0	0.0
C+ / 6.7	9.0	1.39	13.63	759	0	82	17	1	3	93.1	-16.5	23	10	250	50	5.8	0.0
B- / 7.1	9.0	1.39	13.57	N/A	0	82	17	1	3	85.4	-16.8	17	10	250	50	0.0	0.0
B- / 7.1	9.1	1.40	13.43	47	0	82	17	1	3	85.0	-16.8	15	10	250	50	0.0	0.0
B- / 7.2	9.0	1.39	13.57	7	0	82	17	1	3	91.6	-16.6	22	10	250	50	0.0	0.0
B- / 7.2	9.0	1.39	13.64	4	0	82	17	1	3	94.4	-16.5	25	10	250	50	0.0	0.0
C+ / 6.1	9.0	1.39	13.63	N/A	0	82	17	1	3	93.1	-16.5	23	10	250	50	0.0	0.0
C+ / 6.8	9.0	1.40	13.41	8	0	82	17	1	3	84.8	-16.7	15	10	250	50	0.0	0.0
C+ / 6.8	9.0	1.40	13.35	516	0	82	17	1	3	85.6	-16.7	16	10	250	50	0.0	0.0
B- / 7.1	9.1	1.40	13.50	34	0	82	17	1	3	88.3	-16.7	19	10	250	50	0.0	0.0
C+ / 6.7	9.0	1.39	13.49	634	0	82	17	1	3	89.7	-16.6	20	10	250	50	0.0	0.0
C+ / 6.7	9.0	1.40	13.60	634	0	82	17	1	3	92.8	-16.4	22	10	250	50	0.0	0.0
C+ / 6.7	9.1	1.40	13.73	349	0	82	17	1	3	96.1	-16.4	25	10	250	50	0.0	0.0
C+ / 6.1	9.0	1.39	13.59	50	0	82	17	1	3	93.5	-16.5	23	10	250	50	0.0	0.0
C+ / 6.7	9.0	1.40	13.68	1,418	0	82	17	1	3	96.4	-16.4	25	10	250	50	0.0	0.0
C+ / 6.7	9.1	1.40	13.33	650	0	82	16	2	2	93.1	-16.4	22	10	250	50	5.8	0.0
B- / 7.1	9.1	1.40	13.34	N/A	0	82	16	2	2	86.5	-16.7	18	10	250	50	0.0	0.0

99 Pct = Best
0 Pct = Worst

Fund Type	Fund Name	Ticker Symbol	Overall Investment Rating	Phone	Performance Rating/Pts	3 Mo	6 Mo	1Yr / Pct	3Yr / Pct	5Yr / Pct	Dividend Yield	Expense Ratio
								Total Return % through 2/28/17			Incl. in Returns	
									Annualized			
AA	American Funds Tgt Dte Ret 2050 C	CCITX	B-	(800) 421-0180	C+ / 5.7	6.35	6.35	19.61 / 50	5.36 / 58	9.56 / 55	0.36	1.54
AA	American Funds Tgt Dte Ret 2050 F1	FAITX	B-	(800) 421-0180	C+ / 6.3	6.49	6.74	20.48 / 55	6.15 / 66	10.27 / 60	0.99	0.79
AA	American Funds Tgt Dte Ret 2050 F2	FBITX	B-	(800) 421-0180	C+ / 6.5	6.56	6.89	20.82 / 56	6.41 / 68	10.55 / 62	1.07	0.53
AA	American Funds Tgt Dte Ret 2050 F3	DITFX	C+	(800) 421-0180	C+ / 6.4	6.56	6.80	20.61 / 55	6.18 / 66	10.42 / 61	0.85	N/A
AA	American Funds Tgt Dte Ret 2050 R1	RAITX	C+	(800) 421-0180	C+ / 5.6	6.30	6.30	19.52 / 49	5.31 / 58	9.54 / 55	0.15	1.57
AA	American Funds Tgt Dte Ret 2050 R2	RBITX	C+	(800) 421-0180	C+ / 5.7	6.30	6.39	19.60 / 50	5.39 / 58	9.63 / 56	0.23	1.53
AA	American Funds Tgt Dte Ret 2050	RBHEX	B-	(800) 421-0180	C+ / 6.0	6.38	6.55	19.95 / 52	5.79 / 62	9.91 / 58	0.71	1.22
AA	American Funds Tgt Dte Ret 2050 R3	RCITX	C+	(800) 421-0180	C+ / 6.0	6.41	6.57	20.09 / 52	5.79 / 62	10.05 / 59	0.59	1.11
AA	American Funds Tgt Dte Ret 2050 R4	RDITX	C+	(800) 421-0180	C+ / 6.3	6.49	6.74	20.47 / 55	6.14 / 65	10.39 / 61	0.86	0.79
AA	American Funds Tgt Dte Ret 2050 R5	REITX	C+	(800) 421-0180	C+ / 6.6	6.54	6.86	20.77 / 56	6.46 / 68	10.73 / 64	1.09	0.49
AA	American Funds Tgt Dte Ret 2050	RHITX	C+	(800) 421-0180	C+ / 6.4	6.48	6.81	20.64 / 56	6.23 / 66	10.46 / 62	1.06	0.58
AA	American Funds Tgt Dte Ret 2050 R6	RFITX	C+	(800) 421-0180	C+ / 6.6	6.59	6.92	20.88 / 57	6.50 / 68	10.78 / 64	1.12	0.43
AA	American Funds Tgt Dte Ret 2055 A	AAMTX	C+	(800) 421-0180	C / 5.1	6.46	6.72	20.50 / 55	6.15 / 66	10.42 / 61	0.74	0.77
AA	American Funds Tgt Dte Ret 2055 B	BBJTX	B-	(800) 421-0180	C+ / 6.0	6.52	6.72	20.32 / 54	5.67 / 61	9.76 / 57	0.10	1.58
AA	American Funds Tgt Dte Ret 2055 C	CCJTX	B-	(800) 421-0180	C+ / 5.6	6.26	6.32	19.58 / 50	5.33 / 58	9.55 / 55	0.23	1.55
AA	American Funds Tgt Dte Ret 2055 F1	FAJTX	B-	(800) 421-0180	C+ / 6.3	6.47	6.74	20.47 / 55	6.15 / 66	10.28 / 60	0.89	0.80
AA	American Funds Tgt Dte Ret 2055 F2	FBJTX	B-	(800) 421-0180	C+ / 6.5	6.61	6.88	20.82 / 56	6.37 / 67	10.57 / 63	0.98	0.54
AA	American Funds Tgt Dte Ret 2055 F3	FCJTX	C+	(800) 421-0180	C+ / 6.4	6.52	6.79	20.57 / 55	6.18 / 66	10.43 / 61	0.78	N/A
AA	American Funds Tgt Dte Ret 2055 R1	RAMTX	C+	(800) 421-0180	C+ / 5.6	6.30	6.30	19.56 / 50	5.30 / 58	9.54 / 55	0.01	1.59
AA	American Funds Tgt Dte Ret 2055 R2	RBMTX	C+	(800) 421-0180	C+ / 5.7	6.29	6.36	19.60 / 50	5.37 / 58	9.60 / 55	0.18	1.54
AA	American Funds Tgt Dte Ret 2055	RBEMX	B-	(800) 421-0180	C+ / 6.0	6.35	6.48	19.91 / 51	5.83 / 63	9.93 / 58	0.64	1.23
AA	American Funds Tgt Dte Ret 2055 R3	RCMTX	C+	(800) 421-0180	C+ / 6.0	6.38	6.58	20.05 / 52	5.77 / 62	10.02 / 58	0.54	1.12
AA	American Funds Tgt Dte Ret 2055 R4	RDJTX	C+	(800) 421-0180	C+ / 6.3	6.54	6.74	20.53 / 55	6.13 / 65	10.39 / 61	0.79	0.81
AA	American Funds Tgt Dte Ret 2055 R5	REKTX	C+	(800) 421-0180	C+ / 6.6	6.60	6.93	20.88 / 57	6.45 / 68	10.71 / 63	1.01	0.50
AA	American Funds Tgt Dte Ret 2055	RHJTX	C+	(800) 421-0180	C+ / 6.4	6.56	6.83	20.72 / 56	6.24 / 66	10.47 / 62	0.99	0.58
AA	American Funds Tgt Dte Ret 2055 R6	RFKTX	C+	(800) 421-0180	C+ / 6.6	6.57	6.90	20.82 / 56	6.48 / 68	10.76 / 64	1.04	0.45
AA	American Funds Tgt Dte Ret 2060 A	AANTX	U	(800) 421-0180	U /	6.55	6.86	20.56 / 55	--	--	0.95	0.97
AA	American Funds Tgt Dte Ret 2060 R2	RBNTX	U	(800) 421-0180	U /	6.24	6.34	19.56 / 50	--	--	0.60	1.73
AA	American Funds Tgt Dte Ret 2060 R3	RCNTX	U	(800) 421-0180	U /	6.42	6.52	20.09 / 52	--	--	0.79	1.30
AA	American Funds Tgt Dte Ret 2060 R4	RDKTX	U	(800) 421-0180	U /	6.46	6.77	20.45 / 55	--	--	1.02	0.95
AA	American Funds Tgt Dte Ret 2060 R6	RFUTX	U	(800) 421-0180	U /	6.65	6.95	20.86 / 57	--	--	1.21	0.60
GI	American Funds Wash Mutl Invs	CWMAX	B+	(800) 421-0180	B / 7.6	6.47	10.17	23.84 / 69	9.29 / 89	12.99 / 84	1.59	0.68
GI	● American Funds Wash Mutl Invs	CWMBX	B+	(800) 421-0180	B / 8.0	6.25	9.73	22.85 / 66	8.43 / 82	12.10 / 75	0.77	1.46
GI	American Funds Wash Mutl Invs	CWMCX	B+	(800) 421-0180	B / 8.0	6.27	9.74	22.88 / 66	8.45 / 82	12.11 / 75	1.01	1.45
GI	American Funds Wash Mutl Invs	CWMEX	A-	(800) 421-0180	B+ / 8.4	6.39	10.04	23.53 / 68	9.02 / 87	12.71 / 81	1.48	0.92
GI	American Funds Wash Mutl Invs	CWMFX	A	(800) 421-0180	B+ / 8.8	6.49	10.26	24.08 / 70	9.53 / 90	13.23 / 86	1.89	0.46
* GI	American Funds Wash Mutl Invs A	AWSHX	B+	(800) 421-0180	B / 7.7	6.50	10.21	23.92 / 70	9.39 / 89	13.09 / 85	1.66	0.58
GI	● American Funds Wash Mutl Invs B	WSHBX	B+	(800) 421-0180	B / 8.1	6.28	9.78	22.97 / 66	8.56 / 83	12.24 / 76	0.91	1.33
GI	American Funds Wash Mutl Invs C	WSHCX	B+	(800) 421-0180	B / 8.0	6.27	9.77	22.93 / 66	8.52 / 83	12.19 / 76	1.07	1.38
GI	American Funds Wash Mutl Invs F1	WSHFX	A-	(800) 421-0180	B+ / 8.6	6.48	10.15	23.82 / 69	9.30 / 89	13.01 / 84	1.69	0.66
GI	American Funds Wash Mutl Invs F2	WMFFX	A	(800) 421-0180	B+ / 8.8	6.53	10.30	24.16 / 70	9.58 / 91	13.30 / 87	1.93	0.41
GI	American Funds Wash Mutl Invs F3	FWMIX	B+	(800) 421-0180	B+ / 8.7	6.52	10.24	23.95 / 70	9.40 / 90	13.09 / 85	1.76	0.30
GI	American Funds Wash Mutl Invs R1	RWMAX	B+	(800) 421-0180	B / 8.0	6.26	9.75	22.94 / 66	8.51 / 83	12.19 / 76	1.06	1.39
GI	American Funds Wash Mutl Invs R2	RWMBX	B+	(800) 421-0180	B / 8.0	6.25	9.76	22.94 / 66	8.54 / 83	12.22 / 76	1.07	1.39
GI	American Funds Wash Mutl Invs R2E	RWEBX	A	(800) 421-0180	B+ / 8.3	6.35	9.93	23.31 / 68	9.00 / 87	12.57 / 80	1.39	1.11
GI	American Funds Wash Mutl Invs R3	RWMCX	A-	(800) 421-0180	B+ / 8.4	6.39	10.00	23.48 / 68	8.99 / 87	12.69 / 81	1.45	0.95
GI	American Funds Wash Mutl Invs R4	RWMEX	A-	(800) 421-0180	B+ / 8.6	6.47	10.16	23.86 / 69	9.32 / 89	13.02 / 84	1.72	0.65
GI	American Funds Wash Mutl Invs R5	RWMFX	A	(800) 421-0180	B+ / 8.8	6.54	10.33	24.23 / 71	9.65 / 91	13.36 / 87	1.98	0.35
GI	American Funds Wash Mutl Invs R5E	RWMHX	B+	(800) 421-0180	B+ / 8.7	6.51	10.27	24.03 / 70	9.44 / 90	13.12 / 85	1.88	0.50
GI	American Funds Wash Mutl Invs R6	RWMGX	A	(800) 421-0180	B+ / 8.9	6.55	10.35	24.26 / 71	9.70 / 92	13.42 / 88	2.02	0.30
GR	American Growth Fund Series One A	AMRAX	C+	(800) 525-2406	C+ / 6.2	6.40	8.80	23.59 / 68	6.77 / 70	11.88 / 73	0.00	6.13
GR	American Growth Fund Series One B	AMRBX	C+	(800) 525-2406	C+ / 6.7	6.14	8.64	22.78 / 66	6.15 / 66	11.03 / 66	0.00	6.82

● Denotes fund is closed to new investors
* Denotes fund is included in Section II

www.thestreetratings.com

Risk Rating/Pts	3 Year Standard Deviation	Beta	NAV As of 2/28/17	Total $(Mil)	Cash %	Stocks %	Bonds %	Other %	Portfolio Turnover Ratio	Last Bull Market Return	Last Bear Market Return	Manager Quality Pct	Manager Tenure (Years)	Initial Purch. $	Additional Purch. $	Front End Load	Back End Load
B- /7.1	9.1	1.41	13.13	41	0	82	16	2	2	85.2	-16.7	16	10	250	50	0.0	0.0
B- /7.2	9.1	1.40	13.27	6	0	82	16	2	2	91.7	-16.5	22	10	250	50	0.0	0.0
B- /7.2	9.0	1.40	13.32	6	0	82	16	2	2	94.4	-16.4	25	10	250	50	0.0	0.0
C+ /6.1	9.1	1.40	13.34	N/A	0	82	16	2	2	93.2	-16.4	22	10	250	50	0.0	0.0
C+ /6.7	9.1	1.40	13.09	9	0	82	16	2	2	85.0	-16.7	16	10	250	50	0.0	0.0
C+ /6.7	9.1	1.40	13.10	380	0	82	16	2	2	85.9	-16.7	16	10	250	50	0.0	0.0
B- /7.1	9.1	1.40	13.19	25	0	82	16	2	2	88.3	-16.6	19	10	250	50	0.0	0.0
C+ /6.7	9.1	1.40	13.20	514	0	82	16	2	2	89.8	-16.6	19	10	250	50	0.0	0.0
C+ /6.7	9.1	1.40	13.30	496	0	82	16	2	2	93.0	-16.4	22	10	250	50	0.0	0.0
C+ /6.7	9.1	1.40	13.42	291	0	82	16	2	2	96.3	-16.4	25	10	250	50	0.0	0.0
C+ /6.1	9.0	1.40	13.29	51	0	82	16	2	2	93.5	-16.4	23	10	250	50	0.0	0.0
C+ /6.6	9.1	1.40	13.38	1,137	0	82	16	2	2	96.8	-16.4	25	10	250	50	0.0	0.0
C+ /6.8	9.1	1.40	16.56	300	0	82	16	2	3	93.3	-16.5	22	5	250	50	5.8	0.0
B- /7.1	9.1	1.41	16.68	N/A	0	82	16	2	3	87.0	-16.8	18	5	250	50	0.0	0.0
B- /7.1	9.1	1.40	16.35	26	0	82	16	2	3	85.2	-16.8	16	5	250	50	0.0	0.0
B- /7.2	9.0	1.40	16.50	3	0	82	16	2	3	91.8	-16.6	22	5	250	50	0.0	0.0
B- /7.2	9.1	1.40	16.57	2	0	82	16	2	3	94.6	-16.5	24	5	250	50	0.0	0.0
C+ /6.1	9.1	1.40	16.57	N/A	0	82	16	2	3	93.4	-16.5	22	5	250	50	0.0	0.0
C+ /6.8	9.1	1.40	16.29	2	0	82	16	2	3	85.1	-16.8	16	5	250	50	0.0	0.0
C+ /6.8	9.1	1.40	16.29	203	0	82	16	2	3	85.8	-16.8	16	5	250	50	0.0	0.0
B- /7.2	9.0	1.40	16.42	10	0	82	16	2	3	88.5	-16.7	20	5	250	50	0.0	0.0
C+ /6.8	9.1	1.40	16.42	228	0	82	16	2	3	89.6	-16.6	19	5	250	50	0.0	0.0
C+ /6.8	9.1	1.40	16.54	229	0	82	16	2	3	93.0	-16.6	22	5	250	50	0.0	0.0
C+ /6.8	9.1	1.40	16.67	126	0	82	16	2	3	96.1	-16.4	25	5	250	50	0.0	0.0
C+ /6.1	9.1	1.40	16.52	21	0	82	16	2	3	93.7	-16.5	23	5	250	50	0.0	0.0
C+ /6.8	9.1	1.40	16.68	404	0	82	16	2	3	96.6	-16.5	25	5	250	50	0.0	0.0
U /	N/A	N/A	10.84	55	0	82	16	2	12	N/A	N/A	N/A	2	250	50	5.8	0.0
U /	N/A	N/A	10.76	31	0	82	16	2	12	N/A	N/A	N/A	2	250	50	0.0	0.0
U /	N/A	N/A	10.81	26	0	82	16	2	12	N/A	N/A	N/A	2	250	50	0.0	0.0
U /	N/A	N/A	10.84	27	0	82	16	2	12	N/A	N/A	N/A	2	250	50	0.0	0.0
U /	N/A	N/A	10.88	54	0	82	16	2	12	N/A	N/A	N/A	2	250	50	0.0	0.0
C+ /6.3	9.8	0.94	42.77	1,978	0	95	4	1	30	117.3	-12.6	67	20	250	50	5.8	0.0
C+ /6.4	9.8	0.94	42.74	2	0	95	4	1	30	108.2	-12.9	57	20	250	50	0.0	0.0
C+ /6.3	9.8	0.94	42.43	473	0	95	4	1	30	108.3	-12.9	57	20	250	50	0.0	0.0
C+ /6.3	9.8	0.94	42.53	100	0	95	4	1	30	114.4	-12.7	64	20	250	50	0.0	0.0
C+ /6.3	9.8	0.94	42.68	126	0	95	4	1	30	119.8	-12.5	70	20	250	50	0.0	0.0
C+ /6.3	9.8	0.94	42.86	54,608	0	95	4	1	30	118.3	-12.5	68	20	250	50	5.8	0.0
C+ /6.4	9.8	0.94	42.68	13	0	95	4	1	30	109.6	-12.8	59	20	250	50	0.0	0.0
C+ /6.3	9.8	0.94	42.30	1,678	0	95	4	1	30	109.1	-12.8	58	20	250	50	0.0	0.0
C+ /6.3	9.8	0.94	42.71	3,140	0	95	4	1	30	117.6	-12.6	67	20	250	50	0.0	0.0
C+ /6.3	9.8	0.94	42.84	9,126	0	95	4	1	30	120.6	-12.5	70	20	250	50	0.0	0.0
C+ /5.7	9.8	0.94	42.87	N/A	0	95	4	1	30	118.4	-12.5	68	20	250	50	0.0	0.0
C+ /6.3	9.9	0.94	42.39	96	0	95	4	1	30	109.1	-12.8	58	20	250	50	0.0	0.0
C+ /6.3	9.8	0.94	42.25	756	0	95	4	1	30	109.5	-12.8	58	20	250	50	0.0	0.0
B- /7.0	9.8	0.94	42.68	23	0	95	4	1	30	112.9	-12.7	64	20	250	50	0.0	0.0
C+ /6.3	9.8	0.94	42.50	1,921	0	95	4	1	30	114.2	-12.7	64	20	250	50	0.0	0.0
C+ /6.3	9.8	0.94	42.65	2,670	0	95	4	1	30	117.7	-12.5	68	20	250	50	0.0	0.0
C+ /6.3	9.8	0.94	42.85	2,138	0	95	4	1	30	121.3	-12.5	71	20	250	50	0.0	0.0
C+ /5.7	9.8	0.94	42.83	N/A	0	95	4	1	30	118.6	-12.5	69	20	250	50	0.0	0.0
C+ /6.3	9.8	0.94	42.89	11,157	0	95	4	1	30	121.9	-12.4	72	20	250	50	0.0	0.0
C+ /6.5	13.0	1.19	4.82	8	0	99	0	1	3	121.1	-24.0	12	6	0	0	5.8	0.0
C+ /6.5	13.1	1.20	4.15	N/A	0	99	0	1	3	113.9	-24.5	8	6	0	0	0.0	0.0

Fund Type	Fund Name	Ticker Symbol	Overall Investment Rating	Phone	Performance Rating/Pts	3 Mo	6 Mo	1Yr / Pct	3Yr / Pct	5Yr / Pct	Dividend Yield	Expense Ratio
GR	American Growth Fund Series One C	AMRCX	C+	(800) 525-2406	C+ / 6.7	6.17	8.40	22.92 /66	6.08 /65	11.10 /67	0.00	6.82
GR	American Growth Fund Series One D	AMRGX	C+	(800) 525-2406	C+ / 6.4	6.47	8.97	23.79 /69	7.11 /73	12.19 /76	0.00	5.83
GR	American Growth Fund Series Two E	AMREX	E-		E- / 0.1	2.30	-5.42	-3.25 / 1	-2.95 / 5	2.34 / 9	0.00	8.94
GL	American Ind JAF Glbl Tact Alloc A	AARMX	C	(866) 410-2006	D / 2.1	6.22	1.62	10.36 /13	3.70 /39	--	1.18	2.55
GL	● American Ind JAF Glbl Tact Alloc C	ACRMX	C	(866) 410-2006	D+ / 2.5	5.96	1.30	9.60 /11	3.04 /32	--	0.38	3.17
GL	American Ind JAF Glbl Tact Alloc I	RMAIX	C+	(866) 410-2006	C- / 3.2	6.18	1.79	10.73 /14	4.05 /44	--	1.68	2.17
GR	American Trust Allegiance Fd	ATAFX	C	(800) 385-7003	C+ / 5.9	9.78	10.23	20.90 /57	4.00 /43	7.77 /40	0.00	1.86
GI	AMF Large Cap Equity H	IICHX	B	(800) 527-3713	B+ / 8.7	7.11	12.33	23.63 /69	9.02 /87	11.64 /71	1.25	1.10
GI	AMF Large Cap Equity Inst	IICAX	B	(800) 527-3713	B+ / 8.6	7.02	12.19	23.38 /68	8.82 /86	11.46 /69	1.01	1.35
AA	AMG CEP Balanced I	MBESX	B-	(800) 548-4539	C / 4.8	5.27	4.86	13.06 /22	5.92 /63	--	1.01	1.05
BA	AMG CEP Balanced N	MBEAX	C+	(800) 548-4539	C / 4.7	5.21	4.82	12.85 /21	5.73 /62	8.30 /45	0.87	1.20
BA	AMG CEP Balanced Z	MBEYX	B-	(800) 548-4539	C / 4.9	5.29	4.98	13.17 /22	6.00 /64	8.57 /47	1.11	0.95
GL	AMG FQ Global Risk-Balanced I	MMASX	C+	(800) 548-4539	C / 4.4	7.16	2.82	17.15 /39	4.34 /47	4.07 /16	1.52	1.23
GL	AMG FQ Global Risk-Balanced N	MMAVX	C+	(800) 548-4539	C- / 4.1	7.09	2.65	16.76 /37	3.93 /42	3.65 /14	0.97	1.64
GL	AMG FQ Global Risk-Balanced Z	MMAFX	C+	(800) 548-4539	C / 4.5	7.20	2.86	17.26 /39	4.43 /48	4.16 /16	1.57	1.14
GI	AMG FQ Tax-Mgnd U.S. Equity I	MFQTX	A-	(800) 548-4539	B / 7.9	7.94	10.43	21.16 /58	8.17 /80	13.23 /86	1.14	1.02
GR	AMG FQ Tax-Mgnd US Equity N	MFQAX	A-	(800) 548-4539	B / 7.7	7.90	10.31	20.88 /57	7.89 /78	12.95 /83	0.88	1.27
GR	AMG FQ US Equity I	MEQFX	B	(800) 548-4539	B- / 7.1	6.98	10.38	20.59 /55	6.99 /72	11.03 /66	1.18	0.72
GR	AMG FQ US Equity N	FQUAX	B	(800) 548-4539	B- / 7.0	6.96	10.28	20.32 /54	6.73 /70	10.76 /64	0.93	1.04
SC	AMG Frontier Small Cap Gr I	MSSCX	E	(800) 548-4539	C / 4.3	4.76	7.61	27.22 /80	1.58 /21	9.22 /52	0.00	1.47
SC	● AMG Frontier Small Cap Gr N	MSSVX	E	(800) 548-4539	C- / 4.1	4.66	7.45	26.86 /79	1.29 /20	8.92 /50	0.00	1.82
SC	AMG Frontier Small Cap Gr Z	MSSYX	E	(800) 548-4539	C / 4.5	4.78	7.77	27.46 /80	1.82 /23	9.49 /55	0.00	1.32
SC	● AMG GW&K Small Cap Core I	GWEIX	B-	(800) 835-3879	B / 7.8	4.89	9.00	29.51 /85	7.00 /72	13.18 /86	0.37	0.96
SC	● AMG GW&K Small Cap Core N	GWETX	C+	(800) 835-3879	B- / 7.5	4.82	8.80	29.04 /84	6.56 /69	12.71 /81	0.00	1.31
SC	● AMG GW&K Small Cap Core S	GWESX	B-	(800) 835-3879	B / 7.7	4.85	8.92	29.32 /85	6.85 /71	13.02 /84	0.18	1.03
SC	● AMG GW&K US Small Cap Gr I	ATSIX	E	(800) 548-4539	C- / 3.5	4.04	9.22	25.59 /75	0.37 /15	6.33 /30	0.00	1.17
SC	● AMG GW&K US Small Cap Gr N	ATASX	E-	(800) 548-4539	C- / 3.2	3.75	9.01	24.97 /73	0.09 /14	6.06 /29	0.00	1.42
GR	AMG Managers Brandywine I	BRWIX	C+	(800) 548-4539	C+ / 6.8	6.77	6.46	24.46 /72	6.29 /67	9.41 /54	0.00	1.11
MC	AMG Mgrs Brandywine Adv MCG N	BWAFX	E+	(800) 548-4539	D / 1.7	6.50	6.16	23.03 /67	-0.43 /12	4.43 /18	0.00	1.14
GR	AMG Mgrs Brandywine Blue I	BLUEX	B	(800) 548-4539	B- / 7.5	9.03	9.18	22.00 /62	7.22 /73	9.00 /51	0.00	1.20
GR	AMG Mgrs Cadence Cap App I	MCFYX	A+	(800) 548-4539	B+ / 8.9	9.14	10.95	22.80 /66	9.45 /90	11.37 /69	0.48	0.90
GR	AMG Mgrs Cadence Cap App N	MPAFX	A+	(800) 548-4539	B+ / 8.8	9.08	10.83	22.61 /65	9.29 /89	11.21 /68	0.40	1.05
GR	AMG Mgrs Cadence Cap App Z	MPCIX	A+	(800) 548-4539	A- / 9.0	9.15	11.07	23.03 /67	9.69 /91	11.64 /71	0.75	0.75
SC	AMG Mgrs Cadence Emerg Cos I	MECIX	A-	(800) 548-4539	A+ / 9.8	4.90	13.34	41.90 /98	11.04 /97	15.75 /98	0.00	1.64
SC	AMG Mgrs Cadence Emerg Cos S	MECAX	A-	(800) 548-4539	A+ / 9.8	4.86	13.21	41.58 /98	10.78 /97	15.48 /98	0.00	1.64
MC	AMG Mgrs Cadence Mid Cap I	MCMYX	C-	(800) 548-4539	C+ / 6.9	7.53	9.91	21.27 /59	6.38 /67	9.80 /57	0.69	0.87
MC	AMG Mgrs Cadence Mid Cap N	MCMAX	C-	(800) 548-4539	C+ / 6.8	7.48	9.80	21.03 /57	6.23 /66	9.63 /56	0.52	1.11
MC	AMG Mgrs Cadence Mid Cap Z	MCMFX	C-	(800) 548-4539	B- / 7.1	7.59	10.05	21.55 /60	6.66 /69	10.07 /59	0.89	0.72
RE	AMG Mgrs CenterSquare RE N	MRESX	B+	(800) 548-4539	B / 7.8	7.54	-1.99	14.99 /30	11.73 /98	11.34 /68	2.23	1.07
SC	AMG Mgrs Emerging Opps I	MIMFX	D+	(800) 548-4539	C+ / 5.8	2.55	9.31	33.79 /93	2.65 /29	12.42 /78	0.00	1.26
SC	AMG Mgrs Emerging Opps S	MMCFX	D	(800) 548-4539	C / 5.5	2.50	9.17	33.47 /92	2.40 /27	12.13 /75	0.00	1.28
SC	AMG Mgrs Essex Sm/Micro Gr N	MBRSX	E+	(800) 548-4539	C- / 3.6	3.36	5.70	26.79 /79	1.17 /19	12.54 /79	0.00	1.58
MC	AMG Mgrs Fairpointe Mid Cap I	ABMIX	B-	(800) 548-4539	A+ / 9.6	7.44	20.55	36.24 /95	7.63 /76	14.54 /96	0.53	0.87
MC	AMG Mgrs Fairpointe Mid Cap N	CHTTX	B-	(800) 548-4539	A+ / 9.6	7.36	20.37	35.89 /95	7.36 /74	14.26 /94	0.30	1.12
GL	AMG Mgrs Guardian Glbl Div I	AGCDX	U	(800) 548-4539	U /	7.46	5.54	13.18 /22	--	--	1.98	3.03
GR	AMG Mgrs Lake Partners LASSO I	ALSOX	D+	(800) 548-4539	D- / 1.1	2.08	2.51	5.34 / 4	0.28 /15	2.61 /10	0.00	2.95
GR	AMG Mgrs Lake Partners LASSO N	ALSNX	D+	(800) 548-4539	D- / 1.0	2.01	2.35	5.00 / 4	0.03 /13	2.35 / 9	0.00	3.20
IN	AMG Mgrs LMCG Small Cap Gr I	ACWIX	D-	(800) 548-4539	C- / 3.9	5.83	7.01	25.35 /74	1.12 /19	10.78 /64	0.00	1.28
IN	AMG Mgrs LMCG Small Cap Gr N	ACWDX	D-	(800) 548-4539	C- / 3.7	5.83	7.03	25.11 /74	0.91 /18	10.52 /62	0.00	1.53
BA	AMG Mgrs M&C Balancd I	MOBIX	D+	(800) 548-4539	D+ / 2.3	4.34	0.37	4.82 / 4	4.04 /43	6.37 /31	0.81	1.33
BA	AMG Mgrs M&C Balancd N	MOBAX	D+	(800) 548-4539	D / 2.2	4.42	0.39	4.78 / 4	3.96 /42	6.28 /30	0.71	1.58
GR	AMG Mgrs M&C Growth I	MCGIX	E	(800) 548-4539	C- / 3.6	5.51	2.37	8.34 / 8	5.35 /58	9.68 /56	0.65	0.81

● Denotes fund is closed to new investors
* Denotes fund is included in Section II

90

www.thestreetratings.com

RISK	3 Year		NET ASSETS		ASSET					BULL / BEAR		FUND MANAGER		MINIMUMS		LOADS	
Risk Rating/Pts	Standard Deviation	Beta	NAV As of 2/28/17	Total $(Mil)	Cash %	Stocks %	Bonds %	Other %	Portfolio Turnover Ratio	Last Bull Market Return	Last Bear Market Return	Manager Quality Pct	Manager Tenure (Years)	Initial Purch. $	Additional Purch. $	Front End Load	Back End Load
C+ / 6.5	13.1	1.20	4.13	3	0	99	0	1	3	112.9	-24.2	8	6	0	0	0.0	0.0
C+ / 6.6	12.9	1.18	5.10	6	0	99	0	1	3	124.7	-24.1	15	6	0	0	5.8	0.0
D- / 1.0	17.8	0.57	4.89	1	1	98	0	1	0	33.7	-23.3	3	59	0	0	5.8	0.0
B / 8.5	7.4	1.02	10.95	51	7	58	33	2	129	N/A	N/A	62	4	5,000	250	5.8	0.0
B / 8.5	7.4	1.03	10.83	5	7	58	33	2	129	N/A	N/A	53	4	5,000	250	0.0	0.0
B / 8.5	7.4	1.01	10.96	52	7	58	33	2	129	N/A	N/A	67	4	3,000,000	5,000	0.0	0.0
C / 5.0	13.3	1.18	26.05	24	3	93	2	2	41	82.4	-18.6	4	20	2,500	250	0.0	0.0
C / 4.5	9.6	0.87	9.01	6	1	98	0	1	76	101.5	-8.8	72	N/A	3,000,000	0	0.0	0.0
C / 4.6	9.6	0.87	9.02	39	1	98	0	1	76	99.8	-8.8	70	N/A	2,500	100	0.0	0.0
B- / 7.8	6.6	1.00	16.25	80	0	0	0	100	105	N/A	N/A	55	17	100,000	100	0.0	0.0
B- / 7.8	6.6	1.01	16.10	93	0	0	0	100	105	68.2	-7.1	52	17	2,000	100	0.0	0.0
B- / 7.8	6.6	1.01	16.25	7	0	0	0	100	105	70.6	-7.1	56	17	5,000,000	1,000	0.0	0.0
B- / 7.8	8.1	0.39	14.47	8	11	14	74	1	71	35.6	-3.6	94	8	100,000	100	0.0	0.0
B- / 7.9	8.1	0.39	14.46	2	11	14	74	1	71	32.6	-3.7	93	8	2,000	100	0.0	0.0
B- / 7.8	8.1	0.39	14.50	59	11	14	74	1	71	36.2	-3.5	94	8	5,000,000	1,000	0.0	0.0
B- / 7.0	9.8	0.90	26.98	58	0	98	0	2	102	132.7	-18.7	59	9	100,000	100	0.0	0.0
B- / 7.1	9.8	0.90	27.00	22	0	98	0	2	102	129.6	-18.8	55	9	2,000	100	0.0	0.0
C+ / 6.2	8.9	0.80	16.71	37	0	99	0	1	178	107.1	-16.4	57	9	100,000	100	0.0	0.0
C+ / 6.2	8.9	0.81	16.73	25	0	99	0	1	178	104.3	-16.5	53	9	2,000	100	0.0	0.0
E / 0.4	17.2	1.04	11.82	10	0	99	0	1	70	96.6	-26.8	12	8	100,000	100	0.0	0.0
E / 0.4	17.2	1.05	11.61	N/A	0	99	0	1	70	93.7	-26.9	10	8	2,000	100	0.0	0.0
E / 0.4	17.2	1.04	12.02	7	0	99	0	1	70	99.1	-26.7	14	8	5,000,000	1,000	0.0	0.0
C / 4.9	13.7	0.85	25.85	392	0	97	1	2	16	130.4	-20.2	81	8	100,000	100	0.0	0.0
C / 4.9	13.7	0.85	25.56	37	0	97	1	2	16	125.4	-20.4	79	8	2,000	100	0.0	0.0
C / 4.9	13.7	0.85	25.79	18	0	97	1	2	16	128.4	-20.3	81	8	100,000	100	0.0	0.0
E / 0.3	15.3	0.92	4.81	9	0	98	1	1	106	74.0	-24.3	10	1	1,000,000	50	0.0	0.0
E / 0.3	15.2	0.92	4.02	30	0	98	1	1	106	71.6	-24.4	9	1	2,500	50	0.0	0.0
C / 5.0	13.1	1.07	39.89	730	1	96	2	1	139	86.6	-28.9	17	7	2,000	100	0.0	0.0
C / 4.4	14.1	1.03	9.99	141	0	93	6	1	195	46.6	-29.2	2	7	2,000	100	0.0	0.0
C+ / 5.8	11.2	0.93	40.09	161	2	93	4	1	139	86.9	-21.5	42	7	2,000	100	0.0	0.0
C+ / 6.8	10.8	1.01	30.07	3	0	99	0	1	22	105.1	-16.0	60	13	100,000	100	0.0	0.0
C+ / 6.8	10.8	1.01	29.63	65	0	99	0	1	22	103.6	-16.1	58	13	2,000	100	0.0	0.0
C+ / 6.8	10.7	1.01	30.72	37	0	99	0	1	22	107.8	-16.0	63	13	1,000,000	1,000	0.0	0.0
C / 4.8	16.3	0.98	48.60	48	0	96	3	1	150	174.9	-25.0	93	13	1,000,000	1,000	0.0	0.0
C / 4.8	16.3	0.98	44.91	10	0	96	3	1	150	171.4	-25.1	92	13	2,000	100	0.0	0.0
C- / 3.3	11.6	0.85	29.45	15	1	97	0	2	149	97.9	-19.8	54	13	100,000	100	0.0	0.0
C- / 3.2	11.5	0.85	28.64	88	1	97	0	2	149	96.3	-19.9	52	13	2,000	100	0.0	0.0
C- / 3.2	11.5	0.85	30.66	25	1	97	0	2	149	100.6	-19.8	57	13	1,000,000	1,000	0.0	0.0
C+ / 6.1	15.0	1.09	11.23	400	0	0	0	100	61	107.3	-16.1	70	13	2,000	100	0.0	0.0
D+ / 2.7	16.9	1.02	42.20	27	2	97	0	1	72	131.0	-25.2	21	10	100,000	100	0.0	0.0
D+ / 2.7	16.9	1.02	41.82	135	2	97	0	1	72	128.2	-25.2	19	10	2,000	100	0.0	0.0
D+ / 2.3	16.4	0.97	24.61	28	0	97	2	1	66	120.7	-28.0	13	15	2,000	100	0.0	0.0
C- / 3.0	15.7	1.15	43.98	2,508	0	96	2	2	24	157.1	-25.7	32	18	1,000,000	50	0.0	0.0
C- / 3.0	15.7	1.15	43.00	1,599	0	96	2	2	24	153.7	-25.7	29	18	2,500	50	0.0	0.0
U /	N/A	N/A	10.42	30	0	99	0	1	36	N/A	N/A	N/A	N/A	1,000,000	50	0.0	2.0
B- / 7.8	3.9	0.35	12.18	61	29	31	37	3	30	23.6	-9.5	30	N/A	100,000	50	0.0	0.0
B- / 7.8	3.9	0.35	12.12	29	29	31	37	3	30	21.9	-9.6	27	N/A	2,500	50	0.0	0.0
C- / 3.3	18.3	1.31	14.34	86	5	94	0	1	138	109.9	N/A	1	7	1,000,000	50	0.0	0.0
C- / 3.3	18.3	1.30	14.15	51	5	94	0	1	138	107.3	-30.2	1	7	2,500	50	0.0	0.0
C+ / 6.5	5.9	0.81	21.07	3	2	63	33	2	85	50.2	-5.9	49	23	1,000,000	50	0.0	0.0
C+ / 6.6	5.9	0.81	21.16	21	2	63	33	2	85	49.4	-6.0	48	23	2,500	50	0.0	0.0
D / 1.6	9.4	0.79	18.45	664	2	95	2	1	64	85.4	-11.6	37	23	1,000,000	50	0.0	0.0

					PERFORMANCE							
99 Pct = Best 0 Pct = Worst			Overall		Perfor-	Total Return % through 2/28/17					Incl. in Returns	
									Annualized		Dividend	Expense
Fund Type	Fund Name	Ticker Symbol	Investment Rating	Phone	mance Rating/Pts	3 Mo	6 Mo	1Yr / Pct	3Yr / Pct	5Yr / Pct	Yield	Ratio
GR	AMG Mgrs M&C Growth N	MCGFX	E	(800) 548-4539	C- / 3.4	5.44	2.23	8.11 / 8	5.10 / 55	9.42 / 54	0.20	1.06
GR	AMG Mgrs M&C Growth R	MCRGX	E	(800) 548-4539	C- / 3.2	5.36	2.14	7.80 / 7	4.84 / 52	9.15 / 52	0.14	1.31
MC	AMG Mgrs M&C Mid Cap Gr N	AMCMX	C-	(800) 548-4539	C / 5.1	5.14	5.14	18.03 / 43	5.28 / 57	8.68 / 48	0.28	2.01
FO	AMG Mgrs Pictet Intl I	APCTX	U	(800) 548-4539	U /	8.69	3.49	15.48 / 32	--	--	1.36	1.58
SC	AMG Mgrs Silvercrest Sm Cap I	ACRTX	A-	(800) 548-4539	A+ / 9.6	2.97	12.28	36.64 / 95	9.68 / 91	13.82 / 92	0.20	1.23
SC	AMG Mgrs Silvercrest Sm Cap N	ASCTX	B+	(800) 548-4539	A / 9.5	2.95	12.20	36.28 / 95	9.41 / 90	13.54 / 89	0.00	1.48
SC	● AMG Mgrs Skyline Special Eq N	SKSEX	B-	(800) 548-4539	B- / 7.1	4.20	12.53	27.85 / 81	6.15 / 66	13.98 / 93	0.00	1.36
SC	AMG Mgrs Special Equity I	MSEIX	C+	(800) 548-4539	B- / 7.3	6.45	10.34	30.49 / 87	5.32 / 58	11.54 / 70	0.00	1.16
SC	AMG Mgrs Special Equity N	MGSEX	C+	(800) 548-4539	B- / 7.1	6.39	10.21	30.16 / 87	5.06 / 55	11.35 / 69	0.00	1.16
GR	AMG Renaissance Large Cap Gr I	MRLSX	B+	(800) 548-4539	A / 9.4	7.81	13.82	24.56 / 72	10.24 / 95	14.16 / 94	0.62	1.12
GR	AMG Renaissance Large Cap Gr N	MRLTX	B+	(800) 548-4539	A / 9.3	7.77	13.74	24.22 / 71	9.86 / 93	13.75 / 91	0.39	1.37
GR	AMG Renaissance Large Cap Gr Z	MRLIX	B+	(800) 548-4539	A / 9.5	7.87	13.95	24.70 / 72	10.39 / 95	14.31 / 95	0.77	0.97
IN	AMG River Road Div ACV I	ARIDX	B+	(800) 548-4539	B+ / 8.5	5.48	9.53	23.97 / 70	9.38 / 89	12.58 / 80	2.42	0.86
IN	AMG River Road Div ACV II I	ADIVX	A	(800) 548-4539	B+ / 8.5	5.59	9.60	23.67 / 69	9.44 / 90	--	2.21	0.90
IN	AMG River Road Div ACV II N	ADVTX	A	(800) 548-4539	B+ / 8.3	5.55	9.49	23.41 / 68	9.15 / 88	--	2.00	1.15
IN	AMG River Road Div ACV N	ARDEX	B	(800) 548-4539	B+ / 8.3	5.44	9.41	23.63 / 69	9.11 / 87	12.32 / 77	2.18	1.11
GL	AMG River Road Long-Short I	ALSIX	C-	(800) 548-4539	D / 2.2	0.86	4.34	11.25 / 15	2.46 / 27	--	0.00	2.43
AA	AMG River Road Long-Short N	ARLSX	C-	(800) 548-4539	D / 2.1	0.87	4.20	11.06 / 15	2.21 / 25	5.14 / 22	0.00	2.68
MC	AMG River Road Select Val I	ARIMX	C+	(800) 548-4539	A / 9.3	6.25	12.30	32.82 / 91	8.73 / 85	12.28 / 77	0.34	1.10
MC	AMG River Road Select Val N	ARSMX	C+	(800) 548-4539	A- / 9.2	6.24	12.25	32.54 / 91	8.45 / 82	12.01 / 74	0.12	1.35
SC	AMG River Road Small Cap Val I	ARSIX	B+	(800) 548-4539	A- / 9.1	5.53	13.02	32.59 / 91	8.25 / 81	12.34 / 77	0.00	1.14
SC	AMG River Road Small Cap Val N	ARSVX	B	(800) 548-4539	A- / 9.0	5.46	12.95	32.29 / 90	7.98 / 79	12.05 / 75	0.00	1.39
SC	AMG SouthernSun Small Cap I	SSSIX	D-	(800) 548-4539	C / 4.5	7.53	11.07	30.56 / 87	0.53 / 16	9.12 / 52	0.23	0.96
SC	AMG SouthernSun Small Cap N	SSSFX	D-	(800) 548-4539	C- / 4.2	7.42	10.91	30.19 / 87	0.27 / 15	8.85 / 49	0.00	1.21
MC	AMG SouthernSun US Equity C	SSECX	D	(800) 548-4539	C- / 3.3	2.11	5.31	24.19 / 71	2.16 / 25	--	0.00	1.97
MC	AMG SouthernSun US Equity I	SSEIX	D+	(800) 548-4539	C- / 4.1	2.42	5.87	25.47 / 75	3.21 / 34	--	0.37	0.97
MC	AMG SouthernSun US Equity N	SSEFX	D+	(800) 548-4539	C- / 3.9	2.34	5.71	25.12 / 74	2.95 / 31	--	0.13	1.22
GR	AMG Systematic Large Cap Val I	MSYSX	C+	(800) 548-4539	B+ / 8.9	5.47	16.25	33.03 / 92	7.07 / 72	11.84 / 73	1.70	0.92
GR	AMG Systematic Large Cap Val N	MSYAX	C+	(800) 548-4539	B+ / 8.8	5.41	16.11	32.60 / 91	6.77 / 70	11.53 / 70	1.47	1.17
MC	AMG Systematic Mid Cap Val I	SYIMX	C+	(800) 548-4539	B / 8.0	4.14	12.77	33.91 / 93	6.02 / 64	11.12 / 67	2.27	0.83
MC	AMG Systematic Mid Cap Val N	SYAMX	C+	(800) 548-4539	B / 7.8	4.14	12.63	33.55 / 92	5.73 / 62	10.83 / 64	1.97	1.08
MC	AMG Systematic Mid Cap Val S	SYCSX	C+	(800) 548-4539	B / 8.0	4.19	12.76	33.83 / 93	5.94 / 64	--	2.17	0.93
GR	AMG TimesSquare All Cap Gr I	MTGIX	C+	(800) 548-4539	B- / 7.4	9.93	8.64	23.49 / 68	6.59 / 69	12.06 / 75	0.21	1.06
GR	AMG TimesSquare All Cap Gr N	MTGVX	C	(800) 548-4539	B- / 7.0	9.82	8.36	22.88 / 66	6.05 / 65	11.52 / 70	0.00	1.65
GR	AMG TimesSquare All Cap Gr S	MTGSX	C+	(800) 548-4539	B- / 7.3	9.87	8.59	23.32 / 68	6.48 / 68	11.93 / 74	0.11	1.25
GL	AMG TimesSquare Intl Sm Cap N	TCMPX	C+	(800) 548-4539	C / 4.3	7.32	1.87	13.98 / 25	5.68 / 61	--	0.51	1.44
GL	AMG TimesSquare Intl Sm Cap Z	TCMIX	C+	(800) 548-4539	C / 4.5	7.48	2.04	14.30 / 27	5.96 / 64	--	0.59	1.19
MC	AMG TimesSquare Mid Cap Gr N	TMDPX	C+	(800) 548-4539	C+ / 6.2	6.29	6.47	22.60 / 65	5.52 / 60	11.60 / 71	0.00	1.14
MC	AMG TimesSquare Mid Cap Gr Z	TMDIX	C+	(800) 548-4539	C+ / 6.4	6.33	6.56	22.87 / 66	5.75 / 62	11.83 / 73	0.05	1.04
SC	● AMG TimesSquare Small Cap Gr N	TSCPX	D+	(800) 548-4539	C / 4.7	2.88	5.78	23.69 / 69	3.72 / 39	11.15 / 67	0.19	1.25
SC	● AMG TimesSquare Small Cap Gr Z	TSCIX	D+	(800) 548-4539	C / 4.8	2.90	5.80	23.88 / 69	3.91 / 42	11.35 / 69	0.36	1.05
EM	AMG Trilogy EM Equity I	TLESX	D-	(800) 548-4539	C- / 3.2	7.58	4.01	27.64 / 81	0.21 / 14	-1.95 / 3	1.07	1.00
EM	AMG Trilogy EM Equity N	TLEVX	E+	(800) 548-4539	D / 1.8	7.57	3.73	27.04 / 79	-0.17 / 13	--	0.84	1.44
EM	AMG Trilogy EM Equity Z	TLEIX	D-	(800) 548-4539	C- / 3.2	7.59	3.87	27.59 / 81	0.31 / 15	-1.83 / 3	1.17	0.94
EM	AMG Trilogy EM Wealth Equity Z	TYWIX	U	(800) 548-4539	U /	4.33	2.05	21.41 / 59	--	--	0.79	1.34
GL	AMG Trilogy Global Equity I	TLGSX	C-	(800) 548-4539	C / 5.1	7.60	9.99	21.99 / 62	2.98 / 32	7.00 / 35	1.05	0.82
GL	AMG Trilogy Global Equity N	TLGVX	C-	(800) 548-4539	C / 4.8	7.47	9.73	21.47 / 60	2.57 / 28	--	0.52	1.22
GL	AMG Trilogy Global Equity Z	TLGIX	C-	(800) 548-4539	C / 5.2	7.61	10.01	22.04 / 62	3.09 / 33	7.11 / 35	1.15	0.72
GR	AMG Trilogy Intl Small Cap I	TLSSX	E+	(800) 548-4539	E+ / 0.7	8.75	2.72	13.79 / 24	-2.26 / 6	4.15 / 16	0.77	1.69
GR	AMG Trilogy Intl Small Cap N	TLSVX	E+	(800) 548-4539	E+ / 0.6	8.72	2.53	13.42 / 23	-2.67 / 5	3.77 / 14	0.39	2.08
GR	AMG Trilogy Intl Small Cap Z	TLSIX	E+	(800) 548-4539	E+ / 0.7	8.75	2.73	13.91 / 25	-2.18 / 6	4.27 / 17	0.89	1.58
GI	AMG Yacktman Focused I	YAFIX	C-	(800) 548-4539	B- / 7.1	7.08	8.02	20.60 / 55	7.93 / 78	10.85 / 65	1.50	1.08

● Denotes fund is closed to new investors

* Denotes fund is included in Section II

92

Risk Rating/Pts	Standard Deviation	Beta	NAV As of 2/28/17	Total $(Mil)	Cash %	Stocks %	Bonds %	Other %	Portfolio Turnover Ratio	Last Bull Market Return	Last Bear Market Return	Manager Quality Pct	Manager Tenure (Years)	Initial Purch. $	Additional Purch. $	Front End Load	Back End Load
D / 1.7	9.4	0.79	18.41	390	2	95	2	1	64	83.0	-11.7	34	23	2,500	50	0.0	0.0
D / 1.6	9.4	0.79	18.01	6	2	95	2	1	64	80.5	-11.8	31	23	2,500	50	0.0	0.0
C / 4.4	10.9	0.82	10.36	5	4	95	0	1	39	88.8	-18.0	42	10	2,500	50	0.0	0.0
U /	N/A	N/A	9.80	1,509	0	99	0	1	38	N/A	N/A	N/A	N/A	1,000,000	50	0.0	2.0
C / 5.0	15.9	0.97	17.97	228	2	97	0	1	32	N/A	N/A	89	6	1,000,000	50	0.0	0.0
C / 5.0	15.9	0.98	17.85	27	2	97	0	1	32	N/A	N/A	88	6	2,500	50	0.0	0.0
C / 5.5	15.6	0.93	43.19	1,461	0	0	0	100	31	156.4	-25.2	71	16	2,000	100	0.0	2.0
C / 4.5	15.7	0.96	106.52	20	0	96	2	2	116	121.1	-23.4	59	11	100,000	100	0.0	0.0
C / 4.5	15.7	0.96	103.75	187	0	96	2	2	116	118.7	-23.5	56	11	2,000	100	0.0	0.0
C / 4.6	11.8	1.07	12.80	15	0	98	1	1	48	148.6	-22.0	62	N/A	100,000	100	0.0	0.0
C / 4.7	11.8	1.07	12.71	5	0	98	1	1	48	144.1	-22.1	57	N/A	2,000	100	0.0	0.0
C / 4.6	11.8	1.07	12.66	61	0	98	1	1	48	150.7	-22.0	63	N/A	5,000,000	1,000	0.0	0.0
C / 5.3	10.0	0.90	12.68	615	7	91	1	1	47	109.6	-11.6	73	12	100,000	50	0.0	0.0
B- / 7.0	9.9	0.89	14.54	125	9	90	0	1	34	N/A	N/A	74	5	1,000,000	50	0.0	0.0
B- / 7.0	9.9	0.90	14.53	4	9	90	0	1	34	N/A	N/A	70	5	2,500	50	0.0	0.0
C / 5.3	10.0	0.90	12.69	332	7	91	1	1	47	106.8	-11.7	70	12	2,500	50	0.0	0.0
B / 8.2	7.5	0.35	11.77	37	53	46	0	1	298	N/A	N/A	88	7	1,000,000	50	0.0	0.0
B / 8.1	7.5	0.73	11.65	8	53	46	0	1	298	39.2	N/A	33	7	2,500	50	0.0	0.0
C- / 3.1	12.8	0.99	7.66	34	0	97	2	1	65	116.7	-17.5	66	10	1,000,000	50	0.0	0.0
C- / 3.1	12.8	0.99	7.54	5	0	97	2	1	65	113.8	-17.7	62	10	2,500	50	0.0	0.0
C / 4.7	12.2	0.71	13.65	272	1	91	7	1	57	115.7	-18.0	91	12	1,000,000	50	0.0	0.0
C / 4.6	12.3	0.71	13.48	27	1	91	7	1	57	112.9	-18.1	90	12	2,500	50	0.0	0.0
D / 2.1	16.8	0.86	23.90	214	4	95	0	1	16	109.9	-23.6	14	14	100,000	100	0.0	2.0
D / 2.1	16.8	0.85	23.59	128	4	95	0	1	16	107.1	-23.7	12	14	2,000	100	0.0	2.0
C / 5.0	14.2	1.04	13.09	40	9	90	0	1	16	N/A	N/A	5	5	2,000	100	0.0	2.0
C / 5.0	14.2	1.04	13.50	751	9	90	0	1	16	N/A	N/A	7	5	100,000	100	0.0	0.0
C / 5.1	14.2	1.03	13.47	46	9	90	0	1	16	N/A	N/A	7	5	2,000	100	0.0	2.0
C- / 3.5	13.1	1.15	11.42	4	0	97	2	1	87	119.7	-24.9	17	15	100,000	100	0.0	0.0
C- / 3.6	13.1	1.15	11.41	16	0	97	2	1	87	116.5	-25.0	15	15	2,000	100	0.0	0.0
C- / 4.1	14.2	1.12	13.97	94	0	98	0	2	122	113.8	-24.8	19	11	1,000,000	1,000	0.0	0.0
C- / 4.1	14.2	1.12	13.96	16	0	98	0	2	122	110.7	-24.8	17	11	2,000	100	0.0	0.0
C- / 4.1	14.2	1.12	13.95	2	0	98	0	2	122	N/A	N/A	19	11	100,000	100	0.0	0.0
C- / 4.2	13.1	1.14	15.30	5	0	99	0	1	116	127.0	-22.7	14	7	100,000	100	0.0	0.0
C- / 4.2	13.1	1.14	14.98	N/A	0	99	0	1	116	121.4	-22.8	11	7	2,000	100	0.0	0.0
C- / 4.2	13.1	1.14	15.33	27	0	99	0	1	116	125.6	-22.8	13	7	100,000	100	0.0	0.0
B- / 7.4	11.4	0.74	13.18	40	0	0	0	100	95	N/A	N/A	96	4	2,000	100	0.0	2.0
B- / 7.5	11.4	0.74	13.25	112	0	0	0	100	95	N/A	N/A	97	4	5,000,000	100,000	0.0	2.0
C+ / 5.8	11.2	0.86	18.36	858	0	0	0	100	47	120.1	-21.1	40	12	2,000	100	0.0	0.0
C+ / 5.8	11.2	0.86	18.74	1,055	0	0	0	100	47	122.5	-21.0	43	12	5,000,000	100,000	0.0	0.0
C- / 4.2	14.4	0.88	15.96	312	0	0	0	100	71	111.6	-21.5	45	17	2,000	100	0.0	0.0
C- / 4.2	14.4	0.88	16.29	786	0	0	0	100	71	113.7	-21.5	47	17	5,000,000	100,000	0.0	0.0
C- / 4.0	15.8	0.95	8.05	2	0	0	0	100	33	9.9	-27.8	57	6	100,000	100	0.0	2.0
C- / 4.1	15.7	0.94	8.07	N/A	0	0	0	100	33	N/A	N/A	51	6	2,000	100	0.0	2.0
C- / 3.9	15.7	0.94	8.00	108	0	0	0	100	33	10.5	-27.8	58	6	1,000,000	1,000	0.0	2.0
U /	N/A	N/A	10.15	36	0	0	0	100	58	N/A	N/A	N/A	2	5,000,000	1,000	0.0	2.0
C / 4.4	11.9	0.88	10.28	40	0	0	0	100	48	74.8	-21.5	91	6	100,000	100	0.0	0.0
C / 4.6	11.8	0.88	10.39	N/A	0	0	0	100	48	N/A	N/A	89	6	2,000	100	0.0	0.0
C / 4.4	11.9	0.88	10.25	11	0	0	0	100	48	75.5	-21.5	91	6	1,000,000	1,000	0.0	0.0
C / 5.1	12.8	0.87	9.74	10	0	0	0	100	80	53.4	-29.5	1	6	100,000	100	0.0	2.0
C / 5.0	12.8	0.87	9.68	N/A	0	0	0	100	80	50.6	N/A	1	6	2,000	100	0.0	2.0
C / 5.1	12.9	0.88	9.75	8	0	0	0	100	80	54.3	-29.5	2	6	1,000,000	1,000	0.0	2.0
C- / 3.3	9.9	0.83	20.81	1,075	0	0	0	100	6	90.4	-9.4	65	15	100,000	100	0.0	2.0

I. Index of Stock Mutual Funds

| | | | | | | Total Return % through 2/28/17 | | | Annualized | | Incl. in Returns | |
Fund Type	Fund Name	Ticker Symbol	Overall Investment Rating	Phone	Performance Rating/Pts	3 Mo	6 Mo	1Yr / Pct	3Yr / Pct	5Yr / Pct	Dividend Yield	Expense Ratio
GI	AMG Yacktman Focused N	YAFFX	C-	(800) 548-4539	C+ / 6.9	7.02	7.91	20.35 /54	7.72 /77	10.67 /63	1.33	1.25
GI	AMG Yacktman I	YACKX	C+	(800) 548-4539	C+ / 6.6	6.46	7.68	19.14 /48	7.43 /75	10.80 /64	1.70	0.74
FO	Amidex 35 Israel Mutual A	AMDAX	E+	(888) 876-3566	E- / 0.2	6.52	1.16	3.57 / 3	-2.66 / 5	1.52 / 7	0.00	3.71
FO	Amidex 35 Israel Mutual C	AMDCX	E+	(888) 876-3566	E / 0.3	6.33	0.84	2.70 / 2	-3.36 / 4	0.77 / 6	0.00	4.46
FO	Amidex 35 Israel Mutual Fd	AMDEX	D-	(888) 876-3566	E / 0.3	6.47	1.11	3.49 / 3	-2.64 / 5	1.55 / 7	0.00	3.71
FS	Anchor Tactical Credit Strgs Inv	ATCSX	U	(855) 282-1100	U /	2.26	1.49	3.27 / 3	--	--	1.63	3.17
GI	Ancora Income Fund Class C	ANICX	C	(866) 626-2672	D+ / 2.9	3.61	-0.83	9.30 /10	5.55 /60	4.46 /18	5.71	2.28
GI	Ancora Income Fund Class I	AAIIX	C+	(866) 626-2672	C- / 3.4	3.69	-0.48	10.02 /12	6.23 /66	5.07 /22	6.03	1.78
SC	Ancora Microcap Fund Class C	ANCCX	D+	(866) 626-2672	C+ / 6.1	4.00	9.11	24.48 /72	5.64 /61	11.83 /73	0.00	2.36
SC	Ancora Microcap Fund I	ANCIX	C-	(866) 626-2672	C+ / 6.7	4.23	9.58	25.51 /75	6.49 /68	12.73 /81	0.20	1.61
SC	Ancora Special Opportunity Fund C	ANSCX	C+	(866) 626-2672	C+ / 6.9	6.05	7.69	27.02 /79	6.45 /68	12.50 /79	0.00	2.89
SC	Ancora Special Opportunity Fund I	ANSIX	C+	(866) 626-2672	B- / 7.5	6.26	8.23	28.19 /82	7.26 /74	13.31 /87	0.00	2.14
MC	Ancora Thelen Small Mid Cap C	AATCX	C-	(866) 626-2672	C / 5.1	6.11	8.37	26.24 /77	3.36 /35	--	0.00	2.07
MC	Ancora Thelen Small Mid Cap I	AATIX	C	(866) 626-2672	C+ / 5.8	6.33	8.79	27.25 /80	4.14 /44	--	0.14	1.31
AA	Angel Oak Multi Strategy Income A	ANGLX	C	(877) 625-3042	D / 1.9	1.15	3.14	8.94 / 9	3.23 /34	6.28 /30	5.06	1.42
MC	APEXcm Small/Mid Cap Growth	APSGX	C-	(888) 575-4800	C / 5.0	4.63	6.72	23.52 /68	3.69 /39	--	0.00	1.22
GI	API Capital Income A	APIGX	D+	(800) 544-6060	C- / 3.1	6.11	5.90	17.66 /41	3.48 /37	6.80 /33	1.66	1.84
GI	API Capital Income Inst	AFAAX	C	(800) 544-6060	C / 4.6	6.20	6.14	18.27 /44	3.99 /43	7.32 /37	2.17	1.34
GI	API Capital Income L	AFDDX	C-	(800) 544-6060	C- / 3.7	5.95	5.61	17.07 /39	2.96 /31	6.26 /30	1.43	2.34
GL	API Growth A	AFGGX	D+	(800) 544-6060	C- / 3.1	6.32	5.26	19.84 /51	3.16 /33	9.67 /56	0.00	1.42
GL	API Growth Inst	APGRX	C-	(800) 544-6060	C- / 4.2	6.29	5.27	19.79 /51	3.16 /33	--	0.00	1.42
GL	API Growth L	APITX	D+	(800) 544-6060	C- / 3.4	6.03	4.73	18.56 /45	2.14 /25	8.58 /47	0.00	2.42
AA	API Master Allocation A	APIFX	D	(800) 544-6060	D / 2.1	4.80	5.06	17.25 /39	1.91 /23	6.86 /34	0.00	2.66
AA	API Master Allocation Inst	APMAX	D+	(800) 544-6060	C- / 3.4	4.90	5.28	17.81 /42	2.41 /27	--	0.00	2.16
AA	API Master Allocation L	APILX	D	(800) 544-6060	D+ / 2.6	4.65	4.77	16.64 /37	1.39 /20	6.32 /30	0.00	3.16
AA	API Multi Asset Income I	APIIX	C-	(800) 544-6060	C / 4.8	5.75	6.71	24.33 /71	2.93 /31	6.06 /29	7.08	2.04
GL	API Short Term Bond A	APIMX	E-	(800) 544-6060	D- / 1.2	2.31	2.21	7.51 / 7	0.91 /18	2.15 / 8	2.36	1.76
GR	API Short Term Bond Inst	APIBX	E-	(800) 544-6060	D- / 1.4	2.30	2.18	7.62 / 7	0.90 /18	--	2.27	1.76
GL	API Short Term Bond L	AFMMX	E-	(800) 544-6060	E+ / 0.9	2.06	1.70	6.64 / 5	-0.09 /13	1.13 / 6	1.77	2.76
GL	Appleseed Fund Institutional	APPIX	D	(800) 408-4682	D / 1.9	6.65	1.65	16.15 /35	0.47 /16	5.34 /24	1.63	1.22
GL	Appleseed Fund Investor	APPLX	D	(800) 408-4682	D / 1.8	6.60	1.48	15.95 /34	0.23 /14	5.10 /22	1.40	1.41
GR	● AQR Diversified Arbitrage I	ADAIX	D	(866) 290-2688	E+ / 0.9	3.41	5.26	9.62 /11	-0.90 /10	0.19 / 5	7.09	2.58
GR	● AQR Diversified Arbitrage N	ADANX	D	(866) 290-2688	E+ / 0.8	3.28	5.12	9.26 /10	-1.17 / 9	-0.08 / 4	6.74	2.83
EM	AQR Emerging Defensive Style I	AZEIX	E+	(866) 290-2688	E+ / 0.7	5.65	-1.96	13.93 /25	-2.14 / 6	--	1.65	1.15
EM	AQR Emerging Defensive Style N	AZENX	E+	(866) 290-2688	E+ / 0.6	5.52	-2.03	13.73 /24	-2.37 / 6	--	1.39	1.43
EM	AQR Emerging Multi-Style I	QEELX	U	(866) 290-2688	U /	9.09	5.12	27.12 /79	--	--	1.90	1.43
EM	AQR Emerging Multi-Style R6	QECRX	U	(866) 290-2688	U /	9.06	5.22	27.39 /80	--	--	1.99	0.93
GR	AQR Equity Market Neutral I	QMNIX	U	(866) 290-2688	U /	1.60	5.75	4.21 / 3	--	--	1.50	2.22
GR	AQR Equity Market Neutral N	QMNNX	U	(866) 290-2688	U /	1.53	5.60	3.97 / 3	--	--	1.17	2.46
GR	AQR Equity Market Neutral R6	QMNRX	U	(866) 290-2688	U /	1.66	5.80	4.36 / 3	--	--	1.56	3.10
GL	AQR Global Equity Fund I	AQGIX	C+	(866) 290-2688	C+ / 6.7	8.20	9.15	21.76 /61	5.80 /62	10.72 /64	2.09	0.91
GL	AQR Global Equity Fund N	AQGNX	C+	(866) 290-2688	C+ / 6.5	8.01	8.96	21.46 /60	5.54 /60	10.41 /61	1.90	1.18
GL	AQR Global Equity Fund R6	AQGRX	B-	(866) 290-2688	C+ / 6.9	8.28	9.22	22.06 /62	6.01 /64	--	2.31	0.72
GR	AQR International Def Style I	ANDIX	D	(866) 290-2688	D / 2.1	5.98	0.79	10.91 /14	1.72 /22	--	1.41	1.13
GR	AQR International Def Style N	ANDNX	D+	(866) 290-2688	D / 1.9	5.93	0.78	10.73 /14	1.47 /21	--	1.30	1.45
FO	AQR International Equity Fund I	AQIIX	D	(866) 290-2688	D+ / 2.8	8.26	5.99	17.13 /39	0.49 /16	6.82 /34	2.96	0.93
FO	AQR International Equity N	AQINX	D	(866) 290-2688	D+ / 2.6	8.24	6.01	16.81 /38	0.22 /14	6.50 /31	2.65	1.22
FO	AQR International Equity R6	AQIRX	C-	(866) 290-2688	D+ / 2.8	8.31	6.06	17.13 /39	0.62 /16	--	2.90	0.86
FO	AQR International Momentum Style I	AIMOX	D-	(866) 290-2688	E / 0.4	5.55	0.20	8.41 / 8	-2.72 / 5	4.26 /17	2.43	0.68
FO	AQR International Momentum Style N	AIONX	D-	(866) 290-2688	E / 0.4	5.58	0.14	8.19 / 8	-2.93 / 5	--	2.15	0.94
FO	AQR International Momentum Style	QIORX	U	(866) 290-2688	U /	5.59	0.31	8.53 / 8	--	--	2.53	0.55
GR	AQR International Multi-Style I	QICLX	D-	(866) 290-2688	E+ / 0.8	7.01	4.89	12.59 /20	-2.09 / 6	--	2.53	0.84

● Denotes fund is closed to new investors
* Denotes fund is included in Section II

RISK	3 Year		NET ASSETS		ASSET					BULL / BEAR		FUND MANAGER		MINIMUMS		LOADS	
Risk Rating/Pts	Standard Deviation	Beta	NAV As of 2/28/17	Total $(Mil)	Cash %	Stocks %	Bonds %	Other %	Portfolio Turnover Ratio	Last Bull Market Return	Last Bear Market Return	Manager Quality Pct	Manager Tenure (Years)	Initial Purch. $	Additional Purch. $	Front End Load	Back End Load
C- /3.4	9.9	0.83	20.83	3,520	0	0	0	100	6	88.9	-9.4	62	15	2,000	100	0.0	2.0
C /5.5	8.8	0.78	22.51	8,758	3	77	18	2	2	91.0	-10.2	65	15	2,500	100	0.0	2.0
C+ /5.9	11.3	0.71	10.45	1	2	97	0	1	11	7.6	-28.8	40	16	500	250	5.5	0.0
C+ /5.8	11.4	0.71	7.22	1	2	97	0	1	11	3.3	-29.0	30	16	500	250	0.0	0.0
C+ /5.9	11.3	0.71	13.65	8	2	97	0	1	11	7.7	-28.7	40	16	500	250	0.0	2.0
U /	N/A	N/A	10.13	125	0	0	0	100	1,832	N/A	N/A	N/A	2	2,500	100	4.8	1.0
B /8.1	4.1	0.19	8.17	12	5	56	38	1	89	31.1	-0.4	92	13	5,000	1,000	0.0	2.0
B /8.2	4.1	0.20	8.29	22	5	56	38	1	89	34.9	-0.2	93	13	5,000	1,000	0.0	2.0
D+ /2.9	15.3	0.84	12.02	1	1	98	0	1	27	102.0	-23.1	73	9	5,000	1,000	0.0	2.0
C- /3.1	15.3	0.84	13.01	17	1	98	0	1	27	110.7	-22.9	79	9	5,000	1,000	0.0	2.0
C /4.7	11.1	0.55	6.62	12	13	83	2	2	200	101.6	-18.8	88	13	5,000	1,000	0.0	2.0
C /4.9	11.1	0.56	7.26	4	13	83	2	2	200	109.5	-18.5	91	13	5,000	1,000	0.0	2.0
C /5.2	13.2	1.02	14.24	1	0	99	0	1	57	N/A	N/A	9	4	5,000	1,000	0.0	2.0
C /5.3	13.2	1.02	14.60	65	0	99	0	1	57	N/A	N/A	13	4	5,000	1,000	0.0	2.0
B+ /9.4	2.7	0.16	11.29	456	7	0	91	2	44	43.5	N/A	86	6	1,000	100	2.3	0.0
C /4.6	15.0	1.13	17.06	287	3	96	0	1	35	N/A	N/A	6	5	2,500	100	0.0	0.0
C+ /6.0	9.5	0.87	43.59	7	1	89	8	2	30	63.1	-15.8	13	29	1,000	100	5.8	0.0
C+ /6.0	9.8	0.88	44.51	20	1	89	8	2	30	67.5	-15.6	15	29	1,000,000	100,000	0.0	0.0
C+ /5.9	9.5	0.87	42.22	16	1	89	8	2	30	58.7	-16.0	9	29	1,000	100	0.0	0.0
C+ /5.8	11.3	0.76	15.60	26	1	98	0	1	47	94.6	-21.5	91	32	1,000	100	5.8	0.0
C+ /5.8	11.3	0.76	16.36	9	1	98	0	1	47	N/A	N/A	91	32	1,000,000	100,000	0.0	0.0
C+ /5.7	11.2	0.76	13.50	27	1	98	0	1	47	84.3	-21.9	87	32	1,000	100	0.0	0.0
C+ /5.7	10.6	1.58	31.28	6	2	97	0	1	1	67.1	-20.7	2	8	1,000	100	5.8	0.0
C+ /5.9	10.6	1.57	32.98	2	2	97	0	1	1	N/A	N/A	3	8	1,000,000	100,000	0.0	0.0
C /5.3	10.7	1.58	29.77	22	2	97	0	1	1	62.6	-20.8	2	8	1,000	100	0.0	0.0
C /5.4	8.4	1.15	10.86	226	0	40	59	1	101	51.3	-12.4	12	20	1,000,000	100,000	0.0	0.0
D- /1.0	3.3	0.21	3.93	10	3	6	90	1	84	16.2	-9.9	80	20	1,000	100	2.3	0.0
D- /1.0	3.4	0.21	4.18	45	3	6	90	1	84	N/A	N/A	58	20	1,000,000	100,000	0.0	0.0
D- /1.0	3.3	0.21	3.61	46	3	6	90	1	84	10.0	-10.2	72	20	1,000	100	0.0	0.0
C+ /5.9	9.8	0.54	12.57	86	26	50	23	1	82	43.8	-11.7	78	11	100,000	0	0.0	2.0
C+ /5.9	9.8	0.55	12.50	99	26	50	23	1	82	42.1	-11.8	76	11	2,500	0	0.0	2.0
B- /7.3	3.7	0.10	9.36	375	9	18	24	49	249	3.2	-0.5	49	8	5,000,000	0	0.0	0.0
B- /7.3	3.8	0.10	9.35	102	9	18	24	49	249	1.8	-0.7	45	8	1,000,000	0	0.0	0.0
C /4.7	13.8	0.80	8.43	53	0	97	1	2	23	N/A	N/A	28	5	5,000,000	0	0.0	0.0
C /4.9	13.8	0.80	8.64	4	0	97	1	2	23	N/A	N/A	26	5	1,000,000	0	0.0	0.0
U /	N/A	N/A	9.04	77	0	98	1	1	94	N/A	N/A	N/A	3	5,000,000	0	0.0	0.0
U /	N/A	N/A	9.05	191	0	98	1	1	94	N/A	N/A	N/A	3	50,000,000	0	0.0	0.0
U /	N/A	N/A	12.00	932	58	17	23	2	383	N/A	N/A	N/A	3	5,000,000	0	0.0	0.0
U /	N/A	N/A	11.98	161	58	17	23	2	383	N/A	N/A	N/A	3	1,000,000	0	0.0	0.0
U /	N/A	N/A	12.01	159	58	17	23	2	383	N/A	N/A	N/A	3	50,000,000	0	0.0	0.0
C /5.3	9.8	0.74	7.93	36	2	88	8	2	78	101.8	-23.7	97	8	5,000,000	0	0.0	0.0
C /5.4	9.7	0.74	7.89	2	2	88	8	2	78	98.7	-23.8	96	8	1,000,000	0	0.0	0.0
B- /7.5	9.7	0.74	7.99	115	2	88	8	2	78	N/A	N/A	97	8	100,000	0	0.0	0.0
C+ /6.3	9.7	0.70	11.76	104	1	92	6	1	83	N/A	N/A	12	5	5,000,000	0	0.0	0.0
C+ /6.6	9.8	0.71	12.06	29	1	92	6	1	83	N/A	N/A	10	5	1,000,000	0	0.0	0.0
C+ /5.6	10.6	0.83	10.12	345	4	89	5	2	62	65.2	-28.0	78	8	5,000,000	0	0.0	0.0
C+ /5.6	10.5	0.83	10.33	38	4	89	5	2	62	62.4	-28.1	77	8	1,000,000	0	0.0	0.0
B- /7.4	10.5	0.83	10.74	21	4	89	5	2	62	N/A	N/A	79	8	100,000	0	0.0	0.0
C+ /5.8	10.2	0.77	13.30	283	2	95	2	1	85	40.3	-26.9	39	8	5,000,000	0	0.0	0.0
C+ /5.8	10.2	0.77	13.29	29	2	95	2	1	85	N/A	N/A	36	8	1,000,000	0	0.0	0.0
U /	N/A	N/A	13.28	37	2	95	2	1	85	N/A	N/A	N/A	8	50,000,000	0	0.0	0.0
C+ /6.0	11.5	0.89	10.31	65	1	95	3	1	106	N/A	N/A	1	4	5,000,000	0	0.0	0.0

I. Index of Stock Mutual Funds

						PERFORMANCE						
								Total Return % through 2/28/17			Incl. in Returns	
	99 Pct = Best *0 Pct = Worst*		Overall Investment		Perfor- mance				Annualized		Dividend	Expense
Fund Type	Fund Name	Ticker Symbol	Rating	Phone	Rating/Pts	3 Mo	6 Mo	1Yr / Pct	3Yr / Pct	5Yr / Pct	Yield	Ratio
GR	AQR International Multi-Style N	QICNX	D-	(866) 290-2688	E+ / 0.7	6.88	4.76	12.23 /19	-2.38 / 6	---	2.31	1.08
GR	AQR International Multi-Style R6	QICRX	U	(866) 290-2688	U /	6.90	4.99	12.60 /20	---	---	2.63	0.68
GI	AQR Large Cap Defensive Style I	AUEIX	A+	(866) 290-2688	A+ / 9.7	9.02	9.37	21.57 /60	13.05 /99	---	1.35	0.55
GI	AQR Large Cap Defensive Style R6	QUERX	U	(866) 290-2688	U /	9.12	9.39	21.70 /61	---	---	1.42	0.45
GR	AQR Large Cap Momentum Style I	AMOMX	C	(866) 290-2688	C+ / 6.2	7.16	6.37	18.88 /46	6.28 /67	12.88 /83	1.49	0.51
GR	AQR Large Cap Momentum Style N	AMONX	C	(866) 290-2688	C+ / 6.0	7.09	6.25	18.63 /46	6.02 /64	---	1.24	0.78
GR	AQR Large Cap Momentum Style R6	QMORX	U	(866) 290-2688	U /	7.18	6.39	18.99 /47	---	---	1.60	0.37
GR	AQR Large Cap Multi-Style I	QCELX	A+	(866) 290-2688	B+ / 8.5	8.50	11.92	22.83 /66	8.46 /83	---	1.20	0.54
GR	AQR Large Cap Multi-Style N	QCENX	A	(866) 290-2688	B+ / 8.3	8.44	11.79	22.55 /65	8.20 /80	---	0.99	0.79
GR	AQR Large Cap Multi-Style R6	QCERX	U	(866) 290-2688	U /	8.50	12.00	22.92 /66	---	---	1.34	0.42
GR	AQR Long Short Equity I	QLEIX	A+	(866) 290-2688	A+ / 9.6	4.89	8.60	15.12 /30	15.19 /99	---	1.79	1.91
GR	AQR Long Short Equity N	QLENX	A+	(866) 290-2688	A+ / 9.6	4.76	8.41	14.76 /29	14.86 /99	---	1.65	2.17
GR	AQR Long Short Equity R6	QLERX	U	(866) 290-2688	U /	4.86	8.64	15.15 /30	---	---	1.84	1.82
GL	AQR Managed Futures Strat HV I	QMHIX	E+	(866) 290-2688	E+ / 0.8	2.81	-9.36	-15.82 / 0	3.98 /43	---	0.01	1.68
GL	AQR Managed Futures Strat HV N	QMHNX	E+	(866) 290-2688	E+ / 0.7	2.71	-9.42	-15.98 / 0	3.73 /40	---	0.01	1.95
GL	AQR Managed Futures Strat HV R6	QMHRX	U	(866) 290-2688	U /	2.80	-9.27	-15.73 / 0	---	---	0.01	1.62
IN	AQR Managed Futures Strategy I	AQMIX	D	(866) 290-2688	E+ / 0.8	1.62	-6.49	-10.71 / 0	2.90 /31	3.24 /12	0.02	1.22
IN	AQR Managed Futures Strategy N	AQMNX	D	(866) 290-2688	E+ / 0.7	1.53	-6.65	-10.91 / 0	2.62 /28	2.96 /11	0.02	1.48
GL	AQR Managed Futures Strategy R6	AQMRX	U	(866) 290-2688	U /	1.62	-6.39	-10.53 / 0	---	---	0.02	1.14
GL	● AQR Multi-Strategy Alternative R6	QSARX	U	(866) 290-2688	U /	2.64	4.36	1.38 / 2	---	---	0.86	2.38
OT	AQR Risk Bal Commodities Strat I	ARCIX	E-	(866) 290-2688	E / 0.3	6.40	12.82	25.13 /74	-8.28 / 1	---	4.45	1.22
OT	AQR Risk Bal Commodities Strat N	ARCNX	E-	(866) 290-2688	E- / 0.2	6.28	12.60	24.82 /73	-8.54 / 1	---	4.33	1.56
OT	AQR Risk Bal Commodities Strat R6	QRCRX	U	(866) 290-2688	U /	6.44	12.85	25.15 /74	---	---	4.49	1.19
AA	AQR Risk Parity I	AQRIX	C-	(866) 290-2688	C- / 3.4	6.82	3.55	13.54 /24	3.29 /35	4.09 /16	2.31	0.99
GL	AQR Risk Parity II HV I	QRHIX	D+	(866) 290-2688	C- / 3.4	8.34	4.22	16.04 /34	2.32 /26	---	1.28	1.48
GL	AQR Risk Parity II HV N	QRHNX	D	(866) 290-2688	C- / 3.2	8.31	4.06	15.73 /33	2.04 /24	---	1.04	1.82
GL	AQR Risk Parity II MV I	QRMIX	D+	(866) 290-2688	D+ / 2.3	5.61	2.93	10.92 /14	2.09 /25	---	0.93	1.15
GL	AQR Risk Parity II MV N	QRMNX	D+	(866) 290-2688	D / 2.2	5.44	2.75	10.65 /13	1.81 /23	---	0.65	1.43
AA	AQR Risk Parity N	AQRNX	C-	(866) 290-2688	C- / 3.2	6.73	3.44	13.23 /22	3.01 /32	3.82 /14	2.02	1.24
GL	AQR Risk Parity R6	AQRRX	U	(866) 290-2688	U /	6.90	3.63	13.62 /24	---	---	2.38	0.91
SC	AQR Small Cap Momentum Style I	ASMOX	C	(866) 290-2688	C+ / 6.7	5.42	11.27	31.49 /89	3.78 /40	12.86 /82	0.76	0.70
SC	AQR Small Cap Momentum Style N	ASMNX	C-	(866) 290-2688	C+ / 6.5	5.38	11.15	31.18 /88	3.52 /37	---	0.00	0.96
SC	AQR Small Cap Multi-Style I	QSMLX	A-	(866) 290-2688	B+ / 8.6	5.53	13.02	32.04 /90	7.20 /73	---	0.90	1.24
SC	AQR Small Cap Multi-Style N	QSMNX	B+	(866) 290-2688	B+ / 8.4	5.39	12.83	31.58 /89	6.90 /71	---	0.68	1.47
SC	AQR Small Cap Multi-Style R6	QSERX	U	(866) 290-2688	U /	5.52	13.08	32.11 /90	---	---	0.97	1.03
GL	● AQR Style Premia Alternative I	QSPIX	B+	(866) 290-2688	C / 4.8	3.56	5.99	2.74 / 2	8.36 /82	---	1.69	2.35
IN	● AQR Style Premia Alternative LV I	QSLIX	U	(866) 290-2688	U /	1.90	3.09	1.90 / 2	---	---	0.27	1.53
IN	● AQR Style Premia Alternative LV N	QSLNX	U	(866) 290-2688	U /	1.81	2.90	1.61 / 2	---	---	0.27	1.97
IN	● AQR Style Premia Alternative LV R6	QSLRX	U	(866) 290-2688	U /	1.90	3.08	1.99 / 2	---	---	0.27	1.64
GL	● AQR Style Premia Alternative N	QSPNX	B+	(866) 290-2688	C / 4.6	3.57	5.90	2.55 / 2	8.10 /80	---	1.70	2.62
GL	● AQR Style Premia Alternative R6	QSPRX	U	(866) 290-2688	U /	3.66	5.98	2.84 / 3	---	---	1.69	2.27
EM	AQR TM Emerging Multi-Style R6	QTERX	U	(866) 290-2688	U /	8.89	5.30	27.59 /81	---	---	2.36	2.51
FO	AQR TM International Multi-Style R6	QIMRX	U	(866) 290-2688	U /	7.19	5.69	13.63 /24	---	---	2.08	1.25
FO	AQR TM Intl Momentum Style I	ATIMX	D-	(866) 290-2688	E / 0.4	5.41	-0.01	7.96 / 7	-2.83 / 5	4.52 /18	2.43	0.95
FO	AQR TM Intl Momentum Style N	ATNNX	D-	(866) 290-2688	E / 0.4	5.38	-0.07	7.84 / 7	-3.02 / 4	---	2.31	1.04
FO	AQR TM Intl Momentum Style R6	QTIRX	U	(866) 290-2688	U /	5.46	0.11	8.11 / 8	---	---	2.56	0.71
GR	AQR TM Large Cap Multi-Style I	QTLLX	U	(866) 290-2688	U /	8.45	11.93	22.62 /65	---	---	1.13	1.68
GR	AQR TM Large Cap Multi-Style R6	QTLRX	U	(866) 290-2688	U /	8.40	11.88	22.68 /65	---	---	1.18	1.43
GR	AQR TM Lg Cap Momentum Style I	ATMOX	C+	(866) 290-2688	C+ / 6.1	6.86	6.61	18.04 /43	6.26 /66	12.71 /81	1.40	0.65
GR	AQR TM Lg Cap Momentum Style N	ATMNX	C+	(866) 290-2688	C+ / 5.9	6.76	6.51	17.89 /42	6.06 /65	---	1.24	0.75
GR	AQR TM Lg Cap Momentum Style R6	QTMRX	U	(866) 290-2688	U /	6.85	6.66	18.19 /44	---	---	1.50	0.43
SC	AQR TM SC Momentum Style I	ATSMX	C+	(866) 290-2688	B- / 7.0	6.41	12.38	31.78 /90	4.05 /43	13.04 /84	0.68	1.37

● Denotes fund is closed to new investors

* Denotes fund is included in Section II

RISK Risk Rating/Pts	3 Year Standard Deviation	Beta	NET ASSETS NAV As of 2/28/17	Total $(Mil)	ASSET Cash %	Stocks %	Bonds %	Other %	Portfolio Turnover Ratio	BULL / BEAR Last Bull Market Return	Last Bear Market Return	FUND MANAGER Manager Quality Pct	Manager Tenure (Years)	MINIMUMS Initial Purch. $	Additional Purch. $	LOADS Front End Load	Back End Load
C+ /6.0	11.5	0.89	10.29	9	1	95	3	1	106	N/A	N/A	1	4	1,000,000	0	0.0	0.0
U /	N/A	N/A	10.29	332	1	95	3	1	106	N/A	N/A	N/A	4	50,000,000	0	0.0	0.0
B- /7.2	8.6	0.77	16.99	598	0	90	9	1	8	N/A	N/A	94	5	5,000,000	0	0.0	0.0
U /	N/A	N/A	16.96	151	0	90	9	1	8	N/A	N/A	N/A	5	50,000,000	0	0.0	0.0
C /5.0	10.7	0.94	20.10	805	0	97	2	1	77	122.9	-20.7	30	8	5,000,000	0	0.0	0.0
C /5.0	10.7	0.94	20.11	57	0	97	2	1	77	N/A	N/A	27	8	1,000,000	0	0.0	0.0
U /	N/A	N/A	20.05	64	0	97	2	1	77	N/A	N/A	N/A	8	50,000,000	0	0.0	0.0
B- /7.1	11.0	1.02	15.43	409	4	95	0	1	80	N/A	N/A	45	4	5,000,000	0	0.0	0.0
B- /7.1	11.0	1.03	15.38	66	4	95	0	1	80	N/A	N/A	41	4	1,000,000	0	0.0	0.0
U /	N/A	N/A	15.42	1,160	4	95	0	1	80	N/A	N/A	N/A	4	50,000,000	0	0.0	0.0
B /8.9	6.4	0.39	13.41	2,231	5	18	75	2	303	N/A	N/A	99	4	5,000,000	0	0.0	0.0
B /8.9	6.4	0.39	13.33	316	5	18	75	2	303	N/A	N/A	99	4	1,000,000	0	0.0	0.0
U /	N/A	N/A	13.43	537	5	18	75	2	303	N/A	N/A	N/A	4	50,000,000	0	0.0	0.0
C /5.0	15.2	-0.36	9.57	414	0	0	0	100	0	N/A	N/A	92	4	5,000,000	0	0.0	0.0
C /4.9	15.3	-0.36	9.51	127	0	0	0	100	0	N/A	N/A	92	4	1,000,000	0	0.0	0.0
U /	N/A	N/A	9.58	218	0	0	0	100	0	N/A	N/A	N/A	4	50,000,000	0	0.0	0.0
B- /7.3	10.2	-0.27	9.49	7,958	25	0	74	1	0	14.5	-5.4	96	7	5,000,000	0	0.0	0.0
B- /7.3	10.1	-0.27	9.38	3,414	25	0	74	1	0	12.8	-5.4	96	7	1,000,000	0	0.0	0.0
U /	N/A	N/A	9.50	1,593	25	0	74	1	0	N/A	N/A	N/A	7	50,000,000	0	0.0	0.0
U /	N/A	N/A	9.68	607	61	12	0	27	208	N/A	N/A	N/A	6	50,000,000	0	0.0	0.0
D+ /2.8	15.4	0.20	6.78	104	60	0	39	1	0	N/A	N/A	2	5	5,000,000	0	0.0	0.0
D+ /2.8	15.3	0.21	6.70	8	60	0	39	1	0	N/A	N/A	1	5	1,000,000	0	0.0	0.0
U /	N/A	N/A	6.79	115	60	0	39	1	0	N/A	N/A	N/A	5	50,000,000	0	0.0	0.0
C+ /6.2	8.7	0.89	9.77	377	24	0	75	1	157	35.3	-6.5	32	7	5,000,000	0	0.0	0.0
C /5.0	11.3	1.12	8.92	53	2	0	97	1	184	N/A	N/A	37	5	5,000,000	0	0.0	0.0
C /5.1	11.3	1.12	8.93	7	2	0	97	1	184	N/A	N/A	33	5	1,000,000	0	0.0	0.0
C+ /6.8	7.5	0.73	9.34	78	17	0	82	1	159	N/A	N/A	59	5	5,000,000	0	0.0	0.0
C+ /6.8	7.5	0.73	9.30	5	17	0	82	1	159	N/A	N/A	55	5	1,000,000	0	0.0	0.0
C+ /6.2	8.7	0.89	9.75	14	24	0	75	1	157	33.4	-6.6	29	7	1,000,000	0	0.0	0.0
U /	N/A	N/A	9.78	38	24	0	75	1	157	N/A	N/A	N/A	7	50,000,000	0	0.0	0.0
C- /3.8	16.2	1.00	22.69	335	0	97	2	1	85	135.8	-26.2	35	8	5,000,000	0	0.0	0.0
C- /3.8	16.2	1.00	22.72	2	0	97	2	1	85	N/A	N/A	32	8	1,000,000	0	0.0	0.0
C+ /6.0	14.7	0.92	15.23	50	0	99	0	1	96	N/A	N/A	80	4	5,000,000	0	0.0	0.0
C+ /6.0	14.7	0.92	15.17	11	0	99	0	1	96	N/A	N/A	78	4	1,000,000	0	0.0	0.0
U /	N/A	N/A	15.24	677	0	99	0	1	96	N/A	N/A	N/A	4	50,000,000	0	0.0	0.0
B+ /9.1	6.9	-0.14	10.23	2,402	25	21	52	2	138	N/A	N/A	98	4	5,000,000	0	0.0	0.0
U /	N/A	N/A	10.58	258	0	0	0	100	213	N/A	N/A	N/A	3	5,000,000	0	0.0	0.0
U /	N/A	N/A	10.54	42	0	0	0	100	213	N/A	N/A	N/A	3	1,000,000	0	0.0	0.0
U /	N/A	N/A	10.60	98	0	0	0	100	213	N/A	N/A	N/A	3	50,000,000	0	0.0	0.0
B+ /9.1	6.9	-0.14	10.20	194	25	21	52	2	138	N/A	N/A	98	4	1,000,000	0	0.0	0.0
U /	N/A	N/A	10.25	1,451	25	21	52	2	138	N/A	N/A	N/A	4	50,000,000	0	0.0	0.0
U /	N/A	N/A	9.34	285	1	98	0	1	181	N/A	N/A	N/A	2	50,000,000	0	0.0	0.0
U /	N/A	N/A	9.63	127	2	94	3	1	135	N/A	N/A	N/A	2	50,000,000	0	0.0	0.0
C+ /5.8	10.2	0.78	11.75	33	0	95	3	2	87	N/A	N/A	37	5	5,000,000	0	0.0	0.0
C+ /5.8	10.3	0.78	11.71	N/A	0	95	3	2	87	N/A	N/A	35	5	1,000,000	0	0.0	0.0
U /	N/A	N/A	11.72	47	0	95	3	2	87	N/A	N/A	N/A	5	50,000,000	0	0.0	0.0
U /	N/A	N/A	11.04	52	1	98	0	1	173	N/A	N/A	N/A	2	5,000,000	0	0.0	0.0
U /	N/A	N/A	11.04	129	1	98	0	1	173	N/A	N/A	N/A	2	50,000,000	0	0.0	0.0
C+ /6.5	10.7	0.95	17.79	74	2	97	0	1	49	N/A	N/A	28	5	5,000,000	0	0.0	0.0
C+ /6.5	10.7	0.96	17.75	N/A	2	97	0	1	49	N/A	N/A	26	5	1,000,000	0	0.0	0.0
U /	N/A	N/A	17.76	81	2	97	0	1	49	N/A	N/A	N/A	5	50,000,000	0	0.0	0.0
C /4.4	16.3	1.00	17.51	40	0	98	1	1	92	N/A	N/A	38	5	5,000,000	0	0.0	0.0

Fund Type	Fund Name	Ticker Symbol	Overall Investment Rating	Phone	PERFORMANCE Perfor- mance Rating/Pts	Total Return % through 2/28/17 3 Mo	6 Mo	1Yr / Pct	Annualized 3Yr / Pct	5Yr / Pct	Incl. in Returns Dividend Yield	Expense Ratio
	99 Pct = Best 0 Pct = Worst											
SC	AQR TM SC Momentum Style N	ATSNX	C	(866) 290-2688	C+ / 6.9	6.34	12.26	31.55 /89	3.84 /41	--	0.54	1.52
GI	AQR US Defensive Equity N	AUENX	A+	(866) 290-2688	A+ / 9.6	9.02	9.23	21.27 /59	12.77 /99	--	1.16	0.81
IN	Aquila Three Peaks Oppty Gro A	ATGAX	C+	(800) 437-1020	C+ / 5.6	5.17	4.13	16.35 /36	8.74 /85	15.38 /97	0.00	1.41
IN	Aquila Three Peaks Oppty Gro C	ATGCX	C+	(800) 437-1020	C+ / 6.2	4.98	3.76	15.52 /32	7.95 /79	14.55 /96	0.00	2.10
IN	Aquila Three Peaks Oppty Gro I	ATRIX	C+	(800) 437-1020	C+ / 6.6	5.19	4.18	16.49 /36	8.93 /86	15.65 /98	0.00	1.32
IN	Aquila Three Peaks Oppty Gro Y	ATGYX	C+	(800) 437-1020	C+ / 6.7	5.27	4.29	16.72 /37	9.07 /87	15.74 /98	0.00	1.10
AA	AR 529 Gift College Inv Csv Gr		C+	(800) 662-7447	D / 1.9	2.57	0.06	6.29 / 5	3.23 /34	3.77 /14	0.00	0.75
AA	AR 529 Gift College Inv Gr		B	(800) 662-7447	C / 5.1	5.89	5.23	17.33 /40	5.27 /57	8.03 /42	0.00	0.75
BA	AR 529 Gift College Inv Mod Gr		B-	(800) 662-7447	C- / 3.3	4.17	2.61	11.71 /17	4.31 /46	5.95 /28	0.00	0.75
GL	Arbitrage Event-Driven A	AGEAX	D	(800) 295-4485	E / 0.3	1.21	1.43	4.55 / 4	-1.84 / 7	--	0.00	2.64
GL	Arbitrage Event-Driven C	AEFCX	D	(800) 295-4485	E / 0.3	0.89	1.00	3.66 / 3	-2.60 / 5	--	0.00	3.39
GR	Arbitrage Event-Driven I	AEDNX	D	(800) 295-4485	E / 0.4	1.20	1.53	4.75 / 4	-1.63 / 8	0.12 / 5	0.00	2.39
GR	Arbitrage Event-Driven R	AEDFX	D	(800) 295-4485	E / 0.4	1.10	1.32	4.43 / 3	-1.88 / 7	-0.12 / 4	0.00	2.64
GR	Arbitrage Fund (The) - A	ARGAX	C	(800) 295-4485	E+ / 0.9	1.12	1.67	2.79 / 3	1.98 /24	--	0.00	1.91
GR	Arbitrage Fund (The) - C	ARBCX	C	(800) 295-4485	D- / 1.0	0.83	1.24	2.07 / 2	1.22 /19	--	0.00	2.66
GI	Arbitrage Fund (The) - Instl	ARBNX	C	(800) 295-4485	D- / 1.2	1.16	1.85	3.11 / 3	2.25 /26	1.48 / 7	0.00	1.66
GI	Arbitrage Fund (The) - Retail	ARBFX	C	(800) 295-4485	D- / 1.1	1.04	1.67	2.79 / 3	1.98 /24	1.23 / 7	0.00	1.91
BA	Archer Balanced Fund	ARCHX	B	(800) 494-2755	C+ / 5.7	5.38	5.21	14.12 /26	7.27 /74	8.39 /45	1.37	1.78
IN	Archer Stock Fund	ARSKX	C-	(800) 494-2755	C / 5.0	6.43	8.06	18.10 /43	4.51 /49	9.72 /56	0.00	1.90
MC	Ariel Appreciation Fund Inst	CAAIX	B-	(800) 292-7435	B / 8.1	7.11	10.06	29.23 /85	6.98 /72	13.73 /91	0.82	0.79
MC	Ariel Appreciation Fund Investor	CAAPX	C+	(800) 292-7435	B / 7.8	7.04	9.93	28.86 /84	6.64 /69	13.39 /88	0.57	1.12
SC	Ariel Discovery Institutional	ADYIX	E-	(800) 292-7435	E / 0.3	2.48	7.35	24.91 /73	-6.81 / 2	3.24 /12	0.00	1.36
GL	Ariel Discovery Investor	ARDFX	E-	(800) 292-7435	E / 0.3	2.41	7.24	24.62 /72	-7.07 / 1	2.96 /11	0.00	2.17
SC	Ariel Focus Institutional	AFOYX	B	(800) 292-7435	A / 9.4	9.07	14.49	39.50 /97	6.46 /68	11.22 /68	1.20	1.07
GR	Ariel Focus Investor	ARFFX	B	(800) 292-7435	A / 9.3	9.04	14.45	39.26 /97	6.21 /66	10.95 /65	0.97	1.37
SC	Ariel Fund Institutional	ARAIX	B	(800) 292-7435	A+ / 9.6	7.48	13.08	32.93 /91	9.30 /89	15.45 /98	0.52	0.72
SC	Ariel Fund Investor	ARGFX	B	(800) 292-7435	A / 9.5	7.40	12.94	32.54 /91	8.98 /87	15.09 /97	0.26	1.02
GL	Ariel Global Institutional	AGLYX	C	(800) 292-7435	C- / 4.1	6.38	3.52	14.56 /28	4.52 /49	8.79 /49	1.92	1.30
GL	Ariel Global Investor	AGLOX	C	(800) 292-7435	C- / 3.9	6.24	3.31	14.17 /26	4.25 /46	8.49 /46	1.44	2.71
FO	Ariel International Institutional	AINIX	D+	(800) 292-7435	D / 1.7	6.77	-0.35	8.71 / 9	1.15 /19	6.08 /29	1.66	2.68
FO	Ariel International Investor	AINTX	D+	(800) 292-7435	D / 1.6	6.59	-0.56	8.32 / 8	0.86 /17	5.81 /27	1.35	3.49
GI	Arin Large Cap Theta Advisor	AVOAX	C-	(800) 773-3863	D- / 1.5	1.09	0.33	5.09 / 4	2.45 /27	--	0.00	4.09
GI	Arin Large Cap Theta Institutional	AVOLX	C-	(800) 773-3863	D / 1.6	1.09	0.42	5.50 / 4	2.65 /29	--	0.00	3.69
GL	Aristotle/Saul Glbl Opportunities I	ARSOX	D+	(888) 661-6691	C- / 3.1	5.49	4.12	19.82 /51	1.79 /23	--	0.62	1.42
GR	Arrow Alter Soltns A	ASFFX	C-	(877) 277-6933	D+ / 2.6	1.89	2.97	11.56 /16	5.59 /60	2.46 / 9	3.18	1.44
GR	Arrow Alter Soltns C	ASFTX	C-	(877) 277-6933	C- / 3.0	1.68	2.50	10.64 /13	4.78 /52	1.68 / 7	2.94	2.19
IN	Arrow Alter Soltns Institutional	ASFNX	C	(877) 277-6933	C- / 3.8	1.94	2.96	11.85 /17	5.89 /63	--	3.69	1.19
IN	Arrow Commodity Strategy A	CSFFX	E	(877) 277-6933	E- / 0.0	2.92	3.68	11.02 /15	-12.15 / 0	-10.12 / 1	0.00	3.98
IN	Arrow Commodity Strategy C	CSFTX	E	(877) 277-6933	E- / 0.0	2.66	3.24	10.18 /12	-12.79 / 0	-10.81 / 0	0.00	4.73
OT	Arrow Commodity Strategy Inst	CSFNX	E	(877) 277-6933	E- / 0.0	2.91	3.66	11.20 /15	-11.96 / 1	--	0.00	3.73
AA	Arrow DWA Balanced A	DWAFX	E+	(877) 277-6933	E+ / 0.7	3.01	-0.08	8.10 / 8	0.68 /17	4.15 /16	0.00	1.71
AA	Arrow DWA Balanced C	DWATX	E+	(877) 277-6933	E+ / 0.8	2.83	-0.50	7.25 / 6	-0.06 /13	3.37 /12	0.00	2.46
BA	Arrow DWA Balanced Institutional	DWANX	D-	(877) 277-6933	D- / 1.3	3.06	0.00	8.38 / 8	0.94 /18	--	0.00	1.46
AA	Arrow DWA Tactical A	DWTFX	C-	(877) 277-6933	D+ / 2.3	6.22	5.69	13.89 /25	2.91 /31	7.73 /40	1.49	1.76
AA	Arrow DWA Tactical C	DWTTX	C-	(877) 277-6933	D+ / 2.7	6.10	5.33	13.09 /22	2.15 /25	6.94 /34	0.94	2.51
AA	Arrow DWA Tactical Inst	DWTNX	C	(877) 277-6933	C- / 3.4	6.39	5.87	14.28 /27	3.19 /34	--	1.84	1.51
GI	Arrow Managed Futures Strategy A	MFTFX	D-	(877) 277-6933	E / 0.3	6.88	-7.94	-7.55 / 0	1.28 /20	-1.23 / 3	8.40	1.43
GI	Arrow Managed Futures Strategy C	MFTTX	D-	(877) 277-6933	E / 0.4	6.65	-8.23	-8.12 / 0	0.53 /16	-1.96 / 3	8.93	2.18
GL	Arrow Managed Futures Strategy Inst	MFTNX	D-	(877) 277-6933	E+ / 0.6	6.90	-7.78	-7.29 / 0	1.51 /21	--	8.91	1.18
EM	Artisan Developing World Adv	APDYX	U	(800) 344-1770	U /	7.85	2.52	28.50 /83	--	--	0.22	1.29
EM	Artisan Developing World Inst	APHYX	U	(800) 344-1770	U /	7.84	2.50	28.56 /83	--	--	0.29	1.20
EM	Artisan Developing World Inv	ARTYX	U	(800) 344-1770	U /	7.76	2.36	28.04 /82	--	--	0.06	1.67

● Denotes fund is closed to new investors

* Denotes fund is included in Section II

www.thestreetratings.com

RISK Risk Rating/Pts	3 Year Standard Deviation	Beta	NET ASSETS NAV As of 2/28/17	Total $(Mil)	ASSET Cash %	Stocks %	Bonds %	Other %	Portfolio Turnover Ratio	BULL Last Bull Market Return	BEAR Last Bear Market Return	FUND MANAGER Manager Quality Pct	Manager Tenure (Years)	MINIMUMS Initial Purch. $	Additional Purch. $	LOADS Front End Load	Back End Load
C /4.4	16.3	1.00	17.44	N/A	0	98	1	1	92	N/A	N/A	35	5	1,000,000	0	0.0	0.0
B- /7.2	8.6	0.77	16.97	222	0	90	9	1	8	N/A	N/A	94	5	1,000,000	0	0.0	0.0
C+ /6.3	9.6	0.82	49.65	139	1	98	0	1	49	150.7	-21.0	74	14	1,000	0	4.3	2.0
C+ /6.2	9.6	0.82	41.68	87	1	98	0	1	49	140.9	-21.2	67	14	1,000	0	0.0	0.0
C+ /6.3	9.6	0.82	51.28	45	1	98	0	1	49	154.0	-20.8	76	14	0	0	0.0	2.0
C+ /6.3	9.6	0.82	52.70	362	1	98	0	1	49	155.0	-20.9	77	14	0	0	0.0	2.0
B+ /9.7	3.4	0.45	16.38	53	0	25	74	1	0	28.0	-1.9	73	12	25	10	0.0	0.0
B /8.3	7.8	1.22	20.51	55	0	74	24	2	0	70.9	-14.2	27	12	25	10	0.0	0.0
B+ /9.4	5.3	0.83	18.50	82	0	50	49	1	0	48.5	-8.3	51	12	25	10	0.0	0.0
B- /7.5	3.7	0.17	9.20	1	34	39	24	3	350	N/A	N/A	49	7	2,000	0	3.3	2.0
B- /7.6	3.6	0.17	9.06	2	34	39	24	3	350	N/A	N/A	38	7	2,000	0	0.0	0.0
B- /7.5	3.6	0.18	9.27	73	34	39	24	3	350	9.6	-4.3	28	7	100,000	0	0.0	2.0
B- /7.5	3.6	0.18	9.19	73	34	39	24	3	350	8.1	-4.2	25	7	2,000	0	0.0	2.0
B+ /9.9	1.9	0.07	12.90	10	45	48	6	1	321	N/A	N/A	82	17	2,000	0	2.5	2.0
B+ /9.9	1.9	0.07	12.40	27	45	48	6	1	321	N/A	N/A	77	17	2,000	0	0.0	0.0
B+ /9.9	1.9	0.07	13.28	1,412	45	48	6	1	321	10.4	1.7	83	17	100,000	0	0.0	2.0
B+ /9.9	1.9	0.07	12.89	349	45	48	6	1	321	8.8	1.7	82	17	2,000	0	0.0	2.0
B /8.1	6.6	1.02	12.29	30	6	64	29	1	26	67.6	-10.7	70	12	2,500	100	0.0	0.5
C /5.4	13.0	1.18	41.57	14	1	98	0	1	88	93.0	-23.5	5	6	2,500	100	0.0	1.0
C /4.5	14.4	1.10	50.03	230	5	94	0	1	14	N/A	N/A	30	15	1,000,000	100	0.0	0.0
C /4.6	14.4	1.10	49.97	1,546	5	94	0	1	14	139.0	-24.9	27	15	1,000	100	0.0	0.0
D- /1.5	17.8	0.99	9.93	31	3	96	0	1	45	N/A	N/A	1	6	1,000,000	100	0.0	0.0
D- /1.5	17.8	0.61	9.77	8	3	96	0	1	45	45.0	-24.3	5	6	1,000	100	0.0	0.0
C- /3.7	13.7	0.71	13.43	13	5	93	0	2	20	N/A	N/A	84	12	1,000,000	100	0.0	0.0
C- /3.7	13.7	1.13	13.48	41	5	93	0	2	20	99.2	-17.3	12	12	1,000	100	0.0	0.0
C- /3.6	16.0	0.94	67.65	675	8	88	2	2	20	N/A	N/A	89	31	1,000,000	100	0.0	0.0
C- /3.7	16.0	0.94	67.60	1,674	8	88	2	2	20	163.6	-31.1	88	31	1,000	100	0.0	0.0
B- /7.1	9.7	0.72	14.15	82	2	97	0	1	31	N/A	N/A	94	6	1,000,000	100	0.0	0.0
B- /7.2	9.7	0.72	14.60	10	2	97	0	1	31	N/A	N/A	94	6	1,000	100	0.0	0.0
B- /7.0	9.9	0.76	12.54	256	8	91	0	1	27	N/A	N/A	82	6	1,000,000	100	0.0	0.0
B- /7.0	9.9	0.76	12.76	59	8	91	0	1	27	N/A	N/A	81	6	1,000	100	0.0	0.0
B /8.6	5.6	0.49	10.13	N/A	28	10	61	1	0	N/A	N/A	40	4	25,000	100	0.0	0.0
B /8.6	5.7	0.49	10.14	5	28	10	61	1	0	N/A	N/A	42	4	25,000	100	0.0	0.0
C+ /5.9	10.2	0.69	12.07	100	0	85	13	2	51	N/A	N/A	85	5	2,500	100	0.0	1.0
B- /7.4	4.3	0.21	8.98	16	14	0	85	1	71	15.7	-7.3	91	10	5,000	250	5.8	1.0
B- /7.4	4.2	0.21	8.58	3	14	0	85	1	71	11.0	-7.6	88	10	5,000	250	0.0	1.0
B- /7.4	4.3	0.21	9.05	141	14	0	85	1	71	N/A	N/A	92	10	1,000,000	0	0.0	1.0
C /4.4	11.9	0.25	5.64	1	15	0	84	1	1,236	-36.2	-20.3	0	7	5,000	250	5.8	1.0
C /4.3	11.9	0.25	5.41	N/A	15	0	84	1	1,236	-38.7	-20.5	0	7	5,000	250	0.0	1.0
C /4.3	11.8	0.24	5.66	7	15	0	84	1	1,236	N/A	N/A	0	7	1,000,000	0	0.0	1.0
C /5.2	7.1	1.04	12.68	54	8	62	28	2	84	35.0	-13.0	6	6	5,000	250	5.8	1.0
C /5.2	7.1	1.04	11.98	65	8	62	28	2	84	29.7	-13.3	4	6	5,000	250	0.0	1.0
C /5.2	7.1	1.04	12.80	17	8	62	28	2	84	N/A	N/A	7	6	1,000,000	0	0.0	1.0
B- /7.1	8.6	1.21	10.40	44	4	70	25	1	169	50.0	-18.4	10	6	5,000	250	5.8	1.0
B- /7.0	8.6	1.21	9.88	57	4	70	25	1	169	44.0	-18.6	6	6	5,000	250	0.0	1.0
B- /7.1	8.7	1.21	10.44	99	4	70	25	1	169	N/A	N/A	11	6	1,000,000	0	0.0	1.0
C+ /6.3	15.3	-0.19	7.84	47	17	0	82	1	0	-12.6	-9.6	91	7	5,000	250	5.8	1.0
C+ /6.3	15.4	-0.19	7.53	6	17	0	82	1	0	-15.9	-9.9	88	7	5,000	250	0.0	1.0
C+ /6.3	15.3	-0.32	7.93	73	17	0	82	1	0	N/A	N/A	83	7	1,000,000	0	0.0	1.0
U /	N/A	N/A	10.58	424	10	89	0	1	48	N/A	N/A	N/A	2	250,000	0	0.0	0.0
U /	N/A	N/A	10.59	297	10	89	0	1	48	N/A	N/A	N/A	2	1,000,000	0	0.0	0.0
U /	N/A	N/A	10.56	305	10	89	0	1	48	N/A	N/A	N/A	2	1,000	0	0.0	0.0

						PERFORMANCE						
	99 Pct = Best					Perfor-	Total Return % through 2/28/17				Incl. in Returns	
	0 Pct = Worst			Overall		mance				Annualized	Dividend	Expense
Fund Type	Fund Name	Ticker Symbol	Investment Rating	Phone		Rating/Pts	3 Mo	6 Mo	1Yr / Pct	3Yr / Pct	5Yr / Pct	Yield	Ratio
EM	Artisan Emerging Markets Inst	APHEX	C	(800) 344-1770		C+ / 6.4	8.58	6.66	32.46 /91	3.28 /34	-0.02 / 4	0.69	1.36
EM	Artisan Emerging Markets Inv	ARTZX	C	(800) 344-1770		C+ / 6.5	8.62	6.75	32.60 /91	3.25 /34	-0.17 / 4	0.94	1.79
GL	Artisan Global Equity Inst	APHHX	U	(800) 344-1770		U /	4.24	0.78	15.85 /34	--	--	0.17	1.15
GL	Artisan Global Equity Inv	ARTHX	D	(800) 344-1770		D / 2.1	4.18	0.67	15.52 /32	1.30 /20	10.11 /59	0.00	1.37
GL	Artisan Global Opportunities Adv	APDRX	U	(800) 344-1770		U /	6.14	4.07	23.17 /67	--	--	0.00	1.14
GR	Artisan Global Opportunities Fd Inv	ARTRX	C+	(800) 344-1770		C+ / 6.5	6.15	4.03	23.07 /67	6.46 /68	11.35 /69	0.00	1.19
GR	Artisan Global Opportunities Inst	APHRX	C+	(800) 344-1770		C+ / 6.7	6.21	4.14	23.40 /68	6.72 /70	11.62 /71	0.00	0.95
GL	Artisan Global Value Adv	APDGX	U	(800) 344-1770		U /	5.52	6.64	21.41 /59	--	--	0.72	1.16
GL	Artisan Global Value Inst	APHGX	C+	(800) 344-1770		C+ / 5.8	5.58	6.79	21.55 /60	5.21 /57	--	0.80	1.04
GL	Artisan Global Value Inv	ARTGX	C+	(800) 344-1770		C / 5.5	5.51	6.59	21.24 /58	4.92 /53	11.18 /67	0.63	1.29
FO	● Artisan International Adv	APDIX	U	(800) 344-1770		U /	5.24	-2.54	4.07 / 3	--	--	1.38	1.02
FO	● Artisan International Fund Inst	APHIX	D-	(800) 344-1770		E / 0.3	5.28	-2.47	4.18 / 3	-3.15 / 4	4.84 /20	1.43	0.95
*FO	● Artisan International Fund Inv	ARTIX	D-	(800) 344-1770		E / 0.3	5.15	-2.63	3.86 / 3	-3.40 / 4	4.59 /19	1.12	1.17
FO	Artisan International Small Cp Inst	APHJX	U	(800) 344-1770		U /	6.14	-4.01	--	--	--	0.00	1.35
FO	● Artisan International Small Cp Inv	ARTJX	E	(800) 344-1770		E- / 0.1	6.05	-4.11	0.96 / 2	-5.98 / 2	5.54 /25	0.00	1.52
FO	Artisan International Value Adv	APDKX	U	(800) 344-1770		U /	6.17	4.25	16.90 /38	--	--	0.90	1.07
FO	● Artisan International Value Inst	APHKX	D+	(800) 344-1770		C- / 3.1	6.15	4.26	16.94 /38	2.07 /24	9.63 /56	0.95	1.00
FO	● Artisan International Value Inv	ARTKX	D+	(800) 344-1770		C- / 3.0	6.10	4.14	16.68 /37	1.83 /23	9.40 /54	0.75	1.21
MC	Artisan Mid Cap Adv	APDMX	U	(800) 344-1770		U /	4.37	2.43	20.98 /57	--	--	0.00	1.05
MC	● Artisan Mid Cap Fund Inst	APHMX	D-	(800) 344-1770		C- / 3.4	4.35	2.46	21.07 /58	2.48 /27	10.08 /59	0.00	0.95
MC	● Artisan Mid Cap Fund Inv	ARTMX	D-	(800) 344-1770		C- / 3.3	4.33	2.33	20.77 /56	2.24 /26	9.81 /57	0.00	1.19
MC	Artisan Mid Cap Value Adv	APDQX	U	(800) 344-1770		U /	4.34	11.92	30.64 /87	--	--	0.77	1.05
MC	Artisan Mid Cap Value Institutional	APHQX	C	(800) 344-1770		B- / 7.3	4.38	12.02	30.79 /88	5.36 /58	10.43 /61	0.86	0.96
MC	Artisan Mid Cap Value Inv	ARTQX	C	(800) 344-1770		B- / 7.1	4.33	11.83	30.49 /87	5.11 /55	10.17 /60	0.67	1.19
SC	● Artisan Small Cap Fund Inst	APHSX	D+	(800) 344-1770		C / 4.8	4.92	4.97	29.95 /86	2.20 /25	--	0.00	1.02
SC	● Artisan Small Cap Fund Inv	ARTSX	D	(800) 344-1770		C / 4.5	4.82	4.80	29.62 /86	1.96 /24	10.46 /62	0.00	1.23
GR	Artisan Value Adv	APDLX	U	(800) 344-1770		U /	5.04	12.52	38.44 /97	--	--	0.59	0.82
GR	Artisan Value Institutional	APHLX	B+	(800) 344-1770		A+ / 9.6	5.03	12.54	38.50 /97	8.60 /84	10.99 /66	0.70	0.75
GR	Artisan Value Investor	ARTLX	B+	(800) 344-1770		A / 9.5	4.95	12.41	38.31 /97	8.38 /82	10.72 /64	0.60	1.00
GL	Ascendant Deep Value Convertibles	AEQAX	D	(855) 527-2363		E- / 0.2	3.16	3.24	4.71 / 4	-2.76 / 5	1.93 / 8	0.39	2.44
GL	Ascendant Deep Value Convertibles	AEQCX	D	(855) 527-2363		E / 0.3	2.94	2.82	3.93 / 3	-3.44 / 4	1.19 / 6	0.24	3.19
GL	Ascendant Deep Value Convertibles I	AEQIX	D	(855) 527-2363		E / 0.4	3.16	3.31	4.96 / 4	-2.52 / 5	2.17 / 8	0.48	2.19
FS	Ascendant Tactical Yield A	ATYAX	U	(855) 527-2363		U /	3.06	4.43	7.41 / 6	--	--	1.22	2.65
EM	Ashmore Em Mkts Frontier Eq Inst	EFEIX	C+	(866) 876-8294		C- / 3.9	9.31	6.66	18.62 /46	1.97 /24	--	1.11	2.46
EM	Ashmore Emerg Mkts Sm-Cap Eqty A	ESSAX	D+	(866) 876-8294		C / 4.4	11.33	10.34	27.30 /80	1.59 /21	2.51 / 9	1.67	2.33
EM	Ashmore Emerg Mkts Sm-Cap Eqty C	ESSCX	D+	(866) 876-8294		C / 4.8	11.05	9.84	26.40 /77	0.78 /17	--	1.19	3.09
EM	Ashmore Emerg Mkts Sm-Cap Eqty	ESCIX	C-	(866) 876-8294		C+ / 5.8	11.29	10.36	27.72 /81	1.91 /23	2.84 /10	1.49	2.08
EM	Ashmore Emerg Mkts Value A	EMEAX	C	(866) 876-8294		C+ / 6.8	13.26	14.97	43.33 /98	0.73 /17	-0.77 / 4	1.41	3.56
EM	Ashmore Emerg Mkts Value Instl	EMFIX	C+	(866) 876-8294		B / 7.9	13.44	15.14	43.74 /98	1.05 /18	-0.27 / 4	1.70	3.31
GI	Aspen Managed Futures Strategy A	MFBPX	D	(855) 845-9444		E / 0.5	-1.13	-0.90	-3.53 / 1	2.39 /27	0.81 / 6	1.14	1.61
GI	Aspen Managed Futures Strategy I	MFBTX	D+	(855) 845-9444		E+ / 0.9	-0.94	-0.94	-3.85 / 1	2.53 /28	1.05 / 6	0.89	1.23
GI	Aspiriant Defensive Allocation	RMDFX	U	(877) 997-9971		U /	3.57	3.16	6.54 / 5	--	--	1.12	1.15
GL	Aspiriant Risk Mgd Eqty Alloc Adv	RMEAX	C-	(877) 997-9971		C- / 3.9	7.09	4.30	14.63 /28	3.71 /39	--	1.65	0.59
GR	Astor Dynamic Allocation A	ASTLX	C+	(877) 738-0333		C- / 3.5	5.19	4.92	15.46 /32	4.79 /52	5.70 /26	0.86	1.97
GR	Astor Dynamic Allocation C	ASTZX	C+	(877) 738-0333		C- / 3.8	4.95	4.51	14.63 /28	4.03 /43	4.92 /21	0.39	2.72
GR	Astor Dynamic Allocation I	ASTIX	B-	(877) 738-0333		C / 4.6	5.14	4.95	15.72 /33	5.04 /55	5.95 /28	1.12	1.72
GR	Astor Dynamic Allocation R	ASTRX	B-	(877) 738-0333		C / 4.4	5.11	4.85	15.50 /32	4.80 /52	5.68 /26	0.91	1.97
GL	Astor Sector Allocation A	ASPGX	C-	(877) 738-0333		C- / 3.5	5.55	7.42	18.91 /47	3.56 /38	8.88 /50	0.00	2.26
GL	Astor Sector Allocation C	CSPGX	C	(877) 738-0333		C- / 3.9	5.40	7.10	18.06 /43	2.83 /30	8.03 /42	0.00	3.01
GL	Astor Sector Allocation I	STARX	C+	(877) 738-0333		C / 4.8	5.64	7.72	19.35 /49	3.86 /41	--	0.00	2.01
IN	AT Disciplined Equity Institutional	AWEIX	A	(855) 328-3863		B+ / 8.8	6.87	8.86	21.99 /62	10.37 /95	13.34 /87	0.85	0.79
AA	AT Income Opportunities Instl	AWIIX	U	(855) 328-3863		U /	5.32	5.63	21.17 /58	--	--	2.73	0.87

● Denotes fund is closed to new investors
* Denotes fund is included in Section II

RISK Rating/Pts	3 Year Standard Deviation	Beta	NET ASSETS NAV As of 2/28/17	Total $(Mil)	ASSET Cash %	Stocks %	Bonds %	Other %	Portfolio Turnover Ratio	BULL/BEAR Last Bull Market Return	Last Bear Market Return	FUND MANAGER Manager Quality Pct	Manager Tenure (Years)	MINIMUMS Initial Purch. $	Additional Purch. $	LOADS Front End Load	Back End Load
C /4.8	17.1	1.02	13.04	7	1	98	0	1	46	21.5	-30.9	84	11	1,000,000	0	0.0	0.0
C /4.8	17.1	1.02	13.11	32	1	98	0	1	46	20.4	-31.0	84	11	1,000	0	0.0	0.0
U /	N/A	N/A	16.48	113	2	97	0	1	96	N/A	N/A	N/A	7	1,000,000	0	0.0	0.0
C /5.4	11.9	0.83	16.45	128	2	97	0	1	96	96.4	-20.0	83	7	1,000	0	0.0	0.0
U /	N/A	N/A	22.11	225	7	92	0	1	35	N/A	N/A	N/A	9	250,000	0	0.0	0.0
C /5.5	12.6	0.97	22.08	793	7	92	0	1	35	112.0	-19.9	28	9	1,000	0	0.0	0.0
C /5.4	12.6	0.97	22.25	897	7	92	0	1	35	114.8	N/A	31	9	1,000,000	0	0.0	0.0
U /	N/A	N/A	15.86	531	9	90	0	1	21	N/A	N/A	N/A	10	250,000	0	0.0	0.0
C+ /6.5	10.8	0.78	15.90	1,168	9	90	0	1	21	N/A	N/A	96	10	1,000,000	0	0.0	0.0
C+ /6.5	10.8	0.78	15.89	769	9	90	0	1	21	101.6	-14.8	95	10	1,000	0	0.0	0.0
U /	N/A	N/A	26.90	2,646	3	95	1	1	65	N/A	N/A	N/A	22	250,000	0	0.0	0.0
C+ /6.2	11.9	0.86	27.10	4,959	3	95	1	1	65	57.6	-24.1	34	22	1,000,000	0	0.0	0.0
C+ /6.2	11.9	0.86	26.94	6,041	3	95	1	1	65	55.6	-24.2	31	22	1,000	0	0.0	0.0
U /	N/A	N/A	20.56	202	0	0	0	100	70	N/A	N/A	N/A	16	1,000,000	0	0.0	0.0
C /4.3	13.7	0.86	20.52	434	0	0	0	100	70	57.4	-23.8	9	16	1,000	0	0.0	0.0
U /	N/A	N/A	33.73	4,269	13	86	0	1	18	N/A	N/A	N/A	15	250,000	0	0.0	0.0
C+ /5.8	10.3	0.78	33.85	3,294	13	86	0	1	18	86.6	-19.8	87	15	1,000,000	0	0.0	0.0
C+ /5.8	10.3	0.78	33.73	4,928	13	86	0	1	18	84.5	-19.9	86	15	1,000	0	0.0	0.0
U /	N/A	N/A	38.95	575	5	94	0	1	40	N/A	N/A	N/A	11	250,000	0	0.0	0.0
C- /3.2	14.4	1.02	41.73	4,073	5	94	0	1	40	101.0	-16.4	6	11	1,000,000	0	0.0	0.0
C- /3.1	14.4	1.02	38.82	2,710	5	94	0	1	40	98.3	-16.5	5	11	1,000	0	0.0	0.0
U /	N/A	N/A	23.09	1,202	6	93	0	1	27	N/A	N/A	N/A	16	250,000	0	0.0	0.0
C- /3.7	11.7	0.91	23.12	749	6	93	0	1	27	N/A	N/A	33	16	1,000,000	0	0.0	0.0
C- /3.7	11.7	0.91	23.14	2,295	6	93	0	1	27	98.6	-17.0	30	16	1,000	0	0.0	0.0
C- /3.6	17.9	0.94	30.51	502	0	0	0	100	27	N/A	N/A	22	13	1,000,000	0	0.0	0.0
C- /3.6	17.9	0.94	30.21	717	0	0	0	100	27	109.8	-16.9	20	13	1,000	0	0.0	0.0
U /	N/A	N/A	14.39	302	2	97	0	1	52	N/A	N/A	N/A	11	250,000	0	0.0	0.0
C /4.7	14.1	1.07	14.42	98	2	97	0	1	52	105.1	N/A	41	11	1,000,000	0	0.0	0.0
C /4.8	14.2	1.07	14.43	507	2	97	0	1	52	102.6	-14.6	37	11	1,000	0	0.0	0.0
B- /7.7	4.0	0.18	11.75	6	48	0	8	44	540	N/A	N/A	36	N/A	1,000	100	5.8	0.0
B- /7.7	3.9	0.18	11.57	N/A	48	0	8	44	540	N/A	N/A	28	N/A	1,000	100	0.0	0.0
B- /7.6	4.0	0.18	11.75	2	48	0	8	44	540	N/A	N/A	40	N/A	1,000,000	25,000	0.0	0.0
U /	N/A	N/A	10.04	33	0	0	0	100	1,676	N/A	N/A	N/A	2	1,000	100	5.8	0.0
B- /7.8	11.5	0.47	9.68	54	0	99	0	1	76	N/A	N/A	82	3	1,000,000	5,000	0.0	0.0
C /4.3	16.9	0.91	9.15	1	2	97	0	1	104	N/A	N/A	74	6	1,000	50	5.3	0.0
C /4.3	16.9	0.91	9.68	N/A	2	97	0	1	104	N/A	N/A	65	6	1,000	50	0.0	0.0
C /4.5	16.8	0.91	11.67	32	2	97	0	1	104	N/A	N/A	76	6	1,000,000	5,000	0.0	0.0
C- /3.9	18.5	1.06	9.17	N/A	1	97	0	2	119	N/A	N/A	61	5	1,000	50	5.3	0.0
C- /3.9	18.5	1.06	8.85	13	1	97	0	2	119	23.4	N/A	65	6	1,000,000	5,000	0.0	0.0
B- /7.7	7.9	-0.05	8.62	7	18	0	81	1	58	-4.1	N/A	89	6	2,500	0	5.5	2.0
B- /7.7	7.9	-0.05	8.77	220	18	0	81	1	58	-2.7	N/A	90	6	100,000	0	0.0	2.0
U /	N/A	N/A	10.29	566	21	32	45	2	0	N/A	N/A	N/A	2	0	0	0.0	0.0
C+ /6.3	8.1	0.58	11.77	760	1	83	14	2	83	N/A	N/A	93	3	0	0	0.0	0.0
B /8.2	7.8	0.74	12.63	11	10	73	15	2	55	N/A	N/A	36	8	1,000	100	4.8	0.0
B /8.2	7.8	0.74	12.23	20	10	73	15	2	55	28.4	-11.9	28	8	1,000	100	0.0	0.0
B /8.2	7.8	0.74	12.64	91	10	73	15	2	55	35.3	-11.4	39	8	50,000	100	0.0	0.0
B /8.2	7.8	0.74	12.61	2	10	73	15	2	55	33.6	-11.5	36	8	1,000	100	0.0	0.0
C+ /6.6	10.6	1.40	15.78	22	1	91	6	2	68	N/A	N/A	36	N/A	5,000	100	4.8	0.0
C+ /6.6	10.5	1.40	15.23	37	1	91	6	2	68	N/A	N/A	28	N/A	5,000	100	0.0	0.0
B- /7.2	10.6	1.40	15.91	28	1	91	6	2	68	N/A	N/A	41	N/A	5,000	100	0.0	0.0
C+ /6.6	10.5	1.00	17.24	838	1	96	1	2	12	127.7	-13.6	71	7	250,000	0	0.0	0.0
U /	N/A	N/A	10.66	279	5	59	34	2	24	N/A	N/A	N/A	3	250,000	0	0.0	0.0

Fund Type	Fund Name	Ticker Symbol	Overall Investment Rating	Phone	PERFORMANCE Performance Rating/Pts	Total Return % through 2/28/17 3 Mo	6 Mo	1Yr / Pct	Annualized 3Yr / Pct	5Yr / Pct	Incl. in Returns Dividend Yield	Expense Ratio
	99 Pct = Best / 0 Pct = Worst											
MC	AT Mid Cap Equity Instl	AWMIX	U	(855) 328-3863	U /	4.86	4.95	17.60 /41	--	--	0.00	0.94
GL	ATAC Inflation Rotation Investor	ATACX	C+	(855) 282-2386	C+/ 6.9	12.65	11.43	28.35 /82	3.91 /42	--	0.00	2.31
GR	Auxier Focus A	AUXAX	C+	(877) 328-9437	C / 4.8	7.06	7.48	17.97 /43	6.50 /68	8.96 /50	0.62	1.41
GR	Auxier Focus Institutional	AUXIX	C+	(877) 328-9437	C+/ 6.3	7.24	7.71	18.38 /45	6.81 /71	--	1.06	1.11
GR	Auxier Focus Inv	AUXFX	C+	(877) 328-9437	C+/ 6.1	7.18	7.60	18.16 /44	6.59 /69	9.02 /51	1.06	1.10
GR	Ave Maria Catholic Values	AVEMX	D	(866) 283-6274	C- / 3.7	4.07	8.71	28.49 /83	0.14 /14	5.47 /25	0.00	1.18
GR	Ave Maria Growth Fund	AVEGX	C+	(866) 283-6274	B- / 7.4	6.96	7.50	21.76 /61	7.90 /78	11.25 /68	0.08	1.17
GI	Ave Maria Rising Dividend Fd	AVEDX	B	(866) 283-6274	B- / 7.5	5.26	7.51	24.31 /71	7.76 /77	12.24 /76	1.48	0.92
GL	Ave Maria World Equity Fund	AVEWX	C-	(866) 283-6274	C / 4.4	6.42	5.39	21.28 /59	3.12 /33	6.70 /33	0.45	1.50
AA	AZ 529 Fidelity CSP 100% Eq Ptf		C+	(800) 544-8544	C+/ 6.6	7.24	7.52	22.51 /65	5.91 /63	10.27 /60	0.00	1.00
AA	AZ 529 Fidelity CSP 70% Eq Ptf		B	(800) 544-8544	C / 5.0	5.62	5.12	17.65 /41	5.03 /54	8.25 /44	0.00	0.93
AA	AZ 529 Fidelity CSP College Ptf		C+	(800) 544-8544	D / 1.8	2.44	1.00	7.47 / 6	2.50 /27	3.18 /11	0.00	0.67
AA	AZ 529 Fidelity CSP Consv Ptf		C	(800) 544-8544	D- / 1.0	0.82	-0.44	2.51 / 2	1.40 /20	1.33 / 7	0.00	0.59
AA	AZ 529 Fidelity CSP Idx 100% Eq Ptf		C+	(800) 544-8544	C+/ 6.8	7.56	8.42	22.84 /66	6.00 /64	10.45 /62	0.00	0.27
AA	AZ 529 Fidelity CSP Idx 70% Eq Ptf		B	(800) 544-8544	C / 4.7	5.61	5.18	16.05 /34	4.88 /53	8.01 /42	0.00	0.30
AA	AZ 529 Fidelity CSP Index Clg Ptf		C+	(800) 544-8544	D- / 1.5	2.05	0.56	4.93 / 4	2.11 /25	2.71 /10	0.00	0.33
AA	AZ 529 Fidelity CSP Index Ptf 2018		C+	(800) 544-8544	D / 1.8	2.49	1.06	6.72 / 5	2.75 /30	4.74 /20	0.00	0.31
AA	AZ 529 Fidelity CSP Index Ptf 2021		C+	(800) 544-8544	D+/ 2.5	3.45	2.25	9.52 /11	3.51 /37	6.14 /29	0.00	0.30
AA	AZ 529 Fidelity CSP Index Ptf 2024		B-	(800) 544-8544	C- / 3.4	4.31	3.46	12.28 /19	4.15 /45	7.44 /38	0.00	0.29
AA	AZ 529 Fidelity CSP Index Ptf 2027		B-	(800) 544-8544	C- / 4.2	5.15	4.58	15.03 /30	4.72 /51	8.50 /46	0.00	0.28
AA	AZ 529 Fidelity CSP Portfolio 2018		C+	(800) 544-8544	D+/ 2.3	2.99	1.59	9.52 /11	3.25 /34	5.28 /23	0.00	0.86
AA	AZ 529 Fidelity CSP Portfolio 2021		C+	(800) 544-8544	C- / 3.2	3.89	2.71	12.24 /19	3.94 /42	6.59 /32	0.00	0.92
AA	AZ 529 Fidelity CSP Portfolio 2024		B-	(800) 544-8544	C- / 3.9	4.68	3.70	14.72 /29	4.47 /48	7.77 /40	0.00	0.97
AA	AZ 529 Fidelity CSP Portfolio 2027		B-	(800) 544-8544	C / 4.8	5.46	4.71	17.17 /39	4.92 /53	8.78 /49	0.00	0.99
MC	Azzad Ethical Fund	ADJEX	D+	(888) 350-3369	C- / 4.0	7.69	7.18	19.54 /50	2.91 /31	8.03 /42	0.09	1.16
GL	Azzad Wise Capital	WISEX	C-	(888) 350-3369	E+/ 0.9	1.13	0.15	2.25 / 2	1.31 /20	2.31 / 9	1.07	1.42
GR	B Riley Diversified Equity Instl	BRDZX	B+	(800) 673-0550	A+/ 9.6	10.47	14.92	39.17 /97	7.06 /72	--	0.58	3.18
FO	Baillie Gifford EAFE 5	BGEVX	U		U /	9.41	5.18	23.60 /68	--	--	0.72	0.47
FO	Baillie Gifford EAFE Choice 2	BGCWX	U		U /	5.40	-0.31	14.17 /26	--	--	1.20	0.65
FO	Baillie Gifford EAFE Fund 2	BGETX	U		U /	9.37	5.10	23.41 /68	--	--	0.59	0.62
FO	Baillie Gifford EAFE Fund 3	BGEUX	U		U /	9.39	5.14	23.50 /68	--	--	0.62	0.55
GL	Baillie Gifford EAFE Pure 2	BGPTX	U		U /	5.22	-0.88	12.03 /18	--	--	1.37	0.66
EM	Baillie Gifford Emerg Markets 2	BGEHX	U		U /	7.77	4.40	29.04 /84	--	--	0.83	0.86
EM	Baillie Gifford Emerg Markets 5	BGEDX	U		U /	7.81	4.46	29.21 /85	--	--	0.88	0.71
GL	Baillie Gifford Global Alpha Eq 2	BGATX	U		U /	7.28	8.09	24.93 /73	--	--	0.50	0.66
GL	Baillie Gifford Global Alpha Eq 3	BGAEX	U		U /	7.30	8.13	25.01 /73	--	--	0.61	0.59
FO	● Baillie Gifford International Eq 2	BGITX	U		U /	6.18	2.51	20.63 /56	--	--	1.29	0.62
FO	● Baillie Gifford International Eq 3	BGIFX	U		U /	6.20	2.55	20.71 /56	--	--	1.45	0.54
FO	● Baillie Gifford International Eq 5	BGIVX	U		U /	6.22	2.59	20.81 /56	--	--	1.54	0.47
FO	Baillie Gifford LT Glbl Gro Eq 2	BGLTX	U		U /	9.99	5.88	24.60 /72	--	--	0.00	0.91
FO	Baillie Gifford LT Glbl Gro Eq 4	BGLFX	U		U /	10.02	5.93	24.72 /72	--	--	0.00	0.81
GR	Baird Large Cap Inst	BHGIX	A	(866) 442-2473	A / 9.5	8.64	13.78	29.57 /85	9.34 /89	12.15 /76	1.36	1.11
GR	Baird Large Cap Inv	BHGSX	A	(866) 442-2473	A / 9.4	8.59	13.64	29.36 /85	9.06 /87	11.88 /73	0.75	1.36
MC	Baird MidCap Inst	BMDIX	C-	(866) 442-2473	C / 4.5	6.08	6.54	20.33 /54	3.27 /34	9.36 /53	0.00	0.81
MC	Baird MidCap Inv	BMDSX	C-	(866) 442-2473	C / 4.3	6.03	6.45	20.03 /52	3.04 /32	9.10 /51	0.00	1.06
SC	Baird SmallCap Value Inst	BSVIX	C	(866) 442-2473	C / 4.4	4.95	7.19	20.69 /56	3.20 /34	--	1.14	1.52
SC	Baird SmallCap Value Inv	BSVSX	C-	(866) 442-2473	C- / 4.2	4.89	7.14	20.41 /54	2.95 /31	--	0.73	1.77
GL	Balter Discretionary Gl Macro Inst	BGMIX	U	(855) 854-7258	U /	-0.61	0.92	-1.40 / 1	--	--	0.00	2.14
FO	Balter European LS Small Cap Inst	BESMX	U	(855) 854-7258	U /	10.12	8.93	7.32 / 6	--	--	0.00	2.62
FS	● Balter Event Driven Institutional	BEVIX	U	(855) 854-7258	U /	2.84	-0.43	1.79 / 2	--	--	0.00	2.43
GR	Balter LS Small Cap Equity Instl	BEQIX	C+	(855) 854-7258	C- / 3.5	3.49	4.95	17.44 /40	3.44 /36	--	0.00	2.93
MC	Baron Asset Fd Retail	BARAX	C+	(800) 992-2766	B / 7.7	9.03	8.12	26.42 /78	6.84 /71	12.98 /83	0.00	1.31

● Denotes fund is closed to new investors
* Denotes fund is included in Section II

102

Risk Rating/Pts	3 Year Standard Deviation	Beta	NAV As of 2/28/17	Total $(Mil)	Cash %	Stocks %	Bonds %	Other %	Portfolio Turnover Ratio	Last Bull Market Return	Last Bear Market Return	Manager Quality Pct	Manager Tenure (Years)	Initial Purch. $	Additional Purch. $	Front End Load	Back End Load
U /	N/A	N/A	12.13	431	3	96	0	1	23	N/A	N/A	N/A	3	250,000	0	0.0	0.0
C /4.6	14.9	0.46	30.02	83	0	99	0	1	2,311	N/A	N/A	93	5	2,500	100	0.0	2.0
C+ /6.8	9.0	0.85	21.38	3	9	89	0	2	6	74.6	-11.6	45	18	2,000	50	5.8	2.0
C+ /6.7	9.0	0.85	21.41	57	9	89	0	2	6	N/A	N/A	49	18	1,000,000	0	0.0	2.0
C+ /6.7	8.9	0.84	21.09	193	9	89	0	2	6	75.0	-11.6	46	18	5,000	50	0.0	2.0
C /4.6	12.9	1.04	19.71	231	7	92	0	1	63	60.3	-19.9	2	15	2,500	0	0.0	0.0
C /4.9	10.3	0.90	28.30	378	5	94	0	1	32	111.0	-19.0	56	4	2,500	0	0.0	0.0
C+ /5.7	10.8	0.96	17.61	897	7	92	0	1	35	111.2	-16.1	45	12	2,500	0	0.0	0.0
C+ /5.8	10.9	0.82	13.80	49	10	89	0	1	35	65.3	-23.8	91	4	2,500	0	0.0	0.0
C+ /6.6	10.5	1.59	20.30	18	2	95	1	2	24	99.6	-23.1	10	12	50	25	0.0	0.0
B /8.1	7.8	1.19	19.93	10	2	67	30	1	24	74.2	-17.3	27	12	50	25	0.0	0.0
B+ /9.9	3.2	0.46	15.10	22	8	21	69	2	43	23.4	-4.4	63	12	50	25	0.0	0.0
B+ /9.5	1.4	0.09	13.49	3	17	0	82	1	34	8.6	0.7	78	12	50	25	0.0	0.0
C+ /6.8	10.3	1.59	17.64	14	1	97	1	1	24	98.0	-19.3	11	11	50	25	0.0	0.0
B /8.9	7.2	1.13	18.08	10	0	68	30	2	33	68.3	-11.2	29	11	50	25	0.0	0.0
B+ /9.9	2.4	0.34	14.46	12	10	19	69	2	36	19.4	-0.3	69	11	50	25	0.0	0.0
B+ /9.8	3.5	0.54	15.24	18	8	26	65	1	33	39.6	-7.2	59	11	50	25	0.0	0.0
B+ /9.6	4.8	0.74	15.88	22	5	39	54	2	25	52.8	-10.5	49	11	50	25	0.0	0.0
B+ /9.2	6.0	0.94	16.46	30	3	51	44	2	18	65.9	-13.6	37	11	50	25	0.0	0.0
B /8.6	7.2	1.13	15.31	28	1	63	34	2	11	77.0	-15.9	28	10	50	25	0.0	0.5
B+ /9.4	4.4	0.66	17.25	28	6	29	63	2	24	45.5	-12.4	54	12	50	25	0.0	0.0
B+ /9.1	5.7	0.87	18.16	35	5	42	52	1	19	59.2	-16.1	42	12	50	25	0.0	0.0
B /8.6	6.9	1.06	18.78	48	4	54	41	1	17	71.8	-19.1	31	12	50	25	0.0	0.0
B /8.1	8.1	1.23	14.67	33	3	66	30	1	16	82.9	-21.2	22	10	50	25	0.0	0.0
C /5.2	12.1	0.91	13.46	67	3	96	0	1	34	82.8	-17.0	12	17	1,000	50	0.0	2.0
B+ /9.4	1.2	0.06	10.44	101	21	7	70	2	19	12.5	-0.6	82	7	4,000	300	0.0	2.0
C /4.8	16.8	1.26	12.78	9	1	98	0	1	203	N/A	N/A	10	3	10,000	2,500	0.0	0.0
U /	N/A	N/A	11.04	849	2	97	0	1	17	N/A	N/A	N/A	9	500,000,000	0	0.0	0.1
U /	N/A	N/A	13.17	288	0	0	0	100	16	N/A	N/A	N/A	N/A	25,000,000	0	0.0	0.1
U /	N/A	N/A	10.99	813	2	97	0	1	17	N/A	N/A	N/A	9	25,000,000	0	0.0	0.1
U /	N/A	N/A	11.02	473	2	97	0	1	17	N/A	N/A	N/A	9	100,000,000	0	0.0	0.1
U /	N/A	N/A	9.99	197	0	0	0	100	18	N/A	N/A	N/A	3	25,000,000	0	0.0	0.1
U /	N/A	N/A	16.76	130	0	0	0	100	46	N/A	N/A	N/A	14	25,000,000	0	0.0	0.4
U /	N/A	N/A	17.28	1,186	0	0	0	100	46	N/A	N/A	N/A	14	500,000,000	0	0.0	0.4
U /	N/A	N/A	15.50	240	0	0	0	100	16	N/A	N/A	N/A	N/A	25,000,000	0	0.0	0.1
U /	N/A	N/A	15.80	634	0	0	0	100	16	N/A	N/A	N/A	2	100,000,000	0	0.0	0.1
U /	N/A	N/A	11.56	614	0	0	0	100	15	N/A	N/A	N/A	2	25,000,000	0	0.0	0.1
U /	N/A	N/A	11.71	957	0	0	0	100	15	N/A	N/A	N/A	2	100,000,000	0	0.0	0.1
U /	N/A	N/A	12.06	178	0	0	0	100	15	N/A	N/A	N/A	2	500,000,000	0	0.0	0.1
U /	N/A	N/A	12.58	36	1	98	0	1	10	N/A	N/A	N/A	N/A	25,000,000	0	0.0	0.1
U /	N/A	N/A	14.49	32	1	98	0	1	10	N/A	N/A	N/A	N/A	200,000,000	0	0.0	0.1
C+ /5.8	12.1	1.13	9.48	42	1	95	2	2	87	124.0	-18.4	42	4	25,000	0	0.0	0.0
C+ /5.9	12.1	1.13	9.46	1	1	95	2	2	87	121.2	-18.6	38	4	2,500	100	0.0	0.0
C+ /5.7	11.5	0.89	16.93	1,193	0	97	2	1	53	102.0	-16.8	15	17	25,000	0	0.0	0.0
C+ /5.7	11.5	0.89	16.18	141	0	97	2	1	53	99.3	-16.9	14	17	2,500	100	0.0	0.0
C+ /6.2	12.7	0.71	14.88	28	7	92	0	1	42	N/A	N/A	54	5	25,000	0	0.0	0.0
C+ /6.3	12.7	0.71	14.86	3	7	92	0	1	42	N/A	N/A	50	5	2,500	100	0.0	0.0
U /	N/A	N/A	9.83	123	0	0	0	100	602	N/A	N/A	N/A	2	50,000	500	0.0	1.0
U /	N/A	N/A	10.12	29	0	0	0	100	0	N/A	N/A	N/A	2	50,000	500	0.0	1.0
U /	N/A	N/A	10.00	26	47	28	23	2	145	N/A	N/A	N/A	2	50,000	500	0.0	1.0
B /8.1	7.5	0.57	11.09	158	53	46	0	1	228	N/A	N/A	43	4	50,000	500	0.0	1.0
C- /4.1	12.3	0.93	63.12	1,855	1	98	0	1	13	122.1	-19.8	49	14	2,000	0	0.0	0.0

I. Index of Stock Mutual Funds

								PERFORMANCE			Incl. in Returns	
	99 Pct = Best 0 Pct = Worst		Overall		Perfor-			Total Return % through 2/28/17				
		Ticker	Investment		mance				Annualized		Dividend	Expense
Fund Type	Fund Name	Symbol	Rating	Phone	Rating/Pts	3 Mo	6 Mo	1Yr / Pct	3Yr / Pct	5Yr / Pct	Yield	Ratio
MC	Baron Asset Inst	BARIX	C+	(800) 992-2766	B / 7.9	9.14	8.30	26.79 /79	7.15 /73	13.29 /87	0.00	1.04
SC	Baron Discovery Fd Inst	BDFIX	C+	(800) 992-2766	A- / 9.2	6.95	12.26	47.35 /99	5.06 /55	--	0.00	1.25
SC	Baron Discovery Fd Retail	BDFFX	C+	(800) 992-2766	A- / 9.1	6.93	12.11	47.03 /99	4.80 /52	--	0.00	1.57
EM	Baron Emerging Markets Inst	BEXIX	D+	(800) 992-2766	D+ / 2.7	6.26	0.80	21.93 /62	0.83 /17	5.08 /22	0.36	1.20
EM	Baron Emerging Markets Retail	BEXFX	D	(800) 992-2766	D+ / 2.5	6.18	0.66	21.60 /60	0.57 /16	4.84 /20	0.14	1.45
EN	Baron Energy and Res Inst	BENIX	E-	(800) 992-2766	E- / 0.2	-3.24	4.68	42.74 /98	-10.15 / 1	-3.09 / 2	0.00	1.29
EN	Baron Energy and Res Retail	BENFX	E-	(800) 992-2766	E- / 0.2	-3.28	4.49	42.35 /98	-10.35 / 1	-3.30 / 2	0.00	1.58
GR	Baron Fifth Avenue Growth Fd	BFTHX	C	(800) 992-2766	C+ / 6.7	10.10	6.53	21.65 /60	5.86 /63	12.02 /74	0.00	1.12
GR	Baron Fifth Avenue Growth Inst	BFTIX	C	(800) 992-2766	C+ / 6.9	10.17	6.65	21.92 /62	6.14 /65	12.29 /77	0.00	0.84
GL	Baron Global Advantage Fund Inst	BGAIX	C-	(800) 992-2766	C+ / 5.6	9.99	7.24	22.59 /65	3.63 /38	--	0.00	2.89
GL	Baron Global Advantage Fund Retail	BGAFX	C-	(800) 992-2766	C / 5.4	9.94	7.16	22.36 /64	3.42 /36	--	0.00	3.19
GR	Baron Growth Fd Retail	BGRFX	C-	(800) 992-2766	C / 5.2	8.00	4.88	22.25 /63	3.97 /43	11.53 /70	0.00	1.29
GR	Baron Growth Inst	BGRIX	C-	(800) 992-2766	C / 5.5	8.07	5.03	22.57 /65	4.23 /46	11.83 /73	0.00	1.04
FO	Baron International Growth Fd Rtl	BIGFX	D	(800) 992-2766	D+ / 2.3	4.86	2.04	14.86 /29	1.53 /21	5.84 /27	0.05	1.59
FO	Baron International Growth Inst	BINIX	D	(800) 992-2766	D+ / 2.5	4.87	2.12	15.11 /30	1.77 /22	6.12 /29	0.05	1.31
TC	Baron Opportunity Inst	BIOIX	E+	(800) 992-2766	C- / 3.5	9.75	6.88	23.23 /67	0.05 /14	8.64 /48	0.00	1.10
TC	Baron Opportunity Retail	BIOPX	E	(800) 992-2766	D / 2.0	9.66	6.73	22.91 /66	-0.23 /12	8.34 /45	0.00	1.38
MC	Baron Partners Retail	BPTRX	C-	(800) 992-2766	C+ / 6.6	9.86	5.63	28.80 /83	4.27 /46	13.82 /92	0.00	1.52
RE	Baron Real Estate Institutional	BREIX	C-	(800) 992-2766	C- / 4.1	8.05	4.61	19.69 /50	2.82 /30	13.79 /92	0.26	1.06
RE	Baron Real Estate Retail	BREFX	D+	(800) 992-2766	C- / 3.9	8.01	4.50	19.39 /49	2.56 /28	13.51 /89	0.00	1.31
GI	Baron Select Focused Growth Inst	BFGIX	D-	(800) 992-2766	D+ / 2.9	8.54	1.88	15.07 /30	1.91 /23	8.12 /43	0.00	1.09
GI	Baron Select Focused Growth Rtl	BFGFX	D-	(800) 992-2766	D+ / 2.7	8.42	1.76	14.76 /29	1.64 /22	7.83 /41	0.00	1.39
MC	Baron Select Partners Inst	BPTIX	C-	(800) 992-2766	C+ / 6.8	9.93	5.78	29.16 /84	4.55 /49	14.12 /94	0.00	1.26
SC	Baron Small Cap Fd Retail	BSCFX	D+	(800) 992-2766	C+ / 6.1	6.38	7.84	29.34 /85	3.71 /39	10.62 /63	0.00	1.30
SC	Baron Small Cap Inst	BSFIX	D+	(800) 992-2766	C+ / 6.4	6.48	7.99	29.66 /86	3.99 /43	10.90 /65	0.00	1.04
SC	Baron Small Cap R6	BSCUX	U	(800) 992-2766	U /	6.48	7.99	29.71 /86	--	--	0.00	1.04
GR	Barrett Growth	BGRWX	C+	(800) 451-2010	C+ / 6.6	6.06	6.78	16.58 /37	7.55 /76	10.28 /60	0.10	2.01
GR	Barrett Opportunity Fund	SAOPX	C+	(800) 451-2010	B+ / 8.9	6.95	11.42	28.46 /83	8.49 /83	10.85 /65	0.96	1.28
GR	Barrow Long/Short Opportunity Inst	BFSLX	C-	(877) 767-6633	D- / 1.0	2.59	-0.19	-4.71 / 1	2.19 /25	--	0.00	4.59
GR	Barrow Value Opportunity Inst	BALIX	C+	(877) 767-6633	C+ / 5.7	6.23	5.54	17.26 /39	6.11 /65	11.89 /73	0.49	1.60
GR	Baywood SKBA ValuePlus Inst	BVPIX	A	(855) 409-2297	B / 7.8	4.71	9.72	26.33 /77	7.68 /77	--	2.01	2.09
GR	Baywood SKBA ValuePlus Inv	BVPNX	A-	(855) 409-2297	B / 7.6	4.67	9.64	25.99 /76	7.39 /75	--	1.80	5.80
GR	Baywood SociallyResponsible Instl	BVSIX	C	(855) 409-2297	C+ / 6.1	4.65	9.64	27.99 /82	3.93 /42	9.25 /53	1.16	0.85
GR	Baywood SociallyResponsible Inv	BVSNX	C	(855) 409-2297	C+ / 5.8	4.55	9.37	27.59 /81	3.70 /39	9.00 /51	1.02	1.22
GR	● BBH Core Select Fund Class N	BBTEX	C+	(800) 625-5759	C / 5.5	6.41	6.95	17.34 /40	6.17 /66	10.69 /63	0.58	1.02
GR	● BBH Core Select Fund Class Retail	BBTRX	C	(800) 625-5759	C / 5.3	6.36	6.84	17.11 /39	5.91 /63	10.41 /61	0.71	1.34
GL	BBH Global Core Select N	BBGNX	C-	(800) 625-5759	D+ / 2.5	6.30	3.07	13.41 /23	2.40 /27	--	0.52	1.35
GL	BBH Global Core Select Retail	BBGRX	D+	(800) 625-5759	D+ / 2.3	6.26	2.93	13.20 /22	2.17 /25	--	0.29	2.97
FO	BBH Partner Fd International Eq I	BBHLX	D	(800) 625-5759	D / 1.7	5.87	0.78	14.14 /26	0.75 /17	4.86 /20	2.21	0.89
FO	Beck Mack & Oliver Partners	BMPEX	E-	(800) 943-6786	D- / 1.2	5.12	8.29	25.06 /73	-1.99 / 7	4.53 /18	1.00	1.44
GR	Becker Value Equity Inst	BVEIX	B+	(800) 551-3998	A- / 9.2	7.56	12.10	31.34 /89	8.82 /86	13.51 /89	1.56	0.80
GR	Becker Value Equity Retail	BVEFX	B+	(800) 551-3998	A- / 9.1	7.54	12.09	31.17 /88	8.65 /84	13.28 /87	1.48	0.70
GR	Beech Hill Total Return A	BHTAX	D	(877) 760-0005	D+ / 2.4	7.23	5.82	19.86 /51	1.18 /19	4.92 /21	0.77	2.59
GR	Beech Hill Total Return C	BHTCX	D	(877) 760-0005	D+ / 2.6	7.00	5.46	19.01 /47	0.41 /15	4.13 /16	0.32	3.34
GR	Beehive Fund	BEEHX	C+	(866) 684-4915	C+ / 6.1	5.77	9.54	20.58 /55	5.37 /58	9.87 /57	0.90	0.98
GR	Berkshire Focus Fund	BFOCX	D+	(877) 526-0707	C / 5.5	11.49	11.43	26.08 /76	2.21 /25	11.93 /74	0.00	1.99
FO	Bernstein International Sm Cp SCB	IRCSX	U	(800) 221-5672	U /	7.98	3.91	17.14 /39	--	--	1.33	N/A
FO	Bernstein International Str EQ SCB	STESX	U	(800) 221-5672	U /	6.89	5.86	15.96 /34	--	--	1.27	N/A
SC	Bernzott US Small Cap Value	BSCVX	B-	(877) 998-9880	B / 8.2	7.05	10.34	30.94 /88	7.58 /76	--	0.41	1.52
GR	Berwyn Cornerstone Fund	BERCX	B+	(800) 992-6757	A- / 9.0	7.43	15.87	40.84 /97	5.42 /59	10.13 /59	1.38	1.94
GR	Berwyn Fund	BERWX	D-	(800) 992-6757	C- / 4.1	0.62	11.92	30.72 /88	0.87 /17	8.37 /45	0.00	1.27
GR	BFS Equity	BFSAX	C+		C+ / 6.4	6.62	6.26	17.60 /41	6.96 /72		0.43	1.86

● Denotes fund is closed to new investors

* Denotes fund is included in Section II

104

www.thestreetratings.com

RISK Risk Rating/Pts	3 Year Standard Deviation	Beta	NAV As of 2/28/17	Total $(Mil)	Cash %	Stocks %	Bonds %	Other %	Portfolio Turnover Ratio	Last Bull Market Return	Last Bear Market Return	Manager Quality Pct	Manager Tenure (Years)	Initial Purch. $	Additional Purch. $	Front End Load	Back End Load
C- / 4.2	12.3	0.93	64.98	805	1	98	0	1	13	125.5	-19.7	53	14	1,000,000	0	0.0	0.0
D+ / 2.7	19.0	1.04	14.47	64	9	90	0	1	91	N/A	N/A	48	4	1,000,000	0	0.0	0.0
D+ / 2.7	19.0	1.04	14.35	27	9	90	0	1	91	N/A	N/A	45	4	2,000	0	0.0	0.0
C+ / 5.7	12.7	0.72	11.88	2,120	12	87	0	1	26	47.3	-18.5	69	7	1,000,000	0	0.0	0.0
C+ / 5.7	12.8	0.72	11.85	892	12	87	0	1	26	45.4	-18.6	66	7	2,000	0	0.0	0.0
D- / 1.3	25.6	1.18	8.95	31	21	78	0	1	48	N/A	N/A	20	6	1,000,000	0	0.0	0.0
D- / 1.3	25.6	1.18	8.84	63	21	78	0	1	48	N/A	N/A	18	6	2,000	0	0.0	0.0
C / 4.3	14.7	1.18	20.06	68	0	99	0	1	19	123.4	-16.7	8	6	2,000	0	0.0	0.0
C / 4.3	14.7	1.18	20.36	82	0	99	0	1	19	126.5	-16.7	9	6	1,000,000	0	0.0	0.0
C- / 4.0	16.8	1.09	15.41	5	10	89	0	1	26	N/A	N/A	93	5	1,000,000	0	0.0	0.0
C- / 4.0	16.9	1.09	15.27	6	10	89	0	1	26	N/A	N/A	92	5	2,000	0	0.0	0.0
C- / 4.2	12.0	0.97	64.26	2,738	3	96	0	1	5	107.0	-19.3	9	23	2,000	0	0.0	0.0
C- / 4.2	12.0	0.97	65.73	3,117	3	96	0	1	5	109.9	-19.2	11	23	1,000,000	0	0.0	0.0
C / 5.4	11.5	0.82	19.20	45	5	94	0	1	43	56.5	-22.9	84	16	2,000	0	0.0	0.0
C / 5.4	11.5	0.81	19.38	53	5	94	0	1	43	58.6	-22.9	86	16	1,000,000	0	0.0	0.0
D / 2.0	17.3	1.28	15.99	41	1	98	0	1	32	76.5	-19.9	1	11	1,000,000	0	0.0	0.0
D / 1.9	17.3	1.28	15.55	177	1	98	0	1	32	74.0	-20.0	1	11	2,000	0	0.0	0.0
C- / 3.3	17.1	1.24	40.12	964	0	100	0	0	17	136.7	-25.1	5	25	2,000	0	0.0	0.0
C / 5.3	14.6	0.72	25.24	523	0	0	0	100	51	147.2	-23.1	16	8	1,000,000	0	0.0	0.0
C / 5.3	14.6	0.72	24.96	406	0	0	0	100	51	143.9	-23.1	14	8	2,000	0	0.0	0.0
C- / 3.8	13.6	1.07	13.34	135	9	90	0	1	12	78.6	-20.8	3	21	1,000,000	0	0.0	0.0
C- / 3.8	13.6	1.07	13.13	39	9	90	0	1	12	76.2	-20.9	3	21	2,000	0	0.0	0.0
C- / 3.3	17.1	1.24	40.84	684	0	100	0	0	17	140.2	-25.0	6	25	1,000,000	0	0.0	0.0
D+ / 2.8	13.8	0.81	27.00	1,695	6	93	0	1	10	106.0	-22.6	51	20	2,000	0	0.0	0.0
D+ / 2.8	13.8	0.81	27.79	1,632	6	93	0	1	10	108.9	-22.5	55	20	1,000,000	0	0.0	0.0
U /	N/A	N/A	27.79	75	6	93	0	1	10	N/A	N/A	N/A	20	5,000,000	0	0.0	0.0
C+ / 6.9	9.8	0.92	17.26	21	3	93	3	1	34	97.9	-17.8	48	13	2,500	50	0.0	0.0
C- / 3.5	10.9	0.96	27.39	59	0	98	1	1	6	103.4	-24.6	55	11	1,000	50	0.0	0.0
B+ / 9.0	5.4	0.15	10.31	34	67	32	0	1	64	N/A	N/A	78	4	2,500	0	0.0	0.0
C+ / 6.7	10.8	0.90	27.38	34	4	95	0	1	84	120.7	-20.2	33	4	2,500	0	0.0	0.0
B- / 7.3	10.0	0.91	16.71	1	2	97	0	1	32	N/A	N/A	51	N/A	100,000	0	0.0	0.0
B- / 7.2	10.0	0.91	16.63	2	2	97	0	1	32	N/A	N/A	47	N/A	2,500	100	0.0	0.0
C / 5.2	12.2	1.08	11.02	6	7	92	0	1	57	84.2	-19.0	5	13	100,000	0	0.0	0.0
C / 5.3	12.1	1.07	10.99	9	7	92	0	1	57	81.8	-19.1	5	13	2,500	100	0.0	0.0
C+ / 6.6	9.1	0.84	21.42	3,204	5	92	2	1	12	96.8	-11.5	41	12	10,000	10,000	0.0	2.0
C+ / 5.7	9.1	0.84	12.51	175	5	92	2	1	12	94.3	-11.6	37	12	5,000	250	0.0	2.0
B- / 7.0	9.3	0.67	11.81	115	1	90	8	1	19	N/A	N/A	88	4	10,000	1,000	0.0	2.0
C+ / 6.9	9.3	0.67	11.76	4	1	90	8	1	19	N/A	N/A	87	4	5,000	250	0.0	2.0
C+ / 6.1	10.8	0.85	14.56	1,026	2	97	0	1	12	42.2	-16.6	80	13	5,000,000	25,000	0.0	2.0
D / 2.0	14.7	0.92	10.31	38	5	94	0	1	50	52.6	-15.5	50	2	2,500	1,000	0.0	2.0
C / 5.3	11.3	1.04	18.76	259	5	94	0	1	34	129.9	N/A	48	14	250,000	100	0.0	1.0
C / 5.3	11.3	1.04	18.70	145	5	94	0	1	34	127.6	-18.5	46	14	2,500	100	0.0	1.0
C / 5.3	11.6	0.99	11.12	1	13	86	0	1	80	46.7	-13.0	3	6	500	250	4.0	1.0
C / 5.3	11.6	0.99	10.85	11	13	86	0	1	80	40.7	-13.3	2	6	500	250	0.0	1.0
C+ / 6.1	13.0	1.21	14.85	125	0	90	9	1	17	95.3	-21.6	6	9	2,500	500	0.0	0.0
D+ / 2.9	19.9	1.24	19.73	55	0	99	0	1	456	107.5	-13.3	2	20	5,000	500	0.0	2.0
U /	N/A	N/A	10.77	51	1	96	2	1	51	N/A	N/A	N/A	2	5,000	0	0.0	0.0
U /	N/A	N/A	10.76	96	0	0	0	100	79	N/A	N/A	N/A	2	10,000	0	0.0	0.0
C / 4.6	13.1	0.76	13.49	75	3	96	0	1	27	N/A	N/A	87	5	25,000	5,000	0.0	2.0
C / 4.9	13.6	1.05	17.71	25	2	89	7	2	30	102.5	-18.7	13	15	1,000	250	0.0	1.0
C- / 3.2	14.9	0.91	29.80	125	5	84	9	2	11	96.6	-24.9	3	33	1,000	250	0.0	1.0
C+ / 6.8	9.8	0.93	12.62	26	2	96	0	2	49	N/A	N/A	39	4	1,000	0	0.0	0.0

99 Pct = Best
0 Pct = Worst

Fund Type	Fund Name	Ticker Symbol	Overall Investment Rating	Phone	Performance Rating/Pts	3 Mo	6 Mo	1Yr / Pct	3Yr / Pct	5Yr / Pct	Dividend Yield	Expense Ratio
GR	Biondo Focus Inv	BFONX	C+	(800) 672-9152	B+ / 8.7	14.94	22.98	37.65 /96	2.79 /30	10.16 /59	0.00	2.62
GR	Biondo Growth Inv	BIONX	C-	(800) 672-9152	C / 5.2	11.08	14.94	23.41 /68	1.80 /23	7.03 /35	0.00	1.72
GR	Bishop Street Dividend Value I	BSLIX	A+	(800) 262-9565	B+ / 8.9	7.61	9.01	21.95 /62	10.20 /94	12.69 /81	1.58	1.38
GR	Bishop Street Strategic Growth Inst	BSRIX	D	(800) 262-9565	C / 5.2	10.42	3.33	22.97 /66	3.61 /38	9.58 /55	0.00	1.40
GI	BlackRock 20/80 Target Alloc Inst	BICPX	C-	(800) 441-7762	D+ / 2.3	3.04	1.31	6.20 / 5	3.85 /41	6.24 /30	1.81	0.75
GI	BlackRock 20/80 Target Alloc Inv A	BACPX	C-	(800) 441-7762	D- / 1.5	2.98	1.13	5.88 / 5	3.46 /37	5.85 /27	1.48	1.02
GI	BlackRock 20/80 Target Alloc Inv C	BCCPX	C-	(800) 441-7762	D / 1.7	2.76	0.79	5.09 / 4	2.71 /29	5.07 /22	0.96	1.75
GI	BlackRock 20/80 Target Alloc R	BRCPX	C-	(800) 441-7762	D / 1.9	2.87	0.92	5.48 / 4	3.17 /33	5.58 /25	1.26	1.33
GI	BlackRock 40/60 Target Alloc Inst	BIMPX	C-	(800) 441-7762	C- / 3.3	4.42	3.20	10.32 /12	4.51 /49	7.62 /39	1.78	0.78
GI	BlackRock 40/60 Target Alloc Inv A	BAMPX	D+	(800) 441-7762	D / 2.2	4.26	3.04	9.89 /11	4.15 /45	7.24 /36	1.44	1.01
GI	BlackRock 40/60 Target Alloc Inv C	BCMPX	C-	(800) 441-7762	D+ / 2.5	4.13	2.70	9.11 /10	3.35 /35	6.43 /31	0.91	1.76
GI	BlackRock 40/60 Target Alloc R	BRMPX	C-	(800) 441-7762	C- / 3.0	4.22	2.89	9.76 /11	3.99 /43	7.10 /35	1.38	1.32
GR	BlackRock 60/40 Target Alloc Inst	BIGPX	C	(800) 441-7762	C- / 4.2	5.33	4.80	13.78 /24	4.81 /52	8.69 /48	1.69	0.70
GR	BlackRock 60/40 Target Alloc Inv A	BAGPX	C-	(800) 441-7762	C- / 3.0	5.26	4.64	13.43 /23	4.46 /48	8.29 /45	1.42	0.96
GR	BlackRock 60/40 Target Alloc Inv C	BCGPX	C-	(800) 441-7762	C- / 3.3	5.06	4.24	12.60 /20	3.68 /39	7.51 /38	0.90	1.72
GR	BlackRock 60/40 Target Alloc R	BRGPX	C-	(800) 441-7762	C- / 3.8	5.15	4.53	13.15 /22	4.24 /46	8.09 /43	1.31	1.29
AG	BlackRock 80/20 Target Alloc Inst	BIAPX	C-	(800) 441-7762	C / 5.4	6.24	6.72	18.49 /45	5.17 /56	9.73 /56	1.60	0.79
AG	BlackRock 80/20 Target Alloc Inv A	BAAPX	D+	(800) 441-7762	C- / 4.0	6.13	6.52	18.02 /43	4.78 /52	9.35 /53	1.35	1.10
AG	BlackRock 80/20 Target Alloc Inv C	BCAPX	D+	(800) 441-7762	C / 4.4	5.94	6.15	17.15 /39	4.02 /43	8.53 /47	0.85	1.85
AG	BlackRock 80/20 Target Alloc R	BRAPX	C-	(800) 441-7762	C / 4.9	6.06	6.36	17.81 /42	4.61 /50	9.15 /52	1.24	1.41
SC	BlackRock Advg Sm Cap Core Inst	BDSIX	B+	(800) 441-7762	A+ / 9.6	5.57	14.17	37.54 /96	8.58 /84	--	0.47	3.52
SC	BlackRock Advg Sm Cap Core Inv A	BDSAX	B	(800) 441-7762	B+ / 8.9	5.50	14.13	37.18 /96	8.34 /82	--	0.23	3.94
SC	BlackRock Advg Sm Cap Core Inv C	BDSCX	B+	(800) 441-7762	A- / 9.2	5.32	13.58	36.15 /95	7.50 /75	--	0.00	4.75
SC	BlackRock Advntg Sm Cap Gr Eq Inst	PSGIX	C-	(800) 441-7762	B- / 7.2	5.73	11.90	32.02 /90	4.52 /49	10.62 /63	0.05	0.72
SC	BlackRock Advntg Sm Cap Gr Eq Inv	CSGEX	D	(800) 441-7762	C+ / 6.0	5.59	11.67	31.63 /89	4.19 /45	10.27 /60	0.00	1.03
SC	BlackRock Advntg Sm Cap Gr Eq Inv	CGICX	D-	(800) 441-7762	C+ / 6.4	5.42	11.33	30.60 /87	3.38 /36	9.40 /54	0.00	1.81
SC	BlackRock Advntg Sm Cap Gr Eq Svc	PCGEX	D+	(800) 441-7762	B- / 7.0	5.63	11.78	31.69 /89	4.23 /46	10.31 /61	0.00	1.02
EN	BlackRock AllCap Energy & Res Inst	BACIX	E-	(800) 441-7762	E- / 0.1	-2.71	5.20	26.88 /79	-9.09 / 1	-4.98 / 2	2.52	1.11
EN	BlackRock AllCap Energy & Res Inv	BACAX	E-	(800) 441-7762	E- / 0.1	-2.80	5.03	26.38 /77	-9.47 / 1	-5.36 / 2	1.96	1.48
EN	● BlackRock AllCap Energy & Res Inv	BACBX	E-	(800) 441-7762	E- / 0.1	-2.96	4.69	25.48 /75	-10.13 / 1	-6.05 / 1	0.00	2.47
EN	BlackRock AllCap Energy & Res Inv	BACCX	E-	(800) 441-7762	E- / 0.1	-2.92	4.72	25.61 /75	-10.09 / 1	-6.04 / 1	1.25	2.18
EN	BlackRock AllCap Energy & Res Svc	BACSX	E-	(800) 441-7762	E- / 0.1	-2.76	5.03	26.52 /78	-9.45 / 1	-5.33 / 2	2.08	1.41
GL	BlackRock Alternative Cap Str Inst	BIMBX	U	(800) 441-7762	U /	2.97	2.37	5.34 / 4	--	--	1.60	1.61
BA	BlackRock Bal Capital Inst	MACPX	B-	(800) 441-7762	C+ / 6.8	6.00	8.45	18.11 /43	7.45 /75	9.74 /56	1.47	0.92
BA	BlackRock Bal Capital Inv A	MDCPX	B-	(800) 441-7762	C+ / 5.6	5.91	8.32	17.79 /42	7.15 /73	9.42 /54	1.15	1.20
BA	● BlackRock Bal Capital Inv B	MBCPX	C+	(800) 441-7762	C / 5.5	5.42	7.34	15.97 /34	5.83 /63	8.18 /43	0.00	2.28
BA	BlackRock Bal Capital Inv C	MCCPX	C+	(800) 441-7762	C+ / 6.0	5.77	7.90	16.93 /38	6.35 /67	8.58 /47	0.72	1.97
BA	BlackRock Bal Capital R	MRBPX	C+	(800) 441-7762	C+ / 6.4	5.80	8.07	17.35 /40	6.78 /70	9.04 /51	1.04	1.53
GI	BlackRock Basic Value Inst	MABAX	C	(800) 441-7762	B / 8.2	3.73	9.38	30.78 /88	7.68 /77	12.43 /78	1.72	0.55
GI	BlackRock Basic Value Inv A	MDBAX	C-	(800) 441-7762	B- / 7.0	3.65	9.19	30.41 /87	7.38 /75	12.12 /75	1.39	0.83
GI	● BlackRock Basic Value Inv B	MBBAX	C-	(800) 441-7762	B- / 7.1	3.33	8.56	29.05 /84	6.28 /67	10.96 /65	0.00	1.90
GI	BlackRock Basic Value Inv C	MCBAX	C-	(800) 441-7762	B- / 7.3	3.44	8.81	29.38 /85	6.53 /69	11.24 /68	0.91	1.62
GI	BlackRock Basic Value K	MBVKX	U	(800) 441-7762	U /	3.76	9.44	30.96 /88	--	--	1.82	0.44
GI	BlackRock Basic Value R	MRBVX	C-	(800) 441-7762	B / 7.7	3.54	9.03	29.98 /86	7.03 /72	11.75 /72	1.29	1.15
GR	BlackRock Capital Appr Inst	MAFGX	C-	(800) 441-7762	B- / 7.3	9.55	7.29	20.86 /57	7.24 /74	11.69 /71	0.00	0.79
GR	BlackRock Capital Appr Inv A	MDFGX	D+	(800) 441-7762	C+ / 6.2	9.47	7.16	20.53 /55	6.94 /71	11.39 /69	0.00	1.07
GR	● BlackRock Capital Appr Inv B	MBFGX	D	(800) 441-7762	C+ / 6.2	9.05	6.45	19.07 /47	5.80 /62	10.21 /60	0.00	2.04
GR	BlackRock Capital Appr Inv C	MCFGX	D+	(800) 441-7762	C+ / 6.5	9.22	6.70	19.48 /49	6.07 /65	10.49 /62	0.00	1.86
GR	BlackRock Capital Appr R	MRFGX	D+	(800) 441-7762	C+ / 6.9	9.38	6.98	20.14 /53	6.65 /69	11.08 /66	0.00	1.32
GR	BlackRock Capital Appreciation K	BFGBX	C-	(800) 441-7762	B- / 7.4	9.59	7.34	21.02 /57	7.35 /74	11.81 /72	0.00	0.68
AA	BlackRock Cmdty Strat Inst	BICSX	E	(800) 441-7762	E- / 0.2	3.95	6.85	24.20 /71	-7.85 / 1	-7.10 / 1	0.92	1.16
AA	BlackRock Cmdty Strat Inv A	BCSAX	E-	(800) 441-7762	E- / 0.1	3.79	6.56	23.83 /69	-8.07 / 1	-7.31 / 1	0.70	1.74

● Denotes fund is closed to new investors
* Denotes fund is included in Section II

www.thestreetratings.com

RISK	3 Year		NET ASSETS		ASSET				Portfolio Turnover Ratio	BULL / BEAR		FUND MANAGER		MINIMUMS		LOADS	
Risk Rating/Pts	Standard Deviation	Beta	NAV As of 2/28/17	Total $(Mil)	Cash %	Stocks %	Bonds %	Other %		Last Bull Market Return	Last Bear Market Return	Manager Quality Pct	Manager Tenure (Years)	Initial Purch. $	Additional Purch. $	Front End Load	Back End Load
C- /3.0	21.9	1.72	16.16	24	0	0	0	100	55	87.5	-28.8	1	7	1,000	100	0.0	2.0
C- /4.2	15.6	1.33	13.23	31	0	89	10	1	46	65.2	-22.0	1	11	1,000	100	0.0	2.0
B- /7.6	9.4	0.89	15.43	42	0	97	2	1	24	116.4	-13.0	79	7	1,000	0	0.0	0.0
D+ /2.3	17.2	1.31	13.25	29	0	98	1	1	55	98.5	-21.0	2	4	1,000	0	0.0	0.0
B- /7.9	3.4	0.26	11.23	36	0	18	80	2	95	50.1	-8.2	81	2	2,000,000	0	0.0	0.0
B- /7.9	3.4	0.27	11.10	159	0	18	80	2	95	47.1	-8.4	79	2	1,000	50	5.3	0.0
B /8.0	3.4	0.27	10.98	138	0	18	80	2	95	41.3	-8.7	73	2	1,000	50	0.0	0.0
B- /7.9	3.4	0.26	11.05	16	0	18	80	2	95	45.0	-8.4	77	2	100	0	0.0	0.0
C+ /6.9	5.2	0.46	11.31	43	12	33	53	2	103	65.1	-12.3	70	2	2,000,000	0	0.0	0.0
C+ /6.9	5.2	0.47	11.22	195	12	33	53	2	103	62.0	-12.5	66	2	1,000	50	5.3	0.0
B- /7.0	5.2	0.47	11.08	152	12	33	53	2	103	55.4	-12.7	56	2	1,000	50	0.0	0.0
B- /7.0	5.2	0.47	11.18	23	12	33	53	2	103	60.8	-12.5	64	2	100	0	0.0	0.0
C+ /6.6	7.0	0.65	12.40	66	16	49	33	2	94	78.8	-16.1	49	2	2,000,000	0	0.0	0.0
C+ /6.6	7.0	0.66	12.22	275	16	49	33	2	94	75.3	-16.4	44	2	1,000	50	5.3	0.0
C+ /6.7	7.0	0.66	11.97	130	16	49	33	2	94	68.6	-16.6	34	2	1,000	50	0.0	0.0
C+ /6.6	7.0	0.66	12.18	20	16	49	33	2	94	73.6	-16.4	41	2	100	0	0.0	0.0
C /4.5	9.0	0.85	11.62	46	5	77	16	2	81	93.8	-20.4	28	2	2,000,000	0	0.0	0.0
C /4.5	9.0	0.85	11.42	139	5	77	16	2	81	90.0	-20.4	24	2	1,000	50	5.3	0.0
C /4.5	8.9	0.85	11.09	47	5	77	16	2	81	82.5	-20.7	18	2	1,000	50	0.0	0.0
C /4.5	9.0	0.85	11.34	11	5	77	16	2	81	88.4	-20.5	23	2	100	0	0.0	0.0
C /4.6	14.8	0.91	12.94	46	0	0	0	100	171	N/A	N/A	87	4	2,000,000	0	0.0	0.0
C /4.5	14.8	0.91	12.91	5	0	0	0	100	171	N/A	N/A	86	4	1,000	50	5.3	0.0
C /4.5	14.8	0.91	12.71	1	0	0	0	100	171	N/A	N/A	82	4	1,000	50	0.0	0.0
D /2.2	15.9	0.98	19.74	496	0	98	0	2	103	123.7	-26.9	47	4	2,000,000	0	0.0	0.0
D- /1.5	15.9	0.98	15.69	203	0	98	0	2	103	119.9	-27.0	42	4	1,000	50	5.3	0.0
E+ /0.6	15.9	0.98	9.73	24	0	98	0	2	103	110.7	-27.2	32	4	1,000	50	0.0	0.0
D /1.7	15.9	0.98	17.08	10	0	98	0	2	103	120.2	-26.9	43	4	5,000	0	0.0	0.0
D- /1.0	21.8	1.10	11.01	25	0	99	0	1	66	-2.5	-33.6	27	4	2,000,000	0	0.0	0.0
D- /1.0	21.7	1.09	10.74	56	0	99	0	1	66	-4.7	-33.7	22	4	1,000	50	5.3	0.0
D- /1.1	21.7	1.09	10.49	N/A	0	99	0	1	66	-8.4	-33.9	16	4	1,000	50	0.0	0.0
D- /1.0	21.8	1.10	10.27	30	0	99	0	1	66	-8.3	-33.9	17	4	1,000	50	0.0	0.0
D- /1.0	21.7	1.10	10.80	1	0	99	0	1	66	-4.5	-33.7	23	4	5,000	0	0.0	0.0
U /	N/A	N/A	9.85	26	0	9	90	1	440	N/A	N/A	N/A	2	2,000,000	0	0.0	0.0
B- /7.0	7.1	1.10	24.77	375	0	56	43	1	39	84.9	-12.8	65	11	2,000,000	0	0.0	0.0
B- /7.0	7.1	1.10	24.70	525	0	56	43	1	39	82.1	-13.0	62	11	1,000	50	5.3	0.0
B- /7.0	7.1	1.09	23.89	N/A	0	56	43	1	39	71.2	-13.3	45	11	1,000	50	0.0	0.0
C+ /6.8	7.1	1.09	22.07	128	0	56	43	1	39	74.6	-13.2	52	11	1,000	50	0.0	0.0
C+ /6.8	7.1	1.10	23.11	15	0	56	43	1	39	78.5	-13.1	57	11	100	0	0.0	0.0
D+ /2.6	13.1	1.16	25.89	1,893	1	97	0	2	42	123.2	-21.1	21	8	2,000,000	0	0.0	0.0
D+ /2.6	13.1	1.16	25.60	1,532	1	97	0	2	42	119.8	-21.2	19	8	1,000	50	5.3	0.0
D+ /2.9	13.1	1.16	26.04	1	1	97	0	2	42	107.8	-21.5	11	8	0	0	0.0	0.0
D+ /2.3	13.1	1.16	22.67	335	1	97	0	2	42	110.6	-21.4	12	8	1,000	50	0.0	0.0
U /	N/A	N/A	25.90	61	1	97	0	2	42	N/A	N/A	N/A	8	1,000,000	0	0.0	0.0
D+ /2.5	13.1	1.16	24.19	18	1	97	0	2	42	116.0	-21.3	16	8	100	0	0.0	0.0
D+ /2.9	13.0	1.08	25.60	449	0	99	0	1	78	107.8	-20.4	24	4	2,000,000	0	0.0	0.0
D+ /2.7	13.0	1.08	23.95	1,460	0	99	0	1	78	104.8	-20.5	21	4	1,000	50	5.3	0.0
D /2.0	13.0	1.08	18.21	1	0	99	0	1	78	93.4	-20.8	13	4	1,000	50	0.0	0.0
D /2.0	13.0	1.09	18.49	470	0	99	0	1	78	95.9	-20.8	14	4	1,000	50	0.0	0.0
D+ /2.3	13.0	1.08	20.41	76	0	99	0	1	78	101.7	-20.6	19	4	100	0	0.0	0.0
D+ /2.9	13.0	1.08	25.72	463	0	99	0	1	78	109.0	-20.4	25	4	5,000,000	0	0.0	0.0
C- /3.5	15.2	0.95	7.58	128	2	49	47	2	132	N/A	N/A	0	6	2,000,000	0	0.0	0.0
C- /3.5	15.1	0.95	7.51	35	2	49	47	2	132	N/A	N/A	0	6	1,000	50	5.3	0.0

Data as of February 28, 2017

I. Index of Stock Mutual Funds

99 Pct = Best
0 Pct = Worst

Fund Type	Fund Name	Ticker Symbol	Overall Investment Rating	Phone	Performance Rating/Pts	3 Mo	6 Mo	1Yr / Pct	3Yr / Pct	5Yr / Pct	Dividend Yield	Expense Ratio
AA	BlackRock Cmdty Strat Inv C	BCSCX	E-	(800) 441-7762	E- / 0.2	3.56	6.29	22.80 /66	-8.76 / 1	-8.00 / 1	0.00	2.45
RE	BlackRock Developed RE Idx K	BKRDX	U	(800) 441-7762	U /	6.11	-3.32	12.52 /20	--	--	2.49	0.29
GL	BlackRock Dynamic Hi Inc Port Instl	BDHIX	U	(800) 441-7762	U /	6.33	5.86	19.34 /49	--	--	6.13	1.45
GL	BlackRock Dynamic Hi Inc Port Inv A	BDHAX	U	(800) 441-7762	U /	6.16	5.73	19.04 /47	--	--	5.58	1.70
EM	BlackRock Emerg Mkt Institutional	MADCX	E+	(800) 441-7762	D / 2.1	8.91	2.40	29.24 /85	-0.43 /12	-0.89 / 4	1.66	1.18
EM	BlackRock Emerg Mkt Inv A	MDDCX	E+	(800) 441-7762	D- / 1.3	8.87	2.24	28.68 /83	-0.88 /10	-1.30 / 3	1.25	1.63
EM	BlackRock Emerg Mkt Inv C	MCDCX	E+	(800) 441-7762	D- / 1.5	8.61	1.83	27.61 /81	-1.70 / 7	-2.13 / 3	0.69	2.45
FO	BlackRock Emerging Mkts Div Inst	BICHX	C	(800) 441-7762	C+ / 5.7	11.55	7.05	31.22 /89	1.66 /22	0.86 / 6	1.14	6.01
FO	BlackRock Emerging Mkts Div Inv A	BACHX	D+	(800) 441-7762	C / 4.4	11.38	6.94	30.83 /88	1.43 /21	0.64 / 6	0.86	7.31
FO	BlackRock Emerging Mkts Div Inv C	BCCHX	C-	(800) 441-7762	C / 4.9	11.20	6.60	29.89 /86	0.69 /17	-0.09 / 4	0.38	8.06
EM	BlackRock Emg Mkt LS Eqty Inst	BLSIX	C-	(800) 441-7762	E / 0.5	2.72	1.24	3.15 / 3	-1.20 / 9	-0.37 / 4	0.00	2.03
EM	BlackRock Emg Mkt LS Eqty Inv A	BLSAX	C-	(800) 441-7762	E / 0.3	2.64	1.14	2.86 / 3	-1.44 / 8	-0.61 / 4	0.00	2.28
EM	BlackRock Emg Mkt LS Eqty Inv C	BLSCX	C-	(800) 441-7762	E / 0.4	2.41	0.65	2.07 / 2	-2.21 / 6	-1.37 / 3	0.00	3.03
EN	BlackRock Energy & Resources Inst	SGLSX	E-	(800) 441-7762	E- / 0.0	-6.20	2.49	34.92 /94	-17.71 / 0	-11.61 / 0	0.00	1.11
EN	BlackRock Energy & Resources Inv A	SSGRX	E-	(800) 441-7762	E- / 0.0	-6.26	2.35	34.48 /93	-17.96 / 0	-11.87 / 0	0.00	1.39
EN	● BlackRock Energy & Resources Inv B	SSGPX	E-	(800) 441-7762	E- / 0.0	-6.39	1.99	33.57 /92	-18.55 / 0	-12.53 / 0	0.00	2.55
EN	BlackRock Energy & Resources Inv C	SSGDX	E-	(800) 441-7762	E- / 0.0	-6.44	1.93	33.43 /92	-18.56 / 0	-12.54 / 0	0.00	2.13
IN	BlackRock Eq Dividend Inst	MADVX	B+	(800) 441-7762	A / 9.3	6.15	11.70	27.20 /80	9.89 /93	11.72 /72	1.77	0.72
* IN	BlackRock Eq Dividend Inv A	MDDVX	B	(800) 441-7762	B+ / 8.3	6.09	11.56	26.94 /79	9.63 /91	11.44 /69	1.50	0.97
IN	● BlackRock Eq Dividend Inv B	MBDVX	B+	(800) 441-7762	B+ / 8.6	5.84	11.11	25.89 /76	8.76 /85	10.58 /63	0.71	1.75
IN	BlackRock Eq Dividend Inv C	MCDVX	B+	(800) 441-7762	B+ / 8.6	5.90	11.15	25.96 /76	8.83 /86	10.64 /63	0.95	1.70
IN	BlackRock Eq Dividend Inv C1	BEDCX	B+	(800) 441-7762	B+ / 8.8	5.96	11.28	26.26 /77	9.05 /87	10.84 /64	1.14	1.50
IN	BlackRock Eq Dividend K	MKDVX	U	(800) 441-7762	U /	6.17	11.76	--	--	--	0.00	0.59
IN	BlackRock Eq Dividend R	MRDVX	B+	(800) 441-7762	B+ / 8.9	6.01	11.40	26.52 /78	9.26 /89	11.09 /67	1.28	1.28
IN	BlackRock Eq Dividend Svc	MSDVX	B+	(800) 441-7762	A- / 9.1	6.09	11.61	26.97 /79	9.57 /91	11.39 /69	1.54	1.05
FO	BlackRock Eurofund Inst	MAEFX	E+	(800) 441-7762	E- / 0.2	7.51	0.80	4.61 / 4	-5.80 / 2	4.05 /15	2.25	1.07
FO	BlackRock Eurofund Inv A	MDEFX	E	(800) 441-7762	E- / 0.1	7.41	0.66	4.29 / 3	-6.00 / 2	3.82 /14	1.88	1.28
FO	BlackRock Eurofund Inv C	MCEFX	E	(800) 441-7762	E- / 0.1	7.32	0.29	3.52 / 3	-6.74 / 2	2.96 /11	1.88	2.09
FO	BlackRock Eurofund R	MREFX	E	(800) 441-7762	E- / 0.1	7.24	0.41	3.82 / 3	-6.45 / 2	3.29 /12	2.28	1.72
GR	BlackRock Event Driven Eqty Inst	BILPX	E-	(800) 441-7762	C- / 3.0	3.75	5.18	4.34 / 3	5.24 /57	9.82 /57	0.00	2.58
GR	BlackRock Event Driven Eqty Inv A	BALPX	E-	(800) 441-7762	D / 2.0	3.63	5.11	4.12 / 3	4.96 /54	9.52 /55	0.00	2.89
GR	BlackRock Event Driven Eqty Inv C	BCLPX	E-	(800) 441-7762	D+ / 2.3	3.38	4.60	3.24 / 3	4.19 /45	8.72 /48	0.00	3.65
GR	● BlackRock Exchange Port BlkRk	STSEX	A-	(800) 441-7762	B / 7.9	6.86	9.47	23.23 /67	8.11 /80	10.63 /63	1.87	0.66
MC	BlackRock Flexible Equity Inst	CMVIX	B	(800) 441-7762	B+ / 8.6	9.20	14.70	28.24 /82	6.75 /70	8.80 /49	0.79	1.12
MC	BlackRock Flexible Equity Inv A	BMCAX	C+	(800) 441-7762	B- / 7.4	9.16	14.61	27.80 /81	6.41 /68	8.46 /46	0.50	1.42
MC	● BlackRock Flexible Equity Inv B	BMCVX	C+	(800) 441-7762	B / 7.7	8.88	14.05	26.83 /79	5.60 /60	7.63 /39	0.00	2.53
MC	BlackRock Flexible Equity Inv C	BMCCX	C+	(800) 441-7762	B / 7.7	8.90	14.15	26.86 /79	5.58 /60	7.62 /39	0.00	2.16
MC	BlackRock Flexible Equity R	BMCRX	B-	(800) 441-7762	B / 8.0	9.08	14.37	27.34 /80	6.04 /64	8.07 /43	0.26	1.70
MC	BlackRock Flexible Equity Svc	CMVSX	B-	(800) 441-7762	B+ / 8.3	9.18	14.58	27.89 /81	6.41 /68	8.48 /46	0.51	1.34
GR	BlackRock Focus Growth Fd Inst	MAFOX	C+	(800) 441-7762	B / 8.1	9.57	7.90	21.58 /60	8.64 /84	13.07 /84	0.00	1.26
GR	BlackRock Focus Growth Fd Inv A	MDFOX	C	(800) 441-7762	B- / 7.0	9.60	7.82	21.25 /58	8.32 /81	12.63 /80	0.00	1.60
GR	BlackRock Focus Growth Fd Inv C	MCFOX	C	(800) 441-7762	B- / 7.2	9.06	7.36	19.91 /51	7.41 /75	11.84 /73	0.00	2.36
FS	BlackRock Glbl Long/Short Crd K	BDMKX	U	(800) 441-7762	U /	1.89	2.71	--	--	--	0.00	2.00
GI	BlackRock Glbl Long/Short Eqty Inst	BDMIX	D+	(800) 441-7762	E / 0.5	2.32	5.16	0.73 / 2	-1.40 / 8	--	0.00	1.83
GI	BlackRock Glbl Long/Short Eqty InvA	BDMAX	D+	(800) 441-7762	E / 0.3	2.15	4.90	0.37 / 1	-1.68 / 7	--	0.00	2.09
GI	BlackRock Glbl Long/Short Eqty InvC	BDMCX	D+	(800) 441-7762	E / 0.3	2.11	4.62	-0.28 / 1	-2.37 / 6	--	0.00	2.86
GL	BlackRock Global Allocation Inst	MALOX	D+	(800) 441-7762	D+ / 2.8	4.64	4.07	12.88 /21	2.68 /29	5.06 /22	1.22	0.87
* GL	BlackRock Global Allocation Inv A	MDLOX	D	(800) 441-7762	D / 1.9	4.58	3.90	12.57 /20	2.40 /27	4.78 /20	0.89	1.14
GL	● BlackRock Global Allocation Inv B	MBLOX	D	(800) 441-7762	D / 2.1	4.37	3.55	11.60 /16	1.57 /21	3.93 /15	0.00	1.92
GL	BlackRock Global Allocation Inv C	MCLOX	D	(800) 441-7762	D / 2.2	4.46	3.59	11.81 /17	1.65 /22	4.00 /15	0.25	1.88
GL	BlackRock Global Allocation K	MKLOX	U	(800) 441-7762	U /	4.68	4.12	--	--	--	0.00	N/A
GL	BlackRock Global Allocation R	MRLOX	D+	(800) 441-7762	D+ / 2.4	4.50	3.79	12.26 /19	2.07 /24	4.42 /18	0.71	1.48

● Denotes fund is closed to new investors
* Denotes fund is included in Section II

RISK			NET ASSETS		ASSET					Portfolio Turnover Ratio	BULL / BEAR		FUND MANAGER		MINIMUMS		LOADS	
	3 Year		NAV As of 2/28/17	Total $(Mil)	Cash %	Stocks %	Bonds %	Other %			Last Bull Market Return	Last Bear Market Return	Manager Quality Pct	Manager Tenure (Years)	Initial Purch. $	Additional Purch. $	Front End Load	Back End Load
Risk Rating/Pts	Standard Deviation	Beta																
C- / 3.4	15.1	0.95	7.27	6	2	49	47	2		132	N/A	N/A	0	6	1,000	50	0.0	0.0
U /	N/A	N/A	10.26	990	12	86	0	2		0	N/A	N/A	N/A	2	5,000,000	0	0.0	0.0
U /	N/A	N/A	9.58	200	25	9	64	2		112	N/A	N/A	N/A	3	2,000,000	0	0.0	0.0
U /	N/A	N/A	9.58	38	25	9	64	2		112	N/A	N/A	N/A	3	1,000	50	5.3	0.0
C- / 4.0	15.9	0.94	18.36	54	0	98	0	2		92	19.4	-24.8	48	8	2,000,000	0	0.0	0.0
C- / 4.0	15.9	0.94	17.71	189	0	98	0	2		92	16.9	-24.8	41	8	1,000	50	5.3	0.0
C- / 4.0	15.9	0.94	15.06	87	0	98	0	2		92	11.7	-25.1	30	8	1,000	50	0.0	0.0
C / 4.8	13.7	0.77	8.36	3	2	96	1	1		117	35.7	-31.0	85	4	2,000,000	0	0.0	0.0
C / 4.8	13.6	0.76	8.33	3	2	96	1	1		117	34.1	-31.1	84	4	1,000	50	5.3	0.0
C / 4.8	13.7	0.77	8.24	1	2	96	1	1		117	28.9	-31.3	80	4	1,000	50	0.0	0.0
B+ / 9.3	4.8	0.09	9.83	143	83	16	0	1		0	N/A	N/A	56	6	2,000,000	0	0.0	0.0
B+ / 9.3	4.7	0.08	9.72	6	83	16	0	1		0	N/A	N/A	53	6	1,000	50	5.3	0.0
B+ / 9.2	4.7	0.08	9.36	5	83	16	0	1		0	N/A	N/A	41	6	1,000	50	0.0	0.0
E / 0.3	29.5	1.43	21.79	75	0	98	0	2		44	-28.5	-37.2	1	4	2,000,000	0	0.0	0.0
E / 0.3	29.5	1.43	18.72	154	0	98	0	2		44	-29.7	-37.3	1	4	1,000	50	5.3	0.0
E- / 0.2	29.5	1.43	13.33	N/A	0	98	0	2		44	-32.4	-37.5	1	4	1,000	50	0.0	0.0
E- / 0.2	29.5	1.43	13.21	34	0	98	0	2		44	-32.4	-37.5	1	4	1,000	50	0.0	0.0
C / 5.2	10.2	0.94	23.39	11,752	3	96	0	1		25	106.1	-13.7	73	16	2,000,000	0	0.0	0.0
C / 5.2	10.2	0.94	23.33	5,997	3	96	0	1		25	103.3	-13.8	70	16	1,000	50	5.3	0.0
C / 5.3	10.2	0.94	23.64	4	3	96	0	1		25	95.0	-14.1	61	16	1,000	50	0.0	0.0
C / 5.1	10.2	0.94	22.59	2,964	3	96	0	1		25	95.6	-14.1	61	16	1,000	50	0.0	0.0
C / 5.1	10.2	0.94	22.56	7	3	96	0	1		25	97.5	N/A	64	16	0	0	0.0	0.0
U /	N/A	N/A	23.39	113	3	96	0	1		25	N/A	N/A	N/A	16	1,000,000	0	0.0	0.0
C / 5.2	10.2	0.94	23.47	862	3	96	0	1		25	100.0	-14.0	66	16	100	0	0.0	0.0
C / 5.2	10.2	0.94	23.32	67	3	96	0	1		25	103.0	-13.8	70	16	5,000	0	0.0	0.0
C / 5.1	11.9	0.92	13.27	134	0	99	0	1		100	45.1	-28.9	10	7	2,000,000	0	0.0	0.0
C / 5.1	11.9	0.91	13.02	153	0	99	0	1		100	43.4	-29.0	9	7	1,000	50	5.3	0.0
C / 4.9	11.9	0.91	9.16	11	0	99	0	1		100	37.1	-29.2	6	7	1,000	50	0.0	0.0
C / 5.0	11.9	0.92	9.86	1	0	99	0	1		100	39.5	-29.1	7	7	100	0	0.0	0.0
E+ / 0.6	7.1	0.42	9.06	80	0	54	45	1		233	100.9	-22.1	80	2	2,000,000	0	0.0	0.0
E / 0.5	7.1	0.42	8.74	33	0	54	45	1		233	97.9	-22.2	78	2	1,000	50	5.3	0.0
E / 0.4	7.1	0.42	7.96	6	0	54	45	1		233	90.2	-22.4	71	2	1,000	50	0.0	0.0
C+ / 6.8	9.8	0.89	965.87	179	0	99	0	1		0	97.8	-15.1	59	4	1,000	50	0.0	0.0
C / 4.5	11.3	0.83	14.00	43	0	98	0	2		36	90.2	-24.3	61	2	2,000,000	0	0.0	0.0
C / 4.4	11.3	0.82	13.47	342	0	98	0	2		36	87.0	-24.4	57	2	1,000	50	5.3	0.0
C- / 4.1	11.3	0.83	11.77	1	0	98	0	2		36	79.4	-24.7	46	2	1,000	50	0.0	0.0
C- / 4.0	11.3	0.83	11.62	64	0	98	0	2		36	79.3	-24.7	45	2	1,000	50	0.0	0.0
C / 4.5	11.3	0.83	13.88	2	0	98	0	2		36	83.4	-24.5	52	2	100	0	0.0	0.0
C / 4.5	11.3	0.83	13.80	N/A	0	98	0	2		36	87.2	-24.4	57	2	5,000	0	0.0	0.0
C / 4.3	12.8	1.02	3.55	26	0	97	2	1		112	116.5	-21.2	48	4	2,000,000	0	0.0	0.0
C- / 4.1	12.6	1.01	3.31	53	0	97	2	1		112	112.9	-21.4	46	4	1,000	50	5.3	0.0
C- / 3.8	12.7	1.02	2.77	28	0	97	2	1		112	103.5	-21.4	33	4	1,000	50	0.0	0.0
U /	N/A	N/A	10.25	31	6	4	84	6		253	N/A	N/A	N/A	6	5,000,000	0	0.0	0.0
B / 8.7	4.9	0.13	11.01	511	23	11	64	2		34	N/A	N/A	36	N/A	2,000,000	0	0.0	0.0
B / 8.6	4.9	0.11	10.92	65	23	11	64	2		34	N/A	N/A	35	N/A	1,000	50	5.3	0.0
B / 8.5	5.0	0.12	10.64	38	23	11	64	2		34	N/A	N/A	26	N/A	1,000	50	0.0	0.0
C+ / 6.2	6.5	0.98	18.94	15,915	4	56	38	2		131	44.5	-13.6	51	28	2,000,000	0	0.0	0.0
C+ / 6.2	6.5	0.98	18.83	12,892	4	56	38	2		131	42.4	-13.7	47	28	1,000	50	5.3	0.0
C+ / 6.2	6.5	0.98	18.36	35	4	56	38	2		131	36.3	-14.0	36	28	1,000	50	0.0	0.0
C+ / 6.0	6.5	0.98	17.13	10,075	4	56	38	2		131	36.8	-14.0	36	28	1,000	50	0.0	0.0
U /	N/A	N/A	18.94	645	4	56	38	2		131	N/A	N/A	N/A	28	5,000,000	0	0.0	0.0
C+ / 6.1	6.5	0.98	18.00	1,108	4	56	38	2		131	39.8	-13.8	42	28	100	0	0.0	0.0

I. Index of Stock Mutual Funds

	99 Pct = Best 0 Pct = Worst				PERFORMANCE						Incl. in Returns	
		Ticker	Overall Investment		Perfor- mance	3 Mo	6 Mo	Total Return % through 2/28/17	Annualized		Dividend	Expense
Fund Type	Fund Name	Symbol	Rating	Phone	Rating/Pts			1Yr / Pct	3Yr / Pct	5Yr / Pct	Yield	Ratio
AA	BlackRock Global Dividend Inst	BIBDX	C+	(800) 441-7762	C / 4.7	7.68	2.86	14.09 /26	5.41 /59	8.51 /46	2.18	0.75
AA	BlackRock Global Dividend Inv A	BABDX	C-	(800) 441-7762	C- / 3.4	7.55	2.64	13.74 /24	5.10 /55	8.21 /44	1.83	1.03
AA	BlackRock Global Dividend Inv C	BCBDX	C	(800) 441-7762	C- / 3.8	7.39	2.25	12.89 /21	4.29 /46	7.39 /37	1.22	1.78
GL	BlackRock Global Dividend K	BKBDX	U	(800) 441-7762	U /	7.61	2.89	--	--	--	0.00	0.69
GL	BlackRock Global Opps Port Inst	BROIX	D+	(800) 441-7762	D+ / 2.9	6.41	4.57	19.35 /49	0.95 /18	7.30 /37	1.99	1.21
GL	BlackRock Global Opps Port Inv A	BROAX	D	(800) 441-7762	D / 2.0	6.33	4.47	19.03 /47	0.68 /17	7.01 /35	1.65	1.48
GL	BlackRock Global Opps Port Inv C	BROCX	D-	(800) 441-7762	D- / 1.5	6.23	4.07	18.13 /43	-0.11 /13	6.16 /29	0.99	2.27
GL	● BlackRock Global Opps Port Inv R	BGORX	D	(800) 441-7762	D+ / 2.5	6.32	4.30	18.62 /46	0.30 /15	6.62 /32	1.36	1.81
GL	BlackRock Global Small Cap Inst	MAGCX	D-	(800) 441-7762	C- / 3.6	5.57	6.02	25.55 /75	0.88 /18	8.58 /47	1.14	1.07
GL	BlackRock Global Small Cap Inv A	MDGCX	E+	(800) 441-7762	D+ / 2.5	5.48	5.85	25.12 /74	0.53 /16	8.22 /44	0.60	1.42
GL	● BlackRock Global Small Cap Inv B	MBGCX	E	(800) 441-7762	D / 1.8	5.21	5.42	24.07 /70	-0.34 /12	7.24 /36	0.00	2.38
GL	BlackRock Global Small Cap Inv C	MCGCX	E	(800) 441-7762	D / 1.8	5.21	5.43	24.10 /70	-0.27 /12	7.35 /37	0.00	2.22
GL	BlackRock Global SmallCap R	MRGSX	E+	(800) 441-7762	C- / 3.1	5.35	5.66	24.62 /72	0.18 /14	7.82 /41	0.20	1.77
HL	BlackRock Health Sci Opps Inst	SHSSX	B-	(800) 441-7762	B+ / 8.6	9.89	5.05	18.53 /45	10.71 /96	19.43 /99	0.00	0.88
HL	BlackRock Health Sci Opps Inv A	SHSAX	C+	(800) 441-7762	B- / 7.5	9.82	4.92	18.19 /44	10.40 /95	19.09 /99	0.00	1.16
HL	● BlackRock Health Sci Opps Inv B	SHSPX	C+	(800) 441-7762	B / 7.8	9.57	4.45	17.22 /39	9.52 /90	18.15 /99	0.00	1.95
HL	BlackRock Health Sci Opps Inv C	SHSCX	C+	(800) 441-7762	B / 7.8	9.60	4.52	17.33 /40	9.61 /91	18.23 /99	0.00	1.88
HL	● BlackRock Health Sci Opps R	BHSRX	C+	(800) 441-7762	B / 8.1	9.72	4.73	17.80 /42	10.06 /94	18.70 /99	0.00	1.46
HL	BlackRock Health Sci Opps Svc	SHISX	B-	(800) 441-7762	B+ / 8.4	9.83	4.92	18.22 /44	10.40 /95	19.09 /99	0.00	1.16
GI	BlackRock Impact US Equity Instl	BIRIX	U	(800) 441-7762	U /	7.78	10.85	27.20 /80	--	--	1.41	1.68
FO	BlackRock International Inst	MAILX	D-	(800) 441-7762	D- / 1.4	7.75	4.82	16.77 /37	-0.69 /11	4.02 /15	1.54	1.26
FO	BlackRock International Inv A	MDILX	E+	(800) 441-7762	E+ / 0.8	7.64	4.65	16.32 /36	-1.08 / 9	3.62 /13	1.18	1.60
FO	BlackRock International Inv C	MCILX	E+	(800) 441-7762	E+ / 0.9	7.35	4.04	15.05 /30	-2.07 / 6	2.58 / 9	0.15	2.46
FO	BlackRock International R	BIFRX	D-	(800) 441-7762	D- / 1.1	7.58	4.42	15.90 /34	-1.41 / 8	3.29 /12	0.90	1.86
FO	BlackRock Intl Index Inst	MAIIX	D-	(800) 441-7762	D- / 1.2	7.32	4.26	15.71 /33	-1.00 / 9	4.92 /21	2.69	0.10
FO	BlackRock Intl Index Inv A	MDIIX	D-	(800) 441-7762	D- / 1.1	7.22	4.15	15.45 /32	-1.25 / 9	4.66 /19	2.49	0.40
FO	BlackRock Intl Index K	BTMKX	D-	(800) 441-7762	D- / 1.2	7.35	4.30	15.74 /33	-0.97 / 9	4.96 /21	2.73	0.10
FO	BlackRock Intl Opps Inst	BISIX	E	(800) 441-7762	E / 0.3	3.47	-0.37	12.46 /20	-3.86 / 3	3.37 /12	4.67	1.27
FO	BlackRock Intl Opps Inv A	BREAX	E	(800) 441-7762	E- / 0.2	3.39	-0.55	12.11 /18	-4.16 / 3	3.05 /11	4.29	1.58
FO	● BlackRock Intl Opps Inv B	BREBX	E	(800) 441-7762	E- / 0.2	3.17	-0.98	11.13 /15	-4.96 / 2	2.18 / 8	1.49	2.48
FO	BlackRock Intl Opps Inv C	BRECX	E	(800) 441-7762	E- / 0.2	3.16	-0.92	11.26 /15	-4.87 / 3	2.28 / 9	3.85	2.32
FO	BlackRock Intl Opps Svc	BRESX	E	(800) 441-7762	E / 0.3	3.39	-0.50	12.12 /18	-4.15 / 3	3.00 /11	4.30	1.53
GR	BlackRock Large Cap Core Inst	MALRX	A+	(800) 441-7762	A / 9.5	9.17	14.60	28.02 /82	9.26 /89	12.77 /82	0.92	0.87
GR	BlackRock Large Cap Core Inv A	MDLRX	A	(800) 441-7762	B+ / 8.7	9.06	14.44	27.69 /81	8.96 /87	12.43 /78	0.61	1.23
GR	● BlackRock Large Cap Core Inv B	MBLRX	A+	(800) 441-7762	B+ / 8.9	8.88	13.98	26.68 /78	8.06 /79	11.49 /70	0.00	2.48
GR	BlackRock Large Cap Core Inv C	MCLRX	A+	(800) 441-7762	B+ / 8.9	8.83	14.00	26.65 /78	8.07 /79	11.48 /70	0.00	1.96
GR	BlackRock Large Cap Core R	MRLRX	A+	(800) 441-7762	A- / 9.2	8.95	14.26	27.28 /80	8.64 /84	12.08 /75	0.34	1.44
GR	BlackRock Large Cap Core Service	MSLRX	A+	(800) 441-7762	A / 9.3	9.08	14.19	27.31 /80	8.79 /85	12.29 /77	0.00	1.21
GR	BlackRock Large Cap Growth Inst	MALHX	A	(800) 441-7762	A+ / 9.6	10.27	12.73	24.52 /72	10.48 /96	13.06 /84	0.58	0.93
GR	BlackRock Large Cap Growth Inv A	MDLHX	A-	(800) 441-7762	B+ / 8.8	10.18	12.60	24.13 /70	10.14 /94	12.75 /81	0.25	1.23
GR	● BlackRock Large Cap Growth Inv B	MBLHX	A-	(800) 441-7762	A- / 9.0	9.93	12.14	23.10 /67	9.26 /89	11.81 /72	0.00	2.05
GR	BlackRock Large Cap Growth Inv C	MCLHX	B+	(800) 441-7762	A- / 9.0	9.96	12.11	23.19 /67	9.26 /89	11.86 /73	0.00	1.99
GR	BlackRock Large Cap Growth R	MRLHX	A	(800) 441-7762	A / 9.3	10.07	12.38	23.83 /69	9.85 /92	12.45 /79	0.04	1.46
GR	BlackRock Large Cap Growth Svc	MSLHX	A	(800) 441-7762	A / 9.5	10.22	12.62	24.18 /70	10.16 /94	12.74 /81	0.26	1.19
GR	BlackRock Large Cap Index Inst	BRGNX	A+	(800) 441-7762	A- / 9.2	7.92	10.00	25.39 /74	10.07 /94	13.82 /92	1.80	0.26
GR	BlackRock Large Cap Index Inv A	BRGAX	A+	(800) 441-7762	A- / 9.0	7.83	9.85	25.04 /73	9.77 /92	13.46 /88	1.57	0.53
GR	BlackRock Large Cap Index K	BRGKX	A+	(800) 441-7762	A- / 9.2	7.89	9.99	25.44 /75	10.09 /94	13.80 /92	1.82	0.18
GR	BlackRock Large Cap Value Inst	MALVX	A+	(800) 441-7762	A+ / 9.7	8.38	15.65	30.99 /88	9.63 /91	12.60 /80	1.31	0.91
GR	BlackRock Large Cap Value Inv A	MDLVX	A+	(800) 441-7762	A- / 9.1	8.27	15.50	30.54 /87	9.30 /89	12.28 /77	0.95	1.22
GR	● BlackRock Large Cap Value Inv B	MBLVX	A+	(800) 441-7762	A- / 9.2	7.99	14.91	29.39 /85	8.37 /82	11.27 /68	0.00	2.06
GR	BlackRock Large Cap Value Inv C	MCLVX	A+	(800) 441-7762	A / 9.3	8.07	15.04	29.60 /85	8.46 /83	11.37 /69	0.18	1.98
GR	BlackRock Large Cap Value R	MRLVX	A+	(800) 441-7762	A / 9.5	8.18	15.29	30.18 /87	9.00 /87	11.94 /74	0.74	1.48

● Denotes fund is closed to new investors
* Denotes fund is included in Section II

www.thestreetratings.com

RISK			NET ASSETS		ASSET						BULL / BEAR		FUND MANAGER		MINIMUMS		LOADS	
	3 Year		NAV							Portfolio	Last Bull	Last Bear	Manager	Manager	Initial	Additional	Front	Back
Risk	Standard		As of	Total	Cash	Stocks	Bonds	Other		Turnover	Market	Market	Quality	Tenure	Purch.	Purch.	End	End
Rating/Pts	Deviation	Beta	2/28/17	$(Mil)	%	%	%	%		Ratio	Return	Return	Pct	(Years)	$	$	Load	Load
C+ / 6.9	9.8	1.39	12.59	1,623	1	97	1	1		31	67.6	-9.7	17	7	2,000,000	0	0.0	0.0
C+ / 6.9	9.8	1.39	12.54	654	1	97	1	1		31	65.2	-9.8	15	7	1,000	50	5.3	0.0
C+ / 6.9	9.8	1.39	12.46	410	1	97	1	1		31	58.6	-10.1	10	7	1,000	50	0.0	0.0
U /	N/A	N/A	12.59	37	1	97	1	1		31	N/A	N/A	N/A	7	5,000,000	0	0.0	0.0
C+ / 5.7	11.1	0.81	14.77	56	0	98	0	2		67	68.5	-23.8	81	11	2,000,000	0	0.0	0.0
C+ / 5.7	11.1	0.81	14.64	148	0	98	0	2		67	66.2	-23.9	80	11	1,000	50	5.3	0.0
C+ / 5.7	11.1	0.81	14.15	41	0	98	0	2		67	59.1	-24.1	N/A	11	1,000	50	0.0	0.0
C+ / 5.7	11.1	0.81	14.61	8	0	98	0	2		67	62.8	N/A	77	11	100	0	0.0	0.0
C- / 3.1	13.4	0.91	24.46	245	0	99	0	1		73	81.4	-23.7	81	12	2,000,000	0	0.0	0.0
C- / 3.0	13.4	0.91	23.57	360	0	99	0	1		73	78.1	-23.8	79	12	1,000	50	5.3	0.0
D+ / 2.8	13.4	0.91	21.60	1	0	99	0	1		73	69.5	-24.1	72	12	1,000	50	0.0	0.0
D+ / 2.7	13.5	0.91	20.39	217	0	99	0	1		73	70.5	-24.1	73	12	1,000	50	0.0	0.0
D+ / 2.9	13.4	0.91	21.90	21	0	99	0	1		73	74.5	-23.9	76	12	100	0	0.0	0.0
C / 4.3	15.2	1.03	51.30	1,620	1	97	1	1		50	175.3	-12.5	71	14	2,000,000	0	0.0	0.0
C / 4.3	15.2	1.03	49.07	2,541	1	97	1	1		50	171.1	-12.6	68	14	1,000	50	5.3	0.0
C / 4.3	15.2	1.03	44.84	3	1	97	1	1		50	159.6	-12.9	58	14	1,000	50	0.0	0.0
C- / 4.2	15.2	1.03	43.72	1,031	1	97	1	1		50	160.6	-12.9	59	14	1,000	50	0.0	0.0
C / 4.3	15.2	1.03	48.27	174	1	97	1	1		50	166.2	N/A	64	14	100	0	0.0	0.0
C / 4.3	15.2	1.03	49.25	30	1	97	1	1		50	171.1	-12.6	68	14	5,000	0	0.0	0.0
U /	N/A	N/A	11.81	27	0	99	0	1		56	N/A	N/A	N/A	2	2,000,000	0	0.0	0.0
C / 5.2	12.4	0.95	14.41	119	0	98	1	1		84	40.2	-24.3	68	10	2,000,000	0	0.0	0.0
C / 5.2	12.4	0.95	14.10	305	0	98	1	1		84	37.4	-24.4	63	10	1,000	50	5.3	0.0
C / 5.2	12.5	0.95	13.13	102	0	98	1	1		84	30.0	-24.7	49	10	1,000	50	0.0	0.0
C / 5.2	12.5	0.96	14.10	21	0	98	1	1		84	34.9	N/A	59	10	100	0	0.0	0.0
C+ / 5.9	11.5	0.93	12.12	744	2	97	0	1		9	47.0	-23.4	64	6	2,000,000	0	0.0	0.0
C+ / 5.9	11.4	0.92	12.05	260	2	97	0	1		9	44.9	-23.5	61	6	1,000	50	0.0	0.0
C+ / 5.9	11.4	0.93	12.13	4,644	2	97	0	1		9	47.2	-23.4	64	6	1	1	0.0	0.0
C- / 3.9	11.2	0.85	31.53	268	0	99	0	1		47	39.1	-25.1	25	18	2,000,000	0	0.0	0.0
C- / 3.8	11.2	0.85	29.75	351	0	99	0	1		47	36.7	-25.2	22	18	1,000	50	5.3	0.0
C- / 3.7	11.2	0.85	27.68	N/A	0	99	0	1		47	30.6	-25.4	15	18	1,000	50	0.0	0.0
C- / 3.7	11.2	0.85	26.75	64	0	99	0	1		47	31.3	-25.5	16	18	1,000	50	0.0	0.0
C- / 3.9	11.2	0.85	30.17	10	0	99	0	1		47	36.3	-25.2	22	18	5,000	0	0.0	0.0
C+ / 6.8	11.7	1.09	19.82	480	1	97	1	1		39	130.2	-22.5	46	7	2,000,000	0	0.0	0.0
C+ / 6.8	11.7	1.09	19.32	810	1	97	1	1		39	126.6	-22.5	42	7	1,000	50	5.3	0.0
C+ / 6.8	11.7	1.09	17.60	1	1	97	1	1		39	116.6	-22.8	31	7	1,000	50	0.0	0.0
C+ / 6.8	11.7	1.09	17.33	331	1	97	1	1		39	116.4	-22.8	31	7	1,000	50	0.0	0.0
C+ / 6.8	11.7	1.09	18.42	38	1	97	1	1		39	122.6	-22.6	38	7	100	0	0.0	0.0
C+ / 6.9	11.7	1.09	19.78	N/A	1	97	1	1		39	125.2	-22.6	40	7	5,000	0	0.0	0.0
C+ / 5.9	11.5	1.08	15.16	416	2	95	1	2		32	134.8	-20.5	63	18	2,000,000	0	0.0	0.0
C+ / 5.8	11.5	1.07	14.42	572	2	95	1	2		32	131.0	-20.6	60	18	1,000	50	5.3	0.0
C+ / 5.6	11.5	1.08	12.43	N/A	2	95	1	2		32	120.9	-20.9	48	18	1,000	50	0.0	0.0
C / 5.5	11.5	1.08	12.28	176	2	95	1	2		32	121.4	-20.9	48	18	1,000	50	0.0	0.0
C+ / 5.7	11.5	1.07	13.53	24	2	95	1	2		32	127.6	-20.6	56	18	100	0	0.0	0.0
C+ / 5.9	11.5	1.07	15.11	2	2	95	1	2		32	130.9	-20.5	60	18	5,000	0	0.0	0.0
C+ / 6.6	10.4	1.01	15.96	24	1	98	0	1		6	133.8	-17.2	67	5	2,000,000	0	0.0	0.0
C+ / 6.6	10.5	1.01	15.87	28	1	98	0	1		6	129.9	-17.3	63	5	1,000	50	0.0	0.0
C+ / 6.6	10.5	1.01	15.90	127	1	98	0	1		6	133.6	-17.2	67	5	1	1	0.0	0.0
C+ / 6.9	11.7	1.07	26.88	159	1	97	1	1		40	125.6	-24.3	54	18	2,000,000	0	0.0	0.0
C+ / 6.9	11.7	1.07	26.38	314	1	97	1	1		40	121.8	-24.3	50	18	1,000	50	5.3	0.0
C+ / 6.9	11.7	1.07	24.74	1	1	97	1	1		40	111.5	-24.6	37	18	1,000	50	0.0	0.0
C+ / 6.9	11.7	1.07	24.54	168	1	97	1	1		40	112.5	-24.5	38	18	1,000	50	0.0	0.0
C+ / 6.9	11.7	1.07	25.41	36	1	97	1	1		40	118.4	-24.4	46	18	100	0	0.0	0.0

Fund Type	Fund Name	Ticker Symbol	Overall Investment Rating	Phone	Performance Rating/Pts	3 Mo	6 Mo	1Yr / Pct	3Yr / Pct	5Yr / Pct	Dividend Yield	Expense Ratio
	99 Pct = Best							Total Return % through 2/28/17	Annualized		Incl. in Returns	
GR	BlackRock Large Cap Value Ret Inst	MKLVX	A-	(800) 441-7762	A+ / 9.7	8.42	15.76	31.29 /89	9.83 /92	12.84 /82	1.27	0.71
GR	BlackRock Large Cap Value Svc	MSLVX	A+	(800) 441-7762	A+ / 9.6	8.25	15.48	30.56 /87	9.30 /89	12.24 /76	0.99	1.20
FO	BlackRock Latin America Inst	MALTX	E	(800) 441-7762	D+ / 2.8	12.22	8.08	42.84 /98	-1.72 / 7	-6.74 / 1	1.28	1.32
FO	BlackRock Latin America Inv A	MDLTX	E	(800) 441-7762	D / 1.9	12.14	7.92	42.40 /98	-2.01 / 7	-6.99 / 1	0.95	1.61
FO	● BlackRock Latin America Inv B	MBLTX	E	(800) 441-7762	D / 1.9	11.67	7.08	40.38 /97	-3.20 / 4	-8.01 / 1	0.00	2.69
FO	BlackRock Latin America Inv C	MCLTX	E	(800) 441-7762	D / 2.1	11.91	7.50	41.21 /98	-2.84 / 5	-7.77 / 1	0.32	2.48
AA	BlackRock LifePath Dyn 2020 Inst	STLCX	C-	(800) 441-7762	D+ / 2.9	3.85	2.65	12.05 /18	3.48 /37	5.23 /23	1.51	0.98
AA	BlackRock LifePath Dyn 2020 Inv A	LPRCX	D+	(800) 441-7762	D / 2.0	3.81	2.54	11.76 /17	3.25 /34	4.98 /21	1.36	1.23
AA	BlackRock LifePath Dyn 2020 Inv C	LPCMX	C-	(800) 441-7762	D / 2.2	3.62	2.17	10.94 /14	2.45 /27	4.19 /16	0.62	2.03
AA	BlackRock LifePath Dyn 2020 K	LPSCX	C-	(800) 441-7762	C- / 3.1	3.93	2.79	12.28 /19	3.80 /40	5.57 /25	1.74	0.78
AA	BlackRock LifePath Dyn 2020 R	LPRMX	C-	(800) 441-7762	D+ / 2.6	3.74	2.42	11.49 /16	2.98 /32	4.72 /19	1.10	1.43
GI	BlackRock LifePath Dyn 2025 Inst	LPBIX	C+	(800) 441-7762	C- / 3.5	4.69	3.68	14.30 /27	3.85 /41	5.90 /28	1.64	1.05
GI	BlackRock LifePath Dyn 2025 Inv A	LPBAX	C	(800) 441-7762	D+ / 2.4	4.54	3.48	13.97 /25	3.56 /38	5.62 /26	1.34	1.30
GI	BlackRock LifePath Dyn 2025 Inv C	LPBCX	C	(800) 441-7762	D+ / 2.7	4.34	3.07	13.01 /22	2.79 /30	4.82 /20	0.62	2.10
GI	BlackRock LifePath Dyn 2025 K	LPBKX	C+	(800) 441-7762	C- / 3.7	4.75	3.79	14.56 /28	4.14 /44	6.07 /29	1.84	0.85
GI	BlackRock LifePath Dyn 2025 R	LPBRX	C	(800) 441-7762	C- / 3.2	4.49	3.38	13.69 /24	3.35 /35	5.38 /24	1.25	1.50
AA	BlackRock LifePath Dyn 2030 Inst	STLDX	C	(800) 441-7762	C- / 4.2	5.43	4.57	16.38 /36	4.17 /45	6.47 /31	1.73	0.98
AA	BlackRock LifePath Dyn 2030 Inv A	LPRDX	C-	(800) 441-7762	C- / 3.0	5.26	4.39	16.01 /34	3.89 /42	6.18 /30	1.49	1.23
AA	BlackRock LifePath Dyn 2030 Inv C	LPCNX	C-	(800) 441-7762	C- / 3.3	5.10	4.02	15.07 /30	3.11 /33	5.38 /24	0.80	2.03
AA	BlackRock LifePath Dyn 2030 K	LPSDX	C	(800) 441-7762	C / 4.4	5.44	4.63	16.59 /37	4.47 /48	6.80 /33	1.95	0.78
AA	BlackRock LifePath Dyn 2030 R	LPRNX	C-	(800) 441-7762	C- / 3.7	5.27	4.26	15.75 /33	3.66 /39	5.94 /28	1.31	1.43
GL	BlackRock LifePath Dyn 2035 Inst	LPJIX	C+	(800) 441-7762	C / 4.8	6.06	5.34	18.35 /44	4.45 /48	6.96 /34	1.82	1.06
GL	BlackRock LifePath Dyn 2035 Inv A	LPJAX	C	(800) 441-7762	C- / 3.5	5.99	5.30	18.00 /43	4.20 /45	6.70 /33	1.51	1.31
GL	BlackRock LifePath Dyn 2035 Inv C	LPJCX	C	(800) 441-7762	C- / 3.9	5.76	4.86	17.07 /39	3.37 /35	5.87 /27	0.87	2.11
GL	BlackRock LifePath Dyn 2035 K	LPJKX	B-	(800) 441-7762	C / 5.0	6.11	5.55	18.60 /45	4.72 /51	7.39 /37	1.99	0.86
GL	BlackRock LifePath Dyn 2035 R	LPJRX	C+	(800) 441-7762	C / 4.3	5.94	5.13	17.79 /42	3.96 /42	6.44 /31	1.50	1.51
AA	BlackRock LifePath Dyn 2040 Inst	STLEX	C	(800) 441-7762	C / 5.3	6.62	6.11	20.10 /53	4.68 /51	7.42 /37	1.76	0.98
AA	BlackRock LifePath Dyn 2040 Inv A	LPREX	C-	(800) 441-7762	C- / 4.0	6.58	6.04	19.83 /51	4.43 /48	7.15 /36	1.62	1.23
AA	BlackRock LifePath Dyn 2040 Inv C	LPCKX	C-	(800) 441-7762	C / 4.4	6.40	5.56	18.78 /46	3.63 /38	6.34 /31	0.86	2.03
AA	BlackRock LifePath Dyn 2040 K	LPSFX	C+	(800) 441-7762	C+ / 5.6	6.72	6.27	20.35 /54	4.98 /54	7.77 /40	1.98	0.78
AA	BlackRock LifePath Dyn 2040 R	LPRKX	C	(800) 441-7762	C / 4.9	6.55	5.93	19.59 /50	4.18 /45	6.91 /34	1.43	1.43
GL	BlackRock LifePath Dyn 2045 Inst	LPHIX	B-	(800) 441-7762	C+ / 5.7	7.07	6.60	21.10 /58	4.85 /52	7.79 /41	1.91	1.11
GL	BlackRock LifePath Dyn 2045 Inv A	LPHAX	C+	(800) 441-7762	C / 4.3	6.92	6.41	20.75 /56	4.59 /50	7.52 /38	1.61	1.36
GL	BlackRock LifePath Dyn 2045 Inv C	LPHCX	C+	(800) 441-7762	C / 4.7	6.77	5.97	19.78 /51	3.76 /40	6.70 /33	0.96	2.16
GL	BlackRock LifePath Dyn 2045 K	LPHKX	B-	(800) 441-7762	C+ / 5.9	7.05	6.66	21.31 /59	5.07 /55	8.13 /43	2.10	0.91
GL	BlackRock LifePath Dyn 2045 R	LPHRX	C+	(800) 441-7762	C / 5.2	6.90	6.33	20.57 /55	4.34 /47	7.27 /36	1.61	1.56
AA	BlackRock LifePath Dyn 2050 Inst	STLFX	C+	(800) 441-7762	C+ / 5.8	7.17	6.71	21.42 /59	4.92 /53	8.10 /43	1.92	0.97
AA	BlackRock LifePath Dyn 2050 Inv A	LPRFX	C-	(800) 441-7762	C / 4.5	7.13	6.60	21.13 /58	4.67 /50	7.84 /41	1.62	1.22
AA	BlackRock LifePath Dyn 2050 Inv C	LPCPX	C	(800) 441-7762	C / 4.9	6.82	6.16	20.16 /53	3.86 /41	7.00 /35	1.01	2.02
AA	BlackRock LifePath Dyn 2050 K	LPSGX	C+	(800) 441-7762	C+ / 6.0	7.22	6.81	21.72 /61	5.23 /57	8.44 /46	2.15	0.77
AA	BlackRock LifePath Dyn 2050 R	LPRPX	C	(800) 441-7762	C / 5.4	7.03	6.45	20.94 /57	4.42 /48	7.59 /39	1.52	1.42
GL	BlackRock LifePath Dyn 2055 Inst	LPVIX	B-	(800) 441-7762	C+ / 5.8	7.15	6.76	21.49 /60	4.95 /53	8.33 /45	1.84	1.31
GL	BlackRock LifePath Dyn 2055 Inv A	LPVAX	C+	(800) 441-7762	C / 4.5	7.09	6.65	21.19 /58	4.70 /51	8.06 /43	1.55	1.56
GL	BlackRock LifePath Dyn 2055 Inv C	LPVCX	C+	(800) 441-7762	C / 4.9	6.89	6.24	20.22 /53	3.90 /42	7.25 /36	0.92	2.36
GL	BlackRock LifePath Dyn 2055 K	LPVKX	B-	(800) 441-7762	C+ / 6.0	7.18	6.88	21.65 /60	5.25 /57	8.72 /48	2.02	1.11
GL	BlackRock LifePath Dyn 2055 R	LPVRX	B-	(800) 441-7762	C / 5.4	7.05	6.50	20.93 /57	4.45 /48	7.80 /41	1.50	1.76
AA	BlackRock LifePath Dyn Ret Inst	STLAX	C	(800) 441-7762	D+ / 2.4	3.29	1.85	10.06 /12	3.24 /34	4.33 /17	1.44	0.98
AA	BlackRock LifePath Dyn Ret Inv A	LPRAX	C-	(800) 441-7762	D / 1.6	3.21	1.78	9.85 /11	2.96 /31	4.07 /16	1.37	1.23
AA	BlackRock LifePath Dyn Ret Inv C	LPCRX	C-	(800) 441-7762	D / 1.9	3.02	1.39	8.93 / 9	2.19 /25	3.27 /12	0.53	2.03
AA	BlackRock LifePath Dyn Ret K	LPSAX	C	(800) 441-7762	D+ / 2.6	3.27	1.89	10.26 /12	3.49 /37	4.64 /19	1.69	0.78
AA	BlackRock LifePath Dyn Ret R	LPRRX	C-	(800) 441-7762	D / 2.2	3.11	1.68	9.65 /11	2.73 /29	3.81 /14	1.11	1.43
AA	BlackRock LifePath Idx 2020 Inst	LIQIX	C+	(800) 441-7762	C- / 3.4	4.20	2.67	11.97 /18	4.40 /47	6.19 /30	1.93	0.25

● Denotes fund is closed to new investors

* Denotes fund is included in Section II

112

www.thestreetratings.com

RISK			NET ASSETS		ASSET				Portfolio	BULL / BEAR		FUND MANAGER		MINIMUMS		LOADS	
Risk Rating/Pts	3 Year		NAV As of 2/28/17	Total $(Mil)	Cash %	Stocks %	Bonds %	Other %	Turnover Ratio	Last Bull Market Return	Last Bear Market Return	Manager Quality Pct	Manager Tenure (Years)	Initial Purch. $	Additional Purch. $	Front End Load	Back End Load
	Standard Deviation	Beta															
C /5.3	11.7	1.07	21.15	194	1	97	1	1	40	128.3	-24.1	56	18	1	1	0.0	0.0
C+ /6.9	11.7	1.07	26.71	14	1	97	1	1	40	121.8	-24.3	50	18	5,000	0	0.0	0.0
D /2.0	25.2	1.09	44.44	56	3	96	0	1	58	-10.0	-29.0	55	15	2,000,000	0	0.0	0.0
D /2.0	25.2	1.09	43.89	100	3	96	0	1	58	-11.3	-29.0	51	15	1,000	50	5.3	0.0
D /2.0	25.2	1.09	40.85	N/A	3	96	0	1	58	-16.4	-29.3	34	15	1,000	50	0.0	0.0
D /2.0	25.2	1.09	40.03	22	3	96	0	1	58	-15.2	-29.3	39	15	1,000	50	0.0	0.0
B- /7.3	5.6	0.86	15.29	112	31	17	51	1	81	45.6	-9.8	36	N/A	2,000,000	0	0.0	0.0
B- /7.1	5.6	0.86	14.16	256	31	17	51	1	81	43.7	-10.0	34	N/A	1,000	50	5.3	0.0
B- /7.3	5.6	0.86	15.09	3	31	17	51	1	81	37.8	-10.2	25	7	1,000	50	0.0	0.0
B- /7.3	5.6	0.86	15.25	30	31	17	51	1	81	48.1	-9.7	41	N/A	5,000	0	0.0	0.0
B- /7.3	5.6	0.86	15.20	4	31	17	51	1	81	41.8	-10.0	31	7	100	0	0.0	0.0
B /8.1	6.6	0.60	13.09	17	31	24	43	2	51	52.3	-11.9	43	7	2,000,000	0	0.0	0.0
B /8.1	6.6	0.60	13.06	29	31	24	43	2	51	50.3	-12.1	40	7	1,000	50	5.3	0.0
B /8.1	6.6	0.60	12.99	2	31	24	43	2	51	44.2	-12.3	30	7	1,000	50	0.0	0.0
B /8.1	6.6	0.60	13.07	3	31	24	43	2	51	53.9	-11.8	47	7	5,000	0	0.0	0.0
B /8.1	6.6	0.60	13.05	3	31	24	43	2	51	48.3	-12.1	37	7	100	0	0.0	0.0
C+ /6.5	7.6	1.17	14.33	112	47	23	29	1	81	58.3	-13.6	20	10	2,000,000	0	0.0	0.0
C+ /6.4	7.6	1.17	13.84	274	47	23	29	1	81	56.1	-13.7	18	10	1,000	50	5.3	0.0
C+ /6.5	7.6	1.17	14.08	3	47	23	29	1	81	49.8	-13.9	12	10	1,000	50	0.0	0.0
C+ /6.5	7.6	1.17	14.31	31	47	23	29	1	81	61.1	-13.4	23	10	5,000	0	0.0	0.0
C+ /6.5	7.5	1.17	14.19	3	47	23	29	1	81	54.1	-13.8	16	10	100	0	0.0	0.0
B- /7.6	8.5	1.30	13.85	10	45	35	19	1	44	63.9	-15.1	55	7	2,000,000	0	0.0	0.0
B- /7.5	8.5	1.30	13.83	31	45	35	19	1	44	61.9	-15.2	51	7	1,000	50	5.3	0.0
B- /7.5	8.5	1.30	13.70	2	45	35	19	1	44	55.2	-15.5	40	7	1,000	50	0.0	0.0
B- /7.5	8.5	1.30	14.04	3	45	35	19	1	44	67.5	-15.0	58	7	5,000	0	0.0	0.0
B- /7.6	8.5	1.30	13.83	3	45	35	19	1	44	59.7	-15.3	48	7	100	0	0.0	0.0
C+ /5.9	9.3	1.43	17.96	91	57	31	10	2	80	69.1	-16.6	10	23	2,000,000	0	0.0	0.0
C+ /5.7	9.3	1.44	16.66	205	57	31	10	2	80	66.8	-16.6	9	23	1,000	50	5.3	0.0
C+ /5.9	9.3	1.43	17.70	3	57	31	10	2	80	60.1	-16.9	6	23	1,000	50	0.0	0.0
C+ /5.9	9.3	1.44	18.05	35	57	31	10	2	80	72.2	-16.4	12	23	5,000	0	0.0	0.0
C+ /5.9	9.3	1.44	17.83	3	57	31	10	2	80	64.8	-16.8	8	23	100	0	0.0	0.0
B- /7.2	9.7	1.48	14.57	8	54	41	3	2	50	73.8	-17.8	49	7	2,000,000	0	0.0	0.0
B- /7.2	9.7	1.49	14.55	18	54	41	3	2	50	71.5	-17.9	45	7	1,000	50	5.3	0.0
B- /7.2	9.8	1.49	14.37	1	54	41	3	2	50	64.5	-18.1	34	7	1,000	50	0.0	0.0
B- /7.2	9.8	1.50	14.71	2	54	41	3	2	50	77.0	-17.8	51	7	5,000	0	0.0	0.0
B- /7.2	9.7	1.48	14.53	2	54	41	3	2	50	69.4	-18.0	42	7	100	0	0.0	0.0
C+ /5.9	9.9	1.53	19.52	19	65	31	3	1	36	77.8	-19.0	8	9	2,000,000	0	0.0	0.0
C+ /5.9	9.9	1.52	19.47	74	65	31	3	1	36	75.4	-19.1	7	9	1,000	50	5.3	0.0
C+ /5.9	9.9	1.53	19.27	1	65	31	3	1	36	68.3	-19.4	5	9	1,000	50	0.0	0.0
C+ /5.9	9.9	1.53	19.58	14	65	31	3	1	36	80.9	-18.9	9	9	5,000	0	0.0	0.0
C+ /5.9	9.9	1.53	19.42	2	65	31	3	1	36	73.3	-19.2	6	9	100	0	0.0	0.0
B- /7.3	9.9	1.52	15.01	4	59	38	2	1	49	80.7	-19.6	48	7	2,000,000	0	0.0	0.0
B- /7.2	10.0	1.52	14.97	10	59	38	2	1	49	78.2	-19.7	45	7	1,000	50	5.3	0.0
B- /7.2	10.0	1.52	14.81	1	59	38	2	1	49	71.0	-20.0	34	7	1,000	50	0.0	0.0
B- /7.3	9.9	1.52	15.19	1	59	38	2	1	49	84.2	-19.4	52	7	5,000	0	0.0	0.0
B- /7.3	10.0	1.52	14.96	1	59	38	2	1	49	75.8	-19.7	41	7	100	0	0.0	0.0
B /8.0	4.6	0.68	11.05	49	20	16	62	2	83	35.4	-5.3	51	10	2,000,000	0	0.0	0.0
B- /7.8	4.6	0.69	9.87	81	20	16	62	2	83	33.5	-5.4	47	10	1,000	50	5.3	0.0
B /8.1	4.6	0.69	10.91	1	20	16	62	2	83	28.0	-5.6	36	10	1,000	50	0.0	0.0
B /8.0	4.6	0.68	11.01	14	20	16	62	2	83	37.6	-5.1	54	10	5,000	0	0.0	0.0
B /8.1	4.6	0.68	10.96	1	20	16	62	2	83	31.8	-5.5	44	10	100	0	0.0	0.0
B+ /9.0	5.6	0.86	11.97	90	2	50	47	1	14	52.5	N/A	49	6	2,000,000	0	0.0	0.0

						PERFORMANCE						
	99 Pct = Best 0 Pct = Worst			Overall		Perfor-	Total Return % through 2/28/17				Incl. in Returns	
				Investment		mance				Annualized	Dividend	Expense
Fund Type	Fund Name	Ticker Symbol	Rating	Phone	Rating/Pts	3 Mo	6 Mo	1Yr / Pct	3Yr / Pct	5Yr / Pct	Yield	Ratio
AA	BlackRock LifePath Idx 2020 Inv A	LIQAX	C+	(800) 441-7762	C- / 3.2	4.14	2.55	11.72 /17	4.15 /45	5.93 /28	1.70	0.50
AA	BlackRock LifePath Idx 2020 K	LIMKX	C+	(800) 441-7762	C- / 3.4	4.22	2.70	12.02 /18	4.45 /48	6.25 /30	1.98	0.19
AA	BlackRock LifePath Idx 2025 Inst	LIBIX	B-	(800) 441-7762	C- / 4.1	4.91	3.62	14.19 /26	4.85 /53	6.89 /34	1.92	0.24
IX	BlackRock LifePath Idx 2025 Inv A	LILAX	B-	(800) 441-7762	C- / 4.0	4.94	3.58	13.93 /25	4.64 /50	6.66 /33	1.69	0.49
IX	BlackRock LifePath Idx 2025 K	LIBKX	B-	(800) 441-7762	C- / 4.2	5.01	3.65	14.23 /27	4.93 /53	6.94 /34	1.96	0.18
AA	BlackRock LifePath Idx 2030 Inst	LINIX	B-	(800) 441-7762	C / 4.8	5.66	4.44	16.27 /35	5.25 /57	7.51 /38	1.98	0.24
AA	BlackRock LifePath Idx 2030 Inv A	LINAX	B-	(800) 441-7762	C / 4.6	5.60	4.32	16.01 /34	4.97 /54	7.25 /36	1.75	0.49
AA	BlackRock LifePath Idx 2030 K	LINKX	B-	(800) 441-7762	C / 4.8	5.60	4.39	16.25 /35	5.27 /57	7.52 /38	2.03	0.18
AA	BlackRock LifePath Idx 2035 Inst	LIJIX	B-	(800) 441-7762	C / 5.5	6.34	5.18	18.14 /43	5.58 /60	8.04 /42	1.98	0.25
AA	BlackRock LifePath Idx 2035 Inv A	LIJAX	B-	(800) 441-7762	C / 5.2	6.29	5.06	17.91 /42	5.32 /58	7.78 /40	1.76	0.50
AA	BlackRock LifePath Idx 2035 K	LIJKX	B-	(800) 441-7762	C / 5.5	6.36	5.21	18.21 /44	5.63 /61	8.09 /43	2.03	0.19
AA	BlackRock LifePath Idx 2040 Inst	LIKIX	B-	(800) 441-7762	C+ / 6.0	6.87	5.78	19.90 /51	5.85 /63	8.54 /47	2.04	0.26
AA	BlackRock LifePath Idx 2040 Inv A	LIKAX	B-	(800) 441-7762	C+ / 5.8	6.90	5.75	19.65 /50	5.62 /61	8.28 /44	1.83	0.51
AA	BlackRock LifePath Idx 2040 K	LIKKX	B-	(800) 441-7762	C+ / 6.1	6.89	5.89	19.95 /52	5.91 /63	8.58 /47	2.09	0.20
AA	BlackRock LifePath Idx 2045 Inst	LIHIX	C+	(800) 441-7762	C+ / 6.4	7.29	6.27	20.93 /57	6.10 /65	8.95 /50	2.03	0.28
AA	BlackRock LifePath Idx 2045 Inv A	LIHAX	C+	(800) 441-7762	C+ / 6.2	7.25	6.07	20.59 /55	5.83 /63	8.67 /48	1.82	0.53
AA	BlackRock LifePath Idx 2045 K	LIHKX	C+	(800) 441-7762	C+ / 6.4	7.30	6.29	20.96 /57	6.14 /65	9.01 /51	2.08	0.22
AA	BlackRock LifePath Idx 2050 Inst	LIPIX	C+	(800) 441-7762	C+ / 6.5	7.38	6.28	21.20 /58	6.20 /66	9.30 /53	2.05	0.28
AA	BlackRock LifePath Idx 2050 Inv A	LIPAX	C+	(800) 441-7762	C+ / 6.3	7.33	6.18	20.87 /57	5.93 /64	9.01 /51	1.85	0.52
AA	BlackRock LifePath Idx 2050 K	LIPKX	C+	(800) 441-7762	C+ / 6.5	7.39	6.31	21.25 /58	6.25 /66	9.34 /53	2.10	0.22
AA	BlackRock LifePath Idx 2055 Inst	LIVIX	C+	(800) 441-7762	C+ / 6.6	7.43	6.41	21.30 /59	6.31 /67	9.60 /55	2.04	0.38
AA	BlackRock LifePath Idx 2055 Inv A	LIVAX	C+	(800) 441-7762	C+ / 6.4	7.38	6.22	20.98 /57	6.05 /65	9.32 /53	1.83	0.61
AA	BlackRock LifePath Idx 2055 K	LIVKX	C+	(800) 441-7762	C+ / 6.6	7.45	6.36	21.25 /58	6.36 /67	9.65 /56	2.08	0.32
GL	BlackRock LifePath Idx Ret Inv A	LIRAX	C+	(800) 441-7762	D+ / 2.6	3.45	1.85	9.81 /11	3.74 /40	4.94 /21	1.63	0.51
GL	BlackRock LifePath Idx Ret Ptf Inst	LIRIX	C+	(800) 441-7762	D+ / 2.9	3.60	2.06	10.16 /12	4.01 /43	5.20 /23	1.86	0.26
GL	BlackRock LifePath Idx Ret Ptf K	LIRKX	C+	(800) 441-7762	D+ / 2.9	3.53	2.00	10.12 /12	4.07 /44	5.25 /23	1.91	0.20
GI	BlackRock LifePath SB 2020 Inst	BLBIX	C	(800) 441-7762	C- / 3.5	4.74	4.23	13.99 /25	3.77 /40	--	1.98	1.22
AA	BlackRock LifePath SB 2020 Inv A	BAPCX	C-	(800) 441-7762	D+ / 2.4	4.64	4.01	13.72 /24	3.51 /37	5.98 /28	1.76	1.51
AA	BlackRock LifePath SB 2020 K	BIPCX	C	(800) 441-7762	C- / 3.6	4.79	4.17	14.05 /26	3.89 /42	6.35 /31	2.22	1.11
AA	BlackRock LifePath SB 2020 R	BRPCX	C-	(800) 441-7762	C- / 3.1	4.54	3.81	13.36 /23	3.24 /34	5.70 /26	1.55	1.73
GI	BlackRock LifePath SB 2025 Inst	BLCIX	C-	(800) 441-7762	C- / 4.1	5.44	4.92	15.87 /34	4.08 /44	--	1.88	1.46
AA	BlackRock LifePath SB 2025 Inv A	BAPDX	D+	(800) 441-7762	C- / 3.0	5.39	4.76	15.65 /33	3.85 /41	6.52 /32	1.54	1.52
AA	BlackRock LifePath SB 2025 K	BIPDX	C-	(800) 441-7762	C- / 4.2	5.52	4.99	16.07 /35	4.21 /45	6.91 /34	1.95	1.14
AA	BlackRock LifePath SB 2025 R	BRPDX	C-	(800) 441-7762	C- / 3.7	5.30	4.66	15.38 /32	3.59 /38	6.28 /30	1.40	1.81
GI	BlackRock LifePath SB 2030 Inst	BLEIX	C-	(800) 441-7762	C / 4.5	6.05	5.61	17.68 /41	4.13 /44	--	1.89	1.35
AA	BlackRock LifePath SB 2030 Inv A	BAPEX	D+	(800) 441-7762	C- / 3.3	6.01	5.45	17.35 /40	3.86 /41	6.75 /33	1.53	1.58
AA	BlackRock LifePath SB 2030 K	BIPEX	C-	(800) 441-7762	C / 4.6	6.02	5.58	17.76 /42	4.21 /45	7.15 /36	1.97	1.22
AA	BlackRock LifePath SB 2030 R	BRPEX	C-	(800) 441-7762	C- / 4.1	6.01	5.44	17.16 /39	3.63 /38	6.50 /31	1.29	1.83
GI	BlackRock LifePath SB 2035 Inst	BLGIX	C	(800) 441-7762	C / 5.0	6.70	6.38	19.76 /51	4.20 /45	--	1.61	1.56
AA	BlackRock LifePath SB 2035 Inv A	BAPGX	C-	(800) 441-7762	C- / 3.7	6.67	6.25	19.50 /49	3.94 /42	6.86 /34	1.29	1.75
AA	BlackRock LifePath SB 2035 K	BIPGX	C	(800) 441-7762	C / 5.1	6.81	6.49	20.03 /52	4.29 /46	7.29 /37	1.72	1.32
AA	BlackRock LifePath SB 2035 R	BRPGX	C	(800) 441-7762	C / 4.6	6.61	6.18	19.28 /48	3.68 /39	6.64 /32	1.16	1.99
GI	BlackRock LifePath SB 2040 Inst	BLHIX	C	(800) 441-7762	C / 5.5	7.08	6.75	21.41 /59	4.44 /48	--	1.44	1.72
AA	BlackRock LifePath SB 2040 Inv A	BAPHX	C-	(800) 441-7762	C- / 4.2	7.08	6.75	21.16 /58	4.21 /45	7.32 /37	1.13	1.87
AA	BlackRock LifePath SB 2040 K	BIPHX	C	(800) 441-7762	C+ / 5.6	7.08	6.87	21.53 /60	4.55 /49	7.70 /40	1.54	1.44
AA	BlackRock LifePath SB 2040 R	BRPHX	C-	(800) 441-7762	C / 5.1	6.99	6.55	20.88 /57	3.97 /43	7.07 /35	0.89	2.11
GI	BlackRock LifePath SB 2045 Inst	BLJIX	C	(800) 441-7762	C+ / 5.6	7.26	6.96	22.18 /63	4.39 /47	--	1.27	1.96
AA	BlackRock LifePath SB 2045 Inv A	BAPJX	C-	(800) 441-7762	C / 4.3	7.29	6.89	21.98 /62	4.14 /44	7.68 /40	0.98	2.24
AA	BlackRock LifePath SB 2045 K	BIPJX	C	(800) 441-7762	C+ / 5.8	7.34	7.14	22.37 /64	4.51 /49	8.10 /43	1.34	1.79
AA	BlackRock LifePath SB 2045 R	BRPJX	C	(800) 441-7762	C / 5.2	7.25	6.74	21.71 /61	3.89 /42	7.43 /38	0.76	2.40
GI	BlackRock LifePath SB 2050 Inst	BLKIX	C	(800) 441-7762	C+ / 5.7	7.30	7.09	22.21 /63	4.42 /48	--	1.34	2.05
AA	BlackRock LifePath SB 2050 Inv A	BAPKX	C-	(800) 441-7762	C / 4.4	7.33	7.11	22.04 /62	4.19 /45	7.85 /41	1.05	2.44

● Denotes fund is closed to new investors
★ Denotes fund is included in Section II

114

www.thestreetratings.com

Risk Rating/Pts	3 Year Standard Deviation	Beta	NAV As of 2/28/17	Total $(Mil)	Cash %	Stocks %	Bonds %	Other %	Portfolio Turnover Ratio	Last Bull Market Return	Last Bear Market Return	Manager Quality Pct	Manager Tenure (Years)	Initial Purch. $	Additional Purch. $	Front End Load	Back End Load
B+ / 9.0	5.6	0.87	11.95	169	2	50	47	1	14	50.4	N/A	45	6	1,000	50	0.0	0.0
B+ / 9.0	5.6	0.86	11.97	1,593	2	50	47	1	14	52.8	N/A	49	6	1	1	0.0	0.0
B / 8.6	6.5	1.02	12.33	83	1	60	37	2	12	59.8	N/A	39	13	2,000,000	0	0.0	0.0
B / 8.6	6.6	0.60	12.32	142	1	60	37	2	12	57.8	N/A	55	13	1,000	50	0.0	0.0
B / 8.6	6.5	0.59	12.34	1,432	1	60	37	2	12	60.2	N/A	59	13	1	1	0.0	0.0
B / 8.1	7.5	1.18	12.49	107	2	71	25	2	12	66.5	N/A	30	6	2,000,000	0	0.0	0.0
B / 8.1	7.5	1.18	12.48	229	2	71	25	2	12	64.3	N/A	27	6	1,000	50	0.0	0.0
B / 8.1	7.5	1.17	12.47	1,831	2	71	25	2	12	66.6	N/A	30	6	1	1	0.0	0.0
B- / 7.6	8.4	1.32	12.75	71	3	81	15	1	10	72.5	N/A	23	6	2,000,000	0	0.0	0.0
B- / 7.6	8.4	1.32	12.72	134	3	81	15	1	10	70.1	N/A	20	6	1,000	50	0.0	0.0
B- / 7.6	8.4	1.31	12.74	1,167	3	81	15	1	10	72.7	N/A	24	6	1	1	0.0	0.0
B- / 7.1	9.2	1.44	12.90	77	3	89	6	2	11	78.3	N/A	17	6	2,000,000	0	0.0	0.0
B- / 7.1	9.2	1.44	12.88	153	3	89	6	2	11	76.0	N/A	16	6	1,000	50	0.0	0.0
B- / 7.1	9.3	1.44	12.90	1,335	3	89	6	2	11	78.7	N/A	18	6	1	1	0.0	0.0
C+ / 6.9	9.7	1.51	13.14	53	3	94	2	1	10	83.2	N/A	15	6	2,000,000	0	0.0	0.0
C+ / 6.9	9.7	1.51	13.11	67	3	94	2	1	10	80.8	N/A	14	6	1,000	50	0.0	0.0
C+ / 6.9	9.7	1.51	13.15	715	3	94	2	1	10	83.7	N/A	16	6	1	1	0.0	0.0
C+ / 6.7	9.8	1.52	13.32	48	3	95	0	2	14	88.1	N/A	15	6	2,000,000	0	0.0	0.0
C+ / 6.7	9.8	1.53	13.29	67	3	95	0	2	14	85.6	N/A	13	6	1,000	50	0.0	0.0
C+ / 6.7	9.8	1.52	13.32	659	3	95	0	2	14	88.5	N/A	16	6	1	1	0.0	0.0
C+ / 6.7	9.9	1.54	13.57	33	3	95	0	2	17	91.8	N/A	15	6	2,000,000	0	0.0	0.0
C+ / 6.7	9.9	1.54	13.54	30	3	95	0	2	17	89.2	N/A	14	6	1,000	50	0.0	0.0
C+ / 6.7	9.9	1.54	13.57	252	3	95	0	2	17	92.2	N/A	16	6	1	1	0.0	0.0
B+ / 9.3	4.6	0.32	11.62	75	1	38	59	2	25	39.2	N/A	92	6	1,000	50	0.0	0.0
B+ / 9.3	4.6	0.32	11.64	71	1	38	59	2	25	41.2	N/A	93	6	2,000,000	0	0.0	0.0
B+ / 9.3	4.6	0.32	11.63	748	1	38	59	2	25	41.4	N/A	93	6	1	1	0.0	0.0
B- / 7.0	5.8	0.53	10.35	N/A	0	0	0	100	30	N/A	N/A	53	1	2,000,000	0	0.0	0.0
B- / 7.0	5.8	0.89	10.25	15	0	0	0	100	30	52.5	-12.2	34	1	1,000	50	5.3	0.0
B- / 7.0	5.8	0.88	10.32	2	0	0	0	100	30	55.5	-11.9	40	1	1	1	0.0	0.0
B- / 7.0	5.8	0.89	10.16	9	0	0	0	100	30	50.4	-12.3	31	1	100	0	0.0	0.0
C+ / 6.1	6.8	0.63	10.24	N/A	0	0	0	100	36	N/A	N/A	42	1	2,000,000	0	0.0	0.0
C+ / 6.2	6.8	1.05	10.18	15	0	0	0	100	36	58.1	-13.5	25	1	1,000	50	5.3	0.0
C+ / 6.1	6.9	1.06	10.25	2	0	0	0	100	36	61.2	-13.2	28	1	1	1	0.0	0.0
C+ / 6.2	6.9	1.05	10.11	11	0	0	0	100	36	56.1	-13.5	23	1	100	0	0.0	0.0
C+ / 5.8	7.9	0.73	9.77	N/A	0	0	0	100	34	N/A	N/A	30	1	2,000,000	0	0.0	0.0
C+ / 5.8	7.9	1.21	9.69	12	0	0	0	100	34	62.1	-15.4	15	1	1,000	50	5.3	0.0
C+ / 5.7	7.8	1.20	9.78	2	0	0	0	100	34	65.2	-15.2	18	1	1	1	0.0	0.0
C+ / 5.8	7.9	1.21	9.66	7	0	0	0	100	34	60.0	-15.5	14	1	100	0	0.0	0.0
C+ / 6.2	8.8	0.82	10.40	N/A	0	0	0	100	37	N/A	N/A	22	1	2,000,000	0	0.0	0.0
C+ / 6.2	8.8	1.35	10.31	9	0	0	0	100	37	66.9	-18.4	10	1	1,000	50	5.3	0.0
C+ / 6.1	8.8	1.35	10.40	2	0	0	0	100	37	70.4	-18.2	12	1	1	1	0.0	0.0
C+ / 6.2	8.8	1.35	10.23	7	0	0	0	100	37	64.9	-18.5	8	1	100	0	0.0	0.0
C / 5.1	9.7	0.91	10.14	N/A	0	0	0	100	35	N/A	N/A	16	1	2,000,000	0	0.0	0.0
C / 5.2	9.7	1.48	10.05	8	0	0	0	100	35	70.3	-18.2	7	1	1,000	50	5.3	0.0
C / 5.1	9.7	1.48	10.14	1	0	0	0	100	35	73.7	-18.0	8	1	1	1	0.0	0.0
C / 5.2	9.7	1.48	10.01	6	0	0	0	100	35	68.1	-18.3	6	1	100	0	0.0	0.0
C+ / 5.6	10.0	0.93	11.20	N/A	0	0	0	100	32	N/A	N/A	14	1	2,000,000	0	0.0	0.0
C+ / 5.6	10.1	1.54	11.04	6	0	0	0	100	32	73.3	-18.2	5	1	1,000	50	5.3	0.0
C / 5.5	10.0	1.52	11.22	1	0	0	0	100	32	76.9	-18.0	7	1	1	1	0.0	0.0
C+ / 5.6	10.1	1.53	10.95	5	0	0	0	100	32	70.9	-18.2	5	1	100	0	0.0	0.0
C+ / 5.7	10.2	0.95	10.45	N/A	0	0	0	100	36	N/A	N/A	13	1	2,000,000	0	0.0	0.0
C+ / 5.7	10.2	1.54	10.34	7	0	0	0	100	36	74.4	-18.3	5	1	1,000	50	5.3	0.0

Fund Type	Fund Name	Ticker Symbol	Overall Investment Rating	Phone	Performance Rating/Pts	3 Mo	6 Mo	1Yr / Pct	3Yr / Pct	5Yr / Pct	Dividend Yield	Expense Ratio
								Total Return % through 2/28/17	Annualized		Incl. in Returns	
AA	BlackRock LifePath SB 2050 K	BIPKX	C+	(800) 441-7762	C+ / 5.8	7.39	7.28	22.56 /65	4.58 /50	8.26 /44	1.42	1.88
AA	BlackRock LifePath SB 2050 R	BRPKX	C	(800) 441-7762	C / 5.2	7.18	6.85	21.69 /61	3.92 /42	7.56 /39	0.85	2.55
GI	BlackRock LifePath SB 2055 Inst	BLLIX	C	(800) 441-7762	C+ / 5.7	7.20	6.79	22.20 /63	4.60 /50	--	1.19	5.66
GI	BlackRock LifePath SB 2055 Inv A	BAPLX	C-	(800) 441-7762	C / 4.4	7.15	6.64	21.97 /62	4.35 /47	--	0.98	5.93
GI	BlackRock LifePath SB 2055 K	BIPLX	C	(800) 441-7762	C+ / 5.8	7.20	6.80	22.32 /64	4.71 /51	--	1.29	5.25
GI	BlackRock LifePath SB 2055 R	BRPLX	C	(800) 441-7762	C / 5.2	7.00	6.38	21.63 /60	4.09 /44	--	0.87	5.92
AA	BlackRock LifePath Smart Beta Ret A	BAPBX	D+	(800) 441-7762	D / 2.0	4.01	3.28	11.59 /16	3.13 /33	5.33 /23	1.88	1.76
BA	BlackRock LifePath Smart Beta Ret I	BLAIX	C-	(800) 441-7762	C- / 3.0	4.12	3.39	11.87 /17	3.42 /36	--	2.30	1.38
AA	BlackRock LifePath Smart Beta Ret K	BIPBX	C-	(800) 441-7762	C- / 3.0	4.07	3.44	11.92 /18	3.48 /37	5.70 /26	2.35	1.41
AA	BlackRock LifePath Smart Beta Ret R	BRPBX	C-	(800) 441-7762	D+ / 2.6	3.97	3.14	11.32 /16	2.86 /30	5.07 /22	1.65	2.07
GL	BlackRock Long-Horizon Eq Inst	MAEGX	E	(800) 441-7762	D / 1.8	7.85	2.62	9.69 /11	0.44 /15	5.55 /25	0.88	0.98
GL	BlackRock Long-Horizon Eq Inv A	MDEGX	E	(800) 441-7762	D- / 1.2	7.83	2.49	9.46 /10	0.19 /14	5.26 /23	0.56	1.25
GL	● BlackRock Long-Horizon Eq Inv B	MBEGX	E	(800) 441-7762	E+ / 0.9	7.60	2.09	8.49 / 8	-0.75 /10	4.30 /17	0.00	2.20
GL	BlackRock Long-Horizon Eq Inv C	MCEGX	E	(800) 441-7762	D- / 1.0	7.69	2.14	8.61 / 9	-0.57 /11	4.46 /18	0.00	2.01
GL	BlackRock Long-Horizon Eq R	MREGX	E	(800) 441-7762	D- / 1.1	7.79	2.36	9.01 / 9	-0.23 /12	4.80 /20	0.06	1.78
MC	BlackRock Mid Cap Growth Eq Inst	CMGIX	C+	(800) 441-7762	B / 7.7	10.48	8.41	27.12 /79	6.33 /67	13.19 /86	0.00	1.06
MC	BlackRock Mid Cap Growth Eq Inv A	BMGAX	C	(800) 441-7762	C+ / 6.6	10.31	8.24	26.73 /78	5.99 /64	12.83 /82	0.00	1.43
MC	● BlackRock Mid Cap Growth Eq Inv B	BMGBX	C	(800) 441-7762	C+ / 6.9	10.15	7.85	25.79 /76	5.17 /56	11.97 /74	0.00	2.75
MC	BlackRock Mid Cap Growth Eq Inv C	BMGCX	C-	(800) 441-7762	C+ / 6.9	10.07	7.85	25.75 /75	5.18 /56	11.97 /74	0.00	2.16
MC	BlackRock Mid Cap Growth Eq R	BMRRX	C	(800) 441-7762	B- / 7.3	10.24	8.07	26.40 /77	5.71 /62	12.52 /79	0.00	1.73
MC	BlackRock Mid Cap Growth Eq Svc	CMGSX	C+	(800) 441-7762	B- / 7.5	10.38	8.32	26.93 /79	5.97 /64	12.73 /81	0.00	1.50
MC	BlackRock Mid Cap Val Opps Inst	MARFX	C+	(800) 441-7762	B+ / 8.9	5.13	12.63	34.70 /94	7.36 /74	11.94 /74	0.63	0.94
MC	BlackRock Mid Cap Val Opps Inv A	MDRFX	C	(800) 441-7762	B / 7.8	5.05	12.49	34.29 /93	7.05 /72	11.60 /71	0.38	1.20
MC	BlackRock Mid Cap Val Opps Inv C	MCRFX	C	(800) 441-7762	B / 8.1	4.86	12.02	33.22 /92	6.19 /66	10.68 /63	0.00	2.00
MC	BlackRock Mid Cap Value Opp R	MRRFX	C	(800) 441-7762	B+ / 8.5	4.99	12.31	33.90 /93	6.73 /70	11.25 /68	0.21	1.50
MC	BlackRock Midcap Index Inst	BRMIX	U	(800) 441-7762	U /	6.44	8.86	26.65 /78	--	--	1.66	0.13
MC	BlackRock Midcap Index K	BRMKX	U	(800) 441-7762	U /	6.45	8.88	26.80 /79	--	--	1.69	0.09
FO	BlackRock Min Vol EAFE Index K	BKEVX	U	(800) 441-7762	U /	5.55	-1.34	--	--	--	0.00	0.23
FO	BlackRock MSCI Asia ex Japan K	BAJKX	U	(800) 441-7762	U /	7.24	5.11	26.62 /78	--	--	1.45	0.77
GL	BlackRock MSCI World Index K	BWIKX	U	(800) 441-7762	U /	7.65	7.71	21.61 /60	--	--	1.99	0.28
BA	BlackRock Multi Asset Inc Ptf C	BCICX	D+	(800) 441-7762	D+ / 2.4	3.67	2.76	10.99 /14	2.62 /28	4.86 /20	3.68	1.73
BA	BlackRock Multi Asset Inc Ptf Inst	BIICX	C-	(800) 441-7762	C- / 3.1	3.91	3.27	12.19 /19	3.69 /39	5.92 /28	4.65	0.73
BA	BlackRock Multi Asset Income Ptf A	BAICX	D+	(800) 441-7762	D / 2.1	3.76	3.05	11.81 /17	3.40 /36	5.64 /26	4.18	0.97
GL	BlackRock Multi-Mgr Alt Str Inst	BMMNX	U	(800) 441-7762	U /	1.87	3.24	6.67 / 5	--	--	1.75	3.58
EN	BlackRock Natural Resource Inst	MAGRX	E-	(800) 441-7762	E- / 0.2	-4.21	4.27	29.92 /86	-7.87 / 1	-3.35 / 2	0.91	0.89
EN	BlackRock Natural Resource Inv A	MDGRX	E-	(800) 441-7762	E- / 0.1	-4.27	4.13	29.59 /85	-8.11 / 1	-3.61 / 2	0.64	1.15
EN	● BlackRock Natural Resource Inv B	MBGRX	E-	(800) 441-7762	E- / 0.1	-4.69	3.44	28.22 /82	-8.95 / 1	-4.45 / 2	0.00	2.08
EN	BlackRock Natural Resource Inv C	MCGRX	E-	(800) 441-7762	E- / 0.2	-4.45	3.73	28.56 /83	-8.83 / 1	-4.36 / 2	0.06	1.95
FO	BlackRock Pacific Inst	MAPCX	C	(800) 441-7762	C+ / 6.2	9.47	8.40	26.49 /78	3.67 /39	7.02 /35	1.41	0.94
FO	BlackRock Pacific Inv A	MDPCX	C-	(800) 441-7762	C / 4.9	9.43	8.28	26.24 /77	3.44 /36	6.80 /33	1.17	1.17
FO	BlackRock Pacific Inv C	MCPCX	C-	(800) 441-7762	C / 5.3	9.14	7.85	25.25 /74	2.64 /29	5.97 /28	1.02	1.95
FO	BlackRock Pacific R	MRPCX	C-	(800) 441-7762	C+ / 5.6	9.27	8.02	25.58 /75	2.96 /31	6.27 /30	1.00	1.63
RE	BlackRock RI Est Securities Inst	BIREX	B	(800) 441-7762	B / 8.2	8.23	-0.66	18.13 /43	11.55 /98	--	1.50	1.39
RE	BlackRock RI Est Securities Inv A	BAREX	C+	(800) 441-7762	B- / 7.1	8.09	-0.87	17.86 /42	11.24 /97	--	1.18	1.76
RE	BlackRock RI Est Securities Inv C	BCREX	B-	(800) 441-7762	B- / 7.5	7.94	-1.18	16.95 /38	10.45 /96	--	0.56	2.61
IX	BlackRock S&P 500 Index Inst	BSPIX	A+	(800) 441-7762	A / 9.3	8.00	9.95	24.84 /73	10.51 /96	13.85 /92	1.75	0.11
IX	BlackRock S&P 500 Index Investor A	BSPAX	A+	(800) 441-7762	A- / 9.2	7.93	9.82	24.53 /72	10.24 /95	13.57 /89	1.54	0.36
IX	BlackRock S&P 500 Index Investor	BSPZX	A+	(800) 441-7762	B+ / 8.7	7.74	9.43	23.64 /69	9.44 /90	12.77 /82	0.88	1.08
IX	BlackRock S&P 500 Index K	WFSPX	A+	(800) 441-7762	A / 9.4	8.02	10.00	24.93 /73	10.57 /96	13.90 /92	1.81	0.04
IX	BlackRock S&P 500 Index Service	BSPSX	A+	(800) 441-7762	A / 9.3	7.97	9.89	24.70 /72	10.38 /95	13.71 /91	1.65	0.23
TC	BlackRock Sci & Tech Opp Inst	BGSIX	A	(800) 441-7762	A+ / 9.7	10.07	11.21	33.80 /93	10.22 /94	15.00 /97	0.00	1.31
TC	BlackRock Sci & Tech Opp Inv A	BGSAX	A-	(800) 441-7762	A / 9.3	9.94	10.97	33.35 /92	9.86 /93	14.64 /96	0.00	1.60

RISK			NET ASSETS		ASSET					BULL / BEAR		FUND MANAGER		MINIMUMS		LOADS	
	3 Year		NAV						Portfolio	Last Bull	Last Bear	Manager	Manager	Initial	Additional	Front	Back
Risk	Standard		As of	Total	Cash	Stocks	Bonds	Other	Turnover	Market	Market	Quality	Tenure	Purch.	Purch.	End	End
Rating/Pts	Deviation	Beta	2/28/17	$(Mil)	%	%	%	%	Ratio	Return	Return	Pct	(Years)	$	$	Load	Load
C+ / 5.7	10.2	1.55	10.47	1	0	0	0	100	36	78.3	-18.2	6	1	1	1	0.0	0.0
C+ / 5.7	10.2	1.55	10.29	5	0	0	0	100	36	72.1	-18.4	5	1	100	0	0.0	0.0
C / 5.3	10.0	0.93	10.94	N/A	0	0	0	100	38	N/A	N/A	16	1	2,000,000	0	0.0	0.0
C / 5.3	10.1	0.93	10.89	1	0	0	0	100	38	N/A	N/A	14	1	1,000	50	5.3	0.0
C / 5.2	10.1	0.93	10.94	3	0	0	0	100	38	N/A	N/A	16	1	1	1	0.0	0.0
C / 5.2	10.0	0.93	10.83	1	0	0	0	100	38	N/A	N/A	12	1	100	0	0.0	0.0
B- / 7.0	4.7	0.71	10.06	9	0	0	0	100	34	46.7	-11.1	47	1	1,000	50	5.3	0.0
C+ / 6.9	4.7	0.70	10.13	1	0	0	0	100	34	N/A	N/A	52	1	2,000,000	0	0.0	0.0
C+ / 6.9	4.7	0.70	10.13	1	0	0	0	100	34	49.6	-11.0	53	1	1	1	0.0	0.0
B- / 7.0	4.7	0.70	10.07	5	0	0	0	100	34	44.7	-11.2	44	1	100	0	0.0	0.0
C- / 3.4	10.9	0.78	11.52	44	0	97	1	2	80	55.3	-19.5	78	5	2,000,000	0	0.0	0.0
C- / 3.5	10.9	0.78	11.52	194	0	97	1	2	80	53.0	-19.6	76	5	1,000	50	5.3	0.0
C- / 3.7	10.9	0.78	11.75	N/A	0	97	1	2	80	45.7	-19.9	67	5	1,000	50	0.0	0.0
C- / 3.6	10.9	0.78	11.48	58	0	97	1	2	80	46.7	-19.8	69	5	1,000	50	0.0	0.0
C- / 3.6	10.9	0.77	11.57	3	0	97	1	2	80	49.5	-19.7	73	5	100	0	0.0	0.0
C- / 4.0	14.2	0.91	19.08	103	0	99	0	1	81	134.1	-21.1	46	4	2,000,000	0	0.0	0.0
C- / 3.9	14.2	0.91	16.69	410	0	99	0	1	81	130.2	-21.2	41	4	1,000	50	5.3	0.0
C- / 3.6	14.2	0.90	13.46	1	0	99	0	1	81	120.8	-21.4	31	4	1,000	50	0.0	0.0
C- / 3.5	14.2	0.91	13.33	54	0	99	0	1	81	120.7	-21.4	31	4	1,000	50	0.0	0.0
C- / 3.9	14.2	0.91	16.47	8	0	99	0	1	81	126.9	-21.2	37	4	100	0	0.0	0.0
C- / 3.9	14.2	0.91	17.44	1	0	99	0	1	81	129.1	-21.2	40	4	5,000	0	0.0	0.0
C- / 3.1	13.2	1.05	21.59	213	1	98	0	1	73	121.4	-21.8	40	8	2,000,000	0	0.0	0.0
C- / 3.1	13.2	1.06	20.80	238	1	98	0	1	73	117.7	-21.9	36	8	1,000	50	5.3	0.0
D+ / 2.7	13.2	1.06	17.36	57	1	98	0	1	73	108.1	-22.3	27	8	1,000	50	0.0	0.0
D+ / 2.8	13.2	1.06	18.59	52	1	98	0	1	73	114.0	-22.0	32	8	100	0	0.0	0.0
U /	N/A	N/A	10.96	304	0	99	0	1	24	N/A	N/A	N/A	2	2,000,000	0	0.0	0.0
U /	N/A	N/A	10.97	2,492	0	99	0	1	24	N/A	N/A	N/A	2	5,000,000	0	0.0	0.0
U /	N/A	N/A	9.68	102	0	0	0	100	0	N/A	N/A	N/A	1	5,000,000	0	0.0	0.0
U /	N/A	N/A	9.65	42	2	97	0	1	11	N/A	N/A	N/A	2	5,000,000	0	0.0	0.0
U /	N/A	N/A	10.42	468	1	97	0	2	10	N/A	N/A	N/A	2	5,000,000	0	0.0	0.0
C+ / 6.9	4.5	0.67	10.83	3,110	17	15	66	2	142	41.5	-7.5	45	6	1,000	50	0.0	0.0
C+ / 6.9	4.5	0.67	10.86	6,836	17	15	66	2	142	49.4	-7.0	59	6	2,000,000	0	0.0	0.0
C+ / 6.9	4.5	0.67	10.84	4,455	17	15	66	2	142	47.1	-7.1	55	6	1,000	50	5.3	0.0
U /	N/A	N/A	9.80	100	62	0	34	4	234	N/A	N/A	N/A	3	2,000,000	0	0.0	0.0
E+ / 0.9	21.4	1.08	45.55	82	1	97	1	1	7	10.2	-30.7	42	N/A	2,000,000	0	0.0	0.0
E+ / 0.9	21.4	1.08	44.09	203	1	97	1	1	7	8.7	-30.8	38	N/A	1,000	50	5.3	0.0
E+ / 0.8	21.4	1.08	38.44	N/A	1	97	1	1	7	3.7	-31.0	27	N/A	1,000	50	0.0	0.0
E+ / 0.8	21.4	1.08	37.79	45	1	97	1	1	7	4.1	-31.0	29	N/A	1,000	50	0.0	0.0
C / 4.8	13.2	0.89	17.52	101	1	96	1	2	89	66.2	-23.7	93	6	2,000,000	0	0.0	0.0
C / 4.8	13.2	0.88	17.33	104	1	96	1	2	89	64.2	-23.8	92	6	1,000	50	5.3	0.0
C / 4.5	13.2	0.89	12.65	19	1	96	1	2	89	57.3	-24.0	89	6	1,000	50	0.0	0.0
C / 4.6	13.3	0.89	14.04	3	1	96	1	2	89	59.8	-24.0	91	6	100	0	0.0	0.0
C / 5.1	15.1	1.10	12.98	15	2	98	0	0	86	N/A	N/A	67	5	2,000,000	0	0.0	0.0
C / 5.1	15.1	1.10	12.95	22	2	98	0	0	86	N/A	N/A	63	5	1,000	50	5.3	0.0
C / 5.1	15.1	1.10	12.86	4	2	98	0	0	86	N/A	N/A	54	5	1,000	50	0.0	0.0
B- / 7.1	10.3	1.00	282.83	4,661	1	96	1	2	3	133.1	-16.3	73	9	2,000,000	0	0.0	0.0
B- / 7.1	10.3	1.00	282.67	1,876	1	96	1	2	3	129.9	-16.4	70	9	1,000	50	0.0	0.0
B- / 7.1	10.3	1.00	282.43	77	1	96	1	2	3	121.4	-16.6	61	9	0	0	0.0	0.0
B- / 7.1	10.3	1.00	282.92	3,029	1	96	1	2	3	133.6	-16.3	73	9	1,000,000	0	0.0	0.0
B- / 7.1	10.3	1.00	282.76	351	1	96	1	2	3	131.5	-16.4	72	9	5,000	0	0.0	0.0
C / 5.4	15.2	1.09	20.20	82	1	97	0	2	84	137.2	-21.4	58	17	2,000,000	0	0.0	0.0
C / 5.4	15.2	1.09	18.89	192	1	97	0	2	84	132.8	-21.4	54	17	1,000	50	5.3	0.0

Fund Type	Fund Name	Ticker Symbol	Overall Investment Rating	Phone	Performance Rating/Pts	3 Mo	6 Mo	1Yr / Pct	3Yr / Pct	5Yr / Pct	Dividend Yield	Expense Ratio
	99 Pct = Best 0 Pct = Worst							Total Return % through 2/28/17	Annualized		Incl. in Returns	
TC	BlackRock Sci & Tech Opp Inv C	BGSCX	A-	(800) 441-7762	A / 9.5	9.82	10.63	32.36 /91	8.99 /87	13.69 /91	0.00	2.40
TC	BlackRock Sci & Tech Opp R	BGSRX	A-	(800) 441-7762	A+ / 9.6	9.88	10.82	33.00 /92	9.55 /91	14.33 /95	0.00	1.86
TC	BlackRock Sci & Tech Opp Svc	BSTSX	A	(800) 441-7762	A+ / 9.7	9.97	11.04	33.46 /92	9.95 /93	14.75 /96	0.00	1.48
SC	BlackRock Small Cap Growth II Inst	MASWX	C-	(800) 441-7762	B- / 7.0	5.52	11.63	31.68 /89	4.34 /47	10.34 /61	0.18	1.39
SC	BlackRock Small Cap Growth II Inv A	MDSWX	D+	(800) 441-7762	C+ / 5.8	5.38	11.51	31.31 /89	4.10 /44	10.04 /59	0.18	1.62
SC	BlackRock Small Cap Growth II Inv C	MCSWX	D+	(800) 441-7762	C+ / 6.2	5.27	11.06	30.19 /87	3.21 /34	9.10 /51	0.24	2.50
SC	BlackRock Small Cap Growth II R	MRUSX	C-	(800) 441-7762	C+ / 6.6	5.39	11.34	30.97 /88	3.82 /41	9.76 /57	0.21	1.88
SC	BlackRock Small Cap Index Class K	BDBKX	B	(800) 441-7762	B+ / 8.9	5.20	12.58	36.06 /95	6.97 /72	12.97 /83	1.17	0.20
SC	BlackRock Small Cap Index Inst	MASKX	B	(800) 441-7762	B+ / 8.8	5.19	12.58	36.10 /95	6.92 /71	12.92 /83	1.15	0.21
SC	BlackRock Small Cap Index Inv A	MDSKX	B	(800) 441-7762	B+ / 8.7	5.13	12.46	35.78 /95	6.66 /69	12.64 /80	0.93	0.52
MC	BlackRock Small/Mid Cap K	BSMKX	U	(800) 441-7762	U /	5.80	10.71	31.81 /90	--	--	1.28	0.70
AA	BlackRock Strategic Inc Opps Inst	BSIIX	C-	(800) 441-7762	D / 1.8	2.14	2.87	6.23 / 5	2.46 /27	3.67 /14	2.93	0.80
AA	BlackRock Strategic Inc Opps Inv A	BASIX	C-	(800) 441-7762	D- / 1.3	2.07	2.72	5.92 / 5	2.15 /25	3.38 /12	2.54	1.15
AA	BlackRock Strategic Inc Opps Inv C	BSICX	C-	(800) 441-7762	D- / 1.4	1.89	2.34	5.13 / 4	1.39 /20	2.61 /10	1.91	1.86
FS	BlackRock Strategic Inc Opps K	BSIKX	U	(800) 441-7762	U /	2.27	2.90	--	--	--	0.00	0.74
AA	BlackRock Tactical Opptys Inst	PBAIX	D+	(800) 441-7762	E+ / 0.9	-0.49	1.96	2.50 / 2	0.56 /16	3.38 /12	1.74	0.92
AA	BlackRock Tactical Opptys Inv A	PCBAX	D	(800) 441-7762	E / 0.5	-0.45	1.87	2.25 / 2	0.26 /15	3.07 /11	1.34	1.22
AA	● BlackRock Tactical Opptys Inv B	CBIBX	D	(800) 441-7762	E / 0.5	-0.67	1.45	1.29 / 2	-0.71 /10	2.09 / 8	0.00	2.35
AA	BlackRock Tactical Opptys Inv C	BRBCX	D	(800) 441-7762	E+ / 0.6	-0.66	1.48	1.48 / 2	-0.42 /12	2.37 / 9	0.63	1.90
GR	BlackRock Tactical Opptys K	PBAKX	U	(800) 441-7762	U /	-0.38	2.07	--	--	--	0.00	N/A
AA	BlackRock Tactical Opptys Svc	PCBSX	D	(800) 441-7762	E+ / 0.8	-0.52	1.87	2.25 / 2	0.22 /14	3.05 /11	1.49	1.29
FS	BlackRock Tot Intl ex US Idx Inst	BDOIX	E+	(800) 441-7762	D- / 1.5	7.51	4.63	19.19 /48	-0.45 /11	3.10 /11	2.53	0.45
FS	BlackRock Tot Intl ex US Idx Inv A	BDOAX	E+	(800) 441-7762	D- / 1.4	7.46	4.65	18.96 /47	-0.72 /10	2.84 /10	2.31	0.43
FS	BlackRock Tot Intl ex US Idx K	BDOKX	E+	(800) 441-7762	D- / 1.5	7.43	4.65	19.13 /48	-0.43 /12	3.58 /13	2.50	0.46
EM	BlackRock Total Emerg Mkt Inst	BEEIX	C	(800) 441-7762	C / 5.0	8.03	1.76	24.00 /70	3.74 /40	--	1.06	1.62
EM	BlackRock Total Emerg Mkt InvA	BEEAX	C-	(800) 441-7762	C- / 3.7	7.96	1.66	23.85 /69	3.48 /37	--	0.93	2.03
EM	BlackRock Total Emerg Mkt InvC	BEECX	C-	(800) 441-7762	C- / 4.1	7.75	1.21	22.82 /66	2.71 /29	--	0.56	2.79
GL	BlackRock Total Factor Inst	BSTIX	C+	(800) 441-7762	C- / 4.0	5.86	3.28	14.45 /28	4.54 /49	--	0.39	1.26
GL	BlackRock Total Factor Inv A	BSTAX	C	(800) 441-7762	D+ / 2.9	5.77	3.18	14.26 /27	4.29 /46	--	0.19	1.68
GL	BlackRock Total Factor Inv C	BSTCX	C+	(800) 441-7762	C- / 3.3	5.55	2.84	13.32 /23	3.53 /37	--	0.00	2.33
GR	BlackRock Total Stock Mkt Idx Inv A	BASMX	U	(800) 441-7762	U /	7.65	10.12	25.91 /76	--	--	1.18	0.40
GR	BlackRock Total Stock Mkt Idx K	BKTSX	U	(800) 441-7762	U /	7.70	10.22	26.26 /77	--	--	1.34	0.20
MC	BlackRock US Opportunities Inst	BMCIX	C	(800) 441-7762	C+ / 6.7	6.06	7.53	24.17 /70	6.10 /65	12.01 /74	0.58	1.18
MC	BlackRock US Opportunities Inv A	BMEAX	D+	(800) 441-7762	C / 5.4	5.98	7.35	23.73 /69	5.68 /61	11.55 /70	0.16	1.45
MC	● BlackRock US Opportunities Inv B	BRMBX	D+	(800) 441-7762	C+ / 5.8	5.78	6.95	22.81 /66	4.87 /53	10.68 /63	0.00	2.23
MC	BlackRock US Opportunities Inv C	BMECX	D+	(800) 441-7762	C+ / 5.8	5.78	6.95	22.81 /66	4.89 /53	10.71 /63	0.00	2.17
MC	BlackRock US Opportunities Svc	BMCSX	C-	(800) 441-7762	C+ / 6.5	5.96	7.34	23.73 /69	5.68 /61	11.55 /70	0.12	1.53
SC	BlackRock Value Opportunities Inst	MASPX	B-	(800) 441-7762	B / 7.7	2.99	10.70	34.16 /93	5.99 /64	12.35 /78	0.00	1.08
SC	BlackRock Value Opportunities Inv A	MDSPX	C+	(800) 441-7762	C+ / 6.7	2.93	10.55	33.82 /93	5.74 /62	12.07 /75	0.00	1.26
SC	● BlackRock Value Opportunities Inv B	MBSPX	C+	(800) 441-7762	C+ / 6.8	2.73	10.10	32.32 /90	4.70 /51	10.93 /65	0.00	2.31
SC	BlackRock Value Opportunities Inv C	MCSPX	C+	(800) 441-7762	C+ / 6.9	2.70	10.11	32.68 /91	4.86 /53	11.11 /67	0.00	2.09
SC	BlackRock Value Opportunities R	MRSPX	C+	(800) 441-7762	B- / 7.3	2.84	10.37	33.38 /92	5.42 /59	11.73 /72	0.00	1.51
GL	Blackstone Alternative Multi Str D	BXMDX	U	(800) 831-5776	U /	3.30	3.92	8.32 / 8	--	--	0.32	3.49
GL	Blackstone Alternative Multi Str I	BXMIX	U	(800) 831-5776	U /	3.32	4.04	8.55 / 8	--	--	0.44	3.24
GL	Blackstone Alternative Multi Str Y	BXMYX	U	(800) 831-5776	U /	3.45	4.18	8.73 / 9	--	--	0.55	3.14
GR	Blue Chip Investor Fund	BCIFX	A	(800) 710-5777	B+ / 8.3	4.28	7.41	23.91 /70	9.64 /91	13.29 /87	0.25	1.49
GL	Blue Current Global Dividend Instl	BCGDX	U		U /	7.22	5.97	17.22 /39	--	--	1.90	1.55
GR	BMO Aggressive Allocation I	BDSHX	C+	(800) 236-3863	C+ / 6.6	7.60	8.38	22.17 /63	5.69 /61	10.09 /59	1.35	0.95
GR	BMO Aggressive Allocation R3	BDSRX	C+	(800) 236-3863	C+ / 6.2	7.41	8.08	21.58 /60	5.20 /56	9.78 /57	0.89	1.45
GR	BMO Aggressive Allocation R-6	BDSQX	C+	(800) 236-3863	C+ / 6.7	7.56	8.46	22.24 /63	5.84 /63	10.18 /60	1.52	0.80
GR	BMO Aggressive Allocation Y	BDSYX	C+	(800) 236-3863	C+ / 6.4	7.54	8.33	21.84 /61	5.46 /59	9.94 /58	1.01	1.20
GI	BMO Alternative Strategies I	BMASX	U	(800) 236-3863	U /	1.83	2.52	6.54 / 5	--	--	0.00	3.68

Risk Rating/Pts	3 Year Standard Deviation	Beta	NAV As of 2/28/17	Total $(Mil)	Cash %	Stocks %	Bonds %	Other %	Portfolio Turnover Ratio	Last Bull Market Return	Last Bear Market Return	Manager Quality Pct	Manager Tenure (Years)	Initial Purch. $	Additional Purch. $	Front End Load	Back End Load
C /5.3	15.2	1.09	16.42	67	1	97	0	2	84	122.7	-21.8	43	17	1,000	50	0.0	0.0
C /5.4	15.2	1.09	19.12	8	1	97	0	2	84	129.4	-21.5	50	17	100	0	0.0	0.0
C /5.4	15.2	1.09	19.28	2	1	97	0	2	84	134.4	-21.4	55	17	5,000	0	0.0	0.0
C- /3.4	15.9	0.97	14.05	52	4	95	0	1	115	120.4	-27.3	45	4	2,000,000	0	0.0	0.0
C- /3.2	15.9	0.98	13.21	60	4	95	0	1	115	117.0	-27.4	41	4	1,000	50	5.3	0.0
D+ /2.7	15.9	0.97	10.48	29	4	95	0	1	115	107.1	-27.7	30	4	1,000	50	0.0	0.0
C- /3.1	15.8	0.97	12.01	21	4	95	0	1	115	114.1	-27.5	37	4	100	0	0.0	0.0
C /4.5	15.7	1.00	18.21	82	3	96	0	1	37	132.7	-25.3	74	5	0	0	0.0	0.0
C /4.5	15.8	1.00	18.18	251	3	96	0	1	37	132.2	-25.3	N/A	5	2,000,000	0	0.0	0.0
C /4.5	15.8	1.00	18.19	124	3	96	0	1	37	129.0	-25.3	71	5	1,000	50	0.0	0.0
U /	N/A	N/A	11.29	59	0	96	3	1	17	N/A	N/A	N/A	2	5,000,000	0	0.0	0.0
B /8.5	1.6	0.16	9.92	18,844	11	0	86	3	1,856	24.0	-2.7	82	6	2,000,000	0	0.0	0.0
B /8.5	1.6	0.16	9.92	3,817	11	0	86	3	1,856	22.1	-2.8	80	6	1,000	50	4.0	0.0
B /8.5	1.6	0.15	9.91	836	11	0	86	3	1,856	17.3	-3.2	75	6	1,000	50	0.0	0.0
U /	N/A	N/A	9.93	3,836	11	0	86	3	1,856	N/A	N/A	N/A	6	5,000,000	0	0.0	0.0
B- /7.6	4.5	0.47	13.44	208	14	45	39	2	359	33.2	-13.0	36	11	2,000,000	0	0.0	0.0
B- /7.6	4.5	0.47	13.39	254	14	45	39	2	359	31.1	-13.1	32	11	1,000	50	5.3	0.0
B- /7.8	4.5	0.47	13.32	1	14	45	39	2	359	24.5	-13.4	22	11	0	0	0.0	0.0
B- /7.7	4.5	0.47	13.07	48	14	45	39	2	359	26.3	-13.4	25	11	1,000	50	0.0	0.0
U /	N/A	N/A	13.43	42	14	45	39	2	359	N/A	N/A	N/A	11	5,000,000	0	0.0	0.0
B- /7.6	4.5	0.47	13.38	2	14	45	39	2	359	30.9	-13.1	31	11	5,000	0	0.0	0.0
C /4.5	11.8	0.55	8.12	68	1	98	0	1	6	35.6	N/A	6	5	2,000,000	0	0.0	0.0
C /4.5	11.8	0.55	8.10	258	1	98	0	1	6	33.8	N/A	5	5	1,000	50	0.0	0.0
C /4.6	11.7	0.55	8.35	154	1	98	0	1	6	38.8	N/A	6	5	1	1	0.0	0.0
C+ /6.2	12.0	0.69	9.75	192	0	39	60	1	22	N/A	N/A	88	4	2,000,000	0	0.0	0.0
C+ /6.2	12.0	0.69	9.71	41	0	39	60	1	22	N/A	N/A	87	4	1,000	50	5.3	0.0
C+ /6.3	12.0	0.69	9.66	4	0	39	60	1	22	N/A	N/A	84	4	1,000	50	0.0	0.0
B /8.1	6.4	0.88	10.01	30	28	0	71	1	11	N/A	N/A	77	5	2,000,000	0	0.0	0.0
B /8.1	6.4	0.87	9.99	2	28	0	71	1	11	N/A	N/A	75	5	1,000	50	5.3	0.0
B /8.2	6.4	0.87	9.94	1	28	0	71	1	11	N/A	N/A	68	5	1,000	50	0.0	0.0
U /	N/A	N/A	11.41	46	0	96	3	1	4	N/A	N/A	N/A	2	1,000	50	0.0	0.0
U /	N/A	N/A	11.42	520	0	96	3	1	4	N/A	N/A	N/A	2	5,000,000	0	0.0	0.0
C- /3.8	12.5	0.97	37.93	699	1	97	1	1	72	114.8	-24.7	34	19	2,000,000	0	0.0	0.0
C- /3.6	12.5	0.97	34.48	353	1	97	1	1	72	110.0	-24.9	30	19	1,000	50	5.3	0.0
C- /3.1	12.5	0.97	27.74	2	1	97	1	1	72	101.3	-25.1	22	19	1,000	50	0.0	0.0
C- /3.1	12.5	0.97	27.74	161	1	97	1	1	72	101.6	-25.1	22	19	1,000	50	0.0	0.0
C- /3.8	12.5	0.97	35.71	22	1	97	1	1	72	110.0	-24.9	29	19	5,000	0	0.0	0.0
C /4.9	15.4	0.95	35.20	154	0	97	1	2	71	127.8	-24.3	68	8	2,000,000	0	0.0	0.0
C /4.9	15.4	0.95	34.09	377	0	97	1	2	71	124.8	-24.4	65	8	1,000	50	5.3	0.0
C /5.2	15.4	0.95	27.53	N/A	0	97	1	2	71	112.7	-24.8	52	8	1,000	50	0.0	0.0
C /4.8	15.4	0.95	25.54	137	0	97	1	2	71	114.5	-24.8	54	8	1,000	50	0.0	0.0
C /4.8	15.4	0.95	27.92	27	0	97	1	2	71	121.1	-24.6	61	8	100	0	0.0	0.0
U /	N/A	N/A	10.44	498	0	0	0	100	172	N/A	N/A	N/A	3	25,000	5,000	0.0	0.0
U /	N/A	N/A	10.46	3,586	0	0	0	100	172	N/A	N/A	N/A	3	1,000,000	200,000	0.0	0.0
U /	N/A	N/A	10.39	420	0	0	0	100	172	N/A	N/A	N/A	3	5,000,000	1,000,000	0.0	0.0
B- /7.1	9.2	0.77	164.96	35	4	94	0	2	20	118.5	-16.0	83	15	5,000	100	0.0	0.0
U /	N/A	N/A	10.58	49	8	91	0	1	58	N/A	N/A	N/A	3	100,000	0	0.0	0.0
C+ /6.9	10.4	0.99	9.36	22	2	96	0	2	33	96.7	-20.6	19	3	2,000,000	0	0.0	0.0
C+ /6.8	10.5	0.99	9.36	20	2	96	0	2	33	94.0	-20.6	15	3	0	0	0.0	0.0
C+ /6.9	10.5	0.99	9.36	121	2	96	0	2	33	97.5	-20.6	20	3	0	0	0.0	0.0
C+ /6.9	10.5	1.00	9.38	42	2	96	0	2	33	95.4	-20.6	17	3	1,000	50	0.0	0.0
U /	N/A	N/A	10.59	105	0	0	0	100	279	N/A	N/A	N/A	3	1,000,000	0	0.0	0.0

Fund Type	Fund Name	Ticker Symbol	Overall Investment Rating	Phone	Performance Rating/Pts	3 Mo	6 Mo	1Yr / Pct	3Yr / Pct	5Yr / Pct	Dividend Yield	Expense Ratio
	99 Pct = Best 0 Pct = Worst				**PERFORMANCE** Total Return % through 2/28/17 — Annualized — Incl. in Returns							
GI	BMO Balanced Allocation I	BGRHX	B-	(800) 236-3863	C / 4.4	5.29	5.29	16.40 /36	4.44 /48	7.32 /37	2.13	0.97
GI	BMO Balanced Allocation R3	BGRRX	C+	(800) 236-3863	C- / 4.0	5.19	5.08	15.80 /33	3.97 /43	7.02 /35	1.51	1.47
GI	BMO Balanced Allocation R6	BGRQX	B-	(800) 236-3863	C / 4.5	5.35	5.35	16.58 /37	4.58 /50	7.40 /37	2.28	0.82
GI	BMO Balanced Allocation Y	BGRYX	C+	(800) 236-3863	C- / 4.2	5.18	5.07	16.03 /34	4.18 /45	7.15 /36	1.82	1.22
AA	BMO Conservative Allocation Fund	BDVSX	C+	(800) 236-3863	D+ / 2.4	2.91	1.86	9.68 /11	3.22 /34	4.34 /17	2.93	0.85
AA	BMO Conservative Allocation I	BDVIX	C+	(800) 236-3863	D+ / 2.3	2.87	1.72	9.53 /11	3.05 /32	4.24 /16	2.78	1.00
AA	BMO Conservative Allocation R3	BDVRX	C	(800) 236-3863	D / 2.0	2.65	1.39	8.95 / 9	2.58 /28	3.95 /15	2.26	1.50
AA	BMO Conservative Allocation Y	BDVYX	C	(800) 236-3863	D / 2.1	2.74	1.58	9.16 /10	2.83 /30	4.10 /16	2.45	1.25
FO	BMO Disciplined International Eq I	BDIQX	U	(800) 236-3863	U /	8.56	6.75	13.63 /24	--	--	2.84	1.20
IN	BMO Dividend Income A	BADIX	A	(800) 236-3863	B / 8.2	7.06	10.86	25.27 /74	9.62 /91	12.26 /77	1.99	1.08
IN	BMO Dividend Income I	MDIVX	A	(800) 236-3863	A- / 9.2	7.17	11.05	25.51 /75	9.93 /93	12.67 /81	2.30	0.83
GL	BMO Global Low Volatility Equity A	BAEGX	C+	(800) 236-3863	C- / 3.2	5.27	0.51	12.86 /21	6.48 /68	--	1.33	1.64
GL	BMO Global Low Volatility Equity I	BGLBX	B-	(800) 236-3863	C / 4.3	5.28	0.54	13.05 /22	6.71 /70	--	1.58	1.39
GI	BMO Growth Allocation I	BABHX	B-	(800) 236-3863	C+ / 5.6	6.51	7.07	19.83 /51	5.04 /55	8.78 /49	1.49	1.09
GI	BMO Growth Allocation R3	BABRX	B-	(800) 236-3863	C / 5.2	6.44	6.88	19.38 /49	4.59 /50	8.50 /46	0.82	1.59
GI	BMO Growth Allocation R6	BABQX	B-	(800) 236-3863	C+ / 5.8	6.58	7.14	20.03 /52	5.19 /56	8.87 /49	1.64	0.94
GI	BMO Growth Allocation Y	BABYX	B-	(800) 236-3863	C / 5.4	6.51	6.95	19.57 /50	4.81 /52	8.64 /47	1.18	1.34
GI	BMO In-Retirement R3	BTRRX	C-	(800) 236-3863	D+ / 2.5	3.64	2.67	11.05 /15	3.05 /32	5.38 /24	2.00	2.13
GI	BMO In-Retirement R6	BTRTX	C-	(800) 236-3863	C- / 3.0	3.81	2.94	11.71 /17	3.73 /40	5.86 /27	2.88	1.48
GI	BMO In-Retirement Y	BTRYX	C-	(800) 236-3863	D+ / 2.7	3.64	2.66	11.17 /15	3.30 /35	5.55 /25	2.41	1.88
GI	BMO Large Cap Value A	BALVX	A-	(800) 236-3863	B / 8.0	8.28	12.70	25.45 /75	8.51 /83	13.10 /85	1.31	1.03
GI	BMO Large Cap Value I	MLVIX	B+	(800) 236-3863	A- / 9.0	8.33	12.82	25.82 /76	8.79 /85	13.52 /89	1.59	0.78
GI	BMO Large Cap Value Y	MREIX	B	(800) 236-3863	B+ / 8.8	8.28	12.70	25.45 /75	8.53 /83	13.22 /86	1.37	1.03
GR	BMO Large-Cap Growth A	BALGX	A+	(800) 236-3863	A- / 9.1	9.67	10.88	22.99 /67	11.43 /98	14.75 /96	0.18	1.06
GR	BMO Large-Cap Growth I	MLCIX	B	(800) 236-3863	A+ / 9.6	9.71	11.06	23.25 /67	11.72 /98	15.16 /97	0.41	0.81
GR	BMO Large-Cap Growth Y	MASTX	B	(800) 236-3863	A+ / 9.6	9.67	10.88	22.99 /67	11.45 /98	14.88 /97	0.19	1.06
EM	BMO LGM Emg Mkts Eqty A	BAEMX	D	(800) 236-3863	D / 2.0	6.62	-4.01	16.38 /36	3.61 /38	1.20 / 6	0.45	1.64
EM	BMO LGM Emg Mkts Eqty I	MIEMX	D	(800) 236-3863	D+ / 2.9	6.62	-3.90	16.64 /37	3.88 /41	1.56 / 7	0.78	1.39
GR	BMO Low Volatility Equity A	BLVAX	B	(800) 236-3863	C+ / 6.8	7.45	5.34	15.53 /32	10.03 /93	--	1.21	1.06
GR	BMO Low Volatility Equity I	MLVEX	A+	(800) 236-3863	B / 7.9	7.47	5.44	15.88 /34	10.39 /95	--	1.45	0.81
MC	BMO Mid-Cap Growth A	BGMAX	D+	(800) 236-3863	C- / 3.6	7.97	9.63	25.62 /75	1.32 /20	7.56 /39	0.13	1.30
MC	BMO Mid-Cap Growth I	MRMIX	E+	(800) 236-3863	C / 4.8	8.02	9.77	25.83 /76	1.59 /21	7.94 /42	0.28	1.05
MC	BMO Mid-Cap Growth R-3	BMGDX	C-	(800) 236-3863	C / 4.3	7.92	9.46	25.20 /74	1.06 /19	7.28 /36	0.00	1.55
MC	BMO Mid-Cap Growth R-6	BMGGX	C	(800) 236-3863	C / 5.0	8.13	9.87	26.04 /76	1.72 /22	7.91 /41	0.44	0.90
MC	BMO Mid-Cap Growth Y	MRMSX	E+	(800) 236-3863	C / 4.6	7.97	9.63	25.62 /75	1.34 /20	7.68 /40	0.14	1.30
MC	BMO Mid-Cap Value A	BAMCX	A-	(800) 236-3863	B / 8.2	6.05	12.50	32.04 /90	8.13 /80	13.34 /87	0.69	1.23
MC	BMO Mid-Cap Value I	MRVIX	C	(800) 236-3863	A- / 9.2	6.15	12.62	32.40 /91	8.41 /82	13.75 /91	0.90	0.98
MC	BMO Mid-Cap Value R-3	BMVDX	A	(800) 236-3863	B+ / 8.9	6.02	12.41	31.83 /90	7.86 /78	13.06 /84	0.49	1.48
MC	BMO Mid-Cap Value R-6	BMVGX	A+	(800) 236-3863	A / 9.3	6.19	12.73	32.59 /91	8.53 /83	13.71 /91	1.02	0.83
MC	BMO Mid-Cap Value Y	MRVEX	C	(800) 236-3863	A- / 9.0	6.05	12.50	32.04 /90	8.15 /80	13.47 /89	0.71	1.23
GI	BMO Moderate Allocation Fund Y	BMBYX	C+	(800) 236-3863	C- / 3.1	4.07	3.43	12.71 /21	3.56 /38	5.65 /26	2.22	1.28
GI	BMO Moderate Allocation I	BMBHX	B-	(800) 236-3863	C- / 3.3	4.08	3.54	12.95 /21	3.80 /40	5.80 /27	2.53	1.03
GI	BMO Moderate Allocation R3	BMBQX	C+	(800) 236-3863	D+ / 2.9	3.85	3.21	12.34 /19	3.29 /35	5.49 /25	2.01	1.53
GI	BMO Moderate Allocation R6	BMBTX	B-	(800) 236-3863	C- / 3.3	4.06	3.52	13.04 /22	3.91 /42	5.87 /27	2.71	0.88
FO	BMO Pyrford International Stock A	BPIAX	D	(800) 236-3863	D- / 1.0	6.76	1.24	11.79 /17	0.14 /14	5.13 /22	1.95	1.31
FO	BMO Pyrford International Stock I	MISNX	D	(800) 236-3863	D / 1.6	6.89	1.38	12.01 /18	0.41 /15	5.54 /25	2.26	1.06
FO	BMO Pyrford International Stock R3	BISDX	D	(800) 236-3863	D- / 1.2	6.65	1.13	11.47 /16	-0.11 /13	4.87 /20	1.79	1.56
FO	BMO Pyrford International Stock R6	BISGX	D+	(800) 236-3863	D / 1.8	6.88	1.46	12.19 /19	0.52 /16	5.48 /25	2.42	0.91
FO	BMO Pyrford International Stock Y	MISYX	D	(800) 236-3863	D- / 1.5	6.76	1.24	11.79 /17	0.16 /14	5.25 /23	2.05	1.31
SC	BMO Small-Cap Core A	BCCAX	A	(800) 236-3863	A / 9.5	6.88	15.56	33.04 /92	10.31 /95	--	0.07	2.54
SC	BMO Small-Cap Core I	BSCNX	A+	(800) 236-3863	A+ / 9.8	6.90	15.63	33.39 /92	10.62 /96	--	0.28	2.29
SC	BMO Small-Cap Growth I	MSGIX	E-	(800) 236-3863	D / 1.9	6.77	8.12	29.56 /85	-1.14 / 9	7.89 /41	0.00	0.92

• Denotes fund is closed to new investors
* Denotes fund is included in Section II

www.thestreetratings.com

RISK Risk Rating/Pts	3 Year Standard Deviation	Beta	NET ASSETS NAV As of 2/28/17	Total $(Mil)	ASSET Cash %	Stocks %	Bonds %	Other %	Portfolio Turnover Ratio	BULL/BEAR Last Bull Market Return	Last Bear Market Return	FUND MANAGER Manager Quality Pct	Manager Tenure (Years)	MINIMUMS Initial Purch. $	Additional Purch. $	LOADS Front End Load	Back End Load
B /8.3	7.3	0.68	9.19	65	9	62	27	2	33	63.5	-13.8	40	3	2,000,000	0	0.0	0.0
B /8.2	7.3	0.68	9.20	27	9	62	27	2	33	61.3	-13.8	34	3	0	0	0.0	0.0
B /8.3	7.3	0.69	9.19	220	9	62	27	2	33	64.1	-13.8	41	3	0	0	0.0	0.0
B /8.2	7.3	0.68	9.19	102	9	62	27	2	33	62.2	-13.8	36	3	1,000	50	0.0	0.0
B+/9.2	3.8	0.55	9.71	88	10	21	68	1	31	34.2	-5.4	63	3	0	0	0.0	0.0
B+/9.2	3.9	0.56	9.70	30	10	21	68	1	31	33.5	-5.4	61	3	2,000,000	0	0.0	0.0
B+/9.2	3.9	0.56	9.71	5	10	21	68	1	31	31.7	-5.4	54	3	0	0	0.0	0.0
B+/9.2	3.8	0.55	9.71	17	10	21	68	1	31	32.6	-5.4	58	3	1,000	50	0.0	0.0
U /	N/A	N/A	9.93	58	0	0	0	100	64	N/A	N/A	N/A	2	1,000,000	0	0.0	2.0
B- /7.3	10.6	1.00	14.08	84	2	97	0	1	51	N/A	N/A	63	4	1,000	50	5.0	0.0
C+ /6.0	10.6	1.00	14.11	37	2	97	0	1	51	N/A	N/A	67	4	1,000,000	0	0.0	0.0
B /8.7	8.1	0.53	12.41	1	0	0	0	100	36	N/A	N/A	97	4	1,000	50	5.0	2.0
B /8.6	8.1	0.53	12.43	46	0	0	0	100	36	N/A	N/A	97	4	1,000,000	0	0.0	2.0
B- /7.6	9.2	0.87	9.65	10	3	85	11	1	38	79.9	-17.5	24	3	2,000,000	0	0.0	0.0
B- /7.5	9.3	0.88	9.67	20	3	85	11	1	38	77.6	-17.5	20	3	0	0	0.0	0.0
B- /7.6	9.2	0.87	9.65	90	3	85	11	1	38	80.7	-17.5	26	3	0	0	0.0	0.0
B- /7.5	9.3	0.88	9.66	19	3	85	11	1	38	78.8	-17.5	22	3	1,000	50	0.0	0.0
C+ /6.8	4.8	0.42	9.09	1	8	36	55	1	44	46.9	-11.0	58	4	0	0	0.0	0.0
C+ /6.6	4.8	0.42	9.04	12	8	36	55	1	44	50.3	-11.0	66	4	0	0	0.0	0.0
C+ /6.7	4.8	0.42	9.05	3	8	36	55	1	44	48.1	-11.0	61	4	1,000	50	0.0	0.0
C+ /6.9	10.5	0.96	15.71	N/A	1	97	0	2	60	125.6	-19.0	54	5	1,000	50	5.0	0.0
C /4.8	10.5	0.97	15.73	157	1	97	0	2	60	130.2	-18.8	58	5	1,000,000	0	0.0	0.0
C /4.8	10.5	0.96	15.71	186	1	97	0	2	60	127.1	-18.9	55	5	1,000	50	0.0	0.0
C+ /6.5	11.2	1.03	16.00	N/A	1	97	0	2	70	145.4	-18.6	77	5	1,000	50	5.0	0.0
C- /3.9	11.2	1.03	16.13	108	1	97	0	2	70	150.4	-18.4	79	5	1,000,000	0	0.0	0.0
C- /3.9	11.2	1.03	16.00	185	1	97	0	2	70	147.0	-18.5	77	5	1,000	50	0.0	0.0
C+ /6.3	12.6	0.64	13.41	50	1	98	0	1	24	22.9	-27.5	88	6	1,000	50	5.0	2.0
C /5.4	12.5	0.64	13.42	92	1	98	0	1	24	25.3	-27.3	89	6	1,000,000	0	0.0	2.0
B /8.8	7.9	0.66	14.25	31	0	98	0	2	40	N/A	N/A	90	5	1,000	50	5.0	0.0
B /8.2	8.0	0.67	14.30	134	0	98	0	2	40	N/A	N/A	91	5	1,000,000	0	0.0	0.0
C+ /5.6	13.7	1.05	13.89	N/A	3	96	0	1	59	85.8	-25.9	3	1	1,000	50	5.0	0.0
E+ /0.8	13.7	1.05	14.43	32	3	96	0	1	59	89.5	-25.7	4	1	1,000,000	0	0.0	0.0
C+ /5.6	13.7	1.04	14.21	N/A	3	96	0	1	59	83.2	-25.9	3	1	0	0	0.0	0.0
C+ /5.6	13.7	1.04	14.49	N/A	3	96	0	1	59	89.1	-25.8	4	1	0	0	0.0	0.0
E+ /0.7	13.7	1.05	13.89	88	3	96	0	1	59	87.0	-25.8	3	1	1,000	50	0.0	0.0
C+ /6.5	12.8	1.01	11.87	N/A	1	97	0	2	24	135.2	-24.3	55	1	1,000	50	5.0	0.0
D /1.7	12.8	1.02	11.84	69	1	97	0	2	24	139.9	-24.1	59	1	1,000,000	0	0.0	0.0
C+ /6.5	12.8	1.02	11.82	N/A	1	97	0	2	24	132.1	-24.4	52	1	0	0	0.0	0.0
C+ /6.5	12.8	1.02	11.84	13	1	97	0	2	24	139.3	-24.2	60	1	0	0	0.0	0.0
D /1.8	12.8	1.01	11.87	148	1	97	0	2	24	136.8	-24.2	56	1	1,000	50	0.0	0.0
B+/9.2	5.5	0.50	9.69	12	10	41	48	1	38	46.9	-9.6	53	3	1,000	50	0.0	0.0
B+/9.2	5.5	0.50	9.68	12	10	41	48	1	38	47.9	-9.6	57	3	2,000,000	0	0.0	0.0
B+/9.2	5.5	0.50	9.69	13	10	41	48	1	38	45.8	-9.6	50	3	0	0	0.0	0.0
B+/9.2	5.5	0.50	9.67	90	10	41	48	1	38	48.4	-9.6	58	3	0	0	0.0	0.0
B- /7.1	10.0	0.76	12.07	N/A	3	96	0	1	12	N/A	N/A	76	6	1,000	50	5.0	2.0
C+ /6.3	10.0	0.76	12.10	517	3	96	0	1	12	N/A	N/A	78	6	1,000,000	0	0.0	2.0
B- /7.1	10.0	0.76	12.09	N/A	3	96	0	1	12	N/A	N/A	74	6	0	0	0.0	0.0
B- /7.1	9.9	0.76	12.10	34	3	96	0	1	12	N/A	N/A	78	6	0	0	0.0	0.0
C+ /6.4	10.0	0.76	12.07	100	3	96	0	1	12	N/A	N/A	76	6	1,000	50	0.0	2.0
C+ /6.0	14.5	0.89	13.16	1	1	98	0	1	70	N/A	N/A	93	4	1,000	50	5.0	0.0
C+ /6.0	14.5	0.89	13.22	18	1	98	0	1	70	N/A	N/A	94	4	1,000,000	0	0.0	0.0
D- /1.3	18.1	1.08	17.97	83	3	95	1	1	63	97.3	-29.2	3	1	1,000,000	0	0.0	0.0

Fund Type	Fund Name	Ticker Symbol	Overall Investment Rating	Phone	Performance Rating/Pts	3 Mo	6 Mo	1Yr / Pct	3Yr / Pct	5Yr / Pct	Dividend Yield	Expense Ratio
	99 Pct = Best 0 Pct = Worst							Total Return % through 2/28/17	Annualized		Incl. in Returns	
SC	BMO Small-Cap Growth Y	MRSCX	E-	(800) 236-3863	D / 1.8	6.62	7.95	29.10 /84	-1.40 / 8	7.61 /39	0.00	1.17
SC	BMO Small-Cap Value A	BACVX	B	(800) 236-3863	B / 7.7	4.57	14.60	35.29 /94	6.28 /67	13.35 /87	0.24	1.40
SC	BMO Small-Cap Value I	MRSNX	B	(800) 236-3863	B+ / 8.8	4.70	14.86	35.66 /95	6.58 /69	13.78 /91	0.55	1.15
SC	BMO Small-Cap Value R3	BSVDX	B+	(800) 236-3863	B+ / 8.4	4.56	14.59	35.03 /94	6.04 /64	13.08 /85	0.25	1.65
SC	BMO Small-Cap Value R6	BSVGX	A-	(800) 236-3863	B+ / 8.9	4.66	14.95	35.91 /95	6.73 /70	13.75 /91	0.67	1.00
GI	BMO Target Retirement 2015 R3	BRTCX	C+	(800) 236-3863	C- / 3.3	4.26	3.48	13.03 /22	3.83 /41	---	1.80	4.99
GI	BMO Target Retirement 2015 R6	BRTDX	B	(800) 236-3863	C- / 3.9	4.51	3.93	13.79 /24	4.56 /49	---	2.41	4.34
GI	BMO Target Retirement 2015 Y	BRTAX	B-	(800) 236-3863	C- / 3.5	4.32	3.64	13.31 /23	4.09 /44	---	1.95	4.74
GI	BMO Target Retirement 2020 R3	BTRFX	C	(800) 236-3863	C- / 3.8	5.06	4.44	15.27 /31	3.82 /41	7.01 /35	1.51	1.58
GI	BMO Target Retirement 2020 R6	BTRGX	C	(800) 236-3863	C / 4.3	5.30	4.89	16.12 /35	4.51 /49	7.51 /38	2.19	0.93
GI	BMO Target Retirement 2020 Y	BTRDX	C	(800) 236-3863	C- / 4.0	5.13	4.62	15.60 /32	4.08 /44	7.19 /36	1.75	1.33
GI	BMO Target Retirement 2025 R3	BRTGX	C+	(800) 236-3863	C / 4.3	5.59	5.19	16.89 /38	4.20 /45	---	1.33	1.96
GI	BMO Target Retirement 2025 R6	BRTHX	B	(800) 236-3863	C / 5.0	5.77	5.57	17.66 /41	4.89 /53	---	1.89	1.31
GI	BMO Target Retirement 2025 Y	BRTEX	B-	(800) 236-3863	C / 4.6	5.61	5.32	17.09 /39	4.50 /49	---	1.46	1.71
GI	BMO Target Retirement 2030 R3	BTRKX	C+	(800) 236-3863	C / 4.6	5.97	5.77	18.04 /43	4.16 /45	8.20 /44	1.10	1.58
GI	BMO Target Retirement 2030 R6	BTRLX	C+	(800) 236-3863	C / 5.2	6.23	6.13	18.89 /47	4.83 /52	8.70 /48	1.78	0.93
GI	BMO Target Retirement 2030 Y	BTRHX	C+	(800) 236-3863	C / 4.8	6.05	5.85	18.35 /44	4.40 /47	8.38 /45	1.35	1.33
GI	BMO Target Retirement 2035 R3	BRTKX	C+	(800) 236-3863	C / 5.0	6.46	6.26	19.23 /48	4.27 /46	---	1.07	1.96
GI	BMO Target Retirement 2035 R6	BRTLX	B-	(800) 236-3863	C / 5.5	6.54	6.54	19.99 /52	4.96 /54	---	1.62	1.31
GI	BMO Target Retirement 2035 Y	BRTIX	B-	(800) 236-3863	C / 5.2	6.55	6.35	19.49 /49	4.58 /50	---	1.26	1.71
GI	BMO Target Retirement 2040 R3	BTRPX	C	(800) 236-3863	C / 5.2	6.67	6.57	20.05 /52	4.42 /48	8.86 /49	0.85	1.68
GI	BMO Target Retirement 2040 R6	BTRQX	C+	(800) 236-3863	C+ / 5.8	6.84	6.84	20.70 /56	5.06 /55	9.34 /53	1.62	1.03
GI	BMO Target Retirement 2040 Y	BTRMX	C+	(800) 236-3863	C / 5.5	6.76	6.76	20.40 /54	4.66 /50	9.05 /51	1.18	1.43
GI	BMO Target Retirement 2045 R3	BRTPX	B-	(800) 236-3863	C+ / 5.6	6.84	6.64	20.37 /54	4.92 /53	---	0.99	2.47
GI	BMO Target Retirement 2045 R6	BRTQX	B-	(800) 236-3863	C+ / 6.2	7.02	7.02	21.14 /58	5.61 /61	---	1.55	1.82
GI	BMO Target Retirement 2045 Y	BRTMX	B-	(800) 236-3863	C+ / 5.8	6.81	6.71	20.63 /56	5.16 /56	---	1.16	2.22
GI	BMO Target Retirement 2050 R3	BTRWX	C+	(800) 236-3863	C / 5.3	6.74	6.55	20.15 /53	4.46 /48	8.86 /49	0.93	1.83
GI	BMO Target Retirement 2050 R6	BTRZX	C+	(800) 236-3863	C+ / 5.9	6.94	6.94	21.03 /57	5.18 /56	9.37 /54	1.62	1.18
GI	BMO Target Retirement 2050 Y	BTRUX	C+	(800) 236-3863	C / 5.5	6.83	6.73	20.59 /55	4.76 /52	9.06 /51	1.10	1.58
GI	BMO Target Retirement 2055 R3	BRTTX	B-	(800) 236-3863	C+ / 5.6	6.69	6.60	20.17 /53	4.93 /53	---	0.96	4.28
GI	BMO Target Retirement 2055 R6	BRTUX	B-	(800) 236-3863	C+ / 6.2	6.96	6.96	20.93 /57	5.62 /61	---	1.43	3.63
GI	BMO Target Retirement 2055 Y	BRTRX	B-	(800) 236-3863	C+ / 5.8	6.90	6.70	20.59 /55	5.18 /56	---	0.99	4.03
GL	BNY Mellon Abs Insight Multi Str I	MAJIX	U	(800) 645-6561	U /	0.00	-0.40	-0.24 / 1	---	---	0.00	N/A
GL	BNY Mellon Abs Insight Multi Str Y	MAJYX	U	(800) 645-6561	U /	0.08	-0.32	-0.16 / 1	---	---	0.00	N/A
BA	BNY Mellon Asset Allocation Fund M	MPBLX	C	(800) 645-6561	C / 4.6	5.72	5.84	15.74 /33	4.66 /50	6.63 /32	1.71	0.97
BA	BNY Mellon Asset Allocation Inv	MIBLX	C	(800) 645-6561	C / 4.3	5.64	5.71	15.38 /32	4.42 /48	6.37 /31	1.51	1.22
EM	BNY Mellon Emerging Markets Inv	MIEGX	D	(800) 645-6561	C- / 3.7	8.71	3.74	28.29 /82	0.16 /14	-1.84 / 3	0.53	1.70
EM	BNY Mellon Emerging Markets M	MEMKX	D	(800) 645-6561	C- / 3.9	8.71	3.86	28.53 /83	0.39 /15	-1.58 / 3	0.75	1.45
GR	BNY Mellon Focused Eqty Opps Inv	MFOIX	B	(800) 645-6561	A+ / 9.6	10.52	13.03	29.86 /86	9.23 /88	12.76 /82	0.95	1.12
GR	BNY Mellon Focused Eqty Opps M	MFOMX	B	(800) 645-6561	A+ / 9.6	10.61	13.18	30.17 /87	9.51 /90	13.05 /84	1.15	0.87
GI	BNY Mellon Income Stock Inv	MIISX	A-	(800) 645-6561	A+ / 9.6	7.95	11.74	28.56 /83	10.76 /97	14.50 /96	1.81	1.06
GI	BNY Mellon Income Stock M	MPISX	A	(800) 645-6561	A+ / 9.7	7.99	11.90	28.79 /83	11.08 /97	14.79 /96	2.07	0.81
FO	BNY Mellon International App Fd Inv	MARIX	D-	(800) 645-6561	D- / 1.3	7.54	4.77	16.47 /36	-0.83 /10	4.52 /18	2.04	1.17
FO	BNY Mellon International App Fd M	MPPMX	D-	(800) 645-6561	D- / 1.4	7.60	4.96	16.84 /38	-0.54 /11	4.79 /20	2.64	0.92
FO	BNY Mellon International Inv	MIINX	D-	(800) 645-6561	D- / 1.0	8.10	4.83	16.02 /34	-1.87 / 7	5.14 /22	1.59	1.28
FO	BNY Mellon International M	MPITX	D-	(800) 645-6561	D- / 1.1	8.06	4.88	16.28 /35	-1.64 / 8	5.42 /24	1.95	1.03
FO	BNY Mellon Internatl Eqty Inc Inv	MLIIX	D-	(800) 645-6561	D- / 1.4	7.37	5.39	18.65 /46	-0.86 /10	1.94 / 8	2.35	1.34
FO	BNY Mellon Internatl Eqty Inc M	MLIMX	D-	(800) 645-6561	D- / 1.5	7.47	5.53	18.95 /47	-0.65 /11	2.21 / 9	2.61	1.09
GR	BNY Mellon Large Cap Mkt Opps Inv	MMOIX	C	(800) 645-6561	B+ / 8.8	8.58	11.26	26.67 /78	8.39 /82	11.89 /73	0.86	1.26
GR	BNY Mellon Large Cap Mkt Opps M	MMOMX	C	(800) 645-6561	A- / 9.0	8.56	11.35	27.00 /79	8.68 /84	12.17 /76	1.44	1.02
GR	BNY Mellon Large Cap Stock Inv	MILCX	B-	(800) 645-6561	B+ / 8.7	8.47	10.90	21.90 /62	9.30 /89	12.02 /74	1.04	1.08
GR	BNY Mellon Large Cap Stock M	MPLCX	B	(800) 645-6561	B+ / 8.8	8.55	10.85	22.23 /63	9.51 /90	12.29 /77	1.26	0.83

● Denotes fund is closed to new investors

* Denotes fund is included in Section II

| RISK | 3 Year | | NET ASSETS | | ASSET | | | | Portfolio | BULL / BEAR | | FUND MANAGER | | MINIMUMS | | LOADS | |
Risk Rating/Pts	Standard Deviation	Beta	NAV As of 2/28/17	Total $(Mil)	Cash %	Stocks %	Bonds %	Other %	Turnover Ratio	Last Bull Market Return	Last Bear Market Return	Manager Quality Pct	Manager Tenure (Years)	Initial Purch. $	Additional Purch. $	Front End Load	Back End Load
D- / 1.3	18.1	1.08	17.39	105	3	95	1	1	63	94.6	-29.3	3	1	1,000	50	0.0	0.0
C+ / 5.8	15.9	0.98	13.66	45	3	95	1	1	39	131.2	-22.2	69	1	1,000	50	5.0	0.0
C / 4.5	15.9	0.97	13.83	23	3	95	1	1	39	136.1	-22.1	72	1	1,000,000	0	0.0	0.0
C+ / 5.8	15.9	0.97	13.66	N/A	3	95	1	1	39	128.3	-22.3	66	1	0	0	0.0	0.0
C+ / 5.8	15.9	0.98	13.88	2	3	95	1	1	39	135.6	-22.1	74	1	0	0	0.0	0.0
B+ / 9.1	5.9	0.54	10.82	N/A	8	48	43	1	49	N/A	N/A	52	4	0	0	0.0	0.0
B+ / 9.1	5.9	0.54	10.88	4	8	48	43	1	49	N/A	N/A	62	4	0	0	0.0	0.0
B+ / 9.1	5.9	0.54	10.83	1	8	48	43	1	49	N/A	N/A	56	4	1,000	50	0.0	0.0
B- / 7.0	6.9	0.64	10.01	10	7	59	32	2	39	63.9	-15.1	37	4	0	0	0.0	0.0
C+ / 6.8	6.9	0.64	9.99	61	7	59	32	2	39	67.7	-15.1	47	4	0	0	0.0	0.0
C+ / 6.9	6.9	0.64	9.99	17	7	59	32	2	39	65.3	-15.1	41	4	1,000	50	0.0	0.0
B / 8.0	7.7	0.72	10.89	1	7	69	23	1	33	N/A	N/A	32	4	0	0	0.0	0.0
B / 8.1	7.7	0.72	10.99	30	7	69	23	1	33	N/A	N/A	41	4	0	0	0.0	0.0
B / 8.1	7.7	0.72	10.94	1	7	69	23	1	33	N/A	N/A	35	4	1,000	50	0.0	0.0
C+ / 6.9	8.4	0.79	10.84	8	6	76	16	2	33	76.9	-18.0	24	4	0	0	0.0	0.0
C+ / 6.8	8.5	0.79	10.83	78	6	76	16	2	33	81.1	-18.0	31	4	0	0	0.0	0.0
C+ / 6.9	8.4	0.79	10.83	18	6	76	16	2	33	78.4	-18.0	27	4	1,000	50	0.0	0.0
B- / 7.5	9.1	0.85	10.88	1	6	83	10	1	29	N/A	N/A	20	4	0	0	0.0	0.0
B- / 7.5	9.1	0.85	10.97	32	6	83	10	1	29	N/A	N/A	26	4	0	0	0.0	0.0
B- / 7.5	9.1	0.85	10.93	1	6	83	10	1	29	N/A	N/A	22	4	1,000	50	0.0	0.0
C+ / 6.2	9.6	0.90	10.80	4	5	89	4	2	31	84.4	-19.2	17	4	0	0	0.0	0.0
C+ / 6.1	9.6	0.90	10.76	51	5	89	4	2	31	88.5	-19.2	22	4	0	0	0.0	0.0
C+ / 6.1	9.6	0.91	10.77	11	5	89	4	2	31	86.0	-19.2	18	4	1,000	50	0.0	0.0
B- / 7.3	9.6	0.90	11.07	1	6	89	4	1	32	N/A	N/A	20	4	0	0	0.0	0.0
B- / 7.3	9.6	0.90	11.16	16	6	89	4	1	32	N/A	N/A	27	4	0	0	0.0	0.0
B- / 7.3	9.6	0.90	11.11	1	6	89	4	1	32	N/A	N/A	23	4	1,000	50	0.0	0.0
C+ / 6.5	9.6	0.90	11.15	4	5	89	4	2	29	84.2	-19.2	17	4	0	0	0.0	0.0
C+ / 6.4	9.6	0.90	11.15	33	5	89	4	2	29	88.6	-19.2	23	4	0	0	0.0	0.0
C+ / 6.4	9.6	0.90	11.16	8	5	89	4	2	29	85.9	-19.2	19	4	1,000	50	0.0	0.0
B- / 7.3	9.6	0.90	11.04	1	6	88	4	2	38	N/A	N/A	21	4	0	0	0.0	0.0
B- / 7.3	9.5	0.89	11.14	8	6	88	4	2	38	N/A	N/A	28	4	0	0	0.0	0.0
B- / 7.3	9.6	0.90	11.10	1	6	88	4	2	38	N/A	N/A	23	4	1,000	50	0.0	0.0
U /	N/A	N/A	12.39	99	0	0	0	100	320	N/A	N/A	N/A	2	1,000	100	0.0	0.0
U /	N/A	N/A	12.40	200	0	0	0	100	320	N/A	N/A	N/A	2	1,000,000	0	0.0	0.0
C+ / 6.3	7.4	1.16	11.72	449	4	61	33	2	23	57.0	-15.0	25	4	10,000	100	0.0	0.0
C+ / 6.3	7.4	1.15	11.80	7	4	61	33	2	23	54.8	-15.1	24	4	10,000	100	0.0	0.0
C- / 4.2	16.3	0.98	9.49	14	0	98	0	2	104	13.3	-28.4	55	7	10,000	100	0.0	0.0
C- / 4.2	16.3	0.98	9.23	668	0	98	0	2	104	14.9	-28.4	58	7	10,000	100	0.0	0.0
C- / 3.6	12.9	1.18	14.99	5	0	99	0	1	48	126.3	-23.1	34	8	10,000	100	0.0	0.0
C- / 3.6	12.9	1.18	15.11	430	0	99	0	1	48	129.6	-23.1	37	8	10,000	100	0.0	0.0
C / 5.3	10.4	0.97	9.45	20	0	95	3	2	54	134.9	-16.2	77	6	10,000	100	0.0	0.0
C / 5.3	10.4	0.97	9.35	1,225	0	95	3	2	54	138.4	-16.1	79	6	10,000	100	0.0	0.0
C+ / 5.7	11.6	0.93	12.35	1	1	98	0	1	3	44.3	-24.4	66	8	10,000	100	0.0	0.0
C+ / 5.7	11.6	0.93	12.45	71	1	98	0	1	3	46.4	-24.3	70	8	10,000	100	0.0	0.0
C+ / 5.7	12.3	0.97	12.29	12	3	96	0	1	87	47.2	-25.1	52	15	10,000	100	0.0	0.0
C+ / 5.6	12.4	0.97	11.53	942	3	96	0	1	87	49.2	-25.0	56	15	10,000	100	0.0	0.0
C+ / 5.6	12.1	0.91	12.93	1	3	95	1	1	78	N/A	N/A	66	6	10,000	100	0.0	0.0
C / 5.5	12.1	0.90	12.80	317	3	95	1	1	78	N/A	N/A	68	6	10,000	100	0.0	0.0
D / 1.7	11.1	1.06	11.98	1	0	97	1	2	19	113.8	-19.6	39	7	10,000	100	0.0	0.0
D / 1.6	11.1	1.05	11.84	70	0	97	1	2	19	115.0	-19.5	44	7	10,000	100	0.0	0.0
C- / 4.1	10.7	1.02	6.01	11	0	99	0	1	50	113.2	-21.3	56	4	10,000	100	0.0	0.0
C- / 4.1	10.7	1.02	6.00	299	0	99	0	1	50	115.7	-21.2	59	4	10,000	100	0.0	0.0

99 Pct = Best
0 Pct = Worst

Fund Type	Fund Name	Ticker Symbol	Overall Investment Rating	Phone	Perfor-mance Rating/Pts	3 Mo	6 Mo	1Yr / Pct	3Yr / Pct	5Yr / Pct	Dividend Yield	Expense Ratio
MC	BNY Mellon MC Multi-Strategy Inv	MIMSX	B	(800) 645-6561	B / 7.6	6.58	9.25	26.33 /77	6.95 /72	11.68 /71	0.45	1.15
MC	BNY Mellon MC Mutli-Strategy M	MPMCX	B	(800) 645-6561	B / 7.8	6.63	9.33	26.59 /78	7.19 /73	11.94 /74	0.64	0.90
SC	BNY Mellon SC Multi-Strategy Inv	MISCX	B-	(800) 645-6561	B+ / 8.9	6.39	15.06	37.68 /96	5.95 /64	12.61 /80	0.00	1.30
SC	BNY Mellon SC Multi-Strategy M	MPSSX	B	(800) 645-6561	A- / 9.0	6.42	15.14	37.92 /96	6.18 /66	12.87 /82	0.00	1.05
GR	BNY Mellon Sm/Mid Cap Mlti-Str Inv	MMCIX	C	(800) 645-6561	B+ / 8.9	7.16	13.69	31.91 /90	7.43 /75	10.18 /60	0.00	1.05
GR	BNY Mellon Sm/Mid Cap Mlti-Str M	MMCMX	C	(800) 645-6561	A- / 9.1	7.23	13.95	32.36 /91	7.74 /77	10.47 /62	0.07	1.30
GR	BNY Mellon Tx Sens LC Mulit-Str Inv	MTSIX	B-	(800) 645-6561	B+ / 8.8	8.01	10.55	25.59 /75	8.93 /86	12.40 /78	1.21	1.15
GR	BNY Mellon Tx Sens LC Mulit-Str M	MTSMX	B	(800) 645-6561	A- / 9.0	8.08	10.67	25.88 /76	9.22 /88	12.37 /78	1.39	0.90
SC	Bogle Inv Mgt Small Cap Gr Inst	BOGIX	C-	(877) 264-5346	B / 7.6	4.50	13.52	34.84 /94	4.75 /51	13.58 /90	0.00	1.42
SC	Bogle Inv Mgt Small Cap Gr Inv	BOGLX	D+	(877) 264-5346	B- / 7.5	4.47	13.43	34.70 /94	4.64 /50	13.46 /88	0.00	1.42
FO	Boston Common International	BCAIX	D-	(877) 777-6944	E+ / 0.7	6.76	2.02	13.27 /23	-1.48 / 8	3.35 /12	1.54	1.12
GR	Boston Common US Equity	BCAMX	B-	(877) 777-6944	C+ / 6.9	7.91	6.51	19.93 /52	7.76 /77	--	0.80	1.40
GR	Boston Partners All Cap Val Inst	BPAIX	A+	(888) 261-4073	A+ / 9.6	6.02	10.79	30.42 /87	10.55 /96	15.06 /97	1.08	0.96
GR	Boston Partners All Cap Val Inv	BPAVX	A+	(888) 261-4073	A / 9.5	5.98	10.68	30.14 /87	10.29 /95	14.83 /97	0.86	1.21
GL	Boston Partners Glbl Lg/Sh Inst	BGLSX	C+	(888) 261-4073	D+ / 2.7	3.25	3.06	8.75 / 9	4.20 /45	--	0.21	2.99
GL	Boston Partners Glbl Lg/Sh Inv	BGRSX	U	(888) 261-4073	U /	3.19	2.90	8.40 / 8	--	--	0.13	3.24
GL	Boston Partners Global Eqty Inst	BPGIX	C+	(888) 261-4073	C+ / 6.2	6.72	6.99	22.99 /67	5.64 /61	10.90 /65	1.82	1.10
AA	● Boston Partners Lg/Sh Equity Inst	BPLSX	A-	(888) 261-4073	B / 7.9	3.26	10.45	20.66 /56	9.99 /93	8.43 /46	0.00	3.57
AA	● Boston Partners Lg/Sh Equity Inv	BPLEX	B+	(888) 261-4073	B / 7.7	3.22	10.32	20.35 /54	9.71 /92	8.17 /43	0.00	3.82
IN	● Boston Partners Lg/Sh Res Inst	BPIRX	C+	(888) 261-4073	C- / 3.7	3.37	4.60	12.03 /18	5.02 /54	7.92 /41	0.00	2.51
IN	● Boston Partners Lg/Sh Res Inv	BPRRX	C+	(888) 261-4073	C- / 3.4	3.30	4.47	11.69 /17	4.75 /51	7.63 /39	0.00	2.76
SC	Boston Partners Sm/Cp Val II Inst	BPSIX	A-	(888) 261-4073	A- / 9.1	4.35	12.52	35.85 /95	8.22 /81	13.86 /92	0.83	1.22
SC	Boston Partners Sm/Cp Val II Inv	BPSCX	A-	(888) 261-4073	A- / 9.0	4.26	12.39	35.48 /94	7.95 /79	13.58 /90	0.64	1.47
BA	Boston Trust Asset Management	BTBFX	B-	(800) 282-8782	C+ / 6.3	5.60	5.28	15.51 /32	7.67 /77	9.17 /52	1.04	0.94
IN	Boston Trust Equity	BTEFX	B+	(800) 282-8782	B / 7.8	7.07	8.10	20.94 /57	8.53 /83	10.93 /65	0.90	0.96
MC	Boston Trust Mid Cap	BTMFX	B+	(800) 282-8782	B / 7.9	7.00	7.34	21.21 /58	8.90 /86	11.22 /68	0.76	1.03
SC	● Boston Trust Small Cap	BOSOX	C+	(800) 282-8782	B / 7.9	5.53	10.56	27.49 /80	7.21 /73	10.63 /63	0.91	1.08
GL	Boston Trust SMID Cap	BTSMX	A-	(800) 282-8782	A- / 9.0	7.70	12.14	29.60 /85	8.19 /80	11.27 /68	1.02	1.73
MC	Boyar Value Fund	BOYAX	B-	(800) 266-5566	C / 5.5	5.22	7.94	16.60 /37	8.04 /79	12.58 /80	0.13	2.14
EN	BP Capital TwinLine Energy A	BPEAX	E+	(855) 402-7227	C / 5.4	-0.83	9.87	53.97 /99	0.23 /14	--	0.00	1.88
EN	BP Capital TwinLine Energy I	BPEIX	D	(855) 402-7227	C+ / 6.8	-0.78	10.06	54.48 /99	0.48 /16	--	0.16	1.55
EN	BP Capital TwinLine MLP A	BPMAX	E	(855) 402-7227	D / 1.9	5.72	7.86	40.92 /98	-0.90 /10	--	5.64	8.04
EN	BP Capital TwinLine MLP I	BPMIX	E	(855) 402-7227	C- / 3.0	5.87	7.99	41.33 /98	-0.63 /11	--	5.93	7.79
FS	Braddock Multi-Strategy Income Inst	BDKNX	U	(800) 207-7108	U /	2.33	2.99	8.77 / 9	--	--	5.78	N/A
FO	Bradesco Latin American Eq Inst	BDEIX	E-	(888) 739-1390	D / 1.7	12.83	9.02	43.06 /98	-3.71 / 3	--	0.36	2.99
EM	Brandes Emerging Markets Value A	BEMAX	D	(800) 237-7119	C / 4.5	8.97	7.95	37.30 /96	0.71 /17	0.44 / 5	1.77	1.39
EM	Brandes Emerging Markets Value C	BEMCX	E+	(800) 237-7119	C- / 3.1	8.82	7.59	36.42 /95	-0.02 /13	--	1.07	2.14
EM	Brandes Emerging Markets Value I	BEMIX	D+	(800) 237-7119	C+ / 6.0	9.12	8.16	37.77 /96	0.98 /18	0.70 / 6	2.05	1.19
EM	Brandes Emerging Markets Value R6	BEMRX	U	(800) 237-7119	U /	9.13	8.45	--	--	--	0.00	N/A
GL	Brandes Global Equity A	BGEAX	D+	(800) 237-7119	C- / 3.5	6.55	9.08	21.59 /60	2.66 /29	8.06 /43	1.74	1.67
GL	Brandes Global Equity C	BGVCX	D+	(800) 237-7119	C- / 4.0	6.34	8.63	20.70 /56	1.89 /23	--	1.14	2.42
GL	Brandes Global Equity I	BGVIX	C-	(800) 237-7119	C / 4.9	6.60	9.21	21.96 /62	2.91 /31	8.34 /45	2.00	1.47
FO	Brandes Intl Equity Fund A	BIEAX	D	(800) 237-7119	D / 1.9	6.21	5.59	18.08 /43	0.70 /17	5.72 /26	3.16	1.18
FO	Brandes Intl Equity Fund C	BIECX	D	(800) 237-7119	D- / 1.5	6.00	5.18	17.14 /39	-0.07 /13	--	2.86	1.93
FO	Brandes Intl Equity Fund I	BIIEX	D+	(800) 237-7119	D+ / 2.8	6.22	5.63	18.22 /44	0.87 /17	5.89 /28	3.48	1.00
FO	Brandes Intl Small Cap Equity A	BISAX	C	(800) 237-7119	C / 4.6	8.14	6.88	18.26 /44	5.45 /59	10.39 /61	1.64	1.40
FO	Brandes Intl Small Cap Equity C	BINCX	C+	(800) 237-7119	C / 5.2	7.89	6.41	17.38 /40	4.68 /51	--	1.47	2.07
FO	Brandes Intl Small Cap Equity I	BISMX	C+	(800) 237-7119	C+ / 6.0	8.24	6.95	18.49 /45	5.68 /61	10.65 /63	1.89	1.15
FO	Brandes Intl Small Cap Equity R6	BISRX	U	(800) 237-7119	U /	8.25	7.05	--	--	--	0.00	N/A
GR	Bread & Butter Fund Inc	BABFX	D+	(888) 476-8585	D / 1.9	5.86	2.79	12.68 /20	0.51 /16	3.98 /15	0.00	2.89
GL	Bretton	BRTNX	B+	(800) 231-2901	B- / 7.1	6.37	11.23	23.62 /69	6.13 /65	9.98 /58	0.00	1.50
FO	Bridge Builder International Equity	BBIEX	U	(855) 823-3611	U /	6.71	3.25	15.15 /30	--	--	1.33	0.70

● Denotes fund is closed to new investors
* Denotes fund is included in Section II

www.thestreetratings.com

Risk Rating/Pts	3 Year Standard Deviation	Beta	NAV As of 2/28/17	Total $(Mil)	Cash %	Stocks %	Bonds %	Other %	Portfolio Turnover Ratio	Last Bull Market Return	Last Bear Market Return	Manager Quality Pct	Manager Tenure (Years)	Initial Purch. $	Additional Purch. $	Front End Load	Back End Load
C / 5.4	11.8	0.94	15.92	72	0	98	0	2	75	114.5	-26.8	49	5	10,000	100	0.0	0.0
C / 5.4	11.8	0.94	16.16	2,623	0	98	0	2	75	117.2	-26.7	52	5	10,000	100	0.0	0.0
C- / 4.1	16.7	1.04	18.39	18	0	97	1	2	101	128.0	-28.0	60	5	10,000	100	0.0	0.0
C- / 4.1	16.7	1.04	19.14	484	0	97	1	2	101	131.0	-27.9	63	5	10,000	100	0.0	0.0
D / 2.0	13.8	1.11	13.95	1	0	97	1	2	99	92.5	-27.7	23	3	10,000	100	0.0	0.0
D / 2.0	13.8	1.11	14.12	329	0	97	1	2	99	95.3	-27.6	26	3	10,000	100	0.0	0.0
C- / 4.1	10.7	1.03	15.93	5	0	98	0	2	14	116.8	-19.2	51	7	10,000	100	0.0	0.0
C- / 4.1	10.7	1.03	15.59	337	0	98	0	2	14	116.7	-18.5	55	7	10,000	100	0.0	0.0
D / 1.8	17.4	1.01	30.65	38	0	98	1	1	380	145.7	-26.8	46	18	1,000,000	0	0.0	0.0
D / 1.7	17.5	1.02	29.89	76	0	98	1	1	380	144.3	-26.8	45	18	10,000	0	0.0	0.0
C+ / 5.7	12.1	0.96	25.78	200	2	97	0	1	32	37.6	-22.8	58	4	100,000	1,000	0.0	2.0
B- / 7.4	9.9	0.93	38.57	30	1	98	0	1	29	N/A	N/A	49	5	100,000	1,000	0.0	2.0
C+ / 6.3	11.9	1.10	24.66	1,174	0	99	0	1	30	149.3	-19.9	62	10	100,000	5,000	0.0	0.0
C+ / 6.3	11.9	1.09	24.56	393	0	99	0	1	30	146.7	-20.1	59	10	2,500	100	0.0	0.0
B+ / 9.8	5.0	0.32	11.21	842	0	0	0	100	137	N/A	N/A	94	3	100,000	5,000	0.0	1.0
U /	N/A	N/A	11.14	33	0	0	0	100	137	N/A	N/A	N/A	3	2,500	100	0.0	1.0
C+ / 6.8	10.8	0.80	16.38	456	5	94	0	1	80	N/A	N/A	96	6	100,000	5,000	0.0	1.0
C+ / 6.7	9.4	0.35	22.19	889	76	23	0	1	72	68.8	-4.2	98	20	100,000	5,000	0.0	2.0
C+ / 6.5	9.4	0.35	20.52	112	76	23	0	1	72	66.6	-4.2	98	20	2,500	100	0.0	2.0
B / 8.5	6.5	0.58	15.93	6,275	52	47	0	1	53	68.2	-10.5	62	7	100,000	5,000	0.0	1.0
B / 8.5	6.6	0.58	15.67	232	52	47	0	1	53	65.9	-10.5	59	7	2,500	100	0.0	1.0
C+ / 5.7	13.9	0.86	25.32	347	1	97	0	2	29	141.5	-23.5	87	19	100,000	5,000	0.0	1.0
C+ / 5.7	13.9	0.86	24.29	133	1	97	0	2	29	138.3	-23.7	86	19	2,500	100	0.0	1.0
B- / 7.6	7.1	1.11	42.97	424	1	76	21	2	12	78.8	-10.2	67	22	100,000	1,000	0.0	0.0
C+ / 6.6	9.3	0.87	21.08	124	0	99	0	1	18	103.4	-15.7	67	14	100,000	1,000	0.0	0.0
C+ / 6.3	9.9	0.79	16.14	53	0	98	1	1	21	109.3	-18.0	82	N/A	100,000	1,000	0.0	0.0
C- / 4.0	13.5	0.82	14.62	343	0	98	1	1	37	106.0	-21.9	84	12	100,000	1,000	0.0	0.0
C+ / 5.7	12.7	0.62	14.10	7	0	99	0	1	50	N/A	N/A	98	6	1,000,000	1,000	0.0	0.0
B- / 7.6	9.7	0.69	24.14	25	13	85	1	1	7	120.0	-16.9	83	19	5,000	1,000	5.0	2.0
E+ / 0.7	24.2	1.16	20.37	19	20	79	0	1	79	N/A	N/A	97	4	3,000	100	5.8	0.0
E+ / 0.7	24.2	1.16	20.48	119	20	79	0	1	79	N/A	N/A	98	4	250,000	100	0.0	0.0
D / 2.2	19.9	0.69	17.21	13	77	19	3	1	96	N/A	N/A	89	4	3,000	100	5.8	0.0
D / 2.2	19.9	0.69	17.36	64	77	19	3	1	96	N/A	N/A	90	4	250,000	100	0.0	0.0
U /	N/A	N/A	10.13	71	0	0	0	100	0	N/A	N/A	N/A	2	1,000,000	100,000	0.0	0.0
E- / 0.0	25.4	1.12	8.35	15	0	0	0	100	77	N/A	N/A	28	4	1,000,000	0	0.0	2.0
D+ / 2.9	20.4	1.16	8.38	326	2	97	0	1	26	26.1	-26.2	59	6	2,500	500	5.8	0.0
D+ / 2.9	20.4	1.16	8.32	23	2	97	0	1	26	N/A	N/A	49	6	2,500	500	0.0	0.0
D+ / 2.9	20.4	1.16	8.42	977	2	97	0	1	26	27.9	-26.1	62	6	100,000	500	0.0	0.0
U /	N/A	N/A	8.43	27	2	97	0	1	26	N/A	N/A	N/A	6	0	0	0.0	0.0
C / 5.1	10.6	0.81	22.83	8	8	91	0	1	16	68.9	-19.1	89	4	2,500	500	5.8	0.0
C / 5.1	10.6	0.81	22.67	2	8	91	0	1	16	N/A	N/A	86	4	2,500	500	0.0	0.0
C / 5.1	10.6	0.81	22.98	57	8	91	0	1	16	71.2	-19.0	90	4	100,000	500	0.0	0.0
C+ / 5.8	12.2	0.94	16.20	18	6	93	0	1	18	49.9	-20.6	80	20	2,500	500	5.8	0.0
C+ / 5.8	12.2	0.94	16.02	13	6	93	0	1	18	N/A	N/A	74	20	2,500	500	0.0	0.0
C+ / 5.8	12.2	0.94	16.23	430	6	93	0	1	18	51.4	-20.7	81	20	100,000	500	0.0	0.0
C+ / 6.7	11.7	0.82	13.75	166	14	85	0	1	21	84.9	-20.1	96	N/A	2,500	500	5.8	0.0
C+ / 6.6	11.7	0.82	13.49	23	14	85	0	1	21	N/A	N/A	95	N/A	2,500	500	0.0	0.0
C+ / 6.7	11.7	0.82	13.80	1,361	14	85	0	1	21	87.0	-20.1	96	N/A	100,000	0	0.0	0.0
U /	N/A	N/A	13.81	57	14	85	0	1	21	N/A	N/A	N/A	N/A	0	0	0.0	0.0
B- / 7.3	8.4	0.70	13.68	2	43	56	0	1	16	36.9	-13.1	6	12	3,000	500	0.0	0.0
B- / 7.1	11.0	0.55	27.30	26	9	90	0	1	27	102.1	-11.7	97	7	5,000	100	0.0	0.0
U /	N/A	N/A	10.05	4,129	4	94	0	2	18	N/A	N/A	N/A	1	0	0	0.0	0.0

Fund Type	Fund Name	Ticker Symbol	Overall Investment Rating	Phone	Performance Rating/Pts	3 Mo	6 Mo	1Yr / Pct	3Yr / Pct	5Yr / Pct	Dividend Yield	Expense Ratio
GR	Bridge Builder Large Cap Growth	BBGLX	U	(855) 823-3611	U /	8.01	6.96	20.73 /56	--	--	0.86	0.50
GR	Bridge Builder Large Cap Value	BBVLX	U	(855) 823-3611	U /	6.19	10.20	26.61 /78	--	--	1.60	0.50
MC	Bridge Builder Small Mid Cap Growth	BBGSX	U	(855) 823-3611	U /	6.84	9.27	28.98 /84	--	--	0.34	0.72
MC	Bridge Builder Small Mid Cap Value	BBVSX	U	(855) 823-3611	U /	5.27	10.89	30.97 /88	--	--	0.80	0.81
GI	Bridges Investment Fund	BRGIX	B+	(866) 934-4700	B / 7.7	7.83	10.96	22.64 /65	7.35 /74	11.17 /67	0.53	0.82
AG	Bridgeway Aggressive Investor 1 Fd	BRAGX	A	(800) 661-3550	A+/ 9.6	7.86	16.32	36.49 /95	8.23 /81	14.91 /97	0.53	0.63
GR	Bridgeway Blue Chip 35 Index Fund	BRLIX	A+	(800) 661-3550	A- / 9.0	6.84	8.52	23.49 /68	10.57 /96	13.42 /88	2.33	0.25
BA	Bridgeway Managed Volatility Fund	BRBPX	C	(800) 661-3550	D / 2.1	2.52	2.95	6.69 / 5	3.11 /33	4.39 /17	0.41	1.07
GR	Bridgeway Omni SCV	BOSVX	A	(800) 661-3550	A / 9.5	2.95	16.86	40.11 /97	7.72 /77	13.63 /90	0.91	0.71
SC	Bridgeway Omni Tax-Mgd SCV	BOTSX	A	(800) 661-3550	A+/ 9.6	2.94	16.51	39.68 /97	7.98 /79	13.39 /88	0.80	0.72
SC	Bridgeway Small-Cap Growth	BRSGX	B+	(800) 661-3550	B+/ 8.4	4.92	7.26	27.24 /80	9.04 /87	14.05 /93	0.32	1.20
SC	Bridgeway Small-Cap Momentum	BRSMX	C	(800) 661-3550	C+/ 6.0	3.73	8.81	28.29 /82	4.86 /53	10.59 /63	1.01	3.96
SC	Bridgeway Small-Cap Value	BRSVX	B+	(800) 661-3550	B+/ 8.4	4.57	15.90	36.30 /95	5.43 /59	12.50 /79	0.97	1.03
SC	● Bridgeway Ultra-SmCo	BRUSX	E-	(800) 661-3550	D- / 1.1	4.77	13.64	24.16 /70	-3.23 / 4	10.35 /61	1.13	1.27
SC	Bridgeway Ultra-SmCo Market Fund	BRSIX	C	(800) 661-3550	B- / 7.2	5.11	15.01	34.23 /93	4.29 /46	13.91 /92	0.96	0.84
GL	Bright Rock Mid Cap Growth Inst	BQMGX	B	(800) 273-7223	B- / 7.4	5.90	6.43	21.22 /58	8.40 /82	9.18 /52	0.06	1.27
GL	Bright Rock Qual Lrg Cap Inst	BQLCX	C+	(800) 273-7223	C+/ 6.1	5.79	4.28	14.64 /28	7.74 /77	11.59 /71	1.24	0.90
SC	Broadview Opportunity	BVAOX	C-	(855) 846-1463	C+/ 6.5	3.37	9.43	31.77 /90	4.21 /45	10.72 /64	0.00	1.23
OT	Brookfield Global Listed Infr A	BGLAX	E	(855) 244-4859	D- / 1.1	7.52	0.84	21.75 /61	-0.38 /12	6.68 /33	3.47	1.41
OT	Brookfield Global Listed Infr C	BGLCX	E	(855) 244-4859	D- / 1.3	7.31	0.44	20.83 /57	-1.12 / 9	--	2.97	2.16
OT	Brookfield Global Listed Infr I	BGLIX	E+	(855) 244-4859	D / 1.7	7.58	0.98	21.99 /62	-0.11 /13	6.92 /34	3.89	1.16
OT	Brookfield Global Listed Infr Y	BGLYX	E+	(855) 244-4859	D / 1.7	7.58	0.90	22.01 /62	-0.11 /13	6.91 /34	3.89	1.16
RE	Brookfield Global Listed Rl Est A	BLRAX	C-	(855) 244-4859	C- / 4.1	6.14	-3.25	16.53 /36	6.99 /72	--	3.30	1.31
RE	Brookfield Global Listed Rl Est C	BLRCX	C	(855) 244-4859	C / 4.4	5.94	-3.65	15.69 /33	6.18 /66	--	2.77	2.06
RE	Brookfield Global Listed Rl Est I	BLRIX	C+	(855) 244-4859	C / 5.3	6.29	-3.11	16.91 /38	7.25 /74	10.12 /59	3.72	1.06
RE	Brookfield Global Listed Rl Est Y	BLRYX	C+	(855) 244-4859	C / 5.3	6.21	-3.10	16.89 /38	7.24 /74	10.14 /59	3.71	1.06
OT	Brookfield Real Assets Securities I	RASIX	U	(855) 244-4859	U /	6.58	0.71	20.63 /56	--	--	3.89	1.87
RE	Brookfield US Listed Real Est A	BRUAX	C	(855) 244-4859	C / 5.4	7.76	-3.79	19.24 /48	8.20 /80	--	2.62	1.78
RE	Brookfield US Listed Real Est C	BRUCX	C	(855) 244-4859	C+/ 5.7	7.57	-4.08	18.30 /44	7.45 /75	--	2.24	2.53
RE	Brookfield US Listed Real Est I	BRUIX	C+	(855) 244-4859	C+/ 6.5	7.81	-3.67	19.57 /50	8.45 /82	--	2.93	1.53
RE	Brookfield US Listed Real Est Y	BRUYX	C+	(855) 244-4859	C+/ 6.6	7.89	-3.57	19.64 /50	8.54 /83	--	2.92	1.53
EM	Brown Adv - Somerset Em Mkts Adv	BAQAX	D	(800) 540-6807	D- / 1.5	6.75	2.36	17.36 /40	-0.11 /13	--	0.74	1.58
EM	Brown Adv - Somerset Em Mkts Inst	BAFQX	D+	(800) 540-6807	D+/ 2.3	6.84	2.57	17.89 /42	0.30 /15	--	1.23	1.18
EM	Brown Adv - Somerset Em Mkts Inv	BIAQX	D+	(800) 540-6807	D / 2.2	6.82	2.42	17.61 /41	0.11 /14	--	1.09	1.33
EM	Brown Advisory Emerging Mkt SC	BAFNX	U	(800) 540-6807	U /	5.63	-6.34	6.88 / 6	--	--	0.00	1.54
IN	Brown Advisory Eqty Inc Adv	BADAX	C+	(800) 540-6807	C+/ 5.8	6.37	5.46	16.94 /38	6.30 /67	10.06 /59	1.31	1.16
IN	Brown Advisory Eqty Inc Inv	BIADX	C+	(800) 540-6807	C+/ 6.0	6.43	5.58	17.19 /39	6.55 /69	10.33 /61	1.53	0.91
IN	Brown Advisory Eqty Inst	BAFDX	C+	(800) 540-6807	C+/ 6.2	6.51	5.70	17.41 /40	6.73 /70	--	1.67	0.76
GR	Brown Advisory Flexible Equity Adv	BAFAX	B+	(800) 540-6807	B / 8.0	7.10	9.18	23.97 /70	8.22 /81	13.02 /84	0.15	1.14
GR	Brown Advisory Flexible Equity Inst	BAFFX	A-	(800) 540-6807	B+/ 8.3	7.16	9.32	24.43 /71	8.64 /84	--	0.56	0.74
GR	Brown Advisory Flexible Equity Inv	BIAFX	A-	(800) 540-6807	B / 8.2	7.17	9.29	24.26 /71	8.48 /83	13.29 /87	0.41	0.89
GL	Brown Advisory Global Leaders Inv	BIALX	U	(800) 540-6807	U /	7.57	4.26	12.41 /19	--	--	0.17	1.42
GR	Brown Advisory Growth Equity Adv	BAGAX	C-	(800) 540-6807	C / 4.8	7.49	3.46	13.67 /24	5.50 /59	9.08 /51	0.00	1.12
GR	Brown Advisory Growth Equity Inst	BAFGX	C-	(800) 540-6807	C / 5.1	7.59	3.72	14.11 /26	5.94 /64	--	0.00	0.72
GR	Brown Advisory Growth Equity Inv	BIAGX	C-	(800) 540-6807	C / 5.0	7.52	3.59	13.96 /25	5.78 /62	9.35 /53	0.00	0.87
SC	Brown Advisory Small-Cap Gr Adv	BASAX	D+	(800) 540-6807	C+/ 6.0	2.74	3.38	25.70 /75	6.12 /65	12.12 /75	0.00	1.39
SC	Brown Advisory Small-Cap Gr Inst	BAFSX	C-	(800) 540-6807	C+/ 6.4	2.79	3.60	26.18 /77	6.52 /69	12.52 /79	0.00	0.99
SC	Brown Advisory Small-Cap Gr Inv	BIASX	D+	(800) 540-6807	C+/ 6.3	2.77	3.50	25.93 /76	6.36 /67	12.36 /78	0.00	1.14
GR	● Brown Advisory SmCP Fund Val Adv	BAUAX	B+	(800) 540-6807	B / 7.8	3.73	11.48	29.36 /85	6.89 /71	13.55 /89	0.00	1.63
GR	● Brown Advisory SmCP Fund Val Inst	BAUUX	B+	(800) 540-6807	B / 8.1	3.84	11.67	29.90 /86	7.31 /74	--	0.35	1.23
GL	● Brown Advisory SmCP Fund Val Inv	BIAUX	B+	(800) 540-6807	B / 8.0	3.78	11.58	29.63 /86	7.15 /73	13.83 /92	0.22	1.38
FS	Brown Advisory Strategic Bond Inv	BIABX	U	(800) 540-6807	U /	1.27	1.17	6.77 / 5	--	--	2.49	0.76

● Denotes fund is closed to new investors
* Denotes fund is included in Section II

RISK			NET ASSETS		ASSET						BULL / BEAR		FUND MANAGER		MINIMUMS		LOADS	
	3 Year		NAV						Portfolio	Last Bull	Last Bear	Manager	Manager	Initial	Additional	Front	Back
Risk Rating/Pts	Standard Deviation	Beta	As of 2/28/17	Total $(Mil)	Cash %	Stocks %	Bonds %	Other %	Turnover Ratio	Market Return	Market Return	Quality Pct	Tenure (Years)	Purch. $	Purch. $	End Load	End Load
U /	N/A	N/A	10.97	3,348	4	95	0	1	45	N/A	N/A	N/A	2	0	0	0.0	0.0
U /	N/A	N/A	11.17	3,778	4	95	0	1	33	N/A	N/A	N/A	2	0	0	0.0	0.0
U /	N/A	N/A	11.04	2,057	3	96	0	1	49	N/A	N/A	N/A	2	0	0	0.0	0.0
U /	N/A	N/A	11.12	2,437	2	97	0	1	49	N/A	N/A	N/A	2	0	0	0.0	0.0
C+ / 6.2	11.6	1.08	55.07	131	0	97	1	2	13	113.1	-16.1	25	20	1,000	0	0.0	0.0
C+ / 5.6	14.1	1.22	66.92	233	1	98	0	1	124	155.7	-31.0	20	23	2,000	100	0.0	0.0
B- / 7.2	10.4	0.99	13.47	561	0	99	0	1	23	128.1	-13.2	74	20	2,000	100	0.0	0.0
B+ / 9.2	3.8	0.52	14.63	46	0	52	47	1	54	40.9	-10.6	65	16	2,000	100	0.0	0.0
C / 5.5	16.4	1.06	18.43	679	0	99	0	1	24	147.6	N/A	31	7	0	0	0.0	0.0
C+ / 5.8	16.3	0.95	17.63	626	0	100	0	0	29	142.0	-26.1	83	7	0	0	0.0	0.0
C+ / 5.6	14.9	0.90	23.49	43	1	98	0	1	137	159.3	-27.8	89	14	2,000	100	0.0	0.0
C / 4.4	14.4	0.87	12.57	5	0	99	0	1	184	114.2	-25.1	61	7	2,000	100	0.0	2.0
C / 5.5	16.2	0.96	25.00	65	0	99	0	1	62	128.4	-24.0	60	14	2,000	100	0.0	0.0
D / 2.1	17.2	0.96	29.59	105	0	99	0	1	101	110.4	-30.0	2	23	2,000	100	0.0	0.0
C- / 3.4	15.3	0.91	14.54	349	0	99	0	1	41	143.4	-26.0	50	20	2,000	100	0.0	2.0
C+ / 5.6	10.6	0.52	14.83	59	1	98	0	1	44	91.2	-23.4	99	5	100,000	5,000	0.0	0.0
C+ / 6.5	9.1	0.55	15.26	216	1	98	0	1	58	115.8	-15.8	98	7	100,000	5,000	0.0	0.0
C- / 3.8	13.5	0.82	36.07	665	5	90	4	1	40	113.6	-24.5	57	20	1,000	100	0.0	0.0
C- / 3.8	12.7	0.82	12.57	20	20	79	0	1	98	N/A	N/A	3	6	1,000	100	4.8	0.0
C- / 3.8	12.7	0.82	12.41	14	20	79	0	1	98	N/A	N/A	2	6	1,000	100	0.0	0.0
C- / 3.8	12.6	0.82	12.61	179	20	79	0	1	98	N/A	N/A	3	6	1,000,000	0	0.0	0.0
C- / 3.8	12.7	0.82	12.60	55	20	79	0	1	98	N/A	N/A	3	6	1,000	100	0.0	0.0
C+ / 6.3	12.9	0.87	13.06	13	12	87	0	1	60	N/A	N/A	43	1	1,000	100	4.8	0.0
C+ / 6.3	12.9	0.87	12.98	7	12	87	0	1	60	N/A	N/A	32	1	1,000	100	0.0	0.0
C+ / 6.3	12.9	0.87	13.08	400	12	87	0	1	60	N/A	N/A	46	1	1,000,000	0	0.0	0.0
C+ / 6.3	12.9	0.87	13.09	1,311	12	87	0	1	60	N/A	N/A	46	1	1,000	100	0.0	0.0
U /	N/A	N/A	9.19	58	8	73	18	1	76	N/A	N/A	N/A	3	1,000,000	0	0.0	0.0
C / 5.2	15.2	1.09	10.72	N/A	4	95	0	1	78	N/A	N/A	28	6	1,000	100	4.8	0.0
C / 5.2	15.2	1.09	10.68	1	4	95	0	1	78	N/A	N/A	21	6	1,000	100	0.0	0.0
C / 5.2	15.2	1.09	10.66	47	4	95	0	1	78	N/A	N/A	30	6	1,000,000	0	0.0	0.0
C / 5.2	15.2	1.09	10.69	1	4	95	0	1	78	N/A	N/A	32	6	1,000	100	0.0	0.0
C+ / 6.4	11.7	0.66	9.14	N/A	7	92	0	1	19	N/A	N/A	58	5	2,000	100	0.0	0.0
C+ / 6.3	11.7	0.66	9.11	360	7	92	0	1	19	N/A	N/A	64	5	1,000,000	100	0.0	0.0
C+ / 6.3	11.7	0.67	9.09	192	7	92	0	1	19	N/A	N/A	61	5	5,000	100	0.0	0.0
U /	N/A	N/A	9.01	189	16	83	0	1	126	N/A	N/A	N/A	3	1,000,000	100	0.0	0.0
C+ / 6.5	9.3	0.86	13.35	3	3	96	0	1	17	N/A	N/A	40	6	2,000	100	0.0	0.0
C+ / 6.5	9.3	0.85	13.37	99	3	96	0	1	17	N/A	N/A	44	6	5,000	100	0.0	0.0
C+ / 6.5	9.2	0.85	13.38	12	3	96	0	1	17	N/A	N/A	47	6	1,000,000	100	0.0	0.0
C+ / 6.5	11.8	1.07	17.81	8	1	95	2	2	15	127.1	-15.5	35	9	2,000	100	0.0	0.0
C+ / 6.4	11.8	1.07	17.81	55	1	95	2	2	15	N/A	N/A	41	9	1,000,000	100	0.0	0.0
C+ / 6.4	11.7	1.07	17.79	348	1	95	2	2	15	130.1	-15.4	38	9	5,000	100	0.0	0.0
U /	N/A	N/A	10.48	33	7	92	0	1	53	N/A	N/A	N/A	2	5,000	100	0.0	0.0
C / 4.9	11.5	0.97	17.90	28	0	97	2	1	24	95.0	-18.5	19	18	2,000	100	0.0	0.0
C / 5.0	11.5	0.98	18.82	250	0	97	2	1	24	N/A	N/A	23	18	1,000,000	100	0.0	0.0
C / 4.9	11.5	0.97	18.69	1,517	0	97	2	1	24	97.6	-18.4	21	18	5,000	100	0.0	0.0
D+ / 2.8	14.0	0.81	16.04	37	3	89	6	2	32	122.2	-24.5	77	18	2,000	100	0.0	0.5
D+ / 2.9	14.0	0.81	33.40	104	3	89	6	2	32	126.6	-24.3	80	18	1,000,000	100	0.0	0.0
D+ / 2.9	14.0	0.81	16.74	319	3	89	6	2	32	125.0	-24.3	79	18	5,000	100	0.0	0.0
C+ / 6.0	12.7	1.00	26.25	30	4	95	0	1	30	129.9	N/A	30	9	2,000	100	0.0	0.0
C+ / 5.9	12.7	0.99	26.37	311	4	95	0	1	30	N/A	N/A	35	9	1,000,000	100	0.0	0.0
C+ / 5.9	12.7	0.58	26.35	832	4	95	0	1	30	133.0	-20.6	98	9	5,000	100	0.0	0.0
U /	N/A	N/A	9.58	80	0	0	99	1	288	N/A	N/A	N/A	6	5,000	100	0.0	0.0

I. Index of Stock Mutual Funds

Spring 2017

Fund Type	Fund Name	Ticker Symbol	Overall Investment Rating	Phone	Performance Rating/Pts	3 Mo	6 Mo	1Yr / Pct	3Yr / Pct	5Yr / Pct	Dividend Yield	Expense Ratio
GR	Brown Advisory Sustain Gro Adv	BAWAX	B	(800) 540-6807	B / 8.2	6.20	5.56	21.78 /61	9.98 /93	--	0.00	1.15
GR	Brown Advisory Sustain Gro Inst	BAFWX	B+	(800) 540-6807	B+ / 8.6	6.33	5.76	22.26 /63	10.44 /96	--	0.00	0.75
GR	Brown Advisory Sustain Gro Inv	BIAWX	B+	(800) 540-6807	B+ / 8.4	6.25	5.68	22.05 /62	10.27 /95	--	0.00	0.90
FO	Brown Advisory WCMJpn Alp Opps	BAFJX	U	(800) 540-6807	U /	6.51	9.69	14.57 /28	--	--	0.00	1.15
FO	Brown Advisory WMC Str Euro Eq	BAHAX	D+	(800) 540-6807	D / 2.1	9.15	1.84	11.82 /17	0.82 /17	--	0.98	1.51
FO	Brown Advisory WMC Str Euro Eq	BAFHX	D+	(800) 540-6807	D+ / 2.3	9.16	2.00	12.29 /19	1.22 /19	--	1.22	1.11
FO	Brown Advisory WMC Str Euro Eq Inv	BIAHX	D+	(800) 540-6807	D / 2.2	9.15	1.89	12.04 /18	1.07 /19	--	1.12	1.26
FO	Brown Capital Mgmt Intl Eq Inst	BCISX	U	(877) 892-4226	U /	5.33	0.17	5.42 / 4	--	--	1.99	1.80
FO	Brown Capital Mgmt Intl Eq Investor	BCIIX	D	(877) 892-4226	E+ / 0.7	5.35	0.10	5.26 / 4	-0.24 /12	6.89 /34	1.77	2.05
MC	Brown Capital Mgmt Mid Company	BCMIX	E-	(877) 892-4226	D- / 1.4	6.30	7.82	17.30 /40	-0.87 /10	6.04 /29	0.00	1.36
MC	Brown Capital Mgmt Mid Company	BCMSX	E-	(877) 892-4226	D- / 1.3	6.30	7.67	17.08 /39	-1.12 / 9	5.74 /27	0.00	1.61
FO	● Brown Capital Mgmt-Small Co Ins	BCSSX	C+	(877) 892-4226	B+ / 8.3	4.14	7.32	29.49 /85	8.55 /83	15.57 /98	0.00	1.07
SC	● Brown Capital Mgmt-Small Co Inv	BCSIX	C+	(877) 892-4226	B / 8.1	4.08	7.21	29.23 /85	8.33 /81	15.34 /97	0.00	1.27
GR	Bruce Fund	BRUFX	B-	(800) 872-7823	C / 4.4	6.27	1.30	10.09 /12	6.38 /67	9.45 /54	1.91	0.70
FS	BTS Tactical Fixed Income I	BTFIX	U	(877) 287-9820	U /	3.46	3.40	10.25 /12	--	--	3.14	1.93
TC	Buffalo Discovery Fund	BUFTX	C+	(800) 492-8332	C+ / 6.6	6.21	6.05	20.30 /54	7.51 /75	13.31 /87	0.00	1.02
IN	Buffalo Dividend Focus	BUFDX	A+	(800) 492-8332	A+ / 9.7	8.96	11.36	24.26 /71	12.49 /98	--	1.19	0.98
SC	● Buffalo Emerging Opportunities	BUFOX	E-	(800) 492-8332	D- / 1.1	3.56	5.72	27.81 /81	-2.18 / 6	11.46 /70	0.00	1.48
BA	Buffalo Flexible Income Fund	BUFBX	C+	(800) 492-8332	C / 4.4	5.84	6.34	17.89 /42	4.44 /48	7.07 /35	2.64	1.01
GL	Buffalo Growth Fund	BUFGX	C-	(800) 492-8332	C+ / 6.1	8.00	5.50	17.93 /42	6.95 /72	11.65 /71	0.69	0.92
FO	Buffalo International Fund	BUFIX	C-	(800) 492-8332	C- / 3.1	9.32	3.49	17.16 /39	2.13 /25	6.12 /29	0.97	1.06
GR	Buffalo Large Cap Fund	BUFEX	B+	(800) 492-8332	B+ / 8.6	7.61	7.27	22.67 /65	10.57 /96	13.83 /92	0.48	0.95
MC	Buffalo Mid Cap Fund	BUFMX	D-	(800) 492-8332	C- / 3.7	3.49	5.16	18.92 /47	3.72 /39	9.13 /52	0.00	1.02
SC	● Buffalo Small Cap Fund	BUFSX	E	(800) 492-8332	C- / 4.2	7.50	9.83	28.78 /83	0.73 /17	9.83 /57	0.00	1.01
GR	Bullfinch Unrestricted Series	BUNRX	B	(888) 285-5346	B- / 7.4	5.37	4.56	16.56 /37	9.85 /92	11.35 /69	0.15	1.48
CV	Calamos Convertible A	CCVIX	D	(800) 582-6959	D+ / 2.3	4.72	5.33	17.70 /41	1.97 /24	5.41 /24	2.59	1.13
CV	● Calamos Convertible B	CALBX	D+	(800) 582-6959	D+ / 2.6	4.46	4.97	16.76 /37	1.21 /19	4.63 /19	1.27	1.88
CV	Calamos Convertible C	CCVCX	D+	(800) 582-6959	D+ / 2.6	4.49	4.96	16.82 /38	1.21 /19	4.63 /19	2.02	1.88
CV	Calamos Convertible I	CICVX	D+	(800) 582-6959	C- / 3.3	4.75	5.44	17.95 /43	2.22 /25	5.68 /26	3.30	0.88
CV	Calamos Convertible R	CCVRX	D+	(800) 582-6959	D+ / 2.9	4.61	5.15	17.34 /40	1.72 /22	5.15 /22	2.51	1.38
GL	Calamos Dividend Growth A	CADVX	C+	(800) 582-6959	C+ / 5.8	7.83	10.03	22.63 /65	5.47 /59	--	0.81	1.74
GL	Calamos Dividend Growth C	CCDVX	C+	(800) 582-6959	C+ / 6.1	7.67	9.60	21.77 /61	4.70 /51	--	0.27	2.51
GL	Calamos Dividend Growth I	CIDVX	C+	(800) 582-6959	C+ / 6.9	7.97	10.15	22.89 /66	5.77 /62	--	1.08	1.49
EM	Calamos Emerging Market Equity A	CEGAX	E+	(800) 582-6959	E- / 0.2	5.89	-2.76	14.65 /28	-5.29 / 2	--	0.00	2.44
EM	Calamos Emerging Market Equity C	CEGCX	E+	(800) 582-6959	E- / 0.2	5.73	-3.03	13.84 /25	-5.98 / 2	--	0.00	3.23
EM	Calamos Emerging Market Equity I	CIEIX	E+	(800) 582-6959	E / 0.3	6.01	-2.64	14.93 /30	-5.05 / 2	--	0.00	2.24
GL	Calamos Evolving World Growth A	CNWGX	E	(800) 582-6959	E- / 0.2	6.01	-2.04	11.33 /16	-4.46 / 3	-1.28 / 3	0.00	1.66
GL	● Calamos Evolving World Growth B	CNWZX	E	(800) 582-6959	E- / 0.2	5.84	-2.31	10.56 /13	-5.16 / 2	-2.00 / 3	0.00	2.41
GL	Calamos Evolving World Growth C	CNWDX	E	(800) 582-6959	E- / 0.2	5.85	-2.40	10.47 /13	-5.17 / 2	-2.02 / 3	0.00	2.41
GL	Calamos Evolving World Growth I	CNWIX	E+	(800) 582-6959	E / 0.3	6.15	-1.87	11.65 /17	-4.21 / 3	-1.03 / 3	0.00	1.41
GL	Calamos Evolving World Growth R	CNWRX	E+	(800) 582-6959	E / 0.3	5.99	-2.06	11.15 /15	-4.69 / 3	-1.53 / 3	0.00	1.91
CV	Calamos Global Convertible Fund A	CAGCX	U	(800) 582-6959	U /	3.62	2.48	13.00 /22	--	--	1.83	2.31
CV	Calamos Global Convertible Fund I	CXGCX	U	(800) 582-6959	U /	3.78	2.71	13.36 /23	--	--	2.15	1.80
GL	Calamos Global Equity A	CAGEX	D-	(800) 582-6959	C- / 3.0	6.93	4.34	18.16 /44	3.04 /32	6.06 /29	0.00	1.35
GL	● Calamos Global Equity B	CBGEX	D-	(800) 582-6959	C- / 3.3	6.73	3.97	17.39 /40	2.27 /26	5.28 /23	0.00	2.10
GL	Calamos Global Equity C	CCGEX	D-	(800) 582-6959	C- / 3.3	6.66	3.90	17.23 /39	2.24 /26	5.25 /23	0.00	2.10
GL	Calamos Global Equity I	CIGEX	D	(800) 582-6959	C- / 4.1	6.97	4.43	18.50 /45	3.30 /35	6.32 /30	0.00	1.10
GL	Calamos Global Equity R	CRGEX	D-	(800) 582-6959	C- / 3.7	6.86	4.21	17.87 /42	2.77 /30	5.79 /27	0.00	1.60
GL	Calamos Global Growth and Income	CVLOX	D-	(800) 582-6959	D / 1.6	4.89	2.44	12.72 /21	1.33 /20	3.81 /14	0.01	1.49
GL	● Calamos Global Growth and Income	CVLDX	D-	(800) 582-6959	D / 1.7	4.62	2.07	11.80 /17	0.54 /16	3.02 /11	0.00	2.24
GL	Calamos Global Growth and Income	CVLCX	E+	(800) 582-6959	D / 1.7	4.61	2.04	11.87 /17	0.56 /16	3.04 /11	0.00	2.24
GL	Calamos Global Growth and Income I	CGCIX	D-	(800) 582-6959	D / 2.2	4.87	2.60	13.02 /22	1.59 /21	4.06 /15	0.32	1.24

● Denotes fund is closed to new investors
★ Denotes fund is included in Section II

128

www.thestreetratings.com

Risk Rating/Pts	3 Year Standard Deviation	Beta	NAV As of 2/28/17	Total $(Mil)	Cash %	Stocks %	Bonds %	Other %	Portfolio Turnover Ratio	Last Bull Market Return	Last Bear Market Return	Manager Quality Pct	Manager Tenure (Years)	Initial Purch. $	Additional Purch. $	Front End Load	Back End Load
C /5.4	11.3	0.94	17.40	174	4	95	0	1	30	N/A	N/A	74	5	2,000	100	0.0	0.0
C /5.5	11.2	0.93	17.75	173	4	95	0	1	30	N/A	N/A	77	5	1,000,000	100	0.0	0.0
C /5.5	11.2	0.94	17.61	34	4	95	0	1	30	N/A	N/A	76	5	5,000	100	0.0	0.0
U /	N/A	N/A	10.30	1,650	8	91	0	1	105	N/A	N/A	N/A	3	1,000,000	100	0.0	0.0
C+ /6.6	11.3	0.85	10.39	2	1	98	0	1	31	N/A	N/A	81	4	2,000	100	0.0	0.0
C+ /6.6	11.3	0.85	10.44	1,002	1	98	0	1	31	N/A	N/A	83	4	1,000,000	100	0.0	0.0
C+ /6.6	11.4	0.85	10.44	7	1	98	0	1	31	N/A	N/A	82	4	5,000	100	0.0	0.0
U /	N/A	N/A	12.02	29	3	96	0	1	2	N/A	N/A	N/A	11	500,000	500	0.0	2.0
C+ /6.7	10.7	0.80	12.03	4	3	96	0	1	2	61.5	-25.2	73	11	5,000	500	0.0	2.0
E /0.4	12.7	0.98	12.17	11	3	96	0	1	37	N/A	N/A	2	15	500,000	500	0.0	0.0
E /0.4	12.7	0.98	11.83	9	3	96	0	1	37	63.6	-20.8	2	15	5,000	500	0.0	0.0
C- /3.5	16.1	0.71	78.68	1,520	0	95	3	2	22	N/A	N/A	99	25	500,000	500	0.0	0.0
C- /3.5	16.1	0.91	77.72	2,009	0	95	3	2	22	144.3	-18.8	86	25	5,000	500	0.0	0.0
B /8.1	7.9	0.47	507.56	581	12	44	37	7	26	74.6	-10.4	83	34	1,000	500	0.0	0.0
U /	N/A	N/A	10.51	288	33	0	66	1	660	N/A	N/A	N/A	4	100,000	1,000	0.0	1.0
C /5.1	11.2	0.93	21.40	1,223	6	84	9	1	59	136.6	-19.1	47	4	2,500	100	0.0	2.0
B- /7.0	10.1	0.93	15.32	55	5	89	4	2	65	N/A	N/A	88	5	2,500	100	0.0	2.0
D- /1.5	19.7	1.12	14.97	83	2	92	4	2	70	126.2	-20.9	2	4	2,500	100	0.0	2.0
B- /7.1	8.2	1.18	14.86	815	2	78	12	8	5	59.7	-6.7	22	14	2,500	100	0.0	2.0
C- /3.8	9.9	0.69	30.58	336	0	97	1	2	42	114.5	-18.1	98	13	2,500	100	0.0	2.0
C+ /6.3	11.2	0.85	12.29	196	1	97	1	1	7	60.5	-23.5	87	9	2,500	100	0.0	2.0
C /5.4	10.6	0.92	26.07	57	2	93	4	1	62	131.9	-19.6	79	13	2,500	100	0.0	2.0
C- /3.1	12.5	0.95	15.61	372	2	94	3	1	46	88.4	-20.0	14	16	2,500	100	0.0	2.0
E- /0.0	16.2	0.93	16.22	563	2	93	3	2	41	108.7	-25.5	11	19	2,500	100	0.0	2.0
C+ /6.1	10.7	0.91	20.07	9	11	88	0	1	2	108.4	-14.8	75	20	2,500	250	0.0	0.0
C+ /6.0	8.8	1.00	16.78	218	4	15	2	79	44	44.7	-13.9	35	32	2,500	50	4.8	0.0
C+ /6.3	8.8	1.00	21.73	3	4	15	2	79	44	38.9	-14.1	27	32	2,500	50	0.0	0.0
C+ /6.0	8.8	1.00	16.62	180	4	15	2	79	44	38.9	-14.1	27	32	2,500	50	0.0	0.0
C+ /5.9	8.8	1.00	15.13	209	4	15	2	79	44	46.6	-13.7	39	32	1,000,000	0	0.0	0.0
C+ /6.0	8.8	1.00	16.71	2	4	15	2	79	44	42.7	-14.0	32	32	0	0	0.0	0.0
C+ /6.6	9.9	0.69	11.54	24	0	99	0	1	12	N/A	N/A	96	4	2,500	50	4.8	0.0
C+ /6.6	9.9	0.68	11.40	1	0	99	0	1	12	N/A	N/A	95	4	2,500	50	0.0	0.0
C+ /6.6	9.9	0.68	11.56	5	0	99	0	1	12	N/A	N/A	96	4	1,000,000	0	0.0	0.0
C+ /5.6	14.7	0.86	8.45	4	0	99	0	1	75	N/A	N/A	6	4	2,500	50	4.8	0.0
C+ /5.6	14.7	0.86	8.31	N/A	0	99	0	1	75	N/A	N/A	4	4	2,500	50	0.0	0.0
C+ /5.6	14.7	0.86	8.47	9	0	99	0	1	75	N/A	N/A	6	4	1,000,000	0	0.0	0.0
C /5.0	12.4	0.81	11.99	87	2	79	1	18	87	8.8	-21.5	20	9	2,500	50	4.8	0.0
C /4.9	12.5	0.81	11.41	N/A	2	79	1	18	87	4.5	-21.7	14	9	2,500	50	0.0	0.0
C /4.9	12.5	0.81	11.40	26	2	79	1	18	87	4.5	-21.7	14	9	2,500	50	0.0	0.0
C /5.0	12.4	0.81	12.08	214	2	79	1	18	87	10.3	-21.4	22	9	1,000,000	0	0.0	0.0
C /5.0	12.5	0.81	11.86	2	2	79	1	18	87	7.4	-21.5	18	9	0	0	0.0	0.0
U /	N/A	N/A	10.18	31	6	9	10	75	38	N/A	N/A	N/A	3	2,500	50	4.8	0.0
U /	N/A	N/A	10.21	49	6	9	10	75	38	N/A	N/A	N/A	3	1,000,000	0	0.0	0.0
C- /3.5	12.6	0.90	12.79	26	2	96	1	1	65	59.3	-17.7	91	10	2,500	50	4.8	0.0
C- /3.2	12.6	0.90	11.87	N/A	2	96	1	1	65	52.9	-17.9	88	10	2,500	50	0.0	0.0
C- /3.2	12.6	0.90	11.83	15	2	96	1	1	65	52.8	-17.9	88	10	2,500	50	0.0	0.0
C- /3.6	12.6	0.90	13.03	80	2	96	1	1	65	61.4	-17.5	92	10	1,000,000	0	0.0	0.0
C- /3.4	12.6	0.90	12.44	4	2	96	1	1	65	57.1	-17.7	90	10	0	0	0.0	0.0
C /4.7	8.8	0.67	8.70	78	1	55	2	42	58	34.6	-12.5	83	21	2,500	50	4.8	0.0
C /4.7	8.8	0.66	8.73	N/A	1	55	2	42	58	29.1	-12.8	78	21	2,500	50	0.0	0.0
C /4.5	8.8	0.66	7.84	83	1	55	2	42	58	29.2	-12.8	79	21	2,500	50	0.0	0.0
C /4.8	8.8	0.66	8.92	71	1	55	2	42	58	36.4	-12.4	85	21	1,000,000	0	0.0	0.0

Fund Type	Fund Name	Ticker Symbol	Overall Investment Rating	Phone	Performance Rating/Pts	3 Mo	6 Mo	1Yr / Pct	3Yr / Pct	5Yr / Pct	Dividend Yield	Expense Ratio
GL	Calamos Global Growth and Income	CVLRX	D-	(800) 582-6959	D / 2.0	4.71	2.35	12.51 /20	1.07 /19	3.55 /13	0.00	1.74
MC	Calamos Growth A	CVGRX	E	(800) 582-6959	C- / 3.8	7.63	7.20	16.23 /35	4.14 /44	8.54 /47	0.00	1.32
GI	Calamos Growth and Income A	CVTRX	C	(800) 582-6959	C / 5.3	6.12	7.43	18.74 /46	6.35 /67	7.25 /36	2.86	1.11
GI	● Calamos Growth and Income B	CVTYX	C+	(800) 582-6959	C+ / 5.6	5.87	6.95	17.77 /42	5.58 /60	6.67 /33	1.58	1.86
GI	Calamos Growth and Income C	CVTCX	C	(800) 582-6959	C+ / 5.6	5.93	7.01	17.87 /42	5.52 /60	6.43 /31	2.26	1.86
GI	Calamos Growth and Income I	CGIIX	C+	(800) 582-6959	C+ / 6.5	6.21	7.56	19.06 /47	6.61 /69	7.51 /38	3.35	0.86
GI	Calamos Growth and Income R	CGNRX	C+	(800) 582-6959	C+ / 6.0	6.07	7.28	18.43 /45	6.10 /65	6.99 /34	2.78	1.36
MC	● Calamos Growth B	CVGBX	E	(800) 582-6959	C- / 4.1	7.45	6.78	15.38 /32	3.36 /35	7.73 /40	0.00	2.07
MC	Calamos Growth C	CVGCX	E	(800) 582-6959	C- / 4.1	7.41	6.81	15.39 /32	3.36 /35	7.73 /40	0.00	2.07
MC	Calamos Growth I	CGRIX	D-	(800) 582-6959	C / 5.0	7.69	7.32	16.53 /36	4.40 /47	8.81 /49	0.00	1.07
MC	Calamos Growth R	CGRRX	E	(800) 582-6959	C / 4.5	7.56	7.04	15.94 /34	3.87 /41	8.27 /44	0.00	1.57
FO	Calamos International Growth A	CIGRX	E	(800) 582-6959	E / 0.4	6.08	0.30	12.05 /18	-2.21 / 6	1.98 / 8	0.00	1.31
FO	● Calamos International Growth B	CIGBX	E	(800) 582-6959	E / 0.5	5.91	-0.13	11.20 /15	-2.94 / 5	1.20 / 6	0.00	2.06
FO	Calamos International Growth C	CIGCX	E	(800) 582-6959	E / 0.5	5.92	-0.13	11.13 /15	-2.94 / 5	1.21 / 7	0.00	2.06
FO	Calamos International Growth I	CIGIX	E	(800) 582-6959	E+ / 0.7	6.15	0.41	12.30 /19	-1.97 / 7	2.23 / 9	0.00	1.06
FO	Calamos International Growth R	CIGFX	E	(800) 582-6959	E+ / 0.6	6.08	0.18	11.73 /17	-2.43 / 6	1.73 / 7	0.00	1.56
IN	Calamos Market Neutral Income A	CVSIX	C	(800) 582-6959	D / 1.6	1.95	2.94	8.62 / 9	2.99 /32	3.49 /13	1.06	1.23
IN	● Calamos Market Neutral Income B	CAMNX	C	(800) 582-6959	D / 1.8	1.76	2.58	7.80 / 7	2.21 /25	2.70 /10	0.08	1.98
IN	Calamos Market Neutral Income C	CVSCX	C	(800) 582-6959	D / 1.8	1.80	2.57	7.82 / 7	2.21 /25	2.72 /10	0.36	1.98
IN	Calamos Market Neutral Income I	CMNIX	C	(800) 582-6959	D+ / 2.3	2.04	3.10	8.91 / 9	3.26 /34	3.74 /14	1.37	0.98
IN	Calamos Market Neutral Income R	CVSRX	C	(800) 582-6959	D / 2.0	1.81	2.74	8.29 / 8	2.73 /29	3.21 /12	0.87	1.48
GR	Calamos Opportunistic Value A	CVAAX	C-	(800) 582-6959	C / 4.7	6.01	9.30	22.74 /66	4.22 /45	9.10 /51	0.65	1.60
GR	● Calamos Opportunistic Value B	CVABX	C-	(800) 582-6959	C / 5.0	5.80	8.92	21.82 /61	3.43 /36	8.29 /45	0.00	2.34
GR	Calamos Opportunistic Value C	CVACX	C-	(800) 582-6959	C / 5.0	5.81	8.89	21.85 /61	3.43 /36	8.28 /44	0.05	2.35
GR	Calamos Opportunistic Value I	CVAIX	C	(800) 582-6959	C+ / 5.9	6.04	9.40	23.08 /67	4.49 /49	9.37 /54	0.91	1.34
GR	Calamos Opportunistic Value R	CVARX	C	(800) 582-6959	C / 5.5	5.93	9.18	22.37 /64	3.97 /43	8.82 /49	0.47	1.86
GL	Calamos Phineus Long Short A	CPLSX	B-	(800) 582-6959	C / 5.0	3.04	13.03	19.62 /50	5.28 /57	6.90 /34	0.00	3.65
GL	Calamos Phineus Long Short C	CPCLX	B	(800) 582-6959	C / 5.3	2.79	12.59	18.70 /46	4.46 /48	6.09 /29	0.00	4.40
GL	Calamos Phineus Long Short I	CPLIX	B-	(800) 582-6959	C+ / 6.2	3.03	13.10	19.93 /52	5.54 /60	7.19 /36	0.00	3.40
AA	Caldwell & Orkin Mkt Opportunity	COAGX	D	(800) 467-7903	E / 0.4	-0.34	-1.71	-7.19 / 0	0.90 /18	2.45 / 9	0.00	2.99
AA	Calvert Aggresive Allocation A	CAAAX	C-	(800) 368-2745	C / 4.5	6.27	7.51	19.13 /48	5.63 /61	9.61 /55	1.83	1.15
AA	Calvert Aggresive Allocation C	CAACX	C-	(800) 368-2745	C / 4.7	6.05	7.12	18.28 /44	4.61 /50	8.44 /46	2.04	1.97
BA	Calvert Balanced Portfolio A	CSIFX	C-	(800) 368-2745	C- / 3.2	4.46	4.46	14.66 /28	5.36 /58	7.55 /39	1.41	0.97
BA	Calvert Balanced Portfolio C	CSGCX	C-	(800) 368-2745	C- / 3.4	4.26	4.03	13.76 /24	4.53 /49	6.69 /33	0.78	1.76
BA	Calvert Balanced Portfolio I	CBAIX	C+	(800) 368-2745	C / 4.9	4.53	4.62	15.10 /30	5.81 /63	8.03 /42	1.82	0.63
BA	Calvert Balanced Portfolio Y	CBAYX	C+	(800) 368-2745	C / 4.7	4.49	4.56	14.96 /30	5.58 /60	7.71 /40	1.73	0.93
MC	Calvert Capital Accumulation A	CCAFX	D-	(800) 368-2745	D+ / 2.7	5.09	7.61	14.87 /29	3.59 /38	8.88 /50	0.45	1.28
MC	Calvert Capital Accumulation C	CCACX	E+	(800) 368-2745	C- / 3.0	4.89	7.21	13.96 /25	2.79 /30	8.04 /42	0.00	2.08
MC	Calvert Capital Accumulation I	CCPIX	D+	(800) 368-2745	C / 4.3	5.19	7.79	15.32 /31	4.13 /44	9.50 /55	0.82	0.85
MC	Calvert Capital Accumulation Y	CCAYX	D	(800) 368-2745	C- / 4.1	5.16	7.75	15.15 /31	3.82 /41	9.13 /52	0.58	1.05
AA	Calvert Conservative Allocation A	CCLAX	C-	(800) 368-2745	D / 1.9	2.92	2.92	9.44 /10	4.05 /44	5.74 /27	2.46	1.05
AA	Calvert Conservative Allocation C	CALCX	C-	(800) 368-2745	D / 2.0	2.75	2.55	8.52 / 8	3.09 /33	4.74 /20	1.55	1.84
AA	Calvert Conservative Allocation Y	CALYX	C	(800) 368-2745	D+ / 2.9	3.04	3.06	9.67 /11	4.12 /44	5.79 /27	2.90	N/A
EM	Calvert Emerging Markets Equity A	CVMAX	D	(800) 368-2745	D+ / 2.8	5.94	3.75	21.09 /58	2.99 /32	--	0.48	2.01
EM	Calvert Emerging Markets Equity C	CVMCX	D	(800) 368-2745	C- / 3.0	5.68	3.29	20.15 /53	2.09 /25	--	0.13	4.83
EM	Calvert Emerging Markets Equity I	CVMIX	C-	(800) 368-2745	C / 4.3	5.97	3.88	21.51 /60	3.34 /35	--	0.79	1.92
EM	Calvert Emerging Markets Equity Y	CVMYX	C-	(800) 368-2745	C / 4.3	6.05	3.89	21.46 /60	3.26 /34	--	0.75	1.90
GR	Calvert Equity Portfolio A	CSIEX	D+	(800) 368-2745	C / 5.3	5.93	4.15	13.99 /25	7.26 /74	11.00 /66	0.13	1.07
GR	Calvert Equity Portfolio C	CSECX	D-	(800) 368-2745	C / 4.7	5.73	3.77	13.11 /22	6.44 /68	10.18 /60	0.00	1.81
GR	Calvert Equity Portfolio I	CEYIX	C-	(800) 368-2745	C+ / 6.1	6.02	4.35	14.43 /27	7.73 /77	11.54 /70	0.56	0.68
GR	Calvert Equity Portfolio Y	CIEYX	C-	(800) 368-2745	C+ / 6.0	5.99	4.31	14.34 /27	7.57 /76	11.37 /69	0.49	0.77
GL	Calvert Global Water A	CFWAX	E+	(800) 368-2745	E+ / 0.9	4.54	4.54	24.13 /70	-0.85 /10	7.56 /39	0.00	1.44

● Denotes fund is closed to new investors
* Denotes fund is included in Section II

RISK	3 Year		NET ASSETS		ASSET				Portfolio	BULL / BEAR		FUND MANAGER		MINIMUMS		LOADS	
Risk Rating/Pts	Standard Deviation	Beta	NAV As of 2/28/17	Total $(Mil)	Cash %	Stocks %	Bonds %	Other %	Turnover Ratio	Last Bull Market Return	Last Bear Market Return	Manager Quality Pct	Manager Tenure (Years)	Initial Purch. $	Additional Purch. $	Front End Load	Back End Load
C /4.7	8.9	0.67	8.56	1	1	55	2	42	58	32.7	-12.6	82	21	0	0	0.0	0.0
E+ /0.7	11.8	0.79	31.43	963	5	92	2	1	90	83.1	-22.6	31	27	2,500	50	4.8	0.0
C+ /5.7	8.8	0.84	31.00	914	3	68	8	21	24	62.8	-13.7	44	29	2,500	50	4.8	0.0
C+ /6.1	8.8	0.84	37.77	3	3	68	8	21	24	57.9	-14.0	34	29	2,500	50	0.0	0.0
C+ /5.7	8.9	0.84	31.11	702	3	68	8	21	24	56.2	-14.0	33	29	2,500	50	0.0	0.0
C+ /5.6	8.9	0.84	29.91	483	3	68	8	21	24	65.0	-13.6	47	29	1,000,000	0	0.0	0.0
C+ /5.7	8.8	0.84	30.75	13	3	68	8	21	24	60.7	-13.8	40	29	0	0	0.0	0.0
E+ /0.6	11.8	0.79	28.25	4	5	92	2	1	90	75.8	-22.9	24	27	2,500	50	0.0	0.0
E+ /0.6	11.8	0.79	21.56	502	5	92	2	1	90	75.9	-22.9	24	27	2,500	50	0.0	0.0
D /1.7	11.8	0.79	39.89	305	5	92	2	1	90	85.6	-22.6	35	27	1,000,000	0	0.0	0.0
E+ /0.6	11.8	0.79	29.69	7	5	92	2	1	90	80.7	-22.7	29	27	0	0	0.0	0.0
C- /4.2	12.0	0.89	16.93	88	0	99	0	1	69	29.5	-20.0	47	12	2,500	50	4.8	0.0
C- /4.0	12.0	0.89	15.59	N/A	0	99	0	1	69	24.3	-20.2	36	12	2,500	50	0.0	0.0
C- /4.0	12.0	0.89	15.57	30	0	99	0	1	69	24.3	-20.2	36	12	2,500	50	0.0	0.0
C- /4.2	12.0	0.89	17.26	171	0	99	0	1	69	31.2	-19.9	51	12	1,000,000	0	0.0	0.0
C- /4.1	12.0	0.89	16.57	5	0	99	0	1	69	27.8	-20.0	44	12	0	0	0.0	0.0
B /8.9	3.2	0.30	13.22	979	29	23	6	42	38	27.8	-4.5	73	27	2,500	50	4.8	0.0
B /8.9	3.2	0.30	14.08	N/A	29	23	6	42	38	22.7	-4.9	63	27	2,500	50	0.0	0.0
B /8.9	3.1	0.29	13.42	314	29	23	6	42	38	22.7	-4.8	64	27	2,500	50	0.0	0.0
B /8.9	3.2	0.30	13.08	2,866	29	23	6	42	38	29.5	-4.4	75	27	1,000,000	0	0.0	0.0
B /8.9	3.2	0.30	13.16	9	29	23	6	42	38	26.0	-4.6	70	27	0	0	0.0	0.0
C /5.3	10.1	0.94	13.98	34	0	98	0	2	41	79.5	-17.4	13	15	2,500	50	4.8	0.0
C /5.4	10.1	0.94	12.95	N/A	0	98	0	2	41	72.2	-17.7	8	15	2,500	50	0.0	0.0
C /5.2	10.1	0.94	12.69	6	0	98	0	2	41	72.3	-17.7	8	15	2,500	50	0.0	0.0
C /5.3	10.1	0.94	14.34	19	0	98	0	2	41	81.8	-17.3	14	15	1,000,000	0	0.0	0.0
C /5.3	10.1	0.94	13.81	N/A	0	98	0	2	41	76.9	-17.5	11	15	0	0	0.0	0.0
B- /7.9	12.3	0.57	11.79	27	0	0	0	100	0	68.9	-14.1	96	15	2,500	50	4.8	0.0
B- /7.9	12.3	0.57	11.71	9	0	0	0	100	0	62.2	-14.4	94	15	2,500	50	0.0	0.0
B- /7.9	12.3	0.57	11.82	112	0	0	0	100	0	71.3	-14.0	96	15	1,000,000	0	0.0	0.0
B- /7.8	6.8	-0.04	20.64	126	23	24	52	1	415	14.5	0.4	82	25	25,000	100	0.0	2.0
C /5.1	9.5	1.44	18.45	106	1	92	5	2	62	86.0	-17.5	16	2	2,000	250	4.8	2.0
C /4.8	9.5	1.44	16.00	18	1	92	5	2	62	75.5	-18.0	9	2	2,000	250	0.0	2.0
C+ /6.7	6.9	1.09	31.69	574	3	60	35	2	146	64.1	-8.2	39	4	2,000	250	4.8	2.0
C+ /6.7	6.9	1.09	30.74	64	3	60	35	2	146	57.1	-8.6	29	4	2,000	250	0.0	2.0
C+ /6.8	6.9	1.09	32.23	44	3	60	35	2	146	68.2	-8.0	45	4	1,000,000	0	0.0	2.0
C+ /6.7	6.9	1.09	31.96	22	3	60	35	2	146	65.3	-8.2	42	4	2,000	250	0.0	0.0
C- /4.1	12.1	0.92	32.15	185	0	98	0	2	199	94.4	-24.0	15	1	2,000	250	4.8	2.0
C- /3.1	12.1	0.92	23.73	22	0	98	0	2	199	86.3	-24.3	10	1	2,000	250	0.0	2.0
C /4.5	12.1	0.92	37.17	135	0	98	0	2	199	100.5	-23.7	20	1	1,000,000	0	0.0	0.0
C- /4.1	12.1	0.92	32.63	13	0	98	0	2	199	96.6	-23.9	17	1	2,000	250	0.0	0.0
B /8.3	4.0	0.61	16.54	124	4	38	57	1	61	42.3	-3.1	68	2	2,000	250	4.8	2.0
B /8.3	4.0	0.61	16.36	34	4	38	57	1	61	35.2	-3.6	56	2	2,000	250	0.0	2.0
B /8.3	4.0	0.61	16.52	8	4	38	57	1	61	42.6	-3.1	69	2	2,000	250	0.0	0.0
C /5.2	13.7	0.80	12.97	30	3	94	1	2	32	N/A	N/A	84	5	2,000	250	4.8	2.0
C /5.2	13.7	0.81	12.79	1	3	94	1	2	32	N/A	N/A	79	5	2,000	250	0.0	2.0
C /5.2	13.7	0.81	13.06	75	3	94	1	2	32	N/A	N/A	86	5	1,000,000	0	0.0	0.0
C /5.2	13.7	0.81	13.18	35	3	94	1	2	32	N/A	N/A	85	5	2,000	250	0.0	0.0
C- /3.8	9.5	0.88	38.95	1,239	3	95	0	2	44	99.5	-16.0	50	2	2,000	250	0.0	2.0
D /1.6	9.5	0.88	24.24	164	3	95	0	2	44	91.7	-16.3	39	2	2,000	250	0.0	2.0
C- /4.2	9.5	0.87	44.35	513	3	95	0	2	44	104.8	-15.8	57	2	1,000,000	0	0.0	0.0
C- /3.8	9.5	0.88	40.07	155	3	95	0	2	44	103.2	-15.9	54	2	2,000	250	0.0	0.0
C /4.4	13.6	0.82	18.21	242	0	99	0	1	103	72.8	-19.0	66	1	2,000	250	4.8	2.0

	99 Pct = Best 0 Pct = Worst				**PERFORMANCE**							
								Total Return % through 2/28/17			Incl. in Returns	
			Overall		Perfor-				Annualized		Dividend	Expense
Fund		Ticker	Investment		mance						Yield	Ratio
Type	Fund Name	Symbol	Rating	Phone	Rating/Pts	3 Mo	6 Mo	1Yr / Pct	3Yr / Pct	5Yr / Pct		
GL	Calvert Global Water C	CFWCX	E+	(800) 368-2745	D- / 1.1	4.35	4.16	23.29 /67	-1.56 / 8	6.72 /33	0.00	2.15
EN	Calvert Global Water I	CFWIX	E+	(800) 368-2745	D / 1.7	4.63	4.75	24.63 /72	-0.34 /12	7.84 /41	0.00	3.71
GL	Calvert Global Water Y	CFWYX	E+	(800) 368-2745	D / 1.7	4.59	4.65	24.46 /72	-0.53 /11	7.89 /41	0.00	1.11
FO	Calvert International Equity A	CWVGX	D-	(800) 368-2745	E- / 0.2	5.12	1.67	8.28 / 8	-2.83 / 5	3.29 /12	2.55	1.45
FO	Calvert International Equity C	CWVCX	D-	(800) 368-2745	E / 0.3	4.92	1.32	7.47 / 6	-3.61 / 4	2.41 / 9	2.04	2.36
FO	Calvert International Equity I	CWVIX	D-	(800) 368-2745	E / 0.5	5.18	1.82	8.70 / 9	-2.35 / 6	3.88 /15	3.19	1.01
FO	Calvert International Equity Y	CWEYX	D-	(800) 368-2745	E / 0.5	5.17	1.83	8.58 / 9	-2.54 / 5	3.63 /14	2.90	1.15
FO	Calvert International Opp A	CIOAX	D-	(800) 368-2745	D- / 1.3	7.05	4.48	14.37 /27	0.08 /14	7.25 /36	0.98	1.51
FO	Calvert International Opp C	COICX	D-	(800) 368-2745	D- / 1.0	6.85	4.07	13.31 /23	-0.82 /10	6.30 /30	0.06	2.54
FO	Calvert International Opp I	COIIX	D	(800) 368-2745	D+ / 2.3	7.17	4.64	14.70 /28	0.50 /16	7.70 /40	1.45	1.12
FO	Calvert International Opp Y	CWVYX	D	(800) 368-2745	D / 2.2	7.12	4.59	14.70 /28	0.34 /15	7.51 /38	1.33	1.24
AA	Calvert Moderate Allocation A	CMAAX	C-	(800) 368-2745	C- / 3.2	4.80	5.44	15.12 /30	4.92 /53	7.73 /40	2.51	1.11
AA	Calvert Moderate Allocation C	CMACX	C-	(800) 368-2745	C- / 3.5	4.64	5.07	14.37 /27	4.15 /45	6.93 /34	2.15	1.89
BA	Calvert Moderate Allocation Y	CMLYX	C	(800) 368-2745	C / 4.6	4.87	5.59	15.40 /32	5.00 /54	7.78 /40	2.86	N/A
SC	Calvert Small Cap A	CCVAX	B-	(800) 368-2745	B / 8.2	5.54	14.09	29.34 /85	9.01 /87	13.91 /92	0.00	1.39
SC	Calvert Small Cap C	CSCCX	B-	(800) 368-2745	B+ / 8.4	5.34	13.63	28.34 /82	8.19 /80	13.00 /84	0.00	2.23
SC	Calvert Small Cap I	CSVIX	B+	(800) 368-2745	A / 9.5	5.67	14.34	29.92 /86	9.53 /91	14.57 /96	0.06	0.93
SC	Calvert Small Cap Y	CSCYX	B+	(800) 368-2745	A / 9.4	5.63	14.22	29.71 /86	9.29 /89	14.14 /94	0.00	1.18
FS	Calvert Unconstrained Bond I	CUBIX	U	(800) 368-2745	U /	1.42	2.50	8.75 / 9	--	--	3.52	1.15
GR	Calvert US LC Core Responsible Ix A	CSXAX	B+	(800) 368-2745	B / 8.0	8.06	10.02	24.77 /72	9.86 /93	13.76 /91	1.02	0.74
GR	Calvert US LC Core Responsible Ix C	CSXCX	B+	(800) 368-2745	B / 8.2	7.84	9.54	23.80 /69	9.00 /87	12.82 /82	0.29	1.54
GR	Calvert US LC Core Responsible Ix I	CISIX	A	(800) 368-2745	A / 9.3	8.13	10.15	25.17 /74	10.33 /95	14.30 /95	1.47	0.38
GR	Calvert US LC Core Responsible Ix Y	CISYX	A	(800) 368-2745	A- / 9.1	8.10	10.11	25.05 /73	9.96 /93	13.89 /92	1.41	0.59
GR	Calvert US LC Gro Responsible Ix I	CGJIX	U	(800) 368-2745	U /	8.57	7.32	20.20 /53	--	--	1.05	7.28
GR	Calvert US LC Val Responsible Ix A	CFJAX	U	(800) 368-2745	U /	7.37	12.88	29.81 /86	--	--	1.52	7.42
GR	Calvert US LC Val Responsible Ix I	CFJIX	U	(800) 368-2745	U /	7.41	13.00	30.25 /87	--	--	1.92	7.00
GL	Cambiar Global Equity Investor	CAMGX	D	(866) 777-8227	D+ / 2.5	2.53	3.69	13.79 /24	2.98 /32	7.80 /41	0.64	3.72
GR	Cambiar Global Ultra Focus Investor	CAMAX	C-	(866) 777-8227	C / 4.3	5.13	11.30	13.34 /23	4.56 /49	10.02 /58	0.23	1.40
FO	Cambiar International Equity Inst	CAMYX	D	(866) 777-8227	D- / 1.3	4.43	1.56	8.54 / 8	0.55 /16	--	1.74	1.03
FO	Cambiar International Equity Inv	CAMIX	D	(866) 777-8227	D- / 1.2	4.43	1.51	8.46 / 8	0.41 /15	5.65 /26	1.65	1.28
GR	Cambiar Opportunity Fund Inst	CAMWX	B	(866) 777-8227	B / 8.2	3.99	9.98	26.69 /78	8.48 /83	11.08 /66	1.79	0.86
GR	Cambiar Opportunity Fund Inv	CAMOX	B	(866) 777-8227	B / 8.0	3.93	9.82	26.36 /77	8.21 /81	10.80 /64	1.54	1.11
SC	Cambiar Small Cap Fund Inst	CAMZX	D-	(866) 777-8227	C- / 4.0	2.34	9.65	26.69 /78	1.97 /24	7.95 /42	0.00	1.10
SC	● Cambiar Small Cap Fund Inv	CAMSX	D-	(866) 777-8227	C- / 3.8	2.29	9.58	26.46 /78	1.73 /22	7.68 /40	0.00	1.35
GR	Cambiar SMID Investor	CAMMX	B+	(866) 777-8227	B+ / 8.5	6.42	16.34	33.12 /92	6.53 /69	12.46 /79	0.50	1.54
SC	Camelot Excalibur Small Cap Inc A	CEXAX	C	(877) 315-5558	C- / 4.0	5.74	9.77	32.16 /90	1.33 /20	--	3.65	2.91
SC	Camelot Excalibur Small Cap Inc C	CEXCX	C+	(877) 315-5558	C / 5.1	5.43	9.84	31.30 /89	1.36 /20	--	3.55	3.66
IN	Camelot Premium Return A	CPRFX	C-	(877) 315-5558	C+ / 5.9	5.79	6.05	30.91 /88	5.43 /59	8.28 /44	2.66	2.56
IN	Camelot Premium Return C	CPRCX	C	(877) 315-5558	C+ / 6.6	5.54	6.25	30.55 /87	4.83 /52	7.52 /38	2.17	3.32
AG	CAN SLIM Select Growth	CANGX	C+	(800) 558-9105	C / 4.5	6.30	8.20	14.68 /28	4.87 /53	10.00 /58	0.06	1.63
EM	Capital Group Emg Mkts Total Oppty	ETOPX	D	(800) 421-0180	D / 1.6	6.95	4.60	18.31 /44	-0.05 /13	0.25 / 5	0.00	1.12
GL	Capital Group Global Equity Fund	CGLOX	C-	(800) 421-0180	C / 4.4	7.23	4.58	18.07 /43	3.82 /41	8.67 /48	1.44	0.86
FO	Capital Group International Equity	CNUSX	D-	(800) 421-0180	D- / 1.2	6.81	1.20	11.88 /17	-0.10 /13	4.51 /18	1.55	0.85
IN	Capital Group U.S. Equity Fund	CUSEX	B+	(800) 421-0180	B / 8.1	7.60	8.16	23.62 /69	8.53 /83	12.01 /74	1.32	0.66
MC	Capital Management Mid-Cap Inst	CMEIX	B	(888) 626-3863	B- / 7.5	4.46	5.83	24.63 /72	8.27 /81	11.95 /74	0.00	1.61
MC	Capital Management Mid-Cap Inv	CMCIX	C	(888) 626-3863	C+ / 6.5	4.26	5.42	23.70 /69	7.55 /76	11.16 /67	0.00	2.36
SC	Capital Management Sm-Cap Inst	CMSSX	E+	(888) 626-3863	D / 1.7	3.97	6.99	26.22 /77	-0.74 /10	7.28 /36	0.00	1.73
SC	Capital Management Sm-Cap Inv	CMSVX	E	(888) 626-3863	D- / 1.3	3.86	6.80	25.82 /76	-1.08 / 9	6.92 /34	0.00	2.48
SC	Cardinal Small Cap Value Instl	CCMSX	U	(866) 777-7818	U /	2.66	10.29	26.68 /78	--	--	0.37	3.40
GL	Castle Focus Fund C	CASTX	C	(877) 743-7820	C- / 3.9	4.31	3.95	14.33 /27	5.14 /56	5.93 /28	0.00	2.62
GL	Castle Focus Fund Inv	MOATX	C+	(877) 743-7820	C / 4.7	4.57	4.42	15.46 /32	6.20 /66	7.01 /35	0.12	1.62
GR	Catalyst Dynamic Alpha A	CPEAX	A-	(866) 447-4228	A+ / 9.7	9.00	12.20	31.75 /90	12.55 /98	17.06 /98	0.00	1.51

● Denotes fund is closed to new investors

* Denotes fund is included in Section II

RISK Risk Rating/Pts	3 Year Standard Deviation	Beta	NET ASSETS NAV As of 2/28/17	Total $(Mil)	ASSET Cash %	Stocks %	Bonds %	Other %	Portfolio Turnover Ratio	BULL/BEAR Last Bull Market Return	Last Bear Market Return	FUND MANAGER Manager Quality Pct	Manager Tenure (Years)	MINIMUMS Initial Purch. $	Additional Purch. $	LOADS Front End Load	Back End Load
C- /4.2	13.6	0.82	16.78	69	0	99	0	1	103	65.4	-19.4	56	1	2,000	250	0.0	2.0
C /4.3	13.6	0.57	18.32	14	0	99	0	1	103	75.1	-19.0	89	1	1,000,000	0	0.0	0.0
C /4.4	13.6	0.82	18.47	118	0	99	0	1	103	75.7	-19.0	69	1	2,000	250	0.0	0.0
C+ /6.3	11.1	0.88	15.09	126	1	96	1	2	94	36.4	-23.3	38	2	2,000	250	4.8	2.0
C+ /6.3	11.1	0.88	13.01	12	1	96	1	2	94	30.2	-23.6	28	2	2,000	250	0.0	2.0
C+ /6.3	11.1	0.88	16.05	79	1	96	1	2	94	40.8	-23.1	45	2	1,000,000	0	0.0	0.0
C+ /6.3	11.1	0.88	15.91	19	1	96	1	2	94	38.9	-23.2	42	2	2,000	250	0.0	0.0
C+ /5.6	11.5	0.86	15.06	98	3	96	0	1	52	66.9	-23.5	75	1	2,000	250	4.8	2.0
C+ /5.7	11.5	0.86	14.80	5	3	96	0	1	52	59.2	-23.7	66	1	2,000	250	0.0	2.0
C+ /5.6	11.5	0.86	14.80	85	3	96	0	1	52	70.8	-23.3	79	1	1,000,000	0	0.0	0.0
C+ /5.6	11.5	0.86	14.40	35	3	96	0	1	52	69.1	-23.4	77	1	2,000	250	0.0	0.0
C+ /6.4	7.2	1.10	17.99	201	2	70	26	2	61	64.4	-11.6	32	3	2,000	250	4.8	2.0
C+ /6.3	7.2	1.11	17.19	42	2	70	26	2	61	57.9	-11.9	24	3	2,000	250	0.0	2.0
C+ /6.5	7.2	1.10	17.99	2	2	70	26	2	61	64.8	-11.6	33	3	2,000	250	0.0	0.0
C /4.7	13.3	0.80	24.33	162	0	99	0	1	150	134.5	-23.7	91	2	2,000	250	4.8	2.0
C /4.4	13.3	0.80	21.47	18	0	99	0	1	150	124.4	-24.0	88	2	2,000	250	0.0	2.0
C /4.8	13.3	0.80	25.97	95	0	99	0	1	150	142.1	-23.4	93	2	1,000,000	0	0.0	0.0
C /4.7	13.3	0.80	24.53	33	0	99	0	1	150	136.9	-23.7	92	2	2,000	250	0.0	0.0
U /	N/A	N/A	15.11	56	6	0	93	1	132	N/A	N/A	N/A	3	1,000,000	0	0.0	0.0
C+ /6.1	10.9	1.05	19.99	343	0	99	0	1	27	132.7	-15.9	60	N/A	5,000	250	4.8	2.0
C+ /6.0	10.9	1.04	18.90	49	0	99	0	1	27	122.4	-16.2	49	N/A	5,000	250	0.0	2.0
C+ /6.0	10.9	1.05	20.44	443	0	99	0	1	27	138.9	-15.7	65	N/A	100,000	0	0.0	0.0
C+ /6.0	10.9	1.04	19.99	65	0	99	0	1	27	134.0	-15.9	61	N/A	10,000	250	0.0	0.0
U /	N/A	N/A	21.98	35	0	99	0	1	43	N/A	N/A	N/A	2	100,000	0	0.0	0.0
U /	N/A	N/A	22.24	26	0	99	0	1	53	N/A	N/A	N/A	2	5,000	250	4.8	0.0
U /	N/A	N/A	22.28	64	0	99	0	1	53	N/A	N/A	N/A	2	100,000	0	0.0	0.0
C /5.1	10.6	0.78	11.81	14	6	93	0	1	59	N/A	N/A	90	6	2,500	100	0.0	2.0
C /5.3	17.7	1.27	19.11	118	10	89	0	1	115	109.8	-39.9	3	10	2,500	100	0.0	2.0
C+ /6.7	10.4	0.81	24.35	1,682	4	95	0	1	39	N/A	N/A	79	20	5,000,000	0	0.0	2.0
C+ /6.7	10.4	0.81	24.30	1,335	4	95	0	1	39	58.3	-24.1	78	20	2,500	100	0.0	2.0
C /5.4	11.9	1.06	24.31	181	2	97	0	1	55	109.0	-26.6	40	19	5,000,000	0	0.0	0.0
C /5.4	11.9	1.06	24.37	180	2	97	0	1	55	106.1	-26.6	37	19	2,500	100	0.0	0.0
C- /3.0	16.6	0.96	19.65	359	0	97	1	2	59	98.6	-26.8	19	13	5,000,000	0	0.0	2.0
D+ /2.9	16.6	0.96	19.21	181	0	97	1	2	59	95.9	-26.9	17	13	2,500	100	0.0	2.0
C+ /6.0	13.7	1.10	15.89	32	12	87	0	1	78	144.2	N/A	17	6	2,500	100	0.0	2.0
C+ /6.8	13.1	0.64	8.80	11	28	71	0	1	23	N/A	N/A	34	4	2,500	50	5.8	0.0
C+ /6.8	12.8	0.63	9.13	N/A	28	71	0	1	23	N/A	N/A	35	4	2,500	50	0.0	0.0
C /4.5	12.8	1.00	10.16	63	2	82	14	2	44	82.8	-17.2	16	7	2,500	50	5.8	0.0
C /4.5	12.8	1.00	10.08	2	2	82	14	2	44	75.9	-17.4	12	7	2,500	50	0.0	0.0
C+ /6.9	9.9	0.89	14.84	73	3	89	7	1	277	76.2	-15.8	21	9	2,500	100	0.0	2.0
C+ /6.5	9.7	0.57	10.92	287	11	51	36	2	51	N/A	N/A	61	6	25,000	0	0.0	0.0
C+ /5.9	9.8	0.73	13.34	501	0	96	2	2	36	79.2	-18.9	93	6	25,000	0	0.0	0.0
C+ /6.0	10.4	0.80	11.37	1,317	1	94	4	1	21	45.1	-20.0	74	6	25,000	0	0.0	0.0
C+ /6.3	10.1	0.95	21.06	228	0	95	4	1	31	112.2	-17.6	56	4	25,000	0	0.0	0.0
C+ /5.6	11.2	0.86	23.90	19	1	97	0	2	25	116.5	-21.5	74	1	25,000	500	0.0	0.0
C /4.6	11.2	0.87	19.07	1	1	97	0	2	25	108.4	-21.7	66	1	1,000	500	3.0	0.0
C- /3.9	13.8	0.80	20.71	15	4	87	7	2	31	69.7	-17.6	8	1	25,000	500	0.0	0.0
C- /3.8	13.8	0.80	19.36	N/A	4	87	7	2	31	66.7	-17.7	7	1	1,000	500	3.0	0.0
U /	N/A	N/A	11.85	37	5	94	0	1	72	N/A	N/A	N/A	3	1,000,000	0	0.0	0.0
B- /7.1	6.7	0.41	20.40	22	33	66	0	1	38	46.8	-6.1	95	7	2,000	100	0.0	2.0
B- /7.2	6.7	0.41	21.48	156	33	66	0	1	38	55.0	-5.7	97	7	4,000	100	0.0	2.0
C /4.9	13.7	1.03	19.13	129	2	97	0	1	119	N/A	N/A	83	6	2,500	50	5.8	0.0

99 Pct = Best

0 Pct = Worst

| Fund Type | Fund Name | Ticker Symbol | Overall Investment Rating | Phone | Performance Rating/Pts | 3 Mo | 6 Mo | 1Yr / Pct | 3Yr / Pct | 5Yr / Pct | Dividend Yield | Expense Ratio |

|---|---|---|---|---|---|---|---|---|---|---|---|---|

| GR | Catalyst Dynamic Alpha C | CPECX | A- | (866) 447-4228 | A+ / 9.8 | 8.84 | 11.82 | 30.79 /88 | 11.70 /98 | 16.18 /98 | 0.00 | 2.26 |

| GR | Catalyst Dynamic Alpha I | CPEIX | U | (866) 447-4228 | U / | 9.01 | 12.32 | 32.05 /90 | -- | -- | 0.00 | 1.26 |

| GR | ● Catalyst Exceed Defined Risk A | CLPAX | D+ | (866) 447-4228 | D / 2.2 | 3.31 | 7.09 | 12.64 /20 | 3.18 /33 | -- | 0.00 | 2.42 |

| GR | ● Catalyst Exceed Defined Risk C | CLPCX | D+ | (866) 447-4228 | D+ / 2.5 | 3.06 | 6.45 | 11.41 /16 | 2.28 /26 | -- | 0.00 | 3.17 |

| IN | Catalyst Hedged Commodity Strat A | CFHAX | U | (866) 447-4228 | U / | 4.52 | 0.80 | 15.65 /33 | -- | -- | 0.93 | 3.70 |

| IN | Catalyst Hedged Commodity Strat I | CFHIX | U | (866) 447-4228 | U / | 4.60 | 0.99 | 15.96 /34 | -- | -- | 1.07 | 3.45 |

| IN | ● Catalyst Hedged Futures Strategy A | HFXAX | D- | (866) 447-4228 | E- / 0.0 | -20.03 | -21.03 | -13.19 / 0 | -2.30 / 6 | 1.47 / 7 | 0.00 | 2.26 |

| IN | ● Catalyst Hedged Futures Strategy C | HFXCX | D- | (866) 447-4228 | E- / 0.1 | -20.27 | -21.42 | -13.92 / 0 | -3.06 / 4 | 0.93 / 6 | 0.00 | 3.01 |

| IN | ● Catalyst Hedged Futures Strategy I | HFXIX | E | (866) 447-4228 | E- / 0.1 | -20.05 | -21.03 | -13.11 / 0 | -2.09 / 6 | 1.62 / 7 | 0.00 | 2.01 |

| IN | Catalyst Insider Buying A | INSAX | C- | (866) 447-4228 | C- / 3.3 | 8.66 | 11.77 | 18.49 /45 | 2.06 /24 | 10.11 /59 | 0.00 | 1.49 |

| IN | Catalyst Insider Buying C | INSCX | C- | (866) 447-4228 | C- / 3.8 | 8.46 | 11.33 | 17.65 /41 | 1.31 /20 | 9.82 /57 | 0.00 | 2.24 |

| GR | Catalyst Insider Long/Short A | CIAAX | E+ | (866) 447-4228 | E / 0.5 | 4.89 | 6.67 | -8.00 / 0 | 1.48 /21 | -- | 0.00 | 4.04 |

| GR | Catalyst Insider Long/Short C | CIACX | E+ | (866) 447-4228 | E+ / 0.7 | 4.59 | 6.05 | -8.81 / 0 | 0.70 /17 | -- | 0.00 | 4.79 |

| EN | Catalyst MLP Infrastructure A | MLXAX | U | (866) 447-4228 | U / | 3.64 | 15.39 | 87.65 /99 | -- | -- | 7.64 | 2.03 |

| EN | Catalyst MLP Infrastructure I | MLXIX | U | (866) 447-4228 | U / | 3.83 | 15.65 | 88.51 /99 | -- | -- | 8.26 | 1.78 |

| SC | Catalyst Small Cap Insider Buying A | CTVAX | E- | (866) 447-4228 | E- / 0.2 | 2.54 | 7.35 | 28.46 /83 | -6.44 / 2 | 4.31 /17 | 0.60 | 1.96 |

| SC | Catalyst Small Cap Insider Buying C | CTVCX | E- | (866) 447-4228 | E / 0.3 | 2.38 | 6.97 | 27.51 /81 | -7.14 / 1 | 3.53 /13 | 0.00 | 2.71 |

| SC | Catalyst Small Cap Insider Buying I | CTVIX | E- | (866) 447-4228 | E / 0.4 | 2.63 | 7.48 | 28.82 /84 | -6.20 / 2 | 4.57 /19 | 1.02 | 1.71 |

| GR | Catalyst/EquityCompass Buyback St | BUYAX | C+ | (866) 447-4228 | C / 5.1 | 5.01 | 9.95 | 21.25 /58 | 5.63 /61 | -- | 0.21 | 2.10 |

| GR | Catalyst/EquityCompass Buyback St | BUYCX | C+ | (866) 447-4228 | C+ / 5.7 | 4.84 | 9.63 | 20.39 /54 | 4.86 /53 | -- | 0.00 | 2.85 |

| GR | Catalyst/EquityCompass Buyback St I | BUYIX | C+ | (866) 447-4228 | C+ / 6.5 | 5.08 | 10.21 | 21.61 /60 | 5.89 /63 | -- | 0.48 | 1.85 |

| IN | Catalyst/Groesbeck Growth of Inc A | CGGAX | D- | (866) 447-4228 | C / 5.5 | 6.97 | 7.48 | 23.90 /69 | 5.75 /62 | 8.41 /45 | 1.81 | 1.74 |

| IN | Catalyst/Groesbeck Growth of Inc C | CGGCX | D | (866) 447-4228 | C+ / 6.1 | 6.88 | 7.12 | 23.13 /67 | 5.00 /54 | 7.64 /39 | 1.04 | 2.49 |

| IN | Catalyst/Groesbeck Growth of Inc I | CGGIX | D+ | (866) 447-4228 | C+ / 6.9 | 7.13 | 7.87 | 24.60 /72 | 6.13 /65 | 8.75 /48 | 2.10 | 1.49 |

| AA | Catalyst/Lyons Tactical Alloc A | CLTAX | C+ | (866) 447-4228 | C+ / 6.9 | 6.81 | 11.67 | 20.60 /55 | 8.18 /80 | -- | 1.21 | 1.74 |

| AA | Catalyst/Lyons Tactical Alloc C | CLTCX | B | (866) 447-4228 | B- / 7.3 | 6.63 | 11.25 | 19.75 /51 | 7.40 /75 | -- | 0.50 | 2.49 |

| GL | Catalyst/MAP Global Balance A | TRXAX | D+ | (866) 447-4228 | D / 1.9 | 4.98 | 3.29 | 9.51 /10 | 3.29 /35 | 5.88 /27 | 1.34 | 1.84 |

| GL | Catalyst/MAP Global Balance C | TRXCX | C- | (866) 447-4228 | D / 2.2 | 4.80 | 2.97 | 8.67 / 9 | 2.54 /28 | 5.10 /22 | 0.80 | 2.59 |

| GL | Catalyst/MAP Global Equity A | CAXAX | C | (866) 447-4228 | C / 4.4 | 8.52 | 6.59 | 19.59 /50 | 4.76 /52 | 8.93 /50 | 0.95 | 1.71 |

| GL | Catalyst/MAP Global Equity C | CAXCX | C+ | (866) 447-4228 | C / 4.9 | 8.28 | 6.17 | 18.65 /46 | 3.95 /42 | 8.11 /43 | 0.36 | 2.46 |

| GL | Catalyst/Millburn Hedge Strategy A | MBXAX | A+ | (866) 447-4228 | A / 9.3 | 7.29 | 5.30 | 19.43 /49 | 14.71 /99 | 10.34 /61 | 1.09 | 2.35 |

| GL | Catalyst/Millburn Hedge Strategy C | MBXCX | A+ | (866) 447-4228 | A+ / 9.6 | 7.09 | 4.95 | 18.56 /45 | 14.37 /99 | 10.14 /59 | 0.91 | 3.10 |

| GL | Catalyst/Millburn Hedge Strategy I | MBXIX | A+ | (866) 447-4228 | A+ / 9.7 | 7.34 | 5.42 | 19.69 /50 | 14.81 /99 | 10.39 /61 | 1.24 | 2.10 |

| GI | Catalyst/SMH Total Return Income A | TRIFX | E | (866) 447-4228 | D- / 1.1 | 7.96 | 10.96 | 45.92 /99 | -4.79 / 3 | 0.94 / 6 | 5.15 | 3.90 |

| GI | Catalyst/SMH Total Return Income C | TRICX | E | (866) 447-4228 | D- / 1.3 | 7.76 | 10.58 | 44.87 /98 | -5.50 / 2 | 0.19 / 5 | 4.81 | 4.64 |

| GL | Catalyst/SMH Total Return Income I | TRIIX | E | (866) 447-4228 | D / 1.7 | 7.78 | 11.11 | 45.95 /99 | -4.61 / 3 | -- | 5.68 | 3.64 |

| EM | Causeway Emerging Mkt Instl | CEMIX | C- | (866) 947-7000 | C / 5.3 | 10.42 | 7.34 | 30.68 /88 | 1.94 /24 | 1.19 / 6 | 1.41 | 1.21 |

| EM | Causeway Emerging Mkt Inv | CEMVX | C- | (866) 947-7000 | C / 5.1 | 10.39 | 7.22 | 30.35 /87 | 1.71 /22 | 0.94 / 6 | 1.18 | 1.48 |

| FO | Causeway Global Absolute Rtn Inst | CGAIX | D- | (866) 947-7000 | E- / 0.2 | -9.54 | -2.66 | -1.33 / 1 | -1.01 / 9 | 0.63 / 5 | 11.99 | 1.87 |

| FO | Causeway Global Absolute Rtn Inv | CGAVX | D- | (866) 947-7000 | E- / 0.2 | -9.60 | -2.75 | -1.61 / 1 | -1.26 / 8 | 0.35 / 5 | 11.77 | 2.12 |

| GL | Causeway Global Value Institutional | CGVIX | D | (866) 947-7000 | C- / 3.1 | 4.26 | 5.73 | 20.11 /53 | 2.19 /25 | 7.73 /40 | 1.34 | 1.10 |

| GL | Causeway Global Value Investor | CGVVX | D | (866) 947-7000 | D+ / 2.9 | 4.11 | 5.58 | 19.76 /51 | 1.91 /23 | 7.49 /38 | 1.18 | 1.35 |

| FO | Causeway International Oppty Instl | CIOIX | D- | (866) 947-7000 | E+ / 0.9 | 6.92 | 5.37 | 16.47 /36 | -1.50 / 8 | 4.27 /17 | 3.77 | 1.19 |

| FO | Causeway International Oppty Inv | CIOVX | D- | (866) 947-7000 | E+ / 0.9 | 6.82 | 5.18 | 16.22 /35 | -1.75 / 7 | 4.00 /15 | 3.58 | 1.46 |

| FO | Causeway International Value Instl | CIVIX | D- | (866) 947-7000 | E+ / 0.6 | 5.88 | 4.67 | 14.26 /27 | -2.46 / 6 | 5.16 /22 | 1.90 | 0.90 |

| FO | Causeway International Value Inv | CIVVX | E+ | (866) 947-7000 | E / 0.5 | 5.79 | 4.49 | 13.97 /25 | -2.71 / 5 | 4.90 /21 | 1.64 | 1.15 |

| GL | Cavalier Dividend Income Advisor | CDVNX | D+ | (877) 773-3863 | D- / 1.0 | 2.67 | 2.44 | 9.82 /11 | -0.30 /12 | -- | 0.46 | 9.58 |

| GL | Cavalier Dividend Income Inst | CDVDX | D+ | (877) 773-3863 | D / 1.7 | 2.99 | 3.04 | 11.04 /15 | 0.75 /17 | -- | 0.74 | 8.58 |

| AA | Cavalier Dynamic Growth Advisor | CADYX | D- | (877) 773-3863 | C- / 3.2 | 5.70 | 5.16 | 13.95 /25 | 2.85 /30 | 7.51 /38 | 0.00 | 2.92 |

| AA | Cavalier Dynamic Growth Inst | CDYGX | D | (877) 773-3863 | C- / 4.0 | 5.93 | 5.62 | 15.10 /30 | 3.85 /41 | 8.57 /47 | 0.00 | 1.92 |

| GL | Cavalier Fundamental Growth | CFGAX | D+ | (877) 773-3863 | D+ / 2.5 | 6.22 | 3.15 | 12.79 /21 | 1.78 /23 | -- | 0.22 | 2.52 |

| GL | Cavalier Fundamental Growth Inst | CAFGX | D+ | (877) 773-3863 | C- / 3.1 | 6.53 | 3.60 | 13.83 /25 | 2.79 /30 | -- | 0.22 | 1.52 |

● Denotes fund is closed to new investors

* Denotes fund is included in Section II

www.thestreetratings.com

Risk Rating/Pts	3 Year Standard Deviation	Beta	NAV As of 2/28/17	Total $(Mil)	Cash %	Stocks %	Bonds %	Other %	Portfolio Turnover Ratio	Last Bull Market Return	Last Bear Market Return	Manager Quality Pct	Manager Tenure (Years)	Initial Purch. $	Additional Purch. $	Front End Load	Back End Load
C /4.8	13.6	1.03	18.35	40	2	97	0	1	119	N/A	N/A	79	6	2,500	50	0.0	0.0
U /	N/A	N/A	19.24	52	2	97	0	1	119	N/A	N/A	N/A	6	2,500	50	0.0	0.0
C+ /6.7	13.0	1.09	9.36	N/A	0	0	0	100	153	N/A	N/A	4	4	2,500	50	5.8	0.0
C+ /6.7	13.0	1.09	9.08	N/A	0	0	0	100	153	N/A	N/A	3	4	2,500	50	0.0	0.0
U /	N/A	N/A	10.94	44	0	0	0	100	194	N/A	N/A	N/A	2	2,500	50	5.8	0.0
U /	N/A	N/A	10.97	55	0	0	0	100	194	N/A	N/A	N/A	2	2,500	50	0.0	0.0
C+ /6.9	13.6	-0.42	8.61	947	0	0	0	100	177	12.7	8.5	85	N/A	2,500	50	5.8	0.0
C+ /6.9	13.6	-0.42	8.36	330	0	0	0	100	177	9.7	8.5	81	N/A	2,500	50	0.0	0.0
C /4.4	13.6	-0.43	8.68	1,783	0	0	0	100	177	13.5	8.5	86	N/A	2,500	50	0.0	0.0
C+ /6.0	11.8	1.02	15.19	49	2	97	0	1	167	96.4	N/A	3	6	2,500	50	5.8	0.0
C+ /6.0	11.7	1.02	15.13	22	2	97	0	1	167	93.2	N/A	3	6	2,500	50	0.0	0.0
C /5.3	16.1	0.32	9.43	3	96	0	3	1	184	N/A	N/A	50	5	2,500	50	5.8	0.0
C /5.1	16.0	0.32	9.11	1	96	0	3	1	184	N/A	N/A	39	5	2,500	50	0.0	0.0
U /	N/A	N/A	7.30	48	34	65	0	1	96	N/A	N/A	N/A	N/A	2,500	50	5.8	0.0
U /	N/A	N/A	7.32	73	34	65	0	1	96	N/A	N/A	N/A	N/A	2,500	50	0.0	0.0
D+ /2.8	18.8	1.01	13.89	15	1	98	0	1	189	45.3	-32.9	1	11	2,500	50	5.8	0.0
D+ /2.8	18.7	1.01	13.35	5	1	98	0	1	189	39.5	-33.1	1	11	2,500	50	0.0	0.0
D+ /2.8	18.8	1.01	13.94	4	1	98	0	1	189	47.3	-32.8	1	11	2,500	50	0.0	0.0
C+ /6.6	12.4	1.00	11.19	4	2	97	0	1	790	N/A	N/A	18	4	2,500	50	5.8	0.0
C+ /6.6	12.4	1.00	11.04	4	2	97	0	1	790	N/A	N/A	12	4	2,500	50	0.0	0.0
C+ /6.6	12.4	1.00	11.23	2	2	97	0	1	790	N/A	N/A	20	4	2,500	50	0.0	0.0
D- /1.5	12.3	1.12	9.71	8	8	91	0	1	45	78.3	-11.1	11	8	2,500	50	5.8	0.0
D- /1.4	12.3	1.12	9.51	N/A	8	91	0	1	45	71.4	-11.4	7	8	2,500	50	0.0	0.0
D- /1.5	12.3	1.12	9.75	N/A	8	91	0	1	45	81.2	-11.0	13	8	2,500	50	0.0	0.0
C+ /6.3	11.1	1.60	15.03	53	0	99	0	1	91	N/A	N/A	27	2	2,500	50	5.8	0.0
C+ /6.3	11.2	1.60	14.82	33	0	99	0	1	91	N/A	N/A	20	2	2,500	50	0.0	0.0
B- /7.4	6.0	0.44	11.65	14	7	55	36	2	15	44.0	N/A	91	6	2,500	50	5.8	0.0
B- /7.4	6.1	0.44	11.56	7	7	55	36	2	15	38.4	N/A	88	6	2,500	50	0.0	0.0
C+ /6.4	9.3	0.66	13.61	22	8	91	0	1	26	70.4	N/A	95	6	2,500	50	5.8	0.0
C+ /6.5	9.3	0.66	13.50	8	8	91	0	1	26	63.6	N/A	93	6	2,500	50	0.0	0.0
B /8.5	10.0	0.25	30.16	265	0	0	0	100	1	75.8	-17.8	99	20	2,500	50	5.8	0.0
B /8.5	10.0	0.25	29.97	140	0	0	0	100	1	74.3	-17.8	99	20	2,500	50	0.0	0.0
B /8.5	10.0	0.25	30.21	1,225	0	0	0	100	1	76.3	-17.8	99	20	2,500	50	0.0	0.0
D+ /2.6	14.9	0.97	4.46	7	19	46	34	1	4	19.7	-19.6	0	9	2,500	50	5.8	0.0
D+ /2.6	14.9	0.98	4.46	9	19	46	34	1	4	15.0	-19.9	0	9	2,500	50	0.0	0.0
D+ /2.6	14.8	0.82	4.45	7	19	46	34	1	4	N/A	N/A	18	9	2,500	50	0.0	0.0
C /4.7	16.0	0.98	11.36	2,656	0	98	1	1	73	33.5	-27.4	76	10	1,000,000	0	0.0	2.0
C /4.7	16.0	0.98	11.45	636	0	98	1	1	73	31.8	-27.4	74	10	5,000	0	0.0	2.0
C+ /6.9	7.2	-0.18	9.11	49	100	0	0	0	0	13.1	-0.7	60	6	1,000,000	0	0.0	2.0
C+ /6.9	7.2	-0.19	9.04	18	100	0	0	0	0	11.4	-0.8	56	6	5,000	0	0.0	2.0
C /5.0	10.8	0.80	11.15	114	0	97	2	1	64	81.3	-22.8	87	9	1,000,000	0	0.0	2.0
C /5.1	10.8	0.80	11.10	3	0	97	2	1	64	79.0	-22.9	86	9	5,000	0	0.0	2.0
C /5.5	11.2	0.90	11.92	76	4	95	0	1	63	49.9	-26.2	57	8	1,000,000	0	0.0	2.0
C /5.5	11.2	0.90	11.85	3	4	95	0	1	63	43.7	-26.3	54	8	5,000	0	0.0	2.0
C+ /5.6	11.0	0.88	14.31	5,668	0	95	3	2	41	55.2	-25.8	43	16	1,000,000	0	0.0	2.0
C+ /5.6	11.0	0.88	14.21	711	0	95	3	2	41	53.2	-25.9	40	16	5,000	0	0.0	2.0
B- /7.5	7.4	0.50	10.81	N/A	3	52	43	2	118	N/A	N/A	71	2	250	50	0.0	0.0
B- /7.6	7.4	0.50	10.69	1	3	52	43	2	118	N/A	N/A	79	2	250	50	0.0	0.0
C- /3.7	11.9	1.54	9.58	1	7	92	0	1	313	62.5	-17.4	3	N/A	250	50	0.0	0.0
C- /3.9	11.9	1.54	10.12	6	7	92	0	1	313	71.1	-17.0	5	N/A	250	50	0.0	0.0
C+ /6.1	12.3	0.56	12.13	3	1	98	0	1	172	N/A	N/A	85	4	250	50	0.0	0.0
C+ /6.1	12.2	0.56	12.39	59	1	98	0	1	172	N/A	N/A	90	4	250	50	0.0	0.0

Fund Type	Fund Name	Ticker Symbol	Overall Investment Rating	Phone	Performance Rating/Pts	3 Mo	6 Mo	1Yr / Pct	3Yr / Pct	5Yr / Pct	Dividend Yield	Expense Ratio
	99 Pct = Best							Total Return % through 2/28/17	Annualized		Incl. in Returns	
GL	Cavalier Global Opportunities Adv	CATDX	C+	(877) 773-3863	C+ / 5.7	7.47	9.28	22.75 /66	3.93 /42	--	0.19	2.49
GL	Cavalier Global Opportunities Inst	CATEX	C+	(877) 773-3863	C+ / 6.6	7.69	9.80	24.03 /70	4.98 /54	--	0.19	1.49
GL	Cavalier Multi Strategist Adv	CMSYX	C	(877) 773-3863	C- / 3.8	7.31	7.41	15.89 /34	2.70 /29	--	0.00	5.50
GL	Cavalier Multi Strategist Inst	CMSFX	C+	(877) 773-3863	C / 4.7	7.62	7.91	17.06 /39	3.72 /39	--	0.00	4.50
GL	Cavalier Tactical Rotation Advisor	CATOX	B-	(877) 773-3863	C / 5.1	5.93	7.91	16.06 /35	5.03 /54	--	0.00	2.79
GL	Cavalier Tactical Rotation Inst	CTROX	B-	(877) 773-3863	C+ / 6.0	6.19	8.39	17.21 /39	6.06 /65	--	0.00	1.79
BA	Cavanal Hill Active Core A	AABAX	C	(800) 762-7085	C- / 3.3	4.29	3.80	11.82 /17	5.18 /56	7.02 /35	1.37	1.04
BA	Cavanal Hill Active Core Instl	AIBLX	C+	(800) 762-7085	C- / 4.2	4.33	3.92	12.19 /19	5.46 /59	7.30 /37	1.63	0.94
BA	Cavanal Hill Active Core Investor	APBAX	C	(800) 762-7085	C- / 4.0	4.28	3.79	11.85 /17	5.28 /57	7.07 /35	1.39	1.19
GI	Cavanal Hill Mult Cap Eqty Inc A	AAEQX	E+	(800) 762-7085	C / 4.4	4.10	6.19	19.07 /47	5.18 /56	9.71 /56	0.43	1.24
GR	Cavanal Hill Mult Cap Eqty Inc Inst	AIEQX	D-	(800) 762-7085	C / 5.4	4.13	6.29	19.36 /49	5.45 /59	9.98 /58	0.68	1.14
GR	Cavanal Hill Mult Cap Eqty Inc Inv	APEQX	E+	(800) 762-7085	C / 5.2	4.03	6.13	19.03 /47	5.22 /57	9.73 /56	0.47	1.38
GL	Cavanal Hill Opportunistic A	AAOPX	C	(800) 762-7085	C- / 4.0	5.06	12.71	16.40 /36	3.61 /38	8.01 /42	0.12	1.64
GL	Cavanal Hill Opportunistic Inst	AIOPX	C+	(800) 762-7085	C / 5.0	5.16	12.90	16.79 /38	3.90 /42	8.28 /44	0.39	1.54
GL	Cavanal Hill Opportunistic Investor	APOPX	C+	(800) 762-7085	C / 4.8	5.08	12.74	16.41 /36	3.62 /38	7.92 /41	0.16	1.79
EN	Cavanal Hill World Energy A	AAWEX	E+	(800) 762-7085	E+ / 0.6	-2.45	7.46	25.23 /74	-3.03 / 4	--	1.00	1.30
EN	Cavanal Hill World Energy C	ACWEX	E+	(800) 762-7085	E+ / 0.7	-2.54	7.13	24.58 /72	-3.71 / 3	--	0.38	2.20
EN	Cavanal Hill World Energy Instl	AIWEX	E+	(800) 762-7085	D- / 1.0	-2.27	7.71	25.78 /76	-2.70 / 5	--	1.27	1.20
EN	Cavanal Hill World Energy Investor	APWEX	E+	(800) 762-7085	E+ / 0.9	-2.35	7.56	25.33 /74	-3.01 / 4	--	1.00	1.45
OT	CBRE Clarion Gbl Infras Val Inst	CGIVX	D+	(866) 777-7818	C / 4.7	7.22	1.74	15.66 /33	6.07 /65	--	2.08	1.43
OT	CBRE Clarion Gbl Infras Val Inv	CGILX	C	(866) 777-7818	C / 4.4	7.14	1.58	15.21 /31	5.75 /62	--	1.80	1.76
RE	CBRE Clarion Long/Short Inst	CLSIX	D-	(855) 520-4227	D- / 1.2	2.03	-2.75	5.09 / 4	2.44 /27	2.53 / 9	0.00	4.08
RE	CBRE Clarion Long/Short Investor	CLSVX	D-	(855) 520-4227	D- / 1.1	1.94	-2.96	4.69 / 4	2.14 /25	2.28 / 9	0.00	4.28
GL	CCA Aggressive Return Inst	RSKIX	D	(800) 595-4866	E+ / 0.7	4.81	2.71	10.37 /13	-1.09 / 9	--	0.41	1.78
GL	CCA Aggressive Return Inv	RSKAX	D	(800) 595-4866	E+ / 0.7	4.69	2.61	10.24 /12	-1.32 / 8	--	0.13	2.04
GL	CCA Core Return Inst	CORIX	D+	(800) 595-4866	D- / 1.5	4.58	0.85	11.12 /15	0.96 /18	--	1.10	2.45
GL	CCA Core Return Inv	CORAX	D+	(800) 595-4866	D- / 1.4	4.56	0.68	10.73 /14	0.68 /17	--	0.75	2.70
GL	CCM Alternative Income Inst	CCMNX	C-	(877) 272-1977	D / 1.9	2.45	2.40	8.15 / 8	2.23 /25	--	4.22	2.83
FS	Cedar Ridge Uncons Credit Inst	CRUMX	C+	(855) 550-5090	D / 2.0	3.66	0.78	7.34 / 6	3.22 /34	--	2.24	3.84
FS	Cedar Ridge Uncons Credit Inv	CRUPX	C+	(855) 550-5090	D / 1.9	3.50	0.65	6.98 / 6	2.93 /31	--	2.01	4.09
GI	Centaur Total Return	TILDX	C	(888) 484-5766	C- / 3.6	3.02	5.83	14.09 /26	4.70 /51	8.34 /45	0.00	2.58
EN	Center Coast MLP Focus A	CCCAX	D	(877) 766-0066	C / 4.3	8.07	10.45	37.04 /96	0.13 /14	3.06 /11	7.34	1.47
EN	Center Coast MLP Focus C	CCCCX	D-	(877) 766-0066	D+ / 2.8	7.92	10.17	36.04 /95	-0.60 /11	2.30 / 9	8.29	2.22
EN	Center Coast MLP Focus Inst	CCCNX	C-	(877) 766-0066	C+ / 5.8	8.20	10.69	37.35 /96	0.39 /15	3.33 /12	7.68	1.22
FO	Centerstone International I	CINTX	U	(877) 314-9006	U /	5.06	1.54	--	--	--	0.00	N/A
GL	Centerstone Investors I	CENTX	U	(877) 314-9006	U /	3.64	1.45	--	--	--	0.00	N/A
GR	Centre American Select Equity Inst	DHANX	C+	(855) 298-4236	C / 5.0	7.73	5.70	12.78 /21	6.27 /66	--	2.41	1.11
GR	Centre American Select Equity Inv	DHAMX	C	(855) 298-4236	C / 4.9	7.73	5.60	12.68 /20	6.17 /66	9.71 /56	2.06	1.33
FS	Century Shares Trust Inst	CENSX	C	(800) 321-1928	C+ / 6.9	8.47	6.63	15.32 /31	8.25 /81	12.08 /75	0.16	1.11
SC	Century Small Cap Select Instl	CSMCX	E	(800) 321-1928	C / 4.4	7.34	8.73	23.22 /67	2.19 /25	8.28 /44	0.00	1.13
SC	Century Small Cap Select Inv	CSMVX	E	(800) 321-1928	C- / 4.1	7.26	8.55	22.87 /66	1.87 /23	7.94 /42	0.00	1.42
AA	CG Core Balanced Institutional	CGBNX	C+		C / 5.1	5.98	8.63	21.89 /62	3.62 /38	--	0.65	11.80
EM	CGCM Emerging Mkts Eqty	TEMUX	C-	(800) 444-4273	C / 5.2	8.84	4.71	29.29 /85	2.19 /25	-0.92 / 3	1.02	1.08
FO	CGCM Intl Equity	TIEUX	D-	(800) 444-4273	E+ / 0.8	6.45	2.52	12.26 /19	-1.72 / 7	3.17 /11	2.65	0.81
GR	CGCM Large Cap Equity	TLGUX	C-	(800) 444-4273	B / 7.8	7.51	8.58	23.91 /70	7.83 /78	12.69 /81	1.46	0.68
SC	CGCM Small Mid Cap Equity	TSGUX	E+	(800) 444-4273	C / 5.3	5.94	10.33	29.10 /84	1.96 /24	10.15 /59	0.30	0.93
AG	CGM Focus	CGMFX	B	(800) 345-4048	A+ / 9.7	11.87	26.87	43.50 /98	4.42 /48	9.20 /52	0.00	2.22
BA	CGM Mutual	LOMMX	B-	(800) 345-4048	B- / 7.3	6.03	16.18	26.87 /79	4.94 /53	7.63 /39	0.00	1.12
RE	CGM Realty	CGMRX	C+	(800) 345-4048	B / 8.1	4.11	12.56	29.73 /86	7.19 /73	8.26 /44	0.35	0.92
GL	Chadwick & D'Amato	CDFFX	D		E+ / 0.6	1.00	-0.09	9.69 /11	-1.42 / 8	2.01 / 8	0.00	2.31
MC	Champlain Mid Cap Fd Institutional	CIPIX	B+	(866) 777-7818	A+ / 9.8	8.36	12.01	34.29 /93	11.19 /97	14.26 /95	0.06	0.96
MC	Champlain Mid Cap Fund	CIPMX	B+	(866) 777-7818	A+ / 9.8	8.28	11.83	33.89 /93	10.99 /97	14.03 /93	0.00	1.21

● Denotes fund is closed to new investors
* Denotes fund is included in Section II

www.thestreetratings.com

Risk Rating/Pts	Standard Deviation	Beta	NAV As of 2/28/17	Total $(Mil)	Cash %	Stocks %	Bonds %	Other %	Portfolio Turnover Ratio	Last Bull Market Return	Last Bear Market Return	Manager Quality Pct	Manager Tenure (Years)	Initial Purch. $	Additional Purch. $	Front End Load	Back End Load
C+ / 6.6	9.5	0.49	13.61	1	3	86	9	2	285	N/A	N/A	93	2	250	50	0.0	0.0
C+ / 6.7	9.5	0.49	13.95	12	3	86	9	2	285	N/A	N/A	95	2	250	50	0.0	0.0
B- / 7.4	7.2	0.49	11.89	1	12	58	29	1	174	N/A	N/A	89	1	250	50	0.0	0.0
B- / 7.6	7.2	0.49	12.28	7	12	58	29	1	174	N/A	N/A	92	1	250	50	0.0	0.0
B- / 7.4	9.4	0.57	12.14	3	0	0	0	100	634	N/A	N/A	95	1	250	50	0.0	0.0
B- / 7.6	9.4	0.57	12.53	86	0	0	0	100	634	N/A	N/A	97	1	250	50	0.0	0.0
B- / 7.3	5.6	0.88	13.31	2	2	55	42	1	69	58.3	N/A	58	12	0	0	3.5	0.0
B- / 7.3	5.6	0.88	13.39	53	2	55	42	1	69	60.6	-9.3	61	12	100,000	100	0.0	0.0
B- / 7.3	5.6	0.89	13.35	7	2	55	42	1	69	58.7	-9.3	58	12	1,000	0	0.0	0.0
E+ / 0.9	11.4	1.06	8.45	N/A	0	99	0	1	79	95.0	N/A	11	11	0	0	3.5	0.0
E+ / 0.9	11.3	1.05	8.54	2	0	99	0	1	79	97.6	-18.8	13	11	100,000	100	0.0	0.0
E+ / 0.9	11.5	1.06	8.44	2	0	99	0	1	79	95.1	-18.9	11	11	1,000	0	0.0	0.0
B- / 7.1	8.8	0.42	14.54	2	6	80	3	11	266	81.9	N/A	92	5	0	0	3.5	0.0
B- / 7.1	8.8	0.42	14.64	34	6	80	3	11	266	84.5	N/A	93	5	100,000	100	0.0	0.0
B- / 7.1	8.7	0.42	14.49	3	6	80	3	11	266	81.3	N/A	92	5	1,000	0	0.0	0.0
C / 5.0	16.6	0.81	9.24	9	5	77	17	1	150	N/A	N/A	82	N/A	0	0	3.5	0.0
C / 5.0	16.6	0.81	9.18	8	5	77	17	1	150	N/A	N/A	78	N/A	0	0	0.0	0.0
C / 5.0	16.6	0.81	9.27	28	5	77	17	1	150	N/A	N/A	84	N/A	100,000	100	0.0	0.0
C / 5.0	16.6	0.81	9.25	12	5	77	17	1	150	N/A	N/A	82	N/A	1,000	0	0.0	0.0
C / 4.5	10.5	0.67	10.25	31	16	83	0	1	88	N/A	N/A	62	4	1,000,000	0	0.0	2.0
C+ / 6.7	10.5	0.67	10.25	1	16	83	0	1	88	N/A	N/A	59	4	5,000	100	0.0	2.0
C / 5.3	9.1	0.61	9.84	422	11	88	0	1	196	N/A	N/A	23	N/A	1,000,000	0	0.0	2.0
C / 5.3	9.2	0.61	9.77	5	11	88	0	1	196	N/A	N/A	20	N/A	5,000	100	0.0	2.0
C+ / 6.7	8.9	0.96	10.76	21	0	99	0	1	457	N/A	N/A	12	5	100,000	100	0.0	2.0
C+ / 6.8	8.9	0.96	10.80	N/A	0	99	0	1	457	N/A	N/A	11	5	2,500	100	0.0	2.0
B- / 7.7	7.2	1.03	10.36	12	4	50	45	1	56	N/A	N/A	26	5	100,000	100	0.0	2.0
B- / 7.6	7.2	1.03	10.24	N/A	4	50	45	1	56	N/A	N/A	24	5	2,500	100	0.0	2.0
B / 8.5	4.0	0.19	9.64	31	24	38	36	2	86	N/A	N/A	87	4	1,000	0	0.0	0.0
B+ / 9.9	3.7	-0.04	10.87	67	37	1	61	1	64	N/A	N/A	92	4	50,000	5,000	0.0	1.0
B+ / 9.9	3.7	-0.04	10.86	20	37	1	61	1	64	N/A	N/A	91	4	4,000	1,000	0.0	1.0
B- / 7.1	6.5	0.54	12.96	27	14	66	17	3	127	71.8	-15.4	63	12	1,500	100	0.0	2.0
C- / 3.6	17.3	0.61	8.78	494	90	9	0	1	51	31.4	-4.5	91	7	2,500	100	5.8	0.0
C- / 3.5	17.3	0.61	8.25	842	90	9	0	1	51	26.2	-4.8	89	7	2,500	100	0.0	0.0
C- / 3.6	17.3	0.61	8.91	1,479	90	9	0	1	51	33.2	-4.4	92	7	1,000,000	100,000	0.0	0.0
U /	N/A	N/A	10.52	37	0	0	0	100	0	N/A	N/A	N/A	1	100,000	100	0.0	2.0
U /	N/A	N/A	10.52	65	0	0	0	100	0	N/A	N/A	N/A	1	100,000	100	0.0	2.0
B- / 7.2	8.1	0.71	11.83	2	2	96	0	2	74	N/A	N/A	61	N/A	1,000,000	10,000	0.0	2.0
C+ / 6.3	8.2	0.71	11.84	123	2	96	0	2	74	N/A	N/A	59	N/A	5,000	1,000	0.0	2.0
C- / 3.7	10.8	0.61	21.20	220	2	94	3	1	44	121.3	-17.3	79	18	100,000	0	0.0	1.0
E+ / 0.7	16.6	0.99	25.15	89	0	95	3	2	82	91.9	-24.2	19	18	100,000	0	0.0	1.0
E+ / 0.6	16.6	0.99	23.48	67	0	95	3	2	82	88.6	-24.3	17	18	2,500	50	0.0	1.0
B- / 7.1	11.6	1.59	11.21	4	0	0	0	100	155	N/A	N/A	4	4	100,000	100	0.0	0.0
C / 4.7	15.1	0.90	12.80	422	2	96	0	2	99	19.1	-27.0	78	8	100	0	0.0	0.0
C+ / 6.1	10.8	0.87	10.80	1,107	1	97	0	2	64	39.5	-25.5	54	3	100	0	0.0	0.0
D+ / 2.6	11.5	1.06	17.89	1,716	1	97	0	2	105	123.7	-18.4	32	1	100	0	0.0	0.0
E+ / 0.7	16.5	0.98	18.82	501	0	96	3	1	151	110.6	-28.1	18	20	100	0	0.0	0.0
C- / 3.5	20.1	1.53	45.89	983	1	98	0	1	268	88.9	-27.5	2	20	2,500	50	0.0	0.0
C / 5.4	12.8	1.47	32.35	401	0	73	25	2	345	71.9	-18.9	10	36	2,500	50	0.0	0.0
C- / 3.3	16.7	0.68	31.49	904	2	97	0	1	224	84.6	-22.5	71	23	2,500	50	0.0	0.0
B- / 7.5	8.8	1.22	11.09	78	36	36	26	2	24	16.6	-14.6	6	7	250	50	0.0	0.0
C / 4.8	11.2	0.86	16.26	671	5	94	0	1	40	137.6	-18.3	89	13	1,000,000	0	0.0	0.0
C / 4.7	11.2	0.86	16.02	748	5	94	0	1	40	134.9	-18.5	88	13	10,000	0	0.0	0.0

Fund Type	Fund Name	Ticker Symbol	Overall Investment Rating	Phone	Performance Rating/Pts	3 Mo	6 Mo	1Yr / Pct	3Yr / Pct	5Yr / Pct	Dividend Yield	Expense Ratio
	99 Pct = Best 0 Pct = Worst							Total Return % through 2/28/17	Annualized		Incl. in Returns	
SC	Chartwell Small Cap Value I	CWSIX	A-	(866) 585-6552	B+ / 8.7	3.72	12.87	34.06 /93	7.91 /78	—	0.47	1.48
GR	Chase Growth Fund	CHASX	C-	(888) 861-7556	C / 5.2	6.16	4.73	14.90 /29	6.67 /70	11.79 /72	0.00	1.30
GR	Chase Growth Fund Institutional	CHAIX	C-	(888) 861-7556	C / 5.4	6.19	4.81	15.03 /30	6.90 /71	12.05 /75	0.00	1.05
MC	Chase Mid-Cap Growth Fund Inst	CHIMX	C-	(888) 861-7556	C+ / 6.0	5.42	6.94	22.26 /63	6.06 /65	10.78 /64	0.00	1.52
MC	Chase Mid-Cap Growth Fund N	CHAMX	C-	(888) 861-7556	C+ / 5.8	5.36	6.85	22.02 /62	5.83 /63	10.54 /62	0.00	1.76
GR	Chesapeake Growth Fund	CHCGX	B	(800) 430-3863	B- / 7.5	6.38	11.04	22.09 /63	7.33 /74	11.83 /73	0.00	1.98
GI	● Chestnut Street Exchange	CHNTX	A	(800) 441-7762	B / 8.0	6.83	8.81	22.49 /64	8.58 /84	12.48 /79	1.80	N/A
GL	Chiron Capital Allocation Fund I	CCAPX	U	(877) 924-4766	U /	4.94	7.87	15.41 /32	—	—	0.75	1.15
GL	Chou Opportunity	CHOEX	E-	(877) 682-6352	E- / 0.1	4.58	3.81	17.40 /40	-9.32 / 1	3.38 /12	6.21	1.28
GR	Christopher Weil & Co Core Inv	CWCFX	C-	(888) 550-9266	C- / 4.1	7.79	8.12	17.32 /40	3.25 /34	10.14 /59	0.00	1.50
AA	Cincinnati Asset Mgmt Br Mkt St Inc	CAMBX	C-	(866) 738-1128	D / 1.6	2.05	-0.74	6.09 / 5	2.63 /28	—	2.99	3.77
GR	Clark Fork Tarkio	TARKX	A-	(866) 738-3629	A+ / 9.8	6.03	17.68	40.24 /97	10.28 /95	14.05 /93	0.03	1.00
GR	Clarkston Institutional	CILGX	U	(866) 759-5679	U /	5.54	7.24	—	—	—	0.00	1.37
GR	Clarkston Partners Founders	CFSMX	U	(866) 759-5679	U /	2.60	5.34	22.42 /64	—	—	0.49	1.09
GR	Clarkston Partners Institutional	CISMX	U	(866) 759-5679	U /	2.48	5.30	22.29 /64	—	—	0.46	1.24
* AG	ClearBridge Aggressive Growth A	SHRAX	C+	(877) 534-4627	C+ / 6.1	8.22	11.84	24.71 /72	5.49 /59	14.04 /93	0.30	1.15
AG	● ClearBridge Aggressive Growth B	SAGBX	C+	(877) 534-4627	C+ / 6.4	7.92	11.22	23.32 /68	4.38 /47	12.88 /83	0.00	2.32
AG	ClearBridge Aggressive Growth C	SAGCX	C+	(877) 534-4627	C+ / 6.6	8.03	11.45	23.83 /69	4.75 /51	13.27 /86	0.00	1.85
AG	ClearBridge Aggressive Growth FI	LMPFX	C+	(877) 534-4627	B- / 7.1	8.23	11.84	24.72 /72	5.49 /59	14.02 /93	0.26	1.14
AG	ClearBridge Aggressive Growth I	SAGYX	B-	(877) 534-4627	B- / 7.3	8.30	12.01	25.08 /74	5.81 /63	14.41 /95	0.51	0.84
AG	ClearBridge Aggressive Growth IS	LSIFX	B-	(877) 534-4627	B- / 7.4	8.33	12.07	25.23 /74	5.93 /64	14.55 /96	0.63	0.72
AG	ClearBridge Aggressive Growth R	LMPRX	C+	(877) 534-4627	C+ / 6.9	8.15	11.68	24.35 /71	5.18 /56	13.74 /91	0.03	1.44
GR	ClearBridge All Cap Value A	SHFVX	B	(877) 534-4627	A- / 9.1	8.06	14.74	37.77 /96	8.22 /81	11.70 /72	0.81	1.29
GR	● ClearBridge All Cap Value B	SFVBX	B	(877) 534-4627	A- / 9.1	7.67	13.85	35.72 /95	6.86 /71	10.39 /61	0.00	2.71
GR	ClearBridge All Cap Value C	SFVCX	B	(877) 534-4627	A / 9.5	7.87	14.38	36.88 /96	7.51 /75	10.99 /66	0.38	1.96
GR	ClearBridge All Cap Value I	SFVYX	B+	(877) 534-4627	A+ / 9.7	8.20	14.99	38.45 /97	8.68 /84	12.19 /76	1.16	0.87
GR	ClearBridge Appreciation A	SHAPX	C+	(877) 534-4627	C+ / 6.7	7.24	7.75	19.52 /49	8.66 /84	12.26 /77	0.89	0.98
GR	● ClearBridge Appreciation B	SAPBX	B-	(877) 534-4627	C+ / 6.8	6.92	7.13	18.05 /43	7.42 /75	11.01 /66	0.00	2.11
GR	ClearBridge Appreciation C	SAPCX	B+	(877) 534-4627	B- / 7.1	7.07	7.38	18.69 /46	7.90 /78	11.48 /70	0.31	1.69
GR	ClearBridge Appreciation FI	LMPIX	A-	(877) 534-4627	B / 7.6	7.23	7.73	19.50 /49	8.64 /84	12.28 /77	0.97	0.97
GR	ClearBridge Appreciation I	SAPYX	A-	(877) 534-4627	B / 7.9	7.34	7.95	19.93 /52	9.00 /87	12.65 /80	1.23	0.68
GR	ClearBridge Appreciation IS	LMESX	A-	(877) 534-4627	B / 7.9	7.32	7.98	19.99 /52	9.09 /87	12.73 /81	1.32	0.58
GR	ClearBridge Appreciation R	LMPPX	B+	(877) 534-4627	B- / 7.4	7.19	7.65	19.23 /48	8.32 /81	11.95 /74	0.66	1.29
IN	● ClearBridge Dividend Strategy 1	LCBOX	A	(877) 534-4627	B / 8.0	6.85	7.59	21.73 /61	9.05 /87	11.94 /74	1.33	0.88
GI	ClearBridge Dividend Strategy A	SOPAX	B-	(877) 534-4627	C+ / 6.9	6.79	7.41	21.43 /59	8.74 /85	11.64 /71	1.03	1.15
GI	● ClearBridge Dividend Strategy B	SOPTX	B+	(877) 534-4627	B- / 7.1	6.49	6.91	20.23 /53	7.82 /78	10.77 /64	0.17	1.95
GI	ClearBridge Dividend Strategy C	SBPLX	B+	(877) 534-4627	B- / 7.3	6.56	7.01	20.55 /55	8.00 /79	10.85 /65	0.50	1.85
AA	ClearBridge Dividend Strategy FI	LBRIX	A-	(877) 534-4627	B / 7.8	6.76	7.37	21.33 /59	8.70 /85	—	0.99	1.16
GI	ClearBridge Dividend Strategy I	SOPYX	A	(877) 534-4627	B / 8.0	6.78	7.51	21.75 /61	9.07 /87	11.99 /74	1.32	0.86
IN	ClearBridge Dividend Strategy IS	LCBEX	A	(877) 534-4627	B / 8.1	6.85	7.60	21.89 /62	9.15 /88	—	1.40	0.90
IN	ClearBridge Dividend Strategy R	LMMRX	A-	(877) 534-4627	B / 7.6	6.71	7.29	21.09 /58	8.47 /83	11.34 /68	1.03	1.43
EN	ClearBridge Energy MLP & Infra A	LCPAX	E-	(877) 534-4627	D / 1.9	3.34	11.03	54.39 /99	-3.15 / 4	—	0.73	2.79
EN	ClearBridge Energy MLP & Infra C	LCPCX	E-	(877) 534-4627	D / 2.2	3.13	10.58	53.35 /99	-3.73 / 3	—	0.43	3.48
EN	ClearBridge Energy MLP & Infra I	LCPIX	E	(877) 534-4627	D+ / 2.7	3.42	11.25	54.97 /99	-3.09 / 4	—	0.97	2.41
EN	ClearBridge Energy MLP & Infra IS	LCPSX	E	(877) 534-4627	D+ / 2.8	3.42	11.27	55.08 /99	-3.07 / 4	—	0.98	2.38
GR	ClearBridge International Growth A	LGGAX	D	(877) 534-4627	D / 1.6	6.44	2.96	12.89 /21	1.19 /19	7.55 /39	0.36	1.19
GR	ClearBridge International Growth C	LMGTX	D	(877) 534-4627	D / 1.8	6.27	2.60	12.07 /18	0.44 /15	6.75 /33	0.00	2.00
GR	ClearBridge International Growth FI	LMGFX	D	(877) 534-4627	D / 2.2	6.43	2.97	12.91 /21	1.19 /19	7.55 /39	0.29	1.27
GR	ClearBridge International Growth I	LMGNX	D	(877) 534-4627	D+ / 2.4	6.52	3.11	13.19 /22	1.44 /21	7.82 /41	0.53	0.96
GR	ClearBridge International Growth R	LMGRX	D	(877) 534-4627	D / 2.1	6.39	2.87	12.64 /20	0.93 /18	7.27 /36	0.28	1.47
FO	ClearBridge International Sm Cap A	LCOAX	D-	(877) 534-4627	E+ / 0.6	7.28	4.88	13.54 /24	-1.39 / 8	9.01 /51	1.76	1.52
FO	ClearBridge International Sm Cap C	LCOCX	D-	(877) 534-4627	E+ / 0.8	7.06	4.56	12.69 /20	-2.14 / 6	8.20 /44	1.04	2.30

● Denotes fund is closed to new investors
* Denotes fund is included in Section II

138

RISK			NET ASSETS		ASSET					BULL / BEAR		FUND MANAGER		MINIMUMS		LOADS	
Risk Rating/Pts	3 Year Standard Deviation	Beta	NAV As of 2/28/17	Total $(Mil)	Cash %	Stocks %	Bonds %	Other %	Portfolio Turnover Ratio	Last Bull Market Return	Last Bear Market Return	Manager Quality Pct	Manager Tenure (Years)	Initial Purch. $	Additional Purch. $	Front End Load	Back End Load
C+ / 6.1	14.8	0.89	18.84	187	3	96	0	1	21	N/A	N/A	84	6	1,000,000	0	0.0	2.0
C- / 4.2	10.2	0.90	12.15	42	3	95	1	1	46	107.8	-15.9	38	20	2,000	250	0.0	2.0
C / 4.3	10.2	0.90	12.59	32	3	95	1	1	46	110.4	-15.8	42	20	1,000,000	1,000	0.0	2.0
C- / 3.8	12.7	0.97	38.48	10	2	97	0	1	90	N/A	N/A	35	15	1,000,000	1,000	0.0	2.0
C- / 3.7	12.7	0.97	37.87	14	2	97	0	1	90	96.8	-15.1	32	15	2,000	250	0.0	2.0
C+ / 6.2	12.4	1.10	27.36	31	5	94	0	1	79	119.1	-22.9	24	23	2,500	500	0.0	0.0
B- / 7.1	10.7	1.01	609.61	211	1	98	0	1	0	117.3	-15.4	49	4	0	0	0.0	0.0
U /	N/A	N/A	11.14	461	0	0	0	100	187	N/A	N/A	N/A	2	100,000	0	0.0	0.0
D / 1.8	18.5	0.66	9.49	85	24	53	22	1	4	41.7	-25.7	2	7	5,000	500	0.0	2.0
C+ / 5.8	11.8	1.01	14.11	34	14	85	0	1	62	N/A	N/A	5	6	3,500	100	0.0	2.0
B- / 7.7	4.0	0.40	9.69	8	6	0	93	1	18	N/A	N/A	70	5	5,000	100	0.0	2.0
C / 5.0	15.6	1.24	17.91	61	0	99	0	1	12	145.9	N/A	38	6	2,500	100	0.0	2.0
U /	N/A	N/A	11.16	27	0	0	0	100	0	N/A	N/A	N/A	2	10,000	0	0.0	0.0
U /	N/A	N/A	11.71	348	27	72	0	1	16	N/A	N/A	N/A	2	100,000,000	0	0.0	0.0
U /	N/A	N/A	11.69	316	27	72	0	1	16	N/A	N/A	N/A	2	25,000	0	0.0	0.0
C / 5.3	13.6	1.16	205.32	5,513	2	97	0	1	3	143.4	-19.7	8	34	1,000	50	5.8	0.0
C / 5.1	13.6	1.16	160.40	69	2	97	0	1	3	130.3	-20.0	5	34	1,000	50	0.0	0.0
C / 5.2	13.6	1.16	167.79	1,433	2	97	0	1	3	134.7	-19.9	5	34	1,000	50	0.0	0.0
C / 5.3	13.6	1.16	206.04	38	2	97	0	1	3	143.2	-19.7	8	34	0	0	0.0	0.0
C / 5.4	13.6	1.16	225.13	3,177	2	97	0	1	3	147.9	-19.5	9	34	1,000,000	0	0.0	0.0
C / 5.4	13.6	1.16	227.36	1,763	2	97	0	1	3	149.5	-19.5	9	34	0	0	0.0	0.0
C / 5.3	13.6	1.16	201.37	107	2	97	0	1	3	140.1	-19.7	7	34	0	0	0.0	0.0
C / 4.3	13.1	1.20	15.11	1,626	0	99	0	1	27	114.3	-24.3	21	2	1,000	50	5.8	0.0
C / 4.3	13.1	1.20	13.11	28	0	99	0	1	27	101.1	-24.7	12	2	1,000	50	0.0	0.0
C- / 4.1	13.1	1.20	13.30	156	0	99	0	1	27	107.2	-24.6	16	2	1,000	50	0.0	0.0
C / 4.4	13.2	1.20	15.93	37	0	99	0	1	27	119.5	-24.2	25	2	1,000,000	0	0.0	0.0
C+ / 6.9	9.9	0.95	22.03	3,830	0	95	4	1	5	114.4	-15.3	58	22	1,000	50	5.8	0.0
B- / 7.0	9.9	0.95	21.03	33	0	95	4	1	5	101.6	-15.8	42	22	1,000	50	0.0	0.0
C+ / 6.9	9.9	0.95	21.29	427	0	95	4	1	5	106.2	-15.5	48	22	1,000	50	0.0	0.0
B- / 7.0	9.9	0.95	22.14	5	0	95	4	1	5	114.4	-15.3	58	22	0	0	0.0	0.0
C+ / 6.9	9.9	0.95	21.90	826	0	95	4	1	5	118.3	-15.2	62	22	1,000,000	0	0.0	0.0
C+ / 6.8	9.9	0.95	21.95	658	0	95	4	1	5	119.2	-15.2	63	22	0	0	0.0	0.0
C+ / 6.9	9.9	0.95	21.96	68	0	95	4	1	5	111.2	-15.5	54	22	0	0	0.0	0.0
B- / 7.2	9.5	0.87	22.07	1,377	7	92	0	1	22	108.2	-11.4	72	8	0	0	0.0	0.0
B- / 7.2	9.5	0.87	22.05	2,915	7	92	0	1	22	105.3	-11.5	69	8	1,000	50	5.8	0.0
B- / 7.2	9.4	0.87	21.69	30	7	92	0	1	22	96.8	-11.7	58	8	1,000	50	0.0	0.0
B- / 7.2	9.5	0.87	21.73	369	7	92	0	1	22	97.4	-11.7	60	8	1,000	50	0.0	0.0
B- / 7.2	9.4	1.46	22.03	N/A	7	92	0	1	22	N/A	N/A	46	8	0	0	0.0	0.0
B- / 7.2	9.5	0.87	22.58	1,016	7	92	0	1	22	108.8	-11.4	72	8	1,000,000	0	0.0	0.0
B- / 7.2	9.5	0.87	22.61	4	7	92	0	1	22	N/A	N/A	73	8	0	0	0.0	0.0
B- / 7.2	9.5	0.87	21.93	20	7	92	0	1	22	N/A	N/A	66	8	0	0	0.0	0.0
D- / 1.1	23.4	0.97	9.92	7	35	64	0	1	37	N/A	N/A	86	4	1,000	50	5.8	0.0
D- / 1.1	23.4	0.97	9.91	1	35	64	0	1	37	N/A	N/A	83	4	1,000	50	0.0	0.0
D / 1.7	23.4	0.97	9.86	10	35	64	0	1	37	N/A	N/A	86	4	1,000,000	0	0.0	0.0
D / 1.7	23.4	0.97	9.85	N/A	35	64	0	1	37	N/A	N/A	86	4	0	0	0.0	0.0
C+ / 5.9	12.4	1.05	33.00	19	1	98	0	1	89	78.0	-17.6	3	4	1,000	50	5.8	0.0
C+ / 5.8	12.4	1.05	31.19	66	1	98	0	1	89	71.0	-17.8	2	4	1,000	50	0.0	0.0
C+ / 5.9	12.4	1.05	34.40	8	1	98	0	1	89	78.1	-17.6	3	4	0	0	0.0	0.0
C+ / 5.9	12.4	1.05	35.58	27	1	98	0	1	89	80.5	-17.5	3	4	1,000,000	0	0.0	0.0
C+ / 5.9	12.4	1.05	33.48	1	1	98	0	1	89	75.6	-17.7	2	4	0	0	0.0	0.0
C+ / 6.0	12.0	0.85	15.65	35	3	96	0	1	44	72.7	-20.9	59	7	1,000	50	5.8	0.0
C+ / 6.0	11.9	0.85	15.48	5	3	96	0	1	44	65.8	-21.1	48	7	1,000	50	0.0	0.0

					PERFORMANCE						Incl. in Returns	
			99 Pct = Best 0 Pct = Worst			Total Return % through 2/28/17						
									Annualized			
Fund Type	Fund Name	Ticker Symbol	Overall Investment Rating	Phone	Perfor- mance Rating/Pts	3 Mo	6 Mo	1Yr / Pct	3Yr / Pct	5Yr / Pct	Dividend Yield	Expense Ratio
FO	ClearBridge International Sm Cap I	LCOIX	D-	(877) 534-4627	D- / 1.1	7.33	5.10	13.93 /25	-1.12 / 9	9.29 /53	2.14	1.23
FO	ClearBridge International Sm Cap IS	CBISX	D	(877) 534-4627	D- / 1.1	7.42	5.18	14.09 /26	-1.04 / 9	9.35 /53	2.29	1.13
FO	ClearBridge International Value A	SBIEX	E+	(877) 534-4627	E / 0.5	7.30	6.30	19.21 /48	-3.23 / 4	5.27 /23	1.36	1.56
FO	ClearBridge International Value C	SBICX	E+	(877) 534-4627	E+ / 0.6	7.13	5.92	18.36 /44	-3.94 / 3	4.49 /18	1.43	2.21
FO	ClearBridge International Value I	SBIYX	E+	(877) 534-4627	E+ / 0.9	7.45	6.55	19.69 /50	-2.81 / 5	5.69 /26	1.81	1.11
FO	ClearBridge International Value IS	LSIUX	E+	(877) 534-4627	E+ / 0.9	7.49	6.61	19.87 /51	-2.74 / 5	5.78 /27	1.85	0.99
FO	ClearBridge International Value R	LIORX	D-	(877) 534-4627	E+ / 0.7	7.30	6.19	18.88 /47	-3.42 / 4	--	1.61	1.87
GR	ClearBridge Large Cap Growth A	SBLGX	B+	(877) 534-4627	B / 7.9	6.57	7.63	21.28 /59	10.90 /97	15.67 /98	0.07	1.19
GR	ClearBridge Large Cap Growth C	SLCCX	B+	(877) 534-4627	B+ / 8.3	6.36	7.22	20.38 /54	10.08 /94	14.82 /96	0.00	1.92
GR	ClearBridge Large Cap Growth I	SBLYX	A	(877) 534-4627	A- / 9.0	6.64	7.77	21.63 /60	11.24 /97	16.10 /98	0.29	0.88
GR	ClearBridge Large Cap Growth IS	LSITX	A	(877) 534-4627	A- / 9.1	6.65	7.79	21.71 /61	11.31 /97	--	0.33	0.79
GR	ClearBridge Large Cap Growth O	LCMMX	U	(877) 534-4627	U /	6.63	7.77	21.65 /60		--	0.29	0.84
GR	ClearBridge Large Cap Growth R	LMPLX	A-	(877) 534-4627	B+ / 8.7	6.51	7.48	20.96 /57	10.58 /96	15.30 /97	0.06	1.45
GI	ClearBridge Large Cap Value 1	LCLIX	A	(877) 534-4627	B+ / 8.6	6.49	11.80	24.55 /72	8.75 /85	--	1.38	0.68
GR	ClearBridge Large Cap Value A	SINAX	B+	(877) 534-4627	B- / 7.4	6.44	11.74	24.37 /71	8.57 /84	12.66 /80	1.16	0.89
GI	ClearBridge Large Cap Value A2	LIVVX	B+	(877) 534-4627	B- / 7.3	6.41	11.62	24.13 /70	8.36 /82	--	1.00	1.06
GR	ClearBridge Large Cap Value C	SINOX	A-	(877) 534-4627	B / 7.8	6.20	11.24	23.35 /68	7.71 /77	11.78 /72	0.59	1.66
GR	ClearBridge Large Cap Value I	SAIFX	A	(877) 534-4627	B+ / 8.7	6.52	11.87	24.67 /72	8.89 /86	13.00 /84	1.48	0.58
GI	ClearBridge Large Cap Value IS	LMLSX	A+	(877) 534-4627	B+ / 8.7	6.54	11.90	24.78 /73	8.95 /86	--	1.54	0.52
GI	ClearBridge Large Cap Value R	LCBVX	A	(877) 534-4627	B / 8.1	6.34	11.52	24.01 /70	8.04 /79	--	1.11	1.45
MC	● ClearBridge Mid Cap 1	SMCPX	B+	(877) 534-4627	B / 8.2	6.86	12.51	26.20 /77	7.46 /75	12.86 /82	0.40	0.90
MC	ClearBridge Mid Cap A	SBMAX	B-	(877) 534-4627	B- / 7.0	6.79	12.33	25.79 /76	7.16 /73	12.60 /80	0.13	1.23
MC	ClearBridge Mid Cap C	SBMLX	B	(877) 534-4627	B- / 7.4	6.62	11.98	24.90 /73	6.41 /68	11.82 /73	0.00	1.93
GL	ClearBridge Mid Cap Growth A	LBGAX	D+	(877) 534-4627	C- / 4.0	6.51	6.24	22.46 /64	3.89 /42	10.87 /65	0.00	1.36
GR	ClearBridge Mid Cap Growth A2	LCBGX	D+	(877) 534-4627	C- / 3.8	6.47	6.15	22.17 /63	3.68 /39	--	0.00	1.62
GL	ClearBridge Mid Cap Growth C	LBGCX	C-	(877) 534-4627	C / 4.5	6.35	5.88	21.45 /59	3.11 /33	10.05 /59	0.00	2.14
GL	ClearBridge Mid Cap Growth I	LBGIX	C	(877) 534-4627	C / 5.4	6.57	6.40	22.76 /66	4.18 /45	11.17 /67	0.00	1.09
GR	ClearBridge Mid Cap Growth IS	LCMIX	C	(877) 534-4627	C / 5.4	6.61	6.44	22.75 /66	4.19 /45	--	0.00	1.11
GR	ClearBridge Mid Cap Growth R	LCMRX	C-	(877) 534-4627	C / 4.9	6.45	6.05	21.99 /62	3.56 /38	--	0.00	1.63
MC	ClearBridge Mid Cap I	SMBYX	B+	(877) 534-4627	B / 8.2	6.87	12.53	26.22 /77	7.53 /76	13.01 /84	0.42	0.89
MC	ClearBridge Mid Cap IS	LSIRX	B+	(877) 534-4627	B+ / 8.3	6.92	12.60	26.35 /77	7.64 /76	13.11 /85	0.48	0.78
MC	ClearBridge Mid Cap R	LMREX	B	(877) 534-4627	B / 7.8	6.71	12.22	25.50 /75	6.89 /71	12.31 /77	0.00	1.49
GL	ClearBridge Select A	LCLAX	C	(877) 534-4627	B / 7.7	12.14	9.56	35.57 /95	5.74 /62	--	0.00	2.78
GL	ClearBridge Select C	LCLCX	C	(877) 534-4627	B / 8.1	11.89	9.32	34.73 /94	4.96 /54	--	0.00	3.74
GL	ClearBridge Select FI	LCBSX	C+	(877) 534-4627	B+ / 8.7	12.14	9.49	35.57 /95	5.74 /62	--	0.00	2.58
GL	ClearBridge Select I	LBFIX	C+	(877) 534-4627	B+ / 8.9	12.24	9.71	36.04 /95	6.09 /65	--	0.00	2.37
GL	ClearBridge Select IS	LCSSX	C+	(877) 534-4627	B+ / 8.9	12.20	9.73	36.16 /95	6.16 /66	--	0.00	2.30
MC	ClearBridge Small Cap A	LMSAX	B	(877) 534-4627	A+ / 9.7	6.69	14.95	42.20 /98	10.15 /94	14.28 /95	0.00	1.26
MC	ClearBridge Small Cap C	LMASX	B	(877) 534-4627	A+ / 9.8	6.48	14.52	41.06 /98	9.27 /89	13.39 /88	0.00	2.06
MC	ClearBridge Small Cap FI	LGASX	B+	(877) 534-4627	A+ / 9.8	6.70	15.00	42.13 /98	9.98 /93	14.08 /94	0.00	1.40
SC	● ClearBridge Small Cap Growth 1	LMPMX	D+	(877) 534-4627	C+ / 5.6	7.05	7.93	31.35 /89	2.20 /25	10.83 /64	0.00	1.00
SC	ClearBridge Small Cap Growth A	SASMX	D	(877) 534-4627	C- / 4.2	7.01	7.82	31.13 /88	2.01 /24	10.66 /63	0.00	1.24
SC	ClearBridge Small Cap Growth C	SCSMX	D	(877) 534-4627	C / 4.8	6.80	7.41	30.11 /87	1.28 /20	9.85 /57	0.00	1.95
SC	ClearBridge Small Cap Growth FI	LMPSX	D+	(877) 534-4627	C / 5.5	7.00	7.86	31.20 /88	2.04 /24	10.67 /63	0.00	1.21
SC	ClearBridge Small Cap Growth I	SBPYX	D+	(877) 534-4627	C+ / 5.7	7.07	7.99	31.53 /89	2.35 /26	11.06 /66	0.00	0.91
SC	ClearBridge Small Cap Growth IS	LMOIX	C-	(877) 534-4627	C+ / 5.8	7.12	8.07	31.69 /89	2.49 /27	11.18 /67	0.00	0.78
SC	● ClearBridge Small Cap Growth R	LMPOX	D+	(877) 534-4627	C / 5.2	6.92	7.67	30.78 /88	1.76 /22	10.40 /61	0.00	1.49
MC	ClearBridge Small Cap I	LMNSX	B+	(877) 534-4627	A+ / 9.8	6.75	15.07	42.52 /98	10.37 /95	14.53 /96	0.00	1.07
MC	ClearBridge Small Cap R	LMARX	B+	(877) 534-4627	A+ / 9.8	6.58	14.78	41.68 /98	9.68 /91	13.77 /91	0.00	1.67
SC	ClearBridge Small Cap Value A	SBVAX	C	(877) 534-4627	B- / 7.3	6.08	12.97	40.91 /98	4.62 /50	10.66 /63	0.00	1.38
SC	ClearBridge Small Cap Value C	SBVLX	C	(877) 534-4627	B / 7.8	5.87	12.58	39.93 /97	3.87 /41	9.85 /57	0.00	2.07
SC	ClearBridge Small Cap Value I	SMCYX	B-	(877) 534-4627	B+ / 8.6	6.16	13.19	41.39 /98	5.00 /54	11.04 /66	0.05	0.99

● Denotes fund is closed to new investors

★ Denotes fund is included in Section II

www.thestreetratings.com

RISK			NET ASSETS		ASSET					BULL / BEAR		FUND MANAGER		MINIMUMS		LOADS	
	3 Year		NAV						Portfolio	Last Bull	Last Bear	Manager	Manager	Initial	Additional	Front	Back
Risk	Standard		As of	Total	Cash	Stocks	Bonds	Other	Turnover	Market	Market	Quality	Tenure	Purch.	Purch.	End	End
Rating/Pts	Deviation	Beta	2/28/17	$(Mil)	%	%	%	%	Ratio	Return	Return	Pct	(Years)	$	$	Load	Load
C+ / 6.0	12.0	0.85	15.77	75	3	96	0	1	44	75.2	-20.8	62	7	1,000,000	0	0.0	0.0
B- / 7.0	12.0	0.85	15.78	16	3	96	0	1	44	75.7	-20.8	63	7	0	0	0.0	0.0
C / 5.0	12.2	0.96	10.16	121	0	94	5	1	32	48.1	-21.5	33	11	1,000	50	5.8	0.0
C / 5.0	12.3	0.96	8.34	18	0	94	5	1	32	42.4	-21.7	25	11	1,000	50	0.0	0.0
C / 5.0	12.2	0.96	10.01	44	0	94	5	1	32	51.4	-21.4	38	11	1,000,000	0	0.0	0.0
C / 5.0	12.3	0.96	10.21	131	0	94	5	1	32	52.2	-21.3	40	11	0	0	0.0	0.0
C+ / 6.3	12.2	0.96	10.08	1	0	94	5	1	32	N/A	N/A	31	11	0	0	0.0	0.0
C+ / 6.2	10.6	0.96	35.98	1,478	0	95	4	1	13	152.6	-15.5	78	8	1,000	50	5.8	0.0
C+ / 6.1	10.6	0.96	29.51	439	0	95	4	1	13	142.8	-15.8	73	8	1,000	50	0.0	0.0
C+ / 6.3	10.6	0.96	39.65	3,238	0	95	4	1	13	157.6	-15.4	80	8	1,000,000	0	0.0	0.0
C+ / 6.3	10.6	0.96	39.67	425	0	95	4	1	13	N/A	N/A	81	8	0	0	0.0	0.0
U /	N/A	N/A	39.67	475	0	95	4	1	13	N/A	N/A	N/A	8	50	0	0.0	0.0
C+ / 6.2	10.6	0.96	34.74	50	0	95	4	1	13	148.3	-15.6	76	8	0	0	0.0	0.0
C+ / 6.9	10.6	0.98	31.26	186	1	98	0	1	5	N/A	N/A	56	13	0	0	0.0	0.0
C+ / 6.9	10.6	0.98	31.27	415	1	98	0	1	5	121.8	-16.7	53	13	1,000	50	5.8	0.0
C+ / 6.9	10.6	0.98	31.24	185	1	98	0	1	5	N/A	N/A	50	13	1,000	50	5.8	0.0
C+ / 6.9	10.6	0.98	30.35	110	1	98	0	1	5	112.6	-17.0	42	13	1,000	50	0.0	0.0
C+ / 6.9	10.6	0.97	31.22	775	1	98	0	1	5	125.5	-16.6	58	13	1,000,000	0	0.0	0.0
B- / 7.1	10.6	0.98	31.24	5	1	98	0	1	5	N/A	N/A	58	13	0	0	0.0	0.0
B- / 7.1	10.5	0.97	31.29	N/A	1	98	0	1	5	N/A	N/A	47	13	0	0	0.0	0.0
C+ / 5.8	12.7	1.00	34.62	4	0	97	2	1	22	139.5	-24.5	48	12	0	0	0.0	0.0
C+ / 5.8	12.6	1.00	33.36	1,021	0	97	2	1	22	136.5	-24.5	45	12	1,000	50	5.8	0.0
C+ / 5.6	12.6	1.00	27.30	200	0	97	2	1	22	127.6	-24.7	35	12	1,000	50	0.0	0.0
C / 5.3	14.4	0.88	25.19	27	1	98	0	1	25	132.7	-25.1	93	7	1,000	50	5.8	0.0
C / 5.5	14.4	1.24	25.02	23	1	98	0	1	25	N/A	N/A	3	7	1,000	50	5.8	0.0
C / 5.2	14.4	0.88	23.95	7	1	98	0	1	25	123.6	-25.4	91	7	1,000	50	0.0	0.0
C / 5.3	14.4	0.88	25.62	41	1	98	0	1	25	136.1	-25.1	94	7	1,000,000	0	0.0	0.0
C / 5.3	14.4	1.24	25.63	9	1	98	0	1	25	N/A	N/A	3	7	0	0	0.0	0.0
C / 5.3	14.4	1.24	24.91	N/A	1	98	0	1	25	N/A	N/A	3	7	0	0	0.0	0.0
C+ / 5.9	12.6	1.00	36.67	621	0	97	2	1	22	141.2	-24.4	50	12	1,000,000	0	0.0	0.0
C+ / 5.9	12.7	1.00	36.96	384	0	97	2	1	22	142.2	-24.4	51	12	0	0	0.0	0.0
C+ / 5.8	12.6	1.00	32.69	52	0	97	2	1	22	133.0	-24.6	41	12	0	0	0.0	0.0
C- / 3.1	17.4	1.00	16.49	1	2	95	0	3	25	N/A	N/A	97	N/A	1,000	50	5.8	0.0
C- / 3.1	17.4	1.00	16.05	N/A	2	95	0	3	25	N/A	N/A	95	N/A	1,000	50	0.0	0.0
C- / 3.1	17.5	1.00	16.49	N/A	2	95	0	3	25	N/A	N/A	97	N/A	0	0	0.0	0.0
C- / 3.2	17.5	1.00	16.82	6	2	95	0	3	25	N/A	N/A	97	N/A	1,000,000	0	0.0	0.0
C- / 3.2	17.4	1.00	16.78	8	2	95	0	3	25	N/A	N/A	97	N/A	0	0	0.0	0.0
C- / 3.8	14.3	1.12	40.00	111	2	96	0	2	35	142.5	-30.3	67	6	1,000	50	5.8	0.0
C- / 3.7	14.3	1.11	38.29	464	2	96	0	2	35	132.5	-30.5	57	6	1,000	50	0.0	0.0
C / 4.6	14.3	1.12	56.07	11	2	96	0	2	35	140.3	-30.3	66	6	0	0	0.0	0.0
C- / 3.5	17.3	0.99	29.41	3	2	97	0	1	9	123.1	-22.6	19	10	0	0	0.0	0.0
C- / 3.5	17.3	1.00	28.81	825	2	97	0	1	9	121.2	-22.7	18	10	1,000	50	5.8	0.0
C- / 3.3	17.2	1.00	23.65	42	2	97	0	1	9	112.3	-23.0	12	10	1,000	50	0.0	0.0
C- / 3.5	17.3	1.00	28.97	11	2	97	0	1	9	121.3	-22.7	18	10	0	0	0.0	0.0
C- / 3.5	17.2	0.99	30.53	991	2	97	0	1	9	125.6	-22.5	20	10	1,000,000	0	0.0	0.0
C- / 3.5	17.3	1.00	30.78	851	2	97	0	1	9	127.0	-22.6	22	10	0	0	0.0	0.0
C- / 3.4	17.2	1.00	28.22	78	2	97	0	1	9	118.4	-22.7	16	10	0	0	0.0	0.0
C / 4.7	14.3	1.11	58.35	167	2	96	0	2	35	145.5	-30.2	70	6	1,000,000	0	0.0	0.0
C / 4.5	14.3	1.11	54.87	5	2	96	0	2	35	136.8	-30.4	62	6	0	0	0.0	0.0
C- / 3.8	16.0	0.97	21.93	118	0	98	1	1	61	108.4	-27.0	49	2	1,000	50	5.8	0.0
C- / 3.4	16.1	0.97	17.99	47	0	98	1	1	61	100.2	-27.2	38	2	1,000	50	0.0	0.0
C- / 3.9	16.1	0.97	23.38	16	0	98	1	1	61	112.1	-26.8	54	2	1,000,000	0	0.0	0.0

I. Index of Stock Mutual Funds

	99 Pct = Best 0 Pct = Worst				**PERFORMANCE**						**Incl. in Returns**	
								Total Return % through 2/28/17				
			Overall		**Perfor-**				Annualized		**Dividend**	**Expense**
Fund		Ticker	**Investment**		**mance**						Yield	Ratio
Type	Fund Name	Symbol	**Rating**	Phone	**Rating/Pts**	3 Mo	6 Mo	1Yr / Pct	3Yr / Pct	5Yr / Pct		
SC	ClearBridge Small Cap Value IS	LCBIX	B-	(877) 534-4627	B+ / 8.7	6.20	13.23	41.56 /98	5.10 /55	--	0.13	0.89
GR	ClearBridge Tactical Div Inc A	CFLGX	D	(877) 534-4627	D+ / 2.8	6.34	5.20	23.48 /68	1.78 /23	7.64 /39	4.65	1.83
IN	ClearBridge Tactical Div Inc A2	LBDAX	D	(877) 534-4627	D+ / 2.8	6.33	5.13	23.31 /68	1.69 /22	7.57 /39	4.55	1.98
GR	ClearBridge Tactical Div Inc C	SMDLX	D+	(877) 534-4627	C- / 3.3	6.21	4.82	22.58 /65	1.13 /19	6.92 /34	4.50	2.58
GR	ClearBridge Tactical Div Inc I	LADIX	D+	(877) 534-4627	C- / 4.1	6.44	5.37	23.84 /69	2.08 /24	7.95 /42	5.14	1.59
IN	ClearBridge Tactical Div Inc IS	LCBDX	C-	(877) 534-4627	C- / 4.2	6.43	5.35	23.76 /69	2.25 /26	--	5.15	1.62
GR	ClearBridge Value A	LGVAX	B	(877) 534-4627	B / 7.7	5.61	10.48	30.74 /88	8.16 /80	13.43 /88	0.84	1.02
GR	ClearBridge Value C	LMVTX	B+	(877) 534-4627	B / 8.2	5.42	10.10	29.85 /86	7.38 /75	12.60 /80	0.10	1.75
GR	ClearBridge Value FI	LMVFX	B+	(877) 534-4627	B+ / 8.7	5.59	10.42	30.65 /87	8.08 /80	13.36 /87	0.55	1.11
GR	ClearBridge Value I	LMNVX	A-	(877) 534-4627	B+ / 8.9	5.67	10.61	31.08 /88	8.40 /82	13.68 /90	0.87	0.82
GR	ClearBridge Value R	LMVRX	B+	(877) 534-4627	B+ / 8.4	5.51	10.28	30.30 /87	7.75 /77	12.98 /83	0.35	1.42
GI	Clearwater Core Equity	QWVPX	B+	(888) 228-0935	B / 8.1	7.21	10.98	24.10 /70	7.97 /79	12.29 /77	1.20	0.90
FO	Clearwater International	QCVAX	D	(888) 228-0935	D / 2.1	6.89	3.64	15.29 /31	0.12 /14	5.66 /26	1.84	1.00
SC	Clearwater Small Companies	QWVOX	C+	(888) 228-0935	B / 8.0	4.57	10.90	30.06 /86	7.09 /73	12.16 /76	0.26	1.35
GR	Clifford Capital Partners Instl	CLIFX	A+	(800) 673-0550	A+ / 9.9	5.72	11.41	42.13 /98	13.52 /99	--	0.51	0.90
GR	Clifford Capital Partners Investor	CLFFX	A+	(800) 673-0550	A+ / 9.9	5.63	11.24	41.73 /98	13.28 /99	--	0.40	1.10
GR	Clipper	CFIMX	A+	(800) 432-2504	A+ / 9.6	4.50	10.57	31.33 /89	11.30 /97	14.00 /93	0.97	0.72
IX	Cloud Capital Strat All Cap Inst	CCILX	D	(877) 670-2227	B / 7.7	4.55	7.33	25.37 /74	8.22 /81	12.23 /76	0.51	1.90
FO	Clough China A	CHNAX	E+	(866) 759-5679	D- / 1.4	3.69	2.18	21.57 /60	0.04 /13	4.04 /15	0.09	1.98
FO	Clough China C	CHNCX	E	(866) 759-5679	D- / 1.1	3.52	1.83	20.67 /56	-0.69 /11	3.27 /12	0.00	2.78
FO	Clough China I	CHNIX	E+	(866) 759-5679	D / 2.2	3.81	2.32	21.92 /62	0.42 /15	4.39 /17	0.27	1.77
GL	Clough Global Long/Short I	CLOIX	U	(877) 256-8445	U /	3.59	1.13	8.87 / 9	--	--	0.00	2.69
GR	CM Advisors	CMAFX	E+	(800) 664-4888	D+ / 2.3	1.34	13.47	42.62 /98	-1.78 / 7	4.11 /16	0.35	1.42
AA	CM Advisors Small Cap Value Fd I	CMOVX	E+	(800) 664-4888	C- / 3.4	0.36	18.17	52.33 /99	-1.69 / 7	6.10 /29	1.01	1.60
GL	CMG Global Equity A	GEFAX	D	(866) 264-9456	E / 0.3	4.72	1.22	1.92 / 2	-1.86 / 7	--	0.00	2.97
GL	CMG Global Equity I	GEFIX	D	(866) 264-9456	E / 0.5	4.80	1.31	2.11 / 2	-1.66 / 7	--	0.00	2.72
AA	CMG Long Short A	SCOTX	E	(866) 264-9456	E- / 0.0	6.58	11.90	-3.64 / 1	-12.26 / 0	-10.23 / 1	0.00	3.76
AA	CMG Long Short I	SCOIX	E	(866) 264-9456	E- / 0.0	6.86	11.91	-3.43 / 1	-11.98 / 0	-9.95 / 1	0.00	3.36
GL	CMG Tactical All Asset Strategy A	CMGQX	U	(866) 264-9456	U /	3.09	1.17	--	--	--	0.00	1.65
IN	CNR Dividend and Income N	RIMHX	A	(888) 889-0799	B / 7.8	7.20	4.42	17.73 /42	9.93 /93	10.84 /64	2.71	1.13
EM	CNR Emerging Markets N	RIMIX	C	(888) 889-0799	C / 5.4	6.20	0.23	22.93 /66	5.44 /59	8.06 /43	0.17	1.65
EM	CNR Emerging Markets Y	CNRYX	U	(888) 889-0799	U /	6.28	0.39	--	--	--	0.00	1.40
GR	CNR US Core Equity Inst	CNRUX	B+	(888) 889-0799	B / 7.8	8.35	8.34	20.87 /57	8.24 /81	--	1.13	0.52
GR	CNR US Core Equity N	CNRWX	B	(888) 889-0799	B- / 7.3	8.23	8.00	20.24 /53	7.66 /76	--	0.69	1.02
GR	CNR US Core Equity Servicing	CNRVX	B	(888) 889-0799	B- / 7.5	8.20	8.12	20.50 /55	7.94 /78	--	0.91	0.77
GR	CO 529 CollegeInvest Agg Gro Port		B+	(800) 662-7447	B- / 7.4	7.65	8.49	23.98 /70	6.93 /71	11.07 /66	0.00	0.52
GI	CO 529 CollegeInvest Csv Growth		C+	(800) 662-7447	D / 2.2	2.63	0.27	6.62 / 5	3.77 /40	4.32 /17	0.00	0.52
GI	CO 529 CollegeInvest Growth Port		B	(800) 662-7447	C+ / 5.7	5.91	5.71	18.00 /43	5.99 /64	8.90 /50	0.00	0.52
GI	CO 529 CollegeInvest Mod Growth		B	(800) 662-7447	C- / 3.8	4.23	2.92	12.17 /19	4.97 /54	6.66 /33	0.00	0.52
GR	CO 529 CollegeInvest Stock Idx Port		A+	(800) 662-7447	A- / 9.0	7.65	10.06	25.86 /76	9.53 /90	13.43 /88	0.00	0.52
GR	Cognios Market Neutral Lg Cap Inst	COGIX	D+	(866) 759-5679	D / 1.9	1.15	-2.54	-5.62 / 0	5.60 /60	--	0.00	5.68
GR	Cognios Market Neutral Lg Cap Inv	COGMX	D	(866) 759-5679	D / 1.8	1.17	-2.67	-5.77 / 0	5.38 /58	--	0.00	5.92
GI	Cohen & Steers Dividend Value A	DVFAX	B+	(800) 330-7348	B+ / 8.7	7.86	13.51	28.81 /84	9.04 /87	12.82 /82	1.20	1.26
GI	Cohen & Steers Dividend Value C	DVFCX	B+	(800) 330-7348	B+ / 8.9	7.63	13.12	27.93 /81	8.31 /81	12.06 /75	0.62	1.91
GI	Cohen & Steers Dividend Value I	DVFIX	A-	(800) 330-7348	A / 9.5	7.91	13.66	29.24 /85	9.41 /90	13.20 /86	1.52	1.01
UT	Cohen & Steers Glbl Infr A	CSUAX	D+	(800) 330-7348	C- / 3.2	9.07	2.88	14.02 /25	3.93 /42	8.68 /48	1.84	1.32
UT	Cohen & Steers Glbl Infr C	CSUCX	C-	(800) 330-7348	C- / 3.4	8.85	2.47	13.29 /23	3.24 /34	7.97 /42	1.33	1.97
UT	Cohen & Steers Glbl Infr I	CSUIX	C-	(800) 330-7348	C- / 4.2	9.14	3.03	14.37 /27	4.22 /45	9.02 /51	2.21	1.05
GL	Cohen & Steers Inst Glbl Realty Shs	GRSIX	C	(800) 330-7348	C / 4.9	6.95	-2.30	13.99 /25	6.82 /71	8.47 /46	4.51	1.02
RE	Cohen & Steers Inst Realty Shrs	CSRIX	C+	(800) 330-7348	B / 8.0	8.36	-1.38	16.75 /37	11.43 /98	11.53 /70	2.93	0.76
FO	Cohen & Steers Intl Realty A	IRFAX	D	(800) 330-7348	D- / 1.2	5.05	-3.84	8.99 / 9	1.88 /23	5.14 /22	5.63	1.47
FO	Cohen & Steers Intl Realty C	IRFCX	D	(800) 330-7348	D- / 1.4	5.00	-4.08	8.27 / 8	1.22 /19	4.47 /18	5.19	2.12

● Denotes fund is closed to new investors

* Denotes fund is included in Section II

www.thestreetratings.com

Risk Rating/Pts	3 Year Standard Deviation	Beta	NAV As of 2/28/17	Total $(Mil)	Cash %	Stocks %	Bonds %	Other %	Portfolio Turnover Ratio	Last Bull Market Return	Last Bear Market Return	Manager Quality Pct	Manager Tenure (Years)	Initial Purch. $	Additional Purch. $	Front End Load	Back End Load
C- / 3.9	16.0	0.97	23.40	9	0	98	1	1	61	N/A	N/A	55	2	0	0	0.0	0.0
C / 5.1	11.7	0.99	17.28	203	29	68	1	2	20	70.8	-21.5	3	5	1,000	50	5.8	0.0
C / 5.1	11.6	0.98	17.23	62	29	68	1	2	20	70.3	-21.5	3	5	1,000	50	5.8	0.0
C / 5.1	11.6	0.98	16.45	229	29	68	1	2	20	64.7	-21.7	3	5	1,000	50	0.0	0.0
C / 5.1	11.6	0.98	17.41	172	29	68	1	2	20	73.5	-21.4	4	5	1,000,000	0	0.0	0.0
C / 5.1	11.6	0.98	17.41	N/A	29	68	1	2	20	N/A	N/A	4	5	0	0	0.0	0.0
C+ / 5.8	13.7	1.25	74.75	449	1	97	0	2	45	129.3	-18.1	17	7	1,000	50	5.8	0.0
C+ / 5.8	13.7	1.25	73.46	1,377	1	97	0	2	45	120.3	-18.4	12	7	1,000	50	0.0	0.0
C+ / 5.8	13.7	1.25	84.94	15	1	97	0	2	45	128.7	-18.2	16	7	0	0	0.0	0.0
C+ / 5.8	13.7	1.25	87.68	547	1	97	0	2	45	132.0	-18.0	18	7	1,000,000	0	0.0	0.0
C+ / 5.8	13.7	1.25	83.77	13	1	97	0	2	45	124.4	-18.3	14	7	0	0	0.0	0.0
C+ / 5.8	10.4	1.00	39.50	489	1	98	0	1	94	116.4	-19.5	42	7	1,000	1,000	0.0	0.0
C+ / 5.8	11.1	0.89	14.68	532	3	96	0	1	18	53.1	-23.4	76	8	1,000	1,000	0.0	0.0
C- / 3.4	14.0	0.88	20.08	346	4	95	0	1	59	125.6	-23.9	81	10	1,000	1,000	0.0	0.0
C+ / 6.5	12.5	0.98	14.41	12	0	92	6	2	55	N/A	N/A	90	3	100,000	100	0.0	0.0
C+ / 6.5	12.5	0.98	14.37	N/A	0	92	6	2	55	N/A	N/A	89	3	2,500	100	0.0	2.0
C+ / 6.6	12.1	1.05	112.44	1,201	1	98	0	1	31	125.2	-14.0	74	11	2,500	25	0.0	0.0
E- / 0.0	10.3	0.92	7.61	9	0	0	0	100	289	117.1	N/A	57	6	1,000,000	0	0.0	0.0
C- / 4.0	18.7	0.88	21.63	16	7	92	0	1	126	45.2	-24.2	75	12	2,500	0	5.5	2.0
C- / 4.0	18.7	0.88	20.61	7	7	92	0	1	126	39.3	-24.4	68	12	2,500	0	0.0	2.0
C- / 4.0	18.7	0.88	22.15	29	7	92	0	1	126	47.7	-24.1	78	12	1,000,000	0	0.0	2.0
U /	N/A	N/A	9.82	46	0	0	0	100	261	N/A	N/A	N/A	2	1,000,000	0	0.0	2.0
C- / 3.3	19.2	1.02	12.83	73	7	92	0	1	62	47.9	-16.8	1	14	2,500	0	0.0	1.0
D+ / 2.3	24.2	1.68	11.37	51	15	84	0	1	68	66.7	-22.2	1	6	2,500	0	0.0	1.0
B- / 7.6	7.0	0.43	10.20	3	12	87	0	1	20	N/A	N/A	50	4	5,000	1,000	5.8	0.0
B- / 7.6	6.9	0.42	10.25	3	12	87	0	1	20	N/A	N/A	53	4	15,000	1,000	0.0	0.0
C / 4.8	11.1	-0.04	5.83	1	26	0	73	1	35	N/A	N/A	1	5	5,000	1,000	5.8	0.0
C / 4.9	11.1	-0.05	5.92	4	26	0	73	1	35	N/A	N/A	1	5	15,000	1,000	0.0	0.0
U /	N/A	N/A	10.24	33	0	0	0	100	0	N/A	N/A	N/A	1	5,000	1,000	5.8	0.0
B- / 7.4	8.5	0.59	41.29	248	5	91	2	2	5	89.0	-8.6	92	14	0	0	0.0	0.0
C / 5.5	14.5	0.75	42.38	108	9	90	0	1	15	N/A	N/A	93	6	0	0	0.0	0.0
U /	N/A	N/A	42.44	1,009	9	90	0	1	15	N/A	N/A	N/A	6	0	0	0.0	0.0
C+ / 6.1	10.5	0.96	14.42	N/A	2	97	0	1	31	N/A	N/A	51	5	1,000,000	0	0.0	0.0
C+ / 6.1	10.5	0.96	14.26	117	2	97	0	1	31	N/A	N/A	44	5	0	0	0.0	0.0
C+ / 6.1	10.5	0.97	14.28	116	2	97	0	1	31	N/A	N/A	47	5	0	0	0.0	0.0
B- / 7.0	10.4	0.99	23.78	419	0	99	0	1	0	105.5	-19.2	31	13	25	15	0.0	0.0
B+ / 9.7	3.4	0.23	18.36	365	0	25	73	2	0	31.6	-1.6	82	13	25	15	0.0	0.0
B / 8.4	7.8	0.74	22.22	454	0	74	24	2	0	78.5	-13.5	53	13	25	15	0.0	0.0
B+ / 9.4	5.3	0.48	20.46	431	0	50	48	2	0	54.1	-7.8	73	13	25	15	0.0	0.0
B- / 7.2	10.6	1.02	27.45	218	0	99	0	1	0	130.3	-17.8	59	13	25	15	0.0	0.0
C+ / 6.5	7.8	0.07	9.71	82	60	36	3	1	250	N/A	N/A	95	5	100,000	0	0.0	0.0
C+ / 6.5	7.8	0.07	9.61	34	60	36	3	1	250	N/A	N/A	94	5	1,000	0	0.0	0.0
C / 5.2	11.1	1.03	15.50	20	0	99	0	1	64	120.7	-16.8	52	13	0	0	4.5	0.0
C / 5.2	11.1	1.03	15.38	26	0	99	0	1	64	112.8	-17.0	42	13	0	0	0.0	0.0
C / 5.2	11.1	1.03	15.53	139	0	99	0	1	64	124.8	-16.7	56	13	100,000	0	0.0	0.0
C+ / 5.8	10.2	0.46	18.13	32	8	90	0	2	86	65.8	-8.1	42	13	1,000	250	4.5	0.0
C+ / 5.9	10.2	0.45	18.06	22	8	90	0	2	86	59.9	-8.4	33	13	1,000	250	0.0	0.0
C+ / 5.8	10.2	0.46	18.19	159	8	90	0	2	86	68.6	-8.0	46	13	100,000	0	0.0	0.0
C+ / 6.5	11.9	0.63	25.62	428	9	90	0	1	77	79.7	-22.1	98	9	1,000,000	10,000	0.0	0.0
C- / 3.9	14.4	1.05	44.95	2,764	1	98	0	1	60	107.2	-17.7	72	10	1,000,000	10,000	0.0	0.0
B- / 7.0	11.6	0.76	10.52	56	19	80	0	1	73	51.6	-23.0	86	9	1,000	250	4.5	0.0
B- / 7.0	11.6	0.76	10.41	46	19	80	0	1	73	46.4	-23.2	83	9	1,000	250	0.0	0.0

Fund Type	Fund Name	Ticker Symbol	Overall Investment Rating	Phone	Performance Rating/Pts	3 Mo	6 Mo	1Yr / Pct	3Yr / Pct	5Yr / Pct	Dividend Yield	Expense Ratio
			99 Pct = Best / 0 Pct = Worst			Total Return % through 2/28/17			Annualized		Incl. in Returns	
FO	Cohen & Steers Intl Realty I	IRFIX	D+	(800) 330-7348	D / 1.8	5.21	-3.63	9.44 /10	2.28 /26	5.52 /25	6.23	1.22
EN	Cohen & Steers MLP & Energy Oppty	MLOAX	E-	(800) 330-7348	D- / 1.5	4.18	8.10	46.41 /99	-3.15 / 4	--	3.28	1.91
EN	Cohen & Steers MLP & Energy Oppty	MLOCX	E	(800) 330-7348	D / 1.7	4.07	7.71	45.61 /99	-3.79 / 3	--	2.92	2.56
EN	Cohen & Steers MLP & Energy Oppty	MLOIX	E	(800) 330-7348	D / 2.1	4.12	8.12	46.75 /99	-2.86 / 5	--	3.69	1.66
EN	Cohen & Steers MLP & Energy Oppty	MLOZX	E	(800) 330-7348	D / 2.2	4.30	8.17	47.06 /99	-2.88 / 5	--	3.74	1.56
* RE	Cohen & Steers Realty Shares	CSRSX	C+	(800) 330-7348	B / 7.8	8.31	-1.55	16.50 /36	11.21 /97	11.27 /68	2.71	0.96
RE	Cohen and Steers Global Rlty Shs A	CSFAX	C-	(800) 330-7348	C- / 3.6	6.84	-2.53	13.50 /23	6.40 /67	8.03 /42	3.94	1.31
RE	Cohen and Steers Global Rlty Shs C	CSFCX	C	(800) 330-7348	C- / 3.9	6.68	-2.83	12.77 /21	5.71 /62	7.33 /37	3.46	1.96
RE	Cohen and Steers Global Rlty Shs I	CSSPX	C	(800) 330-7348	C / 4.8	6.94	-2.36	13.90 /25	6.77 /70	8.40 /45	4.47	1.03
GL	Cohen and Steers Real Assets A	RAPAX	D-	(800) 330-7348	E / 0.5	3.58	1.95	15.51 /32	-2.06 / 6	-1.23 / 3	2.36	1.57
OT	Cohen and Steers Real Assets C	RAPCX	D-	(800) 330-7348	E+ / 0.6	3.48	1.72	14.94 /30	-2.71 / 5	-1.89 / 3	1.81	2.22
TC	Cohen and Steers Real Assets I	RAPIX	D-	(800) 330-7348	E+ / 0.9	3.80	2.29	16.14 /35	-1.73 / 7	-0.88 / 4	2.80	1.26
GL	Cohen and Steers Real Assets R	RAPRX	D-	(800) 330-7348	E+ / 0.7	3.55	1.93	15.48 /32	-2.22 / 6	-1.38 / 3	1.67	1.72
GL	Cohen and Steers Real Assets Z	RAPZX	D-	(800) 330-7348	E+ / 0.9	3.81	2.18	16.03 /34	-1.76 / 7	-1.00 / 3	2.81	1.22
RE	Cohen and Steers Real Estate Sec A	CSEIX	C	(800) 330-7348	B+ / 8.3	8.22	-1.10	17.83 /42	13.31 /99	13.07 /84	2.44	1.22
RE	Cohen and Steers Real Estate Sec C	CSCIX	C+	(800) 330-7348	B+ / 8.6	8.07	-1.45	17.15 /39	12.58 /98	12.33 /77	2.21	1.87
RE	Cohen and Steers Real Estate Sec I	CSDIX	C+	(800) 330-7348	A- / 9.2	8.32	-0.98	18.19 /44	13.61 /99	13.37 /88	2.68	0.97
RE	Cohen and Steers Real Estate Sec Z	CSZIX	U	(800) 330-7348	U /	8.39	-0.90	18.29 /44	--	--	2.70	0.87
IN	Coho Relative Value Equity Adv	COHOX	A-		B- / 7.1	6.44	5.95	18.11 /43	9.13 /88	--	1.41	1.08
IN	Coho Relative Value Equity Inst	COHIX	U		U /	6.52	6.03	18.28 /44	--	--	1.49	0.93
RE	Cole Real Estate Income Strategy		B+	(866) 907-2653	C- / 4.2	0.84	1.52	4.52 / 4	7.88 /78	9.58 /55	5.36	N/A
FS	Collins Long/Short Credit Inst	CCLIX	U	(855) 552-5863	U /	1.71	1.98	8.42 / 8	--	--	3.25	5.67
IN	Columbia Abs Rtn Currency & Inc R4	CARCX	A	(800) 345-6611	B / 8.0	4.88	4.88	9.64 /11	12.53 /98	5.45 /24	0.00	1.50
IN	Columbia Abs Rtn Currency & Inc R5	COUIX	A+	(800) 345-6611	B / 8.0	4.84	4.84	9.67 /11	12.56 /98	5.40 /24	0.00	1.39
IN	Columbia Abs Rtn Currency & Inc Y	CABYX	A	(800) 345-6611	B / 8.1	4.83	4.83	9.76 /11	12.66 /98	5.55 /25	0.00	1.34
MC	Columbia Acorn A	LACAX	E+	(800) 345-6611	C / 5.5	6.24	10.22	29.35 /85	4.20 /45	9.35 /53	0.00	1.07
MC	Columbia Acorn C	LIACX	D-	(800) 345-6611	C+ / 6.1	6.12	9.92	28.51 /83	3.47 /37	8.57 /47	0.00	1.82
EM	Columbia Acorn Emg Mkts A	CAGAX	E	(800) 345-6611	E- / 0.1	5.25	-2.16	13.26 /23	-6.39 / 2	0.11 / 5	0.66	1.80
EM	Columbia Acorn Emg Mkts C	CGMCX	E	(800) 345-6611	E- / 0.1	5.04	-2.61	12.39 /19	-7.11 / 1	-0.64 / 4	0.00	2.55
EM	Columbia Acorn Emg Mkts I	CATIX	E	(800) 345-6611	E- / 0.2	5.34	-2.04	13.79 /24	-6.06 / 2	0.47 / 5	1.08	1.39
EM	Columbia Acorn Emg Mkts R4	CAERX	E	(800) 345-6611	E- / 0.2	5.38	-2.04	13.68 /24	-6.12 / 2	0.42 / 5	0.96	1.55
EM	Columbia Acorn Emg Mkts R5	CANRX	E	(800) 345-6611	E- / 0.2	5.30	-2.04	13.70 /24	-6.08 / 2	0.45 / 5	1.06	1.44
EM	Columbia Acorn Emg Mkts Y	CPHRX	E	(800) 345-6611	E- / 0.2	5.36	-1.95	13.72 /24	-6.02 / 2	0.51 / 5	1.08	1.39
EM	Columbia Acorn Emg Mkts Z	CEFZX	E	(800) 345-6611	E- / 0.2	5.31	-2.08	13.65 /24	-6.15 / 2	0.36 / 5	0.95	1.55
FO	Columbia Acorn European A	CAEAX	D-	(800) 345-6611	E / 0.4	9.01	0.06	10.23 /12	-1.65 / 7	7.41 /37	0.75	2.06
FO	Columbia Acorn European C	CAECX	D-	(800) 345-6611	E+ / 0.6	8.78	-0.27	9.37 /10	-2.38 / 6	6.62 /32	0.18	2.83
FO	Columbia Acorn European I	CAFIX	D-	(800) 345-6611	E+ / 0.8	9.15	0.28	10.61 /13	-1.33 / 8	7.74 /40	1.11	1.70
FO	Columbia Acorn European R4	CLOFX	D	(800) 345-6611	E+ / 0.8	9.09	0.19	10.46 /13	-1.39 / 8	7.68 /40	1.03	1.84
FO	Columbia Acorn European R5	CAEEX	D-	(800) 345-6611	E+ / 0.8	9.07	0.29	10.52 /13	-1.37 / 8	7.69 /40	1.05	1.75
FO	Columbia Acorn European Z	CAEZX	D-	(800) 345-6611	E+ / 0.8	9.13	0.26	10.51 /13	-1.39 / 8	7.68 /40	1.03	1.79
SC	Columbia Acorn I	CANIX	D	(800) 345-6611	C+ / 6.9	6.33	10.41	29.81 /86	4.57 /49	9.73 /56	0.00	0.74
FO	Columbia Acorn International A	LAIAX	E+	(800) 345-6611	E / 0.4	7.06	-0.28	10.72 /14	-1.34 / 8	4.86 /20	0.34	1.24
FO	● Columbia Acorn International B	LIABX	E+	(800) 345-6611	E+ / 0.6	6.91	-0.51	10.21 /12	-2.09 / 6	4.08 /16	0.00	1.63
FO	Columbia Acorn International C	LAICX	E+	(800) 345-6611	E+ / 0.6	6.86	-0.67	9.90 /11	-2.07 / 6	4.08 /16	0.00	1.99
FO	Columbia Acorn International I	CARIX	E+	(800) 345-6611	E+ / 0.9	7.15	-0.14	11.10 /15	-0.98 / 9	5.25 /23	0.70	0.88
FO	Columbia Acorn International R	CACRX	E+	(800) 345-6611	E+ / 0.7	7.00	-0.41	10.40 /13	-1.69 / 7	4.49 /18	0.04	1.49
FO	Columbia Acorn International R4	CCIRX	E+	(800) 345-6611	E+ / 0.8	7.12	-0.18	10.95 /14	-1.14 / 9	5.10 /22	0.54	0.99
FO	Columbia Acorn International R5	CAIRX	E+	(800) 345-6611	E+ / 0.9	7.13	-0.17	11.03 /15	-1.03 / 9	5.20 /23	0.65	0.93
FO	Columbia Acorn International Sel A	LAFAX	E	(800) 345-6611	E+ / 0.7	9.64	3.51	16.66 /37	-1.35 / 8	4.49 /18	0.66	1.56
FO	Columbia Acorn International Sel C	LFFCX	E	(800) 345-6611	E+ / 0.9	9.37	3.12	15.74 /33	-2.10 / 6	3.68 /14	0.00	2.31
FO	Columbia Acorn International Sel I	CRSIX	E+	(800) 345-6611	D- / 1.3	9.74	3.74	17.17 /39	-0.97 / 9	4.87 /20	1.09	1.19
FO	Columbia Acorn International Sel R4	CILRX	E+	(800) 345-6611	D- / 1.3	9.72	3.66	16.98 /38	-1.08 / 9	4.77 /20	0.92	1.31

● Denotes fund is closed to new investors
* Denotes fund is included in Section II

www.thestreetratings.com

RISK			NET ASSETS		ASSET				Portfolio Turnover Ratio	BULL / BEAR		FUND MANAGER		MINIMUMS		LOADS	
Risk Rating/Pts	3 Year Standard Deviation	Beta	NAV As of 2/28/17	Total $(Mil)	Cash %	Stocks %	Bonds %	Other %		Last Bull Market Return	Last Bear Market Return	Manager Quality Pct	Manager Tenure (Years)	Initial Purch. $	Additional Purch. $	Front End Load	Back End Load
C+ / 6.9	11.6	0.76	10.59	488	19	80	0	1	73	54.6	-22.9	88	9	100,000	0	0.0	0.0
D / 2.1	21.3	0.90	8.71	13	31	68	0	1	81	N/A	N/A	84	4	0	0	4.5	0.0
D / 2.0	21.3	0.90	8.67	11	31	68	0	1	81	N/A	N/A	80	4	0	0	0.0	0.0
D / 2.1	21.3	0.90	8.72	81	31	68	0	1	81	N/A	N/A	86	4	100,000	0	0.0	0.0
D / 2.0	21.3	0.90	8.72	N/A	31	68	0	1	81	N/A	N/A	85	4	0	0	0.0	0.0
C- / 3.9	14.5	1.05	68.29	5,230	1	98	0	1	58	105.0	-17.7	69	10	10,000	500	0.0	0.0
C+ / 6.5	11.8	0.79	50.85	51	9	90	0	1	82	76.0	-22.3	46	10	1,000	250	4.5	0.0
C+ / 6.5	11.8	0.79	50.46	59	9	90	0	1	82	70.0	-22.5	37	10	1,000	250	0.0	0.0
C+ / 6.5	11.8	0.79	51.08	349	9	90	0	1	82	79.3	-22.1	51	10	100,000	0	0.0	0.0
C+ / 6.0	9.4	1.05	8.89	13	13	56	30	1	101	N/A	N/A	6	5	1,000	250	4.5	0.0
C+ / 6.0	9.4	0.54	8.86	9	13	56	30	1	101	N/A	N/A	3	5	1,000	250	0.0	0.0
C+ / 6.0	9.4	0.54	8.92	153	13	56	30	1	101	N/A	N/A	5	5	100,000	0	0.0	0.0
C+ / 6.0	9.4	1.06	8.97	N/A	13	56	30	1	101	N/A	N/A	5	5	100	0	0.0	0.0
C+ / 6.0	9.3	1.06	8.90	2	13	56	30	1	101	N/A	N/A	7	5	250	25	0.0	0.0
C- / 3.1	14.0	1.02	14.65	684	3	95	0	2	95	121.5	-17.2	85	11	1,000	250	4.5	0.0
D+ / 2.8	14.0	1.02	13.31	353	3	95	0	2	95	113.9	-17.4	82	11	1,000	250	0.0	0.0
C- / 3.2	14.0	1.02	15.40	1,803	3	95	0	2	95	125.1	-17.1	86	11	100,000	0	0.0	0.0
U /	N/A	N/A	15.41	127	3	95	0	2	95	N/A	N/A	N/A	11	0	0	0.0	0.0
B- / 7.4	9.1	0.84	13.33	227	3	96	0	1	24	N/A	N/A	75	4	100,000	100	0.0	0.0
U /	N/A	N/A	13.35	238	3	96	0	1	24	N/A	N/A	N/A	4	1,000,000	100	0.0	0.0
B+ / 9.9	1.6	0.04	18.07	240	0	0	0	100	0	N/A	N/A	98	6	0	0	0.0	0.0
U /	N/A	N/A	9.99	77	0	0	0	100	93	N/A	N/A	N/A	2	1,000,000	1,000	0.0	0.0
B- / 7.4	11.6	0.14	11.29	1	98	0	1	1	0	36.0	-3.2	99	11	0	0	0.0	0.0
B- / 7.6	11.6	0.14	11.35	N/A	98	0	1	1	0	35.7	-3.2	99	11	0	0	0.0	0.0
B- / 7.4	11.5	0.14	11.33	N/A	98	0	1	1	0	36.6	-3.2	99	11	0	0	0.0	0.0
E+ / 0.6	13.5	1.06	14.15	943	1	98	0	1	21	95.5	-22.2	11	18	2,000	0	5.8	0.0
E+ / 0.6	13.5	1.07	8.83	302	1	98	0	1	21	88.2	-22.5	7	18	2,000	0	0.0	0.0
C / 4.4	13.6	0.79	10.49	48	1	98	0	1	58	23.7	N/A	4	6	2,000	0	5.8	0.0
C / 4.4	13.6	0.79	10.43	16	1	98	0	1	58	18.9	N/A	3	6	2,000	0	0.0	0.0
C / 4.3	13.6	0.79	10.52	N/A	1	98	0	1	58	26.4	N/A	4	6	0	0	0.0	0.0
C / 4.3	13.6	0.79	10.58	1	1	98	0	1	58	25.9	N/A	4	6	0	0	0.0	0.0
C / 4.3	13.7	0.79	10.57	1	1	98	0	1	58	26.1	N/A	4	6	0	0	0.0	0.0
C / 4.3	13.7	0.79	10.48	N/A	1	98	0	1	58	26.5	N/A	4	6	0	0	0.0	0.0
C / 4.4	13.6	0.79	10.51	39	1	98	0	1	58	25.6	N/A	4	6	2,000	0	0.0	0.0
C+ / 6.4	12.5	0.89	15.02	26	1	98	0	1	37	67.1	N/A	55	6	2,000	0	5.8	0.0
C+ / 6.4	12.5	0.88	14.87	8	1	98	0	1	37	60.6	N/A	45	6	2,000	0	0.0	0.0d
C+ / 6.4	12.5	0.89	15.02	N/A	1	98	0	1	37	69.9	N/A	60	6	0	0	0.0	0.0
C+ / 6.5	12.5	0.89	15.09	N/A	1	98	0	1	37	69.5	N/A	59	6	0	0	0.0	0.0
C+ / 6.4	12.5	0.88	15.17	1	1	98	0	1	37	69.5	N/A	59	6	0	0	0.0	0.0
C+ / 6.4	12.5	0.88	15.03	12	1	98	0	1	37	69.5	N/A	59	6	2,000	0	0.0	0.0
E+ / 0.6	13.5	0.82	16.33	11	1	98	0	1	21	99.3	-22.1	62	18	0	0	0.0	0.0
C / 5.1	11.0	0.80	40.12	596	4	95	0	1	50	46.8	-21.5	59	18	2,000	0	5.8	0.0
C / 5.1	11.0	0.80	38.68	N/A	4	95	0	1	50	41.0	-21.7	48	18	2,000	0	0.0	0.0
C / 5.1	11.0	0.80	38.45	65	4	95	0	1	50	40.9	-21.7	49	18	2,000	0	0.0	0.0
C / 5.1	11.0	0.80	40.21	21	4	95	0	1	50	49.7	-21.3	64	18	0	0	0.0	0.0
C / 5.1	11.0	0.80	40.11	5	4	95	0	1	50	44.0	-21.5	54	18	0	0	0.0	0.0
C / 5.1	11.0	0.80	40.48	102	4	95	0	1	50	48.7	-21.3	61	18	0	0	0.0	0.0
C / 5.0	11.0	0.80	40.15	312	4	95	0	1	50	49.4	-21.3	63	18	0	0	0.0	0.0
C- / 4.1	11.8	0.78	22.97	23	0	100	0	0	59	41.6	-18.6	59	16	2,000	0	5.8	0.0
C- / 4.0	11.8	0.78	21.47	5	0	100	0	0	59	35.8	-18.9	48	16	2,000	0	0.0	0.0
C- / 4.1	11.8	0.78	23.25	N/A	0	100	0	0	59	44.4	-18.4	64	16	0	0	0.0	0.0
C- / 4.1	11.8	0.78	23.43	1	0	100	0	0	59	43.7	-18.5	62	16	0	0	0.0	0.0

					PERFORMANCE							
	99 Pct = Best 0 Pct = Worst		Ticker	Overall Investment	Perfor- mance		Total Return % through 2/28/17			Annualized	Incl. in Returns	
Fund Type	Fund Name		Symbol	Rating	Phone	Rating/Pts	3 Mo	6 Mo	1Yr / Pct	3Yr / Pct	5Yr / Pct	Dividend Yield	Expense Ratio

Fund Type	Fund Name	Ticker Symbol	Overall Investment Rating	Phone	Performance Rating/Pts	3 Mo	6 Mo	1Yr / Pct	3Yr / Pct	5Yr / Pct	Dividend Yield	Expense Ratio
FO	Columbia Acorn International Sel R5	CRIRX	E+	(800) 345-6611	D- / 1.3	9.74	3.73	17.06 / 39	-1.00 / 9	4.83 / 20	0.98	1.24
FO	Columbia Acorn International Sel Y	CSIRX	E+	(800) 345-6611	D- / 1.3	9.73	3.72	17.17 / 39	-0.95 / 10	4.87 / 20	1.05	1.19
FO	Columbia Acorn International Sel Z	ACFFX	E+	(800) 345-6611	D- / 1.3	9.72	3.67	16.99 / 38	-1.05 / 9	4.79 / 20	0.95	1.31
FO	Columbia Acorn International Y	CCYIX	E+	(800) 345-6611	E+ / 0.9	7.15	-0.14	11.11 / 15	-0.98 / 9	5.24 / 23	0.70	0.88
FO	Columbia Acorn International Z	ACINX	E+	(800) 345-6611	E+ / 0.9	7.10	-0.17	10.99 / 14	-1.07 / 9	5.16 / 22	0.61	0.99
SC	Columbia Acorn R4	CEARX	D	(800) 345-6611	C+ / 6.8	6.35	10.39	29.77 / 86	4.42 / 48	9.60 / 55	0.00	0.82
SC	Columbia Acorn R5	CRBRX	D	(800) 345-6611	C+ / 6.9	6.30	10.39	29.79 / 86	4.52 / 49	9.69 / 56	0.00	0.79
MC	Columbia Acorn Select A	LTFAX	D-	(800) 345-6611	C+ / 6.4	5.63	11.44	27.73 / 81	5.89 / 63	9.83 / 57	0.00	1.33
MC	Columbia Acorn Select C	LTFCX	D	(800) 345-6611	C+ / 6.8	5.41	11.01	26.81 / 79	5.11 / 55	9.02 / 51	0.00	2.08
MC	Columbia Acorn Select I	CACIX	D	(800) 345-6611	B / 7.6	5.75	11.60	28.14 / 82	6.28 / 67	10.23 / 60	0.00	0.97
MC	Columbia Acorn Select R4	CSSRX	D	(800) 345-6611	B- / 7.5	5.68	11.54	28.04 / 82	6.14 / 65	10.09 / 59	0.00	1.08
MC	Columbia Acorn Select R5	CSLRX	D	(800) 345-6611	B / 7.6	5.72	11.63	28.17 / 82	6.23 / 66	10.16 / 59	0.00	1.02
MC	Columbia Acorn Select Y	CSLYX	D	(800) 345-6611	B / 7.6	5.68	11.61	28.21 / 82	6.27 / 66	10.21 / 60	0.00	0.97
MC	Columbia Acorn Select Z	ACTWX	D	(800) 345-6611	B- / 7.5	5.67	11.50	28.01 / 82	6.17 / 66	10.12 / 59	0.00	1.08
SC	Columbia Acorn USA A	LAUAX	D-	(800) 345-6611	C+ / 6.7	5.93	11.38	34.01 / 93	5.13 / 56	10.73 / 64	0.00	1.43
SC	Columbia Acorn USA C	LAUCX	D	(800) 345-6611	B- / 7.1	5.77	10.95	32.97 / 92	4.40 / 47	9.96 / 58	0.00	2.18
SC	Columbia Acorn USA I	CAUIX	D+	(800) 345-6611	B / 8.0	6.11	11.68	34.62 / 94	5.60 / 60	11.19 / 67	0.00	1.03
SC	Columbia Acorn USA R4	CUSAX	D+	(800) 345-6611	B / 7.8	6.02	11.56	34.31 / 93	5.38 / 58	11.01 / 66	0.00	1.18
SC	Columbia Acorn USA R5	CYSRX	D+	(800) 345-6611	B / 7.9	6.03	11.61	34.50 / 93	5.49 / 59	11.08 / 66	0.00	1.08
SC	Columbia Acorn USA Y	CUSYX	D+	(800) 345-6611	B / 8.0	6.07	11.67	34.57 / 94	5.56 / 60	11.14 / 67	0.00	1.03
SC	Columbia Acorn USA Z	AUSAX	D+	(800) 345-6611	B / 7.9	6.02	11.55	34.34 / 93	5.39 / 59	11.00 / 66	0.00	1.18
SC	Columbia Acorn Y	CRBYX	D	(800) 345-6611	C+ / 6.9	6.32	10.38	29.84 / 86	4.57 / 49	9.73 / 56	0.00	0.74
MC	Columbia Acorn Z	ACRNX	D	(800) 345-6611	C+ / 6.9	6.31	10.41	29.78 / 86	4.50 / 49	9.66 / 56	0.00	0.82
AA	Columbia Adaptive Risk Alloc A	CRAAX	C+	(800) 345-6611	D+ / 2.6	5.28	2.38	13.95 / 25	4.28 / 46	--	0.93	1.28
AA	Columbia Adaptive Risk Alloc C	CRACX	C+	(800) 345-6611	C- / 3.1	5.15	1.97	13.12 / 22	3.49 / 37	--	0.29	2.03
AA	● Columbia Adaptive Risk Alloc K	CRFRX	B-	(800) 345-6611	C- / 3.7	5.26	2.27	13.91 / 25	4.38 / 47	--	1.08	1.18
AA	Columbia Adaptive Risk Alloc R	CRKRX	C+	(800) 345-6611	C- / 3.5	5.26	2.24	13.65 / 24	4.02 / 43	--	0.75	1.53
GR	Columbia Adaptive Risk Alloc R4	CARRX	B	(800) 345-6611	C- / 3.9	5.39	2.52	14.24 / 27	4.50 / 49	--	1.22	1.03
AA	Columbia Adaptive Risk Alloc R5	CRDRX	B-	(800) 345-6611	C- / 3.9	5.35	2.47	14.17 / 26	4.65 / 50	--	1.27	0.93
AA	Columbia Adaptive Risk Alloc W	CRAWX	B-	(800) 345-6611	C- / 3.7	5.26	2.27	13.93 / 25	4.31 / 46	--	0.99	1.28
GR	Columbia Adaptive Risk Alloc Y	CARYX	B	(800) 345-6611	C- / 3.9	5.41	2.54	14.34 / 27	4.61 / 50	--	1.34	0.88
AA	Columbia Adaptive Risk Alloc Z	CRAZX	B-	(800) 345-6611	C- / 3.8	5.29	2.42	14.13 / 26	4.53 / 49	--	1.22	1.03
GL	Columbia Alternative Beta W	CLAWX	U	(800) 345-6611	U /	2.13	-0.82	-0.18 / 1	--	--	0.46	1.65
FO	Columbia Asia Pacific ex-Japan A	CAJAX	E	(800) 345-6611	D+ / 2.8	6.17	2.59	23.29 / 67	2.34 / 26	3.47 / 13	0.85	1.96
FO	Columbia Asia Pacific ex-Japan C	CAJCX	E+	(800) 345-6611	C- / 3.2	5.98	2.15	22.27 / 63	1.56 / 21	2.69 / 10	0.22	2.71
FO	Columbia Asia Pacific ex-Japan I	CAPIX	D-	(800) 345-6611	C- / 4.2	6.20	2.72	23.68 / 69	2.80 / 30	3.92 / 15	1.28	1.49
FO	Columbia Asia Pacific ex-Japan R	CAJRX	E+	(800) 345-6611	C- / 3.6	6.07	2.35	22.94 / 66	2.08 / 24	3.17 / 11	0.68	2.21
FO	Columbia Asia Pacific ex-Japan R5	TAPRX	D-	(800) 345-6611	C- / 4.2	6.22	2.75	23.62 / 69	2.73 / 29	3.85 / 14	1.23	1.54
FO	Columbia Asia Pacific ex-Japan Z	CAJZX	D-	(800) 345-6611	C- / 4.0	6.13	2.65	23.46 / 68	2.59 / 28	3.71 / 14	1.13	1.71
BA	Columbia Balanced A	CBLAX	C+	(800) 345-6611	C- / 4.2	4.92	4.05	13.68 / 24	6.91 / 71	9.59 / 55	0.92	1.00
BA	● Columbia Balanced B	CBLBX	B-	(800) 345-6611	C / 4.7	4.72	3.67	12.83 / 21	6.11 / 65	8.77 / 49	0.28	1.75
BA	Columbia Balanced C	CBLCX	B-	(800) 345-6611	C / 4.7	4.71	3.64	12.82 / 21	6.13 / 65	8.78 / 49	0.28	1.75
BA	● Columbia Balanced K	CLRFX	B	(800) 345-6611	C / 5.4	4.92	4.07	13.75 / 24	7.01 / 72	9.69 / 56	1.07	0.96
BA	Columbia Balanced R	CBLRX	B	(800) 345-6611	C / 5.1	4.85	3.91	13.39 / 23	6.66 / 69	9.33 / 53	0.74	1.25
BA	Columbia Balanced R4	CBDRX	B	(800) 345-6611	C+ / 5.6	4.97	4.17	13.94 / 25	7.20 / 73	9.88 / 57	1.20	0.75
BA	Columbia Balanced R5	CLREX	B	(800) 345-6611	C+ / 5.7	4.98	4.23	14.05 / 26	7.31 / 74	9.99 / 58	1.30	0.71
BA	Columbia Balanced Y	CBDYX	B	(800) 345-6611	C+ / 5.7	5.01	4.24	14.10 / 26	7.35 / 74	10.02 / 58	1.34	0.66
BA	Columbia Balanced Z	CBALX	B	(800) 345-6611	C+ / 5.6	4.96	4.18	13.95 / 25	7.18 / 73	9.86 / 57	1.21	0.75
BA	Columbia Capital Alloc Mod Aggr A	NBIAX	C-	(800) 345-6611	C- / 3.6	5.52	5.19	16.30 / 35	5.01 / 54	7.53 / 38	1.19	1.16
BA	● Columbia Capital Alloc Mod Aggr B	NLBBX	C-	(800) 345-6611	C- / 4.1	5.40	4.77	15.48 / 32	4.22 / 45	6.73 / 33	0.75	1.91
BA	Columbia Capital Alloc Mod Aggr C	NBICX	C-	(800) 345-6611	C- / 4.1	5.39	4.78	15.40 / 32	4.23 / 46	6.73 / 33	0.74	1.91
GL	● Columbia Capital Alloc Mod Aggr K	CAMKX	C	(800) 345-6611	C / 4.8	5.57	5.18	16.28 / 35	5.08 / 55	7.61 / 39	1.35	1.07

● Denotes fund is closed to new investors
★ Denotes fund is included in Section II

146

Risk Rating/Pts	3 Year Standard Deviation	Beta	NAV As of 2/28/17	Total $(Mil)	Cash %	Stocks %	Bonds %	Other %	Portfolio Turnover Ratio	Last Bull Market Return	Last Bear Market Return	Manager Quality Pct	Manager Tenure (Years)	Initial Purch. $	Additional Purch. $	Front End Load	Back End Load
C- / 4.1	11.9	0.79	23.42	1	0	100	0	0	59	44.1	-18.5	63	16	0	0	0.0	0.0
C- / 4.1	11.9	0.79	23.40	N/A	0	100	0	0	59	44.4	-18.5	64	16	0	0	0.0	0.0
C- / 4.1	11.8	0.78	23.26	76	0	100	0	0	59	43.9	-18.5	63	16	2,000	0	0.0	0.0
C / 5.1	11.0	0.80	40.48	259	4	95	0	1	50	49.7	-21.3	64	18	0	0	0.0	0.0
C / 5.0	11.0	0.80	40.17	3,479	4	95	0	1	50	49.1	-21.3	62	18	2,000	0	0.0	0.0
E+ / 0.6	13.5	0.82	16.79	35	1	98	0	1	21	98.1	-22.1	60	18	0	0	0.0	0.0
E+ / 0.6	13.5	0.82	16.90	47	1	98	0	1	21	98.9	-22.1	61	18	0	0	0.0	0.0
E+ / 0.7	12.4	0.94	13.85	122	2	97	0	1	55	103.8	-27.3	35	15	2,000	0	5.8	0.0
E+ / 0.7	12.4	0.95	9.71	27	2	97	0	1	55	95.7	-27.5	26	15	2,000	0	0.0	0.0
E+ / 0.7	12.4	0.94	15.59	11	2	97	0	1	55	107.8	-27.1	40	15	0	0	0.0	0.0
E+ / 0.7	12.4	0.94	15.96	1	2	97	0	1	55	106.5	-27.2	38	15	0	0	0.0	0.0
E+ / 0.8	12.4	0.94	16.03	1	2	97	0	1	55	107.2	-27.2	39	15	0	0	0.0	0.0
E+ / 0.8	12.4	0.95	16.15	4	2	97	0	1	55	107.6	-27.2	40	15	0	0	0.0	0.0
E+ / 0.7	12.4	0.94	15.42	147	2	97	0	1	55	106.8	-27.2	38	15	2,000	0	0.0	0.0
E+ / 0.6	15.4	0.95	15.60	72	3	96	0	1	35	110.2	-24.8	57	3	2,000	0	5.8	0.0
E+ / 0.6	15.4	0.95	10.47	12	3	96	0	1	35	102.3	-25.1	48	3	2,000	0	0.0	0.0
E+ / 0.6	15.4	0.95	18.25	N/A	3	96	0	1	35	115.0	-24.7	63	3	0	0	0.0	0.0
E+ / 0.6	15.4	0.95	18.72	6	3	96	0	1	35	113.1	-24.7	61	3	0	0	0.0	0.0
E+ / 0.6	15.4	0.95	18.81	14	3	96	0	1	35	113.8	-24.7	62	3	0	0	0.0	0.0
E+ / 0.6	15.4	0.95	18.94	41	3	96	0	1	35	114.4	-24.7	63	3	0	0	0.0	0.0
E+ / 0.6	15.4	0.95	17.95	502	3	96	0	1	35	113.0	-24.7	61	3	2,000	0	0.0	0.0
E+ / 0.6	13.5	0.82	17.00	77	1	98	0	1	21	99.3	-22.1	62	18	0	0	0.0	0.0
E+ / 0.6	13.5	1.07	16.21	3,503	1	98	0	1	21	98.6	-22.1	12	18	2,000	0	0.0	0.0
B+ / 9.0	6.3	0.86	10.58	208	54	8	37	1	254	N/A	N/A	48	5	2,000	0	5.8	0.0
B / 8.9	6.3	0.85	10.32	86	54	8	37	1	254	N/A	N/A	38	5	2,000	0	0.0	0.0
B+ / 9.0	6.3	0.85	10.59	N/A	54	8	37	1	254	N/A	N/A	50	5	0	0	0.0	0.0
B / 8.9	6.3	0.85	10.50	6	54	8	37	1	254	N/A	N/A	45	5	0	0	0.0	0.0
B+ / 9.2	6.3	0.46	10.65	10	54	8	37	1	254	N/A	N/A	71	5	0	0	0.0	0.0
B+ / 9.0	6.3	0.85	10.66	3	54	8	37	1	254	N/A	N/A	53	5	0	0	0.0	0.0
B+ / 9.0	6.3	0.85	10.59	1,277	54	8	37	1	254	N/A	N/A	49	5	500	0	0.0	0.0
B+ / 9.3	6.3	0.46	10.68	N/A	54	8	37	1	254	N/A	N/A	72	5	0	0	0.0	0.0
B+ / 9.0	6.2	0.84	10.64	83	54	8	37	1	254	N/A	N/A	53	5	2,000	0	0.0	0.0
U /	N/A	N/A	9.22	326	28	4	66	2	32	N/A	N/A	N/A	2	500	0	0.0	0.0
D / 2.2	13.9	0.84	10.83	1	1	98	0	1	20	44.1	-27.2	88	8	2,000	0	5.8	0.0
D / 2.2	13.9	0.84	10.71	N/A	1	98	0	1	20	38.2	-27.5	85	8	2,000	0	0.0	0.0
D / 2.1	13.9	0.84	10.82	14	1	98	0	1	20	47.4	-27.1	90	8	0	0	0.0	0.0
D / 2.2	14.0	0.84	10.74	N/A	1	98	0	1	20	41.8	-27.3	87	8	0	0	0.0	0.0
D / 2.2	13.9	0.84	10.87	14	1	98	0	1	20	46.9	-27.0	90	8	0	0	0.0	0.0
D / 2.2	13.9	0.84	10.83	N/A	1	98	0	1	20	45.8	-27.2	89	8	2,000	0	0.0	0.0
B / 8.1	6.5	1.03	38.70	3,349	4	62	32	2	60	82.4	-10.9	65	20	2,000	0	5.8	0.0
B / 8.1	6.5	1.03	38.55	4	4	62	32	2	60	75.1	-11.2	55	20	2,000	0	0.0	0.0
B / 8.1	6.5	1.03	38.57	1,431	4	62	32	2	60	75.3	-11.2	55	20	2,000	0	0.0	0.0
B / 8.1	6.5	1.03	38.63	1	4	62	32	2	60	83.4	-10.9	66	20	0	0	0.0	0.0
B / 8.1	6.5	1.03	38.70	87	4	62	32	2	60	80.2	-11.0	62	20	0	0	0.0	0.0
B / 8.1	6.5	1.03	38.99	156	4	62	32	2	60	85.0	-10.9	68	20	0	0	0.0	0.0
B / 8.1	6.5	1.03	38.67	233	4	62	32	2	60	86.0	-10.8	70	20	0	0	0.0	0.0
B / 8.1	6.5	1.03	39.00	154	4	62	32	2	60	86.2	-10.9	70	20	0	0	0.0	0.0
B / 8.1	6.5	1.03	38.64	1,011	4	62	32	2	60	84.9	-10.9	68	20	0	0	0.0	0.0
C+ / 6.0	7.6	1.18	12.28	1,695	14	56	28	2	16	65.5	-13.4	27	N/A	2,000	0	5.8	0.0
C+ / 6.0	7.6	1.18	12.10	14	14	56	28	2	16	58.9	-13.7	20	N/A	2,000	0	0.0	0.0
C+ / 6.0	7.6	1.17	12.31	219	14	56	28	2	16	58.9	-13.7	20	N/A	2,000	0	0.0	0.0
C+ / 6.0	7.6	1.15	12.23	N/A	14	56	28	2	16	66.1	-13.4	71	8	0	0	0.0	0.0

| | | | | | | Total Return % through 2/28/17 | | | Annualized | | Incl. in Returns | |
Fund Type	Fund Name	Ticker Symbol	Overall Investment Rating	Phone	Perfor-mance Rating/Pts	3 Mo	6 Mo	1Yr / Pct	3Yr / Pct	5Yr / Pct	Dividend Yield	Expense Ratio
BA	Columbia Capital Alloc Mod Aggr R	CLBRX	C	(800) 345-6611	C / 4.6	5.55	5.07	16.03 /34	4.78 /52	7.29 /37	1.03	1.41
GL	Columbia Capital Alloc Mod Aggr R4	CGBRX	C	(800) 345-6611	C / 5.0	5.63	5.28	16.55 /36	5.26 /57	7.78 /40	1.48	0.91
GL	Columbia Capital Alloc Mod Aggr R5	CLHRX	C	(800) 345-6611	C / 5.1	5.65	5.34	16.68 /37	5.37 /58	7.86 /41	1.57	0.82
BA	● Columbia Capital Alloc Mod Aggr V	CGGTX	C-	(800) 345-6611	C- / 3.6	5.52	5.19	16.30 /35	4.99 /54	7.50 /38	1.19	1.16
GL	Columbia Capital Alloc Mod Aggr Y	CPHNX	C	(800) 345-6611	C / 5.1	5.70	5.39	16.80 /38	5.42 /59	7.78 /40	1.65	0.77
BA	Columbia Capital Alloc Mod Aggr Z	NBGPX	C	(800) 345-6611	C / 5.0	5.59	5.25	16.52 /36	5.25 /57	7.79 /41	1.49	0.91
GI	Columbia Capital Alloc Mod Consv A	NLGAX	C-	(800) 345-6611	D / 1.9	3.48	2.21	10.11 /12	3.59 /38	5.16 /22	1.39	1.05
GI	● Columbia Capital Alloc Mod Consv B	NLIBX	C-	(800) 345-6611	D / 2.2	3.31	1.84	9.24 /10	2.80 /30	4.38 /17	0.76	1.80
GI	Columbia Capital Alloc Mod Consv C	NIICX	C-	(800) 345-6611	D / 2.2	3.34	1.85	9.32 /10	2.82 /30	4.39 /17	0.77	1.80
AA	● Columbia Capital Alloc Mod Consv K	CCAKX	C-	(800) 345-6611	D+ / 2.7	3.55	2.27	10.14 /12	3.67 /39	5.23 /23	1.57	0.99
GI	Columbia Capital Alloc Mod Consv R	CLIRX	C-	(800) 345-6611	D+ / 2.5	3.51	2.17	9.81 /11	3.33 /35	4.92 /21	1.23	1.30
AA	Columbia Capital Alloc Mod Consv	CHWRX	C-	(800) 345-6611	D+ / 2.8	3.58	2.36	10.37 /13	3.85 /41	5.39 /24	1.72	0.80
AA	Columbia Capital Alloc Mod Consv	CLRRX	C-	(800) 345-6611	D+ / 2.9	3.59	2.38	10.43 /13	3.93 /42	5.46 /24	1.77	0.74
AA	Columbia Capital Alloc Mod Consv Y	CPDGX	C-	(800) 345-6611	D+ / 2.9	3.55	2.44	10.51 /13	3.99 /43	5.51 /25	1.85	0.69
GI	Columbia Capital Alloc Mod Consv Z	NIPAX	C-	(800) 345-6611	D+ / 2.8	3.50	2.37	10.30 /12	3.84 /41	5.42 /24	1.73	0.80
AA	Columbia Capital Allocation Aggr A	AXBAX	C-	(800) 345-6611	C / 4.3	6.34	6.34	18.63 /46	5.36 /58	8.74 /48	1.04	1.20
AA	● Columbia Capital Allocation Aggr B	AXPBX	C-	(800) 345-6611	C / 4.8	6.10	5.92	17.70 /41	4.54 /49	7.93 /41	0.47	1.95
AA	Columbia Capital Allocation Aggr C	RBGCX	C-	(800) 345-6611	C / 4.8	6.13	5.95	17.75 /42	4.54 /49	7.93 /41	0.48	1.95
AA	● Columbia Capital Allocation Aggr K	CAGRX	C	(800) 345-6611	C+ / 5.6	6.39	6.39	18.76 /46	5.43 /59	8.86 /49	1.15	1.13
GR	Columbia Capital Allocation Aggr R	CPARX	C	(800) 345-6611	C / 5.3	6.33	6.24	18.31 /44	5.09 /55	8.47 /46	0.89	1.45
GR	Columbia Capital Allocation Aggr R4	CPDAX	C	(800) 345-6611	C+ / 5.8	6.43	6.52	18.95 /47	5.62 /61	8.97 /50	1.33	0.95
GR	Columbia Capital Allocation Aggr R5	CPANX	C	(800) 345-6611	C+ / 5.8	6.41	6.50	19.04 /47	5.68 /61	9.05 /51	1.39	0.88
GI	Columbia Capital Allocation Aggr Y	CPDIX	C	(800) 345-6611	C+ / 5.9	6.46	6.55	19.10 /48	5.76 /62	9.09 /51	1.43	0.83
GR	Columbia Capital Allocation Aggr Z	CPAZX	C	(800) 345-6611	C+ / 5.8	6.43	6.52	18.87 /46	5.60 /60	9.01 /51	1.31	0.95
AA	Columbia Capital Allocation Consv Y	CPDHX	C	(800) 345-6611	D / 2.1	2.76	1.11	7.96 / 7	3.20 /34	4.17 /16	1.86	0.68
AA	Columbia Capital Allocation Csv A	ABDAX	C-	(800) 345-6611	D- / 1.4	2.65	0.93	7.63 / 7	2.84 /30	3.84 /14	1.43	1.04
AA	● Columbia Capital Allocation Csv B	ABBDX	C-	(800) 345-6611	D / 1.6	2.36	0.55	6.86 / 6	2.07 /24	3.07 /11	0.77	1.79
AA	Columbia Capital Allocation Csv C	RPCCX	C-	(800) 345-6611	D / 1.6	2.47	0.55	6.87 / 6	2.07 /24	3.08 /11	0.78	1.79
AA	● Columbia Capital Allocation Csv K	CPVRX	C-	(800) 345-6611	D / 2.0	2.69	0.97	7.67 / 7	2.91 /31	3.94 /15	1.58	0.98
AA	Columbia Capital Allocation Csv R	CBVRX	C-	(800) 345-6611	D / 1.8	2.48	0.80	7.37 / 6	2.55 /28	3.60 /13	1.26	1.29
AA	Columbia Capital Allocation Csv R4	CPCYX	C-	(800) 345-6611	D / 2.1	2.62	1.05	7.94 / 7	3.04 /32	4.07 /16	1.75	0.79
AA	Columbia Capital Allocation Csv R5	CPAOX	C-	(800) 345-6611	D / 2.1	2.64	1.09	7.91 / 7	3.12 /33	4.14 /16	1.82	0.73
AA	Columbia Capital Allocation Csv Z	CBVZX	C-	(800) 345-6611	D / 2.1	2.72	1.05	7.90 / 7	3.10 /33	4.11 /16	1.74	0.79
AA	Columbia Capital Allocation Modt A	ABUAX	C-	(800) 345-6611	D+ / 2.8	4.59	3.70	13.53 /24	4.51 /49	6.69 /33	1.74	1.08
AA	● Columbia Capital Allocation Modt B	AURBX	C-	(800) 345-6611	C- / 3.2	4.42	3.33	12.66 /20	3.72 /39	5.88 /28	1.15	1.83
AA	Columbia Capital Allocation Modt C	AMTCX	C-	(800) 345-6611	C- / 3.2	4.43	3.43	12.69 /20	3.75 /40	5.90 /28	1.15	1.83
AA	● Columbia Capital Allocation Modt K	CBRRX	C-	(800) 345-6611	C- / 3.9	4.61	3.82	13.61 /24	4.59 /50	6.77 /33	1.90	1.03
AA	Columbia Capital Allocation Modt R	CBMRX	C-	(800) 345-6611	C- / 3.6	4.54	3.67	13.18 /22	4.26 /46	6.41 /31	1.61	1.33
BA	Columbia Capital Allocation Modt R4	CPCZX	C	(800) 345-6611	C- / 4.0	4.71	3.87	13.76 /24	4.78 /52	6.93 /34	2.10	0.83
BA	Columbia Capital Allocation Modt R5	CPAMX	C	(800) 345-6611	C- / 4.1	4.72	3.90	13.93 /25	4.87 /53	7.00 /35	2.15	0.78
BA	Columbia Capital Allocation Modt Y	CPDMX	C	(800) 345-6611	C- / 4.1	4.74	3.92	13.87 /25	4.94 /53	7.05 /35	2.20	0.73
AA	Columbia Capital Allocation Modt Z	CBMZX	C	(800) 345-6611	C- / 4.0	4.66	3.83	13.83 /25	4.78 /52	6.95 /34	2.08	0.83
OT	Columbia Commodity Strategy A	CCSAX	E-	(800) 345-6611	E- / 0.0	1.47	5.33	15.69 /33	-13.45 / 0	-10.69 / 0	0.00	1.48
OT	Columbia Commodity Strategy C	CCSCX	E-	(800) 345-6611	E- / 0.0	1.52	4.91	15.09 /30	-14.08 / 0	-11.35 / 0	0.00	2.23
OT	Columbia Commodity Strategy I	CCIYX	E-	(800) 345-6611	E- / 0.0	1.80	5.61	16.26 /35	-13.13 / 0	-10.34 / 1	0.00	1.05
OT	Columbia Commodity Strategy R	CCSRX	E-	(800) 345-6611	E- / 0.0	1.67	5.39	15.64 /33	-13.63 / 0	-10.89 / 0	0.00	1.73
OT	Columbia Commodity Strategy R4	CCOMX	E-	(800) 345-6611	E- / 0.0	1.62	5.43	16.08 /35	-13.24 / 0	-10.50 / 1	0.00	1.23
OT	Columbia Commodity Strategy R5	CADLX	E-	(800) 345-6611	E- / 0.0	1.62	5.61	16.26 /35	-13.17 / 0	-10.50 / 1	0.00	1.10
OT	Columbia Commodity Strategy W	CCSWX	E-	(800) 345-6611	E- / 0.0	1.65	5.53	15.93 /34	-13.42 / 0	-10.69 / 0	0.00	1.48
OT	Columbia Commodity Strategy Y	CCFYX	E+	(800) 345-6611	E- / 0.0	1.62	5.60	16.22 /35	-13.16 / 0	-10.53 / 1	0.00	1.05
OT	Columbia Commodity Strategy Z	CCSZX	E-	(800) 345-6611	E- / 0.0	1.64	5.47	15.98 /34	-13.28 / 0	-10.49 / 1	0.00	1.23
GR	Columbia Contrarian Core A	LCCAX	B+	(800) 345-6611	B- / 7.5	7.31	7.74	21.66 /60	9.82 /92	13.98 /93	0.60	1.06

● Denotes fund is closed to new investors

* Denotes fund is included in Section II

Risk Rating/Pts	Standard Deviation	Beta	NAV As of 2/28/17	Total $(Mil)	Cash %	Stocks %	Bonds %	Other %	Portfolio Turnover Ratio	Last Bull Market Return	Last Bear Market Return	Manager Quality Pct	Manager Tenure (Years)	Initial Purch. $	Additional Purch. $	Front End Load	Back End Load
C+ / 6.0	7.6	1.18	12.27	4	14	56	28	2	16	63.4	-13.6	25	N/A	0	0	0.0	0.0
C+ / 6.0	7.5	1.14	12.38	2	14	56	28	2	16	67.4	-13.4	73	8	0	0	0.0	0.0
C+ / 6.0	7.6	1.15	12.37	6	14	56	28	2	16	68.1	-13.4	N/A	8	0	0	0.0	0.0
C+ / 6.0	7.6	1.18	12.28	88	14	56	28	2	16	65.2	-13.5	27	6	2,000	0	5.8	0.0
C+ / 6.0	7.6	1.15	12.12	1	14	56	28	2	16	67.4	-13.4	74	8	0	0	0.0	0.0
C+ / 6.0	7.5	1.17	12.26	122	14	56	28	2	16	67.6	-13.3	31	N/A	2,000	0	0.0	0.0
B- / 7.6	4.8	0.43	10.78	496	9	34	55	2	21	41.2	-6.4	63	N/A	2,000	0	5.8	0.0
B- / 7.6	4.8	0.43	10.71	4	9	34	55	2	21	35.5	-6.6	53	N/A	2,000	0	0.0	0.0
B- / 7.6	4.8	0.43	10.63	87	9	34	55	2	21	35.6	-6.6	53	N/A	2,000	0	0.0	0.0
B- / 7.5	4.8	0.74	10.62	N/A	9	34	55	2	21	41.7	-6.4	51	8	0	0	0.0	0.0
B- / 7.6	4.8	0.43	10.80	3	9	34	55	2	21	39.4	-6.5	60	N/A	0	0	0.0	0.0
B- / 7.5	4.8	0.74	10.69	3	9	34	55	2	21	42.7	-6.4	53	8	0	0	0.0	0.0
B- / 7.5	4.8	0.74	10.69	2	9	34	55	2	21	43.2	-6.4	55	8	0	0	0.0	0.0
B- / 7.5	4.8	0.74	10.56	N/A	9	34	55	2	21	43.5	-6.4	56	8	0	0	0.0	0.0
B- / 7.5	4.8	0.43	10.64	21	9	34	55	2	21	43.0	-6.2	67	N/A	2,000	0	0.0	0.0
C / 5.2	9.0	1.38	12.43	594	10	73	15	2	12	78.3	-16.5	17	13	2,000	0	5.8	0.0
C / 5.3	9.0	1.38	12.39	7	10	73	15	2	12	71.0	-16.7	12	13	2,000	0	0.0	0.0
C / 5.3	9.0	1.38	12.16	77	10	73	15	2	12	71.1	-16.7	12	13	2,000	0	0.0	0.0
C / 5.2	9.0	1.38	12.46	N/A	10	73	15	2	12	79.1	-16.3	18	13	0	0	0.0	0.0
C / 5.3	9.0	0.84	12.34	2	10	73	15	2	12	75.7	-16.4	28	7	0	0	0.0	0.0
C / 5.2	8.9	0.84	12.21	1	10	73	15	2	12	80.2	-16.5	34	7	0	0	0.0	0.0
C / 5.2	8.9	0.84	12.20	2	10	73	15	2	12	80.9	-16.5	35	7	0	0	0.0	0.0
C / 5.2	9.0	0.84	12.20	2	10	73	15	2	12	81.2	-16.5	35	7	0	0	0.0	0.0
C / 5.2	8.9	0.84	12.38	3	10	73	15	2	12	80.7	-16.3	34	7	2,000	0	0.0	0.0
B / 8.4	3.6	0.52	9.89	1	13	18	67	2	24	31.0	-4.2	66	7	0	0	0.0	0.0
B / 8.4	3.6	0.53	9.96	214	13	18	67	2	24	28.9	-4.2	61	13	2,000	0	4.8	0.0
B / 8.4	3.6	0.53	9.92	2	13	18	67	2	24	23.9	-4.6	51	13	2,000	0	0.0	0.0
B / 8.4	3.6	0.52	9.90	42	13	18	67	2	24	23.9	-4.5	51	13	2,000	0	0.0	0.0
B / 8.4	3.5	0.51	9.86	N/A	13	18	67	2	24	29.6	-4.2	63	13	0	0	0.0	0.0
B / 8.4	3.6	0.52	9.95	N/A	13	18	67	2	24	27.2	-4.4	57	7	0	0	0.0	0.0
B / 8.4	3.6	0.53	9.90	1	13	18	67	2	24	30.4	-4.2	63	7	0	0	0.0	0.0
B / 8.4	3.6	0.52	9.90	N/A	13	18	67	2	24	30.8	-4.2	65	7	0	0	0.0	0.0
B / 8.4	3.6	0.53	9.96	4	13	18	67	2	24	30.6	-4.1	64	7	2,000	0	0.0	0.0
C+ / 6.5	6.1	0.95	11.20	1,324	6	45	47	2	17	55.1	-10.5	42	13	2,000	0	5.8	0.0
C+ / 6.6	6.1	0.95	11.13	13	6	45	47	2	17	49.0	-10.8	32	13	2,000	0	0.0	0.0
C+ / 6.6	6.0	0.94	11.11	188	6	45	47	2	17	49.0	-10.8	33	13	2,000	0	0.0	0.0
C+ / 6.5	6.1	0.95	11.19	N/A	6	45	47	2	17	55.8	-10.4	43	13	0	0	0.0	0.0
C+ / 6.6	6.0	0.94	11.17	2	6	45	47	2	17	53.0	-10.5	39	7	0	0	0.0	0.0
C+ / 6.5	6.1	0.95	11.08	N/A	6	45	47	2	17	56.9	-10.5	46	7	0	0	0.0	0.0
C+ / 6.5	6.1	0.95	11.08	6	6	45	47	2	17	57.4	-10.5	47	7	0	0	0.0	0.0
C+ / 6.5	6.1	0.95	11.08	4	6	45	47	2	17	57.8	-10.5	48	7	0	0	0.0	0.0
C+ / 6.5	6.0	0.94	11.19	4	6	45	47	2	17	57.1	-10.3	46	7	2,000	0	0.0	0.0
D+ / 2.4	14.3	0.29	5.53	3	99	0	0	1	0	-36.6	N/A	0	6	2,000	0	5.8	0.0
D+ / 2.4	14.4	0.30	5.34	N/A	99	0	0	1	0	-39.1	N/A	0	6	2,000	0	0.0	0.0
D+ / 2.5	14.3	0.29	5.65	296	99	0	0	1	0	-35.3	N/A	0	6	0	0	0.0	0.0
D+ / 2.4	14.3	0.30	5.47	N/A	99	0	0	1	0	-37.4	N/A	0	6	0	0	0.0	0.0
D+ / 2.5	14.2	0.29	5.63	15	99	0	0	1	0	-35.9	N/A	0	6	0	0	0.0	0.0
D+ / 2.5	14.3	0.29	5.65	1	99	0	0	1	0	-35.9	N/A	0	6	100,000	0	0.0	0.0
D+ / 2.4	14.3	0.30	5.53	N/A	99	0	0	1	0	-36.6	N/A	0	6	500	0	0.0	0.0
C+ / 6.0	14.3	0.29	5.66	N/A	99	0	0	1	0	-36.0	N/A	0	6	0	0	0.0	0.0
D+ / 2.5	14.3	0.30	5.59	2	99	0	0	1	0	-35.9	N/A	0	6	2,000	0	0.0	0.0
C+ / 6.3	10.4	0.99	23.68	2,914	0	99	0	1	47	137.7	-18.2	67	12	2,000	0	5.8	0.0

Fund Type	Fund Name	Ticker Symbol	Overall Investment Rating	Phone	PERFORMANCE Perfor-mance Rating/Pts	Total Return % through 2/28/17 3 Mo	6 Mo	1Yr / Pct	Annualized 3Yr / Pct	5Yr / Pct	Incl. in Returns Dividend Yield	Expense Ratio
	99 Pct = Best 0 Pct = Worst											
GR	● Columbia Contrarian Core B	LCCBX	B+	(800) 345-6611	B / 7.9	7.14	7.35	20.71 /56	9.02 /87	13.13 /85	0.00	1.81
GR	Columbia Contrarian Core C	LCCCX	B+	(800) 345-6611	B / 7.9	7.13	7.39	20.72 /56	9.01 /87	13.14 /85	0.00	1.81
GR	Columbia Contrarian Core I	CCCIX	A	(800) 345-6611	B+ / 8.8	7.44	7.96	22.16 /63	10.31 /95	14.48 /95	1.00	0.67
GR	● Columbia Contrarian Core K	CCRFX	A-	(800) 345-6611	B+ / 8.6	7.38	7.86	21.81 /61	9.99 /93	14.13 /94	0.73	0.97
GR	Columbia Contrarian Core R	CCCRX	A-	(800) 345-6611	B+ / 8.3	7.29	7.63	21.35 /59	9.56 /91	13.69 /91	0.41	1.31
GI	Columbia Contrarian Core R4	CORRX	A	(800) 345-6611	B+ / 8.7	7.38	7.90	21.96 /62	10.12 /94	14.27 /95	0.84	0.81
GI	Columbia Contrarian Core R5	COFRX	A	(800) 345-6611	B+ / 8.8	7.41	7.97	22.11 /63	10.25 /95	14.40 /95	0.94	0.72
GR	● Columbia Contrarian Core V	SGIEX	B+	(800) 345-6611	B- / 7.5	7.32	7.76	21.64 /60	9.83 /92	13.95 /93	0.60	1.06
GR	Columbia Contrarian Core W	CTRWX	A-	(800) 345-6611	B+ / 8.5	7.36	7.79	21.65 /60	9.84 /92	13.98 /93	0.63	1.06
GI	Columbia Contrarian Core Y	COFYX	A	(800) 345-6611	B+ / 8.8	7.45	8.02	22.16 /63	10.31 /95	14.45 /95	0.99	0.67
GR	Columbia Contrarian Core Z	SMGIX	A-	(800) 345-6611	B+ / 8.7	7.41	7.93	21.95 /62	10.11 /94	14.26 /95	0.85	0.81
CV	Columbia Convertible Securities A	PACIX	C-	(800) 345-6611	C / 5.1	5.84	8.64	26.68 /78	4.47 /48	9.04 /51	2.10	1.22
CV	● Columbia Convertible Securities B	NCVBX	C	(800) 345-6611	C+ / 5.6	5.71	8.24	25.69 /75	3.69 /39	8.23 /44	1.60	1.97
CV	Columbia Convertible Securities C	PHIKX	C	(800) 345-6611	C+ / 5.6	5.66	8.21	25.70 /75	3.68 /39	8.22 /44	1.57	1.97
CV	Columbia Convertible Securities I	CCSIX	C+	(800) 345-6611	C+ / 6.6	5.98	8.88	27.16 /80	4.90 /53	9.50 /55	2.58	0.81
CV	Columbia Convertible Securities R	CVBRX	C	(800) 345-6611	C+ / 6.0	5.78	8.51	26.32 /77	4.19 /45	8.76 /48	2.01	1.47
CV	Columbia Convertible Securities R4	COVRX	C+	(800) 345-6611	C+ / 6.5	5.96	8.80	27.00 /79	4.74 /51	9.29 /53	2.43	0.97
CV	Columbia Convertible Securities R5	COCRX	C+	(800) 345-6611	C+ / 6.5	5.93	8.80	27.08 /79	4.83 /52	9.38 /54	2.52	0.86
CV	Columbia Convertible Securities W	CVBWX	C+	(800) 345-6611	C+ / 6.3	5.85	8.66	26.69 /78	4.44 /48	9.04 /51	2.24	1.22
CV	Columbia Convertible Securities Y	CSFYX	B-	(800) 345-6611	C+ / 6.5	5.96	8.82	27.14 /80	4.81 /52	9.25 /53	2.54	0.81
CV	Columbia Convertible Securities Z	NCIAX	C+	(800) 345-6611	C+ / 6.5	5.95	8.75	26.94 /79	4.72 /51	9.31 /53	2.45	0.97
GI	Columbia Disciplined Core A	AQEAX	A-	(800) 345-6611	B / 7.6	7.00	9.79	21.22 /58	9.90 /93	12.93 /83	1.14	1.04
GI	● Columbia Disciplined Core B	AQEBX	A	(800) 345-6611	B / 8.0	6.82	9.30	20.36 /54	9.08 /87	12.08 /75	0.55	1.79
GI	Columbia Disciplined Core C	RDCEX	A	(800) 345-6611	B / 8.1	6.81	9.32	20.41 /54	9.09 /87	12.08 /75	0.55	1.79
GI	Columbia Disciplined Core I	ALEIX	A+	(800) 345-6611	B+ / 8.9	7.11	9.99	21.74 /61	10.38 /95	13.42 /88	1.54	0.66
GI	● Columbia Disciplined Core K	RQEYX	A+	(800) 345-6611	B+ / 8.7	7.03	9.81	21.30 /59	10.03 /93	13.07 /84	1.28	0.96
GI	Columbia Disciplined Core R	CLQRX	A+	(800) 345-6611	B+ / 8.5	6.96	9.65	20.94 /57	9.64 /91	12.67 /81	0.99	1.29
GR	Columbia Disciplined Core R4	CLCQX	A+	(800) 345-6611	B+ / 8.8	7.07	9.84	21.54 /60	10.19 /94	13.15 /85	1.42	0.79
GI	Columbia Disciplined Core R5	RSIPX	A+	(800) 345-6611	B+ / 8.9	7.10	9.88	21.67 /61	10.30 /95	13.38 /88	1.50	0.71
GI	Columbia Disciplined Core W	RDEWX	A+	(800) 345-6611	B+ / 8.7	7.06	9.72	21.32 /59	9.91 /93	12.92 /83	1.20	1.04
GR	Columbia Disciplined Core Y	CCQYX	A+	(800) 345-6611	B+ / 8.8	7.11	9.99	21.75 /61	10.16 /94	13.09 /85	1.53	0.66
GR	Columbia Disciplined Core Z	CCRZX	A+	(800) 345-6611	B+ / 8.8	7.10	9.88	21.51 /60	10.19 /94	13.22 /86	1.43	0.79
GR	Columbia Disciplined Growth A	RDLAX	B	(800) 345-6611	B+ / 8.7	8.13	10.44	21.23 /58	11.50 /98	13.74 /91	0.46	1.27
GR	● Columbia Disciplined Growth B	CGQBX	B+	(800) 345-6611	A- / 9.0	7.90	9.99	20.22 /53	10.63 /96	12.90 /83	0.00	2.02
GR	Columbia Disciplined Growth C	RDLCX	B+	(800) 345-6611	A- / 9.0	7.96	10.07	20.38 /54	10.66 /96	12.91 /83	0.00	2.02
GR	Columbia Disciplined Growth I	RDLIX	B+	(800) 345-6611	A+ / 9.6	8.29	10.68	21.58 /60	11.95 /98	14.26 /95	0.85	0.81
GR	● Columbia Disciplined Growth K	RDLFX	B+	(800) 345-6611	A / 9.5	8.19	10.59	21.35 /59	11.69 /98	13.95 /93	0.65	1.11
GR	Columbia Disciplined Growth R	CGQRX	B+	(800) 345-6611	A / 9.3	8.11	10.28	20.87 /57	11.19 /97	13.46 /88	0.27	1.52
GR	Columbia Disciplined Growth R4	CGQFX	A+	(800) 345-6611	A / 9.5	8.11	10.53	21.41 /59	11.65 /98	13.84 /92	0.72	1.02
GR	Columbia Disciplined Growth R5	CQURX	B+	(800) 345-6611	A / 9.5	8.21	10.56	21.55 /60	11.91 /98	14.15 /94	0.79	0.86
GR	Columbia Disciplined Growth W	RDLWX	B+	(800) 345-6611	A / 9.4	8.09	10.38	21.09 /58	11.43 /98	13.72 /91	0.49	1.27
GR	Columbia Disciplined Growth Y	CGQYX	A+	(800) 345-6611	A / 9.5	8.31	10.71	21.80 /61	11.80 /98	13.93 /93	0.85	0.81
GR	Columbia Disciplined Growth Z	CLQZX	B+	(800) 345-6611	A / 9.5	8.21	10.63	21.49 /60	11.77 /98	14.04 /93	0.71	1.02
SC	Columbia Disciplined Small Core A	LSMAX	E	(800) 345-6611	C- / 3.5	3.65	9.89	26.73 /78	2.15 /25	8.51 /46	0.22	1.41
SC	● Columbia Disciplined Small Core B	LSMBX	E	(800) 345-6611	C- / 4.0	3.44	9.42	25.83 /76	1.40 /20	7.71 /40	0.00	2.16
SC	Columbia Disciplined Small Core C	LSMCX	E	(800) 345-6611	C- / 4.0	3.43	9.40	25.76 /75	1.40 /20	7.70 /40	0.00	2.16
SC	Columbia Disciplined Small Core I	CPOIX	E+	(800) 345-6611	C / 5.1	3.84	10.11	27.29 /80	2.64 /29	9.02 /51	0.54	0.95
SC	Columbia Disciplined Small Core R4	CFFRX	E+	(800) 345-6611	C / 5.0	3.84	10.01	27.11 /79	2.45 /27	8.80 /49	0.41	1.16
SC	Columbia Disciplined Small Core R5	CLLRX	E+	(800) 345-6611	C / 5.1	3.84	10.06	27.18 /80	2.58 /28	8.94 /50	0.49	1.00
SC	● Columbia Disciplined Small Core V	SSCEX	E	(800) 345-6611	C- / 3.6	3.82	10.01	26.92 /79	2.20 /25	8.50 /46	0.22	1.41
SC	Columbia Disciplined Small Core W	CSCWX	E+	(800) 345-6611	C / 4.7	3.65	9.89	26.73 /78	2.18 /25	8.51 /46	0.22	1.41
SC	Columbia Disciplined Small Core Y	CPFRX	E+	(800) 345-6611	C / 5.2	3.80	10.14	27.37 /80	2.66 /29	8.99 /51	0.53	0.95

● Denotes fund is closed to new investors

* Denotes fund is included in Section II

150

RISK			NET ASSETS		ASSET				Portfolio Turnover Ratio	BULL / BEAR		FUND MANAGER		MINIMUMS		LOADS	
	3 Year		NAV As of 2/28/17	Total $(Mil)	Cash %	Stocks %	Bonds %	Other %		Last Bull Market Return	Last Bear Market Return	Manager Quality Pct	Manager Tenure (Years)	Initial Purch. $	Additional Purch. $	Front End Load	Back End Load
Risk Rating/Pts	Standard Deviation	Beta															
C+ / 6.2	10.4	0.99	21.55	4	0	99	0	1	47	128.2	-18.5	57	12	2,000	0	0.0	0.0
C+ / 6.3	10.4	0.99	21.60	717	0	99	0	1	47	128.2	-18.5	57	12	2,000	0	0.0	0.0
C+ / 6.3	10.4	0.99	23.82	329	0	99	0	1	47	143.3	-18.1	72	12	0	0	0.0	0.0
C+ / 6.3	10.4	0.99	23.83	6	0	99	0	1	47	139.3	-18.1	69	12	0	0	0.0	0.0
C+ / 6.3	10.4	0.99	23.71	113	0	99	0	1	47	134.6	-18.3	64	12	0	0	0.0	0.0
C+ / 6.3	10.4	0.99	24.22	470	0	99	0	1	47	141.0	-18.1	70	12	0	0	0.0	0.0
C+ / 6.3	10.4	0.99	24.20	638	0	99	0	1	47	142.3	-18.1	72	12	0	0	0.0	0.0
C+ / 6.3	10.4	0.99	23.47	150	0	99	0	1	47	137.2	-18.2	67	12	2,000	0	5.8	0.0
C+ / 6.3	10.4	0.99	23.69	37	0	99	0	1	47	137.6	-18.1	67	12	500	0	0.0	0.0
C+ / 6.3	10.4	0.99	24.21	423	0	99	0	1	47	143.0	-18.1	72	12	0	0	0.0	0.0
C+ / 6.3	10.4	0.99	23.84	4,492	0	99	0	1	47	140.9	-18.1	70	12	0	0	0.0	0.0
C / 5.3	9.7	1.11	18.64	289	7	23	0	70	71	78.8	-16.7	62	11	2,000	0	5.8	0.0
C / 5.3	9.8	1.11	18.24	N/A	7	23	0	70	71	71.7	-17.0	52	11	2,000	0	0.0	0.0
C / 5.4	9.7	1.11	18.57	42	7	23	0	70	71	71.6	-17.0	52	11	2,000	0	0.0	0.0
C / 5.3	9.7	1.11	18.70	85	7	23	0	70	71	82.8	-16.6	67	11	0	0	0.0	0.0
C / 5.4	9.7	1.11	18.62	3	7	23	0	70	71	76.4	-16.8	59	11	0	0	0.0	0.0
C / 5.3	9.7	1.11	18.82	12	7	23	0	70	71	80.8	-16.7	65	11	0	0	0.0	0.0
C / 5.3	9.7	1.11	18.80	65	7	23	0	70	71	81.6	-16.7	66	11	0	0	0.0	0.0
C / 5.3	9.7	1.11	18.59	N/A	7	23	0	70	71	78.7	-16.7	62	11	500	0	0.0	0.0
B- / 7.0	9.7	1.11	18.94	1	7	23	0	70	71	80.5	-16.7	66	11	0	0	0.0	0.0
C / 5.3	9.7	1.11	18.67	229	7	23	0	70	71	81.2	-16.7	65	11	2,000	0	0.0	0.0
B- / 7.2	10.7	1.01	10.81	3,566	0	99	0	1	77	128.9	-14.6	65	7	2,000	0	5.8	0.0
B- / 7.2	10.7	1.01	10.76	19	0	99	0	1	77	119.7	-14.9	55	7	2,000	0	0.0	0.0
B- / 7.2	10.7	1.01	10.62	59	0	99	0	1	77	119.8	-14.9	55	7	2,000	0	0.0	0.0
B- / 7.2	10.7	1.01	10.88	299	0	99	0	1	77	134.3	-14.5	70	7	0	0	0.0	0.0
B- / 7.2	10.7	1.02	10.87	22	0	99	0	1	77	130.6	-14.7	66	7	0	0	0.0	0.0
B- / 7.2	10.7	1.02	10.81	5	0	99	0	1	77	126.1	-14.8	61	7	0	0	0.0	0.0
B- / 7.2	10.7	1.01	10.90	7	0	99	0	1	77	131.2	-14.6	68	7	0	0	0.0	0.0
B- / 7.1	10.7	1.02	10.83	105	0	99	0	1	77	133.7	-14.4	69	7	0	0	0.0	0.0
B- / 7.2	10.7	1.02	10.88	13	0	99	0	1	77	128.7	-14.6	64	7	500	0	0.0	0.0
B- / 7.2	10.7	1.01	10.87	1	0	99	0	1	77	130.6	-14.6	67	7	0	0	0.0	0.0
B- / 7.1	10.7	1.02	10.86	37	0	99	0	1	77	132.1	-14.7	67	7	2,000	0	0.0	0.0
C / 4.9	11.3	1.04	8.78	145	0	99	0	1	86	137.0	-15.9	77	7	2,000	0	5.8	0.0
C / 4.9	11.3	1.03	8.57	N/A	0	99	0	1	86	127.4	-16.1	70	7	2,000	0	0.0	0.0
C / 4.9	11.4	1.04	8.51	23	0	99	0	1	86	127.6	-16.2	70	7	2,000	0	0.0	0.0
C / 4.9	11.3	1.04	8.94	227	0	99	0	1	86	142.4	-15.7	80	7	0	0	0.0	0.0
C / 4.9	11.3	1.03	8.93	N/A	0	99	0	1	86	139.2	-15.9	78	7	0	0	0.0	0.0
C / 5.0	11.3	1.04	8.81	1	0	99	0	1	86	133.8	-16.0	75	7	0	0	0.0	0.0
C+ / 6.8	11.3	1.03	8.82	3	0	99	0	1	86	137.9	-15.9	78	7	0	0	0.0	0.0
C / 4.9	11.3	1.04	9.10	3	0	99	0	1	86	141.2	-15.9	80	7	0	0	0.0	0.0
C / 4.9	11.3	1.04	8.83	22	0	99	0	1	86	136.3	-15.9	77	7	500	0	0.0	0.0
C+ / 6.8	11.3	1.04	8.92	N/A	0	99	0	1	86	138.9	-15.9	79	7	0	0	0.0	0.0
C / 4.9	11.4	1.04	8.85	40	0	99	0	1	86	140.1	-15.8	78	7	2,000	0	0.0	0.0
D- / 1.0	15.3	0.94	8.58	65	3	96	0	1	112	88.9	-23.6	22	12	2,000	0	5.8	0.0
D- / 1.0	15.4	0.94	5.29	N/A	3	96	0	1	112	81.5	-23.9	16	12	2,000	0	0.0	0.0
D- / 1.0	15.4	0.94	5.31	13	3	96	0	1	112	81.3	-23.9	16	12	2,000	0	0.0	0.0
D- / 1.0	15.4	0.94	9.59	47	3	96	0	1	112	93.8	-23.5	26	12	0	0	0.0	0.0
D- / 1.0	15.3	0.94	9.64	2	3	96	0	1	112	91.7	-23.6	25	12	0	0	0.0	0.0
D- / 1.0	15.3	0.94	9.70	3	3	96	0	1	112	93.0	-23.6	26	12	0	0	0.0	0.0
D- / 1.0	15.3	0.94	8.15	60	3	96	0	1	112	88.9	-23.7	22	12	2,000	0	5.8	0.0
D- / 1.0	15.3	0.94	8.58	N/A	3	96	0	1	112	88.9	-23.6	22	12	500	0	0.0	0.0
D- / 1.0	15.4	0.94	9.80	5	3	96	0	1	112	93.4	-23.6	26	12	0	0	0.0	0.0

					PERFORMANCE								
99 Pct = Best						Total Return % through 2/28/17						Incl. in Returns	
0 Pct = Worst									Annualized			Dividend	Expense
Fund Type	Fund Name	Ticker Symbol	Overall Investment Rating	Phone	Perfor- mance Rating/Pts	3 Mo	6 Mo	1Yr / Pct	3Yr / Pct	5Yr / Pct		Yield	Ratio
SC	Columbia Disciplined Small Core Z	SMCEX	E+	(800) 345-6611	C / 5.0	3.72	9.98	27.11 /79	2.43 /27	8.79 /49		0.41	1.16
GR	Columbia Disciplined Value A	RLCAX	B+	(800) 345-6611	B / 7.7	6.05	10.53	25.35 /74	9.27 /89	13.33 /87		1.39	1.20
GR ●	Columbia Disciplined Value B	CVQBX	B+	(800) 345-6611	B / 8.2	5.93	10.22	24.54 /72	8.45 /82	12.49 /79		0.82	1.95
GR	Columbia Disciplined Value C	RDCCX	B+	(800) 345-6611	B / 8.2	5.91	10.14	24.38 /71	8.46 /83	12.47 /79		0.83	1.95
GR	Columbia Disciplined Value I	CLQIX	A	(800) 345-6611	A- / 9.0	6.17	10.84	25.85 /76	9.75 /92	13.80 /92		1.83	0.77
GR ●	Columbia Disciplined Value K	RLCYX	A	(800) 345-6611	B+ / 8.9	6.12	10.70	25.61 /75	9.44 /90	13.47 /89		1.57	1.07
GR	Columbia Disciplined Value R	RLCOX	A-	(800) 345-6611	B+ / 8.5	5.91	10.38	25.01 /73	8.99 /87	13.03 /84		1.25	1.45
GR	Columbia Disciplined Value R4	COLEX	A+	(800) 345-6611	B+ / 8.9	6.12	10.69	25.69 /75	9.46 /90	13.44 /88		1.68	0.95
GR	Columbia Disciplined Value R5	COLVX	A+	(800) 345-6611	B+ / 8.9	6.14	10.71	25.73 /75	9.47 /90	13.45 /88		1.79	0.82
GR ●	Columbia Disciplined Value V	CVQTX	B+	(800) 345-6611	B / 7.8	6.06	10.55	25.41 /75	9.27 /89	13.29 /87		1.39	1.20
GR	Columbia Disciplined Value W	RLCWX	A-	(800) 345-6611	B+ / 8.7	6.01	10.46	25.32 /74	9.25 /88	13.30 /87		1.47	1.20
GR	Columbia Disciplined Value Y	COLYX	A+	(800) 345-6611	B+ / 8.9	6.16	10.84	25.86 /76	9.53 /91	13.49 /89		1.82	0.77
GR	Columbia Disciplined Value Z	CVQZX	A	(800) 345-6611	B+ / 8.9	6.12	10.67	25.66 /75	9.57 /91	13.62 /90		1.68	0.95
GL	Columbia Diversified Abslt Rtn I	CDUIX	U	(800) 345-6611	U /	2.13	0.00	-0.31 / 1	--	--		0.00	1.94
IN	Columbia Diversified Equity Inc A	INDZX	B	(800) 345-6611	B / 8.1	6.96	11.00	28.07 /82	9.06 /87	12.32 /77		1.20	1.04
IN ●	Columbia Diversified Equity Inc B	IDEBX	B	(800) 345-6611	B+ / 8.5	6.82	10.64	27.14 /80	8.25 /81	11.49 /70		0.62	1.79
IN	Columbia Diversified Equity Inc C	ADECX	B	(800) 345-6611	B+ / 8.5	6.78	10.63	27.12 /79	8.25 /81	11.50 /70		0.62	1.79
IN	Columbia Diversified Equity Inc I	ADIIX	B+	(800) 345-6611	A / 9.3	7.15	11.24	28.62 /83	9.51 /90	12.80 /82		1.62	0.66
IN ●	Columbia Diversified Equity Inc K	IDQYX	B+	(800) 345-6611	A- / 9.1	7.05	11.04	28.14 /82	9.17 /88	12.44 /78		1.33	0.96
IN	Columbia Diversified Equity Inc R	RDEIX	B+	(800) 345-6611	B+ / 8.9	7.01	10.94	27.84 /81	8.79 /85	12.05 /75		1.06	1.29
IN	Columbia Diversified Equity Inc R4	RDERX	B+	(800) 345-6611	A- / 9.2	7.10	11.14	28.38 /82	9.34 /89	12.56 /80		1.48	0.79
IN	Columbia Diversified Equity Inc R5	RSEDX	B+	(800) 345-6611	A- / 9.2	7.11	11.26	28.57 /83	9.44 /90	12.73 /81		1.55	0.71
IN	Columbia Diversified Equity Inc W	CDEWX	B+	(800) 345-6611	A- / 9.0	7.02	11.05	28.08 /82	9.03 /87	12.32 /77		1.24	1.04
IN	Columbia Diversified Equity Inc Y	CDEYX	B+	(800) 345-6611	A / 9.3	7.13	11.25	28.62 /83	9.49 /90	12.74 /81		1.58	0.66
IN	Columbia Diversified Equity Inc Z	CDVZX	B+	(800) 345-6611	A- / 9.2	7.11	11.23	28.40 /83	9.34 /89	12.62 /80		1.48	0.79
GI	Columbia Dividend Income A	LBSAX	B+	(800) 345-6611	B / 7.9	7.68	9.16	22.08 /63	10.30 /95	12.65 /80		1.50	1.02
GI ●	Columbia Dividend Income B	LBSBX	A-	(800) 345-6611	B+ / 8.3	7.49	8.74	21.15 /58	9.46 /90	11.80 /72		0.94	1.77
GI	Columbia Dividend Income C	LBSCX	A-	(800) 345-6611	B+ / 8.3	7.49	8.75	21.16 /58	9.46 /90	11.81 /72		0.94	1.77
IN	Columbia Dividend Income I	CDVIX	A+	(800) 345-6611	A- / 9.2	7.77	9.31	22.54 /65	10.76 /97	13.12 /85		1.96	0.59
GI	Columbia Dividend Income R	CDIRX	A	(800) 345-6611	B+ / 8.7	7.61	8.96	21.71 /61	10.00 /93	12.37 /78		1.36	1.27
IN	Columbia Dividend Income R4	CVIRX	A	(800) 345-6611	A- / 9.0	7.72	9.25	22.31 /64	10.57 /96	12.93 /83		1.78	0.77
IN	Columbia Dividend Income R5	CDDRX	A+	(800) 345-6611	A- / 9.1	7.76	9.32	22.48 /64	10.70 /96	13.06 /84		1.89	0.64
GI ●	Columbia Dividend Income V	GEQAX	B+	(800) 345-6611	B / 7.9	7.62	9.10	22.01 /62	10.26 /95	12.61 /80		1.50	1.02
IN	Columbia Dividend Income W	CDVWX	A	(800) 345-6611	B+ / 8.9	7.63	9.11	21.96 /62	10.27 /95	12.63 /80		1.59	1.02
IN	Columbia Dividend Income Y	CDDYX	A+	(800) 345-6611	A- / 9.2	7.77	9.34	22.52 /65	10.76 /97	13.11 /85		1.93	0.59
GI	Columbia Dividend Income Z	GSFTX	A	(800) 345-6611	A- / 9.0	7.74	9.29	22.35 /64	10.56 /96	12.93 /83		1.81	0.77
IN	Columbia Dividend Opportunity A	INUTX	C+	(800) 345-6611	C+ / 6.4	7.59	6.99	20.07 /52	8.05 /79	10.96 /65		3.47	1.01
IN ●	Columbia Dividend Opportunity B	IUTBX	C+	(800) 345-6611	C+ / 6.8	7.35	6.66	19.14 /48	7.23 /73	10.15 /59		3.02	1.76
IN	Columbia Dividend Opportunity C	ACUIX	C+	(800) 345-6611	C+ / 6.8	7.43	6.62	19.22 /48	7.22 /73	10.15 /59		3.05	1.76
IN	Columbia Dividend Opportunity I	RSOIX	B-	(800) 345-6611	B / 7.7	7.75	7.26	20.67 /56	8.48 /83	11.43 /69		4.01	0.62
IN ●	Columbia Dividend Opportunity K	RSORX	B-	(800) 345-6611	B- / 7.4	7.57	7.11	20.19 /53	8.15 /80	11.08 /66		3.73	0.92
IN	Columbia Dividend Opportunity R	RSOOX	C+	(800) 345-6611	B- / 7.2	7.53	6.86	19.80 /51	7.74 /77	10.70 /63		3.45	1.26
IN	Columbia Dividend Opportunity R4	CDORX	B-	(800) 345-6611	B / 7.6	7.64	7.23	20.40 /54	8.30 /81	11.19 /67		3.84	0.76
IN	Columbia Dividend Opportunity R5	RSDFX	B-	(800) 345-6611	B / 7.6	7.74	7.23	20.46 /55	8.42 /82	11.38 /69		3.96	0.67
IN	Columbia Dividend Opportunity W	CDOWX	B-	(800) 345-6611	B- / 7.4	7.69	7.09	20.16 /53	8.04 /79	10.98 /66		3.67	1.01
IN	Columbia Dividend Opportunity Y	CDOYX	B-	(800) 345-6611	B / 7.6	7.65	7.17	20.51 /55	8.45 /82	11.33 /68		3.96	0.62
IN	Columbia Dividend Opportunity Z	CDOZX	B-	(800) 345-6611	B- / 7.5	7.62	7.20	20.40 /54	8.29 /81	11.25 /68		3.89	0.76
EM	Columbia Emerging Markets A	EEMAX	D-	(800) 345-6611	D- / 1.1	7.68	1.00	22.30 /64	-0.10 /13	0.89 / 6		0.00	1.69
EM ●	Columbia Emerging Markets B	CEBMX	D-	(800) 345-6611	D- / 1.4	7.52	0.63	21.42 /59	-0.86 /10	0.12 / 5		0.00	2.44
EM	Columbia Emerging Markets C	EEMCX	D-	(800) 345-6611	D- / 1.4	7.39	0.52	21.39 /59	-0.85 /10	0.12 / 5		0.00	2.44
EM	Columbia Emerging Markets I	CEHIX	D	(800) 345-6611	D+ / 2.8	7.79	1.19	22.78 /66	0.34 /15	1.33 / 7		0.00	1.22
EM ●	Columbia Emerging Markets K	CEKMX	D	(800) 345-6611	D+ / 2.6	7.76	1.00	22.46 /64	0.07 /14	1.06 / 6		0.00	1.52

● Denotes fund is closed to new investors

* Denotes fund is included in Section II

152

RISK			NET ASSETS		ASSET					Portfolio Turnover Ratio	BULL / BEAR		FUND MANAGER		MINIMUMS		LOADS	
Risk Rating/Pts	3 Year		NAV As of 2/28/17	Total $(Mil)	Cash %	Stocks %	Bonds %	Other %			Last Bull Market Return	Last Bear Market Return	Manager Quality Pct	Manager Tenure (Years)	Initial Purch. $	Additional Purch. $	Front End Load	Back End Load
	Standard Deviation	Beta																
D- / 1.0	15.3	0.94	9.44	53	3	96	0	1	112	91.6	-23.6	24	12	0	0	0.0	0.0
C+ / 6.1	10.9	1.02	10.04	90	0	99	0	1	82	129.6	-18.6	56	7	2,000	0	5.8	0.0
C+ / 6.2	10.9	1.02	9.98	N/A	0	99	0	1	82	120.6	-18.9	45	7	2,000	0	0.0	0.0
C+ / 6.2	10.9	1.02	9.83	16	0	99	0	1	82	120.7	-18.9	46	7	2,000	0	0.0	0.0
C+ / 6.1	10.9	1.02	10.13	443	0	99	0	1	82	135.0	-18.5	62	7	0	0	0.0	0.0
C+ / 6.1	10.9	1.02	10.10	N/A	0	99	0	1	82	131.4	-18.5	58	7	0	0	0.0	0.0
C+ / 6.2	10.9	1.02	10.06	3	0	99	0	1	82	126.4	-18.7	52	7	0	0	0.0	0.0
B- / 7.3	10.9	1.02	10.12	5	0	99	0	1	82	130.8	-18.6	58	7	0	0	0.0	0.0
B- / 7.3	10.9	1.02	10.10	N/A	0	99	0	1	82	130.8	-18.6	59	7	0	0	0.0	0.0
C+ / 6.2	10.9	1.03	10.02	83	0	99	0	1	82	129.3	-18.6	56	7	2,000	0	5.8	0.0
C+ / 6.2	10.9	1.02	10.10	48	0	99	0	1	82	129.3	-18.5	56	7	500	0	0.0	0.0
B- / 7.3	10.9	1.02	10.12	2	0	99	0	1	82	131.3	-18.6	59	7	0	0	0.0	0.0
C+ / 6.1	10.9	1.02	10.13	119	0	99	0	1	82	132.8	-18.5	60	7	2,000	0	0.0	0.0
U /	N/A	N/A	9.58	81	84	6	9	1	196	N/A	N/A	N/A	2	0	0	0.0	0.0
C / 5.0	10.8	1.02	13.90	2,224	2	96	0	2	43	117.2	-21.6	54	4	2,000	0	5.8	0.0
C / 5.0	10.8	1.02	13.95	13	2	96	0	2	43	108.6	-21.8	44	4	2,000	0	0.0	0.0
C / 5.0	10.9	1.02	13.86	69	2	96	0	2	43	108.6	-21.9	43	4	2,000	0	0.0	0.0
C / 5.0	10.9	1.02	13.88	N/A	2	96	0	2	43	122.3	-21.4	59	4	0	0	0.0	0.0
C / 5.0	10.8	1.02	13.91	36	2	96	0	2	43	118.6	-21.5	55	4	0	0	0.0	0.0
C / 5.0	10.8	1.02	13.82	6	2	96	0	2	43	114.3	-21.6	50	4	0	0	0.0	0.0
C / 5.0	10.8	1.02	13.90	9	2	96	0	2	43	119.5	-21.7	57	4	0	0	0.0	0.0
C / 5.0	10.8	1.02	13.91	38	2	96	0	2	43	121.6	-21.4	59	4	0	0	0.0	0.0
C / 5.0	10.8	1.02	13.93	N/A	2	96	0	2	43	117.0	-21.5	54	4	500	0	0.0	0.0
C / 5.0	10.8	1.02	14.05	N/A	2	96	0	2	43	121.3	-21.6	59	4	0	0	0.0	0.0
C / 5.0	10.8	1.02	13.89	26	2	96	0	2	43	120.3	-21.5	58	4	2,000	0	0.0	0.0
C+ / 6.4	9.5	0.89	20.07	2,589	1	97	0	2	25	115.1	-12.6	80	16	2,000	0	5.8	0.0
C+ / 6.4	9.5	0.89	19.47	3	1	97	0	2	25	106.5	-12.8	N/A	16	2,000	0	0.0	0.0
C+ / 6.4	9.5	0.89	19.46	773	1	97	0	2	25	106.6	-12.9	74	16	2,000	0	0.0	0.0
C+ / 6.4	9.5	0.89	20.11	112	1	97	0	2	25	119.9	-12.4	82	16	0	0	0.0	0.0
C+ / 6.4	9.5	0.89	20.07	98	1	97	0	2	25	112.1	-12.7	78	16	0	0	0.0	0.0
C+ / 6.4	9.4	0.89	20.39	354	1	97	0	2	25	117.9	-12.4	81	16	0	0	0.0	0.0
C+ / 6.4	9.5	0.89	20.38	509	1	97	0	2	25	119.2	-12.4	82	16	0	0	0.0	0.0
C+ / 6.4	9.5	0.89	20.07	79	1	97	0	2	25	114.6	-12.5	79	16	2,000	0	5.8	0.0
C+ / 6.4	9.4	0.89	20.05	N/A	1	97	0	2	25	115.0	-12.6	80	16	500	0	0.0	0.0
C+ / 6.4	9.4	0.89	20.40	383	1	97	0	2	25	119.6	-12.4	82	16	0	0	0.0	0.0
C+ / 6.4	9.5	0.89	20.09	5,374	1	97	0	2	25	117.9	-12.4	81	16	2,000	0	0.0	0.0
C / 5.1	9.5	0.83	9.92	2,782	3	92	4	1	85	101.2	-14.3	66	13	2,000	0	5.8	0.0
C / 5.1	9.5	0.83	9.82	7	3	92	4	1	85	93.4	-14.6	57	13	2,000	0	0.0	0.0
C / 5.1	9.5	0.83	9.72	413	3	92	4	1	85	93.4	-14.6	56	13	2,000	0	0.0	0.0
C / 5.1	9.5	0.83	9.98	53	3	92	4	1	85	105.8	-14.1	71	13	0	0	0.0	0.0
C / 5.1	9.5	0.83	9.97	4	3	92	4	1	85	102.5	-14.2	67	13	0	0	0.0	0.0
C / 5.1	9.5	0.83	9.91	45	3	92	4	1	85	98.5	-14.3	62	13	0	0	0.0	0.0
C / 5.1	9.5	0.83	10.08	108	3	92	4	1	85	103.3	-14.3	70	13	0	0	0.0	0.0
C / 5.1	9.5	0.82	9.98	255	3	92	4	1	85	105.4	-14.2	71	13	0	0	0.0	0.0
C / 5.1	9.5	0.83	9.94	N/A	3	92	4	1	85	101.2	-14.3	66	13	500	0	0.0	0.0
C / 5.1	9.5	0.83	10.10	77	3	92	4	1	85	104.6	-14.3	70	13	0	0	0.0	0.0
C / 5.1	9.5	0.83	9.96	649	3	92	4	1	85	104.1	-14.2	69	13	2,000	0	0.0	0.0
C / 5.1	14.0	0.81	10.09	240	1	98	0	1	81	27.1	-25.8	55	9	2,000	0	5.8	0.0
C / 5.0	14.0	0.82	9.58	1	1	98	0	1	81	22.0	-26.0	45	9	2,000	0	0.0	0.0
C / 5.0	14.0	0.81	9.59	18	1	98	0	1	81	21.9	-26.0	45	9	2,000	0	0.0	0.0
C / 5.1	14.0	0.81	10.24	245	1	98	0	1	81	30.3	-25.7	61	9	0	0	0.0	0.0
C / 5.1	14.0	0.82	10.14	N/A	1	98	0	1	81	28.4	-25.7	57	9	0	0	0.0	0.0

					PERFORMANCE							
99 Pct = Best			Overall		Perfor-	Total Return % through 2/28/17					Incl. in Returns	
0 Pct = Worst			Investment		mance				Annualized		Dividend	Expense
Fund Type	Fund Name	Ticker Symbol	Rating	Phone	Rating/Pts	3 Mo	6 Mo	1Yr / Pct	3Yr / Pct	5Yr / Pct	Yield	Ratio
EM	Columbia Emerging Markets R	CEMRX	D-	(800) 345-6611	D / 1.6	7.55	0.81	22.03 /62	-0.37 /12	0.62 / 5	0.00	1.94
EM	Columbia Emerging Markets R4	CEMHX	D	(800) 345-6611	D+ / 2.7	7.78	1.08	22.61 /65	0.16 /14	1.13 / 6	0.00	1.44
EM	Columbia Emerging Markets R5	CEKRX	D	(800) 345-6611	D+ / 2.8	7.79	1.19	22.78 /66	0.32 /15	1.26 / 7	0.00	1.27
EM	Columbia Emerging Markets W	CEMWX	D-	(800) 345-6611	D / 1.7	7.58	0.90	22.33 /64	-0.10 /13	0.87 / 6	0.00	1.69
EM	Columbia Emerging Markets Y	CEKYX	D	(800) 345-6611	D+ / 2.8	7.86	1.18	22.94 /66	0.36 /15	1.32 / 7	0.00	1.22
EM	Columbia Emerging Markets Z	UMEMX	D	(800) 345-6611	D+ / 2.7	7.72	1.09	22.65 /65	0.16 /14	1.13 / 6	0.00	1.44
FO	Columbia European Equity A	AXEAX	E	(800) 345-6611	E- / 0.1	5.66	-0.49	4.94 / 4	-5.23 / 2	4.25 /17	1.96	1.35
FO	● Columbia European Equity B	AEEBX	E	(800) 345-6611	E- / 0.1	5.58	-0.96	4.13 / 3	-5.92 / 2	3.45 /13	1.31	2.10
FO	Columbia European Equity C	REECX	E	(800) 345-6611	E- / 0.1	5.50	-0.98	4.03 / 3	-5.93 / 2	3.46 /13	1.34	2.10
FO	Columbia European Equity I	CEEIX	E	(800) 345-6611	E- / 0.2	5.76	-0.37	5.40 / 4	-4.82 / 3	4.71 /19	2.52	0.92
FO	● Columbia European Equity K	CEQRX	E	(800) 345-6611	E- / 0.2	5.64	-0.53	4.92 / 4	-5.16 / 2	4.40 /18	2.22	1.22
FO	Columbia European Equity R4	CADJX	E	(800) 345-6611	E- / 0.2	5.81	-0.37	5.26 / 4	-4.99 / 2	4.41 /18	2.38	1.10
FO	Columbia European Equity R5	CADKX	E	(800) 345-6611	E- / 0.2	5.88	-0.43	5.34 / 4	-4.84 / 3	4.51 /18	2.46	0.97
FO	Columbia European Equity W	CEEWX	E	(800) 345-6611	E- / 0.2	5.70	-0.65	4.97 / 4	-5.22 / 2	4.23 /16	2.10	1.35
FO	Columbia European Equity Y	CEEUX	E+	(800) 345-6611	E- / 0.2	5.75	-0.36	5.32 / 4	-5.11 / 2	4.33 /17	2.60	0.92
FO	Columbia European Equity Z	CEEZX	E	(800) 345-6611	E- / 0.2	5.79	-0.56	5.24 / 4	-5.00 / 2	4.50 /18	2.35	1.10
AA	Columbia Flexible Cap Inc A	CFIAX	C+	(800) 345-6611	C+ / 6.1	6.20	8.34	28.86 /84	5.61 /61	8.45 /46	4.42	1.18
AA	Columbia Flexible Cap Inc C	CFIGX	C+	(800) 345-6611	C+ / 6.5	5.95	7.90	27.89 /81	4.82 /52	7.63 /39	4.05	1.93
AA	Columbia Flexible Cap Inc I	CFIIX	B	(800) 345-6611	B- / 7.4	6.28	8.54	29.44 /85	6.07 /65	8.87 /49	5.06	0.80
AA	Columbia Flexible Cap Inc R	CFIRX	C+	(800) 345-6611	C+ / 6.9	6.14	8.30	28.58 /83	5.35 /58	8.17 /43	4.47	1.43
GL	Columbia Flexible Cap Inc R4	CFCRX	B	(800) 345-6611	B- / 7.3	6.30	8.49	29.17 /84	5.89 /63	8.68 /48	4.88	0.93
GL	Columbia Flexible Cap Inc R5	CFXRX	B	(800) 345-6611	B- / 7.3	6.31	8.52	29.24 /85	5.96 /64	8.74 /48	4.94	0.85
AA	Columbia Flexible Cap Inc W	CFIWX	B	(800) 345-6611	B- / 7.1	6.20	8.34	28.74 /83	5.60 /61	8.43 /46	4.70	1.18
AA	Columbia Flexible Cap Inc Z	CFIZX	B	(800) 345-6611	B- / 7.3	6.26	8.47	29.18 /84	5.88 /63	8.72 /48	4.91	0.93
GR	Columbia FS Lrg Cap Idx Port Dir		A+	(800) 345-6611	A / 9.3	7.99	9.87	24.72 /72	10.43 /96	13.77 /91	0.00	0.34
MC	Columbia FS Mid Cap Indx Port Dir		A+	(800) 345-6611	A / 9.4	6.59	11.30	31.47 /89	9.42 /90	13.58 /90	0.00	0.34
SC	Columbia FS Sm Cap Indx Port Dir		A+	(800) 345-6611	A+ / 9.6	4.58	13.08	34.72 /94	9.46 /90	14.65 /96	0.00	0.41
EN	Columbia Gl Energy and Nat Res A	EENAX	E-	(800) 345-6611	E / 0.3	0.91	7.13	27.06 /79	-5.27 / 2	-2.04 / 3	1.42	1.35
EN	● Columbia Gl Energy and Nat Res B	CEGBX	E-	(800) 345-6611	E / 0.4	0.71	6.67	26.02 /76	-5.99 / 2	-2.78 / 2	1.22	2.10
EN	Columbia Gl Energy and Nat Res C	EENCX	E-	(800) 345-6611	E / 0.4	0.71	6.73	26.10 /76	-5.99 / 2	-2.77 / 2	1.22	2.10
EN	Columbia Gl Energy and Nat Res I	CERIX	E-	(800) 345-6611	E+ / 0.6	1.06	7.36	27.68 /81	-4.82 / 3	-1.56 / 3	1.70	0.90
EN	● Columbia Gl Energy and Nat Res K	CEGFX	E-	(800) 345-6611	E / 0.5	0.88	7.14	27.11 /79	-5.13 / 2	-1.87 / 3	1.57	1.20
EN	Columbia Gl Energy and Nat Res R	CETRX	E-	(800) 345-6611	E / 0.5	0.86	6.98	26.67 /78	-5.51 / 2	-2.28 / 3	1.40	1.60
EN	Columbia Gl Energy and Nat Res R4	CENRX	E-	(800) 345-6611	E+ / 0.6	1.00	7.23	27.38 /80	-5.03 / 2	-1.79 / 3	1.58	1.10
EN	Columbia Gl Energy and Nat Res R5	CNRRX	E-	(800) 345-6611	E+ / 0.6	1.03	7.35	27.59 /81	-4.87 / 3	-1.64 / 3	1.66	0.95
EN	Columbia Gl Energy and Nat Res Z	UMESX	E-	(800) 345-6611	E+ / 0.6	0.96	7.23	27.34 /80	-5.03 / 2	-1.79 / 3	1.61	1.34
GR	● Columbia Globa Equity Value K	AEVYX	C-	(800) 345-6611	C / 4.9	6.24	9.01	20.25 /53	3.46 /37	8.72 /48	2.31	1.04
MC	Columbia Global Dividend Opp A	CSVAX	D-	(800) 345-6611	D / 1.7	6.75	4.50	15.47 /32	0.63 /16	5.45 /24	2.96	1.53
MC	● Columbia Global Dividend Opp B	CSVBX	E+	(800) 345-6611	D- / 1.4	6.53	4.06	14.63 /28	-0.12 /13	4.65 /19	2.59	2.28
MC	Columbia Global Dividend Opp C	CSRCX	E+	(800) 345-6611	D- / 1.4	6.52	4.06	14.61 /28	-0.12 /13	4.65 /19	2.59	2.28
MC	Columbia Global Dividend Opp I	CEVIX	D	(800) 345-6611	D+ / 2.7	6.86	4.68	16.06 /35	1.11 /19	5.92 /28	3.58	0.91
MC	Columbia Global Dividend Opp R	CSGRX	D-	(800) 345-6611	D / 2.2	6.63	4.31	15.14 /30	0.38 /15	5.18 /23	2.91	1.78
GR	Columbia Global Dividend Opp R4	CGOLX	D	(800) 345-6611	D+ / 2.5	6.76	4.59	15.76 /33	0.88 /18	5.71 /26	3.35	1.28
GR	Columbia Global Dividend Opp R5	CADPX	D	(800) 345-6611	D+ / 2.6	6.85	4.71	16.00 /34	1.07 /19	5.83 /27	3.53	0.96
MC	Columbia Global Dividend Opp W	CTVWX	D-	(800) 345-6611	D+ / 2.4	6.69	4.44	15.42 /32	0.69 /17	5.47 /25	3.15	1.53
MC	Columbia Global Dividend Opp Y	CLSYX	D	(800) 345-6611	D+ / 2.7	6.85	4.73	16.03 /34	1.14 /19	5.93 /28	3.57	0.91
MC	Columbia Global Dividend Opp Z	CSVFX	D	(800) 345-6611	D+ / 2.5	6.79	4.61	15.77 /33	0.88 /18	5.71 /26	3.36	1.28
GR	Columbia Global Equity Value A	IEVAX	D+	(800) 345-6611	C- / 3.6	6.23	8.89	20.08 /52	3.31 /35	8.57 /47	2.07	1.18
GR	● Columbia Global Equity Value B	INEGX	C-	(800) 345-6611	C- / 4.1	6.08	8.51	19.26 /48	2.57 /28	7.77 /40	1.51	1.93
GR	Columbia Global Equity Value C	REVCX	C-	(800) 345-6611	C- / 4.1	6.10	8.58	19.32 /49	2.56 /28	7.78 /40	1.53	1.93
GR	Columbia Global Equity Value I	CEQIX	C-	(800) 345-6611	C / 5.2	6.34	9.20	20.79 /56	3.82 /41	9.07 /51	2.66	0.74
GR	Columbia Global Equity Value R	REVRX	C-	(800) 345-6611	C / 4.5	6.18	8.77	19.82 /51	3.06 /32	8.30 /45	1.98	1.43

● Denotes fund is closed to new investors
* Denotes fund is included in Section II

www.thestreetratings.com

Risk Rating/Pts	Standard Deviation	Beta	NAV As of 2/28/17	Total $(Mil)	Cash %	Stocks %	Bonds %	Other %	Portfolio Turnover Ratio	Last Bull Market Return	Last Bear Market Return	Manager Quality Pct	Manager Tenure (Years)	Initial Purch. $	Additional Purch. $	Front End Load	Back End Load
C /5.1	14.0	0.82	9.97	10	1	98	0	1	81	25.5	-25.8	52	9	0	0	0.0	0.0
C /5.1	14.0	0.81	10.25	3	1	98	0	1	81	28.8	-25.7	59	9	0	0	0.0	0.0
C /5.1	14.0	0.81	10.24	104	1	98	0	1	81	29.7	-25.7	61	9	0	0	0.0	0.0
C /5.1	14.0	0.82	10.08	21	1	98	0	1	81	27.0	-25.8	55	9	500	0	0.0	0.0
C /5.1	14.0	0.81	10.29	23	1	98	0	1	81	30.1	-25.7	61	9	0	0	0.0	0.0
C /5.1	14.0	0.81	10.18	577	1	98	0	1	81	28.8	-25.7	59	9	0	0	0.0	0.0
C /4.9	11.9	0.89	6.02	97	0	99	0	1	55	45.4	-25.6	14	8	2,000	0	5.8	0.0
C /5.0	12.0	0.90	5.99	N/A	0	99	0	1	55	39.7	-25.8	9	8	2,000	0	0.0	0.0
C /5.0	12.0	0.90	5.88	13	0	99	0	1	55	39.4	-25.7	9	8	2,000	0	0.0	0.0
C /4.9	12.0	0.90	6.03	202	0	99	0	1	55	49.3	-25.4	17	8	0	0	0.0	0.0
C /4.9	11.9	0.90	5.99	N/A	0	99	0	1	55	46.8	-25.5	14	8	0	0	0.0	0.0
C /4.9	12.0	0.90	5.99	N/A	0	99	0	1	55	46.6	-25.6	15	8	0	0	0.0	0.0
C /4.9	12.0	0.90	6.03	N/A	0	99	0	1	55	47.2	-25.6	16	8	0	0	0.0	0.0
C /4.9	12.0	0.90	5.99	N/A	0	99	0	1	55	45.3	-25.6	14	8	500	0	0.0	0.0
C /5.0	11.9	0.90	5.87	N/A	0	99	0	1	55	46.0	-25.6	14	8	0	0	0.0	0.0
C /4.9	12.0	0.90	5.99	55	0	99	0	1	55	47.1	-25.4	15	8	2,000	0	0.0	0.0
C+ /6.3	8.9	1.26	12.45	251	7	47	25	21	63	76.9	N/A	27	6	2,000	0	5.8	0.0
C+ /6.3	8.9	1.26	12.37	128	7	47	25	21	63	69.9	N/A	20	6	2,000	0	0.0	0.0
C+ /6.3	8.9	1.26	12.48	N/A	7	47	25	21	63	80.8	N/A	32	6	0	0	0.0	0.0
C+ /6.3	8.9	1.26	12.44	1	7	47	25	21	63	74.5	N/A	25	6	0	0	0.0	0.0
C+ /6.3	8.9	1.26	12.54	20	7	47	25	21	63	78.8	N/A	N/A	6	0	0	0.0	0.0
C+ /6.3	8.9	1.26	12.55	6	7	47	25	21	63	79.3	N/A	74	6	0	0	0.0	0.0
C+ /6.3	8.9	1.26	12.45	N/A	7	47	25	21	63	76.9	N/A	27	6	500	0	0.0	0.0
C+ /6.3	8.9	1.26	12.45	84	7	47	25	21	63	79.3	N/A	30	6	0	0	0.0	0.0
B- /7.4	10.3	1.00	26.49	42	1	98	0	1	12	131.9	-16.4	72	N/A	250	50	0.0	0.0
C+ /6.4	12.1	1.00	38.31	34	2	97	0	1	24	137.4	-22.7	72	N/A	250	50	0.0	0.0
C+ /6.0	14.7	0.92	28.09	16	2	97	0	1	0	152.3	-22.1	90	N/A	250	50	0.0	0.0
D /2.0	17.7	0.85	17.70	96	2	97	0	1	45	14.6	-30.5	63	6	2,000	0	5.8	0.0
D /2.0	17.7	0.85	16.75	N/A	2	97	0	1	45	9.9	-30.7	53	6	2,000	0	0.0	0.0
D /2.0	17.7	0.85	16.76	15	2	97	0	1	45	10.1	-30.7	53	6	2,000	0	0.0	0.0
D /2.0	17.7	0.85	18.04	17	2	97	0	1	45	17.7	-30.4	69	6	0	0	0.0	0.0
D /2.0	17.7	0.85	17.86	N/A	2	97	0	1	45	15.6	-30.5	65	6	0	0	0.0	0.0
D /2.0	17.7	0.85	17.58	9	2	97	0	1	45	13.1	-30.6	60	6	0	0	0.0	0.0
D /2.0	17.7	0.85	18.22	7	2	97	0	1	45	16.2	-30.4	67	6	0	0	0.0	0.0
D /2.0	17.7	0.85	18.30	8	2	97	0	1	45	17.1	-30.4	69	6	0	0	0.0	0.0
D /2.0	17.7	0.85	17.91	92	2	97	0	1	45	16.2	-30.4	67	6	0	0	0.0	0.0
C /5.2	11.1	1.02	12.34	N/A	0	99	0	1	143	86.4	-22.3	6	1	0	0	0.0	0.0
C /4.9	9.7	0.57	17.46	106	8	91	0	1	115	59.1	-24.5	18	1	2,000	0	5.8	0.0
C /4.8	9.7	0.57	16.36	N/A	8	91	0	1	115	52.7	-24.7	12	1	2,000	0	0.0	0.0
C /4.8	9.7	0.57	16.38	9	8	91	0	1	115	52.8	-24.8	12	1	2,000	0	0.0	0.0
C /4.9	9.7	0.57	17.48	63	8	91	0	1	115	63.0	-24.4	22	1	0	0	0.0	0.0
C /4.9	9.7	0.57	17.43	2	8	91	0	1	115	56.9	-24.6	16	1	0	0	0.0	0.0
C /4.9	9.7	0.83	17.60	1	8	91	0	1	115	61.3	-24.4	4	1	0	0	0.0	0.0
C /4.9	9.7	0.83	17.48	N/A	8	91	0	1	115	62.2	-24.4	5	1	100,000	0	0.0	0.0
C /4.9	9.7	0.57	17.45	N/A	8	91	0	1	115	59.2	-24.4	18	1	500	0	0.0	0.0
C /4.9	9.7	0.57	17.51	1	8	91	0	1	115	63.2	-24.4	22	1	0	0	0.0	0.0
C /4.9	9.7	0.57	17.52	419	8	91	0	1	115	61.3	-24.4	20	1	0	0	0.0	0.0
C /5.2	11.1	1.02	12.29	689	0	99	0	1	143	84.9	-22.3	5	1	2,000	0	5.8	0.0
C /5.2	11.1	1.02	12.38	2	0	99	0	1	143	77.7	-22.6	4	1	2,000	0	0.0	0.0
C /5.2	11.1	1.02	12.16	21	0	99	0	1	143	77.8	-22.6	4	1	2,000	0	0.0	0.0
C /5.1	11.2	1.03	11.96	N/A	0	99	0	1	143	89.5	-22.2	7	1	0	0	0.0	0.0
C /5.1	11.1	1.02	12.27	1	0	99	0	1	143	82.6	-22.4	5	1	0	0	0.0	0.0

Fund Type	Fund Name	Ticker Symbol	Overall Investment Rating	Phone	Performance Rating/Pts	3 Mo	6 Mo	1Yr / Pct	3Yr / Pct	5Yr / Pct	Dividend Yield	Expense Ratio
GR	Columbia Global Equity Value R4	RSEVX	C-	(800) 345-6611	C / 5.0	6.35	9.07	20.49 /55	3.61 /38	8.82 /49	2.42	0.93
GR	Columbia Global Equity Value R5	RSEYX	C-	(800) 345-6611	C / 5.1	6.33	9.19	20.64 /56	3.71 /39	8.96 /50	2.54	0.79
GR	Columbia Global Equity Value W	CEVWX	C-	(800) 345-6611	C / 4.8	6.27	8.91	20.14 /53	3.32 /35	8.56 /47	2.19	1.18
GI	Columbia Global Equity Value Y	CEVYX	C-	(800) 345-6611	C / 5.2	6.32	9.17	20.61 /55	3.78 /40	8.96 /50	2.68	0.74
GI	Columbia Global Equity Value Z	CEVZX	C-	(800) 345-6611	C / 5.0	6.28	9.11	20.45 /55	3.59 /38	8.85 /49	2.42	0.93
GR	Columbia Global Infrastructure A	RRIAX	E-	(800) 345-6611	D / 1.7	5.10	4.48	16.58 /37	1.03 /18	8.53 /47	2.27	1.20
GR ●	Columbia Global Infrastructure B	RRIBX	E-	(800) 345-6611	D+ / 2.5	5.06	4.40	16.54 /36	1.04 /18	8.28 /44	2.57	1.95
GR	Columbia Global Infrastructure C	RRICX	E-	(800) 345-6611	D+ / 2.5	5.16	4.60	16.91 /38	0.87 /18	8.11 /43	2.83	1.95
GR	Columbia Global Infrastructure I	RRIIX	E-	(800) 345-6611	D+ / 2.7	5.19	4.59	17.02 /38	1.42 /21	8.96 /50	2.72	0.81
GR ●	Columbia Global Infrastructure K	RRIYX	E-	(800) 345-6611	D+ / 2.6	5.16	4.54	16.66 /37	1.14 /19	8.65 /48	2.48	1.11
GR	Columbia Global Infrastructure R	RRIRX	E-	(800) 345-6611	D+ / 2.3	5.08	4.35	16.24 /35	0.80 /17	8.26 /44	2.23	1.45
OT	Columbia Global Infrastructure R4	CRRIX	E-	(800) 345-6611	D+ / 2.7	5.12	4.60	16.90 /38	1.31 /20	8.76 /48	2.58	0.86
GR	Columbia Global Infrastructure R5	RRIZX	E-	(800) 345-6611	D+ / 2.7	5.16	4.63	16.93 /38	1.37 /20	8.92 /50	2.67	0.86
GR	Columbia Global Infrastructure Z	CRIZX	E-	(800) 345-6611	D+ / 2.6	5.16	4.55	16.84 /38	1.28 /20	8.80 /49	2.60	0.95
AA	Columbia Global Opportunities A	IMRFX	C-	(800) 345-6611	D / 1.6	4.70	1.93	11.81 /17	2.33 /26	5.01 /21	2.52	1.21
AA ●	Columbia Global Opportunities B	IMRBX	C-	(800) 345-6611	D / 1.9	4.49	1.56	10.98 /14	1.55 /21	4.22 /16	2.01	1.96
AA	Columbia Global Opportunities C	RSSCX	C-	(800) 345-6611	D / 1.9	4.52	1.57	10.94 /14	1.56 /21	4.24 /16	2.02	1.96
AA ●	Columbia Global Opportunities K	IDRYX	C	(800) 345-6611	D+ / 2.4	4.68	2.01	11.85 /17	2.43 /27	5.13 /22	2.75	1.12
AA	Columbia Global Opportunities R	CSARX	C	(800) 345-6611	D / 2.2	4.66	1.87	11.53 /16	2.02 /24	4.71 /19	2.46	1.46
AA	Columbia Global Opportunities R4	CSDRX	C	(800) 345-6611	D+ / 2.5	4.75	2.08	12.11 /18	2.55 /28	5.21 /23	2.90	0.96
AA	Columbia Global Opportunities R5	CLNRX	C	(800) 345-6611	D+ / 2.6	4.81	2.16	12.16 /18	2.67 /29	5.33 /23	2.97	0.87
AA	Columbia Global Opportunities W	CGOPX	D+	(800) 345-6611	D+ / 2.3	4.63	1.86	11.66 /17	2.24 /26	4.96 /21	2.69	1.21
AA	Columbia Global Opportunities Z	CSAZX	C	(800) 345-6611	D+ / 2.5	4.76	2.09	12.14 /18	2.59 /28	5.28 /23	2.91	0.96
GR	Columbia Global Strategic Equity A	NLGIX	D-	(800) 345-6611	C- / 4.2	6.97	6.44	20.15 /53	4.61 /50	8.80 /49	0.09	1.27
GR ●	Columbia Global Strategic Equity B	NLGBX	D-	(800) 345-6611	C / 4.7	6.79	6.09	19.23 /48	3.84 /41	7.99 /42	0.00	2.02
GR	Columbia Global Strategic Equity C	NLGCX	D-	(800) 345-6611	C / 4.7	6.77	6.07	19.26 /48	3.82 /41	7.98 /42	0.00	2.02
GR ●	Columbia Global Strategic Equity K	CGRUX	D	(800) 345-6611	C / 5.5	6.95	6.53	20.26 /53	4.72 /51	8.92 /50	0.14	1.17
GR	Columbia Global Strategic Equity R	CLGRX	D	(800) 345-6611	C / 5.1	6.83	6.30	19.78 /51	4.35 /47	8.52 /46	0.02	1.52
GR	Columbia Global Strategic Equity R4	CWPRX	D+	(800) 345-6611	C+ / 5.6	6.99	6.57	20.44 /55	4.88 /53	9.03 /51	0.20	1.02
GR	Columbia Global Strategic Equity R5	CGPRX	D+	(800) 345-6611	C+ / 5.7	6.98	6.56	20.47 /55	4.98 /54	9.16 /52	0.24	0.92
GR	Columbia Global Strategic Equity Z	NGPAX	D+	(800) 345-6611	C+ / 5.6	7.02	6.60	20.40 /54	4.87 /53	9.08 /51	0.20	1.02
TC	Columbia Global Technology Gro 5	CTHRX	A+	(800) 345-6611	A+ / 9.9	11.58	15.08	37.64 /96	15.32 /99	19.47 /99	0.00	1.34
TC	Columbia Global Technology Gro A	CTCAX	A	(800) 345-6611	A+ / 9.9	11.48	14.90	37.09 /96	14.87 /99	19.01 /99	0.00	2.09
TC ●	Columbia Global Technology Gro B	CTCBX	A	(800) 345-6611	A+ / 9.9	11.27	14.45	36.04 /95	14.00 /99	18.11 /99	0.00	2.09
TC	Columbia Global Technology Gro C	CTHCX	A	(800) 345-6611	A+ / 9.9	11.30	14.47	36.10 /95	14.01 /99	18.14 /99	0.00	0.96
TC	Columbia Global Technology Gro I	CONIX	A	(800) 345-6611	A+ / 9.9	11.56	15.09	37.68 /96	15.28 /99	19.39 /99	0.00	1.09
TC	Columbia Global Technology Gro R4	CTYRX	A	(800) 345-6611	A+ / 9.9	11.51	15.03	37.43 /96	15.15 /99	19.32 /99	0.00	1.01
TC	Columbia Global Technology Gro Y	CGTUX	A-	(800) 345-6611	A+ / 9.9	11.60	15.14	37.74 /96	15.24 /99	19.37 /99	0.00	0.96
TC	Columbia Global Technology Gro Z	CMTFX	A	(800) 345-6611	A+ / 9.9	11.57	15.03	37.46 /96	15.16 /99	19.32 /99	0.00	1.09
FO	Columbia Greater China A	NGCAX	E	(800) 345-6611	D / 2.1	3.78	0.60	18.83 /46	2.51 /28	4.66 /19	0.00	1.62
FO ●	Columbia Greater China B	NGCBX	E	(800) 345-6611	D+ / 2.4	3.59	0.22	17.93 /43	1.74 /22	3.87 /15	0.00	2.37
FO	Columbia Greater China C	NGCCX	E	(800) 345-6611	D+ / 2.4	3.59	0.21	17.93 /43	1.75 /22	3.87 /15	0.00	2.37
FO	Columbia Greater China I	CCINX	E+	(800) 345-6611	C- / 3.3	3.91	0.81	19.34 /49	2.97 /32	5.12 /22	0.00	1.18
FO	Columbia Greater China R4	CGCHX	E+	(800) 345-6611	C- / 3.1	3.83	0.70	19.11 /48	2.76 /30	4.85 /20	0.00	1.37
FO	Columbia Greater China R5	CGCRX	E+	(800) 345-6611	C- / 3.2	3.88	0.77	19.28 /48	2.92 /31	5.01 /21	0.00	1.23
FO	Columbia Greater China W	CGCWX	E+	(800) 345-6611	D+ / 2.9	3.78	0.57	18.79 /46	2.51 /28	4.68 /19	0.00	1.62
FO	Columbia Greater China Z	LNGZX	E+	(800) 345-6611	C- / 3.1	3.85	0.71	19.12 /48	2.77 /30	4.92 /21	0.00	1.37
GI	Columbia Income Builder A	RBBAX	C-	(800) 345-6611	D+ / 2.6	3.35	3.30	13.42 /23	4.25 /46	5.43 /24	2.73	1.02
GI ●	Columbia Income Builder B	RBBBX	C	(800) 345-6611	D+ / 2.9	3.14	2.90	12.61 /20	3.46 /37	4.65 /19	2.13	1.77
GI	Columbia Income Builder C	RBBCX	C	(800) 345-6611	D+ / 2.9	3.14	2.90	12.53 /20	3.43 /36	4.63 /19	2.13	1.77
GI ●	Columbia Income Builder K	CIPRX	C	(800) 345-6611	C- / 3.5	3.28	3.34	13.51 /24	4.31 /46	5.50 /25	2.96	0.97
AA	Columbia Income Builder R	CBURX	C	(800) 345-6611	C- / 3.2	3.27	3.15	13.06 /22	3.97 /43	5.16 /22	2.61	1.27

● Denotes fund is closed to new investors
* Denotes fund is included in Section II

156

RISK			NET ASSETS		ASSET					BULL / BEAR		FUND MANAGER		MINIMUMS		LOADS	
	3 Year		NAV						Portfolio	Last Bull	Last Bear	Manager	Manager	Initial	Additional	Front	Back
Risk Rating/Pts	Standard Deviation	Beta	As of 2/28/17	Total $(Mil)	Cash %	Stocks %	Bonds %	Other %	Turnover Ratio	Market Return	Market Return	Quality Pct	Tenure (Years)	Purch. $	Purch. $	End Load	End Load
C /5.1	11.1	1.02	12.35	N/A	0	99	0	1	143	86.9	-22.4	6	1	0	0	0.0	0.0
C /5.1	11.1	1.02	12.29	N/A	0	99	0	1	143	88.7	-22.2	6	1	0	0	0.0	0.0
C /5.2	11.1	1.02	12.38	N/A	0	99	0	1	143	84.6	-22.4	5	1	500	0	0.0	0.0
C /5.1	11.1	1.02	12.00	N/A	0	99	0	1	143	88.3	-22.3	6	1	0	0	0.0	0.0
C /5.1	11.1	1.02	12.31	90	0	99	0	1	143	87.7	-22.2	6	1	2,000	0	0.0	0.0
E+ /0.8	9.9	0.87	12.08	142	6	75	12	7	60	101.9	-32.8	4	10	2,000	0	5.8	0.0
E+ /0.8	9.9	0.87	11.33	4	6	75	12	7	60	98.9	-33.0	4	10	2,000	0	0.0	0.0
E+ /0.8	9.9	0.87	11.29	24	6	75	12	7	60	97.2	-33.0	4	10	2,000	0	0.0	0.0
E+ /0.8	9.9	0.87	12.35	25	6	75	12	7	60	106.3	-32.7	5	10	0	0	0.0	0.0
E+ /0.8	9.9	0.87	12.16	N/A	6	75	12	7	60	103.2	-32.7	4	10	0	0	0.0	0.0
E+ /0.8	9.9	0.86	11.76	1	6	75	12	7	60	99.2	-32.8	4	10	0	0	0.0	0.0
E+ /0.8	9.9	0.87	12.40	1	6	75	12	7	60	104.0	-32.8	5	4	0	0	0.0	0.0
E+ /0.8	9.9	0.87	12.30	2	6	75	12	7	60	105.8	-32.7	5	10	0	0	0.0	0.0
E+ /0.8	9.9	0.86	12.30	16	6	75	12	7	60	104.5	-32.7	5	4	2,000	0	0.0	0.0
B /8.4	6.5	0.92	12.01	567	3	53	43	1	127	48.6	-11.8	20	7	2,000	0	5.8	0.0
B /8.4	6.5	0.93	11.73	3	3	53	43	1	127	42.6	-12.1	14	7	2,000	0	0.0	0.0
B /8.4	6.5	0.92	11.66	26	3	53	43	1	127	42.8	-12.2	14	7	2,000	0	0.0	0.0
B /8.4	6.5	0.92	12.06	N/A	3	53	43	1	127	49.4	-11.7	21	7	0	0	0.0	0.0
B /8.4	6.5	0.92	11.92	1	3	53	43	1	127	46.4	-11.9	17	7	0	0	0.0	0.0
B /8.4	6.5	0.92	12.08	N/A	3	53	43	1	127	49.9	-11.8	22	7	0	0	0.0	0.0
B /8.4	6.6	0.93	12.11	N/A	3	53	43	1	127	50.9	-11.8	23	7	0	0	0.0	0.0
C+ /6.2	6.4	0.91	11.96	N/A	3	53	43	1	127	48.2	-11.8	20	7	500	0	0.0	0.0
B /8.4	6.5	0.92	12.05	5	3	53	43	1	127	50.8	-11.7	22	7	2,000	0	0.0	0.0
D+ /2.7	10.4	0.96	13.05	529	2	94	0	4	75	84.5	-20.0	14	N/A	2,000	0	5.8	0.0
D+ /2.4	10.4	0.96	11.33	5	2	94	0	4	75	77.1	-20.3	9	N/A	2,000	0	0.0	0.0
D+ /2.4	10.4	0.96	11.19	75	2	94	0	4	75	77.1	-20.3	9	N/A	2,000	0	0.0	0.0
D+ /2.8	10.4	0.96	13.38	N/A	2	94	0	4	75	85.6	-20.1	14	6	0	0	0.0	0.0
D+ /2.7	10.3	0.96	12.83	1	2	94	0	4	75	81.9	-20.1	12	N/A	0	0	0.0	0.0
D+ /2.8	10.3	0.96	13.62	N/A	2	94	0	4	75	86.4	-20.0	16	8	0	0	0.0	0.0
D+ /2.8	10.4	0.96	13.64	1	2	94	0	4	75	87.5	-20.0	17	8	0	0	0.0	0.0
D+ /2.8	10.4	0.96	13.41	23	2	94	0	4	75	86.9	-20.0	16	N/A	2,000	0	0.0	0.0
C+ /5.6	13.9	1.14	25.61	26	1	98	0	1	55	184.9	-24.7	89	5	0	0	0.0	0.0
C+ /5.6	14.0	1.14	24.26	201	1	98	0	1	55	179.3	-24.8	88	5	2,000	0	5.8	0.0
C+ /5.6	13.9	1.14	21.91	N/A	1	98	0	1	55	168.1	-25.0	84	5	2,000	0	0.0	0.0
C+ /5.6	14.0	1.14	21.96	75	1	98	0	1	55	168.1	-25.0	84	5	2,000	0	0.0	0.0
C /5.5	14.0	1.14	26.43	35	1	98	0	1	55	184.0	-24.7	89	5	0	0	0.0	0.0
C+ /5.6	14.0	1.14	25.46	8	1	98	0	1	55	183.2	-24.7	89	5	0	0	0.0	0.0
C /4.8	14.0	1.14	25.67	2	1	98	0	1	55	183.7	-24.7	89	5	0	0	0.0	0.0
C+ /5.6	13.9	1.14	25.15	251	1	98	0	1	55	183.1	-24.7	89	5	0	0	0.0	0.0
D+ /2.3	19.4	1.03	35.41	54	1	98	0	1	39	54.6	-32.2	89	12	2,000	0	5.8	0.0
D /2.1	19.3	1.03	32.03	N/A	1	98	0	1	39	48.4	-32.4	86	12	2,000	0	0.0	0.0
D /2.2	19.3	1.03	32.88	9	1	98	0	1	39	48.5	-32.4	86	12	2,000	0	0.0	0.0
D+ /2.5	19.3	1.03	38.50	N/A	1	98	0	1	39	58.4	-32.1	91	12	0	0	0.0	0.0
D+ /2.6	19.4	1.03	39.01	3	1	98	0	1	39	56.1	-32.2	90	12	0	0	0.0	0.0
D+ /2.6	19.4	1.03	39.10	1	1	98	0	1	39	57.3	-32.2	91	12	0	0	0.0	0.0
D+ /2.3	19.4	1.03	35.40	N/A	1	98	0	1	39	54.8	-32.2	89	12	500	0	0.0	0.0
D+ /2.5	19.4	1.03	38.32	34	1	98	0	1	39	56.7	-32.1	90	12	0	0	0.0	0.0
B- /7.6	4.9	0.41	11.74	942	0	17	79	4	26	43.8	-5.9	74	11	2,000	0	4.8	0.0
B- /7.6	4.9	0.41	11.80	3	0	17	79	4	26	38.1	-6.2	65	11	2,000	0	0.0	0.0
B- /7.6	4.9	0.41	11.78	235	0	17	79	4	26	37.9	-6.2	64	11	2,000	0	0.0	0.0
B- /7.6	4.9	0.41	11.75	N/A	0	17	79	4	26	44.3	-5.9	74	11	0	0	0.0	0.0
B- /7.6	4.8	0.70	11.80	2	0	17	79	4	26	41.8	-6.0	60	7	0	0	0.0	0.0

Data as of February 28, 2017

Fund Type	Fund Name	Ticker Symbol	Overall Investment Rating	Phone	Perfor-mance Rating/Pts	3 Mo	6 Mo	1Yr / Pct	3Yr / Pct	5Yr / Pct	Dividend Yield	Expense Ratio
								Total Return % through 2/28/17	Annualized		Incl. in Returns	
AA	Columbia Income Builder R4	CNMRX	C	(800) 345-6611	C- / 3.6	3.40	3.41	13.66 /24	4.50 /49	5.65 /26	3.10	0.77
AA	Columbia Income Builder R5	CKKRX	C	(800) 345-6611	C- / 3.7	3.41	3.44	13.71 /24	4.56 /49	5.71 /26	3.15	0.72
AA	Columbia Income Builder W	CINDX	C+	(800) 345-6611	C- / 3.4	3.34	3.29	13.42 /23	4.24 /46	5.42 /24	2.86	1.02
AA	Columbia Income Builder Z	CBUZX	C	(800) 345-6611	C- / 3.6	3.41	3.42	13.70 /24	4.48 /48	5.69 /26	3.11	0.77
GR	Columbia Large Cap Enh Core A	NMIAX	A+	(800) 345-6611	B+ / 8.8	7.11	9.74	22.62 /65	9.81 /92	13.37 /88	1.30	1.24
GI	Columbia Large Cap Enh Core I	CCEIX	A+	(800) 345-6611	A- / 9.0	7.27	9.95	23.13 /67	10.26 /95	13.82 /92	1.65	0.80
GR	Columbia Large Cap Enh Core R	CCERX	A+	(800) 345-6611	B+ / 8.6	7.09	9.58	22.36 /64	9.55 /91	13.11 /85	1.08	1.49
GI	Columbia Large Cap Enh Core R4	CECFX	A+	(800) 345-6611	B+ / 8.9	7.19	9.85	22.98 /67	9.97 /93	13.46 /88	1.53	0.99
GI	Columbia Large Cap Enh Core R5	CLNCX	A+	(800) 345-6611	A- / 9.0	7.24	9.93	23.08 /67	10.18 /94	13.60 /90	1.60	0.85
GR	Columbia Large Cap Enh Core Y	CECYX	A+	(800) 345-6611	A- / 9.0	7.21	9.94	23.11 /67	10.25 /95	13.82 /92	1.64	0.80
GR	Columbia Large Cap Enh Core Z	NMIMX	A+	(800) 345-6611	B+ / 8.9	7.23	9.87	22.94 /66	10.09 /94	13.68 /90	1.52	0.99
GR	Columbia Large Cap Growth A	LEGAX	C+	(800) 345-6611	B- / 7.4	8.31	7.70	21.38 /59	9.54 /91	13.33 /87	0.19	1.10
GR	● Columbia Large Cap Growth B	LEGBX	C+	(800) 345-6611	B / 7.8	8.10	7.28	20.48 /55	8.71 /85	12.48 /79	0.00	1.85
GR	Columbia Large Cap Growth C	LEGCX	C+	(800) 345-6611	B / 7.8	8.13	7.31	20.49 /55	8.73 /85	12.49 /79	0.00	1.85
GR	● Columbia Large Cap Growth E	CLGEX	C+	(800) 345-6611	B / 7.6	8.30	7.65	21.30 /59	9.43 /90	13.22 /86	0.11	1.20
GR	● Columbia Large Cap Growth F	CLGFX	C+	(800) 345-6611	B / 7.8	8.14	7.31	20.53 /55	8.72 /85	12.49 /79	0.00	1.85
GR	Columbia Large Cap Growth I	CLGIX	B	(800) 345-6611	B+ / 8.7	8.43	7.94	21.91 /62	9.99 /93	13.82 /92	0.55	0.69
GR	Columbia Large Cap Growth III A	NFEAX	D+	(800) 345-6611	C+ / 5.8	8.37	7.78	20.85 /57	6.47 /68	11.68 /71	0.00	1.22
GR	● Columbia Large Cap Growth III B	NFEBX	D	(800) 345-6611	C+ / 6.2	8.08	7.37	19.79 /51	5.64 /61	10.83 /64	0.00	1.97
GR	Columbia Large Cap Growth III C	NFECX	D	(800) 345-6611	C+ / 6.3	8.08	7.38	19.89 /51	5.67 /61	10.85 /65	0.00	1.97
GR	Columbia Large Cap Growth III I	CMRIX	C-	(800) 345-6611	B- / 7.1	8.47	8.00	21.31 /59	6.97 /72	12.20 /76	0.00	0.78
GR	Columbia Large Cap Growth III R	CLGPX	C+	(800) 345-6611	C+ / 6.7	8.30	7.66	20.57 /55	6.20 /66	11.41 /69	0.00	N/A
GR	Columbia Large Cap Growth III R4	CSFRX	C-	(800) 345-6611	B- / 7.0	8.43	7.96	21.11 /58	6.73 /70	11.92 /74	0.00	0.97
GR	Columbia Large Cap Growth III R5	CADRX	B-	(800) 345-6611	B- / 7.1	8.43	7.96	21.23 /58	6.87 /71	11.96 /74	0.00	0.83
GR	Columbia Large Cap Growth III W	CLCPX	C+	(800) 345-6611	C+ / 6.9	8.36	7.84	20.92 /57	6.48 /68	11.70 /72	0.00	N/A
GR	Columbia Large Cap Growth III Z	NFEPX	C-	(800) 345-6611	B- / 7.0	8.40	7.99	21.19 /58	6.74 /70	11.97 /74	0.00	0.97
GR	● Columbia Large Cap Growth K	CLRUX	B	(800) 345-6611	B+ / 8.5	8.34	7.75	21.52 /60	9.67 /91	13.48 /89	0.29	0.99
GR	Columbia Large Cap Growth R	CGWRX	B-	(800) 345-6611	B / 8.2	8.24	7.56	21.10 /58	9.27 /89	13.05 /84	0.00	1.35
GR	Columbia Large Cap Growth R4	CCGRX	B	(800) 345-6611	B+ / 8.6	8.40	7.82	21.70 /61	9.84 /92	13.63 /90	0.41	0.85
GR	Columbia Large Cap Growth R5	CLWFX	B	(800) 345-6611	B+ / 8.7	8.40	7.87	21.82 /61	9.93 /93	13.77 /91	0.50	0.74
GR	● Columbia Large Cap Growth V	GAEGX	C+	(800) 345-6611	B- / 7.4	8.32	7.70	21.42 /59	9.53 /91	13.31 /87	0.20	1.10
GR	Columbia Large Cap Growth W	CLGWX	B	(800) 345-6611	B+ / 8.4	8.29	7.68	21.41 /59	9.55 /91	13.35 /87	0.21	1.10
GR	Columbia Large Cap Growth Y	CGFYX	B	(800) 345-6611	B+ / 8.7	8.43	7.90	21.90 /62	9.99 /93	13.83 /92	0.55	0.69
GR	Columbia Large Cap Growth Z	GEGTX	B	(800) 345-6611	B+ / 8.6	8.36	7.80	21.68 /61	9.80 /92	13.61 /90	0.42	0.85
IX	Columbia Large Cap Index A	NEIAX	A+	(800) 345-6611	A- / 9.1	7.91	9.74	24.40 /71	10.15 /94	13.51 /89	1.61	0.45
IX	● Columbia Large Cap Index B	CLIBX	A+	(800) 345-6611	B+ / 8.7	7.73	9.35	23.49 /68	9.35 /89	12.67 /81	0.94	1.20
GR	Columbia Large Cap Index I	CCXIX	A+	(800) 345-6611	A / 9.3	7.99	9.89	24.73 /72	10.42 /95	13.80 /92	1.83	0.20
GI	Columbia Large Cap Index R5	CLXRX	A+	(800) 345-6611	A / 9.3	7.98	9.90	24.73 /72	10.42 /95	13.80 /92	1.80	0.20
IX	Columbia Large Cap Index Z	NINDX	A+	(800) 345-6611	A / 9.3	7.99	9.89	24.72 /72	10.43 /96	13.79 /92	1.83	0.20
MC	Columbia Mid Cap Growth A	CBSAX	D	(800) 345-6611	C / 4.8	7.14	7.74	19.83 /51	5.38 /58	9.57 /55	0.00	1.20
MC	● Columbia Mid Cap Growth B	CBSBX	D	(800) 345-6611	C / 5.3	6.94	7.34	18.91 /47	4.59 /50	8.76 /48	0.00	1.95
MC	Columbia Mid Cap Growth C	CMCCX	D	(800) 345-6611	C / 5.3	6.95	7.34	18.91 /47	4.59 /50	8.75 /48	0.00	1.95
MC	Columbia Mid Cap Growth I	CMTIX	C-	(800) 345-6611	C+ / 6.4	7.25	7.94	20.30 /54	5.86 /63	10.06 /59	0.00	0.81
MC	● Columbia Mid Cap Growth K	CMCKX	D+	(800) 345-6611	C+ / 6.1	7.16	7.81	19.94 /52	5.51 /60	9.75 /57	0.00	1.11
MC	Columbia Mid Cap Growth R	CMGRX	D+	(800) 345-6611	C+ / 5.8	7.09	7.62	19.48 /49	5.12 /55	9.30 /53	0.00	1.45
MC	Columbia Mid Cap Growth R4	CPGRX	C-	(800) 345-6611	C+ / 6.2	7.24	7.88	20.10 /53	5.66 /61	9.84 /57	0.00	0.95
MC	Columbia Mid Cap Growth R5	CMGVX	C-	(800) 345-6611	C+ / 6.3	7.26	7.95	20.28 /54	5.78 /62	9.99 /58	0.00	0.86
MC	● Columbia Mid Cap Growth V	CBSTX	D	(800) 345-6611	C / 4.8	7.13	7.73	19.80 /51	5.37 /58	9.54 /55	0.00	1.20
MC	Columbia Mid Cap Growth W	CMRWX	D+	(800) 345-6611	C+ / 6.0	7.14	7.74	19.77 /51	5.38 /58	9.57 /55	0.00	1.20
MC	Columbia Mid Cap Growth Y	CMGYX	C-	(800) 345-6611	C+ / 6.4	7.24	7.96	20.29 /54	5.84 /63	10.03 /59	0.00	0.81
MC	Columbia Mid Cap Growth Z	CLSPX	C-	(800) 345-6611	C+ / 6.2	7.19	7.88	20.09 /52	5.65 /61	9.85 /57	0.00	0.95
MC	Columbia Mid Cap Index A	NTIAX	B+	(800) 345-6611	A / 9.3	6.47	11.10	31.10 /88	9.12 /88	13.30 /87	0.97	0.64

● Denotes fund is closed to new investors
* Denotes fund is included in Section II

www.thestreetratings.com

RISK			NET ASSETS		ASSET				Portfolio Turnover Ratio	BULL / BEAR		FUND MANAGER		MINIMUMS		LOADS	
Risk Rating/Pts	3 Year		NAV As of 2/28/17	Total $(Mil)	Cash %	Stocks %	Bonds %	Other %		Last Bull Market Return	Last Bear Market Return	Manager Quality Pct	Manager Tenure (Years)	Initial Purch. $	Additional Purch. $	Front End Load	Back End Load
	Standard Deviation	Beta															
B- /7.6	4.9	0.70	11.77	6	0	17	79	4	26	45.3	-5.9	66	11	0	0	0.0	0.0
B- /7.6	4.9	0.70	11.78	3	0	17	79	4	26	45.7	-5.9	66	11	0	0	0.0	0.0
B /8.5	4.8	0.70	11.73	N/A	0	17	79	4	26	43.7	-5.9	63	11	500	0	0.0	0.0
B- /7.6	4.9	0.70	11.74	45	0	17	79	4	26	45.7	-5.8	66	7	2,000	0	0.0	0.0
B- /7.0	10.7	1.02	23.81	80	1	98	0	1	89	131.2	-15.2	62	8	2,000	0	0.0	0.0
B- /7.0	10.7	1.02	23.76	11	1	98	0	1	89	136.0	-15.1	67	8	0	0	0.0	0.0
B- /7.0	10.7	1.02	23.78	38	1	98	0	1	89	128.2	-15.4	59	8	0	0	0.0	0.0
B- /7.0	10.7	1.02	23.58	N/A	1	98	0	1	89	132.2	-15.2	64	8	0	0	0.0	0.0
B- /7.0	10.7	1.03	23.69	7	1	98	0	1	89	133.5	-15.2	66	8	0	0	0.0	0.0
B- /7.0	10.7	1.03	23.77	5	1	98	0	1	89	136.0	-15.1	67	8	1,000,000	0	0.0	0.0
B- /7.0	10.7	1.02	23.77	256	1	98	0	1	89	134.5	-15.2	65	8	2,000	0	0.0	0.0
C /4.6	13.1	1.15	35.74	1,787	3	96	0	1	45	127.9	-18.6	41	12	2,000	0	5.8	0.0
C /4.3	13.1	1.15	30.54	7	3	96	0	1	45	118.8	-18.9	31	12	2,000	0	0.0	0.0
C /4.3	13.1	1.15	30.58	102	3	96	0	1	45	118.8	-18.8	31	12	2,000	0	0.0	0.0
C /4.6	13.1	1.15	35.63	15	3	96	0	1	45	126.6	-18.6	40	12	0	0	4.5	0.0
C /4.3	13.1	1.15	30.54	1	3	96	0	1	45	118.8	-18.8	31	12	0	0	0.0	0.0
C /4.7	13.1	1.15	37.05	143	3	96	0	1	45	133.3	-18.4	47	12	0	0	0.0	0.0
D+ /2.9	12.9	1.08	15.74	841	0	99	0	1	102	112.1	-17.6	18	2	2,000	0	5.8	0.0
D /1.6	12.9	1.08	11.45	2	0	99	0	1	102	103.4	-17.9	12	2	2,000	0	0.0	0.0
D /1.6	12.9	1.08	11.58	427	0	99	0	1	102	103.7	-17.9	12	2	2,000	0	0.0	0.0
C- /3.2	12.9	1.08	17.10	N/A	0	99	0	1	102	117.4	-17.4	22	2	0	0	0.0	0.0
C /4.8	12.9	1.08	15.87	26	0	99	0	1	102	109.2	-17.7	16	2	0	0	0.0	0.0
C- /3.3	12.9	1.08	17.30	25	0	99	0	1	102	114.3	-17.6	20	2	0	0	0.0	0.0
C+ /5.8	12.9	1.08	17.44	9	0	99	0	1	102	114.7	-17.6	21	2	100,000	0	0.0	0.0
C /4.9	12.9	1.08	15.89	N/A	0	99	0	1	102	112.2	-17.6	18	2	0	0	0.0	0.0
C- /3.2	12.9	1.08	16.84	452	0	99	0	1	102	115.0	-17.5	20	2	2,000	0	0.0	0.0
C /4.6	13.1	1.15	36.83	N/A	3	96	0	1	45	129.5	-18.5	43	12	0	0	0.0	0.0
C /4.6	13.1	1.15	35.58	28	3	96	0	1	45	124.8	-18.7	37	12	0	0	0.0	0.0
C /4.7	13.1	1.15	37.72	9	3	96	0	1	45	131.1	-18.5	45	12	0	0	0.0	0.0
C /4.6	13.1	1.15	36.98	22	3	96	0	1	45	132.7	-18.4	46	12	0	0	0.0	0.0
C /4.6	13.1	1.15	35.45	183	3	96	0	1	45	127.5	-18.6	41	12	2,000	0	5.8	0.0
C /4.6	13.1	1.15	35.81	27	3	96	0	1	45	128.0	-18.6	41	12	500	0	0.0	0.0
C /4.6	13.1	1.15	37.06	32	3	96	0	1	45	133.4	-18.4	47	12	1,000,000	0	0.0	0.0
C /4.6	13.1	1.15	36.97	945	3	96	0	1	45	131.0	-18.5	45	12	2,000	0	0.0	0.0
B- /7.0	10.3	1.00	45.16	1,072	0	99	0	1	11	129.2	-16.4	69	6	2,000	0	0.0	0.0
B- /7.0	10.3	1.00	45.25	N/A	0	99	0	1	11	120.1	-16.7	60	6	2,000	0	0.0	0.0
B- /7.0	10.3	1.00	45.37	N/A	0	99	0	1	11	132.4	-16.3	72	6	0	0	0.0	0.0
B- /7.0	10.3	1.00	45.98	361	0	99	0	1	11	132.4	-16.3	72	6	0	0	0.0	0.0
B- /7.0	10.3	1.00	45.38	2,275	0	99	0	1	11	132.4	-16.3	72	6	2,000	0	0.0	0.0
C- /3.0	12.3	0.90	25.43	869	3	96	0	1	130	93.7	-23.1	33	11	2,000	0	5.8	0.0
D+ /2.5	12.3	0.90	21.61	3	3	96	0	1	130	85.9	-23.4	25	11	2,000	0	0.0	0.0
D+ /2.5	12.3	0.91	21.74	45	3	96	0	1	130	85.9	-23.4	25	11	2,000	0	0.0	0.0
C- /3.1	12.3	0.90	27.23	N/A	3	96	0	1	130	98.3	-23.0	39	11	0	0	0.0	0.0
C- /3.1	12.3	0.90	26.85	N/A	3	96	0	1	130	95.3	-23.0	35	11	0	0	0.0	0.0
D+ /2.9	12.3	0.90	24.54	15	3	96	0	1	130	91.0	-23.2	30	11	0	0	0.0	0.0
C- /3.2	12.3	0.90	27.63	28	3	96	0	1	130	96.1	-23.0	37	11	0	0	0.0	0.0
C- /3.1	12.3	0.90	27.11	41	3	96	0	1	130	97.7	-23.0	38	11	0	0	0.0	0.0
C- /3.0	12.3	0.90	25.34	22	3	96	0	1	130	93.3	-23.1	33	11	2,000	0	5.8	0.0
C- /3.0	12.3	0.91	25.43	N/A	3	96	0	1	130	93.6	-23.1	33	11	500	0	0.0	0.0
C- /3.1	12.3	0.90	27.11	12	3	96	0	1	130	98.0	-23.0	39	11	0	0	0.0	0.0
C- /3.1	12.3	0.90	26.92	803	3	96	0	1	130	96.3	-23.0	36	11	0	0	0.0	0.0
C /5.2	12.0	1.00	16.05	1,601	1	98	0	1	20	134.6	-22.7	69	6	2,000	0	0.0	0.0

Fund Type	Fund Name	Ticker Symbol	Overall Investment Rating	Phone	Performance Rating/Pts	Total Return % through 2/28/17			Annualized		Incl. in Returns	
	99 Pct = Best / 0 Pct = Worst					3 Mo	6 Mo	1Yr / Pct	3Yr / Pct	5Yr / Pct	Dividend Yield	Expense Ratio
MC	Columbia Mid Cap Index I	CIDIX	A-	(800) 345-6611	A / 9.4	6.57	11.29	31.52 /89	9.46 /90	13.64 /90	1.19	0.21
MC	Columbia Mid Cap Index R5	CPXRX	A-	(800) 345-6611	A / 9.4	6.59	11.23	31.35 /89	9.40 /90	13.61 /90	1.17	0.26
MC	Columbia Mid Cap Index Z	NMPAX	A-	(800) 345-6611	A / 9.4	6.57	11.30	31.45 /89	9.42 /90	13.59 /90	1.19	0.39
MC	Columbia Mid Cap Value A	CMUAX	C-	(800) 345-6611	C+ / 6.5	6.22	9.88	27.41 /80	6.44 /68	12.73 /81	0.63	1.17
MC	● Columbia Mid Cap Value B	CMUBX	C	(800) 345-6611	C+ / 6.9	6.08	9.57	26.47 /78	5.65 /61	11.91 /73	0.25	1.92
MC	Columbia Mid Cap Value C	CMUCX	C	(800) 345-6611	B- / 7.0	6.04	9.58	26.48 /78	5.66 /61	11.91 /73	0.25	1.92
MC	Columbia Mid Cap Value I	CMVUX	C+	(800) 345-6611	B / 7.8	6.33	10.19	27.95 /82	6.93 /71	13.24 /86	1.05	0.74
MC	● Columbia Mid Cap Value K	CMUFX	C	(800) 345-6611	B / 7.6	6.23	9.99	27.66 /81	6.61 /69	12.92 /83	0.80	1.04
MC	Columbia Mid Cap Value R	CMVRX	C	(800) 345-6611	B- / 7.3	6.11	9.77	27.10 /79	6.17 /66	12.45 /79	0.46	1.42
MC	Columbia Mid Cap Value R4	CFDRX	C+	(800) 345-6611	B / 7.7	6.27	10.06	27.70 /81	6.71 /70	13.02 /84	0.86	0.92
MC	Columbia Mid Cap Value R5	CVERX	C+	(800) 345-6611	B / 7.8	6.30	10.12	27.86 /81	6.84 /71	13.15 /85	0.98	0.79
MC	Columbia Mid Cap Value W	CMUWX	C	(800) 345-6611	B- / 7.5	6.22	9.88	27.41 /80	6.44 /68	12.73 /81	0.67	1.17
MC	Columbia Mid Cap Value Y	CMVYX	C+	(800) 345-6611	B / 7.8	6.33	10.19	27.94 /81	6.91 /71	13.21 /86	1.04	0.74
MC	Columbia Mid Cap Value Z	NAMAX	C+	(800) 345-6611	B / 7.7	6.27	10.06	27.74 /81	6.72 /70	13.02 /84	0.88	0.92
GL	Columbia Mlti-Mgr Growth Strat A	CSLGX	C-	(800) 345-6611	C+ / 5.8	8.50	3.12	22.19 /63	5.16 /56	--	0.00	1.12
GL	Columbia Mlti-Mgr Growth Strat Z	CZMGX	C-	(800) 345-6611	C+ / 5.8	8.53	3.15	22.22 /63	5.17 /56	--	0.00	0.87
GL	Columbia Mlti-Mgr Value Strat A	CDEIX	A+	(800) 345-6611	A / 9.3	7.70	11.93	28.57 /83	9.20 /88	--	1.72	1.15
IN	Columbia Mlti-Mgr Value Strat Z	CZMVX	A-	(800) 345-6611	A / 9.3	7.74	11.97	28.62 /83	9.22 /88	--	1.72	0.90
IN	Columbia MMrg Alternative Strat A	CPASX	D	(800) 345-6611	E / 0.5	1.32	-2.54	-0.11 / 1	-0.56 /11	--	0.00	1.80
GI	Columbia MMrg Alternative Strat Z	CZAMX	C-	(800) 345-6611	E / 0.5	1.43	-2.43	--	-0.53 /11	--	0.00	1.55
GL	Columbia MMrg SC Eqty Strat A	CSCEX	C+	(800) 345-6611	B / 7.6	4.02	12.17	32.22 /90	5.67 /61	--	0.07	1.52
SC	Columbia MMrg SC Eqty Strat Z	CZMSX	C+	(800) 345-6611	B / 7.6	4.02	12.18	32.23 /90	5.67 /61	--	0.07	1.27
IN	Columbia Mortgage Opportunities I	CLMIX	U	(800) 345-6611	U /	1.67	4.01	11.40 /16	--	--	3.71	0.74
AA	Columbia Multi-Asset Income I	CLNIX	U	(800) 345-6611	U /	5.41	2.96	14.30 /27	--	--	5.16	0.95
FO	Columbia Overseas Value A	COAVX	D	(800) 345-6611	D- / 1.0	6.67	7.19	16.25 /35	-0.21 /13	5.59 /25	1.61	1.39
FO	● Columbia Overseas Value B	COBVX	D	(800) 345-6611	D- / 1.2	6.31	6.70	15.31 /31	-0.98 / 9	4.78 /20	1.12	2.14
FO	Columbia Overseas Value C	COCVX	D	(800) 345-6611	D- / 1.2	6.32	6.71	15.32 /31	-0.98 / 9	4.78 /20	1.13	2.14
FO	Columbia Overseas Value I	COVIX	D+	(800) 345-6611	D+ / 2.6	6.72	7.37	16.87 /38	0.28 /15	6.04 /29	2.12	0.92
FO	● Columbia Overseas Value K	COKVX	D	(800) 345-6611	D / 1.6	6.59	7.25	16.45 /36	-0.03 /13	5.78 /27	1.88	1.22
FO	Columbia Overseas Value R	COVUX	D-	(800) 345-6611	D- / 1.4	6.61	7.02	16.06 /35	-0.45 /11	5.30 /23	1.56	1.64
FO	Columbia Overseas Value R4	COSVX	C-	(800) 345-6611	D+ / 2.4	6.64	7.17	16.55 /36	0.04 /13	5.82 /27	1.91	1.14
FO	Columbia Overseas Value R5	COSSX	C-	(800) 345-6611	D+ / 2.5	6.72	7.25	16.79 /38	0.12 /14	5.87 /27	2.10	0.97
FO	Columbia Overseas Value W	COVWX	D	(800) 345-6611	D- / 1.5	6.67	7.20	16.27 /35	-0.22 /13	5.58 /25	1.71	1.39
FO	Columbia Overseas Value Y	COSYX	C-	(800) 345-6611	D+ / 2.6	6.74	7.40	16.95 /38	0.19 /14	5.91 /28	2.12	0.92
FO	Columbia Overseas Value Z	COSZX	D+	(800) 345-6611	D+ / 2.5	6.75	7.28	16.63 /37	0.05 /14	5.82 /27	1.91	1.14
FO	Columbia Pacific/Asia A	CASAX	C-	(800) 345-6611	C- / 3.5	5.63	3.35	18.98 /47	4.51 /49	5.68 /26	0.19	1.50
FO	Columbia Pacific/Asia C	CASCX	C-	(800) 345-6611	C- / 3.9	5.38	2.86	18.01 /43	3.73 /40	4.89 /21	0.04	2.25
FO	Columbia Pacific/Asia I	CPCIX	C	(800) 345-6611	C / 5.0	5.74	3.57	19.43 /49	4.99 /54	6.15 /29	0.60	1.06
FO	Columbia Pacific/Asia R4	CPRAX	C	(800) 345-6611	C / 4.8	5.68	3.41	19.16 /48	4.75 /51	5.95 /28	0.42	1.25
FO	Columbia Pacific/Asia W	CPAWX	C	(800) 345-6611	C / 4.6	5.53	3.25	18.88 /47	4.51 /49	5.68 /26	0.21	1.50
FO	Columbia Pacific/Asia Z	USPAX	C	(800) 345-6611	C / 4.8	5.69	3.43	19.18 /48	4.78 /52	5.97 /28	0.43	1.25
RE	Columbia Real Estate Equity A	CREAX	C	(800) 345-6611	C+ / 5.8	7.85	-2.56	13.04 /22	10.37 /95	10.19 /60	1.72	1.24
RE	● Columbia Real Estate Equity B	CREBX	C	(800) 345-6611	C+ / 6.3	7.63	-2.93	12.19 /19	9.56 /91	9.36 /53	1.09	1.99
RE	Columbia Real Estate Equity C	CRECX	C	(800) 345-6611	C+ / 6.3	7.65	-2.94	12.22 /19	9.55 /91	9.37 /54	1.09	1.99
RE	Columbia Real Estate Equity I	CREIX	C+	(800) 345-6611	B- / 7.2	7.99	-2.34	13.53 /24	10.86 /97	10.71 /63	2.22	0.80
RE	● Columbia Real Estate Equity K	CRRFX	C+	(800) 345-6611	B- / 7.0	7.86	-2.49	13.15 /22	10.52 /96	10.37 /61	1.95	1.10
RE	Columbia Real Estate Equity R	CRSRX	C+	(800) 345-6611	C+ / 6.7	7.79	-2.69	12.78 /21	10.10 /94	9.92 /58	1.58	1.49
RE	Columbia Real Estate Equity R4	CRERX	C+	(800) 345-6611	B- / 7.1	7.90	-2.40	13.35 /23	10.64 /96	10.47 /62	2.01	0.99
RE	Columbia Real Estate Equity R5	CRRVX	C+	(800) 345-6611	B- / 7.2	7.96	-2.37	13.48 /23	10.81 /97	10.58 /63	2.19	0.85
RE	Columbia Real Estate Equity W	CREWX	C+	(800) 345-6611	C+ / 6.9	7.84	-2.56	13.03 /22	10.36 /95	10.18 /60	1.81	1.24
RE	Columbia Real Estate Equity Z	CREEX	C+	(800) 345-6611	B- / 7.1	7.97	-2.43	13.36 /23	10.65 /96	10.48 /62	2.05	0.99
GL	Columbia Select Global Equity A	IGLGX	D+	(800) 345-6611	D+ / 2.7	9.43	1.91	14.84 /29	3.35 /35	7.64 /39	0.00	1.40

● Denotes fund is closed to new investors
* Denotes fund is included in Section II

www.thestreetratings.com

RISK			NET ASSETS		ASSET				Portfolio Turnover Ratio	BULL / BEAR		FUND MANAGER		MINIMUMS		LOADS	
Risk Rating/Pts	3 Year Standard Deviation	Beta	NAV As of 2/28/17	Total $(Mil)	Cash %	Stocks %	Bonds %	Other %		Last Bull Market Return	Last Bear Market Return	Manager Quality Pct	Manager Tenure (Years)	Initial Purch. $	Additional Purch. $	Front End Load	Back End Load
C / 5.1	12.1	1.00	16.00	N/A	1	98	0	1	20	138.3	-22.6	72	6	0	0	0.0	0.0
C / 5.2	12.0	1.00	16.28	748	1	98	0	1	20	138.0	-22.6	72	6	0	0	0.0	0.0
C / 5.1	12.1	1.00	15.99	2,109	1	98	0	1	20	137.8	-22.6	72	6	2,000	0	0.0	0.0
C- / 3.7	11.2	0.89	15.19	888	1	97	0	2	47	124.2	-23.2	48	13	2,000	0	5.8	0.0
C- / 3.5	11.1	0.89	14.20	1	1	97	0	2	47	115.4	-23.5	38	13	2,000	0	0.0	0.0
C- / 3.6	11.1	0.89	14.29	100	1	97	0	2	47	115.4	-23.4	38	13	2,000	0	0.0	0.0
C- / 3.7	11.1	0.89	15.20	N/A	1	97	0	2	47	129.8	-23.1	56	13	0	0	0.0	0.0
C- / 3.7	11.2	0.90	15.26	N/A	1	97	0	2	47	126.4	-23.2	50	13	0	0	0.0	0.0
C- / 3.7	11.1	0.89	15.14	54	1	97	0	2	47	121.3	-23.3	45	13	0	0	0.0	0.0
C- / 3.8	11.1	0.89	15.57	105	1	97	0	2	47	127.4	-23.1	53	13	0	0	0.0	0.0
C- / 3.8	11.1	0.89	15.57	89	1	97	0	2	47	128.7	-23.1	54	13	0	0	0.0	0.0
C- / 3.7	11.2	0.89	15.19	N/A	1	97	0	2	47	124.2	-23.2	48	13	500	0	0.0	0.0
C- / 3.7	11.1	0.89	15.20	80	1	97	0	2	47	129.4	-23.1	55	13	1,000,000	0	0.0	0.0
C- / 3.7	11.1	0.89	15.23	1,423	1	97	0	2	47	127.3	-23.1	52	13	2,000	0	0.0	0.0
C- / 3.8	15.1	0.98	12.86	2,214	1	98	0	1	39	N/A	N/A	96	5	100	0	0.0	0.0
C / 4.5	15.1	0.98	12.69	N/A	1	98	0	1	39	N/A	N/A	96	5	100	0	0.0	0.0
C+ / 6.3	10.3	0.67	13.00	2,531	3	95	0	2	67	N/A	N/A	99	1	500	0	0.0	0.0
C+ / 5.6	10.3	0.96	12.90	N/A	3	95	0	2	67	N/A	N/A	63	1	100	0	0.0	0.0
B- / 7.6	4.4	0.14	9.21	604	57	27	14	2	289	N/A	N/A	47	5	100	0	0.0	0.0
B+ / 9.1	4.4	0.14	9.19	N/A	57	27	14	2	289	N/A	N/A	47	5	100	0	0.0	0.0
C / 4.7	15.0	0.63	14.84	936	2	97	0	1	115	N/A	N/A	96	5	100	0	0.0	0.0
C / 4.5	15.0	0.95	14.77	N/A	2	97	0	1	115	N/A	N/A	64	5	100	0	0.0	0.0
U /	N/A	N/A	9.87	249	0	0	100	0	743	N/A	N/A	N/A	3	0	0	0.0	0.0
U /	N/A	N/A	9.78	126	25	9	64	2	70	N/A	N/A	N/A	2	0	0	0.0	0.0
C+ / 6.4	11.4	0.89	8.52	244	0	99	0	1	68	52.6	-22.6	73	9	2,000	100	5.8	0.0
C+ / 6.4	11.4	0.89	8.48	1	0	99	0	1	68	46.4	-22.8	64	9	2,000	100	0.0	0.0
C+ / 6.4	11.4	0.89	8.48	21	0	99	0	1	68	46.4	-22.8	64	9	2,000	100	0.0	0.0
C+ / 6.3	11.4	0.89	8.53	274	0	99	0	1	68	56.1	-22.5	77	9	0	0	0.0	0.0
C+ / 6.3	11.4	0.89	8.52	N/A	0	99	0	1	68	54.2	-22.5	75	9	0	0	0.0	0.0
C / 5.3	11.4	0.89	8.33	1	0	99	0	1	68	50.3	-22.6	71	9	0	0	0.0	0.0
B- / 7.4	11.4	0.89	8.49	24	0	99	0	1	68	54.4	-22.5	75	9	0	0	0.0	0.0
B- / 7.4	11.4	0.89	8.48	30	0	99	0	1	68	54.8	-22.5	76	9	0	0	0.0	0.0
C+ / 6.4	11.4	0.89	8.51	24	0	99	0	1	68	52.6	-22.6	73	9	500	0	0.0	0.0
B- / 7.4	11.4	0.89	8.49	14	0	99	0	1	68	55.1	-22.5	76	9	0	0	0.0	0.0
C+ / 6.3	11.4	0.89	8.53	58	0	99	0	1	68	54.5	-22.5	75	9	2,000	0	0.0	0.0
C+ / 6.3	11.9	0.76	9.48	3	6	93	0	1	73	48.9	-18.9	94	9	2,000	0	5.8	0.0
C+ / 6.3	11.9	0.76	9.31	1	6	93	0	1	73	43.1	-19.0	93	9	2,000	0	0.0	0.0
C+ / 6.3	11.8	0.75	9.51	145	6	93	0	1	73	52.6	-18.7	95	9	0	0	0.0	0.0
C+ / 6.3	11.9	0.76	9.53	N/A	6	93	0	1	73	51.0	-18.7	95	9	0	0	0.0	0.0
C+ / 6.3	11.9	0.75	9.47	N/A	6	93	0	1	73	48.8	-18.8	94	9	500	0	0.0	0.0
C+ / 6.3	11.9	0.76	9.52	62	6	93	0	1	73	51.1	-18.7	95	9	2,000	0	0.0	0.0
C / 4.9	14.7	1.07	15.89	116	1	98	0	1	32	95.8	-16.4	57	11	2,000	0	5.8	0.0
C / 4.9	14.7	1.07	15.91	1	1	98	0	1	32	88.0	-16.8	47	11	2,000	0	0.0	0.0
C / 4.9	14.7	1.07	15.87	17	1	98	0	1	32	87.9	-16.7	46	11	2,000	0	0.0	0.0
C / 4.9	14.7	1.07	15.97	132	1	98	0	1	32	100.8	-16.2	62	11	0	0	0.0	0.0
C / 4.9	14.7	1.07	15.94	N/A	1	98	0	1	32	97.5	-16.4	59	11	0	0	0.0	0.0
C / 4.8	14.8	1.07	15.87	8	1	98	0	1	32	93.2	-16.6	53	11	0	0	0.0	0.0
C / 4.9	14.7	1.07	16.19	N/A	1	98	0	1	32	98.5	-16.6	60	11	0	0	0.0	0.0
C / 4.8	14.7	1.07	15.89	8	1	98	0	1	32	99.7	-16.3	62	11	0	0	0.0	0.0
C / 4.9	14.7	1.07	15.90	N/A	1	98	0	1	32	95.7	-16.4	57	11	500	0	0.0	0.0
C / 4.9	14.7	1.07	15.93	286	1	98	0	1	32	98.6	-16.6	60	11	2,000	0	0.0	0.0
C+ / 6.4	11.2	0.78	10.68	304	1	98	0	1	66	75.4	-23.0	92	4	2,000	0	5.8	0.0

I. Index of Stock Mutual Funds

99 Pct = Best
0 Pct = Worst

Fund Type	Fund Name	Ticker Symbol	Overall Investment Rating	Phone	Performance Rating/Pts	3 Mo	6 Mo	1Yr / Pct	3Yr / Pct	5Yr / Pct	Dividend Yield	Expense Ratio
GL	● Columbia Select Global Equity B	IDGBX	C-	(800) 345-6611	C- / 3.1	9.21	1.57	13.82 /25	2.56 /28	6.83 /34	0.00	2.15
GL	Columbia Select Global Equity C	RGCEX	C-	(800) 345-6611	C- / 3.1	9.22	1.48	13.88 /25	2.56 /28	6.84 /34	0.00	2.15
GL	Columbia Select Global Equity I	CGEIX	C	(800) 345-6611	C / 4.1	9.60	2.17	15.30 /31	3.81 /41	8.13 /43	0.00	0.95
GL	● Columbia Select Global Equity K	IDGYX	C-	(800) 345-6611	C- / 3.8	9.42	1.98	14.89 /29	3.48 /37	7.82 /41	0.00	1.25
GL	Columbia Select Global Equity R	CGERX	C-	(800) 345-6611	C- / 3.5	9.31	1.81	14.47 /28	3.09 /33	7.36 /37	0.00	1.65
GL	Columbia Select Global Equity R5	RGERX	C	(800) 345-6611	C- / 4.0	9.49	2.17	15.20 /31	3.77 /40	8.09 /43	0.00	1.00
GL	Columbia Select Global Equity W	CGEWX	C-	(800) 345-6611	C- / 3.6	9.39	1.90	14.65 /28	3.26 /34	7.61 /39	0.00	1.40
GL	Columbia Select Global Equity Z	CGEZX	C-	(800) 345-6611	C- / 3.9	9.53	2.08	15.14 /30	3.60 /38	7.92 /41	0.00	1.15
GL	Columbia Select Global Growth A	COGAX	D-	(800) 345-6611	D / 2.2	7.24	0.08	18.89 /47	2.20 /25	9.87 /57	0.00	1.56
GL	Columbia Select Global Growth C	COGCX	D-	(800) 345-6611	D+ / 2.6	7.02	-0.34	17.86 /42	1.43 /21	9.05 /51	0.00	2.31
GL	Columbia Select Global Growth R	COGRX	D-	(800) 345-6611	C- / 3.0	7.20	0.00	18.63 /46	1.97 /24	9.61 /55	0.00	1.81
GL	Columbia Select Global Growth R4	CADHX	D	(800) 345-6611	C- / 3.3	7.28	0.24	19.15 /48	2.46 /27	10.03 /59	0.00	1.31
GL	Columbia Select Global Growth R5	CADIX	D	(800) 345-6611	C- / 3.3	7.26	0.24	19.20 /48	2.53 /28	10.07 /59	0.00	1.20
GL	Columbia Select Global Growth Z	COGZX	D	(800) 345-6611	C- / 3.3	7.28	0.16	19.14 /48	2.46 /27	10.14 /59	0.00	1.15
FO	Columbia Select Intl Eqty A	NIIAX	E+	(800) 345-6611	E- / 0.2	6.49	2.59	8.98 / 9	-3.60 / 4	1.94 / 8	1.01	1.42
FO	● Columbia Select Intl Eqty B	NIENX	E+	(800) 345-6611	E / 0.3	6.23	2.25	8.12 / 8	-4.34 / 3	1.17 / 6	0.29	2.17
FO	Columbia Select Intl Eqty C	NITRX	E+	(800) 345-6611	E / 0.3	6.21	2.18	8.02 / 7	-4.34 / 3	1.16 / 6	0.29	2.17
FO	Columbia Select Intl Eqty I	CUAIX	D-	(800) 345-6611	E / 0.5	6.62	2.83	9.91 /11	-3.00 / 4	2.51 / 9	1.49	0.94
FO	● Columbia Select Intl Eqty K	CMEFX	D-	(800) 345-6611	E / 0.4	6.45	2.62	9.08 /10	-3.46 / 4	2.11 / 8	1.23	1.24
FO	Columbia Select Intl Eqty R	CIERX	D-	(800) 345-6611	E / 0.3	6.36	2.43	8.66 / 9	-3.85 / 3	1.70 / 7	0.81	1.67
FO	Columbia Select Intl Eqty R4	CQYRX	D-	(800) 345-6611	E / 0.4	6.49	2.68	9.18 /10	-3.38 / 4	2.18 / 8	1.29	1.17
FO	Columbia Select Intl Eqty R5	CQQRX	D-	(800) 345-6611	E / 0.4	6.54	2.75	9.33 /10	-3.20 / 4	2.34 / 9	1.46	0.99
FO	Columbia Select Intl Eqty W	CMAWX	D-	(800) 345-6611	E / 0.4	6.49	2.59	8.88 / 9	-3.60 / 4	1.94 / 8	1.07	1.42
FO	Columbia Select Intl Eqty Y	CMIYX	D-	(800) 345-6611	E / 0.5	6.56	2.84	9.42 /10	-3.14 / 4	2.43 / 9	1.53	0.94
FO	Columbia Select Intl Eqty Z	NIEQX	D-	(800) 345-6611	E / 0.4	6.53	2.70	9.25 /10	-3.35 / 4	2.20 / 8	1.31	1.17
GR	Columbia Select Large Cap Equity A	NSGAX	B	(800) 345-6611	B / 8.1	7.73	9.94	23.66 /69	10.17 /94	13.32 /87	0.81	1.24
GR	● Columbia Select Large Cap Equity B	NSIBX	B+	(800) 345-6611	B+ / 8.5	7.50	9.50	22.64 /65	9.32 /89	12.46 /79	0.29	1.99
GR	Columbia Select Large Cap Equity C	NSGCX	B+	(800) 345-6611	B+ / 8.5	7.50	9.50	22.66 /65	9.32 /89	12.47 /79	0.29	1.99
GR	Columbia Select Large Cap Equity I	CLPIX	A-	(800) 345-6611	A / 9.3	7.86	10.17	24.07 /70	10.59 /96	13.78 /91	1.21	0.81
GR	Columbia Select Large Cap Equity R5	CLCRX	A-	(800) 345-6611	A / 9.3	7.79	10.13	24.09 /70	10.55 /96	13.71 /91	1.15	0.86
GR	Columbia Select Large Cap Equity W	CLCWX	A-	(800) 345-6611	A- / 9.0	7.74	9.94	23.57 /68	10.15 /94	13.33 /87	0.86	1.24
GR	Columbia Select Large Cap Equity Z	NSEPX	A-	(800) 345-6611	A- / 9.2	7.75	10.06	23.83 /69	10.42 /95	13.59 /90	1.09	0.99
GR	Columbia Select Large Cap Gr A	ELGAX	D-	(800) 345-6611	C / 4.4	10.74	3.58	23.77 /69	3.91 /42	11.44 /69	0.00	1.07
GR	Columbia Select Large Cap Gr C	ELGCX	D-	(800) 345-6611	C / 4.9	10.55	3.18	22.90 /66	3.14 /33	10.63 /63	0.00	1.82
GR	Columbia Select Large Cap Gr I	CSPIX	D	(800) 345-6611	C+ / 6.0	10.90	3.83	24.33 /71	4.36 /47	11.94 /74	0.00	0.65
GR	Columbia Select Large Cap Gr R	URLGX	D-	(800) 345-6611	C / 5.4	10.66	3.43	23.55 /68	3.66 /39	11.18 /67	0.00	1.32
GR	Columbia Select Large Cap Gr R4	CSRRX	D	(800) 345-6611	C+ / 5.8	10.83	3.72	24.09 /70	4.17 /45	11.74 /72	0.00	0.82
GR	Columbia Select Large Cap Gr R5	CGTRX	D	(800) 345-6611	C+ / 5.9	10.80	3.71	24.25 /71	4.30 /46	11.86 /73	0.00	0.70
GR	Columbia Select Large Cap Gr W	CSLWX	D	(800) 345-6611	C+ / 5.6	10.74	3.58	23.77 /69	3.90 /42	11.44 /69	0.00	1.07
GR	Columbia Select Large Cap Gr Y	CCWRX	D	(800) 345-6611	C+ / 6.0	10.83	3.73	24.26 /71	4.34 /47	11.92 /74	0.00	0.65
GR	Columbia Select Large Cap Gr Z	UMLGX	D	(800) 345-6611	C+ / 5.8	10.75	3.68	24.07 /70	4.16 /45	11.73 /72	0.00	0.82
GR	Columbia Select Large-Cap Value A	SLVAX	A	(800) 345-6611	A- / 9.2	7.16	14.96	34.96 /94	9.23 /88	14.01 /93	0.97	1.20
GR	● Columbia Select Large-Cap Value B	SLVBX	A	(800) 345-6611	A / 9.5	6.96	14.51	33.99 /93	8.41 /82	13.16 /85	0.43	1.95
GR	Columbia Select Large-Cap Value C	SVLCX	A	(800) 345-6611	A / 9.5	6.97	14.52	34.01 /93	8.41 /82	13.17 /86	0.43	1.95
GR	Columbia Select Large-Cap Value I	CLVIX	A+	(800) 345-6611	A+ / 9.7	7.29	15.17	35.53 /94	9.66 /91	14.47 /95	1.31	0.79
GR	● Columbia Select Large-Cap Value K	SLVTX	A+	(800) 345-6611	A+ / 9.7	7.17	14.98	35.13 /94	9.33 /89	14.13 /94	1.08	1.09
GR	Columbia Select Large-Cap Value R	SLVRX	A+	(800) 345-6611	A+ / 9.6	7.12	14.79	34.67 /94	8.96 /87	13.74 /91	0.83	1.45
GI	Columbia Select Large-Cap Value R4	CSERX	A+	(800) 345-6611	A+ / 9.7	7.23	15.11	35.32 /94	9.51 /90	14.27 /95	1.18	0.95
GR	Columbia Select Large-Cap Value R5	SLVIX	A+	(800) 345-6611	A+ / 9.7	7.23	15.14	35.42 /94	9.59 /91	14.42 /95	1.27	0.84
GR	Columbia Select Large-Cap Value W	CSVWX	A+	(800) 345-6611	A+ / 9.7	7.16	14.95	35.01 /94	9.24 /88	13.99 /93	1.03	1.20
GI	Columbia Select Large-Cap Value Y	CSRYX	A+	(800) 345-6611	A+ / 9.7	7.30	15.20	35.51 /94	9.61 /91	14.25 /94	1.29	0.79
GR	Columbia Select Large-Cap Value Z	CSVZX	A+	(800) 345-6611	A+ / 9.7	7.24	15.06	35.33 /94	9.50 /90	14.29 /95	1.20	0.95

● Denotes fund is closed to new investors
* Denotes fund is included in Section II

www.thestreetratings.com

RISK Rating/Pts	3 Year Standard Deviation	Beta	NAV As of 2/28/17	Total $(Mil)	Cash %	Stocks %	Bonds %	Other %	Portfolio Turnover Ratio	Last Bull Market Return	Last Bear Market Return	Manager Quality Pct	Manager Tenure (Years)	Initial Purch. $	Additional Purch. $	Front End Load	Back End Load
C+ / 6.4	11.1	0.77	9.72	1	1	98	0	1	66	68.5	-23.4	89	4	2,000	0	0.0	0.0
C+ / 6.4	11.2	0.77	9.60	13	1	98	0	1	66	68.4	-23.3	89	4	2,000	0	0.0	0.0
C+ / 6.5	11.1	0.77	10.85	63	1	98	0	1	66	79.9	-23.0	93	4	0	0	0.0	0.0
C+ / 6.5	11.1	0.77	10.80	N/A	1	98	0	1	66	77.2	-23.1	92	4	0	0	0.0	0.0
C+ / 6.4	11.1	0.77	10.68	N/A	1	98	0	1	66	73.1	-23.2	91	4	0	0	0.0	0.0
C+ / 6.5	11.1	0.77	10.84	N/A	1	98	0	1	66	79.6	-23.1	93	4	0	0	0.0	0.0
C+ / 6.5	11.1	0.77	10.72	N/A	1	98	0	1	66	75.1	-23.1	91	4	500	0	0.0	0.0
C+ / 6.5	11.2	0.77	10.80	3	1	98	0	1	66	78.0	-23.1	92	4	2,000	0	0.0	0.0
C- / 4.0	13.8	0.92	12.44	36	1	98	0	1	154	93.1	-23.6	88	2	2,000	0	5.8	0.0
C- / 3.8	13.8	0.92	11.74	11	1	98	0	1	154	85.6	-23.9	84	2	2,000	0	0.0	0.0
C- / 3.9	13.8	0.92	12.21	1	1	98	0	1	154	90.6	-23.7	87	2	0	0	0.0	0.0
C- / 4.0	13.8	0.92	12.67	2	1	98	0	1	154	94.5	-23.6	89	2	0	0	0.0	0.0
C- / 4.0	13.8	0.92	12.70	N/A	1	98	0	1	154	94.9	-23.6	89	2	100,000	0	0.0	0.0
C- / 4.0	13.8	0.92	12.67	6	1	98	0	1	154	95.8	-23.6	89	2	2,000	0	0.0	0.0
C+ / 5.9	12.2	0.95	12.30	221	1	98	0	1	131	32.6	-25.2	29	2	2,000	0	5.8	0.0
C+ / 5.8	12.2	0.95	10.91	N/A	1	98	0	1	131	27.2	-25.5	21	2	2,000	0	0.0	0.0
C+ / 5.8	12.2	0.95	10.77	14	1	98	0	1	131	27.2	-25.4	21	2	2,000	0	0.0	0.0
C+ / 5.9	12.1	0.95	12.72	N/A	1	98	0	1	131	36.5	-25.0	36	2	0	0	0.0	0.0
C+ / 5.9	12.2	0.95	12.54	N/A	1	98	0	1	131	33.7	-25.1	30	2	0	0	0.0	0.0
C+ / 5.8	12.2	0.95	12.20	1	1	98	0	1	131	30.8	-25.3	26	2	0	0	0.0	0.0
C+ / 5.9	12.2	0.96	12.64	N/A	1	98	0	1	131	34.3	-25.1	31	2	0	0	0.0	0.0
C+ / 5.9	12.2	0.95	12.70	N/A	1	98	0	1	131	35.3	-25.1	33	2	0	0	0.0	0.0
C+ / 5.8	12.2	0.95	12.30	19	1	98	0	1	131	32.5	-25.2	29	2	500	0	0.0	0.0
C+ / 5.9	12.2	0.95	12.67	10	1	98	0	1	131	36.0	-25.0	34	2	0	0	0.0	0.0
C+ / 5.9	12.2	0.95	12.57	70	1	98	0	1	131	34.4	-25.1	31	2	2,000	0	0.0	0.0
C / 5.5	10.7	1.02	13.16	137	2	96	0	2	102	128.2	-18.1	67	13	2,000	0	5.8	0.0
C / 5.4	10.6	1.02	12.19	N/A	2	96	0	2	102	119.2	-18.5	57	13	2,000	0	0.0	0.0
C / 5.4	10.7	1.02	12.18	6	2	96	0	2	102	119.1	-18.4	57	13	2,000	0	0.0	0.0
C / 5.5	10.6	1.02	13.08	304	2	96	0	2	102	133.2	-18.1	72	13	0	0	0.0	0.0
C / 5.5	10.7	1.02	13.41	N/A	2	96	0	2	102	132.4	-18.1	71	13	0	0	0.0	0.0
C / 5.5	10.7	1.02	13.15	N/A	2	96	0	2	102	128.3	-18.2	67	13	500	0	0.0	0.0
C / 5.5	10.7	1.02	13.06	160	2	96	0	2	102	131.3	-18.1	70	13	2,000	0	0.0	0.0
D / 1.9	17.2	1.30	14.98	956	0	99	0	1	56	109.6	-18.6	3	14	2,000	0	5.8	0.0
D / 1.6	17.2	1.30	13.66	163	0	99	0	1	56	101.4	-18.9	2	14	2,000	0	0.0	0.0
D / 1.9	17.2	1.30	15.59	167	0	99	0	1	56	114.7	-18.5	3	14	0	0	0.0	0.0
D / 1.7	17.2	1.30	14.16	14	0	99	0	1	56	106.9	-18.7	2	14	0	0	0.0	0.0
D / 2.0	17.2	1.31	15.78	26	0	99	0	1	56	112.6	-18.6	3	14	0	0	0.0	0.0
D / 2.0	17.2	1.31	15.84	698	0	99	0	1	56	113.7	-18.6	3	14	0	0	0.0	0.0
D / 1.9	17.2	1.30	14.98	2	0	99	0	1	56	109.6	-18.6	3	14	500	0	0.0	0.0
D / 2.0	17.2	1.30	15.99	23	0	99	0	1	56	114.3	-18.6	3	14	0	0	0.0	0.0
D / 1.9	17.2	1.30	15.38	2,550	0	99	0	1	56	112.5	-18.6	3	14	2,000	0	0.0	0.0
C+ / 5.9	12.6	1.15	23.94	240	1	98	0	1	13	144.2	-22.6	38	20	2,000	0	5.8	0.0
C+ / 5.9	12.6	1.15	22.06	1	1	98	0	1	13	134.3	-22.8	29	20	2,000	0	0.0	0.0
C+ / 5.9	12.6	1.15	22.05	73	1	98	0	1	13	134.4	-22.9	29	20	2,000	0	0.0	0.0
C+ / 5.9	12.6	1.15	24.76	124	1	98	0	1	13	149.7	-22.5	44	20	0	0	0.0	0.0
C+ / 5.9	12.6	1.15	24.68	N/A	1	98	0	1	13	145.6	-22.6	39	20	0	0	0.0	0.0
C+ / 5.9	12.6	1.15	23.59	24	1	98	0	1	13	140.8	-22.7	35	20	0	0	0.0	0.0
C+ / 5.9	12.6	1.15	25.09	29	1	98	0	1	13	146.9	-22.6	41	20	0	0	0.0	0.0
C+ / 5.9	12.6	1.15	24.79	27	1	98	0	1	13	148.8	-22.5	43	20	0	0	0.0	0.0
C+ / 5.9	12.5	1.14	23.80	6	1	98	0	1	13	143.9	-22.6	38	20	500	0	0.0	0.0
C+ / 6.6	12.6	1.15	25.15	1	1	98	0	1	13	146.7	-22.6	43	20	0	0	0.0	0.0
C+ / 5.9	12.5	1.14	24.78	252	1	98	0	1	13	147.4	-22.5	42	20	2,000	0	0.0	0.0

99 Pct = Best
0 Pct = Worst

Fund Type	Fund Name	Ticker Symbol	Overall Investment Rating	Phone	Performance Rating/Pts	3 Mo	6 Mo	1Yr / Pct	3Yr / Pct	5Yr / Pct	Dividend Yield	Expense Ratio
SC	Columbia Select Smaller-Cap Val A	SSCVX	D	(800) 345-6611	C / 5.0	5.44	9.19	23.87 /69	4.91 /53	11.73 /72	0.00	1.33
SC	● Columbia Select Smaller-Cap Val B	SSCBX	D	(800) 345-6611	C / 5.5	5.26	8.80	22.96 /66	4.14 /44	10.89 /65	0.00	2.08
SC	Columbia Select Smaller-Cap Val C	SVMCX	D	(800) 345-6611	C / 5.5	5.25	8.78	22.91 /66	4.13 /44	10.89 /65	0.00	2.08
SC	Columbia Select Smaller-Cap Val I	CSSIX	C-	(800) 345-6611	C+ / 6.5	5.56	9.40	24.37 /71	5.38 /58	12.23 /76	0.00	0.90
SC	● Columbia Select Smaller-Cap Val K	SSLRX	C-	(800) 345-6611	C+ / 6.3	5.42	9.20	23.95 /70	5.05 /55	11.88 /73	0.00	1.20
SC	Columbia Select Smaller-Cap Val R	SSVRX	D+	(800) 345-6611	C+ / 6.0	5.39	9.09	23.56 /68	4.65 /50	11.45 /69	0.00	1.58
SC	Columbia Select Smaller-Cap Val R4	CSPRX	C-	(800) 345-6611	C+ / 6.4	5.53	9.32	24.17 /70	5.17 /56	11.97 /74	0.00	1.08
SC	Columbia Select Smaller-Cap Val R5	SSVIX	C-	(800) 345-6611	C+ / 6.5	5.54	9.40	24.32 /71	5.32 /58	12.16 /76	0.00	0.95
SC	Columbia Select Smaller-Cap Val Y	CSSYX	C+	(800) 345-6611	C+ / 6.5	5.54	9.39	24.34 /71	5.26 /57	11.94 /74	0.00	0.90
SC	Columbia Select Smaller-Cap Val Z	CSSZX	C-	(800) 345-6611	C+ / 6.4	5.50	9.29	24.15 /70	5.18 /56	12.01 /74	0.00	1.08
TC	Columbia Seligman Comm & Info A	SLMCX	B+	(800) 345-6611	A+ / 9.9	12.18	16.62	35.52 /94	19.14 /99	14.82 /96	0.00	1.35
TC	● Columbia Seligman Comm & Info B	SLMBX	B	(800) 345-6611	A+ / 9.9	12.19	16.63	35.52 /94	19.14 /99	14.68 /96	0.00	2.10
TC	Columbia Seligman Comm & Info C	SCICX	B	(800) 345-6611	A+ / 9.9	11.97	16.20	34.52 /93	18.25 /99	13.97 /93	0.00	2.10
TC	Columbia Seligman Comm & Info I	CSFIX	B+	(800) 345-6611	A+ / 9.9	12.29	16.83	36.08 /95	19.65 /99	15.31 /97	0.00	0.92
TC	● Columbia Seligman Comm & Info K	SCIFX	B+	(800) 345-6611	A+ / 9.9	12.18	16.65	35.63 /95	19.27 /99	14.96 /97	0.00	1.22
TC	Columbia Seligman Comm & Info R	SCIRX	B+	(800) 345-6611	A+ / 9.9	12.11	16.48	35.18 /94	18.84 /99	14.54 /96	0.00	1.60
TC	Columbia Seligman Comm & Info R4	SCIOX	B+	(800) 345-6611	A+ / 9.9	12.25	16.77	35.84 /95	19.44 /99	15.05 /97	0.00	1.10
TC	Columbia Seligman Comm & Info R5	SCMIX	B+	(800) 345-6611	A+ / 9.9	12.26	16.79	35.98 /95	19.58 /99	15.25 /97	0.00	0.97
TC	Columbia Seligman Comm & Info Z	CCIZX	B+	(800) 345-6611	A+ / 9.9	12.25	16.77	35.85 /95	19.43 /99	15.11 /97	0.00	1.10
TC	Columbia Seligman Global Tech A	SHGTX	A-	(800) 345-6611	A+ / 9.9	12.07	16.46	36.39 /95	19.38 /99	15.63 /98	0.00	1.42
TC	● Columbia Seligman Global Tech B	SHTBX	B+	(800) 345-6611	A+ / 9.9	11.89	16.03	35.39 /94	18.48 /99	14.76 /96	0.00	2.17
TC	Columbia Seligman Global Tech C	SHTCX	B+	(800) 345-6611	A+ / 9.9	11.89	16.03	35.35 /94	18.49 /99	14.77 /96	0.00	2.17
TC	Columbia Seligman Global Tech I	CSYIX	A-	(800) 345-6611	A+ / 9.9	12.19	16.68	36.92 /96	19.88 /99	16.13 /98	0.00	0.97
TC	● Columbia Seligman Global Tech K	SGTSX	A-	(800) 345-6611	A+ / 9.9	12.09	16.51	36.54 /95	19.53 /99	15.80 /98	0.00	1.27
TC	Columbia Seligman Global Tech R	SGTRX	A-	(800) 345-6611	A+ / 9.9	12.01	16.30	36.04 /95	19.07 /99	15.33 /97	0.00	1.67
TC	Columbia Seligman Global Tech R4	CCHRX	A-	(800) 345-6611	A+ / 9.9	12.15	16.59	36.73 /96	19.66 /99	15.88 /98	0.00	1.17
TC	Columbia Seligman Global Tech R5	SGTTX	A-	(800) 345-6611	A+ / 9.9	12.16	16.64	36.88 /96	19.85 /99	16.10 /98	0.00	1.02
TC	Columbia Seligman Global Tech Z	CSGZX	A-	(800) 345-6611	A+ / 9.9	12.13	16.56	36.71 /96	19.66 /99	15.92 /98	0.00	1.17
SC	Columbia Small Cap Growth I A	CGOAX	E+	(800) 345-6611	C+ / 5.7	5.96	11.23	32.08 /90	3.72 /39	10.39 /61	0.00	1.41
SC	● Columbia Small Cap Growth I B	CGOBX	D-	(800) 345-6611	C+ / 6.2	5.76	10.86	31.16 /88	2.94 /31	9.57 /55	0.00	2.16
SC	Columbia Small Cap Growth I C	CGOCX	D-	(800) 345-6611	C+ / 6.2	5.76	10.78	31.16 /88	2.94 /31	9.57 /55	0.00	2.16
SC	Columbia Small Cap Growth I I	CSWIX	D	(800) 345-6611	B- / 7.1	6.10	11.51	32.63 /91	4.19 /45	10.89 /65	0.00	0.97
SC	● Columbia Small Cap Growth I K	CSCKX	D-	(800) 345-6611	C+ / 6.9	5.98	11.27	32.28 /90	3.87 /41	10.57 /63	0.00	1.27
SC	Columbia Small Cap Growth I R	CCRIX	D-	(800) 345-6611	C+ / 6.6	5.93	11.10	31.80 /90	3.47 /37	10.12 /59	0.00	1.66
SC	Columbia Small Cap Growth I R4	CHHRX	D-	(800) 345-6611	C+ / 6.9	6.09	11.38	32.45 /91	3.99 /43	10.69 /63	0.00	1.16
SC	Columbia Small Cap Growth I R5	CSCRX	D	(800) 345-6611	B- / 7.1	6.07	11.46	32.57 /91	4.23 /46	10.86 /65	0.00	1.02
SC	Columbia Small Cap Growth I Y	CSGYX	D	(800) 345-6611	B- / 7.1	6.06	11.47	32.62 /91	4.16 /45	10.87 /65	0.00	0.97
SC	Columbia Small Cap Growth I Z	CMSCX	D-	(800) 345-6611	C+ / 6.9	6.07	11.40	32.43 /91	3.99 /43	10.67 /63	0.00	1.16
SC	Columbia Small Cap Index A	NMSAX	B+	(800) 345-6611	A / 9.5	4.49	12.92	34.40 /93	9.18 /88	14.39 /95	0.75	0.45
SC	● Columbia Small Cap Index B	CIDBX	B+	(800) 345-6611	A- / 9.1	4.29	12.46	33.37 /92	8.36 /82	13.53 /89	0.16	1.20
SC	Columbia Small Cap Index I	CSIIX	B+	(800) 345-6611	A+ / 9.6	4.54	13.05	34.76 /94	9.49 /90	14.70 /96	0.96	0.20
SC	● Columbia Small Cap Index K	CIDUX	B+	(800) 345-6611	A / 9.5	4.47	12.87	34.37 /93	9.17 /88	14.38 /95	0.75	0.45
SC	Columbia Small Cap Index R5	CXXRX	B+	(800) 345-6611	A+ / 9.6	4.56	13.03	34.73 /94	9.45 /90	14.64 /96	0.93	0.20
SC	Columbia Small Cap Index W	CSMWX	A-	(800) 345-6611	A / 9.5	4.48	12.93	34.41 /93	9.19 /88	14.40 /95	0.75	0.45
SC	Columbia Small Cap Index Z	NMSCX	B+	(800) 345-6611	A+ / 9.6	4.57	13.05	34.74 /94	9.46 /90	14.67 /96	0.95	0.20
SC	Columbia Small Cap Value I A	CSMIX	B	(800) 345-6611	A+ / 9.6	5.49	16.48	43.51 /98	8.75 /85	12.35 /78	0.31	1.35
SC	● Columbia Small Cap Value I B	CSSBX	C+	(800) 345-6611	A+ / 9.7	5.31	16.04	42.47 /98	7.93 /78	11.51 /70	0.00	2.10
SC	Columbia Small Cap Value I C	CSSCX	C+	(800) 345-6611	A+ / 9.7	5.29	16.06	42.45 /98	7.94 /78	11.52 /70	0.00	2.10
SC	Columbia Small Cap Value I I	CVUIX	B	(800) 345-6611	A+ / 9.8	5.60	16.74	44.14 /98	9.24 /88	12.86 /82	0.61	0.90
SC	Columbia Small Cap Value I R	CSVRX	B	(800) 345-6611	A+ / 9.7	5.43	16.35	43.16 /98	8.49 /83	12.08 /75	0.19	1.60
SC	Columbia Small Cap Value I R4	CVVRX	B	(800) 345-6611	A+ / 9.8	5.56	16.65	43.90 /98	9.03 /87	12.61 /80	0.45	1.10
SC	Columbia Small Cap Value I R5	CUURX	B	(800) 345-6611	A+ / 9.8	5.60	16.72	44.11 /98	9.19 /88	12.75 /81	0.56	0.95

● Denotes fund is closed to new investors
* Denotes fund is included in Section II

164

Risk Rating/Pts	Standard Deviation	Beta	NAV As of 2/28/17	Total $(Mil)	Cash %	Stocks %	Bonds %	Other %	Portfolio Turnover Ratio	Last Bull Market Return	Last Bear Market Return	Manager Quality Pct	Manager Tenure (Years)	Initial Purch. $	Additional Purch. $	Front End Load	Back End Load
C- /3.4	15.8	0.96	18.50	540	1	98	0	1	27	129.1	-27.7	54	20	2,000	0	5.8	0.0
D+ /2.6	15.8	0.96	14.08	2	1	98	0	1	27	120.0	-27.9	43	20	2,000	0	0.0	0.0
D+ /2.7	15.8	0.96	14.11	40	1	98	0	1	27	120.1	-28.0	43	20	2,000	0	0.0	0.0
C- /3.7	15.8	0.96	21.14	14	1	98	0	1	27	134.9	-27.6	60	20	0	0	0.0	0.0
C- /3.6	15.8	0.96	20.51	1	1	98	0	1	27	131.0	-27.6	56	20	0	0	0.0	0.0
C- /3.2	15.8	0.96	17.50	12	1	98	0	1	27	126.0	-27.7	50	20	0	0	0.0	0.0
C- /3.7	15.8	0.96	21.08	5	1	98	0	1	27	131.6	-27.7	57	20	0	0	0.0	0.0
C- /3.7	15.8	0.96	21.02	18	1	98	0	1	27	134.1	-27.6	59	20	0	0	0.0	0.0
C+ /5.7	15.8	0.96	21.62	N/A	1	98	0	1	27	131.3	-27.7	58	20	0	0	0.0	0.0
C- /3.7	15.8	0.96	20.78	85	1	98	0	1	27	132.2	-27.6	57	20	2,000	0	0.0	0.0
C /4.4	15.1	1.12	65.38	3,224	3	96	0	1	48	153.9	-17.5	97	27	2,000	0	5.8	0.0
C- /3.5	15.1	1.12	47.19	9	3	96	0	1	48	151.5	-17.7	97	27	2,000	0	0.0	0.0
C- /3.7	15.1	1.12	47.13	880	3	96	0	1	48	143.8	-17.7	96	27	2,000	0	0.0	0.0
C /4.4	15.1	1.12	71.02	N/A	3	96	0	1	48	159.9	-17.3	97	27	0	0	0.0	0.0
C /4.4	15.1	1.12	69.61	N/A	3	96	0	1	48	155.6	-17.4	97	27	0	0	0.0	0.0
C /4.3	15.1	1.12	62.58	62	3	96	0	1	48	150.5	-17.6	97	27	0	0	0.0	0.0
C- /4.2	15.1	1.12	63.59	55	3	96	0	1	48	156.3	-17.5	97	27	0	0	0.0	0.0
C /4.4	15.1	1.12	70.80	104	3	96	0	1	48	159.1	-17.3	97	27	0	0	0.0	0.0
C /4.5	15.1	1.12	70.55	525	3	96	0	1	48	157.4	-17.4	97	27	2,000	0	0.0	0.0
C /4.7	15.0	1.11	34.91	631	3	96	0	1	55	159.7	-17.8	97	23	2,000	0	5.8	0.0
C /4.4	15.0	1.11	27.54	2	3	96	0	1	55	149.3	-18.0	97	23	2,000	0	0.0	0.0
C /4.4	15.0	1.11	27.53	119	3	96	0	1	55	149.4	-18.1	97	23	2,000	0	0.0	0.0
C /4.7	15.0	1.11	35.81	N/A	3	96	0	1	55	166.1	-17.6	98	23	0	0	0.0	0.0
C /4.7	15.0	1.11	35.28	N/A	3	96	0	1	55	162.1	-17.7	97	23	0	0	0.0	0.0
C /4.7	15.0	1.11	33.74	11	3	96	0	1	55	156.2	-17.9	97	23	0	0	0.0	0.0
C /4.7	15.0	1.11	35.99	11	3	96	0	1	55	162.6	-17.8	98	23	0	0	0.0	0.0
C /4.7	15.0	1.11	35.65	5	3	96	0	1	55	165.2	-17.6	98	23	0	0	0.0	0.0
C /4.7	15.0	1.11	35.48	78	3	96	0	1	55	163.3	-17.7	98	23	2,000	0	0.0	0.0
E /0.3	17.0	0.99	17.68	181	7	92	0	1	142	106.4	-28.5	35	11	2,000	0	5.8	0.0
E /0.3	17.0	0.99	14.91	N/A	7	92	0	1	142	98.3	-28.7	27	11	2,000	0	0.0	0.0
E /0.3	17.0	0.99	14.91	14	7	92	0	1	142	98.3	-28.7	26	11	2,000	0	0.0	0.0
E /0.3	17.0	0.99	18.96	35	7	92	0	1	142	111.5	-28.4	41	11	0	0	0.0	0.0
E /0.3	17.0	0.99	18.47	N/A	7	92	0	1	142	108.3	-28.4	37	11	0	0	0.0	0.0
E /0.3	17.0	0.98	17.38	1	7	92	0	1	142	103.7	-28.6	32	11	0	0	0.0	0.0
E /0.3	17.0	0.98	19.41	2	7	92	0	1	142	109.4	-28.4	39	11	0	0	0.0	0.0
E /0.3	17.0	0.99	18.76	14	7	92	0	1	142	111.0	-28.4	42	11	0	0	0.0	0.0
E /0.3	17.0	0.99	18.92	12	7	92	0	1	142	111.3	-28.3	41	11	0	0	0.0	0.0
E /0.3	17.0	0.98	18.60	149	7	92	0	1	142	109.3	-28.4	39	11	0	0	0.0	0.0
C /4.7	14.7	0.92	23.83	1,638	2	97	0	1	19	149.3	-22.2	89	6	2,000	0	0.0	0.0
C /4.7	14.7	0.92	23.63	2	2	97	0	1	19	139.2	-22.4	85	6	2,000	0	0.0	0.0
C /4.7	14.7	0.92	23.87	N/A	2	97	0	1	19	152.9	-22.2	90	6	0	0	0.0	0.0
C /4.7	14.7	0.92	23.92	5	2	97	0	1	19	149.2	-22.2	89	6	0	0	0.0	0.0
C /4.7	14.7	0.92	24.43	437	2	97	0	1	19	152.1	-22.2	90	6	0	0	0.0	0.0
C /5.5	14.7	0.92	23.63	13	2	97	0	1	19	149.4	-22.2	89	6	500	0	0.0	0.0
C /4.7	14.7	0.92	23.96	1,668	2	97	0	1	19	152.7	-22.1	90	6	2,000	0	0.0	0.0
C- /3.4	16.6	0.99	41.81	262	0	99	0	1	65	121.9	-24.0	85	12	2,000	0	5.8	0.0
D /2.2	16.6	0.99	26.37	N/A	0	99	0	1	65	113.1	-24.3	81	12	2,000	0	0.0	0.0
D+ /2.6	16.6	0.99	30.04	30	0	99	0	1	65	113.1	-24.3	81	12	2,000	0	0.0	0.0
C- /3.6	16.6	0.99	45.99	59	0	99	0	1	65	127.4	-23.9	87	12	0	0	0.0	0.0
C- /3.4	16.6	0.99	41.84	3	0	99	0	1	65	119.1	-24.1	84	12	0	0	0.0	0.0
C- /3.7	16.6	0.99	47.09	6	0	99	0	1	65	124.5	-24.0	86	12	0	0	0.0	0.0
C- /3.7	16.6	0.99	47.07	9	0	99	0	1	65	125.9	-24.0	87	12	0	0	0.0	0.0

Fund Type	Fund Name	Ticker Symbol	Overall Investment Rating	Phone	Performance Rating/Pts	3 Mo	6 Mo	1Yr / Pct	3Yr / Pct	5Yr / Pct	Dividend Yield	Expense Ratio
	99 Pct = Best 0 Pct = Worst							Total Return % through 2/28/17	Annualized		Incl. in Returns	
SC	Columbia Small Cap Value I Y	CSVYX	B	(800) 345-6611	A+ / 9.8	5.62	16.75	44.16 /98	9.25 /88	12.87 /82	0.60	0.90
SC	Columbia Small Cap Value I Z	CSCZX	B	(800) 345-6611	A+ / 9.8	5.57	16.65	43.89 /98	9.03 /87	12.63 /80	0.46	1.10
SC	● Columbia Small Cap Value II A	COVAX	B	(800) 345-6611	B+ / 8.5	5.13	15.39	34.98 /94	7.95 /79	13.39 /88	0.16	1.27
SC	● Columbia Small Cap Value II B	COVBX	B	(800) 345-6611	B+ / 8.9	4.98	14.97	33.99 /93	7.14 /73	12.56 /80	0.02	2.02
SC	● Columbia Small Cap Value II C	COVCX	B	(800) 345-6611	B+ / 8.9	4.93	14.91	33.93 /93	7.12 /73	12.55 /79	0.02	2.02
SC	Columbia Small Cap Value II I	CSLIX	B+	(800) 345-6611	A / 9.5	5.23	15.66	35.53 /94	8.45 /82	13.92 /93	0.54	0.84
SC	Columbia Small Cap Value II R	CCTRX	B	(800) 345-6611	A- / 9.2	5.07	15.26	34.67 /94	7.68 /77	13.12 /85	0.08	1.52
SC	Columbia Small Cap Value II R4	CLURX	B+	(800) 345-6611	A / 9.4	5.20	15.52	35.21 /94	8.21 /81	13.63 /90	0.35	1.02
SC	Columbia Small Cap Value II R5	CRRRX	B+	(800) 345-6611	A / 9.5	5.24	15.62	35.42 /94	8.36 /82	13.77 /91	0.47	0.89
SC	Columbia Small Cap Value II Y	CRRYX	B+	(800) 345-6611	A / 9.5	5.27	15.62	35.55 /95	8.42 /82	13.83 /92	0.51	0.84
SC	● Columbia Small Cap Value II Z	NSVAX	B+	(800) 345-6611	A / 9.5	5.19	15.51	35.26 /94	8.22 /81	13.69 /91	0.37	1.02
MC	Columbia Small/Mid Cap Value A	AMVAX	C	(800) 345-6611	B / 7.6	7.32	15.21	33.01 /92	6.08 /65	11.77 /72	0.22	1.25
MC	● Columbia Small/Mid Cap Value B	AMVBX	C	(800) 345-6611	B / 7.9	7.06	14.63	31.84 /90	5.26 /57	10.93 /65	0.00	2.00
MC	Columbia Small/Mid Cap Value C	AMVCX	C+	(800) 345-6611	B / 7.9	7.07	14.65	31.88 /90	5.27 /57	10.94 /65	0.00	2.00
MC	Columbia Small/Mid Cap Value I	RMCIX	B-	(800) 345-6611	B+ / 8.9	7.37	15.37	33.54 /92	6.50 /68	12.27 /77	0.58	0.84
MC	● Columbia Small/Mid Cap Value K	RMCVX	C+	(800) 345-6611	B+ / 8.6	7.34	15.15	33.05 /92	6.17 /66	11.91 /73	0.32	1.14
MC	Columbia Small/Mid Cap Value R	RMVTX	C+	(800) 345-6611	B+ / 8.3	7.23	14.90	32.50 /91	5.78 /62	11.49 /70	0.03	1.50
MC	Columbia Small/Mid Cap Value R4	RMCRX	B-	(800) 345-6611	B+ / 8.8	7.41	15.29	33.37 /92	6.33 /67	12.01 /74	0.43	1.00
MC	Columbia Small/Mid Cap Value R5	RSCMX	B-	(800) 345-6611	B+ / 8.8	7.41	15.29	33.41 /92	6.41 /68	12.18 /76	0.52	0.89
MC	Columbia Small/Mid Cap Value W	CVOWX	C+	(800) 345-6611	B+ / 8.5	7.24	15.06	32.79 /91	6.03 /64	11.75 /72	0.22	1.25
MC	Columbia Small/Mid Cap Value Y	CPHPX	B-	(800) 345-6611	B+ / 8.8	7.45	15.33	33.42 /92	6.45 /68	12.05 /75	0.56	0.84
MC	Columbia Small/Mid Cap Value Z	CMOZX	B-	(800) 345-6611	B+ / 8.7	7.35	15.28	33.24 /92	6.33 /67	12.05 /75	0.42	1.00
GI	Columbia Thermostat A	CTFAX	C-	(800) 345-6611	D- / 1.3	1.76	0.79	7.25 / 6	3.07 /32	5.15 /22	0.48	1.04
GI	Columbia Thermostat C	CTFDX	C	(800) 345-6611	D / 1.6	1.51	0.34	6.37 / 5	2.27 /26	4.35 /17	0.33	1.79
AA	Columbia Thermostat R4	CTORX	C	(800) 345-6611	D / 2.1	1.82	0.91	7.50 / 7	3.33 /35	5.41 /24	0.75	0.79
AA	Columbia Thermostat R5	CQTRX	C	(800) 345-6611	D / 2.1	1.76	0.85	7.51 / 7	3.34 /35	5.43 /24	0.76	0.77
AA	Columbia Thermostat Y	CYYYX	C	(800) 345-6611	D / 2.1	1.81	0.91	7.57 / 7	3.37 /35	5.46 /24	0.81	0.72
GI	Columbia Thermostat Z	COTZX	C	(800) 345-6611	D / 2.0	1.76	0.85	7.47 / 7	3.30 /35	5.40 /24	0.76	0.79
GR	Commerce Growth	CFGRX	B-	(800) 995-6365	A / 9.4	9.39	7.56	21.06 /58	11.87 /98	13.47 /89	0.80	0.82
MC	Commerce Mid Cap Growth	CFAGX	B-	(800) 995-6365	B / 8.1	7.46	6.89	20.98 /57	9.32 /89	12.13 /75	0.48	0.90
GI	Commerce Value	CFVLX	A	(800) 995-6365	A- / 9.2	5.13	9.81	25.71 /75	10.62 /96	13.93 /93	2.34	0.75
EM	Commonwealth Africa	CAFRX	E	(888) 345-1898	D / 1.8	12.64	13.52	33.10 /92	-3.17 / 4	-2.56 / 2	0.60	3.76
GL	Commonwealth Global	CNGLX	D-	(888) 345-1898	D- / 1.3	7.80	5.38	16.67 /37	-1.03 / 9	3.22 /12	0.00	2.74
FO	Commonwealth Japan	CNJFX	C	(888) 345-1898	C- / 3.2	5.57	4.60	7.57 / 7	4.25 /46	4.47 /18	0.00	3.13
FO	Commonwealth-Australia/New	CNZLX	B-	(888) 345-1898	B- / 7.5	7.81	8.70	31.45 /89	5.47 /59	6.88 /34	2.38	2.75
RE	Commonwealth-Real Estate	CNREX	C	(888) 345-1898	C+ / 5.8	7.17	2.03	18.70 /46	6.47 /68	8.25 /44	0.00	2.80
IN	Comstock Capital Value A	DRCVX	E	(800) 422-3554	E- / 0.0	-8.57	-14.16	-29.33 / 0	-15.66 / 0	-17.86 / 0	0.00	2.94
IN	Comstock Capital Value AAA	COMVX	E	(800) 422-3554	E- / 0.0	-8.56	-14.26	-29.29 / 0	-15.61 / 0	-17.83 / 0	0.00	2.94
IN	Comstock Capital Value C	CPCCX	E	(800) 422-3554	E- / 0.0	-8.71	-14.46	-29.75 / 0	-16.37 / 0	-18.51 / 0	0.00	3.69
IN	Comstock Capital Value R	CPCRX	E	(800) 422-3554	E- / 0.0	-8.38	-13.99	-29.00 / 0	-15.56 / 0	-17.67 / 0	0.00	2.69
GR	Concorde Wealth Management	CONWX	D+	(800) 294-1699	C- / 3.7	2.98	4.07	16.84 /38	3.86 /41	7.42 /37	0.00	1.37
GL	Conductor Global Equity Value I	RAILX	B+	(844) 467-2459	B- / 7.2	6.71	11.19	25.61 /75	5.89 /63	--	0.00	2.02
SC	Conestoga Small Cap Institutional	CCALX	U	(800) 344-2716	U /	1.82	8.87	29.21 /85	--	--	0.00	1.09
SC	Conestoga Small Cap Investor	CCASX	C	(800) 344-2716	C+ / 6.8	1.78	8.75	28.93 /84	5.94 /64	12.51 /79	0.00	1.50
GL	Conestoga SMid Cap Investor	CCSMX	C-	(800) 344-2716	C / 5.3	4.62	8.13	28.97 /84	2.67 /29	--	0.00	2.25
GR	Congress All Cap Opportunity Inst	IACOX	B-	(888) 688-1299	B+ / 8.4	5.55	12.18	29.40 /85	7.92 /78	--	0.26	1.63
GR	Congress All Cap Opportunity Retail	CACOX	B-	(888) 688-1299	B / 8.2	5.50	12.02	29.11 /84	7.67 /77	--	0.13	1.90
GR	Congress Large Cap Growth I	CMLIX	C+	(888) 688-1299	C+ / 6.3	6.86	7.15	16.77 /37	7.02 /72	10.32 /61	0.78	1.08
GR	Congress Large Cap Growth R	CAMLX	C+	(888) 688-1299	C+ / 6.0	6.82	7.02	16.52 /36	6.76 /70	10.06 /59	0.49	1.33
MC	Congress Mid Cap Growth Inst	IMIDX	A+	(888) 688-1299	B+ / 8.8	8.04	9.60	24.24 /71	9.78 /92	--	0.17	0.87
MC	Congress Mid Cap Growth Retail	CMIDX	A	(888) 688-1299	B+ / 8.7	7.98	9.48	23.95 /70	9.48 /90	--	0.01	1.12
GL	Context Macro Opportunities Instl	CMOTX	U	(855) 612-2257	U /	0.46	0.06	0.36 / 1	--	--	0.55	2.97

● Denotes fund is closed to new investors

* Denotes fund is included in Section II

166

Risk Rating/Pts	3 Year Standard Deviation	Beta	NAV As of 2/28/17	Total $(Mil)	Cash %	Stocks %	Bonds %	Other %	Portfolio Turnover Ratio	Last Bull Market Return	Last Bear Market Return	Manager Quality Pct	Manager Tenure (Years)	Initial Purch. $	Additional Purch. $	Front End Load	Back End Load
C- /3.6	16.6	0.99	46.04	5	0	99	0	1	65	127.5	-23.9	87	12	0	0	0.0	0.0
C- /3.6	16.6	0.99	45.89	232	0	99	0	1	65	125.0	-23.9	86	12	2,000	0	0.0	0.0
C /4.5	14.4	0.90	18.01	202	2	97	0	1	57	140.6	-26.8	85	15	2,000	0	0.0	0.0
C- /4.2	14.4	0.90	16.15	N/A	2	97	0	1	57	131.1	-27.1	80	15	2,000	0	5.8	0.0
C- /4.2	14.4	0.89	16.13	12	2	97	0	1	57	131.1	-27.1	80	15	2,000	0	0.0	0.0
C /4.5	14.4	0.90	18.28	N/A	2	97	0	1	57	146.6	-26.7	87	15	0	0	0.0	0.0
C /4.4	14.5	0.90	17.77	11	2	97	0	1	57	137.5	-26.9	83	15	0	0	0.0	0.0
C /4.5	14.4	0.90	18.61	70	2	97	0	1	57	143.1	-26.8	86	15	0	0	0.0	0.0
C /4.5	14.4	0.89	18.63	78	2	97	0	1	57	144.6	-26.8	86	15	0	0	0.0	0.0
C /4.5	14.4	0.89	18.68	204	2	97	0	1	57	145.3	-26.8	87	15	0	0	0.0	0.0
C /4.5	14.4	0.90	18.25	1,104	2	97	0	1	57	144.0	-26.8	86	15	2,000	0	0.0	0.0
C- /3.8	14.0	1.14	10.31	709	3	96	0	1	69	118.7	-25.4	19	4	2,000	0	5.8	0.0
C- /3.5	14.0	1.14	9.40	3	3	96	0	1	69	109.9	-25.6	13	4	2,000	0	0.0	0.0
C- /3.5	14.0	1.14	9.39	31	3	96	0	1	69	109.7	-25.6	13	4	2,000	0	0.0	0.0
C- /3.9	14.0	1.14	10.62	N/A	3	96	0	1	69	123.8	-25.2	22	4	0	0	0.0	0.0
C- /3.8	14.0	1.14	10.41	38	3	96	0	1	69	120.1	-25.4	20	4	0	0	0.0	0.0
C- /3.7	14.0	1.14	10.12	7	3	96	0	1	69	115.4	-25.4	16	4	0	0	0.0	0.0
C- /3.8	13.9	1.13	10.33	18	3	96	0	1	69	120.9	-25.4	21	4	0	0	0.0	0.0
C- /3.8	14.0	1.14	10.47	41	3	96	0	1	69	123.0	-25.2	21	4	0	0	0.0	0.0
C- /3.8	13.9	1.13	10.40	N/A	3	96	0	1	69	118.7	-25.3	19	4	500	0	0.0	0.0
C- /3.8	13.9	1.13	10.32	2	3	96	0	1	69	121.5	-25.4	22	4	0	0	0.0	0.0
C- /3.8	14.0	1.14	10.56	37	3	96	0	1	69	121.5	-25.2	21	4	2,000	0	0.0	0.0
B /8.9	3.4	0.28	14.79	392	0	23	76	1	69	48.4	-8.1	75	N/A	2,000	0	5.8	0.0
B+ /9.0	3.4	0.28	14.79	326	0	23	76	1	69	42.4	-8.4	67	N/A	2,000	0	0.0	0.0
B /8.9	3.4	0.49	14.67	16	0	23	76	1	69	50.4	-8.0	70	14	0	0	0.0	0.0
B /8.9	3.4	0.48	14.68	13	0	23	76	1	69	50.5	-8.0	71	14	0	0	0.0	0.0
B /8.9	3.4	0.49	14.66	N/A	0	23	76	1	69	50.8	-8.0	71	14	0	0	0.0	0.0
B /8.9	3.4	0.27	14.59	334	0	23	76	1	69	50.3	-8.0	77	N/A	2,000	0	0.0	0.0
C- /3.4	10.1	0.94	29.07	99	1	98	0	1	37	134.2	-18.0	85	N/A	1,000	250	0.0	0.0
C /4.8	9.7	0.75	36.50	124	1	98	0	1	39	117.8	-22.1	86	N/A	1,000	250	0.0	0.0
C+ /6.0	9.6	0.86	32.67	323	1	98	0	1	41	126.9	-11.8	83	13	1,000	250	0.0	0.0
C- /3.0	19.2	0.97	8.66	3	4	94	0	2	13	N/A	N/A	16	6	200	0	0.0	0.0
C /5.1	10.8	0.75	14.39	15	0	99	0	1	45	37.5	-23.2	63	15	200	0	0.0	0.0
B- /7.4	10.0	0.61	3.41	5	1	98	0	1	4	23.6	-0.4	94	20	200	0	0.0	0.0
C /5.3	14.0	0.82	12.92	21	2	94	3	1	26	60.8	-13.1	96	26	200	0	0.0	0.0
C /5.4	11.2	0.72	15.55	10	0	98	1	1	12	84.4	-22.5	58	13	200	0	0.0	0.0
C- /3.7	13.2	-1.22	5.76	22	35	0	64	1	155	-71.3	22.6	15	30	1,000	0	5.8	0.0
C- /3.8	13.2	-1.22	5.77	2	35	0	64	1	155	-71.2	22.0	16	30	1,000	0	0.0	0.0
C- /3.6	13.2	-1.22	5.03	4	35	0	64	1	155	-72.5	22.8	10	30	1,000	0	0.0	0.0
C- /3.9	13.1	-1.21	5.90	N/A	35	0	64	1	155	-70.8	22.4	15	30	1,000	0	0.0	0.0
C /5.3	10.0	0.87	14.73	19	8	54	36	2	17	72.2	-21.3	15	30	500	100	0.0	0.0
B- /7.2	9.7	0.66	11.92	47	2	94	3	1	123	N/A	N/A	97	4	100,000	1,000	0.0	0.0
U /	N/A	N/A	41.21	381	5	94	0	1	24	N/A	N/A	N/A	15	250,000	0	0.0	0.0
C /4.6	16.3	0.95	40.98	568	5	94	0	1	24	116.1	-18.0	67	15	2,500	0	0.0	0.0
C /4.6	15.0	0.67	10.64	2	0	100	0	0	21	N/A	N/A	89	3	2,500	0	0.0	0.0
C /4.3	13.9	1.15	16.39	17	9	90	0	1	37	N/A	N/A	24	3	500,000	250	0.0	1.0
C /4.3	13.9	1.15	16.31	7	9	90	0	1	37	N/A	N/A	21	3	2,000	250	0.0	1.0
C+ /6.3	10.2	0.95	23.39	38	3	96	0	1	31	98.9	-15.3	37	8	500,000	250	0.0	1.0
C+ /6.3	10.2	0.95	23.40	10	3	96	0	1	31	96.3	-15.4	34	8	2,000	250	0.0	1.0
C+ /6.9	11.4	0.89	17.29	639	6	93	0	1	24	N/A	N/A	82	5	500,000	250	0.0	1.0
C+ /6.9	11.4	0.89	17.18	54	6	93	0	1	24	N/A	N/A	80	5	2,000	250	0.0	1.0
U /	N/A	N/A	10.07	103	0	0	0	100	410	N/A	N/A	N/A	2	1,000,000	0	0.0	2.0

99 Pct = Best
0 Pct = Worst

Fund Type	Fund Name	Ticker Symbol	Overall Investment Rating	Phone	Performance Rating/Pts	3 Mo	6 Mo	1Yr / Pct	3Yr / Pct	5Yr / Pct	Dividend Yield	Expense Ratio
GL	Convergence Core Plus Fund Inst	MARNX	A-	(877) 677-9414	B+ / 8.3	5.14	13.30	22.52 /65	8.68 /84	12.57 /80	0.91	2.24
GL	Convergence Core Plus Fund Inv	MARVX	B+	(877) 677-9414	B / 8.1	5.07	13.13	22.14 /63	8.41 /82	---	0.57	2.50
SC	Convergence Opportunities Instl	CIPOX	B	(877) 677-9414	B- / 7.2	2.54	12.43	24.18 /70	6.86 /71	---	0.00	2.63
GL	Cook & Bynum	COBYX	C-	(877) 839-2629	D / 1.6	1.96	0.09	5.14 / 4	3.27 /34	5.30 /23	0.00	1.75
FO	Copeland Intl Risk Mgd Div Gro A	IDVGX	D	(888) 926-7352	E- / 0.1	5.48	-3.46	-0.62 / 1	-3.35 / 4	---	0.55	2.06
FO	Copeland Intl Risk Mgd Div Gro C	IDVCX	D	(888) 926-7352	E- / 0.2	5.18	-3.97	-1.46 / 1	-4.22 / 3	---	0.00	2.82
FO	Copeland Intl Risk Mgd Div Gro I	IDVIX	D	(888) 926-7352	E- / 0.2	5.48	-3.62	-0.61 / 1	-3.19 / 4	---	1.05	1.91
GL	Copeland Risk Managed Div Gro A	CDGRX	D-	(888) 926-7352	E+ / 0.7	8.60	7.55	10.04 /12	-0.38 /12	6.48 /31	0.65	1.49
IN	Copeland Risk Managed Div Gro C	CDCRX	D+	(888) 926-7352	D+ / 2.5	8.41	7.16	9.23 /10	1.80 /23	7.56 /39	0.00	2.25
IN	Copeland Risk Managed Div Gro I	CDIVX	D	(888) 926-7352	D- / 1.2	8.61	7.65	10.14 /12	-0.20 /13	---	1.04	1.25
IN	Copley	COPLX	A	(800) 424-8570	B / 7.6	7.11	7.30	15.81 /33	9.43 /90	10.54 /62	0.00	1.14
BA	CornerCap Balanced	CBLFX	C	(888) 813-8637	C / 5.4	5.16	7.60	19.04 /47	5.34 /58	7.84 /41	1.38	1.22
SC	CornerCap Large/Mid-Cap Value	CMCRX	C+	(888) 813-8637	B / 8.1	7.86	12.22	27.33 /80	7.16 /73	11.08 /66	0.83	1.30
GR	CornerCap Sm Cap Value Inv	CSCVX	A-	(888) 813-8637	A+ / 9.6	4.10	14.16	34.64 /94	10.35 /95	14.68 /96	0.18	1.30
SC	CornerCap Small Cap Value Inst	CSCJX	U	(888) 813-8637	U /	4.23	14.34	35.09 /94	---	---	0.47	1.00
GL	Cornerstone Advisors Glb Pb Eq Inst	CAGLX	C		C+ / 5.9	7.32	7.50	21.60 /60	4.92 /53	---	0.99	0.99
AA	Cornerstone Advisors Pb Alt Inst	CAALX	C		D / 1.9	2.62	1.89	1.08 / 2	4.06 /44	---	0.50	2.57
AA	Cornerstone Advisors Real Asst Inst	CAREX	E+		E+ / 0.7	4.76	7.56	21.73 /61	-3.77 / 3	---	1.65	0.99
SC	Cortina Small Cap Growth Inst	CRSGX	D+	(855) 612-3936	C+ / 6.1	4.01	12.78	41.07 /98	1.25 /20	8.49 /46	0.00	1.54
SC	Cortina Small Cap Value Inst	CRSVX	C+	(855) 612-3936	B- / 7.1	7.46	14.46	34.39 /93	3.61 /38	12.74 /81	0.16	1.51
SC	Cove Street Capital Sm Cap Val Inst	CSCAX	C-	(866) 497-0097	C+ / 5.7	3.24	7.67	25.51 /75	5.20 /56	12.25 /77	1.28	1.42
GL	Covered Bridge A	TCBAX	B-	(800) 639-3935	C / 4.7	4.97	7.12	19.76 /51	6.11 /65	---	0.65	2.34
GL	Covered Bridge I	TCBIX	B-	(800) 639-3935	C+ / 6.1	5.06	7.27	20.07 /52	6.38 /67	---	1.01	2.09
SC	Cozad Small Cap Value I	COZIX	U	(800) 437-1686	U /	6.04	15.30	30.60 /87	---	---	0.96	2.03
GR	Crawford Dividend Growth C	CDGCX	C-	(800) 408-4682	C+ / 5.6	5.04	6.08	21.79 /61	5.10 /55	8.60 /47	0.45	1.92
GR	Crawford Dividend Growth I	CDGIX	C	(800) 408-4682	C+ / 6.4	5.17	6.48	22.95 /66	6.14 /65	9.66 /56	1.38	0.92
IN	Crawford Dividend Opportunity	CDOFX	A+	(800) 408-4682	A+ / 9.7	5.69	12.30	34.35 /93	10.86 /97	---	1.28	1.35
OT	Credit Suisse Comdty ACCESS Strat	CRCAX	E-	(877) 927-2874	E- / 0.0	2.58	7.74	25.17 /74	-16.93 / 0	---	0.00	1.85
OT	Credit Suisse Comdty ACCESS Strat	CRCCX	E-	(877) 927-2874	E- / 0.0	2.47	7.37	24.19 /71	-17.55 / 0	---	0.00	2.60
OT	Credit Suisse Comdty ACCESS Strat	CRCIX	E-	(877) 927-2874	E- / 0.0	2.55	7.85	25.39 /74	-16.75 / 0	---	0.00	1.60
EM	Credit Suisse Emerg Mkts Equity A	CSNAX	D+	(877) 927-2874	D+ / 2.8	8.66	6.22	29.86 /86	0.08 /14	---	1.62	2.72
EM	Credit Suisse Emerg Mkts Equity C	CSNCX	D	(877) 927-2874	D / 1.8	8.60	5.78	28.92 /84	-0.67 /11	---	1.01	3.47
EM	Credit Suisse Emerg Mkts Equity I	CSNIX	C-	(877) 927-2874	C- / 3.9	8.69	6.25	30.01 /86	0.30 /15	---	1.94	2.47
IN	Credit Suisse Mgd Fut Str A	CSAAX	D+	(877) 927-2874	D- / 1.4	-1.37	-1.73	-4.49 / 1	5.78 /62	---	0.00	1.70
IN	Credit Suisse Mgd Fut Str C	CSACX	D+	(877) 927-2874	D / 1.6	-1.50	-2.05	-5.21 / 1	4.99 /54	---	0.00	2.45
IN	Credit Suisse Mgd Fut Str I	CSAIX	C-	(877) 927-2874	D / 2.1	-1.36	-1.72	-4.30 / 1	6.03 /64	---	0.00	1.45
AA	Credit Suisse Mltialtern Strategy A	CSQAX	C	(877) 677-2874	D- / 1.0	1.57	2.16	5.12 / 4	1.82 /23	---	0.10	1.87
AA	Credit Suisse Mltialtern Strategy C	CSQCX	C	(877) 927-2874	D- / 1.1	1.29	1.70	4.28 / 3	0.99 /18	---	0.00	2.62
AA	Credit Suisse Mltialtern Strategy I	CSQIX	C	(877) 927-2874	D- / 1.5	1.52	2.21	5.36 / 4	2.01 /24	---	0.35	1.62
GR	CRM All Cap Value Inst	CRIEX	D+	(800) 276-2883	B- / 7.3	5.14	7.05	24.89 /73	7.40 /75	11.52 /70	0.59	1.52
GR	CRM All Cap Value Inv	CRMEX	D	(800) 276-2883	B- / 7.2	5.18	7.00	24.78 /73	7.15 /73	11.26 /68	0.36	1.77
FO	CRM International Opportunity Inst	CRIIX	D-	(800) 276-2883	D / 1.6	6.54	0.33	9.04 /10	1.28 /20	3.12 /11	1.09	2.53
FO	CRM International Opportunity Inv	CRMIX	D-	(800) 276-2883	D- / 1.5	6.47	0.23	8.79 / 9	1.05 /18	2.89 /10	0.84	2.80
MC	CRM Large Cap Opportunity Inst	CRIGX	C	(800) 276-2883	B+ / 8.8	6.19	10.11	27.68 /81	8.83 /86	12.47 /79	0.90	1.05
MC	CRM Large Cap Opportunity Inv	CRMGX	C	(800) 276-2883	B+ / 8.5	6.06	9.87	27.28 /80	8.53 /83	12.18 /76	0.67	1.34
GL	CRM Long/Short Opportunities Inst	CRIHX	U	(800) 276-2883	U /	-1.39	-0.60	---	---	---	0.00	N/A
MC	CRM Mid Cap Value Instl	CRIMX	D	(800) 276-2883	B / 7.7	4.89	6.85	28.92 /84	7.48 /75	12.44 /78	0.16	0.96
MC	CRM Mid Cap Value Inv	CRMMX	D	(800) 276-2883	B / 7.6	4.83	6.71	28.66 /83	7.28 /74	12.22 /76	0.01	1.14
SC	CRM Small Cap Value Inst	CRISX	C	(800) 276-2883	B+ / 8.8	2.13	11.52	32.43 /91	8.54 /83	13.40 /88	0.57	0.90
SC	CRM Small Cap Value Inv	CRMSX	C-	(800) 276-2883	B+ / 8.7	2.08	11.39	32.13 /90	8.30 /81	13.14 /85	0.44	1.13
SC	CRM Small/Mid Cap Value Inst	CRIAX	D	(800) 276-2883	C+ / 5.6	2.93	7.12	26.42 /78	4.34 /47	10.45 /62	2.30	0.91
SC	CRM Small/Mid Cap Value Inv	CRMAX	D	(800) 276-2883	C / 5.4	2.88	6.99	26.22 /77	4.11 /44	10.19 /60	2.09	1.13

● Denotes fund is closed to new investors
* Denotes fund is included in Section II

RISK			NET ASSETS		ASSET						BULL / BEAR		FUND MANAGER		MINIMUMS		LOADS	
	3 Year		NAV							Portfolio	Last Bull	Last Bear	Manager	Manager	Initial	Additional	Front	Back
Risk	Standard		As of	Total	Cash	Stocks	Bonds	Other		Turnover	Market	Market	Quality	Tenure	Purch.	Purch.	End	End
Rating/Pts	Deviation	Beta	2/28/17	$(Mil)	%	%	%	%		Ratio	Return	Return	Pct	(Years)	$	$	Load	Load
C+ / 6.4	11.3	0.62	18.61	128	1	98	0	1		251	129.3	-19.6	99	8	100,000	5,000	0.0	0.0
C+ / 6.4	11.3	0.62	18.57	4	1	98	0	1		251	N/A	N/A	99	8	2,500	100	0.0	0.0
C+ / 6.5	13.5	0.78	12.12	78	1	98	0	1		320	N/A	N/A	83	4	100,000	5,000	0.0	0.0
B / 8.3	6.4	0.28	15.08	139	1	62	36	1		9	41.9	-2.5	91	8	5,000	1,000	0.0	2.0
B- / 7.8	7.4	0.45	10.41	3	81	18	0	1		323	N/A	N/A	30	5	2,500	500	5.8	1.0
B- / 7.6	7.4	0.45	10.15	2	81	18	0	1		323	N/A	N/A	21	5	2,500	500	0.0	1.0
B- / 7.8	7.4	0.45	10.39	11	81	18	0	1		323	N/A	N/A	32	5	250,000	500	0.0	1.0
C+ / 6.4	10.1	0.37	12.84	75	7	53	38	2		142	47.9	-7.8	70	7	1,000	500	5.8	1.0
C+ / 6.3	8.6	0.63	12.63	42	7	53	38	2		142	N/A	N/A	18	7	1,000	500	0.0	1.0
C+ / 6.3	10.1	0.70	12.76	76	7	53	38	2		142	N/A	N/A	5	7	250,000	500	0.0	1.0
B- / 7.5	9.0	0.43	82.86	83	0	100	0	0		0	79.8	-3.2	95	39	1,000	100	0.0	0.0
C / 5.5	7.7	1.10	14.13	31	3	58	38	1		70	65.9	-13.3	38	20	2,000	250	0.0	1.0
C- / 3.8	12.3	0.65	12.66	25	1	94	4	1		97	106.5	-23.0	88	21	2,000	250	0.0	1.0
C / 5.1	15.1	1.04	16.75	79	0	0	0	100		144	156.8	-28.0	66	25	2,000	250	0.0	1.0
U /	N/A	N/A	16.77	29	0	0	0	100		144	N/A	N/A	N/A	25	1,000,000	0	0.0	1.0
C / 5.2	10.4	0.77	12.48	982	3	96	0	1		49	N/A	N/A	95	5	2,000	0	0.0	0.0
B / 8.9	3.5	0.03	9.90	519	51	17	28	4		92	N/A	N/A	92	5	2,000	0	0.0	0.0
C / 5.1	11.1	0.96	8.28	204	37	9	53	1		36	N/A	N/A	2	5	2,000	0	0.0	0.0
C- / 3.1	16.9	1.00	17.38	24	3	96	0	1		93	90.3	N/A	12	6	25,000	0	0.0	2.0
C / 5.1	14.9	0.92	20.34	44	6	93	0	1		109	132.2	N/A	40	6	25,000	0	0.0	2.0
C / 4.5	15.1	0.84	35.72	129	7	78	13	2		85	142.1	-19.8	67	19	10,000	100	0.0	2.0
B- / 7.7	8.3	0.55	10.21	10	1	98	0	1		193	N/A	N/A	97	4	5,000	1,000	5.3	1.0
B- / 7.8	8.2	0.55	10.20	36	1	98	0	1		193	N/A	N/A	97	4	1,000,000	1,000	0.0	1.0
U /	N/A	N/A	21.83	36	1	98	0	1		62	N/A	N/A	N/A	7	10,000	100	0.0	0.0
C / 4.4	10.4	0.95	10.24	6	0	97	2	1		24	81.4	-17.2	18	2	2,500	0	0.0	0.0
C / 4.4	10.4	0.95	10.33	31	0	97	2	1		24	91.2	-16.8	27	2	10,000	0	0.0	0.0
C+ / 5.9	12.1	0.91	40.12	147	2	97	0	1		37	N/A	N/A	81	5	10,000	0	0.0	0.0
D- / 1.4	20.0	0.59	5.57	1	0	0	0	100		137	N/A	N/A	0	N/A	2,500	100	4.8	0.0
D- / 1.3	19.9	0.59	5.39	N/A	0	0	0	100		137	N/A	N/A	0	N/A	2,500	100	0.0	0.0
D- / 1.4	19.9	0.59	5.63	33	0	0	0	100		137	N/A	N/A	0	N/A	250,000	100,000	0.0	0.0
C+ / 6.1	16.4	0.99	9.28	1	5	94	0	1		61	N/A	N/A	54	4	2,500	100	5.3	2.0
C+ / 6.1	16.5	0.99	9.27	1	5	94	0	1		61	N/A	N/A	43	4	2,500	100	0.0	2.0
C+ / 6.1	16.5	0.99	9.28	24	5	94	0	1		61	N/A	N/A	57	4	250,000	100,000	0.0	2.0
B- / 7.2	9.9	-0.22	10.58	45	0	0	0	100		0	N/A	N/A	98	5	2,500	100	5.3	0.0
B- / 7.1	9.9	-0.22	10.28	4	0	0	0	100		0	N/A	N/A	98	5	2,500	100	0.0	0.0
B- / 7.2	9.9	-0.22	10.64	149	0	0	0	100		0	N/A	N/A	98	5	250,000	100,000	0.0	0.0
B+ / 9.6	3.7	0.51	10.33	1	88	9	1	2		1,021	N/A	N/A	49	5	2,500	100	5.3	0.0
B+ / 9.6	3.7	0.52	10.06	N/A	88	9	1	2		1,021	N/A	N/A	36	5	2,500	100	0.0	0.0
B+ / 9.6	3.7	0.51	10.38	119	88	9	1	2		1,021	N/A	N/A	51	5	250,000	100,000	0.0	0.0
D- / 1.1	11.0	0.98	9.01	4	2	95	2	1		91	108.9	-24.5	37	7	1,000,000	0	0.0	0.0
D- / 1.1	11.1	0.98	8.90	19	2	95	2	1		91	106.3	-24.7	34	7	2,500	100	0.0	0.0
C / 4.9	10.8	0.81	12.42	4	2	92	5	1		88	42.4	-27.5	83	N/A	1,000,000	0	0.0	1.5
C / 4.9	10.8	0.81	12.37	8	2	92	5	1		88	40.7	-27.6	82	N/A	2,500	100	0.0	1.5
D / 2.1	11.0	0.83	9.68	82	1	96	2	1		121	117.9	-19.5	80	12	1,000,000	0	0.0	0.0
D / 2.1	11.0	0.82	9.66	13	1	96	2	1		121	114.9	-19.6	78	12	2,500	100	0.0	0.0
U /	N/A	N/A	9.91	372	0	0	0	100		0	N/A	N/A	N/A	11	100,000,000	0	0.0	0.0
E / 0.5	11.4	0.88	23.03	237	1	96	1	2		76	116.3	-23.1	63	19	1,000,000	0	0.0	0.0
E / 0.5	11.4	0.88	22.30	313	1	96	1	2		76	114.0	-23.2	61	19	2,500	100	0.0	0.0
D / 1.8	14.7	0.90	19.78	364	0	96	2	2		68	127.2	-28.1	87	6	1,000,000	0	0.0	0.0
D- / 1.4	14.7	0.90	17.51	72	0	96	2	2		68	124.5	-28.1	86	6	2,500	100	0.0	0.0
D / 2.1	12.7	0.76	14.41	550	2	95	2	1		72	110.3	-24.3	63	13	1,000,000	0	0.0	0.0
D / 2.1	12.7	0.76	14.17	43	2	95	2	1		72	107.8	-24.3	61	13	2,500	100	0.0	0.0

I. Index of Stock Mutual Funds

					PERFORMANCE							
	99 Pct = Best				Perfor-	Total Return % through 2/28/17					Incl. in Returns	
	0 Pct = Worst		Overall		mance				Annualized		Dividend	Expense
Fund Type	Fund Name	Ticker Symbol	Investment Rating	Phone	Rating/Pts	3 Mo	6 Mo	1Yr / Pct	3Yr / Pct	5Yr / Pct	Yield	Ratio
GR	Croft Value I	CIVFX	D+	(800) 551-0990	B- / 7.2	8.42	13.17	30.61 /87	4.68 /51	--	0.00	1.23
GR	Croft Value R	CLVFX	D+	(800) 551-0990	B- / 7.0	8.32	13.01	30.27 /87	4.41 /48	8.26 /44	0.00	1.49
GL	Crow Point Def Risk Glbl Eqty Inc A	CGHAX	D	(855) 754-7940	E+ / 0.6	4.52	3.07	6.15 / 5	-0.57 /11	--	2.58	4.15
GL	Crow Point Def Risk Glbl Eqty Inc I	CGHIX	D	(855) 754-7940	E+ / 0.8	4.68	3.18	6.45 / 5	-0.34 /12	--	2.83	4.89
FO	● CSTG&E Intl Social Core Equity	DFCCX	D	(800) 984-9472	D / 1.7	7.71	6.66	20.07 /52	-0.31 /12	5.34 /24	2.62	0.54
AA	CT 529 CHET Adv AB Ptf 14-15 A		C	(888) 843-7824	D / 1.9	4.25	4.25	14.38 /27	2.12 /25	5.13 /22	0.00	1.25
AA	CT 529 CHET Adv AB Ptf 14-15 C		C	(888) 843-7824	D / 2.2	3.99	3.84	13.49 /23	1.35 /20	4.34 /17	0.00	2.00
AA	CT 529 CHET Adv AB Ptf 14-15 E		C+	(888) 843-7824	D+ / 2.8	4.25	4.40	14.64 /28	2.37 /26	5.39 /24	0.00	1.00
AA	CT 529 CHET Adv AB Ptf 16-17 A		C	(888) 843-7824	D- / 1.4	2.73	2.24	9.13 /10	1.60 /22	3.09 /11	0.00	1.20
AA	CT 529 CHET Adv AB Ptf 16-17 C		C	(888) 843-7824	D- / 1.4	2.61	1.92	8.36 / 8	0.86 /17	2.33 / 9	0.00	1.95
AA	CT 529 CHET Adv AB Ptf 16-17 E		C	(888) 843-7824	D / 1.8	2.77	2.36	9.43 /10	1.86 /23	3.35 /12	0.00	0.95
AA	CT 529 CHET Adv AB Ptf 18+ A		C	(888) 843-7824	E+ / 0.9	1.70	1.07	5.67 / 4	0.87 /17	1.47 / 7	0.00	1.17
AA	CT 529 CHET Adv AB Ptf 18+ C		C	(888) 843-7824	E+ / 0.9	1.50	0.65	4.84 / 4	0.09 /14	0.70 / 6	0.00	1.92
AA	CT 529 CHET Adv AB Ptf 18+ E		C	(888) 843-7824	D- / 1.3	1.67	1.14	5.87 / 5	1.10 /19	1.71 / 7	0.00	0.92
AA	CT 529 CHET Adv AB Ptf 9-13 A		C	(888) 843-7824	D+ / 2.4	4.98	5.41	16.68 /37	2.45 /27	6.30 /30	0.00	1.27
AA	CT 529 CHET Adv AB Ptf 9-13 C		C	(888) 843-7824	D+ / 2.7	4.79	5.01	15.79 /33	1.69 /22	5.51 /25	0.00	2.02
AA	CT 529 CHET Adv AB Ptf 9-13 E		C+	(888) 843-7824	C- / 3.5	5.04	5.47	16.99 /38	2.70 /29	6.56 /32	0.00	1.02
AA	CT 529 CHET Adv Age-Based 0-8 A		C	(888) 843-7824	C- / 3.3	6.04	6.64	19.41 /49	3.39 /36	8.06 /43	0.00	1.32
AA	CT 529 CHET Adv Age-Based 0-8 C		C	(888) 843-7824	C- / 3.8	5.86	6.21	18.51 /45	2.62 /28	7.26 /36	0.00	2.07
AA	CT 529 CHET Adv Age-Based 0-8 E		C+	(888) 843-7824	C / 4.7	6.13	6.80	19.71 /51	3.66 /39	8.33 /45	0.00	1.07
AG	CT 529 CHET Adv Aggr Growth A		C+	(888) 843-7824	C+ / 5.7	7.12	8.25	23.01 /67	4.14 /44	9.83 /57	0.00	1.37
AG	CT 529 CHET Adv Aggr Growth C		C+	(888) 843-7824	C / 5.0	6.91	7.76	22.01 /62	3.35 /35	9.01 /51	0.00	2.12
AG	CT 529 CHET Adv Aggr Growth E		C+	(888) 843-7824	C+ / 5.9	7.13	8.36	23.21 /67	4.39 /47	10.10 /59	0.00	1.12
BA	CT 529 CHET Adv Balanced Ptf A		C+	(888) 843-7824	C- / 3.3	5.03	5.41	16.69 /37	2.46 /27	5.57 /25	0.00	N/A
BA	CT 529 CHET Adv Balanced Ptf C		C	(888) 843-7824	D+ / 2.8	4.82	5.06	15.91 /34	1.71 /22	4.78 /20	0.00	N/A
AA	CT 529 CHET Adv Checks & Bals Ptf		B	(888) 843-7824	C / 4.5	5.65	6.43	17.27 /40	6.04 /65	9.26 /53	0.00	1.23
AA	CT 529 CHET Adv Checks & Bals Ptf		B	(888) 843-7824	C / 5.0	5.41	6.02	16.29 /35	5.23 /57	8.44 /46	0.00	1.98
AA	CT 529 CHET Adv Checks & Bals Ptf		B	(888) 843-7824	C+ / 5.9	5.69	6.51	17.50 /41	6.30 /67	9.53 /55	0.00	0.98
AA	CT 529 CHET Adv Consv Ptf A		C	(888) 843-7824	D / 1.7	2.72	2.15	9.11 /10	1.61 /22	3.10 /11	0.00	N/A
AA	CT 529 CHET Adv Consv Ptf C		C	(888) 843-7824	D- / 1.4	2.51	1.83	8.33 / 8	0.86 /17	2.34 / 9	0.00	N/A
AA	CT 529 CHET Adv Consv Ptf E		C	(888) 843-7824	D / 1.8	2.76	2.36	9.40 /10	1.88 /23	3.37 /12	0.00	N/A
GR	CT 529 CHET Adv Growth A		C+	(888) 843-7824	C / 4.4	6.05	6.65	19.43 /49	3.42 /36	8.08 /43	0.00	N/A
GR	CT 529 CHET Adv Growth C		C	(888) 843-7824	C- / 3.8	5.87	6.29	18.52 /45	2.65 /29	7.28 /36	0.00	N/A
GR	CT 529 CHET Adv Growth E		C+	(888) 843-7824	C / 4.7	6.14	6.80	19.72 /51	3.68 /39	8.35 /45	0.00	N/A
BA	CT 529 CHET Advisor Balanced Ptf E		C+	(888) 843-7824	C- / 3.5	5.09	5.54	17.02 /38	2.73 /29	5.84 /27	0.00	N/A
GR	CT 529 Hartford Cap App 529 Ptf A		C+	(888) 843-7824	C+ / 5.8	7.94	9.15	22.11 /63	6.02 /64	12.44 /78	0.00	1.29
GR	CT 529 Hartford Cap App 529 Ptf C		C+	(888) 843-7824	C+ / 6.3	7.73	8.74	21.19 /58	5.23 /57	11.60 /71	0.00	2.04
GR	CT 529 Hartford Cap App 529 Ptf E		B	(888) 843-7824	B- / 7.0	8.04	9.29	22.43 /64	6.29 /67	12.72 /81	0.00	1.04
GI	'CT 529 Hartford Eqty Inc 529 Ptf A		A+	(888) 843-7824	B / 8.2	7.55	11.62	26.07 /76	9.35 /89	12.69 /81	0.00	1.26
GI	'CT 529 Hartford Eqty Inc 529 Ptf C		A+	(888) 843-7824	B+ / 8.6	7.33	11.17	25.08 /73	8.52 /83	11.85 /73	0.00	2.01
GI	'CT 529 Hartford Eqty Inc 529 Ptf E		A+	(888) 843-7824	A- / 9.2	7.64	11.71	26.37 /77	9.62 /91	12.97 /83	0.00	1.01
GR	CT 529 Hartford Gro Oppty 529 Ptf A		C	(888) 843-7824	C+ / 6.1	6.49	3.88	19.98 /52	8.29 /81	14.23 /94	0.00	1.36
GR	CT 529 Hartford Gro Oppty 529 Ptf C		C+	(888) 843-7824	C+ / 6.5	6.27	3.49	19.02 /47	7.48 /75	13.38 /88	0.00	2.11
GR	CT 529 Hartford Gro Oppty 529 Ptf E		C+	(888) 843-7824	B- / 7.2	6.57	4.00	20.26 /53	8.56 /83	14.52 /96	0.00	1.11
FO	CT 529 Hartford Itl Oppty 529 Ptf A		D	(888) 843-7824	D- / 1.5	6.56	3.98	14.14 /26	0.47 /16	5.09 /22	0.00	1.42
FO	CT 529 Hartford Itl Oppty 529 Ptf C		D	(888) 843-7824	D- / 1.3	6.37	3.59	13.30 /23	-0.28 /12	4.31 /17	0.00	2.17
FO	CT 529 Hartford Itl Oppty 529 Ptf E		D+	(888) 843-7824	D+ / 2.3	6.62	4.08	14.47 /28	0.72 /17	5.35 /24	0.00	1.17
MC	CT 529 Hartford MidCap 529 Ptf A		B	(888) 843-7824	B- / 7.3	6.64	11.23	26.42 /78	7.75 /77	14.04 /93	0.00	1.38
MC	CT 529 Hartford MidCap 529 Ptf C		B	(888) 843-7824	B / 7.6	6.40	10.80	25.45 /75	6.94 /72	13.18 /86	0.00	2.13
MC	CT 529 Hartford MidCap 529 Ptf E		B+	(888) 843-7824	B+ / 8.4	6.73	11.41	26.73 /78	8.02 /79	14.32 /95	0.00	1.13
SC	CT 529 Hartford SmCap Gr 529 Ptf A		C+	(888) 843-7824	C+ / 6.8	5.53	10.49	30.66 /87	6.15 /66	11.95 /74	0.00	1.47
SC	CT 529 Hartford SmCap Gr 529 Ptf C		C+	(888) 843-7824	B- / 7.1	5.30	10.03	29.66 /86	5.36 /58	11.11 /67	0.00	2.22

● Denotes fund is closed to new investors
* Denotes fund is included in Section II

www.thestreetratings.com

RISK			NET ASSETS		ASSET				Portfolio Turnover Ratio	BULL / BEAR		FUND MANAGER		MINIMUMS		LOADS	
Risk Rating/Pts	3 Year Standard Deviation	Beta	NAV As of 2/28/17	Total $(Mil)	Cash %	Stocks %	Bonds %	Other %		Last Bull Market Return	Last Bear Market Return	Manager Quality Pct	Manager Tenure (Years)	Initial Purch. $	Additional Purch. $	Front End Load	Back End Load
D / 1.6	14.2	1.30	21.52	19	1	98	0	1	39	N/A	N/A	3	22	500,000	0	0.0	2.0
D / 1.7	14.2	1.30	21.24	45	1	98	0	1	39	88.4	-25.6	3	22	2,000	100	0.0	2.0
C+ / 6.8	5.7	0.71	8.34	5	14	85	0	1	160	N/A	N/A	25	4	2,500	250	2.3	1.0
C+ / 6.8	5.7	0.36	8.40	3	14	85	0	1	160	N/A	N/A	70	4	100,000	0	0.0	1.0
C+ / 5.9	12.0	0.95	8.67	86	5	94	0	1	8	50.4	-24.6	72	7	0	0	0.0	0.0
B / 8.6	6.4	0.92	14.48	24	11	48	39	2	0	46.0	-10.6	18	7	50	25	5.5	0.0
B / 8.5	6.4	0.92	13.80	10	11	48	39	2	0	40.1	-10.9	13	7	50	25	0.0	0.0
B / 8.6	6.4	0.91	14.72	3	11	48	39	2	0	47.9	-10.5	21	7	50	25	0.0	0.0
B+ / 9.3	4.1	0.58	12.79	21	23	24	51	2	0	25.9	-4.3	39	7	50	25	3.0	0.0
B+ / 9.2	4.1	0.58	12.19	12	23	24	51	2	0	20.9	-4.6	30	7	50	25	0.0	0.0
B+ / 9.4	4.1	0.58	13.00	4	23	24	51	2	0	27.6	-4.2	43	7	50	25	0.0	0.0
B+ / 9.9	2.6	0.32	11.37	13	38	9	51	2	0	12.3	-1.6	54	7	50	25	3.0	0.0
B+ / 9.9	2.6	0.33	10.83	12	38	9	51	2	0	7.8	-2.0	43	7	50	25	0.0	0.0
B+ / 9.9	2.6	0.32	11.54	2	38	9	51	2	0	13.7	-1.6	57	7	50	25	0.0	0.0
B / 8.2	7.6	1.10	15.39	59	12	63	23	2	0	57.0	-13.5	11	7	50	25	5.5	0.0
B / 8.1	7.6	1.10	14.67	19	12	63	23	2	0	50.8	-13.7	7	7	50	25	0.0	0.0
B / 8.2	7.6	1.10	15.63	8	12	63	23	2	0	59.1	-13.4	13	7	50	25	0.0	0.0
B- / 7.6	8.9	1.31	16.86	53	10	77	11	2	0	75.3	-17.7	8	7	50	25	5.5	0.0
B- / 7.6	8.9	1.31	16.07	18	10	77	11	2	0	68.4	-17.9	6	7	50	25	0.0	0.0
B- / 7.6	8.9	1.31	17.13	7	10	77	11	2	0	77.7	-17.6	10	7	50	25	0.0	0.0
C+ / 6.7	10.5	0.94	18.50	9	3	95	1	1	0	97.3	-22.6	12	7	50	25	0.0	0.0
C+ / 6.7	10.4	0.94	17.63	4	3	95	1	1	0	89.4	-22.9	8	7	50	25	0.0	0.0
C+ / 6.7	10.4	0.94	18.79	5	3	95	1	1	0	99.9	-22.6	14	7	50	25	0.0	0.0
B / 8.2	7.6	1.10	14.82	11	13	63	23	1	0	48.8	-10.3	11	7	50	25	0.0	0.0
B / 8.1	7.6	1.11	14.13	8	13	63	23	1	0	42.9	-10.6	7	7	50	25	0.0	0.0
B / 8.5	7.5	1.18	17.38	4	0	62	37	1	0	79.3	-14.0	38	7	50	25	5.5	0.0
B / 8.5	7.5	1.18	16.56	3	0	62	37	1	0	72.2	-14.2	30	7	50	25	0.0	0.0
B / 8.6	7.5	1.18	17.66	1	0	62	37	1	0	81.8	-13.9	43	7	50	25	0.0	0.0
B+ / 9.3	4.1	0.57	12.82	4	23	24	51	2	0	26.2	-4.2	40	7	50	25	0.0	0.0
B+ / 9.2	4.1	0.58	12.23	3	23	24	51	2	0	21.2	-4.5	30	7	50	25	0.0	0.0
B+ / 9.4	4.1	0.57	13.03	1	23	24	51	2	0	27.9	-4.1	43	7	50	25	0.0	0.0
B- / 7.6	8.9	0.80	16.84	18	10	77	11	2	0	75.3	-17.7	17	7	50	25	0.0	0.0
B- / 7.6	8.9	0.80	16.06	7	10	77	11	2	0	68.4	-17.9	12	7	50	25	0.0	0.0
B- / 7.6	8.9	0.80	17.12	3	10	77	11	2	0	77.7	-17.6	19	7	50	25	0.0	0.0
B / 8.2	7.6	1.10	15.06	2	13	63	23	1	0	50.9	-10.2	13	7	50	25	0.0	0.0
C+ / 6.3	12.0	1.12	19.44	5	0	99	0	1	0	121.8	-25.7	12	7	50	25	5.5	0.0
C+ / 6.2	12.0	1.12	18.53	3	0	99	0	1	0	112.9	-25.9	8	7	50	25	0.0	0.0
C+ / 6.3	12.0	1.12	19.76	2	0	99	0	1	0	124.8	-25.6	14	7	50	25	0.0	0.0
B- / 7.6	10.4	0.99	21.52	9	3	96	0	1	0	118.2	-17.4	61	7	50	25	5.5	0.0
B- / 7.5	10.4	0.99	20.50	11	3	96	0	1	0	109.5	-17.7	51	7	50	25	0.0	0.0
B- / 7.6	10.4	0.99	21.85	3	3	96	0	1	0	121.2	-17.3	64	7	50	25	0.0	0.0
C / 5.2	13.2	1.08	23.30	6	1	98	0	1	0	138.4	-23.1	36	N/A	50	25	5.5	0.0
C / 5.2	13.2	1.08	22.21	2	1	98	0	1	0	128.9	-23.3	27	N/A	50	25	0.0	0.0
C / 5.2	13.2	1.08	23.68	1	1	98	0	1	0	141.7	-23.0	39	N/A	50	25	0.0	0.0
C+ / 6.2	10.6	0.84	13.32	3	2	97	0	1	0	52.1	-23.2	78	7	50	25	5.5	0.0
C+ / 6.2	10.6	0.84	12.69	2	2	97	0	1	0	46.1	-23.5	72	7	50	25	0.0	0.0
C+ / 6.2	10.6	0.84	13.53	1	2	97	0	1	0	54.2	-23.2	80	7	50	25	0.0	0.0
C+ / 6.0	12.9	1.03	22.49	4	0	99	0	1	0	143.3	-25.7	49	7	50	25	5.5	0.0
C+ / 6.0	12.9	1.03	21.44	3	0	99	0	1	0	133.6	-25.9	38	7	50	25	0.0	0.0
C+ / 6.0	12.9	1.03	22.85	2	0	99	0	1	0	146.6	-25.6	53	7	50	25	0.0	0.0
C / 4.7	15.9	0.98	22.12	4	1	98	0	1	0	118.5	-24.9	67	7	50	25	5.5	0.0
C / 4.7	15.9	0.98	21.07	1	1	98	0	1	0	109.7	-25.1	58	7	50	25	0.0	0.0

I. Index of Stock Mutual Funds

Fund Type	Fund Name	Ticker Symbol	Overall Investment Rating	Phone	Perfor-mance Rating/Pts	3 Mo	6 Mo	1Yr / Pct	3Yr / Pct	5Yr / Pct	Dividend Yield	Expense Ratio
SC	CT 529 Hartford SmCap Gr 529 Ptf E		B-	(888) 843-7824	B / 7.9	5.59	10.58	30.94 /88	6.42 /68	12.23 /76	0.00	1.22
GR	CT 529 Hartford Value 529 Ptf A		A	(888) 843-7824	B / 7.6	7.06	9.03	24.74 /72	9.03 /87	12.49 /79	0.00	1.30
GR	CT 529 Hartford Value 529 Ptf C		A+	(888) 843-7824	B / 7.9	6.87	8.58	23.82 /69	8.21 /80	11.65 /71	0.00	2.05
GR	CT 529 Hartford Value 529 Ptf E		A+	(888) 843-7824	B+ / 8.7	7.10	9.09	25.04 /73	9.29 /89	12.76 /82	0.00	1.05
EM	Cullen Emerging Mrkts High Div C	CEMGX	D	(877) 485-8586	D+ / 2.4	6.71	1.80	19.61 /50	0.22 /14	--	2.67	2.36
EM	Cullen Emerging Mrkts High Div I	CEMFX	D	(877) 485-8586	C- / 3.1	6.98	2.39	20.90 /57	1.30 /20	--	3.39	1.37
EM	Cullen Emerging Mrkts High Div Rtl	CEMDX	D	(877) 485-8586	D+ / 2.9	6.84	2.17	20.63 /56	0.99 /18	--	3.20	1.61
GI	Cullen High Dividend Equity C	CHVCX	B+	(877) 485-8586	B / 7.6	8.43	6.51	20.72 /56	8.25 /81	10.60 /63	1.62	2.08
GI	Cullen High Dividend Equity I	CHDVX	A	(877) 485-8586	B+ / 8.3	8.73	6.79	21.74 /61	9.25 /88	11.66 /71	2.51	1.08
GI	Cullen High Dividend Equity Retail	CHDEX	A-	(877) 485-8586	B / 8.1	8.61	6.66	21.37 /59	8.99 /87	11.38 /69	2.28	1.33
FO	Cullen Intl High Dividend C	CIHCX	D-	(877) 485-8586	E / 0.4	6.00	0.77	10.06 /12	-3.19 / 4	2.25 / 9	2.03	2.20
FO	Cullen Intl High Dividend I	CIHIX	D-	(877) 485-8586	E+ / 0.6	6.30	1.37	11.16 /15	-2.17 / 6	3.28 /12	2.99	1.20
FO	Cullen Intl High Dividend Retail	CIHDX	D-	(877) 485-8586	E+ / 0.6	6.16	1.14	10.84 /14	-2.47 / 6	3.01 /11	2.76	1.45
SC	Cullen Small Cap Value C	CUSCX	E+	(877) 485-8586	D+ / 2.4	4.68	16.48	24.98 /73	-0.07 /13	4.21 /16	0.00	6.30
SC	Cullen Small Cap Value I	CUSIX	D	(877) 485-8586	C / 4.8	4.89	17.03	26.21 /77	0.84 /17	5.20 /23	0.08	5.29
SC	Cullen Small Cap Value Retail	CUSRX	D	(877) 485-8586	C / 4.7	4.82	16.96	25.84 /76	0.65 /16	4.98 /21	0.01	5.54
GI	Cullen Value Fund C	CVLFX	A	(877) 485-8586	B / 8.0	7.63	10.68	26.37 /77	7.28 /74	--	2.31	2.99
GI	Cullen Value Fund I	CVLVX	A+	(877) 485-8586	B+ / 8.8	7.88	11.22	27.68 /81	8.37 /82	--	3.19	1.98
GI	Cullen Value Fund Retail	CVLEX	A+	(877) 485-8586	B+ / 8.7	7.87	11.20	27.44 /80	8.16 /80	--	3.04	2.22
GI	Cutler Equity	CALEX	C+	(888) 288-5374	C+ / 6.7	3.68	6.70	19.47 /49	7.69 /77	10.89 /65	1.54	1.15
GI	CVR Dynamic Allocation Inst	CVRAX	B-	(855) 328-7691	C / 5.1	6.48	12.06	20.31 /54	3.14 /33	--	0.05	2.39
GR	Dana Large Cap Equity A	DLCAX	B+		B- / 7.1	9.97	11.43	22.13 /63	8.10 /80	11.71 /72	1.21	1.25
GR	Dana Large Cap Equity Institutional	DLCIX	A		B / 8.2	10.08	11.61	22.46 /64	8.42 /82	--	1.49	1.00
GR	Dana Large Cap Equity N	DLCEX	A		B / 8.0	10.01	11.46	22.15 /63	8.09 /80	11.82 /73	1.26	1.25
AA	Davenport Balanced Income	DBALX	U	(800) 281-2317	U /	4.34	4.53	13.46 /23	--	--	1.01	2.25
GR	Davenport Core	DAVPX	A-	(800) 281-2317	B+ / 8.4	8.34	9.18	23.73 /69	8.75 /85	12.66 /80	0.48	0.92
GR	Davenport Equity Opportunities	DEOPX	C-	(800) 281-2317	C / 4.8	4.75	4.19	16.81 /38	5.39 /58	11.73 /72	0.00	0.95
SC	Davenport Small Cap Focus Fund	DSCPX	U	(800) 281-2317	U /	3.90	11.40	36.24 /95	--	--	0.00	1.17
IN	Davenport Value and Income Fund	DVIPX	A-	(800) 281-2317	B / 7.9	6.37	7.64	21.90 /62	8.83 /86	13.04 /84	1.79	0.93
GR	Davidson Multi Cap Equity Fund A	DFMAX	B	(877) 332-0529	B- / 7.1	4.45	6.77	26.73 /78	8.48 /83	12.86 /82	0.17	1.34
GR	Davidson Multi Cap Equity Fund C	DFMCX	B	(877) 332-0529	B- / 7.4	4.27	6.38	25.82 /76	7.67 /77	12.03 /75	0.00	2.09
GR	Davidson Multi Cap Equity Fund I	DFMIX	A-	(877) 332-0529	B / 8.1	4.55	6.92	27.07 /79	8.76 /85	--	0.43	1.09
GI	Davis Appreciation & Income A	RPFCX	D+	(800) 279-0279	D+ / 2.8	4.16	6.07	23.64 /69	1.56 /21	6.23 /30	1.00	0.87
GI	● Davis Appreciation & Income B	DCSBX	D+	(800) 279-0279	D+ / 2.8	3.92	5.54	22.24 /63	0.48 /16	5.15 /22	0.16	1.93
GI	Davis Appreciation & Income C	DCSCX	D+	(800) 279-0279	C- / 3.0	4.00	5.68	22.62 /65	0.71 /17	5.36 /24	0.31	1.72
GI	Davis Appreciation & Income Y	DCSYX	C-	(800) 279-0279	C- / 3.8	4.26	6.25	23.94 /70	1.76 /22	6.44 /31	1.26	0.68
FS	Davis Financial A	RPFGX	A+	(800) 279-0279	A+ / 9.8	7.90	16.11	33.82 /93	12.34 /98	14.42 /95	0.58	0.86
FS	● Davis Financial B	DFIBX	A	(800) 279-0279	A+ / 9.8	7.62	15.51	32.30 /90	11.10 /97	13.14 /85	0.00	1.96
FS	Davis Financial C	DFFCX	A+	(800) 279-0279	A+ / 9.8	7.70	15.70	32.78 /91	11.39 /98	13.41 /88	0.00	1.75
FS	Davis Financial Y	DVFYX	A+	(800) 279-0279	A+ / 9.8	7.97	16.25	34.12 /93	12.54 /98	14.62 /96	0.77	0.71
GL	Davis Global Fund A	DGFAX	C-	(800) 279-0279	C / 4.3	4.19	5.95	24.64 /72	4.86 /53	10.95 /65	0.00	0.97
GL	Davis Global Fund B	DGFBX	D+	(800) 279-0279	C- / 4.1	3.81	5.24	22.92 /66	3.48 /37	9.48 /54	0.00	2.36
GL	Davis Global Fund C	DGFCX	C-	(800) 279-0279	C / 4.5	3.99	5.51	23.59 /68	3.99 /43	9.97 /58	0.00	1.80
GL	Davis Global Fund Y	DGFYX	C	(800) 279-0279	C / 5.5	4.29	6.11	24.89 /73	5.13 /56	11.24 /68	0.00	0.73
FO	Davis International Fund A	DILAX	E+	(800) 279-0279	E+ / 0.8	4.54	1.35	18.51 /45	-0.41 /12	5.15 /22	0.03	1.14
FO	Davis International Fund B	DILBX	E+	(800) 279-0279	E+ / 0.8	4.23	0.76	17.05 /39	-1.63 / 8	3.96 /15	0.00	4.69
FO	Davis International Fund C	DILCX	E+	(800) 279-0279	E+ / 0.8	4.21	0.76	17.13 /39	-1.50 / 8	4.04 /15	0.00	2.18
FO	Davis International Fund Y	DILYX	E+	(800) 279-0279	D- / 1.2	4.54	1.42	18.81 /46	-0.11 /13	5.50 /25	0.27	0.80
* GR	Davis New York Venture Fund A	NYVTX	C	(800) 279-0279	B / 7.8	4.89	10.00	30.46 /87	8.22 /81	12.24 /76	0.65	0.89
GR	Davis New York Venture Fund B	NYVBX	C	(800) 279-0279	B / 7.8	4.66	9.48	29.19 /84	7.20 /73	11.19 /67	0.04	1.85
GR	Davis New York Venture Fund C	NYVCX	C	(800) 279-0279	B / 8.0	4.71	9.61	29.49 /85	7.39 /75	11.37 /69	0.15	1.66
GR	Davis New York Venture Fund R	NYVRX	C+	(800) 279-0279	B+ / 8.4	4.80	9.86	30.08 /87	7.90 /78	11.91 /73	0.45	1.18

● Denotes fund is closed to new investors
* Denotes fund is included in Section II

www.thestreetratings.com

Risk Rating/Pts	3 Year Standard Deviation	Beta	NAV As of 2/28/17	Total $(Mil)	Cash %	Stocks %	Bonds %	Other %	Portfolio Turnover Ratio	Last Bull Market Return	Last Bear Market Return	Manager Quality Pct	Manager Tenure (Years)	Initial Purch. $	Additional Purch. $	Front End Load	Back End Load
C /4.7	15.8	0.98	22.47	1	1	98	0	1	0	121.5	-24.8	71	7	50	25	0.0	0.0
B- /7.8	9.9	0.93	21.38	4	2	97	0	1	0	123.2	-20.4	66	7	50	25	5.5	0.0
B- /7.7	9.9	0.93	20.38	2	2	97	0	1	0	114.4	-20.7	56	7	50	25	0.0	0.0
B- /7.8	9.9	0.93	21.72	1	2	97	0	1	0	126.2	-20.4	69	7	50	25	0.0	0.0
C /5.1	13.5	0.81	9.82	3	6	88	4	2	69	N/A	N/A	60	5	1,000	100	0.0	0.0
C /5.1	13.5	0.81	9.98	257	6	88	4	2	69	N/A	N/A	73	5	1,000,000	100	0.0	0.0
C /5.1	13.5	0.81	9.92	15	6	88	4	2	69	N/A	N/A	69	5	1,000	100	0.0	0.0
C+ /6.9	9.8	0.87	18.12	91	1	94	3	2	12	87.5	-8.8	63	14	1,000	100	0.0	0.0
C+ /6.9	9.9	0.87	18.23	1,502	1	94	3	2	12	97.6	-8.4	N/A	14	1,000,000	100	0.0	0.0
C+ /6.9	9.8	0.87	18.22	341	1	94	3	2	12	94.9	-8.5	72	14	1,000	100	0.0	0.0
C+ /6.1	10.4	0.80	9.54	3	0	92	6	2	38	25.5	-21.0	33	12	1,000	100	0.0	0.0
C+ /6.1	10.3	0.80	9.66	156	0	92	6	2	38	32.5	-20.7	47	12	1,000,000	100	0.0	0.0
C+ /6.1	10.3	0.80	9.58	36	0	92	6	2	38	30.4	-20.7	43	12	1,000	100	0.0	0.0
D+ /2.9	16.8	0.85	13.45	N/A	1	98	0	1	42	58.1	-23.5	10	8	1,000	100	0.0	0.0
C- /3.1	16.8	0.85	14.39	4	1	98	0	1	42	66.3	-23.1	16	8	1,000,000	100	0.0	0.0
C- /3.1	16.8	0.85	14.17	1	1	98	0	1	42	64.2	-23.2	14	8	1,000	100	0.0	0.0
B- /7.4	9.9	0.90	15.08	1	19	80	0	1	3	N/A	N/A	48	5	1,000	100	0.0	0.0
B- /7.4	9.9	0.90	15.11	33	19	80	0	1	3	N/A	N/A	61	5	1,000,000	100	0.0	0.0
B- /7.4	9.9	0.90	15.12	1	19	80	0	1	3	N/A	N/A	59	5	1,000	100	0.0	0.0
C+ /6.6	9.8	0.89	18.28	143	3	96	0	1	11	99.2	-13.0	54	14	2,500	0	0.0	0.0
B- /7.5	9.5	0.79	11.11	21	15	84	0	1	129	N/A	N/A	15	2	100,000	0	0.0	0.0
B- /7.1	10.6	0.99	20.04	1	1	98	0	1	69	110.8	-18.0	46	9	1,000	250	5.0	2.0
B- /7.3	10.6	0.99	20.08	105	1	98	0	1	69	N/A	N/A	50	9	1,000,000	1,000	0.0	2.0
B- /7.1	10.6	0.99	20.08	36	1	98	0	1	69	112.0	-18.0	46	9	1,000	250	0.0	2.0
U /	N/A	N/A	11.08	78	3	60	35	2	0	N/A	N/A	N/A	2	5,000	0	0.0	0.0
C+ /6.3	10.4	0.98	21.20	398	0	99	0	1	23	122.0	-16.2	55	19	5,000	0	0.0	0.0
C /5.5	12.2	1.02	15.67	352	4	95	0	1	29	117.2	-17.1	14	7	5,000	0	0.0	0.0
U /	N/A	N/A	11.73	71	7	92	0	1	48	N/A	N/A	N/A	3	5,000	0	0.0	0.0
C+ /6.7	9.2	0.86	16.16	564	3	96	0	1	25	122.3	-12.7	72	7	5,000	0	0.0	0.0
C+ /6.1	11.8	1.09	24.01	55	0	98	1	1	25	124.3	-19.3	36	9	2,500	0	5.0	0.0
C+ /6.1	11.8	1.09	23.21	22	0	98	1	1	25	115.4	-19.5	27	9	2,500	0	0.0	0.0
C+ /6.6	11.8	1.09	24.00	40	0	98	1	1	25	N/A	N/A	40	9	250,000	0	0.0	0.0
C+ /5.7	12.9	1.01	35.71	93	9	61	29	1	32	60.3	-21.6	3	1	1,000	25	4.8	0.0
C+ /5.6	12.9	1.01	35.16	1	9	61	29	1	32	51.7	-21.9	2	1	1,000	25	0.0	0.0
C+ /5.6	12.9	1.01	35.80	46	9	61	29	1	32	53.3	-21.9	2	1	1,000	25	0.0	0.0
C+ /5.7	12.9	1.01	35.89	63	9	61	29	1	32	61.9	-21.5	3	1	5,000,000	25	0.0	0.0
C+ /6.1	12.6	0.94	47.12	551	16	83	0	1	5	131.9	-19.8	78	26	1,000	25	4.8	0.0
C+ /5.7	12.6	0.95	37.66	2	16	83	0	1	5	118.2	-20.1	68	26	1,000	25	0.0	0.0
C+ /5.8	12.6	0.94	39.54	155	16	83	0	1	5	121.0	-20.1	71	26	1,000	25	0.0	0.0
C+ /6.1	12.6	0.95	48.52	396	16	83	0	1	5	134.2	-19.7	79	26	5,000,000	25	0.0	0.0
C /5.1	12.9	0.88	20.64	132	6	93	0	1	53	103.1	-26.0	95	13	1,000	25	4.8	2.0
C /4.9	12.9	0.88	19.09	1	6	93	0	1	53	89.3	-26.4	92	13	1,000	25	0.0	2.0
C /5.0	12.9	0.88	19.54	90	6	93	0	1	53	93.7	-26.3	94	13	1,000	25	0.0	2.0
C /5.1	12.9	0.88	20.67	437	6	93	0	1	53	106.0	-25.9	96	13	5,000,000	25	0.0	2.0
C /4.9	14.6	1.01	10.27	10	11	88	0	1	47	54.4	-31.5	71	11	1,000	25	4.8	2.0
C /4.9	14.6	1.01	9.69	N/A	11	88	0	1	47	45.4	-32.9	56	11	1,000	25	0.0	2.0
C /4.9	14.6	1.01	9.72	1	11	88	0	1	47	46.1	-33.0	58	11	1,000	25	0.0	2.0
C /4.9	14.6	1.01	10.14	98	11	88	0	1	47	57.6	-32.5	74	11	5,000,000	25	0.0	2.0
C- /3.2	12.6	1.11	31.75	6,521	1	98	0	1	25	115.8	-20.2	31	22	1,000	25	4.8	0.0
D+ /2.9	12.6	1.11	28.46	43	1	98	0	1	25	105.2	-20.6	21	22	1,000	25	0.0	0.0
C- /3.0	12.6	1.11	29.18	2,325	1	98	0	1	25	107.0	-20.5	23	22	1,000	25	0.0	0.0
C- /3.3	12.6	1.11	31.86	201	1	98	0	1	25	112.4	-20.3	28	22	500,000	25	0.0	0.0

Fund Type	Fund Name	Ticker Symbol	Overall Investment Rating	Phone	Performance Rating/Pts	3 Mo	6 Mo	1Yr / Pct	3Yr / Pct	5Yr / Pct	Dividend Yield	Expense Ratio
GR	Davis New York Venture Fund Y	DNVYX	C+	(800) 279-0279	B+ / 8.8	4.97	10.16	30.81 / 88	8.49 / 83	12.52 / 79	0.92	0.63
MC	Davis Opportunity A	RPEAX	C-	(800) 279-0279	C+ / 6.6	2.62	6.21	25.81 / 76	7.98 / 79	14.29 / 95	0.00	0.96
MC	● Davis Opportunity B	RPFEX	D	(800) 279-0279	C+ / 6.6	2.34	5.64	24.40 / 71	6.85 / 71	13.12 / 85	0.00	1.98
MC	Davis Opportunity C	DGOCX	D+	(800) 279-0279	C+ / 6.8	2.42	5.78	24.83 / 73	7.13 / 73	13.38 / 88	0.00	1.75
MC	Davis Opportunity Y	DGOYX	C	(800) 279-0279	B- / 7.5	2.72	6.35	26.17 / 77	8.25 / 81	14.57 / 96	0.00	0.73
RE	Davis Real Estate A	RPFRX	C+	(800) 279-0279	C+ / 6.5	6.79	-1.93	16.31 / 35	10.51 / 96	9.62 / 55	1.50	0.94
RE	● Davis Real Estate B	DREBX	C+	(800) 279-0279	C+ / 6.5	6.53	-2.43	15.03 / 30	9.31 / 89	8.43 / 46	0.55	2.02
RE	Davis Real Estate C	DRECX	C+	(800) 279-0279	C+ / 6.6	6.58	-2.34	15.28 / 31	9.55 / 91	8.67 / 48	0.73	1.81
RE	Davis Real Estate Y	DREYX	B-	(800) 279-0279	B- / 7.4	6.82	-1.83	16.55 / 36	10.75 / 96	9.86 / 57	1.77	0.74
OT	Davis Research Fund Class A	DRFAX	B-	(800) 279-0279	C+ / 6.7	6.37	8.38	21.73 / 61	7.96 / 79	11.77 / 72	0.39	0.70
AA	Day Hagan Tact Alloc Fd of ETFs A	DHAAX	D+	(877) 329-4246	E+ / 0.9	1.07	1.88	9.34 / 10	1.07 / 19	3.66 / 14	0.00	2.04
AA	Day Hagan Tact Alloc Fd of ETFs C	DHACX	D+	(877) 329-4246	D- / 1.2	0.94	1.51	8.58 / 9	0.34 / 15	2.91 / 10	0.00	2.79
IN	Day Hagan Tactical Dividend I	DHQIX	U	(877) 329-4246	U /	2.38	3.59	13.19 / 22	--	--	0.47	1.47
AA	DE 529 Fidelity CIP 100% Eq Ptf		C+	(800) 544-8544	C+ / 6.6	7.21	7.54	22.46 / 64	5.90 / 63	10.28 / 60	0.00	1.00
AA	DE 529 Fidelity CIP 70% Eq Ptf		B	(800) 544-8544	C / 5.0	5.63	5.13	17.66 / 41	5.04 / 55	8.24 / 44	0.00	0.93
AA	DE 529 Fidelity CIP College Ptf		C+	(800) 544-8544	D / 1.8	2.41	0.99	7.42 / 6	2.51 / 28	3.17 / 11	0.00	0.67
AA	DE 529 Fidelity CIP Consv Ptf		C-	(800) 544-8544	D- / 1.0	0.79	-0.45	2.40 / 2	1.34 / 20	1.30 / 7	0.00	0.59
AA	DE 529 Fidelity CIP Idx 100% Eq Ptf		C+	(800) 544-8544	C+ / 6.8	7.57	8.42	22.91 / 66	6.00 / 64	10.46 / 62	0.00	0.27
AA	DE 529 Fidelity CIP Idx 70% Eq Ptf		B	(800) 544-8544	C / 4.6	5.59	5.16	15.97 / 34	4.88 / 53	7.98 / 42	0.00	0.30
AA	DE 529 Fidelity CIP Idx Consv Ptf		C	(800) 544-8544	E+ / 0.9	0.53	-0.90	0.68 / 2	1.16 / 19	0.93 / 6	0.00	0.34
AA	DE 529 Fidelity CIP Index Clg Ptf		C	(800) 544-8544	D- / 1.5	1.99	0.56	4.90 / 4	2.11 / 25	2.72 / 10	0.00	0.33
AA	DE 529 Fidelity CIP Index Ptf 2018		C+	(800) 544-8544	D / 1.8	2.49	1.06	6.72 / 5	2.77 / 30	4.74 / 20	0.00	0.31
AA	DE 529 Fidelity CIP Index Ptf 2021		C+	(800) 544-8544	D+ / 2.5	3.39	2.26	9.54 / 11	3.49 / 37	6.13 / 29	0.00	0.30
AA	DE 529 Fidelity CIP Index Ptf 2024		B-	(800) 544-8544	C- / 3.4	4.33	3.47	12.27 / 19	4.17 / 45	7.44 / 38	0.00	0.29
AA	DE 529 Fidelity CIP Index Ptf 2027		B-	(800) 544-8544	C / 4.3	5.15	4.57	15.02 / 30	4.72 / 51	8.50 / 46	0.00	0.28
GL	DE 529 Fidelity CIP Portfolio 2018		C+	(800) 544-8544	D+ / 2.3	2.99	1.60	9.49 / 10	3.25 / 34	5.27 / 23	0.00	0.86
AA	DE 529 Fidelity CIP Portfolio 2021		C+	(800) 544-8544	C- / 3.1	3.87	2.66	12.18 / 19	3.94 / 42	6.59 / 32	0.00	0.92
AA	DE 529 Fidelity CIP Portfolio 2024		B-	(800) 544-8544	C- / 3.9	4.68	3.70	14.78 / 29	4.47 / 48	7.78 / 40	0.00	0.97
AA	DE 529 Fidelity CIP Portfolio 2027		B-	(800) 544-8544	C / 4.8	5.46	4.70	17.24 / 39	4.92 / 53	8.79 / 49	0.00	0.99
GR	Dean Mid Cap Value	DALCX	A+	(888) 899-8343	A- / 9.0	5.70	9.27	27.76 / 81	9.63 / 91	12.96 / 83	0.41	1.81
SC	Dean Small Cap Value	DASCX	A	(888) 899-8343	A / 9.5	3.32	12.99	35.69 / 95	9.26 / 89	13.34 / 87	1.06	1.20
IN	Dearborn Partners Rising Dividend A	DRDAX	B-	(888) 983-3380	C+ / 5.9	6.99	4.58	17.02 / 38	8.22 / 81	--	0.79	1.40
IN	Dearborn Partners Rising Dividend C	DRDCX	B-	(888) 983-3380	C+ / 6.3	6.80	4.26	16.14 / 35	7.42 / 75	--	0.21	2.15
IN	Dearborn Partners Rising Dividend I	DRDIX	B+	(888) 983-3380	B- / 7.0	7.05	4.70	17.27 / 40	8.49 / 83	--	1.06	1.15
SC	Delafield	DEFIX	E-	(800) 697-3863	D+ / 2.7	5.26	10.40	33.90 / 93	-0.25 / 12	6.16 / 29	0.00	1.26
EM	● Delaware Emerging Markets	DPEMX	E+	(800) 523-1918	D / 1.6	8.45	3.01	21.27 / 59	-0.24 / 12	-1.39 / 3	3.38	1.19
EM	Delaware Emerging Markets A	DEMAX	D+	(800) 523-1918	C+ / 5.7	10.18	6.74	41.19 / 98	1.76 / 22	3.23 / 12	0.60	1.73
EM	Delaware Emerging Markets C	DEMCX	D+	(800) 523-1918	C+ / 6.2	9.97	6.36	40.15 / 97	1.00 / 18	2.46 / 9	0.07	2.48
EM	Delaware Emerging Markets I	DEMIX	C-	(800) 523-1918	B- / 7.0	10.23	6.95	41.55 / 98	2.04 / 24	3.48 / 13	0.85	1.48
EM	Delaware Emerging Markets II	DPEGX	E+	(800) 523-1918	D+ / 2.5	9.54	5.49	31.24 / 89	-0.14 / 13	1.14 / 6	1.11	1.35
EM	Delaware Emerging Markets R	DEMRX	C-	(800) 523-1918	C+ / 6.6	10.07	6.65	40.80 / 97	1.52 / 21	2.96 / 11	0.42	1.98
AA	Delaware Foundation Consv All A	DFIAX	D+	(800) 523-1918	D / 1.6	2.93	2.27	9.81 / 11	3.03 / 32	4.65 / 19	1.70	1.36
AA	Delaware Foundation Consv All C	DFICX	D+	(800) 523-1918	D / 1.9	2.84	1.99	9.10 / 10	2.25 / 26	3.88 / 15	1.08	2.11
AA	Delaware Foundation Consv All Inst	DFIIX	C-	(800) 523-1918	D+ / 2.5	3.09	2.50	10.18 / 12	3.28 / 34	4.92 / 21	2.04	1.11
AA	Delaware Foundation Consv All R	DFIRX	D+	(800) 523-1918	D / 2.2	2.97	2.25	9.67 / 11	2.77 / 30	4.41 / 18	1.57	1.61
AA	Delaware Foundation Growth All A	DFGAX	D	(800) 523-1918	D+ / 2.7	4.98	4.23	15.86 / 34	3.66 / 39	6.77 / 33	1.23	1.50
AA	Delaware Foundation Growth All C	DFGCX	D+	(800) 523-1918	C- / 3.1	4.66	3.78	15.01 / 30	2.86 / 30	5.97 / 28	0.65	2.25
AA	Delaware Foundation Growth All Inst	DFGIX	D+	(800) 523-1918	C- / 3.9	4.93	4.29	16.16 / 35	3.90 / 42	7.04 / 35	1.53	1.25
AA	Delaware Foundation Growth All R	DFGRX	D+	(800) 523-1918	C- / 3.5	4.83	4.07	15.59 / 32	3.37 / 35	6.50 / 31	1.08	1.75
AA	Delaware Foundation Modt All A	DFBAX	D+	(800) 523-1918	D / 2.2	3.94	3.24	13.09 / 22	3.45 / 36	5.86 / 27	1.70	1.17
AA	Delaware Foundation Modt All C	DFBCX	D+	(800) 523-1918	D+ / 2.5	3.75	2.95	12.25 / 19	2.66 / 29	5.05 / 22	1.09	1.93
AA	Delaware Foundation Modt All Inst	DFFIX	C-	(800) 523-1918	C- / 3.2	4.00	3.36	13.34 / 23	3.69 / 39	6.11 / 29	2.03	0.93

● Denotes fund is closed to new investors
* Denotes fund is included in Section II

Risk Rating/Pts	Standard Deviation	Beta	NAV As of 2/28/17	Total $(Mil)	Cash %	Stocks %	Bonds %	Other %	Portfolio Turnover Ratio	Last Bull Market Return	Last Bear Market Return	Manager Quality Pct	Manager Tenure (Years)	Initial Purch. $	Additional Purch. $	Front End Load	Back End Load
C- /3.3	12.6	1.11	32.40	2,774	1	98	0	1	25	118.8	-20.2	34	22	5,000,000	25	0.0	0.0
C- /3.1	12.9	0.90	31.75	286	2	66	31	1	39	132.5	-18.3	67	18	1,000	25	4.8	0.0
D /1.8	12.9	0.90	24.11	1	2	66	31	1	39	120.1	-18.7	53	18	1,000	25	0.0	0.0
D /2.2	12.9	0.90	26.33	107	2	66	31	1	39	122.8	-18.7	57	18	1,000	25	0.0	0.0
C- /3.2	12.9	0.90	33.23	228	2	66	31	1	39	135.7	-18.3	70	18	5,000,000	25	0.0	0.0
C /5.4	13.8	1.00	39.75	145	6	93	0	1	93	91.7	-14.3	68	15	1,000	25	4.8	0.0
C /5.4	13.8	1.00	39.14	2	6	93	0	1	93	80.7	-14.7	53	15	1,000	25	0.0	0.0
C /5.4	13.7	1.00	39.69	22	6	93	0	1	93	83.0	-14.6	56	15	1,000	25	0.0	0.0
C /5.4	13.8	1.00	40.29	45	6	93	0	1	93	94.0	-14.2	70	15	5,000,000	25	0.0	0.0
B- /7.3	9.9	0.91	19.12	39	43	56	0	1	29	109.2	-16.1	54	16	1,000	25	4.8	0.0
B /8.0	6.6	0.99	11.36	11	13	62	24	1	59	35.7	-14.0	8	8	1,000	50	5.8	0.0
B- /7.9	6.5	0.99	10.76	6	13	62	24	1	59	30.3	-14.2	6	8	1,000	50	0.0	0.0
U /	N/A	N/A	11.45	123	19	80	0	1	73	N/A	N/A	N/A	3	1,000	50	0.0	0.0
C+ /6.6	10.5	1.59	20.83	43	2	95	2	1	42	99.5	-23.0	10	12	50	25	0.0	0.0
B /8.1	7.8	1.19	22.32	19	2	67	30	1	44	74.1	-17.3	27	12	50	25	0.0	0.0
B+ /9.9	3.2	0.46	20.40	104	8	21	70	1	145	23.3	-4.4	63	12	50	25	0.0	0.0
B+ /9.3	1.5	0.09	15.33	7	14	0	85	1	131	8.5	0.6	78	12	50	25	0.0	0.0
C+ /6.8	10.3	1.60	17.76	11	1	97	1	1	42	98.0	-19.3	11	11	50	25	0.0	0.0
B /8.9	7.2	1.13	17.94	9	0	68	30	2	21	68.3	-11.3	30	11	50	25	0.0	0.0
B+ /9.7	1.4	0.02	13.24	3	19	0	80	1	219	5.3	4.4	80	11	50	25	0.0	0.0
B+ /9.9	2.4	0.34	14.35	9	10	19	69	2	297	19.4	-0.3	69	11	50	25	0.0	0.0
B+ /9.8	3.6	0.54	15.25	12	8	26	65	1	28	39.7	-7.2	59	11	50	25	0.0	0.0
B+ /9.6	4.8	0.75	15.85	14	5	39	54	2	21	52.8	-10.6	48	11	50	25	0.0	0.0
B+ /9.2	6.0	0.94	16.38	15	3	51	44	2	9	66.0	-13.6	38	11	50	25	0.0	0.0
B /8.7	7.2	1.13	15.32	10	1	63	34	2	3	76.9	-15.8	28	10	50	25	0.0	0.0
B+ /9.4	4.4	0.67	20.99	148	6	29	64	1	43	45.5	-12.4	75	12	50	25	0.0	0.0
B+ /9.1	5.7	0.86	21.19	102	4	42	52	2	34	59.2	-16.1	42	12	50	25	0.0	0.0
B /8.6	6.9	1.06	18.79	45	3	54	41	2	38	71.9	-19.1	31	12	50	25	0.0	0.0
B /8.1	8.1	1.23	14.69	18	2	66	30	2	0	82.9	-21.2	22	10	50	25	0.0	0.0
B- /7.5	9.8	0.85	19.02	26	2	96	0	2	39	137.0	-23.9	78	9	1,000	0	0.0	0.0
C /5.5	14.2	0.85	16.96	277	1	98	0	1	148	147.2	-25.8	91	9	1,000	0	0.0	0.0
B- /7.4	9.6	0.83	13.27	71	6	93	0	1	18	N/A	N/A	68	4	5,000	500	5.0	0.0
B- /7.4	9.6	0.84	13.20	81	6	93	0	1	18	N/A	N/A	58	4	5,000	500	0.0	0.0
B- /7.4	9.7	0.84	13.29	54	6	93	0	1	18	N/A	N/A	70	4	500,000	500	0.0	0.0
E+ /0.9	17.4	0.94	25.36	416	5	74	20	1	39	80.0	-27.4	7	24	1,000	100	0.0	0.0
C- /4.1	14.2	0.83	7.72	135	1	98	0	1	28	16.2	-20.6	53	N/A	1,000,000	0	0.6	0.6
C- /3.1	20.5	1.20	15.94	495	2	97	0	1	12	44.5	-30.4	71	11	1,000	100	5.8	0.0
C- /3.1	20.5	1.20	14.90	128	2	97	0	1	12	38.8	-30.7	62	11	1,000	100	0.0	0.0
C- /3.1	20.5	1.20	16.04	2,023	2	97	0	1	12	46.5	-30.3	74	11	0	0	0.0	0.0
D+ /2.8	18.0	1.07	8.18	38	0	99	0	1	20	28.5	-28.8	49	7	1,000,000	0	0.0	0.0
C- /3.1	20.5	1.20	16.06	42	2	97	0	1	12	42.5	-30.5	68	11	0	0	0.0	0.0
C+ /6.9	4.5	0.68	9.58	43	0	37	62	1	168	38.2	-7.7	49	13	1,000	100	5.8	0.0
C+ /6.9	4.5	0.68	9.60	26	0	37	62	1	168	32.8	-7.9	38	13	1,000	100	0.0	0.0
C+ /6.9	4.6	0.69	9.61	12	0	37	62	1	168	40.2	-7.6	51	13	0	0	0.0	0.0
C+ /6.9	4.6	0.69	9.58	4	0	37	62	1	168	36.4	-7.7	45	13	0	0	0.0	0.0
C /5.3	8.1	1.24	9.72	35	0	73	26	1	87	62.1	-16.4	13	13	1,000	100	5.8	0.0
C /5.3	8.0	1.23	9.43	12	0	73	26	1	87	55.5	-16.7	9	13	1,000	100	0.0	0.0
C /5.3	8.0	1.23	9.78	14	0	73	26	1	87	64.2	-16.3	15	13	0	0	0.0	0.0
C /5.3	8.1	1.24	9.64	3	0	73	26	1	87	59.9	-16.5	11	13	0	0	0.0	0.0
C+ /6.5	6.3	0.97	11.39	171	0	55	43	2	131	50.9	-12.3	27	13	1,000	100	5.8	0.0
C+ /6.5	6.3	0.96	11.38	23	0	55	43	2	131	44.8	-12.5	20	13	1,000	100	0.0	0.0
C+ /6.5	6.3	0.96	11.40	79	0	55	43	2	131	52.8	-12.2	30	13	0	0	0.0	0.0

| | | | | | | Total Return % through 2/28/17 | | | Annualized | | Incl. in Returns | |
Fund Type	Fund Name	Ticker Symbol	Overall Investment Rating	Phone	Perfor-mance Rating/Pts	3 Mo	6 Mo	1Yr / Pct	3Yr / Pct	5Yr / Pct	Dividend Yield	Expense Ratio
AA	Delaware Foundation Modt All R	DFBRX	C-	(800) 523-1918	D+ / 2.9	3.81	3.13	12.75 /21	3.16 /33	5.57 /25	1.57	1.43
RE	Delaware Global RE Opps A	DGRPX	D+	(800) 523-1918	D+ / 2.4	5.52	-4.40	11.24 /15	5.53 /60	8.36 /45	1.96	1.72
RE	Delaware Global RE Opps Inst	DGROX	C-	(800) 523-1918	C- / 3.5	5.60	-4.27	11.53 /16	5.80 /62	8.63 /47	2.34	1.47
RE	Delaware Global Real Estate Opps C	DLPCX	C-	(800) 523-1918	D+ / 2.8	5.32	-4.78	10.43 /13	4.80 /52	--	1.35	2.47
RE	Delaware Global Real Estate Opps R	DLPRX	C-	(800) 523-1918	C- / 3.2	5.45	-4.52	11.00 /14	5.28 /57	--	1.85	1.97
GL	Delaware Global Value A	DABAX	D+	(800) 523-1918	D+ / 2.8	5.53	6.93	19.27 /48	2.39 /27	6.88 /34	1.57	1.80
GL	Delaware Global Value C	DABCX	C-	(800) 523-1918	C- / 3.2	5.28	6.51	18.38 /45	1.61 /22	6.06 /29	1.01	2.55
GL	Delaware Global Value I	DABIX	C-	(800) 523-1918	C- / 4.0	5.57	7.06	19.48 /49	2.64 /29	7.14 /35	1.89	1.55
HL	Delaware Healthcare Fund A	DLHAX	C-	(800) 523-1918	C+ / 6.3	8.76	5.87	19.90 /51	7.80 /77	17.14 /98	0.82	1.35
HL	Delaware Healthcare Fund C	DLHCX	C	(800) 523-1918	C+ / 6.7	8.51	5.44	18.97 /47	6.99 /72	16.28 /98	0.21	2.10
HL	Delaware Healthcare Fund I	DLHIX	C+	(800) 523-1918	B- / 7.4	8.77	5.95	20.12 /53	8.03 /79	17.43 /98	1.09	1.10
HL	Delaware Healthcare Fund R	DLRHX	C	(800) 523-1918	B- / 7.0	8.64	5.72	19.56 /50	7.51 /75	16.86 /98	0.64	1.60
GL	Delaware International Sml Cap A	DGGAX	E-	(800) 523-1918	D / 2.2	5.88	1.59	15.77 /33	2.83 /30	6.55 /32	0.00	1.44
GL	Delaware International Sml Cap C	DGGCX	E-	(800) 523-1918	D+ / 2.6	5.80	1.39	15.03 /30	2.09 /25	5.79 /27	0.00	2.19
GL	Delaware International Sml Cap Inst	DGGIX	E	(800) 523-1918	C- / 3.2	5.85	1.66	16.00 /34	3.05 /32	6.82 /34	0.00	1.19
GL	Delaware International Sml Cap R	DGGRX	E-	(800) 523-1918	C- / 3.0	5.88	1.59	15.58 /32	2.60 /28	6.31 /30	0.00	1.69
FO	Delaware Intl Value Equity A	DEGIX	D-	(800) 523-1918	E+ / 0.9	5.46	3.54	17.24 /39	-0.47 /11	4.54 /18	1.89	1.36
FO	Delaware Intl Value Equity C	DEGCX	D-	(800) 523-1918	D- / 1.1	5.37	3.25	16.38 /36	-1.21 / 9	3.76 /14	1.33	2.11
FO	Delaware Intl Value Equity Inst	DEQIX	D	(800) 523-1918	D- / 1.4	5.61	3.70	17.55 /41	-0.21 /13	4.82 /20	2.24	1.11
FO	Delaware Intl Value Equity R	DIVRX	D-	(800) 523-1918	D- / 1.3	5.47	3.46	16.91 /38	-0.72 /10	4.29 /17	1.78	1.61
GI	Delaware Large Cap Value Eqty Port	DPDEX	A-	(800) 523-1918	A- / 9.0	5.91	7.16	24.33 /71	10.66 /96	14.44 /95	1.79	0.65
MC	Delaware Mid Cap Value A	DLMAX	B-	(800) 523-1918	A- / 9.2	7.15	14.18	34.73 /94	9.30 /89	11.95 /74	0.45	3.94
MC	Delaware Mid Cap Value C	DLMCX	B-	(800) 523-1918	A / 9.4	6.89	13.72	33.87 /93	8.45 /82	11.11 /67	0.00	4.69
MC	Delaware Mid Cap Value Inst	DLMIX	B	(800) 523-1918	A+ / 9.7	7.20	14.23	35.04 /94	9.56 /91	12.22 /76	0.70	3.69
MC	Delaware Mid Cap Value R	DLMRX	B	(800) 523-1918	A+ / 9.6	7.12	14.16	34.44 /93	8.99 /87	11.67 /71	0.27	4.19
FO	Delaware Pooled Tr-Labor Sel Itl Eq	DELPX	E+	(800) 523-1918	D- / 1.1	7.94	3.25	13.45 /23	-1.04 / 9	4.38 /17	2.89	0.87
RE	Delaware RE Inv A	DPREX	D	(800) 523-1918	C / 4.9	6.17	-2.80	12.23 /19	9.48 /90	9.94 /58	1.53	1.32
RE	Delaware RE Inv C	DPRCX	D+	(800) 523-1918	C / 5.4	5.95	-3.14	11.33 /16	8.67 /84	9.12 /52	0.93	2.07
RE	Delaware RE Inv Inst	DPRSX	C-	(800) 523-1918	C+ / 6.3	6.21	-2.68	12.53 /20	9.76 /92	10.21 /60	1.82	1.07
RE	Delaware RE Inv R	DPRRX	D+	(800) 523-1918	C+ / 5.9	6.13	-2.90	11.99 /18	9.21 /88	9.69 /56	1.38	1.57
AG	● Delaware Select Growth A	DVEAX	E	(800) 523-1918	D / 1.8	4.92	2.97	11.57 /16	2.68 /29	7.68 /40	0.00	1.23
AG	● Delaware Select Growth C	DVECX	E-	(800) 523-1918	D / 2.1	4.70	2.59	10.72 /14	1.90 /23	6.87 /34	0.00	1.98
AG	● Delaware Select Growth I	VAGGX	E+	(800) 523-1918	D+ / 2.8	4.98	3.07	11.82 /17	2.93 /31	7.95 /42	0.00	0.98
AG	● Delaware Select Growth R	DFSRX	E	(800) 523-1918	D+ / 2.4	4.88	2.86	11.28 /15	2.42 /27	7.41 /37	0.00	1.48
SC	Delaware Small Cap Core A	DCCAX	B+	(800) 523-1918	B+ / 8.5	4.02	14.25	34.75 /94	8.41 /82	14.26 /95	0.00	1.27
SC	Delaware Small Cap Core C	DCCCX	B+	(800) 523-1918	B+ / 8.9	3.85	13.80	33.74 /93	7.59 /76	13.40 /88	0.00	2.02
SC	Delaware Small Cap Core I	DCCIX	A-	(800) 523-1918	A / 9.4	4.10	14.40	35.11 /94	8.69 /85	14.55 /96	0.06	1.02
SC	Delaware Small Cap Core R	DCCRX	B+	(800) 523-1918	A- / 9.2	3.94	14.11	34.41 /93	8.12 /80	13.96 /93	0.00	1.52
SC	Delaware Small Cap Value A	DEVLX	B+	(800) 523-1918	A+ / 9.7	6.87	18.06	43.22 /98	9.58 /91	12.65 /80	0.47	1.21
SC	Delaware Small Cap Value C	DEVCX	B+	(800) 523-1918	A+ / 9.8	6.68	17.60	42.14 /98	8.76 /85	11.81 /73	0.04	1.96
SC	Delaware Small Cap Value I	DEVIX	A-	(800) 523-1918	A+ / 9.8	6.94	18.22	43.55 /98	9.85 /92	12.93 /83	0.67	0.96
SC	Delaware Small Cap Value R	DVLRX	A-	(800) 523-1918	A+ / 9.8	6.80	17.90	42.84 /98	9.30 /89	12.37 /78	0.32	1.46
SC	Delaware Small Cap Value R6	DVZRX	U	(800) 523-1918	U /	6.99	18.31	--	--	--	0.00	N/A
MC	● Delaware Smid Cap Growth A	DFCIX	E-	(800) 523-1918	D / 1.9	5.48	-5.09	7.29 / 6	5.28 /57	9.17 /52	0.00	1.19
MC	● Delaware Smid Cap Growth C	DEEVX	E-	(800) 523-1918	D / 2.2	5.28	-5.47	6.46 / 5	4.48 /48	8.34 /45	0.00	1.94
MC	● Delaware Smid Cap Growth I	DFDIX	E	(800) 523-1918	D+ / 2.9	5.55	-4.97	7.52 / 7	5.54 /60	9.43 /54	0.02	0.94
MC	● Delaware Smid Cap Growth R	DFRIX	E-	(800) 523-1918	D+ / 2.5	5.46	-5.18	7.01 / 6	5.02 /54	8.90 /50	0.00	1.44
IN	Delaware US Growth A	DUGAX	D-	(800) 523-1918	D+ / 2.6	6.15	2.70	9.14 /10	4.90 /53	10.31 /61	0.00	1.04
IN	Delaware US Growth C	DEUCX	D	(800) 523-1918	C- / 3.0	5.96	2.33	8.31 / 8	4.12 /44	9.50 /55	0.00	1.79
IN	Delaware US Growth I	DEUIX	D+	(800) 523-1918	C- / 3.8	6.21	2.82	9.41 /10	5.15 /56	10.58 /63	0.17	0.79
IN	Delaware US Growth R	DEURX	D	(800) 523-1918	C- / 3.4	6.07	2.56	8.85 / 9	4.64 /50	10.03 /59	0.00	1.29
GR	● Delaware Value A	DDVAX	A-	(800) 523-1918	B / 7.8	5.78	6.94	23.92 /70	10.36 /95	14.05 /93	1.32	0.97

● Denotes fund is closed to new investors
* Denotes fund is included in Section II

www.thestreetratings.com

RISK Rating/Pts	3 Year Standard Deviation	Beta	NAV As of 2/28/17	Total $(Mil)	Cash %	Stocks %	Bonds %	Other %	Portfolio Turnover Ratio	Last Bull Market Return	Last Bear Market Return	Manager Quality Pct	Manager Tenure (Years)	Initial Purch. $	Additional Purch. $	Front End Load	Back End Load
C+ / 6.5	6.3	0.97	11.34	2	0	55	43	2	131	48.8	-12.4	25	13	0	0	0.0	0.0
C+ / 6.8	11.7	0.83	7.36	23	16	82	0	2	193	77.7	-18.1	30	10	1,000	100	5.8	0.0
C+ / 6.8	11.7	0.83	7.36	44	16	82	0	2	193	79.7	-17.9	33	10	0	0	0.0	0.0
C+ / 6.8	11.7	0.83	7.35	3	16	82	0	2	193	N/A	N/A	23	10	1,000	100	0.0	0.0
C+ / 6.8	11.8	0.83	7.35	N/A	16	82	0	2	193	N/A	N/A	27	10	0	0	0.0	0.0
C+ / 6.5	11.3	0.83	11.89	13	1	98	0	1	14	64.0	-23.7	88	11	1,000	100	5.8	0.0
C+ / 6.5	11.3	0.83	11.67	4	1	98	0	1	14	57.3	-23.9	85	11	1,000	100	0.0	0.0
C+ / 6.5	11.2	0.82	11.92	2	1	98	0	1	14	66.1	-23.6	89	11	0	0	0.0	0.0
C- / 4.2	14.6	1.07	19.19	172	0	100	0	0	46	163.1	-17.5	31	10	1,000	100	5.8	0.0
C- / 4.2	14.6	1.07	18.37	59	0	100	0	0	46	152.7	-17.8	23	10	1,000	100	0.0	0.0
C- / 4.2	14.6	1.07	19.26	141	0	100	0	0	46	166.6	-17.4	33	10	0	0	0.0	0.0
C- / 4.2	14.6	1.07	18.98	5	0	100	0	0	46	159.6	-17.6	28	10	0	0	0.0	0.0
E / 0.5	13.0	0.93	6.03	9	2	96	0	2	41	67.3	-16.8	90	1	1,000	100	5.8	0.0
E / 0.5	13.0	0.92	5.19	4	2	96	0	2	41	60.8	-17.0	87	1	1,000	100	0.0	0.0
E / 0.5	13.0	0.92	6.28	5	2	96	0	2	41	69.4	-16.7	91	1	0	0	0.0	0.0
E / 0.5	13.0	0.92	5.76	N/A	2	96	0	2	41	65.0	-16.9	89	1	0	0	0.0	0.0
C+ / 6.0	11.7	0.93	13.37	59	3	96	0	1	13	45.1	-28.1	70	11	1,000	100	5.8	0.0
C+ / 6.0	11.8	0.93	13.19	20	3	96	0	1	13	39.4	-28.3	61	11	1,000	100	0.0	0.0
C+ / 6.0	11.7	0.92	13.42	178	3	96	0	1	13	47.3	-28.0	73	11	0	0	0.0	0.0
C+ / 6.0	11.7	0.92	13.34	2	3	96	0	1	13	43.2	-28.1	67	11	0	0	0.0	0.0
C+ / 6.0	10.0	0.90	27.57	227	1	98	0	1	13	137.3	-13.6	81	11	1,000,000	0	0.0	0.0
C- / 3.7	12.8	1.00	5.83	8	3	96	0	1	49	122.4	-25.2	70	9	1,000	100	5.8	0.0
C- / 3.4	12.8	1.01	5.46	2	3	96	0	1	49	113.3	-25.4	60	9	1,000	100	0.0	0.0
C- / 3.6	12.8	1.00	5.83	3	3	96	0	1	49	125.1	-25.0	74	9	0	0	0.0	0.0
C- / 3.7	12.8	1.00	5.83	N/A	3	96	0	1	49	118.4	-25.2	67	9	0	0	0.0	0.0
C / 5.1	11.2	0.87	13.16	446	1	98	0	1	22	36.1	-16.2	63	N/A	1,000,000	0	0.0	0.0
C- / 3.2	14.3	1.04	11.92	82	4	95	0	1	111	94.7	-15.4	50	20	1,000	100	5.8	0.0
C- / 3.2	14.3	1.04	11.86	19	4	95	0	1	111	86.9	-15.6	40	20	1,000	100	0.0	0.0
C- / 3.3	14.2	1.03	11.97	35	4	95	0	1	111	97.4	-15.2	55	20	0	0	0.0	0.0
C- / 3.2	14.3	1.04	11.91	10	4	95	0	1	111	92.0	-15.4	47	20	0	0	0.0	0.0
D / 2.2	12.6	1.01	34.32	232	0	100	0	0	33	78.6	-12.0	4	12	1,000	100	5.8	0.0
E+ / 0.8	12.6	1.01	24.99	53	0	100	0	0	33	71.5	-12.2	3	12	1,000	100	0.0	0.0
D+ / 2.5	12.6	1.00	37.09	144	0	100	0	0	33	81.0	-11.9	5	12	0	0	0.0	0.0
D / 2.0	12.6	1.01	32.46	9	0	100	0	0	33	76.2	-12.1	4	12	0	0	0.0	0.0
C / 5.3	14.9	0.93	22.88	306	3	96	0	1	38	151.0	-24.2	85	13	1,000	100	5.8	0.0
C / 5.2	14.9	0.93	20.90	137	3	96	0	1	38	141.0	-24.5	82	13	1,000	100	0.0	0.0
C / 5.3	14.9	0.93	23.33	1,704	3	96	0	1	38	154.3	-24.1	87	13	0	0	0.0	0.0
C / 5.3	14.9	0.93	22.27	32	3	96	0	1	38	147.4	-24.3	84	13	0	0	0.0	0.0
C / 4.8	14.5	0.88	61.84	887	2	97	0	1	20	132.3	-22.4	91	20	1,000	100	5.8	0.0
C / 4.6	14.5	0.88	51.55	116	2	97	0	1	20	123.0	-22.7	88	20	1,000	100	0.0	0.0
C / 4.9	14.5	0.87	65.13	2,411	2	97	0	1	20	135.5	-22.4	92	20	0	0	0.0	0.0
C / 4.8	14.5	0.87	60.04	89	2	97	0	1	20	129.2	-22.5	90	20	0	0	0.0	0.0
U /	N/A	N/A	65.15	106	2	97	0	1	20	N/A	N/A	N/A	20	0	0	0.0	0.0
E / 0.3	13.2	0.81	17.73	678	0	99	0	1	24	92.0	-15.7	43	1	1,000	100	5.8	0.0
E / 0.3	13.2	0.81	9.17	52	0	99	0	1	24	84.4	-16.0	33	1	1,000	100	0.0	0.0
D- / 1.0	13.2	0.81	23.69	227	0	99	0	1	24	94.6	-15.6	47	1	0	0	0.0	0.0
E / 0.3	13.2	0.81	16.39	17	0	99	0	1	24	89.5	-15.8	40	1	0	0	0.0	0.0
C / 4.7	11.9	0.96	22.28	153	0	99	0	1	22	104.8	-12.4	16	12	1,000	100	5.8	0.0
C / 4.5	11.9	0.96	19.74	72	0	99	0	1	22	96.7	-12.7	11	12	1,000	100	0.0	0.0
C / 4.8	11.9	0.96	24.00	2,496	0	99	0	1	22	107.6	-12.3	18	12	0	0	0.0	0.0
C / 4.7	11.9	0.96	21.50	21	0	99	0	1	22	102.1	-12.5	14	12	0	0	0.0	0.0
B- / 7.1	9.9	0.89	20.45	3,604	4	95	0	1	12	132.9	-14.5	80	13	1,000	100	5.8	0.0

Fund Type	Fund Name	Ticker Symbol	Overall Investment Rating	Phone	Performance Rating/Pts	3 Mo	6 Mo	1Yr / Pct	3Yr / Pct	5Yr / Pct	Dividend Yield	Expense Ratio
								Total Return % through 2/28/17	Annualized		Incl. in Returns	
GR	● Delaware Value C	DDVCX	A	(800) 523-1918	B / 8.2	5.60	6.56	23.02 /67	9.54 /91	13.20 /86	0.73	1.72
GR	● Delaware Value Institutional	DDVIX	A+	(800) 523-1918	B+ / 8.9	5.84	7.07	24.22 /71	10.62 /96	14.32 /95	1.63	0.72
GR	● Delaware Value R	DDVRX	A+	(800) 523-1918	B+ / 8.6	5.72	6.81	23.64 /69	10.09 /94	13.74 /91	1.18	1.22
GI	● Delaware Value R6	DDZRX	U	(800) 523-1918	U /	5.82	7.13	--	--	--	0.00	N/A
BA	Delaware Wealth Builder A	DDIAX	C	(800) 523-1918	C- / 3.3	4.41	3.33	15.44 /32	5.21 /57	8.61 /47	2.01	1.08
BA	Delaware Wealth Builder C	DDICX	C+	(800) 523-1918	C- / 3.8	4.22	2.95	14.65 /28	4.45 /48	7.81 /41	1.40	1.83
BA	Delaware Wealth Builder Inst	DDIIX	C+	(800) 523-1918	C / 4.6	4.48	3.46	15.73 /33	5.48 /59	8.89 /50	2.37	0.83
BA	Delaware Wealth Builder R	DDDRX	C+	(800) 523-1918	C- / 4.2	4.43	3.21	15.25 /31	4.95 /53	8.35 /45	1.89	1.33
GL	Destra Dividend Total Return A	DHDAX	D+	(877) 287-9646	D+ / 2.7	5.80	4.30	18.98 /47	2.42 /27	6.56 /32	1.79	2.36
GL	Destra Dividend Total Return C	DHDCX	D+	(877) 287-9646	C- / 3.0	5.64	3.92	18.12 /43	1.61 /22	5.73 /27	1.38	2.61
GL	Destra Dividend Total Return I	DHDIX	D+	(877) 287-9646	C- / 3.4	5.86	4.38	19.32 /49	2.74 /29	6.93 /34	2.12	1.57
GL	Destra Flhrty and Cr Pref and Inc A	DPIAX	B+	(877) 287-9646	C / 4.4	5.51	1.32	11.76 /17	7.67 /77	7.26 /36	4.21	2.12
AA	Destra Flhrty and Cr Pref and Inc C	DPICX	B+	(877) 287-9646	C / 4.7	5.30	0.88	10.88 /14	6.89 /71	6.70 /33	3.66	2.69
GL	Destra Flhrty and Cr Pref and Inc I	DPIIX	A-	(877) 287-9646	C / 5.2	5.60	1.39	12.03 /18	8.07 /79	7.87 /41	4.68	1.47
GL	Destra Focused Equity A	DFOAX	D	(877) 287-9646	D / 2.2	7.72	6.33	5.72 / 4	4.42 /48	8.50 /46	0.00	2.22
GR	Destra Focused Equity C	DFOCX	D	(877) 287-9646	D+ / 2.4	7.48	5.92	4.92 / 4	3.65 /39	7.68 /40	0.00	2.72
GL	Destra Focused Equity I	DFOIX	D+	(877) 287-9646	D+ / 2.7	7.76	6.44	5.98 / 5	4.74 /51	8.84 /49	0.00	1.37
GL	Destra Wolverine Alt Oppty I	DWAIX	U	(877) 287-9646	U /	4.06	2.84	9.39 /10	--	--	2.77	1.78
GR	Deutsche Capital Growth A	SDGAX	C+	(800) 728-3337	B / 8.1	9.34	9.06	22.98 /67	10.03 /93	13.19 /86	0.20	0.97
GR	Deutsche Capital Growth C	SDGCX	C+	(800) 728-3337	B+ / 8.5	9.13	8.63	21.96 /62	9.14 /88	12.29 /77	0.00	1.78
GR	Deutsche Capital Growth Inst	SDGTX	B	(800) 728-3337	A- / 9.2	9.41	9.20	23.30 /67	10.32 /95	13.51 /89	0.47	0.70
GR	Deutsche Capital Growth R	SDGRX	B-	(800) 728-3337	B+ / 8.8	9.24	8.87	22.50 /64	9.59 /91	12.75 /81	0.00	1.37
GR	Deutsche Capital Growth S	SCGSX	B	(800) 728-3337	A- / 9.2	9.41	9.21	23.30 /67	10.31 /95	13.48 /89	0.46	0.71
TC	Deutsche Communication A	TISHX	C	(800) 728-3337	C- / 3.1	6.92	1.08	12.28 /19	5.43 /59	10.27 /60	3.96	1.69
TC	Deutsche Communication C	FTICX	C	(800) 728-3337	C- / 3.6	6.73	0.71	11.50 /16	4.64 /50	9.45 /54	3.45	2.54
TC	Deutsche Communication Inst	FLICX	C+	(800) 728-3337	C / 4.4	7.01	1.22	12.57 /20	5.70 /61	10.56 /62	4.46	1.42
GI	Deutsche Core Equity A	SUWAX	B+	(800) 728-3337	B / 8.2	6.79	10.17	25.81 /76	9.98 /93	14.12 /94	0.83	0.87
GI	Deutsche Core Equity C	SUWCX	B+	(800) 728-3337	B+ / 8.6	6.59	9.75	24.85 /73	9.14 /88	13.24 /86	0.20	1.64
GI	Deutsche Core Equity Inst	SUWIX	A	(800) 728-3337	A / 9.3	6.89	10.32	26.22 /77	10.34 /95	14.53 /96	1.17	0.54
GI	Deutsche Core Equity R	SUWTX	A-	(800) 728-3337	B+ / 8.9	6.71	9.96	25.35 /74	9.53 /91	--	0.64	1.08
GI	Deutsche Core Equity S	SCDGX	A-	(800) 728-3337	A / 9.3	6.89	10.32	26.16 /77	10.30 /95	14.46 /95	1.13	0.59
GR	Deutsche CROCI Equity Dividend A	KDHAX	B+	(800) 728-3337	B- / 7.4	8.05	9.22	24.78 /73	8.63 /84	10.85 /65	1.61	1.16
GR	Deutsche CROCI Equity Dividend C	KDHCX	A-	(800) 728-3337	B / 7.9	7.85	8.79	23.83 /69	7.82 /78	10.03 /59	1.03	1.92
GR	Deutsche CROCI Equity Dividend Inst	KDHIX	A+	(800) 728-3337	B+ / 8.7	8.13	9.35	25.08 /74	8.90 /86	11.16 /67	1.94	0.89
GR	Deutsche CROCI Equity Dividend R	KDHRX	A	(800) 728-3337	B / 8.2	7.98	9.06	24.45 /71	8.36 /82	10.57 /63	1.48	1.56
GR	Deutsche CROCI Equity Dividend S	KDHSX	A+	(800) 728-3337	B+ / 8.7	8.13	9.35	25.09 /74	8.90 /86	11.13 /67	1.94	0.94
FO	Deutsche CROCI International A	SUIAX	D-	(800) 728-3337	D / 1.7	8.76	8.87	12.58 /20	0.03 /13	5.27 /23	3.17	1.14
FO	Deutsche CROCI International C	SUICX	D-	(800) 728-3337	D- / 1.3	8.52	8.44	11.69 /17	-0.72 /10	4.47 /18	2.61	1.89
FO	Deutsche CROCI International Inst	SUIIX	D	(800) 728-3337	D+ / 2.6	8.79	9.01	12.89 /21	0.33 /15	5.64 /26	3.68	0.83
FO	Deutsche CROCI International S	SCINX	D	(800) 728-3337	D+ / 2.5	8.80	8.96	12.82 /21	0.26 /15	5.54 /25	3.59	0.92
GL	Deutsche CROCI Sector Opps A	DSOAX	U	(800) 728-3337	U /	7.31	5.14	13.57 /24	--	--	1.04	1.53
GL	Deutsche CROCI Sector Opps Inst	DSOIX	U	(800) 728-3337	U /	7.33	5.16	13.85 /25	--	--	1.34	1.26
GL	Deutsche CROCI Sector Opps S	DSOSX	U	(800) 728-3337	U /	7.35	5.18	13.60 /24	--	--	1.25	1.40
GR	Deutsche CROCI US A	DCUAX	U	(800) 728-3337	U /	8.12	8.58	20.49 /55	--	--	0.05	4.40
GR	Deutsche CROCI US S	DCUSX	U	(800) 728-3337	U /	8.17	8.74	20.67 /56	--	--	0.20	4.15
FO	Deutsche EAFE Equity Index Inst	BTAEX	E-	(800) 728-3337	D- / 1.1	7.18	4.53	15.15 /31	-1.05 / 9	4.87 /20	3.25	0.58
EM	Deutsche Emerging Markets Eqty A	SEKAX	D+	(800) 728-3337	C- / 4.2	8.06	5.46	30.42 /87	2.33 /26	-0.24 / 4	0.26	1.97
EM	Deutsche Emerging Markets Eqty C	SEKCX	C-	(800) 728-3337	C / 4.7	7.90	5.08	29.52 /85	1.58 /21	-0.98 / 3	0.00	2.76
EM	Deutsche Emerging Markets Eqty Inst	SEKIX	C-	(800) 728-3337	C+ / 5.6	8.16	5.59	30.79 /88	2.60 /28	0.02 / 4	0.50	1.53
EM	Deutsche Emerging Markets Eqty S	SEMGX	C-	(800) 728-3337	C+ / 5.6	8.16	5.59	30.77 /88	2.60 /28	--	0.50	1.74
EN	Deutsche Enhanced Comdty Strat A	SKNRX	E+	(800) 728-3337	E- / 0.1	1.81	4.96	12.29 /19	-6.26 / 2	-5.63 / 1	6.32	1.44
EN	Deutsche Enhanced Comdty Strat C	SKCRX	E+	(800) 728-3337	E- / 0.2	1.64	4.45	11.43 /16	-6.98 / 1	-6.37 / 1	6.30	2.22

● Denotes fund is closed to new investors
* Denotes fund is included in Section II

RISK			NET ASSETS		ASSET				Portfolio Turnover Ratio	BULL / BEAR		FUND MANAGER		MINIMUMS		LOADS	
	3 Year		NAV							Last Bull	Last Bear	Manager	Manager	Initial	Additional	Front	Back
Risk Rating/Pts	Standard Deviation	Beta	As of 2/28/17	Total $(Mil)	Cash %	Stocks %	Bonds %	Other %	Portfolio Turnover Ratio	Market Return	Market Return	Quality Pct	Tenure (Years)	Purch. $	Purch. $	End Load	End Load
B- / 7.1	9.9	0.89	20.39	797	4	95	0	1	12	123.6	-14.7	75	13	1,000	100	0.0	0.0
B- / 7.1	9.9	0.89	20.45	10,181	4	95	0	1	12	135.8	-14.4	81	13	0	0	0.0	0.0
B- / 7.1	9.9	0.89	20.43	179	4	95	0	1	12	129.7	-14.6	78	13	0	0	0.0	0.0
U /	N/A	N/A	20.45	26	4	95	0	1	12	N/A	N/A	N/A	13	0	0	0.0	0.0
B- / 7.8	6.8	1.04	14.15	254	10	56	23	11	67	73.5	-13.3	42	11	1,000	100	5.8	0.0
B- / 7.8	6.8	1.04	14.17	284	10	56	23	11	67	66.7	-13.6	32	11	1,000	100	0.0	0.0
B- / 7.8	6.8	1.04	14.15	190	10	56	23	11	67	76.1	-13.3	45	11	0	0	0.0	0.0
B- / 7.8	6.8	1.05	14.15	3	10	56	23	11	67	71.4	-13.4	38	11	0	0	0.0	0.0
C+ / 5.9	11.1	0.75	20.42	7	20	79	0	1	40	60.4	N/A	88	1	2,500	0	4.5	0.0
C+ / 5.8	11.2	0.75	18.12	9	20	79	0	1	40	N/A	N/A	85	1	2,500	0	0.0	0.0
C+ / 5.9	11.1	0.75	20.46	14	20	79	0	1	40	62.9	N/A	90	1	100,000	0	0.0	2.0
B+ / 9.8	4.1	0.37	18.12	63	2	69	28	1	13	54.6	-1.1	96	6	2,500	0	4.5	0.0
B+ / 9.8	4.1	0.33	18.19	28	2	69	28	1	13	N/A	N/A	94	6	2,500	0	0.0	0.0
B+ / 9.8	4.2	0.37	18.06	125	2	69	28	1	13	59.3	-1.0	97	6	1,000,000	0	0.0	2.0
C+ / 5.9	11.0	0.63	20.29	6	1	98	0	1	52	80.0	-13.1	94	6	2,500	0	4.5	0.0
C+ / 5.7	11.0	0.93	19.19	4	1	98	0	1	52	N/A	N/A	10	6	2,500	0	0.0	0.0
C+ / 6.0	11.0	0.63	20.61	34	1	98	0	1	52	82.6	-12.9	95	6	1,000,000	0	0.0	2.0
U /	N/A	N/A	10.19	52	0	0	0	100	424	N/A	N/A	N/A	2	1,000,000	0	0.0	2.0
C- / 4.1	12.1	1.09	71.82	587	0	98	0	2	33	131.0	-19.5	56	1	1,000	50	5.8	0.0
C- / 3.8	12.1	1.09	63.07	25	0	98	0	2	33	121.3	-19.8	44	1	1,000	50	0.0	0.0
C- / 4.1	12.1	1.09	72.40	208	0	98	0	2	33	134.6	-19.4	59	1	1,000,000	0	0.0	0.0
C- / 4.1	12.1	1.09	70.95	7	0	98	0	2	33	126.5	-19.4	50	1	0	0	0.0	0.0
C- / 4.1	12.1	1.09	72.47	719	0	98	0	2	33	134.3	-19.4	59	1	2,500	50	0.0	0.0
B- / 7.4	10.8	0.77	25.82	99	3	95	0	2	15	82.7	-15.3	41	1	1,000	50	5.8	0.0
B- / 7.4	10.8	0.77	23.69	5	3	95	0	2	15	75.4	-15.5	31	1	1,000	50	0.0	0.0
B- / 7.4	10.8	0.77	26.37	2	3	95	0	2	15	85.1	-15.3	45	1	1,000,000	0	0.0	0.0
C+ / 5.7	11.2	1.06	25.12	340	0	99	0	1	27	136.7	-19.3	60	4	1,000	50	5.8	0.0
C+ / 5.6	11.2	1.06	24.06	42	0	99	0	1	27	127.1	-19.6	50	4	1,000	50	0.0	0.0
C+ / 5.7	11.2	1.06	25.43	66	0	99	0	1	27	141.4	-19.2	64	4	1,000,000	0	0.0	0.0
C+ / 5.7	11.2	1.06	25.34	1	0	99	0	1	27	N/A	N/A	54	4	0	0	0.0	0.0
C+ / 5.7	11.2	1.06	25.38	2,921	0	99	0	1	27	140.5	-19.2	64	4	2,500	50	0.0	0.0
B- / 7.1	11.2	1.00	52.03	886	0	99	0	1	55	104.7	-19.5	51	3	1,000	50	5.8	0.0
B- / 7.1	11.1	1.00	51.84	138	0	99	0	1	55	96.5	-19.7	41	3	1,000	50	0.0	0.0
B- / 7.1	11.1	1.00	52.06	34	0	99	0	1	55	107.9	-19.4	55	3	1,000,000	0	0.0	0.0
B- / 7.1	11.2	1.00	51.90	3	0	99	0	1	55	101.8	-19.5	48	3	0	0	0.0	0.0
B- / 7.1	11.2	1.00	52.05	46	0	99	0	1	55	107.5	-19.4	55	3	2,500	50	0.0	0.0
C / 5.1	11.0	0.74	42.75	224	2	95	1	2	87	51.4	-26.3	75	3	1,000	50	5.8	0.0
C / 5.1	11.0	0.74	42.47	70	2	95	1	2	87	45.2	-26.5	67	3	1,000	50	0.0	0.0
C / 5.1	11.0	0.74	42.71	61	2	95	1	2	87	54.4	-26.1	77	3	1,000,000	0	0.0	0.0
C / 5.1	11.0	0.74	42.91	727	2	95	1	2	87	53.6	-26.2	77	3	2,500	50	0.0	0.0
U /	N/A	N/A	9.24	42	0	95	4	1	164	N/A	N/A	N/A	3	1,000	50	5.8	0.0
U /	N/A	N/A	9.24	30	0	95	4	1	164	N/A	N/A	N/A	3	1,000,000	0	0.0	0.0
U /	N/A	N/A	9.24	26	0	95	4	1	164	N/A	N/A	N/A	3	2,500	50	0.0	0.0
U /	N/A	N/A	10.32	165	0	0	0	100	98	N/A	N/A	N/A	2	1,000	50	5.8	0.0
U /	N/A	N/A	10.32	701	0	0	0	100	98	N/A	N/A	N/A	2	2,500	50	0.0	0.0
D- / 1.0	11.6	0.95	5.64	57	4	95	0	1	127	46.5	-23.4	63	4	1,000,000	0	0.0	0.0
C / 4.7	15.9	0.96	16.15	7	2	96	1	1	72	21.1	-30.0	79	3	1,000	50	5.8	0.0
C / 4.7	15.9	0.96	14.48	2	2	96	1	1	72	16.2	-30.2	73	3	1,000	50	0.0	0.0
C / 4.7	15.9	0.97	16.35	1	2	96	1	1	72	22.8	-29.8	80	3	1,000,000	0	0.0	0.0
C / 4.7	15.9	0.97	16.36	48	2	96	1	1	72	22.6	-29.9	80	3	2,500	50	0.0	0.0
C+ / 5.7	9.8	0.32	11.63	130	3	0	96	1	92	-21.4	-20.1	16	7	1,000	50	5.8	0.0
C+ / 5.7	9.9	0.33	10.50	30	3	0	96	1	92	-24.6	-20.4	11	7	1,000	50	0.0	0.0

						PERFORMANCE							
	99 Pct = Best 0 Pct = Worst			**Overall**		**Perfor-** **mance**	Total Return % through 2/28/17					Incl. in Returns	
				Investment						Annualized		Dividend	Expense
Fund Type	Fund Name	Ticker Symbol	**Rating**	Phone	**Rating/Pts**	3 Mo	6 Mo	1Yr / Pct	3Yr / Pct	5Yr / Pct	Yield	Ratio
EN	Deutsche Enhanced Comdty Strat	SKIRX	E+	(800) 728-3337	E- / 0.2	1.92	5.10	12.66 /20	-5.96 / 2	-5.31 / 2	7.04	1.16
EN	Deutsche Enhanced Comdty Strat S	SKSRX	E+	(800) 728-3337	E- / 0.2	1.87	5.00	12.49 /20	-6.07 / 2	-5.42 / 2	6.87	1.25
IX	Deutsche Equity 500 Index Inst	BTIIX	A	(800) 728-3337	A- / 9.2	7.95	9.85	24.61 /72	10.33 /95	13.69 /91	1.74	0.27
IX	Deutsche Equity 500 Index S	BTIEX	A	(800) 728-3337	A- / 9.2	7.94	9.83	24.55 /72	10.28 /95	13.63 /90	1.69	0.35
RE	Deutsche Gl Real Est Sec A	RRGAX	D+	(800) 728-3337	D+ / 2.6	6.39	-3.59	10.19 /12	5.97 /64	8.15 /43	3.60	1.53
RE	Deutsche Gl Real Est Sec C	RRGCX	C-	(800) 728-3337	C- / 3.1	6.15	-3.91	9.42 /10	5.17 /56	7.32 /37	3.04	2.31
RE	Deutsche Gl Real Est Sec Inst	RRGIX	C-	(800) 728-3337	C- / 3.9	6.44	-3.43	10.51 /13	6.28 /67	8.51 /46	4.09	1.24
RE	Deutsche Gl Real Est Sec S	RRGTX	C-	(800) 728-3337	C- / 3.7	6.45	-3.44	10.38 /13	6.04 /65	8.26 /44	3.98	1.37
GL	Deutsche Glb Infrastructure A	TOLLX	D-	(800) 728-3337	D / 1.8	5.63	-0.72	12.07 /18	3.08 /33	8.50 /46	0.93	1.38
GL	Deutsche Glb Infrastructure C	TOLCX	D	(800) 728-3337	D / 2.1	5.43	-1.16	11.26 /15	2.30 /26	7.68 /40	0.59	2.15
GL	Deutsche Glb Infrastructure Inst	TOLIX	D	(800) 728-3337	D+ / 2.7	5.66	-0.64	12.38 /19	3.35 /35	8.81 /49	1.29	1.09
GL	Deutsche Glb Infrastructure S	TOLSX	D	(800) 728-3337	D+ / 2.7	5.70	-0.64	12.31 /19	3.27 /34	8.69 /48	1.16	1.20
FO	Deutsche Global Equity A	DBISX	D+	(800) 728-3337	D+ / 2.4	5.65	4.33	17.14 /39	2.48 /27	6.59 /32	0.00	2.06
FO	Deutsche Global Equity C	DBICX	D+	(800) 728-3337	D+ / 2.8	5.47	3.96	16.38 /36	1.75 /22	5.82 /27	0.00	2.79
FO	Deutsche Global Equity Inst	MGINX	C-	(800) 728-3337	C- / 3.6	5.79	4.55	17.59 /41	2.75 /30	6.90 /34	0.00	1.61
FO	Deutsche Global Equity R	DBITX	C-	(800) 728-3337	C- / 3.2	5.61	4.24	16.91 /38	2.24 /26	6.34 /31	0.00	2.32
FO	Deutsche Global Equity S	DBIVX	C-	(800) 728-3337	C- / 3.5	5.68	4.44	17.50 /41	2.68 /29	6.79 /33	0.00	1.79
GL	Deutsche Global Growth A	SGQAX	D	(800) 728-3337	D- / 1.4	6.71	3.96	14.47 /28	0.19 /14	5.93 /28	0.00	1.51
GL	Deutsche Global Growth C	SGQCX	D-	(800) 728-3337	D- / 1.2	6.53	3.61	13.66 /24	-0.55 /11	5.14 /22	0.00	2.24
GL	Deutsche Global Growth Inst	SGQIX	D	(800) 728-3337	D / 2.2	6.81	4.14	14.84 /29	0.47 /16	6.22 /30	0.16	1.17
GL	Deutsche Global Growth R	SGQRX	D	(800) 728-3337	D- / 1.4	6.64	3.84	14.18 /26	-0.06 /13	5.65 /26	0.00	1.84
GL	Deutsche Global Growth S	SCOBX	D	(800) 728-3337	D / 2.2	6.75	4.08	14.73 /29	0.44 /15	6.19 /30	0.13	1.21
BA	Deutsche Global Income Builder A	KTRAX	D+	(800) 728-3337	D+ / 2.7	5.93	5.81	16.97 /38	2.95 /31	5.83 /27	2.49	0.91
BA	Deutsche Global Income Builder C	KTRCX	D+	(800) 728-3337	C- / 3.2	5.84	5.39	16.20 /35	2.16 /25	4.99 /21	1.89	1.70
BA	Deutsche Global Income Builder Inst	KTRIX	C-	(800) 728-3337	C- / 3.9	6.00	5.94	17.26 /39	3.18 /33	6.08 /29	2.85	0.68
BA	Deutsche Global Income Builder S	KTRSX	C-	(800) 728-3337	C- / 3.9	5.99	5.92	17.20 /39	3.16 /33	6.04 /29	2.83	0.71
GL	Deutsche Global Small Cap A	KGDAX	E	(800) 728-3337	E+ / 0.8	4.85	5.13	16.54 /36	-0.52 /11	6.83 /34	0.00	1.53
GL	Deutsche Global Small Cap C	KGDCX	E	(800) 728-3337	D- / 1.1	4.64	4.74	15.67 /33	-1.26 / 8	6.03 /28	0.00	2.30
GL	Deutsche Global Small Cap Inst	KGDIX	E+	(800) 728-3337	D- / 1.4	4.90	5.28	16.84 /38	-0.22 /13	7.16 /36	0.00	1.19
GL	Deutsche Global Small Cap S	SGSCX	E+	(800) 728-3337	D- / 1.4	4.90	5.25	16.82 /38	-0.26 /12	7.10 /35	0.00	1.26
PM	Deutsche Gold & Prec Metals Fund A	SGDAX	E-	(800) 728-3337	E- / 0.2	10.91	-9.71	19.17 /48	-5.25 / 2	-15.57 / 0	2.58	1.80
PM	Deutsche Gold & Prec Metals Fund C	SGDCX	E-	(800) 728-3337	E- / 0.2	10.72	-10.07	18.24 /44	-5.97 / 2	-16.21 / 0	2.08	2.51
PM	Deutsche Gold & Prec Metals Fund I	SGDIX	E-	(800) 728-3337	E / 0.3	11.11	-9.45	19.67 /50	-4.99 / 2	-15.34 / 0	2.96	1.42
PM	Deutsche Gold & Prec Metals Fund S	SCGDX	E-	(800) 728-3337	E / 0.3	10.94	-9.59	19.49 /49	-5.00 / 2	-15.36 / 0	2.96	1.52
HL	Deutsche Health and Wellness A	SUHAX	D	(800) 728-3337	C / 4.6	10.17	3.82	13.39 /23	6.55 /69	16.32 /98	0.01	1.35
HL	Deutsche Health and Wellness C	SUHCX	D	(800) 728-3337	C / 5.1	9.96	3.42	12.53 /20	5.77 /62	15.46 /98	0.00	2.10
HL	Deutsche Health and Wellness Inst	SUHIX	C-	(800) 728-3337	C+ / 6.0	10.23	3.94	13.69 /24	6.82 /71	16.62 /98	0.25	1.10
HL	Deutsche Health and Wellness S	SCHLX	C-	(800) 728-3337	C+ / 6.0	10.25	3.95	13.67 /24	6.84 /71	16.62 /98	0.24	1.08
GR	Deutsche Large Cap Focus Gro A	SGGAX	C+	(800) 728-3337	B+ / 8.6	10.65	9.32	23.26 /67	10.51 /96	12.74 /81	0.00	1.25
GR	Deutsche Large Cap Focus Gro C	SGGCX	C+	(800) 728-3337	B+ / 8.9	10.47	8.91	22.33 /64	9.69 /92	11.90 /73	0.00	1.97
GR	Deutsche Large Cap Focus Gro Inst	SGGIX	B	(800) 728-3337	A / 9.5	10.75	9.45	23.57 /68	10.80 /97	13.05 /84	0.17	1.00
GR	Deutsche Large Cap Focus Gro S	SCQGX	B	(800) 728-3337	A / 9.5	10.71	9.45	23.55 /68	10.79 /97	13.02 /84	0.16	0.98
FO	Deutsche Latin America Equity A	SLANX	E-	(800) 728-3337	D / 1.9	10.52	1.87	43.22 /98	-1.22 / 9	-4.66 / 2	1.34	1.91
FO	Deutsche Latin America Equity C	SLAPX	E-	(800) 728-3337	D / 2.2	10.33	1.54	42.22 /98	-1.95 / 7	-5.36 / 2	0.76	2.72
FO	Deutsche Latin America Equity S	SLAFX	E	(800) 728-3337	D+ / 2.9	10.55	2.00	43.57 /98	-0.97 / 9	-4.42 / 2	1.65	1.61
MC	Deutsche Mid Cap Growth A	SMCAX	D	(800) 728-3337	C / 4.4	7.20	6.51	25.09 /74	3.87 /41	8.77 /49	0.00	1.25
MC	Deutsche Mid Cap Growth C	SMCCX	D	(800) 728-3337	C / 4.9	7.01	6.15	24.15 /70	3.07 /32	7.93 /41	0.00	2.05
MC	Deutsche Mid Cap Growth Inst	BTEAX	D+	(800) 728-3337	C+ / 5.9	7.30	6.64	25.51 /75	4.16 /45	9.11 /52	0.00	0.97
MC	Deutsche Mid Cap Growth S	SMCSX	D+	(800) 728-3337	C+ / 5.9	7.24	6.64	25.45 /75	4.15 /45	9.08 /51	0.00	0.98
MC	Deutsche Mid Cap Value A	MIDVX	C+	(800) 728-3337	C+ / 6.2	4.66	7.50	21.83 /61	7.83 /78	12.94 /83	0.82	1.25
MC	Deutsche Mid Cap Value C	MIDZX	C+	(800) 728-3337	C+ / 6.6	4.48	7.08	20.89 /57	7.01 /72	12.10 /75	0.13	2.00
MC	Deutsche Mid Cap Value Inst	MIDIX	B-	(800) 728-3337	B- / 7.4	4.81	7.65	22.15 /63	8.11 /80	13.26 /86	1.11	0.96

● Denotes fund is closed to new investors

* Denotes fund is included in Section II

RISK Rating/Pts	3 Year Standard Deviation	Beta	NAV As of 2/28/17	Total $(Mil)	Cash %	Stocks %	Bonds %	Other %	Portfolio Turnover Ratio	Last Bull Market Return	Last Bear Market Return	Manager Quality Pct	Manager Tenure (Years)	Initial Purch. $	Additional Purch. $	Front End Load	Back End Load
C+ / 5.7	9.9	0.32	11.82	2,184	3	0	96	1	92	-20.1	-19.9	19	7	1,000,000	0	0.0	0.0
C+ / 5.7	9.9	0.33	11.78	329	3	0	96	1	92	-20.6	-19.9	18	7	2,500	50	0.0	0.0
C+ / 6.2	10.3	1.00	222.42	399	1	97	0	2	3	131.4	-16.3	71	10	1,000,000	0	0.0	0.0
C+ / 6.1	10.3	1.00	219.80	439	1	97	0	2	3	130.8	-16.4	70	10	2,500	50	0.0	0.0
C+ / 6.3	11.9	0.84	8.90	483	7	91	0	2	142	76.0	-20.4	34	11	1,000	50	5.8	0.0
C+ / 6.3	12.0	0.84	8.94	18	7	91	0	2	142	68.8	-20.7	25	11	1,000	50	0.0	0.0
C+ / 6.3	11.9	0.84	8.88	651	7	91	0	2	142	79.1	-20.3	38	11	1,000,000	0	0.0	0.0
C+ / 6.2	12.0	0.84	8.88	69	7	91	0	2	142	77.6	-20.4	34	11	2,500	50	0.0	0.0
C / 5.3	10.1	0.49	14.06	907	8	89	2	1	136	68.3	-3.7	91	9	1,000	50	5.8	0.0
C / 5.2	10.0	0.49	13.87	594	8	89	2	1	136	61.5	-4.1	88	9	1,000	50	0.0	0.0
C / 5.2	10.1	0.49	14.00	653	8	89	2	1	136	70.9	-3.6	91	9	1,000,000	0	0.0	0.0
C / 5.2	10.1	0.49	14.01	1,379	8	89	2	1	136	70.0	-3.7	91	9	2,500	50	0.0	0.0
C+ / 6.4	10.0	0.74	9.16	10	1	98	0	1	42	57.4	-23.1	89	4	1,000	50	5.8	0.0
C+ / 6.3	10.0	0.74	8.67	3	1	98	0	1	42	51.2	-23.4	85	4	1,000	50	0.0	0.0
C+ / 6.4	10.1	0.75	8.96	2	1	98	0	1	42	59.7	-23.0	90	4	1,000,000	0	0.0	0.0
C+ / 6.4	10.1	0.75	8.85	1	1	98	0	1	42	55.5	-23.3	88	4	0	0	0.0	0.0
C+ / 6.4	10.0	0.74	8.93	4	1	98	0	1	42	59.1	-23.1	89	4	2,500	50	0.0	0.0
C+ / 6.1	11.0	0.79	29.91	51	2	93	3	2	39	60.6	-26.1	76	4	1,000	50	5.8	0.0
C+ / 6.0	11.0	0.79	28.38	18	2	93	3	2	39	54.3	-26.3	69	4	1,000	50	0.0	0.0
C+ / 6.1	11.0	0.79	29.90	14	2	93	3	2	39	63.1	-26.0	78	4	1,000,000	0	0.0	0.0
C+ / 6.0	11.0	0.79	29.72	4	2	93	3	2	39	58.4	-26.2	74	4	0	0	0.0	0.0
C+ / 6.1	11.0	0.79	29.88	498	2	93	3	2	39	62.8	-25.9	78	4	2,500	50	0.0	0.0
C+ / 5.9	7.2	1.04	9.44	598	0	62	37	1	123	50.2	-12.5	18	5	1,000	50	5.8	0.0
C+ / 5.9	7.3	1.05	9.43	21	0	62	37	1	123	44.0	-12.9	12	5	1,000	50	0.0	0.0
C+ / 5.8	7.2	1.04	9.43	9	0	62	37	1	123	52.2	-12.5	20	5	1,000,000	0	0.0	0.0
C+ / 5.9	7.3	1.05	9.44	189	0	62	37	1	123	51.8	-12.5	19	5	2,500	50	0.0	0.0
C / 4.3	12.6	0.80	35.93	73	0	98	0	2	31	63.1	-21.0	70	15	1,000	50	5.8	0.0
C- / 4.0	12.6	0.79	30.07	10	0	98	0	2	31	56.6	-21.3	60	15	1,000	50	0.0	0.0
C / 4.4	12.6	0.80	37.70	70	0	98	0	2	31	65.9	-20.9	73	15	1,000,000	0	0.0	0.0
C / 4.4	12.6	0.79	37.68	226	0	98	0	2	31	65.4	-21.0	72	15	2,500	50	0.0	0.0
E- / 0.0	45.1	2.50	6.82	24	1	97	1	1	55	-55.7	-17.0	67	1	1,000	50	5.8	0.0
E- / 0.0	45.0	2.49	6.45	10	1	97	1	1	55	-57.5	-17.3	57	1	1,000	50	0.0	2.0
E- / 0.0	45.0	2.49	6.90	2	1	97	1	1	55	-55.2	-16.9	70	1	1,000,000	0	0.0	0.0
E- / 0.0	45.0	2.49	6.89	75	1	97	1	1	55	-55.2	-16.9	70	1	2,500	50	0.0	0.0
C- / 3.2	15.7	1.11	34.72	70	1	96	1	2	56	152.2	-13.8	16	16	1,000	50	5.8	0.0
D+ / 2.7	15.7	1.11	27.93	14	1	96	1	2	56	142.4	-14.1	11	16	1,000	50	0.0	0.0
C- / 3.4	15.7	1.11	38.43	3	1	96	1	2	56	155.7	-13.6	18	16	1,000,000	0	0.0	0.0
C- / 3.3	15.7	1.11	37.01	218	1	96	1	2	56	155.8	-13.6	18	16	2,500	50	0.0	0.0
C- / 3.7	12.5	1.11	39.04	25	0	97	1	2	55	126.2	-20.1	60	1	1,000	50	5.8	0.0
C- / 3.2	12.5	1.10	33.53	6	0	97	1	2	55	117.2	-20.3	50	1	1,000	50	0.0	0.0
C- / 3.8	12.5	1.10	41.09	8	0	97	1	2	55	129.6	-20.0	63	1	1,000,000	0	0.0	0.0
C- / 3.8	12.5	1.11	40.56	185	0	97	1	2	55	129.2	-20.0	63	1	2,500	50	0.0	0.0
D- / 1.2	27.8	1.22	22.53	12	4	95	0	1	108	N/A	-27.7	62	4	1,000	50	5.8	0.0
D- / 1.2	27.8	1.22	21.36	3	4	95	0	1	108	-4.0	-28.0	52	4	1,000	50	0.0	0.0
D- / 1.2	27.8	1.22	22.50	253	4	95	0	1	108	1.3	-27.7	66	4	2,500	50	0.0	0.0
C- / 3.0	14.4	1.11	17.48	159	1	96	2	1	60	86.9	-22.1	7	11	1,000	50	5.8	0.0
D+ / 2.6	14.5	1.11	15.01	8	1	96	2	1	60	79.3	-22.4	5	11	1,000	50	0.0	0.0
C- / 3.2	14.5	1.11	18.42	2	1	96	2	1	60	90.2	-22.1	8	11	1,000,000	0	0.0	0.0
C- / 3.1	14.4	1.11	18.11	151	1	96	2	1	60	89.7	-22.0	8	11	2,500	50	0.0	0.0
C / 5.5	12.2	0.92	17.74	89	1	94	3	2	62	127.6	-23.7	62	4	1,000	50	5.8	0.0
C / 5.4	12.1	0.92	17.34	27	1	94	3	2	62	118.4	-23.9	52	4	1,000	50	0.0	0.0
C / 5.4	12.2	0.92	17.73	34	1	94	3	2	62	131.0	-23.6	66	4	1,000,000	0	0.0	0.0

Fund Type	Fund Name	Ticker Symbol	Overall Investment Rating	Phone	Performance Rating/Pts	3 Mo	6 Mo	1Yr / Pct	3Yr / Pct	5Yr / Pct	Dividend Yield	Expense Ratio
MC	Deutsche Mid Cap Value R	MIDQX	C+	(800) 728-3337	B- / 7.0	4.65	7.37	21.57 /60	7.55 /76	12.68 /81	0.59	1.64
MC	Deutsche Mid Cap Value S	MIDTX	B-	(800) 728-3337	B- / 7.4	4.78	7.68	22.21 /63	8.10 /80	13.23 /86	1.08	1.02
AA	Deutsche Multi-Asset Consv Alloc A	SPDAX	C-	(800) 728-3337	D- / 1.5	4.15	2.77	9.46 /10	2.30 /26	4.66 /19	1.64	1.37
AA	Deutsche Multi-Asset Consv Alloc C	SPDCX	C	(800) 728-3337	D / 1.8	3.95	2.46	8.65 / 9	1.56 /21	3.89 /15	1.02	2.11
AA	Deutsche Multi-Asset Consv Alloc S	SPBAX	C	(800) 728-3337	D+ / 2.3	4.22	2.98	9.75 /11	2.59 /28	4.94 /21	1.99	1.09
GI	Deutsche Multi-Asset Global Alloc A	SUPAX	D+	(800) 728-3337	D- / 1.1	4.87	2.72	9.78 /11	0.67 /16	4.18 /16	2.93	1.57
GI	Deutsche Multi-Asset Global Alloc C	SUPCX	D+	(800) 728-3337	D- / 1.1	4.74	2.42	8.97 / 9	-0.06 /13	3.41 /12	2.34	2.31
GI	Deutsche Multi-Asset Global Alloc S	SPGRX	C-	(800) 728-3337	D / 1.8	4.92	2.84	10.06 /12	0.91 /18	4.44 /18	3.36	1.32
GR	Deutsche Multi-Asset Modt Alloc A	PLUSX	D	(800) 728-3337	D / 2.1	4.60	4.93	13.78 /24	2.75 /30	6.32 /30	1.48	1.74
GR	Deutsche Multi-Asset Modt Alloc C	PLSCX	D+	(800) 728-3337	D+ / 2.5	4.46	4.68	13.04 /22	2.03 /24	5.55 /25	0.82	2.44
GR	Deutsche Multi-Asset Modt Alloc S	PPLSX	C-	(800) 728-3337	C- / 3.2	4.76	5.09	14.09 /26	3.02 /32	6.57 /32	1.81	1.47
AA	Deutsche Real Assets A	AAAAX	D	(800) 728-3337	E / 0.4	5.12	-0.59	7.95 / 7	-0.72 /10	0.98 / 6	1.34	1.38
AA	Deutsche Real Assets C	AAAPX	D+	(800) 728-3337	E+ / 0.6	4.93	-0.91	7.31 / 6	-1.43 / 8	0.25 / 5	1.04	2.11
AA	Deutsche Real Assets Institutional	AAAZX	D+	(800) 728-3337	E+ / 0.9	5.16	-0.46	8.37 / 8	-0.35 /12	1.35 / 7	1.75	1.08
AA	Deutsche Real Assets R	AAAQX	D+	(800) 728-3337	E+ / 0.7	5.01	-0.77	7.78 / 7	-0.92 /10	0.80 / 6	1.19	1.76
AA	Deutsche Real Assets S	AAASX	D+	(800) 728-3337	E+ / 0.8	5.04	-0.58	8.19 / 8	-0.54 /11	1.14 / 6	1.58	1.20
RE	Deutsche Real Est Secs A	RRRAX	C-	(800) 728-3337	C+ / 6.2	8.19	-1.89	13.74 /24	10.73 /96	10.70 /63	2.39	0.98
RE	Deutsche Real Est Secs C	RRRCX	C	(800) 728-3337	C+ / 6.7	7.97	-2.25	12.94 /21	9.97 /93	9.93 /58	1.85	1.66
RE	Deutsche Real Est Secs Inst	RRRRX	C+	(800) 728-3337	B- / 7.5	8.25	-1.76	14.11 /26	11.10 /97	11.09 /67	2.88	0.62
RE	Deutsche Real Est Secs R	RRRSX	C	(800) 728-3337	B- / 7.0	8.05	-2.10	13.37 /23	10.37 /95	10.35 /61	2.21	1.31
RE	Deutsche Real Est Secs R6	RRRZX	U	(800) 728-3337	U /	8.27	-1.71	14.21 /26	--	--	2.97	0.53
RE	Deutsche Real Est Secs S	RRREX	C+	(800) 728-3337	B- / 7.4	8.23	-1.81	14.00 /25	11.01 /97	10.97 /66	2.81	0.69
IX	Deutsche S&P 500 Index A	SXPAX	A-	(800) 728-3337	B+ / 8.3	7.86	9.66	24.19 /71	9.92 /93	13.26 /86	1.37	0.64
IX	Deutsche S&P 500 Index C	SXPCX	A	(800) 728-3337	B+ / 8.5	7.65	9.26	23.31 /68	9.16 /88	12.49 /79	0.81	1.32
IX	Deutsche S&P 500 Index S	SCPIX	A+	(800) 728-3337	A- / 9.2	7.92	9.79	24.52 /72	10.24 /95	13.60 /90	1.69	0.34
TC	Deutsche Science and Tech A	KTCAX	C	(800) 728-3337	B+ / 8.4	10.23	11.56	29.60 /85	8.57 /84	11.11 /67	0.00	0.99
TC	Deutsche Science and Tech C	KTCCX	C-	(800) 728-3337	B+ / 8.7	9.96	11.07	28.43 /83	7.61 /76	10.13 /59	0.00	1.86
TC	Deutsche Science and Tech Inst	KTCIX	B-	(800) 728-3337	A / 9.4	10.33	11.75	29.99 /86	8.83 /86	11.42 /69	0.00	0.77
TC	Deutsche Science and Tech S	KTCSX	C+	(800) 728-3337	A / 9.4	10.30	11.62	29.80 /86	8.74 /85	11.26 /68	0.00	0.86
GR	Deutsche Select Alt Allocation Inst	SELIX	D+	(800) 728-3337	D- / 1.4	3.52	1.03	8.99 / 9	0.68 /17	2.00 / 8	3.16	1.55
GR	Deutsche Select Alternative Alloc A	SELAX	D+	(800) 728-3337	E+ / 0.9	3.53	0.94	8.79 / 9	0.43 /15	1.71 / 7	2.71	1.82
GR	Deutsche Select Alternative Alloc C	SELEX	D+	(800) 728-3337	E+ / 0.9	3.32	0.54	7.96 / 7	-0.35 /12	0.94 / 6	2.11	2.57
AA	Deutsche Select Alternative Alloc R	SELRX	D+	(800) 728-3337	D- / 1.2	3.43	0.85	8.35 / 8	0.10 /14	--	2.50	2.19
GR	Deutsche Select Alternative Alloc S	SELSX	D+	(800) 728-3337	D- / 1.4	3.52	0.94	8.89 / 9	0.57 /16	1.86 / 8	3.06	1.64
SC	Deutsche Small Cap Core A	SZCAX	B	(800) 728-3337	B / 8.2	4.74	12.16	32.52 /91	8.53 /83	13.56 /89	0.35	1.42
SC	Deutsche Small Cap Core C	SZCCX	B	(800) 728-3337	B+ / 8.6	4.52	11.72	31.51 /89	7.72 /77	12.71 /81	0.00	2.21
SC	Deutsche Small Cap Core S	SSLCX	B+	(800) 728-3337	A- / 9.2	4.79	12.28	32.82 /91	8.80 /85	13.84 /92	0.59	1.13
SC	Deutsche Small Cap Growth A	SSDAX	D+	(800) 728-3337	C / 4.8	5.63	10.11	28.01 /82	3.48 /37	9.97 /58	0.00	1.40
SC	Deutsche Small Cap Growth C	SSDCX	D+	(800) 728-3337	C / 5.3	5.45	9.74	27.02 /79	2.70 /29	9.15 /52	0.00	2.14
SC	Deutsche Small Cap Growth Inst	SSDIX	C-	(800) 728-3337	C+ / 6.2	5.68	10.23	28.35 /82	3.77 /40	10.35 /61	0.00	1.08
SC	Deutsche Small Cap Growth R	SSDGX	C-	(800) 728-3337	C+ / 5.8	5.53	9.94	27.65 /81	3.22 /34	--	0.00	1.71
SC	Deutsche Small Cap Growth S	SSDSX	C-	(800) 728-3337	C+ / 6.2	5.68	10.25	28.33 /82	3.73 /40	10.24 /60	0.00	1.15
SC	Deutsche Small Cap Value A	KDSAX	D	(800) 728-3337	C- / 4.0	3.28	9.53	25.29 /74	3.50 /37	8.75 /48	0.00	1.17
SC	Deutsche Small Cap Value C	KDSCX	D	(800) 728-3337	C / 4.6	3.15	9.19	24.43 /71	2.72 /29	7.94 /42	0.00	1.94
SC	Deutsche Small Cap Value Inst	KDSIX	C-	(800) 728-3337	C+ / 5.6	3.37	9.78	25.75 /75	3.86 /41	9.14 /52	0.28	0.81
SC	Deutsche Small Cap Value S	KDSSX	D+	(800) 728-3337	C / 5.5	3.35	9.77	25.69 /75	3.78 /40	9.00 /51	0.13	0.94
FO	Deutsche World Dividend A	SERAX	D+	(800) 728-3337	D+ / 2.5	5.63	4.15	15.82 /33	3.02 /32	6.99 /35	1.27	1.27
FO	Deutsche World Dividend C	SERCX	D+	(800) 728-3337	D+ / 2.9	5.40	3.76	14.94 /30	2.26 /26	6.20 /30	0.66	2.00
FO	Deutsche World Dividend Inst	SERNX	C-	(800) 728-3337	C- / 3.7	5.71	4.31	16.11 /35	3.32 /35	7.30 /37	1.62	0.96
FO	Deutsche World Dividend S	SCGEX	C-	(800) 728-3337	C- / 3.6	5.68	4.27	16.12 /35	3.27 /34	7.22 /36	1.59	1.07
GR	DF Dent MidCap Growth	DFDMX	C-	(800) 754-8757	C / 4.8	6.07	4.21	21.52 /60	4.61 /50	12.25 /77	0.00	1.84
GR	DF Dent Premier Growth	DFDPX	C-	(866) 233-3368	C+ / 6.3	6.76	5.68	22.40 /64	5.81 /63	10.78 /64	0.00	1.20

● Denotes fund is closed to new investors

★ Denotes fund is included in Section II

www.thestreetratings.com

RISK			NET ASSETS		ASSET					BULL / BEAR		FUND MANAGER		MINIMUMS		LOADS	
	3 Year		NAV						Portfolio	Last Bull	Last Bear	Manager	Manager	Initial	Additional	Front	Back
Risk Rating/Pts	Standard Deviation	Beta	As of 2/28/17	Total $(Mil)	Cash %	Stocks %	Bonds %	Other %	Turnover Ratio	Market Return	Market Return	Quality Pct	Tenure (Years)	Purch. $	Purch. $	End Load	End Load
C /5.5	12.2	0.92	17.73	30	1	94	3	2	62	125.1	-23.8	59	4	0	0	0.0	0.0
C /5.4	12.2	0.92	17.72	167	1	94	3	2	62	130.6	-23.6	66	4	2,500	50	0.0	0.0
B /8.7	5.4	0.81	12.46	35	1	25	73	1	162	41.8	-12.3	27	N/A	1,000	50	5.8	0.0
B /8.7	5.3	0.81	12.45	9	1	25	73	1	162	36.2	-12.5	20	N/A	1,000	50	0.0	0.0
B /8.7	5.3	0.81	12.45	52	1	25	73	1	162	43.9	-12.2	31	N/A	2,500	50	0.0	0.0
B- /7.9	7.1	0.60	14.55	37	6	50	43	1	259	40.7	-14.2	12	4	1,000	50	5.8	0.0
B /8.0	7.1	0.60	14.49	8	6	50	43	1	259	35.2	-14.5	8	4	1,000	50	0.0	0.0
B- /7.8	7.1	0.60	14.55	55	6	50	43	1	259	42.6	-14.1	13	4	2,500	50	0.0	0.0
C+ /6.1	7.1	0.65	9.41	21	10	58	31	1	161	60.5	-18.5	25	4	1,000	50	5.8	0.0
C+ /6.3	7.1	0.65	9.42	5	10	58	31	1	161	54.2	-18.7	18	4	1,000	50	0.0	0.0
C+ /6.1	7.2	0.65	9.40	8	10	58	31	1	161	62.6	-18.4	27	4	2,500	50	0.0	0.0
B- /7.9	6.3	0.72	8.77	66	34	37	20	9	51	14.0	-11.2	9	4	1,000	50	5.8	0.0
B /8.0	6.4	0.73	8.72	41	34	37	20	9	51	9.5	-11.5	6	4	1,000	50	0.0	0.0
B- /7.9	6.4	0.72	8.71	44	34	37	20	9	51	16.2	-11.1	11	4	1,000,000	0	0.0	0.0
B- /7.9	6.4	0.73	8.83	2	34	37	20	9	51	12.9	N/A	8	4	0	0	0.0	0.0
B- /7.9	6.4	0.74	8.70	52	34	37	20	9	51	15.0	-11.0	9	4	2,500	50	0.0	0.0
C- /4.2	14.8	1.08	20.83	287	0	99	0	1	150	102.2	-17.3	60	13	1,000	50	5.8	0.0
C- /4.2	14.8	1.08	21.06	47	0	99	0	1	150	94.6	-17.5	51	13	1,000	50	0.0	0.0
C- /4.2	14.8	1.08	20.81	571	0	99	0	1	150	105.9	-17.1	65	13	1,000,000	0	0.0	0.0
C- /4.2	14.8	1.08	20.82	36	0	99	0	1	150	98.4	-17.2	56	13	0	0	0.0	0.0
U /	N/A	N/A	20.82	208	0	99	0	1	150	N/A	N/A	N/A	13	0	0	0.0	0.0
C- /4.2	14.8	1.07	20.96	333	0	99	0	1	150	104.7	-17.1	64	13	2,500	50	0.0	0.0
C+ /6.6	10.3	1.00	28.25	203	1	97	0	2	3	126.8	-16.5	66	10	1,000	50	4.5	0.0
C+ /6.6	10.3	1.00	28.16	76	1	97	0	2	3	118.4	-16.7	58	10	1,000	50	0.0	0.0
C+ /6.6	10.3	1.00	28.32	666	1	97	0	2	3	130.3	-16.3	70	10	2,500	50	0.0	0.0
D+ /2.9	14.2	1.17	18.03	549	0	98	0	2	171	109.0	-16.8	27	3	1,000	50	5.8	0.0
D /1.7	14.2	1.18	12.74	18	0	98	0	2	171	99.2	-17.1	18	3	1,000	50	0.0	0.0
C- /3.1	14.2	1.17	19.58	3	0	98	0	2	171	112.1	-16.6	30	3	1,000,000	0	0.0	0.0
D+ /2.9	14.2	1.18	18.24	103	0	98	0	2	171	110.3	-16.7	29	3	2,500	50	0.0	0.0
B- /7.9	4.9	0.33	10.59	10	10	24	58	8	34	19.0	-8.5	38	4	1,000,000	0	0.0	0.0
B- /7.9	4.9	0.33	10.60	136	10	24	58	8	34	17.1	-8.7	35	4	1,000	50	5.8	0.0
B /8.0	4.9	0.33	10.60	18	10	24	58	8	34	12.3	-8.9	26	4	1,000	50	0.0	0.0
B /8.0	4.9	0.62	10.66	2	10	24	58	8	34	N/A	N/A	20	4	0	0	0.0	0.0
B- /7.9	4.9	0.33	10.59	34	10	24	58	8	34	18.1	-8.5	37	4	2,500	50	0.0	0.0
C /5.2	14.8	0.90	28.73	21	0	98	1	1	51	145.9	-25.4	87	4	1,000	50	5.8	0.0
C /4.8	14.8	0.90	24.50	6	0	98	1	1	51	136.1	-25.7	83	4	1,000	50	0.0	0.0
C /5.3	14.8	0.90	29.96	137	0	98	1	1	51	149.2	-25.3	88	4	2,500	50	0.0	0.0
C- /4.0	16.2	0.98	30.39	31	0	97	1	2	50	106.8	-21.3	33	11	1,000	50	5.8	0.0
C- /3.6	16.2	0.98	26.14	7	0	97	1	2	50	98.5	-21.5	25	11	1,000	50	0.0	0.0
C- /4.1	16.2	0.98	32.01	17	0	97	1	2	50	110.7	-21.1	36	11	1,000,000	0	0.0	0.0
C- /3.9	16.2	0.98	29.96	4	0	97	1	2	50	N/A	N/A	30	11	0	0	0.0	0.0
C- /4.1	16.2	0.98	31.62	73	0	97	1	2	50	109.6	-21.2	36	11	2,500	50	0.0	0.0
C- /3.8	15.2	0.92	25.17	264	0	98	0	2	29	91.6	-27.1	38	1	1,000	50	5.8	0.0
C- /3.3	15.2	0.92	20.32	50	0	98	0	2	29	84.0	-27.3	29	1	1,000	50	0.0	0.0
C- /3.8	15.3	0.92	25.77	26	0	98	0	2	29	95.4	-27.0	43	1	1,000,000	0	0.0	0.0
C- /3.8	15.3	0.92	25.62	55	0	98	0	2	29	93.8	-27.1	42	1	2,500	50	0.0	0.0
C+ /6.0	9.6	0.62	29.55	57	7	82	10	1	33	58.3	-15.6	90	7	1,000	50	5.8	0.0
C+ /6.1	9.6	0.62	29.30	25	7	82	10	1	33	52.2	-15.9	88	7	1,000	50	0.0	0.0
C+ /6.0	9.6	0.62	29.85	21	7	82	10	1	33	60.9	-15.5	91	7	1,000,000	0	0.0	0.0
C+ /6.0	9.6	0.62	29.61	169	7	82	10	1	33	60.2	-15.6	91	7	2,500	50	0.0	0.0
C /4.9	13.0	1.08	16.67	33	8	91	0	1	29	127.9	N/A	7	6	2,500	500	0.0	2.0
C- /3.8	12.6	1.09	26.02	141	0	99	0	1	20	111.7	-18.9	12	16	2,500	500	0.0	0.0

					PERFORMANCE						Incl. in Returns	
99 Pct = Best						Total Return % through 2/28/17						
0 Pct = Worst			Overall		Perfor-				Annualized		Dividend	Expense
Fund Type	Fund Name	Ticker Symbol	Investment Rating	Phone	mance Rating/Pts	3 Mo	6 Mo	1Yr / Pct	3Yr / Pct	5Yr / Pct	Yield	Ratio
SC	DF Dent Small Cap Growth	DFDSX	C	(800) 754-8757	C+ / 5.7	1.52	4.02	27.18 / 80	6.01 / 64	--	0.00	5.16
FO	DFA Asia Pacif Sm Comp Ptf Inst	DFRSX	D	(800) 984-9472	C- / 3.7	6.23	3.94	25.64 / 75	1.28 / 20	2.14 / 8	3.53	0.65
IN	DFA Commodity Strategy Port	DCMSX	E	(800) 984-9472	E- / 0.1	3.02	6.94	18.21 / 44	-11.53 / 1	-8.25 / 1	1.15	0.34
FO	DFA Continental Small Co Inst	DFCSX	C-	(800) 984-9472	C / 4.3	10.97	6.20	20.12 / 53	2.04 / 24	10.88 / 65	1.93	0.65
GR	DFA CSTG&E US Soc Core Eq 2	DFCUX	A+	(800) 984-9472	A- / 9.1	6.32	13.23	30.47 / 87	8.42 / 82	13.06 / 84	1.60	0.34
GL	DFA Dimensional 2015 TDR Inc Inst	DRIQX	U		U /	3.07	1.00	8.68 / 9	--	--	1.86	0.21
GL	DFA Dimensional 2020 TDR Inc Inst	DRIRX	U		U /	3.60	1.03	11.03 / 15	--	--	1.99	0.23
GL	DFA Dimensional 2025 TDR Inc Inst	DRIUX	U		U /	4.44	1.94	13.78 / 24	--	--	2.06	0.25
GL	DFA Dimensional 2030 TDR Inc Inst	DRIWX	U		U /	5.21	3.56	16.24 / 35	--	--	2.01	0.27
GL	DFA Dimensional 2035 TDR Inc Inst	DRIGX	U		U /	5.96	5.95	18.21 / 44	--	--	1.90	0.28
GL	DFA Dimensional 2040 TDR Inc Inst	DRIHX	U		U /	6.83	7.56	21.19 / 58	--	--	1.92	0.29
GL	DFA Dimensional 2045 TDR Inc Inst	DRIIX	U		U /	7.44	8.25	22.80 / 66	--	--	1.94	0.29
EM	DFA Emerging Markets II Inst	DFETX	C-	(800) 984-9472	C / 5.2	9.53	5.41	29.23 / 85	1.98 / 24	0.32 / 5	2.19	0.44
* EM	DFA Emerging Markets Inst	DFEMX	C-	(800) 984-9472	C / 5.0	9.51	5.30	28.98 / 84	1.76 / 22	0.09 / 5	1.75	0.67
* FO	DFA Emerging Markets Sm Cap Inst	DEMSX	B-	(800) 984-9472	B / 7.6	12.01	6.49	31.94 / 90	5.14 / 56	3.45 / 13	2.28	0.93
EM	DFA Emerging Markets Val Inst	DFEVX	C+	(800) 984-9472	B / 7.8	11.64	11.59	40.28 / 97	2.84 / 30	-0.34 / 4	1.79	0.66
EM	DFA Emerging Markets Val R2	DFEPX	C+	(800) 984-9472	B / 7.7	11.54	11.44	39.91 / 97	2.59 / 28	-0.59 / 4	1.89	0.91
* EM	DFA Emerging Markts Core Eqty Inst	DFCEX	C	(800) 984-9472	C+ / 5.9	10.53	6.04	30.67 / 87	2.49 / 27	0.63 / 6	1.80	0.62
EM	DFA Emerging Mkts Socl Core Eq	DFESX	C	(800) 984-9472	C+ / 6.0	10.50	6.24	31.12 / 88	2.44 / 27	0.36 / 5	1.86	0.65
GR	DFA Enhanced US Large Co Inst	DFELX	A-	(800) 984-9472	A / 9.4	8.03	9.76	25.23 / 74	10.64 / 96	14.12 / 94	0.68	0.24
* RE	DFA GI Real Estate Securities Port	DFGEX	C	(800) 984-9472	C / 5.4	7.23	-3.41	12.46 / 20	8.21 / 81	9.71 / 56	4.57	0.38
GL	DFA Global Allocation 25/75 Inst	DGTSX	C+	(800) 984-9472	D / 1.9	2.26	2.16	7.36 / 6	2.67 / 29	3.62 / 13	1.48	0.43
GL	DFA Global Allocation 25/75 R2	DFGPX	C+	(800) 984-9472	D / 1.8	2.24	2.06	7.18 / 6	2.30 / 26	3.28 / 12	1.61	0.68
GL	DFA Global Allocation 60/40 Inst	DGSIX	B-	(800) 984-9472	C / 4.3	4.83	5.55	16.54 / 36	4.35 / 47	6.98 / 34	1.81	0.52
GL	DFA Global Allocation 60/40 R2	DFPRX	B-	(800) 984-9472	C- / 4.1	4.70	5.42	16.21 / 35	4.10 / 44	6.71 / 33	1.80	0.77
GL	DFA Global Equity Inst	DGEIX	B+	(800) 984-9472	B- / 7.2	7.17	9.73	26.16 / 77	6.07 / 65	10.58 / 63	1.81	0.60
GL	DFA Global Equity R2	DGERX	B	(800) 984-9472	B- / 7.1	7.09	9.58	25.79 / 76	5.81 / 63	10.29 / 60	1.72	0.86
FO	DFA International Large Cap Gr Inst	DILRX	D-	(800) 984-9472	D- / 1.1	7.07	1.75	11.24 / 15	-0.42 / 12	--	2.29	0.34
* FO	DFA International Sm Cap Val Inst	DISVX	C	(800) 984-9472	C / 5.3	9.00	10.43	24.32 / 71	2.28 / 26	9.38 / 54	2.39	0.69
FO	DFA International Small Cap Gr Inst	DISMX	C-	(800) 984-9472	C- / 3.9	7.99	3.89	16.11 / 35	3.36 / 35	--	1.96	0.67
* FO	DFA International Small Co Inst	DFISX	C-	(800) 984-9472	C- / 4.1	8.43	6.74	20.53 / 55	2.11 / 25	8.10 / 43	2.39	0.54
EM	DFA International Value II Inst	DIVTX	D-	(800) 984-9472	D / 1.8	6.90	10.51	26.17 / 77	-1.09 / 9	4.81 / 20	8.34	0.47
EM	DFA International Value III Inst	DFVIX	D-	(800) 984-9472	D / 1.8	6.94	10.09	25.94 / 76	-1.17 / 9	4.76 / 20	3.31	0.45
EM	DFA International Value Inst	DFIVX	D-	(800) 984-9472	D / 1.7	6.99	10.12	25.88 / 76	-1.32 / 8	4.60 / 19	3.25	0.63
EM	DFA International Value IV Inst	DFVFX	D-	(800) 984-9472	D / 1.7	6.80	9.90	25.70 / 75	-1.25 / 9	4.70 / 19	3.68	0.47
EM	DFA International Value R2	DFIPX	D-	(800) 984-9472	D / 1.6	6.91	9.98	25.62 / 75	-1.56 / 8	4.32 / 17	3.26	0.88
FO	DFA International Vector Eq Inst	DFVQX	C-	(800) 984-9472	C- / 3.6	8.11	7.77	22.29 / 64	0.65 / 16	6.45 / 31	2.58	0.50
GR	DFA Internatl Soc Cre Eqty Ptf Inst	DSCLX	D+	(800) 984-9472	C- / 3.0	7.62	6.95	20.96 / 57	0.16 / 14	--	2.63	0.46
* FO	DFA Intl Core Equity Port Inst	DFIEX	D+	(800) 984-9472	C- / 3.1	7.78	6.61	20.30 / 54	0.46 / 16	6.14 / 29	2.63	0.38
RE	DFA Intl Real Estate Sec Port Inst	DFITX	D	(800) 984-9472	D / 1.7	5.95	-5.78	5.95 / 5	3.08 / 33	7.06 / 35	8.35	0.29
FO	DFA Intl Sustainability Core 1	DFSPX	D	(800) 984-9472	D- / 1.5	7.61	5.03	16.88 / 38	-0.28 / 12	5.48 / 25	2.37	0.48
FO	DFA Japanese Small Co Inst	DFJSX	A+	(800) 984-9472	A+ / 9.7	8.70	13.59	28.62 / 83	10.53 / 96	10.00 / 58	1.82	0.64
FO	DFA Large Cap International Inst	DFALX	D-	(800) 984-9472	D- / 1.4	7.25	5.09	17.44 / 40	-0.62 / 11	4.88 / 20	2.76	0.29
FO	DFA LWAS Intl Hi Bk to Mkt Port	DFHBX	E+	(800) 984-9472	D / 1.7	6.92	9.98	25.65 / 75	-1.39 / 8	4.51 / 18	3.21	0.67
GR	DFA LWAS US High Bk to Mkt Port	DFBMX	B+	(800) 984-9472	B+ / 8.8	7.08	14.01	33.01 / 92	6.80 / 70	13.25 / 86	1.78	0.42
* RE	DFA Real Estate Securities Ptf Inst	DFREX	B-	(800) 984-9472	B / 7.8	7.98	-2.02	16.15 / 35	11.39 / 98	11.38 / 69	3.03	0.19
GL	DFA Select Hedged Global Eq Inst	DSHGX	B+	(800) 984-9472	B- / 7.4	7.52	10.67	26.93 / 79	6.00 / 64	9.55 / 55	2.06	0.66
* GR	DFA TA US Core Equity 2 Inst	DFTCX	A+	(800) 984-9472	B+ / 8.9	6.54	11.95	28.31 / 82	8.71 / 85	13.81 / 92	1.52	0.24
FO	DFA TA World ex US Core Eq Inst	DFTWX	C-	(800) 984-9472	C- / 3.6	8.49	6.60	22.54 / 65	0.78 / 17	4.70 / 19	2.26	0.45
FO	DFA Tax Managed Intl Val Inst	DTMIX	D-	(800) 984-9472	D / 1.6	6.89	9.88	25.60 / 75	-1.59 / 8	4.21 / 16	2.85	0.53
SC	DFA Tax Managed US Sm Cap Inst	DFTSX	B+	(800) 984-9472	B+ / 8.9	4.10	13.82	32.32 / 90	7.89 / 78	14.29 / 95	0.85	0.52
MC	DFA Tax Mgd US MktWide Val Inst	DTMMX	A+	(800) 984-9472	A / 9.5	6.74	13.40	30.40 / 87	9.35 / 89	15.04 / 97	1.59	0.57

● Denotes fund is closed to new investors

* Denotes fund is included in Section II

www.thestreetratings.com

RISK Risk Rating/Pts	3 Year Standard Deviation	Beta	NET ASSETS NAV As of 2/28/17	Total $(Mil)	ASSET Cash %	Stocks %	Bonds %	Other %	Portfolio Turnover Ratio	BULL / BEAR Last Bull Market Return	Last Bear Market Return	FUND MANAGER Manager Quality Pct	Manager Tenure (Years)	MINIMUMS Initial Purch. $	Additional Purch. $	LOADS Front End Load	Back End Load
C /5.0	14.6	0.81	12.68	8	4	95	0	1	39	N/A	N/A	77	4	2,500	500	0.0	2.0
C /4.5	15.9	0.97	21.34	263	0	100	0	0	10	39.7	-28.0	84	13	0	0	0.0	0.0
C- /3.8	13.8	0.28	6.06	1,709	8	0	91	1	159	-31.0	-19.7	0	7	0	0	0.0	0.0
C+ /5.9	13.1	0.97	22.86	347	0	99	0	1	14	93.0	-32.9	87	19	0	0	0.0	0.0
C+ /6.5	12.0	1.08	16.16	98	0	99	0	1	17	131.9	-22.4	37	5	0	0	0.0	0.0
U /	N/A	N/A	10.59	29	0	0	0	100	0	N/A	N/A	N/A	2	0	0	0.0	0.0
U /	N/A	N/A	10.70	71	0	0	0	100	0	N/A	N/A	N/A	2	0	0	0.0	0.0
U /	N/A	N/A	10.79	81	0	0	0	100	0	N/A	N/A	N/A	2	0	0	0.0	0.0
U /	N/A	N/A	10.82	68	0	0	0	100	0	N/A	N/A	N/A	2	0	0	0.0	0.0
U /	N/A	N/A	10.77	47	0	0	0	100	0	N/A	N/A	N/A	2	0	0	0.0	0.0
U /	N/A	N/A	10.87	40	0	0	0	100	0	N/A	N/A	N/A	N/A	0	0	0.0	0.0
U /	N/A	N/A	10.94	27	0	0	0	100	0	N/A	N/A	N/A	2	0	0	0.0	0.0
C- /4.2	15.6	0.95	23.79	84	1	98	0	1	9	25.0	-25.7	76	13	0	0	0.0	0.0
C /4.5	15.6	0.96	24.89	5,331	1	98	0	1	9	23.5	-25.7	75	13	0	0	0.0	0.0
C /4.9	15.4	0.90	20.66	6,081	1	98	0	1	18	46.6	-27.1	96	13	0	0	0.0	0.0
C- /3.8	18.2	1.10	26.62	17,388	0	99	0	1	12	23.0	-31.1	81	13	0	0	0.0	0.0
C- /3.8	18.2	1.10	26.46	105	0	99	0	1	12	21.3	-31.2	79	13	0	0	0.0	0.0
C /4.6	15.7	0.96	19.14	20,486	1	98	0	1	3	28.1	-27.4	80	12	0	0	0.0	0.0
C /4.7	15.8	0.96	12.23	1,161	5	94	0	1	12	27.0	-28.1	79	11	0	0	0.0	0.0
C /5.5	10.4	1.01	13.26	267	1	0	98	1	119	136.0	-16.1	73	16	0	0	0.0	0.0
C /5.2	12.8	0.92	10.73	5,413	0	99	0	1	3	86.9	-17.2	51	N/A	0	0	0.0	0.0
B+ /9.7	2.9	0.20	13.12	787	3	24	71	2	0	27.2	-4.7	89	N/A	0	0	0.0	0.0
B+ /9.7	3.0	0.20	13.09	1	3	24	71	2	0	25.0	-4.9	87	N/A	0	0	0.0	0.0
B /8.6	6.7	0.48	16.77	3,441	1	59	38	2	54	60.3	-13.8	94	N/A	0	0	0.0	0.0
B /8.6	6.7	0.48	16.86	6	1	59	38	2	54	58.2	-14.0	93	N/A	0	0	0.0	0.0
C+ /6.6	10.8	0.76	20.44	5,479	5	94	0	1	15	102.3	-23.1	97	N/A	0	0	0.0	0.0
C+ /6.6	10.7	0.76	20.56	26	5	94	0	1	15	99.5	-23.1	97	N/A	0	0	0.0	0.0
C+ /6.1	10.4	0.81	11.19	253	0	99	0	1	20	N/A	N/A	71	5	0	0	0.0	0.0
C+ /5.9	12.6	0.93	20.10	13,966	1	98	0	1	19	85.0	-26.1	88	13	0	0	0.0	0.0
C+ /6.5	11.4	0.84	13.13	126	0	99	0	1	29	N/A	N/A	92	5	0	0	0.0	0.0
C+ /6.1	11.6	0.87	18.28	11,092	17	82	0	1	18	70.4	-23.3	87	13	0	0	0.0	0.0
C /4.4	13.8	0.64	4.62	12	0	99	0	1	21	46.2	-26.8	45	19	0	0	0.0	0.0
C /4.6	13.7	0.63	14.71	2,218	0	99	0	1	21	46.1	-26.8	44	19	0	0	0.0	0.0
C /4.9	13.7	0.64	17.36	7,987	0	99	0	1	21	44.9	-26.9	42	19	0	0	0.0	0.0
C /4.5	13.8	0.63	13.14	201	0	99	0	1	21	45.6	-26.8	43	19	0	0	0.0	0.0
C /4.9	13.8	0.64	17.31	4	0	99	0	1	21	42.9	-27.0	38	19	0	0	0.0	0.0
C+ /5.8	12.0	0.95	11.41	2,055	1	98	0	1	4	59.1	-25.8	80	5	0	0	0.0	0.0
C+ /5.8	11.9	0.91	11.79	613	0	99	0	1	8	N/A	N/A	3	5	0	0	0.0	0.0
C+ /5.9	11.7	0.93	12.24	19,345	0	92	7	1	2	56.9	-25.1	78	11	0	0	0.0	0.0
C+ /6.3	11.8	0.63	4.85	4,447	34	65	0	1	1	58.5	-18.8	27	10	0	0	0.0	0.0
C+ /6.0	11.5	0.92	9.32	587	1	98	0	1	24	51.5	-24.4	73	5	0	0	0.0	0.0
B- /7.6	10.9	0.61	23.74	517	0	99	0	1	10	64.3	3.5	99	13	0	0	0.0	0.0
C+ /5.8	11.4	0.92	20.50	3,896	1	98	0	1	10	47.4	-23.5	69	13	0	0	0.0	0.0
C /4.3	13.7	1.06	7.59	55	0	99	0	1	21	44.3	-26.9	59	19	0	0	0.0	0.0
C /5.2	13.9	1.16	19.01	59	0	99	0	1	15	135.1	-24.0	14	13	0	0	0.0	0.0
C /5.0	15.0	1.09	35.61	7,920	0	99	0	1	3	107.6	-16.1	66	5	0	0	0.0	0.0
C+ /6.3	10.7	0.78	14.67	324	2	97	0	1	0	N/A	N/A	97	6	0	0	0.0	0.0
C+ /6.6	11.5	1.05	16.31	7,238	1	98	0	1	7	139.2	-22.0	45	5	0	0	0.0	0.0
C+ /5.9	12.0	0.93	9.91	2,643	2	97	0	1	7	49.1	-26.0	81	9	0	0	0.0	0.0
C /4.9	13.8	1.06	14.28	3,290	1	98	0	1	18	43.0	-27.0	57	13	0	0	0.0	0.0
C /5.3	14.5	0.91	41.24	2,651	0	99	0	1	10	146.8	-24.6	84	5	0	0	0.0	0.0
C+ /6.8	11.8	0.89	28.81	4,554	0	99	0	1	9	154.8	-23.8	79	13	0	0	0.0	0.0

Fund Type	Fund Name	Ticker Symbol	Overall Investment Rating	Phone	Performance Rating/Pts	3 Mo	6 Mo	1Yr / Pct	3Yr / Pct	5Yr / Pct	Dividend Yield	Expense Ratio
	99 Pct = Best							Total Return % through 2/28/17	Annualized		Incl. in Returns	
SC	DFA Tax Mgd US Target Val Inst	DTMVX	A-	(800) 984-9472	A- / 9.1	4.33	15.40	32.79 /91	8.07 /79	14.70 /96	0.93	0.44
IN	DFA Tax-Managed US Eq Inst	DTMEX	A+	(800) 984-9472	A- / 9.2	7.63	10.60	26.02 /76	9.84 /92	13.76 /91	1.63	0.22
IN	DFA U.S: Vector Equity Port Inst	DFVEX	A-	(800) 984-9472	A- / 9.0	5.53	14.01	32.64 /91	7.85 /78	13.69 /91	1.27	0.32
FO	DFA United Kingdom Small Co Inst	DFUKX	E	(800) 984-9472	E- / 0.2	6.70	0.87	2.57 / 2	-4.18 / 3	8.94 /50	3.94	0.69
* IN	DFA US Core Equity 1 Ptf Inst	DFEOX	A+	(800) 984-9472	A- / 9.0	7.07	11.31	27.39 /80	9.13 /88	13.82 /92	1.63	0.19
* IN	DFA US Core Equity 2 Ptf Inst	DFQTX	A	(800) 984-9472	B+ / 8.9	6.46	11.93	28.65 /83	8.54 /83	13.75 /91	1.54	0.22
GR	DFA US Large Cap Equity Inst	DUSQX	A+	(800) 984-9472	A- / 9.1	7.67	10.92	25.74 /75	9.53 /91	---	1.70	0.19
GR	DFA US Large Cap Growth Inst	DUSLX	A+	(800) 984-9472	B+ / 8.5	7.65	8.43	20.92 /57	9.83 /92	---	1.62	0.20
GR	DFA US Large Cap Value I Inst	DFLVX	A+	(800) 984-9472	A+ / 9.7	7.11	14.07	33.10 /92	9.96 /93	15.28 /97	1.78	0.37
GR	DFA US Large Cap Value II Inst	DFCVX	A+	(800) 984-9472	A+ / 9.7	7.14	14.14	33.26 /92	10.07 /94	15.42 /97	1.99	0.25
GR	DFA US Large Cap Value III Inst	DFUVX	A+	(800) 984-9472	A+ / 9.7	7.16	14.15	33.29 /92	10.11 /94	15.44 /98	1.92	0.23
* GR	DFA US Large Company Portfolio	DFUSX	A+	(800) 984-9472	A / 9.4	8.08	10.04	24.92 /73	10.57 /96	13.95 /93	1.95	0.09
* SC	DFA US Micro Cap Portfolio Inst	DFSCX	B+	(800) 984-9472	B+ / 8.6	3.26	13.56	32.30 /90	7.48 /75	14.24 /94	0.71	0.52
SC	DFA US Small Cap Growth Inst	DSCGX	B	(800) 984-9472	B- / 7.5	4.15	9.56	26.37 /77	7.21 /73	---	0.83	0.40
* SC	DFA US Small Cap Port Inst	DFSTX	B+	(800) 984-9472	B+ / 8.9	4.14	13.24	32.06 /90	7.97 /79	14.12 /94	0.94	0.37
* SC	DFA US Small Cap Value I Inst	DFSVX	B+	(800) 984-9472	B+ / 8.9	3.19	16.20	36.30 /95	6.87 /71	13.81 /92	0.76	0.52
GR	DFA US Social Core Eq 2 Inst	DFUEX	A	(800) 984-9472	B+ / 8.9	6.52	12.70	29.75 /86	8.11 /80	13.06 /84	1.43	0.29
GR	DFA US Sustainability Core 1 Inst	DFSIX	A+	(800) 984-9472	B+ / 8.9	7.18	11.26	26.62 /78	8.97 /87	13.69 /91	1.39	0.32
GR	DFA US Targeted Value Port Inst	DFFVX	B+	(800) 984-9472	A- / 9.2	4.01	15.87	35.77 /95	7.53 /76	14.08 /94	0.96	0.37
GR	DFA US Targeted Value Portfolio R1	DFTVX	B+	(800) 984-9472	A- / 9.1	4.00	15.83	35.72 /95	7.43 /75	13.98 /93	0.97	0.47
GR	DFA US Targeted Value Portfolio R2	DFTPX	B+	(800) 984-9472	A- / 9.1	3.96	15.75	35.54 /95	7.27 /74	13.80 /92	0.94	0.63
FO	DFA Wld ex US Val Institutional	DFWVX	D	(800) 984-9472	D+ / 2.6	8.30	10.46	28.91 /84	-0.01 /13	3.88 /15	2.76	0.75
GL	DFA World Core Eqty Inst	DREIX	C+	(800) 984-9472	C+ / 6.6	7.69	8.96	24.90 /73	5.04 /55	---	1.97	0.65
FO	DFA World ex US Core Eqty Port Inst	DFWIX	C-	(800) 984-9472	C- / 3.6	8.32	6.49	22.63 /65	0.78 /17	---	2.44	0.49
GR	DFA World ex US Tgtd Val Port Inst	DWUSX	C+	(800) 984-9472	C+ / 6.3	10.09	10.28	28.78 /83	2.88 /31	---	1.79	0.64
GR	DGHM All-Cap Value C	DGACX	D+	(800) 673-0550	B / 7.8	5.20	10.89	31.17 /88	6.17 /66	10.36 /61	1.65	2.38
GR	DGHM All-Cap Value Inst	DGAIX	C-	(800) 673-0550	B+ / 8.5	5.45	11.27	32.44 /91	7.24 /74	11.50 /70	2.51	1.30
GR	DGHM All-Cap Value Investor	DGHMX	C-	(800) 673-0550	B / 8.2	5.47	11.20	31.94 /90	6.86 /71	11.13 /67	1.96	1.71
SC	DGHM V2000 Small Cap Value Inst	DGIVX	A+	(800) 673-0550	B+ / 8.7	4.92	13.18	31.97 /90	7.40 /75	12.14 /75	0.55	1.70
SC	DGHM V2000 Small Cap Value	DGSMX	A	(800) 673-0550	B+ / 8.3	4.80	12.83	31.30 /89	6.90 /71	11.76 /72	0.48	2.18
GR	Diamond Hill All Cap Select Fund A	DHTAX	B-	(614) 255-3333	B- / 7.5	8.16	13.04	24.03 /70	7.88 /78	13.19 /86	0.00	1.19
GR	Diamond Hill All Cap Select Fund C	DHTCX	B-	(614) 255-3333	B / 7.8	7.93	12.58	23.10 /67	7.06 /72	12.33 /77	0.00	1.94
GR	Diamond Hill All Cap Select Fund I	DHLTX	B+	(614) 255-3333	B+ / 8.6	8.30	13.25	24.43 /71	8.18 /80	13.47 /89	0.09	0.89
GR	Diamond Hill All Cap Select Fund Y	DHTYX	B+		B+ / 8.7	8.33	13.26	24.52 /72	8.29 /81	13.63 /90	0.19	0.79
FS	Diamond Hill Financial Lng-Sht A	BANCX	A	(614) 255-3333	A+ / 9.8	9.21	22.11	42.96 /98	9.53 /91	14.48 /95	0.00	1.80
FS	Diamond Hill Financial Lng-Sht C	BSGCX	A	(614) 255-3333	A+ / 9.8	8.98	21.63	41.88 /98	8.71 /85	13.61 /90	0.00	2.55
FS	Diamond Hill Financial Lng-Sht I	DHFSX	A+		A+ / 9.9	9.24	22.32	43.38 /98	9.82 /92	14.77 /96	0.00	1.50
GR	Diamond Hill Large Cap A	DHLAX	A	(614) 255-3333	A- / 9.0	8.57	12.74	28.71 /83	10.00 /93	13.67 /90	0.89	0.99
GR	Diamond Hill Large Cap C	DHLCX	A+	(614) 255-3333	A / 9.3	8.32	12.34	27.75 /81	9.16 /88	12.82 /82	0.40	1.74
GR	Diamond Hill Large Cap I	DHLRX	A+	(614) 255-3333	A+ / 9.6	8.59	12.91	29.10 /84	10.28 /95	13.97 /93	1.18	0.69
GR	Diamond Hill Large Cap Y	DHLYX	A+		A+ / 9.6	8.64	12.96	29.20 /85	10.42 /95	14.12 /94	1.27	0.59
GR	● Diamond Hill Long-Short Fd Cl A	DIAMX	B	(614) 255-3333	C / 5.5	4.95	10.22	19.33 /49	6.38 /67	8.65 /48	0.00	1.91
GR	● Diamond Hill Long-Short Fd Cl C	DHFCX	B-	(614) 255-3333	C+ / 5.9	4.75	9.84	18.49 /45	5.59 /60	7.85 /41	0.00	2.66
GR	● Diamond Hill Long-Short Fd Cl I	DHLSX	B	(614) 255-3333	C+ / 6.7	5.04	10.40	19.69 /50	6.69 /70	8.95 /50	0.00	1.61
GR	● Diamond Hill Long-Short Fd Cl Y	DIAYX	B		C+ / 6.8	5.02	10.44	19.82 /51	6.80 /70	9.09 /51	0.00	1.51
MC	Diamond Hill Mid Cap A	DHPAX	A		B+ / 8.4	6.27	11.53	27.01 /79	9.76 /92	---	0.13	1.09
MC	Diamond Hill Mid Cap I	DHPIX	A+		A / 9.4	6.36	11.69	27.37 /80	10.06 /94	---	0.40	0.79
MC	Diamond Hill Mid Cap Y	DHPYX	A+		A / 9.4	6.37	11.69	27.57 /81	10.19 /94	---	0.42	0.69
GR	Diamond Hill Rsrch Opptys A	DHROX	C		C / 5.4	7.59	12.09	19.80 /51	5.15 /56	9.27 /53	0.00	1.78
GR	Diamond Hill Rsrch Opptys C	DROCX	C		C+ / 5.7	7.41	11.64	18.92 /47	4.37 /47	8.47 /46	0.00	2.53
GR	Diamond Hill Rsrch Opptys I	DROIX	C+		C+ / 6.6	7.67	12.19	20.11 /53	5.43 /59	9.55 /55	0.00	1.48
GR	Diamond Hill Rsrch Opptys Y	DROYX	C+		C+ / 6.7	7.71	12.29	20.26 /53	5.57 /60	9.71 /56	0.00	1.38

● Denotes fund is closed to new investors
* Denotes fund is included in Section II

RISK			NET ASSETS		ASSET					BULL / BEAR		FUND MANAGER		MINIMUMS		LOADS	
	3 Year		NAV						Portfolio	Last Bull	Last Bear	Manager	Manager	Initial	Additional	Front	Back
Risk Rating/Pts	Standard Deviation	Beta	As of 2/28/17	Total $(Mil)	Cash %	Stocks %	Bonds %	Other %	Turnover Ratio	Market Return	Market Return	Quality Pct	Tenure (Years)	Purch. $	Purch. $	End Load	End Load
C+ / 5.7	14.3	0.88	35.86	4,331	0	98	0	2	20	155.8	-26.6	86	5	0	0	0.0	0.0
C+ / 6.9	10.6	1.02	25.69	2,994	0	98	0	2	4	133.2	-17.4	63	5	0	0	0.0	0.0
C+ / 5.8	13.1	1.10	18.06	4,427	0	99	0	1	10	141.1	-24.8	28	5	0	0	0.0	0.0
C- / 3.6	15.4	0.90	28.06	39	3	96	0	1	15	87.4	-22.8	22	13	0	0	0.0	0.0
C+ / 6.7	11.1	1.04	20.25	18,041	1	98	0	1	4	137.5	-20.2	52	12	0	0	0.0	0.0
C+ / 6.4	11.6	1.06	19.42	19,751	0	98	0	2	4	138.8	-22.0	41	5	0	0	0.0	0.0
C+ / 6.9	10.7	1.02	14.67	992	0	99	0	1	12	N/A	N/A	59	4	0	0	0.0	0.0
B- / 7.2	10.4	1.00	16.55	1,315	0	99	0	1	14	N/A	N/A	66	5	0	0	0.0	0.0
C+ / 6.3	12.0	1.09	36.67	20,772	0	99	0	1	15	157.1	-24.0	56	13	0	0	0.0	0.0
C+ / 6.7	12.0	1.09	18.12	178	0	99	0	1	15	158.6	-23.9	57	13	0	0	0.0	0.0
C+ / 5.9	12.0	1.09	25.77	3,433	0	99	0	1	15	159.1	-24.0	57	13	0	0	0.0	0.0
B- / 7.0	10.3	1.00	18.44	7,392	0	99	0	1	9	134.0	-16.3	74	N/A	0	0	0.0	0.0
C / 5.1	15.1	0.93	20.73	5,790	1	98	0	1	15	145.5	-24.0	81	5	0	0	0.0	0.0
C+ / 5.6	14.0	0.87	16.63	392	0	99	0	1	47	N/A	N/A	82	5	0	0	0.0	0.0
C / 5.2	14.5	0.91	34.24	15,230	0	98	0	2	10	145.6	-24.7	84	5	0	0	0.0	0.0
C / 5.0	15.9	0.97	37.31	14,467	1	97	1	1	19	145.9	-27.8	75	5	0	0	0.0	0.0
C+ / 6.3	11.9	1.08	14.48	825	0	99	0	1	17	132.7	-22.9	33	5	0	0	0.0	0.0
C+ / 6.6	11.1	1.04	18.78	938	0	99	0	1	26	136.8	-20.1	49	5	0	0	0.0	0.0
C / 5.2	15.0	1.12	24.29	9,529	0	98	0	2	28	149.0	-27.4	23	5	0	0	0.0	0.0
C / 5.2	15.0	1.13	24.29	52	0	98	0	2	28	147.9	-27.5	22	5	0	0	0.0	0.0
C / 5.2	15.0	1.13	24.17	181	0	98	0	2	28	145.7	-27.5	20	5	0	0	0.0	0.0
C / 5.1	13.7	1.04	11.01	209	0	100	0	0	0	42.6	-27.8	75	7	0	0	0.0	0.0
C+ / 6.5	10.7	0.81	14.30	433	2	97	0	1	0	N/A	N/A	95	N/A	0	0	0.0	0.0
C+ / 5.9	12.1	0.94	10.46	2,031	1	98	0	1	1	N/A	N/A	81	4	0	0	0.0	0.0
C+ / 6.0	13.2	0.94	13.02	343	1	98	0	1	28	N/A	N/A	6	5	0	0	0.0	0.0
D- / 1.2	12.4	1.07	8.02	2	2	97	0	1	50	96.2	-21.8	16	10	1,000	500	0.0	0.0
D- / 1.2	12.3	1.07	8.79	4	2	97	0	1	50	107.6	-21.4	26	10	100,000	500	0.0	0.0
D- / 1.2	12.3	1.07	8.78	9	2	97	0	1	50	103.8	-21.5	22	10	2,500	500	0.0	0.0
C+ / 6.9	13.3	0.81	13.44	61	0	0	0	100	38	114.0	-22.3	85	7	100,000	500	0.0	0.0
B- / 7.0	13.3	0.81	12.61	1	0	0	0	100	38	109.9	-22.2	82	7	2,500	500	0.0	0.0
C / 5.2	12.3	0.96	14.11	16	2	93	4	1	89	125.4	-18.5	47	4	2,500	100	5.0	0.0
C / 5.1	12.3	0.96	13.40	13	2	93	4	1	89	116.5	-18.8	36	4	2,500	100	0.0	0.0
C / 5.2	12.3	0.96	14.18	100	2	93	4	1	89	128.6	-18.4	51	4	2,500	100	0.0	0.0
C / 5.2	12.3	0.96	14.20	19	2	93	4	1	89	130.1	-18.5	53	4	500,000	100	0.0	0.0
C+ / 5.7	15.3	1.09	23.36	11	18	79	1	2	63	146.2	-23.6	28	16	2,500	100	5.0	0.0
C+ / 5.7	15.3	1.08	21.48	2	18	79	1	2	63	136.6	-23.9	20	16	2,500	100	0.0	0.0
C+ / 5.7	15.3	1.08	23.40	22	18	79	1	2	63	149.9	-23.5	31	16	2,500	100	0.0	0.0
C+ / 6.4	11.8	1.10	24.62	1,274	0	99	0	1	20	132.0	-17.1	54	15	2,500	100	5.0	0.0
C+ / 6.4	11.8	1.10	23.39	102	0	99	0	1	20	122.7	-17.3	43	15	2,500	100	0.0	0.0
C+ / 6.4	11.8	1.10	24.77	2,366	0	99	0	1	20	135.3	-17.0	57	15	2,500	100	0.0	0.0
C+ / 6.4	11.8	1.10	24.79	744	0	99	0	1	20	136.9	-17.1	60	15	500,000	100	0.0	0.0
B / 8.0	8.7	0.74	25.85	463	37	53	9	1	81	77.1	-12.1	58	17	2,500	100	5.0	0.0
B- / 7.9	8.7	0.74	23.33	145	37	53	9	1	81	70.2	-12.4	48	17	2,500	100	0.0	0.0
B / 8.0	8.7	0.74	26.41	3,824	37	53	9	1	81	79.8	-12.1	62	17	2,500	100	0.0	0.0
B / 8.0	8.7	0.74	26.51	242	37	53	9	1	81	80.9	-12.1	63	17	500,000	100	0.0	0.0
B- / 7.0	10.6	0.84	13.00	7	6	93	0	1	29	N/A	N/A	84	4	2,500	100	5.0	0.0
B- / 7.0	10.6	0.84	13.04	38	6	93	0	1	29	N/A	N/A	86	4	2,500	100	0.0	0.0
B- / 7.0	10.6	0.84	13.07	25	6	93	0	1	29	N/A	N/A	86	4	500,000	100	0.0	0.0
C / 5.3	10.7	0.82	22.63	6	14	82	2	2	147	89.2	-12.5	31	6	2,500	100	5.0	0.0
C / 5.2	10.7	0.82	21.69	2	14	82	2	2	147	82.1	-12.5	23	6	2,500	100	0.0	0.0
C / 5.3	10.7	0.82	22.82	31	14	82	2	2	147	91.7	-12.5	35	6	2,500	100	0.0	0.0
C / 5.3	10.6	0.82	22.85	18	14	82	2	2	147	93.1	-12.5	36	6	500,000	100	0.0	0.0

Data as of February 28, 2017

					PERFORMANCE						Incl. in Returns	
99 Pct = Best			**Overall**		**Perfor-**	Total Return % through 2/28/17			Annualized		Dividend	Expense
0 Pct = Worst		**Ticker**	**Investment**		**mance**						Yield	Ratio
Fund Type	Fund Name	Symbol	Rating	Phone	**Rating/Pts**	3 Mo	6 Mo	1Yr / Pct	3Yr / Pct	5Yr / Pct		
SC	● Diamond Hill Small Cap A	DHSCX	C+	(614) 255-3333	C / 4.9	4.18	9.55	21.96 /62	5.23 /57	10.85 /65	0.00	1.31
SC	● Diamond Hill Small Cap C	DHSMX	C+	(614) 255-3333	C / 5.3	4.04	9.19	21.10 /58	4.46 /48	10.04 /59	0.00	2.06
SC	● Diamond Hill Small Cap I	DHSIX	C+	(614) 255-3333	C+ / 6.3	4.28	9.73	22.33 /64	5.53 /60	11.15 /67	0.21	1.01
SC	● Diamond Hill Small Cap Y	DHSYX	C+		C+ / 6.4	4.30	9.77	22.45 /64	5.65 /61	11.30 /68	0.28	0.91
SC	Diamond Hill Small-Mid Cap Fd A	DHMAX	A-	(614) 255-3333	B+ / 8.3	5.81	10.71	27.70 /81	9.59 /91	14.12 /94	0.05	1.25
SC	Diamond Hill Small-Mid Cap Fd C	DHMCX	A-	(614) 255-3333	B+ / 8.6	5.59	10.29	26.76 /78	8.77 /85	13.26 /86	0.00	2.00
SC	Diamond Hill Small-Mid Cap Fd I	DHMIX	A+	(614) 255-3333	A- / 9.2	5.88	10.88	28.05 /82	9.89 /93	14.43 /95	0.31	0.95
MC	Diamond Hill Small-Mid Cap Fd Y	DHMYX	A+		A / 9.3	5.89	10.94	28.22 /82	10.02 /93	14.57 /96	0.37	0.85
AA	Direxion Hilton Tactical Inc A	HCYAX	C	(800) 851-0511	C- / 3.1	4.89	4.50	13.57 /24	5.26 /57	--	3.19	1.73
AA	Direxion Hilton Tactical Inc Instl	HCYIX	B-	(800) 851-0511	C / 4.4	4.95	4.63	13.92 /25	5.55 /60	--	3.61	1.48
IN	Direxion Idx Managed Futrs Stg Inst	DXMIX	D-	(800) 851-0511	E / 0.4	-5.37	-5.68	-6.79 / 0	1.22 /19	-1.12 / 3	1.63	1.28
IN	Direxion Idx Managed Futures Stg A	DXMAX	D-	(800) 851-0511	E- / 0.2	-5.43	-5.78	-7.02 / 0	0.97 /18	-1.35 / 3	1.29	1.53
IN	Direxion Idx Managed Futures Stg C	DXMCX	D-	(800) 851-0511	E / 0.3	-5.59	-6.14	-7.72 / 0	0.20 /14	-2.10 / 3	0.50	2.28
OT	Direxion Indexed Commodity Stg A	DXCTX	D-	(800) 851-0511	E- / 0.1	-0.78	0.20	4.63 / 4	-7.01 / 1	-6.14 / 1	0.00	1.35
OT	Direxion Indexed Commodity Stg C	DXSCX	D-	(800) 851-0511	E- / 0.1	-0.95	-0.20	3.91 / 3	-7.71 / 1	-6.84 / 1	0.00	2.10
OT	Direxion Indexed Commodity Stg Inst	DXCIX	D-	(800) 851-0511	E- / 0.1	-0.76	0.26	4.91 / 4	-6.80 / 2	-5.92 / 1	0.00	1.10
CV	Direxion Indexed CVT Strategy	DXCBX	D	(800) 851-0511	D- / 1.2	5.71	-4.21	8.88 / 9	0.49 /16	--	0.39	1.56
GR	Direxion Mo 25+Yr Trs Br 1.35X Inv	DXSTX	U	(800) 851-0511	U /	-2.49	12.04	2.73 / 2	--	--	0.00	1.23
FO	Direxion Mo China Bull 2X Inv	DXHLX	C-	(800) 851-0511	A+ / 9.6	5.72	7.94	60.49 /99	4.75 /51	-2.36 / 2	0.00	1.40
FO	Direxion Mo Emerg Mkts Bull 2X Inv	DXELX	E-	(800) 851-0511	D+ / 2.9	16.00	8.73	56.15 /99	-3.90 / 3	-7.82 / 1	0.00	1.37
GR	Direxion Mo Hi Yld Bull 1.2X Inv	DXHYX	U	(800) 851-0511	U /	4.71	5.26	19.80 /51	--	--	2.91	1.59
GR	Direxion Mo NASDAQ-100 Bull 2X	DXQLX	B+	(800) 851-0511	A+ / 9.9	21.98	23.89	57.83 /99	25.17 /99	30.71 /99	0.00	1.39
GR	Direxion Mo S&P 500 Bear 2X Inv	DXSSX	E-	(800) 851-0511	E- / 0.0	-14.91	-18.43	-38.18 / 0	-21.97 / 0	-26.81 / 0	0.00	1.41
GR	Direxion Mo S&P 500 Bull 2X Inv	DXSLX	B+	(800) 851-0511	A+ / 9.9	15.65	18.94	50.67 /99	18.17 /99	25.43 /99	0.00	1.41
SC	Direxion Mo Small Cap Bear 2X Inv	DXRSX	E-	(800) 851-0511	E- / 0.0	-10.43	-25.98	-51.71 / 0	-21.24 / 0	-28.82 / 0	0.00	1.40
SC	Direxion Mo Small Cap Bull 2X Inv	DXRLX	C-	(800) 851-0511	A+ / 9.9	9.94	23.76	77.27 /99	9.79 /92	22.88 /99	0.00	1.41
BA	Disciplined Growth Investors I	DGIFX	B-	(855) 344-3863	C / 5.4	3.03	4.60	19.45 /49	6.76 /70	9.86 /57	0.59	0.78
✱ BA	Dodge & Cox Balanced Fund	DODBX	A+	(800) 621-3979	B+ / 8.4	5.16	12.00	27.47 /80	8.12 /80	12.35 /78	2.10	0.53
✱ GL	Dodge & Cox Global Stock	DODWX	B+	(800) 621-3979	A / 9.3	8.40	15.09	37.70 /96	6.51 /68	12.04 /75	1.09	0.63
✱ FO	● Dodge & Cox International Stock	DODFX	D-	(800) 621-3979	D+ / 2.6	8.15	9.14	29.88 /86	-0.02 /13	6.61 /32	2.09	0.64
✱ GI	Dodge & Cox Stk Fund	DODGX	A+	(800) 621-3979	A+ / 9.8	6.67	18.01	38.12 /96	10.05 /94	15.91 /98	1.49	0.52
GR	Domini Impact Equity A	DSEPX	D-	(800) 498-1351	C+ / 6.1	6.83	10.84	23.74 /69	6.58 /69	10.21 /60	7.14	1.41
GR	Domini Impact Equity Inst	DIEQX	C	(800) 498-1351	B- / 7.3	6.98	11.10	24.17 /70	7.00 /72	10.65 /63	2.51	0.81
GR	Domini Impact Equity Inv	DSEFX	C+	(800) 498-1351	B- / 7.0	6.90	10.93	23.76 /69	6.63 /69	10.22 /60	0.92	1.14
GR	Domini Impact Equity R	DSFRX	D	(800) 498-1351	B- / 7.3	7.06	11.16	24.18 /70	6.98 /72	10.59 /63	9.53	0.82
FO	Domini Impact International Eq A	DOMAX	D+	(800) 498-1351	D+ / 2.6	9.36	6.69	17.70 /41	1.91 /23	8.25 /44	1.57	1.59
FO	Domini Impact International Eq Inst	DOMOX	C-	(800) 498-1351	C- / 3.8	9.57	7.06	18.23 /44	2.36 /26	--	2.28	1.10
FO	Domini Impact International Eq Inv	DOMIX	C-	(800) 498-1351	C- / 3.4	9.46	6.80	17.76 /42	1.91 /23	8.25 /44	1.77	1.52
OT	DoubleLine Infrastructure Income I	BILDX	U	(877) 354-6311	U /	1.76	-0.56	--	--	--	0.00	1.18
AA	DoubleLine Multi-Asset Growth A	DMLAX	C	(877) 354-6311	C- / 4.1	6.03	7.57	18.14 /43	4.73 /51	3.98 /15	2.89	1.66
AA	DoubleLine Multi-Asset Growth I	DMLIX	C+	(877) 354-6311	C / 5.2	6.07	7.68	18.50 /45	4.98 /54	4.26 /17	3.24	1.41
IN	DoubleLine Shiller Enhanced CAPE I	DSEEX	A+	(877) 354-6311	A+ / 9.9	9.11	12.71	32.53 /91	15.94 /99	--	1.90	0.64
IN	DoubleLine Shiller Enhanced CAPE	DSENX	A+	(877) 354-6311	A+ / 9.9	9.06	12.59	32.13 /90	15.64 /99	--	1.69	0.89
MC	Dreyfus Active MidCap A	DNLDX	B+	(800) 782-6620	B- / 7.4	6.75	11.15	20.94 /57	9.25 /88	13.84 /92	0.27	1.13
MC	Dreyfus Active MidCap C	DNLCX	B+	(800) 782-6620	B / 7.7	6.54	10.70	19.94 /52	8.32 /81	12.87 /82	0.00	1.98
MC	Dreyfus Active MidCap I	DNLRX	A	(800) 782-6620	B+ / 8.5	6.80	11.26	21.17 /58	9.46 /90	14.06 /94	0.54	0.93
GI	Dreyfus Alternative Dvfsr Strat Y	DRYNX	U	(800) 645-6561	U /	2.40	0.02	2.73 / 2	--	--	0.57	2.08
GR	Dreyfus Appreciation I	DGIGX	U	(800) 645-6561	U /	8.86	7.48	--	--	--	0.00	N/A
GR	Dreyfus Appreciation Inv	DGAGX	D+	(800) 645-6561	C+ / 6.7	8.80	7.41	18.93 /47	6.64 /69	8.36 /45	1.28	0.92
GR	Dreyfus Appreciation Y	DGYGX	C-	(800) 645-6561	B- / 7.0	8.88	7.58	19.32 /49	7.02 /72	--	1.59	0.57
BA	Dreyfus Balanced Opport A	DBOAX	C+	(800) 645-6561	C / 5.2	5.29	8.01	19.32 /49	6.55 /69	9.38 /54	0.98	1.27
BA	Dreyfus Balanced Opport C	DBOCX	C+	(800) 645-6561	C+ / 5.7	5.12	7.64	18.44 /45	5.76 /62	8.54 /47	0.31	2.02

● Denotes fund is closed to new investors

✱ Denotes fund is included in Section II

www.thestreetratings.com

Risk Rating/Pts	3 Year Standard Deviation	Beta	NAV As of 2/28/17	Total $(Mil)	Cash %	Stocks %	Bonds %	Other %	Portfolio Turnover Ratio	Last Bull Market Return	Last Bear Market Return	Manager Quality Pct	Manager Tenure (Years)	Initial Purch. $	Additional Purch. $	Front End Load	Back End Load
C+ / 6.6	10.4	0.61	35.08	429	6	84	9	1	17	103.8	-21.7	81	17	5,000	100	5.0	0.0
C+ / 6.4	10.4	0.61	30.88	54	6	84	9	1	17	95.8	-22.0	75	17	5,000	100	0.0	0.0
C+ / 6.5	10.4	0.61	35.59	1,056	6	84	9	1	17	106.8	-21.6	82	17	5,000	100	0.0	0.0
C+ / 6.5	10.4	0.61	35.61	228	6	84	9	1	17	108.1	-21.7	83	17	500,000	100	0.0	0.0
C+ / 6.3	11.1	0.65	21.84	296	4	89	6	1	21	140.2	-21.4	95	10	2,500	100	5.0	0.0
C+ / 6.3	11.1	0.65	20.18	44	4	89	6	1	21	130.5	-21.6	93	10	2,500	100	0.0	0.0
C+ / 6.3	11.1	0.65	22.06	1,022	4	89	6	1	21	143.5	-21.2	95	10	2,500	100	0.0	0.0
C+ / 6.3	11.1	0.87	22.10	1,066	4	89	6	1	21	145.2	-21.4	84	10	500,000	100	0.0	0.0
B / 8.2	4.9	0.65	16.18	4	10	65	20	5	84	N/A	N/A	77	4	2,500	100	5.5	1.0
B / 8.2	4.9	0.65	16.20	86	10	65	20	5	84	N/A	N/A	79	4	250,000	100	0.0	1.0
C+ / 6.6	11.3	-0.19	35.21	14	69	0	30	1	0	N/A	N/A	90	5	5,000,000	0	0.0	1.0
C+ / 6.6	11.3	-0.19	34.86	6	69	0	30	1	0	N/A	N/A	89	5	2,500	0	5.5	1.0
C+ / 6.5	11.3	-0.19	33.75	4	69	0	30	1	0	N/A	N/A	86	5	2,500	0	0.0	0.0
C+ / 6.8	7.0	0.06	15.36	20	57	0	42	1	0	-32.7	-25.4	4	9	2,500	0	5.5	1.0
C+ / 6.7	7.0	0.06	14.63	2	57	0	42	1	0	-35.4	-25.7	3	9	2,500	0	0.0	0.0
C+ / 6.9	7.0	0.06	15.61	45	57	0	42	1	0	-31.8	-25.4	4	9	5,000,000	0	0.0	1.0
C+ / 6.9	13.0	1.20	42.86	34	62	0	37	1	947	N/A	N/A	13	3	25,000	500	0.0	0.0
U /	N/A	N/A	18.80	121	0	0	0	100	0	N/A	N/A	N/A	2	25,000	500	0.0	0.0
E- / 0.0	44.4	1.95	35.50	3	28	0	71	1	0	45.7	-56.1	96	10	25,000	500	0.0	0.0
E- / 0.1	32.5	1.88	38.85	6	66	0	33	1	0	2.3	-53.8	28	12	25,000	500	0.0	0.0
U /	N/A	N/A	23.90	273	0	0	0	100	165	N/A	N/A	N/A	1	25,000	500	0.0	0.0
C- / 3.7	27.7	2.34	79.86	169	27	0	72	1	0	463.3	-21.3	62	11	25,000	500	0.0	0.0
E+ / 0.8	21.7	-2.06	18.72	8	19	0	80	1	0	-86.7	37.8	20	11	25,000	500	0.0	0.0
C / 4.5	20.8	1.99	113.80	55	62	0	37	1	0	349.4	-31.5	31	11	25,000	500	0.0	0.0
E- / 0.0	33.1	-2.04	19.31	5	20	0	79	1	0	-89.8	64.8	2	13	25,000	500	0.0	0.0
E / 0.5	32.3	2.00	63.18	24	27	0	72	1	0	336.3	-45.8	24	13	25,000	500	0.0	0.0
B- / 7.1	8.7	1.16	17.81	152	2	67	29	2	13	95.6	N/A	51	6	10,000	0	0.0	2.0
B / 8.6	8.8	1.23	107.49	15,593	2	67	29	2	20	111.2	-16.2	62	25	2,500	100	0.0	0.0
C / 5.1	13.2	0.96	12.68	7,307	2	97	0	1	20	112.4	-24.3	97	9	2,500	100	0.0	0.0
C- / 4.2	14.5	1.10	40.22	56,393	0	99	0	1	18	61.6	-25.7	75	13	2,500	100	0.0	0.0
C+ / 6.1	12.8	1.13	194.15	63,420	2	97	0	1	15	156.9	-21.6	51	25	2,500	100	0.0	0.0
E+ / 0.8	11.4	1.05	7.05	9	0	99	0	1	91	99.4	-16.1	22	8	2,500	100	4.8	2.0
C- / 3.5	11.3	1.04	23.90	186	0	99	0	1	91	103.5	-15.9	26	8	1,000,000	0	0.0	2.0
C / 4.9	11.3	1.04	45.35	682	0	99	0	1	91	99.2	-16.1	23	8	2,500	100	0.0	2.0
E+ / 0.8	11.3	1.04	5.77	45	0	99	0	1	91	102.9	-15.9	26	8	0	0	0.0	2.0
C+ / 6.2	11.6	0.90	8.21	68	4	95	0	1	89	70.9	-24.4	86	8	2,500	100	4.8	2.0
C+ / 6.1	11.6	0.91	7.81	202	4	95	0	1	89	N/A	N/A	88	8	1,000,000	0	0.0	2.0
C+ / 6.2	11.6	0.91	7.81	453	4	95	0	1	89	71.0	-24.5	86	8	2,500	100	0.0	2.0
U /	N/A	N/A	10.05	208	0	0	0	100	0	N/A	N/A	N/A	1	100,000	100	0.0	0.0
C+ / 6.4	6.8	0.97	9.79	120	21	17	61	1	56	24.3	-0.1	43	7	2,000	100	4.3	1.0
C+ / 6.4	6.7	0.96	9.82	47	21	17	61	1	56	25.9	N/A	47	7	100,000	100	0.0	1.0
B- / 7.6	11.5	1.07	14.68	2,195	6	0	93	1	67	N/A	N/A	93	4	100,000	100	0.0	0.0
B- / 7.6	11.4	1.07	14.67	624	6	0	93	1	67	N/A	N/A	93	4	2,000	100	0.0	0.0
C+ / 6.6	11.6	0.92	62.60	517	0	99	0	1	61	138.1	-24.0	77	5	1,000	100	5.8	0.0
C+ / 6.6	11.6	0.92	58.34	11	0	99	0	1	61	127.3	-24.3	69	5	1,000	100	0.0	0.0
C+ / 6.6	11.6	0.92	63.01	100	0	99	0	1	61	140.6	-24.0	78	5	1,000	100	0.0	0.0
U /	N/A	N/A	12.42	484	27	34	37	2	61	N/A	N/A	N/A	3	1,000,000	0	0.0	0.0
U /	N/A	N/A	35.48	35	0	99	0	1	6	N/A	N/A	N/A	27	1,000	100	0.0	0.0
D+ / 2.6	10.2	0.94	35.50	1,838	0	99	0	1	6	79.6	-12.5	33	27	2,500	100	0.0	0.0
D+ / 2.5	10.2	0.94	35.52	71	0	99	0	1	6	N/A	N/A	38	27	1,000,000	0	0.0	0.0
C+ / 6.7	7.5	1.12	22.31	190	0	68	31	1	114	80.0	-14.4	51	10	1,000	100	5.8	0.0
C+ / 6.8	7.5	1.12	22.36	29	0	68	31	1	114	72.9	-14.7	41	10	1,000	100	0.0	0.0

					PERFORMANCE							
							Total Return % through 2/28/17				Incl. in Returns	
									Annualized		Dividend	Expense
Fund Type	Fund Name	Ticker Symbol	Overall Investment Rating	Phone	Perfor-mance Rating/Pts	3 Mo	6 Mo	1Yr / Pct	3Yr / Pct	5Yr / Pct	Yield	Ratio
BA	Dreyfus Balanced Opport I	DBORX	C+	(800) 645-6561	C+ / 6.6	5.37	8.19	19.68 /50	6.84 /71	9.65 /56	1.27	1.02
BA	● Dreyfus Balanced Opport J	THPBX	C+	(800) 645-6561	C+ / 6.6	5.37	8.19	19.68 /50	6.84 /71	9.64 /56	1.27	1.00
BA	Dreyfus Balanced Opport Z	DBOZX	C+	(800) 645-6561	C+ / 6.6	5.34	8.12	19.55 /50	6.75 /70	9.51 /55	1.21	1.12
GI	Dreyfus Conservative Allocation Fd	SCALX	C	(800) 645-6561	D+ / 2.9	4.39	3.24	11.87 /17	3.29 /35	4.93 /21	1.49	1.19
GR	Dreyfus Core Equity A	DLTSX	C-	(800) 645-6561	C / 5.4	8.63	7.40	19.13 /48	6.26 /66	7.86 /41	0.98	1.36
GR	Dreyfus Core Equity C	DPECX	C-	(800) 645-6561	C+ / 5.9	8.50	7.02	18.24 /44	5.47 /59	7.07 /35	0.35	2.11
GR	Dreyfus Core Equity I	DPERX	C	(800) 645-6561	C+ / 6.6	8.54	7.35	19.23 /48	6.47 /68	8.10 /43	1.23	1.11
GI	Dreyfus Disciplined Stock Fund	DDSTX	B+	(800) 645-6561	A / 9.5	8.63	12.28	28.22 /82	9.82 /92	12.56 /80	1.06	1.01
FO	Dreyfus Divers Intl A	DFPAX	D-	(800) 782-6620	E+ / 0.8	6.85	2.22	13.73 /24	-0.13 /13	4.06 /15	0.93	2.46
FO	Dreyfus Divers Intl C	DFPCX	D-	(800) 782-6620	D- / 1.0	6.65	1.81	12.76 /21	-0.88 /10	3.28 /12	0.00	2.37
FO	Dreyfus Divers Intl I	DFPIX	D	(800) 782-6620	D / 1.9	6.96	2.42	13.94 /25	0.20 /14	4.40 /18	1.35	0.92
FO	Dreyfus Divers Intl Y	DDIFX	U	(800) 782-6620	U /	6.86	2.33	14.06 /26	--	--	1.43	0.92
EM	Dreyfus Diversified Emerg Mkt A	DBEAX	D-	(800) 645-6561	D+ / 2.6	7.98	3.72	27.18 /80	1.03 /18	-0.30 / 4	0.07	1.89
EM	Dreyfus Diversified Emerg Mkt C	DBECX	D-	(800) 645-6561	D+ / 2.9	7.68	3.17	25.87 /76	0.24 /14	-1.06 / 3	0.00	2.55
EM	Dreyfus Diversified Emerg Mkt I	SBCEX	D	(800) 645-6561	C- / 3.9	8.07	3.91	27.64 /81	1.41 /20	0.10 / 5	0.41	1.46
EM	Dreyfus Diversified Emerg Mkt Y	SBYEX	D+	(800) 645-6561	C- / 3.9	8.10	3.94	27.71 /81	1.52 /21	--	0.49	1.40
GL	Dreyfus Dynamic Total Return A	AVGAX	C-	(800) 782-6620	D- / 1.5	3.53	1.74	7.32 / 6	2.98 /32	5.19 /23	0.00	1.56
GL	Dreyfus Dynamic Total Return C	AVGCX	C-	(800) 782-6620	D / 1.7	3.33	1.36	6.51 / 5	2.22 /25	4.41 /18	0.00	2.31
GL	Dreyfus Dynamic Total Return I	AVGRX	C-	(800) 782-6620	D / 2.2	3.58	1.83	7.58 / 7	3.25 /34	5.48 /25	0.00	1.29
GL	Dreyfus Dynamic Total Return Y	AVGYX	C-	(800) 782-6620	D+ / 2.3	3.58	1.89	7.65 / 7	3.34 /35	--	0.00	1.21
EM	Dreyfus Emerging Markets A	DRFMX	C	(800) 782-6620	B- / 7.0	10.17	9.81	42.56 /98	3.87 /41	-0.91 / 3	0.64	2.20
EM	Dreyfus Emerging Markets C	DCPEX	C+	(800) 782-6620	B- / 7.4	10.05	9.55	41.51 /98	3.12 /33	-1.66 / 3	0.01	2.90
EM	Dreyfus Emerging Markets I	DRPEX	C+	(800) 782-6620	B / 8.1	10.22	9.98	42.83 /98	4.11 /44	-0.68 / 4	0.93	1.76
EM	Dreyfus Emerging Markets Y	DYPEX	C+	(800) 782-6620	B+ / 8.4	10.30	10.06	43.15 /98	4.49 /49	--	1.09	1.68
IN	Dreyfus Equity Income A	DQIAX	B+	(800) 782-6620	B / 7.8	7.66	9.33	23.95 /70	9.52 /90	12.27 /77	2.64	1.21
IN	Dreyfus Equity Income C	DQICX	A-	(800) 782-6620	B / 8.2	7.47	8.95	23.03 /67	8.69 /85	11.45 /69	1.94	1.92
IN	Dreyfus Equity Income I	DQIRX	A	(800) 782-6620	B+ / 8.9	7.70	9.50	24.25 /71	9.79 /92	12.57 /80	3.24	0.92
IN	Dreyfus Equity Income Y	DQIYX	A	(800) 782-6620	B+ / 8.9	7.72	9.46	24.22 /71	9.74 /92	--	3.25	0.84
GI	Dreyfus Fund Incorporated	DREVX	B-	(800) 645-6561	B / 7.6	7.74	8.66	22.42 /64	7.73 /77	12.28 /77	0.93	0.75
EM	Dreyfus Global Emerging Markets A	DGEAX	D-	(800) 645-6561	D / 2.1	6.58	-0.14	22.93 /66	1.82 /23	--	0.00	1.82
EM	Dreyfus Global Emerging Markets C	DGECX	D	(800) 645-6561	D+ / 2.4	6.40	-0.51	22.04 /62	1.03 /18	--	0.00	2.67
EM	Dreyfus Global Emerging Markets I	DGIEX	D	(800) 645-6561	C- / 3.1	6.67	0.04	23.28 /67	1.97 /24	--	0.03	1.35
EM	Dreyfus Global Emerging Markets Y	DGEYX	D	(800) 645-6561	C- / 3.1	6.64	-0.03	23.27 /67	2.09 /25	--	0.03	1.28
GL	Dreyfus Global Equity Income A	DEQAX	C-	(800) 782-6620	C- / 3.6	6.64	2.40	12.97 /22	6.04 /65	8.67 /48	1.80	1.28
GL	Dreyfus Global Equity Income C	DEQCX	C	(800) 782-6620	C- / 4.2	6.55	2.10	12.14 /18	5.30 /58	7.87 /41	0.72	2.03
GL	Dreyfus Global Equity Income I	DQEIX	C+	(800) 782-6620	C / 5.0	6.74	2.56	13.22 /22	6.33 /67	8.96 /50	2.40	1.03
GL	Dreyfus Global Equity Income Y	DEQYX	C+	(800) 782-6620	C / 5.1	6.89	2.64	13.45 /23	6.45 /68	--	2.50	0.95
RE	Dreyfus Global Real Estate Sec A	DRLAX	D+	(800) 645-6561	C- / 3.1	6.74	-3.24	12.47 /20	6.16 /66	7.69 /40	3.87	1.64
RE	Dreyfus Global Real Estate Sec C	DGBCX	C-	(800) 645-6561	C- / 3.5	6.46	-3.71	11.64 /17	5.33 /58	6.89 /34	3.35	2.25
RE	Dreyfus Global Real Estate Sec I	DRLIX	C	(800) 645-6561	C / 4.3	6.79	-3.19	12.87 /21	6.41 /68	8.00 /42	4.46	1.03
RE	Dreyfus Global Real Estate Sec Y	DRLYX	C	(800) 645-6561	C / 4.3	6.81	-3.18	12.75 /21	6.42 /68	--	4.47	1.01
GL	Dreyfus Global Real Return A	DRRAX	D+	(800) 782-6620	E+ / 0.6	2.12	-3.56	0.13 / 1	1.66 /22	3.06 /11	2.60	1.15
GL	Dreyfus Global Real Return C	DRRCX	D+	(800) 782-6620	E+ / 0.7	2.04	-3.85	-0.57 / 1	0.93 /18	2.29 / 9	2.25	1.91
GL	Dreyfus Global Real Return I	DRRIX	D+	(800) 782-6620	D- / 1.1	2.25	-3.35	0.48 / 1	1.99 /24	3.37 /12	2.95	0.86
GL	Dreyfus Global Real Return Y	DRRYX	D+	(800) 782-6620	D- / 1.1	2.21	-3.31	0.51 / 2	1.99 /24	--	2.98	0.83
GL	Dreyfus Global Stock CL A	DGLAX	C-	(800) 782-6620	C- / 3.3	6.12	3.63	15.98 /34	4.74 /51	7.61 /39	0.45	1.23
GL	Dreyfus Global Stock CL C	DGLCX	C-	(800) 782-6620	C- / 3.8	5.96	3.24	15.15 /31	3.95 /42	6.80 /33	0.00	1.99
GL	Dreyfus Global Stock CL I	DGLRX	C	(800) 782-6620	C / 4.7	6.22	3.77	16.36 /36	5.08 /55	7.97 /42	0.78	0.91
GL	Dreyfus Global Stock CL Y	DGLYX	C	(800) 782-6620	C / 4.8	6.26	3.86	16.42 /36	5.10 /55	--	0.81	0.90
GI	Dreyfus Growth Allocation Fund	SGALX	C+	(800) 645-6561	C / 4.8	5.72	5.96	16.80 /38	4.69 /51	7.50 /38	0.96	1.41
GI	Dreyfus Growth and Income	DGRIX	B	(800) 645-6561	B+ / 8.4	7.59	10.50	25.73 /75	8.23 /81	13.56 /89	0.93	0.91
IX	Dreyfus Instl S&P 500 Stock Index I	DSPIX	A+	(800) 645-6561	A / 9.3	7.99	9.92	24.73 /72	10.42 /95	13.80 /92	1.75	0.21

● Denotes fund is closed to new investors
* Denotes fund is included in Section II

RISK Risk Rating/Pts	3 Year Standard Deviation	Beta	NAV As of 2/28/17	Total $(Mil)	Cash %	Stocks %	Bonds %	Other %	Portfolio Turnover Ratio	Last Bull Market Return	Last Bear Market Return	Manager Quality Pct	Manager Tenure (Years)	Initial Purch. $	Additional Purch. $	Front End Load	Back End Load
C+ /6.7	7.5	1.12	22.35	20	0	68	31	1	114	82.6	-14.4	55	10	1,000	100	0.0	0.0
C+ /6.7	7.5	1.12	22.35	18	0	68	31	1	114	82.4	-14.4	55	10	1,000	100	0.0	0.0
C+ /6.7	7.5	1.12	22.22	36	0	68	31	1	114	81.0	-14.4	54	10	1,000	100	0.0	0.0
B /8.1	5.4	0.49	15.01	33	1	40	57	2	11	40.1	-8.6	52	8	2,500	100	0.0	0.0
C /4.3	10.3	0.96	17.70	71	0	99	0	1	4	75.3	-12.7	28	19	1,000	100	5.8	0.0
C /4.3	10.3	0.96	17.23	77	0	99	0	1	4	68.4	-13.0	20	19	1,000	100	0.0	0.0
C /4.4	10.3	0.96	18.20	37	0	99	0	1	4	77.4	-12.6	30	19	1,000	100	0.0	0.0
C /4.8	11.4	1.07	36.32	604	0	99	0	1	49	118.1	-21.0	56	2	2,500	100	0.0	0.0
C+ /6.2	11.0	0.88	11.19	6	2	96	1	1	11	41.8	-23.3	74	8	1,000	100	5.8	0.0
C+ /6.2	11.0	0.88	11.22	N/A	2	96	1	1	11	36.1	-23.4	65	8	1,000	100	0.0	0.0
C+ /6.2	11.0	0.88	11.19	16	2	96	1	1	11	44.2	-23.2	76	8	1,000	100	0.0	0.0
U /	N/A	N/A	11.17	729	2	96	1	1	11	N/A	N/A	N/A	8	1,000,000	0	0.0	0.0
C- /4.1	15.1	0.91	20.23	1	0	98	0	2	63	19.1	-29.1	68	3	1,000	100	5.8	2.0
C- /4.1	15.0	0.91	19.22	N/A	0	98	0	2	63	14.2	-29.3	58	3	1,000	100	0.0	2.0
C- /4.1	15.1	0.91	20.14	2	0	98	0	2	63	21.9	-28.9	72	3	1,000	100	0.0	2.0
C /5.3	15.1	0.91	20.16	147	0	98	0	2	63	N/A	N/A	74	3	1,000,000	0	0.0	2.0
B /8.0	7.0	0.91	15.80	165	3	0	96	1	11	44.3	-11.4	59	7	1,000	100	5.8	0.0
B- /7.9	7.0	0.91	14.86	107	3	0	96	1	11	38.5	-11.6	49	7	1,000	100	0.0	0.0
B /8.0	7.0	0.91	16.16	396	3	0	96	1	11	46.5	-11.2	63	7	1,000	100	0.0	0.0
B /8.0	7.0	0.91	16.16	720	3	0	96	1	11	N/A	N/A	64	7	1,000,000	0	0.0	0.0
C- /4.0	19.5	1.17	9.82	56	1	98	0	1	80	19.3	-28.1	85	10	1,000	100	5.8	2.0
C- /4.0	19.5	1.17	9.65	7	1	98	0	1	80	14.5	-28.4	82	10	1,000	100	0.0	2.0
C- /4.1	19.5	1.17	10.08	37	1	98	0	1	80	20.8	-28.0	86	10	1,000	100	0.0	2.0
C- /3.9	19.4	1.17	9.83	36	1	98	0	1	80	N/A	N/A	88	10	1,000,000	0	0.0	2.0
C+ /6.4	9.2	0.84	18.45	182	0	99	0	1	65	108.6	-10.3	79	6	1,000	100	5.8	0.0
C+ /6.4	9.2	0.83	18.23	25	0	99	0	1	65	100.3	-10.5	73	6	1,000	100	0.0	0.0
C+ /6.4	9.1	0.83	18.48	116	0	99	0	1	65	111.5	-10.1	81	6	1,000	100	0.0	0.0
C+ /6.4	9.1	0.83	18.45	2	0	99	0	1	65	N/A	N/A	80	6	1,000,000	0	0.0	0.0
C /4.9	10.7	1.00	11.21	1,173	0	98	1	1	56	116.1	-20.2	39	12	2,500	100	0.0	0.0
C /5.1	15.5	0.82	14.10	N/A	0	98	1	1	51	N/A	N/A	77	3	1,000	100	5.8	2.0
C /5.1	15.6	0.82	13.79	N/A	0	98	1	1	51	N/A	N/A	70	3	1,000	100	0.0	2.0
C /5.1	15.6	0.81	14.16	3	0	98	1	1	51	N/A	N/A	78	3	1,000	100	0.0	2.0
C /5.1	15.6	0.82	14.22	103	0	98	1	1	51	N/A	N/A	79	3	1,000,000	0	0.0	2.0
C+ /6.8	9.0	0.57	12.76	64	3	93	3	1	28	73.3	-13.3	97	5	1,000	100	5.8	0.0
C+ /6.9	9.0	0.58	13.06	58	3	93	3	1	28	66.6	-13.5	96	5	1,000	100	0.0	0.0
C+ /6.8	9.0	0.57	12.26	280	3	93	3	1	28	75.8	-13.2	97	5	1,000	100	0.0	0.0
C+ /6.8	9.0	0.58	12.26	35	3	93	3	1	28	N/A	N/A	97	5	1,000,000	0	0.0	0.0
C+ /6.2	12.5	0.88	8.94	7	10	88	0	2	61	73.6	-19.2	31	11	1,000	100	5.8	0.0
C+ /6.2	12.4	0.87	8.77	1	10	88	0	2	61	66.7	-19.3	23	11	1,000	100	0.0	0.0
C+ /6.2	12.5	0.88	8.81	161	10	88	0	2	61	76.4	-18.9	33	11	1,000,000	0	0.0	0.0
C+ /6.2	12.4	0.87	8.81	593	10	88	0	2	61	N/A	N/A	35	11	1,000,000	0	0.0	0.0
B /8.1	5.1	0.14	14.00	149	4	51	44	1	57	22.3	-7.2	84	7	1,000	100	5.8	0.0
B /8.1	5.1	0.14	13.68	35	4	51	44	1	57	17.5	-7.5	80	7	1,000	100	0.0	0.0
B /8.1	5.1	0.14	14.06	609	4	51	44	1	57	24.3	-7.1	86	7	1,000	100	0.0	0.0
B /8.1	5.1	0.14	14.06	741	4	51	44	1	57	N/A	N/A	86	7	1,000,000	0	0.0	0.0
C+ /6.4	9.3	0.68	18.42	24	0	96	3	1	11	70.7	-14.1	95	11	1,000	100	5.8	0.0
C+ /6.5	9.3	0.68	17.98	13	0	96	3	1	11	63.8	-14.4	93	11	1,000	100	0.0	0.0
C+ /6.4	9.3	0.68	18.64	944	0	96	3	1	11	73.8	-14.0	95	11	1,000	100	0.0	0.0
C+ /6.4	9.3	0.68	18.62	310	0	96	3	1	11	N/A	N/A	95	11	1,000,000	0	0.0	0.0
B- /7.1	7.8	0.74	17.03	22	2	68	28	2	13	66.5	-15.7	36	8	2,500	100	0.0	0.0
C /4.8	11.3	1.06	20.84	881	0	98	1	1	52	133.5	-20.4	37	9	2,500	100	0.0	0.0
B- /7.0	10.3	1.00	47.82	2,468	0	98	1	1	5	132.5	-16.3	72	15	10,000	1,000	0.0	0.0

Fund Type	Fund Name	Ticker Symbol	Overall Investment Rating	Phone	Performance Rating/Pts	3 Mo	6 Mo	1Yr / Pct	3Yr / Pct	5Yr / Pct	Dividend Yield	Expense Ratio
	99 Pct = Best							Total Return % through 2/28/17	Annualized		Incl. in Returns	
FO	Dreyfus International Small Cap Y	DYYPX	U	(800) 782-6620	U /	7.96	4.28	15.97 /34	--	--	1.71	1.22
FO	Dreyfus Intl Equity A	DIEAX	D-	(800) 782-6620	E+ / 0.7	8.16	4.95	16.06 /35	-1.51 / 8	6.23 /30	1.55	1.37
FO	Dreyfus Intl Equity C	DIECX	D-	(800) 782-6620	E+ / 0.9	7.94	4.54	15.16 /31	-2.26 / 6	5.41 /24	0.78	2.14
FO	Dreyfus Intl Equity I	DIERX	D-	(800) 782-6620	D- / 1.2	8.22	5.09	16.36 /36	-1.22 / 9	6.53 /32	1.72	1.03
FO	Dreyfus Intl Equity Y	DIEYX	U	(800) 782-6620	U /	8.23	5.06	16.37 /36	--	--	1.73	1.01
FO	Dreyfus Intl Stk CL A	DISAX	D	(800) 782-6620	D / 1.6	5.77	0.46	14.78 /29	1.72 /22	3.80 /14	0.77	1.26
FO	Dreyfus Intl Stk CL C	DISCX	D+	(800) 782-6620	D / 1.9	5.52	0.07	13.85 /25	0.94 /18	3.02 /11	0.00	2.03
FO	Dreyfus Intl Stk CL I	DISRX	D+	(800) 782-6620	D+ / 2.6	5.86	0.65	15.14 /30	2.06 /24	4.16 /16	1.18	0.94
FO	Dreyfus Intl Stk CL Y	DISYX	D+	(800) 782-6620	D+ / 2.5	5.82	0.62	15.13 /30	1.94 /24	--	1.22	0.91
FO	Dreyfus Intl Stock Index I	DINIX	U	(800) 645-6561	U /	7.62	4.36	--	--	--	0.00	N/A
FO	Dreyfus Intl Stock Index Inv	DIISX	D-	(800) 645-6561	D- / 1.1	7.60	4.19	15.39 /32	-1.15 / 9	4.64 /19	2.77	0.61
GR	Dreyfus Inv Core Value I		B+	(800) 645-6561	A+ / 9.7	6.91	15.51	33.79 /93	9.85 /92	14.87 /97	0.85	0.83
GR	Dreyfus Inv Core Value S		B+	(800) 645-6561	A+ / 9.7	6.86	15.44	33.48 /92	9.58 /91	14.59 /96	0.60	1.08
MC	Dreyfus Inv MidCap Stock I		B	(800) 645-6561	B+ / 8.5	6.18	10.29	24.28 /71	8.97 /87	13.72 /91	0.93	0.85
MC	Dreyfus Inv MidCap Stock S		B	(800) 645-6561	B+ / 8.3	6.10	10.17	23.98 /70	8.70 /85	13.43 /88	0.74	1.10
GR	Dreyfus Inv Tech Growth Fund I		B	(800) 645-6561	B+ / 8.6	10.91	9.13	28.03 /82	7.59 /76	12.02 /74	0.00	1.07
GR	Dreyfus Inv Tech Growth Fund S		B-	(800) 645-6561	B+ / 8.4	10.83	9.03	27.75 /81	7.32 /74	11.75 /72	0.00	1.32
GR	Dreyfus LgCap Eq A	DLQAX	B+	(800) 782-6620	B+ / 8.5	8.83	11.59	27.57 /81	9.44 /90	13.14 /85	0.61	1.09
GR	Dreyfus LgCap Eq C	DEYCX	A-	(800) 782-6620	B+ / 8.9	8.68	11.21	26.65 /78	8.59 /84	12.29 /77	0.00	1.93
GR	Dreyfus LgCap Eq I	DLQIX	A	(800) 782-6620	A / 9.5	8.95	11.75	28.00 /82	9.79 /92	13.53 /89	0.87	0.75
GR	Dreyfus LgCap Eq Y	DLACX	U	(800) 782-6620	U /	8.94	11.74	27.94 /81	--	--	0.93	0.75
GR	Dreyfus Lrg Cap Gr A	DAPAX	B	(800) 645-6561	B / 7.9	9.17	10.10	24.54 /72	9.18 /88	13.70 /91	0.51	1.40
GR	Dreyfus Lrg Cap Gr C	DGTCX	B	(800) 645-6561	B+ / 8.3	8.98	9.70	23.76 /69	8.37 /82	12.88 /83	0.00	2.20
GR	Dreyfus Lrg Cap Gr Inst	DAPIX	B+	(800) 645-6561	A- / 9.0	9.20	10.22	24.84 /73	9.43 /90	14.05 /93	0.61	1.10
MC	Dreyfus Mid Cap Growth A	FRSDX	C-	(800) 645-6561	C / 4.8	7.53	8.06	22.62 /65	4.73 /51	9.89 /57	0.00	1.35
MC	Dreyfus Mid Cap Growth C	FRSCX	C-	(800) 645-6561	C / 5.4	7.51	7.67	21.70 /61	3.95 /42	9.06 /51	0.00	2.12
MC	● Dreyfus Mid Cap Growth F	FRSPX	C	(800) 645-6561	C+ / 6.2	7.67	8.06	22.86 /66	4.97 /54	10.13 /59	0.00	1.14
MC	Dreyfus Mid Cap Growth I	FRSRX	C	(800) 645-6561	C+ / 6.3	7.68	8.19	22.89 /66	5.02 /54	10.18 /60	0.00	1.11
MC	Dreyfus Midcap Index I	DMIDX	U	(800) 645-6561	U /	6.54	11.19	--	--	--	0.00	N/A
MC	Dreyfus Midcap Index Inv	PESPX	B+	(800) 645-6561	A / 9.3	6.47	11.09	31.11 /88	9.15 /88	13.31 /87	0.95	0.51
BA	Dreyfus Moderate Allocation Fund	SMDAX	C	(800) 645-6561	C- / 3.8	5.03	4.59	14.29 /27	3.98 /43	6.15 /29	1.26	1.08
EN	Dreyfus Natural Resources A	DNLAX	E	(800) 782-6620	D / 1.6	2.84	13.87	35.70 /95	-1.45 / 8	2.01 / 8	1.15	1.47
EN	Dreyfus Natural Resources C	DLDCX	E	(800) 782-6620	D / 1.9	2.65	13.50	34.70 /94	-2.17 / 6	1.24 / 7	0.70	2.16
EN	Dreyfus Natural Resources I	DLDRX	E+	(800) 782-6620	D+ / 2.4	2.88	14.05	36.07 /95	-1.19 / 9	2.27 / 9	1.40	1.17
FO	Dreyfus Newton Intl Equity Fd A	NIEAX	D-	(800) 645-6561	E / 0.4	6.52	0.38	8.17 / 8	-1.21 / 9	4.45 /18	0.92	1.19
FO	Dreyfus Newton Intl Equity Fd C	NIECX	D-	(800) 645-6561	E / 0.5	6.38	0.03	7.32 / 6	-1.96 / 7	3.64 /14	0.08	2.01
FO	Dreyfus Newton Intl Equity Fd I	SNIEX	D-	(800) 645-6561	E+ / 0.8	6.62	0.54	8.47 / 8	-0.90 /10	4.77 /20	1.35	0.90
FO	Dreyfus Newton Intl Equity Fd Y	NIEYX	D-	(800) 645-6561	E+ / 0.8	6.65	0.60	8.58 / 9	-0.83 /10	--	1.41	0.89
MC	Dreyfus Opportunistic Midcap Val A	DMCVX	C-	(800) 645-6561	B- / 7.3	8.15	14.50	32.89 /91	5.53 /60	13.19 /86	0.02	1.21
MC	Dreyfus Opportunistic Midcap Val C	DVLCX	C-	(800) 645-6561	B / 7.7	7.95	14.04	31.89 /90	4.75 /51	12.34 /77	0.00	1.94
MC	Dreyfus Opportunistic Midcap Val I	DVLIX	C	(800) 645-6561	B+ / 8.5	8.26	14.69	33.27 /92	5.84 /63	13.47 /89	0.34	0.90
MC	Dreyfus Opportunistic Midcap Val Y	DMCYX	C	(800) 645-6561	B+ / 8.7	8.25	14.70	33.37 /92	6.03 /64	--	0.45	0.78
SC	● Dreyfus Opportunistic Small Cap Inv	DSCVX	B-	(800) 645-6561	A+ / 9.8	10.99	21.06	43.17 /98	6.88 /71	14.23 /94	0.00	1.11
GR	Dreyfus Opportunistic US Stock A	DOSAX	C+	(800) 645-6561	C+ / 6.2	8.00	11.98	26.20 /77	5.37 /58	14.17 /94	0.00	1.60
GR	Dreyfus Opportunistic US Stock C	DOSCX	C+	(800) 645-6561	C+ / 6.7	7.77	11.54	25.19 /74	4.59 /50	13.29 /87	0.00	2.41
GR	Dreyfus Opportunistic US Stock I	DOSIX	B-	(800) 645-6561	B- / 7.4	8.04	12.09	26.46 /78	5.65 /61	14.42 /95	0.23	1.32
GR	Dreyfus Research Growth A	DWOAX	C	(800) 645-6561	C / 5.3	8.16	6.50	18.91 /47	6.53 /69	12.27 /77	0.12	1.16
GR	Dreyfus Research Growth C	DWOCX	C+	(800) 645-6561	C+ / 5.9	7.99	6.08	18.04 /43	5.73 /62	11.42 /69	0.00	1.90
GR	Dreyfus Research Growth I	DWOIX	C+	(800) 645-6561	C+ / 6.7	8.22	6.64	19.25 /48	6.83 /71	12.57 /80	0.57	0.88
GR	Dreyfus Research Growth Y	DRYQX	C+	(800) 645-6561	C+ / 6.8	8.30	6.73	19.34 /49	6.89 /71	--	0.70	0.79
GR	● Dreyfus Research Growth Z	DREQX	C+	(800) 645-6561	C+ / 6.7	8.26	6.63	19.17 /48	6.77 /70	12.50 /79	0.46	0.91
GL	Dreyfus Research LngSht Equity A	DLSAX	D+	(800) 645-6561	E / 0.3	2.29	1.71	6.30 / 5	-1.38 / 8	--	0.00	3.24

● Denotes fund is closed to new investors

* Denotes fund is included in Section II

I. Index of Stock Mutual Funds

RISK Risk Rating/Pts	3 Year Standard Deviation	Beta	NET ASSETS NAV As of 2/28/17	Total $(Mil)	ASSET Cash %	Stocks %	Bonds %	Other %	Portfolio Turnover Ratio	BULL/BEAR Last Bull Market Return	Last Bear Market Return	FUND MANAGER Manager Quality Pct	Manager Tenure (Years)	MINIMUMS Initial Purch. $	Additional Purch. $	LOADS Front End Load	Back End Load
U /	N/A	N/A	13.52	696	4	95	0	1	118	N/A	N/A	N/A	2	1,000,000	0	0.0	0.0
C+ / 5.8	12.2	0.96	33.72	135	2	96	0	2	80	59.0	-24.9	57	7	1,000	100	5.8	0.0
C+ / 5.8	12.2	0.96	33.98	14	2	96	0	2	80	52.5	-25.1	47	7	1,000	100	0.0	0.0
C+ / 5.8	12.2	0.96	34.19	148	2	96	0	2	80	61.5	-24.8	61	7	1,000	100	0.0	0.0
U /	N/A	N/A	34.17	293	2	96	0	2	80	N/A	N/A	N/A	7	1,000,000	0	0.0	0.0
C+ / 6.5	10.8	0.82	15.49	27	0	97	1	2	17	38.7	-18.5	85	11	1,000	100	5.8	0.0
C+ / 6.5	10.9	0.82	15.29	13	0	97	1	2	17	33.2	-18.8	81	11	1,000	100	0.0	0.0
C+ / 6.4	10.9	0.82	15.56	1,618	0	97	1	2	17	41.4	-18.4	87	11	1,000	100	0.0	0.0
C+ / 6.4	10.8	0.82	15.38	1,709	0	97	1	2	17	N/A	N/A	86	11	1,000,000	0	0.0	0.0
U /	N/A	N/A	15.33	98	1	97	0	2	6	N/A	N/A	N/A	10	1,000	100	0.0	0.0
C+ / 5.7	11.6	0.94	15.34	420	1	97	0	2	6	45.6	-23.4	62	10	2,500	100	0.0	0.0
C / 4.6	12.2	1.09	18.40	18	0	99	0	1	105	149.7	-24.5	54	13	0	0	0.0	0.0
C / 4.6	12.2	1.09	18.54	12	0	99	0	1	105	146.7	-24.7	51	13	0	0	0.0	0.0
C / 5.0	11.7	0.95	20.79	125	0	99	0	1	80	143.0	-23.1	72	5	0	0	0.0	0.0
C / 5.0	11.7	0.95	20.69	65	0	99	0	1	80	139.8	-23.1	70	5	0	0	0.0	0.0
C / 4.4	14.9	1.18	19.73	96	0	99	0	1	70	117.8	-19.3	18	10	0	0	0.0	0.0
C / 4.3	14.9	1.18	18.83	257	0	99	0	1	70	114.9	-19.4	16	10	0	0	0.0	0.0
C+ / 5.8	11.4	1.06	18.18	3	0	99	0	1	51	127.0	-20.4	52	14	1,000	100	5.8	0.0
C+ / 5.9	11.4	1.06	18.40	1	0	99	0	1	51	117.6	-20.6	41	14	1,000	100	0.0	0.0
C+ / 5.8	11.4	1.07	19.15	49	0	99	0	1	51	131.2	-20.2	57	14	1,000	100	0.0	0.0
U /	N/A	N/A	19.14	469	0	99	0	1	51	N/A	N/A	N/A	14	1,000,000	0	0.0	0.0
C / 5.2	12.1	1.09	10.29	7	0	99	0	1	64	128.1	-18.8	45	12	1,000	100	5.8	0.0
C / 5.1	12.1	1.10	9.95	2	0	99	0	1	64	119.6	-19.3	34	12	1,000	100	0.0	0.0
C / 5.2	12.1	1.10	10.58	19	0	99	0	1	64	131.8	-18.7	47	12	1,000	100	0.0	0.0
C / 5.0	12.0	0.90	8.71	17	0	98	0	2	158	97.4	-16.7	26	7	1,000	100	5.8	0.0
C / 4.9	12.0	0.91	7.44	10	0	98	0	2	158	89.8	-17.1	19	7	1,000	100	0.0	0.0
C / 5.1	12.0	0.90	9.12	94	0	98	0	2	158	99.7	-16.9	29	7	1,000	100	0.0	0.0
C / 5.0	12.0	0.91	9.11	12	0	98	0	2	158	100.4	-16.8	29	7	1,000	100	0.0	0.0
U /	N/A	N/A	36.46	887	0	98	1	1	22	N/A	N/A	N/A	17	1,000	100	0.0	0.0
C / 4.4	12.1	1.00	36.54	2,881	0	98	1	1	22	134.5	-22.7	69	17	2,500	100	0.0	0.0
B- / 7.6	6.5	1.01	16.07	63	2	54	43	1	10	52.1	-12.0	29	8	2,500	100	0.0	0.0
C- / 3.0	15.7	0.62	29.15	82	0	98	1	1	108	36.8	-27.2	85	8	1,000	100	5.8	0.0
C- / 3.0	15.7	0.62	26.99	12	0	98	1	1	108	31.4	-27.5	81	8	1,000	100	0.0	0.0
C- / 3.0	15.7	0.62	29.94	230	0	98	1	1	108	38.7	-27.2	87	8	1,000	100	0.0	0.0
C+ / 5.9	10.5	0.81	18.61	3	1	98	0	1	35	42.2	-21.9	61	12	1,000	100	5.8	0.0
C+ / 5.9	10.5	0.81	18.26	1	1	98	0	1	35	36.3	-22.2	50	12	1,000	100	0.0	0.0
C+ / 5.9	10.5	0.81	18.44	83	1	98	0	1	35	44.5	-21.9	65	12	1,000	100	0.0	0.0
C+ / 5.8	10.5	0.81	18.36	880	1	98	0	1	35	N/A	N/A	66	12	1,000,000	0	0.0	0.0
D+ / 2.6	14.3	1.10	34.74	789	0	98	0	2	102	136.8	-27.9	18	14	1,000	100	5.8	0.0
D+ / 2.3	14.3	1.10	31.14	76	0	98	0	2	102	127.2	-28.1	12	14	1,000	100	0.0	0.0
D+ / 2.6	14.3	1.10	34.59	492	0	98	0	2	102	140.0	-27.8	20	14	1,000	100	0.0	0.0
D+ / 2.6	14.3	1.09	34.64	7	0	98	0	2	102	N/A	N/A	22	14	1,000,000	0	0.0	0.0
C- / 3.0	19.4	1.15	35.76	1,063	0	0	0	100	82	162.6	-34.1	61	12	2,500	100	0.0	0.0
C / 5.2	13.2	1.13	21.87	12	0	99	0	1	200	N/A	N/A	8	6	1,000	100	5.8	0.0
C / 5.1	13.2	1.13	21.07	4	0	99	0	1	200	N/A	N/A	6	6	1,000	100	0.0	0.0
C / 5.2	13.2	1.13	22.05	10	0	99	0	1	200	N/A	N/A	9	6	1,000	100	0.0	0.0
C+ / 5.9	11.3	1.02	14.53	487	0	98	1	1	54	118.8	-19.3	24	12	1,000	100	5.8	0.0
C+ / 5.8	11.3	1.03	13.59	119	0	98	1	1	54	110.0	-19.6	17	12	1,000	100	0.0	0.0
C+ / 5.8	11.3	1.03	14.56	448	0	98	1	1	54	122.0	-19.2	26	12	1,000	100	0.0	0.0
C+ / 5.8	11.3	1.03	14.55	229	0	98	1	1	54	N/A	N/A	26	12	1,000,000	0	0.0	0.0
C+ / 5.9	11.4	1.03	14.77	430	0	98	1	1	54	121.0	-19.1	25	12	1,000	100	0.0	0.0
B / 8.6	4.5	0.22	12.49	1	64	35	0	1	268	N/A	N/A	56	4	1,000	100	5.8	0.0

Data as of February 28, 2017

Fund Type	Fund Name	Ticker Symbol	Overall Investment Rating	Phone	Performance Rating/Pts	3 Mo	6 Mo	1Yr / Pct	3Yr / Pct	5Yr / Pct	Dividend Yield	Expense Ratio
	99 Pct = Best 0 Pct = Worst				**PERFORMANCE**			Total Return % through 2/28/17	Annualized		Incl. in Returns	
GL	Dreyfus Research LngSht Equity C	DLSCX	D+	(800) 645-6561	E / 0.4	2.10	1.33	5.56 / 4	-2.10 / 6	--	0.00	4.09
GL	Dreyfus Research LngSht Equity I	DLSYX	D+	(800) 645-6561	E+ / 0.7	2.35	1.86	6.59 / 5	-1.12 / 9	--	0.00	2.95
GL	Dreyfus Research LngSht Equity Y	DLYYX	D+	(800) 645-6561	E+ / 0.7	2.35	1.86	6.59 / 5	-1.12 / 9	--	0.00	2.95
IX	Dreyfus S&P 500 Index Fund	PEOPX	A-	(800) 645-6561	A- / 9.1	7.90	9.75	24.34 /71	10.08 /94	13.46 /88	1.62	0.51
GR	Dreyfus Select Managers L/S Y	DBNYX	U	(800) 645-6561	U /	1.30	2.73	3.75 / 3	--	--	0.00	2.80
GR	Dreyfus Select Managers SmCap Gro	DSGAX	E+	(800) 782-6620	D+ / 2.9	5.34	8.23	26.59 /78	0.96 /18	9.60 /55	0.00	1.29
GR	Dreyfus Select Managers SmCap Gro	DSGCX	E+	(800) 782-6620	C- / 3.4	5.08	7.77	25.65 /75	0.19 /14	8.77 /49	0.00	2.39
GR	Dreyfus Select Managers SmCap Gro	DSGIX	D-	(800) 782-6620	C / 4.3	5.40	8.37	27.02 /79	1.27 /20	9.94 /58	0.00	0.98
SC	Dreyfus Select Managers SmCap Gro	DSGYX	D-	(800) 782-6620	C / 4.3	5.40	8.37	27.03 /79	1.29 /20	--	0.00	0.96
SC	Dreyfus Select Managers SmCap Val	DMVAX	C-	(800) 645-6561	C+ / 6.7	4.42	12.92	32.76 /91	5.39 /58	11.72 /72	0.30	1.29
SC	Dreyfus Select Managers SmCap Val	DMECX	C	(800) 645-6561	B- / 7.1	4.26	12.56	31.87 /90	4.66 /50	10.92 /65	0.00	2.42
SC	Dreyfus Select Managers SmCap Val	DMVIX	C+	(800) 645-6561	B / 7.9	4.51	13.14	33.24 /92	5.74 /62	12.10 /75	0.54	0.97
SC	Dreyfus Select Managers SmCap Val	DMVYX	C+	(800) 645-6561	B / 7.9	4.51	13.14	33.26 /92	5.75 /62	--	0.58	0.95
SC	Dreyfus Small Cap Eqty A	DSEAX	C-	(800) 782-6620	B- / 7.0	6.09	13.07	27.72 /81	6.69 /70	11.41 /69	0.00	1.55
SC	Dreyfus Small Cap Eqty C	DSECX	D+	(800) 782-6620	B- / 7.3	5.90	12.59	26.64 /78	5.80 /62	10.50 /62	0.00	2.31
SC	Dreyfus Small Cap Eqty I	DSERX	C	(800) 782-6620	B / 8.1	6.16	13.18	28.07 /82	6.95 /72	11.71 /72	0.00	1.26
SC	Dreyfus Smallcap Stock Index I	DISIX	U	(800) 645-6561	U /	4.47	12.95	--	--	--	0.00	N/A
SC	Dreyfus Smallcap Stock Index Inv	DISSX	B+	(800) 645-6561	A / 9.5	4.41	12.82	34.04 /93	9.28 /89	14.47 /95	0.87	0.51
GR	Dreyfus Socially Resp Growth I		C+	(800) 645-6561	B / 7.6	7.22	9.22	22.68 /65	7.68 /77	11.39 /69	1.14	0.86
GR	Dreyfus Socially Resp Growth S		C+	(800) 645-6561	B- / 7.4	7.13	9.09	22.36 /64	7.41 /75	11.11 /67	0.92	1.11
GI	Dreyfus Stock Index Fund I		A+	(800) 645-6561	A- / 9.2	7.97	9.91	24.68 /72	10.36 /95	13.73 /91	1.76	0.27
GI	Dreyfus Stock Index Fund S		A+	(800) 645-6561	A- / 9.1	7.92	9.76	24.38 /71	10.09 /94	13.45 /88	1.54	0.52
GR	Dreyfus Strategic Value A	DAGVX	B	(800) 782-6620	A / 9.4	6.89	15.51	33.75 /93	9.86 /93	14.77 /96	1.12	1.12
GR	Dreyfus Strategic Value C	DCGVX	B	(800) 782-6620	A+ / 9.6	6.69	15.09	32.76 /91	9.03 /87	13.91 /92	0.57	1.89
GR	Dreyfus Strategic Value I	DRGVX	B+	(800) 782-6620	A+ / 9.7	6.99	15.68	34.08 /93	10.14 /94	15.06 /97	1.35	0.89
GR	Dreyfus Strategic Value Y	DRGYX	B+	(800) 782-6620	A+ / 9.7	6.99	15.68	34.08 /93	10.14 /94	--	1.35	0.79
MC	Dreyfus Structure Midcap A	DPSAX	C+	(800) 782-6620	B / 7.7	6.85	12.78	25.90 /76	8.53 /83	13.26 /86	0.67	1.29
MC	Dreyfus Structure Midcap C	DPSCX	C+	(800) 782-6620	B / 8.2	6.64	12.36	25.00 /73	7.74 /77	12.44 /78	0.14	2.00
MC	Dreyfus Structure Midcap I	DPSRX	B	(800) 782-6620	B+ / 8.9	6.96	12.95	26.25 /77	8.80 /85	13.55 /89	1.04	1.09
MC	Dreyfus Structure Midcap Y	DPSYX	B	(800) 782-6620	A- / 9.0	6.96	12.99	26.44 /78	8.95 /86	--	1.37	0.87
GR	Dreyfus Tax Mgd Growth A	DTMGX	C	(800) 782-6620	C / 5.0	8.64	7.18	17.97 /43	5.90 /63	7.48 /38	0.92	1.36
GR	Dreyfus Tax Mgd Growth C	DPTAX	C+	(800) 782-6620	C / 5.5	8.41	6.80	17.10 /39	5.11 /55	6.67 /33	0.36	2.11
GR	Dreyfus Tax Mgd Growth I	DPTRX	C+	(800) 782-6620	C+ / 6.4	8.73	7.35	18.28 /44	6.17 /66	7.75 /40	1.21	1.11
TC	Dreyfus Tech Growth A	DTGRX	C-	(800) 782-6620	B- / 7.5	10.86	8.96	28.74 /83	7.33 /74	11.80 /72	0.00	1.28
TC	Dreyfus Tech Growth C	DTGCX	C-	(800) 782-6620	B / 7.9	10.64	8.52	27.68 /81	6.46 /68	10.88 /65	0.00	2.10
TC	Dreyfus Tech Growth I	DGVRX	C+	(800) 782-6620	B+ / 8.7	10.95	9.12	29.09 /84	7.61 /76	12.11 /75	0.00	1.03
GR	Dreyfus Third Century A	DTCAX	C+	(800) 782-6620	C+ / 6.4	7.12	9.01	22.16 /63	7.30 /74	10.94 /65	0.78	1.23
GR	Dreyfus Third Century C	DTCCX	C+	(800) 782-6620	C+ / 6.8	6.85	8.60	21.18 /58	6.48 /68	10.09 /59	0.25	1.98
GR	Dreyfus Third Century I	DRTCX	B+	(800) 782-6620	B / 7.6	7.25	9.19	22.61 /65	7.63 /76	11.30 /68	1.11	0.91
GR	● Dreyfus Third Century Z	DRTHX	B+	(800) 782-6620	B- / 7.5	7.21	9.15	22.47 /64	7.55 /76	11.19 /67	1.00	1.03
EM	Dreyfus Total Emerging Markets A	DTMAX	D+	(800) 645-6561	C- / 3.5	10.23	3.97	28.44 /83	2.05 /24	0.51 / 5	1.28	1.72
EM	Dreyfus Total Emerging Markets C	DTMCX	D+	(800) 645-6561	C- / 4.0	10.07	3.59	27.46 /80	1.28 /20	-0.24 / 4	0.65	2.46
EM	Dreyfus Total Emerging Markets I	DTEIX	C-	(800) 645-6561	C / 4.9	10.34	4.10	28.75 /83	2.32 /26	0.76 / 6	1.57	1.36
EM	Dreyfus Total Emerging Markets Y	DTMYX	C-	(800) 645-6561	C / 4.9	10.31	4.16	28.83 /84	2.34 /26	--	1.54	1.38
IN	● Dreyfus US Equity Fd A	DPUAX	C-	(800) 782-6620	C+ / 5.7	6.81	7.22	20.89 /57	6.78 /70	9.98 /58	0.49	1.16
IN	● Dreyfus US Equity Fd C	DPUCX	C	(800) 782-6620	C+ / 6.2	6.60	6.79	19.92 /52	5.97 /64	9.12 /52	0.00	2.04
IN	● Dreyfus US Equity Fd I	DPUIX	C+	(800) 782-6620	B- / 7.0	6.88	7.35	21.20 /58	7.14 /73	10.36 /61	0.75	0.80
GR	● Dreyfus US Equity Fd Y	DPUYX	C+	(800) 782-6620	B- / 7.0	6.93	7.45	21.32 /59	7.19 /73	--	0.79	0.79
GL	Dreyfus Wrldwde Growth A	PGROX	C-	(800) 782-6620	C / 4.5	9.51	6.51	16.87 /38	5.34 /58	7.55 /39	1.13	1.17
GL	Dreyfus Wrldwde Growth C	PGRCX	C	(800) 782-6620	C / 5.1	9.32	6.12	16.00 /34	4.56 /49	6.76 /33	0.58	1.91
GL	Dreyfus Wrldwde Growth I	DPWRX	C+	(800) 782-6620	C+ / 6.0	9.59	6.67	17.20 /39	5.62 /61	7.84 /41	1.62	0.90
GL	Dreyfus Wrldwde Growth Y	DPRIX	C+	(800) 782-6620	C+ / 6.0	9.63	6.70	17.28 /40	5.70 /61	--	1.78	0.84

● Denotes fund is closed to new investors

* Denotes fund is included in Section II

www.thestreetratings.com

I. Index of Stock Mutual Funds

RISK			NET ASSETS		ASSET				Portfolio	BULL / BEAR		FUND MANAGER		MINIMUMS		LOADS	
Risk Rating/Pts	3 Year Standard Deviation	Beta	NAV As of 2/28/17	Total $(Mil)	Cash %	Stocks %	Bonds %	Other %	Portfolio Turnover Ratio	Last Bull Market Return	Last Bear Market Return	Manager Quality Pct	Manager Tenure (Years)	Initial Purch. $	Additional Purch. $	Front End Load	Back End Load
B /8.4	4.5	0.22	12.16	N/A	64	35	0	1	268	N/A	N/A	46	4	1,000	100	0.0	0.0
B /8.6	4.6	0.22	12.61	3	64	35	0	1	268	N/A	N/A	60	4	1,000	100	0.0	0.0
B /8.6	4.6	0.23	12.61	70	64	35	0	1	268	N/A	N/A	60	4	1,000,000	0	0.0	0.0
C+ /5.7	10.3	1.00	51.52	2,676	0	99	0	1	4	128.7	-16.4	68	17	2,500	100	0.0	0.0
U /	N/A	N/A	12.44	419	77	22	0	1	369	N/A	N/A	N/A	3	1,000,000	0	0.0	0.0
D+ /2.9	16.7	1.19	23.66	3	2	97	0	1	125	93.8	-20.4	2	N/A	1,000	100	5.8	0.0
D+ /2.7	16.7	1.19	22.34	N/A	2	97	0	1	125	86.2	-20.7	1	N/A	1,000	100	0.0	0.0
D+ /2.9	16.7	1.19	24.21	12	2	97	0	1	125	97.0	-20.3	2	N/A	1,000	100	0.0	0.0
D+ /2.9	16.7	1.00	24.20	607	2	97	0	1	125	N/A	N/A	12	N/A	1,000,000	0	0.0	0.0
C- /3.8	15.2	0.94	23.65	2	3	96	0	1	65	121.3	-25.6	61	9	1,000	100	5.8	0.0
C- /3.6	15.2	0.94	22.05	N/A	3	96	0	1	65	112.8	-25.8	52	9	1,000	100	0.0	0.0
C- /3.8	15.2	0.94	24.00	24	3	96	0	1	65	125.4	-25.4	65	9	1,000	100	0.0	0.0
C- /3.8	15.2	0.94	23.98	844	3	96	0	1	65	N/A	N/A	66	9	1,000,000	0	0.0	0.0
D+ /2.4	12.0	0.73	25.06	31	0	99	0	1	64	121.6	-26.3	84	17	1,000	100	5.8	0.0
D- /1.5	12.0	0.73	20.45	8	0	99	0	1	64	111.9	-26.5	79	17	1,000	100	0.0	0.0
D+ /2.6	12.0	0.73	26.50	12	0	99	0	1	64	124.7	-26.2	85	17	1,000	100	0.0	0.0
U /	N/A	N/A	30.38	135	0	98	0	2	24	N/A	N/A	N/A	17	1,000	100	0.0	0.0
C /4.3	14.7	0.92	30.41	2,242	0	98	0	2	24	150.7	-22.2	89	17	2,500	100	0.0	0.0
C /4.8	10.7	1.02	39.80	229	0	99	0	1	60	110.8	-16.6	36	5	0	0	0.0	0.0
C /4.8	10.7	1.02	39.36	11	0	99	0	1	60	107.9	-16.7	33	5	0	0	0.0	0.0
C+ /6.8	10.3	1.00	48.57	2,102	0	98	1	1	4	131.7	-16.4	71	17	0	0	0.0	0.0
C+ /6.8	10.3	1.00	48.61	206	0	98	1	1	4	128.6	-16.5	69	17	0	0	0.0	0.0
C- /4.1	12.2	1.09	40.56	864	0	99	0	1	81	148.2	-24.5	54	16	1,000	100	5.8	0.0
C- /4.1	12.2	1.09	38.08	50	0	99	0	1	81	138.3	-24.8	43	16	1,000	100	0.0	0.0
C- /4.1	12.2	1.09	40.64	798	0	99	0	1	81	151.5	-24.4	58	16	1,000	100	0.0	0.0
C- /4.1	12.2	1.09	40.64	207	0	99	0	1	81	N/A	N/A	58	16	1,000,000	0	0.0	0.0
C /4.6	12.3	1.00	30.71	97	0	99	0	1	71	138.1	-23.2	62	6	1,000	100	5.8	0.0
C /4.3	12.3	1.00	27.40	32	0	99	0	1	71	128.9	-23.4	52	6	1,000	100	0.0	0.0
C /4.6	12.3	1.00	31.35	73	0	99	0	1	71	141.0	-23.1	65	6	1,000	100	0.0	0.0
C /4.6	12.3	1.00	31.32	17	0	99	0	1	71	N/A	N/A	67	6	1,000,000	0	0.0	0.0
C+ /6.3	10.1	0.94	26.19	64	0	99	0	1	11	71.8	-11.0	26	20	1,000	100	5.8	0.0
C+ /6.2	10.1	0.94	24.74	28	0	99	0	1	11	65.0	-11.4	19	20	1,000	100	0.0	0.0
C+ /6.3	10.1	0.94	26.24	72	0	99	0	1	11	74.2	-11.0	29	20	1,000	100	0.0	0.0
D+ /2.9	15.2	1.20	42.16	216	0	97	1	2	38	117.0	-19.6	14	10	1,000	100	5.8	0.0
D+ /2.3	15.2	1.21	33.69	25	0	97	1	2	38	107.6	-19.8	9	10	1,000	100	0.0	0.0
C- /3.2	15.2	1.20	46.08	19	0	97	1	2	38	120.3	-19.4	17	10	1,000	100	0.0	0.0
C+ /6.8	10.7	1.02	12.88	20	0	98	1	1	61	106.1	-16.7	32	5	1,000	100	5.8	0.0
C+ /6.8	10.6	1.01	11.32	5	0	98	1	1	61	97.7	-17.0	24	5	1,000	100	0.0	0.0
C+ /6.8	10.6	1.01	13.13	13	0	98	1	1	61	109.6	-16.5	36	5	1,000	100	0.0	0.0
C+ /6.8	10.7	1.02	13.13	276	0	98	1	1	61	108.5	-16.6	35	5	1,000	100	0.0	0.0
C /5.2	13.4	0.78	11.72	1	0	72	26	2	80	21.7	-21.1	79	6	1,000	100	5.8	2.0
C /5.2	13.4	0.78	11.53	1	0	72	26	2	80	17.0	-21.3	73	6	1,000	100	0.0	2.0
C /5.2	13.4	0.78	11.76	105	0	72	26	2	80	23.4	-21.0	81	6	1,000	100	0.0	2.0
C /5.2	13.4	0.78	11.77	1	0	72	26	2	80	N/A	N/A	81	6	1,000,000	0	0.0	2.0
C /4.7	9.3	0.87	17.95	1	0	98	1	1	14	93.6	-14.2	45	9	1,000	100	5.8	0.0
C /4.7	9.4	0.87	17.05	N/A	0	98	1	1	14	85.5	-14.5	34	9	1,000	100	0.0	0.0
C /4.7	9.4	0.87	18.00	17	0	98	1	1	14	97.4	-14.0	49	9	1,000	100	0.0	0.0
C /4.6	9.3	0.87	18.00	488	0	98	1	1	14	N/A	N/A	50	9	1,000,000	0	0.0	0.0
C+ /5.9	10.4	0.73	50.56	389	0	99	0	1	6	72.6	-14.2	96	24	1,000	100	5.8	0.0
C+ /5.8	10.4	0.73	45.12	51	0	99	0	1	6	65.8	-14.5	94	24	1,000	100	0.0	0.0
C+ /5.9	10.4	0.73	50.92	116	0	99	0	1	6	75.1	-14.1	96	24	1,000	100	0.0	0.0
C+ /5.9	10.4	0.73	50.90	36	0	99	0	1	6	N/A	N/A	96	24	1,000,000	0	0.0	0.0

Data as of February 28, 2017

Fund Type	Fund Name	Ticker Symbol	Overall Investment Rating	Phone	Performance Rating/Pts	3 Mo	6 Mo	1Yr / Pct	3Yr / Pct	5Yr / Pct	Dividend Yield	Expense Ratio
FS	Dreyfus Yield Enhancement Strat Y	DABJX	U	(800) 645-6561	U /	2.68	1.05	8.75 / 9	--	--	4.19	0.72
SC	Dreyfus/Boston Co Sm Cap Growth I	SSETX	D	(800) 645-6561	B- / 7.4	2.41	9.19	37.06 /96	5.10 /55	12.15 /76	0.00	1.40
SC	Dreyfus/Boston Co Sm Cap Growth Y	SSYGX	D	(800) 645-6561	B- / 7.4	2.41	9.18	37.01 /96	5.12 /55	--	0.00	1.40
SC	Dreyfus/Boston Co Sm Cap Value I	STSVX	C	(800) 645-6561	B+ / 8.6	4.42	13.92	33.99 /93	6.85 /71	12.55 /79	0.39	0.97
SC	Dreyfus/Boston Co Sm/Mid Cap Gro	DBMAX	C-	(800) 645-6561	C+ / 5.8	6.78	8.65	27.25 /80	5.38 /58	11.06 /66	0.00	1.03
SC	Dreyfus/Boston Co Sm/Mid Cap Gro	DBMCX	C-	(800) 645-6561	C+ / 6.4	6.66	8.28	26.34 /77	4.57 /49	10.16 /59	0.00	1.81
SC	Dreyfus/Boston Co Sm/Mid Cap Gro I	SDSCX	C	(800) 645-6561	B- / 7.1	6.90	8.78	27.56 /81	5.65 /61	11.34 /68	0.00	0.79
SC	Dreyfus/Boston Co Sm/Mid Cap Gro	DBMYX	C	(800) 645-6561	B- / 7.2	6.93	8.87	27.76 /81	5.77 /62	--	0.00	0.68
GI	Driehaus Active Income Fund	LCMAX	D+	(800) 560-6111	D- / 1.3	0.12	1.94	8.03 / 7	0.96 /18	1.86 / 8	3.13	1.05
EM	Driehaus Emerging Markets Growth	DREGX	E+	(800) 560-6111	D- / 1.0	6.75	0.36	20.39 /54	-1.26 / 8	1.61 / 7	0.37	1.65
EM	Driehaus Emg Mkts Sm Cap Growth	DRESX	E+	(800) 560-6111	E- / 0.1	4.50	-5.52	2.98 / 3	-5.04 / 2	3.11 /11	0.15	1.69
IN	Driehaus Event Driven	DEVDX	D	(800) 560-6111	E+ / 0.7	1.31	2.60	13.93 /25	-1.71 / 7	--	1.21	1.86
EM	Driehaus Frontier Emerging Markets	DRFRX	U	(800) 560-6111	U /	5.83	3.08	16.39 /36	--	--	0.54	3.91
FO	● Driehaus Intl SmCap Gr Fd	DRIOX	D-	(800) 560-6111	D- / 1.3	5.73	-1.20	9.32 /10	0.90 /18	7.23 /36	0.00	1.71
SC	Driehaus Micro Cap Growth	DMCRX	D	(800) 560-6111	B- / 7.2	1.68	7.69	40.00 /97	5.25 /57	17.51 /98	0.00	1.53
GI	Dunham Appreciation & Income A	DAAIX	E+	(888) 338-6426	D- / 1.1	3.74	2.22	11.35 /16	0.60 /16	4.17 /16	2.64	1.59
GI	Dunham Appreciation & Income C	DCAIX	E+	(888) 338-6426	D- / 1.0	3.44	1.89	10.45 /13	-0.19 /13	3.36 /12	2.24	2.34
GI	Dunham Appreciation & Income N	DNAIX	E+	(888) 338-6426	D / 1.7	3.64	2.25	11.51 /16	0.83 /17	4.42 /18	3.08	1.34
GR	Dunham Dynamic Macro A	DAAVX	D+	(888) 338-6426	E / 0.5	2.59	-0.63	4.73 / 4	0.13 /14	-0.08 / 4	0.00	2.51
GR	Dunham Dynamic Macro C	DCAVX	D+	(888) 338-6426	E+ / 0.6	2.34	-1.08	3.84 / 3	-0.61 /11	-0.83 / 4	0.00	3.26
GR	Dunham Dynamic Macro N	DNAVX	C-	(888) 338-6426	D- / 1.0	2.58	-0.52	4.94 / 4	0.42 /15	0.17 / 5	0.00	2.26
EM	Dunham Emerging Markets Stock A	DAEMX	D+	(888) 338-6426	C- / 4.0	12.00	9.14	31.29 /89	0.33 /15	-0.63 / 4	1.50	2.05
EM	Dunham Emerging Markets Stock C	DCEMX	D	(888) 338-6426	D+ / 2.5	11.75	8.65	30.18 /87	-0.45 /11	-1.41 / 3	1.16	2.80
EM	Dunham Emerging Markets Stock N	DNEMX	C-	(888) 338-6426	C / 5.5	12.09	9.20	31.55 /89	0.58 /16	-0.41 / 4	1.78	1.80
GR	Dunham Focused Large Cap Growth	DAFGX	D-	(888) 338-6426	D+ / 2.8	7.66	4.37	16.50 /36	3.17 /33	9.42 /54	0.00	1.59
GR	Dunham Focused Large Cap Growth	DCFGX	D	(888) 338-6426	C- / 3.3	7.48	4.01	15.66 /33	2.43 /27	8.61 /47	0.00	2.34
GR	Dunham Focused Large Cap Growth	DNFGX	D+	(888) 338-6426	C- / 4.1	7.69	4.44	16.74 /37	3.44 /36	9.70 /56	0.00	1.34
FO	Dunham International Stock A	DAINX	D-	(888) 338-6426	D- / 1.0	7.62	6.47	19.09 /48	-0.56 /11	5.10 /22	0.00	2.29
FO	Dunham International Stock C	DCINX	D-	(888) 338-6426	D- / 1.3	7.50	6.07	18.23 /44	-1.30 / 8	4.34 /17	0.00	3.04
FO	Dunham International Stock N	DNINX	D	(888) 338-6426	D / 1.7	7.73	6.59	19.35 /49	-0.31 /12	5.38 /24	0.00	2.04
GI	Dunham Large Cap Value A	DALVX	C-	(888) 338-6426	C+ / 6.5	6.72	10.00	23.46 /68	7.18 /73	10.78 /64	1.34	1.50
GI	Dunham Large Cap Value C	DCLVX	C-	(888) 338-6426	C+ / 6.9	6.48	9.62	22.41 /64	6.38 /67	9.97 /58	0.91	2.25
GI	Dunham Large Cap Value N	DNLVX	C	(888) 338-6426	B / 7.7	6.77	10.21	23.76 /69	7.45 /75	11.07 /66	1.63	1.25
IN	Dunham Monthly Distribution Class A	DAMDX	D+	(888) 338-6426	D- / 1.2	3.04	4.13	8.40 / 8	1.54 /21	3.05 /11	2.48	2.44
IN	Dunham Monthly Distribution Class C	DCMDX	D+	(888) 338-6426	D- / 1.5	2.91	3.87	7.65 / 7	0.74 /17	2.25 / 9	3.18	3.19
IN	Dunham Monthly Distribution Class N	DNMDX	C-	(888) 338-6426	D / 1.8	3.08	3.92	8.37 / 8	1.69 /22	3.25 /12	2.57	2.19
RE	Dunham Real Estate Stock A	DAREX	C-	(888) 338-6426	C+ / 5.7	6.91	-3.07	14.21 /26	10.16 /94	10.84 /64	1.30	1.89
RE	Dunham Real Estate Stock C	DCREX	C-	(888) 338-6426	C+ / 6.2	6.72	-3.45	13.39 /23	9.33 /89	10.00 /58	1.15	2.64
RE	Dunham Real Estate Stock N	DNREX	C	(888) 338-6426	C+ / 6.9	6.98	-2.97	14.51 /28	10.43 /96	11.10 /67	1.93	1.64
SC	Dunham Small Cap Growth A	DADGX	E+	(888) 338-6426	C- / 3.1	4.61	6.63	27.56 /81	1.44 /21	10.31 /61	0.00	1.83
SC	Dunham Small Cap Growth C	DCDGX	E+	(888) 338-6426	C- / 3.5	4.33	6.19	26.60 /78	0.66 /16	9.49 /55	0.00	2.58
SC	Dunham Small Cap Growth N	DNDGX	D-	(888) 338-6426	C / 4.3	4.64	6.73	27.84 /81	1.68 /22	10.59 /63	0.00	1.58
SC	Dunham Small Cap Value A	DASVX	B+	(888) 338-6426	B+ / 8.6	5.14	14.90	35.15 /94	8.12 /80	11.84 /73	0.39	2.05
SC	Dunham Small Cap Value C	DCSVX	B+	(888) 338-6426	A- / 9.0	5.03	14.47	34.21 /93	7.35 /74	10.98 /66	0.00	2.80
SC	Dunham Small Cap Value N	DNSVX	A-	(888) 338-6426	A / 9.5	5.21	15.05	35.45 /94	8.40 /82	12.09 /75	0.58	1.80
EM	Dupont Capital Emerging Mkts I	DCMEX	E+	(888) 739-1390	D- / 1.2	10.14	7.98	29.36 /85	-2.84 / 5	-3.40 / 2	1.36	1.66
GR	Eagle Capital Appreciation A	HRCPX	C+	(800) 421-4184	B / 8.0	8.60	8.51	19.30 /49	10.51 /96	13.68 /90	0.06	1.19
GR	Eagle Capital Appreciation C	HRCCX	C+	(800) 421-4184	B / 8.2	8.40	8.08	18.36 /44	9.65 /91	12.81 /82	0.00	1.96
GR	Eagle Capital Appreciation I	HRCIX	B	(800) 421-4184	A- / 9.0	8.67	8.67	19.67 /50	10.83 /97	14.01 /93	0.30	0.90
GR	Eagle Capital Appreciation R3	HRCLX	B-	(800) 421-4184	B+ / 8.6	8.54	8.35	18.89 /47	10.15 /94	13.29 /87	0.00	1.51
GR	Eagle Capital Appreciation R5	HRCMX	B	(800) 421-4184	A- / 9.0	8.69	8.66	19.65 /50	10.82 /97	14.00 /93	0.33	0.95
GR	Eagle Capital Appreciation R6	HRCUX	U	(800) 421-4184	U /	8.73	8.73	19.76 /51	--	--	0.47	0.82

RISK Risk Rating/Pts	3 Year Standard Deviation	Beta	NET ASSETS NAV As of 2/28/17	Total $(Mil)	ASSET Cash %	Stocks %	Bonds %	Other %	Portfolio Turnover Ratio	BULL / BEAR Last Bull Market Return	Last Bear Market Return	FUND MANAGER Manager Quality Pct	Manager Tenure (Years)	MINIMUMS Initial Purch. $	Additional Purch. $	LOADS Front End Load	Back End Load
U /	N/A	N/A	12.26	432	17	0	82	1	16	N/A	N/A	N/A	3	1,000,000	0	0.0	0.0
E- / 0.0	17.9	1.07	28.04	6	1	98	0	1	197	122.4	-22.9	46	4	1,000	100	0.0	0.0
E- / 0.0	17.9	1.07	28.07	N/A	1	98	0	1	197	N/A	N/A	46	4	1,000,000	0	0.0	0.0
D+ / 2.6	14.3	0.88	24.37	223	0	99	0	1	79	138.2	-24.8	79	17	1,000	100	0.0	0.0
C- / 3.8	13.4	0.78	17.66	226	0	95	4	1	121	117.7	-18.1	74	12	1,000	100	5.8	0.0
C- / 3.6	13.4	0.78	16.04	36	0	95	4	1	121	108.3	-18.5	65	12	1,000	100	0.0	0.0
C- / 3.9	13.4	0.78	18.15	464	0	95	4	1	121	120.8	-18.1	76	12	1,000	100	0.0	0.0
C- / 3.9	13.4	0.78	18.23	353	0	95	4	1	121	N/A	N/A	77	12	1,000,000	0	0.0	0.0
B / 8.0	3.1	0.23	10.15	2,233	30	15	48	7	76	17.8	-9.1	56	12	25,000	5,000	0.0	0.0
C / 5.1	12.7	0.75	29.92	1,392	3	96	0	1	257	27.9	-22.2	40	9	10,000	2,000	0.0	2.0
C / 5.5	10.9	0.49	11.31	270	6	93	0	1	306	27.8	-18.0	9	6	10,000	2,000	0.0	2.0
C+ / 6.7	6.9	0.39	10.30	260	30	67	1	2	400	N/A	N/A	10	4	10,000	2,000	0.0	2.0
U /	N/A	N/A	9.86	76	9	89	0	2	66	N/A	N/A	N/A	2	250,000	50,000	0.0	2.0
C / 5.2	11.0	0.71	9.83	260	4	95	0	1	251	58.4	-22.4	81	10	10,000	2,000	0.0	2.0
E+ / 0.9	22.3	1.24	12.74	395	3	96	0	1	183	181.0	-35.0	33	4	10,000	2,000	0.0	2.0
C / 4.3	8.3	0.63	8.12	3	1	5	1	93	96	39.1	-14.5	10	N/A	5,000	100	5.8	0.0
C / 4.3	8.3	0.63	7.97	3	1	5	1	93	96	33.4	-14.9	6	N/A	5,000	100	0.0	0.0
C- / 4.2	8.3	0.63	8.12	15	1	5	1	93	96	40.9	-14.5	11	N/A	100,000	0	0.0	0.0
B / 8.4	6.5	0.45	9.52	4	8	46	45	1	54	11.3	-7.9	19	N/A	5,000	100	5.8	0.0
B / 8.3	6.5	0.45	9.20	2	8	46	45	1	54	6.8	-8.1	14	N/A	5,000	100	0.0	0.0
B / 8.5	6.5	0.45	9.55	30	8	46	45	1	54	12.8	-7.7	22	N/A	100,000	0	0.0	0.0
C / 4.9	14.8	0.87	13.03	7	1	98	0	1	97	15.5	-30.6	60	4	5,000	100	5.8	0.0
C / 4.9	14.8	0.87	12.39	3	1	98	0	1	97	10.7	-30.9	49	4	5,000	100	0.0	0.0
C / 4.8	14.8	0.87	13.30	47	1	98	0	1	97	16.9	-30.6	63	4	100,000	0	0.0	0.0
C / 4.4	15.1	1.10	16.73	12	0	99	0	1	29	N/A	N/A	4	6	5,000	100	5.8	0.0
C / 4.3	15.1	1.10	16.10	6	0	99	0	1	29	N/A	N/A	3	6	5,000	100	0.0	0.0
C / 4.4	15.1	1.10	16.95	54	0	99	0	1	29	N/A	N/A	4	6	100,000	0	0.0	0.0
C+ / 5.8	12.2	0.91	14.97	11	2	96	1	1	143	46.6	-23.6	69	9	5,000	100	5.8	0.0
C+ / 5.8	12.2	0.91	14.33	6	2	96	1	1	143	40.9	-23.8	60	9	5,000	100	0.0	0.0
C+ / 5.8	12.2	0.91	15.05	80	2	96	1	1	143	48.7	-23.4	72	9	100,000	0	0.0	0.0
C- / 3.0	10.7	1.00	13.42	7	0	97	2	1	59	99.7	-18.4	32	2	5,000	100	5.8	0.0
D+ / 2.9	10.7	1.00	12.89	5	0	97	2	1	59	91.8	-18.7	25	2	5,000	100	0.0	0.0
D+ / 2.9	10.7	1.00	13.46	49	0	97	2	1	59	102.6	-18.4	35	2	100,000	0	0.0	0.0
B- / 7.9	4.5	0.37	35.72	44	13	68	18	1	208	25.1	-6.3	44	9	5,000	100	5.8	0.0
B- / 7.7	4.5	0.37	29.47	37	13	68	18	1	208	19.9	-6.6	33	9	5,000	100	0.0	0.0
B / 8.0	4.5	0.37	36.61	157	13	68	18	1	208	26.4	-6.2	46	9	100,000	0	0.0	0.0
C- / 3.7	14.8	1.08	15.98	4	0	98	1	1	110	102.4	-17.9	54	2	5,000	100	5.8	0.0
C- / 3.6	14.8	1.08	15.15	3	0	98	1	1	110	94.3	-18.1	43	2	5,000	100	0.0	0.0
C- / 3.6	14.8	1.08	15.84	26	0	98	1	1	110	105.2	-17.8	57	2	100,000	0	0.0	0.0
D+ / 2.3	16.7	0.94	16.57	7	3	94	2	1	181	101.3	-27.8	16	13	5,000	100	5.8	0.0
D / 2.0	16.7	0.94	14.23	3	3	94	2	1	181	93.3	-28.0	11	13	5,000	100	0.0	0.0
D+ / 2.4	16.6	0.93	17.13	28	3	94	2	1	181	104.1	-27.7	18	13	100,000	0	0.0	0.0
C / 5.5	14.4	0.88	16.39	4	0	99	0	1	129	112.4	-20.5	86	4	5,000	100	5.8	0.0
C / 5.3	14.4	0.88	14.92	3	0	99	0	1	129	103.6	-20.7	82	4	5,000	100	0.0	0.0
C / 5.5	14.4	0.88	16.52	21	0	99	0	1	129	114.7	-20.4	87	4	100,000	0	0.0	0.0
C- / 4.0	15.1	0.90	7.60	30	3	96	0	1	53	3.9	-24.5	20	3	1,000,000	100,000	0.0	2.0
C / 4.5	10.9	0.99	36.45	148	2	97	0	1	35	135.0	-17.6	74	4	1,000	0	4.8	0.0
C- / 3.5	10.9	0.99	27.37	64	2	97	0	1	35	125.6	-17.9	65	4	1,000	0	0.0	0.0
C / 4.6	10.9	0.99	38.05	106	2	97	0	1	35	138.8	-17.5	76	4	2,500,000	0	0.0	0.0
C / 4.4	10.9	0.99	35.23	1	2	97	0	1	35	130.7	-17.7	70	4	0	0	0.0	0.0
C / 4.6	10.9	0.99	37.91	8	2	97	0	1	35	138.5	-17.5	76	4	0	0	0.0	0.0
U /	N/A	N/A	37.77	32	2	97	0	1	35	N/A	N/A	N/A	4	0	0	0.0	0.0

Fund Type	Fund Name	Ticker Symbol	Overall Investment Rating	Phone	Performance Rating/Pts	3 Mo	6 Mo	1Yr / Pct	3Yr / Pct	5Yr / Pct	Dividend Yield	Expense Ratio
								Total Return % through 2/28/17	Annualized		Incl. in Returns	
GI	Eagle Growth and Income A	HRCVX	B+	(800) 421-4184	B- / 7.1	8.06	7.66	23.86 /69	8.03 /79	11.87 /73	1.62	1.02
GI	Eagle Growth and Income C	HIGCX	B+	(800) 421-4184	B- / 7.3	7.90	7.29	22.98 /67	7.23 /73	11.03 /66	1.10	1.79
GI	Eagle Growth and Income I	HIGJX	A	(800) 421-4184	B / 8.1	8.15	7.85	24.27 /71	8.33 /81	12.18 /76	1.97	0.76
GI	Eagle Growth and Income R3	HIGRX	A-	(800) 421-4184	B / 7.6	7.99	7.56	23.60 /68	7.64 /76	11.47 /70	1.48	1.44
GI	Eagle Growth and Income R5	HIGSX	A-	(800) 421-4184	B / 8.0	8.17	7.86	24.26 /71	8.16 /80	12.09 /75	1.98	0.79
GI	Eagle Growth and Income R6	HIGUX	A	(800) 421-4184	B / 8.1	8.20	7.91	24.39 /71	8.34 /82	12.22 /76	2.07	0.65
FO	Eagle International Stock A	EISAX	D	(800) 421-4184	D / 1.8	8.54	6.80	13.46 /23	0.26 /15	—	1.14	4.04
FO	Eagle International Stock C	EISDX	D	(800) 421-4184	D- / 1.3	8.33	6.35	12.51 /20	-0.55 /11	—	1.03	4.96
FO	Eagle International Stock I	EISIX	D+	(800) 421-4184	D+ / 2.7	8.73	7.14	14.11 /26	0.75 /17	—	2.20	3.83
FO	Eagle International Stock R3	EISRX	D+	(800) 421-4184	D+ / 2.3	8.56	6.75	13.40 /23	0.14 /14	—	2.08	4.39
FO	Eagle International Stock R5	EISSX	D+	(800) 421-4184	D+ / 2.7	8.66	7.07	14.03 /25	0.72 /17	—	2.20	3.60
FO	Eagle International Stock R6	EISVX	D+	(800) 421-4184	D+ / 2.8	8.73	7.22	14.17 /26	0.83 /17	—	2.27	3.81
GR	Eagle Mid Cap Growth A	HAGAX	C+	(800) 421-4184	C+ / 6.7	7.13	8.20	25.77 /75	6.99 /72	12.35 /78	0.00	1.14
GR	Eagle Mid Cap Growth C	HAGCX	C+	(800) 421-4184	B- / 7.0	6.93	7.79	24.90 /73	6.24 /66	11.55 /70	0.00	1.88
GR	Eagle Mid Cap Growth I	HAGIX	B-	(800) 421-4184	B / 7.8	7.21	8.37	26.22 /77	7.36 /74	12.73 /81	0.00	0.83
GR	Eagle Mid Cap Growth R3	HAREX	C+	(800) 421-4184	B- / 7.3	7.06	8.05	25.46 /75	6.71 /70	12.04 /75	0.00	1.42
GR	Eagle Mid Cap Growth R5	HARSX	B-	(800) 421-4184	B / 7.8	7.24	8.40	26.22 /77	7.31 /74	12.70 /81	0.01	0.83
GR	Eagle Mid Cap Growth R6	HRAUX	B-	(800) 421-4184	B / 7.9	7.24	8.44	26.37 /77	7.48 /75	12.84 /82	0.02	0.74
MC	Eagle Mid Cap Stock A	HMCAX	C-	(800) 421-4184	C+ / 5.6	6.24	7.33	23.37 /68	5.94 /64	9.45 /54	0.00	1.24
MC	Eagle Mid Cap Stock C	HMCCX	C-	(800) 421-4184	C+ / 6.0	6.10	6.94	22.49 /64	5.15 /56	8.64 /48	0.00	1.99
MC	Eagle Mid Cap Stock I	HMCJX	C	(800) 421-4184	C+ / 6.8	6.34	7.49	23.77 /69	6.25 /66	9.76 /57	0.00	1.06
MC	Eagle Mid Cap Stock R3	HMRRX	C	(800) 421-4184	C+ / 6.4	6.20	7.20	23.00 /67	5.60 /61	9.11 /52	0.00	1.59
MC	Eagle Mid Cap Stock R5	HMRSX	C	(800) 421-4184	C+ / 6.8	6.35	7.49	23.81 /69	6.25 /66	9.84 /57	0.00	0.99
MC	Eagle Mid Cap Stock R6	HMRUX	C	(800) 421-4184	C+ / 6.9	6.40	7.54	23.87 /69	6.38 /67	9.89 /57	0.00	0.83
EN	Eagle MLP Strategy A	EGLAX	E-	(800) 421-4184	E+ / 0.7	2.82	11.56	57.32 /99	-7.48 / 1	—	5.95	1.75
EN	Eagle MLP Strategy C	EGLCX	E-	(800) 421-4184	E+ / 0.9	2.51	11.04	56.21 /99	-8.19 / 1	—	5.66	2.50
EN	Eagle MLP Strategy I	EGLIX	E-	(800) 421-4184	D- / 1.3	2.76	11.69	57.88 /99	-7.24 / 1	—	6.54	1.51
SC	Eagle Small Cap Gr A	HRSCX	C	(800) 421-4184	B / 7.6	8.01	11.21	32.99 /92	6.37 /67	10.97 /66	0.00	1.10
SC	Eagle Small Cap Gr C	HSCCX	C	(800) 421-4184	B / 7.9	7.84	10.85	32.09 /90	5.63 /61	10.19 /60	0.00	1.82
SC	Eagle Small Cap Gr I	HSIIX	C+	(800) 421-4184	B+ / 8.7	8.08	11.39	33.43 /92	6.72 /70	11.32 /68	0.00	0.78
SC	Eagle Small Cap Gr R3	HSRRX	C+	(800) 421-4184	B / 8.2	7.96	11.11	32.66 /91	6.09 /65	10.67 /63	0.00	1.38
SC	Eagle Small Cap Gr R5	HSRSX	C+	(800) 421-4184	B+ / 8.7	8.10	11.42	33.48 /92	6.75 /70	11.35 /69	0.00	0.75
SC	Eagle Small Cap Gr R6	HSRUX	C+	(800) 421-4184	B+ / 8.8	8.14	11.49	33.61 /92	6.87 /71	11.47 /70	0.00	0.66
SC	Eagle Smaller Company A	EGEAX	D-	(800) 421-4184	C+ / 6.4	5.97	10.72	30.16 /87	5.18 /56	10.42 /61	0.00	1.60
SC	Eagle Smaller Company C	EGECX	D-	(800) 421-4184	C+ / 6.7	5.72	10.33	29.28 /85	4.41 /48	9.62 /55	0.00	2.35
SC	Eagle Smaller Company I	EGEIX	D	(800) 421-4184	B / 7.7	6.07	10.97	30.77 /88	5.89 /63	11.05 /66	0.00	1.27
SC	Eagle Smaller Company R3	EGERX	D	(800) 421-4184	B- / 7.0	5.87	10.52	29.82 /86	4.90 /53	10.11 /59	0.00	2.07
SC	Eagle Smaller Company R5	EGESX	D	(800) 421-4184	B / 7.6	6.08	10.96	30.80 /88	5.69 /61	10.94 /65	0.00	1.14
SC	Eagle Smaller Company R6	EGEUX	D	(800) 421-4184	B / 7.6	6.12	10.98	31.05 /88	5.75 /62	11.02 /66	0.00	1.20
GR	EAS Crow Point Alternatives A	EASAX	D+		E / 0.3	0.94	0.00	0.26 / 1	-0.23 /12	1.60 / 7	0.24	3.24
GR	EAS Crow Point Alternatives C	EASYX	C-		E / 0.4	0.84	-0.24	-0.36 / 1	-0.90 /10	0.89 / 6	0.00	4.17
GR	Eaton Vance Atlanta Cap Focusd Gr	EAALX	D	(800) 262-1122	C / 4.4	6.26	5.85	15.93 /34	6.24 /66	9.14 /52	0.00	1.13
GR	Eaton Vance Atlanta Cap Focusd Gr	EAGCX	D+	(800) 262-1122	C / 5.0	6.09	5.41	15.04 /30	5.44 /59	8.32 /45	0.00	1.88
GR	Eaton Vance Atlanta Cap Focusd Gr I	EILGX	D+	(800) 262-1122	C+ / 5.8	6.31	5.96	16.12 /35	6.49 /68	9.40 /54	0.24	0.88
GR	Eaton Vance Atlanta Cap Sel Eq A	ESEAX	B+	(800) 262-1122	B- / 7.0	8.46	7.29	17.42 /40	9.60 /91	12.88 /83	0.00	1.35
GR	Eaton Vance Atlanta Cap Sel Eq C	ESECX	B+	(800) 262-1122	B- / 7.4	8.29	6.90	16.56 /37	8.76 /85	12.03 /75	0.00	2.10
GR	Eaton Vance Atlanta Cap Sel Eq I	ESEIX	A	(800) 262-1122	B / 8.1	8.49	7.39	17.72 /42	9.85 /92	13.15 /85	0.00	1.10
SC	● Eaton Vance Atlanta Cap SMID Cap	EAASX	B	(800) 262-1122	B / 7.7	6.84	6.80	20.65 /56	10.65 /96	14.00 /93	0.00	1.22
SC	● Eaton Vance Atlanta Cap SMID Cap	ECASX	B+	(800) 262-1122	B / 8.0	6.64	6.42	19.71 /51	9.82 /92	13.15 /85	0.00	1.97
SC	● Eaton Vance Atlanta Cap SMID Cap I	EISMX	A-	(800) 262-1122	B+ / 8.8	6.91	6.94	20.95 /57	10.93 /97	14.28 /95	0.00	0.97
SC	● Eaton Vance Atlanta Cap SMID Cap	ERSMX	B+	(800) 262-1122	B+ / 8.5	6.78	6.70	20.35 /54	10.38 /95	13.72 /91	0.00	1.47
SC	● Eaton Vance Atlanta Cap SMID Cap	ERASX	A	(800) 262-1122	B+ / 8.9	6.92	7.00	21.07 /58	11.04 /97	14.35 /95	0.00	0.97

● Denotes fund is closed to new investors

* Denotes fund is included in Section II

www.thestreetratings.com

RISK			NET ASSETS		ASSET					BULL / BEAR		FUND MANAGER		MINIMUMS		LOADS	
	3 Year		NAV						Portfolio	Last Bull	Last Bear	Manager	Manager	Initial	Additional	Front	Back
Risk Rating/Pts	Standard Deviation	Beta	As of 2/28/17	Total $(Mil)	Cash %	Stocks %	Bonds %	Other %	Turnover Ratio	Market Return	Market Return	Quality Pct	Tenure (Years)	Purch. $	Purch. $	End Load	End Load
B- / 7.0	10.4	0.97	19.29	159	0	99	0	1	15	104.5	-14.3	47	6	1,000	0	4.8	0.0
B- / 7.0	10.4	0.97	18.50	189	0	99	0	1	15	96.4	-14.5	37	6	1,000	0	0.0	0.0
B- / 7.0	10.4	0.97	19.26	226	0	99	0	1	15	107.7	-14.1	52	6	2,500,000	0	0.0	0.0
B- / 7.0	10.4	0.97	19.20	3	0	99	0	1	15	100.7	-14.4	43	6	0	0	0.0	0.0
B- / 7.0	10.5	0.97	19.28	N/A	0	99	0	1	15	106.7	-14.3	49	6	0	0	0.0	0.0
C+ / 6.9	10.3	0.96	19.22	38	0	99	0	1	15	107.9	N/A	53	6	0	0	0.0	0.0
C+ / 6.1	11.6	0.91	15.82	4	3	96	0	1	100	N/A	N/A	77	4	1,000	0	4.8	0.0
C+ / 6.1	11.6	0.91	15.56	5	3	96	0	1	100	N/A	N/A	70	4	1,000	0	0.0	0.0
C+ / 6.1	11.6	0.91	15.78	6	3	96	0	1	100	N/A	N/A	80	4	2,500,000	0	0.0	0.0
C+ / 6.1	11.7	0.92	15.69	1	3	96	0	1	100	N/A	N/A	76	4	0	0	0.0	0.0
C+ / 6.1	11.6	0.91	15.78	N/A	3	96	0	1	100	N/A	N/A	80	4	0	0	0.0	0.0
C+ / 6.1	11.6	0.91	15.81	N/A	3	96	0	1	100	N/A	N/A	81	4	0	0	0.0	0.0
C / 4.9	13.2	1.14	47.78	350	0	98	1	1	34	123.8	-24.1	17	19	1,000	0	4.8	0.0
C / 4.6	13.2	1.14	38.87	123	0	98	1	1	34	115.5	-24.3	12	19	1,000	0	0.0	0.0
C / 5.0	13.2	1.14	50.11	486	0	98	1	1	34	128.0	-23.9	20	19	2,500,000	0	0.0	0.0
C / 4.8	13.2	1.14	46.57	24	0	98	1	1	34	120.6	-24.1	15	19	0	0	0.0	0.0
C / 5.0	13.2	1.14	49.99	172	0	98	1	1	34	127.6	-23.9	20	19	0	0	0.0	0.0
C / 5.0	13.2	1.14	50.36	433	0	98	1	1	34	129.2	N/A	21	19	0	0	0.0	0.0
C / 4.3	11.3	0.89	26.29	122	1	96	2	1	44	92.8	-23.0	42	5	1,000	0	4.8	0.0
C- / 3.5	11.3	0.89	19.56	91	1	96	2	1	44	85.2	-23.2	32	5	1,000	0	0.0	0.0
C / 4.4	11.3	0.89	27.73	52	1	96	2	1	44	95.9	-22.9	46	5	2,500,000	0	0.0	0.0
C- / 4.2	11.3	0.89	25.27	2	1	96	2	1	44	89.6	-23.0	37	5	0	0	0.0	0.0
C / 4.4	11.3	0.89	27.90	N/A	1	96	2	1	44	96.5	-22.9	46	5	0	0	0.0	0.0
C / 4.4	11.3	0.89	28.00	1	1	96	2	1	44	96.9	N/A	48	5	0	0	0.0	0.0
D- / 1.5	26.5	1.11	8.58	67	45	54	0	1	30	N/A	N/A	51	5	2,500	100	5.8	0.0
D- / 1.5	26.6	1.12	8.55	32	45	54	0	1	30	N/A	N/A	40	5	2,500	100	0.0	0.0
D- / 1.5	26.6	1.12	8.59	764	45	54	0	1	30	N/A	N/A	55	5	100,000	100	0.0	0.0
C- / 3.5	15.9	0.94	56.84	886	0	99	0	1	32	112.5	-21.9	72	24	1,000	0	4.8	0.0
D+ / 2.9	16.0	0.94	43.54	182	0	99	0	1	32	104.6	-22.1	64	24	1,000	0	0.0	0.0
C- / 3.5	15.9	0.94	59.31	1,423	0	99	0	1	32	115.6	-21.7	75	24	2,500,000	0	0.0	0.0
C- / 3.4	15.9	0.94	55.30	100	0	99	0	1	32	109.5	-21.8	70	24	0	0	0.0	0.0
C- / 3.5	15.9	0.94	59.56	444	0	99	0	1	32	116.4	-21.7	75	24	0	0	0.0	0.0
C- / 3.6	15.9	0.94	59.94	1,628	0	99	0	1	32	117.7	N/A	76	24	0	0	0.0	0.0
E / 0.4	12.9	0.79	13.50	17	0	96	2	2	46	103.9	-21.7	71	3	1,000	0	4.8	0.0
E / 0.4	12.9	0.79	11.85	19	0	96	2	2	46	96.1	-22.0	62	3	1,000	0	0.0	0.0
E / 0.4	12.9	0.79	14.51	9	0	96	2	2	46	110.2	-21.5	77	3	2,500,000	0	0.0	0.0
E / 0.4	12.9	0.79	13.02	1	0	96	2	2	46	100.9	-21.8	68	3	0	0	0.0	0.0
E / 0.4	12.9	0.79	14.33	N/A	0	96	2	2	46	109.1	-21.6	76	3	0	0	0.0	0.0
E / 0.4	12.9	0.79	14.40	3	0	96	2	2	46	109.8	N/A	76	3	0	0	0.0	0.0
B+ / 9.0	3.5	0.24	8.63	13	24	31	44	1	149	11.9	-11.4	38	8	2,500	500	5.5	2.0
B+ / 9.0	3.4	0.23	8.41	1	24	31	44	1	149	7.6	-11.7	30	8	2,500	500	0.0	2.0
C- / 3.8	11.1	1.02	11.76	50	2	97	0	1	39	86.6	-18.2	21	15	1,000	0	5.8	0.0
C- / 3.7	11.1	1.02	11.36	2	2	97	0	1	39	79.1	-18.4	15	15	1,000	0	0.0	0.0
C- / 3.4	11.1	1.02	10.81	9	2	97	0	1	39	89.1	-18.2	23	15	250,000	0	0.0	0.0
B- / 7.2	10.2	0.92	18.89	103	5	94	0	1	16	N/A	N/A	72	5	1,000	0	5.8	0.0
B- / 7.1	10.3	0.93	18.32	22	5	94	0	1	16	N/A	N/A	62	5	1,000	0	0.0	0.0
B- / 7.2	10.3	0.93	19.09	205	5	94	0	1	16	N/A	N/A	74	5	250,000	0	0.0	0.0
C+ / 6.0	11.7	0.66	26.70	1,843	4	95	0	1	17	142.5	-19.2	96	15	1,000	0	5.8	0.0
C+ / 5.9	11.7	0.66	25.06	237	4	95	0	1	17	132.8	-19.4	95	15	1,000	0	0.0	0.0
C+ / 6.1	11.7	0.66	29.26	5,376	4	95	0	1	17	145.8	-19.0	97	15	250,000	0	0.0	0.0
C+ / 5.9	11.7	0.66	26.15	388	4	95	0	1	17	139.3	-19.2	96	15	1,000	0	0.0	0.0
C+ / 6.4	11.7	0.66	29.35	1,121	4	95	0	1	17	146.5	-19.0	97	15	1,000,000	0	0.0	0.0

| | | | Overall | | PERFORMANCE | Total Return % through 2/28/17 | | | Annualized | | Incl. in Returns | |
| | | | | | Perfor- | | | | | | Dividend | Expense |
Fund Type	Fund Name	Ticker Symbol	Investment Rating	Phone	mance Rating/Pts	3 Mo	6 Mo	1Yr / Pct	3Yr / Pct	5Yr / Pct	Yield	Ratio
BA	Eaton Vance Balanced A	EVIFX	C	(800) 262-1122	C- / 3.2	4.56	2.94	11.21 /15	6.00 /64	9.05 /51	1.33	1.02
BA	● Eaton Vance Balanced B	EMIFX	C	(800) 262-1122	C- / 3.7	4.46	2.63	10.43 /13	5.25 /57	8.23 /44	0.63	1.77
BA	Eaton Vance Balanced C	ECIFX	C	(800) 262-1122	C- / 3.7	4.47	2.68	10.42 /13	5.25 /57	8.24 /44	0.76	1.77
BA	Eaton Vance Balanced I	EIIFX	C+	(800) 262-1122	C / 4.5	4.75	3.08	11.47 /16	6.29 /67	9.30 /53	1.64	0.77
BA	Eaton Vance Balanced R	ERIFX	C	(800) 262-1122	C- / 4.2	4.63	2.93	11.40 /16	5.88 /63	8.87 /50	1.34	N/A
BA	Eaton Vance Balanced R6	ESIFX	C+	(800) 262-1122	C / 4.7	4.64	3.11	11.91 /18	6.43 /68	9.39 /54	1.68	N/A
OT	Eaton Vance Commodity Strategy A	EACSX	E	(800) 262-1122	E- / 0.0	3.89	7.26	21.03 /57	-12.00 /0	-9.76 /1	2.63	1.85
OT	Eaton Vance Commodity Strategy C	ECCSX	E	(800) 262-1122	E- / 0.1	3.68	6.95	20.20 /53	-12.64 /0	-10.42 /1	0.96	2.60
OT	Eaton Vance Commodity Strategy I	EICSX	E	(800) 262-1122	E- / 0.1	3.94	7.31	21.32 /59	-11.76 /1	-9.54 /1	3.42	1.58
UT	Eaton Vance Dividend Builder Fd A	EVTMX	C+	(800) 262-1122	C+ / 6.4	6.51	5.79	17.91 /42	9.05 /87	11.36 /69	1.72	1.04
UT	Eaton Vance Dividend Builder Fd C	ECTMX	C+	(800) 262-1122	C+ / 6.8	6.29	5.36	16.94 /38	8.22 /81	10.52 /62	1.11	1.79
UT	Eaton Vance Dividend Builder Fd I	EIUTX	B+	(800) 262-1122	B / 7.6	6.59	5.93	18.22 /44	9.33 /89	11.63 /71	2.05	0.79
FO	Eaton Vance Focused Growth Oppty	EAFGX	B	(800) 262-1122	B- / 7.5	8.04	7.32	23.60 /68	9.40 /90	13.80 /92	0.00	1.20
FO	Eaton Vance Focused Growth Oppty	ECFGX	B	(800) 262-1122	B / 7.9	7.80	6.91	22.62 /65	8.56 /83	12.94 /83	0.00	1.95
FO	Eaton Vance Focused Growth Oppty I	EIFGX	B+	(800) 262-1122	B+ / 8.7	8.07	7.48	23.94 /70	9.67 /91	14.09 /94	0.00	0.95
FO	Eaton Vance Focused Value Oppty A	EAFVX	C+	(800) 262-1122	C+ / 5.8	7.98	8.21	19.67 /50	6.74 /70	11.96 /74	1.09	1.30
FO	Eaton Vance Focused Value Oppty C	ECFVX	C+	(800) 262-1122	C+ / 6.3	7.79	7.79	18.69 /46	5.97 /64	11.13 /67	0.82	2.05
FO	Eaton Vance Focused Value Oppty I	EIFVX	B	(800) 262-1122	B- / 7.0	8.10	8.41	19.93 /52	7.03 /72	12.26 /77	1.40	1.05
GL	Eaton Vance Glb Mac Abs Ret Adv A	EGRAX	C-	(800) 262-1122	D+ / 2.3	1.76	0.96	7.66 /7	5.66 /61	3.39 /12	1.39	1.60
GL	Eaton Vance Glb Mac Abs Ret Adv C	EGRCX	C-	(800) 262-1122	D+ / 2.6	1.65	0.63	6.88 /6	4.95 /53	2.67 /10	0.83	2.30
GL	Eaton Vance Glb Mac Abs Ret Adv I	EGRIX	C	(800) 262-1122	C- / 3.4	1.88	1.18	8.05 /7	6.02 /64	3.70 /14	1.77	1.30
GL	Eaton Vance Glb Mac Abs Ret Adv R	EGRRX	C-	(800) 262-1122	C- / 3.0	1.73	0.82	7.35 /6	5.46 /59	3.18 /11	1.32	1.79
IN	Eaton Vance Global Income Builder A	EDIAX	C-	(800) 262-1122	D+ / 2.7	5.85	4.07	13.68 /24	4.04 /43	7.91 /41	3.61	1.25
IN	Eaton Vance Global Income Builder C	EDICX	C-	(800) 262-1122	C- / 3.2	5.71	3.72	12.83 /21	3.26 /34	7.10 /35	3.14	2.00
IN	Eaton Vance Global Income Builder I	EDIIX	C	(800) 262-1122	C- / 4.0	5.92	4.21	14.01 /25	4.30 /46	8.20 /44	4.10	1.01
IN	Eaton Vance Global Income Builder R	EDIRX	C	(800) 262-1122	C- / 3.5	5.79	3.93	13.41 /23	3.75 /40	7.64 /39	3.57	1.50
GL	Eaton Vance Global Macro Cap Opps	EACOX	D	(800) 262-1122	D- / 1.1	6.73	5.87	23.45 /68	-0.96 /9	--	0.30	1.81
GL	Eaton Vance Global Macro Cap Opps	EICOX	D+	(800) 262-1122	D / 1.7	6.86	6.01	23.72 /69	-0.75 /10	--	0.55	1.56
SC	Eaton Vance Global Small Cap A	EAVSX	E+	(800) 262-1122	C- / 3.3	7.29	9.65	21.75 /61	2.02 /24	8.12 /43	0.97	1.77
SC	Eaton Vance Global Small Cap C	ECVSX	E+	(800) 262-1122	C- / 3.8	7.09	9.16	20.83 /57	1.25 /20	7.31 /37	0.45	2.52
SC	Eaton Vance Global Small Cap I	EIVSX	D-	(800) 262-1122	C / 4.7	7.29	9.76	22.20 /63	2.27 /26	8.38 /45	1.25	1.52
FO	Eaton Vance Greater China Gr A	EVCGX	D-	(800) 262-1122	D+ / 2.3	3.64	2.12	24.47 /72	1.72 /22	5.07 /22	0.82	1.96
FO	● Eaton Vance Greater China Gr B	EMCGX	D-	(800) 262-1122	D+ / 2.8	3.49	1.79	23.64 /69	1.02 /18	4.33 /17	0.70	2.66
FO	Eaton Vance Greater China Gr C	ECCGX	D-	(800) 262-1122	D+ / 2.8	3.51	1.75	23.60 /68	1.01 /18	4.34 /17	0.71	2.66
FO	Eaton Vance Greater China Gr I	EICGX	D	(800) 262-1122	C- / 3.6	3.77	2.25	24.90 /73	2.04 /24	5.37 /24	0.95	1.66
EM	Eaton Vance Greater India A	ETGIX	B+	(800) 262-1122	A+ / 9.7	10.20	-1.98	34.49 /93	14.73 /99	7.07 /35	0.47	1.65
EM	● Eaton Vance Greater India B	EMGIX	B+	(800) 262-1122	A+ / 9.8	10.03	-2.34	33.51 /92	13.93 /99	6.31 /30	0.00	2.35
EM	Eaton Vance Greater India C	ECGIX	B+	(800) 262-1122	A+ / 9.8	10.01	-2.34	33.51 /92	13.92 /99	6.31 /30	0.00	2.35
EM	Eaton Vance Greater India I	EGIIX	B+	(800) 262-1122	A+ / 9.8	10.28	-1.85	34.88 /94	15.07 /99	7.39 /37	0.78	1.35
GR	Eaton Vance Growth A	EALCX	B-	(800) 262-1122	B- / 7.5	8.34	7.09	22.12 /63	9.72 /92	13.24 /86	0.33	1.12
GR	Eaton Vance Growth C	ECLCX	B	(800) 262-1122	B / 8.0	8.19	6.76	21.22 /58	8.90 /86	12.39 /78	0.00	1.87
GR	Eaton Vance Growth I	ELCIX	B+	(800) 262-1122	B+ / 8.7	8.45	7.23	22.39 /64	9.99 /93	13.52 /89	0.54	0.87
GR	Eaton Vance Growth R	ELCRX	B	(800) 262-1122	B+ / 8.3	8.27	7.00	21.80 /61	9.44 /90	12.95 /83	0.02	1.37
IN	Eaton Vance Hedged Stock A	EROAX	D+	(800) 262-1122	D- / 1.2	3.00	1.28	6.36 /5	2.52 /28	3.80 /14	0.74	1.79
IN	Eaton Vance Hedged Stock C	EROCX	C-	(800) 262-1122	D- / 1.5	2.84	0.85	5.58 /4	1.76 /22	3.43 /13	0.00	2.54
IN	Eaton Vance Hedged Stock I	EROIX	C-	(800) 262-1122	D / 1.9	3.15	1.43	6.76 /5	2.84 /30	3.93 /15	1.05	1.54
EM	Eaton Vance Hexavest EM Eq A	EHEAX	E	(800) 262-1122	E+ / 0.6	7.87	3.01	20.90 /57	-2.46 /6	--	2.11	4.38
EM	Eaton Vance Hexavest EM Eq I	EHEIX	E+	(800) 262-1122	D- / 1.0	7.93	3.10	21.16 /58	-2.24 /6	--	2.44	4.13
GL	Eaton Vance Hexavest Global Eq A	EHGAX	C+	(800) 262-1122	C / 4.6	6.25	4.76	17.64 /41	6.32 /67	--	0.43	1.45
GL	Eaton Vance Hexavest Global Eq C	EHGCX	C+	(800) 262-1122	C / 5.1	6.11	4.43	16.82 /38	5.54 /60	--	0.65	2.20
GL	Eaton Vance Hexavest Global Eq I	EHGIX	C+	(800) 262-1122	C+ / 6.1	6.36	4.96	18.05 /43	6.60 /69	--	0.65	1.20
FO	Eaton Vance Hexavest Intl Eq A	EHIAX	D-	(800) 262-1122	E+ / 0.6	6.08	1.50	12.01 /18	-0.57 /11	--	1.64	3.16

● Denotes fund is closed to new investors
* Denotes fund is included in Section II

Risk Rating/Pts	3 Year Standard Deviation	Beta	NAV As of 2/28/17	Total $(Mil)	Cash %	Stocks %	Bonds %	Other %	Portfolio Turnover Ratio	Last Bull Market Return	Last Bear Market Return	Manager Quality Pct	Manager Tenure (Years)	Initial Purch. $	Additional Purch. $	Front End Load	Back End Load
B- /7.6	6.3	0.98	8.69	377	0	60	38	2	2	75.1	-10.6	59	10	1,000	0	5.8	0.0
B- /7.6	6.3	0.98	8.70	5	0	60	38	2	2	68.3	-11.0	48	10	1,000	0	0.0	0.0
B- /7.6	6.3	0.98	8.72	263	0	60	38	2	2	68.3	-10.9	48	10	1,000	0	0.0	0.0
B- /7.6	6.3	0.99	8.70	215	0	60	38	2	2	77.1	-10.6	62	10	250,000	0	0.0	0.0
C+ /6.5	6.3	0.98	8.68	N/A	0	60	38	2	2	73.5	-10.7	57	10	1,000	0	0.0	0.0
C+ /6.9	6.3	0.98	8.70	2	0	60	38	2	2	77.8	-10.6	63	10	1,000,000	0	0.0	0.0
C- /3.8	13.6	0.29	5.52	8	12	3	84	1	15	-36.7	-20.2	0	2	1,000	0	4.8	0.0
C- /3.8	13.6	0.29	5.38	3	12	3	84	1	15	-39.2	-20.5	0	2	1,000	0	0.0	0.0
C- /3.8	13.5	0.29	5.52	23	12	3	84	1	15	-35.9	-20.1	0	2	250,000	0	0.0	0.0
C+ /6.5	9.4	0.15	13.99	692	1	98	0	1	99	104.5	-14.6	97	10	1,000	0	5.8	0.0
C+ /6.5	9.4	0.15	14.05	165	1	98	0	1	99	96.3	-14.9	97	10	1,000	0	0.0	0.0
C+ /6.5	9.4	0.15	13.98	119	1	98	0	1	99	107.5	-14.6	98	10	250,000	0	0.0	0.0
C+ /5.7	12.5	0.82	17.60	39	1	98	0	1	87	132.2	-20.7	99	6	1,000	0	5.8	0.0
C+ /5.7	12.5	0.82	16.86	15	1	98	0	1	87	122.8	-21.0	99	6	1,000	0	0.0	0.0
C+ /5.7	12.5	0.82	17.81	145	1	98	0	1	87	135.4	-20.6	99	6	250,000	0	0.0	0.0
C+ /6.6	9.7	0.64	14.98	4	1	98	0	1	90	113.3	-19.9	97	6	1,000	0	5.8	0.0
C+ /6.6	9.6	0.64	14.78	1	1	98	0	1	90	104.8	-20.1	97	6	1,000	0	0.0	0.0
C+ /6.6	9.7	0.64	15.01	62	1	98	0	1	90	116.5	-19.9	98	6	250,000	0	0.0	0.0
B- /7.2	3.8	0.18	10.07	306	16	2	80	2	97	24.3	-4.2	96	7	1,000	0	4.8	0.0
B- /7.3	3.8	0.18	9.90	50	16	2	80	2	97	19.8	-4.5	95	7	1,000	0	0.0	0.0
B- /7.2	3.8	0.18	10.17	1,565	16	2	80	2	97	26.5	-4.1	97	7	250,000	0	0.0	0.0
B- /7.2	3.8	0.18	9.97	3	16	2	80	2	97	23.0	-4.3	96	7	1,000	0	0.0	0.0
C+ /6.9	8.6	0.77	8.47	167	1	93	5	1	72	71.2	-18.8	25	5	1,000	0	5.8	0.0
C+ /6.9	8.5	0.77	8.39	121	1	93	5	1	72	64.6	-19.1	18	5	1,000	0	0.0	0.0
B- /7.0	8.6	0.77	8.46	71	1	93	5	1	72	73.7	-18.7	28	5	250,000	0	0.0	0.0
C+ /6.9	8.6	0.77	8.45	1	1	93	5	1	72	69.0	-18.9	22	5	1,000	0	0.0	0.0
C+ /6.9	12.0	0.76	9.19	19	3	95	0	2	40	N/A	N/A	64	3	1,000	0	5.8	0.0
C+ /6.9	12.0	0.76	9.20	109	3	95	0	2	40	N/A	N/A	66	3	250,000	0	0.0	0.0
D+ /2.3	11.5	0.67	13.31	12	0	99	0	1	150	81.0	-23.0	40	4	1,000	0	5.8	0.0
D /1.8	11.5	0.67	11.81	6	0	99	0	1	150	73.8	-23.2	31	4	1,000	0	0.0	0.0
D+ /2.4	11.5	0.67	13.63	2	0	99	0	1	150	83.5	-22.9	44	4	250,000	0	0.0	0.0
C /4.4	16.7	0.92	20.62	64	3	96	0	1	78	56.2	-28.3	85	2	1,000	0	5.8	0.0
C /4.3	16.7	0.91	19.66	1	3	96	0	1	78	50.5	-28.5	82	2	1,000	0	0.0	0.0
C /4.3	16.6	0.92	19.59	13	3	96	0	1	78	50.5	-28.5	82	2	1,000	0	0.0	0.0
C /4.4	16.7	0.92	20.76	6	3	96	0	1	78	58.8	-28.2	87	2	250,000	0	0.0	0.0
C /4.3	18.6	0.65	29.54	168	1	98	0	1	30	51.0	-23.3	99	1	1,000	0	5.8	0.0
C- /4.2	18.6	0.65	25.90	3	1	98	0	1	30	45.3	-23.5	99	1	1,000	0	0.0	0.0
C- /4.2	18.6	0.65	25.82	25	1	98	0	1	30	45.3	-23.6	99	1	1,000	0	0.0	0.0
C /4.3	18.6	0.64	30.08	30	1	98	0	1	30	53.4	-23.2	99	1	250,000	0	0.0	0.0
C /5.4	12.0	1.07	24.16	202	4	95	0	1	55	124.4	-17.8	55	15	1,000	0	5.8	0.0
C /5.1	12.0	1.07	21.01	43	4	95	0	1	55	115.5	-18.0	44	15	1,000	0	0.0	0.0
C /5.4	11.9	1.07	24.77	61	4	95	0	1	55	127.5	-17.7	58	15	250,000	0	0.0	0.0
C /5.3	12.0	1.07	23.70	4	4	95	0	1	55	121.3	-17.8	51	15	1,000	0	0.0	0.0
B- /7.8	6.0	0.53	8.41	18	0	99	0	1	118	27.4	-7.5	35	9	1,000	0	5.8	0.0
B- /7.8	5.9	0.53	8.32	7	0	99	0	1	118	24.8	-7.8	27	9	1,000	0	0.0	0.0
B- /7.8	6.0	0.53	8.44	19	0	99	0	1	118	28.3	-7.4	39	9	250,000	0	0.0	0.0
C- /4.2	14.2	0.86	8.70	N/A	5	94	0	1	39	N/A	N/A	24	5	1,000	0	5.8	0.0
C- /4.2	14.2	0.86	8.76	5	5	94	0	1	39	N/A	N/A	26	5	250,000	0	0.0	0.0
B- /7.0	8.2	0.56	12.28	13	14	85	0	1	83	N/A	N/A	97	5	1,000	0	5.8	0.0
C+ /6.5	8.2	0.56	12.24	2	14	85	0	1	83	N/A	N/A	96	5	1,000	0	0.0	0.0
C+ /6.9	8.2	0.56	12.30	80	14	85	0	1	83	N/A	N/A	97	5	250,000	0	0.0	0.0
C+ /6.3	9.4	0.74	10.63	1	11	88	0	1	88	N/A	N/A	69	5	1,000	0	5.8	0.0

99 Pct = Best
0 Pct = Worst

Fund Type	Fund Name	Ticker Symbol	Overall Investment Rating	Phone	Performance Rating/Pts	3 Mo	6 Mo	1Yr / Pct	3Yr / Pct	5Yr / Pct	Dividend Yield	Expense Ratio
FO	Eaton Vance Hexavest Intl Eq I	EHIIX	D	(800) 262-1122	D- / 1.1	6.19	1.72	12.33 /19	-0.33 /12	--	1.95	2.91
GI	Eaton Vance Large-Cap Value A	EHSTX	D	(800) 262-1122	C+ / 6.2	7.45	9.14	20.92 /57	7.17 /73	11.71 /72	1.21	1.05
GI	Eaton Vance Large-Cap Value C	ECSTX	D+	(800) 262-1122	C+ / 6.7	7.24	8.78	20.03 /52	6.37 /67	10.87 /65	0.60	1.80
GI	Eaton Vance Large-Cap Value I	EILVX	C-	(800) 262-1122	B- / 7.4	7.54	9.30	21.27 /59	7.44 /75	11.99 /74	1.51	0.80
GI	Eaton Vance Large-Cap Value R	ERSTX	D+	(800) 262-1122	B- / 7.0	7.40	9.03	20.69 /56	6.91 /71	11.43 /69	1.06	1.30
GI	Eaton Vance Large-Cap Value R6	ERLVX	B+	(800) 262-1122	B- / 7.4	7.50	9.35	21.37 /59	7.48 /75	11.91 /73	1.59	0.71
AA	Eaton Vance Multi-Strat All Mkt A	EAAMX	C-	(800) 262-1122	D / 2.2	4.16	2.39	11.08 /15	3.72 /39	3.38 /12	2.68	1.61
AA	Eaton Vance Multi-Strat All Mkt C	ECAMX	C-	(800) 262-1122	D+ / 2.4	3.88	1.93	10.23 /12	2.96 /31	2.60 /10	2.13	2.36
AA	Eaton Vance Multi-Strat All Mkt I	EIAMX	C	(800) 262-1122	C- / 3.1	4.13	2.42	11.25 /15	3.99 /43	3.61 /13	3.06	1.36
RE	Eaton Vance Real Estate Fund A	EAREX	C+	(800) 262-1122	C+ / 6.2	7.29	-1.35	12.19 /19	11.14 /97	10.60 /63	2.64	1.55
RE	Eaton Vance Real Estate Fund I	EIREX	B-	(800) 262-1122	B- / 7.4	7.35	-1.23	12.46 /20	11.41 /98	10.86 /65	3.04	1.30
AA	Eaton Vance Richard B A Asst Str A	EARAX	C	(800) 262-1122	D+ / 2.6	5.50	4.86	14.89 /29	3.49 /37	6.02 /28	0.43	1.38
AA	Eaton Vance Richard B A Asst Str C	ECRAX	C	(800) 262-1122	C- / 3.1	5.26	4.44	14.04 /26	2.70 /29	5.24 /23	0.00	2.13
AA	Eaton Vance Richard B A Asst Str I	EIRAX	C+	(800) 262-1122	C- / 3.8	5.59	4.95	15.22 /31	3.73 /40	6.30 /30	0.70	1.13
IN	Eaton Vance Richard Bern Eq St A	ERBAX	C+	(800) 262-1122	C / 4.9	7.00	9.24	22.10 /63	4.79 /52	10.02 /58	0.70	1.25
IN	Eaton Vance Richard Bern Eq St C	ERBCX	C+	(800) 262-1122	C / 5.4	6.81	8.86	21.22 /58	4.00 /43	9.21 /52	0.01	2.00
IN	Eaton Vance Richard Bern Eq St I	ERBIX	C+	(800) 262-1122	C+ / 6.3	7.07	9.38	22.41 /64	5.04 /55	10.30 /61	1.00	1.00
GL	Eaton Vance Small Cap A	ETEGX	C-	(800) 262-1122	B- / 7.5	5.54	12.87	30.17 /87	7.38 /75	11.68 /71	0.00	1.43
GL	● Eaton Vance Small Cap B	EBSMX	C-	(800) 262-1122	B / 7.9	5.39	12.54	29.25 /85	6.58 /69	10.86 /65	0.00	2.18
GL	Eaton Vance Small Cap C	ECSMX	C-	(800) 262-1122	B / 7.9	5.46	12.55	29.19 /84	6.58 /69	10.87 /65	0.00	2.18
GL	Eaton Vance Small Cap Inst	EISGX	C	(800) 262-1122	B+ / 8.7	5.69	13.04	30.56 /87	7.65 /75	11.97 /74	0.00	1.18
GL	Eaton Vance Small Cap R	ERSGX	C-	(800) 262-1122	B+ / 8.3	5.55	12.74	29.84 /86	7.12 /73	11.42 /69	0.00	1.68
SC	Eaton Vance Special Eq A	EVSEX	C-	(800) 262-1122	C+ / 6.0	6.28	10.57	25.51 /75	5.72 /62	9.68 /56	0.00	1.32
SC	Eaton Vance Special Eq C	ECSEX	C-	(800) 262-1122	C+ / 6.5	6.13	10.20	24.57 /72	4.93 /53	8.86 /49	0.00	2.06
SC	Eaton Vance Special Eq I	EISEX	C	(800) 262-1122	B- / 7.2	6.37	10.70	25.81 /76	5.99 /64	9.96 /58	0.00	1.07
GR	Eaton Vance Stock A	EAERX	C+	(800) 262-1122	C+ / 6.4	6.85	6.58	18.52 /45	8.65 /84	12.88 /83	0.79	1.14
GR	Eaton Vance Stock C	ECERX	C+	(800) 262-1122	C+ / 6.8	6.66	6.18	17.59 /41	7.84 /78	12.03 /75	0.21	1.89
GR	Eaton Vance Stock I	EIERX	B	(800) 262-1122	B / 7.6	6.89	6.69	18.80 /46	8.93 /86	13.16 /85	1.07	0.89
SC	Eaton Vance Tax Mgd Glbl Sm Cap A	ESVAX	E	(800) 262-1122	C- / 3.5	7.30	9.58	21.44 /59	2.55 /28	9.27 /53	0.00	1.76
SC	Eaton Vance Tax Mgd Glbl Sm Cap C	ESVCX	E	(800) 262-1122	C- / 4.1	7.17	9.21	20.60 /55	1.78 /23	8.46 /46	0.00	2.51
SC	Eaton Vance Tax Mgd Glbl Sm Cap I	ESVIX	E+	(800) 262-1122	C / 4.9	7.33	9.73	21.80 /61	2.81 /30	9.55 /55	0.00	1.51
SC	Eaton Vance Tax Mgd SmCap A	ETMGX	C+	(800) 262-1122	B- / 7.2	5.49	12.21	29.91 /86	6.98 /72	11.46 /70	0.00	1.19
SC	● Eaton Vance Tax Mgd SmCap B	EMMGX	C+	(800) 262-1122	B / 7.6	5.30	11.77	28.95 /84	6.16 /66	10.63 /63	0.00	1.94
SC	Eaton Vance Tax Mgd SmCap C	ECMGX	C+	(800) 262-1122	B / 7.6	5.32	11.78	28.97 /84	6.17 /66	10.63 /63	0.00	1.94
SC	Eaton Vance Tax Mgd SmCap I	EIMGX	B	(800) 262-1122	B+ / 8.4	5.59	12.36	30.26 /87	7.23 /73	11.74 /72	0.00	0.94
AA	Eaton Vance Tax-Mgd Eqty A-Alloc A	EAEAX	C+	(800) 262-1122	C / 5.5	6.89	7.70	20.49 /55	6.40 /67	10.75 /64	0.83	1.91
AA	● Eaton Vance Tax-Mgd Eqty A-Alloc B	EBEAX	C+	(800) 262-1122	C+ / 6.0	6.75	7.34	19.60 /50	5.62 /61	9.92 /58	0.00	2.66
AA	Eaton Vance Tax-Mgd Eqty A-Alloc C	ECEAX	C+	(800) 262-1122	C+ / 6.0	6.73	7.26	19.64 /50	5.61 /61	9.91 /58	0.26	2.66
GR	Eaton Vance Tax-Mgd Eqty A-Alloc I	EIEAX	C+	(800) 262-1122	C+ / 6.7	6.98	7.80	20.84 /57	6.51 /69	10.82 /64	1.12	1.64
IN	Eaton Vance Tax-Mgd Gl Div Inc A	EADIX	C-	(800) 262-1122	D+ / 2.9	6.91	5.44	15.07 /30	3.61 /38	7.79 /41	3.54	1.18
IN	● Eaton Vance Tax-Mgd Gl Div Inc B	EBDIX	C-	(800) 262-1122	C- / 3.3	6.72	4.95	14.12 /26	2.83 /30	7.00 /35	3.02	1.93
IN	Eaton Vance Tax-Mgd Gl Div Inc C	ECDIX	C-	(800) 262-1122	C- / 3.4	6.73	5.05	14.13 /26	2.84 /30	6.98 /34	3.03	1.93
IN	Eaton Vance Tax-Mgd Gl Div Inc I	EIDIX	C	(800) 262-1122	C- / 4.2	6.97	5.58	15.35 /31	3.86 /41	8.08 /43	3.99	0.93
IN	● Eaton Vance Tax-Mgd Growth 1.0	CAPEX	A+	(800) 262-1122	B+ / 8.8	7.51	9.29	22.97 /66	9.88 /93	13.25 /86	1.33	0.45
GR	● Eaton Vance Tax-Mgd Growth 1.1 A	ETTGX	A-	(800) 262-1122	B / 7.6	7.42	9.13	22.61 /65	9.53 /91	12.89 /83	0.95	0.82
GR	● Eaton Vance Tax-Mgd Growth 1.1 B	EMTGX	A	(800) 262-1122	B / 8.0	7.23	8.74	21.72 /61	8.71 /85	12.05 /75	0.13	1.57
GR	● Eaton Vance Tax-Mgd Growth 1.1 C	ECTGX	A	(800) 262-1122	B / 8.0	7.24	8.74	21.70 /61	8.71 /85	12.05 /75	0.46	1.57
GR	● Eaton Vance Tax-Mgd Growth 1.1 I	EITMX	A+	(800) 262-1122	B+ / 8.8	7.47	9.25	22.91 /66	9.80 /92	13.18 /86	1.32	0.56
GR	Eaton Vance Tax-Mgd Growth 1.2 A	EXTGX	B+	(800) 262-1122	B- / 7.4	7.36	9.04	22.40 /64	9.34 /89	12.72 /81	0.81	0.97
GR	● Eaton Vance Tax-Mgd Growth 1.2 B	EYTGX	A-	(800) 262-1122	B / 7.9	7.21	8.67	21.52 /60	8.55 /83	11.87 /73	0.00	1.72
GR	Eaton Vance Tax-Mgd Growth 1.2 C	EZTGX	A-	(800) 262-1122	B / 7.9	7.24	8.66	21.54 /60	8.54 /83	11.87 /73	0.21	1.72
GR	Eaton Vance Tax-Mgd Growth 1.2 I	EITGX	A+	(800) 262-1122	B+ / 8.7	7.42	9.20	22.76 /66	9.65 /91	12.98 /83	1.08	0.72

● Denotes fund is closed to new investors
* Denotes fund is included in Section II

www.thestreetratings.com

RISK Risk Rating/Pts	3 Year Standard Deviation	Beta	NET ASSETS NAV As of 2/28/17	Total $(Mil)	ASSET Cash %	Stocks %	Bonds %	Other %	Portfolio Turnover Ratio	BULL/BEAR Last Bull Market Return	Last Bear Market Return	FUND MANAGER Manager Quality Pct	Manager Tenure (Years)	MINIMUMS Initial Purch. $	Additional Purch. $	LOADS Front End Load	Back End Load
C+ / 6.3	9.4	0.74	10.67	6	11	88	0	1	88	N/A	N/A	71	5	250,000	0	0.0	0.0
D / 2.0	9.9	0.93	18.73	930	1	98	0	1	98	108.1	-19.0	41	8	1,000	0	5.8	0.0
D / 2.1	9.9	0.94	18.72	298	1	98	0	1	98	99.8	-19.2	31	8	1,000	0	0.0	0.0
D / 2.0	9.9	0.94	18.81	1,570	1	98	0	1	98	111.0	-18.9	44	8	250,000	0	0.0	0.0
D / 2.0	9.9	0.94	18.68	102	1	98	0	1	98	105.4	-19.1	37	8	1,000	0	0.0	0.0
B- / 7.0	9.9	0.93	18.82	38	1	98	0	1	98	110.0	-19.0	45	8	1,000,000	0	0.0	0.0
B / 8.0	4.9	0.66	10.25	30	15	28	56	1	49	N/A	N/A	60	6	1,000	0	4.8	0.0
B / 8.0	4.9	0.67	10.20	2	15	28	56	1	49	N/A	N/A	48	6	1,000	0	0.0	0.0
B / 8.0	4.9	0.66	10.24	13	15	28	56	1	49	N/A	N/A	63	6	250,000	0	0.0	0.0
C / 5.5	14.4	1.04	14.01	22	1	98	0	1	72	99.0	-15.1	70	11	1,000	0	5.8	0.0
C / 5.5	14.4	1.04	14.02	27	1	98	0	1	72	101.7	-15.0	73	11	250,000	0	0.0	0.0
B / 8.1	6.2	0.92	13.63	96	9	65	25	1	51	44.7	N/A	31	6	1,000	0	5.8	0.0
B / 8.1	6.2	0.92	13.40	130	9	65	25	1	51	38.8	N/A	23	6	1,000	0	0.0	0.0
B / 8.1	6.2	0.92	13.68	341	9	65	25	1	51	46.6	N/A	35	6	250,000	0	0.0	0.0
C+ / 6.7	9.6	0.87	15.66	162	8	91	0	1	57	82.1	-19.6	22	7	1,000	0	5.8	0.0
C+ / 6.8	9.6	0.87	15.51	182	8	91	0	1	57	74.9	-19.9	16	7	1,000	0	0.0	0.0
C+ / 6.7	9.6	0.88	15.67	522	8	91	0	1	57	84.5	-19.5	24	7	250,000	0	0.0	0.0
D / 2.1	13.3	0.54	13.09	31	0	99	0	1	71	113.0	-25.3	98	2	1,000	0	5.8	0.0
D / 1.8	13.3	0.54	12.07	1	0	99	0	1	71	104.7	-25.5	97	2	1,000	0	0.0	0.0
D / 1.6	13.3	0.54	11.34	11	0	99	0	1	71	104.6	-25.5	97	2	1,000	0	0.0	0.0
D+ / 2.4	13.3	0.54	14.23	37	0	99	0	1	71	116.0	-25.2	98	2	250,000	0	0.0	0.0
D / 2.0	13.3	0.54	12.69	1	0	99	0	1	71	110.1	-25.4	98	2	1,000	0	0.0	0.0
C- / 4.1	12.5	0.75	21.85	33	0	99	0	1	83	90.1	-21.2	78	2	1,000	0	5.8	0.0
C- / 3.9	12.5	0.75	19.76	3	0	99	0	1	83	82.6	-21.5	71	2	1,000	0	0.0	0.0
C- / 4.1	12.5	0.75	22.23	9	0	99	0	1	83	92.9	-21.2	79	2	250,000	0	0.0	0.0
C+ / 5.9	9.9	0.94	16.50	61	1	98	0	1	96	122.4	-17.9	60	10	1,000	0	5.8	0.0
C+ / 5.9	9.9	0.94	16.14	16	1	98	0	1	96	113.4	-18.0	49	10	1,000	0	0.0	0.0
C+ / 5.9	9.9	0.94	16.51	24	1	98	0	1	96	125.3	-17.7	63	10	250,000	0	0.0	0.0
D- / 1.1	12.0	0.70	12.35	14	0	99	0	1	92	91.4	-21.3	45	2	1,000	0	5.8	0.0
E+ / 0.8	12.0	0.70	9.72	5	0	99	0	1	92	83.9	-21.5	35	2	1,000	0	0.0	0.0
D- / 1.2	12.0	0.70	12.74	4	0	99	0	1	92	94.0	-21.1	49	2	250,000	0	0.0	0.0
C / 4.7	13.2	0.80	25.26	74	3	96	0	1	66	111.2	-25.1	83	2	1,000	0	5.8	0.0
C / 4.6	13.2	0.80	21.39	N/A	3	96	0	1	66	102.7	-25.4	78	2	1,000	0	0.0	0.0
C / 4.6	13.1	0.80	21.29	23	3	96	0	1	66	102.7	-25.4	79	2	1,000	0	0.0	0.0
C / 4.8	13.1	0.80	25.80	17	3	96	0	1	66	114.2	-25.1	84	2	250,000	0	0.0	0.0
C+ / 6.0	9.5	1.45	18.27	244	1	94	3	2	6	102.1	-20.2	21	4	1,000	0	5.8	0.0
C+ / 6.1	9.5	1.46	17.25	3	1	94	3	2	6	94.1	-20.5	15	4	1,000	0	0.0	0.0
C+ / 6.0	9.5	1.46	17.03	173	1	94	3	2	6	94.2	-20.5	15	4	1,000	0	0.0	0.0
C+ / 6.9	9.4	0.90	18.23	32	1	94	3	2	6	102.7	-20.2	37	4	250,000	0	0.0	0.0
C+ / 6.6	9.3	0.84	11.51	366	2	92	5	1	134	68.4	-16.7	15	7	1,000	0	5.8	0.0
C+ / 6.7	9.2	0.83	11.48	10	2	92	5	1	134	61.6	-16.9	11	7	1,000	0	0.0	0.0
C+ / 6.7	9.2	0.83	11.48	250	2	92	5	1	134	61.7	-17.0	11	7	1,000	0	0.0	0.0
C+ / 6.6	9.3	0.84	11.52	122	2	92	5	1	134	70.8	-16.6	17	7	250,000	0	0.0	0.0
B- / 7.1	10.4	1.00	1,000.22	869	2	97	0	1	9	126.2	-16.1	66	11	0	0	0.0	0.0
B- / 7.0	10.5	1.01	44.69	1,116	2	97	0	1	9	122.4	-16.2	61	11	1,000	0	5.8	0.0
B- / 7.1	10.5	1.01	43.88	3	2	97	0	1	9	113.6	-16.5	51	11	1,000	0	0.0	0.0
B- / 7.1	10.5	1.01	40.15	276	2	97	0	1	9	113.5	-16.4	51	11	1,000	0	0.0	0.0
B- / 7.0	10.4	1.00	41.78	75	2	97	0	1	9	125.5	-16.1	65	11	250,000	0	0.0	0.0
B- / 7.0	10.5	1.01	20.09	419	2	97	0	1	9	120.3	-16.2	59	11	1,000	0	5.8	0.0
B- / 7.1	10.4	1.00	19.93	3	2	97	0	1	9	111.6	-16.5	49	11	1,000	0	0.0	0.0
B- / 7.1	10.4	1.00	19.55	183	2	97	0	1	9	111.8	-16.5	49	11	1,000	0	0.0	0.0
B- / 7.0	10.5	1.01	20.14	85	2	97	0	1	9	123.4	-16.2	62	11	250,000	0	0.0	0.0

						PERFORMANCE							
	99 Pct = Best					Perfor-	Total Return % through 2/28/17					Incl. in Returns	
	0 Pct = Worst			Overall		mance				Annualized		Dividend	Expense
Fund		Ticker	Investment			Rating/Pts	3 Mo	6 Mo	1Yr / Pct	3Yr / Pct	5Yr / Pct	Yield	Ratio
Type	Fund Name	Symbol	Rating	Phone									
GR	Eaton Vance Tax-Mgd MultiCap Gr A	EACPX	C+	(800) 262-1122		C+ / 5.9	7.96	6.72	22.52 /65	6.57 /69	10.53 /62	0.00	1.40
GR	Eaton Vance Tax-Mgd MultiCap Gr C	ECCPX	C+	(800) 262-1122		C+ / 6.4	7.82	6.35	21.61 /60	5.77 /62	9.70 /56	0.00	2.15
GR	Eaton Vance Tax-Mgd Value A	EATVX	C+	(800) 262-1122		C+ / 6.0	7.31	9.23	21.02 /57	6.86 /71	11.67 /71	1.00	1.19
GR	Eaton Vance Tax-Mgd Value C	ECTVX	C+	(800) 262-1122		C+ / 6.5	7.11	8.80	20.15 /53	6.06 /65	10.83 /64	0.41	1.94
GR	Eaton Vance Tax-Mgd Value Cl I	EITVX	B-	(800) 262-1122		B- / 7.2	7.42	9.40	21.37 /59	7.10 /73	11.93 /74	1.30	0.94
HL	Eaton Vance WW Health Sciences A	ETHSX	E	(800) 262-1122		D / 1.9	10.29	0.19	6.71 / 5	4.24 /46	15.20 /97	0.00	1.34
HL	● Eaton Vance WW Health Sciences B	EMHSX	E	(800) 262-1122		D / 2.2	10.02	-0.18	5.84 / 5	3.46 /37	14.35 /95	0.00	2.10
HL	Eaton Vance WW Health Sciences C	ECHSX	E	(800) 262-1122		D / 2.2	9.90	-0.27	5.79 / 5	3.43 /36	14.32 /95	0.00	2.09
HL	Eaton Vance WW Health Sciences I	EIHSX	E+	(800) 262-1122		D+ / 2.8	10.19	0.28	6.88 / 6	4.47 /48	15.47 /98	0.00	1.09
HL	Eaton Vance WW Health Sciences R	ERHSX	E+	(800) 262-1122		D+ / 2.5	10.17	0.09	6.40 / 5	3.97 /43	14.90 /97	0.00	1.59
GR	Edgar Lomax Value Fund	LOMAX	B	(888) 263-6443		B+ / 8.9	6.19	9.63	24.68 /72	9.96 /93	12.47 /79	2.04	1.31
GR	Edgewood Growth Fund Inst	EGFIX	A-	(866) 777-7818		A+ / 9.7	11.59	10.76	26.65 /78	11.89 /98	16.13 /98	0.00	1.09
GR	Edgewood Growth Fund Retail	EGFFX	B+	(866) 777-7818		A+ / 9.7	11.50	10.54	26.17 /77	11.46 /98	15.86 /98	0.00	1.48
IN	EIC Value A	EICVX	C+	(888) 739-1390		C / 4.5	4.90	6.43	18.44 /45	6.54 /69	9.00 /51	0.70	1.28
IN	EIC Value C	EICCX	C+	(888) 739-1390		C / 4.9	4.69	6.01	17.58 /41	5.73 /62	8.20 /44	0.01	2.03
IN	EIC Value Fund Inst	EICIX	B-	(888) 739-1390		C+ / 5.9	5.02	6.55	18.71 /46	6.80 /70	9.28 /53	1.01	1.03
RE	EII Global Property Inst	EIIGX	E	(888) 323-8912		C- / 3.5	7.76	-1.55	12.58 /20	4.54 /49	6.36 /31	9.21	2.06
RE	EII International Property I	EIIPX	E-	(888) 323-8912		E / 0.4	5.25	-4.48	6.21 / 5	-1.94 / 7	3.00 /11	7.52	1.98
RE	EII Realty Sec Inst	EIIRX	C+	(888) 323-8912		B / 7.6	7.64	-1.25	16.31 /35	10.87 /97	11.41 /69	2.51	1.93
EN	EIP Growth and Income I	EIPIX	D+			D- / 1.1	3.89	4.09	16.85 /38	-0.95 /10	1.51 / 7	0.77	N/A
AA	Elfun Diversified	ELDFX	C-	(800) 843-2639		C- / 3.7	4.88	3.85	14.27 /27	4.00 /43	6.74 /33	1.90	0.43
FO	Elfun International	EGLBX	D-	(800) 843-2639		E+ / 0.9	5.72	2.69	14.08 /26	-1.58 / 8	4.26 /17	2.12	0.36
GI	Elfun Trusts	ELFNX	B+	(800) 843-2639		A- / 9.2	10.41	9.97	24.44 /71	9.83 /92	14.20 /94	1.28	0.19
FS	Emerald Banking and Finance A	HSSAX	A+	(855) 828-9909		A+ / 9.9	11.83	29.96	51.05 /99	16.40 /99	21.78 /99	0.00	1.49
FS	Emerald Banking and Finance C	HSSCX	A+	(855) 828-9909		A+ / 9.9	11.61	29.53	50.06 /99	15.65 /99	20.98 /99	0.00	2.14
FS	Emerald Banking and Finance Inst	HSSIX	A+	(855) 828-9909		A+ / 9.9	11.88	30.17	51.52 /99	16.77 /99	--	0.00	1.19
FS	Emerald Banking and Finance Inv	FFBFX	A+	(855) 828-9909		A+ / 9.9	11.80	29.92	50.96 /99	16.37 /99	21.76 /99	0.00	1.54
SC	● Emerald Growth A	HSPGX	D+	(855) 828-9909		C / 5.4	4.09	10.67	28.99 /84	4.21 /45	13.08 /85	0.00	1.16
SC	● Emerald Growth C	HSPCX	C-	(855) 828-9909		C+ / 5.9	3.96	10.33	28.19 /82	3.56 /38	12.36 /78	0.00	1.82
SC	● Emerald Growth Institutional	FGROX	C-	(855) 828-9909		C+ / 6.7	4.15	10.85	29.46 /85	4.54 /49	13.44 /88	0.00	0.86
GR	● Emerald Growth Investor	FFGRX	C-	(855) 828-9909		C+ / 6.4	4.06	10.66	28.97 /84	4.18 /45	13.04 /84	0.00	1.23
SC	Emerald Small Cap Value Inst	LSRYX	B+	(855) 828-9909		B+ / 8.9	5.60	14.65	32.67 /91	7.28 /74	--	0.00	1.77
SC	Emerald Small Cap Value Inv	LSRIX	B+	(855) 828-9909		B+ / 8.8	5.69	14.64	32.53 /91	7.09 /73	--	0.00	2.02
EM	Emerging Markets Growth	EMRGX	E+	(800) 421-0180		D / 2.0	8.06	6.85	30.01 /86	-1.08 / 9	-1.49 / 3	1.05	0.82
GL	Empiric 2500 A	EMCAX	D	(800) 880-0324		C- / 3.0	4.87	7.49	25.74 /75	1.58 /21	9.17 /52	0.00	1.82
GL	Empiric 2500 C	EMCCX	D	(800) 880-0324		C- / 3.5	4.70	7.11	24.80 /73	0.82 /17	8.35 /45	0.00	2.57
GR	Entrepreneur All Cap Institutional	IMPAX	B+	(877) 271-8811		B / 7.6	5.89	12.30	31.84 /90	5.21 /57	--	0.17	0.91
GL	EntrepreneurShares Global Inst	ENTIX	C+	(877) 271-8811		C+ / 6.7	8.87	8.43	27.74 /81	4.38 /47	8.37 /45	0.00	2.53
GR	EntrepreneurShares US Lg Cap Inst	IMPLX	U	(877) 271-8811		U /	6.06	7.58	20.92 /57	--	--	0.52	0.83
AA	EnTrustPermal Alternative Core A	LPTAX	C-	(877) 534-4627		D- / 1.4	2.12	2.49	8.49 / 8	2.68 /29	4.91 /21	0.23	2.47
AA	EnTrustPermal Alternative Core C	LPTCX	C-	(877) 534-4627		D / 1.6	1.90	2.05	7.60 / 7	1.90 /23	4.13 /16	0.25	3.19
AA	EnTrustPermal Alternative Core FI	LPTFX	C-	(877) 534-4627		D / 2.0	2.07	2.44	8.38 / 8	2.66 /29	4.90 /21	0.24	2.65
AA	EnTrustPermal Alternative Core I	LPTIX	C-	(877) 534-4627		D / 2.1	2.11	2.56	8.64 / 9	2.90 /31	5.17 /23	0.25	2.23
AA	EnTrustPermal Alternative Core IS	LPTSX	C-	(877) 534-4627		D / 2.2	2.16	2.60	8.75 / 9	2.93 /31	5.18 /23	0.24	2.33
FO	EP Emerging Markets Small Co A	EPASX	E+	(888) 558-5851		E+ / 0.8	6.28	1.03	23.79 /69	-1.10 / 9	6.12 /29	0.00	2.71
FO	EP Emerging Markets Small Co I	EPEIX	D-	(888) 558-5851		D- / 1.3	6.31	1.11	24.03 /70	-0.85 /10	--	0.00	2.46
GR	● Epiphany FFV A	EPVNX	C			C / 5.5	6.71	7.19	19.29 /48	5.55 /60	10.14 /59	0.33	1.68
AA	Epiphany FFV Strat Income A	EPIAX	C			E+ / 0.6	1.47	-0.93	2.50 / 2	1.82 /23	2.01 / 8	1.81	1.73
AA	Epiphany FFV Strat Income C	EPICX	C			E+ / 0.7	1.27	-1.41	1.68 / 2	1.11 /19	1.27 / 7	0.02	2.51
GL	Epoch Gl Eqty Shareholder Yld Adv	TDGIX	C-			C- / 3.4	7.49	3.03	12.58 /20	3.54 /37	--	2.21	4.78
GL	Epoch Gl Eqty Shareholder Yld Inst	TDGEX	C-			C- / 3.4	7.41	3.05	12.60 /20	3.54 /37	--	2.23	4.24
IN	Epoch US Eqty Shareholder Yld Adv	TDUEX	A+			B+ / 8.3	7.32	6.51	18.94 /47	10.39 /95	--	1.99	5.84

● Denotes fund is closed to new investors
* Denotes fund is included in Section II

204

www.thestreetratings.com

RISK	3 Year		NET ASSETS		ASSET					BULL / BEAR		FUND MANAGER		MINIMUMS		LOADS	
Risk Rating/Pts	Standard Deviation	Beta	NAV As of 2/28/17	Total $(Mil)	Cash %	Stocks %	Bonds %	Other %	Portfolio Turnover Ratio	Last Bull Market Return	Last Bear Market Return	Manager Quality Pct	Manager Tenure (Years)	Initial Purch. $	Additional Purch. $	Front End Load	Back End Load
C+ / 5.6	12.7	1.12	23.18	52	1	98	0	1	33	105.0	-20.7	15	4	1,000	0	5.8	0.0
C / 5.5	12.8	1.13	20.26	22	1	98	0	1	33	96.7	-20.9	10	4	1,000	0	0.0	0.0
C+ / 5.6	9.5	0.89	23.52	309	0	99	0	1	45	108.8	-18.3	43	8	1,000	0	5.8	0.0
C+ / 5.7	9.5	0.89	22.60	144	0	99	0	1	45	100.4	-18.5	33	8	1,000	0	0.0	0.0
C+ / 5.6	9.5	0.89	23.41	120	0	99	0	1	45	111.5	-18.2	47	8	250,000	0	0.0	0.0
D+ / 2.6	16.2	1.06	9.89	725	0	99	0	1	70	123.3	-9.7	7	1	1,000	0	5.8	0.0
D+ / 2.6	16.2	1.05	10.15	7	0	99	0	1	70	114.6	-10.1	5	1	1,000	0	0.0	0.0
D+ / 2.6	16.2	1.05	10.05	243	0	99	0	1	70	114.4	-10.1	5	1	1,000	0	0.0	0.0
D+ / 2.7	16.2	1.06	10.10	142	0	99	0	1	70	126.3	-9.6	8	1	250,000	0	0.0	0.0
D+ / 2.8	16.2	1.05	10.55	59	0	99	0	1	70	120.3	-9.8	6	1	1,000	0	0.0	0.0
C / 4.3	9.8	0.88	14.16	86	1	94	3	2	56	108.4	-10.3	78	20	2,500	100	0.0	0.0
C / 4.9	13.8	1.14	24.63	7,450	0	99	0	1	31	156.5	-11.9	71	11	100,000	0	0.0	0.0
C / 4.8	13.8	1.15	23.84	353	0	99	0	1	31	154.3	-12.4	66	11	3,000	0	0.0	0.0
B- / 7.2	8.4	0.77	14.34	55	13	86	0	1	34	78.4	N/A	55	6	2,500	250	5.5	2.0
B- / 7.2	8.4	0.77	14.19	48	13	86	0	1	34	71.3	N/A	44	6	2,500	250	0.0	2.0
B- / 7.1	8.4	0.78	14.37	203	13	86	0	1	34	80.8	-8.5	58	6	100,000	0	0.0	2.0
E+ / 0.9	11.8	0.80	3.76	2	12	86	1	1	135	61.5	-18.5	23	11	100,000	0	0.0	0.0
D- / 1.5	11.9	0.56	11.95	10	27	67	5	1	79	35.2	-22.3	4	3	100,000	0	0.0	0.0
C- / 4.0	14.0	1.02	4.38	19	0	96	3	1	98	109.3	-15.1	70	13	100,000	0	0.0	0.0
B- / 7.8	12.6	0.35	16.08	18	0	0	0	100	0	19.7	-6.3	80	11	1,000,000	0	0.0	0.0
C+ / 6.3	7.2	1.10	18.56	203	1	56	41	2	123	59.0	-13.8	23	N/A	500	100	0.0	0.0
C / 5.5	12.6	1.01	19.32	211	1	97	0	2	24	45.2	-25.9	57	N/A	500	100	0.0	0.0
C / 4.7	12.5	1.15	57.89	2,512	1	97	1	1	11	141.4	-17.0	46	29	500	100	0.0	0.0
C+ / 6.5	17.1	1.10	42.64	159	0	98	1	1	30	228.5	-20.2	88	20	2,000	100	4.8	0.0
C+ / 6.5	17.1	1.10	38.25	78	0	98	1	1	30	217.2	-20.3	85	20	2,000	100	0.0	0.0
C+ / 6.5	17.1	1.10	43.32	103	0	98	1	1	30	N/A	N/A	89	20	1,000,000	0	0.0	0.0
C+ / 6.5	17.1	1.10	40.82	122	0	98	1	1	30	228.9	-20.0	88	20	2,000	100	0.0	0.0
C- / 3.5	17.9	1.03	21.36	306	0	97	1	2	45	147.2	-26.9	37	25	2,000	100	4.8	0.0
C- / 3.4	17.9	1.03	18.37	37	0	97	1	2	45	138.7	-27.1	30	25	2,000	100	0.0	0.0
C- / 3.6	17.9	1.04	22.06	572	0	97	1	2	45	151.3	-26.8	41	25	1,000,000	0	0.0	0.0
C- / 3.5	17.9	1.14	21.28	116	0	97	1	2	45	146.7	N/A	5	25	2,000	100	0.0	0.0
C / 5.3	15.4	0.92	16.04	5	4	95	0	1	31	N/A	N/A	80	5	1,000,000	0	0.0	0.0
C / 5.3	15.4	0.91	15.97	1	4	95	0	1	31	N/A	N/A	79	5	2,000	100	0.0	0.0
C- / 3.3	16.2	0.98	6.58	2,740	3	94	2	1	48	11.5	-28.2	38	27	100,000	0	0.0	0.0
C / 4.6	15.3	0.89	33.17	22	0	97	1	2	171	79.7	-24.0	85	22	2,500	100	5.8	0.0
C / 4.4	15.4	0.90	30.29	1	0	97	1	2	171	72.5	-24.2	81	22	2,500	100	0.0	0.0
C+ / 6.4	14.3	1.18	11.66	157	0	0	0	100	67	N/A	N/A	6	4	2,500	0	0.0	0.0
C+ / 6.0	11.9	0.79	13.63	25	0	0	0	100	71	83.0	-24.8	94	7	2,500	0	0.0	0.0
U /	N/A	N/A	11.81	100	1	98	0	1	77	N/A	N/A	N/A	4	2,500	0	0.0	0.0
B- / 7.9	4.0	0.52	13.99	50	57	18	23	2	105	40.0	-12.4	60	N/A	1,000	50	5.8	0.0
B / 8.0	4.0	0.52	13.93	28	57	18	23	2	105	34.4	-12.6	49	N/A	1,000	50	0.0	0.0
B / 8.0	4.0	0.52	14.28	N/A	57	18	23	2	105	39.9	-12.4	60	N/A	0	0	0.0	0.0
B- / 7.9	4.0	0.52	14.01	234	57	18	23	2	105	41.7	-12.2	63	N/A	1,000,000	0	0.0	0.0
B- / 7.9	4.0	0.52	14.22	N/A	57	18	23	2	105	41.8	-12.2	63	N/A	0	0	0.0	0.0
C / 5.1	12.8	0.59	11.70	60	16	83	0	1	79	58.3	-25.1	61	N/A	2,500	250	4.5	2.0
C / 5.1	12.8	0.59	11.81	N/A	16	83	0	1	79	N/A	N/A	65	N/A	15,000	2,500	0.0	2.0
C+ / 5.6	11.2	1.03	12.15	21	3	96	0	1	63	96.1	-17.8	15	9	1,000	250	0.0	2.0
B+ / 9.9	2.1	0.19	10.40	28	8	21	70	1	52	15.7	-1.8	76	7	1,000	250	5.0	2.0
B+ / 9.9	2.1	0.20	10.45	1	8	21	70	1	52	11.2	-2.1	69	7	1,000	250	0.0	2.0
C+ / 6.4	9.4	0.61	11.17	N/A	0	0	0	100	39	N/A	N/A	92	4	0	0	0.0	0.0
C+ / 6.4	9.4	0.62	11.17	12	0	0	0	100	39	N/A	N/A	92	4	0	0	0.0	0.0
B / 8.2	8.9	0.75	13.93	1	0	0	0	100	19	N/A	N/A	88	4	0	0	0.0	0.0

Fund Type	Fund Name	Ticker Symbol	Overall Investment Rating	Phone	Performance Rating/Pts	3 Mo	6 Mo	1Yr / Pct	3Yr / Pct	5Yr / Pct	Dividend Yield	Expense Ratio
	99 Pct = Best							Total Return % through 2/28/17			Incl. in Returns	
	0 Pct = Worst								Annualized			
IN	Epoch US Eqty Shareholder Yld Inst	TDUIX	A+		B+ / 8.5	7.45	6.68	19.12 / 48	10.48 / 96	--	2.08	5.05
MC	Epoch US Sm Md Cp Equity Adv	TDUAX	A-		B+ / 8.8	7.30	12.83	32.10 / 90	7.23 / 73	--	0.52	1.37
MC	Epoch US Sm Md Cp Equity Inst	TDUSX	A-		B+ / 8.8	7.30	12.83	32.11 / 90	7.24 / 74	--	0.53	1.12
GR	Equinox BH-DG Strategy I	EBHIX	C-	(888) 643-3431	D+ / 2.3	1.97	-1.04	-5.96 / 0	6.36 / 67	--	0.00	N/A
AA	Equinox Campbell Strategy A	EBSAX	D-	(888) 643-3431	E / 0.4	1.56	-6.32	-13.44 / 0	2.82 / 30	--	0.00	1.24
AA	Equinox Campbell Strategy C	EBSCX	D	(888) 643-3431	E / 0.5	1.37	-6.61	-14.12 / 0	2.10 / 25	--	0.00	1.99
AA	Equinox Campbell Strategy I	EBSIX	D-	(888) 643-3431	E+ / 0.7	1.54	-6.18	-13.28 / 0	3.11 / 33	--	0.00	0.99
AA	Equinox Campbell Strategy P	EBSPX	D-	(888) 643-3431	E+ / 0.7	1.65	-6.18	-13.20 / 0	3.11 / 33	--	0.00	1.00
IN	Equinox Chesapeake Strat I	EQCHX	C-	(888) 643-3431	C- / 3.6	3.71	0.34	-5.40 / 0	8.30 / 81	--	0.00	1.38
IN	Equinox Crabel Strategy I	EQCRX	D+	(888) 643-3431	E / 0.3	-4.78	-8.63	-7.77 / 0	-0.33 / 12	--	5.88	5.66
GR	Equinox EquityHedge US Strategy A	EEHAX	C	(888) 643-3431	C- / 4.2	6.80	4.12	15.22 / 31	6.50 / 68	--	2.35	4.08
GR	Equinox EquityHedge US Strategy C	EEHCX	C	(888) 643-3431	C / 4.7	6.65	3.80	14.46 / 28	5.70 / 61	--	2.23	4.77
GR	Equinox EquityHedge US Strategy I	EEHIX	C+	(888) 643-3431	C+ / 5.6	6.81	4.26	15.52 / 32	6.76 / 70	--	2.72	3.77
IN	Equinox IPM Systematic Macro I	EQIPX	U	(888) 643-3431	U /	-1.58	0.64	-4.51 / 1	--	--	0.00	2.08
GR	Equinox MutualHedge Futures Str A	MHFAX	D	(866) 643-3431	D- / 1.5	2.63	-1.06	-4.39 / 1	6.02 / 64	1.81 / 8	2.71	2.05
GR	Equinox MutualHedge Futures Str C	MHFCX	D+	(866) 643-3431	D / 1.8	2.40	-1.54	-5.19 / 1	5.22 / 57	1.04 / 6	2.15	2.80
GR	Equinox MutualHedge Futures Str I	MHFIX	D+	(866) 643-3431	D+ / 2.3	2.64	-1.02	-4.12 / 1	6.30 / 67	2.07 / 8	3.12	1.80
IN	Equinox Systematica Macro I	EBCIX	U	(888) 643-3431	U /	0.70	-10.15	-15.33 / 0	--	--	10.76	0.95
EN	EuroPac Gold A	EPGFX	E-	(888) 558-5851	D+ / 2.3	8.46	-6.61	52.45 / 99	-0.29 / 12	--	16.92	1.81
FO	EuroPac International Div Inc A	EPDPX	D-	(888) 558-5851	E- / 0.1	6.11	-2.96	11.13 / 15	-4.79 / 3	--	2.03	1.73
FO	EuroPac International Div Inc I	EPDIX	D-	(888) 558-5851	E- / 0.2	6.28	-2.73	11.51 / 16	-4.53 / 3	--	2.34	1.48
FO	EuroPac International Value A	EPIVX	E-	(888) 558-5851	E- / 0.1	9.17	-2.52	17.14 / 39	-6.68 / 2	-3.99 / 2	0.62	2.00
FO	EuroPac International Value I	EPVIX	E-	(888) 558-5851	E- / 0.2	9.20	-2.47	17.48 / 41	-6.49 / 2	--	0.79	1.75
FO	European Gro and Inc Direct	EUGIX	E+	(800) 955-9988	E+ / 0.8	10.02	5.44	15.80 / 33	-3.03 / 4	3.68 / 14	2.67	1.30
FO	European Gro and Inc K	EUGKX	E+	(800) 955-9988	E+ / 0.7	10.14	5.40	15.41 / 32	-3.19 / 4	3.38 / 12	2.40	1.80
GL	E-Valuator Aggressive Grwth RMS	EVAGX	U	(800) 673-0550	U /	6.00	7.01	--	--	--	0.00	1.09
GL	E-Valuator Conservativ RMS Inst	EVCLX	U	(800) 673-0550	U /	3.41	2.20	--	--	--	0.00	1.04
GL	E-Valuator Growth RMS Institutional	EVGLX	U	(800) 673-0550	U /	6.11	6.31	--	--	--	0.00	1.05
GL	E-Valuator Growth RMS Investor	EVGRX	U	(800) 673-0550	U /	6.07	6.17	--	--	--	0.00	1.30
GL	E-Valuator Moderate RMS Inst	EVMLX	U	(800) 673-0550	U /	5.56	4.85	--	--	--	0.00	1.05
GL	E-Valuator Moderate RMS Inv	EVFMX	U	(800) 673-0550	U /	5.40	4.69	--	--	--	0.00	1.30
GR	Eventide Gilead A	ETAGX	D+	(877) 453-7877	C / 5.1	5.40	10.04	27.91 / 81	4.13 / 44	15.00 / 97	0.00	1.48
GR	Eventide Gilead C	ETCGX	C-	(877) 453-7877	C+ / 5.7	5.19	9.59	26.92 / 79	3.35 / 35	14.12 / 94	0.00	2.23
GR	Eventide Gilead I	ETILX	C	(877) 453-7877	C+ / 6.5	5.43	10.12	28.19 / 82	4.39 / 47	15.29 / 97	0.00	1.23
GR	Eventide Gilead N	ETGLX	C-	(877) 453-7877	C+ / 6.4	5.39	10.01	27.98 / 82	4.17 / 45	15.05 / 97	0.00	1.43
HL	Eventide Healthcare & Life Sci A	ETAHX	D-	(877) 453-7877	C+ / 6.6	5.14	11.85	33.49 / 92	5.34 / 58	--	0.00	1.60
HL	Eventide Healthcare & Life Sci C	ETCHX	D	(877) 453-7877	C+ / 6.9	4.90	11.45	32.49 / 91	4.55 / 49	--	2.00	2.35
HL	Eventide Healthcare & Life Sci I	ETIHX	D	(877) 453-7877	B / 7.7	5.18	11.99	33.81 / 93	5.59 / 60	--	0.00	1.35
HL	Eventide Healthcare & Life Sci N	ETNHX	D	(877) 453-7877	B- / 7.5	5.13	11.87	33.51 / 92	5.38 / 58	--	0.00	1.55
GL	Eventide Multi-Asset Income I	ETIMX	U	(877) 453-7877	U /	4.10	1.34	14.13 / 26	--	--	2.50	1.83
GR	Evercore Equity	EWMCX	B-	(800) 443-4693	B- / 7.5	8.01	10.55	21.95 / 62	7.21 / 73	11.42 / 69	0.17	1.07
GL	Evermore Global Value Inst	EVGIX	A	(866) 383-7667	B+ / 8.8	5.86	17.61	34.19 / 93	6.75 / 70	10.83 / 64	1.02	1.53
GL	Evermore Global Value Inv	EVGBX	B+	(866) 383-7667	B / 7.7	5.73	17.36	33.76 / 93	6.49 / 68	10.54 / 62	0.77	1.78
GR	Fairholme	FAIRX	E+	(866) 202-2263	C+ / 5.6	-5.00	20.04	41.66 / 98	0.96 / 18	9.32 / 53	1.78	1.04
AA	Fairholme Allocation	FAAFX	E-	(866) 202-2263	E+ / 0.9	-1.53	14.90	33.46 / 92	-4.41 / 3	4.54 / 18	1.81	1.01
IN	Fallen Angels Income Fund	FAINX	C+	(888) 999-1395	C / 4.4	5.72	4.90	18.41 / 45	4.01 / 43	7.49 / 38	0.86	2.37
IN	FAM Equity-Income Inv	FAMEX	A+	(800) 932-3271	A / 9.3	6.00	10.77	26.90 / 79	10.37 / 95	13.06 / 84	0.92	1.27
SC	FAM Small Cap Instl	FAMDX	U	(800) 932-3271	U /	2.17	9.33	23.95 / 70	--	--	0.00	1.27
GR	FAM Small Cap Investor	FAMFX	A	(800) 932-3271	B / 7.7	2.17	9.29	23.83 / 69	8.68 / 84	--	0.00	1.37
SC	FAM Value Inv	FAMVX	A-	(800) 932-3271	B+ / 8.6	5.30	9.75	23.51 / 68	9.70 / 92	13.24 / 86	0.00	1.19
BA	FBP Appreciation and Income Opps	FBPBX	C+	(800) 443-4249	C+ / 6.0	4.00	9.24	23.94 / 70	4.86 / 53	8.57 / 47	1.60	1.08
GR	FBP Equity and Dividend Plus	FBPEX	B+	(800) 443-4249	B / 7.8	4.99	10.93	26.83 / 79	7.26 / 74	10.66 / 63	2.14	1.19

● Denotes fund is closed to new investors

✻ Denotes fund is included in Section II

RISK			NET ASSETS		ASSET					BULL / BEAR		FUND MANAGER		MINIMUMS		LOADS	
	3 Year		NAV						Portfolio	Last Bull	Last Bear	Manager	Manager	Initial	Additional	Front	Back
Risk Rating/Pts	Standard Deviation	Beta	As of 2/28/17	Total $(Mil)	Cash %	Stocks %	Bonds %	Other %	Turnover Ratio	Market Return	Market Return	Quality Pct	Tenure (Years)	Purch. $	Purch. $	End Load	End Load
B /8.2	8.9	0.75	13.95	7	0	0	0	100	19	N/A	N/A	88	4	0	0	0.0	0.0
C+ /5.8	13.7	1.10	12.93	N/A	0	0	0	100	50	N/A	N/A	33	4	0	0	0.0	0.0
C+ /5.8	13.7	1.10	12.93	106	0	0	0	100	50	N/A	N/A	33	4	0	0	0.0	0.0
B- /7.7	11.3	-0.11	11.37	N/A	100	0	0	0	0	N/A	N/A	98	4	25,000	0	0.0	0.0
C+ /6.0	12.7	0.18	9.79	39	12	15	72	1	0	N/A	N/A	83	4	2,500	500	5.8	0.0
B- /7.2	12.7	0.18	9.61	36	12	15	72	1	0	N/A	N/A	79	4	2,500	500	0.0	0.0
C+ /6.0	12.7	0.18	9.86	371	12	15	72	1	0	N/A	N/A	85	4	100,000	0	0.0	0.0
C+ /6.0	12.7	0.18	9.86	62	12	15	72	1	0	N/A	N/A	85	4	2,500	0	0.0	0.0
C+ /6.3	15.2	-0.04	11.73	50	24	0	75	1	0	N/A	N/A	99	5	25,000	0	0.0	0.0
B /8.1	7.2	0.09	8.37	2	40	0	59	1	0	N/A	N/A	57	4	25,000	0	0.0	0.0
C+ /6.4	9.5	0.72	10.27	4	41	0	58	1	31	N/A	N/A	62	4	2,500	500	5.8	1.0
C+ /6.3	9.6	0.72	9.97	N/A	41	0	58	1	31	N/A	N/A	51	4	2,500	500	0.0	1.0
C+ /6.4	9.6	0.72	10.34	3	41	0	58	1	31	N/A	N/A	65	4	1,000,000	0	0.0	1.0
U /	N/A	N/A	9.73	499	0	0	0	100	0	N/A	N/A	N/A	2	200,000,000	0	0.0	0.0
C+ /6.7	9.8	0.01	8.51	100	33	0	66	1	20	6.7	-0.2	96	8	2,500	500	5.8	1.0
C+ /6.7	9.8	0.01	8.23	40	33	0	66	1	20	2.5	-0.6	95	8	2,500	500	0.0	1.0
C+ /6.7	9.8	0.01	8.57	144	33	0	66	1	20	8.2	N/A	97	8	1,000,000	0	0.0	1.0
U /	N/A	N/A	8.21	33	29	0	70	1	0	N/A	N/A	N/A	3	25,000	0	0.0	0.0
E- /0.0	41.5	0.71	8.82	74	2	97	0	1	21	N/A	N/A	92	4	2,500	250	4.5	2.0
C+ /6.5	13.3	0.79	7.92	60	20	79	0	1	25	N/A	N/A	17	4	2,500	250	4.5	2.0
C+ /6.5	13.4	0.79	7.93	2	20	79	0	1	25	N/A	N/A	19	4	15,000	2,000	0.0	2.0
D /2.2	19.7	0.96	7.46	61	13	86	0	1	40	-1.4	-23.6	6	7	2,500	250	4.5	2.0
D /2.2	19.6	0.96	7.47	1	13	86	0	1	40	N/A	N/A	7	7	15,000	2,500	0.0	2.0
C /5.2	12.3	0.94	8.33	6	2	97	0	1	0	39.5	-26.9	35	14	1,000	100	0.0	0.0
C /5.2	12.3	0.94	8.36	4	2	97	0	1	0	37.3	-27.1	34	14	1,000	100	0.0	0.0
U /	N/A	N/A	11.10	42	0	0	0	100	0	N/A	N/A	N/A	1	10,000	100	0.0	0.0
U /	N/A	N/A	10.37	39	0	0	0	100	0	N/A	N/A	N/A	1	10,000	100	0.0	0.0
U /	N/A	N/A	10.98	161	0	0	0	100	0	N/A	N/A	N/A	1	10,000	100	0.0	0.0
U /	N/A	N/A	10.99	34	0	0	0	100	0	N/A	N/A	N/A	1	10,000	100	0.0	0.0
U /	N/A	N/A	10.76	108	0	0	0	100	0	N/A	N/A	N/A	1	10,000	100	0.0	0.0
U /	N/A	N/A	10.76	32	0	0	0	100	0	N/A	N/A	N/A	1	10,000	100	0.0	0.0
C- /4.0	17.6	1.40	27.50	520	17	81	0	2	28	166.3	-25.5	2	9	1,000	50	5.8	0.0
C- /3.9	17.6	1.41	25.93	191	17	81	0	2	28	155.4	-25.7	2	9	1,000	50	0.0	0.0
C- /4.0	17.6	1.40	27.97	278	17	81	0	2	28	169.7	-25.4	2	9	100,000	50	0.0	0.0
C- /4.0	17.6	1.40	27.58	312	17	81	0	2	28	166.8	-25.4	2	9	1,000	50	0.0	0.0
E+ /0.7	34.3	2.03	22.08	157	3	96	0	1	28	N/A	N/A	0	5	1,000	50	5.8	1.0
E+ /0.6	34.3	2.03	21.41	49	3	96	0	1	28	N/A	N/A	0	5	1,000	50	0.0	1.0
E+ /0.7	34.3	2.03	22.32	94	3	96	0	1	28	N/A	N/A	0	5	100,000	50	0.0	1.0
E+ /0.7	34.3	2.03	22.15	38	3	96	0	1	28	N/A	N/A	0	5	1,000	50	0.0	1.0
U /	N/A	N/A	10.62	30	34	49	15	2	18	N/A	N/A	N/A	2	100,000	50	0.0	0.0
C /5.3	11.8	1.09	14.98	120	4	95	0	1	24	113.1	-16.8	23	7	1,000	100	0.0	0.0
C+ /6.4	11.7	0.72	13.54	355	3	94	1	2	57	91.2	-30.0	97	8	1,000,000	100	0.0	2.0
C+ /6.4	11.7	0.72	13.46	63	3	94	1	2	57	88.5	-30.1	97	8	5,000	100	5.0	2.0
E- /0.0	22.5	1.13	21.51	2,740	5	51	42	2	40	97.7	-30.6	2	18	10,000	1,000	0.0	2.0
D /1.9	21.0	1.50	8.89	223	11	70	17	2	39	71.5	-25.6	0	7	25,000	2,500	0.0	2.0
B- /7.4	8.6	0.79	10.76	10	2	84	10	4	27	63.2	-11.4	23	11	10,000	1,000	0.0	0.0
C+ /6.8	10.2	0.83	27.78	199	11	88	0	1	16	125.0	-14.4	84	21	500	50	0.0	0.0
U /	N/A	N/A	17.56	34	0	0	0	100	27	N/A	N/A	N/A	5	1,000,000	0	0.0	0.0
B- /7.4	14.5	0.95	17.53	111	0	0	0	100	27	N/A	N/A	59	5	5,000	50	0.0	0.0
C+ /6.3	10.9	0.64	68.66	1,100	0	0	0	100	9	125.0	-18.4	95	30	500	50	0.0	0.0
C+ /6.6	10.1	1.39	18.92	35	10	75	13	2	23	76.3	-18.1	13	28	5,000	0	0.0	0.0
C+ /6.5	10.5	0.94	26.30	28	7	92	0	1	21	99.8	-25.3	42	24	5,000	0	0.0	0.0

I. Index of Stock Mutual Funds

99 Pct = Best
0 Pct = Worst

Fund Type	Fund Name	Ticker Symbol	Overall Investment Rating	Phone	Performance Rating/Pts	3 Mo	6 Mo	1Yr / Pct	3Yr / Pct	5Yr / Pct	Dividend Yield	Expense Ratio
GI	FDP BlackRock Invesco Value Instl	MAVVX	A-	(800) 441-7762	B+ / 8.8	5.22	13.80	32.86 / 91	7.26 / 74	12.56 / 80	2.27	0.97
GI	FDP BlackRock Invesco Value Inv A	MDVVX	B+	(800) 441-7762	B / 7.7	5.18	13.71	32.52 / 91	7.01 / 72	12.29 / 77	1.96	1.22
GI	FDP BlackRock Invesco Value Inv C	MCVVX	B+	(800) 441-7762	B / 8.0	4.98	13.22	31.51 / 89	6.18 / 66	11.44 / 69	1.38	1.98
GR	FDP BlackRock Janus Growth Instl	MADDX	C-	(800) 441-7762	C / 5.4	8.09	6.65	18.35 / 44	4.71 / 51	9.97 / 58	0.00	1.12
GR	FDP BlackRock Janus Growth Inv A	MDDDX	D+	(800) 441-7762	C- / 4.0	8.01	6.45	18.02 / 43	4.43 / 48	9.69 / 56	0.00	1.37
GR	FDP BlackRock Janus Growth Inv C	MCDDX	D+	(800) 441-7762	C / 4.4	7.73	6.08	17.12 / 39	3.63 / 38	8.85 / 49	0.00	2.13
FO	FDP BlackRock MFS Rsrch Intl Instl	MAIQX	D-	(800) 441-7762	E+ / 0.7	5.94	1.84	13.49 / 23	-2.22 / 6	3.17 / 11	1.39	1.24
FO	FDP BlackRock MFS Rsrch Intl Inv A	MDIQX	E+	(800) 441-7762	E / 0.4	5.88	1.77	13.17 / 22	-2.46 / 6	2.92 / 11	1.08	1.48
FO	FDP BlackRock MFS Rsrch Intl Inv C	MCIQX	E+	(800) 441-7762	E / 0.5	5.74	1.33	12.34 / 19	-3.19 / 4	2.14 / 8	0.33	2.24
AA	Federated Absolute Return A	FMAAX	C-	(800) 341-7400	E / 0.4	2.85	-0.31	-3.09 / 1	0.37 / 15	0.10 / 5	0.00	1.64
AA	● Federated Absolute Return B	FMBBX	C-	(800) 341-7400	E / 0.5	2.80	-0.62	-3.73 / 1	-0.35 / 12	-0.65 / 4	0.00	2.39
AA	Federated Absolute Return C	FMRCX	C-	(800) 341-7400	E / 0.5	2.71	-0.63	-3.85 / 1	-0.35 / 12	-0.65 / 4	0.00	2.39
AA	Federated Absolute Return Inst	FMIIX	C-	(800) 341-7400	E+ / 0.7	3.04	-0.10	-2.77 / 1	0.66 / 16	0.35 / 5	0.00	1.40
GI	Federated Capital Income A	CAPAX	D+	(800) 341-7400	D / 1.7	4.73	4.14	13.45 / 23	1.78 / 23	5.18 / 23	3.81	1.08
GI	Federated Capital Income B	CAPBX	D+	(800) 341-7400	D / 2.0	4.39	3.61	12.42 / 19	0.97 / 18	4.36 / 17	3.29	1.86
GI	Federated Capital Income C	CAPCX	D+	(800) 341-7400	D / 2.0	4.53	3.75	12.43 / 20	1.02 / 18	4.37 / 17	3.30	1.82
GI	Federated Capital Income F	CAPFX	D+	(800) 341-7400	D+ / 2.3	4.73	4.14	13.30 / 23	1.77 / 22	5.15 / 22	3.99	1.09
AA	Federated Capital Income Inst	CAPSX	C-	(800) 341-7400	D+ / 2.6	4.79	4.27	13.71 / 24	2.03 / 24	5.45 / 24	4.27	0.84
AA	Federated Capital Income R	CAPRX	C-	(800) 341-7400	D+ / 2.3	4.67	4.04	13.17 / 22	1.57 / 21	4.93 / 21	3.80	1.41
SC	Federated Clover Small Value A	VSFAX	B	(800) 341-7400	B+ / 8.3	6.94	15.04	36.20 / 95	6.92 / 71	11.50 / 70	0.47	1.42
SC	Federated Clover Small Value C	VSFCX	B	(800) 341-7400	B+ / 8.7	6.75	14.62	35.19 / 94	6.12 / 65	10.68 / 63	0.00	2.20
SC	Federated Clover Small Value Inst	VSFIX	B+	(800) 341-7400	A / 9.3	7.01	15.20	36.56 / 95	7.18 / 73	11.79 / 72	0.72	1.14
SC	Federated Clover Small Value R	VSFRX	B+	(800) 341-7400	A- / 9.1	6.92	15.08	36.18 / 95	6.82 / 71	11.35 / 69	0.51	1.66
SC	Federated Clover Small Value R6	VSFSX	B+	(800) 341-7400	A / 9.3	7.02	15.25	36.45 / 95	6.99 / 72	11.54 / 70	0.74	1.06
GR	Federated Clover Value Fund A	VFCAX	C-	(800) 341-7400	C / 4.7	6.17	12.62	25.68 / 75	3.07 / 32	9.63 / 56	1.40	1.32
GR	Federated Clover Value Fund B	VFCBX	C	(800) 341-7400	C / 5.1	6.01	12.18	24.79 / 73	2.33 / 26	8.85 / 49	1.05	2.15
GR	Federated Clover Value Fund C	VFCCX	C	(800) 341-7400	C / 5.1	5.95	12.17	24.77 / 72	2.31 / 26	8.84 / 49	1.02	2.11
GR	Federated Clover Value Fund I	VFCIX	C+	(800) 341-7400	C+ / 6.0	6.26	12.77	26.05 / 76	3.34 / 35	9.92 / 58	1.64	1.02
GR	Federated Clover Value Fund R	VFCKX	C	(800) 341-7400	C+ / 5.6	6.13	12.46	25.43 / 75	2.86 / 30	9.42 / 54	1.35	1.74
GL	Federated Emerging Markets Eq Inst	FGLEX	E-	(800) 341-7400	D- / 1.2	8.03	3.98	25.35 / 74	-2.52 / 5	2.97 / 11	0.82	2.92
IN	Federated Equity Income A	LEIFX	C+	(800) 341-7400	C+ / 5.9	6.84	11.90	23.92 / 70	5.42 / 59	9.84 / 57	1.96	1.13
IN	Federated Equity Income B	LEIBX	C+	(800) 341-7400	C+ / 6.3	6.65	11.46	22.91 / 66	4.58 / 50	8.98 / 50	1.35	1.92
IN	Federated Equity Income C	LEICX	C+	(800) 341-7400	C+ / 6.3	6.65	11.46	22.92 / 66	4.61 / 50	9.00 / 51	1.38	1.89
IN	Federated Equity Income F	LFEIX	C+	(800) 341-7400	C+ / 6.5	6.77	11.71	23.60 / 68	5.16 / 56	9.57 / 55	1.83	1.37
IN	Federated Equity Income Inst	LEISX	B	(800) 341-7400	B- / 7.0	6.90	11.99	24.25 / 71	5.70 / 61	10.10 / 59	2.30	0.87
IN	Federated Equity Income R	FDERX	C+	(800) 341-7400	C+ / 6.8	6.80	11.78	23.73 / 69	5.25 / 57	--	1.93	1.54
BA	Federated Global Allocation A	FSTBX	D	(800) 341-7400	D / 1.6	4.40	2.82	12.10 / 18	1.83 / 23	5.44 / 24	1.71	1.33
BA	Federated Global Allocation B	FSBBX	D+	(800) 341-7400	D / 1.8	4.17	2.41	11.17 / 15	1.01 / 18	4.58 / 19	1.05	2.13
BA	Federated Global Allocation C	FSBCX	D+	(800) 341-7400	D / 1.8	4.20	2.39	11.23 / 15	1.06 / 19	4.63 / 19	1.13	2.10
BA	Federated Global Allocation Inst	SBFIX	D+	(800) 341-7400	D+ / 2.4	4.44	2.92	12.37 / 19	2.12 / 25	5.73 / 27	2.09	1.05
BA	Federated Global Allocation R	FSBKX	D+	(800) 341-7400	D / 2.0	4.35	2.64	11.67 / 17	1.41 / 20	5.00 / 21	1.42	1.77
FO	Federated Intercontinental Fund A	RIMAX	E+	(800) 341-7400	E / 0.3	7.86	3.34	10.61 / 13	-3.30 / 4	0.97 / 6	1.64	1.61
FO	● Federated Intercontinental Fund B	ICFBX	D-	(800) 341-7400	E / 0.4	7.66	2.95	9.76 / 11	-4.06 / 3	0.17 / 5	0.71	2.47
FO	Federated Intercontinental Fund C	ICFFX	D-	(800) 341-7400	E / 0.4	7.66	2.96	9.77 / 11	-4.05 / 3	0.18 / 5	0.91	2.36
FO	Federated Intercontinental Fund I	ICFIX	D-	(800) 341-7400	E+ / 0.6	7.95	3.53	11.01 / 14	-2.97 / 5	1.29 / 7	2.18	1.27
FO	Federated Intercontinental Fund R6	ICRSX	D-	(800) 341-7400	E+ / 0.6	7.95	3.54	11.02 / 15	-2.97 / 5	1.18 / 6	2.18	1.23
FO	Federated International Div Strat	FIDPX	U	(800) 341-7400	U /	4.41	-2.83	7.76 / 7	--	--	4.29	1.70
FO	Federated International Sm-Mid A	ISCAX	E	(800) 341-7400	E / 0.3	6.47	1.51	8.39 / 8	-1.97 / 7	4.37 / 17	0.00	1.96
FO	● Federated International Sm-Mid B	ISCBX	E	(800) 341-7400	E / 0.4	6.26	1.09	7.54 / 7	-2.75 / 5	3.50 / 13	0.00	2.71
FO	Federated International Sm-Mid C	ISCCX	E	(800) 341-7400	E / 0.4	6.26	1.09	7.54 / 7	-2.74 / 5	3.50 / 13	0.00	2.71
FO	Federated International Sm-Mid Inst	ISCIX	E	(800) 341-7400	E / 0.5	6.51	1.57	8.58 / 9	-1.77 / 7	4.58 / 19	0.00	1.71
FO	Federated International Str VD A	IVFAX	E+	(800) 341-7400	E / 0.3	7.05	-1.89	8.29 / 8	-2.43 / 6	2.51 / 9	2.66	1.25

● Denotes fund is closed to new investors
* Denotes fund is included in Section II

208

RISK			NET ASSETS		ASSET				Portfolio Turnover Ratio	BULL / BEAR		FUND MANAGER		MINIMUMS		LOADS	
	3 Year		NAV As of 2/28/17	Total $(Mil)	Cash %	Stocks %	Bonds %	Other %		Last Bull Market Return	Last Bear Market Return	Manager Quality Pct	Manager Tenure (Years)	Initial Purch. $	Additional Purch. $	Front End Load	Back End Load
Risk Rating/Pts	Standard Deviation	Beta															
C+ /6.1	12.9	1.14	17.14	5	3	96	0	1	15	122.1	-19.8	19	12	2,000,000	0	0.0	0.0
C+ /6.1	12.9	1.14	16.99	50	3	96	0	1	15	119.3	-19.9	17	12	1,000	50	5.3	0.0
C+ /6.2	12.9	1.14	16.70	64	3	96	0	1	15	110.3	-20.2	12	12	1,000	50	0.0	0.0
C /4.9	11.8	1.01	15.55	5	0	99	0	1	128	98.3	-18.2	11	2	2,000,000	0	0.0	0.0
C /4.8	11.8	1.02	15.01	50	0	99	0	1	128	95.4	-18.3	9	2	1,000	50	5.3	0.0
C /4.6	11.8	1.01	13.44	62	0	99	0	1	128	87.6	-18.5	6	2	1,000	50	0.0	0.0
C+ /5.6	11.5	0.91	11.60	5	2	97	0	1	37	34.1	-22.0	47	N/A	2,000,000	0	0.0	0.0
C+ /5.6	11.4	0.91	11.53	55	2	97	0	1	37	32.3	-22.1	44	N/A	1,000	50	5.3	0.0
C+ /5.6	11.4	0.91	11.42	70	2	97	0	1	37	27.0	-22.4	33	N/A	1,000	50	0.0	0.0
B+ /9.4	4.1	0.34	9.73	61	14	72	12	2	132	2.0	-0.5	46	8	1,500	100	5.5	0.0
B+ /9.3	4.1	0.34	9.54	4	14	72	12	2	132	-2.0	-0.8	35	8	1,500	100	0.0	0.0
B+ /9.3	4.1	0.34	9.49	43	14	72	12	2	132	-2.1	-0.8	36	8	1,500	100	0.0	0.0
B+ /9.5	4.1	0.34	9.84	71	14	72	12	2	132	3.5	-0.4	50	8	1,000,000	0	0.0	0.0
B- /7.0	6.4	0.53	7.89	745	16	40	40	4	71	43.3	-7.2	27	17	1,500	100	5.5	0.0
B- /7.0	6.4	0.54	7.90	94	16	40	40	4	71	37.3	-7.5	18	17	1,500	100	0.0	0.0
B- /7.0	6.4	0.54	7.89	741	16	40	40	4	71	37.5	-7.5	19	17	1,500	100	0.0	0.0
B- /7.0	6.5	0.55	7.88	199	16	40	40	4	71	43.1	-7.2	25	17	1,500	100	1.0	0.0
B- /7.0	6.4	0.92	7.90	358	16	40	40	4	71	45.2	-7.2	18	17	1,000,000	0	0.0	0.0
B- /7.0	6.4	0.92	7.90	1	16	40	40	4	71	41.4	-7.4	14	17	0	0	0.0	0.0
C /4.8	13.7	0.84	27.92	138	0	96	3	1	89	116.5	-24.9	81	N/A	1,500	100	5.5	0.0
C /4.8	13.7	0.84	26.84	24	0	96	3	1	89	107.9	-25.1	76	N/A	1,500	100	0.0	0.0
C /4.8	13.7	0.84	28.01	510	0	96	3	1	89	119.5	-24.8	83	N/A	1,000,000	0	0.0	0.0
C /4.8	13.7	0.84	27.56	15	0	96	3	1	89	114.7	-25.0	81	7	0	0	0.0	0.0
C /4.8	13.7	0.84	27.90	9	0	96	3	1	89	116.9	-24.9	82	8	0	0	0.0	0.0
C+ /5.7	12.6	1.15	23.56	521	1	91	7	1	78	97.9	-20.0	3	11	1,500	100	5.5	0.0
C+ /5.7	12.6	1.15	23.30	20	1	91	7	1	78	90.2	-20.2	3	11	1,500	100	0.0	0.0
C+ /5.7	12.6	1.15	23.33	33	1	91	7	1	78	90.1	-20.2	3	11	1,500	100	0.0	0.0
C+ /5.7	12.6	1.15	23.61	115	1	91	7	1	78	100.7	-19.9	3	11	1,000,000	0	0.0	0.0
C+ /5.7	12.6	1.15	23.55	23	1	91	7	1	78	95.7	-20.1	3	11	0	0	0.0	0.0
D /2.1	13.9	0.79	9.07	21	4	87	8	1	53	42.2	-23.7	42	7	1,000,000	0	0.0	0.0
C+ /6.3	10.8	1.01	23.98	879	0	94	5	1	133	91.8	-12.2	16	15	1,500	100	5.5	0.0
C+ /6.3	10.8	1.01	23.90	46	0	94	5	1	133	83.7	-12.5	11	15	1,500	100	0.0	0.0
C+ /6.3	10.8	1.00	23.93	91	0	94	5	1	133	84.0	-12.5	11	15	1,500	100	0.0	0.0
C+ /6.3	10.8	1.01	23.99	53	0	94	5	1	133	89.1	-12.3	14	15	1,500	100	1.0	0.0
C+ /6.3	10.9	1.01	23.97	109	0	94	5	1	133	94.1	-12.2	18	15	1,000,000	0	0.0	0.0
C+ /6.3	10.8	1.01	23.98	22	0	94	5	1	133	N/A	N/A	15	15	250	100	0.0	0.0
C+ /6.7	7.6	1.14	18.13	167	11	60	27	2	105	47.5	-13.4	7	10	1,500	100	5.5	0.0
C+ /6.6	7.6	1.14	17.67	16	11	60	27	2	105	41.2	-13.7	5	10	1,500	100	0.0	0.0
C+ /6.6	7.6	1.14	17.61	82	11	60	27	2	105	41.6	-13.7	5	10	1,500	100	0.0	0.0
C+ /6.7	7.6	1.13	18.23	94	11	60	27	2	105	49.8	-13.3	8	10	1,000,000	0	0.0	0.0
C+ /6.7	7.6	1.14	18.00	56	11	60	27	2	105	44.2	-13.6	6	10	0	0	0.0	0.0
C+ /5.9	11.2	0.85	46.30	43	2	96	1	1	56	26.1	-27.9	32	10	1,500	100	5.5	0.0
C+ /5.9	11.2	0.85	46.32	2	2	96	1	1	56	20.8	-28.2	24	10	1,500	100	0.0	0.0
C+ /5.9	11.2	0.85	46.00	19	2	96	1	1	56	20.9	-28.2	24	10	1,500	100	0.0	0.0
C+ /5.8	11.2	0.85	45.99	60	2	96	1	1	56	28.3	-27.8	36	10	1,000,000	0	0.0	0.0
C+ /5.8	11.2	0.85	46.11	7	2	96	1	1	56	27.4	-27.9	36	10	0	0	0.0	0.0
U /	N/A	N/A	8.23	100	0	99	0	1	9	N/A	N/A	N/A	2	0	0	0.0	0.0
C- /4.0	13.4	1.01	33.24	90	1	96	1	2	39	54.9	-29.4	51	18	1,500	100	5.5	2.0
C- /3.3	13.4	1.01	26.49	2	1	96	1	2	39	48.1	-29.6	40	18	1,500	100	0.0	2.0
C- /3.3	13.4	1.01	26.46	17	1	96	1	2	39	48.1	-29.6	40	18	1,500	100	0.0	2.0
C- /4.0	13.4	1.01	33.84	33	1	96	1	2	39	56.5	-29.3	54	18	1,000,000	0	0.0	2.0
C+ /5.6	11.1	0.70	3.57	168	2	97	0	1	39	27.3	-15.9	43	9	1,500	100	5.5	0.0

I. Index of Stock Mutual Funds

Spring 2017

					PERFORMANCE						Incl. in Returns	
	99 Pct = Best 0 Pct = Worst		Overall		Perfor-		Total Return % through 2/28/17					
		Ticker	Investment		mance				Annualized		Dividend	Expense
Fund Type	Fund Name	Symbol	Rating	Phone	Rating/Pts	3 Mo	6 Mo	1Yr / Pct	3Yr / Pct	5Yr / Pct	Yield	Ratio
FO	Federated International Str VD C	IVFCX	E+	(800) 341-7400	E / 0.3	6.60	-2.21	7.31 / 6	-3.25 / 4	1.72 / 7	2.15	2.00
FO	Federated International Str VD I	IVFIX	E+	(800) 341-7400	E / 0.5	6.80	-1.79	8.22 / 8	-2.29 / 6	2.76 /10	3.05	1.00
FO	Federated Intl Leaders A	FGFAX	E+	(800) 341-7400	E / 0.5	8.03	6.84	16.00 /34	-2.51 / 5	5.80 /27	1.93	1.44
FO	Federated Intl Leaders B	FGFBX	E+	(800) 341-7400	E+ / 0.7	7.85	6.43	15.16 /31	-3.23 / 4	5.01 /21	1.42	2.23
FO	Federated Intl Leaders C	FGFCX	E+	(800) 341-7400	E+ / 0.7	7.86	6.43	15.16 /31	-3.23 / 4	5.01 /21	1.30	2.24
FO	Federated Intl Leaders Instl	FGFLX	E+	(800) 341-7400	D- / 1.0	8.10	6.96	16.32 /36	-2.26 / 6	6.06 /29	2.35	1.17
FO	Federated Intl Leaders R	FGFRX	E+	(800) 341-7400	E+ / 0.8	7.95	6.73	15.76 /33	-2.69 / 5	5.52 /25	1.94	1.83
FO	Federated Intl Leaders R6	FGRSX	E+	(800) 341-7400	D- / 1.0	8.13	6.98	16.35 /36	-2.21 / 6	6.03 /28	2.40	1.09
GR	Federated Kaufman Large Cap IS	KLCIX	B-	(800) 341-7400	B- / 7.3	7.68	6.43	22.34 /64	7.51 /75	14.19 /94	0.00	1.05
GR	Federated Kaufman Large Cap R	KLCKX	C+	(800) 341-7400	C+ / 6.8	7.48	6.10	21.52 /60	6.83 /71	13.44 /88	0.00	1.75
GR	Federated Kaufman Large Cap R6	KLCSX	B	(800) 341-7400	B- / 7.3	7.67	6.42	22.37 /64	7.56 /76	14.22 /94	0.00	0.90
MC	Federated Kaufmann A	KAUAX	D+	(800) 341-7400	C+ / 6.5	5.41	7.36	29.36 /85	6.52 /69	12.86 /82	0.00	2.04
MC	Federated Kaufmann B	KAUBX	D+	(800) 341-7400	C+ / 6.9	5.15	6.94	28.55 /83	5.88 /63	12.22 /76	0.00	2.55
MC	Federated Kaufmann C	KAUCX	D+	(800) 341-7400	B- / 7.0	5.40	6.97	28.58 /83	5.97 /64	12.24 /76	0.00	2.55
GR	Federated Kaufmann Large Cap A	KLCAX	C+	(800) 341-7400	C+ / 6.2	7.62	6.29	22.02 /62	7.24 /74	13.90 /92	0.00	1.33
GR	Federated Kaufmann Large Cap C	KLCCX	C+	(800) 341-7400	C+ / 6.6	7.43	5.89	21.10 /58	6.42 /68	13.01 /84	0.00	2.08
MC	Federated Kaufmann R	KAUFX	C-	(800) 341-7400	B- / 7.3	5.40	7.34	29.29 /85	6.51 /69	12.84 /82	0.00	2.28
SC	Federated Kaufmann Sm Cap A	FKASX	D	(800) 341-7400	B- / 7.0	6.39	8.72	36.12 /95	5.55 /60	12.26 /77	0.00	2.08
SC	Federated Kaufmann Sm Cap B	FKBSX	D+	(800) 341-7400	B- / 7.5	6.26	8.46	35.45 /94	4.97 /54	11.65 /71	0.00	2.63
SC	Federated Kaufmann Sm Cap C	FKCSX	D+	(800) 341-7400	B- / 7.5	6.26	8.46	35.37 /94	4.97 /54	11.65 /71	0.00	2.59
SC	Federated Kaufmann Sm Cap Inst	FKAIX	C-	(800) 341-7400	B / 8.1	6.52	8.98	36.76 /96	5.74 /62	12.38 /78	0.00	N/A
SC	Federated Kaufmann Sm Cap R	FKKSX	C-	(800) 341-7400	B / 7.9	6.41	8.77	36.23 /95	5.59 /60	12.32 /77	0.00	2.22
GR	Federated Max-Cap Index C	MXCCX	B-	(800) 341-7400	B+ / 8.5	7.56	9.20	23.44 /68	9.14 /88	12.62 /80	0.72	1.48
GR	Federated Max-Cap Index Inst	FISPX	B	(800) 341-7400	A- / 9.2	7.86	9.83	24.75 /72	10.32 /95	13.82 /92	1.62	0.45
GR	Federated Max-Cap Index R	FMXKX	B	(800) 341-7400	B+ / 8.8	7.64	9.43	23.83 /69	9.51 /90	12.98 /83	0.99	1.17
GR	Federated Max-Cap Index Svc	FMXSX	B	(800) 341-7400	A- / 9.0	7.84	9.66	24.42 /71	10.01 /93	13.49 /89	1.37	1.02
GR	Federated MDT All Cap Core Fd A	QAACX	B+	(800) 341-7400	B- / 7.2	7.05	11.17	25.47 /75	7.78 /77	13.73 /91	0.75	1.39
GR	Federated MDT All Cap Core Fd C	QCACX	A-	(800) 341-7400	B / 7.6	6.89	10.81	24.51 /72	6.96 /72	12.85 /82	0.16	2.15
GR	Federated MDT All Cap Core Fd Inst	QIACX	A	(800) 341-7400	B+ / 8.4	7.14	11.36	25.82 /76	8.09 /80	14.04 /93	1.06	1.08
GR	Federated MDT All Cap Core Fd R6	QKACX	A-	(800) 341-7400	B / 8.0	7.16	11.24	25.26 /74	7.40 /75	13.27 /86	0.00	1.04
BA	Federated MDT Balanced Fund A	QABGX	C	(800) 341-7400	C- / 3.2	4.78	5.35	14.85 /29	4.72 /51	8.29 /45	1.47	1.44
BA	Federated MDT Balanced Fund C	QCBGX	C+	(800) 341-7400	C- / 3.7	4.56	4.94	14.02 /25	3.94 /42	7.47 /38	0.84	2.17
BA	Federated MDT Balanced Fund Inst	QIBGX	B-	(800) 341-7400	C / 4.5	4.85	5.48	15.11 /30	4.97 /54	8.56 /47	1.80	1.14
BA	Federated MDT Balanced Fund R6	QKBGX	C+	(800) 341-7400	C- / 4.2	4.80	5.43	14.81 /29	4.54 /49	8.02 /42	1.46	1.14
GR	Federated MDT Large Cap Gr Fd A	QALGX	C	(800) 341-7400	C+ / 5.7	8.21	10.64	21.35 /59	5.74 /62	11.58 /71	0.00	1.58
GR	Federated MDT Large Cap Gr Fd B	QBLGX	C	(800) 341-7400	C+ / 6.2	7.99	10.20	20.50 /55	4.94 /53	10.76 /64	0.00	2.34
GR	Federated MDT Large Cap Gr Fd C	QCLGX	C	(800) 341-7400	C+ / 6.2	8.05	10.24	20.55 /55	4.94 /53	10.77 /64	0.00	2.33
GR	Federated MDT Large Cap Gr Fd Inst	QILGX	C+	(800) 341-7400	B- / 7.0	8.25	10.73	21.75 /61	6.01 /64	11.87 /73	0.00	1.33
GI	Federated MDT Large Cap Value A	FSTRX	A-	(800) 341-7400	B / 7.7	5.89	11.74	27.17 /80	8.43 /82	14.20 /94	1.27	1.23
GI	Federated MDT Large Cap Value IS	FMSTX	B+	(800) 341-7400	B+ / 8.8	5.94	11.91	27.49 /80	8.67 /84	14.48 /95	1.55	0.99
GI	Federated MDT Large Cap Value R6	FSTLX	U	(800) 341-7400	U /	5.92	11.92	--	--	--	0.00	0.94
GI	Federated MDT Large Cap Value SS	FSTKX	B+	(800) 341-7400	B+ / 8.6	5.88	11.78	27.15 /80	8.43 /82	14.22 /94	1.35	1.25
MC	Federated MDT MidCap Growth A	FGSAX	C-	(800) 341-7400	B- / 7.0	8.10	11.96	23.98 /70	7.27 /74	11.24 /68	0.04	1.30
MC	● Federated MDT MidCap Growth B	FGSBX	D+	(800) 341-7400	B- / 7.4	7.90	11.52	23.06 /67	6.46 /68	10.41 /61	0.00	2.12
MC	Federated MDT MidCap Growth C	FGSCX	D+	(800) 341-7400	B- / 7.4	7.89	11.52	23.06 /67	6.46 /68	10.41 /61	0.00	2.07
MC	Federated MDT MidCap Growth Inst	FGSIX	C	(800) 341-7400	B / 8.1	8.15	12.06	24.27 /71	7.53 /76	11.47 /70	0.26	1.03
MC	Federated MDT MidCap Growth R6	FGSKX	C-	(800) 341-7400	B / 7.7	8.17	12.06	23.78 /69	6.87 /71	10.78 /64	0.00	1.73
SC	Federated MDT Small Cap Gr Fd A	QASGX	B-	(800) 341-7400	A+ / 9.6	7.48	13.33	38.83 /97	9.78 /92	13.96 /93	0.00	2.00
SC	● Federated MDT Small Cap Gr Fd B	QBSGX	B-	(800) 341-7400	A+ / 9.7	7.28	12.89	37.74 /96	8.96 /87	13.11 /85	0.00	2.74
SC	Federated MDT Small Cap Gr Fd C	QCSGX	B-	(800) 341-7400	A+ / 9.7	7.27	12.85	37.80 /96	8.95 /86	13.11 /85	0.00	2.75
SC	Federated MDT Small Cap Gr Fd Inst	QISGX	B	(800) 341-7400	A+ / 9.8	7.55	13.44	39.14 /97	10.05 /94	14.25 /94	0.00	1.74
SC	Federated MDT Small Cp Core Fd A	QASCX	B+	(800) 341-7400	A+ / 9.8	5.30	16.06	45.52 /99	11.56 /98	16.72 /98	0.00	2.09

● Denotes fund is closed to new investors

* Denotes fund is included in Section II

RISK			NET ASSETS		ASSET					BULL / BEAR		FUND MANAGER		MINIMUMS		LOADS	
	3 Year		NAV						Portfolio	Last Bull	Last Bear	Manager	Manager	Initial	Additional	Front	Back
Risk	Standard		As of	Total	Cash	Stocks	Bonds	Other	Turnover	Market	Market	Quality	Tenure	Purch.	Purch.	End	End
Rating/Pts	Deviation	Beta	2/28/17	$(Mil)	%	%	%	%	Ratio	Return	Return	Pct	(Years)	$	$	Load	Load
C+ / 5.6	10.9	0.69	3.54	93	2	97	0	1	39	22.2	-16.3	32	9	1,500	100	0.0	0.0
C+ / 5.7	10.9	0.69	3.57	554	2	97	0	1	39	28.8	-15.8	45	9	1,000,000	0	0.0	0.0
C / 5.0	13.5	1.04	30.60	373	2	93	3	2	2	66.1	-29.5	43	19	1,500	100	5.5	0.0
C / 5.0	13.5	1.04	28.63	20	2	93	3	2	2	59.5	-29.7	33	19	1,500	100	0.0	0.0
C / 5.0	13.5	1.04	28.54	94	2	93	3	2	2	59.5	-29.7	33	19	1,500	100	0.0	0.0
C / 5.0	13.5	1.04	30.63	865	2	93	3	2	2	68.4	-29.4	47	19	1,000,000	0	0.0	0.0
C / 5.0	13.5	1.04	30.42	54	2	93	3	2	2	63.6	-29.6	41	19	0	0	0.0	0.0
C / 5.0	13.5	1.04	30.59	147	2	93	3	2	2	67.9	-29.5	48	19	0	0	0.0	0.0
C / 5.5	11.6	0.98	21.03	1,544	3	90	6	1	34	147.3	-20.3	39	10	1,000,000	0	0.0	0.0
C / 5.5	11.6	0.99	19.82	78	3	90	6	1	34	138.8	-20.5	30	10	250	100	0.0	0.0
C+ / 5.9	11.6	0.98	21.06	91	3	90	6	1	34	147.7	-20.3	39	10	0	0	0.0	0.0
D / 2.0	15.7	1.10	5.26	1,348	3	87	8	2	55	127.7	-25.6	25	31	1,500	100	5.5	0.0
D / 1.6	15.7	1.10	4.48	71	3	87	8	2	55	120.9	-25.7	20	31	1,500	100	0.0	0.0
D / 1.6	15.7	1.10	4.48	337	3	87	8	2	55	121.1	-25.7	21	31	1,500	100	0.0	0.0
C / 5.5	11.6	0.98	20.61	597	3	90	6	1	34	143.9	-20.4	35	10	1,500	100	5.5	0.0
C / 5.4	11.6	0.98	19.23	460	3	90	6	1	34	133.8	-20.7	26	10	1,500	100	0.0	0.0
D / 2.0	15.7	1.10	5.27	3,378	3	87	8	2	55	127.9	-25.6	25	31	250	100	0.0	0.2
D- / 1.4	18.5	1.02	26.64	353	0	96	2	2	48	139.0	-29.2	56	15	1,500	100	5.5	0.0
D- / 1.0	18.5	1.03	23.42	16	0	96	2	2	48	132.0	-29.3	48	15	1,500	100	0.0	0.0
D- / 1.0	18.5	1.02	23.42	146	0	96	2	2	48	132.0	-29.3	48	15	1,500	100	0.0	0.0
D / 2.1	18.5	1.02	26.78	111	0	96	2	2	48	140.2	-29.2	59	15	1,000,000	0	0.0	0.0
D- / 1.4	18.5	1.02	26.73	41	0	96	2	2	48	139.4	-29.2	57	15	250	100	0.0	0.0
C / 4.3	10.3	1.00	13.82	41	0	94	4	2	31	119.3	-16.7	57	5	1,500	100	0.0	0.0
C / 4.3	10.3	1.00	14.12	204	0	94	4	2	31	132.2	-16.3	70	5	1,000,000	0	0.0	0.0
C / 4.3	10.3	1.00	13.98	51	0	94	4	2	31	123.2	-16.6	61	5	250	100	0.0	0.0
C / 4.3	10.3	1.00	14.00	187	0	94	4	2	31	128.7	-16.5	67	5	1,000,000	0	0.0	0.0
B- / 7.0	11.3	1.04	24.09	33	0	98	0	2	62	136.0	-23.0	34	9	1,500	100	5.5	0.0
B- / 7.0	11.3	1.05	22.92	40	0	98	0	2	62	126.2	-23.3	25	9	1,500	100	0.0	0.0
C+ / 6.9	11.3	1.05	24.34	54	0	98	0	2	62	139.6	-23.0	37	9	1,000,000	0	0.0	0.0
B- / 7.0	11.3	1.05	23.95	17	0	98	0	2	62	131.0	-23.2	29	9	250	100	0.0	0.0
B / 8.0	6.9	1.07	17.17	60	6	54	38	2	98	70.5	-14.8	33	N/A	1,500	100	5.5	0.0
B / 8.1	6.9	1.07	16.99	29	6	54	38	2	98	63.7	-15.0	25	N/A	1,500	100	0.0	0.0
B / 8.0	6.9	1.07	17.20	39	6	54	38	2	98	72.8	-14.7	36	N/A	1,000,000	0	0.0	0.0
B / 8.1	6.9	1.07	17.17	10	6	54	38	2	98	68.0	-15.0	31	N/A	250	100	0.0	0.0
C / 5.3	11.4	1.05	16.69	46	0	98	1	1	69	114.1	-18.8	15	9	1,500	100	5.5	0.0
C / 5.1	11.4	1.05	15.50	15	0	98	1	1	69	105.5	-18.9	10	9	1,500	100	0.0	0.0
C / 5.1	11.4	1.05	15.12	11	0	98	1	1	69	105.6	-19.1	10	9	1,500	100	0.0	0.0
C / 5.4	11.4	1.05	17.28	8	0	98	1	1	69	116.9	-18.7	17	9	1,000,000	0	0.0	0.0
B- / 7.3	11.5	1.03	28.30	25	0	97	1	2	88	150.7	-22.3	44	8	1,500	100	5.5	0.0
C+ / 5.6	11.5	1.03	28.32	396	0	97	1	2	88	154.1	-22.2	47	8	1,000,000	0	0.0	0.0
U /	N/A	N/A	28.32	43	0	97	1	2	88	N/A	N/A	N/A	8	0	0	0.0	0.0
C+ / 5.6	11.5	1.04	28.32	300	0	97	1	2	88	151.0	-22.3	43	8	1,000,000	0	0.0	0.0
D+ / 2.4	12.7	0.94	38.48	228	0	98	1	1	115	108.2	-22.7	54	4	1,500	100	5.5	0.0
D- / 1.4	12.7	0.94	28.23	2	0	98	1	1	115	99.9	-23.0	43	4	1,500	100	0.0	0.0
D- / 1.4	12.7	0.94	28.82	11	0	98	1	1	115	99.9	-22.9	43	4	1,500	100	0.0	0.0
D+ / 2.5	12.7	0.93	39.25	19	0	98	1	1	115	110.6	-22.6	57	4	1,000,000	0	0.0	0.0
D / 2.2	12.7	0.94	36.38	36	0	98	1	1	115	103.5	-22.9	49	4	250	100	0.0	0.0
C- / 3.3	16.5	1.00	20.09	37	0	97	1	2	198	155.7	-27.2	89	9	1,500	100	5.5	0.0
C- / 3.1	16.5	1.00	18.69	2	0	97	1	2	198	145.5	-27.4	86	9	1,500	100	0.0	0.0
C- / 3.0	16.5	1.00	18.12	7	0	97	1	2	198	145.4	-27.4	86	9	1,500	100	0.0	0.0
C- / 3.4	16.5	1.00	20.79	72	0	97	1	2	198	159.1	-27.1	90	9	1,000,000	0	0.0	0.0
C / 4.6	16.5	1.01	17.91	32	2	97	0	1	189	181.7	-29.3	94	9	1,500	100	5.5	0.0

I. Index of Stock Mutual Funds

					PERFORMANCE						Incl. in Returns	
99 Pct = Best 0 Pct = Worst			Overall		Perfor-			Total Return % through 2/28/17				
		Ticker	Investment		mance				Annualized		Dividend	Expense
Fund Type	Fund Name	Symbol	Rating	Phone	Rating/Pts	3 Mo	6 Mo	1Yr / Pct	3Yr / Pct	5Yr / Pct	Yield	Ratio
SC	Federated MDT Small Cp Core Fd C	QCSCX	B+	(800) 341-7400	A+ / 9.8	5.08	15.65	44.38 /98	10.72 /96	15.85 /98	0.00	2.85
SC	Federated MDT Small Cp Core Fd	QISCX	B+	(800) 341-7400	A+ / 9.9	5.34	16.25	45.93 /99	11.85 /98	17.02 /98	0.03	1.85
MC	Federated Mid-Cap Index Inst	FMCRX	B	(800) 341-7400	A / 9.4	6.52	11.22	31.32 /89	9.37 /89	13.62 /90	1.18	0.41
MC	Federated Mid-Cap Index Svc	FMDCX	B	(800) 341-7400	A- / 9.2	6.45	11.08	30.99 /88	9.10 /87	13.35 /87	0.97	0.66
AA	Federated Muni & Stock Advtd Inst	FMUIX	C+	(800) 341-7400	C- / 3.3	4.47	2.89	10.07 /12	4.49 /49	6.24 /30	2.44	0.82
GR	Federated Prudent Bear Fund A	BEARX	E+	(800) 341-7400	E- / 0.0	-6.24	-9.64	-20.72 / 0	-12.33 / 0	-14.98 / 0	0.00	3.28
GR	Federated Prudent Bear Fund C	PBRCX	E+	(800) 341-7400	E- / 0.0	-6.41	-9.94	-21.31 / 0	-12.94 / 0	-15.64 / 0	0.00	4.03
GR	Federated Prudent Bear Fund IS	PBRIX	E+	(800) 341-7400	E- / 0.0	-6.18	-9.51	-20.53 / 0	-12.08 / 0	-14.77 / 0	0.00	2.98
IN	Federated Strategic Value Div A	SVAAX	C+	(800) 341-7400	C+ / 5.6	8.06	2.30	12.81 /21	8.98 /87	11.38 /69	2.55	1.19
IN	Federated Strategic Value Div C	SVACX	C+	(800) 341-7400	C+ / 6.0	7.68	1.75	11.78 /17	8.11 /80	10.55 /62	1.97	1.94
IN	Federated Strategic Value Div Inst	SVAIX	C+	(800) 341-7400	C+ / 6.8	8.10	2.41	12.84 /21	9.22 /88	11.66 /71	2.93	0.94
IN	Federated Strategic Value Div R6	SVALX	U	(800) 341-7400	U /	8.10	2.42	--	--	--	0.00	0.87
GR	Fidelity 100 Index F	FOHJX	A+	(800) 544-8544	A / 9.5	8.63	10.23	24.62 /72	11.08 /97	13.60 /90	2.17	0.05
GR	Fidelity 100 Index FD	FOHIX	A+	(800) 544-8544	A / 9.5	8.57	10.17	24.55 /72	11.02 /97	13.56 /89	2.12	0.05
IX	Fidelity 500 Index Inst	FXSIX	A+	(800) 544-8544	A / 9.4	8.03	10.01	24.94 /73	10.61 /96	13.98 /93	1.87	0.04
IX	Fidelity 500 Index Inv	FUSEX	A+	(800) 544-8544	A / 9.3	8.02	9.96	24.88 /73	10.54 /96	13.91 /92	1.82	0.09
IX	Fidelity 500 Index IP	FXAIX	A+	(800) 544-8544	A / 9.4	8.03	10.02	24.97 /73	10.63 /96	14.00 /93	1.89	0.02
IX	Fidelity 500 Index Pr	FUSVX	A+	(800) 544-8544	A / 9.4	8.03	9.99	24.91 /73	10.59 /96	13.96 /93	1.86	0.05
AA	Fidelity Adv 529 100% Equity A	FFAGX	C	(800) 522-7297	C / 4.7	7.40	7.29	21.84 /61	4.86 /53	9.72 /56	0.00	1.26
AA	Fidelity Adv 529 100% Equity C	FFCGX	C+	(800) 522-7297	C / 5.2	7.20	6.84	20.89 /57	4.08 /44	8.89 /50	0.00	2.01
AA	Fidelity Adv 529 100% Equity D	FFRGX	C+	(800) 522-7297	C+ / 5.7	7.35	7.19	21.61 /60	4.61 /50	9.44 /54	0.00	1.51
AA	Fidelity Adv 529 100% Equity Old-A	FFOGX	C+	(800) 522-7297	C / 5.2	7.41	7.31	21.89 /62	4.87 /53	9.73 /56	0.00	1.26
AA	Fidelity Adv 529 100% Equity P	FFPGX	C+	(800) 522-7297	C / 5.5	7.29	7.00	21.21 /58	4.33 /47	9.17 /52	0.00	1.76
AA	Fidelity Adv 529 2016 A	FPCAX	C	(800) 522-7297	D- / 1.1	2.43	0.89	7.29 / 6	2.25 /26	3.98 /15	0.00	1.10
AA	Fidelity Adv 529 2016 C	FPJCX	C	(800) 522-7297	D- / 1.4	2.19	0.49	6.46 / 5	1.49 /21	3.20 /12	0.00	1.85
AA	Fidelity Adv 529 2016 D	FPCDX	C	(800) 522-7297	D / 1.6	2.34	0.75	6.98 / 6	2.00 /24	3.73 /14	0.00	1.35
AA	Fidelity Adv 529 2016 Old-A	FPCOX	C	(800) 522-7297	D- / 1.4	2.43	0.89	7.27 / 6	2.25 /26	3.99 /15	0.00	1.10
AA	Fidelity Adv 529 2016 P	FPCPX	C	(800) 522-7297	D- / 1.5	2.31	0.60	6.72 / 5	1.74 /22	3.47 /13	0.00	1.60
AA	Fidelity Adv 529 2019 A		C	(800) 522-7297	D / 1.6	3.22	1.74	9.94 /11	2.90 /31	5.34 /24	0.00	1.16
AA	Fidelity Adv 529 2019 C	FPLCX	C	(800) 522-7297	D / 1.9	3.10	1.41	9.14 /10	2.15 /25	4.58 /19	0.00	1.91
AA	Fidelity Adv 529 2019 D	FPDDX	C	(800) 522-7297	D / 2.1	3.23	1.65	9.72 /11	2.66 /29	5.09 /22	0.00	1.41
AA	Fidelity Adv 529 2019 Old-A	FAAPX	C	(800) 522-7297	D / 1.8	3.27	1.74	9.99 /12	2.91 /31	5.35 /24	0.00	1.16
AA	Fidelity Adv 529 2019 P	FPPCX	C	(800) 522-7297	D / 2.0	3.12	1.48	9.38 /10	2.39 /27	4.83 /20	0.00	1.66
AA	Fidelity Adv 529 2022 A	FPIAX	C	(800) 522-7297	D / 2.1	4.14	2.79	12.54 /20	3.44 /36	6.59 /32	0.00	1.21
AA	Fidelity Adv 529 2022 C	FPICX	C	(800) 522-7297	D+ / 2.4	3.92	2.39	11.68 /17	2.66 /29	5.80 /27	0.00	1.96
AA	Fidelity Adv 529 2022 D	FADPX	C+	(800) 522-7297	D+ / 2.8	4.06	2.67	12.28 /19	3.18 /33	6.32 /30	0.00	1.46
AA	Fidelity Adv 529 2022 Old-A	FPKAX	C	(800) 522-7297	D+ / 2.4	4.13	2.79	12.57 /20	3.45 /36	6.59 /32	0.00	1.21
AA	Fidelity Adv 529 2022 P	FAEPX	C+	(800) 522-7297	D+ / 2.6	4.01	2.53	11.99 /18	2.94 /31	6.07 /29	0.00	1.71
AA	Fidelity Adv 529 2025 A	FPGAX	C	(800) 522-7297	D+ / 2.6	4.94	3.79	15.03 /30	3.83 /41	7.67 /40	0.00	1.25
AA	Fidelity Adv 529 2025 C	FPHCX	C+	(800) 522-7297	C- / 3.1	4.76	3.44	14.16 /26	3.05 /32	6.87 /34	0.00	2.00
AA	Fidelity Adv 529 2025 P	FPFPX	C+	(800) 522-7297	C- / 3.3	4.83	3.61	14.47 /28	3.32 /35	7.15 /36	0.00	1.75
AA	Fidelity Adv 529 70% Equity A	FMAFX	C	(800) 522-7297	C- / 3.2	5.69	4.91	16.99 /38	4.22 /45	7.78 /40	0.00	1.21
AA	Fidelity Adv 529 70% Equity C	FMCGX	C+	(800) 522-7297	C- / 3.7	5.49	4.51	16.13 /35	3.45 /36	6.98 /34	0.00	1.96
AA	Fidelity Adv 529 70% Equity D	FMGDX	C+	(800) 522-7297	C- / 4.2	5.67	4.81	16.76 /37	3.96 /42	7.52 /38	0.00	1.46
AA	Fidelity Adv 529 70% Equity Old-A	FMGOX	C+	(800) 522-7297	C- / 3.7	5.73	4.90	17.01 /38	4.22 /45	7.78 /40	0.00	1.21
AA	Fidelity Adv 529 70% Equity P	FBBBX	C+	(800) 522-7297	C- / 3.9	5.56	4.67	16.42 /36	3.71 /39	7.24 /36	0.00	1.71
AA	Fidelity Adv 529 College A	FACAX	C	(800) 522-7297	D- / 1.1	2.38	0.84	7.03 / 6	2.07 /24	2.84 /10	0.00	0.98
AA	Fidelity Adv 529 College C	FCCLX	C	(800) 522-7297	D- / 1.3	2.21	0.48	6.25 / 5	1.32 /20	2.08 / 8	0.00	1.73
AA	Fidelity Adv 529 College D	FCDLX	C+	(800) 522-7297	D- / 1.5	2.36	0.69	6.77 / 5	1.83 /23	2.59 /10	0.00	1.23
AA	Fidelity Adv 529 College Old-A	FCPOX	C	(800) 522-7297	D- / 1.3	2.38	0.84	7.03 / 6	2.07 /24	2.84 /10	0.00	0.98
AA	Fidelity Adv 529 College P	FCPLX	C	(800) 522-7297	D- / 1.4	2.25	0.59	6.47 / 5	1.56 /21	2.33 / 9	0.00	1.48
FO	Fidelity Adv 529 Diversified Intl A	FDAPX	D-	(800) 522-7297	D- / 1.1	6.50	1.24	10.68 /13	0.19 /14	6.57 /32	0.00	1.44

● Denotes fund is closed to new investors
* Denotes fund is included in Section II

Risk Rating/Pts	Standard Deviation	Beta	NAV As of 2/28/17	Total $(Mil)	Cash %	Stocks %	Bonds %	Other %	Portfolio Turnover Ratio	Last Bull Market Return	Last Bear Market Return	Manager Quality Pct	Manager Tenure (Years)	Initial Purch. $	Additional Purch. $	Front End Load	Back End Load
C / 4.4	16.6	1.01	16.18	11	2	97	0	1	189	170.6	-29.5	92	9	1,500	100	0.0	0.0
C / 4.7	16.6	1.01	18.48	108	2	97	0	1	189	185.7	-29.2	94	9	1,000,000	0	0.0	0.0
C- / 4.2	12.0	1.00	26.08	183	1	96	2	1	33	137.8	-22.7	72	7	1,000,000	0	0.0	0.0
C- / 4.2	12.0	1.00	26.09	735	1	96	2	1	33	135.0	-22.7	69	7	1,000,000	0	0.0	0.0
B / 8.9	4.5	0.64	12.87	252	0	40	58	2	55	48.6	-0.4	71	14	1,000,000	0	0.0	0.0
C+ / 6.0	9.6	-0.84	17.72	110	56	0	43	1	430	-64.4	16.1	16	9	1,500	100	5.5	0.0
C+ / 6.0	9.4	-0.82	15.77	23	56	0	43	1	430	-65.8	15.5	10	9	1,500	100	0.0	0.0
C+ / 6.1	9.5	-0.83	18.08	128	56	0	43	1	430	-63.9	16.0	17	9	1,000,000	0	0.0	0.0
C+ / 6.7	9.8	0.59	6.12	3,158	2	97	0	1	21	88.0	-4.1	89	11	1,500	100	5.5	0.0
C+ / 6.7	9.9	0.60	6.12	2,210	2	97	0	1	21	80.1	-4.4	85	11	1,500	100	0.0	0.0
C+ / 6.7	9.8	0.58	6.14	9,212	2	97	0	1	21	90.5	-4.2	90	11	1,000,000	0	0.0	0.0
U /	N/A	N/A	6.14	54	2	97	0	1	21	N/A	N/A	N/A	11	0	0	0.0	0.0
B- / 7.1	10.5	1.01	15.40	1,800	1	98	0	1	10	130.7	-14.9	76	10	0	0	0.0	0.0
B- / 7.1	10.5	1.01	15.40	1,657	1	98	0	1	10	130.4	-14.9	76	10	0	0	0.0	0.0
B / 8.2	10.3	1.00	83.00	31,891	0	0	0	100	5	134.4	N/A	74	13	5,000,000	0	0.0	0.0
B / 8.2	10.3	1.00	82.98	3,815	0	0	0	100	5	133.7	-16.3	73	13	2,500	0	0.0	0.0
B / 8.2	10.3	1.00	83.00	14,852	0	0	0	100	5	134.7	N/A	N/A	13	200,000,000	0	0.0	0.0
B / 8.2	10.3	1.00	82.99	66,055	0	0	0	100	5	134.3	-16.3	74	13	10,000	0	0.0	0.0
C+ / 6.4	10.7	1.61	21.48	117	2	95	1	2	21	93.3	-21.4	6	12	1,000	50	5.8	0.0
C+ / 6.4	10.7	1.61	19.21	44	2	95	1	2	21	85.6	-21.7	4	12	1,000	50	0.0	0.0
C+ / 6.4	10.7	1.61	20.88	10	2	95	1	2	21	90.7	-21.5	5	12	1,000	50	0.0	0.0
C+ / 6.4	10.7	1.61	21.44	26	2	95	1	2	21	93.3	-21.5	6	12	1,000	50	3.5	0.0
C+ / 6.4	10.7	1.61	20.17	2	2	95	1	2	21	88.2	-21.6	5	12	1,000	50	0.0	0.0
B+ / 9.5	3.6	0.52	18.11	279	8	21	69	2	21	34.0	-9.4	54	12	1,000	50	5.8	0.0
B+ / 9.5	3.6	0.52	16.32	106	8	21	69	2	21	28.6	-9.7	44	12	1,000	50	0.0	0.0
B+ / 9.5	3.6	0.52	17.47	26	8	21	69	2	21	32.2	-9.6	50	12	1,000	50	0.0	0.0
B+ / 9.5	3.6	0.52	18.14	79	8	21	69	2	21	33.9	-9.4	54	12	1,000	50	3.5	0.0
B+ / 9.5	3.6	0.53	16.83	8	8	21	69	2	21	30.4	-9.7	46	12	1,000	50	0.0	0.0
B+ / 9.3	4.9	0.73	19.25	475	5	33	60	2	22	47.1	-12.9	42	12	1,000	50	5.8	0.0
B+ / 9.2	4.9	0.73	17.31	160	5	33	60	2	22	41.2	-13.1	32	12	1,000	50	0.0	0.0
B+ / 9.3	4.9	0.74	18.51	35	5	33	60	2	22	45.1	-12.8	38	12	1,000	50	0.0	0.0
B+ / 9.3	4.9	0.74	19.27	119	5	33	60	2	22	47.1	-12.8	41	12	1,000	50	3.5	0.0
B+ / 9.2	4.9	0.74	17.85	13	5	33	60	2	22	43.1	-13.0	34	12	1,000	50	0.0	0.0
B / 8.9	6.1	0.94	24.68	577	4	46	48	2	22	59.8	-16.0	30	12	1,000	50	5.8	0.0
B / 8.8	6.2	0.94	22.28	161	4	46	48	2	22	53.4	-16.2	22	12	1,000	50	0.0	0.0
B / 8.9	6.2	0.94	23.86	4	4	46	48	2	22	57.7	-16.1	27	12	1,000	50	0.0	0.0
B / 8.9	6.1	0.94	24.71	14	4	46	48	2	22	59.7	-16.0	30	12	1,000	50	3.5	0.0
B / 8.8	6.1	0.94	23.07	10	4	46	48	2	22	55.6	-16.1	25	12	1,000	50	0.0	0.0
B / 8.4	7.4	1.13	16.99	346	3	58	37	2	20	71.3	-18.6	20	12	1,000	50	5.8	0.0
B / 8.3	7.4	1.13	15.64	97	3	58	37	2	20	64.5	-18.8	14	12	1,000	50	0.0	0.0
B / 8.4	7.4	1.12	16.06	5	3	58	37	2	20	66.8	-18.7	16	12	1,000	50	0.0	0.0
B / 8.0	7.8	1.20	22.66	81	2	67	30	1	28	69.6	-16.1	19	12	1,000	50	5.8	0.0
B / 8.0	7.8	1.19	20.16	46	2	67	30	1	28	62.8	-16.3	13	12	1,000	50	0.0	0.0
B / 8.0	7.9	1.20	21.81	10	2	67	30	1	28	67.4	-16.2	17	12	1,000	50	0.0	0.0
B / 8.0	7.9	1.20	22.70	20	2	67	30	1	28	69.7	-16.1	19	12	1,000	50	3.5	0.0
B / 8.0	7.9	1.20	21.06	1	2	67	30	1	28	65.2	-16.3	15	12	1,000	50	0.0	0.0
B+ / 9.9	3.2	0.45	16.75	141	8	21	69	2	20	21.1	-4.2	58	12	1,000	50	5.8	0.0
B+ / 9.9	3.2	0.46	14.80	69	8	21	69	2	20	16.4	-4.4	47	12	1,000	50	0.0	0.0
B+ / 9.9	3.2	0.46	16.08	25	8	21	69	2	20	19.5	-4.2	54	12	1,000	50	0.0	0.0
B+ / 9.9	3.2	0.45	16.75	49	8	21	69	2	20	21.0	-4.1	58	12	1,000	50	3.5	0.0
B+ / 9.9	3.2	0.46	15.47	5	8	21	69	2	20	17.8	-4.3	51	12	1,000	50	0.0	0.0
C+ / 6.1	11.1	0.87	22.79	62	1	98	0	1	0	61.3	-24.7	76	12	1,000	50	5.8	0.0

					PERFORMANCE							
	99 Pct = Best 0 Pct = Worst			Overall	Perfor-	Total Return % through 2/28/17					Incl. in Returns	
				Investment	mance				Annualized		Dividend	Expense
Fund		Ticker	Investment	Rating	Rating/Pts	3 Mo	6 Mo	1Yr / Pct	3Yr / Pct	5Yr / Pct	Yield	Ratio
Type	Fund Name	Symbol	Rating	Phone								
FO	Fidelity Adv 529 Diversified Intl C	FDIIX	D-	(800) 522-7297	D- / 1.0	6.23	0.84	9.82 / 11	-0.56 / 11	5.77 / 27	0.00	2.19
FO	Fidelity Adv 529 Diversified Intl D	FDIPX	D-	(800) 522-7297	D- / 1.1	6.44	1.10	10.45 / 13	-0.06 / 13	6.32 / 30	0.00	1.69
FO	Fidelity Adv 529 Diversified Intl P	FDPPX	D-	(800) 522-7297	D- / 1.0	6.37	0.95	10.12 / 12	-0.31 / 12	6.04 / 29	0.00	1.94
GR	Fidelity Adv 529 Dividend Growth A	FDGAX	B-	(800) 522-7297	C+ / 5.9	6.91	8.12	19.13 / 48	7.27 / 74	11.00 / 66	0.00	1.21
GR	Fidelity Adv 529 Dividend Growth C	FDGGX	B-	(800) 522-7297	C+ / 6.4	6.74	7.75	18.28 / 44	6.46 / 68	10.17 / 60	0.00	1.96
GR	Fidelity Adv 529 Dividend Growth D	FDGDX	B-	(800) 522-7297	C+ / 6.7	6.79	7.99	18.81 / 46	6.99 / 72	10.71 / 63	0.00	1.46
GR	Fidelity Adv 529 Dividend Growth P	FDGPX	B-	(800) 522-7297	C+ / 6.6	6.80	7.88	18.54 / 45	6.73 / 70	10.45 / 62	0.00	1.71
GR	Fidelity Adv 529 Equity Growth A	FEGAX	C+	(800) 522-7297	C+ / 6.1	10.58	8.29	20.92 / 57	6.36 / 67	12.35 / 78	0.00	1.25
GR	Fidelity Adv 529 Equity Growth C	FEGCX	C+	(800) 522-7297	C+ / 6.5	10.35	7.90	20.05 / 52	5.56 / 60	11.52 / 70	0.00	2.00
GR	Fidelity Adv 529 Equity Growth D	FEGDX	C+	(800) 522-7297	C+ / 6.9	10.51	8.18	20.63 / 56	6.11 / 65	12.09 / 75	0.00	1.50
GR	Fidelity Adv 529 Equity Growth P	FEGPX	C+	(800) 522-7297	C+ / 6.7	10.47	8.06	20.34 / 54	5.84 / 63	11.80 / 72	0.00	1.75
IN	Fidelity Adv 529 Equity Income A	FEIZX	B+	(800) 522-7297	B- / 7.1	5.67	10.05	27.24 / 80	7.82 / 78	11.62 / 71	0.00	1.17
IN	Fidelity Adv 529 Equity Income C	FEPCX	A-	(800) 522-7297	B / 7.6	5.49	9.66	26.36 / 77	7.03 / 72	10.80 / 64	0.00	1.92
IN	Fidelity Adv 529 Equity Income D	FEIDX	A	(800) 522-7297	B / 8.0	5.66	9.95	26.97 / 79	7.57 / 76	11.35 / 69	0.00	1.42
IN	Fidelity Adv 529 Equity Income P	FEIPX	A-	(800) 522-7297	B / 7.8	5.57	9.79	26.66 / 78	7.29 / 74	11.06 / 66	0.00	1.67
GR	Fidelity Adv 529 New Insights C	FNPCX	C+	(800) 522-7297	C+ / 6.5	7.75	7.32	21.35 / 59	5.85 / 63	11.04 / 66	0.00	2.06
GR	Fidelity Adv 529 New Insights P	FNPPX	C+	(800) 522-7297	C+ / 6.7	7.83	7.47	21.69 / 61	6.13 / 65	11.33 / 68	0.00	1.81
SC	Fidelity Adv 529 Small Cap A	FSLAX	C	(800) 522-7297	C / 5.0	4.97	8.32	20.83 / 57	5.89 / 63	9.41 / 54	0.00	1.48
SC	Fidelity Adv 529 Small Cap C	FSZPX	C+	(800) 522-7297	C / 5.5	4.79	7.92	19.91 / 51	5.09 / 55	8.59 / 47	0.00	2.23
SC	Fidelity Adv 529 Small Cap D	FSPDX	C+	(800) 522-7297	C+ / 6.0	4.90	8.20	20.50 / 55	5.62 / 61	9.13 / 52	0.00	1.73
SC	Fidelity Adv 529 Small Cap P	FSPPX	C+	(800) 522-7297	C+ / 5.7	4.83	8.05	20.22 / 53	5.35 / 58	8.86 / 49	0.00	1.98
MC	Fidelity Adv 529 Stock Select MC A	FBBEX	C+	(800) 522-7297	C+ / 6.7	8.18	11.04	27.11 / 79	6.25 / 66	11.45 / 69	0.00	1.24
MC	Fidelity Adv 529 Stock Select MC C	FBBFX	B-	(800) 522-7297	B- / 7.1	7.95	10.63	26.12 / 77	5.45 / 59	10.62 / 63	0.00	1.99
MC	Fidelity Adv 529 Stock Select MC D	FSSDX	B	(800) 522-7297	B- / 7.5	8.08	10.91	26.78 / 79	5.98 / 64	11.18 / 67	0.00	1.49
MC	Fidelity Adv 529 Stock Select MC P	FSMPX	B-	(800) 522-7297	B- / 7.3	8.02	10.76	26.47 / 78	5.73 / 62	10.90 / 65	0.00	1.74
AA	Fidelity Adv 529 Value Strat A	FVASX	B-	(800) 522-7297	B- / 7.0	8.77	9.74	28.51 / 83	6.62 / 69	11.77 / 72	0.00	1.25
AA	Fidelity Adv 529 Value Strat C	FVSCX	B	(800) 522-7297	B- / 7.4	8.59	9.32	27.53 / 81	5.82 / 63	10.94 / 65	0.00	2.00
AA	Fidelity Adv 529 Value Strat D	FVSDX	B+	(800) 522-7297	B / 7.8	8.73	9.62	28.23 / 82	6.36 / 67	11.49 / 70	0.00	1.50
AA	Fidelity Adv 529 Value Strat P	FVSPX	B	(800) 522-7297	B / 7.6	8.67	9.46	27.88 / 81	6.09 / 65	11.21 / 68	0.00	1.75
AA	Fidelity Adv Asset Manager 20% A	FTAWX	C-	(800) 522-7297	D- / 1.2	2.46	1.08	7.17 / 6	2.56 / 28	3.48 / 13	1.21	0.84
AA	Fidelity Adv Asset Manager 20% C	FTCWX	C-	(800) 522-7297	D- / 1.5	2.28	0.65	6.43 / 5	1.78 / 23	2.69 / 10	0.57	1.60
AA	Fidelity Adv Asset Manager 20% I	FTIWX	C	(800) 522-7297	D / 1.9	2.52	1.14	7.47 / 7	2.83 / 30	3.75 / 14	1.56	0.58
AA	Fidelity Adv Asset Manager 20% T	FTDWX	C-	(800) 522-7297	D- / 1.3	2.41	0.90	6.93 / 6	2.30 / 26	3.21 / 12	1.01	1.10
GI	Fidelity Adv Asset Manager 30% A	FTAAX	C-	(800) 522-7297	D / 1.6	3.23	1.85	9.57 / 11	3.17 / 33	4.57 / 19	1.26	0.86
GI	Fidelity Adv Asset Manager 30% C	FCANX	C	(800) 522-7297	D / 2.0	3.09	1.54	8.77 / 9	2.41 / 27	3.77 / 14	0.67	1.62
GI	Fidelity Adv Asset Manager 30% I	FTINX	C	(800) 522-7297	D+ / 2.5	3.29	1.97	9.74 / 11	3.43 / 36	4.82 / 20	1.58	0.61
GI	Fidelity Adv Asset Manager 30% T	FTTNX	C-	(800) 522-7297	D / 1.8	3.19	1.73	9.31 / 10	2.92 / 31	4.30 / 17	1.05	1.12
GI	Fidelity Adv Asset Manager 40% A	FFNAX	C-	(800) 522-7297	D / 2.1	3.98	2.76	11.59 / 16	3.64 / 38	5.50 / 25	1.24	0.85
GI	Fidelity Adv Asset Manager 40% C	FFNCX	C	(800) 522-7297	D+ / 2.4	3.79	2.39	10.69 / 13	2.84 / 30	4.69 / 19	0.59	1.62
GI	Fidelity Adv Asset Manager 40% I	FFNIX	C+	(800) 522-7297	C- / 3.2	4.05	2.91	11.88 / 17	3.93 / 42	5.77 / 27	1.57	0.59
GI	Fidelity Adv Asset Manager 40% T	FFNTX	C	(800) 522-7297	D / 2.2	4.01	2.72	11.38 / 16	3.38 / 36	5.23 / 23	1.00	1.13
AA	Fidelity Adv Asset Manager 50% A	FFAMX	C-	(800) 544-8544	D+ / 2.5	4.76	3.69	13.64 / 24	3.98 / 43	6.32 / 30	1.14	0.97
AA	Fidelity Adv Asset Manager 50% C	FFCMX	C-	(800) 544-8544	C- / 3.0	4.53	3.26	12.73 / 21	3.17 / 33	5.51 / 25	0.49	1.73
AA	Fidelity Adv Asset Manager 50% I	FFIMX	C	(800) 544-8544	C- / 3.7	4.82	3.76	13.90 / 25	4.24 / 46	6.59 / 32	1.44	0.71
AA	Fidelity Adv Asset Manager 50% T	FFTMX	C-	(800) 544-8544	D+ / 2.7	4.71	3.50	13.29 / 23	3.68 / 39	6.04 / 29	0.92	1.23
GI	Fidelity Adv Asset Manager 60% A	FSAAX	C-	(800) 522-7297	C- / 3.1	5.53	4.58	15.64 / 33	4.28 / 46	7.11 / 35	0.94	1.04
GI	Fidelity Adv Asset Manager 60% C	FSCNX	C	(800) 522-7297	C- / 3.5	5.27	4.12	14.76 / 29	3.49 / 37	6.28 / 30	0.34	1.79
GI	Fidelity Adv Asset Manager 60% I	FSNIX	C+	(800) 522-7297	C / 4.4	5.65	4.72	15.95 / 34	4.57 / 49	7.38 / 37	1.30	0.76
GI	Fidelity Adv Asset Manager 60% T	FSATX	C-	(800) 522-7297	C- / 3.3	5.50	4.45	15.33 / 31	4.01 / 43	6.83 / 34	0.75	1.30
AA	Fidelity Adv Asset Manager 85% A	FEYAX	C-	(800) 522-7297	C / 4.5	7.31	6.91	20.46 / 55	4.97 / 54	9.08 / 51	0.68	1.07
AA	Fidelity Adv Asset Manager 85% C	FEYCX	C	(800) 522-7297	C / 5.1	7.12	6.52	19.54 / 50	4.17 / 45	8.25 / 44	0.04	1.82
AA	Fidelity Adv Asset Manager 85% I	FEYIX	C	(800) 522-7297	C+ / 6.0	7.43	7.10	20.84 / 57	5.27 / 57	9.40 / 54	0.92	0.77

● Denotes fund is closed to new investors

* Denotes fund is included in Section II

Risk Rating/Pts	3 Year Standard Deviation	Beta	NAV As of 2/28/17	Total $(Mil)	Cash %	Stocks %	Bonds %	Other %	Portfolio Turnover Ratio	Last Bull Market Return	Last Bear Market Return	Manager Quality Pct	Manager Tenure (Years)	Initial Purch. $	Additional Purch. $	Front End Load	Back End Load
C+ / 6.0	11.2	0.87	20.47	22	1	98	0	1	0	54.8	-25.0	69	12	1,000	50	0.0	0.0
C+ / 6.1	11.2	0.87	21.99	1	1	98	0	1	0	59.1	-24.8	74	12	1,000	50	0.0	0.0
C+ / 6.0	11.1	0.87	21.21	1	1	98	0	1	0	57.0	-24.9	72	12	1,000	50	0.0	0.0
B- / 7.2	9.9	0.95	23.98	49	1	95	3	1	10	113.2	-24.8	40	12	1,000	50	5.8	0.0
B- / 7.1	9.9	0.95	21.55	19	1	95	3	1	10	104.7	-25.0	30	12	1,000	50	0.0	0.0
B- / 7.2	9.9	0.95	23.12	1	1	95	3	1	10	110.2	-24.8	36	12	1,000	50	0.0	0.0
B- / 7.1	9.9	0.95	22.31	1	1	95	3	1	10	107.5	-24.9	33	12	1,000	50	0.0	0.0
C+ / 6.1	11.7	0.96	26.13	46	2	91	6	1	5	120.1	-18.2	28	12	1,000	50	5.8	0.0
C+ / 6.0	11.7	0.96	23.35	17	2	91	6	1	5	111.3	-18.5	21	12	1,000	50	0.0	0.0
C+ / 6.1	11.7	0.96	25.14	2	2	91	6	1	5	117.5	-18.4	26	12	1,000	50	0.0	0.0
C+ / 6.1	11.6	0.96	24.26	1	2	91	6	1	5	114.3	-18.4	24	12	1,000	50	0.0	0.0
B- / 7.1	10.1	0.94	24.43	47	6	89	3	2	4	107.7	-17.9	49	12	1,000	50	5.8	0.0
B- / 7.0	10.1	0.94	21.91	19	6	89	3	2	4	99.5	-18.2	39	12	1,000	50	0.0	0.0
B- / 7.1	10.1	0.94	23.54	N/A	6	89	3	2	4	105.1	-18.1	46	12	1,000	50	0.0	0.0
B- / 7.1	10.1	0.94	22.76	1	6	89	3	2	4	102.1	-18.1	42	12	1,000	50	0.0	0.0
C+ / 6.5	10.4	0.94	21.54	77	6	93	0	1	0	100.4	-14.8	25	12	1,000	50	0.0	0.0
C+ / 6.5	10.4	0.95	22.16	1	6	93	0	1	0	102.9	-14.7	27	12	1,000	50	0.0	0.0
C+ / 6.1	12.8	0.79	34.63	44	1	95	2	2	3	93.4	-24.0	77	12	1,000	50	5.8	0.0
C+ / 6.1	12.8	0.79	31.08	14	1	95	2	2	3	85.7	-24.2	70	12	1,000	50	0.0	0.0
C+ / 6.1	12.8	0.79	33.39	1	1	95	2	2	3	90.7	-24.0	75	12	1,000	50	0.0	0.0
C+ / 6.1	12.8	0.79	32.35	1	1	95	2	2	3	88.2	-24.1	73	12	1,000	50	0.0	0.0
C+ / 5.7	12.3	0.99	29.77	54	0	98	1	1	2	114.8	-21.2	34	12	1,000	50	5.8	0.0
C+ / 5.6	12.3	0.99	26.75	20	0	98	1	1	2	106.3	-21.4	26	12	1,000	50	0.0	0.0
C+ / 5.7	12.3	0.99	28.88	1	0	98	1	1	2	112.0	-21.3	31	12	1,000	50	0.0	0.0
C+ / 5.7	12.3	0.99	28.00	1	0	98	1	1	2	109.1	-21.3	29	12	1,000	50	0.0	0.0
C+ / 5.9	12.4	1.76	32.23	25	2	97	0	1	7	123.4	-26.9	8	12	1,000	50	5.8	0.0
C+ / 5.9	12.4	1.76	29.32	8	2	97	0	1	7	114.5	-27.1	5	12	1,000	50	0.0	0.0
C+ / 5.9	12.4	1.76	30.89	N/A	2	97	0	1	7	120.3	-27.0	7	12	1,000	50	0.0	0.0
C+ / 5.9	12.4	1.76	30.09	1	2	97	0	1	7	117.4	-27.1	6	12	1,000	50	0.0	0.0
B / 8.9	3.1	0.44	13.23	39	30	18	50	2	19	25.6	-3.4	65	8	2,500	0	5.8	0.0
B+ / 9.0	3.1	0.44	13.15	28	30	18	50	2	19	20.5	-3.6	56	8	2,500	0	0.0	0.0
B / 8.9	3.1	0.44	13.24	41	30	18	50	2	19	27.3	-3.2	69	8	2,500	0	0.0	0.0
B+ / 9.0	3.1	0.44	13.20	24	30	18	50	2	19	23.8	-3.5	63	8	2,500	0	3.5	0.0
B / 8.7	4.1	0.34	10.72	21	19	29	50	2	24	34.9	-5.7	69	8	2,500	0	5.8	0.0
B / 8.7	4.1	0.34	10.66	21	19	29	50	2	24	29.6	-6.0	60	8	2,500	0	0.0	0.0
B / 8.7	4.0	0.34	10.72	16	19	29	50	2	24	36.8	-5.6	73	8	2,500	0	0.0	0.0
B / 8.7	4.1	0.34	10.71	12	19	29	50	2	24	33.0	-5.8	66	8	2,500	0	3.5	0.0
B / 8.4	5.0	0.44	11.13	37	16	38	45	1	22	43.8	-8.2	63	8	2,500	0	5.8	0.0
B / 8.4	5.0	0.44	11.08	22	16	38	45	1	22	37.9	-8.5	53	8	2,500	0	0.0	0.0
B / 8.4	5.0	0.44	11.13	15	16	38	45	1	22	45.8	-8.1	67	8	2,500	0	0.0	0.0
B / 8.4	5.0	0.44	11.12	11	16	38	45	1	22	41.8	-8.3	59	8	2,500	0	3.5	0.0
B- / 7.2	6.0	0.92	17.28	75	11	47	40	2	19	51.9	-10.7	37	8	2,500	0	5.8	0.0
B- / 7.2	6.0	0.92	17.16	42	11	47	40	2	19	45.8	-11.0	28	8	2,500	0	0.0	0.0
B- / 7.2	6.0	0.92	17.31	38	11	47	40	2	19	54.0	-10.6	41	8	2,500	0	0.0	0.0
B- / 7.2	6.0	0.92	17.26	34	11	47	40	2	19	49.8	-10.8	34	8	2,500	0	3.5	0.0
B- / 7.1	7.0	0.64	11.56	56	10	57	32	1	21	60.3	-13.2	44	8	2,500	0	5.8	0.0
B- / 7.2	7.0	0.64	11.39	34	10	57	32	1	21	53.8	-13.5	33	8	2,500	0	0.0	0.0
B- / 7.1	7.0	0.64	11.60	24	10	57	32	1	21	62.7	-13.1	48	8	2,500	0	0.0	0.0
B- / 7.1	7.0	0.64	11.51	19	10	57	32	1	21	58.1	-13.3	40	8	2,500	0	3.5	0.0
C / 5.4	9.5	1.45	17.31	83	5	82	12	1	22	83.4	-19.4	11	8	2,500	0	5.8	0.0
C / 5.5	9.5	1.45	17.05	41	5	82	12	1	22	76.0	-19.7	7	8	2,500	0	0.0	0.0
C / 5.4	9.5	1.44	17.40	26	5	82	12	1	22	86.1	-19.3	13	8	2,500	0	0.0	0.0

	99 Pct = Best 0 Pct = Worst				PERFORMANCE						Incl. in Returns	
							Total Return % through 2/28/17					
			Overall		Perfor-				Annualized		Dividend	Expense
Fund Type	Fund Name	Ticker Symbol	Investment Rating	Phone	mance Rating/Pts	3 Mo	6 Mo	1Yr / Pct	3Yr / Pct	5Yr / Pct	Yield	Ratio
AA	Fidelity Adv Asset Manager 85% T	FEYTX	C-	(800) 522-7297	C / 4.7	7.24	6.78	20.16 /53	4.65 /50	8.77 /49	0.38	1.34
GI	Fidelity Adv Asset Mang 70% A	FAASX	C-	(800) 522-7297	C- / 3.6	6.22	5.57	17.64 /41	4.55 /49	7.87 /41	0.90	1.03
GI	Fidelity Adv Asset Mang 70% C	FCASX	C-	(800) 522-7297	C- / 4.1	6.01	5.19	16.72 /37	3.75 /40	7.06 /35	0.25	1.79
GI	Fidelity Adv Asset Mang 70% I	FTASX	C-	(800) 522-7297	C- / 3.9	6.18	5.48	17.34 /40	4.28 /46	7.60 /39	0.70	1.29
GI	Fidelity Adv Asset Mang 70% T	FAAIX	C	(800) 522-7297	C / 5.1	6.29	5.75	18.00 /43	4.83 /52	8.18 /43	1.28	0.75
BA	Fidelity Adv Balanced A	FABLX	C+	(800) 522-7297	C / 5.0	6.48	6.14	17.96 /43	6.57 /69	9.26 /53	1.07	0.90
BA	Fidelity Adv Balanced C	FABCX	B-	(800) 522-7297	C / 5.5	6.27	5.72	17.06 /39	5.77 /62	8.44 /46	0.47	1.65
BA	Fidelity Adv Balanced Inst	FAIOX	B-	(800) 522-7297	C+ / 6.4	6.60	6.28	18.26 /44	6.85 /71	9.56 /55	1.34	0.64
BA	Fidelity Adv Balanced T	FAIGX	B-	(800) 522-7297	C / 5.2	6.45	6.05	17.66 /41	6.31 /67	9.02 /51	0.87	1.14
BA	Fidelity Adv Balanced Z	FZAAX	B-	(800) 522-7297	C+ / 6.5	6.63	6.35	18.43 /45	7.00 /72	--	1.47	0.50
HL	Fidelity Adv Biotechnology A	FBTAX	E	(800) 522-7297	C / 4.9	9.66	10.82	26.09 /76	3.05 /32	20.98 /99	0.00	1.05
HL	Fidelity Adv Biotechnology C	FBTCX	E+	(800) 522-7297	C / 5.4	9.43	10.40	25.12 /74	2.27 /26	20.10 /99	0.00	1.80
HL	Fidelity Adv Biotechnology I	FBTIX	D-	(800) 522-7297	C+ / 6.3	9.71	10.96	26.43 /78	3.33 /35	21.34 /99	0.00	0.78
HL	Fidelity Adv Biotechnology T	FBTTX	E	(800) 522-7297	C / 5.1	9.55	10.60	25.62 /75	2.72 /29	20.60 /99	0.00	1.37
FO	Fidelity Adv Canada A	FACNX	E	(800) 522-7297	E+ / 0.8	2.71	3.52	20.26 /53	-0.30 /12	1.88 / 8	0.86	1.43
FO	Fidelity Adv Canada C	FCCNX	E	(800) 522-7297	D- / 1.0	2.54	3.17	19.41 /49	-1.03 / 9	1.13 / 6	0.22	2.19
FO	Fidelity Adv Canada I	FICCX	E	(800) 522-7297	D / 2.0	2.80	3.71	20.70 /56	0.02 /13	2.21 / 9	1.33	1.13
FO	Fidelity Adv Canada T	FTCNX	E	(800) 522-7297	E+ / 0.9	2.64	3.39	19.94 /52	-0.60 /11	1.58 / 7	0.66	1.75
GR	Fidelity Adv Capital Devp Class A	FDTTX	C+	(800) 522-7297	B+ / 8.4	6.84	12.61	32.58 /91	8.41 /82	12.06 /75	1.06	0.89
GR	Fidelity Adv Capital Devp Class C	FDECX	B-	(800) 522-7297	B+ / 8.6	6.59	12.04	31.27 /89	7.32 /74	10.96 /65	0.51	1.89
GR	Fidelity Adv Capital Devp Class I	FDEIX	B	(800) 522-7297	A / 9.3	6.92	12.64	32.75 /91	8.55 /83	12.20 /76	1.25	0.75
GR	Fidelity Adv Capital Devp Class O	FDETX	B	(800) 522-7297	A / 9.4	6.90	12.72	32.94 /92	8.71 /85	12.40 /78	1.34	0.59
GR	Fidelity Adv Capital Devp Class T	FDTZX	C+	(800) 522-7297	B+ / 8.3	6.70	12.29	31.75 /90	7.79 /77	11.46 /70	0.70	1.44
FO	Fidelity Adv China Region Fd A	FHKAX	E	(800) 522-7297	D+ / 2.6	5.74	4.90	26.70 /78	1.34 /20	5.85 /27	0.65	1.28
FO	Fidelity Adv China Region Fd C	FCHKX	E	(800) 522-7297	C- / 3.1	5.57	4.54	25.79 /76	0.60 /16	5.08 /22	0.00	2.05
FO	Fidelity Adv China Region Fd I	FHKIX	E+	(800) 522-7297	C- / 3.9	5.84	5.09	27.13 /79	1.68 /22	6.22 /30	1.07	0.97
FO	Fidelity Adv China Region Fd T	FHKTX	E	(800) 522-7297	D+ / 2.8	5.67	4.74	26.30 /77	1.00 /18	5.52 /25	0.41	1.62
TC	Fidelity Adv Commu Equipment A	FDMAX	C+	(800) 522-7297	C+ / 6.4	5.38	10.48	28.55 /83	6.26 /66	8.84 /49	0.37	2.10
TC	Fidelity Adv Commu Equipment C	FDMCX	C+	(800) 522-7297	C+ / 6.8	5.24	10.03	27.53 /81	5.49 /59	8.06 /43	0.00	2.86
TC	Fidelity Adv Commu Equipment I	FDMIX	B-	(800) 522-7297	B / 7.6	5.45	10.62	28.87 /84	6.54 /69	9.12 /52	0.56	1.69
TC	Fidelity Adv Commu Equipment T	FDMTX	C+	(800) 522-7297	C+ / 6.6	5.33	10.37	28.21 /82	6.00 /64	8.57 /47	0.17	2.41
GR	Fidelity Adv Consumer Discre A	FCNAX	C-	(800) 522-7297	C / 4.5	4.27	4.37	14.61 /28	7.28 /74	13.33 /87	0.40	1.10
GR	Fidelity Adv Consumer Discre C	FCECX	C	(800) 522-7297	C / 5.0	4.08	3.96	13.78 /24	6.49 /68	12.48 /79	0.00	1.86
GR	Fidelity Adv Consumer Discre I	FCNIX	C+	(800) 522-7297	C+ / 5.9	4.31	4.49	14.92 /30	7.58 /76	13.66 /90	0.59	0.84
GR	Fidelity Adv Consumer Discre T	FACPX	C	(800) 522-7297	C / 4.7	4.21	4.21	14.27 /27	6.97 /72	12.99 /84	0.36	1.40
GR	Fidelity Adv Consumer Staples A	FDAGX	C+	(800) 522-7297	C+ / 6.3	11.00	3.37	11.91 /18	9.61 /91	11.35 /69	1.30	1.04
GR	Fidelity Adv Consumer Staples C	FDCGX	C+	(800) 522-7297	C+ / 6.7	10.80	2.99	11.07 /15	8.79 /85	10.52 /62	0.75	1.80
GR	Fidelity Adv Consumer Staples I	FDIGX	B+	(800) 522-7297	B- / 7.5	11.08	3.50	12.21 /19	9.89 /93	11.63 /71	1.62	0.78
GR	Fidelity Adv Consumer Staples T	FDTGX	C+	(800) 522-7297	C+ / 6.5	10.94	3.24	11.61 /16	9.31 /89	11.04 /66	1.11	1.32
GR	Fidelity Adv Divers Stk A	FDTOX	B	(800) 522-7297	B / 8.1	7.20	11.30	31.47 /89	8.33 /81	13.12 /85	1.20	0.87
GR	Fidelity Adv Divers Stk C	FDTCX	B	(800) 522-7297	B+ / 8.5	6.94	10.86	30.30 /87	7.34 /74	12.07 /75	0.53	1.80
GR	Fidelity Adv Divers Stk I	FDTIX	B+	(800) 522-7297	A- / 9.2	7.22	11.43	31.71 /89	8.55 /83	13.31 /87	1.35	0.67
GR	Fidelity Adv Divers Stk O	FDESX	B+	(800) 522-7297	A / 9.3	7.31	11.55	31.94 /90	8.71 /85	13.50 /89	1.55	0.50
GR	Fidelity Adv Divers Stk T	FDTEX	B	(800) 522-7297	B / 8.2	7.08	11.11	30.93 /88	7.89 /78	12.64 /80	0.92	1.27
GR	Fidelity Adv Divers Stk Z	FZACX	B+	(800) 522-7297	A / 9.3	7.29	11.53	31.95 /90	8.69 /85	--	1.49	0.54
FO	Fidelity Adv Diversified Intl A	FDVAX	D-	(800) 522-7297	D- / 1.1	6.51	1.34	10.88 /14	0.36 /15	6.74 /33	0.89	1.23
FO	Fidelity Adv Diversified Intl C	FADCX	D-	(800) 522-7297	D- / 1.0	6.31	0.96	10.00 /12	-0.40 /12	5.94 /28	0.16	1.98
FO	Fidelity Adv Diversified Intl I	FDVIX	D	(800) 522-7297	D / 1.8	6.58	1.44	11.17 /15	0.63 /16	7.05 /35	1.24	0.94
FO	Fidelity Adv Diversified Intl T	FADIX	D-	(800) 522-7297	D- / 1.2	6.45	1.19	10.55 /13	0.09 /14	6.47 /31	0.63	1.49
FO	Fidelity Adv Diversified Intl Z	FZABX	D	(800) 522-7297	D / 1.8	6.59	1.50	11.30 /15	0.79 /17	--	1.39	0.79
GR	Fidelity Adv Dividend Growth A	FADAX	C+	(800) 522-7297	C+ / 6.0	6.94	8.16	19.37 /49	7.48 /75	11.20 /68	1.08	1.01
GR	Fidelity Adv Dividend Growth C	FDGCX	C+	(800) 522-7297	C+ / 6.5	6.68	7.75	18.40 /45	6.66 /69	10.37 /61	0.47	1.76

● Denotes fund is closed to new investors

* Denotes fund is included in Section II

216

RISK			NET ASSETS		ASSET				Portfolio Turnover Ratio	BULL / BEAR		FUND MANAGER		MINIMUMS		LOADS	
Risk Rating/Pts	3 Year Standard Deviation	Beta	NAV As of 2/28/17	Total $(Mil)	Cash %	Stocks %	Bonds %	Other %		Last Bull Market Return	Last Bear Market Return	Manager Quality Pct	Manager Tenure (Years)	Initial Purch. $	Additional Purch. $	Front End Load	Back End Load
C /5.4	9.5	1.44	17.23	21	5	82	12	1	22	80.3	-19.4	9	8	2,500	0	3.5	0.0
C+ /6.2	8.0	0.73	20.54	142	9	63	26	2	21	69.2	-15.8	35	8	2,500	0	5.8	0.0
C+ /6.3	8.0	0.74	20.46	58	9	63	26	2	21	62.3	-16.1	26	8	2,500	0	0.0	0.0
C+ /6.3	8.0	0.73	20.56	49	9	63	26	2	21	66.8	-15.9	31	8	2,500	0	3.5	0.0
C+ /6.2	8.0	0.73	20.57	72	9	63	26	2	21	71.7	-15.7	38	8	2,500	0	0.0	0.0
B- /7.4	7.6	1.19	20.14	574	6	64	28	2	63	77.3	-10.5	45	9	2,500	0	5.8	0.0
B- /7.4	7.6	1.19	19.99	433	6	64	28	2	63	70.1	-10.8	35	9	2,500	0	0.0	0.0
B- /7.4	7.6	1.19	20.51	323	6	64	28	2	63	79.7	-10.4	48	9	2,500	0	0.0	0.0
B- /7.4	7.6	1.19	20.35	1,124	6	64	28	2	63	75.1	-10.6	41	9	2,500	0	3.5	0.0
B- /7.4	7.6	1.19	20.51	42	6	64	28	2	63	N/A	N/A	50	9	0	0	0.0	0.0
E- /0.1	31.5	1.80	23.05	981	0	98	0	2	29	236.7	-12.0	0	12	2,500	0	0.0	0.0
E- /0.1	31.4	1.80	20.07	611	0	98	0	2	29	223.2	-12.2	0	12	2,500	0	5.8	0.0
E- /0.2	31.5	1.80	24.30	903	0	98	0	2	29	241.6	-11.9	0	12	2,500	0	0.0	0.0
E- /0.1	31.5	1.80	21.92	126	0	98	0	2	29	230.6	-12.0	0	12	2,500	0	3.5	0.0
C- /3.2	13.5	0.72	49.28	43	2	96	1	1	44	24.3	-23.9	72	3	2,500	0	5.8	1.5
C- /3.3	13.5	0.72	48.25	18	2	96	1	1	44	19.5	-24.1	63	3	2,500	0	0.0	1.5
C- /3.2	13.5	0.72	49.33	42	2	96	1	1	44	26.5	-23.8	75	3	2,500	0	0.0	1.5
C- /3.3	13.5	0.72	49.07	12	2	96	1	1	44	22.4	-24.0	68	3	2,500	0	3.5	1.5
C- /4.1	12.5	1.15	15.22	415	2	97	0	1	29	110.7	-19.6	29	4	2,500	0	5.8	0.0
C- /4.1	12.5	1.15	14.38	3	2	97	0	1	29	99.7	-19.8	19	4	2,500	0	0.0	0.0
C- /4.2	12.5	1.15	15.77	3	2	97	0	1	29	112.0	-19.5	30	4	2,500	0	0.0	0.0
C- /4.1	12.5	1.15	15.70	2,647	2	97	0	1	29	114.1	-19.4	32	4	0	0	0.0	0.0
C- /4.1	12.5	1.14	14.86	3	2	97	0	1	29	104.7	-19.7	23	4	2,500	0	3.5	0.0
D- /1.5	22.9	1.13	26.22	22	0	98	1	1	70	63.5	-27.2	84	6	2,500	0	5.8	1.5
D /1.6	22.9	1.13	25.73	9	0	98	1	1	70	57.1	-27.4	80	6	2,500	0	0.0	1.5
D- /1.5	22.9	1.13	26.32	19	0	98	1	1	70	66.6	-27.1	86	6	2,500	0	0.0	1.5
D /1.6	22.9	1.13	26.15	6	0	98	1	1	70	60.8	-27.2	82	6	2,500	0	3.5	1.5
C /5.0	15.9	1.29	13.44	7	0	98	1	1	29	80.1	-32.4	6	3	2,500	0	5.8	0.8
C /4.9	15.8	1.29	11.92	3	0	98	1	1	29	72.9	-32.6	4	3	2,500	0	0.0	0.8
C /5.0	15.8	1.29	13.95	6	0	98	1	1	29	82.6	-32.4	6	3	2,500	0	0.0	0.8
C /5.0	15.8	1.29	12.96	4	0	98	1	1	29	77.9	-32.5	5	3	2,500	0	3.5	0.8
C+ /5.9	11.4	0.99	21.75	128	0	98	0	2	59	132.4	-16.6	34	3	2,500	0	5.8	0.0
C+ /5.7	11.5	1.00	17.84	63	0	98	0	2	59	123.3	-16.9	26	3	2,500	0	0.0	0.0
C+ /5.9	11.4	1.00	23.35	68	0	98	0	2	59	136.3	-16.5	38	3	2,500	0	0.0	0.0
C+ /5.8	11.4	0.99	20.40	26	0	98	0	2	59	128.7	-16.7	31	3	2,500	0	3.5	0.0
C+ /6.7	10.5	0.66	96.18	522	0	99	0	1	63	95.8	-6.7	88	13	2,500	0	5.8	0.0
C+ /6.7	10.5	0.66	93.89	308	0	99	0	1	63	88.0	-7.0	85	13	2,500	0	0.0	0.0
C+ /6.7	10.5	0.66	96.81	272	0	99	0	1	63	98.5	-6.7	89	13	2,500	0	0.0	0.0
C+ /6.7	10.5	0.66	95.42	90	0	99	0	1	63	92.9	-6.8	87	13	2,500	0	3.5	0.0
C /4.9	11.6	1.06	23.84	252	4	94	1	1	46	130.0	-18.3	38	11	2,500	0	5.8	0.0
C /4.9	11.6	1.07	23.19	29	4	94	1	1	46	118.7	-18.7	27	11	2,500	0	0.0	0.0
C /5.0	11.6	1.07	25.19	44	4	94	1	1	46	131.9	-18.2	40	11	2,500	0	0.0	0.0
C /4.9	11.6	1.07	24.43	1,626	4	94	1	1	46	134.2	-18.2	43	11	0	0	0.0	0.0
C /4.9	11.6	1.06	23.68	36	4	94	1	1	46	124.6	-18.5	33	11	2,500	0	3.5	0.0
C /4.9	11.6	1.06	24.98	N/A	4	94	1	1	46	N/A	N/A	43	11	0	0	0.0	0.0
C+ /6.0	11.1	0.87	19.78	562	1	98	0	1	31	62.6	-24.7	78	8	2,500	0	5.8	0.0
C+ /6.0	11.1	0.87	18.96	196	1	98	0	1	31	56.1	-24.9	71	8	2,500	0	0.0	0.0
C+ /6.0	11.1	0.87	20.09	770	1	98	0	1	31	65.2	-24.6	79	8	2,500	0	0.0	0.0
C+ /6.0	11.1	0.87	19.65	217	1	98	0	1	31	60.3	-24.7	76	8	2,500	0	3.5	0.0
C+ /6.0	11.1	0.87	20.07	95	1	98	0	1	31	N/A	N/A	80	8	0	0	0.0	0.0
C /5.4	9.9	0.95	17.86	375	3	93	2	2	56	115.1	-24.7	42	3	2,500	0	5.8	0.0
C /5.4	9.9	0.95	17.05	160	3	93	2	2	56	106.5	-24.9	32	3	2,500	0	0.0	0.0

Fund Type	Fund Name	Ticker Symbol	Overall Investment Rating	Phone	Performance Rating/Pts	3 Mo	6 Mo	1Yr / Pct	3Yr / Pct	5Yr / Pct	Dividend Yield	Expense Ratio
	99 Pct = Best 0 Pct = Worst							Total Return % through 2/28/17	Annualized		Incl. in Returns	
GR	Fidelity Adv Dividend Growth I	FDGIX	B-	(800) 522-7297	B- / 7.2	7.01	8.36	19.66 /50	7.74 /77	11.49 /70	1.30	0.76
GR	Fidelity Adv Dividend Growth T	FDGTX	C+	(800) 522-7297	C+ / 6.3	6.83	8.05	19.01 /47	7.22 /73	10.93 /65	0.88	1.24
GR	Fidelity Adv Dividend Growth Z	FZADX	B-	(800) 522-7297	B- / 7.3	6.99	8.38	19.80 /51	7.91 /78	--	1.40	0.59
EM	Fidelity Adv Emerg Mkts Discv A	FEDAX	C	(800) 522-7297	C / 4.9	9.58	5.76	30.17 /87	3.78 /40	3.63 /14	0.48	1.88
EM	Fidelity Adv Emerg Mkts Discv C	FEDGX	C	(800) 522-7297	C / 5.4	9.36	5.37	29.16 /84	3.03 /32	2.86 /10	0.04	2.64
EM	Fidelity Adv Emerg Mkts Discv I	FEDIX	C+	(800) 522-7297	C+ / 6.3	9.67	5.88	30.46 /87	4.06 /44	3.91 /15	0.79	1.54
EM	Fidelity Adv Emerg Mkts Discv T	FEDTX	C	(800) 522-7297	C / 5.1	9.51	5.59	29.82 /86	3.54 /37	3.38 /12	0.34	2.16
EM	Fidelity Adv Emerging Asia A	FEAAX	D+	(800) 522-7297	C- / 3.7	6.43	2.23	24.69 /72	4.29 /46	4.13 /16	0.75	1.42
EM	Fidelity Adv Emerging Asia C	FERCX	C-	(800) 522-7297	C- / 4.2	6.25	1.88	23.77 /69	3.52 /37	3.21 /12	0.27	2.16
EM	Fidelity Adv Emerging Asia I	FERIX	C-	(800) 522-7297	C / 5.2	6.52	2.41	25.07 /73	4.61 /50	4.28 /17	0.97	1.11
EM	Fidelity Adv Emerging Asia T	FEATX	D+	(800) 522-7297	C- / 3.9	6.37	2.09	24.29 /71	3.97 /43	3.76 /14	0.57	1.72
EM	Fidelity Adv Emerging EMEA A	FMEAX	E+	(800) 522-7297	D / 1.8	8.40	10.48	32.74 /91	-0.02 /13	0.32 / 5	0.94	1.61
EM	Fidelity Adv Emerging EMEA C	FEMCX	E+	(800) 522-7297	D / 2.2	8.29	10.11	31.86 /90	-0.77 /10	-0.45 / 4	0.39	2.41
EM	Fidelity Adv Emerging EMEA Fd	FEMEX	D+	(800) 522-7297	C / 4.8	8.47	10.69	33.17 /92	0.25 /14	0.56 / 5	1.19	1.39
EM	Fidelity Adv Emerging EMEA I	FIEMX	D+	(800) 522-7297	C / 4.9	8.57	10.80	33.13 /92	0.36 /15	0.66 / 6	1.28	1.25
EM	Fidelity Adv Emerging EMEA T	FEMTX	E+	(800) 522-7297	D / 2.0	8.47	10.42	32.54 /91	-0.26 /12	0.05 / 4	0.78	1.92
EM	Fidelity Adv Emerging Markets A	FAMKX	D-	(800) 522-7297	D / 1.8	7.98	0.79	20.71 /56	0.93 /18	0.80 / 6	0.03	1.51
EM	Fidelity Adv Emerging Markets C	FMCKX	D	(800) 522-7297	D / 2.1	7.74	0.37	19.79 /51	0.17 /14	0.03 / 4	0.00	2.26
EM	Fidelity Adv Emerging Markets I	FIMKX	D	(800) 522-7297	D+ / 2.8	8.09	0.94	21.13 /58	1.29 /20	1.15 / 6	0.41	1.16
EM	Fidelity Adv Emerging Markets T	FTMKX	D-	(800) 522-7297	D / 1.9	7.90	0.63	20.34 /54	0.67 /16	0.54 / 5	0.00	1.77
EM	Fidelity Adv Emerging Markets Z	FZAEX	D	(800) 522-7297	C- / 3.0	8.14	1.03	21.31 /59	1.44 /21	--	0.58	1.01
EN	Fidelity Adv Energy A	FANAX	E-	(800) 522-7297	E / 0.4	-6.41	4.07	35.34 /94	-4.68 / 3	0.10 / 5	0.00	1.12
EN	Fidelity Adv Energy C	FNRCX	E-	(800) 522-7297	E / 0.5	-6.61	3.69	34.34 /93	-5.38 / 2	-0.64 / 4	0.00	1.84
EN	Fidelity Adv Energy I	FANIX	E-	(800) 522-7297	E+ / 0.7	-6.36	4.19	35.66 /95	-4.42 / 3	0.37 / 5	0.21	0.85
EN	Fidelity Adv Energy T	FAGNX	E-	(800) 522-7297	E / 0.4	-6.49	3.92	34.94 /94	-4.92 / 2	-0.14 / 4	0.00	1.38
GR	Fidelity Adv Equity Growth A	EPGAX	C+	(800) 522-7297	C+ / 6.2	10.62	8.42	21.16 /58	6.54 /69	12.52 /79	0.00	1.05
GR	Fidelity Adv Equity Growth C	EPGCX	C+	(800) 522-7297	C+ / 6.7	10.41	8.00	20.24 /53	5.74 /62	11.68 /71	0.00	1.81
GR	Fidelity Adv Equity Growth I	EQPGX	B	(800) 522-7297	B- / 7.4	10.70	8.56	21.49 /60	6.84 /71	12.86 /82	0.00	0.78
GR	Fidelity Adv Equity Growth T	FAEGX	C+	(800) 522-7297	C+ / 6.5	10.56	8.28	20.88 /57	6.31 /67	12.29 /77	0.00	1.27
GR	Fidelity Adv Equity Growth Z	FZAFX	B	(800) 522-7297	B- / 7.5	10.74	8.65	21.67 /61	6.99 /72	--	0.00	0.64
IN	Fidelity Adv Equity Income A	FEIAX	B	(800) 522-7297	B- / 7.3	5.75	10.16	27.54 /81	8.04 /79	11.83 /73	1.71	1.03
IN	Fidelity Adv Equity Income C	FEICX	B	(800) 522-7297	B / 7.7	5.55	9.74	26.55 /78	7.21 /73	10.98 /66	1.13	1.80
IN	Fidelity Adv Equity Income I	EQPIX	B+	(800) 522-7297	B+ / 8.5	5.80	10.29	27.81 /81	8.31 /81	12.12 /75	1.97	0.77
IN	Fidelity Adv Equity Income T	FEIRX	B	(800) 522-7297	B- / 7.5	5.70	10.02	27.23 /80	7.78 /77	11.59 /71	1.51	1.26
IN	Fidelity Adv Equity Income Z	FZAGX	B+	(800) 522-7297	B+ / 8.6	5.87	10.41	28.04 /82	8.47 /83	--	2.09	0.62
GR	Fidelity Adv Equity Value A	FAVAX	A	(800) 522-7297	B / 7.9	8.19	11.93	24.35 /71	9.03 /87	13.49 /89	0.70	1.24
GR	Fidelity Adv Equity Value C	FAVCX	A	(800) 522-7297	B+ / 8.3	7.95	11.57	23.33 /68	8.22 /81	12.63 /80	0.14	2.00
GR	Fidelity Adv Equity Value I	FAIVX	A+	(800) 522-7297	A- / 9.1	8.30	12.12	24.69 /72	9.38 /89	13.84 /92	0.96	0.93
GR	Fidelity Adv Equity Value T	FAVTX	A	(800) 522-7297	B / 8.1	8.10	11.85	24.03 /70	8.75 /85	13.21 /86	0.48	1.50
FS	Fidelity Adv Financial Serv A	FAFDX	A+	(800) 522-7297	A+ / 9.7	9.11	20.36	38.17 /96	9.86 /93	13.68 /90	0.19	1.15
FS	Fidelity Adv Financial Serv C	FAFCX	A+	(800) 522-7297	A+ / 9.8	8.90	19.93	37.24 /96	9.08 /87	12.85 /82	0.01	1.90
FS	Fidelity Adv Financial Serv I	FFSIX	A+	(800) 522-7297	A+ / 9.8	9.21	20.57	38.66 /97	10.23 /94	14.06 /94	0.31	0.85
FS	Fidelity Adv Financial Serv T	FAFSX	A+	(800) 522-7297	A+ / 9.8	9.03	20.23	37.82 /96	9.56 /91	13.38 /88	0.10	1.45
AA	Fidelity Adv Freedom 2005 A	FFAVX	C	(800) 522-7297	D / 1.9	3.67	2.52	11.07 /15	3.37 /35	4.51 /18	1.41	0.80
AA	Fidelity Adv Freedom 2005 C	FCFVX	C	(800) 522-7297	D+ / 2.3	3.52	2.28	10.35 /12	2.63 /28	3.73 /14	0.76	1.55
AA	Fidelity Adv Freedom 2005 I	FFIVX	C+	(800) 522-7297	D+ / 2.9	3.76	2.71	11.38 /16	3.65 /39	4.77 /20	1.73	0.55
AA	Fidelity Adv Freedom 2005 T	FFTVX	C	(800) 522-7297	D / 2.0	3.57	2.42	10.82 /14	3.10 /33	4.24 /16	1.22	1.05
AA	Fidelity Adv Freedom 2010 A	FACFX	C-	(800) 522-7297	D+ / 2.3	4.27	3.32	12.90 /21	3.78 /40	5.44 /24	1.42	0.85
AA	Fidelity Adv Freedom 2010 C	FCFCX	C	(800) 522-7297	D+ / 2.7	4.08	2.96	12.11 /18	3.00 /32	4.66 /19	0.82	1.60
AA	Fidelity Adv Freedom 2010 I	FCIFX	C+	(800) 522-7297	C- / 3.5	4.38	3.53	13.35 /23	4.07 /44	5.72 /26	1.76	0.60
AA	Fidelity Adv Freedom 2010 T	FCFTX	C	(800) 522-7297	D+ / 2.5	4.25	3.22	12.76 /21	3.55 /38	5.20 /23	1.23	1.10
AA	Fidelity Adv Freedom 2015 A	FFVAX	C	(800) 522-7297	D+ / 2.8	4.86	4.09	14.76 /29	4.18 /45	5.85 /27	1.38	0.89

Risk Rating/Pts	3 Year Standard Deviation	Beta	NAV As of 2/28/17	Total $(Mil)	Cash %	Stocks %	Bonds %	Other %	Portfolio Turnover Ratio	Last Bull Market Return	Last Bear Market Return	Manager Quality Pct	Manager Tenure (Years)	Initial Purch. $	Additional Purch. $	Front End Load	Back End Load
C /5.5	9.9	0.95	18.69	130	3	93	2	2	56	118.3	-24.6	46	3	2,500	0	0.0	0.0
C /5.4	9.9	0.95	17.79	366	3	93	2	2	56	112.3	-24.7	39	3	2,500	0	3.5	0.0
C+ /5.6	9.9	0.95	18.93	N/A	3	93	2	2	56	N/A	N/A	48	3	0	0	0.0	0.0
C+ /5.8	13.8	0.81	12.60	7	3	96	0	1	60	N/A	N/A	88	3	2,500	0	5.8	2.0
C+ /5.8	13.8	0.81	12.34	3	3	96	0	1	60	N/A	N/A	84	3	2,500	0	0.0	2.0
C+ /5.8	13.8	0.81	12.68	10	3	96	0	1	60	N/A	N/A	89	3	2,500	0	0.0	2.0
C+ /5.8	13.8	0.81	12.55	4	3	96	0	1	60	N/A	N/A	86	3	2,500	0	3.5	2.0
C /5.1	15.3	0.88	30.78	116	2	96	1	1	75	48.9	-25.5	89	1	2,500	0	5.8	1.5
C /5.1	15.3	0.88	28.08	41	2	96	1	1	75	42.1	-25.8	86	1	2,500	0	0.0	1.5
C /5.0	15.3	0.88	31.71	33	2	96	1	1	75	50.2	-25.4	90	1	2,500	0	0.0	1.5
C /5.1	15.3	0.88	29.93	35	2	96	1	1	75	46.1	-25.6	88	1	2,500	0	3.5	1.5
C- /3.8	17.0	0.88	8.54	9	0	98	1	1	54	25.7	-26.8	55	9	2,500	0	5.8	1.5
C- /3.9	16.9	0.88	8.51	7	0	98	1	1	54	20.7	-27.0	44	9	2,500	0	0.0	1.5
C- /3.8	16.9	0.87	8.55	85	0	98	1	1	54	27.5	-26.7	59	9	2,500	0	0.0	1.5
C- /3.8	16.9	0.87	8.54	8	0	98	1	1	54	28.2	-26.7	60	9	2,500	0	0.0	1.5
C- /3.9	16.9	0.87	8.53	3	0	98	1	1	54	24.0	-26.8	52	9	2,500	0	3.5	1.5
C /5.3	13.7	0.79	22.41	113	1	97	0	2	85	24.5	-28.5	69	5	2,500	0	5.8	1.5
C /5.2	13.7	0.79	21.43	41	1	97	0	2	85	19.5	-28.7	60	5	2,500	0	0.0	1.5
C /5.3	13.7	0.79	22.49	240	1	97	0	2	85	26.8	-28.4	73	5	2,500	0	0.0	1.5
C /5.3	13.7	0.79	22.25	43	1	97	0	2	85	22.7	-28.6	66	5	2,500	0	3.5	1.5
C /5.3	13.7	0.79	22.46	6	1	97	0	2	85	N/A	N/A	74	5	0	0	0.0	1.5
D- /1.5	22.3	1.11	33.94	383	5	94	0	1	85	30.3	-31.0	82	11	2,500	0	5.8	0.0
D- /1.5	22.3	1.11	31.22	268	5	94	0	1	85	25.2	-31.2	77	11	2,500	0	0.0	0.0
D- /1.5	22.3	1.11	35.73	285	5	94	0	1	85	32.3	-30.9	83	11	2,500	0	0.0	0.0
D- /1.5	22.3	1.11	34.72	153	5	94	0	1	85	28.7	-31.1	80	11	2,500	0	3.5	0.0
C+ /5.7	11.7	0.96	99.93	843	0	99	0	1	63	121.9	-18.2	30	11	2,500	0	5.8	0.0
C+ /5.6	11.7	0.96	87.16	171	0	99	0	1	63	113.2	-18.5	22	11	2,500	0	0.0	0.0
C+ /5.8	12.9	0.89	108.32	451	0	99	0	1	63	125.6	-18.1	43	11	2,500	0	0.0	0.0
C+ /5.7	11.7	0.96	98.41	1,190	0	99	0	1	63	119.5	-18.3	27	11	2,500	0	3.5	0.0
C+ /5.8	11.7	0.96	108.90	44	0	99	0	1	63	N/A	N/A	35	11	0	0	0.0	0.0
C+ /5.8	10.1	0.94	33.18	734	5	90	2	3	53	109.9	-17.9	52	6	2,500	0	5.8	0.0
C+ /5.8	10.1	0.94	33.35	208	5	90	2	3	53	101.4	-18.1	41	6	2,500	0	0.0	0.0
C+ /5.9	10.1	0.94	34.51	467	5	90	2	3	53	112.9	-17.8	56	6	2,500	0	0.0	0.0
C+ /5.8	10.1	0.94	33.83	819	5	90	2	3	53	107.4	-17.9	49	6	2,500	0	3.5	0.0
C+ /5.8	10.1	0.94	34.51	17	5	90	2	3	53	N/A	N/A	58	6	0	0	0.0	0.0
B- /7.1	10.0	0.92	17.67	85	7	89	3	1	49	131.7	-21.2	66	5	2,500	0	5.8	0.0
B- /7.1	10.0	0.92	17.29	36	7	89	3	1	49	122.3	-21.4	56	5	2,500	0	0.0	0.0
B- /7.1	10.0	0.92	17.95	24	7	89	3	1	49	135.6	-21.1	70	5	2,500	0	0.0	0.0
B- /7.2	10.0	0.92	17.67	42	7	89	3	1	49	128.3	-21.2	63	5	2,500	0	3.5	0.0
C+ /6.3	13.4	1.02	19.00	151	2	96	1	1	63	144.3	-28.2	41	4	2,500	0	5.8	0.0
C+ /6.3	13.4	1.02	17.88	88	2	96	1	1	63	134.6	-28.3	32	4	2,500	0	0.0	0.0
C+ /6.3	13.4	1.02	19.53	76	2	96	1	1	63	148.6	-28.0	46	4	2,500	0	0.0	0.0
C+ /6.3	13.4	1.02	18.82	43	2	96	1	1	63	140.9	-28.3	37	4	2,500	0	3.5	0.0
B /8.6	4.7	0.71	11.79	121	7	37	55	1	30	36.0	-8.5	50	14	2,500	0	5.8	0.0
B /8.7	4.6	0.70	11.78	6	7	37	55	1	30	30.7	-8.8	41	14	2,500	0	0.0	0.0
B /8.6	4.7	0.71	11.87	60	7	37	55	1	30	38.0	-8.4	54	14	2,500	0	0.0	0.0
B /8.6	4.7	0.71	11.78	28	7	37	55	1	30	34.2	-8.6	46	14	2,500	0	3.5	0.0
B /8.1	5.5	0.84	12.28	272	6	45	47	2	21	44.9	-10.4	43	14	2,500	0	5.8	0.0
B /8.2	5.5	0.85	12.17	29	6	45	47	2	21	39.1	-10.6	32	14	2,500	0	0.0	0.0
B /8.1	5.5	0.85	12.34	131	6	45	47	2	21	47.0	-10.4	46	14	2,500	0	0.0	0.0
B /8.2	5.5	0.84	12.25	85	6	45	47	2	21	43.0	-10.5	39	14	2,500	0	3.5	0.0
B- /7.9	6.3	0.96	12.36	668	5	54	39	2	20	48.0	-10.6	36	14	2,500	0	5.8	0.0

Fund Type	Fund Name	Ticker Symbol	Overall Investment Rating	Phone	Performance Rating/Pts	3 Mo	6 Mo	1Yr / Pct	3Yr / Pct	5Yr / Pct	Dividend Yield	Expense Ratio
	99 Pct = Best 0 Pct = Worst							Total Return % through 2/28/17	Annualized		Incl. in Returns	
AA	Fidelity Adv Freedom 2015 C	FFVCX	C	(800) 522-7297	C- / 3.3	4.67	3.71	13.95 /25	3.40 /36	5.07 /22	0.78	1.64
AA	Fidelity Adv Freedom 2015 I	FFVIX	C+	(800) 522-7297	C- / 4.1	4.94	4.26	15.14 /30	4.45 /48	6.13 /29	1.70	0.64
AA	Fidelity Adv Freedom 2015 T	FFVTX	C	(800) 522-7297	C- / 3.0	4.77	3.99	14.51 /28	3.91 /42	5.60 /25	1.19	1.14
AA	Fidelity Adv Freedom 2020 A	FDAFX	C	(800) 522-7297	C- / 3.1	5.21	4.55	15.98 /34	4.42 /48	6.31 /30	1.33	0.91
AA	Fidelity Adv Freedom 2020 C	FDCFX	C+	(800) 522-7297	C- / 3.6	5.06	4.24	15.15 /31	3.67 /39	5.51 /25	0.72	1.66
AA	Fidelity Adv Freedom 2020 I	FDIFX	C+	(800) 522-7297	C / 4.5	5.29	4.72	16.33 /36	4.68 /51	6.56 /32	1.63	0.66
AA	Fidelity Adv Freedom 2020 T	FDTFX	C	(800) 522-7297	C- / 3.4	5.18	4.44	15.69 /33	4.16 /45	6.05 /29	1.13	1.16
AA	Fidelity Adv Freedom 2025 A	FATWX	C	(800) 522-7297	C- / 3.6	5.67	5.17	17.34 /40	4.69 /51	7.13 /35	1.27	0.94
AA	Fidelity Adv Freedom 2025 C	FCTWX	C+	(800) 522-7297	C- / 4.1	5.51	4.74	16.39 /36	3.92 /42	6.33 /30	0.72	1.69
AA	Fidelity Adv Freedom 2025 I	FITWX	C+	(800) 522-7297	C / 5.0	5.74	5.24	17.57 /41	4.97 /54	7.39 /37	1.56	0.69
AA	Fidelity Adv Freedom 2025 T	FTTWX	C	(800) 522-7297	C- / 3.8	5.54	4.96	16.92 /38	4.42 /48	6.85 /34	1.08	1.19
AA	Fidelity Adv Freedom 2030 A	FAFEX	C	(800) 522-7297	C / 4.5	6.58	6.42	20.26 /53	5.14 /56	7.67 /40	1.16	0.99
AA	Fidelity Adv Freedom 2030 C	FCFEX	C+	(800) 522-7297	C / 5.0	6.41	6.08	19.38 /49	4.36 /47	6.88 /34	0.70	1.74
AA	Fidelity Adv Freedom 2030 I	FEFIX	C+	(800) 522-7297	C+ / 5.9	6.66	6.58	20.52 /55	5.41 /59	7.94 /42	1.45	0.74
AA	Fidelity Adv Freedom 2030 T	FTFEX	C+	(800) 522-7297	C / 4.7	6.56	6.32	19.98 /52	4.91 /53	7.42 /37	0.99	1.24
AA	Fidelity Adv Freedom 2035 A	FATHX	C+	(800) 522-7297	C / 5.1	7.18	7.44	22.09 /63	5.44 /59	8.33 /45	1.09	1.02
AA	Fidelity Adv Freedom 2035 C	FCTHX	C+	(800) 522-7297	C+ / 5.7	7.04	7.04	21.24 /58	4.68 /51	7.52 /38	0.68	1.77
AA	Fidelity Adv Freedom 2035 I	FITHX	C+	(800) 522-7297	C+ / 6.5	7.26	7.59	22.47 /64	5.71 /62	8.58 /47	1.32	0.77
AA	Fidelity Adv Freedom 2035 T	FTTHX	C	(800) 522-7297	C / 5.4	7.13	7.30	21.85 /61	5.20 /56	8.06 /43	0.96	1.27
AA	Fidelity Adv Freedom 2040 A	FAFFX	C+	(800) 522-7297	C / 5.1	7.27	7.51	22.15 /63	5.47 /59	8.39 /45	1.09	1.02
AA	Fidelity Adv Freedom 2040 C	FCFFX	C+	(800) 522-7297	C+ / 5.7	7.09	7.09	21.28 /59	4.67 /50	7.58 /39	0.68	1.77
AA	Fidelity Adv Freedom 2040 I	FIFFX	C+	(800) 522-7297	C+ / 6.5	7.35	7.58	22.42 /64	5.73 /62	8.66 /48	1.34	0.77
AA	Fidelity Adv Freedom 2040 T	FTFFX	C+	(800) 522-7297	C / 5.4	7.17	7.33	21.89 /62	5.19 /56	8.12 /43	0.95	1.27
AA	Fidelity Adv Freedom 2045 A	FFFZX	C+	(800) 522-7297	C / 5.1	7.22	7.43	22.11 /63	5.48 /59	8.52 /46	1.08	1.02
AA	Fidelity Adv Freedom 2045 C	FFFJX	C+	(800) 522-7297	C+ / 5.7	7.09	7.09	21.22 /58	4.68 /51	7.72 /40	0.68	1.77
AA	Fidelity Adv Freedom 2045 I	FFFIX	C+	(800) 522-7297	C+ / 6.5	7.37	7.58	22.43 /64	5.72 /62	8.79 /49	1.31	0.77
AA	Fidelity Adv Freedom 2045 T	FFFTX	C+	(800) 522-7297	C / 5.4	7.19	7.29	21.81 /61	5.22 /57	8.25 /44	0.96	1.27
AA	Fidelity Adv Freedom 2050 A	FFFLX	C+	(800) 522-7297	C / 5.1	7.21	7.42	22.19 /63	5.47 /59	8.56 /47	1.08	1.02
AA	Fidelity Adv Freedom 2050 C	FFFYX	C+	(800) 522-7297	C+ / 5.7	7.05	7.05	21.29 /59	4.67 /50	7.76 /40	0.66	1.77
AA	Fidelity Adv Freedom 2050 I	FFFPX	C+	(800) 522-7297	C+ / 6.5	7.36	7.66	22.45 /64	5.74 /62	8.84 /49	1.33	0.77
AA	Fidelity Adv Freedom 2050 T	FFFQX	C+	(800) 522-7297	C / 5.3	7.16	7.26	21.77 /61	5.19 /56	8.30 /45	0.95	1.27
GL	Fidelity Adv Freedom 2055 A	FHFAX	C+	(800) 522-7297	C / 5.1	7.24	7.43	22.10 /63	5.47 /59	8.71 /48	1.06	1.02
GL	Fidelity Adv Freedom 2055 C	FHFCX	C+	(800) 522-7297	C+ / 5.7	7.05	7.05	21.18 /58	4.69 /51	7.90 /41	0.67	1.77
GL	Fidelity Adv Freedom 2055 I	FHFIX	C+	(800) 522-7297	C+ / 6.5	7.30	7.58	22.52 /65	5.76 /62	9.00 /51	1.30	0.77
GL	Fidelity Adv Freedom 2055 T	FHFTX	C+	(800) 522-7297	C / 5.4	7.18	7.37	21.86 /61	5.22 /57	8.47 /46	0.94	1.27
AA	Fidelity Adv Freedom Income A	FAFAX	C	(800) 522-7297	D- / 1.4	2.84	1.62	8.56 / 9	2.74 /29	3.35 /12	1.33	0.74
AA	Fidelity Adv Freedom Income C	FCAFX	C	(800) 522-7297	D / 1.7	2.66	1.26	7.80 / 7	1.99 /24	2.60 /10	0.72	1.49
AA	Fidelity Adv Freedom Income I	FIAFX	C	(800) 522-7297	D / 2.2	2.90	1.74	8.78 / 9	3.01 /32	3.63 /14	1.63	0.49
AA	Fidelity Adv Freedom Income T	FTAFX	C	(800) 522-7297	D- / 1.5	2.77	1.49	8.28 / 8	2.48 /27	3.11 /11	1.12	0.99
GL	Fidelity Adv Glb Commodity Stk A	FFGAX	E-	(800) 522-7297	E+ / 0.7	4.77	11.41	37.54 /96	-4.74 / 3	-4.53 / 2	0.63	1.34
GL	Fidelity Adv Glb Commodity Stk C	FCGCX	E-	(800) 522-7297	E+ / 0.8	4.68	11.08	36.51 /95	-5.45 / 2	-5.24 / 2	0.10	2.12
GL	Fidelity Adv Glb Commodity Stk Fd	FFGCX	E-	(800) 544-8544	D- / 1.2	4.92	11.54	37.93 /96	-4.50 / 3	-4.29 / 2	0.90	1.12
GL	Fidelity Adv Glb Commodity Stk I	FFGIX	E-	(800) 522-7297	D- / 1.2	4.94	11.68	37.97 /96	-4.44 / 3	-4.23 / 2	1.01	1.09
GL	Fidelity Adv Glb Commodity Stk T	FFGTX	E-	(800) 522-7297	E+ / 0.7	4.72	11.26	37.06 /96	-4.99 / 2	-4.78 / 2	0.42	1.63
GL	Fidelity Adv Global Cap App-Cl A	FGEAX	C-	(800) 522-7297	C- / 3.9	6.46	4.71	19.40 /49	5.13 /56	11.79 /72	0.00	1.55
GL	Fidelity Adv Global Cap App-Cl C	FEUCX	C	(800) 522-7297	C / 4.4	6.27	4.29	18.53 /45	4.36 /47	10.96 /65	0.00	2.31
GL	Fidelity Adv Global Cap App-Cl I	FEUIX	C+	(800) 522-7297	C / 5.4	6.57	4.82	19.78 /51	5.41 /59	12.14 /75	0.00	1.23
GL	Fidelity Adv Global Cap App-Cl T	FGETX	C-	(800) 522-7297	C- / 4.2	6.39	4.57	19.14 /48	4.89 /53	11.52 /70	0.00	1.86
AA	Fidelity Adv Global Strat A	FDASX	C-	(800) 522-7297	D+ / 2.6	5.55	3.88	14.06 /26	3.74 /40	4.99 /21	1.08	1.46
AA	Fidelity Adv Global Strat C	FDCSX	C-	(800) 522-7297	C- / 3.0	5.40	3.47	13.20 /22	2.95 /31	4.20 /16	0.62	2.21
AA	Fidelity Adv Global Strat I	FDYIX	C	(800) 522-7297	C- / 3.8	5.58	3.92	14.31 /27	4.01 /43	5.23 /23	1.40	1.21
AA	Fidelity Adv Global Strat T	FDTSX	C-	(800) 522-7297	D+ / 2.7	5.43	3.64	13.70 /24	3.45 /36	4.70 /19	0.89	1.71

● Denotes fund is closed to new investors

* Denotes fund is included in Section II

RISK			NET ASSETS		ASSET					BULL / BEAR		FUND MANAGER		MINIMUMS		LOADS	
	3 Year		NAV						Portfolio	Last Bull	Last Bear	Manager	Manager	Initial	Additional	Front	Back
Risk Rating/Pts	Standard Deviation	Beta	As of 2/28/17	Total $(Mil)	Cash %	Stocks %	Bonds %	Other %	Turnover Ratio	Market Return	Market Return	Quality Pct	Tenure (Years)	Purch. $	Purch. $	End Load	End Load
B /8.0	6.3	0.97	12.26	62	5	54	39	2	20	42.1	-10.9	27	14	2,500	0	0.0	0.0
B- /7.9	6.3	0.97	12.46	326	5	54	39	2	20	50.1	-10.6	39	14	2,500	0	0.0	0.0
B- /7.9	6.3	0.96	12.34	180	5	54	39	2	20	46.1	-10.7	33	14	2,500	0	3.5	0.0
B- /7.8	6.9	1.06	13.22	1,343	5	60	34	1	20	53.2	-12.6	31	14	2,500	0	5.8	0.0
B- /7.8	6.8	1.05	13.13	102	5	60	34	1	20	47.2	-12.9	24	14	2,500	0	0.0	0.0
B- /7.7	6.9	1.06	13.32	755	5	60	34	1	20	55.4	-12.6	34	14	2,500	0	0.0	0.0
B- /7.8	6.9	1.06	13.22	403	5	60	34	1	20	51.2	-12.7	28	14	2,500	0	3.5	0.0
B- /7.5	7.6	1.17	13.07	1,527	4	65	29	2	24	62.1	-15.0	25	14	2,500	0	5.8	0.0
B- /7.5	7.6	1.17	12.90	98	4	65	29	2	24	55.6	-15.2	18	14	2,500	0	0.0	0.0
B- /7.5	7.6	1.17	13.18	894	4	65	29	2	24	64.4	-14.9	28	14	2,500	0	0.0	0.0
B- /7.5	7.6	1.17	13.09	418	4	65	29	2	24	59.9	-15.1	23	14	2,500	0	3.5	0.0
C+ /6.8	9.0	1.38	14.01	1,435	3	79	16	2	22	67.2	-15.8	16	14	2,500	0	5.8	0.0
C+ /6.9	9.0	1.37	13.82	95	3	79	16	2	22	60.6	-16.1	11	14	2,500	0	0.0	0.0
C+ /6.8	8.9	1.37	14.09	879	3	79	16	2	22	69.4	-15.7	18	14	2,500	0	0.0	0.0
C+ /6.8	9.0	1.38	13.96	443	3	79	16	2	22	64.9	-15.9	14	14	2,500	0	3.5	0.0
C+ /6.4	9.7	1.48	13.49	1,131	3	89	7	1	22	75.0	-18.1	13	14	2,500	0	5.8	0.0
C+ /6.4	9.7	1.49	13.21	60	3	89	7	1	22	68.0	-18.3	8	14	2,500	0	0.0	0.0
C+ /6.4	9.7	1.48	13.58	694	3	89	7	1	22	77.2	-17.9	14	14	2,500	0	0.0	0.0
C+ /6.4	9.7	1.49	13.39	335	3	89	7	1	22	72.6	-18.1	11	14	2,500	0	3.5	0.0
C+ /6.4	9.7	1.49	14.44	984	3	89	7	1	21	75.8	-18.3	12	14	2,500	0	5.8	0.0
C+ /6.4	9.7	1.48	14.16	80	3	89	7	1	21	68.8	-18.6	8	14	2,500	0	0.0	0.0
C+ /6.3	9.7	1.48	14.52	651	3	89	7	1	21	78.2	-18.3	14	14	2,500	0	0.0	0.0
C+ /6.4	9.7	1.49	14.39	324	3	89	7	1	21	73.5	-18.4	11	14	2,500	0	3.5	0.0
C+ /6.4	9.7	1.48	11.16	561	3	89	7	1	26	77.7	-18.9	13	11	2,500	0	5.8	0.0
C+ /6.4	9.7	1.48	10.99	27	3	89	7	1	26	70.7	-19.2	8	11	2,500	0	0.0	0.0
C+ /6.4	9.7	1.48	11.23	425	3	89	7	1	26	80.1	-18.8	14	11	2,500	0	0.0	0.0
C+ /6.4	9.7	1.49	11.09	186	3	89	7	1	26	75.2	-18.9	11	11	2,500	0	3.5	0.0
C+ /6.4	9.7	1.48	11.10	400	3	89	7	1	24	79.0	-19.7	13	11	2,500	0	5.8	0.0
C+ /6.5	9.7	1.48	10.96	28	3	89	7	1	24	71.9	-20.0	8	11	2,500	0	0.0	0.0
C+ /6.4	9.7	1.48	11.17	354	3	89	7	1	24	81.5	-19.7	14	11	2,500	0	0.0	0.0
C+ /6.4	9.7	1.48	11.05	147	3	89	7	1	24	76.6	-19.9	11	11	2,500	0	3.5	0.0
C+ /6.6	9.7	0.72	12.08	169	5	88	5	2	24	80.7	N/A	96	6	2,500	0	5.8	0.0
C+ /6.7	9.7	0.72	12.01	8	5	88	5	2	24	73.6	N/A	95	6	2,500	0	0.0	0.0
C+ /6.6	9.7	0.72	12.13	162	5	88	5	2	24	83.2	N/A	96	6	2,500	0	0.0	0.0
C+ /6.7	9.7	0.72	12.04	57	5	88	5	2	24	78.3	N/A	96	6	2,500	0	3.5	0.0
B+ /9.2	3.4	0.49	10.92	92	8	25	66	1	30	24.5	-3.9	63	14	2,500	0	5.8	Load
B+ /9.2	3.5	0.50	10.89	15	8	25	66	1	30	19.7	-4.2	53	14	2,500	0	0.0	0.0
B+ /9.2	3.4	0.49	10.95	81	8	25	66	1	30	26.3	-3.8	66	14	2,500	0	0.0	0.0
B+ /9.2	3.4	0.49	10.91	39	8	25	66	1	30	23.0	-4.0	60	14	2,500	0	3.5	0.0
D /2.0	19.2	1.08	11.64	40	0	97	1	2	85	-3.3	-29.7	18	8	2,500	0	5.8	1.0
D /2.1	19.2	1.08	11.55	15	0	97	1	2	85	-7.2	-29.9	12	8	2,500	0	0.0	1.0
D /2.0	19.2	1.08	11.66	277	0	97	1	2	85	-2.0	-29.6	20	8	2,500	0	0.0	1.0
D /2.0	19.2	1.08	11.65	96	0	97	1	2	85	-1.6	-29.6	20	8	2,500	0	0.0	1.0
D /2.1	19.2	1.08	11.64	7	0	97	1	2	85	-4.7	-29.8	16	8	2,500	0	3.5	1.0
C+ /6.2	10.6	0.78	17.01	40	0	99	0	1	122	98.9	-23.0	96	7	2,500	0	5.8	1.0
C+ /6.1	10.6	0.78	14.94	20	0	99	0	1	122	90.9	-23.3	94	7	2,500	0	0.0	1.0
C+ /6.2	10.6	0.78	17.78	52	0	99	0	1	122	102.1	-22.9	96	7	2,500	0	0.0	1.0
C+ /6.1	10.6	0.78	16.34	22	0	99	0	1	122	96.0	-23.1	95	7	2,500	0	3.5	1.0
B- /7.0	6.8	1.02	9.01	26	7	60	31	2	37	44.1	-16.1	26	3	2,500	0	5.8	0.0
B- /7.0	6.8	1.02	8.86	25	7	60	31	2	37	38.4	-16.4	19	3	2,500	0	0.0	0.0
C+ /6.9	6.8	1.01	9.04	17	7	60	31	2	37	46.1	-16.1	30	3	2,500	0	0.0	0.0
B- /7.0	6.8	1.01	8.97	19	7	60	31	2	37	42.0	-16.1	24	3	2,500	0	3.5	0.0

	99 Pct = Best 0 Pct = Worst				PERFORMANCE						Incl. in Returns	
							Total Return % through 2/28/17					
			Overall		Perfor-				Annualized		Dividend	Expense
Fund Type	Fund Name	Ticker Symbol	Investment Rating	Phone	mance Rating/Pts	3 Mo	6 Mo	1Yr / Pct	3Yr / Pct	5Yr / Pct	Yield	Ratio
PM	Fidelity Adv Gold A	FGDAX	E-	(800) 522-7297	E+ / 0.7	12.15	-9.33	19.97 /52	-1.19 / 9	-14.09 / 0	0.00	1.23
PM	Fidelity Adv Gold C	FGDCX	E-	(800) 522-7297	E+ / 0.8	11.99	-9.65	19.19 /48	-1.90 / 7	-14.71 / 0	0.00	1.97
PM	Fidelity Adv Gold I	FGDIX	E-	(800) 522-7297	D- / 1.2	12.27	-9.15	20.41 /54	-0.87 /10	-13.80 / 0	0.00	0.92
PM	Fidelity Adv Gold T	FGDTX	E-	(800) 522-7297	E+ / 0.7	12.05	-9.50	19.62 /50	-1.48 / 8	-14.34 / 0	0.00	1.52
GR	Fidelity Adv Gr Opportunity A	FAGAX	C	(800) 522-7297	C+ / 6.6	11.06	9.63	22.97 /66	6.45 /68	12.34 /77	0.00	1.05
GR	Fidelity Adv Gr Opportunity C	FACGX	C	(800) 522-7297	B- / 7.0	10.84	9.22	22.04 /62	5.66 /61	11.51 /70	0.00	1.80
GR	Fidelity Adv Gr Opportunity I	FAGCX	C+	(800) 522-7297	B / 7.7	11.13	9.77	23.32 /68	6.75 /70	12.66 /80	0.00	0.77
GR	Fidelity Adv Gr Opportunity T	FAGOX	C	(800) 522-7297	C+ / 6.8	10.98	9.49	22.68 /65	6.20 /66	12.09 /75	0.00	1.28
GR	Fidelity Adv Gr Opportunity Z	FZAHX	C+	(800) 522-7297	B / 7.8	11.18	9.86	23.48 /68	6.89 /71	--	0.00	0.64
GI	Fidelity Adv Growth and Income A	FGIRX	B	(800) 522-7297	B+ / 8.3	6.34	11.82	29.62 /86	9.12 /88	13.12 /85	1.37	1.01
GI	Fidelity Adv Growth and Income C	FGIUX	B+	(800) 522-7297	B+ / 8.7	6.12	11.44	28.67 /83	8.31 /81	12.30 /77	0.90	1.75
GI	Fidelity Adv Growth and Income I	FGIOX	B+	(800) 522-7297	A / 9.4	6.39	11.99	29.96 /86	9.43 /90	13.47 /89	1.62	0.73
GI	Fidelity Adv Growth and Income T	FGITX	B	(800) 522-7297	B+ / 8.5	6.24	11.68	29.29 /85	8.85 /86	12.85 /82	1.18	1.25
HL	Fidelity Adv Health Care A	FACDX	C-	(800) 522-7297	C+ / 5.7	12.79	3.72	15.86 /34	7.23 /73	19.51 /99	0.00	1.04
HL	Fidelity Adv Health Care C	FHCCX	C-	(800) 522-7297	C+ / 6.2	12.60	3.32	14.99 /30	6.43 /68	18.63 /99	0.00	1.79
HL	Fidelity Adv Health Care I	FHCIX	C	(800) 522-7297	C+ / 6.9	12.88	3.83	16.15 /35	7.50 /75	19.82 /99	0.00	0.78
HL	Fidelity Adv Health Care T	FACTX	C-	(800) 522-7297	C+ / 5.9	12.72	3.55	15.51 /32	6.94 /72	19.19 /99	0.00	1.31
AA	● Fidelity Adv Inc Replacement 2018 A	FRKAX	C-	(800) 522-7297	E+ / 0.7	0.64	0.54	2.98 / 3	1.46 /21	3.09 /11	0.48	0.60
AA	● Fidelity Adv Inc Replacement 2018 C	FRKCX	C	(800) 522-7297	E+ / 0.9	0.45	0.17	2.21 / 2	0.70 /17	2.32 / 9	0.03	1.35
AA	● Fidelity Adv Inc Replacement 2018 I	FRKIX	C	(800) 522-7297	D- / 1.2	0.70	0.66	3.23 / 3	1.71 /22	3.35 /12	0.76	0.35
AA	● Fidelity Adv Inc Replacement 2018 T	FRKTX	C-	(800) 522-7297	E+ / 0.7	0.56	0.40	2.72 / 2	1.21 /19	2.83 /10	0.25	0.85
AA	● Fidelity Adv Inc Replacement 2020 A	FILAX	C	(800) 522-7297	D- / 1.1	1.68	1.33	6.55 / 5	2.49 /27	4.32 /17	0.97	0.71
AA	● Fidelity Adv Inc Replacement 2020 C	FILCX	C	(800) 522-7297	D- / 1.4	1.50	0.96	5.75 / 5	1.72 /22	3.55 /13	0.33	1.46
AA	● Fidelity Adv Inc Replacement 2020 I	FILIX	C	(800) 522-7297	D / 1.8	1.76	1.47	6.82 / 6	2.75 /30	4.59 /19	1.28	0.46
AA	● Fidelity Adv Inc Replacement 2020 T	FILTX	C	(800) 522-7297	D- / 1.3	1.61	1.20	6.28 / 5	2.23 /25	4.06 /15	0.76	0.96
AA	● Fidelity Adv Inc Replacement 2022 A	FRAMX	C	(800) 522-7297	D / 1.6	2.60	2.16	8.86 / 9	3.13 /33	5.20 /23	1.21	0.77
AA	● Fidelity Adv Inc Replacement 2022 C	FRCMX	C+	(800) 522-7297	D / 1.8	2.41	1.76	8.06 / 7	2.36 /26	4.42 /18	0.57	1.52
AA	● Fidelity Adv Inc Replacement 2022 I	FRIMX	C+	(800) 522-7297	D+ / 2.4	2.65	2.27	9.13 /10	3.39 /36	5.46 /25	1.53	0.52
AA	● Fidelity Adv Inc Replacement 2022 T	FRTMX	C	(800) 522-7297	D / 1.7	2.54	2.01	8.60 / 9	2.87 /30	4.95 /21	1.00	1.02
AA	● Fidelity Adv Inc Replacement 2024 A	FRNAX	C	(800) 522-7297	D / 1.9	3.21	2.97	10.77 /14	3.62 /38	5.86 /27	1.21	0.80
AA	● Fidelity Adv Inc Replacement 2024 C	FRNCX	C+	(800) 522-7297	D+ / 2.3	3.00	2.58	9.95 /11	2.85 /30	5.07 /22	0.60	1.55
AA	● Fidelity Adv Inc Replacement 2024 I	FRNIX	C+	(800) 522-7297	C- / 3.0	3.26	3.08	11.04 /15	3.88 /41	6.13 /29	1.54	0.55
AA	● Fidelity Adv Inc Replacement 2024 T	FRNTX	C	(800) 522-7297	D / 2.1	3.13	2.82	10.48 /13	3.36 /35	5.60 /26	1.02	1.05
AA	● Fidelity Adv Inc Replacement 2026 A	FIOAX	C	(800) 522-7297	D+ / 2.3	3.66	3.56	12.16 /18	3.97 /43	6.33 /30	1.23	0.83
AA	● Fidelity Adv Inc Replacement 2026 C	FIOCX	C+	(800) 522-7297	D+ / 2.7	3.45	3.16	11.32 /16	3.19 /34	5.55 /25	0.64	1.58
AA	● Fidelity Adv Inc Replacement 2026 I	FIOIX	B-	(800) 522-7297	C- / 3.4	3.72	3.69	12.43 /20	4.23 /46	6.60 /32	1.54	0.58
AA	Fidelity Adv Inc Replacement 2026 T	FIOTX	C+	(800) 522-7297	D+ / 2.5	3.59	3.43	11.89 /18	3.71 /39	6.07 /29	1.03	1.08
AA	● Fidelity Adv Inc Replacement 2028 A	FARPX	C+	(800) 522-7297	D+ / 2.5	3.99	4.00	13.16 /22	4.20 /45	6.66 /33	1.26	0.85
AA	● Fidelity Adv Inc Replacement 2028 C	FCRPX	C+	(800) 522-7297	C- / 3.0	3.80	3.63	12.33 /19	3.43 /36	5.86 /27	0.67	1.60
AA	● Fidelity Adv Inc Replacement 2028 I	FRAPX	B-	(800) 522-7297	C- / 3.7	4.04	4.13	13.44 /23	4.46 /48	6.93 /34	1.58	0.60
AA	● Fidelity Adv Inc Replacement 2028 T	FTRPX	C+	(800) 522-7297	D+ / 2.7	3.94	3.88	12.88 /21	3.95 /42	6.40 /31	1.06	1.10
AA	● Fidelity Adv Inc Replacement 2030 A	FRQAX	C	(800) 522-7297	D+ / 2.7	4.21	4.28	13.81 /25	4.35 /47	6.89 /34	1.26	0.86
AA	● Fidelity Adv Inc Replacement 2030 C	FRQCX	C+	(800) 522-7297	C- / 3.2	4.03	3.90	12.95 /21	3.57 /38	6.10 /29	0.67	1.61
AA	● Fidelity Adv Inc Replacement 2030 I	FRQIX	B-	(800) 522-7297	C- / 4.0	4.27	4.40	14.09 /26	4.61 /50	7.16 /36	1.58	0.61
AA	● Fidelity Adv Inc Replacement 2030 T	FRQTX	C+	(800) 522-7297	D+ / 2.9	4.15	4.15	13.52 /24	4.09 /44	6.64 /32	1.08	1.11
AA	● Fidelity Adv Inc Replacement 2032 A	FIARX	C+	(800) 522-7297	D+ / 2.9	4.39	4.49	14.28 /27	4.46 /48	7.09 /35	1.26	0.87
AA	● Fidelity Adv Inc Replacement 2032 C	FICRX	C+	(800) 522-7297	C- / 3.3	4.19	4.09	13.42 /23	3.68 /39	6.29 /30	0.71	1.62
AA	● Fidelity Adv Inc Replacement 2032 I	FIIRX	B-	(800) 522-7297	C- / 4.2	4.45	4.61	14.56 /28	4.73 /51	7.36 /37	1.57	0.62
AA	● Fidelity Adv Inc Replacement 2032 T	FTIRX	C+	(800) 522-7297	C- / 3.1	4.32	4.35	14.00 /25	4.20 /45	6.82 /34	1.04	1.12
AA	● Fidelity Adv Inc Replacement 2034 A	FARSX	C+	(800) 522-7297	C- / 3.0	4.51	4.63	14.66 /28	4.52 /49	7.23 /36	1.29	0.88
AA	● Fidelity Adv Inc Replacement 2034 C	FCRSX	C+	(800) 522-7297	C- / 3.4	4.31	4.23	13.79 /25	3.73 /40	6.44 /31	0.73	1.63
AA	● Fidelity Adv Inc Replacement 2034 I	FRASX	B-	(800) 522-7297	C / 4.3	4.57	4.76	14.96 /30	4.78 /52	7.51 /38	1.61	0.63

● Denotes fund is closed to new investors
* Denotes fund is included in Section II

www.thestreetratings.com

RISK			NET ASSETS		ASSET				Portfolio Turnover Ratio	BULL / BEAR		FUND MANAGER		MINIMUMS		LOADS	
Risk Rating/Pts	3 Year		NAV As of 2/28/17	Total $(Mil)	Cash %	Stocks %	Bonds %	Other %		Last Bull Market Return	Last Bear Market Return	Manager Quality Pct	Manager Tenure (Years)	Initial Purch. $	Additional Purch. $	Front End Load	Back End Load
	Standard Deviation	Beta															
E- /0.1	42.9	2.41	20.54	84	5	94	0	1	20	-52.2	-13.7	92	10	2,500	0	5.8	0.0
E- /0.1	42.9	2.41	19.36	101	5	94	0	1	20	-54.1	-14.0	89	10	2,500	0	0.0	0.0
E- /0.1	42.9	2.41	21.02	59	5	94	0	1	20	-51.3	-13.6	93	10	2,500	0	0.0	0.0
E- /0.1	42.9	2.41	20.19	25	5	94	0	1	20	-52.9	-13.8	91	10	2,500	0	3.5	0.0
C- /4.0	14.1	1.21	56.72	507	0	99	0	1	51	124.7	-16.3	9	2	2,500	0	5.8	0.0
C- /3.8	14.1	1.21	50.27	177	0	99	0	1	51	115.8	-16.5	6	2	2,500	0	0.0	0.0
C- /4.1	14.1	1.21	60.40	524	0	99	0	1	51	128.3	-16.1	11	2	2,500	0	0.0	0.0
C- /4.0	14.1	1.21	56.41	1,334	0	99	0	1	51	122.1	-16.3	8	2	2,500	0	3.5	0.0
C- /4.1	14.1	1.21	60.76	8	0	99	0	1	51	N/A	N/A	11	2	0	0	0.0	0.0
C /5.1	11.7	1.09	27.73	257	2	97	0	1	35	128.6	-16.9	44	6	2,500	0	5.8	0.0
C /5.1	11.8	1.09	26.19	85	2	97	0	1	35	119.7	-17.2	34	6	2,500	0	0.0	0.0
C /5.1	11.8	1.09	28.24	39	2	97	0	1	35	132.5	-16.8	48	6	2,500	0	0.0	0.0
C /5.2	11.8	1.09	27.75	186	2	97	0	1	35	125.7	-17.0	40	6	2,500	0	3.5	0.0
C- /3.6	16.7	1.11	38.80	1,007	0	99	0	1	67	189.2	-14.9	21	9	2,500	0	5.8	0.0
C- /3.4	16.7	1.11	31.45	614	0	99	0	1	67	177.8	-15.1	15	9	2,500	0	0.0	0.0
C- /3.7	16.7	1.11	41.99	665	0	99	0	1	67	193.4	-14.8	24	9	2,500	0	0.0	0.0
C- /3.6	16.7	1.11	36.42	262	0	99	0	1	67	185.1	-15.0	19	9	2,500	0	3.5	0.0
B+ /9.6	1.6	0.24	55.23	N/A	22	6	70	2	105	25.3	-6.4	70	10	25,000	0	5.8	0.0
B+ /9.6	1.6	0.24	54.85	N/A	22	6	70	2	105	20.3	-6.7	60	10	25,000	0	0.0	0.0
B+ /9.6	1.6	0.24	55.25	N/A	22	6	70	2	105	27.0	-6.3	73	10	25,000	0	0.0	0.0
B+ /9.6	1.6	0.24	55.24	N/A	22	6	70	2	105	23.6	-6.5	67	10	25,000	0	3.5	0.0
B+ /9.5	2.9	0.44	55.31	1	15	16	67	2	66	34.8	-8.0	65	10	25,000	0	5.8	0.0
B+ /9.5	2.9	0.44	55.16	1	15	16	67	2	66	29.4	-8.3	55	10	25,000	0	0.0	0.0
B+ /9.5	2.9	0.44	55.32	N/A	15	16	67	2	66	36.7	-7.9	68	10	25,000	0	0.0	0.0
B+ /9.5	2.9	0.44	55.32	N/A	15	16	67	2	66	33.0	-8.1	62	10	25,000	0	3.5	0.0
B+ /9.6	3.8	0.58	59.83	N/A	11	26	61	2	47	41.9	-9.2	60	10	25,000	0	5.8	0.0
B+ /9.6	3.8	0.58	59.71	N/A	11	26	61	2	47	36.3	-9.5	49	10	25,000	0	0.0	0.0
B+ /9.6	3.8	0.58	59.80	N/A	11	26	61	2	47	43.8	-9.1	63	10	25,000	0	0.0	0.0
B+ /9.6	3.8	0.58	59.88	N/A	11	26	61	2	47	40.1	-9.3	56	10	25,000	0	3.5	0.0
B+ /9.2	4.5	0.70	59.84	N/A	10	34	54	2	49	47.5	-10.0	55	10	25,000	0	5.8	0.0
B+ /9.2	4.5	0.70	59.60	N/A	10	34	54	2	49	41.6	-10.3	44	10	25,000	0	0.0	0.0
B+ /9.2	4.5	0.70	59.82	N/A	10	34	54	2	49	49.4	-9.9	58	10	25,000	0	0.0	0.0
B+ /9.2	4.5	0.70	59.82	N/A	10	34	54	2	49	45.5	-10.1	51	10	25,000	0	3.5	0.0
B+ /9.1	5.0	0.78	61.74	1	9	40	49	2	45	51.4	-10.6	51	10	25,000	0	5.8	0.0
B+ /9.1	5.0	0.79	61.47	N/A	9	40	49	2	45	45.4	-10.9	40	10	25,000	0	0.0	0.0
B+ /9.1	5.0	0.79	61.75	N/A	9	40	49	2	45	53.4	-10.5	54	10	25,000	0	0.0	0.0
B+ /9.1	5.0	0.79	61.78	N/A	9	40	49	2	45	49.3	-10.7	47	10	25,000	0	3.5	0.0
B /8.9	5.4	0.85	62.68	N/A	8	45	46	1	47	54.3	-11.1	48	10	25,000	0	5.8	0.0
B /8.9	5.4	0.85	62.42	N/A	8	45	46	1	47	48.2	-11.4	37	10	25,000	0	0.0	0.0
B /8.9	5.4	0.85	62.67	N/A	8	45	46	1	47	56.4	-11.0	52	10	25,000	0	0.0	0.0
B /8.9	5.4	0.85	62.68	N/A	8	45	46	1	47	52.2	-11.2	45	10	25,000	0	3.5	0.0
B /8.7	5.7	0.89	61.83	N/A	8	48	43	1	26	56.5	-11.6	46	10	25,000	0	5.8	0.0
B /8.6	5.7	0.89	61.47	N/A	8	48	43	1	26	50.3	-11.8	35	10	25,000	0	0.0	0.0
B /8.7	5.7	0.89	61.83	N/A	8	48	43	1	26	58.7	-11.5	49	10	25,000	0	0.0	0.0
B /8.7	5.7	0.89	61.94	N/A	8	48	43	1	26	54.5	-11.6	42	10	25,000	0	3.5	0.0
B /8.6	5.9	0.92	58.74	N/A	7	50	41	2	24	58.4	-11.9	44	10	25,000	0	5.8	0.0
B /8.6	5.9	0.92	58.48	N/A	7	50	41	2	24	52.1	-12.2	34	10	25,000	0	0.0	0.0
B /8.6	5.9	0.92	58.76	N/A	7	50	41	2	24	60.5	-11.8	47	10	25,000	0	0.0	0.0
B /8.6	5.9	0.92	58.79	N/A	7	50	41	2	24	56.2	-12.0	40	10	25,000	0	3.5	0.0
B /8.4	6.1	0.95	62.04	N/A	7	52	40	1	33	59.9	-12.3	41	10	25,000	0	5.8	0.0
B /8.4	6.1	0.95	61.74	N/A	7	52	40	1	33	53.5	-12.6	32	10	25,000	0	0.0	0.0
B /8.4	6.1	0.95	62.03	N/A	7	52	40	1	33	62.1	-12.2	45	10	25,000	0	0.0	0.0

						PERFORMANCE					Incl. in Returns	
	99 Pct = Best						Total Return % through 2/28/17					
	0 Pct = Worst			Overall		Perfor-				Annualized		
Fund		Ticker	Investment			mance					Dividend	Expense
Type	Fund Name	Symbol	Rating	Phone		Rating/Pts	3 Mo	6 Mo	1Yr / Pct	3Yr / Pct	5Yr / Pct	Yield	Ratio
AA	● Fidelity Adv Inc Replacement 2034 T	FTRSX	C+	(800) 522-7297		C- / 3.2	4.42	4.46	14.35 / 27	4.24 / 46	6.96 / 34	0.99	1.13
AA	● Fidelity Adv Inc Replacement 2036 A	FURAX	C+	(800) 522-7297		C- / 3.1	4.62	4.75	14.95 / 30	4.57 / 49	7.39 / 37	1.28	0.89
AA	● Fidelity Adv Inc Replacement 2036 C	FURCX	C+	(800) 522-7297		C- / 3.5	4.43	4.36	14.08 / 26	3.79 / 40	6.59 / 32	0.74	1.64
AA	● Fidelity Adv Inc Replacement 2036 I	FURIX	B-	(800) 522-7297		C / 4.4	4.69	4.90	15.28 / 31	4.88 / 53	7.69 / 40	1.59	0.64
AA	● Fidelity Adv Inc Replacement 2036 T	FURTX	C+	(800) 522-7297		C- / 3.3	4.55	4.62	14.65 / 28	4.31 / 46	7.12 / 35	1.05	1.14
AA	● Fidelity Adv Inc Replacement 2038 A	FARVX	C+	(800) 522-7297		C- / 3.1	4.73	4.86	15.23 / 31	4.62 / 50	7.54 / 39	1.21	0.90
AA	● Fidelity Adv Inc Replacement 2038 C	FCRVX	C+	(800) 522-7297		C- / 3.6	4.53	4.46	14.39 / 27	3.84 / 41	6.73 / 33	0.76	1.65
AA	● Fidelity Adv Inc Replacement 2038 I	FIIVX	B-	(800) 522-7297		C / 4.5	4.79	4.99	15.54 / 32	4.88 / 53	7.81 / 41	1.60	0.65
AA	● Fidelity Adv Inc Replacement 2038 T	FTRVX	C+	(800) 522-7297		C- / 3.3	4.67	4.74	14.95 / 30	4.35 / 47	7.27 / 36	1.09	1.15
AA	● Fidelity Adv Inc Replacement 2040 A	FARWX	C+	(800) 522-7297		C- / 3.2	4.84	4.96	15.54 / 32	4.67 / 50	7.74 / 40	1.29	0.91
AA	● Fidelity Adv Inc Replacement 2040 C	FCRWX	C+	(800) 522-7297		C- / 3.7	4.64	4.57	14.69 / 28	3.88 / 41	6.92 / 34	0.77	1.66
AA	● Fidelity Adv Inc Replacement 2040 I	FIIWX	B-	(800) 522-7297		C / 4.6	4.89	5.09	15.83 / 34	4.93 / 53	8.00 / 42	1.60	0.66
AA	● Fidelity Adv Inc Replacement 2040 T	FTRWX	C+	(800) 522-7297		C- / 3.4	4.76	4.83	15.25 / 31	4.40 / 47	7.46 / 38	1.09	1.16
AA	● Fidelity Adv Inc Replacement 2042 A	FARFX	C+	(800) 522-7297		C- / 3.3	4.94	5.06	15.88 / 34	4.73 / 51	7.95 / 42	1.28	0.92
AA	● Fidelity Adv Inc Replacement 2042 C	FCRFX	C+	(800) 522-7297		C- / 3.8	4.77	4.68	15.03 / 30	3.96 / 42	7.15 / 36	0.76	1.67
AA	● Fidelity Adv Inc Replacement 2042 I	FIRFX	B-	(800) 522-7297		C / 4.7	5.02	5.19	16.19 / 35	5.00 / 54	8.23 / 44	1.59	0.67
AA	● Fidelity Adv Inc Replacement 2042 T	FITTX	C+	(800) 522-7297		C- / 3.5	4.89	4.95	15.61 / 32	4.47 / 48	7.69 / 40	1.08	1.17
GR	Fidelity Adv Industrials A	FCLAX	C+	(800) 522-7297		C+ / 6.9	4.99	11.21	25.11 / 74	7.62 / 76	12.86 / 82	0.38	1.06
GR	Fidelity Adv Industrials C	FCLCX	C+	(800) 522-7297		B- / 7.2	4.80	10.78	24.14 / 70	6.81 / 71	12.01 / 74	0.00	1.82
GR	Fidelity Adv Industrials I	FCLIX	B	(800) 522-7297		B / 8.0	5.09	11.37	25.43 / 75	7.91 / 78	13.17 / 86	0.61	0.80
GR	Fidelity Adv Industrials T	FCLTX	C+	(800) 522-7297		B- / 7.0	4.93	11.05	24.77 / 73	7.34 / 74	12.56 / 80	0.20	1.33
FO	Fidelity Adv International Disc A	FAIDX	D-	(800) 522-7297		E / 0.4	5.27	0.39	8.09 / 8	-1.31 / 8	5.61 / 26	1.17	1.33
FO	Fidelity Adv International Disc C	FCADX	D-	(800) 522-7297		E / 0.5	5.08	0.03	7.30 / 6	-2.05 / 7	4.82 / 20	0.36	2.09
FO	Fidelity Adv International Disc I	FIADX	D-	(800) 522-7297		E+ / 0.8	5.38	0.55	8.49 / 8	-0.97 / 9	5.97 / 28	1.60	1.00
FO	Fidelity Adv International Disc T	FTADX	D-	(800) 522-7297		E / 0.4	5.21	0.25	7.83 / 7	-1.54 / 8	5.35 / 24	0.95	1.57
FO	Fidelity Adv International Disc Z	FZAIX	D-	(800) 522-7297		E+ / 0.8	5.42	0.65	8.62 / 9	-0.83 / 10	--	1.76	0.86
FO	Fidelity Adv International Gr A	FIAGX	D	(800) 522-7297		D- / 1.3	7.37	0.52	11.05 / 15	0.95 / 18	5.88 / 28	0.86	1.26
FO	Fidelity Adv International Gr C	FIGCX	D	(800) 522-7297		D / 1.6	7.21	0.15	10.19 / 12	0.17 / 14	5.05 / 22	0.14	2.06
FO	Fidelity Adv International Gr Inst	FIIIX	D	(800) 522-7297		D / 2.0	7.47	0.66	11.35 / 16	1.24 / 19	6.19 / 30	1.21	0.98
FO	Fidelity Adv International Gr T	FITGX	D	(800) 522-7297		D- / 1.4	7.36	0.40	10.72 / 14	0.64 / 16	5.56 / 25	0.60	1.58
FO	Fidelity Adv International Gr Z	FZAJX	D+	(800) 522-7297		D / 2.1	7.50	0.70	11.47 / 16	1.39 / 20	--	1.32	0.84
FO	Fidelity Adv International Sm Cap A	FIASX	D+	(800) 522-7297		C- / 3.4	7.19	4.88	21.24 / 58	3.92 / 42	9.75 / 57	1.06	1.59
FO	Fidelity Adv International Sm Cap C	FICSX	D+	(800) 522-7297		C- / 3.9	6.98	4.50	20.31 / 54	3.14 / 33	8.94 / 50	0.34	2.37
FO	Fidelity Adv International Sm Cap I	FIXIX	C-	(800) 522-7297		C / 4.8	7.26	5.05	21.61 / 60	4.28 / 46	10.15 / 59	1.47	1.25
FO	Fidelity Adv International Sm Cap T	FTISX	D+	(800) 522-7297		C- / 3.6	7.08	4.72	20.88 / 57	3.62 / 38	9.46 / 54	0.73	1.87
FO	Fidelity Adv International Val A	FIVMX	D-	(800) 522-7297		E / 0.3	5.20	2.66	10.67 / 13	-2.46 / 6	4.75 / 20	1.98	1.37
FO	Fidelity Adv International Val C	FIVOX	D-	(800) 522-7297		E / 0.4	4.96	2.16	9.84 / 11	-3.22 / 4	3.95 / 15	1.35	2.15
FO	Fidelity Adv International Val I	FIVQX	D-	(800) 522-7297		E+ / 0.6	5.10	2.71	10.85 / 14	-2.24 / 6	5.04 / 22	2.40	1.14
FO	Fidelity Adv International Val T	FIVPX	D-	(800) 522-7297		E / 0.3	5.02	2.48	10.33 / 12	-2.72 / 5	4.47 / 18	1.73	1.66
FO	Fidelity Adv Intl Cap Apprec A	FCPAX	D	(800) 522-7297		D- / 1.5	7.29	-1.16	9.94 / 11	2.32 / 26	7.41 / 37	0.10	1.50
FO	Fidelity Adv Intl Cap Apprec C	FCPCX	D	(800) 522-7297		D / 1.8	7.04	-1.49	9.06 / 10	1.54 / 21	6.59 / 32	0.00	2.27
FO	Fidelity Adv Intl Cap Apprec I	FCPIX	D+	(800) 522-7297		D+ / 2.3	7.37	-0.94	10.28 / 12	2.58 / 28	7.69 / 40	0.35	1.21
FO	Fidelity Adv Intl Cap Apprec T	FIATX	D	(800) 522-7297		D / 1.6	7.26	-1.23	9.66 / 11	2.08 / 24	7.14 / 35	0.00	1.76
FO	Fidelity Adv Intl Real Estate A	FIRAX	D	(800) 522-7297		D- / 1.3	4.89	-1.57	10.55 / 13	2.64 / 29	8.24 / 44	1.22	1.35
FO	Fidelity Adv Intl Real Estate C	FIRCX	D+	(800) 522-7297		D / 1.6	4.79	-1.87	9.81 / 11	1.90 / 23	7.46 / 38	0.86	2.10
FO	Fidelity Adv Intl Real Estate I	FIRIX	D+	(800) 522-7297		D / 2.1	5.07	-1.30	11.10 / 15	3.00 / 32	8.61 / 47	1.54	0.97
FO	Fidelity Adv Intl Real Estate T	FIRTX	D+	(800) 522-7297		D- / 1.4	4.82	-1.64	10.33 / 12	2.36 / 26	7.95 / 42	1.11	1.66
FO	Fidelity Adv Japan A	FPJAX	D+	(800) 544-8544		D+ / 2.7	5.09	4.74	19.13 / 48	3.43 / 36	5.67 / 26	0.45	1.10
FO	Fidelity Adv Japan C	FJPCX	C-	(800) 544-8544		C- / 3.2	4.84	4.40	18.25 / 44	2.68 / 29	4.92 / 21	0.00	1.81
FO	Fidelity Adv Japan I	FJPIX	C	(800) 544-8544		C- / 4.0	5.17	5.00	19.50 / 49	3.76 / 40	6.03 / 28	0.87	0.80
FO	Fidelity Adv Japan T	FJPTX	C-	(800) 544-8544		D+ / 2.9	5.00	4.65	18.73 / 46	3.10 / 33	5.34 / 24	0.08	1.43
GR	Fidelity Adv Large Cap Fund A	FALAX	B+	(800) 522-7297		B+ / 8.4	7.03	12.96	33.21 / 92	8.24 / 81	14.27 / 95	0.98	1.15

● Denotes fund is closed to new investors
* Denotes fund is included in Section II

Risk Rating/Pts	3 Year Standard Deviation	Beta	NAV As of 2/28/17	Total $(Mil)	Cash %	Stocks %	Bonds %	Other %	Portfolio Turnover Ratio	Last Bull Market Return	Last Bear Market Return	Manager Quality Pct	Manager Tenure (Years)	Initial Purch. $	Additional Purch. $	Front End Load	Back End Load
B /8.4	6.1	0.95	62.11	N/A	7	52	40	1	33	57.7	-12.4	38	10	25,000	0	3.5	0.0
B /8.4	6.3	0.98	62.43	1	7	54	38	1	27	61.4	-12.7	40	10	25,000	0	5.8	0.0
B /8.4	6.3	0.98	62.01	N/A	7	54	38	1	27	55.0	-13.0	30	10	25,000	0	0.0	0.0
B /8.4	6.3	0.98	62.55	N/A	7	54	38	1	27	63.9	-12.6	44	10	25,000	0	0.0	0.0
B /8.4	6.3	0.98	62.41	1	7	54	38	1	27	59.2	-12.8	36	10	25,000	0	3.5	0.0
B /8.3	6.5	1.00	60.10	N/A	7	55	37	1	23	63.1	-13.2	38	10	25,000	0	5.8	0.0
B /8.3	6.5	1.00	59.66	N/A	7	55	37	1	23	56.6	-13.5	29	10	25,000	0	0.0	0.0
B /8.3	6.5	1.00	60.06	N/A	7	55	37	1	23	65.3	-13.1	41	10	25,000	0	0.0	0.0
B /8.3	6.5	1.00	60.04	N/A	7	55	37	1	23	60.9	-13.3	35	10	25,000	0	3.5	0.0
B /8.2	6.7	1.03	61.30	N/A	6	57	36	1	29	65.4	-13.8	36	10	25,000	0	5.8	0.0
B /8.2	6.7	1.03	60.82	N/A	6	57	36	1	29	58.7	-14.1	27	10	25,000	0	0.0	0.0
B /8.2	6.7	1.03	61.26	N/A	6	57	36	1	29	67.6	-13.7	39	10	25,000	0	0.0	0.0
B /8.2	6.7	1.03	61.36	1	6	57	36	1	29	63.1	-13.9	33	10	25,000	0	3.5	0.0
B /8.1	6.9	1.06	61.41	1	6	58	34	2	29	67.5	-14.1	34	10	25,000	0	5.8	0.0
B /8.1	6.9	1.06	61.02	1	6	58	34	2	29	60.9	-14.4	25	10	25,000	0	0.0	0.0
B /8.1	6.9	1.06	61.43	N/A	6	58	34	2	29	69.8	-14.0	37	10	25,000	0	0.0	0.0
B /8.1	6.9	1.06	61.43	1	6	58	34	2	29	65.3	-14.2	31	10	25,000	0	3.5	0.0
C /5.0	13.4	1.16	37.66	353	0	97	1	2	53	137.6	-26.1	21	10	2,500	0	5.8	0.0
C /4.9	13.4	1.16	33.99	137	0	97	1	2	53	128.1	-26.4	14	10	2,500	0	0.0	0.0
C /5.1	13.4	1.16	39.52	245	0	97	1	2	53	141.1	-26.0	23	10	2,500	0	0.0	0.0
C /5.0	13.4	1.16	36.85	96	0	97	1	2	53	134.3	-26.2	18	10	2,500	0	3.5	0.0
C+ /6.0	11.0	0.85	37.82	229	1	97	0	2	50	50.5	-24.6	60	12	2,500	0	5.8	0.0
C+ /6.0	11.0	0.85	37.43	24	1	97	0	2	50	44.6	-24.8	49	12	2,500	0	0.0	0.0
C+ /6.0	11.0	0.85	37.95	572	1	97	0	2	50	53.4	-24.5	64	12	2,500	0	0.0	0.0
C+ /6.0	11.0	0.85	37.63	32	1	97	0	2	50	48.6	-24.7	56	12	2,500	0	3.5	0.0
C+ /6.0	11.0	0.84	37.92	41	1	97	0	2	50	N/A	N/A	66	12	0	0	0.0	0.0
C+ /6.3	10.5	0.80	11.24	214	3	94	1	2	29	60.3	-22.0	81	10	2,500	0	5.8	0.0
C+ /6.3	10.5	0.80	11.09	55	3	94	1	2	29	53.7	-22.3	76	10	2,500	0	0.0	0.0
C+ /6.3	10.5	0.80	11.29	385	3	94	1	2	29	62.9	-22.0	83	10	2,500	0	0.0	0.0
C+ /6.4	10.5	0.80	11.23	29	3	94	1	2	29	57.9	-22.2	79	10	2,500	0	3.5	0.0
C+ /6.3	10.5	0.80	11.30	24	3	94	1	2	29	N/A	N/A	84	10	0	0	0.0	0.0
C /5.4	10.5	0.75	24.27	43	5	94	0	1	29	80.8	-21.7	93	3	2,500	0	5.8	2.0
C /5.4	10.5	0.75	23.54	13	5	94	0	1	29	73.5	-21.9	91	3	2,500	0	0.0	2.0
C /5.5	10.5	0.75	24.83	48	5	94	0	1	29	84.4	-21.6	94	3	2,500	0	0.0	2.0
C /5.4	10.5	0.75	24.17	14	5	94	0	1	29	78.1	-21.8	92	3	2,500	0	3.5	2.0
C+ /6.1	10.6	0.84	7.91	8	1	98	0	1	47	41.4	-27.7	43	6	2,500	0	5.8	1.0
C+ /6.1	10.6	0.85	7.91	4	1	98	0	1	47	35.6	-28.0	33	6	2,500	0	0.0	1.0
C+ /6.0	10.6	0.85	7.91	2	1	98	0	1	47	43.5	-27.7	46	6	2,500	0	0.0	1.0
C+ /6.1	10.6	0.84	7.91	4	1	98	0	1	47	39.4	-27.9	39	6	2,500	0	3.5	1.0
C+ /6.4	10.7	0.78	15.55	136	0	98	0	2	167	78.7	-26.0	88	9	2,500	0	5.8	0.0
C+ /6.3	10.7	0.78	13.84	45	0	98	0	2	167	71.5	-26.3	84	9	2,500	0	0.0	0.0
C+ /6.4	10.8	0.78	16.58	251	0	98	0	2	167	81.2	-26.0	89	9	2,500	0	0.0	0.0
C+ /6.4	10.7	0.78	15.21	63	0	98	0	2	167	76.4	-26.1	87	9	2,500	0	3.5	0.0
B- /7.0	10.5	0.73	9.86	12	15	81	2	2	71	78.7	-25.3	89	7	2,500	0	5.8	1.5
B- /7.0	10.5	0.73	9.63	5	15	81	2	2	71	71.7	-25.5	86	7	2,500	0	0.0	1.5
B- /7.0	10.5	0.73	9.94	73	15	81	2	2	71	81.7	-25.2	90	7	2,500	0	0.0	1.5
B- /7.0	10.5	0.73	9.79	4	15	81	2	2	71	76.0	-25.3	88	7	2,500	0	3.5	1.5
C+ /6.4	12.3	0.81	12.65	22	2	97	0	1	15	40.7	-10.4	92	3	2,500	0	5.8	1.5
C+ /6.4	12.3	0.81	12.57	14	2	97	0	1	15	35.4	-10.7	89	3	2,500	0	0.0	1.5
C+ /6.4	12.3	0.81	12.65	5	2	97	0	1	15	43.4	-10.3	93	3	2,500	0	0.0	1.5
C+ /6.5	12.3	0.81	12.67	4	2	97	0	1	15	38.4	-10.5	91	3	2,500	0	3.5	1.5
C+ /5.8	12.6	1.15	31.77	492	2	97	0	1	31	144.1	-19.3	27	12	2,500	0	5.8	0.0

Fund Type	Fund Name	Ticker Symbol	Overall Investment Rating	Phone	Performance Rating/Pts	3 Mo	6 Mo	1Yr / Pct	3Yr / Pct	5Yr / Pct	Dividend Yield	Expense Ratio
	99 Pct = Best / 0 Pct = Worst							Total Return % through 2/28/17 / Annualized			Incl. in Returns	
GR	Fidelity Adv Large Cap Fund C	FLCCX	A-	(800) 522-7297	B+ / 8.8	6.85	12.52	32.21 /90	7.42 /75	13.42 /88	0.52	1.90
GR	Fidelity Adv Large Cap Fund I	FALIX	A	(800) 522-7297	A / 9.4	7.13	13.11	33.57 /92	8.51 /83	14.59 /96	1.21	0.89
GR	Fidelity Adv Large Cap Fund T	FALGX	B+	(800) 522-7297	B+ / 8.6	6.95	12.78	32.84 /91	7.95 /79	13.98 /93	0.77	1.41
GR	Fidelity Adv Leveraged Co Stk A	FLSAX	C	(800) 522-7297	C+ / 5.9	7.75	11.22	28.35 /82	4.47 /48	11.78 /72	0.52	1.08
GR	Fidelity Adv Leveraged Co Stk C	FLSCX	C+	(800) 522-7297	C+ / 6.4	7.56	10.83	27.39 /80	3.70 /39	10.96 /65	0.00	1.82
GR	Fidelity Adv Leveraged Co Stk I	FLVIX	C+	(800) 522-7297	B- / 7.1	7.83	11.39	28.69 /83	4.75 /51	12.08 /75	0.78	0.81
GR	Fidelity Adv Leveraged Co Stk T	FLSTX	C	(800) 522-7297	C+ / 6.1	7.69	11.09	28.03 /82	4.23 /46	11.53 /70	0.32	1.32
GR	Fidelity Adv Leveraged Co Stk Z	FZAKX	C+	(800) 522-7297	B- / 7.2	7.85	11.45	28.84 /84	4.89 /53	--	0.91	0.68
PM	Fidelity Adv Materials A	FMFAX	D	(800) 522-7297	C / 4.5	7.20	10.32	30.18 /87	2.10 /25	7.00 /35	0.73	1.06
PM	Fidelity Adv Materials C	FMFCX	D+	(800) 522-7297	C / 5.0	7.00	9.90	29.21 /85	1.33 /20	6.20 /30	0.25	1.81
PM	Fidelity Adv Materials I	FMFEX	C-	(800) 522-7297	C+ / 5.9	7.27	10.46	30.55 /87	2.38 /27	7.30 /37	0.98	0.78
PM	Fidelity Adv Materials T	FMFTX	D	(800) 522-7297	C / 4.7	7.13	10.15	29.78 /86	1.78 /23	6.68 /33	0.54	1.38
MC	Fidelity Adv Mid Cap II A	FIIAX	C	(800) 522-7297	C+ / 6.5	6.64	10.19	26.70 /78	6.29 /67	11.04 /66	0.20	1.06
MC	Fidelity Adv Mid Cap II C	FIICX	C	(800) 522-7297	C+ / 6.9	6.43	9.82	25.69 /75	5.50 /59	10.21 /60	0.00	1.82
MC	Fidelity Adv Mid Cap II I	FIIMX	C+	(800) 522-7297	B / 7.6	6.67	10.34	27.03 /79	6.58 /69	11.32 /68	0.44	0.77
MC	Fidelity Adv Mid Cap II T	FITIX	C	(800) 522-7297	C+ / 6.7	6.53	10.03	26.39 /77	6.04 /65	10.79 /64	0.01	1.29
MC	Fidelity Adv Mid Cap II Z	FZAMX	B-	(800) 522-7297	B / 7.8	6.77	10.44	27.27 /80	6.75 /70	--	0.58	0.64
MC	Fidelity Adv Mid Cap Value A	FMPAX	B	(800) 522-7297	B- / 7.4	7.34	10.93	24.79 /73	8.39 /82	14.06 /94	1.00	1.14
MC	Fidelity Adv Mid Cap Value C	FMPEX	B+	(800) 522-7297	B / 7.8	7.16	10.57	23.85 /69	7.59 /76	13.22 /86	0.46	1.89
MC	Fidelity Adv Mid Cap Value I	FMPOX	B+	(800) 522-7297	B+ / 8.6	7.37	11.07	25.10 /74	8.71 /85	14.39 /95	1.31	0.87
MC	Fidelity Adv Mid Cap Value T	FMPTX	B	(800) 522-7297	B / 7.6	7.24	10.80	24.42 /71	8.09 /80	13.75 /91	0.83	1.42
* GR	Fidelity Adv New Insights A	FNIAX	C+	(800) 522-7297	C+ / 6.2	7.99	7.87	22.51 /65	6.85 /71	12.09 /75	0.12	0.92
GR	Fidelity Adv New Insights C	FNICX	C+	(800) 522-7297	C+ / 6.6	7.79	7.44	21.59 /60	6.06 /65	11.24 /68	0.00	1.67
GR	Fidelity Adv New Insights I	FINSX	B	(800) 522-7297	B- / 7.3	8.08	7.97	22.82 /66	7.13 /73	12.37 /78	0.37	0.66
GR	Fidelity Adv New Insights T	FNITX	C+	(800) 522-7297	C+ / 6.4	7.92	7.71	22.20 /63	6.58 /69	11.81 /73	0.00	1.17
GR	Fidelity Adv New Insights Z	FZANX	B	(800) 522-7297	B- / 7.4	8.09	8.06	23.00 /67	7.26 /74	--	0.49	0.53
FO	Fidelity Adv Overseas Fund A	FAOAX	D-	(800) 522-7297	E / 0.3	6.72	0.93	8.71 / 9	-2.16 / 6	5.13 /22	0.90	1.36
FO	Fidelity Adv Overseas Fund C	FAOCX	D-	(800) 522-7297	E / 0.4	6.54	0.52	7.85 / 7	-2.93 / 5	4.32 /17	0.04	2.16
FO	Fidelity Adv Overseas Fund I	FAOIX	D-	(800) 522-7297	E+ / 0.7	6.84	1.17	9.12 /10	-1.83 / 7	5.50 /25	1.35	1.04
FO	Fidelity Adv Overseas Fund T	FAERX	D-	(800) 522-7297	E / 0.4	6.65	0.85	8.47 / 8	-2.36 / 6	4.93 /21	0.67	1.56
RE	Fidelity Adv Real Estate A	FHEAX	C	(800) 522-7297	C+ / 5.7	7.65	-2.19	13.76 /24	9.95 /93	10.43 /61	1.45	1.09
RE	Fidelity Adv Real Estate C	FHECX	C	(800) 522-7297	C+ / 6.2	7.41	-2.58	12.90 /21	9.12 /88	9.59 /55	0.86	1.86
RE	Fidelity Adv Real Estate I	FHEIX	C+	(800) 522-7297	C+ / 6.9	7.72	-2.06	14.08 /26	10.22 /94	10.71 /63	1.77	0.84
RE	Fidelity Adv Real Estate Income A	FRINX	B	(800) 522-7297	C / 4.3	4.24	1.85	14.55 /28	7.14 /73	8.59 /47	3.80	1.03
RE	Fidelity Adv Real Estate Income C	FRIOX	B	(800) 522-7297	C / 4.4	3.95	1.39	13.63 /24	6.31 /67	7.77 /40	3.26	1.79
RE	Fidelity Adv Real Estate Income I	FRIRX	B+	(800) 522-7297	C / 5.3	4.24	1.92	14.84 /29	7.42 /75	8.87 /50	4.22	0.77
RE	Fidelity Adv Real Estate Income T	FRIQX	B	(800) 522-7297	C- / 4.2	4.15	1.74	14.50 /28	7.11 /73	8.56 /47	3.77	1.07
RE	Fidelity Adv Real Estate T	FHETX	C	(800) 522-7297	C+ / 5.9	7.57	-2.29	13.51 /24	9.69 /92	10.17 /60	1.27	1.33
TC	Fidelity Adv Semiconductors A	FELAX	B+	(800) 522-7297	A+ / 9.9	8.67	16.14	51.50 /99	22.10 /99	18.34 /99	0.21	1.31
TC	Fidelity Adv Semiconductors C	FELCX	B+	(800) 522-7297	A+ / 9.9	8.49	15.69	50.26 /99	21.18 /99	17.44 /98	0.00	2.08
TC	Fidelity Adv Semiconductors I	FELIX	B+	(800) 522-7297	A+ / 9.9	8.73	16.24	51.88 /99	22.49 /99	18.67 /99	0.41	0.98
TC	Fidelity Adv Semiconductors T	FELTX	B+	(800) 522-7297	A+ / 9.9	8.56	15.85	50.82 /99	21.68 /99	17.98 /99	0.00	1.65
GR	Fidelity Adv Series Growth and Inc	FMALX	A	(800) 522-7297	A / 9.3	6.51	12.03	30.03 /86	9.35 /89	--	1.58	0.68
SC	Fidelity Adv Small Cap A	FSCDX	C-	(800) 522-7297	C / 5.1	5.00	8.44	21.03 /58	6.06 /65	9.58 /55	0.28	1.26
SC	Fidelity Adv Small Cap C	FSCEX	C-	(800) 522-7297	C+ / 5.7	4.79	8.00	20.09 /52	5.25 /57	8.75 /48	0.00	2.02
SC	Fidelity Adv Small Cap Growth A	FCAGX	C+	(800) 522-7297	B / 7.6	8.03	9.98	32.52 /91	7.51 /76	13.62 /90	0.00	1.38
SC	Fidelity Adv Small Cap Growth C	FCCGX	C+	(800) 522-7297	B / 7.9	7.81	9.57	31.47 /89	6.69 /70	12.76 /82	0.00	2.17
SC	Fidelity Adv Small Cap Growth I	FCIGX	B	(800) 522-7297	B+ / 8.8	8.14	10.12	32.84 /91	7.82 /78	13.97 /93	0.00	1.10
SC	Fidelity Adv Small Cap Growth T	FCTGX	C+	(800) 522-7297	B / 7.7	7.99	9.86	32.16 /90	7.23 /74	13.32 /87	0.00	1.67
SC	Fidelity Adv Small Cap I	FSCIX	C	(800) 522-7297	C+ / 6.6	5.06	8.56	21.35 /59	6.35 /67	9.90 /58	0.53	0.99
SC	Fidelity Adv Small Cap T	FSCTX	C-	(800) 522-7297	C / 5.4	4.91	8.31	20.79 /56	5.82 /63	9.34 /53	0.10	1.49
SC	Fidelity Adv Small Cap Value A	FCVAX	C+	(800) 522-7297	C+ / 6.9	3.55	11.03	24.10 /70	8.85 /86	13.73 /91	0.48	1.45

● Denotes fund is closed to new investors

* Denotes fund is included in Section II

www.thestreetratings.com

RISK			NET ASSETS		ASSET					BULL / BEAR		FUND MANAGER		MINIMUMS		LOADS	
	3 Year		NAV						Portfolio	Last Bull	Last Bear	Manager	Manager	Initial	Additional	Front	Back
Risk	Standard		As of	Total	Cash	Stocks	Bonds	Other	Turnover	Market	Market	Quality	Tenure	Purch.	Purch.	End	End
Rating/Pts	Deviation	Beta	2/28/17	$(Mil)	%	%	%	%	Ratio	Return	Return	Pct	(Years)	$	$	Load	Load
C+ / 5.8	12.6	1.15	29.03	196	2	97	0	1	31	134.4	-19.6	20	12	2,500	0	0.0	0.0
C+ / 5.8	12.6	1.15	33.12	489	2	97	0	1	31	147.9	-19.2	30	12	2,500	0	0.0	0.0
C+ / 5.9	12.6	1.15	31.72	188	2	97	0	1	31	140.7	-19.4	24	12	2,500	0	3.5	0.0
C / 5.1	13.7	1.15	51.65	989	4	92	3	1	9	132.8	-30.1	5	1	10,000	0	5.8	0.0
C / 5.1	13.7	1.16	47.54	396	4	92	3	1	9	123.7	-30.4	4	1	10,000	0	0.0	0.0
C / 5.1	13.7	1.15	52.54	800	4	92	3	1	9	136.2	-30.1	5	1	10,000	0	0.0	0.0
C / 5.1	13.7	1.15	50.41	580	4	92	3	1	9	129.9	-30.2	4	1	10,000	0	3.5	0.0
C / 5.1	13.7	1.15	52.54	22	4	92	3	1	9	N/A	N/A	6	1	0	0	0.0	0.0
C- / 3.7	16.4	0.03	81.27	229	0	98	0	2	64	84.5	-28.4	86	9	2,500	0	5.8	0.0
C- / 3.7	16.4	0.03	78.72	80	0	98	0	2	64	77.1	-28.6	82	9	2,500	0	0.0	0.0
C- / 3.7	16.4	0.03	81.49	335	0	98	0	2	64	87.3	-28.3	88	9	2,500	0	0.0	0.0
C- / 3.7	16.4	0.03	80.66	41	0	98	0	2	64	81.5	-28.5	85	9	2,500	0	3.5	0.0
C / 4.7	12.4	0.99	19.55	800	0	99	0	1	27	99.1	-20.5	34	13	2,500	0	5.8	0.0
C / 4.4	12.4	0.99	17.66	243	0	99	0	1	27	91.2	-20.8	26	13	2,500	0	0.0	0.0
C / 4.7	12.4	0.99	20.11	946	0	99	0	1	27	101.8	-20.4	38	13	2,500	0	0.0	0.0
C / 4.6	12.4	0.99	19.10	386	0	99	0	1	27	96.6	-20.6	32	13	2,500	0	3.5	0.0
C / 4.7	12.4	0.99	20.12	21	0	99	0	1	27	N/A	N/A	40	13	0	0	0.0	0.0
C+ / 5.8	11.2	0.88	25.59	304	2	96	0	2	83	140.9	-23.2	74	4	2,500	0	5.8	0.0
C+ / 5.8	11.2	0.88	24.84	155	2	96	0	2	83	131.4	-23.5	65	4	2,500	0	0.0	0.0
C+ / 5.8	11.2	0.88	25.71	382	2	96	0	2	83	144.7	-23.1	76	4	2,500	0	0.0	0.0
C+ / 5.9	11.2	0.88	25.48	63	2	96	0	2	83	137.3	-23.3	70	4	2,500	0	3.5	0.0
C+ / 5.8	10.4	0.94	28.11	7,165	2	96	1	1	47	110.8	-14.5	36	14	2,500	0	5.8	0.0
C / 5.5	10.4	0.94	25.12	3,643	2	96	1	1	47	102.4	-14.8	27	14	2,500	0	0.0	0.0
C+ / 5.7	10.4	0.94	28.67	12,323	2	96	1	1	47	113.7	-14.4	39	14	2,500	0	0.0	0.0
C+ / 5.7	10.4	0.94	27.33	1,928	2	96	1	1	47	107.9	-14.6	33	14	2,500	0	3.5	0.0
C+ / 5.7	10.4	0.94	28.70	549	2	96	1	1	47	N/A	N/A	41	14	0	0	0.0	0.0
C+ / 6.0	12.0	0.93	20.79	59	0	98	0	2	94	52.2	-27.6	48	12	2,500	0	5.8	0.0
C+ / 6.0	12.0	0.93	20.25	15	0	98	0	2	94	45.9	-27.8	37	12	2,500	0	0.0	0.0
C+ / 6.0	12.0	0.93	21.20	269	0	98	0	2	94	55.0	-27.5	53	12	2,500	0	0.0	0.0
C+ / 6.0	12.0	0.93	21.35	237	0	98	0	2	94	50.6	-27.7	45	12	2,500	0	3.5	0.0
C / 4.9	14.8	1.08	23.04	306	0	99	0	1	62	103.0	-18.9	50	13	2,500	0	5.8	0.0
C / 4.9	14.8	1.08	22.58	72	0	99	0	1	62	94.9	-19.2	40	13	2,500	0	0.0	0.0
C / 4.9	14.8	1.08	23.25	300	0	99	0	1	62	105.8	-18.8	54	13	2,500	0	0.0	0.0
B / 8.9	5.2	0.36	12.06	552	6	51	37	6	26	68.0	-6.5	90	14	2,500	0	4.0	0.8
B / 8.9	5.2	0.36	11.94	289	6	51	37	6	26	61.3	-6.8	87	14	2,500	0	0.0	0.8
B / 8.9	5.2	0.36	12.08	1,491	6	51	37	6	26	70.5	-6.4	91	14	2,500	0	0.0	0.8
B / 8.9	5.2	0.36	12.06	63	6	51	37	6	26	67.8	-6.5	90	14	2,500	0	4.0	0.8
C / 4.9	14.8	1.08	23.02	172	0	99	0	1	62	100.5	-19.0	47	13	2,500	0	3.5	0.0
C / 4.4	17.1	1.26	20.18	67	1	96	1	2	185	196.6	-23.5	98	8	2,500	0	5.8	0.8
C / 4.3	17.0	1.26	17.93	37	1	96	1	2	185	184.3	-23.6	97	8	2,500	0	0.0	0.8
C / 4.5	17.0	1.26	21.08	70	1	96	1	2	185	200.9	-23.4	98	8	2,500	0	0.0	0.8
C / 4.4	17.0	1.26	19.46	16	1	96	1	2	185	191.8	-23.6	98	8	2,500	0	3.5	0.8
C+ / 5.9	11.8	1.09	14.62	1,169	2	97	0	1	33	N/A	N/A	47	5	0	0	0.0	0.0
C / 4.6	12.8	0.79	26.46	933	1	95	2	2	33	95.0	-23.9	78	12	2,500	0	5.8	0.0
C- / 4.0	12.8	0.79	20.88	283	1	95	2	2	33	87.2	-24.1	72	12	2,500	0	0.0	0.0
C / 4.5	14.7	0.86	21.23	223	3	96	0	1	143	136.8	-24.6	84	6	2,500	0	5.8	1.5
C / 4.4	14.7	0.86	19.30	90	3	96	0	1	143	127.1	-24.9	79	6	2,500	0	0.0	1.5
C / 4.5	14.7	0.86	22.04	243	3	96	0	1	143	140.7	-24.5	85	6	2,500	0	0.0	1.5
C / 4.5	14.7	0.86	20.67	59	3	96	0	1	143	133.5	-24.7	82	6	2,500	0	3.5	1.5
C / 4.8	12.8	0.79	28.64	658	1	95	2	2	33	98.0	-23.8	80	12	2,500	0	0.0	0.0
C / 4.4	12.8	0.79	24.77	770	1	95	2	2	33	92.6	-23.9	77	12	2,500	0	3.5	0.0
C / 4.7	12.3	0.73	18.58	216	0	99	0	1	33	144.1	-23.8	92	4	2,500	0	5.8	1.5

99 Pct = Best
0 Pct = Worst

Fund Type	Fund Name	Ticker Symbol	Overall Investment Rating	Phone	Performance Rating/Pts	Total Return % through 2/28/17			Annualized		Incl. in Returns	
						3 Mo	6 Mo	1Yr / Pct	3Yr / Pct	5Yr / Pct	Dividend Yield	Expense Ratio
SC	Fidelity Adv Small Cap Value C	FCVCX	C+	(800) 522-7297	B- / 7.3	3.34	10.63	23.14 /67	8.04 /79	12.87 /82	0.20	2.22
SC	Fidelity Adv Small Cap Value I	FCVIX	B-	(800) 522-7297	B / 8.1	3.60	11.20	24.42 /71	9.15 /88	14.04 /93	0.75	1.18
SC	Fidelity Adv Small Cap Value T	FCVTX	C+	(800) 522-7297	B- / 7.1	3.48	10.89	23.78 /69	8.59 /84	13.46 /88	0.34	1.70
SC	Fidelity Adv Small Cap Z	FZAOX	C+	(800) 522-7297	C+ / 6.7	5.09	8.63	21.55 /60	6.50 /68	—	0.69	0.84
GR	Fidelity Adv Srs Stock Selector LCV	FMMLX	B+	(800) 544-8544	A / 9.3	7.24	11.92	27.61 /81	9.59 /91	—	1.39	0.77
MC	Fidelity Adv Stk Selector Mid Cap	FSSMX	B	(800) 522-7297	B / 8.0	8.27	11.27	27.60 /81	6.76 /70	11.93 /74	0.69	0.75
MC	Fidelity Adv Stk Selector Mid Cap A	FMCDX	C+	(800) 522-7297	C+ / 6.9	8.20	11.11	27.29 /80	6.49 /68	11.69 /71	0.50	0.98
MC	Fidelity Adv Stk Selector Mid Cap C	FMCEX	B-	(800) 522-7297	B- / 7.3	7.99	10.73	26.35 /77	5.71 /62	10.85 /65	0.00	1.74
MC	Fidelity Adv Stk Selector Mid Cap I	FMCCX	B	(800) 522-7297	B / 8.0	8.28	11.27	27.65 /81	6.73 /70	11.95 /74	0.73	0.83
MC	Fidelity Adv Stk Selector Mid Cap T	FMCAX	B-	(800) 522-7297	B- / 7.1	8.14	11.02	26.97 /79	6.25 /66	11.44 /69	0.29	1.22
GR	Fidelity Adv Stock Sel Lg Cap Val A	FLUAX	A-	(800) 522-7297	B / 7.7	6.57	10.74	25.89 /76	8.96 /87	13.08 /85	0.96	1.10
GR	Fidelity Adv Stock Sel Lg Cap Val C	FLUEX	A-	(800) 522-7297	B / 8.1	6.37	10.26	24.84 /73	8.05 /79	12.17 /76	0.39	1.93
GR	Fidelity Adv Stock Sel Lg Cap Val I	FLUIX	A+	(800) 522-7297	B+ / 8.9	6.63	10.79	26.20 /77	9.23 /88	13.39 /88	1.24	0.82
GR	Fidelity Adv Stock Sel Lg Cap Val T	FLUTX	A-	(800) 522-7297	B / 7.8	6.53	10.53	25.52 /75	8.59 /84	12.73 /81	0.68	1.42
SC	Fidelity Adv Stock Select Sm Cap A	FCDAX	C	(800) 522-7297	C+ / 6.1	5.52	11.34	28.68 /83	5.82 /63	11.05 /66	0.23	1.01
SC	Fidelity Adv Stock Select Sm Cap C	FCDCX	C+	(800) 522-7297	C+ / 6.5	5.32	10.91	27.61 /81	4.95 /54	10.17 /60	0.00	1.84
SC	Fidelity Adv Stock Select Sm Cap I	FCDIX	C+	(800) 522-7297	B- / 7.3	5.62	11.54	29.07 /84	6.13 /65	11.43 /69	0.44	0.74
SC	Fidelity Adv Stock Select Sm Cap T	FCDTX	C	(800) 522-7297	C+ / 6.3	5.46	11.18	28.26 /82	5.47 /59	10.70 /63	0.00	1.35
GR	Fidelity Adv Stock Selector AC A	FMAMX	C+	(800) 544-8544	B- / 7.4	8.94	9.74	26.30 /77	7.83 /78	12.62 /80	0.40	1.06
GR	Fidelity Adv Stock Selector AC C	FLACX	B-	(800) 544-8544	B / 7.8	8.73	9.31	25.32 /74	7.00 /72	11.75 /72	0.00	1.83
GR	Fidelity Adv Stock Selector AC I	FBRNX	B	(800) 544-8544	B+ / 8.6	8.99	9.87	26.64 /78	8.13 /80	12.92 /83	0.70	0.79
GR	Fidelity Adv Stock Selector AC T	FSJHX	B-	(800) 544-8544	B- / 7.5	8.86	9.59	25.96 /76	7.55 /76	12.33 /77	0.18	1.32
GR	Fidelity Adv Stock Selector AC Z	FZAPX	B+	(800) 544-8544	B+ / 8.7	9.05	9.96	26.82 /79	8.29 /81	—	0.83	0.64
GI	Fidelity Adv Strat Div and Inc A	FASDX	B-	(800) 522-7297	C+ / 6.1	5.98	5.13	19.53 /50	8.32 /81	10.45 /62	2.26	1.05
GI	Fidelity Adv Strat Div and Inc C	FCSDX	B-	(800) 522-7297	C+ / 6.5	5.72	4.67	18.59 /45	7.47 /75	9.61 /55	1.71	1.80
GI	Fidelity Adv Strat Div and Inc I	FSIDX	A-	(800) 522-7297	B- / 7.2	5.95	5.26	19.75 /51	8.59 /84	10.73 /64	2.62	0.79
GI	Fidelity Adv Strat Div and Inc T	FTSDX	B-	(800) 522-7297	C+ / 6.3	5.91	4.99	19.15 /48	8.02 /79	10.17 /60	2.08	1.30
GL	Fidelity Adv Strat Real Return A	FSRAX	D+	(800) 522-7297	E+ / 0.8	2.69	3.07	11.81 /17	-0.31 /12	0.90 / 6	1.78	1.08
GL	Fidelity Adv Strat Real Return C	FCSRX	D+	(800) 522-7297	E+ / 0.8	2.51	2.67	10.95 /14	-1.09 / 9	0.13 / 5	1.13	1.85
GL	Fidelity Adv Strat Real Return I	FSIRX	C-	(800) 522-7297	D- / 1.2	2.77	3.22	12.25 /19	-0.03 /13	1.14 / 6	2.13	0.80
GL	Fidelity Adv Strat Real Return T	FSRTX	D+	(800) 522-7297	E+ / 0.7	2.69	3.05	11.77 /17	-0.33 /12	0.86 / 6	1.76	1.11
TC	Fidelity Adv Technology A	FADTX	A-	(800) 522-7297	A+ / 9.8	13.71	13.71	38.37 /97	11.98 /98	14.18 /94	0.00	1.09
TC	Fidelity Adv Technology C	FTHCX	A-	(800) 522-7297	A+ / 9.8	13.49	13.29	37.32 /96	11.14 /97	13.33 /87	0.00	1.85
TC	Fidelity Adv Technology I	FATIX	A-	(800) 522-7297	A+ / 9.9	13.82	13.90	38.81 /97	12.35 /98	14.55 /96	0.00	0.75
TC	Fidelity Adv Technology T	FATEX	A-	(800) 522-7297	A+ / 9.8	13.65	13.59	37.99 /96	11.69 /98	13.89 /92	0.00	1.35
TC	Fidelity Adv Telecom A	FTUAX	C+	(800) 522-7297	C+ / 6.9	6.36	6.04	18.65 /46	9.85 /92	11.87 /73	1.44	1.15
TC	Fidelity Adv Telecom C	FTUCX	B+	(800) 522-7297	B- / 7.3	6.15	5.63	17.77 /42	9.05 /87	11.07 /66	0.96	1.89
TC	Fidelity Adv Telecom I	FTUIX	A-	(800) 522-7297	B / 8.1	6.44	6.21	19.03 /47	10.20 /94	12.22 /76	1.78	0.82
TC	Fidelity Adv Telecom T	FTUTX	B+	(800) 522-7297	B- / 7.0	6.27	5.85	18.26 /44	9.50 /90	11.52 /70	0.97	1.47
EM	Fidelity Adv Total Emerg Mkts A	FTEDX	C-	(800) 522-7297	C- / 3.8	8.14	4.37	25.29 /74	3.58 /38	2.85 /10	0.98	1.93
EM	Fidelity Adv Total Emerg Mkts C	FTEFX	C-	(800) 522-7297	C / 4.3	7.93	3.95	24.39 /71	2.80 /30	2.07 / 8	0.49	2.68
EM	Fidelity Adv Total Emerg Mkts I	FTEJX	C	(800) 522-7297	C / 5.3	8.12	4.45	25.66 /75	3.84 /41	3.09 /11	1.19	1.58
EM	Fidelity Adv Total Emerg Mkts T	FTEHX	C-	(800) 522-7297	C- / 4.0	7.98	4.13	24.98 /73	3.31 /35	2.58 / 9	0.72	2.27
FO	Fidelity Adv Total Intl Eq A	FTAEX	D	(800) 522-7297	D- / 1.1	6.55	1.24	13.42 /23	0.05 /14	4.71 /19	1.00	1.48
FO	Fidelity Adv Total Intl Eq C	FTCEX	D-	(800) 522-7297	E+ / 0.9	6.26	0.82	12.49 /20	-0.76 /10	3.91 /15	0.29	2.26
FO	Fidelity Adv Total Intl Eq Inst	FTEIX	D	(800) 522-7297	D / 1.7	6.52	1.20	13.56 /24	0.27 /15	4.96 /21	1.27	1.17
FO	Fidelity Adv Total Intl Eq T	FTTEX	D-	(800) 522-7297	E+ / 0.8	6.29	1.01	13.11 /22	-0.23 /12	4.42 /18	0.81	1.70
UT	Fidelity Adv Utilities A	FUGAX	C+	(800) 522-7297	C+ / 6.6	12.27	8.39	17.60 /41	7.64 /76	11.55 /70	1.66	1.13
UT	Fidelity Adv Utilities C	FUGCX	B-	(800) 522-7297	B- / 7.0	12.07	8.02	16.74 /37	6.84 /71	10.74 /64	1.08	1.88
UT	Fidelity Adv Utilities I	FUGIX	B	(800) 522-7297	B / 7.8	12.34	8.53	17.90 /42	7.95 /79	11.89 /73	1.96	0.84
UT	Fidelity Adv Utilities T	FAUFX	C+	(800) 522-7297	C+ / 6.7	12.15	8.23	17.23 /39	7.33 /74	11.24 /68	1.41	1.43
GR	Fidelity Adv Value A	FAVFX	B-	(800) 522-7297	B- / 7.0	7.02	10.59	28.20 /82	6.93 /71	13.23 /86	0.54	1.24

● Denotes fund is closed to new investors
* Denotes fund is included in Section II

RISK			NET ASSETS		ASSET					Portfolio Turnover Ratio	BULL / BEAR		FUND MANAGER		MINIMUMS		LOADS	
	3 Year		NAV								Last Bull	Last Bear	Manager	Manager	Initial	Additional	Front	Back
Risk Rating/Pts	Standard Deviation	Beta	As of 2/28/17	Total $(Mil)	Cash %	Stocks %	Bonds %	Other %			Market Return	Market Return	Quality Pct	Tenure (Years)	Purch. $	Purch. $	End Load	End Load
C /4.5	12.2	0.73	17.02	56	0	99	0	1		33	134.3	-24.0	90	4	2,500	0	0.0	1.5
C /4.7	12.3	0.73	18.91	440	0	99	0	1		33	147.7	-23.6	93	4	2,500	0	0.0	1.5
C /4.7	12.2	0.73	18.17	83	0	99	0	1		33	140.8	-23.8	91	4	2,500	0	3.5	1.5
C /4.8	12.8	0.79	28.58	47	1	95	2	2		33	N/A	N/A	81	12	0	0	0.0	0.0
C /5.2	10.5	0.98	13.16	1,134	4	95	0	1		64	N/A	N/A	66	5	0	0	0.0	0.0
C+ /5.6	12.3	0.99	37.11	241	1	96	1	2		109	119.4	-21.2	41	6	2,500	0	0.0	0.0
C+ /5.6	12.3	0.99	35.64	571	1	96	1	2		109	117.1	-21.1	37	6	2,500	0	5.8	0.0
C+ /5.6	12.3	0.99	32.70	146	1	96	1	2		109	108.6	-21.4	28	6	2,500	0	0.0	0.0
C+ /5.6	12.3	0.99	37.17	573	1	96	1	2		109	120.1	-21.0	40	6	2,500	0	0.0	0.0
C+ /5.6	12.3	0.99	35.84	613	1	96	1	2		109	114.6	-21.2	34	6	2,500	0	3.5	0.0
C+ /6.9	10.2	0.95	19.31	32	3	93	3	1		67	128.0	-20.3	62	5	2,500	0	5.8	0.0
C+ /6.8	10.2	0.95	18.90	11	3	93	3	1		67	118.3	-20.5	51	5	2,500	0	0.0	0.0
C+ /6.9	10.2	0.95	19.35	12	3	93	3	1		67	131.3	-20.2	65	5	2,500	0	0.0	0.0
C+ /6.9	10.2	0.95	19.29	11	3	93	3	1		67	124.1	-20.3	57	5	2,500	0	3.5	0.0
C /5.0	13.8	0.86	26.47	14	4	95	0	1		57	113.6	-25.5	72	8	2,500	0	5.8	1.5
C /4.9	13.8	0.86	24.77	5	4	95	0	1		57	104.5	-25.7	62	8	2,500	0	0.0	1.5
C /5.0	13.8	0.86	27.01	46	4	95	0	1		57	117.5	-25.5	75	8	2,500	0	0.0	1.5
C /5.0	13.8	0.87	25.91	3	4	95	0	1		57	110.0	-25.6	69	8	2,500	0	3.5	1.5
C /5.1	11.2	1.05	39.05	196	3	96	0	1		14	123.0	-21.2	34	8	2,500	0	5.8	0.0
C /5.1	11.2	1.05	38.75	65	3	96	0	1		14	113.9	-21.5	25	8	2,500	0	0.0	0.0
C /5.0	11.2	1.05	39.03	333	3	96	0	1		14	126.2	-21.1	37	8	2,500	0	0.0	0.0
C /5.1	11.2	1.05	39.04	122	3	96	0	1		14	119.9	-21.3	31	8	2,500	0	3.5	0.0
C /5.0	11.2	1.05	38.94	7	3	96	0	1		14	N/A	N/A	39	8	0	0	0.0	0.0
B- /7.7	7.6	0.68	15.05	744	2	66	13	19		55	91.2	-11.7	81	14	2,500	0	5.8	0.0
B- /7.7	7.5	0.68	14.97	421	2	66	13	19		55	83.4	-12.0	76	14	2,500	0	0.0	0.0
B- /7.7	7.6	0.68	15.10	458	2	66	13	19		55	93.9	-11.5	83	14	2,500	0	0.0	0.0
B- /7.7	7.5	0.68	15.04	267	2	66	13	19		55	88.6	-11.7	80	14	2,500	0	3.5	0.0
B /8.2	4.9	0.22	8.87	56	53	15	30	2		15	12.4	-7.8	70	11	2,500	0	4.0	0.0
B /8.3	4.9	0.22	8.78	29	53	15	30	2		15	7.8	-8.2	60	11	2,500	0	0.0	0.0
B /8.2	4.9	0.22	8.89	193	53	15	30	2		15	14.0	-7.8	73	11	2,500	0	0.0	0.0
B /8.2	4.9	0.22	8.88	12	53	15	30	2		15	12.3	-7.9	70	11	2,500	0	4.0	0.0
C /4.8	15.1	1.20	43.77	548	0	99	0	1		102	139.4	-21.7	64	12	2,500	0	5.8	0.0
C /4.7	15.1	1.20	37.80	190	0	99	0	1		102	130.0	-22.0	54	12	2,500	0	0.0	0.0
C /4.9	15.1	1.20	46.73	255	0	99	0	1		102	143.7	-21.7	69	12	2,500	0	0.0	0.0
C /4.8	15.1	1.21	41.73	229	0	99	0	1		102	136.1	-21.8	61	12	2,500	0	3.5	0.0
C+ /6.8	10.9	0.74	69.61	32	0	98	0	2		51	96.1	-16.7	86	4	2,500	0	5.8	0.0
C+ /6.8	10.9	0.74	69.24	14	0	98	0	2		51	88.6	-16.9	82	4	2,500	0	0.0	0.0
C+ /6.8	10.9	0.74	69.82	15	0	98	0	2		51	99.4	-16.6	87	4	2,500	0	0.0	0.0
C+ /6.8	10.9	0.74	69.33	7	0	98	0	2		51	92.8	-16.8	84	4	2,500	0	3.5	0.0
C+ /5.9	11.6	0.69	11.55	24	4	52	42	2		57	N/A	N/A	88	6	2,500	0	5.8	1.5
C+ /6.0	11.5	0.69	11.51	15	4	52	42	2		57	N/A	N/A	84	6	2,500	0	0.0	1.5
C+ /5.8	11.6	0.69	11.54	80	4	52	42	2		57	N/A	N/A	89	6	2,500	0	0.0	1.5
C+ /5.9	11.6	0.69	11.57	4	4	52	42	2		57	N/A	N/A	86	6	2,500	0	3.5	1.5
C+ /6.2	10.5	0.83	7.83	9	1	96	1	2		51	47.2	-25.3	75	10	2,500	0	5.8	1.0
C+ /6.2	10.5	0.83	7.85	3	1	96	1	2		51	41.3	-25.6	67	10	2,500	0	0.0	1.0
C+ /6.2	10.4	0.82	7.80	2	1	96	1	2		51	49.3	-25.3	77	10	2,500	0	0.0	1.0
C+ /6.2	10.5	0.83	7.86	14	1	96	1	2		51	45.1	-25.3	73	10	2,500	0	3.5	1.0
C+ /5.7	12.6	0.80	27.69	157	3	96	0	1		73	81.4	-2.6	28	11	2,500	0	5.8	0.0
C+ /5.7	12.6	0.80	27.16	59	3	96	0	1		73	74.3	-2.9	20	11	2,500	0	0.0	0.0
C+ /5.7	12.6	0.80	28.22	37	3	96	0	1		73	84.3	-2.5	31	11	2,500	0	0.0	0.0
C+ /5.7	12.6	0.80	27.75	48	3	96	0	1		73	78.6	-2.7	25	11	2,500	0	3.5	0.0
C+ /5.7	12.1	1.08	24.08	62	4	93	2	1		77	132.9	-24.8	21	7	2,500	0	5.8	0.0

Fund Type	Fund Name	Ticker Symbol	Overall Investment Rating	Phone	Performance Rating/Pts	3 Mo	6 Mo	1Yr / Pct	3Yr / Pct	5Yr / Pct	Dividend Yield	Expense Ratio
GR	Fidelity Adv Value C	FCVFX	B	(800) 522-7297	B- / 7.4	6.80	10.19	27.19 /80	6.13 /65	12.39 /78	0.00	2.03
GR	Fidelity Adv Value I	FVIFX	B+	(800) 522-7297	B / 8.2	7.07	10.74	28.58 /83	7.23 /74	13.55 /89	0.84	0.94
GR	Fidelity Adv Value Leaders A	FVLAX	A	(800) 522-7297	B / 8.1	9.62	12.01	23.78 /69	9.31 /89	12.63 /80	0.40	1.47
GR	Fidelity Adv Value Leaders C	FVLCX	A+	(800) 522-7297	B+ / 8.6	9.47	11.58	22.91 /66	8.52 /83	11.79 /72	0.00	2.29
GR	Fidelity Adv Value Leaders I	FVLIX	A+	(800) 522-7297	A- / 9.2	9.68	12.11	24.12 /70	9.60 /91	12.94 /83	0.65	1.18
GR	Fidelity Adv Value Leaders T	FVLTX	A+	(800) 522-7297	B+ / 8.3	9.55	11.86	23.51 /68	9.06 /87	12.36 /78	0.21	1.77
MC	Fidelity Adv Value Strategies A	FSOAX	C+	(800) 522-7297	B- / 7.1	8.84	9.85	28.78 /83	6.83 /71	11.97 /74	1.23	0.93
MC	Fidelity Adv Value Strategies C	FVCSX	C+	(800) 522-7297	B / 7.6	8.67	9.43	27.81 /81	6.03 /64	11.12 /67	0.76	1.70
MC	Fidelity Adv Value Strategies Fd	FSLSX	B	(800) 522-7297	B+ / 8.3	8.91	10.01	29.16 /84	7.13 /73	12.29 /77	1.38	0.67
MC	Fidelity Adv Value Strategies I	FASOX	B	(800) 522-7297	B+ / 8.3	8.90	9.98	29.07 /84	7.10 /73	12.26 /77	1.44	0.68
MC	Fidelity Adv Value Strategies T	FASPX	C+	(800) 522-7297	B- / 7.4	8.78	9.73	28.49 /83	6.61 /69	11.74 /72	0.99	1.15
GR	Fidelity Adv Value T	FTVFX	B-	(800) 522-7297	B- / 7.2	6.96	10.46	27.84 /81	6.67 /70	12.94 /83	0.36	1.52
CV	Fidelity Advisor Convertible Sec A	FACVX	D-	(800) 522-7297	D / 1.8	4.27	4.45	17.28 /40	1.16 /19	6.72 /33	2.77	0.84
CV	Fidelity Advisor Convertible Sec C	FCCVX	D	(800) 522-7297	D / 2.1	4.08	4.03	16.42 /36	0.40 /15	5.90 /28	2.19	1.60
CV	Fidelity Advisor Convertible Sec I	FICVX	D	(800) 522-7297	D+ / 2.7	4.34	4.56	17.62 /41	1.43 /21	6.99 /35	3.20	0.58
CV	Fidelity Advisor Convertible Sec T	FTCVX	D-	(800) 522-7297	D / 1.9	4.20	4.29	16.97 /38	0.87 /18	6.40 /31	2.56	1.12
FO	Fidelity Advisor Europe A	FHJUX	D-	(800) 544-8544	E- / 0.2	5.37	-3.77	5.28 / 4	-3.59 / 4	5.26 /23	0.61	1.33
FO	Fidelity Advisor Europe C	FHJTX	D-	(800) 544-8544	E- / 0.2	5.17	-4.15	4.47 / 3	-4.34 / 3	4.45 /18	0.00	2.13
FO	Fidelity Advisor Europe I	FHJMX	D-	(800) 544-8544	E / 0.3	5.48	-3.59	5.67 / 4	-3.23 / 4	5.59 /25	1.18	0.98
FO	Fidelity Advisor Europe T	FHJVX	D-	(800) 544-8544	E- / 0.2	5.29	-3.91	4.97 / 4	-3.86 / 3	4.97 /21	0.25	1.61
GL	Fidelity Advisor Glbl Eq Inc A	FBLYX	C-	(800) 522-7297	C- / 3.1	5.90	4.57	13.26 /23	4.74 /51	--	0.83	2.13
GL	Fidelity Advisor Glbl Eq Inc C	FGTNX	C	(800) 522-7297	C- / 3.6	5.71	4.19	12.52 /20	3.96 /42	--	0.28	2.93
GL	Fidelity Advisor Glbl Eq Inc I	FBUSX	C	(800) 522-7297	C / 4.4	5.96	4.69	13.50 /23	5.01 /54	--	1.09	1.68
GL	Fidelity Advisor Glbl Eq Inc T	FGABX	C-	(800) 522-7297	C- / 3.3	5.83	4.43	12.97 /22	4.48 /48	--	0.60	2.46
GL	Fidelity Advisor Global Balanced A	FGLAX	D-	(800) 522-7297	E / 0.5	4.11	-1.23	8.28 / 8	-0.34 /12	4.39 /17	0.02	1.30
GL	Fidelity Advisor Global Balanced C	FGLCX	D-	(800) 522-7297	E+ / 0.6	3.89	-1.65	7.39 / 6	-1.15 / 9	3.55 /13	0.00	2.11
GL	Fidelity Advisor Global Balanced I	FGLIX	D	(800) 522-7297	E+ / 0.9	4.21	-1.04	8.60 / 9	-0.05 /13	4.69 /19	0.07	1.01
GL	Fidelity Advisor Global Balanced T	FGLTX	D-	(800) 522-7297	E / 0.5	4.04	-1.39	7.93 / 7	-0.62 /11	4.10 /16	0.00	1.58
FO	Fidelity Advisor Intl SC Opp A	FOPAX	D+	(800) 522-7297	D / 1.7	7.60	1.63	11.02 /15	2.69 /29	8.96 /50	0.73	1.52
FO	Fidelity Advisor Intl SC Opp C	FOPCX	D+	(800) 522-7297	D / 1.9	7.41	1.23	10.05 /12	1.90 /23	8.13 /43	0.00	2.27
FO	Fidelity Advisor Intl SC Opp I	FOPIX	C-	(800) 522-7297	D+ / 2.6	7.67	1.76	11.28 /15	3.02 /32	9.28 /53	1.14	1.19
FO	Fidelity Advisor Intl SC Opp T	FOPTX	D+	(800) 522-7297	D / 1.8	7.56	1.47	10.69 /13	2.40 /27	8.67 /48	0.35	1.80
EM	Fidelity Advisor Latin America Fd A	FLFAX	E-	(800) 544-8544	E+ / 0.6	11.43	2.93	39.87 /97	-5.06 / 2	-10.20 / 1	1.88	1.40
EM	Fidelity Advisor Latin America Fd C	FLFCX	E-	(800) 544-8544	E+ / 0.8	11.26	2.58	38.90 /97	-5.76 / 2	-10.86 / 0	1.28	2.15
EM	Fidelity Advisor Latin America Fd I	FLFIX	E-	(800) 544-8544	D- / 1.1	11.54	3.17	40.45 /97	-4.73 / 3	-9.89 / 1	2.28	1.06
EM	Fidelity Advisor Latin America Fd T	FLFTX	E-	(800) 544-8544	E+ / 0.7	11.40	2.81	39.55 /97	-5.31 / 2	-10.44 / 1	1.66	1.67
GI	Fidelity Advisor Mega Cap Stock A	FGTAX	B+	(800) 544-8544	B / 8.0	6.37	11.44	27.78 /81	8.97 /87	13.14 /85	1.13	0.95
GI	Fidelity Advisor Mega Cap Stock C	FGRCX	A-	(800) 544-8544	B+ / 8.4	6.19	10.99	26.84 /79	8.21 /81	12.30 /77	0.53	1.70
GI	Fidelity Advisor Mega Cap Stock I	FTRIX	A	(800) 544-8544	A- / 9.1	6.44	11.60	28.12 /82	9.31 /89	13.44 /88	1.41	0.68
GI	Fidelity Advisor Mega Cap Stock T	FTGRX	B+	(800) 544-8544	B / 8.2	6.30	11.24	27.41 /80	8.73 /85	12.86 /82	0.95	1.21
GI	Fidelity Advisor Mega Cap Stock Z	FZALX	A	(800) 544-8544	A- / 9.2	6.48	11.66	28.27 /82	9.45 /90	--	1.55	0.54
GL	Fidelity Advisor Series Equity Gro	FMFMX	U	(800) 522-7297	U /	10.74	8.80	22.18 /63	--	--	0.11	0.74
GR	Fidelity Advisor Series Equity Inc	FLMLX	A+	(800) 544-8544	A- / 9.2	6.12	10.93	28.99 /84	9.54 /91	--	2.04	0.74
GL	Fidelity Advisor Series Growth Opp	FAOFX	B	(800) 522-7297	B / 7.6	11.08	9.43	22.62 /65	6.79 /70	--	0.32	0.74
GL	Fidelity Advisor Series Small Cap	FSSFX	C+	(800) 522-7297	C+ / 6.4	5.10	8.68	21.43 /59	6.00 /64	--	0.83	0.94
GR	Fidelity Advisor Srs Opp Insights	FAMGX	B-	(800) 522-7297	B- / 7.5	9.04	7.53	19.92 /52	7.90 /78	--	0.00	0.94
FO	Fidelity Advisor Worldwide A	FWAFX	D-	(800) 522-7297	D / 1.7	6.43	3.41	14.08 /26	1.36 /20	8.81 /49	0.50	1.27
FO	Fidelity Advisor Worldwide C	FWCFX	D-	(800) 522-7297	D / 2.0	6.26	3.04	13.24 /22	0.59 /16	8.00 /42	0.00	2.07
FO	Fidelity Advisor Worldwide I	FWIFX	D	(800) 522-7297	D+ / 2.6	6.50	3.59	14.37 /27	1.64 /22	9.10 /51	0.80	0.98
FO	Fidelity Advisor Worldwide T	FWTFX	D-	(800) 522-7297	D / 1.8	6.36	3.28	13.73 /24	1.07 /19	8.51 /46	0.13	1.57
AA	Fidelity Asset Manager 20%	FASIX	C	(800) 544-8544	D / 2.0	2.53	1.25	7.58 / 7	2.87 /30	3.79 /14	1.59	0.53
GI	Fidelity Asset Manager 30%	FTANX	C	(800) 544-8544	D+ / 2.5	3.32	2.01	9.79 /11	3.50 /37	4.88 /21	1.63	0.54

99 Pct = Best
0 Pct = Worst

• Denotes fund is closed to new investors
∗ Denotes fund is included in Section II

www.thestreetratings.com

RISK			NET ASSETS		ASSET					BULL / BEAR		FUND MANAGER		MINIMUMS		LOADS	
Risk Rating/Pts	3 Year Standard Deviation	Beta	NAV As of 2/28/17	Total $(Mil)	Cash %	Stocks %	Bonds %	Other %	Portfolio Turnover Ratio	Last Bull Market Return	Last Bear Market Return	Manager Quality Pct	Manager Tenure (Years)	Initial Purch. $	Additional Purch. $	Front End Load	Back End Load
C+ / 5.7	12.1	1.08	22.92	19	4	93	2	1	77	123.4	-25.0	15	7	2,500	0	0.0	0.0
C+ / 5.7	12.1	1.08	24.29	20	4	93	2	1	77	136.3	-24.7	24	7	2,500	0	0.0	0.0
B- / 7.3	10.7	0.98	18.41	19	8	88	2	2	63	118.1	-23.9	62	3	2,500	0	5.8	0.0
B- / 7.3	10.7	0.98	17.92	6	8	88	2	2	63	109.5	-24.1	52	3	2,500	0	0.0	0.0
B- / 7.3	10.7	0.98	18.54	3	8	88	2	2	63	121.4	-23.8	66	3	2,500	0	0.0	0.0
B- / 7.4	10.7	0.98	18.46	8	8	88	2	2	63	115.0	-23.9	59	3	2,500	0	3.5	0.0
C / 4.8	12.4	0.92	35.34	209	2	96	0	2	9	125.5	-26.8	50	1	2,500	0	5.8	0.0
C / 4.7	12.4	0.92	31.14	46	2	96	0	2	9	116.5	-27.1	39	1	2,500	0	0.0	0.0
C / 5.0	12.4	0.93	40.61	476	2	96	0	2	9	129.1	-26.8	53	1	2,500	0	0.0	0.0
C / 4.9	12.4	0.93	38.32	79	2	96	0	2	9	128.8	-26.8	53	1	2,500	0	0.0	0.0
C / 4.9	12.4	0.93	37.02	270	2	96	0	2	9	123.0	-26.9	47	1	2,500	0	3.5	0.0
C+ / 5.7	12.1	1.08	23.87	20	4	93	2	1	77	129.7	-24.9	19	7	2,500	0	3.5	0.0
C / 5.3	9.8	1.05	27.36	29	9	28	7	56	19	62.9	-19.9	24	1	2,500	0	5.8	0.0
C / 5.3	9.8	1.05	27.19	23	9	28	7	56	19	56.3	-20.1	17	1	2,500	0	0.0	0.0
C / 5.3	9.8	1.05	27.42	50	9	28	7	56	19	65.2	-19.8	27	1	2,500	0	0.0	0.0
C / 5.3	9.8	1.05	27.37	7	9	28	7	56	19	60.3	-20.0	21	1	2,500	0	3.5	0.0
C+ / 6.1	13.1	0.99	34.47	16	0	99	0	1	62	54.0	-29.4	29	4	2,500	0	5.8	0.0
C+ / 6.1	13.1	0.99	34.39	8	0	99	0	1	62	47.7	-29.6	21	4	2,500	0	0.0	0.0
C+ / 6.1	13.1	0.99	34.44	5	0	99	0	1	62	56.6	-29.3	33	4	2,500	0	0.0	0.0
C+ / 6.1	13.1	0.99	34.54	7	0	99	0	1	62	51.8	-29.5	26	4	2,500	0	3.5	0.0
C+ / 6.9	8.9	0.67	13.10	6	5	94	0	1	43	N/A	N/A	95	5	2,500	0	5.8	0.0
C+ / 6.9	8.9	0.67	13.04	4	5	94	0	1	43	N/A	N/A	93	5	2,500	0	0.0	0.0
C+ / 6.9	8.9	0.67	13.12	5	5	94	0	1	43	N/A	N/A	95	5	2,500	0	0.0	0.0
C+ / 6.9	8.9	0.67	13.09	3	5	94	0	1	43	N/A	N/A	94	5	2,500	0	3.5	0.0
C+ / 6.7	7.4	1.06	22.63	40	1	58	39	2	155	36.6	-13.0	14	10	2,500	0	5.8	0.0
C+ / 6.6	7.4	1.06	21.90	26	1	58	39	2	155	30.7	-13.3	9	10	2,500	0	0.0	0.0
C+ / 6.7	7.4	1.06	22.87	5	1	58	39	2	155	38.7	-12.9	16	10	2,500	0	0.0	0.0
C+ / 6.7	7.4	1.06	22.41	14	1	58	39	2	155	34.6	-13.1	12	10	2,500	0	3.5	0.0
B- / 7.1	10.1	0.71	15.22	44	7	92	0	1	24	80.8	-20.5	89	9	2,500	0	5.8	2.0
B- / 7.1	10.1	0.71	14.78	12	7	92	0	1	24	73.4	-20.7	86	9	2,500	0	0.0	2.0
B- / 7.1	10.1	0.71	15.35	160	7	92	0	1	24	83.6	-20.4	91	9	2,500	0	0.0	2.0
B- / 7.1	10.1	0.71	15.13	11	7	92	0	1	24	78.1	-20.6	88	9	2,500	0	3.5	2.0
D / 2.0	24.4	1.29	21.38	18	0	100	0	0	108	-26.9	-24.9	5	2	2,500	0	5.8	1.5
D / 2.0	24.4	1.29	21.66	5	0	100	0	0	108	-29.8	-25.1	4	2	2,500	0	0.0	1.5
D / 1.9	24.4	1.29	21.29	5	0	100	0	0	108	-25.6	-24.8	5	2	2,500	0	0.0	1.5
D / 2.0	24.4	1.29	21.45	6	0	100	0	0	108	-28.0	-25.0	4	2	2,500	0	3.5	1.5
C+ / 6.3	11.7	1.10	18.04	73	0	99	0	1	25	130.8	-16.1	41	8	2,500	0	5.8	0.0
C+ / 6.3	11.7	1.10	17.81	35	0	99	0	1	25	121.9	-16.4	32	8	2,500	0	0.0	0.0
C+ / 6.3	11.7	1.10	18.20	154	0	99	0	1	25	134.2	-16.0	46	8	2,500	0	0.0	0.0
C+ / 6.3	11.7	1.10	18.03	29	0	99	0	1	25	127.7	-16.2	38	8	2,500	0	3.5	0.0
C+ / 6.3	11.7	1.09	18.13	3	0	99	0	1	25	N/A	N/A	48	8	0	0	0.0	0.0
U /	N/A	N/A	12.41	961	4	95	0	1	65	N/A	N/A	N/A	3	0	0	0.0	0.0
C+ / 6.3	10.2	0.95	13.42	1,685	8	91	0	1	42	N/A	N/A	69	5	0	0	0.0	0.0
C+ / 5.6	13.8	0.92	11.37	633	0	99	0	1	50	N/A	N/A	98	2	0	0	0.0	0.0
C+ / 6.8	12.8	0.60	11.39	458	9	89	0	2	35	N/A	N/A	97	4	0	0	0.0	0.0
C / 5.2	11.3	0.94	16.06	883	0	99	0	1	47	N/A	N/A	49	5	0	0	0.0	0.0
C / 5.1	10.9	0.78	22.80	28	0	99	0	1	117	77.1	-20.1	84	11	2,500	0	5.8	0.0
C / 5.2	10.9	0.78	22.41	10	0	99	0	1	117	70.1	-20.3	79	11	2,500	0	0.0	0.0
C / 5.1	10.9	0.78	22.93	14	0	99	0	1	117	79.8	-19.9	85	11	2,500	0	0.0	0.0
C / 5.1	10.9	0.78	22.71	9	0	99	0	1	117	74.6	-20.2	82	11	2,500	0	3.5	0.0
B+ / 9.0	3.1	0.45	13.25	4,780	30	18	50	2	19	27.7	-3.2	69	8	2,500	0	0.0	0.0
B / 8.7	4.0	0.34	10.72	981	19	29	50	2	24	37.2	-5.6	73	8	2,500	0	0.0	0.0

I. Index of Stock Mutual Funds

99 Pct = Best
0 Pct = Worst

Fund Type	Fund Name	Ticker Symbol	Overall Investment Rating	Phone	Perfor-mance Rating/Pts	3 Mo	6 Mo	1Yr / Pct	3Yr / Pct	5Yr / Pct	Dividend Yield	Expense Ratio
GI	Fidelity Asset Manager 40%	FFANX	C+	(800) 544-8544	C- / 3.2	4.06	2.92	11.93 /18	3.94 /42	5.84 /27	1.61	0.55
AA	Fidelity Asset Manager 50%	FASMX	C	(800) 544-8544	C- / 3.8	4.83	3.84	13.93 /25	4.28 /46	6.64 /32	1.49	0.66
GI	Fidelity Asset Manager 60%	FSANX	C+	(800) 544-8544	C / 4.4	5.58	4.74	15.98 /34	4.61 /50	7.43 /38	1.32	0.72
AA	Fidelity Asset Manager 70%	FASGX	C	(800) 544-8544	C / 5.1	6.26	5.78	17.98 /43	4.85 /53	8.21 /44	1.25	0.73
AG	Fidelity Asset Manager 85%	FAMRX	C	(800) 544-8544	C+ / 6.0	7.36	7.10	20.79 /56	5.28 /57	9.41 /54	0.99	0.76
AA	Fidelity AZ Conservative Index		C	(800) 544-8544	E+ / 0.9	0.53	-0.90	0.69 / 2	1.16 /19	0.93 / 6	0.00	0.34
GL	Fidelity AZ International Index		D	(800) 544-8544	D- / 1.2	7.43	4.40	15.71 /33	-0.80 /10	5.07 /22	0.00	0.35
AA	Fidelity AZ Spartan 500 Index		A+	(800) 544-8544	A / 9.3	8.00	9.98	24.85 /73	10.46 /96	13.80 /92	0.00	0.25
AA	Fidelity AZ Ttl Mkt Index		A+	(800) 544-8544	A- / 9.1	7.73	10.28	26.18 /77	9.72 /92	13.62 /90	0.00	0.25
* BA	Fidelity Balanced Fd	FBALX	B-	(800) 544-8544	C+ / 6.3	6.48	6.11	17.95 /43	6.84 /71	9.61 /55	1.51	0.55
BA	Fidelity Balanced K	FBAKX	B-	(800) 544-8544	C+ / 6.4	6.50	6.17	18.07 /43	6.95 /72	9.72 /56	1.60	0.46
* GR	Fidelity Blue Chip Growth Fd	FBGRX	B	(800) 544-8544	B+ / 8.4	9.59	9.01	23.25 /67	8.64 /84	14.12 /94	0.20	0.82
GR	Fidelity Blue Chip Growth K	FBGKX	B	(800) 544-8544	B+ / 8.5	9.63	9.09	23.40 /68	8.77 /85	14.26 /95	0.35	0.70
GR	Fidelity Blue Chip Value	FBCVX	A+	(800) 544-8544	A / 9.4	9.88	12.41	24.99 /73	9.90 /93	13.21 /86	0.98	0.88
FO	Fidelity Canada Fund	FICDX	E	(800) 544-8544	D- / 1.4	2.80	3.69	20.67 /56	-0.01 /13	2.19 / 8	1.23	1.15
* GI	Fidelity Capital and Income	FAGIX	C+	(800) 544-8544	C+ / 5.6	6.10	6.49	19.34 /49	5.61 /61	7.66 /39	3.99	0.75
* GR	Fidelity Capital Appreciation Fd	FDCAX	C-	(800) 544-8544	C+ / 5.8	5.59	8.28	18.03 /43	5.66 /61	12.53 /79	1.13	0.83
GR	Fidelity Capital Appreciation K	FCAKX	C-	(800) 544-8544	C+ / 5.9	5.60	8.35	18.16 /44	5.78 /62	12.67 /81	1.23	0.72
FO	Fidelity China Region Fund	FHKCX	E+	(800) 544-8544	C- / 3.9	5.85	5.10	27.11 /79	1.66 /22	6.19 /30	1.02	0.99
* GR	Fidelity Contrafund Fd	FCNTX	B+	(800) 544-8544	B / 7.7	8.97	8.25	20.21 /53	8.19 /80	12.97 /83	0.27	0.71
GR	Fidelity Contrafund K	FCNKX	B+	(800) 544-8544	B / 7.8	9.00	8.31	20.34 /54	8.30 /81	13.09 /85	0.36	0.61
CV	Fidelity Convertible Securities	FCVSX	D	(800) 544-8544	D+ / 2.7	4.34	4.56	17.61 /41	1.44 /21	7.01 /35	3.21	0.56
GL	Fidelity DE International Index		D	(800) 544-8544	D- / 1.3	7.33	4.36	15.70 /33	-0.81 /10	5.08 /22	0.00	0.35
AA	Fidelity DE Spartan 500 Index		A+	(800) 544-8544	A / 9.3	8.00	9.98	24.81 /73	10.46 /96	13.81 /92	0.00	0.25
AA	Fidelity DE Total Market Index		A+	(800) 544-8544	A- / 9.1	7.73	10.22	26.15 /77	9.71 /92	13.62 /90	0.00	0.25
GR	Fidelity Disciplined Equity Fd	FDEQX	B	(800) 544-8544	B- / 7.2	7.62	8.66	19.38 /49	7.66 /76	12.78 /82	1.38	0.89
GR	Fidelity Disciplined Equity K	FDEKX	B	(800) 544-8544	B- / 7.3	7.67	8.72	19.49 /49	7.77 /77	12.90 /83	1.48	0.79
* FO	Fidelity Diversified Intl Fd	FDIVX	D-	(800) 544-8544	D- / 1.1	6.49	0.78	10.10 /12	-0.05 /13	6.10 /29	1.10	1.00
FO	Fidelity Diversified Intl K	FDIKX	D	(800) 544-8544	D- / 1.5	6.52	0.84	10.25 /12	0.08 /14	6.25 /30	1.23	0.92
* GR	Fidelity Dividend Growth Fd	FDGFX	C+	(800) 544-8544	B- / 7.3	7.05	8.43	19.89 /51	7.84 /78	11.58 /71	1.50	0.62
GR	Fidelity Dividend Growth K	FDGKX	C+	(800) 544-8544	B- / 7.4	7.08	8.50	20.05 /52	7.97 /79	11.73 /72	1.62	0.50
EM	Fidelity EM Index Inst	FPMIX	D+	(800) 544-8544	C / 5.0	8.84	5.29	29.26 /85	2.26 /26	-0.45 / 4	1.54	0.11
EM	Fidelity EM Index Inv	FPEMX	D+	(800) 544-8544	C / 4.8	8.77	5.10	29.05 /84	2.07 /24	-0.65 / 4	1.36	0.30
EM	Fidelity EM Index IP	FPADX	D+	(800) 544-8544	C / 5.0	8.74	5.20	29.14 /84	2.29 /26	-0.44 / 4	1.56	0.09
EM	Fidelity EM Index Pr	FPMAX	D+	(800) 544-8544	C / 4.9	8.82	5.27	29.26 /85	2.20 /25	-0.54 / 4	1.51	0.14
EM	Fidelity Emerg Mkts Discv	FEDDX	C+	(800) 522-7297	C+ / 6.3	9.68	5.97	30.55 /87	4.06 /44	3.91 /15	0.72	1.56
FO	Fidelity Emerging Asia Fund	FSEAX	C	(800) 544-8544	C / 5.2	6.52	2.46	24.87 /73	4.65 /50	4.23 /16	1.00	1.09
EM	Fidelity Emerging Markets Fd	FEMKX	D	(800) 544-8544	D+ / 2.9	8.10	1.03	21.25 /58	1.41 /20	1.27 / 7	0.61	1.05
EM	Fidelity Emerging Markets K	FKEMX	D	(800) 544-8544	C- / 3.1	8.13	1.12	21.50 /60	1.62 /22	1.47 / 7	0.77	0.85
* IN	Fidelity Equity Dividend Income	FEQTX	A+	(800) 544-8544	B+ / 8.7	5.80	9.62	25.33 /74	9.46 /90	12.62 /80	1.78	0.66
IN	Fidelity Equity Dividend Income K	FETKX	A+	(800) 544-8544	B+ / 8.8	5.84	9.64	25.46 /75	9.57 /91	12.75 /81	1.88	0.55
IN	Fidelity Equity Income I	FEQIX	B+	(800) 544-8544	B+ / 8.6	6.11	10.46	27.87 /81	8.46 /83	12.23 /76	2.24	0.71
IN	Fidelity Equity Income K	FEIKX	B+	(800) 544-8544	B+ / 8.7	6.12	10.51	28.02 /82	8.59 /84	12.37 /78	2.34	0.59
FO	Fidelity Europe	FIEUX	E+	(800) 544-8544	E / 0.3	5.46	-3.61	5.62 / 4	-3.27 / 4	5.57 /25	1.11	1.03
FS	Fidelity Event Driven Opportunities	FARNX	A	(800) 544-8544	A+ / 9.8	8.85	19.92	34.95 /94	10.13 /94	--	0.89	1.14
FS	Fidelity Event Drvn Opp A	FCHSX	A+	(800) 544-8544	A / 9.5	8.32	19.24	33.50 /92	9.22 /88	--	0.30	2.84
FS	Fidelity Event Drvn Opp C	FATJX	A+	(800) 544-8544	A+ / 9.6	8.02	18.77	32.47 /91	8.40 /82	--	0.11	3.54
FS	Fidelity Event Drvn Opp I	FMRMX	A+	(800) 544-8544	A+ / 9.8	8.36	19.33	33.76 /93	9.47 /90	--	0.37	2.25
FS	Fidelity Event Drvn Opp T	FJPDX	A+	(800) 544-8544	A / 9.5	8.12	19.07	33.00 /92	8.90 /86	--	0.24	3.06
GR	Fidelity Export and Multination	FEXPX	B	(800) 544-8544	B / 8.1	7.69	9.99	20.89 /57	8.80 /85	11.54 /70	1.12	0.77
GR	Fidelity Export and Multination K	FEXKX	B	(800) 544-8544	B / 8.2	7.70	10.04	21.01 /57	8.94 /86	11.69 /71	1.23	0.64
GR	Fidelity Ext Mkt Idx Inv	FSEMX	B	(800) 544-8544	B+ / 8.5	6.52	11.52	32.50 /91	6.88 /71	13.00 /84	1.22	0.10

● Denotes fund is closed to new investors
* Denotes fund is included in Section II

232

www.thestreetratings.com

| RISK | | | NET ASSETS | | ASSET | | | | Portfolio | BULL / BEAR | | FUND MANAGER | | MINIMUMS | | LOADS | |
| Risk Rating/Pts | 3 Year | | NAV As of 2/28/17 | Total $(Mil) | Cash % | Stocks % | Bonds % | Other % | Turnover Ratio | Last Bull Market Return | Last Bear Market Return | Manager Quality Pct | Manager Tenure (Years) | Initial Purch. $ | Additional Purch. $ | Front End Load | Back End Load |
	Standard Deviation	Beta															
B /8.4	5.0	0.44	11.13	1,188	16	38	45	1	22	46.1	-8.0	67	8	2,500	0	0.0	0.0
B- /7.2	6.0	0.92	17.34	7,798	11	47	40	2	19	54.5	-10.6	42	8	2,500	0	0.0	0.0
B- /7.1	6.9	0.63	11.59	1,618	10	57	32	1	21	63.0	-13.0	49	8	2,500	0	0.0	0.0
C+ /6.2	8.0	1.22	20.56	4,263	9	63	26	2	21	72.0	-15.7	23	8	2,500	0	0.0	0.0
C /5.4	9.5	0.88	17.44	1,628	5	82	12	1	22	86.2	-19.2	26	8	2,500	0	0.0	0.0
B+ /9.9	1.4	0.03	13.22	3	55	0	44	1	46	5.3	4.5	80	11	50	25	0.0	0.0
C+ /6.2	11.4	1.65	11.86	7	1	97	0	2	3	47.7	-23.0	3	11	50	25	0.0	1.0
B- /7.3	10.3	1.62	21.05	30	0	99	0	1	2	132.3	-16.3	52	11	50	25	0.0	0.0
B- /7.0	10.7	1.66	21.45	21	0	99	0	1	0	132.1	-17.7	39	11	50	25	0.0	0.0
B- /7.0	7.6	1.18	23.15	21,728	4	63	31	2	64	80.3	-10.4	49	9	2,500	0	0.0	0.0
B- /7.0	7.6	1.18	23.15	8,216	4	63	31	2	64	81.4	-10.3	51	9	0	0	0.0	0.0
C /4.9	12.7	1.07	73.36	14,615	0	99	0	1	50	138.2	-17.2	41	8	2,500	0	0.0	0.0
C /4.9	12.6	1.07	73.45	5,181	0	99	0	1	50	139.9	-17.1	43	8	0	0	0.0	0.0
B- /7.3	10.7	0.97	18.45	432	8	89	2	1	54	124.0	-23.9	70	3	2,500	0	0.0	0.0
C- /3.2	13.5	0.72	49.45	1,233	2	96	1	1	44	26.4	-23.8	74	3	2,500	0	0.0	1.5
C+ /6.0	6.1	0.48	10.07	11,124	1	20	78	1	35	62.8	-12.8	78	14	2,500	0	0.0	1.0
C /4.3	12.5	1.08	33.44	4,982	1	98	0	1	120	122.0	-17.0	12	12	2,500	0	0.0	0.0
C /4.3	12.5	1.08	33.50	2,122	1	98	0	1	120	123.6	-16.9	13	12	0	0	0.0	0.0
D- /1.5	22.9	1.13	26.49	950	0	98	1	1	70	66.4	-27.1	85	6	2,500	0	0.0	1.5
C+ /6.0	10.3	0.91	106.03	77,315	0	99	0	1	35	120.7	-14.4	58	27	2,500	0	0.0	0.0
C+ /6.0	10.3	0.91	105.97	30,099	0	99	0	1	35	122.0	-14.4	60	27	0	0	0.0	0.0
C /5.3	9.7	1.05	27.46	1,501	9	28	7	56	19	65.4	-19.8	27	1	2,500	0	0.0	0.0
C+ /6.2	11.4	1.66	11.72	5	1	97	0	2	8	47.8	-23.1	3	11	50	25	0.0	0.0
B- /7.3	10.3	1.62	20.93	15	0	99	0	1	22	132.6	-16.5	52	11	50	25	0.0	0.0
B- /7.0	10.7	1.66	21.47	10	0	99	0	1	24	132.1	-17.7	39	11	50	25	0.0	0.0
C+ /5.9	10.4	0.99	35.21	1,216	0	98	0	2	179	123.8	-21.9	40	4	2,500	0	0.0	0.0
C+ /5.9	10.4	0.99	35.16	112	0	98	0	2	179	125.4	-21.9	41	4	0	0	0.0	0.0
C+ /5.8	11.2	0.88	34.88	10,130	1	97	1	1	24	57.8	-24.5	74	16	2,500	0	0.0	0.0
C+ /5.8	11.2	0.87	34.81	8,042	1	97	1	1	24	59.0	-24.5	75	16	0	0	0.0	0.0
C /4.8	10.0	0.96	33.84	5,973	2	94	2	2	30	119.1	-24.6	47	3	2,500	0	0.0	0.0
C /4.8	10.0	0.96	33.81	1,661	2	94	2	2	30	120.7	-24.5	48	3	0	0	0.0	0.0
C /4.3	16.1	0.99	9.22	180	4	94	0	2	25	19.9	N/A	78	6	0	0	0.0	1.5
C /4.3	16.1	0.99	9.21	25	4	94	0	2	25	18.6	N/A	77	6	2,500	0	0.0	1.5
C /4.3	16.1	0.99	9.21	136	4	94	0	2	25	20.0	N/A	78	6	0	0	0.0	1.5
C /4.3	16.2	0.99	9.21	560	4	94	0	2	25	19.4	N/A	77	6	10,000	0	0.0	1.5
C+ /5.8	13.8	0.81	12.66	76	3	96	0	1	60	N/A	N/A	89	3	2,500	0	0.0	2.0
C /5.3	15.1	0.87	33.95	888	2	96	0	2	68	49.9	-25.4	95	1	2,500	0	0.0	1.5
C /5.3	13.7	0.79	24.26	3,043	1	98	0	1	79	27.2	-28.3	74	5	2,500	0	0.0	1.5
C /5.2	13.7	0.79	24.27	678	1	98	0	1	79	28.7	-28.2	76	5	0	0	0.0	1.5
C+ /6.9	9.8	0.92	27.77	5,558	7	92	0	1	49	121.8	-22.3	71	6	2,500	0	0.0	0.0
C+ /6.9	9.8	0.92	27.77	308	7	92	0	1	49	123.2	-22.3	72	6	0	0	0.0	0.0
C+ /5.8	10.1	0.93	59.57	6,886	5	90	2	3	46	115.5	-22.3	58	6	2,500	0	0.0	0.0
C+ /5.8	10.1	0.93	59.54	1,844	5	90	2	3	46	117.0	-22.2	60	6	0	0	0.0	0.0
C /5.4	13.1	0.99	34.44	1,046	0	99	0	1	62	56.4	-29.3	33	4	2,500	0	0.0	0.0
C+ /5.6	15.3	0.95	13.76	280	17	81	0	2	111	N/A	N/A	56	4	2,500	0	0.0	0.0
C+ /6.3	15.3	0.95	13.25	6	0	0	0	100	113	N/A	N/A	45	4	2,500	0	5.8	0.0
C+ /6.2	15.3	0.95	13.06	3	0	0	0	100	113	N/A	N/A	34	4	2,500	0	0.0	0.0
C+ /6.3	15.3	0.95	13.30	10	0	0	0	100	113	N/A	N/A	48	4	2,500	0	0.0	0.0
C+ /6.3	15.3	0.94	13.19	2	0	0	0	100	113	N/A	N/A	41	4	2,500	0	3.5	0.0
C /4.9	9.8	0.93	22.26	1,556	4	95	0	1	84	106.8	-18.5	62	3	2,500	0	0.0	0.0
C /4.9	9.8	0.93	22.22	170	4	95	0	1	84	108.3	-18.4	65	3	0	0	0.0	0.0
C /4.8	13.6	1.14	58.10	815	0	99	0	1	12	133.5	-23.6	17	13	2,500	0	0.0	0.0

Fund Type	Fund Name	Ticker Symbol	Overall Investment Rating	Phone	PERFORMANCE Perfor-mance Rating/Pts	Total Return % through 2/28/17 3 Mo	6 Mo	1Yr / Pct	Annualized 3Yr / Pct	5Yr / Pct	Incl. in Returns Dividend Yield	Expense Ratio
GI	Fidelity Ext Mkt Idx IP	FSMAX	B	(800) 544-8544	B+ / 8.5	6.55	11.56	32.58 /91	6.93 /71	13.05 /84	1.27	0.05
GR	Fidelity Ext Mkt Idx Pr	FSEVX	B	(800) 544-8544	B+ / 8.5	6.54	11.56	32.56 /91	6.91 /71	13.04 /84	1.25	0.07
GR	Fidelity Focused Stock Fund	FTQGX	D+	(800) 544-8544	C- / 3.9	7.24	4.53	17.83 /42	3.02 /32	11.44 /69	0.52	0.73
AA	Fidelity Four In One Index	FFNOX	B-	(800) 544-8544	C+ / 6.2	6.62	6.90	19.68 /50	6.05 /65	9.83 /57	1.99	0.13
AA	Fidelity Freedom 2005	FFFVX	C+	(800) 544-8544	D+ / 2.9	3.58	2.72	11.39 /16	3.75 /40	4.88 /21	1.68	0.56
AA	Fidelity Freedom 2010	FFFCX	C+	(800) 544-8544	C- / 3.6	4.23	3.48	13.40 /23	4.22 /45	5.86 /27	1.67	0.60
* AA	Fidelity Freedom 2015	FFVFX	C+	(800) 544-8544	C- / 4.2	4.77	4.26	15.21 /31	4.64 /50	6.28 /30	1.65	0.64
* AA	Fidelity Freedom 2020	FFFDX	B-	(800) 544-8544	C / 4.6	5.06	4.71	16.45 /36	4.88 /53	6.73 /33	1.62	0.67
* AA	Fidelity Freedom 2025	FFTWX	B-	(800) 544-8544	C / 5.1	5.53	5.29	17.76 /42	5.18 /56	7.56 /39	1.54	0.69
* AA	Fidelity Freedom 2030	FFFEX	B-	(800) 544-8544	C+ / 6.1	6.39	6.59	20.71 /56	5.69 /61	8.15 /43	1.45	0.75
* AA	Fidelity Freedom 2035	FFTHX	C+	(800) 544-8544	C+ / 6.6	6.94	7.60	22.71 /65	6.00 /64	8.79 /49	1.29	0.77
* AA	Fidelity Freedom 2040	FFFFX	C+	(800) 544-8544	C+ / 6.7	7.01	7.71	22.80 /66	6.04 /65	8.88 /50	1.34	0.77
AA	Fidelity Freedom 2045	FFFGX	C+	(800) 544-8544	C+ / 6.6	6.98	7.60	22.63 /65	6.01 /64	8.98 /50	1.33	0.77
AA	Fidelity Freedom 2050	FFFHX	C+	(800) 544-8544	C+ / 6.7	7.03	7.65	22.74 /66	6.03 /64	9.03 /51	1.31	0.77
GL	Fidelity Freedom 2055	FDEEX	C+	(800) 544-8544	C+ / 6.6	6.90	7.55	22.60 /65	6.01 /64	9.16 /52	1.29	0.77
GL	Fidelity Freedom 2060	FDKVX	U	(800) 522-7297	U /	6.90	7.63	22.62 /65	--	--	1.19	0.78
BA	Fidelity Freedom Income	FFFAX	C	(800) 544-8544	D / 2.2	2.86	1.81	8.90 / 9	3.13 /33	3.70 /14	1.63	0.49
GI	Fidelity Freedom Index 2005 Inv	FJIFX	C+	(800) 544-8544	D+ / 2.3	3.02	2.13	8.75 / 9	3.32 /35	4.13 /16	1.53	0.24
GI	Fidelity Freedom Index 2005 IP	FFGFX	C+	(800) 544-8544	D+ / 2.4	3.06	2.09	8.81 / 9	3.35 /35	4.15 /16	1.59	0.14
GI	Fidelity Freedom Index 2010 Inv	FKIFX	C+	(800) 544-8544	D+ / 2.9	3.69	2.93	10.76 /14	3.80 /40	5.12 /22	1.61	0.24
GI	Fidelity Freedom Index 2010 IP	FFWTX	B-	(800) 544-8544	C- / 3.0	3.66	2.90	10.84 /14	3.85 /41	5.14 /22	1.68	0.14
GL	Fidelity Freedom Index 2015 Inv	FLIFX	B-	(800) 544-8544	C- / 3.6	4.34	3.74	12.86 /21	4.32 /47	5.58 /25	1.70	0.23
GI	Fidelity Freedom Index 2015 IP	FIWFX	B-	(800) 544-8544	C- / 3.6	4.31	3.78	12.94 /21	4.33 /47	5.59 /25	1.77	0.13
GL	Fidelity Freedom Index 2020 Inv	FPIFX	B-	(800) 544-8544	C- / 4.0	4.75	4.31	14.26 /27	4.62 /50	6.04 /29	1.73	0.23
GI	Fidelity Freedom Index 2020 IP	FIWTX	C+	(800) 544-8544	C- / 4.1	4.73	4.29	14.26 /27	4.64 /50	6.05 /29	1.80	0.13
GL	Fidelity Freedom Index 2025 Inv	FQIFX	B	(800) 544-8544	C / 4.6	5.15	4.80	15.70 /33	4.99 /54	6.92 /34	1.76	0.23
GI	Fidelity Freedom Index 2025 IP	FFEDX	B	(800) 544-8544	C / 4.6	5.12	4.84	15.77 /33	5.03 /54	6.94 /34	1.82	0.13
GL	Fidelity Freedom Index 2030 Inv	FXIFX	B-	(800) 544-8544	C+ / 5.7	6.18	6.25	19.12 /48	5.61 /61	7.54 /39	1.82	0.24
GI	Fidelity Freedom Index 2030 IP	FFEGX	B-	(800) 544-8544	C+ / 5.8	6.23	6.29	19.27 /48	5.65 /61	7.57 /39	1.87	0.14
GL	Fidelity Freedom Index 2035 Inv	FIHFX	B-	(800) 544-8544	C+ / 6.5	6.85	7.39	21.50 /60	5.99 /64	8.28 /44	1.81	0.24
GI	Fidelity Freedom Index 2035 IP	FFEZX	B-	(800) 544-8544	C+ / 6.5	6.90	7.44	21.64 /60	6.05 /65	8.31 /45	1.87	0.14
GL	Fidelity Freedom Index 2040 Inv	FBIFX	B-	(800) 544-8544	C+ / 6.5	6.85	7.39	21.48 /60	5.99 /64	8.35 /45	1.84	0.24
GI	Fidelity Freedom Index 2040 IP	FFIZX	B-	(800) 544-8544	C+ / 6.5	6.90	7.44	21.64 /60	6.03 /64	8.38 /45	1.90	0.14
GL	Fidelity Freedom Index 2045 Inv	FIOFX	B-	(800) 544-8544	C+ / 6.5	6.89	7.42	21.56 /60	6.00 /64	8.44 /46	1.85	0.24
GI	Fidelity Freedom Index 2045 IP	FFOLX	B-	(800) 544-8544	C+ / 6.5	6.87	7.40	21.54 /60	6.04 /65	8.47 /46	1.90	0.14
GL	Fidelity Freedom Index 2050 Inv	FIPFX	B-	(800) 544-8544	C+ / 6.5	6.89	7.42	21.52 /60	6.00 /64	8.49 /46	1.94	0.24
GI	Fidelity Freedom Index 2050 IP	FFOPX	B-	(800) 544-8544	C+ / 6.5	6.93	7.46	21.67 /61	6.04 /65	8.51 /46	1.99	0.14
GL	Fidelity Freedom Index 2055 Inv	FDEWX	B-	(800) 544-8544	C+ / 6.5	6.88	7.38	21.52 /60	5.98 /64	8.64 /48	2.15	0.24
GI	Fidelity Freedom Index 2055 IP	FFLDX	B-	(800) 544-8544	C+ / 6.5	6.87	7.45	21.61 /60	6.02 /64	8.67 /48	2.15	0.14
GI	Fidelity Freedom Index 2060 Inv	FDKLX	U	(800) 522-7297	U /	6.88	7.50	21.62 /60	--	--	2.00	0.24
GL	Fidelity Freedom Index Income Inv	FIKFX	C+	(800) 544-8544	D / 1.7	2.19	1.10	5.98 / 5	2.55 /28	2.89 /10	1.45	0.24
GI	Fidelity Freedom Index Income IP	FFGZX	C+	(800) 544-8544	D / 1.7	2.30	1.13	6.14 / 5	2.58 /28	2.91 /10	1.51	0.14
GI	Fidelity Freedom K 2005	FFKVX	C+	(800) 544-8544	C- / 3.0	3.63	2.75	11.57 /16	3.84 /41	4.95 /21	1.82	0.49
GI	Fidelity Freedom K 2010	FFKCX	C	(800) 544-8544	C- / 3.6	4.28	3.55	13.43 /23	4.31 /46	5.94 /28	1.83	0.53
* GI	Fidelity Freedom K 2015	FKVFX	C+	(800) 544-8544	C- / 4.2	4.74	4.27	15.33 /31	4.71 /51	6.36 /31	1.81	0.56
* GI	Fidelity Freedom K 2020	FFKDX	C+	(800) 544-8544	C / 4.7	5.18	4.81	16.55 /36	5.01 /54	6.83 /34	1.74	0.58
* GI	Fidelity Freedom K 2025	FKTWX	B-	(800) 544-8544	C / 5.2	5.56	5.34	17.85 /42	5.28 /57	7.67 /40	1.65	0.61
* GL	Fidelity Freedom K 2030	FFKEX	C+	(800) 544-8544	C+ / 6.1	6.37	6.66	20.82 /56	5.80 /62	8.26 /44	1.56	0.65
* GI	Fidelity Freedom K 2035	FKTHX	C+	(800) 544-8544	C+ / 6.7	6.98	7.67	22.74 /66	6.11 /65	8.91 /50	1.42	0.67
* GI	Fidelity Freedom K 2040	FFKFX	C+	(800) 544-8544	C+ / 6.7	7.03	7.66	22.78 /66	6.13 /65	9.01 /51	1.43	0.67
* GI	Fidelity Freedom K 2045	FFKGX	C+	(800) 544-8544	C+ / 6.8	7.05	7.72	22.84 /66	6.14 /65	9.12 /52	1.42	0.67
* GL	Fidelity Freedom K 2050	FFKHX	C+	(800) 544-8544	C+ / 6.7	6.99	7.67	22.79 /66	6.14 /65	9.15 /52	1.42	0.67

● Denotes fund is closed to new investors
★ Denotes fund is included in Section II

www.thestreetratings.com

RISK			NET ASSETS		ASSET					BULL / BEAR		FUND MANAGER		MINIMUMS		LOADS	
	3 Year		NAV						Portfolio	Last Bull	Last Bear	Manager	Manager	Initial	Additional	Front	Back
Risk	Standard		As of	Total	Cash	Stocks	Bonds	Other	Turnover	Market	Market	Quality	Tenure	Purch.	Purch.	End	End
Rating/Pts	Deviation	Beta	2/28/17	$(Mil)	%	%	%	%	Ratio	Return	Return	Pct	(Years)	$	$	Load	Load
C /4.8	13.6	1.14	58.09	2,221	0	99	0	1	12	134.1	-23.6	17	13	100,000,000	0	0.0	0.0
C /4.8	13.6	1.14	58.11	16,224	0	99	0	1	12	133.9	-23.6	17	13	10,000	0	0.0	0.0
C /4.8	11.8	0.96	19.60	1,564	1	97	1	1	141	104.7	-17.3	6	10	2,500	0	0.0	0.0
B- /7.1	8.8	1.38	39.99	4,797	0	84	15	1	9	88.1	-16.0	23	18	2,500	0	0.0	0.0
B /8.8	4.7	0.71	12.14	582	7	37	55	1	22	38.5	-8.5	56	12	2,500	0	0.0	0.0
B /8.4	5.5	0.85	15.47	4,162	6	44	48	2	17	47.7	-10.3	48	12	2,500	0	0.0	0.0
B /8.1	6.3	0.97	12.74	5,322	5	54	39	2	17	51.0	-10.5	41	12	2,500	0	0.0	0.0
B- /7.9	6.9	1.06	15.58	12,231	5	58	35	2	17	56.5	-12.6	35	12	2,500	0	0.0	0.0
B- /7.6	7.7	1.18	13.39	9,642	4	66	29	1	17	65.5	-14.9	29	12	2,500	0	0.0	0.0
B- /7.0	9.0	1.38	16.56	11,194	4	77	17	2	16	71.0	-15.8	20	12	2,500	0	0.0	0.0
C+ /6.5	9.8	1.50	13.73	6,800	3	89	7	1	15	78.9	-18.1	15	12	2,500	0	0.0	0.0
C+ /6.5	9.8	1.50	9.64	7,177	3	89	7	1	16	79.9	-18.4	16	12	2,500	0	0.0	0.0
C+ /6.4	9.8	1.49	10.88	3,434	3	89	7	1	17	81.5	-19.0	16	10	2,500	0	0.0	0.0
C+ /6.4	9.8	1.50	10.94	2,838	3	89	7	1	17	83.0	-19.9	15	11	2,500	0	0.0	0.0
C+ /6.6	9.8	0.73	12.27	897	5	89	5	1	20	84.4	N/A	97	6	2,500	0	0.0	0.0
U /	N/A	N/A	10.90	108	5	89	5	1	31	N/A	N/A	N/A	3	2,500	0	0.0	0.0
B+ /9.1	3.5	0.50	11.54	2,136	8	24	66	2	20	26.8	-3.9	67	12	2,500	0	0.0	0.0
B+ /9.7	4.0	0.36	12.90	47	22	37	39	2	28	32.5	-6.9	70	N/A	2,500	0	0.0	0.0
B+ /9.8	4.0	0.36	12.90	45	22	37	39	2	28	32.6	-6.9	70	2	0	0	0.0	0.0
B+ /9.3	4.9	0.44	13.67	206	17	46	36	1	22	41.4	-8.6	65	N/A	2,500	0	0.0	0.0
B+ /9.7	4.8	0.44	13.67	273	17	46	36	1	22	41.6	-8.6	65	2	0	0	0.0	0.0
B+ /9.0	5.7	0.88	14.05	517	13	53	33	1	22	45.0	-8.8	75	8	2,500	0	0.0	0.0
B+ /9.3	5.7	0.53	14.04	490	13	53	33	1	22	45.0	-8.8	60	2	0	0	0.0	0.0
B /8.7	6.3	0.98	14.63	1,314	10	59	30	1	16	50.0	-10.6	74	8	2,500	0	0.0	0.0
B- /7.9	6.3	0.59	14.62	1,885	10	59	30	1	16	50.1	-10.6	56	2	0	0	0.0	0.0
B /8.4	7.0	1.08	15.41	1,245	5	68	26	1	17	59.0	-12.7	74	8	2,500	0	0.0	0.0
B /8.4	7.1	0.66	15.41	1,332	5	68	26	1	17	59.2	-12.7	51	2	0	0	0.0	0.0
B- /7.7	8.5	1.29	15.96	1,335	4	80	15	1	13	64.5	-13.5	70	8	2,500	0	0.0	0.0
B- /7.9	8.5	0.80	15.96	1,897	4	80	15	1	13	64.7	-13.5	40	2	0	0	0.0	0.0
B- /7.2	9.3	1.42	16.66	923	3	86	9	2	11	72.9	-15.7	67	8	2,500	0	0.0	0.0
B- /7.5	9.3	0.88	16.67	1,046	3	86	9	2	11	73.2	-15.7	34	2	0	0	0.0	0.0
B- /7.2	9.3	1.41	16.76	897	3	86	9	2	9	73.7	-15.9	67	8	2,500	0	0.0	0.0
B- /7.5	9.3	0.88	16.76	1,344	3	86	9	2	9	73.9	-15.9	34	2	0	0	0.0	0.0
B- /7.2	9.3	1.42	16.90	572	4	85	9	2	8	74.9	-16.3	67	8	2,500	0	0.0	0.0
B- /7.5	9.3	0.88	16.90	689	4	85	9	2	8	75.1	-16.3	34	2	0	0	0.0	0.0
B- /7.2	9.3	1.41	17.01	529	4	85	9	2	7	76.1	-17.2	67	8	2,500	0	0.0	0.0
B- /7.5	9.3	0.88	17.01	654	4	85	9	2	7	76.3	-17.2	34	2	0	0	0.0	0.0
B- /7.2	9.3	0.68	13.42	199	4	85	9	2	7	77.9	N/A	97	6	2,500	0	0.0	0.0
B- /7.5	9.3	0.88	13.43	171	4	85	9	2	7	78.1	N/A	34	2	0	0	0.0	0.0
U /	N/A	N/A	10.96	39	0	0	0	100	8	N/A	N/A	N/A	3	2,500	0	0.0	0.0
B+ /9.9	2.7	0.40	11.61	123	32	22	45	1	22	20.8	-2.6	78	8	2,500	0	0.0	0.0
B+ /9.9	2.8	0.22	11.60	133	32	22	45	1	22	20.9	-2.6	75	3	0	0	0.0	0.0
B /8.6	4.7	0.41	13.02	413	15	37	47	1	27	39.1	-8.5	69	N/A	0	0	0.0	0.0
B- /7.7	5.5	0.50	13.03	2,674	12	46	41	1	19	48.4	-10.4	64	N/A	0	0	0.0	0.0
B- /7.8	6.3	0.58	13.65	5,147	9	54	35	2	18	51.7	-10.6	59	N/A	0	0	0.0	0.0
B- /7.7	6.9	0.63	14.51	16,609	7	60	31	2	21	57.3	-12.6	55	N/A	0	0	0.0	0.0
B- /7.5	7.7	0.71	15.21	14,407	7	66	26	1	19	66.5	-15.0	48	N/A	0	0	0.0	0.0
C+ /6.9	9.0	1.37	15.61	16,906	4	80	15	1	19	72.0	-15.9	68	8	0	0	0.0	0.0
C+ /6.4	9.8	0.91	16.24	11,546	4	89	5	2	17	79.9	-18.0	31	N/A	0	0	0.0	0.0
C+ /6.3	9.8	0.91	16.27	12,161	4	89	5	2	17	81.0	-18.4	31	N/A	0	0	0.0	0.0
C+ /6.4	9.8	0.91	16.76	7,545	4	89	5	2	16	82.9	-18.9	31	N/A	0	0	0.0	0.0
C+ /6.5	9.8	1.47	16.89	6,442	5	88	5	2	15	84.0	-19.8	66	8	0	0	0.0	0.0

I. Index of Stock Mutual Funds

Fund Type	Fund Name	Ticker Symbol	Overall Investment Rating	Phone	Performance Rating/Pts	3 Mo	6 Mo	1Yr / Pct	3Yr / Pct	5Yr / Pct	Dividend Yield	Expense Ratio
	99 Pct = Best / 0 Pct = Worst							Total Return % through 2/28/17	Annualized		Incl. in Returns	
GL	Fidelity Freedom K 2055	FDENX	C+	(800) 544-8544	C+ / 6.7	6.97	7.60	22.74 / 66	6.14 / 65	9.28 / 53	1.38	0.67
GL	Fidelity Freedom K 2060	FDKNX	U	(800) 522-7297	U /	6.96	7.69	22.79 / 66	--	--	1.29	0.67
GI	Fidelity Freedom K Income	FFKAX	C+	(800) 544-8544	D+ / 2.3	2.90	1.79	8.93 / 9	3.18 / 33	3.74 / 14	1.75	0.44
GR	Fidelity Fund Fd	FFIDX	B	(800) 544-8544	B- / 7.4	7.61	7.92	20.08 / 52	8.00 / 79	12.13 / 75	0.94	0.52
GR	Fidelity Fund K	FFDKX	B	(800) 544-8544	B- / 7.5	7.62	7.95	20.18 / 53	8.11 / 80	12.27 / 77	1.04	0.41
FO	Fidelity Gl ex US Idx Inst	FSGSX	D-	(800) 544-8544	D / 1.6	7.41	4.71	19.12 / 48	-0.28 / 12	3.50 / 13	1.93	0.09
FO	Fidelity Gl ex US Idx Inv	FSGUX	D-	(800) 544-8544	D- / 1.5	7.32	4.62	19.03 / 47	-0.40 / 12	3.40 / 12	1.84	0.18
FO	Fidelity Gl ex US Idx IP	FSGGX	D-	(800) 544-8544	D / 1.6	7.34	4.65	19.15 / 48	-0.28 / 12	3.52 / 13	1.96	0.06
FO	Fidelity Gl ex US Idx Pr	FSGDX	D-	(800) 544-8544	D / 1.6	7.29	4.60	19.12 / 48	-0.33 / 12	3.44 / 13	1.91	0.11
GL	Fidelity Global Balanced Fund	FGBLX	D	(800) 544-8544	E+ / 0.9	4.20	-1.08	8.57 / 9	-0.06 / 13	4.69 / 19	0.07	1.02
GL	Fidelity Global Equity Income	FGILX	C	(800) 522-7297	C- / 4.2	5.98	4.74	13.83 / 25	4.99 / 54	--	1.21	1.15
AA	Fidelity Global Strategies	FDYSX	C	(800) 544-8544	C- / 3.8	5.70	4.04	14.31 / 27	4.01 / 43	5.25 / 23	1.40	1.21
* GI	Fidelity Growth and Income	FGRIX	A+	(800) 544-8544	A / 9.4	6.44	12.07	30.09 / 87	9.51 / 90	13.63 / 90	1.73	0.65
GI	Fidelity Growth and Income K	FGIKX	A+	(800) 544-8544	A / 9.4	6.48	12.11	30.23 / 87	9.63 / 91	13.78 / 91	1.84	0.53
* GR ●	Fidelity Growth Company Fd	FDGRX	B+	(800) 544-8544	A+ / 9.6	9.60	12.21	29.85 / 86	9.95 / 93	14.74 / 96	0.06	0.88
GR ●	Fidelity Growth Company K	FGCKX	B+	(800) 544-8544	A+ / 9.6	9.62	12.27	29.98 / 86	10.07 / 94	14.87 / 97	0.15	0.77
GR	Fidelity Growth Discovery Fd	FDSVX	B	(800) 544-8544	B- / 7.5	10.74	8.63	21.61 / 60	7.04 / 72	13.00 / 84	0.08	0.78
GR	Fidelity Growth Discovery K	FGDKX	B+	(800) 544-8544	B / 7.6	10.76	8.70	21.78 / 61	7.16 / 73	13.16 / 85	0.14	0.66
AG	Fidelity Growth Strategies Fd	FDEGX	B+	(800) 544-8544	B- / 7.3	8.66	7.20	17.05 / 39	8.32 / 81	12.12 / 75	0.50	0.91
AG	Fidelity Growth Strategies K	FAGKX	B+	(800) 544-8544	B- / 7.4	8.68	7.27	17.23 / 39	8.49 / 83	12.33 / 77	0.63	0.76
AA ●	Fidelity Inc Replacement 2018	FIRKX	C	(800) 544-8544	D- / 1.2	0.68	0.66	3.23 / 3	1.71 / 22	3.35 / 12	0.76	0.35
AA ●	Fidelity Inc Replacement 2020	FIRLX	C	(800) 544-8544	D / 1.8	1.74	1.46	6.80 / 6	2.74 / 29	4.58 / 19	1.28	0.46
AA ●	Fidelity Inc Replacement 2022	FIRMX	C+	(800) 544-8544	D+ / 2.4	2.67	2.27	9.13 / 10	3.39 / 36	5.46 / 25	1.53	0.52
AA ●	Fidelity Inc Replacement 2024	FIRNX	C+	(800) 544-8544	C- / 3.0	3.27	3.10	11.05 / 15	3.88 / 41	6.13 / 29	1.54	0.55
AA ●	Fidelity Inc Replacement 2026	FIROX	B-	(800) 544-8544	C- / 3.4	3.72	3.69	12.43 / 20	4.23 / 46	6.60 / 32	1.54	0.58
AA ●	Fidelity Inc Replacement 2028	FIRPX	B-	(800) 544-8544	C- / 3.7	4.04	4.13	13.44 / 23	4.46 / 48	6.93 / 34	1.58	0.60
AA ●	Fidelity Inc Replacement 2030	FIRQX	B-	(800) 544-8544	C- / 4.0	4.27	4.42	14.09 / 26	4.61 / 50	7.16 / 36	1.58	0.61
AA ●	Fidelity Inc Replacement 2032	FIRRX	B-	(800) 544-8544	C- / 4.2	4.45	4.61	14.58 / 28	4.73 / 51	7.36 / 37	1.57	0.62
AA ●	Fidelity Inc Replacement 2034	FIRSX	B-	(800) 544-8544	C / 4.3	4.59	4.78	14.96 / 30	4.79 / 52	7.51 / 38	1.61	0.63
AA ●	Fidelity Inc Replacement 2036	FIRUX	B-	(800) 544-8544	C / 4.3	4.68	4.88	15.23 / 31	4.83 / 52	7.66 / 39	1.59	0.64
AA ●	Fidelity Income Replacement 2038 Fd	FIRVX	B-	(800) 544-8544	C / 4.4	4.78	4.97	15.54 / 32	4.87 / 53	7.81 / 41	1.60	0.65
AA ●	Fidelity Income Replacement 2040 Fd	FIRWX	B-	(800) 544-8544	C / 4.5	4.89	5.08	15.82 / 34	4.93 / 53	8.00 / 42	1.60	0.66
AA ●	Fidelity Income Replacement 2042 Fd	FIXRX	B-	(800) 544-8544	C / 4.7	5.02	5.21	16.18 / 35	5.00 / 54	8.23 / 44	1.59	0.67
GR	Fidelity Independence Fd	FDFFX	D+	(800) 544-8544	C / 4.6	7.65	8.30	20.30 / 54	2.74 / 29	11.33 / 68	0.49	0.86
GR	Fidelity Independence K	FDFKX	D+	(800) 544-8544	C / 4.7	7.72	8.36	20.44 / 55	2.83 / 30	11.44 / 69	0.57	0.78
FO	Fidelity International Cap App Fd	FIVFX	D+	(800) 544-8544	D+ / 2.4	7.42	-0.95	10.39 / 13	2.71 / 29	7.76 / 40	0.63	1.13
FO	Fidelity International Discovery Fd	FIGRX	D-	(800) 522-7297	E+ / 0.8	5.39	0.57	8.49 / 8	-0.96 / 9	5.97 / 28	1.61	0.99
FO	Fidelity International Discovery K	FIDKX	D-	(800) 522-7297	E+ / 0.8	5.40	0.63	8.60 / 9	-0.84 / 10	6.13 / 29	1.75	0.86
FO	Fidelity International Growth Fund	FIGFX	D	(800) 522-7297	D / 2.0	7.42	0.62	11.28 / 15	1.24 / 19	6.19 / 30	1.17	0.97
GL	Fidelity International Real Estate	FIREX	D+	(800) 544-8544	D / 2.1	4.94	-1.39	10.83 / 14	2.90 / 31	8.52 / 46	1.44	1.13
FO	Fidelity International Small Cap	FISMX	C-	(800) 544-8544	C / 4.8	7.26	5.04	21.58 / 60	4.21 / 45	10.07 / 59	1.36	1.32
FO	Fidelity International Value Fund	FIVLX	D-	(800) 522-7297	E+ / 0.6	5.22	2.82	11.13 / 15	-2.09 / 6	5.12 / 22	2.50	1.02
FO	Fidelity Intl Enhanced Index Fd	FIENX	D+	(800) 544-8544	D+ / 2.7	8.06	5.96	17.31 / 40	0.82 / 17	6.57 / 32	2.32	0.63
FO	Fidelity Intl Index Inst	FSPNX	D-	(800) 544-8544	D- / 1.3	7.38	4.43	15.87 / 34	-0.61 / 11	5.32 / 23	2.85	0.06
FO	Fidelity Intl Index Inv	FSIIX	D-	(800) 544-8544	D- / 1.3	7.35	4.36	15.72 / 33	-0.74 / 10	5.18 / 23	2.72	0.19
FO	Fidelity Intl Index IP	FSPSX	D-	(800) 544-8544	D- / 1.3	7.36	4.41	15.85 / 34	-0.61 / 11	5.32 / 23	2.86	0.05
FO	Fidelity Intl Index Pr	FSIVX	D-	(800) 544-8544	D- / 1.2	7.34	4.41	15.84 / 34	-0.89 / 10	5.12 / 22	2.82	0.08
FO	Fidelity Intl Sm Cp Opp Fd	FSCOX	C-	(800) 522-7297	D+ / 2.6	7.74	1.83	11.36 / 16	3.01 / 32	9.28 / 53	1.09	1.23
FO	Fidelity Japan Fund	FJPNX	C	(800) 544-8544	C- / 4.0	5.18	5.01	19.49 / 49	3.75 / 40	6.01 / 28	0.88	0.80
FO	Fidelity Japan Small Companies	FJSCX	A+	(800) 544-8544	B / 7.9	7.13	9.70	19.77 / 51	9.37 / 89	14.45 / 95	1.07	1.00
GR	Fidelity Large Cap Gro Idx Inst	FSWIX	U	(800) 544-8544	U /	9.03	9.24	--	--	--	0.00	0.06
GR	Fidelity Large Cap Gro Idx Premium	FSUPX	U	(800) 544-8544	U /	9.03	9.24	--	--	--	0.00	0.07

● Denotes fund is closed to new investors
* Denotes fund is included in Section II

www.thestreetratings.com

Risk Rating/Pts	3 Year Standard Deviation	Beta	NAV As of 2/28/17	Total $(Mil)	Cash %	Stocks %	Bonds %	Other %	Portfolio Turnover Ratio	Last Bull Market Return	Last Bear Market Return	Manager Quality Pct	Manager Tenure (Years)	Initial Purch. $	Additional Purch. $	Front End Load	Back End Load
C+ / 6.6	9.7	0.72	12.54	2,066	5	89	5	1	13	85.7	N/A	97	6	0	0	0.0	0.0
U /	N/A	N/A	10.98	238	5	89	5	1	18	N/A	N/A	N/A	3	0	0	0.0	0.0
B+ / 9.3	3.5	0.28	11.85	1,628	19	25	54	2	23	27.2	-3.9	75	N/A	0	0	0.0	0.0
C+ / 5.9	10.6	0.99	43.72	3,883	3	95	0	2	67	110.1	-18.4	44	15	2,500	0	0.0	0.0
C+ / 5.9	10.6	0.99	43.70	573	3	95	0	2	67	111.5	-18.4	46	15	0	0	0.0	0.0
C+ / 5.6	11.7	0.92	11.45	475	7	91	0	2	1	39.7	N/A	73	6	5,000,000	0	0.0	0.0
C+ / 5.6	11.7	0.92	11.44	36	7	91	0	2	1	38.8	N/A	71	6	2,500	0	0.0	0.0
C+ / 5.6	11.7	0.92	11.45	750	7	91	0	2	1	39.8	N/A	73	6	100,000,000	0	0.0	0.0
C+ / 5.6	11.7	0.92	11.44	967	7	91	0	2	1	39.3	N/A	72	6	10,000	0	0.0	0.0
C+ / 6.7	7.4	1.06	22.93	371	1	58	39	2	155	38.7	-12.9	16	10	2,500	0	0.0	0.0
C+ / 6.6	8.9	0.67	12.71	74	5	94	0	1	64	N/A	N/A	95	5	2,500	0	0.0	1.0
C+ / 6.9	6.8	1.02	9.04	81	7	60	31	2	37	46.1	-16.1	29	3	2,500	0	0.0	0.0
C+ / 6.5	11.8	1.09	34.36	6,354	3	96	0	1	29	134.2	-16.9	49	6	2,500	0	0.0	0.0
C+ / 6.5	11.7	1.09	34.33	906	3	96	0	1	29	135.8	-16.9	51	6	0	0	0.0	0.0
C / 4.8	14.2	1.23	147.85	21,436	0	99	0	1	18	148.5	-16.9	36	20	2,500	0	0.0	0.0
C / 4.8	14.2	1.23	147.71	14,728	0	99	0	1	18	150.0	-16.9	37	20	0	0	0.0	0.0
C+ / 6.1	11.7	0.97	27.97	1,041	0	98	0	2	57	126.1	-17.6	35	10	2,500	0	0.0	0.0
C+ / 6.1	11.7	0.97	27.98	180	0	98	0	2	57	127.8	-17.5	36	10	0	0	0.0	0.0
C+ / 6.7	10.6	0.95	36.59	2,292	0	98	0	2	40	119.0	-23.7	54	4	2,500	0	0.0	0.0
C+ / 6.7	10.7	0.95	36.84	376	0	98	0	2	40	121.3	-23.6	56	4	0	0	0.0	0.0
B+ / 9.6	1.7	0.24	55.24	4	22	6	70	2	105	27.0	-6.3	73	10	25,000	0	0.0	0.0
B+ / 9.5	2.9	0.44	55.31	7	15	16	67	2	66	36.6	-7.9	68	10	25,000	0	0.0	0.0
B+ / 9.6	3.8	0.58	59.82	13	11	26	61	2	47	43.9	-9.1	63	10	25,000	0	0.0	0.0
B+ / 9.2	4.5	0.70	59.83	10	10	34	54	2	49	49.4	-9.9	58	10	25,000	0	0.0	0.0
B+ / 9.1	5.0	0.79	61.75	10	9	40	49	2	45	53.4	-10.5	54	10	25,000	0	0.0	0.0
B / 8.9	5.4	0.85	62.67	24	8	45	46	1	47	56.4	-11.0	52	10	25,000	0	0.0	0.0
B / 8.7	5.7	0.89	61.83	13	8	48	43	1	26	58.7	-11.5	49	10	25,000	0	0.0	0.0
B / 8.6	5.9	0.92	58.76	7	7	50	41	2	24	60.5	-11.8	47	10	25,000	0	0.0	0.0
B / 8.4	6.2	0.95	62.03	6	7	52	40	1	33	62.1	-12.2	45	10	25,000	0	0.0	0.0
B / 8.4	6.3	0.98	62.44	9	7	54	38	1	27	63.6	-12.6	43	10	25,000	0	0.0	0.0
B / 8.3	6.5	1.00	60.06	4	7	55	37	1	23	65.3	-13.1	41	10	25,000	0	0.0	0.0
B / 8.2	6.7	1.03	61.25	8	6	57	36	1	29	67.6	-13.7	39	10	25,000	0	0.0	0.0
B / 8.1	6.9	1.06	61.44	26	6	58	34	2	29	69.9	-14.1	37	10	25,000	0	0.0	0.0
C / 4.4	14.5	1.21	35.88	3,343	2	95	1	2	48	116.9	-25.5	2	1	2,500	0	0.0	0.0
C / 4.4	14.5	1.21	35.90	344	2	95	1	2	48	118.1	-25.4	3	1	0	0	0.0	0.0
C+ / 6.1	10.8	0.78	17.05	1,726	0	99	0	1	187	81.7	-25.9	90	9	2,500	0	0.0	0.0
C+ / 6.0	11.0	0.85	38.04	6,182	1	97	0	2	50	53.4	-24.5	64	13	2,500	0	0.0	0.0
C+ / 6.0	11.0	0.85	37.94	1,781	1	97	0	2	50	54.6	-24.4	66	13	0	0	0.0	0.0
C+ / 6.3	10.5	0.80	11.31	1,034	3	94	1	2	29	62.7	-21.9	83	10	2,500	0	0.0	0.0
B- / 7.0	10.5	0.73	9.98	286	15	81	2	2	71	80.9	-25.2	90	7	2,500	0	0.0	1.5
C / 5.4	10.5	0.75	24.66	1,042	5	94	0	1	29	83.5	-21.6	94	3	2,500	0	0.0	2.0
C+ / 6.0	10.7	0.85	7.90	310	1	98	0	1	47	44.2	-27.7	49	6	2,500	0	0.0	1.0
C+ / 6.4	11.4	0.92	8.48	271	2	96	1	1	77	57.9	-22.4	81	10	2,500	0	0.0	1.0
C+ / 5.9	11.4	0.93	36.89	2,096	0	0	0	100	1	49.6	-23.0	69	13	5,000,000	0	0.0	0.0
C+ / 5.9	11.4	0.93	36.88	741	0	0	0	100	1	48.6	-23.0	67	13	2,500	0	0.0	0.0
C+ / 5.9	11.4	0.93	36.88	4,738	0	0	0	100	1	49.6	-23.0	69	13	100,000,000	0	0.0	0.0
C+ / 5.9	11.4	0.92	36.88	8,719	0	0	0	100	1	48.2	-23.0	65	13	10,000	0	0.0	0.0
B- / 7.1	10.1	0.71	15.37	746	7	92	0	1	24	83.5	-20.4	90	9	2,500	0	0.0	2.0
C+ / 6.4	12.3	0.81	12.67	365	2	97	0	1	15	43.2	-10.3	93	3	2,500	0	0.0	1.5
B- / 7.9	10.6	0.50	15.60	598	1	98	0	1	30	104.6	-6.4	99	3	2,500	0	0.0	1.5
U /	N/A	N/A	11.22	66	0	0	0	100	0	N/A	N/A	N/A	1	5,000,000	0	0.0	0.0
U /	N/A	N/A	11.22	239	0	0	0	100	0	N/A	N/A	N/A	1	10,000	0	0.0	0.0

Fund Type	Fund Name	Ticker Symbol	Overall Investment Rating	Phone	Performance Rating/Pts	3 Mo	6 Mo	1Yr / Pct	3Yr / Pct	5Yr / Pct	Dividend Yield	Expense Ratio
	99 Pct = Best *0 Pct = Worst*					**PERFORMANCE** Total Return % through 2/28/17 / Annualized						Incl. in Returns	
GR	Fidelity Large Cap Stock Fund	FLCSX	A	(800) 544-8544	A / 9.4	7.05	12.89	33.28 /92	8.54 /83	14.48 /95	1.30	0.78
GI	Fidelity Large Cap Val Idx Inst	FLCMX	U	(800) 544-8544	U /	6.97	11.11	--	--	--	0.00	0.06
GI	Fidelity Large Cap Val Idx Prm	FLCHX	U	(800) 544-8544	U /	6.96	11.10	--	--	--	0.00	0.07
EM	Fidelity Latin American Fund	FLATX	E-	(800) 544-8544	D- / 1.1	11.52	3.10	40.32 /97	-4.80 / 3	-9.93 / 1	2.23	1.13
GR	Fidelity Leveraged Company Stock	FLVCX	C-	(800) 544-8544	C+ / 6.4	7.49	10.02	27.30 /80	4.02 /43	11.26 /68	0.84	0.80
GR	Fidelity Leveraged Company Stock K	FLCKX	C-	(800) 544-8544	C+ / 6.5	7.53	10.09	27.47 /80	4.14 /44	11.40 /69	0.95	0.68
GR	Fidelity LgCp Core Enh Idx Fd	FLCEX	A+	(800) 544-8544	B+ / 8.8	7.52	9.99	23.09 /67	9.56 /91	13.47 /89	1.49	0.45
GR	Fidelity LgCp Gr Enh Idx Fd	FLGEX	A+	(800) 544-8544	B+ / 8.9	8.42	9.76	21.33 /59	10.23 /94	13.59 /90	0.94	0.45
GR	Fidelity LgCp Val Enh Idx Fd	FLVEX	A+	(800) 544-8544	A / 9.5	7.07	12.26	28.30 /82	10.16 /94	14.42 /95	1.71	0.45
* MC	Fidelity Low-Priced Stock Fd	FLPSX	C+	(800) 544-8544	C+ / 5.8	3.94	7.94	17.95 /43	6.07 /65	11.44 /69	1.13	0.88
MC	Fidelity Low-Priced Stock K	FLPKX	C+	(800) 544-8544	C+ / 5.8	3.97	7.98	18.05 /43	6.17 /66	11.55 /70	1.22	0.78
GL	Fidelity MA Intl Index		D	(800) 544-8544	D- / 1.2	7.31	4.35	15.65 /33	-0.81 /10	5.08 /22	0.00	0.35
AA	Fidelity MA Spart 500 Index		A+	(800) 544-8544	A / 9.3	8.04	9.98	24.82 /73	10.45 /96	13.80 /92	0.00	0.25
* GR	Fidelity Magellan Fund	FMAGX	B+	(800) 544-8544	B / 8.1	7.60	8.95	21.78 /61	8.81 /85	13.57 /89	0.55	0.85
GR	Fidelity Magellan Fund K	FMGKX	B+	(800) 544-8544	B / 8.2	7.61	8.99	21.89 /62	8.91 /86	13.69 /91	0.63	0.75
GI	Fidelity Mega Cap Stock Fund	FGRTX	A	(800) 544-8544	A- / 9.1	6.45	11.55	28.16 /82	9.30 /89	13.45 /88	1.41	0.69
MC	Fidelity Mid Cap Enhanced Index Fd	FMEIX	A-	(800) 544-8544	B+ / 8.4	6.23	10.79	24.85 /73	8.58 /84	14.14 /94	1.24	0.60
MC	Fidelity Mid Cap Idx Inst	FSTPX	B+	(800) 544-8544	B+ / 8.3	6.49	8.88	26.77 /79	8.42 /82	13.57 /89	1.25	0.14
MC	Fidelity Mid Cap Idx Inv	FSCLX	B+	(800) 544-8544	B / 8.2	6.48	8.81	26.62 /78	8.26 /81	13.40 /88	1.12	0.33
MC	Fidelity Mid Cap Idx IP	FSMDX	B+	(800) 544-8544	B+ / 8.4	6.50	8.89	26.80 /79	8.45 /83	13.60 /90	1.27	0.12
MC	Fidelity Mid Cap Idx Pr	FSCKX	B+	(800) 544-8544	B+ / 8.3	6.49	8.87	26.75 /78	8.40 /82	13.55 /89	1.24	0.20
MC	Fidelity Mid Cap Value	FSMVX	B+	(800) 522-7297	B+ / 8.7	7.42	11.10	25.14 /74	8.72 /85	14.43 /95	1.29	0.86
* MC	Fidelity Mid-Cap Stock Fund	FMCSX	C+	(800) 544-8544	B- / 7.1	6.22	7.67	27.16 /80	6.11 /65	12.16 /76	0.68	0.73
MC	Fidelity Mid-Cap Stock Fund K	FKMCX	C+	(800) 544-8544	B- / 7.2	6.30	7.75	27.38 /80	6.24 /66	12.31 /77	0.79	0.61
GR	Fidelity NASDAQ Composite Index	FNCMX	A+	(800) 544-8544	A+ / 9.8	9.66	12.22	29.21 /85	11.79 /98	15.71 /98	0.84	0.42
MC	Fidelity New Millennium	FMILX	C+	(800) 544-8544	B- / 7.4	6.67	9.62	28.58 /83	6.03 /64	12.36 /78	1.08	0.74
AA	Fidelity NH International Index		D	(800) 544-8544	D- / 1.2	7.39	4.40	15.72 /33	-0.79 /10	5.10 /22	0.00	0.35
AA	Fidelity NH Spart 500 Index		A+	(800) 544-8544	A / 9.3	8.03	9.97	24.85 /73	10.46 /96	13.81 /92	0.00	0.25
AA	Fidelity NH Ttl Mkt Index		A+	(800) 544-8544	A- / 9.1	7.75	10.27	26.17 /77	9.71 /92	13.62 /90	0.00	0.25
FO	Fidelity Nordic Fund	FNORX	D-	(800) 544-8544	E+ / 0.7	6.42	-4.94	2.00 / 2	0.42 /15	9.91 /58	1.43	1.00
* SC	Fidelity OTC Portfolio Fd	FOCPX	B+	(800) 544-8544	A+ / 9.8	12.65	11.10	33.90 /93	10.93 /97	15.94 /98	0.00	0.91
SC	Fidelity OTC Portfolio K	FOCKX	B+	(800) 544-8544	A+ / 9.8	12.68	11.16	34.06 /93	11.06 /97	16.09 /98	0.00	0.79
FO	Fidelity Overseas Fd	FOSFX	D+	(800) 544-8544	D+ / 2.5	6.90	2.00	12.46 /20	1.93 /23	8.27 /44	1.74	1.04
FO	Fidelity Overseas K	FOSKX	D+	(800) 544-8544	D+ / 2.5	6.97	2.08	12.62 /20	2.07 /24	8.43 /46	1.86	0.91
FO	Fidelity Pacific Basin	FPBFX	C-	(800) 544-8544	C / 4.5	4.79	0.70	17.67 /41	5.81 /63	9.69 /56	0.60	1.17
* GI	Fidelity Puritan Fd	FPURX	B-	(800) 544-8544	C+ / 5.9	6.44	5.79	16.43 /36	6.54 /69	9.54 /55	1.63	0.56
GI	Fidelity Puritan K	FPUKX	B-	(800) 544-8544	C+ / 6.0	6.47	5.85	16.57 /37	6.66 /69	9.66 /56	1.73	0.46
RE	Fidelity Real Est Idx Inst	FSRNX	B-	(800) 544-8544	B- / 7.4	7.35	-2.03	15.01 /30	11.20 /97	11.08 /66	2.49	0.07
RE	Fidelity Real Est Idx Inv	FRXIX	B-	(800) 544-8544	B- / 7.2	7.33	-2.11	14.79 /29	11.05 /97	10.91 /65	2.29	0.23
RE	Fidelity Real Est Idx Pr	FSRVX	B-	(800) 544-8544	B- / 7.3	7.41	-2.05	14.98 /30	11.18 /97	11.05 /66	2.47	0.09
RE	Fidelity Real Estate High Income Fd		C+	(800) 544-8544	D+ / 2.4	2.11	0.58	6.78 / 6	4.47 /48	7.25 /36	4.59	0.80
RE	Fidelity Real Estate Income	FRIFX	B+	(800) 544-8544	C / 5.3	4.30	1.89	14.83 /29	7.36 /74	8.84 /49	4.16	0.82
RE	Fidelity Real Estate Investment	FRESX	B-	(800) 522-7297	B- / 7.5	6.60	-3.12	14.24 /27	11.67 /98	11.37 /69	1.65	0.78
EM	Fidelity SAI Emerging Markets Index	FERGX	U	(800) 544-8544	U /	8.75	5.14	28.13 /82	--	--	1.02	0.17
FO	Fidelity SAI International Index	FIONX	U	(800) 544-8544	U /	7.19	4.17	15.25 /31	--	--	1.10	0.13
FO	Fidelity SAI Intl Min Volatility Ix	FSKLX	U	(800) 544-8544	U /	5.61	-0.63	9.09 /10	--	--	2.24	0.32
RE	Fidelity SAI Real Estate Index	FESIX	U	(800) 544-8544	U /	7.39	-2.11	14.89 /29	--	--	2.40	0.15
MC	Fidelity SAI Small-Mid Cap 500 Idx	FZFLX	U	(800) 544-8544	U /	6.31	9.14	28.25 /82	--	--	0.77	0.35
GI	Fidelity SAI US Large Cap Index	FLCPX	U	(800) 544-8544	U /	7.97	10.00	24.91 /73	--	--	0.71	0.09
GR	Fidelity SAI US Min Volatility Idx	FSUVX	U	(800) 544-8544	U /	8.40	5.31	17.42 /40	--	--	2.11	0.23
GI	Fidelity SAI US Qual Idx	FUQIX	U	(800) 544-8544	U /	8.07	9.09	20.63 /56	--	--	1.20	0.25
GR	Fidelity Sel Defense and Aerospace	FSDAX	A+	(800) 544-8888	A+ / 9.8	5.92	16.46	34.37 /93	10.37 /95	15.46 /98	0.80	0.80

● Denotes fund is closed to new investors

* Denotes fund is included in Section II

www.thestreetratings.com

RISK Rating/Pts	3 Year Standard Deviation	Beta	NET ASSETS NAV As of 2/28/17	Total $(Mil)	Cash %	Stocks %	Bonds %	Other %	Portfolio Turnover Ratio	Last Bull Market Return	Last Bear Market Return	Manager Quality Pct	Manager Tenure (Years)	Initial Purch. $	Additional Purch. $	Front End Load	Back End Load
C+ / 5.7	12.6	1.15	30.81	3,046	2	96	1	1	31	146.7	-19.3	30	12	2,500	0	0.0	0.0
U /	N/A	N/A	11.43	118	0	0	0	100	0	N/A	N/A	N/A	1	5,000,000	0	0.0	0.0
U /	N/A	N/A	11.43	232	0	0	0	100	0	N/A	N/A	N/A	1	10,000	0	0.0	0.0
D / 1.9	24.4	1.29	21.31	538	0	100	0	0	108	-25.8	-24.8	5	2	2,500	0	0.0	1.5
C- / 3.8	14.1	1.19	35.45	2,699	2	92	4	2	9	126.9	-30.1	4	1	10,000	0	0.0	0.0
C- / 3.8	14.1	1.19	35.52	520	2	92	4	2	9	128.5	-30.1	4	1	0	0	0.0	0.0
C+ / 6.9	10.3	0.99	13.21	526	0	98	0	2	84	128.5	-15.1	64	10	2,500	0	0.0	0.0
C+ / 6.8	10.7	1.01	16.65	824	1	98	0	1	89	132.2	-15.1	69	10	2,500	0	0.0	0.0
B- / 7.0	10.7	0.99	12.53	2,887	1	97	1	1	88	137.8	-17.5	70	10	2,500	0	0.0	0.0
C+ / 6.8	9.3	0.71	51.14	28,068	5	89	5	1	9	109.5	-17.6	66	28	2,500	0	0.0	0.0
C+ / 6.8	9.3	0.71	51.10	10,938	5	89	5	1	9	110.7	-17.6	67	28	0	0	0.0	0.0
C+ / 6.2	11.4	1.66	11.75	52	1	97	0	2		47.8	-23.1	3	11	50	25	0.0	1.0
B- / 7.3	10.3	1.62	20.82	162	0	99	0	1	0	132.4	-16.3	52	11	50	25	0.0	0.0
C+ / 5.7	11.4	1.06	97.24	13,562	1	98	0	1	78	129.4	-24.3	44	6	2,500	0	0.0	0.0
C+ / 5.7	11.4	1.06	97.11	1,938	1	98	0	1	78	130.7	-24.2	46	6	0	0	0.0	0.0
C+ / 6.3	11.7	1.10	18.18	3,500	0	99	0	1	25	134.6	-16.0	46	8	2,500	0	0.0	0.0
C+ / 6.2	11.1	0.89	14.77	1,176	0	98	0	2	88	139.6	-21.5	74	10	2,500	0	0.0	0.0
C+ / 5.9	11.3	0.91	19.13	808	0	99	0	1	16	134.4	N/A	71	6	0	0	0.0	0.0
C+ / 5.9	11.3	0.91	19.11	64	0	99	0	1	16	132.4	N/A	69	6	2,500	200	0.0	0.0
C+ / 5.9	11.2	0.91	19.13	12	0	99	0	1	16	134.7	N/A	71	6	0	0	0.0	0.0
C+ / 5.9	11.3	0.91	19.13	2,414	0	99	0	1	16	134.2	N/A	70	6	10,000	0	0.0	0.0
C+ / 5.8	11.2	0.88	25.91	2,485	2	96	0	2	83	144.9	-23.1	76	4	2,500	0	0.0	0.0
C / 4.8	10.9	0.87	36.16	5,648	9	90	0	1	23	117.1	-18.8	47	6	2,500	0	0.0	0.0
C / 4.8	10.9	0.87	36.18	2,174	9	90	0	1	23	118.7	-18.7	49	6	0	0	0.0	0.0
C+ / 6.0	13.2	1.18	76.54	3,510	0	99	0	1	9	156.0	-15.6	65	13	2,500	0	0.0	0.0
C / 4.6	11.2	0.84	37.74	3,210	3	95	1	1	57	116.3	-15.4	50	11	2,500	0	0.0	0.0
C+ / 6.6	11.5	1.51	11.63	105	1	97	0	2	0	47.8	-23.1	1	11	50	25	0.0	1.0
B- / 7.3	10.3	1.62	20.85	401	0	99	0	1	0	132.4	-16.3	52	11	50	25	0.0	0.0
B- / 7.0	10.6	1.66	21.26	262	0	99	0	1	0	132.1	-17.7	39	11	50	25	0.0	0.5
C+ / 6.6	12.0	0.79	45.33	353	0	99	0	1	63	95.9	-31.8	78	13	2,500	0	0.0	1.5
C- / 4.1	16.4	0.74	92.25	10,608	0	99	0	1	56	155.7	-17.4	96	8	2,500	0	0.0	0.0
C- / 4.1	16.4	0.74	93.35	3,273	0	99	0	1	56	157.5	-17.4	96	8	0	0	0.0	0.0
C+ / 6.5	11.1	0.87	41.41	4,709	0	98	0	2	33	81.0	-27.5	86	5	2,500	0	0.0	0.0
C+ / 6.4	11.1	0.87	41.32	827	0	98	0	2	33	82.5	-27.5	87	5	0	0	0.0	0.0
C+ / 6.0	11.6	0.74	28.24	726	1	97	0	2	30	82.1	-21.3	97	4	2,500	0	0.0	1.5
B- / 7.1	7.6	0.70	21.67	19,933	0	66	32	2	36	81.3	-11.8	65	10	2,500	0	0.0	0.0
B- / 7.1	7.6	0.70	21.66	6,075	0	66	32	2	36	82.4	-11.8	66	10	0	0	0.0	0.0
C / 5.5	15.0	1.09	15.85	29	1	98	0	1	5	104.9	N/A	64	6	5,000,000	0	0.0	0.8
C / 5.5	15.0	1.09	15.84	34	1	98	0	1	5	103.1	N/A	63	6	2,500	0	0.0	0.8
C / 5.5	15.0	1.09	15.85	857	1	98	0	1	5	104.6	N/A	64	6	10,000	0	0.0	0.8
B+ / 9.9	2.7	0.11	8.59	1,041	2	4	93	1	20	52.2	-1.5	91	17	1,000,000	0	0.0	0.0
B / 8.9	5.2	0.36	12.12	2,578	6	51	37	6	26	70.1	-6.4	91	14	2,500	0	0.0	0.8
C / 5.5	14.9	1.09	42.47	4,619	1	96	1	2	24	110.8	-16.9	70	20	2,500	0	0.0	0.0
U /	N/A	N/A	12.14	2,316	0	0	0	100	0	N/A	N/A	N/A	1	0	0	0.0	0.0
U /	N/A	N/A	10.58	2,572	0	0	0	100	0	N/A	N/A	N/A	1	0	0	0.0	0.0
U /	N/A	N/A	9.65	1,150	2	97	0	1	22	N/A	N/A	N/A	N/A	0	0	0.0	0.0
U /	N/A	N/A	11.17	99	0	0	0	100	0	N/A	N/A	N/A	1	0	0	0.0	0.0
U /	N/A	N/A	11.05	956	0	0	0	100	99	N/A	N/A	N/A	2	0	0	0.0	0.0
U /	N/A	N/A	12.62	5,761	0	0	0	100	0	N/A	N/A	N/A	1	0	0	0.0	0.0
U /	N/A	N/A	11.59	674	0	99	0	1	37	N/A	N/A	N/A	N/A	0	0	0.0	0.0
U /	N/A	N/A	11.67	4,615	0	99	0	1	25	N/A	N/A	N/A	2	0	0	0.0	0.0
C+ / 6.0	13.2	1.02	138.34	1,584	2	95	2	1	52	155.1	-15.4	70	2	2,500	0	0.0	0.0

					PERFORMANCE							
99 Pct = Best					Perfor-	Total Return % through 2/28/17					Incl. in Returns	
0 Pct = Worst			Overall		mance				Annualized		Dividend	Expense
Fund		Ticker	Investment		Rating/Pts	3 Mo	6 Mo	1Yr / Pct	3Yr / Pct	5Yr / Pct	Yield	Ratio
Type	Fund Name	Symbol	Rating	Phone								
GR	Fidelity Select Air Transport	FSAIX	A+	(800) 544-8888	A+ / 9.7	4.32	20.53	26.31 /77	11.81 /98	18.53 /99	0.33	0.83
GR	Fidelity Select Automotive Fund	FSAVX	E	(800) 544-8888	D+ / 2.5	8.87	5.62	16.80 /38	0.32 /15	9.11 /52	1.33	0.87
FS	Fidelity Select Banking Port	FSRBX	A-	(800) 544-8888	A+ / 9.9	10.49	29.94	56.16 /99	12.86 /99	17.00 /98	0.73	0.79
* HL	Fidelity Select Biotech Port	FBIOX	D-	(800) 544-8888	B- / 7.0	10.24	11.27	29.67 /86	3.91 /42	22.19 /99	0.00	0.73
FS	Fidelity Select Brkg and Inv Mgmt	FSLBX	C	(800) 544-8888	B- / 7.0	6.66	16.71	31.76 /90	3.26 /34	11.50 /70	1.17	0.79
GR	Fidelity Select Chemicals Port	FSCHX	A-	(800) 544-8888	A+ / 9.7	10.49	16.69	38.01 /96	8.27 /81	13.39 /88	1.00	0.80
TC	Fidelity Select Commun Equip Port	FSDCX	B-	(800) 544-8888	B / 7.7	5.53	10.83	29.24 /85	6.73 /70	9.50 /55	1.07	0.90
TC	Fidelity Select Computers Port	FDCPX	B+	(800) 544-8888	A+ / 9.8	13.66	18.99	41.57 /98	7.98 /79	9.78 /57	1.01	0.80
GR	Fidelity Select Constn and Housing	FSHOX	B	(800) 544-8888	B- / 7.4	6.90	4.57	20.23 /53	8.93 /86	15.34 /97	0.71	0.81
GR	Fidelity Select Consu Staples Port	FDFAX	B+	(800) 544-8888	B- / 7.5	11.10	3.52	12.24 /19	9.91 /93	11.66 /71	1.60	0.77
GR	Fidelity Select Consumer Discr	FSCPX	C+	(800) 544-8888	C+ / 6.3	4.37	4.46	15.29 /31	8.08 /80	14.00 /93	0.86	0.77
FS	Fidelity Select Consumer Finance	FSVLX	B-	(800) 544-8888	A- / 9.2	8.42	15.46	33.57 /92	7.34 /74	13.76 /91	1.64	0.90
EN	Fidelity Select Energy	FSENX	E-	(800) 544-8888	E+ / 0.7	-6.40	4.29	36.05 /95	-4.39 / 3	0.38 / 5	0.53	0.80
EN	Fidelity Select Energy Svcs	FSESX	E-	(800) 544-8888	E / 0.5	4.63	21.79	46.38 /99	-9.69 / 1	-2.73 / 2	0.43	0.85
EN	Fidelity Select Envir and Alt Ener	FSLEX	B+	(800) 544-8888	B+ / 8.7	8.25	13.81	33.02 /92	6.70 /70	12.08 /75	0.67	0.95
FS	Fidelity Select Financial Services	FIDSX	A+	(800) 544-8888	A+ / 9.8	9.20	20.54	38.78 /97	10.04 /93	13.85 /92	0.96	0.76
PM	Fidelity Select Gold	FSAGX	E-	(800) 544-8888	D- / 1.2	12.28	-9.19	20.38 /54	-0.90 /10	-13.85 / 0	0.00	0.97
* HL	Fidelity Select Health Care	FSPHX	C-	(800) 544-8888	B- / 7.0	12.95	3.97	16.43 /36	7.52 /76	20.06 /99	0.11	0.73
HL	Fidelity Select Health Care Srvcs	FSHCX	A	(800) 544-8888	A+ / 9.6	7.89	11.77	19.71 /51	12.48 /98	14.53 /96	0.14	0.77
GR	Fidelity Select Ind Equipment	FSCGX	C	(800) 544-8888	C+ / 6.0	3.79	7.15	21.11 /58	6.24 /66	10.45 /62	0.64	0.83
GR	Fidelity Select Industrials Port	FCYIX	B	(800) 544-8888	B / 7.9	5.06	11.28	25.18 /74	7.67 /77	13.04 /84	0.53	0.77
FS	Fidelity Select Insurance	FSPCX	A+	(800) 544-8888	A+ / 9.8	6.68	14.04	31.60 /89	13.17 /99	17.52 /98	1.09	0.80
GR	Fidelity Select IT Serv Portfolio	FBSOX	A-	(800) 544-8888	B+ / 8.8	8.05	9.31	21.05 /58	10.18 /94	17.31 /98	0.30	0.81
GR	Fidelity Select Leisure	FDLSX	C	(800) 544-8888	C / 4.7	2.18	6.85	11.26 /15	6.63 /69	11.92 /74	0.98	0.79
GR	Fidelity Select Materials Port	FSDPX	C-	(800) 544-8888	C+ / 5.9	7.27	10.45	30.52 /87	2.36 /26	7.29 /37	0.98	0.81
GR	Fidelity Select Medical Eqpmnt Sys	FSMEX	B	(800) 544-8888	A+ / 9.9	14.50	1.55	30.13 /87	16.02 /99	19.54 /99	0.00	0.76
GR	Fidelity Select Multimedia	FBMPX	B+	(800) 544-8888	A- / 9.0	10.13	17.15	26.86 /79	7.59 /76	16.90 /98	0.39	0.81
EN	Fidelity Select Natural Gas	FSNGX	E-	(800) 544-8888	E / 0.4	-5.44	9.10	56.75 /99	-9.69 / 1	-2.06 / 3	0.55	0.89
EN	Fidelity Select Natural Resources	FNARX	E-	(800) 544-8888	E / 0.4	-5.67	3.01	34.54 /93	-5.97 / 2	-1.73 / 3	0.37	0.86
HL	Fidelity Select Pharmaceuticals	FPHAX	E	(800) 544-8888	D- / 1.3	7.04	-4.42	0.57 / 2	2.30 /26	13.13 /85	1.01	0.78
GR	Fidelity Select Retailing	FSRPX	A	(800) 544-8888	A- / 9.1	5.50	5.73	17.20 /39	13.05 /99	18.48 /99	0.13	0.81
TC	Fidelity Select Semiconductor Port	FSELX	B+	(800) 544-8888	A+ / 9.9	8.74	16.37	51.79 /99	22.41 /99	18.88 /99	0.65	0.77
TC	Fidelity Select Sware and IT Svcs	FSCSX	A-	(800) 544-8888	A+ / 9.7	9.24	9.29	31.86 /90	11.23 /97	17.29 /98	0.03	0.77
TC	Fidelity Select Technology	FSPTX	B+	(800) 544-8888	A+ / 9.9	13.88	14.07	38.53 /97	12.25 /98	14.58 /96	0.05	0.78
TC	Fidelity Select Telecommunications	FSTCX	A-	(800) 544-8888	B / 8.1	6.44	6.22	19.06 /47	10.21 /94	12.24 /76	1.79	0.82
GR	Fidelity Select Transportation	FSRFX	A-	(800) 544-8888	A+ / 9.7	4.24	19.41	29.40 /85	11.16 /97	16.85 /98	0.40	0.81
UT	Fidelity Select Utilities	FSUTX	B	(800) 544-8888	B / 7.8	12.32	8.55	18.21 /44	8.00 /79	11.92 /74	2.30	0.80
TC	Fidelity Select Wireless Fund	FWRLX	C+	(800) 544-8888	B / 7.6	13.00	11.58	24.09 /70	5.88 /63	10.90 /65	0.92	0.86
GR	Fidelity Series 1000 Value Index	FIOOX	A+	(800) 544-8544	A / 9.4	6.91	11.01	29.02 /84	9.80 /92	--	1.55	0.10
GR	Fidelity Series 1000 Value Index F	FSIOX	A+	(800) 544-8544	A / 9.4	6.94	11.05	29.06 /84	9.86 /93	--	1.58	0.05
GR	Fidelity Series Blue Chip Growth	FSBDX	B+	(800) 544-8544	B+ / 8.6	9.52	9.14	23.36 /68	8.89 /86	--	0.26	0.73
GR	Fidelity Series Blue Chip Growth F	FSBEX	B+	(800) 544-8544	B+ / 8.7	9.51	9.13	23.56 /68	9.07 /87	--	0.41	0.57
* GR	Fidelity Series Equity Income	FNKLX	A	(800) 544-8544	A- / 9.1	5.99	10.83	28.80 /83	9.46 /90	--	1.92	0.70
GR	Fidelity Series Equity Income F	FRLLX	A+	(800) 544-8544	A / 9.3	6.03	10.91	28.98 /84	9.67 /91	--	2.06	0.54
FO	Fidelity Series Global ex US Idx Fd	FSGEX	D-	(800) 544-8544	D / 1.6	7.36	4.72	19.28 /48	-0.30 /12	3.52 /13	2.38	0.06
GR	Fidelity Series Growth and Income	FGLGX	A	(800) 522-7297	A / 9.3	6.41	11.95	29.89 /86	9.37 /89	--	1.61	0.64
GR	Fidelity Series Growth and Income F	FTBTX	A	(800) 522-7297	A / 9.4	6.52	12.10	30.12 /87	9.55 /91	--	1.74	0.47
GR	Fidelity Series Growth Company	FCGSX	A-	(800) 544-8544	A+ / 9.6	9.63	12.29	29.50 /85	9.88 /93	--	0.10	0.79
GR	Fidelity Series Growth Company F	FFGSX	A-	(800) 544-8544	A+ / 9.6	9.71	12.46	29.67 /86	10.09 /94	--	0.24	0.63
CV	● Fidelity Series High Income	FSHNX	C+	(800) 544-8544	C / 5.1	5.96	6.28	22.61 /65	3.85 /41	5.99 /28	5.43	0.69
CV	● Fidelity Series High Income F	FSHFX	C+	(800) 544-8544	C / 5.2	5.99	6.33	22.74 /66	3.96 /42	6.10 /29	5.53	0.58
FO	Fidelity Series International Gr	FIGSX	D	(800) 544-8544	D / 1.9	7.06	0.27	10.72 /14	1.16 /19	6.05 /29	1.16	0.92

● Denotes fund is closed to new investors

* Denotes fund is included in Section II

240

RISK	3 Year		NET ASSETS		ASSET				Portfolio Turnover Ratio	BULL / BEAR		FUND MANAGER		MINIMUMS		LOADS	
Risk Rating/Pts	Standard Deviation	Beta	NAV As of 2/28/17	Total $(Mil)	Cash %	Stocks %	Bonds %	Other %		Last Bull Market Return	Last Bear Market Return	Manager Quality Pct	Manager Tenure (Years)	Initial Purch. $	Additional Purch. $	Front End Load	Back End Load
C+ /5.9	14.4	1.00	76.05	394	1	96	1	2	97	182.1	-18.1	82	5	2,500	0	0.0	0.8
D /2.1	18.2	1.40	36.78	54	2	95	2	1	80	104.3	-33.1	1	4	2,500	0	0.0	0.8
C /5.1	18.5	1.30	33.63	1,261	2	95	1	2	63	187.5	-25.9	33	5	2,500	0	0.0	0.8
E- /0.1	32.9	1.90	203.21	9,578	0	99	0	1	35	253.6	-12.5	0	12	2,500	0	0.0	0.0
C- /3.8	19.2	1.36	71.13	405	2	96	0	2	67	121.1	-30.1	1	2	2,500	0	0.0	0.8
C /4.9	16.3	1.29	162.40	1,627	1	97	1	1	79	156.2	-26.7	15	1	2,500	0	0.0	0.0
C /4.9	15.9	1.30	34.12	205	0	99	0	1	30	87.7	-31.9	7	3	2,500	0	0.0	0.8
C /4.6	16.9	1.35	83.01	472	0	97	1	2	31	109.2	-20.4	9	4	2,500	0	0.0	0.8
C+ /5.7	14.4	1.05	61.70	405	0	98	0	2	80	184.2	-23.4	48	1	2,500	0	0.0	0.8
C+ /6.7	10.5	0.66	97.01	1,666	0	99	0	1	63	98.7	-6.6	89	13	2,500	0	0.0	0.0
C+ /6.2	11.8	1.04	37.00	833	2	94	2	2	69	139.6	-16.2	38	3	2,500	0	0.0	0.0
C- /3.3	14.6	1.03	14.02	102	0	99	0	1	48	135.9	-15.9	16	5	2,500	0	0.0	0.8
D /1.6	22.4	1.11	44.10	2,291	4	94	0	2	79	32.2	-30.9	84	11	2,500	0	0.0	0.0
E /0.4	26.8	1.26	54.71	736	4	93	2	1	58	14.4	-36.4	29	4	2,500	0	0.0	0.8
C /5.1	13.1	0.44	23.89	137	2	95	1	2	20	103.5	-29.0	99	N/A	2,500	0	0.0	0.8
C+ /6.2	13.4	1.02	103.05	1,019	2	96	1	1	55	146.0	-28.3	43	4	2,500	0	0.0	0.0
E- /0.1	42.9	2.41	21.02	1,275	5	94	0	1	20	-51.5	-13.6	93	10	2,500	0	0.0	0.0
C- /3.4	17.1	1.14	208.91	6,629	0	99	0	1	76	197.3	-14.9	21	9	2,500	0	0.0	0.0
C+ /6.0	13.5	0.78	89.93	760	0	99	0	1	39	146.4	-17.6	93	5	2,500	0	0.0	0.8
C /4.6	13.3	1.13	40.61	186	1	98	0	1	72	123.9	-28.5	12	5	2,500	0	0.0	0.8
C /5.4	13.3	1.15	33.72	1,003	1	97	1	1	75	139.5	-26.1	21	10	2,500	0	0.0	0.0
C+ /6.7	12.3	0.90	80.60	649	3	93	2	2	25	173.2	-22.5	86	4	2,500	0	0.0	0.8
C+ /5.8	13.5	1.08	44.84	1,665	0	99	0	1	24	174.2	-17.3	60	8	2,500	0	0.0	0.0
C+ /5.8	11.0	0.83	141.37	404	2	96	1	1	48	124.5	-12.1	49	4	2,500	0	0.0	0.8
C- /3.7	16.4	1.32	81.64	883	0	98	0	2	64	87.2	-28.3	2	9	2,500	0	0.0	0.0
C- /3.5	15.0	0.91	41.48	3,130	0	99	0	1	46	171.9	-15.9	96	10	2,500	0	0.0	0.0
C /5.2	15.2	1.26	80.76	680	0	99	0	1	42	179.6	-22.5	13	4	2,500	0	0.0	0.8
E+ /0.6	29.4	1.41	27.76	482	5	93	1	1	62	11.8	-28.0	39	5	2,500	0	0.0	0.8
D- /1.5	22.5	1.11	29.13	912	4	94	0	2	78	17.5	-31.0	71	11	2,500	0	0.0	0.8
C- /3.8	14.6	0.91	18.11	1,002	0	99	0	1	77	114.0	-10.4	6	4	2,500	0	0.0	0.0
C+ /5.9	11.9	0.94	115.63	1,926	0	98	0	2	11	174.9	-8.4	90	1	2,500	0	0.0	0.0
C /4.3	17.1	1.25	101.24	3,011	2	95	2	1	179	203.3	-22.9	98	8	2,500	0	0.0	0.8
C /5.2	14.6	1.14	140.90	4,165	1	97	1	1	36	183.7	-15.4	65	3	2,500	0	0.0	0.0
C /4.3	14.9	1.19	146.96	4,113	0	99	0	1	130	143.8	-21.6	69	10	2,500	0	0.0	0.0
C+ /6.8	10.9	0.74	69.97	693	0	98	0	2	51	99.6	-16.6	87	4	2,500	0	0.0	0.0
C /5.0	15.6	1.11	92.98	645	1	97	1	1	80	171.7	-23.3	67	5	2,500	0	0.0	0.8
C+ /5.8	12.6	0.80	77.05	697	3	96	0	1	74	84.5	-2.4	32	11	2,500	0	0.0	0.0
C /4.6	11.6	0.93	9.11	239	0	99	0	1	78	88.5	-15.6	27	1	2,500	0	0.0	0.8
B- /7.0	10.5	0.98	12.17	1,582	1	98	0	1	20	N/A	N/A	67	4	0	0	0.0	0.0
B- /7.0	10.5	0.99	12.17	2,169	1	98	0	1	20	N/A	N/A	68	4	0	0	0.0	0.0
C+ /5.6	12.7	1.07	12.41	2,223	0	99	0	1	55	N/A	N/A	45	4	0	0	0.0	0.0
C+ /5.6	12.7	1.07	12.41	3,455	0	99	0	1	55	N/A	N/A	46	4	0	0	0.0	0.0
C+ /6.4	10.2	0.94	13.42	5,216	9	90	0	1	41	N/A	N/A	68	5	0	0	0.0	0.0
C+ /6.4	10.2	0.94	13.43	8,121	9	90	0	1	41	N/A	N/A	71	5	0	0	0.0	0.0
C /5.5	11.7	0.92	11.21	3,945	5	94	0	1	2	39.5	-24.2	72	8	0	0	0.0	0.0
C+ /6.0	11.7	1.09	14.79	3,694	2	96	0	2	36	N/A	N/A	48	5	0	0	0.0	0.0
C+ /6.0	11.8	1.09	14.82	5,749	2	96	0	2	36	N/A	N/A	50	5	0	0	0.0	0.0
C /5.1	14.2	1.23	14.44	4,323	0	99	0	1	18	N/A	N/A	35	4	0	0	0.0	0.0
C /5.2	14.1	1.22	14.45	6,669	0	99	0	1	18	N/A	N/A	38	4	0	0	0.0	0.0
B- /7.1	6.4	0.58	9.65	1,972	4	1	93	2	34	51.4	-8.4	80	6	0	0	0.0	0.0
B- /7.1	6.4	0.58	9.65	2,241	4	1	93	2	34	52.4	-8.4	81	6	0	0	0.0	0.0
C+ /6.0	10.5	0.80	13.57	6,214	4	95	0	1	24	61.7	-22.4	83	8	0	0	0.0	0.0

Data as of February 28, 2017

	99 Pct = Best 0 Pct = Worst		Overall		**PERFORMANCE**							
					Perfor-	Total Return % through 2/28/17					Incl. in Returns	
		Ticker	Investment		mance				Annualized		Dividend	Expense
Fund Type	Fund Name	Symbol	Rating	Phone	Rating/Pts	3 Mo	6 Mo	1Yr / Pct	3Yr / Pct	5Yr / Pct	Yield	Ratio
* FO	Fidelity Series International Gr F	FFIGX	D	(800) 544-8544	D / 2.0	7.12	0.35	10.86 /14	1.33 /20	6.24 /30	1.30	0.75
FO	Fidelity Series International SC	FSTSX	D+	(800) 544-8544	D+ / 2.3	7.20	1.48	10.70 /13	2.06 /24	8.50 /46	1.00	1.10
FO	Fidelity Series International SC F	FFSTX	D+	(800) 544-8544	D+ / 2.4	7.21	1.57	10.85 /14	2.24 /26	8.69 /48	1.15	0.94
FO	Fidelity Series International Val	FINVX	E+	(800) 544-8544	E+ / 0.7	5.19	2.73	11.00 /14	-2.10 / 6	5.20 /23	2.37	0.89
* FO	Fidelity Series International Val F	FFVNX	D-	(800) 544-8544	E+ / 0.7	5.22	2.77	11.27 /15	-1.92 / 7	5.37 /24	2.51	0.73
GR	Fidelity Series Intrinsic Opp	FDMLX	A-	(800) 522-7297	B / 7.8	4.66	8.16	21.92 /62	8.89 /86	--	1.22	0.79
GR	Fidelity Series Intrinsic Opp F	FGLLX	A-	(800) 522-7297	B / 7.9	4.73	8.24	22.17 /63	9.09 /87	--	1.36	0.63
GR	Fidelity Series Opp Insights	FVWSX	B-	(800) 522-7297	B- / 7.0	8.55	6.84	18.43 /45	7.58 /76	--	0.03	0.90
GR	Fidelity Series Opp Insights F	FWWEX	B-	(800) 522-7297	B- / 7.1	8.57	6.86	18.51 /45	7.74 /77	--	0.17	0.74
SC	Fidelity Series Sm Cap Discovery	FJACX	B	(800) 544-8544	B- / 7.0	2.12	9.69	24.51 /72	7.13 /73	--	0.45	0.96
SC	Fidelity Series Sm Cap Discovery F	FJAKX	B	(800) 544-8544	B- / 7.2	2.14	9.71	24.70 /72	7.29 /74	--	0.60	0.80
SC	Fidelity Sm Cap Enhanced Index Fd	FCPEX	A-	(800) 544-8544	A- / 9.1	5.06	14.31	31.15 /88	8.45 /83	13.90 /92	0.66	0.68
* SC ●	Fidelity Small Cap Discovery Fund	FSCRX	B-	(800) 544-8544	B- / 7.2	3.13	10.74	26.10 /76	7.17 /73	13.54 /89	0.43	1.01
SC	Fidelity Small Cap Growth Fund	FCPGX	B	(800) 522-7297	B+ / 8.8	8.16	10.15	32.86 /91	7.82 /78	13.98 /93	0.00	1.13
SC	Fidelity Small Cap Idx Inst	FSSSX	B+	(800) 544-8544	A- / 9.0	5.21	12.74	36.43 /95	7.18 /73	13.08 /85	1.18	0.17
SC	Fidelity Small Cap Idx Inv	FSSPX	B+	(800) 544-8544	B+ / 8.9	5.20	12.61	36.21 /95	7.01 /72	12.90 /83	1.05	0.36
SC	Fidelity Small Cap Idx IP	FSSNX	B+	(800) 544-8544	A- / 9.0	5.16	12.69	36.38 /95	7.19 /73	13.09 /85	1.20	0.15
SC	Fidelity Small Cap Idx Pr	FSSVX	B+	(800) 544-8544	A- / 9.0	5.20	12.67	36.34 /95	7.15 /73	13.06 /84	1.17	0.23
SC	Fidelity Small Cap Opp Fd	FSOPX	B-	(800) 544-8544	B- / 7.4	5.73	11.62	29.10 /84	5.63 /61	10.80 /64	0.46	0.85
SC	Fidelity Small Cap Stock Fund	FSLCX	C+	(800) 544-8544	B- / 7.1	5.07	8.87	22.54 /65	7.77 /77	10.68 /63	0.02	1.00
SC ●	Fidelity Small Cap Value Fund	FCPVX	B-	(800) 544-8544	B / 8.1	3.65	11.23	24.38 /71	9.14 /88	14.04 /93	0.72	1.22
GR	Fidelity Srs All-Sector Equity Fd	FSAEX	B	(800) 544-8544	A- / 9.0	8.49	10.43	25.84 /76	9.19 /88	13.41 /88	1.22	0.73
GR	Fidelity Srs All-Sector Equity Fd F	FSFFX	B	(800) 544-8544	A- / 9.1	8.49	10.52	26.04 /76	9.38 /89	13.62 /90	1.42	0.57
GR	Fidelity Srs Broad Market Opps Fd	FBMAX	B+	(800) 544-8544	B+ / 8.4	8.92	9.98	26.41 /77	7.91 /78	12.73 /81	0.45	1.06
OT	Fidelity Srs Commodity Strat Fund	FCSSX	E-	(800) 544-8544	E- / 0.0	2.07	5.85	15.29 /31	-13.60 / 0	-10.39 / 1	0.00	0.65
OT	Fidelity Srs Commodity Strat Fund F	FCSFX	E-	(800) 544-8544	E- / 0.0	2.23	5.97	15.55 /32	-13.40 / 0	-10.18 / 1	0.00	0.45
* EM	Fidelity Srs Emerging Markets Fd	FEMSX	C-	(800) 544-8544	C / 5.5	9.95	6.15	31.30 /89	1.85 /23	1.51 / 7	1.12	1.04
EM	Fidelity Srs Emerging Markets Fd F	FEMFX	C	(800) 544-8544	C+ / 5.7	10.02	6.23	31.48 /89	2.04 /24	1.69 / 7	1.26	0.88
RE	Fidelity Srs Real Estate Equity	FREDX	C+	(800) 544-8544	B- / 7.0	7.69	-1.98	14.19 /26	10.32 /95	10.80 /64	1.93	0.76
RE	Fidelity Srs Real Estate Equity F	FREFX	C+	(800) 544-8544	B- / 7.1	7.74	-1.95	14.28 /27	10.50 /96	10.97 /66	2.09	0.59
AA	Fidelity Srs Real Estate Income	FSREX	B	(800) 544-8544	C / 4.6	3.48	1.76	12.47 /20	6.62 /69	8.25 /44	4.70	0.77
AA	Fidelity Srs Real Estate Income F	FSRWX	B	(800) 544-8544	C / 4.7	3.53	1.86	12.53 /20	6.75 /70	8.41 /45	4.85	0.61
SC	Fidelity Srs Small Cap Opp Fd F	FSOFX	B-	(800) 544-8544	B- / 7.5	5.69	11.73	29.33 /85	5.78 /62	10.96 /65	0.61	0.69
GR	Fidelity Srs Stock Selector LCV	FBLEX	B+	(800) 544-8544	A- / 9.1	7.00	11.26	26.81 /79	9.36 /89	--	1.24	0.73
GR	Fidelity Srs Stock Selector LCV F	FRGEX	B+	(800) 544-8544	A- / 9.1	7.04	11.30	26.95 /79	9.53 /91	--	1.36	0.57
GR	Fidelity Stock Sel Lg Cap Val LCV	FSLVX	A+	(800) 522-7297	B+ / 8.9	6.65	10.85	26.27 /77	9.26 /89	13.42 /88	1.23	0.81
GR	Fidelity Stock Selector All Cap	FDSSX	B	(800) 544-8544	B+ / 8.6	8.99	9.91	26.69 /78	8.19 /80	12.99 /84	0.75	0.73
GR	Fidelity Stock Selector All Cap K	FSSKX	B+	(800) 544-8544	B+ / 8.7	9.05	9.96	26.85 /79	8.30 /81	13.10 /85	0.82	0.64
SC	Fidelity Stock Selector Small Cap	FDSCX	C+	(800) 522-7297	B- / 7.3	5.64	11.54	29.11 /84	6.10 /65	11.36 /69	0.45	0.77
GL	Fidelity Strat Adv Core Mlt Mngr	FLAUX	B	(800) 544-8544	B+ / 8.5	6.99	9.34	23.59 /68	9.23 /88	12.69 /81	0.75	1.20
GL	Fidelity Strat Adv Core Mlt Mngr F	FHJSX	B+	(800) 544-8544	B+ / 8.6	7.05	9.38	23.69 /69	9.32 /89	12.55 /80	0.75	1.10
GL	Fidelity Strat Adv Core Mlt Mngr L	FQAPX	A+	(800) 544-8544	B+ / 8.5	6.99	9.34	23.59 /68	9.20 /88	12.69 /81	0.75	1.20
GL	Fidelity Strat Adv Core Mlt Mngr N	FQAQX	A	(800) 544-8544	B+ / 8.3	6.93	9.18	23.31 /68	8.94 /86	12.31 /77	0.53	1.45
EM	Fidelity Strat Adv Emg Mkts FOF	FLILX	D+	(800) 544-8544	C / 4.3	9.31	5.39	29.08 /84	1.04 /18	--	0.92	2.24
EM	Fidelity Strat Adv Emg Mkts FOF F	FSWPX	D+	(800) 544-8544	C / 4.3	9.31	5.51	29.08 /84	1.04 /18	--	0.92	2.19
EM	Fidelity Strat Adv Emg Mkts FOF L	FQAAX	C-	(800) 544-8544	C / 4.3	9.31	5.39	29.08 /84	1.04 /18	--	0.92	2.23
EM	Fidelity Strat Adv Emg Mkts FOF N	FQABX	C-	(800) 544-8544	C- / 4.0	9.22	5.30	28.68 /83	0.77 /17	--	0.73	2.48
GL	Fidelity Strat Adv Gro Mlt Mng	FMELX	B-	(800) 544-8544	B / 7.6	8.35	7.68	20.93 /57	8.05 /79	12.38 /78	0.49	0.87
GL	Fidelity Strat Adv Gro Mlt Mng F	FFSPX	B-	(800) 544-8544	B / 7.6	8.32	7.66	20.95 /57	8.11 /80	12.34 /78	0.58	0.76
GL	Fidelity Strat Adv Gro Mlt Mng L	FQACX	B+	(800) 544-8544	B / 7.6	8.36	7.69	20.95 /57	8.02 /79	12.38 /78	0.50	0.86
GL	Fidelity Strat Adv Gro Mlt Mng N	FQAEX	B+	(800) 544-8544	B- / 7.4	8.28	7.53	20.57 /55	7.76 /77	11.90 /73	0.28	1.11
FO	Fidelity Strat Adv Intl M-M	FMJDX	D-	(800) 544-8544	D- / 1.1	5.95	2.50	12.84 /21	-0.33 /12	--	1.47	1.11

● Denotes fund is closed to new investors
* Denotes fund is included in Section II

RISK Risk Rating/Pts	3 Year Standard Deviation	Beta	NET ASSETS NAV As of 2/28/17	Total $(Mil)	ASSET Cash %	Stocks %	Bonds %	Other %	Portfolio Turnover Ratio	BULL/BEAR Last Bull Market Return	Last Bear Market Return	FUND MANAGER Manager Quality Pct	Manager Tenure (Years)	MINIMUMS Initial Purch. $	Additional Purch. $	LOADS Front End Load	Back End Load
C+ / 6.0	10.5	0.80	13.60	7,596	4	95	0	1	24	63.3	-22.3	84	8	0	0	0.0	0.0
C+ / 6.3	10.5	0.75	14.98	1,425	3	96	0	1	16	77.1	-20.9	87	8	0	0	0.0	0.0
C+ / 6.3	10.5	0.75	15.01	1,743	3	96	0	1	16	78.8	-20.8	88	8	0	0	0.0	0.0
C / 5.5	10.7	0.85	9.40	6,135	2	97	0	1	44	44.7	-27.6	49	6	0	0	0.0	0.0
C / 5.5	10.7	0.85	9.42	7,501	2	97	0	1	44	46.1	-27.5	51	6	0	0	0.0	0.0
C+ / 6.8	9.6	0.85	15.85	3,146	0	99	0	1	14	N/A	N/A	73	5	0	0	0.0	0.0
C+ / 6.8	9.7	0.85	15.87	5,008	0	99	0	1	14	N/A	N/A	75	5	0	0	0.0	0.0
C+ / 5.6	11.1	0.93	15.90	2,430	1	97	0	2	35	N/A	N/A	47	5	0	0	0.0	0.0
C+ / 5.6	11.0	0.93	15.92	3,776	1	97	0	2	35	N/A	N/A	49	5	0	0	0.0	0.0
C+ / 6.3	14.0	0.84	11.50	636	2	97	0	1	35	N/A	N/A	82	1	0	0	0.0	0.0
C+ / 6.3	14.0	0.84	11.50	986	2	97	0	1	35	N/A	N/A	83	1	0	0	0.0	0.0
C / 5.4	15.1	0.94	14.32	1,209	0	96	3	1	87	145.4	-23.5	85	8	2,500	0	0.0	0.0
C / 5.4	13.8	0.84	31.85	5,761	0	99	0	1	25	148.5	-24.4	83	1	2,500	0	0.0	1.5
C / 4.5	14.7	0.86	21.99	2,043	3	96	0	1	143	140.7	-24.5	85	6	2,500	0	0.0	1.5
C / 5.0	15.8	1.00	18.80	479	3	95	0	2	13	133.6	N/A	76	6	0	0	0.0	0.0
C / 5.0	15.8	1.00	18.77	42	3	95	0	2	13	131.8	N/A	74	6	2,500	0	0.0	0.0
C / 5.0	15.8	1.00	18.79	157	3	95	0	2	13	133.8	N/A	76	6	0	0	0.0	0.0
C / 5.0	15.8	1.00	18.79	2,080	3	95	0	2	13	133.2	N/A	75	6	10,000	0	0.0	0.0
C / 5.1	13.7	0.86	14.41	2,459	4	95	0	1	58	110.9	-25.4	71	10	0	0	0.0	0.0
C / 5.1	12.4	0.76	19.23	1,813	0	98	0	2	59	109.4	-32.4	88	6	2,500	0	0.0	2.0
C / 4.7	12.2	0.73	18.91	2,747	0	99	0	1	33	147.8	-23.6	93	4	2,500	0	0.0	1.5
C / 4.6	10.8	1.04	12.81	2,838	3	96	0	1	66	127.1	-18.7	53	9	0	0	0.0	0.0
C / 4.6	10.8	1.04	12.79	3,381	3	96	0	1	66	129.2	-18.5	56	9	0	0	0.0	0.0
C / 5.5	11.3	1.06	16.81	13	1	97	1	1	12	124.8	-21.4	34	8	0	0	0.0	0.0
D+ / 2.5	14.0	0.27	5.43	1,777	100	0	0	0	237	-39.1	-20.5	0	8	0	0	0.0	0.0
D+ / 2.5	13.9	0.28	5.50	1,892	100	0	0	0	237	-38.3	-20.5	0	8	0	0	0.0	0.0
C / 4.9	14.8	0.90	17.26	7,366	2	97	0	1	64	34.2	-28.3	76	8	0	0	0.0	0.0
C / 4.8	14.8	0.90	17.31	8,855	2	97	0	1	64	35.6	-28.2	77	8	0	0	0.0	0.0
C / 4.5	14.8	1.08	13.31	560	2	97	0	1	64	N/A	N/A	56	6	0	0	0.0	0.0
C / 4.5	14.8	1.08	13.31	695	2	97	0	1	64	N/A	N/A	58	6	0	0	0.0	0.0
B+ / 9.0	3.7	0.41	11.15	410	4	40	49	7	24	N/A	N/A	92	6	0	0	0.0	0.0
B+ / 9.0	3.7	0.41	11.15	471	4	40	49	7	24	N/A	N/A	92	6	0	0	0.0	0.0
C / 5.1	13.7	0.86	14.49	2,967	4	95	0	1	58	112.8	-25.3	72	10	0	0	0.0	0.0
C / 5.2	10.5	0.97	12.95	3,747	5	94	0	1	64	N/A	N/A	63	5	0	0	0.0	0.0
C / 5.2	10.5	0.97	12.96	5,833	5	94	0	1	64	N/A	N/A	66	5	0	0	0.0	0.0
C+ / 6.8	10.2	0.95	19.45	710	3	93	3	1	67	131.5	-20.1	66	5	2,500	0	0.0	0.0
C / 5.0	11.2	1.05	39.01	6,642	3	96	0	1	14	126.9	-21.1	38	8	2,500	0	0.0	0.0
C / 5.0	11.2	1.05	39.03	83	3	96	0	1	14	128.1	-21.1	39	8	0	0	0.0	0.0
C / 5.0	13.8	0.86	26.94	1,522	4	95	0	1	57	116.8	-25.4	75	8	2,500	0	0.0	1.5
C / 5.1	10.4	0.70	12.50	57	7	92	0	1	143	N/A	N/A	99	4	0	0	0.0	0.0
C / 5.1	10.4	0.70	12.56	4	7	92	0	1	143	N/A	N/A	99	4	0	0	0.0	0.0
B- / 7.1	10.4	0.70	12.50	N/A	7	92	0	1	143	N/A	N/A	99	4	0	0	0.0	0.0
B- / 7.1	10.4	0.70	12.49	N/A	7	92	0	1	143	N/A	N/A	99	4	0	0	0.0	0.0
C / 4.5	15.3	0.93	9.61	11	1	98	0	1	61	N/A	N/A	67	5	0	0	0.0	1.5
C / 4.5	15.3	0.93	9.61	2	1	98	0	1	61	N/A	N/A	67	5	0	0	0.0	1.5
C+ / 6.2	15.3	0.94	9.61	N/A	1	98	0	1	61	N/A	N/A	68	5	0	0	0.0	1.5
C+ / 6.2	15.3	0.93	9.60	N/A	1	98	0	1	61	N/A	N/A	64	5	0	0	0.0	1.5
C / 5.1	11.1	0.76	12.90	59	6	93	0	1	46	N/A	N/A	98	5	0	0	0.0	0.0
C / 5.1	11.1	0.75	12.89	3	6	93	0	1	46	N/A	N/A	98	6	0	0	0.0	0.0
C+ / 6.5	11.2	0.76	12.89	N/A	6	93	0	1	46	N/A	N/A	98	6	0	0	0.0	0.0
C+ / 6.5	11.1	0.76	12.88	N/A	6	93	0	1	46	N/A	N/A	98	6	0	0	0.0	0.0
C+ / 6.0	10.3	0.83	11.41	58	10	89	0	1	42	N/A	N/A	72	5	0	0	0.0	1.0

I. Index of Stock Mutual Funds

				PERFORMANCE								
						Total Return % through 2/28/17					Incl. in Returns	
99 Pct = Best		Overall							Annualized		Dividend	Expense
0 Pct = Worst		Investment		Perfor-mance								
Fund Type	Fund Name	Ticker Symbol	Rating	Phone	Rating/Pts	3 Mo	6 Mo	1Yr / Pct	3Yr / Pct	5Yr / Pct	Yield	Ratio
FO	Fidelity Strat Adv Intl M-M F	FMBKX	D-	(800) 544-8544	D- / 1.1	5.94	2.58	12.92 /21	-0.26 /12	--	1.46	1.02
FO	Fidelity Strat Adv Intl M-M L	FQAHX	D	(800) 544-8544	D- / 1.1	5.96	2.50	12.85 /21	-0.34 /12	--	1.47	1.12
FO	Fidelity Strat Adv Intl M-M N	FQAIX	D	(800) 544-8544	D- / 1.0	5.84	2.38	12.52 /20	-0.60 /11	--	1.27	1.36
AA	Fidelity Strat Adv Mlt Mng 2005	FEHPX	C+	(800) 544-8544	D+ / 2.8	3.64	2.84	11.06 /15	3.52 /37	--	1.41	0.81
AA	Fidelity Strat Adv Mlt Mng 2005 L	FMJRX	B-	(800) 544-8544	D+ / 2.7	3.53	2.73	11.06 /15	3.46 /37	--	1.41	0.84
AA	Fidelity Strat Adv Mlt Mng 2005 N	FMJSX	C+	(800) 544-8544	D+ / 2.6	3.54	2.64	10.78 /14	3.23 /34	--	1.16	1.09
AA	Fidelity Strat Adv Mlt Mng 2010	FEMPX	C+	(800) 544-8544	C- / 3.4	4.20	3.61	13.15 /22	3.95 /42	--	1.61	0.86
AA	Fidelity Strat Adv Mlt Mng 2010 L	FMJTX	B-	(800) 544-8544	C- / 3.3	4.11	3.62	13.04 /22	3.90 /42	--	1.62	0.87
AA	Fidelity Strat Adv Mlt Mng 2010 N	FMJUX	B-	(800) 544-8544	C- / 3.2	4.11	3.52	12.76 /21	3.68 /39	--	1.38	1.12
GI	Fidelity Strat Adv Mlt Mng 2015	FEJPX	C+	(800) 544-8544	C- / 4.0	4.80	4.41	14.99 /30	4.31 /46	--	1.36	0.94
GI	Fidelity Strat Adv Mlt Mng 2015 L	FMJVX	C+	(800) 544-8544	C- / 4.0	4.80	4.41	14.87 /29	4.29 /46	--	1.36	0.94
GI	Fidelity Strat Adv Mlt Mng 2015 N	FMJWX	C+	(800) 544-8544	C- / 3.8	4.80	4.31	14.71 /29	4.04 /43	--	1.13	1.19
GI	Fidelity Strat Adv Mlt Mng 2020	FEKPX	C+	(800) 544-8544	C / 4.4	5.21	4.92	16.24 /35	4.53 /49	--	1.23	0.97
GI	Fidelity Strat Adv Mlt Mng 2020 L	FMJYX	C+	(800) 544-8544	C / 4.4	5.21	4.92	16.24 /35	4.55 /49	--	1.23	0.97
GI	Fidelity Strat Adv Mlt Mng 2020 N	FMJZX	C+	(800) 544-8544	C- / 4.1	5.12	4.73	15.85 /34	4.26 /46	--	1.00	1.22
GI	Fidelity Strat Adv Mlt Mng 2025	FEDPX	C+	(800) 544-8544	C / 4.8	5.52	5.52	17.50 /41	4.77 /52	--	1.18	1.03
GI	Fidelity Strat Adv Mlt Mng 2025 L	FMJAX	C+	(800) 544-8544	C / 4.8	5.53	5.43	17.49 /41	4.78 /52	--	1.19	1.01
GI	Fidelity Strat Adv Mlt Mng 2025 N	FMJBX	C+	(800) 544-8544	C / 4.6	5.44	5.34	17.23 /39	4.50 /49	--	0.96	1.26
GI	Fidelity Strat Adv Mlt Mng 2030	FECPX	C+	(800) 544-8544	C+ / 5.8	6.49	6.78	20.49 /55	5.23 /57	--	1.08	1.10
GI	Fidelity Strat Adv Mlt Mng 2030 L	FMJIX	C+	(800) 544-8544	C+ / 5.8	6.49	6.89	20.62 /56	5.23 /57	--	1.08	1.08
GI	Fidelity Strat Adv Mlt Mng 2030 N	FMJJX	C+	(800) 544-8544	C+ / 5.6	6.40	6.69	20.22 /53	4.98 /54	--	0.85	1.33
GI	Fidelity Strat Adv Mlt Mng 2035	FENPX	C+	(800) 544-8544	C+ / 6.4	6.93	7.80	22.41 /64	5.52 /60	--	0.92	1.16
GI	Fidelity Strat Adv Mlt Mng 2035 L	FMJCX	C+	(800) 544-8544	C+ / 6.4	7.02	7.90	22.51 /65	5.54 /60	--	0.92	1.10
GI	Fidelity Strat Adv Mlt Mng 2035 N	FMJEX	C+	(800) 544-8544	C+ / 6.2	6.93	7.71	22.13 /63	5.24 /57	--	0.72	1.35
GI	Fidelity Strat Adv Mlt Mng 2040	FEWPX	C+	(800) 544-8544	C+ / 6.5	7.12	7.91	22.65 /65	5.53 /60	--	0.82	1.21
GI	Fidelity Strat Adv Mlt Mng 2040 L	FJMVX	C+	(800) 544-8544	C+ / 6.4	7.00	7.88	22.49 /64	5.54 /60	--	0.79	1.11
GI	Fidelity Strat Adv Mlt Mng 2040 N	FMJKX	C+	(800) 544-8544	C+ / 6.2	6.91	7.70	22.19 /63	5.25 /57	--	0.62	1.36
GI	Fidelity Strat Adv Mlt Mng 2045	FEZPX	C+	(800) 544-8544	C+ / 6.4	7.03	7.90	22.50 /65	5.53 /60	--	0.89	1.20
GI	Fidelity Strat Adv Mlt Mng 2045 L	FMJFX	C+	(800) 544-8544	C+ / 6.4	7.02	7.79	22.49 /64	5.51 /60	--	0.88	1.10
GI	Fidelity Strat Adv Mlt Mng 2045 N	FMJGX	C+	(800) 544-8544	C+ / 6.2	6.93	7.70	22.26 /63	5.25 /57	--	0.71	1.35
GI	Fidelity Strat Adv Mlt Mng 2050	FEYPX	C+	(800) 544-8544	C+ / 6.4	7.05	7.84	22.59 /65	5.51 /60	--	0.98	1.22
GI	Fidelity Strat Adv Mlt Mng 2050 L	FMJLX	B-	(800) 544-8544	C+ / 6.4	7.04	7.83	22.44 /64	5.50 /59	--	0.96	1.11
GI	Fidelity Strat Adv Mlt Mng 2050 N	FMJMX	B-	(800) 544-8544	C+ / 6.2	6.96	7.74	22.20 /63	5.26 /57	--	0.78	1.36
GI	Fidelity Strat Adv Mlt Mng 2055	FESPX	C+	(800) 544-8544	C+ / 6.4	7.01	7.88	22.56 /65	5.51 /60	--	0.92	1.25
GI	Fidelity Strat Adv Mlt Mng 2055 L	FMJNX	B-	(800) 544-8544	C+ / 6.4	7.01	7.78	22.55 /65	5.50 /60	--	0.92	1.11
GI	Fidelity Strat Adv Mlt Mng 2055 N	FMJOX	B-	(800) 544-8544	C+ / 6.2	6.92	7.69	22.25 /63	5.25 /57	--	0.74	1.36
AA	Fidelity Strat Adv Mlt Mng Inc	FEBPX	C+	(800) 544-8544	D / 2.1	2.82	1.79	8.59 / 9	2.92 /31	--	1.45	0.71
AA	Fidelity Strat Adv Mlt Mng Inc L	FMJPX	C+	(800) 544-8544	D / 2.1	2.83	1.80	8.59 / 9	2.91 /31	--	1.45	0.71
AA	Fidelity Strat Adv Mlt Mng Inc N	FMJQX	C+	(800) 544-8544	D / 2.0	2.86	1.77	8.32 / 8	2.69 /29	--	1.21	0.96
GR	Fidelity Strat Adv SmMid Cp MM	FNAPX	C-	(800) 544-8544	B / 7.6	6.44	11.40	31.35 /89	6.04 /65	11.23 /68	0.03	1.43
GR	Fidelity Strat Adv SmMid Cp MM F	FARMX	C-	(800) 544-8544	B / 7.7	6.40	11.44	31.46 /89	6.14 /65	11.02 /66	0.03	1.33
GR	Fidelity Strat Adv SmMid Cp MM L	FQAJX	B	(800) 544-8544	B / 7.6	6.44	11.41	31.39 /89	6.04 /65	11.24 /68	0.03	1.42
GR	Fidelity Strat Adv SmMid Cp MM N	FQAKX	B	(800) 544-8544	B- / 7.5	6.37	11.36	31.00 /88	5.79 /62	10.77 /64	0.00	1.67
GL	Fidelity Strat Adv Value Mlt Mngr	FKMOX	A+	(800) 544-8544	A / 9.4	7.78	13.33	29.40 /85	9.23 /88	13.17 /86	1.35	1.32
GL	Fidelity Strat Adv Value Mlt Mngr F	FGWBX	A+	(800) 544-8544	A / 9.5	7.82	13.42	29.53 /85	9.35 /89	12.74 /81	1.34	1.19
GL	Fidelity Strat Adv Value Mlt Mngr L	FQALX	A+	(800) 544-8544	A / 9.4	7.79	13.33	29.40 /85	9.23 /88	13.17 /86	1.35	1.29
GL	Fidelity Strat Adv Value Mlt Mngr N	FQAMX	A+	(800) 544-8544	A / 9.3	7.71	13.18	29.11 /84	8.94 /86	12.69 /81	1.13	1.54
EM	Fidelity Strategic Adv Emerg Mkt	FSAMX	D+	(800) 544-8544	C / 4.8	9.11	5.38	29.40 /85	1.31 /20	0.05 / 4	1.06	1.36
* IN	Fidelity Strategic Advisers Core	FCSAX	A-	(800) 544-8544	B+ / 8.8	7.73	10.36	25.22 /74	9.18 /88	13.02 /84	1.12	0.81
* GR	Fidelity Strategic Advisers Growth	FSGFX	B	(800) 544-8544	B / 8.0	8.49	8.63	22.09 /63	8.46 /83	12.75 /81	0.80	0.72
* FO	Fidelity Strategic Advisers Intl	FILFX	D-	(800) 544-8544	D- / 1.3	6.38	3.73	14.33 /27	-0.12 /13	5.54 /25	1.87	1.02
FO	Fidelity Strategic Advisers Intl II	FUSIX	D-	(800) 544-8544	D- / 1.1	6.28	1.65	11.11 /15	-0.19 /13	5.97 /28	1.49	1.19

● Denotes fund is closed to new investors

* Denotes fund is included in Section II

Risk Rating/Pts	3 Year Standard Deviation	Beta	NAV As of 2/28/17	Total $(Mil)	Cash %	Stocks %	Bonds %	Other %	Portfolio Turnover Ratio	Last Bull Market Return	Last Bear Market Return	Manager Quality Pct	Manager Tenure (Years)	Initial Purch. $	Additional Purch. $	Front End Load	Back End Load
C+ / 6.0	10.3	0.83	11.43	4	10	89	0	1	42	N/A	N/A	73	5	0	0	0.0	1.0
B- / 7.2	10.2	0.82	11.40	N/A	10	89	0	1	42	N/A	N/A	72	5	0	0	0.0	1.0
B- / 7.2	10.3	0.83	11.38	N/A	10	89	0	1	42	N/A	N/A	69	5	0	0	0.0	1.0
B / 8.8	4.7	0.72	10.51	N/A	52	35	11	2	48	N/A	N/A	51	5	0	0	0.0	0.0
B+ / 9.8	4.7	0.72	10.50	N/A	52	35	11	2	48	N/A	N/A	50	5	0	0	0.0	0.0
B+ / 9.8	4.6	0.71	10.50	N/A	52	35	11	2	48	N/A	N/A	48	5	0	0	0.0	0.0
B / 8.4	5.5	0.86	10.72	N/A	46	44	9	1	32	N/A	N/A	43	5	0	0	0.0	0.0
B+ / 9.5	5.5	0.86	10.72	N/A	46	44	9	1	32	N/A	N/A	43	5	0	0	0.0	0.0
B+ / 9.5	5.5	0.86	10.72	N/A	46	44	9	1	32	N/A	N/A	39	5	0	0	0.0	0.0
B / 8.2	6.4	0.59	11.03	1	40	51	7	2	37	N/A	N/A	52	5	0	0	0.0	0.0
B- / 7.8	6.3	0.59	11.03	N/A	40	51	7	2	37	N/A	N/A	52	5	0	0	0.0	0.0
B- / 7.7	6.4	0.59	11.03	N/A	40	51	7	2	37	N/A	N/A	48	5	0	0	0.0	0.0
B- / 7.8	7.0	0.65	11.08	5	36	57	6	1	29	N/A	N/A	45	5	0	0	0.0	0.0
B- / 7.8	6.9	0.65	11.08	N/A	36	57	6	1	29	N/A	N/A	47	5	0	0	0.0	0.0
B- / 7.9	6.9	0.64	11.07	N/A	36	57	6	1	29	N/A	N/A	43	5	0	0	0.0	0.0
B- / 7.6	7.7	0.73	11.23	2	30	64	5	1	17	N/A	N/A	38	5	0	0	0.0	0.0
B- / 7.6	7.7	0.73	11.24	N/A	30	64	5	1	17	N/A	N/A	38	5	0	0	0.0	0.0
B- / 7.6	7.7	0.72	11.23	N/A	30	64	5	1	17	N/A	N/A	35	5	0	0	0.0	0.0
C+ / 6.5	9.1	0.86	11.20	2	18	77	4	1	54	N/A	N/A	28	5	0	0	0.0	0.0
C+ / 6.5	9.1	0.86	11.20	N/A	18	77	4	1	54	N/A	N/A	28	5	0	0	0.0	0.0
C+ / 6.5	9.1	0.86	11.19	N/A	18	77	4	1	54	N/A	N/A	26	5	0	0	0.0	0.0
C+ / 6.3	9.9	0.93	11.48	3	10	84	4	2	18	N/A	N/A	23	5	0	0	0.0	0.0
C+ / 6.3	9.9	0.93	11.49	N/A	10	84	4	2	18	N/A	N/A	23	5	0	0	0.0	0.0
C+ / 6.3	9.9	0.93	11.47	N/A	10	84	4	2	18	N/A	N/A	21	5	0	0	0.0	0.0
C+ / 6.2	9.9	0.94	11.50	2	10	84	4	2	18	N/A	N/A	23	5	0	0	0.0	0.0
C+ / 6.2	9.9	0.93	11.50	N/A	10	84	4	2	18	N/A	N/A	23	5	0	0	0.0	0.0
C+ / 6.2	9.9	0.93	11.48	N/A	10	84	4	2	18	N/A	N/A	21	5	0	0	0.0	0.0
C+ / 6.3	9.9	0.93	11.60	2	10	84	4	2	23	N/A	N/A	23	5	0	0	0.0	0.0
C+ / 6.3	9.9	0.93	11.60	N/A	10	84	4	2	23	N/A	N/A	23	5	0	0	0.0	0.0
C+ / 6.3	9.9	0.93	11.59	N/A	10	84	4	2	23	N/A	N/A	20	5	0	0	0.0	0.0
C+ / 6.1	9.9	0.93	11.34	2	10	84	4	2	31	N/A	N/A	23	5	0	0	0.0	0.0
B- / 7.2	9.9	0.93	11.34	N/A	10	84	4	2	31	N/A	N/A	23	5	0	0	0.0	0.0
B- / 7.2	9.9	0.93	11.33	N/A	10	84	4	2	31	N/A	N/A	21	5	0	0	0.0	0.0
C+ / 6.2	9.9	0.93	11.66	2	10	84	4	2	15	N/A	N/A	23	5	0	0	0.0	0.0
B- / 7.2	9.9	0.93	11.66	N/A	10	84	4	2	15	N/A	N/A	23	5	0	0	0.0	0.0
B- / 7.2	9.9	0.93	11.64	N/A	10	84	4	2	15	N/A	N/A	20	5	0	0	0.0	0.0
B+ / 9.6	3.4	0.50	10.29	1	62	23	13	2	44	N/A	N/A	64	5	0	0	0.0	0.0
B+ / 9.9	3.4	0.50	10.29	N/A	62	23	13	2	44	N/A	N/A	64	5	0	0	0.0	0.0
B+ / 9.9	3.4	0.51	10.29	N/A	62	23	13	2	44	N/A	N/A	61	5	0	0	0.0	0.0
D+ / 2.7	13.7	1.14	9.71	13	9	90	0	1	89	N/A	N/A	11	6	0	0	0.0	1.5
D+ / 2.7	13.7	1.14	9.76	2	9	90	0	1	89	N/A	N/A	12	6	0	0	0.0	1.5
C+ / 6.0	13.7	1.14	9.70	N/A	9	90	0	1	89	N/A	N/A	11	6	0	0	0.0	1.5
C+ / 6.0	13.7	1.14	9.65	N/A	9	90	0	1	89	N/A	N/A	10	6	0	0	0.0	1.5
C+ / 6.4	11.4	0.71	15.07	16	16	83	0	1	41	N/A	N/A	99	6	0	0	0.0	0.0
C+ / 6.4	11.4	0.70	15.15	4	16	83	0	1	41	N/A	N/A	99	6	0	0	0.0	0.0
B- / 7.3	11.4	0.71	15.07	N/A	16	83	0	1	41	N/A	N/A	99	6	0	0	0.0	0.0
B- / 7.3	11.4	0.70	15.06	N/A	16	83	0	1	41	N/A	N/A	99	6	0	0	0.0	0.0
C- / 4.0	15.3	0.94	9.14	4,600	14	85	0	1	41	22.1	-24.8	71	7	0	0	0.0	0.0
C+ / 6.0	10.7	1.03	16.80	24,090	3	95	0	2	85	126.0	-18.8	54	8	0	0	0.0	0.0
C / 5.4	11.4	1.05	16.88	11,187	1	97	0	2	30	123.5	-17.6	42	7	0	0	0.0	0.0
C / 5.1	10.8	0.87	9.78	16,141	12	86	0	2	28	52.9	-22.8	74	N/A	0	0	0.0	0.0
C / 5.4	10.6	0.84	8.94	3,590	17	82	0	1	16	55.6	-24.6	73	N/A	0	0	0.0	0.0

Fund Type	Fund Name	Ticker Symbol	Overall Investment Rating	Phone	Performance Rating/Pts	3 Mo	6 Mo	1Yr / Pct	3Yr / Pct	5Yr / Pct	Dividend Yield	Expense Ratio
* GR	Fidelity Strategic Advisers Sm-Mid	FSCFX	C+	(800) 544-8544	B- / 7.5	5.61	10.95	30.11 /87	5.89 /63	11.34 /68	0.31	1.09
* GR	Fidelity Strategic Advisers Val Fd	FVSAX	A	(800) 544-8544	A / 9.4	7.16	13.02	28.73 /83	9.54 /91	13.60 /90	1.68	0.74
GI	Fidelity Strategic Div and Inc	FSDIX	A-	(800) 544-8544	B- / 7.2	5.95	5.25	19.72 /51	8.59 /84	10.74 /64	2.63	0.78
GL	Fidelity Strategic Real Return Fund	FSRRX	C-	(800) 544-8544	D- / 1.2	2.87	3.20	12.19 /19	-0.02 /13	1.18 / 6	2.11	0.82
UT	Fidelity Telecom and Utilities	FIUIX	B+	(800) 544-8544	B / 7.7	10.06	7.05	18.53 /45	8.45 /83	11.98 /74	2.57	0.76
EM	Fidelity Total Emerg Mkts	FTEMX	C	(800) 522-7297	C / 5.2	8.09	4.43	25.60 /75	3.82 /41	3.09 /11	1.17	1.72
FO	Fidelity Total International Equity	FTIEX	D	(800) 522-7297	D / 1.8	6.49	1.33	13.81 /25	0.39 /15	5.06 /22	1.39	1.07
FO	Fidelity Total Internatl Idx Inst	FTIUX	U	(800) 544-8544	U /	7.39	4.52	--	--	--	0.00	0.09
FO	Fidelity Total Internatl Idx Prm	FTIPX	U	(800) 544-8544	U /	7.38	4.51	--	--	--	0.00	0.11
GI	Fidelity Total Mkt Idx F	FFSMX	A+	(800) 544-8544	A- / 9.2	7.76	10.30	26.33 /77	9.87 /93	13.79 /92	1.71	0.02
GI	Fidelity Total Mkt Idx Ins	FSKTX	A+	(800) 544-8544	A- / 9.2	7.74	10.29	26.30 /77	9.86 /93	13.79 /92	1.70	0.04
GI	Fidelity Total Mkt Idx Inv	FSTMX	A+	(800) 544-8544	A- / 9.2	7.75	10.26	26.22 /77	9.80 /92	13.73 /91	1.64	0.09
GI	Fidelity Total Mkt Idx IP	FSKAX	A+	(800) 544-8544	A- / 9.2	7.76	10.31	26.32 /77	9.88 /93	13.80 /92	1.71	0.02
GI	Fidelity Total Mkt Idx Pr	FSTVX	A+	(800) 544-8544	A- / 9.2	7.75	10.28	26.28 /77	9.85 /92	13.77 /91	1.69	0.05
GR	Fidelity Trend Fund	FTRNX	B	(800) 544-8544	B+ / 8.3	8.99	8.60	22.65 /65	8.65 /84	13.56 /89	0.40	0.77
GI	Fidelity Value Discovery Fd	FVDFX	A+	(800) 544-8544	A- / 9.1	8.19	12.01	24.60 /72	9.51 /90	13.96 /93	1.08	0.86
GI	Fidelity Value Discovery K	FVDKX	A+	(800) 544-8544	A- / 9.2	8.23	12.08	24.73 /72	9.65 /91	14.14 /94	1.18	0.70
* GI	Fidelity Value Fd	FDVLX	B	(800) 544-8544	B+ / 8.3	7.21	10.96	28.86 /84	7.34 /74	13.77 /91	1.17	0.84
GI	Fidelity Value K	FVLKX	B	(800) 544-8544	B+ / 8.4	7.24	11.01	28.99 /84	7.46 /75	13.91 /92	1.27	0.73
MC	Fidelity Value Strategies Fund K	FVSKX	B	(800) 522-7297	B+ / 8.5	8.97	10.09	29.32 /85	7.29 /74	12.46 /79	1.50	0.51
FO	Fidelity Worldwide Fund	FWWFX	D	(800) 544-8544	D+ / 2.6	6.52	3.59	14.42 /27	1.68 /22	9.17 /52	0.85	0.96
GL	Fiera Capital Diversified Alt Inst	FCAIX	U	(866) 777-7818	U /	-0.31	-1.75	-0.94 / 1	--	--	0.00	3.59
MC	First Eagle Fund of America A	FEFAX	D	(800) 334-2143	D / 2.1	6.38	5.36	12.89 /21	2.21 /25	9.87 /57	0.17	1.30
MC	First Eagle Fund of America C	FEAMX	D	(800) 334-2143	D+ / 2.4	6.18	4.95	12.03 /18	1.44 /21	9.04 /51	0.00	2.05
GR	First Eagle Fund of America I	FEAIX	D+	(800) 334-2143	C- / 3.1	6.45	5.48	13.21 /22	2.50 /27	10.10 /59	0.47	1.00
MC	● First Eagle Fund of America Y	FEAFX	D	(800) 334-2143	D+ / 2.9	6.37	5.37	12.89 /21	2.21 /25	9.86 /57	0.21	1.31
* GL	First Eagle Global A	SGENX	C	(800) 334-2143	C- / 3.6	4.97	4.36	17.16 /39	4.90 /53	7.16 /36	0.33	1.11
GL	First Eagle Global C	FESGX	C	(800) 334-2143	C- / 4.0	4.78	3.96	16.28 /35	4.12 /44	6.35 /31	0.00	1.86
GL	First Eagle Global I	SGIIX	C+	(800) 334-2143	C / 4.9	5.05	4.48	17.46 /40	5.18 /56	7.43 /38	0.59	0.84
GL	First Eagle Global Income Builder A	FEBAX	C-	(800) 334-2143	D+ / 2.5	5.03	3.47	16.56 /37	2.97 /32	--	2.80	1.19
GL	First Eagle Global Income Builder C	FEBCX	C-	(800) 334-2143	D+ / 2.8	4.84	3.07	15.71 /33	2.19 /25	--	2.21	1.96
GL	First Eagle Global Income Builder I	FEBIX	C-	(800) 334-2143	C- / 3.5	5.11	3.59	16.89 /38	3.19 /34	--	3.19	0.94
PM	First Eagle Gold A	SGGDX	E-	(800) 334-2143	E / 0.5	8.98	-8.21	17.35 /40	-1.09 / 9	-11.21 / 0	0.00	1.33
PM	First Eagle Gold C	FEGOX	E-	(800) 334-2143	E+ / 0.6	8.83	-8.51	16.51 /36	-1.88 / 7	-11.90 / 0	0.00	2.14
PM	First Eagle Gold I	FEGIX	E-	(800) 334-2143	E+ / 0.9	9.04	-8.09	17.70 /41	-0.82 /10	-10.97 / 0	0.00	1.03
FO	● First Eagle Overseas A	SGOVX	C-	(800) 334-2143	D / 2.0	5.32	1.61	12.76 /21	2.84 /30	5.42 /24	1.03	1.16
FO	● First Eagle Overseas C	FESOX	C-	(800) 334-2143	D / 2.2	5.18	1.28	11.97 /18	2.08 /24	4.65 /19	0.38	1.89
FO	● First Eagle Overseas I	SGOIX	C-	(800) 334-2143	D+ / 2.9	5.40	1.77	13.09 /22	3.12 /33	5.70 /26	1.32	0.88
FO	First Eagle Overseas Variable Fund	FEOVX	D	(800) 334-2143	D+ / 2.4	5.42	1.28	12.55 /20	2.34 /26	5.63 /26	0.55	1.30
SC	First Eagle US Value A	FEVAX	C+	(800) 334-2143	C / 5.2	4.41	6.97	20.35 /54	6.44 /68	8.21 /44	0.15	1.14
SC	First Eagle US Value C	FEVCX	C+	(800) 334-2143	C+ / 5.6	4.25	6.55	19.45 /49	5.65 /61	7.40 /37	0.00	1.90
SC	First Eagle US Value I	FEVIX	C+	(800) 334-2143	C+ / 6.5	4.46	7.09	20.65 /56	6.72 /70	8.49 /46	0.40	0.87
AA	First Inv Balanced Income A	FBIJX	U	(800) 423-4026	U /	3.08	1.20	9.08 /10	--	--	1.74	1.39
GR	First Inv Covered Call Strat Adv	FRCDX	U	(800) 423-4026	U /	6.13	6.52	--	--	--	0.00	N/A
IN	First Inv Equity Income A	FIUTX	C+	(800) 423-4026	C+ / 6.3	5.89	7.78	22.04 /62	7.57 /76	10.83 /64	1.49	1.22
IN	● First Inv Equity Income Adv	FIUUX	B+	(800) 423-4026	B- / 7.5	6.07	8.05	22.65 /65	7.96 /79	--	1.87	0.85
IN	First Inv Equity Income B	FIUBX	C+	(800) 423-4026	C+ / 6.6	5.70	7.32	21.11 /58	6.66 /69	9.94 /58	0.90	2.07
IN	First Inv Equity Income Inst	FIUVX	B+	(800) 423-4026	B / 7.6	6.12	8.01	22.72 /65	8.03 /79	--	1.90	0.82
GL	First Inv Global A	FIISX	D	(800) 423-4026	C- / 3.7	6.65	6.51	17.71 /42	4.40 /47	8.25 /44	0.14	1.52
GL	● First Inv Global Adv	FIITX	D+	(800) 423-4026	C / 5.2	6.77	6.63	18.33 /44	4.80 /52	--	0.23	1.11
GL	First Inv Global B	FIBGX	D	(800) 423-4026	C- / 4.2	6.42	6.06	16.95 /38	3.59 /38	7.41 /37	0.02	2.33
GL	First Inv Global Inst	FIIUX	C-	(800) 423-4026	C / 5.3	6.90	6.75	18.42 /45	4.88 /53	--	0.25	1.07

● Denotes fund is closed to new investors
* Denotes fund is included in Section II

246

www.thestreetratings.com

RISK			NET ASSETS		ASSET				Portfolio Turnover Ratio	BULL / BEAR		FUND MANAGER		MINIMUMS		LOADS	
	3 Year		NAV							Last Bull	Last Bear	Manager	Manager	Initial	Additional	Front	Back
Risk Rating/Pts	Standard Deviation	Beta	As of 2/28/17	Total $(Mil)	Cash %	Stocks %	Bonds %	Other %		Market Return	Market Return	Quality Pct	Tenure (Years)	Purch. $	Purch. $	End Load	End Load
C / 4.5	13.6	1.12	14.19	7,049	3	93	2	2	71	114.9	-24.1	11	7	0	0	0.0	0.0
C+ / 5.9	11.0	1.03	19.50	11,132	1	96	1	2	39	130.6	-18.6	59	9	0	0	0.0	0.0
B- / 7.7	7.5	0.68	15.13	3,581	2	66	13	19	55	93.8	-11.5	83	14	2,500	0	0.0	0.0
B / 8.2	4.9	0.21	8.91	497	53	15	30	2	15	14.2	-7.7	73	11	2,500	0	0.0	0.0
C+ / 6.8	10.3	0.49	26.02	1,012	1	98	0	1	65	89.6	-5.8	83	12	2,500	0	0.0	0.0
C+ / 5.8	11.5	0.69	11.55	143	4	52	42	2	57	N/A	N/A	88	6	2,500	0	0.0	1.5
C+ / 6.2	10.5	0.83	7.83	307	1	96	1	2	51	49.9	-25.2	78	10	2,500	0	0.0	1.0
U /	N/A	N/A	10.53	41	0	0	0	100	0	N/A	N/A	N/A	1	5,000,000	0	0.0	1.0
U /	N/A	N/A	10.53	134	0	0	0	100	0	N/A	N/A	N/A	1	10,000	0	0.0	1.0
B- / 7.7	10.7	1.03	68.21	9,200	0	0	0	100	3	134.3	-17.7	63	13	0	0	0.0	0.0
B- / 7.7	10.6	1.02	68.19	2,344	0	0	0	100	3	134.2	-17.7	63	13	5,000,000	0	0.0	0.0
B- / 7.7	10.6	1.02	68.20	737	0	0	0	100	3	133.5	-17.7	62	13	2,500	0	0.0	0.0
B- / 7.7	10.7	1.03	68.19	4,716	0	0	0	100	3	134.3	-17.7	63	13	100,000,000	0	0.0	0.0
B- / 7.7	10.6	1.03	68.20	23,277	0	0	0	100	3	134.0	-17.7	63	13	10,000	0	0.0	0.0
C / 5.1	11.7	1.04	89.35	1,605	0	99	0	1	140	129.0	-17.0	45	5	2,500	0	0.0	0.0
B- / 7.0	9.9	0.92	27.15	2,168	6	90	2	2	41	137.0	-21.0	72	5	2,500	0	0.0	0.0
B- / 7.0	9.9	0.92	27.15	136	6	90	2	2	41	139.1	-21.0	73	5	0	0	0.0	0.0
C / 4.7	12.2	1.09	115.37	7,434	3	94	1	2	72	138.7	-24.7	25	7	2,500	0	0.0	0.0
C / 4.7	12.2	1.09	115.47	1,021	3	94	1	2	72	140.3	-24.6	26	7	0	0	0.0	0.0
C / 5.0	12.4	0.93	40.58	68	2	96	0	2	9	131.0	-26.7	56	1	2,500	0	0.0	0.0
C / 5.1	10.9	0.78	23.03	1,414	0	99	0	1	117	80.3	-19.9	85	11	2,500	0	0.0	0.0
U /	N/A	N/A	9.52	57	93	6	0	1	796	N/A	N/A	N/A	3	10,000	0	0.0	0.0
C / 5.3	12.7	0.87	34.11	754	7	92	0	1	55	97.3	-19.9	10	30	2,500	100	5.0	0.0
C / 5.1	12.7	0.87	27.91	463	7	92	0	1	55	89.4	-20.1	7	30	2,500	100	0.0	0.0
C / 5.3	12.7	1.09	34.90	741	7	92	0	1	55	99.4	-19.9	3	30	1,000,000	100	0.0	0.0
C / 5.4	12.8	0.87	34.91	386	7	92	0	1	55	97.3	-19.9	10	30	2,500	100	0.0	0.0
B- / 7.3	7.9	0.57	56.57	16,128	25	72	1	2	12	61.0	-11.4	95	9	2,500	100	5.0	0.0
B- / 7.3	7.9	0.57	54.66	11,384	25	72	1	2	12	54.5	-11.7	94	9	2,500	100	0.0	0.0
B- / 7.3	7.9	0.57	56.83	25,340	25	72	1	2	12	63.2	-11.3	96	9	1,000,000	100	0.0	0.0
C+ / 6.9	7.5	1.05	11.35	357	13	51	34	2	30	N/A	N/A	51	5	2,500	100	5.0	0.0
C+ / 6.9	7.5	1.05	11.32	332	13	51	34	2	30	N/A	N/A	40	5	2,500	100	0.0	0.0
C+ / 6.9	7.5	1.05	11.32	554	13	51	34	2	30	N/A	N/A	53	5	1,000,000	100	0.0	0.0
E / 0.5	35.7	2.04	17.11	515	30	68	1	1	16	-43.7	-11.3	90	4	2,500	100	5.0	2.0
E / 0.4	35.7	2.04	16.02	188	30	68	1	1	16	-46.1	-11.6	86	4	2,500	100	0.0	2.0
E+ / 0.6	35.7	2.04	17.49	532	30	68	1	1	16	-42.9	-11.2	91	4	1,000,000	100	0.0	2.0
B- / 7.4	8.8	0.62	23.40	3,445	25	71	2	2	9	43.6	-11.7	90	9	2,500	100	5.0	0.0
B- / 7.4	8.8	0.62	22.56	948	25	71	2	2	9	37.9	-12.0	87	9	2,500	100	0.0	0.0
B- / 7.4	8.8	0.62	23.90	11,760	25	71	2	2	9	45.6	-11.6	91	9	1,000,000	100	0.0	0.0
C / 5.2	9.2	0.64	26.62	453	24	72	2	2	12	45.5	-13.0	88	9	0	0	0.0	0.0
C+ / 6.7	8.6	0.43	20.12	828	26	72	1	1	11	72.3	-10.3	91	8	2,500	100	5.0	0.0
C+ / 6.6	8.6	0.43	19.53	527	26	72	1	1	11	65.4	-10.6	89	8	2,500	100	0.0	0.0
C+ / 6.6	8.6	0.43	20.41	906	26	72	1	1	11	74.7	-10.2	92	8	1,000,000	100	0.0	0.0
U /	N/A	N/A	10.77	42	0	0	0	100	57	N/A	N/A	N/A	2	1,000	0	5.8	0.0
U /	N/A	N/A	10.97	66	0	0	0	100	83	N/A	N/A	N/A	1	1,000	0	0.0	0.0
C+ / 6.5	9.5	0.91	10.29	556	0	93	5	2	22	102.4	-17.8	50	6	1,000	0	5.8	0.0
C+ / 6.5	9.6	0.91	10.32	64	0	93	5	2	22	N/A	N/A	54	6	1,000	0	0.0	0.0
C+ / 6.5	9.6	0.91	10.06	3	0	93	5	2	22	93.8	-18.0	37	6	1,000	0	0.0	0.0
C+ / 6.5	9.6	0.91	10.37	7	0	93	5	2	22	N/A	N/A	55	6	2,000,000	0	0.0	0.0
C- / 4.0	11.5	0.86	7.71	349	0	95	4	1	94	81.3	-22.6	94	17	1,000	0	5.8	0.0
C- / 4.0	11.5	0.86	7.85	194	0	95	4	1	94	N/A	N/A	95	17	1,000	0	0.0	0.0
C- / 3.3	11.6	0.86	6.15	3	0	95	4	1	94	73.8	-22.8	92	17	1,000	0	0.0	0.0
C- / 4.1	11.5	0.86	7.89	3	0	95	4	1	94	N/A	N/A	95	17	2,000,000	0	0.0	0.0

Fund Type	Fund Name	Ticker Symbol	Overall Investment Rating	Phone	Performance Rating/Pts	3 Mo	6 Mo	1Yr / Pct	3Yr / Pct	5Yr / Pct	Dividend Yield	Expense Ratio
GI	First Inv Growth & Income A	FGINX	C	(800) 423-4026	C / 5.4	6.55	7.29	22.65 /65	5.93 /64	11.28 /68	1.19	1.15
GI	● First Inv Growth & Income Adv	FGIPX	C+	(800) 423-4026	C+ / 6.9	6.65	7.49	23.12 /67	6.42 /68	--	1.44	0.75
GI	First Inv Growth & Income B	FGIBX	C+	(800) 423-4026	C+ / 5.9	6.33	6.80	21.67 /61	5.10 /55	10.43 /61	0.64	1.93
GI	First Inv Growth & Income Inst	FGIQX	C+	(800) 423-4026	C+ / 6.8	6.64	7.49	23.15 /67	6.36 /67	--	1.53	0.75
GR	First Inv Hedged US Eqty Oppty A	FHEJX	U	(800) 423-4026	U /	4.23	4.44	--	--	--	0.00	N/A
GR	First Inv Hedged US Eqty Oppty Adv	FHEKX	U	(800) 423-4026	U /	4.35	4.56	--	--	--	0.00	N/A
FO	First Inv International A	FIINX	D	(800) 423-4026	E+ / 0.9	8.68	-1.30	6.86 / 6	1.38 /20	4.14 /16	0.48	1.64
FO	● First Inv International Adv	FIIPX	D	(800) 423-4026	D / 1.6	8.74	-1.13	7.20 / 6	1.79 /23	--	0.58	1.24
FO	First Inv International B	FIIOX	D	(800) 423-4026	D- / 1.2	8.44	-1.72	5.89 / 5	0.88 /18	3.53 /13	0.36	2.47
FO	First Inv International Inst	FIIQX	D	(800) 423-4026	D / 1.6	8.79	-1.05	7.34 / 6	1.88 /23	--	0.64	1.14
MC	First Inv Opportunity A	FIUSX	C-	(800) 423-4026	C / 4.7	5.83	7.44	20.86 /57	5.29 /57	12.02 /74	0.52	1.21
MC	● First Inv Opportunity Adv	FIVUX	C	(800) 423-4026	C+ / 6.1	5.92	7.59	21.23 /58	5.61 /61	--	0.60	0.92
MC	First Inv Opportunity B	FIMBX	C-	(800) 423-4026	C / 5.2	5.66	7.08	19.98 /52	4.49 /49	11.19 /67	0.56	1.98
MC	First Inv Opportunity Inst	FIVVX	C	(800) 423-4026	C+ / 6.2	5.95	7.68	21.40 /59	5.74 /62	--	0.64	0.79
RE	First Inv Real Estate A	FIRDX	U	(800) 423-4026	U /	8.25	-0.85	13.45 /23	--	--	1.87	1.70
RE	First Inv Real Estate Advisor	FIRGX	U	(800) 423-4026	U /	8.32	-0.70	13.82 /25	--	--	2.44	1.41
AG	First Inv Select Growth A	FICGX	C	(800) 423-4026	C+ / 6.6	7.39	8.72	20.00 /52	8.19 /80	11.94 /74	0.24	1.25
GR	● First Inv Select Growth Advisor	FICHX	B-	(800) 423-4026	B / 7.9	7.53	9.03	20.56 /55	8.71 /85	--	0.34	0.84
AG	First Inv Select Growth B	FIGBX	C	(800) 423-4026	B- / 7.0	7.21	8.40	19.06 /47	7.38 /75	11.10 /67	0.14	2.03
GR	First Inv Select Growth Inst	FICIX	B-	(800) 423-4026	B / 7.9	7.51	9.01	20.59 /55	8.67 /84	--	0.36	0.82
SC	First Inv Special Situations A	FISSX	C+	(800) 423-4026	B- / 7.1	4.86	11.13	28.66 /83	7.39 /75	9.74 /56	0.52	1.34
SC	● First Inv Special Situations Adv	FISTX	B	(800) 423-4026	B+ / 8.3	4.93	11.28	29.04 /84	7.74 /77	--	0.61	1.05
SC	First Inv Special Situations B	FISBX	C+	(800) 423-4026	B- / 7.5	4.65	10.67	27.65 /81	6.52 /69	8.87 /50	0.58	2.15
SC	First Inv Special Situations Inst	FISUX	B	(800) 423-4026	B+ / 8.4	5.00	11.36	29.21 /85	7.87 /78	--	0.63	0.90
BA	First Inv Total Return A	FITRX	C-	(800) 423-4026	D+ / 2.6	4.27	3.64	13.74 /24	4.14 /44	7.36 /37	1.40	1.18
BA	● First Inv Total Return Adv	FITUX	C+	(800) 423-4026	C- / 3.8	4.14	3.78	14.16 /26	4.54 /49	--	1.73	0.78
BA	First Inv Total Return B	FBTRX	C	(800) 423-4026	C- / 3.0	4.04	3.21	12.81 /21	3.32 /35	6.53 /32	0.79	1.96
BA	First Inv Total Return Inst	FITVX	C+	(800) 423-4026	C- / 3.9	4.35	3.83	14.19 /26	4.57 /49	--	1.73	0.77
AA	First Investors Strategic Inc A	FSIFX	C-	(800) 423-4026	D- / 1.0	2.33	1.19	6.76 / 5	1.68 /22	--	2.80	1.27
GI	First Trust Pref Sec and Inc A	FPEAX	B+	(800) 621-1675	C- / 4.2	4.28	2.66	12.10 /18	7.23 /74	5.97 /28	5.06	1.49
GI	First Trust Pref Sec and Inc C	FPECX	B+	(800) 621-1675	C / 4.5	4.08	2.23	11.19 /15	6.52 /69	5.24 /23	4.56	2.15
GI	First Trust Pref Sec and Inc F	FPEFX	A	(800) 621-1675	C / 5.2	4.32	2.69	12.20 /19	7.32 /74	6.05 /29	5.34	1.92
GI	First Trust Pref Sec and Inc I	FPEIX	A	(800) 621-1675	C / 5.3	4.38	2.78	12.32 /19	7.50 /75	6.23 /30	5.52	1.15
GI	First Trust Pref Sec and Inc R3	FPERX	A-	(800) 621-1675	C / 4.9	4.22	2.54	11.83 /17	6.95 /72	5.65 /26	5.06	6.56
IN	First Trust/Confluence SCV A	FOVAX	A-	(800) 621-1675	B+ / 8.7	7.60	11.19	30.21 /87	9.41 /90	12.67 /81	0.00	7.82
IN	First Trust/Confluence SCV C	FOVCX	A-	(800) 621-1675	B+ / 8.9	7.34	10.57	28.95 /84	8.44 /82	11.80 /72	0.00	9.14
IN	First Trust/Confluence SCV I	FOVIX	A	(800) 621-1675	A / 9.4	7.55	11.02	30.26 /87	9.50 /90	12.95 /83	0.00	8.67
EN	Firsthand Alternative Energy Fd	ALTEX	E-	(888) 884-2675	E- / 0.1	9.75	8.27	6.03 / 5	-8.46 / 1	3.68 /14	0.00	1.98
TC	Firsthand Technology Opportunities	TEFQX	C	(888) 884-2675	A / 9.3	11.89	9.47	32.64 /91	7.86 /78	12.44 /78	0.00	1.85
GR	FMC Strategic Value Fund	FMSVX	E	(866) 777-7818	E / 0.3	3.32	5.14	17.70 /41	-5.25 / 2	2.97 /11	0.00	1.20
SC	FMI Common Stock Investor	FMIMX	C+	(800) 811-5311	B- / 7.3	4.53	10.66	26.30 /77	6.60 /69	10.58 /63	0.01	1.07
* FO	FMI International Investor	FMIJX	B-	(800) 811-5311	C+ / 5.9	5.14	5.07	16.45 /36	6.96 /72	11.00 /66	2.92	0.98
GR	FMI Large Cap Investor	FMIHX	B+	(800) 811-5311	B+ / 8.7	5.96	9.71	24.18 /71	9.56 /91	12.83 /82	1.04	0.87
AA	Footprints Discover Value A	DAVAX	E-	(855) 445-9339	E- / 0.1	0.24	14.90	23.52 /68	-9.61 / 1	--	0.38	3.85
FO	Forester Discovery	INTLX	D+	(800) 388-0365	E / 0.4	3.86	-2.11	0.33 / 1	-1.35 / 8	1.70 / 7	0.62	1.36
IX	Forester Value I	FVILX	D+	(800) 388-0365	E- / 0.2	0.79	-3.39	-7.01 / 0	-2.39 / 6	-0.54 / 4	1.06	1.00
IX	Forester Value N	FVALX	D+	(800) 388-0365	E- / 0.2	0.69	-3.51	-7.22 / 0	-2.64 / 5	-0.76 / 4	0.42	1.26
GR	Forester Value R	FVRLX	D+	(800) 388-0365	E- / 0.2	0.61	-3.65	-7.49 / 0	-2.81 / 5	-0.85 / 4	0.09	1.51
GR	FormulaFolios US Equity Inst	FFILX	U	(855) 907-3233	U /	7.40	8.52	16.46 /36	--	--	0.16	N/A
GI	Fort Pitt Capital Total Return Fd	FPCGX	A	(800) 471-5827	A- / 9.1	7.92	12.66	28.22 /82	9.49 /90	11.75 /72	0.86	1.43
SC	Foundry Partners Fdm Sm Cp Val	DRISX	B+	(800) 408-4682	A+ / 9.6	4.74	14.99	36.42 /95	9.05 /87	13.54 /89	0.77	1.45
SC	Foundry Partners Fdm Sm Cp Val Inv	DRSVX	B	(800) 408-4682	A / 9.5	4.69	14.83	36.20 /95	8.80 /85	13.29 /87	0.53	1.20

99 Pct = Best
0 Pct = Worst

● Denotes fund is closed to new investors
* Denotes fund is included in Section II

www.thestreetratings.com

RISK Risk Rating/Pts	3 Year Standard Deviation	Beta	NET ASSETS NAV As of 2/28/17	Total $(Mil)	ASSET Cash %	Stocks %	Bonds %	Other %	Portfolio Turnover Ratio	BULL/BEAR Last Bull Market Return	Last Bear Market Return	FUND MANAGER Manager Quality Pct	Manager Tenure (Years)	MINIMUMS Initial Purch. $	Additional Purch. $	LOADS Front End Load	Back End Load
C+ / 5.9	11.4	1.07	22.18	1,648	0	99	0	1	23	114.9	-18.8	15	15	1,000	0	5.8	0.0
C+ / 6.0	11.4	1.07	22.37	152	0	99	0	1	23	N/A	N/A	19	15	1,000	0	0.0	0.0
C+ / 5.9	11.4	1.06	20.49	16	0	99	0	1	23	106.3	-19.1	10	15	1,000	0	0.0	0.0
C+ / 5.9	11.4	1.07	22.27	11	0	99	0	1	23	N/A	N/A	18	15	2,000,000	0	0.0	0.0
U /	N/A	N/A	10.35	32	0	0	0	100	0	N/A	N/A	N/A	1	1,000	0	5.8	0.0
U /	N/A	N/A	10.36	33	0	0	0	100	0	N/A	N/A	N/A	1	1,000	0	0.0	0.0
C+ / 6.4	10.8	0.74	13.37	201	1	93	5	1	28	44.5	-14.2	84	N/A	1,000	0	5.8	0.0
C+ / 6.5	10.8	0.74	13.54	91	1	93	5	1	28	N/A	N/A	86	N/A	1,000	0	0.0	0.0
C+ / 6.3	10.8	0.74	12.53	1	1	93	5	1	28	39.8	-14.4	81	N/A	1,000	0	0.0	0.0
C+ / 6.4	10.8	0.74	13.57	3	1	93	5	1	28	N/A	N/A	86	N/A	2,000,000	0	0.0	0.0
C / 5.0	11.9	0.94	38.63	935	0	96	3	1	36	123.5	-20.9	29	13	1,000	0	5.8	0.0
C / 5.1	11.9	0.94	39.20	86	0	96	3	1	36	N/A	N/A	32	13	1,000	0	0.0	0.0
C / 4.7	11.9	0.94	30.37	8	0	96	3	1	36	114.6	-21.1	21	13	1,000	0	0.0	0.0
C / 5.1	11.9	0.94	39.12	5	0	96	3	1	36	N/A	N/A	34	13	2,000,000	0	0.0	0.0
U /	N/A	N/A	10.00	38	1	98	0	1	31	N/A	N/A	N/A	N/A	1,000	0	5.8	0.0
U /	N/A	N/A	10.02	63	1	98	0	1	31	N/A	N/A	N/A	N/A	1,000	0	0.0	0.0
C / 4.7	11.1	1.00	10.58	398	0	98	1	1	59	114.4	-16.5	46	10	1,000	0	5.8	0.0
C / 4.7	11.1	1.00	10.73	78	0	98	1	1	59	N/A	N/A	53	10	1,000	0	0.0	0.0
C / 4.4	11.1	1.00	8.99	3	0	98	1	1	59	106.0	-16.9	35	10	1,000	0	0.0	0.0
C / 4.8	11.1	1.00	10.78	4	0	98	1	1	59	N/A	N/A	51	10	2,000,000	0	0.0	0.0
C / 5.0	13.1	0.80	28.62	512	0	97	1	2	39	98.5	-19.7	85	4	1,000	0	5.8	0.0
C / 5.0	13.2	0.80	28.83	68	0	97	1	2	39	N/A	N/A	86	4	1,000	0	0.0	0.0
C / 4.7	13.1	0.80	21.75	3	0	97	1	2	39	90.1	-20.0	80	4	1,000	0	0.0	0.0
C / 5.0	13.1	0.80	28.99	8	0	97	1	2	39	N/A	N/A	87	4	2,000,000	0	0.0	0.0
B- / 7.7	6.8	1.05	19.32	864	1	59	39	1	63	66.8	-10.6	28	16	1,000	0	5.8	0.0
B- / 7.7	6.8	1.05	19.41	1	1	59	39	1	63	N/A	N/A	32	16	1,000	0	0.0	0.0
B- / 7.8	6.8	1.05	18.97	8	1	59	39	1	63	59.9	-10.8	20	16	1,000	0	0.0	0.0
B- / 7.7	6.8	1.06	19.46	34	1	59	39	1	63	N/A	N/A	32	16	2,000,000	0	0.0	0.0
B+ / 9.3	3.2	0.39	9.47	157	9	4	85	2	49	N/A	N/A	59	4	1,000	0	5.8	0.0
B+ / 9.9	3.4	0.16	21.67	36	1	33	65	1	71	46.3	-0.6	96	6	2,500	50	4.5	0.0
B+ / 9.9	3.4	0.16	21.71	51	1	33	65	1	71	40.9	-0.6	95	6	2,500	50	0.0	0.0
B+ / 9.9	3.4	0.16	21.86	5	1	33	65	1	71	48.1	-0.7	96	6	2,500	50	0.0	0.0
B+ / 9.9	3.4	0.16	21.75	109	1	33	65	1	71	48.4	-0.4	96	6	1,000,000	0	0.0	0.0
B+ / 9.9	3.4	0.16	21.65	1	1	33	65	1	71	44.0	-1.1	95	6	0	0	0.0	0.0
C+ / 5.9	12.0	0.96	31.64	5	4	95	0	1	15	115.4	-19.3	66	6	2,500	50	5.5	0.0
C+ / 5.8	11.9	0.95	29.01	4	4	95	0	1	15	104.4	-19.3	55	6	2,500	50	0.0	0.0
C+ / 5.9	11.9	0.95	32.28	4	4	95	0	1	15	119.0	-18.8	68	6	1,000,000	0	0.0	0.0
C- / 3.4	17.4	0.40	5.63	5	4	95	0	1	5	22.1	-40.8	6	10	2,000	50	0.0	0.0
D / 1.6	16.5	1.15	7.11	83	0	98	0	2	19	103.1	-18.0	24	18	2,000	50	0.0	0.0
C- / 3.9	14.3	1.12	23.43	123	0	90	9	1	42	51.9	-30.2	0	19	10,000	1,000	0.0	0.0
C / 4.3	11.7	0.68	26.83	869	4	83	12	1	17	106.2	-17.6	85	20	1,000	100	0.0	0.0
B- / 7.2	7.2	0.48	30.98	5,287	6	82	10	2	16	97.4	-13.7	98	N/A	2,500	100	0.0	0.0
C / 5.5	10.1	0.92	20.78	4,676	7	90	2	1	17	118.1	-15.4	72	16	1,000	100	0.0	0.0
D- / 1.1	26.6	1.97	6.73	8	7	92	0	1	51	N/A	N/A	0	5	10,000	100	5.8	1.0
B / 8.4	5.6	0.40	13.21	5	7	54	37	2	10	14.9	-10.1	57	18	2,500	100	0.0	0.0
B / 8.3	4.1	0.03	11.53	31	8	68	22	2	6	-0.9	-5.3	37	18	25,000	100	0.0	0.0
B / 8.4	4.0	0.02	11.29	25	8	68	22	2	6	-2.2	-5.4	34	18	2,500	100	0.0	0.0
B / 8.4	4.1	0.02	11.60	2	8	68	22	2	6	-2.2	-5.6	32	18	2,500	100	0.0	0.0
U /	N/A	N/A	10.85	156	26	37	35	2	0	N/A	N/A	N/A	2	50,000	500	0.0	2.0
C+ / 6.3	10.7	0.98	23.04	67	1	94	4	1	5	104.9	-11.8	64	16	2,500	100	0.0	2.0
C- / 4.1	13.6	0.82	23.22	110	5	94	0	1	13	137.6	-26.8	91	14	100,000	1,000	0.0	0.0
C- / 4.1	13.6	0.82	23.13	45	5	94	0	1	13	135.2	-27.0	90	14	2,500	1,000	0.0	1.0

I. Index of Stock Mutual Funds

					PERFORMANCE						Incl. in Returns	
	99 Pct = Best					Total Return % through 2/28/17						
	0 Pct = Worst		Overall		Perfor-				Annualized		Dividend	Expense
Fund		Ticker	Investment		mance				3Yr / Pct	5Yr / Pct		
Type	Fund Name	Symbol	Rating	Phone	Rating/Pts	3 Mo	6 Mo	1Yr / Pct			Yield	Ratio
GR	● FPA Capital Inc	FPPTX	E	(800) 982-4372	D- / 1.4	0.19	10.48	29.39 /85	-1.76 / 7	3.56 /13	0.26	0.77
* BA	FPA Crescent	FPACX	B-	(800) 982-4372	C+ / 5.8	5.27	8.57	21.03 /57	5.80 /62	8.85 /49	0.82	1.11
FO	FPA International Value	FPIVX	D-	(800) 982-4372	D- / 1.4	8.52	9.41	19.90 /51	-0.97 / 9	5.28 /23	2.71	1.25
GI	FPA Paramount Inc	FPRAX	D+	(800) 982-4372	C- / 3.5	6.99	8.17	21.29 /59	1.57 /21	7.51 /38	0.95	1.32
GR	FPA US Value Inc	FPPFX	E	(800) 982-4372	D+ / 2.8	6.99	6.03	9.82 /11	3.22 /34	9.54 /55	0.00	0.97
GR	Frank Value C	FNKCX	D	(866) 706-9790	D- / 1.0	1.84	0.87	3.84 / 3	0.34 /15	6.64 /32	0.00	2.29
GR	Frank Value Instl	FNKIX	D+	(866) 706-9790	D- / 1.3	2.03	1.34	4.80 / 4	1.36 /20	7.72 /40	0.00	1.29
GR	Frank Value Investor	FRNKX	D+	(866) 706-9790	D- / 1.2	1.97	1.28	4.52 / 4	1.10 /19	7.44 /38	0.00	1.54
GI	Franklin Balance Sheet Investmt A	FRBSX	C-	(800) 342-5236	B- / 7.3	6.35	16.91	33.69 /92	5.21 /57	10.76 /64	0.42	0.96
GI	Franklin Balance Sheet Investmt Adv	FBSAX	C	(800) 321-8563	B+ / 8.5	6.42	17.07	34.04 /93	5.48 /59	11.03 /66	0.67	0.71
GI	Franklin Balance Sheet Investmt C	FCBSX	C-	(800) 342-5236	B / 7.7	6.18	16.50	32.73 /91	4.44 /48	9.94 /58	0.00	1.71
GI	Franklin Balance Sheet Investmt R	FBSRX	C	(800) 342-5236	B / 8.1	6.32	16.81	33.39 /92	4.96 /54	10.49 /62	0.23	1.21
GR	Franklin Balance Sheet Investmt R6	FBSIX	C	(800) 342-5236	B+ / 8.6	6.49	17.13	34.21 /93	5.64 /61	11.09 /67	0.67	0.52
BA	Franklin Balanced A	FBLAX	C+	(800) 342-5236	C- / 4.0	4.27	4.98	17.12 /39	5.83 /63	7.52 /38	2.77	1.04
BA	Franklin Balanced Adv	FBFZX	B-	(800) 321-8563	C / 5.5	4.32	5.19	17.46 /40	6.17 /66	7.83 /41	3.16	0.79
BA	Franklin Balanced C	FBMCX	C+	(800) 342-5236	C / 4.6	4.12	4.64	16.33 /36	5.09 /55	6.76 /33	2.27	1.79
BA	Franklin Balanced R		B-	(800) 342-5236	C / 5.0	4.19	4.93	16.91 /38	5.61 /61	7.29 /37	2.71	1.29
BA	Franklin Balanced R6	FBFRX	B-	(800) 342-5236	C+ / 5.6	4.44	5.25	17.59 /41	6.27 /66	7.92 /41	3.26	0.68
HL	● Franklin Biotechnology Discvry A	FBDIX	D-	(800) 342-5236	C+ / 6.4	10.21	13.29	30.89 /88	3.79 /40	20.85 /99	1.07	1.00
HL	● Franklin Biotechnology Discvry Adv	FTDZX	D	(800) 321-8563	B- / 7.5	10.28	13.43	31.22 /89	4.05 /44	21.17 /99	1.34	0.76
HL	Franklin Biotechnology Discvry C	FBTDX	U	(800) 342-5236	U /	10.01	12.88	29.97 /86	--	--	0.87	1.72
HL	● Franklin Biotechnology Discvry R6	FRBRX	D	(800) 342-5236	B / 7.6	10.32	13.52	31.44 /89	4.21 /45	21.32 /99	1.48	0.61
GL	Franklin Conservative Alloc A	FTCIX	C-	(800) 342-5236	D / 1.7	4.17	3.66	11.84 /17	2.35 /26	4.29 /17	0.97	1.26
GL	Franklin Conservative Alloc Adv	FTCZX	C	(800) 321-8563	D+ / 2.6	4.25	3.83	12.24 /19	2.62 /28	4.56 /18	1.23	1.01
GL	Franklin Conservative Alloc C	FTCCX	C-	(800) 342-5236	D / 2.0	3.95	3.24	11.01 /14	1.58 /21	3.50 /13	0.33	2.01
GL	Franklin Conservative Alloc R	FTCRX	C-	(800) 342-5236	D+ / 2.3	4.11	3.54	11.61 /16	2.10 /25	4.02 /15	0.79	1.51
GL	Franklin Conservative Alloc R6		C	(800) 342-5236	D+ / 2.7	4.28	3.86	12.32 /19	2.73 /29	4.59 /19	1.36	0.93
CV	Franklin Convertible Securities A	FISCX	C	(800) 342-5236	C- / 3.8	6.53	4.50	19.19 /48	4.73 /51	9.03 /51	2.37	0.86
CV	Franklin Convertible Securities Adv	FCSZX	C+	(800) 321-8563	C / 5.3	6.63	4.65	19.48 /49	5.00 /54	9.31 /53	2.75	0.61
CV	Franklin Convertible Securities C	FROTX	C	(800) 342-5236	C / 4.4	6.36	4.16	18.32 /44	3.96 /42	8.22 /44	1.85	1.61
GI	Franklin Corefolio 529 Port A		B-	(800) 342-5236	C+ / 5.6	8.13	9.14	24.33 /71	5.24 /57	10.11 /59	0.00	1.44
GI	● Franklin Corefolio 529 Port B		B-	(800) 342-5236	C+ / 6.1	7.93	8.76	23.40 /68	4.46 /48	9.28 /53	0.00	2.19
GI	Franklin Corefolio 529 Port C		B-	(800) 342-5236	C+ / 6.1	7.94	8.75	23.42 /68	4.46 /48	9.28 /53	0.00	2.19
GI	Franklin Corefolio Allocation A	FTCOX	C+	(800) 342-5236	C+ / 5.8	8.21	9.30	24.62 /72	5.46 /59	10.37 /61	0.83	1.02
GI	Franklin Corefolio Allocation Adv	FCAZX	B-	(800) 321-8563	B- / 7.1	8.28	9.43	24.96 /73	5.75 /62	10.69 /63	1.11	0.77
GI	Franklin Corefolio Allocation C	FTCLX	C+	(800) 342-5236	C+ / 6.3	7.96	8.87	23.68 /69	4.69 /51	9.59 /55	0.20	1.77
GI	Franklin Corefolio Allocation R		C	(800) 342-5236	C / 5.3	8.14	9.17	19.55 /50	3.86 /41	9.27 /53	0.68	1.27
TC	Franklin DynaTech A	FKDNX	C+	(800) 342-5236	B- / 7.2	10.75	8.36	27.39 /80	7.25 /74	13.25 /86	0.00	0.89
TC	Franklin DynaTech Adv	FDYZX	B	(800) 321-8563	B+ / 8.5	10.82	8.48	27.72 /81	7.52 /76	13.54 /89	0.00	0.64
TC	Franklin DynaTech C	FDYNX	C+	(800) 342-5236	B / 7.7	10.56	7.95	26.45 /78	6.45 /68	12.41 /78	0.00	1.64
TC	Franklin DynaTech R	FDNRX	B-	(800) 342-5236	B / 8.0	10.69	8.20	27.06 /79	6.98 /72	12.97 /83	0.00	1.14
GR	Franklin DynaTech R6	FDTRX	B	(800) 342-5236	B+ / 8.6	10.86	8.57	27.93 /81	7.69 /77	13.61 /90	0.00	0.48
IN	Franklin Equity Inc A	FISEX	C+	(800) 342-5236	C+ / 6.1	5.98	7.64	21.45 /60	7.47 /75	11.17 /67	2.23	0.86
IN	Franklin Equity Inc Adv	FEIFX	B+	(800) 321-8563	B- / 7.3	6.02	7.75	21.68 /61	7.72 /77	11.45 /69	2.60	0.61
IN	Franklin Equity Inc C	FRETX	C+	(800) 342-5236	C+ / 6.6	5.81	7.24	20.52 /55	6.66 /70	10.33 /61	1.70	1.61
IN	Franklin Equity Inc R	FREIX	C+	(800) 342-5236	C+ / 6.9	5.92	7.51	21.13 /58	7.20 /73	10.88 /65	2.16	1.11
IN	Franklin Equity Inc R6	FEIQX	B+	(800) 342-5236	B- / 7.4	6.06	7.82	21.87 /61	7.87 /78	11.43 /69	2.70	2.88
GR	Franklin Focused Core Equity A	FCEQX	C	(800) 342-5236	C+ / 5.6	5.47	9.55	21.01 /57	6.48 /68	11.64 /71	0.00	1.45
GR	Franklin Focused Core Equity Adv	FCEZX	C+	(800) 342-5236	C+ / 6.9	5.55	9.73	21.27 /59	6.74 /70	11.94 /74	0.00	1.20
GR	Franklin Focused Core Equity C	FCEDX	C	(800) 342-5236	C+ / 6.1	5.29	9.15	20.03 /52	5.67 /61	10.85 /65	0.00	2.20
GR	Franklin Focused Core Equity R	FCERX	C+	(800) 342-5236	C+ / 6.6	5.47	9.51	20.73 /56	6.24 /66	11.42 /69	0.00	1.70
GR	Franklin Focused Core Equity R6	FEFCX	C+	(800) 342-5236	B- / 7.0	5.61	9.78	21.50 /60	6.92 /71	12.08 /75	0.00	1.04

● Denotes fund is closed to new investors

* Denotes fund is included in Section II

www.thestreetratings.com

RISK	3 Year		NET ASSETS		ASSET				Portfolio Turnover Ratio	BULL / BEAR		FUND MANAGER		MINIMUMS		LOADS	
Risk Rating/Pts	Standard Deviation	Beta	NAV As of 2/28/17	Total $(Mil)	Cash %	Stocks %	Bonds %	Other %		Last Bull Market Return	Last Bear Market Return	Manager Quality Pct	Manager Tenure (Years)	Initial Purch. $	Additional Purch. $	Front End Load	Back End Load
C- /3.1	14.1	0.88	36.82	811	10	60	29	1	45	49.5	-22.2	2	10	1,500	100	0.0	2.0
B- /7.0	7.5	1.04	33.93	17,381	6	57	35	2	48	75.3	-11.6	50	24	1,500	100	0.0	2.0
C /5.4	11.4	0.80	12.90	292	21	66	12	1	39	N/A	N/A	64	6	1,500	100	0.0	2.0
C /5.1	12.6	0.94	18.41	155	11	88	0	1	52	82.7	-24.1	4	6	1,500	100	0.0	2.0
D- /1.4	13.5	1.06	9.49	125	7	92	0	1	109	101.2	-24.8	4	2	1,500	100	0.0	2.0
B- /7.1	6.1	0.39	12.30	3	63	36	0	1	51	68.1	-14.7	27	13	1,500	100	0.0	0.0
B- /7.3	6.1	0.39	13.13	7	63	36	0	1	51	77.5	-14.4	39	13	1,000,000	500	0.0	0.0
B- /7.3	6.1	0.39	13.00	18	63	36	0	1	51	75.0	-14.4	36	13	1,500	100	0.0	0.0
D+ /2.5	13.0	1.02	38.99	893	16	83	0	1	30	103.7	-22.7	13	27	1,000	0	5.8	0.0
D+ /2.5	13.0	1.02	40.16	93	16	83	0	1	30	106.4	-22.6	15	27	1,000,000	0	0.0	0.0
D+ /2.4	13.0	1.02	37.46	70	16	83	0	1	30	95.6	-22.9	9	27	1,000	0	0.0	0.0
D+ /2.5	13.0	1.02	39.08	10	16	83	0	1	30	101.0	-22.8	12	27	1,000	0	0.0	0.0
D+ /2.5	13.0	1.02	40.13	N/A	16	83	0	1	30	106.8	-22.7	16	27	1,000,000	0	0.0	0.0
B- /7.9	7.1	1.09	12.08	2,609	3	53	32	12	46	67.1	-10.8	46	11	1,000	0	5.8	0.0
B- /7.9	7.1	1.08	12.11	168	3	53	32	12	46	69.8	-10.8	50	11	1,000,000	0	0.0	0.0
B- /7.9	7.1	1.09	11.98	659	3	53	32	12	46	61.0	-11.1	36	11	1,000	0	0.0	0.0
B- /7.9	7.1	1.08	12.11	5	3	53	32	12	46	65.3	-11.0	43	11	1,000	0	0.0	0.0
B- /7.9	7.1	1.09	12.11	N/A	3	53	32	12	46	70.5	-10.8	51	11	1,000,000	0	0.0	0.0
E+ /0.7	28.7	1.72	147.85	1,133	4	95	0	1	22	229.6	-15.6	1	20	1,000	0	5.8	0.0
E+ /0.7	28.7	1.72	150.78	120	4	95	0	1	22	234.5	-15.5	1	20	1,000	0	0.0	0.0
U /	N/A	N/A	144.77	47	4	95	0	1	22	N/A	N/A	N/A	20	1,000	0	0.0	0.0
E+ /0.8	28.7	1.72	151.57	8	4	95	0	1	22	236.5	-15.5	1	20	1,000,000	0	0.0	0.0
B- /7.9	5.6	0.85	14.16	806	3	39	55	3	18	34.5	-8.4	55	17	1,000	0	5.8	0.0
B- /7.9	5.6	0.85	14.17	28	3	39	55	3	18	36.4	-8.3	58	17	1,000	0	0.0	0.0
B- /7.9	5.6	0.85	13.87	467	3	39	55	3	18	29.2	-8.7	44	17	1,000	0	0.0	0.0
B- /7.9	5.6	0.85	14.10	125	3	39	55	3	18	32.8	-8.5	51	17	1,000	0	0.0	0.0
B- /7.9	5.6	0.41	14.16	2	3	39	55	3	18	36.4	-8.4	89	17	1,000,000	0	0.0	0.0
C+ /6.6	8.3	0.92	18.87	759	12	12	1	75	28	78.4	-18.4	75	15	1,000	0	5.8	0.0
C+ /6.6	8.4	0.92	18.88	1,162	12	12	1	75	28	81.0	-18.3	77	15	1,000,000	0	0.0	0.0
C+ /6.6	8.4	0.92	18.60	297	12	12	1	75	28	71.4	-18.7	67	15	1,000	0	0.0	0.0
B- /7.2	10.8	1.00	30.46	95	0	0	0	100	0	95.9	-19.0	15	14	250	0	5.8	0.0
B- /7.2	10.8	1.00	26.95	3	0	0	0	100	0	88.1	-19.2	10	14	250	0	0.0	0.0
B- /7.2	10.9	1.01	27.46	36	0	0	0	100	0	88.1	-19.3	10	14	250	0	0.0	0.0
C+ /5.6	10.8	1.00	18.14	521	2	94	3	1	1	98.6	-18.9	16	14	1,000	0	5.8	0.0
C+ /5.6	10.8	1.00	18.18	24	2	94	3	1	1	101.5	-18.8	19	14	1,000	0	0.0	0.0
C+ /5.7	10.8	1.00	17.90	164	2	94	3	1	1	91.0	-19.2	11	14	1,000	0	0.0	0.0
C+ /5.6	11.3	1.01	18.14	2	2	94	3	1	1	88.7	-19.0	7	14	1,000	0	0.0	0.0
C /4.7	14.6	1.11	53.14	2,032	0	99	0	1	22	124.6	-16.8	21	49	1,000	0	5.8	0.0
C /4.7	14.6	1.11	54.47	286	0	99	0	1	22	127.7	-16.8	24	49	1,000	0	0.0	0.0
C /4.6	14.6	1.11	45.24	305	0	99	0	1	22	115.6	-17.1	15	49	1,000	0	0.0	0.0
C /4.6	14.6	1.11	51.87	37	0	99	0	1	22	121.6	-16.9	19	49	1,000	0	0.0	0.0
C /4.7	14.6	1.11	54.83	356	0	99	0	1	22	128.1	-16.8	25	49	1,000,000	0	0.0	0.0
C+ /6.6	9.3	0.88	23.62	1,752	4	86	0	10	50	103.3	-15.6	52	12	1,000	0	5.8	0.0
C+ /6.6	9.2	0.88	23.65	99	4	86	0	10	50	106.1	-15.5	56	12	1,000,000	0	0.0	0.0
C+ /6.6	9.2	0.88	23.43	273	4	86	0	10	50	95.2	-15.8	42	12	1,000	0	0.0	0.0
C+ /6.6	9.2	0.88	23.61	7	4	86	0	10	50	100.5	-15.6	49	12	1,000	0	0.0	0.0
C+ /6.6	9.3	0.88	23.66	11	4	86	0	10	50	105.8	-15.6	57	12	1,000,000	0	0.0	0.0
C /5.0	12.7	1.11	15.03	81	0	100	0	0	36	111.4	-20.8	16	8	1,000	0	5.8	0.0
C /5.0	12.8	1.11	15.22	19	0	100	0	0	36	114.8	-20.6	17	8	1,000	0	0.0	0.0
C /5.0	12.7	1.11	14.32	20	0	100	0	0	36	103.8	-21.0	11	8	1,000	0	0.0	0.0
C /5.0	12.7	1.11	14.85	N/A	0	100	0	0	36	109.5	-20.9	14	8	1,000	0	0.0	0.0
C /5.0	12.7	1.11	15.26	20	0	100	0	0	36	116.0	-20.6	19	8	1,000,000	0	0.0	0.0

I. Index of Stock Mutual Funds

Fund Type	Fund Name	Ticker Symbol	Overall Investment Rating	Phone	Performance Rating/Pts	3 Mo	6 Mo	1Yr / Pct	3Yr / Pct	5Yr / Pct	Dividend Yield	Expense Ratio
GI	Franklin Founding Funds 529 Port A		C+	(800) 342-5236	C / 4.5	6.72	9.27	25.05 / 73	3.52 / 37	8.55 / 47	0.00	1.32
GI	● Franklin Founding Funds 529 Port B		C+	(800) 342-5236	C / 5.0	6.49	8.84	24.09 / 70	2.73 / 29	7.74 / 40	0.00	2.07
GI	Franklin Founding Funds 529 Port C		C+	(800) 342-5236	C / 5.0	6.56	8.92	24.11 / 70	2.73 / 29	7.75 / 40	0.00	2.07
GI	Franklin Founding Funds Alloc A	FFALX	C	(800) 342-5236	C / 4.6	6.72	9.36	25.14 / 74	3.70 / 39	8.77 / 49	1.97	1.00
GI	Franklin Founding Funds Alloc Adv	FFAAX	C+	(800) 321-8563	C+ / 6.0	6.82	9.45	25.39 / 74	3.94 / 42	9.03 / 51	2.31	0.75
GI	Franklin Founding Funds Alloc C	FFACX	C	(800) 342-5236	C / 5.1	6.49	8.92	24.15 / 70	2.90 / 31	7.96 / 42	1.43	1.75
GI	Franklin Founding Funds Alloc R	FFARX	C+	(800) 342-5236	C / 5.5	6.64	9.19	24.69 / 72	3.42 / 36	8.48 / 46	1.86	1.25
OT	Franklin Global Listed Infra A	FLGIX	D+	(800) 342-5236	C- / 3.3	7.88	1.07	17.26 / 40	4.58 / 50	—	1.65	2.24
OT	Franklin Global Listed Infra Adv	FLGZX	C-	(800) 342-5236	C / 4.7	8.00	1.15	17.54 / 41	4.86 / 53	—	2.01	1.99
OT	Franklin Global Listed Infra C		C-	(800) 342-5236	C- / 3.8	7.74	0.69	16.40 / 36	3.81 / 41	—	1.14	2.99
OT	Franklin Global Listed Infra R		C-	(800) 342-5236	C- / 4.2	7.82	0.94	17.00 / 38	4.32 / 47	—	1.62	2.49
OT	Franklin Global Listed Infra R6		C	(800) 342-5236	C / 4.8	7.96	1.23	17.72 / 42	4.98 / 54	—	2.15	2.26
IX	Franklin Global Real Estate A	FGRRX	D+	(800) 342-5236	D+ / 2.3	6.74	-4.00	9.68 / 11	5.38 / 58	7.22 / 36	3.24	1.54
IX	Franklin Global Real Estate Adv	FVGRX	C-	(800) 342-5236	C- / 3.5	6.84	-3.82	9.94 / 11	5.70 / 62	7.53 / 38	3.70	1.29
IX	Franklin Global Real Estate C	FCGRX	D+	(800) 342-5236	D+ / 2.8	6.58	-4.29	8.93 / 9	4.67 / 50	6.48 / 31	2.68	2.29
RE	Franklin Global Real Estate R6		C-	(800) 342-5236	C- / 3.6	6.80	-3.78	10.11 / 12	5.83 / 63	7.64 / 39	3.85	1.23
PM	Franklin Gold & Precious Metals A	FKRCX	E-	(800) 342-5236	D- / 1.3	11.36	-7.21	32.77 / 91	-0.71 / 10	-13.34 / 0	7.35	1.11
PM	Franklin Gold & Precious Metals Adv	FGADX	E-	(800) 321-8563	D / 2.0	11.46	-7.03	33.11 / 92	-0.46 / 11	-13.12 / 0	7.48	0.86
PM	Franklin Gold & Precious Metals C	FRGOX	E-	(800) 342-5236	D- / 1.5	11.16	-7.51	31.74 / 89	-1.45 / 8	-13.98 / 0	7.75	1.86
PM	Franklin Gold & Precious Metals R6	FGPMX	E-	(800) 342-5236	D / 2.1	11.58	-6.93	33.48 / 92	-0.18 / 13	-12.95 / 0	7.65	0.62
GI	Franklin Gr and Inc 529 Port A		C	(800) 342-5236	D / 2.0	4.81	4.53	12.55 / 20	2.59 / 28	5.29 / 23	0.00	1.34
GI	● Franklin Gr and Inc 529 Port B		C	(800) 342-5236	D+ / 2.3	4.60	4.13	11.70 / 17	1.80 / 23	4.50 / 18	0.00	2.09
GI	Franklin Gr and Inc 529 Port C		C	(800) 342-5236	D+ / 2.3	4.61	4.14	11.69 / 17	1.81 / 23	4.51 / 18	0.00	2.09
GI	Franklin Growth 529 Port A		A+	(800) 342-5236	B / 7.9	8.63	9.61	23.21 / 67	9.77 / 92	12.44 / 78	0.00	1.29
GI	● Franklin Growth 529 Port B		A+	(800) 342-5236	B+ / 8.4	8.42	9.18	22.29 / 64	8.94 / 86	11.59 / 71	0.00	2.04
GI	Franklin Growth 529 Port C		A+	(800) 342-5236	B+ / 8.4	8.45	9.21	22.31 / 64	8.91 / 86	11.58 / 71	0.00	2.04
* GR	Franklin Growth A	FKGRX	A-	(800) 342-5236	B / 8.1	8.69	9.71	23.48 / 68	10.02 / 93	12.76 / 82	0.44	0.88
GR	Franklin Growth Adv	FCGAX	A+	(800) 321-8563	A- / 9.2	8.77	9.85	23.79 / 69	10.30 / 95	13.04 / 84	0.71	0.63
GI	Franklin Growth Allocation A	FGTIX	C-	(800) 342-5236	C- / 3.3	6.54	5.75	17.52 / 41	3.79 / 40	7.22 / 36	0.71	1.35
GI	Franklin Growth Allocation Adv	FGTZX	C	(800) 321-8563	C / 4.6	6.59	5.86	17.88 / 42	4.05 / 44	7.49 / 38	0.98	1.10
GI	Franklin Growth Allocation C	FTGTX	C-	(800) 342-5236	C- / 3.8	6.36	5.36	16.73 / 37	3.01 / 32	6.43 / 31	0.06	2.10
GI	Franklin Growth Allocation R	FGTRX	C	(800) 342-5236	C- / 4.2	6.43	5.63	17.28 / 40	3.53 / 37	6.95 / 34	0.48	1.60
AA	Franklin Growth Allocation R6		C	(800) 342-5236	C / 4.7	6.65	5.92	18.01 / 43	4.18 / 45	7.54 / 39	1.14	0.97
GR	Franklin Growth C	FRGSX	A	(800) 342-5236	B+ / 8.6	8.49	9.30	22.54 / 65	9.20 / 88	11.91 / 73	0.00	1.63
AG	Franklin Growth Opportunities A	FGRAX	C-	(800) 342-5236	C / 4.8	10.06	6.91	19.04 / 47	5.11 / 55	10.77 / 64	0.00	1.03
AG	Franklin Growth Opportunities Adv	FRAAX	C	(800) 321-8563	C+ / 6.3	10.16	7.04	19.37 / 49	5.39 / 58	11.08 / 66	0.00	0.78
AG	Franklin Growth Opportunities C	FKACX	C-	(800) 342-5236	C / 5.4	9.90	6.56	18.18 / 44	4.35 / 47	9.97 / 58	0.00	1.78
AG	Franklin Growth Opportunities R	FKARX	C	(800) 342-5236	C+ / 5.8	10.00	6.77	18.77 / 46	4.87 / 53	10.53 / 62	0.00	1.28
GR	Franklin Growth Opportunities R6	FOPPX	C	(800) 342-5236	C+ / 6.4	10.21	7.15	19.63 / 50	5.59 / 60	11.24 / 68	0.00	0.57
GR	Franklin Growth R	FGSRX	A+	(800) 342-5236	B+ / 8.9	8.63	9.58	23.17 / 67	9.75 / 92	12.48 / 79	0.24	1.13
GR	Franklin Growth R6	FIFRX	A+	(800) 342-5236	A / 9.3	8.81	9.94	23.99 / 70	10.49 / 96	13.13 / 85	0.84	0.46
GI	Franklin Income 529 Port A		C+	(800) 342-5236	C- / 4.1	6.22	7.55	23.15 / 67	3.27 / 34	6.92 / 34	0.00	1.21
GI	● Franklin Income 529 Port B		C+	(800) 342-5236	C / 4.3	6.03	7.17	22.22 / 63	2.51 / 28	6.12 / 29	0.00	1.96
GI	Franklin Income 529 Port C		C+	(800) 342-5236	C / 4.3	6.07	7.22	22.28 / 63	2.51 / 28	6.14 / 29	0.00	1.96
* GL	Franklin Income A	FKINX	C-	(800) 342-5236	C / 4.3	6.27	7.71	23.37 / 68	3.63 / 38	7.31 / 37	4.87	0.61
GL	Franklin Income Adv	FRIAX	C+	(800) 321-8563	C / 5.5	6.35	7.83	23.76 / 69	3.80 / 40	7.53 / 38	5.24	0.46
GL	Franklin Income C	FCISX	C	(800) 342-5236	C / 4.9	6.05	7.80	23.00 / 67	3.20 / 34	6.78 / 33	4.54	1.11
GL	Franklin Income R	FISRX	C	(800) 342-5236	C / 5.1	6.28	7.64	23.42 / 68	3.32 / 35	6.96 / 34	4.85	0.96
AA	Franklin Income R6	FNCFX	C+	(800) 342-5236	C / 5.5	6.36	7.86	23.82 / 69	3.87 / 41	7.53 / 38	5.30	0.38
EM	Franklin India Growth Fund A	FINGX	A+	(800) 342-5236	A+ / 9.8	9.89	-1.32	30.84 / 88	15.88 / 99	7.75 / 40	0.00	2.04
EM	Franklin India Growth Fund Adv	FIGZX	A+	(800) 321-8563	A+ / 9.8	9.90	-1.22	31.05 / 88	16.19 / 99	8.06 / 43	0.00	1.79
EM	Franklin India Growth Fund C	FINDX	A+	(800) 342-5236	A+ / 9.8	9.61	-1.71	29.71 / 86	15.04 / 99	6.96 / 34	0.00	2.79

99 Pct = Best
0 Pct = Worst

PERFORMANCE — Total Return % through 2/28/17 — Annualized — Incl. in Returns

● Denotes fund is closed to new investors
* Denotes fund is included in Section II

www.thestreetratings.com

RISK			NET ASSETS		ASSET				Portfolio Turnover Ratio	BULL / BEAR		FUND MANAGER		MINIMUMS		LOADS	
	3 Year		NAV							Last Bull Market Return	Last Bear Market Return	Manager Quality Pct	Manager Tenure (Years)	Initial Purch. $	Additional Purch. $	Front End Load	Back End Load
Risk Rating/Pts	Standard Deviation	Beta	As of 2/28/17	Total $(Mil)	Cash %	Stocks %	Bonds %	Other %									
B- / 7.2	10.1	0.90	18.27	176	0	0	0	100	0	76.5	-17.6	11	12	250	0	5.8	0.0
B- / 7.1	10.0	0.89	16.74	7	0	0	0	100	0	69.4	-17.8	8	12	250	0	0.0	0.0
B- / 7.1	10.1	0.90	16.73	77	0	0	0	100	0	69.5	-17.8	7	12	250	0	0.0	0.0
C+ / 6.2	10.0	0.89	13.98	3,333	2	74	18	6	0	78.5	-17.4	13	14	1,000	0	5.8	0.0
C+ / 6.2	10.0	0.89	14.06	131	2	74	18	6	0	80.9	-17.4	14	14	1,000	0	0.0	0.0
C+ / 6.3	9.9	0.88	13.75	1,405	2	74	18	6	0	71.3	-17.7	9	14	1,000	0	0.0	0.0
C+ / 6.3	9.9	0.88	13.99	11	2	74	18	6	0	76.1	-17.6	11	14	1,000	0	0.0	0.0
C+ / 5.7	11.4	0.71	12.00	28	12	87	0	1	64	N/A	N/A	38	4	1,000	0	5.8	0.0
C+ / 5.7	11.4	0.71	12.02	2	12	87	0	1	64	N/A	N/A	41	4	0	0	0.0	0.0
C+ / 5.7	11.4	0.72	11.92	6	12	87	0	1	64	N/A	N/A	28	4	1,000	0	0.0	0.0
C+ / 5.7	11.4	0.72	11.98	N/A	12	87	0	1	64	N/A	N/A	34	4	1,000	0	0.0	0.0
C+ / 5.7	11.4	0.72	12.02	N/A	12	87	0	1	64	N/A	N/A	43	4	1,000,000	0	0.0	0.0
C+ / 6.5	12.3	0.69	8.77	83	10	89	0	1	28	68.7	-19.0	51	7	1,000	0	5.8	0.0
C+ / 6.5	12.3	0.69	8.81	47	10	89	0	1	28	71.3	-18.9	56	7	0	0	0.0	0.0
C+ / 6.5	12.3	0.69	8.67	17	10	89	0	1	28	62.4	-19.3	42	7	1,000	0	0.0	0.0
C+ / 6.5	12.2	0.86	8.80	N/A	10	89	0	1	28	72.2	-18.9	30	7	1,000,000	0	0.0	0.0
E+ / 0.6	41.6	2.29	17.66	857	1	98	0	1	17	-48.1	-21.1	92	18	1,000	0	5.8	0.0
E+ / 0.6	41.6	2.29	18.72	162	1	98	0	1	17	-47.3	-21.1	93	18	0	0	0.0	0.0
E+ / 0.6	41.6	2.29	16.37	162	1	98	0	1	17	-50.1	-21.4	90	18	1,000	0	0.0	0.0
E+ / 0.6	41.6	2.29	18.86	4	1	98	0	1	17	-46.9	-21.1	94	18	1,000,000	0	0.0	0.0
B / 8.9	6.1	0.56	23.31	79	0	0	0	100	0	44.2	-10.8	33	12	250	0	5.8	0.0
B / 8.8	6.1	0.56	20.91	2	0	0	0	100	0	38.4	-11.0	25	12	250	0	0.0	0.0
B / 8.8	6.1	0.56	20.63	41	0	0	0	100	0	38.5	-11.0	25	12	250	0	0.0	0.0
B / 8.3	10.2	0.95	30.10	68	0	0	0	100	0	119.7	-16.1	71	14	250	0	5.8	0.0
B / 8.2	10.2	0.95	26.39	2	0	0	0	100	0	111.0	-16.4	61	14	250	0	0.0	0.0
B / 8.2	10.2	0.95	28.23	21	0	0	0	100	0	110.8	-16.4	61	14	250	0	0.0	0.0
C+ / 6.7	10.2	0.95	82.45	7,478	4	95	0	1	8	123.3	-16.0	73	9	1,000	0	5.8	0.0
C+ / 6.6	10.2	0.95	82.59	2,129	4	95	0	1	8	126.3	-15.9	75	9	1,000	0	0.0	0.0
C+ / 6.6	8.5	0.78	18.31	827	3	78	17	2	20	63.1	-15.1	22	17	1,000	0	5.8	0.0
C+ / 6.6	8.5	0.78	18.38	40	3	78	17	2	20	65.4	-15.0	24	17	1,000	0	0.0	0.0
C+ / 6.7	8.5	0.78	17.83	311	3	78	17	2	20	56.6	-15.3	15	17	1,000	0	0.0	0.0
C+ / 6.7	8.5	0.78	18.08	113	3	78	17	2	20	60.9	-15.1	19	17	1,000	0	0.0	0.0
C+ / 6.6	8.5	1.31	18.37	3	3	78	17	2	20	65.5	-15.1	13	17	1,000,000	0	0.0	0.0
C+ / 6.7	10.2	0.95	76.16	862	4	95	0	1	8	114.3	-16.2	65	9	1,000	0	0.0	0.0
C / 4.9	13.2	1.07	33.59	2,231	0	99	0	1	26	108.2	-20.0	10	10	1,000	0	5.8	0.0
C / 4.9	13.2	1.07	35.70	482	0	99	0	1	26	111.5	-19.9	11	10	1,000	0	0.0	0.0
C / 4.8	13.2	1.07	29.11	383	0	99	0	1	26	100.2	-20.2	7	10	1,000	0	0.0	0.0
C / 4.9	13.2	1.07	32.36	50	0	99	0	1	26	105.7	-20.0	8	10	1,000	0	0.0	0.0
C / 5.0	13.2	1.08	35.97	276	0	99	0	1	26	113.0	-19.9	12	10	1,000,000	0	0.0	0.0
C+ / 6.7	10.2	0.95	82.14	480	4	95	0	1	8	120.2	-16.1	71	9	1,000	0	0.0	0.0
C+ / 6.6	10.2	0.95	82.51	1,352	4	95	0	1	8	126.9	-16.0	77	9	1,000,000	0	0.0	0.0
B- / 7.6	8.7	0.71	27.50	126	0	0	0	100	0	57.5	-11.9	23	12	250	0	4.3	0.0
B- / 7.5	8.7	0.71	24.97	3	0	0	0	100	0	51.2	-12.1	17	12	250	0	0.0	0.0
B- / 7.5	8.7	0.71	24.81	60	0	0	0	100	0	51.3	-12.2	17	12	250	0	0.0	0.0
C+ / 6.0	8.8	1.23	2.36	46,472	4	46	38	12	61	61.4	-11.7	48	15	1,000	0	4.3	0.0
C+ / 6.0	8.7	1.22	2.34	9,063	4	46	38	12	61	62.5	-11.7	51	15	1,000	0	0.0	0.0
C+ / 6.0	8.6	1.19	2.39	24,044	4	46	38	12	61	56.9	-11.7	45	15	1,000	0	0.0	0.0
C+ / 6.0	8.8	1.22	2.32	396	4	46	38	12	61	58.0	-11.5	44	15	1,000	0	0.0	0.0
C+ / 6.0	8.8	1.20	2.34	1,771	4	46	38	12	61	63.0	-11.7	16	15	1,000,000	0	0.0	0.0
C+ / 6.5	17.9	0.62	13.45	53	98	1	0	1	22	56.5	-18.5	99	9	1,000	0	5.8	0.0
C+ / 6.5	17.9	0.62	13.76	25	98	1	0	1	22	58.7	-18.4	99	9	1,000,000	0	0.0	0.0
C+ / 6.4	17.9	0.62	12.66	16	98	1	0	1	22	50.3	-18.7	99	9	1,000	0	0.0	0.0

Fund Type	Fund Name	Ticker Symbol	Overall Investment Rating	Phone	Performance Rating/Pts	3 Mo	6 Mo	1Yr / Pct	3Yr / Pct	5Yr / Pct	Dividend Yield	Expense Ratio
				99 Pct = Best				Total Return % through 2/28/17	Annualized		Incl. in Returns	
FO	Franklin India Growth Fund R6	FIGEX	A+	(800) 342-5236	A+ / 9.9	9.94	-1.14	31.24 /89	16.36 /99	8.18 /43	0.00	1.63
FO	● Franklin Inter Small Cap Growth A	FINAX	E+	(800) 342-5236	E / 0.5	7.76	5.07	11.64 /17	-1.91 / 7	8.70 /48	0.89	1.38
FO	● Franklin Inter Small Cap Growth Adv	FKSCX	E+	(800) 342-5236	E+ / 0.9	7.89	5.20	11.89 /18	-1.68 / 7	8.98 /50	1.16	1.14
FO	● Franklin Inter Small Cap Growth C	FCSMX	E+	(800) 342-5236	E+ / 0.6	7.62	4.65	10.76 /14	-2.64 / 5	7.90 /41	0.12	2.14
FO	● Franklin Inter Small Cap Growth R	FISDX	E+	(800) 342-5236	E+ / 0.8	7.80	4.93	11.35 /16	-2.16 / 6	8.45 /46	0.62	1.64
FO	● Franklin Inter Small Cap Growth R6	FCAPX	E+	(800) 342-5236	E+ / 0.9	7.93	5.24	12.12 /18	-1.53 / 8	9.08 /51	1.41	0.99
FO	Franklin International Growth A	FNGAX	D	(800) 342-5236	D / 1.8	8.94	3.53	15.76 /33	0.75 /17	4.52 /18	0.47	1.46
FO	Franklin International Growth Adv	FNGZX	D	(800) 321-8563	D+ / 2.8	9.10	3.62	16.12 /35	1.02 /18	4.82 /20	0.84	1.21
FO	Franklin International Growth C		D	(800) 342-5236	D / 2.2	8.81	3.15	14.99 /30	0.04 /13	3.79 /14	0.00	2.21
FO	Franklin International Growth R		D	(800) 342-5236	D+ / 2.5	9.00	3.46	15.50 /32	0.53 /16	4.31 /17	0.10	1.71
FO	Franklin International Growth R6	FILRX	D+	(800) 342-5236	D+ / 2.9	9.11	3.74	16.34 /36	1.22 /19	4.95 /21	1.12	0.82
GL	Franklin K2 Alternative Strat A	FAAAX	C-	(800) 342-5236	D- / 1.2	2.98	2.79	7.27 / 6	1.84 /23	--	0.42	3.40
GL	Franklin K2 Alternative Strat Adv	FABZX	C	(800) 342-5236	D / 1.8	3.01	2.91	7.49 / 7	2.14 /25	--	0.75	3.15
GL	Franklin K2 Alternative Strat C	FASCX	C-	(800) 342-5236	D- / 1.4	2.73	2.35	6.45 / 5	1.11 /19	--	0.00	4.15
GL	Franklin K2 Alternative Strat R	FSKKX	C	(800) 342-5236	D / 1.6	2.81	2.62	6.97 / 6	1.45 /21	--	0.47	3.65
GL	Franklin K2 Alternative Strat R6	FASRX	C	(800) 342-5236	D / 1.9	3.02	2.92	7.60 / 7	2.16 /25	--	0.85	3.06
FS	Franklin K2 Long Short Credit A	FKLSX	U	(800) 342-5236	U /	2.23	3.60	10.92 /14	--	--	2.86	3.61
GR	Franklin Large Cap Growth VIP 2		C-	(800) 342-5236	B / 7.8	9.88	8.57	20.91 /57	7.98 /79	10.89 /65	0.00	1.03
GL	Franklin LifeSmart 2020 Ret Tgt A	FLRMX	C-	(800) 342-5236	D / 1.7	4.39	3.91	12.55 /20	2.15 /25	--	1.40	1.75
GL	Franklin LifeSmart 2020 Ret Tgt Adv	FLROX	C	(800) 342-5236	D+ / 2.7	4.55	4.04	12.91 /21	2.46 /27	--	1.72	1.50
GL	Franklin LifeSmart 2020 Ret Tgt C	FLRQX	C-	(800) 342-5236	D / 2.1	4.29	3.53	11.80 /17	1.44 /21	--	0.78	2.50
GL	Franklin LifeSmart 2020 Ret Tgt R	FLRVX	C	(800) 342-5236	D+ / 2.4	4.42	3.87	12.37 /19	1.92 /23	--	1.21	2.00
GL	Franklin LifeSmart 2020 Ret Tgt R6	FRTSX	C	(800) 342-5236	D+ / 2.7	4.47	4.07	12.96 /21	2.48 /27	--	1.77	1.38
GL	Franklin LifeSmart 2025 Ret Tgt A	FTRTX	D+	(800) 342-5236	D / 2.0	5.28	4.63	14.36 /27	2.14 /25	6.23 /30	1.04	1.47
GL	Franklin LifeSmart 2025 Ret Tgt Adv	FLRFX	C-	(800) 342-5236	C- / 3.0	5.35	4.78	14.70 /29	2.44 /27	6.53 /32	1.34	1.22
GL	Franklin LifeSmart 2025 Ret Tgt C	FTTCX	C-	(800) 342-5236	D+ / 2.4	5.14	4.27	13.63 /24	1.42 /21	5.50 /25	0.38	2.22
GL	Franklin LifeSmart 2025 Ret Tgt R	FRELX	C-	(800) 342-5236	D+ / 2.6	5.15	4.51	14.07 /26	1.91 /23	5.99 /28	0.89	1.72
GL	Franklin LifeSmart 2025 Ret Tgt R6	FTLMX	C-	(800) 342-5236	C- / 3.1	5.36	4.83	14.74 /29	2.49 /27	6.58 /32	1.38	1.09
GL	Franklin LifeSmart 2030 Ret Tgt A	FLRSX	C-	(800) 342-5236	D+ / 2.4	5.73	5.06	15.47 /32	2.83 /30	--	0.69	1.90
GL	Franklin LifeSmart 2030 Ret Tgt Adv	FLRZX	C	(800) 342-5236	C- / 3.6	5.76	5.19	15.69 /33	3.09 /33	--	0.94	1.65
GL	Franklin LifeSmart 2030 Ret Tgt C	FLRTX	C-	(800) 342-5236	D+ / 2.8	5.46	4.60	14.54 /28	2.09 /25	--	0.09	2.65
GL	Franklin LifeSmart 2030 Ret Tgt R	FLRWX	C	(800) 342-5236	C- / 3.2	5.69	4.93	15.14 /30	2.58 /28	--	0.51	2.15
GL	Franklin LifeSmart 2030 Ret Tgt R6	FLERX	C	(800) 342-5236	C- / 3.6	5.80	5.14	15.72 /33	3.13 /33	--	0.99	1.43
GL	Franklin LifeSmart 2035 Ret Tgt A	FRTAX	D+	(800) 342-5236	D+ / 2.4	6.06	5.35	16.35 /36	2.57 /28	6.84 /34	0.72	1.55
GL	Franklin LifeSmart 2035 Ret Tgt Adv	FLRHX	C-	(800) 342-5236	C- / 3.6	6.09	5.47	16.60 /37	2.83 /30	7.13 /35	0.98	1.30
GL	Franklin LifeSmart 2035 Ret Tgt C	FTRCX	C-	(800) 342-5236	D+ / 2.8	5.79	4.88	15.39 /32	1.79 /23	6.06 /29	0.08	2.30
GL	Franklin LifeSmart 2035 Ret Tgt R	FLRGX	C-	(800) 342-5236	C- / 3.2	5.91	5.19	16.00 /34	2.33 /26	6.61 /32	0.61	1.80
GL	Franklin LifeSmart 2035 Ret Tgt R6	FMTLX	C-	(800) 342-5236	C- / 3.6	6.06	5.44	16.68 /37	2.87 /30	7.16 /36	1.04	1.12
GL	Franklin LifeSmart 2040 Ret Tgt A	FLADX	C-	(800) 342-5236	D+ / 2.6	6.13	5.47	16.48 /36	2.92 /31	--	0.67	2.14
GL	Franklin LifeSmart 2040 Ret Tgt Adv	FLSHX	C	(800) 342-5236	C- / 3.9	6.17	5.51	16.69 /37	3.24 /34	--	0.77	1.89
GL	Franklin LifeSmart 2040 Ret Tgt C	FLOLX	C-	(800) 342-5236	C- / 3.1	6.00	5.05	15.59 /32	2.21 /25	--	0.52	2.89
GL	Franklin LifeSmart 2040 Ret Tgt R	FLSGX	C	(800) 342-5236	C- / 3.5	6.09	5.24	16.13 /35	2.72 /29	--	0.65	2.39
GL	Franklin LifeSmart 2040 Ret Tgt R6	FLREX	C	(800) 342-5236	C- / 3.9	6.27	5.62	16.80 /38	3.29 /35	--	0.78	1.58
GL	Franklin LifeSmart 2045 Ret Tgt A	FTTAX	D+	(800) 342-5236	D+ / 2.5	6.25	5.53	16.78 /38	2.61 /28	7.03 /35	0.73	1.73
GL	Franklin LifeSmart 2045 Ret Tgt Adv	FLRLX	C-	(800) 342-5236	C- / 3.7	6.25	5.63	17.00 /38	2.88 /31	7.33 /37	0.97	1.48
GL	Franklin LifeSmart 2045 Ret Tgt C	FLRIX	C-	(800) 342-5236	C- / 3.0	6.09	5.17	15.86 /34	1.89 /23	6.27 /30	0.09	2.48
GL	Franklin LifeSmart 2045 Ret Tgt R	FLRJX	C-	(800) 342-5236	C- / 3.3	6.14	5.33	16.40 /36	2.36 /26	6.79 /33	0.57	1.98
GL	Franklin LifeSmart 2045 Ret Tgt R6	FMLTX	C-	(800) 342-5236	C- / 3.8	6.31	5.69	17.06 /39	2.96 /31	7.39 /37	1.02	1.20
GI	Franklin LifeSmart 2050 Ret Tgt A	FLSJX	C-	(800) 342-5236	D+ / 2.9	6.29	5.63	16.94 /38	3.28 /34	--	0.68	2.55
GI	Franklin LifeSmart 2050 Ret Tgt Adv	FLSOX	C	(800) 342-5236	C- / 4.2	6.36	5.70	17.17 /39	3.55 /38	--	0.89	2.30
GI	Franklin LifeSmart 2050 Ret Tgt C	FLSKX	C	(800) 342-5236	C- / 3.3	6.10	5.16	15.96 /34	2.50 /27	--	0.10	3.30
GI	Franklin LifeSmart 2050 Ret Tgt R	FLSNX	C	(800) 342-5236	C- / 3.7	6.17	5.42	16.60 /37	3.03 /32	--	0.52	2.80

● Denotes fund is closed to new investors
* Denotes fund is included in Section II

Risk Rating/Pts	Standard Deviation	Beta	NAV As of 2/28/17	Total $(Mil)	Cash %	Stocks %	Bonds %	Other %	Portfolio Turnover Ratio	Last Bull Market Return	Last Bear Market Return	Manager Quality Pct	Manager Tenure (Years)	Initial Purch. $	Additional Purch. $	Front End Load	Back End Load
C+ / 6.5	17.9	0.67	13.82	12	98	1	0	1	22	59.5	-18.4	99	9	1,000,000	0	0.0	0.0
C / 4.9	12.9	0.84	17.32	144	5	94	0	1	22	72.6	-20.3	51	11	1,000	0	5.8	0.0
C / 4.8	12.9	0.84	17.35	612	5	94	0	1	22	75.0	-20.2	54	11	0	0	0.0	0.0
C / 4.9	13.0	0.84	17.16	20	5	94	0	1	22	65.9	-20.5	41	11	1,000	0	0.0	0.0
C / 4.9	13.0	0.84	17.38	4	5	94	0	1	22	70.3	-20.4	48	11	1,000	0	0.0	0.0
C / 4.8	13.0	0.84	17.34	434	5	94	0	1	22	75.8	-20.2	57	11	1,000,000	0	0.0	0.0
C+ / 5.6	12.3	0.95	11.41	168	1	98	0	1	27	48.7	-25.1	80	9	1,000	0	5.8	0.0
C+ / 5.6	12.3	0.95	11.45	106	1	98	0	1	27	51.1	-25.0	82	9	0	0	0.0	0.0
C / 5.5	12.3	0.95	11.12	6	1	98	0	1	27	43.1	-25.2	75	9	1,000	0	0.0	0.0
C+ / 5.6	12.3	0.95	11.40	N/A	1	98	0	1	27	47.0	-25.1	79	9	1,000	0	0.0	0.0
C+ / 5.6	12.3	0.95	11.45	47	1	98	0	1	27	52.0	-25.0	83	9	1,000,000	0	0.0	0.0
B / 8.9	4.1	0.24	11.02	139	33	34	14	19	230	N/A	N/A	85	4	1,000	0	5.8	0.0
B / 8.9	4.1	0.25	11.03	633	33	34	14	19	230	N/A	N/A	86	4	1,000,000	0	0.0	0.0
B / 8.9	4.2	0.25	10.90	61	33	34	14	19	230	N/A	N/A	81	4	1,000	0	0.0	0.0
B / 8.9	4.2	0.25	11.05	1	33	34	14	19	230	N/A	N/A	83	4	1,000	0	0.0	0.0
B / 8.9	4.1	0.25	11.03	259	33	34	14	19	230	N/A	N/A	87	4	0	0	0.0	0.0
U /	N/A	N/A	10.41	37	0	0	0	100	512	N/A	N/A	N/A	2	1,000	0	5.8	0.0
D / 1.8	12.6	1.09	19.13	119	0	99	0	1	23	106.1	-17.3	31	3	0	0	0.0	0.0
B / 8.1	6.9	0.51	11.04	19	12	54	33	1	48	N/A	N/A	87	4	1,000	0	5.8	0.0
B / 8.1	6.9	0.51	11.07	N/A	12	54	33	1	48	N/A	N/A	88	4	1,000	0	0.0	0.0
B / 8.1	6.9	0.51	10.97	5	12	54	33	1	48	N/A	N/A	84	4	1,000	0	0.0	0.0
B / 8.1	6.9	0.51	11.02	3	12	54	33	1	48	N/A	N/A	86	4	1,000	0	0.0	0.0
B / 8.1	6.8	0.50	11.07	8	12	54	33	1	48	N/A	N/A	88	4	1,000,000	0	0.0	0.0
B- / 7.0	7.9	1.17	11.97	74	6	58	34	2	36	54.5	-14.4	32	11	1,000	0	5.8	0.0
B- / 7.0	7.9	1.18	12.00	1	6	58	34	2	36	56.9	-14.2	35	11	1,000	0	0.0	0.0
B- / 7.0	7.9	1.18	11.78	27	6	58	34	2	36	48.8	-14.7	24	11	1,000	0	0.0	0.0
B- / 7.0	7.9	1.17	11.91	8	6	58	34	2	36	52.8	-14.5	29	11	1,000	0	0.0	0.0
B- / 7.0	7.9	0.58	12.01	14	6	58	34	2	36	57.3	-14.2	88	11	1,000,000	0	0.0	0.0
B- / 7.4	8.3	0.61	11.59	17	13	70	15	2	44	N/A	N/A	90	4	1,000	0	5.8	0.0
B- / 7.4	8.3	0.61	11.62	N/A	13	70	15	2	44	N/A	N/A	91	4	1,000	0	0.0	0.0
B- / 7.4	8.3	0.61	11.46	5	13	70	15	2	44	N/A	N/A	87	4	1,000	0	0.0	0.0
B- / 7.4	8.4	0.62	11.56	2	13	70	15	2	44	N/A	N/A	89	4	1,000	0	0.0	0.0
B- / 7.4	8.3	0.61	11.63	15	13	70	15	2	44	N/A	N/A	91	4	1,000,000	0	0.0	0.0
C+ / 6.8	8.8	1.30	12.44	57	6	69	22	3	34	60.2	-15.3	30	11	1,000	0	5.8	0.0
C+ / 6.8	8.7	1.29	12.53	2	6	69	22	3	34	62.6	-15.3	34	11	1,000	0	0.0	0.0
C+ / 6.8	8.7	1.29	12.16	19	6	69	22	3	34	54.1	-15.7	23	11	1,000	0	0.0	0.0
C+ / 6.8	8.7	1.29	12.41	6	6	69	22	3	34	58.3	-15.5	28	11	1,000	0	0.0	0.0
C+ / 6.8	8.8	0.64	12.52	23	6	69	22	3	34	62.8	-15.3	90	11	1,000,000	0	0.0	0.0
B- / 7.2	8.8	0.65	11.76	14	14	75	9	2	42	N/A	N/A	90	4	1,000	0	5.8	0.0
B- / 7.2	8.9	0.65	11.82	N/A	14	75	9	2	42	N/A	N/A	91	4	1,000	0	0.0	0.0
B- / 7.2	8.8	0.65	11.59	3	14	75	9	2	42	N/A	N/A	87	4	1,000	0	0.0	0.0
B- / 7.2	8.8	0.65	11.72	2	14	75	9	2	42	N/A	N/A	89	4	1,000	0	0.0	0.0
B- / 7.2	8.8	0.65	11.83	15	14	75	9	2	42	N/A	N/A	91	4	1,000,000	0	0.0	0.0
C+ / 6.7	9.0	1.33	12.45	45	8	71	19	2	34	62.0	-15.6	29	11	1,000	0	5.8	0.0
C+ / 6.7	9.0	1.33	12.54	1	8	71	19	2	34	64.5	-15.5	32	11	1,000	0	0.0	0.0
C+ / 6.7	9.0	1.33	12.14	13	8	71	19	2	34	55.8	-15.9	22	11	1,000	0	0.0	0.0
C+ / 6.7	9.0	1.33	12.39	5	8	71	19	2	34	59.9	-15.7	27	11	1,000	0	0.0	0.0
C+ / 6.7	9.0	0.66	12.54	11	8	71	19	2	34	64.9	-15.5	90	11	1,000,000	0	0.0	0.0
B- / 7.1	8.9	0.81	11.87	11	14	77	7	2	49	N/A	N/A	15	4	1,000	0	5.8	0.0
B- / 7.1	8.9	0.81	11.93	N/A	14	77	7	2	49	N/A	N/A	17	4	1,000	0	0.0	0.0
B- / 7.2	8.9	0.81	11.79	3	14	77	7	2	49	N/A	N/A	10	4	1,000	0	0.0	0.0
B- / 7.1	8.9	0.81	11.86	1	14	77	7	2	49	N/A	N/A	13	4	1,000	0	0.0	0.0

99 Pct = Best
0 Pct = Worst

Fund Type	Fund Name	Ticker Symbol	Overall Investment Rating	Phone	Performance Rating/Pts	3 Mo	6 Mo	1Yr / Pct	3Yr / Pct (Annualized)	5Yr / Pct (Annualized)	Dividend Yield	Expense Ratio
GI	Franklin LifeSmart 2050 Ret Tgt R6	FRLEX	C	(800) 342-5236	C- / 4.2	6.41	5.76	17.23 /39	3.59 /38	--	0.94	1.76
GL	Franklin LifeSmart Ret Income A	FTRAX	D	(800) 342-5236	D- / 1.5	3.03	3.27	11.98 /18	1.81 /23	4.48 /18	3.34	1.57
GL	Franklin LifeSmart Ret Income Adv	FLRDX	D+	(800) 342-5236	D+ / 2.3	3.17	3.48	12.32 /19	2.09 /25	4.80 /20	3.78	1.32
GL	Franklin LifeSmart Ret Income R	FBRLX	D	(800) 342-5236	D / 2.0	2.97	3.15	11.73 /17	1.58 /21	4.27 /17	3.29	1.82
GL	Franklin LifeSmart Ret Income R6	FLMTX	D+	(800) 342-5236	D+ / 2.3	3.18	3.51	12.38 /19	2.15 /25	4.86 /20	3.83	1.21
GL	Franklin LifeSmart Retirement Inc C	FRTCX	D	(800) 342-5236	D / 1.7	2.86	2.91	11.12 /15	1.08 /19	3.75 /14	2.79	2.32
SC	Franklin MicroCap Value A	FRMCX	D	(800) 342-5236	C / 4.4	0.31	9.54	28.26 /82	4.06 /44	11.52 /70	0.29	1.21
SC	Franklin MicroCap Value Adv	FVRMX	C-	(800) 321-8563	C+ / 5.9	0.40	9.72	28.62 /83	4.32 /47	11.79 /72	0.54	0.97
SC	Franklin MicroCap Value R6	FMCVX	C-	(800) 342-5236	C+ / 6.0	0.43	9.77	28.77 /83	4.48 /48	11.86 /73	0.65	0.82
MC	Franklin MidCap Value A	FMVAX	C	(800) 342-5236	C+ / 5.9	5.68	9.33	26.82 /79	5.73 /62	10.70 /63	0.66	1.56
MC	Franklin MidCap Value Adv	FMVZX	C+	(800) 321-8563	B- / 7.1	5.73	9.50	27.12 /79	6.01 /64	11.03 /66	0.94	1.31
MC	Franklin MidCap Value C	FMVCX	C	(800) 342-5236	C+ / 6.4	5.43	8.92	25.85 /76	4.96 /54	9.91 /58	0.06	2.31
MC	Franklin MidCap Value R	FMVRX	C+	(800) 342-5236	C+ / 6.8	5.63	9.20	26.47 /78	5.49 /59	10.47 /62	0.46	1.81
GL	Franklin Moderate Allocation A	FMTIX	C-	(800) 342-5236	D+ / 2.4	5.35	4.72	14.79 /29	3.13 /33	5.60 /26	0.74	1.29
GL	Franklin Moderate Allocation Adv	FMTZX	C	(800) 321-8563	C- / 3.6	5.47	4.90	15.05 /30	3.40 /36	5.87 /27	1.02	1.04
GL	Franklin Moderate Allocation C	FTMTX	C-	(800) 342-5236	D+ / 2.9	5.19	4.39	13.93 /25	2.36 /26	4.82 /20	0.05	2.04
GL	Franklin Moderate Allocation R	FTMRX	C	(800) 342-5236	C- / 3.2	5.34	4.63	14.50 /28	2.87 /30	5.34 /24	0.50	1.54
GL	Franklin Moderate Allocation R6		C	(800) 342-5236	C- / 3.7	5.47	4.91	15.22 /31	3.51 /37	5.90 /28	1.15	0.94
GI	Franklin Mutual Beacon A	TEBIX	B-	(800) 342-5236	B / 7.8	9.01	11.16	29.99 /86	7.71 /77	11.34 /68	1.83	1.09
GI	Franklin Mutual Beacon C	TEMEX	B	(800) 342-5236	B / 8.2	8.72	10.67	28.99 /84	6.90 /71	10.54 /62	1.26	1.84
GI	Franklin Mutual Beacon R		B	(800) 342-5236	B+ / 8.7	8.88	10.98	29.65 /86	7.46 /75	11.10 /67	1.76	1.34
GR	Franklin Mutual Beacon R6	FMBRX	B+	(800) 321-8563	A- / 9.1	9.09	11.35	30.49 /87	8.10 /80	11.75 /72	2.24	0.74
GI	Franklin Mutual Beacon Z	BEGRX	B+	(800) 321-8563	A- / 9.0	9.00	11.19	30.30 /87	7.98 /79	11.65 /71	2.16	0.84
FO	Franklin Mutual European A	TEMIX	E	(800) 342-5236	E+ / 0.8	7.08	8.11	15.02 /30	-0.91 /10	6.42 /31	2.02	1.30
FO	Franklin Mutual European C	TEURX	E	(800) 342-5236	D- / 1.0	6.82	7.67	14.18 /26	-1.63 / 8	5.66 /26	1.31	2.05
FO	Franklin Mutual European R		E	(800) 342-5236	D- / 1.2	6.96	7.94	14.71 /29	-1.14 / 9	6.19 /30	1.78	1.55
FO	Franklin Mutual European R6	FMEUX	E	(800) 321-8563	D- / 1.5	7.19	8.36	15.54 /32	-0.48 /11	6.86 /34	2.53	0.89
FO	Franklin Mutual European Z	MEURX	E	(800) 321-8563	D- / 1.4	7.12	8.23	15.33 /31	-0.63 /11	6.73 /33	2.36	1.05
FS	Franklin Mutual Financial Svcs A	TFSIX	A+	(800) 342-5236	A- / 9.1	5.81	15.54	28.54 /83	10.54 /96	13.48 /89	1.03	1.38
FS	Franklin Mutual Financial Svcs C	TMFSX	A+	(800) 342-5236	A / 9.4	5.57	15.04	27.52 /81	9.74 /92	12.66 /80	0.41	2.13
FS	Franklin Mutual Financial Svcs R6	FMFVX	A+	(800) 321-8563	A+ / 9.7	5.83	15.72	29.01 /84	11.02 /97	13.94 /93	1.45	1.16
FS	Franklin Mutual Financial Svcs Z	TEFAX	A+	(800) 321-8563	A+ / 9.7	5.85	15.65	28.82 /84	10.85 /97	13.80 /92	1.31	1.13
* GL	Franklin Mutual Global Discovery A	TEDIX	C	(800) 342-5236	C+ / 5.8	6.64	10.92	25.00 /73	5.37 /58	9.47 /54	1.73	1.24
GL	Franklin Mutual Global Discovery C	TEDSX	C	(800) 342-5236	C+ / 6.3	6.42	10.51	24.09 /70	4.60 /50	8.68 /48	1.14	1.99
GL	Franklin Mutual Global Discovery R	TEDRX	C+	(800) 342-5236	C+ / 6.7	6.56	10.78	24.70 /72	5.12 /55	9.23 /52	1.64	1.49
GL	Franklin Mutual Global Discovery R6	FMDRX	C+	(800) 321-8563	B- / 7.1	6.73	11.14	25.49 /75	5.80 /63	9.91 /58	2.18	0.84
GL	Franklin Mutual Global Discovery Z	MDISX	C+	(800) 321-8563	B- / 7.0	6.68	11.05	25.32 /74	5.65 /61	9.78 /57	2.04	0.99
FO	Franklin Mutual International A	FMIAX	D	(800) 342-5236	D / 2.0	5.42	6.76	17.79 /42	0.98 /18	4.95 /21	1.52	1.49
FO	Franklin Mutual International C	FCMIX	D	(800) 342-5236	D+ / 2.4	5.35	6.48	17.03 /38	0.27 /15	4.22 /16	0.85	2.24
FO	Franklin Mutual International R	FRMIX	D	(800) 342-5236	D+ / 2.7	5.41	6.68	17.58 /41	0.76 /17	4.73 /20	1.44	1.74
FO	Franklin Mutual International R6	FIMFX	D+	(800) 342-5236	C- / 3.2	5.56	7.04	18.38 /45	1.40 /20	5.38 /24	2.03	1.06
FO	Franklin Mutual International Z	FMIZX	D+	(800) 342-5236	C- / 3.1	5.54	6.94	18.10 /43	1.25 /20	5.26 /23	1.87	1.24
GI	Franklin Mutual Quest A	TEQIX	D	(800) 342-5236	C- / 4.1	4.94	8.03	22.17 /63	4.26 /46	8.73 /48	5.75	1.07
GI	Franklin Mutual Quest C	TEMQX	D+	(800) 342-5236	C / 4.7	4.73	7.61	21.21 /58	3.50 /37	7.95 /42	5.47	1.82
GI	Franklin Mutual Quest R	FMQSX	C-	(800) 342-5236	C / 5.1	4.84	7.91	21.88 /62	4.01 /43	8.49 /46	5.90	1.32
GL	Franklin Mutual Quest R6	FMQRX	C-	(800) 321-8563	C+ / 5.7	5.02	8.21	22.60 /65	4.62 /50	9.10 /51	6.35	0.74
GI	Franklin Mutual Quest Z	MQIFX	C-	(800) 321-8563	C+ / 5.6	5.00	8.19	22.48 /64	4.57 /49	9.05 /51	6.26	0.82
GI	Franklin Mutual Shares 529 Port A		B-	(800) 342-5236	C+ / 6.9	6.94	10.85	27.29 /80	6.98 /72	10.79 /64	0.00	1.41
GI	● Franklin Mutual Shares 529 Port B		A-	(800) 342-5236	B- / 7.3	6.75	10.45	26.33 /77	6.18 /66	9.97 /58	0.00	2.16
GI	Franklin Mutual Shares 529 Port C		A-	(800) 342-5236	B- / 7.3	6.76	10.45	26.31 /77	6.17 /66	9.97 /58	0.00	2.16
GI	Franklin Mutual Shares A	TESIX	B-	(800) 342-5236	B- / 7.1	7.03	11.01	27.52 /81	7.21 /73	11.09 /67	1.76	1.06
GI	Franklin Mutual Shares C	TEMTX	B	(800) 342-5236	B- / 7.5	6.82	10.57	26.59 /78	6.44 /68	10.30 /61	1.21	1.81

● Denotes fund is closed to new investors
* Denotes fund is included in Section II

www.thestreetratings.com

RISK Risk Rating/Pts	3 Year Standard Deviation	Beta	NET ASSETS NAV As of 2/28/17	Total $(Mil)	ASSET Cash %	Stocks %	Bonds %	Other %	Portfolio Turnover Ratio	BULL/BEAR Last Bull Market Return	Last Bear Market Return	FUND MANAGER Manager Quality Pct	Manager Tenure (Years)	MINIMUMS Initial Purch. $	Additional Purch. $	LOADS Front End Load	Back End Load
B- /7.1	8.9	0.81	11.93	9	14	77	7	2	49	N/A	N/A	18	4	1,000,000	0	0.0	0.0
C+ /6.3	5.5	0.80	11.08	38	5	15	77	3	38	38.1	-10.5	50	11	1,000	0	5.8	0.0
C+ /6.3	5.5	0.80	11.13	2	5	15	77	3	38	40.3	-10.3	54	11	1,000	0	0.0	0.0
C+ /6.3	5.5	0.80	11.04	5	5	15	77	3	38	36.4	-10.5	47	11	1,000	0	0.0	0.0
C+ /6.3	5.5	0.39	11.14	4	5	15	77	3	38	40.7	-10.3	87	11	1,000,000	0	0.0	0.0
C+ /6.3	5.5	0.79	10.95	17	5	15	77	3	38	32.9	-10.7	40	11	1,000	0	0.0	0.0
C- /3.8	13.9	0.73	32.58	261	4	95	0	1	12	98.4	-15.9	63	22	1,000	0	5.8	0.0
C- /3.8	13.9	0.73	32.75	73	4	95	0	1	12	101.1	-15.8	66	22	1,000,000	0	0.0	0.0
C- /3.8	13.9	0.73	32.88	23	4	95	0	1	12	101.4	-15.9	68	22	1,000,000	0	0.0	0.0
C /4.9	11.4	0.91	15.87	149	3	96	0	1	87	101.5	-22.7	37	12	1,000	0	5.8	0.0
C /4.9	11.4	0.90	15.93	7	3	96	0	1	87	104.7	-22.6	41	12	1,000,000	0	0.0	0.0
C /4.9	11.4	0.91	15.60	27	3	96	0	1	87	94.0	-22.9	29	12	1,000	0	0.0	0.0
C /5.0	11.4	0.90	15.89	1	3	96	0	1	87	99.3	-22.7	35	12	1,000	0	0.0	0.0
B- /7.5	6.9	1.06	15.47	1,414	3	59	36	2	22	46.3	-10.9	52	17	1,000	0	5.8	0.0
B- /7.5	6.9	1.06	15.49	39	3	59	36	2	22	48.3	-10.8	56	17	1,000	0	0.0	0.0
B- /7.5	6.9	1.06	15.05	594	3	59	36	2	22	40.5	-11.2	41	17	1,000	0	0.0	0.0
B- /7.5	6.9	1.06	15.42	157	3	59	36	2	22	44.4	-11.0	48	17	1,000	0	0.0	0.0
B- /7.5	7.0	1.07	15.48	4	3	59	36	2	22	48.3	-10.9	57	17	1,000,000	0	0.0	0.0
C /4.8	10.6	0.94	16.08	1,011	0	90	8	2	36	105.1	-17.3	48	10	1,000	0	5.8	0.0
C /4.9	10.6	0.94	15.93	281	0	90	8	2	36	97.2	-17.5	37	10	1,000	0	0.0	0.0
C /4.8	10.6	0.94	15.89	2	0	90	8	2	36	102.6	-17.3	44	10	1,000	0	0.0	0.0
C /4.8	10.6	0.94	16.22	1	0	90	8	2	36	109.0	-17.1	53	10	1,000,000	0	0.0	0.0
C /4.8	10.6	0.94	16.21	2,638	0	90	8	2	36	108.1	-17.1	51	10	1,000	0	0.0	0.0
C- /3.4	11.7	0.81	18.91	793	0	90	9	1	33	58.8	-20.8	65	13	1,000	0	5.8	0.0
C- /3.5	11.7	0.81	18.93	204	0	90	9	1	33	52.8	-21.0	55	13	1,000	0	0.0	0.0
C- /3.3	11.7	0.81	18.59	1	0	90	9	1	33	57.0	-20.8	62	13	1,000	0	0.0	0.0
C- /3.4	11.6	0.81	19.46	308	0	90	9	1	33	62.3	-20.7	70	13	1,000,000	0	0.0	0.0
C- /3.4	11.7	0.81	19.47	1,177	0	90	9	1	33	61.3	-20.7	68	13	1,000	0	0.0	0.0
B- /7.1	11.3	0.80	22.14	352	1	94	4	1	25	115.7	-19.8	78	8	1,000	0	5.8	0.0
B- /7.2	11.3	0.80	22.00	130	1	94	4	1	25	107.6	-20.1	73	8	1,000	0	0.0	0.0
B- /7.1	11.3	0.80	22.23	3	1	94	4	1	25	120.4	-19.7	81	8	1,000,000	0	0.0	0.0
B- /7.1	11.3	0.80	22.09	168	1	94	4	1	25	119.1	-19.7	80	8	1,000	0	0.0	0.0
C /5.0	9.7	0.72	31.68	10,517	0	89	10	1	22	83.4	-17.3	96	12	1,000	0	5.8	0.0
C /5.1	9.8	0.72	31.28	2,755	0	89	10	1	22	76.4	-17.5	95	12	1,000	0	0.0	0.0
C /5.0	9.7	0.72	31.25	446	0	89	10	1	22	81.2	-17.3	96	12	1,000	0	0.0	0.0
C /5.0	9.7	0.72	32.28	536	0	89	10	1	22	87.3	-17.1	97	12	1,000,000	0	0.0	0.0
C /5.0	9.7	0.72	32.27	8,567	0	89	10	1	22	86.2	-17.1	96	12	1,000	0	0.0	0.0
C /5.4	10.7	0.80	14.53	82	0	97	2	1	29	50.4	-21.2	82	8	1,000	0	5.8	0.0
C /5.5	10.8	0.80	14.34	26	0	97	2	1	29	44.8	-21.4	77	8	1,000	0	0.0	0.0
C /5.4	10.8	0.80	14.46	1	0	97	2	1	29	48.5	-21.2	80	8	1,000	0	0.0	0.0
C /5.4	10.8	0.80	14.61	17	0	97	2	1	29	53.6	-21.1	84	8	1,000,000	0	0.0	0.0
C /5.4	10.8	0.80	14.60	43	0	97	2	1	29	52.8	-21.1	83	8	1,000	0	0.0	0.0
C- /4.2	7.8	0.65	15.61	1,228	2	42	55	1	31	74.6	-14.9	42	14	1,000	0	5.8	0.0
C /4.3	7.8	0.65	15.33	343	2	42	55	1	31	67.9	-15.2	33	14	1,000	0	0.0	0.0
C- /4.2	7.8	0.65	15.42	1	2	42	55	1	31	72.5	-15.0	39	14	1,000	0	0.0	0.0
C- /4.2	7.8	0.55	15.81	53	2	42	55	1	31	77.8	-14.8	94	14	1,000,000	0	0.0	0.0
C- /4.2	7.8	0.65	15.83	3,738	2	42	55	1	31	77.4	-14.8	47	14	1,000	0	0.0	0.0
B- /7.6	9.7	0.89	29.43	67	0	0	0	100	0	98.7	-17.8	45	12	250	0	5.8	0.0
B- /7.5	9.7	0.89	26.10	2	0	0	0	100	0	90.8	-18.0	35	12	250	0	0.0	0.0
B- /7.5	9.7	0.89	26.21	22	0	0	0	100	0	90.8	-18.0	35	12	250	0	0.0	0.0
C+ /5.6	9.7	0.89	29.21	4,753	0	85	13	2	20	101.7	-17.6	48	31	1,000	0	5.8	0.0
C+ /5.6	9.7	0.89	28.87	1,126	0	85	13	2	20	94.1	-17.9	38	31	1,000	0	0.0	0.0

					PERFORMANCE						Incl. in Returns	
99 Pct = Best / 0 Pct = Worst			Overall		Perfor-	Total Return % through 2/28/17						
			Investment		mance				Annualized		Dividend	Expense
Fund Type	Fund Name	Ticker Symbol	Rating	Phone	Rating/Pts	3 Mo	6 Mo	1Yr / Pct	3Yr / Pct	5Yr / Pct	Yield	Ratio
GI	Franklin Mutual Shares R	TESRX	B	(800) 342-5236	B / 7.9	6.98	10.86	27.25 / 80	6.98 / 72	10.85 / 65	1.62	1.31
GI	Franklin Mutual Shares R6	FMSHX	B+	(800) 321-8563	B+ / 8.4	7.13	11.18	27.98 / 82	7.63 / 76	11.51 / 70	2.19	0.69
GI	Franklin Mutual Shares VIP 2		B-	(800) 342-5236	B / 8.1	7.15	11.18	28.20 / 82	6.97 / 72	10.99 / 66	1.80	0.98
GI	Franklin Mutual Shares Z	MUTHX	B+	(800) 321-8563	B+ / 8.3	7.09	11.14	27.89 / 81	7.52 / 76	11.41 / 69	2.09	0.81
EN	Franklin Natural Resources A	FRNRX	E-	(800) 342-5236	E- / 0.1	-1.50	8.71	38.47 / 97	-9.62 / 1	-6.66 / 1	0.98	1.15
EN	Franklin Natural Resources Adv	FNRAX	E-	(800) 321-8563	E- / 0.2	-1.44	8.87	38.85 / 97	-9.36 / 1	-6.40 / 1	1.26	0.88
EN	Franklin Natural Resources C	FNCRX	E-	(800) 342-5236	E- / 0.2	-1.70	8.34	37.41 / 96	-10.26 / 1	-7.32 / 1	0.52	1.88
OT	Franklin Pelagos Comdty Strat A	FLSQX	D-	(800) 342-5236	E- / 0.0	2.18	5.81	16.11 / 35	-11.49 / 1	-8.64 / 1	0.00	2.34
OT	Franklin Pelagos Comdty Strat Adv	FSLPX	D-	(800) 342-5236	E- / 0.1	2.29	6.01	16.32 / 36	-11.27 / 1	-8.15 / 1	0.00	2.09
OT	Franklin Pelagos Comdty Strat C	FLSVX	D-	(800) 342-5236	E- / 0.1	2.07	5.43	15.29 / 31	-12.14 / 0	-9.30 / 1	0.00	3.09
OT	Franklin Pelagos Comdty Strat R	FLSWX	D-	(800) 342-5236	E- / 0.1	2.03	5.84	15.81 / 33	-11.67 / 1	-8.82 / 1	0.00	2.59
OT	Franklin Pelagos Comdty Strat R6	FPELX	D-	(800) 342-5236	E- / 0.1	2.31	6.06	16.67 / 37	-11.08 / 1	-8.29 / 1	0.00	1.31
RE	Franklin Real Estate Sec A	FREEX	C	(800) 342-5236	C+ / 5.6	7.62	-3.03	13.10 / 22	10.23 / 94	10.50 / 62	3.05	1.00
RE	Franklin Real Estate Sec Adv	FRLAX	C+	(800) 321-8563	C+ / 6.9	7.66	-2.95	13.35 / 23	10.48 / 96	10.78 / 64	3.47	0.75
RE	Franklin Real Estate Sec C	FRRSX	C+	(800) 342-5236	C+ / 6.1	7.39	-3.40	12.24 / 19	9.39 / 89	9.67 / 56	2.61	1.75
RE	Franklin Real Estate Sec R6	FSERX	C+	(800) 342-5236	B- / 7.1	7.77	-2.79	13.60 / 24	10.71 / 96	10.88 / 65	3.64	0.54
* GI	Franklin Rising Dividends A	FRDPX	C+	(800) 342-5236	C+ / 6.0	4.89	5.50	21.61 / 60	7.96 / 79	11.57 / 71	1.44	0.92
GI	Franklin Rising Dividends Adv	FRDAX	B+	(800) 321-8563	B- / 7.2	4.96	5.64	21.92 / 62	8.23 / 81	11.84 / 73	1.76	0.67
GI	Franklin Rising Dividends C	FRDTX	C+	(800) 342-5236	C+ / 6.5	4.71	5.12	20.72 / 56	7.15 / 73	10.73 / 64	0.88	1.67
GI	Franklin Rising Dividends R	FRDRX	C+	(800) 342-5236	C+ / 6.9	4.82	5.36	21.29 / 59	7.68 / 77	11.29 / 68	1.31	1.17
GI	Franklin Rising Dividends R6	FRISX	B+	(800) 342-5236	B- / 7.3	4.99	5.70	22.08 / 63	8.39 / 82	11.91 / 73	1.88	0.52
GI	Franklin S&P 500 Index 529 Port A		A+	(800) 342-5236	B / 8.1	7.89	9.75	24.12 / 70	10.05 / 94	13.26 / 86	0.00	0.85
GI	● Franklin S&P 500 Index 529 Port B		A+	(800) 342-5236	B+ / 8.6	7.70	9.34	23.19 / 67	9.22 / 88	12.41 / 78	0.00	1.60
GI	Franklin S&P 500 Index 529 Port C		A+	(800) 342-5236	B+ / 8.6	7.73	9.33	23.26 / 67	9.24 / 88	12.42 / 78	0.00	1.60
SC	● Franklin Small Cap Growth A	FSGRX	D-	(800) 342-5236	C- / 3.9	3.74	6.42	31.26 / 89	2.36 / 26	11.55 / 70	0.00	1.14
SC	● Franklin Small Cap Growth Adv	FSSAX	D	(800) 342-5236	C / 5.3	3.82	6.49	31.59 / 89	2.63 / 28	11.87 / 73	0.00	0.89
SC	● Franklin Small Cap Growth C	FCSGX	D-	(800) 342-5236	C / 4.4	3.56	5.95	30.29 / 87	1.60 / 22	10.73 / 64	0.00	1.89
SC	● Franklin Small Cap Growth R	FSSRX	D	(800) 342-5236	C / 4.9	3.69	6.30	30.98 / 88	2.12 / 25	11.30 / 68	0.00	1.39
SC	● Franklin Small Cap Growth R6	FSMLX	D+	(800) 342-5236	C / 5.5	3.89	6.65	31.98 / 90	2.87 / 30	12.06 / 75	0.00	0.64
SC	Franklin Small Cap Value A	FRVLX	C	(800) 342-5236	B- / 7.0	3.07	9.98	35.11 / 94	6.39 / 67	11.77 / 72	0.20	1.13
SC	Franklin Small Cap Value Adv	FVADX	C+	(800) 321-8563	B / 8.2	3.12	10.10	35.43 / 94	6.67 / 70	12.09 / 75	0.44	0.88
SC	Franklin Small Cap Value C	FRVFX	C	(800) 342-5236	B- / 7.4	2.88	9.58	34.13 / 93	5.62 / 61	10.98 / 66	0.00	1.88
SC	Franklin Small Cap Value R	FVFRX	C+	(800) 342-5236	B / 7.8	3.01	9.85	34.78 / 94	6.15 / 66	11.53 / 70	0.00	1.38
GI	Franklin Small Cap Value R6	FRCSX	C+	(800) 342-5236	B+ / 8.4	3.19	10.22	35.74 / 95	6.93 / 71	12.21 / 76	0.59	0.63
GI	Franklin Small-Mid Cap Growth 529 A		C-	(800) 342-5236	C- / 3.9	6.23	5.54	22.81 / 66	3.88 / 41	9.59 / 55	0.00	1.49
GI	● Franklin Small-Mid Cap Growth 529 B		C-	(800) 342-5236	C / 4.4	6.03	5.14	21.86 / 61	3.10 / 33	8.79 / 49	0.00	2.24
GI	Franklin Small-Mid Cap Growth 529 C		C-	(800) 342-5236	C / 4.4	6.02	5.16	21.87 / 62	3.09 / 33	8.78 / 49	0.00	2.24
MC	Franklin Small-Mid Cap Growth A	FRSGX	D-	(800) 342-5236	C- / 4.1	6.26	5.63	23.07 / 67	4.12 / 44	9.93 / 58	0.00	0.97
MC	Franklin Small-Mid Cap Growth Adv	FSGAX	D	(800) 321-8563	C / 5.5	6.35	5.80	23.40 / 68	4.39 / 47	10.21 / 60	0.00	0.72
MC	Franklin Small-Mid Cap Growth C	FRSIX	D-	(800) 342-5236	C / 4.6	6.07	5.25	22.20 / 63	3.34 / 35	9.11 / 52	0.00	1.72
MC	Franklin Small-Mid Cap Growth R	FSMRX	D	(800) 342-5236	C / 5.1	6.20	5.53	22.78 / 66	3.86 / 41	9.65 / 56	0.00	1.22
SC	Franklin Small-Mid Cap Growth R6	FMGGX	D+	(800) 342-5236	C+ / 5.7	6.40	5.91	23.74 / 69	4.63 / 50	10.33 / 61	0.00	0.49
FO	Franklin Templeton Growth 529 A		D+	(800) 342-5236	D+ / 2.7	7.09	9.50	24.79 / 73	0.29 / 15	7.83 / 41	0.00	1.43
FO	● Franklin Templeton Growth 529 B		D	(800) 342-5236	D / 1.9	6.86	9.04	23.80 / 69	-0.49 / 11	7.01 / 35	0.00	2.18
FO	Franklin Templeton Growth 529 C		D	(800) 342-5236	D / 1.9	6.89	9.09	23.85 / 69	-0.46 / 11	7.02 / 35	0.00	2.18
UT	Franklin Utilities A	FKUTX	B+	(800) 342-5236	B / 8.1	10.22	6.94	17.33 / 40	10.94 / 97	11.98 / 74	2.44	0.73
UT	Franklin Utilities Adv	FRUAX	A	(800) 321-8563	B+ / 8.9	10.24	7.03	17.57 / 41	11.11 / 97	12.15 / 76	2.67	0.58
UT	Franklin Utilities C	FRUSX	A-	(800) 342-5236	B+ / 8.4	10.07	6.69	16.77 / 37	10.40 / 95	11.42 / 69	2.10	1.23
UT	Franklin Utilities R	FRURX	A-	(800) 342-5236	B+ / 8.6	10.16	6.83	16.99 / 38	10.57 / 96	11.59 / 71	2.23	1.08
UT	Franklin Utilities R6	FUFRX	A	(800) 342-5236	A- / 9.0	10.28	7.09	17.63 / 41	11.24 / 97	12.20 / 76	2.77	0.47
OT	Frontier MFG Core Infra Inst	FMGIX	C	(888) 825-2100	C- / 4.0	7.85	-0.36	9.03 / 9	6.67 / 70	9.84 / 57	2.51	0.84
GL	Frontier MFG Global Equity Inst	FMGEX	C+	(888) 825-2100	C / 5.3	7.18	6.57	15.41 / 32	6.20 / 66	12.25 / 77	0.83	0.87

● Denotes fund is closed to new investors
* Denotes fund is included in Section II

RISK			NET ASSETS		ASSET				Portfolio Turnover Ratio	BULL / BEAR		FUND MANAGER		MINIMUMS		LOADS	
Risk Rating/Pts	3 Year		NAV As of 2/28/17	Total $(Mil)	Cash %	Stocks %	Bonds %	Other %		Last Bull Market Return	Last Bear Market Return	Manager Quality Pct	Manager Tenure (Years)	Initial Purch. $	Additional Purch. $	Front End Load	Back End Load
	Standard Deviation	Beta															
C+ /5.6	9.7	0.89	29.06	124	0	85	13	2	20	99.4	-17.7	45	31	1,000	0	0.0	0.0
C /5.5	9.7	0.89	29.48	1,914	0	85	13	2	20	105.8	-17.5	54	31	1,000,000	0	0.0	0.0
C /4.8	9.8	0.89	20.98	3,638	1	84	13	2	20	101.2	-17.5	44	16	0	0	0.0	0.0
C /5.5	9.7	0.89	29.49	7,794	0	85	13	2	20	104.8	-17.5	52	31	1,000	0	0.0	0.0
E+ /0.9	24.7	1.19	26.69	474	4	95	0	1	36	-8.0	-32.6	26	18	1,000	0	5.8	0.0
E+ /0.8	24.7	1.19	28.49	99	4	95	0	1	36	-6.5	-32.5	29	18	1,000	0	0.0	0.0
E+ /0.9	24.7	1.19	25.84	115	4	95	0	1	36	-11.4	-32.8	19	18	1,000	0	0.0	0.0
C+ /6.3	13.8	0.23	6.56	5	1	21	77	1	28	N/A	N/A	0	6	1,000	0	5.8	0.0
C+ /6.3	13.8	0.23	6.70	2	1	21	77	1	28	N/A	N/A	1	6	0	0	0.0	0.0
C+ /6.2	13.8	0.24	6.41	1	1	21	77	1	28	N/A	N/A	0	6	1,000	0	0.0	0.0
C+ /6.3	13.8	0.23	6.52	N/A	1	21	77	1	28	N/A	N/A	0	6	1,000	0	0.0	0.0
C+ /6.3	13.7	0.24	6.65	127	1	21	77	1	28	N/A	N/A	1	6	1,000,000	0	0.0	0.0
C /5.4	15.0	1.09	23.12	351	0	99	0	1	24	98.8	-15.5	52	7	1,000	0	5.8	0.0
C /5.4	15.0	1.09	23.30	31	0	99	0	1	24	101.5	-15.4	56	7	1,000	0	0.0	0.0
C /5.4	15.0	1.09	22.28	77	0	99	0	1	24	90.8	-15.8	41	7	1,000	0	0.0	0.0
C /5.4	15.0	1.09	23.31	2	0	99	0	1	24	102.3	-15.5	58	7	1,000,000	0	0.0	0.0
C+ /6.6	10.2	0.95	54.92	11,389	0	98	0	2	2	102.1	-11.9	49	30	1,000	0	5.8	0.0
C+ /6.6	10.2	0.95	54.89	2,484	0	98	0	2	2	104.9	-11.9	52	30	1,000	0	0.0	0.0
C+ /6.6	10.2	0.96	53.93	2,912	0	98	0	2	2	94.1	-12.2	38	30	1,000	0	0.0	0.0
C+ /6.6	10.2	0.95	54.73	243	0	98	0	2	2	99.4	-12.0	45	30	1,000	0	0.0	0.0
C+ /6.6	10.2	0.95	54.89	595	0	98	0	2	2	105.2	-11.9	54	30	1,000,000	0	0.0	0.0
B /8.4	10.3	1.00	31.85	52	0	0	0	100	0	126.5	-16.6	68	14	250	0	5.8	0.0
B /8.3	10.3	1.00	27.15	2	0	0	0	100	0	117.4	-16.8	59	14	250	0	0.0	0.0
B /8.3	10.3	1.00	29.41	21	0	0	0	100	0	117.4	-16.8	59	14	250	0	0.0	0.0
C- /3.0	18.5	1.10	19.40	756	1	98	0	1	44	119.7	-22.6	15	17	1,000	0	5.8	0.0
C- /3.0	18.5	1.09	20.66	814	1	98	0	1	44	122.9	-22.4	17	17	1,000	0	0.0	0.0
D+ /2.9	18.5	1.10	16.56	148	1	98	0	1	44	111.0	-22.7	10	17	1,000	0	0.0	0.0
C- /3.0	18.6	1.10	18.56	81	1	98	0	1	44	117.0	-22.6	14	17	1,000	0	0.0	0.0
C- /3.0	18.5	1.10	20.84	1,031	1	98	0	1	44	124.8	-22.4	19	17	1,000,000	0	0.0	0.0
C- /3.8	14.7	0.87	55.20	1,277	8	91	0	1	42	129.6	-25.7	77	21	1,000	0	5.8	0.0
C- /3.8	14.7	0.87	57.51	1,022	8	91	0	1	42	133.1	-25.6	79	21	1,000,000	0	0.0	0.0
C- /3.5	14.7	0.87	49.54	247	8	91	0	1	42	120.9	-25.9	70	21	1,000	0	0.0	0.0
C- /3.8	14.7	0.87	54.63	237	8	91	0	1	42	127.0	-25.7	75	21	1,000	0	0.0	0.0
C- /3.8	14.7	1.12	57.49	137	8	91	0	1	42	134.1	-25.7	18	21	1,000,000	0	0.0	0.0
C+ /6.1	12.9	1.06	35.81	46	0	0	0	100	0	99.8	-24.1	6	14	250	0	5.8	0.0
C+ /6.0	12.9	1.06	32.33	2	0	0	0	100	0	92.0	-24.4	4	14	250	0	0.0	0.0
C+ /6.0	12.9	1.06	32.21	13	0	0	0	100	0	92.0	-24.4	4	14	250	0	0.0	0.0
D+ /2.6	12.9	0.98	33.86	2,249	3	96	0	1	39	103.3	-23.9	15	25	1,000	0	5.8	0.0
D+ /2.8	12.9	0.98	36.57	555	3	96	0	1	39	106.1	-23.8	17	25	1,000	0	0.0	0.0
D /1.6	12.9	0.98	25.26	368	3	96	0	1	39	95.1	-24.2	10	25	1,000	0	0.0	0.0
D+ /2.4	12.9	0.98	31.43	83	3	96	0	1	39	100.5	-24.0	14	25	1,000	0	0.0	0.0
D+ /2.9	12.9	0.73	36.96	208	3	96	0	1	39	107.0	-23.9	69	25	1,000,000	0	0.0	0.0
C+ /5.9	12.7	0.99	25.82	56	0	0	0	100	0	74.7	-23.0	77	14	250	0	5.8	0.0
C+ /5.8	12.7	0.98	23.04	2	0	0	0	100	0	67.7	-23.3	70	14	250	0	0.0	0.0
C+ /5.8	12.7	0.98	22.80	16	0	0	0	100	0	67.8	-23.3	71	14	250	0	0.0	0.0
C+ /6.3	12.8	0.86	18.69	4,061	1	98	0	1	7	88.8	1.6	56	19	1,000	0	4.3	0.0
C+ /6.3	12.8	0.86	18.83	730	1	98	0	1	7	90.4	1.7	59	19	1,000	0	0.0	0.0
C+ /6.3	12.8	0.86	18.59	1,017	1	98	0	1	7	83.7	1.5	50	19	1,000	0	0.0	0.0
C+ /6.3	12.8	0.86	18.62	97	1	98	0	1	7	85.3	1.5	52	19	1,000	0	0.0	0.0
C+ /6.3	12.8	0.86	18.83	225	1	98	0	1	7	90.7	1.6	60	19	1,000,000	0	0.0	0.0
B- /7.1	10.4	0.42	14.58	161	8	91	0	1	15	N/A	N/A	87	5	100,000	1,000	0.0	2.0
B- /7.0	9.6	0.67	16.21	1,125	2	97	0	1	38	N/A	N/A	97	6	1,000,000	1,000	0.0	2.0

	99 Pct = Best 0 Pct = Worst				PERFORMANCE							
								Total Return % through 2/28/17			Incl. in Returns	
									Annualized			
Fund Type	Fund Name	Ticker Symbol	Overall Investment Rating	Phone	Perfor- mance Rating/Pts	3 Mo	6 Mo	1Yr / Pct	3Yr / Pct	5Yr / Pct	Dividend Yield	Expense Ratio
GL	Frontier MFG Global Plus Inst	FMGPX	U	(888) 825-2100	U /	7.90	6.84	15.26 /31	--	--	0.16	2.05
GL	Frontier MFG Global Plus Svc	FMPSX	U	(888) 825-2100	U /	7.88	6.82	--	--	--	0.00	1.40
SC	Frontier Netols Small Cap Val Fd	FNSVX	D	(888) 825-2100	C+ / 6.7	3.85	10.40	26.51 /78	5.36 /58	11.10 /67	0.04	1.21
SC	Frontier Netols Small Cap Value Y	FNSYX	D	(888) 825-2100	C+ / 6.6	3.76	10.35	26.40 /77	5.28 /57	10.79 /64	0.04	1.61
SC	Frontier Phocas Sm Cap Val Fd Inst	FPSVX	A	(888) 825-2100	A / 9.4	4.88	13.92	33.54 /92	8.73 /85	13.64 /90	0.39	1.49
GL	Frontier Silk Inv New Horizons Inst	FSNHX	U	(888) 825-2100	U /	5.99	5.88	--	--	--	0.00	N/A
IN	Frontier Timpani SCG Instl	FTSGX	E	(888) 825-2100	D- / 1.2	3.77	6.31	18.93 /47	-1.41 / 8	10.53 /62	0.00	1.32
IN	Frontier Timpani SCG Y	FTSYX	E-	(888) 825-2100	D- / 1.0	3.68	6.11	18.43 /45	-1.79 / 7	--	0.00	1.70
GR	Frost Growth Equity Inst	FICEX	C+	(866) 777-7818	B / 7.8	8.43	9.39	18.94 /47	8.42 /82	11.42 /69	0.15	0.80
GR	Frost Growth Equity Inv	FACEX	C+	(866) 777-7818	B- / 7.0	8.31	9.27	18.70 /46	8.14 /80	11.14 /67	0.00	1.05
GI	Frost Kempner MC Deep Val Eqty	FIKDX	C	(866) 777-7818	C+ / 6.6	6.78	11.93	28.23 /82	3.95 /42	8.52 /46	1.93	0.78
GI	Frost Kempner MC Deep Val Eqty Inv	FAKDX	C-	(866) 777-7818	C+ / 5.8	6.64	11.83	27.83 /81	3.69 /39	8.26 /44	1.68	1.03
SC	Frost Mid Cap Equity Inst	FIKSX	D	(866) 777-7818	C+ / 6.3	6.69	11.12	25.76 /75	4.04 /43	9.55 /55	0.00	1.41
GR	Frost Mid Cap Equity Inv	FAKSX	D-	(866) 777-7818	C+ / 6.2	6.66	11.14	25.82 /76	3.83 /41	9.37 /54	0.00	1.66
GL	● Frost Moderate Allocation Inst	FIBTX	C+	(866) 777-7818	C- / 3.6	4.73	3.88	13.64 /24	4.02 /43	6.36 /31	2.73	1.04
GL	Frost Moderate Allocation Inv	FASTX	C+	(866) 777-7818	C- / 3.4	4.63	3.71	13.33 /23	3.73 /40	6.07 /29	2.30	1.29
GI	Frost Value Equity Inst	FIDVX	B-	(866) 777-7818	B- / 7.5	6.84	7.86	19.89 /51	8.33 /81	10.99 /66	1.61	0.80
GI	Frost Value Equity Inv	FADVX	C+	(866) 777-7818	B- / 7.3	6.77	7.72	19.60 /50	8.04 /79	10.70 /63	1.37	1.05
AA	FT 529 Age-Based Csv AA Age		C	(800) 342-5236	E+ / 0.7	1.99	1.64	4.61 / 4	0.95 /18	1.10 / 6	0.00	1.21
AA	● FT 529 Age-Based Csv AA Age		C	(800) 342-5236	E+ / 0.9	1.72	1.17	3.70 / 3	0.18 /14	0.34 / 5	0.00	1.96
AA	FT 529 Age-Based Csv AA Age		C	(800) 342-5236	E+ / 0.9	1.81	1.26	3.79 / 3	0.18 /14	0.34 / 5	0.00	1.96
AA	FT 529 Age-Based Csv AA Age 17+		C-	(800) 342-5236	E / 0.4	0.91	0.60	1.93 / 2	0.20 /14	0.28 / 5	0.00	1.04
AA	● FT 529 Age-Based Csv AA Age 17+		C	(800) 342-5236	E+ / 0.6	0.74	0.32	1.28 / 2	-0.52 /11	-0.43 / 4	0.00	1.79
AA	FT 529 Age-Based Csv AA Age 17+		C	(800) 342-5236	E / 0.5	0.63	0.21	1.17 / 2	-0.55 /11	-0.46 / 4	0.00	1.79
AA	FT 529 Age-Based Csv AA Age 9-12		C	(800) 342-5236	D- / 1.3	3.35	2.96	8.31 / 8	2.18 /25	3.48 /13	0.00	1.29
AA	● FT 529 Age-Based Csv AA Age 9-12		C	(800) 342-5236	D / 1.6	3.20	2.63	7.51 / 7	1.41 /20	2.72 /10	0.00	2.04
AA	FT 529 Age-Based Csv AA Age 9-12		C	(800) 342-5236	D / 1.6	3.12	2.63	7.52 / 7	1.41 /20	2.71 /10	0.00	2.04
AA	FT 529 Age-Based Csv AA Age		C	(800) 342-5236	D / 2.0	4.76	4.47	12.44 /20	2.66 /29	5.38 /24	0.00	1.37
AA	● FT 529 Age-Based Csv AA Age		C	(800) 342-5236	D+ / 2.3	4.64	4.11	11.69 /17	1.89 /23	4.61 /19	0.00	2.12
AA	FT 529 Age-Based Csv AA Age		C	(800) 342-5236	D+ / 2.3	4.64	4.12	11.61 /16	1.90 /23	4.59 /19	0.00	2.12
GL	FT 529 Age-Based Gro AA Age 13-16		C	(800) 342-5236	D / 2.0	4.79	4.56	12.55 /20	2.65 /29	5.33 /24	0.00	1.37
GL	● FT 529 Age-Based Gro AA Age 13-16		C	(800) 342-5236	D+ / 2.3	4.59	4.13	11.66 /17	1.88 /23	4.53 /18	0.00	2.12
GL	FT 529 Age-Based Gro AA Age 13-16		C	(800) 342-5236	D+ / 2.3	4.59	4.13	11.64 /17	1.88 /23	4.53 /18	0.00	2.12
GL	FT 529 Age-Based Gro AA Age 17 +		C	(800) 342-5236	D- / 1.3	3.37	3.09	8.59 / 9	1.87 /23	3.25 /12	0.00	1.29
GL	● FT 529 Age-Based Gro AA Age 17 +		C	(800) 342-5236	D / 1.6	3.16	2.73	7.82 / 7	1.10 /19	2.49 / 9	0.00	2.04
GL	FT 529 Age-Based Gro AA Age 17 +		C	(800) 342-5236	D / 1.6	3.17	2.74	7.87 / 7	1.10 /19	2.49 / 9	0.00	2.04
GI	FT 529 Age-Based Gro AA Age 9-12		C	(800) 342-5236	C- / 3.0	6.24	5.95	16.59 /37	3.49 /37	7.28 /37	0.00	1.44
GI	● FT 529 Age-Based Gro AA Age 9-12		C+	(800) 342-5236	C- / 3.5	6.06	5.60	15.77 /33	2.72 /29	6.47 /31	0.00	2.19
GI	FT 529 Age-Based Gro AA Age 9-12		C+	(800) 342-5236	C- / 3.5	6.06	5.61	15.73 /33	2.73 /29	6.48 /31	0.00	2.19
GL	FT 529 Age-Based Gro AA Age		C+	(800) 342-5236	C / 4.4	7.80	7.61	21.10 /58	4.40 /47	9.34 /53	0.00	1.55
GL	● FT 529 Age-Based Gro AA Age		C+	(800) 342-5236	C / 4.9	7.60	7.24	20.17 /53	3.60 /38	8.52 /46	0.00	2.30
GL	FT 529 Age-Based Gro AA Age		C+	(800) 342-5236	C / 4.9	7.57	7.21	20.15 /53	3.60 /38	8.53 /47	0.00	2.30
AA	FT 529 Age-Based Mdt AA Age 13-16		C	(800) 342-5236	D- / 1.3	3.40	3.00	8.43 / 8	1.78 /23	3.20 /12	0.00	1.30
AA	● FT 529 Age-Based Mdt AA Age 13-16		C	(800) 342-5236	D- / 1.5	3.25	2.58	7.62 / 7	1.02 /18	2.43 / 9	0.00	2.05
AA	FT 529 Age-Based Mdt AA Age 13-16		C	(800) 342-5236	D- / 1.5	3.25	2.67	7.63 / 7	1.02 /18	2.44 / 9	0.00	2.05
AA	FT 529 Age-Based Mdt AA Age 17+		C	(800) 342-5236	E+ / 0.7	1.98	1.63	4.59 / 4	1.01 /18	1.21 / 7	0.00	1.21
AA	● FT 529 Age-Based Mdt AA Age 17+		C	(800) 342-5236	E+ / 0.9	1.72	1.26	3.78 / 3	0.27 /15	0.45 / 5	0.00	1.96
AA	FT 529 Age-Based Mdt AA Age 17+		C	(800) 342-5236	E+ / 0.9	1.72	1.26	3.78 / 3	0.24 /14	0.45 / 5	0.00	1.96
AA	FT 529 Age-Based Mdt AA Age 9-12		C	(800) 342-5236	D / 2.0	4.82	4.53	12.60 /20	2.74 /29	5.23 /23	0.00	1.38
AA	● FT 529 Age-Based Mdt AA Age 9-12		C	(800) 342-5236	D+ / 2.4	4.63	4.17	11.68 /17	1.97 /24	4.45 /18	0.00	2.13
AA	FT 529 Age-Based Mdt AA Age 9-12		C	(800) 342-5236	D+ / 2.3	4.62	4.16	11.66 /17	1.94 /24	4.45 /18	0.00	2.13
AA	FT 529 Age-Based Mdt AA Age		C	(800) 342-5236	C- / 3.0	6.25	5.99	16.56 /37	3.50 /37	7.29 /37	0.00	1.46

● Denotes fund is closed to new investors
* Denotes fund is included in Section II

Risk Rating/Pts	Standard Deviation	Beta	NAV As of 2/28/17	Total $(Mil)	Cash %	Stocks %	Bonds %	Other %	Portfolio Turnover Ratio	Last Bull Market Return	Last Bear Market Return	Manager Quality Pct	Manager Tenure (Years)	Initial Purch. $	Additional Purch. $	Front End Load	Back End Load
U /	N/A	N/A	10.80	105	16	83	0	1	30	N/A	N/A	N/A	2	1,000,000	1,000	0.0	2.0
U /	N/A	N/A	10.80	66	16	83	0	1	30	N/A	N/A	N/A	2	10,000	1,000	0.0	2.0
E+ /0.9	14.8	0.91	9.49	69	1	97	1	1	25	120.2	-28.8	64	12	100,000	1,000	0.0	0.0
E+ /0.7	14.8	0.91	8.90	N/A	1	97	1	1	25	116.9	-29.0	62	12	1,000	50	0.0	0.0
C+ /5.7	14.2	0.86	40.17	39	0	98	1	1	49	135.7	-24.5	89	7	100,000	1,000	0.0	0.0
U /	N/A	N/A	9.88	33	0	83	15	2	0	N/A	N/A	N/A	1	100,000	1,000	0.0	2.0
C- /3.0	19.1	1.34	16.52	38	5	94	0	1	156	111.7	-27.9	0	6	100,000	1,000	0.0	0.0
D /1.9	19.1	1.34	16.32	4	5	94	0	1	156	N/A	N/A	0	6	1,000	50	0.0	0.0
C /4.5	11.7	1.02	13.41	273	0	94	4	2	23	110.4	-17.1	45	15	1,000,000	0	0.0	0.0
C /4.5	11.7	1.02	13.31	44	0	94	4	2	23	107.5	-17.1	42	15	2,500	500	3.3	0.0
C /4.6	10.9	0.95	10.33	70	0	86	13	1	10	77.0	-18.2	10	15	1,000,000	0	0.0	0.0
C /4.6	10.8	0.95	10.32	16	0	86	13	1	10	74.7	-18.3	9	15	2,500	500	3.3	0.0
D- /1.2	14.2	0.79	10.28	10	0	94	2	4	102	93.9	-24.2	57	2	1,000,000	0	0.0	0.0
D- /1.1	14.3	1.20	10.16	5	0	94	2	4	102	N/A	N/A	3	2	2,500	500	0.0	0.0
B /8.2	6.9	0.50	12.94	1	9	58	31	2	66	53.7	-12.9	93	11	1,000,000	0	0.0	0.0
B /8.2	6.9	0.50	12.94	4	9	58	31	2	66	51.4	-13.0	93	11	2,500	500	0.0	0.0
C /5.2	11.8	1.09	10.18	250	0	98	1	1	52	96.3	-17.9	35	15	1,000,000	0	0.0	0.0
C /5.2	11.8	1.09	10.17	40	0	98	1	1	52	93.6	-18.0	31	15	2,500	500	0.0	0.0
B+ /9.9	2.5	0.28	11.81	13	0	0	0	100	0	8.8	0.5	60	7	250	0	5.8	0.0
B+ /9.9	2.5	0.28	11.21	N/A	0	0	0	100	0	4.4	0.2	49	7	250	0	0.0	0.0
B+ /9.9	2.5	0.27	11.22	6	0	0	0	100	0	4.4	0.2	50	7	250	0	0.0	0.0
B+ /9.9	1.3	0.14	10.03	18	0	0	0	100	0	1.2	-0.3	63	7	250	0	5.8	0.0
B+ /9.9	1.3	0.13	9.53	N/A	0	0	0	100	0	-2.8	-0.6	54	7	250	0	0.0	0.0
B+ /9.9	1.2	0.14	9.52	12	0	0	0	100	0	-2.9	-0.6	53	7	250	0	0.0	0.0
B+ /9.7	4.1	0.61	13.56	12	0	0	0	100	0	27.2	-5.5	44	7	250	0	5.8	0.0
B+ /9.6	4.1	0.60	12.89	N/A	0	0	0	100	0	22.2	-5.8	34	7	250	0	0.0	0.0
B+ /9.6	4.1	0.61	12.87	3	0	0	0	100	0	22.1	-5.8	34	7	250	0	0.0	0.0
B /8.9	6.2	0.93	15.19	15	0	0	0	100	0	44.3	-10.8	22	7	250	0	5.8	0.0
B /8.8	6.2	0.94	14.43	N/A	0	0	0	100	0	38.6	-11.1	16	7	250	0	0.0	0.0
B /8.8	6.2	0.93	14.42	4	0	0	0	100	0	38.5	-11.0	16	7	250	0	0.0	0.0
B /8.9	6.0	0.91	23.85	331	0	0	0	100	0	44.4	-10.9	55	12	250	0	5.8	0.0
B /8.8	6.0	0.91	21.17	16	0	0	0	100	0	38.6	-11.2	44	14	250	0	0.0	0.0
B /8.8	6.0	0.91	21.19	111	0	0	0	100	0	38.6	-11.1	44	14	250	0	0.0	0.0
B+ /9.6	4.1	0.61	18.70	229	0	0	0	100	0	25.9	-5.2	62	12	250	0	5.8	0.0
B+ /9.5	4.2	0.62	16.96	11	0	0	0	100	0	21.0	-5.5	52	14	250	0	0.0	0.0
B+ /9.5	4.2	0.61	17.27	109	0	0	0	100	0	20.9	-5.5	52	14	250	0	0.0	0.0
B /8.2	8.0	0.73	27.41	344	0	0	0	100	0	64.8	-16.1	24	12	250	0	5.8	0.0
B /8.1	8.0	0.73	24.52	19	0	0	0	100	0	58.3	-16.4	17	14	250	0	0.0	0.0
B /8.1	8.0	0.73	24.87	92	0	0	0	100	0	58.3	-16.4	17	14	250	0	0.0	0.0
B- /7.4	10.1	1.51	31.80	270	0	0	0	100	0	89.2	-21.3	41	14	250	0	5.8	0.0
B- /7.4	10.1	1.50	28.60	8	0	0	0	100	0	81.6	-21.6	31	14	250	0	0.0	0.0
B- /7.4	10.1	1.50	28.98	65	0	0	0	100	0	81.6	-21.6	31	14	250	0	0.0	0.0
B+ /9.6	4.2	0.61	13.37	74	0	0	0	100	0	25.3	-5.5	38	7	250	0	5.8	0.0
B+ /9.5	4.2	0.62	12.71	2	0	0	0	100	0	20.4	-5.9	29	7	250	0	0.0	0.0
B+ /9.5	4.1	0.61	12.70	35	0	0	0	100	0	20.4	-5.8	29	7	250	0	0.0	0.0
B+ /9.9	2.5	0.28	11.84	41	0	0	0	100	0	9.2	0.5	61	7	250	0	5.8	0.0
B+ /9.9	2.5	0.27	11.25	1	0	0	0	100	0	4.9	0.1	51	7	250	0	0.0	0.0
B+ /9.9	2.5	0.27	11.25	37	0	0	0	100	0	4.9	0.1	51	7	250	0	0.0	0.0
B /8.9	6.1	0.92	15.01	72	0	0	0	100	0	43.4	-10.8	24	7	250	0	5.8	0.0
B /8.8	6.0	0.91	14.25	2	0	0	0	100	0	37.7	-11.1	18	7	250	0	0.0	0.0
B /8.8	6.0	0.91	14.27	21	0	0	0	100	0	37.6	-11.0	18	7	250	0	0.0	0.0
B /8.2	8.0	1.21	16.82	96	0	0	0	100	0	64.3	-15.9	13	7	250	0	5.8	0.0

Fund Type	Fund Name	Ticker Symbol	Overall Investment Rating	Phone	Performance Rating/Pts	3 Mo	6 Mo	1Yr / Pct	3Yr / Pct	5Yr / Pct	Dividend Yield	Expense Ratio
	99 Pct = Best							Total Return % through 2/28/17	Annualized		Incl. in Returns	
AA	● FT 529 Age-Based Mdt AA Age		C+	(800) 342-5236	C- / 3.5	6.11	5.55	15.72 /33	2.73 /29	6.49 /31	0.00	2.21
AA	FT 529 Age-Based Mdt AA Age		C+	(800) 342-5236	C- / 3.5	6.05	5.56	15.76 /33	2.74 /29	6.49 /31	0.00	2.21
GL	Fulcrum Dvsfd Abs Ret Super Inst	FARYX	U	(855) 538-5278	U /	0.91	2.28	3.14 / 3	--	--	0.40	1.46
GR	Fuller and Thaler Beh SmCp Eq Inst	FTHSX	C+	(888) 912-4562	A+ / 9.8	6.15	16.29	38.70 /97	11.99 /98	15.91 /98	0.40	2.87
GR	Fuller and Thaler Beh SmCp Eq Inv	FTHNX	A+	(888) 912-4562	A+ / 9.8	6.14	16.22	38.49 /97	11.82 /98	15.71 /98	0.35	3.12
GR	Fuller and Thaler Beh SmCp Eq R6	FTHFX	C+	(888) 912-4562	A+ / 9.9	6.22	16.43	38.88 /97	12.16 /98	16.09 /98	0.40	2.67
AG	Fund *X Aggressive Upgrader	HOTFX	D	(866) 455-3863	D+ / 2.4	4.11	3.10	15.30 /31	1.67 /22	8.51 /46	0.28	1.93
GR	Fund *X Conservative Upgrader	RELAX	C	(866) 455-3863	C- / 4.2	4.27	5.71	15.06 /30	4.46 /48	7.67 /40	1.42	1.89
BA	Fund *X Flexible Income	INCMX	C	(866) 455-3863	D / 1.8	2.76	1.47	7.05 / 6	2.46 /27	3.61 /13	2.65	1.50
GR	Fund *X Upgrader	FUNDX	C+	(866) 455-3863	C / 5.0	4.92	6.94	18.76 /46	4.67 /50	10.11 /59	0.49	1.79
GR	FundX Tactical Upgrader	TACTX	C	(866) 455-3863	C- / 3.7	3.16	5.38	17.43 /40	3.41 /36	4.17 /16	0.33	1.70
AA	Gabelli ABC Fund AAA	GABCX	C	(800) 422-3554	D- / 1.4	0.99	1.58	3.70 / 3	2.08 /24	2.87 /10	0.71	0.59
AA	Gabelli ABC Fund Advisor	GADVX	C-	(800) 422-3554	D- / 1.3	0.95	1.54	3.48 / 3	1.85 /23	2.62 /10	0.47	0.84
GR	Gabelli Asset A	GATAX	D+	(800) 422-3554	C / 4.3	5.99	7.15	21.68 /61	4.65 /50	10.43 /61	0.63	1.35
GR	Gabelli Asset AAA	GABAX	C-	(800) 422-3554	C+ / 5.6	6.00	7.15	21.67 /61	4.66 /50	10.43 /61	0.67	1.35
GR	Gabelli Asset C	GATCX	D+	(800) 422-3554	C / 4.9	5.81	6.74	20.77 /56	3.88 /41	9.61 /55	0.00	2.10
GR	Gabelli Asset I	GABIX	C-	(800) 422-3554	C+ / 5.8	6.05	7.27	21.98 /62	4.92 /53	10.71 /63	0.91	1.10
GR	Gabelli Capital Asset Fund		D+	(800) 422-3554	C / 5.5	6.46	9.44	24.94 /73	3.36 /35	10.56 /62	0.55	1.20
GL	Gabelli Dividend Growth A	GBCAX	C	(800) 422-3554	C / 5.5	6.71	9.79	25.22 /74	5.04 /55	9.62 /55	0.37	1.91
GL	Gabelli Dividend Growth AAA	GABBX	C+	(800) 422-3554	C+ / 6.6	6.74	9.82	25.22 /74	5.03 /54	9.61 /55	0.39	1.91
GL	Gabelli Dividend Growth C	GBCCX	C	(800) 422-3554	C+ / 6.0	6.55	9.46	24.30 /71	4.26 /46	8.78 /49	0.00	2.66
GL	Gabelli Dividend Growth I	GBCIX	C+	(800) 422-3554	C+ / 6.9	6.94	10.24	25.90 /76	5.38 /58	9.95 /58	0.80	1.66
GR	Gabelli Enterprise Mrgrs & Acq A	EMAAX	C-	(800) 422-3554	D / 1.9	2.23	4.86	11.25 /15	3.24 /34	5.59 /25	0.00	1.67
GR	Gabelli Enterprise Mrgrs & Acq AAA	EAAAX	C	(800) 422-3554	D+ / 2.9	2.27	4.94	11.51 /16	3.48 /37	5.81 /27	0.00	1.47
GR	Gabelli Enterprise Mrgrs & Acq C	EMACX	C-	(800) 422-3554	D+ / 2.4	2.10	4.54	10.61 /13	2.68 /29	5.00 /21	0.00	2.22
GR	Gabelli Enterprise Mrgrs & Acq Y	EMAYX	C	(800) 422-3554	C- / 3.1	2.37	5.14	11.73 /17	3.72 /39	6.06 /29	0.00	1.22
IN	Gabelli Equity Income A	GCAEX	C-	(800) 422-3554	C / 4.7	6.29	6.92	21.17 /58	5.21 /57	10.01 /58	3.38	1.37
IN	Gabelli Equity Income AAA	GABEX	C	(800) 422-3554	C+ / 5.9	6.31	6.93	21.18 /58	5.21 /57	10.01 /58	3.55	1.37
IN	Gabelli Equity Income C	GCCEX	C-	(800) 422-3554	C / 5.2	6.11	6.52	20.27 /54	4.41 /48	9.18 /52	4.04	2.12
IN	Gabelli Equity Income I	GCIEX	C+	(800) 422-3554	C+ / 6.1	6.40	7.08	21.47 /60	5.48 /59	10.29 /60	3.45	1.12
SC	Gabelli Focus Five A	GWSAX	E	(800) 422-3554	E / 0.5	4.82	0.32	10.85 /14	-0.99 / 9	8.18 /43	0.00	1.37
SC	Gabelli Focus Five AAA	GWSVX	E	(800) 422-3554	E+ / 0.8	4.87	0.32	10.87 /14	-0.97 / 9	8.18 /43	0.00	1.37
SC	Gabelli Focus Five C	GWSCX	E	(800) 422-3554	E+ / 0.6	4.64	-0.07	10.03 /12	-1.73 / 7	7.38 /37	0.00	2.12
SC	Gabelli Focus Five I	GWSIX	E	(800) 422-3554	E+ / 0.9	4.90	0.46	11.20 /15	-0.74 /10	8.47 /46	0.00	1.12
CV	Gabelli Global Rising Inc & Div A	GAGAX	C	(800) 422-3554	D+ / 2.7	5.62	4.43	14.16 /26	3.80 /40	5.36 /24	0.87	1.75
CV	Gabelli Global Rising Inc & Div AAA	GAGCX	C+	(800) 422-3554	C- / 3.7	5.61	4.46	14.16 /26	3.89 /42	5.38 /24	0.98	1.75
CV	Gabelli Global Rising Inc & Div C	GACCX	C	(800) 422-3554	C- / 3.1	5.44	4.03	13.30 /23	3.03 /32	3.90 /15	0.54	2.50
CV	Gabelli Global Rising Inc & Div I	GAGIX	C+	(800) 422-3554	C- / 4.0	5.81	4.71	14.65 /28	4.14 /44	5.62 /26	1.32	1.50
PM	Gabelli Gold A	GLDAX	E-	(800) 422-3554	D+ / 2.7	12.45	-8.81	24.83 /73	2.66 /29	-10.34 / 1	1.88	1.62
PM	Gabelli Gold AAA	GOLDX	E	(800) 422-3554	C- / 3.7	12.35	-8.87	24.75 /72	2.65 /29	-10.36 / 1	1.96	1.62
PM	Gabelli Gold C	GLDCX	E-	(800) 422-3554	C- / 3.2	12.23	-9.14	23.84 /69	1.89 /23	-11.01 / 0	1.60	2.37
PM	Gabelli Gold I	GLDIX	E	(800) 422-3554	C- / 3.9	12.43	-8.73	25.07 /73	2.90 /31	-10.13 / 1	2.19	1.37
SC	Gabelli Small Cap Growth A	GCASX	C+	(800) 422-3554	C+ / 6.3	5.37	10.57	27.20 /80	6.18 /66	12.40 /78	0.00	1.38
SC	Gabelli Small Cap Growth AAA	GABSX	B	(800) 422-3554	B- / 7.3	5.37	10.57	27.22 /80	6.18 /66	12.40 /78	0.00	1.38
SC	Gabelli Small Cap Growth C	GCCSX	C+	(800) 422-3554	C+ / 6.8	5.16	10.16	26.26 /77	5.39 /58	11.56 /70	0.00	2.13
SC	Gabelli Small Cap Growth I	GACIX	B	(800) 422-3554	B- / 7.5	5.42	10.71	27.52 /81	6.44 /68	12.68 /81	0.12	1.13
GR	Gabelli SRI Inc A	SRIAX	C	(800) 422-3554	C- / 4.2	4.42	3.77	18.66 /46	6.15 /66	8.77 /49	0.00	1.68
GR	Gabelli SRI Inc AAA	SRIGX	C+	(800) 422-3554	C / 5.5	4.41	3.77	18.65 /46	6.14 /65	8.76 /48	0.00	1.68
GR	Gabelli SRI Inc C	SRICX	C	(800) 422-3554	C / 4.8	4.21	3.38	17.79 /42	5.36 /58	7.96 /42	0.00	2.43
GR	Gabelli SRI Inc I	SRIDX	C+	(800) 422-3554	C+ / 5.7	4.53	3.97	19.01 /47	6.43 /68	9.05 /51	0.00	1.43
UT	Gabelli Utilities A	GAUAX	C	(800) 422-3554	C / 4.9	7.81	6.75	18.11 /43	5.96 /64	8.59 /47	7.46	1.39
UT	Gabelli Utilities AAA	GABUX	C+	(800) 422-3554	C+ / 6.1	7.81	6.73	18.13 /43	5.97 /64	8.60 /47	8.02	1.39

● Denotes fund is closed to new investors
* Denotes fund is included in Section II

RISK Risk Rating/Pts	3 Year Standard Deviation	Beta	NET ASSETS NAV As of 2/28/17	Total $(Mil)	ASSET Cash %	Stocks %	Bonds %	Other %	Portfolio Turnover Ratio	BULL/BEAR Last Bull Market Return	Last Bear Market Return	FUND MANAGER Manager Quality Pct	Manager Tenure (Years)	MINIMUMS Initial Purch. $	Additional Purch. $	LOADS Front End Load	Back End Load
B /8.1	8.1	1.21	15.97	2	0	0	0	100	0	57.8	-16.2	9	7	250	0	0.0	0.0
B /8.1	8.0	1.21	15.94	25	0	0	0	100	0	57.7	-16.2	9	7	250	0	0.0	0.0
U /	N/A	N/A	9.79	207	23	0	76	1	54	N/A	N/A	N/A	2	25,000,000	1,000	0.0	0.0
D+ /2.5	12.7	1.06	21.58	23	1	98	0	1	194	162.3	N/A	79	N/A	100,000	50	0.0	0.0
C+ /6.7	12.6	1.06	21.46	27	1	98	0	1	194	159.8	N/A	78	N/A	1,000	50	0.0	0.0
D+ /2.5	12.7	1.06	21.73	3	1	98	0	1	194	164.3	N/A	80	N/A	1,000,000	0	0.0	0.0
C+ /5.8	12.6	1.08	58.28	46	1	98	0	1	226	77.3	-22.2	3	15	1,000	100	0.0	0.0
C+ /6.6	7.1	0.66	38.45	57	2	65	31	2	140	61.3	-14.3	44	15	1,000	100	0.0	0.0
B /8.8	2.7	0.30	28.24	100	2	14	82	2	130	23.9	-4.4	75	15	1,000	100	0.0	0.0
C+ /6.4	11.3	1.04	53.66	229	1	94	3	2	172	90.3	-21.0	9	16	1,000	100	0.0	0.0
B- /7.2	9.7	0.88	23.43	39	1	97	1	1	220	30.2	-3.7	11	9	1,000	100	0.0	0.0
B+ /9.1	1.7	0.21	10.20	629	4	34	61	1	276	20.2	-3.1	77	24	10,000	0	0.0	0.0
B+ /9.1	1.7	0.20	10.11	798	4	34	61	1	276	18.8	-3.4	76	24	10,000	0	0.0	0.0
C /4.5	11.0	1.02	55.27	54	0	99	0	1	8	97.9	-19.0	10	31	1,000	0	5.8	0.0
C /4.5	11.0	1.02	55.82	1,991	0	99	0	1	8	97.8	-19.0	10	31	1,000	0	0.0	0.0
C /4.3	11.0	1.02	51.98	73	0	99	0	1	8	90.0	-19.3	7	31	1,000	0	0.0	0.0
C /4.4	11.0	1.02	55.73	516	0	99	0	1	8	100.6	-18.9	12	31	500,000	0	0.0	0.0
C- /3.5	12.4	1.10	20.54	105	0	99	0	1	1	103.5	-21.1	4	22	0	0	0.0	0.0
C /5.4	12.8	0.90	18.67	4	2	97	0	1	45	94.7	-19.3	95	18	1,000	0	5.8	0.0
C /5.4	12.8	0.90	18.71	18	2	97	0	1	45	94.8	-19.4	95	18	1,000	0	0.0	0.0
C /5.3	12.9	0.90	17.39	2	2	97	0	1	45	87.0	-19.6	94	18	1,000	0	0.0	0.0
C /5.3	12.8	0.90	18.82	5	2	97	0	1	45	98.0	-19.3	96	18	100,000	0	0.0	0.0
B- /7.9	5.6	0.46	14.24	52	0	85	14	1	151	39.3	-6.7	55	16	1,000	0	5.8	0.0
B- /7.9	5.6	0.46	14.44	4	0	85	14	1	151	40.9	-6.5	58	16	1,000	0	0.0	0.0
B- /7.9	5.6	0.46	13.13	45	0	85	14	1	151	35.2	-6.8	48	16	1,000	0	0.0	0.0
B- /7.9	5.5	0.46	15.14	66	0	85	14	1	151	42.8	-6.4	62	16	500,000	0	0.0	0.0
C /5.5	10.2	0.97	24.99	150	0	98	0	2	14	91.0	-16.3	18	25	1,000	0	5.8	0.0
C /5.5	10.2	0.97	25.10	775	0	98	0	2	14	91.1	-16.3	18	25	1,000	0	0.0	0.0
C /5.1	10.2	0.96	21.72	292	0	98	0	2	14	83.4	-16.6	12	25	1,000	0	0.0	0.0
C+ /5.6	10.2	0.97	25.92	470	0	98	0	2	14	93.8	-16.3	20	25	500,000	0	0.0	0.0
C- /3.9	14.9	0.64	13.26	33	1	98	0	1	60	86.2	-27.8	13	5	1,000	0	5.8	0.0
C- /3.9	14.9	0.64	13.13	24	1	98	0	1	60	86.2	-27.8	13	5	1,000	0	0.0	0.0
C- /3.7	14.9	0.64	11.50	42	1	98	0	1	60	78.8	-28.1	9	5	1,000	0	0.0	0.0
C- /4.0	14.9	0.64	13.48	76	1	98	0	1	60	88.8	-27.8	15	5	500,000	0	0.0	0.0
B- /7.9	6.8	0.68	23.77	1	0	67	29	4	167	35.5	-11.3	77	23	1,000	0	5.8	0.0
B- /7.9	6.8	0.68	23.71	5	0	67	29	4	167	35.6	-11.1	77	23	1,000	0	0.0	0.0
B- /7.8	6.8	0.68	20.10	1	0	67	29	4	167	25.9	-11.6	70	23	1,000	0	0.0	0.0
B- /7.9	6.8	0.68	23.83	41	0	67	29	4	167	37.6	-11.2	79	23	100,000	0	0.0	0.0
E- /0.1	44.2	2.49	14.52	18	0	98	1	1	18	-40.1	-12.2	98	23	1,000	0	5.8	0.0
E- /0.1	44.3	2.49	14.48	184	0	98	1	1	18	-40.2	-12.3	98	23	1,000	0	0.0	0.0
E- /0.0	44.3	2.49	13.40	18	0	98	1	1	18	-42.6	-12.5	97	23	1,000	0	0.0	0.0
E- /0.1	44.3	2.49	14.76	109	0	98	1	1	18	-39.4	-12.2	98	23	500,000	0	0.0	0.0
C+ /5.9	12.1	0.75	52.98	272	0	96	3	1	14	117.2	-21.0	81	26	1,000	0	5.8	0.0
C+ /5.9	12.1	0.75	53.00	1,846	0	96	3	1	14	117.2	-21.0	81	26	1,000	0	0.0	0.0
C+ /5.8	12.1	0.75	47.26	234	0	96	3	1	14	108.6	-21.2	75	26	1,000	0	0.0	0.0
C+ /5.9	12.1	0.75	54.04	1,300	0	96	3	1	14	120.2	-20.9	82	26	500,000	0	0.0	0.0
C+ /6.5	10.5	0.95	15.37	21	0	97	1	2	14	70.7	-28.5	28	6	1,000	0	5.8	0.0
C+ /6.5	10.5	0.95	15.38	16	0	97	1	2	14	70.8	-28.5	27	6	1,000	0	5.8	0.0
C+ /6.4	10.5	0.94	14.37	11	0	97	1	2	14	64.0	-28.8	21	6	1,000	0	0.0	0.0
C+ /6.5	10.5	0.94	15.69	24	0	97	1	2	14	73.2	-28.4	31	6	100,000	0	0.0	0.0
C+ /6.4	10.1	0.53	9.63	838	0	99	0	1	8	65.8	-8.7	54	18	1,000	0	5.8	0.0
C+ /6.4	10.1	0.54	9.49	370	0	99	0	1	8	65.7	-8.7	54	18	1,000	0	0.0	0.0

					PERFORMANCE							
99 Pct = Best 0 Pct = Worst							Total Return % through 2/28/17				Incl. in Returns	
Fund Type	Fund Name	Ticker Symbol	Overall Investment Rating	Phone	Perfor- mance Rating/Pts					Annualized		Dividend	Expense
						3 Mo	6 Mo	1Yr / Pct	3Yr / Pct	5Yr / Pct	Yield	Ratio
UT	Gabelli Utilities C	GAUCX	C+	(800) 422-3554	C / 5.4	7.49	6.37	17.25 /39	5.14 /56	7.78 /40	10.83	2.14
UT	Gabelli Utilities I	GAUIX	C+	(800) 422-3554	C+ / 6.3	7.84	6.80	18.29 /44	6.25 /66	8.88 /50	7.72	1.14
AG	Gabelli Value 25 A	GABVX	D-	(800) 422-3554	C- / 3.4	5.74	7.88	22.65 /65	2.75 /30	9.32 /53	0.40	1.39
GR	Gabelli Value 25 AAA	GVCAX	D	(800) 422-3554	C / 4.6	5.75	7.90	22.55 /65	2.75 /30	9.31 /53	0.42	1.39
AG	Gabelli Value 25 C	GVCCX	D-	(800) 422-3554	C- / 3.9	5.63	7.48	21.70 /61	1.98 /24	8.51 /46	0.00	2.14
AG	Gabelli Value 25 I	GVCIX	D	(800) 422-3554	C / 4.8	5.85	8.06	22.95 /66	3.03 /32	9.60 /55	0.70	1.14
GL	GAMCO Global Growth A	GGGAX	D	(800) 422-3554	D+ / 2.7	8.27	5.08	15.66 /33	2.89 /31	8.37 /45	0.43	1.68
GL	GAMCO Global Growth AAA	GICPX	D+	(800) 422-3554	C- / 3.8	8.29	5.10	15.68 /33	2.90 /31	8.36 /45	0.44	1.68
GL	GAMCO Global Growth C	GGGCX	D	(800) 422-3554	C- / 3.2	8.08	4.70	14.82 /29	2.13 /25	7.55 /39	0.00	2.43
GL	GAMCO Global Growth I	GGGIX	C-	(800) 422-3554	C / 4.3	8.47	5.50	16.50 /36	3.54 /37	8.88 /50	1.15	1.43
GL	GAMCO Global Opportunity A	GOCAX	D+	(800) 422-3554	D / 2.0	8.51	3.84	13.99 /25	1.68 /22	5.97 /28	1.01	2.67
GL	GAMCO Global Opportunity AAA	GABOX	C-	(800) 422-3554	D+ / 2.8	8.52	3.82	13.97 /25	1.70 /22	5.98 /28	1.14	2.67
GL	GAMCO Global Opportunity C	GGLCX	D+	(800) 422-3554	D+ / 2.5	8.41	3.71	13.66 /24	1.07 /19	5.27 /23	1.07	3.42
GL	GAMCO Global Opportunity I	GLOIX	C-	(800) 422-3554	C- / 3.3	8.71	4.03	14.39 /27	2.37 /26	6.51 /32	1.46	2.42
TC	GAMCO Global Telecom A	GTCAX	D-	(800) 422-3554	D / 1.6	7.46	2.59	9.85 /11	1.93 /23	5.84 /27	0.39	1.63
TC	GAMCO Global Telecom AAA	GABTX	D	(800) 422-3554	D+ / 2.3	7.48	2.62	10.03 /12	1.98 /24	5.87 /27	1.27	1.63
TC	GAMCO Global Telecom C	GTCCX	D	(800) 422-3554	D / 1.9	7.27	2.21	9.20 /10	1.21 /19	5.08 /22	0.44	2.38
TC	GAMCO Global Telecom I	GTTIX	D	(800) 422-3554	D+ / 2.5	7.59	2.78	10.36 /13	2.25 /26	6.16 /29	1.55	1.38
GR	GAMCO Growth A	GGCAX	C+	(800) 422-3554	C+ / 6.3	8.80	7.18	18.80 /46	7.81 /78	11.97 /74	0.00	1.43
GR	GAMCO Growth AAA	GABGX	B-	(800) 422-3554	B- / 7.2	8.78	7.16	18.78 /46	7.80 /77	11.96 /74	0.00	1.43
GR	GAMCO Growth C	GGCCX	C+	(800) 422-3554	C+ / 6.7	8.59	6.77	17.90 /42	6.99 /72	11.13 /67	0.00	2.18
GR	GAMCO Growth I	GGCIX	B-	(800) 422-3554	B- / 7.4	8.88	7.32	19.09 /48	8.08 /80	12.25 /77	0.00	1.18
FO	GAMCO International Growth A	GAIGX	E+	(800) 422-3554	E / 0.4	8.23	-0.60	10.28 /12	-2.06 / 6	2.17 / 8	1.43	2.12
FO	GAMCO International Growth AAA	GIGRX	E+	(800) 422-3554	E+ / 0.6	8.26	-0.59	10.29 /12	-2.06 / 6	2.15 / 8	1.56	2.12
FO	GAMCO International Growth C	GCIGX	E+	(800) 422-3554	E / 0.5	8.07	-0.89	9.48 /10	-2.79 / 5	1.42 / 7	0.83	2.87
FO	GAMCO International Growth I	GIIGX	D-	(800) 422-3554	E+ / 0.9	8.55	-0.05	11.50 /16	-1.12 / 9	2.87 /10	2.66	1.87
GR	GAMCO Mathers Fund	MATRX	E+	(800) 422-3554	E- / 0.0	-7.38	-10.10	-22.14 / 0	-10.03 / 1	-10.06 / 1	0.00	4.84
GI	Gateway A	GATEX	C	(800) 225-5478	D+ / 2.3	2.99	4.68	10.55 /13	4.27 /46	4.66 /19	1.26	1.01
GI	Gateway C	GTECX	C	(800) 225-5478	D+ / 2.8	2.81	4.30	9.73 /11	3.72 /39	4.01 /15	0.61	1.76
GR	Gateway Equity Call Premium Y	GCPYX	U	(800) 225-5478	U /	3.62	6.27	15.18 /31	--	--	1.12	1.45
GI	Gateway Y	GTEYX	C+	(800) 225-5478	C- / 3.5	3.05	4.80	10.81 /14	4.76 /52	5.05 /22	1.56	0.76
SC	Gator Focus Institutional	GFFIX	E	(855) 270-2678	E+ / 0.7	6.45	12.17	34.71 /94	-6.27 / 2	--	0.98	3.50
SC	Gator Focus Investor	GFFAX	E-	(855) 270-2678	E+ / 0.6	6.42	12.08	34.49 /93	-6.48 / 2	--	0.73	3.99
GL	Gavekal KL Allocation Advisor	GAVAX	C-	(888) 998-9890	D+ / 2.4	2.76	-1.62	7.95 / 7	4.48 /48	7.54 /39	0.26	1.47
GL	Gavekal KL Allocation Institutional	GAVIX	C-	(888) 998-9890	D+ / 2.6	2.81	-1.52	8.25 / 8	4.73 /51	7.81 /41	0.47	1.22
* GI	GE RSP US Equity	GESSX	B	(800) 242-0134	B+ / 8.9	8.89	10.57	26.39 /77	8.79 /85	13.19 /86	1.66	0.17
GR	Geneva Advisors All Cap Gr- Retail	GNVRX	D-	(877) 343-6382	C- / 3.7	6.88	3.31	20.59 /55	2.98 /32	6.63 /32	0.00	1.70
GR	Geneva Advisors All Cap Growth Inst	GNVIX	D-	(877) 343-6382	C- / 4.0	7.01	3.52	21.04 /58	3.34 /35	7.01 /35	0.00	1.38
GR	Geneva Advisors Equity Income I	GNEIX	C+	(877) 343-6382	C+ / 5.9	7.88	9.41	23.33 /68	4.68 /51	8.33 /45	0.90	1.42
GR	Geneva Advisors Equity Income R	GNERX	C+	(877) 343-6382	C+ / 5.6	7.78	9.24	22.89 /66	4.31 /46	7.96 /42	0.65	1.76
GL	Geneva Advisors Internatl Growth I	GNFIX	E+	(877) 343-6382	E / 0.5	6.20	1.57	13.59 /24	-2.61 / 5	--	0.38	2.30
GL	Geneva Advisors Internatl Growth R	GNFRX	E+	(877) 343-6382	E / 0.4	6.14	1.45	13.15 /22	-2.95 / 5	--	1.31	2.65
SC	Geneva Advisors Small Cap Opptys I	GNOIX	D-	(877) 343-6382	D+ / 2.8	4.15	4.05	22.19 /63	1.48 /21	--	0.00	2.87
SC	Geneva Advisors Small Cap Opptys	GNORX	D-	(877) 343-6382	D+ / 2.6	4.04	3.83	21.77 /61	1.13 /19	--	0.00	3.29
AA	George Putnam Balanced A	PGEOX	B-	(800) 225-1581	C / 4.9	5.83	6.27	17.26 /40	6.77 /70	9.09 /51	1.08	1.02
AA	George Putnam Balanced B	PGEBX	B-	(800) 225-1581	C / 5.5	5.65	5.89	16.38 /36	5.96 /64	8.26 /44	0.46	1.77
AA	George Putnam Balanced C	PGPCX	B-	(800) 225-1581	C / 5.4	5.57	5.81	16.31 /35	5.96 /64	8.26 /44	0.46	1.77
AA	George Putnam Balanced M	PGEMX	B-	(800) 225-1581	C / 4.9	5.67	5.98	16.66 /37	6.23 /66	8.54 /47	0.68	1.52
AA	George Putnam Balanced R	PGPRX	B-	(800) 225-1581	C+ / 5.9	5.70	6.08	16.95 /38	6.49 /68	8.80 /49	0.97	1.27
BA	George Putnam Balanced R5	PGELX	B-	(800) 225-1581	C+ / 6.5	6.22	6.73	17.95 /43	7.16 /73	--	1.33	0.73
BA	George Putnam Balanced R6	PGEJX	B-	(800) 225-1581	C+ / 6.4	5.91	6.45	17.68 /41	7.15 /73	--	1.48	0.63
AA	George Putnam Balanced Y	PGEYX	B-	(800) 225-1581	C+ / 6.4	5.88	6.39	17.55 /41	7.03 /72	9.36 /53	1.38	0.77

RISK Risk Rating/Pts	3 Year		NET ASSETS		ASSET				Portfolio Turnover Ratio	BULL / BEAR		FUND MANAGER		MINIMUMS		LOADS	
	Standard Deviation	Beta	NAV As of 2/28/17	Total $(Mil)	Cash %	Stocks %	Bonds %	Other %		Last Bull Market Return	Last Bear Market Return	Manager Quality Pct	Manager Tenure (Years)	Initial Purch. $	Additional Purch. $	Front End Load	Back End Load
C+ / 6.1	10.0	0.53	7.00	799	0	99	0	1	8	59.2	-9.0	44	18	1,000	0	0.0	0.0
C+ / 6.5	10.1	0.53	9.87	174	0	99	0	1	8	67.9	-8.6	59	18	500,000	0	0.0	0.0
C- / 3.1	12.0	1.07	15.42	399	0	98	0	2	3	88.6	-19.7	4	28	1,000	0	5.8	0.0
C- / 3.1	12.0	1.08	15.36	4	0	98	0	2	3	88.5	-19.7	4	28	1,000	0	0.0	0.0
D+ / 2.5	12.0	1.07	12.36	11	0	98	0	2	3	81.1	-19.9	3	28	1,000	0	0.0	0.0
C- / 3.1	12.0	1.07	15.40	50	0	98	0	2	3	91.4	-19.6	4	28	500,000	0	0.0	0.0
C / 5.1	10.8	0.81	28.33	3	1	98	0	1	53	93.6	-22.5	90	23	1,000	0	5.8	0.0
C / 5.1	10.8	0.81	28.34	67	1	98	0	1	53	93.6	-22.4	90	23	1,000	0	0.0	0.0
C / 4.9	10.8	0.81	24.64	1	1	98	0	1	53	85.9	-22.7	87	23	1,000	0	0.0	0.0
C / 5.1	10.8	0.81	28.58	4	1	98	0	1	53	98.4	-22.3	92	23	500,000	0	0.0	0.0
C+ / 6.5	10.8	0.79	23.93	N/A	0	99	0	1	7	61.6	-22.7	85	19	1,000	0	5.8	0.0
C+ / 6.5	10.7	0.79	24.01	8	0	99	0	1	7	61.5	-22.6	85	19	1,000	0	0.0	0.0
C+ / 6.5	10.8	0.79	23.03	N/A	0	99	0	1	7	55.8	-22.9	82	19	1,000	0	0.0	0.0
C+ / 6.6	10.8	0.79	24.35	2	0	99	0	1	7	65.9	-22.6	88	19	500,000	0	0.0	0.0
C / 5.5	11.7	0.89	21.36	1	0	94	5	1	5	48.1	-18.6	5	24	1,000	0	5.8	0.0
C / 5.5	11.7	0.89	21.21	85	0	94	5	1	5	48.3	-18.6	5	24	1,000	0	0.0	0.0
C / 5.6	11.7	0.88	20.58	N/A	0	94	5	1	5	42.4	-18.9	4	24	1,000	0	0.0	0.0
C / 5.4	11.7	0.89	21.19	10	0	94	5	1	5	50.5	-18.5	6	24	100,000	0	0.0	0.0
C / 5.4	11.6	1.07	50.05	3	0	99	0	1	67	122.7	-19.9	31	22	1,000	0	5.8	0.0
C / 5.4	11.6	1.07	50.03	488	0	99	0	1	67	122.6	-19.9	31	22	1,000	0	0.0	0.0
C / 5.3	11.6	1.07	44.74	2	0	99	0	1	67	113.8	-20.2	23	22	1,000	0	0.0	0.0
C / 5.5	11.6	1.07	50.87	40	0	99	0	1	67	125.7	-19.8	34	22	500,000	0	0.0	0.0
C / 5.3	11.9	0.88	21.18	1	2	97	0	1	15	32.9	-20.9	49	22	1,000	0	5.8	0.0
C / 5.3	11.8	0.88	20.78	17	2	97	0	1	15	32.7	-20.9	49	22	1,000	0	0.0	0.0
C / 5.1	11.8	0.88	19.04	N/A	2	97	0	1	15	27.6	-21.1	39	22	1,000	0	0.0	0.0
C / 5.3	11.8	0.88	21.07	8	2	97	0	1	15	37.6	-20.8	62	22	500,000	0	0.0	0.0
C+ / 6.0	8.5	-0.80	5.52	11	41	0	58	1	0	-44.5	0.6	38	44	1,000	0	0.0	0.0
B / 8.3	4.2	0.38	31.57	1,803	2	97	0	1	10	35.2	-6.0	76	11	2,500	100	5.8	0.0
B / 8.3	4.2	0.38	31.41	361	2	97	0	1	10	30.6	-6.3	71	11	2,500	100	0.0	0.0
U /	N/A	N/A	11.20	67	1	98	0	1	38	N/A	N/A	N/A	3	100,000	100	0.0	0.0
B / 8.3	4.2	0.38	31.57	5,629	2	97	0	1	10	37.9	-5.9	79	11	100,000	100	0.0	0.0
C- / 3.0	17.1	0.97	10.95	2	10	89	0	1	52	N/A	N/A	1	4	100,000	2,000	0.0	1.0
D+ / 2.9	17.1	0.97	10.88	N/A	10	89	0	1	52	N/A	N/A	1	4	5,000	1,000	0.0	1.0
B- / 7.2	7.3	0.44	13.85	59	15	74	10	1	104	62.0	-2.3	94	7	2,500	250	0.0	0.0
B- / 7.2	7.3	0.44	14.02	434	15	74	10	1	104	64.4	-2.2	95	7	500,000	25,000	0.0	0.0
C- / 4.1	11.7	1.11	52.73	5,184	3	96	0	1	37	129.9	-18.6	37	10	0	0	0.0	0.0
C- / 3.0	13.7	1.06	24.33	4	0	99	0	1	46	64.1	-18.8	4	10	1,000	100	0.0	2.0
C- / 3.2	13.7	1.06	25.25	130	0	99	0	1	46	67.3	-18.7	5	10	100,000	1,000	0.0	2.0
C+ / 5.9	11.1	1.04	34.08	104	16	83	0	1	41	81.6	-13.1	9	14	100,000	1,000	0.0	2.0
C+ / 5.9	11.1	1.04	33.94	2	16	83	0	1	41	78.3	-13.3	8	14	1,000	100	0.0	2.0
C / 5.3	12.4	0.88	21.79	17	2	97	0	1	60	N/A	N/A	41	4	100,000	1,000	0.0	2.0
C / 5.3	12.5	0.89	21.28	N/A	2	97	0	1	60	N/A	N/A	36	4	1,000	100	0.0	2.0
C / 4.4	16.1	0.91	21.09	13	5	94	0	1	82	N/A	N/A	18	4	100,000	1,000	0.0	2.0
C / 4.4	16.0	0.91	20.86	N/A	5	94	0	1	82	N/A	N/A	15	4	1,000	100	0.0	2.0
B- / 7.9	7.1	1.12	18.34	965	3	62	34	1	154	75.3	-10.5	55	3	500	0	5.8	0.0
B- / 7.9	7.1	1.12	18.15	22	3	62	34	1	154	68.3	-10.9	44	3	500	0	0.0	0.0
B- / 7.9	7.1	1.13	18.22	45	3	62	34	1	154	68.2	-10.9	43	3	500	0	0.0	0.0
B- / 7.9	7.1	1.12	18.10	70	3	62	34	1	154	70.6	-10.7	47	3	500	0	3.5	0.0
B- / 7.9	7.1	1.13	18.28	1	3	62	34	1	154	72.8	-10.7	50	3	500	0	0.0	0.0
B- / 7.8	7.2	1.13	18.47	N/A	3	62	34	1	154	N/A	N/A	59	3	500	0	0.0	0.0
B- / 7.8	7.1	1.12	18.40	13	3	62	34	1	154	N/A	N/A	60	3	500	0	0.0	0.0
B- / 7.9	7.1	1.13	18.40	70	3	62	34	1	154	77.7	-10.5	57	3	500	0	0.0	0.0

I. Index of Stock Mutual Funds

99 Pct = Best
0 Pct = Worst

Fund Type	Fund Name	Ticker Symbol	Overall Investment Rating	Phone	Perfor-mance Rating/Pts	3 Mo	6 Mo	1Yr / Pct	3Yr / Pct	5Yr / Pct	Dividend Yield	Expense Ratio
									Annualized		Incl. in Returns	
RE	Gerstein Fisher Mlt-Fac Gl RE Sec	GFMRX	C+	(800) 473-1155	C / 5.2	6.98	-2.45	12.61 /20	7.97 /79	--	3.12	1.03
GL	Gerstein Fisher Mlt-Fac Intl Gr Ety	GFIGX	D-	(800) 473-1155	E+ / 0.8	8.43	3.21	9.06 /10	-1.19 / 9	6.89 /34	1.00	1.19
GL	GF Multi-Factor Growth Equity Fd I	GFMGX	A-	(800) 473-1155	B+ / 8.5	8.19	10.39	23.03 /67	9.24 /88	13.29 /87	0.53	1.05
AA	Ginkgo Multi-Strategy Inv	GNKIX	D-	(855) 289-4656	E- / 0.2	2.84	1.29	-3.68 / 1	-3.62 / 4	1.34 / 7	0.00	2.37
GL	GKE Asian Opportunities Fund Inst	GKEAX	D+	(866) 759-5679	D / 1.9	4.87	-0.61	10.29 /12	2.68 /29	--	1.51	3.69
FO	Glenmede International Port	GTCIX	D-	(800) 442-8299	E+ / 0.7	6.42	3.39	10.77 /14	-2.20 / 6	2.69 /10	1.76	1.24
FO	Glenmede Intl Sec Opt Ptfl	NOVIX	D	(800) 442-8299	D- / 1.0	6.58	4.15	13.31 /23	-1.21 / 9	--	2.24	0.89
GR	Glenmede Large Cap Core Advisor	GTLOX	A+	(800) 442-8299	A / 9.4	8.14	10.68	25.08 /74	10.64 /96	15.34 /97	1.01	0.87
GR	Glenmede Large Cap Core Inst	GTLIX	U	(800) 442-8299	U /	8.22	10.82	25.42 /75	--	--	1.19	0.65
GR	Glenmede Large Cap Growth Advisor	GTLLX	A+	(800) 442-8299	A- / 9.1	8.00	8.40	20.41 /54	11.29 /97	15.12 /97	0.54	0.87
GR	Glenmede Large Cap Growth Port	GTILX	U	(800) 442-8299	U /	8.04	8.49	20.67 /56	--	--	0.70	0.67
GR	Glenmede Large Cap Value Port	GTMEX	B	(800) 442-8299	A+ / 9.6	6.33	12.95	32.99 /92	9.61 /91	13.53 /89	1.65	0.91
IN	Glenmede Long/Short Portfolio	GTAPX	C+	(800) 442-8299	D+ / 2.8	2.56	6.08	7.02 / 6	4.04 /43	5.37 /24	0.00	2.64
IN	Glenmede Secured Options Advisor	GTSOX	C+	(800) 442-8299	C- / 4.2	1.36	4.49	13.03 /22	5.89 /63	7.49 /38	0.00	0.84
SC	● Glenmede Small Cap Equity Adv	GTCSX	B	(800) 442-8299	B / 7.9	6.09	12.15	29.35 /85	6.50 /68	13.51 /89	0.12	0.91
SC	● Glenmede Small Cap Equity Inst	GTSCX	B	(800) 442-8299	B / 8.1	6.12	12.26	29.59 /85	6.71 /70	13.73 /91	0.22	0.71
GR	Glenmede Strategic Equity	GTCEX	A-	(800) 442-8299	A+ / 9.6	8.27	10.75	26.30 /77	11.04 /97	12.68 /81	0.86	0.84
FO	Glenmede Total Market Port	GTTMX	A	(800) 442-8299	B / 8.2	6.68	13.16	23.29 /67	7.96 /79	13.02 /84	0.53	2.29
SC	Glenmede US Emerging Growth Port	GTGSX	B-	(800) 442-8299	B- / 7.5	5.33	10.53	28.24 /82	6.38 /67	10.72 /64	0.30	0.94
EM	Global Strategic Income A	VEEEX	D	(800) 673-0550	E / 0.4	7.40	0.41	5.52 / 4	-0.85 /10	0.99 / 6	0.00	3.88
EM	Global Strategic Income C	VEECX	D	(800) 673-0550	E+ / 0.6	7.22	0.04	4.75 / 4	-1.59 / 8	0.23 / 5	0.00	4.63
GL	GMG Defensive Beta	MPDAX	E+	(877) 464-3111	E / 0.4	2.29	-1.22	0.40 / 1	-1.74 / 7	2.17 / 8	0.00	2.42
GL	GMO Alpha Only III	GGHEX	D		E / 0.3	1.68	-1.79	-1.94 / 1	-1.57 / 8	-1.00 / 3	3.01	0.72
GL	GMO Alpha Only IV	GAPOX	D		E / 0.3	1.66	-1.77	-1.89 / 1	-1.51 / 8	-0.95 / 3	3.04	0.66
AA	GMO Asset Allocation Bond III	GMOBX	D		E+ / 0.7	0.73	-0.58	-0.05 / 1	0.27 /15	0.39 / 5	0.00	0.45
AA	GMO Asset Allocation Bond VI	GABFX	D		E+ / 0.7	0.82	-0.54	0.09 / 1	0.39 /15	0.49 / 5	0.00	0.36
IN	GMO Benchmark-Free Alloca Srs R6	GBMRX	C-		D / 1.9	4.72	3.33	11.41 /16	1.04 /18	--	1.51	1.00
★ AA	GMO Benchmark-Free Allocation III	GBMFX	C-		D / 2.0	4.80	3.35	11.66 /17	1.14 /19	3.83 /14	1.54	1.09
AA	GMO Benchmark-Free Allocation IV	GBMBX	C-		D / 2.0	4.84	3.39	11.71 /17	1.19 /19	--	1.59	1.04
EM	● GMO Emerging Countries III	GMCEX	C		C+ / 6.7	10.73	7.23	36.00 /95	2.52 /28	-1.16 / 3	1.19	2.10
EM	● GMO Emerging Markets II	GMEMX	C-		C+ / 5.9	10.37	6.05	34.47 /93	2.22 /25	-1.19 / 3	2.01	1.13
EM	● GMO Emerging Markets III	GMOEX	C-		C+ / 6.0	10.39	6.08	34.67 /94	2.28 /26	-1.14 / 3	2.06	1.07
EM	● GMO Emerging Markets IV	GMEFX	C-		C+ / 6.0	10.41	6.10	34.61 /94	2.34 /26	-1.08 / 3	2.12	1.02
EM	● GMO Emerging Markets V	GEMVX	C-		C+ / 6.0	10.43	6.11	34.67 /94	2.34 /26	-1.03 / 3	2.16	1.01
EM	● GMO Emerging Markets VI	GEMMX	C-		C+ / 6.1	10.46	6.15	34.88 /94	2.42 /27	-1.01 / 3	2.18	0.98
EM	GMO Emg Domestic Opportunities II	GEDTX	D+		C- / 3.1	6.72	0.28	20.62 /56	2.30 /26	3.68 /14	2.85	1.22
EM	GMO Emg Domestic Opportunities III	GEDSX	D+		C- / 3.1	6.74	0.29	20.73 /56	2.37 /26	--	2.89	1.15
EM	GMO Emg Domestic Opportunities IV	GEDIX	D+		C- / 3.2	6.78	0.33	20.80 /56	2.43 /27	--	2.95	1.11
EM	GMO Emg Domestic Opportunities VI	GEDFX	D+		C- / 3.2	6.76	0.35	21.32 /59	2.49 /27	3.86 /14	2.79	1.06
FO	GMO Foreign II	GMFRX	D-		D- / 1.4	6.45	6.07	15.62 /33	-0.41 /12	4.87 /20	2.60	1.01
FO	GMO Foreign III	GMOFX	D-		D- / 1.4	6.52	6.15	15.81 /33	-0.31 /12	4.96 /21	2.66	0.93
FO	GMO Foreign IV	GMFFX	D-		D- / 1.5	6.46	6.19	15.95 /34	-0.26 /12	4.99 /21	2.58	0.88
FO	GMO Foreign Small Companies Fund	GFSFX	D-		E+ / 0.9	7.12	3.28	14.34 /27	-1.48 / 8	6.63 /32	2.48	0.87
FO	● GMO Foreign Small Companies III	GMFSX	D-		E+ / 0.9	7.07	3.24	14.25 /27	-1.55 / 8	6.57 /32	2.43	0.92
GL	GMO Global Asset Allocation III	GMWAX	D+		D+ / 2.4	5.05	3.83	13.33 /23	1.75 /22	4.69 /19	2.40	0.55
GL	GMO Global Asset Allocation Srs R6	GATRX	D		D+ / 2.3	5.01	3.70	13.01 /22	1.62 /22	--	2.43	0.60
AA	GMO Global Develope Eqty Alloc III	GWOAX	D		C- / 3.8	7.69	7.12	20.03 /52	1.85 /23	7.55 /39	2.74	0.56
GL	GMO Global Eq Allocation III	GMGEX	D+		C- / 4.1	8.05	6.97	21.93 /62	1.94 /24	6.50 /31	3.00	0.65
GL	GMO Global Equity Allocation Srs R6	GGASX	D		C- / 3.7	8.01	6.87	21.58 /60	1.23 /19	--	2.90	0.71
GL	● GMO International Eq Alloc III	GIEAX	E+		D- / 1.3	8.04	5.79	21.57 /60	-1.64 / 8	3.57 /13	3.27	0.80
FO	GMO International Eq Alloc Srs R6	GEARX	E+		D- / 1.3	7.92	5.71	21.25 /58	-1.67 / 7	--	3.25	0.84
FO	GMO International Equity II	GMICX	E		E+ / 0.6	6.86	5.57	15.45 /32	-3.44 / 4	4.23 /16	3.77	0.76

● Denotes fund is closed to new investors
★ Denotes fund is included in Section II

www.thestreetratings.com

RISK Risk Rating/Pts	3 Year Standard Deviation	Beta	NET ASSETS NAV As of 2/28/17	Total $(Mil)	ASSET Cash %	Stocks %	Bonds %	Other %	Portfolio Turnover Ratio	BULL / BEAR Last Bull Market Return	Last Bear Market Return	FUND MANAGER Manager Quality Pct	Manager Tenure (Years)	MINIMUMS Initial Purch. $	Additional Purch. $	LOADS Front End Load	Back End Load
C+ / 6.8	11.9	0.84	10.84	110	14	85	0	1	9	N/A	N/A	60	3	2,500	100	0.0	1.0
C+ / 5.8	12.5	0.96	12.94	146	0	99	0	1	30	N/A	N/A	62	5	2,500	100	0.0	1.0
C+ / 6.1	11.4	0.68	19.21	280	0	99	0	1	40	130.5	-16.8	99	8	2,500	100	0.0	1.0
C+ / 6.0	6.9	0.69	9.42	21	0	0	0	100	1,837	10.7	N/A	3	1	250	50	0.0	1.0
C+ / 6.6	9.6	1.14	10.50	17	13	57	29	1	232	N/A	N/A	41	4	100,000	0	0.0	2.0
C+ / 6.3	11.1	0.89	13.33	419	0	99	0	1	121	36.7	-27.6	47	3	1,000	0	0.0	0.0
C+ / 6.6	9.7	0.77	9.99	16	46	53	0	1	70	N/A	N/A	61	5	1,000	0	0.0	0.0
B- / 7.8	10.7	1.01	25.34	1,991	0	0	0	100	111	154.4	-18.4	73	13	1,000	0	0.0	0.0
U /	N/A	N/A	25.36	360	0	0	0	100	111	N/A	N/A	N/A	13	10,000,000	0	0.0	0.0
B / 8.2	11.0	1.03	27.71	3,420	0	0	0	100	88	156.3	-18.4	77	13	1,000	0	0.0	0.0
U /	N/A	N/A	27.72	80	0	0	0	100	88	N/A	N/A	N/A	13	10,000,000	0	0.0	0.0
C- / 4.0	12.5	1.13	10.80	82	0	99	0	1	110	134.4	-26.6	45	9	1,000	0	0.0	0.0
B+ / 9.5	4.6	0.32	12.04	267	70	29	0	1	98	42.3	-5.1	79	11	1,000	0	0.0	0.0
B- / 7.9	6.8	0.54	12.25	661	0	0	0	100	0	69.5	-10.4	76	1	1,000	0	0.0	0.0
C+ / 5.6	15.4	0.96	29.65	1,541	2	97	0	1	58	136.7	-23.6	73	21	1,000	0	0.0	0.0
C+ / 5.6	15.4	0.96	30.91	1,670	2	97	0	1	58	139.2	-23.6	74	21	10,000,000	0	0.0	0.0
C / 5.3	10.6	1.01	22.26	189	2	97	0	1	22	124.8	-18.3	76	N/A	1,000	0	0.0	0.0
C+ / 6.8	11.3	0.64	16.73	68	0	99	0	1	88	130.0	-21.0	98	11	1,000	0	0.0	0.0
C / 5.4	14.6	0.91	10.93	62	0	99	0	1	100	114.9	-24.6	75	12	1,000	0	0.0	0.0
C+ / 6.9	10.4	0.37	24.66	13	8	91	0	1	73	19.7	-29.5	54	2	2,500	50	5.8	0.0
C+ / 6.9	10.4	0.37	22.29	N/A	8	91	0	1	73	14.9	-29.8	44	2	2,500	50	0.0	0.0
C / 5.0	6.6	0.39	9.89	17	21	73	5	1	53	30.4	-16.9	52	8	1,000	250	0.0	0.0
B- / 7.6	3.8	0.08	20.96	8	5	88	6	1	85	-7.8	6.1	48	21	0	0	0.0	0.0
B- / 7.6	3.7	0.08	20.97	226	5	88	6	1	85	-7.6	6.1	48	21	125,000,000	0	0.0	0.0
B- / 7.4	5.9	0.21	22.15	282	0	0	99	1	177	3.4	0.5	58	8	0	0	0.0	0.0
B- / 7.5	5.9	0.21	22.23	1,212	0	0	99	1	177	4.0	0.5	60	8	300,000,000	0	0.0	0.0
B- / 7.5	6.3	0.48	9.96	218	20	51	28	1	27	N/A	N/A	24	4	10,000,000	0	0.0	0.0
B- / 7.6	6.3	0.83	25.78	5,178	7	46	46	1	53	31.1	-4.0	16	N/A	0	0	0.1	0.1
B- / 7.6	6.3	0.83	25.78	2,663	7	46	46	1	53	N/A	N/A	16	14	125,000,000	0	0.1	0.1
C- / 3.8	16.7	1.01	27.06	28	2	97	0	1	59	15.6	-27.2	79	20	0	0	0.0	0.0
C- / 3.9	16.9	1.03	29.98	499	1	96	1	2	104	14.6	-26.5	77	24	0	0	0.8	0.8
C- / 3.9	17.0	1.03	30.05	302	1	96	1	2	104	14.9	-26.5	78	24	50,000,000	0	0.8	0.8
C- / 3.9	17.0	1.03	29.78	582	1	96	1	2	104	15.3	-26.5	78	24	125,000,000	0	0.8	0.8
C- / 3.9	17.0	1.03	29.70	110	1	96	1	2	104	15.5	-26.5	78	24	250,000,000	0	0.8	0.8
C- / 3.9	17.0	1.03	29.78	3,524	1	96	1	2	104	15.7	-26.5	79	24	300,000,000	0	0.8	0.8
C / 5.5	11.3	0.63	22.64	608	4	95	0	1	250	39.2	-17.9	82	6	0	0	0.8	0.8
C / 5.5	11.3	0.63	22.64	129	4	95	0	1	250	N/A	N/A	82	6	50,000,000	0	0.8	0.8
C / 5.5	11.3	0.64	22.65	335	4	95	0	1	250	N/A	N/A	83	6	125,000,000	0	0.8	0.8
C / 5.5	11.5	0.64	22.76	15	4	95	0	1	250	40.5	N/A	83	6	300,000,000	0	0.8	0.8
C+ / 5.6	10.9	0.84	11.76	64	0	98	1	1	113	46.0	-23.2	71	33	0	0	0.0	0.0
C+ / 5.6	10.9	0.84	11.85	76	0	98	1	1	113	46.6	-23.2	72	33	0	0	0.0	0.0
C+ / 5.6	10.9	0.84	12.19	3	0	98	1	1	113	46.9	-23.1	73	33	125,000,000	0	0.0	0.0
C / 5.4	11.9	0.89	14.38	571	2	94	3	1	60	58.5	-24.2	57	6	125,000,000	0	0.5	0.5
C / 5.4	11.9	0.89	14.41	247	2	94	3	1	60	57.9	-24.2	57	6	0	0	0.5	0.5
C+ / 6.6	6.9	1.00	30.48	2,424	3	54	42	1	20	37.5	-7.9	37	N/A	0	0	0.1	0.1
C / 5.3	6.8	0.99	8.95	180	4	53	42	1	7	N/A	N/A	36	21	10,000,000	0	0.0	0.0
C / 4.3	10.8	1.54	19.60	992	1	97	1	1	14	64.7	-14.2	3	12	0	0	0.1	0.1
C / 4.4	11.2	1.66	22.84	2,207	1	97	1	1	15	57.8	-15.6	11	N/A	0	0	0.1	0.1
C / 4.6	11.2	0.85	9.73	15	1	97	1	1	18	N/A	N/A	83	21	10,000,000	0	0.0	0.0
C / 4.5	12.5	1.74	27.49	1,086	2	96	1	1	14	36.3	-21.9	2	N/A	0	0	0.2	0.2
C- / 4.0	12.4	0.94	9.00	225	2	96	0	2	4	N/A	N/A	55	5	10,000,000	0	0.0	0.0
C / 4.5	11.9	0.93	20.18	10	2	96	0	2	75	36.7	-21.8	30	2	0	0	0.0	0.0

| 99 Pct = Best 0 Pct = Worst | | | | | PERFORMANCE | | | | | | |
| | | | | | Perfor-mance Rating/Pts | Total Return % through 2/28/17 | | | Annualized | | Incl. in Returns |
Fund Type	Fund Name	Ticker Symbol	Overall Investment Rating	Phone		3 Mo	6 Mo	1Yr / Pct	3Yr / Pct	5Yr / Pct	Dividend Yield	Expense Ratio
FO	GMO International Equity III	GMOIX	E		E+ / 0.6	6.89	5.56	15.53 / 32	-3.39 / 4	4.29 / 17	3.85	0.69
FO	GMO International Equity IV	GMCFX	E		E+ / 0.6	6.89	5.61	15.57 / 32	-3.33 / 4	4.36 / 17	3.92	0.63
FO	● GMO International Small Co III	GMISX	E		E+ / 0.9	7.14	3.70	14.35 / 27	-1.38 / 8	8.01 / 42	4.71	0.94
GL	GMO Intl Developed Equity Alloc III	GIOTX	E+		E+ / 0.8	7.19	5.63	17.37 / 40	-2.72 / 5	4.96 / 21	3.87	0.66
FO	GMO Intl Large/Mid Cap Eqty III	GMIEX	E		E / 0.5	6.62	4.78	14.70 / 29	-3.85 / 3	4.27 / 17	5.43	0.60
FO	GMO Intl Large/Mid Cap Eqty IV	GMIRX	E		E / 0.5	6.64	4.79	14.79 / 29	-3.79 / 3	4.34 / 17	5.58	0.54
FO	GMO Intl Large/Mid Cap Eqty VI	GCEFX	E		E / 0.5	6.65	4.82	14.81 / 29	-3.76 / 3	4.36 / 17	5.67	0.51
IN	GMO Quality Equity III	GQETX	B		B+ / 8.7	9.14	6.86	20.25 / 53	10.24 / 95	12.26 / 77	1.57	0.50
IN	GMO Quality Equity IV	GQEFX	B		A- / 9.1	9.17	6.89	21.98 / 62	10.80 / 97	12.62 / 80	2.89	0.46
IN	GMO Quality Equity V	GQLFX	B		A- / 9.1	9.18	6.90	22.05 / 62	10.83 / 97	12.65 / 80	2.94	0.44
IN	GMO Quality Equity VI	GQLOX	B		A- / 9.1	9.16	6.88	22.04 / 62	10.84 / 97	12.68 / 81	2.96	0.41
EN	GMO Resources III	GOFIX	D-		C / 4.9	7.37	22.73	51.75 / 99	-0.60 / 11	-0.29 / 4	2.74	0.87
EN	GMO Resources IV	GOVIX	D-		C / 4.9	7.34	22.67	51.72 / 99	-0.57 / 11	--	2.80	0.83
GL	GMO Risk Premium III	GMRPX	C+		C+ / 6.4	4.77	8.34	19.51 / 49	6.64 / 69	--	0.00	0.65
GL	GMO Risk Premium VI	GMOKX	C+		C+ / 6.5	4.79	8.38	19.63 / 50	6.75 / 70	--	0.00	0.60
GL	GMO SGM Major Markets III	GSMFX	C		D / 1.6	2.88	-1.51	5.15 / 4	2.80 / 30	3.08 / 11	2.99	1.04
GL	GMO SGM Major Markets VI	GSMHX	U		U /	2.94	-1.48	5.25 / 4	--	--	3.45	0.99
GL	GMO Special Opportunities VI	GSOFX	U		U /	4.50	2.48	15.32 / 31	--	--	3.36	1.34
AA	GMO Strategic Opps Alloc III	GBATX	D+		C- / 3.2	6.04	4.78	16.66 / 37	2.27 / 26	6.79 / 33	2.71	0.56
FO	GMO Tax-Managed Intl Equities III	GTMIX	E+		E / 0.5	7.73	5.10	15.05 / 30	-4.00 / 3	4.20 / 16	3.87	0.80
IN	GMO US Equity Allocation III	GMUEX	B		B+ / 8.4	6.55	10.50	23.59 / 68	9.16 / 88	12.30 / 77	2.05	0.48
IN	GMO US Equity Allocation IV	GMRTX	B		B+ / 8.5	6.60	10.49	23.69 / 69	9.25 / 88	12.38 / 78	1.78	0.43
IN	GMO US Equity Allocation VI	GMCQX	B+		B+ / 8.7	6.60	10.57	23.77 / 69	9.28 / 89	12.42 / 78	2.15	0.39
PM	Gold Bullion Strategy Fund Investor	QGLDX	E+	(855) 747-9555	E- / 0.1	4.38	-7.74	-2.99 / 1	-4.27 / 3	--	0.00	1.62
GI	Goldman Sachs Abslt Ret Tracker A	GARTX	C-	(800) 526-7384	D- / 1.4	2.65	3.22	8.20 / 8	2.21 / 25	2.76 / 10	0.00	1.71
GI	Goldman Sachs Abslt Ret Tracker C	GCRTX	C-	(800) 526-7384	D / 1.6	2.47	2.84	7.33 / 6	1.45 / 21	2.00 / 8	0.00	2.46
GI	Goldman Sachs Abslt Ret Tracker I	GJRTX	C	(800) 526-7384	D / 2.1	2.82	3.38	8.61 / 9	2.61 / 28	3.18 / 11	0.23	1.31
GI	Goldman Sachs Abslt Ret Tracker IR	GSRTX	C	(800) 526-7384	D / 2.1	2.74	3.31	8.57 / 9	2.49 / 27	3.01 / 11	0.14	1.46
GI	Goldman Sachs Abslt Ret Tracker R	GRRTX	C-	(800) 526-7384	D / 1.8	2.59	3.06	7.88 / 7	1.95 / 24	2.49 / 9	0.00	1.96
FO	Goldman Sachs Asia Equity A	GSAGX	D	(800) 526-7384	D / 2.0	4.94	-0.19	17.21 / 39	2.37 / 26	3.09 / 11	0.00	1.99
FO	Goldman Sachs Asia Equity C	GSACX	D	(800) 526-7384	D+ / 2.3	4.72	-0.51	16.40 / 36	1.60 / 22	2.32 / 9	0.00	2.76
FO	Goldman Sachs Asia Equity Inst	GSAIX	D+	(800) 526-7384	C- / 3.1	5.06	0.04	17.70 / 41	2.77 / 30	3.51 / 13	0.00	1.61
FO	Goldman Sachs Asia Equity IR	GSAEX	D+	(800) 526-7384	D+ / 2.9	4.99	-0.04	17.54 / 41	2.62 / 28	--	0.00	1.75
AA	Goldman Sachs Balanced Strat A	GIPAX	C-	(800) 526-7384	D / 1.7	3.96	2.52	10.29 / 12	2.70 / 29	4.46 / 18	0.98	1.40
AA	Goldman Sachs Balanced Strat C	GIPCX	C-	(800) 526-7384	D / 1.9	3.74	2.13	9.46 / 10	1.91 / 23	3.68 / 14	0.38	2.15
AA	Goldman Sachs Balanced Strat Inst	GIPIX	C	(800) 526-7384	D+ / 2.6	4.08	2.74	10.72 / 14	3.08 / 33	4.87 / 20	1.42	1.00
AA	Goldman Sachs Balanced Strat IR	GIPTX	C	(800) 526-7384	D+ / 2.5	4.05	2.67	10.61 / 13	2.94 / 31	4.73 / 20	1.28	1.15
AA	Goldman Sachs Balanced Strat R	GIPRX	C	(800) 526-7384	D / 2.2	3.91	2.41	9.97 / 12	2.50 / 27	4.25 / 17	0.82	1.65
AA	Goldman Sachs Balanced Strat Svc	GIPSX	C	(800) 526-7384	D+ / 2.4	3.98	2.53	10.16 / 12	2.83 / 30	4.51 / 18	0.92	1.50
GR	Goldman Sachs Capital Growth A	GSCGX	C	(800) 526-7384	B- / 7.1	10.47	8.83	21.17 / 58	8.14 / 80	12.31 / 77	0.05	1.51
GR	Goldman Sachs Capital Growth C	GSPCX	C	(800) 526-7384	B- / 7.4	10.27	8.44	20.28 / 54	7.32 / 74	11.47 / 70	0.00	2.26
GR	Goldman Sachs Capital Growth Inst	GSPIX	B-	(800) 526-7384	B+ / 8.3	10.58	9.03	21.68 / 61	8.56 / 83	12.75 / 81	0.40	1.11
GR	Goldman Sachs Capital Growth IR	GSPTX	C+	(800) 526-7384	B / 8.2	10.51	8.93	21.48 / 60	8.38 / 82	12.58 / 80	0.31	1.26
GR	Goldman Sachs Capital Growth R	GSPRX	C+	(800) 526-7384	B / 7.8	10.38	8.69	20.85 / 57	7.85 / 78	12.01 / 74	0.00	1.76
GR	Goldman Sachs Capital Growth Svc	GSPSX	C+	(800) 526-7384	B / 7.9	10.40	8.74	21.00 / 57	8.01 / 79	12.19 / 76	0.00	1.61
GI	Goldman Sachs Commodity Strat A	GSCAX	E-	(800) 526-7384	E- / 0.0	3.33	9.08	18.16 / 44	-20.24 / 0	-14.38 / 0	0.52	1.10
GI	Goldman Sachs Commodity Strat C	GSCCX	E-	(800) 526-7384	E- / 0.0	3.10	8.70	17.29 / 40	-20.85 / 0	-15.02 / 0	0.00	1.85
GI	Goldman Sachs Commodity Strat I	GCCIX	E-	(800) 526-7384	E- / 0.0	3.37	9.26	18.54 / 45	-19.96 / 0	-14.11 / 0	0.85	0.76
GI	Goldman Sachs Commodity Strat IR	GCCTX	E-	(800) 526-7384	E- / 0.0	3.30	9.19	18.31 / 44	-20.05 / 0	-14.18 / 0	0.76	0.85
GI	Goldman Sachs Commodity Strat R	GCCRX	E-	(800) 526-7384	E- / 0.0	3.20	8.93	17.82 / 42	-20.45 / 0	-14.60 / 0	0.39	1.36
GR	Goldman Sachs Concentrated Gr A	GCGAX	D+	(800) 526-7384	C+ / 5.7	10.23	6.79	18.78 / 46	6.50 / 68	10.91 / 65	0.18	1.63
GR	Goldman Sachs Concentrated Gr C	GCGCX	D+	(800) 526-7384	C+ / 6.1	9.99	6.39	17.86 / 42	5.68 / 61	10.07 / 59	0.00	2.38

● Denotes fund is closed to new investors

* Denotes fund is included in Section II

www.thestreetratings.com

Risk Rating/Pts	3 Year Standard Deviation	Beta	NAV As of 2/28/17	Total $(Mil)	Cash %	Stocks %	Bonds %	Other %	Portfolio Turnover Ratio	Last Bull Market Return	Last Bear Market Return	Manager Quality Pct	Manager Tenure (Years)	Initial Purch. $	Additional Purch. $	Front End Load	Back End Load
C /4.5	11.9	0.93	20.41	731	2	96	0	2	75	37.2	-21.8	31	2	0	0	0.0	0.0
C /4.5	11.9	0.93	20.38	5,072	2	96	0	2	75	37.6	-21.8	32	2	125,000,000	0	0.0	0.0
C- /3.4	12.3	0.93	21.53	127	6	92	1	1	64	65.5	-22.9	59	5	0	0	0.5	0.5
C /5.0	12.0	1.66	14.72	602	1	97	0	2	14	42.7	-20.3	2	N/A	0	0	0.1	0.1
C- /4.0	11.9	0.93	25.44	39	0	98	0	2	88	38.8	-21.2	26	5	0	0	0.0	0.0
C- /4.0	11.9	0.93	25.40	146	0	98	0	2	88	39.3	-21.2	26	5	125,000,000	0	0.0	0.0
C- /4.0	11.9	0.93	25.38	1	0	98	0	2	88	39.4	-21.2	27	5	300,000,000	0	0.0	0.0
C /4.4	9.7	0.87	22.05	3,618	0	98	1	1	37	108.9	-6.9	80	13	0	0	0.0	0.0
C /4.4	9.9	0.89	22.08	1,223	0	98	1	1	37	112.3	-6.8	83	13	125,000,000	0	0.0	0.0
C /4.4	9.9	0.89	22.08	463	0	98	1	1	37	112.7	-6.8	83	13	250,000,000	0	0.0	0.0
C /4.4	9.9	0.89	22.05	3,361	0	98	1	1	37	112.9	-6.8	83	13	300,000,000	0	0.0	0.0
D /1.7	23.6	0.95	17.31	23	0	98	1	1	130	N/A	N/A	94	6	0	0	0.3	0.3
D /1.7	23.5	0.95	17.25	190	0	98	1	1	130	N/A	N/A	94	6	125,000,000	0	0.3	0.3
C+ /6.3	8.3	0.51	29.93	5	0	0	100	0	112	N/A	N/A	97	5	0	0	0.2	0.2
C+ /6.3	8.3	0.52	30.07	155	0	0	100	0	112	N/A	N/A	97	5	300,000,000	0	0.2	0.2
B+ /9.4	6.6	0.11	32.68	6	0	0	0	100	0	18.3	-11.7	89	N/A	0	0	0.0	0.0
U /	N/A	N/A	32.57	1,446	0	0	0	100	0	N/A	N/A	N/A	N/A	300,000,000	0	0.0	0.0
U /	N/A	N/A	20.39	993	3	54	40	3	69	N/A	N/A	N/A	3	300,000,000	0	0.5	0.5
C+ /5.7	8.2	1.14	19.76	2,021	0	67	32	1	65	55.2	-9.8	9	12	0	0	0.1	0.1
C /4.8	12.4	0.97	14.28	116	1	97	0	2	79	37.5	-21.3	24	5	0	0	0.0	0.0
C /5.1	10.7	1.01	15.14	110	0	97	2	1	89	111.1	-10.3	56	4	0	0	0.0	0.8
C /5.1	10.6	1.01	15.16	17	0	97	2	1	89	111.9	-10.3	58	4	125,000,000	0	0.0	0.8
C /5.0	10.7	1.01	15.06	1,474	0	97	2	1	89	112.2	-10.2	58	4	300,000,000	0	0.0	0.0
C /5.3	16.7	1.09	23.36	45	0	0	0	100	319	N/A	N/A	43	4	5,000	1,000	0.0	0.0
B /8.5	4.0	0.36	9.17	28	30	17	51	2	213	19.8	-8.3	55	4	1,000	50	5.5	0.0
B /8.4	4.0	0.36	8.56	13	30	17	51	2	213	15.0	-8.6	44	4	1,000	50	0.0	0.0
B /8.5	4.0	0.36	9.40	1,027	30	17	51	2	213	22.3	-8.1	60	4	1,000,000	0	0.0	0.0
B /8.5	4.0	0.36	9.33	29	30	17	51	2	213	21.3	-8.2	59	4	0	0	0.0	0.0
B /8.5	4.0	0.36	8.96	2	30	17	51	2	213	18.1	-8.5	52	4	0	0	0.0	0.0
C+ /5.9	13.6	0.79	21.25	11	0	100	0	0	111	38.5	-24.6	88	4	1,000	50	5.5	0.0
C+ /5.8	13.6	0.79	19.52	2	0	100	0	0	111	33.1	-24.8	85	4	1,000	50	0.0	0.0
C+ /5.9	13.6	0.79	22.41	49	0	100	0	0	111	41.6	-24.5	90	4	1,000,000	0	0.0	0.0
C+ /6.3	13.6	0.79	22.32	N/A	0	100	0	0	111	N/A	N/A	89	4	0	0	0.0	0.0
B /8.4	5.1	0.74	11.13	128	6	36	56	2	48	34.9	-10.0	38	N/A	1,000	50	5.5	0.0
B /8.4	5.1	0.74	11.11	47	6	36	56	2	48	29.4	-10.3	29	N/A	1,000	50	0.0	0.0
B /8.4	5.0	0.73	11.14	327	6	36	56	2	48	37.8	-9.9	44	N/A	1,000,000	0	0.0	0.0
B /8.4	5.0	0.73	11.09	4	6	36	56	2	48	36.6	-9.9	42	10	0	0	0.0	0.0
B /8.4	5.0	0.73	11.09	6	6	36	56	2	48	33.3	-10.1	36	10	0	0	0.0	0.0
B /8.5	4.8	0.70	11.25	1	6	36	56	2	48	35.1	-10.1	44	N/A	0	0	0.0	0.0
C- /4.1	12.2	1.12	25.91	639	0	99	0	1	45	123.2	-16.7	29	17	1,000	50	5.5	0.0
C- /3.3	12.2	1.12	19.90	69	0	99	0	1	45	114.2	-17.0	22	17	1,000	50	0.0	0.0
C /4.3	12.2	1.12	28.25	146	0	99	0	1	45	127.9	-16.6	34	17	1,000,000	0	0.0	0.0
C- /4.1	12.2	1.12	26.22	7	0	99	0	1	45	126.1	-16.6	32	17	0	0	0.0	0.0
C- /4.0	12.2	1.12	25.12	4	0	99	0	1	45	120.0	-16.8	27	17	0	0	0.0	0.0
C- /4.0	12.2	1.11	25.09	2	0	99	0	1	45	121.8	-16.7	28	17	0	0	0.0	0.0
D- /1.3	20.1	0.47	11.53	54	0	19	80	1	506	-46.0	-22.9	0	10	1,000	50	4.5	0.0
D- /1.3	20.0	0.49	10.99	4	0	19	80	1	506	-48.1	-23.2	0	10	1,000	50	0.0	0.0
D- /1.3	20.0	0.47	11.65	327	0	19	80	1	506	-45.0	-22.8	0	10	1,000,000	0	0.0	0.0
D- /1.3	20.0	0.47	11.65	14	0	19	80	1	506	-45.3	-22.8	0	10	0	0	0.0	0.0
D- /1.3	20.1	0.49	11.35	4	0	19	80	1	506	-46.7	-23.0	0	10	0	0	0.0	0.0
C- /3.3	11.9	1.06	15.98	6	1	98	0	1	55	107.9	-16.9	20	15	1,000	50	5.5	0.0
D+ /2.7	11.9	1.06	13.59	2	1	98	0	1	55	99.6	-17.1	14	15	1,000	50	0.0	0.0

Data as of February 28, 2017

Fund Type	Fund Name	Ticker Symbol	Overall Investment Rating	Phone	Performance Rating/Pts	3 Mo	6 Mo	1Yr / Pct	3Yr / Pct	5Yr / Pct	Dividend Yield	Expense Ratio
	99 Pct = Best 0 Pct = Worst					Total Return % through 2/28/17			Annualized		Incl. in Returns	
GR	Goldman Sachs Concentrated Gr Inst	GCRIX	C-	(800) 526-7384	B- / 7.0	10.33	7.00	19.19 /48	6.90 /71	11.36 /69	0.58	1.23
GR	Goldman Sachs Concentrated Gr IR	GGCTX	C-	(800) 526-7384	C+ / 6.9	10.23	6.91	18.98 /47	6.73 /70	11.17 /67	0.49	1.38
GR	Goldman Sachs Concentrated Gr R	GGCRX	C-	(800) 526-7384	C+ / 6.5	10.08	6.62	18.34 /44	6.20 /66	10.62 /63	0.00	1.89
GL	Goldman Sachs Dynamic Alloc A	GDAFX	D+	(800) 526-7384	D- / 1.3	3.64	3.64	10.70 /13	1.14 /19	2.14 / 8	0.00	1.49
GL	Goldman Sachs Dynamic Alloc C	GDCFX	D+	(800) 526-7384	D- / 1.5	3.39	3.17	9.80 /11	0.37 /15	1.36 / 7	0.00	2.24
GL	Goldman Sachs Dynamic Alloc Inst	GDIFX	C-	(800) 526-7384	D / 2.0	3.70	3.80	11.02 /15	1.50 /21	2.53 / 9	0.00	1.09
GL	Goldman Sachs Dynamic Alloc IR	GDHFX	C-	(800) 526-7384	D / 1.9	3.61	3.71	10.94 /14	1.36 /20	2.37 / 9	0.00	1.24
GL	Goldman Sachs Dynamic Alloc R	GDRFX	D+	(800) 526-7384	D / 1.7	3.59	3.48	10.37 /13	0.89 /18	1.88 / 8	0.00	1.71
GR	Goldman Sachs Dynamic US Eqty A	GAGVX	C-	(800) 526-7384	C+ / 6.5	9.02	9.60	23.48 /68	6.57 /69	11.80 /72	0.46	3.60
GR	Goldman Sachs Dynamic US Eqty C	GCGVX	C	(800) 526-7384	C+ / 6.9	8.82	9.16	22.48 /64	5.77 /62	10.97 /66	0.00	4.33
GR	Goldman Sachs Dynamic US Eqty	GINGX	C	(800) 526-7384	B / 7.7	9.09	9.75	23.86 /69	6.99 /72	12.24 /76	0.94	3.16
GR	Goldman Sachs Dynamic US Eqty IR	GIRGX	C	(800) 526-7384	B / 7.6	9.09	9.67	23.68 /69	6.81 /71	12.06 /75	0.74	3.54
GR	Goldman Sachs Dynamic US Eqty R	GRGVX	C	(800) 526-7384	B- / 7.2	8.91	9.41	23.04 /67	6.30 /67	11.52 /70	0.00	3.70
EM	Goldman Sachs EM Eqty Insights A	GERAX	C	(800) 526-7384	C+ / 5.8	9.90	6.91	31.34 /89	3.97 /43	1.41 / 7	0.88	1.67
EM	Goldman Sachs EM Eqty Insights C	GERCX	C+	(800) 526-7384	C+ / 6.2	9.61	6.46	30.31 /87	3.18 /33	0.62 / 5	0.31	2.42
EM	Goldman Sachs EM Eqty Insights Inst	GERIX	C+	(800) 526-7384	B- / 7.1	10.00	7.13	31.84 /90	4.40 /47	1.78 / 8	1.21	1.27
EM	Goldman Sachs EM Eqty Insights IR	GIRPX	C+	(800) 526-7384	B- / 7.0	10.03	7.03	31.72 /89	4.29 /46	1.66 / 7	1.13	1.42
EM	Goldman Sachs EM Eqty Insights R	GRRPX	C+	(800) 526-7384	C+ / 6.7	9.91	6.75	31.08 /88	3.74 /40	--	0.74	1.93
EM	Goldman Sachs Emerg Mkts Eq A	GEMAX	D+	(800) 526-7384	C- / 3.3	6.09	2.44	21.83 /61	3.54 /37	1.13 / 6	0.63	1.92
EM	Goldman Sachs Emerg Mkts Eq C	GEMCX	D+	(800) 526-7384	C- / 3.7	5.95	2.10	20.94 /57	2.77 /30	0.39 / 5	0.00	2.67
EM	Goldman Sachs Emerg Mkts Eq Inst	GEMIX	C-	(800) 526-7384	C / 4.7	6.19	2.64	22.34 /64	3.94 /42	1.54 / 7	1.00	1.52
EM	Goldman Sachs Emerg Mkts Eq IR	GIRMX	C-	(800) 526-7384	C / 4.6	6.19	2.56	22.13 /63	3.77 /40	1.39 / 7	0.98	1.67
EM	Goldman Sachs Emerg Mkts Eq Svc	GEMSX	C-	(800) 526-7384	C / 4.3	6.12	2.41	21.71 /61	3.43 /36	1.03 / 6	0.71	2.02
GL	Goldman Sachs Enhanced Div GE A	GADGX	C+	(800) 526-7384	C / 4.4	5.51	7.29	21.61 /60	4.81 /52	7.73 /40	1.85	1.48
GL	Goldman Sachs Enhanced Div GE	GIDGX	B-	(800) 526-7384	C+ / 5.9	5.56	7.46	22.00 /62	5.23 /57	8.16 /43	2.20	1.08
AA	Goldman Sachs Equity Gr Strat A	GAPAX	C+	(800) 526-7384	C / 5.0	7.90	7.83	21.90 /62	4.94 /53	8.97 /50	1.04	1.42
AA	Goldman Sachs Equity Gr Strat C	GAXCX	C+	(800) 526-7384	C / 5.4	7.70	7.40	20.97 /57	4.16 /45	8.15 /43	0.42	2.17
AA	Goldman Sachs Equity Gr Strat Inst	GAPIX	C+	(800) 526-7384	C+ / 6.4	7.98	8.05	22.34 /64	5.36 /58	9.40 /54	1.47	1.02
AA	Goldman Sachs Equity Gr Strat IR	GAPTX	C+	(800) 526-7384	C+ / 6.3	7.96	7.96	22.14 /63	5.20 /56	9.25 /53	1.37	1.17
AA	Goldman Sachs Equity Gr Strat R	GAPRX	C+	(800) 526-7384	C+ / 5.9	7.81	7.66	21.54 /60	4.66 /50	8.70 /48	0.97	1.67
AA	Goldman Sachs Equity Gr Strat Svc	GAPSX	C+	(800) 526-7384	C+ / 6.0	7.83	7.76	21.72 /61	4.83 /52	8.85 /49	1.01	1.52
FS	Goldman Sachs FI Mac Str C	GAANX	C-	(800) 526-7384	E / 0.4	1.15	0.57	0.46 / 1	-1.72 / 7	--	0.00	4.03
FS	Goldman Sachs FI Mac Str Inst	GAAOX	C-	(800) 526-7384	E / 0.5	1.38	1.04	1.61 / 2	-1.05 / 9	--	1.49	2.94
FS	Goldman Sachs FI Mac Str IR	GAAPX	C-	(800) 526-7384	E / 0.5	1.50	1.16	1.62 / 2	-1.06 / 9	--	1.04	3.03
FS	Goldman Sachs FI Mac Str R	GAAQX	C-	(800) 526-7384	E / 0.4	1.26	0.80	1.03 / 2	-1.42 / 8	--	0.91	3.53
FS	Goldman Sachs FI Macro Str A	GAAMX	C-	(800) 526-7384	E / 0.3	1.47	1.01	1.36 / 2	-1.23 / 9	--	0.97	3.28
GR	Goldman Sachs Flexible Cap Gr A	GALLX	C	(800) 526-7384	C+ / 6.9	10.55	7.44	21.16 /58	7.96 /79	12.44 /78	0.00	3.07
GR	Goldman Sachs Flexible Cap Gr C	GCLLX	C	(800) 526-7384	B- / 7.2	10.33	7.03	20.29 /54	7.16 /73	11.59 /71	0.00	3.82
GR	Goldman Sachs Flexible Cap Gr I	GILLX	B-	(800) 526-7384	B / 8.1	10.68	7.72	21.71 /61	8.40 /82	12.90 /83	0.00	2.68
GR	Goldman Sachs Flexible Cap Gr IR	GSLLX	C+	(800) 526-7384	B / 8.0	10.69	7.59	21.48 /60	8.26 /81	12.72 /81	0.00	2.76
GR	Goldman Sachs Flexible Cap Gr R	GRLLX	C+	(800) 526-7384	B / 7.6	10.49	7.30	20.84 /57	7.70 /77	12.17 /76	0.00	3.33
GL	Goldman Sachs Focused Growth A	GFGAX	C-	(800) 526-7384	C / 4.9	10.99	6.10	15.99 /34	5.76 /62	11.21 /68	0.58	2.35
GL	Goldman Sachs Focused Growth C	GFGCX	C-	(800) 526-7384	C / 5.4	10.78	5.73	15.21 /31	4.96 /54	10.39 /61	0.00	3.14
GL	Goldman Sachs Focused Growth Inst	GFGSX	C+	(800) 526-7384	C+ / 6.4	11.09	6.34	16.47 /36	6.16 /66	11.68 /71	0.96	1.91
GL	Goldman Sachs Focused Growth IR	GFGIX	C+	(800) 526-7384	C+ / 6.2	11.03	6.27	16.33 /36	6.01 /64	11.51 /70	0.95	1.90
GL	Goldman Sachs Focused Growth R	GFGRX	C	(800) 526-7384	C+ / 5.8	10.89	6.04	15.74 /33	5.50 /60	10.95 /65	0.41	2.56
FO	Goldman Sachs Focused Intl Eqty A	GSIFX	E+	(800) 526-7384	E / 0.3	6.91	1.84	11.58 /16	-3.64 / 4	4.45 /18	2.56	1.64
FO	Goldman Sachs Focused Intl Eqty C	GSICX	E+	(800) 526-7384	E / 0.3	6.65	1.40	10.70 /13	-4.37 / 3	3.67 /14	2.22	2.39
FO	Goldman Sachs Focused Intl Eqty I	GSIEX	E+	(800) 526-7384	E / 0.5	6.96	1.98	12.02 /18	-3.26 / 4	4.87 /20	3.11	1.24
FO	Goldman Sachs Focused Intl Eqty IR	GIRNX	E+	(800) 526-7384	E / 0.5	6.97	1.97	11.84 /17	-3.40 / 4	4.71 /19	2.93	1.39
FO	Goldman Sachs Focused Intl Eqty	GSISX	E+	(800) 526-7384	E / 0.4	6.87	1.80	11.48 /16	-3.75 / 3	4.34 /17	0.00	1.73
RE	Goldman Sachs Global RE Secs Inst	GARSX	U	(800) 526-7384	U /	6.14	-3.93	10.00 /12	--	--	3.22	13.24

● Denotes fund is closed to new investors
* Denotes fund is included in Section II

I. Index of Stock Mutual Funds

RISK	3 Year		NET ASSETS		ASSET				Portfolio	BULL / BEAR		FUND MANAGER		MINIMUMS		LOADS	
Risk Rating/Pts	Standard Deviation	Beta	NAV As of 2/28/17	Total $(Mil)	Cash %	Stocks %	Bonds %	Other %	Portfolio Turnover Ratio	Last Bull Market Return	Last Bear Market Return	Manager Quality Pct	Manager Tenure (Years)	Initial Purch. $	Additional Purch. $	Front End Load	Back End Load
C- / 3.5	11.9	1.06	16.88	123	1	98	0	1	55	112.4	-16.7	23	15	1,000,000	0	0.0	0.0
C- / 3.3	11.9	1.06	16.18	1	1	98	0	1	55	110.5	-16.7	22	15	0	0	0.0	0.0
C- / 3.2	11.9	1.06	15.55	N/A	1	98	0	1	55	105.0	-17.0	17	15	0	0	0.0	0.0
B- / 7.5	6.4	0.87	10.24	21	51	41	6	2	241	19.1	-9.8	36	7	1,000	50	5.5	0.0
B- / 7.4	6.3	0.87	9.75	19	51	41	6	2	241	14.3	-10.2	28	7	1,000	50	0.0	0.0
B- / 7.4	6.3	0.87	10.38	482	51	41	6	2	241	21.6	-9.7	42	7	1,000,000	0	0.0	0.0
B- / 7.4	6.3	0.87	10.34	10	51	41	6	2	241	20.6	-9.7	40	7	0	0	0.0	0.0
B- / 7.4	6.3	0.86	10.11	N/A	51	41	6	2	241	17.4	-9.9	34	7	0	0	0.0	0.0
C- / 3.6	11.8	1.11	14.26	2	4	95	0	1	49	112.0	-19.9	17	8	1,000	50	5.5	0.0
C- / 3.6	11.8	1.10	13.85	N/A	4	95	0	1	49	103.5	-20.1	12	8	1,000	50	0.0	0.0
C- / 3.6	11.8	1.11	14.31	5	4	95	0	1	49	116.7	-19.7	20	8	1,000,000	0	0.0	0.0
C- / 3.6	11.8	1.11	14.32	N/A	4	95	0	1	49	114.6	-19.7	18	8	0	0	0.0	0.0
C- / 3.7	11.8	1.11	14.32	N/A	4	95	0	1	49	109.1	-19.9	15	8	0	0	0.0	0.0
C / 5.2	15.7	0.95	8.93	62	0	99	0	1	216	35.2	-26.8	87	9	1,000	50	5.5	0.0
C / 5.2	15.7	0.95	8.87	2	0	99	0	1	216	29.7	-27.0	84	9	1,000	50	0.0	0.0
C / 5.1	15.7	0.95	8.91	856	0	99	0	1	216	38.1	-26.7	89	9	1,000,000	0	0.0	0.0
C / 5.1	15.6	0.95	8.91	11	0	99	0	1	216	37.1	-26.8	89	9	0	0	0.0	0.0
C+ / 6.3	15.7	0.95	8.84	11	0	99	0	1	216	N/A	N/A	86	9	0	0	0.0	0.0
C / 5.4	14.0	0.82	16.23	78	0	99	0	1	92	26.1	-26.4	86	2	1,000	50	5.5	0.0
C / 5.4	14.0	0.83	14.61	28	0	99	0	1	92	21.0	-26.6	83	2	1,000	50	0.0	0.0
C / 5.4	14.0	0.82	17.34	479	0	99	0	1	92	28.8	-26.3	88	2	1,000,000	0	0.0	0.0
C / 5.4	14.0	0.82	17.23	22	0	99	0	1	92	27.7	-26.3	87	2	0	0	0.0	0.0
C / 5.4	14.0	0.83	15.70	20	0	99	0	1	92	25.4	-26.4	86	2	0	0	0.0	0.0
B- / 7.6	9.4	0.70	11.25	7	14	79	6	1	19	72.2	-17.2	95	13	1,000	50	5.5	0.0
B- / 7.6	9.4	0.69	11.34	573	14	79	6	1	19	75.8	-16.9	96	13	1,000,000	0	0.0	0.0
C+ / 6.7	10.3	1.55	16.16	129	2	97	0	1	18	83.7	-22.2	7	N/A	1,000	50	5.5	0.0
C+ / 6.7	10.3	1.56	15.44	77	2	97	0	1	18	76.4	-22.4	5	N/A	1,000	50	0.0	0.0
C+ / 6.7	10.3	1.55	16.31	128	2	97	0	1	18	87.7	-22.1	9	N/A	1,000,000	0	0.0	0.0
C+ / 6.7	10.3	1.56	15.94	6	2	97	0	1	18	86.1	-22.0	8	N/A	0	0	0.0	0.0
C+ / 6.7	10.3	1.55	16.05	2	2	97	0	1	18	81.2	-22.3	6	N/A	0	0	0.0	0.0
C+ / 6.7	10.3	1.55	16.09	1	2	97	0	1	18	82.6	-22.2	7	N/A	0	0	0.0	0.0
B+ / 9.5	4.8	0.06	8.81	N/A	39	0	60	1	472	N/A	N/A	41	4	1,000	50	0.0	0.0
B+ / 9.5	4.7	0.06	8.80	56	39	0	60	1	472	N/A	N/A	50	4	1,000,000	0	0.0	0.0
B+ / 9.5	4.7	0.06	8.82	N/A	39	0	60	1	472	N/A	N/A	50	4	0	0	0.0	0.0
B+ / 9.5	4.7	0.06	8.78	N/A	39	0	60	1	472	N/A	N/A	45	4	0	0	0.0	0.0
B+ / 9.5	4.7	0.06	8.80	N/A	39	0	60	1	472	N/A	N/A	48	4	1,000	50	3.8	0.0
C / 4.3	11.9	1.08	12.60	5	1	98	0	1	46	123.9	-19.1	32	9	1,000	50	5.5	0.0
C- / 4.0	12.0	1.08	11.45	1	1	98	0	1	46	115.0	-19.4	24	9	1,000	50	0.0	0.0
C / 4.4	11.9	1.08	13.29	10	1	98	0	1	46	129.0	-19.0	37	9	1,000,000	0	0.0	0.0
C / 4.3	11.9	1.08	13.07	1	1	98	0	1	46	127.0	-19.0	35	9	0	0	0.0	0.0
C- / 4.2	11.9	1.08	12.24	N/A	1	98	0	1	46	121.1	-19.2	29	9	0	0	0.0	0.0
C / 5.2	12.4	0.82	14.83	N/A	1	98	0	1	55	N/A	N/A	97	5	1,000	50	5.5	0.0
C / 5.1	12.4	0.82	14.39	N/A	1	98	0	1	55	N/A	N/A	95	5	1,000	50	0.0	0.0
C / 5.2	12.4	0.82	15.01	16	1	98	0	1	55	N/A	N/A	97	5	1,000,000	0	0.0	0.0
C / 5.2	12.4	0.82	14.97	N/A	1	98	0	1	55	N/A	N/A	97	5	0	0	0.0	0.0
C / 5.2	12.4	0.82	14.75	N/A	1	98	0	1	55	N/A	N/A	96	5	0	0	0.0	0.0
C / 5.1	12.9	1.02	16.92	35	0	100	0	0	78	41.4	-24.9	28	5	1,000	50	5.5	0.0
C / 5.1	12.9	1.02	15.69	17	0	100	0	0	78	35.8	-25.2	21	5	1,000	50	0.0	0.0
C / 5.1	12.9	1.02	17.20	196	0	100	0	0	78	44.6	-24.8	33	5	1,000,000	0	0.0	0.0
C / 5.1	12.9	1.02	17.15	2	0	100	0	0	78	43.4	-24.9	31	5	0	0	0.0	0.0
C / 5.1	12.9	1.02	17.58	N/A	0	100	0	0	78	40.7	-25.0	27	5	0	0	0.0	0.0
U /	N/A	N/A	10.38	27	0	0	0	100	0	N/A	N/A	N/A	2	1,000,000	0	0.0	0.0

	99 Pct = Best 0 Pct = Worst				PERFORMANCE						Incl. in Returns	
			Overall		Perfor-	Total Return % through 2/28/17					Dividend	Expense
Fund		Ticker	Investment		mance				Annualized			
Type	Fund Name	Symbol	Rating	Phone	Rating/Pts	3 Mo	6 Mo	1Yr / Pct	3Yr / Pct	5Yr / Pct	Yield	Ratio
AA	Goldman Sachs Gr and Inc Strat A	GOIAX	C	(800) 526-7384	D+ / 2.5	5.33	4.44	14.16 /26	3.34 /35	5.87 /27	0.89	1.37
AA	Goldman Sachs Gr and Inc Strat C	GOICX	C	(800) 526-7384	D+ / 2.9	5.15	4.09	13.29 /23	2.58 /28	5.07 /22	0.62	2.12
AA	Goldman Sachs Gr and Inc Strat Inst	GOIIX	C+	(800) 526-7384	C- / 3.7	5.43	4.66	14.57 /28	3.72 /39	6.26 /30	1.32	0.97
AA	Goldman Sachs Gr and Inc Strat IR	GPITX	C+	(800) 526-7384	C- / 3.6	5.43	4.61	14.42 /27	3.59 /38	6.13 /29	1.19	1.12
AA	Goldman Sachs Gr and Inc Strat R	GPIRX	C	(800) 526-7384	C- / 3.2	5.30	4.35	13.85 /25	3.07 /32	5.59 /25	0.77	1.62
AA	Goldman Sachs Gr and Inc Strat Svc	GOISX	C+	(800) 526-7384	C- / 3.3	5.31	4.40	14.00 /25	3.25 /34	5.76 /27	0.87	1.47
GI	Goldman Sachs Growth & Income A	GSGRX	B+	(800) 526-7384	B- / 7.3	6.78	10.78	26.25 /77	8.02 /79	12.87 /82	1.63	1.27
GI	Goldman Sachs Growth & Income C	GSGCX	B+	(800) 526-7384	B / 7.7	6.60	10.37	25.29 /74	7.05 /72	11.92 /74	1.15	2.02
GI	Goldman Sachs Growth & Income	GSIIX	A	(800) 526-7384	B+ / 8.5	6.90	11.02	26.77 /79	8.24 /81	13.19 /86	2.05	0.87
GI	Goldman Sachs Growth & Income IR	GRGTX	A	(800) 526-7384	B+ / 8.5	6.84	10.92	26.54 /78	8.28 /81	13.15 /85	1.96	1.02
GI	Goldman Sachs Growth & Income R	GRGRX	A-	(800) 526-7384	B / 8.1	6.71	10.66	25.90 /76	7.74 /77	12.58 /80	1.51	1.52
GI	Goldman Sachs Growth & Income	GSGSX	A-	(800) 526-7384	B / 8.2	6.78	10.75	26.13 /77	7.91 /78	12.76 /82	1.64	1.37
MC	Goldman Sachs Growth Opps A	GGOAX	E	(800) 526-7384	D+ / 2.9	6.98	3.13	18.60 /45	3.17 /33	9.47 /54	0.00	1.42
MC	Goldman Sachs Growth Opps C	GGOCX	E	(800) 526-7384	C- / 3.3	6.79	2.72	17.68 /41	2.41 /27	8.65 /48	0.00	2.17
MC	Goldman Sachs Growth Opps Inst	GGOIX	D-	(800) 526-7384	C- / 4.2	7.12	3.35	19.02 /47	3.58 /38	9.90 /58	0.00	1.02
MC	Goldman Sachs Growth Opps IR	GGOTX	E+	(800) 526-7384	C- / 4.1	7.06	3.30	18.91 /47	3.44 /36	9.75 /57	0.00	1.17
MC	Goldman Sachs Growth Opps R	GGORX	E+	(800) 526-7384	C- / 3.7	6.97	3.05	18.32 /44	2.93 /31	9.20 /52	0.00	1.67
MC	Goldman Sachs Growth Opps R6	GGOUX	U	(800) 526-7384	U /	7.07	3.31	19.02 /47	--	--	0.00	1.01
MC	Goldman Sachs Growth Opps Svc	GGOSX	E+	(800) 526-7384	C- / 3.8	6.94	3.06	18.39 /45	3.06 /32	9.35 /53	0.00	1.52
AA	Goldman Sachs Growth Strategy A	GGSAX	C	(800) 526-7384	C- / 3.6	6.61	6.29	17.86 /42	4.09 /44	7.29 /37	0.83	1.40
AA	Goldman Sachs Growth Strategy C	GGSCX	C+	(800) 526-7384	C / 4.0	6.36	5.88	17.00 /38	3.29 /35	6.48 /31	0.13	2.15
AA	Goldman Sachs Growth Strategy Inst	GGSIX	B-	(800) 526-7384	C / 5.0	6.66	6.50	18.38 /45	4.50 /49	7.71 /40	1.28	0.99
AA	Goldman Sachs Growth Strategy IR	GGSTX	C+	(800) 526-7384	C / 4.9	6.61	6.44	18.20 /44	4.33 /47	7.56 /39	1.16	1.15
AA	Goldman Sachs Growth Strategy R	GGSRX	C+	(800) 526-7384	C / 4.4	6.48	6.08	17.54 /41	3.79 /40	7.01 /35	0.70	1.65
AA	Goldman Sachs Growth Strategy Svc	GGSSX	C+	(800) 526-7384	C / 4.6	6.49	6.17	17.67 /41	3.98 /43	7.18 /36	0.82	1.50
BA	Goldman Sachs Income Builder A	GSBFX	C-	(800) 526-7384	D+ / 2.7	4.75	4.60	16.21 /35	3.53 /37	7.08 /35	3.42	1.10
BA	Goldman Sachs Income Builder C	GSBCX	C-	(800) 526-7384	C- / 3.1	4.60	4.25	15.38 /32	2.77 /30	6.28 /30	2.98	1.85
BA	Goldman Sachs Income Builder Inst	GSBIX	C	(800) 526-7384	C- / 4.1	4.90	4.85	16.75 /37	3.96 /42	7.52 /38	3.92	0.70
BA	Goldman Sachs Income Builder IR	GKIRX	C	(800) 526-7384	C- / 3.9	4.78	4.70	16.53 /36	3.80 /40	7.35 /37	3.80	0.85
FO	Goldman Sachs Intl Eq Div and Prm	GIDAX	E+	(800) 526-7384	E / 0.4	6.17	3.69	14.77 /29	-2.33 / 6	2.66 /10	2.37	1.37
FO	Goldman Sachs Intl Eq Div and Prm	GIDCX	E+	(800) 526-7384	E+ / 0.6	6.03	3.28	13.92 /25	-3.07 / 4	1.90 / 8	1.89	2.12
FO	Goldman Sachs Intl Eq Div and Prm I	GIDHX	E+	(800) 526-7384	E+ / 0.9	6.22	3.82	15.12 /30	-1.99 / 7	3.06 /11	2.94	0.97
FO	Goldman Sachs Intl Eq Dv and Prm	GIRVX	E+	(800) 526-7384	E+ / 0.8	6.20	3.59	14.84 /29	-2.13 / 6	2.85 /10	2.83	1.12
FO	Goldman Sachs Intl Eq Insights A	GCIAX	D+	(800) 526-7384	D+ / 2.6	8.88	7.22	17.66 /41	1.47 /21	6.80 /33	2.00	1.37
FO	Goldman Sachs Intl Eq Insights C	GCICX	D+	(800) 526-7384	D+ / 2.9	8.55	6.65	16.62 /37	0.70 /17	5.99 /28	1.53	2.12
FO	Goldman Sachs Intl Eq Insights Inst	GCIIX	C-	(800) 526-7384	C- / 3.8	8.89	7.27	18.01 /43	1.88 /23	7.21 /36	2.37	0.97
FO	Goldman Sachs Intl Eq Insights IR	GCITX	C-	(800) 526-7384	C- / 3.7	8.86	7.27	17.91 /42	1.72 /22	7.06 /35	2.45	1.13
FO	Goldman Sachs Intl Eq Insights R	GCIRX	C-	(800) 526-7384	C- / 3.3	8.74	7.04	17.34 /40	1.22 /19	6.52 /32	2.22	1.62
FO	Goldman Sachs Intl Eq Insights R6	GCIUX	U	(800) 526-7384	U /	9.03	7.40	18.05 /43	--	--	2.40	0.93
FO	Goldman Sachs Intl Eq Insights Svc	GCISX	C-	(800) 526-7384	C- / 3.4	8.83	7.08	17.40 /40	1.37 /20	6.67 /33	1.95	1.47
RE	Goldman Sachs Intl Rel Est Sec A	GIRAX	D	(800) 526-7384	E+ / 0.7	4.78	-4.52	8.15 / 8	0.42 /15	5.09 /22	3.92	1.62
RE	Goldman Sachs Intl Rel Est Sec C	GIRCX	D	(800) 526-7384	E+ / 0.7	4.62	-4.84	7.25 / 6	-0.33 /12	4.31 /17	3.32	2.37
RE	Goldman Sachs Intl Rel Est Sec Inst	GIRIX	D	(800) 526-7384	D- / 1.2	4.82	-4.43	8.33 / 8	0.82 /17	5.47 /25	4.74	1.22
RE	Goldman Sachs Intl Rel Est Sec IR	GIRTX	D	(800) 526-7384	D- / 1.2	4.79	-4.42	8.35 / 8	0.66 /16	5.39 /24	4.48	1.37
FO	Goldman Sachs Intl SC Insights A	GICAX	C-	(800) 526-7384	D+ / 2.9	8.15	5.73	17.33 /40	2.74 /30	9.28 /53	2.10	1.39
FO	Goldman Sachs Intl SC Insights C	GICCX	C-	(800) 526-7384	C- / 3.4	7.98	5.38	16.49 /36	1.99 /24	8.46 /46	1.55	2.14
FO	Goldman Sachs Intl SC Insights Inst	GICIX	C	(800) 526-7384	C / 4.3	8.29	5.97	17.82 /42	3.16 /33	9.71 /56	2.62	0.99
FO	Goldman Sachs Intl SC Insights IR	GIRLX	C	(800) 526-7384	C- / 4.2	8.21	5.88	17.66 /41	3.00 /32	9.54 /55	2.52	1.14
FO	Goldman Sachs Intl SC Insights R6	GICUX	U	(800) 526-7384	U /	8.31	6.09	17.94 /43	--	--	2.65	0.96
FO	Goldman Sachs Intl Tax Mgd Eq A	GATMX	D	(800) 526-7384	D / 1.8	7.68	5.70	15.48 /32	0.58 /16	6.12 /29	1.36	1.39
FO	Goldman Sachs Intl Tax Mgd Eq C	GCTMX	D	(800) 526-7384	D- / 1.4	7.51	5.35	14.55 /28	-0.16 /13	5.33 /24	0.79	2.13
FO	Goldman Sachs Intl Tax Mgd Eq Inst	GHTMX	D+	(800) 526-7384	D+ / 2.9	7.95	5.96	15.98 /34	1.00 /18	6.56 /32	1.75	0.99

● Denotes fund is closed to new investors
★ Denotes fund is included in Section II

272

RISK			NET ASSETS		ASSET					BULL / BEAR		FUND MANAGER		MINIMUMS		LOADS	
	3 Year		NAV						Portfolio	Last Bull	Last Bear	Manager	Manager	Initial	Additional	Front	Back
Risk	Standard		As of	Total	Cash	Stocks	Bonds	Other	Turnover	Market	Market	Quality	Tenure	Purch.	Purch.	End	End
Rating/Pts	Deviation	Beta	2/28/17	$(Mil)	%	%	%	%	Ratio	Return	Return	Pct	(Years)	$	$	Load	Load
B /8.1	6.7	1.01	12.65	302	7	57	34	2	40	48.7	-14.2	23	N/A	1,000	50	5.5	0.0
B /8.1	6.7	1.01	12.36	122	7	57	34	2	40	42.9	-14.5	17	N/A	1,000	50	0.0	0.0
B /8.1	6.7	1.01	12.69	499	7	57	34	2	40	51.9	-14.1	27	N/A	1,000,000	0	0.0	0.0
B /8.1	6.7	1.00	12.60	6	7	57	34	2	40	50.7	-14.1	26	10	0	0	0.0	0.0
B /8.1	6.7	1.01	12.56	3	7	57	34	2	40	46.7	-14.3	21	10	0	0	0.0	0.0
B /8.1	6.7	1.01	12.62	3	7	57	34	2	40	48.1	-14.3	23	N/A	0	0	0.0	0.0
C+ /6.7	10.8	1.01	35.70	360	1	98	0	1	61	122.2	-21.8	42	16	1,000	50	5.5	0.0
C+ /6.7	10.9	1.01	34.02	23	1	98	0	1	61	112.5	-22.1	30	16	1,000	50	0.0	0.0
C+ /6.7	10.9	1.01	36.30	38	1	98	0	1	61	125.8	-21.7	44	16	1,000,000	0	0.0	0.0
C+ /6.7	10.8	1.01	35.65	2	1	98	0	1	61	125.3	-21.7	45	16	0	0	0.0	0.0
C+ /6.7	10.8	1.01	35.51	2	1	98	0	1	61	119.2	-21.9	38	16	0	0	0.0	0.0
C+ /6.7	10.8	1.01	35.71	N/A	1	98	0	1	61	121.0	-21.8	41	16	0	0	0.0	0.0
D /1.9	12.2	0.90	21.80	528	1	98	0	1	55	104.1	-23.3	14	18	1,000	50	5.5	0.0
D- /1.1	12.2	0.90	16.39	107	1	98	0	1	55	96.0	-23.5	9	18	1,000	50	0.0	0.0
D+ /2.4	12.2	0.90	25.01	1,949	1	98	0	1	55	108.5	-23.1	17	18	1,000,000	0	0.0	0.0
D /2.0	12.2	0.90	22.62	136	1	98	0	1	55	106.9	-23.2	16	18	0	0	0.0	0.0
D /1.8	12.2	0.90	21.05	60	1	98	0	1	55	101.4	-23.3	13	18	0	0	0.0	0.0
U /	N/A	N/A	25.01	101	1	98	0	1	55	N/A	N/A	N/A	18	0	0	0.0	0.0
D /1.8	12.2	0.89	20.98	33	1	98	0	1	55	102.9	-23.3	13	18	0	0	0.0	0.0
B- /7.6	8.4	1.27	14.05	307	8	78	12	2	38	64.4	-18.9	14	N/A	1,000	50	5.5	0.0
B- /7.6	8.4	1.28	14.01	145	8	78	12	2	38	58.0	-19.2	9	N/A	1,000	50	0.0	0.0
B- /7.5	8.5	1.28	14.04	377	8	78	12	2	38	68.1	-18.9	16	N/A	1,000,000	0	0.0	0.0
B- /7.5	8.4	1.27	13.85	5	8	78	12	2	38	66.7	-18.9	15	10	0	0	0.0	0.0
B- /7.6	8.4	1.27	13.71	3	8	78	12	2	38	62.2	-19.1	12	10	0	0	0.0	0.0
B- /7.6	8.4	1.28	14.00	2	8	78	12	2	38	63.5	-18.9	13	N/A	0	0	0.0	0.0
C+ /6.8	6.3	0.92	22.40	563	2	38	58	2	80	59.3	-8.4	32	5	1,000	50	5.5	0.0
C+ /6.8	6.3	0.92	22.05	674	2	38	58	2	80	53.0	-8.7	24	5	1,000	50	0.0	0.0
C+ /6.9	6.3	0.92	22.87	775	2	38	58	2	80	62.9	-8.2	37	5	1,000,000	0	0.0	0.0
C+ /6.9	6.3	0.92	22.80	154	2	38	58	2	80	61.5	-8.3	35	5	0	0	0.0	0.0
C /5.2	10.8	0.86	6.75	5	2	97	0	1	100	30.1	-22.2	45	7	1,000	50	5.5	0.0
C /5.2	10.8	0.86	6.52	3	2	97	0	1	100	24.9	-22.4	35	7	1,000	50	0.0	0.0
C /5.2	10.8	0.86	6.64	336	2	97	0	1	100	32.9	-22.1	50	7	1,000,000	0	0.0	0.0
C /5.2	10.7	0.86	6.62	4	2	97	0	1	100	31.5	-22.1	48	7	0	0	0.0	0.0
C+ /6.3	11.0	0.87	10.99	117	1	98	0	1	176	60.2	-26.5	84	20	1,000	50	5.5	0.0
C+ /6.3	10.9	0.87	10.80	7	1	98	0	1	176	53.7	-26.7	80	20	1,000	50	0.0	0.0
C+ /6.3	11.0	0.87	11.27	485	1	98	0	1	176	63.5	-26.4	86	20	1,000,000	0	0.0	0.0
C+ /6.3	11.0	0.87	10.78	30	1	98	0	1	176	62.2	-26.4	85	20	0	0	0.0	0.0
C+ /6.3	11.0	0.87	10.72	3	1	98	0	1	176	58.0	-26.6	83	20	0	0	0.0	0.0
U /	N/A	N/A	11.27	49	1	98	0	1	176	N/A	N/A	N/A	20	0	0	0.0	0.0
C+ /6.4	11.0	0.87	11.10	3	1	98	0	1	176	59.2	-26.5	84	20	0	0	0.0	0.0
C+ /6.8	11.8	0.59	5.93	5	19	80	0	1	45	52.9	-24.4	10	6	1,000	50	5.5	0.0
C+ /6.8	11.7	0.58	5.93	1	19	80	0	1	45	46.7	-24.4	7	6	1,000	50	0.0	0.0
C+ /6.7	11.7	0.58	5.74	284	19	80	0	1	45	56.1	-24.2	13	6	1,000,000	0	0.0	0.0
C+ /6.8	11.8	0.58	5.88	N/A	19	80	0	1	45	54.9	-24.2	12	6	0	0	0.0	0.0
B- /7.0	10.9	0.81	11.07	241	1	98	0	1	140	77.9	-21.9	90	10	1,000	50	5.5	0.0
B- /7.0	10.9	0.80	10.76	44	1	98	0	1	140	71.0	-22.1	87	10	1,000	50	0.0	0.0
B- /7.0	10.9	0.81	11.07	1,227	1	98	0	1	140	82.1	-21.8	91	10	1,000,000	0	0.0	0.0
B- /7.0	10.9	0.81	11.02	109	1	98	0	1	140	80.5	-21.8	91	10	0	0	0.0	0.0
U /	N/A	N/A	11.09	26	1	98	0	1	140	N/A	N/A	N/A	10	0	0	0.0	0.0
C+ /6.4	10.6	0.84	9.10	4	0	99	0	1	113	55.9	-23.8	79	7	1,000	50	5.5	0.0
C+ /6.4	10.5	0.84	8.85	1	0	99	0	1	113	49.6	-24.0	74	7	1,000	50	0.0	0.0
C+ /6.4	10.6	0.84	9.03	530	0	99	0	1	113	59.2	-23.6	82	7	1,000,000	0	0.0	0.0

I. Index of Stock Mutual Funds

					PERFORMANCE							
	99 Pct = Best 0 Pct = Worst				Perfor- mance	Total Return % through 2/28/17					Incl. in Returns	
			Overall						Annualized		Dividend	Expense
Fund Type	Fund Name	Ticker Symbol	Investment Rating	Phone	Rating/Pts	3 Mo	6 Mo	1Yr / Pct	3Yr / Pct	5Yr / Pct	Yield	Ratio
FO	Goldman Sachs Intl Tax Mgd Eq IR	GITRX	D+	(800) 526-7384	D+ / 2.7	7.85	5.87	15.68 /33	0.82 /17	6.38 /31	1.59	1.13
GR	Goldman Sachs Large Cap Value A	GSLAX	C+	(800) 526-7384	C+ / 6.6	5.97	9.93	26.08 /76	6.77 /70	12.32 /77	1.51	1.23
GR	Goldman Sachs Large Cap Value C	GSVCX	C+	(800) 526-7384	C+ / 6.9	5.79	9.49	25.14 /74	5.98 /64	11.47 /70	1.07	1.98
GR	Goldman Sachs Large Cap Value Inst	GSLIX	B-	(800) 526-7384	B / 7.8	6.05	10.10	26.53 /78	7.19 /73	12.75 /81	2.00	0.83
GR	Goldman Sachs Large Cap Value IR	GSVTX	B-	(800) 526-7384	B / 7.7	6.07	10.02	26.42 /78	7.04 /72	12.58 /80	1.80	0.98
GR	Goldman Sachs Large Cap Value R	GSVRX	C+	(800) 526-7384	B- / 7.3	5.93	9.76	25.75 /75	6.50 /68	12.03 /75	1.40	1.48
GR	Goldman Sachs Large Cap Value R6	GSVUX	U	(800) 526-7384	U /	6.08	10.13	26.56 /78	--	--	2.03	0.81
GR	Goldman Sachs Large Cap Value Svc	GSVSX	B-	(800) 526-7384	B- / 7.4	5.98	9.82	25.97 /76	6.67 /70	12.19 /76	1.46	1.33
GR	Goldman Sachs LC Gro Insights A	GLCGX	A+	(800) 526-7384	B+ / 8.8	9.12	9.90	23.64 /69	11.06 /97	14.55 /96	0.40	1.16
GR	Goldman Sachs LC Gro Insights C	GLCCX	A+	(800) 526-7384	A- / 9.1	8.89	9.44	22.66 /65	10.22 /94	13.69 /91	0.00	1.91
GR	Goldman Sachs LC Gro Insights Inst	GCGIX	A+	(800) 526-7384	A+ / 9.6	9.21	10.09	24.11 /70	11.50 /98	15.01 /97	0.71	0.76
GR	Goldman Sachs LC Gro Insights IR	GLCTX	A+	(800) 526-7384	A+ / 9.6	9.17	10.00	23.93 /70	11.32 /97	14.84 /97	0.68	0.91
GR	Goldman Sachs LC Gro Insights R	GLCRX	A+	(800) 526-7384	A / 9.4	9.05	9.75	23.28 /67	10.78 /97	14.26 /95	0.30	1.41
GR	Goldman Sachs LC Gro Insights Svc	GSCLX	A+	(800) 526-7384	A / 9.4	9.12	9.86	23.49 /68	10.95 /97	14.45 /95	0.51	1.26
GI	Goldman Sachs LC Val Insights A	GCVAX	A	(800) 526-7384	B+ / 8.7	6.93	12.43	30.39 /87	9.36 /89	13.75 /91	1.03	1.12
GI	Goldman Sachs LC Val Insights C	GCVCX	A+	(800) 526-7384	A- / 9.0	6.72	11.99	29.36 /85	8.52 /83	12.91 /83	0.44	1.87
GI	Goldman Sachs LC Val Insights Inst	GCVIX	A+	(800) 526-7384	A+ / 9.6	7.04	12.67	30.84 /88	9.78 /92	14.23 /94	1.44	0.72
GI	Goldman Sachs LC Val Insights IR	GCVTX	A+	(800) 526-7384	A / 9.5	7.02	12.62	30.67 /88	9.63 /91	14.04 /93	1.33	0.87
GI	Goldman Sachs LC Val Insights R	GCVRX	A+	(800) 526-7384	A / 9.3	6.86	12.26	29.99 /86	9.07 /87	13.48 /89	0.91	1.37
GI	Goldman Sachs LC Val Insights Svc	GCLSX	A+	(800) 526-7384	A / 9.4	6.93	12.37	30.27 /87	9.25 /88	13.65 /90	0.99	1.22
GL	Goldman Sachs Long Short Instl	GSLSX	U	(800) 526-7384	U /	1.74	1.98	-0.57 / 1	--	--	0.00	2.71
IN	Goldman Sachs Mgd Fut Strat A	GMSAX	C-	(800) 526-7384	E+ / 0.7	0.59	-1.36	-5.22 / 0	3.01 /32	1.28 / 7	0.00	1.98
IN	Goldman Sachs Mgd Fut Strat C	GMSCX	C-	(800) 526-7384	E+ / 0.9	0.41	-1.80	-6.03 / 0	2.21 /25	0.50 / 5	0.00	2.87
IN	Goldman Sachs Mgd Fut Strat Inst	GMSSX	C-	(800) 526-7384	D- / 1.3	0.69	-1.23	-4.86 / 1	3.43 /36	1.67 / 7	0.11	1.73
IN	Goldman Sachs Mgd Fut Strat IR	GFIRX	C-	(800) 526-7384	D- / 1.2	0.69	-1.34	-5.00 / 1	3.27 /34	1.52 / 7	0.00	1.87
IN	Goldman Sachs Mgd Fut Strat R	GFFRX	C-	(800) 526-7384	D- / 1.0	0.60	-1.57	-5.46 / 0	2.74 /30	1.02 / 6	0.00	2.38
MC	Goldman Sachs Mid Cap Val R6	GCMUX	U	(800) 526-7384	U /	4.85	9.73	28.65 /83	--	--	1.46	0.74
MC	Goldman Sachs Mid Cap Value A	GCMAX	D+	(800) 526-7384	C+ / 5.7	4.70	9.49	28.09 /82	5.22 /57	11.28 /68	0.93	1.16
MC	Goldman Sachs Mid Cap Value C	GCMCX	D+	(800) 526-7384	C+ / 6.2	4.54	9.11	27.15 /80	4.44 /48	10.45 /62	0.44	1.91
MC	Goldman Sachs Mid Cap Value Inst	GSMCX	C-	(800) 526-7384	B- / 7.1	4.84	9.75	28.63 /83	5.64 /61	11.73 /72	1.43	0.76
MC	Goldman Sachs Mid Cap Value IR	GCMTX	C-	(800) 526-7384	C+ / 6.9	4.78	9.65	28.41 /83	5.49 /59	11.56 /70	1.33	0.91
MC	Goldman Sachs Mid Cap Value Svc	GSMSX	C-	(800) 526-7384	C+ / 6.7	4.70	9.48	27.99 /82	5.12 /55	11.18 /67	0.86	1.26
MC	Goldman Sachs MidCap Val R	GCMRX	D+	(800) 526-7384	C+ / 6.6	4.68	9.40	27.80 /81	4.96 /54	11.01 /66	0.86	1.41
EN	Goldman Sachs MLP Energy Infr A	GLPAX	E-	(800) 526-7384	E / 0.5	7.43	7.57	36.23 /95	-5.96 / 2	--	3.33	1.44
EN	Goldman Sachs MLP Energy Infr C	GLPCX	E-	(800) 526-7384	E+ / 0.6	7.13	6.99	34.93 /94	-6.68 / 2	--	3.64	2.19
EN	Goldman Sachs MLP Energy Infr Inst	GMLPX	E	(800) 526-7384	D- / 1.1	7.43	9.27	38.69 /97	-5.13 / 2	--	4.67	1.04
EN	Goldman Sachs MLP Energy Infr IR	GLPIX	E	(800) 526-7384	E+ / 0.8	7.35	7.62	36.35 /95	-5.73 / 2	--	3.48	1.19
EN	Goldman Sachs MLP Energy Infr R	GLPRX	E-	(800) 526-7384	E+ / 0.7	7.12	7.25	35.71 /95	-6.25 / 2	--	3.56	1.71
GL	Goldman Sachs Multi-Mgr Alt A	GMAMX	D+	(800) 526-7384	E+ / 0.8	1.67	2.36	7.59 / 7	0.60 /16	--	1.28	2.89
GL	Goldman Sachs Multi-Mgr Alt C	GMCMX	D+	(800) 526-7384	E+ / 0.8	1.42	1.93	6.70 / 5	-0.16 /13	--	0.43	3.64
GL	Goldman Sachs Multi-Mgr Alt Inst	GSMMX	C-	(800) 526-7384	D- / 1.4	1.77	2.56	7.98 / 7	1.02 /18	--	1.94	2.49
GL	Goldman Sachs Multi-Mgr Alt IR	GIMMX	C-	(800) 526-7384	D- / 1.4	1.63	2.42	7.85 / 7	0.86 /17	--	1.81	2.64
GL	Goldman Sachs Multi-Mgr Alt R	GRMMX	C-	(800) 526-7384	D- / 1.2	1.52	2.21	7.26 / 6	0.33 /15	--	1.02	3.16
GL	● Goldman Sachs N-11 Equity A	GSYAX	E	(800) 526-7384	E- / 0.1	6.20	-5.72	3.00 / 3	-6.61 / 2	-2.26 / 3	0.00	2.07
GL	● Goldman Sachs N-11 Equity C	GSYCX	E	(800) 526-7384	E- / 0.1	6.04	-6.04	2.36 / 2	-7.28 / 1	-2.99 / 2	0.00	2.82
GL	● Goldman Sachs N-11 Equity Inst	GSYIX	E	(800) 526-7384	E- / 0.1	6.45	-5.44	3.64 / 3	-6.19 / 2	-1.85 / 3	0.04	1.68
GL	● Goldman Sachs N-11 Equity IR	GSYRX	E	(800) 526-7384	E- / 0.1	6.30	-5.60	3.37 / 3	-6.38 / 2	-2.02 / 3	0.00	1.82
RE	Goldman Sachs Real Estate Sec A	GREAX	C	(800) 526-7384	C+ / 5.6	7.14	-2.41	13.05 /22	10.01 /93	10.29 /60	1.85	1.51
RE	Goldman Sachs Real Estate Sec C	GRECX	C	(800) 526-7384	C+ / 6.1	7.02	-2.75	12.23 /19	9.21 /88	9.46 /54	1.34	2.26
RE	Goldman Sachs Real Estate Sec Inst	GREIX	C+	(800) 526-7384	C+ / 6.9	7.25	-2.22	13.47 /23	10.44 /96	10.72 /64	2.28	1.11
RE	Goldman Sachs Real Estate Sec IR	GRETX	C+	(800) 526-7384	C+ / 6.8	7.22	-2.28	13.36 /23	10.29 /95	10.57 /63	2.18	1.26
RE	Goldman Sachs Real Estate Sec R	GRERX	C+	(800) 526-7384	C+ / 6.5	7.13	-2.51	12.84 /21	9.75 /92	10.03 /59	1.75	1.77

● Denotes fund is closed to new investors

* Denotes fund is included in Section II

www.thestreetratings.com

RISK Rating/Pts	3 Year Standard Deviation	Beta	NAV As of 2/28/17	Total $(Mil)	Cash %	Stocks %	Bonds %	Other %	Portfolio Turnover Ratio	Last Bull Market Return	Last Bear Market Return	Manager Quality Pct	Manager Tenure (Years)	Initial Purch. $	Additional Purch. $	Front End Load	Back End Load
C+ /6.4	10.6	0.84	9.09	4	0	99	0	1	113	57.7	-23.7	81	7	0	0	0.0	0.0
C /5.1	11.7	1.08	17.39	194	1	97	0	2	116	118.1	-22.6	20	16	1,000	50	5.5	0.0
C /5.1	11.7	1.09	16.71	45	1	97	0	2	116	109.5	-22.9	14	16	1,000	50	0.0	0.0
C /5.1	11.7	1.09	17.53	744	1	97	0	2	116	122.8	-22.5	24	16	1,000,000	0	0.0	0.0
C /5.2	11.7	1.09	17.40	7	1	97	0	2	116	121.1	-22.6	22	16	0	0	0.0	0.0
C /5.1	11.7	1.09	17.02	7	1	97	0	2	116	115.1	-22.7	17	16	0	0	0.0	0.0
U /	N/A	N/A	17.53	129	1	97	0	2	116	N/A	N/A	N/A	16	0	0	0.0	0.0
C /5.1	11.7	1.09	17.30	3	1	97	0	2	116	117.0	-22.7	19	16	0	0	0.0	0.0
C+ /6.8	11.3	1.06	26.18	292	4	94	0	2	254	143.4	-15.1	71	6	1,000	50	5.5	0.0
C+ /6.8	11.3	1.06	23.76	56	4	94	0	2	254	133.8	-15.4	62	6	1,000	50	0.0	0.0
C+ /6.7	11.3	1.06	26.99	635	4	94	0	2	254	148.7	-15.0	75	6	1,000,000	0	0.0	0.0
C+ /6.7	11.3	1.06	25.85	88	4	94	0	2	254	146.7	-15.1	N/A	6	0	0	0.0	0.0
C+ /6.7	11.3	1.06	25.62	26	4	94	0	2	254	140.2	-15.2	69	6	0	0	0.0	0.0
C+ /6.7	11.3	1.06	25.83	15	4	94	0	2	254	142.1	-15.1	70	6	0	0	0.0	0.0
C+ /6.7	11.4	1.06	19.64	60	2	97	0	1	229	130.8	-17.4	51	6	1,000	50	5.5	0.0
C+ /6.7	11.4	1.06	19.46	15	2	97	0	1	229	121.7	-17.7	41	6	1,000	50	0.0	0.0
C+ /6.7	11.3	1.06	19.63	382	2	97	0	1	229	135.9	-17.3	57	6	1,000,000	0	0.0	0.0
C+ /6.7	11.3	1.06	19.59	21	2	97	0	1	229	134.0	-17.3	55	6	0	0	0.0	0.0
C+ /6.6	11.3	1.06	19.53	2	2	97	0	1	229	127.7	-17.5	48	6	0	0	0.0	0.0
C+ /6.7	11.4	1.06	19.72	7	2	97	0	1	229	129.5	-17.5	50	6	0	0	0.0	0.0
U /	N/A	N/A	8.77	47	42	57	0	1	468	N/A	N/A	N/A	3	1,000,000	0	0.0	0.0
B /8.7	8.4	-0.26	10.16	9	91	0	8	1	196	N/A	N/A	96	5	1,000	50	5.5	0.0
B /8.7	8.4	-0.26	9.81	4	91	0	8	1	196	N/A	N/A	95	5	1,000	50	0.0	0.0
B /8.8	8.4	-0.26	10.34	115	91	0	8	1	196	N/A	N/A	97	5	1,000,000	0	0.0	0.0
B /8.8	8.4	-0.25	10.27	31	91	0	8	1	196	N/A	N/A	96	5	0	0	0.0	0.0
B /8.8	8.3	-0.26	10.04	N/A	91	0	8	1	196	N/A	N/A	96	5	0	0	0.0	0.0
U /	N/A	N/A	38.53	442	3	96	0	1	111	N/A	N/A	N/A	16	0	0	0.0	0.0
D+ /2.7	11.8	0.92	38.21	1,059	3	96	0	1	111	108.0	-22.3	30	16	1,000	50	5.5	0.0
D+ /2.4	11.8	0.92	34.76	132	3	96	0	1	111	99.7	-22.5	22	16	1,000	50	0.0	0.0
D+ /2.6	11.8	0.92	38.55	2,722	3	96	0	1	111	112.5	-22.1	34	16	1,000,000	0	0.0	0.0
D+ /2.6	11.8	0.92	37.46	198	3	96	0	1	111	110.8	-22.2	33	16	0	0	0.0	0.0
D+ /2.7	11.8	0.92	37.58	107	3	96	0	1	111	106.9	-22.3	29	16	0	0	0.0	0.0
D+ /2.6	11.8	0.92	37.28	40	3	96	0	1	111	105.2	-22.3	27	16	0	0	0.0	0.0
D+ /2.8	22.0	0.81	8.43	312	89	10	0	1	96	N/A	N/A	51	4	1,000	50	5.5	0.0
D+ /2.8	21.9	0.81	8.16	180	89	10	0	1	96	N/A	N/A	40	4	1,000	50	0.0	0.0
D+ /2.9	22.0	0.82	8.58	2,050	89	10	0	1	96	N/A	N/A	63	4	1,000,000	0	0.0	0.0
D+ /2.9	22.0	0.81	8.52	132	89	10	0	1	96	N/A	N/A	54	4	0	0	0.0	0.0
D+ /2.8	21.9	0.81	8.33	2	89	10	0	1	96	N/A	N/A	46	4	0	0	0.0	0.0
B /8.3	4.8	0.65	10.38	82	31	28	38	3	73	N/A	N/A	43	4	1,000	50	5.5	0.0
B /8.3	4.8	0.65	10.21	43	31	28	38	3	73	N/A	N/A	32	4	1,000	50	0.0	0.0
B /8.3	4.8	0.64	10.42	947	31	28	38	3	73	N/A	N/A	49	4	1,000,000	0	0.0	0.0
B /8.3	4.8	0.65	10.39	109	31	28	38	3	73	N/A	N/A	46	4	0	0	0.0	0.0
B /8.3	4.8	0.64	10.33	N/A	31	28	38	3	73	N/A	N/A	39	4	0	0	0.0	0.0
C /5.0	12.9	0.69	8.57	14	0	99	0	1	27	-3.0	-19.9	6	2	1,000	50	5.5	0.0
C /4.9	12.9	0.69	8.25	4	0	99	0	1	27	-6.8	-20.2	5	2	1,000	50	0.0	0.0
C /4.9	12.9	0.69	8.63	47	0	99	0	1	27	-0.7	-19.8	8	2	1,000,000	0	0.0	0.0
C /4.9	12.9	0.69	8.60	12	0	99	0	1	27	-1.6	-19.8	7	2	0	0	0.0	0.0
C /5.3	14.2	1.03	18.88	51	0	100	0	0	41	99.9	-16.2	58	7	1,000	50	5.5	0.0
C /5.3	14.2	1.03	18.24	15	0	100	0	0	41	92.0	-16.4	48	7	1,000	50	0.0	0.0
C /5.4	14.2	1.03	19.31	394	0	100	0	0	41	104.2	-16.0	63	7	1,000,000	0	0.0	0.0
C /5.3	14.2	1.03	18.99	13	0	100	0	0	41	102.6	-16.1	62	7	0	0	0.0	0.0
C /5.3	14.2	1.03	18.74	4	0	100	0	0	41	97.4	-16.3	55	7	0	0	0.0	0.0

	99 Pct = Best 0 Pct = Worst		Overall		PERFORMANCE						Incl. in Returns	
					Perfor-	Total Return % through 2/28/17						
					mance				Annualized		Dividend	Expense
Fund Type	Fund Name	Ticker Symbol	Investment Rating	Phone	Rating/Pts	3 Mo	6 Mo	1Yr / Pct	3Yr / Pct	5Yr / Pct	Yield	Ratio
RE	Goldman Sachs Real Estate Sec Svc	GRESX	C+	(800) 526-7384	C+ / 6.6	7.13	-2.44	12.98 /22	9.89 /93	10.16 /59	1.85	1.61
GI	Goldman Sachs Rising Div Gr A	GSRAX	C	(800) 526-7384	C- / 4.0	7.43	5.90	17.16 /39	4.96 /54	9.25 /53	1.25	1.15
IN	Goldman Sachs Rising Div Gr C	GSRCX	C	(800) 526-7384	C / 4.5	7.21	5.48	16.28 /35	4.17 /45	8.45 /46	0.61	1.90
GI	Goldman Sachs Rising Div Gr Inst	GSRLX	C+	(800) 526-7384	C+ / 5.6	7.54	6.15	17.69 /41	5.39 /58	9.69 /56	1.66	0.74
IN	Goldman Sachs Rising Div Gr IR	GSRIX	C+	(800) 526-7384	C / 5.4	7.50	6.07	17.47 /40	5.24 /57	9.52 /55	1.52	0.89
IN	Goldman Sachs Rising Div Gr R	GSRRX	C+	(800) 526-7384	C / 5.0	7.38	5.78	16.93 /38	4.71 /51	8.99 /51	1.12	1.39
GL	Goldman Sachs Satellite Strat A	GXSAX	D+	(800) 526-7384	D / 1.6	5.51	1.45	14.59 /28	1.46 /21	3.07 /11	3.00	1.46
GL	Goldman Sachs Satellite Strat C	GXSCX	D+	(800) 526-7384	D / 1.9	5.32	1.06	13.84 /25	0.73 /17	2.31 / 9	2.46	2.21
GL	Goldman Sachs Satellite Strat I	GXSIX	C-	(800) 526-7384	D+ / 2.5	5.65	1.69	15.10 /30	1.88 /23	3.50 /13	3.59	1.06
GL	Goldman Sachs Satellite Strat IR	GXSTX	C-	(800) 526-7384	D+ / 2.4	5.60	1.61	14.92 /30	1.73 /22	3.35 /12	3.44	1.21
GL	Goldman Sachs Satellite Strat R	GXSRX	C-	(800) 526-7384	D / 2.2	5.61	1.34	14.39 /27	1.26 /20	2.84 /10	2.96	1.71
AA	Goldman Sachs Satellite Strat R6	GXSUX	U	(800) 526-7384	U /	5.66	1.58	14.96 /30	--	--	3.61	1.04
GL	Goldman Sachs Satellite Strat Svc	GXSSX	C-	(800) 526-7384	D / 2.2	5.63	1.41	14.45 /28	1.39 /20	3.00 /11	3.03	1.56
SC	Goldman Sachs SC Eqty Insights A	GCSAX	B+	(800) 526-7384	B / 8.2	3.49	11.86	33.47 /92	8.69 /85	12.22 /76	0.25	1.45
SC	Goldman Sachs SC Eqty Insights C	GCSCX	B+	(800) 526-7384	B+ / 8.6	3.32	11.48	32.49 /91	7.88 /78	11.37 /69	0.00	2.20
SC	Goldman Sachs SC Eqty Insights Inst	GCSIX	A	(800) 526-7384	A / 9.3	3.58	12.10	34.02 /93	9.12 /88	12.66 /80	0.60	1.05
SC	Goldman Sachs SC Eqty Insights IR	GDSTX	A	(800) 526-7384	A / 9.3	3.55	12.04	33.84 /93	8.96 /87	12.51 /79	0.58	1.21
SC	Goldman Sachs SC Eqty Insights R	GDSRX	A-	(800) 526-7384	A- / 9.0	3.44	11.76	33.18 /92	8.42 /82	11.95 /74	0.11	1.70
SC	Goldman Sachs SC Eqty Insights Svc	GCSSX	A-	(800) 526-7384	A- / 9.0	3.44	11.83	33.40 /92	8.58 /84	12.10 /75	0.17	1.56
SC	Goldman Sachs SC Gro Insights A	GSAOX	C	(800) 526-7384	C+ / 6.8	3.98	9.84	29.52 /85	6.95 /72	12.07 /75	0.00	1.59
SC	Goldman Sachs SC Gro Insights C	GSCOX	C	(800) 526-7384	B- / 7.2	3.78	9.41	28.60 /83	6.14 /65	11.23 /68	0.00	2.35
SC	Goldman Sachs SC Gro Insights Inst	GSIOX	C+	(800) 526-7384	B / 8.0	4.09	10.05	30.09 /87	7.38 /75	12.52 /79	0.19	1.19
SC	Goldman Sachs SC Gro Insights IR	GSTOX	C+	(800) 526-7384	B / 7.9	4.04	9.95	29.84 /86	7.21 /73	12.34 /78	0.19	1.32
SC	Goldman Sachs SC Gro Insights R	GSROX	C+	(800) 526-7384	B- / 7.5	3.94	9.72	29.23 /85	6.68 /70	11.78 /72	0.00	1.84
SC	Goldman Sachs SC Val Insights A	GSATX	A-	(800) 526-7384	A / 9.4	3.71	15.17	39.10 /97	9.62 /91	12.39 /78	0.53	1.51
SC	Goldman Sachs SC Val Insights C	GSCTX	A-	(800) 526-7384	A+ / 9.6	3.52	14.77	38.12 /96	8.81 /85	11.55 /70	0.23	2.26
SC	Goldman Sachs SC Val Insights Inst	GSITX	A	(800) 526-7384	A+ / 9.8	3.82	15.41	39.68 /97	10.06 /94	12.83 /82	0.71	1.11
SC	Goldman Sachs SC Val Insights IR	GTTTX	A	(800) 526-7384	A+ / 9.7	3.79	15.31	39.48 /97	9.89 /93	12.66 /80	0.86	1.26
SC	Goldman Sachs SC Val Insights R	GTTRX	A	(800) 526-7384	A+ / 9.7	3.66	15.04	38.79 /97	9.35 /89	12.10 /75	0.42	1.76
MC	Goldman Sachs Sm Mid Cap Value A	GMVAX	B+	(800) 526-7384	B / 7.7	6.31	12.20	32.19 /90	7.17 /73	--	0.55	2.25
MC	Goldman Sachs Sm Mid Cap Value C	GMVCX	B+	(800) 526-7384	B / 8.0	6.07	11.76	31.04 /88	6.42 /68	--	0.20	2.99
MC	Goldman Sachs Sm Mid Cap Value	GSMVX	A	(800) 526-7384	B+ / 8.9	6.39	12.33	32.66 /91	7.67 /77	--	0.87	1.84
MC	Goldman Sachs Sm Mid Cap Value	GMVIX	A-	(800) 526-7384	B+ / 8.8	6.36	12.23	32.39 /91	7.44 /75	--	0.65	2.03
MC	Goldman Sachs Sm Mid Cap Value R	GMVRX	A-	(800) 526-7384	B+ / 8.4	6.15	11.96	31.68 /89	6.90 /71	--	0.26	2.50
SC	● Goldman Sachs Small Cap Value A	GSSMX	B	(800) 526-7384	B+ / 8.6	5.41	12.93	36.95 /96	8.06 /79	13.51 /89	0.36	1.41
SC	● Goldman Sachs Small Cap Value C	GSSCX	B	(800) 526-7384	A- / 9.0	5.23	12.51	35.96 /95	7.25 /74	12.66 /80	0.00	2.16
SC	● Goldman Sachs Small Cap Value Inst	GSSIX	B+	(800) 526-7384	A / 9.5	5.50	13.16	37.51 /96	8.49 /83	13.96 /93	0.67	1.01
SC	● Goldman Sachs Small Cap Value IR	GSQTX	B+	(800) 526-7384	A / 9.5	5.50	13.09	37.33 /96	8.33 /81	13.80 /92	0.61	1.16
SC	● Goldman Sachs Small Cap Value R	GSQRX	B+	(800) 526-7384	A / 9.3	5.35	12.80	36.62 /95	7.79 /77	13.23 /86	0.19	1.66
SC	● Goldman Sachs Small Cap Value R6	GSSUX	U	(800) 526-7384	U /	5.53	13.19	37.55 /96	--	--	0.70	1.00
SC	● Goldman Sachs Small Cap Value Svc	GSSSX	B+	(800) 526-7384	A / 9.3	5.38	12.88	36.82 /96	7.95 /79	13.39 /88	0.30	1.51
MC	Goldman Sachs Small/Mid-Cap Gr A	GSMAX	D	(800) 526-7384	C- / 3.9	7.14	4.60	21.42 /59	4.18 /45	11.22 /68	0.00	1.45
MC	Goldman Sachs Small/Mid-Cap Gr C	GSMGX	D	(800) 526-7384	C / 4.4	6.95	4.24	20.55 /55	3.39 /36	10.39 /61	0.00	2.20
MC	Goldman Sachs Small/Mid-Cap Gr	GSMYX	C-	(800) 526-7384	C / 5.4	7.22	4.76	21.85 /61	4.56 /49	11.65 /71	0.00	1.05
MC	Goldman Sachs Small/Mid-Cap Gr IR	GTMTX	C-	(800) 526-7384	C / 5.3	7.20	4.73	21.74 /61	4.43 /48	11.49 /70	0.00	1.20
MC	Goldman Sachs Small/Mid-Cap Gr R	GTMRX	D+	(800) 526-7384	C / 4.9	7.06	4.46	21.12 /58	3.91 /42	10.94 /65	0.00	1.70
MC	Goldman Sachs Small/Mid-Cap Gr	GSMQX	D+	(800) 526-7384	C / 5.0	7.13	4.54	21.31 /59	4.07 /44	11.09 /67	0.00	1.55
GR	Goldman Sachs Strategic Gr A	GGRAX	C	(800) 526-7384	C+ / 6.8	10.22	7.62	19.91 /51	8.01 /79	12.56 /80	0.28	1.54
GR	Goldman Sachs Strategic Gr C	GGRCX	C	(800) 526-7384	B- / 7.1	10.02	7.27	19.06 /47	7.23 /74	11.72 /72	0.00	2.29
GR	Goldman Sachs Strategic Gr Inst	GSTIX	B-	(800) 526-7384	B / 8.0	10.35	7.91	20.38 /54	8.44 /82	13.01 /84	0.63	1.14
GR	Goldman Sachs Strategic Gr IR	GSTTX	C+	(800) 526-7384	B / 7.9	10.30	7.86	20.23 /53	8.30 /81	12.85 /82	0.51	1.29
GR	Goldman Sachs Strategic Gr R	GSTRX	C+	(800) 526-7384	B- / 7.5	10.10	7.57	19.58 /50	7.77 /77	12.32 /77	0.39	1.79

● Denotes fund is closed to new investors
* Denotes fund is included in Section II

RISK			NET ASSETS		ASSET				Portfolio Turnover Ratio	BULL / BEAR		FUND MANAGER		MINIMUMS		LOADS	
Risk Rating/Pts	3 Year		NAV As of 2/28/17	Total $(Mil)	Cash %	Stocks %	Bonds %	Other %		Last Bull Market Return	Last Bear Market Return	Manager Quality Pct	Manager Tenure (Years)	Initial Purch. $	Additional Purch. $	Front End Load	Back End Load
	Standard Deviation	Beta															
C /5.3	14.2	1.03	19.00	3	0	100	0	0	41	98.7	-16.2	57	7	0	0	0.0	0.0
C+ /6.8	10.4	0.96	21.59	676	18	81	0	1	16	81.2	-12.4	16	7	1,000	50	5.5	0.0
C+ /6.8	10.4	0.96	21.72	559	18	81	0	1	16	74.1	-12.5	11	7	1,000	50	0.0	0.0
C+ /6.8	10.4	0.96	22.07	898	18	81	0	1	16	85.2	-12.1	19	7	1,000,000	0	0.0	0.0
C+ /6.8	10.4	0.96	22.05	260	18	81	0	1	16	N/A	N/A	18	7	0	0	0.0	0.0
C+ /6.8	10.4	0.96	21.56	5	18	81	0	1	16	N/A	N/A	14	7	0	0	0.0	0.0
B- /7.3	7.9	1.08	7.92	76	0	54	45	1	22	32.6	-13.6	29	10	1,000	50	5.5	0.0
B- /7.3	8.0	1.09	7.87	52	0	54	45	1	22	27.5	-14.0	21	10	1,000	50	0.0	0.0
B- /7.3	8.0	1.09	7.91	529	0	54	45	1	22	35.6	-13.5	33	10	1,000,000	0	0.0	0.0
B- /7.3	7.9	1.08	7.91	58	0	54	45	1	22	34.5	-13.6	32	10	0	0	0.0	0.0
B- /7.3	7.9	1.09	7.89	3	0	54	45	1	22	31.1	-13.7	27	10	0	0	0.0	0.0
U /	N/A	N/A	7.91	35	0	54	45	1	22	N/A	N/A	N/A	10	0	0	0.0	0.0
B- /7.3	7.9	1.09	7.91	N/A	0	54	45	1	22	32.1	-13.7	28	10	0	0	0.0	0.0
C+ /5.8	15.2	0.95	22.75	35	2	97	0	1	144	124.7	-22.8	86	6	1,000	50	5.5	0.0
C+ /5.7	15.2	0.95	19.90	14	2	97	0	1	144	116.0	-23.1	82	6	1,000	50	0.0	0.0
C+ /5.8	15.2	0.95	23.57	199	2	97	0	1	144	129.8	-22.7	88	6	1,000,000	0	0.0	0.0
C+ /5.8	15.2	0.95	22.57	11	2	97	0	1	144	127.8	-22.7	87	6	0	0	0.0	0.0
C+ /5.8	15.3	0.95	22.35	12	2	97	0	1	144	121.9	-23.0	85	6	0	0	0.0	0.0
C+ /5.8	15.3	0.95	22.44	1	2	97	0	1	144	123.6	-22.9	85	6	0	0	0.0	0.0
C- /4.2	15.7	0.98	32.38	63	3	96	0	1	139	128.7	-23.4	75	6	1,000	50	5.5	0.0
C- /3.9	15.7	0.98	25.81	9	3	96	0	1	139	119.6	-23.6	67	6	1,000	50	0.0	0.0
C /4.4	15.7	0.98	37.42	121	3	96	0	1	139	133.6	-23.2	78	6	1,000,000	0	0.0	0.0
C- /4.2	15.7	0.98	33.02	109	3	96	0	1	139	131.8	-23.3	77	6	0	0	0.0	0.0
C- /4.2	15.7	0.98	31.39	5	3	96	0	1	139	125.6	-23.5	73	6	0	0	0.0	0.0
C /5.5	15.1	0.93	44.05	105	2	97	0	1	129	123.6	-21.9	90	6	1,000	50	5.5	0.0
C /5.3	15.1	0.93	33.14	18	2	97	0	1	129	114.7	-22.1	87	6	1,000	50	0.0	0.0
C+ /5.7	15.1	0.93	56.35	54	2	97	0	1	129	128.5	-21.8	92	6	1,000,000	0	0.0	0.0
C /5.5	15.1	0.93	43.86	7	2	97	0	1	129	126.6	-21.8	91	6	0	0	0.0	0.0
C /5.5	15.1	0.93	43.44	8	2	97	0	1	129	120.5	-22.0	89	6	0	0	0.0	0.0
C+ /6.2	12.4	1.01	12.47	1	1	98	0	1	109	N/A	N/A	43	3	1,000	50	5.5	0.0
C+ /6.2	12.4	1.01	12.28	1	1	98	0	1	109	N/A	N/A	34	3	1,000	50	0.0	0.0
C+ /6.2	12.4	1.01	12.57	45	1	98	0	1	109	N/A	N/A	50	3	1,000,000	0	0.0	0.0
C+ /6.2	12.4	1.01	12.52	3	1	98	0	1	109	N/A	N/A	47	3	0	0	0.0	0.0
C+ /6.2	12.4	1.00	12.45	N/A	1	98	0	1	109	N/A	N/A	40	3	0	0	0.0	0.0
C /4.7	14.2	0.89	57.33	971	1	98	0	1	46	142.9	-22.8	85	11	1,000	50	5.5	0.0
C /4.4	14.2	0.89	45.22	48	1	98	0	1	46	133.3	-23.1	81	11	1,000	50	0.0	0.0
C /4.8	14.2	0.89	61.41	4,949	1	98	0	1	46	148.2	-22.7	87	11	1,000,000	0	0.0	0.0
C /4.7	14.2	0.89	56.95	197	1	98	0	1	46	146.3	-22.8	86	11	0	0	0.0	0.0
C /4.7	14.2	0.89	56.36	137	1	98	0	1	46	139.7	-22.9	84	11	0	0	0.0	0.0
U /	N/A	N/A	61.40	579	1	98	0	1	46	N/A	N/A	N/A	11	0	0	0.0	0.0
C /4.7	14.2	0.89	55.75	131	1	98	0	1	46	141.7	-22.9	85	11	0	0	0.0	0.0
C- /4.0	14.7	1.06	20.05	589	0	99	0	1	67	119.8	-22.9	11	12	1,000	50	5.5	0.0
C- /3.9	14.7	1.06	17.78	227	0	99	0	1	67	110.9	-23.1	7	12	1,000	50	0.0	0.0
C- /4.1	14.7	1.06	21.17	1,095	0	99	0	1	67	124.4	-22.8	13	12	1,000,000	0	0.0	0.0
C- /4.1	14.6	1.05	20.64	254	0	99	0	1	67	122.7	-22.7	13	12	0	0	0.0	0.0
C- /4.0	14.6	1.05	19.49	30	0	99	0	1	67	116.8	-22.9	10	12	0	0	0.0	0.0
C- /4.0	14.7	1.06	19.63	15	0	99	0	1	67	118.5	-22.9	10	12	0	0	0.0	0.0
C /4.4	11.7	1.06	12.39	46	6	93	0	1	56	122.1	-15.7	34	17	1,000	50	5.5	0.0
C- /4.0	11.8	1.06	10.34	10	6	93	0	1	56	113.2	-15.9	26	17	1,000	50	0.0	0.0
C /4.5	11.7	1.06	13.16	298	6	93	0	1	56	127.0	-15.5	40	17	1,000,000	0	0.0	0.0
C /4.6	11.8	1.06	13.16	1	6	93	0	1	56	125.2	-15.7	37	17	0	0	0.0	0.0
C /4.4	11.7	1.06	12.20	N/A	6	93	0	1	56	119.5	-15.7	32	17	0	0	0.0	0.0

Fund Type	Fund Name	Ticker Symbol	Overall Investment Rating	Phone	Perfor-mance Rating/Pts	3 Mo	6 Mo	1Yr / Pct	3Yr / Pct	5Yr / Pct	Dividend Yield	Expense Ratio
			99 Pct = Best 0 Pct = Worst						Annualized		Incl. in Returns	
GR	Goldman Sachs Strategic Gr Svc	GSTSX	C+	(800) 526-7384	B / 7.6	10.12	7.61	19.85 /51	7.90 /78	12.45 /79	0.33	1.64
FO	Goldman Sachs Strategic Intl Eq A	GSAKX	E+	(800) 526-7384	E / 0.3	7.26	1.44	10.67 /13	-2.55 / 5	4.27 /17	1.83	1.82
FO	Goldman Sachs Strategic Intl Eq C	GSCKX	E+	(800) 526-7384	E / 0.4	7.03	1.04	9.86 /11	-3.27 / 4	3.50 /13	1.35	2.57
FO	Goldman Sachs Strategic Intl Eq I	GSIKX	E+	(800) 526-7384	E+ / 0.7	7.39	1.66	11.20 /15	-2.17 / 6	4.70 /19	2.26	1.42
FO	Goldman Sachs Strategic Intl Eq IR	GSTKX	E+	(800) 526-7384	E+ / 0.6	7.42	1.68	11.12 /15	-2.28 / 6	4.55 /18	2.23	1.56
FO	Goldman Sachs Strategic Intl Eq R	GSRKX	E+	(800) 526-7384	E / 0.5	7.20	1.34	10.49 /13	-2.78 / 5	4.00 /15	1.75	2.07
AA	Goldman Sachs Target Date 2020 R6	GTZHX	U	(800) 526-7384	U /	3.20	1.66	8.02 / 7	--	--	1.76	0.64
AA	Goldman Sachs Target Date 2030 R6	GTZJX	U	(800) 526-7384	U /	4.83	4.20	12.99 /22	--	--	1.90	0.64
AA	Goldman Sachs Target Date 2040 R6	GTZMX	U	(800) 526-7384	U /	5.40	5.18	15.37 /31	--	--	1.98	0.64
AA	Goldman Sachs Target Date 2050 R6	GTZSX	U	(800) 526-7384	U /	5.92	6.34	17.95 /43	--	--	1.95	0.64
GL	Goldman Sachs Tax-Advtg GE A	TAGGX	C+	(800) 526-7384	C / 5.1	7.00	9.07	22.13 /63	5.02 /54	9.72 /56	0.59	1.44
GL	Goldman Sachs Tax-Advtg GE Inst	TIGGX	B-	(800) 526-7384	C+ / 6.6	7.12	9.37	22.73 /66	5.45 /59	10.17 /60	1.07	1.04
TC	Goldman Sachs Tech Oppty A	GITAX	B-	(800) 526-7384	A- / 9.0	9.25	9.83	32.12 /90	9.61 /91	12.82 /82	0.00	1.55
TC	Goldman Sachs Tech Oppty C	GITCX	B-	(800) 526-7384	A- / 9.2	8.99	9.39	31.09 /88	8.77 /85	11.98 /74	0.00	2.30
TC	Goldman Sachs Tech Oppty Inst	GITIX	B	(800) 526-7384	A+ / 9.6	9.37	10.01	32.63 /91	10.04 /93	13.27 /86	0.00	1.15
TC	Goldman Sachs Tech Oppty IR	GISTX	B	(800) 526-7384	A+ / 9.6	9.26	9.92	32.40 /91	9.87 /93	13.09 /85	0.00	1.30
TC	Goldman Sachs Tech Oppty Svc	GITSX	B	(800) 526-7384	A / 9.5	9.18	9.71	31.97 /90	9.48 /90	12.70 /81	0.00	1.65
IN	Goldman Sachs US Eqty Divi & Pre A	GSPAX	B+	(800) 526-7384	B- / 7.2	5.49	7.44	21.54 /60	9.72 /92	11.19 /67	1.37	1.20
IN	Goldman Sachs US Eqty Divi & Pre C	GSPQX	B+	(800) 526-7384	B / 7.6	5.24	7.00	20.61 /55	8.91 /86	10.36 /61	0.83	1.95
IN	Goldman Sachs US Eqty Divi & Pre I	GSPKX	A	(800) 526-7384	B+ / 8.5	5.59	7.65	22.02 /62	10.17 /94	11.65 /71	1.79	0.80
IN	Goldman Sachs US Eqty Divi & Pre	GVIRX	A	(800) 526-7384	B+ / 8.4	5.55	7.57	21.85 /61	10.00 /93	11.49 /70	1.68	0.95
GI	Goldman Sachs US Eqty Insights A	GSSQX	A-	(800) 526-7384	B+ / 8.5	8.02	11.49	26.62 /78	9.72 /92	13.82 /92	0.63	1.17
GI	Goldman Sachs US Eqty Insights C	GSUSX	A	(800) 526-7384	B+ / 8.8	7.80	11.05	25.66 /75	8.89 /86	12.97 /83	0.04	1.92
GI	Goldman Sachs US Eqty Insights Inst	GSELX	A+	(800) 526-7384	A / 9.5	8.10	11.71	27.12 /79	10.16 /94	14.27 /95	1.00	0.77
GI	Goldman Sachs US Eqty Insights IR	GSUTX	A+	(800) 526-7384	A / 9.4	8.06	11.62	26.93 /79	9.99 /93	14.10 /94	0.99	0.92
GI	Goldman Sachs US Eqty Insights R	GSURX	A+	(800) 526-7384	A- / 9.1	7.95	11.34	26.29 /77	9.44 /90	13.54 /89	0.50	1.42
GI	Goldman Sachs US Eqty Insights Svc	GSESX	A+	(800) 526-7384	A- / 9.2	7.99	11.42	26.50 /78	9.61 /91	13.71 /91	0.68	1.27
GR	Goldman Sachs US Tax Mgd Eq A	GCTAX	B+	(800) 526-7384	B- / 7.4	7.41	10.88	24.26 /71	8.33 /81	13.57 /89	0.51	1.17
GR	Goldman Sachs US Tax Mgd Eq C	GCTCX	B+	(800) 526-7384	B / 7.8	7.18	10.46	23.28 /67	7.54 /76	12.72 /81	0.00	1.92
GR	Goldman Sachs US Tax Mgd Eq Inst	GCTIX	A	(800) 526-7384	B+ / 8.7	7.48	11.13	24.74 /72	8.79 /85	14.02 /93	0.91	0.77
GR	Goldman Sachs US Tax Mgd Eq IR	GQIRX	A	(800) 526-7384	B+ / 8.5	7.44	11.04	24.57 /72	8.60 /84	13.85 /92	0.82	1.27
GR	Goldman Sachs US Tax Mgd Eq Svc	GCTSX	A-	(800) 526-7384	B / 8.2	7.31	10.83	24.09 /70	8.22 /81	13.44 /88	0.13	0.92
GL	Golub Group Equity Fund	GGEFX	B+	(866) 954-6682	A- / 9.0	7.84	11.17	24.58 /72	9.56 /91	12.72 /81	0.23	1.41
AA	Good Harbor Tactical Core US A	GHUAX	D-	(877) 270-2848	E / 0.4	4.27	6.82	19.29 /48	-3.35 / 4	--	0.00	1.53
AA	Good Harbor Tactical Core US C	GHUCX	D-	(877) 270-2848	E / 0.5	3.96	6.35	18.27 /44	-4.06 / 3	--	0.00	2.28
AA	Good Harbor Tactical Core US I	GHUIX	D-	(877) 270-2848	E+ / 0.7	4.22	6.86	19.48 /49	-3.11 / 4	--	0.00	1.28
GL	GoodHaven	GOODX	E	(855) 654-6639	E / 0.5	0.17	3.81	23.73 /69	-3.53 / 4	3.33 /12	0.00	1.10
GR	Goodwood SMID Long/Short Adv	GAMAX	E	(800) 773-3863	E- / 0.1	-5.17	4.51	12.10 /18	-4.93 / 2	3.82 /14	0.00	3.07
IN	Gotham Absolute Return Inst	GARIX	C	(888) 739-1390	D+ / 2.9	3.56	7.80	13.06 /22	2.77 /30	--	0.00	2.95
GR	Gotham Enhanced Return Inst	GENIX	B	(888) 739-1390	B / 7.6	6.49	12.43	23.49 /68	7.24 /74	--	0.00	3.36
IX	Gotham Index Plus Inst	GINDX	U	(888) 739-1390	U /	7.60	14.94	27.45 /80	--	--	0.46	4.51
GR	Gotham Neutral Inst	GONIX	C-	(888) 739-1390	E+ / 0.9	0.87	5.03	5.03 / 4	0.40 /15	--	0.00	3.38
GR	Government Street Equity Fund	GVEQX	C+	(866) 738-1125	C+ / 6.5	6.83	7.52	18.32 /44	6.64 /69	9.95 /58	1.03	0.85
MC	Government Street Mid-Cap Fund	GVMCX	A	(866) 738-1125	B+ / 8.5	7.93	10.37	23.74 /69	8.76 /85	12.15 /76	0.55	1.10
GL	Grand Prix Investors		D	(800) 453-6556	D / 2.0	4.54	4.19	12.80 /21	1.14 /19	5.25 /23	0.00	2.22
EM	● Grandeur Peak Em Mkts Opptys Inst	GPEIX	C+	(855) 377-7325	C / 4.6	5.38	3.01	23.80 /69	4.21 /45	--	0.52	1.56
EM	● Grandeur Peak Em Mkts Opptys Inv	GPEOX	C+	(855) 377-7325	C / 4.4	5.33	2.85	23.56 /68	4.01 /43	--	0.37	1.81
FO	● Grandeur Peak Global Micro Cap Inst	GPMCX	U	(855) 377-7325	U /	5.39	6.57	23.15 /67	--	--	0.21	2.30
GL	● Grandeur Peak Global Oppts Inst	GPGIX	C	(855) 377-7325	C / 5.2	5.61	5.28	21.19 /58	5.25 /57	12.63 /80	0.14	1.38
GL	● Grandeur Peak Global Oppts Investor	GPGOX	C	(855) 377-7325	C / 5.0	5.51	5.18	21.24 /58	5.01 /54	12.38 /78	0.00	1.63
GL	● Grandeur Peak Global Reach Inst	GPRIX	C+	(855) 377-7325	C+ / 5.7	5.45	6.10	23.86 /69	5.47 /59	--	0.28	1.30
GL	● Grandeur Peak Global Reach Inv	GPROX	C+	(855) 377-7325	C / 5.5	5.44	5.93	23.48 /68	5.21 /57	--	0.13	1.55

● Denotes fund is closed to new investors
* Denotes fund is included in Section II

RISK			NET ASSETS		ASSET					BULL / BEAR		FUND MANAGER		MINIMUMS		LOADS	
	3 Year		NAV						Portfolio	Last Bull	Last Bear	Manager	Manager	Initial	Additional	Front	Back
Risk	Standard		As of	Total	Cash	Stocks	Bonds	Other	Turnover	Market	Market	Quality	Tenure	Purch.	Purch.	End	End
Rating/Pts	Deviation	Beta	2/28/17	$(Mil)	%	%	%	%	Ratio	Return	Return	Pct	(Years)	$	$	Load	Load
C /4.4	11.8	1.06	12.32	N/A	6	93	0	1	56	121.1	-15.7	33	17	0	0	0.0	0.0
C /5.4	11.6	0.93	12.28	18	0	99	0	1	68	42.1	-23.8	42	5	1,000	50	5.5	0.0
C /5.4	11.6	0.93	11.05	4	0	99	0	1	68	36.4	-24.0	32	5	1,000	50	0.0	0.0
C /5.4	11.7	0.93	12.84	34	0	99	0	1	68	45.2	-23.6	48	5	1,000,000	0	0.0	0.0
C /5.4	11.7	0.93	12.27	1	0	99	0	1	68	44.2	-23.6	46	5	0	0	0.0	0.0
C /5.4	11.7	0.93	12.38	N/A	0	99	0	1	68	40.3	-23.9	39	5	0	0	0.0	0.0
U /	N/A	N/A	9.62	54	0	0	0	100	204	N/A	N/A	N/A	3	0	0	0.0	0.0
U /	N/A	N/A	9.78	78	0	0	0	100	176	N/A	N/A	N/A	3	0	0	0.0	0.0
U /	N/A	N/A	9.59	52	0	0	0	100	174	N/A	N/A	N/A	3	0	0	0.0	0.0
U /	N/A	N/A	9.96	26	0	0	0	100	191	N/A	N/A	N/A	3	0	0	0.0	0.0
B- /7.4	10.0	0.74	13.99	1	10	84	5	1	19	91.2	-18.5	95	9	1,000	50	5.5	0.0
B- /7.4	10.0	0.74	13.91	2,033	10	84	5	1	19	95.6	-18.4	96	9	1,000,000	0	0.0	0.0
C- /3.8	15.3	1.23	19.59	232	1	98	0	1	22	133.5	-23.6	32	18	1,000	50	5.5	0.0
C- /3.6	15.2	1.23	16.60	53	1	98	0	1	22	124.1	-23.9	24	18	1,000	50	0.0	0.0
C- /3.9	15.3	1.23	21.34	83	1	98	0	1	22	138.4	-23.5	37	18	1,000,000	0	0.0	0.0
C- /3.9	15.2	1.23	21.09	23	1	98	0	1	22	136.4	-23.6	35	18	0	0	0.0	0.0
C- /3.8	15.3	1.23	19.25	13	1	98	0	1	22	132.1	-23.6	30	18	0	0	0.0	0.0
C+ /6.9	8.8	0.85	12.59	310	0	99	0	1	39	103.4	-13.0	79	7	1,000	50	5.5	0.0
C+ /6.9	8.9	0.85	12.53	156	0	99	0	1	39	95.4	-13.4	73	7	1,000	50	0.0	0.0
C+ /6.9	8.8	0.85	12.57	2,252	0	99	0	1	39	107.9	-12.9	81	7	1,000,000	0	0.0	0.0
C+ /6.9	8.9	0.85	12.58	188	0	99	0	1	39	106.3	-13.0	80	7	0	0	0.0	0.0
C+ /6.5	10.8	1.04	44.40	265	1	97	0	2	213	131.6	-15.3	59	6	1,000	50	5.5	0.0
C+ /6.5	10.9	1.04	40.45	34	1	97	0	2	213	122.5	-15.6	49	6	1,000	50	0.0	0.0
C+ /6.5	10.8	1.04	45.60	195	1	97	0	2	213	136.7	-15.2	64	6	1,000,000	0	0.0	0.0
C+ /6.5	10.9	1.04	43.87	31	1	97	0	2	213	134.8	-15.3	62	6	0	0	0.0	0.0
C+ /6.5	10.9	1.04	43.72	33	1	97	0	2	213	128.5	-15.4	56	6	0	0	0.0	0.0
C+ /6.5	10.8	1.04	44.20	6	1	97	0	2	213	130.4	-15.4	58	6	0	0	0.0	0.0
C+ /6.6	11.2	1.07	19.77	47	0	99	0	1	96	132.1	-16.7	37	7	1,000	50	5.5	0.0
C+ /6.6	11.2	1.07	18.80	23	0	99	0	1	96	122.7	-17.0	29	7	1,000	50	0.0	0.0
C+ /6.6	11.3	1.07	20.08	1,135	0	99	0	1	96	137.0	-16.5	43	7	1,000,000	0	0.0	0.0
C+ /6.6	11.2	1.07	20.07	17	0	99	0	1	96	135.0	-16.5	41	7	0	0	0.0	0.0
C+ /6.6	11.2	1.07	19.89	1	0	99	0	1	96	130.7	-16.7	36	7	0	0	0.0	0.0
C /5.3	11.5	0.75	18.39	56	6	91	2	1	43	120.0	-13.5	99	8	1,000	0	0.0	0.0
C+ /6.4	9.0	0.78	10.02	24	9	78	11	2	412	N/A	N/A	3	5	2,500	250	5.8	1.0
C+ /6.3	8.9	0.78	9.71	43	9	78	11	2	412	N/A	N/A	2	5	2,500	250	0.0	1.0
C+ /6.4	9.0	0.78	10.12	30	9	78	11	2	412	N/A	N/A	3	5	5,000,000	10,000	0.0	1.0
C /4.4	13.2	0.61	23.41	269	27	72	0	1	18	36.0	-6.1	28	6	10,000	2,500	0.0	2.0
C- /3.6	20.8	1.18	8.80	7	0	85	14	1	581	40.7	-15.8	0	4	2,500	100	4.5	2.0
B- /7.6	7.5	0.62	13.68	961	39	60	0	1	272	N/A	N/A	28	5	250,000	5,000	0.0	1.0
C+ /5.7	12.0	1.03	13.30	1,037	0	99	0	1	248	N/A	N/A	29	4	250,000	5,000	0.0	1.0
U /	N/A	N/A	12.24	133	0	0	0	100	234	N/A	N/A	N/A	2	250,000	5,000	0.0	1.0
B /8.4	5.5	0.16	10.44	787	74	25	0	1	303	N/A	N/A	58	4	250,000	5,000	0.0	1.0
C+ /6.4	10.3	0.99	66.87	66	3	96	0	1	17	95.5	-16.3	28	26	5,000	0	0.0	0.0
C+ /6.7	10.1	0.80	24.32	49	6	93	0	1	20	114.3	-18.8	81	14	5,000	0	0.0	0.0
C+ /6.3	11.1	1.52	12.03	2	13	86	0	1	165	37.1	-13.4	10	7	1,000	100	0.0	1.0
B- /7.1	12.4	0.72	10.92	379	8	91	0	1	40	N/A	N/A	90	4	100,000	0	0.0	2.0
B- /7.1	12.4	0.72	10.88	17	8	91	0	1	40	N/A	N/A	89	4	2,000	0	0.0	2.0
U /	N/A	N/A	11.34	35	1	98	0	1	8	N/A	N/A	N/A	2	2,000	0	0.0	2.0
C+ /5.6	10.6	0.73	3.36	478	0	99	0	1	32	N/A	N/A	96	6	2,000	0	0.0	2.0
C+ /5.6	10.8	0.73	3.33	175	0	99	0	1	32	N/A	N/A	95	6	2,000	0	0.0	2.0
C+ /6.2	10.9	0.76	13.72	243	0	99	0	1	46	N/A	N/A	96	4	2,000	0	0.0	2.0
C+ /6.2	10.9	0.75	13.70	65	0	99	0	1	46	N/A	N/A	96	4	2,000	0	0.0	2.0

I. Index of Stock Mutual Funds

Fund Type	Fund Name	Ticker Symbol	Overall Investment Rating	Phone	Perfor-mance Rating/Pts	3 Mo	6 Mo	1Yr / Pct	3Yr / Pct	5Yr / Pct	Dividend Yield	Expense Ratio
GL	Grandeur Peak Global Stalwarts Inst	GGSYX	U	(855) 377-7325	U /	6.01	4.82	21.78 /61	--	--	0.21	1.84
GL	Grandeur Peak Global Stalwarts Inv	GGSOX	U	(855) 377-7325	U /	5.97	4.69	21.43 /59	--	--	0.08	2.09
FO	● Grandeur Peak Internatl Oppts Inst	GPIIX	C-	(855) 377-7325	C- /4.2	6.63	4.01	19.39 /49	4.02 /43	11.75 /72	0.64	1.38
FO	● Grandeur Peak Internatl Oppts Inv	GPIOX	C-	(855) 377-7325	C- /4.0	6.47	3.85	19.26 /48	3.84 /41	11.52 /70	0.48	1.63
FO	Grandeur Peak Intrntl Stalwart Inst	GISYX	U	(855) 377-7325	U /	5.94	1.91	19.71 /51	--	--	0.44	1.20
FO	Grandeur Peak Intrntl Stalwart Inv	GISOX	U	(855) 377-7325	U /	5.94	1.82	19.40 /49	--	--	0.27	1.45
GL	Granite Value Fund	GVFIX	C-	(888) 442-9893	C- /3.6	4.20	5.67	20.50 /55	2.95 /31	7.46 /38	0.86	2.53
GI	Grant Park Mgd Future Strategy A	GPFAX	D+	(855) 501-4758	D- /1.3	6.29	1.13	1.67 / 2	3.72 /39	-0.09 / 4	5.04	2.31
GI	Grant Park Mgd Future Strategy C	GPFCX	C-	(855) 501-4758	D- /1.5	6.17	0.83	1.05 / 2	2.96 /31	-0.83 / 4	4.50	3.04
GI	Grant Park Mgd Future Strategy I	GPFIX	C-	(855) 501-4758	D /2.0	6.39	1.26	2.01 / 2	4.01 /43	0.17 / 5	5.68	2.01
GI	Grant Park Mgd Future Strategy N	GPFNX	C-	(855) 501-4758	D /1.8	6.38	1.20	1.85 / 2	3.75 /40	-0.07 / 4	5.43	2.30
GL	Grant Park Multi Alt Strat A	GPAAX	C-	(855) 501-4758	D- /1.0	4.65	-3.19	-2.06 / 1	4.02 /43	--	1.55	1.96
GL	Grant Park Multi Alt Strat C	GPACX	C-	(855) 501-4758	D- /1.3	4.39	-3.54	-2.84 / 1	3.26 /34	--	1.18	2.72
GL	Grant Park Multi Alt Strat I	GPAIX	C	(855) 501-4758	D /1.6	4.75	-3.06	-1.84 / 1	4.30 /46	--	1.85	1.72
GL	Grant Park Multi Alt Strat N	GPANX	C	(855) 501-4758	D /1.6	4.65	-3.18	-2.04 / 1	4.05 /44	--	1.65	1.96
FO	Gratry International Growth Inst	GGIGX	E+	(855) 447-2879	E /0.5	6.87	4.92	10.88 /14	-2.79 / 5	--	1.56	2.11
GR	Great Lakes Disciplined Eq Inst	GLDNX	B+	(855) 278-2020	B+ /8.3	6.27	8.53	23.27 /67	9.28 /89	13.71 /91	0.94	0.98
FO	Great Lakes Large Cap Value Inst	GLLIX	A+	(855) 278-2020	A /9.4	6.27	12.14	28.17 /82	10.09 /94	--	1.55	1.02
SC	Great Lakes Small Cap Oppty Inst	GLSIX	C-	(855) 278-2020	C+ /6.9	3.46	11.86	28.87 /84	5.15 /56	11.63 /71	0.57	0.89
SC	Great Lakes Small Cap Oppty Inv	GLSCX	C-	(855) 278-2020	C+ /6.7	3.34	11.67	28.48 /83	4.88 /53	11.34 /68	0.35	1.14
RE	Great West Real Estate Idx Initial	MXREX	C+	(866) 831-7129	B- /7.0	7.17	-2.31	14.12 /26	10.50 /96	--	1.85	0.70
RE	Great West Real Estate Idx Inst	MXSFX	U	(866) 831-7129	U /	7.36	-2.11	14.55 /28	--	--	3.04	0.35
MC	Greater Western New York Series	BWNYX	C	(888) 285-5346	C /4.9	3.66	7.60	13.65 /24	5.76 /62	10.06 /59	0.00	1.54
GR	Great-West Aggressive Prof I Init	MXPPX	C+	(866) 831-7129	B- /7.2	6.67	8.17	23.36 /68	7.01 /72	11.12 /67	1.97	1.32
GR	Great-West Aggressive Prof II Init	MXAPX	C+	(866) 831-7129	B- /7.3	6.65	8.27	23.62 /69	7.18 /73	11.29 /68	2.33	1.16
GR	Great-West Aggressive Prof II Inst	MXGTX	U	(866) 831-7129	U /	6.74	8.44	24.02 /70	--	--	1.26	0.81
GR	Great-West Aggressive Prof II L	MXEPX	B-	(866) 831-7129	B- /7.2	6.66	8.18	23.39 /68	6.94 /72	11.00 /66	1.44	1.41
MC	Great-West Ariel Mid Cap Val Init	MXMCX	B	(866) 831-7129	B /7.8	7.34	9.99	28.42 /83	6.66 /70	13.73 /91	1.31	1.07
MC	Great-West Ariel Mid Cap Val L	MXAMX	B+	(866) 831-7129	B /7.7	6.87	9.80	28.08 /82	6.49 /68	--	0.00	1.34
GL	Great-West Consv Prof I Init	MXVPX	C	(866) 831-7129	D+ /2.7	3.34	2.92	10.46 /13	3.49 /37	4.75 /20	1.62	1.06
AA	Great-West Consv Prof II Init	MXCPX	C+	(866) 831-7129	D+ /2.8	3.25	2.94	10.69 /13	3.63 /38	4.89 /21	1.91	0.90
AA	Great-West Consv Prof II L	MXIPX	C	(866) 831-7129	D+ /2.6	3.24	2.83	10.43 /13	3.41 /36	4.64 /19	1.40	1.15
MC	Great-West Goldman Sachs MC V	MXMVX	B+	(866) 831-7129	A+ /9.7	6.20	13.32	33.92 /93	10.75 /97	14.62 /96	1.86	1.25
MC	Great-West Goldman Sachs MC V	MXKJX	U	(866) 831-7129	U /	6.23	13.39	34.30 /93	--	--	3.46	0.90
FO	Great-West International Index Init	MXINX	D-	(866) 831-7129	D- /1.1	7.10	4.06	15.24 /31	-1.21 / 9	4.66 /19	1.63	0.70
FO	Great-West International Index Inst	MXPBX	U	(866) 831-7129	U /	7.19	4.18	15.60 /32	--	--	2.50	0.35
SC	Great-West Invesco SC Value Init	MXSVX	B	(866) 831-7129	A /9.4	5.93	16.96	36.47 /95	7.17 /73	13.36 /87	0.19	1.40
SC	Great-West Invesco SC Value Inst	MXMYX	U	(866) 831-7129	U /	6.03	17.24	36.95 /96	--	--	0.99	1.05
GI	Great-West Lifetime 2015 L	MXABX	U	(866) 831-7129	U /	4.00	3.29	--	--	--	0.00	N/A
GI	Great-West Lifetime 2015 T	MXLYX	C	(866) 831-7129	C- /3.7	4.16	3.46	13.44 /23	4.46 /48	6.52 /32	1.82	0.90
GI	Great-West Lifetime 2015 T1	MXLZX	C	(866) 831-7129	C- /3.6	4.10	3.40	13.33 /23	4.38 /47	6.43 /31	1.72	1.00
GI	Great-West Lifetime 2025 Inst	MXQBX	U	(866) 831-7129	U /	5.16	4.80	17.03 /38	--	--	3.16	0.57
GI	Great-West Lifetime 2025 L	MXANX	U	(866) 831-7129	U /	5.05	4.44	--	--	--	0.00	N/A
GI	Great-West Lifetime 2025 T	MXELX	C	(866) 831-7129	C /4.7	4.99	4.51	16.55 /37	5.10 /55	8.14 /43	1.80	0.92
GI	Great-West Lifetime 2025 T1	MXFLX	C	(866) 831-7129	C /4.6	5.01	4.45	16.44 /36	4.96 /54	8.01 /42	1.71	1.02
GL	Great-West Lifetime 2035 Inst	MXTBX	U	(866) 831-7129	U /	6.13	6.14	20.60 /55	--	--	2.87	0.59
GL	Great-West Lifetime 2035 L	MXAZX	U	(866) 831-7129	U /	6.06	5.86	--	--	--	0.00	N/A
GL	Great-West Lifetime 2035 T	MXKLX	C-	(866) 831-7129	C+ /5.8	6.06	5.99	20.17 /53	5.63 /61	9.27 /53	1.66	0.94
GL	Great-West Lifetime 2035 T1	MXLLX	C-	(866) 831-7129	C+ /5.7	6.07	5.92	19.99 /52	5.48 /59	9.12 /52	1.60	1.04
GI	Great-West Lifetime 2045 L	MXBHX	U	(866) 831-7129	U /	6.57	6.47	--	--	--	0.00	N/A
GR	Great-West Lifetime 2045 T	MXQLX	D+	(866) 831-7129	C+ /6.1	6.55	6.62	21.52 /60	5.53 /60	9.23 /52	1.58	0.96
GR	Great-West Lifetime 2045 T1	MXRLX	D	(866) 831-7129	C+ /6.1	6.54	6.53	21.40 /59	5.51 /60	9.18 /52	1.55	1.06

● Denotes fund is closed to new investors
* Denotes fund is included in Section II

www.thestreetratings.com

RISK Rating/Pts	3 Year Standard Deviation	Beta	NAV As of 2/28/17	Total $(Mil)	Cash %	Stocks %	Bonds %	Other %	Portfolio Turnover Ratio	Last Bull Market Return	Last Bear Market Return	Manager Quality Pct	Manager Tenure (Years)	Initial Purch. $	Additional Purch. $	Front End Load	Back End Load
U /	N/A	N/A	12.09	43	0	0	0	100	24	N/A	N/A	N/A	2	2,000	0	0.0	2.0
U /	N/A	N/A	12.06	55	0	0	0	100	24	N/A	N/A	N/A	2	2,000	0	0.0	2.0
C+ /6.0	10.8	0.76	3.31	654	6	93	0	1	34	N/A	N/A	93	6	2,000	0	0.0	2.0
C+ /6.0	11.0	0.76	3.30	75	6	93	0	1	34	N/A	N/A	93	6	2,000	0	0.0	2.0
U /	N/A	N/A	12.01	244	0	0	0	100	59	N/A	N/A	N/A	2	2,000	0	0.0	2.0
U /	N/A	N/A	12.00	27	0	0	0	100	59	N/A	N/A	N/A	2	2,000	0	0.0	2.0
C+ /6.2	11.0	0.70	13.78	10	0	99	0	1	31	N/A	N/A	90	6	10,000	0	0.0	2.0
B- /7.9	9.5	0.22	9.08	6	54	0	45	1	21	-3.7	-2.8	83	6	2,500	100	5.8	1.0
B- /7.9	9.5	0.22	8.83	3	54	0	45	1	21	-7.5	-3.0	78	6	5,000	100	0.0	1.0
B- /7.8	9.5	0.22	9.13	17	54	0	45	1	21	-2.3	-2.7	85	6	100,000	1,000	0.0	1.0
B- /7.8	9.5	0.22	9.07	2	54	0	45	1	21	-3.6	-2.8	83	6	5,000	100	0.0	1.0
B+ /9.0	7.6	0.07	10.67	41	62	37	0	1	17	N/A	N/A	93	4	2,500	100	5.8	1.0
B+ /9.0	7.6	0.07	10.54	10	62	37	0	1	17	N/A	N/A	91	4	2,500	100	0.0	1.0
B+ /9.0	7.6	0.07	10.72	167	62	37	0	1	17	N/A	N/A	94	4	100,000	1,000	0.0	1.0
B+ /9.0	7.6	0.07	10.69	35	62	37	0	1	17	N/A	N/A	93	4	2,500	100	0.0	1.0
C /5.3	11.7	0.83	10.17	9	3	96	0	1	87	N/A	N/A	38	4	100,000	5,000	0.0	1.0
C+ /5.9	10.3	0.97	15.79	52	1	97	1	1	112	129.4	-15.1	63	8	100,000	100	0.0	0.0
C+ /6.7	10.8	0.65	15.32	51	4	95	0	1	66	N/A	N/A	99	5	100,000	100	0.0	0.0
C- /3.4	15.3	0.88	17.53	73	5	91	3	1	102	129.1	-25.2	63	7	100,000	100	0.0	0.0
C- /3.4	15.3	0.88	17.26	10	5	91	3	1	102	125.9	-25.2	60	7	1,000	200	0.0	0.0
C /5.0	15.0	1.09	12.12	87	0	99	0	1	38	N/A	N/A	56	5	0	0	0.0	0.0
U /	N/A	N/A	9.48	229	0	99	0	1	38	N/A	N/A	N/A	5	0	0	0.0	0.0
C+ /6.5	10.3	0.74	22.28	2	11	88	0	1	4	92.0	-15.8	60	20	2,500	250	0.0	0.0
C /4.3	10.0	0.95	9.43	91	1	97	0	2	27	105.6	-20.6	37	3	0	0	0.0	0.0
C- /4.2	10.0	0.94	6.79	511	1	97	0	2	28	107.4	-20.6	40	18	0	0	0.0	0.0
U /	N/A	N/A	9.71	52	1	97	0	2	28	N/A	N/A	N/A	18	0	0	0.0	0.0
C /5.3	10.0	0.94	11.90	75	1	97	0	2	28	104.4	N/A	37	18	0	0	0.0	0.0
C /5.4	14.0	1.07	1.76	149	5	92	1	2	25	144.2	-25.2	30	18	0	0	0.0	0.0
C+ /6.4	14.1	1.08	11.99	23	5	92	1	2	25	N/A	N/A	28	18	0	0	0.0	0.0
B /8.2	4.1	0.29	8.06	46	24	30	44	2	23	37.1	-6.7	92	20	0	0	0.0	0.0
B+ /9.5	4.1	0.63	8.12	236	23	30	45	2	33	38.1	-6.5	62	18	0	0	0.0	0.0
B /8.5	4.0	0.61	9.32	308	23	30	45	2	33	36.3	N/A	61	18	0	0	0.0	0.0
C /4.4	11.5	0.92	13.02	42	2	97	0	1	224	144.4	-20.5	85	6	0	0	0.0	0.0
U /	N/A	N/A	10.34	520	2	97	0	1	224	N/A	N/A	N/A	6	0	0	0.0	0.0
C+ /5.7	11.4	0.93	10.43	155	2	97	0	1	5	44.6	-23.4	61	N/A	0	0	0.0	0.0
U /	N/A	N/A	9.04	697	2	97	0	1	5	N/A	N/A	N/A	N/A	0	0	0.0	0.0
C- /3.8	15.8	0.95	11.79	14	0	99	0	1	82	132.0	-24.5	78	9	0	0	0.0	0.0
U /	N/A	N/A	10.59	60	0	99	0	1	82	N/A	N/A	N/A	9	0	0	0.0	0.0
U /	N/A	N/A	10.33	209	0	0	0	100	46	N/A	N/A	N/A	8	0	0	0.0	0.0
B- /7.6	5.8	0.52	13.65	108	0	0	0	100	46	57.1	-12.4	63	8	0	0	0.0	0.0
B- /7.5	5.8	0.52	13.55	674	0	0	0	100	46	56.4	-12.4	62	8	0	0	0.0	0.0
U /	N/A	N/A	9.75	46	3	67	28	2	35	N/A	N/A	N/A	3	0	0	0.0	0.0
U /	N/A	N/A	10.41	149	3	67	28	2	35	N/A	N/A	N/A	3	0	0	0.0	0.0
C+ /6.0	7.5	0.69	14.47	201	3	67	28	2	35	74.9	-16.9	47	3	0	0	0.0	0.0
C+ /6.0	7.5	0.69	14.39	1,397	3	67	28	2	35	73.9	-17.0	46	3	0	0	0.0	0.0
U /	N/A	N/A	9.82	34	24	64	10	2	27	N/A	N/A	N/A	8	0	0	0.0	0.0
U /	N/A	N/A	10.55	129	24	64	10	2	27	N/A	N/A	N/A	8	0	0	0.0	0.0
C /4.3	9.3	0.66	14.35	181	24	64	10	2	27	87.6	-19.2	96	8	0	0	0.0	0.0
C- /4.1	9.2	0.66	14.15	1,223	24	64	10	2	27	86.3	-19.2	96	8	0	0	0.0	0.0
U /	N/A	N/A	10.66	66	0	0	0	100	28	N/A	N/A	N/A	8	0	0	0.0	0.0
D+ /2.6	9.8	0.91	14.24	96	0	0	0	100	28	87.6	-19.7	25	8	0	0	0.0	0.0
D /2.2	9.7	0.91	13.79	691	0	0	0	100	28	87.0	-19.7	25	8	0	0	0.0	0.0

					PERFORMANCE						Incl. in Returns	
	99 Pct = Best 0 Pct = Worst		Overall					Total Return % through 2/28/17				
					Perfor-				Annualized		Dividend	Expense
Fund Type	Fund Name	Ticker Symbol	Investment Rating	Phone	mance Rating/Pts	3 Mo	6 Mo	1Yr / Pct	3Yr / Pct	5Yr / Pct	Yield	Ratio
GR	Great-West Lifetime 2055 T	MXWLX	C	(866) 831-7129	C+ / 6.0	6.57	6.53	21.49 /60	5.33 /58	9.01 /51	1.60	0.98
GR	Great-West Lifetime 2055 T1	MXXLX	C	(866) 831-7129	C+ / 5.9	6.54	6.50	21.44 /59	5.24 /57	8.89 /50	1.55	1.08
GL	Great-West Lifetime Csv 2015 T	MXLTX	C	(866) 831-7129	D+ / 2.8	3.36	2.36	10.71 /14	3.72 /39	4.96 /21	1.52	0.88
GL	Great-West Lifetime Csv 2015 T1	MXLUX	C	(866) 831-7129	D+ / 2.7	3.28	2.34	10.59 /13	3.63 /38	4.85 /20	1.39	0.98
GI	Great-West Lifetime Csv 2025 T	MXALX	C	(866) 831-7129	C- / 3.5	4.08	3.18	13.09 /22	4.24 /46	6.10 /29	1.89	0.90
GI	Great-West Lifetime Csv 2025 T1	MXBLX	C	(866) 831-7129	C- / 3.4	3.98	3.07	12.90 /21	4.12 /44	6.01 /28	1.74	1.00
GI	Great-West Lifetime Csv 2035 T	MXGLX	C	(866) 831-7129	C / 4.6	5.00	4.49	16.50 /36	4.89 /53	7.68 /40	1.82	0.92
GI	Great-West Lifetime Csv 2035 T1	MXHLX	C	(866) 831-7129	C / 4.5	5.02	4.43	16.45 /36	4.80 /52	7.57 /39	1.64	1.02
GI	Great-West Lifetime Csv 2045 T	MXMLX	C	(866) 831-7129	C / 5.5	5.94	5.78	19.64 /50	5.33 /58	8.50 /46	1.61	0.96
GI	Great-West Lifetime Csv 2045 T1	MXNLX	C	(866) 831-7129	C / 5.4	5.95	5.71	19.47 /49	5.19 /56	8.39 /45	1.53	1.06
GI	Great-West Lifetime Csv 2055 T	MXSLX	C+	(866) 831-7129	C+ / 5.6	6.19	6.06	20.32 /54	5.20 /56	8.42 /46	1.74	0.97
GI	Great-West Lifetime Csv 2055 T1	MXTLX	C+	(866) 831-7129	C / 5.5	6.14	6.01	20.22 /53	5.09 /55	8.32 /45	1.57	1.07
SC	Great-West Loomis Sayles SCV Init	MXLSX	B	(866) 831-7129	A / 9.5	5.21	12.92	35.09 /94	9.02 /87	13.16 /85	0.07	1.11
SC	Great-West Loomis Sayles SCV Inst	MXTFX	U	(866) 831-7129	U /	5.41	13.17	35.58 /95	--	--	0.75	0.74
FO	Great-West MFS Internatl Gro Init	MXIGX	D-	(866) 831-7129	D- / 1.3	7.06	3.08	13.35 /23	-0.27 /12	4.93 /21	0.24	1.20
FO	Great-West MFS Internatl Gro Inst	MXHTX	U	(866) 831-7129	U /	7.19	3.31	13.87 /25	--	--	1.43	0.85
FO	Great-West MFS Internatl Value Init	MXIVX	C	(866) 831-7129	C- / 3.7	6.53	0.17	12.80 /21	4.70 /51	7.05 /35	0.60	1.10
FO	Great-West MFS Internatl Value Inst	MXJVX	U	(866) 831-7129	U /	6.56	0.41	13.24 /22	--	--	1.39	0.72
FO	Great-West MFS Internatl Value L	MXMIX	C-	(866) 831-7129	C- / 3.4	6.41	0.02	12.47 /20	4.35 /47	--	0.00	1.63
GR	Great-West Mlti-Mgr Lg Cap Gro Init	MXLGX	B-	(866) 831-7129	B- / 7.5	8.65	8.20	18.08 /43	8.36 /82	11.79 /72	0.15	1.00
GR	Great-West Mlti-Mgr Lg Cap Gro Inst	MXGSX	U	(866) 831-7129	U /	8.84	8.44	18.56 /45	--	--	0.50	0.65
SC	Great-West Mlti-Mgr Sm Cap Gro Inst	MXMSX	U	(866) 831-7129	U /	5.49	9.76	31.28 /89	--	--	0.09	0.90
GR	Great-West Mod Aggr Prof I Init	MXRPX	C+	(866) 831-7129	C+ / 5.6	5.40	6.23	18.34 /44	5.71 /62	8.71 /48	2.05	1.22
GR	Great-West Mod Aggr Prof II Init	MXBPX	C+	(866) 831-7129	C+ / 5.7	5.43	6.23	18.56 /45	5.86 /63	8.88 /50	1.57	1.06
GR	Great-West Mod Aggr Prof II Inst	MXHRX	U	(866) 831-7129	U /	5.49	6.44	18.94 /47	--	--	1.20	0.71
GR	Great-West Mod Aggr Prof II L	MXFPX	C+	(866) 831-7129	C / 5.5	5.31	6.09	18.20 /44	5.62 /61	8.60 /47	1.16	1.31
BA	Great-West Mod Consv Prof I Init	MXTPX	C-	(866) 831-7129	C- / 3.6	3.95	4.04	13.09 /22	4.28 /46	6.11 /29	1.75	1.10
BA	Great-West Mod Consv Prof II Init	MXDPX	C+	(866) 831-7129	C- / 3.7	3.98	4.16	13.37 /23	4.47 /48	6.29 /30	1.72	0.95
BA	Great-West Mod Consv Prof II L	MXHPX	C+	(866) 831-7129	C- / 3.6	4.08	4.09	13.19 /22	4.24 /46	6.03 /29	1.37	1.20
GL	Great-West Moderate Prof I Init	MXOPX	C	(866) 831-7129	C / 4.6	4.67	5.11	15.90 /34	5.04 /55	7.44 /38	1.42	1.16
AA	Great-West Moderate Prof II Init	MXMPX	C+	(866) 831-7129	C / 4.8	4.68	5.18	16.17 /35	5.21 /57	7.63 /39	1.66	1.01
AA	Great-West Moderate Prof II Inst	MXITX	U	(866) 831-7129	U /	4.88	5.56	16.63 /37	--	--	1.00	0.66
AA	Great-West Moderate Prof II L	MXGPX	C+	(866) 831-7129	C / 4.6	4.78	5.28	15.96 /34	4.99 /54	7.37 /37	1.04	1.26
GI	Great-West Putnam Equity Inc Init	MXQIX	B+	(866) 831-7129	B+ / 8.8	7.81	10.89	26.53 /78	8.61 /84	12.94 /83	0.30	1.10
IN	Great-West Putnam Equity Inc Inst	MXQCX	U	(866) 831-7129	U /	7.93	11.10	27.02 /79	--	--	1.53	0.75
IX	Great-West S&P 500 Index Init	MXVIX	A+	(866) 831-7129	A- / 9.0	7.90	9.68	24.18 /71	9.95 /93	13.34 /87	0.84	0.60
IX	Great-West S&P 500 Index Inst	MXKWX	U	(866) 831-7129	U /	7.91	9.87	24.67 /72	--	--	2.79	0.25
IX	Great-West S&P 500 Index L	MXVJX	A+	(866) 831-7129	B+ / 8.9	7.80	9.60	23.91 /70	9.68 /91	13.05 /84	1.17	0.85
MC	Great-West S&P MC 400 Index Init	MXMDX	A-	(866) 831-7129	A- / 9.2	6.44	11.03	30.92 /88	8.99 /87	13.15 /85	0.51	0.60
MC	Great-West S&P MC 400 Index Inst	MXNZX	U	(866) 831-7129	U /	6.49	11.22	31.29 /89	--	--	1.61	0.25
SC	Great-West S&P SC 600 Index Init	MXISX	B+	(866) 831-7129	A / 9.5	4.43	12.84	34.28 /93	9.13 /88	14.32 /95	0.88	0.60
SC	Great-West S&P SC 600 Index Inst	MXERX	U	(866) 831-7129	U /	4.54	13.08	34.71 /94	--	--	1.80	0.25
SC	Great-West S&P SC 600 Index L	MXNSX	B+	(866) 831-7129	A / 9.4	4.43	12.76	33.99 /93	8.86 /86	14.04 /93	0.40	0.85
GL	Great-West SecureFndtn Bal ETF A	SFBPX	C+	(866) 831-7129	C- / 3.7	4.68	4.63	15.89 /34	5.31 /58	7.63 /39	1.81	0.72
GL	Great-West SecureFndtn Balanced G	MXSBX	B	(866) 831-7129	C / 4.6	4.41	4.63	15.17 /31	5.32 /58	7.57 /39	1.77	0.66
GL	Great-West SecureFndtn Balanced	MXSHX	B	(866) 831-7129	C / 4.5	4.46	4.68	15.15 /31	5.23 /57	7.48 /38	1.57	0.76
GL	Great-West SecureFndtn Balanced	MXCJX	U	(866) 831-7129	U /	4.62	4.85	15.58 /32	--	--	2.93	0.31
GL	Great-West SecureFndtn Balanced L	MXLDX	B-	(866) 831-7129	C / 4.4	4.41	4.55	14.95 /30	5.08 /55	7.32 /37	1.91	0.91
GI	Great-West SecureFndtn LT 2015 G	MXSJX	C+	(866) 831-7129	C- / 3.9	4.31	3.82	13.55 /24	4.71 /51	6.91 /34	1.96	0.68
GI	Great-West SecureFndtn LT 2015 G1	MXSKX	C+	(866) 831-7129	C- / 3.8	4.27	3.78	13.40 /23	4.62 /50	6.81 /33	1.74	0.78
GI	Great-West SecureFndtn LT 2015 L	MXLEX	C+	(866) 831-7129	C- / 3.7	4.28	3.72	13.37 /23	4.48 /48	6.67 /33	1.90	0.93
GI	Great-West SecureFndtn LT 2020 G	MXSMX	B-	(866) 831-7129	C- / 3.9	4.32	3.83	13.50 /23	4.72 /51	6.93 /34	1.92	0.68

● Denotes fund is closed to new investors
* Denotes fund is included in Section II

Risk Rating/Pts	3 Year Standard Deviation	Beta	NAV As of 2/28/17	Total $(Mil)	Cash %	Stocks %	Bonds %	Other %	Portfolio Turnover Ratio	Last Bull Market Return	Last Bear Market Return	Manager Quality Pct	Manager Tenure (Years)	Initial Purch. $	Additional Purch. $	Front End Load	Back End Load
C /5.4	9.8	0.91	16.79	41	0	0	0	100	26	85.6	-19.8	23	6	0	0	0.0	0.0
C /5.1	9.8	0.91	16.35	253	0	0	0	100	26	84.5	-19.8	22	6	0	0	0.0	0.0
B /8.0	4.4	0.29	12.05	7	0	0	0	100	40	40.7	-7.7	92	8	0	0	0.0	0.0
B /8.0	4.4	0.30	12.09	109	0	0	0	100	40	40.0	-7.8	92	8	0	0	0.0	0.0
B- /7.4	5.4	0.48	12.82	26	0	0	0	100	36	52.3	-11.4	66	8	0	0	0.0	0.0
B- /7.4	5.4	0.47	12.83	198	0	0	0	100	36	51.5	-11.5	65	8	0	0	0.0	0.0
C+ /6.3	7.2	0.66	13.76	22	0	0	0	100	37	69.2	-15.6	50	8	0	0	0.0	0.0
C+ /6.4	7.2	0.66	13.78	165	0	0	0	100	37	68.4	-15.6	48	8	0	0	0.0	0.0
C+ /5.8	8.6	0.80	14.50	11	0	0	0	100	33	78.4	-17.5	35	8	0	0	0.0	0.0
C+ /5.9	8.6	0.80	14.48	99	0	0	0	100	33	77.2	-17.5	34	8	0	0	0.0	0.0
C+ /6.1	9.0	0.83	14.35	4	1	81	16	2	38	78.0	-17.9	30	8	0	0	0.0	0.0
C+ /6.1	9.0	0.83	14.34	34	1	81	16	2	38	77.0	-17.9	29	8	0	0	0.0	0.0
C- /4.1	14.7	0.91	27.64	107	1	98	0	1	25	135.4	-23.7	89	17	0	0	0.0	0.0
U /	N/A	N/A	9.67	143	1	98	0	1	25	N/A	N/A	N/A	17	0	0	0.0	0.0
C /5.2	11.3	0.90	11.01	32	1	98	0	1	32	50.6	-23.2	73	14	0	0	0.0	0.0
U /	N/A	N/A	8.67	296	1	98	0	1	32	N/A	N/A	N/A	14	0	0	0.0	0.0
B- /7.0	9.4	0.69	12.22	304	0	97	1	2	29	73.3	-22.5	95	8	0	0	0.0	0.0
U /	N/A	N/A	9.99	774	0	97	1	2	29	N/A	N/A	N/A	8	0	0	0.0	0.0
B- /7.0	9.4	0.69	11.87	20	0	97	1	2	29	N/A	N/A	94	8	0	0	0.0	0.0
C /5.2	11.2	1.00	9.14	174	2	97	0	1	31	115.6	-20.3	48	4	0	0	0.0	0.0
U /	N/A	N/A	9.52	626	2	97	0	1	31	N/A	N/A	N/A	4	0	0	0.0	0.0
U /	N/A	N/A	10.57	48	3	96	0	1	0	N/A	N/A	N/A	2	0	0	0.0	0.0
C+ /6.2	7.6	0.72	9.15	157	10	71	17	2	25	77.1	-15.4	52	3	0	0	0.0	0.0
C+ /6.5	7.6	0.71	8.04	323	10	70	18	2	29	78.4	-15.3	55	11	0	0	0.0	0.0
U /	N/A	N/A	9.85	41	10	70	18	2	29	N/A	N/A	N/A	11	0	0	0.0	0.0
C+ /6.9	7.6	0.72	9.31	131	10	70	18	2	29	76.0	N/A	51	11	0	0	0.0	0.0
C+ /6.6	5.2	0.81	7.97	53	23	43	32	2	28	49.8	-9.7	52	20	0	0	0.0	0.0
B- /7.9	5.3	0.82	8.69	114	22	44	32	2	28	51.1	-9.6	54	18	0	0	0.0	0.0
B /8.1	5.2	0.81	9.59	144	22	44	32	2	28	49.2	N/A	52	18	0	0	0.0	0.0
C+ /6.3	6.5	0.46	8.24	197	18	58	22	2	23	63.2	-12.6	95	20	0	0	0.0	0.0
C+ /6.7	6.6	1.03	7.16	866	16	59	24	1	27	64.5	-12.5	43	18	0	0	0.0	0.0
U /	N/A	N/A	9.88	75	16	59	24	1	27	N/A	N/A	N/A	18	0	0	0.0	0.0
B- /7.5	6.5	1.02	10.30	281	16	59	24	1	27	62.6	N/A	41	18	0	0	0.0	0.0
C /5.5	10.4	0.98	14.50	38	2	97	0	1	28	130.3	N/A	53	5	0	0	0.0	0.0
U /	N/A	N/A	9.85	561	2	97	0	1	28	N/A	N/A	N/A	5	0	0	0.0	0.0
C+ /6.8	10.3	1.00	20.15	1,436	0	99	0	1	10	127.4	-16.4	67	N/A	0	0	0.0	0.0
U /	N/A	N/A	10.38	1,069	0	99	0	1	10	N/A	N/A	N/A	N/A	0	0	0.0	0.0
C+ /6.7	10.3	1.00	16.03	236	0	99	0	1	10	124.4	N/A	64	N/A	0	0	0.0	0.0
C /5.5	12.0	1.00	16.01	344	1	98	0	1	25	132.7	-22.7	67	1	0	0	0.0	0.0
U /	N/A	N/A	9.95	450	1	98	0	1	25	N/A	N/A	N/A	1	0	0	0.0	0.0
C /4.7	14.7	0.92	13.35	540	0	99	0	1	25	148.3	-22.2	89	1	0	0	0.0	0.0
U /	N/A	N/A	9.94	351	0	99	0	1	25	N/A	N/A	N/A	1	0	0	0.0	0.0
C /4.9	14.7	0.92	16.89	37	0	99	0	1	25	145.1	N/A	88	1	0	0	0.0	0.0
B /8.5	6.6	0.98	13.51	52	2	59	37	2	37	N/A	N/A	79	3	10,000	500	5.0	0.0
B /8.4	6.3	0.94	13.08	239	6	58	34	2	13	64.1	-11.2	80	8	0	0	0.0	0.0
B /8.4	6.3	0.94	13.23	70	6	58	34	2	13	63.3	-11.2	80	8	0	0	0.0	0.0
U /	N/A	N/A	9.82	53	6	58	34	2	13	N/A	N/A	N/A	8	0	0	0.0	0.0
B /8.3	6.3	0.94	11.64	192	6	58	34	2	13	62.0	-11.2	79	8	0	0	0.0	0.0
B- /7.9	5.8	0.54	11.11	54	5	54	40	1	23	57.5	-10.7	63	8	0	0	0.0	0.0
B- /7.9	5.8	0.53	11.26	39	5	54	40	1	23	56.7	-10.8	63	8	0	0	0.0	0.0
B- /7.7	5.8	0.54	9.96	10	5	54	40	1	23	55.4	-10.9	61	8	0	0	0.0	0.0
B /8.6	5.8	0.54	12.08	65	5	55	38	2	17	57.6	-10.7	64	6	0	0	0.0	0.0

					PERFORMANCE						
						Total Return % through 2/28/17				Incl. in Returns	
99 Pct = Best					Perfor-				Annualized	Dividend	Expense
0 Pct = Worst			Ticker	Overall Investment	mance						
Fund Type	Fund Name		Symbol	Rating	Phone	Rating/Pts	3 Mo	6 Mo	1Yr / Pct	3Yr / Pct	5Yr / Pct	Dividend Yield	Expense Ratio

Fund Type	Fund Name	Ticker Symbol	Overall Investment Rating	Phone	Performance Rating/Pts	3 Mo	6 Mo	1Yr / Pct	3Yr / Pct	5Yr / Pct	Dividend Yield	Expense Ratio
GI	Great-West SecureFndtn LT 2020 G1	MXSPX	C+	(866) 831-7129	C- / 3.8	4.26	3.76	13.48 /23	4.63 /50	6.80 /33	1.84	0.78
GI	Great-West SecureFndtn LT 2020 L	MXLFX	C+	(866) 831-7129	C- / 3.7	4.23	3.72	13.32 /23	4.46 /48	6.65 /32	1.66	0.93
GI	Great-West SecureFndtn LT 2025 G	MXSNX	C+	(866) 831-7129	C- / 3.9	4.36	3.88	13.59 /24	4.75 /51	7.29 /37	1.98	0.68
GI	Great-West SecureFndtn LT 2025 G1	MXSOX	C+	(866) 831-7129	C- / 3.8	4.29	3.82	13.48 /23	4.64 /50	7.16 /36	1.80	0.78
GI	Great-West SecureFndtn LT 2025 L	MXLHX	C+	(866) 831-7129	C- / 3.7	4.23	3.68	13.28 /23	4.49 /49	7.00 /35	1.88	0.93
GI	Great-West SecureFndtn LT 2030 G	MXSQX	B-	(866) 831-7129	C / 4.6	4.89	4.78	16.06 /35	5.00 /54	8.06 /43	1.94	0.70
GI	Great-West SecureFndtn LT 2030 G1	MXASX	B-	(866) 831-7129	C / 4.5	4.87	4.76	15.97 /34	4.91 /53	7.96 /42	1.74	0.80
GI	Great-West SecureFndtn LT 2030 L	MXLIX	B-	(866) 831-7129	C / 4.4	4.81	4.62	15.75 /33	4.78 /52	7.87 /41	1.64	0.95
GI	Great-West SecureFndtn LT 2035 G	MXSRX	C+	(866) 831-7129	C / 5.4	5.63	5.95	18.80 /46	5.33 /58	8.77 /49	1.98	0.72
GI	Great-West SecureFndtn LT 2035 G1	MXSSX	C+	(866) 831-7129	C / 5.3	5.60	5.92	18.70 /46	5.23 /57	8.65 /48	1.79	0.82
GI	Great-West SecureFndtn LT 2035 L	MXLJX	C+	(866) 831-7129	C / 5.3	5.55	5.88	18.73 /46	5.29 /57	8.62 /47	2.20	0.97
GI	Great-West SecureFndtn LT 2040 G	MXDSX	B-	(866) 831-7129	C+ / 6.0	6.21	6.79	20.83 /57	5.49 /59	9.07 /51	1.96	0.73
GI	Great-West SecureFndtn LT 2040 G1	MXESX	B-	(866) 831-7129	C+ / 5.9	6.12	6.80	20.75 /56	5.42 /59	9.00 /51	1.83	0.83
GI	Great-West SecureFndtn LT 2040 L	MXLKX	B-	(866) 831-7129	C+ / 6.0	6.22	6.89	20.90 /57	5.55 /60	9.11 /52	1.93	0.98
GI	Great-West SecureFndtn LT 2045 G	MXSTX	C+	(866) 831-7129	C+ / 6.3	6.51	7.37	21.97 /62	5.57 /60	9.15 /52	0.56	0.74
GI	Great-West SecureFndtn LT 2045 G1	MXSWX	C+	(866) 831-7129	C+ / 6.1	6.43	7.22	21.82 /61	5.45 /59	9.01 /51	0.51	0.84
GI	Great-West SecureFndtn LT 2045 L	MXLNX	C+	(866) 831-7129	C+ / 6.1	6.40	7.17	21.79 /61	5.47 /59	9.06 /51	0.50	0.99
GI	Great-West SecureFndtn LT 2050 G	MXFSX	C+	(866) 831-7129	C+ / 6.3	6.55	7.42	22.33 /64	5.50 /60	9.03 /51	1.98	0.74
GI	Great-West SecureFndtn LT 2050 G1	MXHSX	C+	(866) 831-7129	C+ / 6.2	6.55	7.42	22.20 /63	5.39 /58	8.92 /50	1.85	0.84
GI	Great-West SecureFndtn LT 2050 L	MXLOX	C+	(866) 831-7129	C+ / 6.2	6.47	7.32	22.16 /63	5.47 /59	8.99 /51	1.92	0.99
GI	Great-West SecureFndtn LT 2055 G	MXSYX	C+	(866) 831-7129	C+ / 6.2	6.59	7.38	22.42 /64	5.38 /58	8.86 /49	2.03	0.74
GI	Great-West SecureFndtn LT 2055 G1	MXSZX	C+	(866) 831-7129	C+ / 6.1	6.53	7.34	22.29 /64	5.28 /57	8.74 /48	1.79	0.84
GI	Great-West SecureFndtn LT 2055 L	MXLPX	C+	(866) 831-7129	C+ / 6.2	6.55	7.35	22.42 /64	5.38 /58	8.85 /49	2.32	0.99
IN	Great-West T Rowe Price Eq Inc Init	MXEQX	B	(866) 831-7129	B / 8.1	5.23	11.34	28.64 /83	7.28 /74	11.54 /70	0.58	0.83
IN	Great-West T Rowe Price Eq Inc Inst	MXVHX	U	(866) 831-7129	U /	5.28	11.53	29.19 /85	--	--	2.98	0.47
IN	Great-West T Rowe Price Eq Inc L	MXTQX	C+	(866) 831-7129	B / 7.8	5.12	11.15	28.23 /82	6.87 /71	11.16 /67	2.03	1.79
MC	Great-West T Rowe Price MC Gr Init	MXMGX	B-	(866) 831-7129	B / 8.0	6.63	7.05	21.66 /60	9.19 /88	13.74 /91	0.05	1.03
MC	Great-West T Rowe Price MC Gr Inst	MXYKX	U	(866) 831-7129	U /	6.69	7.20	22.09 /63	--	--	0.21	0.67
MC	Great-West T Rowe Price MC Gr L	MXTMX	D+	(866) 831-7129	B / 7.8	6.42	6.87	21.18 /58	8.85 /86	13.41 /88	0.21	1.42
BA	Green Century Balanced Indiv Inv	GCBLX	C	(800) 221-5519	C- / 3.7	4.64	4.08	14.85 /29	4.66 /50	8.53 /47	0.12	1.48
GR	Green Century Equity Individual Inv	GCEQX	A-	(800) 221-5519	B / 7.8	7.68	8.00	21.99 /62	8.99 /87	12.82 /82	0.74	1.25
GL	Green Owl Intrinsic Value	GOWLX	A+	(888) 695-3729	A+ / 9.6	7.54	18.56	36.03 /95	8.06 /79	13.19 /86	0.33	1.37
BA	Greenspring	GRSPX	C	(800) 366-3863	C / 4.7	2.98	8.46	24.41 /71	3.68 /39	6.24 /30	1.25	0.96
GR	Growth 529 Port A		C+	(800) 342-5236	C / 4.3	7.68	7.57	21.04 /58	4.30 /46	9.29 /53	0.00	1.48
GR	● Growth 529 Port B		C+	(800) 342-5236	C / 4.9	7.48	7.16	20.13 /53	3.52 /37	8.47 /46	0.00	2.23
GR	Growth 529 Port C		C+	(800) 342-5236	C / 4.9	7.49	7.13	20.09 /52	3.52 /37	8.49 /46	0.00	2.23
IN	Guggenheim Alpha Opportunity A	SAOAX	B	(800) 820-0888	C / 4.7	5.67	10.93	11.57 /16	6.41 /68	10.67 /63	0.00	3.92
IN	Guggenheim Alpha Opportunity C	SAOCX	B+	(800) 820-0888	C / 5.0	5.49	10.52	10.72 /14	5.62 /61	9.84 /57	0.00	4.81
IN	Guggenheim Alpha Opportunity Instl	SAOIX	B	(800) 820-0888	C+ / 6.1	5.87	11.49	12.29 /19	6.83 /71	11.17 /67	0.00	2.80
IX	Guggenheim Capital Stewardship Inst	GFCIX	U	(800) 820-0888	U /	7.31	8.48	20.46 /55	--	--	1.28	1.15
AA	Guggenheim Dir Alloc A	TVRAX	C-	(800) 345-7999	C / 5.2	7.54	9.89	23.10 /67	4.47 /48	--	0.00	1.50
AA	Guggenheim Dir Alloc C	TVRCX	C	(800) 345-7999	C+ / 5.6	7.38	9.54	22.36 /64	3.80 /40	--	0.00	2.10
AA	Guggenheim Dir Alloc I	TVRIX	C+	(800) 345-7999	C+ / 6.5	7.64	10.04	23.54 /68	4.83 /52	--	0.00	1.10
AA	Guggenheim Dir Alloc P	TVFRX	C+	(800) 345-7999	C+ / 6.3	7.58	9.92	23.27 /67	4.58 /50	--	0.00	1.35
GL	Guggenheim Event Dr Distr Strat A	RYDOX	D+	(800) 820-0888	D- / 1.1	1.95	2.64	10.98 /14	0.62 /16	3.68 /14	3.15	2.13
GL	Guggenheim Event Dr Distr Strat C	RYDQX	D+	(800) 820-0888	D- / 1.0	1.74	2.22	10.11 /12	-0.14 /13	2.90 /10	3.51	2.88
GL	Guggenheim Event Dr Distr Strat I	RYDTX	C-	(800) 820-0888	D / 1.6	2.03	2.79	11.25 /15	0.87 /18	3.94 /15	3.25	1.88
GL	Guggenheim Event Dr Distr Strat P	RYDSX	C-	(800) 820-0888	D- / 1.5	1.95	2.64	10.98 /14	0.61 /16	3.68 /14	3.31	2.13
GI	Guggenheim Large Cap Value A	SECIX	A-	(800) 820-0888	A- / 9.1	7.56	14.17	33.71 /92	8.83 /86	12.58 /80	1.19	1.35
GI	Guggenheim Large Cap Value C	SEGIX	A-	(800) 820-0888	A / 9.3	7.37	13.74	32.71 /91	8.03 /79	11.74 /72	0.66	2.16
GI	Guggenheim Large Cap Value Inst	GILCX	A	(800) 820-0888	A+ / 9.6	7.65	14.31	34.03 /93	9.10 /87	--	2.36	0.98
FS	Guggenheim Limited Duration A	GILDX	C-	(800) 820-0888	D- / 1.4	1.03	1.75	5.41 / 4	2.65 /29	--	2.72	0.99

● Denotes fund is closed to new investors
* Denotes fund is included in Section II

RISK			NET ASSETS		ASSET				Portfolio	BULL / BEAR		FUND MANAGER		MINIMUMS		LOADS	
	3 Year		NAV							Last Bull	Last Bear	Manager	Manager	Initial	Additional	Front	Back
Risk Rating/Pts	Standard Deviation	Beta	As of 2/28/17	Total $(Mil)	Cash %	Stocks %	Bonds %	Other %	Turnover Ratio	Market Return	Market Return	Quality Pct	Tenure (Years)	Purch. $	Purch. $	End Load	End Load
B /8.6	5.9	0.54	12.10	10	5	55	38	2	17	56.8	-10.7	62	6	0	0	0.0	0.0
B /8.6	5.8	0.54	12.15	2	5	55	38	2	17	55.7	-10.7	60	6	0	0	0.0	0.0
B- /7.9	5.9	0.55	11.32	34	4	56	39	1	22	62.2	-13.4	63	8	0	0	0.0	0.0
B- /7.9	5.9	0.55	11.42	44	4	56	39	1	22	61.3	-13.4	62	8	0	0	0.0	0.0
B- /7.7	5.9	0.55	10.09	1	4	56	39	1	22	60.0	-13.5	60	8	0	0	0.0	0.0
B /8.1	7.1	0.66	12.62	92	2	67	29	2	15	71.6	-15.8	51	6	0	0	0.0	0.0
B /8.1	7.1	0.66	12.66	9	2	67	29	2	15	70.8	-15.8	49	6	0	0	0.0	0.0
B /8.1	7.1	0.66	12.74	N/A	2	67	29	2	15	70.1	-15.8	48	6	0	0	0.0	0.0
B- /7.1	8.3	0.77	12.17	40	1	79	19	1	17	79.8	-17.7	39	8	0	0	0.0	0.0
B- /7.1	8.3	0.77	12.27	28	1	79	19	1	17	78.9	-17.7	38	8	0	0	0.0	0.0
C+ /6.9	8.3	0.78	10.78	N/A	1	79	19	1	17	78.6	-17.7	38	8	0	0	0.0	0.0
B- /7.0	9.1	0.85	12.88	70	0	85	13	2	13	84.0	-18.6	31	6	0	0	0.0	0.0
B- /7.1	9.0	0.85	12.88	7	0	85	13	2	13	83.2	-18.6	31	6	0	0	0.0	0.0
B- /7.1	9.1	0.85	13.00	N/A	0	85	13	2	13	84.1	-18.5	32	6	0	0	0.0	0.0
C+ /6.4	9.4	0.88	12.28	16	0	88	10	2	15	85.0	-19.0	29	8	0	0	0.0	0.0
C+ /6.4	9.5	0.88	12.27	15	0	88	10	2	15	83.9	-19.0	27	8	0	0	0.0	0.0
C+ /6.3	9.5	0.88	10.66	N/A	0	88	10	2	15	84.3	-19.0	27	8	0	0	0.0	0.0
C+ /6.8	9.6	0.89	12.95	18	1	89	8	2	13	84.4	-19.3	27	6	0	0	0.0	0.0
C+ /6.8	9.6	0.89	12.93	3	1	89	8	2	13	83.3	-19.3	26	6	0	0	0.0	0.0
C+ /6.8	9.5	0.89	13.00	N/A	1	89	8	2	13	83.9	-19.2	27	6	0	0	0.0	0.0
C+ /6.2	9.6	0.90	12.34	4	0	89	9	2	15	83.0	-19.4	25	8	0	0	0.0	0.0
C+ /6.2	9.7	0.90	12.36	3	0	89	9	2	15	81.9	-19.5	24	8	0	0	0.0	0.0
C+ /6.0	9.6	0.90	10.75	N/A	0	89	9	2	15	82.9	-19.5	25	8	0	0	0.0	0.0
C /5.3	11.1	1.02	19.83	296	1	98	0	1	41	109.9	-18.3	31	2	0	0	0.0	0.0
U /	N/A	N/A	9.11	562	1	98	0	1	41	N/A	N/A	N/A	2	0	0	0.0	0.0
C- /4.0	11.1	1.02	10.23	4	1	98	0	1	41	106.1	N/A	27	2	0	0	0.0	0.0
C /4.8	12.0	0.92	23.60	731	1	92	5	2	35	133.4	-20.3	77	20	0	0	0.0	0.0
U /	N/A	N/A	8.66	383	1	92	5	2	35	N/A	N/A	N/A	20	0	0	0.0	0.0
D- /1.3	12.0	0.92	7.32	40	1	92	5	2	35	130.0	N/A	N/A	20	0	0	0.0	0.0
B- /7.2	8.2	1.21	24.56	210	7	65	27	1	24	71.1	-11.7	22	12	2,500	100	0.0	2.0
B- /7.1	10.7	1.01	35.86	185	0	100	0	0	19	119.0	-15.2	53	7	2,500	100	0.0	2.0
C+ /6.1	13.0	0.74	17.76	72	5	94	0	1	21	N/A	N/A	98	N/A	2,500	0	0.0	0.0
C+ /6.0	8.5	0.98	25.02	328	6	64	29	1	25	53.1	-10.0	29	30	5,000	100	0.0	2.0
B- /7.4	10.1	0.92	31.70	99	0	0	0	100	0	88.6	-21.2	14	14	250	0	5.8	0.0
B- /7.3	10.1	0.92	28.58	3	0	0	0	100	0	81.1	-21.5	9	14	250	0	0.0	0.0
B- /7.3	10.1	0.92	28.69	33	0	0	0	100	0	81.1	-21.4	10	14	250	0	0.0	0.0
B /8.9	6.1	0.27	21.17	21	28	71	0	1	235	115.7	-24.5	92	N/A	2,500	100	4.8	0.0
B /8.8	6.1	0.27	18.76	2	28	71	0	1	235	107.0	-24.7	89	N/A	2,500	100	0.0	0.0
B /8.9	6.2	0.27	29.85	70	28	71	0	1	235	120.7	-24.4	93	N/A	2,000,000	0	0.0	0.0
U /	N/A	N/A	27.55	224	0	0	0	100	209	N/A	N/A	N/A	3	2,000,000	0	0.0	0.0
C /5.3	11.1	1.63	14.55	137	0	99	0	1	227	N/A	N/A	5	5	2,500	100	4.8	0.0
C /5.2	11.1	1.64	14.12	259	0	99	0	1	227	N/A	N/A	4	5	5,000	100	0.0	0.0
C /5.3	11.1	1.63	14.80	244	0	99	0	1	227	N/A	N/A	6	5	2,000,000	0	0.0	0.0
C /5.3	11.1	1.64	14.62	37	0	99	0	1	227	N/A	N/A	5	5	5,000	100	0.0	0.0
B /8.1	6.0	0.39	26.45	1	73	4	22	1	32	34.4	-12.9	78	2	2,500	0	4.8	0.0
B /8.0	6.0	0.39	24.95	1	73	4	22	1	32	29.0	-13.1	72	2	2,500	0	0.0	0.0
B /8.2	6.0	0.39	26.95	9	73	4	22	1	32	36.2	-12.7	80	2	2,000,000	0	0.0	0.0
B /8.1	6.0	0.39	26.45	1	73	4	22	1	32	34.4	-12.9	78	2	0	0	0.0	0.0
C+ /5.7	11.0	0.99	45.45	63	0	96	3	1	56	122.8	-22.2	54	2	2,500	100	4.8	0.0
C+ /5.6	11.0	1.00	42.10	4	0	96	3	1	56	114.0	-22.4	44	2	2,500	100	0.0	0.0
C+ /5.6	11.0	1.00	45.01	2	0	96	3	1	56	N/A	N/A	58	2	2,000,000	0	0.0	0.0
B /8.8	1.0	0.03	24.74	284	6	0	93	1	39	N/A	N/A	87	4	2,500	100	2.3	0.0

I. Index of Stock Mutual Funds

Fund Type	Fund Name	Ticker Symbol	Overall Investment Rating	Phone	Performance Rating/Pts	3 Mo	6 Mo	1Yr / Pct	3Yr / Pct	5Yr / Pct	Dividend Yield	Expense Ratio
FS	Guggenheim Limited Duration C	GILFX	C-	(800) 820-0888	D- / 1.3	0.84	1.34	4.59 / 4	1.85 /23	--	2.05	1.76
FS	Guggenheim Limited Duration Inst	GILHX	C	(800) 820-0888	D / 1.7	1.09	1.84	5.63 / 4	2.88 /31	--	3.03	0.73
AG	Guggenheim Long Short Equity A	RYAMX	C-	(800) 820-0888	D- / 1.0	1.91	2.24	6.32 / 5	1.35 /20	4.29 /17	0.00	2.53
AG	Guggenheim Long Short Equity C	RYISX	C-	(800) 820-0888	D- / 1.1	1.78	1.85	5.47 / 4	0.59 /16	3.50 /13	0.00	3.24
GR	Guggenheim Long Short Equity Inst	RYQTX	C-	(800) 820-0888	D- / 1.5	2.00	2.32	6.61 / 5	1.61 /22	4.54 /18	0.00	2.27
AG	Guggenheim Long Short Equity P	RYSRX	C-	(800) 820-0888	D- / 1.4	1.91	2.23	6.30 / 5	1.34 /20	4.27 /17	0.00	2.50
FS	Guggenheim Macro Opportunities P	GIOPX	U	(800) 820-0888	U /	2.53	4.70	14.31 /27	--	--	4.76	1.48
OT	Guggenheim Managed Futures Strat	RYMTX	E+	(800) 820-0888	E- / 0.2	2.74	-4.19	-14.83 / 0	-0.85 /10	-2.03 / 3	4.86	1.82
OT	Guggenheim Managed Futures Strat	RYMZX	E+	(800) 820-0888	E- / 0.2	2.56	-4.58	-15.47 / 0	-1.61 / 8	-2.76 / 2	5.54	2.57
OT	Guggenheim Managed Futures Strat I	RYIFX	E+	(800) 820-0888	E / 0.3	2.85	-4.03	-14.60 / 0	-0.60 /11	-1.77 / 3	5.01	1.57
OT	Guggenheim Managed Futures Strat	RYMFX	E+	(800) 820-0888	E- / 0.2	2.79	-4.19	-14.83 / 0	-0.87 /10	-2.03 / 3	5.10	1.82
MC	Guggenheim Mid Cap Value A	SEVAX	C	(800) 820-0888	B / 8.1	5.87	16.75	36.56 /95	6.06 /65	11.16 /67	1.03	1.42
MC	Guggenheim Mid Cap Value C	SEVSX	C-	(800) 820-0888	B+ / 8.3	5.64	16.28	35.49 /94	5.27 /57	10.35 /61	0.73	2.12
MC	Guggenheim Mid Cap Value Inst Fd	SVUIX	B-	(800) 820-0888	A- / 9.2	5.94	17.06	36.66 /96	6.66 /70	11.64 /71	4.44	1.05
GL	Guggenheim Multi-Hedge Strat A	RYMQX	C-	(800) 820-0888	E+ / 0.7	0.36	-0.10	-0.76 / 1	2.04 /24	1.58 / 7	0.14	2.81
GL	Guggenheim Multi-Hedge Strat C	RYMRX	C	(800) 820-0888	E+ / 0.8	0.12	-0.52	-1.54 / 1	1.27 /20	0.81 / 6	0.16	3.56
GL	Guggenheim Multi-Hedge Strat I	RYIMX	C	(800) 820-0888	D- / 1.1	0.39	0.02	-0.51 / 1	2.29 /26	1.83 / 8	0.15	2.56
GL	Guggenheim Multi-Hedge Strat P	RYMSX	C	(800) 820-0888	D- / 1.0	0.32	-0.14	-0.80 / 1	2.03 /24	1.57 / 7	0.15	2.81
OT	Guggenheim Municipal Income C	GIJCX	C	(800) 820-0888	D- / 1.2	1.35	-3.61	-1.10 / 1	2.91 /31	2.54 / 9	1.31	1.87
EN	Guggenheim Municipal Income Inst	GIJIX	C	(800) 820-0888	D / 1.6	1.60	-3.13	-0.11 / 1	3.94 /42	3.57 /13	2.34	0.89
IN	Guggenheim RBP Dividend A	TVEAX	B-	(800) 345-7999	B- / 7.4	9.57	8.44	23.82 /69	8.14 /80	11.63 /71	1.25	1.74
IN	Guggenheim RBP Dividend C	TVECX	B-	(800) 345-7999	B / 7.7	9.32	7.99	22.93 /66	7.45 /75	10.95 /65	0.78	2.34
IN	Guggenheim RBP Dividend I	TVEIX	B	(800) 345-7999	B+ / 8.5	9.68	8.61	24.20 /71	8.55 /83	12.07 /75	1.79	1.34
IN	Guggenheim RBP Dividend P	TVEFX	B	(800) 345-7999	B / 8.2	9.59	8.46	23.84 /69	8.26 /81	11.79 /72	1.27	1.59
GR	Guggenheim RBP LgCp Defensive A	TVDAX	D+	(800) 345-7999	C / 5.1	7.37	5.76	17.83 /42	6.60 /69	10.80 /64	0.19	1.56
GR	Guggenheim RBP LgCp Defensive C	TVDCX	C-	(800) 345-7999	C+ / 5.7	7.15	5.32	17.03 /38	5.93 /64	10.13 /59	0.00	2.16
GR	Guggenheim RBP LgCp Defensive I	TVIDX	C	(800) 345-7999	C+ / 6.5	7.36	5.79	18.16 /44	6.96 /72	11.21 /68	0.56	1.16
GR	Guggenheim RBP LgCp Defensive P	TVFDX	C-	(800) 345-7999	C+ / 6.3	7.37	5.69	17.84 /42	6.72 /70	10.94 /65	0.00	1.41
GR	Guggenheim RBP LgCp Market A	TVMAX	D+	(888) 727-6885	C+ / 6.2	7.25	8.82	23.82 /69	6.29 /67	11.59 /71	0.00	1.53
GR	Guggenheim RBP LgCp Market C	TVMCX	D+	(888) 727-6885	C+ / 6.5	7.04	8.32	22.82 /66	5.60 /61	10.89 /65	0.00	2.13
GR	Guggenheim RBP LgCp Market I	TVIMX	C-	(888) 727-6885	B- / 7.3	7.42	8.93	24.16 /70	6.68 /70	12.02 /74	0.00	1.13
GR	Guggenheim RBP LgCp Market P	TVFMX	C-	(888) 727-6885	B- / 7.1	7.38	8.81	23.93 /70	6.41 /68	11.73 /72	0.00	1.38
GR	Guggenheim RBP LgCp Value A	TVVAX	C+	(888) 727-6885	B- / 7.4	7.57	11.22	25.25 /74	8.25 /81	12.44 /78	2.00	5.10
GR	Guggenheim RBP LgCp Value C	TVVCX	C+	(888) 727-6885	B / 7.9	7.40	10.77	24.44 /71	7.48 /75	11.66 /71	0.75	5.70
GR	Guggenheim RBP LgCp Value I	TVVIX	B-	(888) 727-6885	B+ / 8.7	7.61	11.40	25.69 /75	8.64 /84	12.84 /82	0.94	4.70
GR	Guggenheim RBP LgCp Value P	TVVFX	B-	(888) 727-6885	B+ / 8.5	7.50	11.22	25.31 /74	8.37 /82	12.54 /79	0.00	4.95
RE	Guggenheim Risk Managed Rl Est	GURIX	U	(800) 820-0888	U /	7.12	2.76	17.88 /42	--	--	1.91	2.70
SC	Guggenheim Small Cap Value A	SSUAX	C-	(800) 820-0888	C+ / 6.7	4.45	15.68	32.05 /90	4.70 /51	10.55 /62	0.53	1.99
SC	Guggenheim Small Cap Value C	SSVCX	C-	(800) 820-0888	C+ / 6.9	4.24	15.28	31.07 /88	3.92 /42	9.73 /56	0.00	2.72
SC	Guggenheim Small Cap Value Inst	SSUIX	C-	(800) 820-0888	B / 7.7	4.57	15.93	32.58 /91	4.96 /54	10.82 /64	0.85	1.70
GR	Guggenheim StylePlus - Lg Cre A	SECEX	B+	(800) 820-0888	A- / 9.2	8.33	10.51	27.11 /79	11.17 /97	12.74 /81	0.65	1.37
GR	Guggenheim StylePlus - Lg Cre C	SFECX	B	(800) 820-0888	A / 9.3	8.14	10.09	26.00 /76	10.15 /94	11.69 /71	0.00	2.30
GR	Guggenheim StylePlus - Lg Cre Inst	GILIX	B+	(800) 820-0888	A+ / 9.7	8.49	10.74	27.52 /81	11.54 /98	--	0.99	1.30
MC	Guggenheim StylePlus - Mid Gro A	SECUX	C	(800) 820-0888	C+ / 6.6	7.20	7.44	23.38 /68	7.28 /74	11.23 /68	0.53	1.52
MC	Guggenheim StylePlus - Mid Gro C	SUFCX	C-	(800) 820-0888	C+ / 6.7	6.97	7.00	22.29 /64	6.36 /67	10.24 /60	0.00	2.36
MC	Guggenheim StylePlus - Mid Gro Inst	GIUIX	C+	(800) 820-0888	B- / 7.4	7.27	7.59	23.48 /68	7.32 /74	--	0.72	1.46
FO	Guggenheim World Equity Income A	SEQAX	C	(800) 820-0888	C- / 3.5	5.48	4.64	15.70 /33	4.73 /51	7.75 /40	2.14	1.49
FO	Guggenheim World Equity Income C	SFGCX	C	(800) 820-0888	C- / 3.8	5.29	4.19	14.84 /29	3.96 /42	6.95 /34	1.77	2.29
FO	Guggenheim World Equity Income	SEWIX	C+	(800) 820-0888	C / 4.7	5.61	4.72	16.03 /34	5.01 /54	8.03 /42	2.60	1.24
GR	GuideMark Emerging Makets Inst	GILVX	B	(888) 278-5809	B- / 7.4	9.50	5.98	29.89 /86	5.73 /62	11.81 /73	0.78	0.89
GR	GuideMark Emerging Markets Svc	GMLVX	B-	(888) 278-5809	B- / 7.0	9.38	5.63	29.21 /85	5.13 /56	11.17 /67	0.32	1.56
GR	GuideMark Large Cap Core Inst	GILGX	B	(888) 278-5809	B- / 7.1	6.85	7.33	20.06 /52	7.68 /77	11.35 /69	1.14	0.65

● Denotes fund is closed to new investors
* Denotes fund is included in Section II

286

RISK	3 Year		NET ASSETS		ASSET				Portfolio	BULL / BEAR		FUND MANAGER		MINIMUMS		LOADS	
Risk Rating/Pts	Standard Deviation	Beta	NAV As of 2/28/17	Total $(Mil)	Cash %	Stocks %	Bonds %	Other %	Portfolio Turnover Ratio	Last Bull Market Return	Last Bear Market Return	Manager Quality Pct	Manager Tenure (Years)	Initial Purch. $	Additional Purch. $	Front End Load	Back End Load
B /8.8	1.0	0.03	24.72	27	6	0	93	1	39	N/A	N/A	83	4	2,500	100	0.0	0.0
B /8.8	1.0	0.03	24.73	789	6	0	93	1	39	N/A	N/A	88	4	2,000,000	0	0.0	0.0
B /8.6	6.6	0.41	15.99	5	50	49	0	1	224	35.4	-19.1	36	15	2,500	0	4.8	0.0
B /8.5	6.6	0.41	14.28	14	50	49	0	1	224	30.1	-19.3	27	15	2,500	0	0.0	0.0
B /8.6	6.6	0.42	16.29	1	50	49	0	1	224	N/A	N/A	38	15	2,000,000	0	0.0	0.0
B /8.6	6.6	0.41	16.04	15	50	49	0	1	224	35.4	-19.1	36	15	2,500	0	0.0	0.0
U /	N/A	N/A	26.59	183	2	1	95	2	61	N/A	N/A	N/A	6	0	0	0.0	0.0
C /5.5	10.2	0.16	19.02	22	91	0	8	1	24	-15.6	-7.8	40	10	2,500	0	4.8	0.0
C /5.3	10.3	0.17	17.52	11	91	0	8	1	24	-19.0	-8.1	30	10	2,500	0	0.0	0.0
C+ /5.6	10.3	0.16	19.39	6	91	0	8	1	24	-14.5	-7.7	43	10	2,000,000	0	0.0	0.0
C /5.5	10.3	0.17	19.02	71	91	0	8	1	24	-15.6	-7.8	39	10	2,500	0	0.0	0.0
C- /3.1	12.5	0.96	33.69	447	0	99	0	1	149	108.8	-24.2	35	20	2,500	100	4.8	0.0
D /2.1	12.5	0.96	25.20	100	0	99	0	1	149	100.6	-24.4	26	20	2,500	100	0.0	0.0
C- /3.5	12.4	0.95	11.21	77	0	99	0	1	149	113.4	-24.4	44	20	2,000,000	0	0.0	0.0
B+ /9.7	3.2	0.04	23.99	11	81	14	3	2	163	8.2	1.5	86	12	2,500	0	4.8	0.0
B+ /9.7	3.3	0.04	21.97	9	81	14	3	2	163	3.9	1.2	82	12	2,500	0	0.0	0.0
B+ /9.7	3.3	0.04	24.42	40	81	14	3	2	163	9.7	1.6	87	12	2,000,000	0	0.0	0.0
B+ /9.7	3.3	0.04	24.00	26	81	14	3	2	163	8.2	1.5	86	12	2,500	0	0.0	0.0
B+ /9.4	3.3	-0.04	12.39	4	6	0	93	1	61	N/A	N/A	91	5	2,500	100	0.0	0.0
B+ /9.4	3.3	-0.04	12.40	17	6	0	93	1	61	N/A	N/A	92	5	2,000,000	0	0.0	0.0
C /5.2	10.2	0.85	12.40	6	0	99	0	1	226	112.2	-16.3	65	4	2,500	100	4.8	0.0
C /5.2	10.3	0.86	12.30	7	0	99	0	1	226	105.2	-16.5	55	4	5,000	100	0.0	0.0
C /5.2	10.3	0.86	12.19	5	0	99	0	1	226	116.7	-16.1	69	4	2,000,000	0	0.0	0.0
C /5.2	10.2	0.85	12.48	5	0	99	0	1	226	113.9	-16.3	66	4	5,000	100	0.0	0.0
C- /3.9	9.7	0.82	10.73	4	0	99	0	1	103	96.4	-11.6	50	7	5,000	100	5.8	0.0
C- /3.9	9.7	0.82	10.55	8	0	99	0	1	103	89.8	-11.7	41	7	5,000	100	0.0	0.0
C- /4.0	9.7	0.82	11.06	10	0	99	0	1	103	100.2	-11.4	55	7	2,000,000	100,000	0.0	0.0
C- /4.0	9.7	0.82	10.98	1	0	99	0	1	103	97.6	-11.5	51	7	5,000	100	0.0	0.0
D+ /2.6	11.8	1.09	10.45	5	0	99	0	1	85	107.3	-16.9	16	4	2,500	100	4.8	0.0
D+ /2.5	11.7	1.08	10.14	9	0	99	0	1	85	100.5	-17.1	12	4	5,000	100	0.0	0.0
D+ /2.8	11.7	1.08	10.94	8	0	99	0	1	85	111.7	-16.9	20	4	2,000,000	0	0.0	0.0
D+ /2.7	11.8	1.09	10.72	N/A	0	99	0	1	85	108.9	-17.0	17	4	5,000	100	0.0	0.0
C- /4.2	10.4	0.94	10.54	N/A	0	100	0	0	119	125.2	-18.9	55	6	5,000	100	5.8	0.0
C- /4.2	10.4	0.95	10.46	1	0	100	0	0	119	117.1	-19.2	44	6	5,000	100	0.0	0.0
C- /4.1	10.4	0.94	10.62	3	0	100	0	0	119	129.7	-18.9	59	6	2,000,000	100,000	0.0	0.0
C- /4.1	10.4	0.94	10.54	N/A	0	100	0	0	119	126.3	-18.9	56	6	5,000	100	0.0	0.0
U /	N/A	N/A	29.27	112	10	89	0	1	133	N/A	N/A	N/A	3	2,000,000	0	0.0	0.0
C- /3.2	13.4	0.80	15.40	13	4	95	0	1	64	114.2	-25.9	65	9	2,500	100	4.8	0.0
D+ /2.9	13.5	0.80	14.26	5	4	95	0	1	64	105.8	-26.1	55	9	2,500	100	0.0	0.0
D /2.0	13.5	0.80	14.18	5	4	95	0	1	64	117.2	-25.8	68	9	2,000,000	0	0.0	0.0
C /4.6	10.5	1.02	23.47	205	72	16	10	2	50	124.4	-20.7	76	4	2,500	100	4.8	0.0
C- /3.8	10.5	1.02	18.46	3	72	16	10	2	50	113.4	-20.9	67	4	2,500	100	0.0	0.0
C /4.5	10.6	1.03	23.34	5	72	16	10	2	50	N/A	N/A	78	4	2,000,000	0	0.0	0.0
C- /4.1	12.1	0.94	43.23	78	71	17	11	1	61	112.4	-20.6	54	4	2,500	100	4.8	0.0
C- /3.0	12.1	0.94	32.70	4	71	17	11	1	61	102.5	-20.8	42	4	2,500	100	0.0	0.0
C- /4.1	12.1	0.94	43.29	N/A	71	17	11	1	61	N/A	N/A	55	4	2,000,000	0	0.0	0.0
B- /7.1	8.4	0.57	14.18	82	4	94	1	1	51	63.3	-21.2	95	4	2,500	100	4.8	0.0
B- /7.2	8.4	0.58	12.14	6	4	94	1	1	51	56.9	-21.5	93	4	2,500	100	0.0	0.0
B- /7.1	8.4	0.57	14.09	3	4	94	1	1	51	64.4	N/A	95	4	2,000,000	0	0.0	0.0
C+ /5.9	12.7	0.86	13.07	9	0	99	0	1	153	114.2	-20.5	32	6	0	0	0.0	0.0
C+ /6.0	12.8	0.87	13.21	99	0	99	0	1	153	107.8	-20.7	26	6	0	0	0.0	0.0
C+ /6.4	10.4	0.95	16.14	46	0	99	0	1	116	117.7	-20.1	46	6	0	0	0.0	0.0

Fund Type	Fund Name	Ticker Symbol	Overall Investment Rating	Phone	Performance Rating/Pts	3 Mo	6 Mo	1Yr / Pct	3Yr / Pct	5Yr / Pct	Dividend Yield	Expense Ratio
			99 Pct = Best 0 Pct = Worst									
GR	GuideMark Large Cap Core Svc	GMLGX	C+	(888) 278-5809	C+ / 6.7	6.72	7.07	19.36 /49	7.06 /72	10.70 /63	0.65	1.23
IN	GuideMark Opportunistic Equity Svc	GMOPX	C-	(888) 278-5809	B- / 7.2	8.16	10.94	21.72 /61	6.50 /68	12.04 /75	0.01	1.60
MC	GuideMark Small/Mid Cap Core Inst	GISMX	C+	(888) 278-5809	B- / 7.4	4.62	9.86	29.18 /84	6.19 /66	12.52 /79	0.67	0.92
MC	GuideMark Small/Mid Cap Core Svc	GMSMX	C+	(888) 278-5809	B- / 7.0	4.49	9.61	28.49 /83	5.54 /60	11.85 /73	0.27	1.55
FO	GuideMark World ex-US Inst	GIWEX	D-	(888) 278-5809	D- / 1.1	7.05	4.10	14.76 /29	-1.01 / 9	3.27 /12	1.94	0.82
FO	GuideMark World ex-US Svc	GMWEX	D-	(888) 278-5809	E+ / 0.9	6.81	3.69	13.98 /25	-1.62 / 8	2.64 /10	1.78	1.43
AA	GuidePath Absolute Return Alloc Ins	GIARX	C+	(888) 278-5809	C- / 3.3	3.34	3.64	11.75 /17	4.29 /46	--	3.86	1.08
AA	GuidePath Absolute Return Alloc Svc	GPARX	C+	(888) 278-5809	D+ / 2.8	3.07	3.27	10.90 /14	3.65 /39	2.75 /10	3.12	1.68
GL	GuidePath Conservative Alloc Inst	GITTX	D	(888) 278-5809	D / 1.7	3.99	0.55	9.30 /10	1.58 /21	--	0.00	1.10
GL	GuidePath Conservative Alloc Svc	GPTCX	D	(888) 278-5809	D- / 1.5	4.00	0.35	8.74 / 9	0.96 /18	4.42 /18	0.00	1.71
GL	GuidePath Growth Allocation Inst	GISRX	C	(888) 278-5809	C / 4.3	6.54	5.87	20.06 /52	3.11 /33	--	1.72	0.92
GL	GuidePath Growth Allocation Svc	GPSTX	C-	(888) 278-5809	C- / 3.8	6.40	5.63	19.40 /49	2.52 /28	6.31 /30	1.23	1.51
GL	GuidePath Managed Fut Str Svc	GPMFX	U	(888) 278-5809	U /	3.46	-6.14	-10.75 / 0	--	--	0.00	2.22
GL	GuidePath MultAsst Inc Alloc Svc	GPMIX	C	(888) 278-5809	D+ / 2.7	4.30	2.20	12.56 /20	2.92 /31	--	2.97	1.76
GL	GuidePath Tactical Alloc Inst	GITUX	C-	(888) 278-5809	D+ / 2.9	6.76	6.87	13.30 /23	1.72 /22	--	1.18	0.88
GL	GuidePath Tactical Alloc Svc	GPTUX	C-	(888) 278-5809	D+ / 2.5	6.62	6.62	12.60 /20	1.13 /19	4.23 /16	1.00	1.48
GL	GuideStone Aggressive Alloc Instl	GAGYX	U	(888) 984-8433	U /	7.18	6.99	21.83 /61	--	--	0.00	N/A
GL	GuideStone Aggressive Alloc Inv	GGBZX	D-	(888) 984-8433	C / 5.2	7.10	6.91	21.53 /60	3.83 /41	8.73 /48	0.00	1.21
BA	GuideStone Balanced Alloc Instl	GBAYX	U	(888) 984-8433	U /	3.86	2.78	13.23 /22	--	--	0.96	N/A
GL	GuideStone Balanced Alloc Inv	GGIZX	D	(888) 984-8433	D+ / 2.5	3.88	2.70	13.05 /22	2.47 /27	5.00 /21	0.71	1.03
AA	GuideStone Conservative All Instl	GCAYX	U	(888) 984-8433	U /	2.37	1.92	8.43 / 8	--	--	1.37	N/A
AA	GuideStone Defnsv Market Str Inst	GDMYX	B-	(888) 984-8433	C+ / 6.9	4.94	5.72	17.09 /39	8.55 /83	10.19 /60	1.25	0.73
AA	GuideStone Defnsv Market Str Inv	GDMZX	B-	(888) 984-8433	C+ / 6.7	4.89	5.58	16.81 /38	8.27 /81	9.92 /58	1.03	1.00
EM	GuideStone Em Mkts Eq Inst	GEMYX	D	(888) 984-8433	D / 2.2	8.68	5.62	30.01 /86	-0.42 /12	--	1.63	1.46
EM	GuideStone Em Mkts Eq Inv	GEMZX	D	(888) 984-8433	D / 2.1	8.84	5.52	29.88 /86	-0.63 /11	--	1.44	1.79
IX	GuideStone Equity Index Inst	GEQYX	A+	(888) 984-8433	A- / 9.2	7.72	9.87	24.96 /73	10.37 /95	13.75 /91	2.12	0.17
IX	GuideStone Equity Index Inv	GEQZX	A+	(888) 984-8433	A- / 9.1	7.66	9.85	24.71 /72	10.13 /94	13.55 /89	1.11	0.43
EN	GuideStone Global Natural Res Eq nv	GNRZX	E-	(888) 984-8433	E- / 0.2	-2.78	6.10	44.96 /98	-11.43 / 1	--	0.21	1.30
GI	GuideStone Growth Alloc Instl	GGRYX	U	(888) 984-8433	U /	5.51	4.69	17.94 /43	--	--	0.98	N/A
GI	GuideStone Growth Alloc Inv	GCOZX	C+	(888) 984-8433	C- / 3.5	5.44	4.52	17.67 /41	2.66 /29	6.61 /32	0.74	1.13
GL	Guidestone Growth Equity Inst	GGEYX	D+	(888) 984-8433	C+ / 6.1	7.78	4.60	18.29 /44	6.36 /67	11.79 /72	0.07	0.76
GL	Guidestone Growth Equity Inv	GGEZX	C-	(888) 984-8433	C+ / 5.9	7.74	4.46	18.04 /43	6.09 /65	11.54 /70	0.00	1.04
FO	GuideStone International Eqty Inv	GIEZX	D-	(888) 984-8433	D- / 1.4	8.07	4.96	16.74 /37	-0.57 /11	4.24 /16	1.70	1.35
FO	GuideStone Intl Equity Index Inst	GIIYX	U	(888) 984-8433	U /	7.55	4.82	15.99 /34	--	--	2.43	0.66
GL	GuideStone My Destination 2015 Inv	GMTZX	D+	(888) 984-8433	D+ / 2.9	4.02	3.27	12.70 /20	3.19 /34	5.44 /24	1.39	1.00
GL	GuideStone My Destination 2025 Inv	GMWZX	C-	(888) 984-8433	C- / 3.6	4.88	4.22	15.90 /34	3.40 /36	6.55 /32	1.23	1.04
GI	GuideStone My Destination 2055 Inv	GMGZX	C-	(888) 984-8433	C / 4.6	6.47	6.56	22.05 /62	3.06 /32	7.80 /41	1.11	1.48
RE	GuideStone Real Est Sec Inst	GREYX	U	(888) 984-8433	U /	6.44	-2.87	11.37 /16	--	--	5.18	0.94
RE	GuideStone Real Est Sec Inv	GREZX	C-	(888) 984-8433	C- / 4.2	6.46	-2.93	11.17 /15	6.49 /68	7.26 /36	4.90	1.18
IN	GuideStone Small Cap Equity Inv	GSCZX	C	(888) 984-8433	C+ / 6.5	3.44	9.30	29.60 /85	4.58 /50	10.79 /64	0.14	1.31
IN	GuideStone Value Equity Inv	GVEZX	B+	(888) 984-8433	B / 8.1	5.77	11.10	26.35 /77	7.78 /77	12.76 /82	1.14	0.87
EN	Guinness Atkinson Alt Energy Fd	GAAEX	E-	(800) 915-6565	E- / 0.0	5.51	-4.63	3.88 / 3	-15.17 / 0	-3.85 / 2	0.00	2.31
FO	Guinness Atkinson Asia Focus	IASMX	C	(800) 915-6565	C+ / 6.1	8.28	5.45	33.17 /92	3.44 /36	-0.64 / 4	1.30	2.00
FO	Guinness Atkinson Asia Pac Div Bldr	GAADX	B	(800) 915-6565	B- / 7.0	7.93	3.87	24.15 /70	7.66 /76	5.35 /24	3.35	3.87
FO	Guinness Atkinson China & HK	ICHKX	D	(800) 915-6565	C+ / 6.4	6.26	8.57	34.61 /94	3.50 /37	1.50 / 7	1.23	1.56
GL	Guinness Atkinson Dividend Builder	GAINX	C-	(800) 915-6565	C- / 3.6	5.69	2.41	13.96 /25	4.13 /44	--	2.95	1.77
EN	Guinness Atkinson Glob Energy	GAGEX	E-	(800) 915-6565	E- / 0.1	-3.21	5.57	29.87 /86	-12.18 / 0	-4.40 / 2	1.21	1.41
GL	Guinness Atkinson Glob Innov Inst	GINNX	U	(800) 915-6565	U /	7.58	9.06	23.58 /68	--	--	0.96	1.07
TC	Guinness Atkinson Glob Innov Inv	IWIRX	B	(800) 915-6565	B- / 7.4	7.56	8.97	23.27 /67	7.12 /73	14.17 /94	0.87	1.27
GL	Guinness Atkinson Renminbi Yuan &	GARBX	D+	(800) 915-6565	E / 0.3	0.71	-2.50	-0.31 / 1	-1.78 / 7	0.37 / 5	1.77	1.05
IN	Hamlin High Dividend Eqty Inst	HHDFX	B	(855) 443-3863	B- / 7.2	5.47	6.28	22.31 /64	7.75 /77	--	2.63	1.20
IN	Hamlin High Dividend Eqty Inv	HHDVX	C+	(855) 443-3863	C+ / 6.9	5.36	6.02	21.85 /61	7.29 /74	--	2.28	1.63

RISK Risk Rating/Pts	3 Year Standard Deviation	Beta	NET ASSETS NAV As of 2/28/17	Total $(Mil)	ASSET Cash %	Stocks %	Bonds %	Other %	Portfolio Turnover Ratio	BULL / BEAR Last Bull Market Return	Last Bear Market Return	FUND MANAGER Manager Quality Pct	Manager Tenure (Years)	MINIMUMS Initial Purch. $	Additional Purch. $	LOADS Front End Load	Back End Load
C+ / 6.5	10.4	0.95	15.95	165	0	99	0	1	116	108.7	-20.4	37	6	0	0	0.0	0.0
C- / 3.0	11.3	1.01	11.25	67	2	97	0	1	93	115.5	-22.7	25	6	0	0	0.0	0.0
C / 5.0	13.4	1.07	18.31	64	0	99	0	1	146	132.4	-26.9	25	2	0	0	0.0	0.0
C / 4.9	13.5	1.07	17.85	51	0	99	0	1	146	125.3	-27.1	20	2	0	0	0.0	0.0
C+ / 5.7	11.1	0.87	8.12	74	1	98	0	1	115	38.7	-25.5	64	N/A	0	0	0.0	0.0
C+ / 5.7	11.1	0.88	8.00	111	1	98	0	1	115	34.4	-25.6	56	N/A	0	0	0.0	0.0
B / 8.6	2.7	0.32	10.30	1	7	9	82	2	200	N/A	N/A	85	6	0	0	0.0	0.0
B / 8.7	2.6	0.31	10.33	130	7	9	82	2	200	18.1	-2.0	82	6	0	0	0.0	0.0
C+ / 6.1	7.4	1.09	9.06	5	5	70	23	2	131	N/A	N/A	30	6	0	0	0.0	0.0
C+ / 6.1	7.4	1.09	9.03	111	5	70	23	2	131	44.0	-15.9	24	6	0	0	0.0	0.0
C+ / 6.2	9.9	1.49	11.20	13	5	94	0	1	85	N/A	N/A	27	6	0	0	0.0	0.0
C+ / 6.2	9.9	1.49	11.16	543	5	94	0	1	85	63.4	-21.3	21	6	0	0	0.0	0.0
U /	N/A	N/A	8.74	82	0	0	0	100	0	N/A	N/A	N/A	1	0	0	0.0	0.0
B / 8.2	5.9	0.86	10.48	120	0	0	0	100	145	N/A	N/A	61	5	0	0	0.0	0.0
B- / 7.1	6.7	0.96	10.24	4	1	69	28	2	348	N/A	N/A	39	6	0	0	0.0	0.0
B- / 7.0	6.7	0.96	10.14	307	1	69	28	2	348	34.3	-13.5	31	6	0	0	0.0	0.0
U /	N/A	N/A	11.07	172	0	0	0	100	103	N/A	N/A	N/A	16	1,000,000	0	0.0	0.0
D / 2.1	11.0	0.83	11.04	744	0	0	0	100	103	85.1	-20.6	93	16	1,000	100	0.0	0.0
U /	N/A	N/A	11.41	334	0	0	0	100	95	N/A	N/A	N/A	16	1,000,000	0	0.0	0.0
C / 5.4	5.9	0.89	11.41	1,190	0	0	0	100	95	42.2	-9.1	53	16	1,000	100	0.0	0.0
U /	N/A	N/A	11.08	86	0	0	0	100	92	N/A	N/A	N/A	N/A	1,000,000	0	0.0	0.0
B- / 7.5	5.9	0.93	12.33	572	18	51	6	25	55	79.6	N/A	84	6	1,000,000	0	0.0	0.0
B- / 7.5	5.9	0.93	12.33	300	18	51	6	25	55	77.1	N/A	82	6	1,000	100	0.0	0.0
C+ / 5.9	16.7	1.02	8.85	303	7	92	0	1	39	N/A	N/A	46	4	1,000,000	0	0.0	0.0
C+ / 5.9	16.7	1.02	8.86	57	7	92	0	1	39	N/A	N/A	43	4	1,000	100	0.0	0.0
C+ / 6.5	10.4	1.01	26.08	375	0	97	1	2	6	131.8	-15.2	71	1	1,000,000	0	0.0	0.0
B- / 7.0	10.4	1.01	26.09	419	0	97	1	2	6	129.7	-15.3	68	1	1,000	100	0.0	0.0
E+ / 0.8	27.5	1.17	7.19	217	1	95	2	2	63	N/A	N/A	9	4	1,000	100	0.0	0.0
U /	N/A	N/A	11.43	253	0	0	0	100	97	N/A	N/A	N/A	N/A	1,000,000	0	0.0	0.0
B / 8.3	8.6	0.77	11.42	877	0	0	0	100	97	61.3	-15.5	14	N/A	1,000	100	0.0	0.0
D+ / 2.4	12.8	0.85	22.86	957	1	96	2	1	79	116.3	-15.8	97	14	1,000,000	0	0.0	0.0
C / 4.4	12.8	0.85	22.84	468	1	96	2	1	79	113.8	-15.9	97	14	1,000	100	0.0	0.0
C+ / 5.8	11.3	0.91	13.89	280	0	0	0	100	43	44.6	-25.0	69	6	1,000	100	0.0	0.0
U /	N/A	N/A	9.23	140	3	94	2	1	4	N/A	N/A	N/A	1	1,000,000	0	0.0	0.0
C+ / 6.4	5.3	0.81	9.82	554	7	42	45	6	108	46.2	-10.2	68	11	1,000	100	0.0	0.0
C+ / 5.7	6.9	1.06	9.61	910	7	56	31	6	110	59.0	-14.0	56	11	1,000	100	0.0	0.0
C / 5.4	10.4	0.95	12.11	72	7	85	6	2	124	N/A	N/A	7	5	1,000	100	0.0	0.0
U /	N/A	N/A	9.42	130	10	86	2	2	137	N/A	N/A	N/A	2	1,000,000	0	0.0	0.0
C / 5.5	11.7	0.82	9.45	103	10	86	2	2	137	73.4	-17.8	43	2	1,000	100	0.0	0.0
C / 4.4	15.0	1.16	17.72	267	0	0	0	100	74	113.1	-23.8	5	16	1,000	100	0.0	0.0
C+ / 5.9	11.4	1.06	21.92	381	0	0	0	100	32	125.3	-19.9	32	16	1,000	100	0.0	0.0
D+ / 2.4	19.8	0.48	2.68	11	0	100	0	0	29	-12.4	-48.3	1	11	5,000	250	0.0	0.0
C / 4.8	17.3	0.95	17.13	16	0	100	0	0	9	19.4	-31.5	92	14	5,000	250	0.0	2.0
C+ / 6.2	13.1	0.72	14.58	7	9	90	0	1	29	59.1	-22.5	98	11	5,000	250	0.0	2.0
D / 1.6	20.6	1.07	21.35	64	0	100	0	0	27	37.6	-34.4	92	19	5,000	250	0.0	2.0
C+ / 6.5	10.1	0.71	15.98	8	2	97	0	1	25	N/A	N/A	94	5	10,000	1,000	0.0	0.0
D- / 1.1	24.2	1.19	21.87	45	1	98	0	1	16	1.4	-34.1	6	13	5,000	250	0.0	0.0
U /	N/A	N/A	36.19	29	1	98	0	1	38	N/A	N/A	N/A	6	100,000	5,000	0.0	0.0
C+ / 5.9	12.9	1.16	36.12	144	1	98	0	1	38	139.1	-21.0	17	6	5,000	250	0.0	0.0
B / 8.4	5.5	0.25	11.29	2	8	0	91	1	16	4.7	N/A	51	6	10,000	1,000	0.0	2.0
C+ / 6.3	11.2	0.96	21.77	754	6	91	1	2	44	N/A	N/A	45	5	100,000	0	0.0	0.0
C+ / 6.3	11.2	0.96	21.78	18	6	91	1	2	44	N/A	N/A	38	5	2,500	0	0.0	0.0

Fund Type	Fund Name	Ticker Symbol	Overall Investment Rating	Phone	Performance Rating/Pts	3 Mo	6 Mo	1Yr / Pct	Annualized 3Yr / Pct	5Yr / Pct	Dividend Yield	Expense Ratio
SC	Hancock Horizon Burkenroad SC D	HYBUX	C+	(888) 346-6300	C+ / 6.7	2.15	10.69	30.76 /88	4.78 /52	11.86 /73	0.00	1.60
SC	Hancock Horizon Burkenroad SC Inst	HIBUX	U	(888) 346-6300	U /	2.26	10.96	--	--	--	0.00	1.10
SC	Hancock Horizon Burkenroad SC Inv	HHBUX	C+	(888) 346-6300	C+ / 5.9	2.22	10.82	31.12 /88	5.05 /55	12.14 /75	0.00	1.35
GL	Hancock Horizon Dvsfd Income C	HHICX	D-	(888) 346-6300	D- / 1.1	4.59	1.81	12.07 /18	-0.38 /12	--	3.69	2.22
GL	Hancock Horizon Dvsfd Income Inst	HHIIX	D	(888) 346-6300	D / 1.8	4.83	2.31	13.16 /22	0.61 /16	--	4.67	1.22
GL	Hancock Horizon Dvsfd Income Inv	HHIAX	D-	(888) 346-6300	D- / 1.3	4.77	2.18	12.88 /21	0.36 /15	--	4.23	1.47
FO	Hancock Horizon Dvsfd Intl C	HHDCX	D-	(888) 346-6300	D- / 1.0	7.50	6.60	21.46 /60	-2.61 / 5	1.33 / 7	0.13	2.16
FO	Hancock Horizon Dvsfd Intl Inst	HHDTX	D-	(888) 346-6300	D- / 1.4	7.74	7.08	22.60 /65	-1.65 / 7	2.34 / 9	1.10	1.16
FO	Hancock Horizon Dvsfd Intl Inv	HHDAX	E+	(888) 346-6300	E+ / 0.8	7.69	6.92	22.24 /63	-1.93 / 7	2.07 / 8	0.68	1.41
GR	Hancock Horizon Quant Lng Sht C	HHQCX	C	(888) 346-6300	D+ / 2.4	2.57	3.84	7.23 / 6	3.50 /37	6.81 /33	0.00	2.73
GR	Hancock Horizon Quant Lng Sht Inst	HHQTX	C+	(888) 346-6300	C- / 3.1	2.83	4.34	8.25 / 8	4.52 /49	7.87 /41	0.00	1.68
GR	Hancock Horizon Quant Lng Sht Inv	HHQAX	C	(888) 346-6300	D / 2.1	2.78	4.21	8.00 / 7	4.27 /46	7.61 /39	0.00	1.96
SC	Hancock Horizon US Small Cap C	HHSCX	C+	(888) 346-6300	C+ / 6.0	1.83	7.95	23.30 /67	5.69 /61	--	0.00	2.46
SC	Hancock Horizon US Small Cap Inst	HSCIX	C+	(888) 346-6300	C+ / 6.8	2.07	8.49	24.54 /72	6.74 /70	--	0.62	1.44
SC	Hancock Horizon US Small Cap Inv	HSCAX	C+	(888) 346-6300	C / 5.5	1.99	8.32	24.24 /71	6.45 /68	--	0.34	1.71
GL	Hanlon Managed Income A	HANAX	U		U /	4.00	0.73	7.56 / 7	--	--	2.81	1.77
GL	Hanlon Managed Income I	HANIX	U		U /	4.11	0.88	7.85 / 7	--	--	3.75	1.52
IN	Hanlon Tactical Div and Mom A	HTDAX	U		U /	4.66	2.01	1.90 / 2	--	--	0.00	1.50
IN	Hanlon Tactical Div and Mom I	HTDIX	U		U /	4.78	2.13	2.13 / 2	--	--	1.25	1.25
IN	Hanlon Tactical Div and Mom R	HTDRX	U		U /	4.69	2.02	1.80 / 2	--	--	0.72	1.65
GR	Harbor Capital Appreciation Admin	HRCAX	C+	(800) 422-1050	B- / 7.3	8.47	8.44	20.70 /56	7.30 /74	12.60 /80	0.00	0.95
GR	Harbor Capital Appreciation Inst	HACAX	C+	(800) 422-1050	B- / 7.5	8.53	8.56	20.99 /57	7.57 /76	12.88 /83	0.09	0.70
GR	Harbor Capital Appreciation Inv	HCAIX	C+	(800) 422-1050	B- / 7.2	8.46	8.38	20.56 /55	7.17 /73	12.47 /79	0.00	1.07
GR	Harbor Capital Appreciation Ret	HNACX	U	(800) 422-1050	U /	8.56	8.60	--	--	--	0.00	0.65
IN	Harbor Commodity Real Rtn Str Adm	HCMRX	E-	(800) 422-1050	E- / 0.0	3.23	7.56	20.73 /56	-13.54 / 0	-10.48 / 1	0.61	1.55
IN	Harbor Commodity Real Rtn Str Inst	HACMX	E-	(800) 422-1050	E- / 0.0	3.21	7.82	20.76 /56	-13.31 / 0	-10.24 / 1	0.74	1.30
CV	Harbor Convertible Sec Adm	HRCSX	C-	(800) 422-1050	D / 2.0	2.55	2.61	12.92 /21	1.96 /24	5.01 /21	1.06	1.02
CV	Harbor Convertible Sec Inst	HACSX	C-	(800) 422-1050	D / 2.2	2.61	2.74	13.19 /22	2.21 /25	5.28 /23	1.30	0.77
CV	Harbor Convertible Sec Inv	HICSX	C-	(800) 422-1050	D / 2.0	2.52	2.54	12.81 /21	1.84 /23	4.89 /21	0.96	1.14
FO	Harbor Diversified Intl All Cp Inst	HAIDX	U	(800) 422-1050	U /	7.14	4.00	14.16 /26	--	--	1.26	1.57
EM	Harbor Emerging Markets Eqty Adm	HREMX	D-	(800) 422-1050	D+ / 2.5	8.60	8.99	36.48 /95	-1.23 / 9	--	0.84	1.74
EM	Harbor Emerging Markets Eqty Inst	HAEMX	D-	(800) 422-1050	D+ / 2.6	8.71	9.10	36.94 /96	-0.96 /10	--	1.05	1.49
EM	Harbor Emerging Markets Eqty Inv	HIEEX	E+	(800) 422-1050	D+ / 2.4	8.65	8.91	36.42 /95	-1.35 / 8	--	0.76	1.86
GL	Harbor Global Growth Admin	HRGAX	D-	(800) 422-1050	D / 2.2	6.01	1.53	10.89 /14	1.94 /24	10.03 /59	0.00	1.28
GL	Harbor Global Growth Inst	HGGAX	D-	(800) 422-1050	D+ / 2.3	6.09	1.61	11.15 /15	2.19 /25	10.30 /61	0.00	1.03
GL	Harbor Global Growth Inv	HGGIX	D-	(800) 422-1050	D / 2.1	6.01	1.50	10.77 /14	1.82 /23	9.90 /58	0.00	1.40
FO	Harbor International Admin	HRINX	E+	(800) 422-1050	E+ / 0.6	5.41	1.56	11.46 /16	-2.46 / 6	2.70 /10	1.61	1.03
FO	Harbor International Growth Admin	HRIGX	D	(800) 422-1050	D / 1.8	5.82	0.01	14.61 /28	0.35 /15	3.85 /14	1.02	1.16
FO	Harbor International Growth Inst	HAIGX	D	(800) 422-1050	D / 1.9	5.85	0.13	14.92 /30	0.61 /16	4.13 /16	1.27	0.91
FO	Harbor International Growth Inv	HIIGX	D	(800) 422-1050	D / 1.8	5.87	0.02	14.52 /28	0.26 /15	3.76 /14	0.89	1.28
FO	Harbor International Inst	HAINX	E+	(800) 422-1050	E+ / 0.6	5.48	1.68	11.74 /17	-2.21 / 6	2.96 /11	1.90	0.78
FO	Harbor International Inv	HIINX	E+	(800) 422-1050	E / 0.5	5.36	1.48	11.30 /15	-2.58 / 5	2.57 / 9	1.48	1.15
FO	Harbor International Retirement	HNINX	U	(800) 422-1050	U /	5.49	1.70	--	--	--	0.00	0.73
GI	Harbor Large Cap Value Admin	HRLVX	A+	(800) 422-1050	A+ / 9.7	7.70	11.05	30.81 /88	10.88 /97	15.07 /97	0.71	0.97
GI	Harbor Large Cap Value Inst	HAVLX	A+	(800) 422-1050	A+ / 9.7	7.74	11.18	31.11 /88	11.15 /97	15.37 /97	0.94	0.72
GI	Harbor Large Cap Value Inv	HILVX	A+	(800) 422-1050	A+ / 9.7	7.70	11.02	30.74 /88	10.76 /97	14.96 /97	0.67	1.09
MC	Harbor Mid Cap Growth Admin	HRMGX	E+	(800) 422-1050	C- / 3.8	4.93	3.59	22.80 /66	2.51 /28	10.04 /59	0.00	1.11
MC	Harbor Mid Cap Growth Inst	HAMGX	E+	(800) 422-1050	C- / 4.0	4.98	3.69	22.94 /66	2.75 /30	10.31 /61	0.00	0.86
MC	Harbor Mid Cap Growth Inv	HIMGX	E	(800) 422-1050	C- / 3.8	4.93	3.56	22.64 /65	2.38 /27	9.89 /57	0.00	1.23
MC	Harbor Mid Cap Value Admin	HRMVX	A+	(800) 422-1050	A+ / 9.6	7.27	15.21	30.53 /87	9.41 /90	15.34 /97	1.32	1.13
MC	Harbor Mid Cap Value Inst	HAMVX	A+	(800) 422-1050	A+ / 9.6	7.35	15.35	30.88 /88	9.67 /91	15.64 /98	1.53	0.88
MC	Harbor Mid Cap Value Inv	HIMVX	A+	(800) 422-1050	A / 9.5	7.23	15.09	30.36 /87	9.25 /88	15.20 /97	1.19	1.25

• Denotes fund is closed to new investors
∗ Denotes fund is included in Section II

290

www.thestreetratings.com

RISK			NET ASSETS		ASSET					BULL / BEAR		FUND MANAGER		MINIMUMS		LOADS	
	3 Year		NAV						Portfolio	Last Bull	Last Bear	Manager	Manager	Initial	Additional	Front	Back
Risk Rating/Pts	Standard Deviation	Beta	As of 2/28/17	Total $(Mil)	Cash %	Stocks %	Bonds %	Other %	Turnover Ratio	Market Return	Market Return	Quality Pct	Tenure (Years)	Purch. $	Purch. $	End Load	End Load
C+ / 5.6	13.9	0.82	64.11	46	0	98	1	1	39	121.8	-19.8	64	16	1,000	100	0.0	0.0
U /	N/A	N/A	66.40	158	0	98	1	1	39	N/A	N/A	N/A	16	1,000	100	0.0	0.0
C+ / 5.6	13.9	0.82	66.28	584	0	98	1	1	39	124.8	-19.7	67	16	1,000	100	5.3	0.0
C+ / 5.9	6.2	0.81	13.46	1	11	33	53	3	77	N/A	N/A	23	5	1,000	100	0.0	0.0
C+ / 5.9	6.2	0.81	13.51	51	11	33	53	3	77	N/A	N/A	33	5	1,000	100	0.0	0.0
C+ / 5.9	6.2	0.81	13.49	7	11	33	53	3	77	N/A	N/A	30	5	1,000	100	4.3	0.0
C / 5.3	12.7	0.98	20.45	N/A	0	96	3	1	15	24.8	-25.1	42	9	1,000	100	0.0	0.0
C / 5.3	12.7	0.98	20.99	246	0	96	3	1	15	31.8	-24.8	56	9	1,000	100	0.0	0.0
C / 5.3	12.7	0.98	21.00	8	0	96	3	1	15	29.9	-24.8	52	9	1,000	100	5.3	0.0
B / 8.3	6.1	0.47	16.77	4	12	54	32	2	159	67.0	-20.4	58	9	1,000	100	0.0	0.0
B / 8.6	6.1	0.47	18.50	102	12	54	32	2	159	76.1	-20.1	70	9	1,000	100	0.0	0.0
B / 8.6	6.1	0.47	18.09	53	12	54	32	2	159	73.7	-20.2	67	9	1,000	100	5.3	0.0
C+ / 6.7	14.3	0.86	17.78	N/A	0	0	0	100	61	N/A	N/A	71	4	1,000	100	0.0	0.0
C+ / 6.7	14.3	0.86	18.16	24	0	0	0	100	61	N/A	N/A	79	4	1,000	100	0.0	0.0
C+ / 6.7	14.2	0.86	18.10	2	0	0	0	100	61	N/A	N/A	78	4	1,000	100	5.3	0.0
U /	N/A	N/A	10.01	46	0	0	0	100	599	N/A	N/A	N/A	2	2,500	500	5.8	0.0
U /	N/A	N/A	9.96	417	0	0	0	100	599	N/A	N/A	N/A	2	100,000	500	0.0	0.0
U /	N/A	N/A	9.65	35	0	0	0	100	579	N/A	N/A	N/A	2	2,500	250	5.8	0.0
U /	N/A	N/A	9.54	168	0	0	0	100	579	N/A	N/A	N/A	2	100,000	500	0.0	0.0
U /	N/A	N/A	9.52	40	0	0	0	100	579	N/A	N/A	N/A	2	2,500	500	0.0	0.0
C / 4.4	13.3	1.09	60.62	434	0	99	0	1	34	120.7	-13.9	24	27	50,000	0	0.0	0.0
C / 4.4	13.3	1.09	61.53	21,900	0	99	0	1	34	123.7	-13.8	26	27	50,000	0	0.0	0.0
C / 4.4	13.3	1.09	59.69	1,489	0	99	0	1	34	119.3	-13.9	23	27	2,500	0	0.0	0.0
U /	N/A	N/A	61.52	1,638	0	99	0	1	34	N/A	N/A	N/A	27	0	0	0.0	0.0
D+ / 2.9	15.7	0.36	3.84	1	0	10	89	1	1,069	-36.8	-19.9	0	9	50,000	0	0.0	0.0
D+ / 2.9	15.6	0.36	3.86	70	0	10	89	1	1,069	-35.9	-19.8	0	9	1,000	0	0.0	0.0
B- / 7.6	5.8	0.64	10.80	N/A	1	0	1	98	102	38.9	N/A	59	6	50,000	0	0.0	1.0
B- / 7.6	5.7	0.63	10.81	344	1	0	1	98	102	40.7	N/A	63	6	1,000	0	0.0	1.0
B- / 7.6	5.7	0.63	10.79	2	1	0	1	98	102	38.0	N/A	58	6	2,500	0	0.0	1.0
U /	N/A	N/A	10.15	211	0	0	0	100	68	N/A	N/A	N/A	2	50,000	0	0.0	0.0
C- / 3.8	18.2	1.10	9.06	N/A	10	89	0	1	49	N/A	N/A	33	4	50,000	0	0.0	0.0
C- / 3.8	18.1	1.10	9.07	43	10	89	0	1	49	N/A	N/A	37	4	50,000	0	0.0	0.0
C- / 3.8	18.1	1.10	9.05	1	10	89	0	1	49	N/A	N/A	32	4	2,500	0	0.0	0.0
C / 4.7	11.9	0.79	21.18	1	6	93	0	1	76	95.2	-24.4	86	8	50,000	0	0.0	0.0
C / 4.7	11.9	0.79	21.43	26	6	93	0	1	76	97.8	-24.3	87	8	50,000	0	0.0	0.0
C / 4.6	11.9	0.79	20.99	9	6	93	0	1	76	93.9	-24.4	86	8	2,500	0	0.0	0.0
C / 5.1	12.6	1.00	60.95	447	1	96	1	2	14	40.6	-25.7	44	8	50,000	0	0.0	0.0
C+ / 5.9	13.0	0.96	12.97	N/A	1	98	0	1	19	45.1	-24.5	78	4	50,000	0	0.0	0.0
C+ / 5.9	13.0	0.96	12.97	287	1	98	0	1	19	47.1	-24.4	79	4	50,000	0	0.0	0.0
C+ / 5.9	12.9	0.96	12.91	13	1	98	0	1	19	44.3	-24.6	77	4	2,500	0	0.0	0.0
C / 5.0	12.6	1.00	61.13	31,202	1	96	1	2	14	42.6	-25.7	48	8	50,000	0	0.0	0.0
C / 5.1	12.6	1.00	60.61	1,986	1	96	1	2	14	39.7	-25.8	42	8	2,500	0	0.0	0.0
U /	N/A	N/A	61.11	1,018	1	96	1	2	14	N/A	N/A	N/A	8	0	0	0.0	0.0
C+ / 6.2	11.2	1.03	13.41	10	7	92	0	1	34	143.9	-17.1	74	5	50,000	0	0.0	0.0
C+ / 6.2	11.2	1.03	13.42	402	7	92	0	1	34	147.3	-17.0	75	5	50,000	0	0.0	0.0
C+ / 6.2	11.1	1.03	13.54	85	7	92	0	1	34	142.6	-17.2	73	5	2,500	0	0.0	0.0
D- / 1.5	15.1	1.08	8.94	178	1	98	0	1	84	96.9	-24.1	5	12	50,000	0	0.0	0.0
D- / 1.5	15.1	1.07	9.27	134	1	98	0	1	84	99.4	-24.0	5	12	50,000	0	0.0	0.0
D- / 1.4	15.1	1.08	8.72	18	1	98	0	1	84	95.5	-24.1	4	12	2,500	0	0.0	0.0
C+ / 6.4	12.3	0.98	23.01	51	1	98	0	1	18	163.2	-25.2	74	13	50,000	0	0.0	0.0
C+ / 6.4	12.3	0.98	22.83	675	1	98	0	1	18	166.8	-25.1	76	13	50,000	0	0.0	0.0
C+ / 6.4	12.3	0.98	22.78	171	1	98	0	1	18	161.3	-25.2	73	13	2,500	0	0.0	0.0

Fund Type	Fund Name	Ticker Symbol	Overall Investment Rating	Phone	Performance Rating/Pts	3 Mo	6 Mo	1Yr / Pct	3Yr / Pct	5Yr / Pct	Dividend Yield	Expense Ratio
	99 Pct = Best							Total Return % through 2/28/17	Annualized		Incl. in Returns	
MC	Harbor Mid Cap Value Retirement	HNMVX	U	(800) 422-1050	U /	7.30	15.35	--	--	--	0.00	0.83
SC	● Harbor Small Cap Growth Admin	HRSGX	C-	(800) 422-1050	B- / 7.3	6.89	11.11	30.12 /87	5.15 /56	12.27 /77	0.00	1.11
SC	● Harbor Small Cap Growth Inst	HASGX	C-	(800) 422-1050	B- / 7.5	6.91	11.26	30.47 /87	5.40 /58	12.55 /80	0.00	0.86
SC	● Harbor Small Cap Growth Inv	HISGX	C-	(800) 422-1050	B- / 7.2	6.83	11.04	30.02 /86	5.02 /54	12.13 /75	0.00	1.23
SC	Harbor Small Cap Growth Opps	HRSOX	D	(800) 422-1050	C+ / 5.7	4.06	5.20	30.84 /88	3.70 /39	--	0.00	1.17
SC	Harbor Small Cap Growth Opps Instl	HASOX	D	(800) 422-1050	C+ / 5.8	4.14	5.47	30.44 /87	3.78 /40	--	0.00	0.92
SC	Harbor Small Cap Growth Opps Inv	HISOX	D	(800) 422-1050	C / 5.4	4.00	5.25	30.03 /86	3.37 /35	--	0.00	1.29
SC	Harbor Small Cap Growth Ret	HNSGX	U	(800) 422-1050	U /	6.90	11.34	--	--	--	0.00	0.81
SC	Harbor Small Cap Value Admin	HSVRX	A	(800) 422-1050	A+ / 9.7	6.16	13.96	35.89 /95	9.53 /91	13.68 /90	0.17	1.12
SC	Harbor Small Cap Value Inst	HASCX	A	(800) 422-1050	A+ / 9.7	6.23	14.12	36.28 /95	9.81 /92	13.98 /93	0.35	0.87
SC	Harbor Small Cap Value Inv	HISVX	A	(800) 422-1050	A+ / 9.7	6.11	13.90	35.78 /95	9.40 /90	13.55 /89	0.05	1.24
AA	Harbor Target Ret 2015 Adm	HARHX	D+	(800) 422-1050	D / 2.2	3.42	2.33	10.45 /13	2.58 /28	4.56 /18	2.74	0.90
AA	Harbor Target Ret 2015 Inst	HARGX	D+	(800) 422-1050	D / 2.2	3.42	2.33	10.33 /12	2.58 /28	4.56 /18	2.74	0.65
AA	Harbor Target Ret 2015 Inv	HARIX	D+	(800) 422-1050	D / 2.2	3.42	2.33	10.34 /12	2.58 /28	4.56 /18	2.74	1.02
AA	Harbor Target Ret 2020 Adm	HARKX	D+	(800) 422-1050	D+ / 2.7	3.95	3.17	12.73 /21	2.90 /31	5.09 /22	2.61	0.93
AA	Harbor Target Ret 2020 Inst	HARJX	D+	(800) 422-1050	D+ / 2.8	3.95	3.17	12.71 /21	2.93 /31	5.11 /22	2.61	0.68
AA	Harbor Target Ret 2020 Inv	HARLX	D+	(800) 422-1050	D+ / 2.7	3.95	3.06	12.59 /20	2.90 /31	5.09 /22	2.61	1.05
AA	Harbor Target Ret 2025 Adm	HARNX	D+	(800) 422-1050	C- / 3.0	4.37	3.75	14.07 /26	2.94 /31	5.47 /25	2.35	0.94
AA	Harbor Target Ret 2025 Inst	HARMX	D+	(800) 422-1050	C- / 3.0	4.28	3.66	14.06 /26	2.93 /31	5.47 /25	2.35	0.69
AA	Harbor Target Ret 2025 Inv	HAROX	D+	(800) 422-1050	C- / 3.0	4.37	3.75	14.07 /26	2.94 /31	5.47 /25	2.35	1.06
AA	Harbor Target Ret 2030 Adm	HARQX	D+	(800) 422-1050	C- / 3.2	4.69	4.20	15.41 /32	2.93 /31	6.02 /28	2.34	0.97
AA	Harbor Target Ret 2030 Inst	HARPX	D+	(800) 422-1050	C- / 3.2	4.68	4.20	15.39 /32	2.96 /31	6.03 /29	2.34	0.72
AA	Harbor Target Ret 2030 Inv	HARTX	D+	(800) 422-1050	C- / 3.2	4.69	4.20	15.41 /32	2.93 /31	6.02 /28	2.34	1.09
AA	Harbor Target Ret 2035 Adm	HARVX	C-	(800) 422-1050	C- / 3.6	5.11	4.79	16.81 /38	3.11 /33	6.73 /33	2.08	0.99
AA	Harbor Target Ret 2035 Inst	HARUX	C-	(800) 422-1050	C- / 3.6	5.11	4.78	16.80 /38	3.11 /33	6.74 /33	2.08	0.74
AA	Harbor Target Ret 2035 Inv	HARWX	C-	(800) 422-1050	C- / 3.6	5.11	4.79	16.81 /38	3.11 /33	6.73 /33	2.08	1.11
AA	Harbor Target Ret 2040 Adm	HARZX	C-	(800) 422-1050	C- / 4.0	5.43	5.18	17.93 /43	3.42 /36	7.48 /38	1.90	1.00
AA	Harbor Target Ret 2040 Inst	HARYX	C-	(800) 422-1050	C- / 4.0	5.43	5.30	17.93 /43	3.42 /36	7.51 /38	1.90	0.75
AA	Harbor Target Ret 2040 Inv	HABBX	C-	(800) 422-1050	C- / 4.0	5.43	5.18	17.93 /43	3.42 /36	7.48 /38	1.90	1.12
AA	Harbor Target Ret 2045 Adm	HADDX	C-	(800) 422-1050	C / 4.3	5.78	5.70	19.12 /48	3.56 /38	8.10 /43	1.53	1.02
AA	Harbor Target Ret 2045 Inst	HACCX	C-	(800) 422-1050	C / 4.4	5.86	5.78	19.21 /48	3.56 /38	8.12 /43	1.53	0.77
AA	Harbor Target Ret 2045 Inv	HAEEX	C-	(800) 422-1050	C / 4.3	5.78	5.70	19.12 /48	3.56 /38	8.10 /43	1.53	1.14
AA	Harbor Target Ret 2050 Adm	HAGGX	D+	(800) 422-1050	C / 4.8	6.21	6.21	20.49 /55	3.85 /41	8.75 /48	1.32	1.03
AA	Harbor Target Ret 2050 Inst	HAFFX	D+	(800) 422-1050	C / 4.8	6.22	6.22	20.37 /54	3.86 /41	8.74 /48	1.33	0.78
AA	Harbor Target Ret 2050 Inv	HAHHX	D+	(800) 422-1050	C / 4.8	6.21	6.21	20.49 /55	3.85 /41	8.75 /48	1.32	1.15
AA	Harbor Target Ret Inc Adm	HARBX	C-	(800) 422-1050	D / 2.1	3.11	1.85	9.02 / 9	2.76 /30	3.95 /15	2.67	0.87
AA	Harbor Target Ret Inc Inst	HARAX	C-	(800) 422-1050	D / 2.1	2.99	1.74	9.01 / 9	2.72 /29	3.95 /15	2.67	0.62
AA	Harbor Target Ret Inc Inv	HARCX	C-	(800) 422-1050	D / 2.1	3.11	1.85	9.02 / 9	2.76 /30	3.95 /15	2.67	0.99
EM	● Harding Loevner Emerg Mrkt Advisor	HLEMX	D+	(877) 435-8105	C / 4.4	8.27	4.10	28.72 /83	2.05 /24	2.90 /10	0.55	1.45
EM	Harding Loevner Frontier EM Inst	HLFMX	E	(877) 435-8105	E / 0.3	5.12	0.61	11.69 /17	-4.49 / 3	2.89 /10	0.98	1.79
EM	Harding Loevner Frontier EM Inv	HLMOX	E	(877) 435-8105	E- / 0.2	5.07	0.39	11.04 /15	-4.90 / 3	2.48 / 9	0.50	2.20
GL	Harding Loevner Global Eq Adv	HLMGX	C+	(877) 435-8105	C+ / 6.7	8.49	7.26	22.00 /62	6.73 /70	8.68 /48	0.00	1.18
GL	Harding Loevner Global Eq Inst	HLMVX	B-	(877) 435-8105	B- / 7.0	8.70	7.54	22.50 /65	7.05 /72	9.00 /51	0.38	0.92
FO	Harding Loevner Intl Equity Inst	HLMIX	C-	(877) 435-8105	C- / 3.9	8.25	3.67	19.84 /51	3.26 /34	6.03 /29	0.93	0.84
FO	Harding Loevner Intl Equity Inv	HLMNX	C-	(877) 435-8105	C- / 3.7	8.15	3.51	19.48 /49	2.93 /31	5.70 /26	0.62	1.16
FO	Harding Loevner Intl Small Co Inst	HLMRX	D+	(877) 435-8105	D / 1.9	7.12	3.44	13.68 /24	0.73 /17	7.35 /37	1.13	1.64
FO	Harding Loevner Intl Small Co Inv	HLMSX	D	(877) 435-8105	D / 1.8	7.06	3.28	13.47 /23	0.50 /16	7.09 /35	1.05	1.93
AA	Hartford Balanced A	ITTAX	C+	(888) 843-7824	C- / 3.9	5.95	4.29	14.42 /27	5.91 /63	8.60 /47	1.18	1.15
AA	● Hartford Balanced B	IHABX	C+	(888) 843-7824	C- / 4.2	5.74	3.84	13.41 /23	4.99 /54	7.66 /39	0.26	2.27
AA	Hartford Balanced C	HAFCX	B-	(888) 843-7824	C / 4.4	5.77	3.93	13.65 /24	5.17 /56	7.84 /41	0.60	1.84
GL	Hartford Balanced HLS IA		B	(888) 843-7824	C / 5.1	5.73	3.96	14.11 /26	6.23 /66	9.10 /51	2.69	0.65
GL	Hartford Balanced HLS IB		B	(888) 843-7824	C / 4.9	5.64	3.85	13.82 /25	5.97 /64	8.83 /49	2.40	0.90

● Denotes fund is closed to new investors
* Denotes fund is included in Section II

RISK			NET ASSETS		ASSET					BULL / BEAR		FUND MANAGER		MINIMUMS		LOADS	
	3 Year		NAV						Portfolio	Last Bull	Last Bear	Manager	Manager	Initial	Additional	Front	Back
Risk	Standard		As of	Total	Cash	Stocks	Bonds	Other	Turnover	Market	Market	Quality	Tenure	Purch.	Purch.	End	End
Rating/Pts	Deviation	Beta	2/28/17	$(Mil)	%	%	%	%	Ratio	Return	Return	Pct	(Years)	$	$	Load	Load
U /	N/A	N/A	22.82	49	1	98	0	1	18	N/A	N/A	N/A	13	0	0	0.0	0.0
D+ /2.4	15.9	0.93	12.87	1	2	97	0	1	89	129.9	-28.7	59	17	50,000	0	0.0	0.0
D+ /2.5	15.9	0.93	13.61	552	2	97	0	1	89	132.6	-28.6	62	17	50,000	0	0.0	0.0
D /2.2	16.0	0.94	12.34	8	2	97	0	1	89	128.0	-28.7	57	17	2,500	0	0.0	0.0
D /2.1	18.2	1.08	11.54	1	2	97	0	1	85	N/A	N/A	28	3	50,000	0	0.0	0.0
D /2.1	18.2	1.09	11.57	202	2	97	0	1	85	N/A	N/A	28	3	50,000	0	0.0	0.0
D /2.1	18.2	1.09	11.43	1	2	97	0	1	85	N/A	N/A	24	3	2,500	0	0.0	0.0
U /	N/A	N/A	13.62	100	2	97	0	1	89	N/A	N/A	N/A	17	0	0	0.0	0.0
C+ /5.6	14.4	0.89	31.58	2	2	97	0	1	10	139.7	-22.6	91	16	50,000	0	0.0	0.0
C /5.5	14.4	0.89	31.68	869	2	97	0	1	10	143.2	-22.5	92	16	50,000	0	0.0	0.0
C /5.5	14.5	0.89	31.01	29	2	97	0	1	10	138.3	-22.6	90	16	2,500	0	0.0	0.0
C+ /6.7	4.8	0.68	10.43	N/A	0	22	77	1	32	39.3	-9.0	42	8	50,000	0	0.0	0.0
C+ /6.7	4.7	0.67	10.43	6	0	22	77	1	32	39.2	-9.0	44	8	1,000	0	0.0	0.0
C+ /6.7	4.7	0.67	10.43	N/A	0	22	77	1	32	39.2	-9.0	43	8	2,500	0	0.0	0.0
C+ /6.2	5.6	0.82	9.25	N/A	0	29	68	3	33	44.5	-10.4	34	8	50,000	0	0.0	0.0
C+ /6.2	5.6	0.81	9.26	26	0	29	68	3	33	44.5	-10.4	34	8	1,000	0	0.0	0.0
C+ /6.2	5.7	0.82	9.25	N/A	0	29	68	3	33	44.5	-10.5	33	8	2,500	0	0.0	0.0
C+ /6.2	6.2	0.91	11.83	N/A	0	34	61	5	25	48.8	-12.6	27	8	50,000	0	0.0	0.0
C+ /6.2	6.2	0.90	11.83	16	0	34	61	5	25	48.8	-12.6	27	8	1,000	0	0.0	0.0
C+ /6.2	6.2	0.91	11.83	N/A	0	34	61	5	25	48.8	-12.6	27	8	2,500	0	0.0	0.0
C+ /5.7	7.0	1.03	8.49	N/A	0	42	54	4	31	55.3	-14.8	18	8	50,000	0	0.0	0.0
C+ /5.7	7.1	1.03	8.50	27	0	42	54	4	31	55.3	-14.8	18	8	1,000	0	0.0	0.0
C+ /5.7	7.0	1.03	8.49	N/A	0	42	54	4	31	55.3	-14.8	18	8	2,500	0	0.0	0.0
C+ /5.8	7.8	1.16	13.10	N/A	0	52	45	3	26	63.2	-16.8	13	8	50,000	0	0.0	0.0
C+ /5.8	7.8	1.16	13.11	12	0	52	45	3	26	63.3	-16.8	13	8	1,000	0	0.0	0.0
C+ /5.8	7.8	1.16	13.10	N/A	0	52	45	3	26	63.2	-16.8	13	8	2,500	0	0.0	0.0
C /5.4	8.7	1.29	8.36	N/A	0	62	37	1	30	71.3	-19.0	9	8	50,000	0	0.0	0.0
C /5.4	8.7	1.29	8.36	21	0	62	37	1	30	71.5	-19.0	9	8	1,000	0	0.0	0.0
C /5.4	8.7	1.29	8.36	N/A	0	62	37	1	30	71.3	-19.0	9	8	2,500	0	0.0	0.0
C+ /5.7	9.6	1.42	13.71	N/A	0	72	27	1	24	78.8	-20.8	6	8	50,000	0	0.0	0.0
C+ /5.7	9.6	1.43	13.72	8	0	72	27	1	24	78.9	-20.8	6	8	1,000	0	0.0	0.0
C+ /5.7	9.6	1.42	13.71	N/A	0	72	27	1	24	78.8	-20.8	6	8	2,500	0	0.0	0.0
C- /4.1	10.5	1.57	9.18	N/A	0	84	16	0	24	85.3	-21.5	4	8	50,000	0	0.0	0.0
C- /4.1	10.5	1.56	9.17	20	0	84	16	0	24	85.5	-21.5	5	8	1,000	0	0.0	0.0
C- /4.1	10.5	1.57	9.18	N/A	0	84	16	0	24	85.3	-21.5	4	8	2,500	0	0.0	0.0
B- /7.3	4.0	0.54	8.93	N/A	0	16	83	1	26	31.9	-5.1	59	8	50,000	0	0.0	0.0
B- /7.2	4.0	0.55	8.93	14	0	16	83	1	26	31.9	-5.1	57	8	1,000	0	0.0	0.0
B- /7.2	4.0	0.55	8.93	N/A	0	16	83	1	26	31.9	-5.1	58	8	2,500	0	0.0	0.0
C /4.4	14.5	0.87	47.56	3,222	2	94	2	2	26	41.2	-24.1	78	12	5,000	0	0.0	2.0
C /4.6	11.3	0.50	7.43	359	0	0	0	100	38	26.1	-19.7	12	9	100,000	0	0.0	2.0
C /4.7	11.2	0.49	7.39	29	0	0	0	100	38	23.5	-19.8	9	9	5,000	0	0.0	2.0
C+ /5.9	11.0	0.82	34.57	58	1	97	0	2	24	79.8	-18.5	98	16	5,000	0	0.0	2.0
C+ /5.9	11.0	0.82	34.57	890	1	97	0	2	24	82.7	-18.4	98	16	100,000	0	0.0	2.0
C+ /5.9	12.4	0.92	18.95	7,383	0	98	0	2	22	57.5	-22.2	92	16	100,000	0	0.0	2.0
C+ /5.9	12.4	0.92	18.92	504	0	98	0	2	22	54.7	-22.3	90	16	5,000	0	0.0	2.0
C+ /6.5	10.3	0.73	13.51	77	8	90	1	1	49	65.5	N/A	80	6	100,000	0	0.0	2.0
C+ /6.5	10.3	0.73	13.44	40	8	90	1	1	49	63.3	-23.2	78	6	5,000	0	0.0	2.0
B /8.2	7.4	1.18	22.21	616	0	67	31	2	26	75.1	-12.2	37	5	2,000	50	5.5	0.0
B /8.3	7.4	1.18	22.12	2	0	67	31	2	26	67.1	-12.5	27	5	0	0	0.0	0.0
B /8.2	7.4	1.18	22.19	169	0	67	31	2	26	68.5	-12.4	29	5	2,000	50	0.0	0.0
B /8.4	7.0	1.05	28.63	2,041	0	62	36	2	18	79.9	-12.1	83	5	0	0	0.0	0.0
B /8.4	7.0	1.05	29.03	275	0	62	36	2	18	77.5	-12.2	81	5	0	0	0.0	0.0

					PERFORMANCE							
99 Pct = Best							Total Return % through 2/28/17				Incl. in Returns	
0 Pct = Worst			Overall		Perfor-				Annualized		Dividend	Expense
Fund		Ticker	Investment		mance						Yield	Ratio
Type	Fund Name	Symbol	Rating	Phone	Rating/Pts	3 Mo	6 Mo	1Yr / Pct	3Yr / Pct	5Yr / Pct		
BA	Hartford Balanced I	ITTIX	U	(888) 843-7824	U /	6.03	4.45	14.79 /29	--	--	1.55	0.86
BA	Hartford Balanced Income A	HBLAX	C+	(888) 843-7824	C- / 4.0	4.41	3.30	15.58 /32	6.40 /67	8.11 /43	2.29	0.95
BA	● Hartford Balanced Income B	HBLBX	B	(888) 843-7824	C / 5.1	4.39	3.24	15.48 /32	6.37 /67	8.05 /43	2.31	1.81
BA	Hartford Balanced Income C	HBLCX	B-	(888) 843-7824	C / 4.5	4.22	2.99	14.75 /29	5.62 /61	7.33 /37	1.79	1.69
BA	Hartford Balanced Income I	HBLIX	B	(888) 843-7824	C / 5.4	4.55	3.51	15.86 /34	6.70 /70	8.40 /45	2.66	0.69
BA	Hartford Balanced Income R3	HBLRX	B	(888) 843-7824	C / 4.9	4.33	3.15	15.20 /31	6.10 /65	7.81 /41	2.14	1.31
BA	Hartford Balanced Income R4	HBLSX	B	(888) 843-7824	C / 5.2	4.40	3.30	15.53 /32	6.42 /68	8.13 /43	2.42	1.01
BA	Hartford Balanced Income R5	HBLTX	B	(888) 843-7824	C / 5.4	4.46	3.42	15.78 /33	6.67 /70	8.40 /45	2.64	0.71
BA	Hartford Balanced Income Y	HBLYX	B	(888) 843-7824	C / 5.4	4.46	3.44	15.87 /34	6.75 /70	8.56 /47	2.70	0.61
AA	Hartford Balanced R3	ITTRX	B	(888) 843-7824	C / 4.8	5.89	4.15	14.17 /26	5.64 /61	8.34 /45	1.06	1.49
AA	Hartford Balanced R4	ITTSX	B	(888) 843-7824	C / 5.1	5.95	4.31	14.45 /28	5.95 /64	8.66 /48	1.28	1.16
AA	Hartford Balanced R5	ITTTX	B	(888) 843-7824	C / 5.3	6.06	4.50	14.81 /29	6.28 /67	8.98 /50	1.55	0.87
AA	Hartford Balanced Y	IHAYX	B	(888) 843-7824	C / 5.4	6.12	4.53	14.93 /30	6.34 /67	9.05 /51	1.60	0.74
GR	Hartford Capital Apprec A	ITHAX	D	(888) 843-7824	C+ / 5.9	8.01	9.25	22.33 /64	6.16 /66	12.57 /80	0.36	1.09
GR	● Hartford Capital Apprec B	IHCAX	D	(888) 843-7824	C+ / 6.3	7.80	8.77	21.25 /59	5.24 /57	11.60 /71	0.00	1.97
GR	Hartford Capital Apprec C	HCACX	D	(888) 843-7824	C+ / 6.4	7.83	8.86	21.47 /60	5.41 /59	11.77 /72	0.00	1.81
GL	Hartford Capital Apprec HLS IA		C-	(888) 843-7824	B- / 7.0	7.63	9.19	23.38 /68	6.10 /65	12.00 /74	0.96	0.67
GL	Hartford Capital Apprec HLS IB		D+	(888) 843-7824	C+ / 6.8	7.57	9.05	23.09 /67	5.84 /63	11.72 /72	0.75	0.92
GR	Hartford Capital Apprec HLS IC	HCPCX	C+	(888) 843-7824	C+ / 6.6	7.49	8.90	22.76 /66	5.59 /60	11.56 /70	0.59	1.17
GR	Hartford Capital Apprec I	ITHIX	D+	(888) 843-7824	B- / 7.2	8.09	9.41	22.69 /65	6.50 /68	12.92 /83	0.68	0.78
GR	Hartford Capital Apprec R3	ITHRX	D+	(888) 843-7824	C+ / 6.7	7.94	9.08	21.98 /62	5.84 /63	12.24 /76	0.03	1.40
GR	Hartford Capital Apprec R4	ITHSX	C-	(888) 843-7824	C+ / 6.9	8.03	9.25	22.32 /64	6.16 /66	12.58 /80	0.16	1.10
GR	Hartford Capital Apprec R5	ITHTX	C-	(888) 843-7824	B- / 7.1	8.10	9.41	22.67 /65	6.47 /68	12.91 /83	0.60	0.80
GR	Hartford Capital Apprec R6	ITHVX	U	(888) 843-7824	U /	8.13	9.46	22.83 /66	--	--	0.68	0.76
GR	Hartford Capital Apprec Y	HCAYX	C-	(888) 843-7824	B- / 7.2	8.11	9.46	22.80 /66	6.57 /69	13.03 /84	0.68	0.70
GI	Hartford Checks and Balances A	HCKAX	C-	(888) 843-7824	C / 4.6	5.71	6.55	17.30 /40	6.11 /65	9.36 /53	1.18	0.98
GI	● Hartford Checks and Balances B	HCKBX	C	(888) 843-7824	C / 5.0	5.48	6.15	16.39 /36	5.25 /57	8.50 /46	0.35	1.79
GI	Hartford Checks and Balances C	HCKCX	C	(888) 843-7824	C / 5.1	5.45	6.09	16.45 /36	5.30 /58	8.54 /47	0.56	1.73
GI	Hartford Checks and Balances I	HCKIX	C+	(888) 843-7824	C+ / 6.0	5.86	6.66	17.65 /41	6.38 /67	9.66 /56	1.44	0.75
GI	Hartford Checks and Balances R3	HCKRX	C	(888) 843-7824	C / 5.5	5.64	6.39	16.99 /38	5.73 /62	9.00 /51	0.94	1.34
GI	Hartford Checks and Balances R4	HCKSX	C+	(888) 843-7824	C+ / 5.7	5.71	6.54	17.31 /40	6.06 /65	9.30 /53	1.20	1.04
GI	Hartford Checks and Balances R5	HCKTX	C+	(888) 843-7824	C+ / 6.0	5.88	6.78	17.70 /41	6.41 /68	9.68 /56	1.47	0.73
AA	Hartford Conservative Alloc A	HCVAX	D+	(888) 843-7824	D- / 1.0	3.42	2.58	10.03 /12	0.56 /16	1.58 / 7	1.25	1.31
AA	● Hartford Conservative Alloc B	HCVBX	D+	(888) 843-7824	D- / 1.0	3.32	2.26	9.21 /10	-0.19 /13	0.78 / 6	0.00	2.18
AA	Hartford Conservative Alloc C	HCVCX	D+	(888) 843-7824	D- / 1.0	3.36	2.30	9.26 /10	-0.16 /13	0.85 / 6	0.53	2.05
AA	Hartford Conservative Alloc I	HCVIX	C-	(888) 843-7824	D / 1.7	3.61	2.78	10.34 /12	0.86 /17	1.87 / 8	1.61	1.02
AA	Hartford Conservative Alloc R3	HCVRX	D+	(888) 843-7824	D- / 1.5	3.53	2.59	9.81 /11	0.28 /15	1.28 / 7	1.13	1.65
AA	Hartford Conservative Alloc R4	HCVSX	C-	(888) 843-7824	D / 1.6	3.48	2.64	10.09 /12	0.60 /16	1.58 / 7	1.38	1.36
AA	Hartford Conservative Alloc R5	HCVTX	C-	(888) 843-7824	D / 1.7	3.59	2.76	10.41 /13	0.89 /18	1.87 / 8	1.69	1.05
GR	Hartford Core Equity A	HAIAX	A-	(888) 843-7824	B- / 7.4	7.88	7.57	18.50 /45	10.21 /94	14.51 /96	0.45	0.98
GR	● Hartford Core Equity B	HGIBX	A	(888) 843-7824	B / 7.8	7.66	7.18	17.59 /41	9.35 /89	13.64 /90	0.00	2.13
GR	Hartford Core Equity C	HGICX	A	(888) 843-7824	B / 7.8	7.67	7.14	17.62 /41	9.40 /90	13.70 /91	0.07	1.68
GI	Hartford Core Equity I	HGIIX	A+	(888) 843-7824	B+ / 8.5	7.93	7.71	18.84 /46	10.41 /95	14.63 /96	0.72	0.61
GR	Hartford Core Equity R3	HGIRX	A	(888) 843-7824	B / 8.1	7.79	7.40	18.15 /44	9.90 /93	14.25 /94	0.38	1.29
GR	Hartford Core Equity R4	HGISX	A+	(888) 843-7824	B+ / 8.4	7.89	7.59	18.51 /45	10.25 /95	14.61 /96	0.53	0.93
GR	Hartford Core Equity R5	HGITX	A+	(888) 843-7824	B+ / 8.6	7.94	7.72	18.88 /47	10.56 /96	14.95 /97	0.74	0.59
GI	Hartford Core Equity R6	HAITX	A+	(888) 843-7824	B+ / 8.7	7.97	7.75	18.91 /47	10.60 /96	14.99 /97	0.79	0.52
GR	Hartford Core Equity Y	HGIYX	A+	(888) 843-7824	B+ / 8.7	7.96	7.75	18.96 /47	10.61 /96	14.99 /97	0.79	0.52
IN	Hartford Div & Growth HLS IA		B-	(888) 843-7824	B+ / 8.6	5.71	9.82	24.67 /72	9.32 /89	12.98 /83	0.12	0.67
IN	Hartford Div & Growth HLS IB		B-	(888) 843-7824	B+ / 8.6	5.93	9.97	24.68 /72	9.15 /88	12.76 /82	0.12	0.92
GI	Hartford Dividend & Gr HLS Fd IA	HIADX	B	(888) 843-7824	A / 9.4	7.64	11.83	26.95 /79	9.98 /93	13.39 /88	1.71	0.67
GI	Hartford Dividend & Gr HLS Fd IB	HDGBX	B	(888) 843-7824	A / 9.3	7.61	11.72	26.66 /78	9.72 /92	13.11 /85	1.50	0.92

● Denotes fund is closed to new investors
∗ Denotes fund is included in Section II

294

RISK			NET ASSETS		ASSET					BULL / BEAR		FUND MANAGER		MINIMUMS		LOADS	
	3 Year		NAV						Portfolio	Last Bull	Last Bear	Manager	Manager	Initial	Additional	Front	Back
Risk	Standard		As of	Total	Cash	Stocks	Bonds	Other	Turnover	Market	Market	Quality	Tenure	Purch.	Purch.	End	End
Rating/Pts	Deviation	Beta	2/28/17	$(Mil)	%	%	%	%	Ratio	Return	Return	Pct	(Years)	$	$	Load	Load
U /	N/A	N/A	22.21	69	0	67	31	2	26	N/A	N/A	N/A	5	2,000	50	0.0	0.0
B /8.1	5.7	0.86	14.19	3,112	2	46	51	1	36	66.1	-5.4	74	11	2,000	50	5.5	0.0
B /8.1	5.7	0.86	14.16	5	2	46	51	1	36	65.1	-5.8	74	11	0	0	0.0	0.0
B /8.1	5.7	0.86	13.99	3,420	2	46	51	1	36	59.7	-5.8	65	11	2,000	50	0.0	0.0
B /8.1	5.7	0.86	14.20	3,278	2	46	51	1	36	68.5	-5.4	76	11	2,000	50	0.0	0.0
B /8.1	5.7	0.85	14.23	195	2	46	51	1	36	63.6	-5.6	71	11	0	0	0.0	0.0
B /8.1	5.7	0.85	14.24	101	2	46	51	1	36	66.3	-5.5	74	11	0	0	0.0	0.0
B /8.1	5.7	0.86	14.26	40	2	46	51	1	36	68.5	-5.3	76	11	0	0	0.0	0.0
B /8.1	5.6	0.85	14.33	99	2	46	51	1	36	69.8	-5.3	77	11	250,000	0	0.0	0.0
B /8.2	7.4	1.18	22.42	3	0	67	31	2	26	72.9	-12.3	34	5	0	0	0.0	0.0
B /8.2	7.4	1.18	22.48	1	0	67	31	2	26	75.6	-12.2	38	5	0	0	0.0	0.0
B /8.2	7.4	1.18	22.51	N/A	0	67	31	2	26	78.6	-12.0	42	5	0	0	0.0	0.0
B /8.2	7.4	1.18	22.53	8	0	67	31	2	26	79.1	-12.0	43	5	250,000	0	0.0	0.0
D /2.0	12.0	1.12	38.06	4,684	1	97	0	2	88	123.2	-25.6	13	N/A	2,000	50	5.5	0.0
D- /1.1	12.0	1.12	30.13	39	1	97	0	2	88	113.1	-25.9	8	N/A	0	0	0.0	0.0
D- /1.1	12.0	1.12	30.72	1,398	1	97	0	2	88	114.7	-25.8	9	N/A	2,000	50	0.0	0.0
D+ /2.4	11.9	0.85	44.74	4,621	4	95	0	1	75	118.6	-24.7	97	10	0	0	0.0	0.0
D+ /2.4	11.9	0.85	44.14	565	4	95	0	1	75	115.6	-24.8	97	10	0	0	0.0	0.0
C+ /6.3	11.9	1.12	44.39	23	4	95	0	1	75	114.1	-24.8	10	10	0	0	0.0	0.0
D /2.0	12.0	1.12	38.15	1,273	1	97	0	2	88	127.0	-25.6	15	N/A	2,000	50	0.0	0.0
D+ /2.3	12.0	1.12	41.36	104	1	97	0	2	88	119.8	-25.7	11	N/A	0	0	0.0	0.0
D+ /2.4	12.0	1.12	42.46	99	1	97	0	2	88	123.4	-25.6	13	N/A	0	0	0.0	0.0
D+ /2.4	12.0	1.11	43.14	49	1	97	0	2	88	127.0	-25.5	15	N/A	0	0	0.0	0.0
U /	N/A	N/A	43.35	64	1	97	0	2	88	N/A	N/A	N/A	N/A	0	0	0.0	0.0
D+ /2.4	12.0	1.12	43.34	854	1	97	0	2	88	128.2	-25.5	16	N/A	250,000	0	0.0	0.0
C+ /5.7	7.4	0.71	9.84	1,379	0	60	39	1	8	80.5	-13.8	59	10	2,000	50	5.5	0.0
C+ /5.7	7.4	0.71	9.79	22	0	60	39	1	8	72.8	-14.2	47	10	0	0	0.0	0.0
C+ /5.7	7.5	0.71	9.76	322	0	60	39	1	8	73.1	-14.1	47	10	2,000	50	0.0	0.0
C+ /5.7	7.5	0.72	9.86	46	0	60	39	1	8	83.0	-13.8	61	9	2,000	50	0.0	0.0
C+ /5.7	7.5	0.71	9.80	16	0	60	39	1	8	77.2	-14.1	53	9	0	0	0.0	0.0
C+ /5.7	7.4	0.71	9.81	5	0	60	39	1	8	80.0	-14.0	57	9	0	0	0.0	0.0
C+ /5.7	7.4	0.71	9.86	2	0	60	39	1	8	83.2	-13.8	62	9	0	0	0.0	0.0
B- /7.7	4.7	0.65	10.02	91	11	39	48	2	80	19.5	-8.2	22	N/A	2,000	50	5.5	0.0
B- /7.7	4.7	0.65	9.96	1	11	39	48	2	80	14.5	-8.5	16	N/A	0	0	0.0	0.0
B- /7.7	4.7	0.65	9.90	29	11	39	48	2	80	14.8	-8.4	15	N/A	2,000	50	0.0	0.0
B- /7.8	4.6	0.64	10.03	1	11	39	48	2	80	21.4	-8.1	25	N/A	2,000	50	0.0	0.0
B- /7.7	4.7	0.64	10.02	9	11	39	48	2	80	17.7	-8.3	20	N/A	0	0	0.0	0.0
B- /7.7	4.6	0.63	10.03	2	11	39	48	2	80	19.5	-8.1	23	N/A	0	0	0.0	0.0
B- /7.8	4.7	0.64	10.05	2	11	39	48	2	80	21.4	-8.0	25	N/A	0	0	0.0	0.0
B- /7.3	9.4	0.88	26.02	645	1	95	2	2	29	137.2	-16.2	80	19	2,000	50	5.5	0.0
B- /7.3	9.4	0.88	24.02	1	1	95	2	2	29	127.7	-16.5	74	19	0	0	0.0	0.0
B- /7.3	9.4	0.88	23.95	321	1	95	2	2	29	128.2	-16.5	74	19	2,000	50	0.0	0.0
B- /7.2	9.4	0.88	26.05	1,003	1	95	2	2	29	138.5	-16.2	81	19	2,000	50	0.0	0.0
B- /7.3	9.4	0.88	26.37	46	1	95	2	2	29	134.5	-16.3	78	19	0	0	0.0	0.0
B- /7.3	9.4	0.88	26.75	167	1	95	2	2	29	138.4	-16.2	80	19	0	0	0.0	0.0
B- /7.3	9.4	0.88	26.23	136	1	95	2	2	29	142.1	-16.1	82	19	0	0	0.0	0.0
B- /7.2	9.4	0.88	26.32	59	1	95	2	2	29	142.6	-16.0	82	19	0	0	0.0	0.0
B- /7.3	9.4	0.88	26.33	405	1	95	2	2	29	142.7	-16.0	82	19	250,000	0	0.0	0.0
C- /4.0	10.5	1.00	23.15	3,001	1	97	1	1	20	122.2	-17.5	60	17	0	0	0.0	0.0
C- /4.0	10.5	1.00	23.06	432	1	97	1	1	20	119.8	-17.6	58	17	0	0	0.0	0.0
C- /4.0	10.6	1.01	23.15	3,089	1	97	1	1	20	126.3	-17.5	66	17	0	0	0.0	0.0
C- /4.0	10.5	1.00	23.06	443	1	97	1	1	20	123.3	-17.6	64	17	0	0	0.0	0.0

					PERFORMANCE						Incl. in Returns	
	99 Pct = Best 0 Pct = Worst		Overall		Perfor-	Total Return % through 2/28/17			Annualized		Dividend	Expense
Fund Type	Fund Name	Ticker Symbol	Investment Rating	Phone	mance Rating/Pts	3 Mo	6 Mo	1Yr / Pct	3Yr / Pct	5Yr / Pct	Yield	Ratio
GI	Hartford Dividend & Growth A	IHGIX	B+	(888) 843-7824	B+ / 8.3	7.58	11.65	26.22 /77	9.49 /90	12.81 /82	1.28	1.02
GI	● Hartford Dividend & Growth B	ITDGX	B+	(888) 843-7824	B+ / 8.5	7.33	11.13	25.07 /73	8.49 /83	11.80 /72	0.42	1.97
GI	Hartford Dividend & Growth C	HDGCX	B+	(888) 843-7824	B+ / 8.7	7.37	11.26	25.28 /74	8.68 /84	11.98 /74	0.76	1.76
GI	Hartford Dividend & Growth I	HDGIX	A-	(888) 843-7824	A / 9.3	7.63	11.77	26.49 /78	9.72 /92	13.06 /84	1.53	0.81
GI	Hartford Dividend & Growth R3	HDGRX	B+	(888) 843-7824	B+ / 8.9	7.49	11.45	25.79 /76	9.12 /88	12.47 /79	1.04	1.35
GI	Hartford Dividend & Growth R4	HDGSX	A-	(888) 843-7824	A- / 9.1	7.56	11.64	26.16 /77	9.46 /90	12.80 /82	1.30	1.04
GI	Hartford Dividend & Growth R5	HDGTX	A-	(888) 843-7824	A / 9.3	7.61	11.81	26.55 /78	9.79 /92	13.14 /85	1.53	0.74
GI	Hartford Dividend & Growth Y	HDGYX	A-	(888) 843-7824	A / 9.4	7.68	11.86	26.70 /78	9.89 /93	13.25 /86	1.64	0.64
GI	Hartford Dscpld Equity HLS IA		D+	(888) 843-7824	B+ / 8.3	7.19	6.89	18.27 /44	10.40 /95	14.94 /97	0.13	0.76
GI	Hartford Dscpld Equity HLS IB		D+	(888) 843-7824	B / 8.2	7.35	6.97	18.23 /44	10.20 /94	14.69 /96	0.13	1.01
EM	Hartford Emg Markets Equity A	HERAX	D	(888) 843-7824	C / 4.6	10.76	7.95	33.46 /92	1.17 /19	0.60 / 5	0.88	1.75
EM	Hartford Emg Markets Equity C	HERCX	D+	(888) 843-7824	C / 5.1	10.59	7.58	32.53 /91	0.45 /15	-0.11 / 4	0.40	2.46
EM	Hartford Emg Markets Equity I	HERIX	C-	(888) 843-7824	C+ / 6.1	10.93	8.11	34.15 /93	1.61 /22	1.01 / 6	1.29	1.30
EM	Hartford Emg Markets Equity R3	HERRX	C-	(888) 843-7824	C / 5.5	10.66	7.83	33.17 /92	0.95 /18	0.36 / 5	0.00	1.98
EM	Hartford Emg Markets Equity R4	HERSX	C-	(888) 843-7824	C+ / 5.8	10.76	8.08	33.61 /92	1.23 /19	0.64 / 6	0.00	1.67
EM	Hartford Emg Markets Equity R5	HERTX	C-	(888) 843-7824	C+ / 6.0	10.96	8.71	33.71 /92	1.37 /20	0.86 / 6	1.15	1.37
EM	Hartford Emg Markets Equity Y	HERYX	C-	(888) 843-7824	C+ / 6.2	10.88	8.21	34.09 /93	1.67 /22	1.08 / 6	1.36	1.28
IN	Hartford Equity Income A	HQIAX	B+	(888) 843-7824	B / 7.7	7.11	9.12	24.89 /73	9.19 /88	12.58 /80	1.55	1.02
IN	● Hartford Equity Income B	HQIBX	A-	(888) 843-7824	B+ / 8.5	7.05	9.01	24.69 /72	9.04 /87	12.23 /76	1.47	1.91
IN	Hartford Equity Income C	HQICX	B+	(888) 843-7824	B / 8.1	6.96	8.72	24.02 /70	8.40 /82	11.77 /72	1.01	1.76
IN	Hartford Equity Income I	HQIIX	A	(888) 843-7824	B+ / 8.8	7.21	9.24	25.19 /74	9.46 /90	12.89 /83	1.88	0.76
IN	Hartford Equity Income R3	HQIRX	A-	(888) 843-7824	B+ / 8.3	7.01	8.87	24.45 /71	8.80 /85	12.21 /76	1.34	1.36
IN	Hartford Equity Income R4	HQISX	A-	(888) 843-7824	B+ / 8.6	7.08	9.02	24.78 /73	9.13 /88	12.53 /79	1.61	1.06
IN	Hartford Equity Income R5	HQITX	A	(888) 843-7824	B+ / 8.8	7.18	9.25	25.22 /74	9.47 /90	12.89 /83	1.86	0.76
IN	Hartford Equity Income Y	HQIYX	A	(888) 843-7824	B+ / 8.9	7.19	9.28	25.36 /74	9.58 /91	13.00 /84	1.95	0.66
GL	Hartford Global All Asset A	HLAAX	D-	(888) 843-7824	D / 2.2	4.86	4.16	15.17 /31	2.76 /30	5.15 /22	1.51	1.59
GL	Hartford Global All Asset C	HLACX	D	(888) 843-7824	D+ / 2.6	4.72	3.91	14.49 /28	2.03 /24	4.38 /17	0.78	2.31
GL	Hartford Global All Asset I	HLAIX	D+	(888) 843-7824	C- / 3.3	4.85	4.35	15.56 /32	3.05 /32	5.41 /24	1.88	1.28
GL	Hartford Global All Asset R3	HLARX	D	(888) 843-7824	C- / 3.0	4.80	4.10	14.99 /30	2.54 /28	4.90 /21	1.36	1.91
GL	Hartford Global All Asset R4	HLASX	D	(888) 843-7824	C- / 3.2	4.85	4.26	15.37 /32	2.84 /30	5.22 /23	1.63	1.62
GL	Hartford Global All Asset R5	HLATX	D	(888) 843-7824	C- / 3.3	5.00	4.51	15.56 /32	2.89 /31	5.35 /24	2.10	1.29
GL	Hartford Global All Asset Y	HLAYX	D+	(888) 843-7824	C- / 3.4	4.94	4.35	15.65 /33	3.14 /33	5.50 /25	1.97	1.20
GR	Hartford Global Capital Apprec A	HCTAX	D-	(888) 843-7824	C- / 3.0	6.63	6.16	20.02 /52	2.46 /27	9.55 /55	0.67	1.27
GR	● Hartford Global Capital Apprec B	HCTBX	D-	(888) 843-7824	C- / 3.3	6.43	5.69	19.09 /48	1.67 /22	8.72 /48	0.00	2.14
GR	Hartford Global Capital Apprec C	HFCCX	D-	(888) 843-7824	C- / 3.4	6.44	5.77	19.11 /48	1.71 /22	8.76 /48	0.03	1.97
GR	Hartford Global Capital Apprec I	HCTIX	D	(888) 843-7824	C- / 4.2	6.68	6.29	20.37 /54	2.76 /30	9.86 /57	0.98	0.94
GR	Hartford Global Capital Apprec R3	HCTRX	D	(888) 843-7824	C- / 3.9	6.64	6.16	19.93 /52	2.36 /26	9.45 /54	0.64	1.55
GR	Hartford Global Capital Apprec R4	HCTSX	D	(888) 843-7824	C- / 4.2	6.70	6.30	20.29 /54	2.67 /29	9.77 /57	0.92	1.25
GR	Hartford Global Capital Apprec R5	HCTTX	D	(888) 843-7824	C- / 4.2	6.75	6.36	20.44 /55	2.76 /30	9.88 /57	0.95	0.96
GR	Hartford Global Capital Apprec Y	HCTYX	D	(888) 843-7824	C- / 4.2	6.74	6.35	20.28 /54	2.82 /30	9.93 /58	1.05	0.84
GL	Hartford Global Equtiy Income A	HLEAX	D+	(888) 843-7824	D+ / 2.9	6.93	5.08	19.34 /49	2.63 /28	8.22 /44	1.96	1.33
GL	● Hartford Global Equtiy Income B	HLEBX	C-	(888) 843-7824	C- / 3.3	6.74	4.68	18.54 /45	1.84 /23	7.42 /37	1.23	2.33
GL	Hartford Global Equtiy Income C	HLECX	C-	(888) 843-7824	C- / 3.3	6.81	4.71	18.51 /45	1.85 /23	7.44 /38	1.42	2.08
GL	Hartford Global Equtiy Income I	HLEJX	C-	(888) 843-7824	C- / 4.1	6.97	5.20	19.76 /51	2.91 /31	8.52 /46	2.33	1.00
GL	Hartford Global Equtiy Income R3	HLERX	C-	(888) 843-7824	C- / 3.8	6.89	5.02	19.18 /48	2.42 /27	8.02 /42	1.94	1.57
GL	Hartford Global Equtiy Income R4	HLESX	C-	(888) 843-7824	C- / 4.0	6.93	5.12	19.43 /49	2.72 /29	8.34 /45	2.20	1.26
GL	Hartford Global Equtiy Income R5	HLETX	C	(888) 843-7824	C- / 4.2	7.02	5.28	19.90 /51	3.03 /32	8.66 /48	2.46	0.95
GL	Hartford Global Equtiy Income Y	HLEYX	C-	(888) 843-7824	C- / 4.2	7.03	5.29	19.86 /51	3.02 /32	8.71 /48	2.82	0.84
GL	Hartford Global Growth HLS IA		C+	(888) 843-7824	C+ / 6.7	7.32	5.51	19.88 /51	7.09 /73	12.61 /80	0.63	0.81
GL	Hartford Global Growth HLS IB		C+	(888) 843-7824	C+ / 6.6	7.25	5.42	19.62 /50	6.83 /71	12.33 /77	0.36	1.06
OT	Hartford Global Real Asset A	HRLAX	E	(888) 843-7824	E / 0.3	2.14	5.37	21.63 /60	-4.28 / 3	-4.05 / 2	0.41	1.68
OT	Hartford Global Real Asset C	HRLCX	E	(888) 843-7824	E / 0.4	1.86	5.03	20.63 /56	-5.00 / 2	-4.79 / 2	0.00	2.41

● Denotes fund is closed to new investors
* Denotes fund is included in Section II

RISK			NET ASSETS		ASSET				Portfolio Turnover Ratio	BULL / BEAR		FUND MANAGER		MINIMUMS		LOADS	
Risk Rating/Pts	3 Year Standard Deviation	Beta	NAV As of 2/28/17	Total $(Mil)	Cash %	Stocks %	Bonds %	Other %		Last Bull Market Return	Last Bear Market Return	Manager Quality Pct	Manager Tenure (Years)	Initial Purch. $	Additional Purch. $	Front End Load	Back End Load
C /5.4	10.4	0.99	25.62	3,710	0	97	1	2	22	119.6	-17.4	63	17	2,000	50	5.5	0.0
C /5.4	10.4	0.99	25.12	14	0	97	1	2	22	109.2	-17.7	50	17	0	0	0.0	0.0
C /5.4	10.4	0.99	24.83	468	0	97	1	2	22	110.9	-17.6	53	17	2,000	50	0.0	0.0
C /5.4	10.4	0.99	25.51	2,023	0	97	1	2	22	122.3	-17.3	65	17	2,000	50	0.0	0.0
C /5.5	10.4	0.99	25.91	84	0	97	1	2	22	116.0	-17.5	59	17	0	0	0.0	0.0
C /5.5	10.4	0.99	26.07	149	0	97	1	2	22	119.4	-17.3	63	17	0	0	0.0	0.0
C /5.5	10.4	0.99	26.17	122	0	97	1	2	22	123.2	-17.3	66	17	0	0	0.0	0.0
C /5.5	10.4	0.99	26.18	1,568	0	97	1	2	22	124.3	-17.2	67	17	250,000	0	0.0	0.0
E+ /0.9	9.6	0.90	15.20	586	0	0	0	100	29	142.6	-16.4	80	19	0	0	0.0	0.0
E+ /0.9	9.6	0.90	15.05	81	0	0	0	100	29	139.9	-16.5	78	19	0	0	0.0	0.0
C- /3.8	16.4	0.99	7.99	11	3	96	0	1	97	27.9	N/A	68	2	2,000	50	5.5	0.0
C- /3.8	16.3	0.99	7.85	3	3	96	0	1	97	23.1	N/A	59	2	2,000	50	0.0	0.0
C- /3.7	16.4	0.99	7.96	5	3	96	0	1	97	30.6	N/A	73	2	2,000	50	0.0	0.0
C- /3.8	16.3	0.99	7.99	N/A	3	96	0	1	97	26.3	N/A	65	2	0	0	0.0	0.0
C- /3.7	16.4	0.99	8.03	N/A	3	96	0	1	97	28.1	N/A	69	2	0	0	0.0	0.0
C- /3.7	16.4	0.99	7.92	N/A	3	96	0	1	97	29.6	N/A	70	2	0	0	0.0	0.0
C- /3.7	16.3	0.99	7.95	70	3	96	0	1	97	31.0	N/A	74	2	250,000	0	0.0	0.0
C+ /6.3	9.9	0.93	19.31	1,735	0	99	0	1	14	118.1	-14.1	67	14	2,000	50	5.5	0.0
C+ /6.3	10.0	0.93	19.33	5	0	99	0	1	14	113.8	-14.4	65	14	0	0	0.0	0.0
C+ /6.3	9.9	0.93	19.20	478	0	99	0	1	14	109.6	-14.3	58	14	2,000	50	0.0	0.0
C+ /6.3	9.9	0.93	19.22	1,230	0	99	0	1	14	121.2	-14.0	70	14	2,000	50	0.0	0.0
C+ /6.3	9.9	0.93	19.32	57	0	99	0	1	14	114.2	-14.2	62	14	0	0	0.0	0.0
C+ /6.3	9.9	0.93	19.35	86	0	99	0	1	14	117.5	-14.0	67	14	0	0	0.0	0.0
C+ /6.3	9.9	0.93	19.45	77	0	99	0	1	14	121.4	-14.0	70	14	0	0	0.0	0.0
C+ /6.3	9.9	0.93	19.49	430	0	99	0	1	14	122.5	-13.9	72	14	250,000	0	0.0	0.0
C /5.0	7.2	1.08	10.83	110	12	58	27	3	95	43.7	-15.6	46	7	5,000	50	5.5	0.0
C /5.0	7.2	1.08	10.71	64	12	58	27	3	95	38.2	-15.9	36	7	5,000	50	0.0	0.0
C /5.0	7.2	1.07	10.87	47	12	58	27	3	95	45.8	-15.5	50	7	5,000	50	0.0	0.0
C /5.1	7.2	1.08	10.84	2	12	58	27	3	95	42.0	-15.8	43	7	0	0	0.0	0.0
C /5.1	7.2	1.08	10.97	1	12	58	27	3	95	44.4	-15.7	47	7	0	0	0.0	0.0
C /5.0	7.3	1.09	10.80	N/A	12	58	27	3	95	45.3	-15.5	47	7	0	0	0.0	0.0
C /5.0	7.3	1.08	10.88	91	12	58	27	3	95	46.4	-15.5	51	7	250,000	0	0.0	0.0
C- /3.6	11.6	1.04	16.69	642	1	97	0	2	100	94.7	-25.5	4	12	2,000	50	5.5	0.0
C- /3.4	11.6	1.04	15.22	3	1	97	0	2	100	86.7	-25.7	3	12	0	0	0.0	0.0
C- /3.4	11.5	1.03	15.30	208	1	97	0	2	100	87.0	-25.7	3	12	2,000	50	0.0	0.0
C- /3.6	11.6	1.04	17.18	124	1	97	0	2	100	97.8	-25.4	4	12	2,000	50	0.0	0.0
C- /3.6	11.6	1.04	16.44	27	1	97	0	2	100	93.6	-25.6	4	12	0	0	0.0	0.0
C- /3.6	11.6	1.04	16.93	19	1	97	0	2	100	96.6	-25.4	4	12	0	0	0.0	0.0
C- /3.6	11.6	1.04	17.29	1	1	97	0	2	100	97.9	-25.4	4	12	0	0	0.0	0.0
C- /3.7	11.6	1.04	17.44	9	1	97	0	2	100	98.5	-25.3	4	12	250,000	0	0.0	0.0
C+ /6.3	10.6	0.82	11.46	109	1	98	0	1	28	79.8	-22.9	89	3	2,000	50	5.5	0.0
C+ /6.3	10.5	0.82	11.24	N/A	1	98	0	1	28	72.9	-23.2	86	3	0	0	0.0	0.0
C+ /6.3	10.5	0.82	11.18	12	1	98	0	1	28	72.8	-23.2	86	3	2,000	50	0.0	0.0
C+ /6.3	10.5	0.82	11.48	23	1	98	0	1	28	82.5	-22.9	90	3	2,000	50	0.0	0.0
C+ /6.3	10.6	0.82	11.45	N/A	1	98	0	1	28	78.2	-23.1	88	3	0	0	0.0	0.0
C+ /6.3	10.5	0.82	11.50	N/A	1	98	0	1	28	80.9	-22.9	90	3	0	0	0.0	0.0
C+ /6.3	10.6	0.82	11.49	N/A	1	98	0	1	28	83.9	-22.9	91	3	0	0	0.0	0.0
C+ /6.2	10.6	0.82	11.36	6	1	98	0	1	28	84.3	-22.8	91	3	250,000	0	0.0	0.0
C /5.2	11.4	0.81	23.75	359	1	98	0	1	67	122.1	-24.8	98	12	0	0	0.0	0.0
C /5.2	11.4	0.81	23.53	76	1	98	0	1	67	119.1	-24.9	98	12	0	0	0.0	0.0
C /4.5	12.7	0.67	8.95	20	20	66	12	2	115	-7.8	-20.2	1	7	5,000	50	5.5	0.0
C /4.4	12.7	0.67	8.77	9	20	66	12	2	115	-11.5	-20.5	1	7	5,000	50	0.0	0.0

					PERFORMANCE						Incl. in Returns	
	99 Pct = Best		Overall		Perfor-		Total Return % through 2/28/17					
	0 Pct = Worst		Investment		mance				Annualized		Dividend	Expense
Fund		Ticker	Rating	Phone	Rating/Pts	3 Mo	6 Mo	1Yr / Pct	3Yr / Pct	5Yr / Pct	Yield	Ratio
Type	Fund Name	Symbol										
OT	Hartford Global Real Asset I	HRLIX	E	(888) 843-7824	E+ / 0.6	2.06	5.53	21.84 /61	-4.04 / 3	-3.82 / 2	0.69	1.30
OT	Hartford Global Real Asset R3	HRLRX	E	(888) 843-7824	E / 0.5	2.06	5.28	21.45 /60	-4.52 / 3	-4.27 / 2	0.24	2.03
OT	Hartford Global Real Asset R4	HRLSX	E	(888) 843-7824	E / 0.5	2.09	5.44	21.70 /61	-4.27 / 3	-4.03 / 2	0.38	1.61
OT	Hartford Global Real Asset R5	HRLTX	E	(888) 843-7824	E+ / 0.6	2.13	5.60	22.06 /62	-4.00 / 3	-3.78 / 2	0.76	1.32
OT	Hartford Global Real Asset Y	HRLYX	E	(888) 843-7824	E+ / 0.6	2.14	5.61	22.06 /62	-3.96 / 3	-3.73 / 2	0.76	1.20
AA	Hartford Growth Alloc A	HRAAX	E+	(888) 843-7824	D+ / 2.5	5.84	6.04	17.39 /40	2.25 /26	6.49 /31	0.39	1.44
AA	● Hartford Growth Alloc B	HRABX	E+	(888) 843-7824	D+ / 2.8	5.54	5.64	16.32 /36	1.36 /20	5.58 /25	0.00	2.34
AA	Hartford Growth Alloc C	HRACX	E+	(888) 843-7824	D+ / 2.9	5.58	5.68	16.58 /37	1.51 /21	5.72 /26	0.00	2.17
AA	Hartford Growth Alloc I	HRAIX	D-	(888) 843-7824	C- / 3.7	5.92	6.22	17.77 /42	2.59 /28	6.83 /34	0.72	1.12
AA	Hartford Growth Alloc R3	HRARX	E+	(888) 843-7824	C- / 3.2	5.64	5.85	16.99 /38	1.93 /23	6.15 /29	0.11	1.76
AA	Hartford Growth Alloc R4	HRASX	E+	(888) 843-7824	C- / 3.4	5.79	5.99	17.28 /40	2.22 /25	6.48 /31	0.42	1.46
AA	Hartford Growth Alloc R5	HRATX	D-	(888) 843-7824	C- / 3.7	5.87	6.27	17.76 /42	2.55 /28	6.81 /33	0.71	1.16
GR	Hartford Growth Opportunities A	HGOAX	D+	(888) 843-7824	C+ / 6.2	6.52	3.93	20.08 /52	8.43 /82	14.37 /95	0.00	1.12
GR	● Hartford Growth Opportunities B	HGOBX	D	(888) 843-7824	C+ / 6.5	6.33	3.46	18.99 /47	7.44 /75	13.40 /88	0.00	2.04
GR	Hartford Growth Opportunities C	HGOCX	D+	(888) 843-7824	C+ / 6.6	6.32	3.53	19.20 /48	7.65 /76	13.55 /89	0.00	1.86
GR	Hartford Growth Opportunities I	HGOIX	C-	(888) 843-7824	B- / 7.3	6.58	4.05	20.35 /54	8.68 /84	14.65 /96	0.00	0.89
GR	Hartford Growth Opportunities R3	HGORX	C-	(888) 843-7824	C+ / 6.9	6.44	3.79	19.73 /51	8.09 /80	14.04 /93	0.00	1.45
GR	Hartford Growth Opportunities R4	HGOSX	C-	(888) 843-7824	B- / 7.1	6.52	3.94	20.09 /52	8.42 /82	14.38 /95	0.00	1.15
GR	Hartford Growth Opportunities R5	HGOTX	C	(888) 843-7824	B- / 7.4	6.64	4.11	20.43 /54	8.74 /85	14.73 /96	0.00	0.84
GR	Hartford Growth Opportunities Y	HGOYX	C	(888) 843-7824	B- / 7.4	6.64	4.14	20.56 /55	8.84 /86	14.83 /97	0.00	0.75
GR	Hartford Growth Opps HLS Fd IA	HAGOX	D+	(888) 843-7824	B- / 7.5	6.46	3.91	20.53 /55	9.09 /87	15.15 /97	0.40	0.65
GR	Hartford Growth Opps HLS Fd IB	HBGOX	D+	(888) 843-7824	B- / 7.3	6.39	3.79	20.21 /53	8.81 /85	14.86 /97	0.14	0.90
GL	Hartford Growth Oppty HLS IA		D+	(888) 843-7824	B- / 7.5	6.46	3.91	20.53 /55	9.09 /87	15.15 /97	0.40	0.65
GL	Hartford Growth Oppty HLS IB		D+	(888) 843-7824	B- / 7.3	6.39	3.79	20.21 /53	8.81 /85	14.86 /97	0.14	0.90
MC	Hartford Growth Oppty HLS IC	HCGOX	C+	(888) 843-7824	B- / 7.1	6.31	3.66	19.95 /52	8.57 /84	14.71 /96	0.24	1.16
HL	Hartford Healthcare A	HGHAX	C	(888) 843-7824	B / 8.0	13.02	8.68	20.40 /54	9.64 /91	19.14 /99	0.00	1.29
HL	● Hartford Healthcare B	HGHBX	C	(888) 843-7824	B+ / 8.3	12.80	8.18	19.37 /49	8.68 /84	18.11 /99	0.00	2.16
HL	Hartford Healthcare C	HGHCX	C	(888) 843-7824	B+ / 8.4	12.86	8.29	19.54 /50	8.85 /86	18.28 /99	0.00	2.03
HL	Hartford Healthcare HLS IA		C-	(888) 843-7824	A / 9.3	13.25	9.10	21.18 /58	10.15 /94	20.04 /99	3.33	0.87
HL	Hartford Healthcare HLS IB		C-	(888) 843-7824	A- / 9.1	13.17	8.90	20.86 /57	9.87 /93	19.73 /99	3.13	1.12
HL	Hartford Healthcare I	HGHIX	C+	(888) 843-7824	A- / 9.1	13.12	8.83	20.77 /56	9.94 /93	19.49 /99	0.00	1.02
HL	Hartford Healthcare R3	HGHRX	C+	(888) 843-7824	B+ / 8.8	12.95	8.51	20.07 /52	9.31 /89	18.81 /99	0.00	1.62
HL	Hartford Healthcare R4	HGHSX	C+	(888) 843-7824	B+ / 8.9	13.04	8.69	20.44 /55	9.64 /91	19.17 /99	0.00	1.31
HL	Hartford Healthcare R5	HGHTX	C+	(888) 843-7824	A- / 9.1	13.12	8.85	20.78 /56	9.96 /93	19.53 /99	0.00	1.02
HL	Hartford Healthcare Y	HGHYX	B-	(888) 843-7824	A- / 9.2	13.14	8.90	20.95 /57	10.08 /94	19.64 /99	0.00	0.91
FO	Hartford International Growth A	HNCAX	D-	(888) 843-7824	E+ / 0.6	6.24	0.49	10.88 /14	-0.42 /12	5.76 /27	1.09	1.51
FO	● Hartford International Growth B	HNCBX	D-	(888) 843-7824	E+ / 0.8	6.03	0.09	10.01 /12	-1.17 / 9	4.97 /21	0.00	2.63
FO	Hartford International Growth C	HNCCX	D-	(888) 843-7824	E+ / 0.8	6.02	0.07	10.01 /12	-1.17 / 9	4.98 /21	0.40	2.22
FO	Hartford International Growth I	HNCJX	D-	(888) 843-7824	D- / 1.1	6.29	0.67	11.16 /15	-0.08 /13	6.11 /29	1.47	1.09
FO	Hartford International Growth R3	HNCRX	D-	(888) 843-7824	E+ / 0.9	6.10	0.32	10.50 /13	-0.65 /11	5.59 /25	0.68	1.75
FO	Hartford International Growth R4	HNCSX	D-	(888) 843-7824	D- / 1.0	6.21	0.44	10.82 /14	-0.31 /12	5.91 /28	1.15	1.39
FO	Hartford International Growth R5	HNCTX	D-	(888) 843-7824	D- / 1.1	6.30	0.65	11.16 /15	-0.03 /13	6.22 /30	1.43	1.08
FO	Hartford International Growth Y	HNCYX	D	(888) 843-7824	D- / 1.5	6.34	0.63	11.28 /15	0.02 /13	6.28 /30	1.48	0.97
FO	Hartford International Value A	HILAX	C	(888) 843-7824	C / 5.3	7.81	11.00	30.52 /87	3.08 /33	9.01 /51	1.64	1.36
FO	Hartford International Value C	HILCX	C+	(888) 843-7824	C+ / 5.9	7.69	10.71	29.75 /86	2.42 /27	8.29 /45	1.11	2.02
FO	Hartford International Value I	HILIX	C+	(888) 843-7824	C+ / 6.8	7.97	11.21	31.04 /88	3.47 /37	9.43 /54	2.12	0.99
FO	Hartford International Value R3	HILRX	C+	(888) 843-7824	C+ / 6.2	7.73	10.82	30.21 /87	2.81 /30	8.76 /49	1.64	1.61
FO	Hartford International Value R4	HILSX	C+	(888) 843-7824	C+ / 6.5	7.83	11.01	30.58 /87	3.15 /33	9.09 /51	1.85	1.31
FO	Hartford International Value R5	HILTX	C+	(888) 843-7824	C+ / 6.7	7.94	11.24	31.01 /88	3.46 /37	9.42 /54	2.10	1.00
FO	Hartford International Value Y	HILYX	C+	(888) 843-7824	C+ / 6.8	7.96	11.29	31.23 /89	3.56 /38	9.85 /57	2.15	0.91
FO	Hartford Intl Opportunities A	IHOAX	D-	(888) 843-7824	D- / 1.5	6.56	3.98	14.25 /27	0.49 /16	5.10 /22	0.94	1.20
FO	● Hartford Intl Opportunities B	HIOBX	E+	(888) 843-7824	D- / 1.2	6.36	3.51	13.29 /23	-0.34 /12	4.25 /17	0.00	2.31

● Denotes fund is closed to new investors
* Denotes fund is included in Section II

www.thestreetratings.com

Risk Rating/Pts	3 Year Standard Deviation	Beta	NAV As of 2/28/17	Total $(Mil)	Cash %	Stocks %	Bonds %	Other %	Portfolio Turnover Ratio	Last Bull Market Return	Last Bear Market Return	Manager Quality Pct	Manager Tenure (Years)	Initial Purch. $	Additional Purch. $	Front End Load	Back End Load
C /4.4	12.7	0.67	8.93	29	20	66	12	2	115	-6.6	-20.1	2	7	5,000	50	0.0	0.0
C /4.5	12.7	0.68	8.99	N/A	20	66	12	2	115	-8.9	-20.3	1	7	0	0	0.0	0.0
C /4.4	12.7	0.68	8.96	1	20	66	12	2	115	-7.7	-20.2	1	7	0	0	0.0	0.0
C /4.4	12.6	0.67	8.94	N/A	20	66	12	2	115	-6.4	-20.1	2	7	0	0	0.0	0.0
C /4.4	12.7	0.67	8.94	257	20	66	12	2	115	-6.1	-20.1	2	7	250,000	0	0.0	0.0
D+ /2.8	9.2	1.37	11.14	508	6	80	12	2	98	61.1	-17.6	4	N/A	2,000	50	5.5	0.0
D+ /2.9	9.2	1.38	11.05	5	6	80	12	2	98	53.8	-17.9	3	N/A	0	0	0.0	0.0
D+ /2.8	9.2	1.38	10.97	151	6	80	12	2	98	54.9	-17.9	3	N/A	2,000	50	0.0	0.0
D+ /2.7	9.2	1.38	11.07	8	6	80	12	2	98	64.0	-17.5	5	N/A	2,000	50	0.0	0.0
D+ /2.7	9.2	1.37	10.88	12	6	80	12	2	98	58.4	-17.7	4	N/A	0	0	0.0	0.0
D+ /2.7	9.2	1.37	11.07	12	6	80	12	2	98	61.1	-17.6	4	N/A	0	0	0.0	0.0
D+ /2.7	9.2	1.37	11.14	5	6	80	12	2	98	63.8	-17.5	5	N/A	0	0	0.0	0.0
D+ /2.9	13.2	1.08	38.61	1,710	0	99	0	1	117	140.0	-23.1	37	16	2,000	50	5.5	0.0
D /1.7	13.2	1.08	25.79	2	0	99	0	1	117	129.2	-23.3	27	16	0	0	0.0	0.0
D /1.8	13.2	1.08	26.16	398	0	99	0	1	117	130.8	-23.3	29	16	2,000	50	0.0	0.0
C- /3.0	13.2	1.08	40.07	1,711	0	99	0	1	117	143.1	-22.9	41	16	0	0	0.0	0.0
D+ /2.9	13.2	1.08	38.90	48	0	99	0	1	117	136.3	-23.1	34	16	0	0	0.0	0.0
C- /3.1	13.2	1.08	40.57	69	0	99	0	1	117	140.2	-23.0	37	16	0	0	0.0	0.0
C- /3.1	13.2	1.08	41.99	11	0	99	0	1	117	144.1	-22.9	41	16	0	0	0.0	0.0
C- /3.2	13.2	1.08	42.47	237	0	99	0	1	117	145.3	-22.9	43	16	250,000	0	0.0	0.0
D /1.8	13.2	1.08	32.14	1,215	0	99	0	1	109	148.6	-22.9	46	16	0	0	0.0	0.0
D /1.7	13.2	1.07	30.96	139	0	99	0	1	109	145.2	-23.0	43	16	0	0	0.0	0.0
D /1.8	13.2	0.86	32.14	1,196	0	99	0	1	109	148.6	-22.9	99	16	0	0	0.0	0.0
D /1.7	13.2	0.86	30.96	139	0	99	0	1	109	145.2	-23.0	99	16	0	0	0.0	0.0
C /5.3	13.2	0.86	31.69	28	0	99	0	1	109	143.6	-23.0	76	16	0	0	0.0	0.0
C- /3.2	16.8	1.15	32.55	768	0	98	1	1	35	180.1	-12.9	43	17	2,000	50	5.5	0.0
D+ /2.9	16.8	1.15	26.97	1	0	98	1	1	35	167.5	-13.2	31	17	0	0	0.0	0.0
D+ /2.8	16.8	1.15	27.12	261	0	98	1	1	35	169.5	-13.2	33	17	2,000	50	0.0	0.0
E+ /0.9	17.1	1.17	24.10	272	1	98	0	1	38	191.9	-12.5	47	17	0	0	0.0	0.0
E+ /0.8	17.1	1.17	23.12	47	1	98	0	1	38	187.9	-12.6	43	17	0	0	0.0	0.0
C- /3.2	16.8	1.15	33.96	242	0	98	1	1	35	184.8	-12.8	47	17	2,000	50	0.0	0.0
C- /3.2	16.8	1.15	33.57	47	0	98	1	1	35	176.2	-13.0	38	17	0	0	0.0	0.0
C- /3.3	16.8	1.15	35.03	38	0	98	1	1	35	180.7	-12.9	43	17	0	0	0.0	0.0
C- /3.3	16.8	1.15	36.38	5	0	98	1	1	35	185.3	-12.8	47	17	0	0	0.0	0.0
C- /3.3	16.8	1.15	36.75	55	0	98	1	1	35	186.6	-12.7	49	17	250,000	0	0.0	0.0
C+ /6.1	10.8	0.80	12.29	103	1	97	0	2	89	52.1	-24.2	71	8	2,000	50	5.5	0.0
C+ /6.1	10.9	0.80	11.43	N/A	1	97	0	2	89	46.0	-24.4	61	8	0	0	0.0	0.0
C+ /6.1	10.8	0.80	11.36	14	1	97	0	2	89	46.1	-24.5	61	8	2,000	50	0.0	0.0
C+ /6.1	10.8	0.80	12.18	43	1	97	0	2	89	54.8	-24.1	74	8	2,000	50	0.0	0.0
C+ /6.1	10.8	0.80	12.43	1	1	97	0	2	89	50.6	-24.3	68	8	0	0	0.0	0.0
C+ /6.1	10.8	0.79	12.60	11	1	97	0	2	89	53.4	-24.2	72	8	0	0	0.0	0.0
C+ /6.1	10.9	0.80	12.69	6	1	97	0	2	89	55.7	-24.1	74	8	0	0	0.0	0.0
C+ /6.1	10.9	0.80	12.73	17	1	97	0	2	89	56.2	-24.0	75	8	250,000	0	0.0	0.0
C+ /5.9	12.7	0.98	15.36	370	6	93	0	1	32	78.5	-22.8	91	4	2,000	50	5.5	0.0
C+ /5.9	12.7	0.98	15.20	33	6	93	0	1	32	72.1	-22.9	89	4	2,000	50	0.0	0.0
C+ /5.9	12.7	0.98	15.50	957	6	93	0	1	32	82.1	-22.6	92	4	2,000	50	0.0	0.0
C+ /6.0	12.8	0.98	15.49	1	6	93	0	1	32	76.1	-22.8	90	4	0	0	0.0	0.0
C+ /6.0	12.7	0.98	15.45	2	6	93	0	1	32	79.2	-22.8	91	4	0	0	0.0	0.0
C+ /6.0	12.7	0.98	15.55	1	6	93	0	1	32	82.1	-22.6	92	4	0	0	0.0	0.0
C+ /5.9	12.7	0.98	15.80	469	6	93	0	1	32	85.8	-22.5	92	4	250,000	0	0.0	0.0
C /4.9	10.6	0.84	14.88	462	1	97	1	1	82	52.4	-23.2	78	17	2,000	50	5.5	0.0
C /4.8	10.7	0.84	13.55	1	1	97	1	1	82	45.9	-23.5	72	17	0	0	0.0	0.0

99 Pct = Best 0 Pct = Worst Fund Type	Fund Name	Ticker Symbol	Overall Investment Rating	Phone	PERFORMANCE Performance Rating/Pts	Total Return % through 2/28/17			Annualized		Incl. in Returns	
						3 Mo	6 Mo	1Yr / Pct	3Yr / Pct	5Yr / Pct	Dividend Yield	Expense Ratio
FO	Hartford Intl Opportunities C	HIOCX	E+	(888) 843-7824	D- / 1.3	6.30	3.54	13.34 /23	-0.24 /12	4.35 /17	0.44	1.93
FO	Hartford Intl Opportunities HLS IA		D+	(888) 843-7824	D+ / 2.5	6.67	4.25	15.07 /30	1.15 /19	5.93 /28	1.56	0.74
FO	Hartford Intl Opportunities HLS IB		D+	(888) 843-7824	D+ / 2.4	6.51	4.06	14.79 /29	0.89 /18	5.66 /26	1.25	0.99
FO	Hartford Intl Opportunities I	IHOIX	D-	(888) 843-7824	D+ / 2.3	6.66	4.15	14.65 /28	0.84 /17	5.48 /25	1.40	0.85
FO	Hartford Intl Opportunities R3	IHORX	D-	(888) 843-7824	D / 2.0	6.46	3.85	13.93 /25	0.26 /15	4.87 /20	0.85	1.45
FO	Hartford Intl Opportunities R4	IHOSX	D-	(888) 843-7824	D / 2.2	6.54	3.97	14.30 /27	0.54 /16	5.18 /23	1.08	1.15
FO	Hartford Intl Opportunities R5	IHOTX	D	(888) 843-7824	D+ / 2.4	6.64	4.16	14.66 /28	0.86 /17	5.50 /25	1.34	0.85
FO	Hartford Intl Opportunities R6	IHOVX	U	(888) 843-7824	U /	6.63	4.17	14.77 /29	--	--	1.42	0.86
FO	Hartford Intl Opportunities Y	HAOYX	D	(888) 843-7824	D+ / 2.4	6.70	4.24	14.76 /29	0.97 /18	5.62 /26	1.42	0.75
FO	Hartford Intl Opps HLS Fd IA	HIAOX	D+	(888) 843-7824	D+ / 2.5	6.67	4.25	15.07 /30	1.15 /19	5.93 /28	1.56	0.74
FO	Hartford Intl Opps HLS Fd IB	HBIOX	D+	(888) 843-7824	D+ / 2.4	6.51	4.06	14.79 /29	0.89 /18	5.66 /26	1.25	0.99
FO	● Hartford Intl Small Company A	HNSAX	E	(888) 843-7824	E+ / 0.7	8.33	3.62	12.16 /18	-1.03 / 9	7.67 /40	0.37	1.47
FO	● Hartford Intl Small Company B	HNSBX	E	(888) 843-7824	E+ / 0.8	8.14	3.19	11.22 /15	-1.76 / 7	6.86 /34	0.00	2.58
FO	● Hartford Intl Small Company C	HNSCX	E	(888) 843-7824	E+ / 0.8	8.21	3.19	11.38 /16	-1.73 / 7	6.90 /34	0.00	2.19
FO	● Hartford Intl Small Company I	HNSJX	E	(888) 843-7824	D- / 1.2	8.44	3.78	12.56 /20	-0.67 /11	8.07 /43	0.78	1.09
FO	● Hartford Intl Small Company R3	HNSRX	E	(888) 843-7824	D- / 1.0	8.32	3.49	11.95 /18	-1.19 / 9	7.52 /38	0.23	1.69
FO	● Hartford Intl Small Company R4	HNSSX	E	(888) 843-7824	D- / 1.1	8.39	3.66	12.25 /19	-0.89 /10	7.83 /41	0.59	1.39
FO	● Hartford Intl Small Company R5	HNSTX	E	(888) 843-7824	D- / 1.2	8.50	3.79	12.60 /20	-0.62 /11	8.15 /43	0.86	1.12
FO	● Hartford Intl Small Company Y	HNSYX	E	(888) 843-7824	D- / 1.2	8.56	3.86	12.75 /21	-0.54 /11	8.22 /44	0.92	0.99
GL	Hartford MidCap A	HFMCX	C+	(888) 843-7824	B- / 7.3	6.66	11.33	26.53 /78	7.87 /78	14.16 /94	0.00	1.16
GL	● Hartford MidCap B	HAMBX	C+	(888) 843-7824	B / 7.6	6.45	10.82	25.41 /75	6.90 /71	13.15 /85	0.00	2.05
GL	Hartford MidCap C	HMDCX	C+	(888) 843-7824	B / 7.8	6.49	10.93	25.67 /75	7.09 /73	13.34 /87	0.00	1.88
GL	Hartford MidCap HLS Fd IA	HIMCX	B-	(888) 843-7824	B+ / 8.7	6.78	11.69	27.39 /80	8.30 /81	14.74 /96	0.15	0.70
GL	Hartford MidCap HLS Fd IB	HBMCX	C+	(888) 843-7824	B+ / 8.5	6.74	11.54	27.09 /79	8.03 /79	14.45 /95	0.03	0.95
MC	Hartford MidCap HLS IA		B-	(888) 843-7824	B+ / 8.6	6.63	11.53	27.20 /80	8.24 /81	14.70 /96	0.03	0.70
MC	Hartford MidCap HLS IB		C+	(888) 843-7824	B+ / 8.5	6.74	11.54	27.09 /79	8.03 /79	14.45 /95	0.03	0.95
GL	Hartford MidCap I	HFMIX	B	(888) 843-7824	B+ / 8.5	6.75	11.40	26.75 /78	8.12 /80	14.43 /95	0.00	1.01
GL	Hartford MidCap R3	HFMRX	B-	(888) 843-7824	B / 8.1	6.60	11.16	26.15 /77	7.52 /76	13.82 /92	0.00	1.47
GL	Hartford MidCap R4	HFMSX	B	(888) 843-7824	B+ / 8.3	6.68	11.34	26.52 /78	7.86 /78	14.17 /94	0.00	1.17
GL	Hartford MidCap R5	HFMTX	B	(888) 843-7824	B+ / 8.6	6.75	11.50	26.93 /79	8.19 /80	14.52 /96	0.00	0.86
MC	Hartford MidCap R6	HFMVX	U	(888) 843-7824	U /	6.76	11.52	27.07 /79	--	--	0.00	0.76
MC	Hartford MidCap Value A	HMVAX	C-	(888) 843-7824	C+ / 6.3	4.72	10.45	27.50 /80	6.08 /65	12.62 /80	0.01	1.25
MC	● Hartford MidCap Value B	HMVBX	C-	(888) 843-7824	C+ / 6.6	4.50	9.92	26.41 /78	5.21 /57	11.69 /71	0.00	2.28
MC	Hartford MidCap Value C	HMVCX	C-	(888) 843-7824	C+ / 6.7	4.52	10.04	26.51 /78	5.33 /58	11.82 /73	0.00	1.97
GL	Hartford MidCap Value HLS IA		C	(888) 843-7824	B / 7.6	4.85	10.68	28.08 /82	6.59 /69	13.28 /87	0.48	0.84
GL	Hartford MidCap Value HLS IB		C-	(888) 843-7824	B- / 7.4	4.80	10.58	27.80 /81	6.32 /67	12.99 /84	0.21	1.09
MC	Hartford MidCap Value I	HMVJX	C+	(888) 843-7824	B- / 7.4	4.80	10.49	27.79 /81	6.42 /68	12.98 /83	0.30	0.92
MC	Hartford MidCap Value R3	HMVRX	C	(888) 843-7824	B- / 7.0	4.60	10.27	27.13 /79	5.80 /63	12.33 /77	0.00	1.52
MC	Hartford MidCap Value R4	HMVSX	C+	(888) 843-7824	B- / 7.2	4.76	10.50	27.54 /81	6.14 /65	12.68 /81	0.02	1.21
MC	Hartford MidCap Value R5	HMVTX	C+	(888) 843-7824	B- / 7.5	4.81	10.63	27.95 /82	6.47 /68	13.02 /84	0.29	0.92
MC	Hartford MidCap Value Y	HMVYX	C+	(888) 843-7824	B / 7.6	4.82	10.68	28.06 /82	6.58 /69	13.15 /85	0.36	0.81
GL	Hartford MidCap Y	HMDYX	B	(888) 843-7824	B+ / 8.6	6.77	11.52	27.03 /79	8.29 /81	14.63 /96	0.00	0.76
AA	Hartford Moderate Allocation A	HBAAX	D	(888) 843-7824	D / 1.7	4.78	4.50	14.09 /26	1.60 /22	3.88 /15	0.86	1.32
AA	● Hartford Moderate Allocation B	HBABX	D	(888) 843-7824	D / 1.9	4.55	3.97	12.94 /21	0.69 /17	2.99 /11	0.00	2.20
AA	Hartford Moderate Allocation C	HBACX	D	(888) 843-7824	D / 2.1	4.71	4.23	13.22 /22	0.88 /18	3.14 /11	0.15	2.06
AA	Hartford Moderate Allocation I	HBAIX	D+	(888) 843-7824	D+ / 2.7	4.91	4.72	14.41 /27	1.92 /23	4.21 /16	1.21	1.01
AA	Hartford Moderate Allocation R3	HBARX	D	(888) 843-7824	D+ / 2.3	4.81	4.42	13.71 /24	1.27 /20	3.55 /13	0.61	1.66
AA	Hartford Moderate Allocation R4	HBASX	D+	(888) 843-7824	D+ / 2.4	4.76	4.48	13.96 /25	1.55 /21	3.84 /14	0.88	1.36
AA	Hartford Moderate Allocation R5	HBATX	D+	(888) 843-7824	D+ / 2.6	4.89	4.60	14.27 /27	1.86 /23	4.15 /16	1.19	1.06
GI	Hartford Multi-Asset Income Y	HAFYX	U	(888) 843-7824	U /	4.69	3.65	14.77 /29	--	--	4.58	0.94
GL	Hartford Real Total Return A	HABMX	D-	(888) 843-7824	E- / 0.1	2.06	1.25	0.35 / 1	-4.28 / 3	--	0.00	1.51
GL	Hartford Real Total Return C	HABNX	E+	(888) 843-7824	E- / 0.1	1.88	0.81	-0.45 / 1	-5.00 / 2	--	0.00	2.27

● Denotes fund is closed to new investors
∗ Denotes fund is included in Section II

RISK			NET ASSETS		ASSET						BULL / BEAR		FUND MANAGER		MINIMUMS		LOADS	
	3 Year		NAV						Portfolio		Last Bull	Last Bear	Manager	Manager	Initial	Additional	Front	Back
Risk Rating/Pts	Standard Deviation	Beta	As of 2/28/17	Total $(Mil)	Cash %	Stocks %	Bonds %	Other %		Turnover Ratio	Market Return	Market Return	Quality Pct	Tenure (Years)	Purch. $	Purch. $	End Load	End Load
C / 4.7	10.6	0.84	13.11	52	1	97	1	1	82	46.5	-23.5	73	17	2,000	50	0.0	0.0
C+ / 6.5	10.8	0.85	14.71	1,119	1	97	0	2	68	58.7	-23.5	83	17	0	0	0.0	0.0
C+ / 6.5	10.8	0.86	14.88	150	1	97	0	2	68	56.5	-23.6	81	17	0	0	0.0	0.0
C / 4.9	10.6	0.84	14.79	366	1	97	1	1	82	55.3	-23.1	81	17	2,000	50	0.0	0.0
C / 5.0	10.5	0.84	15.12	62	1	97	1	1	82	50.5	-23.2	77	17	0	0	0.0	0.0
C / 5.0	10.6	0.84	15.36	147	1	97	1	1	82	53.0	-23.2	79	17	0	0	0.0	0.0
C / 5.0	10.6	0.84	15.49	149	1	97	1	1	82	55.6	-23.1	81	17	0	0	0.0	0.0
U /	N/A	N/A	15.56	51	1	97	1	1	82	N/A	N/A	N/A	17	0	0	0.0	0.0
C / 5.0	10.6	0.84	15.57	1,214	1	97	1	1	82	56.4	-23.0	82	17	250,000	0	0.0	0.0
C+ / 6.5	10.8	0.85	14.71	1,118	1	97	0	2	68	58.7	-23.5	83	17	0	0	0.0	0.0
C+ / 6.5	10.8	0.86	14.88	149	1	97	0	2	68	56.5	-23.6	81	17	0	0	0.0	0.0
C- / 3.6	11.8	0.84	14.24	57	1	97	0	2	43	65.7	-21.4	63	15	2,000	50	5.5	0.0
C- / 3.5	11.8	0.85	13.28	N/A	1	97	0	2	43	59.0	-21.7	53	15	0	0	0.0	0.0
C- / 3.3	11.8	0.84	12.92	11	1	97	0	2	43	59.3	-21.7	54	15	2,000	50	0.0	0.0
C- / 3.5	11.8	0.85	14.12	54	1	97	0	2	43	69.1	-21.3	68	15	2,000	50	0.0	0.0
C- / 3.6	11.7	0.84	14.35	8	1	97	0	2	43	64.2	-21.4	61	15	0	0	0.0	0.0
C- / 3.6	11.8	0.84	14.39	8	1	97	0	2	43	67.1	-21.4	65	15	0	0	0.0	0.0
C- / 3.6	11.8	0.84	14.46	2	1	97	0	2	43	69.6	-21.2	69	15	0	0	0.0	0.0
C- / 3.6	11.8	0.84	14.47	239	1	97	0	2	43	70.3	-21.3	69	15	250,000	0	0.0	0.0
C / 4.6	12.9	0.75	26.89	2,280	0	99	0	1	31	144.7	-25.6	98	13	2,000	50	5.5	0.0
C- / 3.8	12.9	0.75	19.46	13	0	99	0	1	31	133.3	-25.9	98	13	0	0	0.0	0.0
C- / 3.9	12.9	0.75	20.18	685	0	99	0	1	31	135.3	-25.8	98	13	2,000	50	0.0	0.0
C- / 3.9	13.0	0.76	35.89	1,825	0	99	0	1	38	151.0	-25.6	99	13	0	0	0.0	0.0
C- / 3.8	13.0	0.76	35.18	99	0	99	0	1	38	147.6	-25.7	98	13	0	0	0.0	0.0
C- / 3.9	13.0	1.03	35.89	1,773	0	99	0	1	38	150.6	-25.6	54	13	0	0	0.0	0.0
C- / 3.8	13.0	1.03	35.18	99	0	99	0	1	38	147.6	-25.7	52	13	0	0	0.0	0.0
C / 4.7	12.9	0.75	27.52	2,591	0	99	0	1	31	147.9	-25.6	98	13	2,000	50	0.0	0.0
C / 4.7	12.9	0.75	29.86	81	0	99	0	1	31	140.8	-25.7	98	13	0	0	0.0	0.0
C / 4.8	12.9	0.75	30.81	193	0	99	0	1	31	144.8	-25.6	98	13	0	0	0.0	0.0
C / 4.9	12.9	0.75	31.47	240	0	99	0	1	31	148.9	-25.5	98	13	0	0	0.0	0.0
U /	N/A	N/A	31.72	38	0	99	0	1	31	N/A	N/A	N/A	13	0	0	0.0	0.0
C- / 4.2	13.2	1.07	14.88	280	1	98	0	1	56	132.4	-25.6	24	16	2,000	50	5.5	0.0
C- / 3.7	13.2	1.07	12.51	1	1	98	0	1	56	122.2	-25.8	17	16	0	0	0.0	0.0
C- / 3.7	13.2	1.07	12.47	41	1	98	0	1	56	123.4	-25.8	18	16	2,000	50	0.0	0.0
D+ / 2.9	13.2	0.72	12.54	299	1	98	0	1	29	139.0	-25.2	97	16	0	0	0.0	0.0
C- / 3.0	13.2	0.72	12.44	92	1	98	0	1	29	135.8	-25.3	97	16	0	0	0.0	0.0
C- / 4.1	13.3	1.07	14.97	152	1	98	0	1	56	136.5	-25.5	27	16	2,000	50	0.0	0.0
C / 4.3	13.2	1.07	15.65	13	1	98	0	1	56	129.2	-25.6	22	16	0	0	0.0	0.0
C / 4.3	13.2	1.07	15.89	12	1	98	0	1	56	133.1	-25.5	25	16	0	0	0.0	0.0
C / 4.3	13.3	1.07	16.05	12	1	98	0	1	56	137.0	-25.4	28	16	0	0	0.0	0.0
C / 4.3	13.3	1.07	16.09	83	1	98	0	1	56	138.3	-25.4	29	16	250,000	0	0.0	0.0
C / 4.9	12.9	0.75	31.71	1,801	0	99	0	1	31	150.2	-25.5	99	13	250,000	0	0.0	0.0
C+ / 5.9	6.9	1.01	11.45	346	10	63	25	2	81	38.4	-13.0	10	N/A	2,000	50	5.5	0.0
C+ / 5.9	6.8	1.01	11.26	3	10	63	25	2	81	32.1	-13.3	7	N/A	0	0	0.0	0.0
C+ / 5.9	6.9	1.01	11.27	105	10	63	25	2	81	33.1	-13.3	7	N/A	2,000	50	0.0	0.0
C+ / 5.9	6.9	1.01	11.48	8	10	63	25	2	81	40.7	-12.9	12	N/A	2,000	50	0.0	0.0
C+ / 5.9	6.8	1.01	11.30	22	10	63	25	2	81	36.0	-13.1	9	N/A	0	0	0.0	0.0
C+ / 6.0	6.9	1.01	11.44	8	10	63	25	2	81	38.1	-13.0	10	N/A	0	0	0.0	0.0
C+ / 5.9	6.8	1.01	11.48	7	10	63	25	2	81	40.3	-12.9	12	N/A	0	0	0.0	0.0
U /	N/A	N/A	9.21	37	9	19	69	3	80	N/A	N/A	N/A	3	250,000	0	0.0	0.0
C+ / 6.1	6.4	0.18	8.91	1	38	42	18	2	239	N/A	N/A	20	4	5,000	50	5.5	0.0
C+ / 5.6	6.4	0.19	8.69	N/A	38	42	18	2	239	N/A	N/A	14	4	5,000	50	0.0	0.0

						PERFORMANCE							
	99 Pct = Best					Perfor-mance Rating/Pts	Total Return % through 2/28/17					Incl. in Returns	
	0 Pct = Worst									Annualized		Dividend	Expense
Fund Type	Fund Name	Ticker Symbol	Overall Investment Rating	Phone			3 Mo	6 Mo	1Yr / Pct	3Yr / Pct	5Yr / Pct	Yield	Ratio
GL	Hartford Real Total Return I	HABOX	D-	(888) 843-7824		E- / 0.2	2.04	1.35	0.68 / 2	-3.99 / 3	--	0.00	1.21
GL	Hartford Real Total Return R3	HABFX	E+	(888) 843-7824		E- / 0.2	1.97	1.03	0.01 / 1	-4.60 / 3	--	0.00	1.84
GL	Hartford Real Total Return R4	HABQX	D-	(888) 843-7824		E- / 0.2	2.06	1.25	0.35 / 1	-4.31 / 3	--	0.00	1.55
GL	Hartford Real Total Return R5	HABRX	D-	(888) 843-7824		E- / 0.2	2.16	1.47	0.68 / 2	-4.00 / 3	--	0.00	1.24
GL	Hartford Real Total Return Y	HABPX	D-	(888) 843-7824		E- / 0.2	2.15	1.35	0.68 / 2	-3.93 / 3	--	0.00	1.11
EM	Hartford Schroders Emg Mkt Eq A	SEMVX	D	(888) 843-7824		C- / 3.3	8.92	5.92	30.38 /87	1.07 /19	0.29 / 5	0.61	1.51
EM	Hartford Schroders Emg Mkt Eq I	SEMNX	C-	(888) 843-7824		C / 4.5	8.93	6.02	30.65 /87	1.30 /20	0.51 / 5	0.87	1.21
EM	Hartford Schroders Emg Mkt Eq SDR	SEMTX	U	(888) 843-7824		U /	9.04	6.13	30.89 /88	--	--	0.89	1.11
FS	Hartford Schroders Gl Strat Bd SDR	SGBJX	U	(888) 843-7824		U /	1.24	2.93	5.59 / 4	--	--	4.15	0.86
FO	Hartford Schroders Intl Alpha A	SCVEX	D-	(888) 843-7824		E / 0.5	6.79	2.38	12.70 /20	-0.93 /10	4.05 /15	1.31	1.35
FO	Hartford Schroders Intl Alpha I	SCIEX	D-	(888) 843-7824		E+ / 0.9	6.80	2.35	12.90 /21	-0.72 /10	4.30 /17	1.69	1.02
FO	Hartford Schroders Intl Alpha SDR	SCIJX	U	(888) 843-7824		U /	6.82	2.47	13.03 /22	--	--	1.71	0.86
FO	Hartford Schroders Itl MltCp VI A	SIDVX	D+	(888) 843-7824		D+ / 2.6	8.59	6.54	21.31 /59	0.94 /18	5.59 /25	1.66	1.32
FO	Hartford Schroders Itl MltCp VI I	SIDNX	D+	(888) 843-7824		C- / 3.4	8.70	6.70	21.52 /60	1.21 /19	5.89 /28	2.01	0.99
FO	Hartford Schroders Itl MltCp VI SDR	SIDRX	U	(888) 843-7824		U /	8.60	6.64	21.70 /61	--	--	2.13	0.85
SC	Hartford Schroders US SmCp Opps A	SCUVX	B-	(888) 843-7824		B+ / 8.3	5.83	12.10	30.63 /87	8.91 /86	12.95 /83	0.23	1.51
SC	Hartford Schroders US SmCp Opps I	SCUIX	B	(888) 843-7824		A- / 9.1	5.86	12.24	30.99 /88	9.20 /88	13.27 /86	0.35	1.18
MC	Hartford Schroders US SMdC Opps A	SMDVX	B-	(888) 843-7824		B+ / 8.8	6.20	10.51	27.49 /80	10.79 /97	13.73 /91	0.14	1.53
MC	Hartford Schroders US SMdC Opps I	SMDIX	B+	(888) 843-7824		A+ / 9.6	6.23	10.64	27.77 /81	11.09 /97	14.03 /93	0.23	1.20
MC	Hartford Small Cap Core A	HSMAX	C-	(888) 843-7824		C+ / 5.6	3.60	10.93	27.96 /82	5.07 /55	11.08 /67	0.74	1.48
MC	● Hartford Small Cap Core B	HSMBX	C-	(888) 843-7824		C+ / 6.1	3.44	10.47	26.95 /79	4.28 /46	10.25 /60	0.00	2.36
MC	Hartford Small Cap Core C	HTSCX	C-	(888) 843-7824		C+ / 6.1	3.41	10.55	27.05 /79	4.29 /46	10.25 /60	0.18	2.22
MC	Hartford Small Cap Core R3	HSMRX	C	(888) 843-7824		C+ / 6.6	3.56	10.69	27.64 /81	4.86 /53	10.85 /65	0.51	1.78
MC	Hartford Small Cap Core R4	HSMSX	C	(888) 843-7824		C+ / 6.8	3.64	10.91	28.16 /82	5.17 /56	11.19 /67	0.61	1.45
MC	Hartford Small Cap Core R5	HSMTX	C	(888) 843-7824		B- / 7.0	3.73	11.07	28.43 /83	5.46 /59	11.50 /70	1.06	1.14
MC	Hartford Small Cap Core Y	HSMYX	C	(888) 843-7824		B- / 7.0	3.73	11.14	28.58 /83	5.54 /60	11.55 /70	1.15	1.04
SC	Hartford Small Company A	IHSAX	E	(888) 843-7824		D+ / 2.8	5.46	8.78	26.91 /79	0.39 /15	8.76 /49	0.00	1.35
SC	● Hartford Small Company B	HSCBX	E-	(888) 843-7824		D / 2.0	5.25	8.35	25.88 /76	-0.39 /12	7.93 /41	0.00	2.31
SC	Hartford Small Company C	HSMCX	E-	(888) 843-7824		D / 2.0	5.26	8.46	25.93 /76	-0.33 /12	7.99 /42	0.00	2.05
GL	● Hartford Small Company HLS IA		E	(888) 843-7824		C- / 4.1	5.45	8.92	27.35 /80	0.74 /17	9.37 /54	0.00	0.72
GL	● Hartford Small Company HLS IB		E	(888) 843-7824		C- / 3.8	5.39	8.75	27.02 /79	0.48 /16	9.10 /51	0.00	0.97
SC	Hartford Small Company I	IHSIX	E	(888) 843-7824		C- / 4.0	5.51	8.88	27.19 /80	0.61 /16	9.01 /51	0.00	1.12
SC	Hartford Small Company R3	IHSRX	E	(888) 843-7824		C- / 3.6	5.42	8.72	26.63 /78	0.20 /14	8.56 /47	0.00	1.55
SC	Hartford Small Company R4	IHSSX	E	(888) 843-7824		C- / 3.9	5.53	8.90	27.05 /79	0.50 /16	8.90 /50	0.00	1.25
SC	Hartford Small Company R5	IHSUX	E+	(888) 843-7824		C- / 4.1	5.59	9.04	27.40 /80	0.80 /17	9.22 /52	0.00	0.98
SC	● Hartford Small Company Y	HSCYX	E+	(888) 843-7824		C- / 4.2	5.60	9.05	27.50 /80	0.89 /18	9.31 /53	0.00	0.86
GL	Hartford Small/Mid Cap Eq HLS Fd IB	HMCVX	D	(888) 843-7824		B- / 7.0	4.33	11.43	27.70 /81	5.59 /60	11.66 /71	0.94	1.21
GL	Hartford Small/Mid Cap Eqty HLS IA		D	(888) 843-7824		B- / 7.2	4.44	11.50	27.95 /82	5.84 /63	11.93 /74	1.25	0.96
GL	Hartford Small/Mid Cap Eqty HLS IB		D	(888) 843-7824		B- / 7.0	4.33	11.43	27.70 /81	5.59 /60	11.66 /71	0.94	1.21
SC	Hartford SmallCap Growth A	HSLAX	C	(888) 843-7824		C+ / 6.8	5.55	10.49	30.66 /87	6.20 /66	12.90 /83	0.00	1.22
SC	● Hartford SmallCap Growth B	HSLBX	C	(888) 843-7824		B- / 7.1	5.32	10.02	29.55 /85	5.32 /58	12.00 /74	0.00	2.21
SC	● Hartford SmallCap Growth C	HSLCX	C	(888) 843-7824		B- / 7.2	5.36	10.10	29.74 /86	5.45 /59	12.11 /75	0.00	1.92
GL	● Hartford SmallCap Growth HLS IA		C	(888) 843-7824		B / 8.0	5.60	10.70	31.07 /88	6.73 /70	13.35 /87	0.13	0.66
GL	● Hartford SmallCap Growth HLS IB		C-	(888) 843-7824		B / 7.9	5.54	10.59	30.82 /88	6.47 /68	13.07 /84	0.00	0.91
SC	● Hartford SmallCap Growth I	HSLIX	C+	(888) 843-7824		B / 7.9	5.60	10.66	31.00 /88	6.50 /68	13.23 /86	0.00	0.93
SC	● Hartford SmallCap Growth R3	HSLRX	C	(888) 843-7824		B- / 7.5	5.45	10.33	30.29 /87	5.91 /63	12.63 /80	0.00	1.49
SC	● Hartford SmallCap Growth R4	HSLSX	C+	(888) 843-7824		B / 7.7	5.53	10.50	30.72 /88	6.25 /66	12.98 /84	0.00	1.18
SC	● Hartford SmallCap Growth R5	HSLTX	C+	(888) 843-7824		B / 8.0	5.63	10.67	31.11 /88	6.57 /69	13.32 /87	0.00	0.88
SC	Hartford SmallCap Growth Y	HSLYX	C+	(888) 843-7824		B / 8.0	5.65	10.73	31.25 /89	6.68 /70	13.42 /88	0.00	0.78
GI	Hartford SMART529 Advisers 529 A		B	(888) 843-7824		C / 4.6	5.72	6.48	17.25 /39	6.10 /65	9.33 /53	0.00	1.85
GI	Hartford SMART529 Advisers 529 B		B+	(888) 843-7824		C / 5.2	5.52	6.16	16.61 /37	5.51 /60	8.72 /48	0.00	2.40
GI	Hartford SMART529 Advisers 529 C		B	(888) 843-7824		C / 5.1	5.50	6.10	16.42 /36	5.31 /58	8.52 /46	0.00	2.59

● Denotes fund is closed to new investors
* Denotes fund is included in Section II

Risk Rating/Pts	Standard Deviation (3 Year)	Beta	NAV As of 2/28/17	Total $(Mil)	Cash %	Stocks %	Bonds %	Other %	Portfolio Turnover Ratio	Last Bull Market Return	Last Bear Market Return	Manager Quality Pct	Manager Tenure (Years)	Initial Purch. $	Additional Purch. $	Front End Load	Back End Load
C+ / 6.5	6.5	0.19	9.00	N/A	38	42	18	2	239	N/A	N/A	22	4	5,000	50	0.0	0.0
C+ / 5.8	6.4	0.19	8.81	N/A	38	42	18	2	239	N/A	N/A	17	4	0	0	0.0	0.0
C+ / 6.2	6.5	0.19	8.90	N/A	38	42	18	2	239	N/A	N/A	19	4	0	0	0.0	0.0
C+ / 6.5	6.5	0.19	8.99	N/A	38	42	18	2	239	N/A	N/A	22	4	0	0	0.0	0.0
C+ / 6.7	6.5	0.19	9.01	105	38	42	18	2	239	N/A	N/A	23	4	250,000	0	0.0	0.0
C / 4.8	14.8	0.90	13.01	41	0	98	0	2	47	26.0	-27.3	69	11	2,000	50	5.5	2.0
C / 4.8	14.8	0.90	12.98	1,443	0	98	0	2	47	27.4	-27.2	71	11	250,000	1,000	0.0	2.0
U /	N/A	N/A	13.00	584	0	98	0	2	47	N/A	N/A	N/A	11	5,000,000	0	0.0	2.0
U /	N/A	N/A	8.93	69	0	0	100	0	140	N/A	N/A	N/A	1	5,000,000	0	0.0	0.0
C+ / 6.0	11.2	0.89	11.24	3	0	98	1	1	53	45.5	-27.2	65	7	2,000	50	5.5	2.0
C+ / 5.7	11.2	0.89	10.87	82	0	98	1	1	53	47.3	-27.1	67	7	250,000	1,000	0.0	2.0
U /	N/A	N/A	10.88	69	0	98	1	1	53	N/A	N/A	N/A	7	5,000,000	0	0.0	2.0
C+ / 5.8	11.2	0.87	9.14	22	2	95	1	2	94	51.1	-22.3	81	11	2,000	50	5.5	0.0
C+ / 5.8	11.2	0.86	9.13	323	2	95	1	2	94	53.2	-22.2	83	11	2,000	50	0.0	2.0
U /	N/A	N/A	9.12	258	2	95	1	2	94	N/A	N/A	N/A	11	5,000,000	0	0.0	2.0
C / 4.5	12.4	0.78	25.77	10	0	90	8	2	51	124.8	-23.0	91	2	2,000	50	5.5	0.0
C / 4.6	12.4	0.78	26.78	134	0	90	8	2	51	128.3	-22.9	92	2	2,000	50	0.0	2.0
C- / 4.1	10.4	0.84	13.14	83	0	89	10	1	72	133.9	-21.0	88	11	2,000	50	5.5	0.0
C / 4.3	10.3	0.84	13.63	385	0	89	10	1	72	137.2	-21.0	90	11	2,000	50	0.0	0.0
C / 4.3	14.5	1.15	13.23	54	0	99	0	1	94	108.3	-22.4	11	5	2,000	50	5.5	0.0
C- / 4.1	14.5	1.15	12.34	1	0	99	0	1	94	100.0	-22.6	7	5	0	0	0.0	0.0
C- / 4.1	14.5	1.15	12.15	12	0	99	0	1	94	100.2	-22.7	7	5	2,000	50	0.0	0.0
C / 4.3	14.5	1.15	13.60	1	0	99	0	1	94	106.0	-22.4	10	5	0	0	0.0	0.0
C / 4.3	14.5	1.15	13.68	N/A	0	99	0	1	94	109.5	-22.3	11	5	0	0	0.0	0.0
C / 4.3	14.5	1.15	13.66	N/A	0	99	0	1	94	112.7	-22.2	13	5	0	0	0.0	0.0
C / 4.3	14.5	1.15	13.69	105	0	99	0	1	94	113.2	-22.2	14	5	250,000	0	0.0	0.0
D- / 1.0	17.0	0.99	17.97	238	0	99	0	1	81	89.1	-24.9	8	18	2,000	50	5.5	0.0
E / 0.5	17.0	0.99	13.23	1	0	99	0	1	81	81.3	-25.1	5	18	0	0	0.0	0.0
E / 0.5	17.0	0.99	13.21	27	0	99	0	1	81	82.0	-25.1	6	18	2,000	50	0.0	0.0
E / 0.5	17.1	0.86	17.22	830	3	96	0	1	88	95.5	-24.5	80	18	0	0	0.0	0.0
E / 0.3	17.1	0.87	16.03	73	3	96	0	1	88	92.9	-24.6	78	18	0	0	0.0	0.0
D- / 1.1	17.0	0.99	18.76	65	0	99	0	1	81	91.5	-24.8	9	18	2,000	50	0.0	0.0
D- / 1.2	17.0	0.99	19.45	31	0	99	0	1	81	87.2	-25.0	7	18	0	0	0.0	0.0
D- / 1.3	17.0	0.99	20.43	29	0	99	0	1	81	90.3	-24.8	8	18	0	0	0.0	0.0
D- / 1.4	17.0	0.99	21.34	6	0	99	0	1	81	93.5	-24.7	10	18	0	0	0.0	0.0
D- / 1.5	17.0	0.99	21.70	70	0	99	0	1	81	94.3	-24.7	10	18	250,000	0	0.0	0.0
D- / 1.0	13.3	0.66	8.19	17	0	0	0	100	80	113.9	-22.4	96	5	0	0	0.0	0.0
D- / 1.0	13.4	0.66	8.24	88	0	0	0	100	80	116.7	-22.3	97	5	0	0	0.0	0.0
D- / 1.0	13.3	0.66	8.19	17	0	0	0	100	80	113.9	-22.4	96	5	0	0	0.0	0.0
C- / 3.8	15.8	0.98	51.15	215	0	98	1	1	45	134.4	-24.1	68	8	2,000	50	5.5	0.0
C- / 3.5	15.9	0.98	40.05	N/A	0	98	1	1	45	124.5	-24.3	57	8	0	0	0.0	0.0
C- / 3.5	15.8	0.97	39.76	40	0	98	1	1	45	125.6	-24.3	59	8	2,000	50	0.0	0.0
D+ / 2.4	15.7	0.74	27.93	992	0	99	0	1	59	139.7	-23.5	97	16	0	0	0.0	0.0
D+ / 2.3	15.7	0.74	27.25	233	0	99	0	1	59	136.5	-23.6	97	16	0	0	0.0	0.0
C- / 3.8	15.8	0.97	52.62	154	0	98	1	1	45	138.3	-24.0	71	8	0	0	0.0	0.0
C- / 3.7	15.8	0.98	50.94	14	0	98	1	1	45	131.4	-24.1	65	8	0	0	0.0	0.0
C- / 3.8	15.8	0.98	52.70	74	0	98	1	1	45	135.4	-24.1	69	8	0	0	0.0	0.0
C- / 3.8	15.8	0.98	54.63	112	0	98	1	1	45	139.2	-23.9	72	8	0	0	0.0	0.0
C- / 3.8	15.8	0.98	55.20	326	0	98	1	1	45	140.4	-23.9	73	8	250,000	0	0.0	0.0
B / 8.6	7.5	0.72	20.87	33	0	62	37	1	7	80.0	-13.9	57	15	250	25	5.5	0.0
B / 8.5	7.5	0.72	19.31	1	0	62	37	1	7	74.7	-14.1	49	15	250	25	0.0	0.0
B / 8.5	7.5	0.72	18.79	5	0	62	37	1	7	72.9	-14.2	47	15	250	25	0.0	0.0

Fund Type	Fund Name	Ticker Symbol	Overall Investment Rating	Phone	PERFORMANCE Performance Rating/Pts	3 Mo	6 Mo	1Yr / Pct	3Yr / Pct	5Yr / Pct	Dividend Yield	Expense Ratio
	99 Pct = Best 0 Pct = Worst							Total Return % through 2/28/17	Annualized		Incl. in Returns	
GI	Hartford SMART529 Advisers 529 E		B	(888) 843-7824	C+ / 6.0	5.73	6.61	17.56 /41	6.36 /67	9.60 /55	0.00	1.19
GR	Hartford SMART529 Age Bsd 0-8 A		C	(888) 843-7824	C- / 3.0	6.22	6.26	18.16 /44	3.02 /32	7.17 /36	0.00	1.85
GR	Hartford SMART529 Age Bsd 0-8 B		C	(888) 843-7824	C- / 3.5	6.05	5.95	17.47 /40	2.45 /27	6.58 /32	0.00	2.40
GR	Hartford SMART529 Age Bsd 0-8 C		C	(888) 843-7824	C- / 3.4	6.02	5.87	17.27 /40	2.26 /26	6.38 /31	0.00	2.59
GR	Hartford SMART529 Age Bsd 0-8 E		C+	(888) 843-7824	C- / 4.2	6.27	6.40	18.47 /45	3.28 /34	7.44 /38	0.00	1.19
BA	Hartford SMART529 Age Bsd 14-18		C-	(888) 843-7824	D / 1.7	4.35	4.41	13.41 /23	1.77 /22	4.39 /17	0.00	1.85
BA	Hartford SMART529 Age Bsd 14-18		C	(888) 843-7824	D / 2.1	4.14	4.09	12.74 /21	1.20 /19	3.80 /14	0.00	2.40
BA	Hartford SMART529 Age Bsd 14-18		C	(888) 843-7824	D / 2.0	4.14	4.03	12.58 /20	1.02 /18	3.62 /14	0.00	2.59
BA	Hartford SMART529 Age Bsd 14-18		C	(888) 843-7824	D+ / 2.6	4.38	4.54	13.68 /24	2.02 /24	4.64 /19	0.00	1.19
AA	Hartford SMART529 Age Bsd 19+ A		C	(888) 843-7824	E+ / 0.7	1.19	1.33	3.96 / 3	0.96 /18	1.76 / 8	0.00	1.85
AA	Hartford SMART529 Age Bsd 19+ B		C	(888) 843-7824	E+ / 0.9	1.06	1.06	3.41 / 3	0.41 /15	1.21 / 7	0.00	2.40
AA	Hartford SMART529 Age Bsd 19+ C		C	(888) 843-7824	E+ / 0.9	1.01	1.01	3.25 / 3	0.22 /14	1.01 / 6	0.00	2.59
AA	Hartford SMART529 Age Bsd 19+ E		C	(888) 843-7824	D- / 1.2	1.21	1.49	4.23 / 3	1.22 /19	2.02 / 8	0.00	1.19
AA	Hartford SMART529 Age Bsd 9-13 A		C-	(888) 843-7824	D / 2.1	5.16	5.37	15.72 /33	2.07 /24	5.44 /24	0.00	1.85
AA	Hartford SMART529 Age Bsd 9-13 B		C	(888) 843-7824	D+ / 2.6	5.03	5.09	15.13 /30	1.52 /21	4.86 /20	0.00	2.40
AA	Hartford SMART529 Age Bsd 9-13 C		C	(888) 843-7824	D+ / 2.5	5.00	5.00	14.90 /29	1.33 /20	4.66 /19	0.00	2.59
AA	Hartford SMART529 Age Bsd 9-13 E		C	(888) 843-7824	C- / 3.2	5.25	5.50	16.05 /35	2.33 /26	5.70 /26	0.00	1.19
GI	Hartford SMART529 Div & Gr 529 A		A+	(888) 843-7824	B / 8.2	7.58	11.58	26.08 /76	9.35 /89	12.69 /81	0.00	1.85
GI	Hartford SMART529 Div & Gr 529 B		A+	(888) 843-7824	B+ / 8.7	7.42	11.30	25.41 /75	8.75 /85	12.07 /75	0.00	2.40
GI	Hartford SMART529 Div & Gr 529 C		A+	(888) 843-7824	B+ / 8.6	7.34	11.18	25.11 /74	8.54 /83	11.86 /73	0.00	2.59
GI	Hartford SMART529 Div & Gr 529 E		A+	(888) 843-7824	A- / 9.2	7.60	11.73	26.36 /77	9.62 /91	12.97 /83	0.00	1.19
GL	Hartford SMART529 Glb Gr 529 A		C	(888) 843-7824	C- / 3.7	7.93	4.77	18.35 /44	4.14 /44	9.79 /57	0.00	1.85
GL	Hartford SMART529 Glb Gr 529 B		C+	(888) 843-7824	C / 4.3	7.81	4.52	17.75 /42	3.58 /38	9.19 /52	0.00	2.40
GL	Hartford SMART529 Glb Gr 529 C		C	(888) 843-7824	C- / 4.1	7.75	4.38	17.49 /41	3.38 /36	8.98 /50	0.00	2.59
GL	Hartford SMART529 Glb Gr 529 E		C+	(888) 843-7824	C / 5.0	8.01	4.87	18.62 /46	4.40 /47	10.06 /59	0.00	1.19
GR	Hartford SMART529 Gr Opp 529 A		C	(888) 843-7824	C+ / 6.1	6.54	3.87	19.92 /52	8.29 /81	14.24 /94	0.00	1.85
GR	Hartford SMART529 Gr Opp 529 B		C+	(888) 843-7824	C+ / 6.7	6.36	3.55	19.25 /48	7.68 /77	13.61 /90	0.00	2.40
GR	Hartford SMART529 Gr Opp 529 C		C+	(888) 843-7824	C+ / 6.5	6.33	3.52	19.09 /48	7.49 /75	13.40 /88	0.00	2.59
GR	Hartford SMART529 Gr Opp 529 E		C+	(888) 843-7824	B- / 7.2	6.55	4.00	20.23 /53	8.55 /83	14.53 /96	0.00	1.19
FO	Hartford SMART529 Intl Gr 529 A		D	(888) 843-7824	D- / 1.5	6.53	3.92	14.10 /26	0.46 /16	5.09 /22	0.00	1.85
FO	Hartford SMART529 Intl Gr 529 B		D	(888) 843-7824	D- / 1.3	6.38	3.62	13.49 /23	-0.09 /13	4.52 /18	0.00	2.40
FO	Hartford SMART529 Intl Gr 529 C		D	(888) 843-7824	D- / 1.3	6.39	3.59	13.39 /23	-0.27 /12	4.33 /17	0.00	2.59
FO	Hartford SMART529 Intl Gr 529 E		D+	(888) 843-7824	D+ / 2.3	6.57	4.02	14.42 /27	0.71 /17	5.35 /24	0.00	1.19
MC	Hartford SMART529 MidCap 529 A		B	(888) 843-7824	B- / 7.2	6.64	11.23	26.39 /77	7.74 /77	14.05 /94	0.00	1.85
MC	Hartford SMART529 MidCap 529 B		B+	(888) 843-7824	B / 7.8	6.50	10.94	25.71 /75	7.15 /73	13.43 /88	0.00	2.40
MC	Hartford SMART529 MidCap 529 C		B	(888) 843-7824	B / 7.7	6.44	10.82	25.46 /75	6.95 /72	13.21 /86	0.00	2.59
MC	Hartford SMART529 MidCap 529 E		B+	(888) 843-7824	B+ / 8.4	6.71	11.38	26.70 /78	8.01 /79	14.34 /95	0.00	1.19
SC	Hartford SMART529 Sm Com 529 A		E+	(888) 843-7824	D+ / 2.8	5.43	8.73	26.84 /79	0.38 /15	8.76 /49	0.00	1.85
SC	Hartford SMART529 Sm Com 529 B		E+	(888) 843-7824	D / 2.1	5.34	8.49	26.14 /77	-0.16 /13	8.17 /43	0.00	2.40
SC	Hartford SMART529 Sm Com 529 C		E+	(888) 843-7824	D / 2.0	5.25	8.39	25.92 /76	-0.36 /12	7.96 /42	0.00	2.59
SC	Hartford SMART529 Sm Com 529 E		D	(888) 843-7824	C- / 4.0	5.53	8.94	27.22 /80	0.64 /16	9.04 /51	0.00	1.19
GR	Hartford SMART529 Stable Val E		D-	(888) 843-7824	D- / 1.0	0.34	0.68	1.36 / 2	1.30 /20	1.52 / 7	0.00	1.17
AG	Hartford SMART529 Static Agg Gr A		C	(888) 843-7824	C- / 4.1	7.12	7.45	21.31 /59	3.87 /41	8.83 /49	0.00	1.85
AG	Hartford SMART529 Static Agg Gr B		C	(888) 843-7824	C / 4.7	6.96	7.16	20.67 /56	3.29 /35	8.23 /44	0.00	2.40
AG	Hartford SMART529 Static Agg Gr C		C	(888) 843-7824	C / 4.6	6.95	7.06	20.42 /54	3.10 /33	8.02 /42	0.00	2.59
AG	Hartford SMART529 Static Agg Gr E		C+	(888) 843-7824	C / 5.5	7.19	7.60	21.66 /61	4.13 /44	9.10 /51	0.00	1.19
BA	Hartford SMART529 Static Bal A		C-	(888) 843-7824	D / 2.2	5.15	5.36	15.76 /33	2.09 /25	5.45 /24	0.00	1.85
BA	Hartford SMART529 Static Bal B		C	(888) 843-7824	D+ / 2.6	5.06	5.12	15.12 /30	1.54 /21	4.88 /21	0.00	2.40
BA	Hartford SMART529 Static Bal C		C	(888) 843-7824	D+ / 2.5	4.97	4.97	14.89 /29	1.34 /20	4.68 /19	0.00	2.59
BA	Hartford SMART529 Static Bal E		C	(888) 843-7824	C- / 3.2	5.25	5.50	16.05 /35	2.35 /26	5.72 /26	0.00	1.19
GR	Hartford SMART529 Static Gr A		C	(888) 843-7824	C- / 3.0	6.18	6.28	18.17 /44	3.03 /32	7.19 /36	0.00	1.85
GR	Hartford SMART529 Static Gr B		C	(888) 843-7824	C- / 3.6	6.08	5.98	17.55 /41	2.47 /27	6.60 /32	0.00	2.40

● Denotes fund is closed to new investors
* Denotes fund is included in Section II

RISK	3 Year		NET ASSETS		ASSET				Portfolio Turnover Ratio	BULL / BEAR		FUND MANAGER		MINIMUMS		LOADS	
Risk Rating/Pts	Standard Deviation	Beta	NAV As of 2/28/17	Total $(Mil)	Cash %	Stocks %	Bonds %	Other %	Portfolio Turnover Ratio	Last Bull Market Return	Last Bear Market Return	Manager Quality Pct	Manager Tenure (Years)	Initial Purch. $	Additional Purch. $	Front End Load	Back End Load
B /8.6	7.5	0.72	21.76	2	0	62	37	1	7	82.4	-13.8	60	15	250	25	0.0	0.0
B- /7.6	8.8	0.80	24.60	90	10	78	11	1	59	68.0	-17.9	14	N/A	250	25	5.5	0.0
B- /7.5	8.8	0.80	22.79	4	10	78	11	1	59	63.1	-18.1	11	N/A	250	25	0.0	0.0
B- /7.5	8.8	0.79	22.20	20	10	78	11	1	59	61.4	-18.2	10	N/A	250	25	0.0	0.0
B- /7.6	8.8	0.80	25.59	5	10	78	11	1	59	70.3	-17.9	16	N/A	250	25	0.0	0.0
B /8.7	6.2	0.90	20.38	114	23	49	27	1	57	40.2	-11.0	17	N/A	250	25	5.5	0.0
B /8.6	6.2	0.90	18.85	7	23	49	27	1	57	36.0	-11.2	13	N/A	250	25	0.0	0.0
B /8.6	6.2	0.90	18.35	18	23	49	27	1	57	34.7	-11.3	12	N/A	250	25	0.0	0.0
B /8.8	6.2	0.90	21.19	9	23	49	27	1	57	42.1	-10.9	19	N/A	250	25	0.0	0.0
B+ /9.9	1.5	0.20	14.45	130	78	9	11	2	88	14.4	-2.9	67	N/A	250	25	4.5	0.0
B+ /9.9	1.5	0.21	13.36	7	78	9	11	2	88	11.1	-3.1	60	N/A	250	25	0.0	0.0
B+ /9.9	1.6	0.21	13.01	32	78	9	11	2	88	9.9	-3.2	57	N/A	250	25	0.0	0.0
B+ /9.9	1.5	0.21	15.03	8	78	9	11	2	88	16.0	-2.8	70	N/A	250	25	0.0	0.0
B /8.2	7.5	1.10	21.20	197	18	63	18	1	58	51.1	-14.6	9	N/A	250	25	5.5	0.0
B /8.1	7.5	1.10	19.63	18	18	63	18	1	58	46.7	-14.8	7	N/A	250	25	0.0	0.0
B /8.1	7.5	1.10	19.12	33	18	63	18	1	58	45.2	-14.9	7	N/A	250	25	0.0	0.0
B /8.2	7.5	1.10	22.05	15	18	63	18	1	58	53.2	-14.5	11	N/A	250	25	0.0	0.0
B- /7.6	10.4	0.99	29.68	160	3	96	0	1	4	118.4	-17.4	61	15	250	25	5.5	0.0
B- /7.6	10.4	0.99	27.49	9	3	96	0	1	4	111.9	-17.6	54	15	250	25	0.0	0.0
B- /7.5	10.4	0.99	26.76	32	3	96	0	1	4	109.8	-17.7	51	15	250	25	0.0	0.0
B- /7.6	10.4	0.99	30.87	20	3	96	0	1	4	121.3	-17.3	64	15	250	25	0.0	0.0
B- /7.2	10.6	0.80	22.19	10	1	98	0	1	7	91.8	-19.9	94	15	250	25	5.5	0.0
B- /7.1	10.6	0.80	20.56	N/A	1	98	0	1	7	86.3	-20.1	92	15	250	25	0.0	0.0
B- /7.1	10.6	0.80	20.02	3	1	98	0	1	7	84.3	-20.2	92	15	250	25	0.0	0.0
B- /7.2	10.6	0.80	23.06	2	1	98	0	1	7	94.4	-19.8	94	15	250	25	0.0	0.0
C /5.2	13.2	1.07	22.82	17	1	98	0	1	19	138.7	-23.0	36	N/A	250	25	5.5	0.0
C /5.2	13.2	1.08	21.56	1	1	98	0	1	19	131.6	-23.2	29	N/A	250	25	0.0	0.0
C /5.2	13.2	1.07	21.15	3	1	98	0	1	19	129.3	-23.3	27	N/A	250	25	0.0	0.0
C /5.2	13.2	1.08	23.42	3	1	98	0	1	19	141.9	-23.0	39	N/A	250	25	0.0	0.0
C+ /6.2	10.6	0.84	10.60	10	2	97	0	1	4	52.2	-23.2	78	N/A	250	25	5.5	0.0
C+ /6.2	10.6	0.84	10.01	N/A	2	97	0	1	4	47.8	-23.4	74	N/A	250	25	0.0	0.0
C+ /6.2	10.6	0.84	9.82	2	2	97	0	1	4	46.3	-23.4	73	N/A	250	25	0.0	0.0
C+ /6.2	10.6	0.84	10.87	2	2	97	0	1	4	54.3	-23.1	80	N/A	250	25	0.0	0.0
C+ /6.0	12.9	1.03	40.80	45	0	99	0	1	8	143.5	-25.6	49	15	250	25	5.5	0.0
C+ /6.0	12.9	1.03	37.84	2	0	99	0	1	8	136.4	-25.8	41	15	250	25	0.0	0.0
C+ /6.0	12.9	1.03	36.86	10	0	99	0	1	8	134.0	-25.9	38	15	250	25	0.0	0.0
C+ /6.0	12.9	1.03	42.47	10	0	99	0	1	8	146.9	-25.6	53	15	250	25	0.0	0.0
C- /3.3	17.0	0.99	18.43	6	3	95	0	2	7	89.1	-24.9	8	N/A	250	25	5.5	0.0
C- /3.3	17.0	0.99	17.37	N/A	3	95	0	2	7	83.6	-25.0	6	N/A	250	25	0.0	0.0
C- /3.3	17.0	0.99	17.05	1	3	95	0	2	7	81.7	-25.1	6	N/A	250	25	0.0	0.0
C- /3.3	17.0	0.99	18.88	1	3	95	0	2	7	91.7	-24.8	9	N/A	250	25	0.0	0.0
C+ /5.9	0.1	N/A	14.86	7	100	0	0	0	20	9.1	1.4	82	15	250	25	0.0	0.0
C+ /6.7	10.3	0.94	24.36	47	2	95	1	2	58	88.4	-22.9	10	N/A	250	25	5.5	0.0
C+ /6.7	10.3	0.94	22.59	4	2	95	1	2	58	82.8	-23.0	8	N/A	250	25	0.0	0.0
C+ /6.6	10.3	0.94	22.00	10	2	95	1	2	58	81.0	-23.1	7	N/A	250	25	0.0	0.0
C+ /6.7	10.3	0.94	25.33	11	2	95	1	2	58	91.0	-22.8	12	N/A	250	25	0.0	0.0
B /8.2	7.5	1.10	20.64	42	18	63	18	1	50	51.2	-14.7	9	N/A	250	25	5.5	0.0
B /8.1	7.5	1.10	19.11	2	18	63	18	1	50	46.8	-14.9	7	N/A	250	25	0.0	0.0
B /8.1	7.5	1.10	18.60	12	18	63	18	1	50	45.3	-14.9	6	N/A	250	25	0.0	0.0
B /8.2	7.5	1.10	21.47	3	18	63	18	1	50	53.3	-14.6	11	N/A	250	25	0.0	0.0
B- /7.6	8.8	0.79	23.35	70	10	78	11	1	55	68.2	-17.9	15	N/A	250	25	5.5	0.0
B- /7.5	8.8	0.80	21.63	3	10	78	11	1	55	63.3	-18.1	11	N/A	250	25	0.0	0.0

Fund Type	Fund Name	Ticker Symbol	Overall Investment Rating	Phone	Performance Rating/Pts	3 Mo	6 Mo	1Yr / Pct	3Yr / Pct	5Yr / Pct	Dividend Yield	Expense Ratio
GR	Hartford SMART529 Static Gr C		C	(888) 843-7824	C- / 3.4	5.99	5.88	17.33 /40	2.27 /26	6.40 /31	0.00	2.59
GR	Hartford SMART529 Static Gr E		C+	(888) 843-7824	C- / 4.2	6.26	6.40	18.45 /45	3.29 /35	7.45 /38	0.00	1.19
GR	Hartford SMART529 Stock 529 A		A	(888) 843-7824	B / 7.6	7.05	9.02	24.76 /72	9.03 /87	12.44 /78	0.00	1.85
GR	Hartford SMART529 Stock 529 B		A+	(888) 843-7824	B / 8.1	6.90	8.70	24.03 /70	8.43 /82	11.82 /73	0.00	2.40
GR	Hartford SMART529 Stock 529 C		A+	(888) 843-7824	B / 7.9	6.83	8.61	23.80 /69	8.22 /81	11.61 /71	0.00	2.59
GR	Hartford SMART529 Stock 529 E		A+	(888) 843-7824	B+ / 8.7	7.14	9.13	25.04 /73	9.30 /89	12.72 /81	0.00	1.19
GL	Hartford Stock HLS IA		B-	(888) 843-7824	C+ / 6.4	5.07	3.47	14.38 /27	8.46 /83	12.00 /74	0.14	0.51
GL	Hartford Stock HLS IB		B-	(888) 843-7824	C+ / 6.3	5.27	3.60	14.39 /27	8.28 /81	11.78 /72	0.14	0.76
GI	Hartford Value HLS Fd IA	HIAVX	B+	(888) 843-7824	B+ / 8.3	6.58	9.24	26.33 /77	8.42 /82	12.48 /79	1.46	0.78
GI	Hartford Value HLS Fd IB	HBVLX	B+	(888) 843-7824	B / 8.1	6.54	9.14	26.00 /76	8.13 /80	12.20 /76	1.25	1.03
GR	Hartford Value HLS IA		B+	(888) 843-7824	B+ / 8.3	6.58	9.24	26.33 /77	8.42 /82	12.48 /79	1.46	0.78
GR	Hartford Value HLS IB		B+	(888) 843-7824	B / 8.1	6.54	9.14	26.00 /76	8.13 /80	12.20 /76	1.25	1.03
GR	Hartford Value Opportunities A	HVOAX	C+	(888) 843-7824	B- / 7.2	4.79	11.03	32.16 /90	6.74 /70	11.83 /73	0.65	1.21
GR	● Hartford Value Opportunities B	HVOBX	C+	(888) 843-7824	B- / 7.5	4.57	10.49	30.99 /88	5.89 /63	10.95 /65	0.00	2.28
GR	Hartford Value Opportunities C	HVOCX	C+	(888) 843-7824	B- / 7.5	4.58	10.57	31.18 /88	5.96 /64	11.02 /66	0.18	1.93
GR	Hartford Value Opportunities I	HVOIX	B-	(888) 843-7824	B+ / 8.4	4.90	11.15	32.59 /91	7.11 /73	12.19 /76	1.04	0.88
GR	Hartford Value Opportunities R3	HVORX	B-	(888) 843-7824	B / 7.9	4.69	10.79	31.67 /89	6.43 /68	11.54 /70	0.39	1.52
GR	Hartford Value Opportunities R4	HVOSX	B-	(888) 843-7824	B / 8.2	4.84	11.00	32.16 /90	6.79 /70	11.91 /73	0.67	1.19
GR	Hartford Value Opportunities R5	HVOTX	B	(888) 843-7824	B+ / 8.4	4.91	11.20	32.54 /91	7.10 /73	12.22 /76	0.96	0.90
GR	Hartford Value Opportunities Y	HVOYX	B	(888) 843-7824	B+ / 8.4	4.90	11.23	32.66 /91	7.19 /73	12.28 /77	1.06	0.79
GR	Hatteras Alpha Hedged Strat A	APHAX	D+	(877) 569-2382	E / 0.3	3.54	2.85	5.88 / 5	-2.56 / 5	0.18 / 5	1.37	5.22
AA	Hatteras Alpha Hedged Strat C	APHCX	D+	(877) 569-2382	E / 0.3	3.35	2.52	5.16 / 4	-3.27 / 4	-0.56 / 4	0.00	5.97
GR	Hatteras Alpha Hedged Strat Inst	ALPIX	D+	(877) 569-2382	E / 0.5	3.62	3.04	6.31 / 5	-2.12 / 6	0.85 / 6	1.03	4.22
GR	Hatteras Disciplined Oppty Inst	HDOIX	C-		C- / 4.0	2.90	4.76	13.06 /22	5.16 /56	--	0.00	2.37
GL	Hatteras Long/Short Debt A	HFIAX	D-	(877) 569-2382	E- / 0.1	1.50	2.68	3.39 / 3	-5.17 / 2	-1.55 / 3	7.95	3.83
FS	Hatteras Long/Short Debt C	HFICX	C-	(877) 569-2382	E- / 0.1	1.31	2.41	2.82 / 3	-5.85 / 2	--	7.40	4.58
GL	Hatteras Long/Short Debt Inst	HFINX	D-	(877) 569-2382	E- / 0.2	1.56	2.91	4.12 / 3	-4.67 / 3	-1.03 / 3	8.52	3.33
IN	Hatteras Long/Short Equity A	HLSAX	D-	(877) 569-2382	E / 0.5	3.70	3.95	5.92 / 5	-0.82 /10	1.54 / 7	0.00	4.42
IN	Hatteras Long/Short Equity Inst	HLSIX	D-	(877) 569-2382	E+ / 0.9	3.75	4.11	6.30 / 5	-0.42 /12	1.98 / 8	0.00	3.92
IN	Hatteras Managed Futures Strat Inst	HMFIX	C-	(877) 569-2382	E+ / 0.6	4.51	-0.78	0.83 / 2	-0.66 /11	--	0.67	2.94
GR	Haverford Quality Gr Stk Fd	HAVGX	C+	(800) 307-4880	C+ / 6.8	7.02	7.52	18.43 /45	7.32 /74	10.28 /60	1.12	0.83
AA	HC Catholic SRI Growth Strategic	HCSRX	U	(800) 242-9596	U /	7.39	6.77	20.68 /56	--	--	2.85	N/A
GR	HC ESG Growth HC Strategic	HCESX	U	(800) 242-9596	U /	7.75	6.15	19.68 /50	--	--	2.69	0.31
IN	HCM Dividend Sector Plus A	HCMNX	U	(855) 959-8464	U /	7.80	17.13	40.90 /97	--	--	1.41	2.25
GR	HCM Tactical Growth Fund A	HCMGX	U	(855) 959-8464	U /	12.32	17.80	35.28 /94	--	--	0.00	2.75
GL	Heartland International Value	HINVX	D+	(800) 432-7856	C / 4.4	10.62	9.76	29.60 /85	0.20 /14	4.06 /15	1.38	1.81
GR	Heartland Select Value Inst	HNSVX	B	(800) 432-7856	B+ / 8.9	5.96	14.24	30.80 /88	7.71 /77	11.63 /71	1.23	0.94
GR	Heartland Select Value Inv	HRSVX	B	(800) 432-7856	B+ / 8.7	5.89	14.13	30.46 /87	7.43 /75	11.31 /68	1.00	1.20
SC	Heartland Value Inst	HNTVX	D-	(800) 432-7856	C- / 3.7	2.94	8.87	26.32 /77	0.92 /18	8.03 /42	0.00	0.91
SC	Heartland Value Inv	HRTVX	D-	(800) 432-7856	C- / 3.6	2.87	8.78	26.11 /77	0.75 /17	7.85 /41	0.00	1.06
GI	● Heartland Value Plus Inst	HNVIX	D+	(800) 432-7856	C+ / 6.5	4.01	18.43	37.68 /96	1.04 /18	7.68 /40	0.75	0.90
GI	● Heartland Value Plus Inv	HRVIX	D+	(800) 432-7856	C+ / 6.4	3.96	18.31	37.57 /96	0.83 /17	7.43 /38	0.65	1.16
GL	Henderson All Asset A	HGAAX	C-	(866) 443-6337	D- / 1.5	3.92	3.10	10.06 /12	2.07 /24	--	0.39	1.40
GL	Henderson All Asset C	HGACX	C-	(866) 443-6337	D / 1.7	3.66	2.72	9.10 /10	1.26 /20	--	0.00	2.16
GL	Henderson All Asset I	HGAIX	C	(866) 443-6337	D / 2.2	3.91	3.19	10.16 /12	2.31 /26	--	0.68	1.13
GL	Henderson All Asset R6	HGARX	U	(866) 443-6337	U /	3.95	3.23	10.21 /12	--	--	0.81	1.09
GL	Henderson Dividend and Inc Bldr A	HDAVX	D+	(866) 443-6337	D / 2.0	6.34	2.79	11.85 /17	2.49 /27	--	2.65	1.28
GL	Henderson Dividend and Inc Bldr C	HDCVX	D+	(866) 443-6337	D / 2.2	6.24	2.46	11.07 /15	1.72 /22	--	2.13	2.05
GL	Henderson Dividend and Inc Bldr I	HDIVX	C-	(866) 443-6337	D+ / 2.8	6.41	2.85	12.12 /18	2.73 /29	--	3.02	1.05
EM	Henderson Emerging Markets A	HEMAX	D+	(866) 443-6337	C- / 3.6	9.27	5.24	24.45 /71	2.38 /27	0.68 / 6	0.62	2.37
EM	Henderson Emerging Markets C	HEMCX	D+	(866) 443-6337	C- / 4.1	9.11	4.82	23.55 /68	1.62 /22	-0.07 / 4	0.16	3.17
EM	Henderson Emerging Markets I	HEMIX	C-	(866) 443-6337	C / 5.0	9.39	5.37	24.84 /73	2.66 /29	0.94 / 6	0.80	2.10

● Denotes fund is closed to new investors
* Denotes fund is included in Section II

www.thestreetratings.com

Risk Rating/Pts	3 Year Standard Deviation	Beta	NAV As of 2/28/17	Total $(Mil)	Cash %	Stocks %	Bonds %	Other %	Portfolio Turnover Ratio	Last Bull Market Return	Last Bear Market Return	Manager Quality Pct	Manager Tenure (Years)	Initial Purch. $	Additional Purch. $	Front End Load	Back End Load
B- /7.5	8.8	0.80	21.06	15	10	78	11	1	55	61.6	-18.2	10	N/A	250	25	0.0	0.0
B- /7.6	8.8	0.79	24.27	5	10	78	11	1	55	70.5	-17.9	16	N/A	250	25	0.0	0.0
B- /7.8	9.9	0.93	23.08	26	2	97	0	1	8	116.5	-14.1	66	15	250	25	5.5	0.0
B- /7.7	9.9	0.93	21.37	1	2	97	0	1	8	110.1	-14.3	59	15	250	25	0.0	0.0
B- /7.7	9.9	0.93	20.81	6	2	97	0	1	8	108.0	-14.4	56	15	250	25	0.0	0.0
B- /7.8	9.9	0.93	24.02	4	2	97	0	1	8	119.4	-14.0	69	15	250	25	0.0	0.0
B- /7.6	9.3	0.52	71.34	1,312	2	97	0	1	23	118.4	-19.4	99	5	0	0	0.0	0.0
B- /7.6	9.3	0.52	71.29	141	2	97	0	1	23	116.0	-19.5	98	5	0	0	0.0	0.0
C+ /6.0	11.3	1.06	15.90	453	0	98	0	2	19	124.4	-20.5	39	16	0	0	0.0	0.0
C+ /6.0	11.3	1.06	15.88	79	0	98	0	2	19	121.5	-20.6	36	16	0	0	0.0	0.0
C+ /6.0	11.3	1.06	15.90	453	0	98	0	2	19	124.4	-20.5	39	16	0	0	0.0	0.0
C+ /6.0	11.3	1.06	15.88	79	0	98	0	2	19	121.5	-20.6	36	16	0	0	0.0	0.0
C /4.6	12.7	1.13	19.85	198	0	98	0	2	41	117.0	-22.1	16	21	2,000	50	5.5	0.0
C /4.5	12.7	1.13	17.43	1	0	98	0	2	41	108.1	-22.4	10	21	0	0	0.0	0.0
C /4.4	12.7	1.13	17.20	24	0	98	0	2	41	108.5	-22.4	11	21	2,000	50	0.0	0.0
C /4.6	12.7	1.13	19.58	26	0	98	0	2	41	120.7	-22.0	19	21	0	0	0.0	0.0
C /4.7	12.6	1.13	20.10	2	0	98	0	2	41	114.0	-22.2	14	21	0	0	0.0	0.0
C /4.7	12.6	1.13	20.30	10	0	98	0	2	41	117.9	-22.1	16	21	0	0	0.0	0.0
C /4.7	12.6	1.13	20.43	N/A	0	98	0	2	41	121.3	-22.0	19	21	0	0	0.0	0.0
C /4.6	12.6	1.13	20.48	1	0	98	0	2	41	121.7	-22.0	19	21	250,000	0	0.0	0.0
B /8.5	4.9	0.38	10.62	12	89	10	0	1	30	5.4	N/A	7	N/A	1,000	250	4.8	0.0
B /8.3	5.0	0.63	10.19	9	89	10	0	1	30	1.3	-5.4	4	N/A	1,000	250	0.0	0.0
B /8.5	5.0	0.39	10.95	42	89	10	0	1	30	12.5	N/A	8	N/A	1,000,000	0	0.0	0.0
C+ /6.0	6.1	0.57	10.65	35	0	0	0	100	75	N/A	N/A	64	N/A	1,000,000	0	0.0	0.0
C+ /6.6	4.4	0.29	7.23	6	100	0	0	0	6	-3.7	N/A	6	6	1,000	250	4.8	0.0
B+ /9.9	4.5	0.16	7.19	3	100	0	0	0	6	N/A	N/A	4	6	1,000	250	0.0	0.0
C+ /6.7	4.4	0.29	7.45	10	100	0	0	0	6	-1.0	N/A	8	6	1,000,000	0	0.0	0.0
C+ /6.4	7.2	0.47	8.87	2	100	0	0	0	42	16.5	N/A	11	6	1,000	250	4.8	0.0
C+ /6.3	7.2	0.47	9.04	11	100	0	0	0	42	19.2	N/A	13	6	1,000,000	0	0.0	0.0
B+ /9.3	6.2	-0.07	7.39	25	1	98	0	1	18	N/A	N/A	73	N/A	1,000,000	0	0.0	0.0
C+ /6.8	10.6	0.99	15.42	184	0	99	0	1	15	98.5	-17.1	36	13	2,500	0	0.0	0.0
U /	N/A	N/A	11.61	27	0	0	0	100	0	N/A	N/A	N/A	1	0	0	0.0	0.0
U /	N/A	N/A	10.25	139	1	98	0	1	36	N/A	N/A	N/A	2	0	0	0.0	0.0
U /	N/A	N/A	12.81	166	2	97	0	1	163	N/A	N/A	N/A	2	2,500	500	5.8	1.0
U /	N/A	N/A	11.12	42	11	88	0	1	238	N/A	N/A	N/A	3	2,500	250	5.8	1.0
C- /4.2	14.2	0.94	9.82	27	4	96	0	0	62	31.0	-20.0	77	4	1,000	100	0.0	2.0
C /4.3	12.6	1.02	29.24	43	0	99	0	1	40	109.4	-21.9	36	13	500,000	100	0.0	0.0
C /4.3	12.6	1.02	29.31	222	0	99	0	1	40	106.1	-22.0	33	13	1,000	100	0.0	0.0
C- /3.4	15.6	0.89	40.73	67	3	96	0	1	52	76.0	-24.1	15	33	500,000	100	0.0	0.0
C- /3.4	15.6	0.89	39.98	740	3	96	0	1	52	74.5	-24.1	13	33	1,000	100	0.0	0.0
D+ /2.6	18.2	1.21	30.27	90	0	99	0	1	22	79.8	-25.0	1	11	500,000	100	0.0	0.0
D+ /2.6	18.2	1.21	30.40	409	0	99	0	1	22	77.5	-25.1	1	11	1,000	100	0.0	0.0
B /8.6	4.8	0.72	10.40	4	38	34	25	3	44	N/A	N/A	59	5	500	0	5.8	0.0
B /8.6	4.8	0.71	10.19	8	38	34	25	3	44	N/A	N/A	48	5	500	0	0.0	0.0
B /8.5	4.7	0.71	10.36	8	38	34	25	3	44	N/A	N/A	62	5	0	0	0.0	0.0
U /	N/A	N/A	10.34	30	38	34	25	3	44	N/A	N/A	N/A	5	0	0	0.0	0.0
C+ /6.9	8.7	0.67	12.35	26	2	84	13	1	39	N/A	N/A	88	5	500	0	5.0	0.0
C+ /6.9	8.7	0.67	12.23	34	2	84	13	1	39	N/A	N/A	85	5	500	0	0.0	0.0
C+ /6.9	8.7	0.67	12.35	69	2	84	13	1	39	N/A	N/A	89	5	0	0	0.0	0.0
C /5.2	13.8	0.80	9.34	14	3	96	0	1	86	34.5	-28.8	81	2	500	0	5.8	0.0
C /5.1	13.8	0.80	9.04	6	3	96	0	1	86	29.3	-29.0	76	2	500	0	0.0	0.0
C /5.2	13.9	0.80	9.38	61	3	96	0	1	86	36.6	-28.7	82	2	0	0	0.0	0.0

Fund Type	Fund Name	Ticker Symbol	Overall Investment Rating	Phone	Performance Rating/Pts	3 Mo	6 Mo	1Yr / Pct	3Yr / Pct	5Yr / Pct	Dividend Yield	Expense Ratio
	99 Pct = Best				PERFORMANCE			Total Return % through 2/28/17			Incl. in Returns	
	0 Pct = Worst								Annualized			
FO	Henderson European Focus A	HFEAX	E+	(866) 443-6337	E- / 0.2	7.72	-0.85	5.23 / 4	-3.82 / 3	4.43 / 18	2.40	1.29
FO	Henderson European Focus C	HFECX	E+	(866) 443-6337	E- / 0.2	7.49	-1.25	4.37 / 3	-4.58 / 3	3.61 / 13	1.77	2.08
FO	Henderson European Focus I	HFEIX	E+	(866) 443-6337	E / 0.3	7.80	-0.74	5.48 / 4	-3.59 / 4	4.71 / 19	3.10	1.05
GL	Henderson Global Equity Income A	HFQAX	D	(866) 443-6337	D / 1.6	7.07	3.03	12.04 / 18	1.47 / 21	6.62 / 32	6.20	1.17
GL	Henderson Global Equity Income C	HFQCX	D+	(866) 443-6337	D / 1.9	6.91	2.66	11.27 / 15	0.71 / 17	5.82 / 27	5.88	1.93
GL	Henderson Global Equity Income I	HFQIX	D+	(866) 443-6337	D+ / 2.5	7.11	3.16	12.46 / 20	1.71 / 22	6.90 / 34	6.81	0.92
TC	Henderson Global Technology A	HFGAX	B-	(866) 443-6337	B+ / 8.8	12.04	11.53	30.73 / 88	8.60 / 84	11.19 / 67	0.00	1.35
TC	Henderson Global Technology C	HFGCX	B-	(866) 443-6337	A- / 9.1	11.79	11.10	29.76 / 86	7.77 / 77	10.34 / 61	0.00	2.12
TC	Henderson Global Technology I	HFGIX	B	(866) 443-6337	A+ / 9.6	12.11	11.71	31.08 / 88	8.87 / 86	11.48 / 70	0.00	1.11
FO	Henderson Internatl Oppty A	HFOAX	D-	(866) 443-6337	E+ / 0.6	6.20	0.54	10.70 / 13	-0.36 / 12	5.91 / 28	1.41	1.36
FO	Henderson Internatl Oppty C	HFOCX	D-	(866) 443-6337	E+ / 0.8	5.94	0.10	9.83 / 11	-1.13 / 9	5.09 / 22	0.86	2.12
FO	Henderson Internatl Oppty I	HFOIX	D	(866) 443-6337	D- / 1.1	6.23	0.65	11.01 / 14	-0.09 / 13	6.20 / 30	1.91	1.07
FO	Henderson Internatl Oppty IF	HFITX	U	(866) 443-6337	U /	6.25	0.68	--	--	--	0.00	1.05
FO	Henderson Internatl Oppty R	HFORX	D-	(866) 443-6337	E+ / 0.9	6.11	0.34	10.28 / 12	-0.66 / 11	5.57 / 25	1.48	1.68
BA	Hennessy Balanced Investor	HBFBX	C+	(800) 966-4354	C- / 3.6	3.06	4.35	12.23 / 19	4.72 / 51	5.48 / 25	0.34	1.68
SC	Hennessy Cornerstone Growth Inst	HICGX	C	(800) 966-4354	C / 4.4	-0.57	4.05	12.92 / 21	6.68 / 70	13.17 / 86	0.00	1.00
SC	Hennessy Cornerstone Growth Inv	HFCGX	C	(800) 966-4354	C- / 4.1	-0.68	3.85	12.50 / 20	6.39 / 67	12.84 / 82	0.00	1.31
GR	Hennessy Cornerstone Large Gro	HILGX	C-	(800) 966-4354	B / 7.7	3.43	12.80	19.81 / 51	8.54 / 83	11.99 / 74	1.30	0.99
GR	Hennessy Cornerstone Large Gro Inv	HFLGX	C-	(800) 966-4354	B- / 7.5	3.23	12.56	19.37 / 49	8.31 / 81	11.74 / 72	1.10	1.24
MC	Hennessy Cornerstone Mid Cap 30	HIMDX	C+	(800) 966-4354	C+ / 6.6	4.50	9.09	14.23 / 27	7.90 / 78	13.37 / 88	0.00	0.97
MC	Hennessy Cornerstone Mid Cap 30	HFMDX	C+	(800) 966-4354	C+ / 6.3	4.44	8.91	13.78 / 24	7.59 / 76	13.00 / 84	0.00	1.33
GL	Hennessy Cornerstone Val Investor	HFCVX	B+	(800) 966-4354	B / 7.8	5.87	9.99	25.31 / 74	7.56 / 76	10.96 / 65	2.17	1.25
GL	Hennessy Cornerstone Value Inst	HICVX	A-	(800) 966-4354	B / 7.9	5.91	10.08	25.68 / 75	7.73 / 77	11.18 / 67	2.46	1.00
BA	Hennessy Equity and Income Inst	HEIIX	B-	(800) 966-4354	C / 5.2	5.45	5.70	14.04 / 26	6.10 / 65	7.82 / 41	1.20	1.09
BA	Hennessy Equity and Income Investor	HEIFX	C+	(800) 966-4354	C / 4.8	5.37	5.49	13.55 / 24	5.72 / 62	7.49 / 38	0.74	1.43
SC	Hennessy Focus Institutional	HFCIX	B+	(800) 966-4354	B- / 7.1	5.85	6.27	17.32 / 40	8.75 / 85	14.23 / 94	0.00	1.12
SC	Hennessy Focus Investor	HFCSX	C+	(800) 966-4354	C+ / 6.9	5.75	6.05	16.88 / 38	8.36 / 82	13.85 / 92	0.00	1.47
EN	Hennessy Gas Utility Investor	GASFX	B-	(800) 966-4354	B- / 7.1	7.71	6.81	21.22 / 58	7.30 / 74	11.66 / 71	1.99	1.02
FO	Hennessy Japan Fund Institutional	HJPIX	A+	(800) 966-4354	A- / 9.2	4.79	5.25	21.21 / 58	12.52 / 98	13.50 / 89	0.00	1.08
FO	Hennessy Japan Fund Investor	HJPNX	A+	(800) 966-4354	A- / 9.0	4.71	5.07	20.73 / 56	12.20 / 98	13.21 / 86	0.00	1.49
FO	Hennessy Japan Small Cap Inv	HJPSX	A+	(800) 966-4354	A+ / 9.9	12.08	15.86	30.37 / 87	13.52 / 99	15.54 / 98	0.98	1.88
FS	Hennessy Large Cap Financial Inv	HLFNX	B	(800) 966-4354	A+ / 9.8	9.35	26.62	40.83 / 97	7.32 / 74	13.99 / 93	0.52	1.58
FS	Hennessy Small Cap Financial Inst	HISFX	A	(800) 966-4354	A+ / 9.9	5.69	23.26	43.49 / 98	13.09 / 99	16.89 / 98	0.96	1.17
FS	Hennessy Small Cap Financial Inv	HSFNX	A	(800) 966-4354	A+ / 9.9	5.51	22.94	42.81 / 98	12.66 / 99	16.50 / 98	0.23	1.50
TC	Hennessy Technology Inst	HTCIX	C-	(800) 966-4354	C / 4.7	8.07	6.00	23.38 / 68	2.62 / 28	8.00 / 42	0.00	2.77
TC	Hennessy Technology Investor	HTECX	C-	(800) 966-4354	C / 4.3	7.96	5.72	22.95 / 66	2.26 / 26	7.68 / 40	0.00	3.14
GR	Hennessy Total Return Investor	HDOGX	C+	(800) 966-4354	C+ / 6.1	3.90	5.25	16.25 / 35	7.54 / 76	8.94 / 50	1.10	1.28
GR	Henssler Equity Institutional	HEQCX	D+	(800) 936-3863	B / 7.7	5.14	9.64	20.33 / 54	8.63 / 84	11.50 / 70	0.86	0.98
GR	Henssler Equity Investor	HEQFX	D	(800) 936-3863	B- / 7.2	4.86	9.24	19.63 / 50	8.03 / 79	10.88 / 65	0.57	1.48
GI	HI 529 CSP Vanguard Csv Growth		C+	(800) 662-7447	D / 1.9	2.62	0.13	6.14 / 5	3.33 / 35	4.02 / 15	0.00	0.75
GI	HI 529 CSP Vanguard Growth Port		B	(800) 662-7447	C+ / 5.7	5.84	5.84	17.62 / 41	5.99 / 64	9.04 / 51	0.00	0.75
GI	HI 529 CSP Vanguard Income Port		C	(800) 662-7447	E+ / 0.9	0.81	-1.50	1.05 / 2	1.17 / 19	0.65 / 6	0.00	0.75
GI	HI 529 CSP Vanguard Mod Growth		B	(800) 662-7447	C- / 3.6	4.21	2.92	11.79 / 17	4.70 / 51	6.54 / 32	0.00	0.75
GI	HI 529 CSP Vanguard Tot Stk Mkt Idx		A+	(800) 662-7447	B+ / 8.8	7.62	9.92	25.48 / 75	9.07 / 87	12.99 / 84	0.00	0.75
EN	Highland Energy MLP A	HEFAX	E-	(877) 665-1287	E- / 0.2	8.04	13.92	82.70 / 99	-16.22 / 0	-5.67 / 1	8.72	2.05
EN	Highland Energy MLP C	HEFCX	E-	(877) 665-1287	E / 0.3	7.88	13.53	81.76 / 99	-16.80 / 0	-6.30 / 1	8.67	2.80
EN	Highland Energy MLP Y	HEFYX	E-	(877) 665-1287	E / 0.3	8.13	14.14	83.69 / 99	-16.17 / 0	-5.48 / 2	9.52	1.80
GR	Highland Global Allocation A	HCOAX	C-	(877) 665-1287	B- / 7.0	7.93	12.73	48.28 / 99	2.03 / 24	9.12 / 52	8.20	1.04
GR	Highland Global Allocation C	HCOCX	C-	(877) 665-1287	B- / 7.5	7.60	12.37	47.22 / 99	1.28 / 20	8.30 / 45	9.23	1.79
GR	Highland Global Allocation Y	HCOYX	C	(877) 665-1287	B / 8.2	7.93	12.93	48.65 / 99	2.25 / 26	9.38 / 54	7.52	0.79
GR	Highland Long/Short Equity A	HEOAX	D-	(877) 665-1287	E / 0.5	1.42	2.06	7.66 / 7	-0.26 / 12	3.89 / 15	0.00	3.64
GR	Highland Long/Short Equity C	HEOCX	D-	(877) 665-1287	E+ / 0.7	1.24	1.72	6.95 / 6	-0.93 / 10	3.21 / 12	0.00	4.29

● Denotes fund is closed to new investors
* Denotes fund is included in Section II

www.thestreetratings.com

RISK			NET ASSETS		ASSET				Portfolio	BULL / BEAR		FUND MANAGER		MINIMUMS		LOADS	
	3 Year		NAV							Last Bull	Last Bear	Manager	Manager	Initial	Additional	Front	Back
Risk Rating/Pts	Standard Deviation	Beta	As of 2/28/17	Total $(Mil)	Cash %	Stocks %	Bonds %	Other %	Turnover Ratio	Market Return	Market Return	Quality Pct	Tenure (Years)	Purch. $	Purch. $	End Load	End Load
C / 5.5	12.9	0.98	30.95	337	4	95	0	1	62	62.9	-33.2	26	16	500	0	5.8	0.0
C / 5.4	12.9	0.98	29.01	201	4	95	0	1	62	56.1	-33.4	19	16	500	0	0.0	0.0
C / 5.4	12.9	0.98	30.83	1,244	4	95	0	1	62	65.3	-33.2	29	16	0	0	0.0	0.0
C+ / 6.5	9.4	0.73	7.32	799	7	92	0	1	145	56.4	-16.1	84	11	500	0	5.8	0.0
C+ / 6.5	9.5	0.73	7.27	994	7	92	0	1	145	50.3	-16.5	80	11	500	0	0.0	0.0
C+ / 6.5	9.4	0.73	7.34	2,390	7	92	0	1	145	58.6	-16.0	85	11	0	0	0.0	0.0
C- / 3.9	14.0	1.11	25.34	84	2	97	0	1	40	102.8	-21.7	35	16	500	0	5.8	0.0
C- / 3.4	14.1	1.11	21.56	58	2	97	0	1	40	94.3	-21.9	27	16	500	0	0.0	0.0
C- / 4.0	14.1	1.11	26.04	69	2	97	0	1	40	105.4	-21.6	38	16	0	0	0.0	0.0
C+ / 6.3	11.4	0.88	26.00	636	3	96	0	1	45	54.6	-24.7	72	16	500	0	5.8	0.0
C+ / 6.3	11.4	0.88	24.31	442	3	96	0	1	45	48.2	-25.0	62	16	500	0	0.0	0.0
C+ / 6.3	11.4	0.88	25.93	2,760	3	96	0	1	45	57.0	-24.6	74	16	0	0	0.0	0.0
U /	N/A	N/A	26.04	485	3	96	0	1	45	N/A	N/A	N/A	16	0	0	0.0	0.0
C+ / 6.3	11.5	0.89	25.45	22	3	96	0	1	45	52.0	-24.8	68	16	0	0	0.0	0.0
B / 8.4	5.6	0.78	12.45	12	4	50	45	1	51	39.7	-3.7	61	21	2,500	0	0.0	0.0
C+ / 6.4	12.6	0.71	21.07	26	5	94	0	1	97	151.5	-32.6	85	17	250,000	0	0.0	0.0
C+ / 6.4	12.6	0.71	20.52	186	5	94	0	1	97	147.5	-32.7	83	17	2,500	0	0.0	0.0
D+ / 2.4	11.7	0.96	11.42	13	5	94	0	1	53	112.4	-16.5	56	13	250,000	0	0.0	0.0
D+ / 2.5	11.7	0.96	11.32	99	5	94	0	1	53	109.8	-16.5	53	13	2,500	0	0.0	0.0
C+ / 5.9	13.0	0.91	20.98	707	4	95	0	1	108	124.1	-20.2	65	14	250,000	0	0.0	0.0
C+ / 5.9	13.0	0.91	20.48	431	4	95	0	1	108	120.3	-20.3	61	14	2,500	0	0.0	0.0
C+ / 6.7	10.8	0.71	19.89	276	2	97	0	1	36	94.4	-11.2	98	21	2,500	0	0.0	0.0
C+ / 6.7	10.8	0.71	19.89	6	2	97	0	1	36	96.7	-11.2	98	21	250,000	0	0.0	0.0
B- / 7.6	6.6	1.01	14.70	120	1	63	34	2	24	64.2	-5.1	57	10	250,000	0	0.0	0.0
B- / 7.6	6.6	1.01	15.55	185	1	63	34	2	24	61.5	-5.2	52	10	2,500	0	0.0	0.0
C+ / 6.7	11.8	0.66	78.85	887	9	90	0	1	2	141.5	-15.4	93	8	250,000	0	0.0	0.0
C+ / 6.7	11.8	0.66	77.07	1,694	9	90	0	1	2	137.3	-15.5	92	8	2,500	0	0.0	0.0
C+ / 5.6	11.9	0.32	29.75	1,472	5	94	0	1	38	97.7	-3.8	99	4	2,500	0	0.0	0.0
C+ / 6.6	12.3	0.68	28.46	101	2	94	3	1	5	95.2	-2.6	99	11	250,000	0	0.0	0.0
C+ / 6.6	12.3	0.68	27.78	71	2	94	3	1	5	92.5	-2.7	99	11	2,500	0	0.0	0.0
B- / 7.3	10.9	0.46	12.14	34	1	98	0	1	22	115.5	-0.4	99	10	2,500	0	0.0	0.0
C- / 3.5	15.9	1.14	20.10	29	0	0	0	100	141	140.8	-25.1	8	20	2,500	0	0.0	0.0
C / 5.2	16.6	1.02	15.36	40	3	96	0	1	46	169.7	-27.5	77	20	250,000	0	0.0	0.0
C / 5.2	16.6	1.02	25.53	216	3	96	0	1	46	165.2	-27.7	74	20	2,500	0	0.0	0.0
C / 5.5	16.0	1.23	17.15	1	3	96	0	1	80	79.6	-23.1	2	15	250,000	0	0.0	0.0
C / 5.4	16.0	1.23	16.82	3	3	96	0	1	80	76.7	-23.2	2	15	2,500	0	0.0	0.0
C+ / 6.7	7.7	0.65	14.10	87	0	53	46	1	44	71.3	-5.7	78	19	2,500	0	0.0	0.0
E+ / 0.8	9.5	0.85	6.39	16	0	97	1	2	155	105.8	N/A	71	19	1,000,000	0	0.0	0.0
E+ / 0.8	9.5	0.85	6.05	28	0	97	1	2	155	99.7	-15.9	64	19	2,000	200	0.0	0.0
B+ / 9.7	3.4	0.23	14.86	18	0	24	74	2	0	29.6	-1.6	80	10	15	15	0.0	0.0
B / 8.4	7.8	0.74	16.49	9	0	74	24	2	0	79.2	-13.6	52	10	15	15	0.0	0.0
B+ / 9.8	2.4	-0.01	12.51	11	25	0	74	1	0	5.0	3.7	82	10	15	15	0.0	0.0
B+ / 9.5	5.3	0.48	15.84	16	0	49	49	2	0	52.6	-7.7	70	10	15	15	0.0	0.0
B- / 7.2	10.7	1.03	19.06	10	0	99	0	1	0	125.6	-18.0	53	10	15	15	0.0	0.0
D- / 1.4	33.5	1.04	5.06	6	68	31	0	1	49	N/A	N/A	1	6	500	100	5.8	0.0
D- / 1.4	33.5	1.04	5.05	4	68	31	0	1	49	N/A	N/A	1	6	500	100	0.0	0.0
D- / 1.4	33.6	1.04	5.04	26	68	31	0	1	49	N/A	N/A	1	6	1,000,000	0	0.0	0.0
D+ / 2.6	16.9	1.03	9.11	324	0	31	68	1	100	89.3	-19.3	3	15	500	100	5.8	0.0
D+ / 2.5	16.8	1.02	8.00	231	0	31	68	1	100	81.7	-19.5	3	15	500	100	0.0	0.0
D+ / 2.6	16.8	1.02	10.82	383	0	31	68	1	100	91.8	-19.3	4	15	1,000,000	0	0.0	0.0
C+ / 6.7	6.9	0.51	11.39	34	30	69	0	1	457	30.1	-6.8	12	9	2,500	50	5.5	0.0
C+ / 6.5	6.9	0.51	10.62	34	30	69	0	1	457	25.8	-7.1	8	9	2,500	50	0.0	0.0

					PERFORMANCE								
99 Pct = Best							Total Return % through 2/28/17					Incl. in Returns	
0 Pct = Worst			Overall		Perfor-					Annualized		Dividend	Expense
Fund Type	Fund Name	Ticker Symbol	Investment Rating	Phone	mance Rating/Pts	3 Mo	6 Mo	1Yr / Pct	3Yr / Pct	5Yr / Pct		Yield	Ratio
GR	Highland Long/Short Equity Z	HEOZX	D	(877) 665-1287	D- / 1.1	1.46	2.16	7.95 / 7	0.05 /14	4.21 /16		0.00	3.29
HL	Highland Long/Short Healthcare A	HHCAX	E	(877) 665-1287	E- / 0.0	-3.46	-4.20	-2.62 / 1	-7.74 / 1	1.55 / 7		0.00	2.87
HL	Highland Long/Short Healthcare C	HHCCX	E	(877) 665-1287	E- / 0.0	-3.57	-4.53	-3.12 / 1	-8.26 / 1	0.95 / 6		0.00	3.52
HL	Highland Long/Short Healthcare Z	HHCZX	E	(877) 665-1287	E- / 0.1	-3.26	-3.90	-2.12 / 1	-7.35 / 1	1.95 / 8		0.00	2.52
FS	Highland Opportunistic Credit Z	HNRZX	E+	(877) 665-1287	E- / 0.2	7.77	12.52	34.05 /93	-10.58 / 1	5.05 /22		0.07	1.79
GR	Highland Premier Growth Equity A	HPEAX	C-	(877) 665-1287	C+ / 6.6	6.02	7.48	18.77 /46	8.88 /86	13.42 /88		0.00	1.13
GR	Highland Premier Growth Equity C	HPECX	D+	(877) 665-1287	B- / 7.0	5.82	7.09	17.90 /42	8.09 /80	12.58 /80		0.00	1.88
GR	Highland Premier Growth Equity Y	HPEYX	C	(877) 665-1287	B / 7.7	6.08	7.62	19.06 /47	9.16 /88	13.70 /91		0.00	0.88
SC	Highland Small-Cap Equity A	HSZAX	B-	(877) 665-1287	A+ / 9.8	10.90	12.67	51.06 /99	10.30 /95	13.44 /88		0.53	1.67
SC	Highland Small-Cap Equity C	HSZCX	C+	(877) 665-1287	A+ / 9.8	10.62	12.14	49.92 /99	9.46 /90	12.58 /80		0.28	2.42
SC	Highland Small-Cap Equity Y	HSZYX	B-	(877) 665-1287	A+ / 9.9	10.92	12.78	51.45 /99	10.55 /95	13.70 /91		0.69	1.42
AA	Highland Total Return A	HTAAX	D+	(877) 665-1287	C- / 3.7	3.88	5.68	19.01 /47	4.90 /53	6.75 /33		1.03	1.41
AA	Highland Total Return C	HTACX	C-	(877) 665-1287	C- / 4.2	3.73	5.26	18.15 /44	4.11 /44	5.95 /28		0.30	2.16
AA	Highland Total Return Y	HTAYX	C	(877) 665-1287	C / 5.1	3.99	5.81	19.39 /49	5.16 /56	7.02 /35		1.32	1.16
AG	Hillman No Load	HCMAX	A+	(800) 773-3863	A / 9.4	6.31	11.41	27.85 /81	10.33 /95	12.28 /77		0.56	1.51
GR	Hodges Blue Chip Equity Income Rtl	HDPBX	B-	(877) 232-1222	B- / 7.0	9.56	10.83	19.01 /47	6.69 /70	12.54 /79		0.91	1.73
GL	Hodges Inst	HDPIX	B+	(877) 232-1222	A+ / 9.8	1.14	14.51	51.96 /99	8.29 /81	17.70 /98		0.00	1.00
GR	Hodges Pure Contrarian Retail	HDPCX	C-	(877) 232-1222	B / 8.2	3.17	11.91	62.04 /99	0.92 /18	10.26 /60		0.00	2.48
GL	Hodges Retail	HDPMX	B+	(877) 232-1222	A+ / 9.7	1.07	14.26	51.41 /99	7.88 /78	17.37 /98		0.00	1.32
SC	Hodges Small Cap Inst	HDSIX	C	(877) 232-1222	C+ / 5.7	2.14	12.07	29.42 /85	3.42 /36	12.31 /77		0.27	0.98
SC	Hodges Small Cap Retail	HDPSX	C-	(877) 232-1222	C / 5.4	2.10	11.92	29.02 /84	3.11 /33	11.97 /74		0.02	1.30
SC	Hodges Small Intrinsic Val Retail	HDSVX	B+	(877) 232-1222	B / 8.1	2.38	11.89	28.00 /82	8.40 /82	--		0.00	1.43
MC	Hodges Small-Mid Cap Retail	HDSMX	A-	(877) 232-1222	B+ / 8.9	3.35	15.11	37.17 /96	7.00 /72	--		0.00	1.79
BA	Holland Balanced	HOLBX	C+		C / 4.8	3.99	5.18	12.27 /19	6.28 /67	8.78 /49		0.00	1.95
GR	Homestead Growth	HNASX	B	(800) 258-3030	B+ / 8.8	9.52	12.44	25.63 /75	8.12 /80	14.40 /95		0.00	0.95
FO	Homestead International Equity	HISIX	E+	(800) 258-3030	D- / 1.2	7.79	3.57	18.91 /47	-1.42 / 8	4.26 /17		0.88	1.45
SC	Homestead Small Company Stock	HSCSX	B	(800) 258-3030	B / 7.9	5.60	13.99	27.51 /81	6.62 /69	12.56 /80		0.32	0.87
IX	Homestead Stock Index	HSTIX	A+	(800) 258-3030	A- / 9.1	7.87	9.72	24.25 /71	10.05 /94	13.39 /88		1.43	0.54
GI	Homestead Value	HOVLX	A	(800) 258-3030	A- / 9.0	7.45	10.33	25.43 /75	9.52 /90	13.56 /89		2.04	0.59
SC	Hood River Small-Cap Growth Inst	HRSMX	B-	(800) 227-6681	B+ / 8.6	5.54	10.37	29.12 /84	8.68 /84	14.92 /97		0.00	1.41
GL	Horizon Active Asset Allocation N	AAANX	C-	(800) 773-3863	C / 4.5	7.52	6.06	18.04 /43	3.62 /38	7.79 /41		0.85	1.70
GL	Horizon Spin-off and Corp Res A	LSHAX	E+	(800) 207-7108	D- / 1.0	3.72	12.09	26.09 /76	-2.11 / 6	8.49 /46		0.00	1.83
GL	Horizon Spin-off and Corp Res C	LSHCX	E+	(800) 754-8757	D- / 1.1	3.53	11.71	25.08 /74	-2.85 / 5	7.77 /40		0.00	2.58
GL	Horizon Spin-off and Corp Res Inst	LSHUX	E+	(800) 426-3750	D- / 1.5	3.71	12.19	26.34 /77	-1.89 / 7	8.76 /49		0.00	1.58
IN	Hotchkis and Wiley Capital Income A	HWIAX	B-	(866) 493-8637	B / 7.8	7.06	12.29	33.19 /92	6.71 /70	11.23 /68		3.73	1.47
IN	Hotchkis and Wiley Capital Income I	HWIIX	B+	(866) 493-8637	A- / 9.0	7.21	12.44	33.64 /92	7.36 /74	11.24 /68		4.28	1.22
GR	Hotchkis and Wiley Divsfd Val A	HWCAX	A-	(866) 493-8637	A- / 9.1	6.17	16.17	37.79 /96	8.00 /79	13.26 /86		4.57	1.28
GR	Hotchkis and Wiley Divsfd Val C	HWCCX	A	(866) 493-8637	A / 9.3	5.99	15.79	36.76 /96	7.19 /73	12.42 /78		4.33	2.03
GR	Hotchkis and Wiley Divsfd Val I	HWCIX	A	(866) 493-8637	A+ / 9.6	6.20	16.30	38.04 /96	8.25 /81	13.55 /89		4.97	1.03
GL	Hotchkis and Wiley Global Value A	HWGAX	C	(866) 493-8637	C+ / 6.2	6.50	13.28	30.92 /88	4.19 /45	--		0.61	4.39
GL	Hotchkis and Wiley Global Value I	HWGIX	C+	(866) 493-8637	B- / 7.3	6.55	13.42	31.20 /88	4.45 /48	--		0.78	4.14
GI	Hotchkis and Wiley Large Cap Val A	HWLAX	A-	(866) 493-8637	A- / 9.0	6.25	14.70	36.27 /95	8.32 /81	14.14 /94		1.53	1.26
GI	Hotchkis and Wiley Large Cap Val C	HWLCX	A	(866) 493-8637	A- / 9.2	6.02	14.22	35.26 /94	7.50 /75	13.28 /87		0.60	2.01
GI	Hotchkis and Wiley Large Cap Val I	HWLIX	A+	(866) 493-8637	A+ / 9.6	6.30	14.82	36.61 /95	8.59 /84	14.42 /95		1.87	1.01
GI	Hotchkis and Wiley Large Cap Val R	HWLRX	A	(866) 493-8637	A / 9.4	6.13	14.50	35.92 /95	8.03 /79	13.85 /92		1.46	1.51
MC	Hotchkis and Wiley Mid-Cap Val A	HWMAX	C	(866) 493-8637	B / 7.7	5.17	17.41	37.86 /96	5.20 /56	13.16 /85		0.17	1.27
MC	Hotchkis and Wiley Mid-Cap Val C	HWMCX	C	(866) 493-8637	B / 8.1	4.99	16.97	36.88 /96	4.42 /48	12.32 /77		0.00	2.02
MC	Hotchkis and Wiley Mid-Cap Val I	HWMIX	C+	(866) 493-8637	B+ / 8.8	5.24	17.55	38.21 /96	5.46 /59	13.44 /88		0.30	1.02
MC	Hotchkis and Wiley Mid-Cap Val R	HWMRX	C+	(866) 493-8637	B+ / 8.5	5.12	17.27	37.54 /96	4.94 /53	12.90 /83		0.09	1.52
SC	● Hotchkis and Wiley Small Cap Val A	HWSAX	B-	(866) 493-8637	A- / 9.2	7.06	20.08	39.26 /97	6.99 /72	14.31 /95		0.00	1.29
SC	● Hotchkis and Wiley Small Cap Val C	HWSCX	C+	(866) 493-8637	A / 9.4	6.87	19.61	38.19 /96	6.19 /66	13.45 /88		0.00	2.04
SC	● Hotchkis and Wiley Small Cap Val I	HWSIX	B	(866) 493-8637	A+ / 9.7	7.13	20.21	39.61 /97	7.26 /74	14.60 /96		0.40	1.04

● Denotes fund is closed to new investors
* Denotes fund is included in Section II

www.thestreetratings.com

RISK	3 Year		NET ASSETS		ASSET					BULL / BEAR		FUND MANAGER		MINIMUMS		LOADS	
Risk Rating/Pts	Standard Deviation	Beta	NAV As of 2/28/17	Total $(Mil)	Cash %	Stocks %	Bonds %	Other %	Portfolio Turnover Ratio	Last Bull Market Return	Last Bear Market Return	Manager Quality Pct	Manager Tenure (Years)	Initial Purch. $	Additional Purch. $	Front End Load	Back End Load
C+ / 6.8	7.0	0.52	11.82	377	30	69	0	1	457	32.2	-6.5	13	9	2,500	50	0.0	0.0
C / 4.9	12.5	0.27	11.17	48	55	38	6	1	901	6.3	N/A	2	7	2,500	50	5.5	0.0
C / 4.8	12.5	0.27	10.54	30	55	38	6	1	901	2.9	-0.2	1	7	2,500	50	0.0	0.0
C / 5.0	12.5	0.28	11.57	75	55	38	6	1	901	8.5	0.2	2	7	2,500	50	0.0	0.0
C+ / 5.9	14.9	0.39	4.34	75	0	0	0	100	83	39.2	-11.7	0	2	2,500	50	0.0	0.0
C- / 3.4	13.2	1.13	28.63	111	0	100	0	0	77	132.1	-17.2	36	1	500	100	5.8	0.0
D / 2.2	13.2	1.12	21.56	16	0	100	0	0	77	123.0	-17.4	28	1	500	100	0.0	0.0
C- / 3.6	13.2	1.13	29.94	32	0	100	0	0	77	135.3	-17.1	40	1	1,000,000	0	0.0	0.0
D+ / 2.7	17.2	0.93	14.79	41	0	99	0	1	107	134.1	-20.7	92	2	500	100	5.8	0.0
D / 1.7	17.2	0.93	10.73	4	0	99	0	1	107	124.7	-20.9	90	2	500	100	0.0	0.0
D+ / 2.9	17.2	0.93	16.07	12	0	99	0	1	107	137.2	-20.6	93	2	1,000,000	0	0.0	0.0
C+ / 5.6	8.2	1.18	22.79	56	7	71	20	2	94	58.6	-14.5	26	2	500	100	5.8	0.0
C / 5.3	8.2	1.17	20.51	6	7	71	20	2	94	52.3	-14.7	19	2	500	100	0.0	0.0
C+ / 5.6	8.2	1.18	23.14	13	7	71	20	2	94	60.8	-14.4	29	2	1,000,000	0	0.0	0.0
B- / 7.1	11.1	0.98	21.01	36	5	91	2	2	48	120.6	-21.8	73	17	5,000	500	0.0	0.0
C+ / 5.8	10.6	0.88	15.29	24	2	97	0	1	51	112.8	-14.6	42	8	1,000	50	0.0	1.0
C- / 4.0	19.2	0.99	47.99	26	8	91	0	1	79	169.6	-24.7	99	18	1,000,000	50	0.0	1.0
D / 1.9	23.1	0.94	14.00	14	9	90	0	1	116	97.2	-28.3	3	8	1,000	50	0.0	1.0
C- / 4.0	19.2	0.99	47.27	408	8	91	0	1	79	165.5	-24.8	98	18	250	50	0.0	1.0
C / 4.8	15.9	0.95	21.11	429	1	98	0	1	49	127.4	-19.0	35	10	1,000,000	50	0.0	1.0
C / 4.8	15.9	0.95	20.54	815	1	98	0	1	49	123.6	-19.1	31	10	1,000	50	0.0	1.0
C+ / 5.8	16.0	0.92	12.89	110	3	94	2	1	79	N/A	N/A	86	4	1,000	50	0.0	1.0
C+ / 5.9	15.9	1.16	12.74	22	6	93	0	1	91	N/A	N/A	25	4	1,000	50	0.0	1.0
B- / 7.4	6.8	0.98	19.47	30	9	64	25	2	28	74.5	-10.1	62	22	1,000	500	0.0	0.0
C / 4.8	13.1	1.07	8.80	129	2	97	0	1	40	144.5	-16.9	34	9	500	0	0.0	0.0
C / 4.5	11.8	0.90	7.08	57	2	97	0	1	62	42.7	-24.3	58	1	500	0	0.0	0.0
C+ / 5.6	14.8	0.87	41.34	1,276	0	97	2	1	16	133.0	-24.4	78	18	500	0	0.0	0.0
B- / 7.1	10.3	1.00	17.65	130	1	96	1	2	3	128.1	-16.5	68	9	500	0	0.0	0.0
C+ / 6.1	12.0	1.11	50.24	1,003	0	98	1	1	8	134.7	-20.7	46	18	500	0	0.0	0.0
C- / 4.1	15.2	0.89	35.03	185	0	96	3	1	170	163.5	-25.3	88	10	25,000	0	0.0	1.0
C / 4.8	10.5	1.56	12.32	350	0	100	0	0	472	N/A	N/A	29	5	2,500	250	0.0	0.0
C / 4.4	14.0	0.81	9.82	6	12	87	0	1	2	80.6	-23.9	48	10	2,500	100	4.8	0.0
C / 4.3	14.0	0.80	9.44	6	12	87	0	1	2	74.3	-24.0	37	10	2,500	100	0.0	0.0
C / 4.4	14.0	0.81	9.84	13	12	87	0	1	2	83.1	-23.9	51	10	1,000,000	100,000	0.0	0.0
C / 5.0	9.8	0.81	12.84	24	3	55	39	3	93	98.6	-10.1	52	7	2,500	100	4.8	0.0
C / 4.9	9.7	0.81	12.36	17	3	55	39	3	93	97.7	-10.0	61	7	1,000,000	100	0.0	0.0
C+ / 5.8	14.1	1.22	16.93	42	1	98	0	1	35	134.3	-21.5	18	13	2,500	100	5.3	0.0
C+ / 5.9	14.1	1.22	16.78	3	1	98	0	1	35	125.1	-21.8	13	13	2,500	100	0.0	0.0
C+ / 5.8	14.1	1.22	16.87	72	1	98	0	1	35	137.5	-21.5	20	13	1,000,000	100	0.0	0.0
C / 4.5	13.2	0.90	12.20	N/A	2	97	0	1	52	N/A	N/A	94	5	2,500	100	5.3	0.0
C / 4.5	13.2	0.89	12.21	7	2	97	0	1	52	N/A	N/A	94	5	1,000,000	100	0.0	0.0
C+ / 6.0	14.0	1.21	29.79	141	2	97	0	1	39	139.1	-20.5	21	29	2,500	100	5.3	0.0
C+ / 6.0	14.0	1.21	29.20	20	2	97	0	1	39	129.4	-20.7	15	29	2,500	100	0.0	0.0
C+ / 6.0	14.0	1.21	29.95	293	2	97	0	1	39	142.3	-20.4	24	29	1,000,000	100	0.0	0.0
C+ / 6.0	14.0	1.21	29.92	16	2	97	0	1	39	135.9	-20.6	19	29	2,500	100	0.0	0.0
D+ / 2.9	17.0	1.21	37.48	316	1	98	0	1	42	167.7	-31.1	9	20	2,500	100	5.3	0.0
D+ / 2.6	17.0	1.21	33.16	61	1	98	0	1	42	157.1	-31.4	6	20	2,500	100	0.0	0.0
D+ / 2.9	17.0	1.21	38.03	1,809	1	98	0	1	42	171.5	-31.1	10	20	1,000,000	100	0.0	0.0
C- / 3.0	17.0	1.21	37.55	13	1	98	0	1	42	164.5	-31.2	8	20	2,500	100	0.0	0.0
C- / 3.5	17.0	0.99	59.56	102	1	98	0	1	45	154.3	-29.2	75	22	2,500	100	5.3	0.0
C- / 3.1	17.0	0.99	50.26	20	1	98	0	1	45	144.2	-29.4	67	22	2,500	100	0.0	0.0
C- / 3.5	17.0	0.99	59.90	711	1	98	0	1	45	157.8	-29.1	77	22	1,000,000	100	0.0	0.0

Fund Type	Fund Name	Ticker Symbol	Overall Investment Rating	Phone	Performance Rating/Pts	3 Mo	6 Mo	1Yr / Pct	3Yr / Pct	5Yr / Pct	Dividend Yield	Expense Ratio
GR	Hotchkis and Wiley Value Opptys A	HWAAX	B	(866) 493-8637	A+ / 9.6	7.80	16.17	39.72 /97	8.84 /86	14.93 /97	1.77	1.25
GR	Hotchkis and Wiley Value Opptys C	HWACX	B	(866) 493-8637	A+ / 9.6	7.59	15.71	38.68 /97	8.02 /79	14.08 /94	1.25	2.00
GR	Hotchkis and Wiley Value Opptys I	HWAIX	B+	(866) 493-8637	A+ / 9.8	7.87	16.29	40.05 /97	9.10 /87	15.21 /97	2.15	1.00
GL	● HSBC Frontier Markets A	HSFAX	D-	(800) 728-8183	D / 2.2	8.47	2.72	20.64 /56	0.87 /18	8.43 /46	1.75	2.23
GL	● HSBC Frontier Markets I	HSFIX	D	(800) 728-8183	C- / 3.3	8.61	2.88	21.06 /58	1.22 /19	8.79 /49	2.23	1.88
CV	HSBC Global Emerging Markets Debt	HCGAX	D	(800) 728-8183	D / 2.1	4.27	-0.93	9.93 /11	4.50 /49	4.20 /16	4.41	1.69
CV	HSBC Global Emerging Markets Debt	HCGIX	D+	(800) 728-8183	C- / 3.1	4.37	-0.68	10.37 /13	4.84 /52	4.56 /18	5.01	1.34
SC	HSBC Opportunity A	HSOAX	D	(800) 728-8183	C / 5.0	8.96	8.65	30.36 /87	2.57 /28	9.91 /58	0.00	1.84
SC	● HSBC Opportunity B	HOPBX	D-	(800) 728-8183	C / 5.4	8.90	8.29	29.40 /85	1.81 /23	9.10 /51	0.00	2.59
SC	HSBC Opportunity C	HOPCX	D-	(800) 728-8183	C / 5.3	8.81	8.22	29.38 /85	1.78 /23	9.10 /51	0.00	2.59
SC	HSBC Opportunity I	RESCX	D+	(800) 728-8183	C+ / 6.5	9.14	8.83	30.97 /88	3.09 /33	10.46 /62	0.00	0.99
EM	HSBC Total Return A	HTRAX	C-	(800) 728-8183	D- / 1.1	2.16	0.71	5.40 / 4	2.39 /27	--	0.00	1.59
EM	HSBC Total Return I	HTRIX	C-	(800) 728-8183	D / 1.8	2.24	0.91	5.80 / 5	2.81 /30	--	0.00	1.24
EM	HSBC Total Return S	HTRSX	C-	(800) 728-8183	D / 1.8	2.35	1.01	5.82 / 5	2.85 /30	--	0.00	1.14
AG	HSBC World Selection Aggr Strat A	HAAGX	D-	(800) 728-8183	C- / 3.5	6.65	6.74	19.95 /52	3.25 /34	6.94 /34	0.84	1.79
AG	● HSBC World Selection Aggr Strat B	HBAGX	D-	(800) 728-8183	C- / 3.9	6.56	6.37	19.09 /48	2.50 /27	6.14 /29	0.35	2.54
AG	● HSBC World Selection Aggr Strat C	HCAGX	D-	(800) 728-8183	C- / 3.9	6.52	6.32	19.13 /48	2.48 /27	6.14 /29	0.35	2.54
GR	HSBC World Selection Bal Strat A	HAGRX	D	(800) 728-8183	C- / 3.1	6.32	5.66	18.36 /44	3.16 /33	6.01 /28	1.50	1.47
GR	● HSBC World Selection Bal Strat B	HSBGX	D	(800) 728-8183	C- / 3.4	6.04	5.19	17.44 /40	2.37 /26	5.21 /23	0.55	2.22
GR	HSBC World Selection Bal Strat C	HCGRX	D	(800) 728-8183	C- / 3.4	6.08	5.24	17.43 /40	2.38 /27	5.21 /23	0.62	2.22
GI	HSBC World Selection Csv Strat A	HACGX	D+	(800) 728-8183	D- / 1.1	3.25	0.37	7.82 / 7	1.77 /22	3.41 /12	1.18	1.73
GI	● HSBC World Selection Csv Strat B	HBCGX	D+	(800) 728-8183	D- / 1.3	3.10	0.07	6.96 / 6	0.99 /18	2.64 /10	0.54	2.48
GI	HSBC World Selection Csv Strat C	HCCGX	D+	(800) 728-8183	D- / 1.3	3.10	0.07	7.03 / 6	1.02 /18	2.65 /10	0.52	2.48
AA	HSBC World Selection Income Strat	HINAX	C-	(800) 728-8183	D- / 1.0	2.61	0.03	5.60 / 4	1.81 /23	--	1.26	10.29
AA	● HSBC World Selection Income Strat	HINBX	C-	(800) 728-8183	D- / 1.1	2.45	-0.33	4.83 / 4	1.05 /18	--	0.60	11.04
AA	HSBC World Selection Income Strat	HINCX	C-	(800) 728-8183	D- / 1.2	2.54	-0.23	4.92 / 4	1.05 /18	--	0.59	11.04
GI	HSBC World Selection Modt Strat A	HSAMX	D+	(800) 728-8183	D / 2.1	4.92	3.15	13.78 /24	2.70 /29	4.80 /20	1.50	1.49
GI	● HSBC World Selection Modt Strat B	HSBMX	D+	(800) 728-8183	D+ / 2.4	4.73	2.75	12.91 /21	1.95 /24	4.01 /15	0.83	2.24
GI	HSBC World Selection Modt Strat C	HSCMX	D+	(800) 728-8183	D+ / 2.4	4.85	2.80	13.00 /22	1.98 /24	4.04 /15	0.94	2.24
GR	Huber Capital Dvsfd Lg Cap Val Inst	HUDEX	C+	(888) 263-6443	C+ / 6.6	8.30	12.02	28.45 /83	3.76 /40	--	1.72	3.59
GR	Huber Capital Dvsfd Lg Cap Val Inv	HUDIX	C+	(888) 263-6443	C+ / 6.3	8.25	11.90	28.05 /82	3.41 /36	--	1.49	4.00
IN	Huber Capital Equity Income Inst	HULEX	C+	(888) 263-6443	C+ / 6.1	8.28	12.23	28.43 /83	2.94 /31	10.24 /60	1.57	1.35
IN	Huber Capital Equity Income Inv	HULIX	C+	(888) 263-6443	C+ / 5.7	8.19	11.98	27.98 /82	2.50 /27	9.77 /57	1.20	1.75
SC	Huber Capital Small Cap Value Inst	HUSEX	E+	(888) 263-6443	D- / 1.5	3.24	11.23	31.58 /89	-2.44 / 6	7.47 /38	1.41	1.59
SC	Huber Capital Small Cap Value Inv	HUSIX	E	(888) 263-6443	D- / 1.3	3.08	11.09	31.41 /89	-2.78 / 5	7.02 /35	1.17	1.99
GR	Hundredfold Select Alternative Inv	HFSAX	C+	(855) 582-8006	C / 4.8	5.87	6.42	15.15 /31	5.08 /55	--	3.46	2.20
GR	Hussman Strategic Growth	HSGFX	E+	(800) 487-7626	E- / 0.0	-7.26	-10.39	-20.42 / 0	-11.06 / 1	-9.36 / 1	0.00	1.20
FO	Hussman Strategic International	HSIEX	D	(800) 487-7626	E- / 0.2	-0.23	-1.78	-2.43 / 1	-3.22 / 4	-1.44 / 3	0.00	2.04
IN	Hussman Strategic Value	HSVLX	D-	(800) 487-7626	E- / 0.1	-5.92	-3.99	-5.12 / 1	-2.76 / 5	-0.28 / 4	1.49	4.75
GR	IA 529 CSI Aggressive Growth Port		B+	(800) 662-7447	B- / 7.1	7.67	8.09	23.54 /68	6.51 /69	10.50 /62	0.00	0.34
GI	IA 529 CSI Conservative Growth Port		B-	(800) 662-7447	C- / 3.1	3.64	1.81	9.97 /12	4.47 /48	5.64 /26	0.00	0.34
GI	IA 529 CSI Growth Port		B	(800) 662-7447	C+ / 5.8	6.26	5.93	18.77 /46	5.87 /63	8.92 /50	0.00	0.34
AA	IA 529 CSI Income Port		C+	(800) 662-7447	D / 2.0	2.29	-0.24	5.64 / 4	3.63 /38	3.91 /15	0.00	0.34
GI	IA 529 CSI Moderate Growth Port		B	(800) 662-7447	C / 4.4	4.94	3.85	14.30 /27	5.22 /57	7.31 /37	0.00	0.34
GR	ICON A	ICNAX	C+	(800) 764-0442	B / 7.6	11.10	18.64	34.83 /94	4.16 /45	8.44 /46	0.00	1.55
GR	ICON C	ICNCX	B-	(800) 764-0442	B / 8.0	10.83	18.15	33.81 /93	3.36 /35	7.62 /39	0.00	2.27
OT	ICON Consumer Discretionary A	ICCAX	D-	(800) 764-0442	D / 2.0	1.83	5.24	8.37 / 8	4.19 /45	10.22 /60	0.00	1.91
OT	ICON Consumer Discretionary S	ICCCX	D	(800) 764-0442	C- / 3.3	2.06	5.57	9.01 / 9	4.72 /51	10.92 /65	0.00	1.43
OT	ICON Consumer Staples A	ICRAX	D	(800) 764-0442	C+ / 6.4	7.90	3.49	10.18 /12	11.19 /97	11.85 /73	0.15	2.12
GR	ICON Consumer Staples S	ICLEX	C-	(800) 764-0442	B / 7.6	8.00	3.74	10.42 /13	11.48 /98	12.19 /76	0.26	1.87
FO	ICON Emerging Markets A	IPCAX	C-	(800) 764-0442	D+ / 2.3	8.95	2.13	16.64 /37	2.13 /25	3.08 /11	0.00	4.75
FO	ICON Emerging Markets S	ICARX	C	(800) 764-0442	C- / 3.4	8.97	2.19	16.90 /38	2.34 /26	3.30 /12	0.00	2.44

● Denotes fund is closed to new investors
* Denotes fund is included in Section II

RISK			NET ASSETS		ASSET				Portfolio Turnover Ratio	BULL / BEAR		FUND MANAGER		MINIMUMS		LOADS	
Risk Rating/Pts	3 Year Standard Deviation	Beta	NAV As of 2/28/17	Total $(Mil)	Cash %	Stocks %	Bonds %	Other %		Last Bull Market Return	Last Bear Market Return	Manager Quality Pct	Manager Tenure (Years)	Initial Purch. $	Additional Purch. $	Front End Load	Back End Load
C- /4.0	13.6	1.11	27.60	141	4	86	7	3	62	158.8	-23.7	38	15	2,500	100	5.3	0.0
C- /3.8	13.6	1.11	25.73	62	4	86	7	3	62	148.5	-23.9	29	15	2,500	100	0.0	0.0
C- /3.9	13.6	1.11	27.56	314	4	86	7	3	62	162.2	-23.6	42	15	1,000,000	100	0.0	0.0
C /4.6	13.0	0.73	12.34	7	3	96	0	1	8	66.0	N/A	81	5	1,000	100	5.0	0.0
C /4.5	13.0	0.73	12.38	34	3	96	0	1	8	69.1	N/A	83	5	1,000,000	0	0.0	0.0
C+ /6.2	6.1	0.35	10.11	N/A	1	0	98	1	91	37.2	-1.1	89	3	1,000	100	4.8	0.0
C+ /6.1	6.1	0.35	10.06	10	1	0	98	1	91	39.8	-0.9	90	3	1,000,000	0	0.0	0.0
D+ /2.5	16.0	0.90	10.01	10	1	98	0	1	96	106.7	-24.9	29	14	1,000	100	5.0	0.0
D- /1.2	15.9	0.89	6.29	N/A	1	98	0	1	96	98.3	-25.1	22	14	1,000	100	0.0	0.0
D- /1.3	15.9	0.89	6.60	1	1	98	0	1	96	98.4	-25.1	22	14	1,000	100	0.0	0.0
D+ /2.3	16.0	0.89	13.67	143	1	98	0	1	96	112.3	-24.7	35	14	5,000,000	0	0.0	0.0
B /8.4	3.7	0.16	9.95	2	37	0	62	1	47	N/A	N/A	86	5	1,000	100	4.8	0.0
B /8.4	3.7	0.16	10.03	28	37	0	62	1	47	N/A	N/A	88	5	1,000,000	0	0.0	0.0
B /8.4	3.7	0.16	10.00	N/A	37	0	62	1	47	N/A	N/A	88	5	25,000,000	0	0.0	0.0
C- /3.1	10.0	0.92	12.29	11	3	91	4	2	50	68.6	-21.9	8	N/A	1,000	100	5.0	0.0
D+ /2.9	10.0	0.92	11.51	2	3	91	4	2	50	62.0	-22.2	6	N/A	1,000	100	0.0	0.0
D+ /2.9	10.0	0.92	11.43	1	3	91	4	2	50	61.9	-22.2	6	N/A	1,000	100	0.0	0.0
C /4.5	8.9	0.81	11.82	28	2	74	23	1	38	56.9	-17.4	15	N/A	1,000	100	5.0	0.0
C /4.6	8.9	0.80	11.84	5	2	74	23	1	38	50.6	-17.7	10	N/A	1,000	100	0.0	0.0
C /4.6	8.9	0.81	11.89	2	2	74	23	1	38	50.7	-17.7	10	N/A	1,000	100	0.0	0.0
B- /7.5	4.6	0.33	10.86	9	2	25	71	2	25	29.9	-8.4	53	N/A	1,000	100	5.0	0.0
B- /7.4	4.7	0.33	10.67	3	2	25	71	2	25	24.8	-8.8	42	N/A	1,000	100	0.0	0.0
B- /7.5	4.7	0.33	11.04	2	2	25	71	2	25	24.9	-8.8	42	N/A	1,000	100	0.0	0.0
B+ /9.2	3.7	0.46	10.18	N/A	0	22	76	2	28	N/A	N/A	54	N/A	1,000	100	4.8	0.0
B+ /9.2	3.8	0.46	10.16	N/A	0	22	76	2	28	N/A	N/A	43	N/A	1,000	100	0.0	0.0
B+ /9.2	3.8	0.46	10.18	N/A	0	22	76	2	28	N/A	N/A	44	N/A	1,000	100	0.0	0.0
C+ /6.3	6.8	0.59	11.44	27	2	53	44	1	33	43.9	-13.4	31	N/A	1,000	100	5.0	0.0
C+ /6.4	6.8	0.59	11.43	4	2	53	44	1	33	38.2	-13.8	23	N/A	1,000	100	0.0	0.0
C+ /6.3	6.8	0.59	10.99	3	2	53	44	1	33	38.3	-13.7	24	N/A	1,000	100	0.0	0.0
C+ /6.1	11.2	0.96	13.16	5	4	95	0	1	26	N/A	N/A	9	5	1,000,000	5,000	0.0	1.0
C+ /6.1	11.3	0.96	13.10	2	4	95	0	1	26	N/A	N/A	7	5	5,000	100	0.0	1.0
C+ /5.8	12.4	1.04	14.53	79	3	96	0	1	16	N/A	N/A	4	10	1,000,000	5,000	0.0	1.0
C+ /5.8	12.4	1.04	14.51	17	3	96	0	1	16	94.0	-16.1	4	10	5,000	100	0.0	1.0
C- /3.9	16.9	0.97	16.17	77	3	96	0	1	15	N/A	N/A	3	10	1,000,000	5,000	0.0	1.0
C- /3.9	16.9	0.97	15.98	27	3	96	0	1	15	82.3	-24.1	3	10	5,000	100	0.0	1.0
B- /7.1	3.9	0.26	23.75	26	26	12	60	2	358	N/A	N/A	87	13	1,000,000	0	0.0	0.0
C /5.5	8.3	-0.72	6.90	412	0	100	0	0	161	-45.3	9.0	18	17	1,000	100	0.0	1.5
B- /7.7	6.1	-0.04	8.84	32	16	83	0	1	10	-11.0	-2.0	30	8	1,000	100	0.0	1.5
B- /7.0	5.2	-0.04	8.41	7	0	99	0	1	118	N/A	N/A	41	5	1,000	100	0.0	1.5
C+ /6.9	10.4	0.98	30.18	891	0	99	0	1	0	101.1	-19.0	28	16	25	25	0.0	0.0
B+ /9.7	4.5	0.38	21.95	398	0	40	58	2	0	44.3	-5.2	77	16	25	25	0.0	0.0
B /8.1	8.3	0.78	23.41	1,010	0	79	19	2	0	80.6	-14.5	46	N/A	25	25	0.0	0.0
B+ /9.7	3.1	0.37	20.59	323	0	19	79	2	0	28.4	N/A	80	16	25	25	0.0	0.0
B+ /9.0	6.3	0.58	22.94	807	0	60	39	1	0	61.9	-9.9	65	16	25	25	0.0	0.0
C /4.8	15.2	1.22	15.91	6	0	99	0	1	31	88.8	-21.4	3	6	1,000	100	5.8	0.0
C /4.8	15.2	1.22	14.84	13	0	99	0	1	31	81.6	-21.3	3	6	1,000	100	0.0	0.0
C /4.5	12.0	1.00	13.07	2	19	80	0	1	158	101.9	-9.1	9	3	1,000	100	5.8	0.0
C /4.6	12.0	1.00	13.63	38	19	80	0	1	158	108.3	-8.7	12	3	1,000	100	0.0	0.0
D /1.7	8.0	0.49	7.34	4	26	73	0	1	125	94.1	-6.7	96	N/A	1,000	100	5.8	0.0
D /1.7	8.0	0.49	7.37	27	26	73	0	1	125	97.3	-7.5	97	N/A	1,000	100	0.0	0.0
B- /7.1	11.4	0.69	14.37	8	20	79	0	1	156	43.2	-26.5	87	N/A	1,000	100	5.8	0.0
B- /7.1	11.4	0.69	14.46	41	20	79	0	1	156	44.9	-26.5	88	N/A	1,000	100	0.0	0.0

I. Index of Stock Mutual Funds

99 Pct = Best
0 Pct = Worst

Fund Type	Fund Name	Ticker Symbol	Overall Investment Rating	Phone	Performance Rating/Pts	3 Mo	6 Mo	1Yr / Pct	3Yr / Pct	5Yr / Pct	Dividend Yield	Expense Ratio
EN	ICON Energy A	ICEAX	E-	(800) 764-0442	E- / 0.1	-3.14	5.64	27.75 /81	-9.48 / 1	-2.86 / 2	0.32	1.66
EN	ICON Energy C	ICEEX	E-	(800) 764-0442	E- / 0.1	-3.28	5.23	26.82 /79	-10.17 / 1	-3.62 / 2	0.16	2.43
EN	ICON Energy S	ICENX	E-	(800) 764-0442	E- / 0.1	-3.04	5.87	28.29 /82	-9.21 / 1	-2.58 / 2	0.42	1.42
IN	ICON Equity Income A	IEQAX	A	(800) 764-0442	B / 7.8	7.36	10.07	24.92 /73	9.34 /89	11.03 /66	2.77	1.87
IN	ICON Equity Income C	IOECX	A	(800) 764-0442	B / 8.2	7.11	9.60	23.96 /70	8.52 /83	10.20 /60	2.24	2.69
IN	ICON Equity Income S	IOEZX	A+	(800) 764-0442	A- / 9.0	7.38	10.14	25.19 /74	9.60 /91	11.31 /68	3.18	1.60
FS	ICON Financial A	ICFAX	A-	(800) 764-0442	A / 9.5	9.58	22.41	39.85 /97	6.95 /72	10.68 /63	0.78	2.26
FS	ICON Financial S	ICFSX	A	(800) 764-0442	A+ / 9.8	9.62	22.67	40.27 /97	7.26 /74	11.04 /66	0.92	1.56
HL	ICON Healthcare A	ICHAX	D	(800) 764-0442	C+ / 6.6	9.70	3.55	19.51 /49	8.70 /85	17.08 /98	0.00	1.62
HL	ICON Healthcare S	ICHCX	D+	(800) 764-0442	B / 7.8	9.75	3.81	19.96 /52	9.08 /87	17.52 /98	0.00	1.36
OT	ICON Industrials A	ICIAX	B	(800) 764-0442	B- / 7.3	6.53	13.59	31.58 /89	6.40 /67	10.60 /63	0.00	2.67
SC	ICON Industrials S	ICTRX	A-	(800) 764-0442	B+ / 8.5	6.61	13.78	31.85 /90	6.65 /69	10.86 /65	0.00	1.53
TC	ICON Information Technology A	ICTTX	A	(800) 764-0442	A+ / 9.8	11.42	12.13	28.79 /83	15.34 /99	13.29 /87	0.00	1.90
TC	ICON Information Technology S	ICTEX	A+	(800) 764-0442	A+ / 9.9	11.56	12.32	29.24 /85	15.71 /99	13.74 /91	0.00	1.44
FO	ICON Intl Equity A	IIQAX	D-	(800) 764-0442	E / 0.3	8.05	0.52	9.67 /11	-2.52 / 5	1.25 / 7	0.00	2.25
FO	ICON Intl Equity C	IIQCX	D-	(800) 764-0442	E / 0.4	7.87	0.09	8.87 / 9	-3.19 / 4	0.52 / 5	0.00	2.96
FO	ICON Intl Equity S	ICNEX	D-	(800) 764-0442	E+ / 0.6	8.10	0.68	10.10 /12	-2.14 / 6	1.62 / 7	0.00	1.41
GR	ICON Long/Short A	ISTAX	B+	(800) 764-0442	B+ / 8.9	11.32	19.93	37.45 /96	6.02 /64	9.34 /53	0.00	1.73
GR	ICON Long/Short C	IOLCX	B+	(800) 764-0442	A- / 9.2	11.10	19.48	36.41 /95	5.22 /57	8.52 /46	0.00	2.53
GR	ICON Long/Short S	IOLZX	A-	(800) 764-0442	A+ / 9.6	11.38	20.04	37.83 /96	6.32 /67	9.65 /56	0.00	1.37
OT	ICON Natural Resources A	ICBAX	D	(800) 764-0442	C / 4.6	4.97	11.53	33.52 /92	1.77 /22	6.54 /32	0.49	1.76
OT	ICON Natural Resources C	ICBCX	D	(800) 764-0442	C / 5.0	4.78	11.09	32.35 /91	0.87 /18	5.67 /26	0.36	2.94
OT	ICON Natural Resources S	ICBMX	D+	(800) 764-0442	C+ / 5.9	5.07	11.59	33.76 /93	1.95 /24	6.81 /33	0.52	1.42
SC	ICON Opportunities	ICONX	A-	(800) 764-0442	A / 9.5	6.52	15.64	35.37 /94	8.01 /79	--	0.00	1.58
GR	ICON Risk-Managed Balanced A	IOCAX	C+	(800) 764-0442	D+ / 2.9	5.35	4.99	12.87 /21	4.43 /48	6.01 /28	1.25	1.78
GR	ICON Risk-Managed Balanced C	IOCCX	C+	(800) 764-0442	C- / 3.3	5.21	4.56	12.02 /18	3.64 /38	5.21 /23	0.74	2.46
GR	ICON Risk-Managed Balanced S	IOCZX	B-	(800) 764-0442	C- / 4.1	5.43	5.07	13.12 /22	4.67 /50	6.25 /30	1.52	1.42
GR	ICON S	ICNZX	B+	(800) 764-0442	B+ / 8.8	11.22	18.91	35.34 /94	4.56 /49	8.87 /50	0.00	1.09
UT	ICON Utilities A	ICTVX	A	(800) 764-0442	B+ / 8.5	9.68	6.97	19.70 /50	11.92 /98	12.03 /75	2.46	1.89
UT	ICON Utilities S	ICTUX	A+	(800) 764-0442	A / 9.5	9.85	7.09	20.03 /52	12.24 /98	12.30 /77	2.75	1.70
GR	ID 529 IDeal CSP Aggr Growth Port		C+	(800) 662-7447	C+ / 6.8	7.59	7.89	23.13 /67	6.08 /65	10.00 /58	0.00	0.86
GI	ID 529 IDeal CSP Csv Growth Port		C+	(800) 662-7447	D / 1.9	2.54	0.07	6.36 / 5	3.30 /35	3.82 /14	0.00	0.83
GI	ID 529 IDeal CSP Growth Port		B	(800) 662-7447	C / 5.1	5.89	5.23	17.45 /40	5.27 /57	8.00 /42	0.00	0.85
GI	ID 529 IDeal CSP Mod Growth Port		B-	(800) 662-7447	C- / 3.4	4.21	2.65	11.85 /17	4.35 /47	5.97 /28	0.00	0.84
GR	Iman Fund	IMANX	B	(877) 417-6161	B+ / 8.5	7.60	8.33	25.76 /75	8.73 /85	11.79 /72	0.02	1.39
GR	IMS Capital Value Inst	IMSCX	C	(800) 934-5550	C+ / 5.7	6.34	7.10	21.33 /59	5.13 /56	7.54 /39	0.00	1.69
AA	IMS Dividend Growth Inst	IMSAX	A-		B / 8.0	6.31	9.28	27.34 /80	7.83 /78	9.50 /55	0.90	2.37
GI	IMS Strategic Income Inst	IMSIX	E-		E- / 0.0	-1.31	-1.33	5.89 / 5	-12.61 / 0	-4.94 / 2	9.60	2.25
IN	Income 529 Port A		C	(800) 342-5236	E+ / 0.8	1.90	1.57	4.50 / 4	0.96 /18	1.14 / 6	0.00	1.21
IN	● Income 529 Port B		C	(800) 342-5236	E+ / 0.9	1.82	1.23	3.77 / 3	0.21 /14	0.39 / 5	0.00	1.96
IN	Income 529 Port C		C	(800) 342-5236	E+ / 0.9	1.74	1.15	3.69 / 3	0.19 /14	0.37 / 5	0.00	1.96
GR	Independent Franch Partners US Eq	IFPUX	A+	(855) 233-0437	A+ / 9.7	10.67	8.27	24.00 /70	12.39 /98	13.92 /93	1.26	0.80
GL	Infinity Q Diversified Alpha Inst	IQDNX	U	(844) 473-8631	U /	4.98	5.08	3.11 / 3	--	--	2.39	2.56
AA	Innealta Capital Country Rotation I	ICCIX	C-	(855) 873-3837	D+ / 2.8	6.88	4.40	18.14 /43	1.62 /22	2.47 / 9	1.81	2.16
AA	Innealta Capital Country Rotation N	ICCNX	C-	(855) 873-3837	D+ / 2.6	6.84	4.25	17.91 /42	1.38 /20	2.22 / 9	1.52	2.42
GR	Innealta Captl Sector Rotation I	ICSIX	A	(855) 873-3837	B- / 7.0	6.37	12.38	23.04 /67	6.59 /69	5.08 /22	4.57	2.39
GR	Innealta Captl Sector Rotation N	ICSNX	B	(855) 873-3837	C+ / 6.9	6.33	12.25	22.75 /66	6.34 /67	4.85 /20	4.18	2.64
AA	Innovator McKinley Income Inst	IMIIX	D+	(877) 386-3890	C- / 3.9	7.78	4.79	18.35 /44	2.71 /29	--	8.78	2.69
AA	Innovator McKinley Income Inv	IMIFX	E+	(877) 386-3890	D- / 1.4	7.76	4.73	18.25 /44	-0.84 /10	--	9.75	2.79
GL	Insignia Macro A	IGMFX	C-	(866) 759-5679	E / 0.5	-0.11	-0.71	-2.94 / 1	1.88 /23	--	0.08	2.46
GL	Insignia Macro I	IGMLX	C-	(866) 759-5679	E+ / 0.8	-0.05	-0.65	-2.88 / 1	1.94 /24	--	0.15	2.25
EM	● Institutional Emerging Markets I	HLMEX	C-	(877) 435-8105	C / 4.4	8.26	4.18	28.52 /83	2.01 /24	2.90 /10	0.57	1.31

● Denotes fund is closed to new investors
* Denotes fund is included in Section II

www.thestreetratings.com

Risk Rating/Pts	3 Year Standard Deviation	Beta	NAV As of 2/28/17	Total $(Mil)	Cash %	Stocks %	Bonds %	Other %	Portfolio Turnover Ratio	Last Bull Market Return	Last Bear Market Return	Manager Quality Pct	Manager Tenure (Years)	Initial Purch. $	Additional Purch. $	Front End Load	Back End Load
E+ /0.8	21.3	1.05	12.90	13	6	93	0	1	99	6.9	-28.2	20	10	1,000	100	5.8	0.0
E+ /0.7	21.2	1.05	12.41	10	6	93	0	1	99	2.4	-28.4	14	10	1,000	100	0.0	0.0
E+ /0.8	21.3	1.05	12.97	312	6	93	0	1	99	8.6	-28.0	23	10	1,000	100	0.0	0.0
B- /7.3	9.9	0.87	17.08	16	0	91	7	2	145	101.5	-16.7	75	15	1,000	100	5.8	0.0
B- /7.3	9.9	0.87	17.26	13	0	91	7	2	145	93.6	-17.0	67	15	1,000	100	0.0	0.0
B- /7.2	9.9	0.87	17.12	55	0	91	7	2	145	104.2	-16.6	77	15	1,000	100	0.0	0.0
C /5.3	16.9	1.24	9.54	2	1	98	0	1	49	109.3	-25.5	4	14	1,000	100	5.8	0.0
C /5.3	16.9	1.24	9.49	43	1	98	0	1	49	113.3	-25.4	4	14	1,000	100	0.0	0.0
D- /1.1	14.4	0.98	15.25	5	15	84	0	1	107	153.7	-11.7	54	4	1,000	100	5.8	0.0
D- /1.1	14.4	0.98	15.86	86	15	84	0	1	107	158.9	-11.6	59	4	1,000	100	0.0	0.0
C+ /6.2	13.1	1.12	14.04	4	10	89	0	1	87	110.5	-26.2	14	N/A	1,000	100	5.8	0.0
C+ /6.2	13.2	0.72	14.20	25	10	89	0	1	87	115.6	-25.9	84	N/A	1,000	100	0.0	0.0
C+ /5.6	12.6	0.99	15.83	3	0	99	0	1	94	135.8	-13.6	94	N/A	1,000	100	5.8	0.0
C+ /5.7	12.6	0.99	16.31	47	0	99	0	1	94	141.0	-13.5	95	N/A	1,000	100	0.0	0.0
C+ /6.6	11.3	0.85	11.68	2	23	76	0	1	198	28.3	-33.2	42	12	1,000	100	5.8	0.0
C+ /6.5	11.3	0.85	10.56	3	23	76	0	1	198	23.5	-33.4	33	12	1,000	100	0.0	0.0
C+ /6.6	11.3	0.85	11.88	42	23	76	0	1	198	31.0	-33.1	48	12	1,000	100	0.0	0.0
C /5.2	15.2	1.20	22.02	6	0	100	0	0	20	92.5	-16.3	8	6	1,000	100	5.8	0.0
C /5.1	15.2	1.20	20.12	5	0	100	0	0	20	84.8	-16.5	5	6	1,000	100	0.0	0.0
C /5.2	15.2	1.20	22.70	9	0	100	0	0	20	95.5	-16.1	9	6	1,000	100	0.0	0.0
C- /3.3	17.3	1.32	14.21	6	12	87	0	1	81	77.0	-27.1	1	10	1,000	100	5.8	0.0
C- /3.2	17.3	1.32	13.78	2	12	87	0	1	81	69.2	-27.3	1	10	1,000	100	0.0	0.0
C- /3.3	17.3	1.32	14.33	72	12	87	0	1	81	79.5	-27.0	1	10	1,000	100	0.0	0.0
C /5.4	16.6	0.99	16.53	18	2	97	0	1	95	N/A	N/A	81	5	1,000	100	0.0	0.0
B /8.8	6.5	0.60	14.86	8	5	55	38	2	109	48.6	-10.7	52	4	1,000	100	5.8	0.0
B /8.8	6.5	0.59	13.95	15	5	55	38	2	109	42.8	-11.0	41	4	1,000	100	0.0	0.0
B /8.8	6.5	0.60	15.23	15	5	55	38	2	109	50.6	-10.6	55	4	1,000	100	0.0	0.0
C /4.8	15.2	1.22	16.85	31	0	99	0	1	31	92.3	-20.8	4	6	1,000	100	0.0	0.0
C+ /6.6	13.5	0.86	9.03	10	3	96	0	1	168	84.6	-0.2	68	3	1,000	100	5.8	0.0
C+ /6.6	13.5	0.86	9.18	40	3	96	0	1	168	87.2	N/A	71	3	1,000	100	0.0	0.0
C+ /6.9	10.4	0.98	15.17	80	0	99	0	1	0	94.7	-19.9	23	10	25	25	0.0	0.0
B+ /9.7	3.4	0.23	14.56	58	0	25	74	1	0	28.2	-2.0	80	10	25	25	0.0	0.0
B /8.3	7.8	0.73	15.28	47	0	74	24	2	0	70.5	-14.3	44	10	25	25	0.0	0.0
B+ /9.4	5.4	0.48	15.10	53	0	49	49	2	0	48.8	-8.3	66	10	25	25	0.0	0.0
C /5.2	11.9	1.10	11.81	76	0	99	0	1	71	110.0	-20.3	38	17	250	50	0.0	0.0
C+ /5.6	11.6	1.02	23.83	41	0	99	0	1	65	91.0	-29.3	13	21	5,000	100	0.0	0.5
C+ /6.8	11.3	1.71	14.47	10	1	98	0	1	7	87.3	-14.7	17	15	5,000	100	0.0	0.5
D+ /2.5	10.5	0.49	3.02	6	2	7	90	1	394	-17.4	-10.5	0	15	5,000	100	0.0	0.5
B+ /9.9	2.5	0.15	15.56	31	0	0	0	100	0	8.9	0.4	66	12	250	0	4.3	0.0
B+ /9.9	2.5	0.15	14.02	1	0	0	0	100	0	4.6	0.2	56	12	250	0	0.0	0.0
B+ /9.9	2.5	0.15	14.06	14	0	0	0	100	0	4.5	0.2	56	12	250	0	0.0	0.0
C+ /6.6	11.1	0.97	16.87	1,753	5	94	0	1	19	N/A	N/A	85	6	3,000,000	250,000	0.0	0.0
U /	N/A	N/A	10.16	148	0	0	0	100	62	N/A	N/A	N/A	3	1,000,000	10,000	0.0	1.0
B- /7.1	8.5	0.94	10.23	45	4	26	69	1	137	N/A	N/A	14	6	100,000	0	0.0	2.0
B- /7.1	8.6	0.95	10.23	10	4	26	69	1	137	N/A	N/A	11	6	5,000	1,000	0.0	2.0
B /8.0	5.9	0.39	11.48	25	7	9	83	1	153	N/A	N/A	88	6	100,000	0	0.0	2.0
B /8.0	5.9	0.39	11.50	9	7	9	83	1	153	N/A	N/A	87	6	5,000	1,000	0.0	2.0
C /4.9	11.0	1.47	17.97	N/A	24	73	2	1	73	N/A	N/A	4	2	3,000,000	10,000	0.0	0.0
C- /4.2	11.2	1.51	16.02	32	24	73	2	1	73	N/A	N/A	1	2	2,000	1,000	0.0	0.0
B+ /9.5	5.2	-0.09	9.93	N/A	35	0	64	1	132	N/A	N/A	85	4	2,500	0	5.5	1.0
B+ /9.5	5.2	-0.09	9.93	53	35	0	64	1	132	N/A	N/A	85	4	250,000	0	0.0	1.0
C /4.9	14.4	0.86	18.15	3,296	2	94	2	2	20	42.0	-24.1	78	12	500,000	0	0.0	2.0

Fund Type	Fund Name	Ticker Symbol	Overall Investment Rating	Phone	Performance Rating/Pts	3 Mo	6 Mo	1Yr / Pct	3Yr / Pct	5Yr / Pct	Dividend Yield	Expense Ratio
EM	● Institutional Emerging Markets II	HLEEX	U	(877) 435-8105	U /	8.36	4.24	28.85 /84	--	--	1.11	1.27
GL	INTECH Global Income Managed Vol	JGDAX	C-	(800) 295-2687	D+ / 2.9	5.47	2.69	10.08 /12	5.52 /60	8.95 /50	2.46	1.48
GL	INTECH Global Income Managed Vol	JGDCX	C	(800) 295-2687	C- / 3.4	5.35	2.37	9.33 /10	4.74 /51	8.14 /43	1.98	2.17
GL	● INTECH Global Income Managed Vol	JGDDX	C+	(800) 295-2687	C- / 4.1	5.56	2.83	10.34 /12	5.70 /62	9.08 /51	2.82	1.33
GL	INTECH Global Income Managed Vol	JGDIX	C+	(800) 295-2687	C- / 4.2	5.62	2.84	10.43 /13	5.82 /63	9.26 /53	2.86	1.18
GL	INTECH Global Income Managed Vol	JGDSX	C+	(800) 295-2687	C- / 4.0	5.49	2.70	10.13 /12	5.60 /61	8.95 /50	2.57	1.79
GL	INTECH Global Income Managed Vol	JDGTX	C+	(800) 295-2687	C- / 4.1	5.61	2.78	10.32 /12	5.63 /61	9.05 /51	2.73	1.31
FO	INTECH International Managed Vol A	JMIAX	E+	(800) 295-2687	E / 0.3	4.92	-0.09	7.32 / 6	-1.59 / 8	6.34 /31	1.62	1.24
FO	INTECH International Managed Vol C	JMICX	E+	(800) 295-2687	E / 0.4	4.83	-0.41	6.56 / 5	-2.27 / 6	6.11 /29	1.20	1.94
FO	● INTECH International Managed Vol D	JIIDX	D	(800) 295-2687	E+ / 0.7	4.93	0.00	7.36 / 6	-1.32 / 8	6.64 /32	1.70	1.17
FO	INTECH International Managed Vol I	JMIIX	E+	(800) 295-2687	E+ / 0.7	4.89	-0.03	7.46 / 6	-1.28 / 8	6.66 /33	1.55	0.87
FO	INTECH International Managed Vol S	JMISX	E+	(800) 295-2687	E+ / 0.6	4.90	-0.23	7.01 / 6	-1.58 / 8	6.36 /31	1.71	1.40
FO	INTECH International Managed Vol T	JRMTX	E+	(800) 295-2687	E+ / 0.6	4.97	0.03	7.40 / 6	-1.45 / 8	6.38 /31	1.73	1.16
GR	● INTECH US Core A	JDOAX	C	(800) 295-2687	C+ / 6.9	7.17	8.86	20.09 /53	8.72 /85	13.39 /88	1.16	0.94
GR	● INTECH US Core C	JLCCX	C+	(800) 295-2687	B- / 7.3	7.07	8.62	19.40 /49	7.97 /79	12.57 /80	0.54	1.73
GR	● INTECH US Core D	JIRMX	C+	(800) 295-2687	B / 8.0	7.23	8.98	20.34 /54	8.91 /86	13.58 /90	1.40	0.79
GR	● INTECH US Core I	JRMCX	C+	(800) 295-2687	B / 8.1	7.28	9.09	20.52 /55	9.03 /87	13.72 /91	1.50	0.68
GR	● INTECH US Core N	JRCNX	A-	(800) 295-2687	B / 8.1	7.30	9.11	20.55 /55	9.04 /87	13.64 /90	1.56	0.57
GR	● INTECH US Core S	JLCIX	C+	(800) 295-2687	B / 7.7	7.17	8.87	19.96 /52	8.55 /83	13.23 /86	1.05	1.12
GR	● INTECH US Core T	JRMSX	C+	(800) 295-2687	B / 7.9	7.25	9.00	20.23 /53	8.82 /86	13.50 /89	1.31	0.87
GR	INTECH US Managed Volatility A	JRSAX	D+	(800) 295-2687	C+ / 6.2	8.14	6.48	16.52 /36	8.38 /82	13.50 /89	1.15	0.93
GR	INTECH US Managed Volatility C	JRSCX	D+	(800) 295-2687	C+ / 6.7	7.97	6.15	15.65 /33	7.68 /77	12.74 /81	0.69	1.66
GR	INTECH US Managed Volatility D	JRSDX	B+	(800) 295-2687	B- / 7.2	8.13	6.55	16.59 /37	8.56 /83	13.74 /91	1.33	0.83
GR	INTECH US Managed Volatility I	JRSIX	C-	(800) 295-2687	B- / 7.4	8.23	6.68	16.87 /38	8.72 /85	13.84 /92	1.40	0.65
GR	INTECH US Managed Volatility N	JRSNX	B+	(800) 295-2687	B- / 7.4	8.21	6.65	16.88 /38	8.77 /85	13.87 /92	1.45	0.61
GR	INTECH US Managed Volatility S	JRSSX	C-	(800) 295-2687	B- / 7.1	8.11	6.44	16.51 /36	8.34 /82	13.48 /89	0.98	1.13
GR	INTECH US Managed Volatility T	JRSTX	C-	(800) 295-2687	B- / 7.2	8.17	6.49	16.65 /37	8.50 /83	13.60 /90	1.26	0.86
IN	Integrity Dividend Harvest A	IDIVX	A+	(800) 601-5593	B+ / 8.8	5.96	8.68	21.96 /62	12.29 /98	--	2.49	1.58
GI	Integrity Growth & Income A	IGIAX	C	(800) 601-5593	C / 5.3	7.48	8.64	20.87 /57	5.54 /60	9.20 /52	1.31	1.85
AA	Intrepid Capital Institutional	ICMVX	C-	(866) 996-3863	C- / 3.8	2.07	4.55	19.85 /51	4.12 /44	6.93 /34	2.98	1.17
GI	Intrepid Capital Investor	ICMBX	C-	(866) 996-3863	C- / 3.5	2.01	4.33	19.44 /49	3.88 /41	6.66 /33	2.74	1.42
GR	Intrepid Disciplined Value Investor	ICMCX	C+	(866) 996-3863	C / 4.3	3.27	4.94	15.21 /31	5.69 /61	7.73 /40	0.53	1.31
SC	Intrepid Endurance Inst	ICMZX	D	(866) 996-3863	E+ / 0.8	-1.00	-0.86	7.73 / 7	0.37 /15	3.80 /14	0.02	1.17
SC	Intrepid Endurance Inv	ICMAX	D	(866) 996-3863	E+ / 0.7	-0.97	-0.97	7.57 / 7	0.12 /14	3.55 /13	0.00	1.42
GR	Invesco All Cap Market Neutral A	CPNAX	C-	(800) 959-4246	D- / 1.5	-2.91	7.01	-4.19 / 1	5.32 /58	--	0.00	2.16
GR	Invesco All Cap Market Neutral C	CPNCX	C-	(800) 959-4246	D / 1.7	-3.07	6.49	-5.01 / 1	4.51 /49	--	0.00	2.91
GR	Invesco All Cap Market Neutral R	CPNRX	C-	(800) 959-4246	D / 2.0	-3.02	6.84	-4.49 / 1	5.02 /54	--	0.00	2.41
GR	Invesco All Cap Market Neutral R5	CPNFX	C	(800) 959-4246	D / 2.2	-2.89	7.07	-4.07 / 1	5.52 /60	--	0.00	1.81
GR	Invesco All Cap Market Neutral R6	CPNSX	C	(800) 959-4246	D / 2.2	-2.80	7.07	-3.98 / 1	5.52 /60	--	0.00	1.81
GR	Invesco All Cap Market Neutral Y	CPNYX	C	(800) 959-4246	D / 2.2	-2.89	7.07	-4.07 / 1	5.52 /60	--	0.00	1.91
* IN	Invesco American Franchise A	VAFAX	C+	(800) 959-4246	B- / 7.2	10.10	9.71	25.64 /75	7.33 /74	12.04 /75	0.00	1.08
IN	● Invesco American Franchise B	VAFBX	B-	(800) 959-4246	B / 8.1	10.07	9.73	25.55 /75	7.32 /74	12.05 /75	0.00	1.08
IN	Invesco American Franchise C	VAFCX	C+	(800) 959-4246	B / 7.6	9.89	9.34	24.69 /72	6.55 /69	11.22 /68	0.00	1.83
GR	Invesco American Franchise R	VAFRX	B-	(800) 959-4246	B / 8.0	10.00	9.61	25.27 /74	7.07 /72	11.76 /72	0.00	1.33
GR	Invesco American Franchise R5	VAFNX	B	(800) 959-4246	B+ / 8.4	10.17	9.91	26.00 /76	7.71 /77	12.44 /78	0.00	0.71
GR	Invesco American Franchise R6	VAFFX	B	(800) 959-4246	B+ / 8.5	10.19	9.93	26.13 /77	7.81 /78	12.48 /79	0.00	0.63
IN	Invesco American Franchise Y	VAFIX	B	(800) 959-4246	B+ / 8.3	10.18	9.86	25.95 /76	7.60 /76	12.32 /77	0.00	0.83
GR	Invesco American Value A	MSAVX	C	(800) 959-4246	B- / 7.1	7.28	11.59	32.59 /91	5.93 /64	11.52 /70	0.19	1.33
GR	● Invesco American Value B	MGAVX	C+	(800) 959-4246	B / 8.1	7.28	11.61	32.59 /91	5.92 /63	11.52 /70	0.22	1.33
GR	Invesco American Value C	MSVCX	C	(800) 959-4246	B- / 7.5	7.10	11.21	31.63 /89	5.15 /56	10.70 /63	0.00	2.07
GR	Invesco American Value R	MSARX	C+	(800) 959-4246	B / 7.9	7.19	11.45	32.24 /90	5.65 /61	11.24 /68	0.00	1.58
GR	Invesco American Value R5	MSAJX	C+	(800) 959-4246	B+ / 8.4	7.37	11.80	33.08 /92	6.31 /67	11.92 /74	0.51	0.96

● Denotes fund is closed to new investors
* Denotes fund is included in Section II

www.thestreetratings.com

RISK			NET ASSETS		ASSET					BULL / BEAR		FUND MANAGER		MINIMUMS		LOADS	
	3 Year		NAV						Portfolio	Last Bull	Last Bear	Manager	Manager	Initial	Additional	Front	Back
Risk	Standard		As of	Total	Cash	Stocks	Bonds	Other	Turnover	Market	Market	Quality	Tenure	Purch.	Purch.	End	End
Rating/Pts	Deviation	Beta	2/28/17	$(Mil)	%	%	%	%	Ratio	Return	Return	Pct	(Years)	$	$	Load	Load
U /	N/A	N/A	10.30	394	2	94	2	2	20	N/A	N/A	N/A	12	25,000,000	0	0.0	2.0
B- /7.4	8.6	0.92	12.83	32	1	98	0	1	41	N/A	N/A	82	6	2,500	0	5.8	0.0
B- /7.4	8.6	0.92	12.75	17	1	98	0	1	41	N/A	N/A	77	6	2,500	0	0.0	0.0
B- /7.4	8.6	0.92	12.80	49	1	98	0	1	41	N/A	N/A	83	6	2,500	100	0.0	0.0
B- /7.4	8.6	0.92	12.87	37	1	98	0	1	41	N/A	N/A	84	6	1,000,000	0	0.0	0.0
B- /7.4	8.6	0.92	12.81	N/A	1	98	0	1	41	N/A	N/A	83	6	2,500	0	0.0	0.0
B- /7.4	8.6	0.92	12.82	61	1	98	0	1	41	N/A	N/A	82	6	2,500	0	0.0	0.0
C /5.2	9.9	0.69	7.81	11	2	97	0	1	74	52.4	-24.8	55	10	2,500	0	5.8	0.0
C /5.2	9.9	0.69	7.67	2	2	97	0	1	74	50.4	-24.9	45	10	2,500	0	0.0	0.0
B- /7.2	9.9	0.69	7.73	3	2	97	0	1	74	54.5	-24.7	59	10	2,500	100	0.0	0.0
C /5.1	9.9	0.69	7.76	22	2	97	0	1	74	54.7	-24.7	60	10	1,000,000	0	0.0	0.0
C /5.2	9.8	0.69	7.82	1	2	97	0	1	74	52.3	-24.7	55	10	2,500	0	0.0	0.0
C /5.2	9.9	0.70	7.73	21	2	97	0	1	74	52.7	-24.8	57	10	2,500	0	0.0	0.0
C- /4.2	9.8	0.89	19.33	25	0	99	0	1	106	128.2	-15.6	66	14	2,500	0	5.8	0.0
C- /4.1	9.8	0.89	19.05	14	0	99	0	1	106	119.2	-15.9	58	14	2,500	0	0.0	0.0
C- /4.2	9.8	0.89	19.36	294	0	99	0	1	106	130.1	-15.5	68	14	2,500	100	0.0	0.0
C- /4.1	9.8	0.89	19.38	109	0	99	0	1	106	131.6	-15.4	70	14	1,000,000	0	0.0	0.0
C+ /6.8	9.8	0.89	19.36	16	0	99	0	1	106	130.7	-15.6	70	14	0	0	0.0	0.0
C- /4.1	9.8	0.89	19.25	32	0	99	0	1	106	126.2	-15.6	65	14	2,500	0	0.0	0.0
C- /4.2	9.8	0.89	19.36	119	0	99	0	1	106	129.3	-15.6	67	14	2,500	0	0.0	0.0
D+ /2.7	8.8	0.67	10.25	41	2	97	0	1	72	127.5	-18.1	82	12	2,500	0	5.8	0.0
D+ /2.6	8.8	0.67	10.00	25	2	97	0	1	72	119.3	-18.4	78	12	2,500	0	0.0	0.0
B- /7.1	8.9	0.67	10.13	20	2	97	0	1	72	130.3	-18.0	83	12	2,500	100	0.0	0.0
D+ /2.6	8.9	0.67	10.25	190	2	97	0	1	72	131.4	-18.0	84	12	1,000,000	0	0.0	0.0
B- /7.0	8.9	0.67	10.21	70	2	97	0	1	72	131.7	-18.0	84	12	0	0	0.0	0.0
D+ /2.6	8.9	0.68	10.24	4	2	97	0	1	72	127.0	-18.1	82	12	2,500	0	0.0	0.0
D+ /2.5	8.9	0.68	10.13	146	2	97	0	1	72	128.5	-18.1	82	12	2,500	0	0.0	0.0
B- /7.5	8.4	0.67	14.83	121	0	100	0	0	38	N/A	N/A	95	5	1,000	50	5.0	0.0
C+ /5.7	10.4	0.95	50.83	34	1	98	0	1	50	96.4	-20.9	21	7	1,000	50	5.0	0.0
C+ /6.3	7.4	0.94	11.66	300	24	47	27	2	43	58.3	-9.5	37	12	250,000	100	0.0	2.0
C+ /6.3	7.4	0.59	11.65	111	24	47	27	2	43	56.1	-9.6	46	12	2,500	100	0.0	2.0
B- /7.1	6.4	0.50	10.62	50	56	43	0	1	32	71.0	-14.7	77	7	2,500	100	0.0	2.0
B- /7.4	4.1	0.15	14.52	69	74	25	0	1	40	36.8	-10.6	65	7	250,000	100	0.0	2.0
B- /7.4	4.1	0.15	14.21	162	74	25	0	1	40	35.1	-10.6	62	7	2,500	100	0.0	2.0
B /8.3	9.4	-0.24	10.16	38	96	0	3	1	168	N/A	N/A	98	4	1,000	50	5.5	0.0
B /8.3	9.4	-0.23	9.93	9	96	0	3	1	168	N/A	N/A	97	4	1,000	50	0.0	0.0
B /8.3	9.4	-0.24	10.08	N/A	96	0	3	1	168	N/A	N/A	98	4	0	0	0.0	0.0
B /8.3	9.4	-0.23	10.22	1	96	0	3	1	168	N/A	N/A	98	4	10,000,000	0	0.0	0.0
B /8.3	9.4	-0.23	10.22	73	96	0	3	1	168	N/A	N/A	98	4	10,000,000	0	0.0	0.0
B /8.3	9.4	-0.23	10.22	43	96	0	3	1	168	N/A	N/A	98	4	1,000	50	0.0	0.0
C /4.8	13.3	1.13	17.89	8,597	0	98	0	2	59	114.3	-19.3	20	7	1,000	50	5.5	0.0
C /4.7	13.3	1.13	17.40	83	0	98	0	2	59	114.3	-19.5	20	7	1,000	50	0.0	0.0
C /4.6	13.3	1.13	16.69	369	0	98	0	2	59	105.9	-19.6	14	7	1,000	50	0.0	0.0
C /4.7	13.3	1.13	17.61	30	0	98	0	2	59	111.3	-19.4	18	7	0	0	0.0	0.0
C /4.8	13.2	1.13	18.22	59	0	98	0	2	59	118.3	-19.2	24	7	10,000,000	0	0.0	0.0
C /4.8	13.3	1.13	18.29	121	0	98	0	2	59	118.5	-19.3	25	7	10,000,000	0	0.0	0.0
C /4.8	13.3	1.13	18.20	175	0	98	0	2	59	117.1	-19.3	23	7	1,000	50	0.0	0.0
C- /3.9	13.5	1.14	39.84	1,106	1	97	0	2	28	121.5	-21.8	10	14	1,000	50	5.5	0.0
C- /3.7	13.5	1.14	35.28	9	1	97	0	2	28	121.6	-21.8	10	14	1,000	50	0.0	0.0
C- /3.5	13.5	1.14	33.59	104	1	97	0	2	28	112.9	-22.0	7	14	1,000	50	0.0	0.0
C- /3.9	13.5	1.14	39.58	52	1	97	0	2	28	118.5	-21.9	9	14	0	0	0.0	0.0
C- /3.9	13.5	1.14	40.15	114	1	97	0	2	28	126.0	-21.6	12	14	10,000,000	0	0.0	0.0

Fund Type	Fund Name	Ticker Symbol	Overall Investment Rating	Phone	Performance Rating/Pts	3 Mo	6 Mo	1Yr / Pct	3Yr / Pct	5Yr / Pct	Dividend Yield	Expense Ratio
MC	Invesco American Value R6	MSAFX	C+	(800) 959-4246	B+ / 8.4	7.39	11.85	33.16 /92	6.41 /68	11.96 /74	0.59	0.87
GR	Invesco American Value Y	MSAIX	C+	(800) 959-4246	B+ / 8.3	7.34	11.75	32.93 /91	6.19 /66	11.80 /72	0.40	1.08
FO	Invesco Asia Pacific Growth A	ASIAX	C-	(800) 959-4246	C- / 3.4	5.89	1.81	20.82 /56	4.19 /45	5.93 /28	0.87	1.46
FO	● Invesco Asia Pacific Growth B	ASIBX	C-	(800) 959-4246	C- / 3.9	5.70	1.47	19.93 /52	3.42 /36	5.14 /22	0.21	2.21
FO	Invesco Asia Pacific Growth C	ASICX	C-	(800) 959-4246	C- / 3.9	5.70	1.45	19.94 /52	3.42 /36	5.13 /22	0.21	2.21
FO	Invesco Asia Pacific Growth Y	ASIYX	C	(800) 959-4246	C / 4.8	5.94	1.97	21.13 /58	4.46 /48	6.19 /30	1.16	1.21
AA	Invesco Balanced Risk Alloc A	ABRZX	D+	(800) 959-4246	D+ / 2.5	4.20	2.92	14.45 /28	3.98 /43	4.23 /16	3.45	1.32
AA	● Invesco Balanced Risk Alloc B	ABRBX	C-	(800) 959-4246	D+ / 2.9	3.97	2.55	13.61 /24	3.21 /34	3.44 /13	2.95	2.07
AA	Invesco Balanced Risk Alloc C	ABRCX	C-	(800) 959-4246	D+ / 2.9	3.97	2.55	13.61 /24	3.21 /34	3.44 /13	2.95	2.07
AA	Invesco Balanced Risk Alloc R	ABRRX	C-	(800) 959-4246	C- / 3.3	4.16	2.87	14.24 /27	3.73 /40	3.97 /15	3.42	1.57
AA	Invesco Balanced Risk Alloc R5	ABRIX	C-	(800) 959-4246	C- / 3.7	4.22	3.05	14.78 /29	4.27 /46	4.51 /18	3.93	1.04
GL	Invesco Balanced Risk Alloc R6	ALLFX	C-	(800) 959-4246	C- / 3.8	4.30	3.13	14.97 /30	4.39 /47	4.57 /19	4.00	0.94
AA	Invesco Balanced Risk Alloc Y	ABRYX	C-	(800) 959-4246	C- / 3.7	4.25	3.07	14.70 /29	4.23 /46	4.48 /18	3.87	1.07
BA	Invesco Balanced-Risk Com Str A	BRCAX	E	(800) 959-4246	E- / 0.1	2.86	6.91	16.42 /36	-7.98 / 1	-8.37 / 1	2.37	1.64
BA	● Invesco Balanced-Risk Com Str B	BRCBX	E	(800) 959-4246	E- / 0.1	2.76	6.64	15.54 /32	-8.66 / 1	-9.03 / 1	2.24	2.39
BA	Invesco Balanced-Risk Com Str C	BRCCX	E	(800) 959-4246	E- / 0.1	2.77	6.65	15.57 /32	-8.67 / 1	-9.06 / 1	2.25	2.39
BA	Invesco Balanced-Risk Com Str R	BRCRX	E	(800) 959-4246	E- / 0.1	2.92	6.86	16.09 /35	-8.19 / 1	-8.58 / 1	2.41	1.89
BA	Invesco Balanced-Risk Com Str R5	BRCNX	E	(800) 959-4246	E- / 0.2	3.03	7.17	16.71 /37	-7.63 / 1	-8.08 / 1	2.67	1.24
OT	Invesco Balanced-Risk Com Str R6	IBRFX	E	(800) 959-4246	E- / 0.2	2.96	7.08	16.95 /38	-7.56 / 1	-8.07 / 1	2.74	1.14
BA	Invesco Balanced-Risk Com Str Y	BRCYX	E	(800) 959-4246	E- / 0.2	3.02	7.17	16.73 /37	-7.75 / 1	-8.13 / 1	2.66	1.39
AA	Invesco Balanced-Risk Ret 2020 A	AFTAX	C-	(800) 959-4246	D / 1.8	3.03	2.22	11.01 /14	3.21 /34	3.61 /13	2.50	1.39
AA	Invesco Balanced-Risk Ret 2020 AX	VRCAX	C-	(800) 959-4246	D / 1.8	3.03	2.22	11.01 /14	3.21 /34	3.61 /13	2.50	1.39
AA	● Invesco Balanced-Risk Ret 2020 B	AFTBX	C-	(800) 959-4246	D / 2.2	3.06	2.01	10.39 /13	2.51 /28	2.86 /10	1.89	2.14
AA	Invesco Balanced-Risk Ret 2020 C	AFTCX	C-	(800) 959-4246	D / 2.2	3.07	2.02	10.41 /13	2.51 /28	2.87 /10	1.89	2.14
AA	● Invesco Balanced-Risk Ret 2020 CX	VRCCX	C-	(800) 959-4246	D / 2.1	2.95	1.79	10.15 /12	2.44 /27	2.84 /10	1.89	2.14
AA	Invesco Balanced-Risk Ret 2020 R	ATFRX	C-	(800) 959-4246	D+ / 2.4	3.13	2.20	10.91 /14	2.98 /32	3.38 /12	2.40	1.64
AA	Invesco Balanced-Risk Ret 2020 R5	AFTSX	C	(800) 959-4246	D+ / 2.7	3.16	2.36	11.36 /16	3.48 /37	3.86 /14	2.88	1.04
GI	Invesco Balanced-Risk Ret 2020 R6	VRCFX	C	(800) 959-4246	D+ / 2.7	3.15	2.36	11.35 /16	3.47 /37	3.86 /15	2.88	0.94
AA	● Invesco Balanced-Risk Ret 2020 RX	VRCRX	C-	(800) 959-4246	D+ / 2.4	3.13	2.20	10.91 /14	2.98 /32	3.38 /12	2.40	1.64
AA	Invesco Balanced-Risk Ret 2020 Y	AFTYX	C	(800) 959-4246	D+ / 2.7	3.17	2.25	11.29 /15	3.49 /37	3.86 /15	2.90	1.14
AA	Invesco Balanced-Risk Ret 2030 A	TNAAX	D+	(800) 959-4246	D+ / 2.9	4.38	3.16	15.52 /32	4.41 /48	4.58 /19	4.44	1.53
AA	● Invesco Balanced-Risk Ret 2030 AX	VREAX	D+	(800) 959-4246	D+ / 2.9	4.38	3.05	15.51 /32	4.45 /48	4.60 /19	4.43	1.53
AA	● Invesco Balanced-Risk Ret 2030 B	TNABX	C-	(800) 959-4246	C- / 3.4	4.33	2.85	14.77 /29	3.66 /39	3.81 /14	3.94	2.28
AA	Invesco Balanced-Risk Ret 2030 C	TNACX	C-	(800) 959-4246	C- / 3.4	4.46	2.85	14.78 /29	3.70 /39	3.83 /14	3.94	2.28
AA	● Invesco Balanced-Risk Ret 2030 CX	VRECX	C-	(800) 959-4246	C- / 3.4	4.46	2.85	14.78 /29	3.70 /39	3.83 /14	3.94	2.28
AA	Invesco Balanced-Risk Ret 2030 R	TNARX	C-	(800) 959-4246	C- / 3.7	4.36	3.01	15.30 /31	4.15 /45	4.34 /17	4.44	1.78
AA	Invesco Balanced-Risk Ret 2030 R5	TNAIX	C-	(800) 959-4246	C- / 4.1	4.38	3.05	15.58 /32	4.67 /50	4.82 /20	4.93	1.16
GI	Invesco Balanced-Risk Ret 2030 R6	TNAFX	C-	(800) 959-4246	C- / 4.1	4.38	3.17	15.73 /33	4.67 /50	4.80 /20	4.93	1.07
AA	● Invesco Balanced-Risk Ret 2030 RX	VRERX	C-	(800) 959-4246	C- / 3.8	4.49	3.02	15.31 /31	4.19 /45	4.34 /17	4.44	1.78
AA	Invesco Balanced-Risk Ret 2030 Y	TNAYX	C-	(800) 959-4246	C- / 4.1	4.39	3.18	15.78 /33	4.68 /51	4.83 /20	4.94	1.28
AA	Invesco Balanced-Risk Ret 2040 A	TNDAX	D+	(800) 959-4246	C- / 3.8	5.15	3.56	18.05 /43	5.21 /57	5.11 /22	4.52	1.73
AA	● Invesco Balanced-Risk Ret 2040 AX	VRGAX	D+	(800) 959-4246	C- / 3.7	5.03	3.56	17.91 /42	5.17 /56	5.11 /22	4.53	1.73
AA	● Invesco Balanced-Risk Ret 2040 B	TNDBX	C-	(800) 959-4246	C- / 4.2	5.09	3.33	17.21 /39	4.43 /48	4.37 /17	4.08	2.48
AA	Invesco Balanced-Risk Ret 2040 C	TNDCX	C-	(800) 959-4246	C / 4.3	5.09	3.33	17.40 /40	4.48 /48	4.37 /17	4.08	2.48
AA	● Invesco Balanced-Risk Ret 2040 CX	VRGCX	C-	(800) 959-4246	C / 4.3	5.10	3.34	17.26 /40	4.44 /48	4.38 /17	4.09	2.48
AA	Invesco Balanced-Risk Ret 2040 R	TNDRX	C-	(800) 959-4246	C / 4.7	5.17	3.56	17.84 /42	4.95 /54	4.87 /20	4.55	1.98
AA	Invesco Balanced-Risk Ret 2040 R5	TNDIX	C-	(800) 959-4246	C / 5.1	5.12	3.66	18.26 /44	5.42 /59	5.38 /24	5.01	1.30
GI	Invesco Balanced-Risk Ret 2040 R6	TNDFX	C-	(800) 959-4246	C / 5.1	5.12	3.66	18.26 /44	5.42 /59	5.36 /24	5.01	1.21
AA	● Invesco Balanced-Risk Ret 2040 RX	VRGRX	C-	(800) 959-4246	C / 4.7	5.17	3.56	17.67 /41	4.91 /53	4.87 /20	4.55	1.98
AA	Invesco Balanced-Risk Ret 2040 Y	TNDYX	C-	(800) 959-4246	C / 5.1	5.13	3.67	18.29 /44	5.43 /59	5.39 /24	5.01	1.48
AA	Invesco Balanced-Risk Ret 2050 A	TNEAX	C-	(800) 959-4246	C / 4.5	5.70	3.93	20.30 /54	5.87 /63	5.60 /26	6.95	2.23
AA	● Invesco Balanced-Risk Ret 2050 AX	VRIAX	C-	(800) 959-4246	C / 4.6	5.69	3.93	20.45 /55	5.87 /63	5.62 /26	6.95	2.23

● Denotes fund is closed to new investors
* Denotes fund is included in Section II

Risk Rating/Pts	3 Year Standard Deviation	Beta	NAV As of 2/28/17	Total $(Mil)	Cash %	Stocks %	Bonds %	Other %	Portfolio Turnover Ratio	Last Bull Market Return	Last Bear Market Return	Manager Quality Pct	Manager Tenure (Years)	Initial Purch. $	Additional Purch. $	Front End Load	Back End Load
C- / 3.9	13.5	1.07	40.18	179	1	97	0	2	28	125.9	-21.8	28	14	10,000,000	0	0.0	0.0
C- / 3.9	13.5	1.14	40.11	381	1	97	0	2	28	124.5	-21.7	12	14	1,000	50	0.0	0.0
C+ / 6.1	12.0	0.77	31.65	455	6	85	7	2	9	60.7	-19.8	94	18	1,000	50	5.5	0.0
C+ / 6.1	12.0	0.77	29.53	3	6	85	7	2	9	54.3	-20.1	92	18	1,000	50	0.0	0.0
C+ / 6.1	12.0	0.77	29.34	69	6	85	7	2	9	54.4	-20.1	92	18	1,000	50	0.0	0.0
C+ / 6.1	12.0	0.76	31.70	314	6	85	7	2	9	62.9	-19.7	94	18	1,000	50	0.0	0.0
C+ / 6.7	5.9	0.66	10.84	1,807	53	0	46	1	96	37.0	1.4	63	8	1,000	50	5.5	0.0
C+ / 6.8	5.9	0.67	10.46	7	53	0	46	1	96	31.6	1.1	52	8	1,000	50	0.0	0.0
C+ / 6.8	5.9	0.67	10.46	1,215	53	0	46	1	96	31.6	1.1	52	8	1,000	50	0.0	0.0
C+ / 6.7	5.9	0.67	10.70	27	53	0	46	1	96	35.2	1.3	59	8	0	0	0.0	0.0
C+ / 6.6	5.9	0.67	10.96	131	53	0	46	1	96	39.0	1.6	66	8	10,000,000	0	0.0	0.0
C+ / 6.6	5.9	0.70	10.97	293	53	0	46	1	96	39.3	1.4	81	8	10,000,000	0	0.0	0.0
C+ / 6.6	5.9	0.67	10.96	1,826	53	0	46	1	96	38.8	1.6	65	8	1,000	50	0.0	0.0
C / 4.7	11.7	0.41	6.89	53	59	0	40	1	98	-25.9	-17.2	1	7	1,000	50	5.5	0.0
C / 4.6	11.6	0.42	6.63	N/A	59	0	40	1	98	-28.8	-17.5	1	7	0	0	0.0	0.0
C / 4.6	11.6	0.41	6.62	8	59	0	40	1	98	-28.9	-17.5	1	7	1,000	50	0.0	0.0
C / 4.7	11.6	0.41	6.82	1	59	0	40	1	98	-26.8	-17.3	1	7	0	0	0.0	0.0
C / 4.8	11.6	0.40	7.02	203	59	0	40	1	98	-24.5	-17.2	2	7	10,000,000	0	0.0	0.0
C / 4.8	11.6	0.24	7.03	8	59	0	40	1	98	-24.7	-17.2	2	7	10,000,000	0	0.0	0.0
C / 4.7	11.6	0.41	7.00	672	59	0	40	1	98	-24.8	-17.1	1	7	1,000	50	0.0	0.0
B- / 7.9	4.8	0.55	8.88	40	43	0	56	1	12	32.1	1.5	64	10	1,000	50	5.5	0.0
B- / 7.9	4.7	0.54	8.88	7	43	0	56	1	12	32.1	1.5	65	7	1,000	50	5.5	0.0
B / 8.0	4.7	0.54	8.79	1	43	0	56	1	12	27.1	1.2	56	10	1,000	50	0.0	0.0
B / 8.0	4.8	0.55	8.77	8	43	0	56	1	12	27.1	1.0	55	10	1,000	50	0.0	0.0
B / 8.0	4.7	0.53	8.76	1	43	0	56	1	12	26.9	1.2	56	7	1,000	50	0.0	0.0
B- / 7.9	4.7	0.54	8.85	8	43	0	56	1	12	30.5	1.3	62	10	0	0	0.0	0.0
B- / 7.8	4.8	0.54	8.93	1	43	0	56	1	12	34.0	1.6	68	10	10,000,000	0	0.0	0.0
B- / 7.8	4.8	0.28	8.94	2	43	0	56	1	12	33.7	1.5	77	8	10,000,000	0	0.0	0.0
B- / 7.9	4.7	0.54	8.85	N/A	43	0	56	1	12	30.5	1.3	62	7	0	0	0.0	0.0
B- / 7.8	4.7	0.54	8.88	4	43	0	56	1	12	34.0	1.5	68	9	1,000	50	0.0	0.0
C+ / 6.1	6.4	0.72	8.40	45	58	0	41	1	17	39.2	1.4	63	10	1,000	50	5.5	0.0
C+ / 6.1	6.4	0.73	8.41	6	58	0	41	1	17	39.4	1.4	62	7	1,000	50	5.5	0.0
C+ / 6.3	6.4	0.73	8.31	1	58	0	41	1	17	33.8	1.1	53	10	1,000	50	0.0	0.0
C+ / 6.3	6.4	0.73	8.31	11	58	0	41	1	17	34.0	1.1	53	10	1,000	50	0.0	0.0
C+ / 6.3	6.4	0.73	8.31	1	58	0	41	1	17	34.0	1.1	53	7	1,000	50	0.0	0.0
C+ / 6.2	6.3	0.72	8.35	9	58	0	41	1	17	37.4	1.3	60	10	0	0	0.0	0.0
C+ / 6.1	6.4	0.72	8.44	1	58	0	41	1	17	41.1	1.6	66	10	10,000,000	0	0.0	0.0
C+ / 6.1	6.4	0.38	8.44	2	58	0	41	1	17	40.7	1.4	79	8	10,000,000	0	0.0	0.0
C+ / 6.2	6.4	0.73	8.35	1	58	0	41	1	17	37.4	1.4	60	7	0	0	0.0	0.0
C+ / 6.1	6.4	0.73	8.42	4	58	0	41	1	17	41.2	1.4	66	9	1,000	50	0.0	0.0
C / 5.4	7.3	0.82	7.67	32	55	0	44	1	28	42.9	1.4	63	10	1,000	50	5.5	0.0
C / 5.4	7.4	0.83	7.66	3	55	0	44	1	28	42.9	1.4	62	7	1,000	50	5.5	0.0
C+ / 5.6	7.4	0.83	7.58	N/A	55	0	44	1	28	37.4	1.1	52	10	1,000	50	0.0	0.0
C+ / 5.6	7.4	0.84	7.57	6	55	0	44	1	28	37.5	1.1	53	10	1,000	50	0.0	0.0
C / 5.5	7.3	0.83	7.56	N/A	55	0	44	1	28	37.3	1.1	53	7	1,000	50	0.0	0.0
C / 5.5	7.3	0.83	7.63	7	55	0	44	1	28	41.1	1.3	59	10	0	0	0.0	0.0
C / 5.4	7.4	0.84	7.70	N/A	55	0	44	1	28	44.8	1.5	64	10	10,000,000	0	0.0	0.0
C / 5.3	7.4	0.43	7.70	2	55	0	44	1	28	44.5	1.4	80	8	10,000,000	0	0.0	0.0
C / 5.5	7.4	0.84	7.63	N/A	55	0	44	1	28	41.1	1.3	58	7	0	0	0.0	0.0
C / 5.3	7.4	0.83	7.69	2	55	0	44	1	28	44.7	1.6	65	9	1,000	50	0.0	0.0
C / 4.8	8.4	0.95	7.49	18	89	0	10	1	22	46.1	1.5	60	10	1,000	50	5.5	0.0
C / 4.9	8.3	0.94	7.50	1	89	0	10	1	22	46.2	1.4	60	7	1,000	50	5.5	0.0

99 Pct = Best
0 Pct = Worst

Fund Type	Fund Name	Ticker Symbol	Overall Investment Rating	Phone	Performance Rating/Pts	\multicolumn{5}{PERFORMANCE Total Return % through 2/28/17}					Incl. in Returns	
						3 Mo	6 Mo	1Yr / Pct	3Yr / Pct (Annualized)	5Yr / Pct (Annualized)	Dividend Yield	Expense Ratio
AA	● Invesco Balanced-Risk Ret 2050 B	TNEBX	C-	(800) 959-4246	C / 5.2	5.72	3.78	19.80 /51	5.11 /55	4.86 /20	6.75	2.98
AA	Invesco Balanced-Risk Ret 2050 C	TNECX	C-	(800) 959-4246	C / 5.2	5.70	3.77	19.73 /51	5.14 /56	4.87 /20	6.73	2.98
AA	● Invesco Balanced-Risk Ret 2050 CX	VRICX	C-	(800) 959-4246	C / 5.1	5.71	3.78	19.58 /50	5.11 /55	4.85 /20	6.74	2.98
AA	Invesco Balanced-Risk Ret 2050 R	TNERX	C-	(800) 959-4246	C / 5.5	5.74	3.96	20.12 /53	5.64 /61	5.38 /24	7.15	2.48
AA	Invesco Balanced-Risk Ret 2050 R5	TNEIX	C	(800) 959-4246	C+ / 5.9	5.64	4.02	20.66 /56	6.12 /65	5.86 /27	7.56	1.69
GI	Invesco Balanced-Risk Ret 2050 R6	TNEFX	C	(800) 959-4246	C+ / 5.9	5.77	4.01	20.63 /56	6.11 /65	5.84 /27	7.55	1.61
AA	● Invesco Balanced-Risk Ret 2050 RX	VRIRX	C-	(800) 959-4246	C / 5.5	5.60	3.83	20.12 /53	5.58 /60	5.34 /24	7.15	2.48
AA	Invesco Balanced-Risk Ret 2050 Y	TNEYX	C	(800) 959-4246	C+ / 5.9	5.65	4.03	20.69 /56	6.08 /65	5.87 /27	7.57	1.98
AA	Invesco Balanced-Risk Ret Now A	IANAX	C-	(800) 959-4246	D- / 1.4	2.45	1.86	8.67 / 9	2.50 /28	2.60 /10	3.20	1.67
AA	● Invesco Balanced-Risk Ret Now AX	VIRAX	C-	(800) 959-4246	D- / 1.4	2.58	1.87	8.69 / 9	2.50 /28	2.61 /10	3.20	1.67
AA	● Invesco Balanced-Risk Ret Now B	IANBX	C-	(800) 959-4246	D / 1.7	2.48	1.63	8.02 / 7	1.76 /22	1.87 / 8	3.01	2.42
AA	Invesco Balanced-Risk Ret Now C	IANCX	C-	(800) 959-4246	D / 1.7	2.48	1.63	8.15 / 8	1.80 /23	1.87 / 8	3.01	2.42
AA	● Invesco Balanced-Risk Ret Now CX	VIRCX	C-	(800) 959-4246	D / 1.7	2.48	1.63	8.02 / 7	1.76 /22	1.87 / 8	3.01	2.42
AA	Invesco Balanced-Risk Ret Now R	IANRX	C-	(800) 959-4246	D / 1.8	2.50	1.78	8.32 / 8	2.23 /25	2.33 / 9	3.26	1.92
AA	Invesco Balanced-Risk Ret Now R5	IANIX	C	(800) 959-4246	D / 2.1	2.53	1.83	8.90 / 9	2.73 /29	2.85 /10	3.51	1.33
AA	Invesco Balanced-Risk Ret Now R6	IANFX	C	(800) 959-4246	D / 2.1	2.53	1.94	8.90 / 9	2.73 /29	2.82 /10	3.51	1.25
AA	● Invesco Balanced-Risk Ret Now RX	VIRRX	C-	(800) 959-4246	D / 1.8	2.50	1.78	8.46 / 8	2.23 /25	2.36 / 9	3.26	1.92
AA	Invesco Balanced-Risk Ret Now Y	IANYX	C	(800) 959-4246	D / 2.1	2.53	1.94	8.90 / 9	2.73 /29	2.83 /10	3.51	1.42
GI	Invesco Charter A	CHTRX	D	(800) 959-4246	C- / 3.5	4.46	5.46	19.93 /52	4.19 /45	9.23 /52	0.80	1.09
GI	● Invesco Charter B	BCHTX	D	(800) 959-4246	C- / 4.0	4.25	5.07	19.00 /47	3.42 /36	8.41 /45	0.08	1.84
GI	Invesco Charter C	CHTCX	D	(800) 959-4246	C- / 4.0	4.23	5.06	19.00 /47	3.41 /36	8.40 /45	0.08	1.84
GI	Invesco Charter R	CHRRX	D+	(800) 959-4246	C / 4.4	4.38	5.40	19.64 /50	3.94 /42	8.96 /50	0.59	1.34
GI	Invesco Charter R5	CHTVX	D+	(800) 959-4246	C / 5.0	4.55	5.68	20.32 /54	4.55 /49	9.60 /55	1.15	0.75
GI	Invesco Charter R6	CHFTX	D+	(800) 959-4246	C / 5.0	4.52	5.70	20.41 /54	4.65 /50	9.64 /56	1.22	0.66
GI	Invesco Charter S	CHRSX	D+	(800) 959-4246	C / 4.7	4.45	5.51	20.05 /52	4.29 /46	9.33 /53	0.94	0.99
GI	Invesco Charter Y	CHTYX	D+	(800) 959-4246	C / 4.9	4.49	5.60	20.23 /53	4.47 /48	9.50 /55	1.09	0.84
* GI	Invesco Comstock A	ACSTX	B	(800) 959-4246	B / 8.2	5.41	14.24	33.48 /92	7.69 /77	12.88 /83	1.81	0.86
GI	● Invesco Comstock B	ACSWX	B+	(800) 959-4246	A- / 9.1	5.42	14.24	33.49 /92	7.67 /77	12.78 /82	1.91	0.86
GI	Invesco Comstock C	ACSYX	B+	(800) 959-4246	B+ / 8.6	5.22	13.78	32.42 /91	6.88 /71	12.03 /75	1.28	1.58
GI	Invesco Comstock R	ACSRX	B+	(800) 959-4246	B+ / 8.9	5.35	14.10	33.09 /92	7.40 /75	12.58 /80	1.70	1.11
GI	Invesco Comstock R5	ACSHX	B+	(800) 959-4246	A / 9.3	5.51	14.44	33.95 /93	8.04 /79	13.27 /87	2.22	0.51
GI	Invesco Comstock R6	ICSFX	B+	(800) 959-4246	A / 9.3	5.54	14.45	34.02 /93	8.15 /80	13.31 /87	2.30	0.41
GI	Invesco Comstock Y	ACSDX	B+	(800) 959-4246	A- / 9.2	5.48	14.34	33.74 /93	7.94 /78	13.16 /85	2.13	0.61
AA	Invesco Cons Alloc A	CAAMX	C-	(800) 959-4246	D / 1.7	3.23	2.82	10.67 /13	2.91 /31	4.32 /17	1.85	1.06
AA	● Invesco Cons Alloc B	CMBAX	C	(800) 959-4246	D / 2.0	3.07	2.45	9.86 /11	2.15 /25	3.54 /13	1.23	1.81
AA	Invesco Cons Alloc C	CACMX	C	(800) 959-4246	D / 2.0	3.06	2.36	9.85 /11	2.15 /25	3.54 /13	1.23	1.81
AA	Invesco Cons Alloc R	CMARX	C	(800) 959-4246	D+ / 2.3	3.26	2.69	10.43 /13	2.66 /29	4.07 /16	1.71	1.31
AA	Invesco Cons Alloc R5	CMAIX	C	(800) 959-4246	D+ / 2.6	3.38	2.96	11.07 /15	3.23 /34	4.63 /19	2.25	0.75
AA	Invesco Cons Alloc S	CMASX	C	(800) 959-4246	D+ / 2.5	3.34	2.86	10.77 /14	3.02 /32	4.43 /18	2.05	0.96
AA	Invesco Cons Alloc Y	CAAYX	C	(800) 959-4246	D+ / 2.6	3.38	2.95	11.06 /15	3.20 /34	4.59 /19	2.20	0.81
CV	Invesco Convertible Securities A	CNSAX	D	(800) 959-4246	D / 1.8	3.86	4.12	15.71 /33	1.68 /22	6.95 /34	3.21	0.88
CV	● Invesco Convertible Securities B	CNSBX	D+	(800) 959-4246	D / 2.1	3.66	3.72	14.81 /29	0.92 /18	6.14 /29	2.67	1.64
CV	Invesco Convertible Securities C	CNSCX	D+	(800) 959-4246	D / 2.1	3.66	3.77	14.86 /29	1.00 /18	6.22 /30	2.71	1.56
CV	Invesco Convertible Securities R5	CNSIX	D+	(800) 959-4246	D+ / 2.7	3.93	4.27	16.01 /34	1.98 /24	7.27 /36	3.65	0.59
CV	Invesco Convertible Securities R6	CNSFX	C-	(800) 959-4246	D+ / 2.8	3.95	4.32	16.12 /35	2.05 /24	7.29 /37	3.74	0.51
CV	Invesco Convertible Securities Y	CNSDX	D+	(800) 959-4246	D+ / 2.7	3.92	4.21	15.92 /34	1.93 /23	7.20 /36	3.63	0.64
EM	● Invesco Developing Markets A	GTDDX	D	(800) 959-4246	C- / 3.8	9.29	3.71	31.99 /90	1.24 /19	0.51 / 5	0.76	1.45
EM	● Invesco Developing Markets B	GTDBX	D+	(800) 959-4246	C- / 4.2	9.13	3.37	31.06 /88	0.49 /16	-0.23 / 4	0.11	2.20
EM	● Invesco Developing Markets C	GTDCX	D+	(800) 959-4246	C- / 4.2	9.11	3.37	31.06 /88	0.49 /16	-0.23 / 4	0.11	2.20
EM	● Invesco Developing Markets R5	GTDIX	D+	(800) 959-4246	C / 5.2	9.41	3.92	32.49 /91	1.64 /22	0.90 / 6	1.14	1.05
EM	● Invesco Developing Markets R6	GTDFX	D+	(800) 959-4246	C / 5.3	9.42	3.94	32.57 /91	1.67 /22	0.90 / 6	1.19	1.02
EM	● Invesco Developing Markets Y	GTDYX	D+	(800) 959-4246	C / 5.1	9.37	3.87	32.35 /91	1.50 /21	0.77 / 6	1.04	1.20

● Denotes fund is closed to new investors
* Denotes fund is included in Section II

www.thestreetratings.com

I. Index of Stock Mutual Funds

| RISK | 3 Year | | NET ASSETS | | ASSET | | | | Portfolio | BULL / BEAR | | FUND MANAGER | | MINIMUMS | | LOADS | |
Risk Rating/Pts	Standard Deviation	Beta	NAV As of 2/28/17	Total $(Mil)	Cash %	Stocks %	Bonds %	Other %	Turnover Ratio	Last Bull Market Return	Last Bear Market Return	Manager Quality Pct	Manager Tenure (Years)	Initial Purch. $	Additional Purch. $	Front End Load	Back End Load
C /5.0	8.3	0.94	7.37	N/A	89	0	10	1	22	40.6	1.2	51	10	1,000	50	0.0	0.0
C /5.0	8.3	0.94	7.39	6	89	0	10	1	22	40.7	1.2	51	10	1,000	50	0.0	0.0
C /5.0	8.3	0.93	7.38	N/A	89	0	10	1	22	40.5	1.2	52	7	1,000	50	0.0	0.0
C /4.9	8.3	0.93	7.45	4	89	0	10	1	22	44.3	1.4	58	10	0	0	0.0	0.0
C /4.8	8.4	0.94	7.52	N/A	89	0	10	1	22	48.2	1.5	63	10	10,000,000	0	0.0	0.0
C /4.8	8.4	0.48	7.53	1	89	0	10	1	22	47.7	1.5	81	8	10,000,000	0	0.0	0.0
C /4.9	8.3	0.94	7.45	N/A	89	0	10	1	22	44.3	1.3	57	7	0	0	0.0	0.0
C /4.8	8.3	0.94	7.51	4	89	0	10	1	22	48.0	1.5	63	9	1,000	50	0.0	0.0
B /8.5	3.6	0.40	8.41	10	36	0	63	1	19	21.4	0.9	68	10	1,000	50	5.5	0.0
B /8.6	3.6	0.41	8.40	9	36	0	63	1	19	21.4	0.8	68	7	1,000	50	5.5	0.0
B /8.5	3.5	0.40	8.15	N/A	36	0	63	1	19	16.7	0.6	59	10	1,000	50	0.0	0.0
B /8.5	3.6	0.42	8.16	4	36	0	63	1	19	16.8	0.6	58	10	1,000	50	0.0	0.0
B /8.5	3.6	0.40	8.15	2	36	0	63	1	19	16.7	0.6	59	7	1,000	50	0.0	0.0
B /8.5	3.5	0.40	8.33	2	36	0	63	1	19	19.6	0.8	65	10	0	0	0.0	0.0
B /8.6	3.5	0.40	8.49	N/A	36	0	63	1	19	22.9	1.0	71	10	10,000,000	0	0.0	0.0
B /8.6	3.5	0.40	8.49	1	36	0	63	1	19	22.7	0.9	71	8	10,000,000	0	0.0	0.0
B /8.5	3.6	0.40	8.32	N/A	36	0	63	1	19	19.8	0.7	65	7	0	0	0.0	0.0
B /8.6	3.5	0.40	8.49	1	36	0	63	1	19	22.9	1.0	71	9	1,000	50	0.0	0.0
C- /4.0	9.9	0.92	17.78	3,514	2	95	2	1	28	82.0	-15.1	13	15	1,000	50	5.5	0.0
C- /4.0	9.9	0.92	16.76	22	2	95	2	1	28	74.8	-15.4	9	15	1,000	50	0.0	0.0
C- /4.0	9.9	0.93	16.82	195	2	95	2	1	28	74.8	-15.5	9	15	1,000	50	0.0	0.0
C- /4.1	9.9	0.92	17.63	35	2	95	2	1	28	79.7	-15.3	12	15	0	0	0.0	0.0
C- /4.1	9.9	0.92	18.53	38	2	95	2	1	28	85.6	-15.0	16	15	10,000,000	0	0.0	0.0
C- /4.1	9.8	0.92	18.52	3	2	95	2	1	28	85.5	-15.1	17	15	10,000,000	0	0.0	0.0
C- /4.0	9.9	0.92	17.78	19	2	95	2	1	28	83.0	-15.1	14	15	0	0	0.0	0.0
C- /4.0	9.9	0.93	17.84	122	2	95	2	1	28	84.6	-15.1	15	15	1,000	50	0.0	0.0
C /5.1	12.9	1.14	24.50	6,720	0	98	0	2	15	125.4	-20.2	23	18	1,000	50	5.5	0.0
C /5.1	12.9	1.14	24.49	49	0	98	0	2	15	124.5	-20.2	23	18	1,000	50	0.0	0.0
C /5.1	12.9	1.14	24.47	537	0	98	0	2	15	116.4	-20.5	16	18	1,000	50	0.0	0.0
C /5.1	12.9	1.14	24.49	339	0	98	0	2	15	122.4	-20.3	20	18	0	0	0.0	0.0
C /5.1	12.9	1.14	24.50	834	0	98	0	2	15	129.9	-20.0	26	18	10,000,000	0	0.0	0.0
C /5.1	12.9	1.14	24.49	690	0	98	0	2	15	129.8	-20.2	27	18	10,000,000	0	0.0	0.0
C /5.1	12.9	1.14	24.50	3,273	0	98	0	2	15	128.4	-20.1	25	18	1,000	50	0.0	0.0
B /8.5	4.7	0.68	11.38	240	2	29	67	2	12	36.3	-4.9	47	1	1,000	50	5.5	0.0
B /8.6	4.7	0.68	11.23	6	2	29	67	2	12	30.9	-5.2	36	1	1,000	50	0.0	0.0
B /8.6	4.7	0.68	11.25	70	2	29	67	2	12	30.9	-5.3	37	1	1,000	50	0.0	0.0
B /8.5	4.7	0.68	11.34	9	2	29	67	2	12	34.5	-4.9	44	1	0	0	0.0	0.0
B /8.5	4.7	0.68	11.44	N/A	2	29	67	2	12	38.4	-4.7	51	1	10,000,000	0	0.0	0.0
B /8.5	4.7	0.69	11.40	2	2	29	67	2	12	37.1	-4.8	48	1	0	0	0.0	0.0
B /8.5	4.7	0.68	11.38	5	2	29	67	2	12	38.1	-4.8	51	1	1,000	50	0.0	0.0
C+ /6.5	7.3	0.83	23.82	788	4	13	0	83	45	58.7	-14.8	43	19	1,000	50	5.5	0.0
C+ /6.5	7.3	0.83	23.86	2	4	13	0	83	45	52.3	-15.0	33	19	1,000	50	0.0	0.0
C+ /6.5	7.3	0.83	23.68	118	4	13	0	83	45	52.9	-15.0	34	19	1,000	50	0.0	0.0
C+ /6.5	7.3	0.83	23.84	4	4	13	0	83	45	61.3	-14.7	47	19	10,000,000	0	0.0	0.0
C+ /6.5	7.3	0.83	23.85	14	4	13	0	83	45	61.2	-14.8	48	19	10,000,000	0	0.0	0.0
C+ /6.5	7.3	0.82	23.85	583	4	13	0	83	45	60.8	-14.7	47	19	1,000	50	0.0	0.0
C- /4.1	16.4	0.95	31.20	815	5	84	10	1	3	23.9	-20.3	70	14	1,000	50	5.5	0.0
C- /4.2	16.5	0.95	30.49	8	5	84	10	1	3	19.0	-20.6	60	14	1,000	50	0.0	0.0
C- /4.2	16.4	0.95	30.45	82	5	84	10	1	3	19.0	-20.6	60	14	1,000	50	0.0	0.0
C- /4.0	16.4	0.95	31.14	347	5	84	10	1	3	26.6	-20.1	74	14	10,000,000	0	0.0	0.0
C- /4.0	16.4	0.95	31.13	186	5	84	10	1	3	26.3	-20.3	74	14	10,000,000	0	0.0	0.0
C- /4.0	16.4	0.95	31.22	1,305	5	84	10	1	3	25.6	-20.2	73	14	1,000	50	0.0	0.0

Fund Type	Fund Name	Ticker Symbol	Overall Investment Rating	Phone	Performance Rating/Pts	3 Mo	6 Mo	1Yr / Pct	3Yr / Pct	5Yr / Pct	Dividend Yield	Expense Ratio
	99 Pct = Best / 0 Pct = Worst				PERFORMANCE — Total Return % through 2/28/17 / Annualized						Incl. in Returns	
* GI	Invesco Diversified Dividend A	LCEAX	B-	(800) 959-4246	C+ / 6.8	5.67	7.19	18.69 /46	9.45 /90	13.73 /91	1.46	0.84
GI	● Invesco Diversified Dividend B	LCEDX	B+	(800) 959-4246	B- / 7.2	5.48	6.80	17.84 /42	8.63 /84	12.89 /83	0.85	1.59
GI	Invesco Diversified Dividend C	LCEVX	B+	(800) 959-4246	B- / 7.2	5.49	6.81	17.86 /42	8.64 /84	12.89 /83	0.85	1.59
GI	Invesco Diversified Dividend Inv	LCEIX	A-	(800) 959-4246	B / 7.8	5.74	7.21	18.74 /46	9.51 /90	13.76 /91	1.58	0.82
GI	Invesco Diversified Dividend R	DDFRX	A-	(800) 959-4246	B- / 7.5	5.59	7.03	18.41 /45	9.18 /88	13.44 /88	1.31	1.09
GI	Invesco Diversified Dividend R5	DDFIX	A	(800) 959-4246	B / 7.9	5.75	7.34	19.09 /48	9.77 /92	14.07 /94	1.81	0.55
GR	Invesco Diversified Dividend R6	LCEFX	A	(800) 959-4246	B / 8.0	5.82	7.39	19.20 /48	9.90 /93	14.13 /94	1.90	0.45
GI	Invesco Diversified Dividend Y	LCEYX	A	(800) 959-4246	B / 7.9	5.73	7.32	19.03 /47	9.72 /92	14.01 /93	1.78	0.59
UT	Invesco Dividend Income A	IAUTX	A+	(800) 959-4246	B / 7.8	6.00	7.13	17.24 /39	11.83 /98	12.99 /84	1.59	1.19
UT	● Invesco Dividend Income B	IBUTX	A+	(800) 959-4246	B / 8.2	5.78	6.71	16.32 /36	11.00 /97	12.16 /76	0.98	1.94
UT	Invesco Dividend Income C	IUTCX	A+	(800) 959-4246	B / 8.2	5.77	6.74	16.32 /36	10.99 /97	12.16 /76	0.98	1.94
UT	● Invesco Dividend Income Investor	FSTUX	A+	(800) 959-4246	B+ / 8.8	5.99	7.12	17.19 /39	11.82 /98	13.00 /84	1.68	1.19
UT	Invesco Dividend Income R5	FSIUX	A+	(800) 959-4246	A- / 9.0	6.08	7.29	17.59 /41	12.17 /98	13.34 /87	1.96	0.87
UT	Invesco Dividend Income R6	IFUTX	A+	(800) 959-4246	A- / 9.0	6.05	7.34	17.68 /41	12.24 /98	13.34 /87	2.05	0.77
UT	Invesco Dividend Income Y	IAUYX	A+	(800) 959-4246	A- / 9.0	6.05	7.25	17.53 /41	12.11 /98	13.29 /87	1.91	0.94
GL	Invesco Em Mkt Equity Y	IEMYX	D+	(800) 959-4246	C- / 3.8	8.25	2.61	23.06 /67	1.75 /22	-2.89 / 2	0.33	2.34
GL	Invesco Em Mkts Equity A	IEMAX	D	(800) 959-4246	D+ / 2.5	8.01	2.36	22.63 /65	1.47 /21	-3.13 / 2	0.09	2.59
GL	Invesco Em Mkts Equity C	IEMCX	D	(800) 959-4246	C- / 3.0	8.09	2.16	21.86 /61	0.76 /17	-3.86 / 2	0.00	3.34
GL	Invesco Em Mkts Equity R	IEMRX	D+	(800) 959-4246	C- / 3.3	8.12	2.28	22.28 /63	1.22 /19	-3.40 / 2	0.00	2.84
GL	Invesco Em Mkts Equity R5	IEMIX	D+	(800) 959-4246	C- / 3.8	8.25	2.61	23.06 /67	1.75 /22	-2.89 / 2	0.33	1.99
EM	Invesco Em Mkts Equity R6	EMEFX	D+	(800) 959-4246	C- / 3.7	8.25	2.47	22.85 /66	1.75 /22	-2.92 / 2	0.33	1.99
MC	Invesco Endeavor A	ATDAX	C	(800) 959-4246	B / 7.8	5.69	16.66	34.59 /94	6.12 /65	10.69 /63	0.00	1.32
MC	● Invesco Endeavor B	ATDBX	C	(800) 959-4246	B / 8.1	5.46	16.20	33.64 /92	5.33 /58	9.87 /57	0.00	2.07
MC	Invesco Endeavor C	ATDCX	C	(800) 959-4246	B / 8.2	5.52	16.26	33.69 /92	5.35 /58	9.87 /57	0.00	2.07
MC	Invesco Endeavor R	ATDRX	C+	(800) 959-4246	B+ / 8.5	5.61	16.50	34.26 /93	5.85 /63	10.42 /61	0.00	1.57
MC	Invesco Endeavor R5	ATDIX	B-	(800) 959-4246	A- / 9.0	5.81	16.91	35.17 /94	6.53 /69	11.12 /67	0.00	0.95
MC	Invesco Endeavor R6	ATDFX	B-	(800) 959-4246	A- / 9.0	5.79	16.96	35.25 /94	6.63 /69	11.15 /67	0.00	0.86
MC	Invesco Endeavor Y	ATDYX	C+	(800) 959-4246	B+ / 8.9	5.75	16.83	35.00 /94	6.41 /68	10.98 /66	0.00	1.07
EN	Invesco Energy A	IENAX	E-	(800) 959-4246	E- / 0.0	-7.06	3.39	29.14 /84	-12.70 / 0	-5.98 / 1	1.12	1.28
EN	● Invesco Energy B	IENBX	E-	(800) 959-4246	E- / 0.0	-7.21	3.05	28.22 /82	-13.35 / 0	-6.68 / 1	0.54	2.03
EN	Invesco Energy C	IEFCX	E-	(800) 959-4246	E- / 0.0	-7.21	3.00	28.19 /82	-13.35 / 0	-6.68 / 1	0.55	2.03
EN	● Invesco Energy Inv	FSTEX	E-	(800) 959-4246	E- / 0.1	-7.02	3.41	29.16 /84	-12.69 / 0	-5.97 / 1	1.18	1.28
EN	Invesco Energy R5	IENIX	E-	(800) 959-4246	E- / 0.1	-6.96	3.64	29.68 /86	-12.33 / 0	-5.61 / 1	1.57	0.86
EN	Invesco Energy Y	IENYX	E-	(800) 959-4246	E- / 0.1	-6.99	3.53	29.44 /85	-12.48 / 0	-5.74 / 1	1.43	1.03
GI	Invesco Equally-Weighted S&P 500 A	VADAX	B+	(800) 959-4246	B / 7.7	6.42	9.20	26.01 /76	9.18 /88	13.87 /92	0.92	0.54
GI	● Invesco Equally-Weighted S&P 500 B	VADBX	A-	(800) 959-4246	B / 8.1	6.22	8.78	25.06 /73	8.36 /82	13.02 /84	0.34	1.29
GI	Invesco Equally-Weighted S&P 500 C	VADCX	A-	(800) 959-4246	B / 8.1	6.19	8.80	25.13 /74	8.40 /82	13.04 /84	0.45	1.23
GI	Invesco Equally-Weighted S&P 500 R	VADRX	A-	(800) 959-4246	B+ / 8.5	6.36	9.09	25.70 /75	8.91 /86	13.59 /90	0.78	0.79
GI	Invesco Equally-Weighted S&P 500	VADFX	A	(800) 959-4246	B+ / 8.9	6.52	9.42	26.47 /78	9.59 /91	14.22 /94	1.28	0.16
GI	Invesco Equally-Weighted S&P 500 Y	VADDX	A	(800) 959-4246	B+ / 8.9	6.47	9.33	26.31 /77	9.45 /90	14.15 /94	1.18	0.29
* GI	Invesco Equity and Income A	ACEIX	C+	(800) 959-4246	C+ / 6.8	4.56	10.53	25.47 /75	7.51 /76	10.96 /66	1.53	0.81
GI	● Invesco Equity and Income B	ACEQX	B	(800) 959-4246	B- / 7.1	4.36	10.14	24.51 /72	6.68 /70	10.16 /60	0.94	1.56
GI	Invesco Equity and Income C	ACERX	B	(800) 959-4246	B- / 7.1	4.35	10.10	24.52 /72	6.70 /70	10.13 /59	0.96	1.54
GI	Invesco Equity and Income R	ACESX	B+	(800) 959-4246	B- / 7.5	4.48	10.34	25.16 /74	7.21 /73	10.66 /63	1.39	1.06
GI	Invesco Equity and Income R5	ACEKX	B+	(800) 959-4246	B / 8.0	4.74	10.70	25.99 /76	7.86 /78	11.31 /68	1.91	0.49
GI	Invesco Equity and Income R6	IEIFX	B+	(800) 959-4246	B / 8.0	4.67	10.76	26.00 /76	7.93 /78	11.36 /69	1.99	0.39
GI	Invesco Equity and Income Y	ACETX	B+	(800) 959-4246	B / 7.9	4.63	10.67	25.78 /76	7.75 /77	11.21 /68	1.84	0.56
FO	Invesco European Growth A	AEDAX	E+	(800) 959-4246	E / 0.5	7.66	1.86	7.89 / 7	-0.80 /10	5.95 /28	1.45	1.39
FO	● Invesco European Growth B	AEDBX	E+	(800) 959-4246	E+ / 0.7	7.47	1.49	7.11 / 6	-1.54 / 8	5.16 /22	0.74	2.14
FO	Invesco European Growth C	AEDCX	E+	(800) 959-4246	E+ / 0.7	7.46	1.46	7.10 / 6	-1.54 / 8	5.16 /22	0.74	2.14
FO	Invesco European Growth Inv	EGINX	D-	(800) 959-4246	E+ / 0.9	7.66	1.87	7.92 / 7	-0.77 /10	5.98 /28	1.57	1.37
FO	Invesco European Growth R	AEDRX	D-	(800) 959-4246	E+ / 0.8	7.61	1.75	7.64 / 7	-1.05 / 9	5.68 /26	1.26	1.64

● Denotes fund is closed to new investors
* Denotes fund is included in Section II

I. Index of Stock Mutual Funds

Risk Rating/Pts	3 Year Standard Deviation	Beta	NAV As of 2/28/17	Total $(Mil)	Cash %	Stocks %	Bonds %	Other %	Portfolio Turnover Ratio	Last Bull Market Return	Last Bear Market Return	Manager Quality Pct	Manager Tenure (Years)	Initial Purch. $	Additional Purch. $	Front End Load	Back End Load
B- /7.2	7.6	0.67	19.83	6,601	4	82	12	2	11	123.4	-15.9	87	15	1,000	50	5.5	0.0
B- /7.2	7.6	0.67	19.59	14	4	82	12	2	11	114.6	-16.2	84	15	1,000	50	0.0	0.0
B- /7.2	7.6	0.67	19.57	875	4	82	12	2	11	114.6	-16.2	84	15	1,000	50	0.0	0.0
B- /7.2	7.6	0.67	19.82	2,229	4	82	12	2	11	123.9	-15.9	87	15	1,000	50	0.0	0.0
B- /7.2	7.6	0.67	19.89	285	4	82	12	2	11	120.4	-16.0	86	15	0	0	0.0	0.0
B- /7.2	7.6	0.67	19.84	3,863	4	82	12	2	11	127.3	-15.8	88	15	10,000,000	0	0.0	0.0
B- /7.2	7.6	0.67	19.85	3,291	4	82	12	2	11	127.3	-15.9	89	15	10,000,000	0	0.0	0.0
B- /7.2	7.6	0.67	19.86	5,032	4	82	12	2	11	126.4	-15.8	88	15	1,000	50	0.0	0.0
B /8.0	7.2	0.31	24.09	1,293	4	81	14	1	9	90.9	0.2	98	8	1,000	50	5.5	0.0
B /8.0	7.2	0.30	24.16	5	4	81	14	1	9	83.3	N/A	97	8	1,000	50	0.0	0.0
B /8.0	7.2	0.31	24.39	313	4	81	14	1	9	83.3	-0.1	97	8	1,000	50	0.0	0.0
B /8.0	7.2	0.30	24.31	99	4	81	14	1	9	90.8	0.3	98	8	1,000	50	0.0	0.0
B /8.0	7.2	0.30	24.10	2	4	81	14	1	9	94.2	0.5	98	8	10,000,000	0	0.0	0.0
B /8.0	7.2	0.30	24.11	89	4	81	14	1	9	93.7	0.3	98	8	10,000,000	0	0.0	0.0
B /8.0	7.2	0.30	24.32	721	4	81	14	1	9	93.6	0.4	98	8	1,000	50	0.0	0.0
C /5.1	14.1	0.80	7.26	6	0	98	0	2	47	6.5	N/A	85	6	1,000	50	0.0	0.0
C /5.2	14.1	0.80	7.24	12	0	98	0	2	47	5.1	N/A	84	6	1,000	50	5.5	0.0
C /5.1	14.0	0.79	7.08	3	0	98	0	2	47	0.9	N/A	80	6	1,000	50	0.0	0.0
C /5.1	14.1	0.79	7.19	1	0	98	0	2	47	3.6	N/A	83	6	0	0	0.0	0.0
C /5.2	14.1	0.79	7.26	2	0	98	0	2	47	6.5	N/A	85	6	10,000,000	0	0.0	0.0
C /5.2	14.0	0.82	7.26	6	0	98	0	2	47	6.3	N/A	76	6	10,000,000	0	0.0	0.0
C- /3.3	12.9	0.90	19.61	141	15	74	10	1	28	100.8	-18.2	44	10	1,000	50	5.5	0.0
D+ /2.9	13.0	0.90	17.29	1	15	74	10	1	28	92.7	-18.4	33	10	1,000	50	0.0	0.0
D+ /2.9	13.0	0.90	17.31	39	15	74	10	1	28	92.9	-18.4	34	10	1,000	50	0.0	0.0
C- /3.2	12.9	0.90	18.93	18	15	74	10	1	28	98.1	-18.2	40	10	0	0	0.0	0.0
C- /3.5	12.9	0.90	20.67	26	15	74	10	1	28	105.2	-18.0	49	10	10,000,000	0	0.0	0.0
C- /3.6	12.9	0.90	20.75	48	15	74	10	1	28	105.0	-18.2	51	10	10,000,000	0	0.0	0.0
C- /3.4	13.0	0.90	20.13	24	15	74	10	1	28	103.6	-18.1	47	10	1,000	50	0.0	0.0
E- /0.2	27.0	1.33	26.02	462	1	96	1	2	22	-4.8	-31.3	7	4	1,000	50	5.5	0.0
E- /0.1	27.0	1.33	22.83	4	1	96	1	2	22	-8.6	-31.5	5	4	1,000	50	0.0	0.0
E- /0.1	27.0	1.33	22.17	134	1	96	1	2	22	-8.6	-31.6	5	4	1,000	50	0.0	0.0
E- /0.2	27.0	1.33	25.92	182	1	96	1	2	22	-4.8	-31.3	7	4	1,000	50	0.0	0.0
E- /0.2	27.0	1.33	26.73	21	1	96	1	2	22	-2.8	-31.2	9	4	10,000,000	0	0.0	0.0
E- /0.2	27.0	1.33	26.10	48	1	96	1	2	22	-3.5	-31.2	8	4	1,000	50	0.0	0.0
C+ /6.5	10.8	1.02	54.88	2,255	0	98	0	2	29	136.4	-19.9	55	7	1,000	50	5.5	0.0
C+ /6.5	10.8	1.02	54.57	4	0	98	0	2	29	126.9	-20.1	44	7	1,000	50	0.0	0.0
C+ /6.5	10.8	1.02	52.71	1,097	0	98	0	2	29	127.1	-20.2	45	7	1,000	50	0.0	0.0
C+ /6.5	10.8	1.02	54.63	132	0	98	0	2	29	133.1	-20.0	52	7	0	0	0.0	0.0
C+ /6.5	10.8	1.02	55.42	737	0	98	0	2	29	140.0	-19.9	60	7	10,000,000	0	0.0	0.0
C+ /6.5	10.8	1.02	55.36	2,961	0	98	0	2	29	139.5	-19.8	58	7	1,000	50	0.0	0.0
C+ /6.3	8.5	0.77	10.89	10,565	2	65	25	8	93	93.6	-15.4	68	18	1,000	50	5.5	0.0
C+ /6.3	8.5	0.76	10.63	142	2	65	25	8	93	86.8	-15.4	59	18	1,000	50	0.0	0.0
C+ /6.3	8.5	0.77	10.69	1,697	2	65	25	8	93	85.8	-15.6	58	18	1,000	50	0.0	0.0
C+ /6.3	8.5	0.77	10.94	227	2	65	25	8	93	90.9	-15.4	65	18	0	0	0.0	0.0
C+ /6.3	8.5	0.77	10.90	489	2	65	25	8	93	96.9	-15.2	72	18	10,000,000	0	0.0	0.0
C+ /6.3	8.5	0.76	10.89	385	2	65	25	8	93	97.1	-15.4	73	18	10,000,000	0	0.0	0.0
C+ /6.3	8.5	0.77	10.89	1,110	2	65	25	8	93	96.2	-15.3	71	18	1,000	50	0.0	0.0
C /5.5	11.0	0.83	34.44	433	1	95	2	2	16	56.9	-20.6	66	20	1,000	50	5.5	0.0
C /5.5	11.0	0.83	32.09	2	1	95	2	2	16	50.7	-20.9	56	20	1,000	50	0.0	0.0
C /5.5	11.0	0.83	32.12	79	1	95	2	2	16	50.6	-20.9	56	20	1,000	50	0.0	0.0
C /5.5	11.0	0.83	34.34	146	1	95	2	2	16	57.2	-20.7	67	20	1,000	50	0.0	0.0
C /5.5	11.0	0.83	34.33	12	1	95	2	2	16	54.8	-20.7	63	20	0	0	0.0	0.0

	99 Pct = Best 0 Pct = Worst				**PERFORMANCE**						**Incl. in Returns**	
			Overall		**Perfor-**		Total Return % through 2/28/17					
					mance				Annualized		Dividend	Expense
Fund Type	**Fund Name**	**Ticker Symbol**	**Investment Rating**	**Phone**	**Rating/Pts**	**3 Mo**	**6 Mo**	**1Yr / Pct**	**3Yr / Pct**	**5Yr / Pct**	**Yield**	**Ratio**
FO	Invesco European Growth Y	AEDYX	D-	(800) 959-4246	D- / 1.0	7.74	1.98	8.17 / 8	-0.55 /11	6.21 /30	1.82	1.14
FO	● Invesco European Small Company A	ESMAX	D+	(800) 959-4246	C- / 3.4	9.25	7.70	19.54 /50	2.55 /28	11.19 /67	1.86	1.48
FO	● Invesco European Small Company B	ESMBX	C-	(800) 959-4246	C- / 3.8	9.04	7.29	18.66 /46	1.79 /23	10.36 /61	1.33	2.23
FO	● Invesco European Small Company C	ESMCX	C-	(800) 959-4246	C- / 3.8	9.03	7.28	18.63 /46	1.78 /23	10.34 /61	1.32	2.23
FO	● Invesco European Small Company Y	ESMYX	C-	(800) 959-4246	C / 4.7	9.34	7.87	19.87 /51	2.81 /30	11.46 /70	2.22	1.23
GI	● Invesco Exchange	ACEHX	D+	(800) 959-4246	C / 5.0	2.95	2.34	22.70 /65	5.03 /54	8.52 /46	1.83	0.49
GL	Invesco Global Core Equity A	AWSAX	D+	(800) 959-4246	C- / 3.3	6.80	5.28	19.92 /52	3.39 /36	6.82 /34	0.89	1.32
GL	● Invesco Global Core Equity B	AWSBX	D+	(800) 959-4246	C- / 3.8	6.65	4.89	18.96 /47	2.62 /28	6.17 /30	0.23	2.07
GL	Invesco Global Core Equity C	AWSCX	D+	(800) 959-4246	C- / 3.8	6.63	4.96	19.00 /47	2.64 /29	6.05 /29	0.23	2.07
GL	Invesco Global Core Equity R	AWSRX	C-	(800) 959-4246	C- / 4.2	6.77	5.18	19.64 /50	3.14 /33	6.57 /32	0.70	1.57
GL	Invesco Global Core Equity R5	AWSIX	C-	(800) 959-4246	C / 4.8	6.92	5.43	20.32 /54	3.77 /40	7.19 /36	1.27	0.95
GL	Invesco Global Core Equity Y	AWSYX	C-	(800) 959-4246	C / 4.7	6.91	5.40	20.13 /53	3.65 /39	7.10 /35	1.19	1.07
GL	Invesco Global Growth A	AGGAX	D	(800) 959-4246	D+ / 2.9	6.88	3.45	15.80 /33	3.64 /38	8.49 /46	0.30	1.42
GL	● Invesco Global Growth B	AGGBX	D+	(800) 959-4246	C- / 3.3	6.71	3.10	14.99 /30	2.89 /31	7.69 /40	0.00	2.17
GL	Invesco Global Growth C	AGGCX	D+	(800) 959-4246	C- / 3.3	6.71	3.10	14.94 /30	2.87 /31	7.68 /40	0.00	2.17
GL	Invesco Global Growth R5	GGAIX	C-	(800) 959-4246	C- / 4.2	7.01	3.70	16.28 /35	4.07 /44	8.93 /50	0.71	0.99
GL	Invesco Global Growth R6	AGGFX	C-	(800) 959-4246	C- / 4.2	7.01	3.70	16.24 /35	4.08 /44	8.91 /50	0.71	0.99
GL	Invesco Global Growth Y	AGGYX	C-	(800) 959-4246	C- / 4.1	6.95	3.59	16.10 /35	3.90 /42	8.76 /49	0.56	1.17
HL	Invesco Global Health Care A	GGHCX	E+	(800) 959-4246	C- / 3.1	9.07	4.79	15.02 /30	3.47 /37	13.69 /91	0.19	1.06
HL	● Invesco Global Health Care B	GTHBX	E+	(800) 959-4246	C- / 3.5	8.86	4.42	14.19 /26	2.70 /29	12.84 /82	0.00	1.81
HL	Invesco Global Health Care C	GTHCX	E+	(800) 959-4246	C- / 3.5	8.85	4.41	14.16 /26	2.69 /29	12.83 /82	0.00	1.81
HL	Invesco Global Health Care Inv	GTHIX	D-	(800) 959-4246	C- / 4.1	9.07	4.79	15.05 /30	3.47 /37	13.69 /91	0.20	1.06
HL	Invesco Global Health Care Y	GGHYX	D-	(800) 959-4246	C / 4.3	9.14	4.93	15.34 /31	3.73 /40	13.97 /93	0.46	0.81
GL	Invesco Global Low Vol Eq Yld A	GTNDX	D-	(800) 959-4246	E+ / 0.7	6.03	1.47	12.68 /20	-0.66 /11	6.36 /31	3.26	1.60
GL	● Invesco Global Low Vol Eq Yld B	GNDBX	D-	(800) 959-4246	E+ / 0.8	5.87	1.15	11.82 /17	-1.39 / 8	5.56 /25	2.73	2.35
GL	Invesco Global Low Vol Eq Yld C	GNDCX	D-	(800) 959-4246	E+ / 0.8	5.79	1.07	11.83 /17	-1.41 / 8	5.56 /25	2.73	2.35
GL	Invesco Global Low Vol Eq Yld R	GTNRX	D-	(800) 959-4246	D- / 1.0	5.96	1.34	12.39 /19	-0.91 /10	6.08 /29	3.21	1.85
GL	Invesco Global Low Vol Eq Yld R5	GNDIX	D-	(800) 959-4246	D- / 1.2	6.15	1.68	13.09 /22	-0.25 /12	6.83 /34	3.84	1.13
GL	Invesco Global Low Vol Eq Yld Y	GTNYX	D-	(800) 959-4246	D- / 1.1	6.08	1.60	12.94 /21	-0.41 /12	6.61 /32	3.70	1.35
GL	Invesco Global Market Neutral A	MKNAX	C-	(800) 959-4246	E / 0.4	-0.80	4.50	-1.87 / 1	0.18 /14	---	0.00	2.99
GL	Invesco Global Market Neutral C	MKNCX	C-	(800) 959-4246	E / 0.5	-1.01	4.15	-2.59 / 1	-0.52 /11	---	0.00	3.74
GL	Invesco Global Market Neutral R	MKNRX	C	(800) 959-4246	E+ / 0.6	-1.00	4.32	-2.08 / 1	-0.07 /13	---	0.00	3.24
GL	Invesco Global Market Neutral R5	MKNFX	C	(800) 959-4246	E+ / 0.7	-0.79	4.69	-1.57 / 1	0.42 /15	---	0.00	2.68
GL	Invesco Global Market Neutral R6	MKNSX	C	(800) 959-4246	E+ / 0.7	-0.79	4.58	-1.57 / 1	0.42 /15	---	0.00	2.68
GL	Invesco Global Market Neutral Y	MKNYX	C	(800) 959-4246	E+ / 0.7	-0.79	4.69	-1.57 / 1	0.42 /15	---	0.00	2.74
GR	Invesco Global Opportunities A	IAOPX	C-	(800) 959-4246	C / 5.2	9.83	11.36	26.96 /79	3.16 /33	---	1.15	2.94
GR	Invesco Global Opportunities C	ICOPX	C-	(800) 959-4246	C+ / 5.7	9.54	10.84	26.02 /76	2.38 /27	---	0.53	3.69
GR	Invesco Global Opportunities R	IROPX	C-	(800) 959-4246	C+ / 6.1	9.70	11.16	26.71 /78	2.89 /31	---	0.99	3.19
GR	Invesco Global Opportunities R5	IIOPX	C	(800) 959-4246	C+ / 6.6	9.90	11.52	27.41 /80	3.42 /36	---	1.45	2.45
GR	Invesco Global Opportunities R6	IFOPX	C	(800) 959-4246	C+ / 6.6	9.83	11.44	27.32 /80	3.42 /36	---	1.46	2.45
GR	Invesco Global Opportunities Y	IYOPX	C	(800) 959-4246	C+ / 6.6	9.91	11.53	27.32 /80	3.40 /36	---	1.46	2.69
RE	Invesco Global Real Estate A	AGREX	D+	(800) 959-4246	D+ / 2.3	6.62	-3.17	11.54 /16	4.73 /51	7.05 /35	3.48	1.43
RE	● Invesco Global Real Estate B	BGREX	D+	(800) 959-4246	D+ / 2.7	6.42	-3.54	10.62 /13	3.96 /42	6.26 /30	2.94	2.18
RE	Invesco Global Real Estate C	CGREX	D+	(800) 959-4246	D+ / 2.6	6.42	-3.61	10.61 /13	3.93 /42	6.24 /30	2.94	2.18
RE	Invesco Global Real Estate Inc A	ASRAX	C-	(800) 959-4246	D / 2.2	4.77	-1.38	8.88 / 9	5.03 /54	6.26 /30	4.13	1.24
RE	● Invesco Global Real Estate Inc B	SARBX	C	(800) 959-4246	D+ / 2.5	4.58	-1.76	7.95 / 7	4.23 /46	5.46 /25	3.62	1.99
RE	Invesco Global Real Estate Inc C	ASRCX	C	(800) 959-4246	D+ / 2.5	4.58	-1.76	7.95 / 7	4.24 /46	5.46 /25	3.62	1.99
RE	Invesco Global Real Estate Inc R5	ASRIX	C+	(800) 959-4246	C- / 3.3	4.86	-1.22	9.23 /10	5.41 /59	6.62 /32	4.69	0.90
RE	Invesco Global Real Estate Inc R6	ASRFX	C+	(800) 959-4246	C- / 3.3	4.88	-1.17	9.33 /10	5.45 /59	6.67 /33	4.78	0.82
RE	Invesco Global Real Estate Inc Y	ASRYX	C	(800) 959-4246	C- / 3.2	4.73	-1.37	9.04 /10	5.30 /58	6.51 /32	4.62	0.99
RE	Invesco Global Real Estate R	RGREX	C-	(800) 959-4246	C- / 3.0	6.55	-3.37	11.17 /15	4.47 /48	6.78 /33	3.44	1.68
RE	Invesco Global Real Estate R5	IGREX	C-	(800) 959-4246	C- / 3.6	6.76	-2.94	12.00 /18	5.28 /57	7.63 /39	4.18	0.91

● Denotes fund is closed to new investors
* Denotes fund is included in Section II

324

www.thestreetratings.com

Risk Rating/Pts	3 Year Standard Deviation	Beta	NAV As of 2/28/17	Total $(Mil)	Cash %	Stocks %	Bonds %	Other %	Portfolio Turnover Ratio	Last Bull Market Return	Last Bear Market Return	Manager Quality Pct	Manager Tenure (Years)	Initial Purch. $	Additional Purch. $	Front End Load	Back End Load
C /5.5	11.0	0.83	34.47	653	1	95	2	2	16	59.0	-20.6	69	20	1,000	50	0.0	0.0
C+ /5.7	10.5	0.69	14.05	193	2	92	5	1	19	90.8	-19.1	89	17	1,000	50	5.5	0.0
C+ /5.7	10.6	0.70	13.14	1	2	92	5	1	19	83.3	-19.5	86	17	1,000	50	0.0	0.0
C+ /5.7	10.6	0.69	13.16	31	2	92	5	1	19	83.3	-19.5	85	17	1,000	50	0.0	0.0
C+ /5.7	10.5	0.69	14.11	281	2	92	5	1	19	93.5	-19.1	90	17	1,000	50	0.0	0.0
C- /4.2	11.4	0.93	538.51	61	0	99	0	1	0	77.4	-18.6	19	7	1,000	25	0.0	0.0
C /5.2	10.7	0.81	14.64	770	0	98	0	2	66	65.0	-24.0	92	3	1,000	50	5.5	0.0
C /5.2	10.8	0.82	13.93	15	0	98	0	2	66	59.7	-24.1	89	3	1,000	50	0.0	0.0
C /5.2	10.8	0.82	13.97	86	0	98	0	2	66	58.4	-24.2	89	3	1,000	50	0.0	0.0
C /5.2	10.8	0.81	14.63	1	0	98	0	2	66	62.8	-24.0	91	3	0	0	0.0	0.0
C /5.2	10.7	0.81	14.83	N/A	0	98	0	2	66	68.0	-23.9	93	3	10,000,000	0	0.0	0.0
C /5.2	10.7	0.81	14.64	29	0	98	0	2	66	67.1	-23.9	93	3	1,000	50	0.0	0.0
C /5.5	11.1	0.84	29.34	318	2	96	1	1	19	78.0	-19.5	93	14	1,000	50	5.5	0.0
C /5.4	11.1	0.84	26.99	2	2	96	1	1	19	71.0	-19.7	90	14	1,000	50	0.0	0.0
C /5.4	11.1	0.84	26.99	24	2	96	1	1	19	71.0	-19.7	90	14	1,000	50	0.0	0.0
C /5.4	11.1	0.84	29.18	N/A	2	96	1	1	19	82.0	-19.3	94	14	10,000,000	0	0.0	0.0
C /5.4	11.1	0.84	29.17	332	2	96	1	1	19	81.4	-19.5	94	14	10,000,000	0	0.0	0.0
C /5.5	11.1	0.84	29.39	14	2	96	1	1	19	80.4	-19.4	93	14	1,000	50	0.0	0.0
D+ /2.8	16.5	1.17	36.23	758	1	95	2	2	21	119.5	-13.8	3	N/A	1,000	50	5.5	0.0
D /2.1	16.5	1.17	26.04	4	1	95	2	2	21	110.8	-14.1	3	N/A	1,000	50	0.0	0.0
D /2.1	16.5	1.17	26.08	64	1	95	2	2	21	110.7	-14.1	3	N/A	1,000	50	0.0	0.0
D+ /2.8	16.5	1.17	36.24	605	1	95	2	2	21	119.5	-13.9	3	N/A	1,000	50	0.0	0.0
D+ /2.9	16.5	1.17	36.78	25	1	95	2	2	21	122.5	-13.8	4	N/A	1,000	50	0.0	0.0
C+ /5.9	11.0	0.75	13.02	93	3	95	0	2	94	59.0	-18.3	68	6	1,000	50	5.5	0.0
C+ /5.9	11.0	0.75	12.31	1	3	95	0	2	94	52.7	-18.6	58	6	1,000	50	0.0	0.0
C+ /6.0	11.0	0.75	12.29	10	3	95	0	2	94	52.6	-18.6	58	6	1,000	50	0.0	0.0
C+ /5.9	11.0	0.75	13.03	2	3	95	0	2	94	56.8	-18.4	65	6	0	0	0.0	0.0
C+ /5.9	11.0	0.75	13.19	1	3	95	0	2	94	63.1	-18.1	72	6	10,000,000	0	0.0	0.0
C+ /5.9	11.0	0.75	13.05	4	3	95	0	2	94	61.0	-18.3	70	6	1,000	50	0.0	0.0
B+ /9.9	4.6	-0.09	9.98	8	96	1	2	1	79	N/A	N/A	74	4	1,000	50	5.5	0.0
B+ /9.9	4.5	-0.09	9.78	N/A	96	1	2	1	79	N/A	N/A	66	4	1,000	50	0.0	0.0
B+ /9.9	4.6	-0.09	9.91	N/A	96	1	2	1	79	N/A	N/A	72	4	0	0	0.0	0.0
B+ /9.9	4.6	-0.09	10.04	1	96	1	2	1	79	N/A	N/A	76	4	10,000,000	0	0.0	0.0
B+ /9.9	4.5	-0.09	10.04	1	96	1	2	1	79	N/A	N/A	76	4	10,000,000	0	0.0	0.0
B+ /9.9	4.6	-0.09	10.04	12	96	1	2	1	79	N/A	N/A	76	4	1,000	50	0.0	0.0
C- /4.1	13.1	1.11	14.14	13	0	100	0	0	52	N/A	N/A	4	4	1,000	50	5.5	0.0
C- /4.1	13.1	1.10	13.91	3	0	100	0	0	52	N/A	N/A	3	4	1,000	50	0.0	0.0
C- /4.1	13.1	1.11	14.07	N/A	0	100	0	0	52	N/A	N/A	3	4	0	0	0.0	0.0
C- /4.1	13.1	1.11	14.18	N/A	0	100	0	0	52	N/A	N/A	4	4	10,000,000	0	0.0	0.0
C- /4.1	13.1	1.11	14.17	N/A	0	100	0	0	52	N/A	N/A	4	4	10,000,000	0	0.0	0.0
C- /4.1	13.1	1.10	14.17	1	0	100	0	0	52	N/A	N/A	4	4	1,000	50	0.0	0.0
C+ /6.5	11.9	0.81	12.83	222	11	87	0	2	84	68.0	-20.1	24	N/A	1,000	50	5.5	0.0
C+ /6.5	11.9	0.81	12.83	1	11	87	0	2	84	61.2	-20.3	17	N/A	1,000	50	0.0	0.0
C+ /6.5	11.9	0.81	12.83	33	11	87	0	2	84	61.2	-20.3	17	N/A	1,000	50	0.0	0.0
B /8.1	7.8	0.54	8.91	329	11	66	21	2	60	50.2	-8.2	64	N/A	1,000	50	5.5	0.0
B /8.1	7.8	0.54	8.89	1	11	66	21	2	60	44.2	-8.5	54	N/A	1,000	50	0.0	0.0
B /8.1	7.8	0.54	8.89	80	11	66	21	2	60	44.2	-8.5	55	N/A	1,000	50	0.0	0.0
B /8.1	7.7	0.53	8.91	7	11	66	21	2	60	53.2	-8.2	69	N/A	10,000,000	0	0.0	0.0
B /8.1	7.8	0.53	8.91	152	11	66	21	2	60	53.2	-8.2	70	N/A	10,000,000	0	0.0	0.0
B /8.1	7.7	0.53	8.88	396	11	66	21	2	60	52.3	-8.1	68	N/A	1,000	50	0.0	0.0
C+ /6.5	11.9	0.81	12.83	20	11	87	0	2	84	65.7	-20.2	21	N/A	0	0	0.0	0.0
C+ /6.5	11.9	0.81	12.81	265	11	87	0	2	84	72.9	-19.8	29	N/A	10,000,000	0	0.0	0.0

99 Pct = Best
0 Pct = Worst

Fund Type	Fund Name	Ticker Symbol	Overall Investment Rating	Phone	Perfor-mance Rating/Pts	PERFORMANCE Total Return % through 2/28/17					Incl. in Returns	
									Annualized		Dividend Yield	Expense Ratio
						3 Mo	6 Mo	1Yr / Pct	3Yr / Pct	5Yr / Pct		
RE	Invesco Global Real Estate R6	FGREX	C-	(800) 959-4246	C- / 3.6	6.77	-2.99	12.07 /18	5.34 /58	7.61 /39	4.23	0.84
RE	Invesco Global Real Estate Y	ARGYX	C-	(800) 959-4246	C- / 3.4	6.69	-3.12	11.72 /17	4.99 /54	7.31 /37	3.94	1.18
GL	Invesco Global Sm and Mid Cp Gro A	AGAAX	D-	(800) 959-4246	D+ / 2.3	5.47	3.35	17.44 /40	2.34 /26	7.34 /37	0.64	1.37
GL	● Invesco Global Sm and Mid Cp Gro B	AGABX	D-	(800) 959-4246	D+ / 2.6	5.27	2.92	16.58 /37	1.57 /21	6.53 /32	0.00	2.12
GL	Invesco Global Sm and Mid Cp Gro C	AGACX	D-	(800) 959-4246	D+ / 2.6	5.26	2.98	16.56 /37	1.59 /21	6.54 /32	0.00	2.12
GL	Invesco Global Sm and Mid Cp Gro	GAIIX	D	(800) 959-4246	C- / 3.4	5.57	3.56	17.90 /42	2.73 /29	7.76 /40	1.06	0.99
GL	Invesco Global Sm and Mid Cp Gro Y	AGAYX	D	(800) 959-4246	C- / 3.3	5.50	3.45	17.73 /42	2.58 /28	7.60 /39	0.92	1.12
GL	Invesco Global Targeted Returns A	GLTAX	C	(800) 959-4246	E+ / 0.6	2.17	-0.68	0.78 / 2	1.51 /21	--	1.21	2.42
GL	Invesco Global Targeted Returns C	GLTCX	C	(800) 959-4246	E+ / 0.8	2.02	-0.99	0.09 / 1	0.75 /17	--	0.61	3.17
GL	Invesco Global Targeted Returns R	GLTRX	C	(800) 959-4246	E+ / 0.9	2.05	-0.72	0.55 / 2	1.24 /20	--	1.06	2.67
GL	Invesco Global Targeted Returns R5	GLTFX	C	(800) 959-4246	D- / 1.1	2.23	-0.51	1.04 / 2	1.76 /22	--	1.54	2.11
GL	Invesco Global Targeted Returns R6	GLTSX	C	(800) 959-4246	D- / 1.1	2.24	-0.51	0.94 / 2	1.73 /22	--	1.54	2.11
GL	Invesco Global Targeted Returns Y	GLTYX	C	(800) 959-4246	D- / 1.1	2.23	-0.51	1.04 / 2	1.76 /22	--	1.54	2.17
PM	Invesco Gold and Precious Mtls A	IGDAX	E-	(800) 959-4246	D- / 1.1	11.91	-6.70	31.79 /90	-1.32 / 8	-11.64 / 0	8.22	1.57
PM	● Invesco Gold and Precious Mtls B	IGDBX	E-	(800) 959-4246	D- / 1.4	11.84	-7.07	31.03 /88	-2.01 / 7	-12.32 / 0	7.99	2.32
PM	Invesco Gold and Precious Mtls C	IGDCX	E-	(800) 959-4246	D- / 1.4	11.77	-7.01	30.90 /88	-2.01 / 7	-12.30 / 0	7.43	2.32
PM	● Invesco Gold and Precious Mtls Iv	FGLDX	E-	(800) 959-4246	D / 1.6	11.82	-6.67	31.88 /90	-1.32 / 8	-11.65 / 0	8.64	1.57
PM	Invesco Gold and Precious Mtls Y	IGDYX	E-	(800) 959-4246	D / 1.7	12.11	-6.58	32.24 /90	-1.11 / 9	-11.44 / 0	8.91	1.32
FO	Invesco Greater China A	AACFX	D	(800) 959-4246	D+ / 2.5	2.87	1.52	25.11 /74	2.03 /24	4.22 /16	0.64	1.88
FO	● Invesco Greater China B	ABCFX	D	(800) 959-4246	D+ / 2.9	2.74	1.16	24.17 /70	1.28 /20	3.44 /13	0.00	2.63
FO	Invesco Greater China C	CACFX	D	(800) 959-4246	D+ / 2.9	2.69	1.16	24.16 /70	1.28 /20	3.44 /13	0.00	2.63
FO	Invesco Greater China R5	IACFX	D+	(800) 959-4246	C- / 3.8	2.99	1.74	25.67 /75	2.52 /28	4.69 /19	1.14	1.41
FO	Invesco Greater China Y	AMCYX	D+	(800) 959-4246	C- / 3.6	2.99	1.69	25.43 /75	2.31 /26	4.48 /18	0.92	1.63
GR	Invesco Growth Allocation A	AADAX	C	(800) 959-4246	C- / 3.3	5.58	6.42	18.19 /44	3.69 /39	6.52 /32	1.02	1.13
GR	● Invesco Growth Allocation B	AAEBX	C	(800) 959-4246	C- / 3.7	5.34	5.95	17.30 /40	2.91 /31	5.69 /26	0.32	1.88
GR	Invesco Growth Allocation C	AADCX	C	(800) 959-4246	C- / 3.7	5.41	5.95	17.29 /40	2.91 /31	5.71 /26	0.32	1.88
GR	Invesco Growth Allocation R	AADRX	C+	(800) 959-4246	C- / 4.1	5.55	6.23	17.94 /43	3.42 /36	6.24 /30	0.83	1.38
GR	Invesco Growth Allocation R5	AADIX	C+	(800) 959-4246	C / 4.7	5.65	6.56	18.64 /46	4.07 /44	6.89 /34	1.44	0.76
GR	Invesco Growth Allocation S	AADSX	C+	(800) 959-4246	C / 4.5	5.62	6.45	18.33 /44	3.80 /40	6.63 /32	1.18	1.03
GR	Invesco Growth Allocation Y	AADYX	C+	(800) 959-4246	C / 4.6	5.63	6.47	18.44 /45	3.94 /42	6.78 /33	1.33	0.88
GI	Invesco Growth and Income A	ACGIX	B+	(800) 959-4246	A / 9.3	5.53	15.63	35.33 /94	9.44 /90	13.72 /91	1.40	0.83
GI	● Invesco Growth and Income B	ACGJX	B+	(800) 959-4246	A+ / 9.7	5.53	15.63	35.33 /94	9.43 /90	13.72 /91	1.48	0.83
GI	Invesco Growth and Income C	ACGKX	B+	(800) 959-4246	A / 9.5	5.35	15.20	34.34 /93	8.63 /84	12.88 /83	0.85	1.55
GI	Invesco Growth and Income R	ACGLX	B+	(800) 959-4246	A+ / 9.6	5.46	15.47	34.96 /94	9.17 /88	13.45 /88	1.27	1.08
GI	Invesco Growth and Income R5	ACGQX	B+	(800) 959-4246	A+ / 9.7	5.61	15.83	35.77 /95	9.83 /92	14.12 /94	1.78	0.48
GI	Invesco Growth and Income R6	GIFFX	B+	(800) 959-4246	A+ / 9.7	5.64	15.84	35.90 /95	9.92 /93	14.16 /94	1.86	0.38
GI	Invesco Growth and Income Y	ACGMX	B+	(800) 959-4246	A+ / 9.7	5.59	15.76	35.69 /95	9.72 /92	14.01 /93	1.70	0.58
FO	Invesco International Alloc A	AINAX	D-	(800) 959-4246	D- / 1.1	7.18	4.24	19.70 /50	-0.24 /12	3.18 /11	1.30	1.39
FO	● Invesco International Alloc B	INABX	D-	(800) 959-4246	D- / 1.3	6.97	3.92	18.87 /46	-0.98 / 9	2.40 / 9	0.62	2.14
FO	Invesco International Alloc C	INACX	D-	(800) 959-4246	D- / 1.3	6.97	3.92	18.87 /46	-0.95 /10	2.40 / 9	0.62	2.14
FO	Invesco International Alloc R	RINAX	D-	(800) 959-4246	D- / 1.5	7.00	4.06	19.38 /49	-0.49 /11	2.90 /10	1.12	1.64
FO	Invesco International Alloc R5	INAIX	D	(800) 959-4246	D+ / 2.7	7.24	4.51	20.26 /53	0.19 /14	3.63 /14	1.81	0.97
FO	Invesco International Alloc Y	AINYX	D	(800) 959-4246	D+ / 2.6	7.16	4.43	19.97 /52	0.03 /13	3.43 /13	1.63	1.14
FO	Invesco International Companies R6	IZISX	U	(800) 959-4246	U /	6.69	1.65	23.03 /67	--	--	1.04	2.38
FO	Invesco International Growth A	AIIEX	D-	(800) 959-4246	D- / 1.0	6.77	0.90	9.43 /10	0.16 /14	4.76 /20	1.11	1.32
FO	● Invesco International Growth B	AIEBX	D-	(800) 959-4246	E+ / 0.9	6.57	0.54	8.63 / 9	-0.58 /11	3.97 /15	0.42	2.07
FO	Invesco International Growth C	AIECX	D-	(800) 959-4246	E+ / 0.9	6.57	0.54	8.62 / 9	-0.59 /11	3.98 /15	0.42	2.07
FO	Invesco International Growth R	AIERX	D-	(800) 959-4246	D- / 1.1	6.71	0.79	9.14 /10	-0.08 /13	4.50 /18	0.92	1.57
FO	Invesco International Growth R5	AIEVX	D	(800) 959-4246	D / 1.6	6.84	1.06	9.79 /11	0.50 /16	5.12 /22	1.51	0.99
FO	Invesco International Growth R6	IGFRX	D	(800) 959-4246	D / 1.7	6.88	1.13	9.89 /11	0.59 /16	5.15 /22	1.60	0.91
FO	Invesco International Growth Y	AIIYX	D	(800) 959-4246	D / 1.6	6.84	1.04	9.71 /11	0.42 /15	5.02 /21	1.44	1.07
EM	Invesco International Small Co A	IEGAX	E	(800) 959-4246	D- / 1.4	9.77	5.29	24.54 /72	-0.31 /12	3.18 /11	1.99	1.54

● Denotes fund is closed to new investors
* Denotes fund is included in Section II

www.thestreetratings.com

Risk Rating/Pts	3 Year Standard Deviation	Beta	NAV As of 2/28/17	Total $(Mil)	Cash %	Stocks %	Bonds %	Other %	Portfolio Turnover Ratio	Last Bull Market Return	Last Bear Market Return	Manager Quality Pct	Manager Tenure (Years)	Initial Purch. $	Additional Purch. $	Front End Load	Back End Load
C+ / 6.5	12.0	0.82	12.81	55	11	87	0	2	84	72.4	-20.1	30	N/A	10,000,000	0	0.0	0.0
C+ / 6.5	11.9	0.81	12.83	1,168	11	87	0	2	84	70.2	-19.9	26	N/A	1,000	50	0.0	0.0
C / 4.4	10.8	0.79	18.36	455	5	90	4	1	22	67.8	-21.9	88	18	1,000	50	5.5	0.0
C- / 4.0	10.8	0.79	15.16	3	5	90	4	1	22	61.1	-22.2	85	18	1,000	50	0.0	0.0
C- / 4.0	10.8	0.79	15.18	23	5	90	4	1	22	61.1	-22.2	85	18	1,000	50	0.0	0.0
C / 4.3	10.8	0.79	18.24	12	5	90	4	1	22	71.5	-21.8	90	18	10,000,000	0	0.0	0.0
C / 4.4	10.8	0.79	18.38	17	5	90	4	1	22	70.0	-21.9	89	18	1,000	50	0.0	0.0
B+ / 9.9	3.3	N/A	9.86	24	0	0	0	100	23	N/A	N/A	83	4	1,000	50	5.5	0.0
B+ / 9.9	3.2	N/A	9.72	15	0	0	0	100	23	N/A	N/A	78	4	1,000	50	0.0	0.0
B+ / 9.9	3.3	N/A	9.82	N/A	0	0	0	100	23	N/A	N/A	82	4	0	0	0.0	0.0
B+ / 9.9	3.3	N/A	9.89	N/A	0	0	0	100	23	N/A	N/A	84	4	10,000,000	0	0.0	0.0
B+ / 9.9	3.3	N/A	9.88	N/A	0	0	0	100	23	N/A	N/A	84	4	10,000,000	0	0.0	0.0
B+ / 9.9	3.3	N/A	9.89	144	0	0	0	100	23	N/A	N/A	84	4	1,000	50	0.0	0.0
E- / 0.1	41.7	2.26	4.41	157	6	86	6	2	23	-42.9	-17.1	90	4	1,000	50	5.5	0.0
E- / 0.1	41.7	2.27	4.15	2	6	86	6	2	23	-45.2	-17.4	88	4	1,000	50	0.0	0.0
E- / 0.1	41.7	2.26	4.46	34	6	86	6	2	23	-45.2	-17.4	87	4	1,000	50	0.0	0.0
E- / 0.1	41.7	2.27	4.44	84	6	86	6	2	23	-42.9	-17.1	90	4	1,000	50	0.0	0.0
E- / 0.1	41.7	2.27	4.50	43	6	86	6	2	23	-42.2	-17.1	91	4	1,000	50	0.0	0.0
C / 4.9	18.5	0.86	22.35	51	1	98	0	1	52	49.5	-29.9	87	2	1,000	50	5.5	0.0
C / 4.9	18.5	0.87	21.78	1	1	98	0	1	52	43.6	-30.1	83	2	1,000	50	0.0	0.0
C / 4.9	18.5	0.86	21.74	11	1	98	0	1	52	43.6	-30.2	83	2	1,000	50	0.0	0.0
C / 4.8	18.5	0.86	22.33	N/A	1	98	0	1	52	53.3	-29.8	89	2	10,000,000	0	0.0	0.0
C / 4.9	18.5	0.86	22.35	5	1	98	0	1	52	51.6	-29.9	88	2	1,000	50	0.0	0.0
B- / 7.6	8.0	0.73	14.68	808	9	70	19	2	15	59.9	-13.6	25	13	1,000	50	5.5	0.0
B- / 7.7	8.0	0.74	14.52	29	9	70	19	2	15	53.4	-13.9	18	13	1,000	50	0.0	0.0
B- / 7.7	8.0	0.74	14.53	146	9	70	19	2	15	53.5	-13.9	18	13	1,000	50	0.0	0.0
B- / 7.7	8.0	0.74	14.64	23	9	70	19	2	15	57.8	-13.7	22	13	0	0	0.0	0.0
B- / 7.6	8.0	0.74	14.74	N/A	9	70	19	2	15	62.9	-13.4	29	13	10,000,000	0	0.0	0.0
B- / 7.6	8.0	0.74	14.67	24	9	70	19	2	15	60.8	-13.5	26	13	0	0	0.0	0.0
B- / 7.6	8.0	0.74	14.65	8	9	70	19	2	15	62.0	-13.5	28	13	1,000	50	0.0	0.0
C / 4.8	12.2	1.06	27.29	4,292	1	97	0	2	18	127.6	-19.7	53	18	1,000	50	5.5	0.0
C / 4.8	12.2	1.06	27.05	28	1	97	0	2	18	127.7	-19.7	53	18	1,000	50	0.0	0.0
C / 4.8	12.2	1.06	26.97	303	1	97	0	2	18	118.8	-20.0	42	18	1,000	50	0.0	0.0
C / 4.8	12.2	1.06	27.31	126	1	97	0	2	18	124.7	-19.8	49	18	0	0	0.0	0.0
C / 4.8	12.1	1.06	27.35	858	1	97	0	2	18	132.1	-19.6	58	18	10,000,000	0	0.0	0.0
C / 4.8	12.2	1.06	27.35	795	1	97	0	2	18	132.1	-19.7	59	18	10,000,000	0	0.0	0.0
C / 4.8	12.2	1.06	27.32	1,853	1	97	0	2	18	130.9	-19.7	56	18	1,000	50	0.0	0.0
C+ / 5.7	11.8	0.91	10.50	103	2	94	2	2	9	34.7	-20.2	73	3	1,000	50	5.5	0.0
C+ / 5.7	11.8	0.91	10.51	1	2	94	2	2	9	29.4	-20.4	64	3	1,000	50	0.0	0.0
C+ / 5.7	11.8	0.91	10.51	22	2	94	2	2	9	29.4	-20.4	65	3	1,000	50	0.0	0.0
C+ / 5.7	11.8	0.91	10.50	4	2	94	2	2	9	32.8	-20.3	70	3	0	0	0.0	0.0
C+ / 5.6	11.8	0.91	10.49	7	2	94	2	2	9	37.9	-20.2	77	3	10,000,000	0	0.0	0.0
C+ / 5.6	11.8	0.91	10.46	6	2	94	2	2	9	36.5	-20.1	75	3	1,000	50	0.0	0.0
U /	N/A	N/A	10.90	54	0	0	0	100	35	N/A	N/A	N/A	2	10,000,000	0	0.0	0.0
C+ / 6.0	10.9	0.85	31.70	2,330	2	94	3	1	12	46.7	-20.3	76	20	1,000	50	5.5	0.0
C+ / 5.9	10.9	0.85	29.17	7	2	94	3	1	12	40.9	-20.6	69	20	1,000	50	0.0	0.0
C+ / 5.9	10.9	0.85	29.20	151	2	94	3	1	12	40.9	-20.5	69	20	1,000	50	0.0	0.0
C+ / 6.0	10.9	0.85	31.34	98	2	94	3	1	12	44.8	-20.4	74	20	0	0	0.0	0.0
C+ / 5.9	10.9	0.85	32.18	1,374	2	94	3	1	12	49.5	-20.1	78	20	10,000,000	0	0.0	0.0
C+ / 5.9	10.9	0.85	32.17	840	2	94	3	1	12	49.5	-20.3	79	20	10,000,000	0	0.0	0.0
C+ / 5.9	10.9	0.85	31.77	3,552	2	94	3	1	12	48.8	-20.2	78	20	1,000	50	0.0	0.0
C- / 3.8	12.7	0.64	16.61	130	6	88	4	2	8	38.0	-17.6	56	17	1,000	50	5.5	0.0

Fund Type	Fund Name	Ticker Symbol	Overall Investment Rating	Phone	Performance Rating/Pts	3 Mo	6 Mo	1Yr / Pct	3Yr / Pct	5Yr / Pct	Dividend Yield	Expense Ratio
	99 Pct = Best				**PERFORMANCE**			Total Return % through 2/28/17			Incl. in Returns	
	0 Pct = Worst								Annualized			
EM	● Invesco International Small Co B	IEGBX	E+	(800) 959-4246	D / 1.6	9.56	4.93	23.64 /69	-1.04 / 9	2.41 / 9	1.42	2.29
EM	Invesco International Small Co C	IEGCX	E+	(800) 959-4246	D / 1.6	9.56	4.87	23.64 /69	-1.06 / 9	2.40 / 9	1.42	2.29
EM	Invesco International Small Co R5	IEGIX	D-	(800) 959-4246	C- / 3.6	9.86	5.48	25.06 /73	0.05 /14	3.54 /13	2.42	1.19
FO	Invesco International Small Co R6	IEGFX	D-	(800) 959-4246	C- / 3.6	9.89	5.51	25.17 /74	0.13 /14	3.57 /13	2.49	1.11
EM	Invesco International Small Co Y	IEGYX	E+	(800) 959-4246	D / 2.1	9.82	5.41	24.88 /73	-0.05 /13	3.43 /13	2.32	1.29
FO	Invesco Intl Core Equity A	IBVAX	D-	(800) 959-4246	D / 1.7	5.56	3.56	16.46 /36	0.76 /17	3.46 /13	1.51	1.61
FO	Invesco Intl Core Equity C	IBVCX	D-	(800) 959-4246	D- / 1.4	5.36	3.21	15.56 /32	-0.03 /13	2.68 /10	0.84	2.36
FO	Invesco Intl Core Equity Inv	IIBCX	D	(800) 959-4246	D+ / 2.3	5.56	3.59	16.52 /36	0.72 /17	3.46 /13	1.57	1.61
FO	Invesco Intl Core Equity R	IIBRX	D	(800) 959-4246	D / 2.2	5.57	3.48	16.22 /35	0.50 /16	3.22 /12	1.34	1.86
FO	Invesco Intl Core Equity R5	IBVIX	D	(800) 959-4246	D+ / 2.6	5.61	3.70	16.82 /38	1.20 /19	4.00 /15	2.01	1.03
FO	Invesco Intl Core Equity R6	IBVFX	D	(800) 959-4246	D+ / 2.6	5.62	3.71	16.83 /38	1.21 /19	3.93 /15	2.02	1.02
FO	Invesco Intl Core Equity Y	IBVYX	D	(800) 959-4246	D+ / 2.5	5.63	3.76	16.82 /38	1.00 /18	3.72 /14	1.83	1.36
GR	Invesco Long/Short Equity A	LSQAX	B-	(800) 959-4246	C+ / 6.8	5.88	15.31	15.42 /32	8.61 /84	--	0.00	2.33
GR	Invesco Long/Short Equity R	LSQRX	B-	(800) 959-4246	C+ / 6.8	5.82	15.19	15.19 /31	8.37 /82	--	0.00	2.58
GR	Invesco Long/Short Equity R5	LSQFX	A-	(800) 959-4246	B / 7.9	5.85	15.33	15.66 /33	8.88 /86	--	0.00	1.95
GR	Invesco Long/Short Equity R6	LSQSX	A-	(800) 959-4246	B / 7.9	5.85	15.33	15.66 /33	8.88 /86	--	0.00	1.95
GR	Invesco Long/Short Equity Y	LSQYX	A-	(800) 959-4246	B / 8.0	5.94	15.43	15.76 /33	8.91 /86	--	0.00	2.08
EM	Invesco Low Volatility Emg Mkts A	LVLAX	D	(800) 959-4246	D / 1.6	11.33	6.38	28.68 /83	-0.63 /11	--	1.12	7.99
EM	Invesco Low Volatility Emg Mkts C	LVLCX	D	(800) 959-4246	D / 1.8	11.22	5.97	27.86 /81	-1.33 / 8	--	0.16	8.74
EM	Invesco Low Volatility Emg Mkts R	LVLRX	D	(800) 959-4246	D / 2.1	11.22	6.25	28.41 /83	-0.85 /10	--	0.86	8.24
EM	Invesco Low Volatility Emg Mkts R5	LVLFX	D+	(800) 959-4246	D+ / 2.4	11.42	6.47	29.10 /84	-0.35 /12	--	1.38	7.64
EM	Invesco Low Volatility Emg Mkts R6	LVLSX	D+	(800) 959-4246	D+ / 2.4	11.43	6.48	29.14 /84	-0.38 /12	--	1.39	7.64
EM	Invesco Low Volatility Emg Mkts Y	LVLYX	D+	(800) 959-4246	D+ / 2.4	11.42	6.47	29.10 /84	-0.35 /12	--	1.38	7.74
GR	Invesco Low Volatility Eq A	SCAUX	C-	(800) 959-4246	C / 4.3	7.45	7.17	17.56 /41	5.01 /54	9.58 /55	2.40	1.20
GR	● Invesco Low Volatility Eq B	SBCUX	C	(800) 959-4246	C / 4.8	7.24	6.85	16.68 /37	4.22 /45	8.75 /48	1.84	1.95
GR	Invesco Low Volatility Eq C	SCCUX	C	(800) 959-4246	C / 4.8	7.26	6.76	16.73 /37	4.22 /45	8.75 /48	1.84	1.95
GR	Invesco Low Volatility Eq Inv	SCNUX	C+	(800) 959-4246	C / 5.5	7.53	7.25	17.63 /41	5.01 /54	9.58 /55	2.53	1.20
GR	Invesco Low Volatility Eq R	SCRUX	C	(800) 959-4246	C / 5.2	7.42	7.06	17.23 /39	4.76 /52	9.32 /53	2.31	1.45
GR	Invesco Low Volatility Eq R5	SCIUX	C+	(800) 959-4246	C+ / 5.8	7.63	7.47	18.08 /43	5.47 /59	10.01 /58	2.94	0.77
GR	Invesco Low Volatility Eq Y	SCAYX	C+	(800) 959-4246	C+ / 5.7	7.48	7.27	17.90 /42	5.27 /57	9.84 /57	2.77	0.95
GL	Invesco Macro Allocation Stratgy A	GMSDX	C-	(800) 959-4246	D / 2.0	1.67	3.16	8.03 / 7	4.54 /49	--	13.09	1.74
GL	Invesco Macro Allocation Stratgy C	GMSEX	C-	(800) 959-4246	D+ / 2.3	1.48	2.88	7.31 / 6	3.77 /40	--	12.89	2.49
GL	Invesco Macro Allocation Stratgy R	GMSJX	C	(800) 959-4246	D+ / 2.6	1.57	3.06	7.81 / 7	4.30 /46	--	13.51	1.99
GL	Invesco Macro Allocation Stratgy R5	GMSKX	C	(800) 959-4246	C- / 3.0	1.64	3.32	8.29 / 8	4.78 /52	--	14.12	1.36
GL	Invesco Macro Allocation Stratgy R6	GMSLX	C	(800) 959-4246	C- / 3.0	1.74	3.33	8.30 / 8	4.78 /52	--	14.14	1.36
GL	Invesco Macro Allocation Stratgy Y	GMSHX	C	(800) 959-4246	C- / 3.0	1.73	3.32	8.41 / 8	4.82 /52	--	14.12	1.49
MC	Invesco Mid Cap Core Equity A	GTAGX	D+	(800) 959-4246	C- / 3.8	5.21	5.21	21.19 /58	4.20 /45	8.41 /45	0.26	1.23
MC	● Invesco Mid Cap Core Equity B	GTABX	D	(800) 959-4246	C- / 4.2	5.00	4.80	20.31 /54	3.43 /36	7.60 /39	0.00	1.98
MC	Invesco Mid Cap Core Equity C	GTACX	D	(800) 959-4246	C- / 4.2	5.02	4.82	20.31 /54	3.42 /36	7.59 /39	0.00	1.98
MC	Invesco Mid Cap Core Equity R	GTARX	C-	(800) 959-4246	C / 4.7	5.10	5.06	20.89 /57	3.95 /42	8.14 /43	0.02	1.48
MC	Invesco Mid Cap Core Equity R5	GTAVX	C-	(800) 959-4246	C / 5.2	5.28	5.36	21.62 /60	4.59 /50	8.80 /49	0.74	0.85
MC	Invesco Mid Cap Core Equity R6	GTAFX	C-	(800) 959-4246	C / 5.3	5.31	5.39	21.71 /61	4.67 /50	8.85 /49	1.05	0.76
MC	Invesco Mid Cap Core Equity Y	GTAYX	C-	(800) 959-4246	C / 5.1	5.22	5.26	21.44 /59	4.45 /48	8.67 /48	0.51	0.98
MC	Invesco Mid Cap Growth A	VGRAX	D	(800) 959-4246	C- / 3.8	6.20	5.15	21.43 /59	4.11 /44	10.09 /59	0.00	1.21
MC	● Invesco Mid Cap Growth B	VGRBX	D+	(800) 959-4246	C / 5.0	6.22	5.15	21.44 /59	4.11 /44	10.09 /59	0.00	1.21
MC	Invesco Mid Cap Growth C	VGRCX	D	(800) 959-4246	C / 4.3	6.03	4.76	20.57 /55	3.36 /35	9.29 /53	0.00	1.93
MC	Invesco Mid Cap Growth R	VGRRX	D+	(800) 959-4246	C / 4.8	6.15	5.01	21.12 /58	3.85 /41	9.82 /57	0.00	1.46
MC	Invesco Mid Cap Growth R5	VGRJX	D+	(800) 959-4246	C / 5.3	6.32	5.34	21.91 /62	4.49 /49	10.51 /62	0.00	0.82
MC	Invesco Mid Cap Growth R6	VGRFX	D+	(800) 959-4246	C / 5.4	6.32	5.40	22.01 /62	4.58 /50	--	0.00	0.73
MC	Invesco Mid Cap Growth Y	VGRDX	D+	(800) 959-4246	C / 5.2	6.26	5.27	21.71 /61	4.36 /47	10.37 /61	0.00	0.96
BA	Invesco Moderate Allocation A	AMKAX	C	(800) 959-4246	D+ / 2.5	4.58	4.77	15.06 /30	3.28 /34	5.47 /25	1.66	1.05
BA	● Invesco Moderate Allocation B	AMKBX	C	(800) 959-4246	D+ / 2.9	4.42	4.32	14.13 /26	2.52 /28	4.68 /19	1.04	1.80

● Denotes fund is closed to new investors
* Denotes fund is included in Section II

www.thestreetratings.com

RISK			NET ASSETS		ASSET					BULL / BEAR		FUND MANAGER		MINIMUMS		LOADS	
	3 Year		NAV						Portfolio	Last Bull	Last Bear	Manager	Manager	Initial	Additional	Front	Back
Risk Rating/Pts	Standard Deviation	Beta	As of 2/28/17	Total $(Mil)	Cash %	Stocks %	Bonds %	Other %	Turnover Ratio	Market Return	Market Return	Quality Pct	Tenure (Years)	Purch. $	Purch. $	End Load	End Load
C- /3.8	12.7	0.64	15.83	1	6	88	4	2	8	32.5	-17.8	46	17	1,000	50	0.0	0.0
C- /3.8	12.7	0.64	15.83	17	6	88	4	2	8	32.5	-17.9	46	17	1,000	50	0.0	0.0
C- /3.7	12.7	0.64	16.50	10	6	88	4	2	8	40.7	-17.5	61	17	10,000,000	0	0.0	0.0
C- /3.7	12.7	0.91	16.49	16	6	88	4	2	8	40.6	-17.6	76	17	10,000,000	0	0.0	0.0
C- /3.7	12.7	0.64	16.64	69	6	88	4	2	8	39.9	-17.5	60	17	1,000	50	0.0	0.0
C+ /5.6	11.4	0.90	10.76	36	1	98	0	1	37	34.8	-22.5	80	3	1,000	50	5.5	0.0
C+ /5.6	11.4	0.90	10.53	9	1	98	0	1	37	29.4	-22.8	75	3	1,000	50	0.0	0.0
C+ /5.6	11.4	0.90	10.94	10	1	98	0	1	37	34.9	-22.5	80	3	1,000	50	0.0	0.0
C+ /5.6	11.4	0.90	10.80	2	1	98	0	1	37	33.1	-22.5	79	3	0	0	0.0	0.0
C /5.5	11.4	0.90	10.68	3	1	98	0	1	37	38.7	-22.3	83	3	10,000,000	0	0.0	0.0
C /5.5	11.4	0.90	10.68	26	1	98	0	1	37	38.0	-22.5	83	3	10,000,000	0	0.0	0.0
C+ /5.6	11.4	0.90	10.94	4	1	98	0	1	37	36.8	-22.5	82	3	1,000	50	0.0	0.0
B- /7.0	11.9	0.68	12.09	15	12	80	6	2	102	N/A	N/A	83	4	1,000	50	5.5	0.0
B- /7.0	11.8	0.68	12.02	N/A	12	80	6	2	102	N/A	N/A	82	4	0	0	0.0	0.0
B- /7.0	11.7	0.68	12.15	1	12	80	6	2	102	N/A	N/A	84	4	10,000,000	0	0.0	0.0
B- /7.0	11.8	0.68	12.15	48	12	80	6	2	102	N/A	N/A	84	4	10,000,000	0	0.0	0.0
B- /7.0	11.8	0.68	12.16	9	12	80	6	2	102	N/A	N/A	84	4	1,000	50	0.0	0.0
C+ /6.2	16.1	0.97	8.64	4	3	96	0	1	63	N/A	N/A	44	4	1,000	50	5.5	0.0
C+ /6.2	16.2	0.97	8.63	N/A	3	96	0	1	63	N/A	N/A	35	4	1,000	50	0.0	0.0
C+ /6.2	16.2	0.97	8.64	N/A	3	96	0	1	63	N/A	N/A	41	4	0	0	0.0	0.0
C+ /6.2	16.1	0.97	8.65	N/A	3	96	0	1	63	N/A	N/A	48	4	10,000,000	0	0.0	0.0
C+ /6.2	16.2	0.97	8.64	38	3	96	0	1	63	N/A	N/A	48	4	10,000,000	0	0.0	0.0
C+ /6.2	16.2	0.97	8.65	2	3	96	0	1	63	N/A	N/A	48	4	1,000	50	0.0	0.0
C+ /6.0	9.7	0.75	10.55	178	0	96	2	2	107	94.4	-17.7	37	6	1,000	50	5.5	0.0
C+ /6.1	9.7	0.75	10.40	2	0	96	2	2	107	86.6	-17.8	29	6	1,000	50	0.0	0.0
C+ /6.0	9.8	0.76	10.37	28	0	96	2	2	107	86.7	-17.8	28	6	1,000	50	0.0	0.0
C+ /6.0	9.8	0.76	10.59	49	0	96	2	2	107	94.5	-17.7	37	6	1,000	50	0.0	0.0
C+ /6.0	9.7	0.76	10.50	N/A	0	96	2	2	107	91.9	-17.7	34	6	0	0	0.0	0.0
C+ /6.0	9.8	0.76	10.62	14	0	96	2	2	107	98.6	-17.5	43	6	10,000,000	0	0.0	0.0
C+ /6.0	9.7	0.75	10.60	9	0	96	2	2	107	97.0	-17.5	41	6	1,000	50	0.0	0.0
B- /7.8	6.7	0.10	9.25	6	56	0	43	1	75	N/A	N/A	94	5	1,000	50	5.5	0.0
B /8.0	6.7	0.10	9.26	6	56	0	43	1	75	N/A	N/A	92	5	1,000	50	0.0	0.0
B- /7.9	6.6	0.09	9.27	N/A	56	0	43	1	75	N/A	N/A	94	5	0	0	0.0	0.0
B- /7.8	6.6	0.09	9.27	N/A	56	0	43	1	75	N/A	N/A	95	5	10,000,000	0	0.0	0.0
B- /7.8	6.6	0.09	9.26	N/A	56	0	43	1	75	N/A	N/A	95	5	10,000,000	0	0.0	0.0
B- /7.8	6.7	0.10	9.27	27	56	0	43	1	75	N/A	N/A	95	5	1,000	50	0.0	0.0
C /4.8	9.9	0.76	22.23	930	7	86	6	1	54	79.0	-20.8	36	19	1,000	50	5.5	0.0
C- /3.7	9.9	0.76	14.46	9	7	86	6	1	54	71.8	-21.1	27	19	1,000	50	0.0	0.0
C- /3.6	9.9	0.76	14.40	108	7	86	6	1	54	71.9	-21.1	27	19	1,000	50	0.0	0.0
C /4.7	9.9	0.76	21.46	63	7	86	6	1	54	76.5	-20.9	32	19	0	0	0.0	0.0
C /5.0	9.9	0.76	24.08	44	7	86	6	1	54	82.6	-20.7	41	19	10,000,000	0	0.0	0.0
C /4.9	9.9	0.76	24.08	4	7	86	6	1	54	82.6	-20.8	42	19	10,000,000	0	0.0	0.0
C /4.8	9.9	0.76	22.56	103	7	86	6	1	54	81.3	-20.8	39	19	1,000	50	0.0	0.0
C- /3.8	13.6	1.01	36.13	2,220	0	98	0	2	60	98.9	-25.9	13	6	1,000	50	5.5	0.0
C- /3.5	13.6	1.01	30.22	28	0	98	0	2	60	99.2	-25.9	13	6	1,000	50	0.0	0.0
C- /3.3	13.6	1.01	27.96	141	0	98	0	2	60	91.3	-26.2	9	6	1,000	50	0.0	0.0
C- /3.8	13.5	1.01	35.20	28	0	98	0	2	60	96.2	-26.0	12	6	0	0	0.0	0.0
C- /3.9	13.5	1.01	37.86	103	0	98	0	2	60	103.1	-25.7	16	6	10,000,000	0	0.0	0.0
C- /3.9	13.5	1.01	37.99	53	0	98	0	2	60	N/A	N/A	17	6	10,000,000	0	0.0	0.0
C- /3.8	13.6	1.01	37.53	99	0	98	0	2	60	101.6	-25.8	15	6	1,000	50	0.0	0.0
B /8.3	6.5	0.99	12.98	585	6	52	41	1	14	48.3	-9.6	24	N/A	1,000	50	5.5	0.0
B /8.3	6.5	1.00	12.87	15	6	52	41	1	14	42.4	-9.9	17	N/A	1,000	50	0.0	0.0

					PERFORMANCE						Incl. in Returns	
	99 Pct = Best 0 Pct = Worst				Perfor-	Total Return % through 2/28/17						
		Ticker	Overall Investment		mance				Annualized		Dividend	Expense
Fund Type	Fund Name	Symbol	Rating	Phone	Rating/Pts	3 Mo	6 Mo	1Yr / Pct	3Yr / Pct	5Yr / Pct	Yield	Ratio
BA	Invesco Moderate Allocation C	AMKCX	C	(800) 959-4246	D+ / 2.9	4.50	4.41	14.23 /27	2.52 /28	4.70 /19	1.04	1.80
BA	Invesco Moderate Allocation R	AMKRX	C+	(800) 959-4246	C- / 3.2	4.61	4.65	14.81 /29	3.03 /32	5.21 /23	1.52	1.30
BA	Invesco Moderate Allocation R5	AMLIX	C+	(800) 959-4246	C- / 3.6	4.72	4.99	15.44 /32	3.53 /37	5.73 /27	2.05	0.74
BA	Invesco Moderate Allocation S	AMKSX	C+	(800) 959-4246	C- / 3.5	4.69	4.82	15.18 /31	3.39 /36	5.57 /25	1.85	0.95
BA	Invesco Moderate Allocation Y	ABKYX	C+	(800) 959-4246	C- / 3.6	4.64	4.89	15.33 /31	3.54 /37	5.73 /27	1.99	0.80
FO	Invesco Pacific Growth A	TGRAX	C-	(800) 959-4246	D+ / 2.6	4.13	0.02	18.12 /43	3.89 /42	4.84 /20	0.19	1.78
FO	● Invesco Pacific Growth B	TGRBX	C-	(800) 959-4246	C- / 3.0	3.92	-0.37	17.23 /39	3.11 /33	4.05 /15	0.00	2.53
FO	Invesco Pacific Growth C	TGRCX	C-	(800) 959-4246	C- / 3.0	3.91	-0.37	17.25 /39	3.12 /33	4.06 /16	0.00	2.53
FO	Invesco Pacific Growth R	TGRRX	C-	(800) 959-4246	C- / 3.4	4.03	-0.12	17.82 /42	3.62 /38	4.55 /18	0.00	2.03
FO	Invesco Pacific Growth R5	TGRSX	C	(800) 959-4246	C- / 3.9	4.22	0.19	18.54 /45	4.29 /46	5.24 /23	0.57	1.39
FO	Invesco Pacific Growth Y	TGRDX	C	(800) 959-4246	C- / 3.8	4.22	0.18	18.42 /45	4.15 /45	5.09 /22	0.46	1.53
RE	Invesco Real Estate A	IARAX	C-	(800) 959-4246	C+ / 6.2	8.36	-1.55	15.74 /33	10.04 /93	10.20 /60	1.57	1.25
RE	● Invesco Real Estate B	AARBX	C-	(800) 959-4246	C+ / 6.6	8.14	-1.95	14.88 /29	9.21 /88	9.37 /54	0.93	2.00
RE	Invesco Real Estate C	IARCX	C-	(800) 959-4246	C+ / 6.6	8.13	-1.92	14.89 /29	9.22 /88	9.37 /54	0.93	2.00
RE	Invesco Real Estate Investor	REINX	C	(800) 959-4246	B- / 7.1	8.33	-1.59	15.73 /33	10.03 /93	10.20 /60	1.66	1.25
RE	Invesco Real Estate R	IARRX	C	(800) 959-4246	B- / 7.0	8.28	-1.72	15.43 /32	9.77 /92	9.92 /58	1.41	1.50
RE	Invesco Real Estate R5	IARIX	C	(800) 959-4246	B- / 7.4	8.47	-1.36	16.17 /35	10.45 /96	10.61 /63	2.00	0.87
RE	Invesco Real Estate R6	IARFX	C	(800) 959-4246	B- / 7.5	8.45	-1.36	16.27 /35	10.54 /96	10.64 /63	2.09	0.78
RE	Invesco Real Estate Y	IARYX	C	(800) 959-4246	B- / 7.3	8.43	-1.46	16.03 /34	10.32 /95	10.48 /62	1.90	1.00
IX	Invesco S&P 500 Index A	SPIAX	A	(800) 959-4246	B / 8.2	7.89	9.67	24.26 /71	9.99 /93	13.36 /87	1.14	0.59
IX	● Invesco S&P 500 Index B	SPIBX	A+	(800) 959-4246	B+ / 8.6	7.69	9.33	23.37 /68	9.18 /88	12.53 /79	0.61	1.34
IX	Invesco S&P 500 Index C	SPICX	A+	(800) 959-4246	B+ / 8.6	7.71	9.32	23.35 /68	9.18 /88	12.53 /79	0.63	1.32
IX	Invesco S&P 500 Index Y	SPIDX	A+	(800) 959-4246	A- / 9.2	7.94	9.84	24.55 /72	10.27 /95	13.64 /90	1.41	0.34
SC	Invesco Select Companies A	ATIAX	D-	(800) 959-4246	C / 5.1	2.20	13.26	29.69 /86	3.73 /40	8.30 /45	0.00	1.23
SC	● Invesco Select Companies B	ATIBX	D-	(800) 959-4246	C+ / 5.6	2.01	12.92	28.70 /83	2.97 /32	7.50 /38	0.00	1.98
SC	Invesco Select Companies C	ATICX	D-	(800) 959-4246	C+ / 5.6	2.02	12.88	28.69 /83	2.96 /31	7.48 /38	0.00	1.98
SC	Invesco Select Companies R	ATIRX	D	(800) 959-4246	C+ / 6.1	2.12	13.17	29.34 /85	3.49 /37	8.02 /42	0.00	1.48
SC	Invesco Select Companies R5	ATIIX	D	(800) 959-4246	C+ / 6.6	2.28	13.49	30.17 /87	4.09 /44	8.65 /48	0.00	0.91
SC	Invesco Select Companies Y	ATIYX	D	(800) 959-4246	C+ / 6.5	2.32	13.49	30.05 /86	4.02 /43	8.57 /47	0.00	0.98
GL	Invesco Select Opportunities A	IZSAX	D-	(800) 959-4246	D / 2.2	3.04	10.22	22.67 /65	0.34 /15	---	0.00	1.75
GL	Invesco Select Opportunities C	IZSCX	D-	(800) 959-4246	D / 1.7	2.84	9.80	21.73 /61	-0.41 /12	---	0.00	2.50
GL	Invesco Select Opportunities R	IZSRX	D	(800) 959-4246	C- / 3.0	2.92	10.09	22.33 /64	0.10 /14	---	0.00	2.00
GL	Invesco Select Opportunities R5	IZSIX	D	(800) 959-4246	C- / 3.3	3.15	10.35	22.99 /67	0.61 /16	---	0.00	1.36
GL	Invesco Select Opportunities R6	IZFSX	D	(800) 959-4246	C- / 3.3	3.16	10.36	23.01 /67	0.61 /16	---	0.00	1.36
GL	Invesco Select Opportunities Y	IZSYX	D	(800) 959-4246	C- / 3.3	3.08	10.36	23.01 /67	0.59 /16	---	0.00	1.50
SC	Invesco Small Cap Discovery A	VASCX	E+	(800) 959-4246	C- / 4.2	7.11	8.65	25.41 /75	3.01 /32	10.09 /59	0.00	1.38
SC	● Invesco Small Cap Discovery B	VBSCX	D-	(800) 959-4246	C / 5.4	7.13	8.62	25.40 /75	3.02 /32	10.09 /59	0.00	1.38
SC	Invesco Small Cap Discovery C	VCSCX	E+	(800) 959-4246	C / 4.7	6.87	8.35	24.60 /72	2.26 /26	9.28 /53	0.00	2.10
SC	Invesco Small Cap Discovery R5	VESCX	D	(800) 959-4246	C+ / 5.8	7.12	8.80	26.03 /76	3.48 /37	---	0.00	0.93
SC	Invesco Small Cap Discovery R6	VFSCX	D	(800) 959-4246	C+ / 5.8	7.21	8.89	26.12 /77	3.51 /37	10.54 /62	0.00	0.88
SC	Invesco Small Cap Discovery Y	VISCX	D	(800) 959-4246	C+ / 5.7	7.19	8.88	25.86 /76	3.31 /35	10.40 /61	0.00	1.13
SC	Invesco Small Cap Equity A	SMEAX	D	(800) 959-4246	C- / 3.9	3.94	8.54	23.16 /67	3.70 /39	9.49 /55	0.00	1.29
SC	● Invesco Small Cap Equity B	SMEBX	D	(800) 959-4246	C / 4.4	3.85	8.24	22.28 /63	2.92 /31	8.68 /48	0.00	2.04
SC	Invesco Small Cap Equity C	SMECX	D	(800) 959-4246	C / 4.3	3.77	8.15	22.19 /63	2.90 /31	8.67 /48	0.00	2.04
SC	Invesco Small Cap Equity R	SMERX	D	(800) 959-4246	C / 4.9	3.94	8.48	22.94 /66	3.44 /36	9.23 /53	0.00	1.54
SC	Invesco Small Cap Equity R5	SMEIX	D+	(800) 959-4246	C / 5.5	4.07	8.79	23.69 /69	4.14 /44	9.96 /58	0.00	0.88
SC	Invesco Small Cap Equity R6	SMEFX	C-	(800) 959-4246	C / 5.5	4.11	8.88	23.73 /69	4.23 /46	9.98 /58	0.00	0.79
SC	Invesco Small Cap Equity Y	SMEYX	D+	(800) 959-4246	C / 5.3	4.04	8.74	23.44 /68	3.94 /42	9.76 /57	0.00	1.04
SC	● Invesco Small Cap Growth A	GTSAX	D+	(800) 959-4246	C+ / 6.1	4.81	8.74	28.60 /83	5.79 /62	12.57 /80	0.00	1.20
SC	● Invesco Small Cap Growth B	GTSBX	D	(800) 959-4246	C+ / 6.5	4.64	8.34	27.63 /81	5.01 /54	11.73 /72	0.00	1.95
SC	● Invesco Small Cap Growth C	GTSDX	D	(800) 959-4246	C+ / 6.5	4.61	8.32	27.65 /81	5.00 /54	11.73 /72	0.00	1.95
SC	● Invesco Small Cap Growth Inv	GTSIX	C-	(800) 959-4246	B- / 7.0	4.80	8.72	28.59 /83	5.79 /62	12.57 /80	0.00	1.20

● Denotes fund is closed to new investors
* Denotes fund is included in Section II

RISK			NET ASSETS		ASSET					BULL / BEAR		FUND MANAGER		MINIMUMS		LOADS	
	3 Year		NAV						Portfolio	Last Bull	Last Bear	Manager	Manager	Initial	Additional	Front	Back
Risk	Standard		As of	Total	Cash	Stocks	Bonds	Other	Turnover	Market	Market	Quality	Tenure	Purch.	Purch.	End	End
Rating/Pts	Deviation	Beta	2/28/17	$(Mil)	%	%	%	%	Ratio	Return	Return	Pct	(Years)	$	$	Load	Load
B /8.3	6.5	0.99	12.87	131	6	52	41	1	14	42.4	-9.9	18	N/A	1,000	50	0.0	0.0
B /8.3	6.5	0.99	12.95	16	6	52	41	1	14	46.4	-9.7	22	N/A	0	0	0.0	0.0
B /8.3	6.6	1.00	13.05	N/A	6	52	41	1	14	50.3	-9.5	26	N/A	10,000,000	0	0.0	0.0
B /8.3	6.5	0.99	12.98	28	6	52	41	1	14	49.1	-9.5	25	N/A	0	0	0.0	0.0
B /8.3	6.5	0.99	13.00	6	6	52	41	1	14	50.3	-9.4	27	N/A	1,000	50	0.0	0.0
C+ /6.7	11.8	0.65	26.05	61	1	98	0	1	31	44.9	-22.2	93	7	1,000	50	5.5	0.0
C+ /6.7	11.8	0.65	24.15	N/A	1	98	0	1	31	39.1	-22.5	91	7	1,000	50	0.0	0.0
C+ /6.7	11.8	0.65	24.20	4	1	98	0	1	31	39.3	-22.5	91	7	1,000	50	0.0	0.0
C+ /6.7	11.8	0.65	25.79	N/A	1	98	0	1	31	42.9	-22.3	92	7	0	0	0.0	0.0
C+ /6.7	11.8	0.65	26.50	N/A	1	98	0	1	31	48.0	-22.1	94	7	10,000,000	0	0.0	0.0
C+ /6.7	11.8	0.65	26.48	7	1	98	0	1	31	46.9	-22.2	94	7	1,000	50	0.0	0.0
C- /3.6	13.8	1.01	21.64	927	0	98	0	2	80	96.1	-16.2	61	22	1,000	50	5.5	0.0
C- /3.6	13.8	1.01	21.61	4	0	98	0	2	80	88.3	-16.5	50	22	1,000	50	0.0	0.0
C- /3.6	13.8	1.01	21.51	117	0	98	0	2	80	88.3	-16.5	50	22	1,000	50	0.0	0.0
C- /3.6	13.8	1.01	21.58	42	0	98	0	2	80	96.0	-16.2	61	22	1,000	50	0.0	0.0
C- /3.6	13.9	1.02	21.66	103	0	98	0	2	80	93.4	-16.3	57	22	0	0	0.0	0.0
C- /3.6	13.8	1.01	21.64	346	0	98	0	2	80	100.2	-16.1	66	22	10,000,000	0	0.0	0.0
C- /3.6	13.8	1.01	21.63	113	0	98	0	2	80	100.0	-16.2	67	22	10,000,000	0	0.0	0.0
C- /3.6	13.8	1.01	21.64	201	0	98	0	2	80	98.8	-16.2	64	22	1,000	50	0.0	0.0
B- /7.1	10.3	1.00	25.56	635	1	97	0	2	6	127.6	-16.5	68	7	1,000	50	5.5	0.0
B- /7.1	10.3	1.00	25.02	2	1	97	0	2	6	118.7	-16.8	58	7	1,000	50	0.0	0.0
B- /7.1	10.3	1.00	24.73	254	1	97	0	2	6	118.7	-16.8	58	7	1,000	50	0.0	0.0
B- /7.1	10.3	1.00	25.85	120	1	97	0	2	6	130.8	-16.4	70	7	1,000	50	0.0	0.0
D /1.7	13.0	0.73	18.30	316	4	89	6	1	20	80.9	-14.8	59	14	1,000	50	5.5	0.0
D- /1.4	13.0	0.73	15.93	2	4	89	6	1	20	73.8	-15.1	48	14	1,000	50	0.0	0.0
D- /1.4	13.1	0.73	15.89	107	4	89	6	1	20	73.6	-15.0	48	14	1,000	50	0.0	0.0
D /1.6	13.1	0.73	17.55	29	4	89	6	1	20	78.5	-14.9	55	14	0	0	0.0	0.0
D /1.8	13.1	0.73	19.45	32	4	89	6	1	20	84.2	-14.6	63	14	10,000,000	0	0.0	0.0
D /1.7	13.1	0.73	18.69	56	4	89	6	1	20	83.5	-14.7	62	14	1,000	50	0.0	0.0
C /5.0	12.2	0.76	14.23	21	22	77	0	1	26	N/A	N/A	77	5	1,000	50	5.5	0.0
C /4.9	12.2	0.76	13.78	20	22	77	0	1	26	N/A	N/A	71	5	1,000	50	0.0	0.0
C /4.9	12.2	0.76	14.08	N/A	22	77	0	1	26	N/A	N/A	75	5	0	0	0.0	0.0
C /5.0	12.2	0.76	14.39	N/A	22	77	0	1	26	N/A	N/A	79	5	10,000,000	0	0.0	0.0
C /5.0	12.2	0.76	14.38	N/A	22	77	0	1	26	N/A	N/A	79	5	10,000,000	0	0.0	0.0
C /5.0	12.2	0.76	14.38	9	22	77	0	1	26	N/A	N/A	79	5	1,000	50	0.0	0.0
D /1.9	15.9	0.95	9.65	397	1	96	1	2	39	104.8	-25.0	30	17	1,000	50	5.5	0.0
D- /1.5	15.9	0.95	8.42	4	1	96	1	2	39	104.8	-25.0	30	17	1,000	50	0.0	0.0
D- /1.1	15.9	0.95	7.63	42	1	96	1	2	39	96.6	-25.2	22	17	1,000	50	0.0	0.0
D /2.1	15.8	0.94	10.24	3	1	96	1	2	39	N/A	N/A	36	17	10,000,000	0	0.0	0.0
D /2.1	15.8	0.95	10.26	78	1	96	1	2	39	109.0	-25.0	36	17	10,000,000	0	0.0	0.0
D /2.0	15.9	0.95	10.15	80	1	96	1	2	39	107.7	-24.9	34	17	1,000	50	0.0	0.0
C- /3.6	14.6	0.90	14.68	560	0	98	0	2	29	100.8	-24.9	43	13	1,000	50	5.5	0.0
C- /3.2	14.5	0.90	12.04	3	0	98	0	2	29	92.8	-25.1	33	13	1,000	50	0.0	0.0
C- /3.2	14.6	0.90	12.03	58	0	98	0	2	29	92.7	-25.0	32	13	1,000	50	0.0	0.0
C- /3.5	14.6	0.90	13.89	76	0	98	0	2	29	98.1	-24.9	39	13	0	0	0.0	0.0
C- /3.8	14.6	0.90	16.02	98	0	98	0	2	29	105.6	-24.7	49	13	10,000,000	0	0.0	0.0
C- /3.8	14.6	0.90	16.10	61	0	98	0	2	29	105.4	-24.9	50	13	10,000,000	0	0.0	0.0
C- /3.7	14.6	0.90	15.11	416	0	98	0	2	29	103.6	-24.8	46	13	1,000	50	0.0	0.0
D+ /2.6	14.2	0.86	34.25	612	1	96	1	2	30	129.0	-23.7	72	13	1,000	50	5.5	0.0
D /1.6	14.2	0.86	24.40	1	1	96	1	2	30	119.9	-23.9	64	13	1,000	50	0.0	0.0
D /1.6	14.2	0.86	24.34	15	1	96	1	2	30	119.9	-23.9	63	13	1,000	50	0.0	0.0
D+ /2.7	14.2	0.86	35.84	233	1	96	1	2	30	128.9	-23.6	72	13	1,000	50	0.0	0.0

Fund Type	Fund Name	Ticker Symbol	Overall Investment Rating	Phone	Perfor-mance Rating/Pts	3 Mo	6 Mo	1Yr / Pct	3Yr / Pct	5Yr / Pct	Dividend Yield	Expense Ratio
	99 Pct = Best 0 Pct = Worst				**PERFORMANCE** Total Return % through 2/28/17 / Annualized						**Incl. in Returns**	
SC	● Invesco Small Cap Growth R	GTSRX	D+	(800) 959-4246	C+ / 6.9	4.75	8.60	28.25 /82	5.52 /60	12.29 /77	0.00	1.45
SC	● Invesco Small Cap Growth R5	GTSVX	C-	(800) 959-4246	B- / 7.3	4.90	8.90	29.06 /84	6.21 /66	13.00 /84	0.32	0.82
SC	● Invesco Small Cap Growth R6	GTSFX	C-	(800) 959-4246	B- / 7.4	4.95	9.00	29.22 /85	6.31 /67	13.05 /84	0.40	0.73
SC	● Invesco Small Cap Growth Y	GTSYX	C-	(800) 959-4246	B- / 7.2	4.86	8.85	28.91 /84	6.05 /65	12.85 /82	0.21	0.95
SC	● Invesco Small Cap Value A	VSCAX	C+	(800) 959-4246	A- / 9.1	9.34	21.30	40.93 /98	5.79 /62	13.10 /85	0.16	1.12
SC	● Invesco Small Cap Value B	VSMBX	C	(800) 959-4246	A / 9.4	9.17	20.91	39.95 /97	5.00 /54	12.30 /77	0.00	1.87
SC	● Invesco Small Cap Value C	VSMCX	C	(800) 959-4246	A / 9.4	9.17	20.85	39.84 /97	5.00 /54	12.26 /77	0.00	1.87
SC	● Invesco Small Cap Value Y	VSMIX	C+	(800) 959-4246	A+ / 9.7	9.43	21.48	41.29 /98	6.06 /65	13.39 /88	0.40	0.87
GR	Invesco Summit A	ASMMX	C	(800) 959-4246	B- / 7.3	9.63	9.43	24.99 /73	7.92 /78	12.64 /80	0.00	1.04
GR	● Invesco Summit B	BSMMX	C+	(800) 959-4246	B / 7.7	9.39	9.04	23.95 /70	7.09 /73	11.79 /72	0.00	1.79
GR	Invesco Summit C	CSMMX	C+	(800) 959-4246	B / 7.7	9.35	9.07	24.04 /70	7.09 /73	11.79 /72	0.00	1.79
GR	Invesco Summit P	SMMIX	C+	(800) 959-4246	B+ / 8.4	9.59	9.46	25.08 /74	8.05 /79	12.79 /82	0.06	0.89
GR	Invesco Summit R5	SMITX	B-	(800) 959-4246	B+ / 8.5	9.63	9.56	25.27 /74	8.26 /81	13.02 /84	0.21	0.68
GR	Invesco Summit S	SMMSX	C+	(800) 959-4246	B+ / 8.4	9.60	9.54	25.04 /73	8.00 /79	12.74 /81	0.01	0.94
GR	Invesco Summit Y	ASMYX	B-	(800) 959-4246	B+ / 8.5	9.66	9.53	25.21 /74	8.16 /80	12.92 /83	0.15	0.79
TC	Invesco Technology A	ITYAX	C	(800) 959-4246	B- / 7.4	10.41	10.78	28.12 /82	6.85 /71	8.87 /50	0.00	1.39
TC	● Invesco Technology B	ITYBX	C	(800) 959-4246	B / 7.8	10.19	10.40	27.19 /80	6.05 /65	8.06 /43	0.00	2.14
TC	Invesco Technology C	ITHCX	C	(800) 959-4246	B / 7.8	10.21	10.39	27.18 /80	6.05 /65	8.06 /43	0.00	2.14
TC	● Invesco Technology Inv	FTCHX	C+	(800) 959-4246	B+ / 8.4	10.42	10.82	28.22 /82	6.94 /72	8.96 /50	0.00	1.30
TC	Invesco Technology R5	FTPIX	C+	(800) 959-4246	B+ / 8.7	10.54	11.07	28.78 /83	7.41 /75	9.47 /54	0.00	0.87
TC	● Invesco Technology Sector A	IFOAX	C+	(800) 959-4246	B- / 7.4	10.38	10.70	27.81 /81	6.92 /71	8.95 /50	0.00	1.58
TC	● Invesco Technology Sector B	IFOBX	B-	(800) 959-4246	B / 7.7	10.13	10.28	26.87 /79	6.12 /65	8.13 /43	0.00	2.33
TC	● Invesco Technology Sector C	IFOCX	B-	(800) 959-4246	B / 7.7	10.13	10.28	26.87 /79	6.12 /65	8.13 /43	0.00	2.33
TC	● Invesco Technology Sector Y	IFODX	B	(800) 959-4246	B+ / 8.5	10.45	10.82	28.10 /82	7.18 /73	9.21 /52	0.00	1.33
TC	Invesco Technology Y	ITYYX	C+	(800) 959-4246	B+ / 8.5	10.49	10.94	28.47 /83	7.11 /73	9.14 /52	0.00	1.14
GI	Invesco Value Opportunities A	VVOAX	C+	(800) 959-4246	B / 8.1	6.90	18.35	35.79 /95	5.93 /64	10.79 /64	0.14	1.26
GI	● Invesco Value Opportunities B	VVOBX	C+	(800) 959-4246	A- / 9.0	6.94	18.41	35.80 /95	5.95 /64	10.80 /64	0.15	1.26
GI	Invesco Value Opportunities C	VVOCX	C+	(800) 959-4246	B+ / 8.5	6.77	17.98	34.89 /94	5.18 /56	10.02 /58	0.00	1.98
GI	Invesco Value Opportunities R	VVORX	C+	(800) 959-4246	B+ / 8.9	6.85	18.27	35.53 /94	5.69 /61	10.53 /62	0.00	1.51
GI	Invesco Value Opportunities R5	VVONX	B-	(800) 959-4246	A / 9.3	7.02	18.65	36.36 /95	6.40 /67	11.30 /68	0.55	0.85
GI	Invesco Value Opportunities Y	VVOIX	B-	(800) 959-4246	A- / 9.2	7.03	18.52	36.14 /95	6.21 /66	11.09 /67	0.40	1.01
MC	Invesco VI American Value I	UMCVX	C	(800) 959-4246	B / 8.1	7.26	11.59	32.74 /91	5.93 /64	11.57 /71	0.32	1.03
MC	Invesco VI American Value II	UMCCX	C	(800) 959-4246	B / 7.9	7.21	11.43	32.35 /91	5.66 /61	11.29 /68	0.10	1.28
IN	Invesco VI Equity and Income II	UEIIX	B	(800) 959-4246	B / 7.6	4.53	10.54	25.40 /75	7.31 /74	10.75 /64	1.49	0.83
GL	Invesco VI Gobal Core Equity I	UGEPX	C	(800) 959-4246	C / 4.8	7.01	5.78	20.10 /53	3.78 /40	7.21 /36	0.97	1.06
BA	InvestEd Balanced A	WBLAX	D	(888) 923-3355	D+ / 2.4	5.16	4.53	13.57 /24	3.35 /35	6.84 /34	0.77	1.02
GR	InvestEd Conservative A	WICAX	D	(888) 923-3355	D- / 1.5	2.80	2.70	9.03 / 9	2.19 /25	4.86 /20	1.18	0.85
GR	InvestEd Growth A	WAGRX	D	(888) 923-3355	C- / 3.4	6.42	5.62	17.38 /40	4.14 /44	8.70 /48	0.21	1.13
GR	Investment House Growth	TIHGX	B	(888) 309-1371	B+ / 8.4	10.55	10.51	22.52 /65	8.28 /81	14.00 /93	0.00	1.44
IN	IPS Strategic Abs Rtn Inst	IPSAX	U	(877) 244-6235	U /	3.38	-0.84	--	--	--	0.00	N/A
GI	IQ Hedge Multi-Strategy Plus A	IQHOX	D	(888) 934-0777	E / 0.3	2.53	-1.52	2.53 / 2	-0.78 /10	1.13 / 6	0.00	2.11
GI	IQ Hedge Multi-Strategy Plus I	IQHIX	D	(888) 934-0777	E+ / 0.7	2.62	-1.31	3.05 / 3	-0.31 /12	1.56 / 7	0.00	1.59
GI	Iron Horse A	IRHAX	D	(855) 241-7514	D / 1.7	3.40	2.18	8.26 / 8	3.37 /35	5.71 /26	0.05	2.37
GI	Iron Horse I	IRHIX	D	(855) 241-7514	D+ / 2.5	3.50	2.28	8.32 / 8	3.65 /39	5.99 /28	0.21	2.12
GL	IronBridge Global	IBGFX	D-	(888) 825-2100	D / 1.8	6.17	1.10	11.64 /17	1.39 /20	6.61 /32	0.95	1.86
GR	IronBridge Large Cap	IBLCX	B+		B / 7.7	6.73	6.65	20.97 /57	8.74 /85	--	0.71	1.18
SC	IronBridge Small Cap	IBSCX	C-	(888) 825-2100	C+ / 6.3	3.63	6.61	26.04 /76	5.48 /59	10.28 /60	0.20	1.10
MC	IronBridge SMID Cap	IBSMX	D+	(888) 825-2100	C+ / 6.1	5.18	6.20	25.10 /74	5.20 /56	10.17 /60	0.26	0.99
GL	Ironclad Managed Risk	IRONX	C-	(888) 979-4766	D / 1.6	1.60	3.01	6.15 / 5	2.57 /28	5.12 /22	0.00	1.28
AA	Issachar Fund N	LIONX	C+	(800) 773-3863	D / 2.0	3.19	1.75	7.27 / 6	2.71 /29	--	2.26	3.03
FO	● IVA Fiduciary Tr IVA Intl A	IVIOX	D+	(866) 941-4482	D- / 1.5	5.04	2.90	10.04 /12	2.42 /27	5.54 /25	0.18	1.25
FO	● IVA Fiduciary Tr IVA Intl C	IVICX	D+	(866) 941-4482	D / 1.7	4.85	2.55	9.27 /10	1.68 /22	4.76 /20	0.00	2.00

● Denotes fund is closed to new investors
∗ Denotes fund is included in Section II

RISK			NET ASSETS		ASSET				Portfolio Turnover Ratio	BULL / BEAR		FUND MANAGER		MINIMUMS		LOADS	
Risk Rating/Pts	3 Year		NAV As of 2/28/17	Total $(Mil)	Cash %	Stocks %	Bonds %	Other %		Last Bull Market Return	Last Bear Market Return	Manager Quality Pct	Manager Tenure (Years)	Initial Purch. $	Additional Purch. $	Front End Load	Back End Load
	Standard Deviation	Beta															
D+ / 2.4	14.2	0.86	32.02	116	1	96	1	2	30	125.8	-23.7	70	13	0	0	0.0	0.0
D+ / 2.9	14.2	0.86	38.08	1,094	1	96	1	2	30	133.8	-23.5	76	13	10,000,000	0	0.0	0.0
D+ / 2.9	14.2	0.86	38.21	222	1	96	1	2	30	133.9	-23.7	77	13	10,000,000	0	0.0	0.0
D+ / 2.7	14.2	0.86	35.12	177	1	96	1	2	30	132.0	-23.6	75	13	1,000	50	0.0	0.0
D+ / 2.5	18.7	1.06	19.83	1,263	1	92	5	2	45	155.6	-29.0	56	7	1,000	50	5.5	0.0
D / 1.8	18.7	1.06	15.75	9	1	92	5	2	45	146.1	-29.1	45	7	1,000	50	0.0	0.0
D / 1.8	18.7	1.06	15.15	103	1	92	5	2	45	145.5	-29.2	45	7	1,000	50	0.0	0.0
D+ / 2.6	18.7	1.06	20.55	1,418	1	92	5	2	45	159.0	-28.9	60	7	1,000	50	0.0	0.0
C- / 4.0	13.5	1.16	17.13	57	0	99	0	1	47	122.0	-18.4	23	5	1,000	50	5.5	0.0
C- / 3.8	13.4	1.16	15.79	N/A	0	99	0	1	47	113.4	-18.6	16	5	1,000	50	0.0	0.0
C- / 3.8	13.4	1.16	15.74	5	0	99	0	1	47	113.1	-18.7	16	5	1,000	50	0.0	0.0
C- / 4.0	13.4	1.16	17.32	1,832	0	99	0	1	47	123.7	-18.3	24	5	0	0	0.0	0.0
C- / 4.0	13.4	1.16	17.33	N/A	0	99	0	1	47	126.2	-18.3	26	5	10,000,000	0	0.0	0.0
C- / 4.0	13.5	1.16	17.21	3	0	99	0	1	47	123.1	-18.3	23	5	0	0	0.0	0.0
C- / 4.0	13.4	1.16	17.27	5	0	99	0	1	47	125.0	-18.3	25	5	1,000	50	0.0	0.0
C- / 3.4	16.1	1.32	37.76	301	1	96	1	2	46	89.6	-17.4	6	3	1,000	50	5.5	0.0
C- / 3.0	16.1	1.32	32.56	4	1	96	1	2	46	82.1	-17.6	5	3	1,000	50	0.0	0.0
D+ / 2.9	16.1	1.32	31.21	29	1	96	1	2	46	82.1	-17.6	5	3	1,000	50	0.0	0.0
C- / 3.4	16.1	1.32	37.52	368	1	96	1	2	46	90.4	-17.4	7	3	1,000	50	0.0	0.0
C- / 3.7	16.1	1.31	43.76	N/A	1	96	1	2	46	95.5	-17.2	8	3	10,000,000	0	0.0	0.0
C / 5.0	16.0	1.31	18.55	76	0	99	0	1	44	93.3	-18.1	7	3	1,000	50	5.5	0.0
C / 4.9	16.0	1.31	15.81	N/A	0	99	0	1	44	85.8	-18.5	5	3	1,000	50	0.0	0.0
C / 4.9	16.0	1.31	15.81	8	0	99	0	1	44	85.8	-18.5	5	3	1,000	50	0.0	0.0
C / 5.0	16.0	1.31	19.49	2	0	99	0	1	44	96.1	-18.1	8	3	1,000	50	0.0	0.0
C- / 3.4	16.1	1.32	38.15	12	1	96	1	2	46	92.2	-17.3	7	3	1,000	50	0.0	0.0
C- / 3.4	16.7	1.32	13.75	673	1	95	3	1	38	108.2	-20.8	4	2	1,000	50	5.5	0.0
C- / 3.4	16.7	1.32	13.52	11	1	95	3	1	38	108.4	-20.9	4	2	1,000	50	0.0	0.0
C- / 3.4	16.7	1.32	13.22	86	1	95	3	1	38	100.2	-21.0	3	2	1,000	50	0.0	0.0
C- / 3.4	16.8	1.32	13.69	16	1	95	3	1	38	105.6	-20.9	4	2	0	0	0.0	0.0
C- / 3.4	16.7	1.32	13.75	3	1	95	3	1	38	113.8	-20.7	5	2	10,000,000	0	0.0	0.0
C- / 3.4	16.8	1.32	13.71	43	1	95	3	1	38	111.2	-20.8	5	2	1,000	50	0.0	0.0
D+ / 2.8	13.7	1.08	17.87	115	1	96	1	2	26	122.1	-21.5	22	14	0	0	0.0	0.0
D+ / 2.8	13.7	1.08	17.69	292	1	96	1	2	26	119.4	-21.6	20	14	0	0	0.0	0.0
C / 5.5	8.5	0.76	18.22	1,351	1	64	27	8	87	91.3	-15.3	66	14	0	0	0.0	0.0
C+ / 5.9	10.9	0.83	9.31	64	1	97	0	2	75	67.6	-23.8	93	N/A	0	0	0.0	0.0
C+ / 5.7	7.9	1.19	11.24	170	0	67	32	1	15	57.7	-13.7	13	15	750	0	5.8	0.0
C+ / 6.6	5.2	0.49	10.39	114	0	39	59	2	34	32.5	-0.3	36	15	750	0	4.3	0.0
C- / 3.9	10.0	0.90	11.44	140	0	86	13	1	17	75.5	-18.1	15	N/A	750	0	5.8	0.0
C / 5.1	12.8	1.11	26.71	82	0	100	0	0	22	144.3	-15.7	31	16	1,000	100	0.0	0.0
U /	N/A	N/A	10.38	90	0	0	0	100	0	N/A	N/A	N/A	1	5,000	200	0.0	0.0
B- / 7.7	4.6	0.34	9.74	5	0	30	53	17	305	13.7	-7.0	21	N/A	25,000	0	5.5	0.0
B- / 7.6	4.6	0.34	9.81	83	0	30	53	17	305	16.2	-6.7	25	N/A	5,000,000	0	0.0	0.0
C+ / 5.8	5.3	0.42	10.33	4	4	95	0	1	279	50.8	N/A	62	6	5,000	500	5.8	0.0
C+ / 5.9	5.2	0.41	10.34	9	4	95	0	1	279	N/A	N/A	66	6	100,000	500	0.0	0.0
C / 5.0	10.1	0.75	8.41	9	4	95	0	1	42	61.1	-19.7	84	8	100,000	1,000	0.0	2.0
C+ / 6.1	9.8	0.94	13.69	32	1	98	0	1	24	N/A	N/A	61	5	100,000	1,000	0.0	0.0
C- / 3.0	13.2	0.81	19.28	449	2	94	3	1	31	104.8	-23.2	73	15	100,000	1,000	0.0	0.0
C- / 3.0	12.0	0.96	11.96	332	1	95	2	2	31	99.2	-23.0	26	13	100,000	1,000	0.0	0.0
B / 8.5	5.0	0.24	10.99	164	70	0	29	1	0	38.8	-3.7	88	7	2,500	500	0.0	2.0
B+ / 9.9	3.7	0.06	10.37	17	0	0	0	100	1,135	N/A	N/A	87	3	1,000	100	0.0	0.0
B- / 7.4	6.2	0.46	16.43	269	8	51	40	1	35	41.4	-9.7	88	9	5,000	100	5.0	2.0
B- / 7.5	6.2	0.46	16.16	61	8	51	40	1	35	35.8	-10.0	85	9	5,000	100	0.0	2.0

			99 Pct = Best 0 Pct = Worst		PERFORMANCE							
			Overall Investment		Perfor- mance		Total Return % through 2/28/17				Incl. in Returns	
		Ticker							Annualized		Dividend	Expense
Fund Type	Fund Name	Symbol	Rating	Phone	Rating/Pts	3 Mo	6 Mo	1Yr / Pct	3Yr / Pct	5Yr / Pct	Yield	Ratio
FO	● IVA Fiduciary Tr IVA Intl I	IVIQX	C-	(866) 941-4482	D / 2.2	5.09	3.08	10.37 / 13	2.70 / 29	5.80 / 27	0.43	1.00
FO	● IVA Fiduciary Tr IVA Worldwide A	IVWAX	C-	(866) 941-4482	D / 1.8	4.63	4.20	12.56 / 20	2.81 / 30	5.34 / 24	0.00	1.25
FO	● IVA Fiduciary Tr IVA Worldwide C	IVWCX	C-	(866) 941-4482	D / 2.1	4.39	3.78	11.70 / 17	2.03 / 24	4.55 / 18	0.00	2.00
FO	● IVA Fiduciary Tr IVA Worldwide I	IVWIX	C	(866) 941-4482	D+ / 2.7	4.68	4.31	12.87 / 21	3.08 / 33	5.61 / 26	0.00	1.00
GL	Ivy Apollo Multi-Asset Income A	IMAAX	U	(800) 777-6472	U /	4.22	2.62	11.39 / 16	--	--	2.71	1.84
GL	Ivy Apollo Multi-Asset Income I	IMAIX	U	(800) 777-6472	U /	4.21	2.78	11.74 / 17	--	--	3.18	1.48
GL	Ivy Asset Strategy A	WASAX	E	(800) 777-6472	E- / 0.1	4.52	1.41	3.61 / 3	-5.69 / 2	2.09 / 8	0.00	0.99
GL	● Ivy Asset Strategy B	WASBX	E	(800) 777-6472	E- / 0.1	4.38	1.05	2.84 / 3	-6.37 / 2	1.33 / 7	0.00	1.76
GL	Ivy Asset Strategy C	WASCX	E	(800) 777-6472	E- / 0.1	4.35	1.09	2.87 / 3	-6.36 / 2	1.35 / 7	0.00	1.71
GL	Ivy Asset Strategy E	IASEX	E	(800) 777-6472	E- / 0.1	4.65	1.50	3.74 / 3	-5.66 / 2	2.08 / 8	0.00	1.14
GL	Ivy Asset Strategy I	IVAEX	E	(800) 777-6472	E- / 0.2	4.65	1.58	3.90 / 3	-5.44 / 2	2.33 / 9	0.00	0.74
GL	Ivy Asset Strategy N	IASTX	D-	(800) 777-6472	E- / 0.2	4.69	1.67	4.04 / 3	-5.33 / 2	2.40 / 9	0.00	0.60
GL	Ivy Asset Strategy R	IASRX	E	(800) 777-6472	E- / 0.1	4.47	1.29	3.30 / 3	-6.01 / 2	1.73 / 7	0.00	1.34
GL	Ivy Asset Strategy Y	WASYX	E	(800) 777-6472	E- / 0.2	4.55	1.46	3.65 / 3	-5.67 / 2	2.09 / 8	0.00	1.00
BA	Ivy Balanced A	IBNAX	C-	(800) 777-6472	D+ / 2.5	4.75	3.68	12.41 / 19	4.11 / 44	7.95 / 42	1.01	1.10
BA	● Ivy Balanced B	IBNBX	C-	(800) 777-6472	D+ / 2.9	4.57	3.29	11.59 / 16	3.35 / 35	7.14 / 35	0.60	1.83
BA	Ivy Balanced C	IBNCX	C-	(800) 777-6472	C- / 3.0	4.61	3.34	11.68 / 17	3.40 / 36	7.21 / 36	0.63	1.79
BA	● Ivy Balanced E	IVYEX	C-	(800) 777-6472	D+ / 2.6	4.81	3.79	12.61 / 20	4.29 / 46	8.21 / 44	1.10	1.16
BA	Ivy Balanced I	IYBIX	C	(800) 777-6472	C- / 3.7	4.81	3.82	12.71 / 21	4.39 / 47	8.23 / 44	1.24	0.84
BA	Ivy Balanced N	IBARX	C	(800) 777-6472	C- / 3.7	4.85	3.89	12.85 / 21	4.45 / 48	8.05 / 43	1.34	0.69
BA	Ivy Balanced R	IYBFX	C-	(800) 777-6472	C- / 3.2	4.71	3.51	12.03 / 18	3.77 / 40	--	0.85	1.44
BA	Ivy Balanced Y	IBNYX	C-	(800) 777-6472	C- / 3.5	4.80	3.69	12.42 / 19	4.13 / 44	7.97 / 42	1.08	1.09
GR	Ivy Core Equity A	WCEAX	D+	(800) 777-6472	C- / 3.5	5.13	5.61	17.52 / 41	4.66 / 50	10.85 / 65	0.33	1.18
GR	● Ivy Core Equity B	WCEBX	D+	(800) 777-6472	C- / 3.9	4.94	5.13	16.34 / 36	3.67 / 39	9.79 / 57	0.00	2.09
GR	Ivy Core Equity C	WTRCX	D+	(800) 777-6472	C- / 4.1	5.00	5.27	16.67 / 37	3.89 / 42	10.01 / 58	0.00	1.91
GR	Ivy Core Equity E	ICFEX	D+	(800) 777-6472	C- / 3.5	5.18	5.65	17.53 / 41	4.56 / 49	10.72 / 64	0.28	1.43
GR	Ivy Core Equity I	ICIEX	C-	(800) 777-6472	C / 5.0	5.28	5.86	17.96 / 43	5.02 / 54	11.23 / 68	0.59	0.90
GR	Ivy Core Equity N	ICEQX	C	(800) 777-6472	C / 5.1	5.23	5.81	17.96 / 43	5.08 / 55	11.27 / 68	0.68	0.75
GR	Ivy Core Equity R	IYCEX	C-	(800) 777-6472	C / 4.4	5.11	5.43	17.11 / 39	4.32 / 47	--	0.09	1.50
GR	Ivy Core Equity Y	WCEYX	C-	(800) 777-6472	C / 5.0	5.21	5.80	17.88 / 42	4.98 / 54	11.16 / 67	0.61	1.15
GL	Ivy Cundill Global Value A	ICDAX	D-	(800) 777-6472	D / 1.7	8.52	14.53	30.13 / 87	-0.85 / 10	5.71 / 26	0.32	1.75
GL	● Ivy Cundill Global Value B	ICDBX	D-	(800) 777-6472	D / 1.8	8.19	13.81	28.44 / 83	-2.03 / 7	4.50 / 18	0.00	2.92
GL	Ivy Cundill Global Value C	ICDCX	D-	(800) 777-6472	D / 2.1	8.41	14.26	29.40 / 85	-1.43 / 8	5.12 / 22	0.00	2.35
GL	Ivy Cundill Global Value E	ICVEX	D-	(800) 777-6472	D / 1.8	8.60	14.71	30.50 / 87	-0.73 / 10	5.88 / 28	0.55	2.13
GL	Ivy Cundill Global Value I	ICVIX	D	(800) 777-6472	D+ / 2.7	8.62	14.77	30.67 / 88	-0.39 / 12	6.24 / 30	0.77	1.29
GL	Ivy Cundill Global Value N	ICNGX	D+	(800) 777-6472	D+ / 2.8	8.68	14.89	30.95 / 88	-0.27 / 12	6.32 / 30	0.90	1.13
GL	Ivy Cundill Global Value R	IYCUX	D-	(800) 777-6472	D+ / 2.4	8.52	14.46	29.98 / 86	-0.97 / 9	--	0.27	1.88
GL	Ivy Cundill Global Value Y	ICDYX	D	(800) 777-6472	D+ / 2.6	8.58	14.71	30.48 / 87	-0.63 / 11	6.00 / 28	0.56	1.55
GI	Ivy Dividend Opportunities A	IVDAX	C-	(800) 777-6472	C / 4.7	6.86	6.92	19.12 / 48	5.62 / 61	9.80 / 57	1.03	1.25
GI	● Ivy Dividend Opportunities B	IVDBX	C-	(800) 777-6472	C / 5.2	6.65	6.51	18.19 / 44	4.81 / 52	8.94 / 50	0.41	2.03
GI	Ivy Dividend Opportunities C	IVDCX	C-	(800) 777-6472	C / 5.3	6.65	6.60	18.34 / 44	4.93 / 53	9.07 / 51	0.49	1.93
GI	Ivy Dividend Opportunities E	IDIEX	C-	(800) 777-6472	C / 4.7	6.90	7.02	19.18 / 48	5.59 / 60	9.74 / 56	1.08	1.56
GI	Ivy Dividend Opportunities I	IVDIX	C	(800) 777-6472	C+ / 6.2	6.96	7.13	19.53 / 50	5.95 / 64	10.17 / 60	1.36	0.94
IN	Ivy Dividend Opportunities N	IDOTX	C+	(800) 777-6472	C+ / 6.3	7.00	7.21	19.68 / 50	6.09 / 65	10.25 / 60	1.50	0.79
IN	Ivy Dividend Opportunities R	IYDVX	C-	(800) 777-6472	C+ / 5.7	6.79	6.85	18.89 / 47	5.35 / 58	--	0.83	1.53
GI	Ivy Dividend Opportunities Y	IVDYX	C	(800) 777-6472	C+ / 6.0	6.91	7.01	19.22 / 48	5.70 / 62	9.89 / 57	1.15	1.19
FO	Ivy Emerging Markets Equity A	IPOAX	C-	(800) 777-6472	C+ / 5.9	10.93	6.96	35.87 / 95	2.96 / 31	3.06 / 11	0.00	1.67
FO	● Ivy Emerging Markets Equity B	IPOBX	C-	(800) 777-6472	C+ / 6.2	10.75	6.42	34.65 / 94	1.92 / 23	1.94 / 8	0.00	2.72
FO	Ivy Emerging Markets Equity C	IPOCX	C	(800) 777-6472	C+ / 6.3	10.83	6.52	34.79 / 94	2.10 / 25	2.23 / 9	0.00	2.35
FO	● Ivy Emerging Markets Equity E	IPOEX	C-	(800) 777-6472	C+ / 6.0	11.05	7.06	36.16 / 95	3.12 / 33	3.33 / 12	0.00	1.42
FO	Ivy Emerging Markets Equity I	IPOIX	C	(800) 777-6472	B- / 7.1	11.08	7.08	36.28 / 95	3.26 / 34	3.46 / 13	0.00	1.22
EM	Ivy Emerging Markets Equity N	IMEGX	C	(800) 777-6472	B- / 7.2	11.16	7.17	36.57 / 95	3.40 / 36	3.54 / 13	0.00	1.09

● Denotes fund is closed to new investors
* Denotes fund is included in Section II

334

RISK Rating/Pts	3 Year Standard Deviation	Beta	NAV As of 2/28/17	Total $(Mil)	Cash %	Stocks %	Bonds %	Other %	Portfolio Turnover Ratio	Last Bull Market Return	Last Bear Market Return	Manager Quality Pct	Manager Tenure (Years)	Initial Purch. $	Additional Purch. $	Front End Load	Back End Load
B- /7.3	6.2	0.46	16.45	3,484	8	51	40	1	35	43.3	-9.6	89	9	1,000,000	100	0.0	2.0
B- /7.8	5.3	0.39	17.77	1,536	9	50	39	2	30	43.8	-11.7	89	9	5,000	100	5.0	2.0
B- /7.9	5.3	0.39	17.50	957	9	50	39	2	30	38.1	-12.1	86	9	5,000	100	0.0	2.0
B- /7.8	5.3	0.39	17.82	5,607	9	50	39	2	30	45.8	-11.7	90	9	1,000,000	100	0.0	2.0
U /	N/A	N/A	10.57	135	0	0	0	100	63	N/A	N/A	N/A	2	750	0	5.8	0.0
U /	N/A	N/A	10.57	363	0	0	0	100	63	N/A	N/A	N/A	2	0	0	0.0	0.0
C- /3.7	9.1	1.24	21.52	1,442	7	61	31	1	68	35.3	-22.1	1	3	750	0	5.8	0.0
C- /3.5	9.1	1.24	20.26	152	7	61	31	1	68	30.0	-22.4	1	3	750	0	0.0	0.0
C- /3.5	9.1	1.24	20.40	1,795	7	61	31	1	68	30.2	-22.3	1	3	750	0	0.0	0.0
C- /3.7	9.1	1.24	21.61	38	7	61	31	1	68	35.3	-22.1	1	3	750	0	5.8	0.0
C- /3.7	9.1	1.24	21.82	1,031	7	61	31	1	68	37.2	-22.0	1	3	0	0	0.0	0.0
C+ /6.7	9.2	1.24	21.89	15	7	61	31	1	68	37.7	-22.0	1	3	0	0	0.0	0.0
C- /3.7	9.1	1.24	21.26	67	7	61	31	1	68	32.8	-22.2	1	3	0	0	0.0	0.0
C- /3.7	9.1	1.24	21.58	249	7	61	31	1	68	35.4	-22.1	1	3	0	0	0.0	0.0
B- /7.0	8.0	1.21	24.36	727	0	58	39	3	56	69.0	-11.7	17	3	750	0	5.8	0.0
B- /7.0	8.0	1.21	24.09	80	0	58	39	3	56	62.3	-12.0	12	3	750	0	0.0	0.0
B- /7.0	8.0	1.22	24.18	748	0	58	39	3	56	62.8	-12.0	12	3	750	0	0.0	0.0
B- /7.0	8.0	1.21	24.49	N/A	0	58	39	3	56	71.1	-11.7	19	3	0	0	5.8	0.0
C+ /6.9	8.0	1.22	24.37	675	0	58	39	3	56	71.4	-11.6	19	3	0	0	0.0	0.0
B- /7.4	8.0	1.21	24.41	9	0	58	39	3	56	69.6	-11.8	20	3	0	0	0.0	0.0
B- /7.0	8.0	1.21	24.32	14	0	58	39	3	56	N/A	N/A	15	3	0	0	0.0	0.0
B- /7.0	8.0	1.21	24.37	81	0	58	39	3	56	69.1	-11.7	17	3	0	0	0.0	0.0
C /4.9	11.6	1.07	13.56	282	0	96	2	2	62	104.4	-17.3	8	11	750	0	5.8	0.0
C /4.7	11.6	1.07	11.44	8	0	96	2	2	62	93.8	-17.6	5	11	750	0	0.0	0.0
C /4.8	11.6	1.07	11.83	118	0	96	2	2	62	95.9	-17.4	6	11	750	0	0.0	0.0
C /5.0	11.6	1.07	13.51	12	0	96	2	2	62	103.1	-17.3	8	11	750	0	5.8	0.0
C /5.1	11.6	1.07	15.03	383	0	96	2	2	62	108.0	-17.1	10	11	0	0	0.0	0.0
C+ /6.1	11.6	1.07	15.04	113	0	96	2	2	62	108.4	-17.1	10	11	0	0	0.0	0.0
C /5.0	11.6	1.07	13.49	3	0	96	2	2	62	N/A	N/A	7	11	0	0	0.0	0.0
C /5.0	11.6	1.07	14.62	66	0	96	2	2	62	107.2	-17.1	9	11	0	0	0.0	0.0
C /4.9	13.6	0.95	17.13	98	0	95	2	3	18	57.7	-23.5	66	1	750	0	5.8	0.0
C /4.8	13.6	0.95	15.58	1	0	95	2	3	18	48.2	-23.8	50	1	750	0	0.0	0.0
C /4.9	13.7	0.95	16.11	14	0	95	2	3	18	52.9	-23.7	59	1	750	0	0.0	0.0
C /4.9	13.7	0.95	17.24	1	0	95	2	3	18	59.1	-23.5	68	1	750	0	5.8	0.0
C /4.9	13.6	0.94	17.50	95	0	95	2	3	18	62.1	-23.4	72	1	0	0	0.0	0.0
C+ /6.3	13.6	0.95	17.54	1	0	95	2	3	18	62.7	-23.4	73	1	0	0	0.0	0.0
C /4.9	13.7	0.95	17.11	N/A	0	95	2	3	18	N/A	N/A	65	1	0	0	0.0	0.0
C /4.9	13.6	0.95	17.37	2	0	95	2	3	18	60.3	-23.4	69	1	0	0	0.0	0.0
C /4.8	10.6	1.00	18.28	143	2	87	9	2	45	98.1	-23.5	18	3	750	0	5.8	0.0
C /4.8	10.7	1.00	17.93	8	2	87	9	2	45	89.7	-23.8	12	3	750	0	0.0	0.0
C /4.8	10.7	1.00	18.03	42	2	87	9	2	45	91.0	-23.7	13	3	750	0	0.0	0.0
C /4.8	10.7	1.00	18.22	5	2	87	9	2	45	97.5	-23.5	17	3	750	0	5.8	0.0
C /4.7	10.7	1.00	18.36	172	2	87	9	2	45	101.5	-23.3	20	3	0	0	0.0	0.0
C+ /6.6	10.6	1.00	18.39	2	2	87	9	2	45	102.3	-23.3	22	3	0	0	0.0	0.0
C /4.8	10.7	1.01	18.26	1	2	87	9	2	45	N/A	N/A	15	3	0	0	0.0	0.0
C /4.8	10.7	1.00	18.32	6	2	87	9	2	45	98.9	-23.4	18	3	0	0	0.0	0.0
C /4.3	17.3	0.99	16.44	275	0	98	1	1	98	42.4	-30.0	91	3	750	0	5.8	0.0
C- /4.2	17.3	0.99	13.60	4	0	98	1	1	98	34.1	-30.3	87	3	750	0	0.0	0.0
C- /4.2	17.3	0.99	14.22	33	0	98	1	1	98	36.3	-30.2	87	3	750	0	0.0	0.0
C /4.3	17.3	0.99	16.68	N/A	0	98	1	1	98	44.5	-29.9	91	3	0	0	5.8	0.0
C /4.3	17.4	0.99	16.94	344	0	98	1	1	98	45.4	-29.8	92	3	0	0	0.0	0.0
C- /3.7	17.3	0.99	17.03	10	0	98	1	1	98	46.0	-29.8	85	3	0	0	0.0	0.0

					PERFORMANCE						Incl. in Returns	
	99 Pct = Best 0 Pct = Worst		Overall Investment Rating		Perfor- mance Rating/Pts	Total Return % through 2/28/17			Annualized		Dividend Yield	Expense Ratio
Fund Type	Fund Name	Ticker Symbol		Phone		3 Mo	6 Mo	1Yr / Pct	3Yr / Pct	5Yr / Pct		
FO	Ivy Emerging Markets Equity R	IYPCX	C	(800) 777-6472	C+ / 6.7	10.94	6.80	35.52 /94	2.62 /28	—	0.00	1.85
FO	Ivy Emerging Markets Equity Y	IPOYX	C	(800) 777-6472	C+ / 6.9	11.00	6.96	35.85 /95	2.97 /32	3.17 /11	0.00	1.47
EN	Ivy Energy A	IEYAX	E-	(800) 777-6472	E / 0.5	-6.38	8.00	42.98 /98	-5.04 / 2	0.46 / 5	0.00	1.49
EN	● Ivy Energy B	IEYBX	E-	(800) 777-6472	E+ / 0.7	-6.52	7.59	41.70 /98	-5.85 / 2	-0.38 / 4	0.00	2.36
EN	Ivy Energy C	IEYCX	E-	(800) 777-6472	E+ / 0.7	-6.48	7.71	42.01 /98	-5.64 / 2	-0.17 / 4	0.00	2.16
EN	● Ivy Energy E	IVEEX	E-	(800) 777-6472	E+ / 0.6	-6.30	8.20	43.38 /98	-4.77 / 3	0.76 / 6	0.00	1.66
EN	Ivy Energy I	IVEIX	E-	(800) 777-6472	D- / 1.0	-6.30	8.19	43.41 /98	-4.69 / 3	0.86 / 6	0.00	1.10
EN	Ivy Energy N	IENRX	E-	(800) 777-6472	D- / 1.1	-6.27	8.31	43.58 /98	-4.55 / 3	0.94 / 6	0.00	0.95
EN	Ivy Energy R	IYEFX	E-	(800) 777-6472	E+ / 0.8	-6.43	7.89	42.57 /98	-5.24 / 2	—	0.00	1.70
EN	Ivy Energy Y	IEYYX	E-	(800) 777-6472	E+ / 0.9	-6.36	8.05	43.02 /98	-4.92 / 2	0.60 / 5	0.00	1.36
FO	Ivy European Opptys A	IEOAX	D-	(800) 777-6472	E / 0.4	5.34	4.20	10.89 /14	-2.38 / 6	4.66 /19	1.24	1.64
FO	● Ivy European Opptys B	IEOBX	D-	(800) 777-6472	E / 0.4	5.07	3.70	9.73 /11	-3.46 / 4	3.49 /13	0.69	2.73
FO	Ivy European Opptys C	IEOCX	D-	(800) 777-6472	E / 0.5	5.18	3.92	10.22 /12	-3.00 / 4	4.00 /15	0.98	2.29
FO	● Ivy European Opptys E	IVEOX	D-	(800) 777-6472	E / 0.4	5.48	4.46	11.33 /16	-2.01 / 7	5.09 /22	1.53	1.32
FO	Ivy European Opptys I	IEOIX	D-	(800) 777-6472	E+ / 0.8	5.48	4.50	11.49 /16	-1.90 / 7	5.22 /23	1.73	1.18
FO	Ivy European Opptys N	IEURX	D	(800) 777-6472	E+ / 0.8	5.51	4.58	11.63 /16	-1.79 / 7	5.29 /23	1.86	1.04
FO	Ivy European Opptys R	IYEUX	D-	(800) 777-6472	E+ / 0.6	5.32	4.21	10.82 /14	-2.49 / 5	—	1.26	1.79
FO	Ivy EuropeanOpptys Y	IEOYX	D-	(800) 777-6472	E+ / 0.7	5.42	4.32	11.14 /15	-2.18 / 6	4.93 /21	1.42	1.47
GL	Ivy Global Equity Income A	IBIAX	D	(800) 777-6472	D / 1.8	5.52	3.08	11.24 /15	2.49 /27	—	3.12	1.46
GL	● Ivy Global Equity Income B	IBIBX	D+	(800) 777-6472	D / 2.2	5.36	2.74	10.53 /13	1.82 /23	—	2.68	2.04
GL	Ivy Global Equity Income C	IBICX	D+	(800) 777-6472	D / 2.2	5.36	2.75	10.44 /13	1.83 /23	—	2.69	2.03
GL	Ivy Global Equity Income I	IBIIX	D+	(800) 777-6472	D+ / 2.8	5.62	3.28	11.64 /17	2.83 /30	—	3.66	1.05
GL	Ivy Global Equity Income N	IICNX	C	(800) 777-6472	D+ / 2.9	5.65	3.35	11.78 /17	2.94 /31	—	3.78	0.91
GL	Ivy Global Equity Income R	IYGEX	D+	(800) 777-6472	D+ / 2.4	5.46	2.95	10.95 /14	2.21 /25	—	3.06	1.66
GL	Ivy Global Equity Income Y	IBIYX	D+	(800) 777-6472	D+ / 2.6	5.55	3.14	11.36 /16	2.59 /28	—	3.41	1.32
FO	Ivy Global Growth A	IVINX	D	(800) 777-6472	D / 1.9	8.12	5.38	13.75 /24	1.42 /21	6.02 /28	0.00	1.47
FO	● Ivy Global Growth B	IVIBX	D	(800) 777-6472	D / 2.1	7.81	4.77	12.45 /20	0.35 /15	4.93 /21	0.00	2.52
FO	Ivy Global Growth C	IVNCX	D	(800) 777-6472	D+ / 2.3	7.92	5.02	12.92 /21	0.68 /17	5.18 /23	0.00	2.22
FO	● Ivy Global Growth E	IIGEX	D	(800) 777-6472	D / 2.1	8.18	5.53	14.05 /26	1.69 /22	6.29 /30	0.00	1.34
FO	Ivy Global Growth I	IGIIX	D+	(800) 777-6472	C- / 3.1	8.21	5.56	14.17 /26	1.79 /23	6.41 /31	0.00	1.09
FO	Ivy Global Growth N	ITGRX	C-	(800) 777-6472	C- / 3.2	8.28	5.67	14.38 /27	1.93 /24	6.50 /31	0.00	0.94
FO	Ivy Global Growth R	IYIGX	D+	(800) 777-6472	D+ / 2.6	8.06	5.28	13.50 /23	1.19 /19	—	0.00	1.68
FO	Ivy Global Growth Y	IVIYX	D+	(800) 777-6472	D+ / 2.9	8.16	5.46	13.90 /25	1.54 /21	6.13 /29	0.00	1.36
GL	Ivy Global Income Allocation A	IVBAX	D+	(800) 777-6472	D+ / 2.3	6.67	4.37	16.07 /35	2.39 /27	4.47 /18	3.53	1.44
GL	● Ivy Global Income Allocation B	IVBBX	D+	(800) 777-6472	D+ / 2.6	6.41	3.85	14.98 /30	1.47 /21	3.52 /13	2.99	2.33
GL	Ivy Global Income Allocation C	IVBCX	D+	(800) 777-6472	D+ / 2.8	6.46	4.04	15.25 /31	1.75 /22	3.80 /14	3.21	2.06
GL	Ivy Global Income Allocation E	IIBEX	D+	(800) 777-6472	D+ / 2.3	6.65	4.35	15.92 /34	2.34 /26	4.44 /18	3.48	1.76
GL	Ivy Global Income Allocation I	IIBIX	C-	(800) 777-6472	C- / 3.5	6.69	4.52	16.41 /36	2.76 /30	4.87 /20	4.04	1.08
GL	Ivy Global Income Allocation N	ILIAX	C	(800) 777-6472	C- / 3.7	6.81	4.67	16.65 /37	2.90 /31	4.96 /21	4.18	0.94
GL	Ivy Global Income Allocation R	IYGBX	C-	(800) 777-6472	C- / 3.1	6.60	4.24	15.79 /33	2.15 /25	—	3.51	1.68
GL	Ivy Global Income Allocation Y	IVBYX	C-	(800) 777-6472	C- / 3.3	6.66	4.41	16.20 /35	2.52 /28	4.62 /19	3.83	1.34
EN	Ivy Global Nat Resource A	IGNAX	E-	(800) 777-6472	E- / 0.2	-0.47	8.59	31.58 /89	-6.95 / 1	-4.80 / 2	0.06	1.66
EN	● Ivy Global Nat Resource B	IGNBX	E-	(800) 777-6472	E / 0.3	-0.78	8.04	30.17 /87	-7.87 / 1	-5.68 / 1	0.00	2.65
EN	Ivy Global Nat Resource C	IGNCX	E-	(800) 777-6472	E / 0.3	-0.63	8.25	30.74 /88	-7.54 / 1	-5.40 / 2	0.00	2.30
EN	Ivy Global Nat Resource E	IGNEX	E-	(800) 777-6472	E / 0.3	-0.35	8.85	32.24 /90	-6.59 / 2	-4.48 / 2	0.41	2.21
EN	Ivy Global Nat Resource I	IGNIX	E-	(800) 777-6472	E / 0.4	-0.32	8.95	32.35 /91	-6.48 / 2	-4.34 / 2	0.53	1.16
EN	Ivy Global Nat Resource N	INRSX	E-	(800) 777-6472	E / 0.5	-0.29	8.93	32.55 /91	-6.36 / 2	-4.26 / 2	0.68	1.00
EN	Ivy Global Nat Resource R	IGNRX	E-	(800) 777-6472	E / 0.4	-0.54	8.56	31.56 /89	-7.05 / 1	-4.90 / 2	0.00	1.75
EN	Ivy Global Nat Resource Y	IGNYX	E-	(800) 777-6472	E / 0.4	-0.35	8.79	31.98 /90	-6.72 / 2	-4.56 / 2	0.30	1.40
FO	Ivy International Core Eq A	IVIAX	D-	(800) 777-6472	D+ / 2.5	8.54	5.70	18.06 /43	1.59 /21	6.14 /29	1.43	1.31
FO	● Ivy International Core Eq B	IIFBX	D	(800) 777-6472	D+ / 2.7	8.25	5.13	16.87 /38	0.67 /16	5.19 /23	0.83	2.20
FO	Ivy International Core Eq C	IVIFX	D	(800) 777-6472	D+ / 2.9	8.34	5.30	17.19 /39	0.90 /18	5.42 /24	1.06	1.98

● Denotes fund is closed to new investors
* Denotes fund is included in Section II

RISK			NET ASSETS		ASSET					BULL / BEAR		FUND MANAGER		MINIMUMS		LOADS	
	3 Year		NAV						Portfolio	Last Bull	Last Bear	Manager	Manager	Initial	Additional	Front	Back
Risk	Standard		As of	Total	Cash	Stocks	Bonds	Other	Turnover	Market	Market	Quality	Tenure	Purch.	Purch.	End	End
Rating/Pts	Deviation	Beta	2/28/17	$(Mil)	%	%	%	%	Ratio	Return	Return	Pct	(Years)	$	$	Load	Load
C / 4.3	17.3	0.99	16.33	10	0	98	1	1	98	N/A	N/A	89	3	0	0	0.0	0.0
C / 4.3	17.3	0.99	16.75	18	0	98	1	1	98	43.3	-29.9	91	3	0	0	0.0	0.0
D- / 1.2	23.7	1.16	13.64	206	4	94	1	1	31	33.1	-31.7	81	11	750	0	5.8	0.0
D- / 1.2	23.7	1.16	12.47	4	4	94	1	1	31	27.1	-31.9	75	11	750	0	0.0	0.0
D- / 1.2	23.7	1.16	12.71	96	4	94	1	1	31	28.5	-31.8	77	11	750	0	0.0	0.0
D- / 1.2	23.8	1.16	13.98	N/A	4	94	1	1	31	35.1	-31.6	83	11	0	0	5.8	0.0
D- / 1.2	23.7	1.16	14.14	196	4	94	1	1	31	35.8	-31.5	83	11	0	0	0.0	0.0
E / 0.4	23.7	1.16	14.20	12	4	94	1	1	31	36.4	-31.5	84	11	0	0	0.0	0.0
D- / 1.2	23.7	1.16	13.53	30	4	94	1	1	31	N/A	N/A	80	11	0	0	0.0	0.0
D- / 1.2	23.7	1.16	13.83	68	4	94	1	1	31	34.0	-31.6	82	11	0	0	0.0	0.0
C+ / 5.9	11.3	0.84	27.44	77	0	99	0	1	91	49.6	-26.7	45	4	750	0	5.8	0.0
C+ / 5.9	11.3	0.85	25.29	1	0	99	0	1	91	40.8	-27.0	30	4	750	0	0.0	0.0
C+ / 5.9	11.3	0.85	25.93	8	0	99	0	1	91	44.5	-26.9	36	4	750	0	0.0	0.0
C+ / 5.9	11.3	0.84	27.64	N/A	0	99	0	1	91	53.0	-26.6	50	4	0	0	5.8	0.0
C+ / 5.9	11.3	0.85	27.68	91	0	99	0	1	91	54.0	-26.5	52	4	0	0	0.0	0.0
C+ / 6.8	11.3	0.85	27.80	1	0	99	0	1	91	54.6	-26.5	53	4	0	0	0.0	0.0
C+ / 5.9	11.3	0.85	27.42	1	0	99	0	1	91	N/A	N/A	43	4	0	0	0.0	0.0
C+ / 5.9	11.3	0.84	27.65	1	0	99	0	1	91	51.8	-26.6	47	4	0	0	0.0	0.0
C+ / 6.5	8.5	0.62	12.34	72	1	98	0	1	73	N/A	N/A	88	5	750	0	5.8	0.0
C+ / 6.5	8.5	0.62	12.32	2	1	98	0	1	73	N/A	N/A	86	5	750	0	0.0	0.0
C+ / 6.5	8.4	0.62	12.32	12	1	98	0	1	73	N/A	N/A	86	5	750	0	0.0	0.0
C+ / 6.4	8.5	0.62	12.35	249	1	98	0	1	73	N/A	N/A	90	5	0	0	0.0	0.0
B- / 7.6	8.5	0.62	12.36	1	1	98	0	1	73	N/A	N/A	90	5	0	0	0.0	0.0
C+ / 6.5	8.5	0.62	12.34	N/A	1	98	0	1	73	N/A	N/A	87	5	0	0	0.0	0.0
C+ / 6.4	8.5	0.62	12.34	4	1	98	0	1	73	N/A	N/A	89	5	0	0	0.0	0.0
C+ / 5.9	11.1	0.83	41.94	114	0	99	0	1	51	60.7	-22.0	84	3	750	0	5.8	0.0
C+ / 5.7	11.1	0.83	36.04	2	0	99	0	1	51	52.0	-22.3	77	3	750	0	0.0	0.0
C+ / 5.8	11.1	0.83	36.37	24	0	99	0	1	51	53.9	-22.3	80	3	750	0	0.0	0.0
C+ / 5.9	11.1	0.83	42.20	N/A	0	99	0	1	51	63.0	-21.9	85	3	0	0	5.8	0.0
C+ / 5.9	11.1	0.83	42.69	274	0	99	0	1	51	64.0	-21.9	86	3	0	0	0.0	0.0
C+ / 6.5	11.1	0.83	42.88	7	0	99	0	1	51	64.7	-21.9	86	3	0	0	0.0	0.0
C+ / 5.8	11.1	0.83	41.69	2	0	99	0	1	51	N/A	N/A	83	3	0	0	0.0	0.0
C+ / 5.9	11.1	0.83	42.13	14	0	99	0	1	51	61.7	-21.9	85	3	0	0	0.0	0.0
C+ / 6.4	8.3	1.22	14.81	213	0	57	42	1	53	40.0	-14.1	32	5	750	0	5.8	0.0
C+ / 6.4	8.3	1.22	14.51	4	0	57	42	1	53	33.2	-14.5	23	5	750	0	0.0	0.0
C+ / 6.4	8.3	1.22	14.61	48	0	57	42	1	53	35.2	-14.4	26	5	750	0	0.0	0.0
C+ / 6.4	8.3	1.22	14.81	3	0	57	42	1	53	40.0	-14.1	32	5	750	0	5.8	0.0
C+ / 6.4	8.3	1.23	14.94	443	0	57	42	1	53	43.0	-14.0	36	5	0	0	0.0	0.0
B- / 7.2	8.3	1.23	14.96	2	0	57	42	1	53	43.6	-14.0	38	5	0	0	0.0	0.0
C+ / 6.4	8.3	1.22	14.80	1	0	57	42	1	53	N/A	N/A	29	5	0	0	0.0	0.0
C+ / 6.4	8.3	1.22	14.88	3	0	57	42	1	53	41.2	-14.1	34	5	0	0	0.0	0.0
D / 2.2	19.9	0.98	15.03	359	11	85	2	2	17	1.6	-40.1	48	4	750	0	5.8	0.0
D / 2.2	19.9	0.98	12.77	8	11	85	2	2	17	-3.3	-40.3	35	4	750	0	0.0	0.0
D / 2.2	19.9	0.98	12.59	110	11	85	2	2	17	-1.8	-40.3	39	4	750	0	0.0	0.0
D+ / 2.3	19.9	0.98	15.38	5	11	85	2	2	17	3.5	-40.1	54	4	750	0	5.8	0.0
D+ / 2.3	19.9	0.98	15.63	198	11	85	2	2	17	4.3	-40.0	56	4	0	0	0.0	0.0
D+ / 2.5	19.9	0.98	15.67	11	11	85	2	2	17	4.7	-40.0	57	4	0	0	0.0	0.0
D / 2.2	19.9	0.98	14.84	29	11	85	2	2	17	1.0	-40.1	47	4	0	0	0.0	0.0
D+ / 2.3	19.8	0.98	15.37	34	11	85	2	2	17	3.0	-40.0	52	4	0	0	0.0	0.0
C / 4.8	11.7	0.93	17.49	731	0	97	2	1	62	58.1	-24.6	85	11	750	0	5.8	0.0
C / 4.7	11.7	0.93	15.56	9	0	97	2	1	62	50.7	-24.9	80	11	750	0	0.0	0.0
C / 4.7	11.7	0.93	15.60	215	0	97	2	1	62	52.5	-24.8	81	11	750	0	0.0	0.0

99 Pct = Best
0 Pct = Worst

Fund Type	Fund Name	Ticker Symbol	Overall Investment Rating	Phone	Performance Rating/Pts	3 Mo	6 Mo	1Yr / Pct	Annualized 3Yr / Pct	Annualized 5Yr / Pct	Dividend Yield	Expense Ratio
FO	Ivy International Core Eq E	IICEX	D-	(800) 777-6472	D+ / 2.4	8.54	5.65	18.00 /43	1.47 /21	6.04 /29	1.36	1.69
FO	Ivy International Core Eq I	ICEIX	D+	(800) 777-6472	C- / 3.7	8.63	5.87	18.47 /45	1.92 /23	6.51 /32	1.81	0.98
FO	Ivy International Core Eq N	IINCX	C	(800) 777-6472	C- / 3.8	8.69	5.94	18.57 /45	2.05 /24	6.60 /32	1.94	0.83
FO	Ivy International Core Eq R	IYITX	D	(800) 777-6472	C- / 3.2	8.39	5.49	17.69 /41	1.32 /20	--	1.26	1.58
FO	Ivy International Core Eq Y	IVVYX	D	(800) 777-6472	C- / 3.5	8.60	5.72	18.14 /43	1.67 /22	6.24 /30	1.55	1.25
GR	Ivy Large Cap Growth A	WLGAX	C+	(800) 777-6472	C+ / 6.2	7.86	7.57	19.71 /51	7.64 /76	12.13 /75	0.00	1.16
GR	● Ivy Large Cap Growth B	WLGBX	C+	(800) 777-6472	C+ / 6.5	7.58	7.00	18.56 /45	6.67 /70	11.09 /67	0.00	2.07
GR	Ivy Large Cap Growth C	WLGCX	C+	(800) 777-6472	C+ / 6.7	7.66	7.19	18.85 /46	6.88 /71	11.31 /68	0.00	1.86
GR	Ivy Large Cap Growth E	ILCEX	C+	(800) 777-6472	C+ / 6.2	7.87	7.58	19.73 /51	7.65 /76	12.13 /75	0.00	1.35
GR	Ivy Large Cap Growth I	IYGIX	B-	(800) 777-6472	B- / 7.4	7.89	7.67	20.01 /52	7.93 /78	12.43 /78	0.00	0.88
GR	Ivy Large Cap Growth N	ILGRX	B	(800) 777-6472	B- / 7.5	7.96	7.80	20.24 /53	8.10 /80	12.53 /79	0.00	0.73
GR	Ivy Large Cap Growth R	WLGRX	C+	(800) 777-6472	B- / 7.0	7.77	7.35	19.29 /48	7.30 /74	11.76 /72	0.00	1.47
GR	Ivy Large Cap Growth Y	WLGYX	B-	(800) 777-6472	B- / 7.2	7.85	7.56	19.76 /51	7.73 /77	12.23 /76	0.00	1.11
RE	Ivy LaSalle Glbl Risk-Managed RE A	IVRAX	C-	(800) 777-6472	D+ / 2.8	6.12	-4.31	7.81 / 7	7.05 /72	--	3.40	1.76
RE	● Ivy LaSalle Glbl Risk-Managed RE B	IVRBX	C-	(800) 777-6472	C- / 3.2	5.92	-4.63	6.84 / 6	6.14 /65	--	2.81	2.33
RE	Ivy LaSalle Glbl Risk-Managed RE C	IVRCX	C-	(800) 777-6472	C- / 3.2	5.93	-4.71	6.82 / 6	6.12 /65	--	2.79	2.35
RE	Ivy LaSalle Glbl Risk-Managed RE I	IVIRX	C	(800) 777-6472	C- / 4.0	6.29	-4.07	8.02 / 7	7.19 /73	--	3.79	1.39
RE	Ivy LaSalle Glbl Risk-Managed RE R	IVRRX	C-	(800) 777-6472	C- / 3.5	6.01	-4.44	7.34 / 6	6.51 /69	--	3.17	1.99
RE	Ivy LaSalle Glbl Risk-Managed RE Y	IVRYX	C	(800) 777-6472	C- / 3.8	6.12	-4.32	7.71 / 7	7.05 /72	--	3.61	1.67
RE	Ivy LaSalle Global Real Estate A	IREAX	D+	(800) 777-6472	D+ / 2.3	6.23	-2.33	10.48 /13	4.91 /53	--	2.52	2.12
RE	● Ivy LaSalle Global Real Estate B	IREBX	D+	(800) 777-6472	D+ / 2.5	6.04	-2.75	9.27 /10	3.79 /40	--	1.57	2.56
RE	Ivy LaSalle Global Real Estate C	IRECX	D+	(800) 777-6472	D+ / 2.4	5.95	-2.84	9.21 /10	3.68 /39	--	1.32	2.74
RE	Ivy LaSalle Global Real Estate I	IRESX	C-	(800) 777-6472	C- / 3.1	6.20	-2.37	10.31 /12	4.81 /52	--	2.52	1.59
RE	Ivy LaSalle Global Real Estate R	IRERX	D+	(800) 777-6472	D+ / 2.8	6.12	-2.56	9.80 /11	4.20 /45	--	1.96	2.20
RE	Ivy LaSalle Global Real Estate Y	IREYX	C-	(800) 777-6472	C- / 3.4	6.16	-2.31	10.94 /14	5.08 /55	--	2.64	1.86
GL	Ivy Managed Intl Opp Class Y	IVTYX	D+	(800) 777-6472	C- / 3.2	8.26	5.74	17.52 /41	1.32 /20	4.47 /18	1.07	1.48
GL	Ivy Managed Intl Opps A	IVTAX	D	(800) 777-6472	D / 2.2	8.28	5.65	17.30 /40	1.21 /19	4.36 /17	0.94	1.54
GL	● Ivy Managed Intl Opps B	IVTBX	D	(800) 777-6472	D+ / 2.5	8.16	5.35	16.62 /37	0.31 /15	3.49 /13	0.42	2.56
GL	Ivy Managed Intl Opps C	IVTCX	D	(800) 777-6472	D+ / 2.6	8.22	5.31	16.80 /38	0.42 /15	3.60 /13	0.50	2.35
GL	● Ivy Managed Intl Opps E	IVTEX	D	(800) 777-6472	D / 2.2	8.24	5.72	17.36 /40	1.28 /20	4.45 /18	1.00	0.44
GL	Ivy Managed Intl Opps I	IVTIX	D+	(800) 777-6472	C- / 3.3	8.27	5.76	17.62 /41	1.48 /21	4.62 /19	1.21	1.24
FO	Ivy Managed Intl Opps R	IYMGX	D+	(800) 777-6472	C- / 3.0	8.17	5.64	17.07 /39	1.06 /19	--	0.87	1.72
SC	Ivy Micro Cap Growth A	IGWAX	E-	(800) 777-6472	E+ / 0.8	-1.42	3.44	32.69 /91	-2.48 / 5	8.52 /46	0.00	1.69
SC	● Ivy Micro Cap Growth B	IGWBX	E-	(800) 777-6472	E+ / 0.9	-1.65	2.98	31.45 /89	-3.36 / 4	7.47 /38	0.00	2.57
SC	Ivy Micro Cap Growth C	IGWCX	E-	(800) 777-6472	D- / 1.0	-1.62	3.03	31.65 /89	-3.21 / 4	7.70 /40	0.00	2.42
SC	Ivy Micro Cap Growth I	IGWIX	E-	(800) 777-6472	D- / 1.4	-1.35	3.62	33.26 /92	-2.08 / 6	8.98 /50	0.00	1.25
SC	Ivy Micro Cap Growth N	IMIGX	E-	(800) 777-6472	D- / 1.4	-1.30	3.73	33.50 /92	-1.92 / 7	9.08 /51	0.00	1.08
SC	Ivy Micro Cap Growth R	IYMRX	E-	(800) 777-6472	D- / 1.1	-1.47	3.36	32.51 /91	-2.64 / 5	--	0.00	1.84
SC	Ivy Micro Cap Growth Y	IGWYX	E-	(800) 777-6472	D- / 1.3	-1.38	3.50	32.89 /91	-2.31 / 6	9.15 /52	0.00	1.50
MC	Ivy Mid Cap Growth A	WMGAX	D-	(800) 777-6472	C- / 3.6	5.80	4.62	22.60 /65	3.68 /39	8.61 /47	0.00	1.29
MC	● Ivy Mid Cap Growth B	WMGBX	D-	(800) 777-6472	C- / 4.1	5.58	4.21	21.59 /60	2.89 /31	7.75 /40	0.00	2.05
MC	Ivy Mid Cap Growth C	WMGCX	D-	(800) 777-6472	C- / 4.1	5.60	4.25	21.69 /61	2.95 /31	7.84 /41	0.00	2.01
MC	Ivy Mid Cap Growth E	IMCEX	D-	(800) 777-6472	C- / 3.5	5.78	4.62	22.58 /65	3.55 /38	8.39 /45	0.00	1.63
MC	Ivy Mid Cap Growth I	IYMIX	D+	(800) 777-6472	C / 5.0	5.87	4.71	22.88 /66	3.99 /43	8.93 /50	0.00	1.00
MC	Ivy Mid Cap Growth N	IGRFX	C	(800) 777-6472	C / 5.2	5.89	4.82	23.13 /67	4.14 /44	9.02 /51	0.00	0.85
MC	Ivy Mid Cap Growth R	WMGRX	D	(800) 777-6472	C / 4.5	5.70	4.39	22.14 /63	3.36 /35	8.29 /45	0.00	1.60
MC	Ivy Mid Cap Growth Y	WMGYX	D	(800) 777-6472	C / 4.8	5.77	4.58	22.63 /65	3.73 /40	8.67 /48	0.00	1.24
MC	Ivy Mid Cap Income Opportunities A	IVOAX	U	(800) 777-6472	U /	3.71	7.15	25.32 /74	--	--	0.83	1.66
MC	Ivy Mid Cap Income Opportunities I	IVOIX	U	(800) 777-6472	U /	3.78	7.20	25.65 /75	--	--	1.07	1.30
RE	Ivy Real Estate Securities A	IRSAX	C-	(800) 777-6472	C+ / 5.6	7.38	-3.03	13.12 /22	10.27 /95	10.20 /60	1.28	1.57
RE	● Ivy Real Estate Securities B	IRSBX	C	(800) 777-6472	C+ / 6.0	7.13	-3.49	12.09 /18	9.25 /88	9.11 /52	0.49	2.47
RE	Ivy Real Estate Securities C	IRSCX	C	(800) 777-6472	C+ / 6.2	7.18	-3.41	12.30 /19	9.47 /90	9.40 /54	0.66	2.28

● Denotes fund is closed to new investors
* Denotes fund is included in Section II

RISK			NET ASSETS		ASSET					Portfolio Turnover Ratio	BULL / BEAR		FUND MANAGER		MINIMUMS		LOADS	
	3 Year		NAV								Last Bull	Last Bear	Manager	Manager	Initial	Additional	Front	Back
Risk Rating/Pts	Standard Deviation	Beta	As of 2/28/17	Total $(Mil)	Cash %	Stocks %	Bonds %	Other %			Market Return	Market Return	Quality Pct	Tenure (Years)	Purch. $	Purch. $	End Load	End Load
C / 4.8	11.7	0.93	17.61	5	0	97	2	1		62	57.4	-24.6	84	11	750	0	5.8	0.0
C / 4.8	11.7	0.93	17.59	2,778	0	97	2	1		62	61.2	-24.5	86	11	0	0	0.0	0.0
C+ / 6.7	11.7	0.93	17.64	431	0	97	2	1		62	61.8	-24.5	87	11	0	0	0.0	0.0
C / 4.8	11.7	0.93	17.48	51	0	97	2	1		62	N/A	N/A	84	11	0	0	0.0	0.0
C / 4.8	11.7	0.93	17.61	389	0	97	2	1		62	58.9	-24.5	85	11	0	0	0.0	0.0
C / 5.3	11.8	1.00	18.97	478	0	99	0	1		38	115.6	-14.8	37	17	750	0	5.8	0.0
C / 4.9	11.8	1.01	14.94	10	0	99	0	1		38	104.9	-15.2	26	17	750	0	0.0	0.0
C / 5.1	11.8	1.01	16.06	97	0	99	0	1		38	107.2	-15.1	29	17	750	0	0.0	0.0
C / 5.3	11.8	1.00	18.95	12	0	99	0	1		38	115.6	-14.8	37	17	750	0	5.8	0.0
C / 5.4	11.8	1.01	19.86	925	0	99	0	1		38	118.7	-14.7	41	17	0	0	0.0	0.0
C+ / 6.0	11.8	1.01	19.96	1	0	99	0	1		38	119.7	-14.7	43	17	0	0	0.0	0.0
C / 5.3	11.8	1.00	18.34	21	0	99	0	1		38	111.9	-15.0	34	17	0	0	0.0	0.0
C / 5.3	11.8	1.00	19.41	37	0	99	0	1		38	116.6	-14.8	38	17	0	0	0.0	0.0
C+ / 6.8	12.1	0.85	10.84	42	10	87	2	1		59	N/A	N/A	47	4	750	0	5.8	0.0
C+ / 6.8	12.1	0.85	10.82	1	10	87	2	1		59	N/A	N/A	35	4	750	0	0.0	0.0
C+ / 6.8	12.2	0.85	10.82	8	10	87	2	1		59	N/A	N/A	34	4	750	0	0.0	0.0
C+ / 6.8	12.1	0.85	10.85	58	10	87	2	1		59	N/A	N/A	48	4	0	0	0.0	0.0
C+ / 6.8	12.1	0.85	10.83	2	10	87	2	1		59	N/A	N/A	39	4	0	0	0.0	0.0
C+ / 6.8	12.2	0.85	10.84	5	10	87	2	1		59	N/A	N/A	46	4	0	0	0.0	0.0
C+ / 6.4	12.1	0.83	10.45	12	9	90	0	1		59	N/A	N/A	24	4	750	0	5.8	0.0
C+ / 6.4	12.1	0.83	10.42	N/A	9	90	0	1		59	N/A	N/A	15	4	750	0	0.0	0.0
C+ / 6.4	12.1	0.83	10.42	1	9	90	0	1		59	N/A	N/A	14	4	750	0	0.0	0.0
C+ / 6.4	12.0	0.83	10.45	19	9	90	0	1		59	N/A	N/A	23	4	0	0	0.0	0.0
C+ / 6.4	12.1	0.84	10.44	1	9	90	0	1		59	N/A	N/A	17	4	0	0	0.0	0.0
C+ / 6.4	12.1	0.83	10.56	1	9	90	0	1		59	N/A	N/A	25	4	0	0	0.0	0.0
C+ / 5.8	11.0	1.57	10.32	1	0	89	9	2		37	47.5	-24.5	10	10	0	0	0.0	0.0
C+ / 5.8	11.0	1.56	10.32	72	0	89	9	2		37	46.7	-24.5	10	10	750	0	5.8	0.0
C+ / 5.7	11.2	1.59	10.09	1	0	89	9	2		37	40.6	-25.1	6	10	750	0	0.0	0.0
C+ / 5.7	11.2	1.59	10.12	4	0	89	9	2		37	41.2	-25.1	6	10	750	0	0.0	0.0
C+ / 5.8	11.0	1.56	10.33	1	0	89	9	2		37	47.3	-24.5	10	10	0	0	5.8	0.0
C+ / 5.8	11.0	1.56	10.36	108	0	89	9	2		37	48.7	-24.3	11	10	0	0	0.0	0.0
C+ / 5.8	11.0	0.85	10.29	1	0	89	9	2		37	N/A	N/A	82	10	0	0	0.0	0.0
D / 1.7	19.4	1.06	22.97	85	0	96	3	1		84	101.1	-28.6	2	N/A	750	0	5.8	0.0
D / 1.7	19.4	1.06	21.57	2	0	96	3	1		84	90.7	-29.0	2	N/A	750	0	0.0	0.0
D / 1.7	19.4	1.06	21.92	7	0	96	3	1		84	93.0	-28.8	2	N/A	750	0	0.0	0.0
D / 1.8	19.4	1.06	23.55	71	0	96	3	1		84	105.9	-28.5	3	N/A	0	0	0.0	0.0
D / 1.7	19.4	1.06	23.70	2	0	96	3	1		84	106.9	-28.5	3	N/A	0	0	0.0	0.0
D / 1.7	19.4	1.06	22.86	1	0	96	3	1		84	N/A	N/A	2	N/A	0	0	0.0	0.0
D / 1.8	19.4	1.06	23.75	1	0	96	3	1		84	107.3	-28.6	2	N/A	0	0	0.0	0.0
C- / 3.3	13.2	1.02	20.67	476	2	97	0	1		38	89.1	-20.7	10	16	750	0	5.8	0.0
C- / 3.0	13.2	1.02	16.92	17	2	97	0	1		38	81.0	-21.0	7	16	750	0	0.0	0.0
C- / 3.1	13.2	1.02	17.98	219	2	97	0	1		38	81.8	-20.9	7	16	750	0	0.0	0.0
C- / 3.3	13.2	1.02	20.20	8	2	97	0	1		38	87.0	-20.7	9	16	750	0	5.8	0.0
C- / 3.4	13.2	1.02	22.07	1,104	2	97	0	1		38	92.2	-20.5	12	16	0	0	0.0	0.0
C / 5.5	13.2	1.02	22.19	62	2	97	0	1		38	93.0	-20.5	13	16	0	0	0.0	0.0
C- / 3.3	13.2	1.02	20.26	55	2	97	0	1		38	86.1	-20.7	8	16	0	0	0.0	0.0
C- / 3.4	13.2	1.02	21.51	328	2	97	0	1		38	89.8	-20.6	10	16	0	0	0.0	0.0
U /	N/A	N/A	12.74	119	1	93	5	1		26	N/A	N/A	N/A	3	750	0	5.8	0.0
U /	N/A	N/A	12.76	151	1	93	5	1		26	N/A	N/A	N/A	3	0	0	0.0	0.0
C / 4.8	15.1	1.10	26.63	271	0	97	1	2		66	97.3	-18.2	52	11	750	0	5.8	0.0
C / 4.8	15.1	1.10	25.80	4	0	97	1	2		66	86.9	-18.6	39	11	750	0	0.0	0.0
C / 4.8	15.1	1.10	26.15	16	0	97	1	2		66	89.7	-18.5	42	11	750	0	0.0	0.0

Fund Type	Fund Name	Ticker Symbol	Overall Investment Rating	Phone	Perfor-mance Rating/Pts	3 Mo	6 Mo	1Yr / Pct	3Yr / Pct	5Yr / Pct	Dividend Yield	Expense Ratio
RE	Ivy Real Estate Securities E	IREEX	C-	(800) 777-6472	C+ / 5.6	7.35	-3.08	13.08 /22	10.17 /94	10.11 /59	1.25	1.87
RE	Ivy Real Estate Securities I	IREIX	C+	(800) 777-6472	B- / 7.0	7.49	-2.89	13.56 /24	10.74 /96	10.72 /64	1.72	1.13
RE	Ivy Real Estate Securities N	IRSEX	C+	(800) 777-6472	B- / 7.1	7.50	-2.83	13.74 /24	10.89 /97	10.81 /64	1.88	0.97
RE	Ivy Real Estate Securities R	IRSRX	C	(800) 777-6472	C+ / 6.6	7.30	-3.18	12.88 /21	10.06 /94	10.03 /59	1.14	1.75
RE	Ivy Real Estate Securities Y	IRSYX	C+	(800) 777-6472	C+ / 6.9	7.44	-2.98	13.33 /23	10.49 /96	10.46 /62	1.50	1.36
TC	Ivy Science and Technology A	WSTAX	D	(800) 777-6472	C- / 4.1	8.64	10.77	27.04 /79	1.80 /23	12.70 /81	0.00	1.28
TC	● Ivy Science and Technology B	WSTBX	D+	(800) 777-6472	C / 4.6	8.44	10.33	26.06 /76	1.03 /18	11.83 /73	0.00	2.02
TC	Ivy Science and Technology C	WSTCX	D+	(800) 777-6472	C / 4.7	8.44	10.37	26.15 /77	1.09 /19	11.91 /73	0.00	1.97
TC	Ivy Science and Technology E	ISTEX	D	(800) 777-6472	C- / 4.0	8.64	10.73	26.97 /79	1.68 /22	12.59 /80	0.00	1.54
TC	Ivy Science and Technology I	ISTIX	C-	(800) 777-6472	C+ / 5.6	8.72	10.91	27.40 /80	2.10 /25	13.04 /84	0.00	0.97
TC	Ivy Science and Technology N	ISTNX	C-	(800) 777-6472	C+ / 5.7	8.76	11.00	27.61 /81	2.23 /25	13.13 /85	0.00	0.83
TC	Ivy Science and Technology R	WSTRX	D+	(800) 777-6472	C / 5.0	8.55	10.58	26.65 /78	1.49 /21	12.36 /78	0.00	1.57
TC	Ivy Science and Technology Y	WSTYX	C-	(800) 777-6472	C / 5.4	8.64	10.77	27.11 /79	1.85 /23	12.76 /82	0.00	1.22
SC	Ivy Small Cap Core A	IYSAX	B	(800) 777-6472	A / 9.5	5.24	12.74	40.27 /97	9.78 /92	13.78 /91	0.00	1.56
SC	● Ivy Small Cap Core B	IYSBX	B-	(800) 777-6472	A+ / 9.6	5.01	12.23	38.97 /97	8.72 /85	12.65 /80	0.00	2.51
SC	Ivy Small Cap Core C	IYSCX	B-	(800) 777-6472	A+ / 9.6	5.10	12.34	39.30 /97	9.04 /87	12.99 /84	0.00	2.23
SC	● Ivy Small Cap Core E	IYVIX	B	(800) 777-6472	A+ / 9.6	5.31	12.86	40.67 /97	10.12 /94	14.17 /94	0.00	1.32
SC	Ivy Small Cap Core I	IVVIX	B	(800) 777-6472	A+ / 9.8	5.34	12.92	40.77 /97	10.23 /94	14.29 /95	0.00	1.12
SC	Ivy Small Cap Core N	ISPVX	A+	(800) 777-6472	A+ / 9.8	5.40	13.05	41.10 /98	10.39 /95	14.40 /95	0.00	0.96
SC	Ivy Small Cap Core R	IYSMX	B	(800) 777-6472	A+ / 9.7	5.21	12.61	40.04 /97	9.58 /91	--	0.00	1.72
SC	Ivy Small Cap Core Y	IYSYX	B	(800) 777-6472	A+ / 9.8	5.33	12.81	40.56 /97	9.96 /93	14.00 /93	0.00	1.37
SC	Ivy Small Cap Growth A	WSGAX	C-	(800) 777-6472	C+ / 6.9	6.35	10.90	32.87 /91	5.83 /63	12.49 /79	0.00	1.44
SC	● Ivy Small Cap Growth B	WSGBX	C-	(800) 777-6472	B- / 7.3	6.11	10.54	31.79 /90	4.95 /54	11.49 /70	0.00	2.32
SC	Ivy Small Cap Growth C	WRGCX	C-	(800) 777-6472	B- / 7.4	6.14	10.54	31.96 /90	5.15 /56	11.75 /72	0.00	2.07
SC	Ivy Small Cap Growth E	ISGEX	C-	(800) 777-6472	C+ / 6.9	6.33	10.86	32.82 /91	5.76 /62	12.38 /78	0.00	1.73
SC	Ivy Small Cap Growth I	IYSIX	C	(800) 777-6472	B / 8.2	6.40	11.07	33.30 /92	6.22 /66	12.90 /83	0.00	1.06
SC	Ivy Small Cap Growth N	IRGFX	B	(800) 777-6472	B+ / 8.3	6.43	11.18	33.58 /92	6.36 /67	12.99 /84	0.00	0.91
SC	Ivy Small Cap Growth R	WSGRX	C	(800) 777-6472	B / 7.7	6.25	10.80	32.52 /91	5.58 /60	12.23 /76	0.00	1.66
SC	Ivy Small Cap Growth Y	WSCYX	C	(800) 777-6472	B / 8.0	6.38	11.01	32.99 /92	5.96 /64	12.63 /80	0.00	1.31
FS	Ivy Targeted Return Bond I	IRBIX	U	(800) 777-6472	U /	1.02	-0.46	3.05 / 3	--	--	1.47	N/A
GR	Ivy Tax-Managed Equity A	IYEAX	C+	(800) 777-6472	C+ / 6.2	9.70	6.95	18.46 /45	7.67 /77	12.31 /77	0.00	1.22
GR	● Ivy Tax-Managed Equity B	IYEBX	C+	(800) 777-6472	C+ / 6.8	9.55	6.64	17.64 /41	6.93 /71	11.59 /71	0.00	1.92
GR	Ivy Tax-Managed Equity C	IYECX	C+	(800) 777-6472	C+ / 6.7	9.53	6.55	17.58 /41	6.87 /71	11.52 /70	0.00	2.01
GR	Ivy Tax-Managed Equity I	WYTMX	B	(800) 777-6472	B- / 7.4	9.82	7.09	18.76 /46	7.94 /78	12.48 /79	0.00	0.99
GR	Ivy Tax-Managed Equity Y	IYEYX	B-	(800) 777-6472	B- / 7.3	9.85	7.10	18.61 /45	7.72 /77	12.36 /78	0.00	1.24
GR	Ivy Value A	IYVAX	C	(800) 777-6472	C+ / 6.8	6.60	12.19	25.73 /75	6.86 /71	11.90 /73	1.36	1.30
GR	● Ivy Value B	IYVBX	C+	(800) 777-6472	B- / 7.0	6.29	11.58	24.42 /71	5.83 /63	10.82 /64	0.66	2.27
GR	Ivy Value C	IYVCX	C+	(800) 777-6472	B- / 7.2	6.38	11.77	24.88 /73	6.13 /65	11.13 /67	0.95	1.98
GR	● Ivy Value E	IVVEX	C+	(800) 777-6472	B- / 7.0	6.65	12.28	25.99 /76	7.12 /73	12.18 /76	1.57	1.22
GR	Ivy Value I	IYAIX	B-	(800) 777-6472	B / 8.0	6.66	12.32	26.10 /76	7.22 /73	12.27 /77	1.74	0.97
GI	Ivy Value N	IVALX	A-	(800) 777-6472	B / 8.2	6.74	12.43	26.35 /77	7.38 /75	12.37 /78	1.88	0.81
GI	Ivy Value R	IYVLX	C+	(800) 777-6472	B / 7.6	6.51	11.98	25.34 /74	6.59 /69	--	1.24	1.56
GR	Ivy Value Y	IYVYX	C+	(800) 777-6472	B / 7.8	6.54	12.16	25.77 /75	6.93 /71	12.00 /74	1.55	1.22
FS	J Hancock Absolute Ret Curr R6	JCURX	C-	(800) 257-3336	D- / 1.2	-1.12	2.96	3.61 / 3	1.52 /21	2.95 /11	0.00	0.97
GI	J Hancock Alpha Opptys NAV		C-	(800) 257-3336	C+ / 5.8	6.11	6.88	21.25 /59	5.12 /55	11.71 /72	2.32	0.99
GL	J Hancock Alt Asst Alloc A	JAAAX	C-	(800) 257-3336	E+ / 0.8	2.29	2.14	6.73 / 5	0.40 /15	2.19 / 8	0.72	1.94
GR	J Hancock Alt Asst Alloc C	JAACX	C-	(800) 257-3336	E+ / 0.8	2.16	1.80	6.05 / 5	-0.28 /12	1.47 / 7	0.08	2.64
GL	J Hancock Alt Asst Alloc I	JAAIX	C-	(800) 257-3336	D- / 1.3	2.30	2.23	7.05 / 6	0.72 /17	2.53 / 9	1.06	1.63
GR	J Hancock Alt Asst Alloc R2	JAAPX	C-	(800) 257-3336	D- / 1.1	2.20	2.06	6.64 / 5	0.26 /15	2.04 / 8	0.67	2.03
AA	J Hancock Alt Asst Alloc R4	JAASX	C-	(800) 257-3336	D- / 1.3	2.29	2.22	6.96 / 6	0.54 /16	--	0.90	1.88
GR	J Hancock Alt Asst Alloc R6	JAARX	C-	(800) 257-3336	D- / 1.4	2.34	2.34	7.17 / 6	0.84 /17	2.58 /10	1.17	1.53
BA	J Hancock Balanced A	SVBAX	C+	(800) 257-3336	C- / 4.2	5.60	5.36	16.91 /38	5.63 /61	8.46 /46	1.55	1.20

● Denotes fund is closed to new investors
* Denotes fund is included in Section II

Risk Rating/Pts	3 Year Standard Deviation	Beta	NAV As of 2/28/17	Total $(Mil)	Cash %	Stocks %	Bonds %	Other %	Portfolio Turnover Ratio	Last Bull Market Return	Last Bear Market Return	Manager Quality Pct	Manager Tenure (Years)	Initial Purch. $	Additional Purch. $	Front End Load	Back End Load
C /4.8	15.1	1.10	26.63	4	0	97	1	2	66	96.6	-18.2	51	11	750	0	5.8	0.0
C /4.8	15.1	1.10	26.80	210	0	97	1	2	66	102.6	-18.0	58	11	0	0	0.0	0.0
C /4.6	15.1	1.10	26.83	3	0	97	1	2	66	103.4	-18.0	59	11	0	0	0.0	0.0
C /4.8	15.1	1.10	26.61	2	0	97	1	2	66	95.8	-18.2	49	11	0	0	0.0	0.0
C /4.8	15.1	1.10	26.66	135	0	97	1	2	66	99.9	-18.1	55	11	0	0	0.0	0.0
C- /4.0	15.8	1.34	54.92	1,102	0	96	3	1	24	124.0	-19.8	1	16	750	0	5.8	0.0
C- /3.9	15.8	1.34	46.25	46	0	96	3	1	24	114.8	-20.1	1	16	750	0	0.0	0.0
C- /3.9	15.8	1.34	47.91	678	0	96	3	1	24	115.5	-20.1	1	16	750	0	0.0	0.0
C- /3.9	15.8	1.34	54.57	23	0	96	3	1	24	122.9	-19.9	1	16	750	0	0.0	0.0
C- /4.0	15.8	1.34	59.98	1,175	0	96	3	1	24	127.6	-19.7	1	16	0	0	0.0	0.0
C /4.7	15.8	1.34	60.22	86	0	96	3	1	24	128.5	-19.7	1	16	0	0	0.0	0.0
C- /3.9	15.8	1.34	53.70	102	0	96	3	1	24	120.4	-19.9	1	16	0	0	0.0	0.0
C- /4.0	15.8	1.34	57.72	635	0	96	3	1	24	124.6	-19.8	1	16	0	0	0.0	0.0
C- /3.5	12.9	0.78	17.84	202	0	95	3	2	135	136.8	-27.1	94	3	750	0	5.8	0.0
C- /3.0	12.9	0.78	14.60	5	0	95	3	2	135	124.1	-27.4	91	3	750	0	0.0	0.0
C- /3.2	12.9	0.78	15.55	30	0	95	3	2	135	128.1	-27.3	92	3	750	0	0.0	0.0
C- /3.6	12.9	0.78	18.49	N/A	0	95	3	2	135	141.4	-27.0	94	3	0	0	5.8	0.0
C- /3.7	12.9	0.78	19.21	209	0	95	3	2	135	142.9	-26.9	94	3	0	0	0.0	0.0
C+ /5.8	12.9	0.78	19.35	7	0	95	3	2	135	144.0	-26.9	95	3	0	0	0.0	0.0
C- /3.5	12.9	0.78	17.76	7	0	95	3	2	135	N/A	N/A	93	3	0	0	0.0	0.0
C- /3.7	12.9	0.78	18.69	21	0	95	3	2	135	139.5	-27.0	94	3	0	0	0.0	0.0
D+ /2.8	15.7	0.95	17.05	242	0	96	3	1	43	116.1	-24.7	66	7	750	0	5.8	0.0
D /2.2	15.7	0.95	12.99	8	0	96	3	1	43	105.8	-25.1	55	7	750	0	0.0	0.0
D+ /2.4	15.7	0.95	14.13	170	0	96	3	1	43	108.7	-25.0	58	7	750	0	0.0	0.0
D+ /2.8	15.7	0.95	16.91	7	0	96	3	1	43	115.2	-24.8	65	7	750	0	5.8	0.0
C- /3.2	15.7	0.95	21.72	259	0	96	3	1	43	120.6	-24.6	70	7	0	0	0.0	0.0
C /4.8	15.7	0.95	21.82	64	0	96	3	1	43	121.5	-24.6	72	7	0	0	0.0	0.0
D+ /2.8	15.7	0.95	16.79	46	0	96	3	1	43	113.5	-24.8	63	7	0	0	0.0	0.0
C- /3.1	15.7	0.95	20.63	129	0	96	3	1	43	117.8	-24.7	68	7	0	0	0.0	0.0
U /	N/A	N/A	9.99	95	0	0	0	100	90	N/A	N/A	N/A	1	0	0	0.0	0.0
C+ /5.7	12.2	1.05	20.92	39	0	90	9	1	21	112.1	-14.9	32	8	750	0	5.8	0.0
C+ /5.6	12.2	1.05	20.07	1	0	90	9	1	21	104.8	-15.2	24	8	750	0	0.0	0.0
C+ /5.6	12.2	1.05	20.00	5	0	90	9	1	21	104.2	-15.2	24	8	750	0	0.0	0.0
C+ /5.6	12.2	1.05	21.14	70	0	90	9	1	21	114.0	-14.8	35	8	0	0	0.0	0.0
C+ /5.6	12.3	1.05	20.97	1	0	90	9	1	21	112.8	-15.0	32	8	0	0	0.0	0.0
C /4.5	12.1	1.09	22.85	116	7	88	3	2	55	115.5	-22.1	20	23	750	0	5.8	0.0
C /4.5	12.1	1.09	21.28	3	7	88	3	2	55	104.2	-22.5	13	23	750	0	0.0	0.0
C /4.6	12.1	1.09	22.08	20	7	88	3	2	55	107.5	-22.3	14	23	750	0	0.0	0.0
C /4.5	12.1	1.09	22.94	N/A	7	88	3	2	55	118.4	-21.9	22	23	0	0	5.8	0.0
C /4.5	12.1	1.09	22.94	164	7	88	3	2	55	119.5	-21.9	23	23	0	0	0.0	0.0
C+ /6.7	12.1	1.09	23.01	9	7	88	3	2	55	120.5	-21.9	24	23	0	0	0.0	0.0
C /4.6	12.1	1.09	22.82	N/A	7	88	3	2	55	N/A	N/A	18	23	0	0	0.0	0.0
C /4.5	12.1	1.09	22.88	1	7	88	3	2	55	116.7	-22.0	21	23	0	0	0.0	0.0
B /8.2	7.2	-0.17	9.75	44	0	0	99	1	0	16.1	-1.0	92	6	1,000,000	0	0.0	0.0
C- /4.0	11.3	1.05	11.53	269	3	96	0	1	95	114.3	-23.2	11	9	0	0	0.0	0.0
B /8.5	3.3	0.47	14.15	163	27	26	45	2	17	19.4	-9.1	51	7	1,000	0	5.0	0.0
B /8.6	3.3	0.27	14.21	83	27	26	45	2	17	15.0	-9.3	33	7	1,000	0	0.0	0.0
B /8.5	3.3	0.46	14.15	481	27	26	45	2	17	21.6	-8.9	56	7	250,000	0	0.0	0.0
B /8.6	3.3	0.27	14.14	7	27	26	45	2	17	18.5	-9.1	41	7	0	0	0.0	0.0
B /8.5	3.3	0.45	14.17	5	27	26	45	2	17	N/A	N/A	37	7	0	0	0.0	0.0
B /8.5	3.3	0.27	14.15	14	27	26	45	2	17	21.9	-9.1	49	7	1,000,000	0	0.0	0.0
B- /7.3	7.1	1.11	19.47	813	1	62	35	2	47	77.3	-14.5	40	11	1,000	0	5.0	0.0

I. Index of Stock Mutual Funds

	99 Pct = Best				PERFORMANCE						Incl. in Returns	
	0 Pct = Worst		Overall		Perfor-		Total Return % through 2/28/17					
		Ticker	Investment		mance				Annualized		Dividend	Expense
Fund Type	Fund Name	Symbol	Rating	Phone	Rating/Pts	3 Mo	6 Mo	1Yr / Pct	3Yr / Pct	5Yr / Pct	Yield	Ratio
BA	● J Hancock Balanced B	SVBBX	C+	(800) 257-3336	C / 4.6	5.37	4.95	16.01 /34	4.89 /53	7.70 /40	0.99	1.90
BA	J Hancock Balanced C	SVBCX	C+	(800) 257-3336	C / 4.6	5.43	4.94	16.06 /35	4.90 /53	7.71 /40	0.99	1.90
BA	J Hancock Balanced I	SVBIX	B-	(800) 257-3336	C / 5.5	5.68	5.47	17.21 /39	5.97 /64	8.81 /49	1.92	0.89
BA	J Hancock Balanced R1	JBAOX	C+	(800) 257-3336	C / 4.9	5.49	5.10	16.44 /36	5.28 /57	8.09 /43	1.31	1.55
BA	J Hancock Balanced R2	JBATX	C+	(800) 257-3336	C / 5.2	5.58	5.26	16.76 /37	5.58 /60	8.49 /46	1.55	1.29
BA	J Hancock Balanced R3	JBAHX	C+	(800) 257-3336	C / 5.0	5.47	5.17	16.53 /36	5.38 /58	8.21 /44	1.41	1.44
BA	J Hancock Balanced R4	JBAFX	B-	(800) 257-3336	C / 5.4	5.61	5.41	17.07 /39	5.82 /63	8.65 /48	1.77	1.15
BA	J Hancock Balanced R5	JBAVX	B-	(800) 257-3336	C+ / 5.6	5.67	5.53	17.33 /40	6.02 /64	8.88 /50	1.95	0.85
BA	J Hancock Balanced R6	JBAWX	B-	(800) 257-3336	C+ / 5.6	5.70	5.52	17.32 /40	6.09 /65	8.94 /50	2.02	0.80
GR	J Hancock Blue Chip Grwth 1	JIBCX	C+	(800) 257-3336	B+ / 8.3	8.76	9.90	22.29 /64	8.66 /84	14.38 /95	0.04	0.87
GI	J Hancock Blue Chip Grwth A	JBGAX	U	(800) 257-3336	U /	8.70	9.74	21.96 /62	--	--	0.00	1.24
GI	J Hancock Blue Chip Grwth C	JBGCX	U	(800) 257-3336	U /	8.49	9.34	21.04 /58	--	--	0.00	1.94
GR	J Hancock Blue Chip Grwth NAV		B-	(800) 257-3336	B+ / 8.4	8.79	9.93	22.36 /64	8.72 /85	14.43 /95	0.06	0.82
GR	J Hancock Capital Appr 1	JICPX	C	(800) 257-3336	B- / 7.4	8.53	8.40	20.77 /56	7.48 /75	12.80 /82	0.06	0.79
GR	J Hancock Capital Appr NAV	JHCPX	C	(800) 257-3336	B- / 7.4	8.57	8.44	20.79 /56	7.53 /76	12.86 /82	0.11	0.74
GR	J Hancock Capital Value Appr NAV		B-	(800) 257-3336	B- / 7.0	5.36	4.81	16.11 /35	9.17 /88	11.70 /72	1.71	0.85
GR	J Hancock Classic Value A	PZFVX	A+	(800) 257-3336	A+ / 9.6	5.58	17.94	39.99 /97	9.02 /87	13.57 /90	1.63	1.19
GR	● J Hancock Classic Value B	JCVBX	A+	(800) 257-3336	A+ / 9.7	5.37	17.51	38.95 /97	8.20 /80	12.72 /81	1.13	1.93
GR	J Hancock Classic Value C	JCVCX	A+	(800) 257-3336	A+ / 9.7	5.40	17.54	38.94 /97	8.21 /81	12.73 /81	1.12	1.94
GR	J Hancock Classic Value I	JCVIX	A+	(800) 257-3336	A+ / 9.8	5.62	18.08	40.36 /97	9.31 /89	13.89 /92	1.93	0.92
GR	J Hancock Classic Value R1	JCVRX	A+	(800) 257-3336	A+ / 9.7	5.49	17.70	39.49 /97	8.61 /84	13.15 /85	1.40	1.57
GR	J Hancock Classic Value R2	JCVSX	A+	(800) 257-3336	A+ / 9.7	5.54	17.89	39.79 /97	8.91 /86	13.57 /90	1.61	1.32
GR	J Hancock Classic Value R3	JCVHX	A+	(800) 257-3336	A+ / 9.7	5.52	17.78	39.62 /97	8.72 /85	13.29 /87	1.48	1.48
GR	J Hancock Classic Value R4	JCVFX	A+	(800) 257-3336	A+ / 9.8	5.62	18.04	40.25 /97	9.25 /88	13.82 /92	1.89	1.18
GR	J Hancock Classic Value R5	JCVVX	A+	(800) 257-3336	A+ / 9.8	5.67	18.17	40.44 /97	9.40 /90	13.98 /93	1.97	0.87
GR	J Hancock Classic Value R6	JCVWX	A+	(800) 257-3336	A+ / 9.8	5.68	18.18	40.51 /97	9.43 /90	14.01 /93	2.02	0.83
GI	J Hancock Disciplined Val 12	JVLTX	B+	(800) 257-3336	B+ / 8.5	6.13	12.91	27.36 /80	7.78 /77	13.22 /86	1.17	0.81
GI	● J Hancock Disciplined Val B	JVLBX	B+	(800) 257-3336	B / 7.7	5.84	12.35	26.06 /76	6.67 /70	12.00 /74	0.29	1.83
GI	J Hancock Disciplined Val C	JVLCX	B+	(800) 257-3336	B / 7.7	5.88	12.37	26.12 /77	6.71 /70	12.05 /75	0.29	1.83
GI	J Hancock Disciplined Val I	JVLIX	B+	(800) 257-3336	B+ / 8.5	6.13	12.91	27.36 /80	7.78 /77	13.23 /86	1.17	0.81
GI	J Hancock Disciplined Val NAV	JDVNX	A-	(800) 257-3336	B+ / 8.6	6.17	13.00	27.51 /81	7.91 /78	13.35 /87	1.26	0.70
GI	J Hancock Disciplined Val R1	JDVOX	B+	(800) 257-3336	B / 7.9	5.95	12.51	26.56 /78	7.06 /72	12.42 /78	0.59	1.47
GI	J Hancock Disciplined Val R2	JDVPX	B+	(800) 257-3336	B / 8.1	6.02	12.69	26.91 /79	7.35 /74	12.73 /81	0.81	1.22
GI	J Hancock Disciplined Val R3	JDVHX	B+	(800) 257-3336	B / 8.0	5.99	12.61	26.76 /78	7.18 /73	12.55 /80	0.68	1.37
GI	J Hancock Disciplined Val R4	JDVFX	B+	(800) 257-3336	B+ / 8.3	6.09	12.87	27.24 /80	7.63 /76	13.03 /84	1.03	1.07
GI	J Hancock Disciplined Val R5	JDVVX	B+	(800) 257-3336	B+ / 8.5	6.16	12.99	27.43 /80	7.86 /78	13.30 /87	1.20	0.77
GI	J Hancock Disciplined Val R6	JDVWX	A-	(800) 257-3336	B+ / 8.5	6.12	12.94	27.53 /81	7.90 /78	13.33 /87	1.26	0.72
GI	J Hancock Disciplined Value A	JVLAX	B	(800) 257-3336	B- / 7.4	6.07	12.78	27.07 /79	7.51 /76	12.90 /83	0.86	1.08
GI	J Hancock Diversified Strategies A	JDSTX	D+	(800) 257-3336	D- / 1.2	2.92	2.11	9.20 /10	1.49 /21	3.77 /14	1.49	1.81
GI	J Hancock Diversified Strategies I	JDSIX	D+	(800) 257-3336	D / 1.9	3.02	2.41	9.63 /11	1.85 /23	4.12 /16	1.87	1.49
MC	● J Hancock Dsp Val Mid Cap A	JVMAX	A-	(800) 257-3336	A- / 9.2	6.06	10.47	31.57 /89	10.77 /97	15.66 /98	0.61	1.13
MC	● J Hancock Dsp Val Mid Cap Adv	JVMVX	A	(800) 257-3336	A+ / 9.6	6.12	10.49	31.57 /89	10.73 /96	15.62 /98	0.64	1.13
MC	● J Hancock Dsp Val Mid Cap C	JVMCX	A	(800) 257-3336	A / 9.4	5.90	10.02	30.60 /87	9.93 /93	14.79 /96	0.00	1.88
MC	● J Hancock Dsp Val Mid Cap Inst	JVMIX	A	(800) 257-3336	A+ / 9.7	6.19	10.60	31.96 /90	11.07 /97	16.00 /98	0.85	0.86
MC	● J Hancock Dsp Val Mid Cap R2	JVMSX	A	(800) 257-3336	A+ / 9.6	6.02	10.34	31.38 /89	10.60 /96	15.51 /98	0.50	1.27
MC	● J Hancock Dsp Val Mid Cap R4	JVMTX	A	(800) 257-3336	A+ / 9.6	6.09	10.50	31.74 /89	10.89 /97	--	0.71	1.12
MC	● J Hancock Dsp Val Mid Cap R6	JVMRX	A	(800) 257-3336	A+ / 9.7	6.18	10.69	32.09 /90	11.17 /97	16.09 /98	0.93	0.77
EM	J Hancock Emerg Mkts A	JEVAX	D+	(800) 257-3336	C- / 3.8	10.08	5.37	28.40 /83	1.51 /21	-0.25 / 4	1.33	1.47
EM	J Hancock Emerg Mkts I	JEVIX	C-	(800) 257-3336	C / 5.1	10.07	5.59	28.70 /83	1.80 /23	0.10 / 5	1.67	1.16
EM	J Hancock Emerg Mkts NAV	JEVNX	C-	(800) 257-3336	C / 5.2	10.07	5.60	28.84 /84	1.94 /24	0.24 / 5	1.77	1.05
EM	J Hancock Emerg Mkts R6	JEVRX	C-	(800) 257-3336	C / 5.2	10.20	5.59	28.87 /84	1.94 /24	0.19 / 5	1.76	1.06
IN	J Hancock Eqty-Inc 1	JIEMX	B	(800) 257-3336	B / 8.1	5.22	11.35	28.76 /83	7.37 /75	11.59 /71	2.32	0.82

● Denotes fund is closed to new investors
★ Denotes fund is included in Section II

Risk Rating/Pts	3 Year Standard Deviation	Beta	NAV As of 2/28/17	Total $(Mil)	Cash %	Stocks %	Bonds %	Other %	Portfolio Turnover Ratio	Last Bull Market Return	Last Bear Market Return	Manager Quality Pct	Manager Tenure (Years)	Initial Purch. $	Additional Purch. $	Front End Load	Back End Load
B- / 7.3	7.1	1.11	19.41	48	1	62	35	2	47	70.7	-14.8	31	11	1,000	0	0.0	0.0
B- / 7.3	7.0	1.11	19.43	522	1	62	35	2	47	70.7	-14.8	32	11	1,000	0	0.0	0.0
B- / 7.3	7.1	1.11	19.46	423	1	62	35	2	47	80.5	-14.4	45	11	250,000	0	0.0	0.0
B- / 7.3	7.0	1.11	19.53	6	1	62	35	2	47	74.2	-14.7	36	11	0	0	0.0	0.0
B- / 7.3	7.0	1.11	19.44	8	1	62	35	2	47	77.5	-14.5	40	11	0	0	0.0	0.0
B- / 7.3	7.0	1.11	19.50	5	1	62	35	2	47	75.1	-14.7	37	11	0	0	0.0	0.0
B- / 7.3	7.1	1.11	19.55	22	1	62	35	2	47	78.9	-14.6	43	11	0	0	0.0	0.0
B- / 7.3	7.0	1.11	19.53	2	1	62	35	2	47	80.9	-14.4	46	11	0	0	0.0	0.0
B- / 7.3	7.0	1.11	19.48	8	1	62	35	2	47	81.5	-14.6	47	11	1,000,000	0	0.0	0.0
C- / 4.1	12.7	1.05	33.55	1,107	0	99	0	1	34	144.0	-14.9	44	12	0	0	0.0	0.0
U /	N/A	N/A	33.37	230	0	99	0	1	34	N/A	N/A	N/A	12	1,000	0	5.0	0.0
U /	N/A	N/A	32.84	35	0	99	0	1	34	N/A	N/A	N/A	12	1,000	0	0.0	0.0
C- / 4.1	12.7	1.05	33.57	1,070	0	99	0	1	34	144.8	-14.9	45	12	0	0	0.0	0.0
C- / 3.4	13.4	1.10	15.90	524	0	99	0	1	32	122.5	-13.8	25	12	0	0	0.0	0.0
C- / 3.4	13.4	1.10	15.93	1,276	0	99	0	1	32	123.2	-13.8	25	12	0	0	0.0	0.0
C+ / 5.6	6.8	0.63	11.55	2,024	15	62	22	1	64	105.7	-12.9	88	6	0	0	0.0	0.0
C+ / 6.0	14.7	1.24	30.39	356	4	95	0	1	21	136.0	-23.6	24	21	1,000	0	5.0	0.0
C+ / 6.0	14.7	1.25	29.96	6	4	95	0	1	21	126.6	-23.9	18	21	1,000	0	0.0	0.0
C+ / 6.0	14.7	1.25	29.96	90	4	95	0	1	21	126.6	-23.8	18	21	1,000	0	0.0	0.0
C+ / 6.0	14.7	1.25	30.43	1,303	4	95	0	1	21	139.7	-23.5	27	21	250,000	0	0.0	0.0
C+ / 6.0	14.7	1.25	30.46	3	4	95	0	1	21	131.3	-23.7	21	21	0	0	0.0	0.0
C+ / 6.0	14.7	1.25	30.35	1	4	95	0	1	21	N/A	N/A	24	21	0	0	0.0	0.0
C+ / 6.0	14.7	1.25	30.34	1	4	95	0	1	21	132.9	-23.6	22	21	0	0	0.0	0.0
C+ / 6.0	14.7	1.25	30.42	N/A	4	95	0	1	21	138.8	-23.6	27	21	0	0	0.0	0.0
C+ / 6.0	14.7	1.24	30.45	N/A	4	95	0	1	21	140.6	-23.5	28	21	0	0	0.0	0.0
C+ / 6.0	14.7	1.25	30.45	3	4	95	0	1	21	140.9	-23.5	28	21	1,000,000	0	0.0	0.0
C+ / 6.0	11.9	1.08	20.26	54	0	98	0	2	61	132.4	-19.8	29	20	250,000	0	0.0	0.0
C+ / 6.1	11.9	1.08	19.67	13	0	98	0	2	61	119.0	-20.2	19	20	1,000	0	0.0	0.0
C+ / 6.1	11.9	1.08	19.73	301	0	98	0	2	61	119.6	-20.2	20	20	1,000	0	0.0	0.0
C+ / 6.0	11.9	1.08	20.26	7,806	0	98	0	2	61	132.5	-19.7	29	20	250,000	0	0.0	0.0
C+ / 6.0	11.9	1.08	20.29	1,258	0	98	0	2	61	133.9	-19.7	31	20	0	0	0.0	0.0
C+ / 6.1	11.9	1.08	20.24	27	0	98	0	2	61	123.6	-20.0	22	20	0	0	0.0	0.0
C+ / 6.1	11.9	1.08	20.25	140	0	98	0	2	61	127.1	-19.9	25	20	0	0	0.0	0.0
C+ / 6.1	11.9	1.09	20.24	23	0	98	0	2	61	124.9	-20.0	23	20	0	0	0.0	0.0
C+ / 6.0	11.9	1.09	20.27	291	0	98	0	2	61	130.1	-19.9	28	20	0	0	0.0	0.0
C+ / 6.0	11.9	1.08	20.29	202	0	98	0	2	61	133.2	-19.8	30	20	0	0	0.0	0.0
C+ / 6.0	11.9	1.08	20.28	3,060	0	98	0	2	61	133.5	-19.7	30	20	1,000,000	0	0.0	0.0
C+ / 6.1	11.9	1.08	20.86	1,543	0	98	0	2	61	128.9	-19.9	27	20	1,000	0	5.0	0.0
B- / 7.3	4.8	0.42	10.21	31	5	43	50	2	55	30.3	N/A	36	6	1,000	0	5.0	0.0
B- / 7.2	4.8	0.43	10.23	10	5	43	50	2	55	32.8	N/A	40	6	250,000	0	0.0	0.0
C+ / 5.7	12.3	0.97	21.74	2,133	0	98	1	1	47	159.5	-21.4	83	7	1,000	0	5.0	0.0
C+ / 5.7	12.3	0.97	21.70	2	0	98	1	1	47	159.1	-21.4	82	7	0	0	0.0	0.0
C+ / 5.7	12.3	0.97	21.92	330	0	98	1	1	47	148.9	-21.6	78	7	1,000	0	0.0	0.0
C+ / 5.7	12.3	0.97	22.53	9,574	0	98	1	1	47	163.5	-21.3	84	7	250,000	0	0.0	0.0
C+ / 5.7	12.3	0.97	22.46	226	0	98	1	1	47	N/A	N/A	82	7	0	0	0.0	0.0
C+ / 5.7	12.3	0.98	22.51	96	0	98	1	1	47	N/A	N/A	83	7	0	0	0.0	0.0
C+ / 5.7	12.3	0.97	22.52	1,764	0	98	1	1	47	164.6	-21.4	85	7	1,000,000	0	0.0	0.0
C / 4.7	15.3	0.94	9.95	274	1	98	0	1	6	21.2	-31.0	73	7	1,000	0	5.0	0.0
C / 4.7	15.3	0.93	9.93	53	1	98	0	1	6	23.6	-30.9	75	7	250,000	0	0.0	0.0
C / 4.7	15.3	0.93	9.93	805	1	98	0	1	6	24.6	-30.9	76	7	0	0	0.0	0.0
C / 4.7	15.3	0.94	9.92	N/A	1	98	0	1	6	24.1	-31.1	76	7	1,000,000	0	0.0	0.0
C / 5.0	11.0	1.01	19.88	271	3	96	0	1	40	110.3	-18.2	33	2	0	0	0.0	0.0

Fund Type	Fund Name	Ticker Symbol	Overall Investment Rating	Phone	Performance Rating/Pts	3 Mo	6 Mo	1Yr / Pct	3Yr / Pct	5Yr / Pct	Dividend Yield	Expense Ratio
IN	J Hancock Eqty-Inc A	JHEIX	U	(800) 257-3336	U /	5.20	11.19	28.38 /82	--	--	1.95	1.20
IN	J Hancock Eqty-Inc NAV		B	(800) 257-3336	B /8.2	5.24	11.39	28.86 /84	7.43 /75	11.64 /71	2.37	0.77
GI	J Hancock Fdm All Cap Core A	JFCAX	B	(800) 257-3336	B+/8.4	8.16	10.52	31.42 /89	8.49 /83	14.51 /96	0.13	1.28
GI	J Hancock Fdm All Cap Core I	JFCIX	B+	(800) 257-3336	A /9.3	8.24	10.65	31.85 /90	8.84 /86	14.91 /97	0.39	0.97
GR	J Hancock Fdm All Cap Core NAV		U	(800) 257-3336	U /	8.22	10.62	31.88 /90	--	--	0.49	0.85
GR	J Hancock Fdm Large Cap Val NAV		B+	(800) 257-3336	B+/8.6	6.93	10.58	29.59 /85	7.79 /77	13.30 /87	2.40	0.68
GR	J Hancock Fdm Large Cap Value A	JFVAX	B-	(800) 257-3336	B- /7.3	6.78	10.37	28.99 /84	7.28 /74	12.70 /81	1.93	1.11
GR	J Hancock Fdm Large Cap Value I	JFVIX	B+	(800) 257-3336	B+/8.5	6.89	10.63	29.53 /85	7.61 /76	13.09 /85	2.30	0.79
FS	J Hancock Financial Indust A	FIDAX	A	(800) 257-3336	A+/9.8	10.19	25.53	45.73 /99	8.53 /83	15.92 /98	0.67	1.42
FS	● J Hancock Financial Indust B	FIDBX	A	(800) 257-3336	A+/9.8	9.99	25.05	44.67 /98	7.73 /77	15.07 /97	0.19	2.12
FS	J Hancock Financial Indust C	FIDCX	A	(800) 257-3336	A+/9.8	9.98	25.08	44.67 /98	7.76 /77	15.08 /97	0.19	2.12
GR	J Hancock Fndmntl Glbl Fran A	JFGAX	C	(800) 257-3336	C /5.5	7.75	0.79	16.23 /35	8.36 /82	--	0.27	1.30
GR	J Hancock Fndmntl Glbl Fran I	JFGIX	C+	(800) 257-3336	C+/6.8	7.82	0.96	16.64 /37	8.73 /85	--	0.57	0.99
GR	J Hancock Fndmntl Glbl Fran NAV		C+	(800) 257-3336	C+/6.9	7.94	1.08	16.86 /38	8.86 /86	--	0.67	0.88
GR	J Hancock Fundamental Lg Cap Cre	TAGRX	A	(800) 257-3336	A- /9.1	8.34	10.88	30.93 /88	10.10 /94	14.18 /94	0.38	1.05
GR	● J Hancock Fundamental Lg Cap Cre	TSGWX	A	(800) 257-3336	A /9.3	8.17	10.47	29.96 /86	9.28 /89	13.33 /87	0.00	1.80
GR	J Hancock Fundamental Lg Cap Cre	JHLVX	A	(800) 257-3336	A /9.3	8.17	10.47	29.97 /86	9.28 /89	13.34 /87	0.00	1.80
GR	J Hancock Fundamental Lg Cap Cre I	JLVIX	A+	(800) 257-3336	A+/9.7	8.46	11.04	31.30 /89	10.41 /95	14.51 /96	0.60	0.79
GR	J Hancock Fundamental Lg Cap Cre	JLCRX	A+	(800) 257-3336	A /9.5	8.24	10.67	30.41 /87	9.67 /91	13.77 /91	0.07	1.44
GR	J Hancock Fundamental Lg Cap Cre	JLCYX	A+	(800) 257-3336	A+/9.6	8.34	10.81	30.75 /88	9.95 /93	14.12 /94	0.27	1.19
GR	J Hancock Fundamental Lg Cap Cre	JLCHX	A+	(800) 257-3336	A /9.5	8.29	10.73	30.57 /87	9.79 /92	13.88 /92	0.15	1.34
GR	J Hancock Fundamental Lg Cap Cre	JLCFX	A+	(800) 257-3336	A+/9.6	8.38	10.94	31.07 /88	10.22 /94	14.32 /95	0.47	1.04
GR	J Hancock Fundamental Lg Cap Cre	JLCVX	A+	(800) 257-3336	A+/9.7	8.44	11.06	31.33 /89	10.44 /96	14.56 /96	0.63	0.74
GR	J Hancock Fundamental Lg Cap Cre	JLCWX	A+	(800) 257-3336	A+/9.7	8.47	11.10	31.43 /89	10.52 /96	14.63 /96	0.68	0.70
RE	J Hancock Glb Real Est Nav		C	(800) 257-3336	C- /4.0	6.50	-3.45	10.70 /13	6.40 /67	8.60 /47	4.86	1.00
GL	J Hancock Glb Shrhldr Yld A	JGYAX	D	(800) 257-3336	D+/2.4	7.39	2.87	12.21 /19	3.20 /34	7.64 /39	2.64	1.29
GL	● J Hancock Glb Shrhldr Yld B	JGYBX	D+	(800) 257-3336	D+/2.6	7.20	2.50	11.42 /16	2.42 /27	6.84 /34	2.10	1.99
GL	J Hancock Glb Shrhldr Yld C	JGYCX	D+	(800) 257-3336	D+/2.7	7.20	2.50	11.41 /16	2.50 /28	6.89 /34	2.10	1.99
GL	J Hancock Glb Shrhldr Yld I	JGYIX	D+	(800) 257-3336	C- /3.4	7.45	3.02	12.51 /20	3.52 /37	7.99 /42	3.07	1.99
GL	J Hancock Glb Shrhldr Yld NAV		C-	(800) 257-3336	C- /3.5	7.48	3.08	12.76 /21	3.65 /39	8.13 /43	3.18	0.86
GL	J Hancock Glb Shrhldr Yld R2	JGSRX	D+	(800) 257-3336	C- /3.1	7.34	2.81	12.04 /18	3.05 /32	7.53 /38	2.66	1.38
GL	J Hancock Glb Shrhldr Yld R6	JGRSX	C-	(800) 257-3336	C- /3.5	7.49	3.08	12.66 /20	3.65 /39	8.08 /43	3.18	0.88
GL	J Hancock Glbl Abs Rtn Strat A	JHAAX	D+	(800) 257-3336	E /0.5	2.22	1.50	0.40 / 1	0.67 /16	1.64 / 7	0.00	1.64
GL	J Hancock Glbl Abs Rtn Strat C	JHACX	D+	(800) 257-3336	E+/0.6	2.03	1.11	-0.30 / 1	-0.04 /13	--	0.00	2.34
GL	J Hancock Glbl Abs Rtn Strat I	JHAIX	D+	(800) 257-3336	E+/0.9	2.31	1.60	0.79 / 2	0.98 /18	2.01 / 8	0.00	1.32
GL	J Hancock Glbl Abs Rtn Strat NAV		D+	(800) 257-3336	D- /1.0	2.41	1.70	0.89 / 2	1.12 /19	2.11 / 8	0.00	1.21
GL	J Hancock Glbl Abs Rtn Strat R2	JHARX	D+	(800) 257-3336	E+/0.8	2.22	1.40	0.30 / 1	0.45 /16	--	0.00	1.73
GL	J Hancock Glbl Abs Rtn Strat R6	JHASX	D+	(800) 257-3336	D- /1.0	2.41	1.69	0.89 / 2	1.13 /19	--	0.00	1.23
FO	J Hancock Greater China Opp A	JCOAX	E	(800) 257-3336	D /1.9	3.42	1.13	23.61 /69	0.61 /16	5.37 /24	1.13	1.76
FO	● J Hancock Greater China Opp B	JCOBX	E	(800) 257-3336	D /1.6	3.21	0.84	22.75 /66	-0.13 /13	4.53 /18	0.57	2.46
FO	J Hancock Greater China Opp C	JCOCX	E	(800) 257-3336	D /1.6	3.27	0.84	22.82 /66	-0.13 /13	4.54 /18	0.57	2.46
FO	J Hancock Greater China Opp I	JCOIX	E+	(800) 257-3336	D+/2.8	3.54	1.36	24.10 /70	1.01 /18	5.82 /27	1.55	1.45
FO	J Hancock Greater China Opp NAV		E+	(800) 257-3336	D+/2.9	3.48	1.38	24.14 /70	1.06 /19	5.86 /27	1.57	1.34
IN	J Hancock Health Sciences NAV		D+	(800) 257-3336	B /8.2	10.04	8.07	16.63 /37	9.77 /92	21.05 /99	0.00	1.10
FO	J Hancock Int Small Comp A	JISAX	D+	(800) 257-3336	D+/2.5	8.28	6.08	19.47 /49	1.13 /19	--	1.81	1.48
FO	J Hancock Int Small Comp I	JSCIX	C-	(800) 257-3336	C- /3.5	8.20	6.11	19.64 /50	1.47 /21	--	2.11	1.17
FO	J Hancock Int Small Comp NAV		C-	(800) 257-3336	C- /3.7	8.33	6.24	19.78 /51	1.59 /21	7.72 /40	2.22	1.05
FO	J Hancock Internatl Val Eq A	JIEAX	E+	(800) 257-3336	E+/0.9	6.99	5.99	16.92 /38	-0.81 /10	3.51 /13	1.51	1.35
FO	J Hancock Internatl Val Eq I	JIEEX	D-	(800) 257-3336	D- /1.4	6.98	5.98	17.22 /39	-0.58 /11	3.78 /14	1.84	1.08
FO	J Hancock Internatl Val Eq NAV		D-	(800) 257-3336	D- /1.5	6.95	6.10	17.35 /40	-0.41 /12	4.00 /15	1.95	0.97
FO	J Hancock Internatl Val Eq R2	JIVSX	E+	(800) 257-3336	D- /1.3	6.74	5.75	16.60 /37	-1.01 / 9	--	1.51	1.49
FO	J Hancock Internatl Val Eq R4	JIVTX	D-	(800) 257-3336	D- /1.4	6.91	6.06	17.13 /39	-0.67 /11	--	1.78	1.34

● Denotes fund is closed to new investors
∗ Denotes fund is included in Section II

344

RISK Rating/Pts	3 Year Standard Deviation	Beta	NAV As of 2/28/17	Total $(Mil)	Cash %	Stocks %	Bonds %	Other %	Portfolio Turnover Ratio	Last Bull Market Return	Last Bear Market Return	Manager Quality Pct	Manager Tenure (Years)	Initial Purch. $	Additional Purch. $	Front End Load	Back End Load
U /	N/A	N/A	19.87	34	3	96	0	1	40	N/A	N/A	N/A	2	1,000	0	5.0	0.0
C /5.0	11.0	1.01	19.86	1,416	3	96	0	1	40	110.9	-18.2	34	2	0	0	0.0	0.0
C /5.2	14.5	1.29	16.72	31	8	91	0	1	40	138.9	N/A	17	6	1,000	0	5.0	0.0
C /5.2	14.5	1.29	16.86	11	8	91	0	1	40	143.8	N/A	19	6	250,000	0	0.0	0.0
U /	N/A	N/A	16.86	113	8	91	0	1	40	N/A	N/A	N/A	6	0	0	0.0	0.0
C /5.4	13.4	1.21	14.10	730	3	96	0	1	21	136.3	N/A	17	6	0	0	0.0	0.0
C /5.5	13.4	1.21	14.05	19	3	96	0	1	21	129.8	N/A	14	6	1,000	0	5.0	0.0
C /5.4	13.4	1.21	14.12	4	3	96	0	1	21	134.1	N/A	16	6	250,000	0	0.0	0.0
C /5.5	16.3	1.19	19.92	348	4	92	3	1	38	171.8	-28.9	10	19	1,000	0	5.0	0.0
C /5.5	16.3	1.19	18.22	6	4	92	3	1	38	161.2	-29.2	7	19	1,000	0	0.0	0.0
C /5.5	16.3	1.19	18.25	50	4	92	3	1	38	161.6	-29.2	7	19	1,000	0	0.0	0.0
C /5.2	11.4	0.91	12.50	N/A	0	92	7	1	38	N/A	N/A	59	5	1,000	0	5.0	0.0
C /5.2	11.4	0.91	12.54	2	0	92	7	1	38	N/A	N/A	64	5	250,000	0	0.0	0.0
C /5.1	11.4	0.91	12.55	572	0	92	7	1	38	N/A	N/A	65	5	0	0	0.0	0.0
C+/6.2	13.0	1.18	46.78	1,534	4	94	1	1	20	134.4	-23.4	44	6	1,000	0	5.0	0.0
C+/6.2	13.0	1.18	42.23	40	4	94	1	1	20	125.2	-23.6	34	6	1,000	0	0.0	0.0
C+/6.2	13.0	1.18	42.22	309	4	94	1	1	20	125.1	-23.6	34	6	1,000	0	0.0	0.0
C+/6.2	13.0	1.18	48.68	1,491	4	94	1	1	20	138.2	-23.3	48	6	250,000	0	0.0	0.0
C+/6.2	13.0	1.18	48.07	9	4	94	1	1	20	129.9	-23.5	38	6	0	0	0.0	0.0
C+/6.2	13.0	1.18	48.55	3	4	94	1	1	20	133.8	-23.4	42	6	0	0	0.0	0.0
C+/6.2	13.0	1.18	48.18	3	4	94	1	1	20	131.1	-23.5	40	6	0	0	0.0	0.0
C+/6.2	13.0	1.18	48.46	3	4	94	1	1	20	135.9	-23.4	46	6	0	0	0.0	0.0
C+/6.2	13.0	1.18	48.74	1	4	94	1	1	20	138.7	-23.3	49	6	0	0	0.0	0.0
C+/6.2	13.0	1.18	48.74	15	4	94	1	1	20	139.5	-23.4	49	6	1,000,000	0	0.0	0.0
C+/6.6	12.0	0.84	9.34	218	9	90	0	1	118	80.6	-20.5	38	11	0	0	0.0	0.0
C+/5.9	9.4	0.61	10.78	382	6	93	0	1	33	63.3	-12.3	91	10	1,000	0	5.0	0.0
C+/5.9	9.4	0.61	10.78	11	6	93	0	1	33	57.0	-12.6	88	10	1,000	0	0.0	0.0
C+/5.9	9.4	0.61	10.79	126	6	93	0	1	33	57.2	-12.5	88	10	1,000	0	0.0	0.0
C+/5.9	9.4	0.61	10.82	1,243	6	93	0	1	33	66.3	-12.0	92	10	250,000	0	0.0	0.0
C+/5.9	9.4	0.61	10.82	536	6	93	0	1	33	67.4	-12.0	92	10	0	0	0.0	0.0
C+/5.9	9.3	0.61	10.82	1	6	93	0	1	33	62.5	-12.3	91	10	0	0	0.0	0.0
C+/5.9	9.3	0.61	10.81	2	6	93	0	1	33	67.0	-12.2	92	10	1,000,000	0	0.0	0.0
B /8.1	3.8	0.16	10.14	321	20	31	47	2	80	N/A	N/A	78	6	1,000	0	5.0	0.0
B /8.2	3.8	0.16	10.06	211	20	31	47	2	80	N/A	N/A	73	6	1,000	0	0.0	0.0
B /8.1	3.8	0.15	10.19	3,902	20	31	47	2	80	N/A	N/A	80	6	250,000	0	0.0	0.0
B /8.0	3.8	0.15	10.19	1,087	20	31	47	2	80	N/A	N/A	81	6	0	0	0.0	0.0
B /8.1	3.8	0.16	10.11	3	20	31	47	2	80	N/A	N/A	77	6	0	0	0.0	0.0
B /8.0	3.8	0.16	10.20	626	20	31	47	2	80	N/A	N/A	81	6	1,000,000	0	0.0	0.0
C- /3.1	18.3	0.93	19.00	27	1	98	0	1	55	56.1	-29.9	79	6	1,000	0	5.0	0.0
C- /3.1	18.3	0.93	18.30	1	1	98	0	1	55	49.5	-30.1	74	6	1,000	0	0.0	0.0
C- /3.1	18.3	0.93	18.31	6	1	98	0	1	55	49.6	-30.1	74	6	1,000	0	0.0	0.0
C- /3.1	18.3	0.93	18.93	5	1	98	0	1	55	59.6	-29.8	82	6	250,000	0	0.0	0.0
C- /3.1	18.3	0.93	19.19	13	1	98	0	1	55	60.2	-29.7	82	6	0	0	0.0	0.0
E+/0.7	17.5	1.10	4.57	219	4	95	0	1	46	215.1	N/A	52	6	0	0	0.0	0.0
C+/6.3	11.8	0.88	10.76	17	0	99	0	1	12	N/A	N/A	83	11	1,000	0	5.0	0.0
C+/6.3	11.8	0.88	10.74	31	0	99	0	1	12	N/A	N/A	84	11	250,000	0	0.0	0.0
C+/6.3	11.8	0.89	10.74	527	0	99	0	1	12	66.5	-23.6	85	11	0	0	0.0	0.0
C /4.8	11.0	0.88	7.81	18	1	98	0	1	18	37.6	-23.5	66	19	1,000	0	5.0	0.0
C /4.8	10.9	0.87	7.81	4	1	98	0	1	18	39.7	-23.4	69	19	250,000	0	0.0	0.0
C /4.8	11.0	0.87	7.81	595	1	98	0	1	18	41.1	-23.5	71	19	0	0	0.0	0.0
C /4.9	11.0	0.88	7.83	1	1	98	0	1	18	N/A	N/A	64	19	0	0	0.0	0.0
C /4.8	11.0	0.88	7.82	N/A	1	98	0	1	18	N/A	N/A	68	19	0	0	0.0	0.0

Fund Type	Fund Name	Ticker Symbol	Overall Investment Rating	Phone	Perfor-mance Rating/Pts	3 Mo	6 Mo	1Yr / Pct	3Yr / Pct	5Yr / Pct	Dividend Yield	Expense Ratio
	99 Pct = Best *0 Pct = Worst*							Total Return % through 2/28/17 (Annualized)			Incl. in Returns	
FO	J Hancock Internatl Val Eq R6	JIVUX	D-	(800) 257-3336	D- / 1.5	6.96	6.11	17.20 /39	-0.41 /12	--	1.95	0.99
FO	J Hancock Intl Gro Stock NAV		D	(800) 257-3336	D / 1.6	6.90	0.85	9.12 /10	0.34 /15	4.99 /21	1.42	0.86
FO	J Hancock Intl Gwth 1	GOIOX	D-	(800) 257-3336	D+ / 2.3	5.84	-0.36	10.04 /12	2.69 /29	8.50 /46	0.95	0.99
FO	J Hancock Intl Gwth A	GOIGX	E+	(800) 257-3336	D- / 1.5	5.74	-0.52	9.62 /11	2.27 /26	8.06 /43	0.55	1.37
FO	● J Hancock Intl Gwth B	GONBX	D-	(800) 257-3336	D / 1.7	5.51	-0.88	8.88 / 9	1.50 /21	7.26 /36	0.00	2.07
FO	J Hancock Intl Gwth C	GONCX	D-	(800) 257-3336	D / 1.7	5.52	-0.88	8.85 / 9	1.53 /21	7.27 /36	0.00	2.07
FO	J Hancock Intl Gwth I	GOGIX	D-	(800) 257-3336	D / 2.2	5.82	-0.38	9.96 /12	2.61 /28	8.42 /46	0.88	1.05
FO	J Hancock Intl Gwth NAV	JIGHX	U	(800) 257-3336	U /	5.85	-0.31	10.10 /12	--	--	1.00	0.94
FO	J Hancock Intl Gwth R6	JIGTX	U	(800) 257-3336	U /	5.83	-0.32	10.08 /12	--	--	0.99	0.96
FO	J Hancock Intl Small Cap 1	JIIMX	D	(800) 257-3336	D- / 1.1	9.03	3.19	12.79 /21	-0.99 / 9	5.10 /22	1.53	1.08
FO	J Hancock Intl Small Cap NAV		D	(800) 257-3336	D- / 1.1	9.02	3.18	12.78 /21	-0.94 /10	5.15 /22	1.58	1.03
FO	J Hancock Intl Value 1	JIVIX	D-	(800) 257-3336	D / 1.7	7.67	8.33	28.26 /82	-1.80 / 7	4.85 /20	2.27	0.90
FO	J Hancock Intl Value NAV	JHVIX	D-	(800) 257-3336	D / 1.7	7.68	8.33	28.23 /82	-1.76 / 7	4.88 /21	2.32	0.85
GR	J Hancock MI Lifestyle Agg 1	JIIOX	B+	(800) 257-3336	B- / 7.2	7.33	8.31	23.82 /69	6.68 /70	--	1.56	0.75
GR	J Hancock MI Lifestyle Agg R6	JIIRX	B+	(800) 257-3336	B- / 7.2	7.36	8.34	23.85 /69	6.69 /70	--	1.59	0.72
BA	J Hancock MI Lifestyle Bal 1	JIBOX	B-	(800) 257-3336	C / 4.7	5.29	4.68	16.42 /36	5.09 /55	--	2.14	0.75
BA	J Hancock MI Lifestyle Bal R6	JIBRX	B-	(800) 257-3336	C / 4.7	5.20	4.70	16.34 /36	5.10 /55	--	2.18	0.71
AA	J Hancock MI Lifestyle Consv 1	JLCGX	C	(800) 257-3336	D / 2.2	2.90	0.72	8.71 / 9	3.35 /35	--	2.40	0.88
AA	J Hancock MI Lifestyle Consv R6	JLCSX	C	(800) 257-3336	D / 2.2	2.90	0.73	8.74 / 9	3.35 /35	--	2.43	0.85
GR	J Hancock MI Lifestyle Growth 1	JLGOX	B-	(800) 257-3336	C+ / 6.1	6.30	6.40	19.97 /52	5.94 /64	--	1.71	0.73
GR	J Hancock MI Lifestyle Growth R6	JLGSX	B-	(800) 257-3336	C+ / 6.1	6.34	6.43	20.00 /52	5.97 /64	--	1.75	0.69
BA	J Hancock MI Lifestyle Mod 1	JLMOX	C+	(800) 257-3336	C- / 3.3	4.04	2.56	12.41 /19	4.12 /44	--	2.30	0.84
BA	J Hancock MI Lifestyle Mod R6	JLMRX	C+	(800) 257-3336	C- / 3.3	4.15	2.67	12.56 /20	4.20 /45	--	2.34	0.80
MC	J Hancock Mid Cap Stock 1	JIMSX	D-	(800) 257-3336	C / 4.3	4.53	3.48	21.82 /61	3.69 /39	10.87 /65	0.00	0.92
MC	J Hancock Mid Cap Stock NAV		D-	(800) 257-3336	C / 4.4	4.55	3.56	21.90 /62	3.75 /40	10.92 /65	0.00	0.87
MC	J Hancock Mid Value Fund NAV		B+	(800) 257-3336	A / 9.5	4.75	10.69	31.47 /89	10.25 /95	14.39 /95	0.84	0.99
AG	J Hancock MM Lifestyle Agg 1	JILAX	C+	(800) 257-3336	C+ / 5.8	6.84	7.52	22.54 /65	4.64 /50	9.16 /52	1.17	1.03
AG	J Hancock MM Lifestyle Agg A	JALAX	C-	(800) 257-3336	C / 4.5	6.70	7.38	22.09 /63	4.27 /46	8.72 /48	0.79	1.41
AG	J Hancock MM Lifestyle Agg B	JBLAX	C	(800) 257-3336	C / 4.9	6.54	6.95	21.27 /59	3.50 /37	7.90 /41	0.15	2.11
AG	J Hancock MM Lifestyle Agg C	JCLAX	C	(800) 257-3336	C / 4.9	6.54	6.95	21.26 /59	3.51 /37	7.94 /42	0.15	2.11
AG	J Hancock MM Lifestyle Agg R1	JPLAX	C	(800) 257-3336	C / 5.1	6.61	7.15	21.65 /60	3.84 /41	8.27 /44	0.51	1.75
GR	J Hancock MM Lifestyle Agg R2	JQLAX	C	(800) 257-3336	C / 5.4	6.63	7.25	21.93 /62	4.13 /44	8.61 /47	0.74	1.50
AG	J Hancock MM Lifestyle Agg R3	JRLAX	C	(800) 257-3336	C / 5.2	6.65	7.20	21.84 /61	3.93 /42	8.38 /45	0.59	1.65
AG	J Hancock MM Lifestyle Agg R4	JSLAX	C	(800) 257-3336	C+ / 5.6	6.74	7.43	22.27 /63	4.32 /47	8.78 /49	0.97	1.35
AG	J Hancock MM Lifestyle Agg R5	JTLAX	C	(800) 257-3336	C+ / 5.8	6.81	7.56	22.55 /65	4.58 /50	9.04 /51	1.15	1.05
GR	J Hancock MM Lifestyle Agg R6	JULAX	C+	(800) 257-3336	C+ / 5.9	6.89	7.64	22.66 /65	4.72 /51	9.22 /52	1.22	1.00
BA	J Hancock MM Lifestyle Bal 1	JILBX	C	(800) 257-3336	C- / 4.1	5.08	4.96	16.62 /37	3.97 /43	7.16 /36	2.03	0.97
BA	J Hancock MM Lifestyle Bal 5	JHLAX	C+	(800) 257-3336	C- / 4.1	5.09	4.98	16.75 /37	4.02 /43	7.22 /36	2.07	0.92
BA	J Hancock MM Lifestyle Bal A	JALBX	C-	(800) 257-3336	D+ / 2.9	4.95	4.74	16.19 /35	3.59 /38	6.75 /33	1.60	1.34
BA	● J Hancock MM Lifestyle Bal B	JBLBX	C	(800) 257-3336	C- / 3.2	4.77	4.44	15.40 /32	2.84 /30	5.98 /28	1.01	2.04
BA	J Hancock MM Lifestyle Bal C	JCLBX	C	(800) 257-3336	C- / 3.2	4.77	4.37	15.39 /32	2.85 /30	5.99 /28	1.02	2.04
BA	J Hancock MM Lifestyle Bal R1	JPLBX	C	(800) 257-3336	C- / 3.5	4.89	4.58	15.79 /33	3.19 /34	6.36 /31	1.36	1.69
BA	J Hancock MM Lifestyle Bal R2	JQLBX	C	(800) 257-3336	C- / 3.7	4.95	4.71	16.08 /35	3.46 /37	6.63 /32	1.59	1.44
BA	J Hancock MM Lifestyle Bal R3	JRLBX	C	(800) 257-3336	C- / 3.6	4.90	4.62	15.95 /34	3.32 /35	6.48 /31	1.45	1.59
BA	J Hancock MM Lifestyle Bal R4	JSLBX	C	(800) 257-3336	C- / 3.9	5.00	4.82	16.39 /36	3.71 /39	6.91 /34	1.82	1.29
BA	J Hancock MM Lifestyle Bal R5	JTSBX	C	(800) 257-3336	C- / 4.0	5.05	4.92	16.59 /37	3.93 /42	7.12 /35	2.00	0.99
BA	J Hancock MM Lifestyle Bal R6	JULBX	C+	(800) 257-3336	C- / 4.1	5.09	4.99	16.67 /37	4.02 /43	7.20 /36	2.07	0.94
AA	J Hancock MM Lifestyle Cons 1	JILCX	C-	(800) 257-3336	D / 2.1	2.96	1.38	9.12 /10	2.78 /30	4.29 /17	2.69	0.89
AA	J Hancock MM Lifestyle Cons A	JALRX	D+	(800) 257-3336	D- / 1.4	2.86	1.19	8.71 / 9	2.40 /27	3.91 /15	2.22	1.27
AA	● J Hancock MM Lifestyle Cons B	JBLCX	C-	(800) 257-3336	D / 1.6	2.75	0.91	8.03 / 7	1.67 /22	3.15 /11	1.63	1.97
AA	J Hancock MM Lifestyle Cons C	JCLCX	C-	(800) 257-3336	D / 1.6	2.67	0.83	7.95 / 7	1.67 /22	3.15 /11	1.63	1.97
AA	J Hancock MM Lifestyle Cons R1	JPLCX	C-	(800) 257-3336	D / 1.7	2.78	1.02	8.35 / 8	1.99 /24	3.47 /13	1.99	1.61

● Denotes fund is closed to new investors

* Denotes fund is included in Section II

www.thestreetratings.com

Risk Rating/Pts	3 Year Standard Deviation	Beta	NAV As of 2/28/17	Total $(Mil)	Cash %	Stocks %	Bonds %	Other %	Portfolio Turnover Ratio	Last Bull Market Return	Last Bear Market Return	Manager Quality Pct	Manager Tenure (Years)	Initial Purch. $	Additional Purch. $	Front End Load	Back End Load
C /4.8	11.0	0.88	7.80	1	1	98	0	1	18	N/A	N/A	71	19	1,000,000	0	0.0	0.0
C+ /6.0	11.0	0.85	12.45	893	6	93	0	1	23	48.6	-20.1	77	7	0	0	0.0	0.0
C /4.5	10.8	0.73	21.71	50	2	98	0	0	82	72.3	-20.4	89	3	0	0	0.0	0.0
C /4.5	10.8	0.74	21.69	426	2	98	0	0	82	68.5	-20.6	88	3	1,000	0	5.0	0.0
C /4.6	10.8	0.73	21.45	2	2	98	0	0	82	61.8	-20.8	84	3	1,000	0	0.0	0.0
C /4.6	10.8	0.73	21.40	145	2	98	0	0	82	61.9	-20.8	84	3	1,000	0	0.0	0.0
C /4.5	10.8	0.73	21.72	2,373	2	98	0	0	82	71.5	-20.4	89	3	250,000	0	0.0	0.0
U /	N/A	N/A	21.71	316	2	98	0	0	82	N/A	N/A	N/A	3	0	0	0.0	0.0
U /	N/A	N/A	21.73	42	2	98	0	0	82	N/A	N/A	N/A	3	1,000,000	0	0.0	0.0
C+ /6.3	11.8	0.88	18.01	71	2	94	2	2	42	49.2	-24.6	64	6	0	0	0.0	0.0
C+ /6.3	11.8	0.88	18.00	530	2	94	2	2	42	49.6	-24.6	65	6	0	0	0.0	0.0
C /4.6	13.8	1.02	15.66	194	1	96	2	1	24	47.1	-24.1	54	12	0	0	0.0	0.0
C /4.6	13.8	1.03	15.61	1,301	1	96	2	1	24	47.5	-24.1	54	12	0	0	0.0	0.0
C+ /6.9	10.3	0.98	11.49	161	3	96	0	1	14	N/A	N/A	29	4	0	0	0.0	0.0
C+ /6.9	10.3	0.98	11.49	N/A	3	96	0	1	14	N/A	N/A	30	4	1,000,000	0	0.0	0.0
B- /7.9	7.0	1.09	11.00	497	1	59	38	2	11	N/A	N/A	35	7	0	0	0.0	0.0
B- /7.8	6.9	1.09	11.00	N/A	1	59	38	2	11	N/A	N/A	36	7	1,000,000	0	0.0	0.0
B /8.8	4.0	0.53	10.49	88	1	21	76	2	21	N/A	N/A	67	4	0	0	0.0	0.0
B /8.8	4.1	0.53	10.49	N/A	1	21	76	2	21	N/A	N/A	67	4	1,000,000	0	0.0	0.0
B- /7.8	8.6	0.81	11.33	407	3	78	17	2	11	N/A	N/A	42	4	0	0	0.0	0.0
B- /7.8	8.6	0.81	11.34	1	3	78	17	2	11	N/A	N/A	42	4	1,000,000	0	0.0	0.0
B /8.9	5.3	0.80	10.71	130	1	39	58	2	15	N/A	N/A	52	4	0	0	0.0	0.0
B /8.9	5.3	0.80	10.72	1	1	39	58	2	15	N/A	N/A	53	4	1,000,000	0	0.0	0.0
D+ /2.5	14.4	1.02	19.43	322	0	97	1	2	79	105.3	-24.4	10	12	0	0	0.0	0.0
D+ /2.5	14.4	1.02	19.59	1,215	0	97	1	2	79	105.9	-24.4	10	12	0	0	0.0	0.0
C /4.3	10.9	0.86	15.98	863	7	92	0	1	56	133.0	-19.6	85	8	0	0	0.0	0.0
C+ /5.6	10.5	0.97	15.46	3,478	6	90	2	2	15	86.8	-20.9	13	N/A	0	0	0.0	0.0
C+ /5.6	10.5	0.96	15.52	437	6	90	2	2	15	82.8	-21.0	11	N/A	1,000	0	5.0	0.0
C+ /5.7	10.6	0.97	15.54	12	6	90	2	2	15	75.5	-21.3	7	N/A	1,000	0	0.0	0.0
C+ /5.7	10.6	0.97	15.55	158	6	90	2	2	15	75.8	-21.3	7	N/A	1,000	0	0.0	0.0
C+ /5.7	10.5	0.96	15.54	7	6	90	2	2	15	78.7	-21.2	9	N/A	0	0	0.0	0.0
C+ /5.7	10.5	0.96	15.43	7	6	90	2	2	15	81.9	-21.0	11	12	0	0	0.0	0.0
C+ /5.7	10.5	0.97	15.48	5	6	90	2	2	15	79.6	-21.2	9	N/A	0	0	0.0	0.0
C+ /5.6	10.5	0.97	15.46	7	6	90	2	2	15	83.2	-21.1	11	N/A	0	0	0.0	0.0
C+ /5.6	10.5	0.97	15.49	7	6	90	2	2	15	85.8	-21.0	13	N/A	0	0	0.0	0.0
C+ /5.6	10.5	0.97	15.48	18	6	90	2	2	15	87.3	N/A	14	6	1,000,000	0	0.0	0.0
B- /7.3	7.1	1.09	14.79	10,188	5	54	39	2	13	62.0	-13.9	24	N/A	0	0	0.0	0.0
B- /7.3	7.2	1.09	14.80	155	5	54	39	2	13	62.4	-13.8	24	N/A	0	0	0.0	0.0
B- /7.3	7.1	1.08	14.87	1,799	5	54	39	2	13	58.5	-14.1	21	N/A	1,000	0	5.0	0.0
B- /7.3	7.1	1.08	14.85	58	5	54	39	2	13	52.4	-14.3	15	N/A	1,000	0	0.0	0.0
B- /7.3	7.2	1.09	14.86	789	5	54	39	2	13	52.5	-14.3	15	N/A	1,000	0	0.0	0.0
B- /7.3	7.1	1.08	14.80	17	5	54	39	2	13	55.5	-14.2	17	N/A	0	0	0.0	0.0
B- /7.3	7.2	1.09	14.79	13	5	54	39	2	13	57.6	-14.1	19	12	0	0	0.0	0.0
B- /7.3	7.2	1.09	14.83	22	5	54	39	2	13	56.4	-14.1	18	N/A	0	0	0.0	0.0
B- /7.3	7.2	1.09	14.84	21	5	54	39	2	13	59.7	-14.0	21	N/A	0	0	0.0	0.0
B- /7.3	7.1	1.08	14.87	17	5	54	39	2	13	61.6	-14.0	24	N/A	0	0	0.0	0.0
B- /7.3	7.2	1.09	14.80	43	5	54	39	2	13	62.2	-13.9	24	6	1,000,000	0	0.0	0.0
B- /7.8	3.7	0.51	12.84	2,129	3	18	77	2	10	33.4	-4.9	62	N/A	0	0	0.0	0.0
B- /7.8	3.7	0.50	12.86	609	3	18	77	2	10	30.6	-5.0	58	N/A	1,000	0	5.0	0.0
B- /7.8	3.7	0.51	12.86	22	3	18	77	2	10	25.6	-5.3	47	N/A	1,000	0	0.0	0.0
B- /7.8	3.7	0.51	12.85	303	3	18	77	2	10	25.6	-5.3	47	N/A	1,000	0	0.0	0.0
B- /7.8	3.7	0.51	12.85	8	3	18	77	2	10	27.6	-5.2	52	N/A	0	0	0.0	0.0

I. Index of Stock Mutual Funds

					PERFORMANCE						Incl. in Returns	
	99 Pct = Best 0 Pct = Worst		Overall		Perfor-	Total Return % through 2/28/17			Annualized		Dividend	Expense
Fund Type	Fund Name	Ticker Symbol	Investment Rating	Phone	mance Rating/Pts	3 Mo	6 Mo	1Yr / Pct	3Yr / Pct	5Yr / Pct	Yield	Ratio
AA	J Hancock MM Lifestyle Cons R2	JQLCX	C-	(800) 257-3336	D /1.9	2.84	1.15	8.62 / 9	2.28 /26	3.80 /14	2.24	1.36
AA	J Hancock MM Lifestyle Cons R3	JRLCX	C-	(800) 257-3336	D /1.8	2.82	1.11	8.59 / 9	2.12 /25	3.60 /13	2.13	1.51
AA	J Hancock MM Lifestyle Cons R4	JSLCX	C-	(800) 257-3336	D /2.0	2.90	1.27	8.89 / 9	2.49 /27	3.96 /15	2.48	1.21
AA	J Hancock MM Lifestyle Cons R5	JTLRX	C-	(800) 257-3336	D /2.1	2.95	1.37	9.10 /10	2.71 /29	4.21 /16	2.68	0.91
AA	J Hancock MM Lifestyle Cons R6	JULCX	C-	(800) 257-3336	D /2.1	2.97	1.41	9.18 /10	2.83 /30	4.34 /17	2.74	0.86
GR	J Hancock MM Lifestyle Gr 1	JILGX	C	(800) 257-3336	C /5.1	6.05	6.39	19.63 /50	4.39 /47	8.42 /46	1.62	1.00
GR	J Hancock MM Lifestyle Gr 5	JHLGX	C+	(800) 257-3336	C /5.1	6.04	6.38	19.72 /51	4.45 /48	8.47 /46	1.67	0.95
GR	J Hancock MM Lifestyle Gr A	JALGX	C-	(800) 257-3336	C- / 3.7	5.91	6.18	19.20 /48	4.02 /43	8.00 /42	1.21	1.37
GR ●	J Hancock MM Lifestyle Gr B	JBLGX	C	(800) 257-3336	C- / 4.1	5.75	5.82	18.39 /45	3.26 /34	7.22 /36	0.58	2.07
GR	J Hancock MM Lifestyle Gr C	JCLGX	C	(800) 257-3336	C- / 4.1	5.69	5.76	18.34 /44	3.26 /34	7.23 /36	0.58	2.07
GR	J Hancock MM Lifestyle Gr R1	JPLGX	C	(800) 257-3336	C /4.4	5.81	6.01	18.80 /46	3.62 /38	7.62 /39	0.94	1.72
GI	J Hancock MM Lifestyle Gr R2	JQLGX	C	(800) 257-3336	C /4.6	5.85	6.12	19.05 /47	3.88 /41	7.88 /41	1.19	1.47
GR	J Hancock MM Lifestyle Gr R3	JRLGX	C	(800) 257-3336	C /4.5	5.86	6.07	18.94 /47	3.72 /39	7.69 /40	1.03	1.62
GR	J Hancock MM Lifestyle Gr R4	JSLGX	C	(800) 257-3336	C /4.8	5.94	6.21	19.40 /49	4.13 /44	8.12 /43	1.41	1.32
GR	J Hancock MM Lifestyle Gr R5	JTLGX	C	(800) 257-3336	C /5.0	6.01	6.34	19.68 /50	4.36 /47	8.36 /45	1.60	1.02
GR	J Hancock MM Lifestyle Gr R6	JULGX	C	(800) 257-3336	C /5.1	5.96	6.37	19.70 /50	4.42 /48	8.46 /46	1.67	0.97
BA	J Hancock MM Lifestyle Mod 1	JILMX	C	(800) 257-3336	C- / 3.1	4.05	3.08	13.00 /22	3.45 /36	5.79 /27	2.48	0.91
BA	J Hancock MM Lifestyle Mod 5	JHLMX	C	(800) 257-3336	C- / 3.1	4.06	3.10	13.07 /22	3.53 /37	5.86 /27	2.53	0.86
BA	J Hancock MM Lifestyle Mod A	JALMX	C-	(800) 257-3336	D /2.1	3.94	2.88	12.56 /20	3.09 /33	5.39 /24	2.02	1.29
BA ●	J Hancock MM Lifestyle Mod B	JBLMX	C-	(800) 257-3336	D+ / 2.3	3.83	2.59	11.87 /17	2.34 /26	4.62 /19	1.44	1.99
BA	J Hancock MM Lifestyle Mod C	JCLMX	C-	(800) 257-3336	D+ / 2.3	3.75	2.51	11.77 /17	2.34 /26	4.63 /19	1.44	1.99
BA	J Hancock MM Lifestyle Mod R1	JPLMX	C-	(800) 257-3336	D+ / 2.5	3.86	2.72	12.23 /19	2.66 /29	4.95 /21	1.82	1.63
AA	J Hancock MM Lifestyle Mod R2	JQLMX	C-	(800) 257-3336	D+ / 2.7	3.93	2.84	12.49 /20	2.95 /31	5.27 /23	2.03	1.38
BA	J Hancock MM Lifestyle Mod R3	JRLMX	C-	(800) 257-3336	D+ / 2.6	3.88	2.75	12.31 /19	2.78 /30	5.06 /22	1.89	1.53
BA	J Hancock MM Lifestyle Mod R4	JSLMX	C	(800) 257-3336	D+ / 2.9	3.99	2.97	12.77 /21	3.17 /33	5.48 /25	2.27	1.23
BA	J Hancock MM Lifestyle Mod R5	JTLMX	C	(800) 257-3336	C- / 3.0	4.04	3.07	12.98 /22	3.40 /36	5.68 /26	2.46	0.93
AA	J Hancock MM Lifestyle Mod R6	JULMX	C	(800) 257-3336	C- / 3.1	4.07	3.11	13.08 /22	3.51 /37	5.83 /27	2.53	0.88
GI	J Hancock Multi-Index 2010 Lft 1	JRLDX	C+	(800) 257-3336	C- / 3.4	4.09	2.73	12.88 /21	4.30 /46	--	2.72	1.32
GI	J Hancock Multi-Index 2010 Lft R6	JRLHX	C+	(800) 257-3336	C- / 3.5	4.04	2.78	12.81 /21	4.35 /47	--	2.77	1.28
GI	J Hancock Multi-Index 2015 Lft 1	JRLIX	C-	(800) 257-3336	C- / 3.8	4.42	3.44	14.18 /26	4.53 /49	--	2.46	1.12
GI	J Hancock Multi-Index 2015 Lft R6	JRLLX	C	(800) 257-3336	C- / 4.0	4.57	3.59	14.35 /27	4.62 /50	--	2.51	1.09
GI	J Hancock Multi-Index 2020 Lft 1	JRLOX	B-	(800) 257-3336	C /4.7	5.08	4.59	16.42 /36	5.10 /55	--	2.31	0.87
GI	J Hancock Multi-Index 2020 Lft R6	JRTAX	B-	(800) 257-3336	C /4.7	5.04	4.55	16.36 /36	5.15 /56	--	2.36	0.84
AA	J Hancock Multi-Index 2020 Psv 1	JRWOX	C	(800) 257-3336	D /2.1	2.60	1.01	7.70 / 7	3.21 /34	4.58 /19	2.11	0.69
GI	J Hancock Multi-Index 2020 Psv R1	JRWQX	C	(800) 257-3336	D /1.8	2.51	0.76	7.23 / 6	2.64 /29	--	1.61	1.41
GI	J Hancock Multi-Index 2020 Psv R2	JRWRX	C	(800) 257-3336	D /1.9	2.56	0.88	7.28 / 6	2.76 /30	--	1.65	1.16
GI	J Hancock Multi-Index 2020 Psv R4	JRWPX	C	(800) 257-3336	D /2.0	2.64	0.97	7.64 / 7	3.04 /32	--	1.98	1.01
GI	J Hancock Multi-Index 2020 Psv R6	JRWSX	C	(800) 257-3336	D /2.1	2.65	1.06	7.75 / 7	3.26 /34	--	2.15	0.66
GI	J Hancock Multi-Index 2025 Lft 1	JRTBX	B	(800) 257-3336	C /5.5	5.70	5.70	18.42 /45	5.62 /61	--	2.18	0.81
GI	J Hancock Multi-Index 2025 Lft R6	JRTFX	B	(800) 257-3336	C /5.5	5.75	5.65	18.48 /45	5.64 /61	--	2.23	0.78
AA	J Hancock Multi-Index 2025 Psv 1	JREOX	C+	(800) 257-3336	C- / 3.3	4.04	3.00	12.06 /18	4.14 /44	6.16 /30	2.09	0.69
GI	J Hancock Multi-Index 2025 Psv R1	JREQX	C+	(800) 257-3336	D+ / 2.8	3.79	2.59	11.16 /15	3.42 /36	--	1.41	1.41
GI	J Hancock Multi-Index 2025 Psv R2	JRERX	C+	(800) 257-3336	C- / 3.0	3.90	2.86	11.62 /16	3.80 /40	--	1.81	1.16
GI	J Hancock Multi-Index 2025 Psv R4	JREPX	C+	(800) 257-3336	C- / 3.1	3.90	2.87	11.80 /17	3.98 /43	--	1.97	1.01
GI	J Hancock Multi-Index 2025 Psv R6	JRESX	C+	(800) 257-3336	C- / 3.3	3.93	2.97	12.03 /18	4.17 /45	--	2.14	0.66
GI	J Hancock Multi-Index 2030 Lft 1	JRTGX	B-	(800) 257-3336	C+ / 6.2	6.33	6.62	20.41 /54	5.98 /64	--	1.98	0.81
GI	J Hancock Multi-Index 2030 Lft R6	JRTJX	B-	(800) 257-3336	C+ / 6.2	6.29	6.68	20.47 /55	6.06 /65	--	2.03	0.78
AA	J Hancock Multi-Index 2030 Psv 1	JRHOX	B-	(800) 257-3336	C /4.6	5.18	4.79	16.17 /35	4.91 /53	7.34 /37	2.06	0.70
GI	J Hancock Multi-Index 2030 Psv R1	JRHQX	C+	(800) 257-3336	C- / 4.0	5.00	4.46	15.33 /31	4.21 /45	--	1.39	1.42
GI	J Hancock Multi-Index 2030 Psv R2	JRHRX	C+	(800) 257-3336	C- / 4.2	5.03	4.64	15.63 /33	4.46 /48	--	1.63	1.17
GI	J Hancock Multi-Index 2030 Psv R4	JRHPX	B-	(800) 257-3336	C /4.5	5.19	4.81	16.04 /34	4.79 /52	--	1.94	1.01
GI	J Hancock Multi-Index 2030 Psv R6	JRHSX	B-	(800) 257-3336	C /4.7	5.23	4.92	16.22 /35	4.99 /54	--	2.11	0.66

● Denotes fund is closed to new investors
* Denotes fund is included in Section II

Risk Rating/Pts	3 Year Standard Deviation	Beta	NAV As of 2/28/17	Total $(Mil)	Cash %	Stocks %	Bonds %	Other %	Portfolio Turnover Ratio	Last Bull Market Return	Last Bear Market Return	Manager Quality Pct	Manager Tenure (Years)	Initial Purch. $	Additional Purch. $	Front End Load	Back End Load
B- /7.8	3.7	0.51	12.84	3	3	18	77	2	10	29.9	-5.0	55	12	0	0	0.0	0.0
B- /7.8	3.7	0.51	12.83	5	3	18	77	2	10	28.6	-5.2	53	N/A	0	0	0.0	0.0
B- /7.8	3.7	0.51	12.84	6	3	18	77	2	10	30.9	-5.0	59	N/A	0	0	0.0	0.0
B- /7.8	3.7	0.51	12.85	7	3	18	77	2	10	32.8	-4.9	61	N/A	0	0	0.0	0.0
B- /7.8	3.7	0.51	12.84	12	3	18	77	2	10	33.6	-4.9	62	6	1,000,000	0	0.0	0.0
C+ /6.3	9.0	0.83	15.40	10,108	7	73	19	1	15	77.0	-18.1	23	N/A	0	0	0.0	0.0
C+ /6.3	9.0	0.83	15.38	273	7	73	19	1	15	77.6	-18.1	23	N/A	0	0	0.0	0.0
C+ /6.4	9.0	0.83	15.46	1,622	7	73	19	1	15	73.3	-18.2	20	N/A	1,000	0	5.0	0.0
C+ /6.5	9.0	0.83	15.49	57	7	73	19	1	15	66.6	-18.4	14	N/A	1,000	0	0.0	0.0
C+ /6.5	9.0	0.83	15.47	676	7	73	19	1	15	66.6	-18.5	14	N/A	1,000	0	0.0	0.0
C+ /6.4	9.0	0.83	15.52	19	7	73	19	1	15	69.9	-18.4	16	N/A	0	0	0.0	0.0
C+ /6.4	9.0	0.83	15.36	17	7	73	19	1	15	72.3	-18.2	19	12	0	0	0.0	0.0
C+ /6.4	9.0	0.83	15.43	14	7	73	19	1	15	70.8	-18.3	17	N/A	0	0	0.0	0.0
C+ /6.4	9.0	0.83	15.44	14	7	73	19	1	15	74.3	-18.2	20	N/A	0	0	0.0	0.0
C+ /6.3	9.0	0.83	15.47	22	7	73	19	1	15	76.6	-18.1	22	N/A	0	0	0.0	0.0
C+ /6.3	9.0	0.83	15.39	40	7	73	19	1	15	77.4	-18.1	23	6	1,000,000	0	0.0	0.0
B- /7.7	5.3	0.79	13.65	2,845	4	36	59	1	11	47.2	-8.7	43	N/A	0	0	0.0	0.0
B- /7.7	5.3	0.79	13.64	58	4	36	59	1	11	47.6	-8.7	44	N/A	0	0	0.0	0.0
B- /7.7	5.3	0.79	13.68	682	4	36	59	1	11	44.1	-8.9	38	N/A	1,000	0	5.0	0.0
B- /7.7	5.3	0.80	13.66	25	4	36	59	1	11	38.5	-9.2	29	N/A	1,000	0	0.0	0.0
B- /7.7	5.3	0.79	13.67	350	4	36	59	1	11	38.6	-9.2	29	N/A	1,000	0	0.0	0.0
B- /7.7	5.3	0.79	13.65	7	4	36	59	1	11	40.9	-9.1	33	N/A	0	0	0.0	0.0
B- /7.7	5.3	0.79	13.63	6	4	36	59	1	11	43.3	-8.9	36	12	0	0	0.0	0.0
B- /7.7	5.3	0.80	13.65	7	4	36	59	1	11	41.7	-9.0	34	N/A	0	0	0.0	0.0
B- /7.7	5.3	0.80	13.63	8	4	36	59	1	11	44.7	-8.9	39	N/A	0	0	0.0	0.0
B- /7.7	5.3	0.79	13.65	9	4	36	59	1	11	46.3	-8.8	43	N/A	0	0	0.0	0.0
B- /7.7	5.3	0.80	13.63	30	4	36	59	1	11	47.5	-8.8	44	6	1,000,000	0	0.0	0.0
B /8.8	5.5	0.48	10.51	29	1	42	55	2	46	N/A	N/A	66	4	0	0	0.0	0.0
B /8.9	5.5	0.48	10.51	N/A	1	42	55	2	46	N/A	N/A	67	4	1,000,000	0	0.0	0.0
C+ /6.2	6.1	0.55	10.71	49	2	50	47	1	26	N/A	N/A	60	4	0	0	0.0	0.0
B- /7.0	6.2	0.55	10.72	N/A	2	50	47	1	26	N/A	N/A	61	4	1,000,000	0	0.0	0.0
B /8.2	7.0	0.65	10.93	136	2	59	37	2	18	N/A	N/A	54	N/A	0	0	0.0	0.0
B /8.2	7.0	0.64	10.93	N/A	2	59	37	2	18	N/A	N/A	55	N/A	1,000,000	0	0.0	0.0
B+ /9.0	3.8	0.54	11.95	936	2	28	69	1	13	37.1	-6.3	65	7	0	0	0.0	0.0
B+ /9.1	3.7	0.29	12.01	N/A	2	28	69	1	13	N/A	N/A	69	7	0	0	0.0	0.0
B+ /9.1	3.7	0.29	12.00	1	2	28	69	1	13	N/A	N/A	71	7	0	0	0.0	0.0
B+ /9.0	3.8	0.29	11.99	N/A	2	28	69	1	13	N/A	N/A	73	7	0	0	0.0	0.0
B+ /9.0	3.7	0.29	11.96	4	2	28	69	1	13	N/A	N/A	75	7	1,000,000	0	0.0	0.0
B /8.1	8.0	0.75	11.11	182	2	71	25	2	12	N/A	N/A	47	4	0	0	0.0	0.0
B /8.1	7.9	0.75	11.11	N/A	2	71	25	2	12	N/A	N/A	47	4	1,000,000	0	0.0	0.0
B /8.7	5.4	0.84	12.90	1,512	3	43	52	2	9	52.9	-10.6	48	7	0	0	0.0	0.0
B /8.7	5.4	0.49	12.93	N/A	3	43	52	2	9	N/A	N/A	54	7	0	0	0.0	0.0
B /8.7	5.4	0.49	12.93	N/A	3	43	52	2	9	N/A	N/A	59	7	0	0	0.0	0.0
B /8.7	5.4	0.49	12.94	N/A	3	43	52	2	9	N/A	N/A	61	7	0	0	0.0	0.0
B /8.7	5.4	0.48	12.89	4	3	43	52	2	9	N/A	N/A	64	7	1,000,000	0	0.0	0.0
B- /7.7	8.8	0.83	11.26	183	2	82	14	2	8	N/A	N/A	39	4	0	0	0.0	0.0
B- /7.7	8.8	0.84	11.26	N/A	2	82	14	2	8	N/A	N/A	40	4	1,000,000	0	0.0	0.0
B /8.0	7.1	1.11	13.55	1,465	3	62	33	2	7	64.6	-13.1	32	7	0	0	0.0	0.0
B /8.1	7.1	0.66	13.59	1	3	62	33	2	7	N/A	N/A	40	7	0	0	0.0	0.0
B /8.0	7.1	0.66	13.57	1	3	62	33	2	7	N/A	N/A	44	7	0	0	0.0	0.0
B /8.0	7.1	0.66	13.62	N/A	3	62	33	2	7	N/A	N/A	48	7	0	0	0.0	0.0
B /8.0	7.1	0.66	13.55	5	3	62	33	2	7	N/A	N/A	51	7	1,000,000	0	0.0	0.0

Fund Type	Fund Name	Ticker Symbol	Overall Investment Rating	Phone	PERFORMANCE Performance Rating/Pts	Total Return % through 2/28/17 3 Mo	6 Mo	1Yr / Pct	Annualized 3Yr / Pct	5Yr / Pct	Incl. in Returns Dividend Yield	Expense Ratio
GI	J Hancock Multi-Index 2035 Lft 1	JRTKX	B-	(800) 257-3336	C+ / 6.7	6.82	7.40	22.00 /62	6.29 /67	--	1.85	0.84
GI	J Hancock Multi-Index 2035 Lft R6	JRTNX	B-	(800) 257-3336	C+ / 6.7	6.78	7.46	22.08 /63	6.33 /67	--	1.90	0.81
AA	J Hancock Multi-Index 2035 Psv 1	JRYOX	B	(800) 257-3336	C / 5.5	5.87	6.02	18.69 /46	5.38 /58	8.03 /42	2.09	0.70
GI	J Hancock Multi-Index 2035 Psv R1	JRYQX	B	(800) 257-3336	C / 4.8	5.74	5.67	17.82 /42	4.67 /50	--	1.42	1.42
GI	J Hancock Multi-Index 2035 Psv R2	JRYRX	B	(800) 257-3336	C / 5.1	5.78	5.78	18.14 /43	4.92 /53	--	1.66	1.17
GI	J Hancock Multi-Index 2035 Psv R4	JRYPX	B	(800) 257-3336	C / 5.3	5.87	5.95	18.55 /45	5.22 /57	--	1.97	1.02
GI	J Hancock Multi-Index 2035 Psv R6	JRYSX	B	(800) 257-3336	C / 5.5	5.92	6.07	18.74 /46	5.43 /59	--	2.13	0.67
GI	J Hancock Multi-Index 2040 Lft 1	JRTTX	B-	(800) 257-3336	C+ / 6.9	7.07	7.85	22.85 /66	6.50 /68	--	1.84	0.89
GI	J Hancock Multi-Index 2040 Lft R6	JRTWX	B+	(800) 257-3336	B- / 7.0	7.13	7.91	22.89 /66	6.59 /69	--	1.89	0.85
AA	J Hancock Multi-Index 2040 Psv 1	JRROX	B	(800) 257-3336	C+ / 5.9	6.36	6.67	20.13 /53	5.62 /61	8.40 /45	2.08	0.70
GI	J Hancock Multi-Index 2040 Psv R1	JRRQX	B	(800) 257-3336	C / 5.4	6.17	6.40	19.44 /49	5.03 /54	--	1.57	1.42
GI	J Hancock Multi-Index 2040 Psv R2	JRRRX	B	(800) 257-3336	C+ / 5.6	6.22	6.52	19.87 /51	5.20 /56	--	1.82	1.17
GI	J Hancock Multi-Index 2040 Psv R4	JRRPX	B	(800) 257-3336	C+ / 5.9	6.36	6.67	19.98 /52	5.49 /59	--	1.96	1.02
GI	J Hancock Multi-Index 2040 Psv R6	JRRSX	B	(800) 257-3336	C+ / 6.0	6.35	6.65	20.12 /53	5.65 /61	--	2.13	0.67
GI	J Hancock Multi-Index 2045 Lft 1	JRLQX	B-	(800) 257-3336	C+ / 6.9	7.10	7.79	22.80 /66	6.43 /68	--	1.82	0.93
GI	J Hancock Multi-Index 2045 Lft R6	JRLVX	B-	(800) 257-3336	C+ / 6.9	7.06	7.84	22.86 /66	6.49 /68	--	1.87	0.90
AA	J Hancock Multi-Index 2045 Psv 1	JRVOX	B-	(800) 257-3336	C+ / 6.2	6.48	6.94	20.76 /56	5.76 /62	8.50 /46	2.08	0.71
GI	J Hancock Multi-Index 2045 Psv R1	JRVQX	B-	(800) 257-3336	C+ / 5.6	6.37	6.60	19.90 /51	5.06 /55	--	1.44	1.42
GI	J Hancock Multi-Index 2045 Psv R2	JRVRX	B-	(800) 257-3336	C+ / 5.8	6.46	6.77	20.19 /53	5.32 /58	--	1.66	1.18
GI	J Hancock Multi-Index 2045 Psv R4	JRVPX	B-	(800) 257-3336	C+ / 6.1	6.48	6.94	20.70 /56	5.63 /61	--	1.96	1.03
GI	J Hancock Multi-Index 2045 Psv R6	JRVSX	B-	(800) 257-3336	C+ / 6.2	6.53	6.91	20.82 /56	5.81 /63	--	2.13	0.68
GI	J Hancock Multi-Index 2050 Lft 1	JRLWX	B-	(800) 257-3336	C+ / 6.9	6.99	7.77	22.74 /66	6.49 /68	--	1.82	1.09
GI	J Hancock Multi-Index 2050 Lft R6	JRLZX	B-	(800) 257-3336	B- / 7.0	7.05	7.83	22.80 /66	6.57 /69	--	1.87	1.06
AA	J Hancock Multi-Index 2050 Psv 1	JRIOX	B-	(800) 257-3336	C+ / 6.2	6.56	6.99	20.87 /57	5.78 /62	8.52 /46	2.09	0.72
GI	J Hancock Multi-Index 2050 Psv R1	JRIQX	B	(800) 257-3336	C+ / 5.7	6.46	6.72	20.13 /53	5.14 /56	--	1.55	1.44
GI	J Hancock Multi-Index 2050 Psv R2	JRINX	B	(800) 257-3336	C+ / 5.9	6.47	6.81	20.44 /55	5.43 /59	--	1.79	1.19
GI	J Hancock Multi-Index 2050 Psv R4	JRIPX	B	(800) 257-3336	C+ / 6.0	6.49	6.92	20.64 /56	5.60 /61	--	1.98	1.04
GI	J Hancock Multi-Index 2050 Psv R6	JRISX	B-	(800) 257-3336	C+ / 6.2	6.53	6.95	20.83 /57	5.80 /63	--	2.14	0.69
GI	J Hancock Multi-Index 2055 Lft 1	JLKZX	U	(800) 257-3336	U /	7.13	7.81	22.78 /66	--	--	1.81	1.15
GI	J Hancock Multi-Index 2055 Psv 1	JRIYX	U	(800) 257-3336	U /	6.51	7.00	20.84 /57	--	--	1.97	0.85
AA	J Hancock Multi-Index Inc Psv 1	JRFOX	C	(800) 257-3336	D- / 1.5	1.87	0.25	4.48 / 3	2.37 /27	2.96 /11	1.83	0.74
GI	J Hancock Multi-Index Inc Psv R1	JRFQX	C	(800) 257-3336	D- / 1.3	1.63	-0.06	3.95 / 3	1.79 /23	--	1.33	1.46
GI	J Hancock Multi-Index Inc Psv R2	JRFNX	C	(800) 257-3336	D- / 1.3	1.71	0.02	4.04 / 3	2.01 /24	--	1.51	1.21
GI	J Hancock Multi-Index Inc Psv R4	JRFPX	C	(800) 257-3336	D- / 1.4	1.74	0.13	4.34 / 3	2.21 /25	--	1.70	1.06
GI	J Hancock Multi-Index Inc Psv R6	JRFSX	C	(800) 257-3336	D- / 1.5	1.83	0.30	4.44 / 3	2.39 /27	--	1.88	0.71
AA	J Hancock Multmgr 2010 Lft 1	JLAOX	C-	(800) 257-3336	C- / 3.3	4.03	3.37	13.40 /23	3.88 /41	6.12 /29	3.09	0.95
AA	J Hancock Multmgr 2010 Lft A	JLAAX	D+	(800) 257-3336	D / 2.2	3.96	3.09	12.97 /22	3.46 /37	5.68 /26	2.59	1.33
AA	J Hancock Multmgr 2010 Lft R1	JLADX	C-	(800) 257-3336	D+ / 2.9	3.88	3.00	12.67 /20	3.17 /33	5.39 /24	2.43	1.67
BA	J Hancock Multmgr 2010 Lft R2	JLAEX	C-	(800) 257-3336	C- / 3.0	3.88	3.12	12.76 /21	3.37 /35	5.63 /26	2.64	1.42
AA	J Hancock Multmgr 2010 Lft R3	JLAFX	C-	(800) 257-3336	D+ / 2.9	3.96	3.08	12.74 /21	3.26 /34	5.48 /25	2.50	1.57
AA	J Hancock Multmgr 2010 Lft R4	JLAGX	C-	(800) 257-3336	C- / 3.2	4.04	3.28	13.19 /22	3.68 /39	5.90 /28	2.90	1.27
AA	J Hancock Multmgr 2010 Lft R5	JLAHX	C-	(800) 257-3336	C- / 3.3	4.03	3.26	13.41 /23	3.88 /41	6.13 /29	3.10	0.97
BA	J Hancock Multmgr 2010 Lft R6	JLAIX	C-	(800) 257-3336	C- / 3.4	4.08	3.42	13.45 /23	3.94 /42	6.18 /30	3.15	0.92
AA	J Hancock Multmgr 2015 Lft 1	JLBOX	C-	(800) 257-3336	C- / 3.8	4.48	4.06	14.83 /29	4.15 /45	6.68 /33	2.90	0.92
AA	J Hancock Multmgr 2015 Lft A	JLBAX	D+	(800) 257-3336	D+ / 2.6	4.39	3.76	14.38 /27	3.76 /40	6.23 /30	2.40	1.30
AA	J Hancock Multmgr 2015 Lft R1	JLBDX	C-	(800) 257-3336	C- / 3.2	4.16	3.54	13.92 /25	3.39 /36	5.90 /28	2.21	1.64
BA	J Hancock Multmgr 2015 Lft R2	JLBKX	C-	(800) 257-3336	C- / 3.4	4.23	3.70	14.11 /26	3.68 /39	6.16 /30	2.46	1.39
AA	J Hancock Multmgr 2015 Lft R3	JLBFX	C-	(800) 257-3336	C- / 3.3	4.37	3.75	14.16 /26	3.53 /37	6.05 /29	2.31	1.54
AA	J Hancock Multmgr 2015 Lft R4	JLBGX	C-	(800) 257-3336	C- / 3.6	4.39	3.86	14.51 /28	3.95 /42	6.46 /31	2.71	1.24
AA	J Hancock Multmgr 2015 Lft R5	JLBHX	C-	(800) 257-3336	C- / 3.8	4.48	4.06	14.83 /29	4.16 /45	6.68 /33	2.90	0.94
AA	J Hancock Multmgr 2015 Lft R6	JLBJX	C-	(800) 257-3336	C- / 3.8	4.42	4.01	14.89 /29	4.20 /45	6.75 /33	2.95	0.89
AA	J Hancock Multmgr 2020 Lft 1	JLDOX	C	(800) 257-3336	C / 4.4	5.06	4.96	16.70 /37	4.53 /49	7.41 /37	2.58	0.91

● Denotes fund is closed to new investors
∗ Denotes fund is included in Section II

RISK	3 Year		NET ASSETS		ASSET					BULL / BEAR		FUND MANAGER		MINIMUMS		LOADS	
Risk Rating/Pts	Standard Deviation	Beta	NAV As of 2/28/17	Total $(Mil)	Cash %	Stocks %	Bonds %	Other %	Portfolio Turnover Ratio	Last Bull Market Return	Last Bear Market Return	Manager Quality Pct	Manager Tenure (Years)	Initial Purch. $	Additional Purch. $	Front End Load	Back End Load
B- /7.4	9.5	0.90	11.37	148	3	88	7	2	10	N/A	N/A	34	4	0	0	0.0	0.0
B- /7.4	9.6	0.91	11.36	N/A	3	88	7	2	10	N/A	N/A	34	4	1,000,000	0	0.0	0.0
B /8.1	8.0	1.26	13.93	1,221	4	70	24	2	7	72.1	-14.5	25	7	0	0	0.0	0.0
B /8.2	8.1	0.76	13.98	1	4	70	24	2	7	N/A	N/A	33	7	0	0	0.0	0.0
B /8.2	8.0	0.75	13.96	N/A	4	70	24	2	7	N/A	N/A	37	7	0	0	0.0	0.0
B /8.1	8.0	0.75	14.00	N/A	4	70	24	2	7	N/A	N/A	40	7	0	0	0.0	0.0
B /8.1	8.0	0.75	13.94	5	4	70	24	2	7	N/A	N/A	43	7	1,000,000	0	0.0	0.0
B- /7.2	9.8	0.93	11.46	114	1	93	4	2	10	N/A	N/A	33	4	0	0	0.0	0.0
B- /7.2	9.8	0.93	11.47	N/A	1	93	4	2	10	N/A	N/A	34	4	1,000,000	0	0.0	0.0
B /8.0	8.6	1.34	14.15	943	4	76	19	1	7	76.0	-15.2	21	7	0	0	0.0	0.0
B /8.0	8.6	0.81	14.19	N/A	4	76	19	1	7	N/A	N/A	31	7	0	0	0.0	0.0
B /8.0	8.6	0.81	14.17	N/A	4	76	19	1	7	N/A	N/A	33	7	0	0	0.0	0.0
B /8.0	8.6	0.81	14.22	N/A	4	76	19	1	7	N/A	N/A	36	7	0	0	0.0	0.0
B /8.0	8.6	0.81	14.13	5	4	76	19	1	7	N/A	N/A	39	7	1,000,000	0	0.0	0.0
B- /7.2	9.8	0.93	11.43	90	3	91	4	2	7	N/A	N/A	32	4	0	0	0.0	0.0
B- /7.2	9.8	0.93	11.43	N/A	3	91	4	2	7	N/A	N/A	33	4	1,000,000	0	0.0	0.0
B- /7.2	8.8	1.37	14.23	719	4	77	17	2	6	76.9	-15.3	21	7	0	0	0.0	0.0
B- /7.2	8.8	0.83	14.27	1	4	77	17	2	6	N/A	N/A	29	7	0	0	0.0	0.0
B- /7.2	8.9	0.84	14.26	N/A	4	77	17	2	6	N/A	N/A	31	7	0	0	0.0	0.0
B- /7.2	8.8	0.83	14.30	N/A	4	77	17	2	6	N/A	N/A	35	7	0	0	0.0	0.0
B- /7.2	8.8	0.83	14.23	3	4	77	17	2	6	N/A	N/A	37	7	1,000,000	0	0.0	0.0
B- /7.2	9.8	0.93	11.47	59	3	91	4	2	8	N/A	N/A	34	4	0	0	0.0	0.0
B- /7.2	9.7	0.92	11.47	N/A	3	91	4	2	8	N/A	N/A	35	4	1,000,000	0	0.0	0.0
B- /7.9	8.8	1.38	12.68	558	4	77	17	2	6	77.0	-15.2	20	6	0	0	0.0	0.0
B /8.0	8.8	0.83	12.72	N/A	4	77	17	2	6	N/A	N/A	30	6	0	0	0.0	0.0
B /8.0	8.8	0.83	12.71	N/A	4	77	17	2	6	N/A	N/A	33	6	0	0	0.0	0.0
B /8.0	8.8	0.83	12.73	N/A	4	77	17	2	6	N/A	N/A	35	6	0	0	0.0	0.0
B- /7.9	8.8	0.83	12.67	4	4	77	17	2	6	N/A	N/A	37	6	1,000,000	0	0.0	0.0
U /	N/A	N/A	11.40	44	4	91	4	1	8	N/A	N/A	N/A	3	0	0	0.0	0.0
U /	N/A	N/A	11.09	186	4	77	17	2	3	N/A	N/A	N/A	3	0	0	0.0	0.0
B+ /9.2	2.4	0.28	11.16	557	0	11	87	2	17	21.8	-0.9	76	7	0	0	0.0	0.0
B+ /9.2	2.4	0.14	11.20	N/A	0	11	87	2	17	N/A	N/A	76	7	0	0	0.0	0.0
B+ /9.2	2.4	0.14	11.18	N/A	0	11	87	2	17	N/A	N/A	78	7	0	0	0.0	0.0
B+ /9.2	2.4	0.14	11.17	N/A	0	11	87	2	17	N/A	N/A	79	7	0	0	0.0	0.0
B+ /9.2	2.4	0.14	11.15	3	0	11	87	2	17	N/A	N/A	80	7	1,000,000	0	0.0	0.0
C+ /6.9	5.4	0.82	9.13	208	4	36	59	1	20	51.9	-11.2	46	N/A	0	0	0.0	0.0
B- /7.0	5.4	0.82	9.13	45	4	36	59	1	20	48.4	-11.4	41	N/A	1,000	0	5.0	0.0
B- /7.0	5.4	0.82	9.10	1	4	36	59	1	20	46.4	-11.4	36	N/A	0	0	0.0	0.0
B- /7.0	5.4	0.81	9.12	N/A	4	36	59	1	20	48.1	-11.4	40	9	0	0	0.0	0.0
B- /7.0	5.4	0.82	9.11	N/A	4	36	59	1	20	47.1	-11.4	37	N/A	0	0	0.0	0.0
C+ /6.9	5.4	0.81	9.12	1	4	36	59	1	20	50.1	-11.3	44	N/A	0	0	0.0	0.0
C+ /6.9	5.5	0.82	9.12	N/A	4	36	59	1	20	51.9	-11.2	46	N/A	0	0	0.0	0.0
C+ /6.9	5.4	0.81	9.13	N/A	4	36	59	1	20	52.4	-11.3	47	6	1,000,000	0	0.0	0.0
C+ /6.5	6.1	0.93	9.65	358	4	42	51	3	19	58.3	-13.1	39	N/A	0	0	0.0	0.0
C+ /6.6	6.1	0.94	9.66	82	4	42	51	3	19	54.7	-13.2	33	N/A	1,000	0	5.0	0.0
C+ /6.7	6.1	0.94	9.63	2	4	42	51	3	19	52.3	-13.3	29	N/A	0	0	0.0	0.0
C+ /6.6	6.1	0.93	9.62	N/A	4	42	51	3	19	54.2	-13.2	33	9	0	0	0.0	0.0
C+ /6.7	6.1	0.93	9.64	5	4	42	51	3	19	53.3	-13.3	31	N/A	0	0	0.0	0.0
C+ /6.6	6.1	0.93	9.63	N/A	4	42	51	3	19	56.5	-13.2	36	N/A	0	0	0.0	0.0
C+ /6.5	6.1	0.93	9.65	1	4	42	51	3	19	58.2	-13.1	39	N/A	0	0	0.0	0.0
C+ /6.5	6.1	0.94	9.65	2	4	42	51	3	19	58.8	-13.2	39	6	1,000,000	0	0.0	0.0
C+ /6.8	7.0	1.08	10.35	867	5	52	41	2	20	66.5	-15.4	30	N/A	0	0	0.0	0.0

	99 Pct = Best 0 Pct = Worst				PERFORMANCE								
							Total Return % through 2/28/17					Incl. in Returns	
			Overall		Perfor-					Annualized		Dividend	Expense
Fund Type	Fund Name	Ticker Symbol	Investment Rating	Phone	mance Rating/Pts	3 Mo	6 Mo	1Yr / Pct	3Yr / Pct	5Yr / Pct		Yield	Ratio
AA	J Hancock Multmgr 2020 Lft A	JLDAX	C-	(800) 257-3336	C- / 3.2	4.96	4.76	16.35 /36	4.11 /44	6.98 /34		2.10	1.28
AA	J Hancock Multmgr 2020 Lft R1	JLDDX	C	(800) 257-3336	C- / 3.8	4.82	4.63	15.90 /34	3.80 /40	6.66 /33		1.90	1.62
GI	J Hancock Multmgr 2020 Lft R2	JLDEX	C	(800) 257-3336	C- / 4.0	4.89	4.69	16.20 /35	4.07 /44	6.95 /34		2.14	1.37
AA	J Hancock Multmgr 2020 Lft R3	JLDFX	C	(800) 257-3336	C- / 3.9	4.83	4.53	16.01 /34	3.88 /41	6.77 /33		2.00	1.52
AA	J Hancock Multmgr 2020 Lft R4	JLDGX	C	(800) 257-3336	C- / 4.2	4.86	4.76	16.39 /36	4.30 /46	7.17 /36		2.39	1.22
AA	J Hancock Multmgr 2020 Lft R5	JLDHX	C	(800) 257-3336	C / 4.4	4.96	4.96	16.70 /37	4.50 /49	7.39 /37		2.58	0.92
AA	J Hancock Multmgr 2020 Lft R6	JLDIX	C	(800) 257-3336	C / 4.4	4.92	4.92	16.67 /37	4.56 /49	7.45 /38		2.64	0.87
AA	J Hancock Multmgr 2025 Lft 1	JLEOX	C+	(800) 257-3336	C / 5.1	5.59	5.88	18.66 /46	4.90 /53	8.17 /43		2.26	0.91
AA	J Hancock Multmgr 2025 Lft A	JLEAX	C	(800) 257-3336	C- / 3.7	5.46	5.65	18.14 /43	4.47 /48	7.70 /40		1.80	1.29
AA	J Hancock Multmgr 2025 Lft R1	JLEDX	C	(800) 257-3336	C / 4.5	5.43	5.43	17.85 /42	4.17 /45	7.40 /37		1.58	1.63
GI	J Hancock Multmgr 2025 Lft R2	JLEEX	C+	(800) 257-3336	C / 4.7	5.51	5.60	18.04 /43	4.40 /47	7.66 /39		1.83	1.37
AA	J Hancock Multmgr 2025 Lft R3	JLEFX	C	(800) 257-3336	C / 4.5	5.44	5.44	17.84 /42	4.24 /46	7.50 /38		1.68	1.53
AA	J Hancock Multmgr 2025 Lft R4	JLEGX	C+	(800) 257-3336	C / 4.9	5.57	5.76	18.41 /45	4.69 /51	7.96 /42		2.07	1.22
AA	J Hancock Multmgr 2025 Lft R5	JLEHX	C+	(800) 257-3336	C / 5.1	5.59	5.88	18.66 /46	4.90 /53	8.18 /43		2.26	0.93
GI	J Hancock Multmgr 2025 Lft R6	JLEIX	C+	(800) 257-3336	C / 5.2	5.65	5.94	18.74 /46	4.96 /54	8.21 /44		2.31	0.88
AA	J Hancock Multmgr 2030 Lft 1	JLFOX	C+	(800) 257-3336	C+ / 5.7	6.13	6.70	20.53 /55	5.15 /56	8.68 /48		1.99	0.91
AA	J Hancock Multmgr 2030 Lft A	JLFAX	C	(800) 257-3336	C- / 4.2	6.00	6.48	20.02 /52	4.72 /51	8.22 /44		1.55	1.29
AA	J Hancock Multmgr 2030 Lft R1	JLFDX	C+	(800) 257-3336	C / 5.0	5.97	6.26	19.61 /50	4.39 /47	7.91 /41		1.33	1.63
GI	J Hancock Multmgr 2030 Lft R2	JLFEX	C+	(800) 257-3336	C / 5.3	6.05	6.44	19.93 /52	4.66 /50	8.16 /43		1.57	1.38
AA	J Hancock Multmgr 2030 Lft R3	JLFFX	C+	(800) 257-3336	C / 5.1	5.98	6.36	19.71 /51	4.50 /49	8.03 /42		1.42	1.53
AA	J Hancock Multmgr 2030 Lft R4	JLFGX	C+	(800) 257-3336	C / 5.5	6.03	6.50	20.20 /53	4.92 /53	8.44 /46		1.80	1.23
AA	J Hancock Multmgr 2030 Lft R5	JLFHX	C+	(800) 257-3336	C+ / 5.6	6.14	6.62	20.43 /54	5.12 /55	8.67 /48		1.99	0.93
GI	J Hancock Multmgr 2030 Lft R6	JLFIX	C+	(800) 257-3336	C+ / 5.7	6.10	6.67	20.49 /55	5.21 /57	8.74 /48		2.04	0.88
AA	J Hancock Multmgr 2035 Lft 1	JLHOX	C+	(800) 257-3336	C+ / 6.1	6.52	7.26	21.81 /61	5.30 /58	9.01 /51		1.79	0.93
AA	J Hancock Multmgr 2035 Lft A	JLHAX	C	(800) 257-3336	C / 4.7	6.52	7.08	21.35 /59	4.90 /53	8.58 /47		1.37	1.30
AA	J Hancock Multmgr 2035 Lft R1	JLHDX	C+	(800) 257-3336	C / 5.4	6.38	6.85	20.90 /57	4.56 /49	8.26 /44		1.13	1.64
GI	J Hancock Multmgr 2035 Lft R2	JLHEX	C+	(800) 257-3336	C+ / 5.7	6.51	6.98	21.29 /59	4.83 /52	8.57 /47		1.37	1.39
AA	J Hancock Multmgr 2035 Lft R3	JLHFX	C+	(800) 257-3336	C / 5.5	6.39	6.95	21.10 /58	4.69 /51	8.38 /45		1.23	1.54
AA	J Hancock Multmgr 2035 Lft R4		C+	(800) 257-3336	C+ / 5.9	6.50	7.06	21.47 /60	5.09 /55	8.78 /49		1.61	1.24
AA	J Hancock Multmgr 2035 Lft R5	JLHHX	C+	(800) 257-3336	C+ / 6.1	6.52	7.17	21.82 /61	5.30 /58	9.03 /51		1.79	0.94
GI	J Hancock Multmgr 2035 Lft R6	JLHIX	C+	(800) 257-3336	C+ / 6.1	6.58	7.23	21.78 /61	5.35 /58	9.07 /51		1.84	0.89
AA	J Hancock Multmgr 2040 Lft 1	JLIOX	C+	(800) 257-3336	C+ / 6.3	6.77	7.52	22.31 /64	5.41 /59	9.16 /52		1.74	0.93
AA	J Hancock Multmgr 2040 Lft A	JLIAX	C	(800) 257-3336	C / 4.9	6.67	7.33	21.94 /62	5.00 /54	8.70 /48		1.32	1.31
AA	J Hancock Multmgr 2040 Lft R1	JLIDX	C+	(800) 257-3336	C+ / 5.7	6.62	7.19	21.60 /60	4.70 /51	8.40 /45		1.08	1.65
GI	J Hancock Multmgr 2040 Lft R2	JLIEX	C+	(800) 257-3336	C+ / 5.9	6.67	7.33	21.91 /62	4.97 /54	8.67 /48		1.31	1.40
AA	J Hancock Multmgr 2040 Lft R3	JLIFX	C+	(800) 257-3336	C+ / 5.7	6.64	7.21	21.63 /60	4.78 /52	8.49 /46		1.17	1.55
AA	J Hancock Multmgr 2040 Lft R4	JLIGX	C+	(800) 257-3336	C+ / 6.1	6.67	7.42	22.03 /62	5.21 /57	8.91 /50		1.55	1.25
AA	J Hancock Multmgr 2040 Lft R5	JLIHX	C+	(800) 257-3336	C+ / 6.2	6.76	7.51	22.29 /64	5.40 /58	9.15 /52		1.74	0.95
AA	J Hancock Multmgr 2040 Lft R6	JLIIX	C+	(800) 257-3336	C+ / 6.3	6.73	7.48	22.39 /64	5.46 /59	9.19 /52		1.79	0.90
AA	J Hancock Multmgr 2045 Lft 1	JLJOX	C+	(800) 257-3336	C+ / 6.3	6.78	7.54	22.36 /64	5.41 /59	9.13 /52		1.73	0.93
AA	J Hancock Multmgr 2045 Lft A	JLJAX	C	(800) 257-3336	C / 4.9	6.70	7.36	21.90 /62	5.01 /54	8.69 /48		1.32	1.31
AA	J Hancock Multmgr 2045 Lft R1	JLJDX	C+	(800) 257-3336	C+ / 5.7	6.65	7.22	21.55 /60	4.71 /51	8.38 /45		1.08	1.65
GI	J Hancock Multmgr 2045 Lft R2	JLJEX	C+	(800) 257-3336	C+ / 5.9	6.60	7.26	21.74 /61	4.95 /54	8.65 /48		1.31	1.40
AA	J Hancock Multmgr 2045 Lft R3	JLJFX	C+	(800) 257-3336	C+ / 5.8	6.66	7.23	21.65 /60	4.81 /52	8.50 /46		1.17	1.55
AA	J Hancock Multmgr 2045 Lft R4	JLJGX	C+	(800) 257-3336	C+ / 6.1	6.78	7.45	22.19 /63	5.22 /57	8.93 /50		1.55	1.25
AA	J Hancock Multmgr 2045 Lft R5	JLJHX	C+	(800) 257-3336	C+ / 6.3	6.78	7.53	22.34 /64	5.41 /59	9.15 /52		1.73	0.95
GI	J Hancock Multmgr 2045 Lft R6	JLJIX	C+	(800) 257-3336	C+ / 6.3	6.75	7.50	22.44 /64	5.47 /59	9.19 /52		1.78	0.90
AA	J Hancock Multmgr 2050 Lft 1	JLKOX	C+	(800) 257-3336	C+ / 6.3	6.79	7.52	22.40 /64	5.44 /59	9.16 /52		1.71	0.99
AA	J Hancock Multmgr 2050 Lft A	JLKAX	C	(800) 257-3336	C / 4.9	6.67	7.31	21.85 /61	4.99 /54	--		1.29	1.36
AA	J Hancock Multmgr 2050 Lft R1	JLKDX	C+	(800) 257-3336	C+ / 5.7	6.65	7.20	21.51 /60	4.71 /51	--		1.09	1.70
AA	J Hancock Multmgr 2050 Lft R2	JLKEX	C+	(800) 257-3336	C+ / 5.9	6.69	7.33	21.87 /62	4.97 /54	--		1.29	1.45
AA	J Hancock Multmgr 2050 Lft R3	JLKFX	C+	(800) 257-3336	C+ / 5.8	6.70	7.25	21.68 /61	4.85 /53	--		1.22	1.60

● Denotes fund is closed to new investors

* Denotes fund is included in Section II

352

Risk Rating/Pts	3 Year Standard Deviation	Beta	NAV As of 2/28/17	Total $(Mil)	Cash %	Stocks %	Bonds %	Other %	Portfolio Turnover Ratio	Last Bull Market Return	Last Bear Market Return	Manager Quality Pct	Manager Tenure (Years)	Initial Purch. $	Additional Purch. $	Front End Load	Back End Load
C+ / 6.9	7.0	1.07	10.37	123	5	52	41	2	20	62.9	-15.6	26	N/A	1,000	0	5.0	0.0
B- / 7.0	7.0	1.08	10.34	4	5	52	41	2	20	60.5	-15.7	23	N/A	0	0	0.0	0.0
C+ / 6.9	7.0	0.65	10.33	1	5	52	41	2	20	62.7	-15.6	40	9	0	0	0.0	0.0
C+ / 6.9	7.0	1.08	10.34	2	5	52	41	2	20	61.2	-15.6	24	N/A	0	0	0.0	0.0
C+ / 6.9	7.0	1.08	10.32	1	5	52	41	2	20	64.6	-15.6	28	N/A	0	0	0.0	0.0
C+ / 6.8	7.0	1.08	10.35	4	5	52	41	2	20	66.4	-15.4	30	N/A	0	0	0.0	0.0
C+ / 6.8	7.0	1.07	10.33	5	5	52	41	2	20	66.9	-15.6	31	6	1,000,000	0	0.0	0.0
C+ / 6.7	8.1	1.24	10.90	1,175	5	63	30	2	21	75.0	-17.5	22	N/A	0	0	0.0	0.0
C+ / 6.8	8.0	1.24	10.94	134	5	63	30	2	21	71.1	-17.6	19	N/A	1,000	0	5.0	0.0
C+ / 6.9	8.0	1.24	10.89	4	5	63	30	2	21	68.5	-17.7	16	N/A	0	0	0.0	0.0
C+ / 6.8	8.0	0.75	10.88	1	5	63	30	2	21	70.8	-17.6	31	9	0	0	0.0	0.0
C+ / 6.9	8.1	1.24	10.89	4	5	63	30	2	21	69.2	-17.6	17	N/A	0	0	0.0	0.0
C+ / 6.8	8.0	1.23	10.91	1	5	63	30	2	21	73.0	-17.5	21	N/A	0	0	0.0	0.0
C+ / 6.7	8.1	1.24	10.90	2	5	63	30	2	21	75.1	-17.5	22	N/A	0	0	0.0	0.0
C+ / 6.7	8.0	0.75	10.89	5	5	63	30	2	21	75.4	-17.6	38	6	1,000,000	0	0.0	0.0
C+ / 6.4	9.1	1.39	11.11	1,091	6	74	19	1	18	81.2	-19.0	15	N/A	0	0	0.0	0.0
C+ / 6.5	9.0	1.38	11.14	137	6	74	19	1	18	76.9	-19.0	12	N/A	1,000	0	5.0	0.0
C+ / 6.6	9.0	1.38	11.09	4	6	74	19	1	18	74.4	-19.2	11	N/A	0	0	0.0	0.0
C+ / 6.5	9.0	0.84	11.08	2	6	74	19	1	18	76.4	-19.0	24	9	0	0	0.0	0.0
C+ / 6.5	9.0	1.38	11.10	3	6	74	19	1	18	75.3	-19.1	11	N/A	0	0	0.0	0.0
C+ / 6.5	9.0	1.38	11.09	1	6	74	19	1	18	79.0	-19.0	14	N/A	0	0	0.0	0.0
C+ / 6.4	9.0	1.38	11.10	2	6	74	19	1	18	81.0	-18.9	15	N/A	0	0	0.0	0.0
C+ / 6.4	9.0	0.85	11.10	5	6	74	19	1	18	81.6	-19.1	29	6	1,000,000	0	0.0	0.0
C+ / 6.2	9.6	1.48	11.48	914	5	82	11	2	18	85.2	-19.7	12	N/A	0	0	0.0	0.0
C+ / 6.3	9.6	1.48	11.43	104	5	82	11	2	18	81.1	-19.9	10	N/A	1,000	0	5.0	0.0
C+ / 6.3	9.7	1.48	11.40	5	5	82	11	2	18	78.1	-19.9	8	N/A	0	0	0.0	0.0
C+ / 6.3	9.6	0.90	11.47	1	5	82	11	2	18	80.9	-19.9	20	9	0	0	0.0	0.0
C+ / 6.3	9.6	1.47	11.42	2	5	82	11	2	18	79.1	-19.8	9	N/A	0	0	0.0	0.0
C+ / 6.2	9.6	1.47	11.47	1	5	82	11	2	18	83.0	-19.8	11	N/A	0	0	0.0	0.0
C+ / 6.2	9.7	1.48	11.48	1	5	82	11	2	18	85.0	-19.6	12	N/A	0	0	0.0	0.0
C+ / 6.2	9.6	0.90	11.47	5	5	82	11	2	18	85.6	-19.8	25	6	1,000,000	0	0.0	0.0
C+ / 6.1	9.8	1.50	11.43	710	6	86	6	2	14	86.1	-19.7	12	N/A	0	0	0.0	0.0
C+ / 6.1	9.8	1.50	11.39	93	6	86	6	2	14	81.9	-19.7	9	N/A	1,000	0	5.0	0.0
C+ / 6.1	9.8	1.50	11.37	3	6	86	6	2	14	79.3	-19.9	8	N/A	0	0	0.0	0.0
C+ / 6.1	9.8	0.92	11.42	1	6	86	6	2	14	81.6	-19.7	19	9	0	0	0.0	0.0
C+ / 6.1	9.8	1.49	11.35	2	6	86	6	2	14	80.1	-19.8	8	N/A	0	0	0.0	0.0
C+ / 6.1	9.8	1.49	11.39	1	6	86	6	2	14	84.0	-19.7	11	N/A	0	0	0.0	0.0
C+ / 6.1	9.8	1.50	11.44	1	6	86	6	2	14	86.1	-19.6	11	N/A	0	0	0.0	0.0
C+ / 6.0	9.8	1.49	11.42	3	6	86	6	2	14	86.5	-19.7	12	6	1,000,000	0	0.0	0.0
C+ / 6.0	9.8	1.49	11.33	662	6	86	6	2	15	86.1	-19.7	12	N/A	0	0	0.0	0.0
C+ / 6.1	9.8	1.49	11.28	85	6	86	6	2	15	82.0	-19.8	10	N/A	1,000	0	5.0	0.0
C+ / 6.1	9.8	1.50	11.26	2	6	86	6	2	15	79.2	-19.8	8	N/A	0	0	0.0	0.0
C+ / 6.1	9.8	0.91	11.31	1	6	86	6	2	15	81.7	-19.8	20	9	0	0	0.0	0.0
C+ / 6.1	9.8	1.49	11.27	2	6	86	6	2	15	80.4	-19.9	9	N/A	0	0	0.0	0.0
C+ / 6.1	9.8	1.50	11.30	1	6	86	6	2	15	84.2	-19.8	11	N/A	0	0	0.0	0.0
C+ / 6.0	9.8	1.49	11.34	2	6	86	6	2	15	86.1	-19.6	12	N/A	0	0	0.0	0.0
C+ / 6.0	9.8	0.91	11.32	3	6	86	6	2	15	86.5	-19.8	24	6	1,000,000	0	0.0	0.0
C+ / 6.3	9.8	1.50	11.80	305	6	86	6	2	11	86.4	-19.6	12	6	0	0	0.0	0.0
C+ / 6.4	9.8	1.50	11.79	32	6	86	6	2	11	N/A	N/A	9	N/A	1,000	0	5.0	0.0
C+ / 6.4	9.8	1.49	11.79	1	6	86	6	2	11	N/A	N/A	8	N/A	0	0	0.0	0.0
C+ / 6.4	9.8	1.50	11.80	1	6	86	6	2	11	N/A	N/A	9	N/A	0	0	0.0	0.0
C+ / 6.4	9.8	1.50	11.79	1	6	86	6	2	11	N/A	N/A	9	N/A	0	0	0.0	0.0

Data as of February 28, 2017

99 Pct = Best
0 Pct = Worst

Fund Type	Fund Name	Ticker Symbol	Overall Investment Rating	Phone	Performance Rating/Pts	3 Mo	6 Mo	1Yr / Pct	3Yr / Pct	5Yr / Pct	Dividend Yield	Expense Ratio
AA	J Hancock Multmgr 2050 Lft R4	JLKGX	C+	(800) 257-3336	C+ / 6.1	6.78	7.42	22.07 /63	5.25 /57	—	1.54	1.30
GI	J Hancock Multmgr 2050 Lft R5	JLKHX	C+	(800) 257-3336	C+ / 6.3	6.82	7.55	22.30 /64	5.44 /59	—	1.74	1.00
GI	J Hancock Multmgr 2050 Lft R6	JLKRX	C+	(800) 257-3336	C+ / 6.3	6.84	7.57	22.44 /64	5.49 /59	—	1.76	0.95
GI	J Hancock Multmgr 2055 Lft 1	JLKUX	U	(800) 257-3336	U /	6.82	7.43	22.22 /63	--	—	1.65	1.22
EN	● J Hancock Natural Resources 1	JINRX	E-	(800) 257-3336	E- / 0.2	-0.87	7.93	40.69 /97	-10.99 / 1	-7.90 / 1	0.93	1.10
EN	● J Hancock Natural Resources A	JNRAX	E-	(800) 257-3336	E- / 0.1	-0.95	7.65	40.18 /97	-11.38 / 1	-8.31 / 1	0.58	1.47
EN	● J Hancock Natural Resources I	JNRIX	E-	(800) 257-3336	E- / 0.2	-0.85	7.86	40.53 /97	-11.19 / 1	-8.12 / 1	0.89	1.16
EN	● J Hancock Natural Resources NAV		E-	(800) 257-3336	E- / 0.2	-0.84	7.94	40.68 /97	-10.94 / 1	-7.84 / 1	0.98	1.05
SC	J Hancock New Oppty 1	JISOX	C	(800) 257-3336	B- / 7.3	3.45	12.42	29.87 /86	5.60 /61	11.93 /74	0.35	1.15
SC	J Hancock New Oppty A	JASOX	U	(800) 257-3336	U /	3.37	12.19	29.26 /85	--	—	0.07	1.52
SC	J Hancock New Oppty NAV		C	(800) 257-3336	B- / 7.3	3.47	12.46	29.61 /86	5.66 /61	11.98 /74	0.39	1.10
RE	J Hancock Real Est Eq Nav		C	(800) 257-3336	C+ / 6.6	5.49	-2.42	12.64 /20	10.36 /95	10.57 /63	1.93	0.93
RE	J Hancock Real Estate Sec 1	JIREX	C+	(800) 257-3336	B- / 7.3	8.21	-1.92	13.84 /25	10.91 /97	10.90 /65	3.55	0.79
GR	J Hancock Redwood A	JTRAX	C	(800) 257-3336	E+ / 0.8	0.88	1.89	6.43 / 5	0.87 /18	—	0.00	1.65
GR	J Hancock Redwood I	JTRIX	C	(800) 257-3336	D- / 1.3	0.97	1.97	6.69 / 5	1.14 /19	—	0.00	1.33
IN	J Hancock Redwood NAV		D+	(800) 257-3336	D- / 1.4	0.97	2.06	6.87 / 6	1.32 /20	2.63 /10	0.00	1.22
GR	J Hancock Redwood R6	JTRRX	C	(800) 257-3336	D- / 1.4	0.97	2.06	6.87 / 6	1.32 /20	—	0.00	1.24
FS	J Hancock Regional Bank A	FRBAX	A+	(800) 257-3336	A+ / 9.9	10.14	31.61	60.84 /99	18.09 /99	20.90 /99	0.56	1.27
FS	● J Hancock Regional Bank B	FRBFX	A+	(800) 257-3336	A+ / 9.9	9.89	31.12	59.70 /99	17.27 /99	20.04 /99	0.10	1.97
FS	J Hancock Regional Bank C	FRBCX	A+	(800) 257-3336	A+ / 9.9	9.92	31.10	59.71 /99	17.27 /99	20.04 /99	0.10	1.97
GR	J Hancock SC Growth NAV		E+	(800) 257-3336	C- / 4.1	6.26	9.34	28.30 /82	0.30 /15	8.89 /50	0.00	1.11
TC	J Hancock Science and Tech NAV		C+	(800) 257-3336	A+ / 9.8	10.51	10.89	33.36 /92	11.75 /98	—	0.18	1.07
SC	J Hancock Small Cap Value A	JSCAX	B-	(800) 257-3336	B- / 7.3	4.62	10.32	26.49 /78	8.19 /80	—	0.27	1.58
SC	J Hancock Small Cap Value I	JSCBX	B+	(800) 257-3336	B+ / 8.4	4.66	10.51	26.88 /79	8.53 /83	—	0.56	1.26
SC	J Hancock Small Cap Value NAV		B+	(800) 257-3336	B+ / 8.5	4.71	10.56	27.02 /79	8.69 /85	13.07 /85	0.66	1.15
SC	J Hancock Small Cap Value R6	JSCCX	B+	(800) 257-3336	B+ / 8.5	4.74	10.59	27.04 /79	8.69 /85	—	0.64	1.17
SC	J Hancock Small Company A	JCSAX	C	(800) 257-3336	C+ / 6.5	4.61	12.24	26.60 /78	6.15 /66	11.13 /67	0.00	1.49
SC	J Hancock Small Company ADV	JCSDX	C+	(800) 257-3336	B- / 7.4	4.65	12.28	26.69 /78	6.24 /66	11.24 /68	0.00	1.44
SC	J Hancock Small Company Grth NAV		C-	(800) 257-3336	B- / 7.1	4.93	8.69	28.47 /83	5.85 /63	12.69 /81	0.00	1.07
SC	J Hancock Small Company I	JCSIX	C+	(800) 257-3336	B- / 7.5	4.72	12.43	27.00 /79	6.47 /68	11.48 /70	0.00	1.17
SC	J Hancock Small Company R1	JCSOX	C	(800) 257-3336	B- / 7.0	4.51	12.08	26.16 /77	5.75 /62	10.74 /64	0.00	1.83
SC	J Hancock Small Company R2	JCSPX	C+	(800) 257-3336	B- / 7.2	4.57	12.19	26.51 /78	6.03 /64	11.03 /66	0.00	1.58
SC	J Hancock Small Company R3	JCSHX	C+	(800) 257-3336	B- / 7.1	4.55	12.11	26.35 /77	5.87 /63	10.85 /65	0.00	1.73
SC	J Hancock Small Company R4	JCSFX	C+	(800) 257-3336	B- / 7.4	4.67	12.41	26.93 /79	6.32 /67	11.31 /68	0.00	1.43
SC	J Hancock Small Company R5	JCSVX	C+	(800) 257-3336	B / 7.6	4.71	12.46	27.07 /79	6.50 /68	11.52 /70	0.00	1.13
SC	J Hancock Small Company R6	JCSWX	C+	(800) 257-3336	B / 7.6	4.72	12.47	27.11 /79	6.60 /69	11.61 /71	0.00	1.08
SC	J Hancock Small Company Val 1	JISVX	C	(800) 257-3336	A / 9.3	4.75	13.47	37.56 /96	7.72 /77	12.11 /75	0.72	1.27
SC	J Hancock Small Company Val NAV		C	(800) 257-3336	A / 9.3	4.74	13.49	37.62 /96	7.77 /77	12.16 /76	0.76	1.22
AA	J Hancock Spectrum Income A	JHSIX	U	(800) 257-3336	U /	2.91	1.02	9.65 /11	--	—	2.69	1.22
GR	J Hancock Spectrum Income Nav		C-	(800) 257-3336	D+ / 2.4	3.00	1.22	10.06 /12	3.37 /35	4.23 /16	3.17	0.80
GL	J Hancock Strat Equity Alloc NAV		B-	(800) 257-3336	B- / 7.0	7.43	8.58	23.63 /69	6.34 /67	—	1.72	0.67
GR	J Hancock Strat Growth A	JSGAX	C+	(800) 257-3336	C+ / 6.2	8.34	8.07	19.67 /50	7.08 /72	12.09 /75	0.23	1.12
GR	J Hancock Strat Growth I	JSGIX	B-	(800) 257-3336	B- / 7.2	8.44	8.23	20.03 /52	7.43 /75	12.46 /79	0.48	0.85
GR	J Hancock Strat Growth NAV		B	(800) 257-3336	B- / 7.3	8.41	8.27	20.14 /53	7.58 /76	12.64 /80	0.58	0.74
GL	J Hancock Technical Opport A	JTCAX	E	(800) 257-3336	E+ / 0.8	5.02	8.51	9.91 /11	-0.33 /12	10.74 /64	0.00	1.66
GL	J Hancock Technical Opport I	JTCIX	E	(800) 257-3336	D- / 1.3	5.04	8.62	10.18 /12	-0.04 /13	11.07 /66	0.00	1.34
GL	J Hancock Technical Opport NAV		E	(800) 257-3336	D / 1.9	5.04	8.67	10.31 /12	0.11 /14	11.28 /68	0.00	1.23
GI	J Hancock Total Return NAV	JHTRX	C	(800) 257-3336	D- / 1.4	1.90	-0.70	3.89 / 3	2.50 /28	2.80 /10	2.71	0.72
GR	J Hancock US Glob Lead Gr A	USGLX	C	(800) 257-3336	C+ / 6.3	8.36	3.89	18.75 /46	8.28 /81	11.72 /72	0.00	1.18
GR	● J Hancock US Glob Lead Gr B	USLBX	C	(800) 257-3336	C+ / 6.6	8.17	3.53	17.86 /42	7.48 /75	10.89 /65	0.00	1.93
GR	J Hancock US Glob Lead Gr C	USLCX	C	(800) 257-3336	C+ / 6.6	8.13	3.50	17.82 /42	7.47 /75	10.88 /65	0.00	1.93
GR	J Hancock US Glob Lead Gr I	USLIX	C+	(800) 257-3336	B- / 7.3	8.42	4.03	19.04 /47	8.57 /84	12.04 /75	0.00	0.91

● Denotes fund is closed to new investors
* Denotes fund is included in Section II

www.thestreetratings.com

RISK			NET ASSETS		ASSET					BULL / BEAR		FUND MANAGER		MINIMUMS		LOADS	
	3 Year		NAV						Portfolio	Last Bull	Last Bear	Manager	Manager	Initial	Additional	Front	Back
Risk Rating/Pts	Standard Deviation	Beta	As of 2/28/17	Total $(Mil)	Cash %	Stocks %	Bonds %	Other %	Turnover Ratio	Market Return	Market Return	Quality Pct	Tenure (Years)	Purch. $	Purch. $	End Load	End Load
C+ / 6.3	9.8	1.49	11.80	1	6	86	6	2	11	N/A	N/A	11	N/A	0	0	0.0	0.0
C+ / 6.3	9.8	0.91	11.81	N/A	6	86	6	2	11	N/A	N/A	24	6	0	0	0.0	0.0
C+ / 6.3	9.8	0.91	11.81	3	6	86	6	2	11	N/A	N/A	24	6	1,000,000	0	0.0	0.0
U /	N/A	N/A	10.75	114	5	87	7	1	7	N/A	N/A	N/A	3	0	0	0.0	0.0
E+ / 0.8	24.7	1.19	12.17	106	4	95	0	1	22	-18.5	-32.5	13	3	0	0	0.0	0.0
E+ / 0.8	24.7	1.19	12.08	3	4	95	0	1	22	-20.5	-32.6	10	3	1,000	0	5.0	0.0
E+ / 0.8	24.7	1.19	12.05	N/A	4	95	0	1	22	-19.6	-32.5	12	3	250,000	0	0.0	0.0
E+ / 0.8	24.6	1.18	12.08	486	4	95	0	1	22	-18.3	-32.5	13	3	0	0	0.0	0.0
C- / 3.2	14.6	0.90	27.44	64	1	97	1	1	49	126.0	-25.8	67	9	0	0	0.0	0.0
U /	N/A	N/A	27.26	313	1	97	1	1	49	N/A	N/A	N/A	9	1,000	0	5.0	0.0
C- / 3.2	14.6	0.90	27.27	131	1	97	1	1	49	126.6	-25.7	68	9	0	0	0.0	0.0
C / 4.7	14.0	1.01	10.41	224	4	94	0	2	14	101.5	-16.4	65	11	0	0	0.0	0.0
C- / 4.1	14.8	1.08	12.98	579	0	99	0	1	141	104.2	-17.1	62	12	0	0	0.0	0.0
B+ / 9.9	4.3	0.38	10.26	N/A	0	67	32	1	82	N/A	N/A	34	6	1,000	0	5.0	0.0
B+ / 9.9	4.3	0.37	10.36	7	0	67	32	1	82	N/A	N/A	38	6	250,000	0	0.0	0.0
B- / 7.5	4.3	0.38	10.42	85	0	67	32	1	82	25.8	N/A	39	6	0	0	0.0	0.0
B+ / 9.9	4.3	0.38	10.42	12	0	67	32	1	82	N/A	N/A	40	6	1,000,000	0	0.0	0.0
C+ / 6.0	17.3	1.15	26.28	1,213	1	92	5	2	11	235.0	-25.7	91	19	1,000	0	0.0	0.0
C+ / 5.9	17.3	1.15	24.94	12	1	92	5	2	11	222.4	-25.9	88	19	1,000	0	5.0	0.0
C+ / 6.0	17.3	1.15	24.99	205	1	92	5	2	11	222.3	-25.9	88	19	1,000	0	0.0	0.0
D- / 1.4	17.5	1.36	8.66	210	3	96	0	1	100	88.0	-25.7	1	9	0	0	0.0	0.0
D / 1.8	14.6	1.23	11.87	641	4	95	0	1	98	N/A	N/A	58	4	0	0	0.0	0.0
C+ / 5.6	14.9	0.90	21.30	90	3	96	0	1	25	N/A	N/A	85	9	1,000	0	5.0	0.0
C+ / 5.6	14.9	0.90	21.32	100	3	96	0	1	25	N/A	N/A	87	9	250,000	0	0.0	0.0
C / 5.5	14.9	0.90	21.31	254	3	96	0	1	25	132.2	-21.4	88	9	0	0	0.0	0.0
C+ / 5.6	14.9	0.90	21.33	N/A	3	96	0	1	25	N/A	N/A	88	9	1,000,000	0	0.0	0.0
C / 4.4	14.1	0.87	28.60	244	1	97	1	1	108	110.5	-25.8	75	2	1,000	0	5.0	0.0
C / 4.4	14.1	0.87	28.81	N/A	1	97	1	1	108	111.9	-25.8	75	2	0	0	0.0	0.0
C- / 3.1	14.2	0.86	18.90	202	0	97	2	1	26	129.9	-23.6	73	12	0	0	0.0	0.0
C / 4.5	14.1	0.87	29.30	89	1	97	1	1	108	114.4	-25.7	77	2	250,000	0	0.0	0.0
C / 4.3	14.1	0.87	27.83	1	1	97	1	1	108	106.7	-26.0	71	2	0	0	0.0	0.0
C / 4.4	14.1	0.87	28.63	1	1	97	1	1	108	109.6	-25.8	N/A	2	0	0	0.0	0.0
C / 4.4	14.1	0.87	28.05	N/A	1	97	1	1	108	107.8	-25.9	72	2	0	0	0.0	0.0
C / 4.5	14.1	0.87	28.89	N/A	1	97	1	1	108	112.4	-25.8	76	2	0	0	0.0	0.0
C / 4.5	14.1	0.87	29.34	N/A	1	97	1	1	108	114.7	-25.7	77	2	0	0	0.0	0.0
C / 4.5	14.1	0.87	29.49	5	1	97	1	1	108	115.7	-25.8	78	2	1,000,000	0	0.0	0.0
D- / 1.5	14.4	0.87	28.74	93	2	97	0	1	29	124.3	-23.4	84	3	0	0	0.0	0.0
D- / 1.5	14.4	0.87	28.70	151	2	97	0	1	29	125.0	-23.4	84	3	0	0	0.0	0.0
U /	N/A	N/A	10.66	37	3	12	83	2	72	N/A	N/A	N/A	6	1,000	0	4.0	0.0
B- / 7.4	3.8	0.25	10.67	899	3	12	83	2	72	32.7	-4.0	79	6	0	0	0.0	0.0
C+ / 5.9	10.4	0.76	12.97	7,190	5	94	0	1	47	N/A	N/A	97	5	0	0	0.0	0.0
C+ / 5.7	11.4	1.02	16.63	344	3	96	0	1	90	N/A	N/A	29	N/A	1,000	0	5.0	0.0
C+ / 5.7	11.4	1.02	16.72	15	3	96	0	1	90	N/A	N/A	33	N/A	250,000	0	0.0	0.0
C+ / 5.6	11.4	1.02	16.73	1,629	3	96	0	1	90	N/A	N/A	35	N/A	0	0	0.0	0.0
C- / 3.1	14.0	0.70	11.08	28	6	93	0	1	349	71.8	-21.1	71	8	1,000	0	5.0	0.0
C- / 3.2	14.0	0.71	11.46	12	6	93	0	1	349	74.7	-21.0	74	8	250,000	0	0.0	0.0
C- / 3.3	14.0	0.71	11.65	578	6	93	0	1	349	76.4	-20.9	75	8	0	0	0.0	0.0
B+ / 9.7	3.2	0.07	13.42	2,104	0	1	98	1	31	20.1	-1.2	85	3	0	0	0.0	0.0
C / 4.3	12.1	1.06	42.10	554	0	98	0	2	44	115.9	-14.4	37	22	1,000	0	5.0	0.0
C- / 3.9	12.1	1.06	36.41	18	0	98	0	2	44	107.3	-14.7	29	22	1,000	0	0.0	0.0
C- / 3.9	12.1	1.06	36.42	113	0	98	0	2	44	107.2	-14.7	29	22	1,000	0	0.0	0.0
C / 4.4	12.1	1.06	44.79	324	0	98	0	2	44	119.4	-14.3	41	22	250,000	0	0.0	0.0

I. Index of Stock Mutual Funds

Fund Type	Fund Name	Ticker Symbol	Overall Investment Rating	Phone	Perfor-mance Rating/Pts	Total Return % through 2/28/17			Annualized		Incl. in Returns	
	99 Pct = Best *0 Pct = Worst*					3 Mo	6 Mo	1Yr / Pct	3Yr / Pct	5Yr / Pct	Dividend Yield	Expense Ratio
GL	J Hancock US Glob Lead Gr R2	USLYX	C+	(800) 257-3336	B- / 7.0	8.32	3.82	18.58 /45	8.13 /80	11.64 /71	0.00	1.31
GR	J Hancock US Glob Lead Gr R6	UGLSX	C+	(800) 257-3336	B- / 7.4	8.44	4.08	19.17 /48	8.69 /85	12.15 /76	0.00	0.82
GR	J Hancock US Growth 1	JHUPX	D+	(800) 257-3336	C+ / 6.9	8.84	5.34	17.92 /42	7.54 /76	--	1.77	0.91
IN	J Hancock US Growth A	JHUAX	D	(800) 257-3336	C+ / 5.6	8.80	5.16	17.56 /41	7.13 /73	10.74 /64	1.39	1.28
IN	J Hancock US Growth I	JHUIX	D+	(800) 257-3336	C+ / 6.8	8.82	5.29	17.86 /42	7.49 /75	11.15 /67	1.72	0.98
IN	J Hancock US Growth NAV		D+	(800) 257-3336	C+ / 6.9	8.74	5.29	17.98 /43	7.59 /76	11.26 /68	1.82	0.86
GR	J Hancock Value NAV		C+	(800) 257-3336	B+ / 8.3	7.42	11.87	33.10 /92	6.12 /65	11.96 /74	1.56	0.85
IX	J Hancock VIT 500 Index B Nav		A+	(800) 257-3336	A- / 9.2	7.96	9.84	24.60 /72	10.36 /95	13.73 /91	1.58	0.49
GR	J Hancock VIT All Cap Core I	JEACX	A-	(800) 257-3336	B / 8.0	6.23	9.82	22.75 /66	8.48 /83	13.00 /84	1.59	0.87
GR	J Hancock VIT All Cap Core II		A-	(800) 257-3336	B / 7.8	6.21	9.75	22.53 /65	8.26 /81	12.78 /82	1.42	1.07
GR	J Hancock VIT All Cap Core NAV		A-	(800) 257-3336	B / 8.0	6.26	9.85	22.83 /66	8.54 /83	13.07 /85	1.63	0.82
AA	J Hancock VIT Amer Ast All I		C+	(800) 257-3336	C+ / 6.1	5.48	6.75	18.12 /43	6.46 /68	9.81 /57	1.06	0.92
GL	J Hancock VIT Amer Growth I		C+	(800) 257-3336	A / 9.3	8.11	10.91	28.26 /82	9.61 /91	12.98 /84	0.26	0.97
GR	J Hancock VIT Amer Growth II		C+	(800) 257-3336	A / 9.3	8.08	10.90	28.15 /82	9.49 /90	12.85 /82	0.22	1.12
GI	J Hancock VIT Amer Growth-Inc I		C+	(800) 257-3336	B+ / 8.6	7.22	10.08	25.46 /75	8.68 /84	13.46 /88	1.16	0.91
GI	J Hancock VIT Amer Growth-Inc II		C	(800) 257-3336	B+ / 8.5	7.16	10.03	25.37 /74	8.55 /83	13.31 /87	1.11	1.06
FO	J Hancock VIT Amer Intl I		D	(800) 257-3336	D+ / 2.5	5.87	3.67	19.90 /51	0.41 /15	5.16 /22	0.96	1.17
FO	J Hancock VIT Amer Intl II		D	(800) 257-3336	D+ / 2.5	5.89	3.64	19.82 /51	0.27 /15	5.02 /21	0.82	1.32
GL	J Hancock VIT Blue Chip Gr I		C	(800) 257-3336	B+ / 8.3	8.78	9.94	22.33 /64	8.66 /84	14.41 /95	0.01	0.87
GL	J Hancock VIT Blue Chip Gr II		C	(800) 257-3336	B / 8.2	8.70	9.85	22.06 /62	8.44 /82	14.18 /94	0.00	1.07
GL	J Hancock VIT Blue Chip Gr NAV		C	(800) 257-3336	B+ / 8.4	8.78	9.98	22.38 /64	8.72 /85	14.47 /95	0.05	0.82
IN	J Hancock VIT Capital App I		C-	(800) 257-3336	B- / 7.5	8.55	8.64	21.01 /57	7.59 /76	12.87 /83	0.00	0.79
IN	J Hancock VIT Capital App II		D+	(800) 257-3336	B- / 7.4	8.54	8.54	20.83 /57	7.39 /75	12.66 /80	0.00	0.99
IN	J Hancock VIT Capital App NAV		C-	(800) 257-3336	B / 7.6	8.62	8.71	21.18 /58	7.67 /77	12.94 /83	0.01	0.74
EM	J Hancock VIT Emerg Mkts Val NAV	JHVTX	C-	(800) 257-3336	C+ / 6.8	11.26	10.12	37.41 /96	1.64 /22	-1.06 / 3	1.91	1.04
GL	J Hancock VIT Equity Income I		C+	(800) 257-3336	B / 8.2	5.24	11.42	28.98 /84	7.48 /75	11.71 /72	1.89	0.83
GL	J Hancock VIT Equity Income II		C+	(800) 257-3336	B / 8.1	5.20	11.29	28.79 /83	7.28 /74	11.48 /70	1.72	1.03
GL	J Hancock VIT Equity Income NAV		C+	(800) 257-3336	B+ / 8.3	5.27	11.44	29.08 /84	7.54 /76	11.76 /72	1.93	0.78
FS	J Hancock VIT Financial Indus I	JEFSX	C	(800) 257-3336	A+ / 9.9	9.83	24.18	44.54 /98	10.18 /94	12.90 /83	1.21	1.07
FS	J Hancock VIT Financial Indus II		C	(800) 257-3336	A+ / 9.9	9.73	24.00	44.30 /98	9.95 /93	12.66 /80	1.06	1.27
FS	J Hancock VIT Financial Indus NAV		C	(800) 257-3336	A+ / 9.9	9.78	24.20	44.48 /98	10.21 /94	12.93 /83	1.25	1.02
GR	J Hancock VIT Fund AC Core I	JEQAX	B+	(800) 257-3336	A / 9.4	8.33	10.76	32.52 /91	9.02 /87	15.17 /97	0.47	0.76
GR	J Hancock VIT Fund AC Core II		B+	(800) 257-3336	A / 9.4	8.30	10.65	32.26 /90	8.79 /85	14.94 /97	0.15	0.96
GR	J Hancock VIT Fund AC Core NAV		B+	(800) 257-3336	A / 9.5	8.39	10.80	32.66 /91	9.08 /87	15.23 /97	0.54	0.71
GR	J Hancock VIT Fund LC Val I	JVFLX	A-	(800) 257-3336	B+ / 8.8	7.21	10.90	30.31 /87	7.90 /78	13.49 /89	2.02	0.71
GR	J Hancock VIT Fund LC Val II		A-	(800) 257-3336	B+ / 8.6	7.16	10.78	30.07 /87	7.68 /77	13.26 /86	1.83	0.91
GR	J Hancock VIT Fund LC Val NAV		A-	(800) 257-3336	B+ / 8.8	7.27	10.94	30.35 /87	7.96 /79	13.55 /89	2.06	0.66
GL	J Hancock VIT Global I	JEFGX	C-	(800) 257-3336	C- / 4.0	6.83	9.60	25.78 /76	0.62 /16	8.32 /45	4.31	0.92
GL	J Hancock VIT Global NAV		C-	(800) 257-3336	C- / 4.1	6.83	9.59	25.80 /76	0.65 /16	8.38 /45	4.36	0.87
HL	J Hancock VIT Hlth Sciences I	JEHSX	D+	(800) 257-3336	B+ / 8.3	10.02	8.03	16.79 /38	9.81 /92	21.15 /99	0.06	1.08
FO	J Hancock VIT Intl Eqty Index B NAV		D-	(800) 257-3336	D / 1.6	7.38	4.54	19.19 /48	-0.39 /12	3.49 /13	2.57	0.61
FO	J Hancock VIT Intl Val I		E+	(800) 257-3336	D- / 1.5	7.46	8.06	27.38 /80	-2.09 / 6	4.77 /20	1.99	0.91
FO	J Hancock VIT Intl Val II		E+	(800) 257-3336	D- / 1.4	7.37	7.98	27.17 /80	-2.27 / 6	4.57 /19	1.82	1.11
FO	J Hancock VIT Intl Val NAV		E+	(800) 257-3336	D- / 1.5	7.43	8.08	27.46 /80	-2.05 / 7	4.81 /20	2.05	0.86
AG	J Hancock VIT Lifestyle Aggr I		D+	(800) 257-3336	D+ / 2.4	7.14	7.80	13.38 /23	0.33 /15	6.31 /30	1.58	0.92
AG	J Hancock VIT Lifestyle Aggr II		D+	(800) 257-3336	D / 2.2	7.06	7.72	13.20 /22	0.13 /14	6.09 /29	1.40	1.12
AG	J Hancock VIT Lifestyle Aggr NAV		D+	(800) 257-3336	D+ / 2.4	7.08	7.85	13.43 /23	0.35 /15	6.33 /30	1.62	0.87
BA	J Hancock VIT Lifestyle Bal I	JELBX	C-	(800) 257-3336	D+ / 2.7	4.65	3.46	11.54 /16	2.86 /30	5.60 /26	1.98	0.78
BA	J Hancock VIT Lifestyle Bal NAV		C-	(800) 257-3336	D+ / 2.7	4.61	3.51	11.66 /17	2.93 /31	5.64 /26	2.02	0.73
AA	J Hancock VIT Lifestyle Csv I	JELCX	C-	(800) 257-3336	D / 2.0	2.67	0.54	7.32 / 6	3.22 /34	4.13 /16	2.37	0.74
AA	J Hancock VIT Lifestyle Csv NAV		C-	(800) 257-3336	D / 2.0	2.62	0.50	7.36 / 6	3.23 /34	4.17 /16	2.42	0.69
GR	J Hancock VIT Lifestyle Gr NAV		C-	(800) 257-3336	D+ / 2.4	6.08	5.75	12.06 /18	1.31 /20	5.82 /27	1.81	0.75

● Denotes fund is closed to new investors
∗ Denotes fund is included in Section II

www.thestreetratings.com

RISK			NET ASSETS		ASSET				Portfolio Turnover Ratio	BULL / BEAR		FUND MANAGER		MINIMUMS		LOADS	
Risk Rating/Pts	3 Year Standard Deviation	Beta	NAV As of 2/28/17	Total $(Mil)	Cash %	Stocks %	Bonds %	Other %		Last Bull Market Return	Last Bear Market Return	Manager Quality Pct	Manager Tenure (Years)	Initial Purch. $	Additional Purch. $	Front End Load	Back End Load
C /4.4	12.1	0.81	44.23	6	0	98	0	2	44	115.1	-14.4	98	22	0	0	0.0	0.0
C /4.4	12.1	1.06	44.95	5	0	98	0	2	44	120.5	-14.4	43	22	1,000,000	0	0.0	0.0
D /1.8	10.5	0.97	8.75	46	0	97	2	1	85	N/A	N/A	41	1	0	0	0.0	0.0
D /1.9	10.5	0.97	8.80	41	0	97	2	1	85	93.9	-9.6	36	1	1,000	0	5.0	0.0
D /1.8	10.4	0.97	8.76	12	0	97	2	1	85	98.0	-9.5	41	1	250,000	0	0.0	0.0
D /1.8	10.4	0.97	8.75	7	0	97	2	1	85	99.0	-9.5	42	1	0	0	0.0	0.0
C- /3.9	13.7	1.16	11.79	338	2	96	0	2	38	126.6	-21.5	10	11	0	0	0.0	0.0
B- /7.0	10.3	1.00	28.89	1,729	3	96	0	1	4	131.6	-16.3	71	4	0	0	0.0	0.0
B- /7.0	11.2	1.01	31.37	72	0	98	1	1	238	127.3	-19.5	48	7	0	0	0.0	0.0
B- /7.0	11.2	1.01	31.30	7	0	98	1	1	238	124.9	-19.6	45	7	0	0	0.0	0.0
B- /7.0	11.2	1.01	31.39	116	0	98	1	1	238	127.9	-19.5	49	7	0	0	0.0	0.0
C+ /6.1	7.6	1.19	13.98	257	0	59	40	1	9	88.1	-13.6	44	10	0	0	0.0	0.0
D+ /2.6	11.3	0.79	20.00	117	0	96	3	1	21	122.4	-19.4	99	14	0	0	0.0	0.0
D+ /2.6	11.4	1.03	19.90	690	0	96	3	1	21	121.0	-19.5	58	14	0	0	0.0	0.0
C- /3.0	10.5	0.99	18.65	257	0	91	7	2	17	125.8	-17.2	53	18	0	0	0.0	0.0
D+ /2.9	10.5	0.99	18.60	604	0	91	7	2	17	124.2	-17.3	51	18	0	0	0.0	0.0
C /5.2	11.5	0.88	18.80	98	0	94	5	1	15	51.5	-25.5	78	14	0	0	0.0	0.0
C /5.2	11.5	0.88	18.79	372	0	94	5	1	15	50.3	-25.5	77	14	0	0	0.0	0.0
D+ /2.6	12.8	0.85	29.86	287	0	99	0	1	29	144.5	-14.8	99	18	0	0	0.0	0.0
D+ /2.5	12.7	0.85	29.23	123	0	99	0	1	29	141.9	-14.9	99	18	0	0	0.0	0.0
D+ /2.6	12.7	0.85	29.86	1,254	0	99	0	1	29	145.2	-14.8	99	18	0	0	0.0	0.0
D /2.0	13.4	1.10	12.70	175	0	99	0	1	30	124.2	-14.2	26	17	0	0	0.0	0.0
D /1.9	13.4	1.10	12.33	62	0	99	0	1	30	121.7	-14.2	24	17	0	0	0.0	0.0
D /2.0	13.4	1.10	12.73	771	0	99	0	1	30	125.0	-14.2	27	17	0	0	0.0	0.0
D+ /2.9	17.8	1.08	8.99	627	0	0	0	100	20	19.5	-31.9	72	7	0	0	0.0	0.0
C- /4.2	11.0	0.69	17.26	276	1	97	0	2	34	111.6	-18.3	98	N/A	0	0	0.0	0.0
C- /4.2	11.0	0.69	17.19	149	1	97	0	2	34	109.4	-18.4	98	N/A	0	0	0.0	0.0
C- /4.2	11.0	0.69	17.19	1,412	1	97	0	2	34	112.2	-18.3	98	N/A	0	0	0.0	0.0
D- /1.2	16.0	1.17	13.74	179	1	92	5	2	27	115.7	-19.7	24	3	0	0	0.0	0.0
D- /1.2	16.0	1.17	13.64	22	1	92	5	2	27	113.4	-19.7	22	3	0	0	0.0	0.0
D- /1.2	16.0	1.17	13.70	34	1	92	5	2	27	116.1	-19.6	24	3	0	0	0.0	0.0
C /4.7	14.8	1.31	22.23	154	4	94	0	2	49	147.0	-20.6	19	6	0	0	0.0	0.0
C /4.7	14.8	1.31	22.18	51	4	94	0	2	49	144.3	-20.7	17	6	0	0	0.0	0.0
C /4.7	14.8	1.31	22.34	1,477	4	94	0	2	49	147.7	-20.6	19	6	0	0	0.0	0.0
C+ /6.1	13.5	1.22	19.32	552	3	96	0	1	9	138.0	-19.9	18	6	0	0	0.0	0.0
C+ /6.1	13.5	1.22	19.45	209	3	96	0	1	9	135.6	-20.0	16	6	0	0	0.0	0.0
C+ /6.1	13.5	1.22	19.33	86	3	96	0	1	9	139.1	-20.0	18	6	0	0	0.0	0.0
C+ /5.6	12.7	0.98	19.56	145	1	97	0	2	23	79.2	-22.7	80	10	0	0	0.0	0.0
C+ /5.6	12.7	0.98	19.54	43	1	97	0	2	23	79.7	-22.7	80	10	0	0	0.0	0.0
E+ /0.7	17.5	1.10	24.48	103	0	99	0	1	43	224.9	-14.7	52	1	0	0	0.0	0.0
C+ /5.6	11.8	0.92	15.57	306	2	96	0	2	4	39.6	-24.5	71	12	0	0	0.0	0.0
C /4.6	13.9	1.03	12.97	113	0	97	2	1	16	46.3	-24.0	49	18	0	0	0.0	0.0
C /4.7	13.9	1.03	12.96	72	0	97	2	1	16	44.8	-24.0	47	18	0	0	0.0	0.0
C /4.6	13.9	1.03	12.87	670	0	97	2	1	16	46.7	-23.9	50	18	0	0	0.0	0.0
C+ /6.4	8.1	0.73	10.39	77	2	95	1	2	16	65.7	-21.3	5	7	0	0	0.0	0.0
C+ /6.4	8.1	0.73	10.36	87	2	95	1	2	16	63.7	-21.3	5	7	0	0	0.0	0.0
C+ /6.4	8.1	0.73	10.39	200	2	95	1	2	16	65.9	-21.2	5	7	0	0	0.0	0.0
B- /7.3	5.6	0.86	12.48	635	0	49	50	1	9	47.1	-9.6	29	7	0	0	0.0	0.0
B- /7.3	5.6	0.86	12.51	1,211	0	49	50	1	9	47.5	-9.7	30	7	0	0	0.0	0.0
B- /7.9	3.4	0.45	11.35	186	0	19	80	1	11	30.1	-2.2	73	N/A	0	0	0.0	0.0
B- /7.9	3.4	0.45	11.37	50	0	19	80	1	11	30.3	-2.2	72	N/A	0	0	0.0	0.0
B- /7.9	6.8	0.61	13.60	704	1	69	29	1	9	53.6	-14.0	15	7	0	0	0.0	0.0

Data as of February 28, 2017

I. Index of Stock Mutual Funds

Fund Type	Fund Name	Ticker Symbol	Overall Investment Rating	Phone	Perfor-mance Rating/Pts	3 Mo	6 Mo	1Yr / Pct	3Yr / Pct	5Yr / Pct	Dividend Yield	Expense Ratio
GR	J Hancock VIT Lifestyle Gro I	JELGX	C-	(800) 257-3336	D+ / 2.4	6.12	5.71	12.03 /18	1.26 /20	5.77 /27	1.76	0.80
GR	J Hancock VIT Lifestyle Gro II		C-	(800) 257-3336	D / 2.2	6.01	5.60	11.76 /17	1.06 /19	5.55 /25	1.58	1.00
BA	J Hancock VIT Lifestyle Modt I	JELMX	C-	(800) 257-3336	D+ / 2.7	3.93	2.45	10.82 /14	3.41 /36	5.52 /25	2.06	0.77
GR	J Hancock VIT Lifestyle Modt NAV		C-	(800) 257-3336	D+ / 2.8	3.98	2.50	10.96 /14	3.46 /37	5.57 /25	2.10	0.72
MC	● J Hancock VIT Mid Cap Index I	JECIX	B+	(800) 257-3336	A / 9.3	6.47	11.12	31.04 /88	9.14 /88	13.36 /87	0.99	0.56
MC	J Hancock VIT Mid Cap Index II		B+	(800) 257-3336	A- / 9.2	6.45	11.00	30.82 /88	8.91 /86	13.14 /85	0.83	0.76
MC	J Hancock VIT Mid Cap Index NAV		B+	(800) 257-3336	A / 9.3	6.52	11.11	31.10 /88	9.19 /88	13.42 /88	1.03	0.51
MC	J Hancock VIT Mid Cap Stock I		E	(800) 257-3336	C / 4.4	4.45	3.59	21.98 /62	3.76 /40	11.08 /67	0.00	0.92
MC	J Hancock VIT Mid Cap Stock II		E	(800) 257-3336	C- / 4.2	4.39	3.41	21.65 /60	3.54 /37	10.84 /64	0.00	1.12
MC	J Hancock VIT Mid Cap Stock NAV		E	(800) 257-3336	C / 4.5	4.47	3.62	22.06 /63	3.82 /41	11.13 /67	0.00	0.87
MC	J Hancock VIT Mid Value II		C+	(800) 257-3336	A / 9.4	4.72	10.56	31.15 /88	10.05 /94	14.18 /94	0.79	1.26
MC	J Hancock VIT Mid Value NAV		B-	(800) 257-3336	A / 9.5	4.83	10.75	31.64 /89	10.34 /95	14.48 /95	1.01	1.01
MC	J Hancock VIT Mid Value Trust I	JEMUX	C+	(800) 257-3336	A / 9.5	4.81	10.74	31.53 /89	10.27 /95	14.43 /95	0.96	1.06
RE	J Hancock VIT Real Est Sec I		C+	(800) 257-3336	B- / 7.3	8.17	-1.96	13.85 /25	10.90 /97	10.93 /65	3.37	0.79
RE	J Hancock VIT Real Est Sec II		C+	(800) 257-3336	B- / 7.2	8.10	-2.03	13.66 /24	10.69 /96	10.72 /64	3.17	0.99
RE	J Hancock VIT Real Est Sec NAV		C+	(800) 257-3336	B- / 7.3	8.17	-1.93	13.94 /25	10.96 /97	11.00 /66	3.44	0.74
TC	J Hancock VIT Science & Tech I	JESTX	B-	(800) 257-3336	A+ / 9.8	10.42	10.82	33.13 /92	11.42 /98	14.62 /96	0.00	1.13
TC	J Hancock VIT Science & Tech II		C+	(800) 257-3336	A+ / 9.8	10.35	10.70	32.89 /91	11.20 /97	14.39 /95	0.00	1.33
TC	J Hancock VIT Science & Tech NAV		B-	(800) 257-3336	A+ / 9.8	10.42	10.86	33.17 /92	11.46 /98	14.66 /96	0.00	1.08
SC	J Hancock VIT Small Cap Gr NAV		E	(800) 257-3336	C / 4.5	6.26	9.76	28.91 /84	0.81 /17	9.24 /53	0.00	1.09
SC	● J Hancock VIT Small Cap Idx I	JESIX	B-	(800) 257-3336	B+ / 8.7	5.16	12.45	35.72 /95	6.69 /70	12.64 /80	0.95	0.58
SC	J Hancock VIT Small Cap Idx II		C+	(800) 257-3336	B+ / 8.5	5.12	12.36	35.49 /94	6.47 /68	12.42 /78	0.79	0.78
SC	J Hancock VIT Small Cap Idx NAV		B-	(800) 257-3336	B+ / 8.7	5.23	12.48	35.84 /95	6.76 /70	12.72 /81	0.99	0.53
SC	J Hancock VIT Small Cap Oppt NAV		C+	(800) 257-3336	B- / 7.4	4.17	12.58	29.62 /86	5.80 /63	12.08 /75	0.46	1.05
SC	J Hancock VIT Small Cap Oppty I		C+	(800) 257-3336	B- / 7.4	4.14	12.59	29.57 /85	5.75 /62	12.02 /74	0.41	1.10
SC	J Hancock VIT Small Cap Oppty II		C+	(800) 257-3336	B- / 7.3	4.11	12.49	29.31 /85	5.55 /60	11.80 /72	0.23	1.30
SC	J Hancock VIT Small Cap Val I	JESVX	C+	(800) 257-3336	B+ / 8.6	4.70	10.89	27.26 /80	8.77 /85	13.11 /85	0.57	1.17
GR	J Hancock VIT Small Cap Val NAV		C+	(800) 257-3336	B+ / 8.7	4.72	10.91	27.34 /80	8.83 /86	13.16 /85	0.61	1.12
SC	J Hancock VIT Small Co Val I		B-	(800) 257-3336	A / 9.3	4.78	13.54	37.68 /96	7.77 /77	12.17 /76	0.61	1.17
SC	J Hancock VIT Small Co Val NAV		B-	(800) 257-3336	A / 9.4	4.74	13.51	37.71 /96	7.81 /78	12.22 /76	0.65	1.12
GR	● J Hancock VIT Tot Stk Mkt Id I	JETSX	A	(800) 257-3336	B+ / 8.8	7.53	10.10	25.95 /76	9.01 /87	13.09 /85	1.29	0.58
GR	J Hancock VIT Tot Stk Mkt Id II		A	(800) 257-3336	B+ / 8.7	7.45	9.97	25.69 /75	8.77 /85	12.85 /82	1.12	0.78
GR	J Hancock VIT Tot Stk Mkt Id NAV		A	(800) 257-3336	B+ / 8.8	7.48	10.09	25.95 /76	9.06 /87	13.13 /85	1.33	0.53
UT	J Hancock VIT Utilities I	JEUTX	D	(800) 257-3336	C / 4.5	9.70	4.52	19.48 /49	3.10 /33	8.19 /44	4.40	0.92
UT	J Hancock VIT Utilities II		D	(800) 257-3336	C / 4.4	9.72	4.54	19.36 /49	2.92 /31	8.00 /42	4.25	1.12
UT	J Hancock VIT Utilities NAV		D	(800) 257-3336	C / 4.6	9.71	4.65	19.66 /50	3.18 /33	8.27 /44	4.45	0.87
GR	Jackson Square Lg-Cap Growth IS	DPLGX	D-	(888) 276-0061	C- / 3.7	6.08	2.85	9.36 /10	5.14 /56	10.76 /64	0.29	0.69
AG	Jackson Square Sel 20 Growth IS	DPCEX	E	(888) 276-0061	D+ / 2.7	4.46	1.45	6.69 / 5	4.29 /46	8.38 /45	0.00	0.90
SC	Jackson Square SMID-Cap Growth IS	DCGTX	C-	(888) 276-0061	C+ / 6.4	4.31	4.22	16.08 /35	8.18 /80	10.88 /65	0.23	0.92
TC	Jacob Internet Fund Investor	JAMFX	D-	(888) 522-6239	C / 4.9	-0.51	-1.87	28.59 /83	5.90 /63	11.57 /71	0.00	2.51
SC	Jacob Micro Cap Growth Inst	JMIGX	E-	(888) 522-6239	E- / 0.0	2.17	-10.49	5.96 / 5	-9.26 / 1	0.51 / 5	0.00	3.81
SC	Jacob Micro Cap Growth Inv	JMCGX	E-	(888) 522-6239	E- / 0.0	2.05	-10.66	5.61 / 4	-9.55 / 1	0.19 / 5	0.00	4.06
SC	Jacob Small Cap Growth Inst	JSIGX	E-	(888) 522-6239	E+ / 0.7	0.57	4.46	32.13 /90	-4.52 / 3	-7.35 / 1	0.00	2.94
SC	Jacob Small Cap Growth Investor	JSCGX	E-	(888) 522-6239	E / 0.5	0.52	4.39	31.69 /89	-4.77 / 3	3.31 /12	0.00	3.14
GR	JAG Large Cap Growth A	JLGAX	C	(855) 552-4596	C+ / 6.2	7.73	6.98	22.75 /66	7.13 /73	11.50 /70	0.00	1.77
GR	JAG Large Cap Growth C	JLGCX	C	(855) 552-4596	C+ / 6.7	7.59	6.60	21.85 /61	6.33 /67	10.65 /63	0.00	2.52
GR	JAG Large Cap Growth I	JLGIX	C+	(855) 552-4596	B- / 7.4	7.83	7.09	23.01 /67	7.37 /75	11.75 /72	0.00	1.52
BA	James Adv Bal Goldn Rainbow Retail	GLRBX	C	(888) 426-7640	D+ / 2.5	3.45	3.42	7.99 / 7	3.47 /37	5.72 /26	1.18	0.97
BA	James Advantage Bal Goldn Rainbow	GLRIX	C	(888) 426-7640	D+ / 2.7	3.51	3.59	8.30 / 8	3.75 /40	5.98 /28	1.43	0.72
GI	James Advantage Long-Short	JAZZX	C-	(888) 426-7640	D+ / 2.7	5.04	6.72	8.38 / 8	2.90 /31	6.70 /33	0.00	2.53
MC	James Advantage Mid-Cap	JAMDX	C-	(888) 426-7640	C- / 3.8	4.76	5.96	11.80 /17	4.45 /48	9.71 /56	0.12	1.51
SC	James Advantage Small Cap Value	JASCX	D+	(888) 426-7640	C- / 3.0	0.30	6.62	16.55 /37	2.77 /30	8.45 /46	0.50	1.51

● Denotes fund is closed to new investors
* Denotes fund is included in Section II

www.thestreetratings.com

I. Index of Stock Mutual Funds

RISK			NET ASSETS		ASSET					BULL / BEAR		FUND MANAGER		MINIMUMS		LOADS	
	3 Year		NAV						Portfolio	Last Bull	Last Bear	Manager	Manager	Initial	Additional	Front	Back
Risk Rating/Pts	Standard Deviation	Beta	As of 2/28/17	Total $(Mil)	Cash %	Stocks %	Bonds %	Other %	Turnover Ratio	Market Return	Market Return	Quality Pct	Tenure (Years)	Purch. $	Purch. $	End Load	End Load
B- / 7.9	6.8	0.61	13.58	691	1	69	29	1	9	53.2	-14.1	15	7	0	0	0.0	0.0
B- / 7.9	6.8	0.61	13.54	8,375	1	69	29	1	9	51.5	-14.1	14	7	0	0	0.0	0.0
B- / 7.1	4.9	0.76	12.00	261	0	40	59	1	10	43.8	-6.8	46	N/A	0	0	0.0	0.0
B- / 7.1	5.0	0.44	12.01	118	0	40	59	1	10	44.1	-6.7	61	12	0	0	0.0	0.0
C / 4.8	12.1	1.00	22.23	863	2	97	0	1	23	135.2	-22.7	69	4	0	0	0.0	0.0
C / 4.8	12.1	1.00	22.13	69	2	97	0	1	23	132.6	-22.8	66	4	0	0	0.0	0.0
C / 4.8	12.0	1.00	22.23	149	2	97	0	1	23	135.9	-22.7	70	4	0	0	0.0	0.0
E+ / 0.6	14.5	1.03	15.02	156	1	98	0	1	78	107.0	-24.3	10	18	0	0	0.0	0.0
E / 0.4	14.5	1.03	14.26	80	1	98	0	1	78	104.8	-24.4	9	18	0	0	0.0	0.0
E+ / 0.7	14.6	1.03	15.19	468	1	98	0	1	78	107.7	-24.3	10	18	0	0	0.0	0.0
C- / 3.0	10.9	0.86	11.99	67	8	91	0	1	93	131.1	-19.5	84	13	0	0	0.0	0.0
D+ / 2.9	10.9	0.86	11.93	431	8	91	0	1	93	134.4	-19.4	86	13	0	0	0.0	0.0
C- / 3.0	10.9	0.87	11.99	353	8	91	0	1	93	133.8	-19.5	85	13	0	0	0.0	0.0
C / 5.1	14.8	1.08	19.32	86	0	99	0	1	152	104.5	-17.1	62	30	0	0	0.0	0.0
C / 5.1	14.8	1.08	19.35	51	0	99	0	1	152	102.3	-17.1	60	30	0	0	0.0	0.0
C / 5.1	14.8	1.08	19.20	256	0	99	0	1	152	105.2	-17.1	63	30	0	0	0.0	0.0
D+ / 2.8	14.6	1.23	25.00	471	4	94	0	2	118	141.1	-20.6	55	8	0	0	0.0	0.0
D+ / 2.7	14.6	1.23	24.10	48	4	94	0	2	118	138.4	-20.6	52	8	0	0	0.0	0.0
D+ / 2.8	14.6	1.22	25.22	38	4	94	0	2	118	141.7	-20.5	56	8	0	0	0.0	0.0
E / 0.5	17.5	1.01	8.66	275	0	98	0	2	87	90.7	-25.5	9	14	0	0	0.0	0.0
C- / 3.9	15.7	1.00	15.08	392	4	95	0	1	19	129.6	-25.3	72	4	0	0	0.0	0.0
C- / 3.9	15.8	1.00	15.00	45	4	95	0	1	19	127.0	-25.4	69	4	0	0	0.0	0.0
C- / 3.9	15.8	1.00	15.10	118	4	95	0	1	19	130.2	-25.2	72	4	0	0	0.0	0.0
C / 4.9	14.5	0.90	31.50	85	1	98	0	1	25	126.9	-26.0	70	9	0	0	0.0	0.0
C / 4.9	14.5	0.90	31.66	98	1	98	0	1	25	126.4	-26.0	69	9	0	0	0.0	0.0
C / 4.9	14.5	0.90	31.16	39	1	98	0	1	25	123.9	-26.1	67	9	0	0	0.0	0.0
C- / 3.1	15.2	0.92	21.37	370	2	97	0	1	22	133.9	-21.3	87	15	0	0	0.0	0.0
C- / 3.1	15.3	1.06	21.31	306	2	97	0	1	22	134.5	-21.2	45	15	0	0	0.0	0.0
C- / 3.5	14.4	0.87	22.15	70	2	97	0	1	35	125.0	-23.4	84	N/A	0	0	0.0	0.0
C- / 3.5	14.4	0.87	22.09	155	2	97	0	1	35	125.7	-23.4	85	N/A	0	0	0.0	0.0
C+ / 6.4	10.6	1.02	20.27	502	6	93	0	1	4	126.4	-17.8	53	4	0	0	0.0	0.0
C+ / 6.4	10.6	1.02	20.19	37	6	93	0	1	4	124.0	-17.8	50	4	0	0	0.0	0.0
C+ / 6.4	10.6	1.02	20.26	137	6	93	0	1	4	127.0	-17.8	53	4	0	0	0.0	0.0
C- / 3.4	12.1	0.46	13.34	285	16	79	3	2	37	68.3	-12.2	31	16	0	0	0.0	0.0
C- / 3.4	12.1	0.46	13.21	15	16	79	3	2	37	66.6	-12.3	28	16	0	0	0.0	0.0
C- / 3.4	12.1	0.46	13.33	29	16	79	3	2	37	68.9	-12.2	31	16	0	0	0.0	0.0
C- / 3.3	11.9	0.96	12.44	161	3	96	0	1	27	109.6	-12.4	18	12	1,000,000	0	0.0	0.0
D- / 1.3	12.5	1.02	7.02	84	5	94	0	1	22	89.6	-8.7	9	12	1,000,000	0	0.0	0.0
C- / 3.1	10.9	0.60	18.68	94	2	97	0	1	21	108.2	-16.0	93	1	1,000,000	0	0.0	0.0
D / 2.1	16.4	0.99	4.11	41	0	98	0	2	43	104.8	-21.8	21	18	2,500	100	0.0	2.0
E- / 0.0	20.2	0.85	10.84	6	0	98	1	1	43	38.6	-30.7	0	5	1,000,000	1,000	0.0	0.0
E- / 0.0	20.1	0.85	9.97	2	0	98	1	1	43	36.3	-30.8	0	5	2,500	100	0.0	2.0
E+ / 0.8	23.2	1.14	17.56	11	0	99	0	1	58	-13.3	-25.2	1	7	1,000,000	1,000	0.0	0.0
E+ / 0.8	23.1	1.14	17.37	5	0	99	0	1	58	44.7	-31.9	1	7	2,500	100	0.0	2.0
C / 4.6	13.0	1.05	15.94	2	1	98	0	1	149	N/A	N/A	27	6	2,500	50	5.8	0.0
C / 4.5	13.0	1.05	15.22	N/A	1	98	0	1	149	N/A	N/A	19	6	2,500	50	0.0	0.0
C / 4.7	13.0	1.05	16.16	46	1	98	0	1	149	N/A	N/A	29	6	250,000	50	0.0	0.0
B / 8.7	5.0	0.73	24.90	2,549	2	44	52	2	46	46.2	-5.4	49	26	2,000	0	0.0	0.0
B / 8.7	5.0	0.74	24.66	1,391	2	44	52	2	46	48.2	-5.3	53	26	50,000	0	0.0	0.0
B- / 7.5	8.8	0.68	13.97	23	0	99	0	1	49	61.3	N/A	24	20	2,000	0	0.0	0.0
C+ / 5.6	10.2	0.75	13.04	15	2	95	1	2	47	95.6	-21.6	41	11	2,000	0	0.0	0.0
C+ / 5.9	14.4	0.81	34.15	76	3	95	1	1	57	87.1	-16.4	38	20	2,000	0	0.0	0.0

	99 Pct = Best 0 Pct = Worst				PERFORMANCE						Incl. in Returns	
			Overall		Perfor-	Total Return % through 2/28/17					Dividend	Expense
			Investment		mance				Annualized			
Fund		Ticker	Rating	Phone	Rating/Pts	3 Mo	6 Mo	1Yr / Pct	3Yr / Pct	5Yr / Pct	Yield	Ratio
Type	Fund Name	Symbol										
FS	James Alpha Hdgd Hi Inc A	INCAX	C-	(866) 759-5679	D / 2.0	3.82	5.98	15.57 /32	2.59 /28	—	4.13	3.69
FS	James Alpha Hdgd Hi Inc C	INCCX	C-	(866) 759-5679	D+ / 2.4	3.68	5.70	14.91 /29	1.97 /24	—	3.83	4.40
FS	James Alpha Hdgd Hi Inc I	INCIX	C-	(866) 759-5679	C- / 3.0	3.83	5.97	15.80 /33	2.93 /31	—	4.57	3.38
GR	James Micro Cap	JMCRX	C	(888) 426-7640	C / 5.5	0.94	8.35	16.48 /36	7.29 /74	13.52 /89	0.00	1.51
GR	Jamestown Equity	JAMEX	C+	(866) 738-1126	C+ / 6.7	7.31	8.75	20.36 /54	6.24 /66	10.83 /64	0.88	1.03
GL	Janus Adaptive Global Allocation N	JAGNX	U	(800) 295-2687	U /	5.11	5.11	12.03 /18	—	—	1.12	1.38
FO	Janus Asia Equity A	JAQAX	C+	(800) 295-2687	C+ / 6.5	7.71	5.74	30.81 /88	6.08 /65	4.55 /18	1.09	2.87
FO	Janus Asia Equity C	JAQCX	C+	(800) 295-2687	C+ / 6.9	7.57	5.46	30.03 /86	5.31 /58	3.77 /14	0.41	3.59
FO	● Janus Asia Equity D	JAQDX	B-	(800) 295-2687	B / 7.6	7.72	5.88	31.12 /88	6.26 /66	4.68 /19	1.11	2.75
FO	Janus Asia Equity I	JAQIX	B-	(800) 295-2687	B / 7.7	7.79	5.95	31.31 /89	6.44 /68	4.89 /21	1.37	2.56
FO	Janus Asia Equity S	JAQSX	B-	(800) 295-2687	B- / 7.5	7.73	5.76	30.97 /88	6.16 /66	4.54 /18	0.99	3.06
FO	Janus Asia Equity T	JAQTX	B-	(800) 295-2687	B / 7.6	7.76	5.89	31.22 /89	6.28 /67	4.71 /19	0.87	2.73
BA	Janus Aspen Balanced Inst	JABLX	B-	(800) 295-2687	C+ / 5.6	6.56	8.03	15.12 /30	5.78 /62	8.71 /48	2.06	0.63
BA	Janus Aspen Balanced Svc		B	(800) 295-2687	C / 5.3	6.51	7.90	14.86 /29	5.51 /60	8.45 /46	1.80	0.89
MC	Janus Aspen Enterprise Inst	JAAGX	B+	(800) 295-2687	A- / 9.0	6.28	6.95	24.90 /73	10.73 /96	14.16 /94	0.13	0.73
MC	Janus Aspen Enterprise Svc		B+	(800) 295-2687	B+ / 8.9	6.23	6.82	24.59 /72	10.45 /96	13.87 /92	0.02	0.99
GR	Janus Aspen Forty Inst	JACAX	C-	(800) 295-2687	B+ / 8.9	9.62	7.94	22.59 /65	10.03 /93	13.86 /92	0.00	0.74
GR	Janus Aspen Forty Svc		D+	(800) 295-2687	B+ / 8.8	9.57	7.81	22.31 /64	9.75 /92	13.57 /90	0.00	0.99
GL	Janus Aspen Global Research Inst	JAWGX	C	(800) 295-2687	C / 4.8	7.00	5.88	20.01 /52	3.75 /40	8.95 /50	1.00	0.85
GL	Janus Aspen Global Research Svc		C-	(800) 295-2687	C / 4.5	6.92	5.73	19.69 /50	3.48 /37	8.68 /48	0.87	1.10
TC	Janus Aspen Global Technology Inst	JGLTX	B	(800) 295-2687	A+ / 9.9	9.63	10.68	39.12 /97	12.72 /99	15.18 /97	0.17	0.81
TC	Janus Aspen Global Technology Svc		B	(800) 295-2687	A+ / 9.9	9.60	10.64	38.77 /97	12.47 /98	14.91 /97	0.08	1.06
FO	Janus Aspen Overseas Inst	JAIGX	E-	(800) 295-2687	E / 0.3	6.50	5.02	18.37 /44	-6.16 / 2	-3.46 / 2	4.49	0.56
FO	Janus Aspen Overseas Svc		E-	(800) 295-2687	E / 0.3	6.43	4.94	18.11 /43	-6.38 / 2	-3.69 / 2	4.48	0.82
MC	Janus Aspen Perkins Mid Cp Val Inst	JAMVX	B+	(800) 295-2687	A- / 9.2	6.46	11.09	30.42 /87	9.12 /88	11.02 /66	0.88	0.64
MC	Janus Aspen Perkins Mid Cp Val Svc		B	(800) 295-2687	A- / 9.1	6.40	10.94	30.12 /87	8.86 /86	10.76 /64	0.76	0.89
BA	Janus Balanced A	JDBAX	C+	(800) 295-2687	C- / 4.1	6.53	7.93	14.90 /29	5.52 /60	8.29 /45	1.76	0.93
BA	Janus Balanced C	JABCX	C+	(800) 295-2687	C / 4.7	6.35	7.57	14.10 /26	4.78 /52	7.51 /38	1.32	1.66
BA	● Janus Balanced D	JANBX	B-	(800) 295-2687	C / 5.5	6.54	8.03	15.11 /30	5.73 /62	8.52 /46	2.03	0.73
BA	Janus Balanced I	JBALX	B-	(800) 295-2687	C+ / 5.6	6.59	8.09	15.21 /31	5.81 /63	8.59 /47	2.09	0.65
BA	Janus Balanced N	JABNX	B-	(800) 295-2687	C+ / 5.7	6.62	8.14	15.31 /31	5.89 /63	8.67 /48	2.15	0.58
BA	Janus Balanced R	JDBRX	C+	(800) 295-2687	C / 5.0	6.42	7.73	14.47 /28	5.10 /55	7.88 /41	1.59	1.32
BA	Janus Balanced S	JABRX	B-	(800) 295-2687	C / 5.2	6.50	7.87	14.76 /29	5.36 /58	8.15 /43	1.75	1.08
BA	Janus Balanced T	JABAX	B-	(800) 295-2687	C / 5.5	6.56	8.02	15.03 /30	5.63 /61	8.42 /46	1.95	0.83
GL	Janus Contrarian A	JCNAX	D	(800) 295-2687	C- / 3.4	4.73	11.85	21.48 /60	2.41 /27	11.68 /71	0.02	1.13
GL	Janus Contrarian C	JCNCX	D	(800) 295-2687	C- / 3.9	4.58	11.51	20.60 /55	1.65 /22	10.79 /64	0.00	1.89
GL	● Janus Contrarian D	JACNX	D+	(800) 295-2687	C / 4.6	4.77	11.98	21.66 /61	2.49 /27	11.81 /73	0.32	0.95
GL	Janus Contrarian I	JCONX	D+	(800) 295-2687	C / 4.8	4.83	12.04	21.85 /61	2.70 /29	12.00 /74	0.37	0.86
GL	Janus Contrarian R	JCNRX	D+	(800) 295-2687	C- / 4.2	4.64	11.65	21.02 /57	2.02 /24	11.24 /68	0.00	1.54
GL	Janus Contrarian S	JCNIX	D+	(800) 295-2687	C / 4.4	4.71	11.77	21.25 /59	2.28 /26	11.53 /70	0.00	1.29
GL	Janus Contrarian T	JSVAX	D+	(800) 295-2687	C / 4.7	4.80	11.96	21.64 /60	2.54 /28	11.82 /73	0.24	1.04
IN	Janus Diversified Alternatives A	JDDAX	C	(800) 295-2687	D / 1.6	1.01	3.62	8.24 / 8	3.29 /35	—	2.60	1.66
IN	Janus Diversified Alternatives C	JDDCX	C	(800) 295-2687	D / 1.9	0.75	3.21	7.34 / 6	2.73 /29	—	2.14	2.40
IN	● Janus Diversified Alternatives D	JDADX	C+	(800) 295-2687	D+ / 2.3	1.02	3.62	8.33 / 8	3.39 /36	—	2.86	1.82
IN	Janus Diversified Alternatives I	JDAIX	C+	(800) 295-2687	D+ / 2.3	1.06	3.75	8.45 / 8	3.50 /37	—	2.99	1.40
IN	Janus Diversified Alternatives N	JDANX	C+	(800) 295-2687	D+ / 2.4	1.03	3.71	8.51 / 8	3.56 /38	—	2.96	1.39
IN	Janus Diversified Alternatives S	JDASX	C+	(800) 295-2687	D / 2.2	0.89	3.50	8.02 / 7	3.23 /34	—	2.94	1.89
IN	Janus Diversified Alternatives T	JDATX	C+	(800) 295-2687	D+ / 2.3	1.03	3.72	8.44 / 8	3.43 /36	—	3.06	1.64
GL	● Janus Enterprise A	JDMAX	B	(800) 295-2687	B- / 7.5	6.10	6.60	23.83 /69	9.81 /92	13.26 /86	0.00	1.14
GL	● Janus Enterprise C	JGRCX	B+	(800) 295-2687	B / 8.0	5.93	6.26	23.05 /67	9.11 /87	12.49 /79	0.00	1.78
GL	● Janus Enterprise D	JANEX	A-	(800) 295-2687	B+ / 8.7	6.18	6.77	24.22 /71	10.14 /94	13.60 /90	0.09	0.84
GL	● Janus Enterprise I	JMGRX	A-	(800) 295-2687	B+ / 8.8	6.19	6.80	24.29 /71	10.20 /94	13.69 /91	0.16	0.74

● Denotes fund is closed to new investors
* Denotes fund is included in Section II

RISK			NET ASSETS		ASSET					BULL / BEAR		FUND MANAGER		MINIMUMS		LOADS	
	3 Year		NAV						Portfolio	Last Bull	Last Bear	Manager	Manager	Initial	Additional	Front	Back
Risk	Standard		As of	Total	Cash	Stocks	Bonds	Other	Turnover	Market	Market	Quality	Tenure	Purch.	Purch.	End	End
Rating/Pts	Deviation	Beta	2/28/17	$(Mil)	%	%	%	%	Ratio	Return	Return	Pct	(Years)	$	$	Load	Load
B- / 7.3	3.9	0.18	9.40	1	11	0	84	5	91	N/A	N/A	76	4	2,500	0	5.8	2.0
B- / 7.3	3.9	0.18	9.40	1	11	0	84	5	91	N/A	N/A	71	4	2,500	0	0.0	2.0
B- / 7.3	3.9	0.18	9.40	13	11	0	84	5	91	N/A	N/A	79	4	1,000,000	0	0.0	2.0
C / 5.4	14.3	0.88	17.25	35	10	89	0	1	44	137.6	-24.3	50	7	10,000	0	0.0	2.0
C+ / 6.0	11.7	1.10	21.04	38	8	91	0	1	50	103.9	-16.5	15	17	5,000	0	0.0	0.0
U /	N/A	N/A	10.09	47	42	53	4	1	122	N/A	N/A	N/A	2	0	0	0.0	0.0
C / 4.9	15.6	0.92	9.70	N/A	4	95	0	1	59	55.3	N/A	97	6	2,500	0	5.8	0.0
C / 4.9	15.7	0.92	9.67	N/A	4	95	0	1	59	49.5	N/A	96	6	2,500	0	0.0	0.0
C / 5.0	15.7	0.92	9.78	7	4	95	0	1	59	56.9	N/A	97	6	2,500	0	0.0	0.0
C / 4.9	15.6	0.92	9.78	3	4	95	0	1	59	58.0	N/A	97	6	1,000,000	0	0.0	0.0
C / 5.0	15.6	0.91	9.73	N/A	4	95	0	1	59	55.1	N/A	97	6	2,500	0	0.0	0.0
C / 4.9	15.7	0.92	9.67	N/A	4	95	0	1	59	56.5	N/A	97	6	2,500	0	0.0	0.0
B- / 7.8	6.8	1.04	31.96	409	2	59	38	1	73	77.4	-12.3	49	12	0	0	0.0	0.0
B- / 7.8	6.8	1.05	33.60	2,261	2	59	38	1	73	75.0	-12.3	45	12	0	0	0.0	0.0
C / 4.9	10.9	0.85	63.02	478	2	97	0	1	22	140.2	-19.2	88	10	0	0	0.0	0.0
C / 4.8	10.9	0.85	59.75	437	2	97	0	1	22	137.0	-19.3	87	10	0	0	0.0	0.0
E / 0.5	12.9	1.08	35.09	271	2	97	0	1	55	139.5	-18.4	58	4	0	0	0.0	0.0
E / 0.3	12.9	1.08	33.55	446	2	97	0	1	55	136.2	-18.5	54	4	0	0	0.0	0.0
C+ / 5.7	11.8	0.87	43.32	487	4	95	0	1	50	85.5	-23.7	93	3	0	0	0.0	0.0
C+ / 5.7	11.8	0.87	42.48	186	4	95	0	1	50	82.9	-23.8	92	3	0	0	0.0	0.0
C- / 3.5	14.5	1.23	9.22	11	1	98	0	1	43	147.1	-19.2	69	6	0	0	0.0	0.0
C- / 3.5	14.4	1.22	9.36	263	1	98	0	1	43	144.0	-19.4	67	6	0	0	0.0	0.0
D / 2.1	17.9	1.26	26.39	164	4	95	0	1	31	4.5	-31.9	8	1	0	0	0.0	0.0
D / 2.1	17.9	1.26	25.41	558	4	95	0	1	31	3.2	-31.9	7	1	0	0	0.0	0.0
C / 4.5	10.1	0.81	17.34	49	5	94	0	1	77	103.1	-19.7	83	15	0	0	0.0	0.0
C / 4.4	10.0	0.80	16.86	73	5	94	0	1	77	100.2	-19.8	82	15	0	0	0.0	0.0
B- / 7.4	6.8	1.05	30.80	900	1	59	38	2	83	73.7	-12.4	45	12	2,500	0	5.8	0.0
B- / 7.4	6.8	1.05	30.54	1,332	1	59	38	2	83	67.1	-12.7	36	12	2,500	0	0.0	0.0
B- / 7.4	6.8	1.05	30.87	1,450	1	59	38	2	83	75.7	-12.3	48	12	2,500	0	0.0	0.0
B- / 7.4	6.8	1.05	30.89	1,601	1	59	38	2	83	76.4	-12.3	49	12	1,000,000	0	0.0	0.0
B- / 7.4	6.8	1.05	30.86	1,924	1	59	38	2	83	76.8	-12.3	50	12	0	0	0.0	0.0
B- / 7.4	6.8	1.05	30.64	338	1	59	38	2	83	70.2	-12.5	40	12	2,500	0	0.0	0.0
B- / 7.4	6.8	1.05	30.79	645	1	59	38	2	83	72.5	-12.4	43	12	2,500	0	0.0	0.0
B- / 7.4	6.8	1.05	30.84	4,613	1	59	38	2	83	74.8	-12.3	47	12	2,500	0	0.0	0.0
C / 4.5	12.4	0.57	20.04	44	7	92	0	1	51	111.2	-26.1	88	6	2,500	0	5.8	0.0
C / 4.4	12.4	0.57	18.99	38	7	92	0	1	51	102.5	-26.3	85	6	2,500	0	0.0	0.0
C / 4.5	12.4	0.57	20.07	1,920	7	92	0	1	51	112.9	-26.1	88	6	2,500	0	0.0	0.0
C / 4.5	12.4	0.57	20.09	97	7	92	0	1	51	114.6	-26.1	89	6	1,000,000	0	0.0	0.0
C / 4.5	12.4	0.57	19.64	1	7	92	0	1	51	107.0	-26.3	86	6	2,500	0	0.0	0.0
C / 4.5	12.4	0.57	20.03	4	7	92	0	1	51	109.9	-26.2	88	6	2,500	0	0.0	0.0
C / 4.5	12.4	0.57	20.07	767	7	92	0	1	51	112.8	-26.1	89	6	2,500	0	0.0	0.0
B+ / 9.4	4.7	0.14	10.16	3	92	7	0	1	0	N/A	N/A	85	5	2,500	0	5.8	0.0
B+ / 9.4	4.7	0.14	9.96	2	92	7	0	1	0	N/A	N/A	82	5	2,500	0	0.0	0.0
B+ / 9.4	4.7	0.14	10.19	5	92	7	0	1	0	N/A	N/A	85	5	2,500	100	0.0	0.0
B+ / 9.5	4.7	0.14	10.23	5	92	7	0	1	0	N/A	N/A	86	5	1,000,000	0	0.0	0.0
B+ / 9.5	4.7	0.14	10.25	45	92	7	0	1	0	N/A	N/A	86	5	0	0	0.0	0.0
B+ / 9.4	4.6	0.13	10.09	1	92	7	0	1	0	N/A	N/A	85	5	2,500	0	0.0	0.0
B+ / 9.5	4.7	0.14	10.17	3	92	7	0	1	0	N/A	N/A	85	5	2,500	0	0.0	0.0
C+ / 6.0	10.8	0.63	98.59	711	5	94	0	1	8	129.8	-19.1	99	10	2,500	0	5.8	0.0
C+ / 5.9	10.8	0.63	92.79	244	5	94	0	1	8	121.4	-19.3	99	10	2,500	0	0.0	0.0
C+ / 6.0	10.8	0.63	100.61	1,518	5	94	0	1	8	133.5	-19.0	99	10	2,500	0	0.0	0.0
C+ / 6.0	10.8	0.63	101.08	3,113	5	94	0	1	8	134.5	-19.0	99	10	1,000,000	0	0.0	0.0

Fund Type	Fund Name	Ticker Symbol	Overall Investment Rating	Phone	Performance Rating/Pts	3 Mo	6 Mo	1Yr / Pct	3Yr / Pct	5Yr / Pct	Dividend Yield	Expense Ratio
MC	● Janus Enterprise N	JDMNX	A-	(800) 295-2687	B+ / 8.8	6.22	6.85	24.40 /71	10.32 /95	13.77 /91	0.21	0.67
GL	● Janus Enterprise R	JDMRX	B+	(800) 295-2687	B / 8.2	6.03	6.45	23.48 /68	9.51 /90	12.94 /83	0.00	1.42
GL	● Janus Enterprise S	JGRTX	B+	(800) 295-2687	B+ / 8.5	6.09	6.58	23.79 /69	9.78 /92	13.23 /86	0.00	1.17
GL	● Janus Enterprise T	JAENX	A-	(800) 295-2687	B+ / 8.7	6.15	6.72	24.11 /70	10.06 /94	13.51 /89	0.06	0.92
GR	Janus Forty A	JDCAX	D+	(800) 295-2687	B / 7.8	9.58	7.90	22.41 /64	9.79 /92	13.56 /89	0.00	1.05
GR	Janus Forty C	JACCX	D+	(800) 295-2687	B+ / 8.4	9.41	7.57	21.66 /61	9.16 /88	12.82 /82	0.00	1.80
GR	Janus Forty I	JCAPX	C-	(800) 295-2687	A- / 9.0	9.69	8.09	22.80 /66	10.15 /94	13.92 /93	0.00	0.75
GR	Janus Forty N	JFRNX	C-	(800) 295-2687	A- / 9.1	9.71	8.11	22.88 /66	10.25 /95	13.98 /93	0.00	0.69
GR	Janus Forty R	JDCRX	D+	(800) 295-2687	B+ / 8.6	9.50	7.73	21.93 /62	9.41 /90	13.16 /85	0.00	1.43
GR	Janus Forty S	JARTX	C-	(800) 295-2687	B+ / 8.8	9.59	7.86	22.29 /64	9.74 /92	13.49 /89	0.00	1.19
GR	Janus Forty T	JACTX	C-	(800) 295-2687	B+ / 8.9	9.62	7.99	22.59 /65	9.98 /93	13.73 /91	0.00	0.95
GR	Janus Fund A	JDGAX	C-	(800) 295-2687	C+ / 6.4	9.22	6.50	17.84 /42	8.33 /81	11.59 /71	0.03	0.98
GR	Janus Fund C	JGOCX	C-	(800) 295-2687	C+ / 6.9	9.02	6.15	17.12 /39	7.55 /76	10.82 /64	0.00	1.72
GR	● Janus Fund D	JANDX	C	(800) 295-2687	B- / 7.5	9.24	6.58	18.10 /43	8.52 /83	11.87 /73	0.30	0.77
GR	Janus Fund I	JGROX	C	(800) 295-2687	B / 7.6	9.24	6.62	18.17 /44	8.59 /84	11.94 /74	0.32	0.72
GR	Janus Fund N	JDGNX	C	(800) 295-2687	B / 7.7	9.29	6.67	18.28 /44	8.69 /85	12.02 /74	0.44	0.64
GR	Janus Fund R	JDGRX	C-	(800) 295-2687	B- / 7.1	9.11	6.30	17.42 /40	7.89 /78	11.21 /68	0.00	1.38
GR	Janus Fund S	JGORX	C-	(800) 295-2687	B- / 7.3	9.16	6.41	17.70 /41	8.16 /80	11.51 /70	0.00	1.11
GR	Janus Fund T	JANSX	C	(800) 295-2687	B- / 7.5	9.22	6.54	17.99 /43	8.43 /82	11.78 /72	0.21	0.87
AA	Janus Global Allocation - Consv A	JCAAX	D+	(800) 295-2687	D- / 1.0	3.47	0.28	7.52 / 7	1.65 /22	4.35 /17	0.38	1.15
AA	Janus Global Allocation - Consv C	JCACX	C-	(800) 295-2687	D / 1.4	3.43	0.18	7.09 / 6	1.20 /19	3.75 /14	0.14	1.88
AA	● Janus Global Allocation - Consv D	JMSCX	C-	(800) 295-2687	D / 1.7	3.56	0.47	7.77 / 7	1.87 /23	4.57 /19	0.90	0.96
AA	Janus Global Allocation - Consv I	JCAIX	C-	(800) 295-2687	D / 1.7	3.57	0.48	7.87 / 7	1.94 /24	4.62 /19	0.99	0.89
AA	Janus Global Allocation - Consv S	JCASX	C-	(800) 295-2687	D- / 1.5	3.46	0.25	7.43 / 6	1.49 /21	4.20 /16	0.54	1.31
AA	Janus Global Allocation - Consv T	JSPCX	C-	(800) 295-2687	D / 1.6	3.49	0.39	7.70 / 7	1.83 /23	4.53 /18	0.83	1.06
GL	Janus Global Allocation - Gr A	JGCAX	D	(800) 295-2687	D / 2.1	5.46	3.77	14.52 /28	2.51 /28	6.25 /30	1.09	1.21
GL	Janus Global Allocation - Gr C	JGCCX	D+	(800) 295-2687	D+ / 2.5	5.30	3.41	13.85 /25	1.91 /23	5.53 /25	0.49	1.99
GL	● Janus Global Allocation - Gr D	JNSGX	C-	(800) 295-2687	C- / 3.1	5.56	3.88	14.75 /29	2.69 /29	6.42 /31	1.27	1.05
GL	Janus Global Allocation - Gr I	JGCIX	C-	(800) 295-2687	C- / 3.1	5.55	3.87	14.82 /29	2.77 /30	6.51 /32	1.33	0.98
GL	Janus Global Allocation - Gr S	JGCSX	D+	(800) 295-2687	D+ / 2.9	5.45	3.66	14.28 /27	2.34 /26	6.09 /29	0.89	1.39
GL	Janus Global Allocation - Gr T	JSPGX	D+	(800) 295-2687	C- / 3.0	5.50	3.74	14.60 /28	2.62 /28	6.37 /31	1.21	1.13
GL	Janus Global Allocation - Modt A	JMOAX	D+	(800) 295-2687	D / 1.6	4.54	2.29	11.08 /15	2.12 /25	5.32 /23	0.85	1.19
GL	Janus Global Allocation - Modt C	JMOCX	D+	(800) 295-2687	D / 1.9	4.40	2.02	10.47 /13	1.55 /21	4.60 /19	0.24	1.94
GL	● Janus Global Allocation - Modt D	JNSMX	C-	(800) 295-2687	D+ / 2.3	4.60	2.36	11.28 /15	2.32 /26	5.49 /25	1.12	1.02
GL	Janus Global Allocation - Modt I	JMOIX	C-	(800) 295-2687	D+ / 2.3	4.57	2.41	11.35 /16	2.36 /26	5.54 /25	1.17	0.97
GL	Janus Global Allocation - Modt S	JMOSX	D+	(800) 295-2687	D / 2.1	4.44	2.17	10.83 /14	1.94 /24	5.11 /22	0.77	1.36
GL	Janus Global Allocation - Modt T	JSPMX	D+	(800) 295-2687	D+ / 2.3	4.52	2.35	11.22 /15	2.26 /26	5.88 /28	1.04	1.11
GL	Janus Global Life Sciences A	JFNAX	D+	(800) 295-2687	C / 5.2	9.70	2.60	15.92 /34	7.29 /74	19.96 /99	0.05	1.04
GL	Janus Global Life Sciences C	JFNCX	D+	(800) 295-2687	C / 5.3	9.47	2.19	15.03 /30	5.82 /63	18.59 /99	0.00	1.81
GL	● Janus Global Life Sciences D	JNGLX	C-	(800) 295-2687	C+ / 6.5	9.74	2.69	16.15 /35	7.50 /75	20.18 /99	0.26	0.85
GL	Janus Global Life Sciences I	JFNIX	C-	(800) 295-2687	C+ / 6.5	9.76	2.72	16.22 /35	7.53 /76	20.24 /99	0.33	0.78
GL	Janus Global Life Sciences S	JFNSX	C-	(800) 295-2687	C+ / 6.2	9.67	2.53	15.77 /33	7.15 /73	19.79 /99	0.01	1.21
GL	Janus Global Life Sciences T	JAGLX	C-	(800) 295-2687	C+ / 6.4	9.71	2.64	16.04 /34	7.40 /75	20.08 /99	0.16	0.95
RE	Janus Global Real Estate A	JERAX	D+	(800) 295-2687	D+ / 2.9	5.21	-0.70	16.67 /37	4.81 /52	8.10 /43	2.91	1.27
RE	Janus Global Real Estate C	JERCX	D+	(800) 295-2687	C- / 3.4	5.06	-1.07	15.93 /34	4.01 /43	7.30 /37	2.60	2.07
RE	● Janus Global Real Estate D	JNGSX	C-	(800) 295-2687	C- / 4.1	5.17	-0.73	16.80 /38	4.95 /54	8.27 /44	3.20	1.44
RE	Janus Global Real Estate I	JERIX	C-	(800) 295-2687	C- / 4.2	5.28	-0.53	17.03 /38	5.09 /55	8.43 /46	3.28	1.02
RE	Janus Global Real Estate S	JERSX	C-	(800) 295-2687	C- / 3.8	5.11	-0.82	16.47 /36	4.61 /50	7.98 /42	3.01	1.02
RE	Janus Global Real Estate T	JERTX	C-	(800) 295-2687	C- / 4.1	5.17	-0.67	16.89 /38	4.93 /53	8.24 /44	3.16	1.18
FO	Janus Global Research A	JDWAX	D+	(800) 295-2687	C- / 3.4	6.88	5.63	19.50 /49	3.48 /37	7.42 /37	0.45	0.98
FO	Janus Global Research C	JWWCX	C-	(800) 295-2687	C- / 3.9	6.72	5.33	18.75 /46	2.73 /29	6.65 /32	0.00	1.74
FO	● Janus Global Research D	JANWX	C-	(800) 295-2687	C / 4.7	6.97	5.81	19.87 /51	3.71 /39	7.69 /40	0.78	0.81

● Denotes fund is closed to new investors
* Denotes fund is included in Section II

www.thestreetratings.com

Risk Rating/Pts	Standard Deviation	Beta	NAV As of 2/28/17	Total $(Mil)	Cash %	Stocks %	Bonds %	Other %	Portfolio Turnover Ratio	Last Bull Market Return	Last Bear Market Return	Manager Quality Pct	Manager Tenure (Years)	Initial Purch. $	Additional Purch. $	Front End Load	Back End Load
C+ / 6.0	10.8	0.84	101.34	2,134	5	94	0	1	8	135.1	-19.1	86	10	0	0	0.0	0.0
C+ / 6.0	10.8	0.63	96.13	158	5	94	0	1	8	126.3	-19.2	99	10	2,500	0	0.0	0.0
C+ / 6.0	10.8	0.63	98.20	519	5	94	0	1	8	129.4	-19.2	99	10	2,500	0	0.0	0.0
C+ / 6.0	10.8	0.63	100.06	3,571	5	94	0	1	8	132.5	-19.1	99	10	2,500	0	0.0	0.0
E+ / 0.6	12.9	1.08	30.48	242	4	95	0	1	40	136.9	-18.5	54	4	2,500	0	5.8	0.0
E / 0.3	12.8	1.07	26.22	243	4	95	0	1	40	128.6	-18.8	47	4	2,500	0	0.0	0.0
E+ / 0.7	12.9	1.08	31.28	753	4	95	0	1	40	140.9	-18.5	59	4	1,000,000	0	0.0	0.0
E+ / 0.7	12.9	1.08	31.34	138	4	95	0	1	40	141.3	-18.6	60	4	0	0	0.0	0.0
E / 0.4	12.9	1.08	27.94	112	4	95	0	1	40	132.4	-18.7	50	4	2,500	0	0.0	0.0
E / 0.5	12.9	1.08	29.53	500	4	95	0	1	40	136.1	-18.6	54	4	2,500	0	0.0	0.0
E+ / 0.6	12.9	1.08	29.90	83	4	95	0	1	40	138.9	-18.5	57	4	2,500	0	0.0	0.0
C- / 3.0	11.6	1.03	35.89	16	4	95	0	1	55	111.2	-18.6	43	6	2,500	0	5.8	0.0
D+ / 2.9	11.6	1.02	34.42	6	4	95	0	1	55	103.5	-18.8	34	6	2,500	0	0.0	0.0
C- / 3.0	11.6	1.03	36.17	5,775	4	95	0	1	55	114.2	-18.5	46	6	2,500	0	0.0	0.0
C- / 3.1	11.6	1.03	36.35	90	4	95	0	1	55	114.8	-18.5	47	6	1,000,000	0	0.0	0.0
C- / 3.0	11.6	1.03	36.22	47	4	95	0	1	55	115.4	-18.5	48	6	0	0	0.0	0.0
C- / 3.0	11.6	1.03	35.31	4	4	95	0	1	55	107.3	-18.7	37	6	2,500	0	0.0	0.0
C- / 3.1	11.6	1.03	36.20	20	4	95	0	1	55	110.3	-18.6	41	6	2,500	0	0.0	0.0
C- / 3.1	11.6	1.03	36.29	1,586	4	95	0	1	55	113.1	-18.5	45	6	2,500	0	0.0	0.0
B- / 7.9	5.2	0.75	12.26	6	10	39	50	1	5	36.0	-7.2	25	12	2,500	0	5.8	0.0
B / 8.0	5.2	0.75	12.04	18	10	39	50	1	5	31.7	-7.6	21	12	2,500	0	0.0	0.0
B- / 7.9	5.2	0.76	12.30	178	10	39	50	1	5	37.5	-7.2	27	12	2,500	100	0.0	0.0
B- / 7.9	5.2	0.76	12.30	4	10	39	50	1	5	37.9	-7.2	27	12	1,000,000	0	0.0	0.0
B- / 7.9	5.2	0.76	12.20	2	10	39	50	1	5	34.8	-7.3	23	12	2,500	0	0.0	0.0
B- / 7.9	5.2	0.75	12.28	26	10	39	50	1	5	37.2	-7.2	27	12	2,500	0	0.0	0.0
C+ / 6.2	8.3	0.62	13.28	5	11	75	13	1	6	58.6	-17.5	89	12	2,500	0	5.8	0.0
C+ / 6.3	8.3	0.62	13.08	5	11	75	13	1	6	52.8	-17.8	86	12	2,500	0	0.0	0.0
C+ / 6.2	8.4	0.62	13.37	205	11	75	13	1	6	60.0	-17.4	89	12	2,500	100	0.0	0.0
C+ / 6.2	8.4	0.63	13.37	5	11	75	13	1	6	60.8	-17.5	90	12	1,000,000	0	0.0	0.0
C+ / 6.2	8.4	0.63	13.22	3	11	75	13	1	6	57.2	-17.5	88	12	2,500	0	0.0	0.0
C+ / 6.2	8.4	0.63	13.35	17	11	75	13	1	6	59.6	-17.5	89	12	2,500	0	0.0	0.0
B- / 7.0	6.8	0.50	12.58	12	13	57	29	1	5	47.0	-12.5	87	12	2,500	0	5.8	0.0
B- / 7.1	6.7	0.49	12.42	8	13	57	29	1	5	41.7	-12.8	84	12	2,500	0	0.0	0.0
B- / 7.0	6.7	0.50	12.65	210	13	57	29	1	5	48.3	-12.5	88	12	2,500	100	0.0	0.0
B- / 7.0	6.7	0.50	12.64	4	13	57	29	1	5	48.8	-12.5	88	12	1,000,000	0	0.0	0.0
B- / 7.0	6.7	0.49	12.49	3	13	57	29	1	5	45.5	-12.6	86	12	2,500	0	0.0	0.0
B- / 7.0	6.7	0.49	12.62	18	13	57	29	1	5	51.2	-12.5	87	12	2,500	0	0.0	0.0
C- / 3.3	18.5	0.93	49.56	231	1	98	0	1	41	199.2	-13.1	98	10	2,500	0	5.8	0.0
C- / 3.2	18.5	0.94	46.41	165	1	98	0	1	41	181.8	-13.3	97	10	2,500	0	0.0	0.0
C- / 3.3	18.5	0.93	50.24	1,218	1	98	0	1	41	202.4	-13.1	98	10	2,500	0	0.0	0.0
C- / 3.3	18.5	0.93	50.28	400	1	98	0	1	41	203.2	-13.0	98	10	1,000,000	0	0.0	0.0
C- / 3.3	18.5	0.93	49.01	15	1	98	0	1	41	197.0	-13.2	98	10	2,500	0	0.0	0.0
C- / 3.3	18.5	0.93	50.09	1,201	1	98	0	1	41	200.9	-13.0	98	10	2,500	0	0.0	0.0
C+ / 5.7	11.4	0.67	10.57	11	14	85	0	1	18	79.2	-23.9	42	10	2,500	0	5.8	0.0
C+ / 5.7	11.4	0.67	10.43	7	14	85	0	1	18	72.3	-24.1	32	10	2,500	0	0.0	0.0
C+ / 5.7	11.4	0.67	10.66	36	14	85	0	1	18	81.0	-23.8	45	8	2,500	0	0.0	0.0
C+ / 5.7	11.4	0.67	10.66	109	14	85	0	1	18	82.3	-23.7	47	10	1,000,000	0	0.0	0.0
C+ / 5.7	11.4	0.67	10.56	3	14	85	0	1	18	78.2	-23.9	40	10	2,500	0	0.0	0.0
C+ / 5.7	11.4	0.67	10.65	57	14	85	0	1	18	80.8	-23.8	44	10	2,500	0	0.0	0.0
C+ / 5.7	11.8	0.87	67.43	19	4	95	0	1	45	76.1	-20.9	92	3	2,500	0	5.8	0.0
C+ / 5.7	11.8	0.87	66.19	9	4	95	0	1	45	69.3	-21.2	90	3	2,500	0	0.0	0.0
C+ / 5.7	11.8	0.87	66.64	1,322	4	95	0	1	45	78.4	-20.9	93	3	2,500	0	0.0	0.0

Fund Type	Fund Name	Ticker Symbol	Overall Investment Rating	Phone	Performance Rating/Pts	3 Mo	6 Mo	1Yr / Pct	3Yr / Pct	5Yr / Pct	Dividend Yield	Expense Ratio
	99 Pct = Best				**PERFORMANCE**			Total Return % through 2/28/17	Annualized		Incl. in Returns	
	0 Pct = Worst											
FO	Janus Global Research I	JWWFX	C	(800) 295-2687	C / 4.8	7.00	5.86	19.98 /52	3.79 /40	7.67 /40	0.86	0.70
FO	Janus Global Research R	JDWRX	C-	(800) 295-2687	C- / 4.2	6.80	5.49	19.18 /48	3.10 /33	7.10 /35	0.23	1.39
FO	Janus Global Research S	JWGRX	C-	(800) 295-2687	C / 4.4	6.90	5.65	19.47 /49	3.37 /35	7.29 /37	0.42	1.13
FO	Janus Global Research T	JAWWX	C-	(800) 295-2687	C / 4.7	6.95	5.77	19.78 /51	3.63 /38	7.53 /38	0.71	0.88
FO	Janus Global Select A	JORAX	C-	(800) 295-2687	C / 4.3	7.91	9.00	23.07 /67	3.56 /38	4.04 /15	0.82	0.97
FO	Janus Global Select C	JORCX	C-	(800) 295-2687	C / 4.8	7.74	8.60	22.09 /63	2.68 /29	3.20 /12	0.10	1.80
FO ●	Janus Global Select D	JANRX	C	(800) 295-2687	C+ / 5.7	7.94	9.12	23.31 /68	3.66 /39	4.23 /16	1.07	0.87
FO	Janus Global Select I	JORFX	C	(800) 295-2687	C+ / 5.8	7.96	9.14	23.39 /68	3.79 /40	4.35 /17	1.18	0.72
FO	Janus Global Select R	JORRX	C	(800) 295-2687	C / 5.2	7.78	8.79	22.56 /65	3.09 /33	3.64 /14	0.55	1.43
FO	Janus Global Select S	JORIX	C	(800) 295-2687	C / 5.4	7.81	8.90	22.88 /66	3.36 /35	3.98 /15	0.74	1.18
FO	Janus Global Select T	JORNX	C	(800) 295-2687	C+ / 5.6	7.95	9.05	23.20 /67	3.60 /38	4.16 /16	1.02	0.92
TC	Janus Global Technology A	JATAX	B-	(800) 295-2687	A+ / 9.8	9.51	10.48	38.45 /97	12.11 /98	14.60 /96	0.00	1.08
TC	Janus Global Technology C	JAGCX	B-	(800) 295-2687	A+ / 9.8	9.37	10.16	37.52 /96	11.37 /97	13.83 /92	0.00	1.79
TC ●	Janus Global Technology D	JNGTX	B-	(800) 295-2687	A+ / 9.8	9.60	10.61	38.71 /97	12.36 /98	14.85 /97	0.00	0.90
TC	Janus Global Technology I	JATIX	B-	(800) 295-2687	A+ / 9.9	9.63	10.67	38.87 /97	12.45 /98	14.93 /97	0.00	0.79
TC	Janus Global Technology S	JATSX	B-	(800) 295-2687	A+ / 9.8	9.48	10.41	38.28 /97	12.00 /98	14.49 /96	0.00	1.20
TC	Janus Global Technology T	JAGTX	B-	(800) 295-2687	A+ / 9.8	9.56	10.52	38.59 /97	12.28 /98	14.79 /96	0.00	0.95
GL	Janus Growth and Income A	JDNAX	A-	(800) 295-2687	B+ / 8.5	8.09	11.88	24.66 /72	10.16 /94	13.01 /84	1.88	0.93
GL	Janus Growth and Income C	JGICX	A	(800) 295-2687	B+ / 8.9	7.90	11.47	23.76 /69	9.34 /89	12.14 /75	1.43	1.71
GL ●	Janus Growth and Income D	JNGIX	A+	(800) 295-2687	A / 9.4	8.12	11.97	24.87 /73	10.33 /95	13.19 /86	2.11	0.79
GL	Janus Growth and Income I	JGINX	A+	(800) 295-2687	A / 9.4	8.14	12.00	24.95 /73	10.41 /95	13.27 /87	2.16	0.71
GL	Janus Growth and Income R	JDNRX	A	(800) 295-2687	A- / 9.1	7.96	11.62	24.10 /70	9.68 /91	12.52 /79	1.66	1.38
GL	Janus Growth and Income S	JADGX	A+	(800) 295-2687	A- / 9.2	8.03	11.78	24.42 /71	9.96 /93	12.81 /82	1.84	1.13
GL	Janus Growth and Income T	JAGIX	A+	(800) 295-2687	A / 9.4	8.12	11.93	24.76 /72	10.25 /95	13.10 /85	2.04	0.87
FO	Janus International Equity A	JAIEX	E	(800) 295-2687	E / 0.3	6.09	2.63	12.00 /18	-2.90 / 5	2.67 /10	1.23	1.05
FO ●	Janus International Equity C	JCIEX	E	(800) 295-2687	E / 0.4	6.00	2.29	11.28 /15	-3.59 / 4	1.89 / 8	0.54	1.84
FO ●	Janus International Equity D	JNISX	E+	(800) 295-2687	E+ / 0.6	6.22	2.74	12.28 /19	-2.70 / 5	2.85 /10	1.65	0.85
FO ●	Janus International Equity I	JIIEX	E+	(800) 295-2687	E+ / 0.6	6.18	2.80	12.33 /19	-2.62 / 5	2.97 /11	1.79	0.78
FO ●	Janus International Equity N	JNIEX	E+	(800) 295-2687	E+ / 0.6	6.27	2.88	12.44 /20	-2.55 / 5	3.04 /11	1.87	0.71
FO ●	Janus International Equity R	JRIEX	E	(800) 295-2687	E / 0.5	6.03	2.42	11.64 /17	-3.27 / 4	2.27 / 9	1.00	1.47
FO ●	Janus International Equity S	JSIEX	E+	(800) 295-2687	E / 0.5	6.14	2.59	11.91 /18	-3.03 / 4	2.82 /10	1.21	1.22
FO ●	Janus International Equity T	JAITX	E+	(800) 295-2687	E+ / 0.6	6.20	2.80	12.20 /19	-2.76 / 5	2.81 /10	1.53	0.97
FO	Janus Overseas A	JDIAX	E-	(800) 295-2687	E- / 0.1	6.21	4.51	17.84 /42	-6.67 / 2	-4.98 / 2	0.74	0.86
FO	Janus Overseas C	JIGCX	E-	(800) 295-2687	E- / 0.2	5.98	4.09	16.91 /38	-7.38 / 1	-5.73 / 1	0.00	1.62
FO ●	Janus Overseas D	JNOSX	E-	(800) 295-2687	E / 0.3	6.29	4.66	18.17 /44	-6.40 / 2	-4.69 / 2	1.24	0.60
FO	Janus Overseas I	JIGFX	E-	(800) 295-2687	E / 0.3	6.23	4.61	18.15 /44	-6.37 / 2	-4.66 / 2	1.20	0.53
FO	Janus Overseas N	JDINX	E-	(800) 295-2687	E / 0.3	6.27	4.64	18.25 /44	-6.27 / 2	-4.58 / 2	1.40	0.43
FO	Janus Overseas R	JDIRX	E-	(800) 295-2687	E- / 0.2	6.14	4.37	17.49 /41	-6.94 / 1	-5.26 / 2	0.59	1.17
FO	Janus Overseas S	JIGRX	E-	(800) 295-2687	E- / 0.2	6.20	4.48	17.79 /42	-6.71 / 2	-5.02 / 2	0.83	0.92
FO	Janus Overseas T	JAOSX	E-	(800) 295-2687	E / 0.3	6.26	4.63	18.08 /43	-6.47 / 2	-4.77 / 2	1.14	0.67
GR	Janus Portfolio Institutional	JAGRX	C	(800) 295-2687	B- / 7.5	9.25	6.52	17.95 /43	8.56 /83	12.09 /75	0.49	0.76
GR	Janus Portfolio Service		C	(800) 295-2687	B- / 7.3	9.15	6.35	17.65 /41	8.28 /81	11.80 /72	0.35	1.02
GL	Janus Real Return A	JURAX	D	(800) 295-2687	D- / 1.0	1.50	0.65	4.59 / 4	2.17 /25	1.80 / 8	3.28	1.76
GL	Janus Real Return C	JURCX	D+	(800) 295-2687	D- / 1.2	1.32	0.27	3.94 / 3	1.42 /21	1.06 / 6	2.70	2.49
GL ●	Janus Real Return D	JURDX	D+	(800) 295-2687	D- / 1.5	1.54	0.72	4.75 / 4	2.26 /26	1.91 / 8	3.60	1.68
GL	Janus Real Return I	JURIX	D+	(800) 295-2687	D- / 1.5	1.58	0.77	4.98 / 4	2.42 /27	2.04 / 8	3.70	1.51
GL	Janus Real Return S	JURSX	D+	(800) 295-2687	D- / 1.4	1.45	0.58	4.47 / 3	2.13 /25	1.74 / 8	3.33	2.00
GL	Janus Real Return T	JURTX	D+	(800) 295-2687	D- / 1.5	1.51	0.69	4.82 / 4	2.28 /26	1.94 / 8	3.55	1.75
GL	Janus Research A	JRAAX	C	(800) 295-2687	C+ / 6.5	8.08	6.68	18.46 /45	8.44 /82	12.76 /82	0.00	1.10
GL	Janus Research C	JRACX	C	(800) 295-2687	C+ / 6.9	7.90	6.34	17.62 /41	7.67 /77	11.94 /74	0.00	1.89
GL ●	Janus Research D	JNRFX	C+	(800) 295-2687	B- / 7.5	8.12	6.77	18.66 /46	8.65 /84	12.99 /84	0.26	0.92
GL	Janus Research I	JRAIX	C+	(800) 295-2687	B / 7.6	8.16	6.82	18.76 /46	8.74 /85	13.09 /85	0.33	0.83

● Denotes fund is closed to new investors
* Denotes fund is included in Section II

364

RISK			NET ASSETS		ASSET					BULL / BEAR		FUND MANAGER		MINIMUMS		LOADS	
	3 Year		NAV						Portfolio	Last Bull	Last Bear	Manager	Manager	Initial	Additional	Front	Back
Risk Rating/Pts	Standard Deviation	Beta	As of 2/28/17	Total $(Mil)	Cash %	Stocks %	Bonds %	Other %	Turnover Ratio	Market Return	Market Return	Quality Pct	Tenure (Years)	Purch. $	Purch. $	End Load	End Load
C+ / 5.7	11.8	0.87	67.55	144	4	95	0	1	45	78.3	-20.8	93	3	1,000,000	0	0.0	0.0
C+ / 5.7	11.8	0.87	66.91	5	4	95	0	1	45	73.5	-20.9	91	3	2,500	0	0.0	0.0
C+ / 5.7	11.7	0.87	67.57	66	4	95	0	1	45	74.9	-21.0	92	3	2,500	0	0.0	0.0
C+ / 5.7	11.8	0.87	66.59	903	4	95	0	1	45	77.1	-20.9	93	3	2,500	0	0.0	0.0
C / 5.4	12.4	0.91	13.89	5	3	96	0	1	58	56.9	-26.1	92	5	2,500	0	5.8	0.0
C / 5.4	12.4	0.91	13.55	3	3	96	0	1	58	50.1	-26.3	90	5	2,500	0	0.0	0.0
C / 5.4	12.5	0.91	13.79	1,376	3	96	0	1	58	58.4	-26.1	93	5	2,500	0	0.0	0.0
C / 5.4	12.4	0.91	13.82	20	3	96	0	1	58	59.3	-26.1	93	5	1,000,000	0	0.0	0.0
C / 5.4	12.5	0.91	13.77	N/A	3	96	0	1	58	53.6	-26.2	91	5	2,500	0	0.0	0.0
C / 5.4	12.5	0.91	13.96	N/A	3	96	0	1	58	56.3	-26.1	92	5	2,500	0	0.0	0.0
C / 5.4	12.4	0.91	13.81	463	3	96	0	1	58	58.0	-26.1	93	5	2,500	0	0.0	0.0
C- / 3.0	14.4	1.23	24.88	16	1	98	0	1	42	140.1	-19.1	63	6	2,500	0	5.8	0.0
D+ / 2.8	14.4	1.22	23.22	7	1	98	0	1	42	131.7	-19.4	54	6	2,500	0	0.0	0.0
C- / 3.0	14.4	1.23	25.33	875	1	98	0	1	42	143.1	-19.0	66	6	2,500	0	0.0	0.0
C- / 3.0	14.5	1.23	25.50	44	1	98	0	1	42	144.0	-19.0	67	6	1,000,000	0	0.0	0.0
C- / 3.0	14.4	1.23	24.60	7	1	98	0	1	42	138.9	-19.1	62	6	2,500	0	0.0	0.0
C- / 3.0	14.4	1.23	25.21	409	1	98	0	1	42	142.2	-19.0	65	6	2,500	0	0.0	0.0
C+ / 6.5	10.2	0.65	48.37	31	0	99	0	1	24	135.3	-21.6	99	10	2,500	0	5.8	0.0
C+ / 6.5	10.2	0.64	47.80	20	0	99	0	1	24	125.6	-21.8	99	10	2,500	0	0.0	0.0
C+ / 6.5	10.2	0.65	48.43	2,875	0	99	0	1	24	137.3	-21.5	99	10	2,500	0	0.0	0.0
C+ / 6.5	10.2	0.65	48.46	71	0	99	0	1	24	138.2	-21.5	99	10	1,000,000	0	0.0	0.0
C+ / 6.5	10.2	0.65	48.12	3	0	99	0	1	24	129.7	-21.7	99	10	2,500	0	0.0	0.0
C+ / 6.5	10.2	0.64	48.34	24	0	99	0	1	24	133.0	-21.6	99	10	2,500	0	0.0	0.0
C+ / 6.5	10.2	0.65	48.40	1,458	0	99	0	1	24	136.2	-21.5	99	10	2,500	0	0.0	0.0
C / 4.7	12.6	0.99	11.50	14	3	96	0	1	42	37.7	-23.9	37	7	2,500	0	5.8	0.0
C / 4.8	12.5	0.98	11.33	8	3	96	0	1	42	32.1	-24.2	29	7	2,500	0	0.0	0.0
C / 4.7	12.5	0.99	11.41	13	3	96	0	1	42	39.1	-23.8	40	7	2,500	0	0.0	0.0
C / 4.7	12.5	0.98	11.41	35	3	96	0	1	42	40.0	-23.8	41	7	1,000,000	0	0.0	0.0
C / 4.6	12.6	0.99	11.39	83	3	96	0	1	42	40.5	-23.8	42	7	0	0	0.0	0.0
C / 4.7	12.6	0.99	11.29	3	3	96	0	1	42	34.9	-24.1	33	7	2,500	0	0.0	0.0
C / 4.7	12.6	0.99	11.80	8	3	96	0	1	42	38.6	-24.0	36	7	2,500	0	0.0	0.0
C / 4.7	12.5	0.98	11.35	4	3	96	0	1	42	38.7	-23.9	39	7	2,500	0	0.0	0.0
C- / 3.0	18.3	1.28	27.23	21	2	97	0	1	85	-2.3	-33.4	6	1	2,500	0	5.8	0.0
C- / 3.0	18.3	1.28	26.75	17	2	97	0	1	85	-6.4	-33.6	5	1	2,500	0	0.0	0.0
D+ / 2.9	18.3	1.28	26.93	651	2	97	0	1	85	-0.7	-33.3	7	1	2,500	0	0.0	0.0
D+ / 2.9	18.3	1.28	27.03	57	2	97	0	1	85	-0.6	-33.3	8	1	1,000,000	0	0.0	0.0
D+ / 2.9	18.3	1.28	26.88	28	2	97	0	1	85	-0.2	-33.4	8	1	0	0	0.0	0.0
C- / 3.0	18.3	1.28	26.75	34	2	97	0	1	85	-3.9	-33.5	6	1	2,500	0	0.0	0.0
D+ / 2.9	18.3	1.28	26.96	148	2	97	0	1	85	-2.5	-33.4	6	1	2,500	0	0.0	0.0
D+ / 2.9	18.3	1.28	26.96	562	2	97	0	1	85	-1.2	-33.4	7	1	2,500	0	0.0	0.0
C- / 3.4	11.7	1.03	31.40	340	1	98	0	1	54	117.5	-18.5	45	6	0	0	0.0	0.0
C- / 3.4	11.7	1.03	30.70	148	1	98	0	1	54	114.5	-18.6	42	6	0	0	0.0	0.0
B- / 7.3	2.1	0.24	9.51	3	10	0	89	1	57	18.6	N/A	81	5	2,500	0	4.8	0.0
B- / 7.3	2.0	0.22	9.47	3	10	0	89	1	57	14.0	N/A	76	5	2,500	0	0.0	0.0
B- / 7.3	2.0	0.23	9.52	9	10	0	89	1	57	19.3	N/A	81	5	2,500	100	0.0	0.0
B- / 7.3	2.1	0.24	9.46	2	10	0	89	1	57	20.2	N/A	82	5	1,000,000	0	0.0	0.0
B- / 7.3	2.0	0.22	9.53	1	10	0	89	1	57	18.2	N/A	81	5	2,500	0	0.0	0.0
B- / 7.3	2.1	0.24	9.49	3	10	0	89	1	57	19.4	N/A	81	5	2,500	0	0.0	0.0
C / 4.5	11.4	0.76	42.87	23	1	98	0	1	38	124.0	-18.6	99	3	2,500	0	5.8	0.0
C / 4.4	11.4	0.75	40.92	19	1	98	0	1	38	115.3	-18.8	98	3	2,500	0	0.0	0.0
C / 4.5	11.4	0.76	43.18	2,563	1	98	0	1	38	126.5	-18.5	99	3	2,500	0	0.0	0.0
C / 4.4	11.4	0.75	43.12	237	1	98	0	1	38	127.5	-18.5	99	3	1,000,000	0	0.0	0.0

www.thestreetratings.com
365
Data as of February 28, 2017

Fund Type	Fund Name	Ticker Symbol	Overall Investment Rating	Phone	Performance Rating/Pts	3 Mo	6 Mo	1Yr / Pct	3Yr / Pct	5Yr / Pct	Dividend Yield	Expense Ratio
								Total Return % through 2/28/17	Annualized		Incl. in Returns	
GR	Janus Research N	JRANX	C+	(800) 295-2687	B / 7.7	8.17	6.86	18.86 /46	8.83 /86	13.17 /86	0.41	0.76
GL	Janus Research S	JRASX	C+	(800) 295-2687	B- / 7.3	8.05	6.61	18.29 /44	8.29 /81	12.63 /80	0.10	1.24
GL	Janus Research T	JAMRX	C+	(800) 295-2687	B- / 7.5	8.11	6.75	18.58 /45	8.58 /84	12.91 /83	0.17	1.00
SC	● Janus Triton A	JGMAX	C+	(800) 295-2687	B- / 7.4	6.05	6.71	26.44 /78	9.02 /87	13.00 /84	0.00	1.10
SC	● Janus Triton C	JGMCX	C+	(800) 295-2687	B / 7.9	5.88	6.40	25.65 /75	8.34 /82	12.24 /76	0.00	1.81
MC	● Janus Triton D	JANIX	B	(800) 295-2687	B+ / 8.6	6.13	6.88	26.88 /79	9.37 /89	13.35 /87	0.13	0.83
SC	● Janus Triton I	JSMGX	B	(800) 295-2687	B+ / 8.7	6.13	6.91	26.92 /79	9.42 /90	13.41 /88	0.16	0.77
MC	● Janus Triton N	JGMNX	B	(800) 295-2687	B+ / 8.8	6.19	6.97	27.11 /79	9.54 /91	13.51 /89	0.22	0.67
SC	● Janus Triton R	JGMRX	B-	(800) 295-2687	B / 8.1	5.97	6.56	26.12 /77	8.71 /85	12.68 /81	0.00	1.42
SC	● Janus Triton S	JGMIX	B-	(800) 295-2687	B+ / 8.3	6.05	6.72	26.44 /78	9.00 /87	12.16 /76	0.00	1.17
SC	● Janus Triton T	JATTX	B	(800) 295-2687	B+ / 8.5	6.10	6.80	26.73 /78	9.26 /89	13.25 /86	0.07	0.92
GR	● Janus Twenty D	JNTFX	C+	(800) 295-2687	B / 7.8	8.70	11.31	18.91 /47	8.20 /80	12.27 /77	1.04	0.72
GR	● Janus Twenty T	JAVLX	C+	(800) 295-2687	B / 7.8	8.65	11.24	18.79 /46	8.10 /80	12.17 /76	0.91	0.82
SC	● Janus Venture A	JVTAX	C	(800) 295-2687	C+ / 6.7	5.95	4.83	26.64 /78	7.92 /78	13.01 /84	0.00	1.04
SC	● Janus Venture C	JVTCX	C	(800) 295-2687	B- / 7.1	5.77	4.45	25.70 /75	7.16 /73	12.27 /77	0.00	1.79
GL	● Janus Venture D	JANVX	C+	(800) 295-2687	B / 7.8	6.01	4.94	26.91 /79	8.18 /80	13.32 /87	0.00	0.82
SC	● Janus Venture I	JVTIX	C+	(800) 295-2687	B / 7.8	6.02	4.96	26.97 /79	8.25 /81	13.40 /88	0.00	0.75
SC	● Janus Venture N	JVTNX	C+	(800) 295-2687	B / 7.9	6.05	5.00	27.08 /79	8.33 /81	13.47 /89	0.00	0.67
SC	● Janus Venture S	JVTSX	C+	(800) 295-2687	B- / 7.5	5.93	4.75	26.46 /78	7.80 /77	12.93 /83	0.00	1.17
GL	● Janus Venture T	JAVTX	C+	(800) 295-2687	B / 7.7	6.00	4.88	26.78 /79	8.08 /80	13.21 /86	0.00	0.92
GR	Jensen Quality Growth I	JENIX	A-	(800) 992-4144	B+ / 8.3	6.39	6.21	19.38 /49	10.56 /96	13.62 /90	1.28	0.64
GR	Jensen Quality Growth J	JENSX	A-	(800) 992-4144	B / 8.2	6.31	6.09	19.05 /47	10.29 /95	13.33 /87	1.05	0.88
GR	Jensen Quality Growth R	JENRX	B+	(800) 992-4144	B / 7.9	6.24	5.90	18.65 /46	9.91 /93	12.96 /83	0.71	1.23
GR	Jensen Quality Value I	JNVIX	D+	(800) 992-4144	C / 4.8	3.11	1.76	19.79 /51	5.56 /60	11.15 /67	1.51	1.48
GR	Jensen Quality Value J	JNVSX	D+	(800) 992-4144	C / 4.7	3.03	1.63	19.55 /50	5.41 /59	10.97 /66	1.31	1.63
FO	JOHCM Asia Ex-Japan Equity Eq I	JOAIX	U	(866) 260-9549	U /	4.98	-1.47	17.63 /41	--	--	0.51	1.50
FO	JOHCM Asia Ex-Japan Equity Inst	JOAMX	U	(866) 260-9549	U /	4.87	-1.48	17.75 /42	--	--	0.59	1.39
EM	JOHCM Emerging Markets Opps I	JOEIX	D+	(866) 260-9549	C- / 4.2	8.40	2.34	26.17 /77	1.90 /23	--	0.74	1.49
EM	JOHCM Emerging Markets Opps II	JOEAX	C-	(866) 260-9549	C- / 4.1	8.32	2.26	25.94 /76	1.80 /23	--	0.57	1.66
EM	JOHCM Emerging Markets Opps Inst	JOEMX	D+	(866) 260-9549	C / 4.3	8.44	2.39	26.33 /77	1.97 /24	--	0.79	1.38
GL	JOHCM Global Equity I	JOGEX	D-	(866) 260-9549	D / 1.6	4.55	1.03	12.08 /18	0.44 /15	--	0.20	1.21
GL	JOHCM Global Equity Inst	JOGIX	D-	(866) 260-9549	D / 1.7	4.49	1.06	12.18 /19	0.53 /16	--	0.30	1.11
FO	● JOHCM International Select I	JOHIX	D+	(866) 260-9549	D+ / 2.8	5.99	1.60	12.87 /21	2.75 /30	9.17 /52	0.68	1.04
FO	● JOHCM International Select II	JOHAX	D+	(866) 260-9549	D+ / 2.6	5.95	1.51	12.56 /20	2.49 /27	8.90 /50	0.50	1.32
FO	JOHCM Intl Small Cap Equity I	JOISX	C	(866) 260-9549	C / 4.3	6.94	6.83	23.80 /69	1.98 /24	--	1.15	1.39
FO	JOHCM Intl Small Cap Equity II	JOSAX	C	(866) 260-9549	C- / 4.2	6.95	6.75	23.58 /68	1.82 /23	--	1.02	1.56
FO	JOHCM Intl Small Cap Equity Inst	JOSMX	C	(866) 260-9549	C / 4.4	7.09	6.88	23.99 /70	2.08 /25	--	1.28	1.28
GL	John Hancock Dscpld Val Intl A	JDIBX	U	(800) 257-3336	U /	6.80	3.65	14.24 /27	--	--	1.07	1.80
GL	John Hancock Dscpld Val Intl I	JDVIX	U	(800) 257-3336	U /	6.77	3.72	14.60 /28	--	--	1.44	1.48
GL	John Hancock Dscpld Val Intl NAV	JDIVX	U	(800) 257-3336	U /	6.89	3.83	14.73 /29	--	--	1.54	1.37
GL	John Hancock Dscpld Val Intl R6	JDIUX	U	(800) 257-3336	U /	6.89	3.83	14.73 /29	--	--	1.54	1.39
EM	John Hancock Emerging Mkts Eq		U	(800) 257-3336	U /	6.89	0.81	21.54 /60	--	--	0.55	1.23
GL	John Hancock Enduring Assets A	JEEBX	C-	(800) 257-3336	D / 2.0	6.81	-0.60	10.74 /14	3.43 /36	--	1.83	1.68
GL	John Hancock Enduring Assets I	JEEIX	C-	(800) 257-3336	D+ / 2.9	6.88	-0.44	11.09 /15	3.70 /39	--	2.16	1.37
GL	John Hancock Enduring Assets NAV		C	(800) 257-3336	C- / 3.0	6.80	-0.39	11.16 /15	3.86 /41	--	2.23	1.27
GL	John Hancock Enduring Assets R6	JEEDX	C	(800) 257-3336	C- / 3.0	6.80	-0.39	11.16 /15	3.84 /41	--	2.23	1.28
GL	John Hancock Glbl Consv Abs Ret A	JHRAX	C-	(800) 257-3336	E / 0.5	0.59	-0.54	2.39 / 2	0.13 /14	--	4.74	1.56
GL	John Hancock Glbl Consv Abs Ret I	JHRIX	C-	(800) 257-3336	E+ / 0.8	0.63	-0.49	2.64 / 2	0.38 /15	--	5.14	1.25
GL	John Hancock Glbl Consv Abs Ret		C	(800) 257-3336	E+ / 0.8	0.64	-0.38	2.75 / 2	0.46 /16	--	5.26	1.13
GL	John Hancock Glbl Consv Abs Ret	JHRRX	C-	(800) 257-3336	E+ / 0.8	0.64	-0.38	2.75 / 3	0.46 /16	--	5.26	1.15
GL	John Hancock Global Foc Strat NAV		U	(800) 257-3336	U /	2.19	-1.03	--	--	--	0.00	1.86
RE	John Hancock Global Real Estate		U	(800) 257-3336	U /	4.72	-4.89	5.37 / 4	--	--	1.67	1.26

I. Index of Stock Mutual Funds

Risk Rating/Pts	3 Year Standard Deviation	Beta	NAV As of 2/28/17	Total $(Mil)	Cash %	Stocks %	Bonds %	Other %	Portfolio Turnover Ratio	Last Bull Market Return	Last Bear Market Return	Manager Quality Pct	Manager Tenure (Years)	Initial Purch. $	Additional Purch. $	Front End Load	Back End Load
C /4.4	11.4	1.04	43.12	204	1	98	0	1	38	128.1	-18.5	48	3	0	0	0.0	0.0
C /4.5	11.4	0.75	42.37	4	1	98	0	1	38	122.4	-18.6	99	3	2,500	0	0.0	0.0
C /4.5	11.4	0.75	43.19	1,376	1	98	0	1	38	125.5	-18.5	99	3	2,500	0	0.0	0.0
C /4.4	13.6	0.82	24.76	605	5	94	0	1	22	131.0	-20.0	91	4	2,500	0	5.8	0.0
C /4.3	13.6	0.82	23.27	215	5	94	0	1	22	122.5	-20.3	88	4	2,500	0	0.0	0.0
C /4.4	13.6	1.07	25.18	945	5	94	0	1	22	134.7	-19.9	63	4	2,500	0	0.0	0.0
C /4.4	13.7	0.82	25.32	1,458	5	94	0	1	22	135.3	-19.9	92	4	1,000,000	0	0.0	0.0
C /4.4	13.7	1.07	25.38	977	5	94	0	1	22	136.3	-20.0	65	4	0	0	0.0	0.0
C /4.4	13.6	0.82	24.19	266	5	94	0	1	22	127.2	-20.2	90	4	2,500	0	0.0	0.0
C /4.4	13.6	0.82	24.57	411	5	94	0	1	22	122.3	-20.1	91	4	2,500	0	0.0	0.0
C /4.4	13.6	0.82	25.04	2,575	5	94	0	1	22	133.6	-20.0	91	4	2,500	0	0.0	0.0
C /4.3	11.5	1.05	59.65	6,015	4	96	0	0	38	125.5	-19.1	38	4	2,500	0	0.0	0.0
C /4.3	11.5	1.05	59.69	2,287	4	96	0	0	38	124.2	-19.1	37	4	2,500	0	0.0	0.0
C- /4.1	15.3	0.91	67.87	34	4	95	0	1	22	128.2	-20.4	84	4	2,500	0	5.8	0.0
C- /4.0	15.3	0.91	64.23	14	4	95	0	1	22	120.2	-20.9	80	4	2,500	0	0.0	0.0
C- /4.1	15.3	0.78	69.35	1,429	4	95	0	1	22	131.5	-20.3	98	4	2,500	0	0.0	0.0
C- /4.1	15.3	0.91	69.56	215	4	95	0	1	22	132.4	-20.3	85	4	1,000,000	0	0.0	0.0
C- /4.1	15.3	0.91	69.85	111	4	95	0	1	22	132.8	-20.3	86	4	0	0	0.0	0.0
C- /4.1	15.3	0.91	67.43	42	4	95	0	1	22	127.3	-20.4	83	4	2,500	0	0.0	0.0
C- /4.1	15.3	0.78	68.64	917	4	95	0	1	22	130.2	-20.3	98	4	2,500	0	0.0	0.0
C+ /6.4	9.9	0.90	41.18	3,089	3	95	1	1	14	122.4	-16.1	81	24	1,000,000	100	0.0	0.0
C+ /6.4	9.9	0.90	41.16	2,524	3	95	1	1	14	119.3	-16.2	79	24	2,500	100	0.0	0.0
C+ /6.4	9.9	0.90	40.96	29	3	95	1	1	14	115.4	-16.3	77	24	2,500	100	0.0	0.0
C- /3.7	10.9	0.93	11.72	29	3	96	0	1	93	99.5	-14.5	23	7	1,000,000	100	0.0	0.0
C- /3.7	10.9	0.93	11.78	3	3	96	0	1	93	98.0	-14.5	22	7	2,500	100	0.0	0.0
U /	N/A	N/A	10.68	32	4	93	2	1	25	N/A	N/A	N/A	N/A	25,000	0	0.0	0.0
U /	N/A	N/A	10.67	314	4	93	2	1	25	N/A	N/A	N/A	N/A	1,000,000	0	0.0	0.0
C- /4.2	16.3	0.95	10.00	44	0	100	0	0	41	N/A	N/A	76	5	25,000	0	0.0	0.0
C+ /5.9	16.3	0.95	10.00	3	0	100	0	0	41	N/A	N/A	75	5	2,000	0	0.0	0.0
C- /4.2	16.3	0.95	10.02	111	0	100	0	0	41	N/A	N/A	76	5	1,000,000	0	0.0	0.0
C /5.5	12.5	0.74	13.50	218	0	100	0	0	124	N/A	N/A	78	4	25,000	0	0.0	0.0
C /5.5	12.5	0.74	13.52	250	0	100	0	0	124	N/A	N/A	78	4	1,000,000	0	0.0	0.0
C+ /5.8	11.8	0.74	19.51	4,467	0	100	0	0	107	87.1	-23.6	90	8	25,000	0	0.0	0.0
C+ /5.8	11.8	0.74	19.55	407	0	100	0	0	107	84.6	-23.6	89	8	2,000	0	0.0	0.0
C+ /6.9	12.0	0.85	10.86	48	1	98	0	1	39	N/A	N/A	87	4	25,000	0	0.0	0.0
C+ /6.9	12.0	0.85	10.93	N/A	1	98	0	1	39	N/A	N/A	86	4	2,000	0	0.0	0.0
C+ /6.9	12.0	0.85	10.85	84	1	98	0	1	39	N/A	N/A	87	4	1,000,000	0	0.0	0.0
U /	N/A	N/A	12.16	118	5	94	0	1	63	N/A	N/A	N/A	6	1,000	0	5.0	0.0
U /	N/A	N/A	12.16	306	5	94	0	1	63	N/A	N/A	N/A	6	250,000	0	0.0	0.0
U /	N/A	N/A	12.16	123	5	94	0	1	63	N/A	N/A	N/A	6	0	0	0.0	0.0
U /	N/A	N/A	12.16	71	5	94	0	1	63	N/A	N/A	N/A	6	1,000,000	0	0.0	0.0
U /	N/A	N/A	9.34	853	0	0	0	100	42	N/A	N/A	N/A	2	0	0	0.0	0.0
B- /7.5	10.4	0.56	11.00	4	4	95	0	1	35	N/A	N/A	92	4	1,000	0	5.0	0.0
B- /7.5	10.3	0.56	11.02	N/A	4	95	0	1	35	N/A	N/A	92	4	250,000	0	0.0	0.0
B- /7.5	10.3	0.56	11.03	107	4	95	0	1	35	N/A	N/A	93	4	0	0	0.0	0.0
B- /7.5	10.4	0.56	11.03	1	4	95	0	1	35	N/A	N/A	93	4	1,000,000	0	0.0	0.0
B+ /9.4	2.2	0.10	9.30	1	16	0	83	1	116	N/A	N/A	74	4	1,000	0	3.0	0.0
B+ /9.3	2.3	0.10	9.32	3	16	0	83	1	116	N/A	N/A	76	4	250,000	0	0.0	0.0
B+ /9.7	2.2	0.09	9.32	65	16	0	83	1	116	N/A	N/A	77	4	0	0	0.0	0.0
B+ /9.3	2.2	0.09	9.32	N/A	16	0	83	1	116	N/A	N/A	77	4	1,000,000	0	0.0	0.0
U /	N/A	N/A	9.64	49	0	0	0	100	36	N/A	N/A	N/A	1	0	0	0.0	0.0
U /	N/A	N/A	10.09	50	0	0	0	100	0	N/A	N/A	N/A	2	0	0	0.0	0.0

Data as of February 28, 2017

Fund Type	Fund Name	Ticker Symbol	Overall Investment Rating	Phone	Perfor-mance Rating/Pts	3 Mo	6 Mo	1Yr / Pct	3Yr / Pct	5Yr / Pct	Dividend Yield	Expense Ratio
	99 Pct = Best							Total Return % through 2/28/17	Annualized		Incl. in Returns	
GL	John Hancock II Global Equity A	JHGEX	C-	(800) 257-3336	C- / 3.9	6.58	5.70	17.04 /38	4.84 /52	--	1.39	1.36
GL	John Hancock II Global Equity I	JGEFX	C+	(800) 257-3336	C / 5.2	6.70	5.82	17.27 /40	5.13 /56	--	1.75	1.05
GL	John Hancock II Global Equity NAV		B-	(800) 257-3336	C / 5.3	6.72	5.94	17.54 /41	5.28 /57	--	1.86	0.93
GR	John Hancock Seaport A	JSFBX	D+	(800) 257-3336	D / 1.6	5.24	3.84	9.23 /10	1.89 /23	--	0.00	3.41
GR	John Hancock Seaport I	JSFDX	C-	(800) 257-3336	D+ / 2.3	5.38	4.00	9.56 /11	2.22 /25	--	0.00	3.09
GR	John Hancock Seaport NAV		C-	(800) 257-3336	D+ / 2.4	5.35	4.07	9.72 /11	2.41 /27	--	0.00	2.98
GR	John Hancock Seaport R6	JSFRX	C-	(800) 257-3336	D+ / 2.4	5.35	4.07	9.72 /11	2.41 /27	--	0.00	3.00
SC	John Hancock Small Cap Core I	JCCIX	A	(800) 257-3336	A+ / 9.7	6.47	12.51	41.14 /98	8.77 /85	--	0.71	1.27
SC	John Hancock Small Cap Core NAV		A	(800) 257-3336	A+ / 9.7	6.57	12.61	41.27 /98	8.86 /86	--	0.80	1.16
GR	John Hancock Value Equity NAV		U	(800) 257-3336	U /	6.54	12.98	27.96 /82	--	--	1.34	0.89
IN	Johnson Enhanced Return	JENHX	A-	(800) 541-0170	A / 9.5	8.16	9.50	25.81 /76	10.94 /97	14.50 /96	1.20	0.36
GI	Johnson Equity Income	JEQIX	C+	(800) 541-0170	B- / 7.0	8.28	7.55	22.86 /66	6.44 /68	11.04 /66	1.24	1.00
GR	Johnson Growth	JGRWX	C+	(800) 541-0170	C+ / 6.7	8.51	8.89	21.64 /60	5.81 /63	10.58 /63	0.50	1.00
FO	Johnson International	JINTX	D	(800) 541-0170	D / 2.2	6.91	3.50	17.03 /38	0.11 /14	3.38 /12	2.02	1.00
MC	Johnson Opportunity	JOPPX	B	(800) 541-0170	B+ / 8.3	5.89	11.41	27.54 /81	7.73 /77	12.49 /79	0.60	1.00
RE	Johnson Realty	JRLTX	C+	(800) 541-0170	B- / 7.2	8.03	-1.61	15.06 /30	10.49 /96	10.15 /59	2.59	1.00
FO	JPMorgan China Region A	JCHAX	E	(800) 480-4111	D+ / 2.9	3.48	1.53	24.13 /70	2.94 /31	4.80 /20	0.36	2.03
FO	JPMorgan China Region C	JCHCX	E	(800) 480-4111	C- / 3.5	3.36	1.28	23.59 /68	2.43 /27	4.28 /17	0.01	2.55
FO	JPMorgan China Region Sel	JCHSX	E+	(800) 480-4111	C- / 4.1	3.63	1.68	24.47 /72	3.21 /34	5.07 /22	0.59	1.61
OT	JPMorgan Commodities Strategy A	CSAFX	E-	(800) 480-4111	E- / 0.0	2.92	6.88	16.69 /37	-13.02 / 0	--	0.00	2.35
OT	JPMorgan Commodities Strategy C	CCSFX	E-	(800) 480-4111	E- / 0.0	2.86	6.78	16.32 /36	-13.41 / 0	--	0.00	2.93
OT	JPMorgan Commodities Strategy R6	CSFVX	E-	(800) 480-4111	E- / 0.1	3.10	7.13	17.23 /39	-12.64 / 0	--	0.00	1.67
OT	JPMorgan Commodities Strategy Sel	CSFSX	E-	(800) 480-4111	E- / 0.0	3.11	7.17	17.19 /39	-12.76 / 0	--	0.00	1.93
GI	JPMorgan Disciplined Equity A	JDEAX	B	(800) 480-4111	B / 7.8	7.94	10.77	25.14 /74	8.77 /85	13.14 /85	1.04	1.02
GI	JPMorgan Disciplined Equity L	JPIEX	A-	(800) 480-4111	B+ / 8.9	8.00	10.92	25.57 /75	9.18 /88	13.59 /90	1.43	0.50
GI	JPMorgan Disciplined Equity R6	JDEUX	A-	(800) 480-4111	A- / 9.0	8.03	10.99	25.70 /75	9.29 /89	13.70 /91	1.52	0.35
GI	JPMorgan Disciplined Equity Sel	JDESX	B+	(800) 480-4111	B+ / 8.9	8.03	10.95	25.49 /75	9.03 /87	13.43 /88	1.31	0.69
BA	JPMorgan Diversified A	JDVAX	C-	(800) 480-4111	C- / 3.4	5.34	4.68	15.75 /33	4.58 /50	7.66 /39	1.62	1.46
BA	JPMorgan Diversified C	JDVCX	C	(800) 480-4111	C- / 3.9	5.18	4.46	15.21 /31	4.05 /44	7.12 /35	1.22	1.92
BA	JPMorgan Diversified L	JPDVX	C	(800) 480-4111	C / 4.8	5.45	4.93	16.33 /36	5.09 /55	8.20 /44	2.15	0.96
BA	JPMorgan Diversified Sel	JDVSX	C	(800) 480-4111	C / 4.5	5.38	4.79	16.03 /34	4.83 /52	7.93 /42	1.92	1.15
IX	JPMorgan Dvsfd Real Return A	JRNAX	D+	(800) 480-4111	D- / 1.4	3.90	2.65	11.59 /16	0.96 /18	0.43 / 5	1.51	2.22
IX	JPMorgan Dvsfd Real Return C	JRNCX	D+	(800) 480-4111	D / 1.6	3.79	2.42	11.03 /15	0.44 /15	-0.08 / 4	0.99	2.64
IX	JPMorgan Dvsfd Real Return R2	JRFRX	D+	(800) 480-4111	D / 1.7	3.87	2.56	11.36 /16	0.71 /17	0.18 / 5	1.33	2.50
IX	JPMorgan Dvsfd Real Return R5	JRLRX	C-	(800) 480-4111	D / 2.0	3.96	2.81	12.00 /18	1.31 /20	0.77 / 6	1.91	1.62
IX	JPMorgan Dvsfd Real Return Sel	JRNSX	C-	(800) 480-4111	D / 1.9	3.94	2.76	11.82 /17	1.19 /19	0.67 / 6	1.81	1.75
EM	JPMorgan Dynamic Emerging Econs	JEEAX	D	(800) 480-4111	C- / 3.6	10.15	7.84	29.86 /86	0.27 /15	-1.67 / 3	1.17	1.99
EM	JPMorgan Dynamic Emerging Econs	JEECX	D-	(800) 480-4111	D+ / 2.4	9.94	7.61	29.20 /85	-0.21 /13	-2.14 / 3	0.53	2.37
EM	JPMorgan Dynamic Emerging Econs	JEERX	C-	(800) 480-4111	C / 5.0	10.24	7.97	30.30 /87	0.72 /17	-1.22 / 3	1.38	1.25
EM	JPMorgan Dynamic Emerging Econs	JEEEX	U	(800) 480-4111	U /	10.22	8.02	30.30 /87	--	--	1.50	1.20
EM	JPMorgan Dynamic Emerging Econs	JEESX	C-	(800) 480-4111	C / 4.8	10.16	7.88	30.02 /86	0.51 /16	-1.42 / 3	1.26	1.46
GR	JPMorgan Dynamic Growth A	DGAAX	C-	(800) 480-4111	C / 5.0	6.90	6.58	23.45 /68	5.09 /55	12.17 /76	0.00	1.44
GR	JPMorgan Dynamic Growth C	DGXCX	C	(800) 480-4111	C+ / 5.7	6.74	6.28	22.80 /66	4.56 /49	11.59 /71	0.00	1.87
GR	JPMorgan Dynamic Growth R5	DGFRX	C+	(800) 480-4111	C+ / 6.5	6.99	6.80	23.98 /70	5.56 /60	12.66 /80	0.00	0.80
GR	JPMorgan Dynamic Growth Select	JDGSX	C+	(800) 480-4111	C+ / 6.3	6.93	6.69	23.74 /69	5.35 /58	12.43 /78	0.00	1.01
SC	● JPMorgan Dynamic Small Cap Gr A	VSCOX	D	(800) 480-4111	B- / 7.2	9.25	11.20	41.79 /98	3.50 /37	11.40 /69	0.00	1.58
SC	● JPMorgan Dynamic Small Cap Gr C	VSCCX	D	(800) 480-4111	B / 7.7	9.09	10.92	41.08 /98	2.98 /32	10.83 /64	0.00	2.19
SC	● JPMorgan Dynamic Small Cap Gr Sel	JDSCX	C-	(800) 480-4111	B / 8.2	9.28	11.32	42.20 /98	3.75 /40	11.70 /72	0.00	1.16
EM	JPMorgan Emerg Mkt Eq A	JFAMX	D+	(800) 480-4111	C- / 3.8	8.41	3.65	29.58 /85	1.92 /23	-0.15 / 4	0.44	1.73
EM	JPMorgan Emerg Mkt Eq C	JEMCX	D+	(800) 480-4111	C / 4.4	8.28	3.39	28.86 /84	1.42 /21	-0.66 / 4	0.03	2.18
EM	JPMorgan Emerg Mkt Eq L	JMIEX	C-	(800) 480-4111	C / 5.2	8.55	3.88	30.07 /87	2.33 /26	0.24 / 5	0.75	1.16
EM	JPMorgan Emerg Mkt Eq R6	JEMWX	C	(800) 480-4111	C / 5.3	8.55	3.93	30.17 /87	2.43 /27	--	0.83	1.01

● Denotes fund is closed to new investors
∗ Denotes fund is included in Section II

RISK				NET ASSETS		ASSET					BULL / BEAR		FUND MANAGER		MINIMUMS		LOADS	
	3 Year			NAV						Portfolio	Last Bull	Last Bear	Manager	Manager	Initial	Additional	Front	Back
Risk Rating/Pts	Standard Deviation	Beta		As of 2/28/17	Total $(Mil)	Cash %	Stocks %	Bonds %	Other %	Turnover Ratio	Market Return	Market Return	Quality Pct	Tenure (Years)	Purch. $	Purch. $	End Load	End Load
C+ / 6.4	9.4	0.67		11.39	47	3	96	0	1	35	N/A	N/A	95	4	1,000	0	5.0	0.0
C+ / 6.4	9.4	0.67		11.39	24	3	96	0	1	35	N/A	N/A	96	4	250,000	0	0.0	0.0
B- / 7.5	9.4	0.67		11.38	748	3	96	0	1	35	N/A	N/A	96	4	0	0	0.0	0.0
B- / 7.6	8.0	0.60		10.94	13	53	46	0	1	403	N/A	N/A	21	4	1,000	0	5.0	0.0
B- / 7.7	8.0	0.60		11.06	405	53	46	0	1	403	N/A	N/A	25	4	250,000	0	0.0	0.0
B- / 7.7	8.0	0.60		11.12	175	53	46	0	1	403	N/A	N/A	26	4	0	0	0.0	0.0
B- / 7.7	8.0	0.60		11.12	6	53	46	0	1	403	N/A	N/A	26	4	1,000,000	0	0.0	0.0
C+ / 5.6	14.8	0.90		12.61	N/A	5	94	0	1	59	N/A	N/A	88	4	250,000	0	0.0	0.0
C+ / 5.6	14.7	0.90		12.61	132	5	94	0	1	59	N/A	N/A	88	4	0	0	0.0	0.0
U /	N/A	N/A		11.61	628	2	97	0	1	27	N/A	N/A	N/A	3	0	0	0.0	0.0
C / 5.3	10.4	1.01		17.27	117	3	0	96	1	58	141.1	-15.8	75	12	1,000,000	100	0.0	0.0
C / 5.3	10.3	0.95		22.92	162	4	95	0	1	39	102.0	-14.9	30	12	2,000	100	0.0	0.0
C / 4.8	10.5	0.97		30.95	46	2	97	0	1	32	99.6	-17.9	23	11	2,000	100	0.0	0.0
C+ / 5.8	11.8	0.91		23.23	15	4	95	0	1	20	42.4	-25.1	76	9	2,000	100	0.0	0.0
C / 5.0	12.0	0.95		41.88	46	6	93	0	1	35	133.5	-30.1	58	14	2,000	100	0.0	0.0
C / 4.9	14.6	1.07		15.93	11	0	99	0	1	2	93.1	-15.1	59	19	2,000	100	0.0	0.0
D- / 1.4	17.9	0.91		15.76	4	0	100	0	0	61	55.1	-30.7	91	9	1,000	50	5.3	0.0
D- / 1.4	17.9	0.92		15.20	2	0	100	0	0	61	51.0	-30.8	89	9	1,000	50	0.0	0.0
D- / 1.5	17.8	0.92		16.31	15	0	100	0	0	61	57.2	-30.6	91	9	1,000,000	0	0.0	0.0
D+ / 2.5	14.0	0.31		9.16	1	0	0	0	100	0	N/A	N/A	0	5	1,000	50	5.3	0.0
D+ / 2.4	14.1	0.30		8.98	N/A	0	0	0	100	0	N/A	N/A	0	5	1,000	50	0.0	0.0
D+ / 2.5	14.0	0.31		9.32	158	0	0	0	100	0	N/A	N/A	0	5	15,000,000	0	0.0	0.0
D+ / 2.5	14.0	0.31		9.27	1	0	0	0	100	0	N/A	N/A	0	5	1,000,000	0	0.0	0.0
C+ / 5.6	11.0	1.04		24.91	463	0	99	0	1	122	126.0	-16.3	47	15	1,000	50	5.3	0.0
C+ / 5.6	11.0	1.05		25.09	857	0	99	0	1	122	130.8	-16.1	52	15	3,000,000	0	0.0	0.0
C+ / 5.6	11.0	1.04		25.10	5,897	0	99	0	1	122	132.0	-16.1	53	15	15,000,000	0	0.0	0.0
C+ / 5.6	11.0	1.04		25.13	255	0	99	0	1	122	129.1	-16.2	50	15	1,000,000	0	0.0	0.0
C+ / 6.6	7.3	1.14		16.75	130	1	64	34	1	57	69.0	-14.2	26	8	1,000	50	4.5	0.0
C+ / 6.6	7.3	1.14		16.62	34	1	64	34	1	57	64.4	-14.4	21	8	1,000	50	0.0	0.0
C+ / 6.6	7.3	1.14		16.82	1,063	1	64	34	1	57	73.5	-14.0	32	8	3,000,000	0	0.0	0.0
C+ / 6.6	7.3	1.13		16.84	87	1	64	34	1	57	71.2	-14.0	29	8	1,000,000	0	0.0	0.0
B- / 7.5	5.2	0.31		14.34	3	11	23	65	1	95	9.6	-7.2	44	6	1,000	50	4.5	0.0
B- / 7.6	5.3	0.31		14.31	N/A	11	23	65	1	95	6.7	-7.3	37	6	1,000	50	0.0	0.0
B- / 7.6	5.3	0.31		14.38	N/A	11	23	65	1	95	8.1	-7.3	41	6	0	0	0.0	0.0
B- / 7.5	5.3	0.31		14.41	63	11	23	65	1	95	11.7	-7.0	49	6	0	0	0.0	0.0
B- / 7.5	5.2	0.31		14.39	16	11	23	65	1	95	11.1	-7.0	48	6	1,000,000	0	0.0	0.0
C / 4.8	15.6	0.95		12.17	147	0	98	1	1	72	17.4	-29.2	57	9	1,000	50	5.3	0.0
C / 4.9	15.6	0.94		12.10	3	0	98	1	1	72	14.4	-29.5	51	9	1,000	50	0.0	0.0
C / 4.9	15.6	0.94		12.41	1	0	98	1	1	72	20.3	-29.1	63	9	0	0	0.0	0.0
U /	N/A	N/A		12.24	1,665	0	98	1	1	72	N/A	N/A	N/A	9	15,000,000	0	0.0	0.0
C / 4.9	15.6	0.94		12.31	57	0	98	1	1	72	19.0	-29.2	61	9	1,000,000	0	0.0	0.0
C / 5.3	13.6	1.08		27.73	51	0	99	0	1	61	122.2	-18.2	9	10	1,000	50	5.3	0.0
C / 5.3	13.6	1.07		26.44	13	0	99	0	1	61	116.3	-18.4	7	10	1,000	50	0.0	0.0
C / 5.3	13.6	1.07		28.93	216	0	99	0	1	61	127.6	-18.0	12	10	0	0	0.0	0.0
C / 5.4	13.6	1.07		28.39	67	0	99	0	1	61	125.2	-18.1	11	10	1,000,000	0	0.0	0.0
E+ / 0.9	20.1	1.17		20.13	62	0	98	1	1	56	122.9	-28.0	20	13	1,000	50	5.3	0.0
E / 0.3	20.1	1.17		15.67	36	0	98	1	1	56	116.8	-28.1	16	13	1,000	50	0.0	0.0
D- / 1.2	20.1	1.17		22.67	63	0	98	1	1	56	126.4	-27.9	22	13	1,000,000	0	0.0	0.0
C / 4.6	15.6	0.90		22.11	409	0	96	2	2	23	21.2	-24.4	77	12	1,000	50	5.3	0.0
C / 4.7	15.6	0.90		21.55	35	0	96	2	2	23	17.9	-24.5	73	12	1,000	50	0.0	0.0
C / 4.6	15.6	0.90		22.77	454	0	96	2	2	23	23.8	-24.2	79	12	3,000,000	0	0.0	0.0
C+ / 5.9	15.6	0.90		22.73	2,066	0	96	2	2	23	N/A	N/A	80	12	15,000,000	0	0.0	0.0

Fund Type	Fund Name	Ticker Symbol	Overall Investment Rating	Phone	Performance Rating/Pts	3 Mo	6 Mo	1Yr / Pct	3Yr / Pct	5Yr / Pct	Dividend Yield	Expense Ratio
EM	JPMorgan Emerg Mkt Eq Sel	JEMSX	C-	(800) 480-4111	C / 5.1	8.48	3.79	29.88 /86	2.17 /25	0.09 / 5	0.61	1.33
GR	JPMorgan Equity Focus A	JPFAX	C+	(800) 480-4111	C+ / 6.6	5.56	9.08	23.41 /68	7.67 /77	13.41 /88	0.03	1.51
GR	JPMorgan Equity Focus C	JPFCX	B-	(800) 480-4111	B- / 7.1	5.40	8.79	22.76 /66	7.12 /73	12.84 /82	0.00	1.92
GR	JPMorgan Equity Focus Select	JPFSX	B	(800) 480-4111	B / 7.7	5.60	9.21	23.69 /69	7.94 /78	13.70 /91	0.25	1.07
IN	JPMorgan Equity Income A	OIEIX	A	(800) 480-4111	B / 7.9	6.69	9.94	24.15 /70	9.63 /91	13.01 /84	1.47	1.12
IN	JPMorgan Equity Income C	OINCX	A+	(800) 480-4111	B+ / 8.4	6.54	9.59	23.56 /68	9.07 /87	12.44 /78	1.20	1.59
IN	JPMorgan Equity Income R2	OIEFX	A+	(800) 480-4111	B+ / 8.6	6.58	9.72	23.82 /69	9.33 /89	12.73 /81	1.37	1.46
IN	JPMorgan Equity Income R5	OIERX	A+	(800) 480-4111	A- / 9.1	6.84	10.14	24.76 /72	10.11 /94	13.51 /89	1.89	0.65
IN	JPMorgan Equity Income R6	OIEJX	A+	(800) 480-4111	A- / 9.1	6.86	10.19	24.79 /73	10.20 /94	13.60 /90	1.98	0.51
IN	JPMorgan Equity Income Sel	HLIEX	A+	(800) 480-4111	A- / 9.0	6.72	10.04	24.43 /71	9.90 /93	13.28 /87	1.71	0.82
IX	JPMorgan Equity Index A	OGEAX	B-	(800) 480-4111	B+ / 8.3	7.90	9.77	24.38 /71	10.12 /94	13.48 /89	1.46	0.73
IX	JPMorgan Equity Index C	OEICX	B	(800) 480-4111	B+ / 8.6	7.72	9.37	23.49 /68	9.30 /89	12.64 /80	0.91	1.22
IX	JPMorgan Equity Index Sel	HLEIX	B	(800) 480-4111	A / 9.3	7.98	9.89	24.68 /72	10.39 /95	13.76 /91	1.75	0.46
GL	JPMorgan Global Allocation A	GAOAX	C-	(800) 480-4111	D+ / 2.9	5.42	4.09	14.23 /27	3.87 /41	6.80 /33	2.38	1.46
GL	JPMorgan Global Allocation C	GAOCX	C	(800) 480-4111	C- / 3.3	5.35	3.88	13.70 /24	3.36 /35	6.27 /30	2.12	1.95
GL	JPMorgan Global Allocation R2	GAONX	C	(800) 480-4111	C- / 3.5	5.37	3.98	13.99 /25	3.62 /38	6.54 /32	2.28	1.83
GL	JPMorgan Global Allocation Sel	GAOSX	C	(800) 480-4111	C- / 3.9	5.52	4.26	14.58 /28	4.15 /45	7.08 /35	2.66	1.22
* GL	JPMorgan Global Rsrch Enh Index	JEITX	C+	(800) 480-4111	C+ / 6.4	7.56	8.13	21.95 /62	5.37 /58	--	2.11	0.57
GL	JPMorgan Global Uncon Eqty A	JFUAX	C+	(800) 480-4111	C / 5.2	6.68	9.74	22.82 /66	4.94 /53	8.82 /49	0.22	7.97
GL	JPMorgan Global Uncon Eqty C	JFECX	C+	(800) 480-4111	C+ / 5.8	6.52	9.53	22.23 /63	4.41 /48	8.27 /44	0.06	10.30
GL	JPMorgan Global Uncon Eqty R5	JFETX	C+	(800) 480-4111	C+ / 6.6	6.76	10.02	23.36 /68	5.40 /58	9.30 /53	0.84	8.11
GL	JPMorgan Global Uncon Eqty R6	JFEUX	C+	(800) 480-4111	C+ / 6.7	6.81	10.01	23.45 /68	5.45 /59	9.37 /54	0.90	8.05
GL	JPMorgan Global Uncon Eqty Select	JMESX	C+	(800) 480-4111	C+ / 6.6	6.82	10.02	23.35 /68	5.29 /57	9.14 /52	0.49	7.32
GR	JPMorgan Growth Advantage A	VHIAX	C+	(800) 480-4111	B- / 7.1	8.46	9.03	23.16 /67	8.01 /79	13.71 /91	0.00	1.35
GR	JPMorgan Growth Advantage C	JGACX	B-	(800) 480-4111	B / 7.6	8.37	8.85	22.59 /65	7.50 /75	13.16 /85	0.00	1.85
GR	JPMorgan Growth Advantage R5	JGVRX	B	(800) 480-4111	B+ / 8.3	8.59	9.28	23.56 /68	8.43 /82	14.15 /94	0.00	0.90
GR	JPMorgan Growth Advantage R6	JGVVX	B+	(800) 480-4111	B+ / 8.4	8.62	9.31	23.73 /69	8.55 /83	--	0.00	0.76
GR	JPMorgan Growth Advantage Sel	JGASX	B	(800) 480-4111	B / 8.1	8.52	9.15	23.38 /68	8.21 /81	13.91 /92	0.00	1.09
GI	JPMorgan Growth and Income A	VGRIX	A-	(800) 480-4111	B / 8.2	5.69	11.13	26.58 /78	9.69 /92	14.05 /94	1.13	1.13
GI	JPMorgan Growth and Income C	VGICX	A	(800) 480-4111	B+ / 8.7	5.56	10.84	25.98 /76	9.14 /88	13.48 /89	0.91	1.62
GI	JPMorgan Growth and Income Sel	VGIIX	A+	(800) 480-4111	A- / 9.2	5.75	11.27	26.89 /79	9.95 /93	14.33 /95	1.33	0.86
GR	JPMorgan Hedged Equity A	JHQAX	B-	(800) 480-4111	C / 4.9	4.83	7.83	17.92 /42	6.29 /67	--	1.02	1.11
GR	JPMorgan Hedged Equity C	JHQCX	B-	(800) 480-4111	C / 5.5	4.66	7.55	17.32 /40	5.74 /62	--	0.66	1.52
GR	JPMorgan Hedged Equity R5	JHQPX	B-	(800) 480-4111	C+ / 6.4	4.92	8.10	18.44 /45	6.76 /70	--	1.48	2.16
GR	JPMorgan Hedged Equity R6	JHQRX	B-	(800) 480-4111	C+ / 6.4	4.93	8.12	18.50 /45	6.79 /70	--	1.53	1.40
GR	JPMorgan Hedged Equity Sel	JHEQX	B-	(800) 480-4111	C+ / 6.2	4.88	7.95	18.17 /44	6.54 /69	--	1.31	0.74
GL	JPMorgan Income Builder A	JNBAX	D+	(800) 480-4111	D+ / 2.7	5.09	3.42	13.99 /25	3.83 /41	6.44 /31	4.00	1.11
GL	JPMorgan Income Builder C	JNBCX	C-	(800) 480-4111	C- / 3.1	4.97	3.05	13.44 /23	3.32 /35	5.91 /28	3.69	1.63
GL	JPMorgan Income Builder Select	JNBSX	C-	(800) 480-4111	C- / 3.7	5.23	3.48	14.24 /27	4.01 /43	6.63 /32	4.32	0.87
FS	JPMorgan Income Select	JMSIX	U	(800) 480-4111	U /	2.73	1.52	10.51 /13	--	--	5.36	1.68
FO	JPMorgan International Eq A	JSEAX	D-	(800) 480-4111	E+ / 0.8	5.68	4.20	18.36 /44	-1.03 / 9	3.67 /14	1.40	1.60
FO	JPMorgan International Eq C	JIECX	D-	(800) 480-4111	D- / 1.1	5.57	3.93	17.83 /42	-1.53 / 8	3.17 /11	1.21	2.07
FO	JPMorgan International Eq R2	JIEZX	D-	(800) 480-4111	D- / 1.2	5.58	4.04	18.13 /43	-1.27 / 8	3.42 /12	1.28	1.94
FO	JPMorgan International Eq R5	JIERX	D-	(800) 480-4111	D- / 1.4	5.84	4.43	18.93 /47	-0.58 /11	4.15 /16	1.87	1.07
FO	JPMorgan International Eq R6	JNEMX	D-	(800) 480-4111	D- / 1.4	5.87	4.47	19.00 /47	-0.53 /11	4.20 /16	1.93	0.92
FO	JPMorgan International Eq Sel	VSIEX	D-	(800) 480-4111	D- / 1.3	5.81	4.34	18.73 /46	-0.78 /10	3.94 /15	1.70	1.20
GL	JPMorgan International Eqty Inc A	JEIAX	D	(800) 480-4111	D- / 1.0	5.04	1.39	8.61 / 9	0.40 /15	5.66 /26	2.98	1.67
GL	JPMorgan International Eqty Inc C	JEICX	D	(800) 480-4111	D- / 1.0	4.92	1.16	7.99 / 7	-0.12 /13	5.13 /22	2.76	2.20
GL	JPMorgan International Eqty Inc R2	JGEZX	D	(800) 480-4111	D- / 1.3	5.03	1.27	8.33 / 8	0.13 /14	5.39 /24	3.03	1.92
GL	JPMorgan International Eqty Inc R5	JEIRX	D	(800) 480-4111	D / 1.6	5.20	1.69	9.08 /10	0.84 /17	6.13 /29	3.52	1.17
GL	JPMorgan International Eqty Inc Sel	JEISX	D	(800) 480-4111	D / 1.6	5.09	1.57	8.90 / 9	0.71 /17	5.96 /28	3.43	1.41
FO	JPMorgan International Value A	JFEAX	E+	(800) 480-4111	E / 0.5	7.13	7.04	18.56 /45	-2.79 / 5	2.99 /11	5.28	1.45

Risk Rating/Pts	Standard Deviation	Beta	NAV As of 2/28/17	Total $(Mil)	Cash %	Stocks %	Bonds %	Other %	Portfolio Turnover Ratio	Last Bull Market Return	Last Bear Market Return	Manager Quality Pct	Manager Tenure (Years)	Initial Purch. $	Additional Purch. $	Front End Load	Back End Load
C /4.6	15.6	0.90	22.63	335	0	96	2	2	23	22.7	-24.3	78	12	1,000,000	0	0.0	0.0
C+ /5.7	11.6	1.02	27.75	3	0	99	0	1	45	133.7	N/A	35	6	1,000	50	5.3	0.0
C+ /5.7	11.6	1.02	27.01	3	0	99	0	1	45	127.4	N/A	29	6	1,000	50	0.0	0.0
C+ /5.7	11.6	1.02	27.96	156	0	99	0	1	45	136.8	N/A	38	6	1,000,000	0	0.0	0.0
B- /7.2	9.7	0.90	15.58	3,675	0	98	1	1	20	121.6	-13.2	74	13	1,000	50	5.3	0.0
B- /7.2	9.7	0.91	15.32	1,448	0	98	1	1	20	115.3	-13.2	68	13	1,000	50	0.0	0.0
B- /7.2	9.7	0.91	15.52	90	0	98	1	1	20	118.4	-13.2	71	13	0	0	0.0	0.0
B- /7.2	9.7	0.91	15.83	962	0	98	1	1	20	126.9	-13.0	77	13	0	0	0.0	0.0
B- /7.2	9.6	0.90	15.82	2,599	0	98	1	1	20	127.4	-13.1	78	13	15,000,000	0	0.0	0.0
B- /7.2	9.7	0.91	15.82	5,863	0	98	1	1	20	124.5	-13.1	76	13	1,000,000	0	0.0	0.0
C /4.4	10.3	1.00	36.55	604	0	99	0	1	4	128.9	-16.4	69	13	1,000	50	5.3	0.0
C /4.4	10.3	1.00	36.19	92	0	99	0	1	4	119.9	-16.7	60	13	1,000	50	0.0	0.0
C /4.4	10.3	1.00	36.60	760	0	99	0	1	4	132.1	-16.3	72	13	1,000,000	0	0.0	0.0
B- /7.4	7.1	1.06	17.05	290	14	48	36	2	64	57.2	N/A	62	6	1,000	50	4.5	0.0
B- /7.3	7.1	1.06	16.86	361	14	48	36	2	64	53.1	N/A	56	6	1,000	50	0.0	0.0
B- /7.4	7.1	1.05	17.02	1	14	48	36	2	64	55.2	N/A	59	6	0	0	0.0	0.0
B- /7.4	7.1	1.05	17.13	906	14	48	36	2	64	59.4	N/A	66	6	1,000	0	0.0	0.0
C+ /6.5	10.4	0.80	19.70	7,457	1	98	0	1	35	N/A	N/A	96	3	1,000,000	0	0.0	0.0
C+ /6.6	12.8	0.94	15.66	1	0	100	0	0	1,256	N/A	N/A	95	3	1,000	50	5.3	0.0
C+ /6.6	12.8	0.94	15.52	N/A	0	100	0	0	1,256	N/A	N/A	94	3	1,000	50	0.0	0.0
C+ /6.6	12.8	0.94	15.71	N/A	0	100	0	0	1,256	N/A	N/A	96	3	0	0	0.0	0.0
C+ /6.6	12.8	0.94	15.70	N/A	0	100	0	0	1,256	N/A	N/A	96	3	15,000,000	0	0.0	0.0
C+ /6.6	12.8	0.95	15.77	1	0	100	0	0	1,256	N/A	N/A	96	3	1,000,000	0	0.0	0.0
C /5.1	13.4	1.12	16.54	1,625	0	97	1	2	46	144.9	-19.1	28	15	1,000	50	5.3	0.0
C /5.0	13.4	1.12	14.76	581	0	97	1	2	46	138.5	-19.3	23	15	1,000	50	0.0	0.0
C /5.1	13.4	1.11	17.20	87	0	97	1	2	46	150.1	-19.0	33	15	0	0	0.0	0.0
C+ /5.7	13.4	1.12	17.26	2,970	0	97	1	2	46	N/A	N/A	34	15	15,000,000	0	0.0	0.0
C /5.1	13.4	1.12	16.94	1,270	0	97	1	2	46	147.4	-19.1	30	15	1,000,000	0	0.0	0.0
C+ /6.4	10.8	1.01	46.82	466	0	98	1	1	39	138.2	-17.9	63	15	1,000	50	5.3	0.0
C+ /6.3	10.8	1.01	42.51	30	0	98	1	1	39	131.8	-18.1	57	15	1,000	50	0.0	0.0
C+ /6.4	10.8	1.01	49.18	51	0	98	1	1	39	141.5	-17.9	66	15	1,000,000	0	0.0	0.0
B- /7.9	6.2	0.55	17.81	102	0	98	1	1	57	N/A	N/A	78	4	1,000	50	5.3	0.0
B- /7.9	6.2	0.55	17.73	15	0	98	1	1	57	N/A	N/A	74	4	1,000	50	0.0	0.0
B- /7.9	6.2	0.55	17.88	N/A	0	98	1	1	57	N/A	N/A	81	4	0	0	0.0	0.0
B- /7.9	6.2	0.55	17.88	N/A	0	98	1	1	57	N/A	N/A	81	4	15,000,000	0	0.0	0.0
B- /7.9	6.2	0.54	17.85	320	0	98	1	1	57	N/A	N/A	80	4	1,000,000	0	0.0	0.0
C+ /6.5	5.9	0.87	10.23	3,964	1	33	64	2	52	54.6	-11.9	71	10	1,000	50	4.5	0.0
C+ /6.5	5.8	0.87	10.20	4,855	1	33	64	2	52	50.4	-12.0	66	10	1,000	50	0.0	0.0
C+ /6.5	5.9	0.88	10.25	3,429	1	33	64	2	52	56.1	-11.8	73	10	1,000,000	0	0.0	0.0
U /	N/A	N/A	9.53	35	0	0	99	1	74	N/A	N/A	N/A	3	1,000,000	0	0.0	0.0
C /5.5	12.3	0.98	14.88	230	0	98	0	2	11	43.2	-23.7	64	18	1,000	50	5.3	0.0
C /5.5	12.4	0.98	14.10	21	0	98	0	2	11	39.4	-23.8	57	18	1,000	50	0.0	0.0
C /5.5	12.3	0.98	14.80	2	0	98	0	2	11	41.2	-23.7	61	18	0	0	0.0	0.0
C /5.5	12.4	0.98	15.12	18	0	98	0	2	11	46.8	-23.6	69	18	0	0	0.0	0.0
C /5.5	12.3	0.98	15.12	3,115	0	98	0	2	11	47.2	-23.5	70	18	15,000,000	0	0.0	0.0
C /5.5	12.3	0.98	15.10	101	0	98	0	2	11	45.2	-23.6	67	18	1,000,000	0	0.0	0.0
C+ /6.7	9.3	0.72	14.85	74	4	92	2	2	162	49.9	-19.4	77	6	1,000	50	5.3	0.0
C+ /6.6	9.3	0.72	14.75	12	4	92	2	2	162	45.9	-19.6	74	6	1,000	50	0.0	0.0
C+ /6.6	9.3	0.72	14.82	1	4	92	2	2	162	47.9	-19.6	75	6	0	0	0.0	0.0
C+ /6.7	9.3	0.72	14.90	2	4	92	2	2	162	53.6	-19.3	81	6	0	0	0.0	0.0
C+ /6.7	9.3	0.72	14.89	62	4	92	2	2	162	52.3	-19.4	80	6	1,000,000	0	0.0	0.0
C /5.2	12.3	0.97	12.40	286	1	98	0	1	61	35.4	-25.4	39	15	1,000	50	5.3	0.0

Fund Type	Fund Name	Ticker Symbol	Overall Investment Rating	Phone	Perfor-mance Rating/Pts	3 Mo	6 Mo	1Yr / Pct	3Yr / Pct	5Yr / Pct	Dividend Yield	Expense Ratio
								Total Return % through 2/28/17	Annualized		Incl. in Returns	
FO	JPMorgan International Value C	JIUCX	E+	(800) 480-4111	E+ / 0.7	7.00	6.74	17.92 /42	-3.28 / 4	2.47 / 9	5.59	1.90
FO	JPMorgan International Value L	JNUSX	E+	(800) 480-4111	D- / 1.0	7.27	7.36	19.17 /48	-2.36 / 6	3.43 /13	6.22	0.99
FO	JPMorgan International Value R2	JPVZX	E+	(800) 480-4111	E+ / 0.8	7.04	6.95	18.22 /44	-3.03 / 4	2.75 /10	5.55	2.02
FO	JPMorgan International Value R6	JNVMX	D-	(800) 480-4111	D- / 1.1	7.26	7.35	19.25 /48	-2.21 / 6	3.57 /13	6.54	0.74
FO	JPMorgan International Value Sel	JIESX	E+	(800) 480-4111	D- / 1.0	7.25	7.17	18.98 /47	-2.48 / 5	3.28 /12	6.13	1.03
FO	JPMorgan International Value SMA	JTIVX	D-	(800) 480-4111	D- / 1.5	8.89	9.37	21.22 /58	-1.47 / 8	3.52 /13	3.08	0.20
FO	JPMorgan Intl Opps A	JIOAX	D-	(800) 480-4111	E+ / 0.8	7.30	3.81	14.87 /29	-0.91 /10	4.42 /18	2.80	1.43
FO	JPMorgan Intl Opps C	JIOCX	D-	(800) 480-4111	D- / 1.0	7.15	3.62	14.25 /27	-1.42 / 8	3.88 /15	2.53	1.84
FO	JPMorgan Intl Opps R6	JIOMX	D-	(800) 480-4111	D- / 1.4	7.45	4.17	15.48 /32	-0.35 /12	5.00 /21	3.51	0.72
FO	JPMorgan Intl Opps Sel	JIOSX	D-	(800) 480-4111	D- / 1.3	7.46	4.08	15.17 /31	-0.62 /11	4.70 /19	3.29	1.02
FO	JPMorgan Intl Res Enh Eq A	OEIAX	E	(800) 480-4111	D- / 1.1	7.41	5.29	17.47 /40	-0.10 /13	5.18 /23	2.03	1.01
FO	JPMorgan Intl Res Enh Eq C	OIICX	E	(800) 480-4111	D- / 1.4	7.26	4.98	16.93 /38	-0.60 /11	4.62 /19	1.68	1.53
FO	JPMorgan Intl Res Enh Eq R2	JEIZX	E	(800) 480-4111	D- / 1.5	7.39	5.15	17.27 /40	-0.35 /12	4.92 /21	2.27	1.42
FO	JPMorgan Intl Res Enh Eq Sel	OIEAX	E+	(800) 480-4111	D+ / 2.5	7.47	5.37	17.77 /42	0.15 /14	5.45 /24	2.43	0.61
GL	JPMorgan Intl Uncons Eqty A	IUAEX	D-	(800) 480-4111	D- / 1.5	6.10	2.48	15.13 /30	0.67 /16	5.51 /25	1.87	2.30
GL	JPMorgan Intl Uncons Eqty C	IUCEX	D-	(800) 480-4111	D / 1.9	5.94	2.16	14.49 /28	0.13 /14	4.96 /21	1.45	2.79
GL	JPMorgan Intl Uncons Eqty R2	IUERX	D-	(800) 480-4111	D / 2.0	5.99	2.37	14.81 /29	0.40 /15	5.23 /23	1.70	5.31
GL	JPMorgan Intl Uncons Eqty R5	IUEFX	D	(800) 480-4111	D+ / 2.4	6.17	2.64	15.60 /32	1.09 /19	5.96 /28	2.35	4.62
GL	JPMorgan Intl Uncons Eqty R6	IUENX	D	(800) 480-4111	D+ / 2.4	6.16	2.69	15.65 /33	1.13 /19	6.02 /28	2.39	2.95
GL	JPMorgan Intl Uncons Eqty Sel	IUESX	D	(800) 480-4111	D+ / 2.3	6.13	2.60	15.48 /32	0.96 /18	5.80 /27	2.26	1.84
GR	JPMorgan Intrepid America A	JIAAX	B	(800) 480-4111	B- / 7.3	6.84	11.08	21.25 /59	8.92 /86	13.14 /85	0.64	1.16
GR	JPMorgan Intrepid America C	JIACX	B+	(800) 480-4111	B / 7.9	6.72	10.79	20.69 /56	8.40 /82	12.58 /80	0.27	1.63
GR	JPMorgan Intrepid America R2	JIAZX	B+	(800) 480-4111	B / 8.1	6.78	10.93	20.99 /57	8.66 /84	12.86 /82	0.50	1.47
GR	JPMorgan Intrepid America R5	JIARX	A-	(800) 480-4111	B+ / 8.6	6.97	11.32	21.81 /61	9.45 /90	13.67 /90	1.19	0.56
GR	JPMorgan Intrepid America R6	JIAPX	U	(800) 480-4111	U /	6.98	11.37	21.94 /62	--	--	1.30	0.51
GR	JPMorgan Intrepid America Sel	JPIAX	B+	(800) 480-4111	B+ / 8.5	6.91	11.24	21.63 /60	9.24 /88	13.45 /88	1.01	0.76
FO	JPMorgan Intrepid Euro A	VEUAX	E+	(800) 480-4111	E / 0.3	7.91	5.81	11.29 /15	-3.92 / 3	7.27 /36	1.75	1.42
FO	JPMorgan Intrepid Euro C	VEUCX	E+	(800) 480-4111	E / 0.4	7.73	5.55	10.71 /14	-4.39 / 3	6.74 /33	1.60	1.92
FO	JPMorgan Intrepid Euro L	JFEIX	E+	(800) 480-4111	E / 0.5	8.00	6.11	11.84 /17	-3.44 / 4	7.80 /41	2.34	0.92
FO	JPMorgan Intrepid Euro Sel	JFESX	E+	(800) 480-4111	E / 0.5	7.98	5.97	11.60 /16	-3.61 / 4	7.59 /39	2.06	1.08
GR	JPMorgan Intrepid Growth A	JIGAX	A-	(800) 480-4111	B / 7.8	8.49	10.30	21.26 /59	9.69 /92	13.35 /87	0.54	1.24
GR	JPMorgan Intrepid Growth C	JCICX	A	(800) 480-4111	B+ / 8.4	8.36	10.04	20.70 /56	9.15 /88	12.80 /82	0.08	1.72
GR	JPMorgan Intrepid Growth R2	JIGZX	A	(800) 480-4111	B+ / 8.6	8.42	10.16	21.00 /57	9.43 /90	13.08 /85	0.51	1.77
GR	JPMorgan Intrepid Growth R5	JGIRX	A+	(800) 480-4111	A- / 9.0	8.62	10.55	21.83 /61	10.19 /94	13.87 /92	1.00	0.75
GR	JPMorgan Intrepid Growth R6	JGISX	U	(800) 480-4111	U /	8.63	10.59	21.88 /62	--	--	1.06	0.62
GR	JPMorgan Intrepid Growth Sel	JPGSX	A+	(800) 480-4111	B+ / 8.9	8.59	10.44	21.57 /60	9.97 /93	13.64 /90	0.83	0.89
FO	JPMorgan Intrepid Int A	JFTAX	D-	(800) 480-4111	E+ / 0.9	7.34	5.71	16.24 /35	-0.74 /10	5.20 /23	1.86	1.44
FO	JPMorgan Intrepid Int C	JIICX	D	(800) 480-4111	D- / 1.1	7.21	5.48	15.69 /33	-1.24 / 9	4.68 /19	1.32	1.87
FO	JPMorgan Intrepid Int R2	JIIZX	D	(800) 480-4111	D- / 1.2	7.28	5.58	15.98 /34	-1.01 / 9	4.93 /21	1.87	1.65
FO	JPMorgan Intrepid Int R6	JIFFX	U	(800) 480-4111	U /	7.50	6.02	16.91 /38	--	--	2.47	0.76
FO	JPMorgan Intrepid Int Sel	JISIX	D	(800) 480-4111	D- / 1.5	7.39	5.88	16.64 /37	-0.44 /12	5.50 /25	2.35	1.07
MC	JPMorgan Intrepid Mid Cap A	PECAX	C	(800) 480-4111	C+ / 6.6	6.24	8.09	24.21 /71	7.53 /76	13.24 /86	0.51	1.45
MC	JPMorgan Intrepid Mid Cap C	ODMCX	C	(800) 480-4111	B- / 7.0	6.06	7.76	23.40 /68	6.84 /71	12.53 /79	0.24	1.97
MC	JPMorgan Intrepid Mid Cap R6	WOOSX	U	(800) 480-4111	U /	6.34	8.39	24.81 /73	--	--	0.87	0.79
MC	JPMorgan Intrepid Mid Cap Sel	WOOPX	C+	(800) 480-4111	B / 7.7	6.28	8.21	24.49 /72	7.79 /77	13.51 /89	0.67	1.14
GR	JPMorgan Intrepid Sustain Ldr A	JICAX	A-	(800) 480-4111	B / 7.7	6.95	10.69	22.53 /65	9.38 /89	13.52 /89	0.85	1.80
GR	JPMorgan Intrepid Sustain Ldr C	JICCX	A	(800) 480-4111	B / 8.2	6.79	10.40	21.91 /62	8.83 /86	12.95 /83	0.37	2.31
GR	JPMorgan Intrepid Sustain Ldr Sel	JIISX	A+	(800) 480-4111	B+ / 8.8	6.98	10.83	22.83 /66	9.63 /91	13.80 /92	1.15	1.50
GR	JPMorgan Intrepid Value A	JIVAX	B-	(800) 480-4111	B- / 7.3	6.08	13.45	26.68 /78	7.35 /74	12.64 /80	1.40	1.19
GR	JPMorgan Intrepid Value C	JIVCX	B	(800) 480-4111	B / 7.8	5.96	13.14	26.05 /76	6.82 /71	12.08 /75	1.08	1.63
GR	JPMorgan Intrepid Value R2	JIVZX	B	(800) 480-4111	B / 8.0	6.02	13.31	26.38 /77	7.09 /73	12.36 /78	1.32	1.76
GR	JPMorgan Intrepid Value R5	JIVRX	B+	(800) 480-4111	B+ / 8.5	6.17	13.62	27.15 /80	7.73 /77	13.05 /84	1.81	0.62

● Denotes fund is closed to new investors
★ Denotes fund is included in Section II

www.thestreetratings.com

RISK			NET ASSETS		ASSET				Portfolio Turnover Ratio	BULL / BEAR		FUND MANAGER		MINIMUMS		LOADS	
Risk Rating/Pts	3 Year		NAV As of 2/28/17	Total $(Mil)	Cash %	Stocks %	Bonds %	Other %		Last Bull Market Return	Last Bear Market Return	Manager Quality Pct	Manager Tenure (Years)	Initial Purch. $	Additional Purch. $	Front End Load	Back End Load
	Standard Deviation	Beta															
C /5.2	12.4	0.97	12.02	23	1	98	0	1	61	31.8	-25.5	32	15	1,000	50	0.0	0.0
C /5.2	12.4	0.97	12.62	542	1	98	0	1	61	38.4	-25.2	45	15	3,000,000	0	0.0	0.0
C /5.2	12.3	0.97	12.20	1	1	98	0	1	61	33.6	-25.4	36	15	0	0	0.0	0.0
C /5.1	12.4	0.97	12.59	30	1	98	0	1	61	39.4	-25.2	47	15	15,000,000	0	0.0	0.0
C /5.2	12.4	0.97	12.69	147	1	98	0	1	61	37.5	-25.3	44	15	1,000,000	0	0.0	0.0
C /5.5	12.9	0.98	11.92	70	3	96	0	1	70	38.7	-25.4	58	10	0	0	0.0	0.0
C+ /5.9	11.4	0.90	14.23	187	2	95	2	1	48	46.5	-24.8	65	17	1,000	50	5.3	0.0
C+ /5.9	11.4	0.90	13.78	2	2	95	2	1	48	42.4	-25.0	58	17	1,000	50	0.0	0.0
C+ /5.9	11.3	0.90	14.46	2,606	2	95	2	1	48	50.7	-24.6	72	17	15,000,000	0	0.0	0.0
C+ /5.9	11.4	0.90	14.43	41	2	95	2	1	48	48.6	-24.7	69	17	1,000,000	0	0.0	0.0
C- /3.2	12.0	0.97	16.19	70	1	96	2	1	24	48.0	-25.7	74	3	1,000	50	5.3	0.0
C- /3.2	12.0	0.97	15.55	13	1	96	2	1	24	43.5	-25.9	69	3	1,000	50	0.0	0.0
C- /3.2	12.0	0.97	15.80	12	1	96	2	1	24	46.1	-25.8	72	3	0	0	0.0	0.0
C- /3.2	12.0	0.97	16.30	1,383	1	96	2	1	24	50.0	-25.6	76	3	1,000,000	0	0.0	0.0
C /5.3	12.1	0.94	17.63	18	0	99	0	1	51	N/A	N/A	80	6	1,000	50	5.3	0.0
C /5.3	12.0	0.94	17.48	4	0	99	0	1	51	N/A	N/A	76	6	1,000	50	0.0	0.0
C /5.3	12.1	0.94	17.63	N/A	0	99	0	1	51	N/A	N/A	78	6	0	0	0.0	0.0
C /5.3	12.1	0.94	17.78	N/A	0	99	0	1	51	N/A	N/A	82	6	0	0	0.0	0.0
C /5.3	12.1	0.94	17.78	101	0	99	0	1	51	N/A	N/A	83	6	15,000,000	0	0.0	0.0
C /5.3	12.1	0.94	17.80	17	0	99	0	1	51	N/A	N/A	82	6	1,000,000	0	0.0	0.0
C+ /5.9	11.2	1.07	38.41	56	0	99	0	1	70	127.5	-18.5	45	12	1,000	50	5.3	0.0
C+ /6.0	11.2	1.07	38.02	11	0	99	0	1	70	121.4	-18.6	38	12	1,000	50	0.0	0.0
C+ /5.9	11.2	1.07	37.58	4	0	99	0	1	70	124.5	-18.6	42	12	0	0	0.0	0.0
C+ /6.0	11.2	1.07	39.20	5	0	99	0	1	70	133.2	-18.3	52	12	0	0	0.0	0.0
U /	N/A	N/A	38.62	3,710	0	99	0	1	70	N/A	N/A	N/A	12	15,000,000	0	0.0	0.0
C+ /6.0	11.3	1.07	39.18	217	0	99	0	1	70	130.8	-18.4	49	12	1,000,000	0	0.0	0.0
C /5.5	11.0	0.84	23.00	152	0	99	0	1	142	69.7	-27.5	25	12	1,000	50	5.3	0.0
C /5.4	10.9	0.84	20.48	45	0	99	0	1	142	65.2	-27.7	20	12	1,000	50	0.0	0.0
C /5.5	11.0	0.84	23.62	437	0	99	0	1	142	74.2	-27.4	30	12	3,000,000	0	0.0	0.0
C /5.5	11.0	0.84	23.43	126	0	99	0	1	142	72.3	-27.4	28	12	1,000,000	0	0.0	0.0
C+ /6.9	11.2	1.05	46.09	96	0	97	1	2	70	128.9	-16.9	57	12	1,000	50	5.3	0.0
C+ /6.9	11.2	1.05	45.33	46	0	97	1	2	70	122.9	-17.1	50	12	1,000	50	0.0	0.0
C+ /6.9	11.2	1.05	45.24	5	0	97	1	2	70	125.9	-17.0	54	12	0	0	0.0	0.0
C+ /6.9	11.2	1.05	46.18	181	0	97	1	2	70	134.6	-16.7	63	12	0	0	0.0	0.0
U /	N/A	N/A	46.16	525	0	97	1	2	70	N/A	N/A	N/A	12	15,000,000	0	0.0	0.0
B- /7.0	11.2	1.05	46.76	174	0	97	1	2	70	132.0	-16.8	61	12	1,000,000	0	0.0	0.0
C+ /6.2	11.3	0.90	19.10	182	1	97	1	1	38	50.8	-25.9	67	12	1,000	50	5.3	0.0
C+ /6.2	11.3	0.90	19.33	2	1	97	1	1	38	46.8	-26.1	61	12	1,000	50	0.0	0.0
C+ /6.2	11.3	0.90	18.95	1	1	97	1	1	38	48.7	-26.0	64	12	0	0	0.0	0.0
U /	N/A	N/A	19.52	2,606	1	97	1	1	38	N/A	N/A	N/A	12	15,000,000	0	0.0	0.0
C+ /6.2	11.3	0.90	19.83	46	1	97	1	1	38	53.1	-25.8	71	12	1,000,000	0	0.0	0.0
C- /3.9	11.3	0.90	21.95	346	0	98	1	1	78	132.2	-23.1	62	9	1,000	50	5.3	0.0
C- /3.5	11.3	0.90	18.80	93	0	98	1	1	78	124.5	-23.3	53	9	1,000	50	0.0	0.0
U /	N/A	N/A	23.04	246	0	98	1	1	78	N/A	N/A	N/A	9	15,000,000	0	0.0	0.0
C- /4.1	11.3	0.90	23.03	305	0	98	1	1	78	135.3	-23.0	65	9	1,000,000	0	0.0	0.0
B- /7.1	11.0	1.05	37.91	8	0	99	0	1	31	136.9	-19.7	53	12	1,000	50	5.3	0.0
B- /7.1	11.0	1.05	37.16	5	0	99	0	1	31	130.5	-19.8	46	12	1,000	50	0.0	0.0
B- /7.1	11.0	1.05	38.10	4	0	99	0	1	31	140.1	-19.6	57	12	1,000,000	0	0.0	0.0
C /5.3	12.0	1.09	35.85	116	0	98	0	2	66	121.2	-19.3	24	12	1,000	50	5.3	0.0
C /5.3	12.0	1.09	35.42	40	0	98	0	2	66	115.2	-19.4	20	12	1,000	50	0.0	0.0
C /5.3	12.0	1.09	35.63	20	0	98	0	2	66	118.2	-19.3	22	12	0	0	0.0	0.0
C /5.3	12.0	1.10	36.11	96	0	98	0	2	66	125.3	-19.1	28	12	0	0	0.0	0.0

					PERFORMANCE						Incl. in Returns	
						Total Return % through 2/28/17						
	99 Pct = Best				Perfor-				Annualized		Dividend	Expense
	0 Pct = Worst		Overall		mance						Yield	Ratio
Fund		Ticker	Investment		Rating/Pts	3 Mo	6 Mo	1Yr / Pct	3Yr / Pct	5Yr / Pct		
Type	Fund Name	Symbol	Rating	Phone								
GR	JPMorgan Intrepid Value R6	JIVMX	B+	(800) 480-4111	B+ / 8.5	6.19	13.68	27.20 /80	7.79 /77	13.10 /85	1.86	0.52
GR	JPMorgan Intrepid Value Sel	JPIVX	B	(800) 480-4111	B+ / 8.3	6.11	13.52	26.87 /79	7.52 /76	12.81 /82	1.62	0.92
AA	JPMorgan Investor Balanced A	OGIAX	C	(800) 480-4111	C- / 3.2	4.35	4.86	14.07 /26	4.60 /50	6.66 /33	1.46	1.28
AA	JPMorgan Investor Balanced C	OGBCX	C+	(800) 480-4111	C- / 3.6	4.26	4.56	13.48 /23	4.05 /44	6.11 /29	1.00	1.77
AA	JPMorgan Investor Balanced Sel	OIBFX	C+	(800) 480-4111	C- / 4.2	4.41	4.98	14.33 /27	4.88 /53	6.93 /34	1.76	1.00
AA	JPMorgan Investor Conserv Gr A	OICAX	C	(800) 480-4111	D / 1.9	3.10	2.57	9.53 /11	3.44 /36	4.75 /20	1.71	1.22
AA	JPMorgan Investor Conserv Gr C	OCGCX	C	(800) 480-4111	D / 2.2	2.87	2.27	8.84 / 9	2.89 /31	4.20 /16	1.21	1.72
AA	JPMorgan Investor Conserv Gr Sel	ONCFX	C	(800) 480-4111	D+ / 2.7	3.14	2.75	9.81 /11	3.69 /39	5.02 /21	1.99	0.97
GI	JPMorgan Investor Gr & Inc A	ONGIX	C+	(800) 480-4111	C / 4.5	5.45	7.02	17.95 /43	5.41 /59	8.20 /44	1.28	1.33
GI	JPMorgan Investor Gr & Inc C	ONECX	C+	(800) 480-4111	C / 5.0	5.32	6.72	17.28 /40	4.85 /53	7.64 /39	0.84	1.83
GI	JPMorgan Investor Gr & Inc Sel	ONGFX	B-	(800) 480-4111	C+ / 5.7	5.53	7.13	18.31 /44	5.67 /61	8.49 /46	1.59	1.04
GR	JPMorgan Investor Growth A	ONGAX	C+	(800) 480-4111	C+ / 6.3	6.65	9.18	22.32 /64	6.70 /70	10.32 /61	0.97	1.34
GR	JPMorgan Investor Growth C	OGGCX	C+	(800) 480-4111	C+ / 6.7	6.55	8.93	21.59 /60	6.14 /65	9.74 /57	0.70	1.83
GR	JPMorgan Investor Growth Sel	ONIFX	B+	(800) 480-4111	B- / 7.2	6.74	9.35	22.61 /65	6.99 /72	10.61 /63	1.22	1.02
GR	JPMorgan Large Cap Growth A	OLGAX	C	(800) 480-4111	C+ / 6.4	9.25	9.63	20.26 /53	6.86 /71	10.90 /65	0.00	1.28
GR	JPMorgan Large Cap Growth C	OLGCX	C+	(800) 480-4111	C+ / 6.9	9.10	9.36	19.68 /50	6.32 /67	10.35 /61	0.00	1.70
GR	JPMorgan Large Cap Growth R2	JLGZX	C+	(800) 480-4111	B- / 7.0	9.16	9.52	19.98 /52	6.59 /69	10.63 /63	0.00	1.56
GR	JPMorgan Large Cap Growth R5	JLGRX	C+	(800) 480-4111	B- / 7.5	9.35	9.82	20.70 /56	7.24 /74	11.31 /68	0.00	0.74
GR	JPMorgan Large Cap Growth R6	JLGMX	B-	(800) 480-4111	B / 7.6	9.37	9.87	20.83 /57	7.33 /74	11.39 /69	0.00	0.61
GR	JPMorgan Large Cap Growth Sel	SEEGX	C+	(800) 480-4111	B- / 7.3	9.29	9.73	20.48 /55	7.04 /72	11.09 /67	0.00	0.94
GR	JPMorgan Large Cap Value A	OLVAX	B+	(800) 480-4111	A+ / 9.8	7.95	19.67	35.37 /94	12.82 /99	15.37 /97	0.90	1.13
GR	JPMorgan Large Cap Value C	OLVCX	B+	(800) 480-4111	A+ / 9.9	7.77	19.40	34.54 /93	12.21 /98	14.78 /96	0.59	1.63
GR	JPMorgan Large Cap Value R2	JLVZX	B+	(800) 480-4111	A+ / 9.9	7.85	19.57	34.97 /94	12.50 /98	15.06 /97	0.74	1.58
GR	JPMorgan Large Cap Value R5	JLVRX	B+	(800) 480-4111	A+ / 9.9	8.00	19.92	35.75 /95	13.19 /99	15.76 /98	1.22	0.61
GR	JPMorgan Large Cap Value R6	JLVMX	B+	(800) 480-4111	A+ / 9.9	8.07	19.99	35.87 /95	13.28 /99	15.84 /98	1.29	0.53
GR	JPMorgan Large Cap Value Sel	HLQVX	B+	(800) 480-4111	A+ / 9.9	7.97	19.74	35.43 /94	12.97 /99	15.54 /98	1.21	0.78
FO	JPMorgan Latin America A	JLTAX	E-	(800) 480-4111	E+ / 0.9	12.16	4.61	36.02 /95	-3.94 / 3	-6.81 / 1	1.55	2.08
FO	JPMorgan Latin America C	JLTCX	E-	(800) 480-4111	D- / 1.2	11.98	4.33	35.34 /94	-4.42 / 3	-7.27 / 1	1.16	2.60
FO	JPMorgan Latin America R6	JLTNX	U	(800) 480-4111	U /	12.35	4.89	36.76 /96	--	--	2.13	1.40
FO	JPMorgan Latin America Sel	JLTSX	E-	(800) 480-4111	D- / 1.4	12.29	4.72	36.34 /95	-3.70 / 3	-6.57 / 1	1.90	1.65
MC	JPMorgan Market Expnsion En Idx A	OMEAX	C+	(800) 480-4111	A- / 9.0	5.85	12.53	32.14 /90	9.97 /93	14.22 /94	0.78	0.98
MC	JPMorgan Market Expnsion En Idx C	OMECX	C+	(800) 480-4111	A / 9.3	5.76	12.17	31.27 /89	9.24 /88	13.46 /88	0.47	1.52
MC	JPMorgan Market Expnsion En Idx	JMEZX	B-	(800) 480-4111	A / 9.5	5.87	12.38	31.82 /90	9.73 /92	13.94 /93	0.66	1.40
MC	JPMorgan Market Expnsion En Idx	PGMIX	B-	(800) 480-4111	A+ / 9.6	5.84	12.52	32.31 /90	10.20 /94	14.48 /96	1.01	0.63
MC	● JPMorgan Mid Cap Equity A	JCMAX	C+	(800) 480-4111	C+ / 6.1	6.02	7.78	22.72 /65	6.91 /71	12.96 /83	0.09	1.44
MC	● JPMorgan Mid Cap Equity C	JMCCX	C+	(800) 480-4111	C+ / 6.7	5.90	7.53	22.12 /63	6.39 /67	12.40 /78	0.00	1.97
GI	JPMorgan Mid Cap Equity R6	JPPEX	U	(800) 480-4111	U /	6.15	8.06	23.33 /68	--	--	0.36	0.78
MC	● JPMorgan Mid Cap Equity Sel	VSNGX	B-	(800) 480-4111	B- / 7.2	6.14	7.99	23.14 /67	7.29 /74	13.36 /87	0.25	1.21
MC	JPMorgan Mid Cap Gr A	OSGIX	D+	(800) 480-4111	C / 4.5	7.04	6.95	20.80 /56	4.72 /51	11.83 /73	0.00	1.41
MC	JPMorgan Mid Cap Gr C	OMGCX	D+	(800) 480-4111	C / 5.1	6.86	6.70	20.16 /53	4.19 /45	11.26 /68	0.00	1.91
MC	JPMorgan Mid Cap Gr R2	JMGZX	C-	(800) 480-4111	C / 5.5	6.98	6.86	20.61 /55	4.56 /49	11.65 /71	0.00	1.72
MC	JPMorgan Mid Cap Gr R5	JMGFX	C-	(800) 480-4111	C+ / 6.0	7.15	7.19	21.37 /59	5.19 /56	12.33 /77	0.00	0.92
MC	JPMorgan Mid Cap Gr R6	JMGMX	C-	(800) 480-4111	C+ / 6.0	7.13	7.21	21.39 /59	5.22 /57	12.39 /78	0.00	0.78
MC	JPMorgan Mid Cap Gr Sel	HLGEX	C-	(800) 480-4111	C+ / 5.9	7.11	7.11	21.16 /58	5.03 /55	12.18 /76	0.00	1.14
MC	● JPMorgan Mid Cap Value A	JAMCX	B-	(800) 480-4111	B- / 7.3	5.06	8.65	24.55 /72	9.06 /87	14.19 /94	0.34	1.42
MC	● JPMorgan Mid Cap Value C	JCMVX	B	(800) 480-4111	B / 7.9	4.96	8.41	23.95 /70	8.51 /83	13.61 /90	0.00	1.84
MC	● JPMorgan Mid Cap Value L	FLMVX	B+	(800) 480-4111	B+ / 8.7	5.20	8.95	25.18 /74	9.60 /91	14.75 /96	0.79	0.95
MC	● JPMorgan Mid Cap Value R2	JMVZX	B	(800) 480-4111	B / 8.0	4.99	8.50	24.22 /71	8.77 /85	13.88 /92	0.18	1.76
MC	● JPMorgan Mid Cap Value Sel	JMVSX	B+	(800) 480-4111	B+ / 8.4	5.11	8.78	24.84 /73	9.32 /89	14.46 /95	0.60	1.12
AA	JPMorgan Multi-Cap Mrkt Netral A	OGNAX	C	(800) 480-4111	E+ / 0.6	0.40	3.05	-1.36 / 1	1.45 /21	0.72 / 6	0.00	2.87
AA	JPMorgan Multi-Cap Mrkt Netral C	OGNCX	C	(800) 480-4111	E+ / 0.8	0.32	2.81	-1.86 / 1	0.93 /18	0.17 / 5	0.00	3.38
AA	JPMorgan Multi-Cap Mrkt Netral Sel	OGNIX	C	(800) 480-4111	D- / 1.0	0.48	3.17	-1.05 / 1	1.72 /22	0.99 / 6	0.00	2.48

● Denotes fund is closed to new investors
* Denotes fund is included in Section II

374

RISK			NET ASSETS		ASSET				Portfolio Turnover Ratio	BULL / BEAR		FUND MANAGER		MINIMUMS		LOADS	
Risk Rating/Pts	3 Year Standard Deviation	Beta	NAV As of 2/28/17	Total $(Mil)	Cash %	Stocks %	Bonds %	Other %		Last Bull Market Return	Last Bear Market Return	Manager Quality Pct	Manager Tenure (Years)	Initial Purch. $	Additional Purch. $	Front End Load	Back End Load
C /5.3	12.0	1.09	36.12	109	0	98	0	2	66	125.9	-19.1	28	12	15,000,000	0	0.0	0.0
C /5.3	12.0	1.09	36.01	892	0	98	0	2	66	122.9	-19.2	26	12	1,000,000	0	0.0	0.0
B /8.1	5.9	0.92	15.02	3,710	3	50	45	2	12	55.7	-10.4	46	12	1,000	50	4.5	0.0
B /8.1	5.9	0.92	14.79	1,130	3	50	45	2	12	51.3	-10.6	38	12	1,000	50	0.0	0.0
B /8.1	5.9	0.92	15.05	450	3	50	45	2	12	57.7	-10.3	49	12	1,000,000	0	0.0	0.0
B /8.7	3.9	0.61	12.60	2,280	3	30	65	2	12	37.2	-6.1	61	21	1,000	50	4.5	0.0
B /8.7	3.9	0.61	12.54	1,659	3	30	65	2	12	33.3	-6.3	54	20	1,000	50	0.0	0.0
B /8.7	3.9	0.61	12.67	141	3	30	65	2	12	39.1	-6.0	64	21	1,000,000	0	0.0	0.0
B- /7.4	7.7	0.73	16.85	2,500	2	67	29	2	13	73.1	-14.1	47	21	1,000	50	4.5	0.0
B- /7.4	7.7	0.73	16.39	413	2	67	29	2	13	68.1	-14.3	39	20	1,000	50	0.0	0.0
B- /7.4	7.7	0.73	16.61	239	2	67	29	2	13	75.4	-14.0	50	21	1,000,000	0	0.0	0.0
C+ /6.5	9.8	0.93	19.55	2,000	1	86	12	1	8	97.4	-18.2	36	21	1,000	50	4.5	0.0
C+ /6.4	9.8	0.93	18.45	287	1	86	12	1	8	91.8	-18.4	30	20	1,000	50	0.0	0.0
C+ /6.5	9.8	0.92	19.94	332	1	86	12	1	8	100.3	-18.1	40	21	1,000,000	0	0.0	0.0
C /4.9	12.8	1.04	34.43	3,664	0	98	0	2	43	105.0	-13.1	25	13	1,000	50	5.3	0.0
C /4.7	12.8	1.04	28.83	490	0	98	0	2	43	99.6	-13.2	20	13	1,000	50	0.0	0.0
C /4.9	12.8	1.04	33.66	170	0	98	0	2	43	102.3	-13.1	22	13	0	0	0.0	0.0
C /5.0	12.8	1.04	35.12	839	0	98	0	2	43	109.2	-12.9	28	13	0	0	0.0	0.0
C /5.0	12.8	1.04	35.28	3,499	0	98	0	2	43	110.0	-12.9	29	13	15,000,000	0	0.0	0.0
C /4.9	12.8	1.04	34.64	3,671	0	98	0	2	43	106.9	-13.0	26	13	1,000,000	0	0.0	0.0
C- /3.9	12.4	1.04	15.40	203	0	97	2	1	219	154.7	-21.5	84	4	1,000	50	5.3	0.0
C- /3.9	12.4	1.04	14.85	35	0	97	2	1	219	147.6	-21.6	81	4	1,000	50	0.0	0.0
C- /3.9	12.4	1.04	15.30	5	0	97	2	1	219	151.0	-21.5	83	4	0	0	0.0	0.0
C- /3.9	12.4	1.04	15.30	8	0	97	2	1	219	159.4	-21.3	86	4	0	0	0.0	0.0
C- /3.9	12.4	1.04	15.22	618	0	97	2	1	219	160.2	-21.3	86	4	15,000,000	0	0.0	0.0
C- /4.0	12.4	1.04	15.17	87	0	97	2	1	219	156.5	-21.3	85	4	1,000,000	0	0.0	0.0
D /2.1	23.4	1.02	13.87	10	1	98	0	1	61	-11.1	-24.6	25	10	1,000	50	5.3	0.0
D /2.1	23.4	1.01	13.57	2	1	98	0	1	61	-13.4	-24.8	20	10	1,000	50	0.0	0.0
U /	N/A	N/A	13.88	28	1	98	0	1	61	N/A	N/A	N/A	10	15,000,000	0	0.0	0.0
D /2.2	23.4	1.01	14.14	6	1	98	0	1	61	-9.8	-24.5	28	10	1,000,000	0	0.0	0.0
C- /3.1	12.7	1.04	11.44	158	0	97	1	2	39	145.6	-23.3	73	4	1,000	50	5.3	0.0
D+ /2.6	12.7	1.04	9.79	38	0	97	1	2	39	136.6	-23.5	65	4	1,000	50	0.0	0.0
C- /3.0	12.7	1.04	11.29	14	0	97	1	2	39	142.4	-23.4	71	4	0	0	0.0	0.0
C- /3.1	12.7	1.04	11.56	826	0	97	1	2	39	148.9	-23.2	75	4	1,000,000	0	0.0	0.0
C /5.4	12.0	0.95	46.60	365	5	94	0	1	39	130.1	-20.6	47	15	1,000	50	5.3	0.0
C /5.4	12.0	0.95	45.27	32	5	94	0	1	39	124.0	-20.8	40	15	1,000	50	0.0	0.0
U /	N/A	N/A	47.19	1,555	5	94	0	1	39	N/A	N/A	N/A	15	15,000,000	0	0.0	0.0
C /5.4	12.0	0.95	47.15	742	5	94	0	1	39	134.5	-20.5	52	15	1,000,000	0	0.0	0.0
C- /4.1	14.4	1.07	26.20	916	1	96	1	2	56	124.0	-23.8	14	13	1,000	50	5.3	0.0
C- /3.8	14.3	1.06	21.22	94	1	96	1	2	56	118.0	-24.0	11	13	1,000	50	0.0	0.0
C- /4.2	14.4	1.07	28.39	35	1	96	1	2	56	122.0	-23.8	13	13	0	0	0.0	0.0
C /4.3	14.4	1.07	29.99	240	1	96	1	2	56	129.4	-23.7	17	13	0	0	0.0	0.0
C /4.3	14.4	1.07	30.08	677	1	96	1	2	56	130.0	-23.7	17	13	15,000,000	0	0.0	0.0
C /4.3	14.4	1.06	29.72	950	1	96	1	2	56	127.7	-23.7	16	13	1,000,000	0	0.0	0.0
C+ /5.6	10.5	0.84	37.26	2,309	1	94	4	1	20	137.3	-17.7	80	20	1,000	50	5.3	0.0
C+ /5.6	10.5	0.84	35.89	537	1	94	4	1	20	130.9	-17.9	77	20	1,000	50	0.0	0.0
C+ /5.6	10.5	0.84	38.09	12,396	1	94	4	1	20	143.7	-17.6	83	20	3,000,000	0	0.0	0.0
C+ /5.6	10.5	0.84	35.84	66	1	94	4	1	20	134.0	-17.8	79	20	0	0	0.0	0.0
C+ /5.6	10.5	0.84	37.65	2,852	1	94	4	1	20	140.5	-17.6	82	20	1,000,000	0	0.0	0.0
B+ /9.9	3.0	N/A	10.15	5	88	2	8	2	258	5.2	-1.0	83	4	1,000	50	5.3	0.0
B+ /9.9	2.9	N/A	9.50	5	88	2	8	2	258	2.0	-1.4	80	4	1,000	50	0.0	0.0
B+ /9.9	2.9	N/A	10.41	138	88	2	8	2	258	6.7	-0.9	84	4	1,000,000	0	0.0	0.0

					PERFORMANCE							
99 Pct = Best / 0 Pct = Worst			**Overall Investment Rating**		**Perfor-mance Rating/Pts**	Total Return % through 2/28/17			Annualized		Incl. in Returns	
Fund Type	**Fund Name**	**Ticker Symbol**		**Phone**		3 Mo	6 Mo	1Yr / Pct	3Yr / Pct	5Yr / Pct	**Dividend Yield**	**Expense Ratio**
GL	JPMorgan Multi-Manager Alt A	JMMAX	U	(800) 480-4111	U /	0.94	0.13	1.55 / 2	--	--	0.00	4.61
GL	JPMorgan Multi-Manager Alt Select	JMMSX	U	(800) 480-4111	U /	1.00	0.27	1.82 / 2	--	--	0.00	4.17
GR	JPMorgan Opportunistic Eqty L/S A	JOELX	U	(800) 480-4111	U /	4.16	1.08	10.86 /14	--	--	0.00	2.81
GR	JPMorgan Opportunistic Eqty L/S Sel	JOEQX	U	(800) 480-4111	U /	4.20	1.25	11.13 /15	--	--	0.00	2.80
RE	JPMorgan Realty Income A	URTAX	C-	(800) 480-4111	C / 4.9	6.77	-3.92	12.44 /20	9.41 /90	9.67 /56	1.93	1.47
RE	JPMorgan Realty Income C	URTCX	C	(800) 480-4111	C+ / 5.6	6.64	-4.15	11.92 /18	8.86 /86	9.12 /52	1.84	1.98
RE	JPMorgan Realty Income L	URTLX	C	(800) 480-4111	C+ / 6.4	6.88	-3.69	12.97 /22	9.85 /92	10.10 /59	2.23	0.98
RE	JPMorgan Realty Income R5	JRIRX	C+	(800) 480-4111	C+ / 6.5	6.92	-3.66	13.02 /22	9.90 /93	10.17 /60	2.32	0.91
RE	JPMorgan Realty Income R6	JPINX	U	(800) 480-4111	U /	6.87	-3.66	13.02 /22	--	--	2.29	0.86
IN	JPMorgan Research Market Neut A	JMNAX	C-	(800) 480-4111	E / 0.3	1.00	2.92	2.92 / 3	-0.97 / 9	0.17 / 5	0.00	3.68
IN	JPMorgan Research Market Neut C	JMNCX	C-	(800) 480-4111	E / 0.5	0.91	2.62	2.39 / 2	-1.45 / 8	-0.32 / 4	0.00	4.11
IN	JPMorgan Research Market Neut L	JPMNX	C-	(800) 480-4111	E+ / 0.7	1.08	3.11	3.32 / 3	-0.53 /11	0.65 / 6	0.00	3.23
IN	JPMorgan Research Market Neut Sel	JMNSX	C-	(800) 480-4111	E+ / 0.6	1.03	3.02	3.16 / 3	-0.71 /10	0.42 / 5	0.00	3.36
RE	JPMorgan Secs Cap US Core RE A	CEEAX	C	(800) 480-4111	C / 4.3	5.85	-1.19	10.95 /14	8.34 /82	8.08 /43	2.24	1.48
RE	JPMorgan Secs Cap US Core RE C	CEECX	C	(800) 480-4111	C / 4.9	5.67	-1.43	10.37 /13	7.79 /77	7.53 /38	1.94	2.15
RE	JPMorgan Secs Cap US Core RE R5	CEEFX	C+	(800) 480-4111	C+ / 5.8	5.90	-1.01	11.37 /16	8.81 /85	8.56 /47	2.77	1.97
RE	JPMorgan Secs Cap US Core RE R6	CEERX	C+	(800) 480-4111	C+ / 5.8	5.91	-0.98	11.42 /16	8.88 /86	8.62 /47	2.82	0.93
RE	JPMorgan Secs Cap US Core RE Sel	CEESX	C+	(800) 480-4111	C+ / 5.6	5.91	-1.06	11.24 /15	8.61 /84	8.34 /45	2.59	1.20
SC	● JPMorgan Small Cap Core R5	VSSCX	B	(800) 480-4111	A / 9.5	5.78	14.42	37.92 /96	7.98 /79	14.39 /95	0.28	0.96
SC	● JPMorgan Small Cap Equity A	VSEAX	B-	(800) 480-4111	B / 8.2	5.61	10.18	30.91 /88	8.97 /87	14.05 /94	0.23	1.39
SC	● JPMorgan Small Cap Equity C	JSECX	B-	(800) 480-4111	B+ / 8.7	5.47	9.90	30.27 /87	8.43 /82	13.49 /89	0.29	1.86
SC	● JPMorgan Small Cap Equity R2	JSEZX	B	(800) 480-4111	B+ / 8.9	5.55	10.06	30.61 /87	8.71 /85	13.77 /91	0.21	1.73
SC	● JPMorgan Small Cap Equity R5	JSERX	B+	(800) 480-4111	A / 9.4	5.73	10.45	31.56 /89	9.52 /90	14.62 /96	0.47	0.87
SC	● JPMorgan Small Cap Equity R6	VSENX	U	(800) 480-4111	U /	5.74	10.48	--	--	--	0.00	0.76
SC	● JPMorgan Small Cap Equity Sel	VSEIX	B+	(800) 480-4111	A- / 9.2	5.69	10.36	31.31 /89	9.31 /89	14.39 /95	0.38	1.15
SC	● JPMorgan Small Cap Growth A	PGSGX	D+	(800) 480-4111	B- / 7.1	9.17	11.33	41.28 /98	3.57 /38	11.59 /71	0.00	1.56
SC	● JPMorgan Small Cap Growth C	OSGCX	D+	(800) 480-4111	B / 7.7	9.09	11.00	40.59 /97	3.04 /32	11.04 /66	0.00	1.97
SC	● JPMorgan Small Cap Growth L	JISGX	C	(800) 480-4111	B+ / 8.3	9.28	11.54	41.79 /98	3.96 /42	12.02 /74	0.00	1.02
SC	● JPMorgan Small Cap Growth R2	JSGZX	C-	(800) 480-4111	B / 7.8	9.09	11.13	40.86 /97	3.30 /35	11.31 /68	0.00	1.91
SC	● JPMorgan Small Cap Growth R6	JGSMX	C	(800) 480-4111	B+ / 8.4	9.28	11.60	41.98 /98	4.07 /44	12.15 /76	0.00	0.83
SC	● JPMorgan Small Cap Growth Sel	OGGFX	C-	(800) 480-4111	B / 8.2	9.29	11.44	41.65 /98	3.82 /41	11.87 /73	0.00	1.24
SC	JPMorgan Small Cap Value A	PSOAX	B-	(800) 480-4111	B / 7.7	2.69	12.68	35.17 /94	7.09 /73	13.09 /85	0.48	1.54
SC	JPMorgan Small Cap Value C	OSVCX	B-	(800) 480-4111	B / 8.1	2.53	12.32	34.38 /93	6.44 /68	12.40 /78	0.27	1.95
SC	JPMorgan Small Cap Value R2	JSVZX	B	(800) 480-4111	B+ / 8.4	2.62	12.53	34.85 /94	6.82 /71	12.79 /82	0.32	1.92
SC	JPMorgan Small Cap Value R5	JSVRX	B+	(800) 480-4111	B+ / 8.8	2.76	12.88	35.63 /95	7.46 /75	13.47 /89	0.76	0.94
SC	JPMorgan Small Cap Value R6	JSVUX	B+	(800) 480-4111	B+ / 8.9	2.82	12.98	35.86 /95	7.59 /76	13.58 /90	0.87	0.78
SC	JPMorgan Small Cap Value Sel	PSOPX	B+	(800) 480-4111	B+ / 8.8	2.73	12.84	35.53 /94	7.36 /74	13.36 /87	0.68	1.19
AA	JPMorgan Smart Ret 2015 A	JSFAX	C	(800) 480-4111	D / 2.0	3.63	2.31	10.45 /13	3.53 /37	5.47 /25	2.00	1.03
AA	JPMorgan Smart Ret 2015 C	JSFCX	C	(800) 480-4111	D+ / 2.3	3.43	1.99	9.76 /11	2.85 /30	4.78 /20	1.47	1.54
AA	JPMorgan Smart Ret 2015 Inst	JSFIX	C+	(800) 480-4111	D+ / 2.9	3.68	2.42	10.67 /13	3.76 /40	5.72 /26	2.31	0.61
AA	JPMorgan Smart Ret 2015 R2	JSFZX	C	(800) 480-4111	D+ / 2.5	3.57	2.19	10.21 /12	3.28 /34	5.21 /23	1.85	1.30
BA	JPMorgan Smart Ret 2015 R6	JSFYX	U	(800) 480-4111	U /	3.65	2.46	10.76 /14	--	--	2.39	0.46
AA	JPMorgan Smart Ret 2015 Sel	JSFSX	C	(800) 480-4111	D+ / 2.8	3.65	2.35	10.54 /13	3.63 /38	5.58 /25	2.18	0.76
AA	JPMorgan Smart Ret 2020 A	JTTAX	C	(800) 480-4111	D+ / 2.9	4.51	3.25	13.40 /23	4.41 /48	6.78 /33	1.95	1.07
AA	JPMorgan Smart Ret 2020 C	JTTCX	C+	(800) 480-4111	C- / 3.2	4.35	2.92	12.65 /20	3.74 /40	6.09 /29	1.41	1.58
AA	JPMorgan Smart Ret 2020 Inst	JTTIX	C+	(800) 480-4111	C- / 3.8	4.55	3.35	13.58 /24	4.65 /50	7.03 /35	2.25	0.64
AA	JPMorgan Smart Ret 2020 R2	JTTZX	C+	(800) 480-4111	C- / 3.5	4.46	3.13	13.10 /22	4.14 /45	6.51 /32	1.82	1.33
GI	JPMorgan Smart Ret 2020 R6	JTTYX	U	(800) 480-4111	U /	4.57	3.39	13.67 /24	--	--	2.32	0.50
AA	JPMorgan Smart Ret 2020 Sel	JTTSX	C+	(800) 480-4111	C- / 3.7	4.52	3.28	13.45 /23	4.52 /49	6.89 /34	2.13	0.81
AA	JPMorgan Smart Ret 2025 A	JNSAX	C+	(800) 480-4111	C- / 3.4	5.11	4.06	15.21 /31	4.83 /52	7.67 /40	1.80	1.08
AA	JPMorgan Smart Ret 2025 C	JNSCX	C+	(800) 480-4111	C- / 3.8	4.95	3.79	14.53 /28	4.15 /45	6.98 /34	1.26	1.61
AA	JPMorgan Smart Ret 2025 Inst	JNSIX	B-	(800) 480-4111	C / 4.5	5.21	4.23	15.55 /32	5.08 /55	7.94 /42	2.09	0.67

● Denotes fund is closed to new investors
* Denotes fund is included in Section II

376

RISK			NET ASSETS		ASSET					BULL / BEAR		FUND MANAGER		MINIMUMS		LOADS	
Risk Rating/Pts	3 Year		NAV As of 2/28/17	Total $(Mil)	Cash %	Stocks %	Bonds %	Other %	Portfolio Turnover Ratio	Last Bull Market Return	Last Bear Market Return	Manager Quality Pct	Manager Tenure (Years)	Initial Purch. $	Additional Purch. $	Front End Load	Back End Load
	Standard Deviation	Beta															
U /	N/A	N/A	15.05	30	0	0	0	100	244	N/A	N/A	N/A	3	1,000	25	5.3	0.0
U /	N/A	N/A	15.14	260	0	0	0	100	244	N/A	N/A	N/A	3	1,000,000	0	0.0	0.0
U /	N/A	N/A	17.76	45	10	52	36	2	463	N/A	N/A	N/A	3	1,000	50	5.3	0.0
U /	N/A	N/A	17.87	146	10	52	36	2	463	N/A	N/A	N/A	3	1,000,000	0	0.0	0.0
C /4.9	14.9	1.09	13.06	174	0	96	2	2	141	93.2	-16.5	42	8	1,000	50	5.3	0.0
C /4.9	14.9	1.09	12.66	8	0	96	2	2	141	87.9	-16.6	35	8	1,000	50	0.0	0.0
C /5.0	14.9	1.09	13.22	104	0	96	2	2	141	97.3	-16.3	48	8	3,000,000	0	0.0	0.0
C /5.0	14.9	1.08	13.29	29	0	96	2	2	141	97.9	-16.2	49	8	0	0	0.0	0.0
U /	N/A	N/A	13.24	2,093	0	96	2	2	141	N/A	N/A	N/A	8	15,000,000	0	0.0	0.0
B+ /9.5	3.1	0.04	14.12	20	88	2	8	2	133	0.2	-3.3	56	3	1,000	50	5.3	0.0
B+ /9.3	3.1	0.03	13.30	13	88	2	8	2	133	-2.4	-3.5	49	3	1,000	50	0.0	0.0
B+ /9.6	3.2	0.03	14.93	190	88	2	8	2	133	2.9	-3.1	62	3	3,000,000	0	0.0	0.0
B+ /9.5	3.2	0.04	14.67	46	88	2	8	2	133	1.6	-3.1	59	3	1,000,000	0	0.0	0.0
C+ /6.2	9.6	0.70	17.92	2	2	77	19	2	85	69.1	N/A	79	6	1,000	50	5.3	0.0
C+ /6.2	9.5	0.69	17.87	1	2	77	19	2	85	64.5	N/A	75	6	1,000	50	0.0	0.0
C+ /6.2	9.5	0.69	17.99	N/A	2	77	19	2	85	73.2	N/A	82	6	0	0	0.0	0.0
C+ /6.2	9.6	0.70	18.00	55	2	77	19	2	85	73.7	N/A	82	6	15,000,000	0	0.0	0.0
C+ /6.2	9.6	0.70	17.97	56	2	77	19	2	85	71.4	N/A	80	6	1,000,000	0	0.0	0.0
C- /3.5	16.7	1.05	51.29	195	0	97	2	1	58	155.3	-27.2	79	13	1,000,000	0	0.0	0.0
C /4.7	12.3	0.76	47.23	1,303	0	96	3	1	32	145.1	-20.5	92	10	1,000	50	5.3	0.0
C- /4.1	12.3	0.76	36.06	176	0	96	3	1	32	138.6	-20.7	90	10	1,000	50	0.0	0.0
C /4.7	12.3	0.76	46.47	12	0	96	3	1	32	141.8	-20.6	91	10	0	0	0.0	0.0
C /4.9	12.3	0.76	54.14	1,249	0	96	3	1	32	151.8	-20.4	93	10	0	0	0.0	0.0
U /	N/A	N/A	54.12	895	0	96	3	1	32	N/A	N/A	N/A	10	15,000,000	0	0.0	0.0
C /4.9	12.3	0.76	54.03	2,577	0	96	3	1	32	149.1	-20.4	93	10	1,000,000	0	0.0	0.0
D /2.0	20.0	1.16	13.57	192	0	98	1	1	47	124.8	-27.9	21	13	1,000	50	5.3	0.0
D /1.6	19.9	1.16	10.31	20	0	98	1	1	47	119.0	-28.1	17	13	1,000	50	0.0	0.0
D /2.2	20.0	1.16	15.18	297	0	98	1	1	47	129.7	-27.8	25	13	3,000,000	0	0.0	0.0
D /2.0	20.0	1.16	13.19	23	0	98	1	1	47	121.8	-28.0	19	13	0	0	0.0	0.0
D /2.2	20.0	1.16	15.30	552	0	98	1	1	47	130.9	-27.8	26	13	15,000,000	0	0.0	0.0
D /2.2	20.0	1.16	14.81	113	0	98	1	1	47	128.0	-27.9	24	13	1,000,000	0	0.0	0.0
C /5.0	15.5	0.95	29.60	588	0	96	2	2	46	136.7	-25.4	78	12	1,000	50	5.3	0.0
C /4.8	15.5	0.94	24.95	46	0	96	2	2	46	129.0	-25.6	73	12	1,000	50	0.0	0.0
C /5.0	15.5	0.95	29.39	58	0	96	2	2	46	133.6	-25.5	76	12	0	0	0.0	0.0
C /5.1	15.5	0.94	31.23	115	0	96	2	2	46	141.2	-25.3	80	12	0	0	0.0	0.0
C /5.1	15.5	0.95	31.27	933	0	96	2	2	46	142.3	-25.3	81	12	15,000,000	0	0.0	0.0
C /5.1	15.5	0.95	31.22	353	0	96	2	2	46	139.9	-25.4	80	12	1,000,000	0	0.0	0.0
B /8.6	4.9	0.74	17.87	674	3	36	60	1	31	48.1	-10.8	50	11	1,000	50	4.5	0.0
B /8.6	4.9	0.74	17.72	25	3	36	60	1	31	43.0	-11.1	40	11	1,000	50	0.0	0.0
B /8.6	4.9	0.73	17.92	1,113	3	36	60	1	31	50.0	-10.7	53	11	3,000,000	0	0.0	0.0
B /8.6	4.9	0.73	17.81	129	3	36	60	1	31	46.1	-10.9	47	11	0	0	0.0	0.0
U /	N/A	N/A	17.92	218	3	36	60	1	31	N/A	N/A	N/A	11	15,000,000	0	0.0	0.0
B /8.6	4.9	0.74	17.90	284	3	36	60	1	31	48.8	-10.7	51	11	1,000,000	0	0.0	0.0
B /8.3	6.2	0.95	18.69	1,695	0	50	48	2	19	60.4	-12.9	40	11	1,000	50	4.5	0.0
B /8.3	6.2	0.96	18.59	52	0	50	48	2	19	54.8	-13.1	31	11	1,000	50	0.0	0.0
B /8.3	6.2	0.95	18.77	3,570	0	50	48	2	19	62.4	-12.8	43	11	3,000,000	0	0.0	0.0
B /8.3	6.2	0.95	18.63	402	0	50	48	2	19	58.1	-12.9	36	11	0	0	0.0	0.0
U /	N/A	N/A	18.78	518	0	50	48	2	19	N/A	N/A	N/A	11	15,000,000	0	0.0	0.0
B /8.3	6.2	0.96	18.75	935	0	50	48	2	19	61.2	-12.8	41	11	1,000,000	0	0.0	0.0
B /8.0	7.1	1.10	18.19	1,761	1	60	38	1	17	70.4	-15.6	32	10	1,000	50	4.5	0.0
B /8.0	7.1	1.11	18.11	52	1	60	38	1	17	64.5	-15.8	24	10	1,000	50	0.0	0.0
B /8.0	7.1	1.10	18.26	3,451	1	60	38	1	17	72.6	-15.5	34	10	3,000,000	0	0.0	0.0

Fund Type	Fund Name	Ticker Symbol	Overall Investment Rating	Phone	Performance Rating/Pts	3 Mo	6 Mo	1Yr / Pct	3Yr / Pct	5Yr / Pct	Dividend Yield	Expense Ratio
AA	JPMorgan Smart Ret 2025 R2	JNSZX	C+	(800) 480-4111	C- / 4.1	5.00	3.95	14.92 /30	4.56 /49	7.40 /37	1.66	1.36
GI	JPMorgan Smart Ret 2025 R6	JNSYX	U	(800) 480-4111	U /	5.17	4.27	15.57 /32	--	--	2.17	0.52
AA	JPMorgan Smart Ret 2025 Sel	JNSSX	C+	(800) 480-4111	C / 4.4	5.18	4.22	15.41 /32	4.94 /53	7.78 /40	1.96	0.83
AA	JPMorgan Smart Ret 2030 A	JSMAX	C	(800) 480-4111	C- / 3.9	5.65	4.84	16.98 /38	5.00 /54	8.28 /44	1.77	1.12
AA	JPMorgan Smart Ret 2030 C	JSMCX	C+	(800) 480-4111	C- / 4.2	5.53	4.55	16.27 /35	4.30 /46	7.59 /39	1.25	1.65
AA	JPMorgan Smart Ret 2030 Inst	JSMIX	B-	(800) 480-4111	C / 5.0	5.73	4.99	17.29 /40	5.23 /57	8.55 /47	2.06	0.69
AA	JPMorgan Smart Ret 2030 R2	JSMZX	C+	(800) 480-4111	C / 4.6	5.60	4.79	16.77 /37	4.73 /51	8.01 /42	1.63	1.38
GI	JPMorgan Smart Ret 2030 R6	JSMYX	U	(800) 480-4111	U /	5.75	5.04	17.38 /40	--	--	2.14	0.54
AA	JPMorgan Smart Ret 2030 Sel	JSMSX	C+	(800) 480-4111	C / 4.9	5.71	4.93	17.11 /39	5.08 /55	8.38 /45	1.94	0.86
AA	JPMorgan Smart Ret 2035 A	SRJAX	C+	(800) 480-4111	C / 4.3	6.11	5.61	18.51 /45	5.19 /56	8.83 /49	1.70	1.15
AA	JPMorgan Smart Ret 2035 C	SRJCX	C+	(800) 480-4111	C / 4.7	5.93	5.26	17.70 /41	4.51 /49	8.12 /43	1.17	1.64
AA	JPMorgan Smart Ret 2035 Inst	SRJIX	B-	(800) 480-4111	C / 5.5	6.19	5.70	18.80 /46	5.46 /59	9.10 /51	1.98	0.72
AA	JPMorgan Smart Ret 2035 R2	SRJZX	C+	(800) 480-4111	C / 5.1	6.06	5.45	18.22 /44	4.94 /53	8.56 /47	1.56	1.42
GI	JPMorgan Smart Ret 2035 R6	SRJYX	U	(800) 480-4111	U /	6.21	5.80	18.96 /47	--	--	2.06	0.56
AA	JPMorgan Smart Ret 2035 Sel	SRJSX	B-	(800) 480-4111	C / 5.4	6.16	5.63	18.59 /45	5.30 /58	8.93 /50	1.86	0.89
AA	JPMorgan Smart Ret 2040 A	SMTAX	C+	(800) 480-4111	C / 4.8	6.56	6.30	20.06 /52	5.42 /59	9.11 /52	1.63	1.20
AA	JPMorgan Smart Ret 2040 C	SMTCX	C+	(800) 480-4111	C / 5.2	6.37	5.94	19.27 /48	4.74 /51	8.40 /45	1.13	1.74
AA	JPMorgan Smart Ret 2040 Inst	SMTIX	C+	(800) 480-4111	C+ / 6.0	6.64	6.38	20.35 /54	5.67 /61	9.37 /54	1.91	0.75
AA	JPMorgan Smart Ret 2040 R2	SMTZX	C+	(800) 480-4111	C+ / 5.6	6.48	6.15	19.77 /51	5.15 /56	8.83 /49	1.50	1.48
GI	JPMorgan Smart Ret 2040 R6	SMTYX	U	(800) 480-4111	U /	6.66	6.43	20.45 /55	--	--	1.99	0.58
AA	JPMorgan Smart Ret 2040 Sel	SMTSX	C+	(800) 480-4111	C+ / 5.9	6.62	6.33	20.18 /53	5.54 /60	9.21 /52	1.79	0.94
AA	JPMorgan Smart Ret 2045 A	JSAAX	C+	(800) 480-4111	C / 4.9	6.63	6.34	20.13 /53	5.44 /59	9.13 /52	1.62	1.24
AA	JPMorgan Smart Ret 2045 C	JSACX	C+	(800) 480-4111	C / 5.3	6.51	6.04	19.39 /49	4.76 /52	8.44 /46	1.11	1.79
AA	JPMorgan Smart Ret 2045 Inst	JSAIX	C+	(800) 480-4111	C+ / 6.1	6.72	6.48	20.44 /55	5.71 /62	9.41 /54	1.90	0.77
AA	JPMorgan Smart Ret 2045 R2	JSAZX	C+	(800) 480-4111	C+ / 5.6	6.59	6.23	19.86 /51	5.19 /56	8.86 /49	1.49	1.52
GI	JPMorgan Smart Ret 2045 R6	JSAYX	U	(800) 480-4111	U /	6.74	6.53	20.53 /55	--	--	1.97	0.59
AA	JPMorgan Smart Ret 2045 Sel	JSASX	C+	(800) 480-4111	C+ / 5.9	6.69	6.42	20.23 /53	5.56 /60	9.26 /53	1.78	0.97
AA	JPMorgan Smart Ret 2050 A	JTSAX	C+	(800) 480-4111	C / 4.9	6.57	6.27	20.07 /52	5.44 /59	9.11 /52	1.62	1.31
AA	JPMorgan Smart Ret 2050 C	JTSCX	C+	(800) 480-4111	C / 5.2	6.45	5.98	19.29 /48	4.76 /52	8.41 /45	1.11	1.86
AA	JPMorgan Smart Ret 2050 Inst	JTSIX	C+	(800) 480-4111	C+ / 6.0	6.65	6.41	20.29 /54	5.69 /61	9.39 /54	1.90	0.79
AA	JPMorgan Smart Ret 2050 R2	JTSZX	C+	(800) 480-4111	C+ / 5.6	6.59	6.23	19.80 /51	5.17 /56	8.84 /49	1.49	1.59
GI	JPMorgan Smart Ret 2050 R6	JTSYX	U	(800) 480-4111	U /	6.67	6.46	20.45 /55	--	--	1.97	0.59
AA	JPMorgan Smart Ret 2050 Sel	JTSSX	C+	(800) 480-4111	C+ / 5.9	6.63	6.36	20.17 /53	5.53 /60	9.22 /52	1.78	1.04
IX	JPMorgan Smart Ret 2055 A	JFFAX	C+	(800) 480-4111	C / 4.9	6.64	6.34	20.09 /53	5.40 /58	9.20 /52	1.60	1.35
GI	JPMorgan Smart Ret 2055 C	JFFCX	C+	(800) 480-4111	C / 5.2	6.43	5.96	19.24 /48	4.71 /51	8.48 /46	1.08	2.11
GI	JPMorgan Smart Ret 2055 Inst	JFFIX	B-	(800) 480-4111	C+ / 6.0	6.68	6.44	20.30 /54	5.65 /61	9.45 /54	1.87	0.81
GI	JPMorgan Smart Ret 2055 R2	JFFRX	B-	(800) 480-4111	C+ / 5.6	6.54	6.17	19.74 /51	5.12 /55	8.92 /50	1.46	1.67
GI	JPMorgan Smart Ret 2055 R6	JFFYX	U	(800) 480-4111	U /	6.70	6.48	20.45 /55	--	--	1.94	0.60
GI	JPMorgan Smart Ret 2055 Select	JFFSX	B-	(800) 480-4111	C+ / 5.9	6.60	6.32	20.17 /53	5.50 /60	9.29 /53	1.76	1.06
GI	JPMorgan Smart Ret Blend 2015 R5	JSBWX	C+	(800) 480-4111	D+ / 2.8	3.55	2.29	10.42 /13	3.82 /41	--	2.34	1.00
GI	JPMorgan Smart Ret Blend 2015 R6	JSBYX	C+	(800) 480-4111	D+ / 2.9	3.63	2.33	10.49 /13	3.87 /41	--	2.40	0.90
GI	JPMorgan Smart Ret Blend 2015 Sel	JSBEX	C+	(800) 480-4111	D+ / 2.7	3.51	2.20	10.20 /12	3.62 /38	--	2.14	1.21
GI	JPMorgan Smart Ret Blend 2020 R5	JBSRX	B-	(800) 480-4111	C- / 3.8	4.55	3.20	13.30 /23	4.71 /51	--	2.34	0.82
GI	JPMorgan Smart Ret Blend 2020 R6	JSYRX	B-	(800) 480-4111	C- / 3.9	4.56	3.24	13.37 /23	4.79 /52	--	2.40	0.73
GI	JPMorgan Smart Ret Blend 2020 Sel	JSSRX	B-	(800) 480-4111	C- / 3.7	4.51	3.11	13.11 /22	4.52 /49	--	2.17	1.01
GI	JPMorgan Smart Ret Blend 2025 R5	JBBSX	B	(800) 480-4111	C / 4.5	5.13	3.98	15.19 /31	5.17 /56	--	2.23	0.84
GI	JPMorgan Smart Ret Blend 2025 R6	JBYSX	B	(800) 480-4111	C / 4.6	5.16	4.03	15.27 /31	5.23 /57	--	2.30	0.74
GI	JPMorgan Smart Ret Blend 2025 Sel	JBSSX	B	(800) 480-4111	C / 4.3	5.09	3.95	15.01 /30	4.98 /54	--	2.07	1.04
GI	JPMorgan Smart Ret Blend 2030 R5	JRBBX	B	(800) 480-4111	C / 5.3	5.80	4.97	17.41 /40	5.58 /60	--	2.17	0.84
GI	JPMorgan Smart Ret Blend 2030 R6	JRBYX	B	(800) 480-4111	C / 5.3	5.76	4.96	17.48 /41	5.62 /61	--	2.23	0.74
GI	JPMorgan Smart Ret Blend 2030 Sel	JRBEX	B	(800) 480-4111	C / 5.1	5.76	4.89	17.22 /39	5.37 /58	--	2.01	1.03
GI	JPMorgan Smart Ret Blend 2035 R5	JPBRX	B	(800) 480-4111	C+ / 5.7	6.18	5.57	18.83 /46	5.82 /63	--	2.13	0.89

● Denotes fund is closed to new investors
∗ Denotes fund is included in Section II

Risk Rating/Pts	3 Year Standard Deviation	Beta	NAV As of 2/28/17	Total $(Mil)	Cash %	Stocks %	Bonds %	Other %	Portfolio Turnover Ratio	Last Bull Market Return	Last Bear Market Return	Manager Quality Pct	Manager Tenure (Years)	Initial Purch. $	Additional Purch. $	Front End Load	Back End Load
B /8.0	7.1	1.10	18.12	389	1	60	38	1	17	68.1	-15.7	29	10	0	0	0.0	0.0
U /	N/A	N/A	18.26	588	1	60	38	1	17	N/A	N/A	N/A	10	15,000,000	0	0.0	0.0
B /8.0	7.1	1.10	18.24	910	1	60	38	1	17	71.4	-15.5	33	10	1,000,000	0	0.0	0.0
B- /7.5	8.1	1.26	19.59	1,900	1	69	29	1	22	77.8	-17.8	22	11	1,000	50	4.5	0.0
B- /7.5	8.1	1.26	19.40	48	1	69	29	1	22	71.6	-18.0	16	11	1,000	50	0.0	0.0
B- /7.5	8.1	1.26	19.69	3,783	1	69	29	1	22	80.1	-17.6	24	11	3,000,000	0	0.0	0.0
B- /7.5	8.1	1.26	19.52	492	1	69	29	1	22	75.5	-17.9	19	11	0	0	0.0	0.0
U /	N/A	N/A	19.69	569	1	69	29	1	22	N/A	N/A	N/A	11	15,000,000	0	0.0	0.0
B- /7.5	8.1	1.26	19.64	1,027	1	69	29	1	22	78.6	-17.7	22	11	1,000,000	0	0.0	0.0
B- /7.2	8.8	1.36	18.84	1,378	1	75	23	1	17	84.6	-19.3	17	10	1,000	50	4.5	0.0
B- /7.2	8.8	1.36	18.67	30	1	75	23	1	17	78.2	-19.5	12	10	1,000	50	0.0	0.0
B- /7.2	8.8	1.36	18.95	2,694	1	75	23	1	17	87.2	-19.2	19	10	3,000,000	0	0.0	0.0
B- /7.2	8.8	1.37	18.78	353	1	75	23	1	17	82.2	-19.4	15	10	0	0	0.0	0.0
U /	N/A	N/A	18.96	469	1	75	23	1	17	N/A	N/A	N/A	10	15,000,000	0	0.0	0.0
B- /7.2	8.8	1.36	18.93	726	1	75	23	1	17	85.7	-19.2	18	10	1,000,000	0	0.0	0.0
C+ /6.8	9.4	1.45	20.27	1,365	1	80	18	1	16	87.3	-19.4	14	11	1,000	50	4.5	0.0
C+ /6.8	9.4	1.46	19.99	30	1	80	18	1	16	80.8	-19.6	10	11	1,000	50	0.0	0.0
C+ /6.8	9.4	1.46	20.38	2,815	1	80	18	1	16	89.7	-19.3	15	11	3,000,000	0	0.0	0.0
C+ /6.8	9.4	1.45	20.16	356	1	80	18	1	16	84.6	-19.5	12	11	0	0	0.0	0.0
U /	N/A	N/A	20.38	434	1	80	18	1	16	N/A	N/A	N/A	11	15,000,000	0	0.0	0.0
C+ /6.8	9.4	1.45	20.33	753	1	80	18	1	16	88.2	-19.3	14	11	1,000,000	0	0.0	0.0
C+ /6.9	9.4	1.45	19.21	851	1	80	18	1	13	87.5	-19.3	14	10	1,000	50	4.5	0.0
C+ /6.9	9.4	1.45	19.06	18	1	80	18	1	13	81.1	-19.5	10	10	1,000	50	0.0	0.0
C+ /6.9	9.4	1.45	19.30	1,736	1	80	18	1	13	89.9	-19.2	16	10	3,000,000	0	0.0	0.0
C+ /6.9	9.4	1.45	19.14	227	1	80	18	1	13	85.0	-19.4	12	10	0	0	0.0	0.0
U /	N/A	N/A	19.30	318	1	80	18	1	13	N/A	N/A	N/A	10	15,000,000	0	0.0	0.0
C+ /6.9	9.4	1.45	19.28	474	1	80	18	1	13	88.6	-19.3	15	10	1,000,000	0	0.0	0.0
C+ /6.9	9.4	1.46	19.17	682	1	80	18	1	16	87.4	-19.4	14	10	1,000	50	4.5	0.0
C+ /6.9	9.4	1.45	19.00	17	1	80	18	1	16	80.9	-19.6	10	10	1,000	50	0.0	0.0
C+ /6.9	9.4	1.45	19.27	1,435	1	80	18	1	16	89.9	-19.3	16	10	3,000,000	0	0.0	0.0
C+ /6.9	9.4	1.45	19.10	194	1	80	18	1	16	84.9	-19.4	12	10	0	0	0.0	0.0
U /	N/A	N/A	19.28	218	1	80	18	1	16	N/A	N/A	N/A	10	15,000,000	0	0.0	0.0
C+ /6.9	9.4	1.46	19.24	448	1	80	18	1	16	88.4	-19.3	14	10	1,000,000	0	0.0	0.0
B- /7.0	9.4	0.87	21.34	204	1	81	16	2	10	N/A	N/A	28	5	1,000	50	4.5	0.0
B- /7.0	9.4	0.87	21.23	3	1	81	16	2	10	N/A	N/A	22	5	1,000	50	0.0	0.0
B- /7.0	9.4	0.87	21.39	410	1	81	16	2	10	N/A	N/A	31	5	3,000,000	0	0.0	0.0
B- /7.0	9.4	0.87	21.29	74	1	81	16	2	10	N/A	N/A	25	5	0	0	0.0	0.0
U /	N/A	N/A	21.40	80	1	81	16	2	10	N/A	N/A	N/A	5	15,000,000	0	0.0	0.0
B- /7.0	9.4	0.87	21.37	124	1	81	16	2	10	N/A	N/A	29	5	1,000,000	0	0.0	0.0
B+ /9.4	4.7	0.41	17.53	15	0	0	0	100	61	N/A	N/A	69	5	0	0	0.0	0.0
B+ /9.4	4.7	0.41	17.54	48	0	0	0	100	61	N/A	N/A	69	5	15,000,000	0	0.0	0.0
B+ /9.5	4.7	0.41	17.52	7	0	0	0	100	61	N/A	N/A	66	5	1,000,000	0	0.0	0.0
B+ /9.0	6.0	0.54	18.68	55	0	0	0	100	48	N/A	N/A	63	5	0	0	0.0	0.0
B+ /9.0	6.1	0.54	18.69	176	0	0	0	100	48	N/A	N/A	64	5	15,000,000	0	0.0	0.0
B+ /9.0	6.0	0.54	18.67	21	0	0	0	100	48	N/A	N/A	61	5	1,000,000	0	0.0	0.0
B /8.7	6.9	0.64	19.47	57	0	0	0	100	45	N/A	N/A	56	5	0	0	0.0	0.0
B /8.7	6.9	0.63	19.47	182	0	0	0	100	45	N/A	N/A	57	5	15,000,000	0	0.0	0.0
B /8.7	6.9	0.63	19.46	21	0	0	0	100	45	N/A	N/A	54	5	1,000,000	0	0.0	0.0
B /8.3	7.8	0.73	20.22	64	0	0	0	100	52	N/A	N/A	49	5	0	0	0.0	0.0
B /8.3	7.8	0.72	20.22	173	0	0	0	100	52	N/A	N/A	50	5	15,000,000	0	0.0	0.0
B /8.3	7.8	0.73	20.20	23	0	0	0	100	52	N/A	N/A	46	5	1,000,000	0	0.0	0.0
B /8.1	8.5	0.79	20.82	43	0	0	0	100	53	N/A	N/A	44	5	0	0	0.0	0.0

Fund Type	Fund Name	Ticker Symbol	Overall Investment Rating	Phone	Performance Rating/Pts	3 Mo	6 Mo	1Yr / Pct	3Yr / Pct	5Yr / Pct	Dividend Yield	Expense Ratio
						PERFORMANCE					Incl. in Returns	
								Total Return % through 2/28/17				
									Annualized			
	99 Pct = Best / 0 Pct = Worst											
GI	JPMorgan Smart Ret Blend 2035 R6	JPYRX	B	(800) 480-4111	C+ / 5.8	6.20	5.62	18.97 /47	5.90 /63	--	2.19	0.78
GI	JPMorgan Smart Ret Blend 2035 Sel	JPSRX	B	(800) 480-4111	C+ / 5.6	6.15	5.49	18.58 /45	5.62 /61	--	1.97	1.11
GI	JPMorgan Smart Ret Blend 2040 R5	JOBBX	B-	(800) 480-4111	C+ / 6.3	6.69	6.32	20.44 /55	6.09 /65	--	2.10	0.91
GI	JPMorgan Smart Ret Blend 2040 R6	JOBYX	B-	(800) 480-4111	C+ / 6.3	6.71	6.37	20.53 /55	6.15 /66	--	2.16	0.79
GI	JPMorgan Smart Ret Blend 2040 Sel	JOBEX	B-	(800) 480-4111	C+ / 6.1	6.65	6.24	20.27 /54	5.88 /63	--	1.94	1.10
GI	JPMorgan Smart Ret Blend 2045 R5	JMBRX	B-	(800) 480-4111	C+ / 6.3	6.70	6.27	20.43 /54	6.09 /65	--	2.08	1.05
GI	JPMorgan Smart Ret Blend 2045 R6	JMYAX	B-	(800) 480-4111	C+ / 6.3	6.72	6.31	20.56 /55	6.17 /66	--	2.15	0.90
GI	JPMorgan Smart Ret Blend 2045 Sel	JMSSX	B-	(800) 480-4111	C+ / 6.1	6.61	6.14	20.19 /53	5.89 /63	--	1.93	1.27
GI	JPMorgan Smart Ret Blend 2050 R5	JNABX	B-	(800) 480-4111	C+ / 6.2	6.70	6.27	20.35 /54	6.08 /65	--	2.07	1.22
GI	JPMorgan Smart Ret Blend 2050 R6	JNYAX	B-	(800) 480-4111	C+ / 6.3	6.72	6.32	20.43 /54	6.14 /66	--	2.14	1.06
GI	JPMorgan Smart Ret Blend 2050 Sel	JNEAX	B-	(800) 480-4111	C+ / 6.1	6.66	6.20	20.18 /53	5.89 /63	--	1.92	1.41
GI	JPMorgan Smart Ret Blend 2055 R5	JTBBX	B-	(800) 480-4111	C+ / 6.3	6.64	6.25	20.37 /54	6.17 /66	--	2.09	1.69
GI	JPMorgan Smart Ret Blend 2055 R6	JTYBX	B-	(800) 480-4111	C+ / 6.4	6.71	6.30	20.50 /55	6.24 /66	--	2.16	1.56
GI	JPMorgan Smart Ret Blend 2055 Sel	JPTBX	B-	(800) 480-4111	C+ / 6.2	6.66	6.18	20.18 /53	5.98 /64	--	1.93	1.89
AA	JPMorgan Smart Ret Blend Inc R5	JIBBX	C+	(800) 480-4111	D+ / 2.7	3.59	2.32	10.40 /13	3.64 /38	--	2.32	1.04
AA	JPMorgan Smart Ret Blend Inc R6	JIYBX	C+	(800) 480-4111	D+ / 2.8	3.61	2.37	10.47 /13	3.70 /39	--	2.39	0.93
AA	JPMorgan Smart Ret Blend Inc Select	JIJSX	C+	(800) 480-4111	D+ / 2.6	3.55	2.18	10.21 /12	3.45 /36	--	2.15	1.22
BA	JPMorgan Smart Ret Inc A	JSRAX	C	(800) 480-4111	D / 2.0	3.66	2.34	10.48 /13	3.33 /35	4.67 /19	2.02	1.03
BA	JPMorgan Smart Ret Inc C	JSRCX	C	(800) 480-4111	D / 2.2	3.49	2.05	9.80 /11	2.66 /29	4.00 /15	1.46	1.53
BA	JPMorgan Smart Ret Inc Inst	JSIIX	C+	(800) 480-4111	D+ / 2.7	3.63	2.43	10.68 /13	3.57 /38	4.92 /21	2.31	0.61
BA	JPMorgan Smart Ret Inc R2	JSIZX	C	(800) 480-4111	D+ / 2.4	3.54	2.21	10.17 /12	3.07 /32	4.41 /18	1.87	1.32
AA	JPMorgan Smart Ret Inc R6	JSIYX	U	(800) 480-4111	U /	3.66	2.47	10.76 /14	--	--	2.38	0.45
BA	JPMorgan Smart Ret Inc Sel	JSRSX	C+	(800) 480-4111	D+ / 2.7	3.67	2.37	10.56 /13	3.44 /36	4.77 /20	2.19	0.77
GR	JPMorgan SmartAllocation Equity A	SAEAX	C+	(800) 480-4111	C / 5.2	7.11	7.11	21.94 /62	5.60 /61	--	1.35	2.17
GR	JPMorgan SmartAllocation Equity C	SAECX	C+	(800) 480-4111	C+ / 5.9	6.93	6.83	21.30 /59	5.05 /55	--	1.06	2.39
GR	JPMorgan SmartAllocation Equity R2	JSMRX	C+	(800) 480-4111	C+ / 6.1	6.99	6.99	21.66 /61	5.32 /58	--	1.10	4.13
GR	JPMorgan SmartAllocation Equity R5	JSRRX	C+	(800) 480-4111	C+ / 6.7	7.21	7.36	22.48 /64	6.07 /65	--	1.74	3.37
GR	JPMorgan SmartAllocation Equity R6	JSARX	C+	(800) 480-4111	C+ / 6.7	7.22	7.37	22.55 /65	6.11 /65	--	1.79	1.21
GR	JPMorgan SmartAllocation Equity Sel	SMESX	C+	(800) 480-4111	C+ / 6.5	7.17	7.27	22.28 /63	5.85 /63	--	1.77	1.63
GI	JPMorgan Systematic Alpha Select	SSALX	C	(800) 480-4111	D- / 1.2	0.39	2.44	0.71 / 2	1.99 /24	--	0.07	1.44
GI	JPMorgan Tax Aware Equity A	JPEAX	A-	(800) 480-4111	B+ / 8.6	8.03	11.34	26.72 /78	9.80 /92	13.82 /92	0.65	0.99
GI	JPMorgan Tax Aware Equity C	JPECX	A	(800) 480-4111	A- / 9.0	7.91	11.09	26.09 /76	9.25 /88	13.25 /86	0.28	1.50
GI	JPMorgan Tax Aware Equity I	JPDEX	A+	(800) 480-4111	A / 9.5	8.16	11.64	27.30 /80	10.29 /95	14.32 /95	1.09	0.55
GI	JPMorgan Tax Aware Equity Sel	JPESX	A	(800) 480-4111	A / 9.5	8.15	11.59	27.16 /80	10.12 /94	14.14 /94	0.97	0.71
GR	JPMorgan US Dynamic Plus A	JPSAX	B	(800) 480-4111	B / 7.8	6.07	12.25	22.90 /66	9.36 /89	12.69 /81	1.37	2.08
GR	JPMorgan US Dynamic Plus C	JPSCX	B+	(800) 480-4111	B+ / 8.3	5.87	11.94	22.24 /63	8.81 /85	12.10 /75	0.97	2.68
GR	JPMorgan US Dynamic Plus Sel	JILSX	A-	(800) 480-4111	B+ / 8.9	6.11	12.40	23.21 /67	9.63 /91	12.96 /83	0.48	1.78
GI	JPMorgan US Equity A	JUEAX	B+	(800) 480-4111	B+ / 8.6	7.73	11.55	27.00 /79	9.77 /92	13.84 /92	0.69	1.14
GI	JPMorgan US Equity C	JUECX	B+	(800) 480-4111	A- / 9.0	7.54	11.25	26.31 /77	9.20 /88	13.27 /87	0.33	1.59
GI	JPMorgan US Equity L	JMUEX	A	(800) 480-4111	A / 9.5	7.79	11.69	27.40 /80	10.12 /94	14.21 /94	1.01	0.68
GI	JPMorgan US Equity R2	JUEZX	A-	(800) 480-4111	A- / 9.2	7.66	11.44	26.66 /78	9.49 /90	13.57 /90	0.53	1.48
GI	JPMorgan US Equity R5	JUSRX	A	(800) 480-4111	A / 9.5	7.80	11.72	27.45 /80	10.17 /94	14.28 /95	1.05	0.63
GI	JPMorgan US Equity R6	JUEMX	A	(800) 480-4111	A / 9.5	7.80	11.73	27.48 /80	10.24 /95	14.34 /95	1.11	0.50
GI	JPMorgan US Equity Sel	JUESX	A-	(800) 480-4111	A / 9.4	7.76	11.70	27.25 /80	9.97 /93	14.06 /94	0.89	0.81
GR	● JPMorgan US LgCap Core Plus A	JLCAX	B+	(800) 480-4111	B+ / 8.6	7.86	12.15	28.14 /82	9.50 /90	13.88 /92	0.04	2.41
GR	● JPMorgan US LgCap Core Plus C	JLPCX	B+	(800) 480-4111	A- / 9.1	7.76	11.87	27.50 /81	8.97 /87	13.31 /87	0.00	2.92
GR	● JPMorgan US LgCap Core Plus R2	JLPZX	B+	(800) 480-4111	A- / 9.2	7.81	12.02	27.83 /81	9.23 /88	13.59 /90	0.00	2.76
GR	● JPMorgan US LgCap Core Plus R5	JCPRX	A-	(800) 480-4111	A / 9.5	8.01	12.39	28.72 /83	9.98 /93	14.38 /95	0.46	1.89
GR	● JPMorgan US LgCap Core Plus Sel	JLPSX	B+	(800) 480-4111	A / 9.5	7.97	12.30	28.43 /83	9.78 /92	14.17 /94	0.30	2.13
SC	JPMorgan US Small Company A	JTUAX	C+	(800) 480-4111	B- / 7.4	3.45	11.35	32.27 /90	7.40 /75	14.01 /93	0.07	1.45
SC	JPMorgan US Small Company C	JTUCX	B-	(800) 480-4111	B / 7.9	3.33	11.04	31.60 /89	6.85 /71	13.43 /88	0.00	1.92
SC	JPMorgan US Small Company L	JUSSX	B	(800) 480-4111	B+ / 8.7	3.55	11.54	32.84 /91	7.86 /78	14.48 /96	0.46	0.91

● Denotes fund is closed to new investors
* Denotes fund is included in Section II

www.thestreetratings.com

RISK			NET ASSETS		ASSET				Portfolio Turnover Ratio	BULL / BEAR		FUND MANAGER		MINIMUMS		LOADS	
	3 Year		NAV							Last Bull	Last Bear	Manager	Manager	Initial	Additional	Front	Back
Risk Rating/Pts	Standard Deviation	Beta	As of 2/28/17	Total $(Mil)	Cash %	Stocks %	Bonds %	Other %		Market Return	Market Return	Quality Pct	Tenure (Years)	Purch. $	Purch. $	End Load	End Load
B /8.1	8.5	0.79	20.83	139	0	0	0	100	53	N/A	N/A	44	5	15,000,000	0	0.0	0.0
B /8.1	8.5	0.79	20.80	12	0	0	0	100	53	N/A	N/A	41	5	1,000,000	0	0.0	0.0
B- /7.8	9.0	0.85	21.19	40	0	0	0	100	56	N/A	N/A	39	5	0	0	0.0	0.0
B- /7.8	9.0	0.85	21.19	132	0	0	0	100	56	N/A	N/A	40	5	15,000,000	0	0.0	0.0
B- /7.8	9.1	0.85	21.17	18	0	0	0	100	56	N/A	N/A	36	5	1,000,000	0	0.0	0.0
B- /7.9	9.0	0.85	21.12	28	0	0	0	100	54	N/A	N/A	39	5	0	0	0.0	0.0
B- /7.9	9.0	0.85	21.14	82	0	0	0	100	54	N/A	N/A	40	5	15,000,000	0	0.0	0.0
B- /7.9	9.0	0.85	21.10	10	0	0	0	100	54	N/A	N/A	37	5	1,000,000	0	0.0	0.0
B- /7.9	9.0	0.84	21.11	19	0	0	0	100	60	N/A	N/A	39	5	0	0	0.0	0.0
B- /7.9	9.0	0.85	21.12	60	0	0	0	100	60	N/A	N/A	40	5	15,000,000	0	0.0	0.0
B- /7.9	9.1	0.85	21.10	11	0	0	0	100	60	N/A	N/A	36	5	1,000,000	0	0.0	0.0
B- /7.9	9.0	0.84	20.79	10	0	0	0	100	53	N/A	N/A	40	5	0	0	0.0	0.0
B- /7.9	9.0	0.84	20.81	22	0	0	0	100	53	N/A	N/A	41	5	15,000,000	0	0.0	0.0
B- /7.9	9.0	0.84	20.78	3	0	0	0	100	53	N/A	N/A	38	5	1,000,000	0	0.0	0.0
B+ /9.5	4.5	0.69	16.98	17	0	0	0	100	52	N/A	N/A	56	5	0	0	0.0	0.0
B+ /9.5	4.5	0.68	16.99	61	0	0	0	100	52	N/A	N/A	57	5	15,000,000	0	0.0	0.0
B+ /9.5	4.5	0.68	16.97	7	0	0	0	100	52	N/A	N/A	54	5	1,000,000	0	0.0	0.0
B /8.8	4.6	0.70	17.85	639	3	36	60	1	29	38.7	-7.5	51	11	1,000	50	4.5	0.0
B /8.8	4.6	0.70	17.76	23	3	36	60	1	29	33.8	-7.7	41	11	1,000	50	0.0	0.0
B /8.7	4.6	0.69	17.91	931	3	36	60	1	29	40.4	-7.4	55	11	3,000,000	0	0.0	0.0
B /8.8	4.6	0.70	17.80	120	3	36	60	1	29	36.8	-7.6	48	11	0	0	0.0	0.0
U /	N/A	N/A	17.91	152	3	36	60	1	29	N/A	N/A	N/A	11	15,000,000	0	0.0	0.0
B /8.8	4.6	0.70	17.88	306	3	36	60	1	29	39.4	-7.5	53	11	1,000,000	0	0.0	0.0
C+ /6.4	10.4	0.98	21.95	1	2	96	0	2	40	N/A	N/A	20	5	1,000	50	5.3	0.0
C+ /6.4	10.4	0.98	21.88	1	2	96	0	2	40	N/A	N/A	15	5	1,000	50	0.0	0.0
C+ /6.5	10.4	0.98	22.20	N/A	2	96	0	2	40	N/A	N/A	18	5	0	0	0.0	0.0
C+ /6.4	10.4	0.98	22.13	N/A	2	96	0	2	40	N/A	N/A	24	5	0	0	0.0	0.0
C+ /6.4	10.4	0.98	22.12	106	2	96	0	2	40	N/A	N/A	24	5	15,000,000	0	0.0	0.0
C+ /6.4	10.4	0.98	22.04	10	2	96	0	2	40	N/A	N/A	22	5	1,000,000	0	0.0	0.0
B+ /9.9	3.1	0.02	15.50	48	0	0	0	100	151	N/A	N/A	84	4	1,000,000	0	0.0	0.0
C+ /6.0	11.5	1.09	31.02	16	0	99	0	1	41	135.4	-18.6	53	9	1,000	50	5.3	0.0
C+ /6.0	11.5	1.09	30.78	7	0	99	0	1	41	129.2	-18.8	46	9	1,000	50	0.0	0.0
C+ /6.0	11.6	1.09	31.17	1,054	0	99	0	1	41	141.0	-18.5	59	9	3,000,000	0	0.0	0.0
C+ /6.0	11.5	1.09	31.14	97	0	99	0	1	41	138.9	-18.6	57	9	1,000,000	0	0.0	0.0
C+ /5.9	12.1	1.13	17.74	224	0	98	1	1	116	121.6	-16.2	41	5	1,000	50	5.3	0.0
C+ /5.9	12.2	1.14	17.14	1	0	98	1	1	116	115.5	-16.4	34	5	1,000	50	0.0	0.0
C+ /5.9	12.2	1.14	18.20	21	0	98	1	1	116	124.6	-16.2	44	5	1,000,000	0	0.0	0.0
C+ /5.6	11.1	1.05	15.46	1,485	0	98	0	2	83	135.4	-17.8	58	16	1,000	50	5.3	0.0
C /5.5	11.2	1.06	15.03	329	0	98	0	2	83	129.2	-18.0	50	16	1,000	50	0.0	0.0
C+ /5.6	11.1	1.05	15.51	3,386	0	98	0	2	83	139.6	-17.7	62	16	3,000,000	0	0.0	0.0
C+ /5.6	11.2	1.06	15.34	228	0	98	0	2	83	132.2	-17.9	54	16	0	0	0.0	0.0
C+ /5.6	11.2	1.06	15.52	866	0	98	0	2	83	140.2	-17.7	62	16	0	0	0.0	0.0
C+ /5.6	11.1	1.05	15.54	6,207	0	98	0	2	83	140.9	-17.7	64	16	15,000,000	0	0.0	0.0
C+ /5.6	11.1	1.05	15.50	1,145	0	98	0	2	83	137.7	-17.7	61	16	1,000,000	0	0.0	0.0
C /5.1	12.1	1.12	29.69	862	0	99	0	1	127	134.6	-18.5	45	12	1,000	50	5.3	0.0
C /5.0	12.1	1.12	28.62	219	0	99	0	1	127	128.4	-18.7	38	12	1,000	50	0.0	0.0
C /5.0	12.1	1.12	29.12	7	0	99	0	1	127	131.5	-18.6	42	12	0	0	0.0	0.0
C /5.0	12.1	1.12	30.09	351	0	99	0	1	127	140.4	-18.4	52	12	0	0	0.0	0.0
C /5.1	12.1	1.12	29.97	8,470	0	99	0	1	127	137.9	-18.5	49	12	1,000,000	0	0.0	0.0
C /4.9	15.9	1.00	18.08	271	0	96	2	2	49	147.7	-26.7	77	13	1,000	50	5.3	0.0
C /4.9	15.9	1.00	17.41	53	0	96	2	2	49	140.9	-26.7	73	13	1,000	50	0.0	0.0
C /4.9	15.9	1.00	18.42	817	0	96	2	2	49	153.3	-26.5	80	13	3,000,000	0	0.0	0.0

Fund Type	Fund Name	Ticker Symbol	Overall Investment Rating	Phone	Performance Rating/Pts	3 Mo	6 Mo	1Yr / Pct	3Yr / Pct	5Yr / Pct	Dividend Yield	Expense Ratio
SC	JPMorgan US Small Company R2	JSCZX	B	(800) 480-4111	B / 8.1	3.37	11.18	31.93 /90	7.12 /73	13.73 /91	0.00	1.76
SC	JPMorgan US Small Company R6	JUSMX	B	(800) 480-4111	B+ / 8.8	3.57	11.62	33.01 /92	7.96 /79	14.58 /96	0.54	0.75
SC	JPMorgan US Small Company Sel	JSCSX	B	(800) 480-4111	B+ / 8.6	3.55	11.48	32.57 /91	7.68 /77	14.30 /95	0.29	1.12
GI	JPMorgan Value Advtg A	JVAAX	A-	(800) 480-4111	B / 8.1	6.43	12.40	28.16 /82	8.69 /85	13.46 /88	0.84	1.44
GI	JPMorgan Value Advtg C	JVACX	A	(800) 480-4111	B+ / 8.6	6.25	12.10	27.49 /80	8.13 /80	12.90 /83	0.51	1.86
GI	JPMorgan Value Advtg L	JVAIX	A+	(800) 480-4111	A- / 9.2	6.55	12.70	28.80 /84	9.23 /88	14.03 /93	1.37	0.89
GI	JPMorgan Value Advtg Sel	JVASX	A+	(800) 480-4111	A- / 9.1	6.47	12.54	28.44 /83	8.95 /86	13.74 /91	1.17	1.06
GR	Kaizen Hedged Premium Spreads I	KZSIX	U	(844) 524-9366	U /	2.33	2.46	10.34 /12	--	--	0.00	1.50
SC	Kalmar Growth With Value Sm Cap	KGSAX	E-	(800) 282-2319	D / 1.6	3.46	6.02	23.21 /67	-0.09 /13	--	0.00	1.28
SC	Kalmar Growth With Value Sm Cap	KGSIX	E-	(800) 282-2319	D+ / 2.4	3.44	6.06	23.36 /68	0.01 /13	--	0.00	1.18
SC	Kalmar Growth With Value Sm Cap	KGSCX	E-	(800) 282-2319	D- / 1.5	3.52	6.09	23.18 /67	-0.18 /13	7.45 /38	0.00	1.36
GR	KCM Macro Trends R1	KCMTX	C	(877) 275-5599	C / 5.3	7.51	10.54	15.51 /32	4.66 /50	8.26 /44	0.00	1.71
GL	KCM Macro Trends R2	KCMBX	C-	(877) 275-5599	C / 4.7	7.39	10.19	14.67 /28	3.90 /42	7.45 /38	0.00	2.46
MC	KEELEY All Cap Value A	KACVX	D+	(800) 533-5344	C / 4.9	4.70	9.84	26.72 /78	3.74 /40	10.82 /64	0.37	1.46
MC	KEELEY All Cap Value I	KACIX	C-	(800) 533-5344	C+ / 6.0	4.74	9.97	26.99 /79	4.01 /43	11.10 /67	0.63	1.21
IN	KEELEY Mid Cap Dividend Value A	KMDVX	A	(800) 533-5344	A / 9.4	4.91	11.05	35.03 /94	10.49 /96	14.58 /96	0.99	1.62
IN	KEELEY Mid Cap Dividend Value I	KMDIX	A	(800) 533-5344	A+ / 9.7	4.97	11.23	35.32 /94	10.77 /97	14.86 /97	1.24	1.37
MC	KEELEY Sm/Md Cap Val A	KSMVX	C-	(800) 533-5344	C+ / 6.0	4.78	12.20	33.50 /92	3.65 /39	11.97 /74	0.10	1.44
MC	KEELEY Sm/Md Cap Val I	KSMIX	C	(800) 533-5344	B- / 7.0	4.87	12.32	33.90 /93	3.91 /42	12.26 /77	0.33	1.19
SC	KEELEY Small Cap Div Value A	KSDVX	B+	(800) 533-5344	B+ / 8.5	4.74	14.38	34.68 /94	7.82 /78	12.02 /74	1.59	1.52
SC	KEELEY Small Cap Div Value I	KSDIX	A-	(800) 533-5344	A / 9.3	4.86	14.56	35.11 /94	8.11 /80	12.30 /77	1.89	1.27
SC	KEELEY Small Cap Value A	KSCVX	D-	(800) 533-5344	C- / 3.7	1.71	10.39	28.03 /82	2.11 /25	9.69 /56	0.42	1.36
SC	KEELEY Small Cap Value I	KSCIX	D+	(800) 533-5344	C / 4.9	1.75	10.52	28.31 /82	2.36 /26	9.96 /58	0.72	1.11
GL	Kellner Merger Inst	GAKIX	D+	(855) 535-5637	E+ / 0.9	0.08	1.35	-1.62 / 1	1.51 /21	--	0.00	2.41
GL	Kellner Merger Inv	GAKAX	D+	(855) 535-5637	E / 0.5	-0.01	1.17	-1.83 / 1	1.10 /19	--	0.00	2.54
GI	Kinetics Alter Inc Inst	KWIIX	C	(800) 930-3828	D- / 1.5	0.87	1.93	5.56 / 4	2.87 /31	3.72 /14	0.11	1.73
GI	Kinetics Alter Inc NL	KWINX	C	(800) 930-3828	D- / 1.5	0.82	1.83	5.35 / 4	2.68 /29	3.53 /13	0.00	1.78
GI	Kinetics Alternative Inc Advisor A	KWIAX	C-	(800) 930-3828	E+ / 0.9	0.75	1.69	5.09 / 4	2.41 /27	3.27 /12	0.00	2.03
GI	Kinetics Alternative Inc Advisor C	KWICX	C	(800) 930-3828	D- / 1.2	0.64	1.45	4.57 / 4	1.91 /23	2.74 /10	0.00	2.53
GL	Kinetics Global Advisor A	KGLAX	E	(800) 930-3828	E- / 0.2	2.15	6.69	18.68 /46	-4.35 / 3	3.81 /14	0.00	3.13
GL	Kinetics Global Advisor C	KGLCX	E	(800) 930-3828	E / 0.3	2.04	6.54	18.21 /44	-4.84 / 3	3.23 /12	0.00	3.63
GL	Kinetics Global No Load	WWWEX	E+	(800) 930-3828	E / 0.4	2.33	7.05	19.27 /48	-4.11 / 3	4.04 /15	0.00	2.88
TC	Kinetics Internet Advisor A	KINAX	E-	(800) 930-3828	E+ / 0.7	4.14	7.83	12.21 /19	-0.03 /13	9.78 /57	0.00	2.07
TC	Kinetics Internet Advisor C	KINCX	E-	(800) 930-3828	D- / 1.0	3.99	7.57	11.65 /17	-0.51 /11	9.24 /53	0.00	2.57
TC	Kinetics Internet NL	WWWFX	E	(800) 930-3828	D / 1.8	4.21	7.96	12.49 /20	0.22 /14	10.05 /59	0.00	1.82
GL	Kinetics Market Opps Advisor A	KMKAX	D+	(800) 930-3828	D+ / 2.5	2.08	14.43	24.13 /70	0.76 /17	9.10 /51	0.00	2.16
GL	Kinetics Market Opps Advisor C	KMKCX	C-	(800) 930-3828	C- / 3.1	1.91	14.16	23.54 /68	0.27 /15	8.53 /47	0.00	2.66
GL	Kinetics Market Opps Inst	KMKYX	C-	(800) 930-3828	C- / 3.8	2.20	14.77	24.71 /72	1.23 /19	9.61 /55	0.00	1.86
GL	Kinetics Market Opps NL	KMKNX	C-	(800) 930-3828	C- / 3.7	2.11	14.61	24.47 /72	1.02 /18	9.35 /53	0.00	1.91
HL	Kinetics Medical Advisor A	KRXAX	D-	(800) 930-3828	D / 2.0	6.29	4.46	13.07 /22	2.91 /31	13.28 /87	0.33	2.24
HL	Kinetics Medical Advisor C	KRXCX	D-	(800) 930-3828	D+ / 2.5	6.16	4.20	12.50 /20	2.40 /27	12.71 /81	0.00	2.74
HL	Kinetics Medical NL	MEDRX	D-	(800) 930-3828	C- / 3.0	6.34	4.58	13.33 /23	3.17 /33	13.55 /89	0.75	1.99
GI	Kinetics Multi-Disciplinary Inc A	KMDAX	D	(800) 930-3828	D / 1.6	2.61	2.46	12.22 /19	3.10 /33	4.12 /16	3.41	2.22
GI	Kinetics Multi-Disciplinary Inc C	KMDCX	D	(800) 930-3828	D / 2.0	2.49	2.21	11.58 /16	2.58 /28	3.59 /13	3.17	2.72
GI	Kinetics Multi-Disciplinary Inc I	KMDYX	D+	(800) 930-3828	D+ / 2.5	2.70	2.76	12.75 /21	3.54 /37	4.57 /19	4.05	1.92
GI	Kinetics Multi-Disciplinary Inc NL	KMDNX	D+	(800) 930-3828	D+ / 2.4	2.66	2.67	12.55 /20	3.35 /35	4.37 /17	3.86	1.97
GR	Kinetics Paradigm Fund A	KNPAX	C-	(800) 930-3828	C / 4.4	2.82	15.38	30.76 /88	2.60 /28	11.17 /67	0.00	1.96
GR	Kinetics Paradigm Fund C	KNPCX	C-	(800) 930-3828	C / 5.2	2.69	15.07	30.08 /87	2.08 /25	10.62 /63	0.00	2.46
GR	Kinetics Paradigm Fund I	KNPYX	C	(800) 930-3828	C+ / 6.1	2.95	15.64	31.32 /89	3.06 /32	11.68 /71	0.00	1.66
GR	Kinetics Paradigm Fund NL	WWNPX	C	(800) 930-3828	C+ / 5.9	2.88	15.52	31.07 /88	2.85 /30	11.45 /69	0.00	1.73
GL	Kinetics Small Cap Opps Advisor A	KSOAX	E+	(800) 930-3828	D / 1.7	1.96	15.30	32.91 /91	-0.08 /13	12.69 /81	0.00	1.98
GL	Kinetics Small Cap Opps Advisor C	KSOCX	D-	(800) 930-3828	D / 2.1	1.82	15.01	32.21 /90	-0.58 /11	12.13 /75	0.00	2.48

• Denotes fund is closed to new investors
* Denotes fund is included in Section II

RISK			NET ASSETS		ASSET				BULL / BEAR		FUND MANAGER		MINIMUMS		LOADS	
	3 Year		NAV													
Risk Rating/Pts	Standard Deviation	Beta	As of 2/28/17	Total $(Mil)	Cash %	Stocks %	Bonds %	Other %	Portfolio Turnover Ratio	Last Bull Market Return	Last Bear Market Return	Manager Quality Pct	Manager Tenure (Years)	Initial Purch. $	Additional Purch. $	Front End Load	Back End Load
C /4.9	15.9	1.00	17.81	45	0	96	2	2	49	144.5	-26.7	75	13	0	0	0.0	0.0
C /4.9	15.9	1.00	18.43	253	0	96	2	2	49	N/A	N/A	81	13	15,000,000	0	0.0	0.0
C /4.9	15.9	1.00	18.44	361	0	96	2	2	49	151.0	-26.5	79	13	1,000,000	0	0.0	0.0
C+ /6.6	10.2	0.93	33.35	1,846	0	96	2	2	26	130.4	-17.4	61	12	1,000	50	5.3	0.0
C+ /6.6	10.2	0.93	33.20	795	0	96	2	2	26	124.2	-17.5	54	12	1,000	50	0.0	0.0
C+ /6.6	10.2	0.93	33.53	3,954	0	96	2	2	26	136.8	-17.2	67	12	3,000,000	0	0.0	0.0
C+ /6.6	10.2	0.93	33.54	1,508	0	96	2	2	26	133.5	-17.3	64	12	1,000,000	0	0.0	0.0
U /	N/A	N/A	7.90	57	0	0	0	100	0	N/A	N/A	N/A	2	10,000	1,000	0.0	0.0
E /0.3	16.1	0.99	12.75	14	0	98	1	1	50	N/A	N/A	6	20	100,000	500	0.0	2.0
E /0.3	16.1	0.99	12.82	65	0	98	1	1	50	N/A	N/A	7	20	250,000	500	0.0	2.0
E /0.3	16.1	0.99	12.70	43	0	98	1	1	50	83.2	-21.4	6	20	2,500	500	0.0	2.0
C /5.5	9.6	0.81	12.88	83	10	86	2	2	437	66.2	-21.7	27	4	5,000	1,000	0.0	0.0
C /5.5	9.7	0.55	12.21	N/A	10	86	2	2	437	59.7	-21.9	93	4	5,000	1,000	0.0	0.0
C- /3.8	12.1	0.94	16.45	20	1	95	2	2	75	111.0	-22.0	15	6	2,500	50	4.5	0.0
C- /3.7	12.1	0.94	16.57	47	1	95	2	2	75	114.1	-22.0	18	6	1,000,000	10,000	0.0	0.0
C+ /5.7	12.0	1.02	20.94	20	3	96	0	1	49	N/A	N/A	71	6	2,500	50	4.5	0.0
C+ /5.7	12.0	1.02	20.95	89	3	96	0	1	49	N/A	N/A	74	6	1,000,000	10,000	0.0	0.0
C- /3.9	13.6	1.10	13.86	46	2	95	2	1	37	134.1	-28.1	7	6	2,500	50	4.5	0.0
C- /3.9	13.7	1.10	14.11	98	2	95	2	1	37	137.3	-28.0	8	6	1,000,000	10,000	0.0	0.0
C /5.4	14.2	0.85	18.63	25	1	96	2	1	27	117.0	-19.5	85	8	2,500	50	4.5	0.0
C /5.4	14.2	0.85	18.67	84	1	96	2	1	27	120.0	-19.4	87	8	1,000,000	10,000	0.0	0.0
C- /3.5	14.4	0.89	33.57	604	1	98	0	1	36	101.7	-26.9	25	6	2,500	50	4.5	0.0
C- /3.5	14.4	0.89	33.96	377	1	98	0	1	36	104.4	-26.9	27	6	1,000,000	10,000	0.0	0.0
B /8.3	3.9	0.02	10.38	151	44	55	0	1	229	N/A	N/A	83	5	100,000	100	0.0	0.0
B /8.2	3.9	0.03	10.20	6	44	55	0	1	229	N/A	N/A	81	5	2,000	100	5.8	0.0
B+ /9.4	2.8	0.23	97.27	18	5	0	94	1	6	37.9	-16.3	77	7	1,000,000	0	0.0	2.0
B+ /9.4	2.8	0.23	95.94	6	5	0	94	1	6	36.6	-16.4	75	7	2,500	0	0.0	2.0
B+ /9.4	2.8	0.23	94.97	3	5	0	94	1	6	34.6	-16.5	73	7	2,500	0	5.8	2.0
B+ /9.4	2.8	0.23	91.77	2	5	0	94	1	6	31.0	-16.6	68	7	2,500	0	0.0	2.0
C /5.0	12.3	0.72	5.26	N/A	33	65	0	2	16	43.9	-20.4	20	18	2,500	0	5.8	2.0
C /4.9	12.3	0.73	5.05	2	33	65	0	2	16	40.0	-20.8	16	18	2,500	0	0.0	2.0
C /5.0	12.4	0.73	5.31	6	33	65	0	2	16	45.6	-20.4	23	18	2,500	0	0.0	2.0
D /2.3	11.4	0.96	39.02	2	22	55	22	1	1	91.2	-22.2	2	18	2,500	0	5.8	2.0
D /1.9	11.5	0.97	35.82	1	22	55	22	1	1	86.3	-22.4	2	18	2,500	0	0.0	2.0
D+ /2.5	11.4	0.97	40.86	111	22	55	22	1	1	93.9	-22.1	2	18	2,500	0	0.0	2.0
C+ /6.5	10.3	0.52	18.16	5	9	57	32	2	2	84.0	-18.7	80	11	2,500	0	5.8	2.0
C+ /6.5	10.3	0.52	17.58	5	9	57	32	2	2	79.2	-18.9	76	11	2,500	0	0.0	2.0
C+ /6.6	10.3	0.52	18.57	3	9	57	32	2	2	88.9	-18.6	83	11	1,000,000	0	0.0	2.0
C+ /6.6	10.3	0.52	18.36	32	9	57	32	2	2	86.5	-18.6	81	11	2,500	0	0.0	2.0
C- /4.2	15.5	1.06	27.05	4	3	94	2	1	12	107.3	-15.5	4	16	2,500	0	5.8	2.0
C- /4.2	15.5	1.06	26.27	N/A	3	94	2	1	12	101.7	-15.6	3	16	2,500	0	0.0	2.0
C /4.3	15.5	1.06	28.02	17	3	94	2	1	12	110.0	-15.3	4	16	2,500	0	0.0	2.0
C+ /6.2	5.1	0.38	11.07	7	0	0	92	8	10	43.4	-12.5	64	9	2,500	0	5.8	2.0
C+ /6.2	5.0	0.37	10.95	8	0	0	92	8	10	39.4	-12.6	58	9	2,500	0	0.0	2.0
C+ /6.2	5.1	0.38	11.15	83	0	0	92	8	10	46.8	-12.3	70	9	1,000,000	0	0.0	2.0
C+ /6.2	5.0	0.37	11.13	7	0	0	92	8	10	45.4	-12.4	68	9	2,500	0	0.0	2.0
C /5.2	12.8	0.98	37.58	105	6	79	13	2	2	105.1	-25.0	5	16	2,500	0	5.8	2.0
C /5.1	12.8	0.98	35.50	113	6	79	13	2	2	99.6	-25.2	4	16	2,500	0	0.0	2.0
C /5.2	12.8	0.98	38.74	276	6	79	13	2	2	110.1	-24.8	6	16	1,000,000	0	0.0	2.0
C /5.2	12.8	0.98	38.56	342	6	79	13	2	2	107.8	-24.9	5	16	2,500	0	0.0	2.0
C /4.3	14.2	0.77	40.02	14	11	79	8	2	2	117.3	-22.1	74	15	2,500	0	5.8	2.0
C- /4.2	14.2	0.77	38.54	9	11	79	8	2	2	111.6	-22.3	69	15	2,500	0	0.0	2.0

					PERFORMANCE						Incl. in Returns	
	99 Pct = Best / 0 Pct = Worst		Overall				Total Return % through 2/28/17		Annualized		Dividend	Expense
Fund Type	Fund Name	Ticker Symbol	Investment Rating	Phone	Perfor-mance Rating/Pts	3 Mo	6 Mo	1Yr / Pct	3Yr / Pct	5Yr / Pct	Yield	Ratio
GL	Kinetics Small Cap Opps Inst	KSCYX	D+	(800) 930-3828	C / 4.6	2.08	15.55	33.50 /92	0.37 /15	13.19 /86	0.00	1.66
GL	Kinetics Small Cap Opps NL	KSCOX	D+	(800) 930-3828	C / 4.4	2.01	15.42	33.24 /92	0.17 /14	12.97 /83	0.00	1.71
MC	Kirr Marbach Parners Value	KMVAX	C	(800) 870-8039	C / 5.1	5.62	11.37	24.00 /70	2.97 /32	10.21 /60	0.00	1.47
GL	Knights of Columbus Intl Eqty Inst	KCIIX	U	(844) 523-8637	U /	6.75	7.16	20.30 /54	--	--	1.59	1.71
GR	Knights of Columbus LC Gro Inst	KCGIX	U	(844) 523-8637	U /	8.32	7.67	17.15 /39	--	--	0.32	1.61
GR	Knights of Columbus LC Val Inst	KCVIX	U	(844) 523-8637	U /	6.92	14.95	27.20 /80	--	--	1.49	1.62
GR	Knights of Columbus Sm Cap Eq Inst	KCSIX	U	(844) 523-8637	U /	5.18	11.09	25.88 /76	--	--	0.22	1.49
GL	Kopernik Global All-Cap A	KGGAX	D+	(866) 777-7818	C+ / 6.9	7.72	6.34	53.98 /99	1.61 /22	--	2.82	1.37
GL	Kopernik Global All-Cap Inst	KGGIX	C-	(866) 777-7818	B / 8.0	7.79	6.40	54.20 /99	1.84 /23	--	3.23	1.13
FO	KP International Equity Instl	KPIEX	C-	(855) 457-3637	D+ / 2.7	8.54	4.65	17.54 /41	0.50 /16	--	1.86	0.50
GR	KP Large Cap Equity Instl	KPLCX	A+	(855) 457-3637	A- / 9.1	8.02	10.83	25.31 /74	9.61 /91	--	1.40	0.35
GI	KP Retirement Path 2015 Instl	KPRAX	C+	(855) 457-3637	D+ / 2.5	3.28	2.32	8.89 / 9	3.52 /37	--	2.12	0.36
GI	KP Retirement Path 2020 Instl	KPRBX	B-	(855) 457-3637	C- / 3.0	3.96	3.18	11.11 /15	3.83 /41	--	2.05	0.38
GI	KP Retirement Path 2025 Instl	KPRCX	C-	(855) 457-3637	C- / 3.8	4.84	4.36	14.03 /26	4.16 /45	--	1.97	0.42
GI	KP Retirement Path 2030 Instl	KPRDX	B-	(855) 457-3637	C / 4.6	5.77	5.49	17.04 /38	4.43 /48	--	1.90	0.47
GI	KP Retirement Path 2035 Instl	KPREX	B	(855) 457-3637	C / 5.2	6.29	6.34	19.00 /47	4.71 /51	--	1.81	0.48
GI	KP Retirement Path 2040 Instl	KPRFX	B-	(855) 457-3637	C+ / 5.6	6.62	6.96	20.23 /53	4.86 /53	--	1.72	0.49
GI	KP Retirement Path 2045 Instl	KPRGX	B-	(855) 457-3637	C+ / 5.8	6.86	7.28	21.01 /57	4.93 /53	--	1.65	0.49
GI	KP Retirement Path 2050 Instl	KPRHX	B-	(855) 457-3637	C+ / 5.9	7.02	7.36	21.08 /58	4.98 /54	--	1.64	0.49
GI	KP Retirement Path 2055 Instl	KPRIX	B-	(855) 457-3637	C+ / 5.9	7.02	7.37	21.05 /58	4.99 /54	--	1.64	0.49
GI	KP Retirement Path 2060 Instl	KPRJX	B-	(855) 457-3637	C+ / 5.9	6.99	7.40	21.09 /58	5.04 /55	--	1.64	0.49
SC	KP Small Cap Equity Instl	KPSCX	B	(855) 457-3637	B / 7.8	4.94	12.01	33.30 /92	5.56 /60	--	0.74	0.55
GL	KS 529 LearningQuest ESP 100% Eq		B+	(800) 345-6488	B- / 7.0	6.98	7.64	23.34 /68	6.67 /70	10.45 /62	0.00	0.99
GL	KS 529 LearningQuest ESP 100% Eq		C+	(800) 345-6488	C / 5.4	6.48	7.27	21.97 /62	6.18 /66	10.31 /61	0.00	1.52
GL	KS 529 LearningQuest ESP 100% Eq		C+	(800) 345-6488	C+ / 6.0	6.39	6.92	21.14 /58	5.42 /59	9.50 /55	0.00	2.27
IX	KS 529 LearningQuest ESP 500 Idx		A+	(800) 345-6488	A / 9.3	8.01	9.92	24.72 /72	10.37 /95	13.74 /91	0.00	0.25
GL	KS 529 LearningQuest ESP Aggr A		C+	(800) 345-6488	C- / 3.2	5.05	4.34	15.47 /32	4.65 /50	7.45 /38	0.00	1.37
GL	KS 529 LearningQuest ESP Aggr C		C+	(800) 345-6488	C- / 3.6	4.69	3.77	14.40 /27	3.87 /41	6.62 /32	0.00	2.12
GL	KS 529 LearningQuest ESP Aggr Idx		B	(800) 345-6488	C+ / 6.4	6.42	6.68	19.66 /50	6.57 /69	9.56 /55	0.00	0.50
GL	KS 529 LearningQuest ESP Aggr		B	(800) 345-6488	C / 4.8	5.32	4.64	16.67 /37	5.17 /56	7.71 /40	0.00	0.82
GL	KS 529 LearningQuest ESP Bal Idx		B	(800) 345-6488	C+ / 5.7	5.08	4.98	15.62 /33	6.87 /71	8.96 /50	0.00	0.28
GL	KS 529 LearningQuest ESP Csv A		C	(800) 345-6488	D / 2.1	3.69	2.67	11.28 /15	3.73 /40	5.63 /26	0.00	1.24
GL	KS 529 LearningQuest ESP Csv C		C+	(800) 345-6488	D+ / 2.4	3.51	2.26	10.41 /13	2.97 /32	4.84 /20	0.00	1.99
GL	KS 529 LearningQuest ESP Csv Idx		B-	(800) 345-6488	C- / 3.0	3.65	2.54	10.04 /12	4.25 /46	5.49 /25	0.00	0.50
GL	KS 529 LearningQuest ESP Csv Port		B-	(800) 345-6488	C- / 3.3	4.03	2.93	12.17 /19	4.16 /45	5.94 /28	0.00	0.75
GL	KS 529 LearningQuest ESP Dsp Gr A		C+	(800) 345-6488	C+ / 6.7	8.16	8.86	21.77 /61	7.75 /77	11.63 /71	0.00	1.49
GL	KS 529 LearningQuest ESP Dsp Gr C		B+	(800) 345-6488	B- / 7.0	7.84	8.47	20.80 /56	6.92 /71	10.80 /64	0.00	2.24
GL	KS 529 LearningQuest ESP Fndl Eq		B-	(800) 345-6488	C+ / 6.6	6.67	8.54	20.99 /57	8.03 /79	11.81 /73	0.00	1.46
GL	KS 529 LearningQuest ESP Fndl Eq		B-	(800) 345-6488	C+ / 6.9	6.42	8.02	19.89 /51	7.24 /74	10.94 /65	0.00	2.21
GL	KS 529 LearningQuest ESP Heritage		D+	(800) 345-6488	C- / 3.5	5.56	3.86	19.95 /52	4.22 /45	9.43 /54	0.00	1.46
GL	KS 529 LearningQuest ESP Heritage		D+	(800) 345-6488	C- / 4.0	5.37	3.56	19.00 /47	3.48 /37	8.60 /47	0.00	2.21
FO	KS 529 LearningQuest ESP Itl Gr A		E+	(800) 345-6488	E- / 0.2	5.14	0.57	7.91 / 7	-3.34 / 4	4.16 /16	0.00	1.83
FO	KS 529 LearningQuest ESP Itl Gr C		E+	(800) 345-6488	E / 0.3	5.07	0.20	7.11 / 6	-4.01 / 3	3.42 /12	0.00	2.58
GL	KS 529 LearningQuest ESP MC Val		A+	(800) 345-6488	A / 9.5	5.16	11.41	30.81 /88	12.36 /98	14.95 /97	0.00	1.45
GL	KS 529 LearningQuest ESP MC Val		A+	(800) 345-6488	A+ / 9.7	4.95	10.98	29.87 /86	11.52 /98	14.13 /94	0.00	2.20
GL	KS 529 LearningQuest ESP Mdt A		C	(800) 345-6488	D+ / 2.5	4.44	3.44	13.25 /23	4.18 /45	6.49 /31	0.00	1.31
GL	KS 529 LearningQuest ESP Mdt C		C+	(800) 345-6488	D+ / 2.9	4.02	2.95	12.20 /19	3.36 /35	5.69 /26	0.00	2.06
GL	KS 529 LearningQuest ESP Mdt Idx		B	(800) 345-6488	C / 4.6	4.94	4.66	14.61 /28	5.35 /58	7.49 /38	0.00	0.50
GL	KS 529 LearningQuest ESP Mdt Port		B-	(800) 345-6488	C- / 4.0	4.73	3.78	14.35 /27	4.67 /50	6.82 /34	0.00	0.79
GL	KS 529 LearningQuest ESP Nw Op II		C-	(800) 345-6488	C+ / 5.8	5.26	9.80	33.29 /92	4.06 /44	10.70 /63	0.00	1.81
GL	KS 529 LearningQuest ESP Nw Op II		C-	(800) 345-6488	C+ / 6.3	5.04	9.38	32.38 /91	3.29 /35	9.89 /57	0.00	2.56
RE	KS 529 LearningQuest ESP Rl Est A		C-	(800) 345-6488	C / 5.1	6.75	-3.55	13.33 /23	9.64 /91	9.96 /58	0.00	1.61

RISK Risk Rating/Pts	3 Year Standard Deviation	Beta	NET ASSETS NAV As of 2/28/17	Total $(Mil)	ASSET Cash %	Stocks %	Bonds %	Other %	Portfolio Turnover Ratio	BULL/BEAR Last Bull Market Return	Last Bear Market Return	FUND MANAGER Manager Quality Pct	Manager Tenure (Years)	MINIMUMS Initial Purch. $	Additional Purch. $	LOADS Front End Load	Back End Load
C /4.3	14.2	0.77	41.68	53	11	79	8	2	2	122.7	-22.0	77	15	1,000,000	0	0.0	2.0
C /4.3	14.2	0.77	41.09	129	11	79	8	2	2	120.3	-22.1	76	15	2,500	0	0.0	2.0
C /5.5	14.1	1.04	23.81	74	1	97	0	2	23	114.2	-25.8	7	30	1,000	100	0.0	1.0
U /	N/A	N/A	9.81	48	0	0	0	100	55	N/A	N/A	N/A	2	25,000	250	0.0	2.0
U /	N/A	N/A	10.81	34	0	0	0	100	75	N/A	N/A	N/A	2	25,000	250	0.0	2.0
U /	N/A	N/A	11.13	36	0	0	0	100	57	N/A	N/A	N/A	2	25,000	250	0.0	2.0
U /	N/A	N/A	10.90	66	0	0	0	100	83	N/A	N/A	N/A	2	25,000	250	0.0	2.0
D /1.6	22.8	1.14	10.47	71	8	88	2	2	39	N/A	N/A	85	4	3,000	250	5.8	0.0
D /1.7	22.8	1.13	10.43	983	8	88	2	2	39	N/A	N/A	86	4	1,000,000	0	0.0	0.0
B- /7.0	11.4	0.91	9.45	1,185	4	95	0	1	21	N/A	N/A	79	3	0	0	0.0	0.0
B- /7.0	10.6	1.01	11.91	1,829	5	93	0	2	126	N/A	N/A	62	3	0	0	0.0	0.0
B+ /9.6	3.8	0.31	10.20	451	4	28	66	2	24	N/A	N/A	76	3	0	0	0.0	0.0
B+ /9.5	4.7	0.41	10.39	785	5	38	56	1	19	N/A	N/A	69	3	0	0	0.0	0.0
C+ /5.7	6.1	0.56	10.51	882	5	51	42	2	12	N/A	N/A	54	3	0	0	0.0	0.0
B /8.2	7.6	0.70	10.57	823	5	66	28	1	9	N/A	N/A	38	3	0	0	0.0	0.0
B- /7.9	8.5	0.78	10.65	901	5	75	19	1	7	N/A	N/A	30	3	0	0	0.0	0.0
B- /7.6	9.1	0.85	10.70	819	4	81	14	1	7	N/A	N/A	25	3	0	0	0.0	0.0
B- /7.4	9.4	0.87	10.71	577	4	84	10	2	9	N/A	N/A	23	3	0	0	0.0	0.0
B- /7.4	9.4	0.88	10.76	284	4	84	10	2	9	N/A	N/A	24	3	0	0	0.0	0.0
B- /7.4	9.4	0.87	10.73	63	4	84	10	2	21	N/A	N/A	24	3	0	0	0.0	0.0
B- /7.4	9.5	0.88	10.79	11	4	84	10	2	100	N/A	N/A	24	3	0	0	0.0	0.0
C+ /5.6	15.1	0.95	11.55	907	5	94	0	1	154	N/A	N/A	63	3	0	0	0.0	0.0
C+ /6.7	10.2	0.73	12.26	59	1	98	0	1	0	100.3	-19.1	97	N/A	500	50	0.0	0.0
C+ /6.7	10.1	0.72	11.66	11	1	98	0	1	0	98.6	-19.6	97	N/A	500	50	5.8	0.0
C+ /6.6	10.1	0.72	10.66	4	1	98	0	1	0	90.7	-19.8	96	N/A	500	50	0.0	0.0
B- /7.2	10.3	1.00	12.41	58	0	99	0	1	0	131.5	-16.4	72	N/A	500	50	0.0	0.0
B /8.5	7.2	0.52	7.69	29	0	68	31	1	0	65.4	-13.1	95	N/A	500	50	5.8	0.0
B /8.5	7.1	0.51	7.15	10	0	68	31	1	0	58.5	-13.3	93	N/A	500	50	0.0	0.0
B /8.0	8.3	0.59	8.46	29	1	79	19	1	0	85.5	-14.6	97	N/A	500	50	0.0	0.0
B /8.4	7.3	0.53	8.12	132	1	68	29	2	0	67.4	-12.1	95	N/A	500	50	0.0	0.0
B /8.6	6.3	0.94	11.18	40	0	60	39	1	0	75.2	-9.0	88	N/A	500	50	0.0	0.0
B+ /9.2	5.3	0.38	7.30	36	0	47	52	1	0	46.3	-8.8	92	N/A	500	50	5.8	0.0
B+ /9.2	5.2	0.37	6.79	15	0	47	52	1	0	40.6	-9.0	90	N/A	500	50	0.0	0.0
B+ /9.6	4.3	0.30	7.67	13	1	39	58	2	0	42.6	-5.9	94	N/A	500	50	0.0	0.0
B+ /9.2	5.3	0.37	7.74	407	1	49	49	1	0	48.0	-7.8	94	N/A	500	50	0.0	0.0
C+ /6.7	10.7	0.72	10.07	1	0	99	0	1	0	117.0	-16.6	98	N/A	100	50	5.8	0.0
C+ /6.7	10.7	0.72	9.35	1	0	99	0	1	0	108.2	-16.9	98	N/A	100	50	0.0	0.0
B- /7.1	10.3	0.67	9.28	1	1	98	0	1	0	114.8	-16.6	98	N/A	100	50	5.8	0.0
B- /7.0	10.3	0.67	8.62	1	1	98	0	1	0	106.2	-16.9	98	N/A	100	50	0.0	0.0
C /5.2	12.4	0.73	9.68	1	0	99	0	1	0	93.2	-21.5	94	N/A	100	50	5.8	0.0
C /5.2	12.4	0.73	9.02	1	0	99	0	1	0	86.0	-21.8	92	N/A	100	50	0.0	0.0
C+ /5.9	11.3	0.87	5.32	1	0	99	0	1	0	42.6	-24.3	31	N/A	100	50	5.8	0.0
C+ /5.9	11.3	0.87	4.97	1	0	99	0	1	0	37.3	-24.6	24	N/A	100	50	0.0	0.0
B- /7.2	10.1	0.55	11.42	1	1	97	0	2	0	141.4	-17.3	99	N/A	100	50	5.8	0.0
B- /7.1	10.1	0.55	10.61	1	1	97	0	2	0	132.2	-17.7	99	N/A	100	50	0.0	0.0
B /8.8	6.2	0.45	7.52	49	0	58	41	1	0	55.4	-10.7	94	N/A	500	50	5.8	0.0
B /8.7	6.3	0.45	6.99	18	0	58	41	1	0	49.0	-11.0	91	N/A	500	50	0.0	0.0
B+ /9.0	6.3	0.45	8.08	19	1	59	39	1	0	62.6	-10.6	96	N/A	500	50	0.0	0.0
B /8.8	6.3	0.45	7.97	283	1	58	39	2	0	57.5	-10.0	95	N/A	500	50	0.0	0.0
C- /3.7	17.0	0.78	9.41	N/A	4	95	0	1	0	115.8	-29.1	94	N/A	500	50	5.8	0.0
C- /3.7	17.0	0.77	8.75	1	4	95	0	1	0	107.4	-29.2	91	N/A	500	50	0.0	0.0
C /5.1	14.5	1.06	6.80	N/A	1	98	0	1	0	95.4	-14.9	49	N/A	100	50	5.8	0.0

I. Index of Stock Mutual Funds

99 Pct = Best
0 Pct = Worst

Fund Type	Fund Name	Ticker Symbol	Overall Investment Rating	Phone	PERFORMANCE Perfor-mance Rating/Pts	3 Mo	6 Mo	1Yr / Pct	Annualized 3Yr / Pct	Annualized 5Yr / Pct	Incl. in Returns Dividend Yield	Incl. in Returns Expense Ratio
RE	KS 529 LearningQuest ESP RI Est C		C	(800) 345-6488	C+ / 5.6	6.41	-3.96	12.28 /19	8.80 /85	9.11 /52	0.00	2.36
GL	KS 529 LearningQuest ESP Tot Gr		A	(800) 345-6488	B / 8.2	7.71	9.35	25.10 /74	8.24 /81	12.13 /75	0.00	0.30
GL	KS 529 LearningQuest ESP Very Agg		B-	(800) 345-6488	C+ / 6.3	6.36	6.64	20.97 /57	6.08 /65	9.47 /54	0.00	0.93
GL	KS 529 LearningQuest ESP Very Agg		C+	(800) 345-6488	C / 4.6	6.01	6.30	19.75 /51	5.60 /61	9.32 /53	0.00	1.47
GL	KS 529 LearningQuest ESP Very Agg		C+	(800) 345-6488	C / 5.1	5.87	5.87	18.75 /46	4.81 /52	8.51 /46	0.00	2.22
GL	KS 529 LearningQuest ESP Very Csv		C+	(800) 345-6488	D / 1.9	2.50	1.61	7.41 / 6	2.73 /29	3.75 /14	0.00	0.70
GL	KS 529 LearningQuest ESP Very Csv		C	(800) 345-6488	D- / 1.3	2.36	1.40	6.90 / 6	2.36 /26	3.47 /13	0.00	1.11
GL	KS 529 LearningQuest ESP Very Csv		C	(800) 345-6488	D- / 1.4	2.02	1.00	5.95 / 5	1.59 /21	2.68 /10	0.00	1.86
GL	KS 529 Schwab CSP Aggressive Port		B-	(800) 345-6488	C+ / 6.1	6.41	8.37	21.89 /62	5.10 /55	9.73 /56	0.00	1.41
GL	KS 529 Schwab CSP Conservative		C+	(800) 345-6488	D- / 1.5	2.01	0.62	5.53 / 4	1.97 /24	2.93 /11	0.00	0.92
GL	KS 529 Schwab CSP Mdt Aggr Port		B	(800) 345-6488	C / 5.1	5.62	6.67	18.62 /46	4.73 /51	8.56 /47	0.00	1.33
GL	KS 529 Schwab CSP Mdt Csv Port		C+	(800) 345-6488	D+ / 2.4	3.36	2.41	10.06 /12	3.07 /32	5.03 /21	0.00	1.13
GL	KS 529 Schwab CSP Moderate Port		B-	(800) 345-6488	C- / 3.7	4.54	4.68	14.54 /28	3.96 /42	6.92 /34	0.00	1.24
GR	Lateef A	LIMAX	E	(866) 499-2151	C- / 3.0	5.80	7.22	15.39 /32	4.09 /44	9.69 /56	0.00	1.41
GR	Lateef C	LIMCX	E	(866) 499-2151	C- / 3.3	5.66	6.80	14.46 /28	3.32 /35	8.88 /50	0.00	2.16
GR	Lateef I	LIMIX	E+	(866) 499-2151	C- / 4.2	5.87	7.36	15.68 /33	4.36 /47	9.98 /58	0.00	1.16
FO	Laudus Internatl MarketMasters Inv	SWOIX	D-	(800) 407-0256	D- / 1.4	7.14	4.21	15.82 /34	-0.40 /12	6.06 /29	0.67	1.59
FO	Laudus Internatl MarketMasters Sel	SWMIX	D-	(800) 407-0256	D- / 1.4	7.17	4.29	16.03 /34	-0.24 /12	6.23 /30	0.82	1.50
EM	Laudus Mondrian Emg Mkts Inst	LEMNX	E+	(800) 407-0256	D- / 1.2	8.34	2.09	20.89 /57	-1.60 / 8	-3.13 / 2	2.47	1.21
EM	Laudus Mondrian Emg Mkts Inv	LEMIX	E+	(800) 407-0256	D- / 1.0	8.05	1.82	20.38 /54	-2.01 / 7	-3.53 / 2	2.09	1.61
EM	Laudus Mondrian Emg Mkts Sel	LEMSX	E+	(800) 407-0256	D- / 1.2	8.24	2.15	20.76 /56	-1.72 / 7	-3.22 / 2	2.39	1.30
FO	Laudus Mondrian Intl Eq Inst	LIEIX	E	(800) 407-0256	D / 2.2	7.71	3.34	13.73 /24	0.54 /16	5.69 /26	2.69	1.05
FO	Laudus Mondrian Intl Eq Inv	LIEQX	E	(800) 407-0256	D / 2.0	7.66	3.06	13.12 /22	0.25 /14	5.37 /24	2.42	1.41
FO	Laudus Mondrian Intl Eq Sel	LIEFX	E	(800) 407-0256	D / 2.1	7.82	3.24	13.45 /23	0.44 /15	5.59 /25	2.60	1.18
SC	Laudus Small-Cap MarketMasters Inv	SWOSX	C+	(800) 407-0256	B / 7.7	6.87	13.96	32.48 /91	4.87 /53	10.09 /59	0.14	1.55
SC	Laudus Small-Cap MarketMasters Sel	SWMSX	C+	(800) 407-0256	B / 7.8	6.92	14.06	32.70 /91	5.03 /55	10.27 /60	0.26	1.51
GR	Laudus US Large Cap Growth	LGILX	C-	(800) 407-0256	B- / 7.4	9.65	7.64	22.01 /62	7.18 /73	12.49 /79	0.00	0.75
GL	Lazard Cap Alloc Srs Opp Stra Open	LCAOX	C-	(800) 821-6474	C- / 3.1	5.25	4.39	15.88 /34	2.65 /29	4.09 /16	1.32	2.07
GL	Lazard Capital Allocator Stra Inst	LCAIX	C-	(800) 821-6474	C- / 3.3	5.31	4.45	16.14 /35	3.09 /33	4.48 /18	1.61	1.59
FO	Lazard Developing Markets Eq Inst	LDMIX	C-	(800) 821-6474	C / 5.1	7.31	6.30	33.81 /93	1.44 /21	-2.30 / 3	0.88	1.20
FO	Lazard Developing Markets Eq Open	LDMOX	D+	(800) 821-6474	C / 4.7	7.07	5.95	33.25 /92	1.04 /18	-2.63 / 2	0.58	1.57
CV	Lazard Emerging Markets Debt Inst	LEDIX	E+	(800) 821-6474	D- / 1.4	6.00	-0.78	11.38 /16	0.06 /14	0.63 / 6	5.91	0.91
CV	Lazard Emerging Markets Debt Open	LEDOX	E+	(800) 821-6474	D- / 1.0	6.00	-0.91	11.11 /15	-0.25 /12	0.38 / 5	5.59	1.70
EM	● Lazard Emerging Markets Inst	LZEMX	C-	(800) 821-6474	C+ / 6.2	10.34	7.40	36.24 /95	1.87 /23	0.23 / 5	1.37	1.10
EM	● Lazard Emerging Markets Open	LZOEX	C-	(800) 821-6474	C+ / 6.0	10.31	7.32	35.94 /95	1.61 /22	-0.04 / 4	1.11	1.37
EM	Lazard Emerging Markets R6	RLEMX	U	(800) 821-6474	U /	10.34	7.41	36.27 /95	--	--	1.37	1.13
EM	Lazard Emerging Mkts Core Eq Inst	ECEIX	C-	(800) 821-6474	C- / 3.1	8.99	3.82	22.28 /63	0.65 /16	--	0.71	1.52
EM	Lazard Emerging Mkts Core Eq Open	ECEOX	C-	(800) 821-6474	D+ / 2.9	8.93	3.74	21.98 /62	0.32 /15	--	0.43	2.35
EM	Lazard Emerging Mkts Eq Blend Inst	EMBIX	D+	(800) 821-6474	C / 4.7	8.66	4.95	30.82 /88	1.35 /20	-1.06 / 3	0.46	1.20
EM	Lazard Emerging Mkts Eq Blend	EMBOX	D+	(800) 821-6474	C / 4.4	8.54	4.73	30.38 /87	1.08 /19	-1.32 / 3	0.18	1.54
GR	Lazard Fundamental Long/Short Inst	LLSIX	U	(800) 821-6474	U /	2.10	2.67	-1.59 / 1	--	--	0.00	3.62
GL	Lazard Global Dynamic Mlt Asst Inst	GDMIX	U	(800) 821-6474	U /	5.79	3.09	--	--	--	0.00	1.10
GL	Lazard Global Equity Select Instl	GESIX	C+	(800) 821-6474	C / 4.7	7.52	5.41	17.23 /39	4.64 /50	--	0.66	2.22
GL	Lazard Global Equity Select Open	GESOX	C	(800) 821-6474	C / 4.5	7.40	5.29	16.88 /38	4.36 /47	--	0.39	7.37
OT	Lazard Global Listed Infr Inst	GLIFX	A+	(800) 821-6474	B+ / 8.7	9.37	8.28	14.53 /28	11.62 /98	16.04 /98	2.29	0.96
OT	Lazard Global Listed Infr Open	GLFOX	A	(800) 821-6474	B+ / 8.5	9.29	8.06	14.22 /26	11.33 /97	15.71 /98	2.06	1.23
RE	Lazard Global Realty Equity Inst	LITIX	D+	(800) 821-6474	C- / 3.8	7.22	-1.65	13.28 /23	5.32 /58	7.69 /40	2.93	4.97
RE	Lazard Global Realty Equity Open	LITOX	D	(800) 821-6474	C- / 3.5	7.13	-1.84	12.87 /21	4.99 /54	7.36 /37	2.64	5.55
FO	Lazard Intl Equity Inst	LZIEX	D-	(800) 821-6474	E / 0.4	4.40	-0.75	6.00 / 5	-1.94 / 7	4.78 /20	1.03	0.87
FO	Lazard Intl Equity Open	LZIOX	D-	(800) 821-6474	E / 0.4	4.28	-0.88	5.72 / 4	-2.20 / 6	4.50 /18	0.50	1.14
FO	Lazard Intl Equity R6	RLIEX	U	(800) 821-6474	U /	4.38	-0.78	6.02 / 5	--	--	1.10	0.92
FO	Lazard Intl Equity Select Inst	LZSIX	D-	(800) 821-6474	E+ / 0.7	6.35	0.67	11.03 /15	-1.62 / 8	3.53 /13	1.10	2.13

● Denotes fund is closed to new investors
* Denotes fund is included in Section II

www.thestreetratings.com

RISK			NET ASSETS		ASSET					Portfolio Turnover Ratio	BULL / BEAR		FUND MANAGER		MINIMUMS		LOADS	
Risk Rating/Pts	3 Year		NAV As of 2/28/17	Total $(Mil)	Cash %	Stocks %	Bonds %	Other %		Last Bull Market Return	Last Bear Market Return	Manager Quality Pct	Manager Tenure (Years)	Initial Purch. $	Additional Purch. $	Front End Load	Back End Load
	Standard Deviation	Beta															
C / 5.0	14.6	1.07	6.31	N/A	1	98	0	1	0	87.2	-15.1	37	N/A	100	50	0.0	0.0
C+ / 6.9	10.5	0.73	12.16	102	0	99	0	1	0	116.0	-18.8	98	N/A	500	50	0.0	0.0
B- / 7.1	9.2	0.66	8.19	84	1	88	9	2	0	88.3	-16.8	97	N/A	500	50	0.0	0.0
B- / 7.3	9.2	0.66	7.76	16	1	87	10	2	0	86.5	-17.3	96	N/A	500	50	5.8	0.0
B- / 7.2	9.1	0.66	7.22	6	1	87	10	2	0	79.2	-17.6	95	N/A	500	50	0.0	0.0
B+ / 9.9	3.3	0.23	6.96	184	35	29	34	2	0	28.7	-4.3	89	N/A	500	50	0.0	0.0
B+ / 9.8	3.3	0.23	6.51	16	34	29	36	1	0	26.7	-4.8	87	N/A	500	50	4.5	0.0
B+ / 9.8	3.2	0.22	6.05	7	34	29	36	1	0	21.7	-5.3	84	N/A	500	50	0.0	0.0
B- / 7.5	10.2	0.71	27.06	541	0	0	0	100	0	91.4	-19.4	95	N/A	1,000	50	0.0	0.0
B+ / 9.9	2.6	0.18	17.75	217	0	0	0	100	0	22.1	-3.3	86	N/A	1,000	50	0.0	0.0
B / 8.2	8.6	0.61	25.74	768	0	0	0	100	0	76.7	-16.1	95	N/A	1,000	50	0.0	0.0
B+ / 9.8	4.5	0.33	21.23	229	0	0	0	100	0	40.3	-7.5	90	N/A	1,000	50	0.0	0.0
B+ / 9.0	6.6	0.47	23.71	482	0	0	0	100	0	58.8	-11.9	93	N/A	1,000	50	0.0	0.0
D- / 1.3	13.6	1.22	9.41	27	1	98	0	1	65	98.9	-15.7	3	10	5,000	250	5.0	2.0
E+ / 0.7	13.7	1.22	8.31	22	1	98	0	1	65	91.0	-16.0	3	10	5,000	250	0.0	2.0
D- / 1.4	13.6	1.22	9.67	80	1	98	0	1	65	101.6	-15.6	4	10	1,000,000	0	0.0	2.0
C / 5.4	11.1	0.86	22.00	441	3	93	3	1	69	59.0	-23.7	71	12	100	0	0.0	0.0
C / 5.4	11.1	0.86	21.97	1,071	3	93	3	1	69	60.3	-23.7	73	12	50,000	0	0.0	0.0
C / 4.4	14.4	0.84	7.42	339	3	96	0	1	28	6.9	-20.9	34	N/A	500,000	0	0.0	0.0
C / 4.4	14.5	0.85	7.43	3	3	96	0	1	28	4.5	-21.0	29	N/A	100	0	0.0	0.0
C / 4.4	14.5	0.84	7.43	5	3	96	0	1	28	6.4	-20.9	32	N/A	50,000	0	0.0	0.0
D / 1.7	10.8	0.84	5.94	123	0	97	2	1	29	44.1	-16.8	79	N/A	500,000	0	0.0	0.0
D / 1.7	10.7	0.83	5.88	7	0	97	2	1	29	41.6	-17.0	77	N/A	100	0	0.0	0.0
D / 1.7	10.8	0.84	5.92	6	0	97	2	1	29	43.4	-16.8	78	N/A	50,000	0	0.0	0.0
C / 4.4	16.0	1.00	19.19	65	1	96	1	2	85	102.0	-25.9	49	5	100	0	0.0	0.0
C / 4.4	16.0	1.00	19.57	111	1	96	1	2	85	103.9	-25.9	52	5	50,000	0	0.0	0.0
D+ / 2.8	13.0	1.09	17.90	1,675	0	98	1	1	82	124.2	-15.4	23	4	100	0	0.0	0.0
B- / 7.1	7.2	0.53	10.07	1	14	39	46	1	255	39.6	-13.0	89	9	2,500	50	0.0	1.0
B- / 7.1	7.2	0.53	10.12	158	14	39	46	1	255	42.5	-12.7	91	9	100,000	50	0.0	1.0
C- / 4.2	17.8	1.02	11.12	206	0	98	1	1	66	14.7	-32.3	84	30	100,000	50	0.0	1.0
C / 4.3	17.8	1.03	11.11	7	0	98	1	1	66	12.7	-32.4	82	30	2,500	50	0.0	1.0
C / 4.7	8.8	0.42	8.14	244	1	0	98	1	162	14.9	-5.8	48	6	100,000	50	0.0	1.0
C / 4.7	8.8	0.42	8.22	8	1	0	98	1	162	13.5	-6.0	43	6	2,500	50	0.0	1.0
C- / 3.7	17.7	1.04	17.21	10,497	0	93	6	1	14	25.4	-23.1	75	23	100,000	50	0.0	1.0
C- / 3.7	17.7	1.04	17.69	1,352	0	93	6	1	14	23.6	-23.2	72	23	2,500	50	0.0	1.0
U /	N/A	N/A	17.20	208	0	93	6	1	14	N/A	N/A	N/A	23	1,000,000	0	0.0	1.0
C+ / 6.5	14.1	0.83	9.55	129	1	98	0	1	46	N/A	N/A	65	4	100,000	50	0.0	1.0
C+ / 6.5	14.1	0.83	9.53	1	1	98	0	1	46	N/A	N/A	61	4	2,500	50	0.0	1.0
C / 4.4	16.3	0.97	10.40	301	1	98	0	1	38	19.1	-27.0	71	7	100,000	50	0.0	1.0
C / 4.5	16.4	0.97	10.41	7	1	98	0	1	38	17.4	-27.2	67	7	2,500	50	0.0	1.0
U /	N/A	N/A	11.16	111	70	29	0	1	183	N/A	N/A	N/A	3	100,000	50	0.0	1.0
U /	N/A	N/A	10.46	50	1	68	30	1	0	N/A	N/A	N/A	1	100,000	50	0.0	1.0
C+ / 6.7	10.8	0.77	11.21	33	1	98	0	1	55	N/A	N/A	95	4	2,500	50	0.0	1.0
C+ / 6.7	10.8	0.78	11.21	1	1	98	0	1	55	N/A	N/A	94	4	100,000	50	0.0	1.0
B- / 7.0	8.0	0.46	14.87	2,991	19	80	0	1	34	127.1	-9.8	97	8	100,000	50	0.0	1.0
B- / 7.0	8.0	0.46	14.89	463	19	80	0	1	34	123.6	-10.1	97	8	2,500	50	0.0	1.0
C / 4.7	11.5	0.74	14.87	3	11	88	0	1	56	77.6	N/A	39	9	100,000	50	0.0	1.0
C / 4.7	11.5	0.74	14.84	2	11	88	0	1	56	74.9	-24.5	35	9	2,500	50	0.0	1.0
C+ / 6.3	10.7	0.83	16.62	1,546	4	95	0	1	30	50.1	-19.6	51	26	100,000	50	0.0	1.0
C+ / 6.4	10.7	0.82	16.80	1,081	4	95	0	1	30	47.7	-19.7	47	26	2,500	50	0.0	1.0
U /	N/A	N/A	16.60	94	4	95	0	1	30	N/A	N/A	N/A	26	1,000,000	0	0.0	1.0
C+ / 5.7	11.1	0.85	9.05	32	0	95	4	1	51	41.9	-19.8	55	16	100,000	50	0.0	1.0

I. Index of Stock Mutual Funds

Fund Type	Fund Name	Ticker Symbol	Overall Investment Rating	Phone	Performance Rating/Pts	3 Mo	6 Mo	1Yr / Pct	3Yr / Pct	5Yr / Pct	Dividend Yield	Expense Ratio
FO	Lazard Intl Equity Select Open	LZESX	D-	(800) 821-6474	E+ / 0.6	6.34	0.55	10.70 /14	-1.96 / 7	3.17 /11	0.81	2.75
FO	Lazard Intl Small Cap Eq Inst	LZISX	D	(800) 821-6474	D- / 1.4	4.79	0.45	7.20 / 6	1.06 /19	8.52 /46	2.84	1.11
FO	Lazard Intl Small Cap Eq Open	LZSMX	D	(800) 821-6474	D- / 1.3	4.71	0.38	6.95 / 6	0.79 /17	8.23 /44	2.33	1.38
FO	Lazard Intl Strategic Equity Inst	LISIX	E+	(800) 821-6474	E / 0.4	4.55	-1.83	4.46 / 3	-2.27 / 6	5.76 /27	1.55	0.82
FO	Lazard Intl Strategic Equity R6	RLITX	U	(800) 821-6474	U /	4.54	-1.83	4.46 / 3	--	--	1.55	1.09
FO	Lazard Intl Strategic EquityOpen	LISOX	E+	(800) 821-6474	E / 0.3	4.49	-1.92	4.16 / 3	-2.53 / 5	5.50 /25	1.29	1.08
GI	Lazard US Eqty Concentrated Inst	LEVIX	A	(800) 821-6474	B+ / 8.4	6.26	3.16	18.11 /43	11.97 /98	14.81 /96	0.31	0.79
GI	Lazard US Eqty Concentrated Open	LEVOX	A	(800) 821-6474	B / 8.2	6.17	3.02	17.78 /42	11.61 /98	14.41 /95	0.07	1.07
RE	Lazard US Realty Equity Inst	LREIX	C+	(800) 821-6474	B / 7.6	8.89	0.47	17.69 /41	10.28 /95	10.94 /65	1.50	1.09
RE	Lazard US Realty Equity Open	LREOX	C+	(800) 821-6474	B- / 7.3	8.82	0.33	17.35 /40	9.96 /93	10.66 /63	1.22	1.32
RE	Lazard US Realty Income Inst	LRIIX	D	(800) 821-6474	C- / 4.1	7.15	0.94	17.95 /43	4.37 /47	7.61 /39	4.06	0.98
RE	Lazard US Realty Income Open	LRIOX	D	(800) 821-6474	C- / 3.9	7.24	0.80	17.67 /41	4.12 /44	7.32 /37	3.80	1.23
SC	Lazard US Sm-Mid Cap Eq Inst	LZSCX	C	(800) 821-6474	B / 7.8	5.03	11.38	26.85 /79	7.54 /76	12.84 /82	0.59	0.91
SC	Lazard US Sm-Mid Cap Eq Open	LZCOX	C	(800) 821-6474	B / 7.6	4.99	11.22	26.49 /78	7.19 /73	12.48 /79	0.36	1.20
GR	Lazard US Strategic Equity Inst	LZUSX	C+	(800) 821-6474	B- / 7.4	7.28	8.41	23.30 /67	7.64 /76	11.52 /70	0.75	0.90
GR	Lazard US Strategic Equity Open	LZUOX	C+	(800) 821-6474	B- / 7.2	7.24	8.27	22.88 /66	7.33 /74	11.18 /67	0.49	1.51
SC	Lebenthal Lisanti Small Cap Growth	ASCGX	D+	(800) 754-8757	C+ / 6.0	4.28	10.57	32.12 /90	3.07 /32	12.16 /76	0.00	2.26
GR	Legg Mason CO Sc Cho Equity 80%		B	(877) 534-4627	C / 5.5	6.27	7.81	20.63 /56	5.76 /62	9.68 /56	0.00	1.16
GR	Legg Mason CO Sc Cho Equity 80%		B	(877) 534-4627	C+ / 5.6	6.08	7.42	19.75 /51	5.02 /54	8.92 /50	0.00	1.86
GR	Legg Mason CO Sc Cho Equity 80%		B	(877) 534-4627	C+ / 5.8	6.17	7.56	20.04 /52	5.24 /57	9.14 /52	0.00	1.66
GR	Legg Mason CO Sc Cho Equity 80%		B	(877) 534-4627	C+ / 6.2	6.31	7.84	20.69 /56	5.78 /62	9.72 /56	0.00	1.09
GR	Legg Mason CO Sch Ch All Equity A		C+	(877) 534-4627	C+ / 6.6	7.25	9.77	24.09 /70	6.27 /66	11.06 /66	0.00	1.23
GR	Legg Mason CO Sch Ch All Equity B		C+	(877) 534-4627	C+ / 6.7	7.04	9.42	23.29 /67	5.52 /60	10.29 /61	0.00	1.93
GR	Legg Mason CO Sch Ch All Equity C		C+	(877) 534-4627	C+ / 6.8	7.06	9.50	23.50 /68	5.73 /62	10.51 /62	0.00	1.73
GR	Legg Mason CO Sch Ch All Equity O		B+	(877) 534-4627	B- / 7.2	7.23	9.80	24.21 /71	6.34 /67	11.17 /67	0.00	1.09
GI	Legg Mason WY Sch Ch Age-Bsd		C	(877) 534-4627	E / 0.5	0.58	0.00	1.23 / 2	0.36 /15	0.32 / 5	0.00	0.86
GI	Legg Mason WY Sch Ch Age-Bsd		C	(877) 534-4627	E / 0.5	0.40	-0.32	0.48 / 2	-0.34 /12	-0.38 / 4	0.00	1.56
GI	Legg Mason WY Sch Ch Age-Bsd		C	(877) 534-4627	E+ / 0.6	0.46	-0.23	0.70 / 2	-0.13 /13	-0.18 / 4	0.00	1.36
GI	Legg Mason WY Sch Ch Age-Bsd		C	(877) 534-4627	E+ / 0.6	0.53	-0.15	0.83 / 2	-0.07 /13	-0.12 / 4	0.00	1.09
GR	Legg Mason WY Sch Ch All Equity A		B-	(877) 534-4627	C+ / 6.6	7.25	9.77	24.09 /70	6.27 /66	11.06 /66	0.00	1.14
GR	Legg Mason WY Sch Ch All Equity B		B-	(877) 534-4627	C+ / 6.7	7.04	9.42	23.29 /67	5.52 /60	10.29 /61	0.00	1.84
GR	Legg Mason WY Sch Ch All Equity C		B-	(877) 534-4627	C+ / 6.8	7.06	9.50	23.50 /68	5.73 /62	10.51 /62	0.00	1.64
GR	Legg Mason WY Sch Ch All Equity O		B+	(877) 534-4627	B- / 7.2	7.23	9.80	24.21 /71	6.34 /67	11.17 /67	0.00	1.09
BA	Legg Mason WY Sch Ch Balanc		B-	(877) 534-4627	C- / 3.5	4.77	4.91	14.96 /30	4.60 /50	7.10 /35	0.00	0.99
BA	Legg Mason WY Sch Ch Balanc		B-	(877) 534-4627	C- / 3.6	4.60	4.55	14.13 /26	3.88 /41	6.35 /31	0.00	1.69
BA	Legg Mason WY Sch Ch Balanc		B-	(877) 534-4627	C- / 3.8	4.64	4.70	14.38 /27	4.09 /44	6.56 /32	0.00	1.49
BA	Legg Mason WY Sch Ch Balanc		B	(877) 534-4627	C- / 4.1	4.76	4.85	14.86 /29	4.50 /49	7.00 /35	0.00	1.09
GR	Legg Mason WY Sch Ch Equity 80%		B	(877) 534-4627	C / 5.5	6.27	7.81	20.63 /56	5.76 /62	9.68 /56	0.00	1.10
GR	Legg Mason WY Sch Ch Equity 80%		B	(877) 534-4627	C+ / 5.6	6.08	7.42	19.75 /51	5.02 /54	8.92 /50	0.00	1.80
GR	Legg Mason WY Sch Ch Equity 80%		B	(877) 534-4627	C+ / 5.8	6.17	7.56	20.04 /52	5.24 /57	9.14 /52	0.00	1.60
GR	Legg Mason WY Sch Ch Equity 80%		B	(877) 534-4627	C+ / 6.2	6.31	7.84	20.69 /56	5.78 /62	9.72 /56	0.00	1.09
GI	Legg Mason WY Schr Ch Age-Bsd		B	(877) 534-4627	C / 4.9	5.88	6.87	18.99 /47	5.45 /59	8.94 /50	0.00	1.06
GI	Legg Mason WY Schr Ch Age-Bsd		B	(877) 534-4627	C / 5.0	5.67	6.51	18.15 /44	4.72 /51	8.19 /44	0.00	1.76
GI	Legg Mason WY Schr Ch Age-Bsd		B	(877) 534-4627	C / 5.2	5.73	6.64	18.40 /45	4.93 /53	8.40 /45	0.00	N/A
GI	Legg Mason WY Schr Ch Age-Bsd		B	(877) 534-4627	C+ / 5.6	5.88	6.86	18.98 /47	5.43 /59	8.93 /50	0.00	1.09
GI	Legg Mason WY Schr Ch Age-Bsd		B	(877) 534-4627	C / 4.3	5.43	5.85	17.29 /40	5.20 /56	8.20 /44	0.00	1.03
GI	Legg Mason WY Schr Ch Age-Bsd		B	(877) 534-4627	C / 4.4	5.26	5.47	16.43 /36	4.47 /48	7.44 /38	0.00	1.73
GI	Legg Mason WY Schr Ch Age-Bsd		B	(877) 534-4627	C / 4.6	5.33	5.63	16.66 /37	4.68 /51	7.66 /39	0.00	1.53
GI	Legg Mason WY Schr Ch Age-Bsd		B+	(877) 534-4627	C / 5.0	5.45	5.82	17.18 /39	5.15 /56	8.15 /43	0.00	1.09
BA	LeggMason CO Sc Ch Balanced		B-	(877) 534-4627	C- / 3.5	4.77	4.91	14.96 /30	4.60 /50	7.10 /35	0.00	1.04
BA	LeggMason CO Sc Ch Balanced		B-	(877) 534-4627	C- / 3.6	4.60	4.55	14.13 /26	3.88 /41	6.35 /31	0.00	1.74
BA	LeggMason CO Sc Ch Balanced		B-	(877) 534-4627	C- / 3.8	4.64	4.70	14.38 /27	4.09 /44	6.56 /32	0.00	1.54

● Denotes fund is closed to new investors
* Denotes fund is included in Section II

www.thestreetratings.com

I. Index of Stock Mutual Funds

Risk Rating/Pts	Standard Deviation	Beta	NAV As of 2/28/17	Total $(Mil)	Cash %	Stocks %	Bonds %	Other %	Portfolio Turnover Ratio	Last Bull Market Return	Last Bear Market Return	Manager Quality Pct	Manager Tenure (Years)	Initial Purch. $	Additional Purch. $	Front End Load	Back End Load
C+ / 5.8	11.1	0.85	9.06	2	0	95	4	1	51	39.5	-20.1	51	16	2,500	50	0.0	1.0
C+ / 6.6	11.3	0.78	10.51	38	0	97	2	1	48	69.8	-20.0	82	26	100,000	50	0.0	1.0
C+ / 6.6	11.2	0.78	10.56	45	0	97	2	1	48	67.3	-20.1	80	26	2,500	50	0.0	1.0
C+ / 5.7	10.7	0.81	12.83	5,254	0	93	6	1	37	56.1	-21.8	46	12	100,000	50	0.0	1.0
U /	N/A	N/A	12.84	105	0	93	6	1	37	N/A	N/A	N/A	12	1,000,000	0	0.0	1.0
C+ / 5.7	10.7	0.81	12.93	1,544	0	93	6	1	37	53.9	-21.9	42	12	2,500	50	0.0	1.0
B- / 7.0	10.6	0.93	14.90	1,283	0	93	6	1	74	147.5	-20.2	86	6	100,000	50	0.0	1.0
B- / 7.1	10.6	0.93	14.99	104	0	93	6	1	74	143.0	-20.3	84	6	2,500	50	0.0	1.0
C / 4.7	12.9	0.93	20.31	20	2	97	0	1	51	118.7	N/A	74	9	100,000	50	0.0	1.0
C / 4.7	12.9	0.93	20.38	58	2	97	0	1	51	115.7	-19.3	71	9	2,500	50	0.0	1.0
C- / 3.8	11.7	0.78	7.63	18	3	96	0	1	60	69.5	N/A	24	9	100,000	50	0.0	1.0
C- / 3.8	11.8	0.79	7.61	23	3	96	0	1	60	67.1	-13.6	20	9	2,500	50	0.0	1.0
C- / 3.5	13.8	0.85	14.76	187	1	98	0	1	91	132.2	-29.1	84	14	100,000	50	0.0	1.0
C- / 3.3	13.7	0.85	13.92	29	1	98	0	1	91	128.3	-29.2	82	14	2,500	50	0.0	1.0
C / 4.6	11.2	1.05	12.25	73	1	97	1	1	75	109.4	-17.0	31	13	100,000	50	0.0	1.0
C / 4.6	11.2	1.05	12.29	1	1	97	1	1	75	106.1	-17.2	28	13	2,500	50	0.0	1.0
D+ / 2.7	17.6	1.00	19.47	24	5	94	0	1	196	115.5	-26.4	27	13	2,000	250	0.0	1.0
B / 8.0	9.1	0.86	23.74	247	0	0	0	100	0	88.3	-15.7	33	18	250	50	3.5	0.0
B / 8.0	9.1	0.86	21.28	4	0	0	0	100	0	81.3	-16.0	26	18	250	50	0.0	0.0
B / 8.0	9.1	0.86	22.04	121	0	0	0	100	0	83.4	-15.9	28	18	250	50	0.0	0.0
B / 8.0	9.1	0.86	23.92	9	0	0	0	100	0	88.6	-15.7	34	18	250	50	0.0	0.0
C+ / 6.7	11.1	1.05	18.65	349	2	96	0	2	0	106.3	-19.4	19	17	250	50	3.5	0.0
C+ / 6.6	11.1	1.04	16.73	13	2	96	0	2	0	98.7	-19.7	14	17	250	50	0.0	0.0
C+ / 6.6	11.1	1.05	17.29	225	2	96	0	2	0	100.8	-19.7	15	17	250	50	0.0	0.0
C+ / 6.7	11.1	1.05	18.83	18	2	96	0	2	0	107.4	-19.4	20	17	250	50	0.0	0.0
B+ / 9.9	1.0	0.01	13.99	142	0	0	0	100	0	2.5	-0.4	75	18	250	50	3.5	0.0
B+ / 9.9	1.0	0.01	12.57	7	0	0	0	100	0	-1.3	-0.7	68	18	250	50	0.0	0.0
B+ / 9.9	0.9	0.01	12.97	140	0	0	0	100	0	-0.2	-0.6	70	18	250	50	0.0	0.0
B+ / 9.9	1.0	0.01	13.32	19	0	0	0	100	0	0.1	-0.6	71	18	250	50	0.0	0.0
B- / 7.3	11.1	1.05	18.65	349	0	0	0	100	0	106.3	-19.4	19	17	250	50	3.5	0.0
B- / 7.2	11.1	1.04	16.73	13	0	0	0	100	0	98.7	-19.7	14	17	250	50	0.0	0.0
B- / 7.3	11.1	1.05	17.29	225	0	0	0	100	0	100.8	-19.7	15	17	250	50	0.0	0.0
B- / 7.3	11.1	1.05	18.83	18	0	0	0	100	0	107.4	-19.4	20	17	250	50	0.0	0.0
B+ / 9.1	6.1	0.95	23.29	424	0	0	0	100	0	59.3	-9.8	43	18	250	50	3.5	0.0
B+ / 9.0	6.1	0.95	20.92	13	0	0	0	100	0	53.3	-10.0	34	18	250	50	0.0	0.0
B+ / 9.1	6.1	0.95	21.63	273	0	0	0	100	0	55.1	-10.0	36	18	250	50	0.0	0.0
B+ / 9.1	6.1	0.95	23.11	24	0	0	0	100	0	58.5	-9.8	42	18	250	50	0.0	0.0
B / 8.0	9.1	0.86	23.74	247	0	0	0	100	0	88.3	-15.7	33	18	250	50	3.5	0.0
B / 8.0	9.1	0.86	21.28	4	0	0	0	100	0	81.3	-16.0	26	18	250	50	0.0	0.0
B / 8.0	9.1	0.86	22.04	121	0	0	0	100	0	83.4	-15.9	28	18	250	50	0.0	0.0
B / 8.0	9.1	0.86	23.92	9	0	0	0	100	0	88.6	-15.7	34	18	250	50	0.0	0.0
B / 8.4	8.1	0.77	24.12	141	0	0	0	100	0	79.5	-13.7	41	18	250	50	3.5	0.0
B / 8.3	8.1	0.77	21.61	1	0	0	0	100	0	72.7	-13.9	32	18	250	50	0.0	0.0
B / 8.3	8.1	0.77	22.33	46	0	0	0	100	0	74.6	-13.8	35	18	250	50	0.0	0.0
B / 8.4	8.1	0.77	24.13	2	0	0	0	100	0	79.4	-13.7	41	18	250	50	0.0	0.0
B / 8.7	7.2	0.68	23.88	196	0	0	0	100	0	70.8	-11.6	51	18	250	50	3.5	0.0
B / 8.6	7.2	0.68	21.40	5	0	0	0	100	0	64.4	-11.9	41	18	250	50	0.0	0.0
B / 8.7	7.2	0.68	22.13	91	0	0	0	100	0	66.1	-11.7	44	18	250	50	0.0	0.0
B / 8.7	7.2	0.68	23.81	5	0	0	0	100	0	70.4	-11.6	50	18	250	50	0.0	0.0
B+ / 9.1	6.1	0.95	23.29	424	0	0	0	100	0	59.3	-9.8	43	18	250	50	3.5	0.0
B+ / 9.0	6.1	0.95	20.92	13	0	0	0	100	0	53.3	-10.0	34	18	250	50	0.0	0.0
B+ / 9.1	6.1	0.95	21.63	273	0	0	0	100	0	55.1	-10.0	36	18	250	50	0.0	0.0

Data as of February 28, 2017

I. Index of Stock Mutual Funds

99 Pct = Best
0 Pct = Worst

Fund Type	Fund Name	Ticker Symbol	Overall Investment Rating	Phone	Performance Rating/Pts	3 Mo	6 Mo	1Yr / Pct	3Yr / Pct	5Yr / Pct	Dividend Yield	Expense Ratio
BA	LeggMason CO Sc Ch Balanced		B	(877) 534-4627	C- / 4.1	4.76	4.85	14.86 /29	4.50 /49	7.00 /35	0.00	1.09
GI	LeggMason CO SC Yr to Enr 10-12 A		B	(877) 534-4627	C / 4.3	5.43	5.85	17.29 /40	5.20 /56	8.20 /44	0.00	1.07
GI	LeggMason CO SC Yr to Enr 10-12 B		B	(877) 534-4627	C / 4.4	5.26	5.47	16.43 /36	4.47 /48	7.44 /38	0.00	1.77
GI	LeggMason CO SC Yr to Enr 10-12 C		B	(877) 534-4627	C / 4.6	5.33	5.63	16.66 /37	4.68 /51	7.66 /39	0.00	1.57
GI	LeggMason CO SC Yr to Enr 10-12 O		B+	(877) 534-4627	C / 5.0	5.45	5.82	17.18 /39	5.15 /56	8.15 /43	0.00	1.09
GI	LeggMason CO SC Yr to Enr 1-3 A		C	(877) 534-4627	D- / 1.4	2.41	2.00	6.26 / 5	2.50 /28	3.49 /13	0.00	0.81
GI	LeggMason CO SC Yr to Enr 1-3 B		C+	(877) 534-4627	D- / 1.5	2.24	1.65	5.48 / 4	1.79 /23	2.77 /10	0.00	1.51
GI	LeggMason CO SC Yr to Enr 1-3 C		C+	(877) 534-4627	D / 1.6	2.23	1.72	5.69 / 4	1.99 /24	2.97 /11	0.00	1.31
GI	LeggMason CO SC Yr to Enr 1-3 O		C+	(877) 534-4627	D / 1.6	2.31	1.89	5.88 / 5	2.17 /25	3.16 /11	0.00	1.09
GI	LeggMason CO SC Yr to Enr 4-6 A		C+	(877) 534-4627	D+ / 2.7	4.06	4.21	12.03 /18	3.95 /42	6.06 /29	0.00	1.12
GI	LeggMason CO SC Yr to Enr 4-6 B		C+	(877) 534-4627	D+ / 2.8	3.91	3.91	11.27 /15	3.24 /34	5.31 /23	0.00	1.65
GI	LeggMason CO SC Yr to Enr 4-6 C		B-	(877) 534-4627	C- / 3.0	3.94	4.00	11.55 /16	3.45 /36	5.53 /25	0.00	1.45
GI	LeggMason CO SC Yr to Enr 4-6 O		B-	(877) 534-4627	C- / 3.2	3.98	4.08	11.81 /17	3.75 /40	5.85 /27	0.00	1.09
GI	LeggMason CO SC Yr to Enr 7-9 A		B-	(877) 534-4627	C- / 3.5	4.77	4.91	14.96 /30	4.60 /50	7.10 /35	0.00	1.07
GI	LeggMason CO SC Yr to Enr 7-9 B		B-	(877) 534-4627	C- / 3.6	4.60	4.55	14.13 /26	3.88 /41	6.35 /31	0.00	1.74
GI	LeggMason CO SC Yr to Enr 7-9 C		B-	(877) 534-4627	C- / 3.8	4.64	4.70	14.38 /27	4.09 /44	6.56 /32	0.00	1.54
GI	LeggMason CO SC Yr to Enr 7-9 O		B	(877) 534-4627	C- / 4.1	4.76	4.85	14.86 /29	4.50 /49	7.00 /35	0.00	1.09
GI	LeggMason CO Sch Ch Age-Bsd		C+	(877) 534-4627	C- / 3.5	4.77	4.91	14.96 /30	4.60 /50	7.10 /35	0.00	1.04
GI	LeggMason CO Sch Ch Age-Bsd		C+	(877) 534-4627	C- / 3.6	4.60	4.55	14.13 /26	3.88 /41	6.35 /31	0.00	1.74
GI	LeggMason CO Sch Ch Age-Bsd		C+	(877) 534-4627	C- / 3.8	4.64	4.70	14.38 /27	4.09 /44	6.56 /32	0.00	1.54
GI	LeggMason CO Sch Ch Age-Bsd		B-	(877) 534-4627	C- / 4.1	4.76	4.85	14.86 /29	4.50 /49	7.00 /35	0.00	1.09
GI	LeggMason CO Sch Ch Age-Bsd		C+	(877) 534-4627	D+ / 2.7	4.06	4.21	12.03 /18	3.95 /42	6.06 /29	0.00	0.95
GI	LeggMason CO Sch Ch Age-Bsd		C+	(877) 534-4627	D+ / 2.8	3.91	3.91	11.27 /15	3.24 /34	5.31 /23	0.00	1.65
GI	LeggMason CO Sch Ch Age-Bsd		C+	(877) 534-4627	C- / 3.0	3.94	4.00	11.55 /16	3.45 /36	5.53 /25	0.00	1.45
GI	LeggMason CO Sch Ch Age-Bsd		C+	(877) 534-4627	C- / 3.2	3.98	4.08	11.81 /17	3.75 /40	5.85 /27	0.00	1.09
GI	LeggMason CO Sch Ch Age-Bsd		C	(877) 534-4627	D- / 1.4	2.41	2.00	6.26 / 5	2.50 /28	3.49 /13	0.00	0.81
GI	LeggMason CO Sch Ch Age-Bsd		C	(877) 534-4627	D- / 1.5	2.24	1.65	5.48 / 4	1.79 /23	2.77 /10	0.00	1.51
GI	LeggMason CO Sch Ch Age-Bsd		C	(877) 534-4627	D / 1.6	2.23	1.72	5.69 / 4	1.99 /24	2.97 /11	0.00	1.31
GI	LeggMason CO Sch Ch Age-Bsd		C	(877) 534-4627	D / 1.6	2.31	1.89	5.88 / 5	2.17 /25	3.16 /11	0.00	1.09
GI	LeggMason CO Sch Ch Age-Bsd 19+		C	(877) 534-4627	E / 0.5	0.58	0.00	1.23 / 2	0.36 /15	0.32 / 5	0.00	0.71
GI	LeggMason CO Sch Ch Age-Bsd 19+		C	(877) 534-4627	E / 0.5	0.40	-0.32	0.48 / 2	-0.34 /12	-0.38 / 4	0.00	1.41
GI	LeggMason CO Sch Ch Age-Bsd 19+		C	(877) 534-4627	E+ / 0.6	0.46	-0.23	0.70 / 2	-0.13 /13	-0.18 / 4	0.00	1.21
GI	LeggMason CO Sch Ch Age-Bsd 19+		C	(877) 534-4627	E+ / 0.6	0.53	-0.15	0.83 / 2	-0.07 /13	-0.12 / 4	0.00	1.09
GR	LeggMason CO Schr Ch Age-Bsd 0-3		B-	(877) 534-4627	C / 5.5	6.27	7.81	20.63 /56	5.76 /62	9.68 /56	0.00	1.16
GR	LeggMason CO Schr Ch Age-Bsd 0-3		B-	(877) 534-4627	C+ / 5.6	6.08	7.42	19.75 /51	5.02 /54	8.92 /50	0.00	1.86
GR	LeggMason CO Schr Ch Age-Bsd 0-3		B-	(877) 534-4627	C+ / 5.8	6.17	7.56	20.04 /52	5.24 /57	9.14 /52	0.00	1.66
GR	LeggMason CO Schr Ch Age-Bsd 0-3		B-	(877) 534-4627	C+ / 6.2	6.31	7.84	20.69 /56	5.78 /62	9.72 /56	0.00	1.09
GI	LeggMason CO Schr Ch Age-Bsd 4-6		B-	(877) 534-4627	C / 4.9	5.88	6.87	18.99 /47	5.45 /59	8.94 /50	0.00	1.12
GI	LeggMason CO Schr Ch Age-Bsd 4-6		B	(877) 534-4627	C / 5.0	5.67	6.51	18.15 /44	4.72 /51	8.19 /44	0.00	1.82
GI	LeggMason CO Schr Ch Age-Bsd 4-6		B	(877) 534-4627	C / 5.2	5.73	6.64	18.40 /45	4.93 /53	8.40 /45	0.00	1.62
GI	LeggMason CO Schr Ch Age-Bsd 4-6		B	(877) 534-4627	C+ / 5.6	5.88	6.86	18.98 /47	5.43 /59	8.93 /50	0.00	1.09
GI	LeggMason CO Schr Ch Age-Bsd 7-9		B-	(877) 534-4627	C / 4.3	5.43	5.85	17.29 /40	5.20 /56	8.20 /44	0.00	1.07
GI	LeggMason CO Schr Ch Age-Bsd 7-9		B-	(877) 534-4627	C / 4.4	5.26	5.47	16.43 /36	4.47 /48	7.44 /38	0.00	1.77
GI	LeggMason CO Schr Ch Age-Bsd 7-9		B-	(877) 534-4627	C / 4.6	5.33	5.63	16.66 /37	4.68 /51	7.66 /39	0.00	1.57
GI	LeggMason CO Schr Ch Age-Bsd 7-9		B	(877) 534-4627	C / 5.0	5.45	5.82	17.18 /39	5.15 /56	8.15 /43	0.00	1.09
GI	LeggMason WY SC Yrs To Enr 10-12		B	(877) 534-4627	C / 4.3	5.43	5.85	17.29 /40	5.20 /56	8.20 /44	0.00	1.03
GI	LeggMason WY SC Yrs To Enr 10-12		B	(877) 534-4627	C / 4.4	5.26	5.47	16.43 /36	4.47 /48	7.44 /38	0.00	1.73
GI	LeggMason WY SC Yrs To Enr 10-12		B	(877) 534-4627	C / 4.6	5.33	5.63	16.66 /37	4.68 /51	7.66 /39	0.00	1.53
GI	LeggMason WY SC Yrs To Enr 10-12		B+	(877) 534-4627	C / 5.1	5.45	5.82	17.18 /39	5.15 /56	8.15 /43	0.00	1.09
GI	LeggMason WY Sch Ch Age-Bsd		B-	(877) 534-4627	C- / 3.5	4.77	4.91	14.96 /30	4.60 /50	7.10 /35	0.00	0.99
GI	LeggMason WY Sch Ch Age-Bsd		B-	(877) 534-4627	C- / 3.6	4.60	4.55	14.13 /26	3.88 /41	6.35 /31	0.00	1.69
GI	LeggMason WY Sch Ch Age-Bsd		B-	(877) 534-4627	C- / 3.8	4.64	4.70	14.38 /27	4.09 /44	6.56 /32	0.00	1.49

● Denotes fund is closed to new investors
∗ Denotes fund is included in Section II

RISK Risk Rating/Pts	3 Year Standard Deviation	Beta	NET ASSETS NAV As of 2/28/17	Total $(Mil)	ASSET Cash %	Stocks %	Bonds %	Other %	Portfolio Turnover Ratio	BULL / BEAR Last Bull Market Return	Last Bear Market Return	FUND MANAGER Manager Quality Pct	Manager Tenure (Years)	MINIMUMS Initial Purch. $	Additional Purch. $	LOADS Front End Load	Back End Load
B+ / 9.1	6.1	0.95	23.11	24	0	0	0	100	0	58.5	-9.8	42	18	250	50	0.0	0.0
B / 8.7	7.2	0.68	23.88	196	0	0	0	100	0	70.8	-11.6	51	18	250	50	3.5	0.0
B / 8.6	7.2	0.68	21.40	5	0	0	0	100	0	64.4	-11.9	41	18	250	50	0.0	0.0
B / 8.7	7.2	0.68	22.13	91	0	0	0	100	0	66.1	-11.7	44	18	250	50	0.0	0.0
B / 8.7	7.2	0.68	23.81	5	0	0	0	100	0	70.4	-11.6	50	18	250	50	0.0	0.0
B+ / 9.9	2.6	0.23	17.82	315	0	0	0	100	0	25.6	-3.3	74	18	250	50	3.5	0.0
B+ / 9.9	2.6	0.22	15.98	15	0	0	0	100	0	21.0	-3.6	67	18	250	50	0.0	0.0
B+ / 9.9	2.5	0.22	16.53	257	0	0	0	100	0	22.3	-3.5	70	18	250	50	0.0	0.0
B+ / 9.9	2.6	0.23	17.28	40	0	0	0	100	0	23.5	-3.5	71	18	250	50	0.0	0.0
B+ / 9.6	4.9	0.46	21.04	386	0	0	0	100	0	48.5	-7.5	64	18	250	50	3.5	0.0
B+ / 9.5	4.9	0.46	18.86	16	0	0	0	100	0	43.0	-7.8	55	18	250	50	0.0	0.0
B+ / 9.6	4.9	0.46	19.51	235	0	0	0	100	0	44.5	-7.7	57	18	250	50	0.0	0.0
B+ / 9.6	4.9	0.46	20.64	18	0	0	0	100	0	47.0	-7.6	62	18	250	50	0.0	0.0
B+ / 9.1	6.1	0.57	23.29	424	0	0	0	100	0	59.3	-9.8	58	18	250	50	3.5	0.0
B+ / 9.0	6.1	0.57	20.92	13	0	0	0	100	0	53.3	-10.0	48	18	250	50	0.0	0.0
B+ / 9.1	6.1	0.57	21.63	273	0	0	0	100	0	55.1	-10.0	51	18	250	50	0.0	0.0
B+ / 9.1	6.1	0.57	23.11	24	0	0	0	100	0	58.5	-9.8	57	18	250	50	0.0	0.0
B / 8.7	6.1	0.57	23.29	424	1	48	50	1	0	59.3	-9.8	58	18	250	50	3.5	0.0
B / 8.6	6.1	0.57	20.92	13	1	48	50	1	0	53.3	-10.0	48	18	250	50	0.0	0.0
B / 8.6	6.1	0.57	21.63	273	1	48	50	1	0	55.1	-10.0	51	18	250	50	0.0	0.0
B / 8.7	6.1	0.57	23.11	24	1	48	50	1	0	58.5	-9.8	57	18	250	50	0.0	0.0
B+ / 9.2	4.9	0.46	21.04	386	12	38	48	2	0	48.5	-7.5	64	18	250	50	3.5	0.0
B+ / 9.2	4.9	0.46	18.86	16	12	38	48	2	0	43.0	-7.8	55	18	250	50	0.0	0.0
B+ / 9.2	4.9	0.46	19.51	235	12	38	48	2	0	44.5	-7.7	57	18	250	50	0.0	0.0
B+ / 9.2	4.9	0.46	20.64	18	12	38	48	2	0	47.0	-7.6	62	18	250	50	0.0	0.0
B+ / 9.6	2.6	0.23	17.82	315	27	17	54	2	0	25.6	-3.3	74	18	250	50	3.5	0.0
B+ / 9.6	2.6	0.22	15.98	15	27	17	54	2	0	21.0	-3.6	67	18	250	50	0.0	0.0
B+ / 9.6	2.5	0.22	16.53	257	27	17	54	2	0	22.3	-3.5	70	18	250	50	0.0	0.0
B+ / 9.6	2.6	0.23	17.28	40	27	17	54	2	0	23.5	-3.5	71	18	250	50	0.0	0.0
B+ / 9.9	1.0	0.01	13.99	142	52	0	47	1	0	2.5	-0.4	75	18	250	50	3.5	0.0
B+ / 9.9	1.0	0.01	12.57	7	52	0	47	1	0	-1.3	-0.7	68	18	250	50	0.0	0.0
B+ / 9.9	0.9	0.01	12.97	140	52	0	47	1	0	-0.2	-0.6	70	18	250	50	0.0	0.0
B+ / 9.9	1.0	0.01	13.32	19	52	0	47	1	0	0.1	-0.6	71	18	250	50	0.0	0.0
B- / 7.7	9.1	0.86	23.74	247	1	77	20	2	0	88.3	-15.7	33	18	250	50	3.5	0.0
B- / 7.6	9.1	0.86	21.28	4	1	77	20	2	0	81.3	-16.0	26	18	250	50	0.0	0.0
B- / 7.7	9.1	0.86	22.04	121	1	77	20	2	0	83.4	-15.9	28	18	250	50	0.0	0.0
B- / 7.7	9.1	0.86	23.92	9	1	77	20	2	0	88.6	-15.7	34	18	250	50	0.0	0.0
B / 8.1	8.1	0.77	24.12	141	1	67	30	2	0	79.5	-13.7	41	18	250	50	3.5	0.0
B / 8.0	8.1	0.77	21.61	1	1	67	30	2	0	72.7	-13.9	32	18	250	50	0.0	0.0
B / 8.0	8.1	0.77	22.33	46	1	67	30	2	0	74.6	-13.8	35	18	250	50	0.0	0.0
B / 8.0	8.1	0.77	24.13	2	1	67	30	2	0	79.4	-13.7	41	18	250	50	0.0	0.0
B / 8.3	7.2	0.68	23.88	196	1	57	40	2	0	70.8	-11.6	51	18	250	50	0.0	0.0
B / 8.3	7.2	0.68	21.40	5	1	57	40	2	0	64.4	-11.9	41	18	250	50	3.5	0.0
B / 8.3	7.2	0.68	22.13	91	1	57	40	2	0	66.1	-11.7	44	18	250	50	0.0	0.0
B / 8.3	7.2	0.68	23.81	5	1	57	40	2	0	70.4	-11.6	50	18	250	50	0.0	0.0
B / 8.7	7.2	0.68	23.88	196	0	0	0	100	0	70.8	-11.6	51	18	250	50	3.5	0.0
B / 8.6	7.2	0.68	21.40	5	0	0	0	100	0	64.4	-11.9	41	18	250	50	0.0	0.0
B / 8.7	7.2	0.68	22.13	91	0	0	0	100	0	66.1	-11.7	44	18	250	50	0.0	0.0
B / 8.7	7.2	0.68	23.81	5	0	0	0	100	0	70.4	-11.6	50	18	250	50	0.0	0.0
B+ / 9.1	6.1	0.57	23.29	424	0	0	0	100	0	59.3	-9.8	58	18	250	50	3.5	0.0
B+ / 9.0	6.1	0.57	20.92	13	0	0	0	100	0	53.3	-10.0	48	18	250	50	0.0	0.0
B+ / 9.1	6.1	0.57	21.63	273	0	0	0	100	0	55.1	-10.0	51	18	250	50	0.0	0.0

						Total Return % through 2/28/17			Annualized		Incl. in Returns	
Fund Type	Fund Name	Ticker Symbol	Overall Investment Rating	Phone	Perfor-mance Rating/Pts	3 Mo	6 Mo	1Yr / Pct	3Yr / Pct	5Yr / Pct	Dividend Yield	Expense Ratio
GI	LeggMason WY Sch Ch Age-Bsd		B	(877) 534-4627	C- / 4.1	4.76	4.85	14.86 /29	4.50 /49	7.00 /35	0.00	1.09
GI	LeggMason WY Sch Ch Age-Bsd		C+	(877) 534-4627	D+ / 2.7	4.06	4.21	12.03 /18	3.95 /42	6.06 /29	0.00	0.96
GI	LeggMason WY Sch Ch Age-Bsd		C+	(877) 534-4627	D+ / 2.8	3.91	3.91	11.27 /15	3.24 /34	5.31 /23	0.00	1.66
GI	LeggMason WY Sch Ch Age-Bsd		B-	(877) 534-4627	C- / 3.0	3.94	4.00	11.55 /16	3.45 /36	5.53 /25	0.00	1.46
GI	LeggMason WY Sch Ch Age-Bsd		B-	(877) 534-4627	C- / 3.2	3.98	4.08	11.81 /17	3.75 /40	5.85 /27	0.00	1.09
GI	LeggMason WY Sch Ch Age-Bsd		C	(877) 534-4627	D- / 1.4	2.41	2.00	6.26 / 5	2.50 /28	3.49 /13	0.00	0.86
GI	LeggMason WY Sch Ch Age-Bsd		C+	(877) 534-4627	D- / 1.5	2.24	1.65	5.48 / 4	1.79 /23	2.77 /10	0.00	1.56
GI	LeggMason WY Sch Ch Age-Bsd		C+	(877) 534-4627	D / 1.6	2.23	1.72	5.69 / 4	1.99 /24	2.97 /11	0.00	1.36
GI	LeggMason WY Sch Ch Age-Bsd		C+	(877) 534-4627	D / 1.6	2.31	1.89	5.88 / 5	2.17 /25	3.16 /11	0.00	1.09
GI	LeggMason WY Sch Ch Yr To Enr		C	(877) 534-4627	D- / 1.4	2.41	2.00	6.26 / 5	2.50 /28	3.49 /13	0.00	0.86
GI	LeggMason WY Sch Ch Yr To Enr		C+	(877) 534-4627	D- / 1.5	2.24	1.65	5.48 / 4	1.79 /23	2.77 /10	0.00	1.56
GI	LeggMason WY Sch Ch Yr To Enr		C+	(877) 534-4627	D / 1.6	2.23	1.72	5.69 / 4	1.99 /24	2.97 /11	0.00	1.36
GI	LeggMason WY Sch Ch Yr To Enr		C+	(877) 534-4627	D / 1.6	2.31	1.89	5.88 / 5	2.17 /25	3.16 /11	0.00	1.09
GI	LeggMason WY Sch Ch Yr To Enr		C+	(877) 534-4627	D+ / 2.7	4.06	4.21	12.03 /18	3.95 /42	6.06 /29	0.00	0.96
GI	LeggMason WY Sch Ch Yr To Enr		C+	(877) 534-4627	D+ / 2.8	3.91	3.91	11.27 /15	3.24 /34	5.31 /23	0.00	1.66
GI	LeggMason WY Sch Ch Yr To Enr		B-	(877) 534-4627	C- / 3.0	3.94	4.00	11.55 /16	3.45 /36	5.53 /25	0.00	1.46
GI	LeggMason WY Sch Ch Yr To Enr		B-	(877) 534-4627	C- / 3.2	3.98	4.08	11.81 /17	3.75 /40	5.85 /27	0.00	1.09
GI	LeggMason WY Sch Ch Yr To Enr		B-	(877) 534-4627	C- / 3.5	4.77	4.91	14.96 /30	4.60 /50	7.10 /35	0.00	0.99
GI	LeggMason WY Sch Ch Yr To Enr		B-	(877) 534-4627	C- / 3.6	4.60	4.55	14.13 /26	3.88 /41	6.35 /31	0.00	1.69
GI	LeggMason WY Sch Ch Yr To Enr		B-	(877) 534-4627	C- / 3.8	4.64	4.70	14.38 /27	4.09 /44	6.56 /32	0.00	1.49
GI	LeggMason WY Sch Ch Yr To Enr		B	(877) 534-4627	C- / 4.1	4.76	4.85	14.86 /29	4.50 /49	7.00 /35	0.00	1.09
GR	LeggMason WY Schr Ch Age-Bsd 0-3		B	(877) 534-4627	C / 5.5	6.27	7.81	20.63 /56	5.76 /62	9.68 /56	0.00	1.10
GR	LeggMason WY Schr Ch Age-Bsd 0-3		B	(877) 534-4627	C+ / 5.6	6.08	7.42	19.75 /51	5.02 /54	8.92 /50	0.00	1.80
GR	LeggMason WY Schr Ch Age-Bsd 0-3		B	(877) 534-4627	C+ / 5.8	6.17	7.56	20.04 /52	5.24 /57	9.14 /52	0.00	1.60
GR	LeggMason WY Schr Ch Age-Bsd 0-3		B	(877) 534-4627	C+ / 6.2	6.31	7.84	20.69 /56	5.78 /62	9.72 /56	0.00	1.09
GI	Leigh Baldwin Total Return	LEBOX	D+	(866) 706-9790	E / 0.4	0.00	-0.71	0.36 / 1	-1.22 / 9	-1.92 / 3	0.22	4.69
IN	Leland Real Asset Opportunities A	GHTAX	D	(877) 270-2848	D / 1.9	6.85	6.92	36.55 /95	-0.06 /13	--	1.40	1.71
IN	Leland Real Asset Opportunities C	GHTCX	D	(877) 270-2848	D / 2.2	6.61	6.50	35.37 /94	-0.85 /10	--	1.18	2.46
IN	Leland Real Asset Opportunities I	GHTIX	C	(877) 270-2848	C / 4.7	6.87	7.04	36.83 /96	0.14 /14	--	2.28	1.46
GI	Leuthold Core Investment Inst	LCRIX	C+	(888) 200-0409	C- / 3.5	4.85	5.38	9.99 /12	4.36 /47	7.19 /36	0.00	1.25
GI	Leuthold Core Investment Retail	LCORX	C+	(888) 200-0409	C- / 3.4	4.85	5.33	9.88 /11	4.25 /46	7.08 /35	0.00	1.35
GL	Leuthold Global Industries Instl	LGIIX	C+	(888) 200-0409	C / 5.5	9.24	10.31	19.59 /50	3.67 /39	10.25 /60	0.96	1.80
GL	Leuthold Global Industries Retail	LGINX	C+	(888) 200-0409	C / 5.3	9.14	10.13	19.29 /48	3.42 /36	9.96 /58	0.72	2.05
GL	Leuthold Global Instl	GLBIX	D+	(888) 200-0409	D+ / 2.3	6.13	4.90	9.08 /10	1.88 /23	5.66 /26	0.07	1.43
GL	Leuthold Global Retail	GLBLX	D+	(888) 200-0409	D / 2.1	6.00	4.76	8.74 / 9	1.65 /22	5.41 /24	0.00	1.68
SC	Leuthold Grizzly Short	GRZZX	E	(888) 200-0409	E- / 0.0	-7.73	-7.00	-26.97 / 0	-8.71 / 1	-13.20 / 0	0.00	2.87
GR	Leuthold Select Industries	LSLTX	B+	(888) 200-0409	B- / 7.1	7.01	10.23	19.25 /48	7.13 /73	13.21 /86	0.10	1.73
SC	Lincoln Baron Growth Opps Svc		D+	(800) 992-2766	C / 5.1	8.32	5.64	21.48 /60	3.78 /40	11.95 /74	0.44	1.30
EM	Lincoln SSgA Emerging Mkts 100 Std		C	(800) 992-2766	B- / 7.3	11.15	12.22	35.56 /95	2.86 /30	-1.12 / 3	2.52	0.46
GR	Linde Hansen Contrarian Value A	LHVAX	D+	(855) 754-7933	D / 2.0	0.31	3.91	15.02 /30	3.40 /36	8.27 /44	0.00	1.77
GR	Linde Hansen Contrarian Value I	LHVIX	C-	(855) 754-7933	D+ / 2.9	0.37	4.02	15.31 /31	3.66 /39	8.54 /47	0.06	1.52
AA	Litman Gregory Masters Alt Str Inst	MASFX	C-	(800) 960-0188	D+ / 2.4	1.87	3.05	10.37 /13	3.24 /34	4.64 /19	2.54	1.94
AA	Litman Gregory Masters Alt Str Inv	MASNX	C-	(800) 960-0188	D / 2.0	1.71	2.82	9.97 /12	2.97 /32	4.39 /17	2.27	2.18
GR	Litman Gregory Masters Equity Inst	MSEFX	C+	(800) 960-0188	B / 7.8	4.97	9.47	26.98 /79	7.57 /76	12.18 /76	0.76	1.28
GR	Litman Gregory Masters Equity Inv	MSENX	C+	(800) 960-0188	B- / 7.3	4.89	9.39	26.64 /78	7.32 /74	11.96 /74	0.52	1.53
FO	Litman Gregory Masters Intl Inst	MSILX	E+	(800) 960-0188	E+ / 0.6	7.71	5.88	10.59 /13	-2.94 / 5	3.28 /12	3.95	1.24
FO	Litman Gregory Masters Intl Inv	MNILX	E+	(800) 960-0188	E / 0.4	7.59	5.73	10.26 /12	-3.19 / 4	3.02 /11	3.55	1.49
SC	Litman Gregory Masters Sm Co Inst	MSSFX	D-	(800) 960-0188	D+ / 2.3	5.19	12.76	30.60 /87	-0.61 /11	8.35 /45	0.00	1.69
AA	LJM Preservation and Growth A	LJMAX	A+	(855) 556-3863	B / 8.2	8.08	11.82	19.43 /49	11.22 /97	--	0.00	2.68
AA	LJM Preservation and Growth I	LJMIX	B-	(855) 556-3863	C / 5.5	0.62	4.17	11.40 /16	8.86 /86	--	0.00	2.43
GI	LK Balanced Institutional	LKBLX	D+	(855) 698-1378	D+ / 2.8	3.00	5.84	16.39 /36	1.89 /23	--	0.71	1.46
IN	LKCM Aquinas Catholic Equity	AQEIX	C-	(800) 688-5526	C / 5.4	5.91	8.29	22.73 /66	4.34 /47	9.55 /55	0.22	1.40

• Denotes fund is closed to new investors
* Denotes fund is included in Section II

RISK			NET ASSETS		ASSET					BULL / BEAR		FUND MANAGER		MINIMUMS		LOADS	
	3 Year		NAV						Portfolio								
Risk Rating/Pts	Standard Deviation	Beta	As of 2/28/17	Total $(Mil)	Cash %	Stocks %	Bonds %	Other %	Turnover Ratio	Last Bull Market Return	Last Bear Market Return	Manager Quality Pct	Manager Tenure (Years)	Initial Purch. $	Additional Purch. $	Front End Load	Back End Load
B+ / 9.1	6.1	0.57	23.11	24	0	0	0	100	0	58.5	-9.8	57	18	250	50	0.0	0.0
B+ / 9.6	4.9	0.46	21.04	386	0	0	0	100	0	48.5	-7.5	64	18	250	50	3.5	0.0
B+ / 9.5	4.9	0.46	18.86	16	0	0	0	100	0	43.0	-7.8	55	18	250	50	0.0	0.0
B+ / 9.6	4.9	0.46	19.51	235	0	0	0	100	0	44.5	-7.7	57	18	250	50	0.0	0.0
B+ / 9.6	4.9	0.46	20.64	18	0	0	0	100	0	47.0	-7.6	62	18	250	50	0.0	0.0
B+ / 9.9	2.6	0.23	17.82	315	0	0	0	100	0	25.6	-3.3	74	18	250	50	3.5	0.0
B+ / 9.9	2.6	0.22	15.98	15	0	0	0	100	0	21.0	-3.6	67	18	250	50	0.0	0.0
B+ / 9.9	2.5	0.22	16.53	257	0	0	0	100	0	22.3	-3.5	70	18	250	50	0.0	0.0
B+ / 9.9	2.6	0.23	17.28	40	0	0	0	100	0	23.5	-3.5	72	18	250	50	0.0	0.0
B+ / 9.9	2.6	0.23	17.82	315	0	0	0	100	0	25.6	-3.3	74	18	250	50	3.5	0.0
B+ / 9.9	2.6	0.22	15.98	15	0	0	0	100	0	21.0	-3.6	67	18	250	50	0.0	0.0
B+ / 9.9	2.5	0.22	16.53	257	0	0	0	100	0	22.3	-3.5	70	18	250	50	0.0	0.0
B+ / 9.9	2.6	0.23	17.28	40	0	0	0	100	0	23.5	-3.5	72	18	250	50	0.0	0.0
B+ / 9.6	4.9	0.46	21.04	386	0	0	0	100	0	48.5	-7.5	64	18	250	50	3.5	0.0
B+ / 9.5	4.9	0.46	18.86	16	0	0	0	100	0	43.0	-7.8	55	18	250	50	0.0	0.0
B+ / 9.6	4.9	0.46	19.51	235	0	0	0	100	0	44.5	-7.7	57	18	250	50	0.0	0.0
B+ / 9.6	4.9	0.46	20.64	18	0	0	0	100	0	47.0	-7.6	62	18	250	50	0.0	0.0
B+ / 9.1	6.1	0.57	23.29	424	0	0	0	100	0	59.3	-9.8	58	18	250	50	3.5	0.0
B+ / 9.0	6.1	0.57	20.92	13	0	0	0	100	0	53.3	-10.0	48	18	250	50	0.0	0.0
B+ / 9.1	6.1	0.57	21.63	273	0	0	0	100	0	55.1	-10.0	51	18	250	50	0.0	0.0
B+ / 9.1	6.1	0.57	23.11	24	0	0	0	100	0	58.5	-9.8	57	18	250	50	0.0	0.0
B / 8.0	9.1	0.86	23.74	247	0	0	0	100	0	88.3	-15.7	33	18	250	50	3.5	0.0
B / 8.0	9.1	0.86	21.28	4	0	0	0	100	0	81.3	-16.0	26	18	250	50	0.0	0.0
B / 8.0	9.1	0.86	22.04	121	0	0	0	100	0	83.4	-15.9	28	18	250	50	0.0	0.0
B / 8.0	9.1	0.86	23.92	9	0	0	0	100	0	88.6	-15.7	34	18	250	50	0.0	0.0
B / 8.2	3.1	0.18	7.00	3	12	84	2	2	478	-5.6	-6.3	32	9	1,000	100	0.0	0.0
C+ / 5.8	13.6	0.93	9.41	15	6	85	7	2	81	N/A	N/A	2	N/A	2,500	250	5.8	1.0
C+ / 5.8	13.6	0.92	9.32	14	6	85	7	2	81	N/A	N/A	2	N/A	2,500	250	0.0	1.0
C+ / 5.8	13.6	0.92	9.27	29	6	85	7	2	81	N/A	N/A	3	N/A	5,000,000	10,000	0.0	1.0
B / 8.3	6.0	0.45	19.04	339	6	63	30	1	109	55.5	-15.3	71	9	1,000,000	100	0.0	0.0
B / 8.3	6.0	0.45	19.01	508	6	63	30	1	109	54.6	-15.4	69	9	10,000	100	0.0	0.0
C+ / 6.5	11.4	0.74	16.50	8	0	100	0	0	111	91.9	-24.7	93	7	1,000,000	100	0.0	0.0
C+ / 6.5	11.4	0.74	16.42	2	0	100	0	0	111	89.1	-24.7	92	7	10,000	100	0.0	0.0
C+ / 6.5	5.9	0.71	9.46	83	10	57	32	1	103	44.4	-14.3	57	9	1,000,000	100	0.0	0.0
C+ / 6.5	5.9	0.71	9.36	28	10	57	32	1	103	42.7	-14.3	54	9	10,000	100	0.0	0.0
C- / 4.2	15.2	-0.77	5.85	168	72	0	27	1	0	-63.8	30.2	21	8	10,000	100	0.0	0.0
C+ / 6.9	12.4	1.04	23.81	14	0	98	1	1	118	125.4	-25.3	28	6	10,000	100	0.0	0.0
C- / 3.9	12.2	0.70	43.35	499	1	97	0	2	12	113.1	-18.5	62	19	0	0	0.0	0.0
C- / 4.0	17.5	1.04	9.13	502	2	97	0	1	51	19.8	-26.6	81	9	0	0	0.0	0.0
B- / 7.1	9.1	0.76	13.77	22	24	75	0	1	16	N/A	N/A	20	5	2,500	250	5.3	1.0
B- / 7.1	9.1	0.76	13.90	25	24	75	0	1	16	N/A	N/A	22	5	1,000,000	1,000	0.0	1.0
B / 8.0	3.2	0.44	11.61	1,475	25	25	46	4	146	34.0	N/A	73	6	100,000	250	0.0	0.0
B / 8.0	3.1	0.43	11.61	185	25	25	46	4	146	32.3	N/A	71	6	1,000	100	0.0	2.0
C / 4.5	12.0	1.09	17.86	325	6	92	0	2	34	113.2	-19.9	27	21	100,000	250	0.0	0.0
C / 4.5	11.9	1.08	17.64	N/A	6	92	0	2	34	110.9	-19.9	25	21	1,000	100	0.0	2.0
C / 5.4	12.4	0.96	15.50	628	0	99	0	1	52	38.6	-26.3	37	20	100,000	250	0.0	0.0
C / 5.4	12.4	0.96	15.40	32	0	99	0	1	52	36.7	-26.4	34	20	1,000	100	0.0	2.0
C / 4.6	14.5	0.76	21.47	37	13	86	0	1	61	94.3	-24.7	10	14	10,000	250	0.0	0.0
B- / 7.4	10.2	0.09	10.40	111	100	0	0	0	0	N/A	N/A	99	5	2,500	500	5.8	1.0
B- / 7.4	9.6	0.05	10.52	305	100	0	0	0	0	N/A	N/A	99	5	100,000	1,000	0.0	1.0
C+ / 6.2	7.5	0.64	44.52	26	1	64	34	1	25	N/A	N/A	18	18	50,000	500	0.0	0.0
C / 4.4	12.5	1.14	16.12	64	0	99	0	1	11	96.0	-19.7	5	23	2,000	500	0.0	1.0

Fund Type	Fund Name	Ticker Symbol	Overall Investment Rating	Phone	Performance Rating/Pts	3 Mo	6 Mo	1Yr / Pct	3Yr / Pct	5Yr / Pct	Dividend Yield	Expense Ratio
								Total Return % through 2/28/17			Incl. in Returns	
									Annualized			
BA	LKCM Balanced Institutional	LKBAX	B-	(800) 688-5526	C / 5.3	4.53	5.57	17.50 /41	6.18 /66	9.38 /54	0.84	1.02
GR	LKCM Equity Institutional	LKEQX	C+	(800) 688-5526	C+ / 6.6	6.49	7.45	23.95 /70	6.03 /64	10.94 /65	0.79	0.93
SC	LKCM Small Cap Equity Adv	LKSAX	E	(800) 688-5526	C- / 3.4	4.15	7.40	25.25 /74	0.91 /18	6.30 /30	0.00	1.22
SC	LKCM Small Cap Equity Inst	LKSCX	E+	(800) 688-5526	C- / 3.6	4.18	7.47	25.57 /75	1.16 /19	6.55 /32	0.00	0.97
IN	LKCM Small-Mid Cap Eq Inst	LKSMX	E+	(800) 688-5526	D- / 1.2	3.49	3.95	17.05 /39	-0.45 /11	5.76 /27	0.00	1.14
GL	LM BW Absolute Return Opptys A	LROAX	C-	(877) 534-4627	D- / 1.5	3.20	2.76	6.24 / 5	2.09 /25	2.80 /10	0.00	1.27
GL	LM BW Absolute Return Opptys C	LAOCX	C-	(877) 534-4627	D- / 1.5	3.05	2.42	5.62 / 4	1.45 /21	2.13 / 8	0.00	1.81
GL	LM BW Absolute Return Opptys C1	LROCX	C-	(877) 534-4627	D- / 1.5	3.04	2.51	5.70 / 4	1.57 /21	2.29 / 9	0.00	1.50
GL	LM BW Absolute Return Opptys I	LROIX	C-	(877) 534-4627	D / 1.9	3.28	2.92	6.68 / 5	2.43 /27	3.17 /11	0.00	0.85
GL	LM BW Absolute Return Opptys IS	LROSX	C-	(877) 534-4627	D / 2.0	3.36	3.00	6.85 / 6	2.59 /28	--	0.00	0.72
GL	LM BW Absolute Return OpptysR	LBARX	C-	(877) 534-4627	D / 1.6	3.20	2.67	6.04 / 5	1.81 /23	2.53 / 9	0.00	1.29
FS	LM BW Alternative Credit A	LMAPX	C-	(877) 534-4627	D / 2.2	4.95	4.41	11.44 /16	2.98 /32	--	0.04	1.63
FS	LM BW Alternative Credit C	LMAQX	C-	(877) 534-4627	D+ / 2.4	4.77	4.02	10.63 /13	2.27 /26	--	0.00	2.32
FS	LM BW Alternative Credit FI	LMAOX	C-	(877) 534-4627	D+ / 2.8	4.85	4.31	11.33 /16	2.92 /31	--	0.04	1.65
FS	LM BW Alternative Credit I	LMANX	C-	(877) 534-4627	C- / 3.1	5.05	4.62	11.80 /17	3.30 /35	--	0.07	1.32
FS	LM BW Alternative Credit IS	LMAMX	C-	(877) 534-4627	C- / 3.1	5.04	4.61	11.92 /18	3.34 /35	6.19 /30	0.07	1.23
GR	LM BW Diversified Large Cap Val A	LBWAX	B+	(877) 534-4627	B+ / 8.5	8.00	12.95	28.13 /82	9.16 /88	12.78 /82	1.20	1.23
GR	LM BW Diversified Large Cap Val A2	LLVAX	B+	(877) 534-4627	B+ / 8.3	8.03	12.90	27.97 /82	9.00 /87	--	1.17	1.30
GR	LM BW Diversified Large Cap Val C	LBWCX	A-	(877) 534-4627	B+ / 8.9	7.85	12.57	27.24 /80	8.36 /82	11.95 /74	0.39	1.97
GR	LM BW Diversified Large Cap Val I	LBWIX	A	(877) 534-4627	A / 9.5	8.11	13.18	28.53 /83	9.49 /90	13.10 /85	1.56	0.90
GR	LM BW Diversified Large Cap Val IS	LBISX	A	(877) 534-4627	A / 9.5	8.14	13.26	28.69 /83	9.57 /91	13.16 /85	1.63	0.81
GR	LM BW Diversified Large Cap Val R	LBDRX	A+	(877) 534-4627	A- / 9.2	7.97	12.88	27.85 /81	8.92 /86	--	1.04	1.45
GR	LM BW Dyn Lg Cap Val IS	LMBGX	B-	(877) 534-4627	C+ / 6.9	3.45	9.44	20.51 /55	7.47 /75	14.26 /95	1.33	1.21
GL	LMCG Global Market Neutral Inst	GMNIX	C	(877) 591-4667	D- / 1.0	-1.29	2.19	-4.62 / 1	2.31 /26	--	0.00	3.74
GL	LMCG Global Market Neutral Inv	GMNRX	C-	(877) 591-4667	E+ / 0.9	-1.29	2.01	-4.90 / 1	2.12 /25	--	0.00	4.09
GR	LMCG Global MultiCap Inst	GMCIX	C+	(877) 591-4667	C+ / 6.9	7.50	8.86	26.43 /78	5.39 /58	--	1.01	16.24
GR	LMCG Global MultiCap Inv	GMCRX	C+	(877) 591-4667	C+ / 6.2	7.36	8.63	25.93 /76	4.14 /45	--	0.96	31.96
OT	LoCorr Lng/Sht Commodities Strat A	LCSAX	C	(855) 523-8637	C- / 3.0	-4.25	-6.06	-8.88 / 0	11.16 /97	2.44 / 9	2.75	3.11
OT	LoCorr Lng/Sht Commodities Strat C	LCSCX	C	(855) 523-8637	C- / 3.4	-4.31	-6.27	-9.42 / 0	10.33 /95	1.69 / 7	2.37	3.86
OT	LoCorr Lng/Sht Commodities Strat I	LCSIX	C+	(855) 523-8637	C / 4.3	-4.13	-5.83	-8.53 / 0	11.45 /98	2.70 /10	3.20	2.86
GR	LoCorr Long/Short Equity A	LEQAX	C	(855) 523-8637	C / 4.3	1.36	5.85	29.50 /85	4.55 /49	--	0.00	3.91
GR	LoCorr Long/Short Equity C	LEQCX	C+	(855) 523-8637	C / 4.9	1.13	5.36	28.49 /83	3.75 /40	--	0.00	4.66
GR	LoCorr Long/Short Equity I	LEQIX	C+	(855) 523-8637	C+ / 5.8	1.43	5.98	29.85 /86	4.80 /52	--	0.00	3.66
GI	LoCorr Managed Futures Strategy A	LFMAX	C	(855) 523-8637	C- / 3.1	3.90	-0.84	1.64 / 2	8.55 /83	3.65 /14	0.00	2.43
GI	LoCorr Managed Futures Strategy C	LFMCX	C+	(855) 523-8637	C- / 3.6	3.68	-1.21	0.89 / 2	7.76 /77	2.89 /10	0.00	3.18
GI	LoCorr Managed Futures Strategy I	LFMIX	C+	(855) 523-8637	C / 4.5	4.09	-0.62	1.95 / 2	8.84 /86	3.92 /15	0.01	2.18
IN	LoCorr Market Trend A	LOTAX	U	(855) 523-8637	U /	1.45	-6.40	-11.67 / 0	--	--	1.61	2.07
IN	LoCorr Market Trend C	LOTCX	U	(855) 523-8637	U /	1.28	-6.74	-12.34 / 0	--	--	1.35	2.82
IN	LoCorr Market Trend I	LOTIX	U	(855) 523-8637	U /	1.49	-6.25	-11.45 / 0	--	--	1.84	1.82
AA	LoCorr Spectrum Income A	LSPAX	D	(855) 523-8637	E / 0.5	6.73	2.35	15.74 /33	-1.42 / 8	--	6.88	3.21
AA	LoCorr Spectrum Income C	LSPCX	D	(855) 523-8637	E+ / 0.7	6.60	2.12	15.07 /30	-2.12 / 6	--	6.33	3.96
AA	LoCorr Spectrum Income I	LSPIX	D	(855) 523-8637	E+ / 0.9	6.82	2.52	16.12 /35	-1.14 / 9	--	7.62	2.96
GR	Logan Capital Large Cap Gro Ins	LGNGX	B	(855) 215-1200	B / 7.6	9.35	8.35	23.64 /69	7.37 /75	--	0.00	1.50
GR	Logan Capital Large Cap Gro Inv	LGNHX	B-	(855) 215-1200	B- / 7.4	9.27	8.19	23.31 /68	7.11 /73	--	0.00	1.75
GR	Logan Capital Long Short Investor	LGNMX	B	(855) 215-1200	C / 4.3	6.47	6.82	10.93 /14	5.22 /57	--	0.00	4.26
IN	Longboard Managed Futures Strat A	WAVEX	D	(855) 294-7540	D / 1.7	2.90	-0.47	-7.80 / 0	6.80 /70	--	0.00	3.12
IN	Longboard Managed Futures Strat I	WAVIX	D	(855) 294-7540	D+ / 2.7	3.06	-0.28	-7.47 / 0	7.11 /73	--	0.00	2.87
GR	Longleaf Partners	LLPFX	D-	(800) 445-9469	C- / 4.2	-1.10	6.36	31.36 /89	1.99 /24	7.72 /40	0.01	0.93
GL	Longleaf Partners Global	LLGLX	C-	(800) 445-9469	C / 5.4	1.55	11.86	40.67 /97	0.27 /15	--	0.47	1.54
FO	Longleaf Partners International	LLINX	E	(800) 445-9469	D- / 1.3	5.50	7.34	31.26 /89	-3.05 / 4	5.04 /22	2.26	1.28
SC	● Longleaf Partners Small-Cap	LLSCX	C	(800) 445-9469	B- / 7.0	1.98	6.64	24.32 /71	7.64 /76	13.87 /92	0.29	0.91
GI	Loomis Sayles Multi Asset Income A	IIDPX	B-	(800) 225-5478	C / 5.0	5.97	5.31	16.19 /35	6.79 /70	7.67 /40	2.75	1.11

RISK	3 Year		NET ASSETS		ASSET					BULL / BEAR		FUND MANAGER		MINIMUMS		LOADS	
Risk Rating/Pts	Standard Deviation	Beta	NAV As of 2/28/17	Total $(Mil)	Cash %	Stocks %	Bonds %	Other %	Portfolio Turnover Ratio	Last Bull Market Return	Last Bear Market Return	Manager Quality Pct	Manager Tenure (Years)	Initial Purch. $	Additional Purch. $	Front End Load	Back End Load
B- /7.5	7.7	1.18	21.11	69	0	70	29	1	16	80.9	-10.6	41	20	2,000	1,000	0.0	1.0
C+ /5.6	11.5	1.07	23.56	308	1	96	1	2	13	105.3	-16.4	15	21	2,000	1,000	0.0	1.0
D- /1.5	15.4	0.94	18.35	1	0	100	0	0	62	71.1	-20.5	12	23	2,000	1,000	0.0	1.0
D /1.7	15.4	0.95	19.46	271	0	100	0	0	62	73.3	-20.4	14	23	2,000	1,000	0.0	1.0
C- /4.0	12.8	1.01	9.92	20	0	0	0	100	70	60.6	N/A	2	6	2,000	1,000	0.0	1.0
B /8.1	4.7	0.37	11.92	226	3	0	96	1	30	20.1	-0.9	76	6	1,000	50	2.3	0.0
B /8.1	4.7	0.17	11.84	10	3	0	96	1	30	15.9	-1.1	83	6	1,000	50	0.0	0.0
B /8.1	4.7	0.38	11.86	2	3	0	96	1	30	16.9	-1.1	71	6	1,000	50	0.0	0.0
B /8.0	4.7	0.37	11.98	798	3	0	96	1	30	22.5	-0.7	79	6	1,000,000	0	0.0	0.0
B /8.0	4.7	0.17	12.01	517	3	0	96	1	30	N/A	N/A	88	6	0	0	0.0	0.0
B /8.1	4.7	0.38	11.93	N/A	3	0	96	1	30	N/A	N/A	74	6	0	0	0.0	0.0
B- /7.3	4.4	0.06	10.17	24	4	0	95	1	156	N/A	N/A	87	4	1,000	50	4.3	0.0
B- /7.3	4.4	0.06	10.10	15	4	0	95	1	156	N/A	N/A	83	4	1,000	50	0.0	0.0
B- /7.3	4.4	0.06	10.16	1	4	0	95	1	156	N/A	N/A	86	4	0	0	0.0	0.0
B- /7.3	4.4	0.06	10.20	224	4	0	95	1	156	N/A	N/A	88	4	1,000,000	0	0.0	0.0
B- /7.3	4.4	0.06	10.21	67	4	0	95	1	156	46.0	4.8	88	4	0	0	0.0	0.0
C+ /5.7	11.5	1.08	19.85	1	0	99	0	1	58	121.5	-15.6	46	7	1,000	50	5.8	0.0
C+ /5.7	11.5	1.08	19.69	18	0	99	0	1	58	N/A	N/A	44	7	1,000	50	5.8	0.0
C+ /5.7	11.6	1.08	19.68	1	0	99	0	1	58	112.8	-15.9	36	7	1,000	50	0.0	0.0
C+ /5.6	11.5	1.08	19.85	11	0	99	0	1	58	125.0	-15.5	51	7	1,000,000	0	0.0	0.0
C+ /5.6	11.6	1.08	19.86	903	0	99	0	1	58	125.8	-15.5	51	7	0	0	0.0	0.0
B- /7.0	11.6	1.08	19.84	N/A	0	99	0	1	58	N/A	N/A	43	7	0	0	0.0	0.0
B- /7.3	11.9	1.08	10.82	36	1	98	0	1	112	143.6	-17.1	27	3	0	0	0.0	0.0
B+ /9.5	5.2	-0.15	10.74	67	99	0	0	1	124	N/A	N/A	87	4	100,000	0	0.0	0.0
B+ /9.5	5.2	-0.15	10.68	6	99	0	0	1	124	N/A	N/A	86	4	2,500	100	0.0	0.0
C+ /6.3	11.0	0.99	11.84	2	2	97	0	1	44	N/A	N/A	17	4	100,000	0	0.0	0.0
C+ /6.3	11.4	1.01	11.80	N/A	2	97	0	1	44	N/A	N/A	8	4	2,500	100	0.0	0.0
B- /7.8	8.3	-0.22	9.18	32	32	0	67	1	164	N/A	N/A	99	4	2,500	500	5.8	1.0
B- /7.9	8.2	-0.21	8.96	7	32	0	67	1	164	N/A	N/A	99	4	2,500	500	0.0	1.0
B- /7.8	8.2	-0.22	9.26	80	32	0	67	1	164	N/A	N/A	99	4	100,000	500	0.0	1.0
C+ /6.7	14.1	0.94	11.94	30	33	44	22	1	269	N/A	N/A	14	4	2,500	500	5.8	1.0
C+ /6.6	14.0	0.94	11.59	12	33	44	22	1	269	N/A	N/A	10	4	2,500	500	0.0	1.0
C+ /6.7	14.0	0.94	12.05	44	33	44	22	1	269	N/A	N/A	16	4	100,000	500	0.0	1.0
B- /7.9	8.7	-0.01	9.16	311	19	0	80	1	53	12.9	-7.2	99	6	2,500	500	5.8	1.0
B- /7.9	8.7	-0.01	8.84	114	19	0	80	1	53	8.3	-7.5	98	6	2,500	500	0.0	1.0
B- /7.8	8.7	-0.01	9.27	521	19	0	80	1	53	14.5	-7.1	99	6	100,000	500	0.0	1.0
U /	N/A	N/A	10.94	124	9	0	90	1	27	N/A	N/A	N/A	3	2,500	500	5.8	1.0
U /	N/A	N/A	10.81	80	9	0	90	1	27	N/A	N/A	N/A	3	2,500	500	0.0	1.0
U /	N/A	N/A	10.98	773	9	0	90	1	27	N/A	N/A	N/A	3	100,000	500	0.0	1.0
B- /7.1	10.5	1.28	7.87	34	37	50	12	1	54	N/A	N/A	2	4	2,500	500	5.8	2.0
B- /7.1	10.5	1.28	7.90	26	37	50	12	1	54	N/A	N/A	1	4	2,500	500	0.0	2.0
B- /7.1	10.5	1.28	7.87	50	37	50	12	1	54	N/A	N/A	2	4	100,000	500	0.0	2.0
C+ /5.6	13.4	1.15	17.78	17	1	98	0	1	14	N/A	N/A	19	5	500,000	50	0.0	1.0
C /5.5	13.4	1.14	17.56	6	1	98	0	1	14	N/A	N/A	18	5	5,000	50	0.0	1.0
B+ /9.0	8.6	0.73	12.86	10	0	0	0	100	83	N/A	N/A	44	5	5,000	50	0.0	1.0
C+ /5.6	12.6	-0.11	10.64	77	53	0	46	1	0	N/A	N/A	98	5	2,500	250	5.8	0.0
C+ /5.6	12.6	-0.10	10.77	403	53	0	46	1	0	N/A	N/A	98	5	10,000	2,500	0.0	0.0
D+ /2.6	15.5	1.24	25.78	3,388	2	81	15	2	46	77.9	-20.7	2	30	10,000	0	0.0	0.0
C- /4.1	17.1	1.19	12.50	192	12	84	2	2	58	N/A	N/A	78	5	10,000	0	0.0	0.0
C- /3.2	17.2	1.24	14.38	1,037	15	79	0	6	53	46.2	-24.5	36	19	10,000	0	0.0	0.0
C- /3.9	11.9	0.54	28.03	4,099	3	73	23	1	47	127.2	-16.7	92	28	10,000	0	0.0	0.0
B- /7.9	6.9	0.48	13.66	60	3	54	40	3	93	62.7	-7.5	84	12	2,500	100	4.3	0.0

Fund Type	Fund Name	Ticker Symbol	Overall Investment Rating	Phone	PERFORMANCE Perfor-mance Rating/Pts	3 Mo	6 Mo	1Yr / Pct	Annualized 3Yr / Pct	5Yr / Pct	Incl. in Returns Dividend Yield	Expense Ratio
	99 Pct = Best											
	0 Pct = Worst											
GI	Loomis Sayles Multi Asset Income C	CIDPX	B	(800) 225-5478	C / 5.3	5.88	5.02	15.39 /32	5.97 /64	6.86 /34	2.17	1.87
AA	Loomis Sayles Multi Asset Income Y	YIDPX	B-	(800) 225-5478	C+ / 6.1	6.07	5.46	16.47 /36	7.03 /72	--	3.12	0.86
SC	● Loomis Sayles Sm Cp Gr Inst	LSSIX	D	(800) 633-3330	C+ / 5.7	6.11	9.35	27.01 /79	3.28 /34	11.55 /70	0.00	0.94
SC	● Loomis Sayles Sm Cp Gr N	LSSNX	D	(800) 633-3330	C+ / 5.8	6.13	9.40	27.14 /80	3.39 /36	--	0.00	0.83
SC	● Loomis Sayles Sm Cp Gr Ret	LCGRX	D	(800) 633-3330	C / 5.5	6.06	9.26	26.68 /78	3.03 /32	11.11 /67	0.00	1.19
SC	● Loomis Sayles SmCp Val Adm	LSVAX	B	(800) 633-3330	A / 9.5	5.15	12.95	35.11 /94	8.90 /86	13.14 /85	0.00	1.47
SC	● Loomis Sayles SmCp Val Inst	LSSCX	B	(800) 633-3330	A+ / 9.6	5.25	13.22	35.78 /95	9.44 /90	13.70 /91	0.36	0.99
SC	● Loomis Sayles SmCp Val N	LSCNX	B	(800) 633-3330	A+ / 9.6	5.29	13.25	35.89 /95	9.50 /90	--	0.43	0.90
SC	● Loomis Sayles SmCp Val Ret	LSCRX	B	(800) 633-3330	A+ / 9.6	5.21	13.06	35.46 /94	9.16 /88	13.42 /88	0.13	1.24
*GI	Lord Abbett Affiliated A	LAFFX	A-	(888) 522-2388	B+ / 8.6	6.89	12.13	28.38 /82	9.71 /92	13.02 /84	2.08	0.74
GI	● Lord Abbett Affiliated B	LAFBX	A	(888) 522-2388	B+ / 8.9	6.59	11.69	27.41 /80	8.88 /86	12.21 /76	1.43	1.49
GI	Lord Abbett Affiliated C	LAFCX	A	(888) 522-2388	B+ / 8.9	6.70	11.79	27.45 /80	8.90 /86	12.22 /76	1.55	1.49
GI	Lord Abbett Affiliated F	LAAFX	A	(888) 522-2388	A / 9.4	6.86	12.22	28.57 /83	9.88 /93	13.21 /86	2.34	0.59
GI	Lord Abbett Affiliated I	LAFYX	A+	(888) 522-2388	A / 9.5	6.92	12.29	28.65 /83	9.97 /93	13.32 /87	2.41	0.49
GI	● Lord Abbett Affiliated P	LAFPX	A	(888) 522-2388	A / 9.4	6.83	12.15	28.33 /82	9.69 /92	13.01 /84	2.20	0.94
GI	Lord Abbett Affiliated R2	LAFQX	A	(888) 522-2388	A- / 9.2	6.72	11.94	27.85 /81	9.33 /89	12.65 /80	1.84	1.09
GI	Lord Abbett Affiliated R3	LAFRX	A	(888) 522-2388	A- / 9.2	6.83	12.01	28.02 /82	9.47 /90	12.79 /82	1.99	0.99
GL	Lord Abbett Alpha Strategy I	ALFYX	D	(888) 522-2388	C / 5.3	4.21	7.20	25.67 /75	3.77 /40	11.07 /66	0.00	1.37
IN	Lord Abbett Calibrated Div Gr A	LAMAX	C+	(888) 522-2388	B- / 7.1	6.03	7.12	21.40 /59	9.62 /91	11.66 /71	1.57	1.07
IN	● Lord Abbett Calibrated Div Gr B	LAMBX	B-	(888) 522-2388	B / 7.6	5.87	6.67	20.47 /55	8.81 /85	10.82 /64	0.93	1.82
IN	Lord Abbett Calibrated Div Gr C	LAMCX	B-	(888) 522-2388	B / 7.6	5.85	6.68	20.39 /54	8.80 /85	10.83 /64	1.03	1.82
IN	Lord Abbett Calibrated Div Gr F	LAMFX	B	(888) 522-2388	B+ / 8.3	6.15	7.22	21.53 /60	9.80 /92	11.84 /73	1.82	0.92
IN	Lord Abbett Calibrated Div Gr I	LAMYX	B	(888) 522-2388	B+ / 8.4	6.19	7.26	21.67 /61	9.92 /93	11.94 /74	1.87	0.82
IN	● Lord Abbett Calibrated Div Gr P	LAMPX	B	(888) 522-2388	B / 8.0	6.01	7.04	21.12 /58	9.40 /90	11.45 /69	1.46	1.27
IN	Lord Abbett Calibrated Div Gr R2	LAMQX	B	(888) 522-2388	B / 7.9	5.97	6.88	20.93 /57	9.23 /88	11.28 /68	1.30	1.42
IN	Lord Abbett Calibrated Div Gr R3	LAMRX	B	(888) 522-2388	B / 8.0	6.00	7.03	21.14 /58	9.39 /89	11.41 /69	1.46	1.32
CV	Lord Abbett Convertible A	LACFX	C-	(888) 522-2388	C / 5.2	6.37	9.66	26.60 /78	3.23 /34	8.43 /46	3.29	1.12
CV	● Lord Abbett Convertible B	LBCFX	C-	(888) 522-2388	C / 5.0	6.21	9.18	25.49 /75	2.42 /27	7.58 /39	2.57	1.92
CV	Lord Abbett Convertible C	LACCX	C-	(888) 522-2388	C / 5.2	6.33	9.37	25.85 /76	2.60 /28	7.77 /40	2.80	1.77
CV	Lord Abbett Convertible F	LBFFX	C	(888) 522-2388	C+ / 5.8	6.40	9.72	26.73 /78	3.34 /35	8.54 /47	3.46	1.02
CV	Lord Abbett Convertible I	LCFYX	C	(888) 522-2388	C+ / 5.9	6.47	9.81	26.79 /79	3.47 /37	8.66 /48	3.53	0.92
CV	● Lord Abbett Convertible P	LCFPX	C	(888) 522-2388	C / 5.5	6.30	9.48	26.32 /77	3.07 /32	8.23 /44	3.17	1.37
CV	Lord Abbett Convertible R2	LBCQX	C-	(888) 522-2388	C / 5.4	6.37	9.50	26.06 /76	2.83 /30	8.01 /42	2.96	1.52
CV	Lord Abbett Convertible R3	LCFRX	C-	(888) 522-2388	C / 5.4	6.32	9.45	26.12 /77	2.92 /31	8.12 /43	3.12	1.42
SC	● Lord Abbett Developing Growth A	LAGWX	E-	(888) 522-2388	E+ / 0.6	5.79	5.04	23.85 /69	-2.68 / 5	9.47 /54	0.00	1.01
SC	● Lord Abbett Developing Growth B	LADBX	E-	(888) 522-2388	E+ / 0.8	5.56	4.64	22.91 /66	-3.39 / 4	8.71 /48	0.00	1.76
SC	● Lord Abbett Developing Growth C	LADCX	E-	(888) 522-2388	E+ / 0.8	5.57	4.66	23.00 /67	-3.38 / 4	8.71 /48	0.00	1.76
SC	● Lord Abbett Developing Growth F	LADFX	E-	(888) 522-2388	D- / 1.1	5.81	5.09	24.10 /70	-2.50 / 5	9.69 /56	0.00	0.86
SC	● Lord Abbett Developing Growth I	LADYX	E-	(888) 522-2388	D- / 1.1	5.84	5.14	24.14 /70	-2.42 / 6	9.80 /57	0.00	0.76
SC	● Lord Abbett Developing Growth P	LADPX	E-	(888) 522-2388	D- / 1.0	5.74	4.97	23.88 /69	-2.67 / 5	9.48 /54	0.00	1.21
SC	● Lord Abbett Developing Growth R2	LADQX	E-	(888) 522-2388	E+ / 0.9	5.68	4.85	23.49 /68	-2.99 / 4	9.14 /52	0.00	1.36
SC	● Lord Abbett Developing Growth R3	LADRX	E-	(888) 522-2388	D- / 1.0	5.71	4.89	23.54 /68	-2.90 / 5	9.25 /53	0.00	1.26
SC	Lord Abbett Developing Growth R6	LADVX	U	(888) 522-2388	U /	5.92	5.22	24.34 /71	--	--	0.00	0.62
GL	Lord Abbett Eq Tr Calib LCV A	LCAAX	B-	(888) 522-2388	B / 8.0	6.29	12.19	29.59 /85	8.45 /83	12.90 /83	1.80	1.00
GL	Lord Abbett Eq Tr Calib LCV C	LCACX	B	(888) 522-2388	B+ / 8.4	6.13	11.76	28.64 /83	7.64 /76	12.07 /75	1.20	1.75
GL	Lord Abbett Eq Tr Calib LCV F	LCAFX	B+	(888) 522-2388	A- / 9.0	6.39	12.30	29.85 /86	8.62 /84	13.08 /85	2.06	0.85
GL	Lord Abbett Eq Tr Calib LCV I	LVCIX	B+	(888) 522-2388	A- / 9.1	6.38	12.32	29.98 /86	8.72 /85	13.18 /86	2.13	0.75
GL	Lord Abbett Eq Tr Calib LCV R2	LCAQX	B+	(888) 522-2388	B+ / 8.7	6.20	11.94	29.14 /84	8.07 /79	12.66 /81	1.61	1.35
GL	Lord Abbett Eq Tr Calib LCV R3	LCARX	B+	(888) 522-2388	B+ / 8.8	6.17	12.02	29.22 /85	8.18 /80	12.66 /81	1.72	1.25
GR	Lord Abbett Eq Tr Calib MCV A	LVMAX	B-	(888) 522-2388	B / 8.1	6.26	11.10	31.04 /88	8.64 /84	13.35 /87	1.40	1.02
GR	Lord Abbett Eq Tr Calib MCV C	LVMCX	B	(888) 522-2388	B+ / 8.6	6.07	10.69	30.05 /86	7.83 /78	12.51 /79	0.83	1.77
GR	Lord Abbett Eq Tr Calib MCV F	LVMFX	B+	(888) 522-2388	A- / 9.2	6.36	11.19	31.26 /89	8.82 /86	13.52 /89	1.62	0.87

● Denotes fund is closed to new investors
* Denotes fund is included in Section II

Risk Rating/Pts	3 Year Standard Deviation	Beta	NAV As of 2/28/17	Total $(Mil)	Cash %	Stocks %	Bonds %	Other %	Portfolio Turnover Ratio	Last Bull Market Return	Last Bear Market Return	Manager Quality Pct	Manager Tenure (Years)	Initial Purch. $	Additional Purch. $	Front End Load	Back End Load
B- / 7.9	6.9	0.49	13.61	47	3	54	40	3	93	56.4	-7.8	80	12	2,500	100	0.0	0.0
B- / 7.9	6.9	0.89	13.59	21	3	54	40	3	93	N/A	N/A	76	12	100,000	100	0.0	0.0
D+ / 2.3	16.8	0.98	23.98	786	2	97	0	1	56	112.6	-22.5	30	12	100,000	0	0.0	0.0
D+ / 2.3	16.9	0.98	24.08	221	2	97	0	1	56	N/A	N/A	32	12	1,000,000	0	0.0	0.0
D / 2.2	16.9	0.98	22.41	107	2	97	0	1	56	108.1	-22.5	28	12	2,500	50	0.0	0.0
C- / 3.8	14.9	0.92	33.93	38	1	98	0	1	22	135.6	-24.0	88	17	0	0	0.0	0.0
C- / 3.8	14.9	0.92	35.53	735	1	98	0	1	22	142.0	-23.9	90	17	100,000	0	0.0	0.0
C- / 3.8	14.9	0.92	35.55	104	1	98	0	1	22	N/A	N/A	90	17	1,000,000	0	0.0	0.0
C- / 3.8	14.9	0.92	35.07	285	1	98	0	1	22	138.7	-23.9	89	17	2,500	50	0.0	0.0
C+ / 6.1	10.3	0.97	16.06	5,808	0	100	0	0	73	128.9	-24.1	68	6	1,000	0	5.8	0.0
C+ / 6.1	10.3	0.97	16.18	17	0	100	0	0	73	120.3	-24.4	58	6	250	0	0.0	0.0
C+ / 6.1	10.3	0.97	16.05	415	0	100	0	0	73	120.4	-24.4	59	6	1,000	0	0.0	0.0
C+ / 6.1	10.3	0.97	16.06	277	0	100	0	0	73	131.2	-24.1	70	6	0	0	0.0	0.0
C+ / 6.1	10.3	0.97	16.12	143	0	100	0	0	73	132.5	-24.1	71	6	1,000,000	0	0.0	0.0
C+ / 6.1	10.3	0.97	16.03	21	0	100	0	0	73	128.8	-24.2	68	6	0	0	0.0	0.0
C+ / 6.1	10.4	0.97	16.06	1	0	100	0	0	73	124.9	-24.2	63	6	0	0	0.0	0.0
C+ / 6.1	10.3	0.97	16.04	52	0	100	0	0	73	126.6	-24.2	65	6	0	0	0.0	0.0
D+ / 2.9	13.2	0.71	26.10	71	2	97	0	1	13	111.4	-25.3	93	13	1,000,000	0	0.0	0.0
C / 5.2	9.5	0.87	14.63	1,635	0	99	0	1	58	109.0	-16.0	77	5	1,000	0	5.8	0.0
C / 5.2	9.5	0.87	14.48	10	0	99	0	1	58	100.9	-16.2	70	5	1,000	0	0.0	0.0
C / 5.2	9.5	0.86	14.44	303	0	99	0	1	58	100.9	-16.2	71	5	1,000	0	0.0	0.0
C / 5.2	9.5	0.87	14.62	356	0	99	0	1	58	111.0	-15.9	78	5	0	0	0.0	0.0
C / 5.3	9.5	0.87	14.76	19	0	99	0	1	58	112.0	-15.9	79	5	1,000,000	0	0.0	0.0
C / 5.3	9.5	0.87	14.70	2	0	99	0	1	58	107.0	-16.0	75	5	0	0	0.0	0.0
C / 5.3	9.5	0.87	14.75	1	0	99	0	1	58	105.3	-16.1	74	5	0	0	0.0	0.0
C / 5.2	9.5	0.87	14.56	23	0	99	0	1	58	106.7	-16.1	75	5	0	0	0.0	0.0
C / 5.0	9.8	1.11	12.16	75	1	24	1	74	223	68.1	-17.3	45	14	1,500	0	2.3	0.0
C / 5.0	9.7	1.11	12.16	1	1	24	1	74	223	61.1	-17.6	35	14	1,000	0	0.0	0.0
C / 5.0	9.8	1.12	12.09	39	1	24	1	74	223	62.6	-17.5	36	14	1,500	0	0.0	0.0
C / 4.9	9.8	1.11	12.16	97	1	24	1	74	223	69.1	-17.3	47	14	0	0	0.0	0.0
C / 5.0	9.8	1.11	12.23	374	1	24	1	74	223	70.1	-17.3	49	14	1,000,000	0	0.0	0.0
C / 5.0	9.8	1.11	12.33	N/A	1	24	1	74	223	66.5	-17.5	44	14	0	0	0.0	0.0
C / 5.0	9.8	1.11	12.32	N/A	1	24	1	74	223	64.6	-17.5	40	14	0	0	0.0	0.0
C / 5.0	9.8	1.11	12.11	3	1	24	1	74	223	65.6	-17.4	41	14	0	0	0.0	0.0
E+ / 0.9	18.5	1.04	19.37	701	0	99	0	1	204	90.3	-23.6	2	16	1,000	0	5.8	0.0
E+ / 0.6	18.5	1.04	14.43	2	0	99	0	1	204	83.3	-23.9	2	16	1,000	0	0.0	0.0
E+ / 0.6	18.5	1.04	14.60	54	0	99	0	1	204	83.3	-23.9	2	16	1,000	0	0.0	0.0
D- / 1.0	18.5	1.04	20.03	100	0	99	0	1	204	92.5	-23.6	2	16	0	0	0.0	0.0
D- / 1.1	18.5	1.04	22.11	937	0	99	0	1	204	93.4	-23.5	3	16	1,000,000	0	0.0	0.0
E+ / 0.9	18.5	1.04	18.78	24	0	99	0	1	204	90.4	-23.6	2	16	0	0	0.0	0.0
E+ / 0.9	18.5	1.04	18.61	7	0	99	0	1	204	87.3	-23.7	2	16	0	0	0.0	0.0
E+ / 0.9	18.5	1.04	18.89	159	0	99	0	1	204	88.4	-23.7	2	16	0	0	0.0	0.0
U /	N/A	N/A	22.17	201	0	99	0	1	204	N/A	N/A	N/A	16	0	0	0.0	0.0
C / 4.9	11.2	0.68	21.29	81	0	99	0	1	68	N/A	N/A	99	6	1,500	0	5.8	0.0
C / 5.0	11.2	0.68	20.95	18	0	99	0	1	68	N/A	N/A	98	6	1,500	0	0.0	0.0
C / 4.9	11.3	0.69	21.31	20	0	99	0	1	68	N/A	N/A	99	6	0	0	0.0	0.0
C / 4.9	11.2	0.68	21.33	349	0	99	0	1	68	N/A	N/A	99	6	1,000,000	0	0.0	0.0
C / 5.0	11.3	0.69	21.41	N/A	0	99	0	1	68	N/A	N/A	98	6	0	0	0.0	0.0
C / 4.9	11.2	0.68	21.17	N/A	0	99	0	1	68	N/A	N/A	98	6	0	0	0.0	0.0
C / 4.8	12.3	1.09	22.07	121	0	99	0	1	83	N/A	N/A	38	6	1,500	0	5.8	0.0
C / 4.8	12.3	1.09	21.67	51	0	99	0	1	83	N/A	N/A	29	6	1,500	0	0.0	0.0
C / 4.8	12.3	1.09	22.09	164	0	99	0	1	83	N/A	N/A	41	6	0	0	0.0	0.0

Fund Type	Fund Name	Ticker Symbol	Overall Investment Rating	Phone	PERFORMANCE Perfor-mance Rating/Pts	3 Mo	6 Mo	1Yr / Pct	3Yr / Pct	5Yr / Pct	Dividend Yield	Expense Ratio

99 Pct = Best
0 Pct = Worst

Total Return % through 2/28/17 — Annualized (3Yr/5Yr). Incl. in Returns.

Fund Type	Fund Name	Ticker Symbol	Overall Investment Rating	Phone	Perf. Rating/Pts	3 Mo	6 Mo	1Yr / Pct	3Yr / Pct	5Yr / Pct	Dividend Yield	Expense Ratio
GR	Lord Abbett Eq Tr Calib MCV I	LVMIX	B+	(888) 522-2388	A- / 9.2	6.34	11.22	31.37 /89	8.90 /86	13.64 /90	1.71	0.77
GR	Lord Abbett Eq Tr Calib MCV R2	LVMQX	B	(888) 522-2388	B+ / 8.9	6.20	10.92	30.57 /87	8.27 /81	13.12 /85	1.25	1.37
GR	Lord Abbett Eq Tr Calib MCV R3	LVMRX	B+	(888) 522-2388	B+ / 8.9	6.24	10.97	30.77 /88	8.39 /82	13.20 /86	1.30	1.27
GI	Lord Abbett Fundamental Equity A	LDFVX	C	(888) 522-2388	C+ / 6.8	5.36	10.57	27.51 /81	7.02 /72	11.28 /68	1.33	0.97
GI	● Lord Abbett Fundamental Equity B	GILBX	C	(888) 522-2388	B- / 7.2	5.16	10.15	26.60 /78	6.24 /66	10.52 /62	0.61	1.72
GI	Lord Abbett Fundamental Equity C	GILAX	C	(888) 522-2388	B- / 7.2	5.23	10.24	26.76 /78	6.25 /66	10.53 /62	0.84	1.72
GI	Lord Abbett Fundamental Equity F	LAVFX	C+	(888) 522-2388	B / 7.9	5.41	10.68	27.79 /81	7.21 /73	11.52 /70	1.57	0.82
GI	Lord Abbett Fundamental Equity I	LAVYX	C+	(888) 522-2388	B / 8.0	5.42	10.71	27.89 /81	7.31 /74	11.63 /71	1.64	0.72
GI	● Lord Abbett Fundamental Equity P	LAVPX	C+	(888) 522-2388	B / 7.7	5.37	10.46	27.36 /80	6.84 /71	11.13 /67	1.25	1.17
GI	Lord Abbett Fundamental Equity R2	LAVQX	C+	(888) 522-2388	B- / 7.5	5.31	10.39	27.13 /80	6.67 /70	10.96 /66	1.09	1.32
GI	Lord Abbett Fundamental Equity R3	LAVRX	C+	(888) 522-2388	B / 7.6	5.28	10.47	27.24 /80	6.78 /70	11.08 /67	1.20	1.22
GL	Lord Abbett Growth Leaders A	LGLAX	C-	(888) 522-2388	C / 4.8	6.57	6.38	17.89 /42	6.15 /66	13.07 /85	0.00	0.99
GR	Lord Abbett Growth Leaders B	GLABX	C-	(888) 522-2388	C / 5.3	6.35	6.02	17.03 /38	5.37 /58	--	0.00	1.74
GL	Lord Abbett Growth Leaders C	LGLCX	C-	(888) 522-2388	C / 5.3	6.38	5.99	17.01 /38	5.37 /58	12.29 /77	0.00	1.74
GL	Lord Abbett Growth Leaders F	LGLFX	C	(888) 522-2388	C+ / 6.1	6.60	6.46	18.06 /43	6.31 /67	13.28 /87	0.00	0.84
GL	Lord Abbett Growth Leaders I	LGLIX	C	(888) 522-2388	C+ / 6.2	6.61	6.52	18.19 /44	6.41 /68	13.40 /88	0.00	0.74
GL	Lord Abbett Growth Leaders R2	LGLQX	C	(888) 522-2388	C+ / 5.6	6.45	6.22	17.46 /40	5.78 /62	12.94 /83	0.00	1.34
GL	Lord Abbett Growth Leaders R3	LGLRX	C	(888) 522-2388	C+ / 5.7	6.48	6.25	17.55 /41	5.87 /63	12.85 /82	0.00	1.24
GR	Lord Abbett Growth Opportunities A	LMGAX	D-	(888) 522-2388	D+ / 2.9	4.64	3.54	17.36 /40	3.86 /41	9.58 /55	0.00	1.28
GR	● Lord Abbett Growth Opportunities B	LMGBX	E+	(888) 522-2388	C- / 3.3	4.44	3.18	16.49 /36	3.09 /33	8.81 /49	0.00	2.03
GR	Lord Abbett Growth Opportunities C	LMGCX	E+	(888) 522-2388	C- / 3.3	4.51	3.18	16.58 /37	3.11 /33	8.83 /49	0.00	2.03
GR	Lord Abbett Growth Opportunities F	LGOFX	D	(888) 522-2388	C- / 4.0	4.69	3.63	17.57 /41	4.03 /43	9.80 /57	0.00	1.13
GR	Lord Abbett Growth Opportunities I	LMGYX	D	(888) 522-2388	C- / 4.1	4.72	3.69	17.65 /41	4.13 /44	9.90 /58	0.00	1.03
GR	● Lord Abbett Growth Opportunities P	LGOPX	D-	(888) 522-2388	C- / 3.8	4.62	3.45	17.13 /39	3.67 /39	9.41 /54	0.00	1.48
GR	Lord Abbett Growth Opportunities R2	LGOQX	D-	(888) 522-2388	C- / 3.6	4.54	3.35	16.95 /38	3.51 /37	9.24 /53	0.00	1.63
GR	Lord Abbett Growth Opportunities R3	LGORX	D-	(888) 522-2388	C- / 3.7	4.58	3.46	17.12 /39	3.61 /38	9.36 /53	0.00	1.53
MC	Lord Abbett Growth Opportunities R6	LGOVX	U	(888) 522-2388	U /	4.71	3.73	17.84 /42	--	--	0.00	0.88
FO	Lord Abbett Intl Core Equity A	LICAX	D-	(888) 522-2388	E- / 0.2	6.28	1.45	10.09 /12	-3.55 / 4	2.12 / 8	2.03	1.29
FO	● Lord Abbett Intl Core Equity B	LICBX	D-	(888) 522-2388	E / 0.3	6.15	1.12	9.40 /10	-4.21 / 3	1.44 / 7	1.09	2.04
FO	Lord Abbett Intl Core Equity C	LICCX	D-	(888) 522-2388	E / 0.3	6.12	1.15	9.38 /10	-4.19 / 3	1.45 / 7	1.37	2.04
FO	Lord Abbett Intl Core Equity F	LICFX	D-	(888) 522-2388	E / 0.4	6.36	1.59	10.39 /13	-3.29 / 4	2.38 / 9	2.37	1.14
FO	Lord Abbett Intl Core Equity I	LICYX	D-	(888) 522-2388	E / 0.4	6.38	1.59	10.46 /13	-3.20 / 4	2.49 / 9	2.44	1.04
FO	● Lord Abbett Intl Core Equity P	LICPX	D-	(888) 522-2388	E / 0.4	6.27	1.36	9.98 /12	-3.70 / 3	1.99 / 8	1.97	1.49
FO	Lord Abbett Intl Core Equity R2	LICQX	D-	(888) 522-2388	E / 0.4	6.23	1.30	9.75 /11	-3.84 / 3	1.85 / 8	1.84	1.64
FO	Lord Abbett Intl Core Equity R3	LICRX	D-	(888) 522-2388	E / 0.4	6.27	1.37	9.94 /11	-3.73 / 3	1.95 / 8	1.99	1.54
FO	Lord Abbett Intl Dividend Inc A	LIDAX	E	(888) 522-2388	E / 0.3	5.38	2.59	13.45 /23	-3.62 / 4	1.43 / 7	3.38	1.15
FO	Lord Abbett Intl Dividend Inc C	LIDCX	E	(888) 522-2388	E / 0.3	5.06	2.21	12.53 /20	-4.35 / 3	0.72 / 6	2.85	1.90
FO	Lord Abbett Intl Dividend Inc F	LIDFX	E	(888) 522-2388	E / 0.5	5.41	2.67	13.61 /24	-3.46 / 4	1.64 / 7	3.73	1.00
FO	Lord Abbett Intl Dividend Inc I	LAIDX	E	(888) 522-2388	E / 0.5	5.42	2.72	13.68 /24	-3.35 / 4	1.77 / 8	3.82	0.90
FO	Lord Abbett Intl Dividend Inc R2	LIDRX	E	(888) 522-2388	E / 0.4	5.32	2.36	13.09 /22	-3.94 / 3	1.13 / 6	3.15	1.50
FO	Lord Abbett Intl Dividend Inc R3	LIRRX	E	(888) 522-2388	E / 0.4	5.26	2.45	13.24 /22	-3.85 / 3	1.23 / 7	3.33	1.40
GL	Lord Abbett Inv Tr-Div Eq Strat A	LDSAX	D	(888) 522-2388	C- / 4.2	5.75	6.98	21.04 /58	4.72 /51	10.22 /60	1.33	1.38
GL	● Lord Abbett Inv Tr-Div Eq Strat B	LDSBX	D+	(888) 522-2388	C / 4.8	5.56	6.58	20.11 /53	3.93 /42	9.37 /54	0.29	2.13
GL	Lord Abbett Inv Tr-Div Eq Strat C	LDSCX	D+	(888) 522-2388	C / 4.8	5.58	6.55	20.11 /53	3.94 /42	9.41 /54	0.70	2.13
GL	Lord Abbett Inv Tr-Div Eq Strat F	LDSFX	C-	(888) 522-2388	C+ / 5.6	5.74	7.04	21.18 /58	4.86 /53	10.36 /61	1.50	1.23
GL	Lord Abbett Inv Tr-Div Eq Strat I	LDSYX	C-	(888) 522-2388	C+ / 5.7	5.80	7.09	21.25 /59	4.96 /54	10.48 /62	1.65	1.13
GL	Lord Abbett Inv Tr-Div Eq Strat R2	LDSQX	D+	(888) 522-2388	C / 4.9	5.69	6.79	20.73 /56	3.97 /43	9.58 /55	0.83	1.73
GL	Lord Abbett Inv Tr-Div Eq Strat R3	LDSRX	D+	(888) 522-2388	C / 5.2	5.67	6.80	20.64 /56	4.45 /48	9.93 /58	1.18	1.63
MC	Lord Abbett Mid Cap Stock A	LAVLX	B	(888) 522-2388	B- / 7.4	4.83	9.77	29.05 /84	8.27 /81	11.93 /74	0.55	1.01
MC	● Lord Abbett Mid Cap Stock B	LMCBX	B+	(888) 522-2388	B / 7.9	4.65	9.40	28.15 /82	7.49 /75	11.16 /67	0.01	1.76
MC	Lord Abbett Mid Cap Stock C	LMCCX	B+	(888) 522-2388	B / 7.9	4.67	9.36	28.12 /82	7.49 /75	11.16 /67	0.01	1.76
MC	Lord Abbett Mid Cap Stock F	LMCFX	A-	(888) 522-2388	B+ / 8.6	4.89	9.87	29.22 /85	8.46 /83	12.15 /76	0.74	0.86

● Denotes fund is closed to new investors
* Denotes fund is included in Section II

RISK			NET ASSETS		ASSET					BULL / BEAR		FUND MANAGER		MINIMUMS		LOADS	
	3 Year		NAV						Portfolio	Last Bull	Last Bear	Manager	Manager	Initial	Additional	Front	Back
Risk Rating/Pts	Standard Deviation	Beta	As of 2/28/17	Total $(Mil)	Cash %	Stocks %	Bonds %	Other %	Turnover Ratio	Market Return	Market Return	Quality Pct	Tenure (Years)	Purch. $	Purch. $	End Load	End Load
C /4.8	12.3	1.09	22.14	661	0	99	0	1	83	N/A	N/A	42	6	1,000,000	0	0.0	0.0
C /4.8	12.3	1.09	22.11	3	0	99	0	1	83	N/A	N/A	35	6	0	0	0.0	0.0
C /4.8	12.3	1.09	22.12	4	0	99	0	1	83	N/A	N/A	36	6	0	0	0.0	0.0
C- /4.2	10.6	0.97	13.36	1,696	1	98	0	1	135	112.1	-22.0	34	7	1,500	0	5.8	0.0
C- /4.1	10.6	0.98	12.22	12	1	98	0	1	135	104.2	-22.2	26	7	1,000	0	0.0	0.0
C- /4.0	10.6	0.98	12.08	551	1	98	0	1	135	104.5	-22.2	26	7	1,500	0	0.0	0.0
C- /4.2	10.6	0.98	13.24	332	1	98	0	1	135	114.4	-21.9	36	7	0	0	0.0	0.0
C- /4.2	10.6	0.98	13.43	146	1	98	0	1	135	115.7	-21.9	37	7	1,000,000	0	0.0	0.0
C- /4.2	10.6	0.98	13.14	11	1	98	0	1	135	110.5	-22.0	31	7	0	0	0.0	0.0
C- /4.2	10.6	0.98	13.10	9	1	98	0	1	135	108.7	-22.0	30	7	0	0	0.0	0.0
C- /4.2	10.6	0.98	13.16	161	1	98	0	1	135	109.8	-22.0	31	7	0	0	0.0	0.0
C /5.0	12.1	0.74	24.18	669	1	98	0	1	246	119.8	N/A	97	6	1,500	0	5.8	0.0
C /5.0	12.1	1.04	23.43	2	1	98	0	1	246	N/A	N/A	13	6	0	0	0.0	0.0
C /5.0	12.1	0.74	23.18	481	1	98	0	1	246	111.6	N/A	96	6	1,500	0	0.0	0.0
C /5.0	12.1	0.74	24.38	902	1	98	0	1	246	122.1	N/A	97	6	0	0	0.0	0.0
C /5.0	12.1	0.74	24.50	103	1	98	0	1	246	123.4	N/A	97	6	1,000,000	0	0.0	0.0
C /5.0	12.1	0.74	24.08	1	1	98	0	1	246	118.7	N/A	97	6	0	0	0.0	0.0
C /5.0	12.1	0.74	23.98	13	1	98	0	1	246	118.0	N/A	97	6	0	0	0.0	0.0
C- /3.3	12.4	1.04	19.18	352	0	99	0	1	97	103.2	-27.6	6	9	1,000	0	5.8	0.0
D+ /2.6	12.4	1.03	14.84	3	0	99	0	1	97	95.6	-27.8	5	9	1,000	0	0.0	0.0
D+ /2.6	12.5	1.04	14.84	48	0	99	0	1	97	95.8	-27.8	5	9	1,000	0	0.0	0.0
C- /3.4	12.4	1.04	19.85	26	0	99	0	1	97	105.3	-27.5	7	9	0	0	0.0	0.0
C- /3.6	12.4	1.03	21.51	44	0	99	0	1	97	106.4	-27.5	7	9	1,000,000	0	0.0	0.0
C- /3.3	12.4	1.04	18.79	3	0	99	0	1	97	101.5	-27.6	6	9	0	0	0.0	0.0
C- /3.2	12.4	1.04	18.41	1	0	99	0	1	97	99.8	-27.6	5	9	0	0	0.0	0.0
C- /3.3	12.4	1.04	18.73	23	0	99	0	1	97	101.0	-27.6	6	9	0	0	0.0	0.0
U /	N/A	N/A	21.57	52	0	99	0	1	97	N/A	N/A	N/A	9	0	0	0.0	0.0
C+ /6.0	10.9	0.86	12.02	235	5	94	0	1	164	29.5	-23.5	29	1	1,500	0	5.8	0.0
C+ /6.1	10.9	0.86	12.02	2	5	94	0	1	164	24.8	-23.7	22	1	1,000	0	0.0	0.0
C+ /6.1	10.9	0.85	11.93	28	5	94	0	1	164	25.0	-23.7	22	1	1,500	0	0.0	0.0
C+ /6.0	10.9	0.85	11.94	62	5	94	0	1	164	31.3	-23.4	32	1	0	0	0.0	0.0
C+ /6.0	10.8	0.85	12.10	163	5	94	0	1	164	31.9	-23.3	33	1	1,000,000	0	0.0	0.0
C+ /6.1	10.9	0.85	12.04	N/A	5	94	0	1	164	28.5	-23.4	27	1	0	0	0.0	0.0
C+ /6.0	10.9	0.86	12.01	1	5	94	0	1	164	27.5	-23.5	26	1	0	0	0.0	0.0
C+ /6.0	10.9	0.86	11.85	14	5	94	0	1	164	28.3	-23.5	27	1	0	0	0.0	0.0
C /4.5	11.5	0.85	6.90	374	6	91	1	2	58	24.6	-22.9	28	9	1,500	0	5.8	0.0
C /4.5	11.5	0.85	6.83	74	6	91	1	2	58	19.9	-23.0	21	9	1,500	0	0.0	0.0
C /4.5	11.6	0.85	6.91	108	6	91	1	2	58	25.9	-22.7	30	9	0	0	0.0	0.0
C /4.5	11.6	0.85	6.93	710	6	91	1	2	58	26.7	-22.7	31	9	1,000,000	0	0.0	0.0
C /4.5	11.6	0.85	7.04	1	6	91	1	2	58	22.6	-22.9	25	9	0	0	0.0	0.0
C /4.5	11.6	0.85	6.96	13	6	91	1	2	58	23.1	-22.9	26	9	0	0	0.0	0.0
C- /4.0	10.5	0.72	17.55	151	2	97	0	1	12	100.3	-23.3	95	2	1,500	0	5.8	0.0
C- /4.1	10.5	0.72	17.25	2	2	97	0	1	12	92.3	-23.5	93	2	1,000	0	0.0	0.0
C- /4.1	10.5	0.72	17.03	52	2	97	0	1	12	92.5	-23.5	93	2	1,500	0	0.0	0.0
C- /4.0	10.5	0.72	17.54	3	2	97	0	1	12	101.8	-23.3	95	2	0	0	0.0	0.0
C- /4.0	10.5	0.72	17.69	20	2	97	0	1	12	103.0	-23.2	95	2	1,000,000	0	0.0	0.0
C- /4.2	10.6	0.73	18.02	N/A	2	97	0	1	12	94.3	-23.4	93	2	0	0	0.0	0.0
C- /4.0	10.5	0.72	17.34	12	2	97	0	1	12	97.6	-23.4	94	2	0	0	0.0	0.0
C+ /6.1	11.7	0.94	29.66	1,171	1	98	0	1	63	121.5	-24.2	66	9	1,000	0	5.8	0.0
C+ /6.2	11.7	0.94	27.69	5	1	98	0	1	63	113.4	-24.4	56	9	1,000	0	0.0	0.0
C+ /6.2	11.7	0.94	27.57	197	1	98	0	1	63	113.4	-24.3	57	9	1,000	0	0.0	0.0
C+ /6.1	11.7	0.94	29.42	153	1	98	0	1	63	124.0	-24.1	68	9	0	0	0.0	0.0

					PERFORMANCE						Incl. in Returns	
	99 Pct = Best 0 Pct = Worst				Perfor-mance			Total Return % through 2/28/17				
									Annualized		Dividend	Expense
Fund Type	Fund Name	Ticker Symbol	Overall Investment Rating	Phone	Rating/Pts	3 Mo	6 Mo	1Yr / Pct	3Yr / Pct	5Yr / Pct	Yield	Ratio
MC	Lord Abbett Mid Cap Stock I	LMCYX	A-	(888) 522-2388	B+ / 8.7	4.90	9.91	29.41 / 85	8.56 / 83	12.26 / 77	0.82	0.76
MC	Lord Abbett Mid Cap Stock P	LMCPX	B+	(888) 522-2388	B+ / 8.3	4.82	9.68	28.80 / 84	8.14 / 80	11.86 / 73	0.41	1.21
MC	Lord Abbett Mid Cap Stock R2	LMCQX	B+	(888) 522-2388	B / 8.2	4.78	9.59	28.63 / 83	7.92 / 78	11.61 / 71	0.33	1.36
MC	Lord Abbett Mid Cap Stock R3	LMCRX	B+	(888) 522-2388	B+ / 8.3	4.78	9.66	28.79 / 83	8.04 / 79	11.73 / 72	0.39	1.26
BA	Lord Abbett Multi Asset Bal Opp A	LABFX	C	(888) 522-2388	C / 4.7	5.09	7.26	20.91 / 57	4.29 / 46	7.56 / 39	3.11	1.23
BA	● Lord Abbett Multi Asset Bal Opp B	LABBX	C	(888) 522-2388	C / 4.4	4.88	6.84	19.96 / 52	3.49 / 37	6.74 / 33	2.43	1.98
BA	Lord Abbett Multi Asset Bal Opp C	BFLAX	C	(888) 522-2388	C / 4.4	4.92	6.82	20.03 / 52	3.50 / 37	6.76 / 33	2.49	1.98
BA	Lord Abbett Multi Asset Bal Opp F	BLAFX	C+	(888) 522-2388	C / 5.3	5.13	7.35	21.11 / 58	4.45 / 48	7.70 / 40	3.33	1.08
BA	Lord Abbett Multi Asset Bal Opp I	LABYX	C+	(888) 522-2388	C / 5.4	5.25	7.49	21.22 / 58	4.55 / 49	7.82 / 41	3.42	0.98
BA	● Lord Abbett Multi Asset Bal Opp P	LABPX	C	(888) 522-2388	C / 5.0	5.06	7.19	20.66 / 56	4.07 / 44	7.33 / 37	3.01	1.43
BA	Lord Abbett Multi Asset Bal Opp R2	BLAQX	C	(888) 522-2388	C / 4.8	5.08	7.12	20.48 / 55	3.92 / 42	7.18 / 36	2.78	1.58
BA	Lord Abbett Multi Asset Bal Opp R3	BLARX	C	(888) 522-2388	C / 4.9	5.04	7.15	20.57 / 55	4.02 / 43	7.28 / 37	2.97	1.48
GL	Lord Abbett Multi Asset Glbl Opp A	LAGEX	D+	(888) 522-2388	D+ / 2.7	5.19	5.98	18.55 / 45	1.60 / 22	4.95 / 21	3.19	1.51
GL	● Lord Abbett Multi Asset Glbl Opp B	LAGBX	D+	(888) 522-2388	D+ / 2.6	5.01	5.57	17.77 / 42	0.87 / 18	4.17 / 16	2.87	2.26
GL	Lord Abbett Multi Asset Glbl Opp C	LAGCX	D+	(888) 522-2388	D+ / 2.6	5.04	5.61	17.72 / 42	0.87 / 18	4.18 / 16	2.93	2.26
GL	Lord Abbett Multi Asset Glbl Opp F	LAGFX	C-	(888) 522-2388	C- / 3.2	5.13	5.96	18.72 / 46	1.75 / 22	5.10 / 22	3.40	1.36
GL	Lord Abbett Multi Asset Glbl Opp I	LGEYX	C-	(888) 522-2388	C- / 3.3	5.21	6.07	18.82 / 46	1.87 / 23	5.21 / 23	3.48	1.26
GL	Lord Abbett Multi Asset Glbl Opp R2	LAGQX	D+	(888) 522-2388	D+ / 2.9	5.09	5.68	18.10 / 43	1.23 / 19	4.58 / 19	2.88	1.86
GL	Lord Abbett Multi Asset Glbl Opp R3	LARRX	D+	(888) 522-2388	C- / 3.0	5.08	5.81	18.27 / 44	1.36 / 20	4.71 / 19	3.01	1.76
GL	Lord Abbett Multi Asset Glbl Opp R6	LARVX	U	(888) 522-2388	U /	5.22	6.09	18.88 / 47	--	--	3.52	1.14
IN	Lord Abbett Multi Asset Income A	ISFAX	C-	(888) 522-2388	C- / 3.1	4.03	5.10	15.68 / 33	3.27 / 34	5.68 / 26	3.91	1.17
IN	● Lord Abbett Multi Asset Income B	ISFBX	C-	(888) 522-2388	D+ / 2.9	3.84	4.69	14.79 / 29	2.51 / 28	4.89 / 21	3.18	1.92
IN	Lord Abbett Multi Asset Income C	ISFCX	C-	(888) 522-2388	D+ / 2.9	3.78	4.70	14.83 / 29	2.49 / 27	4.88 / 21	3.20	1.92
IN	Lord Abbett Multi Asset Income F	LIGFX	C-	(888) 522-2388	C- / 3.5	4.00	5.10	15.78 / 33	3.40 / 36	5.82 / 27	4.15	1.02
IN	Lord Abbett Multi Asset Income I	ISFYX	C-	(888) 522-2388	C- / 3.6	4.04	5.26	15.98 / 34	3.52 / 37	5.92 / 28	4.26	0.92
IN	Lord Abbett Multi Asset Income R2	LIGQX	C-	(888) 522-2388	C- / 3.2	3.91	4.93	15.26 / 31	2.91 / 31	5.30 / 23	3.54	1.52
IN	Lord Abbett Multi Asset Income R3	LIXRX	C-	(888) 522-2388	C- / 3.3	3.96	4.97	15.40 / 32	3.02 / 32	5.41 / 24	3.76	1.42
GL	Lord Abbett Multi-Asset Growth A	LWSAX	C	(888) 522-2388	C / 5.5	5.20	7.96	22.35 / 64	5.22 / 57	8.55 / 47	2.64	1.23
GL	● Lord Abbett Multi-Asset Growth B	LWSBX	C	(888) 522-2388	C / 5.3	5.01	7.50	21.36 / 59	4.42 / 48	7.74 / 40	1.95	1.98
GL	Lord Abbett Multi-Asset Growth C	LWSCX	C	(888) 522-2388	C / 5.3	4.99	7.57	21.44 / 59	4.44 / 48	7.76 / 40	2.03	1.98
GL	Lord Abbett Multi-Asset Growth F	LGXFX	C+	(888) 522-2388	C+ / 6.1	5.24	8.04	22.53 / 65	5.40 / 58	8.73 / 48	2.84	1.08
GL	Lord Abbett Multi-Asset Growth I	LWSYX	C+	(888) 522-2388	C+ / 6.2	5.24	8.06	22.60 / 65	5.47 / 59	8.82 / 49	2.92	0.98
GL	● Lord Abbett Multi-Asset Growth P	LWSPX	C+	(888) 522-2388	C+ / 5.9	5.15	7.85	22.12 / 63	5.08 / 55	8.39 / 45	2.55	1.43
GL	Lord Abbett Multi-Asset Growth R2	LGIQX	C+	(888) 522-2388	C+ / 5.7	5.07	7.76	21.88 / 62	4.85 / 53	8.18 / 43	2.36	1.58
GL	Lord Abbett Multi-Asset Growth R3	LGIRX	C+	(888) 522-2388	C+ / 5.8	5.15	7.86	22.06 / 63	4.99 / 54	8.31 / 45	2.50	1.48
GL	Lord Abbett Sec Tr-Alpha Stratg A	ALFAX	D-	(888) 522-2388	C- / 3.9	4.16	7.08	25.37 / 74	3.52 / 37	10.79 / 64	0.00	1.62
GL	● Lord Abbett Sec Tr-Alpha Stratg B	ALFBX	D-	(888) 522-2388	C / 4.4	3.97	6.70	24.44 / 71	2.75 / 30	9.96 / 58	0.00	2.37
GL	Lord Abbett Sec Tr-Alpha Stratg C	ALFCX	D-	(888) 522-2388	C / 4.5	3.99	6.71	24.46 / 72	2.75 / 30	9.96 / 58	0.00	2.37
GL	Lord Abbett Sec Tr-Alpha Stratg F	ALFFX	D	(888) 522-2388	C / 5.2	4.19	7.14	25.55 / 75	3.67 / 39	10.95 / 65	0.00	1.47
GL	Lord Abbett Sec Tr-Alpha Stratg R2	ALFQX	D	(888) 522-2388	C / 4.8	4.03	6.89	24.92 / 73	3.15 / 33	10.40 / 61	0.00	1.97
GL	Lord Abbett Sec Tr-Alpha Stratg R3	ALFRX	D	(888) 522-2388	C / 4.9	4.05	6.94	25.04 / 73	3.26 / 34	10.51 / 62	0.00	1.87
FO	Lord Abbett Sec Tr-Intl Opp A	LAIEX	D	(888) 522-2388	D- / 1.4	6.99	2.83	12.64 / 20	0.72 / 17	7.71 / 40	0.64	1.33
FO	Lord Abbett Sec Tr-Intl Opp C	LINCX	D	(888) 522-2388	D- / 1.3	6.83	2.45	11.84 / 17	-0.01 / 13	6.96 / 34	0.00	2.08
FO	Lord Abbett Sec Tr-Intl Opp F	LINFX	D	(888) 522-2388	D / 2.1	7.10	2.90	12.87 / 21	0.88 / 18	7.92 / 41	0.83	1.18
FO	Lord Abbett Sec Tr-Intl Opp I	LINYX	D	(888) 522-2388	D / 2.2	7.11	2.98	12.97 / 22	0.99 / 18	8.03 / 42	0.92	1.08
FO	● Lord Abbett Sec Tr-Intl Opp P	LINPX	D	(888) 522-2388	D / 2.0	6.99	2.71	12.46 / 20	0.52 / 16	7.53 / 38	0.37	1.53
FO	Lord Abbett Sec Tr-Intl Opp R2	LINQX	D	(888) 522-2388	D / 1.9	6.95	2.66	12.37 / 19	0.39 / 15	7.39 / 37	0.55	1.68
FO	Lord Abbett Sec Tr-Intl Opp R3	LINRX	D	(888) 522-2388	D / 2.0	6.99	2.70	12.44 / 20	0.51 / 16	7.51 / 38	0.57	1.58
SC	Lord Abbett Small Cap Value A	LRSCX	D-	(888) 522-2388	C+ / 6.2	2.25	9.02	28.61 / 83	6.67 / 70	10.26 / 60	0.00	1.21
SC	● Lord Abbett Small Cap Value B	LRSBX	D-	(888) 522-2388	C+ / 6.7	2.05	8.56	27.63 / 81	5.88 / 63	9.47 / 54	0.00	1.96
SC	Lord Abbett Small Cap Value C	LSRCX	D-	(888) 522-2388	C+ / 6.7	2.05	8.61	27.66 / 81	5.89 / 63	9.48 / 54	0.00	1.96
SC	Lord Abbett Small Cap Value F	LRSFX	D	(888) 522-2388	B- / 7.3	2.25	9.09	28.83 / 84	6.83 / 71	10.45 / 62	0.00	1.06

● Denotes fund is closed to new investors

* Denotes fund is included in Section II

Risk Rating/Pts	Standard Deviation	Beta	NAV As of 2/28/17	Total $(Mil)	Cash %	Stocks %	Bonds %	Other %	Portfolio Turnover Ratio	Last Bull Market Return	Last Bear Market Return	Manager Quality Pct	Manager Tenure (Years)	Initial Purch. $	Additional Purch. $	Front End Load	Back End Load
C+ / 6.1	11.7	0.94	29.45	704	1	98	0	1	63	125.2	-24.0	69	9	1,000,000	0	0.0	0.0
C+ / 6.1	11.7	0.94	28.77	73	1	98	0	1	63	120.8	-24.2	64	9	0	0	0.0	0.0
C+ / 6.2	11.7	0.94	29.24	1	1	98	0	1	63	118.0	-24.2	62	9	0	0	0.0	0.0
C+ / 6.2	11.7	0.94	29.35	38	1	98	0	1	63	119.4	-24.2	63	9	0	0	0.0	0.0
C+ / 6.3	7.7	1.14	11.67	1,431	1	55	34	10	25	69.1	-16.6	23	2	1,500	0	2.3	0.0
C+ / 6.3	7.7	1.15	11.67	10	1	55	34	10	25	62.4	-17.0	16	2	1,000	0	0.0	0.0
C+ / 6.3	7.7	1.15	11.60	357	1	55	34	10	25	62.3	-16.8	16	2	1,500	0	0.0	0.0
C+ / 6.3	7.7	1.14	11.66	71	1	55	34	10	25	70.5	-16.7	25	2	0	0	0.0	0.0
C+ / 6.3	7.7	1.15	11.67	12	1	55	34	10	25	71.3	-16.5	25	2	1,000,000	0	0.0	0.0
C+ / 6.3	7.7	1.15	11.62	1	1	55	34	10	25	67.2	-16.7	21	2	0	0	0.0	0.0
C+ / 6.3	7.7	1.14	11.90	1	1	55	34	10	25	65.9	-16.8	20	2	0	0	0.0	0.0
C+ / 6.3	7.7	1.15	11.64	37	1	55	34	10	25	66.7	-16.7	20	2	0	0	0.0	0.0
C+ / 6.1	8.6	0.64	11.03	135	4	64	30	2	22	48.7	-19.8	85	2	1,000	0	2.3	0.0
C+ / 6.0	8.7	0.64	9.94	1	4	64	30	2	22	42.9	-20.1	81	2	1,000	0	0.0	0.0
C+ / 6.0	8.7	0.64	9.93	33	4	64	30	2	22	42.9	-20.0	81	2	1,000	0	0.0	0.0
C+ / 6.1	8.7	0.65	11.03	5	4	64	30	2	22	49.8	-19.8	85	2	0	0	0.0	0.0
C+ / 6.1	8.7	0.64	11.11	11	4	64	30	2	22	50.7	-19.7	86	2	1,000,000	0	0.0	0.0
C+ / 6.1	8.7	0.64	11.25	N/A	4	64	30	2	22	46.2	-19.9	83	2	0	0	0.0	0.0
C+ / 6.1	8.6	0.64	11.09	6	4	64	30	2	22	46.8	-19.8	83	2	0	0	0.0	0.0
U /	N/A	N/A	11.11	45	4	64	30	2	22	N/A	N/A	N/A	2	0	0	0.0	0.0
C+ / 6.6	5.2	0.43	14.53	824	2	20	68	10	27	48.0	-9.8	59	N/A	1,500	0	2.3	0.0
C+ / 6.6	5.2	0.43	14.74	3	2	20	68	10	27	42.0	-10.0	49	N/A	1,000	0	0.0	0.0
C+ / 6.6	5.2	0.43	14.73	575	2	20	68	10	27	42.0	-10.1	49	N/A	1,500	0	0.0	0.0
C+ / 6.6	5.2	0.43	14.52	303	2	20	68	10	27	49.0	-9.7	61	10	0	0	0.0	0.0
C+ / 6.6	5.2	0.44	14.45	11	2	20	68	10	27	49.9	-9.7	62	N/A	1,000,000	0	0.0	0.0
C+ / 6.6	5.2	0.43	14.90	N/A	2	20	68	10	27	45.1	-9.9	54	10	0	0	0.0	0.0
C+ / 6.6	5.2	0.43	14.53	19	2	20	68	10	27	45.9	-9.8	56	10	0	0	0.0	0.0
C+ / 5.7	8.5	0.60	17.37	772	2	68	29	1	21	79.9	-18.7	96	12	1,500	0	2.3	0.0
C+ / 5.7	8.5	0.60	17.25	7	2	68	29	1	21	72.6	-19.0	94	12	1,000	0	0.0	0.0
C+ / 5.7	8.5	0.59	17.20	201	2	68	29	1	21	72.8	-18.9	94	12	1,500	0	0.0	0.0
C+ / 5.7	8.5	0.60	17.37	46	2	68	29	1	21	81.4	-18.6	96	12	0	0	0.0	0.0
C+ / 5.7	8.5	0.59	17.46	12	2	68	29	1	21	82.3	-18.6	96	12	1,000,000	0	0.0	0.0
C+ / 5.7	8.5	0.59	17.58	N/A	2	68	29	1	21	78.4	-18.7	95	12	0	0	0.0	0.0
C+ / 5.8	8.5	0.60	17.70	N/A	2	68	29	1	21	76.6	-18.8	95	12	0	0	0.0	0.0
C+ / 5.7	8.5	0.59	17.32	28	2	68	29	1	21	77.6	-18.8	95	12	0	0	0.0	0.0
D+ / 2.9	13.2	0.71	25.63	506	2	97	0	1	13	108.6	-25.4	92	19	1,500	0	5.8	0.0
D+ / 2.7	13.2	0.70	22.66	3	2	97	0	1	13	100.3	-25.6	90	19	1,000	0	0.0	0.0
D+ / 2.6	13.2	0.71	22.29	257	2	97	0	1	13	100.3	-25.6	90	19	1,500	0	0.0	0.0
D+ / 2.9	13.2	0.71	25.72	258	2	97	0	1	13	110.3	-25.3	93	10	0	0	0.0	0.0
D+ / 2.9	13.2	0.71	24.93	3	2	97	0	1	13	104.7	-25.5	91	10	0	0	0.0	0.0
D+ / 2.9	13.2	0.71	25.07	36	2	97	0	1	13	105.7	-25.4	91	10	0	0	0.0	0.0
C+ / 6.2	12.4	0.90	16.54	133	1	98	0	1	82	71.7	-24.3	80	14	1,500	0	5.8	0.0
C+ / 6.1	12.4	0.90	15.49	24	1	98	0	1	82	65.4	-24.5	75	14	1,500	0	0.0	0.0
C+ / 6.1	12.4	0.90	16.39	89	1	98	0	1	82	73.6	-24.2	81	14	0	0	0.0	0.0
C+ / 6.2	12.4	0.90	16.96	267	1	98	0	1	82	74.5	-24.2	82	14	1,000,000	0	0.0	0.0
C+ / 6.2	12.4	0.90	16.87	N/A	1	98	0	1	82	70.3	-24.3	79	14	0	0	0.0	0.0
C+ / 6.1	12.4	0.90	16.31	3	1	98	0	1	82	69.1	-24.4	78	14	0	0	0.0	0.0
C+ / 6.2	12.4	0.90	16.26	15	1	98	0	1	82	70.0	-24.3	79	14	0	0	0.0	0.0
E+ / 0.7	13.8	0.86	22.08	406	2	97	0	1	44	115.8	-28.3	79	4	1,000	0	5.8	0.0
E+ / 0.6	13.8	0.86	13.75	1	2	97	0	1	44	107.4	-28.5	74	4	1,000	0	0.0	0.0
E+ / 0.6	13.8	0.86	13.78	33	2	97	0	1	44	107.6	-28.5	74	4	1,000	0	0.0	0.0
E+ / 0.7	13.8	0.86	22.16	48	2	97	0	1	44	117.8	-28.2	80	4	0	0	0.0	0.0

Fund Type	Fund Name	Ticker Symbol	Overall Investment Rating	Phone	Performance Rating/Pts	3 Mo	6 Mo	1Yr / Pct	3Yr / Pct	5Yr / Pct	Dividend Yield	Expense Ratio
								Total Return % through 2/28/17	Annualized		Incl. in Returns	
SC	Lord Abbett Small Cap Value I	LRSYX	D+	(888) 522-2388	B- / 7.4	2.30	9.15	28.90 /84	6.94 /72	10.57 /63	0.00	0.96
SC	● Lord Abbett Small Cap Value P	LRSPX	D	(888) 522-2388	B- / 7.1	2.20	8.90	28.36 /82	6.47 /68	10.07 /59	0.00	1.41
SC	Lord Abbett Small Cap Value R2	LRSQX	D	(888) 522-2388	B- / 7.0	2.13	8.86	28.18 /82	6.30 /67	9.90 /58	0.00	1.56
SC	Lord Abbett Small Cap Value R3	LRSRX	D	(888) 522-2388	B- / 7.1	2.19	8.91	28.36 /82	6.44 /68	10.04 /59	0.00	1.46
SC	Lord Abbett Small Cap Value R6	LRSVX	U	(888) 522-2388	U /	2.34	9.21	29.10 /84	--	--	0.00	0.87
MC	Lord Abbett Value Opportunities A	LVOAX	C	(888) 522-2388	C+ / 5.9	3.21	8.12	25.57 /75	6.66 /70	11.85 /73	0.00	1.17
MC	● Lord Abbett Value Opportunities B	LVOBX	C	(888) 522-2388	C+ / 6.4	2.97	7.69	24.60 /72	5.88 /63	11.05 /66	0.00	1.92
MC	Lord Abbett Value Opportunities C	LVOCX	C	(888) 522-2388	C+ / 6.4	3.03	7.75	24.67 /72	5.90 /63	11.08 /67	0.00	1.92
MC	Lord Abbett Value Opportunities F	LVOFX	C+	(888) 522-2388	B- / 7.0	3.26	8.20	25.77 /75	6.84 /71	12.06 /75	0.10	1.02
MC	Lord Abbett Value Opportunities I	LVOYX	C+	(888) 522-2388	B- / 7.1	3.25	8.24	25.82 /76	6.94 /72	12.17 /76	0.17	0.92
MC	● Lord Abbett Value Opportunities P	LVOPX	C+	(888) 522-2388	C+ / 6.8	3.10	8.02	25.27 /74	6.47 /68	11.68 /71	0.00	1.37
MC	Lord Abbett Value Opportunities R2	LVOQX	C	(888) 522-2388	C+ / 6.7	3.11	7.94	25.14 /74	6.30 /67	11.51 /70	0.00	1.52
MC	Lord Abbett Value Opportunities R3	LVORX	C+	(888) 522-2388	C+ / 6.8	3.13	8.04	25.26 /74	6.42 /68	11.62 /71	0.00	1.42
MC	Lord Abbett Value Opportunities R5	LVOTX	U	(888) 522-2388	U /	3.25	8.24	25.89 /76	--	--	0.18	0.92
MC	Lord Abbett Value Opportunities R6	LVOVX	U	(888) 522-2388	U /	3.30	8.35	25.99 /76	--	--	0.19	0.80
GL	LS Opportunity	LSOFX	C-	(866) 954-6682	C- / 3.4	4.00	7.11	14.41 /27	3.76 /40	6.71 /33	0.00	3.92
GR	LS Theta Institutional	LQTIX	U	(844) 854-7843	U /	1.61	2.88	8.79 / 9	--	--	0.00	3.67
GR	LSV Conservative Value Eq Inst	LSVVX	A	(866) 777-7818	A / 9.5	7.61	13.84	29.27 /85	9.64 /91	14.41 /95	2.27	0.60
SC	LSV Small Cap Value Inst	LSVQX	A+	(866) 777-7818	A+ / 9.7	3.75	14.50	35.27 /94	10.47 /96	--	1.19	0.93
GR	LSV US Managed Volatility Inst	LSVMX	U	(866) 777-7818	U /	6.61	5.33	16.91 /38	--	--	1.66	1.19
GR	LSV Value Equity Inst	LSVEX	A+	(866) 777-7818	A+ / 9.7	7.78	15.51	31.35 /89	10.39 /95	15.98 /98	1.96	0.66
GI	LSV Value Equity Inv	LVAEX	U	(866) 777-7818	U /	7.74	15.40	31.05 /88	--	--	1.79	0.92
GR	Lyrical US Value Equity Inst	LYRIX	A	(888) 884-8099	A / 9.5	7.19	14.71	33.05 /92	8.55 /83	--	1.34	1.42
GR	Lyrical US Value Equity Inv	LYRBX	A	(888) 884-8099	A / 9.4	7.16	14.51	32.67 /91	8.24 /81	--	0.97	1.72
GR	M Fund M Large Cap Value	MBOVX	B-	(800) 237-7119	B / 8.2	7.10	13.54	25.48 /75	7.35 /74	12.32 /77	1.76	0.69
AA	MA 529 Fidelity UF CIP 100% Eq Ptf		C+	(800) 544-8544	C+ / 6.6	7.21	7.54	22.49 /64	5.89 /63	10.27 /60	0.00	1.00
AA	MA 529 Fidelity UF CIP 70% Eq Ptf		B	(800) 544-8544	C / 5.0	5.69	5.15	17.65 /41	5.04 /55	8.25 /44	0.00	0.94
AA	MA 529 Fidelity UF CIP College Ptf		C+	(800) 544-8544	D / 1.8	2.42	0.93	7.40 / 6	2.48 /27	3.18 /11	0.00	0.77
AA	MA 529 Fidelity UF CIP Consv Ptf		C	(800) 544-8544	D- / 1.0	0.79	-0.45	2.40 / 2	1.36 /20	1.31 / 7	0.00	0.59
AA	MA 529 Fidelity UF CIP Idx 100% Eq		C+	(800) 544-8544	C+ / 6.8	7.50	8.42	22.84 /66	6.00 /64	10.45 /62	0.00	0.27
AA	MA 529 Fidelity UF CIP Idx 70% Eq		B	(800) 544-8544	C / 4.7	5.55	5.18	15.96 /34	4.88 /53	7.99 /42	0.00	0.30
AA	MA 529 Fidelity UF CIP Idx College		C+	(800) 544-8544	D- / 1.5	2.05	0.56	4.93 / 4	2.14 /25	2.73 /10	0.00	0.33
AA	MA 529 Fidelity UF CIP Idx Consv		C	(800) 544-8544	E+ / 0.9	0.53	-0.90	0.69 / 2	1.16 /19	0.94 / 6	0.00	0.34
AA	MA 529 Fidelity UF CIP Idx Ptf 2018		C+	(800) 544-8544	D / 1.8	2.50	1.06	6.75 / 5	2.76 /30	4.74 /20	0.00	0.31
AA	MA 529 Fidelity UF CIP Idx Ptf 2021		C+	(800) 544-8544	D+ / 2.6	3.42	2.27	9.53 /11	3.52 /37	6.13 /29	0.00	0.30
AA	MA 529 Fidelity UF CIP Idx Ptf 2024		B-	(800) 544-8544	C- / 3.4	4.29	3.43	12.28 /19	4.15 /45	7.43 /38	0.00	0.29
AA	MA 529 Fidelity UF CIP Idx Ptf 2027		B-	(800) 544-8544	C / 4.3	5.16	4.59	15.06 /30	4.73 /51	8.50 /46	0.00	0.28
AA	MA 529 Fidelity UF CIP Port 2018		C+	(800) 544-8544	D+ / 2.3	2.98	1.57	9.51 /10	3.25 /34	5.30 /23	0.00	0.87
AA	MA 529 Fidelity UF CIP Port 2021		C+	(800) 544-8544	C- / 3.2	3.90	2.68	12.19 /19	3.95 /42	6.61 /32	0.00	0.93
AA	MA 529 Fidelity UF CIP Port 2024		B-	(800) 544-8544	C- / 3.9	4.67	3.68	14.73 /29	4.47 /48	7.81 /41	0.00	0.97
AA	MA 529 Fidelity UF CIP Port 2027		B-	(800) 544-8544	C / 4.8	5.44	4.76	17.26 /40	4.93 /53	8.82 /49	0.00	0.99
AA	MA 529 Fidelity UF CIP Tot Mkt Idx		A+	(800) 544-8544	A- / 9.1	7.76	10.28	26.19 /77	9.72 /92	13.62 /90	0.00	0.25
AA	Madison Aggressive Alloc A	MAGSX	C-	(800) 877-6089	C- / 4.1	5.84	5.74	16.67 /37	5.57 /60	8.65 /48	1.02	1.15
AA	● Madison Aggressive Alloc B	MAGBX	C	(800) 877-6089	C / 4.6	5.67	5.48	15.76 /33	4.80 /52	7.84 /41	0.56	1.90
AA	Madison Aggressive Alloc C	MAACX	C	(800) 877-6089	C / 4.6	5.76	5.47	15.86 /34	4.79 /52	7.85 /41	0.56	1.90
AA	Madison Conservative Alloc A	MCNAX	C-	(800) 877-6089	D / 1.6	3.29	1.35	7.86 / 7	3.36 /35	4.70 /19	1.79	1.13
AA	● Madison Conservative Alloc B	MCNBX	C	(800) 877-6089	D / 1.8	3.05	0.94	6.98 / 6	2.59 /28	3.91 /15	1.04	1.88
AA	Madison Conservative Alloc C	MCOCX	C	(800) 877-6089	D / 1.9	3.05	1.04	7.08 / 6	2.59 /28	3.91 /15	1.04	1.88
IN	Madison Covered Call and Eq Inc A	MENAX	C-	(800) 877-6089	D+ / 2.5	2.52	3.31	12.72 /21	4.60 /50	5.74 /27	4.05	1.28
IN	Madison Covered Call and Eq Inc C	MENCX	C-	(800) 877-6089	D+ / 2.9	2.25	2.95	11.87 /17	3.83 /41	--	4.44	2.03
IN	Madison Covered Call and Eq Inc R6	MENRX	C	(800) 877-6089	C- / 3.8	2.53	3.52	13.12 /22	4.99 /54	--	4.26	0.90
IN	Madison Covered Call and Eq Inc Y	MENYX	C	(800) 877-6089	C- / 3.6	2.43	3.43	12.95 /21	4.83 /52	5.98 /28	4.28	1.03

● Denotes fund is closed to new investors
* Denotes fund is included in Section II

www.thestreetratings.com

RISK			NET ASSETS		ASSET					BULL / BEAR		FUND MANAGER		MINIMUMS		LOADS	
	3 Year		NAV						Portfolio	Last Bull	Last Bear	Manager	Manager	Initial	Additional	Front	Back
Risk	Standard		As of	Total	Cash	Stocks	Bonds	Other	Turnover	Market	Market	Quality	Tenure	Purch.	Purch.	End	End
Rating/Pts	Deviation	Beta	2/28/17	$(Mil)	%	%	%	%	Ratio	Return	Return	Pct	(Years)	$	$	Load	Load
D- /1.2	13.8	0.86	25.59	643	2	97	0	1	44	118.9	-28.2	81	4	1,000,000	0	0.0	0.0
E+ /0.6	13.9	0.86	21.16	43	2	97	0	1	44	113.7	-28.4	78	4	0	0	0.0	0.0
E+ /0.6	13.8	0.86	21.01	N/A	2	97	0	1	44	111.9	-28.4	77	4	0	0	0.0	0.0
E+ /0.6	13.8	0.86	21.25	9	2	97	0	1	44	113.4	-28.3	77	4	0	0	0.0	0.0
U /	N/A	N/A	25.66	42	2	97	0	1	44	N/A	N/A	N/A	4	0	0	0.0	0.0
C /4.8	11.3	0.91	19.91	1,081	2	97	0	1	37	116.4	-23.0	49	12	1,500	0	5.8	0.0
C /4.5	11.3	0.92	18.03	6	2	97	0	1	37	108.4	-23.2	38	12	1,000	0	0.0	0.0
C /4.5	11.3	0.91	18.04	372	2	97	0	1	37	108.5	-23.2	39	12	1,500	0	0.0	0.0
C /4.8	11.3	0.91	20.26	925	2	97	0	1	37	118.8	-22.9	51	12	0	0	0.0	0.0
C /4.9	11.3	0.91	20.63	442	2	97	0	1	37	120.0	-22.9	53	12	1,000,000	0	0.0	0.0
C /4.7	11.3	0.92	19.61	38	2	97	0	1	37	114.9	-23.1	46	12	0	0	0.0	0.0
C /4.7	11.3	0.91	19.25	7	2	97	0	1	37	113.1	-23.1	44	12	0	0	0.0	0.0
C /4.7	11.3	0.92	19.42	103	2	97	0	1	37	114.2	-23.0	45	12	0	0	0.0	0.0
U /	N/A	N/A	20.64	50	2	97	0	1	37	N/A	N/A	N/A	12	0	0	0.0	0.0
U /	N/A	N/A	20.68	82	2	97	0	1	37	N/A	N/A	N/A	12	0	0	0.0	0.0
B- /7.0	7.7	0.79	13.26	40	33	66	0	1	90	46.4	-11.3	74	2	5,000	100	0.0	2.0
U /	N/A	N/A	51.54	61	26	0	73	1	0	N/A	N/A	N/A	3	100,000	1,000	0.0	2.0
C+ /5.7	10.9	1.00	12.30	106	1	98	0	1	17	141.9	-21.1	63	10	100,000	0	0.0	0.0
C+ /6.4	14.6	0.88	15.23	237	2	97	0	1	23	N/A	N/A	94	4	100,000	0	0.0	0.0
U /	N/A	N/A	11.97	69	0	98	0	2	12	N/A	N/A	N/A	3	100,000	0	0.0	0.0
B- /7.0	11.5	1.04	27.34	2,005	0	100	0	0	15	164.2	-23.3	66	18	100,000	0	0.0	0.0
U /	N/A	N/A	27.26	25	0	100	0	0	15	N/A	N/A	N/A	18	1,000	0	0.0	0.0
C+ /5.6	14.1	1.21	17.54	1,134	0	99	0	1	21	N/A	N/A	24	4	100,000	0	0.0	0.0
C+ /6.0	14.1	1.21	17.52	60	0	99	0	1	21	N/A	N/A	21	4	2,500	0	0.0	0.0
C /4.7	12.1	1.09	13.36	93	0	99	0	1	66	117.5	-19.3	25	4	0	0	0.0	0.0
C+ /6.6	10.5	1.59	20.97	262	2	95	1	2	18	99.5	-23.0	10	12	50	25	0.0	0.0
B /8.1	7.8	1.19	22.46	115	2	67	30	1	21	74.2	-17.3	27	12	50	25	0.0	0.0
B+ /9.9	3.2	0.46	19.44	691	8	21	69	2	19	23.4	-4.4	63	12	50	25	0.0	0.0
B+ /9.9	1.5	0.09	15.34	38	14	0	85	1	20	8.6	0.6	78	12	50	25	0.0	0.0
C+ /6.8	10.3	1.59	17.64	102	1	97	1	1	26	98.0	-19.4	11	11	50	25	0.0	0.0
B /8.9	7.2	1.13	17.87	67	0	68	30	2	40	68.3	-11.3	30	11	50	25	0.0	0.0
B+ /9.9	2.4	0.34	14.46	94	10	19	69	2	49	19.5	-0.3	69	11	50	25	0.0	0.0
B+ /9.7	1.4	0.03	13.19	33	19	0	80	1	38	5.3	4.4	80	11	50	25	0.0	0.0
B+ /9.8	3.5	0.53	15.19	152	8	26	65	1	27	39.6	-7.3	59	11	50	25	0.0	0.0
B+ /9.6	4.7	0.74	15.74	157	5	39	54	2	24	52.8	-10.5	49	11	50	25	0.0	0.0
B+ /9.2	6.0	0.94	16.27	186	3	51	44	2	20	66.0	-13.7	38	11	50	25	0.0	0.0
B /8.6	7.3	1.14	15.28	158	1	63	34	2	14	76.9	-15.8	28	10	50	25	0.0	0.0
B+ /9.4	4.4	0.66	19.35	1,015	6	29	64	1	18	45.7	-12.5	54	12	50	25	0.0	0.0
B+ /9.1	5.7	0.86	21.07	784	4	42	52	2	16	59.6	-16.1	43	12	50	25	0.0	0.0
B /8.6	6.9	1.05	18.61	399	3	54	41	2	14	72.6	-19.1	31	12	50	25	0.0	0.0
B /8.1	8.1	1.24	14.74	197	2	66	30	2	11	83.6	-21.2	22	10	50	25	0.0	0.0
B- /7.0	10.6	1.66	21.25	126	0	99	0	1	0	132.2	-17.8	39	11	50	25	0.0	0.5
C+ /6.1	7.8	1.24	11.53	49	4	79	15	2	98	72.6	-13.3	29	9	1,000	50	5.8	0.0
C+ /6.1	7.8	1.23	11.26	11	4	79	15	2	98	65.8	-13.6	21	9	1,000	50	0.0	0.0
C+ /6.1	7.8	1.24	11.27	2	4	79	15	2	98	65.7	-13.6	21	9	1,000	50	0.0	0.0
B /8.7	4.0	0.59	10.51	44	4	34	60	2	82	35.7	-5.2	62	9	1,000	50	5.8	0.0
B /8.8	3.9	0.58	10.58	9	4	34	60	2	82	30.2	-5.4	53	9	1,000	50	0.0	0.0
B /8.8	4.0	0.58	10.59	20	4	34	60	2	82	30.3	-5.5	53	9	1,000	50	0.0	0.0
B- /7.4	5.4	0.48	9.16	19	5	70	24	1	135	61.6	-11.2	70	8	1,000	50	5.8	0.0
B- /7.3	5.4	0.48	8.80	14	5	70	24	1	135	N/A	N/A	60	8	1,000	50	0.0	0.0
B- /7.5	5.4	0.47	9.38	3	5	70	24	1	135	N/A	N/A	74	8	500,000	50,000	0.0	0.0
B- /7.5	5.4	0.48	9.32	79	5	70	24	1	135	63.8	-11.2	72	8	25,000	50	0.0	0.0

					PERFORMANCE						Incl. in Returns	
								Total Return % through 2/28/17				
									Annualized		Dividend	Expense
Fund Type	Fund Name	Ticker Symbol	Overall Investment Rating	Phone	Perfor-mance Rating/Pts	3 Mo	6 Mo	1Yr / Pct	3Yr / Pct	5Yr / Pct	Yield	Ratio
BA	Madison Diversified Income A	MBLAX	C+	(800) 877-6089	C- / 3.4	4.39	3.46	13.01 / 22	6.00 / 64	7.57 / 39	1.60	1.10
BA	● Madison Diversified Income B	MBLNX	B-	(800) 877-6089	C- / 3.9	4.23	3.12	12.16 / 18	5.20 / 56	6.77 / 33	0.97	1.85
GI	Madison Diversified Income C	MBLCX	B-	(800) 877-6089	C- / 3.9	4.23	3.12	12.17 / 19	5.20 / 56	--	0.97	1.85
BA	Madison Dividend Income Y	BHBFX	A-	(800) 877-6089	B / 8.0	7.02	7.71	21.33 / 59	8.98 / 87	12.25 / 77	1.33	1.10
FO	Madison International Stock A	MINAX	D-	(800) 877-6089	E- / 0.2	4.41	-0.83	5.39 / 4	-2.46 / 6	4.10 / 16	1.11	1.60
FO	● Madison International Stock B	MINBX	D-	(800) 877-6089	E / 0.3	4.20	-1.24	4.56 / 4	-3.20 / 4	3.30 / 12	0.58	2.35
FO	Madison International Stock Y	MINYX	D-	(800) 877-6089	E / 0.4	4.44	-0.70	5.70 / 4	-2.22 / 6	4.34 / 17	1.38	1.35
GI	Madison Investors A	MNVAX	C	(800) 877-6089	B- / 7.3	7.26	7.37	21.89 / 62	9.53 / 91	--	0.00	1.20
GI	Madison Investors R6	MNVRX	C+	(800) 877-6089	B+ / 8.7	7.33	7.60	22.43 / 64	10.03 / 93	--	0.38	0.77
GR	Madison Investors Y	MINVX	C+	(800) 877-6089	B+ / 8.5	7.33	7.49	22.19 / 63	9.81 / 92	13.10 / 85	0.21	0.95
GR	Madison Large Cap Value A	MGWAX	C-	(800) 877-6089	C+ / 6.3	5.08	8.78	20.94 / 57	7.92 / 78	11.45 / 69	1.03	1.16
GR	● Madison Large Cap Value B	MGWBX	C	(800) 877-6089	C+ / 6.7	4.88	8.32	20.05 / 52	7.09 / 73	10.61 / 63	0.34	1.91
GR	Madison Large Cap Value Y	MYLVX	C	(800) 877-6089	B- / 7.5	5.09	8.86	21.19 / 58	8.17 / 80	11.73 / 72	1.33	0.91
MC	Madison Mid Cap A	MERAX	C	(800) 877-6089	C+ / 6.6	5.80	8.27	19.55 / 50	8.64 / 84	--	0.00	1.40
MC	● Madison Mid Cap B	MERBX	C	(800) 877-6089	B- / 7.0	5.66	8.00	18.83 / 46	7.87 / 78	--	0.00	2.15
MC	Madison Mid Cap Y	GTSGX	B-	(800) 877-6089	B / 7.8	5.82	8.44	20.07 / 52	8.98 / 87	12.22 / 76	0.00	0.98
AA	Madison Moderate Alloc A	MMDAX	C-	(800) 877-6089	D+ / 2.8	4.73	3.90	12.64 / 20	4.63 / 50	6.92 / 34	1.25	1.15
AA	● Madison Moderate Alloc B	MMDRX	C	(800) 877-6089	C- / 3.2	4.44	3.42	11.67 / 17	3.82 / 41	6.10 / 29	0.60	1.90
AA	Madison Moderate Alloc C	MMDCX	C	(800) 877-6089	C- / 3.2	4.53	3.41	11.77 / 17	3.84 / 41	6.12 / 29	0.60	1.90
SC	Madison Small Cap A	MASVX	B-	(800) 877-6089	B- / 7.2	4.55	10.70	26.64 / 78	8.20 / 80	12.42 / 78	0.13	1.55
SC	● Madison Small Cap B	MBSVX	B	(800) 877-6089	B / 7.6	4.42	10.35	25.73 / 75	7.39 / 75	11.57 / 71	0.00	2.30
SC	Madison Small Cap Y	MYSVX	B+	(800) 877-6089	B+ / 8.4	4.62	10.81	26.98 / 79	8.47 / 83	12.70 / 81	0.39	1.30
BA	MAI Managed Volatility Inst	MAIPX	C	(877) 414-7884	D+ / 2.9	3.26	3.52	9.97 / 12	3.97 / 43	5.14 / 22	0.48	1.23
BA	MAI Managed Volatility Inv	DIVPX	C	(877) 414-7884	D+ / 2.7	3.17	3.36	9.71 / 11	3.71 / 39	4.92 / 21	0.00	4.40
EN	MainGate MLP A	AMLPX	E	(855) 657-3863	D / 2.2	5.24	10.20	46.38 / 99	-1.27 / 8	5.29 / 23	5.79	1.66
EN	MainGate MLP C	MLCPX	U	(855) 657-3863	U /	4.98	9.87	45.20 / 98	--	--	6.23	2.41
EN	MainGate MLP I	IMLPX	E+	(855) 657-3863	C- / 3.3	5.34	10.44	46.72 / 99	-1.00 / 9	5.57 / 25	6.03	1.41
GI	MainStay Absolute Rtn Multi-Str I	MSNIX	U	(800) 624-6782	U /	0.77	0.97	1.57 / 2	--	--	1.79	3.20
BA	MainStay Balanced A	MBNAX	C	(800) 624-6782	C- / 4.0	3.69	5.41	16.20 / 35	5.96 / 64	9.27 / 53	1.20	1.16
BA	● MainStay Balanced B	MBNBX	C+	(800) 624-6782	C / 4.3	3.44	4.92	15.17 / 31	5.02 / 54	8.28 / 44	0.43	2.05
BA	MainStay Balanced C	MBACX	C+	(800) 624-6782	C / 4.3	3.45	4.93	15.18 / 31	5.01 / 54	8.28 / 45	0.43	2.05
BA	MainStay Balanced I	MBAIX	B-	(800) 624-6782	C / 5.3	3.75	5.52	16.48 / 36	6.22 / 66	9.54 / 55	1.50	0.91
BA	MainStay Balanced Inv	MBINX	C	(800) 624-6782	C- / 3.8	3.65	5.32	16.02 / 34	5.79 / 62	9.09 / 51	1.06	1.30
BA	MainStay Balanced R1	MBNRX	C+	(800) 624-6782	C / 5.2	3.69	5.44	16.35 / 36	6.12 / 65	9.43 / 54	1.41	1.01
BA	MainStay Balanced R2	MBCRX	C+	(800) 624-6782	C / 5.0	3.64	5.32	16.06 / 35	5.85 / 63	9.15 / 52	1.18	1.26
BA	MainStay Balanced R3	MBDRX	C+	(800) 624-6782	C / 4.8	3.61	5.19	15.79 / 33	5.59 / 60	8.89 / 50	0.95	1.51
GI	MainStay Common Stock A	MSOAX	B+	(800) 624-6782	B- / 7.0	7.06	8.69	20.41 / 54	8.81 / 86	13.57 / 90	1.09	0.99
GI	● MainStay Common Stock B	MOPBX	B+	(800) 624-6782	B- / 7.1	6.81	8.18	19.20 / 48	7.73 / 77	12.38 / 78	0.19	1.95
GI	MainStay Common Stock C	MGOCX	B+	(800) 624-6782	B- / 7.1	6.81	8.18	19.21 / 48	7.73 / 77	12.37 / 78	0.19	1.95
GI	MainStay Common Stock I	MSOIX	A	(800) 624-6782	B / 8.1	7.10	8.82	20.71 / 56	9.08 / 87	13.87 / 92	1.39	0.74
GI	MainStay Common Stock Inv	MCSSX	B-	(800) 624-6782	C+ / 6.8	6.99	8.56	20.10 / 53	8.55 / 83	13.22 / 86	0.86	1.20
AA	MainStay Conservative Alloc A	MCKAX	C-	(800) 624-6782	D / 2.1	3.94	3.64	12.88 / 21	3.14 / 33	5.76 / 27	1.79	1.22
AA	● MainStay Conservative Alloc B	MCKBX	C-	(800) 624-6782	D+ / 2.3	3.73	3.19	11.85 / 17	2.23 / 25	4.82 / 20	1.05	2.11
AA	MainStay Conservative Alloc C	MCKCX	C-	(800) 624-6782	D+ / 2.3	3.73	3.28	11.85 / 17	2.23 / 26	4.82 / 20	1.05	2.11
AA	MainStay Conservative Alloc I	MCKIX	C	(800) 624-6782	C- / 3.1	3.97	3.82	13.15 / 22	3.39 / 36	6.01 / 28	2.11	0.97
AA	MainStay Conservative Alloc Inv	MCKNX	C-	(800) 624-6782	D / 2.0	3.91	3.57	12.73 / 21	2.99 / 32	5.60 / 26	1.66	1.36
CV	MainStay Convertible A	MCOAX	C	(800) 624-6782	C+ / 5.6	5.79	8.11	23.78 / 69	6.07 / 65	9.23 / 53	1.47	0.99
CV	● MainStay Convertible B	MCSVX	C+	(800) 624-6782	C+ / 6.0	5.58	7.65	22.69 / 65	5.10 / 55	8.22 / 44	0.73	1.90
CV	MainStay Convertible C	MCCVX	C+	(800) 624-6782	C+ / 6.0	5.58	7.66	22.72 / 65	5.11 / 55	8.21 / 44	0.73	1.90
CV	MainStay Convertible I	MCNVX	C+	(800) 624-6782	C+ / 6.9	5.85	8.23	24.12 / 70	6.33 / 67	9.50 / 55	1.78	0.74
CV	MainStay Convertible Inv	MCINX	C	(800) 624-6782	C / 5.5	5.75	8.02	23.59 / 68	5.87 / 63	9.02 / 51	1.33	1.15
GR	MainStay CornerStone Growth A	KLGAX	C-	(800) 624-6782	C / 5.0	7.37	8.17	20.70 / 56	5.29 / 57	7.95 / 42	0.00	1.19

● Denotes fund is closed to new investors
* Denotes fund is included in Section II

www.thestreetratings.com

RISK			NET ASSETS		ASSET				Portfolio Turnover Ratio	BULL / BEAR		FUND MANAGER		MINIMUMS		LOADS	
Risk Rating/Pts	3 Year Standard Deviation	Beta	NAV As of 2/28/17	Total $(Mil)	Cash %	Stocks %	Bonds %	Other %		Last Bull Market Return	Last Bear Market Return	Manager Quality Pct	Manager Tenure (Years)	Initial Purch. $	Additional Purch. $	Front End Load	Back End Load
B /8.6	5.5	0.84	15.13	132	1	57	41	1	35	58.3	-5.0	71	19	1,000	50	5.8	0.0
B /8.6	5.5	0.84	15.23	14	1	57	41	1	35	52.1	-5.3	62	19	1,000	50	0.0	0.0
B /8.6	5.4	0.49	15.22	14	1	57	41	1	35	N/A	N/A	74	19	1,000	50	0.0	0.0
C+ /6.6	9.4	1.43	24.20	107	0	98	0	2	33	100.8	-9.7	52	27	25,000	50	0.0	0.0
C+ /6.1	10.7	0.82	12.12	18	2	95	2	1	34	43.4	-20.4	43	20	1,000	50	5.8	0.0
C+ /6.2	10.6	0.82	11.86	1	2	95	2	1	34	37.7	-20.6	33	20	1,000	50	0.0	0.0
C+ /6.1	10.7	0.82	12.13	10	2	95	2	1	34	45.3	-20.2	47	20	25,000	50	0.0	0.0
C- /3.7	9.3	0.85	20.99	73	7	92	0	1	33	N/A	N/A	78	27	1,000	50	5.8	0.0
C- /3.7	9.3	0.85	21.12	7	7	92	0	1	33	N/A	N/A	81	27	500,000	50,000	0.0	0.0
C- /3.6	9.3	0.85	21.02	215	7	92	0	1	33	120.4	-15.0	80	27	25,000	50	0.0	0.0
C- /3.8	9.2	0.83	14.65	68	0	97	1	2	74	106.2	-14.5	65	8	1,000	50	5.8	0.0
C- /3.9	9.2	0.83	14.32	4	0	97	1	2	74	97.9	-14.8	55	8	1,000	50	0.0	0.0
C- /3.8	9.2	0.82	14.63	33	0	97	1	2	74	108.9	-14.4	69	8	25,000	50	0.0	0.0
C /4.8	10.9	0.85	8.89	58	7	92	0	1	27	N/A	N/A	77	7	1,000	50	5.8	0.0
C- /4.2	10.9	0.85	7.42	3	7	92	0	1	27	N/A	N/A	71	7	1,000	50	0.0	0.0
C /4.9	10.8	0.85	9.23	263	7	92	0	1	27	118.9	-18.5	80	7	25,000	50	0.0	0.0
B- /7.4	5.9	0.94	11.29	108	4	59	35	2	97	55.9	-9.5	44	9	1,000	50	5.8	0.0
B- /7.5	5.9	0.94	11.21	25	4	59	35	2	97	49.4	-9.7	34	9	1,000	50	0.0	0.0
B- /7.5	5.9	0.93	11.22	9	4	59	35	2	97	49.6	-9.8	35	9	1,000	50	0.0	0.0
C /5.5	15.1	0.91	16.63	4	1	96	2	1	19	126.8	-22.0	85	11	1,000	50	5.8	0.0
C /5.4	15.1	0.91	15.65	1	1	96	2	1	19	117.8	-22.3	81	11	1,000	50	0.0	0.0
C /5.5	15.2	0.91	16.67	105	1	96	2	1	19	129.9	-21.9	86	11	25,000	50	0.0	0.0
B- /7.9	5.1	0.79	10.88	109	12	50	37	1	85	43.3	-7.3	51	7	50,000	5,000	0.0	0.0
B- /7.9	5.1	0.79	11.04	1	12	50	37	1	85	41.6	-7.4	47	7	2,500	100	0.0	0.0
D+ /2.7	22.2	0.83	10.25	215	83	16	0	1	58	49.8	-6.9	91	6	2,500	100	5.8	0.0
U /	N/A	N/A	10.12	76	83	16	0	1	58	N/A	N/A	N/A	6	2,500	100	0.0	0.0
D+ /2.7	22.1	0.83	10.45	1,751	83	16	0	1	58	51.9	-6.7	92	6	1,000,000	10,000	0.0	0.0
U /	N/A	N/A	10.05	127	0	0	0	100	164	N/A	N/A	N/A	2	5,000,000	0	0.0	0.0
B- /7.2	6.9	1.03	32.73	250	43	16	40	1	271	77.7	-11.2	53	9	25,000	0	5.5	0.0
B- /7.2	6.9	1.03	32.58	29	43	16	40	1	271	69.1	-11.5	40	9	1,000	50	0.0	0.0
B- /7.2	6.9	1.03	32.56	106	43	16	40	1	271	69.1	-11.6	40	9	1,000	50	0.0	0.0
B- /7.2	6.9	1.03	32.81	321	43	16	40	1	271	80.1	-11.1	56	9	5,000,000	0	0.0	0.0
B- /7.2	6.8	1.03	32.74	86	43	16	40	1	271	76.1	-11.3	51	9	1,000	50	5.5	0.0
B- /7.2	6.9	1.03	32.76	2	43	16	40	1	271	79.1	-11.2	55	9	0	0	0.0	0.0
B- /7.2	6.9	1.03	32.71	30	43	16	40	1	271	76.7	-11.2	52	9	0	0	0.0	0.0
B- /7.2	6.9	1.03	32.69	4	43	16	40	1	271	74.3	-11.3	48	9	0	0	0.0	0.0
B- /7.0	10.5	1.01	21.94	42	0	99	0	1	164	130.2	-17.3	52	10	25,000	0	5.5	0.0
B- /7.0	10.5	1.01	20.20	7	0	99	0	1	164	117.1	-17.7	38	10	1,000	50	0.0	0.0
B- /7.0	10.5	1.01	20.19	17	0	99	0	1	164	117.0	-17.7	38	10	1,000	50	0.0	0.0
B- /7.0	10.5	1.01	22.00	100	0	99	0	1	164	133.2	-17.2	56	10	5,000,000	0	0.0	0.0
B- /7.0	10.5	1.01	21.95	24	0	99	0	1	164	126.0	-17.5	49	10	1,000	50	5.5	0.0
B- /7.9	5.4	0.82	12.01	259	13	40	46	1	44	48.3	-8.5	36	12	25,000	0	5.5	0.0
B- /7.9	5.3	0.81	11.95	33	13	40	46	1	44	41.3	-8.9	27	12	1,000	50	0.0	0.0
B- /7.9	5.4	0.82	11.95	76	13	40	46	1	44	41.3	-8.8	26	12	1,000	50	0.0	0.0
B- /7.9	5.3	0.81	12.11	14	13	40	46	1	44	50.3	-8.4	40	12	5,000,000	0	0.0	0.0
B- /7.9	5.4	0.82	12.01	77	13	40	46	1	44	47.0	-8.5	34	12	1,000	50	5.5	0.0
C+ /5.6	9.5	1.06	16.98	411	13	14	2	71	24	83.4	-19.6	79	16	25,000	0	5.5	0.0
C+ /5.6	9.5	1.07	16.90	23	13	14	2	71	24	74.2	-19.9	72	16	1,000	50	0.0	0.0
C+ /5.6	9.5	1.06	16.88	84	13	14	2	71	24	74.2	-19.9	72	16	1,000	50	0.0	0.0
C+ /5.6	9.5	1.07	17.01	388	13	14	2	71	24	85.9	-19.5	81	16	5,000,000	0	0.0	0.0
C+ /5.6	9.5	1.07	16.97	85	13	14	2	71	24	81.4	-19.6	78	16	1,000	50	0.0	0.0
C /4.4	13.2	1.15	29.33	272	0	99	0	1	137	86.2	-18.6	7	1	25,000	0	5.5	0.0

			Overall		PERFORMANCE								
			Investment		Perfor-mance	Total Return % through 2/28/17						Incl. in Returns	
			Rating						Annualized				
Fund Type	Fund Name	Ticker Symbol		Phone	Rating/Pts	3 Mo	6 Mo	1Yr / Pct	3Yr / Pct	5Yr / Pct		Dividend Yield	Expense Ratio

99 Pct = Best
0 Pct = Worst

Fund Type	Fund Name	Ticker Symbol	Overall Investment Rating	Phone	Performance Rating/Pts	3 Mo	6 Mo	1Yr / Pct	3Yr / Pct	5Yr / Pct	Dividend Yield	Expense Ratio
GR	● MainStay CornerStone Growth B	KLGBX	C-	(800) 624-6782	C / 5.3	7.09	7.62	19.53 / 50	4.31 / 46	--	0.00	2.07
GR	MainStay CornerStone Growth C	KLGCX	C-	(800) 624-6782	C / 5.3	7.09	7.58	19.49 / 49	4.31 / 46	--	0.00	2.07
GR	MainStay CornerStone Growth I	KLGIX	C	(800) 624-6782	C+ / 6.3	7.44	8.26	20.94 / 57	5.54 / 60	8.21 / 44	0.00	0.94
GR	MainStay CornerStone Growth Inv	KLGNX	D+	(800) 624-6782	C / 4.8	7.29	8.02	20.44 / 55	5.10 / 55	--	0.00	1.32
GR	MainStay CornerStone Growth R2	KLGRX	C-	(800) 624-6782	C+ / 6.0	7.34	8.18	20.59 / 55	5.16 / 56	--	0.00	1.29
EN	MainStay Cushing Energy Income A	CURAX	E-	(800) 624-6782	E- / 0.0	1.83	8.78	47.25 / 99	-30.77 / 0	--	4.17	1.60
EN	MainStay Cushing Energy Income C	CURCX	E-	(800) 624-6782	E- / 0.0	1.72	8.49	46.00 / 99	-31.31 / 0	--	3.92	2.41
EN	MainStay Cushing Energy Income I	CURZX	E-	(800) 624-6782	E- / 0.0	1.86	9.04	47.61 / 99	-30.58 / 0	--	4.57	1.33
IN	MainStay Cushing MLP Premier A	CSHAX	E	(800) 624-6782	D / 1.9	9.50	11.54	55.65 / 99	-4.01 / 3	1.00 / 6	9.09	1.50
IN	MainStay Cushing MLP Premier C	CSHCX	E	(800) 624-6782	D / 2.2	9.27	11.09	54.46 / 99	-4.74 / 3	0.23 / 5	10.26	2.25
IN	MainStay Cushing MLP Premier I	CSHZX	E+	(800) 624-6782	D+ / 2.8	9.61	11.68	56.09 / 99	-3.77 / 3	1.27 / 7	9.43	1.25
EN	MainStay Cushing Ren Adv A	CRZAX	E	(800) 624-6782	D / 1.7	1.99	13.27	39.43 / 97	-1.46 / 8	--	2.49	1.74
EN	MainStay Cushing Ren Adv C	CRZCX	E	(800) 624-6782	D / 2.0	1.81	12.77	38.25 / 97	-2.28 / 6	--	2.73	2.60
EN	MainStay Cushing Ren Adv I	CRZZX	E+	(800) 624-6782	D+ / 2.6	2.07	13.43	39.82 / 97	-1.19 / 9	--	2.61	1.46
EM	Mainstay Emerging Markets Eqty A	MEOAX	C-	(800) 624-6782	C / 4.3	10.73	6.98	30.60 / 87	1.49 / 21	--	3.01	1.96
EM	Mainstay Emerging Markets Eqty C	MEOCX	C	(800) 624-6782	C / 4.5	10.29	6.38	29.46 / 85	0.47 / 16	--	2.44	2.95
EM	Mainstay Emerging Markets Eqty I	MEOIX	C+	(800) 624-6782	C+ / 5.7	10.84	7.22	31.02 / 88	1.73 / 22	--	3.40	1.71
EM	Mainstay Emerging Markets Eqty Inv	MEOVX	C-	(800) 624-6782	C- / 4.1	10.66	6.90	30.23 / 87	1.23 / 19	--	2.84	2.20
GL	MainStay Epoch Capital Growth I	MECFX	U	(800) 624-6782	U /	7.88	5.51	--	--	--	0.00	1.20
GL	MainStay Epoch Global Choice A	EPAPX	D	(800) 624-6782	D / 1.8	8.44	4.05	12.67 / 20	1.25 / 20	7.57 / 39	0.73	1.34
GL	MainStay Epoch Global Choice C	EPAKX	D	(800) 624-6782	D / 1.9	8.13	3.50	11.57 / 16	0.25 / 14	6.51 / 32	0.00	2.33
GL	MainStay Epoch Global Choice I	EPACX	D	(800) 624-6782	D+ / 2.6	8.53	4.14	12.97 / 22	1.50 / 21	7.83 / 41	1.00	1.09
GL	MainStay Epoch Global Choice Inv	EPAIX	D-	(800) 624-6782	D / 1.7	8.34	3.92	12.38 / 19	0.98 / 18	7.30 / 37	0.50	1.58
GL	MainStay Epoch Global Equity R2	EPSZX	C	(800) 624-6782	C- / 3.3	7.40	2.91	12.44 / 20	3.33 / 35	--	2.73	1.19
GL	MainStay Epoch Global Equity R6	EPSRX	C-	(800) 624-6782	C- / 3.6	7.54	3.15	12.97 / 22	3.80 / 40	--	3.18	0.74
GL	MainStay Epoch Global Equity Yd A	EPSPX	D+	(800) 624-6782	D+ / 2.4	7.43	2.96	12.54 / 20	3.42 / 36	7.93 / 42	2.66	1.09
GL	MainStay Epoch Global Equity Yd C	EPSKX	D+	(800) 624-6782	D+ / 2.8	7.22	2.59	11.68 / 17	2.64 / 29	7.10 / 35	2.11	1.86
GL	MainStay Epoch Global Equity Yd I	EPSYX	C-	(800) 624-6782	C- / 3.5	7.45	3.09	12.77 / 21	3.67 / 39	8.19 / 44	3.06	0.84
GL	MainStay Epoch Global Equity Yd Inv	EPSIX	D+	(800) 624-6782	D+ / 2.4	7.38	2.96	12.50 / 20	3.40 / 36	7.90 / 41	2.67	1.11
FO	MainStay Epoch Intl Small Cap A	EPIPX	E+	(800) 624-6782	E / 0.3	7.12	3.06	11.69 / 17	-3.17 / 4	5.22 / 23	0.44	1.68
FO	MainStay Epoch Intl Small Cap C	EPIKX	E+	(800) 624-6782	E / 0.4	6.93	2.67	10.70 / 14	-4.10 / 3	4.23 / 16	0.00	2.66
FO	MainStay Epoch Intl Small Cap I	EPIEX	D-	(800) 624-6782	E+ / 0.6	7.20	3.22	11.97 / 18	-2.93 / 5	5.48 / 25	0.73	1.43
FO	MainStay Epoch Intl Small Cap Inv	EPIIX	E+	(800) 624-6782	E / 0.3	7.11	2.99	11.46 / 16	-3.37 / 4	5.02 / 21	0.24	1.91
GR	MainStay Epoch US All Cap A	MAAAX	C+	(800) 624-6782	B / 8.0	8.36	11.83	25.81 / 76	8.65 / 84	11.88 / 73	1.63	1.13
GR	● MainStay Epoch US All Cap B	MAWBX	C+	(800) 624-6782	B / 8.0	8.08	11.27	24.51 / 72	7.50 / 75	10.64 / 63	0.93	2.20
GR	MainStay Epoch US All Cap C	MAWCX	C+	(800) 624-6782	B / 8.0	8.02	11.21	24.50 / 72	7.48 / 75	10.63 / 63	0.93	2.20
GR	MainStay Epoch US All Cap I	MATIX	B	(800) 624-6782	A- / 9.0	8.42	11.94	26.12 / 77	8.91 / 86	12.15 / 76	1.75	0.88
GR	MainStay Epoch US All Cap Investor	MAWNX	C+	(800) 624-6782	B / 7.7	8.32	11.75	25.51 / 75	8.30 / 81	11.47 / 70	1.38	1.45
GR	MainStay Epoch US Equity Yield A	EPLPX	B+	(800) 624-6782	B- / 7.1	7.24	6.33	18.56 / 45	9.98 / 93	12.16 / 76	1.65	1.66
GR	MainStay Epoch US Equity Yield C	EPLKX	B+	(800) 624-6782	B- / 7.4	7.04	5.88	17.41 / 40	9.01 / 87	11.20 / 68	1.05	2.52
GR	MainStay Epoch US Equity Yield I	EPLCX	A	(800) 624-6782	B+ / 8.3	7.38	6.48	18.88 / 47	10.28 / 95	12.44 / 78	2.00	1.41
GR	MainStay Epoch US Equity Yield Inv	EPLIX	B+	(800) 624-6782	B- / 7.0	7.24	6.21	18.30 / 44	9.81 / 92	12.03 / 75	1.52	1.77
SC	MainStay Epoch US Small Cap A	MOPAX	B	(800) 624-6782	B- / 7.4	6.77	12.33	29.12 / 84	7.20 / 73	11.84 / 73	0.34	1.25
SC	● MainStay Epoch US Small Cap B	MOTBX	B	(800) 624-6782	B / 7.6	6.51	11.76	27.82 / 81	6.11 / 65	10.69 / 63	0.00	2.26
SC	MainStay Epoch US Small Cap C	MOPCX	B	(800) 624-6782	B / 7.6	6.51	11.76	27.83 / 81	6.12 / 65	10.70 / 63	0.00	2.26
SC	MainStay Epoch US Small Cap I	MOPIX	B+	(800) 624-6782	B+ / 8.6	6.84	12.50	29.49 / 85	7.47 / 75	12.12 / 75	0.56	1.00
SC	MainStay Epoch US Small Cap Inv	MOINX	B	(800) 624-6782	B- / 7.2	6.71	12.18	28.82 / 84	6.91 / 71	11.52 / 70	0.12	1.51
SC	MainStay Epoch US Small Cap R1	MOPRX	B+	(800) 624-6782	B+ / 8.5	6.79	12.42	29.32 / 85	7.36 / 75	--	0.50	1.10
SC	MainStay Epoch US Small Cap R2	MOTRX	B+	(800) 624-6782	B+ / 8.3	6.72	12.25	28.98 / 84	7.09 / 73	--	0.29	1.35
AA	MainStay Growth Allocation A	MGXAX	C	(800) 624-6782	C / 5.1	7.32	9.23	23.49 / 68	4.66 / 50	9.72 / 56	0.78	1.68
AA	● MainStay Growth Allocation B	MGXBX	C	(800) 624-6782	C / 5.4	7.09	8.75	22.43 / 64	3.72 / 39	8.75 / 48	0.02	2.60
AA	MainStay Growth Allocation C	MGXCX	C	(800) 624-6782	C / 5.4	7.08	8.73	22.39 / 64	3.71 / 39	8.73 / 48	0.01	2.60

● Denotes fund is closed to new investors
* Denotes fund is included in Section II

www.thestreetratings.com

Risk Rating/Pts	Standard Deviation	Beta	NAV As of 2/28/17	Total $(Mil)	Cash %	Stocks %	Bonds %	Other %	Portfolio Turnover Ratio	Last Bull Market Return	Last Bear Market Return	Manager Quality Pct	Manager Tenure (Years)	Initial Purch. $	Additional Purch. $	Front End Load	Back End Load
C /4.3	13.2	1.15	28.00	34	0	99	0	1	137	N/A	N/A	5	1	2,500	50	0.0	0.0
C /4.3	13.2	1.15	27.99	5	0	99	0	1	137	N/A	N/A	5	1	2,500	50	0.0	0.0
C /4.5	13.2	1.15	29.95	43	0	99	0	1	137	88.7	-18.5	8	1	5,000,000	0	0.0	0.0
C /4.4	13.2	1.15	29.07	212	0	99	0	1	137	N/A	N/A	7	1	2,500	50	5.5	0.0
C /4.4	13.2	1.15	29.17	N/A	0	99	0	1	137	N/A	N/A	7	1	0	0	0.0	0.0
D- /1.4	32.9	1.34	4.64	40	63	36	0	1	95	N/A	N/A	0	5	25,000	0	5.5	0.0
D- /1.4	32.9	1.34	4.47	18	63	36	0	1	95	N/A	N/A	0	5	2,500	50	0.0	0.0
D- /1.4	32.9	1.34	4.70	20	63	36	0	1	95	N/A	N/A	0	5	5,000,000	0	0.0	0.0
D+ /2.5	22.6	1.32	15.09	327	81	18	0	1	32	17.6	-8.2	0	7	25,000	0	5.5	0.0
D+ /2.5	22.6	1.32	14.15	587	81	18	0	1	32	12.8	-8.4	0	7	2,500	50	0.0	0.0
D+ /2.5	22.6	1.33	15.40	629	81	18	0	1	32	19.3	-8.1	0	7	5,000,000	0	0.0	0.0
D+ /2.7	19.8	0.85	21.23	34	18	81	0	1	149	N/A	N/A	90	4	25,000	0	5.5	0.0
D+ /2.6	19.8	0.85	20.55	26	18	81	0	1	149	N/A	N/A	87	4	2,500	50	0.0	0.0
D+ /2.7	19.8	0.85	21.43	169	18	81	0	1	149	N/A	N/A	91	4	5,000,000	0	0.0	0.0
C+ /6.1	16.8	1.02	8.85	3	2	97	0	1	149	N/A	N/A	71	4	25,000	0	5.5	0.0
C+ /6.1	16.8	1.01	8.77	1	2	97	0	1	149	N/A	N/A	59	4	2,500	50	0.0	0.0
C+ /6.1	16.8	1.01	8.87	123	2	97	0	1	149	N/A	N/A	74	4	5,000,000	0	0.0	0.0
C+ /6.1	16.8	1.01	8.83	1	2	97	0	1	149	N/A	N/A	68	4	2,500	50	5.5	0.0
U /	N/A	N/A	11.00	92	2	97	0	1	0	N/A	N/A	N/A	1	5,000,000	0	0.0	0.0
C+ /5.6	10.7	0.77	18.06	4	2	97	0	1	70	67.1	-17.2	83	8	25,000	0	5.5	0.0
C+ /5.6	10.7	0.77	17.16	1	2	97	0	1	70	58.4	-17.6	77	8	2,500	50	0.0	0.0
C+ /5.7	10.7	0.77	18.60	170	2	97	0	1	70	69.3	-17.1	84	8	5,000,000	0	0.0	0.0
C+ /5.7	10.7	0.77	17.98	1	2	97	0	1	70	64.9	-17.3	82	8	2,500	50	5.5	0.0
B- /7.6	9.4	0.62	18.37	N/A	2	97	0	1	21	N/A	N/A	91	8	0	0	0.0	0.0
C+ /6.0	9.4	0.62	18.35	48	2	97	0	1	21	N/A	N/A	93	8	250,000	0	0.0	0.0
C+ /6.0	9.4	0.62	18.37	864	2	97	0	1	21	65.6	-12.2	92	8	25,000	0	5.5	0.0
C+ /6.0	9.4	0.62	18.23	209	2	97	0	1	21	58.8	-12.5	89	8	2,500	50	0.0	0.0
C+ /6.0	9.4	0.62	18.34	2,842	2	97	0	1	21	67.7	-12.2	92	8	5,000,000	0	0.0	0.0
C+ /6.0	9.4	0.62	18.33	11	2	97	0	1	21	65.4	-12.2	92	8	2,500	50	5.5	0.0
C+ /5.8	12.9	0.94	20.85	4	2	97	0	1	43	48.7	-28.2	34	11	25,000	0	5.5	0.0
C+ /5.8	12.9	0.94	20.38	1	2	97	0	1	43	41.3	-28.4	23	11	2,500	50	0.0	0.0
C+ /5.8	12.9	0.94	21.49	28	2	97	0	1	43	50.7	-28.1	37	11	5,000,000	0	0.0	0.0
C+ /5.8	12.9	0.94	20.81	1	2	97	0	1	43	47.1	-28.2	31	11	2,500	50	5.5	0.0
C /4.4	11.9	1.12	25.44	25	2	97	0	1	45	119.5	-20.9	35	8	25,000	0	4.8	0.0
C- /4.2	11.9	1.12	22.13	4	2	95	0	1	45	106.7	-21.3	23	8	1,000	50	0.0	0.0
C- /4.2	11.9	1.12	22.14	4	2	97	0	1	45	106.4	-21.3	23	8	1,000	50	0.0	0.0
C /4.6	11.9	1.12	28.08	798	2	97	0	1	45	122.4	-20.8	38	8	5,000,000	0	0.0	0.0
C /4.4	11.9	1.12	25.04	13	2	97	0	1	45	115.1	-21.0	31	8	1,000	50	5.5	0.0
B- /7.1	8.8	0.74	15.39	35	4	95	0	1	14	117.4	-19.0	86	9	25,000	0	5.5	0.0
B- /7.1	8.8	0.74	14.90	10	4	95	0	1	14	107.6	-19.3	82	9	2,500	50	0.0	0.0
B- /7.1	8.8	0.74	15.53	100	4	95	0	1	14	120.3	-18.9	87	9	5,000,000	0	0.0	0.0
B- /7.1	8.8	0.74	15.32	4	4	95	0	1	14	116.0	-19.1	85	9	2,500	50	5.5	0.0
C+ /5.8	13.4	0.83	30.72	131	1	98	0	1	65	119.4	-21.8	83	8	25,000	0	5.5	0.0
C+ /5.7	13.4	0.83	27.66	20	1	98	0	1	65	107.6	-22.2	77	8	1,000	50	0.0	0.0
C+ /5.7	13.4	0.83	27.65	21	1	98	0	1	65	107.6	-22.2	77	8	1,000	50	0.0	0.0
C+ /5.8	13.4	0.83	31.45	349	1	98	0	1	65	122.5	-21.8	84	8	5,000,000	0	0.0	0.0
C+ /5.8	13.4	0.83	30.36	90	1	98	0	1	65	116.1	-21.9	82	8	1,000	50	5.5	0.0
C+ /5.8	13.4	0.83	31.39	1	1	98	0	1	65	N/A	N/A	84	8	0	0	0.0	0.0
C+ /5.8	13.4	0.83	30.64	N/A	1	98	0	1	65	N/A	N/A	83	8	0	0	0.0	0.0
C+ /5.7	11.1	1.67	15.39	142	3	96	0	1	25	94.3	-20.2	5	12	25,000	0	5.5	0.0
C+ /5.7	11.0	1.67	15.02	49	3	96	0	1	25	85.1	-20.5	3	12	1,000	50	0.0	0.0
C+ /5.7	11.1	1.67	15.04	28	3	96	0	1	25	85.1	-20.5	3	12	1,000	50	0.0	0.0

I. Index of Stock Mutual Funds

Spring 2017

Fund Type	Fund Name	Ticker Symbol	Overall Investment Rating	Phone	Performance Rating/Pts	3 Mo	6 Mo	1Yr / Pct	3Yr / Pct	5Yr / Pct	Dividend Yield	Expense Ratio
AA	MainStay Growth Allocation I	MGXIX	C+	(800) 624-6782	C+ / 6.5	7.39	9.42	23.86 /69	4.94 /53	10.03 /59	1.03	1.43
AA	MainStay Growth Allocation Inv	MGXNX	C	(800) 624-6782	C / 4.9	7.27	9.18	23.28 /67	4.48 /49	9.54 /55	0.66	1.85
GR	MainStay ICAP Equity Fd A	ICAUX	C-	(800) 624-6782	C+ / 6.0	8.61	8.44	21.18 /58	6.47 /68	10.58 /63	0.93	1.13
GR	MainStay ICAP Equity Fd C	ICAVX	C-	(800) 624-6782	C+ / 6.2	8.34	7.93	20.00 /52	5.46 /59	9.51 /55	0.15	2.08
GR	MainStay ICAP Equity Fd I	ICAEX	C	(800) 624-6782	B- / 7.1	8.67	8.59	21.47 /60	6.74 /70	10.86 /65	1.21	0.88
GR	MainStay ICAP Equity Fd Inv	ICANX	C-	(800) 624-6782	C+ / 5.8	8.55	8.33	20.89 /57	6.25 /66	10.34 /61	0.73	1.33
GR	MainStay ICAP Equity Fd R1	ICAWX	C	(800) 624-6782	B- / 7.1	8.65	8.52	21.34 /59	6.64 /69	10.76 /64	1.11	0.98
GR	MainStay ICAP Equity Fd R2	ICAYX	C-	(800) 624-6782	C+ / 6.9	8.58	8.41	21.06 /58	6.37 /67	10.47 /62	0.87	1.23
GR	MainStay ICAP Equity Fd R3	ICAZX	C-	(800) 624-6782	C+ / 6.7	8.51	8.27	20.74 /56	6.10 /65	10.19 /60	0.65	1.48
FO	MainStay ICAP International Fd A	ICEVX	E+	(800) 624-6782	E / 0.3	7.06	2.02	14.04 /26	-3.08 / 4	2.76 /10	2.91	1.22
FO	MainStay ICAP International Fd C	ICEWX	E+	(800) 624-6782	E / 0.4	6.81	1.57	13.02 /22	-3.93 / 3	1.86 / 8	2.22	2.11
FO	MainStay ICAP International Fd I	ICEUX	E+	(800) 624-6782	E+ / 0.6	7.16	2.19	14.42 /27	-2.79 / 5	3.08 /11	3.44	0.97
FO	MainStay ICAP International Fd Inv	ICELX	E+	(800) 624-6782	E / 0.3	7.05	1.97	13.92 /25	-3.21 / 4	2.63 /10	2.84	1.36
FO	MainStay ICAP International Fd R1	ICETX	E+	(800) 624-6782	E+ / 0.6	7.13	2.15	14.28 /27	-2.90 / 5	2.97 /11	3.31	1.07
FO	MainStay ICAP International Fd R2	ICEYX	E+	(800) 624-6782	E+ / 0.6	7.08	2.03	14.03 /26	-3.13 / 4	2.69 /10	3.03	1.32
FO	MainStay ICAP International Fd R3	ICEZX	E+	(800) 624-6782	E / 0.5	6.98	1.83	13.65 /24	-3.41 / 4	2.41 / 9	2.72	1.57
GR	MainStay ICAP Select Equity Fd A	ICSRX	D	(800) 624-6782	C / 4.9	8.96	8.73	20.66 /56	4.66 /50	9.31 /53	0.84	1.22
GR	● MainStay ICAP Select Equity Fd B	ICSQX	D	(800) 624-6782	C / 5.2	8.74	8.25	19.54 /50	3.70 /39	8.29 /45	0.15	2.09
GR	MainStay ICAP Select Equity Fd C	ICSVX	D	(800) 624-6782	C / 5.2	8.71	8.22	19.52 /49	3.69 /39	8.28 /45	0.15	2.09
GR	MainStay ICAP Select Equity Fd I	ICSLX	D+	(800) 624-6782	C+ / 6.3	9.04	8.87	21.03 /58	4.97 /54	9.62 /55	1.15	0.97
GR	MainStay ICAP Select Equity Fd Inv	ICSOX	D-	(800) 624-6782	C / 4.7	8.94	8.63	20.42 /54	4.47 /48	9.09 /51	0.66	1.34
GR	MainStay ICAP Select Equity Fd R1	ICSWX	D+	(800) 624-6782	C+ / 6.2	9.03	8.78	20.85 /57	4.85 /53	9.49 /55	1.05	1.07
GR	MainStay ICAP Select Equity Fd R2	ICSYX	D+	(800) 624-6782	C+ / 6.0	8.94	8.67	20.57 /55	4.59 /50	9.22 /52	0.79	1.32
GR	MainStay ICAP Select Equity Fd R3	ICSZX	D	(800) 624-6782	C+ / 5.6	8.86	8.50	20.14 /53	4.23 /46	8.86 /49	0.44	1.57
GR	MainStay ICAP Select Equity R6	ICSDX	D+	(800) 624-6782	C+ / 6.3	9.07	8.91	21.09 /58	5.04 /55	--	1.21	0.82
BA	MainStay Income Builder A	MTRAX	C-	(800) 624-6782	C- / 3.1	5.60	3.26	14.83 /29	4.66 /50	8.32 /45	3.21	1.02
BA	● MainStay Income Builder B	MKTRX	C-	(800) 624-6782	C- / 3.4	5.35	2.81	13.84 /25	3.71 /39	7.29 /37	2.39	1.93
BA	MainStay Income Builder C	MCTRX	C-	(800) 624-6782	C- / 3.4	5.42	2.81	13.86 /25	3.71 /39	7.29 /37	2.40	1.93
BA	MainStay Income Builder I	MTOIX	C	(800) 624-6782	C / 4.3	5.66	3.40	15.09 /30	4.92 /53	8.59 /47	3.65	0.77
BA	MainStay Income Builder Inv	MTINX	C-	(800) 624-6782	C- / 3.0	5.60	3.17	14.71 /29	4.48 /49	8.09 /43	3.06	1.18
FO	MainStay Intl Equity A	MSEAX	D	(800) 624-6782	D- / 1.3	8.43	-0.44	11.03 /15	0.78 /17	4.61 /19	0.25	1.33
FO	● MainStay Intl Equity B	MINEX	D	(800) 624-6782	D- / 1.0	8.21	-0.96	9.84 /11	-0.32 /12	3.48 /13	0.00	2.43
FO	MainStay Intl Equity C	MIECX	D-	(800) 624-6782	D- / 1.0	8.21	-0.96	9.84 /11	-0.32 /12	3.46 /13	0.00	2.43
FO	MainStay Intl Equity I	MSIIX	D+	(800) 624-6782	D / 2.0	8.52	-0.30	11.37 /16	1.05 /18	4.88 /21	0.51	1.08
FO	MainStay Intl Equity Inv	MINNX	D	(800) 624-6782	D- / 1.2	8.42	-0.58	10.68 /13	0.44 /15	4.25 /17	0.00	1.68
FO	MainStay Intl Equity R1	MIERX	D+	(800) 624-6782	D / 1.9	8.53	-0.35	11.22 /15	0.94 /18	4.78 /20	0.41	1.18
FO	MainStay Intl Equity R2	MIRRX	D	(800) 624-6782	D / 1.8	8.53	-0.48	10.95 /14	0.71 /17	4.51 /18	0.15	1.43
FO	MainStay Intl Equity R3	MIFRX	D	(800) 624-6782	D / 1.7	8.33	-0.65	10.67 /13	0.44 /15	4.24 /16	0.00	1.68
FO	MainStay Intl Opportunities A	MYITX	D-	(800) 624-6782	D- / 1.0	8.04	8.04	16.27 /35	-0.40 /12	7.48 /38	2.61	3.34
FO	MainStay Intl Opportunities C	MYICX	D-	(800) 624-6782	D- / 1.2	7.81	7.67	15.23 /31	-1.28 / 8	6.55 /32	1.87	4.23
FO	MainStay Intl Opportunities I	MYIIX	D	(800) 624-6782	D / 1.6	8.15	8.15	16.63 /37	-0.18 /13	7.71 /40	3.01	3.13
FO	MainStay Intl Opportunities Inv	MYINX	D-	(800) 624-6782	D- / 1.0	8.05	8.05	16.17 /35	-0.54 /11	7.31 /37	2.47	3.51
GR	MainStay Large Cap Growth Fd A	MLAAX	D+	(800) 624-6782	C+ / 5.6	9.38	6.24	19.32 /49	6.61 /69	11.22 /68	0.00	0.99
GR	● MainStay Large Cap Growth Fd B	MLABX	D+	(800) 624-6782	C+ / 6.1	9.10	5.83	18.50 /45	5.77 /62	10.32 /61	0.00	1.79
GR	MainStay Large Cap Growth Fd C	MLACX	D+	(800) 624-6782	C+ / 6.1	9.12	5.83	18.53 /45	5.78 /62	10.34 /61	0.00	1.79
GR	MainStay Large Cap Growth Fd I	MLAIX	C	(800) 624-6782	C+ / 6.9	9.32	6.34	19.66 /50	6.86 /71	11.49 /70	0.00	0.74
GR	MainStay Large Cap Growth Fd Inv	MLINX	D+	(800) 624-6782	C+ / 5.6	9.35	6.18	19.24 /48	6.55 /69	11.14 /67	0.00	1.04
GR	MainStay Large Cap Growth Fd R1	MLRRX	C-	(800) 624-6782	C+ / 6.9	9.51	6.46	19.66 /50	6.80 /70	11.40 /69	0.00	0.84
GR	MainStay Large Cap Growth Fd R2	MLRTX	C-	(800) 624-6782	C+ / 6.6	9.28	6.14	19.23 /48	6.47 /68	11.11 /67	0.00	1.09
GR	MainStay Large Cap Growth Fd R3	MLGRX	C-	(800) 624-6782	C+ / 6.5	9.25	6.12	18.99 /47	6.22 /66	10.82 /64	0.00	1.34
GR	MainStay Large Cap Growth R6	MLRSX	C	(800) 624-6782	B- / 7.0	9.40	6.42	19.83 /51	6.98 /72	--	0.00	0.62
GI	MainStay MAP Equity A	MAPAX	C-	(800) 624-6782	C+ / 6.7	8.19	10.40	24.66 /72	6.72 /70	10.84 /64	1.13	1.11

● Denotes fund is closed to new investors
* Denotes fund is included in Section II

408

www.thestreetratings.com

Risk Rating/Pts	Standard Deviation	Beta	NAV As of 2/28/17	Total $(Mil)	Cash %	Stocks %	Bonds %	Other %	Portfolio Turnover Ratio	Last Bull Market Return	Last Bear Market Return	Manager Quality Pct	Manager Tenure (Years)	Initial Purch. $	Additional Purch. $	Front End Load	Back End Load
C+ /5.6	11.1	1.67	15.61	5	3	96	0	1	25	97.1	-20.1	5	12	5,000,000	0	0.0	0.0
C+ /5.7	11.1	1.67	15.37	139	3	96	0	1	25	92.8	-20.3	4	12	1,000	50	5.5	0.0
C- /3.6	11.9	1.12	43.67	38	2	97	0	1	76	103.1	-19.0	15	N/A	25,000	0	5.5	0.0
C- /3.5	11.9	1.12	42.78	9	2	97	0	1	76	92.7	-19.3	9	N/A	1,000	50	0.0	0.0
C- /3.6	11.9	1.12	43.77	495	2	97	0	1	76	106.0	-18.9	17	N/A	5,000,000	0	0.0	0.0
C- /3.6	11.9	1.12	43.57	14	2	97	0	1	76	100.7	-19.1	13	N/A	1,000	50	5.5	0.0
C- /3.6	11.9	1.12	43.81	1	2	97	0	1	76	104.9	-18.9	16	N/A	0	0	0.0	0.0
C- /3.6	11.9	1.12	43.68	3	2	97	0	1	76	102.1	-19.0	14	N/A	0	0	0.0	0.0
C- /3.6	11.9	1.12	43.54	3	2	97	0	1	76	99.3	-19.1	13	N/A	0	0	0.0	0.0
C /5.2	13.3	1.04	30.65	32	1	98	0	1	46	35.0	-22.9	35	N/A	25,000	0	5.5	0.0
C /5.2	13.3	1.04	30.17	11	1	98	0	1	46	28.7	-23.2	25	N/A	1,000	50	0.0	0.0
C /5.1	13.3	1.04	30.65	688	1	98	0	1	46	37.3	-22.8	39	N/A	5,000,000	0	0.0	0.0
C /5.2	13.3	1.04	30.64	8	1	98	0	1	46	34.1	-23.0	34	N/A	1,000	50	5.5	0.0
C /5.1	13.3	1.04	30.61	1	1	98	0	1	46	36.6	-22.9	38	N/A	0	0	0.0	0.0
C /5.2	13.3	1.04	30.65	27	1	98	0	1	46	34.5	-23.0	35	N/A	0	0	0.0	0.0
C /5.2	13.3	1.04	30.47	9	1	98	0	1	46	32.5	-23.0	31	N/A	0	0	0.0	0.0
D+ /2.6	12.5	1.17	38.99	311	1	98	0	1	82	92.3	-20.2	5	N/A	25,000	0	5.5	0.0
D+ /2.6	12.5	1.17	38.36	30	1	98	0	1	82	82.7	-20.5	4	N/A	1,000	50	0.0	0.0
D+ /2.6	12.5	1.17	38.34	50	1	98	0	1	82	82.7	-20.5	4	N/A	1,000	50	0.0	0.0
D+ /2.6	12.5	1.17	39.08	838	1	98	0	1	82	95.2	-20.1	6	N/A	5,000,000	0	0.0	0.0
D+ /2.6	12.4	1.17	38.98	168	1	98	0	1	82	90.2	-20.3	5	N/A	1,000	50	5.5	0.0
D+ /2.6	12.5	1.17	39.09	8	1	98	0	1	82	94.0	-20.2	5	N/A	0	0	0.0	0.0
D+ /2.6	12.5	1.17	39.00	8	1	98	0	1	82	91.5	-20.2	5	N/A	0	0	0.0	0.0
D+ /2.6	12.5	1.17	38.93	3	1	98	0	1	82	88.0	-20.3	4	N/A	0	0	0.0	0.0
D+ /2.6	12.4	1.16	39.07	21	1	98	0	1	82	N/A	N/A	6	N/A	250,000	0	0.0	0.0
C+ /6.8	7.5	1.13	18.96	556	10	42	46	2	27	70.5	-11.0	27	8	25,000	0	5.5	0.0
C+ /6.8	7.5	1.13	19.08	43	10	42	46	2	27	61.8	-11.4	19	8	1,000	50	0.0	0.0
C+ /6.8	7.6	1.13	19.05	257	10	42	46	2	27	61.8	-11.3	19	8	1,000	50	0.0	0.0
C+ /6.8	7.6	1.13	19.12	636	10	42	46	2	27	72.8	-10.9	30	8	5,000,000	0	0.0	0.0
C+ /6.8	7.5	1.13	18.97	157	10	42	46	2	27	68.4	-11.0	26	8	1,000	50	5.5	0.0
C+ /6.6	11.6	0.81	13.84	40	3	96	0	1	33	47.6	-25.6	80	6	25,000	0	5.5	0.0
C+ /6.5	11.6	0.81	12.39	7	3	96	0	1	33	39.1	-25.9	72	6	1,000	50	0.0	0.0
C+ /6.5	11.7	0.81	12.39	7	3	96	0	1	33	39.1	-25.9	72	6	1,000	50	0.0	0.0
C+ /6.6	11.6	0.81	13.90	184	3	96	0	1	33	49.5	-25.5	82	6	5,000,000	0	0.0	0.0
C+ /6.6	11.6	0.81	13.78	31	3	96	0	1	33	44.8	-25.6	78	6	1,000	50	5.5	0.0
C+ /6.6	11.6	0.81	13.83	2	3	96	0	1	33	48.8	-25.6	81	6	0	0	0.0	0.0
C+ /6.6	11.6	0.81	13.89	1	3	96	0	1	33	46.8	-25.6	80	6	0	0	0.0	0.0
C+ /6.6	11.6	0.81	13.79	1	3	96	0	1	33	44.7	-25.7	78	6	0	0	0.0	0.0
C+ /5.8	11.7	0.91	8.31	50	1	98	0	1	137	68.7	-24.3	71	10	25,000	0	5.5	0.0
C+ /5.8	11.6	0.91	8.05	33	1	98	0	1	137	60.8	-24.5	60	10	1,000	50	0.0	0.0
C+ /5.8	11.7	0.92	8.36	430	1	98	0	1	137	71.0	-24.3	74	10	5,000,000	0	0.0	0.0
C+ /5.8	11.7	0.92	8.28	4	1	98	0	1	137	67.3	-24.2	70	10	1,000	50	5.5	0.0
C- /3.5	12.9	1.10	8.81	834	1	98	0	1	84	110.1	-17.7	18	12	25,000	0	5.5	0.0
C- /3.1	13.0	1.10	7.64	36	1	98	0	1	84	101.2	-18.1	11	12	1,000	50	0.0	0.0
C- /3.1	13.0	1.10	7.63	263	1	98	0	1	84	101.4	-18.1	12	12	1,000	50	0.0	0.0
C- /3.6	13.0	1.10	9.34	7,749	1	98	0	1	84	112.9	-17.7	19	12	5,000,000	0	0.0	0.0
C- /3.5	12.9	1.10	8.72	174	1	98	0	1	84	109.6	-17.8	17	12	1,000	50	5.5	0.0
C- /3.6	13.0	1.11	9.16	1,632	1	98	0	1	84	112.2	-17.8	18	12	0	0	0.0	0.0
C- /3.5	13.0	1.10	8.79	331	1	98	0	1	84	109.0	-17.8	16	12	0	0	0.0	0.0
C- /3.4	13.0	1.10	8.45	79	1	98	0	1	84	106.3	-17.9	14	12	0	0	0.0	0.0
C- /3.7	12.9	1.10	9.39	1,851	1	98	0	1	84	N/A	N/A	21	12	250,000	0	0.0	0.0
C- /3.7	11.7	1.11	39.50	305	2	97	0	1	42	105.2	-19.8	17	N/A	25,000	0	5.5	0.0

					PERFORMANCE						Incl. in Returns	
	99 Pct = Best 0 Pct = Worst				Perfor-	Total Return % through 2/28/17					Dividend	Expense
			Overall		mance				Annualized			
Fund		Ticker	Investment		Rating/							
Type	Fund Name	Symbol	Rating	Phone	Pts	3 Mo	6 Mo	1Yr / Pct	3Yr / Pct	5Yr / Pct	Yield	Ratio
GI	● MainStay MAP Equity B	MAPBX	C	(800) 624-6782	C+ / 6.9	7.95	9.87	23.44 /68	5.75 /62	9.82 /57	0.37	2.00
GI	MainStay MAP Equity C	MMPCX	C	(800) 624-6782	C+ / 6.9	7.95	9.87	23.44 /68	5.75 /62	9.81 /57	0.37	2.00
GI	MainStay MAP Equity I	MUBFX	C+	(800) 624-6782	B / 7.8	8.28	10.55	24.97 /73	6.99 /72	11.11 /67	1.40	0.86
GI	MainStay MAP Equity Inv	MSMIX	C-	(800) 624-6782	C+ / 6.6	8.13	10.28	24.40 /71	6.54 /69	10.63 /63	0.96	1.25
GI	MainStay MAP Equity R1	MAPRX	C+	(800) 624-6782	B / 7.7	8.25	10.48	24.83 /73	6.88 /71	10.99 /66	1.31	0.96
GI	MainStay MAP Equity R2	MPRRX	C	(800) 624-6782	B- / 7.5	8.16	10.34	24.49 /72	6.61 /69	10.72 /64	1.08	1.21
GI	MainStay MAP Equity R3	MMAPX	C	(800) 624-6782	B- / 7.3	8.09	10.19	24.21 /71	6.34 /67	10.44 /62	0.85	1.46
AA	MainStay Moderate Allocation A	MMRAX	C-	(800) 624-6782	C- / 3.0	5.26	5.51	16.35 /36	3.85 /41	7.39 /37	1.73	1.35
AA	● MainStay Moderate Allocation B	MMRBX	C	(800) 624-6782	C- / 3.3	5.00	5.08	15.36 /31	2.90 /31	6.41 /31	0.94	2.27
AA	MainStay Moderate Allocation C	MMRCX	C	(800) 624-6782	C- / 3.3	5.08	5.08	15.36 /31	2.90 /31	6.41 /31	0.94	2.27
AA	MainStay Moderate Allocation I	MMRIX	C	(800) 624-6782	C / 4.3	5.33	5.73	16.72 /37	4.11 /44	7.66 /39	2.05	1.10
AA	MainStay Moderate Allocation Inv	MMRDX	C-	(800) 624-6782	D+ / 2.9	5.17	5.41	16.16 /35	3.65 /39	7.19 /36	1.57	1.52
AA	MainStay Moderate Gr Allocation A	MGDAX	C	(800) 624-6782	C- / 4.2	6.23	7.73	20.67 /56	4.44 /48	8.85 /49	1.25	1.50
AA	MainStay Moderate Gr Allocation B	MGDBX	C	(800) 624-6782	C / 4.6	6.00	7.22	19.56 /50	3.49 /37	7.86 /41	0.45	2.43
AA	MainStay Moderate Gr Allocation C	MGDCX	C	(800) 624-6782	C / 4.6	6.00	7.22	19.56 /50	3.51 /37	7.86 /41	0.45	2.43
AA	MainStay Moderate Gr Allocation I	MGDIX	C+	(800) 624-6782	C+ / 5.6	6.27	7.84	20.91 /57	4.71 /51	9.13 /52	1.54	1.25
AA	MainStay Moderate Gr Allocation Inv	MGDNX	C	(800) 624-6782	C- / 4.1	6.27	7.63	20.46 /55	4.29 /46	8.67 /48	1.10	1.68
BA	MainStay Retirement 2010 A	MYRAX	C-	(800) 624-6782	D / 2.0	3.53	2.42	10.81 /14	3.61 /38	5.74 /27	2.41	1.25
BA	MainStay Retirement 2010 I	MYRIX	C	(800) 624-6782	C- / 3.0	3.64	2.54	11.09 /15	3.88 /41	6.01 /28	2.76	1.00
BA	MainStay Retirement 2010 Inv	MYRDX	C-	(800) 624-6782	D / 1.9	3.52	2.32	10.65 /13	3.51 /37	5.63 /26	2.32	1.47
BA	MainStay Retirement 2010 R2	MYRWX	C	(800) 624-6782	D+ / 2.7	3.54	2.33	10.69 /13	3.52 /37	5.65 /26	2.08	1.35
BA	MainStay Retirement 2010 R3	MYREX	C	(800) 624-6782	D+ / 2.5	3.54	2.26	10.45 /13	3.26 /34	5.39 /24	1.91	1.60
GI	MainStay Retirement 2020 A	MYROX	C	(800) 624-6782	D+ / 2.8	4.77	4.18	14.28 /27	4.15 /45	6.91 /34	1.91	1.14
GI	MainStay Retirement 2020 I	MYRTX	C+	(800) 624-6782	C- / 4.0	4.88	4.29	14.56 /28	4.44 /48	7.19 /36	2.22	0.89
GI	MainStay Retirement 2020 Inv	MYRYX	C	(800) 624-6782	D+ / 2.7	4.86	4.17	14.25 /27	4.07 /44	6.82 /34	1.81	1.30
GI	MainStay Retirement 2020 R2	MYRVX	C+	(800) 624-6782	C- / 3.7	4.82	4.13	14.22 /27	4.05 /44	6.80 /33	1.25	1.24
GI	MainStay Retirement 2020 R3	MYRZX	C+	(800) 624-6782	C- / 3.5	4.75	4.07	13.94 /25	3.80 /40	6.53 /32	1.03	1.49
GI	MainStay Retirement 2030 A	MRTTX	C	(800) 624-6782	C- / 3.8	5.96	5.86	17.88 /42	4.73 /51	8.15 /43	1.65	1.18
GI	MainStay Retirement 2030 I	MRTIX	C+	(800) 624-6782	C / 5.1	6.02	6.02	18.19 /44	4.94 /53	8.42 /46	1.92	0.93
GI	MainStay Retirement 2030 Inv	MRTFX	C	(800) 624-6782	C- / 3.7	5.96	5.86	17.75 /42	4.58 /50	8.03 /42	1.56	1.40
GI	MainStay Retirement 2030 R2	MRTUX	C+	(800) 624-6782	C / 4.8	5.97	5.87	17.68 /41	4.57 /49	8.04 /42	1.38	1.28
GI	MainStay Retirement 2030 R3	MRTVX	C+	(800) 624-6782	C / 4.6	5.85	5.65	17.41 /40	4.31 /46	7.76 /40	1.15	1.53
GI	MainStay Retirement 2040 A	MSRTX	C	(800) 624-6782	C / 4.3	6.62	6.82	19.78 /51	4.89 /53	8.80 /49	1.44	1.24
GI	MainStay Retirement 2040 I	MSRYX	C+	(800) 624-6782	C+ / 5.8	6.75	7.04	20.24 /53	5.19 /56	9.08 /51	1.68	0.99
GI	MainStay Retirement 2040 Inv	MSRUX	C	(800) 624-6782	C / 4.3	6.69	6.88	19.80 /51	4.81 /52	8.71 /48	1.35	1.49
GI	MainStay Retirement 2040 R2	MSRQX	C+	(800) 624-6782	C / 5.4	6.62	6.81	19.74 /51	4.81 /52	8.70 /48	1.27	1.34
GI	MainStay Retirement 2040 R3	MSRZX	C+	(800) 624-6782	C / 5.2	6.64	6.74	19.42 /49	4.56 /49	8.44 /46	1.07	1.59
GI	MainStay Retirement 2050 A	MSRLX	C	(800) 624-6782	C / 4.5	6.99	7.09	20.31 /54	4.94 /53	9.03 /51	1.25	1.50
GI	MainStay Retirement 2050 I	MSRMX	C+	(800) 624-6782	C+ / 5.9	7.07	7.17	20.67 /56	5.21 /57	9.30 /53	1.52	1.25
GI	MainStay Retirement 2050 Inv	MSRVX	C	(800) 624-6782	C / 4.4	7.01	7.01	20.25 /53	4.81 /52	8.91 /50	1.18	1.71
GI	MainStay Retirement 2050 R2	MSRPX	C+	(800) 624-6782	C+ / 5.6	6.93	7.03	20.24 /53	4.80 /52	8.92 /50	1.18	1.60
GI	MainStay Retirement 2050 R3	MSRWX	C+	(800) 624-6782	C / 5.4	6.95	6.95	19.96 /52	4.57 /49	8.66 /48	0.97	1.85
GR	MainStay S&P 500 Index A	MSXAX	A-	(800) 624-6782	B+ / 8.6	7.86	9.71	24.21 /71	9.99 /93	13.34 /87	2.00	0.60
GR	MainStay S&P 500 Index I	MSPIX	A+	(800) 624-6782	A- / 9.2	7.93	9.82	24.50 /72	10.26 /95	13.62 /90	2.26	0.35
GR	MainStay S&P 500 Index Inv	MYSPX	A-	(800) 624-6782	B+ / 8.5	7.85	9.65	24.11 /70	9.88 /93	13.22 /86	1.95	0.81
FS	MainStay Unconstrained Bond R2	MSIRX	D+	(800) 624-6782	D / 1.9	2.35	2.31	11.83 /17	1.53 /21	--	3.96	1.11
GI	MainStay US Eqty Opportunities A	MYCTX	A-	(800) 624-6782	A- / 9.1	6.75	12.89	24.02 /70	11.84 /98	15.60 /98	0.00	2.42
GI	MainStay US Eqty Opportunities C	MYCCX	A-	(800) 624-6782	A / 9.3	6.47	12.38	23.02 /67	10.83 /97	14.53 /96	0.00	3.30
GI	MainStay US Eqty Opportunities I	MYCIX	A	(800) 624-6782	A+ / 9.7	6.70	13.02	24.37 /71	12.09 /98	15.87 /98	0.12	2.17
GI	MainStay US Eqty Opportunities Inv	MYCNX	A-	(800) 624-6782	A- / 9.1	6.61	12.83	23.97 /70	11.65 /98	15.39 /97	0.00	2.55
BA	Mairs & Power Balanced Fund	MAPOX	B	(800) 304-7404	C / 5.2	4.45	4.04	16.15 /35	6.23 /66	9.57 /55	2.19	0.73
GR	Mairs & Power Growth Fund	MPGFX	B	(800) 304-7404	B- / 7.2	6.09	6.32	20.90 /57	7.98 /79	13.76 /91	1.30	0.65

● Denotes fund is closed to new investors
∗ Denotes fund is included in Section II

Risk Rating/Pts	Standard Deviation	Beta	NAV As of 2/28/17	Total $(Mil)	Cash %	Stocks %	Bonds %	Other %	Portfolio Turnover Ratio	Last Bull Market Return	Last Bear Market Return	Manager Quality Pct	Manager Tenure (Years)	Initial Purch. $	Additional Purch. $	Front End Load	Back End Load
C- /3.6	11.7	1.11	35.82	42	2	97	0	1	42	95.1	-20.1	11	N/A	1,000	50	0.0	0.0
C- /3.6	11.7	1.11	35.82	93	2	97	0	1	42	95.1	-20.1	11	N/A	1,000	50	0.0	0.0
C- /3.8	11.7	1.11	40.56	774	2	97	0	1	42	108.0	-19.7	19	N/A	5,000,000	0	0.0	0.0
C- /3.8	11.7	1.11	39.48	152	2	97	0	1	42	103.2	-19.8	16	N/A	1,000	50	5.5	0.0
C- /3.7	11.7	1.11	39.74	3	2	97	0	1	42	106.8	-19.7	18	N/A	0	0	0.0	0.0
C- /3.8	11.7	1.11	39.68	4	2	97	0	1	42	104.0	-19.8	16	N/A	0	0	0.0	0.0
C- /3.8	11.7	1.11	39.54	1	2	97	0	1	42	101.2	-19.9	14	N/A	0	0	0.0	0.0
B- /7.0	7.3	1.12	13.21	362	11	59	28	2	37	65.2	-12.7	20	12	25,000	0	5.5	0.0
B- /7.2	7.3	1.12	13.08	74	11	59	28	2	37	57.4	-13.1	13	12	1,000	50	0.0	0.0
B- /7.2	7.3	1.13	13.08	71	11	59	28	2	37	57.2	-13.0	13	12	1,000	50	0.0	0.0
B- /7.0	7.3	1.12	13.29	14	11	59	28	2	37	67.6	-12.6	23	12	5,000,000	0	0.0	0.0
B- /7.0	7.3	1.12	13.21	180	11	59	28	2	37	63.7	-12.8	19	12	1,000	50	5.5	0.0
C+ /6.4	9.3	1.42	14.64	317	9	78	11	2	32	82.4	-17.1	10	12	25,000	0	5.5	0.0
C+ /6.5	9.3	1.42	14.46	85	9	78	11	2	32	73.7	-17.5	6	12	1,000	50	0.0	0.0
C+ /6.5	9.3	1.42	14.46	54	9	78	11	2	32	73.7	-17.5	6	12	1,000	50	0.0	0.0
C+ /6.3	9.3	1.41	14.78	8	9	78	11	2	32	85.0	-17.1	11	12	5,000,000	0	0.0	0.0
C+ /6.4	9.3	1.42	14.64	243	9	78	11	2	32	80.9	-17.2	9	12	1,000	50	5.5	0.0
B /8.1	4.7	0.73	10.06	8	5	30	64	1	45	50.4	-10.6	51	10	25,000	0	5.5	0.0
B /8.1	4.7	0.73	10.14	39	5	30	64	1	45	52.4	-10.4	55	10	5,000,000	0	0.0	0.0
B /8.1	4.7	0.73	10.11	2	5	30	64	1	45	49.5	-10.6	50	10	1,000	50	5.5	0.0
B /8.2	4.7	0.74	10.12	3	5	30	64	1	45	49.6	-10.6	50	10	0	0	0.0	0.0
B /8.2	4.7	0.74	10.31	N/A	5	30	64	1	45	47.7	-10.7	46	10	0	0	0.0	0.0
B- /7.9	6.7	0.63	10.62	22	5	50	43	2	48	62.4	-13.9	44	10	25,000	0	5.5	0.0
B- /7.9	6.6	0.62	10.68	124	5	50	43	2	48	64.8	-13.8	49	10	5,000,000	0	0.0	0.0
B- /7.9	6.6	0.62	10.65	9	5	50	43	2	48	61.7	-13.9	43	10	1,000	50	5.5	0.0
B- /7.9	6.6	0.62	10.70	3	5	50	43	2	48	61.6	-14.0	43	10	0	0	0.0	0.0
B /8.0	6.6	0.62	10.81	N/A	5	50	43	2	48	59.4	-14.0	40	10	0	0	0.0	0.0
B- /7.3	8.5	0.81	10.81	25	5	67	27	1	43	76.3	-17.3	28	10	25,000	0	5.5	0.0
B- /7.3	8.5	0.81	10.90	213	5	67	27	1	43	78.6	-17.3	30	10	5,000,000	0	0.0	0.0
B- /7.3	8.5	0.81	10.82	16	5	67	27	1	43	75.3	-17.4	27	10	1,000	50	5.5	0.0
B- /7.3	8.5	0.80	10.82	5	5	67	27	1	43	75.2	-17.4	27	10	0	0	0.0	0.0
B- /7.4	8.5	0.80	10.96	N/A	5	67	27	1	43	72.7	-17.4	24	10	0	0	0.0	0.0
C+ /6.8	9.7	0.92	11.02	15	5	78	15	2	38	83.8	-18.9	19	10	25,000	0	5.5	0.0
C+ /6.8	9.8	0.92	11.15	170	5	78	15	2	38	86.4	-18.8	21	10	5,000,000	0	0.0	0.0
C+ /6.8	9.8	0.92	11.08	16	5	78	15	2	38	82.9	-18.9	18	10	1,000	50	5.5	0.0
C+ /6.8	9.7	0.92	11.08	6	5	78	15	2	38	83.0	-18.9	18	10	0	0	0.0	0.0
C+ /6.8	9.7	0.92	11.18	N/A	5	78	15	2	38	80.6	-19.0	16	10	0	0	0.0	0.0
C+ /6.5	10.1	0.96	10.96	5	5	83	10	2	38	86.8	-19.7	16	10	25,000	0	5.5	0.0
C+ /6.5	10.1	0.95	11.03	87	5	83	10	2	38	89.4	-19.6	18	10	5,000,000	0	0.0	0.0
C+ /6.5	10.2	0.96	10.94	10	5	83	10	2	38	85.9	-19.8	15	10	1,000	50	5.5	0.0
C+ /6.5	10.1	0.96	10.97	4	5	83	10	2	38	85.8	-19.8	15	10	0	0	0.0	0.0
C+ /6.6	10.2	0.96	11.04	N/A	5	83	10	2	38	83.4	-19.8	14	10	0	0	0.0	0.0
C+ /6.4	10.3	1.00	48.45	495	0	96	3	1	4	127.5	-16.5	68	21	25,000	0	3.0	0.0
C+ /6.4	10.3	1.00	48.97	753	0	96	3	1	4	130.6	-16.4	71	21	5,000,000	0	0.0	0.0
C+ /6.4	10.3	1.00	48.40	55	0	96	3	1	4	126.2	-16.5	66	21	1,000	50	3.0	0.0
B- /7.2	4.2	0.21	8.81	1	7	0	92	1	15	N/A	N/A	62	8	0	0	0.0	0.0
C+ /5.6	10.9	0.99	9.65	114	0	100	0	0	159	152.3	-16.5	82	10	25,000	0	5.5	0.0
C /5.3	11.0	1.00	8.55	97	0	100	0	0	159	139.9	-16.9	75	10	1,000	50	0.0	0.0
C+ /5.7	10.9	0.99	9.74	768	0	100	0	0	159	155.5	-16.5	84	10	5,000,000	0	0.0	0.0
C+ /5.6	10.8	0.98	9.51	6	0	100	0	0	159	149.6	-16.6	82	10	1,000	50	5.5	0.0
B- /7.9	6.8	1.05	89.99	927	2	63	33	2	14	83.7	-11.5	55	11	2,500	100	0.0	0.0
C+ /6.2	10.4	0.94	119.00	4,586	0	98	0	2	10	137.3	-18.1	51	11	2,500	100	0.0	0.0

Fund Type	Fund Name	Ticker Symbol	Overall Investment Rating	Phone	Performance Rating/Pts	3 Mo	6 Mo	1Yr / Pct	3Yr / Pct	5Yr / Pct	Dividend Yield	Expense Ratio
								Total Return % through 2/28/17	Annualized		Incl. in Returns	
SC	● Mairs & Power Small Cap	MSCFX	A+	(800) 304-7404	A / 9.4	5.45	11.51	35.18 /94	9.10 /87	16.54 /98	0.31	1.06
GR	Managed Account Series Glbl SC	MGCSX	D	(800) 441-7762	C / 4.5	5.81	6.54	26.59 /78	1.95 /24	9.75 /57	2.00	1.14
GR	Managed Account Series MCV Opp	MMCVX	B-	(800) 441-7762	A / 9.4	5.35	12.99	35.35 /94	8.38 /82	12.99 /84	1.40	0.83
IN	Manning & Napier Disciplined Val I	MNDFX	B+	(800) 466-3863	A- / 9.0	6.91	9.23	25.39 /74	10.00 /93	12.05 /75	2.30	0.54
IN	Manning & Napier Disciplined Val S	MDFSX	B	(800) 466-3863	B+ / 8.9	6.80	9.04	25.02 /73	9.73 /92	--	3.09	0.79
GR	Manning & Napier Equity Series S	EXEYX	D	(800) 466-3863	C+ / 6.1	7.82	6.33	22.40 /64	5.10 /55	10.78 /64	0.00	1.09
FO	Manning & Napier International I	MNIIX	E+	(800) 466-3863	D / 1.6	4.78	-1.72	16.33 /36	0.05 /14	--	0.75	0.88
FO	Manning & Napier Overseas Srs I	EXOSX	E	(800) 466-3863	E+ / 0.6	7.52	1.73	12.78 /21	-2.79 / 5	2.94 /11	1.63	0.75
GI	Manning & Napier ProBlend Csv Tm I	MNCIX	C-	(800) 466-3863	D / 2.0	3.57	1.58	9.20 /10	2.34 /26	4.38 /17	1.80	0.70
AA	Manning & Napier ProBlend Csv Tm	MNCRX	C-	(800) 466-3863	D / 1.8	3.46	1.39	8.80 / 9	1.85 /23	3.87 /15	1.27	1.20
GI	Manning & Napier ProBlend Csv Tm	MNCCX	C-	(800) 466-3863	D / 1.6	3.32	1.04	8.14 / 8	1.31 /20	3.33 /12	0.87	1.70
GI	Manning & Napier ProBlend Csv Tm	EXDAX	C-	(800) 466-3863	D / 1.9	3.47	1.47	8.96 / 9	2.11 /25	4.16 /16	1.18	0.90
GI	Manning & Napier ProBlend Ext Tm I	MNBIX	D	(800) 466-3863	D+ / 2.7	5.78	2.59	13.39 /23	2.44 /27	6.50 /32	1.20	0.83
GI	Manning & Napier ProBlend Ext Tm R	MNBRX	D	(800) 466-3863	D+ / 2.4	5.64	2.37	12.76 /21	1.90 /23	5.97 /28	0.49	1.33
GI	Manning & Napier ProBlend Ext Tm	MNECX	D	(800) 466-3863	D / 2.1	5.47	2.09	12.18 /19	1.41 /20	5.45 /24	0.14	1.83
GI	Manning & Napier ProBlend Ext Tm S	MNBAX	C-	(800) 466-3863	D+ / 2.6	5.73	2.52	13.10 /22	2.18 /25	6.24 /30	0.43	1.08
GL	Manning & Napier ProBlend Max Tm I	MNHIX	D	(800) 466-3863	C- / 4.1	7.53	4.01	17.59 /41	3.39 /36	8.79 /49	0.42	0.84
GL	Manning & Napier ProBlend Max Tm	MNHRX	D	(800) 466-3863	C- / 3.7	7.41	3.69	16.95 /38	2.88 /31	8.24 /44	0.01	1.34
GL	Manning & Napier ProBlend Max Tm	MNHCX	D	(800) 466-3863	C- / 3.3	7.32	3.48	16.42 /36	2.38 /27	7.71 /40	0.00	1.84
GL	Manning & Napier ProBlend Max Tm	EXHAX	C-	(800) 466-3863	C- / 3.9	7.49	3.83	17.23 /39	3.14 /33	8.52 /47	0.05	1.09
GI	Manning & Napier ProBlend Mdt Tm I	MNMIX	D+	(800) 466-3863	D / 2.0	4.62	1.77	10.46 /13	1.76 /22	5.08 /22	1.26	0.82
GI	Manning & Napier ProBlend Mdt Tm	MNMRX	D+	(800) 466-3863	D / 1.7	4.45	1.45	9.85 /11	1.22 /19	4.55 /18	0.66	1.32
GI	Manning & Napier ProBlend Mdt Tm	EXBAX	C-	(800) 466-3863	D / 1.9	4.59	1.64	10.18 /12	1.48 /21	4.82 /20	0.71	1.07
GI	Manning & Napier ProBlend Mod Tm	MNMCX	D+	(800) 466-3863	D- / 1.5	4.35	1.14	9.31 /10	0.71 /17	4.03 /15	0.25	1.82
RE	Manning & Napier Real Estate I	MNRIX	C	(800) 466-3863	B+ / 8.5	8.83	-0.01	17.81 /42	11.83 /98	--	3.91	0.84
RE	Manning & Napier Real Estate S	MNREX	C+	(800) 466-3863	B+ / 8.3	8.80	-0.11	17.41 /40	11.55 /98	11.85 /73	1.75	1.09
AA	Manning & Napier Strat Inc Cons I	MSCIX	C	(800) 466-3863	D+ / 2.9	3.05	1.76	9.71 /11	4.36 /47	--	3.21	1.09
AA	Manning & Napier Strat Inc Cons S	MSCBX	C	(800) 466-3863	D+ / 2.7	2.87	1.53	9.34 /10	4.07 /44	--	2.97	1.34
GI	Manning & Napier Strat Inc Mod I	MSMAX	C+	(800) 466-3863	C / 4.4	4.01	3.66	14.34 /27	5.48 /59	--	3.42	1.25
GI	Manning & Napier Strat Inc Mod S	MSMSX	C+	(800) 466-3863	C- / 4.2	4.03	3.53	14.06 /26	5.22 /57	--	3.18	1.50
GI	Manning & Napier Target 2015 I	MTJIX	D	(800) 466-3863	D / 1.9	4.30	1.64	10.09 /12	1.62 /22	--	1.54	2.00
GI	Manning & Napier Target 2015 K	MTJKX	D	(800) 466-3863	D / 1.7	4.17	1.41	9.74 /11	1.34 /20	--	1.31	2.25
GI	Manning & Napier Target 2015 R	MTJRX	D	(800) 466-3863	D / 1.6	4.13	1.37	9.45 /10	1.11 /19	--	0.16	2.50
GI	Manning & Napier Target 2020 I	MTNIX	D	(800) 466-3863	D / 2.1	4.82	1.86	10.94 /14	1.85 /23	5.65 /26	1.53	0.90
GI	Manning & Napier Target 2020 K	MTNKX	D	(800) 466-3863	D / 1.9	4.69	1.73	10.58 /13	1.57 /21	5.39 /24	1.30	1.15
GI	Manning & Napier Target 2020 R	MTNRX	D-	(800) 466-3863	D / 1.8	4.68	1.68	10.38 /13	1.37 /20	5.13 /22	1.02	1.40
GI	Manning & Napier Target 2025 I	MTOAX	D	(800) 466-3863	D+ / 2.5	5.42	2.28	12.55 /20	2.17 /25	--	1.61	1.26
GI	Manning & Napier Target 2025 K	MTOKX	D	(800) 466-3863	D+ / 2.3	5.26	2.13	12.13 /18	1.87 /23	--	1.37	1.51
GI	Manning & Napier Target 2025 R	MTORX	D	(800) 466-3863	D / 2.1	5.27	1.97	11.90 /18	1.63 /22	--	1.02	1.76
GI	Manning & Napier Target 2030 I	MTPIX	D-	(800) 466-3863	D+ / 2.9	6.12	2.85	14.20 /26	2.54 /28	7.40 /37	1.55	0.91
GI	Manning & Napier Target 2030 K	MTPKX	D-	(800) 466-3863	D+ / 2.7	6.03	2.74	13.79 /25	2.26 /26	7.11 /35	1.33	1.16
GI	Manning & Napier Target 2030 R	MTPRX	D-	(800) 466-3863	D+ / 2.6	6.01	2.56	13.56 /24	2.01 /24	6.84 /34	1.05	1.41
GI	Manning & Napier Target 2035 I	MTQIX	D	(800) 466-3863	C- / 3.3	6.56	3.23	15.20 /31	2.80 /30	--	1.38	1.40
GI	Manning & Napier Target 2035 K	MTQKX	D	(800) 466-3863	C- / 3.1	6.44	3.10	14.88 /29	2.53 /28	--	1.16	1.65
GI	Manning & Napier Target 2035 R	MTQRX	D	(800) 466-3863	D+ / 2.8	6.34	2.83	14.51 /28	2.24 /26	--	0.73	1.90
GI	Manning & Napier Target 2040 I	MTTIX	E+	(800) 466-3863	C- / 3.6	6.96	3.50	16.33 /36	3.01 /32	8.26 /44	1.26	0.96
GI	Manning & Napier Target 2040 K	MTTKX	E+	(800) 466-3863	C- / 3.4	6.88	3.39	15.91 /34	2.72 /29	7.98 /42	1.04	1.21
GI	Manning & Napier Target 2040 R	MTTRX	E+	(800) 466-3863	C- / 3.2	6.78	3.26	15.59 /32	2.47 /27	7.70 /40	0.81	1.46
GI	Manning & Napier Target 2045 I	MTUIX	D	(800) 466-3863	C- / 3.9	7.34	3.84	17.17 /39	3.27 /34	--	1.09	2.09
GI	Manning & Napier Target 2045 K	MTUKX	D	(800) 466-3863	C- / 3.7	7.31	3.71	16.94 /38	3.01 /32	--	0.89	2.34
GI	Manning & Napier Target 2045 R	MTURX	D	(800) 466-3863	C- / 3.6	7.33	3.61	16.72 /37	2.77 /30	--	0.56	2.59
GI	Manning & Napier Target 2050 I	MTYIX	E+	(800) 466-3863	C- / 4.0	7.49	3.93	17.49 /41	3.35 /35	8.74 /48	1.11	1.14

● Denotes fund is closed to new investors
* Denotes fund is included in Section II

www.thestreetratings.com

RISK	3 Year		NET ASSETS		ASSET				Portfolio	BULL / BEAR		FUND MANAGER		MINIMUMS		LOADS	
Risk Rating/Pts	Standard Deviation	Beta	NAV As of 2/28/17	Total $(Mil)	Cash %	Stocks %	Bonds %	Other %	Portfolio Turnover Ratio	Last Bull Market Return	Last Bear Market Return	Manager Quality Pct	Manager Tenure (Years)	Initial Purch. $	Additional Purch. $	Front End Load	Back End Load
C+ / 6.2	13.7	0.83	24.94	420	2	97	0	1	23	189.3	N/A	91	6	2,500	100	0.0	1.0
C- / 3.3	13.2	1.09	13.79	115	0	99	0	1	86	91.8	-23.2	3	12	0	0	0.0	0.0
C- / 3.4	12.9	1.07	14.63	111	0	99	0	1	91	132.6	-21.4	37	8	0	0	0.0	0.0
C / 5.2	9.7	0.90	15.62	149	0	97	1	2	39	104.8	-10.6	77	9	1,000,000	0	0.0	0.0
C- / 4.2	9.7	0.89	10.71	26	0	97	1	2	39	N/A	N/A	76	9	2,000	0	0.0	0.0
D / 1.7	12.4	1.08	12.51	85	0	96	3	1	40	99.8	-19.9	9	15	2,000	0	0.0	0.0
C- / 4.2	12.3	0.87	10.18	67	6	93	0	1	33	N/A	N/A	75	2	1,000,000	0	0.0	0.0
C- / 4.0	12.4	0.91	21.54	893	1	96	2	1	37	37.5	-27.0	39	15	1,000,000	0	0.0	0.0
B / 8.1	4.5	0.37	10.43	288	0	0	0	100	51	32.6	-4.0	56	22	1,000,000	0	0.0	0.0
B / 8.1	4.5	0.65	10.03	16	0	0	0	100	51	29.1	-4.2	35	22	2,000	0	0.0	0.0
B / 8.1	4.5	0.37	10.02	120	0	0	0	100	51	25.7	-4.5	40	22	2,000	0	0.0	0.0
B / 8.5	4.5	0.37	13.53	681	0	0	0	100	51	31.2	-4.1	52	22	2,000	0	0.0	0.0
C / 5.4	7.6	0.63	9.63	377	0	0	0	100	66	55.9	-13.2	24	22	1,000,000	0	0.0	0.0
C+ / 5.9	7.7	0.63	11.04	22	0	0	0	100	66	51.7	-13.2	19	22	2,000	0	0.0	0.0
C+ / 5.7	7.6	0.62	10.34	139	0	0	0	100	66	47.7	-13.4	15	22	2,000	0	0.0	0.0
C+ / 6.8	7.7	0.63	16.98	449	0	0	0	100	66	53.8	-13.2	21	22	2,000	0	0.0	0.0
C- / 4.0	10.7	0.79	10.39	296	0	0	0	100	59	79.9	-20.0	92	22	1,000,000	0	0.0	0.0
C / 4.7	10.6	0.79	12.80	21	0	0	0	100	59	75.2	-20.2	90	22	2,000	0	0.0	0.0
C- / 4.2	10.7	0.79	10.89	54	0	0	0	100	59	70.6	-20.4	88	22	2,000	0	0.0	0.0
C+ / 5.7	10.7	0.79	19.41	335	0	0	0	100	59	77.6	-20.2	91	22	2,000	0	0.0	0.0
C+ / 6.9	6.0	0.48	10.16	295	0	0	0	100	56	42.8	-9.9	33	24	1,000,000	0	0.0	0.0
B- / 7.1	6.0	0.48	10.67	27	0	0	0	100	56	38.9	-10.1	27	24	2,000	0	0.0	0.0
B- / 7.5	6.0	0.48	13.42	470	0	0	0	100	56	40.9	-10.0	29	24	2,000	0	0.0	0.0
B- / 7.0	6.0	0.48	10.28	124	0	0	0	100	56	35.2	-10.3	22	24	2,000	0	0.0	0.0
D / 2.2	13.5	0.98	7.34	30	2	97	0	1	57	N/A	N/A	80	8	1,000,000	0	0.0	0.0
C- / 4.2	13.5	0.98	15.11	288	2	97	0	1	57	116.6	-17.2	78	8	2,000	0	0.0	0.0
B / 8.3	4.0	0.59	10.27	8	3	30	66	1	90	N/A	N/A	73	5	1,000,000	0	0.0	0.0
B / 8.3	4.0	0.59	10.26	16	3	30	66	1	90	N/A	N/A	70	5	2,000	0	0.0	0.0
B- / 7.5	5.7	0.51	10.90	8	2	54	43	1	74	N/A	N/A	74	5	1,000,000	0	0.0	0.0
B- / 7.5	5.7	0.51	10.90	21	2	54	43	1	74	N/A	N/A	72	5	2,000	0	0.0	0.0
C+ / 6.4	5.9	0.48	10.64	3	4	40	54	2	49	N/A	N/A	31	5	1,000,000	0	0.0	0.0
C+ / 6.4	5.9	0.48	10.60	4	4	40	54	2	49	N/A	N/A	28	5	2,000	0	0.0	0.0
C+ / 6.5	5.8	0.47	10.73	N/A	4	40	54	2	49	N/A	N/A	26	5	2,000	0	0.0	0.0
C / 5.4	6.4	0.52	8.91	47	4	44	50	2	16	48.4	-12.0	29	9	1,000,000	0	0.0	0.0
C / 5.4	6.4	0.51	8.87	82	4	44	50	2	16	46.5	-12.1	27	9	2,000	0	0.0	0.0
C / 5.4	6.4	0.52	8.77	4	4	44	50	2	16	44.6	-12.2	24	9	2,000	0	0.0	0.0
C+ / 5.6	7.5	0.62	11.19	16	5	55	39	1	51	N/A	N/A	22	5	1,000,000	0	0.0	0.0
C+ / 5.6	7.5	0.62	11.22	14	5	55	39	1	51	N/A	N/A	19	5	2,000	0	0.0	0.0
C+ / 5.7	7.6	0.63	11.27	1	5	55	39	1	51	N/A	N/A	17	5	2,000	0	0.0	0.0
C- / 3.7	8.3	0.70	8.91	53	5	64	30	1	22	63.1	-14.7	18	9	1,000,000	0	0.0	0.0
C- / 3.7	8.3	0.70	8.82	81	5	64	30	1	22	60.8	-14.8	16	9	2,000	0	0.0	0.0
C- / 3.7	8.3	0.70	8.75	7	5	64	30	1	22	58.5	-14.8	14	9	2,000	0	0.0	0.0
C / 4.8	9.1	0.78	11.65	12	4	72	22	2	22	N/A	N/A	14	5	1,000,000	0	0.0	0.0
C / 4.8	9.1	0.78	11.61	13	4	72	22	2	22	N/A	N/A	13	5	2,000	0	0.0	0.0
C / 4.8	9.1	0.78	11.66	1	4	72	22	2	22	N/A	N/A	11	5	2,000	0	0.0	0.0
D+ / 2.5	9.8	0.85	9.16	29	4	81	13	2	26	75.6	-20.2	11	9	1,000,000	0	0.0	0.0
D+ / 2.5	9.9	0.85	9.08	60	4	81	13	2	26	72.9	-20.2	9	9	2,000	0	0.0	0.0
D+ / 2.5	9.9	0.85	9.02	5	4	81	13	2	26	70.7	-20.3	8	9	2,000	0	0.0	0.0
C- / 4.0	10.6	0.92	12.10	6	4	90	5	1	26	N/A	N/A	8	5	1,000,000	0	0.0	0.0
C- / 4.0	10.7	0.93	12.08	7	4	90	5	1	26	N/A	N/A	7	5	2,000	0	0.0	0.0
C- / 4.0	10.7	0.93	12.03	1	4	90	5	1	26	N/A	N/A	6	5	2,000	0	0.0	0.0
D / 2.0	10.7	0.93	9.94	15	4	90	5	1	31	79.4	-20.1	8	9	1,000,000	0	0.0	0.0

						PERFORMANCE					Incl. in Returns	
	99 Pct = Best 0 Pct = Worst				Perfor- mance Rating/Pts	Total Return % through 2/28/17			Annualized		Dividend Yield	Expense Ratio
Fund Type	Fund Name	Ticker Symbol	Overall Investment Rating	Phone		3 Mo	6 Mo	1Yr / Pct	3Yr / Pct	5Yr / Pct		
GI	Manning & Napier Target 2050 K	MTYKX	E+	(800) 466-3863	C- / 3.8	7.41	3.82	17.21 /39	3.08 /33	8.48 /46	0.88	1.39
GI	Manning & Napier Target 2050 R	MTYRX	E+	(800) 466-3863	C- / 3.6	7.46	3.72	17.04 /38	2.84 /30	8.19 /44	0.70	1.64
GI	Manning & Napier Target 2055 I	MTZIX	D	(800) 466-3863	C- / 4.0	7.45	3.96	17.53 /41	3.21 /34	—	1.04	4.56
GI	Manning & Napier Target 2055 K	MTZKX	D	(800) 466-3863	C- / 3.7	7.39	3.79	17.24 /39	2.96 /31	—	0.86	4.81
GI	Manning & Napier Target 2055 R	MTZRX	D	(800) 466-3863	C- / 3.6	7.46	3.73	16.99 /38	2.74 /30	—	0.62	5.06
AA	Manning & Napier Target Income I	MTDIX	D+	(800) 466-3863	D / 2.0	3.63	1.56	9.16 /10	2.30 /26	4.33 /17	1.76	0.89
AA	Manning & Napier Target Income K	MTDKX	D+	(800) 466-3863	D / 1.8	3.50	1.42	8.80 / 9	2.02 /24	4.06 /16	1.52	1.14
AA	Manning & Napier Target Income R	MTDRX	D+	(800) 466-3863	D / 1.7	3.49	1.39	8.69 / 9	1.78 /23	3.82 /14	1.24	1.39
FO	Manning & Napier World Oppty A	EXWAX	E	(800) 466-3863	E / 0.4	7.36	1.66	11.82 /17	-3.57 / 4	2.25 / 9	1.56	1.09
MC	Manning and Napier Dynamic Opp I	MDOIX	D	(800) 466-3863	D+ / 2.3	3.16	1.37	16.64 /37	1.71 /22	—	0.00	0.88
MC	Manning and Napier Dynamic Opp S	MDOSX	D	(800) 466-3863	D / 2.2	3.18	1.27	16.48 /36	1.51 /21	—	0.00	1.08
EM	Manning and Napier Emerging Mkts I	MNIEX	D-	(800) 466-3863	E / 0.5	5.37	0.26	16.69 /37	-3.26 / 4	—	0.15	1.01
EM	Manning and Napier Emerging Mkts	MNEMX	E	(800) 466-3863	E / 0.5	5.27	0.15	16.48 /36	-3.47 / 4	-0.08 / 4	0.15	1.27
IN	Manning and Napier Equity Income I	MNEIX	B+	(800) 466-3863	B / 7.7	5.10	7.74	23.29 /67	8.37 /82	—	2.26	1.11
IN	Manning and Napier Equity Income S	MNESX	B+	(800) 466-3863	B- / 7.5	5.10	7.55	22.96 /66	8.15 /80	—	2.08	1.32
GR	Manor Fund	MNRMX	C+	(800) 787-3334	C+ / 6.8	7.18	10.20	19.64 /50	6.42 /68	10.73 /64	0.50	1.50
GR	Manor Growth Fund	MNRGX	C+	(800) 787-3334	C+ / 6.3	6.01	7.93	16.77 /37	6.73 /70	11.17 /67	0.06	1.50
GR	Mar Vista Strategic Growth	MVSGX	A	(800) 227-6681	B / 7.9	8.75	6.42	17.92 /42	9.78 /92	12.93 /83	0.64	1.75
GR	Marathon Value Portfolio	MVPFX	A-	(800) 788-6086	B / 7.9	8.01	8.58	24.16 /70	7.88 /78	10.90 /65	0.47	1.10
GR	Marketfield A	MFADX	D-	(800) 624-6782	E- / 0.1	2.03	2.31	4.13 / 3	-7.78 / 1	—	0.00	2.62
GR	Marketfield C	MFCDX	D-	(800) 624-6782	E- / 0.1	1.80	1.95	3.37 / 3	-8.49 / 1	—	0.00	3.37
IN	Marketfield I	MFLDX	D-	(800) 624-6782	E- / 0.1	2.07	2.43	4.38 / 3	-7.57 / 1	0.46 / 5	0.00	2.34
GR	Marketfield R6	MFRIX	D-	(800) 624-6782	E- / 0.1	2.13	2.56	4.58 / 4	-7.42 / 1	—	0.00	2.33
GR	MarketGrader 100 Enhanced Idx I	KHMIX	U	(844) 524-9366	U /	7.15	6.47	16.15 /35	—	—	0.00	1.66
SC	Marketocracy Masters 100	MOFQX	E	(888) 884-8482	E / 0.3	5.87	1.35	14.61 /28	-5.41 / 2	-0.08 / 4	0.00	2.04
MC	Marsico 21ST Century Fund	MXXIX	C-	(888) 860-8686	C / 5.0	9.06	5.93	19.49 /49	3.75 /40	10.79 /64	0.00	1.33
GI	Marsico Flexible Capital Fd	MFCFX	D	(888) 860-8686	C- / 3.3	7.90	3.37	13.40 /23	2.96 /31	10.34 /61	1.54	1.27
GR	Marsico Focus Fund	MFOCX	E+	(888) 860-8686	C- / 3.4	8.26	4.16	10.88 /14	3.47 /37	9.86 /57	0.00	1.19
GL	Marsico Global Fd	MGLBX	E+	(888) 860-8686	D / 2.0	5.81	1.35	10.68 /13	1.58 /21	9.73 /56	0.00	1.60
GR	Marsico Growth Fd	MGRIX	E	(888) 860-8686	C- / 3.7	8.97	4.74	14.26 /27	3.05 /32	9.12 /52	0.00	1.27
FO	Marsico International Oppty	MIOFX	E+	(888) 860-8686	D- / 1.0	8.00	0.99	9.71 /11	-0.63 /11	3.73 /14	0.00	1.60
BA	MassMutual Premier Balanced A	MMBDX	C-	(800) 542-6767	C- / 4.2	5.37	6.23	16.83 /38	5.70 /62	7.86 /41	1.33	1.22
BA	MassMutual Premier Balanced Adm	MMBLX	C	(800) 542-6767	C+ / 5.6	5.42	6.35	17.10 /39	5.96 /64	8.12 /43	1.64	0.97
BA	MassMutual Premier Balanced I	MBBIX	B-	(800) 542-6767	C+ / 6.3	5.50	6.43	17.45 /40	7.09 /73	8.95 /50	1.87	0.67
BA	MassMutual Premier Balanced R5	MBLDX	C+	(800) 542-6767	C+ / 5.7	5.48	6.41	17.31 /40	6.15 /66	8.39 /45	1.76	0.77
BA	MassMutual Premier Balanced Svc	MBAYX	C+	(800) 542-6767	C+ / 5.6	5.41	6.30	17.11 /39	6.04 /65	8.24 /44	1.53	0.87
GR	MassMutual Premier Dsp Growth A	MPGAX	C+	(800) 542-6767	B- / 7.2	8.38	9.60	20.83 /57	8.90 /86	12.99 /84	0.80	1.05
GR	MassMutual Premier Dsp Growth	MPGLX	B	(800) 542-6767	B+ / 8.4	8.46	9.74	21.15 /58	9.19 /88	13.28 /87	1.06	0.80
GR	MassMutual Premier Dsp Growth I	MPDIX	A+	(800) 542-6767	B+ / 8.8	8.44	9.93	21.38 /59	9.88 /93	13.82 /92	1.36	0.50
GR	MassMutual Premier Dsp Growth R5	MPGSX	B	(800) 542-6767	B+ / 8.6	8.50	9.89	21.33 /59	9.43 /90	13.54 /89	1.26	0.60
GR	MassMutual Premier Dsp Growth Svc	DEIGX	B	(800) 542-6767	B+ / 8.5	8.43	9.82	21.22 /58	9.27 /89	13.40 /88	1.14	0.70
GR	MassMutual Premier Dsp Value A	MEPAX	A-	(800) 542-6767	B / 8.0	7.10	12.79	27.92 /81	8.59 /84	12.98 /84	2.44	1.08
GR	MassMutual Premier Dsp Value Adm	MPILX	A+	(800) 542-6767	A- / 9.1	7.20	12.95	28.32 /82	8.90 /86	13.27 /87	2.66	0.83
GR	MassMutual Premier Dsp Value I	MPIVX	A+	(800) 542-6767	A / 9.4	7.23	13.05	28.60 /83	9.39 /89	13.69 /91	3.00	0.53
GR	MassMutual Premier Dsp Value R3	MPINX	A+	(800) 542-6767	B+ / 8.9	7.05	12.70	27.79 /81	8.46 /83	12.75 /81	2.17	1.23
GR	MassMutual Premier Dsp Value R5	MEPSX	A+	(800) 542-6767	A / 9.3	7.20	13.07	28.53 /83	9.11 /88	13.52 /89	2.91	0.63
GR	MassMutual Premier Dsp Value Svc	DENVX	A+	(800) 542-6767	A- / 9.2	7.21	12.99	28.38 /83	8.99 /87	13.39 /88	2.78	0.73
GL	MassMutual Premier Global A	MGFAX	D+	(800) 542-6767	C / 4.3	8.51	9.00	22.16 /63	3.52 /37	9.19 /52	0.65	1.39
GL	MassMutual Premier Global Adm	MGFLX	C	(800) 542-6767	C+ / 5.7	8.61	9.18	22.51 /65	3.77 /40	9.48 /55	0.98	1.14
GL	MassMutual Premier Global I	MGFZX	C+	(800) 542-6767	C+ / 6.2	8.64	9.21	22.83 /66	4.43 /48	10.00 /58	1.29	0.84
GL	MassMutual Premier Global R3	MGFNX	C-	(800) 542-6767	C / 5.4	8.46	8.87	22.04 /62	3.37 /35	9.05 /51	0.70	1.54
GL	MassMutual Premier Global R5	MGFSX	C	(800) 542-6767	C+ / 5.9	8.59	9.24	22.77 /66	3.99 /43	9.73 /56	1.18	0.94

RISK	3 Year		NET ASSETS		ASSET					BULL / BEAR		FUND MANAGER		MINIMUMS		LOADS	
Risk Rating/Pts	Standard Deviation	Beta	NAV As of 2/28/17	Total $(Mil)	Cash %	Stocks %	Bonds %	Other %	Portfolio Turnover Ratio	Last Bull Market Return	Last Bear Market Return	Manager Quality Pct	Manager Tenure (Years)	Initial Purch. $	Additional Purch. $	Front End Load	Back End Load
D / 2.0	10.7	0.93	9.87	16	4	90	5	1	31	76.9	-20.2	7	9	2,000	0	0.0	0.0
D / 1.9	10.7	0.93	9.77	3	4	90	5	1	31	74.7	-20.3	6	9	2,000	0	0.0	0.0
C- / 4.2	10.7	0.93	12.25	3	4	90	5	1	30	N/A	N/A	8	5	1,000,000	0	0.0	0.0
C- / 4.2	10.7	0.94	12.14	3	4	90	5	1	30	N/A	N/A	7	5	2,000	0	0.0	0.0
C- / 4.2	10.7	0.93	12.04	1	4	90	5	1	30	N/A	N/A	6	5	2,000	0	0.0	0.0
C+ / 6.8	4.5	0.64	9.52	12	1	34	63	2	6	32.3	-4.0	42	9	1,000,000	0	0.0	0.0
C+ / 6.8	4.5	0.65	9.48	65	1	34	63	2	6	30.4	-4.2	38	9	2,000	0	0.0	0.0
C+ / 6.8	4.5	0.65	9.39	1	1	34	63	2	6	28.7	-4.3	35	9	2,000	0	0.0	0.0
C- / 3.9	12.5	0.92	7.15	811	1	96	1	2	71	32.4	-27.1	29	21	2,000	0	0.0	0.0
C / 5.1	13.6	0.86	9.78	1	2	97	0	1	85	N/A	N/A	8	4	1,000,000	0	0.0	0.0
C / 5.1	13.6	0.86	9.72	173	2	97	0	1	85	N/A	N/A	7	4	2,000	0	0.0	0.0
C+ / 5.8	15.2	0.86	9.03	5	5	94	0	1	61	N/A	N/A	17	N/A	2,000,000	0	0.0	0.0
C- / 3.5	15.2	0.86	8.99	108	5	94	0	1	61	N/A	N/A	15	N/A	2,000	0	0.0	0.0
C+ / 6.7	10.4	0.97	11.33	54	0	98	1	1	58	N/A	N/A	52	4	1,000,000	0	0.0	0.0
C+ / 6.7	10.4	0.97	11.32	26	0	98	1	1	58	N/A	N/A	50	4	2,000	0	0.0	0.0
C / 5.5	12.6	1.11	23.26	7	0	97	2	1	16	97.9	-15.4	16	22	1,000	25	0.0	0.0
C+ / 6.4	11.1	1.00	21.38	10	2	94	2	2	19	103.8	-15.7	27	18	1,000	25	0.0	0.0
B- / 7.6	9.8	0.90	16.69	29	0	0	0	100	40	N/A	N/A	75	6	25,000	0	0.0	0.8
B- / 7.1	10.0	0.93	26.27	69	1	94	4	1	6	99.7	-14.3	51	17	2,500	100	0.0	0.0
C+ / 6.7	6.6	0.32	14.61	96	48	51	0	1	93	N/A	N/A	1	10	25,000	0	5.5	0.0
C+ / 6.6	6.6	0.33	14.13	113	48	51	0	1	93	N/A	N/A	1	10	2,500	50	0.0	0.0
C+ / 6.8	6.6	0.32	14.76	350	48	51	0	1	93	13.3	-7.0	1	10	5,000,000	0	0.0	0.0
C+ / 6.8	6.6	0.32	14.84	3	48	51	0	1	93	N/A	N/A	2	10	250,000	0	0.0	0.0
U /	N/A	N/A	11.50	55	0	0	0	100	0	N/A	N/A	N/A	2	10,000	1,000	0.0	2.0
C- / 4.0	16.4	0.94	9.02	4	12	69	17	2	219	17.7	-21.0	1	16	10,000	50	0.0	0.0
C / 4.8	12.5	0.80	23.24	224	1	98	0	1	44	104.6	-25.5	27	6	2,500	100	0.0	0.0
C / 4.4	10.3	0.86	14.60	273	1	86	11	2	35	98.8	-18.0	10	5	2,500	100	0.0	0.0
D / 2.2	12.4	0.98	16.51	535	6	93	0	1	45	95.8	-17.7	7	20	2,500	100	0.0	0.0
C- / 3.7	12.4	0.83	12.02	35	6	93	0	1	82	91.9	-24.3	85	10	2,500	100	0.0	0.0
D- / 1.1	12.1	1.00	16.08	256	0	100	0	0	52	89.9	-17.4	5	20	2,500	100	0.0	0.0
C / 4.8	14.2	0.95	15.25	54	0	100	0	0	223	44.7	-25.2	69	7	2,500	100	0.0	0.0
C+ / 5.8	7.2	1.14	11.49	36	0	65	34	1	176	66.4	-10.4	38	17	0	0	5.8	0.0
C+ / 5.8	7.2	1.14	11.79	13	0	65	34	1	176	68.6	-10.3	41	17	0	0	0.0	0.0
B- / 7.9	7.3	1.14	11.74	2	0	65	34	1	176	75.5	-10.1	57	17	0	0	0.0	0.0
C+ / 5.7	7.2	1.14	11.75	52	0	65	34	1	176	70.9	-10.1	45	17	0	0	0.0	0.0
C+ / 5.9	7.2	1.14	12.30	10	0	65	34	1	176	69.7	-10.2	43	17	0	0	0.0	0.0
C / 5.0	11.1	1.05	11.65	39	1	98	0	1	124	128.0	-16.0	47	17	0	0	5.8	0.0
C / 5.0	11.1	1.05	11.93	39	1	98	0	1	124	131.2	-15.8	51	17	0	0	0.0	0.0
C+ / 6.8	11.1	1.05	11.77	112	1	98	0	1	124	136.8	-15.8	60	17	0	0	0.0	0.0
C / 5.0	11.1	1.05	11.79	89	1	98	0	1	124	133.9	-15.8	55	17	0	0	0.0	0.0
C / 5.0	11.1	1.05	11.82	72	1	98	0	1	124	132.4	-15.8	53	17	0	0	0.0	0.0
C+ / 6.7	10.6	0.99	16.79	11	0	99	0	1	109	122.8	-18.5	53	17	0	0	5.8	0.0
C+ / 6.7	10.6	0.99	17.23	6	0	99	0	1	109	126.1	-18.4	56	17	0	0	0.0	0.0
B- / 7.1	10.6	0.99	17.01	78	0	99	0	1	109	130.4	-18.3	62	17	0	0	0.0	0.0
C+ / 6.7	10.6	0.98	16.97	2	0	99	0	1	109	120.3	-18.6	51	17	0	0	0.0	0.0
C+ / 6.6	10.6	0.98	17.04	60	0	99	0	1	109	128.7	-18.3	60	17	0	0	0.0	0.0
C+ / 6.6	10.6	0.98	16.93	53	0	99	0	1	109	127.3	-18.3	58	17	0	0	0.0	0.0
C / 4.8	13.0	0.97	13.85	30	0	98	0	2	25	82.3	-23.3	92	13	0	0	5.8	0.0
C / 4.7	13.0	0.97	13.98	96	0	98	0	2	25	85.0	-23.1	93	13	0	0	0.0	0.0
C+ / 6.4	13.0	0.97	13.97	30	0	98	0	2	25	89.5	-23.1	94	13	0	0	0.0	0.0
C / 4.7	13.0	0.97	13.81	9	0	98	0	2	25	81.2	-23.3	92	13	0	0	0.0	0.0
C / 4.7	12.9	0.96	13.98	113	0	98	0	2	25	87.2	-23.1	94	13	0	0	0.0	0.0

Fund Type	Fund Name	Ticker Symbol	Overall Investment Rating	Phone	Performance Rating/Pts	3 Mo	6 Mo	1Yr / Pct	3Yr / Pct	5Yr / Pct	Dividend Yield	Expense Ratio
	99 Pct = Best 0 Pct = Worst						Total Return % through 2/28/17 (Annualized)				Incl. in Returns	
GL	MassMutual Premier Global Svc	MGFYX	C	(800) 542-6767	C+ / 5.9	8.67	9.24	22.69 /65	3.91 /42	9.59 /55	1.05	1.04
FO	MassMutual Premier Intl Equity A	MMIAX	E	(800) 542-6767	E / 0.3	6.18	-1.44	6.58 / 5	-1.93 / 7	5.23 /23	0.69	1.51
FO	MassMutual Premier Intl Equity Adm	MIELX	E	(800) 542-6767	E+ / 0.6	6.32	-1.27	6.90 / 6	-1.68 / 7	5.51 /25	1.00	1.26
FO	MassMutual Premier Intl Equity I	MIZIX	D-	(800) 542-6767	E+ / 0.7	6.41	-1.12	7.19 / 6	-1.23 / 9	5.88 /28	1.30	0.96
FO	MassMutual Premier Intl Equity R5	MIEDX	E	(800) 542-6767	E+ / 0.6	6.29	-1.23	7.07 / 6	-1.50 / 8	5.70 /26	1.18	1.06
FO	MassMutual Premier Intl Equity Svc	MYIEX	E	(800) 542-6767	E+ / 0.6	6.30	-1.24	6.89 / 6	-1.59 / 8	5.63 /26	1.10	1.16
GR	MassMutual Premier Main Street A	MSSAX	C-	(800) 542-6767	B / 7.7	7.88	9.55	23.59 /68	9.39 /89	12.97 /83	0.80	1.21
GR	MassMutual Premier Main Street	MMSLX	C	(800) 542-6767	B+ / 8.9	7.90	9.66	23.91 /70	9.65 /91	13.26 /86	1.04	0.96
GR	MassMutual Premier Main Street I	MSZIX	A+	(800) 542-6767	A- / 9.2	8.02	9.88	24.27 /71	10.28 /95	13.74 /91	1.33	0.66
GR	MassMutual Premier Main Street R3	MMSNX	C-	(800) 542-6767	B+ / 8.6	7.91	9.48	23.45 /68	9.23 /88	12.73 /81	0.99	1.36
GR	MassMutual Premier Main Street R5	MMSSX	C	(800) 542-6767	A- / 9.0	8.02	9.77	24.15 /70	9.88 /93	13.49 /89	1.24	0.76
GR	MassMutual Premier Main Street Svc	MMSYX	C	(800) 542-6767	A- / 9.0	7.98	9.79	24.12 /70	9.78 /92	13.41 /88	0.96	0.86
SC	MassMutual Premier Sm Cap Opp A	DLBMX	C	(800) 542-6767	B / 7.7	6.75	12.93	30.89 /88	7.30 /74	13.48 /89	0.65	1.24
SC	MassMutual Premier Sm Cap Opp	MSCLX	C+	(800) 542-6767	B+ / 8.9	6.82	13.04	31.29 /89	7.59 /76	13.75 /91	0.92	0.99
SC	MassMutual Premier Sm Cap Opp I	MSOOX	A	(800) 542-6767	A- / 9.2	6.87	13.20	31.62 /89	8.39 /82	14.37 /95	1.14	0.69
SC	MassMutual Premier Sm Cap Opp R5	MSCDX	C+	(800) 542-6767	A- / 9.0	6.86	13.11	31.44 /89	7.78 /77	13.98 /93	1.06	0.79
SC	MassMutual Premier Sm Cap Opp	MSVYX	C+	(800) 542-6767	B+ / 8.9	6.79	13.06	31.31 /89	7.67 /77	13.86 /92	0.99	0.89
EM	MassMutual Premier Str Em Mkts A	MPASX	E	(800) 542-6767	E+ / 0.8	6.31	3.27	21.74 /61	-1.49 / 8	-3.01 / 2	0.18	1.92
EM	MassMutual Premier Str Em Mkts	MPLSX	E+	(800) 542-6767	D- / 1.3	6.47	3.54	22.03 /62	-1.26 / 9	-2.76 / 2	0.97	1.67
EM	MassMutual Premier Str Em Mkts I	MPZSX	E+	(800) 542-6767	D- / 1.5	6.48	3.64	22.37 /64	-0.93 /10	-2.43 / 2	1.14	1.37
EM	MassMutual Premier Str Em Mkts R5	MPSMX	E+	(800) 542-6767	D- / 1.4	6.45	3.56	22.25 /63	-1.07 / 9	-2.56 / 2	1.01	1.47
EM	MassMutual Premier Str Em Mkts Svc	MPEYX	E+	(800) 542-6767	D- / 1.4	6.46	3.52	22.13 /63	-1.16 / 9	-2.65 / 2	0.94	1.57
GR	MassMutual Premier Value A	MCEAX	B+	(800) 542-6767	B- / 7.5	6.86	12.36	28.25 /82	7.73 /77	11.48 /70	1.07	1.28
GR	MassMutual Premier Value Adm	DLBVX	A-	(800) 542-6767	B+ / 8.7	6.89	12.49	28.58 /83	7.99 /79	11.77 /72	1.38	1.03
GR	MassMutual Premier Value I	MCZIX	A	(800) 542-6767	A- / 9.0	6.97	12.63	28.92 /84	8.54 /83	12.19 /76	1.65	0.73
GR	MassMutual Premier Value R3	MCENX	A-	(800) 542-6767	B+ / 8.4	6.80	12.23	28.01 /82	7.55 /76	11.23 /68	1.05	1.43
GR	MassMutual Premier Value R5	MVEDX	A-	(800) 542-6767	B+ / 8.9	6.96	12.58	28.80 /84	8.21 /81	11.99 /74	1.56	0.83
GR	MassMutual Premier Value Svc	MCEYX	A-	(800) 542-6767	B+ / 8.8	6.94	12.54	28.69 /83	8.10 /80	11.89 /73	1.47	0.93
AA	MassMutual RetireSMART 2010 A	MRXAX	C-	(800) 542-6767	D / 1.6	3.59	2.35	10.78 /14	2.43 /27	4.60 /19	2.38	1.42
AA	MassMutual RetireSMART 2010 Adm	MRXYX	C	(800) 542-6767	D+ / 2.4	3.59	2.53	11.12 /15	2.69 /29	4.88 /21	2.79	1.17
AA	MassMutual RetireSMART 2010 R3	MRXNX	C	(800) 542-6767	D / 2.1	3.46	2.29	10.57 /13	2.28 /26	4.37 /17	2.48	1.57
AA	MassMutual RetireSMART 2010 Svc	MRXSX	C	(800) 542-6767	D+ / 2.4	3.57	2.52	11.17 /15	2.80 /30	5.01 /21	2.86	1.07
GL	MassMutual RetireSMART 2015 A	MMJAX	C-	(800) 542-6767	D / 1.7	3.85	2.84	11.85 /17	2.60 /28	5.40 /24	1.61	1.37
GL	MassMutual RetireSMART 2015 Adm	MMJYX	C	(800) 542-6767	D+ / 2.6	3.88	2.97	12.13 /18	2.84 /30	5.69 /26	1.92	1.12
GL	MassMutual RetireSMART 2015 R3	MMJNX	U	(800) 542-6767	U /	3.74	2.73	11.68 /17	--	--	1.50	1.52
GL	MassMutual RetireSMART 2015 Svc	MMJSX	C	(800) 542-6767	D+ / 2.7	3.91	3.00	12.23 /19	2.95 /31	5.78 /27	1.95	1.02
AA	MassMutual RetireSMART 2020 A	MRTAX	C-	(800) 542-6767	D / 2.1	4.57	3.96	14.36 /27	2.85 /30	6.24 /30	1.57	1.21
AA	MassMutual RetireSMART 2020	MRTYX	C	(800) 542-6767	C- / 3.2	4.74	4.13	14.68 /28	3.13 /33	6.56 /32	1.92	0.96
AA	MassMutual RetireSMART 2020 R3	MRTNX	C	(800) 542-6767	C- / 3.0	4.61	3.97	14.25 /27	2.72 /29	6.02 /28	1.63	1.36
AA	MassMutual RetireSMART 2020 R4	MRTHX	U	(800) 542-6767	U /	4.64	4.01	14.45 /28	--	--	1.86	1.11
AA	MassMutual RetireSMART 2020 Svc	MRTSX	C	(800) 542-6767	C- / 3.3	4.74	4.22	14.76 /29	3.22 /34	6.65 /32	2.01	0.86
GL	MassMutual RetireSMART 2025 A	MMSDX	C-	(800) 542-6767	D+ / 2.7	5.35	5.17	16.78 /38	3.15 /33	6.92 /34	1.49	1.30
GL	MassMutual RetireSMART 2025	MMIYX	C	(800) 542-6767	C- / 3.9	5.39	5.30	17.03 /38	3.38 /36	7.23 /36	1.81	1.05
GL	MassMutual RetireSMART 2025 R3	MMNRX	U	(800) 542-6767	U /	5.27	5.10	16.55 /37	--	--	1.50	1.45
GI	MassMutual RetireSMART 2025 R4	MMNZX	U	(800) 542-6767	U /	5.38	5.20	16.96 /38	--	--	1.69	1.20
GL	MassMutual RetireSMART 2025	MMISX	C	(800) 542-6767	C- / 4.0	5.41	5.32	17.13 /39	3.49 /37	7.31 /37	1.84	0.95
AA	MassMutual RetireSMART 2030 A	MRYAX	C-	(800) 542-6767	C- / 3.0	5.77	5.68	18.13 /43	3.21 /34	7.23 /36	1.47	1.25
AA	MassMutual RetireSMART 2030 Adm	MRYYX	C	(800) 542-6767	C / 4.3	5.90	5.90	18.50 /45	3.49 /37	7.56 /39	1.78	1.00
AA	MassMutual RetireSMART 2030 R3	MRYNX	C	(800) 542-6767	C- / 3.9	5.72	5.63	17.97 /43	3.06 /32	7.00 /35	1.52	1.40
AA	MassMutual RetireSMART 2030 R4	MRYZX	U	(800) 542-6767	U /	5.79	5.79	18.21 /44	--	--	1.72	1.15
AA	MassMutual RetireSMART 2030 R5	MRYTX	U	(800) 542-6767	U /	5.89	5.98	18.70 /46	--	--	2.01	0.80
AA	MassMutual RetireSMART 2030 Svc	MRYSX	C	(800) 542-6767	C / 4.3	5.91	6.00	18.60 /45	3.59 /38	7.65 /39	1.87	0.90

● Denotes fund is closed to new investors
* Denotes fund is included in Section II

RISK	3 Year		NET ASSETS		ASSET				Portfolio Turnover Ratio	BULL / BEAR		FUND MANAGER		MINIMUMS		LOADS	
Risk Rating/Pts	Standard Deviation	Beta	NAV As of 2/28/17	Total $(Mil)	Cash %	Stocks %	Bonds %	Other %		Last Bull Market Return	Last Bear Market Return	Manager Quality Pct	Manager Tenure (Years)	Initial Purch. $	Additional Purch. $	Front End Load	Back End Load
C /4.7	13.0	0.97	13.88	23	0	98	0	2	25	86.2	-23.2	93	13	0	0	0.0	0.0
C- /3.7	11.7	0.90	11.00	38	0	97	1	2	36	51.3	-20.9	51	19	0	0	5.8	0.0
C- /3.7	11.7	0.90	11.32	20	0	97	1	2	36	53.4	-20.8	55	19	0	0	0.0	0.0
C+ /6.5	11.7	0.90	11.40	199	0	97	1	2	36	56.2	-20.7	61	19	0	0	0.0	0.0
C- /3.7	11.7	0.90	11.40	195	0	97	1	2	36	54.9	-20.7	57	19	0	0	0.0	0.0
C- /3.7	11.7	0.90	11.37	17	0	97	1	2	36	54.4	-20.7	56	19	0	0	0.0	0.0
D /1.6	10.3	0.99	10.87	13	3	96	0	1	38	125.1	-15.5	62	8	0	0	5.8	0.0
D /1.6	10.3	0.99	11.00	32	3	96	0	1	38	127.8	-15.3	65	8	0	0	0.0	0.0
B- /7.0	10.3	0.99	11.01	2	3	96	0	1	38	133.2	-15.2	72	8	0	0	0.0	0.0
D /1.6	10.3	0.99	10.89	1	3	96	0	1	38	122.3	-15.5	60	8	0	0	0.0	0.0
D /1.6	10.3	0.99	11.01	82	3	96	0	1	38	130.6	-15.2	68	8	0	0	0.0	0.0
D /1.8	10.3	0.99	11.36	1	3	96	0	1	38	129.8	-15.3	66	8	0	0	0.0	0.0
C- /3.4	14.4	0.89	14.76	75	4	95	0	1	57	144.0	-23.5	81	8	0	0	5.8	0.0
C- /3.5	14.4	0.89	15.03	23	4	95	0	1	57	147.2	-23.4	83	8	0	0	0.0	0.0
C+ /5.9	14.2	0.88	15.15	8	4	95	0	1	57	154.1	-23.4	87	8	0	0	0.0	0.0
C- /3.4	14.4	0.89	15.13	69	4	95	0	1	57	149.8	-23.4	84	8	0	0	0.0	0.0
C- /3.4	14.4	0.89	15.10	15	4	95	0	1	57	148.5	-23.4	83	8	0	0	0.0	0.0
C /4.4	14.8	0.86	10.80	N/A	7	92	0	1	33	3.6	-27.8	35	4	0	0	5.8	0.0
C /4.4	14.7	0.86	10.82	1	7	92	0	1	33	5.0	-27.7	38	4	0	0	0.0	0.0
C /4.4	14.7	0.86	10.77	175	7	92	0	1	33	7.1	-27.6	42	4	0	0	0.0	0.0
C /4.4	14.7	0.86	10.92	3	7	92	0	1	33	6.1	-27.6	40	4	0	0	0.0	0.0
C /4.4	14.7	0.86	10.76	N/A	7	92	0	1	33	5.6	-27.7	39	4	0	0	0.0	0.0
C+ /6.1	11.6	1.08	23.93	6	2	97	0	1	62	104.8	-21.1	30	4	0	0	5.8	0.0
C+ /6.1	11.6	1.08	23.92	13	2	97	0	1	62	107.7	-21.0	33	4	0	0	0.0	0.0
C+ /6.5	11.6	1.07	23.84	N/A	2	97	0	1	62	112.0	-21.0	39	4	0	0	0.0	0.0
C+ /6.1	11.6	1.08	23.78	N/A	2	97	0	1	62	102.1	-21.2	28	4	0	0	0.0	0.0
C+ /6.1	11.6	1.07	23.84	51	2	97	0	1	62	110.0	-21.0	35	4	0	0	0.0	0.0
C+ /6.1	11.5	1.07	23.93	N/A	2	97	0	1	62	108.9	-21.0	34	4	0	0	0.0	0.0
B /8.5	5.2	0.79	11.66	18	0	36	63	1	74	39.8	-10.0	30	14	0	0	5.8	0.0
B /8.5	5.3	0.79	11.74	15	0	36	63	1	74	42.0	-9.9	33	14	0	0	0.0	0.0
B /8.4	5.3	0.79	11.45	11	0	36	63	1	74	38.0	-10.0	28	14	0	0	0.0	0.0
B /8.5	5.2	0.78	11.77	20	0	36	63	1	74	42.7	-9.7	35	14	0	0	0.0	0.0
B /8.1	5.7	0.42	11.42	14	0	41	58	1	76	49.3	-13.3	89	7	0	0	5.8	0.0
B /8.0	5.8	0.42	11.49	15	0	41	58	1	76	51.6	-13.2	90	7	0	0	0.0	0.0
U /	N/A	N/A	11.36	30	0	41	58	1	76	N/A	N/A	N/A	N/A	0	0	0.0	0.0
B /8.1	5.8	0.42	11.53	7	0	41	58	1	76	52.2	-13.2	90	7	0	0	0.0	0.0
B- /7.8	7.1	1.09	12.13	72	0	55	44	1	69	57.8	-15.7	14	14	0	0	5.8	0.0
B- /7.7	7.1	1.09	12.20	116	0	55	44	1	69	60.4	-15.6	17	14	0	0	0.0	0.0
B- /7.7	7.1	1.09	11.82	85	0	55	44	1	69	56.0	-15.8	14	14	0	0	0.0	0.0
U /	N/A	N/A	11.98	58	0	55	44	1	69	N/A	N/A	N/A	11	0	0	0.0	0.0
B- /7.7	7.1	1.09	12.22	127	0	55	44	1	69	61.2	-15.6	17	14	0	0	0.0	0.0
B- /7.4	8.1	0.60	12.22	32	0	66	33	1	69	65.5	-17.7	91	7	0	0	5.8	0.0
B- /7.3	8.1	0.60	12.31	43	0	66	33	1	69	68.2	-17.6	92	7	0	0	0.0	0.0
U /	N/A	N/A	12.15	85	0	66	33	1	69	N/A	N/A	N/A	N/A	0	0	0.0	0.0
U /	N/A	N/A	12.18	55	0	66	33	1	69	N/A	N/A	N/A	7	0	0	0.0	0.0
B- /7.3	8.1	0.60	12.34	22	0	66	33	1	69	68.8	-17.6	92	7	0	0	0.0	0.0
C+ /6.8	8.8	1.35	12.24	77	2	71	25	2	69	68.8	-18.4	7	14	0	0	5.8	0.0
C+ /6.7	8.8	1.35	12.32	115	2	71	25	2	69	71.5	-18.2	8	14	0	0	0.0	0.0
C+ /6.7	8.8	1.34	12.02	107	2	71	25	2	69	66.7	-18.4	6	14	0	0	0.0	0.0
U /	N/A	N/A	12.17	60	2	71	25	2	69	N/A	N/A	N/A	11	0	0	0.0	0.0
U /	N/A	N/A	12.30	30	2	71	25	2	69	N/A	N/A	N/A	11	0	0	0.0	0.0
C+ /6.7	8.7	1.34	12.33	138	2	71	25	2	69	72.5	-18.3	8	14	0	0	0.0	0.0

Fund Type	Fund Name	Ticker Symbol	Overall Investment Rating	Phone	Performance Rating/Pts	3 Mo	6 Mo	1Yr / Pct	3Yr / Pct	5Yr / Pct	Dividend Yield	Expense Ratio
GL	MassMutual RetireSMART 2035 A	MMXAX	C-	(800) 542-6767	C- / 3.1	6.03	6.12	18.84 /46	3.29 /35	7.44 /38	1.31	1.36
GL	MassMutual RetireSMART 2035	MMXYX	C	(800) 542-6767	C / 4.5	6.07	6.24	19.17 /48	3.55 /38	7.76 /40	1.62	1.11
GL	MassMutual RetireSMART 2035 R3	MMXNX	U	(800) 542-6767	U /	5.98	6.07	18.74 /46	--	--	1.33	1.51
GI	MassMutual RetireSMART 2035 R4	MMXZX	U	(800) 542-6767	U /	6.02	6.19	18.95 /47	--	--	1.52	1.26
GL	MassMutual RetireSMART 2035 Svc	MMXSX	C+	(800) 542-6767	C / 4.5	6.04	6.21	19.31 /49	3.66 /39	7.84 /41	1.68	1.01
AA	MassMutual RetireSMART 2040 A	MRFAX	C-	(800) 542-6767	C- / 3.2	6.11	6.21	19.07 /47	3.31 /35	7.47 /38	1.29	1.28
AA	MassMutual RetireSMART 2040 Adm	MRFYX	C	(800) 542-6767	C / 4.5	6.22	6.31	19.42 /49	3.57 /38	7.77 /40	1.58	1.03
AA	MassMutual RetireSMART 2040 R3	MFRNX	C-	(800) 542-6767	C- / 4.1	6.00	6.09	18.87 /46	3.14 /33	7.22 /36	1.35	1.43
AA	MassMutual RetireSMART 2040 R4	MRFZX	U	(800) 542-6767	U /	6.13	6.22	19.16 /48	--	--	1.52	1.18
AA	MassMutual RetireSMART 2040 Svc	MFRSX	C	(800) 542-6767	C / 4.6	6.21	6.40	19.48 /49	3.68 /39	7.90 /41	1.67	0.93
GL	MassMutual RetireSMART 2045 A	MMKAX	C-	(800) 542-6767	C- / 3.3	6.17	6.34	19.47 /49	3.37 /35	7.91 /41	1.22	1.47
GL	MassMutual RetireSMART 2045 adm	MMKYX	C	(800) 542-6767	C / 4.6	6.28	6.45	19.79 /51	3.63 /38	8.23 /44	1.51	1.22
GL	MassMutual RetireSMART 2045 R3	MMKNX	U	(800) 542-6767	U /	6.12	6.21	19.27 /48	--	--	1.23	1.62
GI	MassMutual RetireSMART 2045 R4	MMKZX	U	(800) 542-6767	U /	6.22	6.40	19.58 /50	--	--	1.41	1.37
GL	MassMutual RetireSMART 2045 Svc	MMKSX	C+	(800) 542-6767	C / 4.7	6.34	6.51	19.92 /52	3.75 /40	8.32 /45	1.57	1.12
AA	MassMutual RetireSMART 2050 A	MMARX	D+	(800) 542-6767	C- / 3.5	6.51	6.76	20.21 /53	3.43 /36	7.96 /42	1.16	1.39
AA	MassMutual RetireSMART 2050	MMRYX	C-	(800) 542-6767	C / 4.9	6.56	6.94	20.63 /56	3.71 /39	8.32 /45	1.43	1.14
AA	MassMutual RetireSMART 2050 R3	MMRNX	C-	(800) 542-6767	C / 4.5	6.50	6.76	20.19 /53	3.29 /35	7.72 /40	1.18	1.54
AA	MassMutual RetireSMART 2050 Svc	MMTSX	C-	(800) 542-6767	C / 5.0	6.53	6.90	20.73 /56	3.80 /40	8.32 /45	1.51	1.04
GI	MassMutual RetireSMART 2055 A	MMWAX	C-	(800) 542-6767	C- / 3.5	6.47	6.78	20.35 /54	3.47 /37	--	1.11	2.38
GI	MassMutual RetireSMART 2055	MMWYX	C	(800) 542-6767	C / 4.9	6.53	6.94	20.75 /56	3.72 /40	--	1.42	2.13
GI	MassMutual RetireSMART 2055 Svc	MMWSX	C+	(800) 542-6767	C / 5.0	6.55	6.96	20.85 /57	3.85 /41	--	1.46	2.03
GL	MassMutual RetireSMART Consv A	MCTAX	C-	(800) 542-6767	D- / 1.3	2.91	1.31	8.38 / 8	2.23 /26	3.64 /14	1.30	1.21
GL	MassMutual RetireSMART Consv	MRCLX	C-	(800) 542-6767	D / 2.0	2.91	1.42	8.73 / 9	2.47 /27	3.92 /15	2.10	0.96
GI	MassMutual RetireSMART Consv I	MRCUX	C+	(800) 542-6767	D / 2.1	3.02	1.53	8.95 / 9	2.84 /30	4.21 /16	2.42	0.66
GI	MassMutual RetireSMART Consv R4	MRCZX	U	(800) 542-6767	U /	2.88	1.38	8.49 / 8	--	--	2.17	1.11
GL	MassMutual RetireSMART Consv R5	MRCSX	C-	(800) 542-6767	D / 2.1	3.03	1.54	8.86 / 9	2.66 /29	4.09 /16	2.32	0.76
GL	MassMutual RetireSMART Consv	MRCYX	C-	(800) 542-6767	D / 2.0	2.88	1.39	8.70 / 9	2.55 /28	4.00 /15	2.18	0.86
GL	MassMutual RetireSMART Growth A	MRRAX	D+	(800) 542-6767	C- / 3.5	6.55	6.87	20.48 /55	3.39 /36	8.04 /42	1.08	1.45
GL	MassMutual RetireSMART Growth	MRGLX	C-	(800) 542-6767	C / 4.9	6.61	7.03	20.78 /56	3.65 /39	8.29 /45	1.40	1.20
GI	MassMutual RetireSMART Growth I	MRGUX	B	(800) 542-6767	C / 5.3	6.65	7.08	21.08 /58	4.21 /45	8.70 /48	1.72	0.90
GL	MassMutual RetireSMART Growth	MRRSX	C-	(800) 542-6767	C / 5.1	6.64	7.06	21.07 /58	3.84 /41	8.47 /46	1.61	1.00
GL	MassMutual RetireSMART Growth	MRGYX	C-	(800) 542-6767	C / 5.0	6.63	7.05	21.04 /58	3.76 /40	8.41 /45	1.51	1.10
AA	MassMutual RetireSMART In Ret A	MRDAX	C-	(800) 542-6767	D- / 1.3	3.13	1.72	9.26 /10	2.19 /25	3.73 /14	1.83	1.40
AA	MassMutual RetireSMART In Ret	MDRYX	C	(800) 542-6767	D / 2.1	3.16	1.86	9.55 /11	2.44 /27	4.03 /15	2.16	1.15
AA	MassMutual RetireSMART In Ret R3	MDRNX	C	(800) 542-6767	D / 1.8	3.04	1.62	9.04 /10	2.03 /24	3.52 /13	1.93	1.55
AA	MassMutual RetireSMART In Ret Svc	MDRSX	C	(800) 542-6767	D / 2.1	3.27	1.97	9.67 /11	2.58 /28	4.13 /16	2.27	1.05
GL	MassMutual RetireSMART Modt A	MRMAX	D+	(800) 542-6767	D / 2.1	4.49	3.83	13.89 /25	2.90 /31	5.68 /26	1.54	1.22
GL	MassMutual RetireSMART Modt Adm	MRMLX	C-	(800) 542-6767	C- / 3.1	4.50	3.95	14.03 /26	3.13 /33	5.94 /28	1.94	0.97
GL	MassMutual RetireSMART Modt Gro	MOGAX	D	(800) 542-6767	C- / 3.1	5.93	6.04	18.76 /46	3.29 /35	7.29 /37	1.41	1.28
GL	MassMutual RetireSMART Modt Gro	MRSLX	C-	(800) 542-6767	C / 4.4	6.03	6.14	19.03 /47	3.54 /37	7.57 /39	1.78	1.03
GI	MassMutual RetireSMART Modt Gro I	MROUX	B-	(800) 542-6767	C / 4.8	6.06	6.39	19.33 /49	4.08 /44	7.94 /42	2.10	0.73
GL	MassMutual RetireSMART Modt Gro	MRSSX	C-	(800) 542-6767	C / 4.6	6.09	6.31	19.24 /48	3.76 /40	7.74 /40	2.02	0.83
GL	MassMutual RetireSMART Modt Gro	MROYX	C-	(800) 542-6767	C / 4.5	6.08	6.30	19.23 /48	3.65 /39	7.67 /40	1.72	0.93
GI	MassMutual RetireSMART Modt I	MRMUX	C+	(800) 542-6767	C- / 3.4	4.62	4.07	14.44 /27	3.59 /38	6.25 /30	2.26	0.67
GI	MassMutual RetireSMART Modt R4	MRMZX	U	(800) 542-6767	U /	4.58	3.91	14.03 /26	--	--	2.01	1.12
GL	MassMutual RetireSMART Modt R5	MROSX	C-	(800) 542-6767	C- / 3.3	4.53	3.98	14.34 /27	3.34 /35	6.10 /29	2.17	0.77
GL	MassMutual RetireSMART Modt Svc	MRMYX	C-	(800) 542-6767	C- / 3.2	4.57	4.02	14.23 /27	3.25 /34	6.03 /29	1.91	0.87
MC	MassMutual Sel S and P MC Idx A	MDKAX	B	(800) 542-6767	B / 8.1	6.34	10.83	30.54 /87	8.75 /85	--	0.90	0.82
MC	MassMutual Sel S and P MC Idx Adm	MDKYX	A-	(800) 542-6767	A- / 9.2	6.42	10.97	30.98 /88	9.02 /87	--	1.16	0.57
MC	MassMutual Sel S and P MC Idx I	MDKZX	A-	(800) 542-6767	A / 9.4	6.49	11.25	31.38 /89	9.41 /90	--	1.45	0.22
MC	MassMutual Sel S and P MC Idx R3	MDKTX	U	(800) 542-6767	U /	6.25	10.76	30.35 /87	--	--	0.98	0.97

● Denotes fund is closed to new investors
★ Denotes fund is included in Section II

www.thestreetratings.com

| RISK | 3 Year | | NET ASSETS | | ASSET | | | | Portfolio | BULL / BEAR | | FUND MANAGER | | MINIMUMS | | LOADS | |
Risk Rating/Pts	Standard Deviation	Beta	NAV As of 2/28/17	Total $(Mil)	Cash %	Stocks %	Bonds %	Other %	Turnover Ratio	Last Bull Market Return	Last Bear Market Return	Manager Quality Pct	Manager Tenure (Years)	Initial Purch. $	Additional Purch. $	Front End Load	Back End Load
C+ / 6.9	9.2	1.38	12.61	28	1	77	20	2	69	71.1	-18.9	34	7	0	0	5.8	0.0
C+ / 6.9	9.2	1.38	12.71	28	1	77	20	2	69	74.0	-18.8	37	7	0	0	0.0	0.0
U /	N/A	N/A	12.55	62	1	77	20	2	69	N/A	N/A	N/A	N/A	0	0	0.0	0.0
U /	N/A	N/A	12.57	44	1	77	20	2	69	N/A	N/A	N/A	7	0	0	0.0	0.0
C+ / 6.9	9.2	1.38	12.74	17	1	77	20	2	69	74.8	-18.8	39	7	0	0	0.0	0.0
C+ / 6.2	9.3	1.42	12.02	44	4	77	18	1	70	71.7	-19.1	6	14	0	0	5.8	0.0
C+ / 6.2	9.3	1.42	12.10	83	4	77	18	1	70	74.6	-19.0	6	14	0	0	0.0	0.0
C+ / 6.1	9.3	1.42	11.78	55	4	77	18	1	70	69.6	-19.2	5	14	0	0	0.0	0.0
U /	N/A	N/A	11.94	39	4	77	18	1	70	N/A	N/A	N/A	11	0	0	0.0	0.0
C+ / 6.2	9.3	1.43	12.13	78	4	77	18	1	70	75.4	-19.0	6	14	0	0	0.0	0.0
C+ / 6.7	9.7	1.45	12.56	16	1	82	15	2	68	77.4	-20.5	31	7	0	0	5.8	0.0
C+ / 6.7	9.7	1.45	12.66	15	1	82	15	2	68	80.3	-20.4	35	7	0	0	0.0	0.0
U /	N/A	N/A	12.49	41	1	82	15	2	68	N/A	N/A	N/A	N/A	0	0	0.0	0.0
U /	N/A	N/A	12.51	25	1	82	15	2	68	N/A	N/A	N/A	7	0	0	0.0	0.0
C+ / 6.7	9.7	1.45	12.69	10	1	82	15	2	68	81.0	-20.3	36	7	0	0	0.0	0.0
C / 5.4	10.0	1.53	8.83	20	6	84	9	1	68	77.3	-20.2	4	N/A	0	0	5.8	0.0
C / 5.4	10.1	1.55	8.89	34	6	84	9	1	68	80.3	-20.0	4	N/A	0	0	0.0	0.0
C / 5.4	10.1	1.54	8.75	34	6	84	9	1	68	75.3	-20.4	4	N/A	0	0	0.0	0.0
C / 5.4	10.0	1.53	8.89	36	6	84	9	1	68	80.8	-20.1	5	N/A	0	0	0.0	0.0
C+ / 6.4	10.0	0.94	10.61	4	4	87	7	2	74	N/A	N/A	9	4	0	0	5.8	0.0
C+ / 6.4	10.1	0.94	10.63	4	4	87	7	2	74	N/A	N/A	10	4	0	0	0.0	0.0
C+ / 6.4	10.0	0.93	10.67	3	4	87	7	2	74	N/A	N/A	11	4	0	0	0.0	0.0
B / 8.1	4.0	0.59	9.65	35	0	25	74	1	69	29.6	N/A	68	6	0	0	5.8	0.0
B / 8.1	4.1	0.59	9.60	52	0	25	74	1	69	31.4	N/A	71	6	0	0	0.0	0.0
B+ / 9.3	4.0	0.32	9.60	2	0	25	74	1	69	33.3	N/A	68	6	0	0	0.0	0.0
U /	N/A	N/A	9.53	89	0	25	74	1	69	N/A	N/A	N/A	6	0	0	0.0	0.0
B / 8.0	4.0	0.59	9.59	10	0	25	74	1	69	32.6	N/A	73	6	0	0	0.0	0.0
B / 8.1	4.0	0.59	9.59	7	0	25	74	1	69	32.0	N/A	72	6	0	0	0.0	0.0
C / 4.9	10.3	0.75	10.56	45	3	88	7	2	70	78.6	N/A	92	6	0	0	5.8	0.0
C / 4.9	10.2	0.75	10.57	32	3	88	7	2	70	81.1	N/A	93	6	0	0	0.0	0.0
B- / 7.7	10.2	0.95	10.55	1	3	88	7	2	70	84.5	N/A	12	6	0	0	0.0	0.0
C / 4.9	10.3	0.76	10.56	5	3	88	7	2	70	82.6	N/A	93	6	0	0	0.0	0.0
C / 4.9	10.2	0.75	10.58	2	3	88	7	2	70	82.2	N/A	93	6	0	0	0.0	0.0
B / 8.8	4.5	0.66	10.99	20	0	28	71	1	75	31.0	-6.5	39	14	0	0	5.8	0.0
B / 8.7	4.5	0.66	11.06	27	0	28	71	1	75	33.0	-6.4	43	14	0	0	0.0	0.0
B / 8.6	4.4	0.65	10.83	15	0	28	71	1	75	29.5	-6.6	37	14	0	0	0.0	0.0
B / 8.7	4.5	0.66	11.07	14	0	28	71	1	75	33.9	-6.3	44	14	0	0	0.0	0.0
C+ / 6.7	6.5	0.48	9.71	122	0	52	47	1	62	50.3	N/A	90	6	0	0	5.8	0.0
C+ / 6.7	6.5	0.48	9.68	106	0	52	47	1	62	52.3	N/A	91	6	0	0	0.0	0.0
C / 5.1	9.0	1.35	9.94	96	2	75	21	2	62	69.1	N/A	36	6	0	0	5.8	0.0
C / 5.1	9.0	1.36	9.91	99	2	75	21	2	62	71.3	N/A	39	6	0	0	0.0	0.0
B- / 7.8	8.9	0.83	9.89	1	2	75	21	2	62	74.4	N/A	20	6	0	0	0.0	0.0
C / 5.1	9.0	1.36	9.89	22	2	75	21	2	62	72.8	N/A	42	6	0	0	0.0	0.0
C / 5.1	9.0	1.36	9.92	6	2	75	21	2	62	72.3	N/A	41	6	0	0	0.0	0.0
B / 8.0	6.6	0.60	9.65	2	0	52	47	1	62	54.6	N/A	40	6	0	0	0.0	0.0
U /	N/A	N/A	9.64	25	0	52	47	1	62	N/A	N/A	N/A	6	0	0	0.0	0.0
C+ / 6.6	6.5	0.48	9.65	40	0	52	47	1	62	53.5	N/A	91	6	0	0	0.0	0.0
C+ / 6.7	6.5	0.48	9.70	5	0	52	47	1	62	53.2	N/A	91	6	0	0	0.0	0.0
C / 5.4	12.0	1.00	13.56	38	2	96	0	2	48	N/A	N/A	65	5	0	0	5.8	0.0
C / 5.4	12.1	1.00	13.59	60	2	96	0	2	48	N/A	N/A	67	5	0	0	0.0	0.0
C / 5.4	12.1	1.00	13.68	94	2	96	0	2	48	N/A	N/A	72	5	0	0	0.0	0.0
U /	N/A	N/A	13.47	44	2	96	0	2	48	N/A	N/A	N/A	5	0	0	0.0	0.0

	99 Pct = Best 0 Pct = Worst				PERFORMANCE							
								Total Return % through 2/28/17			Incl. in Returns	
			Overall		Perfor-				Annualized		Dividend	Expense
Fund Type	Fund Name	Ticker Symbol	Investment Rating	Phone	mance Rating/Pts	3 Mo	6 Mo	1Yr / Pct	3Yr / Pct	5Yr / Pct	Yield	Ratio
MC	MassMutual Sel S and P MC Idx R4	MDKFX	U	(800) 542-6767	U /	6.32	10.90	30.67 /88	--	--	1.12	0.72
MC	MassMutual Sel S and P MC Idx R5	MDKIX	A-	(800) 542-6767	A /9.3	6.50	11.11	31.27 /89	9.28 /89	--	1.38	0.32
MC	MassMutual Sel S and P MC Idx Svc	MDKSX	A-	(800) 542-6767	A /9.3	6.47	11.10	31.14 /88	9.15 /88	--	1.27	0.47
SC	MassMutual Sel Small Cap Val Eq A	MMQAX	B	(800) 542-6767	B /8.0	4.31	13.27	31.92 /90	8.14 /80	13.24 /86	0.01	1.50
SC	MassMutual Sel Small Cap Val Eq	MMQLX	A-	(800) 542-6767	A- /9.1	4.40	13.40	32.26 /90	8.41 /82	13.54 /89	0.28	1.25
SC	MassMutual Sel Small Cap Val Eq I	MMQIX	A	(800) 542-6767	A /9.4	4.43	13.54	32.65 /91	9.20 /88	14.14 /94	0.42	0.95
SC	MassMutual Sel Small Cap Val Eq R5	MMQSX	A-	(800) 542-6767	A- /9.2	4.44	13.47	32.47 /91	8.64 /84	13.79 /92	0.32	1.05
SC	MassMutual Sel Small Cap Val Eq	MMQYX	A-	(800) 542-6767	A- /9.1	4.35	13.43	32.30 /90	8.51 /83	13.68 /90	0.25	1.15
GL	MassMutual Select BlackRock GA A	MGJAX	D	(800) 542-6767	D /1.7	4.59	3.96	12.36 /19	2.08 /25	4.44 /18	0.33	1.51
GL	MassMutual Select BlackRock GA	MGSLX	D+	(800) 542-6767	D+ /2.6	4.56	4.06	12.62 /20	2.32 /26	4.70 /19	0.56	1.26
GL	MassMutual Select BlackRock GA I	MGJIX	C	(800) 542-6767	D+ /2.9	4.66	4.25	12.97 /22	2.78 /30	5.09 /22	0.92	0.96
GL	MassMutual Select BlackRock GA R5	MGSSX	D+	(800) 542-6767	D+ /2.7	4.69	4.18	12.89 /21	2.50 /28	4.92 /21	0.81	1.06
GL	MassMutual Select BlackRock GA	MGSYX	D+	(800) 542-6767	D+ /2.7	4.64	4.12	12.72 /21	2.45 /27	4.85 /20	0.70	1.16
GR	MassMutual Select Blue Chip Gr A	MBCGX	C	(800) 542-6767	C+ /6.8	7.83	7.27	21.33 /59	8.41 /82	14.11 /94	0.06	1.22
GR	MassMutual Select Blue Chip Gr Adm	MBCLX	C+	(800) 542-6767	B /7.9	7.85	7.38	21.61 /60	8.67 /84	14.36 /95	0.29	0.97
GR	MassMutual Select Blue Chip Gr I	MBCZX	B+	(800) 542-6767	B+ /8.4	7.92	7.47	21.92 /62	9.59 /91	15.04 /97	0.57	0.67
GR	MassMutual Select Blue Chip Gr R3	MBCNX	C	(800) 542-6767	B /7.6	7.82	7.15	21.08 /58	8.24 /81	13.86 /92	0.19	1.37
GR	MassMutual Select Blue Chip Gr R4	MBGFX	U	(800) 542-6767	U /	7.81	7.26	21.39 /59	--	--	0.28	1.12
GR	MassMutual Select Blue Chip Gr R5	MBCSX	C+	(800) 542-6767	B /8.1	7.95	7.49	21.81 /61	8.89 /86	14.61 /96	0.47	0.77
GR	MassMutual Select Blue Chip Gr Svc	MBCYX	C+	(800) 542-6767	B /8.0	7.89	7.36	21.72 /61	8.77 /85	14.51 /96	0.36	0.87
FO	MassMutual Select Dvsfd Intl A	MMZAX	E+	(800) 542-6767	E /0.5	6.43	6.43	17.91 /42	-2.81 / 5	3.00 /11	4.85	1.74
FO	MassMutual Select Dvsfd Intl Adm	MMZLX	D-	(800) 542-6767	E+ /0.9	6.50	6.66	18.24 /44	-2.54 / 5	3.15 /11	5.41	1.49
FO	MassMutual Select Dvsfd Intl I	MMZIX	D	(800) 542-6767	D- /1.1	6.63	6.80	18.44 /45	-1.98 / 7	3.70 /14	5.81	1.19
FO	MassMutual Select Dvsfd Intl Svc	MMZYX	D-	(800) 542-6767	E+ /0.9	6.58	6.74	18.28 /44	-2.47 / 6	3.35 /12	5.47	1.39
GI	MassMutual Select Dvsfd Value A	MDDAX	B+	(800) 542-6767	B /7.7	7.37	12.04	27.48 /80	8.15 /80	12.96 /83	1.53	1.14
GI	MassMutual Select Dvsfd Value Adm	MDDLX	A+	(800) 542-6767	B+ /8.9	7.43	12.21	27.82 /81	8.45 /83	13.28 /87	1.88	0.89
GI	MassMutual Select Dvsfd Value I	MDDIX	A+	(800) 542-6767	A- /9.1	7.55	12.35	28.26 /82	8.91 /86	13.65 /90	2.14	0.59
GI	MassMutual Select Dvsfd Value R3	MDVNX	A	(800) 542-6767	B+ /8.6	7.31	11.98	27.33 /80	8.00 /79	12.72 /81	1.61	1.29
GI	MassMutual Select Dvsfd Value R5	MDVSX	A+	(800) 542-6767	A- /9.0	7.47	12.27	28.06 /82	8.65 /84	13.49 /89	1.96	0.69
GI	MassMutual Select Dvsfd Value Svc	MDVYX	A+	(800) 542-6767	A- /9.0	7.50	12.23	28.02 /82	8.54 /83	13.41 /88	1.92	0.79
GR	MassMutual Select Focused Value A	MFVAX	C+	(800) 542-6767	A+ /9.6	9.32	16.57	37.82 /96	8.98 /87	13.61 /90	0.67	1.28
GR	MassMutual Select Focused Value	MMFVX	C+	(800) 542-6767	A+ /9.8	9.39	16.75	38.17 /96	9.24 /88	13.89 /92	0.99	1.03
MC	MassMutual Select Focused Value I	MFVZX	C+	(800) 542-6767	A+ /9.8	9.45	16.89	38.57 /97	9.58 /91	14.27 /95	1.25	0.73
GR	MassMutual Select Focused Value	MFVNX	C+	(800) 542-6767	A+ /9.7	9.28	16.49	37.59 /96	8.80 /85	13.36 /87	0.85	1.43
GR	MassMutual Select Focused Value	MFVSX	C+	(800) 542-6767	A+ /9.8	9.43	16.85	38.38 /97	9.48 /90	14.14 /94	1.16	0.83
GR	MassMutual Select Focused Value	MMFYX	C+	(800) 542-6767	A+ /9.8	9.36	16.76	38.27 /97	9.35 /89	14.02 /93	1.08	0.93
IN	MassMutual Select Fundamental G A	MOTAX	C	(800) 542-6767	C+ /6.6	8.72	8.43	18.36 /44	8.36 /82	11.17 /67	0.46	1.36
IN	MassMutual Select Fundamental G	MOTLX	C+	(800) 542-6767	B /7.8	8.83	8.55	18.58 /45	8.60 /84	11.46 /70	0.73	1.11
GR	MassMutual Select Fundamental G I	MOTZX	A-	(800) 542-6767	B /8.2	8.83	8.70	18.85 /46	9.38 /89	12.01 /74	0.99	0.81
IN	MassMutual Select Fundamental G	MOTNX	C+	(800) 542-6767	B- /7.4	8.66	8.35	18.12 /43	8.15 /80	10.94 /65	0.68	1.51
IN	MassMutual Select Fundamental G	MOTCX	B-	(800) 542-6767	B /7.9	8.84	8.56	18.84 /46	8.83 /86	11.67 /71	0.89	0.91
IN	MassMutual Select Fundamental G	MOTYX	C+	(800) 542-6767	B /7.8	8.75	8.47	18.61 /45	8.68 /84	11.55 /70	0.82	1.01
IN	MassMutual Select Fundamental V A	MFUAX	C+	(800) 542-6767	B- /7.0	6.44	9.02	25.79 /76	7.83 /78	11.77 /72	1.19	1.18
IN	MassMutual Select Fundamental V	MFULX	B-	(800) 542-6767	B /8.2	6.53	9.17	26.17 /77	8.11 /80	12.07 /75	1.54	0.93
GR	MassMutual Select Fundamental V I	MFUZX	B	(800) 542-6767	B+ /8.4	6.55	9.28	26.50 /78	8.41 /82	12.44 /78	1.84	0.63
IN	MassMutual Select Fundamental V	MFUNX	B-	(800) 542-6767	B /7.8	6.43	8.95	25.57 /75	7.66 /76	11.54 /70	1.27	1.33
IN	MassMutual Select Fundamental V	MVUSX	B-	(800) 542-6767	B+ /8.3	6.59	9.23	26.38 /77	8.31 /81	12.27 /77	1.74	0.73
IN	MassMutual Select Fundamental V	MFUYX	B-	(800) 542-6767	B /8.2	6.48	9.13	26.22 /77	8.18 /80	12.19 /76	1.62	0.83
AG	MassMutual Select Growth Opps A	MMAAX	E+	(800) 542-6767	D+ /2.7	8.03	3.93	14.01 /25	3.40 /36	10.56 /62	0.00	1.29
AG	MassMutual Select Growth Opps	MAGLX	D-	(800) 542-6767	C- /3.9	8.11	4.12	14.25 /27	3.65 /39	10.84 /65	0.00	1.04
GR	MassMutual Select Growth Opps I	MMAZX	D	(800) 542-6767	C- /4.1	8.13	4.17	14.62 /28	3.95 /42	11.23 /68	0.00	0.74
AG	MassMutual Select Growth Opps R3	MMANX	D-	(800) 542-6767	C- /3.5	7.94	3.83	13.77 /24	3.21 /34	10.30 /61	0.00	1.44

- Denotes fund is closed to new investors
- Denotes fund is included in Section II

www.thestreetratings.com

Risk Rating/Pts	3 Year Standard Deviation	Beta	NAV As of 2/28/17	Total $(Mil)	Cash %	Stocks %	Bonds %	Other %	Portfolio Turnover Ratio	Last Bull Market Return	Last Bear Market Return	Manager Quality Pct	Manager Tenure (Years)	Initial Purch. $	Additional Purch. $	Front End Load	Back End Load
U /	N/A	N/A	13.51	49	2	96	0	2	48	N/A	N/A	N/A	5	0	0	0.0	0.0
C /5.4	12.0	1.00	13.64	27	2	96	0	2	48	N/A	N/A	71	5	0	0	0.0	0.0
C /5.4	12.0	1.00	13.59	28	2	96	0	2	48	N/A	N/A	69	5	0	0	0.0	0.0
C /5.5	14.6	0.90	17.29	10	5	94	0	1	26	153.2	-27.4	85	8	0	0	5.8	0.0
C /5.5	14.6	0.90	17.34	9	5	94	0	1	26	156.4	-27.4	87	8	0	0	0.0	0.0
C+ /5.7	14.5	0.89	17.38	126	5	94	0	1	26	163.6	-27.2	90	8	0	0	0.0	0.0
C /5.5	14.6	0.90	17.40	44	5	94	0	1	26	159.6	-27.2	87	8	0	0	0.0	0.0
C /5.5	14.6	0.90	17.43	8	5	94	0	1	26	158.4	-27.2	87	8	0	0	0.0	0.0
C+ /6.3	6.4	0.97	10.39	5	1	53	42	4	171	39.9	-14.1	43	8	0	0	5.8	0.0
C+ /6.3	6.4	0.97	10.75	10	1	53	42	4	171	41.5	-13.6	46	8	0	0	0.0	0.0
B- /7.6	6.4	0.97	10.44	519	1	53	42	4	171	44.6	-14.0	53	8	0	0	0.0	0.0
C+ /6.4	6.4	0.97	10.58	7	1	53	42	4	171	43.4	-14.0	49	8	0	0	0.0	0.0
C+ /6.2	6.5	0.98	10.43	11	1	53	42	4	171	42.8	-14.0	48	8	0	0	0.0	0.0
C- /3.9	12.5	1.05	15.86	153	0	99	0	1	30	140.5	-14.9	41	N/A	0	0	5.8	0.0
C- /3.9	12.5	1.05	16.50	243	0	99	0	1	30	143.5	-14.8	44	N/A	0	0	0.0	0.0
C+ /5.9	12.5	1.05	16.87	835	0	99	0	1	30	151.2	-14.8	56	N/A	0	0	0.0	0.0
C- /3.7	12.5	1.05	14.91	30	0	99	0	1	30	137.6	-15.0	38	N/A	0	0	0.0	0.0
U /	N/A	N/A	15.83	56	0	99	0	1	30	N/A	N/A	N/A	N/A	0	0	0.0	0.0
C- /3.9	12.5	1.05	16.86	392	0	99	0	1	30	146.4	-14.8	47	N/A	0	0	0.0	0.0
C- /3.9	12.5	1.05	16.71	116	0	99	0	1	30	145.3	-14.8	45	N/A	0	0	0.0	0.0
C /5.4	12.3	0.96	6.44	N/A	4	95	0	1	84	35.0	-26.1	39	6	0	0	5.8	0.0
C /5.3	12.3	0.96	6.71	N/A	4	95	0	1	84	36.3	-26.2	43	6	0	0	0.0	0.0
B- /7.0	12.4	0.96	6.46	22	4	95	0	1	84	40.0	-26.0	51	6	0	0	0.0	0.0
C /5.3	12.4	0.97	6.63	N/A	4	95	0	1	84	37.4	-26.3	44	6	0	0	0.0	0.0
C+ /6.8	11.5	1.08	15.82	18	1	98	0	1	39	124.7	-18.9	33	7	0	0	5.8	0.0
C+ /6.7	11.5	1.08	15.92	8	1	98	0	1	39	128.2	-18.9	37	7	0	0	0.0	0.0
C+ /6.9	11.5	1.08	15.83	285	1	98	0	1	39	132.1	-18.8	43	7	0	0	0.0	0.0
C+ /6.7	11.5	1.08	15.79	2	1	98	0	1	39	122.2	-19.1	32	7	0	0	0.0	0.0
C+ /6.7	11.5	1.08	15.85	50	1	98	0	1	39	130.4	-18.8	39	7	0	0	0.0	0.0
C+ /6.7	11.6	1.08	15.85	13	1	98	0	1	39	129.4	-18.8	38	7	0	0	0.0	0.0
D+ /2.5	15.7	1.39	19.88	128	5	94	0	1	36	144.4	-20.9	12	2	0	0	5.8	0.0
D+ /2.6	15.7	1.40	20.57	88	5	94	0	1	36	147.8	-20.8	14	2	0	0	0.0	0.0
D+ /2.6	15.7	1.13	21.01	244	5	94	0	1	36	152.3	-20.7	59	2	0	0	0.0	0.0
D+ /2.3	15.7	1.40	18.89	4	5	94	0	1	36	141.6	-21.0	11	2	0	0	0.0	0.0
D+ /2.6	15.7	1.39	21.07	219	5	94	0	1	36	150.8	-20.7	15	2	0	0	0.0	0.0
D+ /2.6	15.7	1.40	20.77	71	5	94	0	1	36	149.5	-20.8	14	2	0	0	0.0	0.0
C /4.5	11.0	1.00	6.97	16	0	99	0	1	49	106.1	-11.0	47	5	0	0	5.8	0.0
C /4.5	10.9	1.00	7.27	10	0	99	0	1	49	108.7	-10.8	51	5	0	0	0.0	0.0
C+ /6.6	10.9	1.00	7.56	57	0	99	0	1	49	114.6	-10.8	60	5	0	0	0.0	0.0
C- /4.2	11.0	1.01	6.54	2	0	99	0	1	49	103.4	-11.0	44	5	0	0	0.0	0.0
C /4.6	11.0	1.00	7.58	23	0	99	0	1	49	111.4	-10.8	53	5	0	0	0.0	0.0
C /4.6	11.0	1.00	7.43	7	0	99	0	1	49	109.8	-10.8	52	5	0	0	0.0	0.0
C /4.7	11.3	1.06	12.34	135	2	97	0	1	16	116.3	-20.7	32	N/A	0	0	5.8	0.0
C /4.7	11.4	1.07	12.49	97	2	97	0	1	16	119.3	-20.5	35	N/A	0	0	0.0	0.0
C /4.6	11.3	1.06	12.41	563	2	97	0	1	16	123.4	-20.4	39	N/A	0	0	0.0	0.0
C /4.7	11.3	1.06	12.18	3	2	97	0	1	16	113.7	-20.7	31	N/A	0	0	0.0	0.0
C /4.6	11.3	1.07	12.46	397	2	97	0	1	16	121.4	-20.5	37	N/A	0	0	0.0	0.0
C /4.6	11.3	1.07	12.41	70	2	97	0	1	16	120.5	-20.5	36	N/A	0	0	0.0	0.0
C- /3.2	13.7	1.10	9.04	89	2	97	0	1	22	108.5	-12.4	4	13	0	0	5.8	0.0
C- /3.4	13.7	1.10	9.62	87	2	97	0	1	22	111.3	-12.2	5	13	0	0	0.0	0.0
C- /3.5	13.7	1.10	10.25	317	2	97	0	1	22	N/A	N/A	5	13	0	0	0.0	0.0
C- /3.1	13.7	1.10	8.44	1	2	97	0	1	22	105.6	-12.4	4	13	0	0	0.0	0.0

						PERFORMANCE							
	99 Pct = Best 0 Pct = Worst			Overall		Perfor-	Total Return % through 2/28/17			Annualized		Incl. in Returns	
Fund Type	Fund Name	Ticker Symbol	Investment Rating	Phone		mance Rating/Pts	3 Mo	6 Mo	1Yr / Pct	3Yr / Pct	5Yr / Pct	Dividend Yield	Expense Ratio
AG	MassMutual Select Growth Opps R5	MGRSX	D	(800) 542-6767		C- / 4.0	8.10	4.21	14.51 /28	3.86 /41	11.09 /67	0.00	0.84
AG	MassMutual Select Growth Opps Svc	MAGYX	D	(800) 542-6767		C- / 3.9	8.07	3.99	14.27 /27	3.74 /40	10.94 /65	0.00	0.94
GR	MassMutual Select Lg Cap Val A	MMLAX	C-	(800) 542-6767		C+ / 6.3	7.43	10.99	26.98 /79	5.55 /60	9.40 /54	1.81	1.22
GR	MassMutual Select Lg Cap Val Adm	MLVLX	C	(800) 542-6767		B- / 7.4	7.41	11.11	27.26 /80	5.80 /63	9.67 /56	2.17	0.97
GI	MassMutual Select Lg Cap Val I	MLVZX	A-	(800) 542-6767		B / 7.7	7.60	11.31	27.66 /81	6.25 /66	10.05 /59	2.47	0.67
GR	MassMutual Select Lg Cap Val R3	MLVNX	C-	(800) 542-6767		B- / 7.2	7.50	11.00	26.98 /79	5.40 /59	9.20 /52	1.73	1.37
GR	MassMutual Select Lg Cap Val R5	MLVSX	C	(800) 542-6767		B / 7.6	7.62	11.32	27.65 /81	6.00 /64	9.89 /57	2.36	0.77
GR	MassMutual Select Lg Cap Val Svc	MMLYX	C	(800) 542-6767		B- / 7.5	7.56	11.25	27.51 /81	5.93 /64	9.81 /57	2.07	0.87
MC	MassMutual Select Mid Cap Val A	MLUAX	C+	(800) 542-6767		B- / 7.5	4.59	11.91	31.83 /90	7.44 /75	11.73 /72	0.85	1.39
MC	MassMutual Select Mid Cap Val Adm	MLULX	B	(800) 542-6767		B+ / 8.7	4.60	12.04	32.20 /90	7.70 /77	12.00 /74	1.22	1.14
MC	MassMutual Select Mid Cap Val I	MLUZX	B	(800) 542-6767		B+ / 8.9	4.70	12.20	32.45 /91	8.02 /79	12.36 /78	1.40	0.84
MC	MassMutual Select Mid Cap Val R3	MLUNX	B-	(800) 542-6767		B+ / 8.4	4.59	11.82	31.70 /89	7.29 /74	11.50 /70	0.80	1.54
MC	MassMutual Select Mid Cap Val R5	MLUSX	B	(800) 542-6767		B+ / 8.8	4.66	12.19	32.41 /91	7.90 /78	12.25 /77	1.31	0.94
MC	MassMutual Select Mid Cap Val Svc	MLUYX	B-	(800) 542-6767		B+ / 8.8	4.66	12.06	32.22 /90	7.81 /78	12.14 /75	1.17	1.04
MC	MassMutual Select Mid Cp GE II A	MEFAX	C	(800) 542-6767		C+ / 6.6	6.73	6.98	21.38 /59	8.33 /82	13.15 /85	0.00	1.30
MC	MassMutual Select Mid Cp GE II Adm	MMELX	B-	(800) 542-6767		B / 7.7	6.75	7.05	21.61 /60	8.59 /84	13.42 /88	0.00	1.05
MC	MassMutual Select Mid Cp GE II I	MEFZX	B-	(800) 542-6767		B / 8.0	6.87	7.26	21.98 /62	8.93 /86	13.81 /92	0.16	0.75
MC	MassMutual Select Mid Cp GE II R3	MEFNX	C+	(800) 542-6767		B- / 7.4	6.67	6.87	21.13 /58	8.17 /80	12.90 /83	0.00	1.45
MC	MassMutual Select Mid Cp GE II R4	MEFFX	U	(800) 542-6767		U /	6.76	7.01	21.44 /59	--	--	0.00	1.20
MC	MassMutual Select Mid Cp GE II R5	MGRFX	B-	(800) 542-6767		B / 7.9	6.87	7.21	21.89 /62	8.84 /86	13.68 /90	0.06	0.85
MC	MassMutual Select Mid Cp GE II Svc	MEFYX	B-	(800) 542-6767		B / 7.8	6.78	7.18	21.75 /61	8.71 /85	13.56 /89	0.00	0.95
GR	MassMutual Select MSCI EAFE Itl A	MKRAX	E+	(800) 542-6767		E+ / 0.7	7.13	4.15	15.34 /31	-1.31 / 8	--	4.36	0.89
GR	MassMutual Select MSCI EAFE Itl	MKRYX	D-	(800) 542-6767		D- / 1.2	7.18	4.38	15.68 /33	-1.05 / 9	--	4.84	0.64
GR	MassMutual Select MSCI EAFE Itl I	MKRZX	D-	(800) 542-6767		D- / 1.3	7.24	4.54	16.12 /35	-0.71 /10	--	5.16	0.29
GR	MassMutual Select MSCI EAFE Itl R3	MKRTX	U	(800) 542-6767		U /	7.03	4.03	15.18 /31	--	--	4.69	1.04
GR	MassMutual Select MSCI EAFE Itl R4	MKRFX	U	(800) 542-6767		U /	7.11	4.21	15.45 /32	--	--	4.86	0.79
GR	MassMutual Select MSCI EAFE Itl R5	MKRIX	D-	(800) 542-6767		D- / 1.3	7.33	4.45	16.01 /34	-0.78 /10	--	5.07	0.39
GR	MassMutual Select MSCI EAFE Itl	MKRSX	D-	(800) 542-6767		D- / 1.2	7.20	4.40	15.80 /33	-0.95 /10	--	4.95	0.54
FO	MassMutual Select Overseas A	MOSAX	D-	(800) 542-6767		E+ / 0.8	7.45	6.34	17.81 /42	-1.06 / 9	5.00 /21	1.54	1.48
FO	MassMutual Select Overseas Admin	MOSLX	D-	(800) 542-6767		D- / 1.4	7.58	6.62	18.20 /44	-0.77 /10	5.25 /23	1.86	1.23
FO	MassMutual Select Overseas I	MOSZX	D-	(800) 542-6767		D- / 1.5	7.53	6.57	18.36 /44	-0.52 /11	5.57 /25	2.16	0.93
FO	MassMutual Select Overseas R3	MOSNX	D-	(800) 542-6767		D- / 1.3	7.45	6.33	17.72 /42	-1.22 / 9	4.76 /20	1.60	1.63
FO	MassMutual Select Overseas R5	MOSSX	D-	(800) 542-6767		D- / 1.5	7.53	6.57	18.16 /44	-0.62 /11	5.39 /24	2.05	1.03
FO	MassMutual Select Overseas Svc	MOSYX	D-	(800) 542-6767		D- / 1.5	7.46	6.50	18.14 /43	-0.70 /10	5.33 /24	1.96	1.13
SC	MassMutual Select Russ 2K SCI A	MCJAX	C+	(800) 542-6767		B- / 7.4	5.02	12.28	35.39 /94	6.35 /67	--	0.83	0.89
SC	MassMutual Select Russ 2K SCI Adm	MCJYX	B-	(800) 542-6767		B+ / 8.6	5.13	12.35	35.59 /95	6.61 /69	--	1.07	0.64
SC	MassMutual Select Russ 2K SCI I	MCJZX	B	(800) 542-6767		B+ / 8.9	5.17	12.61	36.16 /95	6.98 /72	--	1.34	0.29
SC	MassMutual Select Russ 2K SCI R3	MCJTX	U	(800) 542-6767		U /	4.98	12.10	35.05 /94	--	--	0.90	1.04
SC	MassMutual Select Russ 2K SCI R4	MCJFX	U	(800) 542-6767		U /	5.10	12.29	35.46 /94	--	--	1.02	0.79
SC	MassMutual Select Russ 2K SCI R5	MCJIX	B	(800) 542-6767		B+ / 8.8	5.17	12.53	36.06 /95	6.90 /71	--	1.27	0.39
SC	MassMutual Select Russ 2K SCI Svc	MCJSX	B-	(800) 542-6767		B+ / 8.7	5.09	12.41	35.84 /95	6.70 /70	--	1.18	0.54
SC	MassMutual Select Small Cap GE A	MMGEX	E	(800) 542-6767		C / 4.7	5.82	9.25	28.19 /82	3.46 /37	11.27 /68	0.00	1.41
SC	MassMutual Select Small Cap GE	MSGLX	D-	(800) 542-6767		C+ / 6.1	5.78	9.35	28.35 /82	3.71 /39	11.53 /70	0.00	1.16
SC	MassMutual Select Small Cap GE I	MSGZX	D-	(800) 542-6767		C+ / 6.4	5.92	9.53	28.92 /84	4.04 /43	11.91 /73	0.00	0.86
SC	MassMutual Select Small Cap GE R3	MSGNX	E+	(800) 542-6767		C+ / 5.8	5.73	9.08	28.00 /82	3.30 /35	11.02 /66	0.00	1.56
SC	MassMutual Select Small Cap GE R5	MSGSX	D-	(800) 542-6767		C+ / 6.3	5.90	9.47	28.70 /83	3.94 /42	11.82 /73	0.00	0.96
SC	MassMutual Select Small Cap GE	MSCYX	D-	(800) 542-6767		C+ / 6.2	5.87	9.43	28.64 /83	3.83 /41	11.69 /71	0.00	1.06
SC	MassMutual Select Small Co Val A	MMYAX	D+	(800) 542-6767		B / 8.0	5.96	15.01	36.27 /95	6.54 /69	11.19 /67	0.45	1.49
SC	MassMutual Select Small Co Val Adm	MMYLX	C-	(800) 542-6767		A- / 9.1	6.01	15.20	36.66 /96	6.81 /71	11.48 /70	0.75	1.24
SC	MassMutual Select Small Co Val I	MSVZX	C	(800) 542-6767		A / 9.3	6.11	15.34	37.00 /96	7.12 /73	11.85 /73	1.00	0.94
SC	MassMutual Select Small Co Val R3	MSVNX	C-	(800) 542-6767		B+ / 8.9	5.85	14.91	36.07 /95	6.37 /67	10.95 /65	0.57	1.64
SC	MassMutual Select Small Co Val R5	MSVSX	C	(800) 542-6767		A- / 9.2	6.08	15.27	36.94 /96	7.01 /72	11.68 /71	0.91	1.04

● Denotes fund is closed to new investors
* Denotes fund is included in Section II

RISK			NET ASSETS		ASSET					BULL / BEAR		FUND MANAGER		MINIMUMS		LOADS	
	3 Year		NAV						Portfolio	Last Bull	Last Bear	Manager	Manager	Initial	Additional	Front	Back
Risk	Standard		As of	Total	Cash	Stocks	Bonds	Other	Turnover	Market	Market	Quality	Tenure	Purch.	Purch.	End	End
Rating/Pts	Deviation	Beta	2/28/17	$(Mil)	%	%	%	%	Ratio	Return	Return	Pct	(Years)	$	$	Load	Load
C- / 3.5	13.7	1.10	10.17	183	2	97	0	1	22	113.7	-12.1	5	13	0	0	0.0	0.0
C- / 3.4	13.7	1.10	9.92	129	2	97	0	1	22	112.3	-12.2	5	13	0	0	0.0	0.0
C- / 3.2	10.8	0.98	7.49	27	3	96	0	1	8	90.2	-20.3	19	5	0	0	5.8	0.0
C- / 3.2	10.7	0.98	7.50	13	3	96	0	1	8	92.6	-20.1	21	5	0	0	0.0	0.0
B- / 7.0	10.8	0.98	7.50	49	3	96	0	1	8	96.3	-20.0	25	5	0	0	0.0	0.0
C- / 3.2	10.7	0.98	7.33	N/A	3	96	0	1	8	88.1	-20.3	18	5	0	0	0.0	0.0
C- / 3.2	10.8	0.98	7.52	98	3	96	0	1	8	94.9	-20.0	23	5	0	0	0.0	0.0
C- / 3.2	10.8	0.98	7.56	3	3	96	0	1	8	94.2	-20.1	22	5	0	0	0.0	0.0
C / 4.3	12.3	0.99	14.78	2	2	97	0	1	96	117.1	-22.0	50	8	0	0	5.8	0.0
C / 4.3	12.3	0.99	14.97	1	2	97	0	1	96	120.1	-22.1	53	8	0	0	0.0	0.0
C- / 4.1	12.3	0.99	14.71	102	2	97	0	1	96	N/A	N/A	57	8	0	0	0.0	0.0
C- / 4.2	12.3	0.99	14.65	N/A	2	97	0	1	96	114.6	-22.1	48	8	0	0	0.0	0.0
C- / 4.2	12.3	0.99	14.81	8	2	97	0	1	96	122.6	-21.8	56	8	0	0	0.0	0.0
C- / 4.2	12.2	0.98	14.77	2	2	97	0	1	96	121.3	-21.8	55	8	0	0	0.0	0.0
C / 4.7	11.9	0.92	17.14	277	5	94	0	1	36	127.1	-20.4	69	N/A	0	0	5.8	0.0
C / 4.8	11.9	0.92	18.33	327	5	94	0	1	36	130.1	-20.3	71	N/A	0	0	0.0	0.0
C / 4.9	11.9	0.92	19.61	2,004	5	94	0	1	36	134.4	-20.2	74	N/A	0	0	0.0	0.0
C / 4.5	11.9	0.92	15.99	19	5	94	0	1	36	124.3	-20.5	67	N/A	0	0	0.0	0.0
U /	N/A	N/A	17.21	70	5	94	0	1	36	N/A	N/A	N/A	N/A	0	0	0.0	0.0
C / 4.9	11.9	0.92	19.47	785	5	94	0	1	36	133.0	-20.2	N/A	N/A	0	0	0.0	0.0
C / 4.9	11.9	0.92	19.07	230	5	94	0	1	36	131.6	-20.2	73	N/A	0	0	0.0	0.0
C / 5.5	11.4	0.90	11.55	16	2	97	0	1	26	N/A	N/A	2	5	0	0	5.8	0.0
C / 5.4	11.4	0.90	11.57	41	2	97	0	1	26	N/A	N/A	2	5	0	0	0.0	0.0
C / 5.4	11.4	0.90	11.62	123	2	97	0	1	26	N/A	N/A	2	5	0	0	0.0	0.0
U /	N/A	N/A	11.46	30	2	97	0	1	26	N/A	N/A	N/A	6	0	0	0.0	0.0
U /	N/A	N/A	11.49	38	2	97	0	1	26	N/A	N/A	N/A	4	0	0	0.0	0.0
C / 5.4	11.4	0.90	11.62	11	2	97	0	1	26	N/A	N/A	2	5	0	0	0.0	0.0
C / 5.4	11.4	0.90	11.58	23	2	97	0	1	26	N/A	N/A	2	5	0	0	0.0	0.0
C / 5.5	12.1	0.97	8.05	52	0	99	0	1	38	51.1	-24.2	63	16	0	0	5.8	0.0
C / 5.5	12.1	0.97	8.22	37	0	99	0	1	38	53.1	-24.0	67	16	0	0	0.0	0.0
C / 5.4	12.1	0.97	8.16	323	0	99	0	1	38	55.8	-23.9	70	16	0	0	0.0	0.0
C / 5.5	12.1	0.97	8.00	2	0	99	0	1	38	49.4	-24.3	61	16	0	0	0.0	0.0
C / 5.5	12.1	0.97	8.19	135	0	99	0	1	38	54.2	-24.0	69	16	0	0	0.0	0.0
C / 5.5	12.1	0.97	8.15	44	0	99	0	1	38	53.6	-24.1	68	16	0	0	0.0	0.0
C- / 4.2	15.8	1.00	12.95	23	0	98	0	2	37	N/A	N/A	68	5	0	0	5.8	0.0
C- / 4.2	15.8	1.00	13.01	46	0	98	0	2	37	N/A	N/A	71	5	0	0	0.0	0.0
C- / 4.2	15.8	1.00	13.07	147	0	98	0	2	37	N/A	N/A	74	5	0	0	0.0	0.0
U /	N/A	N/A	12.86	31	0	98	0	2	37	N/A	N/A	N/A	5	0	0	0.0	0.0
U /	N/A	N/A	12.91	40	0	98	0	2	37	N/A	N/A	N/A	5	0	0	0.0	0.0
C- / 4.2	15.8	1.00	13.07	14	0	98	0	2	37	N/A	N/A	74	5	0	0	0.0	0.0
C- / 4.2	15.8	1.00	12.98	18	0	98	0	2	37	N/A	N/A	72	5	0	0	0.0	0.0
E / 0.4	15.6	0.94	11.46	36	0	99	0	1	85	114.1	-27.4	36	16	0	0	5.8	0.0
E+ / 0.6	15.6	0.94	12.63	29	0	99	0	1	85	116.8	-27.2	39	16	0	0	0.0	0.0
E+ / 0.8	15.6	0.94	14.13	289	0	99	0	1	85	120.9	-27.1	43	16	0	0	0.0	0.0
E / 0.3	15.6	0.95	10.33	2	0	99	0	1	85	111.4	-27.4	33	16	0	0	0.0	0.0
E+ / 0.8	15.6	0.94	13.99	125	0	99	0	1	85	119.8	-27.2	42	16	0	0	0.0	0.0
E+ / 0.7	15.6	0.94	13.34	34	0	99	0	1	85	118.3	-27.2	40	16	0	0	0.0	0.0
D- / 1.3	14.3	0.89	12.25	26	2	97	0	1	60	114.2	-24.3	77	3	0	0	5.8	0.0
D- / 1.3	14.3	0.89	12.59	16	2	97	0	1	60	117.3	-24.3	79	3	0	0	0.0	0.0
D- / 1.3	14.3	0.89	12.78	134	2	97	0	1	60	121.1	-24.1	80	3	0	0	0.0	0.0
D- / 1.2	14.3	0.89	11.53	N/A	2	97	0	1	60	111.8	-24.5	75	3	0	0	0.0	0.0
D- / 1.3	14.3	0.89	12.84	116	2	97	0	1	60	119.6	-24.2	80	3	0	0	0.0	0.0

Data as of February 28, 2017

Fund Type	Fund Name	Ticker Symbol	Overall Investment Rating	Phone	Perfor-mance Rating/Pts	Total Return % through 2/28/17					Incl. in Returns	
	99 Pct = Best 0 Pct = Worst					3 Mo	6 Mo	1Yr / Pct	Annualized 3Yr / Pct	5Yr / Pct	Dividend Yield	Expense Ratio
SC	MassMutual Select Small Co Val Svc	MMVYX	C	(800) 542-6767	A- / 9.1	5.98	15.22	36.73 /96	6.90 /71	11.59 /71	0.80	1.14
IN	Matisse Discounted CE Strategy A	MDCAX	C+	(800) 773-3863	C+ / 6.5	8.23	6.47	29.44 /85	6.12 /65	--	2.92	3.52
IN	Matisse Discounted CE Strategy Inst	MDCEX	B-	(800) 773-3863	B / 7.7	8.39	6.59	29.84 /86	6.40 /68	--	3.11	3.27
GI	Matrix Advisor Value Fund	MAVFX	B	(800) 366-6223	B / 7.6	4.50	9.05	30.08 /87	6.87 /71	11.15 /67	2.32	1.16
GI	Matthew 25 Fund	MXXVX	A-	(888) 625-3863	A+ / 9.8	8.77	24.95	44.67 /98	8.33 /82	14.32 /95	0.82	1.06
FO	● Matthews Asia Dividend Fund Instl	MIPIX	C+	(800) 789-2742	C / 4.8	4.41	0.64	17.73 /42	5.85 /63	7.34 /37	1.90	0.93
FO	Matthews Asia Dividend Fund Inv	MAPIX	C	(800) 789-2742	C / 4.7	4.32	0.60	17.58 /41	5.73 /62	7.21 /36	1.78	1.06
FO	Matthews Asia Focus Institutional	MIFSX	D+	(800) 789-2742	D+ / 2.9	7.13	1.34	17.93 /43	1.81 /23	--	1.46	1.91
FO	Matthews Asia Focus Investor	MAFSX	D+	(800) 789-2742	D+ / 2.7	7.02	1.22	17.69 /41	1.53 /21	--	1.35	2.07
FO	Matthews Asia Growth Fund Inst	MIAPX	D+	(800) 789-2742	D+ / 2.6	4.64	-0.44	13.13 /22	3.13 /33	6.41 /31	1.24	0.91
FO	Matthews Asia Growth Fund Inv	MPACX	D	(800) 789-2742	D+ / 2.5	4.56	-0.51	12.95 /21	2.93 /31	6.20 /30	1.05	1.11
TC	Matthews Asia Innovators Inst	MITEX	D	(800) 789-2742	C / 4.3	8.82	1.49	15.55 /32	4.34 /47	--	0.00	0.97
TC	Matthews Asia Innovators Investor	MATFX	D	(800) 789-2742	C- / 4.1	8.76	1.41	15.29 /31	4.14 /45	9.81 /57	0.00	1.18
CV	Matthews Asian Growth & Income	MICSX	D	(800) 789-2742	D / 1.8	4.72	-0.72	12.37 /19	1.27 /20	4.60 /19	2.98	0.92
CV	Matthews Asian Growth & Income Inv	MACSX	D	(800) 789-2742	D / 1.7	4.64	-0.79	12.18 /19	1.09 /19	4.43 /18	2.83	1.09
FO	Matthews Asian Small Companies	MISMX	D-	(800) 789-2742	D / 1.6	3.44	-0.01	13.07 /22	1.33 /20	--	0.66	1.30
FO	Matthews Asian Small Companies Inv	MSMLX	D-	(800) 789-2742	D- / 1.5	3.37	-0.17	12.82 /21	1.08 /19	4.12 /16	0.40	1.48
FO	Matthews China Dividend Fund Instl	MICDX	C+	(800) 789-2742	C+ / 6.9	1.25	2.92	24.42 /71	8.39 /82	9.26 /53	2.03	1.00
FO	Matthews China Dividend Fund Inv	MCDFX	C+	(800) 789-2742	C+ / 6.8	1.24	2.91	24.19 /71	8.24 /81	9.06 /51	1.86	1.19
FO	Matthews China Fund Institutional	MICFX	D	(800) 789-2742	C+ / 6.8	6.13	11.00	31.87 /90	3.75 /40	2.31 / 9	1.46	0.99
FO	Matthews China Investor	MCHFX	D	(800) 789-2742	C+ / 6.7	6.15	10.95	31.80 /90	3.63 /38	2.16 / 8	1.33	1.14
FO	Matthews China Small Companies	MCSMX	D	(800) 789-2742	C- / 3.6	5.13	4.32	21.46 /60	2.83 /30	6.33 /30	0.30	2.10
EM	Matthews Emerging Asia Inst	MIASX	A+	(800) 789-2742	B / 8.0	4.48	3.46	27.02 /79	9.75 /92	--	1.13	1.57
EM	Matthews Emerging Asia Investor	MEASX	A+	(800) 789-2742	B / 7.8	4.47	3.36	26.78 /79	9.51 /90	--	0.95	1.75
FO	Matthews India Fund Institutional	MIDNX	A-	(800) 789-2742	A+ / 9.9	8.06	-0.03	24.44 /71	21.17 /99	12.08 /75	0.00	0.90
FO	Matthews India Fund Inv	MINDX	A-	(800) 789-2742	A+ / 9.9	8.06	-0.10	24.26 /71	20.97 /99	11.88 /73	0.00	1.11
FO	● Matthews Japan Fund Institutional	MIJFX	C+	(800) 789-2742	C+ / 6.1	4.30	2.91	13.83 /25	8.39 /82	11.59 /71	0.94	0.87
FO	● Matthews Japan Fund Inv	MJFOX	C+	(800) 789-2742	C+ / 6.0	4.24	2.80	13.66 /24	8.25 /81	11.45 /69	0.83	0.99
FO	Matthews Korea Fund Institutional	MIKOX	C+	(800) 789-2742	C+ / 5.9	10.81	2.03	16.21 /35	6.39 /67	8.38 /45	1.46	0.93
FO	Matthews Korea Fund Inv	MAKOX	C+	(800) 789-2742	C+ / 6.0	11.08	2.22	16.32 /36	6.31 /67	8.27 /44	1.31	1.10
FO	Matthews Pacific Tiger Fund Instl	MIPTX	C-	(800) 789-2742	C+ / 5.6	6.10	-1.57	19.69 /50	6.74 /70	6.21 /30	0.68	0.91
FO	Matthews Pacific Tiger Fund Inv	MAPTX	C-	(800) 789-2742	C / 5.4	6.07	-1.64	19.51 /49	6.55 /69	6.03 /29	0.50	1.09
IN	MD Sass Equity Income Plus Inst	MDEIX	C-	(855) 637-3863	C- / 3.4	4.91	5.54	12.27 /19	3.65 /39	--	1.07	1.03
IN	MD Sass Equity Income Plus Inv	MDEPX	C-	(855) 637-3863	C- / 3.1	4.73	5.26	11.79 /17	3.26 /34	--	0.82	1.38
AG	Meeder Aggressive Growth Retail	FLAGX	C	(800) 325-3539	C+ / 6.0	3.64	7.98	19.76 /51	6.08 /65	10.25 /60	0.85	1.68
GR	Meeder Balanced Retail	FLDFX	C	(800) 325-3539	C- / 3.6	5.07	4.78	13.07 /22	3.89 /42	6.99 /35	1.07	1.73
IN	Meeder Dividend Opportunities Rtl	FLDOX	U	(800) 325-3539	U /	5.23	8.02	23.19 /67	--	--	1.49	1.85
GR	Meeder Dynamic Growth Retail	FLDGX	C+	(800) 325-3539	C+ / 6.6	7.16	7.77	20.10 /53	6.46 /68	10.71 /63	0.92	1.63
GR	Meeder Global Opportunities Retail	FLFGX	D	(800) 325-3539	C- / 3.2	6.35	5.35	17.72 /42	1.83 /23	6.23 /30	1.09	1.72
UT	Meeder Infrastructure Retail	FLRUX	E	(800) 325-3539	C- / 3.6	3.17	2.76	23.76 /69	2.32 /26	7.15 /36	0.97	2.01
GR	Meeder Muirfield Retail	FLMFX	C+	(800) 325-3539	C+ / 5.7	6.49	7.50	17.70 /41	5.51 /60	9.73 /56	0.69	1.45
IX	Meeder Quantex Retail	FLCGX	C	(800) 325-3539	B- / 7.5	2.35	7.07	30.55 /87	7.17 /73	13.14 /85	0.46	1.75
GL	Meeder Spectrum Retail	FLSPX	U	(800) 325-3539	U /	6.68	8.69	16.93 /38	--	--	0.18	2.25
GR	Meehan Focus Fund	MEFOX	C+	(866) 884-5968	C+ / 6.8	8.31	12.86	23.81 /69	4.84 /52	9.62 /56	1.27	1.02
EM	Mercer Emerging Markets Equity Y-3	MEMQX	C-	(800) 428-0980	C- / 3.8	8.98	5.44	27.08 /79	0.96 /18	--	1.94	1.00
GR	Merger Fund Institutional	MERIX	C-	(800) 343-8959	D- / 1.3	1.34	2.00	4.29 / 3	1.41 /20	--	0.89	1.57
GR	Merger Fund Investor	MERFX	C-	(800) 343-8959	D- / 1.2	1.28	1.87	3.95 / 3	1.11 /19	2.02 / 8	0.32	1.90
GR	Meridian Contrarian A	MFCAX	C+	(800) 446-6662	C+ / 5.9	3.39	9.31	27.97 /82	6.56 /69	--	0.00	1.60
GR	Meridian Contrarian Investor	MFCIX	B-	(800) 446-6662	B- / 7.1	3.44	9.46	28.31 /82	6.84 /71	--	0.00	1.35
GR	Meridian Contrarian Legacy	MVALX	C-	(800) 446-6662	B- / 7.2	3.49	9.54	28.56 /83	7.05 /72	12.20 /76	0.03	1.13
IN	Meridian Equity Income A	MRAEX	B	(800) 446-6662	B- / 7.0	5.62	8.76	28.45 /83	6.33 /67	--	0.43	1.64
IN	Meridian Equity Income Investor	MRIEX	B	(800) 446-6662	B- / 7.2	5.59	8.79	28.61 /83	6.54 /69	--	0.61	1.39

● Denotes fund is closed to new investors

* Denotes fund is included in Section II

RISK			NET ASSETS		ASSET				Portfolio Turnover Ratio	BULL / BEAR		FUND MANAGER		MINIMUMS		LOADS	
Risk Rating/Pts	3 Year		NAV As of 2/28/17	Total $(Mil)	Cash %	Stocks %	Bonds %	Other %		Last Bull Market Return	Last Bear Market Return	Manager Quality Pct	Manager Tenure (Years)	Initial Purch. $	Additional Purch. $	Front End Load	Back End Load
	Standard Deviation	Beta															
D- / 1.3	14.4	0.89	12.78	14	2	97	0	1	60	118.6	-24.2	79	3	0	0	0.0	0.0
C / 5.2	11.2	0.92	9.52	5	0	45	47	8	135	N/A	N/A	30	5	1,000	100	0.0	0.0
C / 5.3	11.2	0.92	10.20	115	0	45	47	8	135	N/A	N/A	33	5	25,000	100	5.8	0.0
C+ / 6.1	13.2	1.17	66.75	59	0	99	0	1	15	109.2	-26.0	14	21	1,000	100	0.0	1.0
C / 4.9	14.9	1.16	31.27	412	14	85	0	1	18	166.7	-16.0	27	22	10,000	100	0.0	2.0
C+ / 6.7	11.1	0.70	16.60	2,207	4	95	0	1	36	59.8	-13.4	97	6	3,000,000	100	0.0	0.0
C+ / 6.7	11.1	0.71	16.60	2,666	4	95	0	1	36	58.8	-13.6	96	6	2,500	100	0.0	0.0
C+ / 6.1	12.9	0.80	9.79	6	7	92	0	1	24	N/A	N/A	86	4	3,000,000	100	0.0	0.0
C+ / 6.1	12.9	0.81	9.77	5	7	92	0	1	24	N/A	N/A	85	4	2,500	100	0.0	0.0
C+ / 5.8	11.8	0.72	22.28	208	2	97	0	1	30	54.4	-17.3	91	10	3,000,000	100	0.0	0.0
C+ / 5.8	11.8	0.72	22.13	424	2	97	0	1	30	52.8	-17.3	90	10	2,500	100	0.0	0.0
C- / 3.5	15.7	1.08	11.29	18	4	95	0	1	73	N/A	N/A	7	11	3,000,000	100	0.0	0.0
C- / 3.4	15.7	1.07	11.24	87	4	95	0	1	73	82.5	-23.5	6	11	2,500	100	0.0	0.0
C+ / 5.6	10.9	0.79	15.95	922	4	87	0	9	16	39.4	-14.6	40	8	3,000,000	100	0.0	0.0
C+ / 5.7	10.9	0.78	15.96	1,701	4	87	0	9	16	38.2	-14.6	38	8	2,500	100	0.0	0.0
C / 5.3	12.7	0.70	20.27	182	5	94	0	1	48	N/A	N/A	83	9	3,000,000	100	0.0	2.0
C / 5.3	12.7	0.70	20.28	251	5	94	0	1	48	40.6	-21.7	82	9	2,500	100	0.0	2.0
C / 4.6	17.7	0.93	14.73	30	6	93	0	1	80	85.7	-19.0	99	5	3,000,000	100	0.0	0.0
C / 4.6	17.7	0.93	14.73	164	6	93	0	1	80	84.0	-19.2	99	5	2,500	100	0.0	0.0
D- / 1.5	21.6	1.07	17.55	17	0	99	0	1	66	35.1	-26.3	93	7	3,000,000	100	0.0	0.0
D- / 1.5	21.6	1.08	17.58	520	0	99	0	1	66	34.0	-26.3	93	7	2,500	100	0.0	0.0
C- / 3.8	20.0	0.99	9.05	17	6	93	0	1	72	61.3	N/A	90	2	2,500	100	0.0	2.0
B / 8.0	8.5	0.35	13.43	112	0	99	0	1	12	N/A	N/A	99	4	3,000,000	100	0.0	2.0
B- / 8.0	8.6	0.35	13.39	155	0	99	0	1	12	N/A	N/A	99	4	2,500	100	0.0	2.0
C / 4.9	17.3	0.52	28.32	565	3	96	0	1	10	85.9	-19.2	99	12	3,000,000	100	0.0	0.0
C / 4.9	17.4	0.52	28.19	1,013	3	96	0	1	10	84.1	-19.3	99	12	2,500	100	0.0	0.0
C+ / 6.6	13.0	0.60	19.93	1,316	3	96	0	1	24	76.7	-5.5	99	11	3,000,000	100	0.0	0.0
C+ / 6.6	13.0	0.60	19.89	1,723	3	96	0	1	24	75.5	-5.5	98	11	2,500	100	0.0	0.0
C+ / 5.9	14.4	0.70	5.86	14	1	98	0	1	20	77.5	-21.8	97	10	3,000,000	100	0.0	0.0
C+ / 5.9	14.3	0.70	5.84	156	1	98	0	1	20	76.6	-21.9	97	10	2,500	100	0.0	0.0
C / 4.6	13.7	0.78	24.91	4,429	3	96	0	1	13	57.1	-17.4	97	9	100,000	100	0.0	0.0
C / 4.6	13.8	0.78	24.93	2,521	3	96	0	1	13	55.7	-17.5	97	9	2,500	100	0.0	0.0
C+ / 6.7	6.7	0.57	10.89	64	0	100	0	0	64	N/A	N/A	46	4	1,000,000	25,000	0.0	0.0
C+ / 6.7	6.8	0.57	10.85	1	0	100	0	0	64	N/A	N/A	40	4	2,500	100	0.0	0.0
C / 4.6	10.9	0.98	10.56	34	0	0	0	100	283	96.0	-21.7	24	12	2,500	100	0.0	0.0
B- / 7.2	6.5	0.60	11.17	206	5	62	31	2	246	57.7	-14.1	44	11	2,500	100	0.0	0.0
U /	N/A	N/A	10.86	49	0	0	0	100	70	N/A	N/A	N/A	2	2,500	100	0.0	0.0
C / 5.4	10.4	0.98	10.25	100	9	90	0	1	245	100.7	-20.3	27	17	2,500	100	0.0	0.0
C- / 4.2	10.7	0.97	10.02	45	0	0	0	100	170	64.4	-23.3	4	11	2,500	100	0.0	0.0
E / 0.4	11.8	0.28	21.60	19	0	0	0	100	54	64.0	-15.8	55	22	2,500	100	0.0	0.0
C+ / 6.6	8.9	0.82	7.15	365	24	75	0	1	277	85.8	-19.8	35	12	2,500	100	0.0	0.0
C- / 3.4	14.1	1.15	33.80	74	16	80	2	2	87	133.7	-23.1	17	12	2,500	100	0.0	0.0
U /	N/A	N/A	10.81	115	0	0	0	100	161	N/A	N/A	N/A	2	2,500	100	0.0	0.0
C+ / 6.3	12.4	1.14	22.24	60	1	98	0	1	44	86.3	-15.1	6	18	5,000	100	0.0	0.0
C+ / 6.3	15.4	0.95	9.52	1,398	8	89	2	1	66	N/A	N/A	66	5	0	0	0.0	2.0
B / 8.7	2.9	0.22	15.67	1,388	37	42	20	1	157	N/A	N/A	64	10	1,000,000	500	0.0	0.0
B / 8.8	2.9	0.22	15.76	1,478	37	42	20	1	157	14.8	-4.1	60	10	2,000	0	0.0	0.0
C+ / 5.7	13.2	1.10	37.66	1	9	90	0	1	73	N/A	N/A	17	16	2,500	50	5.8	2.0
C+ / 5.7	13.2	1.10	38.03	3	9	90	0	1	73	N/A	N/A	19	16	2,500	50	0.0	2.0
D+ / 2.6	13.2	1.10	38.17	583	9	90	0	1	73	124.5	-20.6	21	16	1,000	50	0.0	2.0
C+ / 6.3	11.6	1.03	13.13	1	7	92	0	1	57	N/A	N/A	21	2	2,500	0	0.0	2.0
C+ / 6.3	11.6	1.03	13.19	N/A	7	92	0	1	57	N/A	N/A	23	2	1,000,000	0	0.0	2.0

Fund Type	Fund Name	Ticker Symbol	Overall Investment Rating	Phone	Performance Rating/Pts	3 Mo	6 Mo	1Yr / Pct	3Yr / Pct	5Yr / Pct	Dividend Yield	Expense Ratio
	99 Pct = Best							Total Return % through 2/28/17	Annualized		Incl. in Returns	
IN	Meridian Equity Income Legacy	MEIFX	C	(800) 446-6662	B- / 7.2	5.67	8.88	28.84 /84	6.66 /70	10.38 /61	0.76	1.29
MC	Meridian Growth A	MRAGX	C+	(800) 446-6662	C+ / 6.7	4.51	7.22	28.93 /84	8.00 /79	—	0.00	1.17
MC	Meridian Growth Institutional	MRRGX	U	(800) 446-6662	U /	4.59	7.41	29.30 /85	--	—	0.00	0.87
MC	Meridian Growth Investor	MRIGX	B	(800) 446-6662	B / 7.9	4.59	7.40	29.19 /85	8.41 /82	—	0.00	0.92
GR	Meridian Growth Legacy	MERDX	C+	(800) 446-6662	B / 8.0	4.59	7.40	29.33 /85	8.60 /84	10.86 /65	0.00	0.86
SC	Meridian Small Cap Growth A	MSGAX	B+	(800) 446-6662	B+ / 8.6	3.52	8.40	34.08 /93	10.66 /96	—	0.00	1.62
SC	Meridian Small Cap Growth C	MSGCX	U	(800) 446-6662	U /	3.31	7.95	33.07 /92	--	—	0.00	2.30
SC	Meridian Small Cap Growth Instl	MSGRX	U	(800) 446-6662	U /	3.55	8.53	34.52 /93	--	—	0.00	1.27
SC	Meridian Small Cap Growth Investor	MISGX	A-	(800) 446-6662	A / 9.5	3.49	8.48	34.30 /93	10.97 /97	—	0.00	1.32
SC	Meridian Small Cap Growth Legacy	MSGGX	A-	(800) 446-6662	A / 9.5	3.48	8.47	34.36 /93	11.05 /97	—	0.00	1.25
GR	Meritage Growth Equity Instl	MPGIX	A+	(855) 261-0104	A / 9.5	9.47	10.82	26.25 /77	10.38 /95	—	0.23	1.63
GR	Meritage Growth Equity Investor	MPGEX	A+	(855) 261-0104	A / 9.4	9.43	10.70	25.99 /76	10.11 /94	—	0.00	1.88
GR	Meritage Value Equity Institutional	MVEBX	B-	(855) 261-0104	C+ / 6.4	6.43	9.41	17.13 /39	6.51 /69	—	0.82	1.71
IN	Meritage Yield Focus Equity Inst	MPYIX	C+	(855) 261-0104	C / 4.5	7.02	6.34	18.48 /45	3.55 /38	—	2.97	1.64
IN	Meritage Yield Focus Equity Inv	MPYEX	C+	(855) 261-0104	C / 4.5	7.28	6.53	18.57 /45	3.40 /36	—	2.74	1.89
OT	Merk Abs Rtn Currency Inst	MAAIX	C-	(866) 637-5386	E / 0.5	-2.03	-1.18	3.49 / 3	-0.62 /11	0.38 / 5	0.00	1.05
OT	Merk Abs Rtn Currency Investor	MABFX	D+	(866) 637-5386	E / 0.5	-2.05	-1.31	3.31 / 3	-0.92 /10	0.10 / 5	0.00	1.30
FS	● Merk Hard Currency Inst	MHCIX	D	(866) 637-5386	E- / 0.1	1.08	-4.28	-2.19 / 1	-6.64 / 2	-4.23 / 2	0.00	1.05
FS	● Merk Hard Currency Investor	MERKX	D	(866) 637-5386	E- / 0.1	0.98	-4.42	-2.52 / 1	-6.91 / 1	-4.51 / 2	0.00	1.30
GL	MFS Absolute Return Fund R6	MRNVX	C-	(800) 225-2606	E+ / 0.9	1.48	0.50	4.45 / 3	0.35 /15	—	0.91	1.12
AG	MFS Aggressive Gr Alloc 529A	EAGTX	C-	(800) 225-2606	C- / 4.0	6.64	4.99	19.61 /50	4.79 /52	9.38 /54	0.86	1.24
AG	MFS Aggressive Gr Alloc 529B	EBAAX	C	(800) 225-2606	C / 4.5	6.46	4.61	18.73 /46	4.01 /43	8.55 /47	0.06	1.99
AG	MFS Aggressive Gr Alloc 529C	ECAAX	C	(800) 225-2606	C / 4.5	6.39	4.57	18.66 /46	4.01 /43	8.55 /47	0.17	1.99
AG	MFS Aggressive Gr Alloc A	MAAGX	C-	(800) 225-2606	C- / 4.0	6.63	5.00	19.64 /50	4.83 /52	9.42 /54	0.88	1.14
AG	MFS Aggressive Gr Alloc B	MBAGX	C	(800) 225-2606	C / 4.5	6.42	4.60	18.73 /46	4.04 /43	8.60 /47	0.19	1.89
AG	MFS Aggressive Gr Alloc C	MCAGX	C	(800) 225-2606	C / 4.6	6.44	4.65	18.79 /46	4.06 /44	8.60 /47	0.24	1.89
AG	MFS Aggressive Gr Alloc I	MIAGX	C+	(800) 225-2606	C / 5.5	6.70	5.14	19.94 /52	5.08 /55	9.69 /56	1.17	0.89
AG	MFS Aggressive Gr Alloc R1	MAAFX	C	(800) 225-2606	C / 4.6	6.44	4.62	18.77 /46	4.05 /44	8.60 /47	0.26	1.89
AG	MFS Aggressive Gr Alloc R2	MAWAX	C+	(800) 225-2606	C / 5.0	6.54	4.87	19.30 /49	4.57 /49	9.14 /52	0.70	1.39
AG	MFS Aggressive Gr Alloc R3	MAAHX	C+	(800) 225-2606	C / 5.2	6.62	5.02	19.66 /50	4.84 /52	9.43 /54	0.93	1.14
AG	MFS Aggressive Gr Alloc R4	MAALX	C+	(800) 225-2606	C / 5.5	6.68	5.15	19.96 /52	5.09 /55	9.71 /56	1.18	0.89
GR	MFS Blended Research Core Eq A	MUEAX	B+	(800) 225-2606	B- / 7.1	7.90	9.02	21.77 /61	8.65 /84	13.03 /84	0.87	0.89
GR	MFS Blended Research Core Eq B	MUSBX	B+	(800) 225-2606	B- / 7.5	7.70	8.61	20.86 /57	7.82 /78	12.17 /76	0.31	1.64
GR	MFS Blended Research Core Eq C	MUECX	B+	(800) 225-2606	B- / 7.5	7.72	8.59	20.85 /57	7.83 /78	12.17 /76	0.31	1.64
GR	MFS Blended Research Core Eq I	MUSEX	A-	(800) 225-2606	B+ / 8.3	7.99	9.14	22.07 /63	8.92 /86	13.31 /87	1.13	0.64
GR	MFS Blended Research Core Eq R1	MUERX	B+	(800) 225-2606	B- / 7.5	7.71	8.59	20.84 /57	7.83 /78	12.19 /76	0.30	1.64
GR	MFS Blended Research Core Eq R2	MUESX	B+	(800) 225-2606	B / 7.9	7.85	8.91	21.47 /60	8.38 /82	12.75 /81	0.76	1.14
GR	MFS Blended Research Core Eq R3	MUETX	A-	(800) 225-2606	B / 8.1	7.93	9.05	21.81 /61	8.65 /84	13.03 /84	0.93	0.89
GR	MFS Blended Research Core Eq R4	MUEUX	A-	(800) 225-2606	B+ / 8.3	7.94	9.14	22.03 /62	8.91 /86	13.31 /87	1.14	0.64
GI	MFS Blended Research Core Eq R6	MUEVX	A	(800) 225-2606	B+ / 8.4	8.00	9.24	22.22 /63	9.05 /87	—	1.23	0.52
GR	MFS Blended Research Growth Eqty	BRWVX	U	(800) 225-2606	U /	8.75	9.78	21.98 /62	--	—	0.38	5.71
FO	MFS Blended Research Intl Eqty R6	BRXVX	U	(800) 225-2606	U /	7.53	5.67	17.63 /41	--	—	0.54	3.34
MC	MFS Blended Research MC Eqty R6	BMSYX	U	(800) 225-2606	U /	6.04	9.24		--	—	0.00	N/A
SC	MFS Blended Research SC Eq Initial		C-	(800) 225-2606	B+ / 8.9	6.01	10.49	33.89 /93	7.75 /77	14.27 /95	1.07	0.54
SC	MFS Blended Research SC Eq		C-	(800) 225-2606	B+ / 8.7	5.99	10.40	33.62 /92	7.49 /75	14.00 /93	0.82	0.79
GR	MFS Blended Research SC Eqty R6	BRSYX	U	(800) 225-2606	U /	5.92	10.15	33.19 /92	--	—	0.31	2.50
GR	MFS Blended Research Value Eqty	BRUNX	U	(800) 225-2606	U /	7.29	11.31	27.51 /81	--	—	0.70	5.43
OT	● MFS Commodity Strategy Fund A	MCSAX	E	(800) 225-2606	E- / 0.0	1.89	5.26	15.28 /31	-12.27 / 0	-9.35 / 1	0.35	1.08
OT	● MFS Commodity Strategy Fund I	MCSIX	E	(800) 225-2606	E- / 0.1	1.80	5.34	15.37 /32	-12.06 / 0	-9.13 / 1	0.61	0.83
OT	MFS Commodity Strategy Fund R6	MCSRX	E	(800) 225-2606	E- / 0.1	1.80	5.34	15.37 /32	-12.09 / 0	—	0.61	0.83
AA	MFS Conservative Alloc 529A	ECLAX	C	(800) 225-2606	D / 1.7	3.51	1.46	9.87 /11	3.19 /34	5.03 /21	1.57	1.04
AA	MFS Conservative Alloc 529B	EBCAX	C	(800) 225-2606	D / 2.0	3.34	1.14	9.11 /10	2.41 /27	4.26 /17	0.95	1.79

● Denotes fund is closed to new investors
* Denotes fund is included in Section II

426

RISK Risk Rating/Pts	3 Year Standard Deviation	Beta	NET ASSETS NAV As of 2/28/17	Total $(Mil)	ASSET Cash %	Stocks %	Bonds %	Other %	Portfolio Turnover Ratio	BULL/BEAR Last Bull Market Return	Last Bear Market Return	FUND MANAGER Manager Quality Pct	Manager Tenure (Years)	MINIMUMS Initial Purch. $	Additional Purch. $	LOADS Front End Load	Back End Load
C- /4.1	11.6	1.03	13.18	48	7	92	0	1	57	95.6	-15.0	24	2	1,000	50	0.0	2.0
C /5.5	13.6	1.05	36.54	14	4	95	0	1	67	N/A	N/A	50	4	2,500	50	5.8	2.0
U /	N/A	N/A	37.28	64	4	95	0	1	67	N/A	N/A	N/A	4	1,000,000	0	0.0	2.0
C /5.5	13.6	1.04	37.04	70	4	95	0	1	67	N/A	N/A	55	4	1,000,000	0	0.0	2.0
C- /3.6	13.6	1.06	37.30	1,217	4	95	0	1	67	110.2	-19.1	42	4	1,000	50	0.0	2.0
C /5.3	14.6	0.86	13.81	78	12	87	0	1	62	N/A	N/A	94	4	2,500	50	5.8	2.0
U /	N/A	N/A	13.72	39	12	87	0	1	62	N/A	N/A	N/A	4	2,500	50	0.0	0.0
U /	N/A	N/A	13.99	110	12	87	0	1	62	N/A	N/A	N/A	4	1,000,000	0	0.0	2.0
C /5.3	14.6	0.86	13.94	390	12	87	0	1	62	N/A	N/A	95	4	1,000,000	0	0.0	2.0
C /5.3	14.6	0.86	13.96	61	12	87	0	1	62	N/A	N/A	95	4	1,000	50	0.0	2.0
C+ /6.7	10.7	0.98	13.26	20	9	90	0	1	73	N/A	N/A	73	N/A	100,000	1,000	0.0	0.0
C+ /6.7	10.7	0.98	13.19	N/A	9	90	0	1	73	N/A	N/A	71	N/A	2,500	100	0.0	0.0
B- /7.2	9.1	0.80	12.01	15	7	92	0	1	67	N/A	N/A	52	4	100,000	1,000	0.0	0.0
B- /7.5	9.9	0.84	10.49	27	20	79	0	1	99	N/A	N/A	15	4	100,000	1,000	0.0	0.0
B- /7.5	10.0	0.85	10.50	1	20	79	0	1	99	N/A	N/A	14	4	2,500	100	0.0	0.0
B /8.9	5.7	-0.09	9.18	14	11	0	88	1	59	3.5	-10.4	75	8	250,000	0	0.0	0.0
B /8.8	5.8	-0.09	9.06	22	11	0	88	1	59	2.0	-10.5	73	8	2,500	100	0.0	0.0
B- /7.5	7.7	-0.05	9.40	18	28	0	71	1	85	-16.3	-7.8	7	12	250,000	0	0.0	0.0
B- /7.4	7.7	-0.05	9.29	94	28	0	71	1	85	-17.6	-8.0	6	12	2,500	100	0.0	0.0
B+ /9.3	3.3	0.09	9.48	199	4	0	95	1	36	N/A	N/A	76	6	0	0	0.0	0.0
C+ /6.4	9.6	0.89	20.46	122	2	91	5	2	5	86.1	-19.0	21	15	250	0	5.8	0.0
C+ /6.5	9.6	0.89	20.09	5	2	91	5	2	5	78.6	-19.3	15	15	250	0	0.0	0.0
C+ /6.5	9.6	0.89	19.84	33	2	91	5	2	5	78.8	-19.3	15	15	250	0	0.0	0.0
C+ /6.4	9.5	0.89	20.59	750	2	91	5	2	5	86.5	-19.0	21	15	1,000	50	5.8	0.0
C+ /6.5	9.6	0.89	20.31	66	2	91	5	2	5	79.1	-19.3	15	15	1,000	50	0.0	0.0
C+ /6.5	9.5	0.89	20.12	277	2	91	5	2	5	79.1	-19.2	15	15	1,000	50	0.0	0.0
C+ /6.4	9.6	0.89	20.90	105	2	91	5	2	5	89.0	-18.9	23	15	0	0	0.0	0.0
C+ /6.5	9.6	0.89	19.84	18	2	91	5	2	5	79.1	-19.2	15	N/A	0	0	0.0	0.0
C+ /6.4	9.5	0.89	20.18	73	2	91	5	2	5	83.9	-19.1	19	14	0	0	0.0	0.0
C+ /6.4	9.5	0.89	20.43	141	2	91	5	2	5	86.5	-19.0	21	N/A	0	0	0.0	0.0
C+ /6.4	9.6	0.89	20.64	69	2	91	5	2	5	89.2	-18.9	24	N/A	0	0	0.0	0.0
C+ /6.7	10.2	0.97	25.05	271	0	99	0	1	43	124.8	-16.9	55	12	1,000	50	5.8	0.0
C+ /6.7	10.2	0.98	24.24	22	0	99	0	1	43	115.8	-17.1	44	12	1,000	50	0.0	0.0
C+ /6.6	10.2	0.97	23.90	80	0	99	0	1	43	115.7	-17.1	44	12	1,000	50	0.0	0.0
C+ /6.7	10.2	0.97	25.36	393	0	99	0	1	43	127.8	-16.8	58	12	0	0	0.0	0.0
C+ /6.6	10.1	0.97	24.01	14	0	99	0	1	43	115.9	-17.1	45	12	0	0	0.0	0.0
C+ /6.7	10.1	0.97	24.14	39	0	99	0	1	43	121.8	-17.0	52	12	0	0	0.0	0.0
C+ /6.7	10.2	0.98	24.96	116	0	99	0	1	43	124.7	-16.8	55	12	0	0	0.0	0.0
C+ /6.7	10.2	0.97	25.13	43	0	99	0	1	43	127.7	-16.8	58	12	0	0	0.0	0.0
C+ /6.7	10.2	0.97	25.39	208	0	99	0	1	43	N/A	N/A	60	12	0	0	0.0	0.0
U /	N/A	N/A	11.59	116	0	99	0	1	28	N/A	N/A	N/A	20	0	0	0.0	0.0
U /	N/A	N/A	10.34	178	0	99	0	1	64	N/A	N/A	N/A	2	0	0	0.0	0.0
U /	N/A	N/A	10.83	183	0	0	0	100	0	N/A	N/A	N/A	1	0	0	0.0	0.0
D- /1.4	13.8	0.86	13.59	29	0	98	0	2	78	146.0	-25.3	85	5	0	0	0.0	0.0
D- /1.3	13.8	0.86	13.27	75	0	98	0	2	78	142.8	-25.5	84	5	0	0	0.0	0.0
U /	N/A	N/A	12.08	45	0	0	0	100	47	N/A	N/A	N/A	N/A	0	0	0.0	0.0
U /	N/A	N/A	12.09	113	0	99	0	1	33	N/A	N/A	N/A	2	0	0	0.0	0.0
C- /4.0	13.1	0.26	6.03	N/A	15	0	84	1	32	-35.3	-21.0	0	7	1,000	50	5.8	0.0
C- /4.0	13.0	0.25	6.02	N/A	15	0	84	1	32	-34.4	-20.9	0	7	0	0	0.0	0.0
C- /4.0	13.0	0.25	6.02	566	15	0	84	1	32	N/A	N/A	0	7	0	0	0.0	0.0
B+ /9.1	4.6	0.69	14.95	103	20	36	43	1	5	39.9	-6.4	50	15	250	0	5.8	0.0
B+ /9.1	4.7	0.70	14.72	7	20	36	43	1	5	34.3	-6.7	38	15	250	0	0.0	0.0

Fund Type	Fund Name	Ticker Symbol	Overall Investment Rating	Phone	Performance Rating/Pts	3 Mo	6 Mo	1Yr / Pct	3Yr / Pct	5Yr / Pct	Dividend Yield	Expense Ratio
AA	MFS Conservative Alloc 529C	ECACX	C	(800) 225-2606	D / 2.0	3.29	1.15	9.09 /10	2.40 /27	4.25 /17	0.97	1.79
AA	MFS Conservative Alloc A	MACFX	C	(800) 225-2606	D / 1.7	3.50	1.53	9.92 /11	3.23 /34	5.08 /22	1.60	0.94
AA	MFS Conservative Alloc B	MACBX	C	(800) 225-2606	D / 2.0	3.30	1.13	9.08 /10	2.45 /27	4.29 /17	0.96	1.69
AA	MFS Conservative Alloc C	MACVX	C	(800) 225-2606	D / 2.0	3.33	1.15	9.10 /10	2.45 /27	4.29 /17	0.98	1.69
AA	MFS Conservative Alloc I	MACIX	C+	(800) 225-2606	D+ / 2.6	3.61	1.66	10.18 /12	3.49 /37	5.34 /24	1.92	0.69
AA	MFS Conservative Alloc R1	MACKX	C	(800) 225-2606	D / 2.0	3.31	1.15	9.12 /10	2.45 /27	4.30 /17	0.99	1.69
AA	MFS Conservative Alloc R2	MCARX	C	(800) 225-2606	D+ / 2.3	3.38	1.37	9.62 /11	2.97 /32	4.82 /20	1.49	1.19
AA	MFS Conservative Alloc R3	MACNX	C+	(800) 225-2606	D+ / 2.4	3.53	1.54	9.93 /11	3.23 /34	5.09 /22	1.70	0.94
AA	MFS Conservative Alloc R4	MACJX	C+	(800) 225-2606	D+ / 2.6	3.57	1.67	10.19 /12	3.49 /37	5.37 /24	1.93	0.69
GR	MFS Core Equity A	MRGAX	B-	(800) 225-2606	B- / 7.5	8.20	9.54	25.46 /75	8.57 /84	13.36 /87	0.52	1.07
GR	MFS Core Equity B	MRGBX	B-	(800) 225-2606	B / 7.9	7.97	9.10	24.48 /72	7.74 /77	12.51 /79	0.00	1.82
GR	MFS Core Equity C	MRGCX	B-	(800) 225-2606	B / 7.9	7.97	9.11	24.50 /72	7.75 /77	12.51 /79	0.00	1.82
GR	MFS Core Equity I	MRGRX	B+	(800) 225-2606	B+ / 8.7	8.25	9.63	25.74 /75	8.83 /86	13.63 /90	0.80	0.82
GR	MFS Core Equity R1	MRGGX	B-	(800) 225-2606	B / 7.9	7.98	9.07	24.46 /72	7.74 /77	12.49 /79	0.00	1.82
GR	MFS Core Equity R2	MRERX	B	(800) 225-2606	B+ / 8.3	8.12	9.36	25.12 /74	8.28 /81	13.07 /85	0.32	1.32
GR	MFS Core Equity R3	MRGHX	B	(800) 225-2606	B+ / 8.5	8.19	9.53	25.42 /75	8.56 /84	13.35 /87	0.54	1.07
GR	MFS Core Equity R4	MRGJX	B	(800) 225-2606	B+ / 8.7	8.24	9.65	25.76 /75	8.84 /86	13.64 /90	0.77	0.82
GI	MFS Core Equity R6	MRGKX	B+	(800) 225-2606	B+ / 8.8	8.28	9.71	25.91 /76	8.94 /86	--	0.84	0.72
AA	MFS Diversified Income Fund A	DIFAX	C+	(800) 225-2606	C- / 4.0	4.70	1.65	13.28 /23	5.30 /58	6.84 /34	3.21	1.03
AA	MFS Diversified Income Fund C	DIFCX	C+	(800) 225-2606	C- / 3.4	4.50	1.35	12.44 /20	4.54 /49	6.07 /29	2.62	1.78
AA	MFS Diversified Income Fund I	DIFIX	C+	(800) 225-2606	C- / 4.2	4.77	1.78	13.56 /24	5.56 /60	7.11 /35	3.60	0.78
AA	MFS Diversified Income Fund R1	DIFDX	C+	(800) 225-2606	C- / 3.4	4.51	1.27	12.36 /19	4.49 /49	6.03 /29	2.62	1.78
AA	MFS Diversified Income Fund R2	DIFEX	C+	(800) 225-2606	C- / 3.8	4.63	1.60	13.00 /22	5.06 /55	6.60 /32	3.11	1.28
AA	MFS Diversified Income Fund R3	DIFFX	C+	(800) 225-2606	C- / 4.0	4.70	1.65	13.28 /23	5.30 /58	6.84 /34	3.35	1.03
AA	MFS Diversified Income Fund R4	DIFGX	C+	(800) 225-2606	C- / 4.2	4.76	1.86	13.55 /24	5.59 /60	7.13 /35	3.59	0.78
AA	MFS Diversified Income Fund R6	DIFHX	C+	(800) 225-2606	C / 4.3	4.83	1.86	13.71 /24	5.67 /61	--	3.73	0.68
EM	MFS Emerging Mkt Equity Fund A	MEMAX	E+	(800) 225-2606	D- / 1.5	7.17	5.21	26.87 /79	-0.07 /13	-1.94 / 3	0.47	1.72
EM	MFS Emerging Mkt Equity Fund B	MEMBX	D-	(800) 225-2606	D / 1.7	6.97	4.81	25.89 /76	-0.82 /10	-2.67 / 2	0.00	2.47
EM	MFS Emerging Mkt Equity Fund C	MEMCX	D-	(800) 225-2606	D / 1.7	6.96	4.80	25.91 /76	-0.83 /10	-2.67 / 2	0.00	2.47
EM	MFS Emerging Mkt Equity Fund I	MEMIX	D	(800) 225-2606	C- / 3.6	7.23	5.33	27.19 /80	0.18 /14	-1.70 / 3	0.72	1.47
EM	MFS Emerging Mkt Equity Fund R1	MEMRX	E+	(800) 225-2606	D / 1.7	6.98	4.80	25.92 /76	-0.82 /10	-2.68 / 2	0.00	2.47
EM	MFS Emerging Mkt Equity Fund R2	MEMFX	D-	(800) 225-2606	D / 2.0	7.08	5.07	26.55 /78	-0.33 /12	-2.19 / 3	0.44	1.97
EM	MFS Emerging Mkt Equity Fund R3	MEMGX	D-	(800) 225-2606	D / 2.1	7.19	5.22	26.88 /79	-0.07 /13	-1.94 / 3	0.45	1.72
EM	MFS Emerging Mkt Equity Fund R4	MEMHX	D	(800) 225-2606	C- / 3.6	7.25	5.32	27.20 /80	0.18 /14	-1.69 / 3	0.75	1.47
EM	MFS Emerging Mkt Equity Fund R6	MEMJX	D	(800) 225-2606	C- / 3.6	7.26	5.36	27.27 /80	0.28 /15	--	0.81	1.35
IN	MFS Equity Income A	EQNAX	B-	(800) 225-2606	C+ / 6.9	8.18	9.36	23.73 /69	7.70 /77	--	1.85	1.23
IN	MFS Equity Income B	EQNBX	B+	(800) 225-2606	B- / 7.3	7.95	8.92	22.70 /65	6.90 /71	--	1.10	1.98
IN	MFS Equity Income C	EQNCX	B+	(800) 225-2606	B- / 7.3	7.95	9.02	22.75 /66	6.88 /71	--	1.14	1.98
IN	MFS Equity Income I	EQNIX	A	(800) 225-2606	B / 8.1	8.24	9.59	24.05 /70	7.98 /79	--	2.28	0.98
IN	MFS Equity Income R1	EQNRX	B+	(800) 225-2606	B- / 7.3	7.99	8.96	22.70 /65	6.87 /71	--	1.11	1.98
IN	MFS Equity Income R2	EQNSX	A-	(800) 225-2606	B / 7.7	8.11	9.22	23.39 /68	7.40 /75	--	1.68	1.48
IN	MFS Equity Income R3	EQNTX	A-	(800) 225-2606	B / 7.9	8.17	9.36	23.71 /69	7.69 /77	--	1.97	1.23
IN	MFS Equity Income R4	EQNUX	A	(800) 225-2606	B / 8.1	8.23	9.56	23.98 /70	7.95 /79	--	2.24	0.98
IN	MFS Equity Income R6	EQNVX	A	(800) 225-2606	B / 8.2	8.29	9.57	24.15 /70	8.19 /80	--	2.39	0.84
GR	MFS Equity Opportunities Class A	SRFAX	C+	(800) 225-2606	C+ / 6.0	6.19	7.97	23.29 /67	6.76 /70	13.37 /88	0.50	1.21
GR	MFS Equity Opportunities Class B	SRFBX	C+	(800) 225-2606	C+ / 6.5	5.98	7.55	22.34 /64	5.95 /64	12.53 /79	0.00	1.96
GR	MFS Equity Opportunities Class C	SRFCX	C+	(800) 225-2606	C+ / 6.5	5.97	7.54	22.36 /64	5.95 /64	12.52 /79	0.00	1.96
GR	MFS Equity Opportunities Class I	SRFIX	B+	(800) 225-2606	B- / 7.2	6.25	8.09	23.59 /68	7.02 /72	13.66 /90	0.77	0.96
GR	MFS Equity Opportunities Class R1	SRFDX	C+	(800) 225-2606	C+ / 6.5	5.99	7.57	22.35 /64	5.96 /64	12.52 /79	0.00	1.96
GR	MFS Equity Opportunities Class R2	SRFEX	C+	(800) 225-2606	C+ / 6.8	6.12	7.84	23.00 /67	6.49 /68	13.09 /85	0.36	1.46
GR	MFS Equity Opportunities Class R3	SRFFX	B+	(800) 225-2606	B- / 7.0	6.17	7.95	23.27 /67	6.74 /70	13.37 /88	0.55	1.21
GR	MFS Equity Opportunities Class R4	SRFGX	B+	(800) 225-2606	B- / 7.2	6.24	8.08	23.60 /68	7.02 /72	13.65 /90	0.77	0.96

● Denotes fund is closed to new investors
★ Denotes fund is included in Section II

RISK			NET ASSETS		ASSET				Portfolio	BULL / BEAR		FUND MANAGER		MINIMUMS		LOADS	
	3 Year		NAV							Last Bull	Last Bear	Manager	Manager	Initial	Additional	Front	Back
Risk Rating/Pts	Standard Deviation	Beta	As of 2/28/17	Total $(Mil)	Cash %	Stocks %	Bonds %	Other %	Turnover Ratio	Market Return	Market Return	Quality Pct	Tenure (Years)	Purch. $	Purch. $	End Load	End Load
B+ / 9.1	4.7	0.70	14.67	45	20	36	43	1	5	34.3	-6.7	38	15	250	0	0.0	0.0
B+ / 9.1	4.6	0.69	15.03	1,331	20	36	43	1	5	40.3	-6.3	50	15	1,000	50	5.8	0.0
B+ / 9.1	4.7	0.70	14.93	141	20	36	43	1	5	34.6	-6.7	39	15	1,000	50	0.0	0.0
B+ / 9.1	4.6	0.70	14.80	685	20	36	43	1	5	34.6	-6.7	39	15	1,000	50	0.0	0.0
B+ / 9.1	4.6	0.69	15.16	257	20	36	43	1	5	42.2	-6.3	53	15	0	0	0.0	0.0
B+ / 9.1	4.6	0.69	14.53	15	20	36	43	1	5	34.7	-6.7	39	N/A	0	0	0.0	0.0
B+ / 9.1	4.6	0.69	14.62	91	20	36	43	1	5	38.4	-6.5	46	14	0	0	0.0	0.0
B+ / 9.1	4.6	0.69	14.91	153	20	36	43	1	5	40.3	-6.4	50	N/A	0	0	0.0	0.0
B+ / 9.1	4.6	0.69	15.04	128	20	36	43	1	5	42.3	-6.3	54	N/A	0	0	0.0	0.0
C / 4.9	10.4	0.98	28.25	952	1	97	1	1	68	126.8	-17.6	53	9	1,000	0	5.8	0.0
C / 4.8	10.4	0.98	25.29	29	1	97	1	1	68	117.8	-17.9	41	9	1,000	0	0.0	0.0
C / 4.8	10.4	0.98	25.02	93	1	97	1	1	68	117.7	-17.9	42	9	1,000	0	0.0	0.0
C / 5.0	10.4	0.98	29.70	131	1	97	1	1	68	129.8	-17.5	56	9	0	0	0.0	0.0
C / 4.8	10.4	0.98	25.00	3	1	97	1	1	68	117.7	-17.9	42	9	0	0	0.0	0.0
C / 5.0	10.4	0.98	27.62	15	1	97	1	1	68	123.6	-17.7	49	9	0	0	0.0	0.0
C / 4.9	10.4	0.98	28.13	29	1	97	1	1	68	126.8	-17.7	52	9	0	0	0.0	0.0
C / 4.9	10.4	0.98	28.44	20	1	97	1	1	68	129.8	-17.6	56	9	0	0	0.0	0.0
C / 5.0	10.4	0.98	29.74	307	1	97	1	1	68	N/A	N/A	57	9	0	0	0.0	0.0
B / 8.2	5.8	0.82	12.28	1,319	31	32	36	1	62	57.0	-8.2	64	11	1,000	0	0.0	0.0
B / 8.2	5.8	0.82	12.28	1,046	31	32	36	1	62	51.0	-8.6	55	11	1,000	0	0.0	0.0
B / 8.2	5.8	0.82	12.28	1,426	31	32	36	1	62	59.2	-8.1	67	11	0	0	0.0	0.0
B / 8.2	5.8	0.82	12.26	1	31	32	36	1	62	50.9	-8.6	54	11	0	0	0.0	0.0
B / 8.2	5.7	0.81	12.28	4	31	32	36	1	62	55.1	-8.3	62	11	0	0	0.0	0.0
B / 8.2	5.8	0.82	12.28	19	31	32	36	1	62	57.2	-8.3	64	11	0	0	0.0	0.0
B / 8.2	5.8	0.82	12.29	6	31	32	36	1	62	59.4	-8.2	68	11	0	0	0.0	0.0
B / 8.2	5.8	0.82	12.28	15	31	32	36	1	62	N/A	N/A	69	11	0	0	0.0	0.0
C / 4.5	14.4	0.86	27.46	104	0	99	0	1	55	11.0	-25.6	55	9	1,000	50	5.8	0.0
C / 4.5	14.4	0.86	25.48	6	0	99	0	1	55	6.6	-25.9	44	9	1,000	50	0.0	0.0
C / 4.5	14.4	0.86	24.88	21	0	99	0	1	55	6.6	-25.9	44	9	1,000	50	0.0	0.0
C / 4.5	14.4	0.86	28.89	29	0	99	0	1	55	12.5	-25.5	58	9	0	0	0.0	0.0
C / 4.4	14.4	0.86	24.68	N/A	0	99	0	1	55	6.6	-25.8	44	9	0	0	0.0	0.0
C / 4.5	14.4	0.86	25.14	4	0	99	0	1	55	9.5	-25.7	51	9	0	0	0.0	0.0
C / 4.5	14.4	0.86	27.35	2	0	99	0	1	55	11.1	-25.6	55	9	0	0	0.0	0.0
C / 4.5	14.4	0.86	27.33	4	0	99	0	1	55	12.6	-25.5	58	9	0	0	0.0	0.0
C / 4.5	14.4	0.86	28.88	727	0	99	0	1	55	N/A	N/A	59	9	0	0	0.0	0.0
B- / 7.0	9.8	0.92	14.71	133	1	98	0	1	43	N/A	N/A	51	5	1,000	0	5.8	Load
B- / 7.0	9.8	0.91	14.68	4	1	98	0	1	43	N/A	N/A	40	5	1,000	0	0.0	0.0
B- / 7.0	9.8	0.91	14.68	22	1	98	0	1	43	N/A	N/A	40	5	1,000	0	0.0	0.0
B- / 7.0	9.8	0.91	14.72	23	1	98	0	1	43	N/A	N/A	55	5	0	0	0.0	0.0
B- / 7.1	9.8	0.91	14.75	N/A	1	98	0	1	43	N/A	N/A	40	5	0	0	0.0	0.0
B- / 7.0	9.8	0.91	14.74	N/A	1	98	0	1	43	N/A	N/A	47	5	0	0	0.0	0.0
B- / 7.0	9.8	0.91	14.73	N/A	1	98	0	1	43	N/A	N/A	51	5	0	0	0.0	0.0
B- / 7.0	9.8	0.91	14.73	N/A	1	98	0	1	43	N/A	N/A	54	5	0	0	0.0	0.0
B- / 7.0	9.8	0.91	14.81	2	1	98	0	1	43	N/A	N/A	58	5	0	0	0.0	0.0
C+ / 6.9	10.2	0.91	33.08	179	2	96	0	2	109	132.2	-18.7	39	7	1,000	0	5.8	0.0
C+ / 6.9	10.2	0.91	31.65	14	2	96	0	2	109	122.9	-19.0	30	7	1,000	0	0.0	0.0
C+ / 6.9	10.2	0.91	31.68	108	2	96	0	2	109	122.8	-19.0	30	7	1,000	0	0.0	0.0
C+ / 6.9	10.2	0.91	33.14	166	2	96	0	2	109	135.4	-18.7	43	7	0	0	0.0	0.0
C+ / 6.9	10.2	0.91	31.58	N/A	2	96	0	2	109	122.9	-19.0	30	7	0	0	0.0	0.0
C+ / 6.9	10.2	0.91	32.23	2	2	96	0	2	109	129.0	-18.8	36	7	0	0	0.0	0.0
C+ / 6.9	10.2	0.91	32.96	2	2	96	0	2	109	132.1	-18.7	39	7	0	0	0.0	0.0
C+ / 6.9	10.2	0.91	33.18	7	2	96	0	2	109	135.2	-18.6	43	7	0	0	0.0	0.0

					PERFORMANCE						Incl. in Returns	
99 Pct = Best					Perfor-	Total Return % through 2/28/17						
0 Pct = Worst			Overall		mance				Annualized		Dividend	Expense
Fund Type	Fund Name	Ticker Symbol	Investment Rating	Phone	Rating/Pts	3 Mo	6 Mo	1Yr / Pct	3Yr / Pct	5Yr / Pct	Yield	Ratio
GR	MFS Equity Opportunities R6	SRFHX	B+	(800) 225-2606	B- / 7.3	6.28	8.16	23.70 /69	7.13 /73	13.74 /91	0.85	0.85
GI	MFS Global Alternative Strategy A	DVRAX	D	(800) 225-2606	E / 0.4	3.14	0.37	1.38 / 2	-0.48 /11	3.10 /11	2.30	1.40
GI	MFS Global Alternative Strategy B	DVRBX	D+	(800) 225-2606	E / 0.4	2.92	-0.02	0.60 / 2	-1.25 / 9	2.32 / 9	1.70	2.15
GI	MFS Global Alternative Strategy C	DVRCX	D+	(800) 225-2606	E / 0.5	3.02	0.07	0.69 / 2	-1.25 / 9	2.33 / 9	1.59	2.15
GI	MFS Global Alternative Strategy I	DVRIX	D+	(800) 225-2606	E+ / 0.7	3.19	0.44	1.54 / 2	-0.27 /12	3.35 /12	2.80	1.15
GI	MFS Global Alternative Strategy R1	DVRFX	D+	(800) 225-2606	E / 0.4	2.92	-0.03	0.59 / 2	-1.26 / 8	2.32 / 9	2.11	2.15
GI	MFS Global Alternative Strategy R2	DVRHX	D+	(800) 225-2606	E+ / 0.6	3.06	0.25	1.17 / 2	-0.75 /10	2.83 /10	2.46	1.65
GI	MFS Global Alternative Strategy R3	DVRJX	D+	(800) 225-2606	E+ / 0.6	3.03	0.37	1.28 / 2	-0.52 /11	3.07 /11	2.74	1.40
GI	MFS Global Alternative Strategy R4	DVRKX	D+	(800) 225-2606	E+ / 0.6	3.17	0.43	1.63 / 2	-0.41 /12	3.26 /12	2.88	1.15
GI	MFS Global Alternative Strategy R6	DVRLX	D+	(800) 225-2606	E+ / 0.7	3.24	0.51	1.71 / 2	-0.15 /13	3.42 /12	2.95	1.07
GL	MFS Global Equity Fund A	MWEFX	C	(800) 225-2606	C- / 4.0	7.98	4.89	18.75 /46	4.62 /50	10.31 /61	0.51	1.22
GL	MFS Global Equity Fund B	MWEBX	C	(800) 225-2606	C / 4.5	7.80	4.50	17.89 /42	3.83 /41	9.48 /54	0.00	1.97
GL	MFS Global Equity Fund C	MWECX	C	(800) 225-2606	C / 4.5	7.80	4.48	17.88 /42	3.83 /41	9.48 /54	0.00	1.97
GL	MFS Global Equity Fund I	MWEIX	C+	(800) 225-2606	C / 5.4	8.06	5.01	19.03 /47	4.87 /53	10.58 /63	0.77	0.97
GL	MFS Global Equity Fund R1	MWEGX	C	(800) 225-2606	C / 4.5	7.82	4.51	17.91 /42	3.83 /41	9.48 /55	0.00	1.97
GL	MFS Global Equity Fund R2	MEQRX	C+	(800) 225-2606	C / 4.9	7.92	4.74	18.44 /45	4.35 /47	10.03 /59	0.31	1.47
GL	MFS Global Equity Fund R3	MWEHX	C+	(800) 225-2606	C / 5.2	8.01	4.90	18.79 /46	4.62 /50	10.31 /61	0.54	1.22
GL	MFS Global Equity Fund R4	MWELX	C+	(800) 225-2606	C / 5.4	8.05	5.03	19.07 /47	4.88 /53	10.58 /63	0.78	0.97
GL	MFS Global Equity Fund R6	MWEMX	C+	(800) 225-2606	C / 5.5	8.08	5.07	19.15 /48	4.97 /54	--	0.85	0.88
GL	MFS Global Growth Fund A	MWOFX	C-	(800) 225-2606	C- / 3.8	8.58	3.38	17.61 /41	4.83 /52	8.15 /43	0.06	1.46
GL	MFS Global Growth Fund B	MWOBX	C-	(800) 225-2606	C / 4.3	8.38	2.97	16.74 /37	4.04 /43	7.35 /37	0.00	2.21
GL	MFS Global Growth Fund C	MWOCX	C-	(800) 225-2606	C / 4.3	8.37	2.97	16.71 /37	4.04 /43	7.34 /37	0.00	2.21
GL	MFS Global Growth Fund I	MWOIX	C	(800) 225-2606	C / 5.2	8.63	3.48	17.90 /42	5.08 /55	8.42 /46	0.33	1.21
GL	MFS Global Growth Fund R1	MWOGX	C-	(800) 225-2606	C / 4.3	8.35	2.97	16.70 /37	4.04 /43	7.34 /37	0.00	2.21
GL	MFS Global Growth Fund R2	MGWRX	C	(800) 225-2606	C / 4.8	8.47	3.23	17.29 /40	4.55 /49	7.88 /41	0.00	1.71
GL	MFS Global Growth Fund R3	MWOHX	C	(800) 225-2606	C / 5.0	8.55	3.36	17.59 /41	4.82 /52	8.15 /43	0.06	1.46
GL	MFS Global Growth Fund R4	MWOJX	C	(800) 225-2606	C / 5.2	8.63	3.47	17.88 /42	5.08 /55	8.41 /45	0.28	1.21
GL	MFS Global Growth Fund R6	MWOKX	C	(800) 225-2606	C / 5.3	8.66	3.51	17.97 /43	5.17 /56	--	0.35	1.13
GL	MFS Global Multi-Asset R6	GLMVX	D+	(800) 225-2606	D / 1.8	3.63	1.84	12.03 /18	1.21 /19	--	0.00	2.22
GL	MFS Global New Discovery A	GLNAX	D+	(800) 225-2606	D+ / 2.4	5.89	3.32	18.16 /44	2.46 /27	8.70 /48	0.12	2.35
GL	MFS Global New Discovery B	GLNBX	D+	(800) 225-2606	D+ / 2.8	5.63	2.97	17.23 /39	1.70 /22	7.87 /41	0.00	3.10
GL	MFS Global New Discovery C	GLNCX	D+	(800) 225-2606	D+ / 2.8	5.70	2.97	17.32 /40	1.68 /22	7.87 /41	0.00	3.10
GL	MFS Global New Discovery I	GLNIX	C-	(800) 225-2606	C- / 3.6	5.98	3.51	18.53 /45	2.73 /29	8.97 /50	0.51	2.10
GL	MFS Global New Discovery R1	GLNJX	D+	(800) 225-2606	D+ / 2.8	5.70	2.97	17.32 /40	1.70 /22	7.87 /41	0.00	3.10
GL	MFS Global New Discovery R2	GLNKX	D+	(800) 225-2606	C- / 3.2	5.81	3.21	17.81 /42	2.18 /25	8.40 /45	0.05	2.60
GL	MFS Global New Discovery R3	GLNLX	C-	(800) 225-2606	C- / 3.4	5.89	3.39	18.23 /44	2.47 /27	8.69 /48	0.25	2.35
GL	MFS Global New Discovery R4	GLNMX	C-	(800) 225-2606	C- / 3.5	5.91	3.44	18.44 /45	2.68 /29	8.94 /50	0.45	2.10
GL	MFS Global New Discovery R6	GLNNX	C-	(800) 225-2606	C- / 3.6	5.96	3.56	18.58 /45	2.82 /30	--	0.56	1.98
RE	MFS Global Real Estate A	MGLAX	C	(800) 225-2606	C / 4.3	6.21	-1.47	14.24 /27	7.77 /77	9.42 /54	3.52	1.46
RE	MFS Global Real Estate I	MGLIX	C+	(800) 225-2606	C+ / 5.7	6.34	-1.34	14.59 /28	8.00 /79	9.67 /56	3.90	1.21
RE	MFS Global Real Estate R6	MGLRX	C+	(800) 225-2606	C+ / 5.8	6.43	-1.24	14.68 /28	8.09 /80	--	3.93	1.16
GL	MFS Global Total Return Fund A	MFWTX	C-	(800) 225-2606	D / 1.7	4.52	0.48	10.55 /13	3.07 /32	6.42 /31	1.03	1.28
GL	MFS Global Total Return Fund B	MFWBX	C-	(800) 225-2606	D / 2.0	4.27	0.08	9.67 /11	2.27 /26	5.62 /26	0.48	2.03
GL	MFS Global Total Return Fund C	MFWCX	C-	(800) 225-2606	D / 2.0	4.28	0.09	9.70 /11	2.28 /26	5.62 /26	0.51	2.03
GL	MFS Global Total Return Fund I	MFWIX	C	(800) 225-2606	D+ / 2.6	4.58	0.62	10.87 /14	3.32 /35	6.70 /33	1.36	1.03
GL	MFS Global Total Return Fund R1	MFWGX	C-	(800) 225-2606	D / 2.0	4.29	0.08	9.73 /11	2.28 /26	5.63 /26	0.50	2.03
GL	MFS Global Total Return Fund R2	MGBRX	C-	(800) 225-2606	D+ / 2.3	4.44	0.32	10.25 /12	2.81 /30	6.16 /30	0.93	1.53
GL	MFS Global Total Return Fund R3	MFWHX	C-	(800) 225-2606	D+ / 2.4	4.49	0.49	10.61 /13	3.09 /33	6.43 /31	1.12	1.28
GL	MFS Global Total Return Fund R4	MFWJX	C	(800) 225-2606	D+ / 2.6	4.52	0.55	10.80 /14	3.32 /35	6.68 /33	1.33	1.03
GL	MFS Global Total Return Fund R6	MFWLX	C	(800) 225-2606	D+ / 2.6	4.61	0.61	10.90 /14	3.42 /36	--	1.44	0.93
AA	MFS Growth Allocation 529A	EAGWX	C	(800) 225-2606	C- / 3.3	5.84	4.30	17.55 /41	4.38 /47	8.12 /43	1.07	1.16
AA	MFS Growth Allocation 529B	EBGWX	C	(800) 225-2606	C- / 3.8	5.66	3.87	16.62 /37	3.60 /38	7.32 /37	0.34	1.91

● Denotes fund is closed to new investors
* Denotes fund is included in Section II

www.thestreetratings.com

RISK			NET ASSETS		ASSET				Portfolio Turnover Ratio	BULL / BEAR		FUND MANAGER		MINIMUMS		LOADS	
Risk Rating/Pts	3 Year Standard Deviation	Beta	NAV As of 2/28/17	Total $(Mil)	Cash %	Stocks %	Bonds %	Other %		Last Bull Market Return	Last Bear Market Return	Manager Quality Pct	Manager Tenure (Years)	Initial Purch. $	Additional Purch. $	Front End Load	Back End Load
C+ / 6.9	10.2	0.91	33.67	12	2	96	0	2	109	136.2	-18.6	44	7	0	0	0.0	0.0
B / 8.0	4.3	0.24	9.82	56	11	66	22	1	51	18.8	1.2	35	10	1,000	0	5.8	0.0
B / 8.1	4.3	0.24	9.63	7	11	66	22	1	51	13.9	1.0	26	10	1,000	0	0.0	0.0
B / 8.1	4.3	0.24	9.63	35	11	66	22	1	51	14.0	0.9	26	10	1,000	0	0.0	0.0
B / 8.0	4.3	0.24	9.89	263	11	66	22	1	51	20.2	1.4	37	10	0	0	0.0	0.0
B / 8.0	4.3	0.24	9.55	N/A	11	66	22	1	51	13.9	1.0	26	10	0	0	0.0	0.0
B / 8.0	4.3	0.24	9.70	1	11	66	22	1	51	17.1	1.1	32	10	0	0	0.0	0.0
B / 8.1	4.2	0.24	9.85	1	11	66	22	1	51	18.6	1.2	34	10	0	0	0.0	0.0
B / 8.0	4.4	0.25	9.91	N/A	11	66	22	1	51	19.7	1.4	35	10	0	0	0.0	0.0
B / 8.0	4.3	0.24	9.94	6	11	66	22	1	51	20.6	1.3	38	10	0	0	0.0	0.0
C+ / 6.7	10.6	0.80	38.30	613	0	98	1	1	8	96.8	-19.7	95	25	1,000	0	5.8	0.0
C+ / 6.7	10.6	0.80	35.48	27	0	98	1	1	8	89.0	-20.0	93	25	1,000	0	0.0	0.0
C+ / 6.7	10.6	0.80	33.99	162	0	98	1	1	8	89.0	-20.0	93	25	1,000	0	0.0	0.0
C+ / 6.7	10.6	0.80	39.24	1,055	0	98	1	1	8	99.4	-19.6	95	25	0	0	0.0	0.0
C+ / 6.7	10.6	0.80	34.73	3	0	98	1	1	8	89.1	-20.0	93	25	0	0	0.0	0.0
C+ / 6.7	10.6	0.80	37.24	50	0	98	1	1	8	94.1	-19.8	94	25	0	0	0.0	0.0
C+ / 6.7	10.6	0.80	38.05	105	0	98	1	1	8	96.8	-19.7	95	25	0	0	0.0	0.0
C+ / 6.7	10.6	0.80	38.40	126	0	98	1	1	8	99.4	-19.7	95	25	0	0	0.0	0.0
C+ / 6.7	10.6	0.80	39.25	632	0	98	1	1	8	N/A	N/A	95	25	0	0	0.0	0.0
C+ / 5.8	11.2	0.81	34.61	175	1	97	0	2	28	79.1	-19.3	95	9	1,000	0	5.8	0.0
C+ / 5.6	11.2	0.81	30.59	5	1	97	0	2	28	72.0	-19.6	94	9	1,000	0	0.0	0.0
C+ / 5.6	11.2	0.81	30.23	13	1	97	0	2	28	72.0	-19.6	94	9	1,000	0	0.0	0.0
C+ / 5.8	11.2	0.81	35.38	31	1	97	0	2	28	81.5	-19.2	95	9	0	0	0.0	0.0
C+ / 5.6	11.2	0.81	30.17	1	1	97	0	2	28	72.0	-19.6	94	9	0	0	0.0	0.0
C+ / 5.8	11.2	0.81	33.61	3	1	97	0	2	28	76.7	-19.4	95	9	0	0	0.0	0.0
C+ / 5.8	11.2	0.81	34.44	4	1	97	0	2	28	79.2	-19.3	95	9	0	0	0.0	0.0
C+ / 5.8	11.2	0.81	34.63	1	1	97	0	2	28	81.5	-19.2	96	9	0	0	0.0	0.0
C+ / 5.8	11.2	0.81	35.38	8	1	97	0	2	28	N/A	N/A	96	9	0	0	0.0	0.0
C+ / 6.7	6.4	0.75	9.23	1	9	34	55	2	54	N/A	N/A	45	6	0	0	0.0	0.0
C+ / 6.0	11.7	0.76	16.19	7	4	95	0	1	37	N/A	N/A	88	6	1,000	0	5.8	0.0
C+ / 5.9	11.7	0.76	15.58	1	4	95	0	1	37	N/A	N/A	85	6	1,000	0	0.0	0.0
C+ / 5.9	11.7	0.76	15.58	5	4	95	0	1	37	N/A	N/A	85	6	1,000	0	0.0	0.0
C+ / 6.1	11.7	0.76	16.33	10	4	95	0	1	37	N/A	N/A	90	6	0	0	0.0	0.0
C+ / 5.9	11.7	0.76	15.58	N/A	4	95	0	1	37	N/A	N/A	85	6	0	0	0.0	0.0
C+ / 6.0	11.7	0.76	15.99	N/A	4	95	0	1	37	N/A	N/A	87	6	0	0	0.0	0.0
C+ / 6.1	11.7	0.76	16.19	N/A	4	95	0	1	37	N/A	N/A	89	6	0	0	0.0	0.0
C+ / 6.1	11.7	0.76	16.34	N/A	4	95	0	1	37	N/A	N/A	89	6	0	0	0.0	0.0
C+ / 6.1	11.7	0.76	16.34	2	4	95	0	1	37	N/A	N/A	90	6	0	0	0.0	0.0
C+ / 6.4	11.4	0.78	15.00	38	17	80	1	2	53	86.2	-19.7	65	8	1,000	0	5.8	0.0
C+ / 6.4	11.4	0.78	15.03	70	17	80	1	2	53	88.4	-19.5	68	8	0	0	0.0	0.0
C+ / 6.4	11.4	0.78	15.06	456	17	80	1	2	53	N/A	N/A	68	8	0	0	0.0	0.0
B / 8.0	6.4	0.46	16.77	750	2	58	38	2	36	49.9	-9.3	90	17	1,000	0	5.8	0.0
B / 8.0	6.4	0.46	17.08	53	2	58	38	2	36	43.9	-9.5	87	17	1,000	0	0.0	0.0
B- / 7.9	6.4	0.46	16.85	349	2	58	38	2	36	43.9	-9.5	87	17	1,000	0	0.0	0.0
B / 8.0	6.4	0.46	16.61	581	2	58	38	2	36	52.0	-9.2	91	17	0	0	0.0	0.0
B- / 7.9	6.4	0.46	16.79	2	2	58	38	2	36	44.0	-9.6	87	17	0	0	0.0	0.0
B / 8.0	6.4	0.46	16.60	23	2	58	38	2	36	48.0	-9.4	90	17	0	0	0.0	0.0
B / 8.0	6.4	0.46	16.72	18	2	58	38	2	36	50.0	-9.3	91	17	0	0	0.0	0.0
B / 8.0	6.4	0.46	16.79	5	2	58	38	2	36	51.9	-9.2	91	17	0	0	0.0	0.0
B / 8.0	6.4	0.95	16.61	198	2	58	38	2	36	N/A	N/A	62	17	0	0	0.0	0.0
B- / 7.3	8.1	1.26	18.81	199	6	73	19	2	3	71.8	-15.3	17	15	250	0	5.8	0.0
B- / 7.4	8.1	1.26	18.62	12	6	73	19	2	3	64.9	-15.4	11	15	250	0	0.0	0.0

Fund Type	Fund Name	Ticker Symbol	Overall Investment Rating	Phone	Performance Rating/Pts	3 Mo	6 Mo	1Yr / Pct	3Yr / Pct	5Yr / Pct	Dividend Yield	Expense Ratio
AA	MFS Growth Allocation 529C	ECGWX	C	(800) 225-2606	C- / 3.8	5.65	3.90	16.68 /37	3.61 /38	7.32 /37	0.43	1.91
AA	MFS Growth Allocation A	MAGWX	C	(800) 225-2606	C- / 3.4	5.89	4.30	17.65 /41	4.43 /48	8.18 /43	1.09	1.06
AA	MFS Growth Allocation B	MBGWX	C	(800) 225-2606	C- / 3.9	5.67	3.90	16.73 /37	3.65 /39	7.37 /37	0.40	1.81
AA	MFS Growth Allocation C	MCGWX	C	(800) 225-2606	C- / 3.9	5.66	3.93	16.70 /37	3.65 /39	7.36 /37	0.45	1.81
AA	MFS Growth Allocation I	MGWIX	C+	(800) 225-2606	C / 4.7	5.88	4.42	17.86 /42	4.67 /50	8.43 /46	1.40	0.81
AA	MFS Growth Allocation R1	MAGMX	C	(800) 225-2606	C- / 3.9	5.63	3.87	16.68 /37	3.64 /38	7.36 /37	0.43	1.81
AA	MFS Growth Allocation R2	MGALX	C+	(800) 225-2606	C / 4.3	5.75	4.13	17.28 /40	4.15 /45	7.90 /41	0.94	1.31
AA	MFS Growth Allocation R3	MAGEX	C+	(800) 225-2606	C / 4.5	5.89	4.29	17.61 /41	4.42 /48	8.18 /43	1.17	1.06
AA	MFS Growth Allocation R4	MAGJX	C+	(800) 225-2606	C / 4.8	5.94	4.41	17.90 /42	4.70 /51	8.43 /46	1.41	0.81
GR	MFS Growth Fund A	MFEGX	C+	(800) 225-2606	C+ / 6.0	8.66	6.27	18.59 /45	7.59 /76	13.06 /84	0.00	1.01
GR	MFS Growth Fund B	MEGBX	C+	(800) 225-2606	C+ / 6.5	8.47	5.87	17.70 /41	6.79 /70	12.22 /76	0.00	1.76
GR	MFS Growth Fund C	MFECX	C+	(800) 225-2606	C+ / 6.5	8.48	5.88	17.70 /41	6.78 /70	12.22 /76	0.00	1.76
GR	MFS Growth Fund I	MFEIX	B	(800) 225-2606	B- / 7.2	8.74	6.40	18.87 /46	7.86 /78	13.33 /87	0.02	0.76
GR	MFS Growth Fund R1	MFELX	C+	(800) 225-2606	C+ / 6.5	8.48	5.90	17.69 /41	6.78 /70	12.22 /76	0.00	1.76
GR	MFS Growth Fund R2	MEGRX	C+	(800) 225-2606	C+ / 6.9	8.61	6.15	18.30 /44	7.32 /74	12.78 /82	0.00	1.26
GR	MFS Growth Fund R3	MFEHX	B	(800) 225-2606	B- / 7.0	8.67	6.28	18.58 /45	7.59 /76	13.06 /84	0.00	1.01
GR	MFS Growth Fund R4	MFEJX	B	(800) 225-2606	B- / 7.2	8.74	6.41	18.88 /47	7.86 /78	13.34 /87	0.00	0.76
GR	MFS Growth R6	MFEKX	B	(800) 225-2606	B- / 7.3	8.76	6.47	18.99 /47	7.96 /79	13.43 /88	0.10	0.66
* FO	MFS Inst Intl Equity Fund	MIEIX	D	(800) 225-2606	D / 2.1	7.20	3.30	14.30 /27	0.24 /14	5.39 /24	1.70	0.71
FO	MFS International Diversifictn A	MDIDX	D	(800) 225-2606	D- / 1.5	6.25	1.27	14.54 /28	0.96 /18	5.05 /22	1.75	1.21
FO	MFS International Diversifictn B	MDIFX	D	(800) 225-2606	D / 1.8	6.09	0.91	13.73 /24	0.21 /14	4.27 /17	1.04	1.96
FO	MFS International Diversifictn C	MDIGX	D	(800) 225-2606	D / 1.7	6.04	0.88	13.67 /24	0.20 /14	4.26 /17	1.14	1.96
FO	MFS International Diversifictn I	MDIJX	D+	(800) 225-2606	D+ / 2.3	6.32	1.39	14.84 /29	1.22 /19	5.31 /23	2.08	0.96
FO	MFS International Diversifictn R1	MDIOX	D	(800) 225-2606	D / 1.7	6.02	0.85	13.68 /24	0.19 /14	4.26 /17	1.18	1.96
FO	MFS International Diversifictn R2	MDIKX	D	(800) 225-2606	D / 2.0	6.19	1.13	14.24 /27	0.70 /17	4.77 /20	1.67	1.46
FO	MFS International Diversifictn R3	MDIHX	D+	(800) 225-2606	D / 2.1	6.25	1.30	14.52 /28	0.96 /18	5.04 /22	1.89	1.21
FO	MFS International Diversifictn R4	MDITX	D+	(800) 225-2606	D+ / 2.3	6.34	1.40	14.82 /29	1.22 /19	5.31 /23	2.09	0.96
FO	MFS International Growth Fund A	MGRAX	D	(800) 225-2606	D- / 1.3	6.51	-0.12	13.09 /22	0.70 /17	4.10 /16	0.91	1.22
FO	MFS International Growth Fund B	MGRBX	D-	(800) 225-2606	D- / 1.1	6.29	-0.48	12.27 /19	-0.06 /13	3.32 /12	0.28	1.97
FO	MFS International Growth Fund C	MGRCX	D-	(800) 225-2606	D- / 1.1	6.27	-0.51	12.25 /19	-0.06 /13	3.31 /12	0.35	1.97
FO	MFS International Growth Fund I	MQGIX	D	(800) 225-2606	D / 2.0	6.56	0.00	13.41 /23	0.95 /18	4.36 /17	1.13	0.97
FO	MFS International Growth Fund R1	MGRRX	D-	(800) 225-2606	D- / 1.1	6.31	-0.48	12.29 /19	-0.06 /13	3.32 /12	0.62	1.97
FO	MFS International Growth Fund R2	MGRQX	D	(800) 225-2606	D / 1.7	6.40	-0.26	12.79 /21	0.43 /15	3.83 /14	0.85	1.47
FO	MFS International Growth Fund R3	MGRTX	D	(800) 225-2606	D / 1.8	6.49	-0.14	13.12 /22	0.69 /17	4.10 /16	0.95	1.22
FO	MFS International Growth Fund R4	MGRVX	D	(800) 225-2606	D / 2.0	6.55	0.02	13.40 /23	0.95 /18	4.36 /17	1.16	0.97
FO	MFS International Growth R6	MGRDX	D	(800) 225-2606	D / 2.0	6.60	0.07	13.53 /24	1.07 /19	4.47 /18	1.39	0.84
FO	● MFS International Value R6	MINJX	C	(800) 225-2606	C- / 4.0	6.10	0.34	13.35 /23	5.19 /56	10.57 /63	1.83	0.66
FO	MFS Intl New Discovery 529A	EAIDX	D	(800) 225-2606	D / 1.6	6.45	1.54	12.65 /20	1.62 /22	6.71 /33	1.23	1.47
FO	MFS Intl New Discovery 529B	EBIDX	D+	(800) 225-2606	D / 2.0	6.32	1.40	12.47 /20	1.11 /19	6.06 /29	1.34	2.22
FO	MFS Intl New Discovery 529C	ECIDX	D+	(800) 225-2606	D / 1.9	6.26	1.15	11.77 /17	0.84 /17	5.89 /28	0.60	2.22
FO	MFS Intl New Discovery A	MIDAX	D	(800) 225-2606	D / 1.6	6.44	1.52	12.62 /20	1.62 /22	6.71 /33	1.18	1.37
FO	MFS Intl New Discovery B	MIDBX	D+	(800) 225-2606	D / 1.9	6.23	1.17	11.78 /17	0.86 /17	5.92 /28	0.47	2.12
FO	MFS Intl New Discovery C	MIDCX	D+	(800) 225-2606	D / 1.9	6.26	1.15	11.77 /17	0.86 /17	5.92 /28	0.58	2.12
FO	MFS Intl New Discovery I	MWNIX	D+	(800) 225-2606	D+ / 2.4	6.51	1.70	12.93 /21	1.89 /23	6.99 /35	1.49	1.12
FO	MFS Intl New Discovery R1	MIDGX	D+	(800) 225-2606	D / 1.9	6.25	1.15	11.81 /17	0.86 /17	5.91 /28	0.71	2.12
FO	MFS Intl New Discovery R2	MIDRX	D+	(800) 225-2606	D / 2.1	6.36	1.39	12.32 /19	1.37 /20	6.44 /31	1.03	1.62
FO	MFS Intl New Discovery R3	MIDHX	D+	(800) 225-2606	D+ / 2.3	6.42	1.54	12.61 /20	1.61 /22	6.71 /33	1.30	1.37
FO	MFS Intl New Discovery R4	MIDJX	D+	(800) 225-2606	D+ / 2.4	6.51	1.67	12.91 /21	1.88 /23	6.98 /34	1.53	1.12
FO	MFS Intl New Discovery R6	MIDLX	D+	(800) 225-2606	D+ / 2.5	6.56	1.75	13.06 /22	2.01 /24	--	1.60	1.00
* FO	● MFS Intl Value Fund A	MGIAX	C-	(800) 225-2606	D+ / 2.7	6.02	0.18	12.94 /21	4.82 /52	10.20 /60	1.36	1.01
FO	● MFS Intl Value Fund B	MGIBX	C-	(800) 225-2606	C- / 3.1	5.84	-0.21	12.09 /18	4.04 /43	9.38 /54	0.76	1.76
FO	● MFS Intl Value Fund C	MGICX	C-	(800) 225-2606	C- / 3.1	5.80	-0.21	12.09 /18	4.03 /43	9.37 /54	0.83	1.76

● Denotes fund is closed to new investors
* Denotes fund is included in Section II

RISK	3 Year Standard Deviation	Beta	NET ASSETS NAV As of 2/28/17	Total $(Mil)	ASSET Cash %	Stocks %	Bonds %	Other %	Portfolio Turnover Ratio	BULL / BEAR Last Bull Market Return	Last Bear Market Return	FUND MANAGER Manager Quality Pct	Manager Tenure (Years)	MINIMUMS Initial Purch. $	Additional Purch. $	LOADS Front End Load	Back End Load
B- /7.4	8.2	1.26	18.38	71	6	73	19	2	3	65.0	-15.6	11	15	250	0	0.0	0.0
B- /7.3	8.1	1.26	18.95	2,734	6	73	19	2	3	72.2	-15.2	17	15	1,000	50	5.8	0.0
B- /7.4	8.2	1.26	18.79	241	6	73	19	2	3	65.3	-15.4	12	15	1,000	50	0.0	0.0
B- /7.4	8.1	1.26	18.60	963	6	73	19	2	3	65.3	-15.5	12	15	1,000	50	0.0	0.0
B- /7.3	8.1	1.26	19.10	137	6	73	19	2	3	74.5	-15.1	19	15	0	0	0.0	0.0
B- /7.4	8.2	1.26	18.24	36	6	73	19	2	3	65.3	-15.5	12	N/A	0	0	0.0	0.0
B- /7.3	8.1	1.26	18.54	182	6	73	19	2	3	69.9	-15.3	15	14	0	0	0.0	0.0
B- /7.3	8.1	1.25	18.79	236	6	73	19	2	3	72.1	-15.2	17	N/A	0	0	0.0	0.0
B- /7.3	8.2	1.26	18.93	232	6	73	19	2	3	74.4	-15.1	19	N/A	0	0	0.0	0.0
C+ /6.0	11.1	0.96	76.46	4,291	0	97	1	2	24	122.1	-14.4	43	15	1,000	50	5.8	0.0
C+ /5.9	11.1	0.96	62.97	131	0	97	1	2	24	113.3	-14.7	33	15	1,000	50	0.0	0.0
C+ /5.9	11.1	0.96	62.51	602	0	97	1	2	24	113.3	-14.7	33	15	1,000	50	0.0	0.0
C+ /6.1	11.1	0.96	80.81	5,059	0	97	1	2	24	125.0	-14.3	46	15	0	0	0.0	0.0
C+ /5.9	11.1	0.96	62.73	13	0	97	1	2	24	113.3	-14.7	33	15	0	0	0.0	0.0
C+ /6.0	11.1	0.96	72.71	180	0	97	1	2	24	119.1	-14.5	39	15	0	0	0.0	0.0
C+ /6.0	11.1	0.96	76.11	573	0	97	1	2	24	122.1	-14.4	43	15	0	0	0.0	0.0
C+ /6.0	11.1	0.96	78.72	763	0	97	1	2	24	125.1	-14.3	46	15	0	0	0.0	0.0
C+ /6.1	11.1	0.96	80.96	2,783	0	97	1	2	24	126.0	N/A	48	15	0	0	0.0	0.0
C+ /6.0	11.3	0.90	21.19	8,082	0	99	0	1	12	54.8	-23.1	77	16	3,000,000	0	0.0	0.0
C+ /6.3	10.5	0.82	16.11	1,526	2	97	0	1	3	48.3	-20.0	81	N/A	1,000	50	5.8	0.0
C+ /6.4	10.6	0.82	15.94	32	2	97	0	1	3	42.3	-20.3	76	N/A	1,000	50	0.0	0.0
C+ /6.3	10.5	0.82	15.77	441	2	97	0	1	3	42.3	-20.2	76	N/A	1,000	50	0.0	0.0
C+ /6.3	10.5	0.82	16.26	3,203	2	97	0	1	3	50.2	-19.9	83	N/A	0	0	0.0	0.0
C+ /6.3	10.6	0.82	15.53	8	2	97	0	1	3	42.3	-20.2	76	N/A	0	0	0.0	0.0
C+ /6.3	10.6	0.82	15.84	68	2	97	0	1	3	46.1	-20.1	80	N/A	0	0	0.0	0.0
C+ /6.3	10.5	0.82	16.00	256	2	97	0	1	3	48.2	-20.0	81	N/A	0	0	0.0	0.0
C+ /6.3	10.5	0.82	16.21	735	2	97	0	1	3	50.2	-19.9	83	N/A	0	0	0.0	0.0
C+ /6.1	11.1	0.85	27.34	290	0	98	0	2	20	45.8	-21.8	80	7	1,000	50	5.8	0.0
C+ /6.1	11.1	0.86	25.68	8	0	98	0	2	20	40.0	-22.1	74	7	1,000	50	0.0	0.0
C+ /6.1	11.1	0.86	25.04	37	0	98	0	2	20	40.0	-22.1	74	7	1,000	50	0.0	0.0
C+ /6.1	11.1	0.86	30.34	1,285	0	98	0	2	20	47.8	-21.7	81	7	0	0	0.0	0.0
C+ /6.0	11.1	0.86	24.61	2	0	98	0	2	20	40.0	-22.1	74	7	0	0	0.0	0.0
C+ /6.1	11.1	0.86	25.11	20	0	98	0	2	20	43.9	-21.9	78	7	0	0	0.0	0.0
C+ /6.1	11.1	0.86	27.16	24	0	98	0	2	20	45.8	-21.8	80	7	0	0	0.0	0.0
C+ /6.1	11.1	0.86	27.39	112	0	98	0	2	20	47.8	-21.8	81	7	0	0	0.0	0.0
C+ /6.1	11.1	0.86	27.37	2,325	0	98	0	2	20	48.5	-21.8	82	7	0	0	0.0	0.0
C+ /6.9	9.4	0.68	36.59	3,995	0	97	1	2	14	82.8	-13.2	96	9	0	0	0.0	0.0
C+ /6.6	10.2	0.77	28.12	6	1	94	3	2	13	62.9	-20.2	85	20	250	0	5.8	0.0
C+ /6.7	10.2	0.77	26.70	N/A	1	94	3	2	13	57.6	-20.4	82	20	250	0	0.0	0.0
C+ /6.6	10.2	0.77	26.44	2	1	94	3	2	13	56.2	-20.4	81	20	250	0	0.0	0.0
C+ /6.6	10.2	0.77	28.56	1,134	1	94	3	2	13	63.0	-20.2	85	20	1,000	50	5.8	0.0
C+ /6.7	10.2	0.77	27.78	15	1	94	3	2	13	56.5	-20.4	81	20	1,000	50	0.0	0.0
C+ /6.6	10.2	0.77	27.28	153	1	94	3	2	13	56.5	-20.4	81	20	1,000	50	0.0	0.0
C+ /6.6	10.2	0.77	29.37	1,860	1	94	3	2	13	65.2	-20.1	86	20	0	0	0.0	0.0
C+ /6.7	10.2	0.77	26.64	3	1	94	3	2	13	56.5	-20.4	81	20	0	0	0.0	0.0
C+ /6.6	10.2	0.77	27.83	51	1	94	3	2	13	60.8	-20.3	84	20	0	0	0.0	0.0
C+ /6.6	10.2	0.77	28.32	153	1	94	3	2	13	63.0	-20.2	85	20	0	0	0.0	0.0
C+ /6.6	10.2	0.77	28.53	302	1	94	3	2	13	65.2	-20.1	86	20	0	0	0.0	0.0
C+ /6.6	10.2	0.77	29.39	1,235	1	94	3	2	13	N/A	N/A	87	20	0	0	0.0	0.0
C+ /6.9	9.4	0.68	36.47	4,961	0	97	1	2	14	79.7	-13.3	95	9	1,000	50	5.8	0.0
C+ /6.9	9.4	0.68	34.80	49	0	97	1	2	14	72.5	-13.5	94	9	1,000	50	0.0	0.0
C+ /6.9	9.4	0.68	33.23	692	0	97	1	2	14	72.5	-13.5	93	9	1,000	50	0.0	0.0

99 Pct = Best
0 Pct = Worst

Fund Type	Fund Name	Ticker Symbol	Overall Investment Rating	Phone	Performance Rating/Pts	3 Mo	6 Mo	1Yr / Pct	3Yr / Pct	5Yr / Pct	Dividend Yield	Expense Ratio
FO	● MFS Intl Value Fund I	MINIX	C	(800) 225-2606	C- / 3.9	6.07	0.27	13.20 /22	5.08 /55	10.47 /62	1.65	0.76
FO	● MFS Intl Value Fund R1	MINRX	C-	(800) 225-2606	C- / 3.1	5.84	-0.19	12.12 /18	4.04 /43	9.38 /54	0.90	1.76
FO	● MFS Intl Value Fund R2	MINFX	C-	(800) 225-2606	C- / 3.5	5.92	0.03	12.62 /20	4.55 /49	9.92 /58	1.34	1.26
FO	● MFS Intl Value Fund R3	MINGX	C	(800) 225-2606	C- / 3.7	6.01	0.16	12.93 /21	4.82 /52	10.20 /60	1.52	1.01
FO	● MFS Intl Value Fund R4	MINHX	C	(800) 225-2606	C- / 3.9	6.06	0.29	13.21 /22	5.08 /55	10.47 /62	1.73	0.76
AA	MFS Lifetime 2020 A	MFLAX	C	(800) 225-2606	D / 1.8	3.39	1.86	10.26 /12	3.44 /36	5.81 /27	1.46	1.07
AA	MFS Lifetime 2020 B	MFLBX	C	(800) 225-2606	D / 2.1	3.17	1.48	9.40 /10	2.66 /29	5.01 /21	0.73	1.82
AA	MFS Lifetime 2020 C	MFLCX	C	(800) 225-2606	D / 2.1	3.14	1.43	9.36 /10	2.65 /29	5.01 /21	0.83	1.82
AA	MFS Lifetime 2020 I	MFLIX	C+	(800) 225-2606	D+ / 2.7	3.47	1.95	10.55 /13	3.69 /39	6.07 /29	1.77	0.82
AA	MFS Lifetime 2020 R1	MFLEX	C	(800) 225-2606	D / 2.1	3.16	1.47	9.38 /10	2.66 /29	5.01 /21	0.58	1.82
AA	MFS Lifetime 2020 R2	MFLGX	C	(800) 225-2606	D+ / 2.4	3.28	1.66	9.92 /11	3.17 /33	5.53 /25	1.35	1.32
AA	MFS Lifetime 2020 R3	MFLHX	C	(800) 225-2606	D+ / 2.5	3.38	1.85	10.24 /12	3.42 /36	5.81 /27	1.53	1.07
AA	MFS Lifetime 2020 R4	MFLJX	C+	(800) 225-2606	D+ / 2.7	3.39	1.95	10.47 /13	3.70 /39	6.06 /29	1.77	0.82
GI	MFS Lifetime 2025 A	LTTAX	C	(800) 225-2606	D+ / 2.6	4.51	3.23	14.03 /26	4.10 /44	--	1.30	1.18
GI	MFS Lifetime 2025 B	LTTBX	C+	(800) 225-2606	C- / 3.0	4.23	2.77	13.21 /22	3.28 /34	--	0.70	1.93
GI	MFS Lifetime 2025 C	LTTCX	C+	(800) 225-2606	C- / 3.0	4.22	2.75	13.14 /22	3.29 /35	--	0.68	1.93
GI	MFS Lifetime 2025 I	LTTIX	C+	(800) 225-2606	C- / 3.8	4.55	3.36	14.34 /27	4.32 /47	--	1.59	0.93
GI	MFS Lifetime 2025 R1	LTTRX	C+	(800) 225-2606	C- / 3.0	4.27	2.82	13.17 /22	3.29 /35	--	1.08	1.93
GI	MFS Lifetime 2025 R2	LTTSX	C+	(800) 225-2606	C- / 3.4	4.40	3.03	13.75 /24	3.81 /41	--	1.35	1.43
GI	MFS Lifetime 2025 R3	LTTTX	C+	(800) 225-2606	C- / 3.6	4.47	3.19	14.08 /26	4.06 /44	--	1.42	1.18
GI	MFS Lifetime 2025 R4	LTTUX	C+	(800) 225-2606	C- / 3.7	4.46	3.28	14.34 /27	4.32 /47	--	1.59	0.93
AA	MFS Lifetime 2030 A	MLTAX	C	(800) 225-2606	C- / 3.7	5.68	4.89	18.26 /44	4.75 /51	8.56 /47	1.17	1.12
AA	MFS Lifetime 2030 B	MLTBX	C+	(800) 225-2606	C- / 4.2	5.45	4.50	17.33 /40	3.94 /42	7.73 /40	0.52	1.87
AA	MFS Lifetime 2030 C	MLTCX	C+	(800) 225-2606	C- / 4.2	5.44	4.48	17.28 /40	3.94 /42	7.74 /40	0.54	1.87
AA	MFS Lifetime 2030 I	MLTIX	B-	(800) 225-2606	C / 4.9	5.52	4.80	18.24 /44	4.91 /53	8.78 /49	1.45	0.87
AA	MFS Lifetime 2030 R1	MLTEX	C+	(800) 225-2606	C- / 4.2	5.46	4.50	17.28 /40	3.94 /42	7.75 /40	0.41	1.87
AA	MFS Lifetime 2030 R2	MLTGX	C+	(800) 225-2606	C / 4.6	5.58	4.78	17.92 /42	4.48 /49	8.28 /44	1.05	1.37
AA	MFS Lifetime 2030 R3	MLTHX	C+	(800) 225-2606	C / 4.8	5.69	4.89	18.20 /44	4.72 /51	8.56 /47	1.24	1.12
AA	MFS Lifetime 2030 R4	MLTJX	B-	(800) 225-2606	C / 5.1	5.67	5.03	18.53 /45	4.99 /54	8.82 /49	1.45	0.87
GI	MFS Lifetime 2035 A	LFEAX	C+	(800) 225-2606	C- / 4.2	6.19	5.62	19.53 /50	5.03 /55	--	1.04	1.25
GI	MFS Lifetime 2035 B	LFEBX	C+	(800) 225-2606	C / 4.7	5.92	5.18	18.66 /46	4.25 /46	--	0.38	2.00
GI	MFS Lifetime 2035 C	LFECX	C+	(800) 225-2606	C / 4.7	5.93	5.19	18.63 /46	4.26 /46	--	0.30	2.00
GI	MFS Lifetime 2035 I	LFEDX	B-	(800) 225-2606	C / 5.4	5.90	5.42	19.55 /50	5.19 /56	--	1.31	1.00
GI	MFS Lifetime 2035 R1	LFERX	C+	(800) 225-2606	C / 4.7	6.02	5.21	18.75 /46	4.27 /46	--	0.95	2.00
GI	MFS Lifetime 2035 R2	LFESX	B-	(800) 225-2606	C / 5.1	6.05	5.40	19.22 /48	4.77 /52	--	1.04	1.50
GI	MFS Lifetime 2035 R3	LFETX	B-	(800) 225-2606	C / 5.3	6.13	5.55	19.54 /50	5.03 /55	--	1.13	1.25
GI	MFS Lifetime 2035 R4	LFEUX	B-	(800) 225-2606	C+ / 5.6	6.23	5.74	19.91 /51	5.32 /58	--	1.30	1.00
AA	MFS Lifetime 2040 A	MLFAX	C	(800) 225-2606	C / 4.4	6.49	5.92	20.40 /54	5.16 /56	9.35 /53	0.94	1.16
AA	MFS Lifetime 2040 B	MLFBX	C+	(800) 225-2606	C / 4.9	6.25	5.52	19.39 /49	4.36 /47	8.52 /46	0.28	1.91
AA	MFS Lifetime 2040 C	MLFCX	C+	(800) 225-2606	C / 4.9	6.19	5.53	19.39 /49	4.37 /47	8.51 /46	0.30	1.91
AA	MFS Lifetime 2040 I	MLFIX	B-	(800) 225-2606	C+ / 5.7	6.32	5.83	20.36 /54	5.35 /58	9.56 /55	1.20	0.91
AA	MFS Lifetime 2040 R1	MLFEX	C+	(800) 225-2606	C / 4.9	6.23	5.50	19.46 /49	4.37 /47	8.52 /46	0.05	1.91
AA	MFS Lifetime 2040 R2	MLFGX	C+	(800) 225-2606	C / 5.3	6.37	5.72	19.94 /52	4.88 /53	9.07 /51	0.78	1.41
AA	MFS Lifetime 2040 R3	MLFHX	B-	(800) 225-2606	C+ / 5.6	6.41	5.91	20.31 /54	5.16 /56	9.34 /53	0.99	1.16
AA	MFS Lifetime 2040 R4	MLFJX	B-	(800) 225-2606	C+ / 5.8	6.48	6.05	20.62 /56	5.42 /59	9.61 /55	1.20	0.91
GI	MFS Lifetime 2045 A	LTMAX	C+	(800) 225-2606	C / 4.4	6.48	5.99	20.35 /54	5.19 /56	--	0.94	1.39
GI	MFS Lifetime 2045 B	LTMBX	C+	(800) 225-2606	C / 5.0	6.25	5.60	19.52 /49	4.39 /47	--	0.33	2.14
GI	MFS Lifetime 2045 C	LTMDX	C+	(800) 225-2606	C / 5.0	6.27	5.61	19.57 /50	4.41 /48	--	0.40	2.14
GI	MFS Lifetime 2045 I	LTMKX	B-	(800) 225-2606	C+ / 6.0	6.68	6.28	20.94 /57	5.49 /59	--	1.19	1.14
GI	MFS Lifetime 2045 R1	LTMRX	C+	(800) 225-2606	C / 5.0	6.25	5.60	19.54 /50	4.39 /47	--	0.49	2.14
GI	MFS Lifetime 2045 R2	LTMSX	B-	(800) 225-2606	C / 5.4	6.38	5.81	20.12 /53	4.92 /53	--	0.95	1.64
GI	MFS Lifetime 2045 R3	LTMTX	B-	(800) 225-2606	C+ / 5.6	6.43	5.94	20.40 /54	5.16 /56	--	1.02	1.39

● Denotes fund is closed to new investors
∗ Denotes fund is included in Section II

Risk Rating/Pts	Standard Deviation	Beta	NAV As of 2/28/17	Total $(Mil)	Cash %	Stocks %	Bonds %	Other %	Portfolio Turnover Ratio	Last Bull Market Return	Last Bear Market Return	Manager Quality Pct	Manager Tenure (Years)	Initial Purch. $	Additional Purch. $	Front End Load	Back End Load
C+ / 6.9	9.4	0.68	38.19	12,693	0	97	1	2	14	82.1	-13.2	95	9	0	0	0.0	0.0
C+ / 6.9	9.4	0.69	33.64	12	0	97	1	2	14	72.5	-13.5	94	9	0	0	0.0	0.0
C+ / 6.9	9.4	0.68	34.20	376	0	97	1	2	14	77.2	-13.3	94	9	0	0	0.0	0.0
C+ / 6.9	9.4	0.68	36.24	1,264	0	97	1	2	14	79.6	-13.3	95	9	0	0	0.0	0.0
C+ / 6.9	9.4	0.68	36.55	1,123	0	97	1	2	14	82.0	-13.1	95	9	0	0	0.0	0.0
B / 8.8	4.7	0.70	12.79	49	22	34	43	1	11	48.6	-10.1	52	12	1,000	50	5.8	0.0
B / 8.9	4.7	0.70	12.71	6	22	34	43	1	11	42.7	-10.3	42	12	1,000	50	0.0	0.0
B / 8.8	4.7	0.70	12.54	17	22	34	43	1	11	42.6	-10.3	41	12	1,000	50	0.0	0.0
B / 8.7	4.7	0.70	12.87	2	22	34	43	1	11	50.7	-10.0	56	12	0	0	0.0	0.0
B / 8.9	4.6	0.70	12.75	4	22	34	43	1	11	42.7	-10.4	42	12	0	0	0.0	0.0
B / 8.8	4.7	0.70	12.70	75	22	34	43	1	11	46.5	-10.1	49	12	0	0	0.0	0.0
B / 8.8	4.6	0.70	12.80	72	22	34	43	1	11	48.6	-10.1	53	12	0	0	0.0	0.0
B / 8.7	4.7	0.70	12.85	186	22	34	43	1	11	50.6	-10.0	56	12	0	0	0.0	0.0
B / 8.4	6.3	0.57	12.18	14	11	54	34	1	10	N/A	N/A	51	5	1,000	50	5.8	0.0
B / 8.5	6.3	0.57	12.10	1	11	54	34	1	10	N/A	N/A	40	5	1,000	50	0.0	0.0
B / 8.5	6.3	0.57	12.05	3	11	54	34	1	10	N/A	N/A	40	5	1,000	50	0.0	0.0
B / 8.4	6.3	0.57	12.21	N/A	11	54	34	1	10	N/A	N/A	54	5	0	0	0.0	0.0
B / 8.6	6.3	0.57	12.17	N/A	11	54	34	1	10	N/A	N/A	40	5	0	0	0.0	0.0
B / 8.5	6.3	0.57	12.12	22	11	54	34	1	10	N/A	N/A	47	5	0	0	0.0	0.0
B / 8.4	6.3	0.57	12.17	36	11	54	34	1	10	N/A	N/A	51	5	0	0	0.0	0.0
B / 8.4	6.3	0.57	12.21	130	11	54	34	1	10	N/A	N/A	54	5	0	0	0.0	0.0
B- / 7.6	8.0	1.24	14.31	54	6	69	23	2	6	76.4	-16.3	21	N/A	1,000	50	5.8	0.0
B- / 7.7	8.0	1.24	14.13	9	6	69	23	2	6	69.3	-16.5	15	N/A	1,000	50	0.0	0.0
B- / 7.7	8.1	1.24	14.05	16	6	69	23	2	6	69.4	-16.6	14	N/A	1,000	50	0.0	0.0
B- / 7.6	8.0	1.24	14.37	2	6	69	23	2	6	78.5	-16.2	22	N/A	0	0	0.0	0.0
B- / 7.7	8.1	1.25	14.20	5	6	69	23	2	6	69.4	-16.6	14	N/A	0	0	0.0	0.0
B- / 7.6	8.1	1.24	14.18	103	6	69	23	2	6	74.1	-16.5	18	N/A	0	0	0.0	0.0
B- / 7.6	8.0	1.24	14.28	102	6	69	23	2	6	76.5	-16.4	20	N/A	0	0	0.0	0.0
B- / 7.6	8.1	1.24	14.37	230	6	69	23	2	6	78.7	-16.2	23	N/A	0	0	0.0	0.0
B- / 7.4	8.5	0.79	13.22	10	7	79	12	2	7	N/A	N/A	34	5	1,000	50	5.8	0.0
B- / 7.4	8.6	0.79	13.14	1	7	79	12	2	7	N/A	N/A	25	5	1,000	50	0.0	0.0
B- / 7.4	8.6	0.79	13.10	2	7	79	12	2	7	N/A	N/A	25	5	1,000	50	0.0	0.0
B- / 7.4	8.6	0.79	13.23	N/A	7	79	12	2	7	N/A	N/A	35	5	0	0	0.0	0.0
B- / 7.5	8.6	0.79	13.20	1	7	79	12	2	7	N/A	N/A	25	5	0	0	0.0	0.0
B- / 7.4	8.6	0.79	13.17	17	7	79	12	2	7	N/A	N/A	30	5	0	0	0.0	0.0
B- / 7.4	8.5	0.79	13.23	32	7	79	12	2	7	N/A	N/A	33	5	0	0	0.0	0.0
B- / 7.4	8.5	0.79	13.27	113	7	79	12	2	7	N/A	N/A	37	5	0	0	0.0	0.0
B- / 7.0	9.0	1.39	14.69	34	4	85	9	2	6	84.9	-18.0	15	N/A	1,000	50	5.8	0.0
B- / 7.1	9.0	1.39	14.57	5	4	85	9	2	6	77.4	-18.2	10	N/A	1,000	50	0.0	0.0
B- / 7.1	9.0	1.39	14.40	11	4	85	9	2	6	77.3	-18.2	10	N/A	1,000	50	0.0	0.0
B- / 7.0	9.0	1.39	14.76	2	4	85	9	2	6	86.9	-17.9	16	N/A	0	0	0.0	0.0
B- / 7.1	9.0	1.39	14.52	5	4	85	9	2	6	77.3	-18.2	10	N/A	0	0	0.0	0.0
B- / 7.0	9.0	1.39	14.57	78	4	85	9	2	6	82.2	-18.1	13	N/A	0	0	0.0	0.0
B- / 7.0	9.0	1.39	14.68	58	4	85	9	2	6	84.8	-18.0	15	N/A	0	0	0.0	0.0
B- / 7.0	9.0	1.39	14.78	204	4	85	9	2	6	87.4	-17.9	17	N/A	0	0	0.0	0.0
B- / 7.1	9.0	0.84	13.49	6	6	87	6	1	6	N/A	N/A	30	5	1,000	50	5.8	0.0
B- / 7.1	9.0	0.84	13.42	1	6	87	6	1	6	N/A	N/A	22	5	1,000	50	0.0	0.0
B- / 7.1	9.1	0.84	13.38	2	6	87	6	1	6	N/A	N/A	22	5	1,000	50	0.0	0.0
B- / 7.1	9.0	0.84	13.54	N/A	6	87	6	1	6	N/A	N/A	33	5	0	0	0.0	0.0
B- / 7.2	9.1	0.84	13.47	N/A	6	87	6	1	6	N/A	N/A	21	5	0	0	0.0	0.0
B- / 7.1	9.1	0.84	13.41	10	6	87	6	1	6	N/A	N/A	26	5	0	0	0.0	0.0
B- / 7.1	9.1	0.84	13.48	21	6	87	6	1	6	N/A	N/A	29	5	0	0	0.0	0.0

Fund Type	Fund Name	Ticker Symbol	Overall Investment Rating	Phone	Perfor-mance Rating/Pts	Total Return % through 2/28/17			Annualized		Incl. in Returns	
						3 Mo	6 Mo	1Yr / Pct	3Yr / Pct	5Yr / Pct	Dividend Yield	Expense Ratio
GI	MFS Lifetime 2045 R4	LTMUX	B-	(800) 225-2606	C+ / 5.9	6.52	6.12	20.76 /56	5.44 /59	--	1.19	1.14
AA	MFS Lifetime 2050 A	MFFSX	C+	(800) 225-2606	C / 4.4	6.50	5.96	20.41 /54	5.17 /56	9.36 /53	0.93	1.33
AA	MFS Lifetime 2050 B	MFFRX	C+	(800) 225-2606	C / 5.0	6.32	5.58	19.50 /49	4.40 /47	8.54 /47	0.29	2.08
AA	MFS Lifetime 2050 C	MFFDX	C+	(800) 225-2606	C / 5.0	6.27	5.59	19.51 /49	4.39 /47	8.52 /46	0.39	2.08
AA	MFS Lifetime 2050 I	MFFIX	B-	(800) 225-2606	C+ / 5.9	6.66	6.19	20.85 /57	5.48 /59	9.65 /56	1.18	1.08
AA	MFS Lifetime 2050 R1	MFFMX	C+	(800) 225-2606	C / 5.0	6.30	5.62	19.58 /50	4.40 /47	8.53 /47	0.43	2.08
AA	MFS Lifetime 2050 R2	MFFNX	B-	(800) 225-2606	C / 5.4	6.46	5.85	20.12 /53	4.93 /53	9.09 /51	0.83	1.58
AA	MFS Lifetime 2050 R3	MFFOX	B-	(800) 225-2606	C+ / 5.6	6.47	5.94	20.38 /54	5.18 /56	9.35 /53	0.99	1.33
AA	MFS Lifetime 2050 R4	MFFPX	B-	(800) 225-2606	C+ / 5.9	6.59	6.12	20.79 /56	5.46 /59	9.63 /56	1.18	1.08
GI	MFS Lifetime 2055 A	LFIAX	C+	(800) 225-2606	C / 4.4	6.46	5.98	20.33 /54	5.17 /56	--	0.88	2.56
GI	MFS Lifetime 2055 B	LFIBX	C+	(800) 225-2606	C / 5.0	6.28	5.56	19.41 /49	4.40 /47	--	0.32	3.31
GI	MFS Lifetime 2055 C	LFICX	C+	(800) 225-2606	C / 4.9	6.20	5.55	19.42 /49	4.39 /47	--	0.28	3.31
GI	MFS Lifetime 2055 I	LFIIX	B-	(800) 225-2606	C+ / 5.6	6.11	5.63	20.16 /53	5.31 /58	--	1.13	2.31
GI	MFS Lifetime 2055 R1	LFIRX	C+	(800) 225-2606	C / 4.9	6.20	5.48	19.35 /49	4.38 /47	--	0.90	3.31
GI	MFS Lifetime 2055 R2	LFISX	B-	(800) 225-2606	C / 5.4	6.32	5.76	19.92 /52	4.91 /53	--	0.86	2.81
GI	MFS Lifetime 2055 R3	LFITX	B-	(800) 225-2606	C+ / 5.6	6.41	5.93	20.26 /53	5.17 /56	--	0.96	2.56
GI	MFS Lifetime 2055 R4	LFIUX	B-	(800) 225-2606	C+ / 5.9	6.57	6.09	20.68 /56	5.46 /59	--	1.12	2.31
AA	MFS Lifetime Income 529A	MLLQX	U	(800) 225-2606	U /	2.66	1.08	7.89 / 7	--	--	1.74	1.13
AA	MFS Lifetime Income 529C	MLLSX	U	(800) 225-2606	U /	2.47	0.70	7.09 / 6	--	--	1.11	1.88
AA	MFS Lifetime Income A	MLLAX	C	(800) 225-2606	D- / 1.4	2.63	1.06	7.87 / 7	2.81 /30	4.09 /16	1.79	1.03
AA	MFS Lifetime Income B	MLLBX	C	(800) 225-2606	D / 1.6	2.43	0.68	7.06 / 6	2.04 /24	3.29 /12	1.16	1.78
AA	MFS Lifetime Income C	MLLCX	C	(800) 225-2606	D / 1.6	2.52	0.68	7.15 / 6	2.04 /24	3.29 /12	1.16	1.78
AA	MFS Lifetime Income I	MLLIX	C+	(800) 225-2606	D / 2.1	2.78	1.27	8.22 / 8	3.10 /33	4.34 /17	2.14	0.78
AA	MFS Lifetime Income R1	MLLEX	C	(800) 225-2606	D / 1.6	2.52	0.76	7.14 / 6	2.07 /24	3.32 /12	1.16	1.78
AA	MFS Lifetime Income R2	MLLGX	C+	(800) 225-2606	D / 1.9	2.65	1.01	7.68 / 7	2.55 /28	3.82 /14	1.65	1.28
AA	MFS Lifetime Income R3	MLLHX	C+	(800) 225-2606	D / 2.0	2.63	1.06	7.86 / 7	2.81 /30	4.06 /16	1.89	1.03
AA	MFS Lifetime Income R4	MLLJX	C+	(800) 225-2606	D / 2.1	2.78	1.27	8.22 / 8	3.10 /33	4.32 /17	2.14	0.78
GR	MFS Low Volatility Equity A	MLVAX	A-	(800) 225-2606	B- / 7.2	7.26	6.35	17.66 /41	10.46 /96	--	1.02	1.57
GR	MFS Low Volatility Equity B	MLVBX	A	(800) 225-2606	B / 7.6	6.96	5.95	16.64 /37	9.61 /91	--	0.33	2.32
GR	MFS Low Volatility Equity C	MLVGX	A	(800) 225-2606	B / 7.6	6.98	5.98	16.75 /37	9.63 /91	--	0.46	2.32
GR	MFS Low Volatility Equity I	MLVHX	A+	(800) 225-2606	B+ / 8.4	7.23	6.48	17.87 /42	10.68 /96	--	1.34	1.32
GR	MFS Low Volatility Equity R1	MLVMX	A	(800) 225-2606	B / 7.6	6.94	5.92	16.72 /37	9.62 /91	--	0.27	2.32
GR	MFS Low Volatility Equity R2	MLVOX	A	(800) 225-2606	B / 8.0	7.14	6.26	17.29 /40	10.21 /94	--	0.70	1.82
GR	MFS Low Volatility Equity R3	MLVPX	A+	(800) 225-2606	B / 8.2	7.23	6.41	17.61 /41	10.45 /96	--	1.01	1.57
GR	MFS Low Volatility Equity R4	MLVRX	A+	(800) 225-2606	B+ / 8.4	7.23	6.48	17.92 /42	10.69 /96	--	1.32	1.32
GR	MFS Low Volatility Equity R6	MLVTX	A+	(800) 225-2606	B+ / 8.4	7.26	6.53	17.95 /43	10.76 /97	--	1.42	1.25
GL	MFS Low Volatility Global Eq R4	MVGMX	B-	(800) 225-2606	C / 4.9	6.43	1.85	13.18 /22	6.42 /68	--	1.52	1.19
GL	MFS Low Volatility Global Equity A	MVGAX	C	(800) 225-2606	C- / 3.6	6.46	1.75	12.96 /22	6.24 /66	--	1.26	1.44
GL	MFS Low Volatility Global Equity B	MVGBX	C+	(800) 225-2606	C- / 4.0	6.17	1.31	12.02 /18	5.37 /58	--	0.54	2.19
GL	MFS Low Volatility Global Equity C	MVGCX	C+	(800) 225-2606	C- / 4.1	6.18	1.39	12.03 /18	5.38 /58	--	0.72	2.19
GL	MFS Low Volatility Global Equity I	MVGIX	B-	(800) 225-2606	C / 5.0	6.53	1.86	13.20 /22	6.43 /68	--	1.53	1.19
GL	MFS Low Volatility Global Equity R1	MVGJX	C+	(800) 225-2606	C- / 4.1	6.24	1.41	12.09 /18	5.40 /58	--	0.57	2.19
GL	MFS Low Volatility Global Equity R2	MVGKX	C+	(800) 225-2606	C / 4.5	6.37	1.59	12.63 /20	5.89 /63	--	1.05	1.69
GL	MFS Low Volatility Global Equity R3	MVGLX	C+	(800) 225-2606	C / 4.7	6.44	1.72	12.89 /21	6.19 /66	--	1.28	1.44
GL	MFS Low Volatility Global Equity R6	MVGNX	B-	(800) 225-2606	C / 5.0	6.45	1.88	13.25 /23	6.45 /68	--	1.57	1.13
GR	MFS Managed Wealth I	MNWIX	U	(800) 225-2606	U /	1.61	-0.21	2.43 / 2	--	--	0.00	1.29
GR	MFS Mass Investors Gr Stk 529A	EISTX	C+	(800) 225-2606	C+ / 6.3	8.98	5.68	18.91 /47	8.10 /80	11.84 /73	0.69	0.84
GR	MFS Mass Investors Gr Stk 529B	EMIVX	C+	(800) 225-2606	C+ / 6.8	8.83	5.34	18.00 /43	7.28 /74	10.99 /66	0.12	1.59
GR	MFS Mass Investors Gr Stk 529C	EMICX	C+	(800) 225-2606	C+ / 6.8	8.83	5.32	18.01 /43	7.28 /74	10.98 /66	0.20	1.59
GR	MFS Mass Investors Gr Stk A	MIGFX	C+	(800) 225-2606	C+ / 6.4	9.03	5.71	18.99 /47	8.15 /80	11.88 /73	0.66	0.74
GR	MFS Mass Investors Gr Stk B	MIGBX	C+	(800) 225-2606	C+ / 6.8	8.76	5.31	18.06 /43	7.32 /74	11.04 /66	0.04	1.49
GR	MFS Mass Investors Gr Stk C	MIGDX	C+	(800) 225-2606	C+ / 6.8	8.77	5.34	18.07 /43	7.32 /74	11.04 /66	0.11	1.49

● Denotes fund is closed to new investors
* Denotes fund is included in Section II

www.thestreetratings.com

Risk Rating/Pts	3 Year Standard Deviation	Beta	NAV As of 2/28/17	Total $(Mil)	Cash %	Stocks %	Bonds %	Other %	Portfolio Turnover Ratio	Last Bull Market Return	Last Bear Market Return	Manager Quality Pct	Manager Tenure (Years)	Initial Purch. $	Additional Purch. $	Front End Load	Back End Load
B- /7.1	9.0	0.84	13.52	81	6	87	6	1	6	N/A	N/A	32	5	0	0	0.0	0.0
B- /7.1	9.0	1.39	16.27	11	6	87	6	1	7	84.8	-17.6	15	7	1,000	50	5.8	0.0
B- /7.1	9.0	1.39	16.11	1	6	87	6	1	7	77.3	-17.9	10	7	1,000	50	0.0	0.0
B- /7.1	9.1	1.40	16.01	2	6	87	6	1	7	77.3	-17.9	10	7	1,000	50	0.0	0.0
B- /7.1	9.1	1.40	16.26	N/A	6	87	6	1	7	87.5	-17.6	17	7	0	0	0.0	0.0
B- /7.2	9.1	1.40	16.05	1	6	87	6	1	7	77.4	-17.9	10	7	0	0	0.0	0.0
B- /7.1	9.1	1.40	16.09	31	6	87	6	1	7	82.4	-17.8	13	7	0	0	0.0	0.0
B- /7.1	9.0	1.39	16.17	25	6	87	6	1	7	84.6	-17.6	15	7	0	0	0.0	0.0
B- /7.1	9.1	1.40	16.24	88	6	87	6	1	7	87.3	-17.6	17	7	0	0	0.0	0.0
B- /7.2	8.9	0.83	13.70	3	4	88	6	2	14	N/A	N/A	30	5	1,000	50	5.8	0.0
B- /7.2	9.0	0.83	13.67	N/A	4	88	6	2	14	N/A	N/A	22	5	1,000	50	0.0	0.0
B- /7.2	9.0	0.83	13.57	1	4	88	6	2	14	N/A	N/A	22	5	1,000	50	0.0	0.0
B- /7.1	8.9	0.83	13.69	N/A	4	88	6	2	14	N/A	N/A	32	5	0	0	0.0	0.0
B- /7.2	8.9	0.83	13.64	N/A	4	88	6	2	14	N/A	N/A	22	5	0	0	0.0	0.0
B- /7.2	8.9	0.83	13.64	6	4	88	6	2	14	N/A	N/A	28	5	0	0	0.0	0.0
B- /7.2	8.9	0.83	13.70	9	4	88	6	2	14	N/A	N/A	30	5	0	0	0.0	0.0
B- /7.2	8.9	0.83	13.75	20	4	88	6	2	14	N/A	N/A	33	5	0	0	0.0	0.0
U /	N/A	N/A	9.96	71	32	25	41	2	10	N/A	N/A	N/A	12	250	0	5.8	0.0
U /	N/A	N/A	9.96	32	32	25	41	2	10	N/A	N/A	N/A	12	250	0	0.0	0.0
B+ /9.6	3.5	0.51	12.10	116	32	25	41	2	10	31.0	-4.1	63	N/A	1,000	50	5.8	0.0
B+ /9.6	3.5	0.51	12.10	16	32	25	41	2	10	25.8	-4.4	52	N/A	1,000	50	0.0	0.0
B+ /9.6	3.5	0.50	12.10	150	32	25	41	2	10	25.8	-4.4	53	N/A	1,000	50	0.0	0.0
B+ /9.6	3.5	0.51	12.11	33	32	25	41	2	10	32.8	-3.9	66	N/A	0	0	0.0	0.0
B+ /9.6	3.6	0.51	12.12	4	32	25	41	2	10	25.9	-4.4	53	N/A	0	0	0.0	0.0
B+ /9.6	3.5	0.51	12.11	31	32	25	41	2	10	29.3	-4.2	60	N/A	0	0	0.0	0.0
B+ /9.6	3.5	0.51	12.10	48	32	25	41	2	10	31.0	-4.1	62	N/A	0	0	0.0	0.0
B+ /9.6	3.5	0.51	12.11	126	32	25	41	2	10	32.8	-3.9	66	N/A	0	0	0.0	0.0
B- /7.4	8.2	0.73	13.24	34	0	99	0	1	38	N/A	N/A	88	4	1,000	0	5.8	0.0
B- /7.4	8.2	0.73	13.21	2	0	99	0	1	38	N/A	N/A	85	4	1,000	0	0.0	0.0
B- /7.4	8.2	0.73	13.18	12	0	99	0	1	38	N/A	N/A	85	4	1,000	0	0.0	0.0
B- /7.4	8.2	0.73	13.25	16	0	99	0	1	38	N/A	N/A	89	4	0	0	0.0	0.0
B- /7.4	8.2	0.73	13.25	N/A	0	99	0	1	38	N/A	N/A	85	4	0	0	0.0	0.0
B- /7.4	8.2	0.73	13.30	N/A	0	99	0	1	38	N/A	N/A	88	4	0	0	0.0	0.0
B- /7.4	8.2	0.73	13.28	N/A	0	99	0	1	38	N/A	N/A	88	4	0	0	0.0	0.0
B- /7.4	8.2	0.73	13.26	N/A	0	99	0	1	38	N/A	N/A	89	4	0	0	0.0	0.0
B- /7.4	8.2	0.73	13.26	2	0	99	0	1	38	N/A	N/A	90	4	0	0	0.0	0.0
B- /7.5	8.5	0.56	12.01	N/A	0	99	0	1	28	N/A	N/A	97	4	0	0	0.0	0.0
B- /7.5	8.6	0.56	12.01	8	0	99	0	1	28	N/A	N/A	97	4	1,000	0	5.8	0.0
B- /7.5	8.5	0.56	11.93	N/A	0	99	0	1	28	N/A	N/A	96	4	1,000	0	0.0	0.0
B- /7.5	8.5	0.56	11.92	2	0	99	0	1	28	N/A	N/A	96	4	1,000	0	0.0	0.0
B- /7.5	8.5	0.56	12.01	30	0	99	0	1	28	N/A	N/A	97	4	0	0	0.0	0.0
B- /7.5	8.5	0.55	11.99	N/A	0	99	0	1	28	N/A	N/A	96	4	0	0	0.0	0.0
B- /7.5	8.5	0.56	12.01	N/A	0	99	0	1	28	N/A	N/A	97	4	0	0	0.0	0.0
B- /7.5	8.5	0.56	12.02	N/A	0	99	0	1	28	N/A	N/A	97	4	0	0	0.0	0.0
B- /7.5	8.6	0.56	12.00	51	0	99	0	1	28	N/A	N/A	97	4	0	0	0.0	0.0
U /	N/A	N/A	9.80	38	11	88	0	1	26	N/A	N/A	N/A	3	0	0	0.0	0.0
C+ /6.1	11.0	1.02	24.65	16	1	97	0	2	24	110.5	-13.2	42	N/A	250	0	5.8	0.0
C+ /6.0	11.0	1.02	21.38	1	1	97	0	2	24	102.0	-13.4	32	N/A	250	0	0.0	0.0
C+ /6.0	11.0	1.02	21.22	5	1	97	0	2	24	102.0	-13.5	32	N/A	250	0	0.0	0.0
C+ /6.1	11.1	1.02	24.98	3,442	1	97	0	2	24	111.0	-13.1	42	N/A	1,000	50	5.8	0.0
C+ /6.1	11.1	1.02	21.93	62	1	97	0	2	24	102.6	-13.5	32	N/A	1,000	50	0.0	0.0
C+ /6.1	11.0	1.02	21.76	243	1	97	0	2	24	102.5	-13.4	32	N/A	1,000	50	0.0	0.0

Fund Type	Fund Name	Ticker Symbol	Overall Investment Rating	Phone	Performance Rating/Pts	3 Mo	6 Mo	1Yr / Pct	3Yr / Pct	5Yr / Pct	Dividend Yield	Expense Ratio
GR	MFS Mass Investors Gr Stk I	MGTIX	B	(800) 225-2606	B- / 7.5	9.07	5.88	19.24 /48	8.40 /82	12.15 /76	0.92	0.49
GR	MFS Mass Investors Gr Stk R1	MIGMX	C+	(800) 225-2606	C+ / 6.8	8.81	5.35	18.08 /43	7.34 /74	11.04 /66	0.13	1.49
GR	MFS Mass Investors Gr Stk R2	MIRGX	B	(800) 225-2606	B- / 7.1	8.95	5.59	18.65 /46	7.87 /78	11.60 /71	0.48	0.99
GR	MFS Mass Investors Gr Stk R3	MIGHX	B	(800) 225-2606	B- / 7.3	8.97	5.72	18.92 /47	8.12 /80	11.87 /73	0.70	0.74
GR	MFS Mass Investors Gr Stk R4	MIGKX	B	(800) 225-2606	B- / 7.5	9.04	5.84	19.24 /48	8.40 /82	12.15 /76	0.92	0.49
GR	MFS Mass Investors Gr Stk R6	MIGNX	B+	(800) 225-2606	B / 7.6	9.13	5.94	19.38 /49	8.52 /83	--	1.01	0.38
GI	MFS Mass Investors Trust 529A	EAMTX	B	(800) 225-2606	B- / 7.4	9.25	9.48	23.96 /70	8.50 /83	13.02 /84	0.80	0.82
GI	MFS Mass Investors Trust 529B	EBMTX	B+	(800) 225-2606	B / 7.9	9.04	9.04	23.33 /68	7.78 /77	12.23 /76	0.49	1.57
GI	MFS Mass Investors Trust 529C	ECITX	B+	(800) 225-2606	B / 7.8	9.03	9.03	22.98 /67	7.66 /76	12.16 /76	0.19	1.57
GI	MFS Mass Investors Trust A	MITTX	B	(800) 225-2606	B- / 7.5	9.24	9.47	23.99 /70	8.53 /83	13.06 /84	0.79	0.72
GI	MFS Mass Investors Trust B	MITBX	B+	(800) 225-2606	B / 7.9	9.04	9.08	23.04 /67	7.71 /77	12.21 /76	0.15	1.47
GI	MFS Mass Investors Trust C	MITCX	B+	(800) 225-2606	B / 7.9	9.03	9.07	23.06 /67	7.72 /77	12.21 /76	0.19	1.47
GI	MFS Mass Investors Trust I	MITIX	A-	(800) 225-2606	B+ / 8.7	9.33	9.64	24.33 /71	8.79 /85	13.33 /87	1.06	0.47
GI	MFS Mass Investors Trust R1	MITGX	B+	(800) 225-2606	B / 7.9	9.05	9.09	23.06 /67	7.72 /77	12.20 /76	0.16	1.47
GI	MFS Mass Investors Trust R2	MIRTX	B+	(800) 225-2606	B+ / 8.3	9.17	9.33	23.68 /69	8.25 /81	12.77 /82	0.62	0.97
GI	MFS Mass Investors Trust R3	MITHX	B+	(800) 225-2606	B+ / 8.5	9.27	9.49	23.99 /70	8.53 /83	13.05 /84	0.83	0.72
GI	MFS Mass Investors Trust R4	MITDX	A-	(800) 225-2606	B+ / 8.7	9.34	9.60	24.31 /71	8.80 /85	13.34 /87	1.03	0.47
GI	MFS Mass Investors Trust R6	MITJX	A-	(800) 225-2606	B+ / 8.7	9.36	9.67	24.44 /71	8.90 /86	--	1.16	0.38
MC	MFS Mid Cap Value 529A	EACVX	B	(800) 225-2606	B- / 7.2	6.28	9.06	26.89 /79	8.17 /80	13.78 /92	1.00	1.29
MC	MFS Mid Cap Value 529B	EBCVX	B	(800) 225-2606	B / 7.7	6.10	8.69	25.92 /76	7.36 /75	12.93 /83	0.30	2.04
MC	MFS Mid Cap Value 529C	ECCVX	B	(800) 225-2606	B / 7.7	6.14	8.66	25.94 /76	7.39 /75	12.95 /83	0.46	2.04
MC	MFS Mid Cap Value A	MVCAX	B	(800) 225-2606	B- / 7.3	6.31	9.10	26.91 /79	8.20 /80	13.83 /92	1.01	1.19
MC	MFS Mid Cap Value B	MCBVX	B	(800) 225-2606	B / 7.7	6.16	8.73	26.04 /76	7.41 /75	12.98 /84	0.43	1.94
MC	MFS Mid Cap Value C	MVCCX	B	(800) 225-2606	B / 7.7	6.11	8.69	25.97 /76	7.39 /75	12.99 /84	0.56	1.94
MC	MFS Mid Cap Value I	MCVIX	B+	(800) 225-2606	B+ / 8.5	6.41	9.24	27.27 /80	8.48 /83	14.12 /94	1.28	0.94
MC	MFS Mid Cap Value Initial		C+	(800) 225-2606	B+ / 8.7	6.51	9.47	27.81 /81	8.63 /84	13.83 /92	0.78	0.82
MC	MFS Mid Cap Value R1	MVCGX	B	(800) 225-2606	B / 7.7	6.10	8.71	26.00 /76	7.41 /75	12.98 /84	0.56	1.94
MC	MFS Mid Cap Value R2	MCVRX	B+	(800) 225-2606	B / 8.1	6.27	8.97	26.66 /78	7.93 /78	13.55 /89	0.92	1.44
MC	MFS Mid Cap Value R3	MVCHX	B+	(800) 225-2606	B+ / 8.3	6.33	9.14	26.95 /79	8.22 /81	13.83 /92	1.08	1.19
MC	MFS Mid Cap Value R4	MVCJX	B+	(800) 225-2606	B+ / 8.5	6.37	9.25	27.27 /80	8.48 /83	14.12 /94	1.29	0.94
MC	MFS Mid Cap Value R6	MVCKX	A-	(800) 225-2606	B+ / 8.6	6.42	9.35	27.46 /80	8.64 /84	--	1.38	0.78
MC	MFS Mid-Cap Growth 529A	EAMCX	C-	(800) 225-2606	C / 4.8	6.44	4.08	18.79 /46	6.51 /69	12.25 /77	0.00	1.34
MC	MFS Mid-Cap Growth 529B	EBCGX	C-	(800) 225-2606	C / 5.3	6.27	3.73	17.92 /42	5.72 /62	11.40 /69	0.00	2.09
MC	MFS Mid-Cap Growth 529C	ECGRX	C-	(800) 225-2606	C / 5.3	6.28	3.76	17.94 /43	5.70 /62	11.38 /69	0.00	2.09
MC	MFS Mid-Cap Growth A	OTCAX	C-	(800) 225-2606	C / 4.9	6.56	4.18	18.86 /46	6.54 /69	12.28 /77	0.00	1.24
MC	MFS Mid-Cap Growth B	OTCBX	C	(800) 225-2606	C / 5.4	6.31	3.74	17.93 /43	5.75 /62	11.43 /69	0.00	1.99
MC	MFS Mid-Cap Growth C	OTCCX	C	(800) 225-2606	C / 5.4	6.31	3.76	17.93 /43	5.75 /62	11.45 /69	0.00	1.99
MC	MFS Mid-Cap Growth I	OTCIX	C+	(800) 225-2606	C+ / 6.3	6.53	4.26	19.09 /48	6.78 /70	12.55 /80	0.00	0.99
MC	MFS Mid-Cap Growth R1	OTCGX	C	(800) 225-2606	C / 5.4	6.34	3.75	18.01 /43	5.75 /62	11.43 /69	0.00	1.99
MC	MFS Mid-Cap Growth R2	MCPRX	C	(800) 225-2606	C+ / 5.8	6.43	4.02	18.60 /45	6.27 /66	11.99 /74	0.00	1.49
MC	MFS Mid-Cap Growth R3	OTCHX	C	(800) 225-2606	C+ / 6.0	6.45	4.14	18.81 /46	6.53 /69	12.28 /77	0.00	1.24
MC	MFS Mid-Cap Growth R4	OTCJX	C+	(800) 225-2606	C+ / 6.3	6.60	4.28	19.18 /48	6.80 /70	12.55 /80	0.00	0.99
MC	MFS Mid-Cap Growth R6	OTCKX	C+	(800) 225-2606	C+ / 6.4	6.57	4.31	19.27 /48	6.89 /71	--	0.00	0.88
AA	MFS Moderate Allocation 529A	EAMDX	C-	(800) 225-2606	D+ / 2.4	4.69	2.76	13.58 /24	3.78 /40	6.64 /32	1.21	1.09
AA	MFS Moderate Allocation 529B	EBMDX	C	(800) 225-2606	D+ / 2.8	4.47	2.38	12.72 /21	3.00 /32	5.84 /27	0.68	1.84
AA	MFS Moderate Allocation 529C	ECMAX	C	(800) 225-2606	D+ / 2.8	4.47	2.37	12.77 /21	3.01 /32	5.84 /27	0.72	1.84
AA	MFS Moderate Allocation A	MAMAX	C-	(800) 225-2606	D+ / 2.4	4.67	2.77	13.70 /24	3.83 /41	6.68 /33	1.24	0.99
AA	MFS Moderate Allocation B	MMABX	C	(800) 225-2606	D+ / 2.8	4.50	2.44	12.82 /21	3.05 /32	5.89 /28	0.69	1.74
AA	MFS Moderate Allocation C	MMACX	C	(800) 225-2606	D+ / 2.8	4.47	2.40	12.84 /21	3.07 /32	5.90 /28	0.70	1.74
AA	MFS Moderate Allocation I	MMAIX	C+	(800) 225-2606	C- / 3.6	4.75	2.93	13.93 /25	4.10 /44	6.96 /34	1.53	0.74
AA	MFS Moderate Allocation R1	MAMFX	C	(800) 225-2606	D+ / 2.8	4.49	2.38	12.83 /21	3.04 /32	5.88 /28	0.71	1.74
AA	MFS Moderate Allocation R2	MARRX	C	(800) 225-2606	C- / 3.2	4.63	2.68	13.42 /23	3.58 /38	6.42 /31	1.09	1.24

• Denotes fund is closed to new investors
∗ Denotes fund is included in Section II

www.thestreetratings.com

I. Index of Stock Mutual Funds

Risk Rating/Pts	3 Year Standard Deviation	Beta	NAV As of 2/28/17	Total $(Mil)	Cash %	Stocks %	Bonds %	Other %	Portfolio Turnover Ratio	Last Bull Market Return	Last Bear Market Return	Manager Quality Pct	Manager Tenure (Years)	Initial Purch. $	Additional Purch. $	Front End Load	Back End Load
C+ / 6.1	11.0	1.02	25.60	794	1	97	0	2	24	113.7	-13.0	45	N/A	0	0	0.0	0.0
C+ / 6.1	11.1	1.02	21.57	31	1	97	0	2	24	102.6	-13.5	32	N/A	0	0	0.0	0.0
C+ / 6.1	11.0	1.02	24.33	198	1	97	0	2	24	108.1	-13.3	38	N/A	0	0	0.0	0.0
C+ / 6.1	11.0	1.02	24.73	464	1	97	0	2	24	111.0	-13.2	42	N/A	0	0	0.0	0.0
C+ / 6.1	11.0	1.02	25.13	767	1	97	0	2	24	113.8	-13.1	46	N/A	0	0	0.0	0.0
C+ / 6.1	11.0	1.02	25.64	636	1	97	0	2	24	N/A	N/A	47	N/A	0	0	0.0	0.0
C+ / 6.0	10.2	0.96	29.27	10	1	98	0	1	18	124.5	-18.0	55	13	250	0	5.8	0.0
C+ / 6.0	10.2	0.96	27.75	1	1	98	0	1	18	116.1	-18.2	46	13	250	0	0.0	0.0
C+ / 6.0	10.2	0.96	27.43	3	1	98	0	1	18	115.3	-18.2	44	13	250	0	0.0	0.0
C+ / 6.1	10.2	0.96	29.92	3,367	1	98	0	1	18	124.9	-17.9	55	13	1,000	50	5.8	0.0
C+ / 6.1	10.2	0.96	29.09	78	1	98	0	1	18	115.8	-18.1	45	13	1,000	50	0.0	0.0
C+ / 6.1	10.2	0.96	28.59	311	1	98	0	1	18	115.8	-18.2	45	13	1,000	50	0.0	0.0
C+ / 6.0	10.2	0.96	29.17	1,683	1	98	0	1	18	127.9	-17.8	59	13	0	0	0.0	0.0
C+ / 6.1	10.2	0.96	28.44	8	1	98	0	1	18	115.8	-18.2	45	13	0	0	0.0	0.0
C+ / 6.0	10.2	0.96	28.65	157	1	98	0	1	18	121.8	-18.0	52	13	0	0	0.0	0.0
C+ / 6.0	10.2	0.96	29.68	333	1	98	0	1	18	124.8	-17.9	55	13	0	0	0.0	0.0
C+ / 6.0	10.2	0.96	30.17	60	1	98	0	1	18	127.9	-17.9	59	13	0	0	0.0	0.0
C+ / 6.0	10.2	0.96	29.19	123	1	98	0	1	18	N/A	N/A	60	13	0	0	0.0	0.0
C+ / 6.0	11.3	0.91	21.80	6	0	98	2	0	27	134.0	-21.0	68	9	250	0	5.8	0.0
C+ / 5.9	11.3	0.91	20.41	N/A	0	98	2	0	27	124.5	-21.2	59	9	250	0	0.0	0.0
C+ / 5.9	11.3	0.91	20.48	2	0	98	2	0	27	124.6	-21.1	60	9	250	0	0.0	0.0
C+ / 6.0	11.3	0.91	22.14	1,070	0	98	2	0	27	134.3	-20.9	69	9	1,000	50	5.8	0.0
C+ / 5.9	11.3	0.91	21.03	22	0	98	2	0	27	125.1	-21.2	60	9	1,000	50	0.0	0.0
C+ / 5.9	11.3	0.91	20.94	168	0	98	2	0	27	125.0	-21.2	59	9	1,000	50	0.0	0.0
C+ / 6.0	11.3	0.91	22.66	1,157	0	98	2	0	27	137.6	-20.8	72	9	0	0	0.0	0.0
C- / 3.3	11.4	0.92	8.67	275	0	99	0	1	51	136.2	-19.8	72	5	0	0	0.0	0.0
C+ / 5.9	11.3	0.91	20.62	13	0	98	2	0	27	125.1	-21.1	59	9	0	0	0.0	0.0
C+ / 6.0	11.3	0.91	21.63	155	0	98	2	0	27	131.3	-21.0	66	9	0	0	0.0	0.0
C+ / 6.0	11.3	0.91	22.07	423	0	98	2	0	27	134.4	-20.9	69	9	0	0	0.0	0.0
C+ / 6.0	11.3	0.91	22.23	566	0	98	2	0	27	137.6	-20.8	72	9	0	0	0.0	0.0
C+ / 6.0	11.3	0.91	22.68	2,683	0	98	2	0	27	N/A	N/A	73	9	0	0	0.0	0.0
C / 5.3	11.1	0.80	14.22	4	0	98	1	1	43	113.3	-19.7	61	9	250	0	5.8	0.0
C / 5.1	11.1	0.80	12.20	N/A	0	98	1	1	43	104.4	-19.8	50	9	250	0	0.0	0.0
C / 5.1	11.1	0.81	11.86	2	0	98	1	1	43	104.5	-20.0	50	9	250	0	0.0	0.0
C / 5.3	11.1	0.81	14.62	497	0	98	1	1	43	113.6	-19.7	61	9	1,000	0	5.8	0.0
C / 5.1	11.1	0.81	12.46	16	0	98	1	1	43	104.9	-20.0	50	9	1,000	0	0.0	0.0
C / 5.1	11.1	0.81	12.13	56	0	98	1	1	43	104.9	-19.9	51	9	1,000	0	0.0	0.0
C / 5.3	11.1	0.81	15.34	209	0	98	1	1	43	116.2	-19.6	64	9	0	0	0.0	0.0
C / 5.1	11.1	0.81	12.41	2	0	98	1	1	43	105.1	-20.0	51	9	0	0	0.0	0.0
C / 5.2	11.1	0.81	13.91	6	0	98	1	1	43	110.6	-19.8	57	9	0	0	0.0	0.0
C / 5.3	11.1	0.81	14.53	25	0	98	1	1	43	113.5	-19.7	61	9	0	0	0.0	0.0
C / 5.3	11.1	0.80	15.03	15	0	98	1	1	43	116.4	-19.6	64	9	0	0	0.0	0.0
C / 5.3	11.1	0.81	15.40	1,301	0	98	1	1	43	N/A	N/A	65	9	0	0	0.0	0.0
B / 8.0	6.3	0.98	16.69	204	7	54	37	2	2	55.6	-10.8	30	15	250	0	5.8	0.0
B / 8.0	6.4	0.98	16.41	15	7	54	37	2	2	49.4	-11.1	22	15	250	0	0.0	0.0
B / 8.0	6.4	0.98	16.31	77	7	54	37	2	2	49.3	-11.1	22	15	250	0	0.0	0.0
B / 8.0	6.4	0.98	16.77	3,063	7	54	37	2	2	56.0	-10.8	30	15	1,000	50	5.8	0.0
B / 8.0	6.4	0.98	16.58	299	7	54	37	2	2	49.8	-11.0	23	15	1,000	50	0.0	0.0
B / 8.0	6.4	0.98	16.47	1,234	7	54	37	2	2	49.7	-11.0	23	15	1,000	50	0.0	0.0
B / 8.0	6.3	0.97	16.99	191	7	54	37	2	2	58.1	-10.7	34	15	0	0	0.0	0.0
B / 8.0	6.4	0.98	16.14	32	7	54	37	2	2	49.7	-11.1	23	N/A	0	0	0.0	0.0
B / 8.0	6.4	0.98	16.43	196	7	54	37	2	2	53.8	-10.8	28	14	0	0	0.0	0.0

Data as of February 28, 2017

I. Index of Stock Mutual Funds

99 Pct = Best
0 Pct = Worst

Fund Type	Fund Name	Ticker Symbol	Overall Investment Rating	Phone	Performance Rating/Pts	3 Mo	6 Mo	1Yr / Pct	3Yr / Pct	5Yr / Pct	Dividend Yield	Expense Ratio
AA	MFS Moderate Allocation R3	MAMHX	C	(800) 225-2606	C- / 3.4	4.71	2.79	13.66 /24	3.83 /41	6.70 /33	1.32	0.99
AA	MFS Moderate Allocation R4	MAMJX	C+	(800) 225-2606	C- / 3.6	4.75	2.91	14.00 /25	4.09 /44	6.96 /34	1.55	0.74
SC	MFS New Discovery 529A	EANDX	D-	(800) 225-2606	C- / 3.4	5.83	6.60	29.37 /85	1.47 /21	8.80 /49	0.00	1.45
SC	MFS New Discovery 529B	EBNDX	D-	(800) 225-2606	C- / 3.9	5.64	6.18	28.38 /82	0.71 /17	7.97 /42	0.00	2.20
SC	MFS New Discovery 529C	ECNDX	D-	(800) 225-2606	C- / 3.9	5.69	6.23	28.38 /82	0.69 /17	7.96 /42	0.00	2.20
SC	MFS New Discovery A	MNDAX	D-	(800) 225-2606	C- / 3.4	5.87	6.66	29.42 /85	1.52 /21	8.83 /49	0.00	1.35
SC	MFS New Discovery B	MNDBX	D-	(800) 225-2606	C- / 4.0	5.71	6.29	28.47 /83	0.77 /17	8.02 /42	0.00	2.10
SC	MFS New Discovery C	MNDCX	D-	(800) 225-2606	C- / 4.0	5.70	6.28	28.48 /83	0.76 /17	8.03 /42	0.00	2.10
SC	MFS New Discovery I	MNDIX	D	(800) 225-2606	C / 4.8	5.92	6.77	29.70 /86	1.77 /22	9.10 /51	0.00	1.10
SC	MFS New Discovery R1	MNDGX	D-	(800) 225-2606	C- / 4.0	5.70	6.23	28.48 /83	0.76 /17	8.03 /42	0.00	2.10
SC	MFS New Discovery R2	MNDRX	D	(800) 225-2606	C / 4.3	5.78	6.47	29.08 /84	1.25 /20	8.56 /47	0.00	1.60
SC	MFS New Discovery R3	MNDHX	D	(800) 225-2606	C / 4.6	5.88	6.62	29.40 /85	1.51 /21	8.83 /49	0.00	1.35
SC	MFS New Discovery R4	MNDJX	D	(800) 225-2606	C / 4.8	5.96	6.80	29.76 /86	1.77 /22	9.11 /52	0.00	1.10
SC	MFS New Discovery R6	MNDKX	D+	(800) 225-2606	C / 4.9	5.96	6.85	29.89 /86	1.89 /23	--	0.00	0.97
GL	MFS New Discovery Value A	NDVAX	A	(800) 225-2606	A / 9.4	6.70	15.08	37.22 /96	9.16 /88	14.36 /95	0.37	1.33
GL	MFS New Discovery Value B	NDVBX	A	(800) 225-2606	A+ / 9.6	6.50	14.66	36.17 /95	8.35 /82	13.52 /89	0.05	2.08
GL	MFS New Discovery Value C	NDVCX	A	(800) 225-2606	A+ / 9.6	6.47	14.67	36.17 /95	8.33 /81	13.51 /89	0.00	2.08
GL	MFS New Discovery Value I	NDVIX	A+	(800) 225-2606	A+ / 9.7	6.74	15.23	37.54 /96	9.42 /90	14.64 /96	0.52	1.08
GL	MFS New Discovery Value R1	NDVRX	A	(800) 225-2606	A+ / 9.6	6.51	14.68	36.19 /95	8.33 /82	13.50 /89	0.00	2.08
GL	MFS New Discovery Value R2	NDVSX	A	(800) 225-2606	A+ / 9.7	6.53	14.91	36.81 /96	8.87 /86	14.09 /94	0.23	1.58
GL	MFS New Discovery Value R3	NDVTX	A	(800) 225-2606	A+ / 9.7	6.61	15.04	37.11 /96	9.15 /88	14.36 /95	0.33	1.33
GL	MFS New Discovery Value R4	NDVUX	A+	(800) 225-2606	A+ / 9.7	6.73	15.21	37.46 /96	9.43 /90	14.66 /96	0.51	1.08
GR	MFS New Discovery Value R6	NDVVX	A+	(800) 225-2606	A+ / 9.7	6.78	15.35	37.68 /96	9.54 /91	--	0.58	1.00
GR	MFS Research A	MFRFX	B-	(800) 225-2606	B- / 7.0	8.15	7.82	23.31 /68	8.36 /82	12.78 /82	0.86	0.82
GR	MFS Research B	MFRBX	B	(800) 225-2606	B- / 7.4	7.97	7.42	22.42 /64	7.55 /76	11.94 /74	0.25	1.57
GR	MFS Research C	MFRCX	B	(800) 225-2606	B- / 7.4	7.95	7.40	22.38 /64	7.55 /76	11.94 /74	0.32	1.57
GR	MFS Research I	MRFIX	B+	(800) 225-2606	B / 8.2	8.24	7.97	23.64 /69	8.63 /84	13.07 /85	1.11	0.57
FO	MFS Research International 529A	EARSX	E+	(800) 225-2606	E / 0.4	5.83	1.83	13.54 /24	-2.10 / 6	3.27 /12	1.85	1.22
FO	MFS Research International 529B	EBRIX	E+	(800) 225-2606	E / 0.5	5.63	1.49	12.78 /21	-2.83 / 5	2.49 / 9	1.79	1.97
FO	MFS Research International 529C	ECRIX	E+	(800) 225-2606	E / 0.5	5.61	1.47	12.72 /21	-2.84 / 5	2.49 / 9	1.84	1.97
FO	MFS Research International A	MRSAX	E+	(800) 225-2606	E / 0.4	5.83	1.88	13.58 /24	-2.07 / 6	3.31 /12	1.55	1.12
FO	MFS Research International B	MRIBX	D-	(800) 225-2606	E+ / 0.6	5.63	1.47	12.73 /21	-2.80 / 5	2.54 / 9	0.72	1.87
FO	MFS Research International C	MRICX	E+	(800) 225-2606	E+ / 0.6	5.67	1.47	12.79 /21	-2.79 / 5	2.53 / 9	0.90	1.87
FO	MFS Research International I	MRSIX	D-	(800) 225-2606	E+ / 0.8	5.89	2.01	13.90 /25	-1.81 / 7	3.56 /13	1.89	0.87
FO	MFS Research International R1	MRSGX	E+	(800) 225-2606	E+ / 0.6	5.64	1.52	12.77 /21	-2.78 / 5	2.54 / 9	0.81	1.87
FO	MFS Research International R2	MRSRX	D-	(800) 225-2606	E+ / 0.7	5.79	1.71	13.34 /23	-2.31 / 6	3.05 /11	1.47	1.37
FO	MFS Research International R3	MRSHX	D-	(800) 225-2606	E+ / 0.7	5.86	1.87	13.62 /24	-2.05 / 7	3.30 /12	1.63	1.12
FO	MFS Research International R4	MRSJX	D-	(800) 225-2606	E+ / 0.8	5.90	1.96	13.88 /25	-1.82 / 7	3.56 /13	1.78	0.87
FO	MFS Research International R6	MRSKX	D-	(800) 225-2606	E+ / 0.8	5.96	2.07	14.06 /26	-1.70 / 7	3.66 /14	2.07	0.77
GR	MFS Research R1	MFRLX	B	(800) 225-2606	B- / 7.5	7.98	7.42	22.40 /64	7.55 /76	11.94 /74	0.33	1.57
GR	MFS Research R2	MSRRX	B+	(800) 225-2606	B / 7.8	8.09	7.66	23.01 /67	8.08 /80	12.49 /79	0.69	1.07
GR	MFS Research R3	MFRHX	B+	(800) 225-2606	B / 8.0	8.16	7.82	23.30 /67	8.35 /82	12.78 /82	0.91	0.82
GR	MFS Research R4	MFRJX	B+	(800) 225-2606	B / 8.2	8.23	7.96	23.60 /68	8.63 /84	13.06 /84	1.13	0.57
GR	MFS Research R6	MFRKX	B+	(800) 225-2606	B+ / 8.3	8.26	8.01	23.76 /69	8.72 /85	13.16 /85	1.22	0.48
TC	MFS Technology A	MTCAX	A-	(800) 225-2606	A / 9.5	9.83	8.94	30.33 /87	11.75 /98	14.79 /96	0.00	1.27
TC	MFS Technology B	MTCBX	A-	(800) 225-2606	A+ / 9.6	9.66	8.56	29.43 /85	10.91 /97	13.94 /93	0.00	2.02
TC	MFS Technology C	MTCCX	A-	(800) 225-2606	A+ / 9.6	9.64	8.54	29.39 /85	10.90 /97	13.93 /93	0.00	2.02
TC	MFS Technology I	MTCIX	A	(800) 225-2606	A+ / 9.8	9.89	9.08	30.64 /87	12.02 /98	15.07 /97	0.00	1.02
TC	MFS Technology R1	MTCKX	A-	(800) 225-2606	A+ / 9.6	9.61	8.56	29.40 /85	10.91 /97	13.93 /93	0.00	2.02
TC	MFS Technology R2	MTERX	A-	(800) 225-2606	A+ / 9.7	9.79	8.82	30.02 /86	11.46 /98	14.50 /96	0.00	1.52
TC	MFS Technology R3	MTCHX	A-	(800) 225-2606	A+ / 9.7	9.83	8.94	30.34 /87	11.74 /98	14.80 /96	0.00	1.27
TC	MFS Technology R4	MTCJX	A	(800) 225-2606	A+ / 9.8	9.89	9.10	30.63 /87	12.03 /98	15.07 /97	0.00	1.02

● Denotes fund is closed to new investors
* Denotes fund is included in Section II

I. Index of Stock Mutual Funds

RISK	3 Year		NET ASSETS		ASSET					BULL / BEAR		FUND MANAGER		MINIMUMS		LOADS	
Risk Rating/Pts	Standard Deviation	Beta	NAV As of 2/28/17	Total $(Mil)	Cash %	Stocks %	Bonds %	Other %	Portfolio Turnover Ratio	Last Bull Market Return	Last Bear Market Return	Manager Quality Pct	Manager Tenure (Years)	Initial Purch. $	Additional Purch. $	Front End Load	Back End Load
B /8.0	6.3	0.98	16.65	343	7	54	37	2	2	56.0	-10.8	31	N/A	0	0	0.0	0.0
B /8.0	6.4	0.98	16.76	256	7	54	37	2	2	58.2	-10.7	33	N/A	0	0	0.0	0.0
C- /3.4	15.8	0.93	24.35	5	2	96	1	1	49	91.0	-27.4	17	4	250	0	5.8	0.0
C- /3.2	15.8	0.93	20.27	N/A	2	96	1	1	49	83.2	-27.6	12	4	250	0	0.0	0.0
C- /3.2	15.8	0.93	20.27	2	2	96	1	1	49	83.1	-27.6	12	4	250	0	0.0	0.0
C- /3.4	15.8	0.93	25.11	377	2	96	1	1	49	91.3	-27.4	17	4	1,000	0	5.8	0.0
C- /3.2	15.8	0.93	20.94	20	2	96	1	1	49	83.7	-27.6	12	4	1,000	0	0.0	0.0
C- /3.2	15.8	0.93	20.98	81	2	96	1	1	49	83.8	-27.6	12	4	1,000	0	0.0	0.0
C- /3.5	15.8	0.93	27.41	150	2	96	1	1	49	93.9	-27.3	19	4	0	0	0.0	0.0
C- /3.2	15.8	0.93	20.80	5	2	96	1	1	49	83.7	-27.6	12	4	0	0	0.0	0.0
C- /3.4	15.8	0.93	23.83	33	2	96	1	1	49	88.7	-27.4	15	4	0	0	0.0	0.0
C- /3.4	15.8	0.93	25.08	54	2	96	1	1	49	91.2	-27.3	17	4	0	0	0.0	0.0
C- /3.5	15.8	0.93	26.19	79	2	96	1	1	49	93.9	-27.3	19	4	0	0	0.0	0.0
C- /3.5	15.8	0.93	27.58	312	2	96	1	1	49	N/A	N/A	20	4	0	0	0.0	0.0
C+ /5.8	13.0	0.62	14.99	189	2	97	0	1	60	159.8	N/A	99	6	1,000	0	5.8	0.0
C+ /5.8	13.1	0.62	14.60	6	2	97	0	1	60	149.5	N/A	99	6	1,000	0	0.0	0.0
C+ /5.8	13.1	0.62	14.54	63	2	97	0	1	60	149.5	N/A	99	6	1,000	0	0.0	0.0
C+ /5.8	13.1	0.62	15.06	241	2	97	0	1	60	163.5	N/A	99	6	0	0	0.0	0.0
C+ /5.8	13.0	0.62	14.61	N/A	2	97	0	1	60	149.5	N/A	99	6	0	0	0.0	0.0
C+ /5.9	13.1	0.62	14.97	1	2	97	0	1	60	156.5	N/A	99	6	0	0	0.0	0.0
C+ /5.8	13.1	0.62	15.03	14	2	97	0	1	60	159.9	N/A	99	6	0	0	0.0	0.0
C+ /5.8	13.1	0.62	15.08	2	2	97	0	1	60	163.3	N/A	99	6	0	0	0.0	0.0
C+ /5.8	13.1	1.02	15.08	347	2	97	0	1	60	N/A	N/A	60	6	0	0	0.0	0.0
C+ /5.8	10.1	0.96	39.75	2,436	1	97	0	2	47	122.4	-16.9	53	9	1,000	50	5.8	0.0
C+ /5.8	10.1	0.96	36.50	24	1	97	0	2	47	113.6	-17.2	42	9	1,000	50	0.0	0.0
C+ /5.8	10.1	0.96	36.24	140	1	97	0	2	47	113.5	-17.2	42	9	1,000	50	0.0	0.0
C+ /5.8	10.1	0.96	40.70	990	1	97	0	2	47	125.5	-16.8	57	9	0	0	0.0	0.0
C /5.5	11.5	0.91	15.58	9	1	97	1	1	40	34.9	-22.0	49	12	250	0	5.8	0.0
C+ /5.6	11.5	0.91	14.73	N/A	1	97	1	1	40	29.4	-22.3	38	12	250	0	0.0	0.0
C+ /5.6	11.5	0.91	14.47	3	1	97	1	1	40	29.4	-22.3	38	12	250	0	0.0	0.0
C /5.5	11.4	0.91	15.86	762	1	97	1	1	40	35.1	-22.0	49	12	1,000	0	5.8	0.0
C+ /5.6	11.4	0.91	15.32	7	1	97	1	1	40	29.7	-22.2	38	12	1,000	0	0.0	0.0
C+ /5.6	11.5	0.91	14.93	54	1	97	1	1	40	29.8	-22.3	39	12	1,000	0	0.0	0.0
C /5.5	11.4	0.91	16.39	2,290	1	97	1	1	40	37.0	-21.9	53	12	0	0	0.0	0.0
C+ /5.6	11.4	0.91	14.73	2	1	97	1	1	40	29.7	-22.2	39	12	0	0	0.0	0.0
C+ /5.6	11.4	0.91	15.34	145	1	97	1	1	40	33.2	-22.1	46	12	0	0	0.0	0.0
C+ /5.6	11.4	0.91	15.70	101	1	97	1	1	40	35.1	-22.0	50	12	0	0	0.0	0.0
C /5.5	11.5	0.91	15.88	108	1	97	1	1	40	36.9	-21.9	53	12	0	0	0.0	0.0
C /5.5	11.4	0.91	15.78	3,033	1	97	1	1	40	37.6	-22.0	54	12	0	0	0.0	0.0
C+ /5.8	10.1	0.96	35.71	4	1	97	0	2	47	113.6	-17.2	42	9	0	0	0.0	0.0
C+ /5.9	10.1	0.96	38.62	29	1	97	0	2	47	119.4	-17.0	49	9	0	0	0.0	0.0
C+ /5.8	10.1	0.96	39.53	50	1	97	0	2	47	122.4	-16.9	53	9	0	0	0.0	0.0
C+ /5.8	10.1	0.96	39.74	50	1	97	0	2	47	125.5	-16.8	57	9	0	0	0.0	0.0
C+ /5.8	10.1	0.96	39.74	1,347	1	97	0	2	47	126.3	-16.9	58	9	0	0	0.0	0.0
C /5.2	13.7	1.11	30.22	323	0	96	2	2	30	139.0	-12.5	73	6	1,000	0	5.8	0.0
C /5.1	13.7	1.11	26.63	29	0	96	2	2	30	129.4	-12.7	64	6	1,000	0	0.0	0.0
C /5.1	13.7	1.11	26.57	85	0	96	2	2	30	129.3	-12.7	64	6	1,000	0	0.0	0.0
C /5.3	13.7	1.11	32.07	140	0	96	2	2	30	142.1	-12.4	75	6	0	0	0.0	0.0
C /5.1	13.7	1.11	26.52	3	0	96	2	2	30	129.5	-12.8	64	6	0	0	0.0	0.0
C /5.2	13.7	1.11	28.99	19	0	96	2	2	30	135.7	-12.6	70	6	0	0	0.0	0.0
C /5.2	13.7	1.11	30.21	34	0	96	2	2	30	138.9	-12.5	73	6	0	0	0.0	0.0
C /5.2	13.7	1.11	31.27	11	0	96	2	2	30	142.1	-12.4	75	6	0	0	0.0	0.0

Fund Type	Fund Name	Ticker Symbol	Overall Investment Rating	Phone	Performance Rating/Pts	3 Mo	6 Mo	1Yr / Pct	3Yr / Pct	5Yr / Pct	Dividend Yield	Expense Ratio
TC	MFS Technology R6	MTCLX	A	(800) 225-2606	A+ / 9.8	9.95	9.14	30.82 / 88	12.14 / 98	--	0.00	0.92
AA	MFS Total Return 529A	EATRX	C+	(800) 225-2606	C- / 3.9	4.68	4.45	14.74 / 29	6.29 / 67	8.75 / 48	1.93	0.84
AA	MFS Total Return 529B	EBTRX	B-	(800) 225-2606	C / 4.5	4.53	4.04	13.87 / 25	5.48 / 59	7.93 / 42	1.30	1.59
AA	MFS Total Return 529C	ECTRX	B-	(800) 225-2606	C / 4.5	4.57	4.08	13.95 / 25	5.50 / 60	7.93 / 42	1.31	1.59
AA	MFS Total Return A	MSFRX	C+	(800) 225-2606	C- / 4.0	4.73	4.46	14.80 / 29	6.35 / 67	8.80 / 49	1.95	0.74
AA	MFS Total Return B	MTRBX	B-	(800) 225-2606	C / 4.5	4.54	4.06	13.92 / 25	5.54 / 60	7.97 / 42	1.35	1.49
AA	MFS Total Return C	MTRCX	B-	(800) 225-2606	C / 4.5	4.52	4.10	13.99 / 25	5.54 / 60	7.99 / 42	1.34	1.49
AA	MFS Total Return I	MTRIX	B	(800) 225-2606	C / 5.4	4.80	4.58	15.09 / 30	6.61 / 69	9.06 / 51	2.31	0.49
AA	MFS Total Return R1	MSFFX	B-	(800) 225-2606	C / 4.5	4.55	4.07	13.96 / 25	5.56 / 60	7.97 / 42	1.35	1.49
AA	MFS Total Return R2	MTRRX	B	(800) 225-2606	C / 5.0	4.71	4.37	14.54 / 28	6.08 / 65	8.52 / 46	1.83	0.99
AA	MFS Total Return R3	MSFHX	B	(800) 225-2606	C / 5.2	4.73	4.45	14.79 / 29	6.34 / 67	8.79 / 49	2.06	0.74
AA	MFS Total Return R4	MSFJX	B	(800) 225-2606	C / 5.4	4.79	4.58	15.14 / 30	6.60 / 69	9.07 / 51	2.30	0.49
BA	MFS Total Return R6	MSFKX	B	(800) 225-2606	C / 5.5	4.82	4.63	15.18 / 31	6.70 / 70	--	2.39	0.41
UT	MFS Utilities A	MMUFX	D	(800) 225-2606	C- / 3.4	9.73	4.66	19.54 / 50	3.13 / 33	8.07 / 43	3.35	1.00
UT	MFS Utilities B	MMUBX	D	(800) 225-2606	C- / 3.9	9.46	4.24	18.61 / 45	2.36 / 26	7.26 / 36	2.83	1.75
UT	MFS Utilities C	MMUCX	D	(800) 225-2606	C- / 3.9	9.46	4.24	18.62 / 46	2.35 / 26	7.26 / 36	2.85	1.75
UT	MFS Utilities I	MMUIX	D+	(800) 225-2606	C / 4.8	9.76	4.77	19.83 / 51	3.38 / 36	8.35 / 45	3.79	0.75
UT	MFS Utilities R1	MMUGX	D	(800) 225-2606	C- / 3.9	9.48	4.20	18.60 / 45	2.35 / 26	7.26 / 36	2.86	1.75
UT	MFS Utilities R2	MURRX	D+	(800) 225-2606	C / 4.3	9.57	4.49	19.24 / 48	2.87 / 31	7.80 / 41	3.33	1.25
UT	MFS Utilities R3	MMUHX	D+	(800) 225-2606	C / 4.5	9.67	4.66	19.55 / 50	3.14 / 33	8.08 / 43	3.56	1.00
UT	MFS Utilities R4	MMUJX	D+	(800) 225-2606	C / 4.8	9.73	4.73	19.83 / 51	3.39 / 36	8.33 / 45	3.80	0.75
UT	MFS Utilities R6	MMUKX	D+	(800) 225-2606	C / 4.8	9.78	4.77	19.94 / 52	3.48 / 37	--	3.88	0.64
GR	MFS Value 529A	EAVLX	A-	(800) 225-2606	B / 7.7	6.83	8.47	24.68 / 72	9.46 / 90	13.67 / 90	1.58	0.96
GR	MFS Value 529B	EBVLX	A	(800) 225-2606	B+ / 8.3	6.80	8.48	24.28 / 71	8.90 / 86	12.96 / 83	1.27	1.71
GR	MFS Value 529C	ECVLX	A-	(800) 225-2606	B / 8.0	6.59	8.02	23.68 / 69	8.59 / 84	12.77 / 82	1.01	1.71
* GR	MFS Value A	MEIAX	A-	(800) 225-2606	B / 7.7	6.80	8.47	24.70 / 72	9.46 / 90	13.68 / 90	1.57	0.86
GR	MFS Value B	MFEBX	A	(800) 225-2606	B / 8.1	6.62	8.08	23.77 / 69	8.65 / 84	12.83 / 82	0.99	1.61
GR	MFS Value C	MEICX	A-	(800) 225-2606	B / 8.1	6.61	8.09	23.78 / 69	8.64 / 84	12.83 / 82	1.02	1.61
GR	MFS Value I	MEIIX	A+	(800) 225-2606	B+ / 8.8	6.89	8.62	25.04 / 73	9.74 / 92	13.96 / 93	1.88	0.61
GR	MFS Value R1	MEIGX	A-	(800) 225-2606	B / 8.1	6.59	8.05	23.77 / 69	8.64 / 84	12.83 / 82	1.01	1.61
GR	MFS Value R2	MVRRX	A	(800) 225-2606	B+ / 8.5	6.74	8.33	24.38 / 71	9.19 / 88	13.39 / 88	1.46	1.11
GR	MFS Value R3	MEIHX	A+	(800) 225-2606	B+ / 8.7	6.80	8.47	24.69 / 72	9.46 / 90	13.68 / 90	1.67	0.86
GR	MFS Value R4	MEIJX	A+	(800) 225-2606	B+ / 8.8	6.88	8.61	25.01 / 73	9.74 / 92	13.96 / 93	1.89	0.61
GR	MFS Value R6	MEIKX	A+	(800) 225-2606	B+ / 8.9	6.90	8.67	25.13 / 74	9.84 / 92	14.08 / 94	1.98	0.51
SC	MH Elite Small Cap Fund of Funds	MHELX	C-	(800) 318-7969	C / 5.5	4.23	9.87	27.29 / 80	3.17 / 33	9.44 / 54	0.00	2.08
PM	Midas Fund	MIDSX	E-	(800) 400-6432	E / 0.4	12.50	-4.55	32.63 / 91	-6.67 / 2	-20.43 / 0	0.00	4.00
AG	Midas Magic Fund	MISEX	D	(800) 400-6432	C / 5.3	4.15	7.62	21.40 / 59	4.95 / 54	11.08 / 67	0.00	3.17
CV	Miller Convertible Bond A	MCFAX	C-	(877) 441-4434	D / 2.1	1.25	2.84	15.71 / 33	3.32 / 35	6.81 / 34	1.79	1.44
CV	Miller Convertible Bond C	MCFCX	C	(877) 441-4434	D+ / 2.6	1.11	2.58	15.16 / 31	2.80 / 30	6.27 / 30	1.44	1.94
CV	Miller Convertible Bond I	MCIFX	C	(877) 441-4434	C- / 3.3	1.40	3.12	16.34 / 36	3.82 / 41	7.17 / 36	2.42	0.94
CV	Miller Convertible Plus I	MCPIX	U	(877) 441-4434	U /	2.56	6.19	27.04 / 79	--	--	1.91	4.33
IN	Miller Howard Income Equity Fund I	MHIEX	U		U /	6.00	6.20	19.53 / 50	--	--	1.89	N/A
AA	Miller Income A	LMCJX	C+	(877) 534-4627	C / 5.5	8.63	13.66	36.76 / 96	1.34 / 20	--	7.08	2.25
AA	Miller Income C	LCMNX	C+	(877) 534-4627	C+ / 6.1	8.47	13.19	35.58 / 95	0.71 / 17	--	6.95	3.03
AA	Miller Income FI	LMCKX	C+	(877) 534-4627	C+ / 6.6	8.56	13.60	36.72 / 96	1.22 / 19	--	7.57	5.15
AA	Miller Income I	LMCLX	C+	(877) 534-4627	C+ / 6.8	8.71	13.84	37.00 / 96	1.54 / 21	--	7.77	2.05
AA	Miller Income IS	LMCMX	C+	(877) 534-4627	C+ / 6.8	8.73	13.88	37.13 / 96	1.59 / 21	--	7.84	1.91
GR	Miller Opportunity Trust A	LGOAX	C	(877) 534-4627	B- / 7.4	11.01	15.45	31.37 / 89	5.20 / 56	18.65 / 99	0.00	1.22
GR	Miller Opportunity Trust C	LMOPX	C+	(877) 534-4627	B / 7.8	10.84	14.97	30.38 / 87	4.40 / 47	17.74 / 99	0.00	1.98
GR	Miller Opportunity Trust FI	LMOFX	C+	(877) 534-4627	B+ / 8.3	11.03	15.45	31.37 / 89	5.15 / 56	18.60 / 99	0.00	1.25
GR	Miller Opportunity Trust I	LMNOX	B-	(877) 534-4627	B+ / 8.6	11.11	15.62	31.81 / 90	5.51 / 60	18.98 / 99	0.00	0.97
GR	Miller Opportunity Trust R	LMORX	C+	(877) 534-4627	B / 8.1	10.93	15.27	30.93 / 88	4.81 / 52	18.18 / 99	0.00	1.55

- Denotes fund is closed to new investors
- * Denotes fund is included in Section II

www.thestreetratings.com

Risk Rating/Pts	3 Year Standard Deviation	Beta	NAV As of 2/28/17	Total $(Mil)	Cash %	Stocks %	Bonds %	Other %	Portfolio Turnover Ratio	Last Bull Market Return	Last Bear Market Return	Manager Quality Pct	Manager Tenure (Years)	Initial Purch. $	Additional Purch. $	Front End Load	Back End Load
C /5.3	13.6	1.11	32.22	68	0	96	2	2	30	N/A	N/A	76	6	0	0	0.0	0.0
B /8.2	5.9	0.94	18.57	22	0	60	39	1	32	72.0	-10.4	65	15	250	0	5.8	0.0
B /8.2	5.9	0.94	18.64	2	0	60	39	1	32	65.0	-10.6	55	15	250	0	0.0	0.0
B /8.2	6.0	0.95	18.72	11	0	60	39	1	32	65.0	-10.7	55	15	250	0	0.0	0.0
B /8.2	6.0	0.95	18.62	4,715	0	60	39	1	32	72.5	-10.4	66	15	1,000	50	5.8	0.0
B /8.2	6.0	0.95	18.64	202	0	60	39	1	32	65.5	-10.6	56	15	1,000	50	0.0	0.0
B /8.2	6.0	0.95	18.73	1,122	0	60	39	1	32	65.5	-10.6	56	15	1,000	50	0.0	0.0
B /8.2	5.9	0.94	18.62	582	0	60	39	1	32	74.8	-10.2	69	15	0	0	0.0	0.0
B /8.2	6.0	0.95	18.60	14	0	60	39	1	32	65.6	-10.6	56	15	0	0	0.0	0.0
B /8.2	6.0	0.95	18.68	214	0	60	39	1	32	70.1	-10.4	62	15	0	0	0.0	0.0
B /8.2	6.0	0.95	18.63	316	0	60	39	1	32	72.4	-10.3	65	15	0	0	0.0	0.0
B /8.2	5.9	0.94	18.64	298	0	60	39	1	32	74.8	-10.2	69	15	0	0	0.0	0.0
B /8.2	6.0	0.95	18.62	202	0	60	39	1	32	N/A	N/A	70	15	0	0	0.0	0.0
C /4.3	12.1	0.47	19.07	2,185	18	79	2	1	27	67.3	-12.3	30	25	1,000	0	5.8	0.0
C /4.3	12.1	0.46	18.97	175	18	79	2	1	27	60.6	-12.6	23	25	1,000	0	0.0	0.0
C /4.3	12.1	0.46	18.97	707	18	79	2	1	27	60.7	-12.6	23	25	1,000	0	0.0	0.0
C /4.3	12.1	0.47	19.14	665	18	79	2	1	27	69.6	-12.2	33	25	0	0	0.0	0.0
C /4.3	12.1	0.47	18.93	9	18	79	2	1	27	60.6	-12.6	23	25	0	0	0.0	0.0
C /4.3	12.1	0.47	19.01	88	18	79	2	1	27	65.0	-12.4	28	25	0	0	0.0	0.0
C /4.3	12.1	0.46	19.06	112	18	79	2	1	27	67.4	-12.3	31	25	0	0	0.0	0.0
C /4.3	12.1	0.47	19.08	87	18	79	2	1	27	69.5	-12.2	33	25	0	0	0.0	0.0
C /4.3	12.1	0.46	19.14	82	18	79	2	1	27	N/A	N/A	35	25	0	0	0.0	0.0
C+ /6.9	10.3	0.98	37.65	21	0	98	1	1	12	130.3	-18.0	64	15	250	0	5.8	0.0
C+ /6.9	10.3	0.98	37.26	1	0	98	1	1	12	122.5	-18.2	57	15	250	0	0.0	0.0
C+ /6.9	10.3	0.98	37.05	6	0	98	1	1	12	120.7	-18.3	53	15	250	0	0.0	0.0
C+ /6.9	10.3	0.98	37.93	8,265	0	98	1	1	12	130.4	-18.0	64	15	1,000	0	5.8	0.0
C+ /6.9	10.3	0.98	37.72	151	0	98	1	1	12	121.2	-18.2	54	15	1,000	0	0.0	0.0
C+ /6.9	10.3	0.98	37.48	1,566	0	98	1	1	12	121.3	-18.2	54	15	1,000	0	0.0	0.0
C+ /6.9	10.3	0.98	38.15	19,643	0	98	1	1	12	133.5	-17.9	67	15	0	0	0.0	0.0
C+ /6.9	10.3	0.98	37.22	29	0	98	1	1	12	121.2	-18.2	54	15	0	0	0.0	0.0
C+ /6.9	10.3	0.98	37.56	639	0	98	1	1	12	127.3	-18.1	61	15	0	0	0.0	0.0
C+ /6.9	10.3	0.98	37.80	2,022	0	98	1	1	12	130.4	-18.0	64	15	0	0	0.0	0.0
C+ /6.9	10.3	0.98	37.94	3,211	0	98	1	1	12	133.5	-17.9	67	15	0	0	0.0	0.0
C+ /6.9	10.3	0.98	37.94	7,199	0	98	1	1	12	134.7	-17.9	68	15	0	0	0.0	0.0
C /4.5	13.6	0.86	6.91	5	7	85	7	1	33	99.0	-25.7	40	N/A	10,000	1,000	0.0	0.0
E- /0.0	42.5	2.26	1.26	20	3	96	0	1	2	-67.4	-26.1	40	15	1,000	100	0.0	1.0
D+ /2.8	12.0	1.10	16.92	14	1	95	2	2	49	110.6	-12.3	8	1	1,000	100	0.0	1.0
B /8.1	7.1	0.75	12.89	117	1	0	7	92	81	57.0	-15.2	70	10	2,500	100	5.8	0.0
B /8.1	7.1	0.75	12.80	73	1	0	7	92	81	52.8	-15.3	63	10	2,500	100	0.0	0.0
B /8.1	7.1	0.75	12.89	752	1	0	7	92	81	60.1	-15.0	74	10	1,000,000	100	0.0	0.0
U /	N/A	N/A	23.79	139	0	0	0	100	109	N/A	N/A	N/A	3	1,000,000	100	0.0	0.0
U /	N/A	N/A	11.09	82	0	0	0	100	38	N/A	N/A	N/A	2	100,000	0	0.0	2.0
C+ /6.5	13.1	1.71	8.62	11	9	80	7	4	53	N/A	N/A	2	3	1,000	50	5.8	0.0
C+ /6.5	13.1	1.70	8.60	26	9	80	7	4	53	N/A	N/A	1	3	1,000	50	0.0	0.0
C+ /6.5	13.2	1.71	8.60	N/A	9	80	7	4	53	N/A	N/A	1	3	0	0	0.0	0.0
C+ /6.5	13.1	1.70	8.61	30	9	80	7	4	53	N/A	N/A	2	3	1,000,000	0	0.0	0.0
C+ /6.5	13.2	1.71	8.61	47	9	80	7	4	53	N/A	N/A	2	3	0	0	0.0	0.0
C- /3.9	23.0	1.79	20.77	232	3	96	0	1	16	211.9	-38.6	1	N/A	1,000	50	5.8	0.0
C- /3.8	23.0	1.79	19.74	694	3	96	0	1	16	199.3	-38.8	1	N/A	1,000	50	0.0	0.0
C- /3.8	23.0	1.79	21.44	24	3	96	0	1	16	211.4	-38.7	1	N/A	0	0	0.0	0.0
C- /3.9	23.0	1.79	22.50	428	3	96	0	1	16	216.6	-38.4	1	N/A	1,000,000	0	0.0	0.0
C- /3.8	23.0	1.79	20.91	9	3	96	0	1	16	204.8	-38.6	1	N/A	0	0	0.0	0.0

Fund Type	Fund Name	Ticker Symbol	Overall Investment Rating	Phone	Performance Rating/Pts	Total Return % through 2/28/17			Annualized		Incl. in Returns	
	99 Pct = Best / 0 Pct = Worst					3 Mo	6 Mo	1Yr / Pct	3Yr / Pct	5Yr / Pct	Dividend Yield	Expense Ratio
FO	Mirae Asia A	MALAX	E+	(888) 335-3417	D / 2.1	5.71	1.29	18.37 /44	2.18 /25	5.84 /27	0.00	5.55
FO	Mirae Asia C	MCLAX	E+	(888) 335-3417	D+ / 2.5	5.59	0.94	17.56 /41	1.41 /20	5.03 /21	0.00	8.41
FO	Mirae Asia I	MILAX	D-	(888) 335-3417	C- / 3.2	5.81	1.37	18.76 /46	2.41 /27	6.09 /29	0.00	2.22
EM	Mirae Emerging Markets A	MALGX	D+	(888) 335-3417	C / 4.4	8.88	7.38	29.68 /86	2.30 /26	1.35 / 7	0.00	6.15
EM	Mirae Emerging Markets C	MCLGX	C-	(888) 335-3417	C / 4.9	8.65	6.97	28.59 /83	1.45 /21	0.53 / 5	0.00	6.30
EM	Mirae Emerging Markets I	MILGX	C	(888) 335-3417	C+ / 5.8	8.98	7.50	29.98 /86	2.51 /28	1.56 / 7	0.00	3.59
EM	Mirae Emg Mkts Great Cnsmr A	MECGX	E	(888) 335-3417	E / 0.4	4.59	-1.97	14.33 /27	-2.05 / 7	1.20 / 6	0.00	1.92
EM	Mirae Emg Mkts Great Cnsmr C	MCCGX	E	(888) 335-3417	E / 0.5	4.41	-2.35	13.40 /23	-2.79 / 5	0.41 / 5	0.00	2.67
EM	Mirae Emg Mkts Great Cnsmr I	MICGX	E	(888) 335-3417	E+ / 0.7	4.62	-1.86	14.57 /28	-1.80 / 7	1.41 / 7	0.00	1.59
FO	Mirae Glbl Asia Great Consumer A	MGCEX	E	(888) 335-3417	E / 0.4	1.34	-6.84	6.30 / 5	0.61 /16	5.31 /23	0.00	1.98
FO	Mirae Glbl Asia Great Consumer C	MGCCX	E	(888) 335-3417	E+ / 0.6	1.13	-7.16	5.59 / 4	-0.13 /13	4.52 /18	0.00	2.83
FO	Mirae Glbl Asia Great Consumer I	MGCIX	E	(888) 335-3417	E+ / 0.9	1.41	-6.67	6.69 / 5	0.87 /18	5.55 /25	0.00	1.61
OT	Mirae Global Great Consumer A	MGUAX	D-	(888) 335-3417	D / 1.6	7.80	3.59	13.62 /24	0.83 /17	7.92 /41	0.00	4.02
OT	Mirae Global Great Consumer C	MGUCX	D-	(888) 335-3417	D / 1.9	7.52	3.16	12.67 /20	0.07 /14	7.09 /35	0.00	4.97
OT	Mirae Global Great Consumer I	MGUIX	D-	(888) 335-3417	D+ / 2.4	7.78	3.70	13.82 /25	1.09 /19	8.17 /43	0.20	2.19
GR	MM S and P 500 Index A	MMFFX	U	(800) 542-6767	U /	7.85	9.62	24.11 /70	--	--	1.54	0.72
GR	MM S and P 500 Index Administrative	MIEYX	A+	(800) 542-6767	A- / 9.1	7.88	9.73	24.38 /71	10.11 /94	13.49 /89	1.82	0.47
GR	MM S and P 500 Index I	MMIZX	A+	(800) 542-6767	A / 9.3	7.98	9.93	24.87 /73	10.51 /96	13.89 /92	2.12	0.12
GR	MM S and P 500 Index R3	MMINX	A	(800) 542-6767	B+ / 8.9	7.81	9.60	23.91 /70	9.69 /92	13.00 /84	1.67	0.87
GR	MM S and P 500 Index R4	MIEAX	A+	(800) 542-6767	A- / 9.0	7.86	9.68	24.18 /71	9.94 /93	13.30 /87	1.71	0.62
GR	MM S and P 500 Index R5	MIEZX	A+	(800) 542-6767	A / 9.3	8.01	9.90	24.73 /72	10.40 /95	13.77 /91	2.01	0.22
GR	MM S and P 500 Index Service	MMIEX	A+	(800) 542-6767	A- / 9.2	7.92	9.81	24.48 /72	10.22 /94	13.57 /90	1.84	0.37
GL	MO 529 MOST CSP Direct Vngd		B+	(800) 662-7447	B- / 7.1	7.62	8.06	23.50 /68	6.47 /68	10.46 /62	0.00	0.55
GI	MO 529 MOST CSP Direct Vngd Csv		B-	(800) 662-7447	C- / 3.0	3.58	1.76	9.95 /12	4.42 /48	5.60 /26	0.00	0.55
GI	MO 529 MOST CSP Direct Vngd		B	(800) 662-7447	C+ / 5.8	6.31	5.94	18.83 /46	5.83 /63	8.84 /49	0.00	0.55
GI	MO 529 MOST CSP Direct Vngd Mdt		B	(800) 662-7447	C / 4.4	4.95	3.86	14.35 /27	5.18 /56	7.27 /36	0.00	0.55
FO	● Mondrian International Equity	DPIEX	D-	(800) 523-1918	D- / 1.0	7.76	3.05	14.10 /26	-0.58 /11	4.97 /21	2.22	0.87
SC	Monetta	MONTX	C+	(800) 241-9772	B- / 7.5	6.04	11.67	22.27 /63	7.32 /74	10.24 /60	0.01	1.42
GR	Monetta Young Investor	MYIFX	B	(800) 241-9772	B+ / 8.6	7.50	11.43	24.26 /71	8.65 /84	12.48 /79	0.53	1.23
GR	Monongahela All Cap Value	MCMVX	A+	(855) 392-9331	A / 9.4	7.46	13.30	31.56 /89	9.21 /88	--	1.16	5.49
AA	Monte Chesapeake Macro Strategies	MHBAX	D-	(855) 542-4642	E- / 0.1	3.44	-0.81	-4.61 / 1	-2.52 / 5	-4.27 / 2	0.00	3.52
AA	Monte Chesapeake Macro Strategies	MHBCX	D-	(855) 542-4642	E- / 0.2	3.25	-1.09	-5.19 / 1	-2.88 / 5	-4.73 / 2	0.00	4.27
AA	Monte Chesapeake Macro Strategies	MHBIX	D-	(855) 542-4642	E / 0.3	3.52	-0.56	-4.21 / 1	-2.22 / 6	-4.01 / 2	0.86	3.27
GR	Monteagle Informed Investor Gr Inst	MIIFX	D	(888) 263-5593	C- / 3.5	5.49	3.90	11.93 /18	4.12 /44	8.27 /44	0.00	1.48
GR	Monteagle Quality Growth Inst	MFGIX	B	(888) 263-5593	B- / 7.1	7.40	7.19	17.92 /42	8.04 /79	9.64 /56	0.33	1.35
GR	Monteagle Select Val Inst	MVEIX	C-	(888) 263-5593	B / 7.8	1.83	12.26	26.76 /78	7.71 /77	14.63 /96	0.50	1.44
GR	Monteagle Texas I	BIGTX	D-	(888) 263-5593	D- / 1.4	2.74	9.80	25.97 /76	-1.75 / 7	--	0.00	1.73
GR	Monteagle Value Inst	MVRGX	C	(888) 263-5593	B- / 7.2	3.88	10.64	30.26 /87	5.65 /61	10.00 /58	1.36	1.38
AA	Morgan Creek Tactical Allocation A	MAGTX	E	(855) 489-9939	E- / 0.1	3.16	2.00	8.37 / 8	-8.64 / 1	--	0.00	3.58
AA	Morgan Creek Tactical Allocation I	MIGTX	E	(855) 489-9939	E- / 0.1	3.27	2.16	8.66 / 9	-8.43 / 1	--	0.00	3.33
SC	Morgan Dempsey Small/Micro Cap	MITYX	C-	(877) 642-7227	C / 5.3	2.86	13.76	27.58 /81	2.96 /31	8.50 /46	0.32	1.58
FO	Morgan Stanley European Eq A	EUGAX	E	(800) 869-6397	E- / 0.1	7.93	1.97	8.51 / 8	-5.89 / 2	2.76 /10	2.15	1.63
FO	● Morgan Stanley European Eq B	EUGBX	E	(800) 869-6397	E- / 0.2	7.89	1.97	8.50 / 8	-5.89 / 2	2.75 /10	2.55	1.59
FO	Morgan Stanley European Eq I	EUGDX	E	(800) 869-6397	E- / 0.2	8.09	2.22	8.99 / 9	-5.54 / 2	3.09 /11	2.68	1.51
FO	● Morgan Stanley European Eq L	EUGCX	E	(800) 869-6397	E- / 0.1	7.77	1.74	7.99 / 7	-6.37 / 2	2.19 / 8	1.94	2.29
MC	Morgan Stanley Multi Cap Gr Tr IS	MCRTX	C-	(800) 869-6397	C+ / 6.7	10.41	6.93	25.95 /76	4.78 /52	--	0.00	15.68
GR	Morgan Stanley Multi Cap Gr Trust A	CPOAX	D	(800) 869-6397	C / 5.3	10.32	6.75	25.52 /75	4.36 /47	12.46 /79	0.00	1.27
GR	● Morgan Stanley Multi Cap Gr Trust B	CPOBX	D	(800) 869-6397	C+ / 5.7	10.10	6.33	24.53 /72	3.56 /38	11.60 /71	0.00	2.19
GR	Morgan Stanley Multi Cap Gr Trust I	CPODX	C-	(800) 869-6397	C+ / 6.7	10.40	6.92	25.90 /76	4.72 /51	12.82 /82	0.00	0.92
GR	● Morgan Stanley Multi Cap Gr Trust L	CPOCX	D+	(800) 869-6397	C+ / 6.0	10.16	6.45	24.79 /73	3.83 /41	11.84 /73	0.00	1.80
GL	Morningstar Agg Gr ETF Asset All I		C+	(866) 432-2926	C+ / 6.4	6.82	7.53	22.84 /66	5.54 /60	8.26 /44	1.44	0.67
GL	Morningstar Agg Gr ETF Asset All II	AGTFX	C+	(866) 432-2926	C+ / 6.2	6.74	7.45	22.58 /65	5.29 /57	8.00 /42	1.16	0.92

● Denotes fund is closed to new investors
* Denotes fund is included in Section II

I. Index of Stock Mutual Funds

RISK			NET ASSETS		ASSET					BULL / BEAR		FUND MANAGER		MINIMUMS		LOADS	
	3 Year		NAV														
Risk Rating/Pts	Standard Deviation	Beta	As of 2/28/17	Total $(Mil)	Cash %	Stocks %	Bonds %	Other %	Portfolio Turnover Ratio	Last Bull Market Return	Last Bear Market Return	Manager Quality Pct	Manager Tenure (Years)	Initial Purch. $	Additional Purch. $	Front End Load	Back End Load
C- /3.7	13.8	0.80	10.18	N/A	1	98	0	1	95	62.3	-30.5	87	7	2,000	100	5.8	0.0
C- /3.6	13.8	0.80	9.64	N/A	1	98	0	1	95	55.8	-30.7	84	7	2,000	100	0.0	0.0
C- /3.8	13.8	0.80	10.38	12	1	98	0	1	95	64.4	-30.4	88	7	250,000	25,000	0.0	0.0
C /4.8	14.4	0.83	10.18	1	3	96	0	1	105	31.3	-28.7	80	7	2,000	100	5.8	0.0
C /4.8	14.5	0.83	9.67	1	3	96	0	1	105	25.6	-28.8	N/A	7	2,000	100	0.0	0.0
C /4.8	14.5	0.83	10.32	13	3	96	0	1	105	32.8	-28.6	81	7	250,000	25,000	0.0	0.0
C- /4.0	14.0	0.80	10.93	13	5	94	0	1	67	27.0	-24.6	29	7	2,000	100	5.8	0.0
C- /3.9	14.0	0.80	10.41	14	5	94	0	1	67	21.9	-24.9	21	7	2,000	100	0.0	0.0
C- /4.0	14.0	0.80	11.09	112	5	94	0	1	67	28.6	-24.5	32	7	250,000	25,000	0.0	0.0
C- /3.9	13.9	0.70	11.31	6	1	98	0	1	57	50.8	-25.1	79	7	2,000	100	0.0	0.0
C- /3.8	14.0	0.70	10.77	4	1	98	0	1	57	44.7	-25.3	74	7	2,000	100	5.8	0.0
C- /3.9	14.0	0.70	11.48	49	1	98	0	1	57	52.7	-25.0	81	7	250,000	25,000	0.0	0.0
C /4.7	11.6	0.97	13.26	N/A	4	95	0	1	46	N/A	N/A	3	1	2,000	100	5.8	0.0
C /4.6	11.6	0.97	12.72	1	4	95	0	1	46	N/A	N/A	2	1	2,000	100	0.0	0.0
C /4.8	11.6	0.97	13.38	10	4	95	0	1	46	N/A	N/A	3	1	250,000	25,000	0.0	0.0
U /	N/A	N/A	19.58	26	1	98	0	1	4	N/A	N/A	N/A	10	0	0	5.8	0.0
C+ /6.7	10.3	1.00	19.84	533	1	98	0	1	4	129.1	-16.5	68	10	0	0	0.0	0.0
C+ /6.6	10.3	1.00	20.04	1,170	1	98	0	1	4	N/A	N/A	73	10	0	0	0.0	0.0
C+ /6.6	10.3	1.00	19.32	124	1	98	0	1	4	123.8	-16.7	64	10	0	0	0.0	0.0
C+ /6.7	10.3	1.00	19.66	656	1	98	0	1	4	126.8	-16.5	67	10	0	0	0.0	0.0
C+ /6.6	10.3	1.00	20.09	771	1	98	0	1	4	132.2	-16.4	72	10	0	0	0.0	0.0
C+ /6.7	10.3	1.00	20.11	533	1	98	0	1	4	129.8	-16.4	70	10	0	0	0.0	0.0
C+ /6.9	10.4	0.77	18.50	467	0	99	0	1	0	99.4	-19.9	97	11	25	25	0.0	0.0
B+ /9.7	4.5	0.38	17.35	443	0	40	59	1	0	43.7	-5.7	77	11	25	25	0.0	0.0
B /8.1	8.3	0.78	18.36	237	0	79	19	2	0	79.1	-15.2	45	11	25	25	0.0	0.0
B+ /9.0	6.3	0.58	18.01	317	0	59	39	2	0	61.0	-10.6	64	11	25	25	0.0	0.0
C /5.3	11.2	0.87	13.84	543	1	98	0	1	20	40.7	-17.1	69	N/A	1,000,000	100	0.0	2.0
C /4.7	11.5	0.59	17.77	56	3	91	4	2	146	97.7	-24.1	91	31	1,000	0	0.0	0.0
C /4.8	10.5	1.00	21.42	125	3	93	3	1	51	117.0	-13.4	52	11	1,000	0	0.0	0.0
B- /7.3	10.6	0.93	13.67	8	7	92	0	1	95	N/A	N/A	67	4	5,000	250	0.0	1.0
C+ /6.8	11.5	0.13	7.82	N/A	59	16	23	2	107	N/A	N/A	28	3	2,500	250	5.5	1.0
C+ /6.7	11.6	0.11	7.63	N/A	59	16	23	2	107	N/A	N/A	25	3	1,000	100	0.0	1.0
C+ /6.8	11.5	0.13	7.86	30	59	16	23	2	107	N/A	N/A	31	3	100,000	10,000	0.0	1.0
C /4.6	11.6	0.71	10.54	11	16	74	9	1	601	83.1	-17.5	32	9	50,000	0	0.0	0.0
C+ /6.2	10.2	0.96	13.20	25	3	95	1	1	34	92.2	-15.9	49	10	50,000	0	0.0	0.0
D /1.8	13.1	1.01	12.98	12	18	81	0	1	25	139.0	-22.9	37	13	50,000	0	0.0	0.0
C /4.9	12.6	0.86	9.75	11	0	0	0	100	48	N/A	N/A	2	4	50,000	0	0.0	0.0
C- /3.5	12.9	1.04	15.11	22	1	97	0	2	40	94.1	-18.9	15	18	50,000	0	0.0	0.0
C- /3.9	9.2	1.14	8.16	1	5	90	3	2	228	N/A	N/A	0	4	2,000	1,000	5.8	0.0
C- /4.0	9.3	1.14	8.53	14	5	90	3	2	228	N/A	N/A	0	4	1,000,000	0	0.0	0.0
C /4.8	14.3	0.82	14.13	21	0	100	0	0	17	82.3	-21.7	40	7	2,500	50	0.0	2.0
C /4.8	12.1	0.94	15.86	7	0	98	0	2	23	35.2	-25.1	9	11	1,000	100	5.3	2.0
C /4.7	12.1	0.94	15.02	96	0	98	0	2	23	35.2	-25.1	9	11	1,000	100	0.0	2.0
C /4.8	12.1	0.94	16.49	4	0	98	0	2	23	37.6	-25.0	11	11	5,000,000	0	0.0	2.0
C /4.8	12.1	0.94	15.17	2	0	98	0	2	23	31.0	-25.3	7	11	1,000	100	0.0	2.0
C- /3.0	16.2	0.86	33.69	N/A	0	97	2	1	46	N/A	N/A	31	15	10,000,000	0	0.0	0.0
D+ /2.9	16.2	1.13	31.27	253	0	97	2	1	46	110.9	-16.8	5	15	1,000	100	5.3	0.0
D+ /2.5	16.2	1.13	24.94	2	0	97	2	1	46	102.4	-17.1	4	15	1,000	100	0.0	0.0
C- /3.0	16.2	1.13	33.60	52	0	97	2	1	46	114.6	-16.7	6	15	5,000,000	0	0.0	0.0
D+ /2.6	16.2	1.13	25.11	24	0	97	2	1	46	104.5	-17.1	4	15	1,000	100	0.0	0.0
C+ /6.6	9.3	0.66	12.23	40	3	81	14	2	27	75.5	-19.1	96	10	0	0	0.0	0.0
C+ /6.6	9.3	0.66	12.13	45	3	81	14	2	27	73.0	-19.1	96	10	0	0	0.0	0.0

Fund Type	Fund Name	Ticker Symbol	Overall Investment Rating	Phone	Performance Rating/Pts	3 Mo	6 Mo	1Yr / Pct	3Yr / Pct	5Yr / Pct	Dividend Yield	Expense Ratio
GL	Morningstar Bal ETF Asset Alloc I		C+	(866) 432-2926	C- / 4.2	5.02	4.47	15.67 /33	4.42 /48	6.30 /30	1.96	0.66
GL	Morningstar Bal ETF Asset Alloc II	BETFX	C+	(866) 432-2926	C- / 3.9	4.92	4.29	15.39 /32	4.13 /44	6.01 /28	1.64	0.91
GL	Morningstar Consv ETF Asset All I		C-	(866) 432-2926	D / 1.7	2.72	0.91	6.84 / 6	2.43 /27	2.88 /10	1.79	0.73
GL	Morningstar Consv ETF Asset All II	CETFX	C-	(866) 432-2926	D / 1.7	2.62	0.80	6.56 / 5	2.20 /25	2.63 /10	1.51	0.98
GL	Morningstar Growth ETF Asset All I		B-	(866) 432-2926	C / 5.5	6.12	6.12	19.91 /51	5.09 /55	7.60 /39	1.65	0.66
GL	Morningstar Growth ETF Asset All II	GETFX	B-	(866) 432-2926	C / 5.3	6.07	5.97	19.64 /50	4.81 /52	7.34 /37	1.38	0.91
GL	Morningstar Inc & G ETF Asst All I		C	(866) 432-2926	D+ / 2.7	3.97	2.71	11.15 /15	3.34 /35	4.52 /18	2.07	0.68
GL	Morningstar Inc & G ETF Asst All II	IETFX	C	(866) 432-2926	D+ / 2.5	3.82	2.62	10.78 /14	3.07 /32	4.25 /17	1.66	0.93
MC	Mosaic Mid Cap R6	MMCRX	B	(800) 877-6089	B / 8.0	5.95	8.66	20.42 /54	9.35 /89	13.80 /92	0.00	0.77
FO	Motley Fool Emerging Markets Inv	TMFEX	D-	(888) 863-8803	D- / 1.2	4.46	0.49	18.02 /43	-0.02 /13	3.16 /11	0.56	1.63
GL	Motley Fool Great America Investor	TMFGX	C	(888) 863-8803	C / 5.1	3.46	7.57	19.62 /50	5.51 /60	11.31 /68	0.00	1.15
GL	Motley Fool Independence Instl	FOIIX	U	(888) 863-8803	U /	6.54	4.03	17.87 /42	--	--	0.42	2.12
GL	Motley Fool Independence Investor	FOOLX	C-	(888) 863-8803	C / 4.5	6.44	3.98	17.70 /41	4.95 /54	8.04 /42	0.19	1.15
GR	Mount Lucas US Focused Eq I	BMLEX	C-	(844) 261-6483	C+ / 6.8	5.37	14.09	22.85 /66	5.38 /58	11.43 /69	4.35	1.31
GR	MP 63 Fund	DRIPX	B+	(877) 676-3386	B / 7.9	6.40	7.02	21.55 /60	9.39 /89	13.33 /87	1.90	0.80
FO	MSIF Active Internatl Allocation A	MSIBX	E+	(800) 354-8185	E / 0.4	7.37	3.72	13.16 /22	-2.36 / 6	3.80 /14	1.80	1.28
FO	MSIF Active Internatl Allocation I	MSACX	D-	(800) 354-8185	E+ / 0.7	7.42	3.87	13.63 /24	-2.02 / 7	4.15 /16	2.33	0.92
FO	● MSIF Active Internatl Allocation L	MSLLX	E+	(800) 354-8185	E / 0.5	7.18	3.33	12.52 /20	-2.88 / 5	--	1.29	1.87
GR	MSIF Advantage A	MAPPX	C+	(800) 354-8185	C+ / 6.8	6.25	4.99	20.45 /55	9.26 /89	13.55 /89	0.00	1.86
GR	MSIF Advantage I	MPAIX	B	(800) 354-8185	B / 7.9	6.31	5.14	20.84 /57	9.61 /91	13.92 /93	0.23	1.48
GR	MSIF Advantage IS	MADSX	B	(800) 354-8185	B / 7.9	6.34	5.16	20.92 /57	9.65 /91	--	0.26	14.51
GR	● MSIF Advantage L	MAPLX	B	(800) 354-8185	B / 7.8	6.27	5.09	20.73 /56	9.50 /90	13.82 /92	0.14	2.31
EM	MSIF Emerging Markets A	MMKBX	E+	(800) 354-8185	D- / 1.0	8.09	0.91	22.81 /66	-0.11 /13	0.30 / 5	0.44	1.41
EM	MSIF Emerging Markets I	MGEMX	D-	(800) 354-8185	D+ / 2.5	8.19	1.14	23.26 /67	0.21 /14	0.60 / 5	0.76	1.10
EM	MSIF Emerging Markets IS	MMMPX	D-	(800) 354-8185	D+ / 2.5	8.15	1.11	23.27 /67	0.27 /15	--	0.82	1.00
EM	MSIF Emerging Markets L	MSELX	E+	(800) 354-8185	D- / 1.5	7.93	0.65	22.19 /63	-0.65 /11	--	0.00	2.43
EM	MSIF Emerging Markets Leaders A	MELAX	D+	(800) 869-6397	D- / 1.2	6.62	-1.15	14.91 /29	0.64 /16	2.10 / 8	0.08	5.89
EM	MSIF Emerging Markets Leaders I	MELIX	D+	(800) 869-6397	D / 1.8	6.72	-0.92	15.34 /31	0.93 /18	2.28 / 9	0.11	2.80
EM	MSIF Emerging Markets Leaders IS	MELSX	C-	(800) 869-6397	D / 1.8	6.72	-0.82	15.34 /31	0.97 /18	2.30 / 9	0.12	2.65
EM	MSIF Frontier Emerging Markets A	MFMPX	D-	(800) 354-8185	E+ / 0.6	8.68	5.26	14.28 /27	-1.13 / 9	--	0.92	2.07
EM	MSIF Frontier Emerging Markets I	MFMIX	D-	(800) 354-8185	D- / 1.1	8.80	5.47	14.64 /28	-0.78 /10	8.63 /47	1.28	1.72
EM	● MSIF Frontier Emerging Markets L	MFMLX	D-	(800) 354-8185	E+ / 0.8	8.58	4.94	13.54 /24	-1.76 / 7	--	0.08	2.73
EM	MSIF Global Advantage A	MIGPX	D	(800) 354-8185	C- / 3.6	7.87	4.76	19.92 /52	3.53 /37	9.39 /54	0.00	5.91
EM	MSIF Global Advantage I	MIGIX	C-	(800) 354-8185	C / 5.0	7.96	4.96	20.44 /55	3.90 /42	9.75 /57	0.00	5.36
EM	● MSIF Global Advantage L	MIGLX	D+	(800) 354-8185	C- / 4.2	7.79	4.53	19.45 /49	3.03 /32	8.86 /49	0.00	6.57
GL	MSIF Global Discovery A	MGDPX	B	(800) 354-8185	A+ / 9.7	8.13	15.51	43.37 /98	9.38 /89	16.22 /98	0.02	3.52
GL	MSIF Global Discovery I	MLDIX	B	(800) 354-8185	A+ / 9.8	8.18	15.71	43.91 /98	9.76 /92	16.59 /98	0.17	3.09
GL	● MSIF Global Discovery L	MGDLX	B	(800) 354-8185	A+ / 9.8	7.92	15.24	42.62 /98	8.82 /86	15.63 /98	0.00	4.55
GL	● MSIF Global Franchise A	MSFBX	C+	(800) 354-8185	C+ / 6.0	10.44	5.57	15.87 /34	7.83 /78	9.69 /56	0.98	1.25
GL	MSIF Global Franchise C	MSGFX	U	(800) 354-8185	U /	10.21	5.17	15.06 /30	--	--	0.62	2.03
GL	MSIF Global Franchise I	MSFAX	B+	(800) 354-8185	B- / 7.2	10.52	5.69	16.19 /35	8.12 /80	9.99 /58	1.22	0.99
GL	● MSIF Global Franchise L	MSFLX	C+	(800) 354-8185	C+ / 6.7	10.32	5.32	15.37 /32	7.34 /74	--	0.46	1.73
OT	MSIF Global Infrastructure A	MTIPX	D-	(800) 354-8185	D / 2.1	2.56	-1.65	17.04 /38	3.61 /38	8.35 /45	2.22	1.35
OT	MSIF Global Infrastructure I	MTIIX	D	(800) 354-8185	C- / 3.2	2.67	-1.53	17.28 /40	3.92 /42	9.02 /51	2.59	1.10
OT	MSIF Global Infrastructure IS	MSGPX	D	(800) 354-8185	C- / 3.2	2.69	-1.45	17.39 /40	3.93 /42	--	2.61	1.41
OT	● MSIF Global Infrastructure L	MTILX	D	(800) 354-8185	D+ / 2.6	2.54	-1.85	16.41 /36	3.04 /32	8.12 /43	1.75	1.95
GL	MSIF Global Insight A	MBPHX	B	(800) 354-8185	A- / 9.1	8.73	12.57	39.62 /97	7.83 /78	12.98 /84	0.00	11.74
GL	MSIF Global Insight I	MBPIX	B+	(800) 354-8185	A+ / 9.7	8.82	12.76	40.03 /97	8.17 /80	13.31 /87	0.22	10.84
GL	● MSIF Global Insight L	MBPLX	B+	(800) 354-8185	A / 9.5	8.60	12.40	38.85 /97	7.27 /74	12.39 /78	0.00	17.24
GL	MSIF Global Opportunity A	MGGPX	B	(800) 354-8185	B / 8.2	9.10	6.79	22.32 /64	10.73 /96	14.11 /94	0.00	1.50
GL	MSIF Global Opportunity C	MSOPX	U	(800) 354-8185	U /	8.97	6.47	21.51 /60	--	--	0.00	2.22
GL	MSIF Global Opportunity I	MGGIX	B+	(800) 354-8185	A / 9.3	9.26	7.07	22.81 /66	11.14 /97	14.51 /96	0.00	1.20

www.thestreetratings.com

Risk Rating/Pts	Standard Deviation	Beta	NAV As of 2/28/17	Total $(Mil)	Cash %	Stocks %	Bonds %	Other %	Portfolio Turnover Ratio	Last Bull Market Return	Last Bear Market Return	Manager Quality Pct	Manager Tenure (Years)	Initial Purch. $	Additional Purch. $	Front End Load	Back End Load
B- /7.9	6.5	0.98	11.17	23	3	54	41	2	29	53.5	-12.2	73	10	0	0	0.0	0.0
B- /7.9	6.5	0.99	11.26	167	3	54	41	2	29	51.2	-12.2	69	10	0	0	0.0	0.0
B /8.6	3.2	0.43	10.95	4	2	17	79	2	37	21.7	-2.6	77	10	0	0	0.0	0.0
B /8.7	3.1	0.42	10.90	32	2	17	79	2	37	20.0	-2.7	75	10	0	0	0.0	0.0
B- /7.5	8.3	0.59	11.54	77	3	73	23	1	28	67.6	-16.8	95	10	0	0	0.0	0.0
B- /7.5	8.3	1.25	11.37	125	3	73	23	1	28	65.3	-16.8	62	10	0	0	0.0	0.0
B /8.0	4.7	0.33	10.28	5	3	35	60	2	24	36.2	-7.5	91	10	0	0	0.0	0.0
B /8.1	4.7	0.33	10.77	78	3	35	60	2	24	34.4	-7.6	90	10	0	0	0.0	0.0
C /5.0	10.9	0.85	9.39	12	7	92	0	1	27	N/A	N/A	82	7	500,000	50,000	0.0	0.0
C /5.0	11.7	0.77	11.84	26	3	96	0	1	54	N/A	N/A	75	6	500	50	0.0	2.0
C+ /6.2	12.5	0.63	20.61	210	4	95	0	1	21	112.3	-17.4	96	7	500	50	0.0	2.0
U /	N/A	N/A	20.93	45	6	93	0	1	26	N/A	N/A	N/A	8	100,000	0	0.0	2.0
C+ /5.9	10.8	0.76	20.94	310	6	93	0	1	26	72.8	-16.1	95	8	500	50	0.0	2.0
C- /3.4	12.7	1.07	9.51	17	0	99	0	1	95	120.6	-23.9	11	10	10,000	0	0.0	0.0
C+ /6.4	9.8	0.90	19.41	62	1	98	0	1	4	119.3	-16.9	73	18	500	50	0.0	1.0
C+ /5.6	11.4	0.92	12.55	58	0	80	19	1	30	36.2	-23.6	45	22	1,000	0	5.3	2.0
C+ /5.6	11.4	0.92	12.28	174	0	80	19	1	30	38.6	-23.6	50	22	5,000,000	0	0.0	2.0
C+ /5.6	11.4	0.92	12.49	6	0	80	19	1	30	N/A	N/A	37	22	1,000	0	0.0	2.0
C /5.2	11.6	0.94	18.58	21	0	95	4	1	51	125.7	-10.7	67	9	1,000	0	5.3	0.0
C /5.2	11.6	0.94	18.81	45	0	95	4	1	51	129.4	-10.6	71	9	5,000,000	0	0.0	0.0
C /5.2	11.7	0.94	18.83	14	0	95	4	1	51	N/A	N/A	71	9	10,000,000	0	0.0	0.0
C /5.2	11.6	0.94	18.80	4	0	95	4	1	51	128.4	-10.6	69	9	1,000	0	0.0	0.0
C /4.4	14.1	0.84	21.91	19	0	96	3	1	40	19.1	-22.8	55	15	1,000	0	5.3	2.0
C /4.3	14.1	0.84	22.48	305	0	96	3	1	40	21.0	-22.8	59	15	5,000,000	0	0.0	2.0
C /4.3	14.1	0.84	22.48	727	0	96	3	1	40	N/A	N/A	60	15	10,000,000	0	0.0	2.0
C /4.4	14.1	0.84	21.64	N/A	0	96	3	1	40	N/A	N/A	47	15	1,000	0	0.0	2.0
B- /7.5	11.8	0.59	10.31	1	0	0	0	100	36	31.6	N/A	69	N/A	1,000	0	5.3	2.0
B- /7.5	11.9	0.59	10.38	27	0	0	0	100	36	32.7	N/A	73	N/A	5,000,000	0	0.0	2.0
B- /7.5	11.8	0.59	10.39	95	0	0	0	100	36	32.9	N/A	73	N/A	10,000,000	0	0.0	2.0
C+ /5.7	11.2	0.47	18.22	100	5	93	0	2	37	N/A	N/A	48	9	1,000	0	5.3	2.0
C+ /5.7	11.2	0.46	18.32	557	5	93	0	2	37	59.2	-21.5	53	9	5,000,000	0	0.0	2.0
C+ /5.7	11.2	0.47	18.14	3	5	93	0	2	37	N/A	N/A	39	9	1,000	0	0.0	2.0
C /4.6	11.7	0.49	12.94	3	0	92	6	2	90	90.6	-15.9	89	7	1,000	0	5.3	0.0
C /4.6	11.7	0.49	13.07	3	0	92	6	2	90	94.0	-15.7	90	7	5,000,000	0	0.0	0.0
C /4.5	11.7	0.49	12.65	N/A	0	92	6	2	90	85.5	-16.0	87	7	1,000	0	0.0	0.0
C- /3.8	12.1	0.74	13.95	23	5	94	0	1	118	169.9	-27.7	99	7	1,000	0	5.3	0.0
C- /3.8	12.2	0.74	14.01	16	5	94	0	1	118	174.3	-27.6	99	7	5,000,000	0	0.0	0.0
C- /3.9	12.2	0.74	13.85	N/A	5	94	0	1	118	162.6	-27.9	99	7	1,000	0	0.0	0.0
C+ /6.6	11.4	0.72	21.65	114	3	96	0	1	37	80.1	-6.5	98	8	1,000	0	5.3	0.0
U /	N/A	N/A	21.33	32	3	96	0	1	37	N/A	N/A	N/A	8	1,000	0	0.0	0.0
C+ /6.6	11.4	0.72	22.09	654	3	96	0	1	37	82.9	-6.5	98	8	5,000,000	0	0.0	0.0
C+ /6.7	11.4	0.72	21.61	8	3	96	0	1	37	N/A	N/A	98	8	1,000	0	0.0	0.0
C /4.8	11.4	0.68	14.10	280	7	92	0	1	48	73.8	-6.8	30	7	1,000	0	5.3	0.0
C /4.8	11.4	0.68	14.14	66	7	92	0	1	48	79.4	-6.7	34	7	5,000,000	0	0.0	0.0
C /4.8	11.4	0.68	14.14	7	7	92	0	1	48	N/A	N/A	34	7	10,000,000	0	0.0	0.0
C /4.8	11.4	0.68	14.05	6	7	92	0	1	48	71.7	-7.0	24	7	1,000	0	0.0	0.0
C /4.3	13.2	0.92	13.55	1	2	97	0	1	62	N/A	N/A	98	6	1,000	0	5.3	0.0
C /4.3	13.2	0.92	13.53	9	2	97	0	1	62	N/A	N/A	98	6	5,000,000	0	0.0	0.0
C /4.3	13.2	0.92	13.35	N/A	2	97	0	1	62	N/A	N/A	98	6	1,000	0	0.0	0.0
C /5.1	13.3	0.85	16.55	367	0	95	4	1	115	131.0	-21.4	99	9	1,000	0	5.3	0.0
U /	N/A	N/A	16.17	38	0	95	4	1	115	N/A	N/A	N/A	9	1,000	0	0.0	0.0
C /5.1	13.3	0.85	17.00	297	0	95	4	1	115	135.2	-21.4	99	9	5,000,000	0	0.0	0.0

Fund Type	Fund Name	Ticker Symbol	Overall Investment Rating	Phone	Perfor-mance Rating/Pts	3 Mo	6 Mo	1Yr / Pct	3Yr / Pct	5Yr / Pct	Dividend Yield	Expense Ratio
			99 Pct = Best 0 Pct = Worst		PERFORMANCE	Total Return % through 2/28/17			Annualized		Incl. in Returns	
GL	MSIF Global Opportunity IS	MGTSX	B+	(800) 354-8185	A / 9.3	9.24	7.06	22.93 /66	11.20 /97	--	0.00	3.56
GL	● MSIF Global Opportunity L	MGGLX	B+	(800) 354-8185	A- / 9.0	9.07	6.81	22.27 /63	10.64 /96	14.05 /94	0.00	2.03
GL	MSIF Global Quality Portfolio A	MGQAX	C+	(800) 354-8185	C / 4.7	10.07	5.34	15.06 /30	5.88 /63	--	1.22	2.52
GL	MSIF Global Quality Portfolio I	MGQIX	B-	(800) 354-8185	C+ / 6.1	10.16	5.45	15.45 /32	6.23 /66	--	1.62	2.21
GL	MSIF Global Quality Portfolio IS	MGQSX	B-	(800) 354-8185	C+ / 6.0	10.13	5.42	15.42 /32	6.23 /66	--	1.68	16.35
GL	● MSIF Global Quality Portfolio L	MGQLX	C+	(800) 354-8185	C / 5.3	9.92	4.98	14.42 /27	5.33 /58	--	0.81	3.06
RE	MSIF Global Real Estate A	MRLBX	D+	(800) 354-8185	D+ / 2.6	6.19	-2.50	11.58 /16	5.21 /57	7.17 /36	3.09	1.34
RE	MSIF Global Real Estate I	MRLAX	C-	(800) 354-8185	C- / 3.7	6.29	-2.34	11.85 /17	5.51 /60	7.51 /38	3.64	1.05
RE	MSIF Global Real Estate IS	MGREX	C-	(800) 354-8185	C- / 3.8	6.23	-2.30	11.99 /18	5.58 /60	--	3.76	0.97
RE	● MSIF Global Real Estate L	MGRLX	C-	(800) 354-8185	C- / 3.1	6.03	-2.69	11.06 /15	4.73 /51	6.69 /33	2.26	1.78
GR	MSIF Growth A	MSEGX	C-	(800) 354-8185	C+ / 6.7	10.08	6.39	25.14 /74	7.01 /72	14.16 /94	0.00	0.96
GR	MSIF Growth I	MSEQX	C+	(800) 354-8185	B / 7.8	10.15	6.55	25.48 /75	7.30 /74	14.45 /95	0.00	0.61
GR	MSIF Growth IS	MGRPX	C+	(800) 354-8185	B / 7.9	10.17	6.58	25.59 /75	7.40 /75	--	0.00	0.54
GR	● MSIF Growth L	MSHLX	C	(800) 354-8185	B- / 7.2	9.96	6.14	24.47 /72	6.45 /68	--	0.00	1.57
GL	MSIF Insight A	MFPHX	B+	(800) 354-8185	A+ / 9.6	5.74	12.10	33.87 /93	11.59 /98	17.13 /98	0.02	8.32
GL	MSIF Insight I	MFPIX	B+	(800) 354-8185	A+ / 9.8	5.76	12.26	34.24 /93	11.97 /98	17.50 /98	0.05	7.50
GL	● MSIF Insight L	MFPLX	B+	(800) 354-8185	A+ / 9.7	5.50	11.73	33.09 /92	11.00 /97	16.54 /98	0.02	10.04
FO	MSIF International Advantage A	MFAPX	C-	(800) 354-8185	C / 5.5	8.78	6.57	18.82 /46	7.09 /73	8.79 /49	0.00	5.73
FO	MSIF International Advantage I	MFAIX	C	(800) 354-8185	C+ / 6.8	8.91	6.79	19.34 /49	7.45 /75	9.13 /52	0.00	4.76
FO	● MSIF International Advantage L	MSALX	C	(800) 354-8185	C+ / 6.1	8.73	6.32	18.26 /44	6.56 /69	8.24 /44	0.00	6.82
FO	MSIF International Equity A	MIQBX	E+	(800) 354-8185	E / 0.4	8.91	2.28	11.65 /17	-1.59 / 8	4.43 /18	0.63	1.32
FO	MSIF International Equity I	MSIQX	D-	(800) 354-8185	E+ / 0.8	8.97	2.44	11.99 /18	-1.24 / 9	4.75 /20	1.02	1.01
FO	MSIF International Equity IS	MIQPX	D-	(800) 354-8185	E+ / 0.8	8.94	2.48	12.04 /18	-1.21 / 9	--	1.06	0.91
FO	● MSIF International Equity L	MSQLX	D-	(800) 354-8185	E+ / 0.6	8.79	2.05	11.14 /15	-2.07 / 6	--	0.13	1.89
FO	MSIF International Opportunity A	MIOPX	C-	(800) 354-8185	C / 4.8	8.36	5.33	19.82 /51	6.10 /65	8.70 /48	0.00	2.26
FO	MSIF International Opportunity I	MIOIX	C	(800) 354-8185	C+ / 6.2	8.42	5.48	20.23 /53	6.50 /68	9.05 /51	0.02	1.92
FO	MSIF International Opportunity IS	MNOPX	C	(800) 354-8185	C+ / 6.2	8.41	5.48	20.31 /54	6.50 /68	--	0.03	15.74
FO	● MSIF International Opportunity L	MIOLX	C-	(800) 354-8185	C / 5.4	8.13	5.04	19.20 /48	5.55 /60	8.15 /43	0.00	3.49
RE	MSIF International Real Estate A	IERBX	D-	(800) 354-8185	E+ / 0.7	5.19	-3.07	9.54 /11	0.63 /16	4.88 /21	4.37	1.70
RE	MSIF International Real Estate I	MSUAX	D	(800) 354-8185	D- / 1.3	5.22	-2.92	9.86 /11	0.97 /18	5.21 /23	5.01	1.29
RE	MSIF International Real Estate IS	MIREX	D	(800) 354-8185	D- / 1.3	5.28	-2.86	10.00 /12	1.01 /18	--	5.07	1.30
RE	● MSIF International Real Estate L	MSOLX	D	(800) 354-8185	D- / 1.0	5.05	-3.28	8.99 / 9	0.12 /14	--	4.20	4.58
GL	MSIF Multi-Asset A	MMPPX	D	(800) 354-8185	E- / 0.1	-1.46	-0.74	-3.83 / 1	-6.22 / 2	--	1.01	1.50
GL	MSIF Multi-Asset I	MMPIX	D	(800) 354-8185	E- / 0.1	-1.35	-0.63	-3.54 / 1	-5.94 / 2	--	1.74	1.17
GL	● MSIF Multi-Asset L	MMPLX	D	(800) 354-8185	E- / 0.1	-1.48	-0.95	-4.21 / 1	-6.66 / 2	--	0.00	1.95
SC	● MSIF Small Company Growth A	MSSMX	E-	(800) 354-8185	E- / 0.1	0.21	-3.58	17.14 /39	-6.62 / 2	7.04 /35	0.00	1.38
SC	● MSIF Small Company Growth I	MSSGX	E-	(800) 354-8185	E- / 0.2	0.19	-3.46	17.44 /40	-6.32 / 2	7.35 /37	0.00	1.11
GL	MSIF Small Company Growth IS	MFLLX	E-	(800) 354-8185	E- / 0.2	0.26	-3.45	17.58 /41	-6.24 / 2	--	0.00	0.99
SC	● MSIF Small Company Growth L	MSSLX	E-	(800) 354-8185	E- / 0.1	0.13	-3.86	16.54 /36	-7.08 / 1	6.49 /31	0.00	2.10
BA	MSIF Trust Global Strategist A	MBAAX	D+	(800) 354-8185	D- / 1.4	4.70	2.82	12.74 /21	0.78 /17	5.55 /25	0.75	1.11
BA	MSIF Trust Global Strategist I	MPBAX	C-	(800) 354-8185	D / 2.1	4.75	2.89	13.10 /22	1.10 /19	5.88 /28	1.11	0.83
BA	● MSIF Trust Global Strategist L	MSDLX	D+	(800) 354-8185	D / 1.7	4.57	2.53	12.14 /18	0.26 /15	--	0.19	1.69
MC	● MSIF Trust Mid Cap Growth A	MACGX	E-	(800) 354-8185	E- / 0.1	5.17	-3.95	11.43 /16	-6.07 / 2	3.44 /13	0.00	1.00
MC	● MSIF Trust Mid Cap Growth I	MPEGX	E-	(800) 354-8185	E- / 0.2	5.25	-3.80	11.74 /17	-5.80 / 2	3.72 /14	0.00	0.74
MC	● MSIF Trust Mid Cap Growth IS	MMCGX	E-	(800) 354-8185	E- / 0.2	5.27	-3.75	11.82 /17	-5.68 / 2	--	0.00	0.61
MC	● MSIF Trust Mid Cap Growth L	MSKLX	E-	(800) 354-8185	E- / 0.1	5.01	-4.25	10.67 /13	-6.60 / 2	--	0.00	1.55
RE	MSIF US Real Estate A	MUSDX	C-	(800) 354-8185	C+ / 5.9	7.01	-1.75	13.51 /24	10.20 /94	10.23 /60	2.63	1.28
RE	MSIF US Real Estate I	MSUSX	C+	(800) 354-8185	B- / 7.0	7.09	-1.60	13.85 /25	10.54 /96	10.56 /62	2.98	0.98
RE	MSIF US Real Estate IS	MURSX	C+	(800) 354-8185	B- / 7.1	7.12	-1.54	14.04 /26	10.64 /96	--	3.08	0.90
RE	● MSIF US Real Estate L	MSULX	C	(800) 354-8185	C+ / 6.4	6.82	-2.03	12.91 /21	9.63 /91	9.66 /56	2.24	1.82
GI	Muhlenkamp Fund	MUHLX	E	(800) 860-3863	D- / 1.1	6.41	9.40	12.64 /20	-1.18 / 9	5.91 /28	0.00	1.24
GR	Mundoval	MUNDX	C-	(800) 595-2877	C / 5.4	8.60	11.53	26.69 /78	1.90 /23	8.18 /43	0.47	1.51

www.thestreetratings.com

Risk Rating/Pts	3 Year Standard Deviation	Beta	NAV As of 2/28/17	Total $(Mil)	Cash %	Stocks %	Bonds %	Other %	Portfolio Turnover Ratio	Last Bull Market Return	Last Bear Market Return	Manager Quality Pct	Manager Tenure (Years)	Initial Purch. $	Additional Purch. $	Front End Load	Back End Load
C /5.1	13.3	0.85	17.03	N/A	0	95	4	1	115	N/A	N/A	99	9	10,000,000	0	0.0	0.0
C /5.1	13.3	0.85	16.36	33	0	95	4	1	115	130.3	-21.5	99	9	1,000	0	0.0	0.0
B- /7.0	10.7	0.72	11.58	2	2	97	0	1	61	N/A	N/A	97	4	1,000	0	5.3	0.0
B- /7.0	10.7	0.72	11.61	4	2	97	0	1	61	N/A	N/A	97	4	5,000,000	0	0.0	0.0
B- /7.0	10.7	0.72	11.60	N/A	2	97	0	1	61	N/A	N/A	97	4	10,000,000	0	0.0	0.0
B- /7.1	10.6	0.72	11.53	2	2	97	0	1	61	N/A	N/A	96	4	1,000	0	0.0	0.0
C+ /6.7	12.2	0.83	11.06	40	8	89	1	2	29	72.9	-21.9	27	11	1,000	0	5.3	0.0
C+ /6.7	12.1	0.83	11.12	458	8	89	1	2	29	75.6	-21.8	30	11	5,000,000	0	0.0	0.0
C+ /6.7	12.1	0.83	11.12	1,301	8	89	1	2	29	N/A	N/A	31	11	10,000,000	0	0.0	0.0
C+ /6.7	12.1	0.83	10.98	2	8	89	1	2	29	68.4	-22.1	23	11	1,000	0	0.0	0.0
C- /3.6	15.6	1.09	38.15	1,518	0	97	2	1	34	128.9	-16.0	22	13	1,000	0	5.3	0.0
C- /3.7	15.6	1.09	39.53	812	0	97	2	1	34	132.2	-15.9	24	13	5,000,000	0	0.0	0.0
C- /3.7	15.6	1.09	39.69	983	0	97	2	1	34	N/A	N/A	25	13	10,000,000	0	0.0	0.0
C- /3.6	15.6	1.09	36.92	81	0	97	2	1	34	N/A	N/A	17	13	1,000	0	0.0	0.0
C- /4.1	11.5	0.65	14.85	12	4	95	0	1	55	N/A	N/A	99	6	1,000	0	5.3	0.0
C- /4.1	11.4	0.65	14.90	16	4	95	0	1	55	N/A	N/A	99	6	5,000,000	0	0.0	0.0
C- /4.1	11.4	0.65	14.51	N/A	4	95	0	1	55	N/A	N/A	99	6	1,000	0	0.0	0.0
C /4.5	11.1	0.79	12.91	11	2	90	6	2	96	84.1	-15.9	98	7	1,000	0	5.3	2.0
C /4.5	11.1	0.79	12.98	40	2	90	6	2	96	87.1	-15.7	98	7	5,000,000	0	0.0	2.0
C /4.5	11.1	0.79	12.73	N/A	2	90	6	2	96	79.3	-16.1	97	7	1,000	0	0.0	2.0
C+ /5.6	11.2	0.87	15.21	1,177	0	98	1	1	29	44.6	-20.1	56	18	1,000	0	5.3	2.0
C+ /5.6	11.2	0.87	15.40	1,762	0	98	1	1	29	46.9	-20.0	61	18	5,000,000	0	0.0	2.0
C+ /5.6	11.2	0.87	15.40	1,097	0	98	1	1	29	N/A	N/A	61	18	10,000,000	0	0.0	2.0
C+ /5.7	11.2	0.87	15.16	7	0	98	1	1	29	N/A	N/A	49	18	1,000	0	0.0	2.0
C /5.1	12.7	0.85	16.20	14	0	96	2	2	51	82.8	-26.2	97	7	1,000	0	5.3	2.0
C /5.1	12.8	0.86	16.36	68	0	96	2	2	51	85.9	-26.1	97	7	5,000,000	0	0.0	2.0
C /5.1	12.7	0.85	16.37	1	0	96	2	2	51	N/A	N/A	97	7	10,000,000	0	0.0	2.0
C /5.0	12.8	0.86	15.83	N/A	0	96	2	2	51	77.7	-26.3	96	7	1,000	0	0.0	2.0
C+ /6.5	12.2	0.59	18.35	2	15	83	0	2	37	55.0	-25.0	11	18	1,000	0	5.3	2.0
C+ /6.5	12.2	0.59	18.34	28	15	83	0	2	37	57.5	-24.9	13	18	5,000,000	0	0.0	2.0
C+ /6.5	12.2	0.59	18.34	12	15	83	0	2	37	N/A	N/A	13	18	10,000,000	0	0.0	2.0
C+ /6.6	12.2	0.59	18.21	N/A	15	83	0	2	37	N/A	N/A	8	18	1,000	0	0.0	2.0
B- /7.4	6.1	0.02	9.42	11	0	38	60	2	355	N/A	N/A	6	5	1,000	0	5.3	0.0
B- /7.4	6.0	0.02	9.47	97	0	38	60	2	355	N/A	N/A	7	5	5,000,000	0	0.0	0.0
B- /7.4	6.0	0.02	9.34	6	0	38	60	2	355	N/A	N/A	5	5	1,000	0	0.0	0.0
E+ /0.8	18.8	1.02	12.00	89	0	98	1	1	42	71.3	-24.7	1	18	1,000	0	5.3	2.0
E+ /0.9	18.7	1.01	13.57	257	0	98	1	1	42	74.0	-24.6	1	18	5,000,000	0	0.0	2.0
E+ /0.9	18.7	0.82	13.61	280	0	98	1	1	42	N/A	N/A	8	18	10,000,000	0	0.0	2.0
E+ /0.8	18.7	1.01	11.60	2	0	98	1	1	42	N/A	N/A	1	18	1,000	0	0.0	2.0
B- /7.5	7.1	1.03	15.88	244	14	45	40	1	103	50.5	-9.4	6	6	1,000	0	5.3	0.0
B- /7.5	7.2	1.03	15.99	75	14	45	40	1	103	53.0	-9.4	7	6	5,000,000	0	0.0	0.0
B- /7.5	7.2	1.03	15.77	21	14	45	40	1	103	N/A	N/A	5	6	1,000	0	0.0	0.0
E- /0.0	16.1	0.90	16.72	317	1	95	2	2	23	39.4	-21.2	0	15	1,000	0	5.3	0.0
E- /0.0	16.1	0.90	18.69	305	1	95	2	2	23	41.4	-21.1	1	15	5,000,000	0	0.0	0.0
E- /0.0	16.0	0.90	18.80	63	1	95	2	2	23	N/A	N/A	1	15	10,000,000	0	0.0	0.0
E- /0.0	16.1	0.91	15.84	8	1	95	2	2	23	N/A	N/A	0	15	1,000	0	0.0	0.0
C /4.5	14.3	1.03	17.16	74	1	97	0	2	24	97.0	-17.5	60	22	1,000	0	5.3	0.0
C /4.5	14.3	1.03	17.65	489	1	97	0	2	24	100.3	-17.4	64	22	5,000,000	0	0.0	0.0
C /4.5	14.3	1.03	17.66	201	1	97	0	2	24	N/A	N/A	65	22	10,000,000	0	0.0	0.0
C /4.5	14.3	1.03	17.13	3	1	97	0	2	24	N/A	N/A	53	22	1,000	0	0.0	0.0
C- /3.5	11.3	1.00	50.98	256	9	85	4	2	19	56.4	-19.0	1	29	1,500	50	0.0	0.0
C /4.9	12.6	0.96	15.67	22	14	85	0	1	11	74.2	-17.3	4	13	10,000	100	0.0	0.0

I. Index of Stock Mutual Funds

Fund Type	Fund Name	Ticker Symbol	Overall Investment Rating	Phone	Performance Rating/Pts	3 Mo	6 Mo	1Yr / Pct	3Yr / Pct	5Yr / Pct	Dividend Yield	Expense Ratio
GR	Mutual of America Inst All Amer	MALLX	C+	(800) 914-8716	B+ / 8.4	6.87	9.16	24.37 /71	8.90 /86	12.58 /80	1.30	2.79
IX	Mutual of America Inst Eqty Idx	MAEQX	C	(800) 914-8716	A / 9.3	7.99	9.93	24.82 /73	10.52 /96	13.91 /92	1.82	1.63
MC	Mutual of America Inst MCE Idx	MAMQX	C+	(800) 914-8716	A+ / 9.9	12.07	17.02	38.28 /97	11.33 /97	14.85 /97	6.41	1.57
SC	Mutual of America Inst SC Gro	MASSX	D	(800) 914-8716	C+ / 5.9	5.29	6.65	27.75 /81	4.17 /45	9.78 /57	0.32	2.51
SC	Mutual of America Inst SC Val	MAVSX	B+	(800) 914-8716	A / 9.3	7.92	14.13	32.41 /91	7.91 /78	11.53 /70	2.88	2.35
GR	NASDAQ-100 Index Direct	NASDX	A+	(800) 955-9988	A+ / 9.8	10.68	11.58	27.11 /79	13.66 /99	16.37 /98	0.69	0.74
GR	NASDAQ-100 Index K	NDXKX	A+	(800) 955-9988	A+ / 9.8	10.51	11.29	26.47 /78	13.07 /99	15.79 /98	0.28	1.24
GI	Nationwide A	NWFAX	A-	(800) 848-0920	B+ / 8.4	8.73	10.61	25.97 /76	9.82 /92	12.71 /81	0.93	1.03
SC	Nationwide Bailard Cognitive Val A	NWHDX	B-	(800) 848-0920	B- / 7.3	3.12	11.94	30.34 /87	7.59 /76	11.36 /69	0.42	1.46
SC	Nationwide Bailard Cognitive Val C	NWHEX	B	(800) 848-0920	B / 7.7	3.02	11.59	29.34 /85	6.79 /70	10.61 /63	0.25	2.22
SC	Nationwide Bailard Cognitive Val IS	NWHHX	B+	(800) 848-0920	B+ / 8.5	3.25	12.17	30.71 /88	7.97 /79	11.73 /72	0.58	1.21
SC	Nationwide Bailard Cognitive Val M	NWHFX	B+	(800) 848-0920	B+ / 8.6	3.28	12.16	30.83 /88	7.96 /79	11.79 /72	0.63	1.13
SC	Nationwide Bailard Cognitive Val R6	NWHGX	B+	(800) 848-0920	B+ / 8.5	3.20	12.08	30.74 /88	7.94 /79	--	0.63	1.13
EM	Nationwide Bailard Em Mkts Eq M	NWWEX	U	(800) 848-0920	U /	10.70	8.50	31.43 /89	--	--	1.51	1.41
EM	Nationwide Bailard Em Mkts Eq R6	NWWCX	U	(800) 848-0920	U /	10.61	8.44	31.32 /89	--	--	1.51	1.56
FO	Nationwide Bailard Intl Eq A	NWHJX	D-	(800) 848-0920	E+ / 0.7	6.21	3.15	11.63 /16	-0.50 /11	5.63 /26	1.73	1.22
FO	Nationwide Bailard Intl Eq C	NWHKX	D-	(800) 848-0920	E+ / 0.8	5.93	2.57	10.61 /13	-1.32 / 8	4.87 /20	1.67	1.96
FO	Nationwide Bailard Intl Eq IS	NWHNX	D	(800) 848-0920	D- / 1.2	6.29	3.22	11.73 /17	-0.27 /12	5.87 /27	1.90	1.00
FO	Nationwide Bailard Intl Eq M	NWHLX	D	(800) 848-0920	D- / 1.2	6.31	3.35	12.01 /18	-0.19 /13	6.01 /28	2.03	0.87
FO	Nationwide Bailard Intl Eq R6	NWHMX	D	(800) 848-0920	D- / 1.2	6.31	3.21	12.01 /18	-0.15 /13	--	2.03	0.87
GR	Nationwide Bailard Tech and Scie A	NWHOX	B+	(800) 848-0920	A+ / 9.8	10.48	14.12	33.37 /92	12.43 /98	14.06 /94	0.12	1.28
GR	Nationwide Bailard Tech and Scie C	NWHPX	B+	(800) 848-0920	A+ / 9.8	10.26	13.69	32.30 /90	11.63 /98	13.27 /87	0.00	2.05
GR	Nationwide Bailard Tech and Scie IS	NWHUX	A-	(800) 848-0920	A+ / 9.9	10.56	14.27	33.65 /92	12.70 /99	14.35 /95	0.21	1.05
GR	Nationwide Bailard Tech and Scie M	NWHQX	A-	(800) 848-0920	A+ / 9.9	10.58	14.31	33.82 /93	12.84 /99	14.47 /95	0.30	0.95
TC	Nationwide Bailard Tech and Scie R6	NWHTX	A-	(800) 848-0920	A+ / 9.9	10.54	14.34	33.83 /93	12.85 /99	--	0.31	0.95
GI	Nationwide C	GTRCX	A	(800) 848-0920	B+ / 8.8	8.54	10.17	24.99 /73	8.95 /86	11.86 /73	0.41	1.79
AA	Nationwide Destination 2010 A	NWDAX	C-	(800) 848-0920	D / 1.9	3.69	2.86	10.66 /13	3.29 /35	4.74 /20	1.62	0.87
AA	Nationwide Destination 2010 C	NWDCX	C-	(800) 848-0920	D / 2.2	3.42	2.32	9.90 /11	2.56 /28	4.11 /16	1.11	1.51
AA	Nationwide Destination 2010 IS	NWDSX	C	(800) 848-0920	D+ / 2.9	3.78	2.99	10.95 /14	3.64 /38	5.20 /23	1.85	0.63
AA	Nationwide Destination 2010 R	NWDBX	C-	(800) 848-0920	D+ / 2.4	3.50	2.61	10.38 /13	2.97 /32	4.44 /18	1.44	1.13
AA	Nationwide Destination 2010 R6	NWDIX	C	(800) 848-0920	C- / 3.0	3.81	3.09	11.16 /15	3.79 /40	5.26 /23	2.16	0.38
AA	Nationwide Destination 2015 A	NWEAX	D+	(800) 848-0920	D / 2.2	4.17	3.48	12.46 /20	3.53 /37	5.49 /25	1.56	0.87
AA	Nationwide Destination 2015 C	NWECX	C-	(800) 848-0920	D+ / 2.6	3.93	3.21	11.80 /17	2.88 /31	4.89 /21	1.15	1.44
AA	Nationwide Destination 2015 IS	NWESX	C-	(800) 848-0920	C- / 3.2	4.23	3.58	12.70 /20	3.74 /40	5.72 /26	1.87	0.64
AA	Nationwide Destination 2015 R	NWEBX	C-	(800) 848-0920	D+ / 2.9	4.11	3.35	12.20 /19	3.21 /34	5.20 /23	1.39	1.14
AA	Nationwide Destination 2015 R6	NWEIX	C-	(800) 848-0920	C- / 3.4	4.29	3.70	12.96 /22	3.99 /43	5.97 /28	2.11	0.39
AA	Nationwide Destination 2020 A	NWAFX	C-	(800) 848-0920	D+ / 2.5	4.74	4.30	14.24 /27	3.66 /39	6.28 /30	1.56	0.87
AA	Nationwide Destination 2020 C	NWFCX	C	(800) 848-0920	C- / 3.0	4.52	3.94	13.47 /23	2.98 /32	5.65 /26	1.08	1.50
AA	Nationwide Destination 2020 IS	NWFSX	C	(800) 848-0920	C- / 3.7	4.79	4.40	14.45 /28	3.88 /41	6.50 /32	1.85	0.64
AA	Nationwide Destination 2020 R	NWFTX	C	(800) 848-0920	C- / 3.3	4.67	4.18	13.95 /25	3.36 /35	5.99 /28	1.38	1.14
AA	Nationwide Destination 2020 R6	NWFIX	C	(800) 848-0920	C- / 3.8	4.84	4.51	14.67 /28	4.12 /44	6.77 /33	2.07	0.40
AA	Nationwide Destination 2025 A	NWHAX	C-	(800) 848-0920	C- / 3.2	5.35	5.40	16.87 /38	4.04 /43	7.24 /36	1.49	0.87
AA	Nationwide Destination 2025 C	NWHCX	C	(800) 848-0920	C- / 3.8	5.24	5.16	16.26 /35	3.42 /36	6.64 /32	1.07	1.46
AA	Nationwide Destination 2025 IS	NWHSX	C+	(800) 848-0920	C / 4.5	5.51	5.61	17.21 /39	4.26 /46	7.48 /38	1.77	0.64
AA	Nationwide Destination 2025 R	NWHBX	C	(800) 848-0920	C- / 4.0	5.29	5.29	16.58 /37	3.71 /39	6.95 /34	1.30	1.14
AA	Nationwide Destination 2025 R6	NWHIX	C+	(800) 848-0920	C / 4.7	5.54	5.71	17.41 /40	4.50 /49	7.76 /40	1.99	0.39
AA	Nationwide Destination 2030 A	NWIAX	C-	(800) 848-0920	C- / 3.7	5.77	6.35	18.86 /46	4.36 /47	8.01 /42	1.42	0.88
AA	Nationwide Destination 2030 C	NWICX	C	(800) 848-0920	C / 4.3	5.56	6.02	18.05 /43	3.78 /40	7.45 /38	1.05	1.44
AA	Nationwide Destination 2030 IS	NWISX	C	(800) 848-0920	C / 5.1	5.82	6.45	19.11 /48	4.62 /50	8.26 /44	1.72	0.65
AA	Nationwide Destination 2030 R	NWBIX	C	(800) 848-0920	C / 4.6	5.72	6.13	18.38 /45	4.10 /44	7.73 /40	1.26	1.15
AA	Nationwide Destination 2030 R6	NWIIX	C+	(800) 848-0920	C / 5.3	5.85	6.54	19.29 /48	4.85 /53	8.53 /47	1.94	0.40
AA	Nationwide Destination 2035 A	NWLAX	C-	(800) 848-0920	C- / 4.1	6.12	6.86	20.13 /53	4.55 /49	8.57 /47	1.40	0.88

● Denotes fund is closed to new investors
∗ Denotes fund is included in Section II

I. Index of Stock Mutual Funds

Risk Rating/Pts	Standard Deviation	Beta	NAV As of 2/28/17	Total $(Mil)	Cash %	Stocks %	Bonds %	Other %	Portfolio Turnover Ratio	Last Bull Market Return	Last Bear Market Return	Manager Quality Pct	Manager Tenure (Years)	Initial Purch. $	Additional Purch. $	Front End Load	Back End Load
C- / 3.5	10.6	1.01	11.43	12	2	96	1	1	14	120.5	-18.3	53	12	25,000	5,000	0.0	0.0
D / 1.6	10.3	1.00	10.68	38	0	97	2	1	6	133.6	-16.3	73	3	25,000	5,000	0.0	0.0
D / 2.0	12.6	1.02	11.65	23	0	99	0	1	27	151.3	-22.6	83	3	25,000	5,000	0.0	0.0
D / 2.2	16.0	0.97	12.16	7	3	93	3	1	66	98.0	-23.9	43	10	25,000	5,000	0.0	0.0
C / 5.2	13.0	0.79	13.49	10	8	90	1	1	20	110.8	-21.7	87	10	25,000	5,000	0.0	0.0
C+ / 6.5	13.6	1.18	13.62	361	3	96	0	1	7	163.7	-10.8	81	14	1,000	100	0.0	0.0
C+ / 6.5	13.6	1.18	13.25	18	3	96	0	1	7	156.4	-11.0	77	14	1,000	100	0.0	0.0
C+ / 6.5	10.6	1.02	24.30	151	0	99	0	1	61	122.5	-18.4	63	4	2,000	100	5.8	0.0
C / 5.4	13.9	0.81	14.21	1	2	97	0	1	95	118.9	-23.3	85	4	2,000	100	5.8	0.0
C / 5.3	13.9	0.81	13.38	N/A	2	97	0	1	95	111.0	-23.5	82	4	2,000	100	0.0	0.0
C / 5.4	13.9	0.81	14.23	1	2	97	0	1	95	122.9	-23.2	87	4	50,000	0	0.0	0.0
C / 5.4	13.9	0.81	14.21	95	2	97	0	1	95	123.5	-23.1	87	4	5,000	100	0.0	0.0
C / 5.4	13.9	0.81	14.20	N/A	2	97	0	1	95	N/A	N/A	87	4	1,000,000	0	0.0	0.0
U /	N/A	N/A	9.36	33	3	96	0	1	96	N/A	N/A	N/A	3	5,000	100	0.0	0.0
U /	N/A	N/A	9.43	125	3	96	0	1	96	N/A	N/A	N/A	3	1,000,000	0	0.0	0.0
C+ / 6.4	10.3	0.81	7.72	11	2	97	0	1	84	53.8	-26.1	70	11	2,000	100	5.8	0.0
C+ / 6.4	10.4	0.82	7.63	4	2	97	0	1	84	48.0	-26.4	60	11	2,000	100	0.0	0.0
C+ / 6.4	10.4	0.81	7.71	47	2	97	0	1	84	55.8	-26.1	72	11	50,000	0	0.0	0.0
C+ / 6.4	10.4	0.82	7.72	166	2	97	0	1	84	56.9	-26.1	73	11	5,000	100	0.0	0.0
C+ / 6.4	10.4	0.81	7.72	157	2	97	0	1	84	N/A	N/A	74	11	1,000,000	0	0.0	0.0
C / 4.7	14.0	1.20	17.99	4	0	99	0	1	29	142.0	-17.6	69	5	2,000	100	5.8	0.0
C / 4.5	14.1	1.21	16.58	1	0	99	0	1	29	133.3	-17.9	60	5	2,000	100	0.0	0.0
C / 4.8	14.0	1.20	18.69	1	0	99	0	1	29	145.5	-17.5	72	5	50,000	0	0.0	0.0
C / 4.7	14.1	1.21	18.71	111	0	99	0	1	29	147.0	-17.5	73	5	5,000	100	0.0	0.0
C / 4.8	14.1	1.21	18.67	2	0	99	0	1	29	N/A	N/A	73	5	1,000,000	0	0.0	0.0
C+ / 6.5	10.7	1.02	22.66	4	0	99	0	1	61	113.6	-18.7	52	4	2,000	100	0.0	0.0
B- / 7.8	4.9	0.75	8.21	6	20	39	39	2	42	36.8	-10.1	45	N/A	2,000	100	5.8	0.0
B- / 7.8	4.9	0.75	8.13	2	20	39	39	2	42	32.5	-10.4	35	N/A	2,000	100	0.0	0.0
B- / 7.8	4.9	0.75	8.22	N/A	20	39	39	2	42	40.2	-10.0	50	N/A	50,000	0	0.0	0.0
B- / 7.8	4.9	0.75	8.18	11	20	39	39	2	42	34.7	-10.2	41	N/A	0	0	0.0	0.0
B- / 7.8	4.9	0.75	8.23	7	20	39	39	2	42	40.5	-10.0	52	N/A	1,000,000	0	0.0	0.0
B- / 7.0	5.7	0.88	8.43	10	17	47	34	2	26	43.6	-11.4	35	N/A	2,000	100	5.8	0.0
B- / 7.0	5.7	0.87	8.37	1	17	47	34	2	26	39.2	-11.6	29	N/A	2,000	100	0.0	0.0
B- / 7.0	5.7	0.89	8.44	34	17	47	34	2	26	45.2	-11.3	37	N/A	50,000	0	0.0	0.0
B- / 7.0	5.7	0.89	8.39	29	17	47	34	2	26	41.4	-11.4	31	N/A	0	0	0.0	0.0
B- / 7.0	5.7	0.88	8.46	32	17	47	34	2	26	47.2	-11.2	41	N/A	1,000,000	0	0.0	0.0
B- / 7.5	6.5	1.01	9.40	22	18	55	26	1	24	50.9	-12.8	26	N/A	2,000	100	5.8	0.0
B- / 7.5	6.5	1.01	9.27	4	18	55	26	1	24	46.2	-13.0	20	N/A	2,000	100	0.0	0.0
B- / 7.5	6.5	1.00	9.42	107	18	55	26	1	24	52.7	-12.7	29	N/A	50,000	0	0.0	0.0
B- / 7.5	6.5	1.01	9.37	66	18	55	26	1	24	48.6	-12.9	23	N/A	0	0	0.0	0.0
B- / 7.5	6.5	1.01	9.46	69	18	55	26	1	24	54.8	-12.7	31	N/A	1,000,000	0	0.0	0.0
B- / 7.0	7.5	1.16	9.70	35	15	64	20	1	19	60.7	-14.8	19	N/A	2,000	100	5.8	0.0
B- / 7.0	7.5	1.16	9.61	3	15	64	20	1	19	55.9	-15.0	15	N/A	2,000	100	0.0	0.0
B- / 7.0	7.6	1.17	9.72	113	15	64	20	1	19	62.8	-14.8	21	N/A	50,000	0	0.0	0.0
B- / 7.0	7.6	1.17	9.67	81	15	64	20	1	19	58.3	-14.8	16	N/A	0	0	0.0	0.0
B- / 7.0	7.6	1.17	9.77	79	15	64	20	1	19	64.9	-14.6	23	N/A	1,000,000	0	0.0	0.0
C+ / 6.2	8.3	1.28	9.38	34	15	71	13	1	17	70.0	-16.8	15	N/A	2,000	100	5.8	0.0
C+ / 6.2	8.3	1.28	9.28	2	15	71	13	1	17	65.1	-17.0	11	N/A	2,000	100	0.0	0.0
C+ / 6.2	8.4	1.28	9.39	105	15	71	13	1	17	72.1	-16.7	17	N/A	50,000	0	0.0	0.0
C+ / 6.2	8.3	1.28	9.32	84	15	71	13	1	17	67.4	-16.8	13	N/A	0	0	0.0	0.0
C+ / 6.3	8.3	1.28	9.44	79	15	71	13	1	17	74.5	-16.6	19	N/A	1,000,000	0	0.0	0.0
C+ / 6.3	9.0	1.38	9.99	31	15	76	7	2	12	77.0	-17.8	12	N/A	2,000	100	5.8	0.0

Fund Type	Fund Name	Ticker Symbol	Overall Investment Rating	Phone	Performance Rating/Pts	3 Mo	6 Mo	1Yr / Pct	3Yr / Pct	5Yr / Pct	Dividend Yield	Expense Ratio
	99 Pct = Best / 0 Pct = Worst							Total Return % through 2/28/17	Annualized		Incl. in Returns	
AA	Nationwide Destination 2035 C	NWLCX	C	(800) 848-0920	C / 4.8	6.06	6.59	19.37 /49	3.94 /42	7.97 /42	1.06	1.49
AA	Nationwide Destination 2035 IS	NWLSX	C+	(800) 848-0920	C / 5.5	6.17	6.96	20.37 /54	4.79 /52	8.83 /49	1.68	0.65
AA	Nationwide Destination 2035 R	NWLBX	C	(800) 848-0920	C / 5.1	6.08	6.76	19.79 /51	4.30 /46	8.29 /45	1.24	1.15
AA	Nationwide Destination 2035 R6	NWLIX	C+	(800) 848-0920	C+ / 5.7	6.31	7.05	20.67 /56	5.06 /55	9.09 /51	1.90	0.40
AA	Nationwide Destination 2040 A	NWMAX	C-	(800) 848-0920	C / 4.3	6.20	7.08	20.77 /56	4.76 /52	8.89 /50	1.40	0.87
AA	Nationwide Destination 2040 C	NWMCX	C	(800) 848-0920	C / 5.1	6.12	6.89	20.14 /53	4.16 /45	8.30 /45	1.05	1.43
AA	Nationwide Destination 2040 IS	NWMSX	C+	(800) 848-0920	C+ / 5.8	6.34	7.26	21.20 /58	5.01 /54	9.15 /52	1.68	0.64
AA	Nationwide Destination 2040 R	NWMDX	C	(800) 848-0920	C / 5.3	6.15	6.97	20.40 /54	4.45 /48	8.59 /47	1.23	1.14
AA	Nationwide Destination 2040 R6	NWMHX	C+	(800) 848-0920	C+ / 6.0	6.38	7.47	21.42 /59	5.25 /57	9.41 /54	1.90	0.39
AA	Nationwide Destination 2045 A	NWNAX	C	(800) 848-0920	C / 4.8	6.49	7.78	22.23 /63	5.00 /54	9.18 /52	1.39	0.87
AA	Nationwide Destination 2045 C	NWNCX	C+	(800) 848-0920	C / 5.4	6.39	7.46	21.40 /59	4.37 /47	8.55 /47	0.99	1.49
AA	Nationwide Destination 2045 IS	NWNSX	C+	(800) 848-0920	C+ / 6.2	6.56	7.80	22.41 /64	5.22 /57	9.43 /54	1.67	0.64
AA	Nationwide Destination 2045 R	NWNBX	C+	(800) 848-0920	C+ / 5.8	6.57	7.70	21.93 /62	4.75 /51	8.89 /50	1.23	1.14
AA	Nationwide Destination 2045 R6	NWNIX	C+	(800) 848-0920	C+ / 6.4	6.69	8.09	22.79 /66	5.51 /60	9.69 /56	1.88	0.39
AA	Nationwide Destination 2050 A	NWOAX	C-	(800) 848-0920	C / 4.9	6.54	7.91	22.55 /65	5.10 /55	9.19 /52	1.39	0.87
AA	Nationwide Destination 2050 C	NWOCX	C	(800) 848-0920	C+ / 5.6	6.49	7.50	21.70 /61	4.50 /49	8.62 /47	1.05	1.44
AA	Nationwide Destination 2050 IS	NWOSX	C+	(800) 848-0920	C+ / 6.3	6.60	8.03	22.69 /65	5.32 /58	9.44 /54	1.68	0.64
AA	Nationwide Destination 2050 R	NWOBX	C	(800) 848-0920	C+ / 5.9	6.54	7.73	22.17 /63	4.80 /52	8.90 /50	1.23	1.14
AA	Nationwide Destination 2050 R6	NWOIX	C+	(800) 848-0920	C+ / 6.5	6.77	8.12	23.05 /67	5.60 /61	9.73 /56	1.89	0.39
AA	Nationwide Destination 2055 A	NTDAX	C	(800) 848-0920	C / 5.2	6.70	8.01	22.73 /66	5.13 /56	9.17 /52	1.42	0.88
AA	Nationwide Destination 2055 C	NTDCX	C+	(800) 848-0920	C+ / 5.7	6.56	7.66	21.94 /62	4.53 /49	8.58 /47	1.05	1.43
AA	Nationwide Destination 2055 IS	NTDSX	C+	(800) 848-0920	C+ / 6.4	6.73	8.09	22.99 /67	5.35 /58	9.44 /54	1.68	0.64
AA	Nationwide Destination 2055 R	NTDTX	C+	(800) 848-0920	C+ / 6.0	6.64	7.89	22.42 /64	4.83 /52	8.89 /50	1.24	1.14
AA	Nationwide Destination 2055 R6	NTDIX	C+	(800) 848-0920	C+ / 6.6	6.79	8.20	23.27 /67	5.63 /61	9.69 /56	1.90	0.39
EM	Nationwide Emg Mktg Debt R6	NWXCX	U	(800) 848-0920	U /	5.29	1.30	11.98 /18	--	--	4.71	N/A
MC	Nationwide Geneva Mid Cap Growth	NWHVX	D-	(800) 848-0920	C- / 3.2	4.66	3.29	15.77 /33	5.01 /54	8.66 /48	0.00	1.15
MC	Nationwide Geneva Mid Cap Growth	NWHWX	D-	(800) 848-0920	C- / 3.7	4.48	2.92	14.91 /29	4.26 /46	7.95 /42	0.00	1.88
MC	Nationwide Geneva Mid Cap Growth	NWHYX	D+	(800) 848-0920	C / 4.6	4.74	3.45	16.05 /35	5.29 /57	8.94 /50	0.00	0.92
MC	Nationwide Geneva Mid Cap Growth	NWKAX	D+	(800) 848-0920	C / 4.7	4.76	3.51	16.20 /35	5.40 /59	--	0.00	0.78
SC	Nationwide Geneva Small Cap Gro A	NWHZX	C+	(800) 848-0920	B- / 7.2	6.63	9.18	27.10 /79	7.84 /78	13.59 /90	0.00	1.37
SC	Nationwide Geneva Small Cap Gro C	NWKBX	C+	(800) 848-0920	B / 7.6	6.45	8.81	26.21 /77	7.09 /73	12.84 /82	0.00	2.09
SC	Nationwide Geneva Small Cap Gro IS	NWKDX	B	(800) 848-0920	B+ / 8.4	6.71	9.35	27.45 /80	8.14 /80	13.90 /92	0.00	1.09
SC	Nationwide Geneva Small Cap Gro	NWKCX	B	(800) 848-0920	B+ / 8.4	6.73	9.40	27.60 /81	8.25 /81	--	0.00	0.99
GL	Nationwide Global Equity A	GGEAX	D+	(800) 848-0920	C- / 3.1	7.84	8.64	24.35 /71	1.04 /18	6.61 /32	1.05	1.57
GL	Nationwide Global Equity C	GGECX	D+	(800) 848-0920	C- / 3.5	7.58	8.20	23.34 /68	0.24 /14	5.86 /27	0.63	2.35
GL	Nationwide Global Equity Inst Svc	GGESX	C-	(800) 848-0920	C / 4.4	7.84	8.77	24.67 /72	1.34 /20	--	1.30	1.28
GL	Nationwide Global Equity R6	GGEIX	C-	(800) 848-0920	C / 4.5	7.96	8.88	24.80 /73	1.43 /21	6.99 /35	1.40	1.17
GR	Nationwide Growth A	NMFAX	C-	(800) 848-0920	C+ / 6.1	8.08	7.99	17.49 /41	7.87 /78	11.40 /69	0.34	1.18
GR	Nationwide Growth C	GCGRX	C-	(800) 848-0920	C+ / 6.6	7.93	7.68	16.54 /36	7.03 /72	10.56 /62	0.06	1.97
GR	Nationwide Growth Institutional Svc	NGISX	C+	(800) 848-0920	B- / 7.2	8.11	8.15	17.68 /41	8.00 /79	11.51 /70	0.45	1.10
GR	Nationwide Growth R	GGFRX	C	(800) 848-0920	B- / 7.0	8.03	7.93	17.78 /42	7.65 /76	11.19 /67	0.60	1.61
GR	Nationwide Growth R6	MUIGX	C+	(800) 848-0920	B- / 7.4	8.17	8.27	17.88 /42	8.23 /81	11.76 /72	0.63	0.86
IN	Nationwide HighMark LC Core Eq A	NWGHX	B	(800) 848-0920	B / 7.8	9.23	9.60	24.72 /72	9.02 /87	12.47 /79	0.68	1.27
IN	Nationwide HighMark LC Core Eq C	NWGIX	B+	(800) 848-0920	B+ / 8.3	9.03	9.25	24.03 /70	8.36 /82	11.79 /72	0.27	1.95
IN	Nationwide HighMark LC Core Eq IS	NWGKX	A-	(800) 848-0920	A- / 9.0	9.23	9.68	24.99 /73	9.31 /89	12.79 /82	0.83	0.94
GR	Nationwide HighMark LC Core Eq R6	NWGJX	A-	(800) 848-0920	A- / 9.0	9.31	9.79	25.24 /74	9.45 /90	--	1.07	0.88
SC	Nationwide HighMark Sm Cp Core A	NWGPX	B+	(800) 848-0920	B+ / 8.9	3.56	14.46	36.62 /95	8.98 /87	14.02 /93	0.00	1.43
SC	Nationwide HighMark Sm Cp Core C	NWGQX	A-	(800) 848-0920	A- / 9.2	3.32	13.99	35.52 /94	8.19 /80	13.24 /86	0.00	2.17
SC	Nationwide HighMark Sm Cp Core IS	NWGSX	A	(800) 848-0920	A+ / 9.6	3.61	14.55	36.93 /96	9.31 /89	14.35 /95	0.00	1.15
SC	Nationwide HighMark Sm Cp Core R6	NWKEX	A	(800) 848-0920	A+ / 9.6	3.63	14.62	37.08 /96	9.37 /89	--	0.00	1.06
GI	Nationwide Inst Service	MUIFX	A+	(800) 848-0920	A / 9.4	8.84	10.73	26.28 /77	10.07 /94	12.97 /83	1.19	0.78
FO	Nationwide Internatl Index A	GIIAX	D-	(800) 848-0920	E+ / 0.7	7.41	4.24	15.46 /32	-1.20 / 9	4.70 /19	2.39	0.71

• Denotes fund is closed to new investors
* Denotes fund is included in Section II

452

RISK			NET ASSETS		ASSET				Portfolio Turnover Ratio	BULL / BEAR		FUND MANAGER		MINIMUMS		LOADS	
Risk Rating/Pts	3 Year		NAV As of 2/28/17	Total $(Mil)	Cash %	Stocks %	Bonds %	Other %		Last Bull Market Return	Last Bear Market Return	Manager Quality Pct	Manager Tenure (Years)	Initial Purch. $	Additional Purch. $	Front End Load	Back End Load
	Standard Deviation	Beta															
C+ / 6.3	8.9	1.37	9.83	2	15	76	7	2	12	71.9	-18.1	9	N/A	2,000	100	0.0	0.0
C+ / 6.3	8.9	1.37	10.00	88	15	76	7	2	12	79.1	-17.7	14	N/A	50,000	0	0.0	0.0
C+ / 6.3	8.9	1.37	9.94	71	15	76	7	2	12	74.5	-17.9	11	N/A	0	0	0.0	0.0
C+ / 6.3	8.9	1.37	10.06	55	15	76	7	2	12	81.7	-17.7	15	N/A	1,000,000	0	0.0	0.0
C+ / 6.1	9.2	1.41	9.65	25	12	80	6	2	15	80.7	-18.9	11	N/A	2,000	100	5.8	0.0
C+ / 6.1	9.2	1.42	9.61	1	12	80	6	2	15	75.5	-19.0	8	N/A	2,000	100	0.0	0.0
C+ / 6.1	9.3	1.42	9.70	62	12	80	6	2	15	82.8	-18.7	13	N/A	50,000	0	0.0	0.0
C+ / 6.1	9.2	1.41	9.60	58	12	80	6	2	15	78.0	-19.0	10	N/A	0	0	0.0	0.0
C+ / 6.1	9.2	1.41	9.73	52	12	80	6	2	15	85.3	-18.7	15	N/A	1,000,000	0	0.0	0.0
C+ / 6.0	9.8	1.50	10.00	23	10	86	3	1	12	83.3	-19.1	9	N/A	2,000	100	5.8	0.0
C+ / 6.0	9.8	1.50	9.90	2	10	86	3	1	12	77.8	-19.2	7	N/A	2,000	100	0.0	0.0
C+ / 6.0	9.8	1.50	9.98	37	10	86	3	1	12	85.6	-19.0	10	N/A	50,000	0	0.0	0.0
C+ / 6.0	9.8	1.50	9.93	45	10	86	3	1	12	80.7	-19.1	8	N/A	0	0	0.0	0.0
C+ / 6.0	9.9	1.51	10.06	41	10	86	3	1	12	88.2	-18.9	12	N/A	1,000,000	0	0.0	0.0
C / 5.2	9.9	1.51	8.51	18	10	87	2	1	15	83.4	-19.2	9	N/A	2,000	100	5.8	0.0
C / 5.2	9.9	1.51	8.37	N/A	10	87	2	1	15	78.4	-19.5	7	N/A	2,000	100	0.0	0.0
C / 5.2	9.9	1.51	8.50	29	10	87	2	1	15	85.8	-19.2	11	N/A	50,000	0	0.0	0.0
C / 5.2	9.9	1.51	8.41	39	10	87	2	1	15	81.0	-19.4	8	N/A	0	0	0.0	0.0
C / 5.2	9.9	1.50	8.53	30	10	87	2	1	15	88.3	-19.2	13	N/A	1,000,000	0	0.0	0.0
C+ / 6.0	10.0	1.52	12.77	11	10	88	0	2	18	83.7	-19.3	9	7	2,000	100	5.0	0.0
C+ / 6.0	10.0	1.53	12.75	N/A	10	88	0	2	18	78.3	-19.4	7	7	2,000	100	0.0	0.0
C+ / 6.0	10.0	1.53	12.82	12	10	88	0	2	18	86.2	-19.2	10	7	50,000	0	0.0	0.0
C+ / 6.0	10.0	1.53	12.75	15	10	88	0	2	18	81.0	-19.4	8	7	0	0	0.0	0.0
C+ / 6.0	10.0	1.52	12.83	14	10	88	0	2	18	88.4	-19.2	12	7	1,000,000	0	0.0	0.0
U /	N/A	N/A	10.23	98	0	0	0	100	99	N/A	N/A	N/A	1	1,000,000	0	0.0	0.0
C- / 3.7	11.3	0.84	23.95	160	1	98	0	1	31	87.7	-17.1	36	8	2,000	100	5.8	0.0
C- / 3.2	11.2	0.84	19.99	53	1	98	0	1	31	81.1	-17.3	28	8	2,000	100	0.0	0.0
C- / 3.8	11.2	0.84	24.66	581	1	98	0	1	31	90.3	-17.0	40	8	50,000	0	0.0	0.0
C- / 3.8	11.2	0.84	24.81	190	1	98	0	1	31	N/A	N/A	42	8	1,000,000	0	0.0	0.0
C / 4.8	13.3	0.75	49.17	90	4	95	0	1	15	128.8	-18.3	88	8	2,000	100	5.8	0.0
C / 4.7	13.3	0.75	46.49	36	4	95	0	1	15	120.8	-18.5	85	8	2,000	100	0.0	0.0
C / 4.8	13.2	0.75	50.35	389	4	95	0	1	15	132.1	-18.2	89	8	50,000	0	0.0	0.0
C / 4.8	13.3	0.75	50.55	39	4	95	0	1	15	N/A	N/A	90	8	1,000,000	0	0.0	0.0
C / 5.5	12.3	0.91	15.89	34	4	95	0	1	147	73.2	-25.5	82	2	2,000	100	5.8	0.0
C / 5.5	12.3	0.91	15.06	11	4	95	0	1	147	66.7	-25.8	77	2	2,000	100	0.0	0.0
C / 5.5	12.3	0.91	16.34	2	4	95	0	1	147	N/A	N/A	84	2	50,000	0	0.0	0.0
C / 5.4	12.2	0.91	16.34	8	4	95	0	1	147	76.4	-25.4	84	2	1,000,000	0	0.0	0.0
C- / 4.2	10.9	0.99	10.86	31	2	97	0	1	100	111.4	-17.0	42	3	2,000	100	5.8	0.0
C- / 3.5	10.9	0.99	8.65	7	2	97	0	1	100	103.3	-17.4	32	3	2,000	100	0.0	0.0
C / 4.4	10.9	0.99	11.44	12	2	97	0	1	100	N/A	N/A	44	3	50,000	0	0.0	0.0
C- / 4.2	11.0	1.00	10.67	N/A	2	97	0	1	100	109.1	-17.2	38	3	0	0	0.0	0.0
C / 4.3	10.9	0.99	11.39	155	2	97	0	1	100	115.2	-17.1	47	3	1,000,000	0	0.0	0.0
C+ / 5.7	10.8	1.03	13.27	26	1	98	0	1	60	120.4	-15.1	52	9	2,000	100	5.8	0.0
C+ / 5.6	10.8	1.03	12.72	4	1	98	0	1	60	113.4	-15.4	43	9	2,000	100	0.0	0.0
C+ / 5.7	10.8	1.03	13.32	4	1	98	0	1	60	124.0	-15.1	56	9	50,000	0	0.0	0.0
C+ / 5.7	10.8	1.04	13.31	44	1	98	0	1	60	N/A	N/A	57	9	1,000,000	0	0.0	0.0
C / 5.4	15.4	0.96	35.87	20	3	96	0	1	70	146.5	-26.0	87	9	2,000	100	5.8	0.0
C / 5.4	15.4	0.96	33.74	9	3	96	0	1	70	137.5	-26.1	84	9	2,000	100	0.0	0.0
C / 5.4	15.4	0.96	36.61	67	3	96	0	1	70	150.4	-25.9	88	9	50,000	0	0.0	0.0
C / 5.4	15.4	0.96	36.69	82	3	96	0	1	70	N/A	N/A	89	9	1,000,000	0	0.0	0.0
C+ / 6.5	10.7	1.02	23.94	858	0	99	0	1	61	125.4	-18.4	65	4	50,000	0	0.0	0.0
C+ / 5.6	11.5	0.93	7.55	155	3	96	0	1	6	45.0	-23.6	61	5	2,000	100	5.8	0.0

Fund Type	Fund Name	Ticker Symbol	Overall Investment Rating	Phone	PERFORMANCE Perfor-mance Rating/Pts	Total Return % through 2/28/17 3 Mo	6 Mo	1Yr / Pct	Annualized 3Yr / Pct	5Yr / Pct	Incl. in Returns Dividend Yield	Expense Ratio
FO	Nationwide Internatl Index C	GIICX	D-	(800) 848-0920	E+ / 0.9	7.07	3.70	14.43 /27	-1.87 / 7	4.01 /15	2.16	1.38
FO	Nationwide Internatl Index R	GIIRX	D-	(800) 848-0920	D- / 1.0	7.19	3.97	15.01 /30	-1.44 / 8	4.51 /18	2.31	1.05
FO	Nationwide Internatl Index R6	GIIXIX	D-	(800) 848-0920	D- / 1.3	7.48	4.43	15.84 /34	-0.79 /10	5.10 /22	2.91	0.30
GL	Nationwide Inv Dest Aggressive A	NDAAX	C	(800) 848-0920	C / 4.8	6.83	7.66	22.35 /64	4.94 /53	9.40 /54	1.67	0.88
GL	Nationwide Inv Dest Aggressive C	NDACX	C	(800) 848-0920	C / 5.3	6.63	7.31	21.42 /59	4.17 /45	8.62 /47	1.22	1.62
GL	Nationwide Inv Dest Aggressive R	GAFRX	C+	(800) 848-0920	C+ / 5.8	6.79	7.57	21.98 /62	4.66 /50	9.08 /51	1.53	1.18
GL	Nationwide Inv Dest Aggressive R6	GAIDX	C+	(800) 848-0920	C+ / 6.4	6.96	7.86	22.89 /66	5.33 /58	9.78 /57	2.07	0.53
GL	Nationwide Inv Dest Aggressive Svc	NDASX	C+	(800) 848-0920	C+ / 6.0	6.81	7.73	22.39 /64	4.92 /53	9.34 /53	1.72	0.92
GL	Nationwide Inv Dest Cons A	NDCAX	C	(800) 848-0920	D- / 1.2	2.04	1.23	6.29 / 5	2.73 /29	3.21 /12	1.79	0.81
GL	Nationwide Inv Dest Cons C	NDCCX	C	(800) 848-0920	D- / 1.5	1.76	0.79	5.45 / 4	1.99 /24	2.47 / 9	1.20	1.56
GL	Nationwide Inv Dest Cons IS	NWWLX	U	(800) 848-0920	U /	2.10	1.24	6.52 / 5	--	--	2.13	0.57
GL	Nationwide Inv Dest Cons R	GCFRX	C	(800) 848-0920	D / 1.7	1.97	1.09	5.96 / 5	2.45 /27	2.90 /10	1.58	1.12
GL	Nationwide Inv Dest Cons R6	GIMCX	C+	(800) 848-0920	D / 1.9	2.11	1.38	6.60 / 5	3.08 /33	3.57 /13	2.21	0.48
GL	Nationwide Inv Dest Cons Svc	NDCSX	C	(800) 848-0920	D / 1.7	2.02	1.09	6.19 / 5	2.66 /29	3.14 /11	1.82	0.87
GL	Nationwide Inv Dest Mdt Aggr A	NDMAX	C-	(800) 848-0920	C- / 4.0	6.15	6.50	19.62 /50	4.55 /49	8.28 /45	1.81	0.90
GL	Nationwide Inv Dest Mdt Aggr C	NDMCX	C	(800) 848-0920	C / 4.5	5.91	6.11	18.74 /46	3.80 /40	7.49 /38	1.31	1.63
GL	Nationwide Inv Dest Mdt Aggr R	GMARX	C	(800) 848-0920	C / 4.9	6.02	6.32	19.31 /49	4.27 /46	7.92 /41	1.68	1.19
GL	Nationwide Inv Dest Mdt Aggr R6	GMIAX	C+	(800) 848-0920	C / 5.5	6.25	6.69	20.06 /52	4.95 /54	8.63 /47	2.24	0.54
GL	Nationwide Inv Dest Mdt Aggr Svc	NDMSX	C+	(800) 848-0920	C / 5.2	6.25	6.50	19.60 /50	4.55 /49	8.20 /44	1.87	0.94
GL	Nationwide Inv Dest Mdt Consv A	NADCX	C	(800) 848-0920	D / 1.9	3.44	3.00	10.62 /13	3.48 /37	4.99 /21	1.90	0.83
GL	Nationwide Inv Dest Mdt Consv C	NCDCX	C	(800) 848-0920	D+ / 2.3	3.26	2.66	9.75 /11	2.73 /29	4.24 /16	1.31	1.57
GL	Nationwide Inv Dest Mdt Consv R	GMMRX	C	(800) 848-0920	D+ / 2.5	3.34	2.83	10.23 /12	3.18 /33	4.67 /19	1.69	1.13
GL	Nationwide Inv Dest Mdt Consv R6	GMIMX	C+	(800) 848-0920	C- / 3.0	3.59	3.23	11.08 /15	3.87 /41	5.36 /24	2.31	0.49
GL	Nationwide Inv Dest Mdt Consv Svc	NSDCX	C	(800) 848-0920	D+ / 2.7	3.40	2.95	10.46 /13	3.45 /36	4.91 /21	1.93	0.88
GL	Nationwide Inv Dest Moderate A	NADMX	C-	(800) 848-0920	D+ / 2.8	4.79	4.80	15.07 /30	3.94 /42	6.59 /32	1.90	0.87
GL	Nationwide Inv Dest Moderate C	NCDMX	C-	(800) 848-0920	C- / 3.3	4.68	4.42	14.30 /27	3.21 /34	5.83 /27	1.36	1.59
GL	Nationwide Inv Dest Moderate R	GMDRX	C	(800) 848-0920	C- / 3.6	4.72	4.67	14.66 /28	3.66 /39	6.26 /30	1.78	1.15
GL	Nationwide Inv Dest Moderate R6	GMDIX	C	(800) 848-0920	C- / 4.1	4.90	5.00	15.43 /32	4.34 /47	6.96 /34	2.35	0.51
GL	Nationwide Inv Dest Moderate Svc	NSDMX	C	(800) 848-0920	C- / 3.8	4.90	4.80	15.08 /30	3.93 /42	6.54 /32	1.97	0.91
MC	Nationwide Mid Cap Market Index A	GMXAX	B-	(800) 848-0920	B+ / 8.3	6.45	10.98	30.82 /88	8.93 /86	13.11 /85	0.84	0.69
MC	Nationwide Mid Cap Market Index C	GMCCX	B	(800) 848-0920	B+ / 8.8	6.29	10.66	29.94 /86	8.20 /80	12.39 /78	0.53	1.36
MC	Nationwide Mid Cap Market Index R	GMXRX	B	(800) 848-0920	A- / 9.0	6.35	10.86	30.49 /87	8.63 /84	12.90 /83	0.69	0.97
MC	Nationwide Mid Cap Market Index R6	GMXIX	B+	(800) 848-0920	A / 9.4	6.58	11.29	31.39 /89	9.39 /90	13.58 /90	1.23	0.27
AA	Nationwide Portfolio Comp A	NWAAX	C-	(800) 848-0920	D- / 1.5	3.49	2.41	10.49 /13	1.10 /19	0.90 / 6	1.79	0.89
AA	Nationwide Portfolio Comp C	NWACX	C-	(800) 848-0920	D- / 1.4	3.22	2.01	9.61 /11	0.35 /15	0.20 / 5	1.12	1.58
AA	Nationwide Portfolio Comp IS	NAASX	C-	(800) 848-0920	D / 1.8	3.48	2.40	10.55 /13	1.31 /20	1.18 / 6	1.93	0.67
AA	Nationwide Portfolio Comp R6	NAAIX	C-	(800) 848-0920	D / 1.8	3.52	2.45	10.72 /14	1.40 /20	1.23 / 7	2.07	0.52
GI	Nationwide R	GNWRX	A	(800) 848-0920	A- / 9.0	8.63	10.34	25.41 /75	9.32 /89	12.29 /77	0.62	1.46
IX	Nationwide S&P 500 Index A	GRMAX	B+	(800) 848-0920	B / 8.1	7.91	9.77	24.28 /71	10.00 /93	13.36 /87	1.30	0.61
IX	Nationwide S&P 500 Index C	GRMCX	B+	(800) 848-0920	B+ / 8.7	7.77	9.36	23.47 /68	9.31 /89	12.65 /80	0.89	1.24
IX	Nationwide S&P 500 Index IS	GRISX	A-	(800) 848-0920	A- / 9.1	7.91	9.80	24.45 /71	10.18 /94	13.54 /89	1.53	0.42
IX	Nationwide S&P 500 Index R	GRMRX	A-	(800) 848-0920	B+ / 8.9	7.83	9.64	23.97 /70	9.71 /92	13.03 /84	1.26	0.92
IX	Nationwide S&P 500 Index R6	GRMIX	A-	(800) 848-0920	A / 9.3	8.03	9.91	24.78 /73	10.47 /96	13.83 /92	1.75	0.17
IX	Nationwide S&P 500 Index Svc	GRMSX	A-	(800) 848-0920	A- / 9.1	7.90	9.77	24.29 /71	10.02 /93	13.38 /88	1.40	0.57
SC	Nationwide Small Cap Index A	GMRAX	C	(800) 848-0920	B- / 7.5	5.01	12.30	35.49 /94	6.48 /68	12.43 /78	0.87	0.68
SC	Nationwide Small Cap Index C	GMRCX	C+	(800) 848-0920	B / 8.0	4.89	11.90	34.53 /93	5.75 /62	11.71 /72	0.53	1.36
SC	Nationwide Small Cap Index R	GMSRX	C+	(800) 848-0920	B+ / 8.4	4.97	12.26	35.26 /94	6.34 /67	12.32 /77	0.83	1.02
SC	Nationwide Small Cap Index R6	GMRIX	C+	(800) 848-0920	B+ / 8.8	5.09	12.53	36.06 /95	6.90 /71	12.89 /83	1.23	0.27
SC	Nationwide Small Company Growth A	NWSAX	D+	(800) 848-0920	B- / 7.2	3.66	8.27	31.57 /89	7.83 /78	14.69 /96	0.00	1.48
SC	Nationwide Small Company Growth	NWSIX	C-	(800) 848-0920	B+ / 8.3	3.71	8.28	31.81 /90	8.03 /79	14.89 /97	0.00	1.33
SC	Nationwide US Sm Cp Val A	NWUAX	C	(800) 848-0920	B- / 7.4	3.73	15.31	34.13 /93	6.28 /67	12.73 /81	0.12	1.44
SC	Nationwide US Sm Cp Val C	NWUCX	C	(800) 848-0920	B / 7.8	3.50	14.92	33.08 /92	5.51 /60	11.92 /74	0.00	2.19

RISK			NET ASSETS		ASSET					BULL / BEAR		FUND MANAGER		MINIMUMS		LOADS	
	3 Year		NAV						Portfolio	Last Bull	Last Bear	Manager	Manager	Initial	Additional	Front	Back
Risk Rating/Pts	Standard Deviation	Beta	As of 2/28/17	Total $(Mil)	Cash %	Stocks %	Bonds %	Other %	Turnover Ratio	Market Return	Market Return	Quality Pct	Tenure (Years)	Purch. $	Purch. $	End Load	End Load
C+ /5.6	11.4	0.92	7.11	5	3	96	0	1	6	39.9	-23.7	52	5	2,000	100	0.0	0.0
C+ /5.6	11.4	0.92	7.55	2	3	96	0	1	6	43.6	-23.5	58	5	0	0	0.0	0.0
C+ /5.6	11.5	0.93	7.59	1,310	3	96	0	1	6	48.1	-23.3	67	5	1,000,000	0	0.0	0.0
C+ /5.7	9.6	1.43	10.22	54	7	86	6	1	16	87.7	-19.6	54	N/A	2,000	100	5.8	0.0
C+ /5.7	9.6	1.43	9.89	61	7	86	6	1	16	80.4	-19.8	43	N/A	2,000	100	0.0	0.0
C+ /5.7	9.6	1.44	10.01	80	7	86	6	1	16	84.4	-19.6	49	N/A	0	0	0.0	0.0
C+ /5.7	9.6	1.44	10.35	174	7	86	6	1	16	91.0	-19.4	58	N/A	1,000,000	0	0.0	0.0
C+ /5.7	9.6	1.44	10.24	722	7	86	6	1	16	87.1	-19.6	53	N/A	50,000	0	0.0	0.0
B+ /9.6	2.5	0.35	10.16	151	6	17	76	1	15	22.9	-2.3	81	N/A	2,000	100	5.8	0.0
B+ /9.6	2.5	0.34	10.10	155	6	17	76	1	15	18.2	-2.6	76	N/A	2,000	100	0.0	0.0
U /	N/A	N/A	10.19	137	6	17	76	1	15	N/A	N/A	N/A	16	50,000	0	0.0	0.0
B+ /9.6	2.5	0.35	10.14	43	6	17	76	1	15	20.8	-2.4	79	N/A	0	0	0.0	0.0
B+ /9.6	2.5	0.34	10.22	84	6	17	76	1	15	25.1	-2.2	83	N/A	1,000,000	0	0.0	0.0
B+ /9.6	2.5	0.35	10.19	148	6	17	76	1	15	22.4	-2.4	81	N/A	50,000	0	0.0	0.0
C+ /6.3	8.5	1.28	10.45	117	8	76	15	1	15	73.5	-16.2	58	N/A	2,000	100	5.8	0.0
C+ /6.2	8.4	1.27	10.16	110	8	76	15	1	15	66.9	-16.4	48	N/A	2,000	100	0.0	0.0
C+ /6.2	8.5	1.28	10.18	170	8	76	15	1	15	70.6	-16.3	54	N/A	0	0	0.0	0.0
C+ /6.3	8.5	1.28	10.44	351	8	76	15	1	15	76.7	-16.1	63	N/A	1,000,000	0	0.0	0.0
C+ /6.3	8.5	1.27	10.43	987	8	76	15	1	15	73.1	-16.3	58	N/A	50,000	0	0.0	0.0
B /8.7	4.3	0.66	10.10	53	7	37	55	1	20	39.1	-6.7	77	N/A	2,000	100	5.8	0.0
B /8.7	4.2	0.64	10.04	61	7	37	55	1	20	33.9	-7.0	71	N/A	2,000	100	0.0	0.0
B /8.7	4.3	0.65	10.12	54	7	37	55	1	20	36.9	-7.0	75	N/A	0	0	0.0	0.0
B /8.7	4.3	0.66	10.22	121	7	37	55	1	20	41.7	-6.6	79	N/A	1,000,000	0	0.0	0.0
B /8.7	4.3	0.65	10.16	199	7	37	55	1	20	38.7	-6.9	77	N/A	50,000	0	0.0	0.0
B- /7.0	6.4	0.97	9.97	129	9	56	34	1	19	55.2	-11.6	68	N/A	2,000	100	5.8	0.0
B- /7.0	6.4	0.97	9.77	122	9	56	34	1	19	49.3	-11.8	58	N/A	2,000	100	0.0	0.0
C+ /6.9	6.4	0.97	9.71	138	9	56	34	1	19	52.6	-11.7	64	N/A	0	0	0.0	0.0
B- /7.0	6.4	0.97	9.93	312	9	56	34	1	19	58.2	-11.5	72	N/A	1,000,000	0	0.0	0.0
B- /7.0	6.4	0.97	9.93	738	9	56	34	1	19	54.8	-11.7	67	N/A	50,000	0	0.0	0.0
C /4.4	12.1	1.00	18.13	365	4	95	0	1	19	132.2	-23.0	66	5	2,000	100	5.8	0.0
C /4.3	12.0	1.00	16.94	16	4	95	0	1	19	124.3	-23.2	58	5	2,000	100	0.0	0.0
C /4.4	12.1	1.00	17.93	21	4	95	0	1	19	129.9	-23.1	63	5	0	0	0.0	0.0
C /4.4	12.1	1.00	18.41	904	4	95	0	1	19	137.5	-22.9	72	5	1,000,000	0	0.0	0.0
B /8.5	5.1	0.57	9.63	1	86	9	3	2	42	14.2	N/A	33	5	2,000	100	2.3	0.0
B /8.4	5.1	0.57	9.45	N/A	86	9	3	2	42	9.8	N/A	25	5	2,000	100	0.0	0.0
B /8.5	5.1	0.56	9.67	N/A	86	9	3	2	42	15.9	N/A	36	5	50,000	0	0.0	0.0
B /8.5	5.2	0.58	9.67	502	86	9	3	2	42	16.1	N/A	36	5	1,000,000	0	0.0	0.0
C+ /6.5	10.7	1.02	23.78	N/A	0	99	0	1	61	118.0	-18.6	57	4	0	0	0.0	0.0
C+ /5.6	10.3	1.00	14.92	114	1	98	0	1	8	127.8	-16.5	67	5	2,000	100	5.8	0.0
C+ /5.6	10.3	1.00	14.61	37	1	98	0	1	8	120.0	-16.7	60	5	2,000	100	0.0	0.0
C+ /5.6	10.3	1.00	15.00	300	1	98	0	1	8	129.6	-16.5	69	5	50,000	0	0.0	0.0
C+ /5.7	10.3	1.00	14.89	31	1	98	0	1	8	123.9	-16.6	65	5	0	0	0.0	0.0
C+ /5.6	10.3	1.00	15.04	1,821	1	98	0	1	8	132.7	-16.4	73	5	1,000,000	0	0.0	0.0
C+ /5.6	10.3	1.00	14.93	317	1	98	0	1	8	127.7	-16.5	68	5	25,000	0	0.0	0.0
C- /3.6	15.8	1.00	14.52	163	1	98	0	1	16	126.6	-25.2	69	5	2,000	100	5.8	0.0
C- /3.5	15.7	1.00	13.93	7	1	98	0	1	16	118.9	-25.4	61	5	2,000	100	0.0	0.0
C- /3.6	15.8	1.00	14.39	3	1	98	0	1	16	125.4	-25.2	68	5	0	0	0.0	0.0
C- /3.6	15.8	1.00	14.77	418	1	98	0	1	16	131.5	-25.0	74	5	1,000,000	0	0.0	0.0
D- /1.5	16.3	0.92	14.62	12	3	96	0	1	14	N/A	N/A	83	5	2,000	100	5.8	0.0
D /1.6	16.3	0.93	14.74	180	3	96	0	1	14	N/A	N/A	84	5	50,000	0	0.0	0.0
C- /3.5	15.0	0.91	13.88	9	0	99	0	1	27	136.5	-26.6	74	5	2,000	100	5.8	0.0
C- /3.3	15.0	0.91	13.08	3	0	99	0	1	27	127.5	-26.9	65	5	2,000	100	0.0	0.0

Data as of February 28, 2017

Fund Type	Fund Name	Ticker Symbol	Overall Investment Rating	Phone	Performance Rating/Pts	3 Mo	6 Mo	1Yr / Pct	3Yr / Pct	5Yr / Pct	Dividend Yield	Expense Ratio
	99 Pct = Best / 0 Pct = Worst							Total Return % through 2/28/17 / Annualized			Incl. in Returns	
SC	Nationwide US Sm Cp Val IS	NWUSX	C+	(800) 848-0920	B+ / 8.5	3.77	15.34	34.25 /93	6.41 /68	12.84 /82	0.19	1.32
SC	Nationwide US Sm Cp Val R6	NWUIX	C+	(800) 848-0920	B+ / 8.7	3.78	15.50	34.57 /94	6.67 /70	13.12 /85	0.39	1.07
IN	Nationwide Ziegler Equity Income A	NWGYX	B-	(800) 848-0920	C+ / 6.8	6.29	8.80	22.93 /66	8.24 /81	11.76 /72	2.26	0.93
IN	Nationwide Ziegler Equity Income C	NWGZX	B+	(800) 848-0920	B- / 7.2	6.09	8.40	21.99 /62	7.44 /75	10.98 /66	1.75	1.67
IN	Nationwide Ziegler Equity Income IS	NWJBX	A	(800) 848-0920	B / 8.0	6.40	8.96	23.30 /67	8.49 /83	12.02 /74	2.59	0.71
IN	Nationwide Ziegler Equity Income R6	NWJAX	A	(800) 848-0920	B / 8.1	6.35	8.95	23.33 /68	8.62 /84	--	2.69	0.60
TC	Nationwide Ziegler NYSE Arc T100 A	NWJCX	A-	(800) 848-0920	B+ / 8.6	9.23	11.68	29.77 /86	8.98 /87	13.81 /92	0.64	0.81
TC	Nationwide Ziegler NYSE Arc T100 C	NWJDX	A-	(800) 848-0920	B+ / 8.9	9.03	11.26	28.82 /84	8.17 /80	13.04 /84	0.41	1.54
TC	Nationwide Ziegler NYSE Arc T100 IS	NWJFX	A	(800) 848-0920	A / 9.5	9.28	11.79	30.05 /86	9.22 /88	14.09 /94	0.86	0.57
TC	Nationwide Ziegler NYSE Arc T100	NWJEX	A	(800) 848-0920	A / 9.5	9.32	11.87	30.25 /87	9.36 /89	--	0.99	0.44
RE	Natixis AEW Real Estate A	NRFAX	C	(800) 225-5478	C+ / 6.1	7.52	-1.60	13.45 /23	10.58 /96	10.55 /62	1.98	1.38
RE	Natixis AEW Real Estate C	NRCFX	C+	(800) 225-5478	C+ / 6.6	7.35	-1.92	12.64 /20	9.77 /92	9.75 /57	1.37	2.13
RE	● Natixis AEW Real Estate N	NRFNX	B-	(800) 225-5478	B- / 7.4	7.69	-1.37	13.90 /25	11.06 /97	--	2.61	1.01
RE	Natixis AEW Real Estate Y	NRFYX	C+	(800) 225-5478	B- / 7.3	7.61	-1.44	13.77 /24	10.86 /97	10.84 /65	2.48	1.13
GL	Natixis ASG Glb Alternatives A	GAFAX	D	(800) 225-5478	E+ / 0.6	4.06	6.33	5.02 / 4	-0.20 /13	2.39 / 9	0.00	1.53
GL	Natixis ASG Glb Alternatives C	GAFCX	D	(800) 225-5478	E+ / 0.7	3.89	5.95	4.23 / 3	-0.94 /10	1.63 / 7	0.00	2.28
GL	Natixis ASG Glb Alternatives N	GAFNX	D	(800) 225-5478	D- / 1.0	4.20	6.54	5.35 / 4	0.06 /14	--	0.00	1.23
GL	Natixis ASG Glb Alternatives Y	GAFYX	D	(800) 225-5478	D- / 1.0	4.09	6.43	5.25 / 4	0.06 /14	2.65 /10	0.00	1.28
IN	Natixis ASG Managed Futures Strat A	AMFAX	D	(800) 225-5478	D- / 1.1	3.09	-6.10	-10.55 / 0	5.70 /62	2.98 /11	0.00	1.73
IN	Natixis ASG Managed Futures Strat	ASFCX	D	(800) 225-5478	D- / 1.3	2.88	-6.50	-11.16 / 0	4.90 /53	2.22 / 9	0.00	2.48
IN	Natixis ASG Managed Futures Strat Y	ASFYX	D+	(800) 225-5478	D / 1.7	3.19	-5.97	-10.25 / 0	5.97 /64	3.25 /12	0.01	1.48
GR	Natixis ASG Tactical US Market A	USMAX	B-	(800) 225-5478	C / 5.2	8.04	8.04	14.50 /28	7.06 /72	--	0.35	1.40
GR	Natixis ASG Tactical US Market C	USMCX	B-	(800) 225-5478	C+ / 5.8	7.79	7.70	13.67 /24	6.26 /66	--	0.00	2.14
GR	Natixis ASG Tactical US Market Y	USMYX	B-	(800) 225-5478	C+ / 6.6	8.17	8.26	14.91 /29	7.32 /74	--	0.68	1.15
GI	Natixis Loomis Sayles Div Inc A	LSCAX	C	(800) 225-5478	C+ / 6.7	7.21	9.05	24.51 /72	7.39 /75	--	2.25	1.60
GI	Natixis Loomis Sayles Div Inc C	LSCCX	C+	(800) 225-5478	B- / 7.1	6.90	8.54	23.58 /68	6.55 /69	--	1.78	2.35
GI	Natixis Loomis Sayles Div Inc Y	LSCYX	C+	(800) 225-5478	B / 7.9	7.26	9.17	24.92 /73	7.65 /76	--	2.60	1.32
GL	Natixis Loomis Sayles Gl Eq & Inc A	LGMAX	C-	(800) 225-5478	C- / 3.1	5.60	3.93	15.54 /32	4.46 /48	6.85 /34	1.14	1.18
GL	Natixis Loomis Sayles Gl Eq & Inc C	LGMCX	C-	(800) 225-5478	C- / 3.6	5.37	3.52	14.65 /28	3.68 /39	6.05 /29	0.44	1.93
GL	Natixis Loomis Sayles Gl Eq & Inc Y	LSWWX	C	(800) 225-5478	C / 4.4	5.67	4.07	15.82 /34	4.73 /51	7.11 /35	1.45	0.93
GR	Natixis Loomis Sayles Growth Fund A	LGRRX	B+	(800) 225-5478	B- / 7.3	6.60	2.64	20.89 /57	10.69 /96	15.26 /97	0.36	0.92
GR	Natixis Loomis Sayles Growth Fund C	LGRCX	B+	(800) 225-5478	B / 7.7	6.40	2.23	19.95 /52	9.85 /92	14.42 /95	0.00	1.67
GR	Natixis Loomis Sayles Growth Fund N	LGRNX	A	(800) 225-5478	B+ / 8.5	6.70	2.81	21.26 /59	11.02 /97	--	0.59	9.82
GR	Natixis Loomis Sayles Growth Fund Y	LSGRX	A	(800) 225-5478	B+ / 8.5	6.71	2.82	21.16 /58	10.98 /97	15.56 /98	0.52	0.67
GI	Natixis Loomis Sayles Value A	LSVRX	D+	(800) 225-5478	C+ / 6.7	6.27	10.64	26.71 /78	6.81 /71	12.74 /81	1.59	0.95
GI	Natixis Loomis Sayles Value Adm	LSAVX	C-	(800) 225-5478	B- / 7.4	6.21	10.55	26.15 /77	6.48 /68	12.41 /78	0.00	1.23
GI	Natixis Loomis Sayles Value C	LSCVX	C-	(800) 225-5478	B- / 7.1	6.11	10.28	25.85 /76	6.02 /64	11.90 /73	0.91	1.70
GI	Natixis Loomis Sayles Value N	LSVNX	C-	(800) 225-5478	B / 8.0	6.39	10.91	27.25 /80	7.22 /73	--	1.98	0.57
GI	Natixis Loomis Sayles Value Y	LSGIX	C-	(800) 225-5478	B / 7.9	6.34	10.75	27.04 /79	7.06 /72	13.01 /84	1.86	0.70
GL	Natixis Mirova Gl Sustainable Eq Y	ESGYX	U	(800) 225-5478	U /	8.18	2.13	--	--	--	0.00	N/A
GR	Natixis Oakmark A	NEFOX	B+	(800) 225-5478	A- / 9.0	5.74	14.06	34.58 /94	9.19 /88	13.27 /87	0.65	1.14
GR	Natixis Oakmark C	NECOX	B+	(800) 225-5478	A / 9.3	5.53	13.65	33.54 /92	8.35 /82	12.43 /78	0.07	1.89
FO	Natixis Oakmark International A	NOIAX	D	(800) 225-5478	C- / 3.3	8.40	12.92	26.95 /79	0.04 /13	7.53 /38	1.52	1.31
FO	Natixis Oakmark International C	NOICX	D-	(800) 225-5478	D / 2.1	8.23	12.45	26.00 /76	-0.71 /10	6.71 /33	0.86	2.06
GR	Natixis Oakmark Y	NEOYX	A-	(800) 225-5478	A+ / 9.6	5.80	14.23	34.94 /94	9.46 /90	13.56 /89	0.87	0.89
GI	Natixis US Equity Opportunities A	NEFSX	C+	(800) 225-5478	B+ / 8.4	5.71	7.77	27.46 /80	10.65 /96	15.06 /97	0.35	1.25
GI	Natixis US Equity Opportunities C	NECCX	C-	(800) 225-5478	B+ / 8.8	5.53	7.37	26.49 /78	9.84 /92	14.21 /94	0.11	2.00
GI	Natixis US Equity Opportunities Y	NESYX	B-	(800) 225-5478	A / 9.4	5.78	7.92	27.75 /81	10.93 /97	15.36 /97	0.51	1.00
SC	● Natixis Vaug Nel Sm Cp Val A	NEFJX	C+	(800) 225-5478	B / 8.1	3.60	11.83	30.21 /87	9.19 /88	14.17 /94	0.06	1.45
SC	● Natixis Vaug Nel Sm Cp Val C	NEJCX	C	(800) 225-5478	B+ / 8.6	3.42	11.48	29.28 /85	8.40 /82	13.31 /87	0.00	2.20
SC	● Natixis Vaug Nel Sm Cp Val Y	NEJYX	B	(800) 225-5478	A- / 9.2	3.68	11.96	30.53 /87	9.47 /90	14.45 /95	0.28	1.20
GR	Natixis Vaughan Nelson Select A	VNSAX	B-	(800) 225-5478	C+ / 6.8	7.33	8.53	22.64 /65	7.94 /79	--	0.04	1.54

● Denotes fund is closed to new investors
* Denotes fund is included in Section II

www.thestreetratings.com

Risk Rating/Pts	Standard Deviation	Beta	NAV As of 2/28/17	Total $(Mil)	Cash %	Stocks %	Bonds %	Other %	Portfolio Turnover Ratio	Last Bull Market Return	Last Bear Market Return	Manager Quality Pct	Manager Tenure (Years)	Initial Purch. $	Additional Purch. $	Front End Load	Back End Load
C- / 3.5	15.1	0.91	13.99	174	0	99	0	1	27	137.5	-26.6	75	5	50,000	0	0.0	0.0
C- / 3.6	15.0	0.91	14.21	6	0	99	0	1	27	140.8	-26.5	77	5	1,000,000	0	0.0	0.0
B- / 7.1	9.7	0.90	14.85	20	0	99	0	1	48	107.5	-14.1	60	12	2,000	100	5.8	0.0
B- / 7.1	9.6	0.89	14.71	8	0	99	0	1	48	100.0	-14.4	50	12	2,000	100	0.0	0.0
B- / 7.1	9.6	0.90	14.91	14	0	99	0	1	48	110.2	-14.1	63	12	50,000	0	0.0	0.0
B- / 7.1	9.7	0.90	14.91	733	0	99	0	1	48	N/A	N/A	64	12	1,000,000	0	0.0	0.0
C+ / 6.0	11.6	1.03	65.70	248	0	99	0	1	28	137.9	-16.5	52	4	2,000	100	5.8	0.0
C+ / 6.0	11.6	1.03	59.01	36	0	99	0	1	28	129.4	-16.7	41	4	2,000	100	0.0	0.0
C+ / 6.0	11.6	1.03	66.32	80	0	99	0	1	28	141.1	-16.4	55	4	50,000	0	0.0	0.0
C+ / 6.0	11.6	1.03	66.31	4	0	99	0	1	28	N/A	N/A	56	4	1,000,000	0	0.0	0.0
C / 5.2	14.7	1.07	16.42	60	3	96	0	1	17	98.8	-15.0	60	17	2,500	100	5.8	0.0
C / 5.2	14.7	1.07	16.45	7	3	96	0	1	17	91.0	-15.2	49	17	2,500	100	0.0	0.0
C / 5.1	14.7	1.07	15.43	6	3	96	0	1	17	N/A	N/A	65	17	1,000,000	0	0.0	0.0
C / 5.1	14.8	1.07	15.39	122	3	96	0	1	17	101.6	-14.8	62	17	100,000	100	0.0	0.0
B- / 7.2	7.1	0.35	10.25	72	21	0	77	2	0	19.2	-9.8	72	9	2,500	100	5.8	0.0
B- / 7.1	7.1	0.35	9.61	36	21	0	77	2	0	14.4	-10.0	63	9	2,500	100	0.0	0.0
B- / 7.3	7.1	0.35	10.43	10	21	0	77	2	0	N/A	N/A	74	9	1,000,000	0	0.0	0.0
B- / 7.3	7.1	0.35	10.43	1,464	21	0	77	2	0	20.8	-9.6	74	9	100,000	100	0.0	0.0
B- / 7.0	11.2	0.03	10.00	461	16	0	83	1	0	13.9	-6.3	96	7	2,500	100	5.8	0.0
C+ / 6.9	11.3	0.03	9.63	69	16	0	83	1	0	9.4	-6.6	94	7	2,500	100	0.0	0.0
B- / 7.0	11.2	0.03	10.06	2,663	16	0	83	1	0	15.5	-6.2	96	7	100,000	100	0.0	0.0
B- / 7.5	9.3	0.82	12.58	10	14	71	13	2	149	N/A	N/A	55	4	2,500	100	5.8	0.0
B- / 7.5	9.3	0.82	12.31	2	14	71	13	2	149	N/A	N/A	45	4	2,500	100	0.0	0.0
B- / 7.5	9.3	0.82	12.63	60	14	71	13	2	149	N/A	N/A	59	4	100,000	100	0.0	0.0
C / 4.6	10.3	0.97	11.43	17	7	80	11	2	51	N/A	N/A	39	5	2,500	100	5.8	0.0
C / 4.6	10.4	0.97	11.36	9	7	80	11	2	51	N/A	N/A	29	5	2,500	100	0.0	0.0
C / 4.6	10.3	0.97	11.44	20	7	80	11	2	51	N/A	N/A	43	5	100,000	100	0.0	0.0
C+ / 6.4	8.1	0.60	19.51	266	2	65	30	3	43	65.2	-16.6	94	21	2,500	100	5.8	0.0
C+ / 6.5	8.1	0.61	19.31	379	2	65	30	3	43	58.6	-16.8	92	21	2,500	100	0.0	0.0
C+ / 6.4	8.2	0.61	19.60	888	2	65	30	3	43	67.4	-16.5	95	21	100,000	100	0.0	0.0
C+ / 6.7	12.1	1.06	12.01	841	1	98	0	1	11	137.1	-13.0	68	7	2,500	100	5.8	0.0
C+ / 6.7	12.1	1.06	11.10	131	1	98	0	1	11	127.5	-13.2	58	7	2,500	100	0.0	0.0
C+ / 6.7	12.1	1.06	12.78	129	1	98	0	1	11	N/A	N/A	71	7	1,000,000	0	0.0	0.0
C+ / 6.7	12.0	1.06	12.79	4,096	1	98	0	1	11	140.3	-12.9	71	7	100,000	100	0.0	0.0
D+ / 2.5	11.8	1.10	22.15	193	0	99	0	1	15	123.1	-21.5	19	12	2,500	100	5.8	0.0
D+ / 2.4	11.8	1.10	22.13	1	0	99	0	1	15	119.8	-21.5	16	12	0	0	0.0	0.0
D+ / 2.6	11.8	1.10	21.94	13	0	99	0	1	15	114.4	-21.7	13	12	2,500	100	0.0	0.0
D+ / 2.5	11.8	1.10	22.19	551	0	99	0	1	15	N/A	N/A	23	12	1,000,000	0	0.0	0.0
D+ / 2.5	11.8	1.10	22.22	523	0	99	0	1	15	126.1	-21.4	21	12	100,000	100	0.0	0.0
U /	N/A	N/A	10.57	53	0	0	0	100	0	N/A	N/A	N/A	1	100,000	100	0.0	0.0
C / 5.0	12.8	1.17	22.24	180	6	93	0	1	23	134.9	-19.1	35	3	2,500	100	5.8	0.0
C / 4.8	12.8	1.17	19.57	60	6	93	0	1	23	125.5	-19.4	26	3	2,500	100	0.0	0.0
C / 4.7	15.2	1.14	12.79	546	2	97	0	1	51	72.9	-22.8	76	7	2,500	100	5.8	0.0
C / 4.7	15.2	1.14	12.57	264	2	97	0	1	51	66.1	-23.1	68	7	2,500	100	0.0	0.0
C / 5.1	12.7	1.17	23.26	31	6	93	0	1	23	138.2	-19.0	38	3	100,000	100	0.0	0.0
C- / 3.1	12.2	1.13	31.78	518	4	95	0	1	20	147.0	-20.1	58	6	2,500	100	5.8	0.0
D / 1.6	12.2	1.13	22.59	83	4	95	0	1	20	137.2	-20.3	48	6	2,500	100	0.0	0.0
C- / 3.6	12.2	1.13	36.52	180	4	95	0	1	20	150.4	-20.0	61	6	100,000	100	0.0	0.0
C- / 3.9	13.6	0.83	20.09	107	2	97	0	1	62	137.8	-23.3	91	13	2,500	100	5.8	0.0
D+ / 2.6	13.6	0.83	13.45	20	2	97	0	1	62	128.4	-23.6	88	13	2,500	100	0.0	0.0
C- / 4.0	13.6	0.83	20.68	190	2	97	0	1	62	140.9	-23.2	92	13	100,000	100	0.0	0.0
B- / 7.0	10.9	1.01	16.24	22	4	95	0	1	35	N/A	N/A	41	5	2,500	100	5.8	0.0

Fund Type	Fund Name	Ticker Symbol	Overall Investment Rating	Phone	Performance Rating/Pts	3 Mo	6 Mo	1Yr / Pct	Annualized 3Yr / Pct	Annualized 5Yr / Pct	Dividend Yield	Expense Ratio
GR	Natixis Vaughan Nelson Select C	VNSCX	B+	(800) 225-5478	B- / 7.2	7.13	8.15	21.69 /61	7.15 /73	--	0.00	2.29
GR	Natixis Vaughan Nelson Select Y	VNSYX	A-	(800) 225-5478	B / 7.9	7.40	8.74	22.97 /67	8.23 /81	--	0.26	1.29
GR	Natixis Vaughan Nelson Val Opp A	VNVAX	D+	(800) 225-5478	C- / 3.9	4.87	6.74	21.73 /61	4.13 /44	11.59 /71	0.21	1.45
GR	Natixis Vaughan Nelson Val Opp C	VNVCX	C-	(800) 225-5478	C / 4.4	4.68	6.38	20.84 /57	3.37 /35	10.76 /64	0.00	2.20
GR	Natixis Vaughan Nelson Val Opp N	VNVNX	C	(800) 225-5478	C / 5.3	4.89	6.89	22.13 /63	4.47 /48	--	0.69	1.11
GR	Natixis Vaughan Nelson Val Opp Y	VNVYX	C	(800) 225-5478	C / 5.3	4.92	6.87	22.04 /62	4.39 /47	11.86 /73	0.58	1.20
GL	Navigator Equity Hedged A	NAVAX	D	(877) 766-2264	D- / 1.3	2.40	5.33	13.93 /25	0.54 /16	1.72 / 7	0.78	1.67
GL	Navigator Equity Hedged C	NAVCX	D	(877) 766-2264	D- / 1.2	2.32	5.00	13.08 /22	-0.19 /13	0.97 / 6	0.00	2.54
GL	Navigator Equity Hedged I	NAVIX	D+	(877) 766-2264	D / 2.0	2.45	5.49	14.20 /26	0.78 /17	1.97 / 8	0.99	1.54
FS	Navigator Tactical Fixed Income A	NTBAX	U	(877) 766-2264	U /	3.99	4.44	16.00 /34	--	--	3.18	1.91
FS	Navigator Tactical Fixed Income I	NTBIX	U	(877) 766-2264	U /	4.14	4.65	16.35 /36	--	--	3.52	1.66
GI	NE 529 State Farm CSP Opp 4-6		C+	(888) 470-0862	D+ / 2.9	5.24	4.23	13.86 /25	4.39 /47	6.93 /34	0.00	1.14
GI	NE 529 State Farm CSP Opp 4-6		C+	(888) 470-0862	C- / 3.3	5.08	3.82	13.00 /22	3.62 /38	6.12 /29	0.00	1.89
GL	NE 529 State Farm CSP Opp		C+	(888) 470-0862	C- / 3.9	6.57	6.06	17.90 /42	4.64 /50	8.41 /45	0.00	1.22
GL	NE 529 State Farm CSP Opp		C+	(888) 470-0862	C / 4.3	6.40	5.61	17.02 /38	3.84 /41	7.61 /39	0.00	1.97
BA	NE 529 State Farm CSP Opp Bal A		C+	(888) 470-0862	D+ / 2.9	5.26	4.16	13.80 /25	4.43 /48	6.93 /34	0.00	1.14
BA	NE 529 State Farm CSP Opp Bal B		C+	(888) 470-0862	C- / 3.3	5.00	3.83	12.93 /21	3.63 /38	6.14 /29	0.00	1.89
GI	NE 529 State Farm CSP Opp Col		C	(888) 470-0862	E+ / 0.6	1.06	0.19	2.44 / 2	1.27 /20	1.43 / 7	0.00	0.92
GI	NE 529 State Farm CSP Opp Col		C	(888) 470-0862	E+ / 0.8	0.83	-0.20	1.67 / 2	0.52 /16	0.67 / 6	0.00	1.67
GL	NE 529 State Farm CSP Opp Gro A		C+	(888) 470-0862	C / 4.8	7.45	7.30	20.35 /54	5.20 /56	9.73 /56	0.00	1.23
GL	NE 529 State Farm CSP Opp Gro B		B-	(888) 470-0862	C / 5.2	7.20	6.89	19.39 /49	4.41 /48	8.89 /50	0.00	1.98
GL	NE 529 State Farm CSP Opp Mdt G		C+	(888) 470-0862	C- / 3.9	6.62	6.10	18.00 /43	4.65 /50	8.43 /46	0.00	1.22
GL	NE 529 State Farm CSP Opp Mdt G		C+	(888) 470-0862	C / 4.3	6.45	5.67	17.13 /39	3.85 /41	7.61 /39	0.00	1.97
GL	NE 529 State Farm CSP		C+	(888) 470-0862	C / 4.8	7.44	7.21	20.21 /53	5.23 /57	9.74 /57	0.00	1.23
GL	NE 529 State Farm CSP		B-	(888) 470-0862	C / 5.2	7.25	6.84	19.35 /49	4.36 /47	8.90 /50	0.00	1.98
GI	NE 529 State Farm CSP		C	(888) 470-0862	D- / 1.5	3.25	2.50	7.99 / 7	2.86 /30	4.44 /18	0.00	1.01
GI	NE 529 State Farm CSP		C+	(888) 470-0862	D / 1.8	3.06	2.08	7.18 / 6	2.09 /25	3.66 /14	0.00	1.76
AG	Needham Aggressive Growth Retail	NEAGX	B-	(800) 625-7071	B- / 7.5	1.67	14.73	28.64 /83	6.84 /71	10.56 /62	0.00	2.44
GR	Needham Growth Fund Retail	NEEGX	D+	(800) 625-7071	C- / 4.2	2.20	8.06	18.86 /46	4.38 /47	9.66 /56	0.00	2.07
SC	Needham Small Cap Growth Retail	NESGX	C+	(800) 625-7071	C+ / 6.6	-0.52	11.98	28.82 /84	6.13 /65	7.45 /38	0.00	2.25
GL	Neiman Balanced Allocation A	NBAFX	C-		D+ / 2.3	4.88	4.97	14.14 /26	2.99 /32	5.72 /26	1.13	2.90
GL	Neiman Balanced Allocation C	NBCFX	C-		D+ / 2.7	4.57	4.48	13.20 /22	2.29 /26	5.00 /21	0.38	3.65
GR	Neiman Large Cap Value A	NEAMX	C+		C+ / 6.4	6.68	10.08	19.85 /51	7.70 /77	--	1.07	1.79
IN	Neiman Large Cap Value NL	NEIMX	B+		B- / 7.4	6.68	10.08	19.85 /51	7.70 /77	9.43 /54	1.13	1.54
GL	Neuberger Berman Abs Ret Mlt-Mgr	NABCX	D+	(800) 877-9700	E / 0.5	1.72	2.66	6.02 / 5	-1.80 / 7	--	0.00	3.84
GL	Neuberger Berman Abs Ret Mlt-Mgr	NRABX	C-	(800) 877-9700	E+ / 0.8	2.04	3.25	7.26 / 6	-0.67 /11	--	0.00	2.68
GL	Neuberger Berman AbsRet MltMgr A	NABAX	D+	(800) 877-9700	E / 0.4	1.96	3.07	6.89 / 6	-1.04 / 9	--	0.00	3.09
GL	Neuberger Berman AbsRet MltMgr	NABIX	D+	(800) 877-9700	E+ / 0.8	2.04	3.25	7.26 / 6	-0.71 /10	--	0.00	2.73
GR	Neuberger Berman AMT Guardian I		D	(800) 877-9700	B- / 7.2	8.52	9.34	22.07 /63	6.64 /69	11.73 /72	0.50	1.15
GR	Neuberger Berman AMT Social Resp		A-	(800) 877-9700	B+ / 8.5	8.34	9.80	24.13 /70	8.64 /84	12.71 /81	0.63	0.98
GR	Neuberger Berman AMT Social Resp		B+	(800) 877-9700	B+ / 8.3	8.30	9.72	23.95 /70	8.44 /82	12.51 /79	0.44	1.23
IN	Neuberger Berman Div Growth Inst	NDGIX	U	(800) 877-9700	U /	6.62	12.77	29.69 /86	--	--	1.77	2.24
EM	Neuberger Berman Emg Mkt Eq A	NEMAX	D+	(800) 877-9700	C- / 3.5	8.48	4.46	28.42 /83	1.69 /22	1.24 / 7	0.31	1.82
EM	Neuberger Berman Emg Mkt Eq C	NEMCX	D+	(800) 877-9700	C- / 4.0	8.33	4.10	27.41 /80	0.92 /18	0.49 / 5	0.00	2.51
EM	Neuberger Berman Emg Mkt Eq I	NEMIX	C-	(800) 877-9700	C / 4.9	8.55	4.55	28.65 /83	1.93 /24	1.48 / 7	0.48	1.44
EM	Neuberger Berman Emg Mkt Eq R3	NEMRX	C-	(800) 877-9700	C / 4.3	8.34	4.17	27.78 /81	1.25 /20	0.81 / 6	0.06	2.06
EM	Neuberger Berman Emg Mkt Eq R6	NREMX	C-	(800) 877-9700	C / 4.9	8.54	4.61	28.82 /84	2.00 /24	--	0.54	1.33
IN	Neuberger Berman Eq Income A	NBHAX	C+	(800) 877-9700	C+ / 5.8	5.25	7.27	20.79 /56	7.34 /74	8.35 /45	2.14	1.08
IN	Neuberger Berman Eq Income C	NBHCX	C+	(800) 877-9700	C+ / 6.3	5.09	6.83	19.84 /51	6.53 /69	7.54 /39	1.59	1.82
IN	Neuberger Berman Eq Income I	NBHIX	B	(800) 877-9700	B- / 7.1	5.41	7.44	21.26 /59	7.73 /77	8.74 /48	2.61	0.70
IN	Neuberger Berman Eq Income R3	NBHRX	C+	(800) 877-9700	C+ / 6.7	5.26	7.13	20.41 /54	7.03 /72	8.03 /42	2.02	1.34
GR	Neuberger Berman Focus A	NFAAX	D+	(800) 877-9700	C+ / 6.5	7.69	8.17	24.63 /72	6.98 /72	12.75 /81	0.51	1.15

● Denotes fund is closed to new investors
* Denotes fund is included in Section II

RISK	3 Year		NET ASSETS		ASSET					BULL / BEAR		FUND MANAGER		MINIMUMS		LOADS	
Risk Rating/Pts	Standard Deviation	Beta	NAV As of 2/28/17	Total $(Mil)	Cash %	Stocks %	Bonds %	Other %	Portfolio Turnover Ratio	Last Bull Market Return	Last Bear Market Return	Manager Quality Pct	Manager Tenure (Years)	Initial Purch. $	Additional Purch. $	Front End Load	Back End Load
C+ / 6.9	10.9	1.01	15.67	8	4	95	0	1	35	N/A	N/A	31	5	2,500	100	0.0	0.0
B- / 7.0	11.0	1.01	16.32	109	4	95	0	1	35	N/A	N/A	44	5	100,000	100	0.0	0.0
C / 5.4	13.1	1.10	21.45	83	1	98	0	1	32	114.4	-23.9	5	9	2,500	100	5.8	0.0
C / 5.4	13.2	1.10	20.35	65	1	98	0	1	32	105.9	-24.2	4	9	2,500	100	0.0	0.0
C / 5.4	13.1	1.10	21.67	144	1	98	0	1	32	N/A	N/A	6	9	1,000,000	0	0.0	0.0
C / 5.4	13.2	1.10	21.69	881	1	98	0	1	32	117.3	-23.9	6	9	100,000	100	0.0	0.0
C+ / 6.7	7.5	0.47	9.13	8	13	86	0	1	363	19.1	-15.4	78	7	5,000	500	5.5	0.0
C+ / 6.7	7.5	0.47	8.82	1	13	86	0	1	363	14.4	-15.8	72	7	5,000	500	0.0	0.0
C+ / 6.7	7.4	0.46	9.17	32	13	86	0	1	363	20.7	-15.4	80	7	25,000	0	0.0	0.0
U /	N/A	N/A	10.43	45	67	5	26	2	302	N/A	N/A	N/A	3	5,000	500	3.8	0.0
U /	N/A	N/A	10.46	599	67	5	26	2	302	N/A	N/A	N/A	3	25,000	0	0.0	0.0
B+ / 9.0	6.7	0.63	14.05	86	0	0	0	100	0	59.3	-11.7	47	9	250	50	5.5	0.0
B / 8.9	6.7	0.63	13.04	2	0	0	0	100	0	52.9	-12.0	37	9	250	50	0.0	0.0
B / 8.1	8.8	0.65	15.41	105	0	0	0	100	0	77.3	-17.7	95	9	250	50	5.5	0.0
B / 8.0	8.8	0.65	14.30	1	0	0	0	100	0	70.2	-18.1	93	9	250	50	0.0	0.0
B+ / 9.1	6.7	1.04	14.02	15	0	0	0	100	0	59.1	-11.6	32	8	250	50	5.5	0.0
B+ / 9.0	6.7	1.04	13.01	N/A	0	0	0	100	0	52.9	-12.0	24	8	250	50	0.0	0.0
B+ / 9.9	1.5	0.10	10.49	42	0	0	0	100	0	10.2	0.6	75	8	250	50	5.5	0.0
B+ / 9.9	1.4	0.09	9.74	2	0	0	0	100	0	5.9	0.3	68	8	250	50	0.0	0.0
B- / 7.5	10.5	0.75	15.73	64	0	0	0	100	0	93.0	-20.3	96	8	250	50	5.5	0.0
B- / 7.5	10.5	0.75	14.59	1	0	0	0	100	0	85.2	-20.4	94	8	250	50	0.0	0.0
B / 8.1	8.9	0.65	15.47	31	0	0	0	100	0	77.2	-17.4	95	8	250	50	5.5	0.0
B / 8.0	8.8	0.65	14.36	1	0	0	0	100	0	70.1	-17.7	93	8	250	50	0.0	0.0
B- / 7.6	10.4	0.75	15.17	40	0	0	0	100	0	92.8	-22.5	96	8	250	50	5.5	0.0
B- / 7.5	10.4	0.75	14.06	N/A	0	0	0	100	0	85.0	-22.8	94	8	250	50	0.0	0.0
B+ / 9.9	4.2	0.40	12.70	72	0	0	0	100	0	35.0	-6.0	59	N/A	250	50	5.5	0.0
B+ / 9.8	4.3	0.40	11.80	2	0	0	0	100	0	29.5	-6.2	48	N/A	250	50	0.0	0.0
C / 5.2	13.4	0.97	22.46	54	0	0	0	100	15	121.9	-30.3	32	7	2,000	100	0.0	2.0
C / 4.7	12.5	0.96	44.67	92	0	97	2	1	13	106.8	-28.5	13	8	2,000	100	0.0	2.0
C / 4.9	14.6	0.77	15.28	31	0	0	0	100	64	83.8	-29.1	79	9	2,000	100	0.0	2.0
B- / 7.3	6.7	0.98	12.22	7	7	51	40	2	77	48.8	-13.2	55	6	2,500	100	5.8	0.0
B- / 7.3	6.7	0.98	12.11	3	7	51	40	2	77	43.2	-13.5	45	6	2,500	100	0.0	0.0
C+ / 6.6	8.5	0.78	26.17	1	10	89	0	1	55	N/A	N/A	69	14	1,000	100	5.8	0.0
C+ / 6.6	8.5	0.78	26.17	24	10	89	0	1	55	83.5	-14.6	69	14	1,000	100	0.0	0.0
B / 8.4	4.0	0.24	10.04	29	54	31	14	1	485	N/A	N/A	50	5	1,000	100	5.8	0.0
B+ / 9.3	4.0	0.24	10.49	3	54	31	14	1	485	N/A	N/A	66	5	0	0	0.0	0.0
B / 8.5	4.0	0.24	10.40	47	54	31	14	1	485	N/A	N/A	61	5	1,000	100	5.8	0.0
B / 8.5	4.0	0.24	10.49	428	54	31	14	1	485	N/A	N/A	65	5	1,000,000	0	0.0	0.0
D- / 1.0	10.1	0.96	15.66	12	2	96	1	1	51	106.8	-20.1	31	2	0	0	0.0	0.0
C+ / 6.1	10.1	0.95	24.04	348	0	97	2	1	24	117.4	-20.8	58	14	0	0	0.0	0.0
C+ / 6.1	10.1	0.95	24.13	82	0	97	2	1	24	115.4	-20.8	55	14	0	0	0.0	0.0
U /	N/A	N/A	12.30	27	0	0	0	100	23	N/A	N/A	N/A	2	1,000,000	0	0.0	0.0
C / 5.2	14.5	0.87	16.57	38	0	95	4	1	43	26.9	-28.0	75	9	1,000	100	5.8	0.0
C / 5.2	14.5	0.87	15.99	6	0	95	4	1	43	22.0	-28.2	67	9	1,000	100	0.0	0.0
C / 5.2	14.5	0.88	16.65	404	0	95	4	1	43	28.7	-27.9	77	9	1,000,000	0	0.0	0.0
C / 5.2	14.5	0.87	16.23	1	0	95	4	1	43	24.0	-28.1	71	9	0	0	0.0	0.0
C / 5.1	14.5	0.87	16.66	110	0	95	4	1	43	N/A	N/A	77	9	0	0	0.0	0.0
C+ / 6.3	8.8	0.78	12.73	236	0	91	1	8	49	66.5	-9.8	64	11	1,000	100	5.8	0.0
C+ / 6.3	8.8	0.78	12.64	316	0	91	1	8	49	60.0	-10.1	54	11	1,000	100	0.0	0.0
C+ / 6.2	8.8	0.78	12.78	1,159	0	91	1	8	49	70.0	-9.7	69	11	1,000,000	0	0.0	0.0
C+ / 6.3	8.8	0.78	12.70	2	0	91	1	8	49	64.0	-10.0	61	11	0	0	0.0	0.0
D+ / 2.7	11.8	1.09	14.66	3	3	96	0	1	89	125.9	-20.5	21	9	1,000	100	5.8	0.0

Fund Type	Fund Name	Ticker Symbol	Overall Investment Rating	Phone	Performance Rating/Pts	3 Mo	6 Mo	1Yr / Pct	3Yr / Pct	5Yr / Pct	Dividend Yield	Expense Ratio
GR	● Neuberger Berman Focus Adv	NBFAX	D	(800) 877-9700	B- / 7.4	7.75	8.16	24.44 /71	6.83 /71	12.59 /80	1.37	1.26
GR	Neuberger Berman Focus C	NFACX	D	(800) 877-9700	C+ / 6.9	7.53	7.82	23.68 /69	6.20 /66	11.93 /74	0.79	1.90
GR	Neuberger Berman Focus Inst	NFALX	C+	(800) 877-9700	B / 7.8	7.83	8.42	25.11 /74	7.39 /75	13.17 /86	0.50	0.76
GR	● Neuberger Berman Focus Inv	NBSSX	C+	(800) 877-9700	B / 7.6	7.81	8.31	24.85 /73	7.19 /73	12.97 /83	0.33	0.94
GR	● Neuberger Berman Focus Tr	NBFCX	C-	(800) 877-9700	B- / 7.5	7.76	8.23	24.70 /72	6.98 /72	12.75 /81	0.49	1.11
SC	Neuberger Berman Genesis Adv	NBGAX	C-	(800) 877-9700	B / 7.9	5.71	10.15	27.69 /81	7.31 /74	11.42 /69	0.27	1.38
SC	Neuberger Berman Genesis Inst	NBGIX	B-	(800) 877-9700	B+ / 8.3	5.82	10.46	28.36 /82	7.89 /78	12.01 /74	0.31	0.85
SC	Neuberger Berman Genesis Inv	NBGNX	C	(800) 877-9700	B / 8.2	5.80	10.35	28.15 /82	7.71 /77	11.82 /73	0.41	1.03
SC	Neuberger Berman Genesis R6	NRGSX	B-	(800) 877-9700	B+ / 8.4	5.84	10.49	28.45 /83	7.96 /79	--	0.37	0.78
SC	Neuberger Berman Genesis Tr	NBGEX	B-	(800) 877-9700	B / 8.1	5.76	10.31	28.04 /82	7.62 /76	11.73 /72	0.05	1.10
GL	Neuberger Berman Global Alloc A	NGLAX	D+	(800) 877-9700	D- / 1.2	4.93	3.23	12.44 /20	0.39 /15	3.94 /15	0.00	3.99
GL	Neuberger Berman Global Alloc C	NGLCX	D	(800) 877-9700	D- / 1.1	4.76	2.82	11.63 /16	-0.35 /12	3.18 /11	0.00	4.75
GL	Neuberger Berman Global Alloc Inst	NGLIX	C-	(800) 877-9700	D / 2.0	5.16	3.47	12.95 /21	0.79 /17	4.31 /17	0.42	3.59
GL	Neuberger Berman Global Equity A	NGQAX	E-	(800) 877-9700	D+ / 2.4	7.24	3.49	14.08 /26	3.13 /33	6.75 /33	0.14	8.92
GL	Neuberger Berman Global Equity C	NGQCX	E	(800) 877-9700	D+ / 2.9	7.07	3.16	13.24 /22	2.40 /27	5.98 /28	0.00	9.60
GL	Neuberger Berman Global Equity Inst	NGQIX	E	(800) 877-9700	C- / 3.7	7.43	3.71	14.57 /28	3.50 /37	7.13 /35	0.53	8.47
FO	Neuberger Berman Grtr China Eq A	NCEAX	C	(800) 877-9700	B / 7.6	4.69	3.42	28.02 /82	10.07 /94	--	0.02	2.19
FO	Neuberger Berman Grtr China Eq C	NCECX	C	(800) 877-9700	B / 7.9	4.50	3.02	27.02 /79	9.08 /87	--	0.00	2.86
FO	Neuberger Berman Grtr China Eq Inst	NCEIX	C+	(800) 877-9700	B+ / 8.8	4.79	3.60	28.53 /83	10.29 /95	--	0.42	1.77
GI	Neuberger Berman Guardian A	NGDAX	D	(800) 877-9700	C+ / 6.1	8.00	9.00	21.96 /62	6.61 /69	11.68 /71	0.81	1.08
GI	● Neuberger Berman Guardian Adv	NBGUX	C-	(800) 877-9700	B- / 7.0	8.22	9.18	22.05 /62	6.35 /67	11.35 /69	0.34	1.31
GI	Neuberger Berman Guardian C	NGDCX	C-	(800) 877-9700	C+ / 6.6	7.85	8.68	21.03 /58	5.79 /62	10.84 /65	0.23	1.86
GI	Neuberger Berman Guardian Inst	NGDLX	C	(800) 877-9700	B- / 7.4	8.17	9.22	22.42 /64	6.98 /72	12.08 /75	0.80	0.73
GI	● Neuberger Berman Guardian Inv	NGUAX	C	(800) 877-9700	B- / 7.2	8.10	9.15	22.22 /63	6.80 /70	11.88 /73	0.60	0.93
GI	Neuberger Berman Guardian R3	NGDRX	C-	(800) 877-9700	C+ / 6.9	7.93	8.90	21.68 /61	6.29 /67	11.38 /69	0.36	1.40
GI	● Neuberger Berman Guardian Tr	NBGTX	D+	(800) 877-9700	B- / 7.1	8.11	9.10	22.01 /62	6.63 /69	11.69 /71	0.85	1.08
FO	Neuberger Berman Intl Equity A	NIQAX	D	(800) 877-9700	D- / 1.2	6.86	1.64	10.83 /14	0.63 /16	5.26 /23	0.18	1.40
FO	Neuberger Berman Intl Equity C	NIQCX	D	(800) 877-9700	D- / 1.1	6.66	1.29	10.01 /12	-0.11 /13	4.47 /18	0.00	2.15
FO	Neuberger Berman Intl Equity Inst	NBIIX	D	(800) 877-9700	D / 2.0	6.93	1.82	11.25 /15	1.00 /18	5.71 /26	1.38	1.04
FO	● Neuberger Berman Intl Equity Inv	NIQVX	D	(800) 877-9700	D / 2.0	7.28	2.12	11.42 /16	0.93 /18	5.52 /25	0.44	1.26
FO	Neuberger Berman Intl Equity R6	NRIQX	D	(800) 877-9700	D / 2.0	6.95	1.80	11.34 /16	1.08 /19	--	1.44	0.96
FO	● Neuberger Berman Intl Equity Trust	NIQTX	D	(800) 877-9700	D / 2.0	7.28	2.06	11.40 /16	0.85 /17	5.46 /25	0.34	1.30
FO	Neuberger Berman Intl Sel A	NBNAX	D-	(800) 877-9700	E+ / 0.6	6.12	0.61	9.76 /11	-0.40 /12	4.24 /16	1.06	1.33
FO	Neuberger Berman Intl Sel C	NBNCX	D-	(800) 877-9700	E+ / 0.8	5.94	0.27	8.86 / 9	-1.14 / 9	3.45 /13	0.34	2.06
FO	Neuberger Berman Intl Sel Inst	NILIX	D-	(800) 877-9700	D- / 1.1	6.17	0.89	10.12 /12	-0.04 /13	4.61 /19	1.47	0.95
FO	Neuberger Berman Intl Sel R3	NBNRX	D-	(800) 877-9700	E+ / 0.9	6.09	0.55	9.43 /10	-0.63 /11	3.98 /15	0.97	1.57
FO	● Neuberger Berman Intl Sel Trust	NILTX	D-	(800) 877-9700	D- / 1.0	6.06	0.60	9.67 /11	-0.39 /12	4.23 /16	1.10	1.39
GR	Neuberger Berman Intrinsic Val A	NINAX	C-	(800) 877-9700	C+ / 5.6	5.24	11.01	25.09 /74	5.31 /58	11.78 /72	0.00	1.49
GR	Neuberger Berman Intrinsic Val C	NINCX	C-	(800) 877-9700	C+ / 6.1	5.09	10.59	24.16 /70	4.53 /49	10.93 /65	0.00	2.21
GR	Neuberger Berman Intrinsic Val Inst	NINLX	C	(800) 877-9700	C+ / 6.9	5.31	11.17	25.59 /75	5.69 /61	12.17 /76	0.00	1.09
GR	Neuberger Berman Large Cap Val A	NPNAX	C	(800) 877-9700	B+ / 8.7	4.52	12.54	38.68 /97	8.11 /80	12.67 /81	0.90	1.09
GR	● Neuberger Berman Large Cap Val	NBPBX	C	(800) 877-9700	A / 9.4	4.53	12.53	38.59 /97	7.99 /79	12.55 /80	1.26	1.22
GR	Neuberger Berman Large Cap Val C	NPNCX	C-	(800) 877-9700	A- / 9.0	4.32	12.19	37.75 /96	7.31 /74	11.84 /73	0.90	1.83
GR	Neuberger Berman Large Cap Val	NBPIX	B	(800) 877-9700	A+ / 9.6	4.57	12.77	39.24 /97	8.53 /83	13.11 /85	0.80	0.71
GR	● Neuberger Berman Large Cap Val Inv	NPRTX	B	(800) 877-9700	A / 9.5	4.55	12.70	38.98 /97	8.35 /82	12.93 /83	0.63	0.90
GR	Neuberger Berman Large Cap Val R3	NPNRX	C	(800) 877-9700	A / 9.3	4.40	12.42	38.34 /97	7.82 /78	12.37 /78	1.12	1.55
GR	● Neuberger Berman Large Cap Val Tr	NBPTX	C+	(800) 877-9700	A / 9.5	4.53	12.61	38.82 /97	8.16 /80	12.72 /81	0.93	1.07
GR	Neuberger Berman Lng Sh MltMgr A	NLMAX	E-	(800) 877-9700	E / 0.4	1.79	1.68	7.19 / 6	-0.93 /10	--	0.00	4.65
GR	Neuberger Berman Lng Sh MltMgr C	NLMCX	E-	(800) 877-9700	E / 0.5	1.61	1.28	6.41 / 5	-1.64 / 8	--	0.00	5.45
GR	Neuberger Berman Lng Sh MltMgr	NLMIX	E-	(800) 877-9700	E+ / 0.8	1.87	1.87	7.59 / 7	-0.57 /11	--	0.00	4.22
GR	Neuberger Berman Long Short A	NLSAX	C-	(800) 877-9700	D- / 1.4	4.11	4.44	10.02 /12	1.58 /21	4.98 /21	0.00	2.05
GR	Neuberger Berman Long Short C	NLSCX	C-	(800) 877-9700	D / 1.7	3.93	4.01	9.20 /10	0.82 /17	4.19 /16	0.00	2.79

RISK			NET ASSETS		ASSET				Portfolio Turnover Ratio	BULL / BEAR		FUND MANAGER		MINIMUMS		LOADS	
Risk Rating/Pts	3 Year		NAV As of 2/28/17	Total $(Mil)	Cash %	Stocks %	Bonds %	Other %		Last Bull Market Return	Last Bear Market Return	Manager Quality Pct	Manager Tenure (Years)	Initial Purch. $	Additional Purch. $	Front End Load	Back End Load
	Standard Deviation	Beta															
E+ / 0.8	11.9	1.09	5.96	4	3	96	0	1	89	123.9	-20.5	20	9	0	0	0.0	0.0
E+ / 0.8	11.8	1.09	5.57	2	3	96	0	1	89	117.0	-20.6	16	9	1,000	100	0.0	0.0
C / 4.4	11.8	1.09	25.53	7	3	96	0	1	89	130.4	-20.4	25	9	1,000,000	0	0.0	0.0
C / 4.4	11.8	1.09	25.50	645	3	96	0	1	89	128.1	-20.4	23	9	1,000	100	0.0	0.0
D+ / 2.8	11.9	1.09	14.85	66	3	96	0	1	89	125.7	-20.4	21	9	0	0	0.0	0.0
D / 1.7	12.3	0.75	23.08	274	1	97	0	2	16	103.7	-17.7	86	23	0	0	0.0	0.0
C / 4.4	12.3	0.75	58.74	3,674	1	97	0	2	16	109.6	-17.5	89	23	1,000,000	0	0.0	0.0
C- / 3.0	12.3	0.75	33.88	1,887	1	97	0	2	16	107.8	-17.6	88	23	1,000	100	0.0	0.0
C / 4.3	12.3	0.75	58.73	3,892	1	97	0	2	16	N/A	N/A	89	23	0	0	0.0	0.0
C / 4.5	12.3	0.75	62.00	1,713	1	97	0	2	16	106.7	-17.6	87	23	0	0	0.0	0.0
B- / 7.3	7.8	1.16	10.85	6	15	59	25	1	176	33.4	-5.9	16	7	1,000	100	5.8	0.0
B- / 7.2	7.8	1.16	10.56	4	15	59	25	1	176	28.2	-6.2	11	7	1,000	100	0.0	0.0
B- / 7.3	7.8	1.16	10.92	10	15	59	25	1	176	36.0	-5.7	19	7	1,000,000	0	0.0	0.0
E+ / 0.8	11.2	0.83	6.74	N/A	0	98	1	1	41	61.4	N/A	91	6	1,000	100	5.8	0.0
E+ / 0.8	11.3	0.83	6.44	N/A	0	98	1	1	41	55.1	N/A	88	6	1,000	100	0.0	0.0
E+ / 0.8	11.3	0.84	6.81	4	0	98	1	1	41	64.5	N/A	92	6	1,000,000	0	0.0	0.0
D+ / 2.9	22.0	0.99	11.89	2	2	93	3	2	120	N/A	N/A	99	4	1,000	100	5.8	0.0
D+ / 2.9	21.9	0.98	11.61	N/A	2	93	3	2	120	N/A	N/A	99	4	1,000	100	0.0	0.0
D+ / 2.9	21.9	0.98	11.86	87	2	93	3	2	120	N/A	N/A	99	4	1,000,000	0	0.0	0.0
D / 2.1	10.1	0.96	9.74	6	2	95	2	1	99	105.8	-20.1	32	2	1,000	100	5.8	0.0
C- / 3.1	10.1	0.96	12.70	N/A	2	95	2	1	99	102.6	-20.2	28	2	0	0	0.0	0.0
C- / 3.0	10.0	0.95	12.18	2	2	95	2	1	99	97.5	-20.3	24	2	1,000	100	0.0	0.0
C- / 3.7	10.0	0.95	15.92	66	2	95	2	1	99	110.0	-20.0	36	2	1,000,000	0	0.0	0.0
C- / 3.8	10.0	0.95	15.89	1,023	2	95	2	1	99	108.0	-20.0	34	2	1,000	100	0.0	0.0
C- / 3.1	10.0	0.95	12.61	1	2	95	2	1	99	102.8	-20.2	29	2	0	0	0.0	0.0
D / 2.2	10.0	0.95	9.90	67	2	95	2	1	99	106.1	-20.1	32	2	0	0	0.0	0.0
C+ / 6.4	10.9	0.83	23.25	82	2	97	0	1	30	46.4	-23.0	79	12	1,000	100	5.8	0.0
C+ / 6.3	10.9	0.83	22.74	13	2	97	0	1	30	40.5	-23.3	74	12	1,000	100	0.0	0.0
C+ / 6.3	10.9	0.83	11.13	1,227	2	97	0	1	30	49.6	-23.0	82	12	1,000,000	0	0.0	0.0
C+ / 6.4	10.9	0.83	20.94	101	2	97	0	1	30	48.3	-23.0	81	12	1,000	100	0.0	0.0
C+ / 6.3	10.9	0.83	11.23	56	2	97	0	1	30	N/A	N/A	82	12	0	0	0.0	0.0
C+ / 6.4	10.9	0.83	23.41	43	2	97	0	1	30	47.9	-23.0	81	12	0	0	0.0	0.0
C+ / 6.2	10.9	0.84	10.74	4	0	96	2	2	22	40.5	-24.6	71	11	1,000	100	5.8	0.0
C+ / 6.3	10.8	0.83	10.63	3	0	96	2	2	22	34.8	-24.7	62	11	1,000	100	0.0	0.0
C+ / 6.2	10.8	0.83	10.79	212	0	96	2	2	22	43.1	-24.4	75	11	1,000,000	0	0.0	0.0
C+ / 6.2	10.8	0.83	10.66	5	0	96	2	2	22	38.5	-24.6	68	11	0	0	0.0	0.0
C+ / 6.2	10.8	0.83	10.82	8	0	96	2	2	22	40.3	-24.5	71	11	1,000	100	0.0	0.0
C / 4.3	14.6	1.16	14.97	45	6	92	0	2	17	118.5	-29.4	7	7	1,000	100	5.8	0.0
C- / 4.2	14.6	1.16	14.15	24	6	92	0	2	17	109.7	-29.6	5	7	1,000	100	0.0	0.0
C / 4.3	14.6	1.16	15.37	655	6	92	0	2	17	122.7	-29.3	8	7	1,000,000	0	0.0	0.0
D / 2.2	13.7	1.12	19.57	3	0	99	0	1	126	116.1	-26.4	29	6	1,000	100	5.8	0.0
D- / 1.5	13.6	1.12	14.35	155	0	99	0	1	126	114.9	-26.5	28	6	0	0	0.0	0.0
D- / 1.4	13.7	1.12	13.55	3	0	99	0	1	126	107.6	-26.7	21	6	1,000	100	0.0	0.0
C- / 3.5	13.7	1.12	30.94	84	0	99	0	1	126	120.7	-26.3	33	6	1,000,000	0	0.0	0.0
C- / 3.5	13.7	1.12	30.73	1,161	0	99	0	1	126	118.8	-26.4	32	6	1,000	100	0.0	0.0
D- / 1.5	13.7	1.12	14.59	N/A	0	99	0	1	126	113.1	-26.5	26	6	0	0	0.0	0.0
D / 2.2	13.7	1.12	19.61	80	0	99	0	1	126	116.6	-26.4	29	6	0	0	0.0	0.0
D- / 1.3	6.2	0.44	9.69	N/A	0	0	0	100	752	N/A	N/A	12	4	1,000	100	5.8	0.0
D- / 1.3	6.3	0.44	9.46	N/A	0	0	0	100	752	N/A	N/A	8	4	1,000	100	0.0	0.0
D / 1.8	6.2	0.44	9.78	16	0	0	0	100	752	N/A	N/A	14	4	1,000,000	0	0.0	0.0
B / 8.2	5.4	0.48	13.18	184	34	50	15	1	86	N/A	N/A	30	6	1,000	100	5.8	0.0
B / 8.1	5.4	0.48	12.70	108	34	50	15	1	86	N/A	N/A	23	6	1,000	100	0.0	0.0

Data as of February 28, 2017

Fund Type	Fund Name	Ticker Symbol	Overall Investment Rating	Phone	Perfor-mance Rating/Pts	3 Mo	6 Mo	1Yr / Pct	3Yr / Pct	5Yr / Pct	Dividend Yield	Expense Ratio
	99 Pct = Best							Total Return % through 2/28/17	(Annualized)		Incl. in Returns	
	0 Pct = Worst											
GR	Neuberger Berman Long Short Inst	NLSIX	C	(800) 877-9700	D+ / 2.3	4.28	4.69	10.48 /13	1.95 /24	5.36 /24	0.00	1.67
MC	Neuberger Berman MC Intrinsc V A	NBRAX	C	(800) 877-9700	B / 7.9	5.81	12.73	29.23 /85	8.36 /82	13.15 /85	0.56	1.50
MC	Neuberger Berman MC Intrinsc V C	NBRCX	C+	(800) 877-9700	B+ / 8.3	5.58	12.30	28.30 /82	7.54 /76	12.31 /77	0.34	2.24
MC	Neuberger Berman MC Intrinsc V Inst	NBRTX	B-	(800) 877-9700	A- / 9.1	5.88	12.91	29.72 /86	8.73 /85	13.57 /90	0.77	1.09
MC	● Neuberger Berman MC Intrinsc V Inv	NBRVX	B-	(800) 877-9700	A- / 9.0	5.87	12.80	29.41 /85	8.51 /83	13.31 /87	0.49	1.31
MC	Neuberger Berman MC Intrinsc V R3	NBRRX	C+	(800) 877-9700	B+ / 8.7	5.79	12.58	28.99 /84	8.09 /80	12.89 /83	0.51	1.76
MC	● Neuberger Berman MC Intrinsc V Tr	NBREX	C+	(800) 877-9700	B+ / 8.9	5.79	12.70	29.25 /85	8.30 /81	13.11 /85	0.59	1.48
MC	Neuberger Berman MidCap Gr A	NMGAX	C-	(800) 877-9700	C / 5.2	6.70	7.90	23.26 /67	5.35 /58	9.93 /58	0.00	1.12
MC	● Neuberger Berman MidCap Gr Adv	NBMBX	C	(800) 877-9700	C+ / 6.2	6.62	7.85	23.06 /67	5.20 /56	9.76 /57	0.00	1.25
MC	Neuberger Berman MidCap Gr C	NMGCX	C-	(800) 877-9700	C+ / 5.7	6.49	7.51	22.36 /64	4.57 /49	9.12 /52	0.00	1.88
MC	Neuberger Berman MidCap Gr Inst	NBMLX	C-	(800) 877-9700	C+ / 6.7	6.79	8.09	23.74 /69	5.74 /62	10.35 /61	0.00	0.76
MC	● Neuberger Berman MidCap Gr Inv	NMANX	C-	(800) 877-9700	C+ / 6.5	6.73	7.98	23.40 /68	5.54 /60	10.11 /59	0.00	0.96
MC	Neuberger Berman MidCap Gr R3	NMGRX	C-	(800) 877-9700	C+ / 6.1	6.63	7.76	22.92 /66	5.08 /55	9.67 /56	0.00	1.39
GR	Neuberger Berman MidCap Gr R6	NRMGX	C-	(800) 877-9700	C+ / 6.7	6.85	8.14	23.85 /69	5.82 /63	--	0.00	0.67
MC	● Neuberger Berman MidCap Gr Tr	NBMTX	C	(800) 877-9700	C+ / 6.5	6.72	7.97	23.40 /68	5.49 /59	10.06 /59	0.00	0.99
GR	Neuberger Berman Mlt-Cp Opps Fd A	NMUAX	A	(800) 877-9700	B+ / 8.7	10.38	13.84	28.78 /83	8.68 /84	14.38 /95	0.38	1.11
GR	Neuberger Berman Mlt-Cp Opps Fd C	NMUCX	A	(800) 877-9700	A- / 9.0	10.20	13.35	27.77 /81	7.87 /78	13.51 /89	0.00	1.85
GR	Neuberger Berman Mlt-Cp Opps Fd	NMULX	A+	(800) 877-9700	A / 9.5	10.52	14.02	29.21 /85	9.08 /87	14.80 /96	0.80	0.76
OT	Neuberger Berman RB Comm Strat A	NRBAX	E	(800) 877-9700	E- / 0.0	4.02	8.00	16.29 /35	-12.24 / 0	--	0.00	1.84
OT	Neuberger Berman RB Comm Strat C	NRBCX	E	(800) 877-9700	E- / 0.0	3.84	6.63	14.42 /27	-13.17 / 0	--	0.00	2.70
OT	Neuberger Berman RB Comm Strat	NRBIX	E	(800) 877-9700	E- / 0.1	4.13	8.05	16.64 /37	-11.97 / 1	--	0.00	1.47
RE	Neuberger Berman Real Est A	NREAX	C-	(800) 877-9700	C+ / 5.7	8.79	-0.91	14.49 /28	9.32 /89	9.21 /52	1.97	1.42
RE	Neuberger Berman Real Est C	NRECX	C	(800) 877-9700	C+ / 6.2	8.62	-1.25	13.67 /24	8.51 /83	8.40 /45	1.32	2.18
RE	Neuberger Berman Real Est Inst	NBRIX	C	(800) 877-9700	B- / 7.0	8.86	-0.79	14.85 /29	9.69 /92	9.58 /55	2.42	1.05
RE	Neuberger Berman Real Est R3	NRERX	C	(800) 877-9700	C+ / 6.6	8.72	-1.05	14.14 /26	9.04 /87	8.92 /50	1.84	1.68
RE	Neuberger Berman Real Est R6	NRREX	C+	(800) 877-9700	B- / 7.1	8.89	-0.68	14.95 /30	9.78 /92	--	2.49	0.98
RE	● Neuberger Berman Real Est Trust	NBRFX	C	(800) 877-9700	C+ / 6.9	8.83	-0.82	14.68 /28	9.51 /90	9.39 /54	2.24	1.41
SC	Neuberger Berman SmallCap Gr A	NSNAX	D	(800) 877-9700	C / 5.4	6.01	11.62	36.48 /95	2.30 /26	10.38 /61	0.00	1.95
SC	● Neuberger Berman SmallCap Gr Adv	NBMVX	D+	(800) 877-9700	C+ / 6.4	5.94	11.49	36.14 /95	2.05 /24	10.10 /59	0.00	2.09
SC	Neuberger Berman SmallCap Gr C	NSNCX	D	(800) 877-9700	C+ / 6.0	5.80	11.19	35.43 /94	1.54 /21	9.57 /55	0.00	2.68
SC	Neuberger Berman SmallCap Gr Inst	NBSMX	C-	(800) 877-9700	C+ / 6.9	6.11	11.82	36.98 /96	2.67 /29	10.79 /64	0.00	1.55
SC	● Neuberger Berman SmallCap Gr Inv	NBMIX	D+	(800) 877-9700	C+ / 6.6	6.02	11.68	36.54 /95	2.36 /26	10.44 /62	0.00	1.87
SC	Neuberger Berman SmallCap Gr R3	NSNRX	D+	(800) 877-9700	C+ / 6.4	5.92	11.51	36.09 /95	2.06 /24	10.13 /59	0.00	2.25
SC	● Neuberger Berman SmallCap Gr Tr	NBMOX	D+	(800) 877-9700	C+ / 6.5	5.98	11.59	36.30 /95	2.19 /25	10.25 /60	0.00	1.94
GR	Neuberger Berman Socially Resp A	NRAAX	C+	(800) 877-9700	B- / 7.5	8.37	9.93	24.37 /71	8.58 /84	12.70 /81	0.98	1.05
GR	Neuberger Berman Socially Resp C	NRACX	C+	(800) 877-9700	B / 7.9	8.13	9.51	23.39 /68	7.77 /77	11.86 /73	0.41	1.79
GR	Neuberger Berman Socially Resp Inst	NBSLX	B+	(800) 877-9700	B+ / 8.8	8.45	10.11	24.81 /73	8.98 /87	13.13 /85	0.78	0.68
GR	● Neuberger Berman Socially Resp Inv	NBSRX	B+	(800) 877-9700	B+ / 8.6	8.39	9.99	24.58 /72	8.78 /85	12.92 /83	0.59	0.86
GR	Neuberger Berman Socially Resp R3	NRARX	C+	(800) 877-9700	B+ / 8.3	8.27	9.73	23.99 /70	8.31 /81	12.43 /78	0.87	1.29
GR	Neuberger Berman Socially Resp R6	NRSRX	B+	(800) 877-9700	B+ / 8.8	8.45	10.15	24.88 /73	9.06 /87	--	0.84	0.61
GR	● Neuberger Berman Socially Resp Tr	NBSTX	B-	(800) 877-9700	B+ / 8.5	8.32	9.92	24.32 /71	8.58 /84	12.72 /81	1.03	1.03
FS	Neuberger Berman Unconstrnd Bd A	NUBAX	D	(800) 877-9700	E+ / 0.8	1.87	1.95	8.61 / 9	0.01 /13	--	1.92	1.76
FS	Neuberger Berman Unconstrnd Bd C	NUBCX	D	(800) 877-9700	E+ / 0.8	1.68	1.57	7.79 / 7	-0.70 /10	--	1.27	2.50
FS	Neuberger Berman Unconstrnd Bd I	NUBIX	D+	(800) 877-9700	D- / 1.3	1.96	2.25	9.13 /10	0.42 /15	--	2.37	1.28
FS	Neuberger Berman Unconstrnd Bd	NRUBX	D+	(800) 877-9700	D- / 1.4	1.98	2.28	9.07 /10	0.52 /16	--	2.43	1.32
GL	Neuberger Berman Value A	NVAAX	B	(800) 877-9700	B+ / 8.5	4.27	12.55	38.87 /97	7.72 /77	12.38 /78	0.37	3.08
GL	Neuberger Berman Value C	NVACX	B+	(800) 877-9700	B+ / 8.9	4.09	12.10	37.92 /96	6.94 /72	11.56 /70	0.54	3.88
GL	Neuberger Berman Value Inst	NLRLX	B+	(800) 877-9700	A / 9.5	4.36	12.73	39.42 /97	8.16 /80	12.83 /82	0.67	2.69
GR	New Alternatives A	NALFX	D	(800) 423-8383	D+ / 2.8	8.56	-0.69	19.21 /48	2.96 /31	9.24 /53	1.23	1.15
GI	New Century Alternative Strategies	NCHPX	C-	(888) 639-0102	D- / 1.1	2.64	2.32	8.32 / 8	0.07 /14	1.95 / 8	0.21	2.40
GI	New Century Balanced	NCIPX	C-	(888) 639-0102	C- / 3.3	5.09	5.52	16.49 /36	3.21 /34	6.41 /31	0.72	2.15
GI	New Century Capital	NCCPX	C-	(888) 639-0102	C / 5.2	6.99	7.24	19.81 /51	4.98 /54	9.33 /53	0.10	1.96

● Denotes fund is closed to new investors
* Denotes fund is included in Section II

462

RISK	3 Year		NET ASSETS		ASSET				Portfolio Turnover Ratio	BULL / BEAR		FUND MANAGER		MINIMUMS		LOADS	
Risk Rating/Pts	Standard Deviation	Beta	NAV As of 2/28/17	Total $(Mil)	Cash %	Stocks %	Bonds %	Other %		Last Bull Market Return	Last Bear Market Return	Manager Quality Pct	Manager Tenure (Years)	Initial Purch. $	Additional Purch. $	Front End Load	Back End Load
B /8.2	5.4	0.48	13.39	2,042	34	50	15	1	86	N/A	N/A	35	6	1,000,000	0	0.0	0.0
C- /3.4	12.6	0.98	18.16	13	6	93	0	1	29	133.0	-25.7	62	6	1,000	100	0.0	0.0
C- /3.4	12.6	0.98	17.77	3	6	93	0	1	29	123.9	-26.0	52	6	1,000	100	5.8	0.0
C- /3.9	12.6	0.98	22.12	26	6	93	0	1	29	137.7	-25.6	67	6	1,000,000	0	0.0	0.0
C- /3.9	12.6	0.98	22.12	40	6	93	0	1	29	134.9	-25.8	64	6	1,000	100	0.0	0.0
C- /3.4	12.6	0.98	18.13	2	6	93	0	1	29	130.2	-25.9	60	6	0	0	0.0	0.0
C- /3.4	12.6	0.98	18.19	11	6	93	0	1	29	132.6	-25.7	62	6	0	0	0.0	0.0
C- /4.2	13.0	0.97	23.33	67	0	95	3	2	63	94.1	-15.1	26	14	1,000	100	5.8	0.0
C- /4.2	12.9	0.97	23.77	12	0	95	3	2	63	92.3	-15.2	25	14	0	0	0.0	0.0
C- /4.2	13.0	0.97	22.91	10	0	95	3	2	63	86.4	-15.3	19	14	1,000	100	0.0	0.0
C- /3.6	12.9	0.97	13.61	302	0	95	3	2	63	98.1	-15.0	31	14	1,000,000	0	0.0	0.0
C- /3.6	12.9	0.97	13.25	431	0	95	3	2	63	95.7	-15.0	29	14	1,000	100	0.0	0.0
C- /4.2	12.9	0.97	23.73	14	0	95	3	2	63	91.6	-15.2	24	14	0	0	0.0	0.0
C- /3.6	13.0	1.06	13.66	225	0	95	3	2	63	N/A	N/A	15	14	0	0	0.0	0.0
C- /4.2	12.9	0.97	23.43	66	0	95	3	2	63	95.2	-15.0	28	14	0	0	0.0	0.0
C+ /6.4	11.3	1.05	17.60	70	1	98	0	1	18	140.1	-17.7	45	8	1,000	100	5.8	0.0
C+ /6.4	11.3	1.05	17.00	41	1	98	0	1	18	130.6	-18.0	35	8	1,000	100	0.0	0.0
C+ /6.4	11.3	1.04	17.70	1,756	1	98	0	1	18	145.0	-17.6	50	8	1,000,000	0	0.0	0.0
C- /3.9	13.6	0.32	6.21	40	19	0	80	1	58	N/A	N/A	0	5	1,000	100	5.8	0.0
C- /3.9	13.5	0.32	5.95	N/A	19	0	80	1	58	N/A	N/A	0	5	1,000	100	0.0	0.0
C- /3.9	13.6	0.33	6.31	65	19	0	80	1	58	N/A	N/A	0	5	1,000,000	0	0.0	0.0
C /4.4	13.5	0.99	13.17	99	1	98	0	1	49	88.7	-16.8	55	12	1,000	100	5.8	0.0
C /4.4	13.5	0.99	13.18	22	1	98	0	1	49	81.2	-17.1	45	12	1,000	100	0.0	0.0
C /4.4	13.6	0.99	13.21	208	1	98	0	1	49	92.3	-16.7	59	12	1,000,000	0	0.0	0.0
C /4.4	13.5	0.99	13.14	22	1	98	0	1	49	86.2	-16.9	52	12	0	0	0.0	0.0
C /4.4	13.5	0.99	13.21	44	1	98	0	1	49	N/A	N/A	61	12	0	0	0.0	0.0
C /4.4	13.6	1.00	13.17	173	1	98	0	1	49	90.4	-16.7	57	12	1,000	100	0.0	0.0
D+ /2.6	18.7	1.06	32.96	3	0	97	1	2	164	98.8	-21.1	17	2	1,000	100	5.8	0.0
D+ /2.3	18.7	1.06	20.87	2	0	97	1	2	164	95.9	-21.2	15	2	0	0	0.0	0.0
D+ /2.3	18.7	1.06	20.07	2	0	97	1	2	164	90.9	-21.3	11	2	1,000	100	0.0	0.0
D+ /2.6	18.7	1.06	30.93	10	0	97	1	2	164	102.7	-21.0	20	2	1,000,000	0	0.0	0.0
D+ /2.6	18.7	1.06	30.12	47	0	97	1	2	164	99.3	-21.1	17	2	1,000	100	0.0	0.0
D+ /2.3	18.7	1.06	20.93	1	0	97	1	2	164	96.1	-21.1	15	2	0	0	0.0	0.0
D+ /2.6	18.7	1.06	32.63	4	0	97	1	2	164	97.4	-21.1	16	2	0	0	0.0	0.0
C- /4.1	10.2	0.96	20.52	122	0	98	1	1	25	116.8	-20.7	56	14	1,000	100	5.8	0.0
C- /4.1	10.2	0.96	19.94	56	0	98	1	1	25	108.2	-20.9	45	14	1,000	100	0.0	0.0
C /5.5	10.2	0.96	36.34	807	0	98	1	1	25	121.3	-20.5	61	14	1,000,000	0	0.0	0.0
C /5.5	10.2	0.96	36.32	741	0	98	1	1	25	119.1	-20.6	58	14	1,000	100	0.0	0.0
C- /4.1	10.2	0.96	20.27	36	0	98	1	1	25	114.0	-20.7	52	14	0	0	0.0	0.0
C /5.5	10.2	0.96	36.35	324	0	98	1	1	25	N/A	N/A	61	14	0	0	0.0	0.0
C- /4.2	10.2	0.96	20.76	251	0	98	1	1	25	117.1	-20.7	56	14	0	0	0.0	0.0
B- /7.2	4.4	0.22	9.30	N/A	6	0	93	1	50	N/A	N/A	39	3	1,000	100	4.3	0.0
B- /7.2	4.4	0.22	9.31	N/A	6	0	93	1	50	N/A	N/A	30	3	1,000	100	0.0	0.0
B- /7.2	4.4	0.22	9.31	10	6	0	93	1	50	N/A	N/A	46	3	1,000,000	0	0.0	0.0
B- /7.2	4.3	0.21	9.32	51	6	0	93	1	50	N/A	N/A	47	3	0	0	0.0	0.0
C /5.1	13.6	0.79	17.51	5	0	100	0	0	118	114.1	-15.8	98	6	1,000	100	5.8	0.0
C /5.1	13.6	0.79	17.09	4	0	100	0	0	118	105.6	-16.1	98	6	1,000	100	0.0	0.0
C /5.0	13.6	0.79	17.60	11	0	100	0	0	118	118.9	-15.8	98	6	1,000,000	0	0.0	0.0
C /4.5	17.5	0.94	50.77	190	9	90	0	1	37	67.3	-24.7	7	35	2,500	250	4.8	0.0
B /8.5	4.7	0.41	12.89	77	27	46	23	4	28	22.2	-12.7	22	17	1,000	0	0.0	2.0
C+ /6.2	7.5	0.70	14.56	52	7	60	29	4	34	55.4	-13.2	24	14	1,000	0	0.0	2.0
C /4.5	10.4	0.98	17.33	89	8	90	1	1	48	87.6	-18.9	14	5	1,000	0	0.0	2.0

Fund Type	Fund Name	Ticker Symbol	Overall Investment Rating	Phone	Performance Rating/Pts	3 Mo	6 Mo	1Yr / Pct	3Yr / Pct	5Yr / Pct	Dividend Yield	Expense Ratio
								Total Return % through 2/28/17	Annualized		Incl. in Returns	
FO	New Century International	NCFPX	E	(888) 639-0102	D- / 1.0	6.15	2.89	12.46 /20	-0.53 /11	3.10 /11	0.91	2.51
GL	New Covenant Balanced Growth	NCBGX	C	(877) 835-4531	C- / 4.2	4.36	4.61	13.44 /23	5.02 /54	7.04 /35	0.93	1.19
BA	New Covenant Balanced Income	NCBIX	C	(877) 835-4531	D+ / 2.5	2.80	2.13	8.32 / 8	3.74 /40	4.75 /20	1.19	1.14
GL	New Covenant Growth	NCGFX	C	(877) 835-4531	B- / 7.1	6.84	8.58	21.99 /62	6.90 /71	10.70 /63	0.63	1.14
GL	Newfound Multi-Asset Income A	NFMAX	U	(855) 394-9777	U /	4.17	1.13	8.58 / 9	--	--	2.41	3.15
GL	Newfound Risk Managed Glbl Sector	NFGIX	U	(855) 394-9777	U /	5.85	5.85	14.89 /29	--	--	0.61	2.06
AA	NH 529 Fidelity UNIQUE CIP 100%		C+	(800) 544-8544	C+ / 6.6	7.20	7.53	22.52 /65	5.89 /63	10.27 /60	0.00	1.00
AA	NH 529 Fidelity UNIQUE CIP 70%E		B	(800) 544-8544	C / 5.0	5.66	5.16	17.64 /41	5.05 /55	8.25 /44	0.00	0.93
AA	NH 529 Fidelity UNIQUE CIP Clg Ptf		C	(800) 544-8544	D / 1.8	2.48	0.98	7.48 / 7	2.50 /28	3.18 /11	0.00	0.67
AA	NH 529 Fidelity UNIQUE CIP Csv Ptf		C	(800) 544-8544	D- / 1.0	0.85	-0.39	2.47 / 2	1.38 /20	1.33 / 7	0.00	0.59
AA	NH 529 Fidelity UNIQUE CIP Idx		C+	(800) 544-8544	C+ / 6.8	7.54	8.47	22.90 /66	6.01 /64	10.46 /62	0.00	0.27
AA	NH 529 Fidelity UNIQUE CIP Idx		C+	(800) 544-8544	D / 1.9	2.51	1.07	6.78 / 6	2.77 /30	4.75 /20	0.00	0.31
AA	NH 529 Fidelity UNIQUE CIP Idx		C+	(800) 544-8544	D+ / 2.6	3.44	2.29	9.59 /11	3.51 /37	6.14 /29	0.00	0.30
AA	NH 529 Fidelity UNIQUE CIP Idx		B-	(800) 544-8544	C- / 3.4	4.29	3.50	12.28 /19	4.18 /45	7.43 /38	0.00	0.29
AA	NH 529 Fidelity UNIQUE CIP Idx		B-	(800) 544-8544	C / 4.3	5.16	4.65	15.14 /30	4.76 /52	8.50 /46	0.00	0.28
AA	NH 529 Fidelity UNIQUE CIP Idx		B	(800) 544-8544	C / 4.6	5.56	5.12	15.98 /34	4.86 /53	7.98 /42	0.00	0.30
AA	NH 529 Fidelity UNIQUE CIP Idx Clg		C+	(800) 544-8544	D- / 1.5	2.05	0.56	4.95 / 4	2.15 /25	2.74 /10	0.00	0.33
AA	NH 529 Fidelity UNIQUE CIP Idx Csv		C	(800) 544-8544	E+ / 0.9	0.53	-0.90	0.69 / 2	1.17 /19	0.94 / 6	0.00	0.34
AA	NH 529 Fidelity UNIQUE CIP Ptf		C+	(800) 544-8544	D+ / 2.3	3.00	1.55	9.51 /10	3.25 /34	5.27 /23	0.00	0.86
AA	NH 529 Fidelity UNIQUE CIP Ptf		C+	(800) 544-8544	C- / 3.2	3.88	2.67	12.20 /19	3.95 /42	6.59 /32	0.00	0.92
AA	NH 529 Fidelity UNIQUE CIP Ptf		B-	(800) 544-8544	C- / 3.9	4.64	3.66	14.72 /29	4.47 /48	7.78 /40	0.00	0.97
AA	NH 529 Fidelity UNIQUE CIP Ptf		B-	(800) 544-8544	C / 4.8	5.46	4.71	17.25 /39	4.92 /53	8.80 /49	0.00	0.99
GR	Nicholas	NICSX	C+	(800) 544-6547	C / 5.4	7.28	6.53	14.81 /29	5.70 /62	12.99 /84	0.65	0.72
IN	Nicholas Equity Income	NSEIX	B+	(800) 544-6547	B / 7.8	7.48	8.30	23.05 /67	8.00 /79	12.41 /78	1.71	0.72
GR	Nicholas High Income I	NCINX	D	(800) 544-6547	D / 2.2	3.16	3.40	11.88 /18	2.05 /24	4.49 /18	4.55	0.71
GR	Nicholas High Income N	NNHIX	D	(800) 544-6547	D / 2.0	3.03	3.18	11.48 /16	1.69 /22	4.12 /16	4.19	1.06
GR	Nicholas II I	NCTWX	C+	(800) 544-6547	B / 7.6	7.78	8.49	21.34 /59	7.82 /78	11.92 /74	0.27	0.61
GR	Nicholas II N	NNTWX	C+	(800) 544-6547	B- / 7.3	7.71	8.31	20.93 /57	7.44 /75	11.53 /70	0.00	0.96
GR	Nicholas Limited Edition I	NCLEX	C+	(800) 544-6547	B- / 7.0	5.22	7.20	26.07 /76	6.58 /69	10.65 /63	0.00	0.86
GR	Nicholas Limited Edition N	NNLEX	C	(800) 544-6547	C+ / 6.8	5.15	7.00	25.65 /75	6.21 /66	10.27 /60	0.00	1.21
EM	Nile Africa Frontier and Emerging A	NAFAX	E	(877) 682-3742	E / 0.3	4.85	12.21	27.68 /81	-5.70 / 2	1.50 / 7	0.00	2.71
EM	Nile Africa Frontier and Emerging C	NAFCX	E	(877) 682-3742	E / 0.4	4.64	11.69	26.63 /78	-6.42 / 2	0.73 / 6	0.00	3.46
EM	Nile Africa Frontier and Emerging I	NAFIX	E	(877) 682-3742	E / 0.5	4.90	12.30	27.90 /81	-5.49 / 2	1.75 / 8	0.00	2.46
GL	NJ 529 NJBest CSP Age-Based 0-8		B-	(800) 342-5236	C+ / 6.0	7.91	7.84	21.59 /60	4.81 /52	9.81 /57	0.00	1.23
GL	NJ 529 NJBest CSP Age-Based		C+	(800) 342-5236	C- / 3.1	4.90	4.72	12.97 /22	3.07 /32	5.77 /27	0.00	1.05
GL	NJ 529 NJBest CSP Age-Based 17 &		C+	(800) 342-5236	D / 2.1	3.48	3.32	9.07 /10	2.28 /26	3.69 /14	0.00	1.02
GL	NJ 529 NJBest CSP Age-Based 9-12		B-	(800) 342-5236	C / 4.4	6.34	6.18	17.05 /39	3.90 /42	7.72 /40	0.00	1.13
GL	NJ 529 NJBest CSP Corefolio Port		B+	(800) 342-5236	B- / 7.0	8.24	9.35	24.82 /73	5.67 /61	10.56 /62	0.00	1.10
GL	NJ 529 NJBest CSP Gro & Inc Port		C+	(800) 342-5236	C- / 3.1	4.93	4.75	13.02 /22	2.99 /32	5.74 /27	0.00	1.09
GL	NJ 529 NJBest CSP Growth Port		B-	(800) 342-5236	C+ / 5.9	7.78	7.78	21.54 /60	4.73 /51	9.76 /57	0.00	1.23
IX	NJ 529 NJBest CSP S&P 500 Idx		A+	(800) 342-5236	A / 9.3	8.02	9.94	24.64 /72	10.48 /96	13.73 /91	0.00	0.85
GR	North Country Equity Growth	NCEGX	B+	(888) 350-2990	B / 7.9	7.74	9.29	21.67 /61	8.28 /81	12.23 /76	0.41	1.03
IN	North Star Dividend I	NSDVX	B	(800) 595-7827	C+ / 6.5	1.05	7.24	21.50 /60	8.02 /79	--	1.79	1.50
SC	North Star Micro Cap I	NSMVX	C	(800) 595-7827	C+ / 6.3	0.67	11.71	31.56 /89	4.71 /51	--	0.00	1.35
AA	North Star Opportunity A	NSOPX	C-	(800) 595-7827	C / 4.7	4.78	8.82	26.83 /79	4.67 /50	8.42 /46	0.57	1.62
AA	North Star Opportunity I	NSOIX	C+	(800) 595-7827	C+ / 6.0	4.86	8.98	27.22 /80	4.66 /50	9.29 /53	0.82	1.37
GR	Northeast Investors Growth	NTHFX	C	(800) 225-6704	C+ / 6.7	8.55	8.14	19.61 /50	6.28 /67	9.47 /54	0.23	1.30
EM	Northern Active M Emg Mkts Eqty	NMMEX	D+	(800) 595-9111	C / 4.6	9.57	7.27	31.53 /89	0.86 /17	0.41 / 5	1.73	1.23
FO	Northern Active M Intl Equity	NMIEX	E+	(800) 595-9111	E / 0.5	6.03	2.48	12.34 /19	-2.62 / 5	2.26 / 9	1.65	0.94
GR	Northern Active M US Equity	NMUSX	U	(800) 595-9111	U /	6.59	8.10	--	--	--	0.00	0.84
EM	Northern Emerg Mkts Eq Idx	NOEMX	D	(800) 595-9111	C- / 4.0	8.72	5.27	28.83 /84	1.00 /18	-0.60 / 4	1.76	0.36
GR	Northern Funds Large Cap Equity	NOGEX	C+	(800) 595-9111	C+ / 6.8	5.69	6.62	19.73 /51	7.35 /74	11.18 /67	0.73	0.98

99 Pct = Best
0 Pct = Worst

● Denotes fund is closed to new investors
★ Denotes fund is included in Section II

www.thestreetratings.com

Risk Rating/Pts	3 Year Standard Deviation	Beta	NAV As of 2/28/17	Total $(Mil)	Cash %	Stocks %	Bonds %	Other %	Portfolio Turnover Ratio	Last Bull Market Return	Last Bear Market Return	Manager Quality Pct	Manager Tenure (Years)	Initial Purch. $	Additional Purch. $	Front End Load	Back End Load
C- /3.7	10.3	0.81	11.62	33	2	94	3	1	45	37.7	-25.0	69	5	1,000	0	0.0	2.0
B- /7.0	6.5	0.96	94.45	291	3	54	41	2	14	61.0	-11.4	78	N/A	500	100	0.0	0.0
B /8.4	3.9	0.61	20.44	79	2	33	63	2	17	38.2	-6.2	65	N/A	500	100	0.0	0.0
C- /3.9	10.9	0.75	38.88	412	6	90	2	2	103	103.4	-19.0	98	2	500	100	0.0	0.0
U /	N/A	N/A	9.85	34	2	22	74	2	443	N/A	N/A	N/A	3	2,500	250	5.8	1.0
U /	N/A	N/A	10.15	40	0	99	0	1	396	N/A	N/A	N/A	3	1,000,000	10,000	0.0	1.0
C+ /6.6	10.5	1.59	20.84	571	2	95	1	2	21	99.4	-23.0	10	12	50	25	0.0	0.0
B /8.1	7.8	1.19	22.21	278	2	67	30	1	24	74.2	-17.3	27	12	50	25	0.0	0.0
B+ /9.5	3.2	0.45	20.70	1,477	8	21	69	2	20	23.4	-4.4	63	12	50	25	0.0	0.0
B+ /9.9	1.4	0.09	15.34	93	14	0	85	1	15	8.6	0.7	78	12	50	25	0.0	0.0
C+ /6.8	10.3	1.59	17.55	213	1	97	1	1	22	98.1	-19.4	11	11	50	25	0.0	0.0
B+ /9.8	3.5	0.54	15.12	288	8	26	65	1	28	39.6	-7.2	60	11	50	25	0.0	0.0
B+ /9.6	4.8	0.75	15.65	318	5	39	54	2	25	52.8	-10.6	48	11	50	25	0.0	0.0
B+ /9.2	6.0	0.94	16.27	329	3	51	44	2	21	66.0	-13.7	38	11	50	25	0.0	0.0
B /8.6	7.3	1.14	15.29	292	1	63	34	2	16	77.0	-15.8	28	10	50	25	0.0	0.0
B /8.9	7.2	1.13	17.85	150	0	68	30	2	29	68.2	-11.3	30	11	50	25	0.0	0.0
B+ /9.9	2.4	0.34	14.42	206	10	19	69	2	37	19.6	-0.3	69	11	50	25	0.0	0.0
B+ /9.7	1.4	0.03	13.17	65	19	0	80	1	22	5.3	4.4	80	11	50	25	0.0	0.0
B+ /9.4	4.4	0.66	20.96	1,914	6	29	64	1	21	45.5	-12.4	54	12	50	25	0.0	0.0
B+ /9.1	5.7	0.87	21.15	1,573	4	42	52	2	20	59.3	-16.2	42	12	50	25	0.0	0.0
B /8.6	6.9	1.06	18.70	832	4	54	41	1	18	71.9	-19.1	31	12	50	25	0.0	0.0
B /8.1	8.1	1.23	14.68	398	3	66	30	1	16	82.8	-21.2	23	10	50	25	0.0	0.0
C+ /6.1	10.4	0.90	65.33	2,883	10	89	0	1	29	125.4	-15.7	28	6	500	100	0.0	0.0
C+ /6.2	10.9	1.01	20.74	535	15	84	0	1	25	109.8	-15.1	42	6	500	100	0.0	0.0
C+ /5.9	4.8	0.32	9.24	102	3	3	93	1	41	38.8	-6.0	58	14	100,000	100	0.0	0.0
C+ /5.9	4.8	0.32	9.38	8	3	3	93	1	41	36.2	-6.2	53	14	500	100	0.0	0.0
C /4.7	11.7	1.04	26.44	660	5	94	0	1	30	118.7	-19.6	35	24	100,000	100	0.0	0.0
C /4.8	11.7	1.04	26.03	99	5	94	0	1	30	114.6	-19.7	31	24	500	100	0.0	0.0
C /4.5	13.3	1.07	24.80	317	9	90	0	1	28	103.5	-19.0	19	24	100,000	100	0.0	0.0
C /4.4	13.3	1.07	23.48	34	9	90	0	1	28	99.7	-19.1	17	24	500	100	0.0	0.0
C- /3.5	17.5	0.82	11.67	12	1	98	0	1	82	35.4	-23.8	5	7	1,000	100	5.8	2.0
C- /3.4	17.4	0.82	11.27	1	1	98	0	1	82	29.9	-24.0	4	7	1,000	100	0.0	2.0
C- /3.5	17.4	0.81	11.78	4	1	98	0	1	82	37.1	-23.7	5	7	250,000	25,000	0.0	2.0
B- /7.5	10.1	0.75	33.29	87	0	0	0	100	0	93.6	-21.2	95	14	25	25	0.0	0.0
B+ /9.0	6.0	0.91	24.83	206	0	0	0	100	0	47.7	-10.7	61	14	25	25	0.0	0.0
B+ /9.7	4.2	0.61	20.21	117	0	0	0	100	0	28.9	-5.0	67	14	25	25	0.0	0.0
B /8.2	8.0	0.60	28.70	217	0	0	0	100	0	68.6	-15.9	93	14	25	25	0.0	0.0
B- /7.3	10.8	0.80	31.93	56	0	0	0	100	0	100.4	-18.9	96	14	25	25	0.0	0.0
B /8.9	6.1	0.46	24.48	42	0	0	0	100	0	47.6	-10.6	90	14	25	25	0.0	0.0
B- /7.5	10.1	0.75	33.24	87	0	0	0	100	0	92.9	-21.0	95	14	25	25	0.0	0.0
B /8.4	10.3	1.00	33.94	109	0	0	0	100	0	131.7	-16.4	73	14	25	25	0.0	0.0
C+ /5.9	10.8	1.01	16.40	125	0	97	2	1	28	113.1	-16.3	45	5	1,000	100	0.0	0.0
B /8.5	8.7	0.47	19.99	71	0	0	0	100	25	N/A	N/A	90	7	5,000	500	0.0	2.0
C /4.9	13.5	0.75	27.29	78	0	0	0	100	34	N/A	N/A	69	20	5,000	500	0.0	2.0
C /5.5	12.3	1.64	12.79	N/A	8	71	19	2	61	N/A	N/A	5	6	2,500	500	5.8	2.0
C /5.5	12.3	1.64	12.75	78	8	71	19	2	61	N/A	N/A	5	6	5,000	500	0.0	2.0
C /4.7	11.2	0.98	15.99	54	0	99	0	1	28	89.7	-20.1	25	37	1,000	0	0.0	0.0
C /4.3	15.7	0.96	17.58	914	4	95	0	1	38	26.2	-25.5	65	5	2,500	50	0.0	2.0
C+ /5.6	11.5	0.91	9.64	1,273	4	95	0	1	70	30.6	-23.3	41	11	2,500	50	0.0	2.0
U /	N/A	N/A	11.41	449	0	0	0	100	0	N/A	N/A	N/A	1	2,500	50	0.0	0.0
C- /4.1	15.9	0.98	10.39	2,037	1	98	0	1	34	20.5	-27.2	66	10	2,500	50	0.0	2.0
C+ /5.8	11.3	1.06	21.28	121	0	99	0	1	28	113.8	-19.4	28	6	2,500	50	0.0	0.0

				PERFORMANCE								
	99 Pct = Best				Perfor-	Total Return % through 2/28/17					Incl. in Returns	
	0 Pct = Worst		Overall		mance				Annualized		Dividend	Expense
Fund		Ticker	Investment		Rating/Pts	3 Mo	6 Mo	1Yr / Pct	3Yr / Pct	5Yr / Pct	Yield	Ratio
Type	Fund Name	Symbol	Rating	Phone								
EM	Northern Glbl Sustainability Index	NSRIX	C+	(800) 595-9111	C / 5.1	6.89	6.18	20.16 / 53	4.87 / 53	9.38 / 54	2.15	0.37
RE	Northern Global Real Estate Index	NGREX	C-	(800) 595-9111	C- / 3.8	6.94	-2.42	13.96 / 25	5.72 / 62	7.43 / 38	4.18	0.53
BA	Northern Global Tactical Asset Allo	BBALX	C+	(800) 637-1380	C- / 3.8	4.83	4.86	15.73 / 33	3.70 / 39	5.93 / 28	2.81	0.84
CV	Northern Income Equity	NOIEX	C	(800) 595-9111	B- / 7.2	6.43	8.08	18.91 / 47	8.11 / 80	10.62 / 63	1.91	1.13
FO	Northern Intl Eqty Index	NOINX	D-	(800) 595-9111	D- / 1.1	7.20	4.35	15.92 / 34	-0.82 / 10	5.09 / 22	3.07	0.29
FO	Northern Intl Equity	NOIGX	E+	(800) 595-9111	E+ / 0.8	4.78	3.93	19.85 / 51	-2.15 / 6	4.11 / 16	1.51	1.22
GR	Northern Large Cap Core	NOLCX	A	(800) 595-9111	B / 8.2	6.84	9.25	22.49 / 64	8.99 / 87	13.53 / 89	1.70	0.59
GR	Northern Large Cap Value	NOLVX	A+	(800) 595-9111	A- / 9.1	6.11	12.77	29.82 / 86	8.74 / 85	12.10 / 75	1.46	1.09
MC	Northern Midcap Index	NOMIX	A-	(800) 595-9111	A / 9.4	6.54	11.25	31.51 / 89	9.44 / 90	13.65 / 90	1.23	0.18
OT	Northern Mlt-Mgr Glb Listed Infra	NMFIX	D+	(800) 595-9111	D+ / 2.9	7.46	1.93	16.61 / 37	2.55 / 28	--	2.42	1.02
RE	Northern Multi Mgr Glbl Rl Estate	NMMGX	E	(800) 595-9111	C- / 3.0	5.75	-3.48	12.94 / 21	4.90 / 53	6.74 / 33	4.75	1.05
SC	Northern Small Cap Core	NSGRX	B	(800) 595-9111	B+ / 8.6	4.68	11.95	32.86 / 91	7.31 / 74	13.31 / 87	0.57	0.93
SC	Northern Small Cap Index	NSIDX	B	(800) 595-9111	B+ / 8.8	5.17	12.54	36.05 / 95	6.81 / 71	12.75 / 81	1.01	0.18
SC	Northern Small Cap Value	NOSGX	A	(800) 595-9111	A+ / 9.6	4.23	14.29	34.96 / 94	9.36 / 89	13.64 / 90	0.90	1.24
* IX	Northern Stock Index	NOSIX	A+	(800) 595-9111	A / 9.3	7.98	9.95	24.83 / 73	10.51 / 96	13.88 / 92	1.93	0.11
TC	Northern Technology	NTCHX	B-	(800) 595-9111	B+ / 8.7	10.12	7.85	27.44 / 80	8.42 / 82	10.36 / 61	0.00	1.37
GR	Northpointe Large Cap Value Inv		U	(866) 777-7818	U /	5.30	7.80	21.96 / 62	--	--	0.94	2.21
GR	NorthQuest Capital	NQCFX	C+	(800) 698-5261	C+ / 5.8	6.86	6.18	17.46 / 40	6.00 / 64	8.31 / 45	0.00	1.87
GR	Nuance Concentrated Value Inst	NCVLX	B+	(855) 682-6233	B / 7.8	5.06	9.75	26.70 / 78	7.43 / 75	13.23 / 86	0.83	1.17
GR	Nuance Concentrated Value Inv	NCAVX	C+	(855) 682-6233	C+ / 6.7	5.02	9.56	26.35 / 77	7.12 / 73	--	0.56	1.42
GR	Nuance Concentrated Value L/S Invt	NCLSX	U	(855) 682-6233	U /	-0.52	5.60	20.14 / 53	--	--	0.00	3.88
MC	Nuance Mid Cap Value Institutional	NMVLX	A+	(855) 682-6233	A / 9.5	6.75	13.96	29.56 / 85	9.84 / 92	--	0.64	1.46
MC	Nuance Mid Cap Value Investor	NMAVX	A+	(855) 682-6233	B+ / 8.9	6.72	13.77	29.27 / 85	9.60 / 91	--	0.45	1.71
GR	Nuveen Concentrated Core A	NCADX	C+	(800) 257-8787	C+ / 6.8	7.06	11.59	20.75 / 56	7.91 / 78	--	1.79	1.23
GR	Nuveen Concentrated Core C	NCAEX	B	(800) 257-8787	B- / 7.2	6.86	11.18	19.87 / 51	7.12 / 73	--	1.22	1.98
GR	Nuveen Concentrated Core I	NCAFX	B+	(800) 257-8787	B / 7.9	7.11	11.68	21.03 / 58	8.18 / 80	--	2.12	0.97
IN	Nuveen Core Dividend A	NCDAX	C+	(800) 257-8787	C+ / 5.6	5.79	7.90	20.08 / 52	6.91 / 71	--	1.73	1.29
IN	Nuveen Core Dividend C	NCCDX	C+	(800) 257-8787	C+ / 6.1	5.57	7.52	19.15 / 48	6.11 / 65	--	1.16	2.04
IN	Nuveen Core Dividend I	NCDIX	C+	(800) 257-8787	C+ / 6.9	5.90	8.08	20.37 / 54	7.18 / 73	--	2.06	1.04
IN	Nuveen Dividend Value A	FFEIX	B	(800) 257-8787	B / 8.2	7.41	12.98	30.29 / 87	8.37 / 82	12.02 / 74	1.35	1.04
IN	Nuveen Dividend Value C	FFECX	B	(800) 257-8787	B+ / 8.7	7.24	12.61	29.38 / 85	7.56 / 76	11.19 / 67	0.78	1.79
IN	Nuveen Dividend Value I	FAQIX	B+	(800) 257-8787	A / 9.3	7.47	13.14	30.62 / 87	8.65 / 84	12.30 / 77	1.63	0.79
IN	Nuveen Dividend Value R3	FEISX	B+	(800) 257-8787	A- / 9.0	7.37	12.88	30.06 / 86	8.10 / 80	11.75 / 72	1.32	1.29
IN	Nuveen Dividend Value R6	FFEFX	B+	(800) 257-8787	A / 9.3	7.45	13.16	30.78 / 88	8.74 / 85	--	1.63	0.70
IX	● Nuveen Equity Index A	FAEIX	A	(800) 257-8787	A- / 9.0	7.83	9.71	24.21 / 71	9.98 / 93	13.31 / 87	1.37	0.71
IX	● Nuveen Equity Index C	FCEIX	A-	(800) 257-8787	B+ / 8.5	7.61	9.26	23.26 / 67	9.17 / 88	12.47 / 79	0.70	1.46
IX	● Nuveen Equity Index I	FEIIX	A	(800) 257-8787	A- / 9.2	7.90	9.85	24.52 / 72	10.27 / 95	13.61 / 90	1.59	0.46
IX	● Nuveen Equity Index R3	FADSX	A-	(800) 257-8787	B+ / 8.9	7.78	9.55	23.88 / 69	9.72 / 92	13.03 / 84	1.26	0.96
GR	Nuveen Equity Long/Short A	NELAX	B-	(800) 257-8787	C+ / 6.2	4.62	13.80	20.57 / 55	6.98 / 72	9.19 / 52	0.00	3.78
GR	Nuveen Equity Long/Short C	NELCX	B-	(800) 257-8787	C+ / 6.7	4.43	13.35	19.65 / 50	6.18 / 66	8.36 / 45	0.00	4.53
GR	Nuveen Equity Long/Short I	NELIX	A-	(800) 257-8787	B- / 7.4	4.69	13.95	20.89 / 57	7.25 / 74	9.46 / 54	0.00	3.52
GR	Nuveen Equity Market Neutral A	NMAEX	C	(800) 257-8787	D- / 1.3	-1.17	5.73	4.00 / 3	3.52 / 37	--	0.00	3.29
GR	Nuveen Equity Market Neutral C	NMECX	C	(800) 257-8787	D / 1.6	-1.37	5.30	3.20 / 3	2.75 / 30	--	0.00	4.06
GR	Nuveen Equity Market Neutral I	NIMEX	C+	(800) 257-8787	D / 2.0	-1.11	5.87	4.29 / 3	3.79 / 40	--	0.00	3.06
GL	Nuveen Global Infrastructure A	FGIAX	D+	(800) 257-8787	C- / 3.4	7.43	1.26	13.82 / 25	5.57 / 60	8.63 / 47	2.75	1.42
GL	Nuveen Global Infrastructure C	FGNCX	D+	(800) 257-8787	C- / 3.7	6.99	0.57	12.63 / 20	4.66 / 50	7.74 / 40	2.17	2.17
GL	Nuveen Global Infrastructure I	FGIYX	C-	(800) 257-8787	C / 4.8	7.52	1.45	14.16 / 26	5.83 / 63	8.90 / 50	3.27	1.17
GL	Nuveen Global Infrastructure R3	FGNRX	C-	(800) 257-8787	C- / 4.2	7.13	0.87	13.30 / 23	5.22 / 57	8.29 / 45	2.66	1.67
AA	Nuveen Gresham Divsfd Comm Str A	NGVAX	E	(800) 257-8787	E- / 0.0	2.56	7.42	16.14 / 35	-13.36 / 0	--	0.00	1.53
AA	Nuveen Gresham Divsfd Comm Str C	NGVCX	E	(800) 257-8787	E- / 0.0	2.37	6.97	15.32 / 31	-13.97 / 0	--	0.00	2.29
AA	Nuveen Gresham Divsfd Comm Str I	NGVIX	E	(800) 257-8787	E- / 0.0	2.61	7.51	16.46 / 36	-13.09 / 0	--	0.00	1.26
AA	Nuveen Gresham Lng Sht Comm Str	NGSAX	D+	(800) 257-8787	E- / 0.2	-1.80	-2.71	-5.71 / 0	-1.58 / 8	--	0.70	3.83

● Denotes fund is closed to new investors
* Denotes fund is included in Section II

466

I. Index of Stock Mutual Funds

Risk Rating/Pts	3 Year Standard Deviation	Beta	NAV As of 2/28/17	Total $(Mil)	Cash %	Stocks %	Bonds %	Other %	Portfolio Turnover Ratio	Last Bull Market Return	Last Bear Market Return	Manager Quality Pct	Manager Tenure (Years)	Initial Purch. $	Additional Purch. $	Front End Load	Back End Load
C+ / 6.5	10.1	0.46	12.44	292	3	96	0	1	17	84.2	-19.3	93	9	2,500	50	0.0	2.0
C+ / 6.5	12.1	0.82	10.08	1,907	11	88	0	1	9	72.3	-20.7	33	9	2,500	50	0.0	2.0
B / 8.1	6.6	0.98	12.33	83	5	56	37	2	20	51.9	-11.2	29	6	2,500	50	0.0	0.0
C- / 3.8	9.1	0.84	13.39	235	1	98	0	1	13	93.5	-15.3	93	3	2,500	50	0.0	0.0
C / 5.5	11.4	0.92	11.04	4,243	2	97	0	1	31	48.4	-23.6	66	10	2,500	50	0.0	2.0
C / 4.8	13.3	1.04	8.78	151	2	97	0	1	13	47.0	-26.1	49	N/A	2,500	50	0.0	2.0
B- / 7.3	10.4	0.99	17.11	131	0	98	0	2	56	131.1	-15.5	56	6	2,500	50	0.0	0.0
C+ / 6.6	11.2	1.02	15.40	96	0	99	0	1	60	122.9	-25.5	50	2	2,500	50	0.0	0.0
C / 5.2	12.1	1.00	18.66	2,146	3	96	0	1	20	138.3	-22.7	72	11	2,500	50	0.0	0.0
C+ / 6.0	10.2	0.69	12.34	1,202	18	81	0	1	57	N/A	N/A	20	5	2,500	50	0.0	0.0
D / 1.8	11.7	0.82	10.72	224	11	88	0	1	94	65.8	-20.0	25	5	2,500	50	0.0	2.0
C / 5.1	14.6	0.92	24.02	529	3	95	0	2	13	134.5	-23.8	80	7	2,500	50	0.0	0.0
C / 4.3	15.8	1.00	12.96	1,154	2	97	0	1	19	130.3	-25.1	73	11	2,500	50	0.0	0.0
C+ / 5.9	14.4	0.88	24.22	3,737	4	94	0	2	25	138.1	-21.4	90	16	2,500	50	0.0	0.0
B- / 7.0	10.3	1.00	28.53	7,788	0	98	0	2	5	133.4	-16.3	73	11	2,500	50	0.0	0.0
C- / 3.9	14.5	1.18	22.51	76	1	98	0	1	54	101.7	-18.9	26	13	2,500	50	0.0	0.0
U /	N/A	N/A	12.14	26	0	97	1	2	126	N/A	N/A	N/A	3	1,000	500	0.0	2.0
C+ / 6.5	9.1	0.76	15.15	3	6	93	0	1	18	80.9	-16.9	50	15	1,000	100	0.0	0.0
C+ / 6.1	10.7	0.83	14.66	512	9	90	0	1	93	123.5	N/A	59	6	1,000,000	100	0.0	0.0
C+ / 6.1	10.7	0.83	14.62	104	9	90	0	1	93	N/A	N/A	55	6	2,500	100	5.0	0.0
U /	N/A	N/A	11.42	48	0	0	0	100	0	N/A	N/A	N/A	1	1,000,000	100	0.0	0.0
B- / 7.2	11.1	0.81	12.11	291	4	95	0	1	105	N/A	N/A	86	6	1,000,000	100	0.0	0.0
B- / 7.2	11.1	0.80	12.08	18	4	95	0	1	105	N/A	N/A	85	6	2,500	100	5.0	0.0
C+ / 6.3	13.1	1.15	28.41	37	0	100	0	0	103	N/A	N/A	24	4	3,000	100	5.8	0.0
C+ / 6.3	13.1	1.15	28.00	22	0	100	0	0	103	N/A	N/A	17	4	3,000	100	0.0	0.0
C+ / 6.3	13.2	1.15	28.42	29	0	100	0	0	103	N/A	N/A	26	4	100,000	0	0.0	0.0
C+ / 6.5	11.6	1.07	26.35	27	0	99	0	1	127	N/A	N/A	22	4	3,000	100	5.8	0.0
C+ / 6.5	11.6	1.07	26.29	7	0	99	0	1	127	N/A	N/A	16	4	3,000	100	0.0	0.0
C+ / 6.5	11.6	1.07	26.36	12	0	99	0	1	127	N/A	N/A	25	4	100,000	0	0.0	0.0
C / 4.9	10.6	0.99	15.00	281	0	99	0	1	67	114.9	-17.0	49	5	3,000	100	5.8	0.0
C / 4.9	10.7	0.99	14.75	45	0	99	0	1	67	106.3	-17.2	38	5	3,000	100	0.0	0.0
C / 4.9	10.6	0.99	15.18	674	0	99	0	1	67	117.8	-16.9	53	5	100,000	0	0.0	0.0
C / 4.9	10.7	0.99	14.94	36	0	99	0	1	67	112.1	-17.1	45	5	0	0	0.0	0.0
C / 4.9	10.6	0.99	15.24	53	0	99	0	1	67	N/A	N/A	54	5	5,000,000	0	0.0	0.0
C+ / 6.1	10.3	1.00	27.92	181	7	91	1	1	2	127.2	-16.5	68	17	3,000	100	0.0	0.0
C+ / 6.1	10.3	1.00	27.52	15	7	91	1	1	2	118.2	-16.7	58	17	3,000	100	0.0	0.0
C+ / 6.1	10.3	1.00	27.92	361	7	91	1	1	2	130.4	-16.4	71	17	100,000	0	0.0	0.0
C+ / 6.1	10.3	1.00	27.89	100	7	91	1	1	2	124.2	-16.6	65	17	0	0	0.0	0.0
B- / 7.4	10.7	0.86	37.11	29	24	75	0	1	224	92.6	-17.5	49	4	3,000	100	5.8	0.0
B- / 7.3	10.7	0.86	34.65	8	24	75	0	1	224	84.8	-17.8	38	4	3,000	100	0.0	0.0
B- / 7.4	10.7	0.86	37.91	56	24	75	0	1	224	95.2	-17.5	53	4	100,000	0	0.0	0.0
B+ / 9.4	6.2	0.19	22.88	10	79	20	0	1	187	N/A	N/A	84	4	3,000	100	5.8	0.0
B+ / 9.4	6.2	0.19	22.25	2	79	20	0	1	187	N/A	N/A	79	4	3,000	100	0.0	0.0
B+ / 9.4	6.2	0.19	23.10	50	79	20	0	1	187	N/A	N/A	85	4	100,000	0	0.0	0.0
C / 5.4	10.5	0.58	10.26	83	19	80	0	1	133	74.5	-15.5	96	10	3,000	100	5.8	0.0
C / 5.5	10.5	0.58	10.17	25	19	80	0	1	133	67.0	-15.7	95	10	3,000	100	0.0	0.0
C / 5.4	10.5	0.58	10.23	330	19	80	0	1	133	77.1	-15.5	97	10	100,000	0	0.0	0.0
C / 5.5	10.4	0.57	10.42	1	19	80	0	1	133	71.9	-16.0	96	10	0	0	0.0	0.0
C- / 3.8	14.0	0.53	12.02	10	11	0	88	1	0	N/A	N/A	0	5	3,000	100	5.8	0.0
C- / 3.8	14.0	0.52	11.67	N/A	11	0	88	1	0	N/A	N/A	0	5	3,000	100	0.0	0.0
C- / 3.8	14.0	0.52	12.17	85	11	0	88	1	0	N/A	N/A	0	5	100,000	0	0.0	0.0
B / 8.7	6.2	-0.23	16.71	N/A	26	0	73	1	28	N/A	N/A	73	5	3,000	100	5.8	0.0

				PERFORMANCE							Incl. in Returns	
						Total Return % through 2/28/17						
									Annualized		Dividend	Expense
Fund Type	Fund Name	Ticker Symbol	Overall Investment Rating	Phone	Performance Rating/Pts	3 Mo	6 Mo	1Yr / Pct	3Yr / Pct	5Yr / Pct	Yield	Ratio
AA	Nuveen Gresham Lng Sht Comm Str	NGSCX	D+	(800) 257-8787	E- / 0.2	-1.97	-3.07	-6.44 / 0	-2.33 / 6	--	0.00	4.67
AA	Nuveen Gresham Lng Sht Comm Str	NGSIX	D+	(800) 257-8787	E / 0.3	-1.77	-2.61	-5.49 / 0	-1.34 / 8	--	1.00	3.68
MC	Nuveen Growth A	NSAGX	C+	(800) 257-8787	C+ / 6.6	6.20	7.62	18.76 /46	8.91 /86	11.74 /72	0.63	1.31
MC	Nuveen Growth C	NSRCX	C+	(800) 257-8787	B- / 7.0	5.99	7.21	17.85 /42	8.09 /80	10.91 /65	0.00	2.06
MC	Nuveen Growth I	NSRGX	B	(800) 257-8787	B / 7.7	6.24	7.72	19.03 /47	9.17 /88	12.03 /75	0.89	1.06
MC	Nuveen Growth R3	NBGRX	B-	(800) 257-8787	B- / 7.4	6.14	7.50	18.45 /45	8.63 /84	11.47 /70	0.43	1.56
FO	Nuveen International Growth A	NBQAX	E+	(800) 257-8787	E- / 0.1	4.67	-0.89	4.82 / 4	-4.09 / 3	6.39 /31	0.00	1.23
FO	Nuveen International Growth C	NBQCX	E+	(800) 257-8787	E- / 0.2	4.48	-1.26	4.04 / 3	-4.81 / 3	5.61 /26	0.00	1.97
FO	Nuveen International Growth I	NBQIX	E+	(800) 257-8787	E / 0.3	4.72	-0.78	5.07 / 4	-3.85 / 3	6.65 /32	0.00	0.97
FO	Nuveen International Growth R3	NBQBX	E+	(800) 257-8787	E- / 0.2	4.60	-1.01	4.57 / 4	-4.33 / 3	6.11 /29	0.00	1.48
FO	Nuveen International Growth R6	NBQFX	U	(800) 257-8787	U /	4.77	-0.72	--	--	--	0.00	0.83
GR	Nuveen Large Cap Core A	NLACX	A-	(800) 257-8787	B / 8.2	6.07	12.46	24.94 /73	9.84 /92	--	0.62	1.07
GR	Nuveen Large Cap Core C	NLCDX	A	(800) 257-8787	B+ / 8.6	5.86	12.02	24.04 /70	9.02 /87	--	0.01	1.82
GR	Nuveen Large Cap Core I	NLCIX	A+	(800) 257-8787	A- / 9.2	6.12	12.55	25.22 /74	10.10 /94	--	0.88	0.82
GR	Nuveen Large Cap Core Plus A	NLAPX	B+	(800) 257-8787	B / 8.0	6.07	13.91	24.00 /70	9.38 /89	--	0.36	2.51
GR	Nuveen Large Cap Core Plus C	NLPCX	A-	(800) 257-8787	B+ / 8.4	5.88	13.49	23.07 /67	8.56 /84	--	0.00	3.25
GR	Nuveen Large Cap Core Plus I	NLPIX	A	(800) 257-8787	A- / 9.1	6.14	14.04	24.32 /71	9.65 /91	--	0.60	2.24
GR	Nuveen Large Cap Growth A	NLAGX	B+	(800) 257-8787	B- / 7.5	6.70	11.80	22.90 /66	9.02 /87	--	0.63	1.17
GR	Nuveen Large Cap Growth C	NLCGX	B+	(800) 257-8787	B / 8.0	6.49	11.39	21.97 /62	8.21 /81	--	0.02	1.93
GR	Nuveen Large Cap Growth I	NLIGX	A	(800) 257-8787	B+ / 8.7	6.78	11.96	23.22 /67	9.29 /89	--	0.89	0.93
GR	Nuveen Large Cap Growth Opps A	FRGWX	D	(800) 257-8787	C+ / 5.6	9.23	7.37	18.23 /44	6.71 /70	11.03 /66	0.00	1.09
GR	Nuveen Large Cap Growth Opps C	FAWCX	D	(800) 257-8787	C+ / 6.2	9.02	7.00	17.38 /40	5.92 /64	10.22 /60	0.00	1.84
GR	Nuveen Large Cap Growth Opps I	FIGWX	C-	(800) 257-8787	C+ / 6.9	9.26	7.48	18.50 /45	6.97 /72	11.31 /68	0.00	0.84
GR	Nuveen Large Cap Growth Opps R3	FLCYX	D+	(800) 257-8787	C+ / 6.5	9.13	7.22	17.93 /43	6.43 /68	10.76 /64	0.00	1.34
GR	Nuveen Large Cap Growth Opps R6	FLCFX	C-	(800) 257-8787	B- / 7.0	9.32	7.54	18.63 /46	7.08 /72	--	0.00	0.75
GR	Nuveen Large Cap Select A	FLRAX	A+	(800) 257-8787	A- / 9.2	8.07	14.72	32.22 /90	9.53 /91	13.78 /92	0.35	1.18
GR	Nuveen Large Cap Select C	FLYCX	A+	(800) 257-8787	A / 9.5	7.91	14.32	31.21 /89	8.72 /85	12.94 /83	0.00	1.93
GR	Nuveen Large Cap Select I	FLRYX	A+	(800) 257-8787	A+ / 9.7	8.16	14.86	32.51 /91	9.81 /92	14.06 /94	0.59	0.93
GR	Nuveen Large Cap Value A	NNGAX	B-	(800) 257-8787	B+ / 8.6	5.87	15.05	32.54 /91	8.60 /84	13.06 /84	1.20	1.04
GR	Nuveen Large Cap Value C	NNGCX	B	(800) 257-8787	A- / 9.0	5.70	14.65	31.55 /89	7.78 /77	12.22 /76	0.63	1.79
GR	Nuveen Large Cap Value I	NNGRX	B+	(800) 257-8787	A / 9.5	5.95	15.17	32.81 /91	8.86 /86	13.34 /87	1.48	0.79
GR	Nuveen Large Cap Value R3	NMMTX	B	(800) 257-8787	A / 9.3	5.82	14.93	32.22 /90	8.33 /82	12.77 /82	1.06	1.29
MC	Nuveen Mid Cap Growth Opps A	FRSLX	D-	(800) 257-8787	C- / 3.2	5.34	5.73	21.45 /60	3.03 /32	9.96 /58	0.00	1.19
MC	Nuveen Mid Cap Growth Opps C	FMECX	E+	(800) 257-8787	C- / 3.7	5.18	5.35	20.55 /55	2.26 /26	9.15 /52	0.00	1.94
MC	Nuveen Mid Cap Growth Opps I	FISGX	D	(800) 257-8787	C / 4.5	5.42	5.85	21.75 /61	3.29 /35	10.24 /60	0.00	0.94
MC	Nuveen Mid Cap Growth Opps R3	FMEYX	D-	(800) 257-8787	C- / 4.1	5.28	5.60	21.15 /58	2.77 /30	9.69 /56	0.00	1.44
MC	Nuveen Mid Cap Growth Opps R6	FMEFX	D	(800) 257-8787	C / 4.6	5.43	5.94	21.93 /62	3.44 /36	--	0.00	0.81
MC	● Nuveen Mid Cap Index A	FDXAX	B+	(800) 257-8787	A- / 9.2	6.49	11.04	30.96 /88	8.95 /86	13.11 /85	0.93	0.79
MC	● Nuveen Mid Cap Index C	FDXCX	B+	(800) 257-8787	B+ / 8.7	6.30	10.61	29.91 /86	8.13 /80	12.26 /77	0.29	1.54
MC	● Nuveen Mid Cap Index I	FIMEX	B+	(800) 257-8787	A / 9.3	6.49	11.14	31.24 /89	9.21 /88	13.38 /88	1.15	0.54
MC	● Nuveen Mid Cap Index R3	FMCYX	B+	(800) 257-8787	A- / 9.0	6.39	10.87	30.60 /87	8.67 /84	12.82 /82	0.72	1.04
MC	Nuveen Mid Cap Value A	FASEX	B+	(800) 257-8787	B / 8.0	7.71	10.56	30.79 /88	8.32 /81	12.75 /81	0.75	1.30
MC	Nuveen Mid Cap Value C	FACSX	A-	(800) 257-8787	B+ / 8.5	7.50	10.15	29.83 /86	7.51 /76	11.90 /73	0.15	2.05
MC	Nuveen Mid Cap Value I	FSEIX	A	(800) 257-8787	A- / 9.1	7.77	10.70	31.13 /88	8.59 /84	13.03 /84	1.01	1.05
MC	Nuveen Mid Cap Value R3	FMVSX	A-	(800) 257-8787	B+ / 8.8	7.63	10.41	30.47 /87	8.04 /79	12.47 /79	0.58	1.55
IN	Nuveen NWQ Global Equity Income	NQGAX	D+	(800) 257-8787	D / 2.2	6.38	3.79	13.66 /24	2.77 /30	7.92 /41	1.97	3.73
IN	Nuveen NWQ Global Equity Income	NQGCX	C-	(800) 257-8787	D+ / 2.6	6.20	3.41	12.81 /21	2.00 /24	7.11 /35	1.53	4.69
IN	Nuveen NWQ Global Equity Income I	NQGIX	C-	(800) 257-8787	C- / 3.3	6.44	3.91	13.94 /25	3.03 /32	8.19 /44	2.33	1.29
IN	Nuveen NWQ Global Equity Income	NQGRX	D	(800) 257-8787	D / 2.2	6.33	3.71	13.40 /23	1.03 /18	6.26 /30	2.01	4.18
FO	Nuveen NWQ Intl Value A	NAIGX	D-	(800) 257-8787	E+ / 0.8	6.54	4.89	14.09 /26	-0.54 /11	2.66 /10	1.72	1.22
FO	Nuveen NWQ Intl Value C	NCIGX	D-	(800) 257-8787	D- / 1.0	6.40	4.56	13.28 /23	-1.29 / 8	1.89 / 8	1.12	1.97
FO	Nuveen NWQ Intl Value I	NGRRX	D-	(800) 257-8787	D- / 1.4	6.64	5.04	14.42 /27	-0.29 /12	2.91 /10	2.07	0.97

● Denotes fund is closed to new investors
* Denotes fund is included in Section II

www.thestreetratings.com

I. Index of Stock Mutual Funds

RISK			NET ASSETS		ASSET					BULL / BEAR		FUND MANAGER		MINIMUMS		LOADS	
Risk Rating/Pts	3 Year Standard Deviation	Beta	NAV As of 2/28/17	Total $(Mil)	Cash %	Stocks %	Bonds %	Other %	Portfolio Turnover Ratio	Last Bull Market Return	Last Bear Market Return	Manager Quality Pct	Manager Tenure (Years)	Initial Purch. $	Additional Purch. $	Front End Load	Back End Load
B /8.7	6.2	-0.23	16.43	N/A	26	0	73	1	28	N/A	N/A	64	5	3,000	100	0.0	0.0
B /8.7	6.2	-0.24	16.79	6	26	0	73	1	28	N/A	N/A	75	5	100,000	0	0.0	0.0
C /5.2	10.8	0.75	27.33	9	0	99	0	1	59	113.9	-16.5	84	5	3,000	100	5.8	0.0
C /5.0	10.8	0.75	24.99	8	0	99	0	1	59	105.6	-16.7	80	5	3,000	100	0.0	0.0
C /5.3	10.8	0.75	27.81	33	0	99	0	1	59	116.9	-16.4	85	5	100,000	0	0.0	0.0
C /5.2	10.8	0.75	27.10	N/A	0	99	0	1	59	111.2	-16.6	83	5	0	0	0.0	0.0
C+ /5.6	11.3	0.81	36.78	60	1	98	0	1	351	58.1	-25.4	23	8	3,000	100	5.8	0.0
C /5.5	11.3	0.81	35.24	15	1	98	0	1	351	51.9	-25.6	17	8	3,000	100	0.0	0.0
C+ /5.6	11.3	0.81	37.07	212	1	98	0	1	351	60.2	-25.3	25	8	100,000	0	0.0	0.0
C+ /5.6	11.3	0.81	36.38	1	1	98	0	1	351	55.9	-25.5	21	8	0	0	0.0	0.0
U /	N/A	N/A	37.10	30	1	98	0	1	351	N/A	N/A	N/A	8	5,000,000	0	0.0	0.0
C+ /6.6	12.5	1.12	30.19	66	0	100	0	0	132	N/A	N/A	49	4	3,000	100	5.8	0.0
C+ /6.6	12.5	1.12	29.84	57	0	100	0	0	132	N/A	N/A	39	4	3,000	100	0.0	0.0
C+ /6.6	12.4	1.12	30.20	204	0	100	0	0	132	N/A	N/A	53	4	100,000	0	0.0	0.0
C+ /6.3	12.9	1.13	29.00	17	0	99	0	1	143	N/A	N/A	42	4	3,000	100	5.8	0.0
C+ /6.3	12.9	1.13	28.43	13	0	99	0	1	143	N/A	N/A	32	4	3,000	100	0.0	0.0
C+ /6.3	12.9	1.13	29.07	53	0	99	0	1	143	N/A	N/A	45	4	100,000	0	0.0	0.0
C+ /6.4	11.8	1.07	28.52	16	0	99	0	1	117	N/A	N/A	46	4	3,000	100	5.8	0.0
C+ /6.4	11.8	1.07	28.12	10	0	99	0	1	117	N/A	N/A	36	4	3,000	100	0.0	0.0
C+ /6.4	11.8	1.07	28.54	51	0	99	0	1	117	N/A	N/A	50	4	100,000	0	0.0	0.0
D+ /2.3	12.3	1.03	28.67	91	1	98	0	1	60	100.1	-15.3	25	15	3,000	100	5.8	0.0
D- /1.4	12.4	1.03	23.03	10	1	98	0	1	60	92.3	-15.6	18	15	3,000	100	0.0	0.0
D+ /2.7	12.3	1.03	31.53	174	1	98	0	1	60	102.9	-15.2	27	15	100,000	0	0.0	0.0
D /2.1	12.3	1.03	27.20	7	1	98	0	1	60	97.4	-15.4	22	15	0	0	0.0	0.0
D+ /2.7	12.3	1.03	31.71	15	1	98	0	1	60	N/A	N/A	29	15	5,000,000	0	0.0	0.0
C+ /6.6	12.0	1.09	24.51	11	0	98	0	2	116	140.0	-23.3	50	14	3,000	100	5.8	0.0
C+ /6.5	12.0	1.09	22.91	1	0	98	0	2	116	130.5	-23.5	40	14	3,000	100	0.0	0.0
C+ /6.5	12.0	1.09	24.68	43	0	98	0	2	116	143.4	-23.2	54	14	100,000	0	0.0	0.0
C- /4.2	13.1	1.16	25.81	265	0	99	0	1	141	125.6	-19.6	29	4	3,000	100	5.8	0.0
C- /4.2	13.1	1.16	24.74	28	0	99	0	1	141	116.6	-19.8	21	4	3,000	100	0.0	0.0
C- /4.2	13.1	1.16	25.95	130	0	99	0	1	141	128.7	-19.5	32	4	100,000	0	0.0	0.0
C /4.3	13.1	1.16	26.00	N/A	0	99	0	1	141	122.6	-19.7	27	4	0	0	0.0	0.0
C- /3.1	13.7	1.00	38.20	276	0	98	0	2	89	94.8	-20.5	8	12	3,000	100	5.8	0.0
D+ /2.3	13.7	1.00	30.00	17	0	98	0	2	89	87.1	-20.7	5	12	3,000	100	0.0	0.0
C- /3.5	13.7	1.01	44.64	473	0	98	0	2	89	97.5	-20.4	9	12	100,000	0	0.0	0.0
D+ /2.9	13.7	1.01	36.02	56	0	98	0	2	89	92.2	-20.6	7	12	0	0	0.0	0.0
C- /3.6	13.7	1.01	44.93	72	0	98	0	2	89	N/A	N/A	10	12	5,000,000	0	0.0	0.0
C /5.2	12.1	1.00	18.90	211	2	93	3	2	13	132.3	-22.7	67	16	3,000	100	5.8	0.0
C /5.2	12.0	1.00	18.11	22	2	93	3	2	13	123.1	-22.9	57	16	3,000	100	0.0	0.0
C /5.2	12.0	1.00	18.95	166	2	93	3	2	13	135.3	-22.6	70	16	100,000	0	0.0	0.0
C /5.2	12.1	1.00	18.63	228	2	93	3	2	13	129.1	-22.7	63	16	0	0	0.0	0.0
C+ /6.1	12.5	0.98	39.14	39	0	98	0	2	44	123.6	-24.2	61	5	3,000	100	5.8	0.0
C+ /6.1	12.5	0.99	37.33	8	0	98	0	2	44	114.7	-24.4	51	5	3,000	100	0.0	0.0
C+ /6.1	12.5	0.98	39.23	58	0	98	0	2	44	126.6	-24.1	65	5	100,000	0	0.0	0.0
C+ /6.0	12.5	0.98	38.86	6	0	98	0	2	44	120.5	-24.3	58	5	0	0	0.0	0.0
B- /7.0	10.2	0.90	26.36	81	5	94	0	1	51	79.3	-20.3	7	1	3,000	100	5.8	0.0
B- /7.0	10.2	0.90	26.27	N/A	5	94	0	1	51	72.2	-20.6	5	1	3,000	100	0.0	0.0
B- /7.0	10.2	0.90	26.38	55	5	94	0	1	51	81.8	-20.3	8	1	100,000	0	0.0	0.0
C /5.3	10.4	0.92	26.31	N/A	5	94	0	1	51	49.3	-21.0	3	1	0	0	0.0	0.0
C+ /6.0	11.1	0.87	23.22	27	1	98	0	1	20	21.9	-18.4	70	N/A	3,000	100	5.8	0.0
C+ /6.0	11.2	0.87	22.16	14	1	98	0	1	20	17.1	-18.7	60	N/A	3,000	100	0.0	0.0
C+ /6.0	11.2	0.87	23.32	168	1	98	0	1	20	23.6	-18.4	72	N/A	100,000	0	0.0	0.0

| | | | 99 Pct = Best | | | | | | | | | |
| | | | 0 Pct = Worst | | | | | | | | | |

Fund Type	Fund Name	Ticker Symbol	Overall Investment Rating	Phone	Performance Rating/Pts	3 Mo	6 Mo	1Yr / Pct	3Yr / Pct	5Yr / Pct	Dividend Yield	Expense Ratio
FO	Nuveen NWQ Intl Value R3	NTITX	D-	(800) 257-8787	D- / 1.2	6.53	4.79	13.87 / 25	-0.79 / 10	2.39 / 9	1.59	1.47
FO	Nuveen NWQ Japan A	NTJAX	C+	(800) 257-8787	C+ / 6.0	7.87	8.65	16.74 / 37	7.66 / 76	7.91 / 41	3.05	2.32
FO	Nuveen NWQ Japan C	NTJCX	B-	(800) 257-8787	C+ / 6.5	7.71	8.25	15.91 / 34	6.86 / 71	7.09 / 35	2.52	3.09
FO	Nuveen NWQ Japan I	NTJIX	B+	(800) 257-8787	B- / 7.2	7.96	8.82	17.08 / 39	7.93 / 78	8.18 / 43	3.47	1.98
GR	Nuveen NWQ Large Cap Value A	NQCAX	D-	(800) 257-8787	C+ / 5.7	5.18	10.95	25.93 / 76	5.37 / 58	8.26 / 44	1.13	1.14
GR	Nuveen NWQ Large Cap Value C	NQCCX	D	(800) 257-8787	C+ / 6.3	5.11	10.66	24.94 / 73	4.62 / 50	7.47 / 38	0.53	1.89
GR	Nuveen NWQ Large Cap Value I	NQCRX	D	(800) 257-8787	B- / 7.0	5.42	11.19	26.32 / 77	5.68 / 61	8.56 / 47	1.41	0.89
GR	Nuveen NWQ Large Cap Value R3	NQCQX	D	(800) 257-8787	C+ / 6.7	5.24	10.93	25.69 / 75	5.13 / 56	8.01 / 42	0.97	1.39
GI	Nuveen NWQ Multi-Cap Value A	NQVAX	C-	(800) 257-8787	C / 4.9	7.31	11.34	26.59 / 78	3.32 / 35	7.81 / 41	0.71	1.26
GI	Nuveen NWQ Multi-Cap Value C	NQVCX	C	(800) 257-8787	C / 5.4	7.16	10.94	25.65 / 75	2.56 / 28	7.01 / 35	0.10	2.01
GI	Nuveen NWQ Multi-Cap Value I	NQVRX	C+	(800) 257-8787	C+ / 6.3	7.43	11.48	26.93 / 79	3.59 / 38	8.10 / 43	0.97	1.01
GI	Nuveen NWQ Multi-Cap Value R3	NMCTX	C+	(800) 257-8787	C+ / 5.9	7.30	11.20	26.28 / 77	3.07 / 32	7.53 / 39	0.53	1.51
SC	Nuveen NWQ Sm and MidCap VL A	NSMAX	C+	(800) 257-8787	C+ / 6.3	6.25	13.79	29.81 / 86	4.67 / 50	10.13 / 59	0.00	1.42
SC	Nuveen NWQ Sm and MidCap VL C	NSMCX	C+	(800) 257-8787	C+ / 6.7	6.06	13.36	28.88 / 84	3.90 / 42	9.31 / 53	0.00	2.17
SC	Nuveen NWQ Sm and MidCap VL I	NSMRX	B	(800) 257-8787	B- / 7.4	6.31	13.92	30.16 / 87	4.94 / 53	10.41 / 61	0.00	1.17
MC	Nuveen NWQ Sm and MidCap VL R3	NWQRX	B-	(800) 257-8787	B- / 7.1	6.18	13.65	29.54 / 85	4.42 / 48	9.85 / 57	0.00	1.68
SC	Nuveen NWQ Small Cap Value A	NSCAX	B	(800) 257-8787	B- / 7.4	5.60	11.50	29.73 / 86	7.58 / 76	14.28 / 95	0.00	1.28
SC	Nuveen NWQ Small Cap Value C	NSCCX	B	(800) 257-8787	B / 7.8	5.40	11.08	28.76 / 83	6.78 / 70	13.43 / 88	0.00	2.03
SC	Nuveen NWQ Small Cap Value I	NSCRX	B+	(800) 257-8787	B+ / 8.6	5.66	11.63	30.06 / 86	7.84 / 78	14.57 / 96	0.00	1.03
SC	Nuveen NWQ Small Cap Value R3	NSCQX	B+	(800) 257-8787	B / 8.2	5.51	11.36	29.40 / 85	7.31 / 74	14.00 / 93	0.00	1.54
SC	Nuveen NWQ Small Cap Value R6	NSCFX	A-	(800) 257-8787	B+ / 8.7	5.69	11.74	30.31 / 87	8.01 / 79	--	0.00	0.88
AA	Nuveen Real Asset Income A	NRIAX	C+	(800) 257-8787	C- / 4.2	5.89	0.70	16.39 / 36	6.85 / 71	8.49 / 46	4.77	1.23
AA	Nuveen Real Asset Income C	NRICX	C+	(800) 257-8787	C / 4.8	5.70	0.34	15.49 / 32	6.06 / 65	7.69 / 40	4.34	1.98
AA	Nuveen Real Asset Income I	NRIIX	B-	(800) 257-8787	C+ / 5.7	5.96	0.83	16.68 / 37	7.11 / 73	8.76 / 49	5.31	0.97
RE	● Nuveen Real Estate Securities A	FREAX	C	(800) 257-8787	C+ / 6.1	7.32	-1.97	14.69 / 28	10.56 / 96	10.87 / 65	2.73	1.30
RE	● Nuveen Real Estate Securities C	FRLCX	C+	(800) 257-8787	C+ / 6.6	7.16	-2.31	13.87 / 25	9.74 / 92	10.04 / 59	2.16	2.05
RE	● Nuveen Real Estate Securities I	FARCX	C+	(800) 257-8787	B- / 7.3	7.39	-1.83	15.00 / 30	10.84 / 97	11.15 / 67	3.12	1.05
RE	● Nuveen Real Estate Securities R3	FRSSX	C+	(800) 257-8787	B- / 7.0	7.25	-2.08	14.43 / 27	10.28 / 95	10.59 / 63	2.76	1.55
RE	Nuveen Real Estate Securities R6	FREGX	B-	(800) 257-8787	B- / 7.5	7.44	-1.73	15.18 / 31	11.01 / 97	--	3.12	0.87
GI	Nuveen Santa Barbara Div Gro A	NSBAX	C+	(800) 257-8787	C+ / 6.6	7.28	6.95	20.72 / 56	8.44 / 82	10.96 / 66	1.37	0.99
GI	Nuveen Santa Barbara Div Gro C	NSBCX	B+	(800) 257-8787	B- / 7.0	7.07	6.54	19.82 / 51	7.63 / 76	10.13 / 59	0.77	1.74
GI	Nuveen Santa Barbara Div Gro I	NSBRX	B+	(800) 257-8787	B / 7.8	7.37	7.07	21.04 / 58	8.71 / 85	11.23 / 68	1.68	0.74
GI	Nuveen Santa Barbara Div Gro R3	NBDRX	B+	(800) 257-8787	B- / 7.4	7.24	6.82	20.44 / 55	8.17 / 80	10.69 / 63	1.34	1.24
IN	Nuveen Santa Barbara Div Gro R6	NSBFX	B+	(800) 257-8787	B / 7.8	7.37	7.11	21.12 / 58	8.80 / 85	--	1.68	0.66
GL	Nuveen Santa Barbara Glb Div Gro A	NUGAX	C	(800) 257-8787	C- / 3.9	6.65	5.12	16.87 / 38	5.12 / 55	--	1.61	1.72
GL	Nuveen Santa Barbara Glb Div Gro C	NUGCX	C	(800) 257-8787	C / 4.4	6.47	4.70	16.02 / 34	4.34 / 47	--	1.01	2.46
GL	Nuveen Santa Barbara Glb Div Gro I	NUGIX	C+	(800) 257-8787	C / 5.3	6.75	5.24	17.20 / 39	5.38 / 58	--	1.94	1.05
GL	Nuveen Santa Barbara Glb Div Gro	NUGRX	C+	(800) 257-8787	C / 4.8	6.60	5.00	16.62 / 37	4.87 / 53	--	1.59	1.98
FO	Nuveen Santa Barbara Intl Div Gr A	NUIAX	D	(800) 257-8787	D- / 1.2	7.37	2.08	12.09 / 18	0.15 / 14	--	2.32	5.52
FO	Nuveen Santa Barbara Intl Div Gr C	NUICX	D	(800) 257-8787	D- / 1.0	7.15	1.71	11.26 / 15	-0.61 / 11	--	1.74	6.23
FO	Nuveen Santa Barbara Intl Div Gr I	NUIIX	D+	(800) 257-8787	D / 1.9	7.47	2.25	12.40 / 19	0.40 / 15	--	2.70	5.33
FO	Nuveen Santa Barbara Intl Div Gr R3	NUIRX	D+	(800) 257-8787	D- / 1.2	7.28	1.96	11.84 / 17	-0.10 / 13	--	2.35	5.86
SC	Nuveen Small Cap Growth Opps A	FRMPX	D+	(800) 257-8787	C+ / 6.3	5.78	9.20	35.11 / 94	4.55 / 49	10.56 / 62	0.00	1.35
SC	Nuveen Small Cap Growth Opps C	FMPCX	D+	(800) 257-8787	C+ / 6.7	5.62	8.78	34.11 / 93	3.76 / 40	9.73 / 56	0.00	2.10
SC	Nuveen Small Cap Growth Opps I	FIMPX	C-	(800) 257-8787	B- / 7.5	5.87	9.32	35.49 / 94	4.81 / 52	10.83 / 64	0.00	1.10
SC	Nuveen Small Cap Growth Opps R3	FMPYX	D+	(800) 257-8787	B- / 7.1	5.73	9.04	34.78 / 94	4.28 / 46	10.27 / 60	0.00	1.60
SC	● Nuveen Small Cap Index A	FMDAX	B-	(800) 257-8787	B+ / 8.4	4.96	12.19	35.32 / 94	6.30 / 67	12.26 / 77	0.91	1.00
SC	● Nuveen Small Cap Index C	FPXCX	C+	(800) 257-8787	B / 7.8	4.79	11.80	34.25 / 93	5.52 / 60	11.40 / 69	0.28	1.75
SC	● Nuveen Small Cap Index I	ASETX	B	(800) 257-8787	B+ / 8.6	5.11	12.40	35.61 / 95	6.59 / 69	12.53 / 79	1.12	0.74
SC	● Nuveen Small Cap Index R3	ARSCX	B-	(800) 257-8787	B / 8.2	4.92	12.07	34.96 / 94	6.03 / 64	11.96 / 74	0.70	1.25
SC	Nuveen Small Cap Select A	EMGRX	C-	(800) 257-8787	B+ / 8.7	5.16	10.93	37.92 / 96	8.48 / 83	11.52 / 70	0.05	1.46
SC	Nuveen Small Cap Select C	FHMCX	C-	(800) 257-8787	A- / 9.1	5.13	10.66	36.96 / 96	7.71 / 77	10.70 / 63	0.00	2.21

● Denotes fund is closed to new investors
* Denotes fund is included in Section II

www.thestreetratings.com

RISK			NET ASSETS		ASSET				Portfolio Turnover Ratio	BULL / BEAR		FUND MANAGER		MINIMUMS		LOADS	
Risk Rating/Pts	3 Year Standard Deviation	Beta	NAV As of 2/28/17	Total $(Mil)	Cash %	Stocks %	Bonds %	Other %		Last Bull Market Return	Last Bear Market Return	Manager Quality Pct	Manager Tenure (Years)	Initial Purch. $	Additional Purch. $	Front End Load	Back End Load
C+ / 6.0	11.2	0.87	23.41	1	1	98	0	1	20	20.3	-18.5	66	N/A	0	0	0.0	0.0
C+ / 6.9	10.8	0.73	27.59	3	2	97	0	1	33	43.9	-2.5	98	N/A	3,000	100	5.8	0.0
B- / 7.0	10.8	0.73	27.30	1	2	97	0	1	33	38.1	-2.7	98	N/A	3,000	100	0.0	0.0
C+ / 6.9	10.8	0.73	27.68	4	2	97	0	1	33	45.8	-2.3	98	N/A	100,000	0	0.0	0.0
D- / 1.1	12.8	1.12	7.69	9	2	97	0	1	32	83.4	-22.8	8	11	3,000	100	5.8	0.0
D- / 1.1	12.7	1.12	7.01	6	2	97	0	1	32	76.2	-23.0	6	11	3,000	100	0.0	0.0
D- / 1.1	12.8	1.12	7.72	80	2	97	0	1	32	86.1	-22.7	10	11	100,000	0	0.0	0.0
D- / 1.1	12.8	1.13	7.63	N/A	2	97	0	1	32	81.0	-22.8	7	11	0	0	0.0	0.0
C / 5.5	13.2	1.12	27.96	29	0	99	0	1	28	86.7	-23.8	4	20	3,000	100	5.8	0.0
C / 5.6	13.2	1.12	26.41	28	0	99	0	1	28	79.2	-24.0	3	20	3,000	100	0.0	0.0
C / 5.5	13.2	1.13	28.11	44	0	99	0	1	28	89.2	-23.7	4	20	100,000	0	0.0	0.0
C / 5.5	13.2	1.12	27.69	N/A	0	99	0	1	28	84.2	-23.9	3	20	0	0	0.0	0.0
C+ / 5.9	15.0	0.90	33.66	10	6	93	0	1	49	106.1	-23.0	56	11	3,000	100	5.8	0.0
C+ / 5.8	15.1	0.90	31.15	3	6	93	0	1	49	97.9	-23.3	46	11	3,000	100	0.0	0.0
C+ / 5.9	15.0	0.90	34.05	54	6	93	0	1	49	109.0	-23.0	60	11	100,000	0	0.0	0.0
C+ / 5.9	15.0	1.17	32.80	1	6	93	0	1	49	103.4	-23.1	7	11	0	0	0.0	0.0
C+ / 5.9	15.9	0.96	49.48	99	4	95	0	1	39	146.3	-21.3	80	13	3,000	100	5.8	0.0
C+ / 5.8	15.9	0.96	45.38	26	4	95	0	1	39	136.5	-21.6	75	13	3,000	100	0.0	0.0
C+ / 5.9	15.9	0.96	50.62	576	4	95	0	1	39	149.7	-21.2	82	13	100,000	0	0.0	0.0
C+ / 5.9	15.9	0.96	48.86	9	4	95	0	1	39	143.1	-21.4	79	13	0	0	0.0	0.0
C+ / 5.9	15.9	0.96	50.93	11	4	95	0	1	39	N/A	N/A	83	13	5,000,000	0	0.0	0.0
B- / 7.2	7.6	0.93	23.47	257	18	57	22	3	82	67.8	N/A	73	6	3,000	100	5.8	0.0
B- / 7.2	7.6	0.92	23.48	197	18	57	22	3	82	61.2	N/A	64	6	3,000	100	0.0	0.0
B- / 7.2	7.6	0.93	23.47	948	18	57	22	3	82	70.0	N/A	75	6	100,000	0	0.0	0.0
C / 5.1	14.5	1.06	22.33	679	4	95	0	1	104	102.4	-16.5	61	12	3,000	100	5.8	0.0
C / 5.1	14.5	1.06	21.72	88	4	95	0	1	104	94.4	-16.7	51	12	3,000	100	0.0	0.0
C / 5.1	14.5	1.06	22.67	3,455	4	95	0	1	104	105.2	-16.4	64	12	100,000	0	0.0	0.0
C / 5.1	14.5	1.06	22.65	51	4	95	0	1	104	99.7	-16.6	58	12	0	0	0.0	0.0
C / 5.1	14.5	1.06	22.83	222	4	95	0	1	104	N/A	N/A	66	12	5,000,000	0	0.0	0.0
C+ / 6.7	10.3	0.98	37.45	617	1	98	0	1	28	102.9	-13.9	52	11	3,000	100	5.8	0.0
C+ / 6.7	10.3	0.98	37.36	545	1	98	0	1	28	94.9	-14.3	41	11	3,000	100	0.0	0.0
C+ / 6.7	10.3	0.98	37.48	1,609	1	98	0	1	28	105.7	-13.9	56	11	100,000	0	0.0	0.0
C+ / 6.7	10.4	0.98	37.68	24	1	98	0	1	28	100.3	-14.1	48	11	0	0	0.0	0.0
C+ / 6.7	10.3	0.97	37.78	36	1	98	0	1	28	N/A	N/A	57	11	5,000,000	0	0.0	0.0
B- / 7.0	10.1	0.76	27.57	7	5	94	0	1	19	N/A	N/A	96	5	3,000	100	5.8	0.0
B- / 7.0	10.1	0.76	27.48	2	5	94	0	1	19	N/A	N/A	94	5	3,000	100	0.0	0.0
B- / 7.0	10.2	0.76	27.58	55	5	94	0	1	19	N/A	N/A	96	5	100,000	0	0.0	0.0
B- / 7.0	10.2	0.76	27.51	N/A	5	94	0	1	19	N/A	N/A	95	5	0	0	0.0	0.0
C+ / 6.5	10.7	0.84	25.10	2	6	93	0	1	53	N/A	N/A	76	5	3,000	100	5.8	0.0
C+ / 6.5	10.7	0.84	24.87	1	6	93	0	1	53	N/A	N/A	69	5	3,000	100	0.0	0.0
C+ / 6.5	10.7	0.84	25.14	2	6	93	0	1	53	N/A	N/A	78	5	100,000	0	0.0	0.0
B- / 7.3	10.7	0.84	25.01	N/A	6	93	0	1	53	N/A	N/A	74	5	0	0	0.0	0.0
D+ / 2.3	17.0	1.03	22.56	34	1	97	1	1	106	116.2	-25.3	42	10	3,000	100	5.8	0.0
D / 1.8	17.0	1.03	18.10	2	1	97	1	1	106	107.6	-25.5	32	10	3,000	100	0.0	0.0
D+ / 2.6	17.0	1.03	26.05	41	1	97	1	1	106	119.1	-25.2	46	10	100,000	0	0.0	0.0
D / 2.2	17.0	1.02	21.48	2	1	97	1	1	106	113.3	-25.4	39	10	0	0	0.0	0.0
C / 4.4	15.8	1.00	15.75	39	0	98	1	1	12	125.1	-25.3	67	16	3,000	100	0.0	0.0
C / 4.4	15.8	1.00	14.95	5	0	98	1	1	12	116.1	-25.5	58	16	3,000	100	0.0	0.0
C / 4.4	15.7	1.00	15.79	29	0	98	1	1	12	128.1	-25.2	71	16	100,000	0	0.0	0.0
C / 4.4	15.8	1.00	15.30	44	0	98	1	1	12	121.9	-25.3	64	16	0	0	0.0	0.0
E+ / 0.7	16.3	1.02	9.68	73	0	98	0	2	66	128.9	-27.1	83	9	3,000	100	5.8	0.0
E+ / 0.7	16.3	1.02	6.75	6	0	98	0	2	66	120.0	-27.3	78	9	3,000	100	0.0	0.0

Fund Type	Fund Name	Ticker Symbol	Overall Investment Rating	Phone	Performance Rating/Pts	3 Mo	6 Mo	1Yr / Pct	3Yr / Pct	5Yr / Pct	Dividend Yield	Expense Ratio
								Total Return % through 2/28/17	Annualized		Incl. in Returns	
SC	Nuveen Small Cap Select I	ARSTX	C	(800) 257-8787	A / 9.5	5.27	11.17	38.29 / 97	8.76 / 85	11.81 / 73	0.26	1.21
SC	Nuveen Small Cap Select R3	ASEIX	C-	(800) 257-8787	A / 9.3	5.09	10.84	37.40 / 96	8.22 / 81	11.24 / 68	0.00	1.71
SC	Nuveen Small Cap Value A	FSCAX	A+	(800) 257-8787	A+ / 9.8	6.37	15.92	42.88 / 98	12.49 / 98	15.54 / 98	0.35	1.46
SC	Nuveen Small Cap Value C	FSCVX	A+	(800) 257-8787	A+ / 9.9	6.15	15.47	41.74 / 98	11.65 / 98	14.68 / 96	0.00	2.21
SC	Nuveen Small Cap Value I	FSCCX	A+	(800) 257-8787	A+ / 9.9	6.43	16.09	43.17 / 98	12.76 / 99	15.82 / 98	0.58	1.21
SC	Nuveen Small Cap Value R3	FSVSX	A+	(800) 257-8787	A+ / 9.9	6.29	15.79	42.49 / 98	12.19 / 98	15.25 / 97	0.17	1.71
SC	Nuveen Small Cap Value R6	FSCWX	U	(800) 257-8787	U /	6.31	15.95	--	--	--	0.00	1.11
AA	Nuveen Strategy Aggr Gro Alloc A	FAAGX	C-	(800) 257-8787	C- / 3.4	5.78	5.85	18.80 / 46	3.92 / 42	7.85 / 41	1.22	1.53
AA	Nuveen Strategy Aggr Gro Alloc C	FSACX	C-	(800) 257-8787	C- / 3.9	5.58	5.51	17.91 / 42	3.15 / 33	7.04 / 35	0.59	2.28
AA	Nuveen Strategy Aggr Gro Alloc I	FSAYX	C	(800) 257-8787	C / 4.8	5.87	6.02	19.13 / 48	4.20 / 45	8.12 / 43	1.52	1.28
AA	Nuveen Strategy Aggr Gro Alloc R3	FSASX	C-	(800) 257-8787	C / 4.3	5.73	5.80	18.58 / 45	3.69 / 39	7.59 / 39	1.06	1.78
AA	Nuveen Strategy Balanced Alloc A	FSGNX	D+	(800) 257-8787	D / 2.0	3.98	2.87	12.21 / 19	3.28 / 34	6.06 / 29	1.50	1.33
AA	Nuveen Strategy Balanced Alloc C	FSKCX	D+	(800) 257-8787	D+ / 2.3	3.74	2.41	11.34 / 16	2.51 / 28	5.30 / 23	0.88	2.08
AA	Nuveen Strategy Balanced Alloc I	FSKYX	C-	(800) 257-8787	C- / 3.0	3.96	2.90	12.41 / 19	3.51 / 37	6.28 / 30	1.83	1.08
AA	Nuveen Strategy Balanced Alloc R3	FSKSX	D+	(800) 257-8787	D+ / 2.6	3.78	2.59	11.88 / 18	3.00 / 32	5.79 / 27	1.48	1.58
AA	Nuveen Strategy Consv Alloc A	FSFIX	C-	(800) 257-8787	D- / 1.2	3.00	0.93	8.25 / 8	2.18 / 25	3.92 / 15	3.41	1.24
AA	Nuveen Strategy Consv Alloc C	FSJCX	C-	(800) 257-8787	D- / 1.5	2.82	0.55	7.48 / 7	1.42 / 21	3.11 / 11	2.88	1.99
AA	Nuveen Strategy Consv Alloc I	FSFYX	C-	(800) 257-8787	D / 1.9	3.05	1.13	8.59 / 9	2.45 / 27	4.13 / 16	3.84	0.99
AA	Nuveen Strategy Consv Alloc R3	FSJSX	C-	(800) 257-8787	D / 1.7	2.94	0.80	7.98 / 7	1.94 / 24	3.61 / 13	3.36	1.49
AA	Nuveen Strategy Growth Alloc A	FSNAX	C-	(800) 257-8787	C- / 3.1	5.07	4.89	16.57 / 37	4.06 / 44	7.30 / 37	1.11	1.44
AA	Nuveen Strategy Growth Alloc C	FSNCX	C-	(800) 257-8787	C- / 3.5	4.86	4.50	15.64 / 33	3.28 / 34	6.48 / 31	0.47	2.19
AA	Nuveen Strategy Growth Alloc I	FSGYX	C	(800) 257-8787	C / 4.3	5.13	5.04	16.77 / 37	4.31 / 46	7.56 / 39	1.41	1.19
AA	Nuveen Strategy Growth Alloc R3	FSNSX	C-	(800) 257-8787	C- / 3.9	4.95	4.78	16.20 / 35	3.80 / 40	7.03 / 35	0.94	1.69
GL	Nuveen Symphony Dynamic Equity A	NQLAX	D+	(800) 257-8787	E / 0.3	3.01	-0.87	-6.16 / 0	0.46 / 16	--	0.00	5.71
GL	Nuveen Symphony Dynamic Equity C	NQLCX	D+	(800) 257-8787	E / 0.4	2.77	-1.28	-6.87 / 0	-0.30 / 12	--	0.00	7.02
GL	Nuveen Symphony Dynamic Equity I	NQLIX	D+	(800) 257-8787	E+ / 0.6	3.03	-0.77	-5.90 / 0	0.71 / 17	--	0.00	5.06
FO	Nuveen Symphony International Eq A	NSIAX	D	(800) 257-8787	D / 1.8	8.32	7.88	15.40 / 32	0.18 / 14	4.86 / 20	1.09	1.84
FO	Nuveen Symphony International Eq C	NSECX	D	(800) 257-8787	D- / 1.4	8.11	7.54	14.56 / 28	-0.57 / 11	4.07 / 16	0.46	2.57
FO	Nuveen Symphony International Eq I	NSIEX	D+	(800) 257-8787	D+ / 2.8	8.34	8.03	15.63 / 33	0.42 / 15	5.11 / 22	1.40	1.54
FO	Nuveen Symphony International Eq	NSREX	D	(800) 257-8787	D / 1.6	8.23	7.73	15.08 / 30	-0.09 / 13	4.60 / 19	0.93	2.05
GR	Nuveen Symphony Large-Cap	NCGAX	C+	(800) 257-8787	C+ / 6.9	8.29	7.97	19.33 / 49	8.79 / 85	11.28 / 68	0.24	1.13
GR	Nuveen Symphony Large-Cap	NCGCX	B	(800) 257-8787	B- / 7.3	8.10	7.59	18.45 / 45	7.99 / 79	10.45 / 62	0.00	1.88
GR	Nuveen Symphony Large-Cap	NSGIX	B+	(800) 257-8787	B / 8.0	8.35	8.10	19.64 / 50	9.06 / 87	11.56 / 70	0.48	0.88
GR	Nuveen Symphony Large-Cap	NSGQX	B+	(800) 257-8787	B / 7.6	8.24	7.85	19.04 / 47	8.52 / 83	11.00 / 66	0.03	1.38
GR	Nuveen Symphony Lw Volatility Eq A	NOPAX	C	(800) 257-8787	C+ / 6.0	6.29	6.29	16.42 / 36	8.52 / 83	12.42 / 78	1.01	1.22
GR	Nuveen Symphony Lw Volatility Eq C	NOPCX	C+	(800) 257-8787	C+ / 6.4	6.09	5.89	15.57 / 32	7.69 / 77	11.57 / 71	0.38	1.97
GR	Nuveen Symphony Lw Volatility Eq I	NOPRX	C+	(800) 257-8787	B- / 7.2	6.35	6.43	16.73 / 37	8.77 / 85	12.70 / 81	1.31	0.97
MC	Nuveen Symphony Mid-Cap Core A	NCCAX	C	(800) 257-8787	C / 5.2	5.96	7.76	20.98 / 57	6.06 / 65	10.18 / 60	0.00	1.51
MC	Nuveen Symphony Mid-Cap Core C	NCCCX	C+	(800) 257-8787	C+ / 5.7	5.74	7.33	20.03 / 52	5.26 / 57	9.34 / 53	0.00	2.26
MC	Nuveen Symphony Mid-Cap Core I	NCCIX	C+	(800) 257-8787	C+ / 6.6	6.02	7.87	21.28 / 59	6.33 / 67	10.45 / 62	0.00	1.25
MC	Nuveen Symphony Mid-Cap Core R3	NMCRX	C+	(800) 257-8787	C+ / 6.2	5.87	7.60	20.73 / 56	5.81 / 63	9.92 / 58	0.00	1.76
SC	Nuveen Symphony Small Cap Core A	NSSAX	B	(800) 257-8787	B- / 7.4	6.92	13.92	31.85 / 90	6.34 / 67	--	0.00	6.85
SC	Nuveen Symphony Small Cap Core C	NSSCX	B	(800) 257-8787	B / 7.8	6.73	13.51	30.82 / 88	5.53 / 60	--	0.00	7.91
SC	Nuveen Symphony Small Cap Core I	NSSIX	B+	(800) 257-8787	B+ / 8.6	7.00	14.06	32.16 / 90	6.58 / 69	--	0.00	6.53
GL	Nuveen Tradewinds Global All-Cap A	NWGAX	D	(800) 257-8787	D / 1.8	6.34	3.75	16.85 / 38	0.95 / 18	1.15 / 6	1.49	1.34
GL	Nuveen Tradewinds Global All-Cap C	NWGCX	D	(800) 257-8787	D / 2.1	6.11	3.34	15.95 / 34	0.19 / 14	0.39 / 5	0.87	2.09
GL	Nuveen Tradewinds Global All-Cap I	NWGRX	D+	(800) 257-8787	D+ / 2.7	6.39	3.89	17.09 / 39	1.21 / 19	1.39 / 7	1.82	1.09
GL	Nuveen Tradewinds Global All-Cap	NGARX	D	(800) 257-8787	D+ / 2.4	6.26	3.63	16.50 / 36	0.70 / 17	0.89 / 6	1.34	1.60
IN	Nuveen Tradewinds Value Opp A	NVOAX	C-	(800) 257-8787	C+ / 5.7	7.09	6.57	20.53 / 55	6.97 / 72	7.50 / 38	2.07	1.18
IN	Nuveen Tradewinds Value Opp C	NVOCX	C-	(800) 257-8787	C+ / 6.2	6.89	6.17	19.65 / 50	6.17 / 66	6.70 / 33	1.49	1.93
IN	Nuveen Tradewinds Value Opp I	NVORX	C	(800) 257-8787	B- / 7.0	7.15	6.67	20.85 / 57	7.24 / 74	7.77 / 40	2.42	0.93
IN	Nuveen Tradewinds Value Opp R3	NTVTX	C-	(800) 257-8787	C+ / 6.6	7.04	6.45	20.26 / 53	6.70 / 70	7.24 / 36	1.95	1.43

99 Pct = Best
0 Pct = Worst

• Denotes fund is closed to new investors
* Denotes fund is included in Section II

www.thestreetratings.com

RISK			NET ASSETS		ASSET				Portfolio Turnover Ratio	BULL / BEAR		FUND MANAGER		MINIMUMS		LOADS	
Risk Rating/Pts	3 Year Standard Deviation	Beta	NAV As of 2/28/17	Total $(Mil)	Cash %	Stocks %	Bonds %	Other %		Last Bull Market Return	Last Bear Market Return	Manager Quality Pct	Manager Tenure (Years)	Initial Purch. $	Additional Purch. $	Front End Load	Back End Load
D- / 1.1	16.3	1.02	12.03	51	0	98	0	2	66	132.2	-27.0	84	9	100,000	0	0.0	0.0
E+ / 0.7	16.3	1.02	8.89	6	0	98	0	2	66	126.0	-27.2	81	9	0	0	0.0	0.0
C+ / 5.9	15.3	0.93	24.70	311	0	97	2	1	40	170.1	-24.2	96	12	3,000	100	5.8	0.0
C+ / 5.9	15.2	0.93	21.05	54	0	97	2	1	40	159.6	-24.5	95	12	3,000	100	0.0	0.0
C+ / 5.9	15.2	0.93	25.54	797	0	97	2	1	40	173.9	-24.2	97	12	100,000	0	0.0	0.0
C+ / 5.9	15.3	0.93	24.17	41	0	97	2	1	40	166.4	-24.2	96	12	0	0	0.0	0.0
U /	N/A	N/A	25.51	37	0	97	2	1	40	N/A	N/A	N/A	12	5,000,000	0	0.0	0.0
C+ / 5.9	9.2	1.40	14.85	45	2	75	21	2	22	74.1	-19.4	8	N/A	3,000	100	5.8	0.0
C+ / 6.0	9.3	1.40	14.27	11	2	75	21	2	22	67.3	-19.6	5	N/A	3,000	100	0.0	0.0
C+ / 5.9	9.2	1.40	14.89	18	2	75	21	2	22	76.7	-19.3	9	N/A	100,000	0	0.0	0.0
C+ / 6.0	9.2	1.40	14.67	3	2	75	21	2	22	71.9	-19.5	7	N/A	0	0	0.0	0.0
C+ / 6.5	6.2	0.94	10.18	140	2	51	45	2	15	53.8	-13.3	27	4	3,000	100	5.8	0.0
C+ / 6.4	6.2	0.94	10.00	29	2	51	45	2	15	47.9	-13.6	20	4	3,000	100	0.0	0.0
C+ / 6.4	6.1	0.94	10.14	98	2	51	45	2	15	55.7	-13.3	30	4	100,000	0	0.0	0.0
C+ / 6.4	6.2	0.95	10.03	4	2	51	45	2	15	51.8	-13.5	24	4	0	0	0.0	0.0
B / 8.3	4.3	0.61	11.19	53	3	30	65	2	11	32.7	-6.4	44	4	3,000	100	5.8	0.0
B / 8.3	4.3	0.61	11.12	18	3	30	65	2	11	27.2	-6.7	34	4	3,000	100	0.0	0.0
B / 8.3	4.3	0.62	11.19	23	3	30	65	2	11	34.2	-6.3	47	4	100,000	0	0.0	0.0
B / 8.3	4.3	0.62	11.16	1	3	30	65	2	11	30.6	-6.5	40	4	0	0	0.0	0.0
C+ / 6.5	8.0	1.23	12.08	81	2	70	26	2	17	66.0	-16.1	16	4	3,000	100	5.8	0.0
C+ / 6.6	8.0	1.23	11.76	20	2	70	26	2	17	59.4	-16.4	11	4	3,000	100	0.0	0.0
C+ / 6.5	8.0	1.22	12.13	35	2	70	26	2	17	68.2	-16.0	18	4	100,000	0	0.0	0.0
C+ / 6.6	7.9	1.22	11.91	4	2	70	26	2	17	63.8	-16.2	15	4	0	0	0.0	0.0
B / 8.3	7.1	0.07	20.56	N/A	52	47	0	1	352	N/A	N/A	77	4	3,000	100	5.8	0.0
B / 8.2	7.2	0.06	20.06	N/A	52	47	0	1	352	N/A	N/A	70	4	3,000	100	0.0	0.0
B / 8.3	7.2	0.07	20.73	23	52	47	0	1	352	N/A	N/A	78	4	100,000	0	0.0	0.0
C+ / 6.1	11.8	0.92	18.32	2	1	98	0	1	82	51.7	-22.3	76	7	3,000	100	5.8	0.0
C+ / 6.1	11.7	0.92	18.15	N/A	1	98	0	1	82	45.7	-22.5	69	7	3,000	100	0.0	0.0
C+ / 6.1	11.8	0.92	18.30	14	1	98	0	1	82	53.7	-22.2	78	7	100,000	0	0.0	0.0
C+ / 6.1	11.8	0.92	18.36	N/A	1	98	0	1	82	49.7	-22.4	74	7	0	0	0.0	0.0
C+ / 6.2	10.9	1.01	34.59	56	1	98	0	1	56	119.2	-16.5	51	7	3,000	100	5.8	0.0
C+ / 6.1	10.9	1.01	32.10	26	1	98	0	1	56	110.5	-16.8	41	7	3,000	100	0.0	0.0
C+ / 6.1	10.9	1.01	35.06	65	1	98	0	1	56	122.2	-16.5	55	7	100,000	0	0.0	0.0
C+ / 6.2	10.9	1.01	34.52	5	1	98	0	1	56	116.3	-16.6	48	7	0	0	0.0	0.0
C / 5.3	9.3	0.87	29.06	39	1	98	0	1	68	113.3	-13.3	66	7	3,000	100	5.8	0.0
C / 5.3	9.3	0.87	28.18	19	1	98	0	1	68	104.7	-13.6	57	7	3,000	100	0.0	0.0
C / 5.3	9.3	0.87	29.09	68	1	98	0	1	68	116.2	-13.3	69	7	100,000	0	0.0	0.0
C+ / 6.1	10.6	0.83	39.85	12	1	98	0	1	70	103.8	-22.8	51	7	3,000	100	5.8	0.0
C+ / 6.0	10.6	0.84	37.04	3	1	98	0	1	70	95.7	-23.0	40	7	3,000	100	0.0	0.0
C+ / 6.1	10.6	0.84	40.70	18	1	98	0	1	70	106.6	-22.7	55	7	100,000	0	0.0	0.0
C+ / 6.1	10.6	0.83	39.49	N/A	1	98	0	1	70	101.1	-22.8	48	7	0	0	0.0	0.0
C+ / 5.7	14.1	0.87	24.88	1	0	99	0	1	54	N/A	N/A	76	4	3,000	100	5.8	0.0
C+ / 5.7	14.1	0.87	24.28	N/A	0	99	0	1	54	N/A	N/A	69	4	3,000	100	0.0	0.0
C+ / 5.7	14.1	0.88	25.07	29	0	99	0	1	54	N/A	N/A	78	4	100,000	0	0.0	0.0
C+ / 6.0	12.1	0.91	26.88	20	3	93	2	2	36	18.4	-14.6	82	1	3,000	100	5.8	0.0
C+ / 6.0	12.1	0.91	26.66	22	3	93	2	2	36	13.6	-14.9	76	1	3,000	100	0.0	0.0
C+ / 6.0	12.1	0.91	26.86	18	3	93	2	2	36	20.0	-14.5	83	1	100,000	0	0.0	0.0
C+ / 6.0	12.1	0.91	26.83	N/A	3	93	2	2	36	16.8	-14.7	80	1	0	0	0.0	0.0
C- / 3.8	11.2	1.03	29.29	71	3	90	1	6	71	66.2	-14.5	27	1	3,000	100	5.8	0.0
C- / 3.8	11.2	1.03	28.18	64	3	90	1	6	71	59.5	-14.8	20	1	3,000	100	0.0	0.0
C- / 3.8	11.2	1.03	29.44	66	3	90	1	6	71	68.4	-14.4	30	1	100,000	0	0.0	0.0
C- / 3.8	11.2	1.03	29.32	2	3	90	1	6	71	64.0	-14.6	25	1	0	0	0.0	0.0

Fund Type	Fund Name	Ticker Symbol	Overall Investment Rating	Phone	Performance Rating/Pts	3 Mo	6 Mo	1Yr / Pct	3Yr / Pct	5Yr / Pct	Dividend Yield	Expense Ratio
	99 Pct = Best *0 Pct = Worst*							Total Return % through 2/28/17	Annualized		Incl. in Returns	
GR	Nuveen Winslow Large-Cap Growth	NWCAX	D+	(800) 257-8787	C+ / 5.8	9.52	6.44	19.61 /50	6.85 /71	11.27 /68	0.00	1.15
GL	Nuveen Winslow Large-Cap Growth	NWCCX	D+	(800) 257-8787	C+ / 6.3	9.31	6.04	18.69 /46	6.05 /65	10.44 /62	0.00	1.89
GR	Nuveen Winslow Large-Cap Growth I	NVLIX	C-	(800) 257-8787	B- / 7.1	9.59	6.57	19.89 /51	7.12 /73	11.54 /70	0.07	0.89
GR	Nuveen Winslow Large-Cap Growth	NWCRX	C-	(800) 257-8787	C+ / 6.7	9.47	6.32	19.29 /49	6.58 /69	10.99 /66	0.00	1.40
GR	Nuveen Winslow Large-Cap Growth	NWCFX	C	(800) 257-8787	B- / 7.2	9.64	6.65	20.07 /52	7.29 /74	--	0.07	0.74
AA	NWM Momentum	MOMOX	U	(888) 331-9609	U /	3.59	2.85	11.58 /16	--	--	1.49	1.66
GL	NY 529 CSP Direct Aggr Gro Port		A	(800) 662-7447	B / 8.2	7.65	8.59	24.25 /71	8.37 /82	12.83 /82	0.00	0.25
GI	NY 529 CSP Direct Csv Gro Port		C+	(800) 662-7447	D+ / 2.3	2.63	0.37	6.83 / 6	4.17 /45	4.84 /20	0.00	0.25
FO	NY 529 CSP Direct Dev Mkts Idx Port		D	(800) 662-7447	D / 1.6	7.27	4.63	17.24 /39	-0.05 /13	5.57 /25	0.00	0.25
GL	NY 529 CSP Direct Gro Stk Idx Port		A	(800) 662-7447	B+ / 8.7	9.33	8.37	22.45 /64	9.49 /90	13.27 /87	0.00	0.25
GI	NY 529 CSP Direct Growth Port		B	(800) 662-7447	C+ / 6.4	5.97	5.80	18.25 /44	7.09 /73	10.23 /60	0.00	0.25
AA	NY 529 CSP Direct Income Port		C	(800) 662-7447	D- / 1.1	0.79	-1.03	1.52 / 2	1.80 /23	1.29 / 7	0.00	0.25
MC	NY 529 CSP Direct MC Stk Idx Port		A-	(800) 662-7447	B+ / 8.3	6.86	8.79	25.91 /76	8.46 /83	13.21 /86	0.00	0.25
BA	NY 529 CSP Direct Mdt Gro Port		B+	(800) 662-7447	C- / 4.2	4.29	3.07	12.44 /20	5.71 /62	7.59 /39	0.00	0.25
SC	NY 529 CSP Direct SC Stk Idx Port		B+	(800) 662-7447	B+ / 8.5	5.89	10.73	31.86 /90	7.28 /74	13.36 /87	0.00	0.25
GI	NY 529 CSP Direct Val Stk Idx Port		A+	(800) 662-7447	A+ / 9.6	7.01	11.53	27.64 /81	10.81 /97	14.18 /94	0.00	0.25
GR	NYSA Fund	NYSAX	E-	(800) 535-9169	E- / 0.0	1.45	-0.24	7.40 / 6	-19.33 / 0	-10.23 / 1	0.00	6.09
TC	Oak Assoc-Black Oak Emerging Tech	BOGSX	B-	(888) 462-5386	B+ / 8.5	5.71	8.46	32.28 /90	7.66 /76	10.77 /64	0.03	1.25
HL	Oak Assoc-Live Oak Health Sciences	LOGSX	B-	(888) 462-5386	B / 7.9	9.92	3.94	16.12 /35	10.12 /94	15.89 /98	3.07	1.08
SC	Oak Assoc-Pin Oak Equity	POGSX	A+	(888) 462-5386	A+ / 9.8	6.63	15.20	34.55 /94	11.91 /98	15.62 /98	0.59	1.10
TC	Oak Assoc-Red Oak Technology	ROGSX	A+	(888) 462-5386	A+ / 9.9	9.77	17.38	42.16 /98	14.41 /99	17.43 /98	0.38	1.11
GR	Oak Assoc-Rock Oak Core Gr Fund	RCKSX	B	(888) 462-5386	B+ / 8.6	9.99	16.31	32.22 /90	5.45 /59	10.42 /61	0.65	1.52
IN	Oak Ridge Dividend Growth A	ORDAX	B+	(855) 551-5521	B- / 7.2	8.03	8.83	22.05 /62	8.84 /86	--	1.24	42.70
IN	Oak Ridge Dividend Growth I	ORDNX	A	(855) 551-5521	B+ / 8.4	8.04	8.99	22.37 /64	9.10 /87	--	1.51	42.45
FO	Oak Ridge International Small Cap I	ORIIX	U	(855) 551-5521	U /	9.88	9.78	21.99 /62	--	--	1.10	2.12
GR	Oak Ridge Lrg Cap Growth A	ORILX	C+	(855) 551-5521	C / 5.2	8.23	6.65	15.69 /33	6.90 /71	10.34 /61	0.00	1.55
GR	Oak Ridge Lrg Cap Growth C	ORLCX	C+	(855) 551-5521	C+ / 5.6	8.06	6.18	14.70 /29	5.96 /64	9.36 /54	0.00	2.25
GR	Oak Ridge Lrg Cap Growth I	PORYX	C+	(855) 551-5521	C+ / 6.4	8.28	6.67	15.77 /33	6.99 /72	10.40 /61	0.00	1.23
SC	Oak Ridge Sm Cap Growth A	ORIGX	E	(855) 551-5521	D / 1.8	2.53	1.81	18.98 /47	1.74 /22	8.82 /49	0.00	1.40
SC	Oak Ridge Sm Cap Growth C	ORICX	E	(855) 551-5521	D / 2.1	2.35	1.45	18.09 /43	0.98 /18	8.01 /42	0.00	2.19
SC	Oak Ridge Sm Cap Growth I	ORIYX	E+	(855) 551-5521	D+ / 2.8	2.60	1.98	19.41 /49	2.08 /25	9.21 /52	0.00	1.12
GR	Oak Ridge Sm Cap Growth K	ORIKX	D-	(855) 551-5521	D+ / 2.9	2.65	2.05	19.53 /50	2.23 /26	9.26 /53	0.00	0.94
* BA	Oakmark Equity and Income Investor	OAKBX	C+	(800) 625-6275	C+ / 6.3	5.97	9.86	20.94 /57	5.52 /60	8.33 /45	1.43	0.89
BA	Oakmark Equity and Income Service	OARBX	C+	(800) 625-6275	C+ / 6.0	5.86	9.70	20.59 /55	5.18 /56	7.99 /42	1.13	1.20
* GR	Oakmark Fund Investor	OAKMX	A+	(800) 625-6275	A+ / 9.6	5.75	14.28	34.15 /93	9.45 /90	14.62 /96	1.00	0.93
GR	Oakmark Fund Service	OARMX	A+	(800) 625-6275	A / 9.5	5.68	14.10	33.74 /93	9.09 /87	14.26 /95	0.67	1.25
GL	Oakmark Global Investor	OAKGX	C+	(800) 625-6275	B- / 7.0	10.07	14.70	30.29 /87	3.12 /33	9.36 /54	1.01	1.23
GL	Oakmark Global Select Investor	OAKWX	B+	(800) 625-6275	B / 8.2	7.26	14.15	29.74 /86	6.23 /66	11.32 /68	0.96	1.22
GL	Oakmark Global Service	OARGX	C+	(800) 625-6275	C+ / 6.8	10.02	14.50	29.85 /86	2.75 /30	8.98 /50	0.74	1.56
* FO	Oakmark International Investor	OAKIX	D+	(800) 625-6275	C / 4.7	8.47	13.03	26.84 /79	0.49 /16	8.22 /44	1.41	1.05
FO	Oakmark International Service	OARIX	D+	(800) 625-6275	C / 4.4	8.42	12.87	26.47 /78	0.12 /14	7.84 /41	1.09	1.39
FO	Oakmark International Small Cap Inv	OAKEX	D	(800) 625-6275	C- / 3.9	8.97	8.81	25.45 /75	0.80 /17	6.25 /30	2.33	1.38
FO	Oakmark International Small Cap Svc	OAREX	D	(800) 625-6275	C- / 3.7	8.94	8.62	25.13 /74	0.52 /16	5.94 /28	2.07	1.69
MC	Oakmark Select Investor	OAKLX	B+	(800) 625-6275	A+ / 9.6	5.63	13.98	36.92 /96	8.65 /84	14.37 /95	0.88	1.05
MC	Oakmark Select Service	OARLX	B+	(800) 625-6275	A / 9.5	5.55	13.80	36.50 /95	8.31 /81	14.04 /93	0.57	1.39
GR	Oakseed Opportunity Institutional	SEDEX	B	(888) 446-4460	B- / 7.0	6.37	8.22	22.19 /63	6.85 /71	--	0.38	1.32
GR	Oakseed Opportunity Investor	SEEDX	C+	(888) 446-4460	C+ / 6.8	6.28	8.15	21.89 /62	6.59 /69	--	0.12	1.57
FO	Oberweis China Opportunities	OBCHX	E-	(800) 245-7311	E- / 0.2	3.15	1.59	15.60 /32	-5.40 / 2	9.70 /56	0.00	1.95
SC	Oberweis Emerging Growth Portfolio	OBEGX	E	(800) 245-7311	D / 1.6	3.08	1.40	15.86 /34	0.07 /14	9.50 /55	0.00	1.51
FO	Oberweis International Opptys Inst	OBIIX	U	(800) 245-7311	U /	6.27	1.39	10.10 /12	--	--	0.38	1.28
FO	Oberweis Internatl Opportunities	OBIOX	D	(800) 245-7311	D / 1.8	6.31	1.06	10.13 /12	1.59 /21	14.03 /93	0.06	1.85
SC	Oberweis Micro Cap Portfolio	OBMCX	B	(800) 245-7311	A+ / 9.6	7.12	16.19	42.39 /98	7.23 /74	16.84 /98	0.00	1.72

● Denotes fund is closed to new investors
✴ Denotes fund is included in Section II

RISK			NET ASSETS		ASSET				Portfolio Turnover Ratio	BULL / BEAR		FUND MANAGER		MINIMUMS		LOADS	
	3 Year		NAV							Last Bull	Last Bear	Manager	Manager	Initial	Additional	Front	Back
Risk Rating/Pts	Standard Deviation	Beta	As of 2/28/17	Total $(Mil)	Cash %	Stocks %	Bonds %	Other %		Market Return	Market Return	Quality Pct	Tenure (Years)	Purch. $	Purch. $	End Load	End Load
C- /3.2	12.9	1.09	36.44	17	1	98	0	1	88	109.8	-17.7	20	8	3,000	100	5.8	0.0
D+ /2.8	12.9	0.84	33.45	2	1	98	0	1	88	101.5	-18.0	97	8	3,000	100	0.0	0.0
C- /3.3	12.9	1.09	37.32	611	1	98	0	1	88	112.6	-17.6	22	8	100,000	0	0.0	0.0
C- /3.1	12.9	1.09	35.47	2	1	98	0	1	88	107.0	-17.8	18	8	0	0	0.0	0.0
C- /3.3	12.9	1.09	37.61	60	1	98	0	1	88	N/A	N/A	24	8	5,000,000	0	0.0	0.0
U /	N/A	N/A	10.22	59	15	0	84	1	1,302	N/A	N/A	N/A	3	5,000	100	0.0	2.0
B- /7.0	10.5	0.73	28.69	2,531	0	99	0	1	0	124.5	-17.8	99	8	25	25	0.0	0.0
B+ /9.7	3.4	0.24	19.09	2,337	0	25	73	2	0	35.3	-1.1	84	8	25	25	0.0	0.0
C+ /6.5	11.4	0.92	20.81	266	1	98	0	1	0	51.8	-23.4	75	8	25	25	0.0	0.0
C+ /6.7	11.5	0.78	29.40	685	0	99	0	1	0	130.4	-15.2	99	8	25	25	0.0	0.0
B /8.5	7.9	0.75	26.82	2,137	0	74	24	2	0	91.0	-12.4	65	8	25	25	0.0	0.0
B+ /9.8	2.2	0.05	15.35	1,896	25	0	74	1	0	8.7	3.9	83	8	25	25	0.0	0.0
C+ /6.3	11.4	0.90	35.04	872	0	99	0	1	0	131.8	-21.4	72	8	25	25	0.0	0.0
B+ /9.5	5.4	0.85	22.86	2,750	0	49	49	2	0	61.4	-7.0	67	8	25	25	0.0	0.0
C+ /5.6	13.6	0.85	34.89	684	0	99	0	1	0	137.7	-24.6	83	8	25	25	0.0	0.0
B- /7.9	10.1	0.94	29.32	775	0	99	0	1	0	134.4	-18.5	79	8	25	25	0.0	0.0
D+ /2.6	19.9	1.01	4.21	2	0	97	2	1	28	-33.0	-21.4	0	4	1,000	250	2.5	0.0
C /4.3	15.7	1.27	4.81	36	0	99	0	1	35	109.5	-28.7	12	11	2,000	25	0.0	0.0
C /5.0	11.9	0.89	19.84	68	1	98	0	1	14	136.3	-10.4	79	16	2,000	25	0.0	0.0
C+ /6.6	13.1	0.69	60.45	209	10	89	0	1	10	160.8	-20.8	97	12	2,000	25	0.0	0.0
C+ /6.3	13.8	1.18	21.70	412	1	98	0	1	6	173.1	-15.6	84	11	2,000	25	0.0	0.0
C /4.9	12.8	1.13	14.68	8	1	98	0	1	11	101.3	-21.6	9	13	2,000	25	0.0	0.0
B- /7.0	10.4	0.98	13.45	N/A	0	92	7	1	11	N/A	N/A	56	4	1,000	100	5.8	0.0
B- /7.0	10.4	0.98	13.54	N/A	0	92	7	1	11	N/A	N/A	59	4	100,000	0	0.0	0.0
U /	N/A	N/A	11.66	38	0	97	1	2	76	N/A	N/A	N/A	2	1,000,000	0	0.0	0.0
C+ /6.7	10.9	0.98	21.82	38	0	98	1	1	23	101.9	-16.4	32	18	1,000	100	5.8	0.0
C+ /6.7	10.9	0.98	19.58	15	0	98	1	1	23	92.3	-16.7	22	18	1,000	500	0.0	0.0
C+ /6.7	10.9	0.98	22.24	13	0	98	1	1	23	102.6	-16.4	33	18	5,000,000	0	0.0	0.0
C- /3.3	15.7	0.92	34.07	264	3	94	2	1	30	81.9	-21.5	20	23	1,000	100	5.8	0.0
C- /3.0	15.7	0.92	26.55	55	3	94	2	1	30	74.7	-21.8	14	23	1,000	500	0.0	0.0
C- /3.3	15.7	0.92	35.12	1,155	3	94	2	1	30	85.5	-21.4	23	23	5,000,000	0	0.0	0.0
C- /3.3	15.7	1.21	34.88	158	3	94	2	1	30	85.6	-21.5	2	23	5,000,000	0	0.0	0.0
C+ /6.2	8.1	1.14	31.76	15,167	0	0	0	100	18	74.5	-13.7	36	22	1,000	100	0.0	0.0
C+ /6.3	8.1	1.15	31.59	691	0	0	0	100	18	71.4	-13.8	32	22	0	0	0.0	0.0
C+ /6.1	12.4	1.13	75.45	15,635	1	94	3	2	20	143.3	-16.3	43	17	1,000	100	0.0	0.0
C+ /6.1	12.4	1.13	75.22	167	1	94	3	2	20	139.4	-16.5	38	17	0	0	0.0	0.0
C /4.8	14.6	1.04	29.96	2,343	2	97	0	1	32	88.5	-21.1	91	14	1,000	100	0.0	0.0
C+ /5.8	13.4	0.99	17.58	2,169	0	0	0	100	17	108.4	-18.4	97	11	1,000	100	0.0	0.0
C /4.8	14.6	1.04	29.20	25	2	97	0	1	32	85.0	-21.3	90	14	0	0	0.0	0.0
C /4.3	15.2	1.15	23.82	26,299	2	96	1	1	44	78.0	-22.8	79	25	1,000	100	0.0	0.0
C /4.3	15.2	1.15	23.96	523	2	96	1	1	44	74.7	-22.9	77	25	0	0	0.0	0.0
C /4.4	13.9	1.04	15.43	2,281	0	0	0	100	38	64.0	-23.8	81	22	1,000	100	0.0	2.0
C /4.5	13.9	1.05	15.36	2	0	0	0	100	38	61.6	-23.9	79	22	0	0	0.0	2.0
C /4.9	13.5	0.91	44.29	4,859	6	93	0	1	38	141.3	-16.9	73	21	1,000	100	0.0	0.0
C /4.9	13.5	0.91	43.77	31	6	93	0	1	38	137.5	-17.0	70	21	0	0	0.0	0.0
C+ /6.0	10.7	0.91	12.47	48	15	84	0	1	86	N/A	N/A	41	5	10,000	250	0.0	0.0
C+ /6.0	10.7	0.90	12.40	7	15	84	0	1	86	N/A	N/A	38	5	2,500	100	0.0	0.0
D- /1.2	22.1	1.00	11.97	96	9	90	0	1	81	94.9	-41.7	13	N/A	1,000	100	0.0	2.0
D+ /2.4	16.9	0.84	25.22	46	0	99	0	1	200	94.2	-32.9	11	N/A	1,000	100	0.0	1.0
U /	N/A	N/A	10.33	711	1	94	3	2	211	N/A	N/A	N/A	3	1,000,000	0	0.0	2.0
C+ /6.5	11.5	0.68	21.46	739	1	97	1	1	214	140.0	-25.4	85	10	1,000	100	0.0	2.0
C- /3.8	15.6	0.91	23.17	73	2	97	0	1	133	169.7	-29.0	80	2	1,000	100	0.0	1.0

					PERFORMANCE							
						Total Return % through 2/28/17					Incl. in Returns	
									Annualized		Dividend	Expense
Fund Type	Fund Name	Ticker Symbol	Overall Investment Rating	Phone	Perfor-mance Rating/Pts	3 Mo	6 Mo	1Yr / Pct	3Yr / Pct	5Yr / Pct	Yield	Ratio
MC	Oberweis Small Cap Opportunity	OBSOX	D	(800) 245-7311	C / 5.5	5.51	10.01	26.28 /77	3.40 /36	10.22 /60	0.00	2.00
PM	OCM Gold Fund Advisor	OCMAX	E-	(800) 628-9403	E+ / 0.9	7.91	-11.87	21.60 /60	-0.79 /10	-11.93 / 0	0.00	2.01
PM	OCM Gold Fund Investor	OCMGX	E-	(800) 628-9403	E / 0.5	7.69	-12.20	20.48 /55	-1.52 / 8	-12.52 / 0	0.00	2.59
GR	OH CollegeAdv 529 BR Cap App Opt		C	(800) 441-7762	C+ / 6.0	9.45	7.09	20.47 /55	6.84 /71	11.26 /68	0.00	1.26
GR	OH CollegeAdv 529 BR Cap App Opt		C+	(800) 441-7762	C+ / 6.5	9.29	6.70	19.57 /50	6.06 /65	10.43 /61	0.00	2.01
AA	OH CollegeAdv 529 BR Csv 0-5 Opt		C+	(800) 441-7762	C- / 4.0	6.06	7.42	18.88 /47	4.53 /49	8.06 /43	0.00	1.40
AA	OH CollegeAdv 529 BR Csv 0-5 Opt		C+	(800) 441-7762	C / 4.5	5.84	7.07	17.95 /43	3.75 /40	7.25 /36	0.00	2.15
AA	OH CollegeAdv 529 BR Csv 10-12		C	(800) 441-7762	D- / 1.0	2.07	2.15	6.66 / 5	1.70 /22	2.80 /10	0.00	1.18
AA	OH CollegeAdv 529 BR Csv 10-12		C	(800) 441-7762	D- / 1.3	1.83	1.83	5.89 / 5	0.93 /18	2.04 / 8	0.00	1.93
AA	OH CollegeAdv 529 BR Csv 13-16		C	(800) 441-7762	E+ / 0.8	1.59	1.77	5.31 / 4	0.94 /18	1.85 / 8	0.00	1.13
AA	OH CollegeAdv 529 BR Csv 13-16		C	(800) 441-7762	D- / 1.0	1.40	1.40	4.51 / 4	0.18 /14	1.08 / 6	0.00	1.88
AA	OH CollegeAdv 529 BR Csv 17Pl Opt		C	(800) 441-7762	E+ / 0.8	1.43	1.71	4.91 / 4	1.14 /19	1.75 / 8	0.00	1.10
AA	OH CollegeAdv 529 BR Csv 17Pl Opt		C	(800) 441-7762	D- / 1.0	1.23	1.23	4.08 / 3	0.34 /15	0.98 / 6	0.00	1.85
AA	OH CollegeAdv 529 BR Csv 6-9 Opt		C	(800) 441-7762	D / 2.1	3.82	3.32	11.66 /17	3.57 /38	5.61 /26	0.00	1.37
AA	OH CollegeAdv 529 BR Csv 6-9 Opt		C+	(800) 441-7762	D+ / 2.4	3.59	2.93	10.84 /14	2.78 /30	4.81 /20	0.00	2.12
IN	OH CollegeAdv 529 BR Eq Div Opt A		A+	(800) 441-7762	B / 8.0	6.00	11.45	26.63 /78	9.36 /89	11.15 /67	0.00	1.26
IN	OH CollegeAdv 529 BR Eq Div Opt C		A+	(800) 441-7762	B+ / 8.4	5.85	11.05	25.65 /75	8.55 /83	10.32 /61	0.00	2.01
GL	OH CollegeAdv 529 BR Glbl All Opt A		C-	(800) 441-7762	D / 1.7	4.52	3.85	12.43 /20	2.20 /25	4.54 /18	0.00	1.35
GL	OH CollegeAdv 529 BR Glbl All Opt C		C-	(800) 441-7762	D / 2.1	4.32	3.46	11.59 /16	1.44 /21	3.76 /14	0.00	2.10
SC	OH CollegeAdv 529 BR ING SmCo		A-	(800) 441-7762	A / 9.3	6.16	13.59	37.91 /96	9.38 /89	13.22 /86	0.00	1.75
SC	OH CollegeAdv 529 BR ING SmCo		A	(800) 441-7762	A / 9.5	5.97	13.17	36.89 /96	8.55 /83	12.37 /78	0.00	2.50
FO	OH CollegeAdv 529 BR Intl Opp Opt		E+	(800) 441-7762	E- / 0.2	3.31	-0.64	11.94 /18	-4.33 / 3	2.84 /10	0.00	1.83
FO	OH CollegeAdv 529 BR Intl Opp Opt		E+	(800) 441-7762	E- / 0.2	3.24	-0.92	11.11 /15	-5.04 / 2	2.09 / 8	0.00	2.58
GR	OH CollegeAdv 529 BR LC Core Opt		A+	(800) 441-7762	B+ / 8.4	9.01	14.29	27.34 /80	8.71 /85	12.20 /76	0.00	1.45
GR	OH CollegeAdv 529 BR LC Core Opt		A+	(800) 441-7762	B+ / 8.8	8.85	13.89	26.46 /78	7.93 /78	11.36 /69	0.00	2.20
AA	OH CollegeAdv 529 BR Mdt 0-5 Opt		C+	(800) 441-7762	C- / 4.0	6.02	7.39	18.81 /46	4.57 /49	8.17 /43	0.00	1.40
AA	OH CollegeAdv 529 BR Mdt 0-5 Opt		C+	(800) 441-7762	C / 4.5	5.80	6.98	17.89 /42	3.79 /40	7.36 /37	0.00	2.15
AA	OH CollegeAdv 529 BR Mdt 10-12		C	(800) 441-7762	D+ / 2.3	4.20	3.86	13.03 /22	3.70 /39	6.09 /29	0.00	1.39
AA	OH CollegeAdv 529 BR Mdt 10-12		C+	(800) 441-7762	D+ / 2.7	4.02	3.45	12.19 /19	2.94 /31	5.29 /23	0.00	2.14
AA	OH CollegeAdv 529 BR Mdt 13-16		C	(800) 441-7762	D- / 1.5	2.78	2.63	9.09 /10	2.62 /28	4.10 /16	0.00	1.27
AA	OH CollegeAdv 529 BR Mdt 13-16		C	(800) 441-7762	D / 1.7	2.62	2.29	8.28 / 8	1.84 /23	3.32 /12	0.00	2.02
AA	OH CollegeAdv 529 BR Mdt 17Pl Op		C	(800) 441-7762	D- / 1.1	2.27	2.35	7.48 / 7	1.95 /24	3.18 /12	0.00	1.21
AA	OH CollegeAdv 529 BR Mdt 17Pl Op		C	(800) 441-7762	D- / 1.4	2.13	1.96	6.78 / 6	1.20 /19	2.42 / 9	0.00	1.96
AA	OH CollegeAdv 529 BR Mdt 6-9 Opt		C+	(800) 441-7762	C- / 3.9	5.76	7.03	18.32 /44	4.66 /50	8.03 /42	0.00	1.40
AA	OH CollegeAdv 529 BR Mdt 6-9 Opt		C+	(800) 441-7762	C / 4.4	5.60	6.61	17.41 /40	3.87 /41	7.22 /36	0.00	2.15
MC	OH CollegeAdv 529 BR Rain MCE		D+	(800) 441-7762	C- / 3.2	5.70	6.35	19.35 /49	3.36 /35	8.37 /45	0.00	1.56
MC	OH CollegeAdv 529 BR Rain MCE		D+	(800) 441-7762	C- / 3.7	5.51	5.94	18.46 /45	2.55 /28	7.53 /39	0.00	2.31
EN	Oil Equip Distr & Serv UltSec ProFd	OEPIX	E-	(888) 776-3637	E- / 0.1	-3.11	14.82	49.36 /99	-15.74 / 0	-6.39 / 1	0.05	1.79
GR	Old Westbury All Cap Core Fund	OWACX	C+	(800) 607-2200	C+ / 5.8	7.20	8.60	22.02 /62	4.35 /47	8.22 /44	1.02	1.01
* FO	Old Westbury Large Cap Strategies	OWLSX	C	(800) 607-2200	C / 4.5	5.71	4.18	16.69 /37	4.67 /50	8.62 /47	0.72	1.15
* GL	Old Westbury Small & Mid Cap Strat	OWSMX	C	(800) 607-2200	C+ / 5.6	5.81	4.70	21.56 /60	5.19 /56	8.91 /50	0.53	1.18
GR	Olstein All Cap Value Adv	OFAFX	B-	(800) 799-2113	B / 7.9	5.13	9.97	24.59 /72	8.02 /79	12.37 /78	0.00	1.26
GR	Olstein All Cap Value C	OFALX	C+	(800) 799-2113	B- / 7.1	4.86	9.46	23.41 /68	6.96 /72	11.35 /69	0.00	2.26
GI	Olstein Strategic Opps Fd A	OFSAX	C	(800) 799-2113	B- / 7.0	2.74	13.05	32.37 /91	6.30 /67	12.47 /79	0.00	1.70
GI	Olstein Strategic Opps Fd Adviser	OFSFX	U	(800) 799-2113	U /	2.79	13.22	32.71 /91	--	--	0.00	1.45
GI	Olstein Strategic Opps Fd C	OFSCX	C	(800) 799-2113	B- / 7.3	2.53	12.64	31.46 /89	5.50 /60	11.64 /71	0.00	2.45
AA	OnTrack Core Fund Adv	OTRGX	C	(855) 747-9555	C- / 3.0	5.06	4.36	14.99 /30	2.36 /26	--	6.63	3.18
AA	OnTrack Core Fund Inv	OTRFX	C	(855) 747-9555	C- / 3.1	5.11	4.48	15.24 /31	2.57 /28	--	6.86	2.94
AA	Oppenheimer 529 BS AgeBsd 0-6yr 4		B	(888) 470-0862	C+ / 6.7	6.95	6.89	19.25 /48	7.03 /72	10.85 /65	0.00	0.60
AA	Oppenheimer 529 BS AgeBsd 0-6yr		B-	(888) 470-0862	C / 4.7	6.73	6.57	18.42 /45	5.05 /55	8.82 /49	0.00	0.96
AA	Oppenheimer 529 BS AgeBsd 0-6yr		B	(888) 470-0862	C / 5.2	6.71	6.46	18.14 /43	4.78 /52	8.55 /47	0.00	1.21
AA	Oppenheimer 529 BS AgeBsd 0-6yr		B	(888) 470-0862	C / 5.4	6.74	6.56	18.40 /45	5.05 /55	8.83 /49	0.00	0.96

• Denotes fund is closed to new investors
* Denotes fund is included in Section II

Risk Rating/Pts	Standard Deviation	Beta	NAV As of 2/28/17	Total $(Mil)	Cash %	Stocks %	Bonds %	Other %	Portfolio Turnover Ratio	Last Bull Market Return	Last Bear Market Return	Manager Quality Pct	Manager Tenure (Years)	Initial Purch. $	Additional Purch. $	Front End Load	Back End Load
D+ /2.8	16.6	1.22	14.59	10	5	94	0	1	134	100.1	-23.4	4	8	1,000	100	0.0	1.0
E- /0.0	45.2	2.56	10.45	8	2	97	0	1	11	-45.4	-11.6	94	21	5,000	50	0.0	1.5
E- /0.0	45.2	2.57	9.88	35	2	97	0	1	11	-47.3	-11.8	92	21	1,000	50	4.5	1.5
C /5.1	13.0	1.08	21.89	74	3	96	0	1	0	103.4	-20.6	21	N/A	25	25	5.8	0.0
C /5.0	13.0	1.09	20.71	22	3	96	0	1	0	95.4	-20.8	15	N/A	25	25	0.0	0.0
B- /7.5	8.9	1.36	18.39	5	2	79	17	2	0	72.8	-16.1	13	N/A	25	25	5.8	0.0
B- /7.5	8.9	1.36	17.41	2	2	79	17	2	0	66.0	-16.4	8	N/A	25	25	0.0	0.0
B+ /9.8	2.8	0.44	12.34	9	48	23	28	1	0	20.5	-4.1	55	N/A	25	25	5.8	0.0
B+ /9.8	2.9	0.44	11.68	3	48	23	28	1	0	15.9	-4.6	44	N/A	25	25	0.0	0.0
B+ /9.9	2.3	0.34	11.51	21	61	18	20	1	0	13.7	-3.3	54	N/A	25	25	5.8	0.0
B+ /9.9	2.3	0.35	10.89	10	61	18	20	1	0	9.1	-3.6	43	N/A	25	25	0.0	0.0
B+ /9.9	2.0	0.31	11.33	34	67	15	17	1	0	12.5	-3.0	60	N/A	25	25	5.8	0.0
B+ /9.9	2.0	0.30	10.71	18	67	15	17	1	0	8.0	-3.2	50	N/A	25	25	0.0	0.0
B+ /9.1	4.9	0.76	15.23	11	0	39	59	2	0	44.4	-7.9	48	N/A	25	25	5.8	0.0
B+ /9.1	4.9	0.76	14.42	3	0	39	59	2	0	38.8	-8.2	37	N/A	25	25	0.0	0.0
B- /7.8	10.2	0.94	23.16	149	3	96	0	1	0	100.5	-13.9	67	N/A	25	25	5.8	0.0
B- /7.7	10.2	0.94	21.90	51	3	96	0	1	0	92.6	-14.3	58	N/A	25	25	0.0	0.0
B /8.2	6.5	0.98	14.56	195	0	57	39	4	0	40.7	-13.8	44	N/A	25	25	5.8	0.0
B /8.1	6.5	0.98	13.77	147	0	57	39	4	0	35.0	-14.1	34	N/A	25	25	0.0	0.0
C+ /5.6	14.2	0.89	25.32	32	3	96	0	1	0	139.3	-24.1	90	N/A	25	25	5.8	0.0
C+ /5.6	14.2	0.89	23.97	9	3	96	0	1	0	129.8	-24.3	87	N/A	25	25	0.0	0.0
C /5.5	11.2	0.85	12.47	36	4	95	0	1	0	35.3	-25.3	21	N/A	25	25	5.8	0.0
C /5.4	11.2	0.85	11.80	12	4	95	0	1	0	30.0	-25.5	15	N/A	25	25	0.0	0.0
B- /7.2	11.7	1.09	22.87	26	1	98	0	1	0	123.8	-22.6	39	N/A	25	25	5.8	0.0
B- /7.2	11.7	1.09	21.65	11	1	98	0	1	0	115.0	-22.8	30	N/A	25	25	0.0	0.0
B- /7.6	8.8	1.34	18.32	89	3	80	16	1	0	73.8	-15.9	14	N/A	25	25	5.8	0.0
B- /7.6	8.8	1.34	17.33	32	3	80	16	1	0	67.0	-16.2	9	8	25	25	0.0	0.0
B /8.8	5.6	0.88	15.87	202	0	45	54	1	0	49.4	-9.3	38	N/A	25	25	5.8	0.0
B /8.8	5.6	0.88	15.00	62	0	45	54	1	0	43.5	-9.6	29	N/A	25	25	0.0	0.0
B+ /9.6	3.8	0.59	13.68	653	26	31	41	2	0	31.0	-6.0	52	N/A	25	25	5.8	0.0
B+ /9.6	3.8	0.59	12.94	121	26	31	41	2	0	25.9	-6.3	41	8	25	25	0.0	0.0
B+ /9.7	3.1	0.48	12.64	472	37	23	38	2	0	23.6	-5.0	54	N/A	25	25	5.8	0.0
B+ /9.7	3.2	0.48	11.97	107	37	23	38	2	0	18.6	-5.3	43	N/A	25	25	0.0	0.0
B- /7.8	8.4	1.29	18.73	135	2	76	20	2	0	71.7	-15.0	17	N/A	25	25	5.8	0.0
B- /7.7	8.4	1.29	17.74	49	2	76	20	2	0	64.7	-15.3	11	N/A	25	25	0.0	0.0
C /5.2	12.7	0.98	22.27	14	1	98	0	1	0	92.2	-24.5	11	N/A	25	25	5.8	0.0
C /5.2	12.7	0.98	21.05	8	1	98	0	1	0	84.3	-24.7	7	N/A	25	25	0.0	0.0
E- /0.0	35.8	1.69	15.63	20	24	74	1	1	229	7.7	-47.1	4	4	15,000	100	0.0	0.0
C+ /6.2	9.8	0.88	14.85	1,381	0	90	8	2	43	60.1	-18.3	18	6	1,000	100	0.0	0.0
C+ /6.4	10.0	0.72	13.47	15,507	0	96	3	1	61	73.2	-25.5	95	6	1,000	100	0.0	0.0
C /5.2	9.9	0.70	15.90	5,733	2	91	6	1	50	84.9	-22.0	96	12	1,000	100	0.0	0.0
C /4.8	12.4	1.11	23.58	196	3	93	3	1	51	124.7	-19.1	29	22	1,000	100	0.0	0.0
C /4.4	12.4	1.11	19.42	499	3	93	3	1	51	114.0	-19.4	19	22	1,000	100	0.0	0.0
C- /3.8	15.6	1.17	16.89	40	1	96	1	2	58	135.5	-24.0	11	11	1,000	100	5.5	0.0
U /	N/A	N/A	16.96	80	1	96	1	2	58	N/A	N/A	N/A	11	1,000	100	0.0	0.0
C- /3.6	15.6	1.17	15.42	37	1	96	1	2	58	126.2	-24.2	7	11	1,000	100	0.0	0.0
B /8.2	5.0	0.20	48.73	5	56	5	38	1	589	N/A	N/A	80	4	1,000	500	0.0	0.0
B /8.1	5.0	0.20	48.50	35	56	5	38	1	589	N/A	N/A	81	4	1,000	500	0.0	0.0
B /8.5	9.1	1.44	20.94	132	0	0	0	100	0	99.4	-14.9	28	10	25	15	0.0	0.0
B- /7.9	9.5	1.47	14.27	100	0	0	0	100	0	82.3	-16.9	11	10	25	15	3.5	0.0
B- /7.9	9.5	1.48	14.00	46	0	0	0	100	0	79.7	-16.9	9	10	25	15	0.0	0.0
B- /7.9	9.5	1.48	18.85	2	0	0	0	100	0	82.1	-16.8	11	10	25	15	0.0	0.0

					PERFORMANCE							
99 Pct = Best						Total Return % through 2/28/17					Incl. in Returns	
0 Pct = Worst			Overall		Perfor-				Annualized		Dividend	Expense
Fund		Ticker	Investment		mance						Yield	Ratio
Type	Fund Name	Symbol	Rating	Phone	Rating/Pts	3 Mo	6 Mo	1Yr / Pct	3Yr / Pct	5Yr / Pct		
AA	Oppenheimer 529 BS AgeBsd 0-6yr		B-	(888) 470-0862	C+ / 5.6	6.80	6.69	18.68 /46	5.32 /58	9.10 /51	0.00	0.71
AA	Oppenheimer 529 BS AgeBsd		B+	(888) 470-0862	C / 4.3	4.86	4.29	13.28 /23	5.23 /57	7.66 /39	0.00	0.59
AA	Oppenheimer 529 BS AgeBsd		C+	(888) 470-0862	D+ / 2.8	4.83	4.23	13.06 /22	3.81 /41	6.21 /30	0.00	0.93
AA	Oppenheimer 529 BS AgeBsd		C+	(888) 470-0862	C- / 3.2	4.78	4.08	12.73 /21	3.55 /38	5.94 /28	0.00	1.18
AA	Oppenheimer 529 BS AgeBsd		B-	(888) 470-0862	C- / 3.5	4.84	4.28	13.10 /22	3.81 /41	6.21 /30	0.00	0.93
AA	Oppenheimer 529 BS AgeBsd		B-	(888) 470-0862	C- / 3.6	4.91	4.36	13.32 /23	4.06 /44	6.47 /31	0.00	0.68
AA	Oppenheimer 529 BS AgeBsd		B	(888) 470-0862	C- / 3.7	4.25	3.95	11.96 /18	4.62 /50	6.57 /32	0.00	0.59
AA	Oppenheimer 529 BS AgeBsd		C+	(888) 470-0862	D+ / 2.5	4.24	3.80	11.82 /17	3.48 /37	5.39 /24	0.00	0.92
AA	Oppenheimer 529 BS AgeBsd		C+	(888) 470-0862	D+ / 2.9	4.21	3.69	11.63 /17	3.21 /34	5.13 /22	0.00	1.17
AA	Oppenheimer 529 BS AgeBsd		C+	(888) 470-0862	C- / 3.1	4.28	3.82	11.90 /18	3.48 /37	5.40 /24	0.00	0.92
AA	Oppenheimer 529 BS AgeBsd		B-	(888) 470-0862	C- / 3.2	4.30	3.92	12.17 /19	3.72 /40	5.66 /26	0.00	0.67
AA	Oppenheimer 529 BS AgeBsd		C+	(888) 470-0862	D / 2.2	2.76	2.42	7.85 / 7	3.15 /33	4.20 /16	0.00	0.55
AA	Oppenheimer 529 BS AgeBsd		C+	(888) 470-0862	D / 1.6	3.01	2.17	8.25 / 8	2.55 /28	3.58 /13	0.00	0.86
AA	Oppenheimer 529 BS AgeBsd		C+	(888) 470-0862	D / 1.9	2.84	2.00	7.98 / 7	2.27 /26	3.32 /12	0.00	1.11
AA	Oppenheimer 529 BS AgeBsd		C+	(888) 470-0862	D / 2.0	2.92	2.16	8.21 / 8	2.52 /28	3.57 /13	0.00	0.86
AA	Oppenheimer 529 BS AgeBsd		C+	(888) 470-0862	D / 2.1	2.98	2.31	8.53 / 8	2.79 /30	3.83 /14	0.00	0.61
AA	Oppenheimer 529 BS AgeBsd 18yr 4		C	(888) 470-0862	D- / 1.2	1.24	0.87	3.75 / 3	1.67 /22	1.81 / 8	0.00	0.48
AA	Oppenheimer 529 BS AgeBsd 18yr A		C	(888) 470-0862	E+ / 0.9	1.36	0.77	3.98 / 3	1.28 /20	1.46 / 7	0.00	0.73
AA	Oppenheimer 529 BS AgeBsd 18yr C		C	(888) 470-0862	D- / 1.1	1.28	0.69	3.74 / 3	1.03 /18	1.21 / 7	0.00	0.98
AA	Oppenheimer 529 BS AgeBsd 18yr G		C	(888) 470-0862	D- / 1.2	1.42	0.82	4.06 / 3	1.28 /20	1.48 / 7	0.00	0.73
AA	Oppenheimer 529 BS AgeBsd 18yr H		C	(888) 470-0862	D- / 1.3	1.46	0.94	4.27 / 3	1.53 /21	1.74 / 8	0.00	0.48
AA	Oppenheimer 529 BS AgeBsd 7-9yr 4		B+	(888) 470-0862	C / 5.2	5.57	5.23	15.42 /32	5.85 /63	8.75 /48	0.00	0.59
AA	Oppenheimer 529 BS AgeBsd 7-9yr		C+	(888) 470-0862	C- / 3.4	5.56	5.15	15.05 /30	4.23 /46	7.07 /35	0.00	0.94
AA	Oppenheimer 529 BS AgeBsd 7-9yr		B-	(888) 470-0862	C- / 3.9	5.45	5.04	14.73 /29	3.96 /42	6.80 /33	0.00	1.19
AA	Oppenheimer 529 BS AgeBsd 7-9yr		B-	(888) 470-0862	C- / 4.1	5.51	5.08	14.95 /30	4.22 /45	7.06 /35	0.00	0.94
AA	Oppenheimer 529 BS AgeBsd 7-9yr		B	(888) 470-0862	C / 4.3	5.56	5.25	15.26 /31	4.48 /49	7.35 /37	0.00	0.69
BA	Oppenheimer 529 BS Bal Port 4		B	(888) 470-0862	C- / 3.7	4.32	3.93	12.16 /18	4.72 /51	6.67 /33	0.00	0.65
BA	Oppenheimer 529 BS Bal Port A		C+	(888) 470-0862	D+ / 2.4	4.22	3.81	11.91 /18	3.42 /36	5.33 /24	0.00	0.88
BA	Oppenheimer 529 BS Bal Port C		C+	(888) 470-0862	D+ / 2.8	4.15	3.64	11.55 /16	3.17 /33	5.05 /22	0.00	1.13
BA	Oppenheimer 529 BS Bal Port G		C+	(888) 470-0862	C- / 3.0	4.24	3.80	11.85 /17	3.41 /36	5.31 /23	0.00	0.88
BA	Oppenheimer 529 BS Bal Port H		B-	(888) 470-0862	C- / 3.2	4.30	3.96	12.12 /18	3.68 /39	5.59 /25	0.00	0.63
GR	Oppenheimer 529 BS Eq Port 4		A+	(888) 470-0862	B- / 7.3	7.55	7.76	21.23 /58	7.54 /76	11.91 /73	0.00	0.63
GR	Oppenheimer 529 BS Eq Port A		B-	(888) 470-0862	C / 5.3	7.39	7.54	20.19 /53	5.35 /58	9.63 /56	0.00	0.94
GR	Oppenheimer 529 BS Eq Port C		B-	(888) 470-0862	C+ / 5.8	7.28	7.36	19.82 /51	5.09 /55	9.33 /53	0.00	1.19
GR	Oppenheimer 529 BS Eq Port G		B-	(888) 470-0862	C+ / 6.0	7.40	7.52	20.23 /53	5.36 /58	9.61 /55	0.00	0.94
GR	Oppenheimer 529 BS Eq Port H		B-	(888) 470-0862	C+ / 6.3	7.44	7.67	20.51 /55	5.63 /61	9.89 /58	0.00	0.69
AA	Oppenheimer 529 BS Idx AB 0-6yr 4		A+	(888) 470-0862	B- / 7.2	6.98	7.91	21.46 /60	7.43 /75	11.08 /67	0.00	0.20
AA	Oppenheimer 529 BS Idx AB 10-11yr		B+	(888) 470-0862	C / 4.6	4.85	4.78	14.17 /26	5.45 /59	7.79 /41	0.00	0.21
AA	Oppenheimer 529 BS Idx AB 12-14yr		B	(888) 470-0862	C- / 3.7	4.18	3.92	11.89 /18	4.76 /52	6.71 /33	0.00	0.21
AA	Oppenheimer 529 BS Idx AB 15-17yr		C+	(888) 470-0862	D / 2.2	2.75	1.91	7.25 / 6	3.36 /35	4.46 /18	0.00	0.22
AA	Oppenheimer 529 BS Idx AB 18 yr 4		C	(888) 470-0862	D- / 1.2	1.29	0.00	2.92 / 3	1.94 /24	2.27 / 9	0.00	0.22
AA	Oppenheimer 529 BS Idx AB 7-9 yr 4		A-	(888) 470-0862	C+ / 5.6	5.63	5.90	16.58 /37	6.10 /65	8.87 /50	0.00	0.21
BA	Oppenheimer 529 BS Idx Bal Port 4		B	(888) 470-0862	C- / 3.7	4.16	3.89	11.88 /18	4.72 /51	6.69 /33	0.00	0.21
AG	Oppenheimer 529 SE Aggressive 3		B-	(888) 470-0862	C+ / 6.4	7.29	8.43	22.00 /62	5.50 /60	9.37 /54	0.00	2.03
AG	Oppenheimer 529 SE Aggressive A		B-	(888) 470-0862	C+ / 6.1	7.50	8.84	22.94 /66	6.30 /67	10.20 /60	0.00	1.19
GR	Oppenheimer 529 SE Cap Apprec A		B	(888) 470-0862	C / 5.1	7.95	6.21	18.25 /44	5.99 /64	10.40 /61	0.00	1.11
GR	Oppenheimer 529 SE Cap Apprec B		B-	(888) 470-0862	C / 5.4	7.76	5.83	17.39 /40	5.20 /56	9.57 /55	0.00	2.06
GR	Oppenheimer 529 SE Cap Apprec C		B-	(888) 470-0862	C / 5.4	7.77	5.84	17.39 /40	5.20 /56	9.57 /55	0.00	2.06
AA	Oppenheimer 529 SE Conserative 3		C+	(888) 470-0862	D+ / 2.6	3.75	3.18	11.45 /16	2.99 /32	4.60 /19	0.00	2.04
AA	Oppenheimer 529 SE Conserative A		C+	(888) 470-0862	D+ / 2.4	3.97	3.60	12.31 /19	3.77 /40	5.40 /24	0.00	1.06
SC	Oppenheimer 529 SE Main St		B-	(888) 470-0862	C+ / 6.8	7.35	9.93	25.96 /76	6.72 /70	11.64 /71	0.00	1.11
SC	Oppenheimer 529 SE Main St		B+	(888) 470-0862	B- / 7.0	7.14	9.49	24.99 /73	5.91 /63	10.79 /64	0.00	2.19

● Denotes fund is closed to new investors
* Denotes fund is included in Section II

www.thestreetratings.com

Risk Rating/Pts	3 Year Standard Deviation	Beta	NAV As of 2/28/17	Total $(Mil)	Cash %	Stocks %	Bonds %	Other %	Portfolio Turnover Ratio	Last Bull Market Return	Last Bear Market Return	Manager Quality Pct	Manager Tenure (Years)	Initial Purch. $	Additional Purch. $	Front End Load	Back End Load
B- / 7.9	9.5	1.47	19.31	1	0	0	0	100	0	84.8	-16.8	12	10	25	15	0.0	0.0
B+ / 9.5	6.1	0.97	19.19	158	0	0	0	100	0	63.6	-8.9	49	10	25	15	0.0	0.0
B+ / 9.0	6.5	1.02	12.81	41	0	0	0	100	0	53.2	-10.9	27	10	25	15	3.5	0.0
B+ / 9.0	6.5	1.02	12.49	42	0	0	0	100	0	51.2	-11.0	24	10	25	15	0.0	0.0
B+ / 9.1	6.5	1.01	17.53	47	0	0	0	100	0	53.4	-10.9	28	10	25	15	0.0	0.0
B+ / 9.1	6.5	1.02	17.95	28	0	0	0	100	0	55.4	-10.8	30	10	25	15	0.0	0.0
B+ / 9.8	5.2	0.83	18.16	350	0	0	0	100	0	52.7	-7.0	56	10	25	15	0.0	0.0
B+ / 9.4	5.5	0.87	12.30	58	0	0	0	100	0	44.9	-9.0	36	10	25	15	3.5	0.0
B+ / 9.4	5.6	0.87	12.38	63	0	0	0	100	0	43.0	-9.0	33	10	25	15	0.0	0.0
B+ / 9.4	5.6	0.87	16.83	127	0	0	0	100	0	44.8	-8.9	36	10	25	15	0.0	0.0
B+ / 9.4	5.6	0.87	17.24	73	0	0	0	100	0	46.9	-8.9	39	10	25	15	0.0	0.0
B+ / 9.9	3.2	0.51	15.66	340	0	0	0	100	0	31.2	-3.8	67	10	25	15	0.0	0.0
B+ / 9.9	3.7	0.57	11.29	46	0	0	0	100	0	28.0	-5.3	53	10	25	15	3.5	0.0
B+ / 9.9	3.6	0.56	11.23	73	0	0	0	100	0	26.2	-5.3	50	10	25	15	0.0	0.0
B+ / 9.9	3.6	0.56	15.16	159	0	0	0	100	0	27.9	-5.2	53	10	25	15	0.0	0.0
B+ / 9.9	3.6	0.56	15.53	89	0	0	0	100	0	29.6	-5.1	57	10	25	15	0.0	0.0
B+ / 9.9	1.4	0.19	13.85	195	0	0	0	100	0	12.2	-0.6	75	10	25	15	0.0	0.0
B+ / 9.9	1.6	0.22	10.44	22	0	0	0	100	0	10.4	-1.3	69	10	25	15	3.5	0.0
B+ / 9.9	1.6	0.22	10.26	53	0	0	0	100	0	8.9	-1.4	66	10	25	15	0.0	0.0
B+ / 9.9	1.6	0.23	13.58	114	0	0	0	100	0	10.5	-1.4	69	10	25	15	0.0	0.0
B+ / 9.9	1.6	0.22	13.91	62	0	0	0	100	0	12.0	-1.2	72	10	25	15	0.0	0.0
B+ / 9.2	7.1	1.13	19.91	159	0	0	0	100	0	75.3	-10.8	42	10	25	15	0.0	0.0
B / 8.7	7.5	1.17	13.68	78	0	0	0	100	0	62.5	-12.9	20	10	25	15	3.5	0.0
B / 8.6	7.5	1.17	13.55	64	0	0	0	100	0	60.2	-13.0	18	10	25	15	0.0	0.0
B / 8.6	7.5	1.17	17.99	16	0	0	0	100	0	62.4	-13.0	20	10	25	15	0.0	0.0
B / 8.7	7.5	1.17	18.43	6	0	0	0	100	0	64.6	-12.8	23	10	25	15	0.0	0.0
B+ / 9.8	5.2	0.83	14.02	79	0	0	0	100	0	53.9	-6.9	56	10	25	15	0.0	0.0
B+ / 9.4	5.6	0.87	10.62	28	0	0	0	100	0	44.1	-8.7	35	10	25	15	3.5	0.0
B+ / 9.3	5.6	0.87	10.53	31	0	0	0	100	0	42.1	-8.7	32	10	25	15	0.0	0.0
B+ / 9.4	5.6	0.88	12.55	24	0	0	0	100	0	44.1	-8.7	34	10	25	15	0.0	0.0
B+ / 9.4	5.6	0.88	12.86	16	0	0	0	100	0	46.0	-8.5	37	10	25	15	0.0	0.0
B / 8.3	10.1	0.97	22.50	426	0	0	0	100	0	112.5	-16.8	40	10	25	15	0.0	0.0
B- / 7.5	10.6	1.00	15.12	72	0	0	0	100	0	91.9	-19.1	16	10	25	15	3.5	0.0
B- / 7.5	10.6	1.00	14.45	69	0	0	0	100	0	89.1	-19.2	14	10	25	15	0.0	0.0
B- / 7.5	10.6	1.00	19.73	215	0	0	0	100	0	91.7	-19.0	16	10	25	15	0.0	0.0
B- / 7.5	10.6	1.00	20.21	99	0	0	0	100	0	94.3	-19.0	18	10	25	15	0.0	0.0
B / 8.4	9.2	1.45	17.32	343	0	0	0	100	0	101.4	-16.2	31	10	25	15	0.0	0.0
B+ / 9.5	6.1	0.97	16.44	177	0	0	0	100	0	64.6	-9.7	52	10	25	15	0.0	0.0
B+ / 9.8	5.1	0.81	16.19	255	0	0	0	100	0	53.9	-7.4	59	10	25	15	0.0	0.0
B+ / 9.9	3.2	0.50	14.94	226	0	0	0	100	0	33.3	-3.2	70	10	25	15	0.0	0.0
B+ / 9.9	1.7	0.18	14.11	158	0	0	0	100	0	15.6	1.6	78	10	25	15	0.0	0.0
B+ / 9.1	7.2	1.14	16.52	320	0	0	0	100	0	76.1	-12.0	44	10	25	15	0.0	0.0
B+ / 9.8	5.1	0.82	16.01	188	0	0	0	100	0	53.8	-7.4	58	10	25	15	0.0	0.0
B- / 7.3	10.9	1.03	40.76	37	0	0	0	100	0	88.4	-20.1	15	12	250	25	0.0	0.0
B- / 7.4	10.9	1.03	46.30	130	0	0	0	100	0	96.3	-19.8	21	12	250	25	4.8	0.0
B / 8.0	11.3	1.02	56.06	13	0	0	0	100	0	99.4	-16.5	19	12	250	25	4.8	0.0
B- / 7.9	11.3	1.02	49.01	N/A	0	0	0	100	0	91.4	-16.8	14	12	250	25	0.0	0.0
B- / 7.9	11.3	1.02	46.04	3	0	0	0	100	0	91.4	-16.8	13	12	250	25	0.0	0.0
B+ / 9.5	5.0	0.77	30.17	10	0	0	0	100	0	38.0	-8.0	39	12	250	25	0.0	0.0
B+ / 9.6	5.0	0.77	34.58	27	0	0	0	100	0	43.8	-7.7	50	12	250	25	4.8	0.0
B- / 7.1	10.8	0.61	89.82	17	0	0	0	100	0	124.8	-23.6	88	12	250	25	4.8	0.0
B- / 7.0	10.8	0.61	80.27	N/A	0	0	0	100	0	115.7	-23.8	85	12	250	25	0.0	0.0

I. Index of Stock Mutual Funds

Fund Type	Fund Name	Ticker Symbol	Overall Investment Rating	Phone	Performance Rating/Pts	3 Mo	6 Mo	1Yr / Pct	3Yr / Pct	5Yr / Pct	Dividend Yield	Expense Ratio
SC	Oppenheimer 529 SE Main St		B+	(888) 470-0862	B- / 7.0	7.15	9.52	25.02 / 73	5.92 / 64	10.80 / 64	0.00	2.19
AA	Oppenheimer 529 SE Moderate 3		B-	(888) 470-0862	C- / 4.0	5.12	4.90	15.59 / 32	4.02 / 43	6.43 / 31	0.00	1.97
AA	Oppenheimer 529 SE Moderate A		B-	(888) 470-0862	C- / 3.7	5.32	5.32	16.46 / 36	4.81 / 52	7.23 / 36	0.00	1.13
AA	Oppenheimer 529 SE Moderately		B	(888) 470-0862	C / 5.2	6.21	6.62	18.69 / 46	4.76 / 52	7.99 / 42	0.00	2.03
AA	Oppenheimer 529 SE Moderately		B	(888) 470-0862	C / 4.9	6.42	7.03	19.59 / 50	5.55 / 60	8.81 / 49	0.00	1.15
GR	Oppenheimer 529 SE Value A		A-	(888) 470-0862	B / 7.6	6.85	12.30	28.07 / 82	7.60 / 76	11.39 / 69	0.00	0.98
GR	Oppenheimer 529 SE Value B		A-	(888) 470-0862	B / 7.9	6.63	11.84	27.11 / 79	6.79 / 70	10.54 / 62	0.00	1.99
GR	Oppenheimer 529 SE Value C		A-	(888) 470-0862	B / 7.9	6.65	11.86	27.12 / 79	6.79 / 70	10.54 / 62	0.00	1.99
AG	Oppenheimer 529 TEP Aggressive		A-	(888) 470-0862	B- / 7.3	7.37	9.20	24.01 / 70	6.65 / 69	10.98 / 66	0.00	0.77
AA	Oppenheimer 529 TEP Cons Portfolio		B-	(888) 470-0862	C- / 3.0	3.59	3.31	10.96 / 14	3.85 / 41	5.43 / 24	0.00	0.67
AA	Oppenheimer 529 TEP Mod Agg Port		B	(888) 470-0862	C+ / 6.0	6.16	7.20	19.70 / 50	5.81 / 63	9.22 / 52	0.00	0.75
AA	Oppenheimer 529 TEP Moderate Port		B	(888) 470-0862	C / 4.5	4.98	5.15	15.38 / 32	4.95 / 54	7.44 / 38	0.00	0.72
AA	Oppenheimer 529 TEP Ultra Cons		C+	(888) 470-0862	D / 1.8	2.15	1.48	6.47 / 5	2.58 / 28	3.26 / 12	0.00	0.61
AA	Oppenheimer Active Alloc A	OAAAX	C-	(888) 470-0862	C- / 3.0	6.04	5.10	16.30 / 35	3.70 / 39	7.57 / 39	0.87	1.22
AA	● Oppenheimer Active Alloc B	OAABX	C	(888) 470-0862	C- / 3.4	5.85	4.73	15.35 / 31	2.90 / 31	6.73 / 33	0.00	1.97
AA	Oppenheimer Active Alloc C	OAACX	C	(888) 470-0862	C- / 3.4	5.83	4.69	15.33 / 31	2.90 / 31	6.77 / 33	0.22	1.97
AA	Oppenheimer Active Alloc R	OAANX	C	(888) 470-0862	C- / 3.8	5.99	4.87	15.92 / 34	3.42 / 36	7.32 / 37	0.69	1.46
AA	Oppenheimer Active Alloc Y	OAAYX	C	(888) 470-0862	C- / 4.2	6.11	5.19	16.56 / 37	3.95 / 42	7.85 / 41	1.20	0.97
GR	Oppenheimer Capital Appr A	OPTFX	C-	(888) 470-0862	C+ / 5.7	9.40	7.64	18.34 / 44	6.81 / 71	10.69 / 63	0.07	1.07
GR	● Oppenheimer Capital Appr B	OTGBX	D+	(888) 470-0862	C+ / 6.2	9.19	7.21	17.43 / 40	5.99 / 64	9.81 / 57	0.00	1.82
GR	Oppenheimer Capital Appr C	OTFCX	D+	(888) 470-0862	C+ / 6.3	9.19	7.21	17.44 / 40	5.99 / 64	9.84 / 57	0.00	1.82
GR	Oppenheimer Capital Appr Fd/VA Svc		C-	(888) 470-0862	C+ / 6.8	9.33	7.58	18.25 / 44	6.78 / 70	10.71 / 63	0.11	1.06
GR	Oppenheimer Capital Appr I	OPTIX	C	(888) 470-0862	B- / 7.1	9.51	7.86	18.84 / 46	7.26 / 74	11.17 / 67	0.44	0.63
GR	Oppenheimer Capital Appr R	OTCNX	C-	(888) 470-0862	C+ / 6.6	9.31	7.50	18.04 / 43	6.53 / 69	10.40 / 61	0.00	1.32
GR	Oppenheimer Capital Appr Y	OTCYX	C	(888) 470-0862	B- / 7.0	9.47	7.75	18.61 / 45	7.06 / 72	11.00 / 66	0.25	0.82
GI	Oppenheimer Capital Income A	OPPEX	C	(888) 470-0862	D / 2.2	3.59	4.04	11.15 / 15	3.95 / 42	5.95 / 28	2.49	1.09
GI	● Oppenheimer Capital Income B	OPEBX	C	(888) 470-0862	D+ / 2.6	3.33	3.56	10.25 / 12	3.12 / 33	5.02 / 21	1.88	1.85
GI	Oppenheimer Capital Income C	OPECX	C	(888) 470-0862	D+ / 2.6	3.40	3.66	10.23 / 12	3.15 / 33	5.12 / 22	2.01	1.85
GL	Oppenheimer Capital Income I	OCIIX	C+	(888) 470-0862	C- / 3.4	3.71	4.16	11.52 / 16	4.37 / 47	--	3.06	0.66
GI	Oppenheimer Capital Income R	OCINX	C+	(888) 470-0862	D+ / 2.9	3.47	3.86	10.82 / 14	3.69 / 39	5.64 / 26	2.45	1.35
GI	Oppenheimer Capital Income Y	OCIYX	C+	(888) 470-0862	C- / 3.3	3.66	4.17	11.31 / 15	4.17 / 45	6.21 / 30	2.87	0.85
AA	Oppenheimer Conservative Inv A	OACIX	C-	(888) 470-0862	D- / 1.5	3.53	1.51	9.60 / 11	2.78 / 30	4.08 / 16	1.99	1.07
AA	● Oppenheimer Conservative Inv B	OBCIX	C-	(888) 470-0862	D / 1.8	3.33	1.19	8.78 / 9	1.99 / 24	3.29 / 12	0.94	1.83
AA	Oppenheimer Conservative Inv C	OCCIX	C-	(888) 470-0862	D / 1.8	3.33	1.17	8.86 / 9	2.01 / 24	3.31 / 12	1.35	1.82
AA	Oppenheimer Conservative Inv R	ONCIX	C	(888) 470-0862	D / 2.1	3.44	1.42	9.27 / 10	2.51 / 28	3.81 / 14	1.91	1.32
AA	Oppenheimer Conservative Inv Y	OYCIX	C	(888) 470-0862	D+ / 2.3	3.65	1.75	9.82 / 11	3.03 / 32	4.33 / 17	2.34	0.82
* EM	● Oppenheimer Developing Mkts A	ODMAX	E	(888) 470-0862	E+ / 0.9	6.41	3.67	22.63 / 65	-1.06 / 9	1.19 / 6	0.20	1.32
EM	● Oppenheimer Developing Mkts B	ODVBX	E+	(888) 470-0862	D- / 1.1	6.23	3.26	21.70 / 61	-1.81 / 7	0.39 / 5	0.00	2.08
EM	● Oppenheimer Developing Mkts C	ODVCX	E	(888) 470-0862	D- / 1.1	6.25	3.28	21.70 / 61	-1.81 / 7	0.46 / 5	0.00	2.07
EM	● Oppenheimer Developing Mkts I	ODVIX	E+	(888) 470-0862	D / 1.6	6.53	3.89	23.18 / 67	-0.63 / 11	1.66 / 7	0.67	0.88
EM	● Oppenheimer Developing Mkts R	ODVNX	E+	(888) 470-0862	D- / 1.3	6.37	3.56	22.33 / 64	-1.31 / 8	0.91 / 6	0.01	1.57
EM	● Oppenheimer Developing Mkts Y	ODVYX	E+	(888) 470-0862	D- / 1.5	6.49	3.78	22.93 / 66	-0.82 / 10	1.48 / 7	0.49	1.07
SC	● Oppenheimer Discovery A	OPOCX	E+	(888) 470-0862	C- / 3.2	5.00	5.64	25.36 / 74	2.31 / 26	11.19 / 68	0.00	1.12
SC	● Oppenheimer Discovery B	ODIBX	E+	(888) 470-0862	C- / 3.7	4.79	5.25	24.40 / 71	1.54 / 21	10.31 / 61	0.00	1.88
SC	● Oppenheimer Discovery C	ODICX	E+	(888) 470-0862	C- / 3.7	4.79	5.24	24.41 / 71	1.54 / 21	10.34 / 61	0.00	1.87
SC	● Oppenheimer Discovery I	ODIIX	D	(888) 470-0862	C / 4.7	5.10	5.87	25.89 / 76	2.76 / 30	11.71 / 72	0.00	0.68
SC	Oppenheimer Discovery Mid Cap Gro	OEGAX	D+	(888) 470-0862	C- / 4.0	6.37	4.10	20.54 / 55	4.78 / 52	11.19 / 68	0.00	1.33
SC	● Oppenheimer Discovery Mid Cap Gro	OEGBX	D+	(888) 470-0862	C / 4.5	6.12	3.73	19.62 / 50	3.99 / 43	10.30 / 61	0.00	2.09
SC	Oppenheimer Discovery Mid Cap Gro	OEGCX	D+	(888) 470-0862	C / 4.5	6.08	3.70	19.64 / 50	3.98 / 43	10.33 / 61	0.00	2.09
GR	Oppenheimer Discovery Mid Cap Gro	OEGIX	C-	(888) 470-0862	C+ / 5.6	6.50	4.35	21.10 / 58	5.26 / 57	--	0.00	0.89
SC	Oppenheimer Discovery Mid Cap Gro	OEGNX	C-	(888) 470-0862	C / 5.0	6.32	3.98	20.25 / 53	4.53 / 49	10.90 / 65	0.00	1.58
SC	Oppenheimer Discovery Mid Cap Gro	OEGYX	C-	(888) 470-0862	C / 5.4	6.40	4.23	20.83 / 57	5.04 / 55	11.53 / 70	0.00	1.08

● Denotes fund is closed to new investors
* Denotes fund is included in Section II

www.thestreetratings.com

Risk Rating/Pts	Std Dev	Beta	NAV As of 2/28/17	Total $(Mil)	Cash %	Stocks %	Bonds %	Other %	Portfolio Turnover Ratio	Last Bull Market Return	Last Bear Market Return	Manager Quality Pct	Manager Tenure (Years)	Initial Purch. $	Additional Purch. $	Front End Load	Back End Load
B- / 7.0	10.8	0.61	82.16	4	0	0	0	100	0	115.8	-23.8	85	12	250	25	0.0	0.0
B / 8.7	7.0	1.09	35.95	24	0	0	0	100	0	55.6	-12.1	24	12	250	25	0.0	0.0
B / 8.8	7.0	1.09	40.41	71	0	0	0	100	0	62.0	-11.8	33	12	250	25	4.8	0.0
B / 8.1	8.9	1.37	41.54	29	0	0	0	100	0	72.9	-17.5	13	12	250	25	0.0	0.0
B / 8.1	8.9	1.37	46.76	95	0	0	0	100	0	80.1	-17.2	19	12	250	25	4.8	0.0
B- / 7.1	11.4	1.06	65.48	10	0	0	0	100	0	103.5	-20.8	30	12	250	25	4.8	0.0
B- / 7.1	11.4	1.06	58.38	N/A	0	0	0	100	0	95.3	-21.1	22	12	250	25	0.0	0.0
B- / 7.1	11.4	1.06	56.95	2	0	0	0	100	0	95.3	-21.1	22	12	250	25	0.0	0.0
B- / 7.5	10.7	1.02	21.85	74	0	0	0	100	0	104.0	-19.7	25	12	250	25	0.0	0.0
B+ / 9.8	4.5	0.70	15.59	9	0	0	0	100	0	42.5	-5.8	58	12	250	25	0.0	0.0
B / 8.3	8.6	1.33	20.84	28	0	0	0	100	0	82.5	-15.0	24	12	250	25	0.0	0.0
B+ / 9.1	6.5	1.02	18.98	16	0	0	0	100	0	62.4	-10.2	41	12	250	25	0.0	0.0
B+ / 9.9	2.6	0.38	12.35	5	0	0	0	100	0	23.1	-1.1	71	12	250	25	0.0	0.0
B- / 7.1	8.6	1.32	12.97	1,675	15	74	9	2	8	63.1	-15.7	9	12	1,000	0	5.8	0.0
B- / 7.2	8.6	1.31	12.85	41	15	74	9	2	8	56.2	-16.0	7	12	1,000	0	0.0	0.0
B- / 7.2	8.6	1.32	12.68	542	15	74	9	2	8	56.6	-16.1	6	12	1,000	0	0.0	0.0
B- / 7.2	8.6	1.31	12.89	120	15	74	9	2	8	60.8	-15.8	8	12	1,000	0	0.0	0.0
B- / 7.1	8.6	1.31	13.10	58	15	74	9	2	8	65.4	-15.7	11	12	1,000	0	0.0	0.0
C- / 3.8	12.2	1.05	54.66	3,115	4	92	2	2	79	102.3	-16.6	23	1	1,000	0	5.8	0.0
C- / 3.0	12.2	1.05	43.08	31	4	92	2	2	79	93.7	-16.9	17	1	1,000	0	0.0	0.0
C- / 3.0	12.2	1.05	42.72	378	4	92	2	2	79	94.0	-16.9	17	1	1,000	0	0.0	0.0
C- / 3.4	12.2	1.05	51.67	316	2	94	2	2	60	103.1	-16.6	23	1	0	0	0.0	0.0
C- / 4.1	12.2	1.05	58.89	1,067	4	92	2	2	79	N/A	N/A	27	1	5,000,000	0	0.0	0.0
C- / 3.7	12.2	1.05	51.94	86	4	92	2	2	79	99.4	-16.7	21	1	1,000	0	0.0	0.0
C- / 4.1	12.2	1.05	58.69	127	4	92	2	2	79	105.5	-16.4	26	1	1,000	0	0.0	0.0
B / 8.6	3.6	0.30	10.09	1,698	1	37	60	2	54	42.9	-4.9	79	8	1,000	0	5.8	0.0
B / 8.6	3.6	0.30	9.86	8	1	37	60	2	54	36.3	-5.3	73	8	1,000	0	0.0	0.0
B / 8.6	3.5	0.30	9.76	407	1	37	60	2	54	36.9	-5.2	74	8	1,000	0	0.0	0.0
B / 8.7	3.6	0.51	10.08	17	1	37	60	2	54	N/A	N/A	86	8	1,000,000	0	0.0	0.0
B / 8.6	3.6	0.31	9.95	35	1	37	60	2	54	40.7	-5.1	77	8	1,000	0	0.0	0.0
B / 8.6	3.6	0.30	10.08	520	1	37	60	2	54	44.8	-4.7	81	8	1,000	0	0.0	0.0
B / 8.4	4.4	0.63	9.15	435	2	28	69	1	10	32.3	-7.3	50	4	1,000	0	5.8	0.0
B / 8.5	4.4	0.63	9.19	6	2	28	69	1	10	26.7	-7.5	39	4	1,000	0	0.0	0.0
B / 8.5	4.4	0.63	9.04	147	2	28	69	1	10	27.0	-7.5	39	4	1,000	0	0.0	0.0
B / 8.5	4.4	0.64	9.13	43	2	28	69	1	10	30.3	-7.3	46	4	1,000	0	0.0	0.0
B / 8.4	4.3	0.63	9.19	6	2	28	69	1	10	34.1	-7.2	54	4	1,000	0	0.0	0.0
C- / 4.1	14.9	0.87	34.60	6,109	3	92	3	2	18	27.0	-23.2	40	10	1,000	0	5.8	0.0
C- / 4.1	14.8	0.87	33.26	29	3	92	3	2	18	21.7	-23.5	31	10	1,000	0	0.0	0.0
C- / 4.1	14.8	0.87	32.47	931	3	92	3	2	18	22.1	-23.4	31	10	1,000	0	0.0	0.0
C- / 4.1	14.8	0.87	34.13	9,032	3	92	3	2	18	N/A	N/A	47	10	5,000,000	0	0.0	0.0
C- / 4.1	14.9	0.87	33.27	607	3	92	3	2	18	25.1	-23.3	37	10	1,000	0	0.0	0.0
C- / 4.1	14.9	0.87	34.13	13,764	3	92	3	2	18	29.0	-23.1	44	10	1,000	0	0.0	0.0
D+ / 2.5	16.4	0.91	72.22	1,186	0	98	1	1	89	105.7	-22.3	26	11	1,000	0	5.8	0.0
D / 2.0	16.4	0.91	52.64	13	0	98	1	1	89	97.0	-22.6	19	11	1,000	0	0.0	0.0
D / 2.0	16.4	0.91	54.66	137	0	98	1	1	89	97.3	-22.6	19	11	1,000	0	0.0	0.0
D+ / 2.7	16.4	0.91	81.10	110	0	98	1	1	89	110.7	-22.3	30	11	5,000,000	0	0.0	0.0
C / 4.6	13.0	0.66	18.39	470	0	98	1	1	128	106.7	-19.7	76	10	1,000	0	5.8	0.0
C- / 4.2	13.0	0.66	15.45	8	0	98	1	1	128	98.0	-20.0	68	10	1,000	0	0.0	0.0
C- / 4.2	13.0	0.66	15.56	123	0	98	1	1	128	98.3	-20.0	68	10	1,000	0	0.0	0.0
C / 4.8	13.0	0.96	20.51	38	0	98	1	1	128	N/A	N/A	18	10	5,000,000	0	0.0	0.0
C / 4.5	13.0	0.66	17.36	40	0	98	1	1	128	103.8	-19.8	74	10	1,000	0	0.0	0.0
C / 4.7	13.0	0.66	20.32	173	0	98	1	1	128	110.4	-19.5	77	10	1,000	0	0.0	0.0

www.thestreetratings.com
481
Data as of February 28, 2017

I. Index of Stock Mutual Funds

99 Pct = Best
0 Pct = Worst

Fund Type	Fund Name	Ticker Symbol	Overall Investment Rating	Phone	PERFORMANCE Perfor-mance Rating/Pts	Total Return % through 2/28/17 3 Mo	6 Mo	1Yr / Pct	Annualized 3Yr / Pct	5Yr / Pct	Incl. in Returns Dividend Yield	Expense Ratio
SC	● Oppenheimer Discovery R	ODINX	D-	(888) 470-0862	C- / 4.1	4.92	5.52	25.03 /73	2.05 /24	10.89 /65	0.00	1.37
SC	● Oppenheimer Discovery Y	ODIYX	D-	(888) 470-0862	C / 4.5	5.04	5.76	25.64 /75	2.56 /28	11.48 /70	0.00	0.87
GR	Oppenheimer Dividend Opportunity A	OSVAX	C+	(888) 470-0862	C+ / 6.6	5.22	8.11	23.57 /68	8.03 /79	9.50 /55	2.64	1.16
GR	● Oppenheimer Dividend Opportunity B	OSVBX	B+	(888) 470-0862	B- / 7.0	4.96	7.65	22.60 /65	7.20 /73	8.64 /48	2.14	1.93
GR	Oppenheimer Dividend Opportunity C	OSCVX	B+	(888) 470-0862	B- / 7.0	5.05	7.73	22.73 /66	7.24 /74	8.67 /48	2.23	1.91
GR	Oppenheimer Dividend Opportunity R	OSVNX	B+	(888) 470-0862	B- / 7.4	5.16	8.01	23.30 /68	7.76 /77	9.24 /53	2.61	1.40
GR	Oppenheimer Dividend Opportunity Y	OSVYX	A-	(888) 470-0862	B / 7.8	5.30	8.25	23.93 /70	8.31 /81	9.84 /57	3.01	0.91
EM	Oppenheimer Em Mkts Innovators A	EMIAX	U	(888) 470-0862	U /	7.53	-0.23	13.90 /25	--	--	0.00	1.77
EM	Oppenheimer Em Mkts Innovators Y	EMIYX	U	(888) 470-0862	U /	7.61	-0.11	14.23 /27	--	--	0.00	1.51
GI	Oppenheimer Equity A	OEQAX	C+	(888) 470-0862	C+ / 6.8	8.11	10.15	23.42 /68	7.34 /74	11.18 /67	0.63	1.03
GI	● Oppenheimer Equity B	OEQBX	C+	(888) 470-0862	B- / 7.1	7.85	9.62	22.42 /64	6.46 /68	10.23 /60	0.00	1.79
GI	Oppenheimer Equity C	OEQCX	C+	(888) 470-0862	B- / 7.1	7.86	9.63	22.42 /64	6.49 /68	10.24 /60	0.01	1.79
GR	Oppenheimer Equity Income A	OAEIX	C	(888) 470-0862	C+ / 6.8	7.23	11.81	29.64 /86	5.79 /62	10.78 /64	2.02	1.02
GR	● Oppenheimer Equity Income B	OBEIX	C	(888) 470-0862	B- / 7.1	7.05	11.41	28.68 /83	4.99 /54	9.87 /57	2.06	1.76
GR	Oppenheimer Equity Income C	OCEIX	C	(888) 470-0862	B- / 7.2	7.07	11.39	28.71 /83	5.01 /54	9.94 /58	2.10	1.76
IN	Oppenheimer Equity Income I	OEIIX	B-	(888) 470-0862	B / 8.1	7.37	12.08	30.24 /87	6.26 /66	11.24 /68	2.54	0.58
GR	Oppenheimer Equity Income R	ONEIX	C+	(888) 470-0862	B- / 7.5	7.20	11.67	29.30 /85	5.52 /60	10.45 /62	2.03	1.26
GL	Oppenheimer Equity Income Y	OYEIX	C+	(888) 470-0862	B / 7.9	7.31	11.96	29.97 /86	6.06 /65	11.08 /67	2.36	0.76
AG	Oppenheimer Equity Inv A	OAAIX	C-	(888) 470-0862	C- / 3.1	6.96	5.50	17.90 /42	3.30 /35	8.58 /47	0.96	1.16
AG	● Oppenheimer Equity Inv B	OBAIX	C-	(888) 470-0862	C- / 3.5	6.73	5.10	17.02 /38	2.52 /28	7.75 /40	0.00	1.91
AG	Oppenheimer Equity Inv C	OCAIX	C-	(888) 470-0862	C- / 3.5	6.70	5.13	17.02 /38	2.52 /28	7.77 /40	0.32	1.91
AG	Oppenheimer Equity Inv R	ONAIX	C-	(888) 470-0862	C- / 4.0	6.90	5.37	17.61 /41	3.05 /32	8.33 /45	0.77	1.41
AG	Oppenheimer Equity Inv Y	OYAIX	C	(888) 470-0862	C / 4.4	7.04	5.66	18.16 /44	3.56 /38	8.90 /50	1.24	0.91
GI	Oppenheimer Equity R	OEQNX	B-	(888) 470-0862	B- / 7.5	8.06	9.96	23.09 /67	7.03 /72	10.81 /64	0.40	1.29
GI	Oppenheimer Equity Y	OEQYX	B	(888) 470-0862	B / 7.9	8.17	10.21	23.68 /69	7.56 /76	11.40 /69	0.86	0.78
GR	Oppenheimer Fundamental Alt A	QVOPX	C-	(888) 470-0862	D- / 1.0	1.79	2.29	3.49 / 3	2.26 /26	4.04 /15	0.24	2.19
GR	● Oppenheimer Fundamental Alt B	QOPBX	C-	(888) 470-0862	D- / 1.2	1.63	1.89	2.71 / 2	1.47 /21	3.20 /12	0.20	2.96
GR	Oppenheimer Fundamental Alt C	QOPCX	C-	(888) 470-0862	D- / 1.2	1.59	1.89	2.71 / 2	1.48 /21	3.25 /12	0.20	2.94
AA	Oppenheimer Fundamental Alt I	QOPIX	C	(888) 470-0862	D / 1.7	1.89	2.48	3.92 / 3	2.71 /29	--	0.71	1.72
GR	Oppenheimer Fundamental Alt R	QOPNX	C-	(888) 470-0862	D- / 1.4	1.74	2.14	3.23 / 3	2.00 /24	3.74 /14	0.22	2.44
GR	Oppenheimer Fundamental Alt Y	QOPYX	C	(888) 470-0862	D / 1.6	1.87	2.39	3.72 / 3	2.50 /28	4.28 /17	0.54	1.89
GL	Oppenheimer Glbl Multi-Asset Gr A	QMGAX	U	(888) 470-0862	U /	7.62	4.06	18.74 /46	--	--	4.44	1.77
GL	Oppenheimer Glbl Multi-Asset Inc A	QMAAX	U	(888) 470-0862	U /	4.41	2.53	14.21 /26	--	--	4.48	1.98
* GL	Oppenheimer Global A	OPPAX	C-	(888) 470-0862	C / 4.7	8.58	9.21	22.79 /66	4.07 /44	9.68 /56	0.60	1.15
BA	Oppenheimer Global Allocation A	QVGIX	C-	(888) 470-0862	D / 1.9	5.46	3.23	12.65 /20	2.56 /28	5.72 /26	3.02	1.34
BA	● Oppenheimer Global Allocation B	QGRBX	C-	(888) 470-0862	D / 2.2	5.22	2.84	11.80 /17	1.77 /22	4.88 /21	2.81	2.09
BA	Oppenheimer Global Allocation C	QGRCX	C-	(888) 470-0862	D+ / 2.3	5.26	2.88	11.87 /17	1.80 /23	4.95 /21	2.87	2.09
AA	Oppenheimer Global Allocation I	QGRIX	C	(888) 470-0862	C- / 3.1	5.54	3.48	13.18 /22	3.02 /32	6.21 /30	3.65	0.88
BA	Oppenheimer Global Allocation R	QGRNX	C-	(888) 470-0862	D+ / 2.6	5.36	3.10	12.41 /19	2.31 /26	5.46 /25	3.08	1.59
BA	Oppenheimer Global Allocation Y	QGRYX	C	(888) 470-0862	D+ / 2.9	5.49	3.39	12.95 /21	2.81 /30	6.03 /29	3.45	1.08
GL	● Oppenheimer Global B	OGLBX	C-	(888) 470-0862	C / 5.3	8.38	8.79	21.84 /61	3.28 /35	8.80 /49	0.00	1.90
GL	Oppenheimer Global C	OGLCX	C-	(888) 470-0862	C / 5.3	8.37	8.78	21.86 /61	3.29 /35	8.87 /50	0.00	1.90
GL	Oppenheimer Global I	OGLIX	C+	(888) 470-0862	C+ / 6.3	8.69	9.44	23.31 /68	4.52 /49	10.17 /60	1.05	0.71
AA	Oppenheimer Global Multi-Alt A	ODAAX	D	(888) 470-0862	E+ / 0.7	2.00	1.68	7.52 / 7	0.31 /15	--	3.49	1.41
AA	Oppenheimer Global Multi-Alt C	ODACX	D	(888) 470-0862	E+ / 0.7	1.81	1.16	6.59 / 5	-0.59 /11	--	2.77	2.16
AA	Oppenheimer Global Multi-Alt I	ODAIX	D+	(888) 470-0862	D- / 1.3	2.01	1.80	7.97 / 7	0.69 /17	--	4.14	0.97
AA	Oppenheimer Global Multi-Alt R	ODANX	D+	(888) 470-0862	E+ / 0.9	1.85	1.42	7.06 / 6	-0.06 /13	--	3.47	1.66
AA	Oppenheimer Global Multi-Alt Y	ODAYX	D+	(888) 470-0862	D- / 1.2	2.07	1.75	7.70 / 7	0.43 /15	--	3.98	1.16
GI	Oppenheimer Global MultiStrat A	OARAX	D-	(888) 470-0862	E / 0.4	0.73	-1.52	3.17 / 3	0.28 /15	2.32 / 9	8.33	1.85
IN	Oppenheimer Global MultiStrat C	OARCX	D-	(888) 470-0862	E / 0.5	0.51	-1.94	2.32 / 2	-0.53 /11	1.49 / 7	7.96	2.72
IN	Oppenheimer Global MultiStrat I	OAIIX	D-	(888) 470-0862	E+ / 0.8	0.78	-1.38	3.42 / 3	0.56 /16	2.60 /10	9.16	1.26
IN	Oppenheimer Global MultiStrat Y	OARYX	D-	(888) 470-0862	E+ / 0.8	0.77	-1.46	3.27 / 3	0.38 /15	2.37 / 9	8.56	1.51

● Denotes fund is closed to new investors
* Denotes fund is included in Section II

RISK				NET ASSETS		ASSET					BULL / BEAR		FUND MANAGER		MINIMUMS		LOADS	
	3 Year			NAV						Portfolio	Last Bull	Last Bear	Manager	Manager	Initial	Additional	Front	Back
Risk	Standard			As of	Total	Cash	Stocks	Bonds	Other	Turnover	Market	Market	Quality	Tenure	Purch.	Purch.	End	End
Rating/Pts	Deviation	Beta		2/28/17	$(Mil)	%	%	%	%	Ratio	Return	Return	Pct	(Years)	$	$	Load	Load
D+ / 2.4	16.4	0.91		67.70	48	0	98	1	1	89	102.7	-22.4	23	11	1,000	0	0.0	0.0
D+ / 2.7	16.4	0.91		80.13	433	0	98	1	1	89	108.9	-22.2	28	11	1,000	0	0.0	0.0
C+ / 6.9	9.2	0.85		22.37	184	2	92	4	2	47	85.1	-24.7	64	4	1,000	0	5.8	0.0
C+ / 6.9	9.1	0.85		21.66	2	2	92	4	2	47	77.2	-24.9	54	4	1,000	0	0.0	0.0
C+ / 6.9	9.2	0.85		21.60	53	2	92	4	2	47	77.6	-25.0	54	4	1,000	0	0.0	0.0
C+ / 6.9	9.2	0.85		22.15	13	2	92	4	2	47	82.8	-24.8	61	4	0	0	0.0	0.0
C+ / 6.9	9.2	0.85		22.36	11	2	92	4	2	47	88.3	-24.5	67	4	0	0	0.0	0.0
U /	N/A	N/A		8.85	58	12	87	0	1	26	N/A	N/A	N/A	3	1,000	0	5.8	0.0
U /	N/A	N/A		8.91	134	12	87	0	1	26	N/A	N/A	N/A	3	1,000	0	0.0	0.0
C / 5.2	11.4	1.07		13.41	1,408	2	96	1	1	57	104.8	-18.8	27	4	1,000	50	5.8	0.0
C / 5.1	11.3	1.06		12.16	7	2	96	1	1	57	95.5	-19.2	20	4	1,000	50	0.0	0.0
C / 5.1	11.4	1.06		12.17	73	2	96	1	1	57	95.8	-19.2	20	4	1,000	50	0.0	0.0
C / 4.6	12.3	1.10		30.90	2,911	3	92	0	5	41	105.8	-22.2	12	10	1,000	0	5.8	0.0
C- / 4.2	12.3	1.10		24.73	55	3	92	0	5	41	96.7	-22.5	8	10	1,000	0	0.0	0.0
C- / 4.2	12.3	1.10		24.75	687	3	92	0	5	41	97.4	-22.4	8	10	1,000	0	0.0	0.0
C / 4.6	12.3	1.10		30.87	104	3	92	0	5	41	N/A	N/A	15	10	1,000,000	0	0.0	0.0
C / 4.5	12.3	1.10		29.58	143	3	92	0	5	41	102.3	-22.3	10	10	1,000	0	0.0	0.0
C / 4.6	12.3	0.80		30.88	333	3	92	0	5	41	108.6	-22.1	97	10	1,000	0	0.0	0.0
C+ / 6.3	10.5	0.96		15.96	549	1	95	2	2	8	78.9	-21.0	7	12	1,000	0	5.8	0.0
C+ / 6.4	10.5	0.96		15.66	13	1	95	2	2	8	71.4	-21.2	5	12	1,000	0	0.0	0.0
C+ / 6.3	10.5	0.96		15.56	183	1	95	2	2	8	71.7	-21.2	5	12	1,000	0	0.0	0.0
C+ / 6.3	10.5	0.96		15.95	46	1	95	2	2	8	76.5	-21.0	6	12	1,000	0	0.0	0.0
C+ / 6.3	10.5	0.96		16.04	20	1	95	2	2	8	81.7	-20.8	8	12	1,000	0	0.0	0.0
C / 5.2	11.4	1.06		13.13	17	2	96	1	1	57	101.1	-18.9	24	4	1,000	50	0.0	0.0
C / 5.2	11.3	1.06		13.41	21	2	96	1	1	57	106.9	-18.8	29	4	0	0	0.0	0.0
B / 8.9	3.0	0.14		27.22	653	21	28	49	2	131	22.3	-10.2	79	6	1,000	0	5.8	0.0
B / 8.9	3.0	0.14		24.16	6	21	28	49	2	131	17.1	-10.5	73	6	1,000	0	0.0	0.0
B / 8.9	3.0	0.14		24.16	129	21	28	49	2	131	17.4	-10.5	73	6	1,000	0	0.0	0.0
B / 8.9	3.0	0.25		27.92	143	21	28	49	2	131	N/A	N/A	79	6	5,000,000	0	0.0	0.0
B / 8.9	3.0	0.14		26.07	21	21	28	49	2	131	20.5	-10.3	77	6	1,000	0	0.0	0.0
B / 8.9	3.0	0.14		27.82	373	21	28	49	2	131	24.0	-10.1	80	6	1,000	0	0.0	0.0
U /	N/A	N/A		10.51	55	7	74	17	2	61	N/A	N/A	N/A	2	1,000	0	5.8	0.0
U /	N/A	N/A		9.67	56	26	20	52	2	71	N/A	N/A	N/A	3	1,000	0	4.8	0.0
C / 5.2	12.9	0.96		80.70	6,348	0	100	0	0	6	86.9	-23.2	94	13	1,000	0	5.8	0.0
B- / 7.8	7.1	1.03		17.93	1,138	1	61	36	2	84	45.1	-15.0	16	4	1,000	0	5.8	0.0
B- / 7.8	7.1	1.03		17.25	14	1	61	36	2	84	39.0	-15.3	10	4	1,000	0	0.0	0.0
B- / 7.8	7.1	1.03		17.26	238	1	61	36	2	84	39.5	-15.2	11	4	1,000	0	0.0	0.0
B- / 7.8	7.1	1.03		17.91	25	1	61	36	2	84	N/A	N/A	19	4	5,000,000	0	0.0	0.0
B- / 7.8	7.1	1.03		17.61	38	1	61	36	2	84	43.1	-15.0	14	4	1,000	0	0.0	0.0
B- / 7.8	7.1	1.03		17.91	71	1	61	36	2	84	47.5	-14.8	18	4	1,000	0	0.0	0.0
C / 5.2	12.9	0.96		73.75	28	0	100	0	0	6	78.9	-23.5	92	13	1,000	0	0.0	0.0
C / 5.2	12.9	0.96		74.81	613	0	100	0	0	6	79.5	-23.4	92	13	1,000	0	0.0	0.0
C / 5.1	12.9	0.96		80.77	736	0	100	0	0	6	91.2	-23.2	95	13	5,000,000	0	0.0	0.0
B- / 7.5	3.8	0.48		9.38	23	16	17	66	1	6	N/A	N/A	31	5	1,000	0	5.8	0.0
B- / 7.6	3.8	0.47		9.27	4	16	17	66	1	6	N/A	N/A	23	5	1,000	0	0.0	0.0
B- / 7.5	3.9	0.48		9.40	N/A	16	17	66	1	6	N/A	N/A	36	5	5,000,000	0	0.0	0.0
B- / 7.6	3.8	0.48		9.30	2	16	17	66	1	6	N/A	N/A	28	5	1,000	0	0.0	0.0
B- / 7.5	3.9	0.49		9.38	3	16	17	66	1	6	N/A	N/A	33	5	1,000	0	0.0	0.0
C+ / 5.8	4.1	0.23		23.05	6	0	12	87	1	72	9.2	-7.2	47	10	1,000	0	5.8	0.0
C+ / 5.9	4.2	0.23		22.66	3	0	12	87	1	72	N/A	N/A	36	10	1,000	0	0.0	0.0
C+ / 5.7	4.2	0.23		23.15	102	0	12	87	1	72	N/A	N/A	51	10	5,000,000	0	0.0	0.0
C+ / 5.8	4.2	0.23		22.96	1	0	12	87	1	72	N/A	N/A	48	10	0	0	0.0	0.0

Fund Type	Fund Name	Ticker Symbol	Overall Investment Rating	Phone	Perfor-mance Rating/Pts	3 Mo	6 Mo	1Yr / Pct	3Yr / Pct	5Yr / Pct	Dividend Yield	Expense Ratio
GL	Oppenheimer Global Opportunities A	OPGIX	B	(888) 470-0862	B+ / 8.7	11.19	9.00	37.86 /96	7.63 /76	12.25 /77	0.23	1.19
GL	● Oppenheimer Global Opportunities B	OGGIX	B+	(888) 470-0862	A- / 9.0	10.96	8.56	36.80 /96	6.80 /71	11.33 /68	0.00	1.94
GL	Oppenheimer Global Opportunities C	OGICX	B+	(888) 470-0862	A- / 9.1	10.97	8.58	36.82 /96	6.81 /71	11.40 /69	0.00	1.94
GL	Oppenheimer Global Opportunities I	OGIIX	B+	(888) 470-0862	A+ / 9.6	11.29	9.22	38.45 /97	8.10 /80	12.74 /81	0.63	0.75
GL	Oppenheimer Global Opportunities R	OGINX	B+	(888) 470-0862	A / 9.4	11.12	8.84	37.53 /96	7.36 /75	11.92 /74	0.11	1.44
GL	Oppenheimer Global Opportunities Y	OGIYX	B+	(888) 470-0862	A / 9.5	11.25	9.13	38.22 /96	7.89 /78	12.54 /79	0.49	0.94
GL	Oppenheimer Global R	OGLNX	C	(888) 470-0862	C+ / 5.7	8.50	9.06	22.47 /64	3.80 /40	9.38 /54	0.40	1.39
RE	Oppenheimer Global Real Estate A	OGRAX	D	(888) 470-0862	D / 1.9	5.94	-4.53	7.77 / 7	4.89 /53	--	4.60	1.58
RE	Oppenheimer Global Real Estate C	OGRCX	D	(888) 470-0862	D / 2.2	5.82	-4.89	7.04 / 6	4.09 /44	--	4.05	2.35
RE	Oppenheimer Global Real Estate I	OIRGX	D+	(888) 470-0862	C- / 3.0	6.16	-4.23	8.39 / 8	5.35 /58	--	5.26	1.07
RE	Oppenheimer Global Real Estate R	OGRNX	D+	(888) 470-0862	D+ / 2.5	5.96	-4.62	7.58 / 7	4.63 /50	--	4.58	1.86
RE	Oppenheimer Global Real Estate Y	OGRYX	D+	(888) 470-0862	D+ / 2.9	6.02	-4.44	8.13 / 8	5.26 /57	--	5.22	1.30
GL	Oppenheimer Global Value A	GLVAX	D-	(888) 470-0862	D+ / 2.5	8.71	7.32	20.71 /56	0.76 /17	8.82 /49	0.00	1.31
GL	Oppenheimer Global Value C	GLVCX	U	(888) 470-0862	U /	8.52	6.91	19.81 /51	--	7.98 /42	0.00	2.06
GL	Oppenheimer Global Value I	GLVIX	D+	(888) 470-0862	C- / 3.8	8.87	7.55	21.25 /59	1.21 /19	9.25 /53	0.00	0.86
GL	Oppenheimer Global Value R	GLVNX	D	(888) 470-0862	C- / 3.3	8.66	7.18	20.40 /54	0.51 /16	8.53 /47	0.00	1.55
GL	Oppenheimer Global Value Y	GLVYX	D	(888) 470-0862	C- / 3.7	8.81	7.45	21.01 /57	1.01 /18	9.12 /52	0.00	1.05
GL	Oppenheimer Global Y	OGLYX	C	(888) 470-0862	C+ / 6.2	8.64	9.32	23.07 /67	4.32 /47	9.96 /58	0.87	0.90
PM	Oppenheimer Gold/Spec Min A	OPGSX	E-	(888) 470-0862	D- / 1.0	12.69	-7.06	32.91 /91	-1.87 / 7	-13.86 / 0	5.94	1.19
PM	● Oppenheimer Gold/Spec Min B	OGMBX	E-	(888) 470-0862	D- / 1.2	12.44	-7.46	31.89 /90	-2.64 / 5	-14.56 / 0	5.42	1.96
PM	Oppenheimer Gold/Spec Min C	OGMCX	E-	(888) 470-0862	D- / 1.2	12.48	-7.41	31.98 /90	-2.61 / 5	-14.52 / 0	6.14	1.95
PM	Oppenheimer Gold/Spec Min I	OGMIX	E-	(888) 470-0862	D / 1.7	12.78	-6.86	33.54 /92	-1.46 / 8	--	6.76	0.75
PM	Oppenheimer Gold/Spec Min R	OGMNX	E-	(888) 470-0862	D- / 1.4	12.60	-7.16	32.55 /91	-2.12 / 6	-14.09 / 0	6.37	1.43
PM	Oppenheimer Gold/Spec Min Y	OGMYX	E-	(888) 470-0862	D / 1.6	12.77	-6.94	33.21 /92	-1.65 / 7	-13.69 / 0	6.60	0.94
FO	Oppenheimer International Equity A	QIVAX	D-	(888) 470-0862	E / 0.5	4.71	1.00	12.19 /19	-0.86 /10	6.61 /32	1.83	1.32
FO	● Oppenheimer International Equity B	QIVBX	D-	(888) 470-0862	E+ / 0.7	4.48	0.54	11.23 /15	-1.64 / 8	5.78 /27	0.81	2.09
FO	Oppenheimer International Equity C	QIVCX	D-	(888) 470-0862	E+ / 0.7	4.52	0.64	11.31 /16	-1.60 / 8	5.79 /27	1.40	2.07
FO	Oppenheimer International Equity I	QIVIX	D	(888) 470-0862	D- / 1.1	4.80	1.19	12.66 /20	-0.43 /12	--	2.41	0.87
FO	Oppenheimer International Equity R	QIVNX	D	(888) 470-0862	E+ / 0.8	4.62	0.87	11.90 /18	-1.12 / 9	6.33 /31	1.71	1.57
FO	Oppenheimer International Equity Y	QIVYX	D	(888) 470-0862	D- / 1.0	4.75	1.13	12.49 /20	-0.61 /11	6.89 /34	2.22	1.07
FO	Oppenheimer Intl Diversified A	OIDAX	D	(888) 470-0862	D- / 1.1	6.08	1.18	12.95 /21	0.06 /14	6.25 /30	0.37	1.26
FO	● Oppenheimer Intl Diversified B	OIDBX	D-	(888) 470-0862	D- / 1.0	5.86	0.78	12.01 /18	-0.69 /11	5.41 /24	0.00	2.01
FO	Oppenheimer Intl Diversified C	OIDCX	D-	(888) 470-0862	D- / 1.0	5.87	0.78	12.13 /18	-0.68 /11	5.46 /25	0.00	2.01
FO	Oppenheimer Intl Diversified I	OIDIX	D	(888) 470-0862	D / 1.9	6.20	1.36	13.38 /23	0.51 /16	6.78 /33	0.83	0.82
FO	Oppenheimer Intl Diversified R	OIDNX	D	(888) 470-0862	D- / 1.2	5.99	1.03	12.68 /20	-0.18 /13	5.96 /28	0.18	1.51
FO	Oppenheimer Intl Diversified Y	OIDYX	D	(888) 470-0862	D / 1.8	6.11	1.26	13.15 /22	0.30 /15	6.52 /32	0.67	1.01
FO	Oppenheimer Intl Growth A	OIGAX	D-	(888) 470-0862	E / 0.3	6.33	-1.15	7.02 / 6	-1.48 / 8	5.63 /26	0.93	1.14
FO	● Oppenheimer Intl Growth B	IGRWX	D-	(888) 470-0862	E / 0.5	6.14	-1.53	6.24 / 5	-2.22 / 6	4.83 /20	0.00	1.89
FO	Oppenheimer Intl Growth C	OIGCX	D-	(888) 470-0862	E / 0.5	6.16	-1.52	6.26 / 5	-2.21 / 6	4.85 /20	0.27	1.89
FO	Oppenheimer Intl Growth I	OIGIX	D-	(888) 470-0862	E+ / 0.7	6.46	-0.93	7.52 / 7	-1.04 / 9	--	1.50	0.70
FO	Oppenheimer Intl Growth R	OIGNX	D-	(888) 470-0862	E+ / 0.6	6.27	-1.29	6.78 / 6	-1.73 / 7	5.37 /24	0.84	1.39
FO	Oppenheimer Intl Growth Svc		E+	(888) 470-0862	E+ / 0.6	6.16	-1.32	6.96 / 6	-1.64 / 8	5.63 /26	0.81	1.33
FO	Oppenheimer Intl Growth Y	OIGYX	D-	(888) 470-0862	E+ / 0.7	6.42	-1.04	7.30 / 6	-1.24 / 9	5.94 /28	1.29	0.89
FO	● Oppenheimer Intl Small Mid Co A	OSMAX	C-	(888) 470-0862	C- / 3.4	7.03	2.95	15.10 /30	5.05 /55	14.24 /94	0.13	1.43
FO	● Oppenheimer Intl Small Mid Co B	OSMBX	C-	(888) 470-0862	C- / 3.9	6.82	2.56	14.24 /27	4.27 /46	13.32 /87	0.00	2.16
FO	● Oppenheimer Intl Small Mid Co C	OSMCX	C-	(888) 470-0862	C- / 3.9	6.85	2.60	14.23 /27	4.27 /46	13.38 /88	0.00	2.18
FO	● Oppenheimer Intl Small Mid Co I	OSCIX	C+	(888) 470-0862	C / 5.0	7.13	3.17	15.59 /32	5.51 /60	14.73 /96	0.57	0.99
FO	● Oppenheimer Intl Small Mid Co R	OSMNX	C	(888) 470-0862	C / 4.3	6.98	2.84	14.83 /29	4.80 /52	13.92 /93	0.00	1.67
FO	● Oppenheimer Intl Small Mid Co Y	OSMYX	C	(888) 470-0862	C / 4.8	7.10	3.10	15.38 /32	5.32 /58	14.56 /96	0.41	1.18
GI	Oppenheimer Main St Select A	OMSOX	C	(888) 470-0862	C+ / 5.6	6.48	9.96	20.62 /56	6.30 /67	10.52 /62	0.97	1.15
GI	● Oppenheimer Main St Select B	OMOBX	C	(888) 470-0862	C+ / 6.1	6.25	9.52	19.71 /51	5.50 /60	9.63 /56	0.00	1.90
GI	Oppenheimer Main St Select C	OMSCX	C	(888) 470-0862	C+ / 6.1	6.23	9.52	19.66 /50	5.49 /59	9.70 /56	0.41	1.90

● Denotes fund is closed to new investors
* Denotes fund is included in Section II

Risk Rating/Pts	3 Year Standard Deviation	Beta	NAV As of 2/28/17	Total $(Mil)	Cash %	Stocks %	Bonds %	Other %	Portfolio Turnover Ratio	Last Bull Market Return	Last Bear Market Return	Manager Quality Pct	Manager Tenure (Years)	Initial Purch. $	Additional Purch. $	Front End Load	Back End Load
C /4.9	17.4	0.95	49.81	2,500	0	98	1	1	26	110.5	-19.5	98	22	1,000	0	5.8	0.0
C /4.9	17.5	0.95	44.40	18	0	98	1	1	26	101.4	-19.9	98	22	1,000	0	0.0	0.0
C /4.9	17.5	0.96	44.46	499	0	98	1	1	26	102.1	-19.8	98	22	1,000	0	0.0	0.0
C /4.9	17.5	1.92	50.39	156	0	98	1	1	26	115.3	-19.5	64	22	5,000,000	0	0.0	0.0
C /4.9	17.5	0.96	48.08	146	0	98	1	1	26	107.2	-19.7	98	22	1,000	0	0.0	0.0
C /4.9	17.5	0.95	50.27	759	0	98	1	1	26	113.5	-19.5	98	22	1,000	0	0.0	0.0
C /5.2	12.9	0.96	80.35	203	0	100	0	0	6	84.1	-23.3	93	13	1,000	0	0.0	0.0
C+ /6.0	12.2	0.86	10.23	17	8	91	0	1	78	N/A	N/A	21	4	1,000	0	5.8	0.0
C+ /6.0	12.2	0.86	10.18	5	8	91	0	1	78	N/A	N/A	15	4	1,000	0	0.0	0.0
C+ /6.0	12.2	0.86	10.26	91	8	91	0	1	78	N/A	N/A	25	4	5,000,000	0	0.0	0.0
C+ /6.0	12.2	0.86	10.21	2	8	91	0	1	78	N/A	N/A	19	4	0	0	0.0	0.0
C+ /6.0	12.2	0.86	10.25	1	8	91	0	1	78	N/A	N/A	24	4	0	0	0.0	0.0
C /4.6	15.4	1.07	44.29	146	0	100	0	0	89	84.1	-22.1	81	10	1,000	0	5.8	0.0
U /	15.4	1.07	41.92	55	0	100	0	0	89	76.6	-22.3	N/A	10	1,000	0	0.0	0.0
C /4.6	15.4	1.07	45.30	76	0	100	0	0	89	87.8	-22.1	83	10	5,000,000	0	0.0	0.0
C /4.5	15.4	1.07	43.43	7	0	100	0	0	89	81.6	-22.1	79	10	0	0	0.0	0.0
C /4.6	15.4	1.07	44.98	90	0	100	0	0	89	86.9	-22.0	82	10	0	0	0.0	0.0
C /5.2	12.9	0.96	80.78	1,193	0	100	0	0	6	89.5	-23.1	94	13	1,000	0	0.0	0.0
E- /0.2	43.8	2.41	16.61	633	0	98	1	1	69	-51.3	-21.1	89	20	1,000	0	0.0	0.0
E- /0.2	43.8	2.41	15.54	4	0	98	1	1	69	-53.4	-21.3	86	20	1,000	0	5.8	0.0
E- /0.2	43.8	2.41	15.25	147	0	98	1	1	69	-53.3	-21.3	86	20	1,000	0	0.0	0.0
E- /0.2	43.8	2.41	16.67	70	0	98	1	1	69	N/A	N/A	91	20	1,000,000	0	0.0	0.0
E- /0.2	43.8	2.41	15.86	151	0	98	1	1	69	-52.0	-21.2	88	20	1,000	0	0.0	0.0
E- /0.2	43.8	2.41	16.57	138	0	98	1	1	69	-50.8	-20.9	90	20	1,000	0	0.0	0.0
C+ /6.5	10.9	0.82	17.86	169	0	96	3	1	79	48.3	-26.8	65	4	1,000	0	5.8	0.0
C+ /6.6	10.9	0.82	16.38	1	0	96	3	1	79	42.1	-27.1	55	4	1,000	0	0.0	0.0
C+ /6.5	10.8	0.82	16.03	32	0	96	3	1	79	42.2	-27.1	56	4	1,000	0	0.0	0.0
C+ /6.5	10.9	0.82	17.75	707	0	96	3	1	79	N/A	N/A	71	4	1,000,000	0	0.0	0.0
C+ /6.5	10.9	0.82	17.69	9	0	96	3	1	79	46.1	-26.9	62	4	1,000	0	0.0	0.0
C+ /6.5	10.9	0.82	18.01	20	0	96	3	1	79	50.5	-26.6	68	4	1,000	0	0.0	0.0
C+ /6.2	10.9	0.84	14.60	1,217	1	94	4	1	3	52.6	-21.3	75	12	1,000	0	5.8	0.0
C+ /6.3	10.9	0.84	14.27	13	1	94	4	1	3	46.2	-21.6	68	12	1,000	0	0.0	0.0
C+ /6.2	10.9	0.84	14.24	377	1	94	4	1	3	46.6	-21.5	68	12	1,000	0	0.0	0.0
C+ /6.2	10.9	0.84	14.79	183	1	94	4	1	3	56.5	-21.3	79	12	1,000,000	0	0.0	0.0
C+ /6.2	10.9	0.84	14.43	167	1	94	4	1	3	50.4	-21.3	73	12	0	0	0.0	0.0
C+ /6.2	10.9	0.84	14.74	709	1	94	4	1	3	54.7	-21.2	77	12	0	0	0.0	0.0
C+ /6.2	11.7	0.90	36.14	4,267	0	95	3	2	9	54.4	-20.4	58	21	1,000	0	5.8	0.0
C+ /6.3	11.7	0.90	34.73	6	0	95	3	2	9	48.1	-20.6	47	21	1,000	0	0.0	0.0
C+ /6.2	11.7	0.90	34.34	438	0	95	3	2	9	48.3	-20.6	47	21	1,000	0	0.0	0.0
C+ /6.2	11.7	0.90	35.96	7,469	0	95	3	2	9	N/A	N/A	63	21	5,000,000	0	0.0	0.0
C+ /6.2	11.7	0.90	35.50	407	0	95	3	2	9	52.2	-20.4	54	21	1,000	0	0.0	0.0
C /5.1	11.7	0.90	2.24	186	0	96	2	2	24	54.7	-20.6	55	18	0	0	0.0	0.0
C+ /6.2	11.7	0.90	35.94	10,570	0	95	3	2	9	56.9	-20.2	61	21	1,000	0	0.0	0.0
C+ /6.6	10.1	0.70	39.35	2,542	1	93	5	1	19	116.7	-18.9	95	5	1,000	0	5.8	0.0
C+ /6.5	10.0	0.69	36.82	4	1	93	5	1	19	107.5	-19.2	94	5	1,000	0	0.0	0.0
C+ /6.5	10.1	0.70	36.36	300	1	93	5	1	19	108.1	-19.2	94	5	1,000	0	0.0	0.0
C+ /6.6	10.0	0.69	39.14	1,416	1	93	5	1	19	N/A	N/A	96	5	5,000,000	0	0.0	0.0
C+ /6.6	10.1	0.69	37.71	72	1	93	5	1	19	113.5	-19.0	95	5	1,000	0	0.0	0.0
C+ /6.6	10.1	0.70	39.07	2,560	1	93	5	1	19	120.3	-18.8	96	5	1,000	0	0.0	0.0
C /5.3	10.1	0.95	18.50	933	0	98	1	1	67	102.0	-14.5	29	3	1,000	0	5.8	0.0
C /5.3	10.1	0.95	16.97	13	0	98	1	1	67	93.3	-14.8	21	3	1,000	50	0.0	0.0
C /5.3	10.1	0.95	17.10	225	0	98	1	1	67	94.0	-14.8	21	3	1,000	50	0.0	0.0

Fund Type	Fund Name	Ticker Symbol	Overall Investment Rating	Phone	Performance Rating/Pts	3 Mo	6 Mo	1Yr / Pct	3Yr / Pct	5Yr / Pct	Dividend Yield	Expense Ratio
GI	Oppenheimer Main St Select R	OMSNX	C+	(888) 470-0862	C+ / 6.6	6.39	9.83	20.33 /54	6.04 /65	10.24 /60	0.82	1.40
GI	Oppenheimer Main St Select Y	OMSYX	C+	(888) 470-0862	C+ / 6.9	6.56	10.08	20.97 /57	6.58 /69	10.82 /64	1.19	0.89
* GI	Oppenheimer Main Street A	MSIGX	B-	(888) 470-0862	B / 8.0	7.93	9.67	23.93 /70	9.81 /92	13.36 /87	0.95	0.94
GI ●	Oppenheimer Main Street B	OMSBX	B	(888) 470-0862	B+ / 8.4	7.73	9.26	22.97 /67	8.97 /87	12.43 /78	0.00	1.70
GI	Oppenheimer Main Street C	MIGCX	B	(888) 470-0862	B+ / 8.4	7.73	9.26	22.99 /67	8.99 /87	12.51 /79	0.41	1.70
GI	Oppenheimer Main Street I	OMSIX	B+	(888) 470-0862	A- / 9.2	8.05	9.89	24.45 /71	10.28 /95	13.84 /92	1.41	0.50
SC	Oppenheimer Main Street Mid Cap A	OPMSX	C-	(888) 470-0862	C+ / 6.7	7.41	9.97	26.07 /76	6.75 /70	11.72 /72	0.76	1.11
SC ●	Oppenheimer Main Street Mid Cap B	OPMBX	C-	(888) 470-0862	B- / 7.1	7.20	9.56	25.08 /74	5.94 /64	10.83 /64	0.00	1.86
SC	Oppenheimer Main Street Mid Cap C	OPMCX	C-	(888) 470-0862	B- / 7.1	7.18	9.56	25.12 /74	5.95 /64	10.88 /65	0.31	1.86
SC	Oppenheimer Main Street Mid Cap I	OPMIX	C+	(888) 470-0862	B / 8.0	7.51	10.21	26.61 /78	7.22 /73	---	1.14	0.67
SC	Oppenheimer Main Street Mid Cap R	OPMNX	C	(888) 470-0862	B- / 7.4	7.34	9.84	25.76 /75	6.48 /68	11.42 /69	0.63	1.36
SC	Oppenheimer Main Street Mid Cap Y	OPMYX	C+	(888) 470-0862	B / 7.8	7.44	10.10	26.36 /77	7.00 /72	12.04 /75	0.96	0.86
GI	Oppenheimer Main Street R	OMGNX	B	(888) 470-0862	B+ / 8.8	7.86	9.53	23.58 /68	9.53 /91	13.06 /84	0.83	1.19
SC	Oppenheimer Main Street Small Cap	OSCAX	B	(888) 470-0862	B / 7.7	6.71	12.90	30.94 /88	7.25 /74	---	0.22	1.26
SC	Oppenheimer Main Street Small Cap	OSCCX	B	(888) 470-0862	B / 8.0	6.52	12.51	29.89 /86	6.39 /67	---	0.00	2.01
SC	Oppenheimer Main Street Small Cap	OSSIX	B+	(888) 470-0862	A- / 9.0	6.88	13.13	31.55 /89	7.72 /77	---	0.56	0.80
SC	Oppenheimer Main Street Small Cap	OSCNX	B+	(888) 470-0862	B+ / 8.4	6.65	12.72	30.54 /87	6.92 /71	---	0.07	1.51
SC	Oppenheimer Main Street Small Cap	OSCYX	B+	(888) 470-0862	B+ / 8.9	6.85	13.11	31.32 /89	7.61 /76	---	0.46	1.00
GI	Oppenheimer Main Street Y	MIGYX	B+	(888) 470-0862	A- / 9.1	8.00	9.80	24.21 /71	10.07 /94	13.67 /90	1.23	0.69
SC	Oppenheimer Mid Cap Value A	QVSCX	A-	(888) 470-0862	B+ / 8.8	7.44	12.37	35.59 /95	8.55 /83	12.73 /81	0.44	1.18
SC ●	Oppenheimer Mid Cap Value B	QSCBX	A	(888) 470-0862	A- / 9.2	7.25	11.94	34.53 /93	7.73 /77	11.84 /73	0.02	1.92
SC	Oppenheimer Mid Cap Value C	QSCCX	A	(888) 470-0862	A- / 9.2	7.26	11.97	34.57 /94	7.74 /77	11.87 /73	0.05	1.92
MC	Oppenheimer Mid Cap Value I	QSCIX	A	(888) 470-0862	A+ / 9.6	7.57	12.62	36.18 /95	9.02 /87	12.99 /84	0.82	0.73
SC	Oppenheimer Mid Cap Value R	QSCNX	A	(888) 470-0862	A / 9.4	7.39	12.23	35.24 /94	8.27 /81	12.44 /78	0.28	1.42
SC	Oppenheimer Mid Cap Value Y	QSCYX	A	(888) 470-0862	A+ / 9.6	7.51	12.50	35.90 /95	8.84 /86	13.05 /84	0.66	0.92
AA	Oppenheimer Moderate Inv A	OAMIX	C-	(888) 470-0862	D+ / 2.5	5.06	4.01	13.94 /25	3.68 /39	6.45 /31	1.47	1.08
AA ●	Oppenheimer Moderate Inv B	OBMIX	C	(888) 470-0862	D+ / 2.9	4.99	3.64	13.12 /22	2.89 /31	5.64 /26	0.39	1.83
AA	Oppenheimer Moderate Inv C	OCMIX	C	(888) 470-0862	C- / 3.0	4.97	3.70	13.16 /22	2.88 /31	5.65 /26	0.85	1.83
AA	Oppenheimer Moderate Inv R	ONMIX	C	(888) 470-0862	C- / 3.3	5.04	3.98	13.76 /24	3.41 /36	6.18 /30	1.34	1.33
AA	Oppenheimer Moderate Inv Y	OYMIX	C+	(888) 470-0862	C- / 3.7	5.20	4.16	14.24 /27	3.93 /42	6.70 /33	1.79	0.83
RE	Oppenheimer Real Estate A	OREAX	C-	(888) 470-0862	C+ / 5.9	6.92	-3.22	14.10 /26	10.56 /96	10.72 /64	2.02	1.43
RE ●	Oppenheimer Real Estate B	OREBX	C	(888) 470-0862	C+ / 6.4	6.72	-3.57	13.26 /23	9.72 /92	9.89 /58	1.36	2.18
RE	Oppenheimer Real Estate C	ORECX	C	(888) 470-0862	C+ / 6.4	6.74	-3.57	13.26 /23	9.73 /92	9.89 /58	1.44	2.18
RE	Oppenheimer Real Estate I	OREIX	C+	(888) 470-0862	B- / 7.2	7.07	-3.02	14.63 /28	11.04 /97	11.17 /67	2.54	0.99
RE	Oppenheimer Real Estate R	ORENX	C	(888) 470-0862	C+ / 6.8	6.87	-3.33	13.84 /25	10.28 /95	10.45 /62	1.89	1.68
RE	Oppenheimer Real Estate Y	OREYX	C+	(888) 470-0862	B- / 7.1	7.00	-3.09	14.39 /27	10.82 /97	11.00 /66	2.34	1.18
GR	Oppenheimer Rising Dividends A	OARDX	C	(888) 470-0862	C / 5.0	7.32	7.30	17.52 /41	6.27 /67	9.78 /57	0.96	1.07
GR ●	Oppenheimer Rising Dividends B	OBRDX	C	(888) 470-0862	C / 5.5	7.16	6.94	16.68 /37	5.47 /59	8.88 /50	0.46	1.83
GR	Oppenheimer Rising Dividends C	OCRDX	C	(888) 470-0862	C / 5.5	7.06	6.85	16.62 /37	5.46 /59	8.95 /50	0.53	1.82
GR	Oppenheimer Rising Dividends I	OIRDX	C+	(888) 470-0862	C+ / 6.5	7.39	7.48	17.95 /43	6.72 /70	10.23 /60	1.38	0.63
GR	Oppenheimer Rising Dividends R	ONRDX	C+	(888) 470-0862	C+ / 6.0	7.23	7.14	17.21 /39	6.00 /64	9.46 /54	0.79	1.32
GR	Oppenheimer Rising Dividends Y	OYRDX	C+	(888) 470-0862	C+ / 6.4	7.37	7.41	17.81 /42	6.53 /69	10.03 /59	1.14	0.82
SC	Oppenheimer Small Cap Value Fund	OVSAX	U	(888) 470-0862	U /	5.10	11.51	38.01 /96	---	---	0.77	3.06
EN	Oppenheimer SteelPath MLP Alp Pls	MLPLX	E	(888) 470-0862	D+ / 2.5	14.23	11.03	65.33 /99	-4.29 / 3	2.49 / 9	7.11	2.30
EN	Oppenheimer SteelPath MLP Alp Pls	MLPMX	E	(888) 470-0862	C- / 3.0	13.98	10.52	64.03 /99	-5.01 / 2	2.10 / 8	7.86	3.05
EN	Oppenheimer SteelPath MLP Alp Pls	OSPPX	E+	(888) 470-0862	C- / 3.9	14.33	11.18	66.06 /99	-3.85 / 3	---	7.38	1.86
EN	Oppenheimer SteelPath MLP Alp Pls	MLPNX	E+	(888) 470-0862	C- / 3.8	14.40	11.10	65.94 /99	-4.03 / 3	2.76 /10	7.41	2.05
GI	Oppenheimer SteelPath MLP Alpha A	MLPAX	E	(888) 470-0862	D- / 1.4	6.58	6.25	40.04 /97	-2.12 / 6	2.53 / 9	6.81	1.63
EN	Oppenheimer SteelPath MLP Alpha C	MLPGX	E	(888) 470-0862	D / 1.7	6.27	5.82	38.96 /97	-2.85 / 5	1.77 / 8	7.55	2.38
EN	Oppenheimer SteelPath MLP Alpha I	OSPAX	E+	(888) 470-0862	D+ / 2.3	6.63	6.43	40.60 /97	-1.76 / 7	---	7.04	1.19
GI	Oppenheimer SteelPath MLP Alpha Y	MLPOX	E+	(888) 470-0862	D / 2.2	6.65	6.45	40.57 /97	-1.87 / 7	2.81 /10	7.07	1.38
GI	Oppenheimer SteelPath MLP Income	MLPDX	E	(888) 470-0862	D / 1.9	5.20	5.62	51.56 /99	-2.38 / 6	0.67 / 6	9.45	1.49

● Denotes fund is closed to new investors
* Denotes fund is included in Section II

486

Risk Rating/Pts	Standard Deviation	Beta	NAV As of 2/28/17	Total $(Mil)	Cash %	Stocks %	Bonds %	Other %	Portfolio Turnover Ratio	Last Bull Market Return	Last Bear Market Return	Manager Quality Pct	Manager Tenure (Years)	Initial Purch. $	Additional Purch. $	Front End Load	Back End Load
	3 Year		**NET ASSETS**		**ASSET**					**BULL / BEAR**		**FUND MANAGER**		**MINIMUMS**		**LOADS**	
C /5.3	10.1	0.95	18.03	62	0	98	1	1	67	99.1	-14.6	26	3	1,000	50	0.0	0.0
C /5.4	10.1	0.95	18.88	30	0	98	1	1	67	105.0	-14.4	32	3	1,000	50	0.0	0.0
C /4.9	10.3	0.98	49.62	5,959	1	96	1	2	39	128.8	-15.1	67	8	1,000	0	5.8	0.0
C /4.9	10.3	0.98	47.67	53	1	96	1	2	39	118.9	-15.5	57	8	1,000	0	0.0	0.0
C /4.9	10.3	0.99	47.20	768	1	96	1	2	39	119.7	-15.4	58	8	1,000	0	0.0	0.0
C /4.8	10.3	0.98	49.15	726	1	96	1	2	39	N/A	N/A	72	8	5,000,000	0	0.0	0.0
C- /3.4	10.8	0.61	28.25	1,580	5	92	2	1	87	125.7	-23.6	88	8	1,000	0	5.8	0.0
C- /3.0	10.8	0.61	23.85	12	5	92	2	1	87	116.1	-23.8	85	8	1,000	0	0.0	0.0
C- /3.0	10.8	0.61	23.99	327	5	92	2	1	87	116.7	-23.8	85	8	1,000	0	0.0	0.0
C- /3.6	10.8	0.61	30.16	419	5	92	2	1	87	N/A	N/A	90	8	5,000,000	0	0.0	0.0
C- /3.4	10.8	0.61	26.98	185	5	92	2	1	87	122.5	-23.7	87	8	1,000	0	0.0	0.0
C- /3.6	10.8	0.61	30.23	588	5	92	2	1	87	129.3	-23.5	89	8	1,000	0	0.0	0.0
C /4.9	10.3	0.98	48.82	151	1	96	1	2	39	125.6	-15.2	64	8	1,000	0	0.0	0.0
C /5.5	14.3	0.89	14.55	103	3	96	0	1	53	N/A	N/A	81	4	1,000	0	5.8	0.0
C /5.5	14.3	0.89	14.21	31	3	96	0	1	53	N/A	N/A	76	4	1,000	0	0.0	0.0
C /5.5	14.3	0.89	14.62	308	3	96	0	1	53	N/A	N/A	84	4	5,000,000	0	0.0	0.0
C /5.5	14.3	0.89	14.44	9	3	96	0	1	53	N/A	N/A	79	4	0	0	0.0	0.0
C /5.5	14.3	0.88	14.61	78	3	96	0	1	53	N/A	N/A	83	4	0	0	0.0	0.0
C /4.8	10.3	0.98	49.22	700	1	96	1	2	39	132.4	-15.0	70	8	1,000	0	0.0	0.0
C+ /5.9	13.2	0.79	56.69	1,057	1	95	2	2	34	117.0	-24.3	90	4	1,000	0	5.8	0.0
C+ /5.9	13.2	0.79	47.36	10	1	95	2	2	34	107.9	-24.6	87	4	1,000	0	0.0	0.0
C+ /5.9	13.2	0.79	47.42	252	1	95	2	2	34	108.1	-24.5	87	4	1,000	0	0.0	0.0
C+ /5.9	13.2	1.05	57.65	1	1	95	2	2	34	119.5	-24.3	61	4	5,000,000	0	0.0	0.0
C+ /5.9	13.2	0.79	54.41	88	1	95	2	2	34	113.9	-24.4	89	4	1,000	0	0.0	0.0
C+ /5.9	13.2	0.79	58.12	88	1	95	2	2	34	120.3	-24.2	91	4	1,000	0	0.0	0.0
B- /7.9	6.8	1.05	11.28	1,066	1	54	44	1	5	52.8	-11.9	24	4	1,000	50	5.8	0.0
B- /7.9	6.7	1.04	11.21	22	1	54	44	1	5	46.6	-12.3	17	4	1,000	50	0.0	0.0
B- /7.9	6.8	1.05	11.06	388	1	54	44	1	5	46.8	-12.2	17	4	1,000	50	0.0	0.0
B- /7.9	6.8	1.05	11.22	108	1	54	44	1	5	50.9	-12.0	21	4	1,000	50	0.0	0.0
B- /7.9	6.8	1.04	11.35	10	1	54	44	1	5	54.7	-11.7	27	4	1,000	50	0.0	0.0
C /4.5	14.8	1.08	25.69	576	0	99	0	1	85	101.3	-17.1	59	5	1,000	0	5.8	0.0
C /4.5	14.8	1.08	25.08	7	0	99	0	1	85	93.3	-17.3	48	5	1,000	0	0.0	0.0
C /4.5	14.8	1.08	24.99	113	0	99	0	1	85	93.3	-17.3	48	5	1,000	0	0.0	0.0
C /4.5	14.8	1.08	25.96	211	0	99	0	1	85	105.4	-17.1	64	5	1,000,000	0	0.0	0.0
C /4.5	14.8	1.08	25.56	110	0	99	0	1	85	98.7	-17.2	55	5	0	0	0.0	0.0
C /4.5	14.8	1.08	25.98	255	0	99	0	1	85	104.2	-16.9	61	5	0	0	0.0	0.0
C+ /5.8	10.5	1.00	19.10	2,231	7	92	0	1	96	93.0	-15.9	24	1	1,000	0	5.8	0.0
C+ /5.6	10.5	1.00	16.57	44	7	92	0	1	96	84.6	-16.2	17	1	1,000	0	0.0	0.0
C /5.5	10.5	1.00	16.41	581	7	92	0	1	96	85.3	-16.1	17	1	1,000	0	0.0	0.0
C+ /5.8	10.5	1.00	19.70	8	7	92	0	1	96	N/A	N/A	28	1	1,000,000	0	0.0	0.0
C+ /5.8	10.5	1.00	18.98	122	7	92	0	1	96	89.9	-16.0	21	1	1,000	0	0.0	0.0
C+ /5.8	10.5	1.00	19.74	490	7	92	0	1	96	95.4	-15.8	26	1	1,000	0	0.0	0.0
U /	N/A	N/A	12.37	29	0	0	0	100	0	N/A	N/A	N/A	2	1,000	0	5.8	0.0
D /2.1	28.2	0.98	8.72	134	96	3	0	1	39	N/A	N/A	80	6	1,000	0	5.8	0.0
D /2.1	28.2	0.98	8.37	61	96	3	0	1	39	N/A	N/A	74	6	1,000	0	0.0	0.0
D /2.1	28.1	0.98	8.91	1	96	3	0	1	39	N/A	N/A	83	6	1,000,000	0	0.0	0.0
D /2.1	28.2	0.98	8.87	98	96	3	0	1	39	N/A	N/A	82	6	1,000	0	0.0	0.0
C- /3.5	18.1	1.08	9.53	1,113	91	8	0	1	36	23.3	-8.9	1	7	1,000	0	5.8	0.0
C- /3.5	18.1	0.66	9.12	805	91	8	0	1	36	18.3	N/A	78	7	1,000	0	0.0	0.0
C- /3.5	18.1	0.66	9.78	150	91	8	0	1	36	N/A	N/A	85	7	1,000,000	0	0.0	0.0
C- /3.5	18.1	1.08	9.75	1,637	91	8	0	1	36	25.0	-8.7	1	7	1,000	0	0.0	0.0
C- /3.2	21.0	1.23	7.73	1,870	98	1	0	1	18	11.8	-12.3	0	7	1,000	0	5.8	0.0

Fund Type	Fund Name	Ticker Symbol	Overall Investment Rating	Phone	Perfor-mance Rating/Pts	3 Mo	6 Mo	1Yr / Pct	Annualized 3Yr / Pct	Annualized 5Yr / Pct	Dividend Yield	Expense Ratio
EN	Oppenheimer SteelPath MLP Income	MLPRX	E+	(888) 470-0862	D / 2.2	5.03	5.33	50.65 /99	-3.08 / 4	-0.08 / 4	10.55	2.24
EN	Oppenheimer SteelPath MLP Income	OSPMX	D+ / 2.9	(888) 470-0862		5.20	5.75	52.16 /99	-2.07 / 6	--	9.78	1.05
GI	Oppenheimer SteelPath MLP Income	MLPZX	E+	(888) 470-0862	D+ / 2.8	5.22	5.77	51.89 /99	-2.15 / 6	0.93 / 6	9.81	1.24
GI	Oppenheimer SteelPath MLP Sel 40	MLPFX	E+	(888) 470-0862	D- / 1.4	7.06	7.49	30.44 /87	-0.98 / 9	2.74 /10	6.85	1.23
EN	Oppenheimer SteelPath MLP Sel 40	MLPEX	E+	(888) 470-0862	D / 1.7	6.76	6.98	29.41 /85	-1.74 / 7	2.00 / 8	7.57	1.98
EN	Oppenheimer SteelPath MLP Sel 40 I	OSPSX	E+	(888) 470-0862	D / 2.2	7.08	7.62	30.89 /88	-0.64 /11	--	7.07	0.80
GI	Oppenheimer SteelPath MLP Sel 40	MLPYX	E+	(888) 470-0862	D / 2.2	7.11	7.53	30.83 /88	-0.76 /10	3.00 /11	7.09	0.98
GI	Oppenheimer SteelPath MLP Sel 40	MLPTX	E+	(888) 470-0862	D / 2.2	7.11	7.53	30.83 /88	-0.76 /10	3.00 /11	7.09	0.98
GR	Oppenheimer Value A	CGRWX	B+	(888) 470-0862	B / 7.6	6.93	12.45	28.39 /83	7.72 /77	11.52 /70	1.40	0.96
GR	● Oppenheimer Value B	CGRBX	B+	(888) 470-0862	B / 8.0	6.72	12.01	27.42 /80	6.90 /71	10.64 /63	0.76	1.71
GR	Oppenheimer Value C	CGRCX	B+	(888) 470-0862	B / 8.0	6.72	12.03	27.42 /80	6.90 /71	10.68 /63	0.90	1.71
GR	Oppenheimer Value I	OGRIX	A	(888) 470-0862	B+ / 8.9	7.06	12.68	28.94 /84	8.19 /80	12.02 /74	1.83	0.51
GR	Oppenheimer Value R	CGRNX	B+	(888) 470-0862	B+ / 8.4	6.87	12.33	28.07 /82	7.45 /75	11.23 /68	1.30	1.20
GR	Oppenheimer Value Y	CGRYX	A-	(888) 470-0862	B+ / 8.8	7.00	12.58	28.70 /83	7.98 /79	11.84 /73	1.66	0.70
FO	Optimum Intl Equity A	OAIEX	D-	(800) 523-1918	E+ / 0.9	8.07	6.37	20.34 /54	-1.09 / 9	4.22 /16	0.81	1.49
FO	Optimum Intl Equity C	OCIEX	D	(800) 523-1918	D- / 1.2	7.72	5.98	19.36 /49	-1.85 / 7	3.47 /13	0.21	2.24
FO	Optimum Intl Equity I	OIIEX	D	(800) 523-1918	D- / 1.5	7.99	6.50	20.49 /55	-0.85 /10	4.49 /18	1.09	1.24
GR	Optimum Large Cap Growth A	OALGX	C+	(800) 523-1918	B- / 7.1	9.56	9.62	21.57 /60	8.25 /81	12.96 /83	0.00	1.37
GR	Optimum Large Cap Growth C	OCLGX	C+	(800) 523-1918	B / 7.6	9.40	9.25	20.69 /56	7.47 /75	12.16 /76	0.00	2.12
GR	Optimum Large Cap Growth I	OILGX	B	(800) 523-1918	B+ / 8.3	9.60	9.74	21.83 /61	8.53 /83	13.29 /87	0.00	1.12
GR	Optimum Large Cap Value A	OALVX	C+	(800) 523-1918	C+ / 5.6	6.71	8.90	24.09 /70	5.65 /61	10.12 /59	0.97	1.34
GR	Optimum Large Cap Value C	OCLVX	C+	(800) 523-1918	C+ / 6.1	6.50	8.44	23.17 /67	4.86 /53	9.33 /53	0.37	2.09
GR	Optimum Large Cap Value I	OILVX	C+	(800) 523-1918	C+ / 6.9	6.75	9.00	24.42 /71	5.92 /64	10.45 /62	1.25	1.09
SC	Optimum Small Mid Cap Growth A	OASGX	E+	(800) 523-1918	C- / 3.5	6.94	8.27	27.33 /80	1.58 /21	8.73 /48	0.00	1.78
SC	Optimum Small Mid Cap Growth C	OCSGX	E+	(800) 523-1918	C- / 4.0	6.74	7.84	26.36 /77	0.82 /17	7.95 /42	0.00	2.53
SC	Optimum Small Mid Cap Growth I	OISGX	D-	(800) 523-1918	C / 4.9	6.98	8.39	27.63 /81	1.83 /23	9.02 /51	0.00	1.53
SC	Optimum Small Mid Cap Value A	OASVX	D+	(800) 523-1918	C / 4.3	6.50	12.26	29.16 /84	1.93 /24	8.24 /44	0.32	1.69
SC	Optimum Small Mid Cap Value C	OCSVX	C-	(800) 523-1918	C / 4.9	6.40	11.92	28.26 /82	1.18 /19	7.47 /38	0.00	2.44
SC	Optimum Small Mid Cap Value I	OISVX	C	(800) 523-1918	C+ / 5.8	6.60	12.39	29.42 /85	2.18 /25	8.54 /47	0.53	1.44
GL	Orinda Income Opportunities Fund A	OIOAX	C-	(855) 467-4632	D+ / 2.9	3.75	1.72	18.90 /47	3.86 /41	--	6.64	2.17
GL	Orinda Income Opportunities Fund D	OIODX	C	(855) 467-4632	C- / 3.3	3.57	1.40	18.10 /43	3.17 /33	--	6.42	2.83
GL	Orinda Income Opportunities Fund I	OIOIX	C	(855) 467-4632	C- / 4.0	3.87	1.92	19.29 /49	4.17 /45	--	7.20	1.87
GR	O'Shaughnessy All Cap Core A	OFAAX	C+	(877) 291-7827	B- / 7.1	6.38	13.76	24.13 /70	8.12 /80	13.06 /84	1.84	1.15
GR	O'Shaughnessy All Cap Core C	OFACX	C+	(877) 291-7827	B- / 7.5	6.23	13.30	22.95 /66	7.50 /75	12.35 /78	1.38	1.90
GR	O'Shaughnessy All Cap Core I	OFAIX	B-	(877) 291-7827	B / 8.1	6.51	13.95	24.22 /71	8.19 /80	13.24 /86	2.21	0.90
IN	O'Shaughnessy Enh Div I	OFDIX	D-	(877) 291-7827	D+ / 2.9	3.90	8.94	25.01 /73	0.06 /14	3.85 /14	2.58	1.40
GR	O'Shaughnessy Market Leader Value	OFVIX	U	(877) 291-7827	U /	4.07	12.65	25.10 /74	--	--	1.01	1.96
GR	O'Shaughnessy S/M Cap Growth I	OFMIX	C-	(877) 291-7827	C / 5.3	3.90	8.91	23.17 /67	4.78 /52	12.18 /76	0.29	1.83
GI	Osterweis	OSTFX	D	(800) 700-3316	C- / 4.2	8.47	8.05	17.14 /39	2.70 /29	9.11 /52	1.04	1.03
GI	Osterweis Institutional Equity Inv	OSTEX	D	(800) 700-3316	C / 5.1	8.67	8.99	20.82 /56	3.18 /34	--	0.35	1.28
GL	Osterweis Strat Invest	OSTVX	C	(800) 700-3316	C / 4.9	6.80	7.70	19.90 /51	3.62 /38	8.84 /49	3.46	1.14
GR	Otter Creek Long/Short Oppty Inst	OTTRX	D+		D- / 1.2	-2.44	-2.44	-6.22 / 0	4.13 /44	--	0.00	2.43
GR	Otter Creek Long/Short Oppty Inv	OTCRX	D		D- / 1.1	-2.54	-2.54	-6.49 / 0	3.92 /42	--	0.00	2.68
GI	Pac Fin Faith and Val Bsd Modt Inv	FVMLX	C	(800) 637-1380	D+ / 2.3	4.16	4.16	12.53 /20	1.79 /23	--	0.00	3.43
GL	PACE Alternatives Strat Invst A	PASIX	C-	(888) 793-8637	E+ / 0.7	2.98	2.29	2.29 / 2	1.38 /20	3.32 /12	0.00	2.10
GL	PACE Alternatives Strat Invst C	PASOX	C-	(888) 793-8637	E+ / 0.9	2.75	1.92	1.51 / 2	0.68 /17	2.59 /10	0.00	2.83
GL	PACE Alternatives Strat Invst P	PASPX	C	(888) 793-8637	D- / 1.2	3.02	2.32	2.52 / 2	1.65 /22	3.58 /13	0.00	1.85
GL	PACE Alternatives Strat Invst Y	PASYX	C	(888) 793-8637	D- / 1.2	2.90	2.31	2.71 / 2	1.67 /22	3.59 /13	0.00	1.77
RE	PACE Glb Real Est Sec Inv Cl A	PREAX	C	(888) 793-8637	C- / 3.5	6.40	-2.53	17.31 /40	5.79 /62	8.16 /43	3.84	1.65
RE	PACE Glb Real Est Sec Inv Cl C	PREEX	C	(888) 793-8637	C- / 3.9	6.14	-2.90	16.49 /36	4.97 /54	7.36 /37	3.46	2.26
RE	PACE Glb Real Est Sec Inv Cl P	PREQX	C+	(888) 793-8637	C / 4.9	6.56	-2.29	17.72 /42	6.10 /65	8.44 /46	4.42	1.59
RE	PACE Glb Real Est Sec Inv Cl Y	PREYX	C+	(888) 793-8637	C / 4.7	6.45	-2.38	17.39 /40	5.99 /64	8.39 /45	4.18	1.50

● Denotes fund is closed to new investors
* Denotes fund is included in Section II

www.thestreetratings.com

I. Index of Stock Mutual Funds

Risk Rating/Pts	Standard Deviation	Beta	NAV As of 2/28/17	Total $(Mil)	Cash %	Stocks %	Bonds %	Other %	Portfolio Turnover Ratio	Last Bull Market Return	Last Bear Market Return	Manager Quality Pct	Manager Tenure (Years)	Initial Purch. $	Additional Purch. $	Front End Load	Back End Load
C- / 3.2	21.1	0.76	7.35	1,307	98	1	0	1	18	7.4	N/A	80	7	1,000	0	0.0	0.0
C- / 3.2	21.1	0.76	7.93	25	98	1	0	1	18	N/A	N/A	86	7	1,000,000	0	0.0	0.0
C- / 3.2	21.0	1.23	7.90	973	98	1	0	1	18	13.4	-12.3	0	7	1,000	0	0.0	0.0
C- / 3.9	15.0	0.96	9.71	679	95	4	0	1	8	24.9	-10.4	2	7	1,000	0	5.8	0.0
C- / 3.9	15.0	0.57	9.32	564	95	4	0	1	8	20.1	N/A	82	7	1,000	0	0.0	0.0
C- / 4.0	15.0	0.57	9.98	375	95	4	0	1	8	N/A	N/A	88	7	1,000,000	0	0.0	0.0
C- / 4.0	15.0	0.96	9.95	7	95	4	0	1	8	26.7	-10.2	2	7	1,000	0	0.0	0.0
C- / 4.0	15.0	0.96	9.95	1,768	95	4	0	1	8	26.7	-10.2	2	7	1,000	0	0.0	0.0
C+ / 6.1	11.5	1.07	35.77	563	0	98	1	1	64	104.7	-20.9	30	4	1,000	0	5.8	0.0
C+ / 6.1	11.5	1.07	35.27	4	0	98	1	1	64	96.1	-21.2	22	4	1,000	0	0.0	0.0
C+ / 6.1	11.5	1.07	34.22	123	0	98	1	1	64	96.5	-21.2	22	4	1,000	0	0.0	0.0
C+ / 6.1	11.5	1.07	36.48	1,324	0	98	1	1	64	109.4	-20.9	35	4	5,000,000	0	0.0	0.0
C+ / 6.1	11.5	1.07	35.10	43	0	98	1	1	64	101.9	-21.0	27	4	1,000	0	0.0	0.0
C+ / 6.1	11.5	1.07	36.53	126	0	98	1	1	64	108.1	-20.7	33	4	1,000	0	0.0	0.0
C+ / 6.3	11.1	0.85	12.08	9	1	98	0	1	47	39.0	-21.0	63	9	1,000	100	5.8	0.0
C+ / 6.3	11.0	0.85	11.79	30	1	98	0	1	47	33.7	-21.2	52	9	1,000	100	0.0	0.0
C+ / 6.3	11.0	0.85	12.15	525	1	98	0	1	47	41.2	-20.9	66	9	0	0	0.0	0.0
C / 4.6	12.3	1.06	16.54	33	2	97	0	1	88	128.0	-18.2	38	9	1,000	100	5.8	0.0
C / 4.4	12.3	1.06	14.57	106	2	97	0	1	88	119.7	-18.5	29	9	1,000	100	0.0	0.0
C / 4.7	12.3	1.05	17.49	1,347	2	97	0	1	88	131.6	-18.1	42	9	0	0	0.0	0.0
C+ / 6.5	10.7	1.01	15.53	30	1	98	0	1	39	97.3	-17.0	18	14	1,000	100	5.8	0.0
C+ / 6.5	10.7	1.01	15.36	98	1	98	0	1	39	89.8	-17.2	12	14	1,000	100	0.0	0.0
C+ / 6.5	10.7	1.01	15.56	1,245	1	98	0	1	39	100.5	-16.9	20	14	0	0	0.0	0.0
D / 2.2	15.4	0.91	13.09	5	2	97	0	1	104	88.7	-24.5	19	1	1,000	100	5.8	0.0
D / 1.8	15.5	0.91	11.41	17	2	97	0	1	104	81.7	-24.7	13	1	1,000	100	0.0	0.0
D+ / 2.4	15.4	0.91	13.95	419	2	97	0	1	104	91.7	-24.4	21	1	0	0	0.0	0.0
C / 4.7	13.5	0.80	13.85	5	0	99	0	1	90	94.1	-25.7	29	2	1,000	100	5.8	0.0
C / 4.5	13.4	0.79	12.30	15	0	99	0	1	90	86.9	-25.9	22	2	1,000	100	0.0	0.0
C / 4.8	13.4	0.79	14.61	414	0	99	0	1	90	97.2	-25.6	32	2	0	0	0.0	0.0
B- / 7.2	6.1	0.69	23.58	101	11	86	1	2	127	N/A	N/A	78	4	5,000	0	5.0	0.0
B- / 7.2	6.0	0.69	23.49	24	11	86	1	2	127	N/A	N/A	74	4	5,000	0	0.0	0.0
B- / 7.2	6.1	0.69	23.66	180	11	86	1	2	127	N/A	N/A	80	4	100,000	0	0.0	0.0
C / 4.7	11.0	0.98	15.58	2	0	99	0	1	104	126.4	-19.7	47	7	2,500	100	5.3	2.0
C / 4.6	10.8	0.97	14.97	6	0	99	0	1	104	118.6	-20.0	40	7	2,500	100	0.0	2.0
C / 4.6	11.0	0.98	15.46	10	0	99	0	1	104	128.2	-19.7	48	7	1,000,000	0	0.0	2.0
C- / 3.8	13.6	0.99	10.65	12	1	98	0	1	48	39.4	-16.7	2	7	1,000,000	0	0.0	2.0
U /	N/A	N/A	12.32	26	0	0	0	100	0	N/A	N/A	N/A	N/A	1,000,000	0	0.0	2.0
C / 4.5	11.5	0.92	15.29	16	0	99	0	1	90	117.7	-28.4	18	7	1,000,000	0	0.0	2.0
C- / 3.2	10.4	0.90	26.33	357	8	81	7	4	20	84.3	-20.6	7	24	5,000	100	0.0	0.0
C- / 3.1	11.4	1.00	10.45	12	11	88	0	1	41	N/A	N/A	6	5	100,000	100	0.0	0.0
C+ / 5.6	8.1	0.56	14.81	207	5	48	43	4	44	76.4	-13.9	92	7	5,000	100	0.0	0.0
B- / 7.2	7.5	-0.06	11.61	289	10	88	0	2	80	N/A	N/A	94	4	100,000	0	0.0	0.0
B- / 7.2	7.5	-0.07	11.53	40	10	88	0	2	80	N/A	N/A	94	4	2,500	0	0.0	1.0
B+ / 9.0	6.0	0.54	10.51	11	0	0	0	100	84	N/A	N/A	26	4	5,000	500	0.0	0.0
B+ / 9.6	3.1	0.16	10.70	9	81	15	3	1	221	26.4	-8.4	83	11	1,000	100	5.5	0.0
B+ / 9.4	3.0	0.16	10.08	11	81	15	3	1	221	21.7	-8.8	78	11	1,000	100	0.0	0.0
B+ / 9.4	3.0	0.16	10.59	646	81	15	3	1	221	28.2	-8.4	84	11	10,000	500	0.0	0.0
B+ / 9.4	3.1	0.16	10.63	1	81	15	3	1	221	28.2	-8.3	84	11	5,000,000	0	0.0	0.0
B- / 7.2	12.9	0.87	7.46	1	3	96	0	1	75	78.6	-20.1	29	8	1,000	100	5.5	0.0
B- / 7.2	12.9	0.87	7.15	N/A	3	96	0	1	75	71.4	-20.4	21	8	1,000	100	0.0	0.0
B- / 7.2	12.9	0.87	7.20	140	3	96	0	1	75	81.2	-20.0	32	8	10,000	500	0.0	0.0
B- / 7.1	12.8	0.86	7.22	N/A	3	96	0	1	75	80.7	-20.1	31	8	5,000,000	0	0.0	0.0

Data as of February 28, 2017

I. Index of Stock Mutual Funds

			99 Pct = Best 0 Pct = Worst Overall Investment		PERFORMANCE		Total Return % through 2/28/17			Annualized		Incl. in Returns	
Fund Type	Fund Name	Ticker Symbol	Rating	Phone	Perfor- mance Rating/Pts	3 Mo	6 Mo	1Yr / Pct	3Yr / Pct	5Yr / Pct	Dividend Yield	Expense Ratio
EM	PACE Intertl Emg Mkts Eq Inve A	PWEAX	D-	(888) 793-8637	D- / 1.1	7.97	3.21	22.75 /66	-0.70 /10	-1.50 / 3	0.74	1.90
EM	PACE Intertl Emg Mkts Eq Inve C	PWECX	D-	(888) 793-8637	D- / 1.3	7.79	2.83	21.81 /61	-1.42 / 8	-2.23 / 3	0.09	2.65
EM	PACE Intertl Emg Mkts Eq Inve P	PCEMX	D-	(888) 793-8637	D / 1.7	8.03	3.37	22.99 /67	-0.48 /11	-1.33 / 3	1.01	1.69
EM	PACE Intertl Emg Mkts Eq Inve Y	PWEYX	D-	(888) 793-8637	D / 1.7	8.03	3.39	23.02 /67	-0.43 /12	-1.25 / 3	1.04	1.63
FO	PACE Intrntl Eq Inve A	PWGAX	D	(888) 793-8637	D- / 1.0	7.68	3.61	15.04 /30	-0.02 /13	5.39 /24	1.84	1.86
FO	PACE Intrntl Eq Inve C	PWGCX	D	(888) 793-8637	D- / 1.1	7.46	3.16	14.09 /26	-0.79 /10	4.54 /18	1.08	2.65
FO	PACE Intrntl Eq Inve P	PCIEX	D+	(888) 793-8637	D / 2.2	7.73	3.72	15.32 /31	0.26 /15	5.68 /26	2.24	1.58
FO	PACE Intrntl Eq Inve Y	PWIYX	D+	(888) 793-8637	D+ / 2.3	7.79	3.78	15.36 /31	0.28 /15	5.68 /26	2.24	1.56
GR	PACE Large Co Gr Eq Inve A	PLAAX	D+	(888) 793-8637	C / 5.1	7.30	4.80	15.65 /33	7.23 /74	11.47 /70	0.12	1.19
GR	PACE Large Co Gr Eq Inve C	PLACX	D+	(888) 793-8637	C / 5.5	7.09	4.39	14.73 /29	6.36 /67	10.56 /62	0.00	2.00
GR	PACE Large Co Gr Eq Inve P	PCLCX	C-	(888) 793-8637	C+ / 6.4	7.35	4.96	15.93 /34	7.51 /76	11.75 /72	0.35	0.93
GR	PACE Large Co Gr Eq Inve Y	PLAYX	C-	(888) 793-8637	C+ / 6.4	7.35	4.94	15.93 /34	7.51 /76	11.76 /72	0.36	0.92
GI	PACE Large Co Val Eq Inve A	PCPAX	B-	(888) 793-8637	B / 8.2	5.94	12.49	28.50 /83	9.13 /88	12.97 /83	1.39	1.48
GI	PACE Large Co Val Eq Inve C	PLVCX	B	(888) 793-8637	B+ / 8.6	5.76	12.06	27.55 /81	8.29 /81	12.09 /75	0.68	2.26
GI	PACE Large Co Val Eq Inve P	PCLVX	B+	(888) 793-8637	A / 9.3	6.00	12.62	28.82 /84	9.40 /90	13.24 /86	1.68	1.24
GI	PACE Large Co Val Eq Inve Y	PLVYX	B+	(888) 793-8637	A / 9.3	5.99	12.63	28.81 /84	9.40 /90	13.25 /86	1.69	1.23
MC	PACE Smal/Med Co Val Eq Inve A	PEVAX	B-	(888) 793-8637	B+ / 8.8	5.85	14.30	34.36 /93	8.55 /83	12.97 /83	1.20	1.24
MC	PACE Smal/Med Co Val Eq Inve C	PEVCX	B-	(888) 793-8637	A- / 9.0	5.67	13.88	33.29 /92	7.72 /77	12.12 /75	0.81	2.01
MC	PACE Smal/Med Co Val Eq Inve P	PCSVX	B	(888) 793-8637	A / 9.5	5.86	14.36	34.48 /93	8.68 /84	13.11 /85	1.35	1.11
MC	PACE Smal/Med Co Val Eq Inve Y	PVEYX	B+	(888) 793-8637	A / 9.5	5.84	14.31	34.50 /93	8.67 /84	13.10 /85	1.24	1.07
MC	PACE Smal/Med Comp Gr Eq Inve A	PQUAX	E	(888) 793-8637	C- / 3.4	5.24	7.36	26.49 /78	2.00 /24	9.15 /52	0.00	1.25
MC	PACE Smal/Med Comp Gr Eq Inve C	PUMCX	E	(888) 793-8637	C- / 3.8	4.94	6.89	25.52 /75	1.20 /19	8.31 /45	0.00	2.02
MC	PACE Smal/Med Comp Gr Eq Inve P	PCSGX	D-	(888) 793-8637	C / 4.6	5.19	7.40	26.62 /78	2.10 /25	9.28 /53	0.00	1.13
MC	PACE Smal/Med Comp Gr Eq Inve Y	PUMYX	D-	(888) 793-8637	C / 4.6	5.24	7.35	26.60 /78	2.09 /25	9.27 /53	0.00	1.09
BA	Pacific Advisors Balanced A	PAABX	E	(800) 282-6693	E- / 0.1	3.92	5.51	10.42 /13	-6.49 / 2	0.87 / 6	0.00	3.27
BA	Pacific Advisors Balanced C	PGBCX	E	(800) 282-6693	E- / 0.1	3.73	5.12	9.59 /11	-7.21 / 1	0.10 / 5	0.00	4.05
GR	Pacific Advisors Large Cap Value A	PAGTX	B-	(800) 282-6693	C+ / 5.9	6.09	8.77	20.51 /55	7.72 /77	10.26 /60	0.00	3.47
GR	Pacific Advisors Large Cap Value C	PGCCX	B-	(800) 282-6693	C+ / 6.4	5.88	8.36	19.60 /50	6.91 /71	9.43 /54	0.00	4.25
GR	Pacific Advisors Mid Cap Value A	PAMVX	E	(800) 282-6693	E- / 0.1	-1.26	11.72	17.73 /42	-6.72 / 2	-0.94 / 3	0.00	3.68
GR	Pacific Advisors Mid Cap Value C	PMVCX	E	(800) 282-6693	E- / 0.2	-1.45	11.30	16.84 /38	-7.43 / 1	-1.68 / 3	0.00	4.46
SC	Pacific Advisors Small Cap Value A	PASMX	E-	(800) 282-6693	E- / 0.1	0.47	23.88	37.16 /96	-10.94 / 1	1.34 / 7	0.00	3.03
SC	Pacific Advisors Small Cap Value C	PGSCX	E-	(800) 282-6693	E- / 0.2	0.28	23.42	36.13 /95	-11.61 / 1	0.59 / 5	0.00	3.88
SC	Pacific Advisors Small Cap Value I	PGISX	E-	(800) 282-6693	E- / 0.2	0.52	23.75	37.18 /96	-10.70 / 1	2.16 / 8	0.00	2.86
IN	Pacific Financial Core Eqty Inst	PFGQX	C+	(888) 451-8734	C+ / 6.8	6.74	9.86	23.80 /69	5.60 /61	10.31 /61	0.00	1.96
IN	Pacific Financial Core Eqty Inv	PFLQX	C+	(888) 451-8734	C+ / 6.2	6.55	9.46	22.89 /66	4.83 /52	9.48 /55	0.00	2.71
GL	Pacific Financial Dyn Alloc Inst	PFGDX	U	(888) 451-8734	U /	4.63	4.13	12.38 /19	--	--	0.59	1.68
GL	Pacific Financial Dyn Alloc Inv	PFLDX	U	(888) 451-8734	U /	4.49	3.79	11.60 /16	--	--	0.16	2.43
OT	Pacific Financial Explorer Inst	PFGPX	C+	(888) 451-8734	C+ / 5.9	6.46	8.18	20.34 /54	5.20 /56	10.49 /62	0.00	1.84
GR	Pacific Financial Explorer Inv	PFLPX	C	(888) 451-8734	C / 5.2	6.34	7.80	19.37 /49	4.44 /48	9.66 /56	0.00	2.59
GL	Pacific Financial Flexible Gl Inv	PFLFX	U	(888) 451-8734	U /	2.27	1.86	6.35 / 5	--	--	0.77	2.53
EM	Pacific Financial Intl Inst	PFGIX	D-	(888) 451-8734	E+ / 0.6	5.47	1.64	10.04 /12	-1.95 / 7	2.84 /10	0.00	2.53
FO	Pacific Financial Intl Investor	PFLIX	D-	(888) 451-8734	E / 0.5	5.16	1.15	9.05 /10	-2.68 / 5	2.09 / 8	0.00	3.28
AA	Pacific Financial Stg Csv Inst	PFGSX	C	(888) 451-8734	D- / 1.0	1.21	-0.69	2.59 / 2	1.16 /19	1.81 / 8	2.03	1.70
AA	Pacific Financial Stg Csv Inv	PFLSX	C	(888) 451-8734	E+ / 0.8	1.11	-0.91	2.12 / 2	0.50 /16	1.13 / 6	1.56	2.20
GI	Pacific Funds Diversified Alt A	PLALX	C	(800) 722-2333	D- / 1.5	2.97	1.94	8.42 / 8	3.00 /32	--	6.14	2.36
GI	Pacific Funds Diversified Alt Adv	PLDLX	C+	(800) 722-2333	D+ / 2.3	2.98	2.06	8.52 / 8	3.20 /34	--	6.71	2.11
GI	Pacific Funds Diversified Alt C	PLCLX	C	(800) 722-2333	D / 1.8	2.90	1.65	7.61 / 7	2.26 /26	--	6.26	3.11
GR	Pacific Funds Small Mid Cap Adv	PFMDX	U	(800) 722-2333	U /	6.96	11.98	27.01 /79	--	--	0.05	4.44
GL	Palmer Square Absolute Return A	PSQAX	D	(866) 933-9033	D / 1.8	2.40	5.51	23.43 /68	0.15 /14	1.32 / 7	6.55	2.29
GL	Palmer Square Absolute Return I	PSQIX	D+	(866) 933-9033	D+ / 2.8	2.49	5.72	23.91 /70	0.32 /15	1.53 / 7	7.26	2.04
CV	Palmer Square SSI Alternative Inc A	PSCAX	C-	(866) 933-9033	E+ / 0.8	1.40	1.40	9.10 /10	0.66 /16	--	0.96	2.35
CV	Palmer Square SSI Alternative Inc I	PSCIX	C	(866) 933-9033	D- / 1.4	1.46	1.57	9.31 /10	0.89 /18	--	1.31	2.10

● Denotes fund is closed to new investors
* Denotes fund is included in Section II

Risk Rating/Pts	3 Year Standard Deviation	Beta	NAV As of 2/28/17	Total $(Mil)	Cash %	Stocks %	Bonds %	Other %	Portfolio Turnover Ratio	Last Bull Market Return	Last Bear Market Return	Manager Quality Pct	Manager Tenure (Years)	Initial Purch. $	Additional Purch. $	Front End Load	Back End Load
C /5.2	14.5	0.88	11.83	4	46	53	0	1	65	14.2	-25.4	45	6	1,000	100	5.5	0.0
C /5.1	14.4	0.88	10.94	1	46	53	0	1	65	9.8	-25.6	35	6	1,000	100	0.0	0.0
C /5.1	14.4	0.88	11.86	411	46	53	0	1	65	15.1	-25.3	48	6	10,000	500	0.0	0.0
C /5.1	14.4	0.88	11.92	7	46	53	0	1	65	15.7	-25.3	49	6	5,000,000	0	0.0	0.0
C+ /6.6	11.1	0.89	14.51	29	45	54	0	1	80	49.8	-22.3	75	4	1,000	100	5.5	0.0
C+ /6.6	11.1	0.89	14.26	2	45	54	0	1	80	43.5	-22.7	66	4	1,000	100	0.0	0.0
C+ /6.6	11.1	0.89	14.41	936	45	54	0	1	80	51.9	-22.2	77	4	10,000	500	0.0	0.0
C+ /6.6	11.1	0.89	14.45	14	45	54	0	1	80	52.1	-22.3	77	4	5,000,000	0	0.0	0.0
C- /3.6	10.8	0.98	22.56	42	3	96	0	1	33	112.7	-17.4	36	10	1,000	100	5.5	0.0
C- /3.0	10.8	0.98	18.70	3	3	96	0	1	33	103.4	-17.7	26	10	1,000	100	0.0	0.0
C- /3.7	10.8	0.98	23.22	1,193	3	96	0	1	33	115.7	-17.3	39	10	10,000	500	0.0	0.0
C- /3.7	10.8	0.98	23.38	13	3	96	0	1	33	115.7	-17.3	39	10	5,000,000	0	0.0	0.0
C /4.6	11.1	1.02	23.38	121	22	77	0	1	65	128.4	-20.6	55	9	1,000	100	5.5	0.0
C /4.8	11.1	1.02	23.47	13	22	77	0	1	65	118.9	-20.9	43	9	1,000	100	0.0	0.0
C /4.6	11.1	1.02	23.31	1,232	22	77	0	1	65	131.2	-20.5	58	9	10,000	500	0.0	0.0
C /4.6	11.1	1.02	23.42	18	22	77	0	1	65	131.4	-20.6	58	9	5,000,000	0	0.0	0.0
C- /4.1	14.0	1.12	21.20	19	27	72	0	1	74	138.6	-27.7	48	10	1,000	100	5.5	0.0
C- /3.7	14.0	1.12	17.89	4	27	72	0	1	74	129.1	-28.0	37	10	1,000	100	0.0	0.0
C- /4.2	14.0	1.12	21.76	537	27	72	0	1	74	140.2	-27.7	49	10	10,000	500	0.0	0.0
C- /4.2	14.0	1.12	22.00	N/A	27	72	0	1	74	140.3	-27.7	49	10	5,000,000	0	0.0	0.0
D /1.6	16.4	1.21	15.47	22	55	44	0	1	98	93.5	-22.9	3	12	1,000	100	5.5	0.0
D- /1.1	16.4	1.21	12.10	3	55	44	0	1	98	85.6	-23.2	2	12	1,000	100	0.0	0.0
D /1.8	16.4	1.21	16.41	454	55	44	0	1	98	94.7	-22.9	3	12	10,000	500	0.0	0.0
D /1.8	16.4	1.21	16.66	N/A	55	44	0	1	98	94.7	-22.9	3	12	5,000,000	0	0.0	0.0
C- /4.0	12.0	1.46	11.63	4	0	69	30	1	28	20.7	-14.6	0	7	1,000	25	5.8	2.0
C- /3.8	12.0	1.46	10.25	2	0	69	30	1	28	15.8	-14.9	0	7	10,000	500	0.0	2.0
B- /7.3	10.9	1.02	15.71	7	0	99	0	1	7	94.1	-10.9	37	7	1,000	25	5.8	2.0
B- /7.2	10.9	1.02	13.49	1	0	99	0	1	7	86.3	-11.2	28	7	10,000	500	0.0	2.0
C- /3.6	17.9	1.27	11.66	6	0	100	0	0	25	29.2	-33.5	0	10	1,000	25	5.8	2.0
C- /3.5	17.9	1.27	10.30	N/A	0	100	0	0	25	24.0	-33.8	0	10	10,000	500	0.0	2.0
D- /1.2	27.1	1.33	26.48	26	0	100	0	0	7	56.3	-30.0	0	24	1,000	25	5.8	2.0
D- /1.2	27.2	1.33	19.22	4	0	100	0	0	7	50.1	-30.2	0	24	10,000	500	0.0	2.0
D- /1.2	27.0	1.33	34.10	N/A	0	100	0	0	7	62.8	-29.9	0	24	250,000	500	0.0	2.0
C+ /6.1	10.6	1.00	10.35	42	1	92	5	2	90	94.3	-22.3	18	10	5,000	250	0.0	0.0
C+ /6.0	10.6	1.00	9.83	444	1	92	5	2	90	86.7	-22.5	13	10	5,000	250	0.0	0.0
U /	N/A	N/A	10.81	30	0	0	0	100	12	N/A	N/A	N/A	2	5,000	500	0.0	0.0
U /	N/A	N/A	10.76	370	0	0	0	100	12	N/A	N/A	N/A	2	5,000	500	0.0	0.0
C+ /6.1	11.0	1.02	10.71	16	0	99	0	1	171	94.9	-25.3	14	10	5,000	250	0.0	0.0
C+ /6.0	11.0	1.02	10.23	134	0	99	0	1	171	87.0	-25.4	9	10	5,000	250	0.0	0.0
U /	N/A	N/A	10.01	123	5	38	55	2	0	N/A	N/A	N/A	2	5,000	500	0.0	0.0
C+ /6.3	9.8	0.40	5.59	5	2	93	4	1	55	26.2	-30.1	38	10	5,000	250	0.0	0.0
C+ /6.3	9.9	0.74	5.30	63	2	93	4	1	55	21.1	-30.2	40	10	5,000	250	0.0	0.0
B+ /9.9	2.0	0.06	9.27	8	0	0	99	1	191	11.5	1.3	79	10	5,000	250	0.0	0.0
B+ /9.9	2.0	0.05	9.25	65	0	0	99	1	191	7.4	1.0	74	10	5,000	250	0.0	0.0
B+ /9.4	3.6	0.26	9.61	3	47	13	39	1	73	N/A	N/A	76	4	1,000	50	5.5	0.0
B+ /9.4	3.6	0.26	9.63	7	47	13	39	1	73	N/A	N/A	77	4	0	0	0.0	0.0
B+ /9.4	3.7	0.26	9.49	1	47	13	39	1	73	N/A	N/A	68	4	1,000	50	0.0	0.0
U /	N/A	N/A	11.89	53	0	0	0	100	11	N/A	N/A	N/A	3	0	0	0.0	0.0
C+ /6.1	7.5	0.23	8.62	4	36	0	62	2	213	8.8	N/A	75	6	2,500	100	5.8	0.0
C+ /6.1	7.5	0.24	8.66	38	36	0	62	2	213	10.0	N/A	76	6	1,000,000	5,000	0.0	0.0
B+ /9.2	2.7	0.21	9.88	5	48	0	0	52	66	N/A	N/A	69	5	2,500	100	5.8	0.0
B+ /9.2	2.7	0.21	9.88	287	48	0	0	52	66	N/A	N/A	71	5	1,000,000	5,000	0.0	0.0

Fund Type	Fund Name	Ticker Symbol	Overall Investment Rating	Phone	Performance Rating/Pts	3 Mo	6 Mo	1Yr / Pct	3Yr / Pct	5Yr / Pct	Dividend Yield	Expense Ratio
FO	Papp Small and Mid Cap Growth	PAPPX	C+	(877) 370-7277	C / 5.3	6.99	4.17	17.03 / 38	5.67 / 61	8.60 / 47	0.00	1.70
GR	Paradigm Micro-Cap	PVIVX	C+	(877) 593-8637	B+ / 8.5	4.78	11.86	39.61 / 97	6.41 / 68	11.13 / 67	0.00	1.25
SC	Paradigm Opportunity	PFOPX	C	(877) 593-8637	C / 5.3	3.41	10.60	19.77 / 51	5.18 / 56	8.38 / 45	0.00	2.00
SC	Paradigm Select	PFSLX	C+	(877) 593-8637	B+ / 8.3	6.04	12.31	27.08 / 79	8.38 / 82	10.42 / 61	0.01	1.50
SC	Paradigm Value	PVFAX	C	(877) 593-8637	B / 7.8	5.26	14.08	30.31 / 87	6.58 / 69	8.41 / 46	0.00	2.00
OT	Parametric Commodity Strategy Inst	EIPCX	E	(800) 262-1122	E- / 0.1	3.30	8.19	19.27 / 48	-9.41 / 1	-7.76 / 1	6.37	0.99
OT	Parametric Commodity Strategy Inv	EAPCX	E	(800) 262-1122	E- / 0.1	3.17	7.91	18.83 / 46	-9.65 / 1	-8.00 / 1	6.29	1.24
EM	● Parametric Emerging Markets C	ECEMX	E+	(800) 262-1122	D / 1.6	9.20	5.42	24.06 / 70	-1.31 / 8	-0.83 / 4	1.07	2.12
EM	Parametric Emerging Markets Inst	EIEMX	D-	(800) 262-1122	D / 2.0	9.44	5.91	25.36 / 74	-0.31 / 12	0.16 / 5	1.66	1.12
EM	Parametric Emerging Markets Inv	EAEMX	D-	(800) 262-1122	D / 1.9	9.39	5.76	25.05 / 73	-0.57 / 11	-0.11 / 4	1.42	1.37
EM	Parametric Emerging Markets R6	EREMX	D+	(800) 262-1122	D / 2.1	9.42	5.89	25.35 / 74	-0.28 / 12	0.17 / 5	1.71	1.07
EM	Parametric Emg Mrkts Core Inst	EIPEX	D	(800) 262-1122	C- / 3.9	9.26	5.41	27.45 / 80	0.25 / 14	--	1.77	3.04
FO	Parametric International Eqty Inst	EIISX	D	(800) 262-1122	D / 2.1	7.45	2.30	13.07 / 22	0.73 / 17	5.90 / 28	1.65	0.95
FO	Parametric International Eqty Inv	EAISX	D	(800) 262-1122	D / 2.0	7.35	2.19	12.85 / 21	0.49 / 16	5.63 / 26	1.52	1.20
FO	Parametric International Eqty R6	ESISX	U	(800) 262-1122	U /	7.56	2.41	13.19 / 22	--	--	1.67	0.92
FO	● Parametric Tax-Mgd Intl Equity C	ECIGX	D-	(800) 262-1122	D- / 1.0	7.06	1.42	11.31 / 16	-0.77 / 10	4.33 / 17	1.03	2.43
FO	Parametric Tax-Mgd Intl Equity Inst	EITIX	D	(800) 262-1122	D / 1.8	7.32	1.97	12.36 / 19	0.25 / 15	5.37 / 24	1.97	1.43
FO	Parametric Tax-Mgd Intl Equity Inv	ETIGX	D	(800) 262-1122	D- / 1.2	7.13	1.68	12.02 / 18	-0.03 / 13	5.10 / 22	1.70	1.68
EM	Parametric TxMg Em Mk Inst	EITEX	D-	(800) 262-1122	D / 2.0	9.29	5.76	24.60 / 72	-0.17 / 13	0.65 / 6	1.55	0.95
GR	Parnassus	PARNX	B+	(800) 999-3505	A / 9.3	7.64	11.09	26.78 / 79	9.75 / 92	15.37 / 97	0.76	0.84
FO	Parnassus Asia	PAFSX	C	(800) 999-3505	C+ / 6.1	4.61	7.07	31.87 / 90	3.57 / 38	--	0.00	2.50
IN	Parnassus Core Equity Inst	PRILX	B+	(800) 999-3505	B / 7.7	6.04	6.19	18.61 / 46	9.42 / 90	14.10 / 94	1.14	0.67
* IN	Parnassus Core Equity Inv	PRBLX	B+	(800) 999-3505	B- / 7.5	6.00	6.06	18.38 / 45	9.20 / 88	13.90 / 92	0.96	0.88
GR	Parnassus Endeavor	PARWX	A+	(800) 999-3505	A+ / 9.9	6.42	13.28	32.69 / 91	15.00 / 99	17.59 / 98	0.92	0.98
GR	Parnassus Endeavor Institutional	PFPWX	U	(800) 999-3505	U /	6.45	13.34	32.92 / 91	--	--	1.04	0.75
GR	Parnassus Institutional	PFPRX	U	(800) 999-3505	U /	7.69	11.17	26.96 / 79	--	--	0.90	0.70
MC	Parnassus Mid Cap	PARMX	A	(800) 999-3505	B+ / 8.7	5.64	6.66	24.41 / 71	10.19 / 94	13.16 / 86	0.36	1.07
MC	Parnassus Mid Cap Institutional	PFPMX	U	(800) 999-3505	U /	5.72	6.81	24.65 / 72	--	--	0.47	0.77
GR	Patriot A	TRFAX	A-	(855) 527-2363	B / 7.6	6.35	10.04	20.06 / 52	10.22 / 94	--	0.00	2.62
GL	Patriot Balanced A	ATBAX	D+	(855) 527-2363	D+ / 2.5	4.48	6.01	16.38 / 36	2.98 / 32	5.87 / 27	0.48	2.28
GL	Patriot Balanced C	ATBTX	C-	(855) 527-2363	C- / 3.0	4.27	5.68	15.48 / 32	2.21 / 25	5.04 / 22	0.00	3.03
GL	Patriot Balanced I	ATBIX	C	(855) 527-2363	C / 4.8	4.56	6.15	16.68 / 37	5.06 / 55	7.25 / 36	0.80	2.03
GR	Patriot C	TRFCX	A	(855) 527-2363	B / 8.0	6.17	9.47	19.16 / 48	9.40 / 90	--	0.00	3.37
GR	Patriot I	TRFTX	A+	(855) 527-2363	B+ / 8.8	6.39	10.04	20.33 / 54	10.51 / 96	--	0.00	2.39
BA	Pax Balanced Ind Inv	PAXWX	C-	(800) 767-1729	C- / 4.2	4.51	3.45	13.38 / 23	5.21 / 57	7.07 / 35	1.23	0.92
BA	Pax Balanced Inst	PAXIX	C	(800) 767-1729	C / 4.4	4.59	3.59	13.69 / 24	5.48 / 59	7.35 / 37	1.46	0.67
BA	Pax Balanced R	PAXRX	C-	(800) 767-1729	C- / 3.9	4.42	3.28	13.10 / 22	4.95 / 54	6.81 / 34	0.98	1.17
GR	Pax Ellevate Glbl Women's Idx Inst	PXWIX	C+	(800) 767-1729	C+ / 5.6	7.85	5.89	17.92 / 42	5.37 / 58	8.52 / 47	1.93	0.66
GR	Pax Ellevate Glbl Women's Idx Inv	PXWEX	C	(800) 767-1729	C / 5.4	7.79	5.77	17.65 / 41	5.12 / 55	8.26 / 44	1.70	0.91
GR	Pax ESG Beta Quality A	PXGAX	C+	(800) 767-1729	C+ / 6.4	7.25	8.08	19.69 / 50	7.86 / 78	10.95 / 65	0.80	0.90
GR	Pax ESG Beta Quality Ind Inv	PXWGX	B+	(800) 767-1729	B- / 7.3	7.33	8.10	19.76 / 51	7.89 / 78	10.95 / 65	0.82	0.90
GR	Pax ESG Beta Quality Instl	PWGIX	B+	(800) 767-1729	B- / 7.5	7.36	8.22	20.08 / 52	8.14 / 80	11.22 / 68	1.04	0.65
GR	Pax ESG Beta Quality R	PXGRX	B	(800) 767-1729	B- / 7.1	7.19	7.96	19.48 / 49	7.59 / 76	10.66 / 63	0.61	1.15
GL	Pax Global Envi Mkts A	PXEAX	C-	(800) 767-1729	C- / 3.8	6.55	5.10	24.90 / 73	3.27 / 34	9.39 / 54	0.45	1.31
GL	Pax Global Envi Mkts Ind Inv	PGRNX	C	(800) 767-1729	C / 5.0	6.55	5.11	24.88 / 73	3.27 / 34	9.38 / 54	0.49	1.31
GL	Pax Global Envi Mkts Inst	PGINX	C	(800) 767-1729	C / 5.2	6.66	5.22	25.21 / 74	3.52 / 37	9.66 / 56	0.71	1.06
GL	Pax Global Envi Mkts R	PGRGX	C	(800) 767-1729	C / 4.8	6.47	5.01	24.62 / 72	3.01 / 32	9.12 / 52	0.27	1.56
MC	Pax Mid Cap Inst	PMIDX	U	(800) 767-1729	U /	6.24	7.55	--	--	--	0.00	0.89
FO	Pax MSCI International ESG Ind Inv	PXINX	D	(800) 767-1729	E+ / 0.9	6.66	2.26	12.86 / 21	-1.25 / 9	5.10 / 22	2.34	0.81
FO	Pax MSCI International ESG Inst	PXNIX	D	(800) 767-1729	D- / 1.0	6.79	2.45	13.24 / 22	-1.01 / 9	5.36 / 24	2.62	0.56
FO	Pax MSCI International ESG R	PXIRX	D	(800) 767-1729	E+ / 0.9	6.62	2.19	12.59 / 20	-1.51 / 8	4.83 / 20	2.15	1.06
GR	Pax Small Cap A	PXSAX	C+	(800) 767-1729	C / 5.4	3.90	9.60	22.42 / 64	6.15 / 66	13.26 / 86	0.63	1.23

● Denotes fund is closed to new investors
* Denotes fund is included in Section II

Risk Rating/Pts	3 Year Standard Deviation	Beta	NAV As of 2/28/17	Total $(Mil)	Cash %	Stocks %	Bonds %	Other %	Portfolio Turnover Ratio	Last Bull Market Return	Last Bear Market Return	Manager Quality Pct	Manager Tenure (Years)	Initial Purch. $	Additional Purch. $	Front End Load	Back End Load
C+ / 6.2	10.1	0.53	18.97	27	1	98	0	1	18	84.1	-19.2	96	N/A	5,000	1,000	0.0	0.0
C- / 3.7	17.9	1.26	30.36	40	2	97	0	1	71	110.5	-21.2	7	6	2,500	100	0.0	2.0
C+ / 5.8	12.7	0.69	36.41	7	1	98	0	1	16	81.8	-19.1	77	4	2,500	100	0.0	2.0
C- / 3.5	12.3	0.73	35.03	25	3	96	0	1	20	103.7	-18.8	91	4	2,500	100	0.0	2.0
D+ / 2.9	14.5	0.86	49.23	62	3	96	0	1	14	83.9	-21.6	79	4	2,500	100	0.0	2.0
C / 4.6	12.3	0.32	5.57	139	22	0	77	1	573	-29.0	N/A	1	3	50,000	0	0.0	0.0
C / 4.6	12.3	0.32	5.51	36	22	0	77	1	573	-30.0	N/A	1	3	1,000	0	0.0	0.0
C / 4.5	14.1	0.85	13.41	9	0	98	0	2	8	13.9	-24.9	37	10	1,000	0	0.0	0.0
C / 4.5	14.1	0.85	13.71	1,887	0	98	0	2	8	20.2	-24.6	52	10	50,000	0	0.0	0.0
C / 4.5	14.1	0.85	13.65	525	0	98	0	2	8	18.5	-24.7	48	10	1,000	0	0.0	0.0
C+ / 6.4	14.2	0.85	13.70	528	0	98	0	2	8	20.3	-24.6	52	10	1,000,000	0	0.0	0.0
C- / 4.0	15.2	0.91	9.09	10	0	93	5	2	14	N/A	N/A	58	4	50,000	0	0.0	0.0
C+ / 5.8	10.7	0.86	11.77	57	2	97	0	1	34	50.1	-21.2	80	7	50,000	0	0.0	0.0
C+ / 5.9	10.7	0.86	11.73	35	2	97	0	1	34	48.0	-21.3	79	7	1,000	0	0.0	0.0
U /	N/A	N/A	11.78	80	2	97	0	1	34	N/A	N/A	N/A	7	1,000,000	0	0.0	0.0
C+ / 6.3	10.5	0.83	9.14	8	3	96	0	1	14	46.8	-28.1	67	5	1,000	0	0.0	0.0
C+ / 6.2	10.4	0.83	9.61	7	3	96	0	1	14	55.1	-27.8	77	5	50,000	0	0.0	0.0
C+ / 6.2	10.4	0.83	9.63	19	3	96	0	1	14	52.8	-27.8	75	5	1,000	0	0.0	0.0
C / 4.5	13.9	0.83	44.97	3,181	1	98	0	1	2	23.1	-24.2	54	10	50,000	0	0.0	0.0
C / 4.6	13.3	1.13	47.07	850	5	94	0	1	69	171.0	-25.9	46	33	2,000	50	0.0	0.0
C / 5.2	14.3	0.93	17.71	9	5	94	0	1	60	N/A	N/A	92	4	2,000	50	0.0	0.0
C+ / 6.7	9.3	0.85	40.92	4,875	2	97	0	1	27	126.5	-14.7	77	16	100,000	0	0.0	0.0
C+ / 6.7	9.3	0.85	40.84	10,582	2	97	0	1	27	124.3	-14.8	75	16	2,000	50	0.0	0.0
C+ / 6.4	11.6	0.99	34.41	3,227	16	83	0	1	63	181.4	-19.9	93	12	2,000	50	0.0	0.0
U /	N/A	N/A	34.44	432	16	83	0	1	63	N/A	N/A	N/A	12	100,000	50	0.0	0.0
U /	N/A	N/A	47.06	94	5	94	0	1	69	N/A	N/A	N/A	33	100,000	50	0.0	0.0
C+ / 6.8	9.6	0.73	30.12	1,762	6	93	0	1	58	129.1	-20.4	90	9	2,000	50	0.0	0.0
U /	N/A	N/A	30.17	343	6	93	0	1	58	N/A	N/A	N/A	9	100,000	50	0.0	0.0
B- / 7.4	9.1	0.84	16.12	11	4	95	0	1	49	N/A	N/A	82	N/A	1,000	100	5.8	0.0
C+ / 6.5	7.1	0.99	13.45	1	7	55	12	26	71	N/A	N/A	55	N/A	1,000	100	5.8	0.0
C+ / 6.5	7.1	0.99	13.09	N/A	7	55	12	26	71	N/A	N/A	44	N/A	1,000	100	0.0	0.0
C+ / 6.4	7.1	0.92	13.48	17	7	55	12	26	71	N/A	N/A	79	N/A	1,000,000	25,000	0.0	0.0
B- / 7.3	9.1	0.84	15.52	1	4	95	0	1	49	N/A	N/A	77	N/A	1,000	100	0.0	0.0
B- / 7.4	9.0	0.84	16.35	23	4	95	0	1	49	N/A	N/A	84	N/A	1,000,000	25,000	0.0	0.0
C+ / 6.2	6.6	1.04	23.09	1,632	3	63	33	1	61	63.9	-15.9	42	19	1,000	50	0.0	0.0
C+ / 6.2	6.6	1.04	23.40	295	3	63	33	1	61	66.2	-15.8	46	19	250,000	0	0.0	0.0
C+ / 6.3	6.6	1.04	23.24	7	3	63	33	1	61	61.7	-15.9	39	19	0	0	0.0	0.0
C+ / 6.0	9.4	0.87	21.89	42	5	94	0	1	50	81.5	-22.2	28	24	250,000	0	0.0	0.0
C+ / 6.0	9.4	0.87	21.79	78	5	94	0	1	50	79.1	-22.2	25	24	1,000	50	0.0	0.0
C+ / 6.4	11.1	1.05	17.77	5	3	96	0	1	26	107.1	-20.1	34	1	1,000	50	5.5	0.0
C+ / 6.4	11.1	1.05	17.82	167	3	96	0	1	26	107.1	-20.1	34	1	1,000	50	0.0	0.0
C+ / 6.4	11.1	1.05	18.29	25	3	96	0	1	26	109.9	-20.0	37	1	250,000	0	0.0	0.0
C+ / 6.4	11.0	1.05	17.69	2	3	96	0	1	26	104.3	-20.2	31	1	0	0	0.0	0.0
C+ / 6.2	12.3	0.84	13.88	14	1	98	0	1	22	91.5	-23.7	91	9	1,000	50	5.5	0.0
C+ / 6.2	12.3	0.84	13.90	130	1	98	0	1	22	91.3	-23.7	92	9	1,000	50	0.0	0.0
C+ / 6.2	12.3	0.84	13.99	241	1	98	0	1	22	94.1	-23.7	92	9	250,000	0	0.0	0.0
C+ / 6.1	12.3	0.84	13.78	3	1	98	0	1	22	88.8	-23.8	91	9	0	0	0.0	0.0
U /	N/A	N/A	11.14	161	0	0	0	100	0	N/A	N/A	N/A	1	250,000	0	0.0	0.0
B- / 7.0	11.2	0.90	8.12	108	1	98	0	1	86	46.1	-21.2	61	6	1,000	50	0.0	0.0
B- / 7.0	11.2	0.90	7.98	397	1	98	0	1	86	48.1	-21.1	64	6	0	0	0.0	0.0
B- / 7.0	11.1	0.89	8.05	1	1	98	0	1	86	44.1	-21.3	57	6	0	0	0.0	0.0
C+ / 6.4	10.8	0.80	15.46	41	4	95	0	1	48	127.1	-23.9	46	9	1,000	50	5.5	0.0

I. Index of Stock Mutual Funds

					PERFORMANCE						Incl. in Returns	
	99 Pct = Best		Overall		Perfor-	Total Return % through 2/28/17					Dividend	Expense
	0 Pct = Worst	Ticker	Investment		mance				Annualized		Yield	Ratio
Fund Type	Fund Name	Symbol	Rating	Phone	Rating/Pts	3 Mo	6 Mo	1Yr / Pct	3Yr / Pct	5Yr / Pct		
SC	Pax Small Cap Ind Inv	PXSCX	C+	(800) 767-1729	C+ / 6.6	3.90	9.58	22.46 /64	6.16 /66	13.26 /86	0.67	1.23
SC	Pax Small Cap Inst	PXSIX	C+	(800) 767-1729	C+ / 6.7	3.94	9.72	22.70 /65	6.41 /68	13.54 /89	0.85	0.98
SC	Pax Small Cap R	PXSRX	C+	(800) 767-1729	C+ / 6.4	3.82	9.41	22.14 /63	5.90 /63	12.96 /83	0.56	1.48
FS	Payden Absolute Rtn Bond Investor	PYARX	U	(888) 409-8007	U /	1.40	1.26	5.43 / 4	--	--	2.54	1.17
GI	Payden Equity Income Adviser	PYVAX	A+	(888) 409-8007	B+ / 8.7	6.29	7.96	21.13 /58	10.46 /96	12.13 /75	2.43	1.05
GI	Payden Equity Income Investor	PYVLX	A+	(888) 409-8007	B+ / 8.8	6.30	8.08	21.41 /59	10.75 /97	12.48 /79	2.58	0.80
IN	Payden Equity Income SI	PYVSX	U	(888) 409-8007	U /	6.38	8.13	21.62 /60	--	--	2.69	0.79
GL	Payden Strategic Income Investor	PYSGX	U	(888) 409-8007	U /	1.76	0.41	4.37 / 3	--	--	2.63	0.90
GL	Payden Strategic Income SI	PYSIX	U	(888) 409-8007	U /	1.80	0.49	4.62 / 4	--	--	2.78	0.90
GR	Payson Total Return	PBFDX	B+	(800) 805-8258	B / 7.6	7.77	10.43	24.68 /72	6.74 /70	8.73 /48	1.34	0.97
EM	Pear Tree PanAgora Emg Mkts Inst	QEMAX	E+	(800) 326-2151	D- / 1.4	8.45	1.64	19.21 /48	-0.67 /11	-1.46 / 3	1.84	1.49
EM	Pear Tree PanAgora Emg Mkts Ord	QFFOX	E+	(800) 326-2151	D- / 1.3	8.37	1.47	18.89 /47	-0.93 /10	-1.71 / 3	1.58	1.74
EM	Pear Tree PanAgora RskPrity EM Inst	EMRPX	E	(800) 326-2151	E+ / 0.7	7.98	0.06	15.16 /31	-2.53 / 5	--	1.23	1.24
EM	Pear Tree PanAgora RskPrity EM	RPEMX	E	(800) 326-2151	E+ / 0.6	7.86	-0.10	14.93 /30	-2.80 / 5	--	0.98	1.49
FO	Pear Tree Polaris Foreign Val Inst	QFVIX	D	(800) 326-2151	D / 1.8	9.11	8.93	19.20 /48	-0.23 /13	7.71 /40	1.24	1.28
FO	Pear Tree Polaris Foreign Val Ord	QFVOX	D	(800) 326-2151	D / 1.7	9.04	8.73	18.89 /47	-0.50 /11	7.43 /38	0.97	1.53
FO	Pear Tree Polaris Foreign VSC Inst	QUSIX	C	(800) 326-2151	C / 4.8	10.71	6.69	19.00 /47	2.99 /32	10.08 /59	1.30	1.31
FO	Pear Tree Polaris Foreign VSC Ord	QUSOX	C	(800) 326-2151	C / 4.6	10.68	6.64	18.78 /46	2.73 /29	9.81 /57	1.04	1.57
SC	Pear Tree Polaris Sm Cap Inst	QBNAX	C+	(800) 326-2151	B- / 7.3	3.81	13.09	32.46 /91	4.87 /53	10.54 /62	0.64	1.22
SC	Pear Tree Polaris Sm Cap Ord	USBNX	C	(800) 326-2151	B- / 7.1	3.73	12.93	32.16 /90	4.62 /50	10.27 /60	0.55	1.22
GI	Pear Tree Quality Inst	QGIAX	B	(800) 326-2151	B+ / 8.3	9.41	6.60	19.32 /49	9.75 /92	11.79 /72	1.20	1.30
GI	Pear Tree Quality Ord	USBOX	B	(800) 326-2151	B / 8.1	9.32	6.41	19.05 /47	9.47 /90	11.46 /70	1.05	1.55
GR	Perkins Discovery Fund	PDFDX	E-	(800) 673-0550	E / 0.4	1.33	0.09	25.93 /76	-4.73 / 3	6.28 /30	0.00	3.27
GL	Perkins Global Value A	JPPAX	D+	(800) 295-2687	D / 2.2	6.47	3.44	12.52 /20	2.97 /32	7.34 /37	1.74	0.97
GL	Perkins Global Value C	JPPCX	D+	(800) 295-2687	D+ / 2.5	6.29	3.11	11.66 /17	2.22 /25	6.66 /33	1.06	1.74
GL	● Perkins Global Value D	JNGOX	C-	(800) 295-2687	C- / 3.2	6.54	3.54	12.71 /21	3.10 /33	7.49 /38	2.03	0.85
GL	Perkins Global Value I	JPPIX	C-	(800) 295-2687	C- / 3.3	6.63	3.66	12.91 /21	3.24 /34	7.64 /39	2.19	0.74
GL	Perkins Global Value N	JPPNX	C-	(800) 295-2687	C- / 3.3	6.57	3.60	12.88 /21	3.31 /35	7.69 /40	2.27	0.63
GL	Perkins Global Value S	JPPSX	D+	(800) 295-2687	C- / 3.0	6.48	3.42	12.36 /19	2.82 /30	7.17 /36	1.21	1.13
GL	Perkins Global Value T	JGVAX	C-	(800) 295-2687	C- / 3.1	6.55	3.55	12.65 /20	3.06 /32	7.44 /38	1.96	0.89
FO	Perkins International Value A	JIFAX	D-	(800) 295-2687	E+ / 0.6	6.08	0.41	10.54 /13	-0.44 /12	--	2.01	2.28
FO	Perkins International Value C	JIFCX	D-	(800) 295-2687	E+ / 0.8	5.95	0.05	9.75 /11	-1.18 / 9	--	1.41	3.02
FO	● Perkins International Value D	JIFDX	D-	(800) 295-2687	D- / 1.0	6.27	0.58	10.75 /14	-0.30 /12	--	2.29	2.14
FO	Perkins International Value I	JIFIX	D-	(800) 295-2687	D- / 1.1	6.24	0.55	10.83 /14	-0.19 /13	--	2.36	2.08
FO	Perkins International Value N	JIFNX	D-	(800) 295-2687	D- / 1.1	6.20	0.52	10.90 /14	-0.15 /13	--	2.43	2.00
FO	Perkins International Value S	JIFSX	D-	(800) 295-2687	D- / 1.0	6.12	0.45	10.46 /13	-0.47 /11	--	2.07	2.50
FO	Perkins International Value T	JIFTX	D-	(800) 295-2687	D- / 1.0	6.20	0.51	10.68 /13	-0.35 /12	--	2.23	2.25
GL	Perkins Lg Cp Value A	JAPAX	C+	(800) 295-2687	C+ / 6.6	7.05	8.56	23.02 /67	7.55 /76	10.78 /64	1.33	0.96
GL	Perkins Lg Cp Value C	JAPCX	B	(800) 295-2687	B- / 7.1	6.83	8.24	22.15 /63	6.92 /71	10.07 /59	0.62	1.75
GL	● Perkins Lg Cp Value D	JNPLX	B+	(800) 295-2687	B / 7.6	7.05	8.64	23.19 /67	7.69 /77	10.97 /66	1.56	0.81
GL	Perkins Lg Cp Value I	JAPIX	B+	(800) 295-2687	B / 7.7	7.03	8.68	23.26 /67	7.76 /77	11.07 /66	1.56	0.73
GR	Perkins Lg Cp Value N	JPLNX	B+	(800) 295-2687	B / 7.7	7.03	8.75	23.36 /68	7.84 /78	11.13 /67	1.67	0.63
GL	Perkins Lg Cp Value S	JAPSX	B+	(800) 295-2687	B- / 7.5	7.02	8.59	22.95 /66	7.52 /76	10.73 /64	1.31	1.14
GL	Perkins Lg Cp Value T	JPLTX	B+	(800) 295-2687	B / 7.6	7.03	8.62	23.11 /67	7.61 /76	10.87 /65	1.48	0.89
GL	● Perkins Mid Cap Value A	JDPAX	C-	(800) 295-2687	B / 8.2	6.70	11.06	30.42 /87	8.88 /86	10.59 /63	0.42	0.82
GL	● Perkins Mid Cap Value C	JMVCX	C	(800) 295-2687	B+ / 8.8	6.56	10.81	29.74 /86	8.27 /81	9.88 /57	0.00	1.52
GL	● Perkins Mid Cap Value D	JNMCX	C	(800) 295-2687	A / 9.3	6.74	11.22	30.77 /88	9.19 /88	10.90 /65	0.78	0.53
GL	● Perkins Mid Cap Value I	JMVAX	C	(800) 295-2687	A / 9.3	6.79	11.26	30.88 /88	9.23 /88	10.92 /65	0.77	0.51
GL	● Perkins Mid Cap Value L	JMIVX	C	(800) 295-2687	A / 9.4	6.80	11.67	31.31 /89	9.29 /88	10.98 /66	0.79	0.63
GR	● Perkins Mid Cap Value N	JDPNX	C	(800) 295-2687	A / 9.4	6.79	11.33	30.94 /88	9.36 /89	11.06 /66	0.91	0.38
GL	● Perkins Mid Cap Value R	JDPRX	C	(800) 295-2687	B+ / 8.9	6.58	10.92	30.00 /86	8.53 /83	10.24 /60	0.21	1.12
GL	● Perkins Mid Cap Value S	JMVIX	C	(800) 295-2687	A- / 9.1	6.69	11.06	30.37 /87	8.82 /86	10.52 /62	0.47	0.87

● Denotes fund is closed to new investors
* Denotes fund is included in Section II

RISK			NET ASSETS		ASSET				Portfolio Turnover Ratio	BULL / BEAR		FUND MANAGER		MINIMUMS		LOADS	
	3 Year		NAV							Last Bull	Last Bear	Manager	Manager	Initial	Additional	Front	Back
Risk Rating/Pts	Standard Deviation	Beta	As of 2/28/17	Total $(Mil)	Cash %	Stocks %	Bonds %	Other %		Market Return	Market Return	Quality Pct	Tenure (Years)	Purch. $	Purch. $	End Load	End Load
C+ / 6.4	10.8	0.66	15.49	272	4	95	0	1	48	127.1	-23.9	84	9	1,000	50	0.0	0.0
C+ / 6.4	10.8	0.66	15.60	520	4	95	0	1	48	130.3	-23.8	85	9	250,000	0	0.0	0.0
C+ / 6.4	10.8	0.66	15.32	5	4	95	0	1	48	124.1	-23.9	83	9	0	0	0.0	0.0
U /	N/A	N/A	10.01	62	1	0	98	1	47	N/A	N/A	N/A	3	100,000	250	0.0	0.0
B- / 7.5	9.0	0.81	15.96	16	6	91	1	2	25	N/A	N/A	85	N/A	5,000	250	0.0	0.0
B- / 7.5	9.0	0.81	15.97	555	6	91	1	2	25	110.9	-5.6	86	N/A	100,000	250	0.0	0.0
U /	N/A	N/A	15.98	326	6	91	1	2	25	N/A	N/A	N/A	N/A	50,000,000	250	0.0	0.0
U /	N/A	N/A	10.02	106	0	1	98	1	52	N/A	N/A	N/A	3	100,000	250	0.0	0.0
U /	N/A	N/A	10.03	31	0	1	98	1	52	N/A	N/A	N/A	3	50,000,000	250	0.0	0.0
C+ / 6.2	11.0	1.02	16.13	78	0	99	0	1	55	88.3	-14.5	26	26	2,000	250	0.0	0.0
C- / 4.0	14.9	0.91	20.16	7	1	98	0	1	82	13.4	-25.0	45	1	1,000,000	0	0.0	0.0
C- / 4.0	14.9	0.91	19.89	102	1	98	0	1	82	11.8	-25.0	41	1	2,500	0	0.0	0.0
C / 4.4	14.2	0.84	8.89	57	0	99	0	1	24	N/A	N/A	24	4	1,000,000	0	0.0	0.0
C / 4.4	14.3	0.84	8.85	2	0	99	0	1	24	N/A	N/A	21	4	2,500	0	0.0	0.0
C+ / 6.0	13.1	0.98	18.72	739	0	99	0	1	13	71.4	-23.6	73	19	1,000,000	0	0.0	0.0
C+ / 6.0	13.0	0.98	18.76	853	0	99	0	1	13	68.9	-23.7	70	19	2,500	0	0.0	0.0
C+ / 6.4	11.4	0.84	13.23	294	0	98	0	2	8	80.6	-22.1	91	9	1,000,000	0	0.0	0.0
C+ / 6.4	11.5	0.84	13.22	263	0	98	0	2	8	78.3	-22.2	90	9	2,500	0	0.0	0.0
C / 4.5	15.3	0.95	30.74	7	2	94	2	2	17	104.2	-21.6	54	2	1,000,000	0	0.0	0.0
C- / 4.2	15.3	0.95	26.31	110	2	94	2	2	17	101.6	-21.7	51	2	2,500	0	0.0	0.0
C / 5.3	9.8	0.88	18.39	7	1	98	0	1	35	105.3	-7.8	77	6	1,000,000	0	0.0	0.0
C / 5.2	9.8	0.88	17.27	113	1	98	0	1	35	101.7	-7.9	75	6	2,500	0	0.0	0.0
D+ / 2.4	20.2	1.17	34.29	7	2	97	0	1	2	53.8	-26.7	0	19	2,500	100	0.0	1.0
C+ / 6.2	7.9	0.59	13.59	15	2	86	11	1	20	58.7	-10.5	90	12	2,500	0	5.8	0.0
C+ / 6.3	7.9	0.59	13.32	8	2	86	11	1	20	53.1	-10.7	87	12	2,500	0	0.0	0.0
C+ / 6.2	7.9	0.59	13.71	83	2	86	11	1	20	59.7	-10.4	91	12	2,500	0	0.0	0.0
C+ / 6.2	7.9	0.59	13.49	33	2	86	11	1	20	61.0	-10.4	91	12	1,000,000	0	0.0	0.0
C+ / 6.2	7.9	0.59	13.42	3	2	86	11	1	20	61.2	-10.5	91	12	0	0	0.0	0.0
C+ / 6.3	7.9	0.59	13.87	N/A	2	86	11	1	20	57.2	-10.6	90	12	2,500	0	0.0	0.0
C+ / 6.2	7.9	0.59	13.69	53	2	86	11	1	20	59.4	-10.5	91	12	2,500	0	0.0	0.0
C+ / 6.0	9.2	0.72	10.18	N/A	17	82	0	1	22	N/A	N/A	70	4	2,500	0	5.8	0.0
C+ / 6.1	9.2	0.72	10.16	N/A	17	82	0	1	22	N/A	N/A	61	4	2,500	0	0.0	0.0
C+ / 6.0	9.2	0.72	10.16	3	17	82	0	1	22	N/A	N/A	72	4	2,500	0	0.0	0.0
C+ / 6.0	9.2	0.72	10.15	7	17	82	0	1	22	N/A	N/A	73	4	1,000,000	0	0.0	0.0
C+ / 6.0	9.2	0.72	10.16	2	17	82	0	1	22	N/A	N/A	73	4	0	0	0.0	0.0
C+ / 6.1	9.2	0.72	10.20	N/A	17	82	0	1	22	N/A	N/A	70	4	2,500	0	0.0	0.0
C+ / 6.0	9.2	0.72	10.16	1	17	82	0	1	22	N/A	N/A	71	4	2,500	0	0.0	0.0
C+ / 6.2	9.8	0.64	16.25	4	5	94	0	1	39	99.6	-17.5	98	9	2,500	0	5.8	0.0
C+ / 6.3	9.7	0.63	16.05	2	5	94	0	1	39	92.7	-17.7	98	9	2,500	0	0.0	0.0
C+ / 6.2	9.8	0.64	16.15	48	5	94	0	1	39	101.4	-17.3	98	9	2,500	100	0.0	0.0
C+ / 6.2	9.8	0.64	16.22	36	5	94	0	1	39	102.6	-17.3	98	9	1,000,000	0	0.0	0.0
C+ / 6.2	9.7	0.92	16.19	72	5	94	0	1	39	103.2	-17.3	52	9	0	0	0.0	0.0
C+ / 6.2	9.7	0.64	16.39	N/A	5	94	0	1	39	99.0	-17.5	98	9	2,500	0	0.0	0.0
C+ / 6.2	9.8	0.64	16.13	5	5	94	0	1	39	100.5	-17.4	98	9	2,500	0	0.0	0.0
D / 1.8	10.1	0.59	17.57	127	6	93	0	1	65	98.4	-19.2	99	6	2,500	0	5.8	0.0
D / 1.9	10.1	0.58	17.26	82	6	93	0	1	65	91.6	-19.4	98	6	2,500	0	0.0	0.0
D / 1.6	10.1	0.59	17.32	844	6	93	0	1	65	101.5	-19.1	99	6	2,500	100	0.0	0.0
D / 1.6	10.1	0.59	17.35	955	6	93	0	1	65	101.7	-19.1	99	6	1,000,000	0	0.0	0.0
D / 1.7	10.1	0.59	17.76	10	6	93	0	1	65	102.1	-19.1	99	6	250,000	0	0.0	0.0
D / 1.6	10.1	0.90	17.28	103	6	93	0	1	65	102.9	-19.2	72	6	0	0	0.0	0.0
D / 1.8	10.1	0.59	17.36	76	6	93	0	1	65	95.1	-19.3	99	6	2,500	0	0.0	0.0
D / 1.8	10.1	0.59	17.53	198	6	93	0	1	65	97.8	-19.3	99	6	2,500	0	0.0	0.0

Fund Type	Fund Name	Ticker Symbol	Overall Investment Rating	Phone	Performance Rating/Pts	3 Mo	6 Mo	1Yr / Pct	3Yr / Pct	5Yr / Pct	Dividend Yield	Expense Ratio
	99 Pct = Best *0 Pct = Worst*							Total Return % through 2/28/17 — Annualized			Incl. in Returns	
GL	● Perkins Mid Cap Value T	JMCVX	C	(800) 295-2687	A / 9.3	6.79	11.25	30.72 /88	9.11 /88	10.81 /64	0.68	0.62
GL	Perkins Select Value A	JVSAX	A-	(800) 295-2687	B+ / 8.4	7.45	11.32	29.67 /86	9.19 /88	10.68 /63	0.80	1.17
GL	Perkins Select Value C	JVSCX	A	(800) 295-2687	B+ / 8.8	7.21	10.87	28.54 /83	8.30 /81	9.83 /57	0.60	1.98
GL	● Perkins Select Value D	JSVDX	A+	(800) 295-2687	A / 9.4	7.48	11.42	29.85 /86	9.43 /90	10.93 /65	0.88	1.00
GL	Perkins Select Value I	JVSIX	A+	(800) 295-2687	A / 9.4	7.54	11.48	29.90 /86	9.52 /90	11.06 /66	0.87	0.88
GL	Perkins Select Value S	JSVSX	A+	(800) 295-2687	A / 9.3	7.42	11.20	29.53 /85	9.21 /88	10.57 /63	0.81	1.27
GL	Perkins Select Value T	JSVTX	A+	(800) 295-2687	A / 9.4	7.45	11.39	29.82 /86	9.35 /89	10.83 /64	0.86	1.02
SC	Perkins Small Cap Value A	JDSAX	C+	(800) 295-2687	A- / 9.0	5.12	12.41	32.78 /91	9.96 /93	11.95 /74	0.18	1.36
SC	Perkins Small Cap Value C	JCSCX	C+	(800) 295-2687	A / 9.4	4.96	12.09	32.00 /90	9.34 /89	11.23 /68	0.01	2.04
SC	Perkins Small Cap Value D	JNPSX	C+	(800) 295-2687	A+ / 9.6	5.19	12.58	33.16 /92	10.31 /95	12.29 /77	0.48	1.05
SC	Perkins Small Cap Value I	JSCOX	C+	(800) 295-2687	A+ / 9.6	5.16	12.56	33.23 /92	10.34 /95	12.31 /77	0.52	0.99
SC	● Perkins Small Cap Value L	JSIVX	C+	(800) 295-2687	A+ / 9.7	5.23	12.68	33.35 /92	10.46 /96	12.44 /78	0.52	1.10
SC	Perkins Small Cap Value N	JDSNX	C+	(800) 295-2687	A+ / 9.7	5.26	12.69	33.45 /92	10.49 /96	12.48 /79	0.56	0.89
SC	Perkins Small Cap Value R	JDSRX	C+	(800) 295-2687	A / 9.5	5.05	12.23	32.42 /91	9.66 /91	11.63 /71	0.11	1.64
SC	Perkins Small Cap Value S	JISCX	C+	(800) 295-2687	A+ / 9.6	5.06	12.39	32.68 /91	9.93 /93	11.90 /73	0.21	1.39
SC	Perkins Small Cap Value T	JSCVX	C+	(800) 295-2687	A+ / 9.6	5.19	12.57	33.12 /92	10.22 /94	12.19 /76	0.41	1.14
GI	Perkins Value Plus Income A	JPVAX	C	(800) 295-2687	C- / 4.0	4.35	5.62	16.50 /36	5.79 /62	7.83 /41	2.08	1.38
GI	Perkins Value Plus Income C	JPVCX	C+	(800) 295-2687	C / 4.5	4.15	5.21	15.65 /33	5.03 /55	7.11 /35	1.45	2.15
GI	● Perkins Value Plus Income D	JPVDX	C+	(800) 295-2687	C / 5.3	4.38	5.77	16.74 /37	5.95 /64	7.97 /42	2.31	1.31
GI	Perkins Value Plus Income I	JPVIX	C+	(800) 295-2687	C / 5.4	4.40	5.81	16.80 /38	6.03 /64	8.07 /43	2.37	1.21
GI	Perkins Value Plus Income S	JPVSX	C+	(800) 295-2687	C / 5.1	4.32	5.56	16.46 /36	5.78 /62	7.76 /40	2.09	1.63
GI	Perkins Value Plus Income T	JPVTX	C+	(800) 295-2687	C / 5.3	4.36	5.64	16.64 /37	5.92 /64	7.93 /42	2.24	1.32
AG	Permanent Portfolio Aggress Gr I	PAGRX	C-	(800) 531-5142	C+ / 5.6	3.53	10.09	26.39 /77	3.60 /38	11.45 /69	0.56	1.21
AA	Permanent Portfolio I	PRPFX	D	(800) 531-5142	D / 1.7	3.59	1.66	11.41 /16	0.89 /18	0.91 / 6	0.79	0.80
FO	Perritt Low Priced Stock Investor	PLOWX	C+	(800) 332-3133	C+ / 6.9	4.78	11.76	27.29 /80	5.81 /63	--	0.00	4.36
SC	Perritt MicroCap Opportunities	PRCGX	C+	(800) 332-3133	C+ / 6.8	3.42	12.27	31.81 /90	4.80 /52	12.08 /75	0.00	1.22
GR	Perritt Ultra MicroCap	PREOX	C-	(800) 332-3133	C / 5.1	4.15	9.02	29.14 /84	3.02 /32	11.53 /70	0.00	1.76
GR	Persimmon Long/Short I	LSEIX	D+	(855) 233-8300	D- / 1.0	3.65	2.94	3.55 / 3	0.83 /17	--	0.00	3.96
GR	PF Comstock P		B-	(800) 722-2333	B+ / 8.9	5.35	13.87	32.64 /91	7.59 /76	12.67 /81	2.18	0.96
MC	PF Developing Growth P		E-	(800) 722-2333	D- / 1.2	5.92	5.43	23.78 /69	-2.28 / 6	5.63 /26	0.00	0.82
EM	PF Emerging Mkts P		E+	(800) 722-2333	D- / 1.5	6.71	3.65	22.10 /63	-0.96 /10	1.30 / 7	0.49	1.23
GL	PF Equity Long/Short P		U	(800) 722-2333	U /	4.77	10.05	17.89 /42	--	--	18.64	1.41
GL	PF Global Absolute Ret P		D+	(800) 722-2333	D / 2.0	0.55	-0.19	5.16 / 4	4.22 /45	--	3.68	1.18
GR	PF Growth P		B	(800) 722-2333	B- / 7.3	8.85	6.45	19.13 /48	7.94 /79	12.45 /79	0.10	0.76
FO	PF International Val P		D-	(800) 722-2333	D- / 1.1	7.33	7.45	19.31 /49	-2.01 / 7	3.68 /14	3.15	0.92
FO	PF Intl Large Cap P		D	(800) 722-2333	D- / 1.3	7.18	3.06	14.00 /25	-0.38 /12	4.92 /21	1.90	1.10
FO	PF Intl Small Cap P		U	(800) 722-2333	U /	8.69	7.56	20.06 /52	--	--	3.78	1.11
GI	PF Large-Cap Growth P		C	(800) 722-2333	B- / 7.3	9.65	7.66	21.95 /62	7.03 /72	12.31 /77	0.00	0.96
GI	PF Large-Cap Value P		B+	(800) 722-2333	B+ / 8.6	6.55	11.87	24.56 /72	8.76 /85	12.78 /82	1.16	0.86
GI	PF Main Street Core P		B-	(800) 722-2333	A- / 9.2	8.07	9.99	24.52 /72	10.19 /94	13.66 /90	1.16	0.66
MC	PF Mid-Cap Equity P		B	(800) 722-2333	A+ / 9.6	8.12	15.87	32.93 /91	8.52 /83	12.38 /78	1.28	0.86
MC	PF Mid-Cap Growth P		D+	(800) 722-2333	C / 4.9	5.73	4.49	22.15 /63	3.96 /43	7.70 /40	1.18	0.91
MC	PF Mid-Cap Value P		U	(800) 722-2333	U /	6.12	10.61	32.20 /90	--	--	1.15	0.93
GR	PF Port Optz Aggr Gro A	POEAX	C	(800) 722-2333	C / 4.7	6.50	8.08	22.07 /63	4.80 /52	7.85 /41	1.08	1.54
GR	PF Port Optz Aggr Gro Adv	POEDX	C+	(800) 722-2333	C+ / 6.1	6.55	8.20	22.35 /64	5.08 /55	8.06 /43	1.31	1.29
GR	PF Port Optz Aggr Gro B	POEBX	C+	(800) 722-2333	C / 5.3	6.34	7.66	21.39 /59	4.07 /44	7.17 /36	0.65	2.29
GR	PF Port Optz Aggr Gro C	POCEX	C+	(800) 722-2333	C / 5.3	6.28	7.68	21.35 /59	4.06 /44	7.17 /36	0.65	2.29
GR	PF Port Optz Aggr Gro R	POERX	C+	(800) 722-2333	C+ / 5.7	6.42	7.93	21.82 /61	4.56 /49	7.61 /39	0.97	1.79
AA	PF Port Optz Consrv Class A	POAAX	C-	(800) 722-2333	D- / 1.5	2.82	1.53	10.02 /12	2.58 /28	3.37 /12	1.84	1.39
AA	PF Port Optz Consrv Class Adv	PLCDX	C-	(800) 722-2333	D / 2.2	2.93	1.73	10.33 /12	2.82 /30	3.55 /13	2.13	1.14
AA	PF Port Optz Consrv Class B	POABX	C-	(800) 722-2333	D / 1.8	2.75	1.24	9.47 /10	1.85 /23	2.65 /10	1.39	2.14
AA	PF Port Optz Consrv Class C	POACX	C-	(800) 722-2333	D / 1.7	2.64	1.14	9.36 /10	1.82 /23	2.64 /10	1.39	2.14

| RISK | | | NET ASSETS | | ASSET | | | | | BULL / BEAR | | FUND MANAGER | | MINIMUMS | | LOADS | |
Risk Rating/Pts	3 Year Standard Deviation	Beta	NAV As of 2/28/17	Total $(Mil)	Cash %	Stocks %	Bonds %	Other %	Portfolio Turnover Ratio	Last Bull Market Return	Last Bear Market Return	Manager Quality Pct	Manager Tenure (Years)	Initial Purch. $	Additional Purch. $	Front End Load	Back End Load
D / 1.7	10.1	0.59	17.41	1,731	6	93	0	1	65	100.6	-19.2	99	6	2,500	0	0.0	0.0
C+ / 6.5	9.6	0.54	13.51	N/A	11	88	0	1	77	N/A	N/A	99	6	2,500	0	0.0	0.0
C+ / 6.5	9.5	0.54	13.27	N/A	11	88	0	1	77	N/A	N/A	99	6	2,500	0	5.8	0.0
C+ / 6.4	9.5	0.54	13.55	33	11	88	0	1	77	N/A	N/A	99	6	2,500	100	0.0	0.0
C+ / 6.4	9.6	0.55	13.57	69	11	88	0	1	77	N/A	N/A	99	6	1,000,000	0	0.0	0.0
C+ / 6.4	9.5	0.54	13.50	N/A	11	88	0	1	77	N/A	N/A	99	6	2,500	0	0.0	0.0
C+ / 6.4	9.6	0.54	13.55	8	11	88	0	1	77	N/A	N/A	99	6	2,500	0	0.0	0.0
D+ / 2.8	11.9	0.73	22.73	53	2	91	5	2	84	111.0	-20.8	95	30	2,500	0	5.8	0.0
D+ / 2.7	11.9	0.73	21.70	19	2	91	5	2	84	103.7	-21.0	93	30	2,500	0	0.0	0.0
D+ / 2.7	11.9	0.73	22.53	154	2	91	5	2	84	114.5	-20.6	95	30	2,500	100	0.0	0.0
D+ / 2.7	11.9	0.73	22.64	937	2	91	5	2	84	114.8	-20.7	95	30	1,000,000	0	0.0	0.0
D+ / 2.8	11.9	0.73	23.19	195	2	91	5	2	84	116.0	-20.6	95	30	250,000	0	0.0	0.0
D+ / 2.7	11.9	0.73	22.60	278	2	91	5	2	84	116.4	-20.6	95	30	0	0	0.0	0.0
D+ / 2.8	11.9	0.73	22.21	28	2	91	5	2	84	107.8	-20.9	94	30	2,500	0	0.0	0.0
D+ / 2.8	11.9	0.73	22.43	73	2	91	5	2	84	110.6	-20.8	94	30	2,500	0	0.0	0.0
D+ / 2.7	11.9	0.73	22.58	791	2	91	5	2	84	113.5	-20.7	95	30	2,500	0	0.0	0.0
B- / 7.1	6.2	0.58	11.57	7	1	58	40	1	77	63.6	-9.3	71	7	2,500	0	5.8	0.0
B- / 7.1	6.2	0.58	11.60	5	1	58	40	1	77	57.7	-9.6	62	7	2,500	0	0.0	0.0
B- / 7.1	6.2	0.58	11.58	33	1	58	40	1	77	64.8	-9.3	72	7	2,500	100	0.0	0.0
B- / 7.1	6.3	0.58	11.59	6	1	58	40	1	77	65.6	-9.2	73	7	1,000,000	0	0.0	0.0
B- / 7.1	6.1	0.57	11.58	2	1	58	40	1	77	62.9	-9.4	72	7	2,500	0	0.0	0.0
B- / 7.1	6.2	0.58	11.58	5	1	58	40	1	77	64.4	-9.3	72	7	2,500	0	0.0	0.0
C- / 4.0	14.3	1.23	59.54	29	0	0	0	100	7	116.8	-25.3	3	14	1,000	100	0.0	0.0
C+ / 6.2	7.5	0.57	39.34	2,795	0	0	0	100	6	14.5	-8.3	31	14	1,000	100	0.0	0.0
C+ / 6.4	14.2	0.64	17.77	6	11	88	0	1	63	N/A	N/A	97	3	1,000	50	0.0	2.0
C / 5.0	13.6	0.78	35.35	264	2	94	2	2	6	125.7	-29.0	67	21	1,000	50	0.0	2.0
C / 4.3	10.4	0.72	16.30	62	0	95	3	2	18	98.8	-22.7	20	13	1,000	50	0.0	2.0
B- / 7.9	5.8	0.44	10.50	22	51	48	0	1	214	N/A	N/A	26	5	100,000	100	0.0	1.0
C- / 3.7	12.8	1.14	15.22	189	5	94	0	1	16	123.5	-20.0	22	14	0	0	0.0	0.0
D- / 1.0	18.6	1.30	11.45	9	4	95	0	1	229	67.9	-26.1	1	3	0	0	0.0	0.0
C- / 3.9	14.7	0.86	13.30	172	4	95	0	1	65	27.8	-23.2	42	10	0	0	0.0	0.0
U /	N/A	N/A	9.72	75	0	0	0	100	0	N/A	N/A	N/A	2	0	0	0.0	0.0
C+ / 6.6	3.9	0.18	9.08	84	14	1	84	1	127	N/A	N/A	94	5	0	0	0.0	0.0
C+ / 5.9	11.2	0.97	20.64	119	0	94	6	0	35	119.4	-18.4	46	4	0	0	0.0	0.0
C / 5.2	12.3	0.96	9.00	171	1	98	0	1	73	40.5	-24.8	50	6	0	0	0.0	0.0
C+ / 6.1	11.2	0.90	17.58	238	1	98	0	1	24	51.3	-23.5	72	13	0	0	0.0	0.0
U /	N/A	N/A	10.20	42	0	0	0	100	51	N/A	N/A	N/A	2	0	0	0.0	0.0
C- / 3.8	13.1	1.10	9.99	121	0	99	0	1	83	122.4	-15.4	21	4	0	0	0.0	0.0
C / 5.2	10.6	0.98	16.71	422	2	97	0	1	10	122.5	-16.4	55	3	0	0	0.0	0.0
C- / 3.7	10.3	0.98	14.00	315	3	96	0	1	50	132.1	-14.9	71	8	0	0	0.0	0.0
C- / 4.0	10.9	0.85	11.07	77	0	98	0	2	184	118.3	-21.5	76	4	0	0	0.0	0.0
C- / 3.6	13.0	1.01	7.07	15	2	97	0	1	43	69.1	-21.5	12	4	0	0	0.0	0.0
U /	N/A	N/A	11.64	162	1	98	0	1	32	N/A	N/A	N/A	2	0	0	0.0	0.0
C+ / 6.5	9.8	0.92	15.68	181	4	91	4	1	35	75.3	-19.4	19	11	1,000	50	5.5	0.0
C+ / 6.5	9.7	0.91	15.70	7	4	91	4	1	35	77.1	-19.4	21	14	0	0	0.0	0.0
C+ / 6.5	10.0	0.94	15.36	30	4	91	4	1	35	70.3	-20.0	12	11	1,000	50	0.0	0.0
C+ / 6.5	10.0	0.93	15.33	101	4	91	4	1	35	70.3	-20.0	12	11	1,000	50	0.0	0.0
C+ / 6.5	9.8	0.92	15.59	7	4	91	4	1	35	73.6	-19.6	16	11	0	0	0.0	0.0
B- / 7.9	4.5	0.65	10.95	138	0	17	82	1	42	26.8	-4.6	45	14	1,000	50	5.5	0.0
B- / 7.9	4.5	0.65	10.97	5	0	17	82	1	42	27.8	-4.6	49	14	0	0	0.0	0.0
B- / 7.9	4.6	0.67	10.75	30	0	17	82	1	42	22.1	-4.9	34	14	1,000	50	0.0	0.0
B- / 7.9	4.5	0.66	10.74	154	0	17	82	1	42	22.1	-4.9	35	14	1,000	50	0.0	0.0

Fund Type	Fund Name	Ticker Symbol	Overall Investment Rating	Phone	Performance Rating/Pts	3 Mo	6 Mo	1Yr / Pct	3Yr / Pct	5Yr / Pct	Dividend Yield	Expense Ratio
AA	PF Port Optz Consrv Class R	POARX	C-	(800) 722-2333	D / 2.0	2.86	1.46	9.80 /11	2.32 /26	3.12 /11	1.79	1.64
GR	PF Port Optz Growth A	PODAX	C	(800) 722-2333	C- / 4.0	5.62	6.35	19.42 /49	4.74 /51	7.43 /38	1.44	1.51
GR	PF Port Optz Growth Advisor	PMADX	C+	(800) 722-2333	C / 5.4	5.73	6.53	19.69 /50	4.99 /54	7.66 /39	1.70	1.26
GR	PF Port Optz Growth B	PODBX	C	(800) 722-2333	C / 4.5	5.47	5.98	18.65 /46	3.99 /43	6.70 /33	1.00	2.26
GR	PF Port Optz Growth C	PODCX	C	(800) 722-2333	C / 4.5	5.48	5.99	18.62 /46	3.97 /43	6.71 /33	1.00	2.26
GR	PF Port Optz Growth R	PODRX	C+	(800) 722-2333	C / 4.9	5.55	6.20	19.12 /48	4.47 /48	7.19 /36	1.31	1.76
GR	PF Port Optz Mod Class A	POCAX	C-	(800) 722-2333	C- / 3.1	4.88	4.96	16.36 /36	4.13 /44	6.23 /30	1.62	1.47
BA	PF Port Optz Mod Class Adv	POMDX	C+	(800) 722-2333	C / 4.3	4.92	5.08	16.56 /37	4.37 /47	6.44 /31	1.90	1.22
GR	PF Port Optz Mod Class B	POMBX	C	(800) 722-2333	C- / 3.5	4.65	4.57	15.52 /32	3.37 /35	5.48 /25	1.18	2.22
GR	PF Port Optz Mod Class C	POMCX	C	(800) 722-2333	C- / 3.5	4.65	4.58	15.54 /32	3.38 /36	5.49 /25	1.18	2.22
GR	PF Port Optz Mod Class R	POCRX	C	(800) 722-2333	C- / 3.9	4.84	4.84	16.07 /35	3.87 /41	5.99 /28	1.52	1.72
GI	PF Port Optz Mod-Consrv A	POBAX	C-	(800) 722-2333	D / 2.1	3.89	3.13	12.65 /20	3.38 /36	4.79 /20	1.80	1.44
AA	PF Port Optz Mod-Consrv Advisor	PMCDX	C	(800) 722-2333	C- / 3.1	3.91	3.16	12.84 /21	3.62 /38	4.96 /21	2.09	1.19
GI	PF Port Optz Mod-Consrv B	POBBX	C-	(800) 722-2333	D+ / 2.4	3.63	2.68	11.83 /17	2.62 /28	4.04 /15	1.38	2.19
GI	PF Port Optz Mod-Consrv C	POBCX	C-	(800) 722-2333	D+ / 2.5	3.70	2.67	11.92 /18	2.65 /29	4.06 /16	1.37	2.19
GI	PF Port Optz Mod-Consrv R	POBRX	C	(800) 722-2333	D+ / 2.8	3.82	2.88	12.33 /19	3.11 /33	4.54 /18	1.74	1.69
RE	PF Real Estate P		C+	(800) 722-2333	C+ / 6.8	7.02	-2.02	13.74 /24	10.06 /94	10.00 /58	2.40	1.12
SC	PF Small-Cap Val P		C+	(800) 722-2333	A+ / 9.8	3.14	14.82	36.30 /95	11.08 /97	13.42 /88	0.55	0.96
RE	Phocas Real Estate	PHREX	B-	(866) 746-2271	B / 8.0	8.16	0.73	18.15 /44	11.12 /97	12.03 /75	1.01	2.30
GR	Piedmont Select Equity	PSVFX	C-	(888) 859-5865	C- / 4.1	6.48	4.35	15.94 /34	3.93 /42	8.49 /46	0.00	1.67
AA	PIMCO All Asset A	PASAX	D	(800) 426-0107	D+ / 2.6	5.86	4.76	19.19 /48	1.85 /23	2.90 /10	2.89	1.53
AA	PIMCO All Asset Admin	PAALX	D+	(800) 426-0107	C- / 3.4	5.92	4.79	19.44 /49	2.07 /24	3.16 /11	3.22	1.33
AA	PIMCO All Asset All Authority A	PAUAX	E	(800) 426-0107	D- / 1.0	5.71	3.97	18.96 /47	-0.37 /12	0.47 / 5	2.90	2.38
AA	PIMCO All Asset All Authority C	PAUCX	E+	(800) 426-0107	D- / 1.2	5.57	3.52	18.08 /43	-1.10 / 9	-0.27 / 4	2.36	3.13
AA	PIMCO All Asset All Authority D	PAUDX	E+	(800) 426-0107	D- / 1.5	5.75	4.02	19.10 /48	-0.28 /12	0.53 / 5	3.13	2.33
AA	PIMCO All Asset All Authority Inst	PAUIX	D-	(800) 426-0107	D+ / 2.4	5.86	4.25	19.65 /50	0.11 /14	0.94 / 6	3.50	1.93
AA	PIMCO All Asset All Authority P	PAUPX	U	(800) 426-0107	U /	5.83	4.07	19.38 /49	---	0.83 / 6	3.40	2.03
AA	PIMCO All Asset C	PASCX	D	(800) 426-0107	D+ / 2.8	5.73	4.32	18.40 /45	1.09 /19	2.15 / 8	2.31	2.28
AA	PIMCO All Asset D	PASDX	D+	(800) 426-0107	C- / 3.4	5.89	4.72	19.31 /49	1.95 /24	3.01 /11	3.09	1.48
AA	PIMCO All Asset Inst	PAAIX	D+	(800) 426-0107	C- / 3.7	6.02	4.95	19.77 /51	2.33 /26	3.42 /12	3.46	1.08
AA	PIMCO All Asset P	PALPX	D+	(800) 426-0107	C- / 3.6	5.98	4.89	19.62 /50	2.22 /25	3.31 /12	3.36	1.18
AA	PIMCO All Asset R	PATRX	D	(800) 426-0107	C- / 3.1	5.82	4.55	18.92 /47	1.59 /21	2.65 /10	2.80	1.78
FS	PIMCO Capital Secs and Fincl Inst	PFINX	U	(800) 426-0107	U /	5.48	5.06	18.06 /43	---	---	5.99	0.79
OT	PIMCO CommoditiesPLUS Strategy	PCLAX	E-	(800) 426-0107	E- / 0.0	4.55	12.22	29.76 /86	-14.64 / 0	-9.61 / 1	0.08	1.41
OT	PIMCO CommoditiesPLUS Strategy	PCPCX	E-	(800) 426-0107	E- / 0.0	4.36	11.67	28.78 /83	-15.29 / 0	-10.30 / 1	0.00	2.21
OT	PIMCO CommoditiesPLUS Strategy	PCLDX	E-	(800) 426-0107	E- / 0.1	4.55	12.19	29.69 /86	-14.63 / 0	-9.61 / 1	0.08	1.41
OT	PIMCO CommoditiesPLUS Strategy	PCLIX	E-	(800) 426-0107	E- / 0.1	4.65	12.41	30.11 /87	-14.25 / 0	-9.18 / 1	0.16	0.96
OT	PIMCO CommoditiesPLUS Strategy	PCLPX	E-	(800) 426-0107	E- / 0.1	4.51	12.28	30.01 /86	-14.35 / 0	-9.28 / 1	0.15	1.06
IN	PIMCO Commodity Real Ret Str A	PCRAX	E	(800) 426-0107	E- / 0.0	2.95	7.08	19.96 /52	-13.58 / 0	-10.58 / 1	0.56	1.53
IN	PIMCO Commodity Real Ret Str Adm	PCRRX	E	(800) 426-0107	E- / 0.0	2.99	7.16	20.18 /53	-13.45 / 0	-10.38 / 1	0.69	1.33
IN	PIMCO Commodity Real Ret Str C	PCRCX	E	(800) 426-0107	E- / 0.0	2.74	6.68	19.17 /48	-14.21 / 0	-11.23 / 0	0.27	2.28
IN	PIMCO Commodity Real Ret Str D	PCRDX	E	(800) 426-0107	E- / 0.0	2.95	7.23	20.10 /53	-13.59 / 0	-10.55 / 1	0.60	1.53
IN	PIMCO Commodity Real Ret Str Inst	PCRIX	E	(800) 426-0107	E- / 0.1	3.02	7.34	20.43 /54	-13.19 / 0	-10.16 / 1	0.90	1.08
IN	PIMCO Commodity Real Ret Str P	PCRPX	E	(800) 426-0107	E- / 0.0	3.00	7.30	20.40 /54	-13.28 / 0	-10.24 / 1	0.83	1.18
OT	PIMCO Commodity Real Ret Str R	PCSRX	E	(800) 426-0107	E- / 0.0	2.82	6.95	19.64 /50	-13.83 / 0	-10.78 / 0	0.46	1.78
GL	PIMCO Div and Inc A	PQIZX	D-	(800) 426-0107	D / 2.0	4.64	6.38	17.44 /40	1.33 /20	5.68 /26	2.40	1.18
GL	PIMCO Div and Inc C	PQICX	D	(800) 426-0107	D+ / 2.4	4.54	5.97	16.63 /37	0.60 /16	4.91 /21	1.94	1.93
GL	PIMCO Div and Inc D	PQIDX	D	(800) 426-0107	D+ / 2.8	4.61	6.24	17.40 /40	1.32 /20	5.66 /26	2.51	1.18
GL	PIMCO Div and Inc Inst	PQIIX	D	(800) 426-0107	C- / 3.1	4.72	6.46	17.87 /42	1.70 /22	6.04 /29	2.81	0.83
GL	PIMCO Div and Inc P	PQIPX	D	(800) 426-0107	C- / 3.1	4.74	6.47	17.84 /42	1.62 /22	5.98 /28	2.71	0.93
GR	PIMCO Eqs Long Short A	PMHAX	C-	(800) 426-0107	D- / 1.0	5.50	3.27	7.64 / 7	0.22 /14	---	2.70	2.79
GR	PIMCO Eqs Long Short C	PMHCX	C-	(800) 426-0107	E+ / 0.9	5.32	2.94	6.85 / 6	-0.52 /11	---	2.53	3.54

● Denotes fund is closed to new investors
* Denotes fund is included in Section II

www.thestreetratings.com

Risk Rating/Pts	3 Year Standard Deviation	Beta	NAV As of 2/28/17	Total $(Mil)	Cash %	Stocks %	Bonds %	Other %	Portfolio Turnover Ratio	Last Bull Market Return	Last Bear Market Return	Manager Quality Pct	Manager Tenure (Years)	Initial Purch. $	Additional Purch. $	Front End Load	Back End Load
B- / 7.9	4.5	0.66	10.88	9	0	17	82	1	42	25.1	-4.6	41	12	0	0	0.0	0.0
C+ / 6.6	8.8	0.82	14.52	565	0	74	25	1	34	68.6	-16.0	26	14	1,000	50	5.5	0.0
C+ / 6.6	8.8	0.83	14.55	13	0	74	25	1	34	70.4	-16.0	29	14	0	0	0.0	0.0
C+ / 6.7	8.9	0.83	14.35	99	0	74	25	1	34	62.9	-16.5	19	14	1,000	50	0.0	0.0
C+ / 6.6	8.9	0.83	14.30	351	0	74	25	1	34	62.8	-16.4	19	14	1,000	50	0.0	0.0
C+ / 6.6	8.8	0.82	14.49	15	0	74	25	1	34	66.5	-16.1	24	12	0	0	0.0	0.0
B- / 7.3	7.2	0.67	13.62	728	0	53	46	1	35	55.0	-12.2	38	14	1,000	50	5.5	0.0
B- / 7.3	7.1	1.10	13.63	16	0	53	46	1	35	56.5	-12.2	26	14	0	0	0.0	0.0
B- / 7.4	7.2	0.68	13.47	136	0	53	46	1	35	49.3	-12.5	28	14	1,000	50	0.0	0.0
B- / 7.4	7.2	0.67	13.45	524	0	53	46	1	35	49.4	-12.6	28	14	1,000	50	0.0	0.0
B- / 7.3	7.2	0.67	13.59	24	0	53	46	1	35	53.1	-12.3	35	12	0	0	0.0	0.0
B- / 7.8	5.5	0.49	12.17	239	0	32	67	1	34	40.0	-8.3	52	14	1,000	50	5.5	0.0
B- / 7.8	5.4	0.83	12.19	5	0	32	67	1	34	41.1	-8.3	42	14	0	0	0.0	0.0
B- / 7.8	5.5	0.50	11.97	46	0	32	67	1	34	34.8	-8.8	41	14	1,000	50	0.0	0.0
B- / 7.8	5.5	0.50	11.97	203	0	32	67	1	34	34.9	-8.8	42	14	1,000	50	0.0	0.0
B- / 7.8	5.4	0.49	12.10	6	0	32	67	1	34	38.1	-8.5	49	12	0	0	0.0	0.0
C / 5.1	14.5	1.05	15.42	66	1	98	0	1	26	96.9	-18.0	57	13	0	0	0.0	0.0
D / 2.2	15.4	0.93	12.19	125	1	98	0	1	55	128.0	-18.5	94	3	0	0	0.0	0.0
C / 4.7	14.5	1.04	33.05	12	0	98	1	1	30	114.6	-18.0	69	11	5,000	200	0.0	1.0
C+ / 5.7	10.3	0.91	15.55	25	11	88	0	1	33	88.1	-14.4	12	11	5,000	250	0.0	0.0
C / 5.2	8.0	0.88	11.62	732	1	4	94	1	40	28.2	-7.5	19	15	1,000	50	3.8	0.0
C / 5.2	8.0	0.88	11.63	196	1	4	94	1	40	29.9	-7.4	21	15	1,000,000	0	0.0	0.0
C- / 4.2	8.9	0.82	8.70	567	0	3	96	1	39	15.6	-7.4	7	14	1,000	50	5.5	0.0
C- / 4.2	8.9	0.83	8.70	757	0	3	96	1	39	11.1	-7.7	5	14	1,000	50	0.0	0.0
C- / 4.2	8.8	0.82	8.67	260	0	3	96	1	39	16.0	-7.4	8	14	1,000	50	0.0	0.0
C- / 4.2	8.9	0.82	8.70	5,724	0	3	96	1	39	18.6	-7.3	9	14	1,000,000	0	0.0	0.0
U /	8.9	0.83	8.70	840	0	3	96	1	39	17.7	-7.2	N/A	14	1,000,000	0	0.0	0.0
C / 5.2	8.0	0.88	11.57	673	1	4	94	1	40	23.1	-7.8	13	15	1,000	50	0.0	0.0
C / 5.2	8.0	0.88	11.61	323	1	4	94	1	40	28.8	-7.4	19	15	1,000	50	0.0	0.0
C / 5.2	8.0	0.88	11.61	16,345	1	4	94	1	40	31.7	-7.4	23	15	1,000,000	0	0.0	0.0
C / 5.2	8.0	0.88	11.63	574	1	4	94	1	40	30.9	-7.3	22	15	1,000,000	0	0.0	0.0
C / 5.2	8.0	0.88	11.55	73	1	4	94	1	40	26.5	-7.6	16	15	0	0	0.0	0.0
U /	N/A	N/A	10.31	32	2	5	91	2	209	N/A	N/A	N/A	2	1,000,000	0	0.0	0.0
D+ / 2.3	19.8	0.64	6.43	48	8	0	91	1	229	-31.1	-21.8	0	7	1,000	50	5.5	0.0
D+ / 2.3	19.7	0.64	6.22	10	8	0	91	1	229	-33.8	-22.1	0	7	1,000	50	0.0	0.0
D+ / 2.3	19.7	0.63	6.44	233	8	0	91	1	229	-31.0	-21.8	0	7	1,000	50	0.0	0.0
D+ / 2.3	19.7	0.63	6.52	2,147	8	0	91	1	229	-29.2	-21.6	0	7	1,000,000	0	0.0	0.0
D+ / 2.3	19.7	0.63	6.49	162	8	0	91	1	229	-29.7	-21.6	0	7	1,000,000	0	0.0	0.0
C / 4.3	15.4	0.36	7.07	297	0	0	100	0	111	-37.0	-20.0	0	10	1,000	50	5.5	0.0
C / 4.3	15.6	0.36	7.10	85	0	0	100	0	111	-36.3	-20.1	0	10	1,000,000	0	0.0	0.0
C / 4.3	15.5	0.37	6.75	107	0	0	100	0	111	-39.4	-20.3	0	10	1,000	50	0.0	0.0
C / 4.3	15.4	0.38	7.09	300	0	0	100	0	111	-36.9	-20.1	0	10	1,000	50	0.0	0.0
C / 4.3	15.5	0.37	7.23	5,286	0	0	100	0	111	-35.4	-19.9	0	10	1,000,000	0	0.0	0.0
C / 4.4	15.5	0.37	7.21	589	0	0	100	0	111	-35.7	-19.9	0	10	1,000,000	0	0.0	0.0
C / 4.3	15.5	0.37	6.93	45	0	0	100	0	111	-37.8	-20.1	0	10	0	0	0.0	0.0
C / 5.0	9.9	0.72	10.76	142	0	92	7	1	114	N/A	N/A	83	6	1,000	50	5.5	0.0
C / 5.0	9.9	0.72	10.73	161	0	92	7	1	114	N/A	N/A	79	6	1,000	50	0.0	0.0
C / 5.0	9.9	0.72	10.76	9	0	92	7	1	114	N/A	N/A	83	6	1,000	50	0.0	0.0
C / 5.0	9.9	0.72	10.77	24	0	92	7	1	114	N/A	N/A	85	6	1,000,000	0	0.0	0.0
C / 5.0	9.9	0.72	10.79	22	0	92	7	1	114	N/A	N/A	85	6	1,000,000	0	0.0	0.0
B / 8.6	6.5	0.31	11.63	99	40	39	20	1	672	N/A	N/A	35	1	1,000	50	5.5	0.0
B / 8.6	6.5	0.31	11.28	104	40	39	20	1	672	N/A	N/A	26	1	1,000	50	0.0	0.0

Fund Type	Fund Name	Ticker Symbol	Overall Investment Rating	Phone	Performance Rating/Pts	3 Mo	6 Mo	1Yr / Pct	3Yr / Pct	5Yr / Pct	Dividend Yield	Expense Ratio
GR	PIMCO Eqs Long Short D	PMHDX	C-	(800) 426-0107	D- / 1.5	5.47	3.24	7.60 / 7	0.21 /14	--	2.74	2.79
GR	PIMCO Eqs Long Short Inst	PMHIX	C-	(800) 426-0107	D / 1.6	5.61	3.50	7.99 / 7	0.57 /16	6.02 /28	2.99	2.44
GR	PIMCO Eqs Long Short P	PMHBX	C-	(800) 426-0107	D / 1.6	5.57	3.45	7.96 / 7	0.50 /16	--	2.94	2.54
GL	PIMCO Global Multi Asset A	PGMAX	C-	(800) 426-0107	C- / 3.1	5.28	4.01	15.84 /34	4.27 /46	1.25 / 7	1.14	1.75
GL	PIMCO Global Multi Asset C	PGMCX	C-	(800) 426-0107	C- / 3.5	5.09	3.59	14.98 /30	3.49 /37	0.48 / 5	0.69	2.50
GL	PIMCO Global Multi Asset D	PGMDX	C	(800) 426-0107	C- / 4.1	5.28	4.01	15.84 /34	4.24 /46	1.25 / 7	1.21	1.75
GL	PIMCO Global Multi Asset I	PGAIX	C+	(800) 426-0107	C / 4.6	5.40	4.21	16.43 /36	4.86 /53	1.84 / 8	1.61	1.30
GL	PIMCO Global Multi Asset P	PGAPX	C	(800) 426-0107	C / 4.5	5.37	4.25	16.35 /36	4.75 /51	1.74 / 8	1.53	1.40
GL	PIMCO Global Multi Asset R	PGMRX	C	(800) 426-0107	C- / 3.8	5.17	3.82	15.48 /32	3.99 /43	0.99 / 6	1.04	2.00
AA	PIMCO Infl Response MultiAsset A	PZRMX	D	(800) 426-0107	D- / 1.3	3.95	2.74	13.33 /23	0.77 /17	0.03 / 4	0.15	1.59
AA	PIMCO Infl Response MultiAsset C	PCRMX	D	(800) 426-0107	D / 1.6	3.87	2.38	12.58 /20	0.07 /14	-0.69 / 4	0.00	2.34
AA	PIMCO Infl Response MultiAsset Inst	PIRMX	D	(800) 426-0107	D / 2.1	4.14	3.05	13.87 /25	1.24 /20	0.51 / 5	0.48	1.14
AA	PIMCO Infl Response MultiAsset P	PPRMX	D	(800) 426-0107	D / 2.1	4.09	3.01	13.96 /25	1.19 /19	0.43 / 5	0.44	1.24
GL	PIMCO Multi Strategy Alt Inst	PXAIX	U	(800) 426-0107	U /	1.80	2.69	6.90 / 6	--	--	5.29	2.03
EM	PIMCO RAE Fdmtl+ EMG A	PEFFX	C+	(800) 426-0107	A+ / 9.8	14.13	18.91	60.93 /99	5.28 /57	--	3.69	1.57
EM	PIMCO RAE Fdmtl+ EMG Admin	PEFAX	C+	(800) 426-0107	A+ / 9.9	14.19	19.01	61.11 /99	5.43 /59	1.79 / 8	3.84	1.42
EM	PIMCO RAE Fdmtl+ EMG C	PEFCX	C+	(800) 426-0107	A+ / 9.8	13.80	18.47	59.75 /99	4.50 /49	--	3.42	2.32
EM	PIMCO RAE Fdmtl+ EMG D	PEFDX	C+	(800) 426-0107	A+ / 9.9	14.12	18.95	61.09 /99	5.28 /57	--	3.86	1.57
EM	PIMCO RAE Fdmtl+ EMG Inst	PEFIX	C+	(800) 426-0107	A+ / 9.9	14.19	19.14	61.54 /99	5.69 /61	2.05 / 8	4.01	1.17
EM	PIMCO RAE Fdmtl+ EMG P	PEFPX	C+	(800) 426-0107	A+ / 9.9	14.22	19.07	61.40 /99	5.60 /61	1.93 / 8	4.02	1.27
GR	PIMCO RAE Fnd+ Intl A	PTSOX	D-	(800) 426-0107	D- / 1.5	9.72	12.29	29.48 /85	-1.96 / 7	--	0.56	1.18
GR	PIMCO RAE Fnd+ Intl C	PTSKX	D-	(800) 426-0107	D- / 1.5	9.43	11.83	28.41 /83	-2.70 / 5	--	0.18	1.93
GR	PIMCO RAE Fnd+ Intl D	PTSLX	D	(800) 426-0107	D / 1.8	9.56	12.27	29.27 /85	-2.01 / 7	--	0.51	1.18
GR	PIMCO RAE Fnd+ Intl Inst	PTSIX	E-	(800) 426-0107	D / 2.0	9.68	12.49	29.76 /86	-1.62 / 8	6.77 /33	0.80	0.83
GR	PIMCO RAE Fndmntl PLUS Sm A	PCFAX	A	(800) 426-0107	A+ / 9.6	5.38	16.77	43.96 /98	8.19 /80	--	0.00	1.22
GR	PIMCO RAE Fndmntl PLUS Sm C	PCFEX	A	(800) 426-0107	A+ / 9.6	5.19	16.27	42.89 /98	7.39 /75	--	0.00	1.97
GR	PIMCO RAE Fndmntl PLUS Sm D	PCFDX	A	(800) 426-0107	A+ / 9.7	5.46	16.73	44.03 /98	8.23 /81	--	0.00	1.22
GR	PIMCO RAE Fndmntl PLUS Sm Inst	PCFIX	C+	(800) 426-0107	A+ / 9.8	5.52	16.95	44.49 /98	8.60 /84	15.45 /98	0.00	0.87
GI	PIMCO RAE Fundamental Advtg	PTFAX	D+	(800) 426-0107	E / 0.5	0.10	3.71	7.71 / 7	-0.72 /10	1.92 / 8	0.00	1.34
GI	PIMCO RAE Fundamental Advtg	PTRCX	D+	(800) 426-0107	E+ / 0.6	-0.10	3.19	6.82 / 6	-1.46 / 8	1.14 / 6	0.00	2.09
GI	PIMCO RAE Fundamental Advtg	PFSDX	C-	(800) 426-0107	E+ / 0.8	0.10	3.73	7.74 / 7	-0.72 /10	1.92 / 8	0.00	1.34
GI	PIMCO RAE Fundamental Advtg	PFATX	C-	(800) 426-0107	E+ / 0.9	0.20	3.84	7.99 / 7	-0.34 /12	2.32 / 9	0.00	0.94
GR	PIMCO RAE Fundamental Advtg	PFAPX	C-	(800) 426-0107	E+ / 0.8	0.20	3.85	8.01 / 7	-0.46 /11	2.26 / 9	0.00	1.04
EM	PIMCO RAE Fundamental Emg Mkts	PEIFX	E-	(800) 426-0107	E- / 0.0	12.29	16.17	52.92 /99	-59.14 / 0	--	2.49	0.95
GL	PIMCO RAE Fundamental Global Inst	PFQIX	U	(800) 426-0107	U /	7.34	10.11	26.65 /78	--	--	2.34	1.16
FO	PIMCO RAE Fundamental GlxUS Inst	PZRIX	U	(800) 426-0107	U /	8.32	10.10	28.00 /82	--	--	2.46	1.31
FO	PIMCO RAE Fundamental Intl Inst	PPYIX	U	(800) 426-0107	U /	7.18	8.50	21.88 /62	--	--	2.23	0.60
IN	PIMCO RAE Fundamental PLUS A	PIXAX	B	(800) 426-0107	A- / 9.1	8.05	13.68	33.46 /92	8.71 /85	14.87 /97	0.00	1.23
IN	PIMCO RAE Fundamental PLUS	PXTAX	B+	(800) 426-0107	A+ / 9.6	8.02	13.69	33.71 /92	8.88 /86	15.04 /97	0.00	1.08
IN	PIMCO RAE Fundamental PLUS C	PIXCX	B	(800) 426-0107	A- / 9.2	7.79	13.24	32.38 /91	7.87 /78	13.99 /93	0.00	1.98
IN	PIMCO RAE Fundamental PLUS D	PIXDX	B+	(800) 426-0107	A / 9.5	7.91	13.54	33.33 /92	8.68 /84	14.83 /97	0.00	1.23
IN	PIMCO RAE Fundamental PLUS Inst	PXTIX	B+	(800) 426-0107	A+ / 9.6	8.16	13.91	34.01 /93	9.14 /88	15.32 /97	0.00	0.83
IN	PIMCO RAE Fundamental PLUS P	PIXPX	B+	(800) 426-0107	A+ / 9.6	8.06	13.66	33.83 /93	9.03 /87	15.18 /97	0.00	0.93
GR	PIMCO RAE Fundamental US Inst	PKAIX	E-	(800) 426-0107	E- / 0.0	5.99	9.86	25.04 /73	-61.51 / 0	-38.95 / 0	2.05	0.50
GR	PIMCO RAE Fundamental US Small	PMJIX	E-	(800) 426-0107	E- / 0.0	3.64	13.18	35.22 /94	-61.96 / 0	-38.90 / 0	1.24	0.60
FO	PIMCO RAE Low Vol PLUS Intl A	PLVBX	C	(800) 426-0107	C- / 3.4	8.65	5.55	18.98 /47	2.69 /29	--	0.41	1.23
FO	PIMCO RAE Low Vol PLUS Intl C	PLVQX	C	(800) 426-0107	C- / 3.5	8.40	5.05	17.96 /43	1.91 /23	--	0.17	1.98
FO	PIMCO RAE Low Vol PLUS Intl Inst	PLVTX	C+	(800) 426-0107	C / 4.5	8.73	5.72	19.30 /49	3.08 /33	--	0.74	0.88
FO	PIMCO RAE Low Vol PLUS Intl P	PLVZX	C+	(800) 426-0107	C / 4.4	8.78	5.63	19.30 /49	2.95 /31	--	0.70	0.98
GI	PIMCO RAE Low Volatility PLUS A	PXLVX	A+	(800) 426-0107	B+ / 8.8	8.52	8.25	24.44 /71	10.70 /96	--	1.35	1.23
GI	PIMCO RAE Low Volatility PLUS C	POLVX	A+	(800) 426-0107	B+ / 8.8	8.20	7.73	23.49 /68	9.88 /93	--	0.94	1.98
EM	PIMCO RAE Low Volatility PLUS	PLVVX	D	(800) 426-0107	C / 4.4	9.92	6.13	32.81 /91	0.97 /18	--	0.72	1.55

● Denotes fund is closed to new investors
* Denotes fund is included in Section II

Risk Rating/Pts	Standard Deviation	Beta	NAV As of 2/28/17	Total $(Mil)	Cash %	Stocks %	Bonds %	Other %	Portfolio Turnover Ratio	Last Bull Market Return	Last Bear Market Return	Manager Quality Pct	Manager Tenure (Years)	Initial Purch. $	Additional Purch. $	Front End Load	Back End Load
B /8.6	6.5	0.31	11.65	36	40	39	20	1	672	N/A	N/A	34	1	1,000	50	0.0	0.0
B /8.6	6.5	0.31	11.82	163	40	39	20	1	672	37.1	-7.6	39	1	1,000,000	0	0.0	0.0
B /8.6	6.6	0.31	11.76	144	40	39	20	1	672	N/A	N/A	38	1	1,000,000	0	0.0	0.0
C+ /6.9	8.2	1.22	11.61	99	0	9	90	1	380	15.4	-10.1	57	3	1,000	50	5.5	0.0
C+ /6.8	8.2	1.22	11.30	109	0	9	90	1	380	10.8	-10.5	47	3	1,000	50	0.0	0.0
C+ /6.9	8.2	1.22	11.61	19	0	9	90	1	380	15.4	-10.1	57	3	1,000	50	0.0	0.0
C+ /6.9	8.2	1.23	11.70	283	0	9	90	1	380	19.2	-10.0	64	3	1,000,000	0	0.0	0.0
C+ /6.9	8.2	1.22	11.69	48	0	9	90	1	380	18.5	-10.0	63	3	1,000,000	0	0.0	0.0
C+ /6.9	8.2	1.22	11.48	6	0	9	90	1	380	13.8	-10.3	53	3	0	0	0.0	0.0
C+ /6.2	7.1	0.58	8.78	9	0	6	93	1	290	7.1	N/A	29	6	1,000	50	5.5	0.0
C+ /6.2	7.1	0.58	8.59	2	0	6	93	1	290	2.8	N/A	21	6	1,000	50	0.0	0.0
C+ /6.2	7.2	0.59	8.85	1,055	0	6	93	1	290	9.6	N/A	34	6	1,000,000	0	0.0	0.0
C+ /6.2	7.1	0.58	8.86	7	0	6	93	1	290	9.2	N/A	33	6	1,000,000	0	0.0	0.0
U /	N/A	N/A	9.81	95	0	0	0	100	115	N/A	N/A	N/A	3	1,000,000	0	0.0	0.0
D /2.0	22.1	1.29	10.16	6	21	0	78	1	482	N/A	N/A	90	3	1,000	50	3.8	0.0
D /2.0	22.1	1.29	10.17	N/A	21	0	78	1	482	41.7	-29.1	91	3	1,000,000	0	0.0	0.0
D /1.9	22.1	1.30	9.92	2	21	0	78	1	482	N/A	N/A	87	3	1,000	50	0.0	0.0
D /1.9	22.1	1.30	10.12	18	21	0	78	1	482	N/A	N/A	90	3	1,000	50	0.0	0.0
D /2.0	22.1	1.29	10.27	1,201	21	0	78	1	482	43.6	-29.0	92	3	1,000,000	0	0.0	0.0
D /2.0	22.1	1.29	10.26	39	21	0	78	1	482	42.8	-29.1	91	3	1,000,000	0	0.0	0.0
C+ /5.7	15.8	1.21	8.81	3	3	0	95	2	465	N/A	N/A	1	3	1,000	50	3.8	0.0
C+ /5.7	15.8	1.22	8.70	1	3	0	95	2	465	N/A	N/A	0	3	1,000	50	0.0	0.0
C+ /5.7	15.8	1.21	8.79	4	3	0	95	2	465	N/A	N/A	1	3	1,000	50	0.0	0.0
E+ /0.8	15.8	1.21	8.82	887	3	0	95	2	465	60.8	N/A	1	3	1,000,000	0	0.0	0.0
C+ /5.8	16.5	1.27	11.56	4	2	0	96	2	526	N/A	N/A	16	3	1,000	50	3.8	0.0
C+ /5.8	16.5	1.27	11.36	3	2	0	96	2	526	N/A	N/A	11	3	1,000	50	0.0	0.0
C+ /5.8	16.5	1.27	11.58	5	2	0	96	2	526	N/A	N/A	16	3	1,000	50	0.0	0.0
D /1.8	16.5	1.27	11.66	65	2	0	96	2	526	165.0	N/A	19	3	1,000,000	0	0.0	0.0
B /8.6	3.3	0.15	10.06	10	0	1	98	1	602	13.6	-5.3	43	3	1,000	50	3.8	0.0
B /8.7	3.3	0.16	10.03	9	0	1	98	1	602	9.1	-5.6	33	3	1,000	50	0.0	0.0
B /8.6	3.3	0.16	10.02	13	0	1	98	1	602	13.6	-5.3	42	3	1,000	50	0.0	0.0
B /8.6	3.3	0.14	10.27	401	0	1	98	1	602	16.0	-5.1	50	3	1,000,000	0	0.0	0.0
B /8.6	3.4	0.16	10.25	6	0	1	98	1	602	15.3	-5.1	47	3	1,000,000	0	0.0	0.0
D- /1.5	213.0	2.21	10.77	1,379	5	94	0	1	30	N/A	N/A	0	2	1,000,000	0	0.0	0.0
U /	N/A	N/A	10.35	406	1	98	0	1	13	N/A	N/A	N/A	N/A	1,000,000	0	0.0	0.0
U /	N/A	N/A	9.82	73	1	98	0	1	8	N/A	N/A	N/A	2	1,000,000	0	0.0	0.0
U /	N/A	N/A	9.47	361	0	99	0	1	39	N/A	N/A	N/A	N/A	1,000,000	0	0.0	0.0
C /4.3	12.3	1.15	6.98	438	3	0	96	1	501	152.9	-18.4	31	3	1,000	50	3.8	0.0
C /4.4	12.3	1.16	7.14	31	3	0	96	1	501	155.2	-18.6	33	3	1,000,000	0	0.0	0.0
C- /4.1	12.3	1.16	6.50	359	3	0	96	1	501	143.1	-18.8	23	3	1,000	50	0.0	0.0
C /4.3	12.3	1.15	6.96	319	3	0	96	1	501	152.9	-18.5	31	3	1,000	50	0.0	0.0
C /4.4	12.2	1.15	7.29	459	3	0	96	1	501	158.6	-18.3	36	3	1,000,000	0	0.0	0.0
C /4.4	12.3	1.16	7.24	258	3	0	96	1	501	156.8	-18.4	35	3	1,000,000	0	0.0	0.0
D- /1.0	235.9	3.78	10.57	571	0	99	0	1	42	-89.8	-17.3	0	2	1,000,000	0	0.0	0.0
E+ /0.8	232.7	3.92	11.18	90	0	99	0	1	85	-89.2	-25.5	0	2	1,000,000	0	0.0	0.0
B- /7.4	12.0	0.92	10.06	2	0	0	100	0	573	N/A	N/A	90	3	1,000	50	3.8	0.0
B- /7.4	12.0	0.92	9.93	1	0	0	100	0	573	N/A	N/A	86	3	1,000	50	0.0	0.0
B- /7.4	12.1	0.92	10.10	1,698	0	0	100	0	573	N/A	N/A	91	3	1,000,000	0	0.0	0.0
B- /7.4	12.1	0.92	10.08	7	0	0	100	0	573	N/A	N/A	91	3	1,000,000	0	0.0	0.0
B /8.1	10.0	0.86	12.46	12	4	0	95	1	551	N/A	N/A	84	3	1,000	50	3.8	0.0
B /8.1	10.0	0.86	12.29	5	4	0	95	1	551	N/A	N/A	79	3	1,000	50	0.0	0.0
C- /3.4	17.5	1.04	9.26	1	7	0	92	1	528	N/A	N/A	65	3	1,000	50	3.8	0.0

					PERFORMANCE							
	99 Pct = Best *0 Pct = Worst*		**Overall**		**Perfor-**	Total Return % through 2/28/17					Incl. in Returns	
		Ticker	**Investment**		**mance**				Annualized		Dividend	Expense
Fund Type	Fund Name	Symbol	**Rating**	Phone	**Rating/Pts**	3 Mo	6 Mo	1Yr / Pct	3Yr / Pct	5Yr / Pct	Yield	Ratio
EM	PIMCO RAE Low Volatility PLUS	PLVOX	D	(800) 426-0107	C / 4.5	9.60	5.70	31.82 /90	0.16 /14	--	0.31	2.30
EM	PIMCO RAE Low Volatility PLUS	PLVLX	D+	(800) 426-0107	C / 5.5	9.89	6.33	33.24 /92	1.33 /20	--	1.00	1.15
EM	PIMCO RAE Low Volatility PLUS	PLVWX	D+	(800) 426-0107	C / 5.5	10.01	6.29	33.20 /92	1.26 /20	--	0.94	1.25
GI	PIMCO RAE Low Volatility PLUS Inst	PILVX	A+	(800) 426-0107	A / 9.5	8.52	8.43	24.88 /73	11.12 /97	--	1.62	0.83
GI	PIMCO RAE Low Volatility PLUS P	PPLVX	A+	(800) 426-0107	A / 9.4	8.55	8.37	24.83 /73	11.02 /97	--	1.55	0.93
GL	PIMCO RAE Worldwide LS PLUS Inst	PWLIX	U	(800) 426-0107	U /	6.96	6.54	16.99 /38	--	--	4.06	1.22
GL	PIMCO RAE Wrldwd FA+ A	PWWAX	C-	(800) 426-0107	D / 1.7	1.99	9.42	15.64 /33	0.12 /14	--	0.00	1.43
GL	PIMCO RAE Wrldwd FA+ C	PWWCX	C-	(800) 426-0107	D- / 1.2	1.80	8.96	14.81 /29	-0.62 /11	--	0.00	2.18
GL	PIMCO RAE Wrldwd FA+ Inst	PWWIX	C	(800) 426-0107	D+ / 2.4	2.07	9.58	16.17 /35	0.53 /16	--	0.00	1.03
GL	PIMCO RAE Wrldwd FA+ P	PWWPX	C-	(800) 426-0107	D+ / 2.3	1.97	9.48	16.08 /35	0.45 /16	--	0.00	1.13
RE	PIMCO RealEstate RlRetrn Str A	PETAX	C	(800) 426-0107	B / 7.9	8.78	-0.66	19.19 /48	12.44 /98	10.78 /64	0.51	1.34
RE	PIMCO RealEstate RlRetrn Str C	PETCX	C	(800) 426-0107	B / 8.2	8.41	-1.10	18.10 /43	11.60 /98	9.94 /58	0.29	2.09
RE	PIMCO RealEstate RlRetrn Str D	PETDX	C+	(800) 426-0107	B+ / 8.9	8.73	-0.65	19.07 /47	12.48 /98	10.75 /64	0.54	1.34
RE	PIMCO RealEstate RlRetrn Str Inst	PRRSX	B-	(800) 426-0107	A- / 9.1	8.73	-0.51	19.58 /50	12.93 /99	11.20 /68	0.64	0.94
RE	PIMCO RealEstate RlRetrn Str P	PETPX	B-	(800) 426-0107	A- / 9.0	8.76	-0.54	19.45 /49	12.84 /99	11.12 /67	0.62	1.04
AA	PIMCO RealPath 2020 A	PTYAX	D+	(800) 426-0107	D / 2.0	4.50	2.70	14.12 /26	2.80 /30	3.25 /12	1.87	1.62
AA	PIMCO RealPath 2020 Admin	PFNAX	C-	(800) 426-0107	C- / 3.1	4.70	2.85	14.52 /28	3.06 /32	3.51 /13	2.10	1.42
AA	PIMCO RealPath 2020 Inst	PRWIX	C-	(800) 426-0107	C- / 3.2	4.63	2.95	14.74 /29	3.31 /35	3.77 /14	2.41	1.17
AA	PIMCO RealPath 2025 A	PENZX	C-	(800) 426-0107	D+ / 2.3	4.97	3.20	16.04 /34	2.96 /31	3.70 /14	3.00	1.66
AA	PIMCO RealPath 2025 Admin	PENMX	C	(800) 426-0107	C- / 3.4	5.05	3.32	16.31 /36	3.21 /34	3.94 /15	3.38	1.46
AA	PIMCO RealPath 2025 Inst	PENTX	C	(800) 426-0107	C- / 3.7	5.13	3.49	16.60 /37	3.51 /37	4.21 /16	3.63	1.21
AA	PIMCO RealPath 2030 A	PEHAX	D+	(800) 426-0107	C- / 3.0	5.82	4.50	18.76 /46	3.35 /35	4.40 /18	3.44	1.69
AA	PIMCO RealPath 2030 Admin	PNLAX	C-	(800) 426-0107	C / 4.3	5.85	4.59	19.05 /47	3.62 /38	4.65 /19	3.82	1.49
AA	PIMCO RealPath 2030 Inst	PRLIX	C-	(800) 426-0107	C / 4.4	5.80	4.63	19.39 /49	3.84 /41	4.92 /21	4.08	1.24
AA	PIMCO RealPath 2035 A	PIVAX	C-	(800) 426-0107	C- / 3.4	6.24	5.25	20.48 /55	3.43 /36	4.82 /20	1.17	1.72
AA	PIMCO RealPath 2035 Admin	PIVNX	C	(800) 426-0107	C / 4.7	6.29	5.38	20.70 /56	3.71 /39	5.07 /22	1.35	1.52
AA	PIMCO RealPath 2040 A	POFAX	D+	(800) 426-0107	C- / 3.4	6.55	5.62	21.01 /57	3.31 /35	4.99 /21	3.25	1.71
AA	PIMCO RealPath 2040 Admin	PEOAX	C-	(800) 426-0107	C / 4.7	6.58	5.68	21.29 /59	3.56 /38	5.23 /23	3.59	1.51
AA	PIMCO RealPath 2040 Inst	PROIX	C-	(800) 426-0107	C / 4.9	6.52	5.74	21.45 /60	3.79 /40	5.49 /25	3.87	1.26
GI	PIMCO RealPath 2045 A	PFZAX	C-	(800) 426-0107	C- / 3.4	6.68	5.83	21.49 /60	3.08 /33	5.22 /23	1.84	1.72
GI	PIMCO RealPath 2045 Admin	PFZMX	C	(800) 426-0107	C / 4.8	6.78	5.93	21.93 /62	3.34 /35	5.48 /25	2.09	1.52
GI	PIMCO RealPath 2045 Inst	PFZIX	C+	(800) 426-0107	C / 4.9	6.80	6.06	22.12 /63	3.57 /38	5.74 /27	1.89	1.27
AA	PIMCO RealPath 2050 A	PFYAX	C-	(800) 426-0107	C- / 3.7	6.82	6.02	21.93 /62	3.44 /36	5.20 /23	3.38	1.71
AA	PIMCO RealPath 2050 Admin	POTAX	C	(800) 426-0107	C / 5.0	6.86	6.12	22.03 /62	3.65 /39	5.45 /24	3.60	1.51
AA	PIMCO RealPath 2050 Inst	PRMIX	C	(800) 426-0107	C / 5.2	6.91	6.12	22.33 /64	3.91 /42	5.71 /26	3.90	1.26
AA	PIMCO RealPath Income A	PTNAX	D+	(800) 426-0107	D / 2.1	4.34	2.90	13.44 /23	3.01 /32	3.35 /12	3.15	1.58
AA	PIMCO RealPath Income Admn	PRNAX	C-	(800) 426-0107	C- / 3.1	4.39	3.00	13.79 /25	3.24 /34	3.59 /13	3.53	1.38
AA	PIMCO RealPath Income Inst	PRIEX	C-	(800) 426-0107	C- / 3.3	4.47	3.17	14.08 /26	3.54 /38	3.86 /15	3.78	1.13
FO	PIMCO StkPlus Intl (DH) P	PIUHX	B-	(800) 426-0107	B / 8.2	9.13	13.87	27.17 /80	6.40 /68	11.33 /68	0.92	0.86
FO	PIMCO StkPlus Intl Unhdg A	PPUAX	E+	(800) 426-0107	D- / 1.3	9.59	7.41	21.97 /62	-0.84 /10	6.14 /29	0.00	1.06
FO	PIMCO StkPlus Intl Unhdg Admin	PSKAX	E+	(800) 426-0107	D- / 1.3	9.77	4.85	18.94 /47	-1.56 / 8	5.90 /28	0.00	0.91
FO	PIMCO StkPlus Intl Unhdg C	PPUCX	E+	(800) 426-0107	D- / 1.4	9.40	7.14	21.02 /57	-1.60 / 8	5.37 /24	0.00	1.81
FO	PIMCO StkPlus Intl Unhdg D	PPUDX	E+	(800) 426-0107	D / 1.7	9.72	7.75	22.04 /62	-0.79 /10	6.20 /30	0.00	1.06
FO	PIMCO StkPlus Intl Unhdg Inst	PSKIX	E+	(800) 426-0107	D / 1.9	9.71	7.77	22.49 /64	-0.44 /12	6.61 /32	0.00	0.66
FO	PIMCO StkPlus Intl Unhdg P	PPLPX	E+	(800) 426-0107	D / 1.9	9.68	7.94	22.65 /65	-0.49 /11	6.51 /32	0.00	0.76
GI	PIMCO StockPlus Long Duration Fd I	PSLDX	B	(800) 426-0107	A+ / 9.9	11.76	3.39	33.07 /92	16.59 /99	18.46 /99	3.90	0.63
IX	PIMCO StocksPLUS A	PSPAX	B-	(800) 426-0107	B+ / 8.8	8.24	10.29	26.67 /78	9.93 /93	14.33 /95	0.71	0.96
IX	PIMCO StocksPLUS Absolute Return	PTOAX	B	(800) 426-0107	A+ / 9.6	9.79	12.66	31.96 /90	10.24 /95	14.72 /96	0.01	1.05
IX	PIMCO StocksPLUS Absolute Return	PSOCX	B	(800) 426-0107	A+ / 9.6	9.66	12.25	30.93 /88	9.39 /90	13.86 /92	0.00	1.80
IX	PIMCO StocksPLUS Absolute Return	PSTDX	B	(800) 426-0107	A+ / 9.7	9.93	12.73	32.05 /90	10.24 /95	14.70 /96	0.00	1.05
IX	PIMCO StocksPLUS Absolute Return	PSPTX	B	(800) 426-0107	A+ / 9.8	10.01	12.96	32.50 /91	10.67 /96	15.18 /97	0.15	0.65
IX	PIMCO StocksPLUS Absolute Return	PTOPX	B	(800) 426-0107	A+ / 9.7	9.90	12.88	32.45 /91	10.55 /96	15.07 /97	0.15	0.75

● Denotes fund is closed to new investors

* Denotes fund is included in Section II

Risk Rating/Pts	3 Year Standard Deviation	Beta	NAV As of 2/28/17	Total $(Mil)	Cash %	Stocks %	Bonds %	Other %	Portfolio Turnover Ratio	Last Bull Market Return	Last Bear Market Return	Manager Quality Pct	Manager Tenure (Years)	Initial Purch. $	Additional Purch. $	Front End Load	Back End Load
C- / 3.3	17.6	1.04	9.13	1	7	0	92	1	528	N/A	N/A	54	3	1,000	50	0.0	0.0
C- / 3.4	17.6	1.04	9.29	3,181	7	0	92	1	528	N/A	N/A	69	3	1,000,000	0	0.0	0.0
C- / 3.4	17.6	1.04	9.28	N/A	7	0	92	1	528	N/A	N/A	68	3	1,000,000	0	0.0	0.0
B / 8.1	10.0	0.86	12.55	206	4	0	95	1	551	N/A	N/A	85	3	1,000,000	0	0.0	0.0
B / 8.1	10.0	0.86	12.53	1	4	0	95	1	551	N/A	N/A	85	3	1,000,000	0	0.0	0.0
U /	N/A	N/A	9.98	1,428	20	0	79	1	529	N/A	N/A	N/A	3	1,000,000	0	0.0	0.0
B / 8.1	5.8	0.29	9.76	N/A	0	0	99	1	530	N/A	N/A	75	3	1,000	50	3.8	0.0
B / 8.1	5.9	0.29	9.61	N/A	0	0	99	1	530	N/A	N/A	66	3	1,000	50	0.0	0.0
B / 8.1	5.9	0.29	9.84	330	0	0	99	1	530	N/A	N/A	78	3	1,000,000	0	0.0	0.0
B / 8.1	5.8	0.29	9.82	1	0	0	99	1	530	N/A	N/A	77	3	1,000,000	0	0.0	0.0
C- / 3.1	17.6	1.26	7.68	224	0	10	89	1	100	112.6	-10.3	55	10	1,000	50	5.5	0.0
D+ / 2.6	17.6	1.26	6.70	93	0	10	89	1	100	103.9	-10.6	44	10	1,000	50	0.0	0.0
C- / 3.2	17.5	1.26	7.72	166	0	10	89	1	100	112.6	-10.3	56	10	1,000	50	0.0	0.0
C- / 3.5	17.6	1.26	8.47	802	0	10	89	1	100	117.1	-10.2	61	10	1,000,000	0	0.0	0.0
C- / 3.5	17.6	1.26	8.32	75	0	10	89	1	100	116.0	-10.1	60	10	1,000,000	0	0.0	0.0
C+ / 6.3	6.4	0.92	8.05	8	0	7	92	1	75	25.5	-4.8	25	N/A	1,000	50	5.5	0.0
C+ / 6.4	6.4	0.91	8.27	15	0	7	92	1	75	27.1	-4.7	27	N/A	1,000,000	0	0.0	0.0
C+ / 6.3	6.5	0.92	8.08	16	0	7	92	1	75	28.7	-4.6	30	N/A	1,000,000	0	0.0	0.0
B- / 7.1	7.4	1.06	9.76	2	13	10	75	2	88	30.6	N/A	17	N/A	1,000	50	5.5	0.0
B- / 7.1	7.4	1.07	9.74	22	13	10	75	2	88	32.1	N/A	19	N/A	1,000,000	0	0.0	0.0
B- / 7.1	7.4	1.07	9.75	14	13	10	75	2	88	34.1	N/A	21	N/A	1,000,000	0	0.0	0.0
C+ / 5.7	8.4	1.22	7.71	4	3	10	85	2	98	33.8	-7.7	12	N/A	1,000	50	5.5	0.0
C+ / 5.7	8.4	1.22	7.76	21	3	10	85	2	98	35.7	-7.7	13	N/A	1,000,000	0	0.0	0.0
C+ / 5.7	8.4	1.23	7.75	22	3	10	85	2	98	37.5	-7.6	14	N/A	1,000,000	0	0.0	0.0
C+ / 6.6	9.3	1.37	10.06	2	14	16	69	1	115	39.7	N/A	7	N/A	1,000	50	5.5	0.0
C+ / 6.6	9.3	1.38	10.09	15	14	16	69	1	115	41.5	N/A	8	N/A	1,000,000	0	0.0	0.0
C / 5.4	9.7	1.43	7.58	4	8	13	78	1	117	40.5	-10.6	5	N/A	1,000	50	5.5	0.0
C / 5.4	9.7	1.43	7.62	11	8	13	78	1	117	42.2	-10.6	6	N/A	1,000,000	0	0.0	0.0
C / 5.4	9.7	1.43	7.62	33	8	13	78	1	117	44.0	-10.4	6	N/A	1,000,000	0	0.0	0.0
C+ / 6.5	10.1	0.88	10.50	1	17	19	62	2	125	N/A	N/A	9	N/A	1,000	50	5.5	0.0
C+ / 6.5	10.1	0.88	10.51	9	17	19	62	2	125	N/A	N/A	11	N/A	1,000,000	0	0.0	0.0
C+ / 6.5	10.1	0.88	10.56	38	17	19	62	2	125	N/A	N/A	12	N/A	1,000,000	0	0.0	0.0
C+ / 5.8	10.2	1.52	7.85	1	11	14	74	1	140	42.4	-12.0	4	N/A	1,000	50	5.5	0.0
C+ / 5.7	10.2	1.52	7.89	11	11	14	74	1	140	44.0	-11.9	5	N/A	1,000,000	0	0.0	0.0
C+ / 5.7	10.2	1.52	7.92	50	11	14	74	1	140	46.1	-11.8	5	N/A	1,000,000	0	0.0	0.0
C+ / 6.4	5.7	0.79	8.42	8	0	6	93	1	74	24.2	-2.0	37	N/A	1,000	50	5.5	0.0
C+ / 6.4	5.8	0.80	8.43	16	0	6	93	1	74	25.8	-1.8	39	N/A	1,000,000	0	0.0	0.0
C+ / 6.4	5.7	0.80	8.44	14	0	6	93	1	74	27.6	-1.7	44	N/A	1,000,000	0	0.0	0.0
C / 4.4	13.8	0.99	7.89	344	2	0	97	1	499	101.3	-19.5	97	2	1,000,000	0	0.0	0.0
C- / 4.1	14.4	1.17	5.94	17	16	0	83	1	566	61.7	-24.7	67	3	1,000	50	3.8	0.0
C- / 4.1	14.6	1.18	5.84	2	16	0	83	1	566	59.8	-24.5	58	3	1,000,000	0	0.0	0.0
C- / 4.1	14.4	1.17	5.70	8	16	0	83	1	566	55.2	-24.7	57	3	1,000	50	0.0	0.0
C- / 4.2	14.4	1.16	5.98	21	16	0	83	1	566	61.9	-24.5	68	3	1,000	50	0.0	0.0
C- / 4.1	14.4	1.17	6.10	1,311	16	0	83	1	566	65.5	-24.5	72	3	1,000,000	0	0.0	0.0
C- / 4.1	14.5	1.17	6.12	32	16	0	83	1	566	64.8	-24.5	71	3	1,000,000	0	0.0	0.0
C- / 3.4	14.0	1.09	7.35	598	0	0	100	0	52	195.5	-5.9	94	10	1,000,000	0	0.0	0.0
C- / 3.9	10.9	1.05	9.36	194	0	0	100	0	525	142.9	-18.8	60	3	1,000	50	3.8	0.0
C- / 3.8	12.5	1.20	10.78	281	28	0	70	2	582	153.2	-19.0	44	3	1,000	50	3.8	0.0
C- / 3.5	12.5	1.20	9.99	177	28	0	70	2	582	143.2	-19.3	33	3	1,000	50	0.0	0.0
C- / 3.7	12.6	1.20	10.63	196	28	0	70	2	582	153.1	-19.1	43	3	1,000	50	0.0	0.0
C- / 3.8	12.5	1.20	10.94	537	28	0	70	2	582	158.9	-18.9	50	3	1,000,000	0	0.0	0.0
C- / 3.8	12.6	1.20	10.83	116	28	0	70	2	582	157.2	-18.9	47	3	1,000,000	0	0.0	0.0

Fund Type	Fund Name	Ticker Symbol	Overall Investment Rating	Phone	Perfor-mance Rating/Pts	3 Mo	6 Mo	1Yr / Pct	3Yr / Pct	5Yr / Pct	Dividend Yield	Expense Ratio
IX	PIMCO StocksPLUS Admin	PPLAX	B	(800) 426-0107	A / 9.4	8.18	10.36	26.79 /79	10.11 /94	14.57 /96	0.89	0.81
IX	PIMCO StocksPLUS C	PSPCX	B-	(800) 426-0107	A- / 9.0	8.03	9.95	26.06 /76	9.39 /90	13.76 /91	0.38	1.46
IX	PIMCO StocksPLUS D	PSPDX	B	(800) 426-0107	A / 9.3	8.31	10.38	26.71 /78	9.97 /93	14.36 /95	0.76	0.96
IX	PIMCO StocksPLUS Inst	PSTKX	B+	(800) 426-0107	A / 9.5	8.33	10.50	27.28 /80	10.40 /95	14.81 /96	0.97	0.56
IX	PIMCO StocksPLUS P	PSKPX	B+	(800) 426-0107	A / 9.5	8.31	10.49	27.14 /80	10.28 /95	14.67 /96	0.92	0.66
IX	PIMCO StocksPLUS R	PSPRX	B	(800) 426-0107	A- / 9.2	8.16	10.15	26.43 /78	9.68 /91	14.07 /94	0.50	1.21
IN	PIMCO StocksPLUS Small A	PCKAX	B-	(800) 426-0107	A+ / 9.6	7.18	16.18	45.14 /98	7.49 /75	14.63 /96	2.96	1.13
IN	PIMCO StocksPLUS Small C	PCKCX	B-	(800) 426-0107	A+ / 9.6	7.05	15.78	43.96 /98	6.66 /70	13.79 /92	2.78	1.88
IN	PIMCO StocksPLUS Small D	PCKDX	B-	(800) 426-0107	A+ / 9.7	7.22	16.29	45.11 /98	7.49 /75	14.63 /96	3.09	1.13
IN	PIMCO StocksPLUS Small I	PSCSX	B-	(800) 426-0107	A+ / 9.8	7.33	16.42	45.78 /99	7.90 /78	15.08 /97	3.29	0.73
IN	PIMCO StocksPLUS Small P	PCKPX	B-	(800) 426-0107	A+ / 9.8	7.31	16.34	45.51 /99	7.80 /77	14.99 /97	3.25	0.83
IN	PIMCO TRENDS Mgd Fut Str A	PQTAX	C-	(800) 426-0107	E+ / 0.6	0.43	-3.30	-6.95 / 0	2.99 /32	--	0.00	1.86
IN	PIMCO TRENDS Mgd Fut Str C	PQTCX	C-	(800) 426-0107	E+ / 0.8	0.33	-3.55	-7.61 / 0	2.20 /25	--	0.00	2.61
IN	PIMCO TRENDS Mgd Fut Str D	PQTDX	C-	(800) 426-0107	D- / 1.0	0.43	-3.31	-6.97 / 0	2.98 /32	--	0.00	1.86
IN	PIMCO TRENDS Mgd Fut Str Inst	PQTIX	C-	(800) 426-0107	D- / 1.1	0.53	-2.98	-6.53 / 0	3.41 /36	--	0.00	1.46
IN	PIMCO TRENDS Mgd Fut Str P	PQTPX	C-	(800) 426-0107	D- / 1.1	0.53	-3.08	-6.82 / 0	3.22 /34	--	0.00	1.56
GL	PineBridge Dyn Asset Alloc Inst	PDAIX	U	(800) 426-9157	U /	5.96	4.44	--	--	--	0.00	N/A
GL	Pinnacle Sherman Multi-Strat Core A	APSHX	U	(877) 369-3705	U /	4.25	5.52	11.86 /17	--	--	0.20	2.09
GL	Pinnacle Sherman Multi-Strat Core I	IPSHX	U	(877) 369-3705	U /	4.36	5.63	12.17 /19	--	--	0.33	1.84
GL	Pinnacle Sherman Tactical Alloc A	PTAFX	D+	(888) 985-9830	E / 0.4	3.46	1.64	5.99 / 5	-0.90 /10	--	0.06	3.26
GL	Pinnacle Sherman Tactical Alloc C	PTCFX	D+	(888) 985-9830	E / 0.5	3.26	1.21	5.30 / 4	-1.66 / 7	--	0.01	4.01
GL	Pinnacle Sherman Tactical Alloc I	PTIFX	D+	(888) 985-9830	E+ / 0.7	3.53	1.81	6.37 / 5	-0.67 /11	--	0.15	3.01
GR	Pinnacle Value Fund	PVFIX	C	(877) 369-3705	C / 4.6	3.93	4.63	21.45 /60	4.44 /48	8.55 /47	0.00	1.67
BA	Pioneer Classic Balanced Fund A	AOBLX	C	(800) 225-6292	C- / 4.0	5.65	5.56	14.35 /27	5.55 /60	8.32 /45	1.86	1.30
BA	Pioneer Classic Balanced Fund C	PCBCX	C	(800) 225-6292	C- / 4.2	5.50	5.18	13.35 /23	4.72 /51	7.45 /38	1.25	2.01
BA	Pioneer Classic Balanced Fund K	PCBKX	B-	(800) 225-6292	C / 5.0	5.72	5.64	14.43 /27	5.61 /61	8.35 /45	2.02	1.06
BA	Pioneer Classic Balanced Fund R	CBPRX	C+	(800) 225-6292	C / 4.7	5.60	5.41	14.06 /26	5.31 /58	8.06 /43	1.80	1.61
BA	Pioneer Classic Balanced Fund Y	AYBLX	C+	(800) 225-6292	C / 5.1	5.75	5.67	14.54 /28	5.79 /62	8.59 /47	2.06	1.03
GR	Pioneer Core Equity A	PIOTX	B+	(800) 225-6292	B- / 7.0	8.58	12.03	23.75 /69	7.34 /74	11.35 /69	1.00	0.93
GR	Pioneer Core Equity C	PCOTX	B+	(800) 225-6292	B- / 7.4	8.34	11.62	22.71 /65	6.45 /68	10.42 /61	0.50	1.74
GR	Pioneer Core Equity Y	PVFYX	A	(800) 225-6292	B / 8.2	8.61	12.15	24.05 /70	7.64 /76	11.67 /71	1.31	0.62
GR	Pioneer Disciplined Growth A	PINDX	C+	(800) 225-6292	C+ / 5.9	7.09	6.80	16.50 /36	8.13 /80	12.08 /75	0.22	1.13
GR	Pioneer Disciplined Growth C	INDCX	C+	(800) 225-6292	C+ / 6.3	6.89	6.37	15.49 /32	7.21 /73	11.12 /67	0.00	1.98
GR	Pioneer Disciplined Growth Y	INYDX	B	(800) 225-6292	B- / 7.1	7.09	6.86	16.73 /37	8.45 /83	12.44 /78	0.45	0.86
GR	Pioneer Disciplined Value A	CVFCX	C	(800) 225-6292	B / 8.2	9.00	14.54	29.31 /85	7.80 /77	11.04 /66	0.84	1.18
GR	Pioneer Disciplined Value C	CVCFX	C+	(800) 225-6292	B+ / 8.6	8.83	14.15	28.47 /83	7.03 /72	10.22 /60	0.17	1.90
GR	Pioneer Disciplined Value R	CVRFX	C+	(800) 225-6292	A- / 9.0	8.95	14.41	29.13 /84	7.56 /76	10.80 /64	0.76	1.58
GR	Pioneer Disciplined Value Y	CVFYX	C+	(800) 225-6292	A / 9.3	9.08	14.66	29.75 /86	8.16 /80	11.43 /69	1.25	0.84
EM	Pioneer Emerging Markets A	PEMFX	E-	(800) 225-6292	E+ / 0.7	8.74	8.47	27.31 /80	-3.67 / 3	-4.08 / 2	0.00	2.18
EM	Pioneer Emerging Markets C	PCEFX	E-	(800) 225-6292	E+ / 0.8	8.42	8.02	26.16 /77	-4.52 / 3	-4.90 / 2	0.00	2.95
EM	Pioneer Emerging Markets R	PEMRX	E-	(800) 225-6292	D- / 1.0	8.64	8.36	27.07 /79	-3.91 / 3	-4.28 / 2	0.00	2.33
EM	Pioneer Emerging Markets Y	PYEFX	E-	(800) 225-6292	D- / 1.2	8.68	8.50	27.48 /80	-3.39 / 4	-3.69 / 2	0.00	1.55
IN	Pioneer Equity Income A	PEQIX	A-	(800) 225-6292	A- / 9.0	6.77	10.62	27.63 /81	11.15 /97	13.41 /88	1.54	1.06
IN	Pioneer Equity Income C	PCEQX	A	(800) 225-6292	A / 9.3	6.57	10.22	26.72 /78	10.35 /95	12.60 /80	0.98	1.80
IN	Pioneer Equity Income K	PEQKX	A	(800) 225-6292	A+ / 9.7	6.87	10.85	28.09 /82	11.59 /98	13.79 /92	1.90	0.67
IN	Pioneer Equity Income R	PQIRX	A	(800) 225-6292	A / 9.5	6.67	10.43	27.17 /80	10.74 /96	13.04 /84	1.24	1.41
IN	Pioneer Equity Income Y	PYEQX	A	(800) 225-6292	A+ / 9.6	6.84	10.79	27.95 /82	11.46 /98	13.77 /91	1.81	0.78
GI	Pioneer Flexible Opportunities A	PMARX	D-	(800) 225-6292	D- / 1.2	2.89	-0.05	10.96 /14	1.11 /19	4.78 /20	1.20	1.29
GI	Pioneer Flexible Opportunities C	PRRCX	D-	(800) 225-6292	D- / 1.3	2.57	-0.49	10.02 /12	0.31 /15	3.97 /15	0.74	2.04
GL	Pioneer Flexible Opportunities R	MUARX	D	(800) 225-6292	D- / 1.3	2.70	-0.32	10.30 /12	0.50 /16	4.29 /17	0.98	2.04
GI	Pioneer Flexible Opportunities Y	PMYRX	D	(800) 225-6292	D / 1.7	2.97	0.12	11.26 /15	1.42 /21	5.07 /22	1.47	1.05
GI	Pioneer Fund A	PIODX	C	(800) 225-6292	B- / 7.2	9.00	10.26	22.77 /66	8.27 /81	11.79 /72	0.89	0.98

Risk Rating/Pts	Standard Deviation	Beta	NAV As of 2/28/17	Total $(Mil)	Cash %	Stocks %	Bonds %	Other %	Portfolio Turnover Ratio	Last Bull Market Return	Last Bear Market Return	Manager Quality Pct	Manager Tenure (Years)	Initial Purch. $	Additional Purch. $	Front End Load	Back End Load
C- /4.0	10.8	1.05	9.44	13	0	0	100	0	525	145.5	-18.7	63	3	1,000,000	0	0.0	0.0
C- /3.7	10.9	1.05	8.90	150	0	0	100	0	525	136.2	-18.9	53	3	1,000	50	0.0	0.0
C- /3.9	10.9	1.05	9.31	33	0	0	100	0	525	142.9	-18.7	61	3	1,000	50	0.0	0.0
C- /4.2	10.9	1.05	10.06	383	0	0	100	0	525	148.1	-18.6	66	3	1,000,000	0	0.0	0.0
C- /4.2	10.9	1.05	10.03	30	0	0	100	0	525	146.9	-18.9	64	3	1,000,000	0	0.0	0.0
C- /4.1	10.9	1.05	9.63	16	0	0	100	0	525	140.0	-18.9	57	3	0	0	0.0	0.0
C- /3.1	17.4	1.38	9.65	265	0	0	100	0	539	160.4	-28.1	6	3	1,000	50	3.8	0.0
D+ /2.9	17.4	1.39	8.97	124	0	0	100	0	539	149.8	-28.2	5	3	1,000	50	0.0	0.0
C- /3.1	17.4	1.39	9.59	186	0	0	100	0	539	160.2	-27.9	6	3	1,000	50	0.0	0.0
C- /3.2	17.4	1.38	9.84	267	0	0	100	0	539	165.7	-27.8	7	3	1,000,000	0	0.0	0.0
C- /3.2	17.4	1.39	9.77	109	0	0	100	0	539	164.5	-28.0	7	3	1,000,000	0	0.0	0.0
B /8.7	8.3	-0.18	9.37	6	21	0	78	1	49	N/A	N/A	95	2	1,000	50	5.5	0.0
B /8.7	8.4	-0.18	9.23	3	21	0	78	1	49	N/A	N/A	93	2	1,000	50	0.0	0.0
B /8.7	8.4	-0.18	9.35	78	21	0	78	1	49	N/A	N/A	95	2	1,000	50	0.0	0.0
B /8.7	8.4	-0.18	9.44	226	21	0	78	1	49	N/A	N/A	96	2	1,000,000	0	0.0	0.0
B /8.7	8.4	-0.19	9.43	1	21	0	78	1	49	N/A	N/A	95	2	1,000,000	0	0.0	0.0
U /	N/A	N/A	10.65	137	0	0	0	100	90	N/A	N/A	N/A	N/A	1,000,000	0	0.0	0.0
U /	N/A	N/A	11.12	58	0	0	0	100	449	N/A	N/A	N/A	2	2,000	500	5.8	1.0
U /	N/A	N/A	11.16	37	0	0	0	100	449	N/A	N/A	N/A	2	1,000,000	5,000	0.0	1.0
B /8.5	6.1	0.63	10.38	19	29	49	20	2	611	N/A	N/A	26	4	2,000	500	5.8	1.0
B /8.4	6.1	0.63	10.15	5	29	49	20	2	611	N/A	N/A	18	4	2,000	500	0.0	1.0
B /8.5	6.1	0.63	10.43	10	29	49	20	2	611	N/A	N/A	28	4	1,000,000	5,000	0.0	1.0
C+ /6.1	8.8	0.50	16.11	68	48	51	0	1	29	61.8	-7.7	65	14	2,500	100	0.0	1.0
B- /7.2	6.7	1.06	9.42	180	1	62	36	1	47	71.5	-12.1	44	12	1,000	100	4.5	0.0
B- /7.2	6.7	1.06	9.34	48	1	62	36	1	47	64.2	-12.4	34	12	1,000	500	0.0	0.0
B- /7.6	6.7	1.06	9.42	N/A	1	62	36	1	47	71.8	-12.1	45	12	5,000,000	0	0.0	0.0
B- /7.5	6.7	1.06	9.40	28	1	62	36	1	47	69.2	-12.1	41	12	0	0	0.0	0.0
B- /7.2	6.7	1.06	9.48	35	1	62	36	1	47	73.9	-11.9	48	12	5,000,000	0	0.0	0.0
B- /7.0	11.0	1.04	19.19	1,507	1	98	0	1	100	109.6	-16.3	29	16	1,000	100	5.8	0.0
B- /7.1	11.0	1.05	17.20	14	1	98	0	1	100	100.2	-16.7	21	16	1,000	500	0.0	0.0
B- /7.0	11.0	1.04	19.37	48	1	98	0	1	100	112.9	-16.3	32	16	5,000,000	0	0.0	0.0
C+ /6.3	11.2	1.05	17.24	1,034	0	99	0	1	118	120.4	-17.6	37	7	1,000	100	5.8	0.0
C+ /6.2	11.2	1.05	15.67	21	0	99	0	1	118	110.4	-17.9	27	7	1,000	500	0.0	0.0
C+ /6.3	11.2	1.05	17.56	45	0	99	0	1	118	124.2	-17.5	41	7	5,000,000	0	0.0	0.0
D+ /2.9	11.2	1.05	16.09	321	0	99	0	1	129	106.4	-18.5	34	6	1,000	100	5.8	0.0
D+ /2.8	11.2	1.05	15.85	119	0	99	0	1	129	97.9	-18.9	26	6	1,000	500	0.0	0.0
D+ /2.7	11.3	1.05	15.63	13	0	99	0	1	129	103.9	-18.6	31	6	0	0	0.0	0.0
D+ /2.9	11.2	1.05	16.15	148	0	99	0	1	129	110.3	-18.5	38	6	5,000,000	0	0.0	0.0
D+ /2.4	17.2	0.90	17.67	68	0	99	0	1	85	-7.3	-27.6	13	4	1,000	100	5.8	0.0
D+ /2.4	17.2	0.90	14.42	12	0	99	0	1	85	-11.5	-27.9	8	4	1,000	500	0.0	0.0
D+ /2.4	17.2	0.90	16.85	21	0	99	0	1	85	-8.5	-27.7	11	4	0	0	0.0	0.0
D+ /2.5	17.2	0.90	19.53	4	0	99	0	1	85	-5.1	-27.5	15	4	5,000,000	0	0.0	0.0
C+ /5.9	10.2	0.92	34.03	882	1	98	0	1	35	121.7	-14.4	83	27	1,000	100	5.8	0.0
C+ /5.8	10.2	0.92	33.42	161	1	98	0	1	35	113.1	-14.7	78	27	1,000	500	0.0	0.0
C+ /5.9	10.2	0.92	34.11	59	1	98	0	1	35	125.4	-14.4	84	27	5,000,000	0	0.0	0.0
C+ /5.9	10.2	0.92	34.56	99	1	98	0	1	35	117.8	-14.6	80	27	0	0	0.0	0.0
C+ /5.9	10.2	0.92	34.43	866	1	98	0	1	35	125.5	-14.3	84	27	5,000,000	0	0.0	0.0
C+ /6.0	9.2	0.63	12.16	141	7	73	18	2	230	39.7	-5.7	13	7	1,000	100	4.5	0.0
C+ /6.0	9.2	0.63	11.99	160	7	73	18	2	230	34.0	-6.0	8	7	1,000	500	0.0	0.0
C+ /6.0	9.2	1.21	12.11	N/A	7	73	18	2	230	36.4	-5.8	15	7	0	0	0.0	0.0
C+ /6.0	9.2	0.64	12.21	323	7	73	18	2	230	41.9	-5.6	14	7	5,000,000	0	0.0	0.0
C- /3.8	10.3	0.98	30.74	4,635	1	98	0	1	50	109.5	-20.2	49	31	1,000	100	5.8	0.0

99 Pct = Best
0 Pct = Worst

Fund Type	Fund Name	Ticker Symbol	Overall Investment Rating	Phone	Performance Rating/Pts	3 Mo	6 Mo	1Yr / Pct	3Yr / Pct	5Yr / Pct	Dividend Yield	Expense Ratio
GI	Pioneer Fund C	PCODX	C	(800) 225-6292	B / 7.7	8.78	9.85	21.84 /61	7.43 /75	10.93 /65	0.35	1.76
GI	Pioneer Fund R	PIORX	C+	(800) 225-6292	B / 8.0	8.84	10.01	22.26 /63	7.88 /78	11.39 /69	0.59	1.30
GI	Pioneer Fund Y	PYODX	C+	(800) 225-6292	B+ / 8.5	9.03	10.35	23.13 /67	8.58 /84	12.13 /75	1.14	0.68
GR	Pioneer Fundamental Growth A	PIGFX	B+	(800) 225-6292	B- / 7.0	8.27	6.74	15.58 /32	10.16 /94	13.11 /85	0.26	1.11
GR	Pioneer Fundamental Growth C	FUNCX	B+	(800) 225-6292	B- / 7.4	8.06	6.34	14.76 /29	9.38 /89	12.28 /77	0.00	1.77
GR	Pioneer Fundamental Growth K	PFGKX	A	(800) 225-6292	B+ / 8.3	8.39	6.96	16.00 /34	10.61 /96	13.50 /89	0.62	0.67
GR	Pioneer Fundamental Growth R	PFGRX	A-	(800) 225-6292	B / 7.7	8.20	6.59	15.17 /31	9.78 /92	12.77 /82	0.06	1.43
GR	Pioneer Fundamental Growth Y	FUNYX	A	(800) 225-6292	B / 8.2	8.40	6.93	15.96 /34	10.50 /96	13.44 /88	0.54	0.79
GL	Pioneer Global Equity A	GLOSX	C	(800) 225-6292	C- / 4.0	8.07	7.43	18.45 /45	4.32 /47	9.13 /52	1.12	1.45
GL	Pioneer Global Equity C	GCSLX	C	(800) 225-6292	C / 4.5	7.89	6.98	17.55 /41	3.52 /37	8.24 /44	0.45	2.16
GL	Pioneer Global Equity K	PGEKX	B-	(800) 225-6292	C+ / 5.6	8.22	7.65	18.96 /47	4.67 /50	9.35 /53	1.67	0.92
GL	Pioneer Global Equity R	PRGEX	C+	(800) 225-6292	C / 5.0	7.92	7.19	18.06 /43	4.08 /44	8.87 /50	1.08	1.68
GL	Pioneer Global Equity Y	PGSYX	C+	(800) 225-6292	C+ / 5.7	8.16	7.68	19.06 /47	4.81 /52	9.66 /56	1.78	1.08
FO	Pioneer International Equity A	PIIFX	D-	(800) 225-6292	E+ / 0.7	6.30	2.65	13.78 /24	-0.58 /11	3.63 /14	0.81	1.71
FO	Pioneer International Equity C	PCITX	D-	(800) 225-6292	E+ / 0.8	6.00	2.09	12.72 /21	-1.49 / 8	2.70 /10	0.10	2.42
FO	Pioneer International Equity Y	INVYX	D-	(800) 225-6292	D- / 1.3	6.37	2.74	14.16 /26	-0.21 /13	4.04 /15	1.22	1.04
MC	Pioneer Mid Cap Value A	PCGRX	B	(800) 225-6292	B+ / 8.5	8.91	13.93	30.65 /87	8.27 /81	11.99 /74	0.37	1.05
MC	Pioneer Mid Cap Value C	PCCGX	B-	(800) 225-6292	B+ / 8.8	8.70	13.47	29.63 /86	7.37 /75	11.06 /66	0.00	1.90
MC	Pioneer Mid Cap Value K	PMCKX	A+	(800) 225-6292	A / 9.5	9.02	14.12	31.16 /88	8.54 /83	12.16 /76	0.71	0.65
MC	Pioneer Mid Cap Value R	PCMRX	B+	(800) 225-6292	A- / 9.1	8.78	13.66	30.16 /87	7.83 /78	11.58 /71	0.05	1.44
MC	Pioneer Mid Cap Value Y	PYCGX	B+	(800) 225-6292	A / 9.4	8.96	14.04	30.99 /88	8.58 /84	12.36 /78	0.57	0.73
GL	Pioneer Multi-Asset Income Fund A	PMAIX	C	(800) 225-6292	C- / 4.2	7.67	7.73	20.91 /57	3.70 /39	7.50 /38	4.94	1.31
GL	Pioneer Multi-Asset Income Fund C	PMACX	C	(800) 225-6292	C / 4.4	7.47	7.30	19.86 /51	2.85 /30	6.61 /32	4.41	2.06
GL	Pioneer Multi-Asset Income Fund K	PMFKX	B-	(800) 225-6292	C+ / 5.8	7.74	8.18	22.07 /63	4.37 /47	7.92 /41	5.38	0.97
GL	Pioneer Multi-Asset Income Fund R	PMFRX	C+	(800) 225-6292	C / 4.9	7.61	7.55	20.25 /53	3.47 /37	7.25 /36	4.71	1.74
GL	Pioneer Multi-Asset Income Fund Y	PMFYX	C+	(800) 225-6292	C / 5.4	7.73	7.94	21.16 /58	3.97 /43	7.70 /40	5.36	1.09
RE	Pioneer Real Estate Shares A	PWREX	C-	(800) 225-6292	C+ / 6.0	7.39	-1.76	13.42 /23	10.49 /96	10.49 /62	2.74	1.41
RE	Pioneer Real Estate Shares C	PCREX	C	(800) 225-6292	C+ / 6.4	7.18	-2.15	12.48 /20	9.57 /91	9.56 /55	2.17	2.24
RE	Pioneer Real Estate Shares Y	PYREX	C+	(800) 225-6292	B- / 7.3	7.47	-1.64	13.78 /24	10.90 /97	10.95 /65	3.20	1.02
MC	Pioneer Sel Mid Cap Growth A	PGOFX	D+	(800) 225-6292	C / 4.6	6.26	6.06	21.85 /61	5.17 /56	11.12 /67	0.00	1.06
MC	Pioneer Sel Mid Cap Growth C	GOFCX	D+	(800) 225-6292	C / 5.1	6.04	5.66	20.91 /57	4.32 /47	10.17 /60	0.00	1.87
MC	Pioneer Sel Mid Cap Growth I	GROYX	C-	(800) 225-6292	C+ / 6.1	6.33	6.22	22.19 /63	5.47 /59	11.48 /70	0.00	0.77
MC	Pioneer Sel Mid Cap Growth K	PSMKX	C+	(800) 225-6292	C+ / 6.1	6.35	6.27	22.33 /64	5.47 /59	11.31 /68	0.00	0.67
MC	Pioneer Sel Mid Cap Growth R	PGRRX	C-	(800) 225-6292	C / 5.5	6.19	5.89	21.46 /60	4.77 /52	--	0.00	1.45
AA	Pioneer Solutions Balanced A	PIALX	D+	(800) 225-6292	D- / 1.4	4.38	2.45	10.21 /12	1.95 /24	5.17 /23	1.99	1.39
AA	Pioneer Solutions Balanced C	PIDCX	D+	(800) 225-6292	D / 1.7	4.07	2.08	9.41 /10	1.24 /20	4.43 /18	1.54	2.09
BA	Pioneer Solutions Balanced R	BALRX	D-	(800) 225-6292	D / 2.0	4.31	2.37	9.85 /11	1.73 /22	4.93 /21	2.03	2.30
AA	Pioneer Solutions Balanced Y	IMOYX	D+	(800) 225-6292	D / 2.2	4.33	2.52	10.38 /13	2.18 /25	5.43 /24	2.36	1.12
AA	Pioneer Solutions Conservative A	PIAVX	D	(800) 225-6292	D- / 1.0	2.74	0.57	6.81 / 6	1.85 /23	3.86 /15	2.16	1.47
AA	Pioneer Solutions Conservative C	PICVX	D	(800) 225-6292	D- / 1.3	2.60	0.25	6.15 / 5	1.12 /19	3.10 /11	1.54	2.20
AA	Pioneer Solutions Conservative R	PSMRX	C	(800) 225-6292	D- / 1.5	2.63	0.47	6.61 / 5	1.63 /22	3.62 /14	2.09	2.11
AA	Pioneer Solutions Conservative Y	IBBCX	D	(800) 225-6292	D- / 1.5	2.79	0.60	6.89 / 6	1.73 /22	3.43 /13	2.53	1.43
AA	Pioneer Solutions Growth A	GRAAX	D+	(800) 225-6292	D+ / 2.4	5.99	4.96	14.00 /25	3.01 /32	6.25 /30	1.16	1.40
AA	Pioneer Solutions Growth C	GRACX	C-	(800) 225-6292	D+ / 2.9	5.86	4.67	13.25 /23	2.30 /26	5.52 /25	0.59	2.10
GI	Pioneer Solutions Growth R	SOGRX	C	(800) 225-6292	C- / 3.2	5.97	4.94	13.73 /24	2.77 /30	6.00 /28	1.19	1.97
AA	Pioneer Solutions Growth Y	IBGYX	C-	(800) 225-6292	C- / 3.5	6.01	5.09	14.22 /27	3.25 /34	6.50 /32	1.50	1.12
BA	Plumb Balanced Fund	PLBBX	B-	(866) 987-7888	C+ / 6.6	8.09	7.47	17.94 /43	6.65 /69	7.71 /40	0.49	1.65
GR	Plumb Equity Fund	PLBEX	B+	(866) 987-7888	A / 9.4	12.05	12.00	25.96 /76	9.38 /89	10.15 /59	0.00	1.82
GL	PMC Diversified Equity	PMDEX	C	(866) 762-7338	C / 5.1	6.28	7.41	19.66 /50	4.12 /44	8.95 /50	0.57	1.49
BA	PNC Balanced Allocation A	PBAAX	C-	(800) 551-2145	D+ / 2.3	4.53	2.68	11.59 /16	3.75 /40	6.52 /32	1.14	1.98
BA	PNC Balanced Allocation C	PBCCX	C-	(800) 551-2145	D+ / 2.6	4.37	2.30	10.77 /14	3.03 /32	5.78 /27	0.57	2.69
BA	PNC Balanced Allocation I	PBLIX	C	(800) 551-2145	C- / 3.2	4.55	2.76	11.85 /17	4.02 /43	6.81 /34	1.46	1.69

● Denotes fund is closed to new investors
* Denotes fund is included in Section II

www.thestreetratings.com

RISK			NET ASSETS		ASSET					BULL / BEAR		FUND MANAGER		MINIMUMS		LOADS	
	3 Year		NAV						Portfolio	Last Bull	Last Bear	Manager	Manager	Initial	Additional	Front	Back
Risk	Standard		As of	Total	Cash	Stocks	Bonds	Other	Turnover	Market	Market	Quality	Tenure	Purch.	Purch.	End	End
Rating/Pts	Deviation	Beta	2/28/17	$(Mil)	%	%	%	%	Ratio	Return	Return	Pct	(Years)	$	$	Load	Load
C- / 3.3	10.3	0.98	27.53	113	1	98	0	1	50	100.8	-20.4	38	31	1,000	500	0.0	0.0
C- / 3.8	10.3	0.98	30.84	54	1	98	0	1	50	105.6	-20.3	44	31	0	0	0.0	0.0
C- / 3.9	10.3	0.98	31.07	117	1	98	0	1	50	113.0	-20.1	53	31	5,000,000	0	0.0	0.0
B- / 7.1	10.4	0.95	20.48	1,246	0	96	2	2	13	123.8	-11.3	75	10	1,000	100	5.8	0.0
B- / 7.0	10.4	0.95	18.90	464	0	96	2	2	13	115.1	-11.6	67	10	1,000	500	0.0	0.0
B- / 7.1	10.4	0.95	20.48	356	0	96	2	2	13	127.7	-11.3	78	10	5,000,000	0	0.0	0.0
B- / 7.1	10.4	0.95	20.20	117	0	96	2	2	13	120.3	-11.4	72	10	0	0	0.0	0.0
B- / 7.1	10.4	0.95	20.65	3,007	0	96	2	2	13	127.6	-11.1	77	10	5,000,000	0	0.0	0.0
C+ / 6.7	11.3	0.82	14.25	72	4	95	0	1	88	87.8	-21.3	94	7	1,000	100	5.8	0.0
C+ / 6.7	11.3	0.82	13.98	12	4	95	0	1	88	79.5	-21.6	92	7	1,000	500	0.0	0.0
B- / 7.2	11.3	0.82	14.25	54	4	95	0	1	88	89.7	-21.3	95	7	5,000,000	0	0.0	0.0
B- / 7.2	11.3	0.82	14.16	17	4	95	0	1	88	85.4	-21.4	94	7	0	0	0.0	0.0
C+ / 6.7	11.3	0.82	14.27	7	4	95	0	1	88	92.6	-21.1	95	7	5,000,000	0	0.0	0.0
C+ / 5.8	11.2	0.88	20.49	68	2	97	0	1	49	39.3	-22.1	69	9	1,000	100	5.8	0.0
C+ / 5.7	11.2	0.88	17.95	10	2	97	0	1	49	32.8	-22.4	57	9	1,000	500	0.0	0.0
C+ / 5.8	11.2	0.88	20.48	78	2	97	0	1	49	42.3	-21.9	73	9	5,000,000	0	0.0	0.0
C / 4.8	12.1	0.97	25.67	886	0	100	0	0	70	116.9	-22.9	62	4	1,000	100	5.8	0.0
C- / 4.0	12.1	0.97	18.49	59	0	100	0	0	70	107.2	-23.2	52	4	1,000	500	0.0	0.0
C+ / 6.6	12.1	0.97	25.67	29	0	100	0	0	70	118.5	-22.9	66	4	5,000,000	0	0.0	0.0
C / 4.7	12.2	0.97	25.17	17	0	100	0	0	70	112.5	-23.1	57	4	0	0	0.0	0.0
C / 4.9	12.1	0.97	27.46	40	0	100	0	0	70	120.8	-22.8	66	4	5,000,000	0	0.0	0.0
C+ / 6.3	7.2	1.02	11.14	220	2	49	48	1	109	N/A	N/A	62	6	1,000	100	4.5	0.0
C+ / 6.2	7.2	1.02	11.11	292	2	49	48	1	109	N/A	N/A	50	6	1,000	500	0.0	0.0
B- / 7.5	7.1	1.02	11.29	1	2	49	48	1	109	N/A	N/A	70	6	5,000,000	0	0.0	0.0
B- / 7.3	7.1	1.03	11.19	2	2	49	48	1	109	N/A	N/A	59	6	0	0	0.0	0.0
C+ / 6.2	7.2	1.02	11.13	226	2	49	48	1	109	N/A	N/A	65	6	5,000,000	0	0.0	0.0
C / 4.4	14.8	1.07	26.46	98	3	96	0	1	22	98.4	-15.7	58	13	1,000	100	5.8	0.0
C / 4.3	14.7	1.07	25.93	13	3	96	0	1	22	89.6	-16.0	47	13	1,000	500	0.0	0.0
C / 4.4	14.8	1.07	26.44	27	3	96	0	1	22	103.0	-15.4	63	13	5,000,000	0	0.0	0.0
C- / 4.1	12.7	0.96	37.33	993	0	99	0	1	91	111.8	-21.0	26	8	1,000	100	5.8	0.0
C- / 3.4	12.7	0.96	28.44	60	0	99	0	1	91	102.0	-21.3	18	8	1,000	500	0.0	0.0
C- / 4.2	12.7	0.96	40.00	236	0	99	0	1	91	115.6	-20.9	29	8	5,000,000	0	0.0	0.0
C+ / 5.8	12.7	0.96	37.66	14	0	99	0	1	91	113.6	-21.0	29	8	5,000,000	0	0.0	0.0
C- / 4.0	12.7	0.96	36.21	39	0	99	0	1	91	N/A	N/A	22	8	0	0	0.0	0.0
B- / 7.1	6.3	0.96	11.39	115	0	54	44	2	16	46.0	-13.4	15	13	1,000	100	5.8	0.0
B- / 7.0	6.4	0.96	10.49	54	0	54	44	2	16	40.4	-13.5	10	13	1,000	500	0.0	0.0
C / 5.2	6.4	0.96	11.34	N/A	0	54	44	2	16	44.2	-13.4	13	3	0	0	0.0	0.0
B- / 7.1	6.4	0.96	11.53	1	0	54	44	2	16	48.1	-13.3	17	13	5,000,000	0	0.0	0.0
C+ / 6.9	3.6	0.51	10.26	44	0	21	77	2	23	31.1	-7.5	49	N/A	1,000	100	5.8	0.0
C+ / 6.9	3.7	0.52	9.95	15	0	21	77	2	23	26.0	-7.8	39	N/A	1,000	500	0.0	0.0
B+ / 9.0	3.7	0.52	10.24	N/A	0	21	77	2	23	29.4	-7.6	45	3	0	0	0.0	0.0
C+ / 6.7	3.7	0.52	9.67	N/A	0	21	77	2	23	28.6	-8.0	47	N/A	5,000,000	0	0.0	0.0
C+ / 6.8	8.4	1.27	12.74	238	0	81	18	1	10	57.3	-16.1	8	13	1,000	100	5.8	0.0
C+ / 6.8	8.4	1.27	12.02	70	0	81	18	1	10	51.3	-16.3	6	13	1,000	500	0.0	0.0
B- / 7.8	8.4	0.77	12.67	N/A	0	81	18	1	10	55.2	-16.2	14	3	0	0	0.0	0.0
C+ / 6.8	8.3	1.26	13.00	1	0	81	18	1	10	59.1	-16.9	9	13	5,000,000	0	0.0	0.0
B- / 7.5	7.6	1.13	24.58	33	1	66	31	2	52	67.4	-13.1	52	10	2,500	100	0.0	0.0
C / 4.6	11.4	1.00	24.40	22	0	99	0	1	41	94.4	-18.8	60	10	2,500	100	0.0	0.0
C+ / 6.1	10.6	0.74	25.02	561	0	97	1	2	49	86.2	-20.8	94	8	1,000	50	0.0	0.0
B- / 7.5	6.1	0.96	13.37	9	0	57	41	2	64	59.5	-12.4	31	2	1,000	50	4.8	0.0
B- / 7.5	6.1	0.96	13.15	1	0	57	41	2	64	53.3	-12.6	24	2	1,000	50	0.0	0.0
B- / 7.5	6.1	0.96	13.32	15	0	57	41	2	64	61.5	-12.3	34	2	0	0	0.0	0.0

I. Index of Stock Mutual Funds

Fund Type	Fund Name	Ticker Symbol	Overall Investment Rating	Phone	Perfor-mance Rating/Pts	3 Mo	6 Mo	1Yr / Pct	3Yr / Pct	5Yr / Pct	Dividend Yield	Expense Ratio
FO	PNC International Equity A	PMIEX	D-	(800) 551-2145	E+ / 0.7	6.82	3.64	15.74 /33	-1.12 / 9	6.96 /34	0.67	1.37
FO	PNC International Equity C	PIUCX	D-	(800) 551-2145	E+ / 0.9	6.60	3.23	14.96 /30	-1.75 / 7	6.26 /30	0.02	2.07
FO	PNC International Equity I	PIUIX	D-	(800) 551-2145	D- / 1.2	6.82	3.73	16.05 /35	-0.84 /10	7.27 /36	0.91	1.07
GR	PNC Large Cap Core A	PLEAX	A-	(800) 551-2145	B- / 7.5	7.74	8.30	18.40 /45	10.29 /95	11.86 /73	0.92	1.59
GR	PNC Large Cap Core C	PLECX	A	(800) 551-2145	B / 7.9	7.57	7.94	17.57 /41	9.52 /90	11.07 /66	0.61	2.29
GR	PNC Large Cap Core I	PLEIX	A+	(800) 551-2145	B+ / 8.7	7.80	8.44	18.75 /46	10.55 /96	12.14 /75	1.14	1.29
GR	PNC Large Cap Growth A	PEWAX	B-	(800) 551-2145	C+ / 6.7	8.11	6.46	15.82 /34	9.44 /90	11.85 /73	0.48	1.39
GR	PNC Large Cap Growth C	PEWCX	B+	(800) 551-2145	B- / 7.2	7.93	6.12	15.05 /30	8.88 /86	11.19 /68	0.00	2.09
GR	PNC Large Cap Growth I	PEWIX	A-	(800) 551-2145	B / 7.8	8.20	6.65	16.21 /35	9.70 /92	12.14 /75	0.72	1.09
GR	PNC Large Cap Value A	PLVAX	B-	(800) 551-2145	C+ / 5.9	6.19	8.17	18.09 /43	7.61 /76	11.59 /71	0.61	1.33
GR	PNC Large Cap Value C	PALVX	B-	(800) 551-2145	C+ / 6.5	5.98	7.79	17.33 /40	7.02 /72	10.91 /65	0.25	2.03
GR	PNC Large Cap Value I	PLIVX	B+	(800) 551-2145	B- / 7.1	6.21	8.28	18.42 /45	7.86 /78	11.89 /73	0.82	1.03
SC	PNC Multi-Factor Small Cap Core A	PLOAX	B	(800) 551-2145	B- / 7.2	3.23	10.48	28.27 /82	8.13 /80	16.08 /98	0.29	1.49
SC	PNC Multi-Factor Small Cap Core I	PLOIX	B+	(800) 551-2145	B+ / 8.4	3.31	10.65	28.70 /83	8.45 /83	16.42 /98	0.53	1.19
SC	PNC Multi-Factor Small Cap Growth	PLWAX	C	(800) 551-2145	C / 5.2	3.65	7.74	21.31 /59	6.42 /68	13.78 /92	0.00	1.75
SC	PNC Multi-Factor Small Cap Growth	PLWCX	C	(800) 551-2145	C+ / 5.7	3.46	7.34	20.51 /55	5.68 /61	12.99 /84	0.00	2.45
SC	PNC Multi-Factor Small Cap Growth I	PLTIX	C+	(800) 551-2145	C+ / 6.5	3.72	7.89	21.66 /61	6.67 /70	14.07 /94	0.00	1.45
SC	PNC Multi-Factor Small Cap Value A	PMRRX	B+	(800) 551-2145	B / 8.2	3.54	13.36	33.85 /93	8.32 /81	13.69 /91	2.21	1.93
SC	PNC Multi-Factor Small Cap Value C	PSVCX	A-	(800) 551-2145	B+ / 8.7	3.36	12.94	32.85 /91	7.65 /76	12.95 /83	2.01	2.63
SC	PNC Multi-Factor Small Cap Value I	PMUIX	A	(800) 551-2145	A- / 9.2	3.58	13.46	34.14 /93	8.52 /83	13.96 /93	2.39	1.63
AA	PNC Retirement Income I	PDTAX	C	(800) 551-2145	D / 2.0	2.60	1.61	7.33 / 6	3.03 /32	--	1.05	5.54
IX	PNC S&P 500 Index A	PIIAX	A+	(800) 551-2145	B+ / 8.7	7.86	9.75	24.24 /71	10.01 /93	13.37 /88	1.17	0.57
IX	PNC S&P 500 Index C	PPICX	A	(800) 551-2145	B+ / 8.6	7.63	9.40	23.37 /68	9.20 /88	12.54 /79	0.70	1.32
IX	PNC S&P 500 Index I	PSXIX	A+	(800) 551-2145	A- / 9.2	7.90	9.85	24.51 /72	10.23 /95	13.65 /90	1.41	0.32
GR	PNC S&P 500 Index R4	PSPEX	A+	(800) 551-2145	A- / 9.1	7.85	9.77	24.32 /71	10.11 /94	13.57 /90	1.28	0.47
GR	PNC S&P 500 Index R5	PSFFX	A+	(800) 551-2145	A- / 9.1	7.88	9.82	24.45 /72	10.20 /94	13.63 /90	1.37	0.37
SC	● PNC Small Cap A	PPCAX	C	(800) 551-2145	C / 5.3	4.14	8.50	23.45 /68	5.87 /63	13.30 /87	0.00	1.35
SC	● PNC Small Cap C	PPCCX	C	(800) 551-2145	C+ / 5.9	4.01	8.08	22.61 /65	5.17 /56	12.54 /79	0.00	2.10
SC	● PNC Small Cap I	PPCIX	C+	(800) 551-2145	C+ / 6.7	4.23	8.59	23.79 /69	6.19 /66	13.62 /90	0.00	1.10
GI	PNC Target 2020 I	PDTCX	C+	(800) 551-2145	D+ / 2.7	3.51	2.51	10.20 /12	3.64 /38	--	1.40	3.23
GI	PNC Target 2030 I	PDTEX	C+	(800) 551-2145	C- / 4.1	4.89	4.20	14.50 /28	4.66 /50	--	1.31	3.14
GI	PNC Target 2040 I	PDTGX	C+	(800) 551-2145	C / 5.2	5.71	5.36	17.15 /39	5.51 /60	--	1.10	5.90
GI	PNC Target 2050 I	PDTIX	D	(800) 551-2145	C+ / 5.7	6.04	6.04	18.41 /45	5.72 /62	--	1.21	15.38
GL	Polaris Global Value	PGVFX	B-	(888) 263-5594	C+ / 6.8	8.16	11.14	23.92 /70	5.55 /60	12.40 /78	1.27	1.27
GR	Polen Growth Inst	POLIX	B+	(888) 678-6024	B / 8.1	6.35	5.97	13.54 /24	12.06 /98	12.38 /78	0.01	1.02
GR	Polen Growth Investor	POLRX	B+	(888) 678-6024	B / 7.9	6.32	5.82	13.24 /23	11.78 /98	12.08 /75	0.00	1.27
AA	Poplar Forest Cornerstone Inst	IPFCX	U	(888) 263-6443	U /	1.42	7.57	24.06 /70	--	--	0.80	3.16
GR	Poplar Forest Partners Fund A	PFPFX	B	(888) 263-6443	B / 7.8	0.39	11.02	35.74 /95	8.04 /79	15.04 /97	0.34	1.31
GR	Poplar Forest Partners Fund Inst	IPFPX	B+	(888) 263-6443	B+ / 8.9	0.47	11.16	36.09 /95	8.31 /81	15.32 /97	0.77	1.06
GL	Port Street Inst Opportunities Inst	PSOFX	U	(855) 369-6220	U /	3.81	3.33	10.42 /13	--	--	0.47	1.86
GR	Port Street Quality Growth Inst	PSQGX	U	(855) 369-6220	U /	4.49	3.47	10.23 /12	--	--	0.02	1.62
GL	Portfolio 21 Global Equity Retail	PORTX	C-	(877) 351-4115	C- / 3.9	6.91	4.39	16.67 /37	3.36 /35	7.69 /40	0.72	1.33
GL	Portfolio 21 Global Equity Inst	PORIX	C-	(877) 351-4115	C- / 4.1	6.98	4.55	16.94 /38	3.64 /38	7.99 /42	0.95	1.08
IN	Power Dividend Index A	PWDAX	B-	(877) 779-7462	C+ / 6.0	4.42	7.03	18.89 /47	8.35 /82	--	1.10	1.61
IN	Power Dividend Index C	PWDCX	U	(877) 779-7462	U /	4.18	6.72	18.01 /43	--	--	0.71	2.36
IN	Power Dividend Index I	PWDIX	A-	(877) 779-7462	B- / 7.0	4.48	7.14	19.17 /48	8.60 /84	--	1.39	1.36
BA	Praxis Genesis Balanced A	MBAPX	C	(800) 977-2947	D+ / 2.3	4.26	3.65	13.53 /24	4.08 /44	6.34 /31	1.23	1.10
GI	Praxis Genesis Conservative A	MCONX	C	(800) 977-2947	D- / 1.3	2.67	0.91	7.22 / 6	3.26 /34	4.24 /16	1.56	1.15
GR	Praxis Genesis Growth A	MGAFX	C-	(800) 977-2947	C- / 3.2	5.23	5.38	17.83 /42	4.46 /48	7.57 /39	0.94	1.21
GR	Praxis Growth Index Fund A	MGNDX	B+	(800) 977-2947	B- / 7.4	8.37	7.56	21.30 /59	10.08 /94	13.53 /89	0.59	0.84
GR	Praxis Growth Index Fund I	MMDEX	A+	(800) 977-2947	B+ / 8.7	8.48	7.79	21.79 /61	10.55 /96	14.06 /94	1.01	0.44
FO	Praxis International Index Fd A	MPLAX	D-	(800) 977-2947	E+ / 0.9	6.69	4.69	19.61 /50	-0.52 /11	2.92 /11	1.29	1.33

● Denotes fund is closed to new investors
* Denotes fund is included in Section II

www.thestreetratings.com

Risk Rating/Pts	3 Year Standard Deviation	Beta	NAV As of 2/28/17	Total $(Mil)	Cash %	Stocks %	Bonds %	Other %	Portfolio Turnover Ratio	Last Bull Market Return	Last Bear Market Return	Manager Quality Pct	Manager Tenure (Years)	Initial Purch. $	Additional Purch. $	Front End Load	Back End Load
C+ / 5.8	11.2	0.87	19.39	61	1	94	4	1	19	66.3	-25.4	62	20	1,000	50	5.5	0.0
C+ / 5.8	11.2	0.87	18.62	3	1	94	4	1	19	60.2	-25.6	54	20	1,000	50	0.0	0.0
C+ / 5.8	11.2	0.87	19.55	856	1	94	4	1	19	68.7	-25.3	66	20	0	0	0.0	0.0
B- / 7.4	10.3	0.96	18.66	3	0	99	0	1	57	111.8	-15.3	75	8	1,000	50	5.5	0.0
B- / 7.4	10.3	0.96	17.19	N/A	0	99	0	1	57	103.8	-15.6	67	8	1,000	50	0.0	0.0
B- / 7.4	10.3	0.96	19.08	20	0	99	0	1	57	114.5	-15.2	76	8	0	0	0.0	0.0
B- / 7.1	10.7	0.96	30.54	42	0	97	1	2	81	115.6	-15.4	66	8	1,000	50	5.5	0.0
B- / 7.1	10.7	0.96	27.75	1	0	97	1	2	81	108.3	-15.6	60	8	1,000	50	0.0	0.0
B- / 7.1	10.7	0.96	31.14	59	0	97	1	2	81	118.4	-15.3	69	8	0	0	0.0	0.0
B- / 7.3	10.1	0.94	23.51	52	0	97	1	2	77	111.4	-17.5	46	4	1,000	50	5.5	0.0
B- / 7.3	10.1	0.94	23.05	N/A	0	97	1	2	77	104.3	-17.8	39	4	1,000	50	0.0	0.0
B- / 7.3	10.1	0.94	23.59	72	0	97	1	2	77	114.2	-17.5	50	4	0	0	0.0	0.0
C+ / 6.0	13.7	0.84	23.99	95	1	95	3	1	77	158.2	-19.9	87	12	1,000	50	5.5	0.0
C+ / 6.0	13.8	0.85	24.17	243	1	95	3	1	77	162.1	-19.8	88	12	0	0	0.0	0.0
C / 5.3	15.1	0.91	21.86	40	0	99	0	1	66	129.1	-20.0	75	12	1,000	50	5.5	0.0
C / 5.3	15.1	0.91	21.21	9	0	99	0	1	66	120.4	-20.2	67	12	1,000	50	0.0	0.0
C / 5.4	15.1	0.91	22.30	71	0	99	0	1	66	132.1	-19.9	76	12	0	0	0.0	0.0
C+ / 6.1	13.3	0.81	21.50	13	1	96	1	2	105	126.0	-19.6	89	12	1,000	50	5.5	0.0
C+ / 6.1	13.3	0.81	19.14	2	1	96	1	2	105	118.0	-19.9	86	12	1,000	50	0.0	0.0
C+ / 6.1	13.3	0.81	23.37	16	1	96	1	2	105	128.6	-19.5	89	12	0	0	0.0	0.0
B+ / 9.0	3.7	0.57	10.30	4	15	30	54	1	104	N/A	N/A	60	5	0	0	0.0	0.0
C+ / 6.9	10.3	1.00	17.63	18	0	99	0	1	7	127.8	-16.5	68	12	1,000	50	2.5	0.0
C+ / 6.9	10.3	1.00	17.43	7	0	99	0	1	7	118.7	-16.6	59	12	1,000	50	0.0	0.0
C+ / 6.9	10.3	1.00	17.70	132	0	99	0	1	7	130.7	-16.4	70	12	0	0	0.0	0.0
C+ / 6.9	10.3	1.00	17.70	3	0	99	0	1	7	129.9	-16.4	69	12	0	0	0.0	0.0
C+ / 6.9	10.3	1.00	17.70	1	0	99	0	1	7	130.5	-16.4	70	12	0	0	0.0	0.0
C / 5.5	15.1	0.90	23.37	55	0	98	0	2	15	142.1	-21.0	70	13	1,000	50	5.5	0.0
C / 5.5	15.0	0.90	21.26	25	0	98	0	2	15	133.1	-21.2	62	13	1,000	50	0.0	0.0
C / 5.5	15.0	0.90	24.14	928	0	98	0	2	15	145.7	-20.9	74	13	0	0	0.0	0.0
B / 8.9	4.9	0.43	11.44	8	8	43	47	2	39	N/A	N/A	64	5	0	0	0.0	0.0
B / 8.1	6.9	0.63	12.46	11	6	65	28	1	18	N/A	N/A	50	5	0	0	0.0	0.0
C+ / 6.9	8.2	0.77	12.60	4	6	78	15	1	27	N/A	N/A	43	5	0	0	0.0	0.0
D / 1.9	8.7	0.81	9.23	1	6	83	9	2	74	N/A	N/A	40	5	0	0	0.0	0.0
B- / 7.0	10.7	0.78	24.35	397	0	99	0	1	5	117.8	-22.5	96	28	2,500	250	0.0	1.0
C+ / 6.1	10.8	0.91	20.81	1,279	3	96	0	1	9	115.0	-8.8	87	7	100,000	0	0.0	2.0
C+ / 6.1	10.7	0.91	20.53	102	3	96	0	1	9	112.1	-8.9	86	7	3,000	100	0.0	2.0
U /	N/A	N/A	26.51	29	0	66	32	2	25	N/A	N/A	N/A	3	1,000,000	1,000	0.0	0.0
C / 5.3	14.7	1.18	50.70	115	1	96	2	1	30	146.0	-21.7	22	8	25,000	1,000	5.0	0.0
C / 5.3	14.7	1.18	50.80	681	1	96	2	1	30	149.4	-21.6	25	8	1,000,000	1,000	0.0	0.0
U /	N/A	N/A	10.91	56	0	0	0	100	0	N/A	N/A	N/A	2	0	0	0.0	0.0
U /	N/A	N/A	11.58	52	19	56	24	1	9	N/A	N/A	N/A	3	2,000	100	0.0	0.0
C / 5.4	10.1	0.75	36.51	257	1	98	0	1	23	65.6	-19.5	92	18	5,000	100	0.0	0.0
C / 5.4	10.1	0.75	36.39	164	1	98	0	1	23	68.2	-19.5	93	18	100,000	1,000	0.0	0.0
B- / 7.8	8.4	0.49	12.05	263	0	99	0	1	99	N/A	N/A	90	4	1,000	100	5.0	1.0
U /	N/A	N/A	11.96	48	0	99	0	1	99	N/A	N/A	N/A	4	2,500	500	0.0	1.0
B- / 7.8	8.4	0.49	12.06	388	0	99	0	1	99	N/A	N/A	91	4	100,000	0	0.0	1.0
B / 8.3	6.2	0.98	12.93	66	0	61	38	1	7	52.8	-10.9	33	N/A	1,000	50	5.3	2.0
B+ / 9.5	3.4	0.28	11.40	22	0	31	68	1	9	31.4	-3.8	76	N/A	1,000	50	5.3	2.0
B- / 7.2	8.4	0.79	13.98	56	0	80	19	1	7	67.5	-15.4	27	N/A	1,000	50	5.3	2.0
C+ / 6.9	10.9	1.03	20.10	72	0	99	0	1	19	129.3	-13.8	65	4	2,500	100	5.3	2.0
C+ / 6.9	10.9	1.03	20.23	149	0	99	0	1	19	135.0	-13.5	70	4	100,000	0	0.0	2.0
C+ / 5.7	11.7	0.92	9.93	20	0	98	0	2	4	36.2	-25.3	70	6	2,500	100	5.3	2.0

Fund Type	Fund Name	Ticker Symbol	Overall Investment Rating	Phone	PERFORMANCE Performance Rating/Pts	Total Return % through 2/28/17 3 Mo	6 Mo	1Yr / Pct	Annualized 3Yr / Pct	5Yr / Pct	Incl. in Returns Dividend Yield	Expense Ratio
FO	Praxis International Index Fd I	MPLIX	D	(800) 977-2947	D+ / 2.3	6.85	5.09	20.22 /53	0.03 /13	3.57 /13	1.84	0.78
SC	Praxis Small Cap Index A	MMSCX	E-	(800) 977-2947	E+ / 0.8	1.12	3.27	19.15 /48	-0.27 /12	5.63 /26	0.00	1.26
SC	Praxis Small Cap Index I	MMSIX	E	(800) 977-2947	D / 1.9	1.34	3.75	20.07 /52	0.34 /15	6.34 /31	0.00	0.51
GR	Praxis Value Index A	MVIAX	B+	(800) 977-2947	B / 7.7	7.23	11.63	28.01 /82	8.67 /84	12.59 /80	1.66	0.94
GR	Praxis Value Index I	MVIIX	A	(800) 977-2947	A- / 9.0	7.40	12.00	28.76 /83	9.18 /88	13.22 /86	2.19	0.45
* AG ●	PRIMECAP Odyssey Agg Growth Fd	POAGX	B+	(800) 729-2307	A / 9.4	6.38	10.98	30.05 /86	9.86 /93	19.60 /99	0.00	0.62
* MC	PRIMECAP Odyssey Growth Fd	POGRX	A	(800) 729-2307	A / 9.5	7.88	12.38	29.60 /85	9.79 /92	16.02 /98	0.43	0.64
* GR	PRIMECAP Odyssey Stock Fd	POSKX	A+	(800) 729-2307	A+ / 9.7	8.45	11.87	28.41 /83	11.07 /97	14.98 /97	1.09	0.65
IN	Princeton Futures Strategy A	PFFAX	D	(888) 868-9501	E- / 0.1	-4.15	-8.81	-6.71 / 0	-2.08 / 6	-4.12 / 2	0.00	2.50
AA	Princeton Futures Strategy C	PFFTX	D-	(888) 868-9501	E- / 0.1	-4.33	-9.29	-7.46 / 0	-2.86 / 5	-4.85 / 2	0.00	3.25
IN	Princeton Futures Strategy I	PFFNX	D	(888) 868-9501	E- / 0.2	-4.21	-8.81	-6.62 / 0	-1.89 / 7	-3.91 / 2	0.00	2.24
GR	Principal Blue Chip A	PBLAX	B+	(800) 222-5852	B / 8.2	8.29	7.65	24.32 /71	10.29 /95	---	0.00	1.39
GR	Principal Blue Chip C	PBLCX	A-	(800) 222-5852	B+ / 8.5	8.04	7.19	23.32 /68	9.46 /90	---	0.00	2.33
GR	Principal Blue Chip Inst	PBCKX	A	(800) 222-5852	A / 9.4	8.40	7.95	25.01 /73	10.95 /97	---	0.43	0.71
GR	Principal Blue Chip P	PBLPX	A	(800) 222-5852	A / 9.3	8.33	7.88	24.79 /73	10.77 /97	---	0.30	1.41
GR	Principal Blue Chip R6	PGBHX	A-	(800) 222-5852	A / 9.4	8.40	7.95	25.01 /73	10.95 /97	---	0.43	N/A
GR	Principal Cap Appreciation Fd A	CMNWX	B+	(800) 222-5852	B / 7.6	8.25	8.78	22.05 /62	9.48 /90	12.88 /83	0.88	0.84
GR	Principal Cap Appreciation Fd C	CMNCX	B+	(800) 222-5852	B / 7.9	8.03	8.32	21.03 /58	8.58 /84	11.94 /74	0.52	1.65
GR	Principal Cap Appreciation Fd Inst	PWCIX	A	(800) 222-5852	B+ / 8.8	8.35	8.99	22.50 /65	9.88 /93	13.33 /87	1.23	0.46
GR	Principal Cap Appreciation Fd P	PCFPX	A-	(800) 222-5852	B+ / 8.7	8.32	8.88	22.32 /64	9.73 /92	13.15 /85	1.11	0.60
GR	Principal Cap Appreciation Fd R1	PCAMX	B+	(800) 222-5852	B / 8.2	8.11	8.50	21.43 /59	8.93 /86	12.34 /78	0.35	1.33
GR	Principal Cap Appreciation Fd R2	PCANX	B+	(800) 222-5852	B+ / 8.3	8.15	8.57	21.59 /60	9.07 /87	12.49 /79	0.60	1.20
GR	Principal Cap Appreciation Fd R3	PCAOX	A-	(800) 222-5852	B+ / 8.4	8.22	8.67	21.83 /61	9.27 /89	12.69 /81	0.76	1.02
GR	Principal Cap Appreciation Fd R4	PCAPX	A-	(800) 222-5852	B+ / 8.6	8.26	8.77	22.05 /62	9.48 /90	12.91 /83	0.91	0.83
GR	Principal Cap Appreciation Fd R5	PCAQX	A-	(800) 222-5852	B+ / 8.7	8.28	8.84	22.20 /63	9.60 /91	13.04 /84	1.02	0.71
FO	Principal Divers Intl A	PRWLX	D-	(800) 222-5852	E+ / 0.7	6.18	2.65	13.35 /23	-0.59 /11	4.55 /18	1.03	1.35
FO	Principal Divers Intl C	PDNCX	D	(800) 222-5852	E+ / 0.9	6.08	2.27	12.52 /20	-1.30 / 8	3.82 /14	0.32	2.23
FO	Principal Divers Intl Inst	PIIIX	D	(800) 222-5852	D- / 1.3	6.32	2.87	13.95 /25	-0.10 /13	5.08 /22	1.62	0.85
FO	Principal Divers Intl J	PIIJX	D	(800) 222-5852	D- / 1.1	6.28	2.81	13.64 /24	-0.43 /12	4.67 /19	1.30	1.18
FO	Principal Divers Intl P	PDIPX	D	(800) 222-5852	D- / 1.2	6.31	2.76	13.65 /24	-0.27 /12	4.88 /21	1.52	1.25
FO	Principal Divers Intl R1	PDVIX	D	(800) 222-5852	D- / 1.0	6.13	2.41	12.91 /21	-0.97 / 9	4.17 /16	0.69	1.73
FO	Principal Divers Intl R2	PINNX	D	(800) 222-5852	D- / 1.0	6.11	2.47	13.01 /22	-0.84 /10	4.31 /17	0.82	1.60
FO	Principal Divers Intl R3	PINRX	D	(800) 222-5852	D- / 1.1	6.19	2.56	13.29 /23	-0.65 /11	4.50 /18	0.99	1.42
FO	Principal Divers Intl R4	PINLX	D	(800) 222-5852	D- / 1.2	6.29	2.70	13.50 /24	-0.47 /11	4.70 /19	1.23	1.23
FO	Principal Divers Intl R5	PINPX	D	(800) 222-5852	D- / 1.2	6.34	2.84	13.78 /24	-0.31 /12	4.85 /20	1.35	1.11
GI	Principal Diversified Real Ast A	PRDAX	D-	(800) 222-5852	E / 0.5	5.01	3.21	13.57 /24	-1.92 / 7	0.68 / 6	2.20	1.26
GI	Principal Diversified Real Ast C	PRDCX	D-	(800) 222-5852	E+ / 0.6	4.87	2.83	12.74 /21	-2.63 / 5	-0.06 / 4	1.29	2.05
GI	Principal Diversified Real Ast Inst	PDRDX	D	(800) 222-5852	E+ / 0.9	5.07	3.45	14.06 /26	-1.53 / 8	1.07 / 6	2.52	0.88
AA	Principal Diversified Real Ast P	PRDPX	D	(800) 222-5852	E+ / 0.9	5.12	3.41	14.04 /26	-1.68 / 7	0.97 / 6	2.30	1.07
GL	Principal Diversified Real Ast R-6	PDARX	U	(800) 222-5852	U /	5.07	3.46	14.07 /26	---	---	2.53	25.59
IN	Principal Equity Inc Fd A	PQIAX	A-	(800) 222-5852	B / 7.6	7.86	9.53	25.09 /74	8.79 /85	11.83 /73	1.63	0.91
IN	Principal Equity Inc Fd C	PEUCX	A-	(800) 222-5852	B / 8.0	7.68	9.14	24.20 /71	7.98 /79	11.01 /66	1.11	1.64
IN	Principal Equity Inc Fd Inst	PEIIX	A+	(800) 222-5852	B+ / 8.9	7.98	9.75	25.63 /75	9.21 /88	12.28 /77	2.06	0.52
IN	Principal Equity Inc Fd P	PEQPX	A+	(800) 222-5852	B+ / 8.8	7.94	9.69	25.47 /75	9.09 /87	12.15 /76	2.00	0.62
IN	Principal Equity Inc Fd R1	PIEMX	A	(800) 222-5852	B / 8.2	7.74	9.23	24.49 /72	8.25 /81	11.29 /68	1.28	1.39
IN	Principal Equity Inc Fd R2	PEINX	A	(800) 222-5852	B+ / 8.3	7.77	9.32	24.66 /72	8.39 /82	11.44 /69	1.39	1.26
IN	Principal Equity Inc Fd R3	PEIOX	A	(800) 222-5852	B+ / 8.4	7.80	9.41	24.86 /73	8.58 /84	11.64 /71	1.56	1.08
IN	Principal Equity Inc Fd R4	PEIPX	A+	(800) 222-5852	B+ / 8.6	7.87	9.50	25.09 /74	8.78 /85	11.85 /73	1.73	0.89
IN	Principal Equity Inc Fd R5	PEIQX	A+	(800) 222-5852	B+ / 8.7	7.93	9.59	25.30 /74	8.93 /86	11.98 /74	1.84	0.77
RE	Principal Glb Real Est Sec A	POSAX	D+	(800) 222-5852	D+ / 2.5	7.05	-3.64	10.90 /14	5.37 /58	8.59 /47	2.90	1.32
RE	Principal Glb Real Est Sec C	POSCX	D+	(800) 222-5852	D+ / 2.9	6.80	-4.01	9.96 /12	4.54 /49	7.75 /40	2.36	2.09
RE	Principal Glb Real Est Sec Inst	POSIX	C-	(800) 222-5852	C- / 3.8	7.06	-3.40	11.24 /15	5.84 /63	9.05 /51	3.27	0.90

● Denotes fund is closed to new investors
★ Denotes fund is included in Section II

www.thestreetratings.com

RISK			NET ASSETS		ASSET					BULL / BEAR		FUND MANAGER		MINIMUMS		LOADS	
	3 Year		NAV						Portfolio	Last Bull	Last Bear	Manager	Manager	Initial	Additional	Front	Back
Risk Rating/Pts	Standard Deviation	Beta	As of 2/28/17	Total $(Mil)	Cash %	Stocks %	Bonds %	Other %	Turnover Ratio	Market Return	Market Return	Quality Pct	Tenure (Years)	Purch. $	Purch. $	End Load	End Load
C+ / 5.7	11.6	0.91	9.99	184	0	98	0	2	4	41.0	-25.3	75	6	100,000	0	0.0	2.0
D / 1.8	14.9	0.91	9.67	5	0	99	0	1	76	65.5	-19.6	7	N/A	2,500	100	5.3	2.0
D / 2.0	14.9	0.91	10.36	42	0	99	0	1	76	71.5	-19.5	10	N/A	100,000	0	0.0	2.0
C+ / 6.5	10.5	0.97	13.26	23	0	99	0	1	21	117.1	-19.5	56	4	2,500	100	5.3	2.0
C+ / 6.4	10.6	0.97	13.19	146	0	99	0	1	21	123.8	-19.2	62	4	100,000	0	0.0	2.0
C / 4.4	15.9	1.27	35.35	7,554	0	95	4	1	15	196.3	-20.5	30	13	2,000	150	0.0	0.0
C+ / 5.9	14.1	0.99	30.75	7,821	0	95	4	1	9	150.4	-20.1	75	13	2,000	150	0.0	0.0
C+ / 6.8	11.4	1.06	27.59	6,894	0	94	5	1	8	139.0	-16.0	72	13	2,000	150	0.0	0.0
B- / 7.3	8.8	-0.11	7.59	4	57	0	42	1	57	-22.5	-7.4	61	7	2,500	100	5.8	0.0
B- / 7.1	8.8	-0.14	7.26	2	57	0	42	1	57	-25.7	N/A	48	7	2,500	100	0.0	0.0
B- / 7.3	8.8	-0.11	7.70	5	57	0	42	1	57	-21.7	-7.3	63	7	100,000	100	0.0	0.0
C+ / 6.2	10.9	0.99	18.04	49	0	100	0	0	36	N/A	N/A	71	5	1,000	100	5.5	0.0
C+ / 6.1	10.9	0.99	17.61	30	0	100	0	0	36	N/A	N/A	62	5	1,000	100	0.0	0.0
C+ / 6.0	11.0	1.00	18.17	1,532	0	100	0	0	36	N/A	N/A	76	5	0	0	0.0	0.0
C+ / 6.2	10.9	0.99	18.15	26	0	100	0	0	36	N/A	N/A	75	5	0	0	0.0	0.0
C / 5.4	11.0	1.00	18.17	N/A	0	100	0	0	36	N/A	N/A	76	5	0	0	0.0	0.0
C+ / 6.2	10.2	0.98	58.27	949	0	98	1	1	35	122.6	-17.6	64	7	1,000	100	5.5	0.0
C+ / 6.0	10.3	0.98	46.36	52	0	98	1	1	35	112.8	-17.9	53	7	1,000	100	0.0	0.0
C+ / 6.2	10.3	0.98	59.22	1,405	0	98	1	1	35	127.4	-17.5	68	7	1,000,000	0	0.0	0.0
C+ / 6.2	10.3	0.98	59.02	25	0	98	1	1	35	125.4	-17.5	67	7	0	0	0.0	0.0
C+ / 6.3	10.3	0.98	58.31	3	0	98	1	1	35	116.9	-17.8	57	7	0	0	0.0	0.0
C+ / 6.3	10.3	0.98	58.37	4	0	98	1	1	35	118.4	-17.7	59	7	0	0	0.0	0.0
C+ / 6.3	10.2	0.98	58.29	33	0	98	1	1	35	120.6	-17.7	61	7	0	0	0.0	0.0
C+ / 6.3	10.3	0.98	58.74	22	0	98	1	1	35	122.9	-17.6	64	7	0	0	0.0	0.0
C+ / 6.2	10.2	0.98	58.89	53	0	98	1	1	35	124.4	-17.6	65	7	0	0	0.0	0.0
C+ / 6.6	10.5	0.82	11.62	221	1	97	1	1	48	46.3	-22.4	69	14	1,000	100	5.5	0.0
C+ / 6.6	10.5	0.82	11.64	13	1	97	1	1	48	40.7	-22.5	60	14	1,000	100	0.0	0.0
C+ / 6.5	10.5	0.82	11.55	8,093	1	97	1	1	48	50.4	-22.2	74	14	1,000,000	0	0.0	0.0
C+ / 6.6	10.5	0.82	11.49	164	1	97	1	1	48	47.2	-22.4	71	14	1,000	100	0.0	1.0
C+ / 6.5	10.5	0.82	11.51	8	1	97	1	1	48	48.9	-22.3	73	14	0	0	0.0	0.0
C+ / 6.6	10.5	0.82	11.59	4	1	97	1	1	48	43.4	-22.5	64	14	0	0	0.0	0.0
C+ / 6.6	10.5	0.82	11.54	6	1	97	1	1	48	44.4	-22.4	66	14	0	0	0.0	0.0
C+ / 6.6	10.5	0.82	11.57	23	1	97	1	1	48	45.8	-22.4	68	14	0	0	0.0	0.0
C+ / 6.6	10.5	0.82	11.72	37	1	97	1	1	48	47.3	-22.3	70	14	0	0	0.0	0.0
C+ / 6.6	10.5	0.82	11.70	62	1	97	1	1	48	48.4	-22.2	72	14	0	0	0.0	0.0
C+ / 6.6	8.0	0.57	11.16	216	28	37	33	2	78	17.1	-12.8	4	7	1,000	100	3.8	0.0
C+ / 6.6	8.1	0.58	10.97	28	28	37	33	2	78	12.5	-13.1	3	7	1,000	100	0.0	0.0
C+ / 6.5	8.0	0.57	11.17	3,773	28	37	33	2	78	19.6	-12.7	5	7	0	0	0.0	0.0
C+ / 6.6	8.0	0.98	11.16	182	28	37	33	2	78	18.8	-12.8	3	7	0	0	0.0	0.0
U /	N/A	N/A	11.17	29	28	37	33	2	78	N/A	N/A	N/A	7	0	0	0.0	0.0
B- / 7.0	9.9	0.92	29.17	951	5	93	0	2	16	108.2	-14.2	63	9	1,000	100	5.5	0.0
B- / 7.0	9.9	0.93	28.46	199	5	93	0	2	16	100.1	-14.5	53	9	1,000	100	0.0	0.0
B- / 7.0	9.9	0.93	29.22	4,594	5	93	0	2	16	112.9	-14.1	68	9	1,000,000	0	0.0	0.0
B- / 7.0	9.9	0.93	29.18	165	5	93	0	2	16	111.4	-14.1	66	9	0	0	0.0	0.0
B- / 7.0	9.9	0.93	29.05	2	5	93	0	2	16	103.0	-14.4	56	9	0	0	0.0	0.0
B- / 7.0	9.9	0.92	29.15	5	5	93	0	2	16	104.4	-14.3	58	9	0	0	0.0	0.0
B- / 7.0	9.9	0.93	29.07	57	5	93	0	2	16	106.4	-14.3	60	9	0	0	0.0	0.0
B- / 7.0	9.8	0.92	29.13	54	5	93	0	2	16	108.5	-14.2	63	9	0	0	0.0	0.0
B- / 7.0	9.9	0.93	29.18	108	5	93	0	2	16	109.9	-14.1	64	9	0	0	0.0	0.0
C+ / 6.2	12.3	0.86	8.41	130	8	90	0	2	55	81.8	-21.0	25	10	1,000	100	5.5	0.0
C+ / 6.2	12.3	0.86	8.15	43	8	90	0	2	55	74.4	-21.2	18	10	1,000	100	0.0	0.0
C+ / 6.2	12.3	0.86	9.00	1,207	8	90	0	2	55	86.1	-20.7	30	10	1,000,000	0	0.0	0.0

I. Index of Stock Mutual Funds

Fund Type	Fund Name	Ticker Symbol	Overall Investment Rating	Phone	Performance Rating/Pts	3 Mo	6 Mo	1Yr / Pct	3Yr / Pct	5Yr / Pct	Dividend Yield	Expense Ratio
								Total Return % through 2/28/17			Incl. in Returns	
									Annualized			
RE	Principal Glb Real Est Sec P	POSPX	C-	(800) 222-5852	C- / 3.7	7.04	-3.46	11.27 /15	5.68 /61	8.90 /50	3.16	1.03
GL	Principal Global Multi-Strat A	PMSAX	C-	(800) 222-5852	D- / 1.4	2.79	2.60	6.56 / 5	2.23 /26	3.09 /11	0.00	2.43
GL	Principal Global Multi-Strat C	PMSCX	C-	(800) 222-5852	D- / 1.4	2.57	2.18	5.68 / 4	1.41 /20	--	0.00	3.25
GL	Principal Global Multi-Strat Inst	PSMIX	C	(800) 222-5852	D / 1.9	2.83	2.73	6.87 / 6	2.57 /28	3.33 /12	0.15	2.11
GL	Principal Global Multi-Strat P	PMSPX	C	(800) 222-5852	D / 1.9	2.81	2.62	6.77 / 5	2.46 /27	3.20 /12	0.03	2.20
GL	Principal Global Opportunities A	PGLAX	C-	(800) 222-5852	D / 2.2	6.85	4.80	12.88 /21	2.59 /28	--	0.99	2.16
GL	Principal Global Opportunities C	PGOCX	C-	(800) 222-5852	D+ / 2.5	6.60	4.35	12.05 /18	1.81 /23	--	0.19	3.51
GL	Principal Global Opportunities Inst	PGOIX	C-	(800) 222-5852	C- / 3.6	7.05	5.11	13.76 /24	3.28 /35	--	1.68	0.84
GL	Principal Global Opportunities P	PGXPX	C	(800) 222-5852	C- / 3.5	7.00	5.06	13.52 /24	3.10 /33	--	1.22	3.55
FO	Principal International Sm Co Inst	PISMX	U	(800) 222-5852	U /	7.30	5.88	17.55 /41	--	--	0.27	4.14
EM	Principal Intl Emrg Mkts A	PRIAX	D	(800) 222-5852	C- / 3.1	8.97	5.91	28.39 /83	0.52 /16	-1.16 / 3	0.81	1.83
EM	Principal Intl Emrg Mkts C	PMKCX	D-	(800) 222-5852	D / 2.0	8.72	5.35	27.05 /79	-0.49 /11	-2.15 / 3	0.00	2.80
EM	Principal Intl Emrg Mkts Inst	PIEIX	C-	(800) 222-5852	C / 4.6	9.08	6.09	28.88 /84	1.02 /18	-0.64 / 4	1.29	1.25
EM	Principal Intl Emrg Mkts J	PIEJX	D+	(800) 222-5852	C / 4.3	9.03	5.95	28.50 /83	0.63 /16	-1.05 / 3	1.01	1.59
EM	Principal Intl Emrg Mkts P	PIEPX	C-	(800) 222-5852	C / 4.5	9.06	6.06	28.80 /84	0.90 /18	-0.77 / 4	1.19	2.20
EM	Principal Intl Emrg Mkts R1	PIXEX	D+	(800) 222-5852	C- / 3.9	8.84	5.64	27.87 /81	0.14 /14	-1.49 / 3	0.45	2.12
EM	Principal Intl Emrg Mkts R2	PEASX	D+	(800) 222-5852	C- / 4.0	8.86	5.70	28.00 /82	0.27 /15	-1.37 / 3	0.63	1.99
EM	Principal Intl Emrg Mkts R3	PEAPX	D+	(800) 222-5852	C- / 4.1	8.97	5.82	28.25 /82	0.46 /16	-1.19 / 3	0.76	1.81
EM	Principal Intl Emrg Mkts R4	PESSX	D+	(800) 222-5852	C / 4.3	8.98	5.89	28.42 /83	0.65 /16	-1.00 / 3	0.97	1.62
EM	Principal Intl Emrg Mkts R5	PEPSX	C-	(800) 222-5852	C / 4.4	9.01	5.97	28.62 /83	0.77 /17	-0.88 / 4	1.04	1.50
FO	Principal Intl Equity Index Inst	PIDIX	D-	(800) 222-5852	D- / 1.2	7.20	4.18	15.42 /32	-1.01 / 9	4.84 /20	2.70	0.33
FO	Principal Intl Equity Index R1	PILIX	D-	(800) 222-5852	E+ / 0.9	6.99	3.76	14.53 /28	-1.85 / 7	3.93 /15	1.84	1.20
FO	Principal Intl Equity Index R2	PINEX	D-	(800) 222-5852	E+ / 0.9	7.15	3.88	14.62 /28	-1.74 / 7	4.07 /16	1.90	1.07
FO	Principal Intl Equity Index R3	PIIOX	D-	(800) 222-5852	D- / 1.0	7.22	3.91	14.94 /30	-1.56 / 8	4.27 /17	2.22	0.89
FO	Principal Intl Equity Index R4	PIIPX	D-	(800) 222-5852	D- / 1.0	7.12	3.96	15.00 /30	-1.38 / 8	4.46 /18	2.39	0.70
FO	Principal Intl Equity Index R5	PIIQX	D-	(800) 222-5852	D- / 1.1	7.19	4.16	15.20 /31	-1.23 / 9	4.59 /19	2.47	0.58
FO	Principal Intl Equity Index R6	PFIEX	D-	(800) 222-5852	D- / 1.2	7.20	4.18	15.42 /32	-1.01 / 9	4.84 /20	2.70	N/A
FO	Principal Intl I Inst	PINIX	D+	(800) 222-5852	D+ / 2.5	6.16	2.60	15.24 /31	1.44 /21	5.77 /27	0.98	0.97
FO	Principal Intl I P	PTRPX	U	(800) 222-5852	U /	6.13	2.57	15.23 /31	--	--	0.96	1.08
FO	Principal Intl I R1	PPISX	D	(800) 222-5852	D / 2.0	5.97	2.15	14.34 /27	0.61 /16	4.88 /21	0.00	1.81
FO	Principal Intl I R2	PSPPX	D	(800) 222-5852	D / 2.1	5.96	2.24	14.48 /28	0.72 /17	5.03 /21	0.31	1.68
FO	Principal Intl I R3	PRPPX	D	(800) 222-5852	D / 2.2	5.99	2.26	14.61 /28	0.90 /18	5.21 /23	0.46	1.50
FO	Principal Intl I R4	PUPPX	D+	(800) 222-5852	D+ / 2.3	6.11	2.46	14.92 /30	1.12 /19	5.43 /24	0.57	1.31
FO	Principal Intl I R5	PTPPX	D+	(800) 222-5852	D+ / 2.3	6.09	2.45	15.00 /30	1.20 /19	5.53 /25	0.77	1.19
GR	Principal LgCap Growth A	PRGWX	D-	(800) 222-5852	C- / 3.2	8.24	4.87	13.34 /23	4.19 /45	10.32 /61	0.09	1.07
GR	Principal LgCap Growth C	PLGCX	D-	(800) 222-5852	C- / 3.5	8.04	4.44	12.32 /19	3.33 /35	9.41 /54	0.00	1.90
GR	Principal LgCap Growth Inst	PGLIX	D+	(800) 222-5852	C / 4.6	8.44	5.10	13.92 /25	4.67 /50	10.88 /65	0.47	0.64
GR	Principal LgCap Growth J	PGLJX	D	(800) 222-5852	C / 4.3	8.40	5.05	13.56 /24	4.33 /47	10.45 /62	0.27	0.96
GR	Principal LgCap Growth P	PGLPX	D	(800) 222-5852	C / 4.5	8.50	5.14	13.79 /25	4.52 /49	10.71 /63	0.29	0.82
GR	Principal LgCap Growth R1	PLSGX	D-	(800) 222-5852	C- / 3.9	8.20	4.67	12.90 /21	3.77 /40	9.91 /58	0.00	1.50
GR	Principal LgCap Growth R2	PCPPX	D	(800) 222-5852	C- / 4.0	8.27	4.80	13.14 /22	3.92 /42	10.08 /59	0.00	1.37
GR	Principal LgCap Growth R3	PLGPX	D	(800) 222-5852	C- / 4.1	8.34	4.86	13.23 /22	4.10 /44	10.27 /60	0.00	1.19
GR	Principal LgCap Growth R4	PEPPX	D	(800) 222-5852	C / 4.3	8.40	5.01	13.43 /23	4.32 /47	10.47 /62	0.11	1.00
GR	Principal LgCap Growth R5	PDPPX	D	(800) 222-5852	C / 4.4	8.33	5.02	13.53 /24	4.42 /48	10.60 /63	0.26	0.88
IX	Principal LgCap S&P 500 A	PLSAX	A+	(800) 222-5852	B+ / 8.9	7.93	9.76	24.38 /71	10.08 /94	13.39 /88	1.53	0.48
IX	Principal LgCap S&P 500 C	PLICX	A+	(800) 222-5852	B+ / 8.6	7.67	9.25	23.31 /68	9.19 /88	12.52 /79	0.91	1.36
IX	Principal LgCap S&P 500 Inst	PLFIX	A+	(800) 222-5852	A / 9.3	7.96	9.86	24.68 /72	10.42 /95	13.80 /92	1.83	0.16
IX	Principal LgCap S&P 500 J	PSPJX	A+	(800) 222-5852	A- / 9.1	7.87	9.72	24.39 /71	10.14 /94	13.44 /88	1.64	0.40
IX	Principal LgCap S&P 500 R1	PLPIX	A+	(800) 222-5852	B+ / 8.8	7.81	9.44	23.64 /69	9.48 /90	12.83 /82	1.00	1.03
IX	Principal LgCap S&P 500 R2	PLFNX	A+	(800) 222-5852	B+ / 8.8	7.75	9.50	23.79 /69	9.63 /91	12.95 /83	1.12	0.90
IX	Principal LgCap S&P 500 R3	PLFMX	A+	(800) 222-5852	B+ / 8.9	7.84	9.60	24.02 /70	9.82 /92	13.16 /86	1.30	0.72
IX	Principal LgCap S&P 500 R4	PLFSX	A+	(800) 222-5852	A- / 9.1	7.88	9.70	24.27 /71	10.02 /93	13.39 /88	1.47	0.53

99 Pct = Best
0 Pct = Worst

● Denotes fund is closed to new investors
∗ Denotes fund is included in Section II

www.thestreetratings.com

RISK			NET ASSETS		ASSET					BULL / BEAR		FUND MANAGER		MINIMUMS		LOADS	
	3 Year		NAV						Portfolio	Last Bull	Last Bear	Manager	Manager	Initial	Additional	Front	Back
Risk Rating/Pts	Standard Deviation	Beta	As of 2/28/17	Total $(Mil)	Cash %	Stocks %	Bonds %	Other %	Turnover Ratio	Market Return	Market Return	Quality Pct	Tenure (Years)	Purch. $	Purch. $	End Load	End Load
C+ / 6.2	12.3	0.86	8.99	281	8	90	0	2	55	84.7	-20.8	28	10	0	0	0.0	0.0
B / 8.9	2.7	0.16	11.05	116	42	27	26	5	234	N/A	N/A	87	6	1,000	100	3.8	0.0
B+ / 9.0	2.7	0.17	10.79	53	42	27	26	5	234	N/A	N/A	83	6	1,000	100	0.0	0.0
B / 8.9	2.7	0.16	11.14	2,415	42	27	26	5	234	N/A	N/A	88	6	0	0	0.0	0.0
B / 8.9	2.7	0.16	11.10	310	42	27	26	5	234	N/A	N/A	88	6	0	0	0.0	0.0
B- / 7.7	9.2	0.70	11.87	5	3	96	0	1	145	N/A	N/A	89	5	1,000	100	5.5	0.0
B- / 7.7	9.2	0.70	11.81	2	3	96	0	1	145	N/A	N/A	86	5	1,000	100	0.0	0.0
C+ / 6.3	9.2	0.70	11.95	1,294	3	96	0	1	145	N/A	N/A	91	5	0	0	0.0	0.0
B- / 7.7	9.2	0.70	11.96	N/A	3	96	0	1	145	N/A	N/A	91	5	0	0	0.0	0.0
U /	N/A	N/A	10.42	631	2	96	0	2	50	N/A	N/A	N/A	3	0	0	0.0	0.0
C / 5.0	15.0	0.91	23.49	77	0	99	0	1	120	16.8	-26.2	62	10	1,000	100	5.5	0.0
C / 5.0	15.0	0.91	22.45	10	0	99	0	1	120	10.6	-26.5	48	10	1,000	100	0.0	0.0
C / 4.9	15.0	0.91	23.24	627	0	99	0	1	120	20.1	-26.0	68	10	1,000,000	0	0.0	0.0
C / 5.0	15.0	0.91	22.62	102	0	99	0	1	120	17.4	-26.2	63	10	1,000	100	0.0	0.0
C / 5.0	15.1	0.91	23.25	2	0	99	0	1	120	19.3	-26.1	66	10	0	0	0.0	0.0
C / 5.0	15.0	0.91	23.22	3	0	99	0	1	120	14.6	-26.3	57	10	0	0	0.0	0.0
C / 5.0	15.0	0.91	23.07	3	0	99	0	1	120	15.4	-26.3	58	10	0	0	0.0	0.0
C / 5.0	15.1	0.91	23.21	10	0	99	0	1	120	16.6	-26.2	61	10	0	0	0.0	0.0
C / 5.0	15.0	0.91	23.29	10	0	99	0	1	120	17.7	-26.2	63	10	0	0	0.0	0.0
C / 5.0	15.0	0.91	23.32	15	0	99	0	1	120	18.5	-26.1	65	10	0	0	0.0	0.0
C / 5.5	11.4	0.92	9.36	871	1	97	0	2	31	46.3	-23.4	64	6	0	0	0.0	0.0
C / 5.5	11.5	0.93	9.09	1	1	97	0	2	31	39.5	-23.5	52	6	0	0	0.0	0.0
C+ / 5.6	11.4	0.93	9.35	1	1	97	0	2	31	40.4	-23.6	54	6	0	0	0.0	0.0
C / 5.5	11.5	0.93	9.21	17	1	97	0	2	31	42.0	-23.5	57	6	0	0	0.0	0.0
C / 5.5	11.4	0.93	9.30	10	1	97	0	2	31	43.3	-23.4	59	6	0	0	0.0	0.0
C / 5.5	11.4	0.93	9.32	25	1	97	0	2	31	44.3	-23.4	61	6	0	0	0.0	0.0
C / 5.4	11.4	0.92	9.36	N/A	1	97	0	2	31	46.3	-23.4	64	6	0	0	0.0	0.0
C+ / 6.2	12.1	0.85	13.33	303	4	95	0	1	70	57.0	-26.0	84	3	1,000,000	0	0.0	0.0
U /	N/A	N/A	13.31	49	4	95	0	1	70	N/A	N/A	N/A	3	0	0	0.0	0.0
C+ / 6.2	12.1	0.85	13.32	3	4	95	0	1	70	49.9	-26.2	79	3	0	0	0.0	0.0
C+ / 6.2	12.1	0.85	13.35	3	4	95	0	1	70	50.9	-26.2	80	3	0	0	0.0	0.0
C+ / 6.2	12.1	0.85	13.32	5	4	95	0	1	70	52.3	-26.1	81	3	0	0	0.0	0.0
C+ / 6.2	12.1	0.85	13.34	3	4	95	0	1	70	54.0	-26.0	82	3	0	0	0.0	0.0
C+ / 6.2	12.1	0.85	13.31	5	4	95	0	1	70	55.0	-26.1	83	3	0	0	0.0	0.0
C- / 3.6	11.9	0.96	8.75	333	0	98	0	2	63	98.7	-16.7	11	8	1,000	100	5.5	0.0
C- / 3.2	12.0	0.97	7.75	14	0	98	0	2	63	90.0	-17.1	7	8	1,000	100	0.0	0.0
C- / 3.8	12.0	0.97	9.19	1,189	0	98	0	2	63	104.4	-16.6	14	8	1,000,000	0	0.0	0.0
C- / 3.4	12.0	0.97	8.17	60	0	98	0	2	63	99.9	-16.7	11	8	1,000	100	0.0	0.0
C- / 3.8	12.0	0.97	9.14	9	0	98	0	2	63	102.6	-16.7	13	8	0	0	0.0	0.0
C- / 3.4	12.1	0.97	8.28	4	0	98	0	2	63	95.0	-16.9	8	8	0	0	0.0	0.0
C- / 3.5	12.0	0.96	8.47	2	0	98	0	2	63	96.5	-16.9	9	8	0	0	0.0	0.0
C- / 3.9	12.0	0.97	9.44	11	0	98	0	2	63	98.3	-16.7	10	8	0	0	0.0	0.0
C- / 3.9	12.0	0.97	9.40	9	0	98	0	2	63	100.5	-16.7	12	8	0	0	0.0	0.0
C- / 3.8	12.0	0.96	9.28	49	0	98	0	2	63	101.6	-16.7	12	8	0	0	0.0	0.0
B- / 7.0	10.3	1.00	16.33	331	0	99	0	1	4	127.8	-16.4	68	6	1,000	100	1.5	0.0
B- / 7.0	10.3	1.00	16.03	50	0	99	0	1	4	118.6	-16.7	58	6	1,000	100	0.0	0.0
C+ / 6.9	10.3	1.00	16.31	3,413	0	99	0	1	4	132.3	-16.3	72	6	1,000,000	0	0.0	0.0
B- / 7.0	10.3	1.00	16.17	600	0	99	0	1	4	128.4	-16.5	70	6	1,000	100	0.0	0.0
B- / 7.0	10.3	1.00	16.29	20	0	99	0	1	4	121.6	-16.5	62	6	0	0	0.0	0.0
B- / 7.0	10.3	1.00	16.40	32	0	99	0	1	4	123.3	-16.6	63	6	0	0	0.0	0.0
B- / 7.0	10.3	1.00	16.35	210	0	99	0	1	4	125.4	-16.5	66	6	0	0	0.0	0.0
B- / 7.0	10.3	1.00	16.39	207	0	99	0	1	4	127.9	-16.5	68	6	0	0	0.0	0.0

I. Index of Stock Mutual Funds

Fund Type	Fund Name	Ticker Symbol	Overall Investment Rating	Phone	Performance Rating/Pts	3 Mo	6 Mo	1Yr / Pct	Annualized 3Yr / Pct	5Yr / Pct	Dividend Yield	Expense Ratio
IX	Principal LgCap S&P 500 R5	PLFPX	A+	(800) 222-5852	A- / 9.1	7.88	9.76	24.47 /72	10.17 /94	13.51 /89	1.59	0.41
GR	Principal LgCap Val Fd A	PCACX	C	(800) 222-5852	C+ / 5.7	6.34	9.31	20.10 /53	6.69 /70	11.66 /71	1.72	0.86
GR	Principal LgCap Val Fd C	PLUCX	C+	(800) 222-5852	C+ / 6.1	6.14	8.91	19.08 /48	5.80 /63	10.72 /64	1.12	1.87
GR	Principal LgCap Val Fd Inst	PVLIX	C+	(800) 222-5852	B- / 7.1	6.46	9.53	20.57 /55	7.15 /73	12.17 /76	2.25	0.42
GR	Principal LgCap Val Fd J	PVLJX	C+	(800) 222-5852	C+ / 6.9	6.36	9.39	20.19 /53	6.76 /70	11.72 /72	2.01	0.72
GR	Principal LgCap Val Fd R1	PLSVX	C+	(800) 222-5852	C+ / 6.5	6.16	9.07	19.52 /49	6.23 /66	11.20 /68	1.38	1.29
GR	Principal LgCap Val Fd R2	PLVNX	C+	(800) 222-5852	C+ / 6.6	6.21	9.11	19.72 /51	6.35 /67	11.34 /69	1.60	1.16
GR	Principal LgCap Val Fd R3	PLVMX	C+	(800) 222-5852	C+ / 6.7	6.34	9.25	19.92 /52	6.57 /69	11.54 /70	1.78	0.98
GR	Principal LgCap Val Fd R4	PLVSX	C+	(800) 222-5852	C+ / 6.8	6.34	9.34	20.14 /53	6.75 /70	11.76 /72	1.86	0.79
GR	Principal LgCap Val Fd R5	PLVPX	C+	(800) 222-5852	C+ / 6.9	6.37	9.34	20.24 /53	6.88 /71	11.88 /73	2.01	0.67
GR	Principal LgCp Gr I A	PLGAX	C	(800) 222-5852	C+ / 6.2	8.56	8.10	19.81 /51	7.17 /73	11.99 /74	0.00	1.28
GR	Principal LgCp Gr I Inst	PLGIX	C+	(800) 222-5852	B / 7.6	8.73	8.46	20.51 /55	7.84 /78	12.59 /80	0.07	0.63
GR	Principal LgCp Gr I J	PLGJX	C	(800) 222-5852	B- / 7.3	8.61	8.29	20.22 /53	7.49 /75	12.15 /76	0.00	0.92
GR	Principal LgCp Gr I R1	PCRSX	C	(800) 222-5852	C+ / 6.9	8.42	7.91	19.46 /49	6.90 /71	11.62 /71	0.00	1.49
GR	Principal LgCp Gr I R2	PPUNX	C	(800) 222-5852	B- / 7.0	8.52	8.11	19.72 /51	7.05 /72	11.78 /72	0.00	1.36
GR	Principal LgCp Gr I R3	PPUMX	C	(800) 222-5852	B- / 7.1	8.50	8.11	19.84 /51	7.23 /74	11.96 /74	0.00	1.18
GR	Principal LgCp Gr I R4	PPUSX	C+	(800) 222-5852	B- / 7.3	8.66	8.28	20.10 /53	7.45 /75	12.18 /76	0.00	0.99
GR	Principal LgCp Gr I R5	PPUPX	C+	(800) 222-5852	B- / 7.4	8.57	8.29	20.29 /54	7.56 /76	12.30 /77	0.00	0.87
GR	Principal LgCp Gr II Inst	PPIIX	C	(800) 222-5852	B / 7.7	8.24	7.70	18.98 /47	8.68 /84	11.89 /73	0.71	0.89
GR	Principal LgCp Gr II J	PPLJX	C-	(800) 222-5852	B- / 7.3	7.90	7.42	18.31 /44	8.20 /80	11.40 /69	0.54	1.25
GR	Principal LgCp Gr II R1	PDASX	C-	(800) 222-5852	B- / 7.0	7.85	7.12	17.74 /42	7.68 /77	10.89 /65	0.00	1.77
GR	Principal LgCp Gr II R2	PPTNX	C-	(800) 222-5852	B- / 7.2	8.03	7.41	18.12 /43	7.88 /78	11.07 /66	0.17	1.64
GR	Principal LgCp Gr II R3	PPTMX	C-	(800) 222-5852	B- / 7.2	7.98	7.39	18.16 /44	8.03 /79	11.25 /68	0.17	1.46
GR	Principal LgCp Gr II R4	PPTSX	C-	(800) 222-5852	B- / 7.4	8.04	7.47	18.44 /45	8.22 /81	11.45 /69	0.27	1.27
GR	Principal LgCp Gr II R5	PPTPX	C-	(800) 222-5852	B- / 7.5	8.07	7.52	18.62 /46	8.39 /82	11.58 /71	0.53	1.15
GR	Principal LgCp Val III Inst	PLVIX	B+	(800) 222-5852	B+ / 8.3	5.98	9.49	24.73 /72	8.78 /85	12.84 /82	1.73	0.77
GR	Principal LgCp Val III J	PLVJX	B+	(800) 222-5852	B / 8.1	5.96	9.37	24.36 /71	8.41 /82	12.40 /78	1.48	1.08
GR	Principal LgCp Val III R1	PESAX	B+	(800) 222-5852	B / 7.7	5.81	9.06	23.68 /69	7.84 /78	11.86 /73	0.89	1.65
GR	Principal LgCp Val III R2	PPSNX	B+	(800) 222-5852	B / 7.8	5.82	9.13	23.79 /69	8.00 /79	12.02 /74	0.98	1.52
GR	Principal LgCp Val III R3	PPSFX	B+	(800) 222-5852	B / 7.9	5.89	9.28	24.06 /70	8.19 /80	12.21 /76	1.15	1.34
GR	Principal LgCp Val III R4	PPSSX	B+	(800) 222-5852	B / 8.0	5.91	9.35	24.24 /71	8.38 /82	12.43 /78	1.36	1.15
GR	Principal LgCp Val III R5	PPSRX	B+	(800) 222-5852	B / 8.1	5.96	9.38	24.41 /71	8.51 /83	12.54 /79	1.49	1.03
AA	Principal LifeTime 2010 A	PENAX	C-	(800) 222-5852	D / 1.9	3.61	2.38	10.27 /12	2.98 /32	5.26 /23	1.57	1.11
AA	Principal LifeTime 2010 Inst	PTTIX	C	(800) 222-5852	D+ / 2.6	3.70	2.61	10.65 /13	3.36 /35	5.65 /26	2.00	0.67
AA	Principal LifeTime 2010 J	PTAJX	C	(800) 222-5852	D+ / 2.5	3.60	2.51	10.40 /13	3.12 /33	5.36 /24	1.83	0.87
AA	Principal LifeTime 2010 R1	PVASX	C	(800) 222-5852	D / 2.1	3.41	2.16	9.69 /11	2.46 /27	4.72 /19	0.98	1.55
AA	Principal LifeTime 2010 R2	PTANX	C	(800) 222-5852	D / 2.2	3.57	2.25	9.86 /11	2.61 /28	4.87 /20	1.13	1.42
AA	Principal LifeTime 2010 R3	PTAMX	C	(800) 222-5852	D+ / 2.3	3.56	2.31	10.04 /12	2.79 /30	5.06 /22	1.40	1.24
AA	Principal LifeTime 2010 R4	PTASX	C	(800) 222-5852	D+ / 2.4	3.53	2.36	10.17 /12	2.97 /32	5.25 /23	1.61	1.05
AA	Principal LifeTime 2010 R5	PTAPX	C	(800) 222-5852	D+ / 2.5	3.64	2.47	10.36 /13	3.10 /33	5.38 /24	1.72	0.93
AA	Principal LifeTime 2015 Inst	LTINX	C-	(800) 222-5852	C- / 3.1	4.24	3.33	12.18 /19	3.63 /38	6.29 /30	1.91	0.68
AA	Principal LifeTime 2015 R1	LTSGX	C-	(800) 222-5852	D+ / 2.5	4.04	2.90	11.24 /15	2.73 /29	5.36 /24	1.08	1.56
AA	Principal LifeTime 2015 R2	LTASX	C-	(800) 222-5852	D+ / 2.6	4.14	3.00	11.44 /16	2.88 /31	5.49 /25	0.99	1.43
AA	Principal LifeTime 2015 R3	LTAPX	C-	(800) 222-5852	D+ / 2.7	4.13	2.99	11.54 /16	3.05 /32	5.68 /26	1.36	1.25
AA	Principal LifeTime 2015 R4	LTSLX	C-	(800) 222-5852	D+ / 2.8	4.10	3.07	11.69 /17	3.24 /34	5.87 /27	1.55	1.06
AA	Principal LifeTime 2015 R5	LTPFX	C-	(800) 222-5852	D+ / 2.9	4.23	3.20	11.93 /18	3.37 /36	6.00 /28	1.68	0.94
AA	Principal LifeTime 2020 A	PTBAX	C-	(800) 222-5852	D+ / 2.4	4.71	3.63	13.38 /23	3.61 /38	6.67 /33	1.42	1.11
AA	Principal LifeTime 2020 Inst	PLWIX	C	(800) 222-5852	C- / 3.6	4.81	3.81	13.80 /25	3.99 /43	7.06 /35	1.87	0.71
AA	Principal LifeTime 2020 J	PLFJX	C	(800) 222-5852	C- / 3.4	4.81	3.72	13.67 /24	3.76 /40	6.78 /33	1.71	0.91
AA	Principal LifeTime 2020 R1	PWASX	C-	(800) 222-5852	D+ / 2.9	4.55	3.30	12.79 /21	3.07 /32	6.13 /29	1.03	1.59
AA	Principal LifeTime 2020 R2	PTBNX	C-	(800) 222-5852	C- / 3.0	4.64	3.39	13.00 /22	3.21 /34	6.26 /30	1.10	1.46
AA	Principal LifeTime 2020 R3	PTBMX	C-	(800) 222-5852	C- / 3.2	4.70	3.53	13.25 /23	3.42 /36	6.46 /31	1.31	1.28

Legend: 99 Pct = Best / 0 Pct = Worst. PERFORMANCE — Total Return % through 2/28/17. Incl. in Returns.

● Denotes fund is closed to new investors
* Denotes fund is included in Section II

RISK			NET ASSETS		ASSET					BULL / BEAR		FUND MANAGER		MINIMUMS		LOADS	
	3 Year		NAV						Portfolio	Last Bull	Last Bear	Manager	Manager	Initial	Additional	Front	Back
Risk Rating/Pts	Standard Deviation	Beta	As of 2/28/17	Total $(Mil)	Cash %	Stocks %	Bonds %	Other %	Turnover Ratio	Market Return	Market Return	Quality Pct	Tenure (Years)	Purch. $	Purch. $	End Load	End Load
B- / 7.0	10.3	1.00	16.52	443	0	99	0	1	4	129.3	-16.4	70	6	0	0	0.0	0.0
C / 5.4	10.2	0.95	12.38	195	0	99	0	1	99	114.5	-19.9	33	3	1,000	100	5.5	0.0
C / 5.4	10.3	0.95	12.08	7	0	99	0	1	99	104.9	-20.0	24	3	1,000	100	0.0	0.0
C / 5.3	10.3	0.95	12.34	1,922	0	99	0	1	99	119.8	-19.7	38	3	1,000,000	0	0.0	0.0
C / 5.3	10.2	0.95	12.13	67	0	99	0	1	99	114.8	-19.8	34	3	1,000	100	0.0	0.0
C / 5.4	10.3	0.95	12.27	1	0	99	0	1	99	109.9	-20.0	28	3	0	0	0.0	0.0
C / 5.4	10.2	0.95	12.31	2	0	99	0	1	99	111.1	-19.9	30	3	0	0	0.0	0.0
C / 5.4	10.3	0.95	12.26	4	0	99	0	1	99	113.4	-19.9	32	3	0	0	0.0	0.0
C / 5.4	10.2	0.95	12.25	2	0	99	0	1	99	115.5	-19.8	34	3	0	0	0.0	0.0
C / 5.4	10.3	0.95	12.37	5	0	99	0	1	99	116.8	-19.8	35	3	0	0	0.0	0.0
C / 4.3	11.9	1.04	12.27	23	3	96	0	1	33	121.1	-17.5	28	N/A	1,000	100	5.5	0.0
C / 4.4	11.9	1.04	12.55	6,532	3	96	0	1	33	127.3	-17.4	35	N/A	1,000,000	0	0.0	0.0
C- / 4.0	11.9	1.04	10.57	117	3	96	0	1	33	122.5	-17.6	31	N/A	1,000	100	0.0	0.0
C- / 4.1	11.9	1.04	11.05	6	3	96	0	1	33	116.7	-17.7	25	N/A	0	0	0.0	0.0
C- / 4.0	11.9	1.04	10.80	11	3	96	0	1	33	118.5	-17.7	26	N/A	0	0	0.0	0.0
C- / 4.2	11.9	1.04	11.59	120	3	96	0	1	33	120.4	-17.5	29	N/A	0	0	0.0	0.0
C- / 4.2	11.9	1.04	11.76	79	3	96	0	1	33	122.7	-17.5	31	N/A	0	0	0.0	0.0
C / 4.3	12.0	1.04	12.14	281	3	96	0	1	33	124.3	-17.5	31	N/A	0	0	0.0	0.0
D+ / 2.9	10.5	0.99	8.41	509	2	96	1	1	46	114.4	-15.7	53	N/A	1,000,000	0	0.0	0.0
D / 2.1	10.4	0.98	6.93	36	2	96	1	1	46	109.3	-15.9	48	N/A	1,000	100	0.0	0.0
D+ / 2.6	10.5	0.99	7.69	1	2	96	1	1	46	104.3	-16.0	40	N/A	0	0	0.0	0.0
D+ / 2.4	10.5	0.98	7.30	2	2	96	1	1	46	105.8	-15.9	44	N/A	0	0	0.0	0.0
D+ / 2.5	10.5	0.98	7.61	4	2	96	1	1	46	107.8	-15.9	45	N/A	0	0	0.0	0.0
D+ / 2.7	10.5	0.99	7.95	2	2	96	1	1	46	109.9	-15.9	47	N/A	0	0	0.0	0.0
D+ / 2.8	10.5	0.98	8.07	6	2	96	1	1	46	111.6	-15.9	50	N/A	0	0	0.0	0.0
C+ / 6.2	10.2	0.97	16.13	1,767	1	96	2	1	35	123.5	-21.2	57	8	1,000,000	0	0.0	0.0
C+ / 6.2	10.2	0.96	15.94	76	1	96	2	1	35	118.8	-21.3	53	8	1,000	100	0.0	0.0
C+ / 6.3	10.2	0.97	16.12	4	1	96	2	1	35	113.3	-21.5	45	8	0	0	0.0	0.0
C+ / 6.3	10.3	0.97	16.17	3	1	96	2	1	35	114.8	-21.4	47	8	0	0	0.0	0.0
C+ / 6.3	10.2	0.97	16.79	12	1	96	2	1	35	116.8	-21.3	50	8	0	0	0.0	0.0
C+ / 6.2	10.2	0.97	16.14	6	1	96	2	1	35	119.2	-21.3	52	8	0	0	0.0	0.0
C+ / 6.2	10.2	0.97	16.25	9	1	96	2	1	35	120.4	-21.3	54	8	0	0	0.0	0.0
B / 8.4	4.8	0.73	13.23	33	7	32	60	1	15	44.2	-10.1	42	12	1,000	100	3.8	0.0
B / 8.3	4.8	0.73	13.14	701	7	32	60	1	15	47.2	-10.0	48	16	0	0	0.0	0.0
B / 8.3	4.8	0.73	13.10	245	7	32	60	1	15	45.0	-10.2	44	16	1,000	100	0.0	0.0
B / 8.4	4.8	0.73	13.13	7	7	32	60	1	15	40.3	-10.3	36	13	0	0	0.0	0.0
B / 8.4	4.8	0.73	13.13	8	7	32	60	1	15	41.4	-10.3	37	16	0	0	0.0	0.0
B / 8.4	4.9	0.74	13.06	46	7	32	60	1	15	42.6	-10.2	39	16	0	0	0.0	0.0
B / 8.4	4.8	0.73	13.08	29	7	32	60	1	15	44.2	-10.1	43	16	0	0	0.0	0.0
B / 8.3	4.8	0.73	13.10	58	7	32	60	1	15	45.1	-10.0	44	16	0	0	0.0	0.0
B- / 7.3	5.5	0.85	10.23	528	8	38	52	2	14	54.9	-12.6	40	9	1,000,000	0	0.0	0.0
B- / 7.4	5.5	0.85	10.01	8	8	38	52	2	14	47.6	-12.8	29	9	0	0	0.0	0.0
B- / 7.4	5.6	0.86	10.07	7	8	38	52	2	14	48.8	-12.8	30	9	0	0	0.0	0.0
B- / 7.3	5.5	0.85	10.03	70	8	38	52	2	14	50.1	-12.8	33	9	0	0	0.0	0.0
B- / 7.3	5.5	0.85	10.09	44	8	38	52	2	14	51.6	-12.6	35	9	0	0	0.0	0.0
B- / 7.3	5.5	0.84	10.11	84	8	38	52	2	14	52.7	-12.6	37	9	0	0	0.0	0.0
B- / 7.1	6.4	0.99	13.65	120	10	47	42	1	12	60.3	-14.7	27	12	1,000	100	5.5	0.0
B- / 7.1	6.4	0.99	13.56	3,881	10	47	42	1	12	63.6	-14.6	31	16	0	0	0.0	0.0
B- / 7.1	6.4	1.00	13.50	923	10	47	42	1	12	61.1	-14.6	29	16	1,000	100	0.0	0.0
B- / 7.2	6.4	1.00	13.49	39	10	47	42	1	12	55.9	-14.8	22	13	0	0	0.0	0.0
B- / 7.2	6.5	1.00	13.47	46	10	47	42	1	12	57.1	-14.8	23	16	0	0	0.0	0.0
B- / 7.1	6.4	0.99	13.45	230	10	47	42	1	12	58.6	-14.8	25	16	0	0	0.0	0.0

99 Pct = Best
0 Pct = Worst

Fund Type	Fund Name	Ticker Symbol	Overall Investment Rating	Phone	Performance Rating/Pts	3 Mo	6 Mo	1Yr / Pct	3Yr / Pct	5Yr / Pct	Dividend Yield	Expense Ratio
AA	Principal LifeTime 2020 R4	PTBSX	C-	(800) 222-5852	C- / 3.3	4.70	3.61	13.40 /23	3.61 /38	6.66 /33	1.53	1.09
AA	Principal LifeTime 2020 R5	PTBPX	C-	(800) 222-5852	C- / 3.4	4.69	3.68	13.54 /24	3.73 /40	6.78 /33	1.60	0.97
AA	Principal LifeTime 2025 Inst	LTSTX	C	(800) 222-5852	C / 4.0	5.32	4.33	15.14 /30	4.22 /45	7.54 /39	1.74	0.73
AA	Principal LifeTime 2025 R1	LTSNX	C-	(800) 222-5852	C- / 3.3	5.15	3.94	14.14 /26	3.34 /35	6.60 /32	0.96	1.60
AA	Principal LifeTime 2025 R2	LTADX	C-	(800) 222-5852	C- / 3.4	5.18	3.97	14.27 /27	3.47 /37	6.74 /33	0.99	1.47
AA	Principal LifeTime 2025 R3	LTVPX	C	(800) 222-5852	C- / 3.6	5.25	4.14	14.56 /28	3.68 /39	6.93 /34	1.24	1.29
AA	Principal LifeTime 2025 R4	LTEEX	C	(800) 222-5852	C- / 3.7	5.22	4.12	14.67 /28	3.85 /41	7.12 /35	1.43	1.10
AA	Principal LifeTime 2025 R5	LTPDX	C	(800) 222-5852	C- / 3.8	5.21	4.21	14.85 /29	3.99 /43	7.26 /36	1.52	0.98
AA	Principal LifeTime 2030 A	PTCAX	C-	(800) 222-5852	C- / 3.0	5.57	4.71	15.64 /33	3.98 /43	7.53 /39	1.26	1.16
AA	Principal LifeTime 2030 Inst	PMTIX	C	(800) 222-5852	C / 4.3	5.73	4.95	16.11 /35	4.39 /47	7.95 /42	1.68	0.73
AA	Principal LifeTime 2030 J	PLTJX	C	(800) 222-5852	C / 4.2	5.70	4.93	15.94 /34	4.15 /45	7.64 /39	1.51	0.95
AA	Principal LifeTime 2030 R1	PXASX	C-	(800) 222-5852	C- / 3.6	5.48	4.55	15.03 /30	3.48 /37	6.99 /35	0.86	1.61
AA	Principal LifeTime 2030 R2	PTCNX	C-	(800) 222-5852	C- / 3.7	5.56	4.62	15.28 /31	3.61 /38	7.13 /35	0.93	1.48
AA	Principal LifeTime 2030 R3	PTCMX	C	(800) 222-5852	C- / 3.9	5.54	4.69	15.43 /32	3.79 /40	7.33 /37	1.14	1.30
AA	Principal LifeTime 2030 R4	PTCSX	C	(800) 222-5852	C / 4.0	5.64	4.81	15.66 /33	4.00 /43	7.54 /39	1.28	1.11
AA	Principal LifeTime 2030 R5	PTCPX	C	(800) 222-5852	C- / 4.1	5.60	4.82	15.81 /33	4.12 /44	7.66 /39	1.41	0.99
AA	Principal LifeTime 2035 Inst	LTIUX	C	(800) 222-5852	C / 4.5	5.85	5.28	16.51 /36	4.42 /48	8.31 /45	1.47	0.69
AA	Principal LifeTime 2035 R1	LTANX	C	(800) 222-5852	C- / 3.7	5.58	4.90	15.52 /32	3.52 /37	7.37 /37	0.72	1.56
AA	Principal LifeTime 2035 R2	LTVIX	C	(800) 222-5852	C- / 3.9	5.65	4.98	15.73 /33	3.68 /39	7.53 /39	0.78	1.43
AA	Principal LifeTime 2035 R3	LTAOX	C	(800) 222-5852	C- / 4.0	5.74	5.07	15.90 /34	3.83 /41	7.71 /40	0.97	1.25
AA	Principal LifeTime 2035 R4	LTSEX	C	(800) 222-5852	C- / 4.2	5.82	5.15	16.12 /35	4.06 /44	7.91 /41	1.15	1.06
AA	Principal LifeTime 2035 R5	LTPEX	C	(800) 222-5852	C / 4.3	5.81	5.15	16.19 /35	4.16 /45	8.03 /42	1.24	0.94
AA	Principal LifeTime 2040 A	PTDAX	C-	(800) 222-5852	C- / 3.4	6.05	5.53	17.07 /39	4.16 /45	8.20 /44	1.07	1.18
AA	Principal LifeTime 2040 Inst	PTDIX	C	(800) 222-5852	C / 4.8	6.16	5.72	17.43 /40	4.54 /49	8.59 /47	1.44	0.71
AA	Principal LifeTime 2040 J	PTDJX	C	(800) 222-5852	C / 4.5	6.07	5.55	17.16 /39	4.22 /45	8.25 /44	1.26	0.94
AA	Principal LifeTime 2040 R1	PYASX	C	(800) 222-5852	C- / 4.0	5.90	5.23	16.48 /36	3.63 /38	7.64 /39	0.63	1.59
AA	Principal LifeTime 2040 R2	PTDNX	C	(800) 222-5852	C- / 4.1	5.95	5.36	16.62 /37	3.75 /40	7.79 /41	0.74	1.46
AA	Principal LifeTime 2040 R3	PTDMX	C	(800) 222-5852	C / 4.3	6.02	5.42	16.82 /38	3.94 /42	7.97 /42	0.92	1.28
AA	Principal LifeTime 2040 R4	PTDSX	C	(800) 222-5852	C / 4.4	6.07	5.55	17.02 /38	4.14 /45	8.19 /44	1.11	1.09
AA	Principal LifeTime 2040 R5	PTDPX	C	(800) 222-5852	C / 4.5	6.04	5.52	17.09 /39	4.26 /46	8.30 /45	1.17	0.97
AA	Principal LifeTime 2045 Inst	LTRIX	C+	(800) 222-5852	C / 5.1	6.36	6.08	18.28 /44	4.66 /50	8.84 /49	1.39	0.73
AA	Principal LifeTime 2045 R1	LTRGX	C	(800) 222-5852	C- / 4.2	6.14	5.57	17.16 /39	3.77 /40	7.89 /41	0.65	1.60
AA	Principal LifeTime 2045 R2	LTRSX	C	(800) 222-5852	C / 4.4	6.22	5.65	17.38 /40	3.91 /42	8.03 /42	0.72	1.47
AA	Principal LifeTime 2045 R3	LTRVX	C	(800) 222-5852	C / 4.5	6.15	5.68	17.55 /41	4.07 /44	8.20 /44	0.94	1.29
AA	Principal LifeTime 2045 R4	LTRLX	C	(800) 222-5852	C / 4.7	6.18	5.81	17.71 /42	4.28 /46	8.44 /46	1.09	1.10
AA	Principal LifeTime 2045 R5	LTRDX	C	(800) 222-5852	C / 4.8	6.31	5.93	17.95 /43	4.41 /48	8.56 /47	1.13	0.98
AA	Principal LifeTime 2050 A	PPEAX	C-	(800) 222-5852	C- / 3.7	6.36	6.06	18.19 /44	4.35 /47	8.63 /47	0.99	1.26
AA	Principal LifeTime 2050 Inst	PPLIX	C+	(800) 222-5852	C / 5.2	6.52	6.29	18.69 /46	4.72 /51	9.04 /51	1.37	0.74
AA	Principal LifeTime 2050 J	PFLJX	C	(800) 222-5852	C / 4.9	6.46	6.14	18.30 /44	4.34 /47	8.57 /47	1.12	1.05
AA	Principal LifeTime 2050 R1	PZASX	C	(800) 222-5852	C / 4.4	6.26	5.80	17.64 /41	3.82 /41	8.08 /43	0.60	1.61
AA	Principal LifeTime 2050 R2	PTENX	C	(800) 222-5852	C / 4.5	6.37	5.91	17.86 /42	3.98 /43	8.23 /44	0.71	1.48
AA	Principal LifeTime 2050 R3	PTERX	C	(800) 222-5852	C / 4.7	6.35	5.96	18.00 /43	4.14 /45	8.42 /46	0.89	1.30
AA	Principal LifeTime 2050 R4	PTESX	C	(800) 222-5852	C / 4.8	6.42	6.03	18.20 /44	4.34 /47	8.62 /47	1.04	1.11
AA	Principal LifeTime 2050 R5	PTEFX	C	(800) 222-5852	C / 4.9	6.43	6.12	18.37 /45	4.46 /48	8.76 /49	1.06	0.99
AA	Principal LifeTime 2055 Inst	LTFIX	C+	(800) 222-5852	C / 5.3	6.70	6.52	19.14 /48	4.83 /52	9.04 /51	1.34	0.75
AA	Principal LifeTime 2055 R1	LTFGX	C	(800) 222-5852	C / 4.6	6.42	6.05	18.14 /43	3.92 /42	8.11 /43	0.68	1.61
AA	Principal LifeTime 2055 R2	LTFSX	C	(800) 222-5852	C / 4.7	6.44	6.07	18.24 /44	4.05 /44	8.23 /44	0.71	1.48
AA	Principal LifeTime 2055 R3	LTFDX	C	(800) 222-5852	C / 4.8	6.48	6.20	18.54 /45	4.22 /45	8.43 /46	0.94	1.30
AA	Principal LifeTime 2055 R4	LTFLX	C+	(800) 222-5852	C / 5.0	6.56	6.29	18.76 /46	4.42 /48	8.63 /47	1.05	1.11
AA	Principal LifeTime 2055 R5	LTFPX	C+	(800) 222-5852	C / 5.1	6.57	6.39	18.94 /47	4.57 /49	8.78 /49	1.08	0.99
GI	Principal LifeTime 2060 Inst	PLTZX	C+	(800) 222-5852	C / 5.3	6.70	6.53	19.07 /47	4.75 /51	--	1.32	0.77
GI	Principal LifeTime 2060 J	PLTAX	C+	(800) 222-5852	C / 5.0	6.60	6.33	18.71 /46	4.43 /48	--	1.04	1.89

● Denotes fund is closed to new investors
* Denotes fund is included in Section II

www.thestreetratings.com

RISK			NET ASSETS		ASSET					BULL / BEAR		FUND MANAGER		MINIMUMS		LOADS	
	3 Year		NAV						Portfolio	Last Bull	Last Bear	Manager	Manager	Initial	Additional	Front	Back
Risk Rating/Pts	Standard Deviation	Beta	As of 2/28/17	Total $(Mil)	Cash %	Stocks %	Bonds %	Other %	Turnover Ratio	Market Return	Market Return	Quality Pct	Tenure (Years)	Purch. $	Purch. $	End Load	End Load
B- /7.1	6.4	0.99	13.47	182	10	47	42	1	12	60.3	-14.7	27	16	0	0	0.0	0.0
B- /7.1	6.4	0.99	13.50	319	10	47	42	1	12	61.3	-14.6	28	16	0	0	0.0	0.0
C+ /6.9	7.0	1.09	10.72	1,286	10	54	34	2	14	68.6	-15.7	26	9	1,000,000	0	0.0	0.0
B- /7.0	7.0	1.09	10.52	16	10	54	34	2	14	60.9	-16.1	18	9	0	0	0.0	0.0
C+ /6.9	7.0	1.09	10.54	18	10	54	34	2	14	61.9	-15.9	19	9	0	0	0.0	0.0
C+ /6.9	7.1	1.10	10.54	171	10	54	34	2	14	63.6	-15.9	21	9	0	0	0.0	0.0
C+ /6.9	7.0	1.09	10.62	102	10	54	34	2	14	65.1	-15.8	22	9	0	0	0.0	0.0
C+ /6.9	7.1	1.09	10.66	147	10	54	34	2	14	66.3	-15.8	24	9	0	0	0.0	0.0
C+ /6.6	7.6	1.18	13.80	124	10	61	27	2	15	69.4	-16.6	18	12	1,000	100	5.5	0.0
C+ /6.6	7.6	1.18	13.76	4,544	10	61	27	2	15	73.0	-16.5	21	16	0	0	0.0	0.0
C+ /6.6	7.6	1.18	13.73	1,123	10	61	27	2	15	70.3	-16.6	19	16	1,000	100	0.0	0.0
C+ /6.7	7.6	1.18	13.68	36	10	61	27	2	15	65.0	-16.9	14	13	0	0	0.0	0.0
C+ /6.7	7.6	1.18	13.71	48	10	61	27	2	15	66.2	-16.8	15	16	0	0	0.0	0.0
C+ /6.7	7.6	1.18	13.71	227	10	61	27	2	15	67.8	-16.7	17	16	0	0	0.0	0.0
C+ /6.7	7.6	1.18	14.15	193	10	61	27	2	15	69.6	-16.7	18	16	0	0	0.0	0.0
C+ /6.6	7.6	1.18	13.75	329	10	61	27	2	15	70.6	-16.6	19	16	0	0	0.0	0.0
C+ /6.8	8.1	1.25	11.32	995	4	71	24	1	15	77.2	-17.5	17	9	1,000,000	0	0.0	0.0
B- /7.0	8.1	1.25	11.14	13	4	71	24	1	15	69.0	-17.8	11	9	0	0	0.0	0.0
C+ /6.9	8.1	1.25	11.13	15	4	71	24	1	15	70.3	-17.8	12	9	0	0	0.0	0.0
C+ /6.9	8.1	1.26	11.17	111	4	71	24	1	15	71.9	-17.7	13	9	0	0	0.0	0.0
C+ /6.9	8.1	1.25	11.24	80	4	71	24	1	15	73.7	-17.6	14	9	0	0	0.0	0.0
C+ /6.9	8.1	1.25	11.27	105	4	71	24	1	15	74.8	-17.6	15	9	0	0	0.0	0.0
C+ /6.5	8.6	1.33	14.23	90	5	75	18	2	18	76.9	-18.3	11	12	1,000	100	5.5	0.0
C+ /6.5	8.6	1.33	14.46	3,118	5	75	18	2	18	80.4	-18.1	14	16	0	0	0.0	0.0
C+ /6.5	8.6	1.33	14.35	672	5	75	18	2	18	77.3	-18.4	12	16	1,000	100	0.0	0.0
C+ /6.6	8.6	1.33	14.35	25	5	75	18	2	18	72.1	-18.5	9	13	0	0	0.0	0.0
C+ /6.6	8.6	1.33	14.35	34	5	75	18	2	18	73.2	-18.4	9	16	0	0	0.0	0.0
C+ /6.5	8.6	1.33	14.30	145	5	75	18	2	18	75.0	-18.4	10	16	0	0	0.0	0.0
C+ /6.5	8.6	1.33	14.32	132	5	75	18	2	18	76.8	-18.3	11	16	0	0	0.0	0.0
C+ /6.5	8.6	1.34	14.40	227	5	75	18	2	18	77.9	-18.3	12	16	0	0	0.0	0.0
C+ /6.5	9.0	1.38	11.62	667	5	79	14	2	15	83.0	-18.5	12	9	1,000,000	0	0.0	0.0
C+ /6.6	9.0	1.38	11.32	7	5	79	14	2	15	74.6	-18.9	8	9	0	0	0.0	0.0
C+ /6.5	9.0	1.38	11.31	11	5	79	14	2	15	75.7	-18.8	8	9	0	0	0.0	0.0
C+ /6.5	9.0	1.39	11.37	72	5	79	14	2	15	77.6	-18.8	9	9	0	0	0.0	0.0
C+ /6.5	8.9	1.38	11.45	49	5	79	14	2	15	79.4	-18.7	10	9	0	0	0.0	0.0
C+ /6.5	9.0	1.39	11.48	68	5	79	14	2	15	80.6	-18.7	11	9	0	0	0.0	0.0
C+ /6.3	9.2	1.42	14.25	72	6	82	10	2	17	81.7	-19.3	9	12	1,000	100	5.5	0.0
C+ /6.2	9.2	1.42	14.18	1,837	6	82	10	2	17	85.6	-19.3	11	16	0	0	0.0	0.0
C+ /6.3	9.2	1.42	13.82	210	6	82	10	2	17	81.2	-19.4	9	16	1,000	100	0.0	0.0
C+ /6.4	9.2	1.42	14.05	17	6	82	10	2	17	76.9	-19.5	7	13	0	0	0.0	0.0
C+ /6.3	9.2	1.42	14.05	22	6	82	10	2	17	78.1	-19.5	7	16	0	0	0.0	0.0
C+ /6.3	9.2	1.42	14.04	78	6	82	10	2	17	80.0	-19.5	8	16	0	0	0.0	0.0
C+ /6.3	9.2	1.42	14.10	67	6	82	10	2	17	81.7	-19.3	9	16	0	0	0.0	0.0
C+ /6.3	9.2	1.42	14.14	114	6	82	10	2	17	83.0	-19.3	10	16	0	0	0.0	0.0
C+ /6.4	9.4	1.45	12.09	255	6	84	9	1	12	85.8	-19.4	10	9	1,000,000	0	0.0	0.0
C+ /6.5	9.4	1.45	11.73	3	6	84	9	1	12	77.4	-19.8	7	9	0	0	0.0	0.0
C+ /6.5	9.4	1.45	11.76	3	6	84	9	1	12	78.5	-19.7	7	9	0	0	0.0	0.0
C+ /6.5	9.5	1.45	11.82	24	6	84	9	1	12	80.3	-19.7	7	9	0	0	0.0	0.0
C+ /6.5	9.4	1.45	11.91	18	6	84	9	1	12	82.0	-19.6	8	9	0	0	0.0	0.0
C+ /6.5	9.4	1.45	11.96	21	6	84	9	1	12	83.3	-19.5	9	9	0	0	0.0	0.0
C+ /6.8	9.4	0.88	12.51	159	10	82	6	2	15	N/A	N/A	21	4	0	0	0.0	0.0
C+ /6.8	9.4	0.88	12.45	7	10	82	6	2	15	N/A	N/A	18	4	1,000	100	0.0	0.0

						PERFORMANCE					Incl. in Returns	
							Total Return % through 2/28/17					
			Overall		Perfor-				Annualized		Dividend	Expense
Fund		Ticker	Investment		mance						Yield	Ratio
Type	Fund Name	Symbol	Rating	Phone	Rating/Pts	3 Mo	6 Mo	1Yr / Pct	3Yr / Pct	5Yr / Pct		
GI	Principal LifeTime 2060 R-1	PLTRX	C	(800) 222-5852	C / 4.6	6.45	6.09	18.10 /43	3.89 /42	--	0.76	1.63
GI	Principal LifeTime 2060 R-2	PLTBX	C+	(800) 222-5852	C / 4.7	6.50	6.14	18.22 /44	4.00 /43	--	0.81	1.50
GI	Principal LifeTime 2060 R-3	PLTCX	C+	(800) 222-5852	C / 4.8	6.57	6.22	18.41 /45	4.18 /45	--	0.93	1.32
GI	Principal LifeTime 2060 R-4	PLTMX	C+	(800) 222-5852	C / 5.0	6.64	6.38	18.69 /46	4.42 /48	--	1.07	1.13
GI	Principal LifeTime 2060 R-5	PLTOX	C+	(800) 222-5852	C / 5.1	6.60	6.43	18.82 /46	4.51 /49	--	1.13	1.01
GL	Principal LifeTime Hybrid 2020 Inst	PHTTX	U	(800) 222-5852	U /	4.54	3.62	13.72 /24	--	--	1.77	0.56
GL	Principal LifeTime Hybrid 2025 Inst	PHTQX	U	(800) 222-5852	U /	4.99	4.27	15.26 /31	--	--	1.67	0.96
GL	Principal LifeTime Hybrid 2030 Inst	PHTNX	U	(800) 222-5852	U /	5.46	4.95	16.70 /37	--	--	1.77	0.57
GL	Principal Lifetime Hybrid 2040 Inst	PLTQX	U	(800) 222-5852	U /	6.18	6.08	19.15 /48	--	--	1.71	0.67
AA	Principal LifeTime Strg Inc A	PALTX	C	(800) 222-5852	D- / 1.5	2.80	1.30	7.57 / 7	2.56 /28	3.87 /15	1.56	1.12
AA	Principal LifeTime Strg Inc Inst	PLSIX	C	(800) 222-5852	D / 2.1	2.92	1.50	7.91 / 7	2.93 /31	4.26 /17	2.06	0.64
AA	Principal LifeTime Strg Inc J	PLSJX	C	(800) 222-5852	D / 1.9	2.89	1.45	7.71 / 7	2.66 /29	3.94 /15	1.85	0.89
AA	Principal LifeTime Strg Inc R1	PLAIX	C	(800) 222-5852	D / 1.7	2.72	1.05	6.98 / 6	2.04 /24	3.34 /12	1.05	1.51
AA	Principal LifeTime Strg Inc R2	PLSNX	C	(800) 222-5852	D / 1.7	2.76	1.09	7.11 / 6	2.17 /25	3.48 /13	1.25	1.38
AA	Principal LifeTime Strg Inc R3	PLSMX	C	(800) 222-5852	D / 1.8	2.78	1.18	7.35 / 6	2.36 /26	3.66 /14	1.50	1.20
AA	Principal LifeTime Strg Inc R4	PLSSX	C	(800) 222-5852	D / 1.9	2.91	1.31	7.57 / 7	2.57 /28	3.87 /15	1.71	1.01
AA	Principal LifeTime Strg Inc R5	PLSPX	C	(800) 222-5852	D / 1.9	2.81	1.31	7.62 / 7	2.66 /29	3.97 /15	1.78	0.89
MC	Principal MdCp Gr III Inst	PPIMX	D	(800) 222-5852	C / 4.8	5.68	5.78	18.84 /46	4.44 /48	9.10 /51	0.00	0.98
MC	Principal MdCp Gr III J	PPQJX	D-	(800) 222-5852	C / 4.5	5.47	5.59	18.44 /45	3.99 /43	8.60 /47	0.00	1.34
MC	Principal MdCp Gr III R1	PHASX	D-	(800) 222-5852	C- / 4.1	5.40	5.28	17.88 /42	3.52 /37	8.15 /43	0.00	1.86
MC	Principal MdCp Gr III R2	PPQNX	D-	(800) 222-5852	C- / 4.2	5.42	5.42	17.98 /43	3.65 /39	8.29 /45	0.00	1.73
MC	Principal MdCp Gr III R3	PPQMX	D-	(800) 222-5852	C / 4.3	5.45	5.45	18.26 /44	3.84 /41	8.47 /46	0.00	1.55
MC	Principal MdCp Gr III R4	PPQSX	D	(800) 222-5852	C / 4.5	5.53	5.64	18.41 /45	4.05 /44	8.68 /48	0.00	1.36
MC	Principal MdCp Gr III R5	PPQPX	D	(800) 222-5852	C / 4.6	5.52	5.63	18.53 /45	4.14 /45	8.80 /49	0.00	1.24
MC	Principal MdCp Value I Inst	PVMIX	C+	(800) 222-5852	B / 8.2	6.03	10.74	29.64 /86	7.23 /74	12.80 /82	1.51	1.00
MC	Principal MdCp Value I J	PVEJX	C+	(800) 222-5852	B / 7.9	5.95	10.55	29.20 /85	6.84 /71	12.35 /78	1.26	1.30
MC	Principal MdCp Value I R1	PLASX	C+	(800) 222-5852	B- / 7.5	5.81	10.22	28.56 /83	6.32 /67	11.83 /73	0.65	1.86
MC	Principal MdCp Value I R2	PABUX	C+	(800) 222-5852	B / 7.7	5.87	10.32	28.73 /83	6.45 /68	11.99 /74	0.81	1.73
MC	Principal MdCp Value I R3	PMPRX	C+	(800) 222-5852	B / 7.8	5.87	10.33	28.83 /84	6.64 /69	12.17 /76	0.96	1.55
MC	Principal MdCp Value I R4	PABWX	C+	(800) 222-5852	B / 7.9	5.95	10.48	29.17 /84	6.83 /71	12.39 /78	1.18	1.36
MC	Principal MdCp Value I R5	PABVX	C+	(800) 222-5852	B / 8.0	5.97	10.56	29.26 /85	6.97 /72	12.53 /79	1.29	1.24
MC	● Principal MidCap A	PEMGX	B	(800) 222-5852	B / 8.1	8.09	8.62	26.18 /77	9.65 /91	14.31 /95	0.12	0.98
MC	● Principal MidCap C	PMBCX	B+	(800) 222-5852	B+ / 8.5	7.90	8.21	25.26 /74	8.84 /86	13.45 /88	0.00	1.71
MC	● Principal MidCap Inst	PCBIX	A-	(800) 222-5852	A- / 9.2	8.18	8.80	26.60 /78	10.00 /93	14.70 /96	0.37	0.67
MC	● Principal MidCap J	PMBJX	B+	(800) 222-5852	A- / 9.1	8.18	8.74	26.46 /78	9.80 /92	14.41 /95	0.27	0.81
MC	● Principal MidCap P	PMCPX	A-	(800) 222-5852	A- / 9.2	8.15	8.77	26.55 /78	9.97 /93	14.63 /96	0.36	0.70
MC	● Principal MidCap R1	PMSBX	B+	(800) 222-5852	B+ / 8.7	7.98	8.39	25.58 /75	9.13 /88	13.76 /91	0.00	1.47
MC	● Principal MidCap R2	PMBNX	B+	(800) 222-5852	B+ / 8.8	8.02	8.42	25.78 /76	9.27 /89	13.91 /93	0.00	1.34
MC	● Principal MidCap R3	PMBMX	B+	(800) 222-5852	B+ / 8.9	8.05	8.54	25.99 /76	9.46 /90	14.12 /94	0.00	1.16
MC	● Principal MidCap R4	PMBSX	B+	(800) 222-5852	A- / 9.0	8.11	8.64	26.23 /77	9.67 /91	14.35 /95	0.09	0.97
MC	● Principal MidCap R5	PMBPX	B+	(800) 222-5852	A- / 9.1	8.09	8.67	26.34 /77	9.80 /92	14.48 /96	0.22	0.85
MC	Principal MidCp Grw Inst	PGWIX	D+	(800) 222-5852	C / 5.5	5.80	5.36	22.16 /63	4.78 /52	11.92 /74	0.32	0.75
MC	Principal MidCp Grw J	PMGJX	D	(800) 222-5852	C / 5.2	5.75	5.20	21.92 /62	4.40 /47	11.44 /69	0.15	1.13
MC	Principal MidCp Grw R1	PMSGX	D-	(800) 222-5852	C / 4.7	5.52	4.82	21.11 /58	3.93 /42	10.99 /66	0.00	1.56
MC	Principal MidCp Grw R2	PGPPX	D	(800) 222-5852	C / 4.8	5.62	4.96	21.33 /59	4.04 /43	11.13 /67	0.00	1.43
MC	Principal MidCp Grw R3	PFPPX	D	(800) 222-5852	C / 5.0	5.60	4.98	21.53 /60	4.26 /46	11.35 /69	0.00	1.25
MC	Principal MidCp Grw R4	PIPPX	D	(800) 222-5852	C / 5.2	5.67	5.08	21.69 /61	4.46 /48	11.56 /70	0.06	1.06
MC	Principal MidCp Grw R5	PHPPX	D	(800) 222-5852	C / 5.2	5.69	5.13	21.66 /61	4.57 /50	11.68 /71	0.13	0.94
MC	Principal MidCp S&P 400 Idx Inst	MPSIX	A-	(800) 222-5852	A / 9.4	6.58	11.22	31.36 /89	9.38 /89	13.55 /89	1.29	0.19
MC	Principal MidCp S&P 400 Idx J	PMFJX	B+	(800) 222-5852	A- / 9.2	6.56	11.09	30.99 /88	9.02 /87	13.14 /85	1.10	0.49
MC	Principal MidCp S&P 400 Idx R1	PMSSX	B+	(800) 222-5852	B+ / 8.9	6.31	10.77	30.19 /87	8.45 /83	12.60 /80	0.44	1.04
MC	Principal MidCp S&P 400 Idx R2	PMFNX	B+	(800) 222-5852	A- / 9.0	6.40	10.85	30.46 /87	8.61 /84	12.75 /81	0.68	0.91

● Denotes fund is closed to new investors
* Denotes fund is included in Section II

518

www.thestreetratings.com

RISK	3 Year		NET ASSETS		ASSET				Portfolio Turnover Ratio	BULL / BEAR		FUND MANAGER		MINIMUMS		LOADS	
Risk Rating/Pts	Standard Deviation	Beta	NAV As of 2/28/17	Total $(Mil)	Cash %	Stocks %	Bonds %	Other %		Last Bull Market Return	Last Bear Market Return	Manager Quality Pct	Manager Tenure (Years)	Initial Purch. $	Additional Purch. $	Front End Load	Back End Load
C+ / 6.8	9.4	0.88	12.27	1	10	82	6	2	15	N/A	N/A	14	4	0	0	0.0	0.0
C+ / 6.8	9.4	0.88	12.31	1	10	82	6	2	15	N/A	N/A	15	4	0	0	0.0	0.0
C+ / 6.8	9.4	0.88	12.41	6	10	82	6	2	15	N/A	N/A	17	4	0	0	0.0	0.0
C+ / 6.8	9.4	0.88	12.42	5	10	82	6	2	15	N/A	N/A	19	4	0	0	0.0	0.0
C+ / 6.8	9.4	0.88	12.45	8	10	82	6	2	15	N/A	N/A	19	4	0	0	0.0	0.0
U /	N/A	N/A	10.40	70	4	55	40	1	15	N/A	N/A	N/A	3	0	0	0.0	0.0
U /	N/A	N/A	10.52	31	2	64	32	2	26	N/A	N/A	N/A	3	0	0	0.0	0.0
U /	N/A	N/A	10.60	64	3	70	26	1	12	N/A	N/A	N/A	3	0	0	0.0	0.0
U /	N/A	N/A	10.77	35	3	80	16	1	13	N/A	N/A	N/A	3	0	0	0.0	0.0
B+ / 9.1	3.5	0.49	12.27	21	5	19	75	1	18	30.2	-4.7	61	10	1,000	100	3.8	0.0
B+ / 9.0	3.5	0.49	12.17	455	5	19	75	1	18	32.9	-4.6	65	10	0	0	0.0	0.0
B+ / 9.1	3.5	0.49	12.12	80	5	19	75	1	18	30.6	-4.7	62	10	1,000	100	0.0	0.0
B+ / 9.1	3.5	0.49	12.21	4	5	19	75	1	18	26.6	-4.9	54	10	0	0	0.0	0.0
B+ / 9.1	3.5	0.49	12.20	6	5	19	75	1	18	27.6	-4.8	56	10	0	0	0.0	0.0
B+ / 9.1	3.5	0.49	12.08	25	5	19	75	1	18	28.9	-4.8	58	10	0	0	0.0	0.0
B+ / 9.1	3.5	0.50	12.10	15	5	19	75	1	18	30.3	-4.7	61	10	0	0	0.0	0.0
B+ / 9.0	3.5	0.49	12.16	34	5	19	75	1	18	31.0	-4.7	62	10	0	0	0.0	0.0
C- / 3.1	11.6	0.91	10.75	1,023	2	95	1	2	65	89.6	-22.4	23	12	1,000,000	0	0.0	0.0
D+ / 2.6	11.6	0.91	9.02	33	2	95	1	2	65	84.9	-22.4	20	12	1,000	100	0.0	0.0
D+ / 2.6	11.7	0.91	9.13	2	2	95	1	2	65	80.7	-22.6	16	12	0	0	0.0	0.0
D+ / 2.7	11.7	0.91	9.48	2	2	95	1	2	65	81.9	-22.5	17	12	0	0	0.0	0.0
C- / 3.0	11.7	0.91	10.20	6	2	95	1	2	65	83.8	-22.5	18	12	0	0	0.0	0.0
C- / 3.1	11.6	0.91	10.45	5	2	95	1	2	65	85.6	-22.4	20	12	0	0	0.0	0.0
C- / 3.2	11.7	0.91	10.84	9	2	95	1	2	65	86.8	-22.4	20	12	0	0	0.0	0.0
C- / 4.1	11.6	0.93	14.73	1,020	1	97	0	2	131	125.3	-22.0	54	N/A	1,000,000	0	0.0	0.0
C- / 4.1	11.6	0.93	14.59	74	1	97	0	2	131	120.3	-22.2	49	N/A	1,000	100	0.0	0.0
C- / 4.0	11.6	0.93	14.20	4	1	97	0	2	131	114.9	-22.3	42	N/A	0	0	0.0	0.0
C- / 4.1	11.6	0.93	14.31	6	1	97	0	2	131	116.5	-22.3	44	N/A	0	0	0.0	0.0
C- / 4.1	11.6	0.93	14.53	20	1	97	0	2	131	118.5	-22.2	46	N/A	0	0	0.0	0.0
C- / 4.1	11.6	0.93	14.56	22	1	97	0	2	131	120.8	-22.2	49	N/A	0	0	0.0	0.0
C- / 4.1	11.6	0.93	14.63	53	1	97	0	2	131	122.2	-22.1	51	N/A	0	0	0.0	0.0
C / 5.4	12.1	0.92	23.75	2,026	1	98	0	1	22	139.5	-15.9	80	17	1,000	100	5.5	0.0
C / 5.3	12.1	0.92	21.84	315	1	98	0	1	22	129.9	-16.1	74	17	1,000	100	0.0	0.0
C / 5.4	12.1	0.91	24.17	6,297	1	98	0	1	22	143.9	-15.7	82	17	1,000,000	0	0.0	0.0
C / 5.4	12.1	0.91	22.87	283	1	98	0	1	22	140.4	-15.8	81	17	1,000	100	0.0	0.0
C / 5.4	12.0	0.91	24.10	3,695	1	98	0	1	22	143.3	-15.7	82	17	0	0	0.0	0.0
C / 5.3	12.1	0.92	22.31	75	1	98	0	1	22	133.5	-16.0	76	17	0	0	0.0	0.0
C / 5.3	12.1	0.92	22.61	29	1	98	0	1	22	135.2	-16.0	77	17	0	0	0.0	0.0
C / 5.4	12.1	0.92	23.33	126	1	98	0	1	22	137.4	-15.9	78	17	0	0	0.0	0.0
C / 5.4	12.1	0.91	24.12	148	1	98	0	1	22	139.9	-15.8	80	17	0	0	0.0	0.0
C / 5.4	12.1	0.91	23.92	329	1	98	0	1	22	141.5	-15.8	81	17	0	0	0.0	0.0
C- / 3.0	14.0	0.99	7.56	47	0	97	2	1	110	110.2	-22.3	20	12	1,000,000	0	0.0	0.0
D+ / 2.4	14.1	0.99	6.05	53	0	97	2	1	110	105.6	-22.4	16	12	1,000	100	0.0	0.0
D+ / 2.5	14.1	0.99	6.31	1	0	97	2	1	110	101.1	-22.5	13	12	0	0	0.0	0.0
D+ / 2.7	14.1	0.99	6.77	4	0	97	2	1	110	102.4	-22.5	14	12	0	0	0.0	0.0
D+ / 2.8	14.1	1.00	7.17	10	0	97	2	1	110	104.5	-22.4	15	12	0	0	0.0	0.0
C- / 3.0	14.1	0.99	7.54	8	0	97	2	1	110	106.8	-22.4	17	12	0	0	0.0	0.0
C- / 3.1	14.0	0.99	7.80	20	0	97	2	1	110	107.9	-22.4	18	12	0	0	0.0	0.0
C / 5.2	12.0	1.00	20.66	743	0	98	0	2	18	137.3	-22.6	72	6	1,000,000	0	0.0	0.0
C / 5.2	12.1	1.00	20.15	129	0	98	0	2	18	132.5	-22.7	68	6	1,000	100	0.0	0.0
C / 5.2	12.0	1.00	20.49	14	0	98	0	2	18	126.7	-22.8	61	6	0	0	0.0	0.0
C / 5.3	12.0	1.00	21.09	18	0	98	0	2	18	128.5	-22.8	63	6	0	0	0.0	0.0

Fund Type	Fund Name	Ticker Symbol	Overall Investment Rating	Phone	Perfor-mance Rating/Pts	3 Mo	6 Mo	1Yr / Pct	3Yr / Pct	5Yr / Pct	Dividend Yield	Expense Ratio
MC	Principal MidCp S&P 400 Idx R3	PMFMX	B+	(800) 222-5852	A- / 9.1	6.43	10.94	30.64 /87	8.79 /85	12.96 /83	0.82	0.73
MC	Principal MidCp S&P 400 Idx R4	PMFSX	B+	(800) 222-5852	A- / 9.2	6.44	11.00	30.88 /88	9.00 /87	13.16 /86	0.89	0.54
MC	Principal MidCp S&P 400 Idx R5	PMFPX	B+	(800) 222-5852	A / 9.3	6.51	11.14	31.09 /88	9.14 /88	13.30 /87	1.08	0.42
MC	Principal MidCp Value III Inst	PVUIX	B	(800) 222-5852	B / 7.9	6.32	11.84	25.82 /76	7.24 /74	13.18 /86	1.33	0.67
MC	Principal MidCp Value III J	PMCJX	B	(800) 222-5852	B / 7.7	6.29	11.72	25.46 /75	6.91 /71	12.78 /82	1.16	0.93
MC	Principal MidCp Value III R1	PMSVX	B-	(800) 222-5852	B- / 7.3	6.11	11.40	24.74 /72	6.33 /67	12.20 /76	0.47	1.53
MC	Principal MidCp Value III R2	PKPPX	B	(800) 222-5852	B- / 7.3	6.14	11.44	24.89 /73	6.45 /69	12.34 /78	0.68	1.40
MC	Principal MidCp Value III R3	PJPPX	B	(800) 222-5852	B- / 7.5	6.19	11.53	25.11 /74	6.64 /69	12.56 /80	0.89	1.22
MC	Principal MidCp Value III R4	PMPPX	B	(800) 222-5852	B / 7.6	6.21	11.60	25.31 /74	6.83 /71	12.77 /82	1.11	1.03
MC	Principal MidCp Value III R5	PLPPX	B	(800) 222-5852	B / 7.7	6.24	11.70	25.43 /75	6.98 /72	12.90 /83	1.19	0.91
EM	Principal Origin Emerging Mkts Inst	POEIX	U	(800) 222-5852	U /	7.62	2.46	24.87 /73	--	--	0.79	1.31
FO	Principal Overseas Institutional	PINZX	E+	(800) 222-5852	E+ / 0.9	6.97	5.72	15.91 /34	-2.22 / 6	4.50 /18	1.95	1.10
FO	Principal Overseas R-1	PINQX	E+	(800) 222-5852	E+ / 0.7	6.74	5.26	14.96 /30	-3.10 / 4	3.58 /13	1.40	1.97
FO	Principal Overseas R-2	PINSX	E+	(800) 222-5852	E+ / 0.7	6.80	5.44	15.28 /31	-2.91 / 5	3.74 /14	1.17	1.84
FO	Principal Overseas R-3	PINTX	E+	(800) 222-5852	E+ / 0.7	6.73	5.37	15.35 /31	-2.79 / 5	3.91 /15	1.40	1.66
FO	Principal Overseas R-4	PINUX	E+	(800) 222-5852	E+ / 0.8	6.84	5.59	15.56 /32	-2.60 / 5	4.12 /16	1.61	1.47
FO	Principal Overseas R-5	PINGX	E+	(800) 222-5852	E+ / 0.8	6.84	5.59	15.68 /33	-2.48 / 6	4.40 /18	1.72	1.35
RE	Principal Real Est Securities A	PRRAX	C+	(800) 222-5852	C+ / 6.5	8.15	-1.90	14.22 /27	11.09 /97	11.51 /70	1.28	1.30
RE	Principal Real Est Securities C	PRCEX	C+	(800) 222-5852	C+ / 6.9	7.94	-2.32	13.29 /23	10.20 /94	10.61 /63	0.71	2.07
RE	Principal Real Est Securities Inst	PIREX	B-	(800) 222-5852	B / 7.8	8.25	-1.72	14.67 /28	11.52 /98	11.98 /74	1.71	0.89
RE	Principal Real Est Securities J	PREJX	C+	(800) 222-5852	B- / 7.5	8.23	-1.86	14.35 /27	11.20 /97	11.59 /71	1.50	1.13
RE	Principal Real Est Securities P	PIRPX	B-	(800) 222-5852	B / 7.7	8.26	-1.77	14.59 /28	11.44 /98	11.88 /73	1.63	0.97
RE	Principal Real Est Securities R1	PRAEX	C+	(800) 222-5852	B- / 7.1	8.08	-2.11	13.72 /24	10.63 /96	11.07 /66	0.95	1.70
RE	Principal Real Est Securities R2	PRENX	C+	(800) 222-5852	B- / 7.2	8.09	-2.06	13.86 /25	10.76 /97	11.20 /68	1.12	1.57
RE	Principal Real Est Securities R3	PRERX	C+	(800) 222-5852	B- / 7.4	8.13	-1.98	14.11 /26	10.97 /97	11.41 /69	1.24	1.39
RE	Principal Real Est Securities R4	PRETX	C+	(800) 222-5852	B- / 7.5	8.17	-1.90	14.30 /27	11.17 /97	11.61 /71	1.42	1.20
RE	Principal Real Est Securities R5	PREPX	C+	(800) 222-5852	B / 7.6	8.23	-1.83	14.44 /27	11.30 /97	11.74 /72	1.57	1.08
BA	Principal SAM Bal Port A	SABPX	C	(800) 222-5852	C- / 3.1	5.21	4.38	14.71 /29	4.49 /49	7.44 /38	1.42	1.37
BA	Principal SAM Bal Port C	SCBPX	C	(800) 222-5852	C- / 3.5	5.02	3.99	13.86 /25	3.73 /40	6.65 /32	0.82	2.11
BA	Principal SAM Bal Port Inst	PSBIX	C+	(800) 222-5852	C / 4.4	5.30	4.56	15.09 /30	4.87 /53	7.80 /41	1.85	1.02
BA	Principal SAM Bal Port J	PSAJX	C+	(800) 222-5852	C- / 4.2	5.28	4.47	14.91 /30	4.60 /50	7.53 /39	1.70	1.22
BA	Principal SAM Bal Port R1	PSBGX	C	(800) 222-5852	C- / 3.6	5.03	4.10	14.05 /26	3.94 /42	6.86 /34	1.02	1.90
BA	Principal SAM Bal Port R2	PSBVX	C	(800) 222-5852	C- / 3.8	5.14	4.19	14.18 /26	4.07 /44	7.00 /35	1.16	1.77
BA	Principal SAM Bal Port R3	PBAPX	C	(800) 222-5852	C- / 3.9	5.15	4.26	14.42 /27	4.27 /46	7.20 /36	1.25	1.59
BA	Principal SAM Bal Port R4	PSBLX	C+	(800) 222-5852	C- / 4.0	5.22	4.30	14.60 /28	4.45 /48	7.40 /37	1.49	1.40
BA	Principal SAM Bal Port R5	PSBFX	C+	(800) 222-5852	C- / 4.2	5.19	4.38	14.77 /29	4.56 /49	7.53 /39	1.63	1.28
BA	Principal SAM Consv Bal A	SAIPX	C	(800) 222-5852	D / 2.2	4.12	3.10	11.68 /17	3.86 /41	5.89 /28	1.91	1.31
BA	Principal SAM Consv Bal C	SCIPX	C	(800) 222-5852	D+ / 2.6	3.97	2.66	10.79 /14	3.08 /33	5.09 /22	1.32	2.06
BA	Principal SAM Consv Bal Inst	PCCIX	C+	(800) 222-5852	C- / 3.4	4.24	3.29	12.04 /18	4.19 /45	6.24 /30	2.34	0.97
BA	Principal SAM Consv Bal J	PCBJX	C+	(800) 222-5852	C- / 3.2	4.21	3.21	11.89 /18	3.96 /43	5.96 /28	2.18	1.16
BA	Principal SAM Consv Bal R1	PCSSX	C	(800) 222-5852	D+ / 2.7	4.04	2.88	11.11 /15	3.28 /35	5.32 /23	1.50	1.84
BA	Principal SAM Consv Bal R2	PCNSX	C	(800) 222-5852	D+ / 2.8	4.04	2.87	11.25 /15	3.42 /36	5.46 /25	1.59	1.71
BA	Principal SAM Consv Bal R3	PCBPX	C	(800) 222-5852	C- / 3.0	4.09	3.00	11.44 /16	3.61 /38	5.64 /26	1.80	1.53
BA	Principal SAM Consv Bal R4	PCBLX	C	(800) 222-5852	C- / 3.1	4.16	3.11	11.65 /17	3.81 /41	5.84 /27	1.99	1.34
BA	Principal SAM Consv Bal R5	PCBFX	C+	(800) 222-5852	C- / 3.2	4.19	3.17	11.78 /17	3.93 /42	5.96 /28	2.11	1.22
AA	Principal SAM Consv Growth A	SAGPX	C-	(800) 222-5852	C- / 4.0	6.31	5.81	17.82 /42	4.99 /54	8.72 /48	1.05	1.42
AA	Principal SAM Consv Growth C	SCGPX	C	(800) 222-5852	C / 4.5	6.11	5.45	17.02 /38	4.23 /46	7.92 /41	0.49	2.18
AA	Principal SAM Consv Growth Inst	PCWIX	C+	(800) 222-5852	C / 5.5	6.43	5.98	18.26 /44	5.37 /58	9.10 /51	1.46	1.08
AA	Principal SAM Consv Growth J	PCGJX	C+	(800) 222-5852	C / 5.3	6.38	5.86	18.05 /43	5.12 /55	8.80 /49	1.30	1.28
AA	Principal SAM Consv Growth R1	PCGGX	C	(800) 222-5852	C / 4.7	6.13	5.48	17.21 /39	4.43 /48	8.14 /43	0.61	1.95
AA	Principal SAM Consv Growth R2	PCGVX	C	(800) 222-5852	C / 4.8	6.17	5.59	17.39 /40	4.57 /50	8.29 /45	0.71	1.82
AA	Principal SAM Consv Growth R3	PCGPX	C	(800) 222-5852	C / 5.0	6.26	5.68	17.57 /41	4.77 /52	8.48 /46	0.84	1.64

● Denotes fund is closed to new investors
* Denotes fund is included in Section II

Risk Rating/Pts	3 Year Standard Deviation	Beta	NAV As of 2/28/17	Total $(Mil)	Cash %	Stocks %	Bonds %	Other %	Portfolio Turnover Ratio	Last Bull Market Return	Last Bear Market Return	Manager Quality Pct	Manager Tenure (Years)	Initial Purch. $	Additional Purch. $	Front End Load	Back End Load
C /5.2	12.0	1.00	21.01	117	0	98	0	2	18	130.8	-22.8	65	6	0	0	0.0	0.0
C /5.2	12.1	1.00	21.06	94	0	98	0	2	18	132.9	-22.7	67	6	0	0	0.0	0.0
C /5.2	12.0	1.00	21.22	236	0	98	0	2	18	134.6	-22.7	69	6	0	0	0.0	0.0
C+ /5.7	11.2	0.90	20.77	1,266	1	95	2	2	74	130.4	-19.9	58	7	1,000,000	0	0.0	0.0
C+ /5.6	11.1	0.90	19.58	107	1	95	2	2	74	125.9	-20.2	54	7	1,000	100	0.0	0.0
C+ /5.6	11.1	0.90	19.72	1	1	95	2	2	74	119.9	-20.3	46	7	0	0	0.0	0.0
C+ /5.7	11.1	0.90	19.85	2	1	95	2	2	74	121.4	-20.3	48	7	0	0	0.0	0.0
C+ /5.6	11.1	0.90	19.68	16	1	95	2	2	74	123.5	-20.2	50	7	0	0	0.0	0.0
C+ /5.6	11.1	0.90	19.48	24	1	95	2	2	74	125.8	-20.2	52	7	0	0	0.0	0.0
C+ /5.6	11.1	0.90	19.67	31	1	95	2	2	74	127.2	-20.1	55	7	0	0	0.0	0.0
U /	N/A	N/A	9.11	641	2	95	1	2	69	N/A	N/A	N/A	2	0	0	0.0	0.0
C /4.6	11.5	0.91	9.78	2,936	3	94	2	1	32	46.4	-24.9	47	9	1,000,000	0	0.0	0.0
C /4.7	11.5	0.92	9.71	N/A	3	94	2	1	32	39.9	-25.0	35	9	0	0	0.0	0.0
C /4.7	11.5	0.92	9.76	N/A	3	94	2	1	32	41.0	-25.0	37	9	0	0	0.0	0.0
C /4.7	11.4	0.91	9.72	N/A	3	94	2	1	32	42.2	-25.0	39	9	0	0	0.0	0.0
C /4.7	11.5	0.92	9.75	1	3	94	2	1	32	43.7	-24.9	42	9	0	0	0.0	0.0
C /4.7	11.5	0.92	9.75	1	3	94	2	1	32	45.7	-24.9	43	9	0	0	0.0	0.0
C /4.9	14.8	1.08	23.38	340	0	97	1	2	25	108.8	-16.3	65	17	1,000	100	5.5	0.0
C /4.8	14.8	1.08	22.96	53	0	97	1	2	25	99.9	-16.6	54	17	1,000	100	0.0	0.0
C /4.9	14.8	1.08	23.41	2,717	0	97	1	2	25	113.8	-16.2	70	17	1,000,000	0	0.0	0.0
C /4.8	14.8	1.08	22.74	184	0	97	1	2	25	109.6	-16.3	66	17	1,000	100	0.0	0.0
C /4.9	14.8	1.08	23.39	127	0	97	1	2	25	112.5	-16.2	69	17	0	0	0.0	0.0
C /4.9	14.8	1.08	23.09	7	0	97	1	2	25	104.3	-16.4	60	17	0	0	0.0	0.0
C /4.8	14.8	1.08	22.29	21	0	97	1	2	25	105.7	-16.4	61	17	0	0	0.0	0.0
C /4.8	14.8	1.08	22.83	61	0	97	1	2	25	107.8	-16.3	63	17	0	0	0.0	0.0
C /4.8	14.8	1.08	22.59	71	0	97	1	2	25	110.0	-16.3	66	17	0	0	0.0	0.0
C /4.8	14.8	1.08	22.64	172	0	97	1	2	25	111.4	-16.3	67	17	0	0	0.0	0.0
B- /7.4	6.6	1.03	15.48	2,095	9	56	33	2	17	63.9	-12.2	34	7	1,000	100	5.5	0.0
B- /7.4	6.6	1.03	15.26	761	9	56	33	2	17	57.4	-12.4	26	7	1,000	100	0.0	0.0
B- /7.4	6.5	1.02	15.26	797	9	56	33	2	17	67.0	-12.1	39	7	1,000,000	0	0.0	0.0
B- /7.4	6.6	1.02	15.01	1,057	9	56	33	2	17	64.6	-12.3	35	7	1,000	100	0.0	0.0
B- /7.4	6.6	1.03	15.21	3	9	56	33	2	17	59.3	-12.4	28	7	0	0	0.0	0.0
B- /7.4	6.6	1.02	15.17	5	9	56	33	2	17	60.4	-12.4	30	7	0	0	0.0	0.0
B- /7.4	6.6	1.02	15.21	35	9	56	33	2	17	62.0	-12.3	32	7	0	0	0.0	0.0
B- /7.4	6.5	1.02	15.23	37	9	56	33	2	17	63.6	-12.3	34	7	0	0	0.0	0.0
B- /7.4	6.6	1.03	15.23	110	9	56	33	2	17	64.7	-12.2	35	7	0	0	0.0	0.0
B /8.2	4.9	0.75	11.93	518	4	41	53	2	17	47.7	-8.4	53	7	1,000	100	5.5	0.0
B /8.2	4.9	0.76	11.80	263	4	41	53	2	17	41.8	-8.7	41	7	1,000	100	0.0	0.0
B /8.2	4.9	0.76	11.83	322	4	41	53	2	17	50.4	-8.3	57	7	1,000,000	0	0.0	0.0
B /8.2	4.9	0.76	11.79	596	4	41	53	2	17	48.2	-8.4	53	7	1,000	100	0.0	0.0
B /8.2	4.9	0.76	11.78	3	4	41	53	2	17	43.4	-8.7	45	7	0	0	0.0	0.0
B /8.2	4.9	0.75	11.86	1	4	41	53	2	17	44.5	-8.6	47	7	0	0	0.0	0.0
B /8.2	4.9	0.76	11.80	14	4	41	53	2	17	45.9	-8.6	48	7	0	0	0.0	0.0
B /8.2	4.9	0.75	11.82	21	4	41	53	2	17	47.4	-8.4	52	7	0	0	0.0	0.0
B /8.2	4.9	0.76	11.82	37	4	41	53	2	17	48.3	-8.3	53	7	0	0	0.0	0.0
C+ /6.3	8.3	1.30	17.38	1,483	10	75	14	1	22	79.6	-16.2	19	7	1,000	100	5.5	0.0
C+ /6.3	8.3	1.30	16.29	535	10	75	14	1	22	72.3	-16.4	14	7	1,000	100	0.0	0.0
C+ /6.2	8.3	1.30	17.02	497	10	75	14	1	22	82.9	-16.0	22	7	1,000,000	0	0.0	0.0
C+ /6.2	8.3	1.30	16.82	526	10	75	14	1	22	80.1	-16.1	20	7	1,000	100	0.0	0.0
C+ /6.3	8.3	1.30	16.81	3	10	75	14	1	22	74.5	-16.4	15	7	0	0	0.0	0.0
C+ /6.3	8.3	1.30	16.83	4	10	75	14	1	22	75.7	-16.3	16	7	0	0	0.0	0.0
C+ /6.2	8.3	1.29	16.82	22	10	75	14	1	22	77.4	-16.2	18	7	0	0	0.0	0.0

Fund Type	Fund Name	Ticker Symbol	Overall Investment Rating	Phone	Performance Rating/Pts	PERFORMANCE Total Return % through 2/28/17 3 Mo	6 Mo	1Yr / Pct	Annualized 3Yr / Pct	5Yr / Pct	Incl. in Returns Dividend Yield	Expense Ratio
	99 Pct = Best 0 Pct = Worst											
AA	Principal SAM Consv Growth R4	PCWSX	C	(800) 222-5852	C / 5.1	6.30	5.78	17.87 /42	4.98 /54	8.69 /48	1.09	1.45
AA	Principal SAM Consv Growth R5	PCWPX	C+	(800) 222-5852	C / 5.2	6.36	5.85	17.96 /43	5.10 /55	8.83 /49	1.26	1.33
AA	Principal SAM Flex Inc A	SAUPX	C	(800) 222-5852	D / 2.1	3.37	2.11	10.23 /12	3.49 /37	5.02 /21	2.52	1.18
AA	Principal SAM Flex Inc C	SCUPX	C	(800) 222-5852	D / 2.1	3.21	1.74	9.40 /10	2.68 /29	4.22 /16	1.89	1.95
AA	Principal SAM Flex Inc Inst	PIFIX	C	(800) 222-5852	D+ / 2.8	3.45	2.27	10.51 /13	3.79 /40	5.35 /24	2.93	0.86
AA	Principal SAM Flex Inc J	PFIJX	C	(800) 222-5852	D+ / 2.6	3.43	2.19	10.37 /13	3.54 /38	5.08 /22	2.77	1.06
AA	Principal SAM Flex Inc R1	PFIGX	C	(800) 222-5852	D / 2.2	3.24	1.84	9.51 /11	2.88 /31	4.44 /18	2.09	1.73
AA	Principal SAM Flex Inc R2	PFIVX	C	(800) 222-5852	D+ / 2.3	3.27	1.89	9.71 /11	3.02 /32	4.58 /19	2.20	1.60
AA	Principal SAM Flex Inc R3	PFIPX	C	(800) 222-5852	D+ / 2.4	3.31	1.99	9.91 /11	3.22 /34	4.78 /20	2.38	1.42
AA	Principal SAM Flex Inc R4	PFILX	C	(800) 222-5852	D+ / 2.5	3.28	2.00	10.12 /12	3.41 /36	4.95 /21	2.57	1.23
AA	Principal SAM Flex Inc R5	PFIFX	C	(800) 222-5852	D+ / 2.6	3.40	2.15	10.26 /12	3.54 /38	5.10 /22	2.69	1.11
AA	Principal SAM Strat Growth A	SACAX	C-	(800) 222-5852	C- / 4.2	6.87	5.89	18.76 /46	5.03 /55	9.47 /54	0.92	1.44
AA	Principal SAM Strat Growth C	SWHCX	C-	(800) 222-5852	C / 4.7	6.67	5.55	17.95 /43	4.25 /46	8.66 /48	0.38	2.19
AA	Principal SAM Strat Growth Inst	PSWIX	C	(800) 222-5852	C+ / 5.7	6.95	6.13	19.25 /48	5.40 /59	9.89 /58	1.35	1.07
AA	Principal SAM Strat Growth J	PSWJX	C	(800) 222-5852	C / 5.5	6.92	6.04	19.07 /47	5.15 /56	9.57 /55	1.17	1.28
AA	Principal SAM Strat Growth R1	PSGGX	C-	(800) 222-5852	C / 5.0	6.80	5.66	18.25 /44	4.51 /49	8.94 /50	0.40	1.94
AA	Principal SAM Strat Growth R2	PSGVX	C-	(800) 222-5852	C / 5.0	6.75	5.68	18.35 /44	4.61 /50	9.06 /51	0.54	1.81
AA	Principal SAM Strat Growth R3	PSGPX	C-	(800) 222-5852	C / 5.2	6.80	5.79	18.55 /45	4.81 /52	9.27 /53	0.73	1.63
AA	Principal SAM Strat Growth R4	PSGLX	C	(800) 222-5852	C / 5.4	6.87	5.93	18.82 /46	5.02 /54	9.48 /55	0.99	1.44
AA	Principal SAM Strat Growth R5	PSGFX	C	(800) 222-5852	C / 5.5	6.94	5.99	19.00 /47	5.14 /56	9.60 /55	1.14	1.32
IN	Principal Small MidCap Div Inc R6	PMDHX	A	(800) 222-5852	A+ / 9.8	7.83	13.74	41.31 /98	11.53 /98	14.61 /96	2.73	N/A
SC	Principal SmallCap A	PLLAX	C+	(800) 222-5852	B- / 7.1	4.74	11.42	31.70 /89	6.64 /69	13.77 /91	0.37	1.28
SC	Principal SmallCap C	PSMCX	C+	(800) 222-5852	B- / 7.4	4.56	10.98	30.57 /87	5.74 /62	12.85 /82	0.00	2.12
SC	Principal SmallCap Institutional	PSLIX	B	(800) 222-5852	B+ / 8.4	4.89	11.70	32.24 /90	7.10 /73	14.31 /95	0.73	0.84
SC	Principal SmallCap J	PSBJX	B-	(800) 222-5852	B / 8.2	4.84	11.63	32.06 /90	6.82 /71	13.94 /93	0.63	1.08
SC	Principal SmallCap R1	PSABX	C+	(800) 222-5852	B / 7.8	4.68	11.27	31.21 /89	6.22 /66	13.37 /88	0.07	1.69
SC	Principal SmallCap R2	PSBNX	C+	(800) 222-5852	B / 7.9	4.75	11.32	31.41 /89	6.36 /67	13.51 /89	0.35	1.56
SC	Principal SmallCap R3	PSBMX	C+	(800) 222-5852	B / 8.0	4.78	11.40	31.61 /89	6.55 /69	13.71 /91	0.33	1.38
SC	Principal SmallCap R4	PSBSX	B-	(800) 222-5852	B / 8.1	4.80	11.51	31.83 /90	6.74 /70	13.92 /93	0.50	1.19
SC	Principal SmallCap R5	PSBPX	B-	(800) 222-5852	B / 8.2	4.83	11.56	32.01 /90	6.87 /71	14.05 /94	0.56	1.07
IN	Principal Small-MidCap Div Inc A	PMDAX	A+	(800) 222-5852	A+ / 9.8	7.80	13.58	40.87 /97	11.14 /97	14.19 /94	2.33	1.60
IN	Principal Small-MidCap Div Inc C	PMDDX	A+	(800) 222-5852	A+ / 9.8	7.59	13.19	39.77 /97	10.29 /95	--	1.84	2.39
IN	Principal Small-MidCap Div Inc Inst	PMDIX	A+	(800) 222-5852	A+ / 9.8	7.83	13.74	41.31 /98	11.53 /98	14.61 /96	2.73	1.30
IN	Principal Small-MidCap Div Inc P	PMDPX	A+	(800) 222-5852	A+ / 9.8	7.81	13.73	41.25 /98	11.47 /98	14.51 /96	2.66	1.32
SC	Principal SmCap S&P 600 Indx Inst	PSSIX	B+	(800) 222-5852	A+ / 9.6	4.57	13.05	34.70 /94	9.47 /90	14.64 /96	0.98	0.20
SC	Principal SmCap S&P 600 Indx J	PSSJX	B+	(800) 222-5852	A / 9.5	4.46	12.89	34.30 /93	9.14 /88	14.24 /94	0.84	0.44
SC	Principal SmCap S&P 600 Indx R1	PSAPX	B+	(800) 222-5852	A- / 9.2	4.33	12.58	33.54 /92	8.55 /83	13.68 /91	0.34	1.04
SC	Principal SmCap S&P 600 Indx R2	PSSNX	B+	(800) 222-5852	A / 9.3	4.36	12.68	33.78 /93	8.70 /85	13.83 /92	0.42	0.91
SC	Principal SmCap S&P 600 Indx R3	PSSMX	B+	(800) 222-5852	A / 9.4	4.42	12.76	33.97 /93	8.89 /86	14.03 /93	0.54	0.73
SC	Principal SmCap S&P 600 Indx R4	PSSSX	B+	(800) 222-5852	A / 9.5	4.46	12.86	34.24 /93	9.10 /87	14.25 /94	0.68	0.54
SC	Principal SmCap S&P 600 Indx R5	PSSPX	B+	(800) 222-5852	A / 9.5	4.48	12.93	34.39 /93	9.23 /88	14.39 /95	0.79	0.42
SC	Principal SmCp Gr I Inst	PGRTX	D	(800) 222-5852	C+ / 6.3	4.96	8.85	30.47 /87	3.84 /41	11.50 /70	0.00	1.10
SC	Principal SmCp Gr I J	PSIJX	D-	(800) 222-5852	C+ / 6.0	4.91	8.67	30.02 /86	3.44 /36	11.00 /66	0.00	1.47
SC	Principal SmCp Gr I R1	PNASX	D-	(800) 222-5852	C / 5.5	4.77	8.40	29.31 /85	2.96 /31	10.54 /62	0.00	1.96
SC	Principal SmCp Gr I R2	PPNNX	D-	(800) 222-5852	C+ / 5.6	4.70	8.42	29.40 /85	3.09 /33	10.68 /63	0.00	1.83
SC	Principal SmCp Gr I R3	PPNMX	D	(800) 222-5852	C+ / 5.8	4.75	8.50	29.63 /86	3.26 /34	10.87 /65	0.00	1.65
SC	Principal SmCp Gr I R4	PPNSX	D	(800) 222-5852	C+ / 6.0	4.88	8.65	29.89 /86	3.46 /37	11.09 /67	0.00	1.46
SC	Principal SmCp Gr I R5	PPNPX	D	(800) 222-5852	C+ / 6.1	4.88	8.70	30.13 /87	3.59 /38	11.22 /68	0.00	1.34
SC	Principal SmCp Value II Inst	PPVIX	B	(800) 222-5852	A / 9.3	3.68	13.83	34.45 /93	8.41 /82	14.02 /93	0.46	1.03
SC	Principal SmCp Value II J	PSMJX	B	(800) 222-5852	A- / 9.0	3.54	13.55	33.88 /93	7.92 /78	13.43 /88	0.18	1.43
SC	Principal SmCp Value II R1	PCPTX	B-	(800) 222-5852	B+ / 8.7	3.38	13.34	33.23 /92	7.46 /75	13.05 /84	0.00	1.90
SC	Principal SmCp Value II R2	PKARX	B-	(800) 222-5852	B+ / 8.8	3.51	13.43	33.44 /92	7.64 /76	13.21 /86	0.00	1.77

● Denotes fund is closed to new investors
* Denotes fund is included in Section II

www.thestreetratings.com

Risk Rating/Pts	3 Year Standard Deviation	Beta	NAV As of 2/28/17	Total $(Mil)	Cash %	Stocks %	Bonds %	Other %	Portfolio Turnover Ratio	Last Bull Market Return	Last Bear Market Return	Manager Quality Pct	Manager Tenure (Years)	Initial Purch. $	Additional Purch. $	Front End Load	Back End Load
C+ / 6.2	8.3	1.30	16.97	19	10	75	14	1	22	79.3	-16.1	19	7	0	0	0.0	0.0
C+ / 6.2	8.3	1.30	16.93	57	10	75	14	1	22	80.5	-16.1	20	7	0	0	0.0	0.0
B / 8.5	4.0	0.59	12.21	936	1	26	71	2	10	39.1	-5.6	63	7	1,000	100	3.8	0.0
B / 8.5	4.0	0.59	12.09	372	1	26	71	2	10	33.4	-5.8	53	7	1,000	100	0.0	0.0
B / 8.5	4.0	0.58	12.17	177	1	26	71	2	10	41.5	-5.4	68	7	1,000,000	0	0.0	0.0
B / 8.5	4.0	0.59	12.11	1,096	1	26	71	2	10	39.4	-5.5	64	7	1,000	100	0.0	0.0
B / 8.5	4.0	0.59	12.12	1	1	26	71	2	10	35.0	-5.7	56	7	0	0	0.0	0.0
B / 8.5	4.0	0.59	12.15	1	1	26	71	2	10	35.9	-5.7	57	7	0	0	0.0	0.0
B / 8.5	4.0	0.59	12.15	7	1	26	71	2	10	37.4	-5.7	60	7	0	0	0.0	0.0
B / 8.5	4.0	0.59	12.15	7	1	26	71	2	10	38.7	-5.5	62	7	0	0	0.0	0.0
B / 8.5	4.0	0.58	12.15	22	1	26	71	2	10	39.6	-5.5	65	7	0	0	0.0	0.0
C / 5.2	9.4	1.45	19.04	971	3	90	6	1	23	90.3	-18.9	11	17	1,000	100	5.5	0.0
C / 5.1	9.4	1.46	17.50	315	3	90	6	1	23	82.8	-19.2	7	15	1,000	100	0.0	0.0
C / 5.1	9.4	1.45	18.62	255	3	90	6	1	23	94.3	-18.8	13	10	1,000,000	0	0.0	0.0
C / 5.1	9.4	1.46	18.45	286	3	90	6	1	23	91.2	-18.9	12	10	1,000	100	0.0	0.0
C / 5.2	9.4	1.46	18.39	2	3	90	6	1	23	85.3	-19.1	8	10	0	0	0.0	0.0
C / 5.2	9.4	1.46	18.45	2	3	90	6	1	23	86.5	-19.0	9	10	0	0	0.0	0.0
C / 5.2	9.4	1.46	18.42	14	3	90	6	1	23	88.4	-19.0	10	10	0	0	0.0	0.0
C / 5.1	9.4	1.46	18.54	14	3	90	6	1	23	90.4	-18.9	11	10	0	0	0.0	0.0
C / 5.1	9.4	1.46	18.48	24	3	90	6	1	23	91.6	-18.9	12	10	0	0	0.0	0.0
C / 5.4	11.9	1.01	16.74	N/A	6	93	0	1	26	146.7	N/A	79	6	0	0	0.0	0.0
C / 4.5	14.6	0.91	22.55	229	0	97	2	1	59	146.7	-24.8	76	11	1,000	100	5.5	0.0
C- / 4.2	14.6	0.91	20.72	31	0	97	2	1	59	136.3	-25.1	68	11	1,000	100	0.0	0.0
C / 4.6	14.6	0.91	23.98	69	0	97	2	1	59	153.3	-24.7	80	11	1,000,000	0	0.0	0.0
C / 4.4	14.6	0.91	21.65	206	0	97	2	1	59	148.9	-24.8	78	11	1,000	100	0.0	0.0
C / 4.4	14.6	0.91	21.66	3	0	97	2	1	59	142.0	-24.9	74	11	0	0	0.0	0.0
C / 4.4	14.6	0.91	21.84	13	0	97	2	1	59	143.7	-24.8	74	11	0	0	0.0	0.0
C / 4.5	14.6	0.91	22.56	15	0	97	2	1	59	146.2	-24.8	76	11	0	0	0.0	0.0
C / 4.5	14.6	0.91	23.32	17	0	97	2	1	59	148.8	-24.8	77	11	0	0	0.0	0.0
C / 4.6	14.6	0.91	23.77	23	0	97	2	1	59	150.3	-24.7	78	11	0	0	0.0	0.0
C+ / 6.4	12.0	1.02	16.67	267	6	93	0	1	26	141.6	N/A	76	6	1,000	100	5.5	0.0
C+ / 6.4	11.9	1.02	16.55	196	6	93	0	1	26	N/A	N/A	68	6	1,000	100	0.0	0.0
C+ / 6.4	11.9	1.01	16.74	1,461	6	93	0	1	26	146.7	N/A	79	6	0	0	0.0	0.0
C+ / 6.4	11.9	1.02	16.91	1,157	6	93	0	1	26	145.6	N/A	78	6	0	0	0.0	0.0
C / 4.6	14.7	0.92	25.86	650	0	98	0	2	21	152.1	-22.1	90	6	1,000,000	0	0.0	0.0
C / 4.6	14.6	0.92	24.62	182	0	98	0	2	21	147.2	-22.2	89	6	1,000	100	0.0	0.0
C / 4.7	14.7	0.92	25.51	15	0	98	0	2	21	141.0	-22.4	86	6	0	0	0.0	0.0
C / 4.7	14.7	0.92	26.16	21	0	98	0	2	21	142.6	-22.3	87	6	0	0	0.0	0.0
C / 4.7	14.7	0.92	26.34	139	0	98	0	2	21	145.1	-22.3	88	6	0	0	0.0	0.0
C / 4.7	14.7	0.92	26.57	92	0	98	0	2	21	147.5	-22.2	89	6	0	0	0.0	0.0
C / 4.7	14.7	0.92	26.69	222	0	98	0	2	21	149.0	-22.1	89	6	0	0	0.0	0.0
D / 2.0	16.8	1.01	12.25	1,375	3	93	2	2	57	123.2	-25.1	35	N/A	1,000,000	0	0.0	0.0
D- / 1.2	16.8	1.01	9.36	52	3	93	2	2	57	117.8	-25.3	30	N/A	1,000	100	0.0	0.0
D- / 1.5	16.8	1.01	10.29	2	3	93	2	2	57	113.0	-25.4	25	N/A	0	0	0.0	0.0
D- / 1.4	16.9	1.01	10.00	5	3	93	2	2	57	114.4	-25.3	26	N/A	0	0	0.0	0.0
D / 1.6	16.8	1.01	10.55	16	3	93	2	2	57	116.5	-25.3	28	N/A	0	0	0.0	0.0
D / 1.7	16.8	1.01	11.13	14	3	93	2	2	57	118.7	-25.2	30	N/A	0	0	0.0	0.0
D / 1.8	16.8	1.01	11.58	38	3	93	2	2	57	120.1	-25.2	32	N/A	0	0	0.0	0.0
C- / 4.0	14.6	0.91	13.18	1,258	3	93	2	2	53	142.7	-25.9	86	12	1,000,000	0	0.0	0.0
C- / 4.0	14.7	0.91	12.88	25	3	93	2	2	53	135.5	-26.1	84	12	1,000	100	0.0	0.0
C- / 3.9	14.6	0.91	12.12	2	3	93	2	2	53	131.5	-26.1	82	12	0	0	0.0	0.0
C- / 3.9	14.6	0.91	12.30	4	3	93	2	2	53	133.4	-26.1	83	12	0	0	0.0	0.0

Fund Type	Fund Name	Ticker Symbol	Overall Investment Rating	Phone	Perfor-mance Rating/Pts	3 Mo	6 Mo	1Yr / Pct	3Yr / Pct	5Yr / Pct	Dividend Yield	Expense Ratio
SC	Principal SmCp Value II R3	PJARX	B-	(800) 222-5852	B+ / 8.9	3.59	13.57	33.69 /92	7.82 /78	13.41 /88	0.03	1.59
SC	Principal SmCp Value II R4	PSTWX	B	(800) 222-5852	A- / 9.0	3.58	13.62	33.99 /93	8.00 /79	13.61 /90	0.14	1.40
SC	Principal SmCp Value II R5	PLARX	B	(800) 222-5852	A- / 9.1	3.63	13.65	34.06 /93	8.14 /80	13.74 /91	0.29	1.28
GL	Principal SystematEx Internatl R-6	PSTMX	U	(800) 222-5852	U /	7.17	5.11	16.13 /35	--	--	2.07	1.00
GL	Private Capital Management Value A	VFPAX	C	(888) 739-1390	C+ / 6.3	8.14	13.43	24.96 /73	5.79 /62	10.08 /59	1.03	1.54
GL	Private Capital Management Value I	VFPIX	C+	(888) 739-1390	B- / 7.2	8.14	13.51	25.17 /74	6.03 /64	10.36 /61	1.34	1.29
GR	Probabilities A	PROAX	C-	(855) 224-7204	C- / 3.1	7.26	7.58	16.90 /38	3.01 /32	--	0.00	2.39
GR	Probabilities C	PROCX	C	(855) 224-7204	C- / 3.5	7.02	7.13	15.98 /34	2.23 /26	--	0.00	3.14
GR	Probabilities I	PROTX	C+	(855) 224-7204	C / 4.4	7.41	7.83	17.23 /39	3.26 /34	--	0.00	2.14
EN	ProFunds Oil Eqpt Svcs & Dist Svc	OEPSX	E-	(888) 776-3637	E- / 0.1	-3.30	14.38	47.90 /99	-16.59 / 0	-7.33 / 1	0.00	2.79
EN	ProFunds Short Oil & Gas Inv	SNPIX	E	(888) 776-3637	E- / 0.1	3.42	-6.66	-25.13 / 0	-1.41 / 8	-6.23 / 1	0.00	2.26
EN	ProFunds Short Oil & Gas Svc	SNPSX	E	(888) 776-3637	E- / 0.1	3.20	-6.98	-25.83 / 0	-2.44 / 6	-7.10 / 1	0.00	3.26
PM	ProFunds Short Precious Metals Inv	SPPIX	E-	(888) 776-3637	E- / 0.0	-11.60	1.18	-32.33 / 0	-13.16 / 0	-1.97 / 3	0.00	1.88
PM	ProFunds Short Precious Metals Svc	SPPSX	E-	(888) 776-3637	E- / 0.0	-11.81	0.40	-33.11 / 0	-14.04 / 0	-2.93 / 2	0.00	2.88
RE	ProFunds Short Real Estate Inv	SRPIX	E	(888) 776-3637	E- / 0.0	-8.89	-1.73	-18.14 / 0	-12.88 / 0	-13.28 / 0	0.00	2.91
RE	ProFunds Short Real Estate Svc	SRPSX	E	(888) 776-3637	E- / 0.0	-9.11	-2.28	-18.98 / 0	-13.70 / 0	-14.11 / 0	0.00	3.91
GR	ProFunds Ultra Short NASDAQ-100	USPIX	E-	(888) 776-3637	E- / 0.0	-19.45	-22.46	-42.54 / 0	-29.79 / 0	-32.38 / 0	0.00	1.75
GR	ProFunds Ultra Short NASDAQ-100	USPSX	E-	(888) 776-3637	E- / 0.0	-19.69	-22.96	-43.32 / 0	-30.48 / 0	-33.03 / 0	0.00	2.75
FS	ProFunds-Banks UltraSector Inv	BKPIX	C+	(888) 776-3637	A+ / 9.9	17.15	50.13	93.81 /99	17.66 /99	24.76 /99	0.00	1.76
FS	ProFunds-Banks UltraSector Svc	BKPSX	C+	(888) 776-3637	A+ / 9.9	16.86	49.39	91.88 /99	16.46 /99	23.53 /99	0.00	2.76
GR	ProFunds-Basic Mat UltraSector Inv	BMPIX	C+	(888) 776-3637	A- / 9.1	8.32	16.23	49.28 /99	3.31 /35	6.60 /32	0.14	1.58
GR	ProFunds-Basic Mat UltraSector Svc	BMPSX	C	(888) 776-3637	B+ / 8.4	8.07	15.68	47.87 /99	2.29 /26	5.55 /25	0.00	2.58
GR	ProFunds-Bear Fund Inv	BRPIX	E+	(888) 776-3637	E- / 0.0	-7.75	-9.87	-21.76 / 0	-12.31 / 0	-14.93 / 0	0.00	1.54
GR	ProFunds-Bear Fund Svc	BRPSX	E+	(888) 776-3637	E- / 0.0	-7.93	-10.38	-22.54 / 0	-13.18 / 0	-15.78 / 0	0.00	2.54
GR	ProFunds-Biotech Ultra Sector Inv	BIPIX	E+	(888) 776-3637	C / 5.1	11.65	4.03	18.47 /45	3.91 /42	31.65 /99	0.00	1.47
GR	ProFunds-Biotech Ultra Sector Svc	BIPSX	E	(888) 776-3637	C- / 4.2	11.40	3.53	17.31 /40	2.88 /31	30.35 /99	0.00	2.47
AG	ProFunds-Bull Inv	BLPIX	A+	(888) 776-3637	B / 8.0	7.47	8.87	22.44 /64	8.55 /83	11.83 /73	0.00	1.58
AG	ProFunds-Bull Svc	BLPSX	A	(888) 776-3637	B- / 7.3	7.21	8.34	21.24 /58	7.47 /75	10.71 /64	0.00	2.58
GR	ProFunds-Consumer Goods Ultra Inv	CNPIX	A+	(888) 776-3637	A+ / 9.7	14.86	3.83	18.76 /46	13.24 /99	17.22 /98	0.00	1.75
GR	ProFunds-Consumer Goods Ultra Svc	CNPSX	A+	(888) 776-3637	A / 9.4	14.57	3.32	17.56 /41	12.12 /98	16.06 /98	0.00	2.75
GR	ProFunds-Consumer Srvs Ultra Inv	CYPIX	A+	(888) 776-3637	A+ / 9.7	8.39	12.31	23.65 /69	12.78 /99	23.26 /99	0.00	1.56
GR	ProFunds-Consumer Srvs Ultra Svc	CYPSX	A	(888) 776-3637	A+ / 9.6	8.13	11.75	22.41 /64	11.66 /98	22.04 /99	0.00	2.56
FO	ProFunds-Europe 30 Inv	UEPIX	E	(888) 776-3637	E+ / 0.9	8.88	7.92	20.06 /52	-3.37 / 4	3.20 /12	3.09	1.84
FO	ProFunds-Europe 30 Svc	UEPSX	E	(888) 776-3637	E+ / 0.6	8.54	7.31	18.78 /46	-4.30 / 3	2.19 / 8	0.00	2.84
FS	ProFunds-Financial UltraSector Inv	FNPIX	A-	(888) 776-3637	A+ / 9.9	13.91	25.42	57.32 /99	15.49 /99	22.06 /99	0.00	1.74
FS	ProFunds-Financial UltraSector Svc	FNPSX	A-	(888) 776-3637	A+ / 9.9	13.63	24.80	55.76 /99	14.35 /99	20.82 /99	0.00	2.74
GR	ProFunds-HlthCare UltraSector Inv	HCPIX	B+	(888) 776-3637	A+ / 9.6	14.22	5.84	22.55 /65	11.55 /98	24.50 /99	0.00	1.53
GR	ProFunds-HlthCare UltraSector Svc	HCPSX	B	(888) 776-3637	A- / 9.2	13.95	5.33	21.35 /59	10.43 /96	23.27 /99	0.00	2.53
GR	ProFunds-Industrial UltraSector Inv	IDPIX	A+	(888) 776-3637	A+ / 9.9	8.31	16.50	43.51 /98	11.84 /98	19.11 /99	0.00	1.70
GR	ProFunds-Industrial UltraSector Svc	IDPSX	A	(888) 776-3637	A+ / 9.8	8.06	15.93	42.07 /98	10.74 /96	17.94 /99	0.00	2.70
SC	ProFunds-Internet UltraSector Inv	INPIX	B-	(888) 776-3637	A+ / 9.9	11.51	12.66	48.06 /99	12.56 /98	27.27 /99	0.00	1.50
SC	ProFunds-Internet UltraSector Svc	INPSX	C+	(888) 776-3637	A+ / 9.9	11.22	12.08	46.58 /99	11.44 /98	25.99 /99	0.00	2.50
GR	ProFunds-Large Cap Growth Inv	LGPIX	A-	(888) 776-3637	B / 7.7	8.26	7.18	19.41 /49	8.66 /84	11.99 /74	0.00	1.67
GR	ProFunds-Large Cap Growth Svc	LGPSX	B+	(888) 776-3637	B- / 7.0	7.99	6.65	18.22 /44	7.60 /76	10.87 /65	0.00	2.67
GR	ProFunds-Large Cap Value Inv	LVPIX	A	(888) 776-3637	B+ / 8.4	6.73	10.78	25.90 /76	8.32 /81	11.63 /71	0.21	1.86
GR	ProFunds-Large Cap Value Svc	LVPSX	B+	(888) 776-3637	B / 7.6	6.47	10.22	24.63 /72	7.23 /74	10.51 /62	0.00	2.86
GR	ProFunds-Mble Telcm UltraSector Inv	WCPIX	C+	(888) 776-3637	A+ / 9.9	21.29	27.68	79.02 /99	13.28 /99	26.96 /99	0.00	2.10
GR	ProFunds-Mble Telcm UltraSector	WCPSX	C+	(888) 776-3637	A+ / 9.9	20.99	27.10	77.35 /99	12.16 /98	25.69 /99	0.00	3.10
GR	ProFunds-Mid Cap Growth Inv	MGPIX	B	(888) 776-3637	B- / 7.3	7.25	7.64	25.05 /73	6.89 /71	10.86 /65	0.00	1.81
GR	ProFunds-Mid Cap Growth Svc	MGPSX	C+	(888) 776-3637	C+ / 6.6	6.99	7.12	23.80 /69	5.81 /63	9.75 /57	0.00	2.81
MC	ProFunds-Mid Cap Inv	MDPIX	A	(888) 776-3637	B+ / 8.4	6.14	10.32	29.42 /85	7.72 /77	11.78 /72	0.00	1.51
MC	ProFunds-Mid Cap Svc	MDPSX	A-	(888) 776-3637	B / 7.6	5.88	9.76	28.10 /82	6.63 /69	10.67 /63	0.00	2.51

• Denotes fund is closed to new investors
* Denotes fund is included in Section II

| RISK | 3 Year | | NET ASSETS | | ASSET | | | | Portfolio | BULL / BEAR | | FUND MANAGER | | MINIMUMS | | LOADS | |
Risk Rating/Pts	Standard Deviation	Beta	NAV As of 2/28/17	Total $(Mil)	Cash %	Stocks %	Bonds %	Other %	Turnover Ratio	Last Bull Market Return	Last Bear Market Return	Manager Quality Pct	Manager Tenure (Years)	Initial Purch. $	Additional Purch. $	Front End Load	Back End Load
C- / 4.0	14.6	0.91	12.72	15	3	93	2	2	53	135.4	-26.0	84	12	0	0	0.0	0.0
C- / 4.0	14.6	0.91	12.87	9	3	93	2	2	53	137.8	-26.0	84	12	0	0	0.0	0.0
C- / 4.0	14.6	0.91	12.99	34	3	93	2	2	53	139.4	-25.9	85	12	0	0	0.0	0.0
U /	N/A	N/A	10.74	67	0	99	0	1	60	N/A	N/A	N/A	2	0	0	0.0	0.0
C / 4.9	13.6	0.57	16.05	6	18	81	0	1	14	100.3	-20.3	96	7	5,000	50	5.0	2.0
C / 4.9	13.6	0.57	16.22	71	18	81	0	1	14	103.0	-20.2	97	7	750,000	0	0.0	2.0
B- / 7.4	11.0	0.89	10.93	22	0	0	0	100	1,798	N/A	N/A	9	3	2,500	100	5.8	0.0
B- / 7.3	11.0	0.89	10.67	6	0	0	0	100	1,798	N/A	N/A	6	3	2,500	100	0.0	0.0
B- / 7.4	11.1	0.89	11.02	45	0	0	0	100	1,798	N/A	N/A	10	3	100,000	100	0.0	0.0
E- / 0.0	35.8	1.69	14.08	1	24	74	1	1	229	2.0	-47.3	3	4	5,000	100	0.0	0.0
C- / 3.7	19.3	-0.99	46.00	3	100	0	0	0	0	-45.8	26.8	6	4	15,000	100	0.0	0.0
C- / 3.6	19.3	-0.99	44.50	N/A	100	0	0	0	0	-48.5	26.2	4	4	5,000	100	0.0	0.0
E- / 0.0	48.0	-2.51	42.01	3	79	0	20	1	0	-19.8	15.3	0	4	15,000	100	0.0	0.0
E- / 0.0	48.0	-2.51	42.33	N/A	79	0	20	1	0	-24.0	14.9	0	4	5,000	100	0.0	0.0
C- / 4.0	13.5	-1.00	15.89	1	82	0	17	1	0	-60.9	13.9	28	4	15,000	100	0.0	0.0
C- / 3.8	13.6	-1.00	14.56	N/A	82	0	17	1	0	-62.9	13.4	19	4	5,000	100	0.0	0.0
E- / 0.0	26.9	-2.27	33.07	13	100	0	0	0	0	-91.3	13.0	1	4	15,000	100	0.0	0.0
E- / 0.0	26.8	-2.26	32.49	N/A	100	0	0	0	0	-91.8	12.5	1	4	5,000	100	0.0	0.0
D / 1.7	30.6	2.11	45.70	57	21	74	3	2	186	335.2	-46.1	3	4	15,000	100	0.0	0.0
D / 1.6	30.6	2.11	42.98	4	21	74	3	2	186	311.7	-46.2	3	4	5,000	100	0.0	0.0
D+ / 2.6	26.9	2.05	60.59	30	27	72	0	1	163	93.3	-45.7	0	4	15,000	100	0.0	0.0
D+ / 2.5	26.9	2.05	55.32	1	27	72	0	1	163	83.2	-46.0	0	4	5,000	100	0.0	0.0
C+ / 5.8	10.0	-0.98	37.36	18	86	0	13	1	0	-64.4	14.8	29	4	15,000	100	0.0	0.0
C+ / 5.6	10.0	-0.97	35.40	3	86	0	13	1	0	-66.3	14.4	19	4	5,000	100	0.0	0.0
E / 0.3	34.2	2.21	56.82	299	15	72	12	1	13	418.8	-16.7	0	4	15,000	100	0.0	0.0
E- / 0.2	34.3	2.21	46.63	13	15	72	12	1	13	391.5	-17.0	0	4	5,000	100	0.0	0.0
B / 8.3	10.3	1.00	108.13	63	27	45	27	1	368	111.4	-17.1	50	4	15,000	100	0.0	0.0
B / 8.2	10.3	1.00	91.73	7	27	45	27	1	368	100.2	-17.4	36	4	5,000	100	0.0	0.0
B- / 7.4	14.7	1.15	101.55	10	35	64	0	1	236	172.6	-13.6	80	4	15,000	100	0.0	0.0
B- / 7.3	14.7	1.15	93.47	1	35	64	0	1	236	158.3	-14.0	73	4	5,000	100	0.0	0.0
C+ / 6.0	17.1	1.48	96.46	49	16	79	3	2	37	280.2	-19.7	36	4	15,000	100	0.0	0.0
C+ / 5.9	17.1	1.48	85.80	1	16	79	3	2	37	260.2	-20.0	25	4	5,000	100	0.0	0.0
C- / 4.2	12.5	0.94	12.51	8	0	100	0	0	718	39.0	-27.7	31	8	15,000	100	0.0	0.0
C / 4.3	12.5	0.93	13.22	N/A	0	100	0	0	718	31.9	-28.0	21	8	5,000	100	0.0	0.0
C / 5.0	19.7	1.51	19.24	49	26	73	0	1	275	272.9	-37.4	32	4	15,000	100	0.0	0.0
C / 5.0	19.7	1.51	16.76	2	26	73	0	1	275	253.6	-37.8	21	4	5,000	100	0.0	0.0
C / 4.4	20.4	1.55	51.25	21	16	79	4	1	7	269.9	-16.7	18	4	15,000	100	0.0	0.0
C / 4.3	20.4	1.55	44.44	2	16	79	4	1	7	250.5	-17.0	11	4	5,000	100	0.0	0.0
C+ / 5.8	18.5	1.66	89.25	36	30	67	1	2	270	245.6	-35.6	12	4	15,000	100	0.0	0.0
C+ / 5.7	18.5	1.66	80.21	1	30	67	1	2	270	227.5	-35.9	7	4	5,000	100	0.0	0.0
D+ / 2.8	26.2	0.98	53.43	81	33	66	0	1	65	333.7	-32.9	96	4	15,000	100	0.0	0.0
D+ / 2.6	26.2	0.98	43.34	5	33	66	0	1	65	310.7	-33.2	94	4	5,000	100	0.0	0.0
B- / 7.1	11.0	1.03	71.63	28	12	87	0	1	460	110.4	-13.7	48	4	15,000	100	0.0	0.0
B- / 7.0	11.0	1.03	61.90	4	12	87	0	1	460	99.4	-14.1	34	4	5,000	100	0.0	0.0
C+ / 6.9	10.4	0.96	60.93	13	1	98	0	1	813	112.2	-20.1	52	4	15,000	100	0.0	0.0
C+ / 6.9	10.4	0.96	55.66	3	1	98	0	1	813	100.9	-20.4	38	4	5,000	100	0.0	0.0
D / 1.7	28.6	1.08	76.39	12	47	45	6	2	962	295.8	-29.8	84	4	15,000	100	0.0	0.0
D / 1.6	28.6	1.08	64.50	1	47	45	6	2	962	275.0	-30.1	78	4	5,000	100	0.0	0.0
C+ / 5.9	11.6	0.96	79.57	10	0	100	0	0	666	105.3	-21.6	34	4	15,000	100	0.0	0.0
C+ / 5.9	11.6	0.96	67.82	1	0	100	0	0	666	94.5	-21.9	23	4	5,000	100	0.0	0.0
B- / 7.1	12.1	1.00	85.87	124	29	64	6	1	1,455	117.6	-23.3	52	4	15,000	100	0.0	0.0
B- / 7.0	12.1	1.00	74.13	2	29	64	6	1	1,455	106.2	-23.6	37	4	5,000	100	0.0	0.0

Fund Type	Fund Name	Ticker Symbol	Overall Investment Rating	Phone	Performance Rating/Pts	3 Mo	6 Mo	1Yr / Pct	3Yr / Pct	5Yr / Pct	Dividend Yield	Expense Ratio
	99 Pct = Best 0 Pct = Worst					Total Return % through 2/28/17			Annualized		Incl. in Returns	
MC	ProFunds-Mid Cap Value Inv	MLPIX	A-	(888) 776-3637	A- / 9.0	4.98	12.54	33.04 /92	8.01 /79	12.34 /78	0.23	1.84
MC	ProFunds-Mid Cap Value Svc	MLPSX	B+	(888) 776-3637	B / 8.2	4.72	11.98	31.66 /89	6.89 /71	11.20 /68	0.00	2.84
AG	ProFunds-Nasdaq-100 Inv	OTPIX	C-	(888) 776-3637	A+ / 9.7	10.57	11.25	25.98 /76	12.00 /98	14.27 /95	0.00	1.54
AG	ProFunds-Nasdaq-100 Svc	OTPSX	C-	(888) 776-3637	A+ / 9.6	10.28	10.72	24.72 /72	10.88 /97	13.11 /85	0.00	2.54
EN	ProFunds-Oil & Gas UltraSector Inv	ENPIX	E-	(888) 776-3637	E- / 0.1	-6.61	4.78	36.66 /96	-11.39 / 1	-2.82 / 2	0.62	1.54
EN	ProFunds-Oil & Gas UltraSector Svc	ENPSX	E-	(888) 776-3637	E- / 0.1	-6.82	4.27	35.37 /94	-12.26 / 0	-3.78 / 2	0.00	2.54
GR	ProFunds-Pharm UltraSector Inv	PHPIX	B-	(888) 776-3637	B- / 7.5	15.32	2.81	15.37 /32	8.36 /82	20.77 /99	0.00	1.64
GR	ProFunds-Pharm UltraSector Svc	PHPSX	C	(888) 776-3637	C+ / 5.8	15.00	2.28	14.18 /26	7.27 /74	19.51 /99	0.00	2.64
PM	ProFunds-Precious Metals Ultra Inv	PMPIX	E-	(888) 776-3637	E- / 0.0	12.81	-18.76	16.84 /38	-16.25 / 0	-26.33 / 0	0.00	1.55
PM	ProFunds-Precious Metals Ultra Svc	PMPSX	E-	(888) 776-3637	E- / 0.0	12.52	-19.19	15.79 /33	-17.10 / 0	-27.06 / 0	0.00	2.55
RE	ProFunds-Real Est UltraSector Inv	REPIX	A-	(888) 776-3637	A / 9.5	12.99	-1.80	24.41 /71	12.53 /98	13.14 /85	3.44	1.61
RE	ProFunds-Real Est UltraSector Svc	REPSX	B+	(888) 776-3637	A- / 9.0	12.69	-2.26	23.19 /67	11.40 /98	12.03 /75	2.92	2.61
FS	ProFunds-Rising Rates Opp 10 Inv	RTPIX	D	(888) 776-3637	E- / 0.2	-1.11	5.56	2.43 / 2	-4.79 / 3	-3.75 / 2	0.00	1.63
FS	ProFunds-Rising Rates Opp 10 Svc	RTPSX	D	(888) 776-3637	E- / 0.1	-1.36	5.06	1.39 / 2	-5.72 / 2	-4.69 / 2	0.00	2.63
OT	ProFunds-Rising Rates Opport Inv	RRPIX	E-	(888) 776-3637	E- / 0.0	-3.24	17.51	3.47 / 3	-11.36 / 1	-7.85 / 1	0.00	1.48
OT	ProFunds-Rising Rates Opport Svc	RRPSX	E-	(888) 776-3637	E- / 0.0	-3.35	17.10	2.55 / 2	-12.25 / 0	-8.80 / 1	0.00	2.48
GR	ProFunds-Rising US Dollar Inv	RDPIX	C+	(888) 776-3637	C- / 3.1	-0.47	5.00	1.86 / 2	6.25 /66	2.98 /11	0.00	1.65
GR	ProFunds-Rising US Dollar Svc	RDPSX	C+	(888) 776-3637	D+ / 2.4	-0.70	4.49	0.86 / 2	5.19 /56	1.96 / 8	0.00	2.65
GR	ProFunds-Semicond UltraSector Inv	SMPIX	B	(888) 776-3637	A+ / 9.9	10.16	20.47	73.81 /99	27.97 /99	21.41 /99	0.14	1.77
GR	ProFunds-Semicond UltraSector Svc	SMPSX	B	(888) 776-3637	A+ / 9.9	9.90	19.91	72.14 /99	26.71 /99	20.19 /99	0.00	2.77
GR	ProFunds-Short OTC Inv	SOPIX	E-	(888) 776-3637	E- / 0.0	-10.41	-11.86	-24.04 / 0	-16.42 / 0	-18.31 / 0	0.00	1.86
GR	ProFunds-Short OTC Svc	SOPSX	E-	(888) 776-3637	E- / 0.0	-10.59	-12.22	-24.75 / 0	-17.16 / 0	-19.09 / 0	0.00	2.86
SC	ProFunds-Short Small Cap Inv	SHPIX	E	(888) 776-3637	E- / 0.0	-5.72	-12.92	-29.76 / 0	-11.09 / 1	-15.89 / 0	0.00	1.74
SC	ProFunds-Short Small Cap Svc	SHPSX	E-	(888) 776-3637	E- / 0.0	-5.91	-13.37	-30.46 / 0	-11.97 / 1	-16.67 / 0	0.00	2.74
SC	ProFunds-Small Cap Growth Inv	SGPIX	B+	(888) 776-3637	B+ / 8.6	5.04	11.32	30.47 /87	7.90 /78	12.89 /83	0.00	1.91
SC	ProFunds-Small Cap Growth Svc	SGPSX	B-	(888) 776-3637	B / 7.8	4.77	10.76	29.15 /84	6.82 /71	11.76 /72	0.00	2.91
SC	ProFunds-Small Cap Inv	SLPIX	B	(888) 776-3637	B- / 7.5	4.78	11.41	33.56 /92	5.08 /55	11.00 /66	0.00	1.93
SC	ProFunds-Small Cap Svc	SLPSX	C+	(888) 776-3637	C+ / 6.8	4.53	10.87	32.20 /90	4.04 /43	9.91 /58	0.00	2.93
SC	ProFunds-Small Cap Value Inv	SVPIX	B+	(888) 776-3637	B+ / 8.5	3.12	12.95	34.33 /93	6.97 /72	12.37 /78	0.00	1.83
SC	ProFunds-Small Cap Value Svc	SVPSX	B	(888) 776-3637	B / 7.7	2.85	12.38	33.02 /92	5.91 /63	11.24 /68	0.00	2.83
TC	ProFunds-Tech UltraSector Inv	TEPIX	A	(888) 776-3637	A+ / 9.9	17.03	20.40	51.72 /99	19.51 /99	17.83 /99	0.00	1.82
TC	ProFunds-Tech UltraSector Svc	TEPSX	A	(888) 776-3637	A+ / 9.9	16.75	19.81	50.25 /99	18.32 /99	16.65 /98	0.00	2.82
GR	ProFunds-Telecom UltraSector Inv	TCPIX	B+	(888) 776-3637	B / 8.2	7.80	1.15	14.30 /27	12.15 /98	13.73 /91	0.00	1.52
GR	ProFunds-Telecom UltraSector Svc	TCPSX	B	(888) 776-3637	B- / 7.5	7.51	0.62	13.09 /22	11.01 /97	12.56 /80	0.00	2.52
GR	ProFunds-Ultra Bear Inv	URPIX	E-	(888) 776-3637	E- / 0.0	-14.46	-18.46	-38.23 / 0	-23.05 / 0	-27.87 / 0	0.00	1.64
GR	ProFunds-Ultra Bear Svc	URPSX	E-	(888) 776-3637	E- / 0.0	-14.59	-18.85	-38.83 / 0	-23.78 / 0	-28.58 / 0	0.00	2.64
AG	ProFunds-Ultra Bull Inv	ULPIX	A	(888) 776-3637	A+ / 9.9	15.70	18.89	50.58 /99	17.27 /99	24.44 /99	0.00	1.46
AG	ProFunds-Ultra Bull Svc	ULPSX	A	(888) 776-3637	A+ / 9.9	15.43	18.31	49.06 /99	16.12 /99	23.23 /99	0.00	2.46
FO	Profunds-Ultra China Inv	UGPIX	E-	(888) 776-3637	D / 2.2	11.01	8.66	35.86 /95	-1.93 / 7	4.02 /15	0.00	1.78
FO	Profunds-Ultra China Svc	UGPSX	E-	(888) 776-3637	D / 1.7	10.71	8.16	34.81 /94	-2.89 / 5	3.00 /11	0.00	2.78
GR	ProFunds-Ultra Dow 30 Inv	UDPIX	A	(888) 776-3637	A+ / 9.9	18.61	28.56	60.91 /99	18.19 /99	21.83 /99	0.00	1.70
GR	ProFunds-Ultra Dow 30 Svc	UDPSX	A-	(888) 776-3637	A+ / 9.9	18.37	27.98	59.39 /99	17.03 /99	20.63 /99	0.00	2.70
EM	Profunds-Ultra Emerging Mkt Inv	UUPIX	D	(888) 776-3637	C+ / 6.5	15.93	11.24	68.36 /99	-0.49 /11	-8.52 / 1	0.00	1.80
EM	Profunds-Ultra Emerging Mkt Svc	UUPSX	D-	(888) 776-3637	C+ / 5.6	15.68	10.72	66.60 /99	-1.51 / 8	-9.46 / 1	0.00	2.80
EM	ProFunds-Ultra Intl Inv	UNPIX	E-	(888) 776-3637	E / 0.3	13.81	6.25	25.66 /75	-7.72 / 1	3.71 /14	0.00	1.81
EM	ProFunds-Ultra Intl Svc	UNPSX	E-	(888) 776-3637	E- / 0.2	13.53	5.62	24.41 /71	-8.64 / 1	2.68 /10	0.00	2.81
FO	ProFunds-Ultra Japan Inv	UJPIX	C-	(888) 776-3637	A+ / 9.8	4.56	26.10	34.70 /94	9.59 /91	20.16 /99	0.00	1.67
FO	ProFunds-Ultra Japan Svc	UJPSX	C-	(888) 776-3637	A+ / 9.7	4.22	25.47	33.28 /92	8.57 /84	19.00 /99	0.00	2.67
FO	ProFunds-Ultra Latin America Inv	UBPIX	E+	(888) 776-3637	C / 4.8	25.66	24.08	129.20 /99	-14.13 / 0	-21.97 / 0	0.25	1.79
FO	ProFunds-Ultra Latin America Svc	UBPSX	E	(888) 776-3637	C- / 3.9	25.35	23.45	126.77 /99	-14.92 / 0	-22.71 / 0	0.00	2.79
AG	ProFunds-Ultra Mid Cap Inv	UMPIX	B	(888) 776-3637	A+ / 9.9	12.60	21.46	65.86 /99	14.87 /99	23.80 /99	0.00	1.50
AG	ProFunds-Ultra Mid Cap Svc	UMPSX	B-	(888) 776-3637	A+ / 9.9	12.40	20.95	64.32 /99	13.75 /99	22.58 /99	0.00	2.50

● Denotes fund is closed to new investors
* Denotes fund is included in Section II

RISK			NET ASSETS		ASSET					BULL / BEAR		FUND MANAGER		MINIMUMS		LOADS	
	3 Year		NAV						Portfolio	Last Bull	Last Bear	Manager	Manager	Initial	Additional	Front	Back
Risk Rating/Pts	Standard Deviation	Beta	As of 2/28/17	Total $(Mil)	Cash %	Stocks %	Bonds %	Other %	Turnover Ratio	Market Return	Market Return	Quality Pct	Tenure (Years)	Purch. $	Purch. $	End Load	End Load
C+ / 6.0	13.2	1.06	78.10	41	0	100	0	0	913	127.2	-24.7	48	4	15,000	100	0.0	0.0
C+ / 5.8	13.2	1.06	67.11	1	0	100	0	0	913	115.0	-25.0	33	4	5,000	100	0.0	0.0
E- / 0.0	13.7	1.19	53.68	68	48	44	7	1	362	138.0	-11.4	67	4	15,000	100	0.0	0.0
E- / 0.0	13.7	1.19	45.05	3	48	44	7	1	362	125.3	-11.8	53	4	5,000	100	0.0	0.0
E / 0.3	29.8	1.50	37.25	26	25	70	4	1	16	22.5	-37.7	23	4	15,000	100	0.0	0.0
E / 0.3	29.8	1.50	31.96	3	25	70	4	1	16	16.2	-38.0	15	4	5,000	100	0.0	0.0
C / 5.4	18.9	1.34	24.92	11	35	58	6	1	79	202.7	-8.4	12	4	15,000	100	0.0	0.0
C / 5.3	18.9	1.34	22.39	1	35	58	6	1	79	186.2	-8.9	7	4	5,000	100	0.0	0.0
E- / 0.0	74.0	3.72	39.97	33	32	65	1	2	167	-76.7	-26.6	2	4	15,000	100	0.0	0.0
E- / 0.0	73.9	3.72	35.50	6	32	65	1	2	167	-77.9	-26.9	1	4	5,000	100	0.0	0.0
C / 5.1	20.9	1.52	42.71	9	20	74	4	2	101	141.2	-26.4	22	4	15,000	100	0.0	0.0
C / 5.0	20.9	1.52	41.05	1	20	74	4	2	101	128.6	-26.7	14	4	5,000	100	0.0	0.0
B- / 7.7	6.2	0.24	15.20	11	82	0	17	1	0	-18.9	-13.8	4	8	15,000	100	0.0	0.0
B- / 7.4	6.1	0.24	14.54	1	82	0	17	1	0	-23.2	-14.2	3	8	5,000	100	0.0	0.0
D+ / 2.7	17.0	0.31	42.96	43	93	0	6	1	0	-34.4	-33.2	0	8	15,000	100	0.0	0.0
D+ / 2.5	16.9	0.30	38.97	5	93	0	6	1	0	-37.9	-33.5	0	8	5,000	100	0.0	0.0
B+ / 9.2	7.1	-0.08	29.59	19	84	0	15	1	0	14.6	6.2	98	8	15,000	100	0.0	0.0
B+ / 9.0	7.1	-0.08	26.99	5	84	0	15	1	0	8.5	5.7	97	8	5,000	100	0.0	0.0
C- / 3.4	27.4	1.88	42.05	156	22	73	3	2	253	261.4	-29.9	97	4	15,000	100	0.0	0.0
C- / 3.3	27.4	1.88	36.23	4	22	73	3	2	253	242.7	-30.2	95	4	5,000	100	0.0	0.0
D+ / 2.7	13.3	-1.14	13.08	10	84	0	15	1	0	-71.4	7.2	6	4	15,000	100	0.0	0.0
D+ / 2.4	13.3	-1.14	12.07	N/A	84	0	15	1	0	-72.9	6.6	4	4	5,000	100	0.0	0.0
C- / 3.8	15.6	-0.99	15.98	10	84	0	15	1	0	-68.6	24.2	13	4	15,000	100	0.0	0.0
C- / 3.6	15.6	-0.99	15.75	2	84	0	15	1	0	-70.1	23.9	7	4	5,000	100	0.0	0.0
C / 5.3	14.6	0.91	78.40	29	0	100	0	0	710	127.8	-22.0	84	4	15,000	100	0.0	0.0
C / 5.1	14.6	0.91	66.10	2	0	100	0	0	710	115.7	-22.3	78	4	5,000	100	0.0	0.0
C+ / 5.6	15.7	1.00	76.53	38	51	38	10	1	190	112.3	-25.2	52	4	15,000	100	0.0	0.0
C / 5.5	15.7	1.00	65.48	2	51	38	10	1	190	101.3	-25.6	38	4	5,000	100	0.0	0.0
C+ / 5.8	15.2	0.93	82.71	43	0	98	0	2	1,206	131.4	-23.2	78	4	15,000	100	0.0	0.0
C+ / 5.7	15.2	0.93	71.35	1	0	98	0	2	1,206	119.0	-23.5	69	4	5,000	100	0.0	0.0
C+ / 5.6	22.0	1.83	83.99	56	25	70	3	2	151	215.2	-20.7	68	4	15,000	100	0.0	0.0
C / 5.5	22.0	1.83	72.57	1	25	70	3	2	151	198.5	-21.0	55	4	5,000	100	0.0	0.0
C+ / 5.8	20.9	0.82	25.57	7	52	42	4	2	330	116.2	-15.3	91	4	15,000	100	0.0	0.0
C+ / 5.7	20.9	0.82	24.19	N/A	52	42	4	2	330	104.6	-15.7	87	4	5,000	100	0.0	0.0
D- / 1.1	20.1	-1.93	34.90	11	86	0	13	1	0	-87.8	28.1	5	4	15,000	100	0.0	0.0
D- / 1.0	20.0	-1.91	32.54	1	86	0	13	1	0	-88.4	27.7	4	4	5,000	100	0.0	0.0
C / 5.5	21.2	2.03	135.07	93	44	55	0	1	165	330.4	-33.2	20	4	15,000	100	0.0	0.0
C / 5.4	21.2	2.03	114.76	2	44	55	0	1	165	308.1	-33.4	12	4	5,000	100	0.0	0.0
E- / 0.0	45.2	2.48	11.29	7	0	0	0	100	323	67.0	-54.1	58	8	15,000	100	0.0	0.0
E- / 0.0	45.2	2.48	10.34	1	0	0	0	100	323	58.4	-54.2	44	8	5,000	100	0.0	0.0
C / 5.1	22.0	2.03	90.88	35	28	65	5	2	20	277.1	-28.5	27	4	15,000	100	0.0	0.0
C / 5.0	22.0	2.03	80.86	4	28	65	5	2	20	257.2	-28.8	18	4	5,000	100	0.0	0.0
D- / 1.3	40.2	2.28	46.72	49	15	83	1	1	402	-7.7	-45.8	21	8	15,000	100	0.0	0.0
D- / 1.3	40.2	2.28	43.90	2	15	83	1	1	402	-12.6	-46.0	13	8	5,000	100	0.0	0.0
D- / 1.4	23.5	1.05	13.76	5	81	0	18	1	0	54.8	-46.5	2	8	15,000	100	0.0	0.0
D- / 1.2	23.5	1.05	12.59	N/A	81	0	18	1	0	46.6	-46.8	2	8	5,000	100	0.0	0.0
E- / 0.0	35.4	1.32	18.36	28	83	0	16	1	0	214.4	-27.4	99	8	15,000	100	0.0	0.0
E- / 0.0	35.4	1.32	16.06	1	83	0	16	1	0	198.0	-27.7	99	8	5,000	100	0.0	0.0
D- / 1.3	60.7	2.59	34.41	38	16	82	1	1	587	-54.4	-47.5	0	8	15,000	100	0.0	0.0
D- / 1.3	60.6	2.59	33.38	1	16	82	1	1	587	-56.7	-47.7	0	8	5,000	100	0.0	0.0
C- / 3.1	24.6	2.06	117.94	98	31	61	7	1	89	341.8	-43.3	6	4	15,000	100	0.0	0.0
C- / 3.0	24.7	2.06	100.35	1	31	61	7	1	89	318.7	-43.6	4	4	5,000	100	0.0	0.0

Fund Type	Fund Name	Ticker Symbol	Overall Investment Rating	Phone	Performance Rating/Pts	3 Mo	6 Mo	1Yr / Pct	3Yr / Pct	5Yr / Pct	Dividend Yield	Expense Ratio
								Total Return % through 2/28/17	Annualized		Incl. in Returns	
GR	ProFunds-Ultra Nasdaq-100 Inv	UOPIX	B+	(888) 776-3637	A+ / 9.9	22.20	23.62	58.10 /99	24.29 /99	29.81 /99	0.00	1.47
GR	ProFunds-Ultra Nasdaq-100 Svc	UOPSX	B+	(888) 776-3637	A+ / 9.9	21.89	23.01	56.53 /99	23.05 /99	28.53 /99	0.00	2.47
EM	Profunds-Ultra Sh Emer Mkt Inv	UVPIX	E-	(888) 776-3637	E- / 0.0	-16.01	-16.71	-50.19 / 0	-17.80 / 0	-9.72 / 1	0.00	1.78
EM	Profunds-Ultra Sh Emer Mkt Svc	UVPSX	E-	(888) 776-3637	E- / 0.0	-16.23	-17.09	-50.69 / 0	-18.58 / 0	-10.59 / 0	0.00	2.78
EM	ProFunds-Ultra Sh Intl Inv	UXPIX	E-	(888) 776-3637	E- / 0.0	-14.01	-10.56	-32.67 / 0	-8.20 / 1	-18.11 / 0	0.00	1.74
EM	ProFunds-Ultra Sh Intl Svc	UXPSX	E-	(888) 776-3637	E- / 0.0	-14.20	-10.97	-33.32 / 0	-9.11 / 1	-18.97 / 0	0.00	2.74
FO	ProFunds-Ultra Sh Latin America Inv	UFPIX	E-	(888) 776-3637	E- / 0.0	-24.74	-31.69	-70.60 / 0	-18.45 / 0	-4.45 / 2	0.00	1.78
FO	ProFunds-Ultra Sh Latin America Svc	UFPSX	E-	(888) 776-3637	E- / 0.0	-24.85	-31.98	-70.86 / 0	-19.19 / 0	-5.36 / 2	0.00	2.78
FO	Profunds-Ultra Short China Inv	UHPIX	E-	(888) 776-3637	E- / 0.0	-12.65	-15.21	-39.47 / 0	-21.92 / 0	-25.22 / 0	0.00	2.13
FO	Profunds-Ultra Short China Svc	UHPSX	E-	(888) 776-3637	E- / 0.0	-12.79	-15.64	-40.01 / 0	-22.67 / 0	-26.02 / 0	0.00	3.13
GR	ProFunds-Ultra Short Dow 30 Inv	UWPIX	E-	(888) 776-3637	E- / 0.0	-16.71	-24.74	-42.28 / 0	-23.94 / 0	-26.04 / 0	0.00	2.01
GR	ProFunds-Ultra Short Dow 30 Svc	UWPSX	E-	(888) 776-3637	E- / 0.0	-16.83	-25.06	-42.80 / 0	-24.73 / 0	-26.83 / 0	0.00	3.01
FO	Profunds-Ultra Short Japan Inv	UKPIX	E-	(888) 776-3637	E- / 0.0	-7.10	-25.23	-41.10 / 0	-28.50 / 0	-35.79 / 0	0.00	2.82
FO	Profunds-Ultra Short Japan Svc	UKPSX	E-	(888) 776-3637	E- / 0.0	-7.24	-25.59	-41.64 / 0	-29.17 / 0	-36.40 / 0	0.00	3.82
MC	ProFunds-Ultra Short Mid-Cap Inv	UIPIX	E-	(888) 776-3637	E- / 0.0	-12.84	-21.44	-45.95 / 0	-23.22 / 0	-28.98 / 0	0.00	2.27
MC	ProFunds-Ultra Short Mid-Cap Svc	UIPSX	E-	(888) 776-3637	E- / 0.0	-12.99	-21.82	-46.49 / 0	-24.06 / 0	-29.67 / 0	0.00	3.27
SC	ProFunds-Ultra Short Small-Cap Inv	UCPIX	E-	(888) 776-3637	E- / 0.0	-11.29	-24.80	-51.34 / 0	-21.89 / 0	-29.83 / 0	0.00	1.78
SC	ProFunds-Ultra Short Small-Cap Svc	UCPSX	E-	(888) 776-3637	E- / 0.0	-11.56	-25.16	-51.85 / 0	-22.71 / 0	-30.58 / 0	0.00	2.78
SC	ProFunds-Ultra Small Cap Inv	UAPIX	C-	(888) 776-3637	A+ / 9.9	9.57	23.83	76.24 /99	8.64 /84	21.52 /99	0.00	1.60
SC	ProFunds-Ultra Small Cap Svc	UAPSX	C-	(888) 776-3637	A+ / 9.9	9.27	23.24	74.55 /99	7.55 /76	20.29 /99	0.00	2.60
UT	ProFunds-Utilities UltraSector Inv	UTPIX	A	(888) 776-3637	A+ / 9.9	16.79	9.56	21.94 /62	15.93 /99	16.23 /98	0.76	1.63
UT	ProFunds-Utilities UltraSector Svc	UTPSX	A-	(888) 776-3637	A+ / 9.8	16.51	9.03	20.74 /56	14.78 /99	15.08 /97	0.00	2.63
IN	Prospector Capital Appreciation Fd	PCAFX	C+	(877) 734-7862	C+ / 6.0	5.13	8.51	22.03 /62	5.84 /63	7.57 /39	1.27	1.89
MC	Prospector Opportunity	POPFX	B-	(877) 734-7862	B+ / 8.5	4.67	10.43	25.72 /75	9.66 /91	12.51 /79	1.06	1.62
GI	Provident Trust Strategy Fd	PROVX	B+	(855) 739-9950	B- / 7.3	7.69	11.14	16.41 /36	7.90 /78	10.38 /61	0.08	1.03
BA	Prudential Balanced A	PIBAX	C	(800) 225-1852	C / 4.3	4.76	5.07	15.00 /30	6.60 /69	8.97 /50	1.11	1.25
BA	● Prudential Balanced B	PBFBX	C+	(800) 225-1852	C / 4.8	4.56	4.68	14.21 /26	5.85 /63	8.21 /44	0.52	1.95
BA	Prudential Balanced C	PABCX	C+	(800) 225-1852	C / 4.8	4.56	4.69	14.21 /26	5.87 /63	8.21 /44	0.52	1.95
BA	Prudential Balanced R	PALRX	C+	(800) 225-1852	C / 5.3	4.69	5.01	14.85 /29	6.41 /68	8.76 /49	0.99	1.70
BA	Prudential Balanced Z	PABFX	C+	(800) 225-1852	C+ / 5.8	4.90	5.28	15.39 /32	6.94 /72	9.31 /53	1.44	0.95
AA	Prudential Conservative Alloc A	JDUAX	C-	(800) 225-1852	D / 1.8	3.64	2.97	10.95 /14	2.89 /31	4.64 /19	1.48	1.52
AA	● Prudential Conservative Alloc B	JDABX	C-	(800) 225-1852	D / 2.1	3.46	2.51	10.09 /12	2.11 /25	3.86 /15	0.85	2.22
AA	Prudential Conservative Alloc C	JDACX	C-	(800) 225-1852	D / 2.1	3.37	2.51	10.09 /12	2.11 /25	3.85 /14	0.85	2.22
AA	Prudential Conservative Alloc R	JDARX	C-	(800) 225-1852	D+ / 2.3	3.56	2.75	10.64 /13	2.62 /28	4.37 /17	1.32	1.22
AA	Prudential Conservative Alloc Z	JDAZX	C-	(800) 225-1852	D+ / 2.6	3.60	3.00	11.18 /15	3.14 /33	4.90 /21	1.79	1.22
FS	Prudential Financial Services A	PFSAX	E	(800) 225-1852	E+ / 0.7	7.93	15.75	26.04 /76	-3.82 / 3	5.30 /23	1.54	1.35
FS	● Prudential Financial Services B	PUFBX	E	(800) 225-1852	E+ / 0.9	7.72	15.28	25.25 /74	-4.49 / 3	4.56 /18	1.23	2.05
FS	Prudential Financial Services C	PUFCX	E	(800) 225-1852	E+ / 0.9	7.72	15.28	25.25 /74	-4.48 / 3	4.57 /19	1.23	2.05
FS	Prudential Financial Services R	PSSRX	E	(800) 225-1852	D- / 1.1	7.83	15.65	25.82 /76	-4.01 / 3	5.11 /22	1.46	1.80
FS	Prudential Financial Services Z	PFSZX	E	(800) 225-1852	D- / 1.3	8.05	15.92	26.51 /78	-3.52 / 4	5.62 /26	1.84	1.05
FS	Prudential Global Abs Rtn Bd Q	PAJQX	U	(800) 225-1852	U /	4.87	3.65	11.83 /17	--	--	5.12	2.60
RE	Prudential Global Real Estate A	PURAX	D	(800) 225-1852	D / 1.8	5.50	-3.71	8.28 / 8	4.52 /49	6.86 /34	2.85	1.27
RE	● Prudential Global Real Estate B	PURBX	D+	(800) 225-1852	D / 2.2	5.31	-4.06	7.51 / 7	3.81 /41	6.11 /29	2.37	1.97
RE	Prudential Global Real Estate C	PURCX	D+	(800) 225-1852	D / 2.2	5.36	-4.01	7.56 / 7	3.81 /41	6.12 /29	2.37	1.97
RE	Prudential Global Real Estate Q	PGRQX	C-	(800) 225-1852	D+ / 2.9	5.64	-3.52	8.75 / 9	5.01 /54	7.30 /37	3.47	0.80
RE	Prudential Global Real Estate R	PURRX	D+	(800) 225-1852	D+ / 2.5	5.46	-3.77	8.08 / 8	4.33 /47	6.65 /32	2.81	1.72
RE	Prudential Global Real Estate Z	PURZX	D+	(800) 225-1852	D+ / 2.8	5.56	-3.58	8.58 / 9	4.83 /52	7.18 /36	3.31	0.97
GR	Prudential Growth Allocation A	JDAAX	C-	(800) 225-1852	C- / 4.0	6.18	7.72	20.50 /55	4.05 /44	8.02 /42	0.98	1.89
GR	● Prudential Growth Allocation B	JDGBX	C-	(800) 225-1852	C / 4.4	5.98	7.31	19.59 /50	3.25 /34	7.22 /36	0.41	2.59
GR	Prudential Growth Allocation C	JDGCX	C-	(800) 225-1852	C / 4.5	5.97	7.30	19.65 /50	3.27 /34	7.22 /36	0.41	2.59
GR	Prudential Growth Allocation R	JGARX	C	(800) 225-1852	C / 4.9	6.11	7.59	20.31 /54	3.78 /40	7.76 /40	0.82	2.34
GR	Prudential Growth Allocation Z	JDGZX	C	(800) 225-1852	C / 5.3	6.22	7.88	20.85 /57	4.28 /46	8.27 /44	1.25	1.59

99 Pct = Best
0 Pct = Worst

● Denotes fund is closed to new investors
* Denotes fund is included in Section II

www.thestreetratings.com

I. Index of Stock Mutual Funds

RISK	3 Year		NET ASSETS		ASSET				Portfolio	BULL / BEAR		FUND MANAGER		MINIMUMS		LOADS	
Risk Rating/Pts	Standard Deviation	Beta	NAV As of 2/28/17	Total $(Mil)	Cash %	Stocks %	Bonds %	Other %	Turnover Ratio	Last Bull Market Return	Last Bear Market Return	Manager Quality Pct	Manager Tenure (Years)	Initial Purch. $	Additional Purch. $	Front End Load	Back End Load
C- /3.9	28.5	2.41	130.02	287	28	68	3	1	6	444.5	-23.3	42	4	15,000	100	0.0	0.0
C- /3.9	28.5	2.41	109.07	10	28	68	3	1	6	416.2	-23.6	29	4	5,000	100	0.0	0.0
E- /0.0	39.1	-2.22	30.11	6	82	0	17	1	0	-64.6	51.8	0	8	15,000	100	0.0	0.0
E- /0.0	39.0	-2.22	28.23	1	82	0	17	1	0	-66.4	51.4	0	8	5,000	100	0.0	0.0
D+ /2.5	22.5	-1.04	19.15	5	82	0	17	1	0	-75.9	47.2	5	8	15,000	100	0.0	0.0
D+ /2.4	22.4	-1.03	17.77	N/A	82	0	17	1	0	-77.2	46.5	4	8	5,000	100	0.0	0.0
E- /0.0	60.4	-2.46	9.55	3	100	0	0	0	0	-57.4	55.6	0	8	15,000	100	0.0	0.0
E- /0.0	60.4	-2.46	8.74	N/A	100	0	0	0	0	-59.5	55.4	0	8	5,000	100	0.0	0.0
E- /0.0	43.0	-2.33	10.43	3	0	0	0	100	0	-86.0	72.5	0	8	15,000	100	0.0	0.0
E- /0.0	43.0	-2.33	9.55	N/A	0	0	0	100	0	-86.8	72.0	0	8	5,000	100	0.0	0.0
E+ /0.9	21.1	-1.94	29.32	3	82	0	17	1	0	-85.5	23.5	4	4	15,000	100	0.0	0.0
E+ /0.9	21.0	-1.93	26.68	1	82	0	17	1	0	-86.3	23.1	3	4	5,000	100	0.0	0.0
E- /0.0	32.2	-1.16	10.46	4	85	0	14	1	0	-92.0	21.7	0	8	15,000	100	0.0	0.0
E- /0.0	32.3	-1.16	9.74	N/A	85	0	14	1	0	-92.4	21.2	0	8	5,000	100	0.0	0.0
E /0.5	23.9	-1.95	29.46	2	100	0	0	0	0	-89.7	43.7	3	4	15,000	100	0.0	0.0
E /0.5	24.0	-1.96	26.97	N/A	100	0	0	0	0	-90.2	43.6	2	4	5,000	100	0.0	0.0
E- /0.0	32.0	-1.98	11.95	13	83	0	16	1	0	-91.0	47.6	1	4	15,000	100	0.0	0.0
E- /0.0	31.9	-1.98	11.48	1	83	0	16	1	0	-91.5	46.5	1	4	5,000	100	0.0	0.0
E /0.5	32.5	2.01	49.93	91	25	37	37	1	123	302.7	-47.5	15	4	15,000	100	0.0	0.0
E /0.4	32.5	2.02	42.31	2	25	37	37	1	123	281.2	-47.7	9	4	5,000	100	0.0	0.0
C /5.2	21.5	1.45	42.50	16	24	71	4	1	229	129.4	0.1	16	4	15,000	100	0.0	0.0
C /5.1	21.5	1.45	40.58	1	24	71	4	1	229	117.4	-0.3	9	4	5,000	100	0.0	0.0
C+ /5.9	8.5	0.74	17.31	26	2	69	5	24	35	62.2	-16.1	51	10	10,000	1,000	0.0	2.0
C- /4.2	9.9	0.76	20.30	107	4	88	5	3	36	111.4	-15.6	87	10	10,000	1,000	0.0	2.0
C+ /6.5	10.5	0.85	12.26	125	7	89	3	1	4	94.0	-15.6	62	15	1,000	100	0.0	0.0
C+ /6.7	6.5	1.05	15.17	332	0	58	41	1	230	76.2	-10.5	60	12	2,500	100	5.5	0.0
C+ /6.8	6.6	1.05	15.25	12	0	58	41	1	230	69.7	-10.8	50	12	2,500	100	0.0	0.0
C+ /6.8	6.5	1.05	15.25	67	0	58	41	1	230	69.7	-10.8	50	12	2,500	100	0.0	0.0
C+ /6.7	6.6	1.05	15.18	1	0	58	41	1	230	74.4	-10.6	57	12	0	0	0.0	0.0
C+ /6.6	6.6	1.05	15.28	120	0	58	41	1	230	79.2	-10.5	64	12	0	0	0.0	0.0
B- /7.8	4.8	0.73	12.47	82	4	38	56	2	25	38.3	-8.1	41	13	2,500	100	5.5	0.0
B- /7.8	4.8	0.73	12.41	14	4	38	56	2	25	32.8	-8.5	32	13	2,500	100	0.0	0.0
B- /7.8	4.8	0.73	12.41	27	4	38	56	2	25	32.8	-8.5	32	13	2,500	100	0.0	0.0
B- /7.8	4.8	0.73	12.51	N/A	4	38	56	2	25	36.4	-8.3	38	10	0	0	0.0	0.0
B- /7.8	4.8	0.73	12.52	8	4	38	56	2	25	40.1	-8.1	45	13	0	0	0.0	0.0
D+ /2.9	17.4	1.10	12.26	81	0	98	0	2	68	64.3	-30.1	0	8	2,500	100	5.5	0.0
D+ /2.8	17.5	1.10	11.02	6	0	98	0	2	68	58.1	-30.2	0	8	2,500	100	0.0	0.0
D+ /2.8	17.5	1.10	11.02	31	0	98	0	2	68	58.1	-30.2	0	8	2,500	100	0.0	0.0
D+ /2.9	17.4	1.10	12.26	14	0	98	0	2	68	62.4	-30.2	0	8	0	0	0.0	0.0
D+ /2.9	17.5	1.10	12.64	45	0	98	0	2	68	67.0	-30.0	0	8	0	0	0.0	0.0
U /	N/A	N/A	10.01	27	0	0	0	100	34	N/A	N/A	N/A	2	0	0	0.0	0.0
C+ /6.4	11.5	0.80	23.32	419	8	91	0	1	80	67.4	-19.0	23	10	2,500	100	5.5	0.0
C+ /6.4	11.5	0.80	22.87	11	8	91	0	1	80	61.1	-19.2	17	10	2,500	100	0.0	0.0
C+ /6.4	11.5	0.80	22.87	126	8	91	0	1	80	61.1	-19.2	17	10	2,500	100	0.0	0.0
C+ /6.4	11.5	0.80	23.42	438	8	91	0	1	80	71.1	-18.9	28	10	0	0	0.0	0.0
C+ /6.4	11.5	0.80	23.27	35	8	91	0	1	80	65.6	-19.1	21	10	0	0	0.0	0.0
C+ /6.4	11.5	0.80	23.42	1,956	8	91	0	1	80	70.1	-18.9	26	10	0	0	0.0	0.0
C+ /5.8	9.6	0.89	16.40	70	4	86	9	1	24	75.5	-18.8	15	13	2,500	100	5.5	0.0
C+ /5.8	9.6	0.89	15.75	12	4	86	9	1	24	68.6	-19.1	10	13	2,500	100	0.0	0.0
C+ /5.8	9.6	0.89	15.77	13	4	86	9	1	24	68.6	-19.1	10	13	2,500	100	0.0	0.0
C+ /5.8	9.6	0.89	16.28	N/A	4	86	9	1	24	73.3	-18.9	13	13	0	0	0.0	0.0
C+ /5.8	9.6	0.89	16.59	2	4	86	9	1	24	77.7	-18.7	16	13	0	0	0.0	0.0

Fund Type	Fund Name	Ticker Symbol	Overall Investment Rating	Phone	Performance Rating/Pts	3 Mo	6 Mo	1Yr / Pct	3Yr / Pct	5Yr / Pct	Dividend Yield	Expense Ratio
	99 Pct = Best							Total Return % through 2/28/17			Incl. in Returns	
	0 Pct = Worst								Annualized			
AA	Prudential Income Builder A	PCGAX	D-	(800) 225-1852	D+ / 2.6	5.64	3.20	15.84 /34	3.14 /33	5.59 /25	4.34	1.42
AA	● Prudential Income Builder B	PBCFX	D-	(800) 225-1852	D+ / 2.8	5.33	2.77	14.91 /30	2.35 /26	4.77 /20	3.91	2.12
AA	Prudential Income Builder C	PCCFX	D-	(800) 225-1852	D+ / 2.8	5.33	2.77	15.05 /30	2.35 /26	4.79 /20	3.91	2.12
AA	Prudential Income Builder R	PCLRX	D	(800) 225-1852	C- / 3.2	5.47	2.97	15.45 /32	2.87 /31	5.31 /23	4.31	1.87
AA	Prudential Income Builder Z	PDCZX	D	(800) 225-1852	C- / 3.6	5.66	3.30	16.15 /35	3.39 /36	5.84 /27	4.76	1.12
GI	Prudential Jennison 20/20 Focus A	PTWAX	D	(800) 225-1852	C / 4.6	6.55	7.62	21.36 /59	4.77 /52	9.37 /54	0.00	1.18
GI	● Prudential Jennison 20/20 Focus B	PTWBX	D	(800) 225-1852	C / 5.1	6.31	7.22	20.50 /55	4.05 /44	8.61 /47	0.00	1.88
GI	Prudential Jennison 20/20 Focus C	PTWCX	D	(800) 225-1852	C / 5.1	6.30	7.21	20.60 /55	4.05 /44	8.62 /47	0.00	1.88
GR	Prudential Jennison 20/20 Focus Q	PJTQX	C-	(800) 225-1852	C+ / 6.1	6.61	7.80	21.87 /62	5.22 /57	9.84 /57	0.20	0.76
GI	Prudential Jennison 20/20 Focus R	JTWRX	D+	(800) 225-1852	C / 5.5	6.43	7.47	21.10 /58	4.56 /49	9.14 /52	0.00	1.63
GI	Prudential Jennison 20/20 Focus Z	PTWZX	C-	(800) 225-1852	C+ / 6.0	6.59	7.78	21.70 /61	5.09 /55	9.70 /56	0.09	0.88
GI	Prudential Jennison Blend A	PBQAX	D+	(800) 225-1852	C+ / 5.6	7.12	10.08	24.70 /72	5.19 /56	10.04 /59	0.77	0.98
GI	● Prudential Jennison Blend B	PBQFX	C-	(800) 225-1852	C+ / 6.2	6.93	9.68	23.83 /69	4.46 /48	9.27 /53	0.30	1.68
GI	Prudential Jennison Blend C	PRECX	C-	(800) 225-1852	C+ / 6.2	6.99	9.74	23.82 /69	4.46 /48	9.28 /53	0.30	1.68
GI	Prudential Jennison Blend Z	PEQZX	C	(800) 225-1852	C+ / 6.9	7.20	10.26	25.10 /74	5.50 /60	10.37 /61	1.07	0.68
GR	Prudential Jennison Conserv Gro A	TBDAX	C+	(800) 225-1852	B- / 7.2	7.78	10.21	24.13 /70	8.10 /80	12.78 /82	0.46	1.33
GR	● Prudential Jennison Conserv Gro B	TBDBX	C+	(800) 225-1852	B / 7.6	7.60	9.86	23.22 /67	7.30 /74	11.96 /74	0.00	2.03
GR	Prudential Jennison Conserv Gro C	TBDCX	C+	(800) 225-1852	B / 7.6	7.49	9.75	23.22 /67	7.30 /74	11.96 /74	0.00	2.03
IN	Prudential Jennison Equity Income A	SPQAX	D	(800) 225-1852	C- / 3.5	6.61	5.64	16.56 /37	4.31 /46	9.39 /54	1.90	1.21
IN	● Prudential Jennison Equity Income B	JEIBX	D+	(800) 225-1852	C- / 3.9	6.41	5.24	15.71 /33	3.53 /37	8.57 /47	1.49	1.91
IN	Prudential Jennison Equity Income C	AGOCX	D+	(800) 225-1852	C- / 3.9	6.36	5.25	15.67 /33	3.54 /38	8.58 /47	1.50	1.91
IN	Prudential Jennison Equity Income Q	PJIQX	C-	(800) 225-1852	C / 4.9	6.70	5.85	16.96 /38	4.70 /51	9.78 /57	2.35	0.79
IN	Prudential Jennison Equity Income R	PJERX	D+	(800) 225-1852	C / 4.3	6.47	5.50	16.20 /35	4.05 /44	9.10 /52	1.77	1.66
IN	Prudential Jennison Equity Income Z	JDEZX	C-	(800) 225-1852	C / 4.8	6.61	5.79	16.77 /37	4.57 /50	9.65 /56	2.24	0.91
GR	Prudential Jennison Equity Oppty A	PJIAX	C+	(800) 225-1852	B / 7.9	6.60	14.37	31.38 /89	7.28 /74	12.51 /79	0.68	1.07
GR	● Prudential Jennison Equity Oppty B	PJIBX	C+	(800) 225-1852	B+ / 8.3	6.43	13.97	30.46 /87	6.52 /69	11.72 /72	0.31	1.77
GR	Prudential Jennison Equity Oppty C	PJGCX	C+	(800) 225-1852	B / 8.2	6.36	13.91	30.38 /87	6.50 /68	11.71 /72	0.31	1.77
GI	Prudential Jennison Equity Oppty Q	PJOQX	A	(800) 225-1852	A- / 9.1	6.69	14.57	31.86 /90	7.70 /77	12.92 /83	1.03	0.66
GR	Prudential Jennison Equity Oppty R	PJORX	B-	(800) 225-1852	B+ / 8.7	6.53	14.22	31.09 /88	7.05 /72	12.28 /77	0.67	1.52
GR	Prudential Jennison Equity Oppty Z	PJGZX	B	(800) 225-1852	A- / 9.0	6.69	14.53	31.75 /90	7.59 /76	12.85 /82	0.94	0.77
OT	Prudential Jennison Global Infra A	PGJAX	D+	(800) 225-1852	C- / 3.1	9.05	3.66	17.54 /41	3.12 /33	--	1.31	1.79
OT	Prudential Jennison Global Infra C	PGJCX	D+	(800) 225-1852	C- / 3.5	8.88	3.26	16.75 /37	2.37 /27	--	0.73	2.49
OT	Prudential Jennison Global Infra Z	PGJZX	C-	(800) 225-1852	C / 4.3	9.19	3.77	17.91 /42	3.39 /36	--	1.61	1.49
IN	Prudential Jennison Global Oppty A	PRJAX	D	(800) 225-1852	D+ / 2.6	8.11	4.65	17.57 /41	2.27 /26	--	0.00	1.54
IN	Prudential Jennison Global Oppty C	PRJCX	D	(800) 225-1852	C- / 3.1	7.92	4.27	16.76 /37	1.52 /21	--	0.00	2.24
GL	Prudential Jennison Global Oppty Q	PRJQX	D+	(800) 225-1852	C- / 3.9	8.21	4.85	18.05 /43	2.60 /28	--	0.00	1.15
IN	Prudential Jennison Global Oppty Z	PRJZX	D+	(800) 225-1852	C- / 3.8	8.22	4.79	17.92 /42	2.53 /28	--	0.00	1.24
GR	Prudential Jennison Growth A	PJFAX	C	(800) 225-1852	C+ / 6.3	8.55	8.40	20.52 /55	7.23 /74	12.54 /79	0.00	1.03
GR	● Prudential Jennison Growth B	PJFBX	C	(800) 225-1852	C+ / 6.8	8.37	8.01	19.66 /50	6.48 /68	11.76 /72	0.00	1.73
GR	Prudential Jennison Growth C	PJFCX	C	(800) 225-1852	C+ / 6.8	8.35	8.04	19.67 /50	6.49 /68	11.75 /72	0.00	1.73
GR	Prudential Jennison Growth R	PJGRX	C+	(800) 225-1852	B- / 7.1	8.46	8.30	20.30 /54	7.02 /72	12.32 /77	0.00	1.48
GR	Prudential Jennison Growth Z	PJFZX	C+	(800) 225-1852	B- / 7.5	8.64	8.57	20.89 /57	7.56 /76	12.89 /83	0.00	0.73
HL	● Prudential Jennison Health Sci A	PHLAX	D	(800) 225-1852	B- / 7.0	12.87	14.10	23.42 /68	5.97 /64	19.39 /99	0.00	1.13
HL	● Prudential Jennison Health Sci B	PHLBX	D	(800) 225-1852	B- / 7.4	12.66	13.68	22.56 /65	5.23 /57	18.56 /99	0.00	1.83
HL	● Prudential Jennison Health Sci C	PHLCX	D	(800) 225-1852	B- / 7.4	12.67	13.69	22.57 /65	5.23 /57	18.56 /99	0.00	1.83
HL	Prudential Jennison Health Sci Q	PHLQX	D	(800) 225-1852	B / 8.2	12.98	14.34	23.95 /70	6.33 /67	19.78 /99	0.00	0.74
HL	● Prudential Jennison Health Sci R	PJHRX	D+	(800) 225-1852	B / 7.8	12.81	13.97	23.18 /67	5.76 /62	19.16 /99	0.00	1.58
HL	● Prudential Jennison Health Sci Z	PHSZX	D+	(800) 225-1852	B / 8.2	12.92	14.25	23.79 /69	6.29 /67	19.75 /99	0.00	0.83
FO	Prudential Jennison Intl Opptys A	PWJAX	E	(800) 225-1852	E- / 0.2	5.75	-0.95	9.36 /10	-3.84 / 3	--	0.00	1.62
FO	Prudential Jennison Intl Opptys C	PWJCX	E	(800) 225-1852	E / 0.3	5.60	-1.31	8.54 / 8	-4.55 / 3	--	0.00	2.32
FO	Prudential Jennison Intl Opptys Q	PWJQX	E+	(800) 225-1852	E / 0.4	5.84	-0.71	9.70 /11	-3.58 / 4	--	0.29	1.29
FO	Prudential Jennison Intl Opptys Z	PWJZX	E	(800) 225-1852	E / 0.3	5.86	-0.78	9.62 /11	-3.60 / 4	--	0.22	1.32

● Denotes fund is closed to new investors
* Denotes fund is included in Section II

Risk Rating/Pts	3 Year Standard Deviation	Beta	NAV As of 2/28/17	Total $(Mil)	Cash %	Stocks %	Bonds %	Other %	Portfolio Turnover Ratio	Last Bull Market Return	Last Bear Market Return	Manager Quality Pct	Manager Tenure (Years)	Initial Purch. $	Additional Purch. $	Front End Load	Back End Load
C / 4.3	6.4	0.90	9.63	161	10	37	50	3	90	43.9	-6.6	29	3	2,500	100	4.5	0.0
C / 4.3	6.3	0.89	9.45	3	10	37	50	3	90	38.2	-7.0	22	3	2,500	100	0.0	0.0
C / 4.3	6.3	0.90	9.45	121	10	37	50	3	90	38.2	-7.0	22	3	2,500	100	0.0	0.0
C / 4.3	6.3	0.89	9.61	1	10	37	50	3	90	41.8	-6.7	27	3	0	0	0.0	0.0
C / 4.3	6.3	0.90	9.69	120	10	37	50	3	90	45.8	-6.5	32	3	0	0	0.0	0.0
C- / 3.3	12.4	1.08	14.67	613	0	99	0	1	55	89.8	-18.6	8	19	2,500	100	5.5	0.0
D+ / 2.6	12.4	1.08	11.16	41	0	99	0	1	55	82.8	-18.8	6	19	2,500	100	0.0	0.0
D+ / 2.6	12.4	1.08	11.17	179	0	99	0	1	55	82.7	-18.8	6	19	2,500	100	0.0	0.0
C- / 3.6	12.4	1.08	16.04	8	0	99	0	1	55	94.2	-18.4	10	19	0	0	0.0	0.0
C- / 3.2	12.4	1.08	14.08	63	0	99	0	1	55	87.7	-18.6	7	19	0	0	0.0	0.0
C- / 3.6	12.4	1.08	15.94	243	0	99	0	1	55	92.8	-18.4	9	19	0	0	0.0	0.0
C- / 3.6	12.2	1.10	19.79	902	0	98	1	1	53	98.9	-21.0	9	12	2,500	100	5.5	0.0
C- / 3.4	12.2	1.10	17.98	10	0	98	1	1	53	91.5	-21.2	6	12	2,500	100	0.0	0.0
C- / 3.4	12.2	1.10	17.99	21	0	98	1	1	53	91.5	-21.2	6	12	2,500	100	0.0	0.0
C- / 3.6	12.2	1.10	19.80	29	0	98	1	1	53	102.0	-20.8	10	12	0	0	0.0	0.0
C / 5.1	11.0	1.04	11.80	168	0	99	0	1	246	118.5	-15.5	39	12	2,500	100	5.5	0.0
C / 4.9	11.0	1.04	10.11	3	0	99	0	1	246	110.1	-15.8	30	12	2,500	100	0.0	0.0
C / 4.9	11.0	1.04	10.11	50	0	99	0	1	246	110.1	-15.8	29	12	2,500	100	0.0	0.0
C / 4.6	10.0	0.92	15.81	802	1	94	2	3	48	85.1	-17.2	14	17	2,500	100	5.5	0.0
C / 4.5	10.0	0.92	14.64	109	1	94	2	3	48	77.8	-17.4	10	17	2,500	100	0.0	0.0
C / 4.5	10.0	0.92	14.60	854	1	94	2	3	48	77.9	-17.5	10	17	2,500	100	0.0	0.0
C / 4.6	10.0	0.92	15.83	4	1	94	2	3	48	88.9	-17.0	18	17	0	0	0.0	0.0
C / 4.6	10.0	0.92	15.80	41	1	94	2	3	48	82.6	-17.3	13	17	0	0	0.0	0.0
C / 4.6	10.0	0.92	15.80	1,224	1	94	2	3	48	87.7	-17.1	16	17	0	0	0.0	0.0
C / 4.3	12.4	1.11	20.25	237	0	97	2	1	59	123.3	-20.0	22	17	2,500	100	5.5	0.0
C- / 4.0	12.4	1.11	17.02	8	0	97	2	1	59	115.2	-20.2	16	17	2,500	100	0.0	0.0
C- / 4.0	12.4	1.11	17.01	40	0	97	2	1	59	115.1	-20.2	16	17	2,500	100	0.0	0.0
C+ / 6.1	12.4	1.10	20.99	17	0	97	2	1	59	127.8	-19.8	26	17	0	0	0.0	0.0
C- / 4.1	12.4	1.11	18.08	7	0	97	2	1	59	121.0	-20.0	20	17	0	0	0.0	0.0
C / 4.3	12.4	1.11	20.98	121	0	97	2	1	59	127.1	-19.8	25	17	0	0	0.0	0.0
C+ / 5.7	11.8	0.77	12.12	10	13	86	0	1	82	N/A	N/A	17	4	2,500	100	5.5	0.0
C+ / 5.6	11.8	0.77	12.05	6	13	86	0	1	82	N/A	N/A	12	4	2,500	100	0.0	0.0
C+ / 5.7	11.8	0.77	12.13	27	13	86	0	1	82	N/A	N/A	19	4	0	0	0.0	0.0
C / 5.1	14.1	0.98	15.99	54	4	95	0	1	88	N/A	N/A	4	5	2,500	100	5.5	0.0
C / 5.0	14.1	0.98	15.40	46	4	95	0	1	88	N/A	N/A	3	5	2,500	100	0.0	0.0
C / 5.2	14.1	0.87	16.22	9	4	95	0	1	88	N/A	N/A	89	5	0	0	0.0	0.0
C / 5.1	14.1	0.98	16.19	160	4	95	0	1	88	N/A	N/A	5	5	0	0	0.0	0.0
C / 4.5	13.3	1.09	30.54	1,026	0	98	1	1	36	120.3	-14.0	24	18	2,500	100	5.5	0.0
C- / 4.2	13.3	1.09	25.05	17	0	98	1	1	36	112.2	-14.3	17	18	2,500	100	0.0	0.0
C- / 4.2	13.3	1.09	25.10	111	0	98	1	1	36	112.1	-14.2	17	18	2,500	100	0.0	0.0
C / 4.3	13.3	1.09	27.10	312	0	98	1	1	36	118.2	-14.1	22	18	0	0	0.0	0.0
C / 4.5	13.3	1.09	32.63	2,093	0	98	1	1	36	124.1	-13.9	27	18	0	0	0.0	0.0
E+ / 0.9	24.2	1.40	41.22	826	0	99	0	1	25	206.0	-14.4	3	18	2,500	100	5.5	0.0
E / 0.5	24.2	1.40	32.21	33	0	99	0	1	25	194.7	-14.6	3	18	2,500	100	0.0	0.0
E / 0.5	24.2	1.40	32.20	201	0	99	0	1	25	194.8	-14.6	3	18	2,500	100	0.0	0.0
E- / 0.0	24.2	1.40	45.07	N/A	0	99	0	1	25	211.4	-14.3	4	18	0	0	0.0	0.0
E+ / 0.9	24.2	1.40	40.68	14	0	99	0	1	25	202.5	-14.5	3	18	0	0	0.0	0.0
D- / 1.0	24.2	1.40	45.01	1,154	0	99	0	1	25	211.0	-14.3	4	18	0	0	0.0	0.0
C / 4.7	13.7	0.92	12.50	2	4	95	0	1	65	N/A	N/A	26	5	2,500	100	5.5	0.0
C / 4.7	13.7	0.93	12.07	1	4	95	0	1	65	N/A	N/A	19	5	2,500	100	0.0	0.0
C / 5.3	13.7	0.92	12.62	24	4	95	0	1	65	N/A	N/A	29	5	0	0	0.0	0.0
C / 4.7	13.8	0.93	12.62	19	4	95	0	1	65	N/A	N/A	29	5	0	0	0.0	0.0

Fund Type	Fund Name	Ticker Symbol	Overall Investment Rating	Phone	Performance Rating/Pts	Total Return % through 2/28/17 3 Mo	6 Mo	1Yr / Pct	Annualized 3Yr / Pct	5Yr / Pct	Incl. in Returns Dividend Yield	Expense Ratio
MC	Prudential Jennison Mid-Cap Gro A	PEEAX	D+	(800) 225-1852	C / 4.8	7.64	8.75	20.70 /56	4.76 /52	9.46 /54	0.00	1.06
MC	● Prudential Jennison Mid-Cap Gro B	PEEBX	D+	(800) 225-1852	C / 5.3	7.46	8.35	19.83 /51	4.04 /43	8.70 /48	0.00	1.76
MC	Prudential Jennison Mid-Cap Gro C	PEGCX	D+	(800) 225-1852	C / 5.3	7.49	8.39	19.87 /51	4.04 /43	8.69 /48	0.00	1.76
MC	Prudential Jennison Mid-Cap Gro Q	PJGQX	C	(800) 225-1852	C+ / 6.3	7.79	9.03	21.28 /59	5.27 /57	9.97 /58	0.00	0.58
MC	Prudential Jennison Mid-Cap Gro R	JDERX	C-	(800) 225-1852	C+ / 5.8	7.63	8.65	20.49 /55	4.57 /50	9.25 /53	0.00	1.51
MC	Prudential Jennison Mid-Cap Gro Z	PEGZX	C-	(800) 225-1852	C+ / 6.2	7.73	8.93	21.08 /58	5.10 /55	9.78 /57	0.00	0.76
EN	Prudential Jennison MLP A	PRPAX	E	(800) 225-1852	D- / 1.3	5.12	7.72	40.72 /97	-2.86 / 5	--	5.55	3.71
EN	Prudential Jennison MLP C	PRPCX	E	(800) 225-1852	D- / 1.5	4.85	7.38	39.63 /97	-3.59 / 4	--	6.04	4.56
EN	Prudential Jennison MLP Z	PRPZX	E	(800) 225-1852	D / 1.9	5.07	7.79	40.95 /98	-2.61 / 5	--	5.83	3.72
EN	Prudential Jennison Natural Res A	PGNAX	E-	(800) 225-1852	E- / 0.1	-1.05	7.82	40.50 /97	-10.24 / 1	-6.57 / 1	1.09	1.22
EN	● Prudential Jennison Natural Res B	PRGNX	E-	(800) 225-1852	E- / 0.2	-1.23	7.46	39.54 /97	-10.87 / 1	-7.22 / 1	1.10	1.92
EN	Prudential Jennison Natural Res C	PNRCX	E-	(800) 225-1852	E- / 0.2	-1.23	7.46	39.52 /97	-10.87 / 1	-7.22 / 1	1.10	1.92
EN	Prudential Jennison Natural Res Q	PJNQX	E-	(800) 225-1852	E- / 0.2	-0.95	8.09	41.20 /98	-9.82 / 1	-6.14 / 1	1.95	0.76
EN	Prudential Jennison Natural Res R	JNRRX	E-	(800) 225-1852	E- / 0.2	-1.12	7.72	40.23 /97	-10.42 / 1	-6.76 / 1	0.98	1.67
EN	Prudential Jennison Natural Res Z	PNRZX	E-	(800) 225-1852	E- / 0.2	-0.98	8.00	40.90 /98	-9.97 / 1	-6.29 / 1	1.62	0.92
GR	Prudential Jennison Select Growth A	SPFAX	D+	(800) 225-1852	C / 4.9	7.63	7.20	18.05 /43	5.90 /63	11.63 /71	0.00	1.46
GR	● Prudential Jennison Select Growth B	SPFBX	D+	(800) 225-1852	C / 5.4	7.46	6.87	17.22 /39	5.12 /55	10.79 /64	0.00	2.16
GR	Prudential Jennison Select Growth C	SPFCX	D+	(800) 225-1852	C / 5.4	7.47	6.88	17.12 /39	5.10 /55	10.80 /64	0.00	2.16
GR	Prudential Jennison Select Growth Q	PSGQX	C-	(800) 225-1852	C+ / 6.3	7.72	7.39	18.38 /45	6.12 /65	11.88 /73	0.00	1.16
GR	Prudential Jennison Select Growth Z	SPFZX	C-	(800) 225-1852	C+ / 6.3	7.70	7.38	18.34 /44	6.16 /66	11.90 /73	0.00	1.16
SC	Prudential Jennison Small Company	PGOAX	C-	(800) 225-1852	C+ / 6.8	7.27	10.87	27.03 /79	6.53 /69	11.13 /67	0.54	1.14
SC	● Prudential Jennison Small Company	CHNDX	D	(800) 225-1852	B- / 7.1	6.95	10.39	25.97 /76	5.73 /62	10.31 /61	0.58	1.84
SC	Prudential Jennison Small Company	PSCCX	D	(800) 225-1852	B- / 7.2	7.07	10.47	26.23 /77	5.74 /62	10.33 /61	0.58	1.84
SC	Prudential Jennison Small Company	PJSQX	C	(800) 225-1852	B / 8.0	7.39	11.04	27.49 /80	7.02 /72	11.66 /71	0.91	0.69
SC	Prudential Jennison Small Company	JSCRX	C-	(800) 225-1852	B / 7.6	7.21	10.74	26.78 /79	6.31 /67	10.91 /65	0.42	1.59
SC	Prudential Jennison Small Company	PSCZX	C	(800) 225-1852	B / 7.9	7.35	11.03	27.52 /81	6.83 /71	11.43 /69	0.77	0.84
UT	Prudential Jennison Utility A	PRUAX	C-	(800) 225-1852	C+ / 5.7	9.77	5.77	19.04 /47	6.84 /71	12.12 /75	1.57	0.84
UT	● Prudential Jennison Utility B	PRUTX	C-	(800) 225-1852	C+ / 6.3	9.56	5.44	18.24 /44	6.13 /65	11.34 /69	1.04	1.54
UT	Prudential Jennison Utility C	PCUFX	C-	(800) 225-1852	C+ / 6.3	9.58	5.45	18.18 /44	6.09 /65	11.32 /68	1.04	1.54
UT	Prudential Jennison Utility R	JDURX	C	(800) 225-1852	C+ / 6.7	9.73	5.75	18.83 /46	6.64 /69	11.88 /73	1.48	1.29
UT	Prudential Jennison Utility Z	PRUZX	C	(800) 225-1852	B- / 7.0	9.82	5.99	19.44 /49	7.18 /73	12.45 /79	1.92	0.54
GR	Prudential Jennison Value A	PBEAX	C	(800) 225-1852	C+ / 6.0	7.61	13.66	27.26 /80	4.38 /47	9.66 /56	1.03	1.12
GR	● Prudential Jennison Value B	PBQIX	C	(800) 225-1852	C+ / 6.5	7.42	13.30	26.39 /77	3.66 /39	8.89 /50	0.53	1.82
GR	Prudential Jennison Value C	PEICX	C	(800) 225-1852	C+ / 6.5	7.43	13.30	26.40 /77	3.67 /39	8.90 /50	0.53	1.82
GR	Prudential Jennison Value Q	PJVQX	C+	(800) 225-1852	B- / 7.3	7.76	13.93	27.86 /81	4.84 /52	10.15 /59	1.48	0.67
GR	Prudential Jennison Value R	JDVRX	C	(800) 225-1852	C+ / 6.8	7.60	13.55	27.03 /79	4.18 /45	9.44 /54	0.92	1.57
GR	Prudential Jennison Value Z	PEIZX	C+	(800) 225-1852	B- / 7.2	7.66	13.82	27.65 /81	4.69 /51	9.99 /58	1.35	0.82
AA	Prudential Moderate Allocation A	JDTAX	C-	(800) 225-1852	D+ / 2.8	4.89	5.34	15.69 /33	3.70 /39	6.52 /32	1.06	1.62
AA	● Prudential Moderate Allocation B	JDMBX	C-	(800) 225-1852	C- / 3.3	4.71	5.01	14.88 /29	2.93 /31	5.73 /27	0.44	2.32
AA	Prudential Moderate Allocation C	JDMCX	C-	(800) 225-1852	C- / 3.2	4.63	5.01	14.80 /29	2.91 /31	5.72 /26	0.44	2.32
AA	Prudential Moderate Allocation R	JMARX	C	(800) 225-1852	C- / 3.6	4.89	5.27	15.49 /32	3.39 /36	6.20 /30	0.89	2.07
AA	Prudential Moderate Allocation Z	JDMZX	C	(800) 225-1852	C- / 4.1	4.99	5.52	16.05 /35	3.96 /43	6.79 /33	1.36	1.32
AA	Prudential QMA Defensive Equity A	PAMGX	C+	(800) 225-1852	C+ / 5.9	7.24	6.32	17.40 /40	7.88 /78	9.66 /56	1.11	1.35
AA	● Prudential QMA Defensive Equity B	DMGBX	C+	(800) 225-1852	C+ / 6.3	7.03	5.96	16.44 /36	7.06 /72	8.85 /49	0.48	2.05
AA	Prudential QMA Defensive Equity C	PIMGX	C+	(800) 225-1852	C+ / 6.4	7.03	5.96	16.53 /36	7.07 /72	8.85 /49	0.48	2.05
AA	Prudential QMA Defensive Equity R	SPMRX	C+	(800) 225-1852	C+ / 6.7	7.14	6.22	17.04 /38	7.62 /76	9.38 /54	0.94	1.80
AA	Prudential QMA Defensive Equity Z	PDMZX	B+	(800) 225-1852	B- / 7.0	7.25	6.42	17.56 /41	8.13 /80	9.93 /58	1.40	1.05
GL	Prudential QMA Global Tact Alloc Q	PTQLX	U	(800) 225-1852	U /	4.93	5.37	10.58 /13	--	--	2.76	2.23
FO	Prudential QMA International Eqty A	PJRAX	D-	(800) 225-1852	E+ / 0.7	7.18	5.35	17.99 /43	-1.76 / 7	4.26 /17	1.80	1.66
FO	● Prudential QMA International Eqty B	PJRBX	D-	(800) 225-1852	E+ / 0.9	6.95	5.04	17.19 /39	-2.44 / 6	3.54 /13	1.34	2.36
FO	Prudential QMA International Eqty C	PJRCX	D-	(800) 225-1852	E+ / 0.9	6.95	5.04	17.20 /39	-2.44 / 6	3.54 /13	1.34	2.36
FO	Prudential QMA International Eqty Z	PJIZX	D-	(800) 225-1852	D- / 1.2	7.27	5.62	18.59 /45	-1.44 / 8	4.58 /19	2.17	1.36

● Denotes fund is closed to new investors
* Denotes fund is included in Section II

www.thestreetratings.com

I. Index of Stock Mutual Funds

Risk Rating/Pts	3 Year Standard Deviation	Beta	NAV As of 2/28/17	Total $(Mil)	Cash %	Stocks %	Bonds %	Other %	Portfolio Turnover Ratio	Last Bull Market Return	Last Bear Market Return	Manager Quality Pct	Manager Tenure (Years)	Initial Purch. $	Additional Purch. $	Front End Load	Back End Load
C- / 4.0	11.7	0.89	35.43	2,263	0	99	0	1	24	93.8	-17.3	28	12	2,500	100	5.5	0.0
C- / 3.5	11.7	0.89	28.74	20	0	99	0	1	24	86.6	-17.5	21	12	2,500	100	0.0	0.0
C- / 3.5	11.7	0.89	28.75	140	0	99	0	1	24	86.5	-17.5	21	12	2,500	100	0.0	0.0
C- / 4.2	11.7	0.89	38.11	1,533	0	99	0	1	24	98.7	-17.1	34	12	0	0	0.0	0.0
C- / 3.9	11.7	0.89	34.45	219	0	99	0	1	24	91.7	-17.3	26	12	0	0	0.0	0.0
C- / 4.1	11.7	0.89	37.79	3,018	0	99	0	1	24	96.9	-17.2	32	12	0	0	0.0	0.0
C- / 3.1	20.7	0.77	8.28	68	78	21	0	1	37	N/A	N/A	82	4	2,500	100	5.5	0.0
C- / 3.1	20.7	0.76	8.06	49	78	21	0	1	37	N/A	N/A	77	4	2,500	100	0.0	0.0
C- / 3.1	20.7	0.77	8.35	300	78	21	0	1	37	N/A	N/A	83	4	0	0	0.0	0.0
E+ / 0.7	25.0	1.21	36.75	608	0	96	2	2	28	-9.2	-33.0	20	11	2,500	100	5.5	0.0
E+ / 0.7	24.9	1.20	29.74	22	0	96	2	2	28	-12.6	-33.2	15	11	2,500	100	0.0	0.0
E+ / 0.7	25.0	1.21	29.75	227	0	96	2	2	28	-12.6	-33.2	15	11	2,500	100	0.0	0.0
E+ / 0.8	25.0	1.21	38.43	121	0	96	2	2	28	-7.0	-32.8	25	11	0	0	0.0	0.0
E+ / 0.7	25.0	1.21	36.21	64	0	96	2	2	28	-10.2	-33.0	19	11	0	0	0.0	0.0
E+ / 0.8	25.0	1.21	38.20	878	0	96	2	2	28	-7.8	-32.9	23	11	0	0	0.0	0.0
C- / 4.1	14.0	1.11	12.42	176	0	99	0	1	45	110.9	-13.0	12	17	2,500	100	5.5	0.0
C- / 3.8	14.0	1.11	10.51	7	0	99	0	1	45	102.6	-13.2	8	17	2,500	100	0.0	0.0
C- / 3.8	14.0	1.10	10.50	47	0	99	0	1	45	102.5	-13.1	8	17	2,500	100	0.0	0.0
C- / 4.2	14.0	1.11	13.12	1	0	99	0	1	45	113.5	-12.8	14	17	0	0	0.0	0.0
C- / 4.2	14.0	1.11	13.14	95	0	99	0	1	45	113.7	-12.8	14	17	0	0	0.0	0.0
D+ / 2.7	13.4	0.81	23.81	815	0	95	3	2	37	114.9	-23.9	80	17	2,500	100	5.5	0.0
D- / 1.0	13.4	0.81	13.86	9	0	95	3	2	37	106.3	-24.0	75	17	2,500	100	0.0	0.0
D- / 1.0	13.4	0.81	14.08	99	0	95	3	2	37	106.6	-24.1	75	17	2,500	100	0.0	0.0
D+ / 2.7	13.3	0.80	25.10	873	0	95	3	2	37	120.6	-25.4	83	17	0	0	0.0	0.0
D+ / 2.6	13.3	0.80	23.27	177	0	95	3	2	37	112.4	-23.9	79	17	0	0	0.0	0.0
D+ / 2.8	13.4	0.81	25.51	1,655	0	95	3	2	37	117.8	-23.6	82	17	0	0	0.0	0.0
C- / 4.1	12.1	0.62	13.65	2,776	7	91	0	2	47	103.3	-12.2	50	17	2,500	100	5.5	0.0
C- / 4.1	12.2	0.62	13.60	40	7	91	0	2	47	95.9	-12.5	40	17	2,500	100	0.0	0.0
C- / 4.1	12.1	0.62	13.58	124	7	91	0	2	47	95.9	-12.5	39	17	2,500	100	0.0	0.0
C- / 4.1	12.1	0.62	13.64	78	7	91	0	2	47	101.3	-12.3	47	17	0	0	0.0	0.0
C- / 4.1	12.1	0.62	13.67	233	7	91	0	2	47	106.7	-12.1	55	17	0	0	0.0	0.0
C / 4.5	12.0	1.09	19.58	442	0	98	1	1	29	93.8	-23.2	6	3	2,500	100	5.5	0.0
C / 4.5	12.0	1.09	18.98	5	0	98	1	1	29	86.7	-23.5	5	3	2,500	100	0.0	0.0
C / 4.5	12.0	1.09	18.97	18	0	98	1	1	29	86.6	-23.4	5	3	2,500	100	0.0	0.0
C / 4.4	12.0	1.09	19.58	10	0	98	1	1	29	98.4	-23.5	8	3	0	0	0.0	0.0
C / 4.5	12.0	1.09	19.54	9	0	98	1	1	29	91.7	-23.2	6	3	0	0	0.0	0.0
C / 4.4	12.0	1.09	19.60	44	0	98	1	1	29	96.9	-23.1	7	3	0	0	0.0	0.0
C+ / 6.8	7.1	1.09	14.12	114	4	62	32	2	20	57.3	-13.6	21	12	2,500	100	5.5	0.0
B- / 7.0	7.1	1.09	14.04	22	4	62	32	2	20	51.1	-13.9	15	12	2,500	100	0.0	0.0
B- / 7.0	7.1	1.09	14.03	28	4	62	32	2	20	51.1	-13.9	15	12	2,500	100	0.0	0.0
C+ / 6.9	7.2	1.10	14.05	N/A	4	62	32	2	20	54.9	-13.7	18	12	0	0	0.0	0.0
C+ / 6.8	7.1	1.09	14.13	3	4	62	32	2	20	59.6	-13.6	24	12	0	0	0.0	0.0
C+ / 6.7	9.2	1.44	13.90	178	4	95	0	1	96	79.9	-12.3	37	4	2,500	100	5.5	0.0
C+ / 6.8	9.2	1.43	13.85	8	4	95	0	1	96	72.7	-12.6	29	4	2,500	100	0.0	0.0
C+ / 6.8	9.2	1.43	13.85	40	4	95	0	1	96	72.7	-12.6	29	4	2,500	100	0.0	0.0
C+ / 6.8	9.2	1.43	13.89	N/A	4	95	0	1	96	77.6	-12.4	35	4	0	0	0.0	0.0
C+ / 6.7	9.2	1.43	13.92	7	4	95	0	1	96	82.4	-12.2	41	4	0	0	0.0	0.0
U /	N/A	N/A	9.94	31	0	0	0	100	0	N/A	N/A	N/A	2	0	0	0.0	0.0
C+ / 5.6	11.8	0.91	6.65	184	2	97	0	1	114	44.9	-24.1	54	14	2,500	100	5.5	0.0
C+ / 5.7	11.8	0.91	6.39	3	2	97	0	1	114	39.5	-24.3	44	14	2,500	100	0.0	0.0
C+ / 5.7	11.8	0.91	6.39	15	2	97	0	1	114	39.5	-24.3	44	14	2,500	100	0.0	0.0
C+ / 5.6	11.8	0.91	6.70	15	2	97	0	1	114	47.4	-24.0	58	14	0	0	0.0	0.0

I. Index of Stock Mutual Funds

99 Pct = Best
0 Pct = Worst

Fund Type	Fund Name	Ticker Symbol	Overall Investment Rating	Phone	Performance Rating/Pts	3 Mo	6 Mo	1Yr / Pct	3Yr / Pct	5Yr / Pct	Dividend Yield	Expense Ratio
GR	Prudential QMA Lg Cap Core Eqty A	PTMAX	B+	(800) 225-1852	B / 7.7	6.86	9.43	22.87 /66	9.65 /91	13.28 /87	0.83	0.92
GR	● Prudential QMA Lg Cap Core Eqty B	PTMBX	B+	(800) 225-1852	B / 8.1	6.65	8.98	21.91 /62	8.84 /86	12.42 /78	0.30	1.62
GR	Prudential QMA Lg Cap Core Eqty C	PTMCX	B+	(800) 225-1852	B / 8.1	6.71	8.97	21.87 /62	8.85 /86	12.43 /78	0.30	1.62
GR	Prudential QMA Lg Cap Core Eqty Z	PTEZX	A-	(800) 225-1852	B+ / 8.8	6.90	9.48	23.12 /67	9.92 /93	13.55 /89	1.08	0.62
GR	Prudential QMA Long Short Equity A	PLHAX	U	(800) 225-1852	U /	2.30	4.90	8.22 / 8	--	--	0.00	2.69
GR	Prudential QMA Long Short Equity C	PLHCX	U	(800) 225-1852	U /	2.07	4.53	7.41 / 6	--	--	0.00	3.39
GR	Prudential QMA Long Short Equity Z	PLHZX	U	(800) 225-1852	U /	2.37	5.05	8.45 / 8	--	--	0.00	2.39
MC	Prudential QMA Mid-Cap Value A	SPRAX	A	(800) 225-1852	A / 9.5	6.68	16.48	34.07 /93	9.86 /93	14.47 /95	1.07	1.34
MC	● Prudential QMA Mid-Cap Value B	SVUBX	A	(800) 225-1852	A+ / 9.6	6.49	16.07	33.11 /92	9.03 /87	13.62 /90	0.72	2.04
MC	Prudential QMA Mid-Cap Value C	NCBVX	A	(800) 225-1852	A+ / 9.6	6.51	16.08	33.11 /92	9.02 /87	13.62 /90	0.72	2.04
MC	Prudential QMA Mid-Cap Value Q	PMVQX	A	(800) 225-1852	A+ / 9.8	6.76	16.70	34.63 /94	10.25 /95	14.94 /97	1.46	0.89
MC	Prudential QMA Mid-Cap Value R	SDVRX	A+	(800) 225-1852	A+ / 9.7	6.60	16.27	33.76 /93	9.51 /90	14.02 /93	0.92	1.79
MC	Prudential QMA Mid-Cap Value Z	SPVZX	A	(800) 225-1852	A+ / 9.7	6.74	16.62	34.43 /93	10.13 /94	14.75 /96	1.33	1.04
SC	Prudential QMA Small-Cap Value A	TSVAX	A+	(800) 225-1852	A+ / 9.7	5.35	18.30	42.83 /98	9.34 /89	13.25 /86	1.30	1.04
SC	Prudential QMA Small-Cap Value C	TRACX	A+	(800) 225-1852	A+ / 9.7	5.15	17.84	41.80 /98	8.52 /83	12.42 /78	0.75	1.74
SC	Prudential QMA Small-Cap Value Q	TSVQX	A+	(800) 225-1852	A+ / 9.8	5.42	18.49	43.25 /98	9.68 /91	13.60 /90	1.63	0.66
SC	Prudential QMA Small-Cap Value R	TSVRX	C	(800) 225-1852	A+ / 9.8	5.31	18.18	42.57 /98	9.07 /87	13.00 /84	1.19	1.49
SC	Prudential QMA Small-Cap Value Z	TASVX	C	(800) 225-1852	A+ / 9.8	5.42	18.44	43.20 /98	9.62 /91	13.56 /89	1.58	0.74
IX	Prudential QMA Stock Index A	PSIAX	A	(800) 225-1852	B+ / 8.6	7.90	9.73	24.30 /71	10.09 /94	13.43 /88	1.45	0.60
IX	Prudential QMA Stock Index C	PSICX	A	(800) 225-1852	B+ / 8.7	7.73	9.38	23.51 /68	9.40 /90	12.72 /81	0.94	1.25
IX	Prudential QMA Stock Index I	PDSIX	A+	(800) 225-1852	A / 9.3	7.97	9.91	24.70 /72	10.46 /96	13.81 /92	1.80	0.26
IX	Prudential QMA Stock Index Z	PSIFX	A+	(800) 225-1852	A / 9.3	7.95	9.87	24.62 /72	10.39 /95	13.75 /91	1.75	0.32
GR	Prudential QMA Strategic Value A	SUVAX	B+	(800) 225-1852	A+ / 9.6	7.22	16.43	35.04 /94	10.48 /96	13.56 /89	1.38	1.29
GR	● Prudential QMA Strategic Value B	SUVBX	B+	(800) 225-1852	A+ / 9.7	6.98	16.10	34.04 /93	9.66 /91	12.72 /81	0.94	1.99
GR	Prudential QMA Strategic Value C	SUVCX	B+	(800) 225-1852	A+ / 9.7	6.99	16.02	34.08 /93	9.64 /91	12.71 /81	0.94	1.99
GR	Prudential QMA Strategic Value R	PRVRX	A+	(800) 225-1852	A+ / 9.8	7.08	16.34	34.69 /94	10.08 /94	13.09 /85	1.21	1.74
GR	Prudential QMA Strategic Value Z	SUVZX	B+	(800) 225-1852	A+ / 9.8	7.26	16.52	35.32 /94	10.75 /97	13.85 /92	1.63	0.99
AA	Prudential Real Assets Fund A	PUDAX	D	(800) 225-1852	E / 0.5	2.72	0.40	9.35 /10	-0.67 /11	0.58 / 5	1.16	1.82
AA	● Prudential Real Assets Fund B	PUDBX	D	(800) 225-1852	E+ / 0.6	2.54	0.15	8.67 / 9	-1.39 / 8	-0.16 / 4	0.69	2.52
AA	Prudential Real Assets Fund C	PUDCX	D	(800) 225-1852	E+ / 0.6	2.54	0.05	8.55 / 8	-1.42 / 8	-0.16 / 4	0.69	2.52
GL	Prudential Real Assets Fund Q	PUDQX	D+	(800) 225-1852	E+ / 0.9	2.70	0.57	9.69 /11	-0.39 /12	0.86 / 6	1.55	1.44
AA	Prudential Real Assets Fund Z	PUDZX	D	(800) 225-1852	E+ / 0.9	2.78	0.63	9.71 /11	-0.41 /12	0.84 / 6	1.46	1.52
FS	Prudential Unconstrained Bond Z	PUCZX	U	(800) 225-1852	U /	3.76	4.38	16.30 /35	--	--	4.91	2.50
GI	Prudential US Real Estate Fund A	PJEAX	C-	(800) 225-1852	C / 5.0	6.93	-1.61	12.56 /20	9.10 /87	9.69 /56	1.90	1.72
GI	● Prudential US Real Estate Fund B	PJEBX	C-	(800) 225-1852	C / 5.5	6.77	-1.99	11.73 /17	8.30 /81	8.86 /49	1.31	2.42
GI	Prudential US Real Estate Fund C	PJECX	C-	(800) 225-1852	C / 5.5	6.78	-1.99	11.76 /17	8.31 /81	8.88 /50	1.31	2.42
GI	Prudential US Real Estate Fund Z	PJEZX	C	(800) 225-1852	C+ / 6.4	7.07	-1.49	12.92 /21	9.40 /90	9.97 /58	2.24	1.42
IN	PSG Tactical Growth	PSGTX	D-	(855) 866-9825	E / 0.5	5.79	4.33	10.43 /13	-3.16 / 4	--	0.57	2.52
IN	PSI All Asset A	FXMAX	D+	(888) 928-9774	E / 0.5	3.92	7.21	9.70 /11	-0.70 /10	-1.55 / 3	0.00	2.64
AA	PSI Calendar Effects A	FXCAX	C-	(888) 928-9774	D- / 1.0	5.39	0.44	6.26 / 5	1.84 /23	--	3.94	2.32
GI	PSI Strategic Growth A	FXSAX	D+	(888) 928-9774	E+ / 0.6	4.37	6.93	3.30 / 3	0.81 /17	2.11 / 8	0.00	2.15
GR	PSI Tactical Growth A	FXTAX	D	(888) 928-9774	E- / 0.2	2.77	-2.11	6.78 / 6	-2.25 / 6	1.43 / 7	0.00	3.08
GL	PSI Total Return A	FXBAX	D+	(888) 928-9774	E- / 0.2	2.05	-2.10	2.90 / 3	-1.35 / 8	-1.01 / 3	0.59	2.83
FO	Putnam Absolute Return 100 P		U	(800) 225-1581	U /	-0.79	-0.40	--	--	--	0.00	N/A
FO	Putnam Absolute Return 100 R6	PRREX	C-	(800) 225-1581	D- / 1.4	1.74	2.14	5.59 / 4	1.38 /20	--	2.71	0.42
FO	Putnam Absolute Return 300 P		U	(800) 225-1581	U /	-0.51	1.14	--	--	--	0.00	N/A
FO	Putnam Absolute Return 300 R6	PTREX	D	(800) 225-1581	D / 1.7	2.77	4.35	9.30 /10	1.20 /19	--	3.32	0.59
FO	Putnam Absolute Return 500 P		U	(800) 225-1581	U /	2.59	2.88	--	--	--	0.00	N/A
FO	Putnam Absolute Return 500 R6	PJMEX	C-	(800) 225-1581	D / 1.7	2.59	2.87	5.31 / 4	2.30 /26	--	0.00	0.82
FO	Putnam Absolute Return 700 P		U	(800) 225-1581	U /	3.70	4.44	--	--	--	0.00	N/A
FO	Putnam Absolute Return 700 R6	PDMEX	D+	(800) 225-1581	D+ / 2.5	3.60	4.34	8.76 / 9	3.18 /34	--	0.00	0.94
FO	● Putnam Asia Pacific Equity Fd A	PAPAX	D-	(800) 225-1581	D / 1.7	4.98	0.40	21.50 /60	0.79 /17	1.75 / 8	0.69	3.51

● Denotes fund is closed to new investors
* Denotes fund is included in Section II

534

RISK			NET ASSETS		ASSET					BULL / BEAR		FUND MANAGER		MINIMUMS		LOADS	
	3 Year		NAV						Portfolio	Last Bull	Last Bear	Manager	Manager	Initial	Additional	Front	Back
Risk Rating/Pts	Standard Deviation	Beta	As of 2/28/17	Total $(Mil)	Cash %	Stocks %	Bonds %	Other %	Turnover Ratio	Market Return	Market Return	Quality Pct	Tenure (Years)	Purch. $	Purch. $	End Load	End Load
C+ / 6.1	10.6	1.02	16.46	97	0	99	0	1	89	131.6	-17.7	61	12	2,500	100	5.5	0.0
C+ / 6.1	10.6	1.02	15.19	3	0	99	0	1	89	122.3	-18.0	51	12	2,500	100	0.0	0.0
C+ / 6.1	10.6	1.02	15.21	38	0	99	0	1	89	122.3	-17.9	52	12	2,500	100	0.0	0.0
C+ / 6.1	10.6	1.02	16.80	51	0	99	0	1	89	134.7	-17.7	65	12	0	0	0.0	0.0
U /	N/A	N/A	11.77	32	66	33	0	1	160	N/A	N/A	N/A	3	2,500	100	5.5	0.0
U /	N/A	N/A	11.52	33	66	33	0	1	160	N/A	N/A	N/A	3	2,500	100	0.0	0.0
U /	N/A	N/A	11.85	266	66	33	0	1	160	N/A	N/A	N/A	3	0	0	0.0	0.0
C+ / 5.6	12.1	0.96	22.16	287	0	99	0	1	87	140.8	-21.2	78	3	2,500	100	5.5	0.0
C / 5.5	12.1	0.96	19.32	8	0	99	0	1	87	131.3	-21.4	72	3	2,500	100	0.0	0.0
C / 5.5	12.0	0.96	19.24	65	0	99	0	1	87	131.2	-21.4	72	3	2,500	100	0.0	0.0
C+ / 5.6	12.1	0.96	22.31	118	0	99	0	1	87	146.2	-21.0	81	3	0	0	0.0	0.0
B- / 7.0	12.1	0.96	22.33	N/A	0	99	0	1	87	135.6	-21.3	76	3	0	0	0.0	0.0
C+ / 5.6	12.1	0.96	22.36	416	0	99	0	1	87	144.0	-21.1	80	3	0	0	0.0	0.0
C+ / 6.1	16.0	0.96	21.69	137	0	99	0	1	72	131.6	-21.9	88	2	2,500	100	5.5	0.0
C+ / 6.1	16.0	0.97	21.75	48	0	99	0	1	72	122.5	-22.1	85	2	2,500	100	0.0	0.0
C+ / 6.1	16.0	0.97	21.67	297	0	99	0	1	72	135.4	-21.8	90	2	0	0	0.0	0.0
D- / 1.2	16.0	0.97	21.45	160	0	99	0	1	72	128.8	-22.0	87	2	0	0	0.0	0.0
D- / 1.2	16.0	0.97	21.66	1,017	0	99	0	1	72	135.0	-21.8	89	2	0	0	0.0	0.0
C+ / 6.5	10.3	1.00	48.07	263	0	96	3	1	4	128.5	-16.5	69	25	2,500	100	3.3	0.0
C+ / 6.5	10.3	1.00	47.80	89	0	96	3	1	4	120.8	-16.6	61	25	2,500	100	0.0	0.0
C+ / 6.4	10.3	1.00	48.17	361	0	96	3	1	4	132.7	-16.3	72	25	0	0	0.0	0.0
C+ / 6.4	10.3	1.00	48.18	424	0	96	3	1	4	132.0	-16.3	72	25	0	0	0.0	0.0
C / 4.7	11.4	0.99	14.47	26	0	99	0	1	153	127.6	-18.3	74	8	2,500	100	5.5	0.0
C / 4.6	11.4	0.99	13.54	1	0	99	0	1	153	118.7	-18.6	65	8	2,500	100	0.0	0.0
C / 4.6	11.4	0.99	13.53	14	0	99	0	1	153	118.6	-18.6	65	8	2,500	100	0.0	0.0
B- / 7.3	11.4	0.99	14.79	245	0	99	0	1	153	122.4	-18.4	70	8	0	0	0.0	0.0
C / 4.7	11.4	0.99	14.78	103	0	99	0	1	153	130.6	-18.2	75	8	0	0	0.0	0.0
B- / 7.3	7.2	0.77	9.48	8	22	40	36	2	99	11.3	-8.0	8	7	2,500	100	5.5	0.0
B- / 7.4	7.2	0.77	9.44	1	22	40	36	2	99	6.9	-8.2	5	7	2,500	100	0.0	0.0
B- / 7.4	7.2	0.76	9.43	3	22	40	36	2	99	6.9	-8.2	6	7	2,500	100	0.0	0.0
B / 8.0	7.2	0.81	9.49	68	22	40	36	2	99	12.9	-7.8	22	7	0	0	0.0	0.0
B- / 7.3	7.2	0.78	9.50	98	22	40	36	2	99	12.9	-7.8	9	7	0	0	0.0	0.0
U /	N/A	N/A	10.15	29	1	0	98	1	38	N/A	N/A	N/A	N/A	0	0	0.0	0.0
C / 4.5	13.9	0.63	12.29	5	1	98	0	1	156	92.1	-18.2	87	7	2,500	100	5.5	0.0
C / 4.5	14.0	0.64	12.09	1	1	98	0	1	156	84.4	-18.5	84	7	2,500	100	0.0	0.0
C / 4.5	14.0	0.63	12.07	2	1	98	0	1	156	84.6	-18.6	84	7	2,500	100	0.0	0.0
C / 4.5	14.0	0.64	12.30	17	1	98	0	1	156	94.8	-18.2	88	7	0	0	0.0	0.0
C+ / 6.4	7.5	0.59	9.77	17	18	63	17	2	115	N/A	N/A	3	5	2,500	250	0.0	0.0
B / 8.0	9.1	-0.12	8.48	25	22	25	52	1	7,886	-10.8	-7.6	77	7	2,500	500	5.8	2.0
B / 8.7	7.5	0.38	9.45	12	22	20	57	1	1,762	N/A	N/A	62	4	2,500	500	5.8	2.0
B / 8.5	7.0	0.25	9.96	22	32	29	38	1	5,232	20.6	-18.6	51	7	2,500	500	5.8	2.0
B- / 7.5	6.8	0.42	9.29	21	34	30	34	2	5,609	13.6	-13.7	7	7	2,500	500	5.8	2.0
B / 8.2	3.9	0.23	8.61	30	15	2	80	3	1,711	-5.3	-0.3	41	7	2,500	500	5.8	2.0
U /	N/A	N/A	10.03	38	4	0	95	1	129	N/A	N/A	N/A	9	500	0	0.0	0.0
B / 8.6	1.4	0.07	10.03	1	4	0	95	1	129	N/A	N/A	83	9	0	0	0.0	0.0
U /	N/A	N/A	9.80	62	0	0	100	0	428	N/A	N/A	N/A	9	500	0	0.0	0.0
C+ / 6.5	3.1	0.16	9.81	6	0	0	100	0	428	N/A	N/A	82	9	0	0	0.0	0.0
U /	N/A	N/A	11.08	99	22	32	45	1	522	N/A	N/A	N/A	9	500	0	0.0	0.0
B- / 7.8	3.3	0.16	11.11	6	22	32	45	1	522	N/A	N/A	87	9	0	0	0.0	0.0
U /	N/A	N/A	11.76	81	0	43	56	1	578	N/A	N/A	N/A	9	500	0	0.0	0.0
C+ / 6.6	4.7	0.25	11.79	8	0	43	56	1	578	N/A	N/A	91	9	0	0	0.0	0.0
C / 5.4	14.2	0.82	10.27	6	3	96	0	1	135	40.1	-32.8	80	6	500	0	5.8	0.0

Data as of February 28, 2017

	99 Pct = Best 0 Pct = Worst				**PERFORMANCE**							
							Total Return % through 2/28/17				Incl. in Returns	
			Overall		Perfor-				Annualized		Dividend	Expense
Fund		Ticker	Investment		mance						Yield	Ratio
Type	Fund Name	Symbol	Rating	Phone	Rating/Pts	3 Mo	6 Mo	1Yr / Pct	3Yr / Pct	5Yr / Pct		
FO	● Putnam Asia Pacific Equity Fd B	PAPBX	D	(800) 225-1581	D / 2.1	4.86	0.04	20.63 / 56	0.05 / 14	1.00 / 6	0.04	4.26
FO	● Putnam Asia Pacific Equity Fd C	PAPCX	D	(800) 225-1581	D / 2.1	4.78	0.05	20.59 / 55	0.02 / 13	0.98 / 6	0.14	4.26
FO	● Putnam Asia Pacific Equity Fd M	PAPMX	D-	(800) 225-1581	D / 1.8	4.84	0.10	20.90 / 57	0.28 / 15	1.23 / 7	0.35	4.01
FO	● Putnam Asia Pacific Equity Fd R	PAPLX	D	(800) 225-1581	D+ / 2.4	5.00	0.31	21.29 / 59	0.53 / 16	1.49 / 7	0.56	3.76
FO	● Putnam Asia Pacific Equity Fd Y	PAPYX	D	(800) 225-1581	D+ / 2.7	5.04	0.56	21.80 / 61	1.05 / 18	2.00 / 8	0.96	3.26
SC	Putnam Capital Opportunities A	PCOAX	C-	(800) 225-1581	C+ / 5.7	5.22	11.65	27.87 / 81	4.77 / 52	9.59 / 55	0.58	1.19
SC	Putnam Capital Opportunities B	POPBX	C-	(800) 225-1581	C+ / 6.2	5.04	11.23	26.90 / 79	3.99 / 43	8.78 / 49	0.05	1.94
SC	Putnam Capital Opportunities C	PCOCX	C-	(800) 225-1581	C+ / 6.2	5.07	11.27	26.91 / 79	3.99 / 43	8.78 / 49	0.08	1.94
SC	Putnam Capital Opportunities M	POPMX	C-	(800) 225-1581	C+ / 5.7	5.07	11.30	27.24 / 80	4.22 / 45	9.04 / 51	0.27	1.69
SC	Putnam Capital Opportunities R	PCORX	C	(800) 225-1581	C+ / 6.6	5.20	11.51	27.50 / 81	4.50 / 49	9.31 / 53	0.36	1.44
SC	Putnam Capital Opportunities R5	POPDX	C	(800) 225-1581	C+ / 6.5	4.28	10.66	26.94 / 79	4.73 / 51	--	0.91	0.85
SC	Putnam Capital Opportunities R6	PCOEX	C	(800) 225-1581	B- / 7.1	5.36	11.86	28.39 / 83	5.19 / 56	--	0.99	0.75
SC	Putnam Capital Opportunities Y	PYCOX	C	(800) 225-1581	B- / 7.0	5.31	11.77	28.15 / 82	5.02 / 54	9.86 / 57	0.82	0.94
GI	Putnam Capital Spectrum Fund A	PVSAX	C-	(800) 225-1581	C- / 3.9	7.81	14.24	18.11 / 43	2.83 / 30	10.86 / 65	0.00	1.37
GI	Putnam Capital Spectrum Fund B	PVSBX	C-	(800) 225-1581	C / 4.4	7.64	13.85	17.26 / 40	2.06 / 24	10.02 / 58	0.00	2.12
GI	Putnam Capital Spectrum Fund C	PVSCX	C-	(800) 225-1581	C / 4.4	7.63	13.84	17.27 / 40	2.07 / 24	10.03 / 59	0.00	2.12
GI	Putnam Capital Spectrum Fund M	PVSMX	D+	(800) 225-1581	C- / 3.9	7.69	13.96	17.53 / 41	2.32 / 26	10.31 / 61	0.00	1.87
GI	Putnam Capital Spectrum Fund R	PVSRX	C-	(800) 225-1581	C / 4.8	7.75	14.12	17.84 / 42	2.57 / 28	10.58 / 63	0.00	1.62
GI	Putnam Capital Spectrum Fund Y	PVSYX	C	(800) 225-1581	C / 5.3	7.89	14.41	18.45 / 45	3.09 / 33	11.13 / 67	0.00	1.12
CV	Putnam Convertible Securities A	PCONX	D+	(800) 225-1581	C- / 3.4	5.80	6.54	21.33 / 59	3.15 / 33	7.99 / 42	1.88	1.06
CV	Putnam Convertible Securities B	PCNBX	C-	(800) 225-1581	C- / 3.8	5.59	6.09	20.45 / 55	2.38 / 27	7.19 / 36	1.33	1.81
CV	Putnam Convertible Securities C	PRCCX	C-	(800) 225-1581	C- / 3.8	5.57	6.12	20.39 / 54	2.36 / 26	7.19 / 36	1.30	1.81
CV	Putnam Convertible Securities M	PCNMX	D+	(800) 225-1581	C- / 3.4	5.65	6.21	20.71 / 56	2.63 / 28	7.45 / 38	1.51	1.56
CV	Putnam Convertible Securities R	PCVRX	C-	(800) 225-1581	C / 4.3	5.75	6.38	21.08 / 58	2.89 / 31	7.73 / 40	1.78	1.31
CV	Putnam Convertible Securities Y	PCGYX	C	(800) 225-1581	C / 4.7	5.82	6.63	21.65 / 60	3.39 / 36	8.27 / 44	2.24	0.81
AA	Putnam Dynamic Asset Alloc Bal A	PABAX	C+	(800) 225-1581	C- / 4.1	5.30	5.85	15.59 / 32	5.96 / 64	8.87 / 50	1.36	0.99
AA	Putnam Dynamic Asset Alloc Bal B	PABBX	C+	(800) 225-1581	C / 4.6	5.06	5.49	14.73 / 29	5.16 / 56	8.06 / 43	0.75	1.74
AA	Putnam Dynamic Asset Alloc Bal C	AABCX	C+	(800) 225-1581	C / 4.6	5.10	5.48	14.69 / 28	5.19 / 56	8.06 / 43	0.81	1.74
AA	Putnam Dynamic Asset Alloc Bal M	PABMX	C+	(800) 225-1581	C- / 4.1	5.11	5.53	14.98 / 30	5.42 / 59	8.32 / 45	0.95	1.49
AA	Putnam Dynamic Asset Alloc Bal P		U	(800) 225-1581	U /	3.90	4.20	--	--	--	0.00	N/A
AA	Putnam Dynamic Asset Alloc Bal R	PAARX	C+	(800) 225-1581	C / 5.1	5.21	5.72	15.23 / 31	5.69 / 61	8.60 / 47	1.26	1.24
AA	Putnam Dynamic Asset Alloc Bal R5	PAADX	B-	(800) 225-1581	C / 5.5	5.28	5.98	15.88 / 34	6.23 / 66	--	1.70	0.74
AA	Putnam Dynamic Asset Alloc Bal R6	PAAEX	B-	(800) 225-1581	C+ / 5.6	5.38	6.11	16.06 / 35	6.35 / 67	--	1.78	0.64
AA	Putnam Dynamic Asset Alloc Bal Y	PABYX	B-	(800) 225-1581	C / 5.5	5.28	5.95	15.81 / 33	6.23 / 66	9.13 / 52	1.65	0.74
AA	Putnam Dynamic Asset Alloc Consv	PACAX	C-	(800) 225-1581	D / 2.1	3.43	2.28	9.07 / 10	4.40 / 47	6.03 / 29	1.64	1.03
AA	Putnam Dynamic Asset Alloc Consv	PACBX	C-	(800) 225-1581	D+ / 2.4	3.26	1.92	8.34 / 8	3.61 / 38	5.26 / 23	1.03	1.78
AA	Putnam Dynamic Asset Alloc Consv	PACCX	C-	(800) 225-1581	D+ / 2.5	3.28	1.94	8.29 / 8	3.62 / 38	5.24 / 23	1.06	1.78
AA	Putnam Dynamic Asset Alloc Consv	PACMX	C-	(800) 225-1581	D / 2.1	3.41	2.13	8.62 / 9	3.90 / 42	5.52 / 25	1.21	1.53
AA	Putnam Dynamic Asset Alloc Consv		U	(800) 225-1581	U /	2.70	1.11	--	--	--	0.00	N/A
AA	Putnam Dynamic Asset Alloc Consv	PACRX	C	(800) 225-1581	D+ / 2.8	3.36	2.19	8.88 / 9	4.12 / 44	5.77 / 27	1.46	1.28
AA	Putnam Dynamic Asset Alloc Consv	PACDX	C	(800) 225-1581	C- / 3.2	3.49	2.42	9.36 / 10	4.70 / 51	--	2.02	0.74
AA	Putnam Dynamic Asset Alloc Consv	PCCEX	C	(800) 225-1581	C- / 3.2	3.50	2.55	9.54 / 11	4.79 / 52	--	2.09	0.67
AA	Putnam Dynamic Asset Alloc Consv	PACYX	C	(800) 225-1581	C- / 3.2	3.58	2.50	9.41 / 10	4.67 / 51	6.31 / 30	1.97	0.78
GR	Putnam Dynamic Asset Alloc Equity A		C	(800) 225-1581	C+ / 6.2	7.27	9.34	22.45 / 64	6.85 / 71	11.42 / 69	1.13	1.38
GR	Putnam Dynamic Asset Alloc Equity P		U	(800) 225-1581	U /	5.93	8.07	--	--	--	0.00	N/A
AA	Putnam Dynamic Asst Alloc Growth A	PAEAX	C	(800) 225-1581	C / 5.4	6.58	7.83	20.30 / 54	6.41 / 68	10.18 / 60	0.34	1.09
AA	Putnam Dynamic Asst Alloc Growth B	PAEBX	C+	(800) 225-1581	C+ / 5.9	6.33	7.38	19.40 / 49	5.61 / 61	9.36 / 54	0.00	1.84
AA	Putnam Dynamic Asst Alloc Growth C	PAECX	C+	(800) 225-1581	C+ / 5.9	6.35	7.44	19.39 / 49	5.61 / 61	9.37 / 54	0.00	1.84
AA	Putnam Dynamic Asst Alloc Growth	PAGMX	C	(800) 225-1581	C / 5.5	6.47	7.60	19.76 / 51	5.90 / 63	9.64 / 56	0.00	1.59
AA	Putnam Dynamic Asst Alloc Growth P		U	(800) 225-1581	U /	4.88	6.29	--	--	--	0.00	N/A
AA	Putnam Dynamic Asst Alloc Growth R	PASRX	C+	(800) 225-1581	C+ / 6.4	6.49	7.69	19.99 / 52	6.13 / 65	9.90 / 58	0.22	1.34
AA	Putnam Dynamic Asst Alloc Growth	PADEX	C+	(800) 225-1581	C+ / 6.8	6.63	7.93	20.61 / 55	6.67 / 70	--	0.58	0.81

● Denotes fund is closed to new investors
* Denotes fund is included in Section II

Risk Rating/Pts	Standard Deviation	Beta	NAV As of 2/28/17	Total $(Mil)	Cash %	Stocks %	Bonds %	Other %	Portfolio Turnover Ratio	Last Bull Market Return	Last Bear Market Return	Manager Quality Pct	Manager Tenure (Years)	Initial Purch. $	Additional Purch. $	Front End Load	Back End Load
C /5.4	14.2	0.83	10.02	N/A	3	96	0	1	135	34.7	-33.0	75	6	500	0	0.0	0.0
C /5.4	14.2	0.83	9.97	1	3	96	0	1	135	34.6	-33.0	75	6	500	0	0.0	0.0
C /5.4	14.2	0.83	10.14	N/A	3	96	0	1	135	36.4	-33.0	77	6	500	0	3.5	0.0
C /5.4	14.2	0.83	10.26	N/A	3	96	0	1	135	38.3	-32.9	79	6	500	0	0.0	0.0
C /5.4	14.2	0.83	10.27	1	3	96	0	1	135	42.0	-32.7	82	6	500	0	0.0	0.0
C /4.3	13.5	0.82	15.52	241	1	98	0	1	55	107.8	-28.4	64	1	500	0	5.8	0.0
C- /4.0	13.5	0.82	13.31	8	1	98	0	1	55	99.6	-28.6	54	1	500	0	0.0	0.0
C- /4.1	13.5	0.82	13.51	21	1	98	0	1	55	99.6	-28.6	54	1	500	0	0.0	0.0
C- /4.2	13.5	0.82	14.14	4	1	98	0	1	55	102.3	-28.5	57	1	500	0	3.5	0.0
C /4.3	13.5	0.81	15.11	11	1	98	0	1	55	104.9	-28.4	61	1	500	0	0.0	0.0
C /4.3	13.5	0.82	15.84	N/A	1	98	0	1	55	N/A	N/A	64	1	500	0	0.0	0.0
C /4.3	13.5	0.82	16.02	11	1	98	0	1	55	N/A	N/A	69	1	500	0	0.0	0.0
C /4.3	13.5	0.82	15.98	48	1	98	0	1	55	110.7	-28.3	67	1	500	0	0.0	0.0
C /5.5	11.6	0.93	35.25	1,066	16	79	3	2	31	108.7	-14.2	6	8	500	0	5.8	0.0
C /5.4	11.6	0.93	33.84	78	16	79	3	2	31	100.4	-14.4	5	8	500	0	0.0	0.0
C /5.4	11.6	0.93	33.76	980	16	79	3	2	31	100.4	-14.4	5	8	500	0	0.0	0.0
C /5.4	11.6	0.93	34.33	8	16	79	3	2	31	103.1	-14.4	5	8	500	0	3.5	0.0
C /5.4	11.6	0.93	34.79	12	16	79	3	2	31	105.9	-14.2	6	8	500	0	0.0	0.0
C /5.5	11.6	0.93	35.58	1,929	16	79	3	2	31	111.6	-14.1	7	8	500	0	0.0	0.0
C+ /5.8	8.7	0.99	24.04	409	8	16	0	76	49	66.5	-16.0	52	11	500	0	5.8	0.0
C+ /5.8	8.7	0.99	23.54	9	8	16	0	76	49	59.8	-16.3	42	11	500	0	0.0	0.0
C+ /5.8	8.7	0.99	23.74	48	8	16	0	76	49	59.8	-16.3	41	11	500	0	0.0	0.0
C+ /5.8	8.7	0.99	23.77	4	8	16	0	76	49	61.9	-16.2	45	11	500	0	3.5	0.0
C+ /5.8	8.7	0.99	23.93	5	8	16	0	76	49	64.2	-16.1	48	11	0	0	0.0	0.0
C+ /5.8	8.7	0.99	24.03	199	8	16	0	76	49	68.7	-15.9	56	11	0	0	0.0	0.0
B- /7.3	7.0	1.11	14.61	1,368	19	51	28	2	374	76.7	-13.8	46	15	500	0	5.8	0.0
B- /7.3	7.0	1.10	14.53	72	19	51	28	2	374	69.7	-14.0	35	15	500	0	0.0	0.0
B- /7.3	7.0	1.10	14.22	295	19	51	28	2	374	69.6	-14.0	35	15	500	0	0.0	0.0
B- /7.3	7.0	1.10	14.56	28	19	51	28	2	374	71.9	-13.9	38	15	500	0	3.5	0.0
U /	N/A	N/A	14.65	178	19	51	28	2	374	N/A	N/A	N/A	15	500	0	0.0	0.0
B- /7.3	7.0	1.10	14.49	28	19	51	28	2	374	74.2	-13.8	42	15	500	0	0.0	0.0
B- /7.3	7.0	1.10	14.64	3	19	51	28	2	374	N/A	N/A	49	15	0	0	0.0	0.0
B- /7.3	7.0	1.10	14.65	177	19	51	28	2	374	N/A	N/A	51	15	0	0	0.0	0.0
B- /7.3	7.0	1.10	14.64	311	19	51	28	2	374	79.1	-13.7	50	15	500	0	0.0	0.0
B- /7.7	4.3	0.65	10.41	490	15	37	47	1	614	46.3	-7.0	69	15	500	0	5.8	0.0
B- /7.7	4.3	0.65	10.33	21	15	37	47	1	614	40.5	-7.3	59	15	500	0	0.0	0.0
B- /7.7	4.2	0.64	10.28	129	15	37	47	1	614	40.4	-7.3	60	15	500	0	0.0	0.0
B- /7.7	4.3	0.65	10.30	11	15	37	47	1	614	42.3	-7.2	63	15	500	0	3.5	0.0
U /	N/A	N/A	10.45	83	15	37	47	1	614	N/A	N/A	N/A	15	0	0	0.0	0.0
B- /7.7	4.3	0.65	10.70	12	15	37	47	1	614	44.3	-7.1	66	15	500	0	0.0	0.0
B- /7.7	4.3	0.65	10.44	1	15	37	47	1	614	N/A	N/A	72	15	0	0	0.0	0.0
B- /7.7	4.3	0.65	10.45	99	15	37	47	1	614	N/A	N/A	73	15	0	0	0.0	0.0
B- /7.7	4.3	0.65	10.45	203	15	37	47	1	614	48.2	-6.8	72	15	500	0	0.0	0.0
C /4.6	10.8	1.02	12.31	N/A	3	96	0	1	109	112.0	-21.6	26	8	500	0	5.8	0.0
U /	N/A	N/A	12.32	76	3	96	0	1	109	N/A	N/A	N/A	8	500	0	0.0	0.0
C /5.5	9.2	1.43	16.38	1,534	21	59	18	2	216	95.1	-19.2	23	15	500	0	5.8	0.0
C+ /5.6	9.2	1.42	16.03	77	21	59	18	2	216	87.4	-19.6	17	15	500	0	0.0	0.0
C /5.5	9.1	1.42	15.48	270	21	59	18	2	216	87.4	-19.5	17	15	500	0	0.0	0.0
C+ /5.6	9.2	1.42	16.02	32	21	59	18	2	216	90.0	-19.5	19	15	500	0	3.5	0.0
U /	N/A	N/A	16.56	235	21	59	18	2	216	N/A	N/A	N/A	15	0	0	0.0	0.0
C /5.5	9.1	1.42	16.05	25	21	59	18	2	216	92.5	-19.4	21	15	500	0	0.0	0.0
C /5.5	9.2	1.42	16.54	4	21	59	18	2	216	N/A	N/A	26	15	0	0	0.0	0.0

	99 Pct = Best / 0 Pct = Worst	Ticker Symbol	Overall Investment Rating	Phone	PERFORMANCE						Incl. in Returns	
					Perfor-mance Rating/Pts	Total Return % through 2/28/17			Annualized		Dividend Yield	Expense Ratio
Fund Type	Fund Name					3 Mo	6 Mo	1Yr / Pct	3Yr / Pct	5Yr / Pct		
AA	Putnam Dynamic Asst Alloc Growth	PAEEX	C+	(800) 225-1581	C+ / 6.8	6.64	8.00	20.75 / 56	6.79 / 70	--	0.71	0.71
AA	Putnam Dynamic Asst Alloc Growth Y	PAGYX	C+	(800) 225-1581	C+ / 6.8	6.61	7.98	20.60 / 55	6.69 / 70	10.47 / 62	0.50	0.84
GL	Putnam Dynamic Risk Allocation A	PDREX	D+	(800) 225-1581	D / 1.8	5.24	4.05	14.64 / 28	1.77 / 22	3.37 / 12	2.17	1.35
GL	Putnam Dynamic Risk Allocation B	PDRBX	D+	(800) 225-1581	D / 2.2	5.03	3.72	13.80 / 25	1.03 / 18	2.62 / 10	1.50	2.10
GL	Putnam Dynamic Risk Allocation C	PDRFX	D+	(800) 225-1581	D / 2.1	4.94	3.73	13.70 / 24	1.00 / 18	2.60 / 10	1.42	2.10
GL	Putnam Dynamic Risk Allocation M	PDRTX	D+	(800) 225-1581	D / 1.8	5.10	3.90	14.05 / 26	1.25 / 20	2.86 / 10	1.83	1.85
GL	Putnam Dynamic Risk Allocation R	PDRRX	C-	(800) 225-1581	D+ / 2.5	5.17	3.97	14.41 / 27	1.51 / 21	3.11 / 11	1.67	1.60
GL	Putnam Dynamic Risk Allocation R6	PDRGX	C-	(800) 225-1581	D+ / 2.9	5.28	4.29	15.04 / 30	2.11 / 25	--	2.71	0.97
GL	Putnam Dynamic Risk Allocation Y	PDRYX	C-	(800) 225-1581	D+ / 2.8	5.32	4.23	14.93 / 30	2.02 / 24	3.65 / 14	2.57	1.10
FO	Putnam Emerging Markets Eq A	PEMMX	D-	(800) 225-1581	D / 2.0	6.91	2.43	24.01 / 70	0.12 / 14	0.12 / 5	0.82	2.24
FO	Putnam Emerging Markets Eq B	PEMBX	D-	(800) 225-1581	D / 1.6	6.62	2.00	23.09 / 67	-0.63 / 11	-0.62 / 4	0.24	2.99
FO	Putnam Emerging Markets Eq C	PEMZX	D-	(800) 225-1581	D / 1.6	6.79	2.03	23.05 / 67	-0.63 / 11	-0.61 / 4	0.26	2.99
FO	Putnam Emerging Markets Eq M	PEMAX	D-	(800) 225-1581	D- / 1.3	6.84	2.15	23.40 / 68	-0.37 / 12	-0.36 / 4	0.39	2.74
FO	Putnam Emerging Markets Eq R	PEMLX	D-	(800) 225-1581	D / 1.8	6.83	2.23	23.64 / 69	-0.14 / 13	-0.13 / 4	0.88	2.49
FO	Putnam Emerging Markets Eq Y	PEMYX	D	(800) 225-1581	C- / 3.0	7.00	2.56	24.36 / 71	0.36 / 15	0.38 / 5	1.10	1.99
IN	Putnam Equity Income A	PEYAX	B+	(800) 225-1581	B / 7.9	7.87	10.95	26.67 / 78	8.89 / 86	13.17 / 86	1.27	0.96
IN	Putnam Equity Income B	PEQNX	B+	(800) 225-1581	B+ / 8.3	7.63	10.59	25.73 / 75	8.07 / 79	12.31 / 77	0.70	1.71
IN	Putnam Equity Income C	PEQCX	B+	(800) 225-1581	B+ / 8.4	7.68	10.59	25.74 / 75	8.08 / 80	12.32 / 77	0.71	1.71
IN	Putnam Equity Income M	PEIMX	B+	(800) 225-1581	B / 8.0	7.75	10.73	26.06 / 76	8.36 / 82	12.62 / 80	0.89	1.46
IN	Putnam Equity Income R	PEQRX	A-	(800) 225-1581	B+ / 8.8	7.76	10.85	26.34 / 77	8.62 / 84	12.88 / 83	1.13	1.21
IN	Putnam Equity Income R5	PEQLX	A-	(800) 225-1581	A- / 9.1	7.94	11.16	27.05 / 79	9.24 / 88	--	1.61	0.65
IN	Putnam Equity Income R6	PEQSX	A	(800) 225-1581	A- / 9.2	7.96	11.21	27.17 / 80	9.36 / 89	--	1.71	0.55
IN	Putnam Equity Income Y	PEIYX	A-	(800) 225-1581	A- / 9.1	7.93	11.14	26.97 / 79	9.18 / 88	13.46 / 89	1.56	0.71
GR	Putnam Equity Spectrum A	PYSAX	U	(800) 225-1581	U /	9.40	17.51	22.52 / 65	--	9.97 / 58	0.00	1.18
GR	Putnam Equity Spectrum B	PYSOX	D-	(800) 225-1581	D / 2.1	9.18	17.06	21.59 / 60	-0.75 / 10	9.14 / 52	0.00	1.93
GR	Putnam Equity Spectrum C	PYSCX	D-	(800) 225-1581	D / 2.1	9.20	17.06	21.60 / 60	-0.75 / 10	9.14 / 52	0.00	1.93
GR	Putnam Equity Spectrum M	PYSMX	E+	(800) 225-1581	D / 1.8	9.28	17.23	21.91 / 62	-0.50 / 11	9.42 / 54	0.00	1.68
GR	Putnam Equity Spectrum R	PYSRX	D-	(800) 225-1581	D+ / 2.3	9.35	17.37	22.22 / 63	-0.25 / 12	9.69 / 56	0.00	1.43
GR	Putnam Equity Spectrum Y	PYSYX	D+	(800) 225-1581	C / 4.7	9.46	17.66	22.83 / 66	0.25 / 15	10.24 / 60	0.00	0.93
FO	Putnam Europe Equity A	PEUGX	E+	(800) 225-1581	E- / 0.2	7.72	2.04	8.65 / 9	-3.69 / 3	6.15 / 29	2.51	1.32
FO	Putnam Europe Equity B	PEUBX	E+	(800) 225-1581	E / 0.3	7.53	1.62	7.83 / 7	-4.42 / 3	5.36 / 24	1.99	2.07
FO	Putnam Europe Equity C	PEECX	E+	(800) 225-1581	E / 0.3	7.55	1.65	7.85 / 7	-4.40 / 3	5.36 / 24	1.84	2.07
FO	Putnam Europe Equity M	PEUMX	E+	(800) 225-1581	E- / 0.2	7.54	1.75	8.08 / 8	-4.18 / 3	5.61 / 26	2.11	1.82
FO	Putnam Europe Equity R	PEERX	E+	(800) 225-1581	E / 0.3	7.69	1.89	8.37 / 8	-3.92 / 3	5.89 / 28	2.49	1.57
FO	Putnam Europe Equity Y	PEUYX	E+	(800) 225-1581	E / 0.4	7.79	2.18	8.95 / 9	-3.45 / 4	6.42 / 31	2.96	1.07
GI	Putnam Fund for Gr & Inc A	PGRWX	B	(800) 225-1581	B- / 7.4	7.73	12.87	30.51 / 87	6.66 / 70	12.38 / 78	1.49	0.94
GI	Putnam Fund for Gr & Inc B	PGIBX	B+	(800) 225-1581	B / 7.8	7.54	12.44	29.55 / 85	5.87 / 63	11.54 / 70	0.94	1.69
GI	Putnam Fund for Gr & Inc C	PGRIX	B+	(800) 225-1581	B / 7.8	7.58	12.46	29.61 / 86	5.88 / 63	11.55 / 70	0.93	1.69
GI	Putnam Fund for Gr & Inc M	PGRMX	B	(800) 225-1581	B- / 7.4	7.63	12.60	29.91 / 86	6.14 / 66	11.82 / 73	1.11	1.44
GI	Putnam Fund for Gr & Inc R	PGCRX	B+	(800) 225-1581	B / 8.2	7.67	12.72	30.17 / 87	6.40 / 68	12.10 / 75	1.36	1.19
GI	Putnam Fund for Gr & Inc R6	PGREX	A-	(800) 225-1581	B+ / 8.7	7.80	13.03	31.03 / 88	7.08 / 72	--	1.91	0.55
GI	Putnam Fund for Gr & Inc Y	PGIYX	A-	(800) 225-1581	B+ / 8.6	7.78	12.98	30.83 / 88	6.93 / 71	12.66 / 81	1.80	0.69
GL	Putnam Glob Telecommunications A	PGBZX	E+	(800) 225-1581	D+ / 2.5	9.21	4.66	11.11 / 15	3.16 / 33	11.43 / 69	3.62	1.60
GL	Putnam Glob Telecommunications B	PGBBX	D-	(800) 225-1581	D+ / 2.9	8.97	4.21	10.27 / 12	2.39 / 27	10.58 / 63	3.33	2.35
GL	Putnam Glob Telecommunications C	PGBNX	D-	(800) 225-1581	D+ / 2.9	9.06	4.27	10.28 / 12	2.40 / 27	10.59 / 63	3.04	2.35
GL	Putnam Glob Telecommunications M	PGBMX	E+	(800) 225-1581	D+ / 2.5	9.11	4.42	10.55 / 13	2.65 / 29	10.86 / 65	2.90	2.10
GL	Putnam Glob Telecommunications R	PGBTX	D-	(800) 225-1581	C- / 3.2	9.10	4.50	10.77 / 14	2.90 / 31	11.13 / 67	1.29	1.85
GL	Putnam Glob Telecommunications Y	PGBYX	D-	(800) 225-1581	C- / 3.6	9.31	4.78	11.36 / 16	3.42 / 36	11.71 / 72	4.10	1.35
OT	Putnam Global Consumer Fund A	PGCOX	C-	(800) 225-1581	C / 5.1	8.36	5.65	17.97 / 43	6.37 / 67	11.81 / 73	0.89	1.54
OT	Putnam Global Consumer Fund B	PGCKX	C-	(800) 225-1581	C+ / 5.6	8.23	5.29	17.17 / 39	5.59 / 60	10.99 / 66	0.36	2.29
OT	Putnam Global Consumer Fund C	PGCNX	C-	(800) 225-1581	C+ / 5.6	8.19	5.30	17.10 / 39	5.59 / 60	10.98 / 66	0.30	2.29
OT	Putnam Global Consumer Fund M	PGCMX	C-	(800) 225-1581	C / 5.1	8.24	5.43	17.39 / 40	5.84 / 63	11.25 / 68	0.51	2.04

● Denotes fund is closed to new investors
* Denotes fund is included in Section II

RISK			NET ASSETS		ASSET					Portfolio	BULL / BEAR		FUND MANAGER		MINIMUMS		LOADS	
	3 Year		NAV								Last Bull	Last Bear	Manager	Manager	Initial	Additional	Front	Back
Risk	Standard		As of	Total	Cash	Stocks	Bonds	Other		Turnover	Market	Market	Quality	Tenure	Purch.	Purch.	End	End
Rating/Pts	Deviation	Beta	2/28/17	$(Mil)	%	%	%	%		Ratio	Return	Return	Pct	(Years)	$	$	Load	Load
C /5.5	9.2	1.42	16.56	167	21	59	18	2	216	N/A	N/A	27	15	0	0	0.0	0.0
C /5.5	9.1	1.42	16.54	234	21	59	18	2	216	97.8	-19.2	26	15	500	0	0.0	0.0
B- /7.0	6.6	0.91	10.77	19	19	38	41	2	300	30.8	N/A	42	6	500	0	5.8	0.0
B- /7.0	6.6	0.92	10.60	3	19	38	41	2	300	25.7	N/A	32	6	500	0	0.0	0.0
B- /7.1	6.6	0.92	10.61	8	19	38	41	2	300	25.6	N/A	32	6	500	0	0.0	0.0
B- /7.1	6.7	0.92	10.77	N/A	19	38	41	2	300	27.4	N/A	35	6	500	0	3.5	0.0
B- /7.0	6.7	0.92	10.75	N/A	19	38	41	2	300	29.1	N/A	38	6	500	0	0.0	0.0
C+ /6.9	6.6	0.91	10.74	100	19	38	41	2	300	N/A	N/A	47	6	0	0	0.0	0.0
B- /7.0	6.6	0.91	10.79	45	19	38	41	2	300	32.8	N/A	46	6	500	0	0.0	0.0
C /5.1	14.4	0.89	9.68	20	2	97	0	1	156	29.5	-34.3	76	9	500	0	5.8	0.0
C /5.1	14.3	0.88	9.38	2	2	97	0	1	156	24.4	-34.6	69	9	500	0	0.0	0.0
C /5.1	14.3	0.88	9.35	3	2	97	0	1	156	24.4	-34.6	69	9	500	0	0.0	0.0
C /5.1	14.3	0.88	9.51	N/A	2	97	0	1	156	26.1	-34.5	72	9	500	0	3.5	0.0
C /5.1	14.4	0.89	9.65	1	2	97	0	1	156	27.7	-34.4	N/A	9	500	0	0.0	0.0
C /5.0	14.3	0.88	9.77	14	2	97	0	1	156	31.2	-34.2	78	9	500	0	0.0	0.0
C+ /5.9	10.3	0.97	22.48	3,446	3	96	0	1	15	132.4	-19.7	58	5	500	0	5.8	0.0
C+ /5.9	10.3	0.97	22.20	112	3	96	0	1	15	123.1	-19.9	48	5	500	0	0.0	0.0
C+ /5.9	10.3	0.97	22.20	389	3	96	0	1	15	123.2	-19.9	47	5	500	0	0.0	0.0
C+ /5.9	10.3	0.97	22.19	53	3	96	0	1	15	126.2	-19.8	51	5	500	0	3.5	0.0
C+ /5.9	10.3	0.97	22.30	121	3	96	0	1	15	129.2	-19.7	55	5	500	0	0.0	0.0
C+ /5.9	10.3	0.97	22.49	108	3	96	0	1	15	N/A	N/A	62	5	0	0	0.0	0.0
C+ /5.9	10.3	0.97	22.50	687	3	96	0	1	15	N/A	N/A	64	5	0	0	0.0	0.0
C+ /5.9	10.3	0.97	22.49	1,635	3	96	0	1	15	135.5	-19.6	62	5	0	0	0.0	0.0
U /	13.2	1.04	38.52	424	18	81	0	1	24	105.1	-14.4	N/A	8	500	0	5.8	0.0
C- /4.2	13.1	1.04	36.50	35	18	81	0	1	24	96.9	-14.7	1	8	500	0	0.0	0.0
C- /4.2	13.1	1.05	36.43	260	18	81	0	1	24	96.8	-14.7	1	8	500	0	0.0	0.0
C /4.3	13.1	1.05	37.22	3	18	81	0	1	24	99.5	-14.6	2	8	500	0	3.5	0.0
C /4.3	13.2	1.05	37.90	9	18	81	0	1	24	102.3	-14.5	2	8	500	0	0.0	0.0
C /4.4	13.1	1.04	39.11	541	18	81	0	1	24	107.8	-14.3	2	8	500	0	0.0	0.0
C /5.4	12.2	0.92	23.50	149	2	97	0	1	66	64.3	-27.8	28	11	500	0	5.8	0.0
C /5.4	12.2	0.92	22.47	4	2	97	0	1	66	57.8	-28.0	20	11	500	0	0.0	0.0
C /5.4	12.2	0.92	22.90	17	2	97	0	1	66	57.8	-28.0	20	11	500	0	0.0	0.0
C /5.4	12.2	0.92	23.29	3	2	97	0	1	66	59.9	-27.9	22	11	500	0	3.5	0.0
C /5.4	12.2	0.92	23.25	N/A	2	97	0	1	66	62.1	-27.9	25	11	500	0	0.0	0.0
C /5.4	12.2	0.92	23.58	38	2	97	0	1	66	66.5	-27.7	30	11	0	0	0.0	0.0
C+ /6.1	11.4	1.06	23.37	4,901	2	97	0	1	42	123.4	-22.2	21	1	500	0	5.8	0.0
C+ /6.1	11.5	1.06	22.92	63	2	97	0	1	42	114.4	-22.4	15	1	500	0	0.0	0.0
C+ /6.1	11.5	1.06	23.24	55	2	97	0	1	42	114.4	-22.4	15	1	500	0	0.0	0.0
C+ /6.1	11.5	1.06	23.16	30	2	97	0	1	42	117.4	-22.3	17	1	500	0	3.5	0.0
C+ /6.1	11.5	1.06	23.24	1	2	97	0	1	42	120.3	-22.2	19	1	500	0	0.0	0.0
C+ /6.1	11.5	1.06	23.44	22	2	97	0	1	42	N/A	N/A	25	1	0	0	0.0	0.0
C+ /6.1	11.4	1.06	23.42	89	2	97	0	1	42	126.3	-22.1	24	1	500	0	0.0	0.0
C- /3.6	11.1	0.74	14.73	16	5	94	0	1	49	88.2	-13.6	91	9	500	0	5.8	0.0
C- /3.6	11.2	0.74	14.29	3	5	94	0	1	49	80.6	-13.8	88	9	500	0	0.0	0.0
C- /3.5	11.2	0.74	14.28	4	5	94	0	1	49	80.7	-13.8	88	9	500	0	0.0	0.0
C- /3.6	11.2	0.74	14.62	N/A	5	94	0	1	49	83.2	-13.8	89	9	500	0	3.5	0.0
C- /3.6	11.1	0.73	14.92	1	5	94	0	1	49	85.5	-13.6	90	9	500	0	0.0	0.0
C- /3.6	11.2	0.74	14.79	4	5	94	0	1	49	90.8	-13.5	92	9	500	0	0.0	0.0
C /4.8	11.7	1.00	19.20	25	3	96	0	1	40	111.8	-17.7	25	9	500	0	5.8	0.0
C /4.7	11.8	1.00	18.50	3	3	96	0	1	40	103.4	-18.0	18	9	500	0	0.0	0.0
C /4.7	11.7	1.00	18.42	6	3	96	0	1	40	103.4	-18.0	18	9	500	0	0.0	0.0
C /4.7	11.7	1.00	18.91	N/A	3	96	0	1	40	106.1	-17.9	20	9	500	0	3.5	0.0

I. Index of Stock Mutual Funds

99 Pct = Best 0 Pct = Worst					PERFORMANCE						Incl. in Returns	
			Overall		Perfor-	Total Return % through 2/28/17			Annualized		Dividend	Expense
Fund		Ticker	Investment		mance							
Type	Fund Name	Symbol	Rating	Phone	Rating/Pts	3 Mo	6 Mo	1Yr / Pct	3Yr / Pct	5Yr / Pct	Yield	Ratio
OT	Putnam Global Consumer Fund R	PGCIX	C	(800) 225-1581	C+ / 6.1	8.32	5.57	17.73 /42	6.11 /65	11.55 /70	0.00	1.79
OT	Putnam Global Consumer Fund Y	PGCYX	C	(800) 225-1581	C+ / 6.5	8.47	5.83	18.31 /44	6.64 /69	12.09 /75	1.17	1.29
GL	Putnam Global Dividend A	PGDEX	C-	(800) 225-1581	C- / 3.2	8.47	5.05	16.76 /37	3.64 /39	---	2.92	2.00
GL	Putnam Global Dividend B	PGDFX	C-	(800) 225-1581	C- / 3.8	8.32	4.69	16.02 /34	2.89 /31	---	2.42	2.75
GL	Putnam Global Dividend C	PGDHX	C-	(800) 225-1581	C- / 3.7	8.30	4.67	15.90 /34	2.88 /31	---	2.40	2.75
GL	Putnam Global Dividend M	PGDMX	C-	(800) 225-1581	C- / 3.3	8.36	4.80	16.28 /35	3.15 /33	---	2.48	2.50
GL	Putnam Global Dividend Y	PGDYX	C	(800) 225-1581	C / 4.6	8.53	5.18	17.14 /39	3.92 /42	---	3.33	1.75
EN	Putnam Global Energy Fund A	PGEAX	E-	(800) 225-1581	E- / 0.0	-1.21	9.18	33.42 /92	-14.99 / 0	-7.86 / 1	0.52	1.72
EN	Putnam Global Energy Fund B	PGEDX	E-	(800) 225-1581	E- / 0.0	-1.28	8.90	32.47 /91	-15.61 / 0	-8.54 / 1	0.00	2.47
EN	Putnam Global Energy Fund C	PGECX	E-	(800) 225-1581	E- / 0.0	-1.28	8.90	32.47 /91	-15.61 / 0	-8.54 / 1	0.00	2.47
EN	Putnam Global Energy Fund M	PGENX	E-	(800) 225-1581	E- / 0.0	-1.16	9.00	32.79 /91	-15.40 / 0	-8.31 / 1	0.23	2.22
EN	Putnam Global Energy Fund R	PGETX	E-	(800) 225-1581	E- / 0.0	-1.18	9.23	33.03 /92	-15.18 / 0	-8.07 / 1	0.34	1.97
EN	Putnam Global Energy Fund Y	PGEIX	E-	(800) 225-1581	E- / 0.1	-1.13	9.31	33.74 /93	-14.78 / 0	-7.62 / 1	0.76	1.47
GL	Putnam Global Equity Fd A	PEQUX	D	(800) 225-1581	D / 1.9	7.04	4.65	16.92 /38	0.85 /17	8.13 /43	1.43	1.23
GL	Putnam Global Equity Fd B	PEQBX	D	(800) 225-1581	D / 2.2	6.82	4.26	16.13 /35	0.11 /14	7.31 /37	0.90	1.98
GL	Putnam Global Equity Fd C	PUGCX	D	(800) 225-1581	D / 2.2	6.85	4.32	16.10 /35	0.10 /14	7.32 /37	0.87	1.98
GL	Putnam Global Equity Fd M	PEQMX	D	(800) 225-1581	D / 1.9	6.85	4.36	16.35 /36	0.36 /15	7.56 /39	1.07	1.73
GL	Putnam Global Equity Fd R	PGLRX	D	(800) 225-1581	D+ / 2.5	7.02	4.53	16.70 /37	0.60 /16	7.86 /41	1.15	1.48
GL	Putnam Global Equity Fd R6	PGLEX	D+	(800) 225-1581	C- / 3.0	7.14	4.92	17.44 /40	1.26 /20	---	1.86	0.84
GL	Putnam Global Equity Fd Y	PEQYX	D+	(800) 225-1581	D+ / 2.8	7.08	4.77	17.21 /39	1.11 /19	8.38 /45	1.71	0.98
FS	Putnam Global Financials Fund A	PGFFX	D-	(800) 225-1581	C- / 4.1	7.29	13.35	26.95 /79	1.63 /22	8.78 /49	1.53	2.26
FS	Putnam Global Financials Fund B	PGFOX	D-	(800) 225-1581	C / 4.7	7.10	12.92	26.01 /76	0.88 /18	7.97 /42	1.02	3.01
FS	Putnam Global Financials Fund C	PGFDX	D-	(800) 225-1581	C / 4.6	7.00	12.88	25.97 /76	0.87 /18	7.96 /42	1.13	3.01
FS	Putnam Global Financials Fund M	PGFMX	D-	(800) 225-1581	C- / 4.1	7.12	13.04	26.27 /77	1.15 /19	8.25 /44	1.19	2.76
FS	Putnam Global Financials Fund R	PGFRX	D	(800) 225-1581	C / 5.1	7.20	13.23	26.61 /78	1.39 /20	8.52 /47	1.39	2.51
FS	Putnam Global Financials Fund Y	PGFYX	D	(800) 225-1581	C / 5.5	7.29	13.40	27.17 /80	1.89 /23	9.04 /51	1.82	2.01
HL	Putnam Global Health Care Fund A	PHSTX	D-	(800) 225-1581	C- / 3.9	9.41	3.28	10.45 /13	6.61 /69	16.37 /98	0.42	1.09
HL	Putnam Global Health Care Fund B	PHSBX	D-	(800) 225-1581	C / 4.4	9.20	2.91	9.64 /11	5.81 /63	15.50 /98	0.00	1.84
HL	Putnam Global Health Care Fund C	PCHSX	D-	(800) 225-1581	C / 4.4	9.20	2.90	9.62 /11	5.81 /63	15.50 /98	0.00	1.84
HL	Putnam Global Health Care Fund M	PHLMX	D-	(800) 225-1581	C- / 3.9	9.26	3.02	9.91 /11	6.08 /65	15.79 /98	0.05	1.59
HL	Putnam Global Health Care Fund R	PHSRX	D	(800) 225-1581	C / 4.8	9.33	3.14	10.17 /12	6.34 /67	16.08 /98	0.16	1.34
HL	Putnam Global Health Care Fund Y	PHSYX	D+	(800) 225-1581	C / 5.3	9.45	3.39	10.72 /14	6.87 /71	16.65 /98	0.66	0.84
GL	Putnam Global Industrials Fund A	PGIAX	C	(800) 225-1581	C+ / 5.7	4.45	8.07	24.30 /71	6.47 /68	14.12 /94	2.02	1.97
GL	Putnam Global Industrials Fund B	PGIVX	C	(800) 225-1581	C+ / 6.3	4.30	7.67	23.34 /68	5.68 /61	13.27 /87	1.96	2.72
GL	Putnam Global Industrials Fund C	PGIEX	C	(800) 225-1581	C+ / 6.2	4.25	7.61	23.31 /68	5.66 /61	13.25 /86	2.03	2.72
GL	Putnam Global Industrials Fund M	PGIHX	C	(800) 225-1581	C+ / 5.7	4.34	7.80	23.65 /69	5.94 /64	13.56 /89	1.74	2.47
GL	Putnam Global Industrials Fund R	PGIOX	C+	(800) 225-1581	C+ / 6.6	4.40	7.94	23.96 /70	6.22 /66	13.85 /92	1.99	2.22
GL	Putnam Global Industrials Fund Y	PGILX	C+	(800) 225-1581	B- / 7.0	4.52	8.17	24.56 /72	6.74 /70	14.40 /95	2.27	1.72
EN	Putnam Global Natural Resources A	EBERX	E-	(800) 225-1581	E- / 0.1	0.68	4.72	21.51 /60	-10.02 / 1	-5.11 / 2	0.00	1.27
EN	Putnam Global Natural Resources B	PNRBX	E-	(800) 225-1581	E- / 0.1	0.43	4.30	20.55 /55	-10.70 / 1	-5.82 / 1	0.00	2.02
EN	Putnam Global Natural Resources C	PGLCX	E-	(800) 225-1581	E- / 0.1	0.42	4.28	20.54 /55	-10.71 / 1	-5.83 / 1	0.00	2.02
EN	Putnam Global Natural Resources M	PGLMX	E-	(800) 225-1581	E- / 0.1	0.53	4.42	20.85 /57	-10.48 / 1	-5.58 / 2	0.00	1.77
EN	Putnam Global Natural Resources R	PGNRX	E-	(800) 225-1581	E- / 0.1	0.57	4.58	21.14 /58	-10.25 / 1	-5.35 / 2	0.00	1.52
EN	Putnam Global Natural Resources Y	PGRYX	E-	(800) 225-1581	E- / 0.1	0.74	4.86	21.74 /61	-9.79 / 1	-4.87 / 2	0.00	1.02
GL	Putnam Global Sector A	PPGAX	D	(800) 225-1581	C- / 4.0	7.19	7.91	21.33 /59	4.08 /44	9.40 /54	1.07	2.85
GL	Putnam Global Sector B	PPGBX	D	(800) 225-1581	C / 4.5	6.88	7.41	20.41 /54	3.30 /35	8.57 /47	0.38	3.60
GL	Putnam Global Sector C	PPGCX	D	(800) 225-1581	C / 4.5	6.87	7.40	20.40 /54	3.32 /35	8.57 /47	0.55	3.60
GL	Putnam Global Sector M	PPGMX	D	(800) 225-1581	C- / 4.0	7.06	7.58	20.76 /56	3.60 /38	8.87 /50	0.11	3.35
GL	Putnam Global Sector R	PPGSX	D+	(800) 225-1581	C / 4.9	6.97	7.70	20.97 /57	3.81 /41	9.12 /52	0.85	3.10
GL	Putnam Global Sector Y	PPGYX	D+	(800) 225-1581	C / 5.4	7.20	8.02	21.66 /61	4.37 /47	9.68 /56	1.34	2.60
TC	Putnam Global Technology Fund A	PGTAX	A	(800) 225-1581	A+ / 9.8	9.64	12.75	33.58 /92	15.00 /99	13.67 /90	0.56	1.56
TC	Putnam Global Technology Fund B	PGTPX	A	(800) 225-1581	A+ / 9.9	9.42	12.34	32.57 /91	14.14 /99	12.82 /82	0.12	2.31

● Denotes fund is closed to new investors
* Denotes fund is included in Section II

Risk Rating/Pts	3 Year Standard Deviation	Beta	NAV As of 2/28/17	Total $(Mil)	Cash %	Stocks %	Bonds %	Other %	Portfolio Turnover Ratio	Last Bull Market Return	Last Bear Market Return	Manager Quality Pct	Manager Tenure (Years)	Initial Purch. $	Additional Purch. $	Front End Load	Back End Load
C /4.7	11.7	1.00	19.11	N/A	3	96	0	1	40	109.1	-17.9	22	9	500	0	0.0	0.0
C /4.7	11.7	1.00	19.29	11	3	96	0	1	40	114.7	-17.7	27	9	500	0	0.0	0.0
C+ /6.2	9.6	0.72	11.27	12	5	94	0	1	22	N/A	N/A	92	4	500	0	5.8	0.0
C+ /6.2	9.5	0.72	11.21	1	5	94	0	1	22	N/A	N/A	90	4	500	0	0.0	0.0
C+ /6.2	9.6	0.72	11.19	2	5	94	0	1	22	N/A	N/A	90	4	500	0	0.0	0.0
C+ /6.2	9.6	0.72	11.24	N/A	5	94	0	1	22	N/A	N/A	91	4	500	0	3.5	0.0
C+ /6.2	9.6	0.72	11.29	7	5	94	0	1	22	N/A	N/A	93	4	500	0	0.0	0.0
E+ /0.7	23.8	1.15	7.95	16	10	89	0	1	180	-16.1	-27.8	2	1	500	0	5.8	0.0
E+ /0.7	23.8	1.15	7.71	3	10	89	0	1	180	-19.4	-28.0	2	1	500	0	0.0	0.0
E+ /0.7	23.8	1.15	7.71	8	10	89	0	1	180	-19.4	-28.1	2	1	500	0	0.0	0.0
E+ /0.7	23.8	1.15	7.83	N/A	10	89	0	1	180	-18.3	-28.0	2	1	500	0	3.5	0.0
E+ /0.7	23.8	1.15	7.85	2	10	89	0	1	180	-17.2	-27.9	2	1	500	0	0.0	0.0
E+ /0.7	23.8	1.15	8.02	5	10	89	0	1	180	-14.9	-27.8	2	1	500	0	0.0	0.0
C+ /5.8	10.7	0.82	12.96	674	3	96	0	1	48	81.9	-23.4	81	6	500	0	5.8	0.0
C+ /5.8	10.7	0.82	11.62	10	3	96	0	1	48	74.7	-23.6	76	6	500	0	0.0	0.0
C+ /5.8	10.7	0.82	12.23	18	3	96	0	1	48	74.7	-23.6	76	6	500	0	0.0	0.0
C+ /5.8	10.7	0.82	12.41	10	3	96	0	1	48	76.8	-23.5	77	6	500	0	3.5	0.0
C+ /5.8	10.7	0.82	12.88	1	3	96	0	1	48	79.4	-23.5	79	6	0	0	0.0	0.0
C+ /5.8	10.7	0.82	13.42	12	3	96	0	1	48	N/A	N/A	83	6	0	0	0.0	0.0
C+ /5.8	10.7	0.81	13.38	30	3	96	0	1	48	84.2	-23.2	82	6	0	0	0.0	0.0
D+ /2.6	14.6	1.01	11.86	9	9	90	0	1	46	94.4	-32.1	2	9	500	0	5.8	0.0
D+ /2.4	14.5	1.02	11.51	1	9	90	0	1	46	86.9	-32.4	2	9	500	0	0.0	0.0
D+ /2.4	14.6	1.02	11.38	3	9	90	0	1	46	86.8	-32.3	2	9	500	0	0.0	0.0
D+ /2.5	14.5	1.01	11.72	N/A	9	90	0	1	46	89.4	-32.3	2	9	500	0	3.5	0.0
D+ /2.5	14.5	1.01	11.72	1	9	90	0	1	46	92.0	-32.2	2	9	500	0	0.0	0.0
D+ /2.6	14.5	1.01	11.92	4	9	90	0	1	46	97.2	-32.1	2	9	500	0	0.0	0.0
C- /3.4	14.8	1.06	54.64	1,272	1	98	0	1	16	144.4	-19.4	21	5	500	0	5.8	1.0
D /2.2	14.8	1.06	35.70	30	1	98	0	1	16	134.6	-19.6	15	5	500	0	0.0	1.0
D+ /2.8	14.8	1.06	42.95	53	1	98	0	1	16	134.6	-19.6	15	5	500	0	0.0	1.0
D+ /2.9	14.8	1.06	44.39	12	1	98	0	1	16	137.8	-19.5	17	5	500	0	3.5	1.0
C- /3.3	14.8	1.06	51.54	3	1	98	0	1	16	141.0	-19.4	19	5	500	0	0.0	1.0
C- /3.6	14.8	1.06	58.00	53	1	98	0	1	16	147.6	-19.3	23	5	500	0	0.0	1.0
C /5.1	10.7	0.63	19.32	27	12	87	0	1	216	145.6	-30.7	97	N/A	500	0	5.8	0.0
C /5.0	10.7	0.63	18.41	4	12	87	0	1	216	136.0	-30.9	96	N/A	500	0	0.0	0.0
C /5.0	10.6	0.63	18.43	6	12	87	0	1	216	136.0	-30.9	96	N/A	500	0	0.0	0.0
C /5.1	10.6	0.63	18.96	N/A	12	87	0	1	216	139.4	-30.9	97	N/A	500	0	3.5	0.0
C /5.1	10.6	0.63	19.19	N/A	12	87	0	1	216	142.5	-30.8	97	N/A	500	0	0.0	0.0
C /5.1	10.6	0.63	19.48	23	12	87	0	1	216	148.9	-30.6	97	N/A	500	0	0.0	0.0
D /1.9	20.0	0.93	16.21	126	4	95	0	1	120	-0.8	-32.6	11	5	500	0	5.8	0.0
D /1.9	20.1	0.93	14.08	4	4	95	0	1	120	-4.8	-32.9	7	5	500	0	0.0	0.0
D /1.9	20.0	0.93	14.38	6	4	95	0	1	120	-4.8	-32.8	7	5	500	0	0.0	0.0
D /1.9	20.0	0.93	15.13	2	4	95	0	1	120	-3.5	-32.8	8	5	500	0	3.5	0.0
D /1.9	20.1	0.93	15.76	7	4	95	0	1	120	-2.1	-32.7	9	5	500	0	0.0	0.0
D /1.9	20.0	0.93	16.41	14	4	95	0	1	120	0.6	-32.6	13	5	500	0	0.0	0.0
C- /3.9	11.4	0.85	10.82	5	6	93	0	1	44	91.7	-24.3	94	6	500	0	5.8	1.0
C- /3.9	11.4	0.85	10.62	1	6	93	0	1	44	84.0	-24.6	92	6	500	0	0.0	1.0
C- /3.8	11.4	0.86	10.60	1	6	93	0	1	44	84.1	-24.6	92	6	500	0	0.0	1.0
C- /3.9	11.4	0.85	10.85	N/A	6	93	0	1	44	86.5	-24.4	93	6	500	0	3.5	1.0
C- /3.9	11.5	0.86	10.82	N/A	6	93	0	1	44	89.1	-24.5	93	6	0	0	0.0	1.0
C- /3.8	11.4	0.85	10.85	2	6	93	0	1	44	94.3	-24.2	94	6	0	0	0.0	1.0
C /5.4	14.0	1.13	27.61	46	6	93	0	1	62	131.8	-15.5	89	5	500	0	5.8	0.0
C /5.4	14.0	1.13	25.98	6	6	93	0	1	62	122.5	-15.7	85	5	500	0	0.0	0.0

I. Index of Stock Mutual Funds

Fund Type	Fund Name	Ticker Symbol	Overall Investment Rating	Phone	Performance Rating/Pts	3 Mo	6 Mo	1Yr / Pct	3Yr / Pct	5Yr / Pct	Dividend Yield	Expense Ratio
TC	Putnam Global Technology Fund C	PGTDX	A	(800) 225-1581	A+ / 9.9	9.41	12.34	32.58 /91	14.12 /99	12.81 /82	0.15	2.31
TC	Putnam Global Technology Fund M	PGTMX	A	(800) 225-1581	A+ / 9.8	9.48	12.48	32.89 /91	14.40 /99	13.09 /85	0.27	2.06
TC	Putnam Global Technology Fund R	PGTRX	A	(800) 225-1581	A+ / 9.9	9.54	12.61	33.23 /92	14.70 /99	13.38 /88	0.49	1.81
TC	Putnam Global Technology Fund Y	PGTYX	A	(800) 225-1581	A+ / 9.9	9.70	12.92	33.89 /93	15.27 /99	13.93 /93	0.76	1.31
UT	Putnam Global Utilities Fund A	PUGIX	D	(800) 225-1581	D- / 1.3	10.58	1.49	7.82 / 7	2.17 /25	5.75 /27	1.65	1.22
UT	Putnam Global Utilities Fund B	PUTBX	D	(800) 225-1581	D / 1.6	10.39	1.18	7.03 / 6	1.42 /21	4.96 /21	1.00	1.97
UT	Putnam Global Utilities Fund C	PUTCX	D	(800) 225-1581	D- / 1.5	10.43	1.08	6.99 / 6	1.42 /21	4.97 /21	1.02	1.97
UT	Putnam Global Utilities Fund M	PUTMX	D	(800) 225-1581	D- / 1.3	10.38	1.17	7.21 / 6	1.66 /22	5.20 /23	1.22	1.72
UT	Putnam Global Utilities Fund R	PULRX	D	(800) 225-1581	D / 1.7	10.52	1.29	7.47 / 7	1.90 /23	5.47 /25	1.51	1.47
UT	Putnam Global Utilities Fund Y	PUTYX	D	(800) 225-1581	D / 2.0	10.65	1.62	8.09 / 8	2.43 /27	6.01 /28	1.99	0.97
GR	Putnam Growth Opportunities A	POGAX	C+	(800) 225-1581	B / 7.6	8.96	9.86	24.81 /73	8.54 /83	13.24 /86	0.01	1.02
GR	Putnam Growth Opportunities B	POGBX	C+	(800) 225-1581	B / 8.0	8.72	9.46	23.87 /69	7.71 /77	12.39 /78	0.00	1.77
GR	Putnam Growth Opportunities C	POGCX	C+	(800) 225-1581	B / 8.0	8.77	9.44	23.89 /69	7.72 /77	12.39 /78	0.00	1.77
GR	Putnam Growth Opportunities M	PGOMX	C+	(800) 225-1581	B / 7.6	8.84	9.59	24.22 /71	8.01 /79	12.68 /81	0.00	1.52
GR	Putnam Growth Opportunities R	PGORX	B-	(800) 225-1581	B+ / 8.4	8.90	9.70	24.50 /72	8.25 /81	12.95 /83	0.00	1.27
GR	Putnam Growth Opportunities R5	PGODX	B	(800) 225-1581	B+ / 8.8	9.04	10.04	25.20 /74	8.86 /86	--	0.00	0.67
GR	Putnam Growth Opportunities R6	PGOEX	B	(800) 225-1581	B+ / 8.9	9.09	10.13	25.34 /74	8.98 /87	--	0.08	0.57
GR	Putnam Growth Opportunities Y	PGOYX	B	(800) 225-1581	B+ / 8.8	9.01	9.97	25.12 /74	8.80 /85	13.52 /89	0.02	0.77
FO	Putnam International Capital Opp A	PNVAX	E+	(800) 225-1581	E / 0.3	7.58	3.74	12.61 /20	-3.53 / 4	3.31 /12	2.24	1.26
FO	Putnam International Capital Opp B	PVNBX	D-	(800) 225-1581	E / 0.4	7.36	3.36	11.79 /17	-4.25 / 3	2.54 / 9	1.48	2.01
FO	Putnam International Capital Opp C	PUVCX	D-	(800) 225-1581	E / 0.4	7.37	3.38	11.78 /17	-4.24 / 3	2.54 / 9	1.54	2.01
FO	Putnam International Capital Opp M	PIVMX	D-	(800) 225-1581	E / 0.3	7.41	3.49	12.03 /18	-4.01 / 3	2.79 /10	1.80	1.76
FO	Putnam International Capital Opp R	PICRX	D-	(800) 225-1581	E / 0.4	7.49	3.63	12.33 /19	-3.77 / 3	3.05 /11	2.12	1.51
FO	Putnam International Capital Opp Y	PIVYX	D-	(800) 225-1581	E / 0.5	7.60	3.85	12.88 /21	-3.29 / 4	3.56 /13	2.65	1.01
FO	Putnam International Equity A	POVSX	E+	(800) 225-1581	E / 0.4	6.88	2.44	12.05 /18	-2.48 / 6	5.18 /23	2.81	1.32
FO	Putnam International Equity B	POVBX	E+	(800) 225-1581	E / 0.5	6.68	2.02	11.19 /15	-3.21 / 4	4.39 /17	2.23	2.07
FO	Putnam International Equity C	PIGCX	E+	(800) 225-1581	E / 0.5	6.68	2.04	11.19 /15	-3.21 / 4	4.39 /17	2.28	2.07
FO	Putnam International Equity M	POVMX	E+	(800) 225-1581	E / 0.4	6.73	2.17	11.48 /16	-2.97 / 5	4.65 /19	2.42	1.82
FO	Putnam International Equity R	PIERX	E+	(800) 225-1581	E+ / 0.6	6.78	2.27	11.76 /17	-2.73 / 5	4.90 /21	2.82	1.57
FO	Putnam International Equity R5	POVDX	D-	(800) 225-1581	E+ / 0.7	7.00	2.62	12.43 /20	-2.18 / 6	--	3.27	0.96
FO	Putnam International Equity R6	POVEX	D-	(800) 225-1581	E+ / 0.7	7.01	2.64	12.54 /20	-2.08 / 6	--	3.38	0.86
FO	Putnam International Equity Y	POVYX	D-	(800) 225-1581	E+ / 0.7	6.91	2.52	12.29 /19	-2.24 / 6	5.44 /24	3.23	1.07
FO	Putnam International Growth A	PINOX	E+	(800) 225-1581	E- / 0.2	5.84	-0.69	9.10 /10	-3.34 / 4	3.73 /14	1.69	1.54
FO	Putnam International Growth B	PINWX	E+	(800) 225-1581	E / 0.3	5.64	-1.02	8.26 / 8	-4.05 / 3	2.96 /11	1.15	2.29
FO	Putnam International Growth C	PIOCX	E+	(800) 225-1581	E / 0.3	5.69	-1.01	8.24 / 8	-4.06 / 3	2.95 /11	1.16	2.29
FO	Putnam International Growth M	PINMX	E+	(800) 225-1581	E- / 0.2	5.71	-0.90	8.58 / 9	-3.82 / 3	3.21 /12	1.37	2.04
FO	Putnam International Growth R	PNPRX	E+	(800) 225-1581	E / 0.3	5.74	-0.80	8.81 / 9	-3.59 / 4	3.47 /13	1.63	1.79
FO	Putnam International Growth Y	PINYX	D-	(800) 225-1581	E / 0.4	5.95	-0.52	9.38 /10	-3.10 / 4	3.99 /15	2.04	1.29
FO	Putnam International Value A	PNGAX	D-	(800) 225-1581	E / 0.4	6.57	4.77	14.93 /30	-2.74 / 5	4.09 /16	2.03	1.36
FO	Putnam International Value B	PGNBX	D-	(800) 225-1581	E / 0.5	6.37	4.45	14.15 /26	-3.48 / 4	3.30 /12	1.27	2.11
FO	Putnam International Value C	PIGRX	D-	(800) 225-1581	E / 0.5	6.41	4.49	14.23 /27	-3.46 / 4	3.32 /12	1.38	2.11
FO	Putnam International Value M	PIGMX	D-	(800) 225-1581	E / 0.4	6.46	4.56	14.44 /27	-3.23 / 4	3.57 /13	1.61	1.86
FO	Putnam International Value R	PIIRX	D-	(800) 225-1581	E+ / 0.6	6.47	4.66	14.66 /28	-3.00 / 4	3.81 /14	2.12	1.61
FO	Putnam International Value R6	PIGWX	D	(800) 225-1581	E+ / 0.8	6.70	5.12	15.50 /32	-2.32 / 6	--	2.58	0.91
FO	Putnam International Value Y	PNGYX	D-	(800) 225-1581	E+ / 0.8	6.55	4.97	15.26 /31	-2.50 / 5	4.35 /17	2.43	1.11
GR	Putnam Investors Fund A	PINVX	A	(800) 225-1581	B / 8.2	7.56	13.18	27.15 /80	8.94 /86	13.34 /87	0.91	1.05
GR	Putnam Investors Fund B	PNVBX	A	(800) 225-1581	B+ / 8.6	7.37	12.72	26.19 /77	8.11 /80	12.50 /79	0.40	1.80
GR	Putnam Investors Fund C	PCINX	A	(800) 225-1581	B+ / 8.6	7.38	12.72	26.20 /77	8.11 /80	12.49 /79	0.38	1.80
GR	Putnam Investors Fund M	PNVMX	A	(800) 225-1581	B / 8.2	7.43	12.88	26.52 /78	8.38 /82	12.77 /82	0.53	1.55
GR	Putnam Investors Fund R	PIVRX	A+	(800) 225-1581	A- / 9.0	7.50	13.06	26.87 /79	8.66 /84	13.06 /84	0.19	1.30
GR	Putnam Investors Fund R6	PIVEX	A+	(800) 225-1581	A / 9.4	7.68	13.39	27.71 /81	9.37 /89	--	1.31	0.65
GR	Putnam Investors Fund Y	PNVYX	A+	(800) 225-1581	A / 9.3	7.65	13.33	27.53 /81	9.22 /88	13.63 /90	1.18	0.80

● Denotes fund is closed to new investors
* Denotes fund is included in Section II

www.thestreetratings.com

RISK	3 Year		NET ASSETS		ASSET					BULL / BEAR		FUND MANAGER		MINIMUMS		LOADS	
Risk Rating/Pts	Standard Deviation	Beta	NAV As of 2/28/17	Total $(Mil)	Cash %	Stocks %	Bonds %	Other %	Portfolio Turnover Ratio	Last Bull Market Return	Last Bear Market Return	Manager Quality Pct	Manager Tenure (Years)	Initial Purch. $	Additional Purch. $	Front End Load	Back End Load
C /5.4	14.0	1.13	25.96	9	6	93	0	1	62	122.4	-15.7	85	5	500	0	0.0	0.0
C /5.4	14.0	1.13	26.53	1	6	93	0	1	62	125.4	-15.6	87	5	500	0	3.5	0.0
C /5.4	14.0	1.13	27.09	N/A	6	93	0	1	62	128.5	-15.5	88	5	500	0	0.0	0.0
C /5.5	14.0	1.13	28.13	34	6	93	0	1	62	134.8	-15.4	90	5	500	0	0.0	0.0
C+ /6.2	11.9	0.71	12.14	151	10	89	0	1	9	37.1	-10.6	4	5	500	0	5.8	0.0
C+ /6.2	11.9	0.71	12.10	4	10	89	0	1	9	31.7	-10.9	3	5	500	0	0.0	0.0
C+ /6.2	11.9	0.71	12.04	5	10	89	0	1	9	31.7	-10.8	3	5	500	0	0.0	0.0
C+ /6.2	11.9	0.70	12.12	1	10	89	0	1	9	33.4	-10.8	4	5	500	0	3.5	0.0
C+ /6.2	11.9	0.70	12.13	N/A	10	89	0	1	9	35.2	-10.7	4	5	500	0	0.0	0.0
C+ /6.2	11.9	0.71	12.14	5	10	89	0	1	9	39.1	-10.6	5	5	500	0	0.0	0.0
C- /4.2	12.0	1.10	26.42	3,337	0	99	0	1	65	135.5	-20.3	36	9	500	0	5.8	0.0
C- /3.9	12.1	1.10	22.68	80	0	99	0	1	65	126.2	-20.6	27	9	500	0	0.0	0.0
C- /4.0	12.1	1.10	23.08	142	0	99	0	1	65	126.1	-20.6	27	9	500	0	0.0	0.0
C- /4.1	12.1	1.10	24.00	27	0	99	0	1	65	129.3	-20.5	30	9	500	0	3.5	0.0
C- /4.1	12.1	1.10	25.56	11	0	99	0	1	65	132.4	-20.4	32	9	500	0	0.0	0.0
C /4.3	12.1	1.10	27.62	11	0	99	0	1	65	N/A	N/A	40	9	0	0	0.0	0.0
C /4.3	12.0	1.10	27.65	69	0	99	0	1	65	N/A	N/A	41	9	0	0	0.0	0.0
C /4.3	12.0	1.10	27.52	310	0	99	0	1	65	138.6	-20.2	39	9	0	0	0.0	0.0
C+ /5.9	12.3	0.89	34.29	322	2	97	0	1	92	39.3	-27.8	29	1	500	0	5.8	0.0
C+ /5.9	12.3	0.89	34.39	6	2	97	0	1	92	33.7	-28.0	22	1	500	0	0.0	0.0
C+ /5.9	12.3	0.89	34.22	23	2	97	0	1	92	33.7	-28.0	22	1	500	0	0.0	0.0
C+ /5.9	12.3	0.89	34.20	5	2	97	0	1	92	35.5	-27.9	24	1	500	0	3.5	0.0
C+ /5.9	12.3	0.89	33.88	18	2	97	0	1	92	37.4	-27.9	27	1	500	0	0.0	1.0
C+ /5.8	12.3	0.89	34.24	43	2	97	0	1	92	41.1	-27.7	32	1	500	0	0.0	0.0
C /5.5	11.7	0.93	21.54	617	1	98	0	1	77	54.1	-26.2	43	6	500	0	5.8	0.0
C+ /5.6	11.7	0.93	20.56	9	1	98	0	1	77	48.0	-26.4	33	6	500	0	0.0	0.0
C /5.5	11.6	0.92	20.82	44	1	98	0	1	77	47.9	-26.4	33	6	500	0	0.0	0.0
C /5.5	11.7	0.92	20.98	10	1	98	0	1	77	50.0	-26.3	36	6	500	0	3.5	0.0
C /5.5	11.7	0.92	21.17	3	1	98	0	1	77	51.9	-26.2	40	6	0	0	0.0	0.0
C /5.5	11.7	0.93	21.84	10	1	98	0	1	77	N/A	N/A	48	6	0	0	0.0	0.0
C /5.5	11.7	0.92	21.86	72	1	98	0	1	77	N/A	N/A	49	6	0	0	0.0	0.0
C /5.5	11.7	0.92	21.78	106	1	98	0	1	77	56.1	-26.1	47	6	0	0	0.0	0.0
C+ /5.8	11.4	0.88	17.70	221	0	99	0	1	146	43.9	-27.8	31	9	500	0	5.8	0.0
C+ /5.7	11.4	0.88	15.97	4	0	99	0	1	146	38.3	-28.1	24	9	500	0	0.0	0.0
C+ /5.7	11.4	0.88	16.35	7	0	99	0	1	146	38.2	-28.1	24	9	500	0	0.0	0.0
C+ /5.7	11.4	0.88	16.56	5	0	99	0	1	146	40.1	-28.0	26	9	500	0	3.5	0.0
C+ /5.7	11.4	0.88	17.34	1	0	99	0	1	146	42.0	-27.9	29	9	500	0	0.0	0.0
C+ /5.8	11.4	0.88	17.86	19	0	99	0	1	146	46.0	-27.8	35	9	500	0	0.0	0.0
C+ /5.8	11.7	0.93	10.32	127	1	98	0	1	20	44.0	-24.8	40	12	500	0	5.8	0.0
C+ /5.9	11.8	0.93	10.32	2	1	98	0	1	20	38.3	-25.1	30	12	500	0	0.0	0.0
C+ /5.9	11.7	0.93	10.27	6	1	98	0	1	20	38.4	-25.1	30	12	500	0	0.0	0.0
C+ /5.9	11.8	0.93	10.36	2	1	98	0	1	20	40.2	-25.0	33	12	500	0	3.5	0.0
C+ /5.9	11.7	0.93	10.21	2	1	98	0	1	20	42.0	-24.9	36	12	500	0	0.0	0.0
C+ /6.9	11.8	0.93	10.36	4	1	98	0	1	20	N/A	N/A	46	12	0	0	0.0	0.0
C+ /5.8	11.7	0.92	10.32	6	1	98	0	1	20	45.9	-24.7	43	12	500	0	0.0	0.0
C+ /6.8	11.1	1.06	24.67	1,519	3	96	0	1	33	132.5	-18.9	47	9	500	0	5.8	0.0
C+ /6.8	11.1	1.06	22.09	34	3	96	0	1	33	123.1	-19.0	36	9	500	0	0.0	0.0
C+ /6.8	11.2	1.06	23.24	61	3	96	0	1	33	123.2	-19.1	36	9	500	0	0.0	0.0
C+ /6.8	11.1	1.06	23.21	19	3	96	0	1	33	126.3	-19.0	39	9	500	0	3.5	0.0
C+ /6.9	11.2	1.06	24.45	1	3	96	0	1	33	129.5	-19.0	43	9	500	0	0.0	0.0
C+ /6.8	11.2	1.06	25.13	20	3	96	0	1	33	N/A	N/A	52	9	0	0	0.0	0.0
C+ /6.8	11.2	1.06	25.03	250	3	96	0	1	33	135.7	-18.7	50	9	0	0	0.0	0.0

Fund Type	Fund Name	Ticker Symbol	Overall Investment Rating	Phone	Performance Rating/Pts	3 Mo	6 Mo	1Yr / Pct	3Yr / Pct	5Yr / Pct	Dividend Yield	Expense Ratio
GI	Putnam Low Volatility Equity A	PLVEX	C-	(800) 225-1581	D+ / 2.5	5.10	4.91	10.41 /13	4.37 /47	--	1.48	1.32
GI	Putnam Low Volatility Equity B	PLVFX	C-	(800) 225-1581	C- / 3.0	4.88	4.58	9.63 /11	3.58 /38	--	0.77	2.07
GI	Putnam Low Volatility Equity C	PLVGX	C-	(800) 225-1581	C- / 3.0	4.93	4.64	9.59 /11	3.62 /38	--	0.73	2.07
GI	Putnam Low Volatility Equity M	PLVHX	C-	(800) 225-1581	D+ / 2.6	5.02	4.73	9.84 /11	3.86 /41	--	1.07	1.82
GI	Putnam Low Volatility Equity Y	PLVKX	C	(800) 225-1581	C- / 3.8	5.23	5.14	10.76 /14	4.65 /50	--	1.78	1.07
GR	Putnam Multi-Cap Core Fund A	PMYAX	A	(800) 225-1581	B+ / 8.6	8.00	14.23	29.52 /85	8.90 /86	14.53 /96	0.84	1.04
GR	Putnam Multi-Cap Core Fund B	PMYBX	A+	(800) 225-1581	A- / 9.0	7.78	13.78	28.52 /83	8.09 /80	13.68 /91	0.33	1.79
GR	Putnam Multi-Cap Core Fund C	PMYCX	A+	(800) 225-1581	A- / 9.0	7.78	13.80	28.50 /83	8.07 /79	13.68 /91	0.22	1.79
GR	Putnam Multi-Cap Core Fund M	PMYMX	A	(800) 225-1581	B+ / 8.6	7.87	13.92	28.90 /84	8.35 /82	13.97 /93	0.38	1.54
GR	Putnam Multi-Cap Core Fund R	PMYZX	A+	(800) 225-1581	A / 9.3	7.97	14.09	29.26 /85	8.62 /84	14.26 /95	0.69	1.29
GR	Putnam Multi-Cap Core Fund Y	PMYYX	A+	(800) 225-1581	A / 9.5	8.03	14.35	29.83 /86	9.17 /88	14.82 /96	1.14	0.79
GR	Putnam Multi-Cap Growth Fund A	PNOPX	C	(800) 225-1581	B- / 7.5	8.65	10.54	26.21 /77	8.04 /79	12.87 /83	0.00	1.05
GR	Putnam Multi-Cap Growth Fund B	PNOBX	C	(800) 225-1581	B / 7.9	8.43	10.12	25.25 /74	7.23 /74	12.02 /74	0.00	1.80
GR	Putnam Multi-Cap Growth Fund C	PNOCX	C	(800) 225-1581	B / 7.9	8.44	10.12	25.24 /74	7.23 /74	12.02 /74	0.00	1.80
GR	Putnam Multi-Cap Growth Fund M	PNOMX	C	(800) 225-1581	B- / 7.5	8.52	10.27	25.57 /75	7.50 /75	12.30 /77	0.00	1.55
GR	Putnam Multi-Cap Growth Fund R	PNORX	C+	(800) 225-1581	B+ / 8.3	8.57	10.39	25.88 /76	7.76 /77	12.58 /80	0.00	1.30
GR	Putnam Multi-Cap Growth Fund Y	PNOYX	B-	(800) 225-1581	B+ / 8.7	8.72	10.67	26.53 /78	8.31 /81	13.15 /85	0.00	0.80
MC	Putnam Multi-Cap Value Fund A	PMVAX	C+	(800) 225-1581	C+ / 6.1	5.77	9.87	23.43 /68	6.71 /70	13.21 /86	0.84	1.08
MC	Putnam Multi-Cap Value Fund B	PMVBX	C+	(800) 225-1581	C+ / 6.6	5.55	9.47	22.50 /65	5.91 /63	12.36 /78	0.27	1.83
MC	Putnam Multi-Cap Value Fund C	PMPCX	C+	(800) 225-1581	C+ / 6.6	5.53	9.41	22.43 /64	5.90 /63	12.36 /78	0.33	1.83
MC	Putnam Multi-Cap Value Fund M	PMCVX	C+	(800) 225-1581	C+ / 6.1	5.61	9.60	22.73 /66	6.17 /66	12.64 /80	0.51	1.58
MC	Putnam Multi-Cap Value Fund R	PMVRX	C+	(800) 225-1581	B- / 7.0	5.71	9.79	23.16 /67	6.45 /68	12.92 /83	0.68	1.33
MC	Putnam Multi-Cap Value Fund Y	PMVYX	B-	(800) 225-1581	B- / 7.3	5.85	10.00	23.69 /69	6.98 /72	13.49 /89	1.12	0.83
GR	Putnam Research Fund A	PNRAX	B+	(800) 225-1581	B / 7.7	8.14	10.50	25.06 /73	8.85 /86	13.38 /88	0.94	1.14
GR	Putnam Research Fund B	PRFBX	A-	(800) 225-1581	B / 8.2	7.95	10.12	24.11 /70	8.04 /79	12.52 /79	0.36	1.89
GR	Putnam Research Fund C	PRACX	A-	(800) 225-1581	B / 8.1	7.92	10.05	24.08 /70	8.02 /79	12.53 /79	0.41	1.89
GR	Putnam Research Fund M	PRFMX	B+	(800) 225-1581	B / 7.7	8.02	10.23	24.45 /72	8.30 /81	12.81 /82	0.54	1.64
GR	Putnam Research Fund R	PRSRX	A-	(800) 225-1581	B+ / 8.6	8.09	10.39	24.74 /72	8.58 /84	13.10 /85	0.71	1.39
GR	Putnam Research Fund Y	PURYX	A	(800) 225-1581	B+ / 8.9	8.22	10.64	25.36 /74	9.11 /88	13.66 /90	1.21	0.89
AA	Putnam Ret Income Fd Lifestyle 1 A	PRMAX	C-	(800) 225-1581	D- / 1.4	2.61	2.63	6.89 / 6	2.37 /27	3.46 /13	1.19	1.25
AA	Putnam Ret Income Fd Lifestyle 1 B	PRMLX	C-	(800) 225-1581	D- / 1.5	2.43	2.25	6.05 / 5	1.59 /21	2.68 /10	0.84	2.00
AA	Putnam Ret Income Fd Lifestyle 1 C	PRMCX	C-	(800) 225-1581	D- / 1.5	2.42	2.23	6.09 / 5	1.61 /22	2.69 /10	0.84	2.00
AA	Putnam Ret Income Fd Lifestyle 1 M	PRMMX	C-	(800) 225-1581	D- / 1.4	2.55	2.44	6.54 / 5	2.10 /25	3.19 /12	0.96	1.50
AA	Putnam Ret Income Fd Lifestyle 1 R	PRMKX	C-	(800) 225-1581	D / 1.7	2.55	2.50	6.63 / 5	2.11 /25	3.20 /12	1.00	1.50
AA	Putnam Ret Income Fd Lifestyle 1 Y	PRMYX	C	(800) 225-1581	D / 1.9	2.65	2.73	7.11 / 6	2.61 /28	3.72 /14	1.46	1.00
AA	Putnam Retirement Ready 2020 A	PRRMX	C-	(800) 225-1581	D / 1.7	3.16	3.33	8.73 / 9	3.26 /34	5.20 /23	0.96	1.20
AA	Putnam Retirement Ready 2020 B		C	(800) 225-1581	D / 2.0	2.94	2.88	7.91 / 7	2.46 /27	4.40 /18	0.29	1.95
AA	Putnam Retirement Ready 2020 C		C	(800) 225-1581	D / 2.0	2.95	2.95	7.91 / 7	2.49 /27	4.41 /18	0.35	1.95
AA	Putnam Retirement Ready 2020 M		C-	(800) 225-1581	D / 1.7	3.03	3.03	8.20 / 8	2.73 /29	4.66 /19	0.56	1.70
AA	Putnam Retirement Ready 2020 R		C	(800) 225-1581	D+ / 2.3	3.08	3.14	8.42 / 8	2.99 /32	4.92 /21	0.76	1.45
AA	Putnam Retirement Ready 2020 Y	PRRNX	C	(800) 225-1581	D+ / 2.6	3.20	3.40	8.96 / 9	3.51 /37	5.45 /24	1.00	0.95
AA	Putnam Retirement Ready 2025 A	PRROX	C	(800) 225-1581	D+ / 2.3	3.79	4.23	11.03 /15	4.05 /44	6.51 /32	1.32	1.24
AA	Putnam Retirement Ready 2025 B		C	(800) 225-1581	D+ / 2.7	3.68	3.89	10.23 /12	3.28 /35	5.72 /27	0.74	1.99
AA	Putnam Retirement Ready 2025 C		C	(800) 225-1581	D+ / 2.7	3.65	3.91	10.27 /12	3.29 /35	5.72 /27	0.85	1.99
AA	Putnam Retirement Ready 2025 M		C	(800) 225-1581	D+ / 2.3	3.70	4.02	10.50 /13	3.54 /38	5.97 /28	1.11	1.74
AA	Putnam Retirement Ready 2025 R		C+	(800) 225-1581	C- / 3.1	3.79	4.16	10.77 /14	3.80 /40	6.25 /30	1.26	1.49
AA	Putnam Retirement Ready 2025 Y	PRRPX	C+	(800) 225-1581	C- / 3.4	3.91	4.40	11.33 /16	4.32 /47	6.78 /33	1.57	0.99
AA	Putnam Retirement Ready 2030 A	PRRQX	C	(800) 225-1581	C- / 3.1	4.61	5.37	13.74 /24	4.75 /51	7.69 /40	0.64	1.23
AA	Putnam Retirement Ready 2030 B		C+	(800) 225-1581	C- / 3.5	4.41	4.94	12.88 /21	3.96 /43	6.88 /34	0.00	1.98
AA	Putnam Retirement Ready 2030 C		C+	(800) 225-1581	C- / 3.5	4.40	4.94	12.89 /21	3.96 /43	6.89 /34	0.03	1.98
AA	Putnam Retirement Ready 2030 M		C	(800) 225-1581	C- / 3.1	4.51	5.09	13.16 /22	4.23 /46	7.15 /36	0.00	1.73
AA	Putnam Retirement Ready 2030 R		C+	(800) 225-1581	C- / 3.9	4.55	5.19	13.45 /23	4.48 /49	7.42 /38	0.42	1.48

● Denotes fund is closed to new investors
* Denotes fund is included in Section II

Risk Rating/Pts	Standard Deviation	Beta	NAV As of 2/28/17	Total $(Mil)	Cash %	Stocks %	Bonds %	Other %	Portfolio Turnover Ratio	Last Bull Market Return	Last Bear Market Return	Manager Quality Pct	Manager Tenure (Years)	Initial Purch. $	Additional Purch. $	Front End Load	Back End Load
B- /7.1	5.9	0.52	11.18	7	2	97	0	1	135	N/A	N/A	62	4	500	0	5.8	0.0
B- /7.1	5.9	0.52	11.05	1	2	97	0	1	135	N/A	N/A	52	4	500	0	0.0	0.0
B- /7.1	6.0	0.52	11.04	1	2	97	0	1	135	N/A	N/A	53	4	500	0	0.0	0.0
B- /7.1	6.0	0.52	11.12	N/A	2	97	0	1	135	N/A	N/A	55	4	500	0	3.5	0.0
B- /7.0	6.0	0.52	11.19	21	2	97	0	1	135	N/A	N/A	65	4	500	0	0.0	0.0
C+ /6.7	11.4	1.06	20.03	155	5	94	0	1	72	148.9	-20.1	46	7	500	0	5.8	0.0
C+ /6.7	11.4	1.06	19.57	14	5	94	0	1	72	139.0	-20.3	36	7	500	0	0.0	0.0
C+ /6.7	11.4	1.06	19.54	112	5	94	0	1	72	138.8	-20.3	35	7	500	0	0.0	0.0
C+ /6.8	11.5	1.07	19.82	1	5	94	0	1	72	142.2	-20.3	38	7	500	0	3.5	0.0
C+ /6.7	11.4	1.06	19.98	2	5	94	0	1	72	145.7	-20.2	42	7	500	0	0.0	0.0
C+ /6.7	11.4	1.06	20.09	219	5	94	0	1	72	152.3	-20.1	49	7	500	0	0.0	0.0
C- /3.7	12.3	1.12	78.79	3,545	0	99	0	1	58	133.2	-22.2	28	7	500	0	5.8	0.0
C- /3.2	12.3	1.12	62.89	62	0	99	0	1	58	123.9	-22.4	21	7	500	0	0.0	0.0
C- /3.4	12.3	1.12	67.98	66	0	99	0	1	58	123.9	-22.4	21	7	500	0	0.0	0.0
C- /3.4	12.3	1.12	69.05	50	0	99	0	1	58	127.0	-22.3	23	7	500	0	3.5	0.0
C- /3.7	12.3	1.12	76.50	7	0	99	0	1	58	130.0	-22.2	26	7	500	0	0.0	0.0
C- /3.8	12.3	1.12	83.90	174	0	99	0	1	58	136.4	-22.1	31	7	0	0	0.0	0.0
C /5.3	10.9	0.86	19.67	350	3	96	0	1	76	132.2	-22.2	57	13	500	0	5.8	0.0
C /5.3	10.9	0.86	18.23	7	3	96	0	1	76	122.7	-22.5	46	13	500	0	0.0	0.0
C /5.2	10.9	0.86	18.11	30	3	96	0	1	76	122.8	-22.5	46	13	500	0	0.0	0.0
C /5.3	10.9	0.86	18.79	5	3	96	0	1	76	126.0	-22.5	50	13	500	0	3.5	0.0
C /5.3	10.9	0.86	19.23	13	3	96	0	1	76	129.2	-22.4	53	13	500	0	0.0	0.0
C /5.3	10.9	0.86	19.69	67	3	96	0	1	76	135.3	-22.2	60	13	500	0	0.0	0.0
C+ /6.4	10.9	1.04	29.03	236	3	96	0	1	75	131.7	-19.0	47	6	500	0	5.8	0.0
C+ /6.5	10.9	1.04	27.25	9	3	96	0	1	75	122.5	-19.3	37	6	500	0	0.0	0.0
C+ /6.5	10.9	1.05	27.23	17	3	96	0	1	75	122.4	-19.3	37	6	500	0	0.0	0.0
C+ /6.4	10.9	1.04	27.91	4	3	96	0	1	75	125.6	-19.2	40	6	500	0	3.5	0.0
C+ /6.4	10.9	1.04	28.76	2	3	96	0	1	75	128.7	-19.1	44	6	500	0	0.0	0.0
C+ /6.4	10.9	1.04	29.22	10	3	96	0	1	75	135.0	-19.0	51	6	500	0	0.0	0.0
B /8.7	2.7	0.39	17.29	71	16	21	61	2	33	24.8	-5.8	68	N/A	500	0	4.0	0.0
B /8.7	2.7	0.38	16.96	1	16	21	61	2	33	19.8	-6.1	59	N/A	500	0	0.0	0.0
B /8.7	2.7	0.39	17.01	2	16	21	61	2	33	19.8	-6.1	59	N/A	500	0	0.0	0.0
B /8.7	2.7	0.38	17.33	1	16	21	61	2	33	23.0	-5.9	65	N/A	500	0	3.3	0.0
B /8.7	2.7	0.39	17.28	1	16	21	61	2	33	23.1	-5.8	64	N/A	500	0	0.0	0.0
B /8.7	2.7	0.39	17.35	4	16	21	61	2	33	26.5	-5.7	71	N/A	500	0	0.0	0.0
B /8.6	3.9	0.59	18.96	172	15	29	54	2	47	41.6	-10.1	60	N/A	500	0	5.8	0.0
B- /8.7	3.9	0.59	18.29	1	15	29	54	2	47	35.9	-10.4	50	N/A	500	0	0.0	0.0
B- /8.7	3.9	0.59	18.28	2	15	29	54	2	47	35.9	-10.4	50	N/A	500	0	0.0	0.0
B- /8.7	3.9	0.59	18.64	N/A	15	29	54	2	47	37.8	-10.3	53	N/A	500	0	3.5	0.0
B- /8.7	3.9	0.59	18.29	2	15	29	54	2	47	39.7	-10.2	57	N/A	500	0	0.0	0.0
B /8.7	3.9	0.59	21.28	1	15	29	54	2	47	43.5	-10.0	63	N/A	500	0	0.0	0.0
B /8.4	5.0	0.78	21.65	74	13	38	48	1	42	54.7	-13.1	52	N/A	500	0	5.8	0.0
B /8.5	5.0	0.78	20.25	1	13	38	48	1	42	48.6	-13.3	42	N/A	500	0	0.0	0.0
B /8.4	5.0	0.78	20.19	2	13	38	48	1	42	48.6	-13.3	42	N/A	500	0	0.0	0.0
B /8.4	5.0	0.78	20.51	N/A	13	38	48	1	42	50.6	-13.2	46	N/A	500	0	3.5	0.0
B /8.5	5.1	0.78	20.33	2	13	38	48	1	42	52.7	-13.2	49	N/A	500	0	0.0	0.0
B /8.4	5.0	0.78	21.77	9	13	38	48	1	42	56.8	-12.9	57	N/A	500	0	0.0	0.0
B /8.1	6.3	0.99	21.63	157	13	46	39	2	47	67.7	-16.0	41	13	500	0	5.8	0.0
B /8.1	6.3	0.98	20.59	1	13	46	39	2	47	61.0	-16.2	32	13	500	0	0.0	0.0
B /8.1	6.3	0.98	20.55	2	13	46	39	2	47	61.0	-16.2	32	13	500	0	0.0	0.0
B /8.1	6.3	0.98	21.07	N/A	13	46	39	2	47	63.2	-16.1	35	13	500	0	3.5	0.0
B /8.1	6.3	0.98	20.57	2	13	46	39	2	47	65.4	-16.0	38	13	500	0	0.0	0.0

						PERFORMANCE					Incl. in Returns	
99 Pct = Best						Perfor-	Total Return % through 2/28/17			Annualized		
0 Pct = Worst			Overall			mance					Dividend	Expense
Fund Type	Fund Name	Ticker Symbol	Investment Rating	Phone		Rating/Pts	3 Mo	6 Mo	1Yr / Pct	3Yr / Pct	5Yr / Pct	Yield	Ratio

Fund Type	Fund Name	Ticker Symbol	Overall Investment Rating	Phone	Perform. Rating/Pts	3 Mo	6 Mo	1Yr / Pct	3Yr / Pct	5Yr / Pct	Dividend Yield	Expense Ratio
AA	Putnam Retirement Ready 2030 Y	PRRTX	B-	(800) 225-1581	C / 4.4	4.70	5.50	14.03 /26	5.02 /54	7.95 /42	0.70	0.98
AA	Putnam Retirement Ready 2035 A	PRRWX	C+	(800) 225-1581	C- / 3.9	5.37	6.38	16.36 /36	5.35 /58	8.70 /48	0.66	1.31
AA	Putnam Retirement Ready 2035 B		C+	(800) 225-1581	C / 4.4	5.18	6.01	15.48 /32	4.56 /49	7.90 /41	0.00	2.06
AA	Putnam Retirement Ready 2035 C		C+	(800) 225-1581	C / 4.4	5.18	6.01	15.52 /32	4.56 /49	7.90 /41	0.03	2.06
AA	Putnam Retirement Ready 2035 M		C+	(800) 225-1581	C- / 3.9	5.25	6.14	15.78 /33	4.83 /52	8.17 /43	0.23	1.81
AA	Putnam Retirement Ready 2035 R		B-	(800) 225-1581	C / 4.9	5.31	6.25	16.07 /35	5.08 /55	8.44 /46	0.49	1.56
AA	Putnam Retirement Ready 2035 Y	PRRYX	B	(800) 225-1581	C / 5.3	5.46	6.50	16.62 /37	5.61 /61	8.97 /50	0.72	1.06
AA	Putnam Retirement Ready 2040 A	PRRZX	C+	(800) 225-1581	C / 4.6	5.95	7.18	18.20 /44	5.77 /62	9.46 /54	0.28	1.31
AA	Putnam Retirement Ready 2040 B		B-	(800) 225-1581	C / 5.1	5.73	6.79	17.27 /40	4.97 /54	8.63 /47	0.00	2.06
AA	Putnam Retirement Ready 2040 C		B-	(800) 225-1581	C / 5.1	5.75	6.83	17.34 /40	4.98 /54	8.63 /47	0.00	2.06
AA	Putnam Retirement Ready 2040 M		C+	(800) 225-1581	C / 4.6	5.83	6.93	17.62 /41	5.24 /57	8.92 /50	0.00	1.81
AA	Putnam Retirement Ready 2040 R		B-	(800) 225-1581	C+ / 5.6	5.91	7.10	17.94 /43	5.50 /60	9.18 /52	0.04	1.56
AA	Putnam Retirement Ready 2040 Y	PRZZX	B-	(800) 225-1581	C+ / 6.0	6.01	7.33	18.47 /45	6.03 /64	9.73 /56	0.37	1.06
AA	Putnam Retirement Ready 2045 A	PRVLX	C+	(800) 225-1581	C / 5.0	6.31	7.82	19.31 /49	5.99 /64	9.83 /57	0.49	1.43
AA	Putnam Retirement Ready 2045 B		B-	(800) 225-1581	C / 5.5	6.14	7.38	18.37 /45	5.20 /56	9.00 /51	0.00	2.18
AA	Putnam Retirement Ready 2045 C		B-	(800) 225-1581	C / 5.5	6.14	7.37	18.35 /44	5.18 /56	9.00 /51	0.00	2.18
AA	Putnam Retirement Ready 2045 M		C+	(800) 225-1581	C / 5.0	6.20	7.53	18.72 /46	5.47 /59	9.28 /53	0.05	1.93
AA	Putnam Retirement Ready 2045 R		B-	(800) 225-1581	C+ / 6.0	6.28	7.70	18.98 /47	5.73 /62	9.55 /55	0.25	1.68
AA	Putnam Retirement Ready 2045 Y	PRVYX	B-	(800) 225-1581	C+ / 6.4	6.37	7.92	19.54 /50	6.26 /66	10.10 /59	0.56	1.18
AA	Putnam Retirement Ready 2050 A	PRRJX	C+	(800) 225-1581	C / 5.2	6.53	8.15	19.75 /51	6.07 /65	10.06 /59	0.59	1.45
AA	Putnam Retirement Ready 2050 B		B-	(800) 225-1581	C+ / 5.7	6.29	7.68	18.86 /46	5.27 /57	9.24 /53	0.00	2.20
AA	Putnam Retirement Ready 2050 C		B-	(800) 225-1581	C+ / 5.7	6.29	7.69	18.83 /46	5.27 /57	9.24 /53	0.00	2.20
AA	Putnam Retirement Ready 2050 M		C+	(800) 225-1581	C / 5.2	6.35	7.83	19.13 /48	5.53 /60	9.51 /55	0.23	1.95
AA	Putnam Retirement Ready 2050 R	PRRKX	B-	(800) 225-1581	C+ / 6.2	6.45	8.03	19.52 /49	5.82 /63	9.79 /57	0.39	1.70
AA	Putnam Retirement Ready 2050 Y	PRRUX	B-	(800) 225-1581	C+ / 6.6	6.58	8.26	20.03 /52	6.34 /67	10.33 /61	0.76	1.20
GL	Putnam Retirement Ready 2055 A	PRRFX	C-	(800) 225-1581	C / 5.3	6.59	8.33	20.03 /52	6.14 /66	10.16 /60	0.73	2.46
GL	Putnam Retirement Ready 2055 B		C	(800) 225-1581	C+ / 5.8	6.45	7.99	19.15 /48	5.34 /58	9.34 /53	0.07	3.21
GL	Putnam Retirement Ready 2055 C		C	(800) 225-1581	C+ / 5.9	6.50	7.95	19.25 /48	5.38 /58	9.36 /54	0.13	3.21
GL	Putnam Retirement Ready 2055 M		C	(800) 225-1581	C / 5.3	6.51	8.04	19.49 /49	5.62 /61	9.61 /55	0.33	2.96
GL	Putnam Retirement Ready 2055 R	PRRVX	C+	(800) 225-1581	C+ / 6.3	6.57	8.31	19.82 /51	5.88 /63	9.89 /58	0.55	2.71
GL	Putnam Retirement Ready 2055 Y	PRTLX	C+	(800) 225-1581	C+ / 6.7	6.71	8.54	20.43 /54	6.41 /68	10.44 /62	0.92	2.21
SC	Putnam Small Cap Growth A	PNSAX	D+	(800) 225-1581	C / 5.0	5.56	11.78	29.03 /84	3.31 /35	11.08 /67	0.00	1.26
SC	Putnam Small Cap Growth B	PNSBX	C-	(800) 225-1581	C / 5.5	5.37	11.34	28.06 /82	2.54 /28	10.25 /60	0.00	2.01
SC	Putnam Small Cap Growth C	PNSCX	C-	(800) 225-1581	C / 5.5	5.35	11.35	28.03 /82	2.54 /28	10.25 /60	0.00	2.01
SC	Putnam Small Cap Growth M	PSGMX	D+	(800) 225-1581	C / 5.0	5.41	11.47	28.41 /83	2.79 /30	10.52 /62	0.00	1.76
SC	Putnam Small Cap Growth R	PSGRX	C-	(800) 225-1581	C+ / 6.0	5.51	11.61	28.68 /83	3.05 /32	10.80 /64	0.00	1.51
SC	Putnam Small Cap Growth Y	PSYGX	C	(800) 225-1581	C+ / 6.4	5.63	11.89	29.37 /85	3.57 /38	11.35 /69	0.22	1.01
SC	Putnam Small Cap Value Fund A	PSLAX	A-	(800) 225-1581	A- / 9.1	5.74	16.54	38.90 /97	8.10 /80	13.37 /88	0.61	1.44
SC	Putnam Small Cap Value Fund B	PSLBX	A-	(800) 225-1581	A / 9.4	5.54	16.10	37.80 /96	7.28 /74	12.50 /79	0.23	2.19
SC	Putnam Small Cap Value Fund C	PSLCX	A-	(800) 225-1581	A / 9.4	5.51	16.10	37.88 /96	7.29 /74	12.51 /79	0.26	2.19
SC	Putnam Small Cap Value Fund M	PSLMX	A-	(800) 225-1581	A- / 9.1	5.59	16.21	38.26 /97	7.55 /76	12.79 /82	0.33	1.94
SC	Putnam Small Cap Value Fund R	PSCRX	A	(800) 225-1581	A+ / 9.6	5.65	16.34	38.55 /97	7.82 /78	13.06 /84	0.48	1.69
SC	Putnam Small Cap Value Fund Y	PYSVX	A	(800) 225-1581	A+ / 9.7	5.81	16.62	39.19 /97	8.38 /82	13.64 /90	0.83	1.19
SC	Putnam Small Cap Value R5	PSLRX	A+	(800) 225-1581	A+ / 9.7	5.77	16.67	39.25 /97	8.47 /83	—	0.92	1.12
SC	Putnam Small Cap Value R6	PSCMX	A+	(800) 225-1581	A+ / 9.7	5.83	16.81	39.54 /97	8.54 /83	—	0.97	1.02
GI	Putnam Strategic Volatility Eq A	PSVEX	C+	(800) 225-1581	C / 4.8	7.72	7.33	15.61 /33	6.33 /67	—	4.47	2.69
GI	Putnam Strategic Volatility Eq B	PSVGX	C+	(800) 225-1581	C / 5.4	7.55	6.94	14.68 /28	5.55 /60	—	4.44	3.44
GI	Putnam Strategic Volatility Eq C	PSVHX	C+	(800) 225-1581	C+ / 6.0	7.48	6.97	14.73 /29	6.53 /69	—	4.28	3.44
GI	Putnam Strategic Volatility Eq M	PSVOX	C+	(800) 225-1581	C / 4.9	7.61	7.11	15.02 /30	5.81 /63	—	4.19	3.19
GI	Putnam Strategic Volatility Eq Y	PSVYX	C+	(800) 225-1581	C+ / 6.3	7.79	7.49	15.89 /34	6.58 /69	—	4.99	2.44
AA	QCI Balanced Institutional	QCIBX	B	(800) 773-3863	C- / 3.5	4.07	4.20	11.69 /17	4.42 /48	—	0.91	1.98
BA	QS Conservative Growth A	SBBAX	C-	(877) 534-4627	D+ / 2.6	5.08	4.27	14.94 /30	3.74 /40	6.65 /33	1.77	1.18

● Denotes fund is closed to new investors
∗ Denotes fund is included in Section II

www.thestreetratings.com

Risk Rating/Pts	3 Year Standard Deviation	Beta	NAV As of 2/28/17	Total $(Mil)	Cash %	Stocks %	Bonds %	Other %	Portfolio Turnover Ratio	Last Bull Market Return	Last Bear Market Return	Manager Quality Pct	Manager Tenure (Years)	Initial Purch. $	Additional Purch. $	Front End Load	Back End Load
B /8.1	6.3	0.98	24.77	5	13	46	39	2	47	69.9	-15.8	45	13	500	0	0.0	0.0
B- /7.7	7.5	1.17	22.03	69	14	54	31	1	38	79.3	-17.8	31	13	500	0	5.8	0.0
B- /7.7	7.5	1.17	20.29	1	14	54	31	1	38	72.0	-18.0	24	13	500	0	0.0	0.0
B- /7.7	7.5	1.17	20.21	2	14	54	31	1	38	72.2	-18.1	24	13	500	0	0.0	0.0
B- /7.8	7.5	1.17	21.25	1	14	54	31	1	38	74.5	-18.0	26	13	500	0	3.5	0.0
B- /7.8	7.5	1.17	21.25	1	14	54	31	1	38	76.9	-17.9	29	13	500	0	0.0	0.0
B- /7.8	7.5	1.17	25.71	7	14	54	31	1	38	81.7	-17.7	35	13	500	0	0.0	0.0
B- /7.4	8.5	1.31	22.00	111	14	57	28	1	48	87.8	-18.8	25	13	500	0	5.8	0.0
B- /7.5	8.5	1.31	20.30	1	14	57	28	1	48	80.3	-19.1	18	13	500	0	0.0	0.0
B- /7.5	8.4	1.31	20.03	1	14	57	28	1	48	80.3	-19.1	18	13	500	0	0.0	0.0
B- /7.5	8.5	1.32	20.69	N/A	14	57	28	1	48	82.8	-19.0	20	13	500	0	3.5	0.0
B- /7.6	8.5	1.31	22.73	2	14	57	28	1	48	85.3	-18.9	22	13	500	0	0.0	0.0
B- /7.5	8.4	1.31	25.81	7	14	57	28	1	48	90.4	-18.8	28	13	500	0	0.0	0.0
B- /7.2	9.0	1.40	20.28	39	10	73	16	1	38	92.3	-19.4	21	N/A	500	0	5.8	0.0
B- /7.2	9.1	1.40	18.49	1	10	73	16	1	38	84.6	-19.6	15	13	500	0	0.0	0.0
B- /7.2	9.1	1.40	18.51	1	10	73	16	1	38	84.7	-19.7	15	13	500	0	0.0	0.0
B- /7.2	9.0	1.40	19.72	N/A	10	73	16	1	38	87.2	-19.6	17	13	500	0	3.5	0.0
B- /7.3	9.0	1.40	20.85	1	10	73	16	1	38	89.8	-19.5	19	13	500	0	0.0	0.0
B- /7.3	9.0	1.40	24.27	5	10	73	16	1	38	94.9	-19.3	24	13	500	0	0.0	0.0
B- /7.1	9.4	1.46	18.31	39	7	79	12	2	41	95.4	-19.8	18	12	500	0	5.8	0.0
B- /7.1	9.4	1.46	18.09	1	7	79	12	2	41	87.5	-20.0	13	12	500	0	0.0	0.0
B- /7.1	9.4	1.45	17.92	1	7	79	12	2	41	87.6	-20.1	13	12	500	0	0.0	0.0
B- /7.1	9.4	1.45	18.49	N/A	7	79	12	2	41	90.1	-20.0	15	12	500	0	3.5	0.0
B- /7.1	9.4	1.45	18.13	N/A	7	79	12	2	41	92.8	-20.0	16	12	500	0	0.0	0.0
B- /7.1	9.4	1.45	18.41	3	7	79	12	2	41	98.1	-19.8	21	12	500	0	0.0	0.0
C /5.2	9.6	1.42	11.22	8	5	85	9	1	38	95.6	-20.6	69	7	500	0	5.8	0.0
C /5.3	9.6	1.42	11.16	N/A	5	85	9	1	38	87.9	-20.8	59	7	500	0	0.0	0.0
C /5.2	9.7	1.43	11.02	1	5	85	9	1	38	88.1	-20.8	59	7	500	0	0.0	0.0
C /5.3	9.6	1.42	11.22	N/A	5	85	9	1	38	90.7	-20.8	62	7	500	0	3.5	0.0
C /5.2	9.6	1.42	11.19	N/A	5	85	9	1	38	93.3	-20.7	66	7	500	0	0.0	0.0
C /5.2	9.6	1.43	11.30	3	5	85	9	1	38	98.6	-20.6	72	7	500	0	0.0	0.0
C /4.3	16.7	1.02	32.85	112	0	99	0	1	66	120.4	-27.5	28	7	500	0	5.8	0.0
C- /4.2	16.7	1.02	29.25	3	0	99	0	1	66	112.3	-27.8	20	7	500	0	0.0	0.0
C- /4.2	16.7	1.02	29.14	10	0	99	0	1	66	111.6	-27.8	20	7	500	0	0.0	0.0
C- /4.2	16.7	1.02	30.42	1	0	99	0	1	66	114.5	-27.7	23	7	500	0	3.5	0.0
C- /4.2	16.8	1.02	31.81	8	0	99	0	1	66	117.4	-27.6	25	7	500	0	0.0	0.0
C /4.3	16.7	1.02	33.88	11	0	99	0	1	66	123.3	-27.5	31	7	0	0	0.0	0.0
C+ /5.6	13.8	0.84	17.69	188	7	92	0	1	62	137.1	-24.8	87	9	500	0	5.8	0.0
C /5.5	13.7	0.84	14.93	3	7	92	0	1	62	127.4	-25.0	83	9	500	0	0.0	0.0
C /5.5	13.8	0.84	14.88	22	7	92	0	1	62	127.7	-25.2	83	9	500	0	0.0	0.0
C /5.5	13.8	0.84	16.12	2	7	92	0	1	62	130.8	-25.1	85	9	500	0	3.5	0.0
C+ /5.6	13.7	0.84	17.40	1	7	92	0	1	62	133.8	-24.9	86	9	500	0	0.0	0.0
C+ /5.6	13.7	0.84	18.33	212	7	92	0	1	62	140.3	-24.8	88	9	0	0	0.0	0.0
C+ /6.3	13.7	0.84	18.39	1	7	92	0	1	62	N/A	N/A	88	9	0	0	0.0	0.0
C+ /6.3	13.7	0.84	18.39	56	7	92	0	1	62	N/A	N/A	89	9	0	0	0.0	0.0
C+ /6.7	8.3	0.72	11.12	4	4	95	0	1	127	N/A	N/A	60	4	500	0	5.8	0.0
C+ /6.6	8.3	0.72	10.90	N/A	4	95	0	1	127	N/A	N/A	50	4	500	0	0.0	0.0
C+ /6.6	8.3	0.71	10.90	N/A	4	95	0	1	127	N/A	N/A	64	4	500	0	0.0	0.0
C+ /6.6	8.3	0.72	11.02	N/A	4	95	0	1	127	N/A	N/A	53	4	500	0	3.5	0.0
C+ /6.6	8.4	0.72	11.13	2	4	95	0	1	127	N/A	N/A	63	4	500	0	0.0	0.0
B+ /9.8	5.0	0.79	11.34	60	0	0	0	100	38	N/A	N/A	56	3	25,000	250	0.0	0.0
B- /7.8	6.4	0.98	14.52	286	1	54	43	2	52	57.6	-11.4	29	21	1,000	50	5.8	0.0

Fund Type	Fund Name	Ticker Symbol	Overall Investment Rating	Phone	Performance Rating/Pts	3 Mo	6 Mo	1Yr / Pct	3Yr / Pct	5Yr / Pct	Dividend Yield	Expense Ratio
	99 Pct = Best / 0 Pct = Worst							Total Return % through 2/28/17 / Annualized			Incl. in Returns	
BA	QS Conservative Growth C	SCBCX	C	(877) 534-4627	C- / 3.1	4.91	3.94	14.14 /26	2.99 /32	5.90 /28	1.14	1.92
AA	QS Defensive Growth A	SBCPX	C	(877) 534-4627	D / 2.2	4.11	2.33	11.57 /16	3.42 /36	5.16 /22	2.23	1.17
AA	QS Defensive Growth C	LWLAX	C	(877) 534-4627	D+ / 2.3	3.85	1.90	10.71 /14	2.66 /29	4.37 /17	1.76	1.85
AA	● QS Defensive Growth C1	SBCLX	C	(877) 534-4627	D+ / 2.4	3.88	2.02	10.94 /14	2.89 /31	4.60 /19	1.79	1.67
AA	QS Defensive Growth I	LMGIX	C+	(877) 534-4627	C- / 3.0	4.12	2.41	11.83 /17	3.66 /39	--	2.61	0.97
GL	QS Glbl Div A	LGDAX	B	(877) 534-4627	C / 5.4	6.86	3.36	13.78 /24	8.65 /84	--	2.07	1.55
GL	QS Glbl Div A2	LMQSX	B	(877) 534-4627	C / 5.4	6.95	3.32	13.83 /25	8.64 /84	--	2.12	1.73
GL	QS Glbl Div C	LGDCX	B	(877) 534-4627	C+ / 6.0	6.72	2.98	12.89 /21	7.84 /78	--	1.67	2.30
GL	QS Glbl Div IS	LDIFX	B	(877) 534-4627	C+ / 6.8	6.96	3.49	14.13 /26	8.98 /87	--	2.55	1.05
GL	● QS Global Equity 1	LMPEX	A-	(877) 534-4627	B- / 7.5	6.61	9.32	21.51 /60	7.85 /78	11.32 /68	1.50	1.39
GL	QS Global Equity A	CFIPX	B-	(877) 534-4627	C+ / 6.6	6.60	9.31	21.54 /60	7.82 /78	11.24 /68	1.37	1.66
GL	QS Global Equity C	SILLX	B+	(877) 534-4627	B- / 7.0	6.48	8.92	20.71 /56	7.02 /72	10.43 /62	0.59	2.36
GL	QS Global Equity I	SMYIX	A	(877) 534-4627	B / 7.8	6.73	9.52	21.99 /62	8.22 /81	11.62 /71	1.76	1.08
GR	QS Growth A	SCHAX	C-	(877) 534-4627	C- / 3.9	6.70	7.86	20.27 /54	3.85 /41	8.72 /48	0.89	1.33
GR	QS Growth C	SCHCX	C	(877) 534-4627	C / 4.4	6.52	7.47	19.45 /49	3.14 /33	8.01 /42	0.39	2.03
GR	QS Growth I	LANIX	C+	(877) 534-4627	C / 5.3	6.82	8.05	20.60 /55	4.15 /45	9.07 /51	1.21	0.99
FO	QS International Eq A	LMEAX	D	(877) 534-4627	D / 1.8	7.46	5.90	15.31 /31	0.72 /17	5.45 /24	2.03	1.19
FO	QS International Eq A2	LIATX	D	(877) 534-4627	D / 1.8	7.44	6.02	15.40 /32	0.78 /17	5.56 /25	2.40	N/A
FO	QS International Eq C	LMGEX	D	(877) 534-4627	D- / 1.4	7.16	5.52	14.38 /27	-0.07 /13	4.66 /19	1.25	2.07
FO	QS International Eq FI	LGFEX	D+	(877) 534-4627	D+ / 2.5	7.40	5.89	15.28 /31	0.67 /16	5.43 /24	2.06	1.27
FO	QS International Eq I	LGIEX	D+	(877) 534-4627	D+ / 2.8	7.47	6.11	15.62 /33	1.01 /18	5.81 /27	2.41	0.96
FO	QS International Eq IS	LIESX	D+	(877) 534-4627	D+ / 2.9	7.52	6.16	15.77 /33	1.13 /19	5.91 /28	2.51	0.86
FO	QS International Eq R	LMIRX	D+	(877) 534-4627	D+ / 2.4	7.28	5.77	14.92 /30	0.42 /15	5.17 /23	1.88	1.58
FO	QS Intl Div IS	LDIVX	D	(877) 534-4627	D+ / 2.3	5.48	-0.68	7.12 / 6	3.65 /39	--	2.78	6.99
GR	QS Moderate Growth A	SCGRX	C-	(877) 534-4627	C- / 3.4	6.04	6.38	18.03 /43	3.97 /43	8.00 /42	1.33	1.25
GR	QS Moderate Growth C	SCGCX	C	(877) 534-4627	C- / 4.0	5.86	6.06	17.28 /40	3.26 /34	7.28 /37	0.67	1.96
GR	QS Moderate Growth I	LLAIX	C+	(877) 534-4627	C / 4.9	6.14	6.62	18.48 /45	4.29 /46	8.29 /45	1.72	0.97
GR	QS S&P 500 Index A	SBSPX	A+	(877) 534-4627	A- / 9.1	7.90	9.72	24.31 /71	10.01 /93	13.38 /88	1.60	0.61
GR	QS S&P 500 Index D	SBSDX	A+	(877) 534-4627	A- / 9.2	7.96	9.82	24.56 /72	10.23 /95	13.60 /90	1.78	0.44
GI	QS Strategic Real Return A	LRRAX	D-	(877) 534-4627	E- / 0.1	4.17	1.18	9.99 /12	-4.98 / 2	-1.76 / 3	0.00	1.43
AA	QS Strategic Real Return A2	LSRAX	D-	(877) 534-4627	E- / 0.1	4.04	1.11	9.70 /11	-5.17 / 2	--	0.00	1.80
GI	QS Strategic Real Return C	LRRCX	E+	(877) 534-4627	E- / 0.2	3.92	0.76	9.05 /10	-5.72 / 2	-2.50 / 2	0.00	2.25
GI	QS Strategic Real Return I	LRRIX	D-	(877) 534-4627	E / 0.3	4.26	1.33	10.26 /12	-4.75 / 3	-1.50 / 3	0.00	1.25
GI	QS Strategic Real Return IS	LRRSX	D-	(877) 534-4627	E / 0.3	4.13	1.35	10.30 /12	-4.66 / 3	-1.42 / 3	0.00	1.17
GR	QS US Large Cap Eq FI	LMUSX	A-	(877) 534-4627	B / 8.2	7.88	10.72	24.23 /71	8.11 /80	12.69 /81	1.36	1.17
GR	QS US Large Cap Eq I	LMTIX	A+	(877) 534-4627	B+ / 8.5	7.97	10.90	24.73 /72	8.45 /83	13.00 /84	1.34	0.80
GR	QS US Large Cap Eq IS	LMISX	A-	(877) 534-4627	B+ / 8.5	8.03	10.89	24.71 /72	8.47 /83	13.01 /84	1.34	0.79
SC	QS US Small Cap Eq A	LMBAX	C+	(877) 534-4627	B- / 7.0	4.28	11.52	29.40 /85	7.08 /73	12.41 /78	0.27	1.16
SC	QS US Small Cap Eq A2	LUSAX	C+	(877) 534-4627	C+ / 6.8	4.18	11.42	29.04 /84	6.83 /71	--	0.15	1.47
SC	QS US Small Cap Eq C	LMBCX	C+	(877) 534-4627	B- / 7.4	4.07	11.15	28.40 /83	6.28 /67	11.57 /71	0.00	1.89
SC	QS US Small Cap Eq FI	LGSCX	B-	(877) 534-4627	B / 7.9	4.16	11.49	29.37 /85	7.01 /72	12.38 /78	0.71	1.17
SC	QS US Small Cap Eq I	LMSIX	B-	(877) 534-4627	B / 8.2	4.28	11.66	29.72 /86	7.47 /75	12.90 /83	0.00	0.77
SC	QS US Small Cap Eq IS	LMBMX	B	(877) 534-4627	B+ / 8.3	4.37	11.78	30.04 /86	7.55 /76	--	0.67	0.76
GR	Quaker Event Arbitrage A	QEAAX	D	(800) 220-8888	C- / 3.0	4.95	5.38	21.07 /58	2.80 /30	4.38 /17	0.49	2.41
GR	Quaker Event Arbitrage C	QEACX	D	(800) 220-8888	C- / 3.4	4.72	4.99	20.15 /53	2.04 /24	3.59 /13	0.14	3.16
GR	Quaker Event Arbitrage Inst	QEAIX	D+	(800) 220-8888	C- / 4.2	5.04	5.48	21.36 /59	3.04 /32	4.64 /19	0.65	2.16
GL	Quaker Global Tactical Alloc A	QTRAX	D-	(800) 220-8888	D- / 1.3	3.59	2.59	10.33 /12	1.41 /21	7.76 /40	0.00	2.10
GL	Quaker Global Tactical Alloc C	QTRCX	D-	(800) 220-8888	D- / 1.5	3.42	2.15	9.54 /11	0.64 /16	6.95 /34	0.00	2.85
GL	Quaker Global Tactical Alloc I	QTRIX	D-	(800) 220-8888	D / 2.0	3.61	2.66	10.68 /13	1.68 /22	8.03 /42	0.00	1.85
MC	Quaker Mid-Cap Value A	QMCVX	B+	(800) 220-8888	B+ / 8.6	7.32	13.99	34.22 /93	7.87 /78	11.42 /69	0.00	2.17
MC	Quaker Mid-Cap Value C	QMCCX	B+	(800) 220-8888	B+ / 8.9	7.13	13.54	33.17 /92	7.07 /72	10.58 /63	0.00	2.92
MC	Quaker Mid-Cap Value Inst	QMVIX	A	(800) 220-8888	A / 9.4	7.39	14.09	34.48 /93	8.13 /80	11.70 /72	0.00	1.92

● Denotes fund is closed to new investors
* Denotes fund is included in Section II

www.thestreetratings.com

RISK			NET ASSETS		ASSET				Portfolio Turnover Ratio	BULL / BEAR		FUND MANAGER		MINIMUMS		LOADS	
Risk Rating/Pts	3 Year		NAV As of 2/28/17	Total $(Mil)	Cash %	Stocks %	Bonds %	Other %		Last Bull Market Return	Last Bear Market Return	Manager Quality Pct	Manager Tenure (Years)	Initial Purch. $	Additional Purch. $	Front End Load	Back End Load
	Standard Deviation	Beta															
B- /7.9	6.3	0.98	15.05	20	1	54	43	2	52	51.6	-11.7	22	21	1,000	50	0.0	0.0
B /8.7	4.7	0.70	13.55	126	17	21	60	2	53	41.9	-7.3	52	21	1,000	50	4.3	0.0
B /8.8	4.7	0.70	13.45	3	17	21	60	2	53	36.3	-7.6	42	14	1,000	50	0.0	0.0
B /8.8	4.7	0.70	13.81	3	17	21	60	2	53	37.8	-7.6	45	21	1,000	50	0.0	0.0
B /8.7	4.7	0.70	13.52	2	17	21	60	2	53	N/A	N/A	55	16	1,000,000	0	0.0	0.0
B /8.0	7.6	0.46	12.16	N/A	2	97	0	1	7	N/A	N/A	99	4	1,000	50	5.8	0.0
B /8.0	7.6	0.46	12.17	3	2	97	0	1	7	N/A	N/A	99	4	1,000	50	5.8	0.0
B /8.0	7.6	0.46	12.12	1	2	97	0	1	7	N/A	N/A	98	4	1,000	50	0.0	0.0
B /8.0	7.6	0.46	12.12	199	2	97	0	1	7	N/A	N/A	99	4	0	0	0.0	0.0
B- /7.4	10.0	0.73	14.80	1	0	99	0	1	33	104.6	-20.4	98	6	0	0	0.0	0.0
B- /7.4	10.0	0.73	14.87	137	0	99	0	1	33	103.9	-20.4	98	6	1,000	50	5.8	0.0
B- /7.4	10.0	0.73	15.08	7	0	99	0	1	33	95.8	-20.6	98	6	1,000	50	0.0	0.0
B- /7.4	10.0	0.73	14.83	8	0	99	0	1	33	107.4	-20.1	98	6	1,000,000	0	0.0	0.0
C+ /6.2	9.7	0.91	16.72	718	27	67	4	2	44	82.3	-18.6	12	21	1,000	50	5.8	0.0
C+ /6.1	9.7	0.91	15.74	20	27	67	4	2	44	76.2	-18.8	8	21	1,000	50	0.0	0.0
C+ /6.1	9.6	0.91	16.66	1	27	67	4	2	44	85.5	-18.6	14	21	1,000,000	0	0.0	0.0
C+ /6.4	10.6	0.84	14.21	7	2	97	0	1	71	50.0	-23.7	80	6	1,000	50	5.8	0.0
C+ /5.6	10.6	0.84	14.16	N/A	2	97	0	1	71	50.8	-23.7	80	6	1,000	50	5.8	0.0
C+ /6.5	10.5	0.84	14.25	38	2	97	0	1	71	44.0	-24.0	74	6	1,000	50	0.0	0.0
C+ /6.4	10.6	0.84	14.75	7	2	97	0	1	71	49.8	-23.7	80	6	0	0	0.0	0.0
C+ /6.4	10.6	0.84	14.73	21	2	97	0	1	71	52.8	-23.6	82	6	1,000,000	0	0.0	0.0
C+ /6.4	10.6	0.84	14.70	272	2	97	0	1	71	53.5	-23.6	83	6	0	0	0.0	0.0
C+ /6.4	10.6	0.84	14.73	1	2	97	0	1	71	48.0	-23.9	78	6	0	0	0.0	0.0
C+ /5.9	8.6	0.60	9.36	2	0	0	0	100	30	N/A	N/A	92	4	0	0	0.0	0.0
C+ /6.9	8.2	0.77	16.37	452	24	55	20	1	47	72.7	-15.4	24	21	1,000	50	5.8	0.0
B- /7.0	8.2	0.77	16.65	22	24	55	20	1	47	66.5	-15.7	18	21	1,000	50	5.8	0.0
C+ /6.9	8.2	0.77	16.25	6	24	55	20	1	47	75.2	-15.4	27	21	1,000,000	0	0.0	0.0
C+ /6.9	10.3	1.00	23.09	242	0	99	0	1	3	127.9	-16.5	67	N/A	0	0	0.0	0.0
C+ /6.9	10.3	1.00	23.24	11	0	99	0	1	3	130.3	-16.4	70	N/A	0	0	0.0	0.0
C+ /6.1	8.4	0.52	11.39	1	9	39	51	1	41	3.9	-13.1	2	6	1,000	50	5.8	0.0
C+ /6.1	8.4	0.89	11.25	1	9	39	51	1	41	N/A	N/A	1	6	1,000	50	5.8	0.0
C+ /6.0	8.4	0.52	11.04	N/A	9	39	51	1	41	-0.2	-13.4	1	6	1,000	50	0.0	0.0
C+ /6.1	8.4	0.52	11.65	2	9	39	51	1	41	5.4	-13.0	2	6	1,000,000	0	0.0	0.0
C+ /6.1	8.4	0.52	11.50	119	9	39	51	1	41	N/A	N/A	2	6	0	0	0.0	0.0
C+ /6.6	11.2	1.07	17.86	N/A	0	0	0	100	86	122.7	-17.6	34	9	0	0	0.0	0.0
B- /7.5	11.3	1.07	17.75	10	0	0	0	100	86	126.1	-17.5	38	9	1,000,000	0	0.0	0.0
C+ /6.4	11.3	1.08	17.76	813	0	0	0	100	86	126.2	-17.5	38	9	0	0	0.0	0.0
C /4.7	15.5	0.97	13.59	21	0	99	0	1	34	128.6	-25.4	77	11	1,000	50	5.8	0.0
C /4.7	15.4	0.97	13.44	33	0	99	0	1	34	N/A	N/A	75	11	1,000	50	5.8	0.0
C /4.6	15.5	0.97	12.75	6	0	99	0	1	34	119.1	-25.6	70	11	1,000	50	0.0	0.0
C /4.7	15.5	0.97	13.04	N/A	0	99	0	1	34	128.1	-25.5	76	11	0	0	0.0	0.0
C /4.7	15.5	0.97	13.86	23	0	99	0	1	34	133.5	-25.3	79	11	1,000,000	0	0.0	0.0
C /4.7	15.5	0.97	13.58	826	0	99	0	1	34	N/A	N/A	80	11	0	0	0.0	0.0
C /5.1	9.4	0.76	12.62	14	9	70	18	3	160	36.0	-11.8	15	14	2,000	100	5.5	0.0
C /5.0	9.4	0.76	12.13	4	9	70	18	3	160	30.6	-12.1	10	14	2,000	100	0.0	0.0
C /5.1	9.4	0.76	12.73	13	9	70	18	3	160	37.9	-11.8	17	14	1,000,000	0	0.0	0.0
C /5.1	11.9	0.82	10.68	2	0	95	4	1	211	67.1	-18.1	84	N/A	2,000	100	5.5	0.0
C /5.0	11.9	0.81	9.99	1	0	95	4	1	211	60.6	-18.4	79	N/A	2,000	100	0.0	0.0
C /5.1	11.9	0.82	12.33	4	0	95	4	1	211	69.6	-18.0	85	N/A	1,000,000	0	0.0	0.0
C+ /5.7	12.8	1.01	28.28	5	0	97	2	1	71	119.9	-23.0	52	9	2,000	100	5.5	0.0
C+ /5.6	12.7	1.01	24.49	2	0	97	2	1	71	111.1	-23.2	42	9	2,000	100	0.0	0.0
C+ /5.7	12.7	1.01	29.80	2	0	97	2	1	71	122.9	-22.9	56	9	1,000,000	0	0.0	0.0

Fund Type	Fund Name	Ticker Symbol	Overall Investment Rating	Phone	Performance Rating/Pts	3 Mo	6 Mo	1Yr / Pct	3Yr / Pct	5Yr / Pct	Dividend Yield	Expense Ratio
	99 Pct = Best 0 Pct = Worst				**PERFORMANCE** Total Return % through 2/28/17 Annualized / Incl. in Returns							
SC	Quaker Small-Cap Value A	QUSVX	C	(800) 220-8888	C+ / 5.9	4.17	11.48	26.21 /77	5.71 /62	10.97 /66	0.00	1.98
SC	Quaker Small-Cap Value C	QSVCX	C	(800) 220-8888	C+ / 6.4	4.00	11.03	25.21 /74	4.91 /53	10.13 /59	0.00	2.73
SC	Quaker Small-Cap Value Inst	QSVIX	C+	(800) 220-8888	B- / 7.1	4.24	11.65	26.49 /78	5.97 /64	11.25 /68	0.00	1.73
GL	Quaker Strategic Growth A	QUAGX	C	(800) 220-8888	C / 4.7	6.31	10.63	19.79 /51	4.75 /51	10.61 /63	0.00	1.87
GL	Quaker Strategic Growth C	QAGCX	C+	(800) 220-8888	C / 5.1	6.11	10.19	18.88 /47	3.96 /43	9.78 /57	0.00	2.62
GL	Quaker Strategic Growth Inst	QAGIX	C+	(800) 220-8888	C+ / 6.1	6.37	10.76	20.13 /53	5.03 /55	10.87 /65	0.00	1.62
GR	Quality Dividend A	QDVAX	B-	(888) 739-1390	C+ / 6.4	7.57	6.93	19.71 /51	8.45 /83	--	2.69	1.38
GR	Quality Dividend C	QDVCX	B-	(888) 739-1390	C+ / 6.8	7.35	6.56	18.81 /46	7.64 /76	--	2.11	1.13
GR	Quantified All Cap Equity Investor	QACFX	B	(855) 747-9555	C / 5.1	5.78	10.43	19.87 /51	3.63 /38	--	0.00	1.65
AA	Quantified Alternative Invest Inv	QALTX	D	(855) 747-9555	E+ / 0.7	2.80	1.35	6.70 / 5	-1.06 / 9	--	0.04	2.07
GL	Quantified Market Leaders Fund Inv	QMLFX	B	(855) 747-9555	B / 7.8	8.07	15.16	31.20 /89	4.79 /52	--	2.14	1.58
AA	Quantified STF Investor	QSTFX	U	(855) 747-9555	U /	22.34	16.41	11.88 /18	--	--	0.01	1.72
SC	Queens Road Small Cap Value Fund	QRSVX	B	(800) 595-3088	C / 4.5	0.19	4.96	15.31 /31	6.00 /64	9.43 /54	0.00	1.26
GI	Queens Road Value Fund	QRVLX	A	(800) 595-3088	B / 8.2	7.84	9.68	22.87 /66	8.44 /82	11.92 /74	1.49	0.96
FO	Rainier International Discv A	RISAX	D	(800) 248-6314	D- / 1.1	4.90	-1.80	5.53 / 4	2.25 /26	--	0.00	1.32
FO	Rainier International Discv Instl	RAIIX	D	(800) 248-6314	D / 1.7	5.00	-1.66	5.84 / 5	2.50 /28	--	0.00	1.65
MC	Rainier Invt Mang Mid Cap Eq Inst	RAIMX	D-	(800) 248-6314	C / 4.7	5.82	6.59	19.96 /52	3.82 /41	8.91 /50	0.00	1.13
MC	Rainier Invt Mang Mid Cap Eq Orig	RIMMX	D-	(800) 248-6314	C / 4.5	5.76	6.46	19.66 /50	3.53 /37	8.62 /47	0.00	1.37
IN	Rainier Large Cap Equity Inst	RAIEX	D-	(800) 248-6314	C+ / 6.1	6.83	7.19	20.44 /55	5.59 /60	10.47 /62	0.01	0.89
IN	Rainier Large Cap Equity Original	RIMEX	D-	(800) 248-6314	C+ / 5.8	6.75	6.96	19.98 /52	5.24 /57	10.14 /59	0.00	1.19
SC	● Rainier Small-Mid Cap Equity Inst	RAISX	D	(800) 248-6314	C+ / 6.0	6.46	11.08	23.72 /69	4.08 /44	9.47 /54	0.00	1.00
SC	● Rainier Small-Mid Cap Equity Orig	RIMSX	D	(800) 248-6314	C+ / 5.7	6.40	10.93	23.37 /68	3.76 /40	9.13 /52	0.00	1.33
AA	Ranger Quest for Inc and Gro Inst	RFIDX	C-	(866) 458-4744	C- / 3.0	4.95	5.12	18.27 /44	1.61 /22	5.78 /27	4.17	1.85
GL	Ranger Quest for Inc and Gro Inv	RFTDX	D+	(866) 458-4744	D+ / 2.8	4.87	4.92	17.93 /43	1.31 /20	--	4.18	2.25
SC	Ranger Small Cap Inst	RFISX	B-	(866) 458-4744	B+ / 8.7	4.53	9.86	30.70 /88	8.55 /83	10.35 /61	0.00	1.38
SC	Rational Defensive Growth A	HSUAX	E-	(800) 253-0412	E+ / 0.6	1.99	4.04	15.99 /34	-1.66 / 7	6.51 /32	1.07	1.82
MC	Rational Defensive Growth C	HSUCX	D-	(800) 253-0412	E+ / 0.7	1.88	3.77	15.33 /31	-2.16 / 6	--	0.45	2.32
SC	Rational Defensive Growth Inst	HSUTX	E-	(800) 253-0412	D- / 1.0	2.06	4.17	16.17 /35	-1.40 / 8	6.79 /33	1.13	1.57
MC	Rational Dividend Capture A	HDCAX	D-	(800) 253-0412	D / 1.8	2.56	1.37	8.28 / 8	3.92 /42	7.45 /38	2.39	1.60
GI	Rational Dividend Capture C	HDCEX	C-	(800) 253-0412	D / 2.2	2.56	1.24	7.88 / 7	3.41 /36	--	2.01	2.10
MC	Rational Dividend Capture Instl	HDCTX	D	(800) 253-0412	D+ / 2.6	2.73	1.60	8.54 / 8	4.17 /45	7.71 /40	2.75	1.35
GI	Rational Real Strategies A	HRSAX	E-	(800) 253-0412	E- / 0.0	-10.60	-8.24	-1.83 / 1	-12.67 / 0	-6.40 / 1	14.25	2.50
GI	Rational Real Strategies Inst	HRSTX	E-	(800) 253-0412	E- / 0.0	-10.80	-8.43	-1.82 / 1	-12.70 / 0	-6.32 / 1	15.43	2.25
FO	Rational Risk Managed Emrg Mkt A	HGSAX	E-	(800) 253-0412	D- / 1.0	2.74	-2.02	10.91 /14	1.09 /19	1.45 / 7	0.81	2.83
FO	Rational Risk Managed Emrg Mkt Inst	HGSIX	E-	(800) 253-0412	D / 1.6	2.86	-1.88	11.16 /15	1.34 /20	1.69 / 7	1.08	2.58
AA	Rational Strategic Allocation A	HBAFX	D	(800) 253-0412	D+ / 2.3	3.11	4.14	14.19 /26	3.22 /34	5.10 /22	1.87	2.10
AA	RBB Free Market Fixed Income Inst	FMFIX	C-	(866) 780-0357	E+ / 0.8	0.48	-0.74	0.51 / 2	0.77 /17	0.59 / 5	0.81	0.79
EM	RBB Free Market Intl Eq Inst	FMNEX	C-	(866) 780-0357	C- / 4.1	8.40	8.87	24.81 /73	0.69 /17	5.72 /27	1.90	1.14
IN	RBB Free Market US Equity Inst	FMUEX	B+	(866) 780-0357	A- / 9.0	5.14	13.65	31.82 /90	8.05 /79	13.74 /91	0.82	0.90
IN	RBC BlueBay Absolute Return A	RABAX	C-	(800) 422-2766	E / 0.4	2.43	3.09	3.97 / 3	-0.44 /12	--	0.00	1.18
IN	RBC BlueBay Absolute Return I	RBARX	D+	(800) 422-2766	E+ / 0.7	2.42	3.18	4.06 / 3	-0.23 /13	--	0.00	0.97
FS	RBC BlueBay Diversified Credit I	RBTRX	U	(800) 422-2766	U /	4.14	0.90	7.84 / 7	--	--	2.61	1.34
CV	RBC BlueBay Global Convertible Bd I	RGCBX	D+	(800) 422-2766	D / 2.2	3.44	3.87	10.12 /12	3.01 /32	5.97 /28	0.63	1.56
EM	RBC Emerging Markets Equity A	REEAX	C-	(800) 422-2766	C- / 3.0	7.28	0.99	20.19 /53	4.13 /44	--	0.63	2.75
EM	RBC Emerging Markets Equity I	REEIX	C	(800) 422-2766	C / 4.3	7.37	0.98	20.48 /55	4.37 /47	--	0.75	1.90
EM	RBC Emerging Markets Sm Cap Eqty	RSMAX	D+	(800) 422-2766	D / 1.8	5.83	0.03	18.17 /44	2.27 /26	--	3.86	5.46
EM	RBC Emerging Markets Sm Cap Eqty	RESIX	C-	(800) 422-2766	D+ / 2.8	5.88	0.19	18.47 /45	2.54 /28	--	4.35	5.21
SC	RBC Enterprise A	TETAX	E+	(800) 422-2766	D+ / 2.6	0.67	8.76	32.46 /91	0.67 /17	10.37 /61	0.02	1.85
SC	RBC Enterprise I	TETIX	D-	(800) 422-2766	C- / 3.9	0.69	8.85	32.83 /91	0.92 /18	11.30 /68	0.24	1.21
SC	RBC Micro Cap Value A	TMVAX	C+	(800) 422-2766	C+ / 6.3	1.66	11.58	29.26 /85	6.89 /71	13.97 /93	0.21	1.71
SC	RBC Micro Cap Value I	RMVIX	B	(800) 422-2766	B- / 7.4	1.71	11.69	29.61 /86	7.15 /73	14.25 /94	0.47	1.24
SC	RBC Mid Cap Value I	RBMVX	C+	(800) 422-2766	B+ / 8.5	4.54	10.91	31.25 /89	8.48 /83	12.57 /80	0.43	3.28

● Denotes fund is closed to new investors
* Denotes fund is included in Section II

550

RISK			NET ASSETS		ASSET				Portfolio Turnover Ratio	BULL / BEAR		FUND MANAGER		MINIMUMS		LOADS	
	3 Year		NAV							Last Bull	Last Bear	Manager	Manager	Initial	Additional	Front	Back
Risk Rating/Pts	Standard Deviation	Beta	As of 2/28/17	Total $(Mil)	Cash %	Stocks %	Bonds %	Other %		Market Return	Market Return	Quality Pct	Tenure (Years)	Purch. $	Purch. $	End Load	End Load
C /4.7	14.5	0.88	23.98	7	0	100	0	0	119	113.5	-24.2	70	21	2,000	100	5.5	0.0
C /4.4	14.5	0.88	19.22	1	0	100	0	0	119	104.9	-24.4	61	21	2,000	100	0.0	0.0
C /4.8	14.5	0.88	25.31	21	0	100	0	0	119	116.4	-24.1	73	21	1,000,000	0	0.0	0.0
C+ /6.6	11.6	0.73	27.48	53	0	100	0	0	211	97.6	-19.3	95	1	2,000	100	5.5	0.0
C+ /6.6	11.6	0.73	23.80	14	0	100	0	0	211	89.6	-19.6	93	1	2,000	100	0.0	0.0
C+ /6.6	11.6	0.73	28.71	9	0	100	0	0	211	100.2	-19.3	95	1	1,000,000	0	0.0	0.0
B- /7.4	9.3	0.79	12.26	36	11	88	0	1	63	N/A	N/A	75	4	1,000	100	5.8	1.0
B- /7.6	9.3	0.79	12.30	26	11	88	0	1	63	N/A	N/A	67	4	1,000	100	0.0	1.0
B /8.0	8.7	0.68	10.80	10	13	73	12	2	961	N/A	N/A	30	4	10,000	1,000	0.0	0.0
C+ /6.7	6.8	0.92	9.29	9	0	0	0	100	687	N/A	N/A	4	4	10,000	1,000	0.0	0.0
C+ /5.8	14.4	1.64	11.16	73	0	0	0	100	687	N/A	N/A	38	4	10,000	1,000	0.0	0.0
U /	N/A	N/A	10.08	85	0	0	0	100	59	N/A	N/A	N/A	2	10,000	1,000	0.0	0.0
B /8.6	9.9	0.59	25.81	154	0	69	29	2	23	75.8	-14.6	85	15	2,500	1,000	0.0	0.0
B- /7.3	8.2	0.76	21.41	43	3	90	5	2	14	98.2	-10.3	77	13	2,500	1,000	0.0	0.0
C+ /6.4	9.7	0.61	15.83	75	4	92	3	1	93	N/A	N/A	87	5	2,500	250	5.8	0.0
C+ /6.4	9.7	0.61	15.96	109	4	92	3	1	93	N/A	N/A	89	5	100,000	1,000	0.0	0.0
D+ /2.5	12.7	0.98	40.03	99	1	98	0	1	144	97.5	-24.3	13	12	100,000	1,000	0.0	0.0
D+ /2.3	12.7	0.98	38.20	35	1	98	0	1	144	94.5	-24.3	12	12	2,500	250	0.0	0.0
E+ /0.8	12.2	1.11	19.62	30	0	99	0	1	63	98.8	-18.7	10	9	100,000	1,000	0.0	0.0
E+ /0.7	12.2	1.11	19.00	82	0	99	0	1	63	95.7	-18.7	8	9	2,500	250	0.0	0.0
D+ /2.4	13.5	0.80	38.99	110	0	99	0	1	153	107.4	-25.1	58	15	100,000	1,000	0.0	0.0
D /2.2	13.5	0.80	36.66	250	0	99	0	1	153	104.1	-25.2	53	15	2,500	250	0.0	0.0
C+ /6.4	9.4	1.33	12.05	15	22	77	0	1	91	51.0	N/A	4	6	250,000	0	0.0	0.0
C+ /6.4	9.4	1.34	11.97	1	22	77	0	1	91	N/A	N/A	17	6	25,000	5,000	0.0	0.0
C- /4.2	15.1	0.89	16.96	22	4	95	0	1	52	121.0	N/A	87	6	250,000	0	0.0	0.0
D- /1.0	11.8	0.70	2.90	16	0	97	2	1	35	74.9	-23.1	7	N/A	1,000	50	4.8	0.0
C+ /6.4	11.9	0.92	2.72	N/A	0	97	2	1	35	N/A	N/A	2	N/A	1,000	50	0.0	0.0
D- /1.0	11.9	0.70	3.79	3	0	97	2	1	35	77.4	-23.0	8	N/A	1,000	500	0.0	0.0
C /4.7	8.1	0.53	8.74	33	4	93	2	1	92	66.0	-11.9	61	1	1,000	50	4.8	0.0
B- /7.4	8.1	0.67	8.73	2	4	93	2	1	92	N/A	N/A	30	1	1,000	50	0.0	0.0
C /4.7	8.1	0.53	8.75	47	4	93	2	1	92	68.4	-11.8	64	1	1,000	500	0.0	0.0
D+ /2.6	13.5	0.57	4.60	1	2	86	11	1	13	-14.3	-24.3	0	N/A	1,000	50	4.8	0.0
D+ /2.6	13.7	0.57	4.55	2	2	86	11	1	13	-13.9	-24.2	0	N/A	1,000	500	0.0	0.0
D- /1.1	11.3	0.59	6.14	4	2	96	0	2	86	26.4	-23.7	82	1	1,000	50	4.8	0.0
D- /1.1	11.4	0.59	6.17	5	2	96	0	2	86	28.0	-23.6	83	1	1,000	500	0.0	0.0
C+ /6.0	5.9	0.88	9.65	15	8	66	25	1	44	44.2	-11.1	32	N/A	1,000	50	4.8	0.0
B+ /9.6	1.4	N/A	10.28	2,297	2	0	97	1	31	3.7	2.0	79	10	0	0	0.0	0.0
C /5.3	12.5	0.64	9.75	1,899	0	100	0	0	1	55.4	-26.3	69	10	0	0	0.0	0.0
C /5.4	12.9	1.08	17.55	2,595	0	98	0	2	1	139.9	-24.1	33	N/A	0	0	0.0	0.0
B+ /9.2	2.4	0.08	9.69	2	40	0	57	3	136	N/A	N/A	57	5	2,500	100	4.3	2.0
B /8.6	2.4	0.09	9.73	78	40	0	57	3	136	N/A	N/A	60	5	1,000,000	10,000	0.0	2.0
U /	N/A	N/A	9.81	68	0	0	0	100	246	N/A	N/A	N/A	3	1,000,000	10,000	0.0	2.0
C+ /6.5	5.6	0.57	10.00	16	0	0	0	100	54	N/A	N/A	75	6	1,000,000	10,000	0.0	2.0
C+ /6.5	12.8	0.75	10.57	4	3	96	0	1	19	N/A	N/A	89	4	1,000	100	5.8	2.0
C+ /6.5	12.7	0.75	10.73	190	3	96	0	1	19	N/A	N/A	90	4	250,000	0	0.0	2.0
B- /7.0	12.1	0.68	9.81	3	6	93	0	1	34	N/A	N/A	81	4	1,000	100	5.8	2.0
B- /7.0	12.1	0.68	9.81	3	6	93	0	1	34	N/A	N/A	83	4	250,000	0	0.0	2.0
C- /3.1	16.8	0.97	23.19	2	0	99	0	1	11	103.8	-22.0	10	18	1,000	100	5.8	2.0
C- /3.1	16.8	0.97	23.91	95	0	99	0	1	11	106.6	-22.0	11	18	250,000	0	0.0	2.0
C+ /6.1	14.5	0.87	30.51	8	0	97	2	1	11	138.5	-20.4	80	8	1,000	100	5.8	2.0
C+ /6.1	14.5	0.87	30.52	145	0	97	2	1	11	141.8	-20.3	82	8	250,000	0	0.0	2.0
C- /3.2	14.1	0.82	11.70	9	0	99	0	1	229	144.1	-26.4	89	8	250,000	0	0.0	2.0

Fund Type	Fund Name	Ticker Symbol	Overall Investment Rating	Phone	Performance Rating/Pts	3 Mo	6 Mo	1Yr / Pct	3Yr / Pct	5Yr / Pct	Dividend Yield	Expense Ratio
	99 Pct = Best 0 Pct = Worst				PERFORMANCE			Total Return % through 2/28/17	Annualized		Incl. in Returns	
SC	RBC Small Cap Core A	TEEAX	C	(800) 422-2766	C+ / 6.3	1.14	8.59	35.20 /94	6.36 /67	11.86 /73	0.00	1.34
SC	RBC Small Cap Core I	RCSIX	B-	(800) 422-2766	B- / 7.5	1.21	8.73	35.57 /95	6.63 /69	12.15 /76	0.17	1.13
GR	RBC Small Cap Value I	RSVIX	U	(800) 422-2766	U /	3.48	12.68	38.24 /97	--	--	0.42	3.50
MC	RBC SMID Cap Growth A	TMCAX	D	(800) 422-2766	C / 5.1	5.89	5.74	24.17 /70	6.22 /66	10.86 /65	0.00	1.45
MC	RBC SMID Cap Growth I	TMCIX	C-	(800) 422-2766	C+ / 6.5	6.04	5.90	24.50 /72	6.49 /68	11.14 /67	0.00	1.07
IN	Redmont Resolute I	RMRGX	C-	(877) 665-1287	D / 1.8	3.12	3.50	8.47 / 8	2.34 /26	3.45 /13	1.18	2.40
MC	Reinhart Mid Cap PMV Adv	RPMVX	A-	(855) 774-3863	B+ / 8.5	4.17	9.87	28.53 /83	8.64 /84	--	0.49	1.32
MC	Reinhart Mid Cap PMV Inv	RPMMX	A-	(855) 774-3863	B+ / 8.3	4.09	9.73	28.24 /82	8.36 /82	--	0.29	1.57
GL	REMS Real Estate Income 50/50 Inst	RREIX	C+	(800) 673-0550	C+ / 6.0	3.28	-2.43	14.18 /26	10.06 /94	9.71 /56	4.37	0.84
GL	REMS Real Estate Income 50/50 Plat	RREFX	C+	(800) 673-0550	C+ / 6.1	3.19	-2.58	13.87 /25	9.78 /92	9.40 /54	4.16	1.09
RE	REMS Real Estate Value Opp Fd Inst	HLRRX	C	(800) 673-0550	C+ / 6.2	4.15	0.27	20.79 /56	7.60 /76	11.69 /71	2.02	1.41
RE	REMS Real Estate Value Opp Fd Plat	HLPPX	C-	(800) 673-0550	C+ / 6.0	4.14	0.22	20.52 /55	7.35 /74	11.42 /69	1.79	1.66
GR	Renaissance Global IPO	IPOSX	E-	(888) 476-3863	E / 0.3	0.88	-3.76	16.22 /35	-3.86 / 3	5.60 /26	0.00	3.86
IN	RESQ Dynamic Allocation A	RQEAX	D-	(877) 940-2526	E / 0.3	7.59	3.96	10.38 /13	-2.38 / 6	--	0.00	2.81
IN	RESQ Dynamic Allocation I	RQEIX	D	(877) 940-2526	E+ / 0.6	7.62	4.15	10.78 /14	-2.00 / 7	--	0.00	2.41
GL	RESQ Strategic Income A	RQIAX	C-	(877) 940-2526	E / 0.5	5.88	1.66	5.08 / 4	0.22 /14	--	0.17	2.92
GL	RESQ Strategic Income I	RQIIX	C-	(877) 940-2526	D- / 1.0	5.99	1.99	5.53 / 4	0.65 /16	--	0.30	2.52
GR	Reynolds Blue Chip Growth	RBCGX	E	(800) 773-9665	D+ / 2.4	6.51	6.49	10.81 /14	1.39 /20	7.75 /40	0.00	1.71
SC	Rice Hall James Micro Cap Port	RHJSX	C+	(866) 777-7818	C+ / 6.8	2.62	13.08	31.09 /88	5.14 /56	11.80 /72	0.00	1.71
SC	Rice Hall James Small Cap Port	RHJMX	E-	(866) 777-7818	C- / 3.0	1.16	4.04	14.46 /28	3.52 /37	8.71 /48	0.00	1.67
MC	Rice Hall James SMID Cap Investor	RHJVX	C-	(866) 777-7818	C / 4.5	7.36	9.01	19.53 /50	2.70 /29	7.21 /36	0.00	2.88
AG	RidgeWorth Aggr Gr Alloc Str A	SLAAX	E+	(888) 784-3863	C- / 3.4	5.76	5.93	17.44 /40	4.21 /45	7.83 /41	0.89	2.28
AG	RidgeWorth Aggr Gr Alloc Str C	CLVLX	E+	(888) 784-3863	C- / 4.0	5.45	5.63	16.62 /37	3.57 /38	7.17 /36	0.16	2.94
AG	RidgeWorth Aggr Gr Alloc Str I	CVMGX	D-	(888) 784-3863	C / 4.7	5.71	6.04	17.60 /41	4.37 /47	8.04 /42	1.12	2.26
GI	RidgeWorth Ceredex Lg Cap Val Eq	SVIIX	C+	(888) 784-3863	B- / 7.3	6.34	10.75	26.77 /79	8.09 /80	12.51 /79	1.21	1.37
GI	RidgeWorth Ceredex Lg Cap Val Eq	SVIFX	B-	(888) 784-3863	B / 8.0	6.15	10.45	26.13 /77	7.58 /76	11.94 /74	0.88	1.71
GI	RidgeWorth Ceredex Lg Cap Val Eq I	STVTX	B	(888) 784-3863	B+ / 8.6	6.38	10.89	27.13 /80	8.39 /82	12.83 /82	1.54	1.09
GI	RidgeWorth Ceredex Lg Cap Val Eq	STVZX	A	(888) 784-3863	B+ / 8.8	6.43	11.06	27.52 /81	8.63 /84	12.98 /84	1.78	0.72
MC	RidgeWorth Ceredex Md Cp Val Eq A	SAMVX	B	(888) 784-3863	B+ / 8.7	6.94	13.42	33.06 /92	8.62 /84	13.17 /86	0.85	1.45
MC	RidgeWorth Ceredex Md Cp Val Eq C	SMVFX	B+	(888) 784-3863	A- / 9.2	6.79	13.24	32.56 /91	8.19 /80	12.70 /81	0.49	1.78
MC	RidgeWorth Ceredex Md Cp Val Eq I	SMVTX	B+	(888) 784-3863	A / 9.5	7.03	13.69	33.49 /92	8.94 /86	13.49 /89	1.16	1.12
MC	RidgeWorth Ceredex Md Cp Val Eq	SMVZX	A+	(888) 784-3863	A+ / 9.6	7.13	13.77	33.87 /93	9.26 /89	13.69 /91	1.46	0.80
SC	● RidgeWorth Ceredex Sm Cap Val Eq	SASVX	D	(888) 784-3863	B- / 7.2	2.96	7.48	31.10 /88	8.30 /81	12.44 /78	0.68	1.55
SC	● RidgeWorth Ceredex Sm Cap Val Eq	STCEX	D+	(888) 784-3863	B / 8.0	2.83	7.31	30.62 /87	7.91 /78	12.01 /74	0.48	1.90
SC	● RidgeWorth Ceredex Sm Cap Val Eq	SCETX	C-	(888) 784-3863	B+ / 8.5	3.01	7.63	31.40 /89	8.63 /84	12.79 /82	0.98	1.21
AA	RidgeWorth Cons Alloc Str A	SVCAX	C-	(888) 784-3863	D- / 1.5	3.13	1.39	7.98 / 7	2.85 /30	4.29 /17	1.81	1.13
AA	RidgeWorth Cons Alloc Str C	SCCLX	C-	(888) 784-3863	D / 1.7	2.96	1.03	7.32 / 6	2.14 /25	3.56 /13	1.31	1.78
AA	RidgeWorth Cons Alloc Str I	SCCTX	C	(888) 784-3863	D / 2.2	3.17	1.44	8.29 / 8	3.14 /33	4.59 /19	2.35	0.90
OT	RidgeWorth Glbl Res and Infra A	INNAX	C-	(888) 990-9950	C+ / 6.1	3.21	16.55	43.26 /98	1.58 /21	--	1.65	2.11
OT	RidgeWorth Glbl Res and Infra C	INNCX	C-	(888) 990-9950	C+ / 6.6	3.00	16.14	42.30 /98	0.83 /17	--	1.79	2.84
OT	RidgeWorth Glbl Res and Infra Inst	INNNX	C	(888) 990-9950	B- / 7.3	3.29	16.71	43.57 /98	1.84 /23	--	1.75	1.87
AA	RidgeWorth Grow Alloc Str A	SGIAX	D+	(888) 784-3863	C- / 3.0	5.22	5.02	15.75 /33	4.13 /44	7.40 /37	0.98	1.33
AA	RidgeWorth Grow Alloc Str C	SGILX	C-	(888) 784-3863	C- / 3.5	4.98	4.57	14.94 /30	3.46 /37	6.72 /33	0.53	1.97
AA	RidgeWorth Grow Alloc Str I	CLVGX	C-	(888) 784-3863	C- / 4.2	5.21	5.01	15.90 /34	4.31 /46	7.60 /39	1.22	1.36
AG	RidgeWorth Innovative Gr Stock A	SAGAX	D	(888) 784-3863	C / 5.2	11.28	10.05	28.00 /82	3.01 /32	12.17 /76	0.00	1.49
AG	RidgeWorth Innovative Gr Stock I	SCATX	D+	(888) 784-3863	C+ / 6.6	11.32	10.14	28.21 /82	3.20 /34	12.39 /78	0.00	1.39
FO	RidgeWorth Intl Equity A	SCIIX	E	(888) 784-3863	E+ / 0.6	7.16	0.44	13.12 /22	-0.72 /10	5.38 /24	0.33	1.78
FO	RidgeWorth Intl Equity I	STITX	E	(888) 784-3863	D- / 1.1	7.22	0.58	13.48 /23	-0.50 /11	5.54 /25	0.38	1.68
AA	RidgeWorth Mod Alloc Str A	SVMAX	D	(888) 784-3863	D / 2.1	4.13	3.14	11.69 /17	3.44 /36	5.86 /27	1.31	1.24
AA	RidgeWorth Mod Alloc Str C	SVGLX	D	(888) 784-3863	D+ / 2.5	3.86	2.74	10.85 /14	2.80 /30	5.21 /23	0.80	1.82
AA	RidgeWorth Mod Alloc Str I	CLVBX	D+	(888) 784-3863	C- / 3.1	4.16	3.28	11.92 /18	3.62 /38	6.04 /29	1.52	1.13
GR	RidgeWorth Silvan LC Gro Stock A	STCIX	D-	(888) 784-3863	C- / 3.6	6.56	5.09	14.88 /29	5.06 /55	10.47 /62	0.00	1.21

● Denotes fund is closed to new investors
* Denotes fund is included in Section II

Risk Rating/Pts	3 Year Standard Deviation	Beta	NAV As of 2/28/17	Total $(Mil)	Cash %	Stocks %	Bonds %	Other %	Portfolio Turnover Ratio	Last Bull Market Return	Last Bear Market Return	Manager Quality Pct	Manager Tenure (Years)	Initial Purch. $	Additional Purch. $	Front End Load	Back End Load
C /5.0	16.9	1.02	36.53	13	0	99	0	1	20	123.7	-24.0	66	26	1,000	100	5.8	2.0
C /5.1	16.9	1.02	37.95	269	0	99	0	1	20	126.8	-23.9	69	26	250,000	0	0.0	2.0
U /	N/A	N/A	12.53	39	3	96	0	1	47	N/A	N/A	N/A	3	250,000	0	0.0	2.0
C- /3.1	11.8	0.92	13.72	11	2	97	0	1	14	108.3	-17.8	42	8	1,000	100	5.8	2.0
C- /3.4	11.8	0.92	15.14	68	2	97	0	1	14	111.1	-17.7	46	8	250,000	0	0.0	2.0
B /8.6	4.4	0.39	11.14	552	36	23	37	4	27	N/A	N/A	53	6	1,000,000	0	0.0	2.0
C+ /6.5	11.1	0.84	15.82	147	7	92	0	1	63	N/A	N/A	78	5	5,000	100	0.0	0.0
C+ /6.5	11.1	0.84	15.78	28	7	92	0	1	63	N/A	N/A	76	5	5,000	100	0.0	0.0
C /5.5	8.6	0.37	12.69	92	2	97	0	1	27	81.4	-9.3	99	7	50,000	5,000	0.0	2.0
C+ /6.1	8.6	0.37	12.54	3	2	97	0	1	27	78.6	-9.4	99	7	2,500	100	0.0	0.0
C /4.4	12.1	0.76	15.36	260	3	96	0	1	51	126.1	-24.1	66	15	50,000	5,000	0.0	0.0
C /4.4	12.1	0.76	15.21	25	3	96	0	1	51	123.1	-24.2	63	15	2,500	100	0.0	0.0
D+ /2.8	16.8	1.12	14.83	6	0	96	3	1	109	54.1	-27.6	0	20	5,000	100	0.0	2.0
C+ /6.9	11.1	0.67	8.93	43	17	82	0	1	907	N/A	N/A	3	4	1,000	0	5.8	2.0
C+ /6.9	11.1	0.68	9.04	1	17	82	0	1	907	N/A	N/A	3	4	100,000	0	0.0	2.0
B+ /9.0	5.0	0.21	9.66	44	4	30	58	8	1,013	N/A	N/A	75	4	1,000	0	4.8	2.0
B /8.9	5.1	0.21	9.69	N/A	4	30	58	8	1,013	N/A	N/A	78	4	100,000	0	0.0	2.0
D+ /2.7	10.6	0.90	51.87	71	3	95	0	2	491	80.7	-22.9	4	29	1,000	100	0.0	0.0
C /5.2	14.5	0.88	32.85	47	2	94	2	2	62	129.7	-23.7	64	23	2,500	100	0.0	2.0
E /0.3	14.0	0.83	10.52	41	0	97	1	2	54	84.8	-19.0	47	21	2,500	100	0.0	0.0
C+ /5.7	12.3	0.99	20.56	5	2	94	2	2	49	77.5	-25.5	7	13	2,500	100	0.0	0.0
D /2.1	9.5	0.89	5.96	3	1	84	14	1	43	78.2	-21.4	16	25	2,000	1,000	5.8	0.0
D /2.0	9.5	0.89	5.70	N/A	1	84	14	1	43	72.4	-21.7	12	25	5,000	1,000	0.0	0.0
D /2.2	9.5	0.90	6.05	3	1	84	14	1	43	80.3	-21.4	17	25	0	0	0.0	0.0
C /4.9	11.1	1.03	17.06	357	1	98	0	1	66	121.6	-19.5	39	22	2,000	1,000	5.8	0.0
C /4.9	11.1	1.03	16.67	19	1	98	0	1	66	115.3	-19.7	33	22	5,000	1,000	0.0	0.0
C /4.9	11.1	1.04	17.19	1,486	1	98	0	1	66	124.9	-19.3	43	22	0	0	0.0	0.0
C+ /6.7	11.1	1.04	17.25	319	1	98	0	1	66	126.4	-19.3	46	22	2,500,000	0	0.0	0.0
C /4.7	12.5	0.98	14.32	377	1	94	3	2	98	139.4	-27.8	65	16	2,000	1,000	5.8	0.0
C /4.7	12.5	0.98	14.01	56	1	94	3	2	98	133.8	-28.1	60	16	5,000	1,000	0.0	0.0
C /4.7	12.5	0.98	14.47	2,724	1	94	3	2	98	143.2	-27.8	69	16	0	0	0.0	0.0
C+ /6.4	12.6	0.98	14.48	284	1	94	3	2	98	145.4	-27.8	72	16	2,500,000	0	0.0	0.0
E+ /0.9	13.7	0.80	12.58	125	0	98	1	1	36	117.6	-20.9	89	23	2,000	1,000	5.8	0.0
E+ /0.8	13.7	0.80	11.46	25	0	98	1	1	36	112.9	-21.1	87	23	5,000	1,000	0.0	0.0
E+ /0.9	13.7	0.80	12.98	807	0	98	1	1	36	121.3	-20.8	90	23	0	0	0.0	0.0
B /8.6	4.4	0.67	12.33	8	0	34	65	1	40	34.6	-5.3	47	14	2,000	1,000	4.8	0.0
B /8.7	4.4	0.67	12.18	17	0	34	65	1	40	29.6	-5.6	37	14	5,000	1,000	0.0	0.0
B /8.6	4.4	0.67	12.31	19	0	34	65	1	40	36.7	-5.2	52	14	0	0	0.0	0.0
C- /3.4	17.3	1.17	11.66	1	9	90	0	1	19	N/A	N/A	2	5	2,500	100	5.8	0.0
C- /3.4	17.3	1.17	11.41	N/A	9	90	0	1	19	N/A	N/A	2	5	2,500	100	0.0	0.0
C- /3.4	17.3	1.17	11.70	8	9	90	0	1	19	N/A	N/A	2	5	1,000,000	100,000	0.0	0.0
C+ /6.2	8.5	1.32	10.31	6	0	73	25	2	29	67.6	-15.4	12	25	2,000	1,000	5.8	0.0
C+ /6.2	8.4	1.31	10.05	2	0	73	25	2	29	61.8	-15.7	9	25	5,000	1,000	0.0	0.0
C+ /6.2	8.4	1.31	10.36	32	0	73	25	2	29	69.3	-15.3	13	25	0	0	0.0	0.0
D /2.2	17.6	1.26	18.44	7	0	99	0	1	59	118.9	-26.2	2	13	2,000	1,000	5.8	0.0
D /2.2	17.6	1.26	19.36	22	0	99	0	1	59	121.3	-26.1	2	13	0	0	0.0	0.0
C- /3.9	10.9	0.78	9.68	14	1	96	1	2	114	56.5	-25.6	67	2	2,000	1,000	5.8	0.0
C- /3.9	11.0	0.79	9.82	49	1	96	1	2	114	58.1	-25.5	70	2	0	0	0.0	0.0
C /5.4	6.3	0.99	8.94	11	0	54	45	1	26	50.5	-10.4	26	25	2,000	1,000	5.8	0.0
C /5.5	6.3	0.99	8.85	10	0	54	45	1	26	45.6	-10.8	20	25	5,000	1,000	0.0	0.0
C /5.4	6.4	0.99	8.99	31	0	54	45	1	26	52.0	-10.3	27	25	0	0	0.0	0.0
C- /3.7	12.9	1.11	7.17	61	2	95	1	2	10	107.0	-16.9	8	10	2,000	1,000	5.8	0.0

Fund Type	Fund Name	Ticker Symbol	Overall Investment Rating	Phone	Performance Rating/Pts	3 Mo	6 Mo	1Yr / Pct	3Yr / Pct	5Yr / Pct	Dividend Yield	Expense Ratio
	99 Pct = Best *0 Pct = Worst*							Total Return % through 2/28/17	Annualized		Incl. in Returns	
GR	RidgeWorth Silvant LC Gro Stock C	STCFX	D-	(888) 784-3863	C- / 4.1	6.50	4.77	14.02 / 25	4.35 / 47	9.76 / 57	0.00	1.89
GR	RidgeWorth Silvant LC Gro Stock I	STCAX	D+	(888) 784-3863	C / 4.9	6.63	5.18	15.15 / 31	5.28 / 57	10.76 / 64	0.00	1.24
GR	RidgeWorth Silvant LC Gro Stock IS	STCZX	C	(888) 784-3863	C / 5.0	6.72	5.16	15.23 / 31	5.37 / 58	10.82 / 64	0.00	0.89
SC	RidgeWorth Silvant SC Gr Stock A	SCGIX	E	(888) 784-3863	C- / 3.6	5.62	8.97	29.16 / 84	1.51 / 21	9.46 / 54	0.00	1.21
SC	RidgeWorth Silvant SC Gr Stock C	SSCFX	E	(888) 784-3863	C- / 4.2	5.33	8.54	28.38 / 83	0.85 / 17	8.73 / 48	0.00	1.89
SC	RidgeWorth Silvant SC Gr Stock I	SSCTX	E+	(888) 784-3863	C / 4.9	5.63	8.88	29.34 / 85	1.58 / 21	9.54 / 55	0.00	1.24
SC	RidgeWorth Silvant SC Gr Stock IS	SCGZX	C-	(888) 784-3863	C / 5.1	5.58	9.03	29.53 / 85	1.80 / 23	9.68 / 56	0.00	0.89
SC	River Oak Discovery Fund	RIVSX	C-	(888) 462-5386	C+ / 5.7	4.65	9.69	22.93 / 66	4.39 / 47	8.82 / 49	0.00	1.45
GR	Riverbridge Growth Institutional	RIVBX	C+	(888) 447-4470	C+ / 5.8	5.18	6.96	21.54 / 60	5.65 / 61	---	0.00	1.42
GR	Riverbridge Growth Investor	RIVRX	C	(888) 447-4470	C+ / 5.6	5.16	6.88	21.23 / 58	5.40 / 59	---	0.00	1.67
AA	RiverFront Consv Inc Bldr A	RCABX	C-	(866) 759-5679	D / 1.6	3.38	2.19	9.62 / 11	2.66 / 29	---	1.75	2.07
AA	RiverFront Consv Inc Bldr C	RCCBX	C-	(866) 759-5679	D / 1.8	3.15	1.88	8.75 / 9	1.91 / 23	---	1.10	2.83
AA	RiverFront Consv Inc Bldr I	RCIBX	C-	(866) 759-5679	D+ / 2.3	3.44	2.32	9.78 / 11	2.92 / 31	---	2.07	1.83
GI	RiverFront Dynamic Equity Income A	RLGAX	D+	(866) 759-5679	C- / 3.7	6.70	6.70	17.10 / 39	4.45 / 48	7.15 / 36	1.32	1.65
GI	RiverFront Dynamic Equity Income C	RLGCX	C-	(866) 759-5679	C- / 4.2	6.52	6.35	16.35 / 36	3.69 / 39	6.36 / 31	0.94	2.40
GI	RiverFront Dynamic Equity Income I	RLIIX	C	(866) 759-5679	C / 5.1	6.77	6.85	17.42 / 40	4.72 / 51	7.42 / 38	1.59	1.40
GI	RiverFront Global Allocation A	RMGAX	D	(866) 759-5679	C- / 3.1	7.24	6.89	17.22 / 39	3.12 / 33	6.56 / 32	1.27	1.76
GI	RiverFront Global Allocation C	RMGCX	D	(866) 759-5679	C- / 3.5	7.03	6.49	16.29 / 35	2.33 / 26	5.76 / 27	1.25	2.51
GI	RiverFront Global Allocation I	RMGIX	D+	(866) 759-5679	C / 4.4	7.31	7.04	17.47 / 40	3.37 / 36	6.82 / 34	1.40	1.51
GL	RiverFront Global Growth A	RLTAX	D	(866) 759-5679	C- / 3.5	7.62	7.31	18.78 / 46	3.34 / 35	7.32 / 37	1.23	1.77
GL	RiverFront Global Growth C	RLTCX	D	(866) 759-5679	C- / 3.9	7.39	6.83	17.80 / 42	2.56 / 28	6.52 / 32	1.22	2.52
GL	RiverFront Global Growth I	RLFIX	D+	(866) 759-5679	C / 4.8	7.68	7.37	19.04 / 47	3.57 / 38	7.56 / 39	1.33	1.53
GL	● RiverFront Global Growth Inv	RLTSX	D+	(866) 759-5679	C / 4.6	7.59	7.27	18.81 / 46	3.34 / 35	7.31 / 37	1.31	1.77
GL	● RiverFront Global Growth L	RLTIX	D+	(866) 759-5679	C / 4.8	7.69	7.38	19.07 / 47	3.61 / 38	7.58 / 39	1.33	1.52
GI	RiverFront Moderate Growth & Inc A	RMIAX	D+	(866) 759-5679	D+ / 2.7	4.82	4.59	13.46 / 23	4.15 / 45	5.89 / 28	1.62	1.57
GI	RiverFront Moderate Growth & Inc C	RMICX	C-	(866) 759-5679	C- / 3.1	4.64	4.23	12.60 / 20	3.35 / 35	5.11 / 22	1.08	2.32
GI	RiverFront Moderate Growth & Inc I	RMIIX	C-	(866) 759-5679	C- / 3.9	4.86	4.72	13.73 / 24	4.38 / 47	6.14 / 29	1.95	1.32
AA	RiverNorth Core Oppty I	RNCIX	U	(888) 848-7549	U /	8.00	6.47	25.26 / 74	---	---	4.60	2.56
IN	RiverNorth Core Oppty R	RNCOX	C+	(888) 848-7549	C+ / 5.9	7.84	6.24	24.96 / 73	4.92 / 53	7.34 / 37	4.37	2.81
GR	RiverPark Focused Value Inst	RFVIX	U	(888) 564-4517	U /	6.97	9.95	15.06 / 30	---	---	0.82	1.25
GR	RiverPark Large Growth Instl	RPXIX	C+	(888) 564-4517	C+ / 5.9	8.01	9.31	22.87 / 66	4.12 / 44	10.88 / 65	0.50	1.00
GR	RiverPark Large Growth Retail	RPXFX	C	(888) 564-4517	C+ / 5.7	7.94	9.20	22.62 / 65	3.79 / 40	10.56 / 62	0.22	1.25
GL	RiverPark Long/Short Oppty Instl	RLSIX	C-	(888) 564-4517	D+ / 2.4	7.41	8.15	13.62 / 24	0.15 / 14	3.07 / 11	0.00	3.01
GL	RiverPark Long/Short Oppty Retail	RLSFX	D+	(888) 564-4517	D- / 1.5	7.38	8.13	13.41 / 23	-0.06 / 13	---	0.00	3.03
AA	RiverPark Strategic Income Inst	RSIIX	C-	(888) 564-4517	C- / 3.1	2.77	4.36	13.81 / 25	3.35 / 35	---	5.54	0.90
AA	RiverPark Strategic Income Rtl	RSIVX	C-	(888) 564-4517	D+ / 2.8	2.71	4.13	13.43 / 23	3.03 / 32	---	5.31	1.19
GR	RiverPark Structural Alpha Instl	RSAIX	C	(888) 564-4517	D- / 1.3	0.23	1.22	2.95 / 3	2.10 / 25	---	0.00	1.90
GR	RiverPark Structural Alpha Retail	RSAFX	C	(888) 564-4517	D- / 1.2	0.13	1.13	2.66 / 2	1.85 / 23	---	0.00	2.24
GR	RiverPark/Wedgewood Instl	RWGIX	C-	(888) 564-4517	C- / 4.0	6.27	7.15	16.21 / 35	3.30 / 35	9.25 / 53	0.16	0.85
GR	RiverPark/Wedgewood Retail	RWGFX	D+	(888) 564-4517	C- / 3.9	6.19	7.07	15.89 / 34	3.22 / 34	9.09 / 51	0.00	1.16
GI	RMB A	RMBHX	D	(800) 601-5228	C / 5.3	8.49	8.64	22.98 / 67	5.53 / 60	8.26 / 44	0.22	1.38
GI	RMB C	RMBJX	D-	(800) 601-5228	C+ / 5.7	8.30	8.27	22.02 / 62	4.74 / 51	7.44 / 38	0.00	2.13
FS	RMB Mendon Financial Long/Short A	RMBFX	A	(800) 462-2392	B / 8.2	4.30	12.59	23.81 / 69	10.92 / 97	14.93 / 97	0.00	2.30
FS	RMB Mendon Financial Long/Short C	RMBCX	A	(800) 462-2392	B+ / 8.5	4.11	12.20	22.95 / 66	10.12 / 94	14.11 / 94	0.00	3.00
FS	RMB Mendon Financial Long/Short I	RMBIX	U	(800) 462-2392	U /	4.39	12.78	24.21 / 71	---	---	0.00	1.80
FS	RMB Mendon Financial Services A	RMBKX	A+	(800) 601-5228	A+ / 9.9	12.14	27.72	49.34 / 99	20.69 / 99	23.00 / 99	0.00	1.79
FS	RMB Mendon Financial Services C	RMBNX	A+	(800) 601-5228	A+ / 9.9	11.91	27.26	48.24 / 99	19.80 / 99	22.07 / 99	0.00	2.54
GI	RNC Genter Dividend Income Fund	GDIIX	B+	(800) 545-4322	B- / 7.2	6.07	7.62	23.23 / 67	7.99 / 79	10.36 / 61	1.78	2.27
GL	Rockefeller Equity Allocation Instl	ROCKX	U	(855) 369-6209	U /	6.98	5.86	17.90 / 42	---	---	0.87	1.43
GR	Roosevelt Multi-Cap Inst	BULRX	D	(877) 322-0576	C / 4.7	6.96	7.41	17.80 / 42	3.77 / 40	---	0.65	0.94
GR	Roosevelt Multi-Cap Investor	BULLX	D	(877) 322-0576	C / 4.4	6.85	7.30	17.46 / 40	3.50 / 37	7.94 / 42	0.36	1.19
GI	Roumell Opportunistic Value A	RAMVX	E	(800) 773-3863	E+ / 0.8	8.31	8.88	27.54 / 81	-3.20 / 4	2.33 / 9	0.16	1.88

● Denotes fund is closed to new investors
* Denotes fund is included in Section II

RISK			NET ASSETS		ASSET						BULL / BEAR		FUND MANAGER		MINIMUMS		LOADS	
	3 Year		NAV							Portfolio	Last Bull	Last Bear	Manager	Manager	Initial	Additional	Front	Back
Risk Rating/Pts	Standard Deviation	Beta	As of 2/28/17	Total $(Mil)	Cash %	Stocks %	Bonds %	Other %		Turnover Ratio	Market Return	Market Return	Quality Pct	Tenure (Years)	Purch. $	Purch. $	End Load	End Load
D /2.2	12.8	1.10	4.60	37	2	95	1	2		10	99.7	-17.1	6	10	5,000	1,000	0.0	0.0
C- /4.2	12.8	1.10	8.87	95	2	95	1	2		10	109.8	-16.7	9	10	0	0	0.0	0.0
C+ /5.6	12.8	1.10	8.90	28	2	95	1	2		10	110.3	-16.7	9	10	2,500,000	0	0.0	0.0
E /0.5	16.4	0.98	7.34	7	0	98	1	1		73	101.4	-25.6	14	10	2,000	1,000	5.8	0.0
E /0.5	16.3	0.98	3.40	5	0	98	1	1		73	94.2	-25.9	10	10	5,000	1,000	0.0	0.0
E /0.5	16.3	0.98	9.02	30	0	98	1	1		73	102.4	-25.5	15	10	0	0	0.0	0.0
C /4.9	16.3	0.98	9.10	3	0	98	1	1		73	103.7	-25.5	17	10	2,500,000	0	0.0	0.0
C- /3.6	13.6	0.79	16.19	14	1	98	0	1		21	100.1	-26.0	61	12	2,000	25	0.0	0.0
C+ /5.7	11.1	0.92	15.27	63	0	97	2	1		25	N/A	N/A	26	5	1,000,000	0	0.0	0.0
C+ /5.7	11.1	0.92	15.12	3	0	97	2	1		25	N/A	N/A	23	5	2,500	100	0.0	1.0
B /8.1	4.6	0.68	10.81	1	5	31	63	1		137	N/A	N/A	43	5	2,500	0	5.5	0.0
B /8.1	4.6	0.68	10.70	11	5	31	63	1		137	N/A	N/A	34	5	2,500	0	0.0	0.0
B /8.1	4.6	0.68	10.64	2	5	31	63	1		137	N/A	N/A	47	5	1,000,000	0	0.0	0.0
C /5.5	9.0	0.81	13.23	19	13	75	10	2		129	61.8	-16.0	25	7	2,500	0	5.5	0.0
C /5.5	9.1	0.81	12.98	31	13	75	10	2		129	55.3	-16.3	18	7	2,500	0	0.0	0.0
C /5.5	9.1	0.81	13.17	28	13	75	10	2		129	64.1	-16.0	28	7	1,000,000	0	0.0	0.0
C /4.7	10.2	0.91	12.67	7	4	87	7	2		124	59.0	-19.0	8	7	2,500	0	5.5	0.0
C /4.7	10.1	0.90	12.34	14	4	87	7	2		124	52.7	-19.3	6	7	2,500	0	0.0	0.0
C /4.7	10.1	0.90	12.48	14	4	87	7	2		124	61.1	-18.9	10	7	1,000,000	0	0.0	0.0
C- /4.1	10.7	0.79	14.46	10	9	90	0	1		113	68.5	-22.1	92	9	2,500	0	5.5	0.0
C- /4.0	10.7	0.79	14.05	11	9	90	0	1		113	61.9	-22.4	89	9	2,500	0	0.0	0.0
C- /4.1	10.8	0.79	14.58	10	9	90	0	1		113	70.6	-22.0	92	9	1,000,000	0	0.0	0.0
C- /4.0	10.8	0.79	14.38	4	9	90	0	1		113	68.6	-22.1	92	9	2,500	0	0.0	0.0
C- /4.1	10.8	0.79	14.56	23	9	90	0	1		113	70.9	-22.0	92	9	1,000,000	0	0.0	0.0
C+ /6.5	6.8	0.62	11.79	20	9	56	34	1		132	48.6	-10.6	45	7	2,500	0	5.5	0.0
C+ /6.5	6.8	0.62	11.68	60	9	56	34	1		132	42.7	-11.0	35	7	2,500	0	0.0	0.0
C+ /6.5	6.8	0.62	11.79	44	9	56	34	1		132	50.7	-10.6	48	7	1,000,000	0	0.0	0.0
U /	N/A	N/A	11.83	157	5	51	42	2		19	N/A	N/A	N/A	11	5,000,000	100	0.0	2.0
C+ /5.6	9.2	0.80	11.82	464	5	51	42	2		19	66.5	-13.9	31	11	5,000	100	0.0	2.0
U /	N/A	N/A	8.59	39	16	83	0	1		26	N/A	N/A	N/A	2	100,000	100	0.0	0.0
C /5.5	12.9	1.15	19.80	19	8	91	0	1		33	110.3	-13.4	4	7	100,000	100	0.0	0.0
C /5.5	12.9	1.15	19.61	30	8	91	0	1		33	107.0	-13.5	4	7	1,000	100	0.0	0.0
B- /7.6	9.9	0.68	11.01	97	66	33	0	1		40	45.0	-6.2	76	5	100,000	100	0.0	0.0
B- /7.6	9.9	0.69	10.91	4	66	33	0	1		40	N/A	N/A	74	5	1,000	100	0.0	0.0
B- /7.3	3.0	0.24	9.54	265	9	0	88	3		69	N/A	N/A	84	4	100,000	100	0.0	0.0
B- /7.3	3.0	0.25	9.52	365	9	0	88	3		69	N/A	N/A	81	4	1,000	100	0.0	0.0
B+ /9.6	2.8	0.23	10.08	13	37	0	62	1		0	N/A	N/A	71	4	100,000	100	0.0	0.0
B+ /9.6	2.8	0.22	9.99	2	37	0	62	1		0	N/A	N/A	68	4	1,000	100	0.0	0.0
C /5.3	10.9	1.00	18.11	1,417	2	97	0	1		24	95.9	-10.4	6	7	100,000	100	0.0	0.0
C /5.3	10.8	0.99	18.01	51	2	97	0	1		24	94.2	-10.5	6	7	1,000	100	0.0	0.0
D /2.1	12.4	1.07	27.73	82	1	98	0	1		17	86.0	-13.4	13	1	2,500	500	5.0	2.0
D /1.6	12.4	1.07	24.59	5	1	98	0	1		17	78.6	-13.7	8	1	2,500	500	0.0	2.0
C+ /6.9	12.6	0.81	18.19	204	24	74	0	2		72	144.3	-24.0	80	13	2,500	500	5.0	2.0
C+ /6.8	12.7	0.81	16.97	28	24	74	0	2		72	134.9	-24.2	75	13	2,500	500	0.0	2.0
U /	N/A	N/A	18.30	83	24	74	0	2		72	N/A	N/A	N/A	13	1,000,000	50,000	0.0	2.0
C+ /6.8	14.6	0.93	42.66	497	10	89	0	1		62	227.8	-20.1	98	18	2,500	500	5.0	2.0
C+ /6.8	14.6	0.93	39.54	55	10	89	0	1		62	214.8	-20.4	98	18	2,500	500	0.0	2.0
C+ /6.9	10.8	0.96	17.47	16	0	99	0	1		25	95.0	-12.2	48	13	2,500	500	0.0	2.0
U /	N/A	N/A	10.72	96	0	0	0	100		57	N/A	N/A	N/A	2	1,000,000	10,000	0.0	0.0
C- /3.1	9.9	0.87	14.59	53	4	95	0	1		89	N/A	N/A	14	16	100,000	0	0.0	0.0
C- /3.1	9.9	0.87	14.44	18	4	95	0	1		89	74.4	-17.0	13	16	1,000	500	0.0	0.0
C- /3.1	12.6	0.75	8.25	1	5	51	43	1		71	13.7	-13.2	2	7	2,500	100	4.5	1.0

I. Index of Stock Mutual Funds

99 Pct = Best
0 Pct = Worst

Fund Type	Fund Name	Ticker Symbol	Overall Investment Rating	Phone	Performance Rating/Pts	3 Mo	6 Mo	1Yr / Pct	3Yr / Pct	5Yr / Pct	Dividend Yield	Expense Ratio
GI	Roumell Opportunistic Value C	RAMDX	E-	(800) 773-3863	E+ / 0.9	8.17	8.51	26.49 /78	-3.93 / 3	--	0.34	2.63
GI	Roumell Opportunistic Value Inst	RAMSX	E	(800) 773-3863	D- / 1.2	8.31	9.02	27.83 /81	-3.01 / 4	2.52 / 9	0.14	1.63
IN	Royce Dividend Value Instl	RDIIX	C	(800) 221-4268	C+ / 6.3	6.01	10.49	25.50 /75	4.32 /47	--	1.55	1.01
GR	Royce Dividend Value Inv	RDVIX	C-	(800) 221-4268	C+ / 6.1	5.95	10.53	25.49 /75	4.34 /47	9.45 /54	1.35	1.14
GR	Royce Dividend Value Svc	RYDVX	C-	(800) 221-4268	C+ / 5.8	5.83	10.18	25.09 /74	4.05 /44	9.14 /52	0.91	1.39
GR	Royce Global Financial Srvcs Svc	RYFSX	C+	(800) 221-4268	B / 7.9	9.40	11.43	30.87 /88	5.90 /63	12.60 /80	0.52	1.85
GR	Royce Heritage Cons	RYGCX	C-	(800) 221-4268	C / 5.2	4.45	8.76	25.09 /74	3.32 /35	6.62 /32	0.00	2.32
GR	Royce Heritage Inv	RHFHX	C	(800) 221-4268	C+ / 6.0	4.82	9.47	26.59 /78	4.52 /49	7.92 /41	0.38	1.01
GR	Royce Heritage R	RHFRX	C-	(800) 221-4268	C+ / 5.6	4.66	9.04	25.62 /75	3.77 /40	7.15 /36	0.00	2.11
GR	Royce Heritage Svc	RGFAX	C	(800) 221-4268	C+ / 5.8	4.77	9.29	26.25 /77	4.25 /46	7.63 /39	0.19	1.37
FO	Royce International Premier Fd Inv	RIPNX	C	(800) 221-4268	C- / 3.5	8.56	2.25	15.57 /32	3.67 /39	--	2.78	1.38
FO	Royce International Premier Fd Svc	RYIPX	C	(800) 221-4268	C- / 3.4	8.65	2.23	15.49 /32	3.48 /37	7.16 /36	2.17	2.35
FO	Royce Intl Micro-Cap Svc	ROIMX	C-	(800) 221-4268	C- / 3.8	7.68	6.52	20.90 /57	2.31 /26	4.67 /19	1.50	3.11
FO	Royce Intl Small Cap Institutional	RISIX	D	(800) 221-4268	E+ / 0.8	7.10	2.51	13.21 /22	-1.92 / 7	--	4.92	2.18
FO	Royce Intl Small Cap Investment	RISNX	D	(800) 221-4268	E+ / 0.7	7.16	2.45	13.13 /22	-1.90 / 7	--	5.06	3.98
FO	Royce Intl Small Cap Service	RYGSX	E+	(800) 221-4268	E+ / 0.6	7.11	2.33	13.00 /22	-2.13 / 6	2.26 / 9	3.36	1.92
SC	Royce Low Priced Stock I	RLPIX	E-	(800) 221-4268	D / 1.9	2.32	8.99	26.39 /77	-0.47 /11	0.99 / 6	0.67	1.12
SC	Royce Low Priced Stock Inv	RLPHX	E-	(800) 221-4268	D / 1.7	2.33	9.01	26.26 /77	-0.57 /11	0.93 / 6	0.67	1.29
SC	Royce Low Priced Stock R	RLPRX	E-	(800) 221-4268	D / 1.6	2.22	8.61	25.62 /75	-1.18 / 9	0.32 / 5	0.12	2.79
SC	Royce Low Priced Stock Svc	RYLPX	E-	(800) 221-4268	D / 1.6	2.23	8.80	26.09 /76	-0.82 /10	0.68 / 6	0.45	1.50
SC	Royce Micro-Cap Cons	RYMCX	E-	(800) 221-4268	D- / 1.5	2.11	10.00	26.51 /78	-1.52 / 8	1.65 / 7	0.00	2.53
SC	Royce Micro-Cap Inv	RYOTX	E	(800) 221-4268	D / 1.9	2.34	10.55	27.83 /81	-0.50 /11	2.71 /10	0.46	1.50
GR	Royce Micro-Cap Opportunity	ROSFX	E	(800) 221-4268	D / 2.1	3.54	9.01	38.22 /96	-1.45 / 8	11.29 /68	0.00	1.39
SC	Royce Micro-Cap Port Inv	RCMCX	E+	(800) 221-4268	D / 2.1	2.22	10.31	26.39 /77	-0.01 /13	2.93 /11	0.64	1.33
SC	Royce Micro-Cap Port Svc	RCMSX	E+	(800) 221-4268	D / 2.0	2.26	10.29	26.25 /77	-0.21 /13	2.69 /10	0.46	1.61
SC	Royce Micro-Cap Svc	RMCFX	E	(800) 221-4268	D / 1.8	2.31	10.49	27.63 /81	-0.63 /11	2.57 / 9	0.31	1.79
SC	Royce Opportunity Fd Cons	ROFCX	C-	(800) 221-4268	B / 7.7	5.25	15.90	41.67 /98	2.72 /29	10.95 /65	0.00	2.26
SC	Royce Opportunity Fd Inst	ROFIX	C	(800) 221-4268	B+ / 8.7	5.63	16.67	43.54 /98	3.99 /43	12.34 /78	0.00	1.05
SC	Royce Opportunity Fd Inv	RYPNX	C	(800) 221-4268	B+ / 8.3	5.58	16.53	43.33 /98	3.86 /41	12.23 /76	0.00	1.17
SC	Royce Opportunity Fd K	ROFKX	C-	(800) 221-4268	B / 8.1	5.51	16.31	42.54 /98	3.33 /35	11.74 /72	0.00	1.62
SC	Royce Opportunity Fd R	ROFRX	C-	(800) 221-4268	B / 8.0	5.44	16.15	42.40 /98	3.19 /34	11.49 /70	0.00	1.82
SC	Royce Opportunity Fd Svc	RYOFX	C-	(800) 221-4268	B / 8.1	5.53	16.45	42.87 /98	3.56 /38	11.87 /73	0.00	1.49
SC	Royce PA Mutual Fd Cons	RYPCX	D-	(800) 221-4268	C+ / 5.9	3.51	11.83	29.52 /85	3.16 /33	8.48 /46	0.00	1.95
SC	Royce PA Mutual Fd Inst	RPMIX	D+	(800) 221-4268	C+ / 6.8	3.83	12.41	30.98 /88	4.29 /46	9.71 /56	0.42	0.82
SC	Royce PA Mutual Fd Inv	PENNX	D+	(800) 221-4268	C+ / 6.6	3.84	12.43	30.90 /88	4.22 /46	9.60 /55	0.34	0.93
SC	Royce PA Mutual Fd K	RPMKX	D	(800) 221-4268	C+ / 6.2	3.64	11.91	29.69 /86	3.47 /37	8.96 /50	0.00	1.52
SC	Royce PA Mutual Fd R	RPMRX	D	(800) 221-4268	C+ / 6.2	3.67	11.99	29.89 /86	3.48 /37	8.87 /50	0.00	1.66
SC	Royce PA Mutual Fd Svc	RYPFX	D	(800) 221-4268	C+ / 6.3	3.75	12.14	30.42 /87	3.88 /41	9.26 /53	0.08	1.24
SC	Royce Premier Cons	RPRCX	C-	(800) 221-4268	B+ / 8.5	9.46	16.39	36.92 /96	4.32 /47	7.47 /38	0.00	2.17
SC	Royce Premier Fd	RYPRX	C-	(800) 221-4268	B+ / 8.9	9.39	16.68	37.94 /96	5.30 /58	8.54 /47	0.21	1.13
SC	Royce Premier Inst	RPFIX	C-	(800) 221-4268	A- / 9.1	9.40	16.72	37.99 /96	5.41 /59	8.65 /48	0.32	1.02
SC	Royce Premier R	RPRRX	C-	(800) 221-4268	B+ / 8.7	9.29	16.46	37.15 /96	4.66 /50	7.86 /41	0.00	1.78
SC	Royce Premier Svc	RPFFX	C-	(800) 221-4268	B+ / 8.7	9.31	16.55	37.47 /96	5.01 /54	8.24 /44	0.21	1.43
SC	Royce Premier W	RPRWX	C-	(800) 221-4268	A- / 9.0	9.42	16.76	37.97 /96	5.32 /58	8.55 /47	0.00	1.12
SC	Royce Small Cap Value Cons	RVFCX	E	(800) 221-4268	D+ / 2.7	2.83	8.21	16.77 /37	1.20 /19	4.83 /20	0.00	2.27
SC	Royce Small Cap Value Inst	RVFIX	D-	(800) 221-4268	C- / 3.6	3.11	8.80	18.15 /44	2.43 /27	6.10 /29	0.97	1.06
SC	Royce Small Cap Value Inv	RVVHX	E+	(800) 221-4268	C- / 3.3	3.01	8.71	17.93 /43	2.26 /26	5.96 /28	0.77	1.23
SC	Royce Small Cap Value K	RVFKX	E	(800) 221-4268	C- / 3.0	2.75	8.24	17.10 /39	1.63 /22	5.38 /24	0.14	1.80
SC	Royce Small Cap Value R	RVVRX	E+	(800) 221-4268	C- / 3.0	2.95	8.43	17.22 /39	1.67 /22	5.30 /23	0.30	1.83
SC	Royce Small Cap Value Svc	RYVFX	E+	(800) 221-4268	C- / 3.1	3.03	8.66	17.67 /41	2.02 /24	5.69 /26	0.58	1.48
GR	Royce Small-Cap Leaders Inv	ROHHX	D	(800) 221-4268	C / 5.4	4.19	11.05	29.56 /85	2.63 /28	7.10 /35	0.76	1.24
GR	Royce Small-Cap Leaders R	ROHRX	D	(800) 221-4268	C / 4.9	3.84	10.52	28.56 /83	1.95 /24	6.40 /31	0.10	2.75

● Denotes fund is closed to new investors
* Denotes fund is included in Section II

Risk Rating/Pts	3 Year Standard Deviation	Beta	NAV As of 2/28/17	Total $(Mil)	Cash %	Stocks %	Bonds %	Other %	Portfolio Turnover Ratio	Last Bull Market Return	Last Bear Market Return	Manager Quality Pct	Manager Tenure (Years)	Initial Purch. $	Additional Purch. $	Front End Load	Back End Load
D+ /2.7	12.6	0.75	6.92	N/A	5	51	43	1	71	N/A	N/A	1	7	2,500	100	0.0	1.0
C- /3.1	12.5	0.75	8.36	53	5	51	43	1	71	14.8	-13.1	2	7	25,000	1,000	0.0	1.0
C- /4.2	12.4	1.03	7.36	1	8	91	0	1	14	N/A	N/A	8	13	1,000,000	0	0.0	0.0
C /4.3	12.4	1.02	7.45	101	8	91	0	1	14	95.5	-21.9	8	13	100,000	50	0.0	1.0
C /4.4	12.4	1.02	7.60	114	8	91	0	1	14	92.6	-22.1	7	13	2,000	50	0.0	1.0
C- /4.3	13.3	1.08	9.52	45	0	0	0	100	46	119.8	-23.5	14	14	2,000	50	0.0	1.0
C- /4.2	12.7	1.07	10.81	12	13	86	0	1	66	73.7	-27.1	4	6	2,000	50	0.0	0.0
C /4.8	12.7	1.06	15.20	88	13	86	0	1	66	85.3	-26.7	7	6	100,000	50	0.0	1.0
C- /4.0	12.7	1.07	9.89	2	13	86	0	1	66	78.3	-27.0	5	6	0	0	0.0	0.0
C /4.9	12.7	1.06	15.15	121	13	86	0	1	66	82.6	-26.8	7	6	2,000	50	0.0	1.0
B- /7.6	11.6	0.84	10.06	21	0	0	0	100	67	N/A	N/A	93	6	100,000	50	0.0	2.0
B- /7.2	11.7	0.84	11.98	40	0	0	0	100	67	65.1	-21.8	92	6	2,000	50	0.0	2.0
C+ /6.5	11.4	0.81	10.66	6	3	96	0	1	94	49.0	-26.5	88	6	2,000	50	0.0	2.0
B- /7.4	11.9	0.83	7.73	2	42	57	0	1	116	N/A	N/A	51	4	1,000,000	0	0.0	0.0
B- /7.4	12.0	0.84	7.51	1	42	57	0	1	116	N/A	N/A	52	4	100,000	50	0.0	2.0
C /4.8	12.0	0.84	9.52	4	42	57	0	1	116	28.2	-24.9	48	4	2,000	50	0.0	2.0
E+ /0.9	16.0	0.89	8.24	12	7	92	0	1	59	29.6	-27.3	7	4	1,000,000	0	0.0	0.0
E+ /0.9	15.9	0.89	8.23	22	7	92	0	1	59	29.1	-27.3	7	4	100,000	50	0.0	1.0
E+ /0.8	16.0	0.89	7.77	1	7	92	0	1	59	24.9	-27.5	5	4	0	0	0.0	0.0
E+ /0.9	16.0	0.89	8.20	275	7	92	0	1	59	27.4	-27.4	6	4	2,000	50	0.0	1.0
D /2.0	15.1	0.90	9.26	32	9	90	0	1	41	33.4	-27.3	4	4	2,000	50	0.0	0.0
D+ /2.6	15.1	0.90	11.75	186	9	90	0	1	41	41.0	-27.1	7	4	2,000	50	0.0	1.0
C- /3.0	19.0	1.28	17.54	45	14	85	0	1	105	124.1	-32.5	1	7	2,000	50	0.0	1.0
C- /3.8	14.5	0.86	10.94	171	11	88	0	1	51	42.2	-27.0	10	4	0	0	0.0	0.0
C- /3.8	14.5	0.86	10.77	34	11	88	0	1	51	40.6	-27.1	9	4	0	0	0.0	0.0
D+ /2.6	15.1	0.90	11.52	17	9	90	0	1	41	40.0	-27.1	6	4	2,000	50	0.0	1.0
D /1.7	17.5	1.05	11.01	20	6	92	0	2	27	124.4	-31.8	21	19	2,000	50	0.0	0.0
D /2.2	17.5	1.05	13.49	581	6	92	0	2	27	140.1	-31.4	33	19	1,000,000	0	0.0	0.0
D /2.2	17.5	1.05	13.24	755	6	92	0	2	27	138.7	-31.5	32	19	2,000	50	0.0	1.0
D /1.7	17.5	1.05	10.91	7	6	92	0	2	27	133.3	-31.6	26	19	0	0	0.0	0.0
D /1.9	17.5	1.05	12.01	38	6	92	0	2	27	130.2	-31.7	25	19	0	0	0.0	0.0
D /2.0	17.5	1.05	12.38	72	6	92	0	2	27	134.8	-31.6	29	19	2,000	50	0.0	1.0
D- /1.4	14.5	0.88	8.99	397	0	99	0	1	21	87.0	-24.5	37	45	2,000	50	0.0	0.0
D /1.9	14.5	0.88	11.17	246	0	99	0	1	21	98.8	N/A	53	45	1,000,000	0	0.0	0.0
D /1.9	14.5	0.88	11.16	1,660	0	99	0	1	21	97.9	-24.2	52	45	2,000	50	0.0	1.0
D- /1.4	14.5	0.87	9.21	3	0	99	0	1	21	91.7	-24.4	42	45	0	0	0.0	0.0
D /1.8	14.5	0.87	10.55	17	0	99	0	1	21	90.7	-24.4	42	45	0	0	0.0	0.0
D /2.0	14.5	0.87	11.16	104	0	99	0	1	21	94.4	-24.3	48	45	2,000	50	0.0	1.0
D- /1.0	14.8	0.87	13.22	32	4	95	0	1	13	79.1	-21.9	54	25	2,000	50	0.0	0.0
D- /1.3	14.8	0.87	16.49	1,786	4	95	0	1	13	88.9	-21.6	66	25	2,000	50	0.0	1.0
D- /1.3	14.8	0.87	16.71	104	4	95	0	1	13	89.9	-21.5	67	25	1,000,000	0	0.0	0.0
D- /1.2	14.8	0.87	15.37	14	4	95	0	1	13	82.6	-21.7	58	25	0	0	0.0	0.0
D- /1.3	14.8	0.87	16.07	49	4	95	0	1	13	86.1	-21.7	62	25	2,000	50	0.0	1.0
D- /1.3	14.8	0.87	16.55	149	4	95	0	1	13	89.0	-21.5	66	25	1,000,000	0	0.0	0.0
D+ /2.5	13.9	0.74	8.82	16	14	85	0	1	60	57.8	-26.2	26	15	2,000	50	0.0	0.0
D+ /2.8	13.9	0.74	9.86	121	14	85	0	1	60	68.4	-25.8	40	15	1,000,000	0	0.0	0.0
D+ /2.9	14.0	0.74	9.86	70	14	85	0	1	60	67.1	-25.8	38	15	100,000	50	0.0	1.0
D /1.9	14.0	0.74	6.80	2	14	85	0	1	60	62.5	-26.0	30	15	0	0	0.0	0.0
D+ /2.8	14.0	0.74	9.46	17	14	85	0	1	60	61.6	-26.1	30	15	0	0	0.0	0.0
D+ /2.9	13.9	0.74	9.81	203	14	85	0	1	60	64.7	-25.9	35	15	2,000	50	0.0	1.0
D /1.9	15.3	1.16	7.14	47	14	86	0	0	64	83.3	-27.0	3	10	100,000	50	0.0	1.0
D+ /2.8	15.4	1.16	9.74	2	14	86	0	0	64	76.7	-27.2	2	10	0	0	0.0	0.0

I. Index of Stock Mutual Funds

Fund Type	Fund Name	Ticker Symbol	Overall Investment Rating	Phone	Performance Rating/Pts	3 Mo	6 Mo	1Yr / Pct	3Yr / Pct	5Yr / Pct	Dividend Yield	Expense Ratio
	99 Pct = Best 0 Pct = Worst							Total Return % through 2/28/17	Annualized		Incl. in Returns	
GR	Royce Small-Cap Leaders Service	RYOHX	D-	(800) 221-4268	C / 5.1	3.97	10.75	29.05 /84	2.30 /26	6.78 /33	0.52	1.54
SC	Royce Small-Cap Port Inv	RCPFX	E+	(800) 221-4268	C- / 3.7	2.34	9.02	17.04 /39	2.99 /32	8.75 /48	1.72	1.06
SC	Royce Small-Cap Port Svc	RCSSX	E	(800) 221-4268	C- / 3.5	2.28	8.87	16.78 /38	2.72 /29	8.48 /46	1.55	1.31
SC	Royce Smaller Companies Cons	RVPCX	E+	(800) 221-4268	C / 5.3	4.41	11.96	26.65 /78	2.62 /28	8.28 /45	0.00	2.33
SC	Royce Smaller Companies Inst	RVPIX	D-	(800) 221-4268	C+ / 6.3	4.62	12.43	28.02 /82	3.78 /40	9.58 /55	0.00	1.11
SC	Royce Smaller Companies Inv	RVPHX	D-	(800) 221-4268	C+ / 6.1	4.68	12.58	28.01 /82	3.67 /39	9.40 /54	0.00	1.33
SC	Royce Smaller Companies R	RVPRX	D-	(800) 221-4268	C+ / 5.7	4.51	12.04	27.15 /80	3.02 /32	8.76 /49	0.00	3.00
SC	Royce Smaller Companies Svc	RYVPX	D-	(800) 221-4268	C+ / 5.8	4.59	12.33	27.62 /81	3.44 /36	9.21 /52	0.00	1.48
SC	Royce Special Equity Cons	RSQCX	C-	(800) 221-4268	C+ / 6.2	1.36	12.00	30.08 /87	3.90 /42	8.38 /45	0.19	2.18
SC	Royce Special Equity Inst	RSEIX	C	(800) 221-4268	B- / 7.0	1.64	12.65	31.56 /89	5.07 /55	9.62 /56	1.01	1.04
SC	Royce Special Equity Inv	RYSEX	C	(800) 221-4268	C+ / 6.8	1.63	12.61	31.43 /89	4.99 /54	9.51 /55	0.92	1.15
GR	Royce Special Equity Multi-Cap Cons	RSMLX	C+	(800) 221-4268	C+ / 5.7	6.15	11.50	22.30 /64	3.83 /41	--	0.83	2.19
GR	Royce Special Equity Multi-Cap Inst	RMUIX	C+	(800) 221-4268	C+ / 6.6	6.41	12.02	23.65 /69	4.95 /54	--	1.16	0.94
GR	Royce Special Equity Multi-Cap Inv	RSMCX	C+	(800) 221-4268	C+ / 6.4	6.41	12.02	23.54 /68	4.88 /53	10.00 /58	1.09	1.01
GR	Royce Special Equity Multi-Cap Svc	RSEMX	C	(800) 221-4268	C+ / 6.2	6.40	11.91	23.31 /68	4.61 /50	9.75 /57	0.88	1.29
SC	Royce Special Equity Svc	RSEFX	C	(800) 221-4268	C+ / 6.6	1.55	12.45	31.14 /88	4.73 /51	9.24 /53	0.75	1.47
GI	Royce Total Return Cons	RYTCX	C	(800) 221-4268	B- / 7.5	4.81	11.23	30.88 /88	5.72 /62	10.22 /60	0.03	2.23
GI	Royce Total Return Fd	RYTRX	C+	(800) 221-4268	B / 8.0	4.99	11.74	32.11 /90	6.74 /70	11.34 /69	1.46	1.22
GI	Royce Total Return Inst	RTRIX	C+	(800) 221-4268	B+ / 8.3	4.97	11.75	32.18 /90	6.88 /71	11.46 /70	1.61	1.10
GI	Royce Total Return K	RTRKX	C-	(800) 221-4268	B / 7.9	4.83	11.49	31.56 /89	6.35 /67	10.94 /65	1.11	1.56
GI	Royce Total Return R	RTRRX	C+	(800) 221-4268	B / 7.8	4.86	11.45	31.38 /89	6.11 /65	10.66 /63	0.52	1.84
GI	Royce Total Return Svc	RYTFX	C+	(800) 221-4268	B / 7.8	4.89	11.60	31.77 /90	6.48 /68	11.03 /66	0.98	1.50
GI	Royce Total Return W	RTRWX	C+	(800) 221-4268	B / 8.2	5.07	11.77	32.12 /90	6.75 /70	11.33 /68	1.36	1.25
GI	RQSI Small Cap Hedged Equity Inst	RQSIX	U	(866) 777-7818	U /	6.00	10.48	21.08 /58	--	--	1.28	1.21
FO	RSQ International Equity Instl	RSQIX	D	(855) 355-4777	E / 0.3	7.17	2.77	8.54 / 8	-4.57 / 3	--	1.47	1.60
FO	RSQ International Equity Inv	RSQVX	D	(855) 355-4777	E / 0.3	7.07	2.66	8.30 / 8	-4.80 / 3	--	1.25	1.85
AA	● Russell 2020 Strategy A	RLLAX	E	(800) 832-6688	D / 1.8	3.44	2.19	10.83 /14	3.28 /35	5.07 /22	2.68	0.84
AA	Russell 2020 Strategy E	RLLEX	E+	(800) 832-6688	D+ / 2.6	3.51	2.26	10.90 /14	3.30 /35	5.08 /22	2.77	0.84
AA	Russell 2020 Strategy R1	RLLRX	E+	(800) 832-6688	D+ / 2.7	3.52	2.33	10.98 /14	3.51 /37	5.33 /24	3.09	0.59
AA	Russell 2020 Strategy R4	RLLUX	C+	(800) 832-6688	D+ / 2.6	3.45	2.19	10.86 /14	3.23 /34	4.95 /21	2.84	0.84
AA	Russell 2020 Strategy R5	RLLVX	C+	(800) 832-6688	D+ / 2.4	3.38	2.17	10.56 /13	2.96 /31	4.68 /19	2.58	1.09
AA	Russell 2020 Strategy S	RLLSX	E+	(800) 832-6688	D+ / 2.7	3.52	2.33	10.98 /14	3.51 /37	5.33 /24	3.09	0.59
AA	Russell 2025 Strategy R1	RPLRX	D	(800) 832-6688	C- / 3.2	4.07	3.28	13.23 /22	3.69 /39	6.07 /29	2.91	0.61
GI	Russell 2025 Strategy R4	RPLUX	B-	(800) 832-6688	C- / 3.1	4.12	3.26	13.07 /22	3.41 /36	5.69 /26	2.66	0.86
GI	Russell 2025 Strategy R5	RPLVX	C+	(800) 832-6688	D+ / 2.9	4.07	3.13	12.83 /21	3.17 /33	5.42 /24	2.42	1.11
AA	● Russell 2030 Strategy A	RRLAX	E+	(800) 832-6688	D+ / 2.7	4.91	4.52	15.88 /34	3.70 /39	6.61 /32	2.26	0.89
AA	Russell 2030 Strategy E	RRLEX	D-	(800) 832-6688	C- / 3.7	4.85	4.45	15.80 /33	3.65 /39	6.57 /32	2.44	0.89
AA	Russell 2030 Strategy R1	RRLRX	D-	(800) 832-6688	C- / 3.9	4.90	4.57	16.04 /34	3.92 /42	6.85 /34	2.66	0.64
AA	Russell 2030 Strategy R4	RRLUX	C+	(800) 832-6688	C- / 3.7	4.84	4.44	15.79 /33	3.61 /38	6.43 /31	2.43	0.89
AA	Russell 2030 Strategy R5	RRLVX	C+	(800) 832-6688	C- / 3.5	4.89	4.42	15.60 /32	3.39 /36	6.20 /30	2.17	1.14
AA	Russell 2030 Strategy S	RRLSX	D-	(800) 832-6688	C- / 4.0	4.91	4.70	16.21 /35	3.94 /42	6.85 /34	2.66	0.64
AA	Russell 2035 Strategy R1	RVLRX	D+	(800) 832-6688	C / 4.7	5.76	6.25	19.29 /49	4.05 /44	7.68 /40	2.21	0.68
GI	Russell 2035 Strategy R4	RVLUX	B-	(800) 832-6688	C / 4.5	5.69	6.11	19.01 /47	3.74 /40	7.27 /36	1.97	0.93
GI	Russell 2035 Strategy R5	RVLVX	B-	(800) 832-6688	C / 4.3	5.64	5.98	18.71 /46	3.49 /37	7.02 /35	1.73	1.18
AA	● Russell 2040 Strategy A	RXLAX	E+	(800) 832-6688	C / 4.3	6.67	7.66	22.26 /63	4.12 /44	7.60 /39	1.56	0.96
AA	Russell 2040 Strategy E	RXLEX	D-	(800) 832-6688	C / 5.5	6.67	7.76	22.23 /63	4.10 /44	7.58 /39	1.62	0.96
AA	Russell 2040 Strategy R1	RXLRX	D	(800) 832-6688	C+ / 5.7	6.74	7.93	22.72 /65	4.41 /48	7.87 /41	1.87	0.71
AA	Russell 2040 Strategy R4	RXLUX	B-	(800) 832-6688	C / 5.5	6.66	7.78	22.40 /64	4.06 /44	7.47 /38	1.64	0.96
AA	Russell 2040 Strategy R5	RXLVX	B	(800) 832-6688	C / 5.2	6.48	7.53	22.00 /62	3.81 /41	7.18 /36	1.40	1.21
AA	Russell 2040 Strategy S	RXLSX	D	(800) 832-6688	C+ / 5.7	6.73	7.78	22.71 /65	4.39 /47	7.86 /41	1.87	0.71
AA	Russell 2045 Strategy R1	RWLRX	C-	(800) 832-6688	C+ / 5.7	6.73	7.81	22.50 /65	4.36 /47	7.88 /41	1.86	0.71
GI	Russell 2045 Strategy R4	RWLUX	B	(800) 832-6688	C / 5.4	6.64	7.64	22.13 /63	4.03 /43	7.47 /38	1.62	0.96

● Denotes fund is closed to new investors

* Denotes fund is included in Section II

Risk Rating/Pts	3 Year Standard Deviation	Beta	NAV As of 2/28/17	Total $(Mil)	Cash %	Stocks %	Bonds %	Other %	Portfolio Turnover Ratio	Last Bull Market Return	Last Bear Market Return	Manager Quality Pct	Manager Tenure (Years)	Initial Purch. $	Additional Purch. $	Front End Load	Back End Load
D /1.9	15.3	1.16	7.04	50	14	86	0	0	64	80.3	-27.0	2	10	2,000	50	0.0	1.0
D /1.6	14.4	0.77	8.26	239	2	97	0	1	59	81.2	-19.3	45	14	0	0	0.0	0.0
D /1.6	14.4	0.77	8.06	258	2	97	0	1	59	78.8	-19.4	41	14	0	0	0.0	0.0
E /0.5	16.8	1.01	10.01	11	8	91	0	1	45	88.8	-26.6	22	9	2,000	50	0.0	0.0
E+ /0.7	16.8	1.01	11.82	20	8	91	0	1	45	101.5	-26.3	34	9	1,000,000	0	0.0	0.0
E+ /0.7	16.8	1.01	11.69	99	8	91	0	1	45	99.6	-26.3	33	9	100,000	50	0.0	1.0
E /0.5	16.8	1.01	10.69	1	8	91	0	1	45	93.4	-26.5	26	9	0	0	0.0	0.0
E+ /0.7	16.8	1.01	11.46	283	8	91	0	1	45	97.6	-26.4	30	9	2,000	50	0.0	1.0
C- /4.1	13.9	0.80	19.54	49	13	86	0	1	15	82.6	-18.4	54	19	2,000	50	0.0	0.0
C- /4.2	13.9	0.81	21.21	203	13	86	0	1	15	94.3	-18.0	69	19	1,000,000	0	0.0	0.0
C- /4.2	13.9	0.81	21.39	1,170	13	86	0	1	15	93.3	-18.0	68	19	2,000	50	0.0	1.0
C+ /6.8	12.5	1.06	9.64	5	8	91	0	1	31	N/A	N/A	6	7	2,000	50	0.0	0.0
C /5.1	12.5	1.06	14.71	39	8	91	0	1	31	N/A	N/A	10	7	1,000,000	0	0.0	0.0
C /5.1	12.5	1.06	14.72	36	8	91	0	1	31	N/A	N/A	9	7	100,000	50	0.0	1.0
C /5.2	12.5	1.06	14.76	30	8	91	0	1	31	90.9	-12.1	8	7	2,000	50	0.0	1.0
C /4.3	13.9	0.80	21.34	122	13	86	0	1	15	90.7	-18.1	65	19	2,000	50	0.0	1.0
C- /3.9	12.8	1.00	14.34	263	4	95	0	1	11	95.3	-19.4	19	24	2,000	50	0.0	0.0
C- /3.7	12.8	0.99	13.96	1,851	4	95	0	1	11	106.2	-19.5	29	24	2,000	50	0.0	0.0
C- /3.7	12.7	0.99	13.80	424	4	95	0	1	11	107.4	-19.4	30	24	1,000,000	0	0.0	1.0
D+ /2.5	12.7	0.99	9.25	40	4	95	0	1	11	102.2	-19.6	25	24	0	0	0.0	0.0
C- /3.8	12.8	0.99	14.37	54	4	95	0	1	11	99.5	-19.7	22	24	0	0	0.0	0.0
C- /3.8	12.8	1.00	14.26	154	4	95	0	1	11	103.0	-19.6	26	24	2,000	50	0.0	1.0
C- /3.7	12.8	0.99	13.95	80	4	95	0	1	11	106.1	-19.4	29	24	1,000,000	0	0.0	0.0
U /	N/A	N/A	10.59	76	9	90	0	1	178	N/A	N/A	N/A	2	1,000,000	0	0.0	0.0
B- /7.1	9.7	0.72	8.38	24	6	93	0	1	219	N/A	N/A	18	4	1,000,000	0	0.0	0.0
B- /7.1	9.7	0.72	8.37	1	6	93	0	1	219	N/A	N/A	16	4	2,500	0	0.0	0.0
D+ /2.9	4.8	0.71	7.55	N/A	2	38	59	1	28	42.3	-10.2	49	N/A	0	0	5.8	0.0
C- /3.0	4.7	0.70	7.57	1	2	38	59	1	28	42.4	-10.2	50	N/A	0	0	0.0	0.0
D+ /2.9	4.7	0.70	7.54	29	2	38	59	1	28	44.3	-10.2	53	N/A	0	0	0.0	0.0
B+ /9.7	4.7	0.70	7.54	9	2	38	59	1	28	41.4	-10.3	49	3	0	0	0.0	0.0
B+ /9.7	4.8	0.71	7.53	9	2	38	59	1	28	39.4	-10.4	45	3	0	0	0.0	0.0
D+ /2.9	4.7	0.71	7.54	5	2	38	59	1	28	44.3	-10.1	53	N/A	0	0	0.0	0.0
C /5.1	5.7	0.86	8.22	15	6	46	47	1	27	52.6	-13.4	39	9	0	0	0.0	0.0
B+ /9.5	5.7	0.51	8.23	7	6	46	47	1	27	49.6	-13.6	51	3	0	0	0.0	0.0
B+ /9.5	5.7	0.50	8.20	6	6	46	47	1	27	47.6	-13.7	49	3	0	0	0.0	0.0
D+ /2.7	6.9	1.06	8.15	1	3	60	35	2	24	60.3	-17.6	24	N/A	0	0	5.8	0.0
D+ /2.6	6.9	1.06	8.04	N/A	3	60	35	2	24	60.0	-17.6	23	N/A	0	0	0.0	0.0
D+ /2.6	6.9	1.05	8.06	38	3	60	35	2	24	62.3	-17.5	26	N/A	0	0	0.0	0.0
B /8.0	6.9	1.06	8.04	10	3	60	35	2	24	58.8	-17.7	23	3	0	0	0.0	0.0
B /8.0	7.0	1.06	8.06	13	3	60	35	2	24	56.9	-17.7	20	3	0	0	0.0	0.0
D+ /2.6	7.0	1.07	8.06	10	3	60	35	2	24	62.3	-17.5	25	N/A	0	0	0.0	0.0
C- /4.2	8.5	1.29	8.73	9	7	70	22	1	29	71.3	-19.0	13	9	0	0	0.0	0.0
B /8.3	8.4	0.77	8.72	7	7	70	22	1	29	67.7	-19.2	22	3	0	0	0.0	0.0
B /8.3	8.3	0.76	8.72	4	7	70	22	1	29	65.6	-19.4	21	3	0	0	0.0	0.0
D /1.8	9.5	1.44	7.67	1	5	87	7	1	31	70.6	-19.1	8	N/A	0	0	5.8	0.0
D /1.8	9.5	1.44	7.67	N/A	5	87	7	1	31	70.4	-19.1	7	N/A	0	0	0.0	0.0
D /1.8	9.6	1.46	7.68	22	5	87	7	1	31	72.9	-19.0	8	N/A	0	0	0.0	0.0
B- /7.9	9.6	1.45	7.68	6	5	87	7	1	31	69.3	-19.2	7	3	0	0	0.0	0.0
B- /7.9	9.5	1.44	7.65	6	5	87	7	1	31	67.0	-19.3	6	3	0	0	0.0	0.0
D /1.8	9.6	1.45	7.68	5	5	87	7	1	31	72.8	-19.0	8	N/A	0	0	0.0	0.0
C- /4.0	9.5	1.45	8.76	5	27	64	8	1	28	72.9	-19.0	8	9	0	0	0.0	0.0
B /8.1	9.5	0.87	8.78	4	27	64	8	1	28	69.4	-19.2	16	3	0	0	0.0	0.0

Fund Type	Fund Name	Ticker Symbol	Overall Investment Rating	Phone	Performance Rating/Pts	3 Mo	6 Mo	1Yr / Pct	Annualized 3Yr / Pct	Annualized 5Yr / Pct	Dividend Yield	Expense Ratio
GI	Russell 2045 Strategy R5	RWLVX	B	(800) 832-6688	C / 5.2	6.49	7.56	21.98 /62	3.79 /40	7.21 /36	1.41	1.21
AA	Russell 2050 Strategy R1	RYLRX	D	(800) 832-6688	C+ / 5.7	6.71	7.95	22.60 /65	4.39 /47	7.88 /41	1.88	0.71
GI	Russell 2050 Strategy R4	RYLUX	B	(800) 832-6688	C / 5.4	6.61	7.77	22.20 /63	4.06 /44	7.47 /38	1.64	0.96
GI	Russell 2050 Strategy R5	RYLWX	B	(800) 832-6688	C / 5.1	6.41	7.51	21.81 /61	3.76 /40	7.20 /36	1.44	1.21
AA	Russell 2055 Strategy R1	RQLRX	C+	(800) 832-6688	C+ / 5.7	6.64	7.81	22.56 /65	4.40 /47	7.87 /41	1.88	0.71
GI	Russell 2055 Strategy R4	RQLUX	B	(800) 832-6688	C / 5.4	6.55	7.65	22.21 /63	4.10 /44	7.48 /38	1.63	0.96
GI	Russell 2055 Strategy R5	RQLVX	B	(800) 832-6688	C / 5.3	6.62	7.67	22.03 /62	3.85 /41	7.19 /36	1.45	1.21
BA	Russell Bal Strat R4	RBLUX	C	(800) 832-6688	C- / 3.8	4.45	4.62	15.69 /33	3.90 /42	5.82 /27	2.55	1.47
BA	Russell Bal Strat R5	RBLVX	C	(800) 832-6688	C- / 3.6	4.39	4.50	15.39 /32	3.63 /38	5.57 /25	2.33	1.72
AA	Russell Cons Strat R4	RCLUX	C	(800) 832-6688	D / 1.9	2.57	0.99	8.09 / 8	2.56 /28	3.24 /12	2.88	1.34
AA	Russell Cons Strat R5	RCLVX	C	(800) 832-6688	D / 1.7	2.48	0.85	7.73 / 7	2.29 /26	2.98 /11	2.60	1.59
GL	Russell Eq Gr Strat R4	RELUX	B	(800) 832-6688	C / 5.4	6.23	7.84	22.08 /63	4.09 /44	7.14 /35	1.96	1.56
GL	Russell Eq Gr Strat R5	RELVX	B	(800) 832-6688	C / 5.2	6.15	7.72	21.85 /61	3.82 /41	6.87 /34	1.75	1.81
GL	Russell Gr Strat R4	RALUX	B-	(800) 832-6688	C / 4.4	5.28	6.33	19.18 /48	3.67 /39	6.33 /31	2.27	1.48
GL	Russell Gr Strat R5	RALVX	C+	(800) 832-6688	C- / 4.2	5.21	6.11	18.88 /47	3.40 /36	6.06 /29	2.04	1.73
GI	● Russell In Ret A	RZLAX	E+	(800) 832-6688	D- / 1.5	2.93	1.49	9.04 /10	3.03 /32	4.26 /17	2.70	0.82
AA	Russell In Ret R1	RZLRX	E+	(800) 832-6688	D+ / 2.4	3.07	1.66	9.39 /10	3.28 /35	4.53 /18	3.18	0.57
GI	Russell In Ret R4	RZLUX	C+	(800) 832-6688	D / 2.2	3.00	1.39	8.95 / 9	2.96 /31	4.12 /16	2.93	0.82
GI	Russell In Ret R5	RZLVX	C+	(800) 832-6688	D / 2.1	2.93	1.38	8.82 / 9	2.74 /30	3.87 /15	2.65	1.07
GL	Russell Investments Bal Str A	RBLAX	C-	(800) 832-6688	D+ / 2.8	4.51	4.71	15.74 /33	3.96 /43	5.91 /28	2.51	1.47
GL	Russell Investments Bal Str C	RBLCX	C-	(800) 832-6688	C- / 3.3	4.28	4.28	14.89 /29	3.17 /33	5.12 /22	2.02	2.22
GL	Russell Investments Bal Str E	RBLEX	C	(800) 832-6688	C- / 3.8	4.36	4.61	15.49 /32	3.87 /41	5.84 /27	2.50	1.47
GL	Russell Investments Bal Str R1	RBLRX	C	(800) 832-6688	C- / 4.0	4.50	4.74	15.97 /34	4.21 /45	6.23 /30	2.79	1.22
GL	Russell Investments Bal Str S	RBLSX	C	(800) 832-6688	C- / 4.0	4.49	4.81	15.90 /34	4.13 /44	6.12 /29	2.74	1.22
OT	Russell Investments Comm Str A	RCSAX	E-	(800) 832-6688	E- / 0.0	2.19	6.45	13.79 /25	-13.64 / 0	-10.93 / 0	0.00	2.13
OT	Russell Investments Comm Str C	RCSCX	E-	(800) 832-6688	E- / 0.0	2.09	5.92	12.82 /21	-14.29 / 0	-11.60 / 0	0.00	2.88
OT	Russell Investments Comm Str E	RCSEX	E-	(800) 832-6688	E- / 0.0	2.19	6.45	13.79 /25	-13.64 / 0	-10.93 / 0	0.00	2.13
OT	Russell Investments Comm Str S	RCCSX	E-	(800) 832-6688	E- / 0.0	2.34	6.55	14.03 /26	-13.43 / 0	-10.70 / 0	0.00	1.88
OT	Russell Investments Comm Str Y	RCSYX	E-	(800) 832-6688	E- / 0.0	2.32	6.69	14.34 /27	-13.28 / 0	-10.54 / 1	0.00	1.68
GL	Russell Investments Cons Stat A	RCLAX	D+	(800) 832-6688	D- / 1.2	2.43	0.92	7.85 / 7	2.44 /27	3.24 /12	2.60	1.34
GL	Russell Investments Cons Stat R1	RCLRX	C-	(800) 832-6688	D / 2.0	2.52	1.12	8.32 / 8	2.86 /30	3.63 /14	3.12	1.09
GL	Russell Investments Cons Strat C	RCLCX	D+	(800) 832-6688	D- / 1.5	2.25	0.53	7.00 / 6	1.67 /22	2.44 / 9	2.04	2.09
GL	Russell Investments Cons Strat E	RCLEX	C-	(800) 832-6688	D / 1.8	2.52	0.92	7.91 / 7	2.47 /27	3.23 /12	2.74	1.34
GL	Russell Investments Cons Strat S	RCLSX	C-	(800) 832-6688	D / 1.9	2.48	1.05	8.17 / 8	2.72 /29	3.49 /13	2.99	1.09
EM	Russell Investments Emerg Mkt A	REMAX	D	(800) 832-6688	C- / 3.8	9.34	7.05	30.65 /87	1.10 /19	-0.06 / 4	0.71	1.77
EM	Russell Investments Emerg Mkt C	REMCX	D+	(800) 832-6688	C / 4.3	9.17	6.63	29.63 /86	0.34 /15	-0.81 / 4	0.10	2.52
EM	Russell Investments Emerg Mkt E	REMEX	C-	(800) 832-6688	C / 5.1	9.43	7.07	30.67 /88	1.11 /19	-0.06 / 4	0.74	1.77
EM	Russell Investments Emerg Mkt S	REMSX	C-	(800) 832-6688	C / 5.3	9.48	7.20	31.00 /88	1.36 /20	0.19 / 5	0.98	1.52
EM	Russell Investments Emerg Mkt Y	REMYX	C-	(800) 832-6688	C / 5.4	9.48	7.27	31.23 /89	1.56 /21	0.38 / 5	1.16	1.32
GL	Russell Investments Eq Gr Str A	REAAX	C	(800) 832-6688	C- / 4.2	6.18	7.83	22.07 /63	4.05 /44	7.14 /35	1.74	1.56
GL	Russell Investments Eq Gr Str C	RELCX	C+	(800) 832-6688	C / 4.6	5.90	7.34	21.12 /58	3.25 /34	6.32 /30	1.40	2.31
GL	Russell Investments Eq Gr Str E	RELEX	B-	(800) 832-6688	C / 5.3	6.14	7.82	22.05 /62	4.04 /43	7.13 /35	1.87	1.56
GL	Russell Investments Eq Gr Str R1	RELRX	B-	(800) 832-6688	C+ / 5.6	6.23	7.97	22.45 /64	4.37 /47	7.52 /38	2.14	1.31
GL	Russell Investments Eq Gr Str S	RELSX	B-	(800) 832-6688	C+ / 5.6	6.21	7.93	22.28 /63	4.30 /46	7.40 /37	2.06	1.31
RE	Russell Investments Glbl RE Sec A	RREAX	D	(800) 832-6688	D+ / 2.5	6.30	-3.03	11.76 /17	5.29 /57	7.45 /38	4.12	1.37
RE	Russell Investments Glbl RE Sec C	RRSCX	D+	(800) 832-6688	C- / 3.0	6.11	-3.38	10.93 /14	4.51 /49	6.65 /33	3.75	2.12
RE	Russell Investments Glbl RE Sec E	RREEX	C-	(800) 832-6688	C- / 3.5	6.32	-3.01	11.79 /17	5.30 /58	7.45 /38	4.34	1.37
RE	Russell Investments Glbl RE Sec S	RRESX	C-	(800) 832-6688	C- / 3.7	6.37	-2.89	12.08 /18	5.56 /60	7.72 /40	4.50	1.12
RE	Russell Investments Glbl RE Sec Y	RREYX	C-	(800) 832-6688	C- / 3.9	6.43	-2.78	12.27 /19	5.77 /62	7.93 /42	4.70	0.92
GL	Russell Investments Global Equity A	RGEAX	C-	(800) 832-6688	C / 5.2	7.13	8.57	23.55 /68	5.10 /55	8.96 /50	1.05	1.49
GL	Russell Investments Global Equity C	RGECX	C	(800) 832-6688	C+ / 5.7	6.91	8.05	22.62 /65	4.30 /46	8.14 /43	0.41	2.24
GL	Russell Investments Global Equity E	RGEEX	C	(800) 832-6688	C+ / 6.3	7.05	8.49	23.42 /68	5.06 /55	8.94 /50	1.15	1.49

● Denotes fund is closed to new investors
* Denotes fund is included in Section II

www.thestreetratings.com

RISK			NET ASSETS		ASSET					BULL / BEAR		FUND MANAGER		MINIMUMS		LOADS	
	3 Year		NAV						Portfolio	Last Bull	Last Bear	Manager	Manager	Initial	Additional	Front	Back
Risk	Standard		As of	Total	Cash	Stocks	Bonds	Other	Turnover	Market	Market	Quality	Tenure	Purch.	Purch.	End	End
Rating/Pts	Deviation	Beta	2/28/17	$(Mil)	%	%	%	%	Ratio	Return	Return	Pct	(Years)	$	$	Load	Load
B /8.1	9.6	0.89	8.73	2	27	64	8	1	28	67.0	-19.3	13	3	0	0	0.0	0.0
D /2.0	9.5	1.44	6.30	7	7	83	9	1	53	72.9	-19.0	8	9	0	0	0.0	0.0
B /8.1	9.5	0.88	6.32	2	7	83	9	1	53	69.4	-19.2	16	3	0	0	0.0	0.0
B /8.0	9.5	0.88	6.29	2	7	83	9	1	53	66.9	-19.2	14	3	0	0	0.0	0.0
C+ /6.2	9.5	1.44	11.61	2	7	82	9	2	76	72.7	-19.0	8	7	0	0	0.0	0.0
B /8.1	9.5	0.88	11.62	1	7	82	9	2	76	69.0	-19.2	16	3	0	0	0.0	0.0
B /8.0	9.5	0.88	11.59	1	7	82	9	2	76	66.6	-19.3	14	3	0	0	0.0	0.0
B- /7.5	6.6	1.00	11.17	86	11	51	37	1	16	50.2	-13.6	29	3	0	0	0.0	0.0
B- /7.5	6.6	1.01	11.19	71	11	51	37	1	16	48.2	-13.6	26	3	0	0	0.0	0.0
B+ /9.2	3.6	0.49	9.71	15	10	20	69	1	18	24.6	-4.3	61	3	0	0	0.0	0.0
B+ /9.2	3.6	0.49	9.79	14	10	20	69	1	18	22.9	-4.4	57	3	0	0	0.0	0.0
B- /7.9	9.4	0.69	12.04	29	9	78	11	2	16	67.9	-20.8	94	3	0	0	0.0	0.0
B- /7.9	9.3	0.69	11.90	23	9	78	11	2	16	65.6	-20.9	93	3	0	0	0.0	0.0
B /8.1	8.4	1.27	12.18	80	9	67	22	2	14	58.1	-17.9	46	3	0	0	0.0	0.0
B /8.1	8.3	1.26	12.18	54	9	67	22	2	14	56.0	-18.1	43	3	0	0	0.0	0.0
C- /3.8	3.9	0.31	7.24	N/A	5	29	65	1	21	33.3	-6.1	72	7	0	0	5.8	0.0
C- /3.6	4.0	0.57	7.07	16	5	29	65	1	21	35.0	-6.0	63	9	0	0	0.0	0.0
B+ /9.7	3.9	0.30	7.07	8	5	29	65	1	21	32.2	-6.2	72	3	0	0	0.0	0.0
B+ /9.7	3.9	0.31	7.06	3	5	29	65	1	21	30.5	-6.2	68	3	0	0	0.0	0.0
B- /7.0	6.6	1.00	11.14	791	11	51	37	1	16	50.8	-13.6	66	N/A	0	0	5.8	0.0
B- /7.0	6.6	1.00	10.93	872	11	51	37	1	16	44.8	-13.8	56	N/A	0	0	0.0	0.0
B- /7.1	6.5	1.00	11.19	18	11	51	37	1	16	50.3	-13.6	65	N/A	0	0	0.0	0.0
B- /7.1	6.6	1.01	11.27	126	11	51	37	1	16	53.3	-13.4	69	N/A	0	0	0.0	0.0
B- /7.1	6.5	1.00	11.27	409	11	51	37	1	16	52.4	-13.4	68	N/A	0	0	0.0	0.0
D+ /2.7	12.8	0.25	5.61	8	100	0	0	0	0	-41.2	-19.5	0	N/A	0	0	5.8	0.0
D+ /2.6	12.8	0.25	5.37	4	100	0	0	0	0	-43.5	-19.8	0	N/A	0	0	0.0	0.0
D+ /2.7	12.8	0.25	5.61	N/A	100	0	0	0	0	-41.2	-19.6	0	N/A	0	0	0.0	0.0
D+ /2.8	12.8	0.24	5.69	525	100	0	0	0	0	-40.3	-19.5	0	N/A	0	0	0.0	0.0
D+ /2.8	12.7	0.26	5.74	199	100	0	0	0	0	-39.8	-19.4	0	N/A	10,000,000	0	0.0	0.0
B- /7.5	3.6	0.51	9.69	85	10	20	69	1	18	24.6	-4.2	74	N/A	0	0	5.8	0.0
B- /7.5	3.6	0.50	9.76	20	10	20	69	1	18	27.2	-4.1	77	N/A	0	0	0.0	0.0
B- /7.5	3.6	0.50	9.58	149	10	20	69	1	18	19.6	-4.5	66	N/A	0	0	0.0	0.0
B- /7.5	3.6	0.50	9.74	12	10	20	69	1	18	24.6	-4.3	75	N/A	0	0	0.0	0.0
B- /7.5	3.6	0.51	9.77	41	10	20	69	1	18	26.3	-4.2	76	N/A	0	0	0.0	0.0
C /4.3	15.9	0.98	17.22	18	1	95	3	1	68	22.8	-26.5	68	N/A	0	0	5.8	0.0
C /4.3	15.9	0.98	16.03	17	1	95	3	1	68	18.0	-26.7	58	N/A	0	0	0.0	0.0
C /4.3	15.9	0.97	17.29	6	1	95	3	1	68	22.9	-26.5	68	N/A	0	0	0.0	0.0
C /4.3	15.9	0.97	17.34	1,780	1	95	3	1	68	24.6	-26.4	71	N/A	0	0	0.0	0.0
C /4.3	15.9	0.98	17.35	481	1	95	3	1	68	25.9	-26.4	73	N/A	10,000,000	0	0.0	0.0
B- /7.2	9.4	1.40	12.28	191	9	78	11	2	16	68.1	-20.8	43	N/A	0	0	5.8	0.0
B- /7.2	9.4	1.40	11.04	243	9	78	11	2	16	61.2	-21.0	33	N/A	0	0	0.0	0.0
B- /7.2	9.3	1.40	12.00	4	9	78	11	2	16	68.1	-20.9	43	N/A	0	0	0.0	0.0
B- /7.2	9.4	1.40	12.34	25	9	78	11	2	16	71.4	-20.6	47	N/A	0	0	0.0	0.0
B- /7.2	9.4	1.40	12.32	136	9	78	11	2	16	70.4	-20.7	47	N/A	0	0	0.0	0.0
C+ /5.8	11.9	0.82	33.29	25	10	89	0	1	79	71.7	-20.7	28	15	0	0	5.8	0.0
C+ /5.7	11.9	0.82	32.11	29	10	89	0	1	79	64.9	-21.0	21	15	0	0	0.0	0.0
C+ /5.8	12.0	0.82	33.35	6	10	89	0	1	79	71.8	-20.7	29	15	0	0	0.0	0.0
C+ /5.8	11.9	0.82	34.12	1,009	10	89	0	1	79	74.1	-20.6	31	15	0	0	0.0	0.0
C+ /5.8	11.9	0.82	34.12	116	10	89	0	1	79	76.0	-20.6	34	15	10,000,000	0	0.0	0.0
C /5.0	11.3	0.85	10.43	13	4	94	0	2	46	84.2	-22.0	96	2	0	0	0.0	0.0
C /5.1	11.2	0.85	10.33	11	4	94	0	2	46	76.9	-22.3	94	2	0	0	5.8	0.0
C /5.1	11.2	0.85	10.44	3	4	94	0	2	46	84.0	-22.0	96	2	0	0	0.0	0.0

I. Index of Stock Mutual Funds

						PERFORMANCE						
	99 Pct = Best							Total Return % through 2/28/17			Incl. in Returns	
	0 Pct = Worst		Overall		Perfor-				Annualized		Dividend	Expense
Fund		Ticker	Investment		mance							
Type	Fund Name	Symbol	Rating	Phone	Rating/Pts	3 Mo	6 Mo	1Yr / Pct	3Yr / Pct	5Yr / Pct	Yield	Ratio
GL	Russell Investments Global Equity S	RGESX	C+	(800) 832-6688	C+ / 6.6	7.19	8.63	23.81 /69	5.34 /58	9.20 /52	1.37	1.24
GL	Russell Investments Global Equity Y	RLGYX	C+	(800) 832-6688	C+ / 6.8	7.29	8.83	24.14 /70	5.58 /60	9.45 /54	1.56	1.04
GL	Russell Investments Global Infra A	RGIAX	D	(800) 832-6688	D+ / 2.7	7.44	1.69	14.44 /28	3.98 /43	7.59 /39	1.98	1.82
GL	Russell Investments Global Infra C	RGCIX	D+	(800) 832-6688	C- / 3.2	7.27	1.29	13.65 /24	3.19 /34	6.78 /33	1.46	2.57
GL	Russell Investments Global Infra E	RGIEX	D+	(800) 832-6688	C- / 3.7	7.44	1.60	14.43 /27	3.94 /42	7.58 /39	2.09	1.82
GL	Russell Investments Global Infra S	RGISX	D+	(800) 832-6688	C- / 4.0	7.50	1.82	14.69 /28	4.23 /46	7.87 /41	2.33	1.57
GL	Russell Investments Global Infra Y	RGIYX	C-	(800) 832-6688	C- / 4.1	7.55	1.82	14.90 /29	4.42 /48	8.04 /43	2.50	1.37
GL	Russell Investments Gr Strat A	RALAX	C	(800) 832-6688	C- / 3.3	5.29	6.25	19.11 /48	3.63 /38	6.34 /31	2.12	1.48
GL	Russell Investments Gr Strat C	RALCX	C	(800) 832-6688	C- / 3.7	5.08	5.80	18.13 /43	2.87 /31	5.55 /25	1.64	2.23
GL	Russell Investments Gr Strat E	RALEX	C+	(800) 832-6688	C / 4.4	5.36	6.31	19.11 /48	3.66 /39	6.37 /31	2.23	1.48
GL	Russell Investments Gr Strat R1	RALRX	C+	(800) 832-6688	C / 4.7	5.40	6.42	19.53 /50	3.99 /43	6.74 /33	2.49	1.23
GL	Russell Investments Gr Strat S	RALSX	C+	(800) 832-6688	C / 4.6	5.39	6.40	19.47 /49	3.90 /42	6.62 /32	2.45	1.23
FO	Russell Investments Int Dev Mkt A	RLNAX	D-	(800) 832-6688	E+ / 0.8	6.56	4.90	16.81 /38	-0.69 /11	5.05 /22	1.88	1.27
FO	Russell Investments Int Dev Mkt C	RLNCX	D-	(800) 832-6688	D- / 1.1	6.35	4.51	15.91 /34	-1.43 / 8	4.26 /17	1.21	2.02
FO	Russell Investments Int Dev Mkt E	RIFEX	D	(800) 832-6688	D- / 1.3	6.53	4.88	16.77 /37	-0.69 /11	5.05 /22	2.01	1.27
FO ●	Russell Investments Int Dev Mkt I	RINSX	D	(800) 832-6688	D- / 1.4	6.62	5.03	17.13 /39	-0.37 /12	5.39 /24	2.32	0.94
FO	Russell Investments Int Dev Mkt S	RINTX	D	(800) 832-6688	D- / 1.4	6.62	4.99	17.07 /39	-0.45 /11	5.31 /23	2.25	1.02
FO	Russell Investments Int Dev Mkt Y	RINYX	D	(800) 832-6688	D- / 1.5	6.66	5.13	17.29 /40	-0.24 /12	5.51 /25	2.44	0.82
GI	Russell Investments Mlt Str Inc S	RMYSX	U	(800) 832-6688	U /	4.91	3.69	15.03 /30	--	--	3.71	1.22
GI	Russell Investments Mlt Str Inc Y	RMYYX	U	(800) 832-6688	U /	4.96	3.89	15.36 /31	--	--	3.87	1.02
GL	Russell Investments Mod Str A	RMLAX	D+	(800) 832-6688	D / 1.9	3.53	2.44	11.45 /16	3.45 /36	4.57 /19	3.05	1.40
GL	Russell Investments Mod Str C	RMLCX	D+	(800) 832-6688	D+ / 2.3	3.37	2.06	10.74 /14	2.67 /29	3.81 /14	2.52	2.15
GL	Russell Investments Mod Str E	RMLEX	C-	(800) 832-6688	D+ / 2.7	3.50	2.38	11.42 /16	3.39 /36	4.54 /18	3.13	1.40
GL	Russell Investments Mod Str R1	RMLRX	C-	(800) 832-6688	C- / 3.0	3.69	2.57	11.78 /17	3.78 /40	4.94 /21	3.45	1.15
GL	Russell Investments Mod Str S	RMLSX	C-	(800) 832-6688	D+ / 2.9	3.57	2.52	11.70 /17	3.64 /39	4.80 /20	3.39	1.15
GR	Russell Investments Str Call Ovr S	ROWSX	B	(800) 832-6688	C+ / 6.4	4.77	8.29	20.95 /57	6.22 /66	--	1.03	1.20
FO	Russell Investments Tx-Mgd Int Eq S	RTNSX	U	(800) 832-6688	U /	7.81	5.36	20.94 /57	--	--	2.13	1.27
GR	Russell Investments Tx-Mgd US LC A	RTLAX	B+	(800) 832-6688	B- / 7.3	7.98	9.39	23.42 /68	8.73 /85	12.14 /75	0.55	1.24
GR	Russell Investments Tx-Mgd US LC C	RTLCX	A-	(800) 832-6688	B / 7.8	7.78	8.99	22.47 /64	7.91 /78	11.30 /68	0.00	1.99
GR	Russell Investments Tx-Mgd US LC E	RTLEX	A	(800) 832-6688	B+ / 8.4	7.99	9.40	23.43 /68	8.72 /85	12.15 /76	0.58	1.24
GR	Russell Investments Tx-Mgd US LC S	RETSX	A	(800) 832-6688	B+ / 8.6	8.07	9.53	23.75 /69	9.00 /87	12.43 /78	0.79	0.99
SC	Russell Investments Tx-Mgd US MSC	RTSAX	C-	(800) 832-6688	C / 4.3	4.34	8.25	23.93 /70	4.19 /45	10.75 /64	0.00	1.57
SC	Russell Investments Tx-Mgd US MSC	RTSCX	C-	(800) 832-6688	C / 4.8	4.17	7.87	23.08 /67	3.44 /36	9.95 /58	0.00	2.32
SC	Russell Investments Tx-Mgd US MSC	RTSEX	C	(800) 832-6688	C / 5.5	4.38	8.28	24.00 /70	4.21 /45	10.77 /64	0.00	1.57
SC	Russell Investments Tx-Mgd US MSC	RTSSX	C	(800) 832-6688	C+ / 5.7	4.43	8.42	24.27 /71	4.48 /49	11.05 /66	0.00	1.32
IX	Russell Investments US Core Eq A	RSQAX	C-	(800) 832-6688	B / 7.6	7.26	10.10	25.55 /75	8.79 /85	12.48 /79	0.89	1.09
IX	Russell Investments US Core Eq C	REQSX	C	(800) 832-6688	B / 8.0	7.04	9.69	24.62 /72	7.98 /79	11.64 /71	0.29	1.84
IX	Russell Investments US Core Eq E	REAEX	C	(800) 832-6688	B+ / 8.6	7.25	10.09	25.56 /75	8.78 /85	12.48 /79	0.94	1.09
IX ●	Russell Investments US Core Eq I	REASX	C+	(800) 832-6688	B+ / 8.9	7.34	10.28	26.00 /76	9.15 /88	12.85 /82	1.24	0.76
IX	Russell Investments US Core Eq S	RLISX	C+	(800) 832-6688	B+ / 8.8	7.34	10.26	25.91 /76	9.06 /87	12.77 /82	1.16	0.84
GR	Russell Investments US Def Eq A	REQAX	A-	(800) 832-6688	B- / 7.0	6.95	7.61	19.24 /48	9.52 /90	11.89 /73	0.91	1.09
GR	Russell Investments US Def Eq C	REQCX	A	(800) 832-6688	B- / 7.4	6.75	7.18	18.34 /44	8.70 /85	11.05 /66	0.27	1.84
GR	Russell Investments US Def Eq E	REQEX	A+	(800) 832-6688	B / 8.0	6.94	7.59	19.24 /48	9.52 /90	11.89 /73	0.96	1.09
GR ●	Russell Investments US Def Eq I	REDSX	A+	(800) 832-6688	B / 8.2	7.03	7.78	19.62 /50	9.89 /93	12.26 /77	1.26	0.76
GR	Russell Investments US Def Eq S	REQTX	A+	(800) 832-6688	B / 8.2	7.00	7.72	19.53 /50	9.79 /92	12.16 /76	1.18	0.84
GR	Russell Investments US Def Eq Y	REUYX	A+	(800) 832-6688	B+ / 8.3	7.05	7.82	19.77 /51	10.01 /93	12.38 /78	1.36	0.64
GR	Russell Investments US Dyn Eq A	RSGAX	C+	(800) 832-6688	A- / 9.0	7.07	14.75	32.47 /91	9.38 /89	--	0.47	1.50
GR	Russell Investments US Dyn Eq C	RSGCX	C+	(800) 832-6688	A / 9.4	6.81	14.26	31.44 /89	8.58 /84	12.30 /77	0.14	2.25
GR	Russell Investments US Dyn Eq E	RSGEX	B-	(800) 832-6688	A+ / 9.6	7.04	14.70	32.52 /91	9.38 /89	13.13 /85	0.50	1.50
GR ●	Russell Investments US Dyn Eq I	RSGIX	B	(800) 832-6688	A+ / 9.7	7.24	14.94	33.05 /92	9.79 /92	13.56 /89	0.72	1.17
GR	Russell Investments US Dyn Eq S	RSGSX	B-	(800) 832-6688	A+ / 9.7	7.17	14.87	32.85 /91	9.65 /91	13.41 /88	0.66	1.25
GR	Russell Investments US Dyn Eq Y	RSGTX	B	(800) 832-6688	A+ / 9.7	7.21	15.08	33.24 /92	9.90 /93	--	0.82	1.05

● Denotes fund is closed to new investors
* Denotes fund is included in Section II

Risk Rating/Pts	3 Year Standard Deviation	Beta	NAV As of 2/28/17	Total $(Mil)	Cash %	Stocks %	Bonds %	Other %	Portfolio Turnover Ratio	Last Bull Market Return	Last Bear Market Return	Manager Quality Pct	Manager Tenure (Years)	Initial Purch. $	Additional Purch. $	Front End Load	Back End Load
C / 5.0	11.3	0.85	10.46	1,789	4	94	0	2	46	86.6	-21.9	96	2	0	0	0.0	0.0
C / 5.0	11.3	0.85	10.48	687	4	94	0	2	46	88.8	-21.9	96	2	10,000,000	0	0.0	0.0
C / 5.2	10.1	0.58	11.27	8	12	87	0	1	102	66.5	-16.1	93	N/A	0	0	5.8	0.0
C / 5.2	10.1	0.58	11.21	7	12	87	0	1	102	60.0	-16.4	91	N/A	0	0	0.0	0.0
C / 5.2	10.1	0.58	11.27	2	12	87	0	1	102	66.4	-16.1	93	N/A	0	0	0.0	0.0
C / 5.2	10.1	0.58	11.29	830	12	87	0	1	102	68.9	-16.0	94	N/A	0	0	0.0	0.0
C / 5.2	10.1	0.58	11.29	210	12	87	0	1	102	70.3	-15.9	94	N/A	10,000,000	0	0.0	0.0
B- / 7.7	8.3	1.26	12.13	587	9	67	22	2	14	58.4	-18.0	46	N/A	0	0	5.8	0.0
B- / 7.6	8.4	1.26	11.76	540	9	67	22	2	14	52.0	-18.2	36	N/A	0	0	0.0	0.0
B- / 7.7	8.4	1.26	12.19	18	9	67	22	2	14	58.4	-17.9	46	N/A	0	0	0.0	0.0
B- / 7.7	8.4	1.27	12.28	76	9	67	22	2	14	61.6	-17.8	51	N/A	0	0	0.0	0.0
B- / 7.7	8.4	1.27	12.28	229	9	67	22	2	14	60.7	-17.9	50	N/A	0	0	0.0	0.0
C+ / 6.0	11.3	0.91	34.99	27	4	93	1	2	68	48.2	-24.6	68	2	0	0	5.8	0.0
C+ / 6.1	11.3	0.91	35.13	26	4	93	1	2	68	42.5	-24.9	58	2	0	0	0.0	0.0
C+ / 6.0	11.3	0.91	35.10	6	4	93	1	2	68	48.4	-24.6	68	2	0	0	0.0	0.0
C+ / 6.0	11.3	0.91	35.04	463	4	93	1	2	68	51.0	-24.5	72	2	100,000	0	0.0	0.0
C+ / 6.0	11.3	0.91	35.00	2,013	4	93	1	2	68	50.4	-24.5	71	2	0	0	0.0	0.0
C+ / 6.0	11.3	0.91	35.01	13	4	93	1	2	68	51.7	-24.5	73	2	10,000,000	0	0.0	0.0
U /	N/A	N/A	9.95	598	0	0	0	100	67	N/A	N/A	N/A	2	0	0	0.0	0.0
U /	N/A	N/A	9.96	271	0	0	0	100	67	N/A	N/A	N/A	2	10,000,000	0	0.0	0.0
C+ / 6.9	4.6	0.68	10.13	175	12	31	55	2	34	37.1	-8.6	76	N/A	0	0	5.8	0.0
C+ / 6.9	4.7	0.68	10.01	207	12	31	55	2	34	31.6	-8.9	68	N/A	0	0	0.0	0.0
B- / 7.0	4.6	0.68	10.16	7	12	31	55	2	34	36.9	-8.7	75	N/A	0	0	0.0	0.0
B- / 7.0	4.6	0.68	10.19	17	12	31	55	2	34	39.6	-8.4	78	N/A	0	0	0.0	0.0
C+ / 6.9	4.6	0.68	10.18	98	12	31	55	2	34	38.6	-8.5	77	N/A	0	0	0.0	0.0
B / 8.6	8.2	0.69	12.63	92	0	0	0	100	4	N/A	N/A	63	5	0	0	0.0	0.0
U /	N/A	N/A	9.52	717	0	0	0	100	85	N/A	N/A	N/A	2	0	0	0.0	0.0
C+ / 6.9	10.7	1.03	35.78	35	7	92	0	1	23	120.5	-18.3	48	10	0	0	5.8	0.0
C+ / 6.9	10.7	1.03	34.06	30	7	92	0	1	23	111.8	-18.6	37	10	0	0	0.0	0.0
C+ / 6.9	10.7	1.03	35.96	3	7	92	0	1	23	120.6	-18.4	48	10	0	0	0.0	0.0
C+ / 6.9	10.7	1.03	36.13	2,061	7	92	0	1	23	123.6	-18.2	52	10	0	0	0.0	0.0
C / 5.5	13.3	0.83	22.84	12	0	95	3	2	70	109.5	-23.0	56	N/A	0	0	5.8	0.0
C / 5.3	13.3	0.83	19.73	13	0	95	3	2	70	101.5	-23.2	46	N/A	0	0	0.0	0.0
C / 5.5	13.3	0.83	22.89	1	0	95	3	2	70	109.9	-23.0	56	N/A	0	0	0.0	0.0
C+ / 5.6	13.3	0.83	23.81	437	0	95	3	2	70	112.7	-22.9	59	N/A	0	0	0.0	0.0
D+ / 2.7	10.7	1.03	32.30	31	3	95	0	2	73	121.2	-19.6	49	6	0	0	5.8	0.0
D+ / 2.7	10.7	1.03	31.60	44	3	95	0	2	73	112.4	-19.9	38	6	0	0	0.0	0.0
D+ / 2.7	10.7	1.03	32.34	6	3	95	0	2	73	121.2	-19.6	49	6	0	0	0.0	0.0
D+ / 2.7	10.7	1.03	32.22	353	3	95	0	2	73	125.2	-19.5	54	6	100,000	0	0.0	0.0
D+ / 2.7	10.7	1.03	32.25	261	3	95	0	2	73	124.2	-19.5	53	6	0	0	0.0	0.0
B- / 7.8	8.8	0.83	50.39	29	10	87	1	2	94	115.6	-16.7	79	3	0	0	5.8	0.0
B- / 7.8	8.8	0.83	50.08	44	10	87	1	2	94	107.0	-17.0	73	3	0	0	0.0	0.0
B- / 7.8	8.8	0.83	50.45	5	10	87	1	2	94	115.6	-16.7	79	3	0	0	0.0	0.0
B- / 7.8	8.8	0.83	50.39	150	10	87	1	2	94	119.4	-16.6	81	3	100,000	0	0.0	0.0
B- / 7.8	8.8	0.83	50.46	188	10	87	1	2	94	118.4	-16.6	80	3	0	0	0.0	0.0
B- / 7.8	8.8	0.83	50.39	209	10	87	1	2	94	120.8	-16.6	82	3	10,000,000	0	0.0	0.0
C- / 3.1	12.8	1.17	10.21	2	4	95	0	1	118	N/A	N/A	37	7	0	0	5.8	0.0
D+ / 2.4	12.9	1.17	8.36	9	4	95	0	1	118	121.3	-17.4	28	7	0	0	0.0	0.0
C- / 3.1	12.9	1.17	10.24	N/A	4	95	0	1	118	130.4	-17.2	36	7	0	0	0.0	0.0
C- / 3.3	12.9	1.17	10.98	13	4	95	0	1	118	135.1	-17.1	42	7	100,000	0	0.0	0.0
C- / 3.2	12.8	1.17	10.76	21	4	95	0	1	118	133.6	-17.1	40	7	0	0	0.0	0.0
C- / 3.3	12.9	1.17	10.93	255	4	95	0	1	118	N/A	N/A	43	7	10,000,000	0	0.0	0.0

I. Index of Stock Mutual Funds

Fund Type	Fund Name	Ticker Symbol	Overall Investment Rating	Phone	Perfor-mance Rating/Pts	3 Mo	6 Mo	1Yr / Pct	3Yr / Pct	5Yr / Pct	Dividend Yield	Expense Ratio
	99 Pct = Best 0 Pct = Worst							Total Return % through 2/28/17	Annualized		Incl. in Returns	
GR	Russell Investments US Lrg Cp Eq A	RLCZX	C+	(800) 832-6688	B- / 7.2	6.92	9.10	24.25 /71	8.56 /84	12.45 /79	0.84	1.26
GR	Russell Investments US Lrg Cp Eq C	RLCCX	B-	(800) 832-6688	B / 7.6	6.67	8.70	23.35 /68	7.74 /77	11.60 /71	0.22	2.01
GR	Russell Investments US Lrg Cp Eq S	RLCSX	B	(800) 832-6688	B+ / 8.4	6.96	9.19	24.57 /72	8.82 /86	12.73 /81	1.10	1.01
MC	Russell Investments US Mid Cp Eq A	RMCAX	C+	(800) 832-6688	B / 7.7	6.98	11.39	29.68 /86	7.90 /78	12.03 /75	0.66	1.40
MC	Russell Investments US Mid Cp Eq C	RMCCX	C+	(800) 832-6688	B / 8.1	6.78	10.97	28.67 /83	7.10 /73	11.19 /68	0.11	2.15
MC	Russell Investments US Mid Cp Eq S	RMCSX	B-	(800) 832-6688	B+ / 8.9	7.03	11.48	29.99 /86	8.16 /80	12.32 /77	0.90	1.15
GR	Russell Investments US Sm Cp Eq A	RLACX	C	(800) 832-6688	B- / 7.1	4.99	12.33	34.20 /93	5.85 /63	12.12 /75	0.25	1.25
GR	Russell Investments US Sm Cp Eq C	RLECX	C+	(800) 832-6688	B- / 7.5	4.81	11.92	33.21 /92	5.06 /55	11.28 /68	0.00	2.00
GR	Russell Investments US Sm Cp Eq E	REBEX	C+	(800) 832-6688	B / 8.0	5.01	12.32	34.22 /93	5.85 /63	12.13 /75	0.22	1.25
GR	● Russell Investments US Sm Cp Eq I	REBSX	B-	(800) 832-6688	B+ / 8.3	5.12	12.52	34.66 /94	6.21 /66	12.50 /79	0.55	0.92
GR	Russell Investments US Sm Cp Eq S	RLESX	B-	(800) 832-6688	B / 8.2	5.10	12.46	34.56 /94	6.12 /65	12.41 /78	0.48	1.00
GR	Russell Investments US Sm Cp Eq Y	REBYX	B-	(800) 832-6688	B+ / 8.4	5.16	12.59	34.85 /94	6.34 /67	12.62 /80	0.66	0.80
GR	Russell Investments US Str Eq A	RSEAX	B	(800) 832-6688	B- / 7.4	7.15	10.54	25.05 /73	8.47 /83	---	0.91	1.31
GR	Russell Investments US Str Eq C	RSECX	B	(800) 832-6688	B / 7.9	6.98	10.16	24.22 /71	7.66 /76	---	0.30	2.06
GR	Russell Investments US Str Eq E	RSEEX	B+	(800) 832-6688	B+ / 8.4	7.16	10.55	25.03 /73	8.47 /83	---	0.98	1.31
GR	Russell Investments US Str Eq S	RSESX	B+	(800) 832-6688	B+ / 8.6	7.14	10.60	25.34 /74	8.75 /85	---	1.21	1.06
AA	Russell Mod Strategy R4	RMLUX	C+	(800) 832-6688	D+ / 2.8	3.53	2.43	11.54 /16	3.44 /36	4.54 /18	3.22	1.40
AA	Russell Mod Strategy R5	RMLVX	C+	(800) 832-6688	D+ / 2.6	3.44	2.28	11.18 /15	3.17 /33	4.24 /16	2.95	1.65
FO	Russell Select International Eq Y	RTIYX	U	(800) 832-6688	U /	6.87	5.25	16.33 /36	---	---	2.30	0.64
GR	Russell Select US Equity Y	RTDYX	U	(800) 832-6688	U /	7.90	10.90	26.17 /77	---	---	1.70	0.42
FS	Rydex Banking A	RYBKX	A	(800) 820-0888	A+ / 9.9	9.54	26.53	54.46 /99	9.74 /92	12.97 /83	0.41	1.59
FS	Rydex Banking C	RYKCX	A	(800) 820-0888	A+ / 9.9	9.32	26.06	53.31 /99	8.92 /86	12.12 /75	0.47	2.35
FS	Rydex Banking H	RYKAX	A	(800) 820-0888	A+ / 9.9	9.53	26.56	54.54 /99	9.67 /91	12.82 /82	0.44	1.68
FS	Rydex Banking Inv	RYKIX	A	(800) 820-0888	A+ / 9.9	9.59	26.67	54.79 /99	10.00 /93	13.24 /86	0.39	1.34
GR	Rydex Basic Materials A	RYBMX	C-	(800) 820-0888	C+ / 6.5	6.13	11.17	39.60 /97	3.12 /33	2.67 /10	1.02	1.60
GR	Rydex Basic Materials C	RYBCX	C-	(800) 820-0888	C+ / 6.8	5.95	10.79	38.58 /97	2.36 /26	1.91 / 8	1.19	2.35
GR	Rydex Basic Materials H	RYBAX	C	(800) 820-0888	B- / 7.2	6.15	11.20	39.63 /97	3.01 /32	2.49 / 9	1.10	1.64
GR	Rydex Basic Materials Inv	RYBIX	C	(800) 820-0888	B- / 7.5	6.20	11.34	39.95 /97	3.39 /36	2.93 /11	1.01	1.35
HL	Rydex Biotechnology A	RYBOX	E+	(800) 820-0888	C- / 3.9	9.08	7.22	21.19 /58	2.91 /31	19.16 /99	0.00	1.57
HL	Rydex Biotechnology C	RYCFX	E+	(800) 820-0888	C- / 4.2	8.88	6.83	20.30 /54	2.14 /25	18.27 /99	0.00	2.33
HL	Rydex Biotechnology H	RYOAX	D-	(800) 820-0888	C / 4.8	9.09	7.23	21.17 /58	2.79 /30	18.96 /99	0.00	1.65
HL	Rydex Biotechnology Inv	RYOIX	D-	(800) 820-0888	C / 5.1	9.14	7.36	21.50 /60	3.17 /33	19.46 /99	0.00	1.32
OT	Rydex Commodities Strgy A	RYMEX	E-	(800) 820-0888	E- / 0.0	3.49	8.44	17.88 /42	-22.76 / 0	-16.20 / 0	0.00	1.77
OT	Rydex Commodities Strgy C	RYMJX	E-	(800) 820-0888	E- / 0.0	3.30	8.08	16.94 /38	-23.32 / 0	-16.80 / 0	0.00	2.51
OT	Rydex Commodities Strgy H	RYMBX	E-	(800) 820-0888	E- / 0.0	3.49	8.37	17.79 /42	-22.77 / 0	-16.19 / 0	0.00	1.77
GR	Rydex Consumer Products A	RYPDX	B-	(800) 820-0888	C+ / 6.0	8.33	0.25	10.77 /14	10.22 /94	12.55 /80	0.90	1.60
GR	Rydex Consumer Products C	RYCPX	B-	(800) 820-0888	C+ / 6.3	8.13	-0.13	9.94 /11	9.39 /90	11.71 /72	1.07	2.35
GR	Rydex Consumer Products H	RYCAX	B-	(800) 820-0888	C+ / 6.8	8.33	0.26	10.74 /14	10.09 /94	12.35 /78	0.98	1.66
GR	Rydex Consumer Products Inv	RYCIX	B+	(800) 820-0888	B- / 7.0	8.39	0.37	11.03 /15	10.49 /96	12.83 /82	0.88	1.34
AG	Rydex Dow 2x Strategy A	RYLDX	B+	(800) 820-0888	A+ / 9.9	18.82	28.74	61.30 /99	18.27 /99	21.91 /99	0.00	1.82
AG	Rydex Dow 2x Strategy C	RYCYX	B+	(800) 820-0888	A+ / 9.9	18.62	28.26	60.10 /99	17.41 /99	21.01 /99	0.00	2.56
AG	Rydex Dow 2x Strategy H	RYCVX	B+	(800) 820-0888	A+ / 9.9	18.81	28.73	61.26 /99	18.26 /99	21.89 /99	0.00	1.82
GR	Rydex Dow Jones Industrial Avg H	RYDHX	U	(800) 820-0888	U /	9.06	13.73	27.61 /81	---	---	0.04	1.55
AG	Rydex Dyn-NASDAQ 100 2x Strgy A	RYVLX	C	(800) 820-0888	A+ / 9.9	22.31	23.72	57.90 /99	24.30 /99	29.92 /99	0.00	1.80
AG	Rydex Dyn-NASDAQ 100 2x Strgy C	RYCCX	C	(800) 820-0888	A+ / 9.9	22.08	23.26	56.72 /99	23.37 /99	28.93 /99	0.00	2.55
AG	Rydex Dyn-NASDAQ 100 2x Strgy H	RYVYX	C	(800) 820-0888	A+ / 9.9	22.31	23.73	57.91 /99	24.31 /99	29.91 /99	0.00	1.80
TC	Rydex Electronics A	RYELX	A-	(800) 820-0888	A+ / 9.9	8.33	15.27	39.94 /97	15.56 /99	14.23 /94	0.00	1.60
TC	Rydex Electronics C	RYSCX	A-	(800) 820-0888	A+ / 9.9	8.14	14.84	38.90 /97	14.70 /99	13.35 /87	0.00	2.35
TC	Rydex Electronics H	RYSAX	A	(800) 820-0888	A+ / 9.9	8.35	15.27	39.82 /97	15.40 /99	14.00 /93	0.00	1.74
TC	Rydex Electronics Inv	RYSIX	A	(800) 820-0888	A+ / 9.9	8.42	15.42	40.24 /97	15.84 /99	14.51 /96	0.00	1.34
EM	Rydex Emerging Mkts 2x Strat A	RYWTX	D-	(800) 820-0888	C / 5.1	16.15	11.09	67.28 /99	-0.96 /10	-8.80 / 1	0.00	1.75
EM	Rydex Emerging Mkts 2x Strat C	RYWUX	D	(800) 820-0888	C / 5.5	15.94	10.67	66.14 /99	-1.68 / 7	-9.33 / 1	0.00	2.46

● Denotes fund is closed to new investors
* Denotes fund is included in Section II

www.thestreetratings.com

RISK			NET ASSETS		ASSET					Portfolio	BULL / BEAR		FUND MANAGER		MINIMUMS		LOADS	
Risk Rating/Pts	3 Year Standard Deviation	Beta	NAV As of 2/28/17	Total $(Mil)	Cash %	Stocks %	Bonds %	Other %		Turnover Ratio	Last Bull Market Return	Last Bear Market Return	Manager Quality Pct	Manager Tenure (Years)	Initial Purch. $	Additional Purch. $	Front End Load	Back End Load
C /5.2	11.0	1.06	13.21	11	5	94	0	1		92	N/A	N/A	42	5	0	0	5.8	0.0
C /5.2	11.0	1.06	13.15	2	5	94	0	1		92	N/A	N/A	32	5	0	0	0.0	0.0
C /5.2	11.0	1.06	13.25	367	5	94	0	1		92	N/A	N/A	44	5	0	0	0.0	0.0
C- /3.9	12.2	0.98	12.00	5	4	95	0	1		127	N/A	N/A	56	4	0	0	5.8	0.0
C- /3.8	12.2	0.98	11.69	3	4	95	0	1		127	N/A	N/A	46	4	0	0	0.0	0.0
C- /3.9	12.2	0.98	12.04	154	4	95	0	1		127	N/A	N/A	60	4	0	0	0.0	0.0
C /4.3	15.3	1.17	31.64	19	4	94	0	2		98	124.7	-24.6	8	N/A	0	0	5.8	0.0
C- /4.2	15.3	1.17	30.12	24	4	94	0	2		98	115.8	-24.9	6	N/A	0	0	0.0	0.0
C /4.3	15.3	1.17	31.81	4	4	94	0	2		98	124.9	-24.6	9	N/A	0	0	0.0	0.0
C- /4.2	15.3	1.17	32.06	162	4	94	0	2		98	128.8	-24.6	10	N/A	100,000	0	0.0	0.0
C- /4.2	15.3	1.17	31.90	1,245	4	94	0	2		98	127.9	-24.6	10	N/A	0	0	0.0	0.0
C- /4.2	15.3	1.17	31.91	403	4	94	0	2		98	130.2	-24.5	11	N/A	10,000,000	0	0.0	0.0
C+ /5.7	10.6	1.01	12.97	6	3	95	0	2		75	N/A	N/A	47	N/A	0	0	5.8	0.0
C+ /5.7	10.6	1.02	12.93	18	3	95	0	2		75	N/A	N/A	35	N/A	0	0	0.0	0.0
C+ /5.7	10.6	1.01	12.99	4	3	95	0	2		75	N/A	N/A	47	N/A	0	0	0.0	0.0
C+ /5.7	10.6	1.01	12.99	3,067	3	95	0	2		75	N/A	N/A	50	N/A	0	0	0.0	0.0
B+ /9.5	4.6	0.67	10.15	25	12	31	55	2		34	36.7	-8.7	56	3	0	0	0.0	0.0
B+ /9.5	4.6	0.66	10.20	16	12	31	55	2		34	34.8	-8.8	53	3	0	0	0.0	0.0
U /	N/A	N/A	8.85	752	0	0	0	100		57	N/A	N/A	N/A	2	10,000,000	0	0.0	0.0
U /	N/A	N/A	12.27	841	0	0	0	100		9	N/A	N/A	N/A	3	10,000,000	0	0.0	0.0
C /5.4	18.2	1.28	73.27	6	0	99	0	1		514	135.0	-30.1	11	19	2,500	0	4.8	0.0
C /5.4	18.2	1.28	66.62	6	0	99	0	1		514	125.6	-30.3	7	19	2,500	0	0.0	0.0
C /5.4	18.2	1.28	71.39	22	0	99	0	1		514	133.2	-30.2	10	19	2,500	0	0.0	0.0
C /5.4	18.2	1.28	79.96	44	0	99	0	1		514	138.0	-30.0	12	19	2,500	0	0.0	0.0
C- /3.8	19.0	1.27	52.84	19	0	99	0	1		471	38.8	-27.3	2	19	2,500	0	4.8	0.0
C- /3.7	19.0	1.27	47.35	6	0	99	0	1		471	33.4	-27.5	2	19	2,500	0	0.0	0.0
C- /3.8	19.1	1.26	51.26	10	0	99	0	1		471	37.5	-27.3	2	19	2,500	0	0.0	0.0
C- /3.8	19.0	1.27	56.15	85	0	99	0	1		471	40.7	-27.2	3	19	2,500	0	0.0	0.0
D /1.9	28.4	1.74	74.87	37	0	99	0	1		83	205.3	-14.5	0	19	2,500	0	4.8	0.0
D /1.8	28.4	1.74	68.03	22	0	99	0	1		83	193.0	-14.8	0	19	2,500	0	0.0	0.0
D /1.9	28.4	1.74	72.86	20	0	99	0	1		83	202.4	-14.6	0	19	2,500	0	0.0	0.0
D /1.9	28.4	1.74	80.47	249	0	99	0	1		83	209.4	-14.5	1	19	2,500	0	0.0	0.0
E+ /0.7	21.9	0.51	84.45	1	100	0	0	0		486	-51.3	-24.0	0	12	2,500	0	4.8	0.0
E+ /0.7	21.9	0.51	77.04	N/A	100	0	0	0		486	-53.2	-24.2	0	12	2,500	0	0.0	0.0
E+ /0.7	21.9	0.51	84.53	12	100	0	0	0		486	-51.3	-24.0	0	12	2,500	0	0.0	0.0
B- /7.2	9.5	0.61	60.72	40	0	99	0	1		104	101.3	-4.7	92	19	2,500	0	4.8	0.0
B- /7.2	9.5	0.61	53.60	29	0	99	0	1		104	93.3	-5.0	89	19	2,500	0	0.0	0.0
B- /7.2	9.5	0.61	58.68	36	0	99	0	1		104	99.4	-4.8	92	19	2,500	0	0.0	0.0
B- /7.3	9.5	0.61	65.52	202	0	99	0	1		104	104.0	-4.6	93	19	2,500	0	0.0	0.0
C /4.6	22.1	2.03	65.73	9	14	85	0	1		1,023	276.5	-28.7	27	13	2,500	0	4.8	0.0
C /4.5	22.1	2.03	59.20	3	14	85	0	1		1,023	261.5	-28.9	20	13	2,500	0	0.0	0.0
C /4.6	22.1	2.03	65.52	24	14	85	0	1		1,023	276.0	-28.8	27	13	2,500	0	0.0	0.0
U /	N/A	N/A	58.72	48	0	0	0	100		0	N/A	N/A	N/A	2	2,500	0	0.0	0.0
E+ /0.9	28.4	2.40	99.83	15	18	79	2	1		114	447.3	-23.4	43	17	2,500	0	4.8	0.0
E+ /0.9	28.4	2.40	83.30	21	18	79	2	1		114	425.2	-23.7	33	17	2,500	0	0.0	0.0
E+ /0.9	28.4	2.40	99.83	231	18	79	2	1		114	447.0	-23.4	44	17	2,500	0	0.0	0.0
C /5.1	18.0	1.27	99.44	5	1	98	0	1		769	135.3	-28.4	85	19	2,500	0	4.8	0.0
C /5.1	18.0	1.27	90.69	2	1	98	0	1		769	125.6	-28.6	80	19	2,500	0	0.0	0.0
C /5.1	18.0	1.27	96.84	21	1	98	0	1		769	132.7	-28.4	84	19	2,500	0	0.0	0.0
C /5.1	18.0	1.27	106.15	43	1	98	0	1		769	138.5	-28.3	86	19	2,500	0	0.0	0.0
D /1.9	39.8	2.27	58.70	1	98	1	0	1		2,874	-7.9	-47.9	18	7	2,500	0	4.8	0.0
D /1.9	39.9	2.27	56.72	N/A	98	1	0	1		2,874	-11.0	-47.5	12	7	2,500	0	0.0	0.0

99 Pct = Best
0 Pct = Worst

Fund Type	Fund Name	Ticker Symbol	Overall Investment Rating	Phone	Performance Rating/Pts	Total Return % through 2/28/17			Annualized		Incl. in Returns	
						3 Mo	6 Mo	1Yr / Pct	3Yr / Pct	5Yr / Pct	Dividend Yield	Expense Ratio
EM	Rydex Emerging Mkts 2x Strat H	RYWVX	D	(800) 820-0888	C+ / 6.0	16.05	10.96	67.12 /99	-1.00 / 9	-8.87 / 1	0.00	1.74
EN	Rydex Energy A	RYENX	E-	(800) 820-0888	E- / 0.1	-5.38	5.62	37.51 /96	-11.20 / 1	-4.47 / 2	0.67	1.60
EN	Rydex Energy C	RYECX	E-	(800) 820-0888	E- / 0.1	-5.56	5.23	36.50 /95	-11.91 / 1	-5.20 / 2	0.78	2.35
EN	Rydex Energy H	RYEAX	E-	(800) 820-0888	E- / 0.1	-5.39	5.55	37.30 /96	-11.35 / 1	-4.65 / 2	0.72	1.70
EN	Rydex Energy Inv	RYEIX	E-	(800) 820-0888	E- / 0.1	-5.33	5.70	37.83 /96	-11.02 / 1	-4.24 / 2	0.66	1.35
EN	Rydex Energy Services A	RYESX	E-	(800) 820-0888	E- / 0.0	-0.19	18.27	34.35 /93	-17.35 / 0	-8.88 / 1	0.74	1.59
EN	Rydex Energy Services C	RYVCX	E-	(800) 820-0888	E- / 0.0	-0.38	17.87	33.35 /92	-17.97 / 0	-9.57 / 1	0.86	2.35
EN	Rydex Energy Services H	RYVAX	E-	(800) 820-0888	E- / 0.0	-0.19	18.27	34.33 /93	-17.49 / 0	-9.07 / 1	0.80	1.67
EN	Rydex Energy Services Inv	RYVIX	E-	(800) 820-0888	E- / 0.0	-0.12	18.44	34.69 /94	-17.15 / 0	-8.66 / 1	0.73	1.35
FO	Rydex Eurp 1.25x Strgy A	RYAEX	E	(800) 820-0888	E- / 0.1	10.82	1.66	11.16 /15	-8.04 / 1	1.64 / 7	0.83	1.67
FO	Rydex Eurp 1.25x Strgy C	RYCEX	E	(800) 820-0888	E- / 0.1	10.62	1.39	10.37 /13	-8.67 / 1	0.68 / 6	1.00	2.42
FO	Rydex Eurp 1.25x Strgy H	RYEUX	E	(800) 820-0888	E- / 0.1	10.85	2.08	11.37 /16	-8.03 / 1	1.48 / 7	0.88	1.66
FS	Rydex Financial Services A	RYFNX	C-	(800) 820-0888	A / 9.4	9.02	14.25	34.99 /94	9.18 /88	12.63 /80	0.68	1.64
FS	Rydex Financial Services C	RYFCX	C	(800) 820-0888	A / 9.5	8.81	13.82	34.00 /93	8.36 /82	11.80 /72	0.79	2.39
FS	Rydex Financial Services H	RYFAX	C	(800) 820-0888	A+ / 9.7	9.02	14.25	34.99 /94	9.05 /87	12.44 /78	0.73	1.69
FS	Rydex Financial Services Inv	RYFIX	C	(800) 820-0888	A+ / 9.7	9.08	14.39	35.34 /94	9.45 /90	12.91 /83	0.67	1.38
HL	Rydex Health Care A	RYHEX	D	(800) 820-0888	C / 4.3	10.05	3.63	14.08 /26	5.71 /62	14.61 /96	0.00	1.59
HL	Rydex Health Care C	RYHCX	D	(800) 820-0888	C / 4.7	9.90	3.26	13.22 /22	4.93 /53	13.74 /91	0.00	2.35
HL	Rydex Health Care H	RYHAX	D+	(800) 820-0888	C / 5.3	10.08	3.67	14.10 /26	5.62 /61	14.43 /95	0.00	1.71
HL	Rydex Health Care Inv	RYHIX	D+	(800) 820-0888	C+ / 5.6	10.15	3.77	14.38 /27	5.97 /64	14.89 /97	0.00	1.34
TC	Rydex Internet A	RYINX	C	(800) 820-0888	C+ / 6.1	7.17	7.88	26.87 /79	5.68 /61	14.98 /97	0.00	1.60
TC	Rydex Internet C	RYICX	C	(800) 820-0888	C+ / 6.4	6.98	7.49	25.94 /76	4.91 /53	14.11 /94	0.00	2.35
TC	Rydex Internet H	RYIAX	C+	(800) 820-0888	C+ / 6.9	7.18	7.91	26.93 /79	5.55 /60	14.78 /96	0.00	1.67
TC	Rydex Internet Inv	RYIIX	C+	(800) 820-0888	B- / 7.2	7.25	8.03	27.20 /80	5.96 /64	15.27 /97	0.00	1.35
AG	Rydex Inv Dow 2x Strategy A	RYIDX	E-	(800) 820-0888	E- / 0.0	-16.89	-24.77	-42.46 / 0	-24.21 / 0	-26.05 / 0	0.00	1.82
AG	Rydex Inv Dow 2x Strategy C	RYCZX	E-	(800) 820-0888	E- / 0.0	-17.02	-25.01	-42.84 / 0	-24.75 / 0	-26.62 / 0	0.00	2.53
AG	Rydex Inv Dow 2x Strategy H	RYCWX	E-	(800) 820-0888	E- / 0.0	-16.80	-24.74	-42.42 / 0	-24.20 / 0	-25.99 / 0	0.00	1.82
MC	Rydex Inv Mid-Cap Stgy A	RYAGX	E	(800) 820-0888	E- / 0.0	-6.37	-10.94	-25.67 / 0	-11.44 / 1	-14.93 / 0	0.00	1.65
MC	Rydex Inv Mid-Cap Stgy C	RYCLX	E	(800) 820-0888	E- / 0.0	-6.55	-11.29	-26.24 / 0	-12.11 / 0	-15.59 / 0	0.00	2.41
MC	Rydex Inv Mid-Cap Stgy H	RYMHX	E	(800) 820-0888	E- / 0.0	-6.37	-10.91	-25.57 / 0	-11.39 / 1	-14.91 / 0	0.00	1.65
AG	Rydex Inv NASDAQ 100 2x Stgy A	RYVTX	E-	(800) 820-0888	E- / 0.0	-19.27	-22.30	-42.38 / 0	-29.59 / 0	-32.13 / 0	0.00	1.79
AG	Rydex Inv NASDAQ 100 2x Stgy C	RYCDX	E-	(800) 820-0888	E- / 0.0	-19.42	-22.42	-42.59 / 0	-29.92 / 0	-32.65 / 0	0.00	2.53
AG	Rydex Inv NASDAQ 100 2x Stgy H	RYVNX	E-	(800) 820-0888	E- / 0.0	-19.28	-22.19	-42.27 / 0	-29.54 / 0	-32.15 / 0	0.00	1.80
AG	Rydex Inv NASDAQ 100 Strgy A	RYAPX	E	(800) 820-0888	E- / 0.0	-10.04	-11.47	-23.36 / 0	-14.84 / 0	-16.74 / 0	0.00	1.69
AG	Rydex Inv NASDAQ 100 Strgy C	RYACX	E-	(800) 820-0888	E- / 0.0	-10.19	-11.81	-24.01 / 0	-15.87 / 0	-17.59 / 0	0.00	2.44
AG	Rydex Inv NASDAQ 100 Strgy Inv	RYAIX	E	(800) 820-0888	E- / 0.0	-9.96	-11.32	-23.24 / 0	-15.03 / 0	-16.72 / 0	0.00	1.44
SC	Rydex Inv Rusl 2000 2x Strtgy A	RYIUX	E-	(800) 820-0888	E- / 0.0	-10.88	-24.21	-50.78 / 0	-21.53 / 0	-29.63 / 0	0.00	1.80
SC	Rydex Inv Rusl 2000 2x Strtgy C	RYIZX	E-	(800) 820-0888	E- / 0.0	-11.02	-24.48	-51.12 / 0	-22.13 / 0	-30.09 / 0	0.00	2.56
SC	Rydex Inv Rusl 2000 2x Strtgy H	RYIRX	E-	(800) 820-0888	E- / 0.0	-10.88	-24.24	-50.80 / 0	-21.57 / 0	-29.60 / 0	0.00	1.81
SC	Rydex Inv Russell 2000 Stgy A	RYAFX	E	(800) 820-0888	E- / 0.0	-5.43	-12.62	-28.99 / 0	-10.39 / 1	-15.17 / 0	0.00	1.70
SC	Rydex Inv Russell 2000 Stgy C	RYCQX	E	(800) 820-0888	E- / 0.0	-5.63	-12.97	-29.51 / 0	-11.05 / 1	-15.80 / 0	0.00	2.45
SC	Rydex Inv Russell 2000 Stgy H	RYSHX	E	(800) 820-0888	E- / 0.0	-5.45	-12.65	-28.98 / 0	-10.39 / 1	-15.15 / 0	0.00	1.70
AG	Rydex Inv S&P 500 2x Strategy A	RYTMX	E-	(800) 820-0888	E- / 0.0	-14.59	-18.46	-38.35 / 0	-23.06 / 0	-27.57 / 0	0.00	1.76
AG	Rydex Inv S&P 500 2x Strategy C	RYCBX	E-	(800) 820-0888	E- / 0.0	-14.79	-18.76	-38.83 / 0	-23.67 / 0	-28.10 / 0	0.00	2.47
AG	Rydex Inv S&P 500 2x Strategy H	RYTPX	E-	(800) 820-0888	E- / 0.0	-14.60	-18.48	-38.39 / 0	-23.07 / 0	-27.56 / 0	0.00	1.76
AG	Rydex Inv S&P 500 Stgry A	RYARX	D-	(800) 820-0888	E- / 0.0	-7.48	-9.55	-20.86 / 0	-11.82 / 1	-14.58 / 0	0.00	1.67
AG	Rydex Inv S&P 500 Stgry C	RYUCX	D-	(800) 820-0888	E- / 0.0	-7.66	-9.86	-21.50 / 0	-12.48 / 0	-15.23 / 0	0.00	2.42
AG	Rydex Inv S&P 500 Stgry Inv	RYURX	D-	(800) 820-0888	E- / 0.0	-7.42	-9.44	-20.70 / 0	-11.60 / 1	-14.37 / 0	0.00	1.42
EM	Rydex Inverse Emg Mkts 2x Str A	RYWWX	E-	(800) 820-0888	E- / 0.0	-15.85	-16.58	-49.84 / 0	-17.38 / 0	-9.47 / 1	0.00	1.75
EM	Rydex Inverse Emg Mkts 2x Str C	RYWZX	E-	(800) 820-0888	E- / 0.0	-15.97	-16.89	-50.15 / 0	-18.07 / 0	-9.92 / 1	0.00	2.50
EM	Rydex Inverse Emg Mkts 2x Str H	RYWYX	E-	(800) 820-0888	E- / 0.0	-15.91	-16.58	-49.84 / 0	-17.57 / 0	-9.60 / 1	0.00	1.74
FO	Rydex Japan 2x Strategy Fd A	RYJSX	B-	(800) 820-0888	A- / 9.2	8.72	7.54	43.02 /98	8.15 /80	11.80 /72	0.00	1.52

● Denotes fund is closed to new investors
* Denotes fund is included in Section II

www.thestreetratings.com

Risk Rating/Pts	Standard Deviation	Beta	NAV As of 2/28/17	Total $(Mil)	Cash %	Stocks %	Bonds %	Other %	Portfolio Turnover Ratio	Last Bull Market Return	Last Bear Market Return	Manager Quality Pct	Manager Tenure (Years)	Initial Purch. $	Additional Purch. $	Front End Load	Back End Load
D /1.9	39.9	2.27	58.71	7	98	1	0	1	2,874	-8.1	-47.7	17	7	2,500	0	0.0	0.0
D- /1.0	25.9	1.29	74.72	5	0	99	0	1	595	4.3	-31.2	15	19	2,500	0	4.8	0.0
E+ /0.9	25.9	1.29	66.91	5	0	99	0	1	595	0.1	-31.5	10	19	2,500	0	0.0	0.0
D- /1.0	25.9	1.29	72.52	4	0	99	0	1	595	3.3	-31.3	14	19	2,500	0	0.0	0.0
D- /1.0	25.9	1.29	79.64	26	0	99	0	1	595	5.7	-31.2	17	19	2,500	0	0.0	0.0
E- /0.2	31.4	1.49	31.95	2	0	99	0	1	1,241	-15.8	-34.8	1	19	2,500	0	4.8	0.0
E- /0.2	31.4	1.49	28.87	4	0	99	0	1	1,241	-19.2	-35.1	1	19	2,500	0	0.0	0.0
E- /0.2	31.4	1.49	30.99	4	0	99	0	1	1,241	-16.7	-34.9	1	19	2,500	0	0.0	0.0
E- /0.2	31.4	1.48	33.89	15	0	99	0	1	1,241	-14.7	-34.8	2	19	2,500	0	0.0	0.0
C /4.5	15.7	1.20	80.59	N/A	41	58	0	1	920	31.8	-31.9	4	17	2,500	0	4.8	0.0
C /4.3	15.7	1.20	70.28	N/A	41	58	0	1	920	25.7	-32.3	3	17	2,500	0	0.0	0.0
C /4.4	15.7	1.20	80.01	3	41	58	0	1	920	30.9	-31.9	4	17	2,500	0	0.0	0.0
D- /1.0	12.3	0.93	63.00	2	0	99	0	1	268	124.9	-26.6	46	19	2,500	0	4.8	0.0
D- /1.0	12.3	0.93	56.69	3	0	99	0	1	268	116.1	-26.8	36	19	2,500	0	0.0	0.0
D- /1.0	12.3	0.93	61.17	7	0	99	0	1	268	122.8	-26.6	45	19	2,500	0	0.0	0.0
D- /1.0	12.3	0.93	66.77	48	0	99	0	1	268	127.9	-26.5	50	19	2,500	0	0.0	0.0
C- /3.6	15.9	1.11	25.74	5	0	99	0	1	249	131.7	-14.6	11	19	2,500	0	4.8	0.0
C- /3.3	16.0	1.11	22.75	5	0	99	0	1	249	122.6	-14.9	7	19	2,500	0	0.0	0.0
C- /3.5	15.9	1.11	24.90	6	0	99	0	1	249	129.9	-14.7	10	19	2,500	0	0.0	0.0
C- /3.7	15.9	1.11	28.00	39	0	99	0	1	249	134.8	-14.5	12	19	2,500	0	0.0	0.0
C /4.7	16.1	1.23	88.07	2	0	99	0	1	520	140.9	-25.0	6	17	2,500	0	4.8	0.0
C /4.6	16.1	1.23	79.09	2	0	99	0	1	520	131.4	-25.3	4	17	2,500	0	0.0	0.0
C /4.7	16.1	1.23	85.55	2	0	99	0	1	520	138.6	-25.2	6	17	2,500	0	0.0	0.0
C /4.7	16.1	1.23	93.53	21	0	99	0	1	520	144.3	-25.0	7	17	2,500	0	0.0	0.0
E+ /0.8	21.1	-1.94	17.52	1	73	0	26	1	0	-85.6	23.4	3	13	2,500	0	4.8	0.0
E+ /0.8	21.1	-1.94	15.80	N/A	73	0	26	1	0	-86.2	22.9	3	13	2,500	0	0.0	0.0
E+ /0.8	21.1	-1.94	17.58	7	73	0	26	1	0	-85.6	23.3	3	13	2,500	0	0.0	0.0
C /4.7	11.9	-0.99	24.84	N/A	100	0	0	0	199	-65.8	22.5	31	13	2,500	0	4.8	0.0
C /4.5	11.9	-0.99	22.40	N/A	100	0	0	0	199	-67.2	22.0	23	13	2,500	0	0.0	0.0
C /4.7	11.8	-0.98	24.83	1	100	0	0	0	199	-65.8	22.5	31	13	2,500	0	0.0	0.0
D /1.9	26.9	-2.27	61.40	N/A	43	0	56	1	0	-91.2	12.5	1	17	2,500	0	4.8	0.0
D /1.9	26.9	-2.27	54.55	1	43	0	56	1	0	-91.5	12.6	1	17	2,500	0	0.0	0.0
D /1.9	27.0	-2.28	61.49	16	43	0	56	1	0	-91.1	12.8	1	17	2,500	0	0.0	0.0
C- /3.9	13.4	-1.16	77.16	2	79	0	20	1	1,674	-68.4	7.8	18	19	2,500	0	4.8	0.0
C- /3.5	13.4	-1.16	66.60	1	79	0	20	1	1,674	-70.1	7.4	10	19	2,500	0	0.0	0.0
C- /3.8	13.4	-1.16	79.24	6	79	0	20	1	1,674	-68.3	8.0	16	19	2,500	0	0.0	0.0
E /0.3	31.8	-1.97	62.99	2	81	0	18	1	0	-90.8	49.4	1	11	2,500	0	4.8	0.0
E- /0.2	31.9	-1.97	57.88	1	81	0	18	1	0	-91.1	49.5	1	11	2,500	0	0.0	0.0
E /0.3	31.8	-1.97	62.73	12	81	0	18	1	0	-90.8	49.6	1	11	2,500	0	0.0	0.0
C- /3.9	15.6	-0.99	23.69	N/A	100	0	0	0	584	-67.1	25.1	18	13	2,500	0	4.8	0.0
C- /3.8	15.6	-0.99	21.47	3	100	0	0	0	584	-68.4	24.7	13	13	2,500	0	0.0	0.0
C- /3.9	15.7	-0.99	23.75	3	100	0	0	0	584	-67.0	25.0	18	13	2,500	0	0.0	0.0
D+ /2.9	20.2	-1.94	59.46	6	18	0	81	1	0	-87.4	28.4	5	17	2,500	0	4.8	0.0
D+ /2.8	20.2	-1.94	52.61	1	18	0	81	1	0	-87.9	28.1	4	17	2,500	0	0.0	0.0
D+ /2.9	20.3	-1.94	59.64	75	18	0	81	1	0	-87.4	28.6	5	17	2,500	0	0.0	0.0
C+ /6.7	10.0	-0.97	65.29	6	40	0	59	1	63	-63.6	14.9	35	23	2,500	0	4.8	0.0
C+ /6.5	10.1	-0.98	59.44	6	40	0	59	1	63	-65.0	14.6	26	23	2,500	0	0.0	0.0
C+ /6.7	10.0	-0.97	70.42	60	40	0	59	1	63	-63.1	15.0	38	23	2,500	0	0.0	0.0
E- /0.0	38.7	-2.20	66.72	N/A	100	0	0	0	0	-64.2	51.9	0	7	2,500	0	4.8	0.0
E- /0.0	38.6	-2.20	67.62	N/A	100	0	0	0	0	-64.7	54.9	0	7	2,500	0	0.0	0.0
E- /0.0	38.6	-2.20	66.27	1	100	0	0	0	0	-64.5	52.0	0	7	2,500	0	0.0	0.0
C- /3.4	22.3	1.30	101.60	N/A	100	0	0	0	543	97.1	-20.5	99	9	2,500	0	4.8	0.0

Fund Type	Fund Name	Ticker Symbol	Overall Investment Rating	Phone	Perfor-mance Rating/Pts	3 Mo	6 Mo	1Yr / Pct	3Yr / Pct	5Yr / Pct	Dividend Yield	Expense Ratio
	99 Pct = Best / 0 Pct = Worst							Total Return % through 2/28/17 (Annualized)			Incl. in Returns	
FO	Rydex Japan 2x Strategy Fd C	RYJTX	B-	(800) 820-0888	A / 9.4	8.53	7.14	41.96 /98	7.45 /75	11.11 /67	0.00	2.25
FO	Rydex Japan 2x Strategy Fd H	RYJHX	B	(800) 820-0888	A+ / 9.6	8.69	8.00	43.41 /98	8.27 /81	11.90 /73	0.00	1.50
GR	Rydex Leisure A	RYLSX	C+	(800) 820-0888	C+ / 6.8	7.30	11.24	19.95 /52	7.85 /78	14.71 /96	0.47	1.60
GR	Rydex Leisure C	RYLCX	B+	(800) 820-0888	B- / 7.1	7.11	10.84	19.05 /47	7.04 /72	13.86 /92	0.54	2.35
GR	Rydex Leisure H	RYLAX	B+	(800) 820-0888	B / 7.6	7.32	11.25	19.96 /52	7.75 /77	14.54 /96	0.50	1.64
GR	Rydex Leisure Inv	RYLIX	A-	(800) 820-0888	B / 7.8	7.40	11.42	20.27 /54	8.13 /80	15.01 /97	0.46	1.34
MC	Rydex Mid Cap 1.5x Strgy A	RYAHX	A	(800) 820-0888	A+ / 9.9	9.57	16.24	47.64 /99	11.80 /98	18.21 /99	0.00	1.65
MC	Rydex Mid Cap 1.5x Strgy C	RYDCX	A	(800) 820-0888	A+ / 9.9	9.38	15.84	46.57 /99	10.98 /97	17.33 /98	0.00	2.40
MC	Rydex Mid Cap 1.5x Strgy H	RYMDX	A	(800) 820-0888	A+ / 9.9	9.66	16.33	47.77 /99	11.91 /98	18.28 /99	0.00	1.66
MC	Rydex MidCap 400 Pure Growth A	RYMGX	D-	(800) 820-0888	D+ / 2.4	6.37	5.76	16.06 /35	2.07 /24	8.31 /45	0.00	1.50
MC	Rydex MidCap 400 Pure Growth C	RYCKX	E+	(800) 820-0888	D+ / 2.7	6.16	5.37	15.21 /31	1.31 /20	7.50 /38	0.00	2.25
MC	Rydex MidCap 400 Pure Growth H	RYBHX	D-	(800) 820-0888	C- / 3.2	6.37	5.77	16.06 /35	2.07 /24	8.31 /45	0.00	1.50
MC	Rydex MidCap 400 Pure Value A	RYMVX	B	(800) 820-0888	B / 8.1	2.46	13.95	37.68 /96	7.07 /72	11.40 /69	0.18	1.50
MC	Rydex MidCap 400 Pure Value C	RYMMX	B+	(800) 820-0888	B+ / 8.4	2.30	13.55	36.71 /96	6.29 /67	10.56 /62	0.22	2.25
MC	Rydex MidCap 400 Pure Value H	RYAVX	B+	(800) 820-0888	B+ / 8.9	2.46	13.94	37.73 /96	7.09 /73	11.40 /69	0.19	1.51
GR	Rydex Mo Rebalance NASDAQ100	RMQHX	U	(800) 820-0888	U /	22.27	24.27	59.04 /99	--	--	0.00	1.67
AG	Rydex NASDAQ 100 A	RYATX	A+	(800) 820-0888	A+ / 9.7	10.65	11.47	26.46 /78	12.71 /99	15.01 /97	0.00	1.51
AG	Rydex NASDAQ 100 C	RYCOX	A+	(800) 820-0888	A+ / 9.7	10.50	11.07	25.64 /75	11.90 /98	14.19 /94	0.00	2.26
GR	Rydex NASDAQ 100 H	RYHOX	U	(800) 820-0888	U /	10.65	11.47	26.58 /78	--	--	0.00	1.51
AG	Rydex NASDAQ 100 Investor	RYOCX	A+	(800) 820-0888	A+ / 9.8	10.74	11.67	26.89 /79	13.03 /99	15.32 /97	0.00	1.25
AG	Rydex Nova A	RYANX	A+	(800) 820-0888	A+ / 9.8	11.58	13.91	36.32 /95	13.35 /99	18.76 /99	0.04	1.51
AG	Rydex Nova C	RYNCX	A+	(800) 820-0888	A+ / 9.9	11.36	13.46	35.24 /94	12.47 /98	17.86 /99	0.04	2.26
GR	Rydex Nova H	RYNHX	U	(800) 820-0888	U /	11.59	13.90	36.23 /95	--	--	0.04	1.51
AG	Rydex Nova Investor	RYNVX	A+	(800) 820-0888	A+ / 9.9	11.65	14.02	36.57 /95	13.59 /99	19.04 /99	0.03	1.25
PM	Rydex Precious Metal A	RYMNX	E-	(800) 820-0888	E / 0.3	6.68	-8.96	27.60 /81	-4.91 / 2	-14.05 / 0	3.70	1.52
PM	Rydex Precious Metal C	RYZCX	E-	(800) 820-0888	E / 0.3	6.48	-9.29	26.64 /78	-5.57 / 2	-14.67 / 0	4.44	2.27
PM	Rydex Precious Metal H	RYMPX	E-	(800) 820-0888	E / 0.4	6.69	-8.95	27.59 /81	-5.01 / 2	-14.19 / 0	4.00	1.61
PM	Rydex Precious Metal Investor	RYPMX	E-	(800) 820-0888	E / 0.5	6.76	-8.82	27.95 /82	-4.63 / 3	-13.81 / 0	3.73	1.27
RE	Rydex Real Estate A	RYREX	C	(800) 820-0888	C+ / 5.7	8.57	0.69	20.15 /53	7.55 /76	8.92 /50	5.60	1.62
RE	Rydex Real Estate C	RYCRX	C	(800) 820-0888	C+ / 6.0	8.37	0.34	19.25 /48	6.73 /70	8.10 /43	6.64	2.36
RE	Rydex Real Estate H	RYHRX	C+	(800) 820-0888	C+ / 6.7	8.57	0.71	20.17 /53	7.54 /76	8.90 /50	5.90	1.62
GR	Rydex Retailing A	RYRTX	D	(800) 820-0888	D- / 1.2	-1.09	-0.12	5.67 / 4	3.28 /35	9.71 /56	0.00	1.60
GR	Rydex Retailing C	RYRCX	D	(800) 820-0888	D- / 1.3	-1.30	-0.52	4.79 / 4	2.47 /27	8.88 /50	0.00	2.35
GR	Rydex Retailing H	RYRAX	D	(800) 820-0888	D / 1.6	-1.04	-0.08	5.68 / 4	3.18 /34	9.59 /55	0.00	1.71
GR	Rydex Retailing Investor	RYRIX	D	(800) 820-0888	D / 1.7	-1.04	0.00	5.87 / 5	3.46 /37	9.95 /58	0.00	1.34
AG	Rydex Russell 2000 1.5x Strgy A	RYAKX	B-	(800) 820-0888	A+ / 9.8	7.32	17.79	54.36 /99	7.51 /76	16.58 /98	0.00	1.70
AG	Rydex Russell 2000 1.5x Strgy C	RYCMX	B-	(800) 820-0888	A+ / 9.8	7.10	17.34	53.20 /99	6.70 /70	15.71 /98	0.00	2.45
AG	Rydex Russell 2000 1.5x Strgy H	RYMKX	B-	(800) 820-0888	A+ / 9.8	7.18	17.62	54.12 /99	7.49 /75	16.58 /98	0.00	1.70
SC	Rydex Russell 2000 2x Strtgy A	RYRUX	C+	(800) 820-0888	A+ / 9.9	9.39	23.46	75.46 /99	8.41 /82	21.08 /99	0.00	1.78
SC	Rydex Russell 2000 2x Strtgy C	RYRLX	C+	(800) 820-0888	A+ / 9.9	9.18	22.99	74.19 /99	7.61 /76	20.21 /99	0.00	2.52
SC	Rydex Russell 2000 2x Strtgy H	RYRSX	C+	(800) 820-0888	A+ / 9.9	9.36	23.41	75.36 /99	8.39 /82	21.05 /99	0.00	1.81
SC	Rydex Russell 2000 A	RYRRX	C+	(800) 820-0888	C+ / 6.7	4.73	11.59	33.68 /92	5.08 /55	10.96 /66	0.00	1.59
SC	Rydex Russell 2000 C	RYROX	C+	(800) 820-0888	C+ / 6.9	4.55	11.18	32.67 /91	4.29 /46	10.10 /59	0.00	2.35
SC	Rydex Russell 2000 H	RYRHX	B-	(800) 820-0888	B- / 7.5	4.75	11.62	33.70 /92	5.06 /55	10.94 /65	0.00	1.60
AG	Rydex S&P 500 2x Strategy A	RYTTX	A	(800) 820-0888	A+ / 9.9	15.69	18.73	50.14 /99	17.30 /99	24.71 /99	0.00	1.76
AG	Rydex S&P 500 2x Strategy C	RYCTX	A	(800) 820-0888	A+ / 9.9	15.50	18.32	49.03 /99	16.43 /99	23.78 /99	0.00	2.51
AG	Rydex S&P 500 2x Strategy H	RYTNX	A	(800) 820-0888	A+ / 9.9	15.68	18.73	50.10 /99	17.28 /99	24.67 /99	0.00	1.76
IX	Rydex S&P 500 A	RYSOX	B+	(800) 820-0888	B- / 7.4	7.58	9.09	22.87 /66	8.80 /85	12.14 /75	0.11	1.55
IX	Rydex S&P 500 C	RYSYX	A-	(800) 820-0888	B / 7.7	7.40	8.67	21.98 /62	7.99 /79	11.29 /68	0.13	2.31
IX	Rydex S&P 500 H	RYSPX	A	(800) 820-0888	B / 8.2	7.56	9.07	22.88 /66	8.80 /85	12.13 /75	0.12	1.55
GR	Rydex S&P500 Pure Growth A	RYLGX	C-	(800) 820-0888	C- / 3.9	5.94	4.34	17.75 /42	5.02 /54	12.47 /79	0.00	1.50
GR	Rydex S&P500 Pure Growth C	RYGRX	C-	(800) 820-0888	C- / 4.2	5.75	3.95	16.85 /38	4.23 /46	11.64 /71	0.00	2.25

● Denotes fund is closed to new investors
* Denotes fund is included in Section II

www.thestreetratings.com

Risk Rating/Pts	3 Year Standard Deviation	Beta	NAV As of 2/28/17	Total $(Mil)	Cash %	Stocks %	Bonds %	Other %	Portfolio Turnover Ratio	Last Bull Market Return	Last Bear Market Return	Manager Quality Pct	Manager Tenure (Years)	Initial Purch. $	Additional Purch. $	Front End Load	Back End Load
C- /3.3	22.3	1.30	95.57	N/A	100	0	0	0	543	90.5	-20.8	98	9	2,500	0	0.0	0.0
C- /3.4	22.3	1.30	102.34	3	100	0	0	0	543	98.0	-20.5	99	9	2,500	0	0.0	0.0
C+ /6.8	11.0	0.99	64.20	2	0	99	0	1	339	150.3	-18.7	42	19	2,500	0	4.8	0.0
C+ /6.7	11.1	0.99	58.59	1	0	99	0	1	339	140.4	-18.9	32	19	2,500	0	0.0	0.0
C+ /6.8	11.1	0.99	62.60	16	0	99	0	1	339	148.1	-18.7	41	19	2,500	0	0.0	0.0
C+ /6.8	11.0	0.99	68.98	21	0	99	0	1	339	153.8	-18.6	46	19	2,500	0	0.0	0.0
C /5.2	18.3	1.50	80.51	2	30	70	0	0	1,506	218.6	-33.8	40	16	2,500	0	4.8	0.0
C /5.1	18.3	1.50	71.00	8	30	70	0	0	1,506	206.2	-33.9	30	16	2,500	0	0.0	0.0
C /5.2	18.2	1.50	80.85	22	30	70	0	0	1,506	220.1	-33.7	41	16	2,500	0	0.0	0.0
C- /3.8	13.0	0.98	50.56	14	0	99	0	1	143	80.6	-18.5	6	13	2,500	0	4.8	0.0
C- /3.5	13.0	0.98	44.62	16	0	99	0	1	143	73.4	-18.7	4	13	2,500	0	0.0	0.0
C- /3.8	13.0	0.98	50.62	71	0	99	0	1	143	80.6	-18.5	6	13	2,500	0	0.0	0.0
C /5.4	17.5	1.28	51.65	3	0	99	0	1	493	120.3	-24.9	16	13	2,500	0	4.8	0.0
C /5.4	17.5	1.28	46.35	5	0	99	0	1	493	111.4	-25.1	11	13	2,500	0	0.0	0.0
C /5.4	17.5	1.28	51.60	30	0	99	0	1	493	120.1	-24.9	16	13	2,500	0	0.0	0.0
U /	N/A	N/A	78.23	29	43	56	0	1	551	N/A	N/A	N/A	3	2,500	0	0.0	0.0
C+ /6.3	13.7	1.18	27.96	53	7	75	16	2	228	146.5	-11.1	74	23	2,500	0	4.8	0.0
C+ /6.2	13.7	1.18	24.95	53	7	75	16	2	228	137.1	-11.4	67	23	2,500	0	0.0	0.0
U /	N/A	N/A	27.95	60	7	75	16	2	228	N/A	N/A	N/A	23	2,500	0	0.0	0.0
C+ /6.3	13.7	1.18	30.10	725	7	75	16	2	228	150.3	-11.0	77	23	2,500	0	0.0	0.0
C+ /6.7	15.7	1.52	56.26	13	25	61	13	1	619	214.0	-25.1	38	21	2,500	0	4.8	0.0
C+ /6.6	15.7	1.52	50.67	10	25	61	13	1	619	201.4	-25.3	29	21	2,500	0	0.0	0.0
U /	N/A	N/A	56.22	34	25	61	13	1	619	N/A	N/A	N/A	21	2,500	0	0.0	0.0
C+ /6.7	15.7	1.52	60.20	307	25	61	13	1	619	217.9	-25.0	41	21	2,500	0	0.0	0.0
E- /0.0	49.6	2.63	30.04	11	0	99	0	1	797	-49.6	-22.6	74	24	2,500	0	4.8	0.0
E- /0.0	49.6	2.63	26.30	8	0	99	0	1	797	-51.6	-22.8	66	24	2,500	0	0.0	0.0
E- /0.0	49.6	2.63	29.17	4	0	99	0	1	797	-50.1	-22.7	73	24	2,500	0	0.0	0.0
E- /0.0	49.6	2.63	31.29	45	0	99	0	1	797	-48.9	-22.5	76	24	2,500	0	0.0	0.0
C /5.1	13.2	0.96	38.24	3	0	99	0	1	880	84.3	-19.7	37	13	2,500	0	4.8	0.0
C /5.0	13.2	0.96	33.91	1	0	99	0	1	880	76.8	-20.0	28	13	2,500	0	0.0	0.0
C /5.1	13.2	0.96	38.14	10	0	99	0	1	880	84.1	-19.7	36	13	2,500	0	0.0	0.0
C+ /6.3	12.0	0.93	25.36	1	0	100	0	0	238	92.0	-11.1	8	19	2,500	0	4.8	0.0
C+ /6.2	12.0	0.93	22.76	2	0	100	0	0	238	84.2	-11.3	6	19	2,500	0	0.0	0.0
C+ /6.3	12.0	0.93	24.75	N/A	0	100	0	0	238	90.6	-11.1	8	19	2,500	0	0.0	0.0
C+ /6.3	12.0	0.93	26.68	13	0	100	0	0	238	94.4	-11.0	9	19	2,500	0	0.0	0.0
C- /3.0	23.9	1.80	55.98	1	30	69	0	1	971	199.1	-37.3	2	17	2,500	0	4.8	0.0
D+ /2.9	23.9	1.80	48.25	2	30	69	0	1	971	187.2	-37.5	1	17	2,500	0	0.0	0.0
C- /3.0	23.8	1.80	55.83	11	30	69	0	1	971	199.1	-37.3	2	17	2,500	0	0.0	0.0
D /1.6	32.4	2.01	124.05	9	71	28	0	1	296	292.5	-47.8	13	11	2,500	0	4.8	0.0
D /1.6	32.4	2.01	113.49	1	71	28	0	1	296	277.4	-47.9	9	11	2,500	0	0.0	0.0
D /1.6	32.4	2.01	123.79	45	71	28	0	1	296	291.8	-47.8	13	11	2,500	0	0.0	0.0
C /5.3	15.7	1.00	41.60	19	28	71	0	1	442	112.7	-25.6	52	11	2,500	0	0.0	0.0
C /5.2	15.7	1.00	37.89	6	28	71	0	1	442	103.9	-25.8	42	11	2,500	0	4.8	0.0
C /5.2	15.8	1.00	41.50	48	28	71	0	1	442	112.4	-25.6	52	11	2,500	0	0.0	0.0
C /5.2	21.2	2.03	89.66	11	29	70	0	1	216	335.1	-33.0	20	17	2,500	0	4.8	0.0
C /5.1	21.2	2.03	78.64	10	29	70	0	1	216	318.2	-33.2	14	17	2,500	0	0.0	0.0
C /5.2	21.2	2.03	89.55	103	29	70	0	1	216	334.6	-33.1	20	17	2,500	0	0.0	0.0
B- /7.0	10.3	1.00	45.53	23	16	75	8	1	181	114.7	-16.8	54	19	2,500	0	4.8	0.0
C+ /6.9	10.3	1.00	41.66	19	16	75	8	1	181	106.1	-17.2	43	19	2,500	0	0.0	0.0
B- /7.0	10.3	1.00	45.52	258	16	75	8	1	181	114.7	-16.8	53	19	2,500	0	0.0	0.0
C+ /5.8	11.3	1.00	57.06	16	0	99	0	1	290	115.8	-18.0	14	13	2,500	0	4.8	0.0
C+ /5.7	11.2	1.00	51.46	10	0	99	0	1	290	107.3	-18.2	9	13	2,500	0	0.0	0.0

I. Index of Stock Mutual Funds

99 Pct = Best
0 Pct = Worst

Fund Type	Fund Name	Ticker Symbol	Overall Investment Rating	Phone	Perfor-mance Rating/Pts	Total Return % through 2/28/17			Annualized		Incl. in Returns	
						3 Mo	6 Mo	1Yr / Pct	3Yr / Pct	5Yr / Pct	Dividend Yield	Expense Ratio
GR	Rydex S&P500 Pure Growth H	RYAWX	C	(800) 820-0888	C / 4.9	5.94	4.34	17.75 /42	5.01 /54	12.48 /79	0.00	1.51
GR	Rydex S&P500 Pure Value A	RYLVX	D+	(800) 820-0888	B / 8.0	6.82	14.56	30.84 /88	7.36 /75	13.91 /93	0.83	1.50
GR	Rydex S&P500 Pure Value C	RYVVX	C-	(800) 820-0888	B+ / 8.3	6.62	14.13	29.86 /86	6.56 /69	13.06 /84	0.99	2.25
GR	Rydex S&P500 Pure Value H	RYZAX	C-	(800) 820-0888	B+ / 8.8	6.82	14.55	30.83 /88	7.36 /75	13.91 /93	0.86	1.50
SC	Rydex SmCp 600 Pure Growth A	RYSGX	C+	(800) 820-0888	B- / 7.5	5.87	12.02	31.79 /90	6.83 /71	11.86 /73	0.00	1.50
SC	Rydex SmCp 600 Pure Growth C	RYWCX	B-	(800) 820-0888	B / 7.8	5.70	11.63	30.83 /88	6.03 /64	11.02 /66	0.00	2.25
SC	Rydex SmCp 600 Pure Growth H	RYWAX	B	(800) 820-0888	B+ / 8.3	5.87	12.04	31.82 /90	6.83 /71	11.86 /73	0.00	1.50
SC	Rydex SmCp 600 Pure Value A	RYSVX	C-	(800) 820-0888	C+ / 5.7	-0.78	14.71	35.65 /95	3.50 /37	10.83 /64	0.00	1.50
SC	Rydex SmCp 600 Pure Value C	RYYCX	C	(800) 820-0888	C+ / 6.0	-0.97	14.27	34.62 /94	2.71 /29	10.00 /58	0.00	2.25
SC	Rydex SmCp 600 Pure Value H	RYAZX	C	(800) 820-0888	C+ / 6.6	-0.78	14.69	35.55 /95	3.47 /37	10.81 /64	0.00	1.50
TC	Rydex Technology A	RYTHX	A-	(800) 820-0888	B+ / 8.9	9.26	11.57	32.76 /91	8.79 /85	12.24 /77	0.00	1.60
TC	Rydex Technology C	RYCHX	A-	(800) 820-0888	A- / 9.1	9.07	11.16	31.78 /90	8.00 /79	11.42 /69	0.00	2.35
TC	Rydex Technology H	RYTAX	A	(800) 820-0888	A / 9.5	9.29	11.61	32.75 /91	8.66 /84	12.07 /75	0.00	1.68
TC	Rydex Technology Investor	RYTIX	A	(800) 820-0888	A+ / 9.6	9.34	11.72	33.09 /92	9.05 /87	12.55 /80	0.00	1.35
TC	Rydex Telecomm A	RYTLX	C-	(800) 820-0888	C- / 4.1	4.66	5.73	20.22 /53	4.71 /51	5.37 /24	2.16	1.59
TC	Rydex Telecomm C	RYCSX	C-	(800) 820-0888	C / 4.4	4.48	5.39	19.36 /49	3.90 /42	4.72 /19	2.50	2.35
TC	Rydex Telecomm H	RYMAX	C	(800) 820-0888	C / 5.0	4.69	5.81	20.27 /54	4.59 /50	5.19 /23	2.32	1.64
TC	Rydex Telecomm Investor	RYMIX	C	(800) 820-0888	C / 5.3	4.73	5.92	20.60 /55	5.03 /55	5.66 /26	2.09	1.34
GR	Rydex Transportation A	RYTSX	B+	(800) 820-0888	B / 7.9	6.99	17.33	28.19 /82	7.16 /73	15.28 /97	0.32	1.60
GR	Rydex Transportation C	RYCNX	B+	(800) 820-0888	B / 8.2	6.78	16.87	27.23 /80	6.34 /67	14.41 /95	0.36	2.35
GR	Rydex Transportation H	RYPAX	A-	(800) 820-0888	B+ / 8.7	7.01	17.34	28.20 /82	7.04 /72	15.09 /97	0.35	1.72
GR	Rydex Transportation Investor	RYPIX	A-	(800) 820-0888	B+ / 8.9	7.06	17.46	28.51 /83	7.41 /75	15.55 /98	0.31	1.34
UT	Rydex Utilities A	RYUTX	B	(800) 820-0888	B- / 7.5	10.26	6.65	17.16 /39	10.08 /94	10.61 /63	2.12	1.60
UT	Rydex Utilities C	RYCUX	B	(800) 820-0888	B / 7.8	10.06	6.30	16.32 /36	9.27 /89	9.79 /57	2.56	2.35
UT	Rydex Utilities H	RYAUX	B+	(800) 820-0888	B+ / 8.3	10.24	6.66	17.17 /39	9.95 /93	10.43 /62	2.29	1.68
UT	Rydex Utilities Investor	RYUIX	B+	(800) 820-0888	B+ / 8.5	10.32	6.79	17.47 /40	10.34 /95	10.89 /65	2.06	1.35
IX	S&P 500 Index Direct	SPFIX	A+	(800) 955-9988	A- / 9.1	7.43	9.54	24.14 /70	10.25 /95	13.60 /90	1.43	0.47
IX	S&P 500 Index K	SPXKX	A+	(800) 955-9988	A- / 9.0	7.73	9.70	24.02 /70	9.85 /93	13.13 /85	1.40	0.97
MC	S&P MidCap Index Direct	SPMIX	B+	(800) 955-9988	A / 9.4	6.04	11.79	31.19 /88	9.39 /90	13.47 /89	0.58	0.62
MC	S&P MidCap Index K	MIDKX	B	(800) 955-9988	A- / 9.2	6.12	11.74	30.79 /88	8.92 /86	12.96 /83	0.42	1.12
SC	S&P SmallCap Index Direct	SMCIX	B+	(800) 955-9988	A+ / 9.6	4.66	12.64	33.53 /92	9.80 /92	14.73 /96	0.73	0.77
SC	S&P SmallCap Index K	SMLKX	B+	(800) 955-9988	A / 9.3	4.28	12.08	32.50 /91	9.16 /88	14.09 /94	0.20	1.28
EM	SA Emerging Markets Value	SAEMX	D+	(800) 366-7266	C+ / 5.9	11.00	9.55	36.65 /96	0.31 /15	-2.34 / 2	1.12	1.72
FO	SA International Sm Comp	SAISX	C-	(800) 366-7266	C- / 3.2	8.15	6.23	19.35 /49	0.86 /17	6.82 /34	1.73	1.57
EM	SA International Value	SAHMX	E+	(800) 366-7266	D- / 1.4	7.26	9.98	24.91 /73	-2.06 / 6	3.66 /14	2.80	1.16
RE	SA Real Estate Securities	SAREX	B+	(800) 366-7266	B- / 7.1	7.78	-2.51	15.27 /31	10.34 /95	10.43 /62	3.00	1.06
GR	SA US Core Market	SAMKX	A+	(800) 366-7266	B+ / 8.5	7.62	9.95	23.77 /69	8.95 /86	12.93 /83	1.18	1.00
SC	SA US Small Company	SAUMX	B	(800) 366-7266	B / 8.0	3.79	12.40	30.82 /88	6.84 /71	13.08 /85	0.30	1.28
GR	SA US Value	SABTX	A	(800) 366-7266	A+ / 9.6	7.02	13.94	32.04 /90	9.37 /89	14.61 /96	1.31	1.05
AA	Salient Adapt Balanced A	AOGAX	D	(800) 999-6809	E / 0.3	3.82	-0.82	7.09 / 6	-2.44 / 6	1.49 / 7	4.75	1.95
AA	Salient Adapt Balanced C	AGGGX	D	(800) 999-6809	E / 0.3	3.65	-1.18	6.39 / 5	-3.07 / 4	0.83 / 6	4.44	2.60
AA	Salient Adapt Balanced Inst	ACGAX	D	(800) 999-6809	E / 0.5	3.86	-0.63	7.45 / 6	-2.09 / 6	1.85 / 8	5.38	1.60
AA	Salient Adapt Balanced Inv	AGALX	D	(800) 999-6809	E / 0.4	3.69	-0.90	6.93 / 6	-2.60 / 5	1.33 / 7	4.89	2.10
AA	Salient Adapt Income A	AILAX	D-	(800) 999-6809	D- / 1.3	3.15	0.41	11.85 /17	0.89 /18	3.83 /14	3.57	2.15
AA	Salient Adapt Income C	AIACX	D	(800) 999-6809	D- / 1.3	2.96	0.07	11.03 /15	0.12 /14	3.05 /11	3.24	2.90
AA	Salient Adapt Income Inst	AIAAX	D	(800) 999-6809	D / 1.7	3.24	0.53	12.19 /19	1.14 /19	4.08 /16	3.85	1.90
AA	Salient Adapt Income Inv	AIAIX	D	(800) 999-6809	D- / 1.5	3.13	0.30	11.68 /17	0.65 /16	3.57 /13	3.55	2.40
SC	Salient Adapt US Eqty Inst	ASMCX	C+	(800) 999-6809	C+ / 6.7	7.66	5.66	17.47 /40	7.40 /75	11.79 /72	1.26	1.27
SC	Salient Adapt US Eqty Inv	ACSIX	C+	(800) 999-6809	C+ / 6.4	7.55	5.45	17.00 /38	6.99 /72	11.37 /69	0.97	1.67
SC	Salient Adapt US Eqty Z		C+	(800) 999-6809	C+ / 6.7	7.67	5.68	17.55 /41	7.51 /76	11.92 /74	1.33	1.17
GL	Salient Adaptive Growth A	SRPAX	E	(866) 667-9228	D+ / 2.6	5.11	-2.47	17.15 /39	4.27 /46	--	2.36	1.67
GL	Salient Adaptive Growth C	SRPCX	E	(866) 667-9228	D+ / 2.8	4.51	-3.18	15.82 /34	3.36 /35	--	1.70	2.42

• Denotes fund is closed to new investors
* Denotes fund is included in Section II

RISK			NET ASSETS		ASSET				Portfolio Turnover Ratio	BULL / BEAR		FUND MANAGER		MINIMUMS		LOADS	
Risk Rating/Pts	3 Year Standard Deviation	Beta	NAV As of 2/28/17	Total $(Mil)	Cash %	Stocks %	Bonds %	Other %		Last Bull Market Return	Last Bear Market Return	Manager Quality Pct	Manager Tenure (Years)	Initial Purch. $	Additional Purch. $	Front End Load	Back End Load
C+ / 5.8	11.3	1.00	57.05	52	0	99	0	1	290	115.9	-17.9	14	13	2,500	0	0.0	0.0
D- / 1.2	13.5	1.18	78.48	9	0	99	0	1	365	142.9	-22.2	17	13	2,500	0	0.0	0.0
D- / 1.2	13.5	1.18	68.98	5	0	99	0	1	365	133.2	-22.4	12	13	2,500	0	4.8	0.0
D- / 1.2	13.5	1.18	78.77	72	0	99	0	1	365	142.9	-22.2	17	13	2,500	0	0.0	0.0
C / 4.9	16.4	1.00	64.88	2	0	99	0	1	309	116.7	-20.4	73	13	2,500	0	4.8	0.0
C / 4.8	16.4	1.00	58.95	4	0	99	0	1	309	108.2	-20.7	65	13	2,500	0	0.0	0.0
C / 4.9	16.4	1.00	64.88	34	0	99	0	1	309	116.8	-20.5	73	13	2,500	0	0.0	0.0
C / 4.6	20.1	1.12	28.08	3	0	99	0	1	417	117.8	-26.2	23	13	2,500	0	4.8	0.0
C / 4.5	20.1	1.12	24.42	3	0	99	0	1	417	109.1	-26.5	17	13	2,500	0	0.0	0.0
C / 4.5	20.2	1.12	27.95	31	0	99	0	1	417	117.5	-26.3	23	13	2,500	0	0.0	0.0
C+ / 5.6	14.5	1.24	69.70	3	0	99	0	1	388	117.3	-22.0	23	19	2,500	0	4.8	0.0
C+ / 5.6	14.5	1.24	63.73	3	0	99	0	1	388	108.7	-22.3	17	19	2,500	0	0.0	0.0
C+ / 5.6	14.5	1.24	68.26	20	0	99	0	1	388	115.3	-22.1	22	19	2,500	0	0.0	0.0
C+ / 5.6	14.5	1.24	74.33	52	0	99	0	1	388	120.4	-21.9	25	19	2,500	0	0.0	0.0
C+ / 5.6	11.7	0.96	44.27	13	0	99	0	1	660	49.2	-23.1	14	19	2,500	0	4.8	0.0
C / 5.5	11.7	0.96	40.08	N/A	0	99	0	1	660	44.3	-23.4	10	19	2,500	0	0.0	0.0
C+ / 5.6	11.7	0.96	43.12	2	0	99	0	1	660	47.7	-23.2	14	19	2,500	0	0.0	0.0
C+ / 5.7	11.7	0.96	47.85	6	0	99	0	1	660	51.3	-23.1	17	19	2,500	0	0.0	0.0
C+ / 5.9	15.7	1.26	50.36	8	0	99	0	1	219	155.9	-26.0	10	19	2,500	0	4.8	0.0
C+ / 5.8	15.7	1.26	46.75	3	0	99	0	1	219	145.5	-26.1	7	19	2,500	0	0.0	0.0
C+ / 5.9	15.7	1.26	48.99	7	0	99	0	1	219	153.4	-26.0	9	19	2,500	0	0.0	0.0
C+ / 5.9	15.7	1.26	54.43	46	0	99	0	1	219	159.2	-25.9	11	19	2,500	0	0.0	0.0
C+ / 5.7	13.8	0.92	36.43	5	0	99	0	1	475	76.0	-2.1	35	17	2,500	0	4.8	0.0
C / 5.5	13.8	0.92	31.17	8	0	99	0	1	475	69.1	-2.5	27	17	2,500	0	0.0	0.0
C+ / 5.7	13.8	0.92	35.11	1	0	99	0	1	475	74.4	-2.2	34	17	2,500	0	0.0	0.0
C+ / 5.8	13.8	0.92	39.33	13	0	99	0	1	475	78.4	-2.0	39	17	2,500	0	0.0	0.0
B- / 7.0	10.3	1.00	46.16	149	1	98	0	1	1	130.2	-16.1	70	14	1,000	100	0.0	0.0
B- / 7.0	10.3	1.00	46.15	9	1	98	0	1	1	125.0	-16.3	66	14	1,000	100	0.0	0.0
C / 4.3	12.0	1.00	25.63	121	1	98	0	1	11	135.3	-22.4	72	14	1,000	100	0.0	0.0
C / 4.3	12.0	1.00	25.32	6	1	98	0	1	11	120.7	-22.5	67	14	1,000	100	0.0	0.0
C / 4.7	14.2	0.89	22.44	59	0	100	0	0	12	147.5	-21.7	92	14	1,000	100	0.0	0.0
C / 4.7	14.2	0.89	21.95	10	0	100	0	0	12	132.8	-21.8	90	14	1,000	100	0.0	0.0
D+ / 2.8	18.4	1.11	9.11	197	0	0	0	100	13	9.6	-30.2	55	5	100,000	0	0.0	0.0
C+ / 6.3	11.7	0.87	20.15	335	0	0	0	100	0	59.9	-23.7	81	5	100,000	0	0.0	0.0
C / 4.3	14.4	0.65	10.55	693	0	0	0	100	21	37.6	-26.3	32	11	100,000	0	0.0	0.0
B- / 7.1	14.9	1.09	11.51	177	0	0	0	100	7	98.7	-16.6	54	5	100,000	0	0.0	0.0
B / 8.0	10.4	1.00	21.06	735	0	0	0	100	11	124.3	-17.7	55	11	100,000	0	0.0	0.0
C / 5.1	14.5	0.91	25.51	410	0	0	0	100	12	133.8	-24.6	78	11	100,000	0	0.0	0.0
C+ / 5.8	11.8	1.07	18.28	586	0	0	0	100	21	149.1	-24.3	50	5	100,000	0	0.0	0.0
B- / 7.3	7.7	1.03	12.48	11	42	36	20	2	52	23.7	-18.3	2	N/A	4,000	100	5.8	0.0
B- / 7.3	7.7	1.03	12.35	10	42	36	20	2	52	19.4	-18.5	2	N/A	4,000	100	0.0	0.0
B- / 7.3	7.7	1.03	12.49	12	42	36	20	2	52	26.0	-18.1	2	N/A	100,000	0	0.0	0.0
B- / 7.3	7.7	1.03	12.48	4	42	36	20	2	52	22.6	-18.3	2	N/A	4,000	100	0.0	0.0
C+ / 6.0	5.7	0.71	13.50	3	10	31	56	3	212	24.9	0.5	21	N/A	4,000	100	3.8	0.0
C+ / 6.0	5.7	0.71	13.39	5	10	31	56	3	212	19.9	0.3	15	N/A	4,000	100	0.0	0.0
C+ / 6.0	5.7	0.71	13.52	4	10	31	56	3	212	26.5	0.6	23	N/A	100,000	0	0.0	0.0
C+ / 6.0	5.7	0.71	13.48	2	10	31	56	3	212	23.2	0.5	19	N/A	4,000	100	0.0	0.0
C+ / 5.7	10.9	0.50	36.48	10	3	95	0	2	42	120.2	-26.7	93	7	100,000	0	0.0	0.0
C / 5.5	10.9	0.50	33.16	2	3	95	0	2	42	115.7	-26.8	92	7	4,000	100	0.0	0.0
C+ / 5.7	10.9	0.50	36.72	7	3	95	0	2	42	121.6	-26.7	93	7	4,000	100	0.0	0.0
D+ / 2.5	14.1	1.42	7.11	4	100	0	0	0	0	N/A	N/A	45	N/A	2,500	100	5.5	0.0
D+ / 2.3	14.1	1.43	6.82	2	100	0	0	0	0	N/A	N/A	33	N/A	2,500	100	0.0	0.0

Fund Type	Fund Name	Ticker Symbol	Overall Investment Rating	Phone	Performance Rating/Pts	3 Mo	6 Mo	1Yr / Pct	3Yr / Pct	5Yr / Pct	Dividend Yield	Expense Ratio
GL	Salient Adaptive Growth I	SRPFX	D-	(866) 667-9228	C- / 3.8	5.23	-2.27	17.60 /41	4.56 /49	--	2.61	1.42
GL	Salient EM Infrastructure A	KGIAX	D-	(800) 999-6809	E+ / 0.7	6.42	-0.97	14.52 /28	-0.27 /12	2.68 /10	2.09	1.92
OT	● Salient EM Infrastructure Adv	FGIMX	D	(800) 999-6809	D / 1.7	6.54	-0.80	14.89 /29	0.08 /14	3.03 /11	2.59	1.57
GL	Salient EM Infrastructure B	KGIBX	D	(800) 999-6809	D- / 1.0	6.30	-1.22	13.90 /25	-0.82 /10	2.08 / 8	1.73	2.47
GL	Salient EM Infrastructure C	KGICX	D	(800) 999-6809	D- / 1.0	6.31	-1.25	13.87 /25	-0.83 /10	2.09 / 8	1.81	2.47
GL	Salient EM Infrastructure Inst	KGIYX	D	(800) 999-6809	D / 1.8	6.57	-0.75	14.99 /30	0.18 /14	3.11 /11	2.61	1.52
OT	Salient EM Infrastructure Inv	FGLRX	D	(800) 999-6809	D- / 1.2	6.44	-0.98	14.54 /28	-0.20 /13	2.72 /10	1.16	1.87
RE	Salient Int Real Estate A	KIRAX	D-	(800) 999-6809	E+ / 0.8	4.41	-0.33	9.03 /10	0.27 /15	3.92 /15	4.80	1.92
RE	● Salient Int Real Estate Adv	FINMX	D	(800) 999-6809	D- / 1.4	4.53	-0.16	9.37 /10	0.62 /16	4.31 /17	5.39	1.57
RE	Salient Int Real Estate C	KIRCX	D-	(800) 999-6809	E+ / 0.9	4.25	-0.63	8.35 / 8	-0.29 /12	3.33 /12	4.70	2.47
RE	Salient Int Real Estate Inst	KIRYX	D	(800) 999-6809	D- / 1.4	4.47	-0.15	9.41 /10	0.66 /16	4.34 /17	5.42	1.52
RE	Salient Int Real Estate Inv	FFIRX	D-	(800) 999-6809	D- / 1.3	4.41	-0.32	9.16 /10	0.34 /15	4.01 /15	4.92	1.87
FO	Salient Intl Dividend Signal A	FFDAX	E+	(800) 999-6809	E- / 0.2	5.54	0.41	10.60 /13	-3.41 / 4	--	3.15	1.77
FO	● Salient Intl Dividend Signal Adv	FIDMX	E+	(800) 999-6809	E / 0.5	5.60	0.65	11.07 /15	-2.98 / 5	2.78 /10	4.52	1.32
FO	Salient Intl Dividend Signal C	FINCX	E+	(800) 999-6809	E / 0.3	5.38	0.20	10.00 /12	-3.83 / 3	--	2.93	2.22
FO	Salient Intl Dividend Signal Inst	FFIEX	E+	(800) 999-6809	E / 0.5	5.63	0.68	10.94 /14	-2.97 / 5	2.82 /10	4.57	1.27
FO	Salient Intl Dividend Signal Inv	FFINX	E+	(800) 999-6809	E / 0.4	5.55	0.42	10.71 /14	-3.29 / 4	2.47 / 9	3.44	1.62
FO	● Salient Intl Small Cap Adv	FNSMX	D+	(800) 999-6809	D / 2.1	6.32	3.11	11.64 /17	1.00 /18	7.70 /40	3.95	1.39
FO	Salient Intl Small Cap Inst	PTSCX	D+	(800) 999-6809	D / 2.1	6.33	3.12	11.72 /17	1.05 /18	7.72 /40	4.02	1.34
FO	Salient Intl Small Cap Inv	PISRX	D+	(800) 999-6809	D / 1.9	6.23	2.96	11.28 /15	0.68 /17	7.36 /37	3.59	1.69
EN	Salient MLP and Energy Infr A	SMAPX	E-	(866) 667-9228	D- / 1.2	1.99	9.98	62.91 /99	-6.22 / 2	--	5.58	1.45
EN	Salient MLP and Energy Infr C	SMFPX	E-	(866) 667-9228	D- / 1.4	1.68	9.47	61.40 /99	-6.98 / 1	--	5.21	2.20
EN	Salient MLP and Energy Infr I	SMLPX	E-	(866) 667-9228	D / 1.8	2.03	10.11	63.07 /99	-6.05 / 2	--	6.15	1.20
RE	Salient Real Estate A	KREAX	C-	(800) 999-6809	B- / 7.5	6.26	1.51	21.76 /61	11.19 /97	11.16 /67	2.35	1.75
RE	Salient Real Estate C	KRECX	C-	(800) 999-6809	B / 8.0	6.13	1.26	21.01 /57	10.56 /96	10.52 /62	1.92	2.30
RE	Salient Real Estate Inst	FPREX	C-	(800) 999-6809	B+ / 8.8	6.36	1.79	22.24 /63	11.68 /98	11.63 /71	3.32	1.35
RE	Salient Real Estate Inv	FFREX	C	(800) 999-6809	B+ / 8.5	6.18	1.49	21.76 /61	11.21 /97	11.18 /67	2.46	1.70
RE	Salient Select Income A	KIFAX	C-	(800) 999-6809	C / 5.1	3.82	1.02	19.16 /48	8.05 /79	9.24 /53	4.23	2.11
RE	● Salient Select Income Adv	FSIMX	C+	(800) 999-6809	C+ / 6.6	3.88	1.21	19.57 /50	8.43 /82	9.63 /56	4.84	1.76
RE	Salient Select Income B	KIFBX	C	(800) 999-6809	C+ / 5.8	3.69	0.78	18.49 /45	7.44 /75	8.63 /47	3.95	2.66
RE	Salient Select Income C	KIFCX	C	(800) 999-6809	C+ / 5.8	3.66	0.73	18.48 /45	7.45 /75	8.63 /47	4.09	2.66
RE	Salient Select Income Inst	KIFYX	C+	(800) 999-6809	C+ / 6.6	3.89	1.19	19.69 /50	8.51 /83	9.70 /56	4.98	1.71
RE	Salient Select Income Inv	FFSLX	C+	(800) 999-6809	C+ / 6.3	3.81	1.06	19.18 /48	8.10 /80	9.29 /53	4.55	2.06
GL	Salient Select Opportunity A	FSONX	D+	(800) 999-6809	C+ / 5.8	8.27	11.02	37.45 /96	2.26 /26	--	2.57	2.62
AA	Salient Select Opportunity C	FSOCX	C+	(800) 999-6809	C+ / 6.5	8.15	10.73	36.85 /96	1.78 /23	--	2.31	3.07
GR	Salient Tactical Growth A	FTAGX	C-	(800) 999-6809	D- / 1.5	3.53	5.80	8.75 / 9	2.07 /24	3.82 /14	0.00	1.98
GR	● Salient Tactical Growth Adv	FTGMX	C	(800) 999-6809	D+ / 2.4	3.63	6.02	9.22 /10	2.54 /28	4.30 /17	0.00	1.53
GR	Salient Tactical Growth C	FTGOX	C	(800) 999-6809	D / 1.9	3.41	5.58	8.26 / 8	1.62 /22	3.35 /12	0.00	2.43
GR	Salient Tactical Growth Inst	FTGWX	C	(800) 999-6809	D+ / 2.5	3.67	6.05	9.25 /10	2.59 /28	4.33 /17	0.00	1.48
GR	Salient Tactical Growth Invest	FFTGX	C	(800) 999-6809	D+ / 2.3	3.57	5.88	8.93 / 9	2.23 /26	3.98 /15	0.00	1.83
GI	Salient Tactical Muni & Credit C	FLSFX	C-	(800) 999-6809	D / 1.6	3.29	-3.23	1.75 / 2	3.52 /37	0.96 / 6	1.91	2.41
GI	Salient Tactical Muni & Credit I	FLSRX	C-	(800) 999-6809	D / 1.9	3.46	-2.93	2.29 / 2	4.14 /45	1.57 / 7	2.45	1.81
GI	Salient Tactical Muni & Credit Inst	FLSIX	C	(800) 999-6809	D / 2.1	3.43	-2.91	2.54 / 2	4.51 /49	1.93 / 8	2.83	1.46
GL	Salient Tactical Plus F	BTPIX	C+	(866) 667-9228	C- / 4.0	4.50	8.07	12.81 /21	4.25 /46	--	0.00	2.85
RE	Salient Tactical Real Estate A	KSRAX	B-	(800) 999-6809	B- / 7.0	4.30	2.65	24.91 /73	9.70 /92	10.49 /62	1.80	2.37
RE	● Salient Tactical Real Estate Adv	FRLSX	B+	(800) 999-6809	B / 8.2	4.37	2.83	25.34 /74	10.09 /94	10.90 /65	2.18	2.02
RE	Salient Tactical Real Estate B	KSRBX	B	(800) 999-6809	B- / 7.5	4.14	2.37	24.23 /71	9.11 /88	9.88 /57	1.35	2.92
RE	Salient Tactical Real Estate C	KSRCX	B	(800) 999-6809	B- / 7.5	4.15	2.37	24.22 /71	9.10 /87	9.87 /57	1.43	2.92
RE	Salient Tactical Real Estate Inst	KSRYX	B+	(800) 999-6809	B / 8.2	4.38	2.85	25.39 /74	10.13 /94	10.92 /65	2.22	1.97
RE	Salient Tactical Real Estate Inv	FFSRX	B+	(800) 999-6809	B / 8.0	4.29	2.68	24.93 /73	9.77 /92	10.54 /62	1.99	2.32
GR	Salient Trend A	SPTAX	E	(866) 667-9228	E / 0.3	-2.69	-8.36	-18.93 / 0	2.96 /31	--	6.34	2.09
GR	Salient Trend C	SPTCX	E	(866) 667-9228	E / 0.3	-2.95	-8.74	-19.56 / 0	2.18 /25	--	5.40	2.84

99 Pct = Best
0 Pct = Worst

● Denotes fund is closed to new investors
* Denotes fund is included in Section II

www.thestreetratings.com

RISK Risk Rating/Pts	3 Year Standard Deviation	Beta	NAV As of 2/28/17	Total $(Mil)	Cash %	Stocks %	Bonds %	Other %	Portfolio Turnover Ratio	Last Bull Market Return	Last Bear Market Return	Manager Quality Pct	Manager Tenure (Years)	Initial Purch. $	Additional Purch. $	Front End Load	Back End Load
D+ /2.5	14.1	1.43	7.21	52	100	0	0	0	0	N/A	N/A	48	N/A	1,000,000	0	0.0	0.0
C+ /6.4	12.5	0.83	22.26	10	15	84	0	1	107	38.8	-21.8	73	10	4,000	100	5.8	0.0
C+ /6.4	12.5	0.82	22.29	2	15	84	0	1	107	41.3	-21.7	4	10	0	0	0.0	0.0
C+ /6.4	12.5	0.83	22.12	N/A	15	84	0	1	107	34.5	-22.1	66	10	4,000	100	0.0	0.0
C+ /6.4	12.5	0.83	22.13	5	15	84	0	1	107	34.5	-22.1	66	10	4,000	100	0.0	0.0
C+ /6.4	12.5	0.83	22.35	7	15	84	0	1	107	41.9	-21.7	76	10	100,000	0	0.0	0.0
C+ /6.4	12.5	0.81	22.40	1	15	84	0	1	107	39.1	N/A	3	10	4,000	100	0.0	0.0
C+ /6.0	12.0	0.46	13.26	9	14	85	0	1	281	56.7	-26.5	18	11	4,000	100	5.8	0.0
C+ /5.9	11.9	0.46	13.19	1	14	85	0	1	281	60.2	N/A	21	11	0	0	0.0	0.0
C+ /6.0	11.9	0.46	13.25	6	14	85	0	1	281	52.0	-26.8	14	11	4,000	100	0.0	0.0
C+ /5.9	11.9	0.46	13.20	5	14	85	0	1	281	60.4	-26.5	21	11	100,000	0	0.0	0.0
C+ /6.0	11.9	0.46	13.31	1	14	85	0	1	281	57.4	N/A	18	11	4,000	100	0.0	0.0
C /5.5	10.1	0.78	7.79	4	0	95	4	1	134	N/A	N/A	30	9	4,000	100	5.8	0.0
C /5.4	10.1	0.79	6.32	25	0	95	4	1	134	33.6	N/A	36	9	0	0	0.0	0.0
C /5.5	10.1	0.78	7.77	10	0	95	4	1	134	N/A	N/A	26	9	4,000	100	0.0	0.0
C /5.4	10.1	0.78	6.32	61	0	95	4	1	134	33.7	-20.3	36	9	100,000	0	0.0	0.0
C /5.5	10.1	0.79	7.79	6	0	95	4	1	134	31.0	-20.3	32	9	4,000	100	0.0	0.0
C+ /6.8	11.1	0.81	17.36	2	4	95	0	1	70	67.5	-26.7	82	16	0	0	0.0	0.0
C+ /6.8	11.1	0.81	17.34	98	4	95	0	1	70	67.6	-26.7	82	16	100,000	0	0.0	0.0
C+ /6.8	11.1	0.81	17.37	25	4	95	0	1	70	64.6	-26.8	80	16	4,000	100	0.0	0.0
D- /1.5	27.2	1.12	9.07	231	39	60	0	1	39	N/A	N/A	69	5	2,500	100	5.5	0.0
D- /1.5	27.1	1.12	9.01	97	39	60	0	1	39	N/A	N/A	59	5	2,500	100	0.0	0.0
D- /1.5	27.2	1.12	9.04	1,255	39	60	0	1	39	N/A	N/A	72	5	1,000,000	0	0.0	0.0
D /2.1	14.3	1.02	12.35	5	13	86	0	1	88	108.8	-19.6	73	7	4,000	100	5.8	0.0
D /2.2	14.4	1.02	12.49	2	13	86	0	1	88	102.2	-19.8	66	7	4,000	100	0.0	0.0
D- /1.2	14.3	1.01	10.05	6	13	86	0	1	88	113.2	-19.4	77	7	100,000	0	0.0	0.0
D /2.2	14.3	1.02	12.52	25	13	86	0	1	88	108.8	-19.6	73	7	4,000	100	0.0	0.0
C /5.2	6.7	0.41	24.30	417	4	78	14	4	39	73.5	-5.4	92	16	4,000	100	5.8	0.0
C /5.2	6.7	0.41	24.25	56	4	78	14	4	39	76.9	-5.3	93	16	0	0	0.0	0.0
C /5.2	6.7	0.41	23.97	1	4	78	14	4	39	68.1	-5.7	90	16	4,000	100	0.0	0.0
C /5.2	6.7	0.41	23.65	207	4	78	14	4	39	68.1	-5.7	90	16	4,000	100	0.0	0.0
C /5.2	6.7	0.41	24.26	378	4	78	14	4	39	77.3	-5.3	93	16	100,000	0	0.0	0.0
C /5.2	6.7	0.41	24.22	42	4	78	14	4	39	N/A	N/A	92	16	4,000	100	0.0	0.0
C- /3.5	13.3	1.46	24.42	4	18	69	3	10	104	N/A	N/A	20	4	4,000	100	5.8	0.0
C+ /5.8	13.3	1.41	24.38	N/A	18	69	3	10	104	N/A	N/A	3	4	4,000	100	0.0	0.0
B /8.8	6.7	0.58	26.06	36	49	50	0	1	349	23.8	-7.0	25	8	4,000	100	5.8	0.0
B /8.9	6.7	0.58	27.09	267	49	50	0	1	349	26.9	-6.8	30	8	0	0	0.0	0.0
B /8.7	6.7	0.58	25.12	41	49	50	0	1	349	20.8	-7.2	20	8	4,000	100	0.0	0.0
B /8.9	6.7	0.58	27.12	26	49	50	0	1	349	27.1	-6.8	30	8	100,000	0	0.0	0.0
B /8.8	6.7	0.58	26.41	13	49	50	0	1	349	24.8	-7.0	26	8	4,000	100	0.0	0.0
B /8.4	3.7	-0.01	7.69	11	4	0	95	1	160	10.8	5.6	92	2	4,000	100	0.0	0.0
B /8.4	3.7	-0.02	7.69	25	4	0	95	1	160	14.4	5.9	94	2	4,000	100	0.0	0.0
B /8.4	3.7	-0.02	7.62	6	4	0	95	1	160	16.6	6.0	94	2	100,000	0	0.0	0.0
B /8.1	9.9	0.44	11.86	18	0	0	0	100	146	N/A	N/A	94	5	0	0	0.0	0.0
C+ /5.7	11.7	0.78	37.41	30	23	75	0	2	77	107.2	-19.4	81	18	4,000	100	5.8	0.0
C+ /5.8	11.7	0.78	38.61	2	23	75	0	2	77	111.5	N/A	83	18	0	0	0.0	0.0
C+ /5.7	11.7	0.78	37.20	N/A	23	75	0	2	77	100.9	-19.6	77	18	4,000	100	0.0	0.0
C+ /5.7	11.7	0.78	37.02	16	23	75	0	2	77	100.8	-19.6	77	18	4,000	100	0.0	0.0
C+ /5.8	11.7	0.78	38.57	24	23	75	0	2	77	111.7	-19.3	84	18	100,000	0	0.0	0.0
C+ /5.7	11.7	0.78	37.35	2	23	75	0	2	77	107.6	N/A	82	18	4,000	100	0.0	0.0
C- /3.5	16.8	-0.06	8.66	3	100	0	0	0	0	N/A	N/A	92	4	2,500	100	5.5	0.0
C- /3.6	16.7	-0.06	8.54	N/A	100	0	0	0	0	N/A	N/A	89	4	2,500	100	0.0	0.0

I. Index of Stock Mutual Funds

Spring 2017

Fund Type	Fund Name	Ticker Symbol	Overall Investment Rating	Phone	Perfor-mance Rating/Pts	3 Mo	6 Mo	1Yr / Pct	3Yr / Pct	5Yr / Pct	Dividend Yield	Expense Ratio
GR	Salient Trend I	SPTIX	E	(866) 667-9228	E / 0.5	-2.68	-8.24	-18.73 / 0	3.20 /34	--	7.03	1.84
AA	Salient US Dividend Signal A	FDYAX	A+	(800) 999-6809	A- / 9.2	8.36	12.01	28.95 /84	10.70 /96	--	0.51	1.96
AA	Salient US Dividend Signal Inst	FDYTX	A+	(800) 999-6809	A+ / 9.7	8.50	12.31	29.61 /86	11.23 /97	--	0.80	1.46
AA	Sandalwood Opportunity A	SANAX	E	(888) 868-9501	E- / 0.0	0.14	-1.63	-11.36 / 0	-7.49 / 1	--	5.56	3.37
AA	Sandalwood Opportunity C	SANCX	D-	(888) 868-9501	E- / 0.0	0.00	-1.94	-11.88 / 0	-7.99 / 1	--	5.18	4.23
AA	Sandalwood Opportunity I	SANIX	E	(888) 868-9501	E- / 0.1	0.28	-1.42	-11.02 / 0	-7.22 / 1	--	6.16	3.15
GL	Sands Global Capital Growth Inst	SCMGX	D+	(866) 777-7818	C / 4.3	7.73	1.99	22.84 /66	3.58 /38	9.00 /51	0.00	1.03
GL	Sands Global Capital Growth Inv	SCGVX	D+	(866) 777-7818	C- / 4.1	7.64	1.90	22.54 /65	3.33 /35	8.71 /48	0.00	1.29
FO	Sanford Bernstein T/M Intl	SNIVX	D	(212) 486-5800	D- / 1.1	6.24	1.80	12.26 /19	-0.32 /12	4.04 /15	1.74	1.16
EM	Sanford C Bernstein Emerg Mkts Val	SNEMX	C-	(212) 486-5800	C / 4.9	7.83	4.80	28.83 /84	2.41 /27	0.09 / 5	0.57	1.49
EM	Sanford C Bernstein Emerg Mkts Z	EGMZX	U		U /	7.86	4.96	29.17 /84	--	--	0.83	N/A
FO	Sanford C Bernstein Internatl II	SIMTX	D	(212) 486-5800	D- / 1.2	6.39	1.99	12.44 /20	-0.31 /12	3.95 /15	1.72	1.21
EN	Saratoga Adv Tr Energy&Basic Mat A	SBMBX	E-	(800) 807-3863	E / 0.1	0.78	9.93	30.86 /88	-10.60 / 1	-4.53 / 2	0.00	3.96
EN	Saratoga Adv Tr Energy&Basic Mat C	SEPCX	E-	(800) 807-3863	E / 0.1	0.63	9.67	30.09 /87	-11.12 / 1	-5.09 / 2	0.00	4.58
EN	Saratoga Adv Tr Energy&Basic Mat I	SEPIX	E-	(800) 807-3863	E / 0.1	0.80	10.12	31.32 /89	-10.26 / 1	-4.16 / 2	0.00	3.56
FS	Saratoga Adv Tr Financial Service A	SFPAX	A-	(800) 807-3863	B+ / 8.5	8.11	17.80	36.57 /95	7.17 /73	10.82 /64	0.00	4.17
FS	Saratoga Adv Tr Financial Service C	SFPCX	A	(800) 807-3863	A- / 9.0	8.00	17.40	35.76 /95	6.55 /69	10.18 /60	0.00	4.82
FS	Saratoga Adv Tr Financial Service I	SFPIX	A+	(800) 807-3863	A / 9.5	8.26	18.00	37.12 /96	7.64 /76	11.27 /68	0.00	3.75
FO	Saratoga Adv Tr Intl Equity A	SIEYX	E	(800) 807-3863	E- / 0.2	5.99	3.95	15.67 /33	-4.99 / 2	0.04 / 4	0.01	3.06
FO	Saratoga Adv Tr Intl Equity C	SIECX	E	(800) 807-3863	E- / 0.2	5.89	3.65	15.01 /30	-5.59 / 2	-0.63 / 4	0.00	3.82
FO	Saratoga Adv Tr Intl Equity I	SIEPX	E+	(800) 807-3863	E / 0.3	6.10	4.17	16.19 /35	-4.64 / 3	0.38 / 5	0.61	2.74
GR	Saratoga Adv Tr Large Cap Value A	SLVYX	D+	(800) 807-3863	C- / 3.6	5.45	9.94	23.90 /69	3.12 /33	11.25 /68	0.00	1.65
GR	Saratoga Adv Tr Large Cap Value C	SLVCX	D+	(800) 807-3863	C- / 4.2	5.28	9.57	23.17 /67	2.52 /28	10.56 /63	0.00	2.25
GR	Saratoga Adv Tr Large Cap Value I	SLCVX	C-	(800) 807-3863	C / 5.1	5.56	10.17	24.43 /71	3.53 /37	11.66 /71	0.00	1.25
MC	Saratoga Adv Tr Mid Cap A	SPMAX	D-	(800) 807-3863	C- / 3.0	4.80	6.38	20.82 /56	3.55 /38	11.01 /66	0.00	2.24
MC	Saratoga Adv Tr Mid Cap C	SPMCX	D	(800) 807-3863	C- / 3.7	4.65	6.17	20.12 /53	3.02 /32	10.40 /61	0.00	2.85
MC	Saratoga Adv Tr Mid Cap I	SMIPX	D+	(800) 807-3863	C / 4.5	4.85	6.63	21.32 /59	3.95 /42	11.45 /69	0.00	1.84
SC	Saratoga Adv Tr Small Cap A	SSCYX	E	(800) 807-3863	C- / 3.0	4.23	11.30	27.65 /81	1.15 /19	7.46 /38	0.00	2.13
SC	Saratoga Adv Tr Small Cap C	SSCCX	E	(800) 807-3863	C- / 3.7	4.41	11.19	27.27 /80	0.60 /16	6.77 /33	0.00	2.81
SC	Saratoga Adv Tr Small Cap I	SSCPX	E	(800) 807-3863	C / 4.4	4.43	11.58	28.23 /82	1.55 /21	7.81 /41	0.00	1.75
TC	Saratoga Adv Tr Technology &	STPAX	B+	(800) 807-3863	A+ / 9.7	10.49	14.31	32.75 /91	11.78 /98	13.91 /93	0.00	2.24
TC	Saratoga Adv Tr Technology &	STPCX	B	(800) 807-3863	A+ / 9.8	10.37	14.01	31.96 /90	11.11 /97	13.23 /86	0.00	2.84
TC	Saratoga Adv Tr Technology &	STPIX	B+	(800) 807-3863	A+ / 9.8	10.58	14.49	33.20 /92	12.20 /98	14.37 /95	0.00	1.84
HL	Saratoga Adv Tr-Health & Biotech A	SHPAX	C	(800) 807-3863	C / 5.5	9.56	2.99	14.48 /28	8.78 /85	14.65 /96	0.00	2.29
HL	Saratoga Adv Tr-Health & Biotech C	SHPCX	C	(800) 807-3863	C+ / 6.1	9.37	2.70	13.76 /24	8.12 /80	13.96 /93	0.00	2.90
HL	Saratoga Adv Tr-Health & Biotech I	SBHIX	C+	(800) 807-3863	C+ / 6.9	9.64	3.19	14.91 /30	9.20 /88	15.10 /97	0.00	1.90
GR	Saratoga Adv Tr-Large Cap Growth A	SLGYX	D+	(800) 807-3863	C / 5.2	6.59	5.71	13.34 /23	8.65 /84	13.93 /93	0.52	1.62
GR	Saratoga Adv Tr-Large Cap Growth C	SLGCX	D+	(800) 807-3863	C+ / 5.9	6.45	5.45	12.68 /20	8.02 /79	13.25 /86	0.60	2.22
GR	Saratoga Adv Tr-Large Cap Growth I	SLCGX	C	(800) 807-3863	C+ / 6.5	6.20	5.45	13.29 /23	8.97 /87	14.31 /95	0.47	1.21
GL	Saratoga James Alpha Macro A	GRRAX	D+	(800) 807-3863	E- / 0.1	0.44	-1.71	-6.79 / 0	-2.03 / 7	-1.38 / 3	0.00	2.33
GL	Saratoga James Alpha Macro C	GRRCX	D+	(800) 807-3863	E- / 0.2	0.23	-1.99	-7.40 / 0	-2.73 / 5	-2.11 / 3	0.00	3.08
GL	Saratoga James Alpha Macro I	GRRIX	D+	(800) 807-3863	E- / 0.2	0.44	-1.61	-6.51 / 0	-1.78 / 7	-1.15 / 3	0.00	2.08
RE	Saratoga JamesAlpha Gl RE Invest A	JAREX	C-	(800) 807-3863	C / 4.8	9.97	3.99	18.18 /44	6.56 /69	9.36 /54	1.91	2.02
RE	Saratoga JamesAlpha Gl RE Invest C	JACRX	C+	(800) 807-3863	B- / 7.2	9.80	7.75	21.98 /62	7.26 /74	9.61 /55	1.26	2.77
RE	Saratoga JamesAlpha Gl RE Invest I	JARIX	C+	(800) 807-3863	C+ / 6.5	10.10	4.24	18.70 /46	7.14 /73	9.98 /58	2.20	1.77
GL	Sarofim Equity	SRFMX	B-	(866) 777-7818	C+ / 6.4	8.37	7.63	19.44 /49	6.56 /69	--	1.59	0.77
SC	Satuit Capital US Emerging Co A	SATMX	E-	(866) 972-8848	E+ / 0.8	5.89	7.76	27.45 /80	-2.26 / 6	6.05 /29	0.00	1.95
AA	Satuit West Shore Real Return A	AWSFX	E-		E- / 0.2	2.81	-1.80	3.94 / 3	-3.02 / 4	--	0.17	2.34
AA	Satuit West Shore Real Return I	IWSFX	E-		E / 0.3	2.83	-1.81	3.97 / 3	-3.03 / 4	--	0.18	1.94
AA	Satuit West Shore Real Return N	NWSFX	E-		E- / 0.2	2.87	-1.90	3.79 / 3	-3.26 / 4	--	0.00	2.19
AA	Satuit West Shore Real Return R	RWSFX	E-		E / 0.3	2.80	-1.80	3.94 / 3	-2.98 / 5	--	0.18	2.44
GL	Saturna Sextant Global High Income	SGHIX	C	(800) 728-8762	C / 5.2	5.75	6.91	26.67 /78	3.08 /33	--	4.31	1.06

● Denotes fund is closed to new investors
* Denotes fund is included in Section II

www.thestreetratings.com

574

RISK			NET ASSETS		ASSET				Portfolio Turnover Ratio	BULL / BEAR		FUND MANAGER		MINIMUMS		LOADS	
Risk Rating/Pts	3 Year Standard Deviation	Beta	NAV As of 2/28/17	Total $(Mil)	Cash %	Stocks %	Bonds %	Other %		Last Bull Market Return	Last Bear Market Return	Manager Quality Pct	Manager Tenure (Years)	Initial Purch. $	Additional Purch. $	Front End Load	Back End Load
C- /3.5	16.8	-0.06	8.67	40	100	0	0	0	0	N/A	N/A	92	4	1,000,000	0	0.0	0.0
B- /7.1	8.5	1.10	29.47	2	4	95	0	1	653	N/A	N/A	87	2	4,000	100	5.8	0.0
B- /7.1	8.5	1.10	29.60	1	4	95	0	1	653	N/A	N/A	89	2	100,000	0	0.0	0.0
C- /3.8	5.8	0.38	7.21	1	11	0	88	1	75	N/A	N/A	2	5	2,500	100	5.8	0.0
B- /7.0	5.8	0.39	7.30	1	11	0	88	1	75	N/A	N/A	1	5	2,500	100	0.0	0.0
C- /3.8	5.8	0.39	7.22	5	11	0	88	1	75	N/A	N/A	2	5	100,000	100	0.0	0.0
C /4.7	14.1	0.93	19.52	1,035	2	97	0	1	18	90.5	-17.4	92	9	1,000,000	0	0.0	2.0
C /4.7	14.1	0.93	19.30	6	2	97	0	1	18	88.0	-17.5	92	9	100,000	0	0.0	2.0
C+ /6.2	11.0	0.86	15.57	3,168	2	97	0	1	69	40.9	-25.5	72	6	10,000	0	0.0	0.0
C /4.4	15.7	0.95	26.75	1,207	1	98	0	1	71	25.5	-30.4	79	5	5,000	0	0.0	1.0
U /	N/A	N/A	26.76	126	1	98	0	1	71	N/A	N/A	N/A	5	0	0	0.0	0.0
C+ /6.2	11.0	0.86	15.52	1,306	2	97	0	1	77	40.3	-25.5	72	18	10,000	0	0.0	0.0
D /1.6	22.6	1.10	11.62	1	1	98	0	1	134	5.4	-34.9	13	2	250	0	5.8	2.0
D /1.6	22.6	1.10	9.64	N/A	1	98	0	1	134	2.1	-35.1	9	2	250	0	0.0	2.0
D /1.6	22.6	1.10	12.62	2	1	98	0	1	134	7.7	-34.8	16	2	250	0	0.0	2.0
C+ /6.3	14.5	1.09	9.86	N/A	1	98	0	1	73	103.3	-26.7	10	2	250	0	5.8	2.0
C+ /6.2	14.5	1.09	8.77	N/A	1	98	0	1	73	97.1	-26.9	7	2	250	0	0.0	2.0
C+ /6.3	14.5	1.09	10.49	2	1	98	0	1	73	107.7	-26.6	12	2	250	0	0.0	2.0
C /5.0	14.0	1.06	9.75	N/A	3	95	1	1	125	16.0	-28.0	16	5	250	0	5.8	2.0
C /4.9	14.0	1.06	8.81	N/A	3	95	1	1	125	11.8	-28.2	11	5	250	0	0.0	2.0
C /4.9	14.0	1.06	9.71	5	3	95	1	1	125	18.1	-27.9	19	5	250	0	0.0	2.0
C /4.8	15.0	1.26	22.24	1	0	99	0	1	79	117.1	-25.3	2	9	250	0	5.8	2.0
C /4.7	15.0	1.26	19.35	1	0	99	0	1	79	109.7	-25.4	2	9	250	0	0.0	2.0
C /4.8	15.0	1.26	22.97	18	0	99	0	1	79	121.3	-25.2	3	9	250	0	0.0	2.0
C- /4.1	13.2	1.03	11.70	2	1	98	0	1	54	108.7	-25.3	9	11	250	0	5.8	2.0
C- /3.7	13.2	1.03	10.03	1	1	98	0	1	54	102.4	-25.4	7	11	250	0	0.0	2.0
C /4.4	13.2	1.03	12.88	11	1	98	0	1	54	113.2	-25.2	11	11	250	0	0.0	2.0
E+ /0.6	14.0	0.85	5.91	N/A	0	99	0	1	112	75.5	-23.0	19	2	250	0	5.8	2.0
E+ /0.6	14.0	0.85	3.08	N/A	0	99	0	1	112	69.3	-23.2	14	2	250	0	0.0	2.0
E+ /0.6	14.1	0.85	6.36	7	0	99	0	1	112	78.6	-22.9	22	2	250	0	0.0	2.0
C- /4.2	13.3	1.12	17.56	17	2	96	1	1	37	136.6	-24.2	73	6	250	0	5.8	2.0
C- /3.6	13.3	1.12	14.65	8	2	96	1	1	37	129.0	-24.4	65	6	250	0	0.0	2.0
C /4.4	13.3	1.12	19.09	24	2	96	1	1	37	141.7	-24.1	76	6	250	0	0.0	2.0
C /5.1	12.2	0.90	27.02	7	0	98	0	2	19	123.9	-10.2	66	12	250	0	5.8	2.0
C /4.6	12.2	0.90	23.24	3	0	98	0	2	19	116.7	-10.4	58	12	250	0	0.0	2.0
C /5.3	12.2	0.90	29.10	11	0	98	0	2	19	128.7	-10.0	71	12	250	0	0.0	2.0
C- /3.9	11.7	1.05	21.76	2	0	99	0	1	160	123.4	-13.4	45	2	250	0	5.8	2.0
C- /3.0	11.7	1.05	17.26	8	0	99	0	1	160	116.3	-13.5	36	2	250	0	0.0	2.0
C- /4.1	11.7	1.04	23.06	28	0	99	0	1	160	127.5	-13.2	49	2	250	0	0.0	2.0
B+ /9.0	4.2	-0.10	9.20	1	80	0	19	1	241	-4.4	-0.5	52	1	2,500	0	5.8	2.0
B /8.8	4.2	-0.10	8.88	1	80	0	19	1	241	N/A	N/A	42	1	2,500	0	0.0	2.0
B /8.9	4.1	-0.10	9.19	9	80	0	19	1	241	-3.2	-0.5	56	1	1,000,000	0	0.0	2.0
C /5.1	12.1	0.73	18.69	99	6	92	0	2	149	90.6	-21.3	57	N/A	2,500	0	5.8	2.0
C /5.1	12.1	0.71	18.83	71	6	92	0	2	149	N/A	N/A	68	N/A	2,500	0	0.0	2.0
C /5.1	12.1	0.73	19.12	275	6	92	0	2	149	96.2	N/A	64	N/A	2,000,000	0	0.0	2.0
B- /7.1	10.1	0.71	10.60	82	3	95	0	2	12	N/A	N/A	97	3	2,500	100	0.0	2.0
D /1.8	16.4	0.97	28.04	31	2	97	0	1	99	67.6	-26.1	3	17	1,000	250	5.8	2.0
D /2.0	6.2	0.42	9.41	N/A	64	33	1	2	28	N/A	N/A	8	4	2,500	500	5.8	1.0
D+ /2.3	6.2	0.42	9.34	26	64	33	1	2	28	N/A	N/A	8	4	100,000	1,000	0.0	1.0
D+ /2.8	6.3	0.42	9.31	N/A	64	33	1	2	28	N/A	N/A	7	4	2,500	500	0.0	1.0
D /1.8	6.2	0.42	9.42	N/A	64	33	1	2	28	N/A	N/A	8	4	2,500	500	0.0	1.0
C /5.3	9.9	1.14	10.23	8	5	47	46	2	40	N/A	N/A	46	5	1,000	25	0.0	0.0

					PERFORMANCE							
	99 Pct = Best *0 Pct = Worst*		Overall		Perfor-mance	Total Return % through 2/28/17			Annualized		Incl. in Returns	
Fund Type	Fund Name	Ticker Symbol	Investment Rating	Phone	Rating/Pts	3 Mo	6 Mo	1Yr / Pct	3Yr / Pct	5Yr / Pct	Dividend Yield	Expense Ratio
AG	SC 529 CO FS Aggressive Growth	CAGGX	B-	(800) 345-6611	C+ / 5.8	6.41	7.36	21.30 /59	6.13 /65	10.20 /60	0.00	1.43
AG	SC 529 CO FS Aggressive Growth B		B-	(800) 345-6611	C+ / 5.8	6.26	7.00	20.41 /54	5.35 /58	9.38 /54	0.00	2.18
AG	SC 529 CO FS Aggressive Growth C	CCGGX	B-	(800) 345-6611	C+ / 5.8	6.24	6.96	20.36 /54	5.34 /58	9.39 /54	0.00	2.18
AG	SC 529 CO FS Aggressive Growth		A+	(800) 345-6611	B- / 7.4	6.77	8.22	22.47 /64	7.49 /75	10.89 /65	0.00	0.50
AG	SC 529 CO FS Aggressive Growth E	CEGGX	B-	(800) 345-6611	C+ / 6.3	6.36	7.25	21.00 /57	5.86 /63	9.94 /58	0.00	1.68
AG	SC 529 CO FS Aggressive Growth Z		B	(800) 345-6611	C+ / 6.7	6.49	7.53	21.60 /60	6.40 /68	10.49 /62	0.00	1.18
GR	SC 529 CO FS Growth AG	CGAGX	B	(800) 345-6611	C / 5.3	6.09	6.66	19.77 /51	5.93 /64	9.45 /54	0.00	1.41
GR	SC 529 CO FS Growth B		B	(800) 345-6611	C / 5.4	5.88	6.29	18.90 /47	5.13 /56	8.65 /48	0.00	2.16
GR	SC 529 CO FS Growth C	CGCGX	B	(800) 345-6611	C / 5.4	5.87	6.25	18.90 /47	5.13 /56	8.64 /48	0.00	2.16
GR	SC 529 CO FS Growth Dir		B	(800) 345-6611	C+ / 6.8	6.22	7.11	20.01 /52	7.13 /73	9.97 /58	0.00	0.51
GR	SC 529 CO FS Growth E	CGAAX	B	(800) 345-6611	C+ / 5.8	6.02	6.55	19.49 /49	5.67 /61	9.18 /52	0.00	1.66
GR	SC 529 CO FS Growth Z		B	(800) 345-6611	C+ / 6.3	6.13	6.77	20.08 /52	6.19 /66	9.73 /56	0.00	1.16
MC	SC 529 CO FS Janus Enterprise AG	CACAX	E-	(800) 345-6611	E- / 0.0	6.06	6.65	-32.85 / 0	-16.33 / 0	-4.21 / 2	0.00	1.29
MC	SC 529 CO FS Janus Enterprise C	CACBX	E-	(800) 345-6611	E- / 0.0	5.91	6.20	-28.09 / 0	-14.82 / 0	-3.46 / 2	0.00	2.04
MC	SC 529 CO FS Janus Enterprise E	CACEX	E-	(800) 345-6611	E- / 0.0	5.98	6.47	-15.42 / 0	-9.80 / 1	0.12 / 5	0.00	1.54
GR	SC 529 CO FS Lg Cp Growth AG	CMRAX	C+	(800) 345-6611	C / 5.3	8.29	7.67	20.54 /55	5.00 /54	10.29 /61	0.00	1.50
GR	SC 529 CO FS Lg Cp Growth B		C+	(800) 345-6611	C / 5.3	8.09	7.31	19.64 /50	4.23 /46	9.47 /54	0.00	2.25
GR	SC 529 CO FS Lg Cp Growth C	CMRCX	C+	(800) 345-6611	C / 5.3	8.09	7.32	19.64 /50	4.24 /46	9.49 /55	0.00	2.25
GR	SC 529 CO FS Lg Cp Growth E	CMREX	C+	(800) 345-6611	C+ / 5.8	8.21	7.55	20.22 /53	4.75 /51	10.02 /58	0.00	1.75
GR	SC 529 CO FS Lg Cp Growth Z		B-	(800) 345-6611	C+ / 6.2	8.34	7.85	20.86 /57	5.28 /57	10.56 /63	0.00	1.25
GI	SC 529 CO FS Mod Conservative AG	MDOCX	C+	(800) 345-6611	D / 1.8	2.72	1.87	8.82 / 9	3.22 /34	4.35 /17	0.00	1.14
GI	SC 529 CO FS Mod Conservative B		C+	(800) 345-6611	D / 1.9	2.54	1.52	8.01 / 7	2.45 /27	3.57 /13	0.00	1.89
GI	SC 529 CO FS Mod Conservative C	CMCNX	C+	(800) 345-6611	D / 1.9	2.53	1.46	8.00 / 7	2.45 /27	3.58 /13	0.00	1.89
GI	SC 529 CO FS Mod Conservative Dir		C+	(800) 345-6611	D+ / 2.5	2.81	1.98	7.99 / 7	3.83 /41	4.73 /20	0.00	0.57
GI	SC 529 CO FS Mod Conservative E	CEGMX	C+	(800) 345-6611	D / 2.1	2.67	1.73	8.60 / 9	2.97 /32	4.11 /16	0.00	1.39
GI	SC 529 CO FS Mod Conservative Z		C+	(800) 345-6611	D+ / 2.4	2.75	1.97	9.08 /10	3.48 /37	4.62 /19	0.00	0.89
BA	SC 529 CO FS Moderate AG	CMAGX	B-	(800) 345-6611	C- / 3.1	4.06	3.52	13.03 /22	4.60 /50	6.58 /32	0.00	1.29
BA	SC 529 CO FS Moderate B		B-	(800) 345-6611	C- / 3.2	3.93	3.18	12.21 /19	3.82 /41	5.78 /27	0.00	2.04
BA	SC 529 CO FS Moderate C	CMCGX	B-	(800) 345-6611	C- / 3.2	3.92	3.18	12.25 /19	3.82 /41	5.79 /27	0.00	2.04
BA	SC 529 CO FS Moderate Dir		B+	(800) 345-6611	C / 4.3	4.27	3.88	12.86 /21	5.49 /59	7.14 /35	0.00	0.60
BA	SC 529 CO FS Moderate E	CMEGX	B	(800) 345-6611	C- / 3.5	4.05	3.42	12.79 /21	4.34 /47	6.32 /30	0.00	1.54
BA	SC 529 CO FS Moderate Growth AG	CGAMX	B-	(800) 345-6611	C- / 4.0	4.91	4.72	15.93 /34	5.23 /57	7.91 /41	0.00	1.36
BA	SC 529 CO FS Moderate Growth B		B-	(800) 345-6611	C- / 4.0	4.72	4.32	15.05 /30	4.43 /48	7.09 /35	0.00	2.11
BA	SC 529 CO FS Moderate Growth C	CMCTX	B-	(800) 345-6611	C- / 4.0	4.70	4.34	15.07 /30	4.44 /48	7.10 /35	0.00	2.11
BA	SC 529 CO FS Moderate Growth Dir		A-	(800) 345-6611	C / 5.2	4.94	4.89	15.32 /31	6.10 /65	8.12 /43	0.00	0.56
BA	SC 529 CO FS Moderate Growth E	CMGEX	B	(800) 345-6611	C / 4.5	4.86	4.62	15.66 /33	4.97 /54	7.65 /39	0.00	1.61
BA	SC 529 CO FS Moderate Growth Z		B+	(800) 345-6611	C / 4.9	4.99	4.84	16.23 /35	5.49 /59	8.17 /43	0.00	1.11
BA	SC 529 CO FS Moderate Z		B	(800) 345-6611	C- / 3.9	4.16	3.65	13.36 /23	4.87 /53	6.85 /34	0.00	1.04
GL	Scharf Alpha Opportunity Rtl	HEDJX	U	(866) 572-4273	U /	1.69	-2.22	0.21 / 1	--	--	0.00	7.24
GI	Scharf Balanced Opportunity Inst	LOGOX	C+	(866) 572-4273	C- / 4.0	4.40	2.06	10.85 /14	5.81 /63	--	0.66	1.46
GL	Scharf Global Opportunity Rtl	WRLDX	U	(866) 572-4273	U /	7.86	5.62	20.00 /52	--	--	0.50	2.36
GL	Scharf Institutional	LOGIX	C+	(866) 572-4273	C+ / 5.6	5.69	3.36	12.82 /21	8.08 /80	11.33 /68	0.16	1.24
GL	Scharf Retail	LOGRX	U	(866) 572-4273	U /	5.61	3.20	12.50 /20	--	--	0.00	1.49
SC	Schneider Small Cap Value	SCMVX	C	(888) 520-3277	A+ / 9.9	8.00	29.26	101.41 /99	3.76 /40	11.39 /69	0.00	2.13
GL	Schroder North American Equity Inv	SNAEX	A	(800) 464-3108	A- / 9.1	7.35	9.90	25.00 /73	10.03 /93	13.14 /85	1.81	0.32
*GI	Schwab 1000 Index Fund	SNXFX	A	(800) 407-0256	A- / 9.1	7.96	9.98	25.06 /73	9.83 /92	13.52 /89	1.68	0.05
BA	Schwab Balanced Fund	SWOBX	B-	(800) 407-0256	C / 5.2	5.39	5.39	15.24 /31	5.86 /63	8.16 /43	1.42	0.68
GR	Schwab Core Equity Fd	SWANX	B-	(800) 407-0256	A- / 9.0	8.46	10.40	25.11 /74	9.41 /90	12.71 /81	1.56	0.74
IN	Schwab Dividend Equity Fund	SWDSX	C+	(800) 407-0256	B+ / 8.5	7.20	11.78	27.02 /79	7.86 /78	11.75 /72	1.61	0.88
RE	Schwab Fundamental Global RI Est	SFREX	U	(800) 407-0256	U /	7.94	0.75	18.28 /44	--	--	3.94	0.81
FO	Schwab Fundm Intl Lg Co Index	SFNNX	D-	(800) 407-0256	D / 1.6	7.14	7.28	20.59 /55	-0.79 /10	5.31 /23	3.09	0.46
FO	Schwab Fundm Intl Sm Co Index	SFILX	C+	(800) 407-0256	C+ / 5.7	7.71	7.53	22.92 /66	4.09 /44	8.36 /45	2.32	0.71

● Denotes fund is closed to new investors
* Denotes fund is included in Section II

RISK			NET ASSETS		ASSET				Portfolio Turnover Ratio	BULL / BEAR		FUND MANAGER		MINIMUMS		LOADS	
	3 Year		NAV							Last Bull	Last Bear	Manager	Manager	Initial	Additional	Front	Back
Risk Rating/Pts	Standard Deviation	Beta	As of 2/28/17	Total $(Mil)	Cash %	Stocks %	Bonds %	Other %		Market Return	Market Return	Quality Pct	Tenure (Years)	Purch. $	Purch. $	End Load	End Load
B- /7.9	9.8	0.92	23.92	140	0	0	0	100	0	98.8	-20.7	30	N/A	250	50	3.5	0.0
B- /7.9	9.8	0.92	29.03	2	0	0	0	100	0	91.0	-20.9	22	N/A	250	50	0.0	0.0
B- /7.9	9.8	0.92	28.43	39	0	0	0	100	0	91.0	-21.0	22	N/A	250	50	0.0	0.0
B /8.2	9.4	0.89	26.33	171	0	0	0	100	0	105.7	-19.4	51	N/A	250	50	0.0	0.0
B- /7.9	9.7	0.92	30.77	8	0	0	0	100	0	96.2	-20.8	27	N/A	250	50	0.0	0.0
B /8.0	9.8	0.92	32.14	5	0	0	0	100	0	101.6	-20.7	33	N/A	250	50	0.0	0.0
B /8.2	9.0	0.85	23.69	187	0	0	0	100	0	88.9	-19.2	36	N/A	250	50	3.5	0.0
B /8.2	9.0	0.85	27.55	3	0	0	0	100	0	81.4	-19.4	28	N/A	250	50	0.0	0.0
B /8.1	9.0	0.85	26.86	64	0	0	0	100	0	81.3	-19.5	27	N/A	250	50	0.0	0.0
B /8.7	8.3	0.79	25.61	143	0	0	0	100	0	94.3	-17.7	60	N/A	250	50	0.0	0.0
B /8.2	9.2	0.87	29.43	9	0	0	0	100	0	86.4	-19.3	31	N/A	250	50	0.0	0.0
B /8.3	9.0	0.85	29.96	6	0	0	0	100	0	91.6	-19.1	40	N/A	250	50	0.0	0.0
E- /0.0	39.4	0.96	11.55	12	0	0	0	100	20	0.8	-22.3	0	N/A	250	50	3.5	0.0
E- /0.0	35.0	0.97	11.47	5	0	0	0	100	20	4.4	-22.6	0	N/A	250	50	0.0	0.0
D- /1.1	26.2	0.98	11.52	1	0	0	0	100	20	25.5	-22.4	0	N/A	250	50	0.0	0.0
B- /7.0	12.6	1.06	28.35	14	0	0	0	100	62	100.9	-18.3	10	N/A	250	50	3.5	0.0
C+ /6.9	12.6	1.06	25.40	N/A	0	0	0	100	62	93.0	-18.5	7	N/A	250	50	0.0	0.0
C+ /6.9	12.6	1.06	24.18	7	0	0	0	100	62	93.0	-18.5	7	N/A	250	50	0.0	0.0
C+ /6.9	12.6	1.06	24.79	1	0	0	0	100	62	98.2	-18.4	8	N/A	250	50	0.0	0.0
B- /7.0	12.6	1.06	23.64	1	0	0	0	100	62	103.6	-18.2	11	N/A	250	50	0.0	0.0
B+ /9.9	3.7	0.34	18.50	129	0	0	0	100	0	34.0	-7.5	70	N/A	250	50	3.5	0.0
B+ /9.9	3.7	0.34	17.39	3	0	0	0	100	0	28.7	-7.8	61	N/A	250	50	0.0	0.0
B+ /9.9	3.7	0.34	17.42	52	0	0	0	100	0	28.7	-7.7	61	N/A	250	50	0.0	0.0
B+ /9.9	3.3	0.29	19.05	88	0	0	0	100	0	36.2	-6.1	79	N/A	250	50	0.0	0.0
B+ /9.9	3.8	0.34	18.81	5	0	0	0	100	0	32.3	-7.6	67	N/A	250	50	0.0	0.0
B+ /9.9	3.7	0.34	20.18	3	0	0	0	100	0	35.8	-7.4	73	N/A	250	50	0.0	0.0
B+ /9.5	5.7	0.90	21.78	268	0	0	0	100	0	55.2	-11.8	48	N/A	250	50	3.5	0.0
B+ /9.4	5.7	0.90	21.42	8	0	0	0	100	0	49.0	-12.1	37	N/A	250	50	0.0	0.0
B+ /9.4	5.7	0.90	21.72	86	0	0	0	100	0	49.0	-12.1	37	N/A	250	50	0.0	0.0
B+ /9.8	5.3	0.84	22.73	168	0	0	0	100	0	58.6	-9.9	65	N/A	250	50	0.0	0.0
B+ /9.5	5.7	0.90	23.90	11	0	0	0	100	0	53.2	-11.9	44	N/A	250	50	0.0	0.0
B+ /9.0	7.0	1.10	23.07	212	0	0	0	100	0	71.4	-16.0	36	N/A	250	50	3.5	0.0
B /8.9	7.0	1.10	24.85	6	0	0	0	100	0	64.6	-16.2	28	N/A	250	50	0.0	0.0
B /8.9	7.0	1.10	24.74	71	0	0	0	100	0	64.5	-16.2	27	N/A	250	50	0.0	0.0
B+ /9.4	6.3	1.00	24.01	156	0	0	0	100	0	72.5	-14.1	58	N/A	250	50	0.0	0.0
B /8.9	7.0	1.10	26.96	10	0	0	0	100	0	69.1	-16.0	34	N/A	250	50	0.0	0.0
B+ /9.0	7.0	1.10	29.22	10	0	0	0	100	0	73.6	-15.9	40	N/A	250	50	0.0	0.0
B+ /9.5	5.7	0.90	25.29	8	0	0	0	100	0	57.3	-11.6	51	N/A	250	50	0.0	0.0
U /	N/A	N/A	24.02	26	0	0	0	100	25	N/A	N/A	N/A	2	10,000	500	0.0	0.0
B- /7.6	7.2	0.66	30.99	56	23	71	3	3	34	N/A	N/A	61	5	5,000,000	0	0.0	0.0
U /	N/A	N/A	28.09	28	6	93	0	1	53	N/A	N/A	N/A	2	10,000	500	0.0	0.0
C+ /6.9	9.5	0.63	42.08	495	0	84	14	2	31	N/A	N/A	98	6	5,000,000	0	0.0	2.0
U /	N/A	N/A	41.95	90	0	84	14	2	31	N/A	N/A	N/A	6	10,000	500	0.0	2.0
D- /1.3	27.6	1.30	17.14	47	1	98	0	1	114	140.1	-37.3	15	19	20,000	2,500	0.0	1.8
C+ /6.4	10.4	0.67	15.71	972	0	99	0	1	70	125.8	-16.5	99	14	250,000	1,000	0.0	0.0
C+ /6.3	10.4	1.01	56.81	7,032	0	99	0	1	3	130.6	-17.2	65	5	0	0	0.0	0.0
B- /7.5	7.1	1.09	14.41	303	0	58	40	2	19	69.6	-10.3	46	N/A	100	0	0.0	0.0
C- /3.5	11.5	1.09	21.80	2,196	0	99	0	1	80	123.6	-19.1	48	5	100	0	0.0	0.0
C- /3.8	11.6	1.07	16.37	1,525	0	99	0	1	74	109.9	-15.1	31	5	100	0	0.0	0.0
U /	N/A	N/A	10.72	93	11	88	0	1	26	N/A	N/A	N/A	N/A	100	0	0.0	0.0
C /5.2	12.0	0.95	8.19	1,081	0	99	0	1	18	49.8	-26.3	67	5	100	0	0.0	0.0
C+ /6.6	10.8	0.84	12.32	540	1	98	0	1	40	67.4	-19.4	94	5	100	0	0.0	0.0

Fund Type	Fund Name	Ticker Symbol	Overall Investment Rating	Phone	Performance Rating/Pts	3 Mo	6 Mo	1Yr / Pct	3Yr / Pct	5Yr / Pct	Dividend Yield	Expense Ratio
							Total Return % through 2/28/17		Annualized		Incl. in Returns	
* GR	Schwab Fundm US Large Co Index	SFLNX	A	(800) 407-0256	B+ / 8.9	6.08	10.14	25.63 / 75	9.58 / 91	13.70 / 91	2.06	0.39
MC	Schwab Fundm US Small Co Index	SFSNX	B+	(800) 407-0256	A / 9.3	5.40	13.07	33.63 / 92	8.39 / 82	13.70 / 91	1.18	0.43
EM	Schwab Fundmntl EM Large Co	SFENX	C+	(800) 407-0256	A- / 9.0	10.54	14.56	49.00 / 99	2.94 / 31	-0.63 / 4	1.98	0.71
RE	Schwab Global Real Estate Fund	SWASX	C+	(800) 407-0256	C / 5.4	8.41	-1.61	14.46 / 28	7.18 / 73	7.86 / 41	4.44	1.13
HL	Schwab Health Care	SWHFX	C	(800) 407-0256	C+ / 6.7	8.74	3.52	13.75 / 24	8.46 / 83	16.51 / 98	0.86	0.79
IN	Schwab Hedged Equity	SWHEX	C+	(800) 407-0256	C+ / 6.8	3.33	9.05	18.09 / 43	7.73 / 77	8.44 / 46	0.00	1.84
FO	Schwab International Core Equity Fd	SICNX	C-	(800) 407-0256	C- / 3.4	8.96	7.42	18.35 / 44	0.98 / 18	7.90 / 41	2.36	0.92
FO	Schwab International Index	SWISX	D-	(800) 407-0256	D- / 1.2	7.28	4.25	15.76 / 33	-0.82 / 10	5.13 / 22	3.05	0.06
GR	Schwab Large-Cap Growth Fund	SWLSX	B-	(800) 407-0256	B+ / 8.4	8.64	8.64	20.70 / 56	9.34 / 89	12.32 / 77	1.00	1.03
GR	Schwab MarketTrack All Eq Port Inv	SWEGX	B-	(800) 407-0256	B- / 7.3	6.86	9.58	26.42 / 78	6.16 / 66	10.75 / 64	1.72	0.59
BA	Schwab MarketTrack Bal Port Inv	SWBGX	C	(800) 407-0256	C / 4.4	4.41	4.88	15.60 / 32	4.85 / 53	7.33 / 37	1.65	0.62
AA	Schwab MarketTrack Consv Port Inv	SWCGX	C	(800) 407-0256	D+ / 2.8	3.24	2.37	10.37 / 13	3.84 / 41	5.35 / 24	1.62	0.67
AA	Schwab MarketTrack Growth Port Inv	SWHGX	C+	(800) 407-0256	C+ / 6.1	5.68	7.45	21.05 / 58	5.73 / 62	9.25 / 53	1.64	0.59
GL	Schwab Monthly Income Fund	SWKRX	C+	(800) 407-0256	D / 2.2	2.98	1.24	7.56 / 7	3.37 / 36	4.15 / 16	2.08	0.69
GL	Schwab Monthly Income Fund	SWLRX	C	(800) 407-0256	D / 1.6	2.01	-0.31	4.43 / 3	2.77 / 30	2.92 / 11	2.17	0.70
GL	Schwab Monthly Income Fund	SWJRX	C	(800) 407-0256	C- / 3.0	4.01	2.73	10.78 / 14	3.96 / 43	5.34 / 24	2.01	0.89
* IX	Schwab S&P 500 Index Fund	SWPPX	A+	(800) 407-0256	A / 9.3	8.01	9.94	24.81 / 73	10.52 / 96	13.89 / 92	1.87	0.03
SC	Schwab Small-Cap Equity Fund	SWSCX	C+	(800) 407-0256	A- / 9.1	4.92	12.85	33.25 / 92	8.20 / 80	14.73 / 96	0.41	1.09
SC	Schwab Small-Cap Index	SWSSX	B	(800) 407-0256	B+ / 8.9	5.16	12.56	36.05 / 95	6.97 / 72	12.91 / 83	1.32	0.05
GR	Schwab Target 2010	SWBRX	C+	(800) 407-0256	D+ / 2.6	3.50	2.11	9.10 / 10	3.64 / 39	5.31 / 23	1.74	0.57
GI	Schwab Target 2015	SWGRX	C	(800) 407-0256	D+ / 2.7	3.65	2.34	9.55 / 11	3.72 / 40	5.91 / 28	1.83	0.52
GR	Schwab Target 2020	SWCRX	C	(800) 407-0256	C- / 3.4	4.42	3.45	12.18 / 19	4.15 / 45	7.01 / 35	1.71	0.52
GI	Schwab Target 2025	SWHRX	C+	(800) 407-0256	C / 4.3	5.30	4.61	14.80 / 29	4.68 / 51	7.96 / 42	1.62	0.60
GR	Schwab Target 2030 Fund	SWDRX	C+	(800) 407-0256	C / 4.9	5.87	5.44	16.69 / 37	5.01 / 54	8.64 / 48	1.58	0.64
GI	Schwab Target 2035	SWIRX	C+	(800) 407-0256	C / 5.5	6.41	6.26	18.41 / 45	5.32 / 58	9.26 / 53	1.52	0.69
GR	Schwab Target 2040	SWERX	C+	(800) 407-0256	C+ / 6.0	6.82	6.96	19.92 / 52	5.53 / 60	9.74 / 57	1.49	0.73
GI	Schwab Target 2045	SWMRX	B-	(800) 407-0256	C+ / 6.3	7.08	7.34	20.81 / 56	5.68 / 61	--	1.39	0.85
GI	Schwab Target 2050	SWNRX	C+	(800) 407-0256	C+ / 6.5	7.29	7.64	21.38 / 59	5.82 / 63	--	1.37	0.89
GI	Schwab Target 2055	SWORX	C+	(800) 407-0256	C+ / 6.6	7.39	7.82	21.90 / 62	5.86 / 63	--	1.33	1.02
* GR	Schwab Total Stock Market Index Fd	SWTSX	A+	(800) 407-0256	A- / 9.2	7.74	10.25	26.22 / 77	9.82 / 92	13.74 / 91	1.74	0.03
GR	Schwartz Value Focused	RCMFX	E+	(888) 449-9240	D- / 1.5	2.86	7.94	23.00 / 67	-1.09 / 9	3.63 / 14	0.00	1.59
EM	Scout Emerging Markets	SEMFX	E+	(800) 996-2862	D- / 1.4	5.04	-1.09	20.34 / 54	-0.39 / 12	--	0.66	2.64
GL	Scout Global Equity	SCGLX	C	(800) 996-2862	C / 5.1	6.61	8.41	16.31 / 36	4.67 / 51	8.88 / 50	0.52	3.23
FO	Scout Internl Fund	UMBWX	E	(800) 996-2862	D+ / 2.5	6.90	3.26	17.71 / 42	0.59 / 16	4.20 / 16	2.20	1.05
MC	Scout Mid Cap Fund	UMBMX	B	(800) 996-2862	A / 9.5	7.95	15.60	32.79 / 91	8.29 / 81	12.46 / 79	0.54	1.04
SC	Scout Small Cap Fund	UMBHX	C+	(800) 996-2862	A- / 9.0	8.61	14.93	28.59 / 83	7.63 / 76	13.01 / 84	0.00	1.13
AA	SCS Tactical Allocation Fund	SCSGX	E	(800) 773-3863	E- / 0.0	2.95	-1.77	-4.85 / 1	-9.62 / 1	0.57 / 5	0.00	5.19
FO	Seafarer Overseas Gr and Inc Inst	SIGIX	C	(855) 732-9220	C / 5.1	8.98	2.19	21.63 / 60	4.90 / 53	5.82 / 27	1.65	0.98
FO	Seafarer Overseas Gr and Inc Inv	SFGIX	C	(855) 732-9220	C / 5.0	8.94	2.13	21.48 / 60	4.76 / 52	5.68 / 26	1.59	1.08
GR	Sector Rotation No Load	NAVFX	C	(800) 525-3863	C+ / 6.4	7.38	7.29	19.21 / 48	6.29 / 67	8.24 / 44	0.00	2.13
GR	Segall Bryant & Hamill All Cap	SBHAX	C+	(866) 490-4999	C+ / 5.8	5.03	6.25	18.31 / 44	6.80 / 71	--	0.03	1.69
EM	Segall Bryant & Hamill Emerg Mkt I	SBEMX	C	(866) 490-4999	C+ / 6.4	12.19	9.78	35.82 / 95	1.43 / 21	0.15 / 5	1.87	4.75
FO	Segall Bryant & Hamill Intl SC I	SBSIX	C+	(866) 490-4999	C / 4.9	8.53	6.85	22.16 / 63	3.16 / 33	10.83 / 64	1.73	1.89
SC	Segall Bryant & Hamill Sm Cap Val	SBHVX	C+	(866) 490-4999	C+ / 6.8	0.38	9.91	29.67 / 86	6.46 / 68	--	0.05	1.68
AA	SEI Asset Alloc Core Mkt Str AI F	SKTAX	B-	(800) 342-5734	C+ / 5.8	6.31	7.90	21.17 / 58	4.97 / 54	9.60 / 55	1.23	1.38
AA	SEI Asset Alloc- Moderate Strgy D	SMSDX	C+	(800) 342-5734	D+ / 2.3	3.48	2.12	8.71 / 9	3.21 / 34	4.18 / 16	1.80	2.05
AA	SEI Asset Alloc- Moderate Strgy F	SMOAX	C+	(800) 342-5734	D+ / 2.9	3.75	2.48	9.49 / 10	4.05 / 44	5.02 / 21	2.52	1.29
AA	SEI Asset Alloc- Moderate Strgy I	SMSIX	C+	(800) 342-5734	D+ / 2.7	3.67	2.37	9.24 / 10	3.78 / 40	4.78 / 20	2.20	1.55
GI	SEI Asset Alloc Tr Tax Mgd Strgy F	SXMAX	B-	(800) 342-5734	C+ / 6.9	6.57	6.11	18.72 / 46	7.87 / 78	11.15 / 67	2.30	1.37
AA	SEI Asset Alloc Trust Cons Strat I	SICIX	C+	(800) 342-5734	D / 1.7	2.24	1.38	5.82 / 5	2.41 / 27	3.17 / 11	1.62	1.41
AA	SEI Asset Alloc-Agg Strgy D	SASDX	C+	(800) 342-5734	C- / 4.1	5.94	4.73	17.78 / 42	3.53 / 37	6.71 / 33	1.88	2.21
AA	SEI Asset Alloc-Agg Strgy F	SSGAX	C+	(800) 342-5734	C / 4.6	6.16	5.15	18.32 / 44	4.20 / 45	7.46 / 38	2.04	1.46

99 Pct = Best
0 Pct = Worst

● Denotes fund is closed to new investors
* Denotes fund is included in Section II

RISK	3 Year		NET ASSETS		ASSET				Portfolio Turnover Ratio	BULL / BEAR		FUND MANAGER		MINIMUMS		LOADS	
Risk Rating/Pts	Standard Deviation	Beta	NAV As of 2/28/17	Total $(Mil)	Cash %	Stocks %	Bonds %	Other %		Last Bull Market Return	Last Bear Market Return	Manager Quality Pct	Manager Tenure (Years)	Initial Purch. $	Additional Purch. $	Front End Load	Back End Load
C+ / 6.4	10.2	0.96	15.84	5,231	0	98	0	2	11	130.9	-18.5	68	5	100	0	0.0	0.0
C / 5.0	13.8	1.12	14.50	1,718	0	98	0	2	30	142.3	-25.5	45	5	100	0	0.0	0.0
C- / 3.1	20.5	1.19	8.34	410	0	98	1	1	20	20.9	-27.2	80	5	100	0	0.0	0.0
B- / 7.0	11.6	0.79	7.37	262	7	92	0	1	91	74.5	-21.4	57	5	100	0	0.0	0.0
C- / 3.8	13.1	0.97	23.33	843	0	99	0	1	54	143.7	-9.6	52	5	100	0	0.0	0.0
C / 5.2	7.5	0.63	17.05	253	40	58	0	2	142	72.2	-14.0	81	5	100	0	0.0	0.0
C+ / 6.6	11.0	0.87	9.64	805	1	98	0	1	90	68.1	-21.3	82	5	100	0	0.0	0.0
C+ / 5.7	11.4	0.92	17.89	3,142	1	98	0	1	4	49.4	-23.9	66	5	0	0	0.0	0.0
C- / 4.2	11.4	1.04	16.14	229	0	99	0	1	84	124.8	-18.8	54	5	100	0	0.0	0.0
C / 5.5	10.8	1.00	16.92	606	3	96	0	1	6	101.5	-20.5	22	9	100	0	0.0	0.0
C+ / 6.8	6.4	1.00	17.87	528	3	59	37	1	15	61.3	-10.9	41	9	100	0	0.0	0.0
B / 8.5	4.5	0.69	15.57	238	3	39	57	1	10	41.8	-6.0	58	9	100	0	0.0	0.0
C+ / 6.0	8.6	1.32	21.59	764	4	79	16	1	12	82.4	-15.8	24	9	100	0	0.0	0.0
B+ / 9.6	3.8	0.55	11.02	93	1	30	67	2	11	29.9	-1.8	79	N/A	100	0	0.0	0.0
B+ / 9.5	2.7	0.32	9.97	47	0	16	83	1	14	19.1	0.6	82	N/A	100	0	0.0	0.0
B / 8.3	5.1	0.76	10.58	46	3	44	51	2	14	41.4	-5.9	77	N/A	100	0	0.0	0.0
C+ / 6.9	10.3	1.00	36.46	25,763	0	99	0	1	2	133.4	-16.2	73	5	0	0	0.0	0.0
D+ / 2.6	15.6	0.97	21.87	635	0	99	0	1	85	155.5	-24.3	83	5	100	0	0.0	0.0
C / 4.3	15.7	1.00	28.75	3,102	0	97	2	1	17	131.3	-23.7	74	5	0	0	0.0	0.0
B+ / 9.5	4.4	0.39	12.69	58	5	36	57	2	14	42.2	-6.7	69	12	100	0	0.0	0.0
B / 8.0	4.6	0.41	11.52	99	5	39	55	1	14	49.3	-9.5	67	N/A	100	0	0.0	0.0
B / 8.3	6.0	0.56	13.72	538	3	51	44	2	9	60.4	-11.8	54	12	100	0	0.0	0.0
B- / 7.6	7.1	0.67	13.54	467	3	62	34	1	5	70.2	-13.6	46	N/A	100	0	0.0	0.0
B- / 7.1	8.0	0.75	14.67	865	3	70	26	1	5	77.8	-15.3	38	12	100	0	0.0	0.0
C+ / 6.8	8.8	0.82	14.10	388	2	77	19	2	3	84.9	-16.5	33	N/A	100	0	0.0	0.0
C+ / 6.4	9.5	0.89	15.39	898	0	84	14	2	4	90.5	-17.5	28	5	100	0	0.0	0.0
B- / 7.0	9.8	0.92	12.44	95	8	84	6	2	1	N/A	N/A	26	4	100	0	0.0	0.0
C+ / 6.9	10.0	0.94	12.55	79	8	86	4	2	1	N/A	N/A	25	4	100	0	0.0	0.0
C+ / 6.7	10.3	0.97	12.61	45	8	88	2	2	1	N/A	N/A	23	4	100	0	0.0	0.0
C+ / 6.6	10.6	1.02	42.01	5,676	2	97	0	1	1	133.6	-17.5	63	5	0	0	0.0	0.0
C / 4.4	11.6	0.81	25.56	21	6	93	0	1	104	41.4	-11.2	3	33	2,500	0	0.0	0.0
C- / 4.2	13.2	0.79	10.30	23	4	95	0	1	51	N/A	N/A	52	5	1,000	100	0.0	0.0
C+ / 6.1	10.5	0.73	13.41	11	5	94	0	1	58	79.9	N/A	95	1	1,000	100	0.0	0.0
D / 1.7	11.4	0.89	21.46	1,220	1	98	0	1	23	46.1	-24.2	79	11	1,000	100	0.0	0.0
C- / 4.0	10.9	0.85	17.58	1,396	2	97	0	1	161	115.0	-15.7	75	11	1,000	100	0.0	0.0
C- / 3.2	15.1	0.91	24.74	218	0	99	0	1	16	136.1	-26.6	82	7	1,000	100	0.0	0.0
C / 4.7	8.8	0.75	9.42	3	4	60	34	2	88	N/A	N/A	0	N/A	2,000	100	4.8	0.0
C+ / 5.9	13.9	0.81	12.01	1,043	7	87	3	3	7	N/A	N/A	95	5	25,000	100	0.0	2.0
C+ / 5.9	13.9	0.82	11.98	729	7	87	3	3	7	N/A	N/A	95	5	2,500	100	0.0	2.0
C / 4.9	9.7	0.87	12.09	22	0	0	0	100	346	68.7	-14.8	38	8	2,500	100	0.0	2.0
C+ / 6.2	10.3	0.92	12.81	57	5	94	0	1	33	N/A	N/A	39	4	2,500	500	0.0	2.0
C- / 4.1	17.2	1.04	8.02	21	3	96	0	1	84	31.7	N/A	70	6	1,000,000	1,000	0.8	0.0
C+ / 6.5	11.8	0.88	12.22	144	3	96	0	1	130	93.7	N/A	91	6	1,000,000	1,000	0.5	0.0
C / 5.2	14.2	0.85	12.02	62	6	93	0	1	57	N/A	N/A	78	4	2,500	100	0.0	2.0
B- / 7.1	9.8	1.49	17.35	26	3	82	14	1	23	91.3	-18.7	9	14	100,000	1,000	0.0	0.0
B+ / 9.4	3.9	0.54	11.71	4	0	0	0	100	15	30.9	-4.2	64	14	150,000	1,000	0.0	0.0
B+ / 9.4	3.9	0.54	11.74	221	0	0	0	100	15	36.8	-3.8	74	14	100,000	1,000	0.0	0.0
B+ / 9.4	3.9	0.54	12.05	4	0	0	0	100	15	35.1	-4.0	71	14	100,000	1,000	0.0	0.0
B- / 7.8	7.6	0.69	19.89	95	2	77	19	2	15	96.5	-12.5	78	14	100,000	1,000	0.0	0.0
B+ / 9.9	2.4	0.31	10.65	4	0	0	0	100	18	21.9	-2.1	74	14	100,000	1,000	0.0	0.0
B- / 7.6	8.4	1.28	13.49	16	0	0	0	100	28	65.7	-17.8	10	14	150,000	1,000	0.0	0.0
B- / 7.6	8.4	1.29	13.60	218	0	0	0	100	28	72.2	-17.5	14	14	100,000	1,000	0.0	0.0

Fund Type	Fund Name	Ticker Symbol	Overall Investment Rating	Phone	Performance Rating/Pts	3 Mo	6 Mo	1Yr / Pct	3Yr / Pct	5Yr / Pct	Dividend Yield	Expense Ratio
AA	SEI Asset Alloc-Agg Strgy I	SEAIX	C+	(800) 342-5734	C / 4.4	6.10	4.99	18.07 /43	3.99 /43	7.21 /36	1.85	1.71
GI	SEI Asset Alloc-Cons Str All F	SMGAX	B+	(800) 342-5734	B- / 7.2	6.50	4.78	18.82 /46	8.68 /85	10.79 /64	3.46	1.35
AA	SEI Asset Alloc-Cons Strat D	SSTDX	C+	(800) 342-5734	D- / 1.5	2.16	1.16	5.30 / 4	1.88 /23	2.57 / 9	1.16	1.91
AA	SEI Asset Alloc-Cons Strat F	SVSAX	C+	(800) 342-5734	D / 1.8	2.35	1.53	6.09 / 5	2.70 /29	3.44 /13	1.90	1.16
GL	SEI Asset Alloc-Core Mrkt Strat F	SOKAX	C	(800) 342-5734	D+ / 2.9	4.27	2.76	12.60 /20	3.22 /34	4.97 /21	2.61	1.37
GL	SEI Asset Alloc-Core Mrkt Strat I	SCMSX	C+	(800) 342-5734	C- / 3.1	4.22	2.62	12.40 /19	3.66 /39	5.14 /22	2.20	1.62
AA	SEI Asset Alloc-Defensive Strat F	SNSAX	C	(800) 342-5734	D- / 1.2	1.18	0.76	3.19 / 3	1.51 /21	1.73 / 7	1.18	1.08
AA	SEI Asset Alloc-Defensive Strat I	SEDIX	C	(800) 342-5734	D- / 1.1	1.11	0.62	2.95 / 3	1.25 /20	1.46 / 7	0.92	1.33
AA	SEI Asset Alloc-Mkt Gr Str Alloc F	SGOAX	B-	(800) 342-5734	C+ / 5.8	6.27	7.89	21.10 /58	4.96 /54	9.62 /56	1.23	1.38
AA	SEI Asset Alloc-Mkt Gr Strgy D	SMKDX	C	(800) 342-5734	D+ / 2.9	4.77	3.37	14.05 /26	2.67 /29	4.83 /20	1.70	2.18
AA	SEI Asset Alloc-Mkt Gr Strgy F	SRWAX	C+	(800) 342-5734	C- / 3.5	5.02	3.78	14.95 /30	3.48 /37	5.67 /26	2.33	1.43
AA	SEI Asset Alloc-Mkt Gr Strgy I	SMGSX	C+	(800) 342-5734	C- / 3.3	4.95	3.71	14.69 /28	3.20 /34	5.40 /24	2.12	1.68
AA	SEI Asset Alloc-Tax Mgd Agg Strgy F	SISAX	B-	(800) 342-5734	C+ / 5.8	6.29	7.86	21.09 /58	4.94 /53	9.61 /55	1.23	1.37
GR	SEI Catholic Values Equity F	CAVAX	U	(800) 342-5734	U /	6.91	9.12	25.03 /73	--	--	0.94	1.32
EM	SEI Inst Intl Emerging Mkts Eqty F	SIEMX	C-	(800) 342-5734	C / 4.8	8.55	5.70	32.30 /90	1.21 /19	-0.34 / 4	0.74	1.84
EM	SEI Inst Intl Emerging Mkts Eqty Y	SEQFX	U	(800) 342-5734	U /	8.60	5.75	32.63 /91	--	--	0.96	1.59
FO	SEI Inst Intl International Eqty F	SEITX	D	(800) 342-5734	D- / 1.1	7.01	4.18	13.17 /22	-0.54 /11	4.77 /20	1.12	1.24
FO	SEI Inst Intl International Eqty I	SEEIX	D	(800) 342-5734	D- / 1.0	6.89	4.05	12.92 /21	-0.80 /10	4.51 /18	0.80	1.49
FO	SEI Inst Intl International Eqty Y	SEFCX	U	(800) 342-5734	U /	7.01	4.19	13.42 /23	--	--	1.33	1.00
GL	SEI Inst Inv Dynamic Asset All A	SDLAX	A+	(800) 342-5734	A+ / 9.8	7.75	11.69	25.30 /74	13.67 /99	15.19 /97	1.52	0.67
EM	SEI Inst Inv Emerging Markets Eq A	SMQFX	U	(800) 342-5734	U /	7.84	3.47	24.30 /71	--	--	2.01	1.28
GL	SEI Inst Inv Extended Mkt Index A	SMXAX	A-	(800) 342-5734	B+ / 8.6	6.34	11.49	32.79 /91	7.02 /72	--	1.38	0.20
GI	SEI Inst Inv Large Cap A	SLCAX	A-	(800) 342-5734	B / 7.7	7.09	9.67	21.55 /60	7.95 /79	12.86 /82	1.48	0.47
GR	SEI Inst Inv Large Cap Index A	LCIAX	A+	(800) 342-5734	A / 9.3	7.93	10.08	25.47 /75	10.18 /94	13.92 /93	1.83	0.25
GR	SEI Inst Inv LC Disciplined Eq A	SCPAX	A+	(800) 342-5734	B+ / 8.9	7.31	9.04	23.38 /68	10.15 /94	13.87 /92	1.72	0.47
IN	SEI Inst Inv Managed Vol Fund A	SVYAX	A	(800) 342-5734	A- / 9.0	7.22	7.73	18.87 /46	11.64 /98	14.82 /96	2.34	0.72
AA	SEI Inst Inv Multi-Asset Rl Rtn A	SEIAX	D+	(800) 342-5734	E / 0.4	0.99	1.60	5.57 / 4	-2.06 / 6	-2.26 / 3	1.73	0.90
IX	SEI Inst Inv S&P 500 Index A	SPINX	A+	(800) 342-5734	A / 9.3	7.97	9.95	24.88 /73	10.58 /96	--	1.86	0.12
SC	SEI Inst Inv Small Cap A	SLPAX	B	(800) 342-5734	B- / 7.1	4.30	10.12	30.52 /87	5.44 /59	11.55 /70	0.87	0.72
SC	SEI Inst Inv Small Cap II A	SECAX	C+	(800) 342-5734	C+ / 6.6	4.08	9.62	28.13 /82	5.06 /55	--	0.71	0.73
MC	SEI Inst Inv Small/Mid Cap Equity A	SSMAX	B	(800) 342-5734	B / 7.7	5.09	10.78	30.17 /87	6.30 /67	12.32 /77	0.79	0.72
GR	SEI Inst Inv Tr-Tax Mgd Volty F	TMMAX	A+	(800) 342-5734	B+ / 8.6	7.83	7.09	17.32 /40	11.08 /97	13.86 /92	1.44	1.23
GR	SEI Inst Inv Tr-Tax Mgd Volty Y	STVYX	U	(800) 342-5734	U /	7.89	7.16	17.61 /41	--	--	1.66	1.06
GL	SEI Inst Mgd Lng Sht Alternative Y	SLSFX	U	(800) 342-5734	U /	5.17	6.03	9.04 /10	--	--	0.00	1.19
AA	SEI Inst Mgd Tr-Dyn Asset Alloc F	SDYAX	U	(800) 342-5734	U /	7.62	11.31	24.51 /72	--	--	0.88	1.25
AA	SEI Inst Mgd Tr-Dyn Asset Alloc Y	SDYYX	U	(800) 342-5734	U /	7.64	11.33	24.64 /72	--	--	1.08	0.96
EM	SEI Inst Screened World Eq Ex-US A	SSEAX	C-	(800) 342-5734	C- / 4.2	8.37	6.93	23.22 /67	1.66 /22	5.38 /24	1.62	0.79
* EM	SEI Inst World Equity Ex US A	WEUSX	C-	(800) 342-5734	D+ / 2.7	7.82	6.00	18.80 /46	0.07 /14	4.53 /18	1.88	0.63
GI	SEI Insti Inv Tr LrgCap Diver Alp A	SCDAX	A-	(800) 342-5734	B- / 7.4	6.86	8.54	20.26 /53	8.04 /79	12.53 /79	1.54	0.48
GR	SEI Instl Managed Tr-Lg Cap Gro F	SELCX	C-	(800) 342-5734	C+ / 5.9	7.88	5.87	15.83 /34	6.48 /68	10.97 /66	0.10	0.98
GR	SEI Instl Managed Tr-Lg Cap Gro I	SPGIX	C-	(800) 342-5734	C+ / 5.7	7.81	5.72	15.58 /32	6.25 /66	10.72 /64	0.00	1.23
GR	SEI Instl Managed Tr-Lg Cap Gro Y	SLRYX	U	(800) 342-5734	U /	7.94	5.96	16.08 /35	--	--	0.35	0.73
GI	SEI Instl Managed Tr-Lg Cap Val F	TRMVX	B-	(800) 342-5734	B / 8.2	6.13	12.26	28.32 /82	7.43 /75	12.32 /77	1.38	0.93
GI	SEI Instl Managed Tr-Lg Cap Val I	SEUIX	B-	(800) 342-5734	B / 8.1	6.07	12.14	28.02 /82	7.19 /73	12.08 /75	1.18	1.18
GI	SEI Instl Managed Tr-Lg Cap Val Y	SVAYX	U	(800) 342-5734	U /	6.19	12.40	28.64 /83	--	--	1.60	0.68
MC	SEI Instl Managed Tr-Mid Cap I	SIPIX	B-	(800) 342-5734	B+ / 8.7	6.89	10.59	28.21 /82	8.66 /84	13.76 /91	0.64	1.23
MC	SEI Instl Managed Tr-MidCap Portf F	SEMCX	B-	(800) 342-5734	B+ / 8.9	6.94	10.74	28.51 /83	8.91 /86	14.03 /93	0.84	0.98
RE	SEI Instl Managed Tr-Real Est F	SETAX	C+	(800) 342-5734	B- / 7.2	7.33	-1.79	15.00 /30	10.89 /97	10.51 /62	1.51	1.23
RE	SEI Instl Managed Tr-Real Est I	SEIRX	C+	(800) 342-5734	B- / 7.0	7.27	-1.90	14.80 /29	10.66 /96	10.26 /60	1.28	1.48
RE	SEI Instl Managed Tr-Real Est Y	SREYX	U	(800) 342-5734	U /	7.40	-1.66	15.28 /31	--	--	1.75	0.98
IX	SEI Instl Managed Tr-S&P 500 Idx E	TRQIX	A+	(800) 342-5734	A- / 9.2	7.98	9.89	24.64 /72	10.39 /95	13.75 /91	1.65	0.29
IX	SEI Instl Managed Tr-S&P 500 Idx F	SSPIX	A	(800) 342-5734	A- / 9.1	7.91	9.79	24.41 /71	10.19 /94	13.55 /89	1.50	0.54

● Denotes fund is closed to new investors
* Denotes fund is included in Section II

www.thestreetratings.com

I. Index of Stock Mutual Funds

Risk Rating/Pts	3 Year Standard Deviation	Beta	NAV As of 2/28/17	Total $(Mil)	Cash %	Stocks %	Bonds %	Other %	Portfolio Turnover Ratio	Last Bull Market Return	Last Bear Market Return	Manager Quality Pct	Manager Tenure (Years)	Initial Purch. $	Additional Purch. $	Front End Load	Back End Load
B- / 7.6	8.4	1.29	13.25	21	0	0	0	100	28	70.0	-17.5	12	14	100,000	1,000	0.0	0.0
B- / 7.2	7.3	0.56	13.69	45	2	64	33	1	24	90.9	-10.2	89	14	100,000	1,000	0.0	0.0
B+ / 9.9	2.4	0.32	10.47	4	0	0	0	100	18	18.0	-2.4	68	14	150,000	1,000	0.0	0.0
B+ / 9.9	2.4	0.32	10.48	88	0	0	0	100	18	23.6	-1.9	76	14	100,000	1,000	0.0	0.0
B / 8.5	5.6	0.81	11.16	107	0	0	0	100	24	43.5	-9.0	68	14	100,000	1,000	0.0	0.0
B / 8.9	5.6	0.81	12.10	N/A	0	0	0	100	24	44.5	-9.1	73	14	100,000	1,000	0.0	0.0
B+ / 9.9	1.3	0.15	9.82	33	0	0	0	100	34	11.0	N/A	76	N/A	100,000	1,000	0.0	0.0
B+ / 9.9	1.3	0.15	9.66	1	0	0	0	100	34	9.5	-0.2	74	14	100,000	1,000	0.0	0.0
B- / 7.1	9.8	1.49	20.89	128	3	82	14	1	13	91.4	-18.5	9	14	100,000	1,000	0.0	0.0
B / 8.2	6.7	0.99	12.15	7	0	0	0	100	20	46.9	-14.0	19	14	150,000	1,000	0.0	0.0
B / 8.2	6.6	0.99	12.21	288	0	0	0	100	20	53.4	-13.6	26	14	100,000	1,000	0.0	0.0
B / 8.2	6.7	1.00	12.03	9	0	0	0	100	20	51.2	-13.6	23	14	100,000	1,000	0.0	0.0
B- / 7.1	9.8	1.49	19.12	64	3	82	14	1	12	91.5	-18.9	9	N/A	100,000	1,000	0.0	0.0
U /	N/A	N/A	10.61	186	2	96	1	1	84	N/A	N/A	N/A	2	500	100	0.0	0.0
C / 4.5	15.9	0.97	10.38	1,583	2	97	0	1	79	20.1	-28.6	69	7	100,000	1,000	0.0	1.3
U /	N/A	N/A	10.38	84	2	97	0	1	79	N/A	N/A	N/A	7	100,000	1,000	0.0	1.3
C+ / 6.4	10.9	0.88	9.72	3,265	8	88	3	1	45	46.1	-24.3	70	8	100,000	1,000	0.0	0.8
C+ / 6.4	10.8	0.87	9.72	4	8	88	3	1	45	44.0	-24.3	66	8	100,000	1,000	0.0	0.8
U /	N/A	N/A	9.72	238	8	88	3	1	45	N/A	N/A	N/A	8	100,000	1,000	0.0	0.8
C+ / 6.3	9.9	1.38	18.02	2,272	1	98	0	1	12	127.6	-9.2	97	5	100,000	1,000	0.0	0.0
U /	N/A	N/A	9.49	1,155	0	0	0	100	105	N/A	N/A	N/A	3	100,000	1,000	0.0	0.0
C+ / 6.0	13.5	0.74	14.13	856	4	94	0	2	27	N/A	N/A	98	4	100,000	1,000	0.0	0.0
C+ / 6.9	10.6	1.01	20.29	2,019	8	90	0	2	73	126.0	-17.7	41	21	100,000	1,000	0.0	0.0
C+ / 6.9	10.4	1.01	178.99	2,231	2	97	0	1	18	134.8	-17.0	68	13	100,000	1,000	0.0	0.0
B- / 7.1	10.2	0.99	13.54	3,571	5	93	0	2	102	135.3	-17.3	71	14	100,000	1,000	0.0	0.0
C+ / 6.3	8.1	0.68	14.68	1,437	1	97	1	1	62	127.7	-9.7	94	8	100,000	1,000	0.0	0.0
B / 8.3	4.4	0.21	8.24	748	0	0	99	1	91	-6.2	N/A	27	6	100,000	1,000	0.0	0.0
B- / 7.0	10.3	1.00	13.09	3,959	3	96	0	1	13	N/A	N/A	74	4	100,000	1,000	0.0	0.0
C+ / 5.9	14.6	0.92	18.10	545	5	94	0	1	115	121.3	-26.1	64	20	100,000	1,000	0.0	0.0
C+ / 5.6	14.9	0.94	12.79	479	10	89	0	1	137	N/A	N/A	57	5	100,000	1,000	0.0	0.0
C+ / 5.9	13.6	1.10	13.34	1,744	3	96	0	1	104	126.3	-24.2	24	14	100,000	1,000	0.0	0.0
B- / 7.4	7.9	0.63	15.41	991	1	96	1	2	32	117.0	-9.4	94	10	100,000	1,000	0.0	0.5
U /	N/A	N/A	15.41	45	1	96	1	2	32	N/A	N/A	N/A	10	100,000	1,000	0.0	0.5
U /	N/A	N/A	10.38	36	0	0	0	100	43	N/A	N/A	N/A	3	100,000	1,000	0.0	0.5
U /	N/A	N/A	11.24	596	0	0	0	100	7	N/A	N/A	N/A	2	100,000	1,000	0.0	0.3
U /	N/A	N/A	11.24	56	0	0	0	100	7	N/A	N/A	N/A	2	100,000	1,000	0.0	0.0
C+ / 6.0	11.7	0.63	9.46	94	6	90	3	1	41	52.5	-24.9	78	9	100,000	1,000	0.0	0.0
C+ / 6.8	11.9	0.62	11.67	7,484	4	93	1	2	50	48.2	-24.2	62	12	100,000	1,000	0.0	0.0
B- / 7.2	10.3	0.98	10.19	54	3	93	3	1	142	121.5	-16.2	46	11	100,000	1,000	0.0	0.0
C- / 4.2	11.5	1.02	31.10	1,345	1	96	2	1	93	108.3	-16.6	24	14	100,000	1,000	0.0	0.5
C- / 4.1	11.5	1.02	30.49	4	1	96	2	1	93	105.8	-16.7	22	14	100,000	1,000	0.0	0.5
U /	N/A	N/A	31.12	85	1	96	2	1	93	N/A	N/A	N/A	14	100,000	1,000	0.0	0.0
C / 4.5	11.9	1.09	23.70	1,334	1	95	2	2	70	120.8	-19.8	25	23	100,000	1,000	0.0	0.5
C / 4.6	11.9	1.09	23.71	6	1	95	2	2	70	118.2	-19.9	23	23	100,000	1,000	0.0	0.5
U /	N/A	N/A	23.70	86	1	95	2	2	70	N/A	N/A	N/A	23	100,000	1,000	0.0	0.0
C- / 4.0	11.9	0.96	26.25	1	6	88	4	2	115	141.0	-23.9	68	24	100,000	1,000	0.0	0.8
C- / 4.0	11.9	0.96	26.29	106	6	88	4	2	115	144.1	-23.8	71	24	100,000	1,000	0.0	0.8
C / 5.1	14.6	1.06	17.87	154	0	98	0	2	84	98.9	-16.4	65	14	100,000	1,000	0.0	1.0
C / 5.1	14.6	1.06	17.86	1	0	98	0	2	84	96.6	-16.5	62	14	100,000	1,000	0.0	1.0
U /	N/A	N/A	17.87	37	0	98	0	2	84	N/A	N/A	N/A	14	100,000	1,000	0.0	1.0
C+ / 6.3	10.3	1.00	56.80	309	3	94	1	2	10	132.1	-16.4	72	6	5,000,000	1,000	0.0	0.2
C+ / 6.3	10.3	1.00	56.41	387	3	94	1	2	10	129.8	-16.4	70	6	100,000	1,000	0.0	0.2

I. Index of Stock Mutual Funds

99 Pct = Best
0 Pct = Worst

Fund Type	Fund Name	Ticker Symbol	Overall Investment Rating	Phone	Performance Rating/Pts	3 Mo	6 Mo	1Yr / Pct	3Yr / Pct	5Yr / Pct	Dividend Yield	Expense Ratio
IX	SEI Instl Managed Tr-S&P 500 Idx I	SPIIX	A	(800) 342-5734	A- / 9.0	7.86	9.66	24.13 /70	9.95 /93	13.30 /87	1.26	0.79
GR	SEI Instl Managed Tr-S&P 500 Idx Y	SETYX	U	(800) 342-5734	U /	7.96	9.88	24.62 /72	--	--	1.68	0.29
SC	SEI Instl Managed Tr-Sm Cap Gr F	SSCGX	C-	(800) 342-5734	C+ / 5.6	4.67	8.53	28.10 /82	3.64 /39	11.04 /66	0.00	1.23
SC	SEI Instl Managed Tr-Sm Cap Gr I	SPWIX	C-	(800) 342-5734	C / 5.3	4.60	8.37	27.76 /81	3.37 /36	10.76 /64	0.00	1.48
GI	SEI Instl Managed Tr-Sm Cap Val F	SESVX	C+	(800) 342-5734	B- / 7.2	3.86	11.32	29.52 /85	5.94 /64	11.07 /66	0.55	1.23
GI	SEI Instl Managed Tr-Sm Cap Val I	SMVIX	C+	(800) 342-5734	B- / 7.0	3.75	11.21	29.21 /85	5.71 /62	10.81 /64	0.36	1.48
SC	SEI Instl Managed Tr-Sm Cap Val Y	SPVYX	U	(800) 342-5734	U /	3.87	11.45	29.83 /86	--	--	0.78	0.98
GR	SEI Instl Managed Tr-T/M Lg Cap F	TMLCX	B+	(800) 342-5734	B- / 7.1	6.54	9.42	22.21 /63	7.05 /72	12.11 /75	0.81	0.98
GR	SEI Instl Managed Tr-T/M Lg Cap Y	STLYX	U	(800) 342-5734	U /	6.60	9.55	22.50 /65	--	--	1.04	0.73
EM	SEI Instl Mgd Tr-Glb Mngd Volty F	SVTAX	B+	(800) 342-5734	B- / 7.3	7.27	4.75	14.10 /26	9.91 /93	11.97 /74	2.75	1.23
EM	SEI Instl Mgd Tr-Glb Mngd Volty I	SGMIX	B	(800) 342-5734	B- / 7.1	7.22	4.56	13.87 /25	9.65 /91	11.71 /72	2.46	1.48
GL	SEI Instl Mgd Tr-Glb Mngd Volty Y	SGLYX	U	(800) 342-5734	U /	7.24	4.82	14.36 /27	--	--	2.99	0.99
GL	SEI Instl Mgd Tr-Mlt-Asst Infl F	SIFAX	D+	(800) 342-5734	E / 0.3	0.80	1.15	4.89 / 4	-2.50 / 5	--	1.16	1.34
GL	SEI Instl Mgd Tr-Mlt-Asst Infl Y	SLFYX	U	(800) 342-5734	U /	0.85	1.32	5.06 / 4	--	--	1.44	1.15
GL	SEI Instl Mgd Tr-Multi-Asset Inc F	SIOAX	C+	(800) 342-5734	C- / 3.8	2.88	3.79	13.69 /24	5.00 /54	--	3.95	1.25
GL	SEI Instl Mgd Tr-Multi-Asset Inc Y	SLIYX	U	(800) 342-5734	U /	2.91	3.84	13.80 /25	--	--	4.04	1.00
AA	SEI Instl Mgd Tr-Multi-Asst Accum F	SAAAX	C-	(800) 342-5734	D+ / 2.8	5.60	1.16	11.39 /16	3.64 /39	--	0.72	1.38
AA	SEI Instl Mgd Tr-Multi-Asst Accum Y	SMOYX	U	(800) 342-5734	U /	5.60	1.18	11.59 /16	--	--	0.93	1.13
AG	SEI Instl Mgd Tr-Multi-Strat Alt F	SMSAX	C-	(800) 342-5734	D- / 1.3	2.03	2.67	6.76 / 5	0.79 /17	1.75 / 8	0.07	2.88
GL	SEI Instl Mgd Tr-T Mlt-Asst Captl F	SCLAX	C	(800) 342-5734	D- / 1.0	1.09	-0.20	1.70 / 2	1.38 /20	--	0.15	0.98
GL	SEI Instl Mgd Tr-T Mlt-Asst Captl Y	SMLYX	U	(800) 342-5734	U /	1.09	-0.01	1.79 / 2	--	--	0.25	0.74
IN	SEI Instl Mgd Tr-US Mgd Volty F	SVOAX	A-	(800) 342-5734	B / 8.2	6.93	6.79	17.52 /41	10.60 /96	13.98 /93	1.38	1.23
IN	SEI Instl Mgd Tr-US Mgd Volty I	SEVIX	A-	(800) 342-5734	B / 8.0	6.88	6.66	17.24 /39	10.31 /95	13.71 /91	1.15	1.48
GR	SEI Instl Mgd Tr-US Mgd Volty Y	SUSYX	U	(800) 342-5734	U /	6.99	6.92	17.87 /42	--	--	1.60	0.99
GI	SEI Large Cap Fund F	SLGAX	C+	(800) 342-5734	B- / 7.3	6.83	9.37	22.05 /62	7.30 /74	12.07 /75	0.89	0.97
GI	SEI Large Cap Fund Y	SLYCX	U	(800) 342-5734	U /	6.81	9.41	22.36 /64	--	--	1.12	0.72
SC	SEI Small Cap F	SLLAX	D+	(800) 342-5734	C / 5.2	4.00	9.10	27.31 /80	3.26 /34	10.42 /61	0.15	1.23
SC	SEI Small Cap Y	SMYFX	U	(800) 342-5734	U /	4.09	9.26	27.63 /81	--	--	0.38	0.99
GI	Selected American Shares D	SLADX	C+	(800) 279-0279	B+ / 8.8	5.00	10.05	30.97 /88	8.48 /83	12.41 /78	0.92	0.61
GI	Selected American Shares S	SLASX	C+	(800) 279-0279	B+ / 8.6	4.91	9.87	30.54 /87	8.12 /80	12.04 /75	0.65	0.95
FO	Selected International Fund D	SLSDX	D-	(800) 279-0279	D+ / 2.3	4.88	1.66	18.57 /45	0.85 /17	6.55 /32	0.37	0.83
FO	Selected International Fund S	SLSSX	D-	(800) 279-0279	D / 2.1	4.79	1.46	17.99 /43	0.38 /15	5.98 /28	0.00	1.41
BA	Sentinel Balanced A	SEBLX	C+	(800) 282-3863	C / 4.4	5.78	5.91	15.47 /32	6.10 /65	8.35 /45	1.19	1.05
BA	Sentinel Balanced C	SBACX	C+	(800) 282-3863	C / 4.7	5.56	5.50	14.58 /28	5.28 /57	7.49 /38	0.56	1.83
BA	Sentinel Balanced I	SIBLX	B-	(800) 282-3863	C+ / 5.6	5.78	6.02	15.67 /33	6.33 /67	8.55 /47	1.50	0.82
GI	Sentinel Common Stock A	SENCX	B+	(800) 282-3863	B / 8.0	8.22	9.90	23.96 /70	9.53 /91	12.55 /80	1.05	0.99
GI	Sentinel Common Stock C	SCSCX	B+	(800) 282-3863	B+ / 8.3	8.00	9.49	23.01 /67	8.68 /85	11.65 /71	0.45	1.78
GI	Sentinel Common Stock I	SICWX	A-	(800) 282-3863	A- / 9.1	8.30	10.07	24.32 /71	9.85 /93	12.87 /83	1.35	0.71
GI	Sentinel Common Stock R6	SCRLX	U	(800) 282-3863	U /	8.31	10.09	24.40 /71	--	--	1.41	1.76
FO	Sentinel International Equity A	SWRLX	E+	(800) 282-3863	D- / 1.1	7.67	-1.00	11.70 /17	0.88 /18	5.88 /28	0.60	1.42
FO	Sentinel International Equity C	SWFCX	E	(800) 282-3863	E+ / 0.8	7.30	-1.56	10.46 /13	-0.39 /12	4.42 /18	0.00	2.71
FO	Sentinel International Equity I	SIIEX	E+	(800) 282-3863	D / 1.8	7.74	-0.82	12.11 /18	1.28 /20	6.38 /31	1.10	1.03
GL	Sentinel Multi-Asset Income A	SECMX	D	(800) 282-3863	D / 2.0	2.92	0.96	10.77 /14	3.87 /41	5.40 /24	2.58	1.07
GL	Sentinel Multi-Asset Income C	SMKCX	D	(800) 282-3863	D / 2.2	2.73	0.57	10.01 /12	3.11 /33	4.62 /19	2.08	1.80
GL	Sentinel Multi-Asset Income I	SCSIX	D	(800) 282-3863	D+ / 2.9	2.98	1.01	10.99 /14	4.15 /45	5.64 /26	2.98	0.80
SC	Sentinel Small Company Fd A	SAGWX	D+	(800) 282-3863	B / 7.9	5.40	11.41	30.98 /88	8.73 /85	12.19 /76	0.00	1.21
SC	Sentinel Small Company Fd C	SSCOX	D+	(800) 282-3863	B / 8.2	5.29	10.85	29.96 /86	7.97 /79	11.35 /69	0.00	1.95
SC	Sentinel Small Company Fd I	SIGWX	C-	(800) 282-3863	A- / 9.0	5.59	11.83	31.45 /89	9.13 /88	12.60 /80	0.00	0.88
SC	Sentinel Small Company R6	SSRRX	U	(800) 282-3863	U /	5.75	11.94	31.73 /89	--	--	0.00	2.97
GR	Sentinel Sustainable Core Oppor A	MYPVX	B+	(800) 282-3863	B- / 7.0	7.67	8.85	22.66 /65	8.18 /80	11.80 /72	0.63	1.21
GR	Sentinel Sustainable Core Oppor I	CVALX	A-	(800) 282-3863	B / 8.1	7.77	9.05	23.02 /67	8.49 /83	12.10 /75	0.90	0.93
GR	● Sequoia Fund	SEQUX	E	(800) 686-6884	E+ / 0.6	5.78	7.39	5.96 / 5	-1.93 / 7	7.11 /35	0.00	1.03

● Denotes fund is closed to new investors
∗ Denotes fund is included in Section II

RISK			NET ASSETS		ASSET				Portfolio	BULL / BEAR		FUND MANAGER		MINIMUMS		LOADS	
	3 Year		NAV						Turnover	Last Bull	Last Bear	Manager	Manager	Initial	Additional	Front	Back
Risk	Standard		As of	Total	Cash	Stocks	Bonds	Other	Ratio	Market	Market	Quality	Tenure	Purch.	Purch.	End	End
Rating/Pts	Deviation	Beta	2/28/17	$(Mil)	%	%	%	%		Return	Return	Pct	(Years)	$	$	Load	Load
C+ / 6.3	10.3	1.00	56.74	7	3	94	1	2	10	127.1	-16.5	67	6	100,000	1,000	0.0	0.2
U /	N/A	N/A	56.41	26	3	94	1	2	10	N/A	N/A	N/A	6	100,000	1,000	0.0	0.0
C- / 4.0	16.1	0.99	30.91	309	1	96	2	1	124	118.6	-26.9	34	6	100,000	1,000	0.0	1.0
C- / 4.0	16.1	0.99	29.78	2	1	96	2	1	124	115.8	-27.0	31	6	100,000	1,000	0.0	1.0
C / 4.8	14.1	1.05	25.27	369	2	94	2	2	87	114.4	-24.6	16	23	100,000	1,000	0.0	1.0
C / 4.8	14.1	1.05	25.07	3	2	94	2	2	87	111.9	-24.7	15	23	100,000	1,000	0.0	1.0
U /	N/A	N/A	25.28	29	2	94	2	2	87	N/A	N/A	N/A	23	100,000	1,000	0.0	0.0
C+ / 6.8	10.8	1.02	22.55	3,242	2	93	3	2	89	118.7	-18.0	29	19	100,000	1,000	0.0	0.5
U /	N/A	N/A	22.56	257	2	93	3	2	89	N/A	N/A	N/A	19	100,000	1,000	0.0	0.5
C+ / 6.5	7.4	0.29	11.24	1,234	9	86	4	1	58	88.4	-4.1	99	11	100,000	1,000	0.0	0.8
C+ / 6.5	7.5	0.29	11.03	2	9	86	4	1	58	85.7	-4.2	99	11	100,000	1,000	0.0	0.8
U /	N/A	N/A	11.25	145	9	86	4	1	58	N/A	N/A	N/A	11	100,000	1,000	0.0	0.8
B / 8.5	4.3	0.14	8.69	830	0	30	69	1	73	N/A	N/A	40	5	100,000	1,000	0.0	0.8
U /	N/A	N/A	8.69	65	0	30	69	1	73	N/A	N/A	N/A	5	100,000	1,000	0.0	0.8
B- / 7.6	2.8	0.31	10.72	708	9	7	82	2	72	N/A	N/A	92	5	100,000	1,000	0.0	0.5
U /	N/A	N/A	10.72	120	9	7	82	2	72	N/A	N/A	N/A	5	100,000	1,000	0.0	0.5
B- / 7.0	8.0	0.87	9.64	2,315	64	7	28	1	55	N/A	N/A	37	5	100,000	1,000	0.0	0.8
U /	N/A	N/A	9.67	232	64	7	28	1	55	N/A	N/A	N/A	5	100,000	1,000	0.0	0.8
B / 8.3	3.3	0.28	9.89	513	31	26	41	2	149	11.4	-5.2	46	2	100,000	1,000	0.0	0.3
B+ / 9.9	2.0	0.19	10.06	677	87	0	11	2	234	N/A	N/A	77	5	100,000	1,000	0.0	0.3
U /	N/A	N/A	10.08	53	87	0	11	2	234	N/A	N/A	N/A	5	100,000	1,000	0.0	0.3
C+ / 6.6	8.0	0.67	17.74	1,128	2	96	1	1	43	119.2	-10.1	91	N/A	100,000	1,000	0.0	0.5
C+ / 6.6	8.0	0.67	17.73	2	2	96	1	1	43	116.3	-10.2	90	N/A	100,000	1,000	0.0	0.5
U /	N/A	N/A	17.75	556	2	96	1	1	43	N/A	N/A	N/A	13	100,000	1,000	0.0	0.5
C / 4.3	10.6	1.01	13.62	2,225	4	94	0	2	68	117.9	-18.0	32	8	100,000	1,000	0.0	0.5
U /	N/A	N/A	13.62	147	4	94	0	2	68	N/A	N/A	N/A	8	100,000	1,000	0.0	0.5
C- / 3.7	15.2	0.96	12.66	561	6	93	0	1	104	110.8	-26.7	32	8	100,000	1,000	0.0	1.0
U /	N/A	N/A	12.70	36	6	93	0	1	104	N/A	N/A	N/A	8	100,000	1,000	0.0	1.0
C- / 3.0	12.3	1.09	37.25	1,424	7	92	0	1	27	117.3	-19.7	36	23	10,000	25	0.0	0.0
C- / 3.0	12.4	1.09	37.18	921	7	92	0	1	27	113.3	-19.8	32	23	1,000	25	0.0	0.0
C / 4.8	14.6	1.01	11.22	53	6	93	0	1	43	65.6	-32.6	81	16	10,000	25	0.0	0.0
C / 4.8	14.6	1.00	11.15	9	6	93	0	1	43	61.0	-32.7	78	16	1,000	25	0.0	0.0
B- / 7.5	6.7	1.06	20.60	272	4	62	33	1	86	73.4	-11.4	52	13	1,000	50	5.0	0.0
B- / 7.5	6.7	1.06	20.65	47	4	62	33	1	86	66.1	-11.7	40	13	1,000	50	0.0	0.0
B- / 7.5	6.7	1.07	20.47	20	4	62	33	1	86	75.0	-11.3	54	13	1,000,000	0	0.0	0.0
C+ / 5.7	10.2	0.98	42.99	1,378	0	98	1	1	11	119.6	-17.0	65	23	1,000	50	5.0	0.0
C+ / 5.6	10.1	0.98	41.00	88	0	98	1	1	11	110.2	-17.3	55	23	1,000	50	0.0	0.0
C+ / 5.7	10.1	0.98	42.97	581	0	98	1	1	11	123.1	-16.8	69	23	1,000,000	0	0.0	0.0
U /	N/A	N/A	43.03	25	0	98	1	1	11	N/A	N/A	N/A	23	1,000,000	0	0.0	0.0
C- / 4.1	12.3	0.92	16.60	119	2	93	4	1	55	55.9	-24.1	81	5	1,000	50	5.0	2.0
C- / 4.1	12.3	0.92	15.73	7	2	93	4	1	55	44.5	-24.5	72	5	1,000	50	0.0	2.0
C- / 4.0	12.3	0.92	16.40	49	2	93	4	1	55	59.8	-24.0	83	5	1,000,000	0	0.0	2.0
C / 5.3	4.7	0.66	12.33	121	4	17	78	1	198	44.2	-8.1	79	8	1,000	50	5.0	0.0
C / 5.3	4.7	0.66	12.26	99	4	17	78	1	198	38.7	-8.4	74	8	1,000	50	0.0	0.0
C / 5.3	4.7	0.66	12.30	81	4	17	78	1	198	46.0	-8.1	81	8	1,000,000	0	0.0	0.0
E+ / 0.9	13.1	0.80	5.04	685	1	95	2	2	70	117.8	-20.3	90	4	1,000	50	5.0	2.0
E+ / 0.6	13.0	0.80	3.14	111	1	95	2	2	70	109.5	-20.6	88	4	1,000	50	0.0	2.0
D- / 1.3	13.0	0.79	5.44	313	1	95	2	2	70	122.1	-20.1	92	4	1,000,000	0	0.0	2.0
U /	N/A	N/A	5.11	29	1	95	2	2	70	N/A	N/A	N/A	4	1,000,000	0	0.0	2.0
C+ / 6.8	10.2	0.98	22.40	354	3	95	1	1	20	113.2	-17.2	48	9	1,000	50	5.0	0.0
C+ / 6.8	10.2	0.98	22.47	28	3	95	1	1	20	116.4	-17.1	52	9	1,000,000	0	0.0	0.0
C- / 3.3	13.1	0.43	170.09	4,191	0	88	11	1	10	71.6	-11.5	7	12	5,000	0	0.0	0.0

I. Index of Stock Mutual Funds

Fund Type	Fund Name	Ticker Symbol	Overall Investment Rating	Phone	Performance Rating/Pts	3 Mo	6 Mo	1Yr / Pct	3Yr / Pct	5Yr / Pct	Dividend Yield	Expense Ratio
GI	Sextant Core Fund	SCORX	C-	(800) 728-8762	D+ / 2.6	5.02	2.25	12.28 / 19	2.67 / 29	4.36 / 17	1.42	1.02
GR	Sextant Growth Fund	SSGFX	C	(800) 728-8762	C / 5.3	7.62	6.59	18.28 / 44	4.76 / 52	10.10 / 59	0.44	0.90
FO	Sextant International Fund	SSIFX	D+	(800) 728-8762	D+ / 2.9	7.91	3.95	17.71 / 42	1.16 / 19	2.04 / 8	1.24	1.05
GL	SFG Futures Strategy A	EFSAX	D	(855) 256-0149	E / 0.3	0.01	-5.23	-6.64 / 0	0.80 / 17	-0.52 / 4	3.77	2.95
GL	SFG Futures Strategy C	EFSCX	D	(855) 256-0149	E / 0.3	-0.13	-5.57	-7.31 / 0	-0.02 / 13	-1.25 / 3	3.60	3.70
GL	SFG Futures Strategy I	EFSIX	D	(855) 256-0149	E / 0.5	0.11	-5.09	-6.33 / 0	1.02 / 18	-0.29 / 4	4.58	2.70
GL	SFG Futures Strategy N	EFSNX	D	(855) 256-0149	E / 0.4	0.01	-5.23	-6.64 / 0	0.80 / 17	-0.82 / 4	3.95	2.95
IN	Shelton Core Value Direct	EQTIX	B+	(800) 955-9988	B / 7.6	4.49	8.24	20.32 / 54	8.92 / 86	12.04 / 75	1.94	0.76
IN	Shelton Core Value K	EQTKX	B+	(800) 955-9988	B- / 7.3	4.43	8.04	19.79 / 51	8.40 / 82	11.50 / 70	1.63	1.28
FO	Shelton Greater China Fund	SGCFX	C-	(800) 955-9988	C / 5.4	6.48	7.35	26.90 / 79	3.84 / 41	3.49 / 13	2.10	2.60
OT	Shelton Green Alpha	NEXTX	D-	(800) 955-9988	D- / 1.2	9.66	5.44	13.99 / 25	-0.92 / 10	--	0.00	1.31
FO	Shelton International Select Eqty A	WHVAX	E-	(888) 739-1390	E- / 0.2	7.96	6.32	20.03 / 52	-6.98 / 1	-1.57 / 3	0.85	1.27
FO	Shelton International Select Eqty I	WHVIX	E-	(888) 739-1390	E / 0.3	8.09	6.51	20.37 / 54	-6.74 / 2	-1.32 / 3	1.25	1.02
AA	Sierra Core Retirement A	SIRAX	C-	(866) 738-4363	D- / 1.0	2.50	-0.28	5.96 / 5	1.96 / 24	2.41 / 9	2.00	2.43
GL	Sierra Core Retirement A1	SIRZX	C-	(866) 738-4363	E+ / 0.9	2.49	-0.35	5.84 / 5	1.72 / 22	--	1.89	2.58
AA	Sierra Core Retirement C	SIRCX	C-	(866) 738-4363	D- / 1.2	2.33	-0.71	5.12 / 4	1.17 / 19	1.63 / 7	1.36	3.18
AA	Sierra Core Retirement I	SIRIX	C-	(866) 738-4363	D- / 1.5	2.51	-0.33	5.91 / 5	1.94 / 24	2.41 / 9	2.12	2.43
GL	Sierra Core Retirement I1	SIRJX	C-	(866) 738-4363	D- / 1.4	2.50	-0.40	5.76 / 5	1.72 / 22	--	1.96	2.58
AA	Sierra Core Retirement R	SIRRX	C-	(866) 738-4363	D- / 1.5	2.59	-0.20	6.23 / 5	2.11 / 25	2.60 / 10	2.39	2.18
GL	SilverPepper Cmdty Str Gl Mac Adv	SPCAX	C-	(855) 554-5540	E- / 0.2	0.00	2.98	4.91 / 4	-3.43 / 4	--	0.00	2.40
GL	SilverPepper Cmdty Str Gl Mac Inst	SPCIX	C-	(855) 554-5540	E / 0.3	0.11	3.08	4.99 / 4	-3.21 / 4	--	0.00	2.15
GI	SilverPepper Merger Arbitrage Adv	SPABX	C	(855) 554-5540	D / 1.9	0.89	1.08	2.30 / 2	4.74 / 51	--	0.00	7.03
GI	SilverPepper Merger Arbitrage Inst	SPAIX	C	(855) 554-5540	D / 2.1	1.07	1.25	2.57 / 2	4.98 / 54	--	0.00	6.78
GI	Sims Total Return Fund Inc	SIMFX	D-	(800) 443-6544	D- / 1.4	1.53	1.27	10.65 / 13	0.75 / 17	4.38 / 17	0.00	2.89
BA	Sit Balanced Fund	SIBAX	B-	(800) 332-5580	C / 5.2	5.76	4.90	12.65 / 20	6.46 / 68	8.32 / 45	1.55	1.02
EM	Sit Developing Mkts Growth Fund	SDMGX	E-	(800) 332-5580	E+ / 0.9	9.23	3.91	24.39 / 71	-3.01 / 4	-2.60 / 2	0.24	2.02
GI	Sit Dividend Growth I	SDVGX	B	(800) 332-5580	B / 8.2	7.67	8.43	21.45 / 60	9.75 / 92	12.27 / 77	1.44	1.07
GI	Sit Dividend Growth S	SDVSX	B-	(800) 332-5580	B / 8.0	7.56	8.25	21.16 / 58	9.47 / 90	11.98 / 74	1.22	1.32
GL	Sit Global Dividend Growth Class I	GDGIX	C-	(800) 332-5580	C- / 3.7	6.26	4.31	15.13 / 30	4.14 / 45	7.49 / 38	2.03	1.27
GL	Sit Global Dividend Growth Class S	GDGSX	D+	(800) 332-5580	C- / 3.5	6.28	4.19	14.86 / 29	3.89 / 42	7.23 / 36	1.80	1.52
FO	Sit International Growth Fund	SNGRX	E+	(800) 332-5580	E / 0.4	6.20	-2.10	6.73 / 5	-1.84 / 7	3.49 / 13	0.48	1.51
GR	Sit Large Cap Growth	SNIGX	D+	(800) 332-5580	B- / 7.3	8.73	8.33	18.13 / 43	8.57 / 84	11.48 / 70	0.47	1.00
MC	Sit Mid Cap Growth Fund	NBNGX	D	(800) 332-5580	C / 4.8	7.84	8.31	19.57 / 50	3.92 / 42	9.40 / 54	0.00	1.25
SC	Sit Small Cap Growth Fund	SSMGX	D-	(800) 332-5580	C- / 3.1	4.84	8.75	20.42 / 54	1.31 / 20	7.75 / 40	0.00	1.50
IN	SkyBridge Dividend Value A	SKYAX	U	(888) 739-1390	U /	0.76	2.56	14.52 / 28	--	--	2.23	1.28
IN	SkyBridge Dividend Value C	SKYCX	U	(888) 739-1390	U /	0.62	2.23	13.72 / 24	--	--	1.81	2.03
IN	SkyBridge Dividend Value I	SKYIX	U	(888) 739-1390	U /	0.86	2.67	14.75 / 29	--	--	2.56	1.03
GR	Small Cap Value Fund Inc	SCAPX	D+	(800) 704-6072	C+ / 5.7	0.92	17.05	41.28 / 98	0.53 / 16	10.38 / 61	0.43	0.95
GR	Smead Value Fund A	SVFAX	B-	(877) 807-4122	C+ / 6.9	9.40	11.85	20.03 / 52	7.78 / 77	--	0.57	1.30
GR	Smead Value Fund I1	SVFFX	A-	(877) 807-4122	B / 8.1	9.49	11.99	20.32 / 54	8.10 / 80	16.28 / 98	0.82	1.07
GR	Smead Value Fund Investor	SMVLX	A-	(877) 807-4122	B / 7.9	9.40	11.82	19.99 / 52	7.80 / 77	15.98 / 98	0.45	1.34
BA	SMI Conservative Allocation	SMILX	D-	(877) 764-3863	E / 0.4	3.08	-2.32	2.75 / 3	-1.49 / 8	4.31 / 17	0.87	1.89
AA	SMI Dynamic Allocation	SMIDX	D+	(877) 764-3863	D- / 1.0	4.80	-1.89	4.11 / 3	1.34 / 20	--	0.24	1.38
GR	Smith Group Lg Cap Core Grow Inst	BSLGX	C+	(877) 764-8465	B+ / 8.3	5.59	8.45	24.40 / 71	9.10 / 87	12.71 / 81	1.03	1.01
GR	Smith Group Lg Cap Core Grow Inv	BSLNX	A+	(877) 764-8465	B / 8.2	5.61	8.47	24.18 / 71	8.87 / 86	--	0.68	1.26
IN	Snow Capital Dividend Plus A	SDPAX	C+	(877) 766-9363	B- / 7.3	5.69	9.88	36.59 / 95	6.23 / 66	--	0.54	29.32
IN	Snow Capital Dividend Plus I	SDPIX	B-	(877) 766-9363	B+ / 8.5	5.77	10.01	36.93 / 96	6.50 / 68	--	0.79	29.07
GR	Snow Capital Focused Value A	SFOAX	D	(877) 766-9363	C / 4.9	5.79	10.43	35.68 / 95	1.84 / 23	--	0.23	29.32
GR	Snow Capital Focused Value I	SFOIX	C-	(877) 766-9363	C+ / 6.2	5.81	10.61	36.03 / 95	2.09 / 25	--	0.46	29.07
GR	Snow Capital Opportunity A	SNOAX	D	(877) 766-9363	C / 5.2	4.86	11.18	42.59 / 98	0.83 / 17	9.23 / 53	0.00	1.59
GR	Snow Capital Opportunity C	SNOCX	D	(877) 766-9363	C+ / 5.6	4.65	10.79	41.53 / 98	0.09 / 14	8.43 / 46	0.00	2.33
GR	Snow Capital Opportunity Inst	SNOIX	D+	(877) 766-9363	C+ / 6.5	4.94	11.36	43.00 / 98	1.10 / 19	9.50 / 55	0.34	1.33

● Denotes fund is closed to new investors
★ Denotes fund is included in Section II

RISK			NET ASSETS		ASSET				Portfolio	BULL / BEAR		FUND MANAGER		MINIMUMS		LOADS	
	3 Year		NAV							Last Bull	Last Bear	Manager	Manager	Initial	Additional	Front	Back
Risk Rating/Pts	Standard Deviation	Beta	As of 2/28/17	Total $(Mil)	Cash %	Stocks %	Bonds %	Other %	Turnover Ratio	Market Return	Market Return	Quality Pct	Tenure (Years)	Purch. $	Purch. $	End Load	End Load
B- / 7.6	6.3	0.57	11.85	10	4	55	39	2	24	37.1	-9.8	33	N/A	1,000	25	0.0	0.0
C / 5.3	11.7	1.08	24.14	37	5	94	0	1	68	90.5	-16.9	8	2	1,000	25	0.0	0.0
C / 5.5	11.4	0.86	15.36	65	6	93	0	1	0	24.7	-15.6	83	22	1,000	25	0.0	0.0
B- / 7.8	8.1	-0.06	9.06	N/A	53	2	39	6	12	N/A	N/A	79	6	2,500	250	4.5	1.0
B- / 7.6	8.1	-0.06	8.72	N/A	53	2	39	6	12	N/A	N/A	72	6	1,000	100	0.0	1.0
B- / 7.6	8.0	-0.06	8.91	26	53	2	39	6	12	N/A	N/A	80	6	500,000	10,000	0.0	1.0
B- / 7.8	8.1	-0.06	9.06	N/A	53	2	39	6	12	N/A	N/A	79	6	2,500	100	0.0	1.0
C+ / 6.6	10.0	0.93	25.03	182	0	91	8	1	20	112.4	-16.7	63	14	1,000	100	0.0	0.0
C+ / 6.6	10.1	0.93	24.78	6	0	91	8	1	20	106.8	-16.8	57	14	1,000	100	0.0	0.0
C- / 4.2	17.3	0.92	7.56	8	0	0	0	100	0	33.3	-26.3	93	5	1,000	100	0.0	2.0
C / 5.4	15.9	1.22	15.32	36	3	96	0	1	13	N/A	N/A	1	4	1,000	100	0.0	0.0
C- / 3.1	15.1	0.97	17.24	5	9	90	0	1	40	14.9	-29.0	5	1	5,000	100	5.8	0.0
C- / 3.1	15.1	0.97	17.25	37	9	90	0	1	40	16.5	-29.0	6	1	500,000	0	0.0	0.0
B / 8.5	3.3	0.24	22.86	46	10	12	77	1	153	14.7	-1.4	75	10	10,000	1,000	5.8	0.0
B / 8.5	3.3	0.11	23.08	3	10	12	77	1	153	N/A	N/A	84	10	10,000	1,000	5.8	0.0
B / 8.5	3.3	0.24	23.00	74	10	12	77	1	153	10.1	-1.7	66	10	10,000	1,000	0.0	0.0
B / 8.5	3.3	0.24	22.82	30	10	12	77	1	153	14.6	-1.5	75	10	10,000	1,000	0.0	0.0
B / 8.5	3.3	0.12	22.97	14	10	12	77	1	153	N/A	N/A	84	10	10,000	1,000	0.0	0.0
B / 8.5	3.3	0.25	22.69	307	10	12	77	1	153	15.8	-1.3	75	10	100,000	1,000	0.0	0.0
B+ / 9.9	4.2	0.06	8.98	132	99	0	0	1	2,213	N/A	N/A	28	4	5,000	100	0.0	2.0
B+ / 9.9	4.3	0.06	9.05	101	99	0	0	1	2,213	N/A	N/A	30	4	500,000	100	0.0	2.0
B / 8.6	2.4	0.05	10.91	6	8	91	0	1	352	N/A	N/A	93	2	5,000	100	0.0	2.0
B / 8.6	2.4	0.05	11.00	53	8	91	0	1	352	N/A	N/A	94	2	500,000	100	0.0	2.0
C / 4.9	10.2	0.75	10.67	9	12	52	34	2	86	43.7	-13.4	6	N/A	500	100	0.0	0.0
B- / 7.8	6.5	1.02	21.92	25	1	63	35	1	54	69.6	-9.4	60	9	5,000	100	0.0	0.0
D+ / 2.7	15.9	0.95	13.41	8	1	97	0	2	28	4.4	-24.4	18	23	5,000	100	0.0	2.0
C / 4.9	9.7	0.93	16.46	974	1	98	0	1	76	116.0	-16.0	73	14	100,000	100	0.0	2.0
C / 4.9	9.7	0.93	16.39	68	1	98	0	1	76	113.0	-16.0	70	14	5,000	100	0.0	2.0
C+ / 5.8	9.5	0.67	14.03	24	3	96	0	1	48	72.0	-19.2	94	9	100,000	100	0.0	0.0
C+ / 5.8	9.4	0.67	14.02	3	3	96	0	1	48	69.7	-19.3	93	9	5,000	100	0.0	0.0
C / 5.3	11.1	0.85	14.72	20	1	97	0	2	38	41.0	-24.4	52	26	5,000	100	0.0	2.0
D / 1.9	10.6	0.98	38.09	117	1	98	0	1	20	109.4	-15.5	53	33	5,000	100	0.0	2.0
D+ / 2.9	11.7	0.89	17.31	151	2	96	0	2	22	102.3	-22.8	20	20	5,000	100	0.0	2.0
C- / 3.3	13.8	0.83	52.43	89	1	98	0	1	27	86.2	-22.0	21	16	5,000	100	0.0	2.0
U /	N/A	N/A	11.41	138	1	98	0	1	104	N/A	N/A	N/A	N/A	1,000	50	5.8	0.0
U /	N/A	N/A	11.34	61	1	98	0	1	104	N/A	N/A	N/A	N/A	1,000	50	0.0	0.0
U /	N/A	N/A	11.41	279	1	98	0	1	104	N/A	N/A	N/A	N/A	50,000	0	0.0	0.0
D+ / 2.9	23.4	1.07	39.05	14	4	95	0	1	48	113.3	-22.0	2	12	100,000	100	0.0	2.0
B- / 7.1	11.8	1.04	41.97	154	4	94	0	2	20	N/A	N/A	35	9	3,000	100	5.8	0.0
C+ / 6.8	11.8	1.04	42.18	805	4	94	0	2	20	164.4	-15.3	38	9	1,000,000	100	0.0	0.0
C+ / 6.9	11.8	1.04	42.23	205	4	94	0	2	20	160.7	-15.4	35	9	3,000	100	0.0	0.0
C+ / 6.9	6.3	0.58	9.41	16	2	58	39	1	378	38.9	-13.2	10	7	2,500	100	0.0	2.0
B- / 7.9	9.0	0.78	11.04	169	1	98	0	1	248	N/A	N/A	21	4	2,500	100	0.0	2.0
C- / 3.2	11.0	1.01	9.19	42	0	0	0	100	61	124.8	-19.1	55	10	25,000	100	0.0	0.0
B- / 7.7	11.0	1.01	9.21	1	0	0	0	100	61	N/A	N/A	52	10	2,500	100	0.0	0.0
C / 4.3	13.5	1.12	22.57	N/A	8	91	0	1	67	N/A	N/A	13	4	2,500	0	5.3	0.5
C- / 4.2	13.5	1.12	22.59	3	8	91	0	1	67	N/A	N/A	15	4	1,000,000	0	0.0	0.5
C- / 3.2	17.0	1.40	21.60	N/A	4	95	0	1	72	N/A	N/A	1	4	2,500	0	5.3	0.5
C- / 3.2	17.0	1.40	21.62	2	4	95	0	1	72	N/A	N/A	1	4	1,000,000	0	0.0	0.5
D+ / 2.7	16.1	1.18	26.55	80	13	82	3	2	68	97.5	-26.9	2	11	2,500	0	5.3	0.5
D+ / 2.7	16.1	1.18	24.74	28	13	82	3	2	68	90.1	-27.0	1	11	2,500	0	0.0	0.5
D+ / 2.7	16.2	1.18	26.83	109	13	82	3	2	68	100.2	-26.8	2	11	1,000,000	0	0.0	0.5

99 Pct = Best
0 Pct = Worst

Fund Type	Fund Name	Ticker Symbol	Overall Investment Rating	Phone	Performance Rating/Pts	3 Mo	6 Mo	1Yr / Pct	Annualized 3Yr / Pct	Annualized 5Yr / Pct	Dividend Yield	Expense Ratio
GL	Snow Capital Small Cap Value A	SNWAX	D-	(877) 766-9363	C- / 3.1	2.34	8.35	29.59 / 85	1.33 / 20	8.51 / 46	0.00	1.93
GL	Snow Capital Small Cap Value C	SNWCX	D-	(877) 766-9363	C- / 3.5	2.14	7.95	28.65 / 83	0.60 / 16	7.71 / 40	0.00	2.42
GL	Snow Capital Small Cap Value Inst	SNWIX	D	(877) 766-9363	C / 4.3	2.40	8.50	29.97 / 86	1.59 / 22	8.79 / 49	0.00	1.67
GR	Sound Mind Investing	SMIFX	D-	(877) 764-3863	C- / 3.2	4.28	6.76	18.50 / 45	2.52 / 28	9.19 / 52	0.00	1.97
GR	Sound Shore Inst	SSHVX	A	(800) 754-8758	B+ / 8.7	6.53	10.66	29.84 / 86	8.07 / 79	--	1.02	0.83
GR	Sound Shore Investor	SSHFX	B	(800) 754-8758	B+ / 8.6	6.48	10.60	29.64 / 86	7.88 / 78	14.00 / 93	0.95	0.93
GR	Sparrow Growth Fd A	SGFFX	E+	(888) 727-3301	E+ / 0.7	6.52	4.17	10.25 / 12	-0.39 / 12	6.54 / 32	0.00	2.45
GR	Sparrow Growth Fd C	SGFCX	E+	(888) 727-3301	E+ / 0.9	6.39	3.88	9.65 / 11	-0.89 / 10	7.17 / 36	0.00	2.93
GR	Sparrow Growth Fd NL	SGNFX	E+	(888) 727-3301	D- / 1.2	6.63	4.32	10.49 / 13	-0.14 / 13	6.80 / 33	0.00	2.18
AA	Spectrum Low Volatility Inv	SVARX	A+	(855) 747-9555	C+ / 6.6	5.67	5.76	20.08 / 52	7.20 / 73	--	6.33	2.90
EN	Spirit of America Energy A	SOAEX	U	(800) 452-4892	U /	9.15	11.77	40.31 / 97	--	--	13.67	1.51
AA	Spirit Of America Inc and Opp A	SOAOX	C-	(800) 452-4892	D / 2.1	4.51	-1.10	12.08 / 18	3.89 / 42	--	4.15	1.28
GR	Spirit Of America Large Cap Value A	SOAVX	C+	(800) 452-4892	C+ / 6.7	8.10	9.66	21.64 / 60	7.47 / 75	10.27 / 60	1.13	1.60
RE	Spirit Of America Real Estate A	SOAAX	C-	(800) 452-4892	C+ / 5.7	8.18	0.39	15.99 / 34	8.70 / 85	9.36 / 54	2.32	1.57
FO	SS Inst Intl Equity Inv	SIEIX	E+	(800) 843-2639	E+ / 0.7	5.66	2.50	13.67 / 24	-1.75 / 7	4.12 / 16	1.81	0.56
FO	SS Inst Intl Equity Svc	SIESX	E+	(800) 843-2639	E+ / 0.6	5.54	2.37	13.48 / 23	-1.99 / 7	3.86 / 15	1.60	0.81
GR	SS Inst Premier Gro Eq Inv	SSPGX	B	(800) 843-2639	A / 9.4	11.42	9.75	23.96 / 70	10.19 / 94	14.53 / 96	0.80	0.38
GR	SS Inst Premier Gro Eq Svc	SSPSX	B	(800) 843-2639	A- / 9.2	11.28	9.60	23.68 / 69	9.89 / 93	14.23 / 94	0.58	0.63
IX	SS Inst S&P 500 Index Inv	SIDIX	A+	(800) 843-2639	A- / 9.2	7.77	9.75	24.64 / 72	10.41 / 95	13.80 / 92	1.60	0.16
IX	SS Inst S&P 500 Index Svc	SIDSX	A+	(800) 843-2639	A- / 9.2	8.00	9.84	24.60 / 72	10.21 / 94	13.56 / 89	1.57	0.41
SC	SS Inst Sm-Cp Eq Inv	SIVIX	B-	(800) 843-2639	A / 9.4	4.82	11.54	36.48 / 95	8.44 / 82	12.92 / 83	0.20	0.89
SC	SS Inst Sm-Cp Eq Svc	SSQSX	B-	(800) 843-2639	A- / 9.2	4.76	11.41	36.19 / 95	8.18 / 80	12.63 / 80	0.04	1.14
AA	SS Inst Strat Invest Inv	SIIVX	C-	(800) 843-2639	C- / 3.7	4.91	3.78	14.30 / 27	4.04 / 43	6.77 / 33	1.98	0.37
AA	SS Inst Strat Invest Svc	SISVX	C-	(800) 843-2639	C- / 3.5	4.86	3.63	14.03 / 26	3.78 / 40	6.50 / 32	1.75	0.62
GR	SS Inst US Equity Inv	SUSIX	C+	(800) 843-2639	B+ / 8.9	8.85	10.47	26.07 / 76	8.76 / 85	12.96 / 83	1.45	0.37
GR	SS Inst US Equity Svc	SUSSX	C+	(800) 843-2639	B+ / 8.7	8.77	10.39	25.72 / 75	8.49 / 83	12.83 / 82	1.13	0.62
GR	SS Inst US Lg Cap Core Eqty Inv	SILCX	C-	(800) 843-2639	B+ / 8.3	8.48	10.71	25.56 / 75	7.76 / 77	12.21 / 76	3.34	0.43
GR	SS Inst US Lg Cap Core Eqty Svc	SSLVX	C-	(800) 843-2639	B / 8.2	8.56	10.67	25.67 / 75	7.60 / 76	11.99 / 74	2.65	0.68
SC	● SSgA Dynamic Small Cap N	SVSCX	B+	(800) 843-2639	B+ / 8.4	3.61	12.16	30.71 / 88	7.65 / 76	14.18 / 94	0.19	2.26
SC	SSgA Enhanced Small Cap K	SSEWX	U	(800) 843-2639	U /	4.16	12.38	31.96 / 90	--	--	1.16	1.43
SC	● SSgA Enhanced Small Cap N	SESPX	C+	(800) 843-2639	B+ / 8.5	4.10	12.32	31.70 / 89	7.41 / 75	13.15 / 85	0.37	1.68
GL	SSgA Intl Stock Selection K	SSIQX	U	(800) 843-2639	U /	7.18	5.69	14.52 / 28	--	--	2.91	1.02
FO	● SSgA Intl Stock Selection N	SSAIX	D	(800) 843-2639	D- / 1.3	7.09	5.60	14.31 / 27	-0.39 / 12	5.37 / 24	2.64	1.27
IX	SSgA S&P 500 Index N	SVSPX	A+	(800) 843-2639	A / 9.3	8.00	9.93	24.79 / 73	10.47 / 96	13.87 / 92	1.25	0.20
GL	STAAR Inv Trust International Fund	SITIX	E	(800) 332-7738	E- / 0.2	6.52	2.84	13.69 / 24	-6.49 / 2	-2.38 / 2	0.00	2.90
AA	STAAR Inv Trust Lg Comp Stock	SITLX	E+	(800) 332-7738	D / 1.9	2.06	0.41	11.59 / 16	2.11 / 25	7.12 / 35	0.00	2.50
SC	STAAR Inv Trust Sm Comp Stock	SITSX	E	(800) 332-7738	E+ / 0.9	2.70	7.98	24.39 / 71	-3.22 / 4	4.03 / 15	0.00	2.81
AA	Stadion Managed Risk 100 A	ETFFX	D-	(866) 383-7636	E+ / 0.7	7.89	7.41	14.61 / 28	-1.65 / 8	0.42 / 5	0.00	2.05
AA	Stadion Managed Risk 100 C	ETFYX	D-	(866) 383-7636	E+ / 0.8	7.64	7.00	13.75 / 24	-2.43 / 6	-0.35 / 4	0.00	2.84
AA	Stadion Managed Risk 100 I	ETFVX	D	(866) 383-7636	D- / 1.1	7.90	7.42	14.79 / 29	-1.50 / 8	0.59 / 5	0.00	1.87
AA	Stadion Tactical Defensive A	ETFRX	C-	(866) 383-7636	D+ / 2.9	6.90	8.88	15.69 / 33	2.86 / 30	5.10 / 22	0.00	2.22
AA	Stadion Tactical Defensive C	ETFZX	C	(866) 383-7636	C- / 3.4	6.77	8.56	14.86 / 29	2.12 / 25	4.29 / 17	0.00	2.99
AA	Stadion Tactical Defensive I	ETFWX	C+	(866) 383-7636	C- / 4.2	6.97	9.00	15.93 / 34	3.14 / 33	5.31 / 23	0.00	2.02
GR	Stadion Tactical Growth A	ETFAX	C	(866) 383-7636	C- / 4.1	4.07	8.03	19.10 / 48	5.05 / 55	--	0.12	1.94
GR	Stadion Tactical Growth C	ETFCX	C+	(866) 383-7636	C / 4.6	3.88	7.63	18.19 / 44	4.24 / 46	--	0.00	2.72
GR	Stadion Tactical Growth I	ETFOX	B-	(866) 383-7636	C / 5.5	4.14	8.22	19.41 / 49	5.30 / 58	7.63 / 39	0.19	1.72
AA	Stadion Trilogy Alternative Ret A	STTGX	C	(866) 383-7636	D- / 1.5	2.27	2.54	8.62 / 9	3.01 / 32	--	0.76	1.93
AA	Stadion Trilogy Alternative Ret C	STTCX	C	(866) 383-7636	D / 1.8	2.03	2.10	7.71 / 7	2.20 / 25	--	0.23	2.75
AA	Stadion Trilogy Alternative Ret I	STTIX	C	(866) 383-7636	D+ / 2.3	2.23	2.56	8.79 / 9	3.23 / 34	--	0.97	1.76
BA	State Farm Balanced	STFBX	C+	(800) 447-4930	C / 5.3	4.93	4.37	14.09 / 26	6.60 / 69	7.57 / 39	2.50	0.13
IX	State Farm Equity & Bond A	NBSAX	B-	(800) 447-4930	C- / 3.9	4.56	4.74	12.40 / 19	6.48 / 68	8.58 / 47	1.06	1.00
IX	State Farm Equity & Bond B	NBSBX	B	(800) 447-4930	C / 4.3	4.37	4.37	11.64 / 17	5.77 / 62	7.87 / 41	0.46	1.71

● Denotes fund is closed to new investors
* Denotes fund is included in Section II

RISK			NET ASSETS		ASSET					BULL / BEAR		FUND MANAGER		MINIMUMS		LOADS	
	3 Year		NAV						Portfolio	Last Bull	Last Bear	Manager	Manager	Initial	Additional	Front	Back
Risk Rating/Pts	Standard Deviation	Beta	As of 2/28/17	Total $(Mil)	Cash %	Stocks %	Bonds %	Other %	Turnover Ratio	Market Return	Market Return	Quality Pct	Tenure (Years)	Purch. $	Purch. $	End Load	End Load
C- /3.2	18.6	0.84	30.61	21	0	100	0	0	61	103.8	-28.4	84	7	2,500	0	5.3	0.5
C- /3.1	18.6	0.84	29.05	9	0	100	0	0	61	95.8	-28.7	79	7	2,500	0	0.0	0.5
C- /3.3	18.6	0.84	31.14	28	0	100	0	0	61	106.6	-28.4	85	7	1,000,000	0	0.0	0.5
C- /3.3	10.7	0.96	11.21	199	2	94	2	2	216	81.3	-21.3	5	12	2,500	100	0.0	2.0
C+ /6.7	12.4	1.15	46.56	537	3	96	0	1	39	N/A	N/A	25	32	1,000,000	0	0.0	0.0
C /4.4	12.4	1.15	46.42	1,502	3	96	0	1	39	141.9	-22.7	24	32	10,000	0	0.0	0.0
C /4.6	13.2	1.01	17.97	6	0	100	0	0	117	71.3	-16.0	2	19	1,000	50	5.8	0.0
C /4.5	13.1	1.01	17.15	N/A	0	100	0	0	117	N/A	N/A	1	19	1,000	50	0.0	0.0
C /4.6	13.2	1.01	17.38	3	0	100	0	0	117	73.8	-15.9	2	19	2,500	100	0.0	0.0
B+ /9.9	4.0	0.33	21.51	50	0	0	0	100	649	N/A	N/A	94	4	1,000	500	0.0	0.0
U /	N/A	N/A	5.17	680	95	4	0	1	15	N/A	N/A	N/A	2	500	50	5.8	0.0
B- /7.7	6.6	0.71	9.71	59	16	40	43	1	8	N/A	N/A	57	4	500	50	4.8	0.0
C+ /6.5	10.6	1.01	20.09	83	1	98	0	1	19	97.7	-17.3	34	9	500	50	5.3	0.0
C /4.4	13.5	0.98	12.03	111	4	94	0	2	37	87.0	-20.4	49	2	500	50	5.3	0.0
C /5.5	12.6	1.00	11.77	1,189	0	96	2	2	33	44.1	-25.8	54	N/A	5,000,000	0	0.0	2.0
C /5.5	12.6	1.00	11.72	17	0	96	2	2	33	42.2	-25.9	51	N/A	5,000,000	0	0.0	2.0
C- /4.2	13.5	1.19	14.03	343	0	98	1	1	21	144.7	-16.8	44	N/A	5,000,000	0	0.0	0.0
C- /4.2	13.5	1.19	13.86	13	0	98	1	1	21	141.3	-16.8	40	N/A	5,000,000	0	0.0	0.0
B- /7.1	10.3	1.00	22.32	9	2	95	2	1	12	132.5	-16.3	72	20	5,000,000	0	0.0	0.0
B- /7.1	10.3	1.00	22.80	8	2	95	2	1	12	129.8	-16.4	70	20	5,000,000	0	0.0	0.0
C- /3.4	14.1	0.88	19.37	1,439	1	94	4	1	33	134.2	-21.7	87	N/A	5,000,000	0	0.0	0.0
C- /3.5	14.0	0.88	19.40	2	1	94	4	1	33	131.0	-21.7	86	N/A	5,000,000	0	0.0	0.0
C+ /6.2	7.1	1.10	12.11	755	1	56	42	1	109	59.3	-13.7	24	N/A	5,000,000	0	0.0	0.0
C+ /6.2	7.1	1.09	12.02	N/A	1	56	42	1	109	57.1	-13.8	22	N/A	5,000,000	0	0.0	0.0
D+ /2.9	11.6	1.10	13.88	634	0	97	1	2	43	127.0	-18.7	38	N/A	5,000,000	0	0.0	0.0
C- /3.1	11.6	1.10	14.66	N/A	0	97	1	2	43	125.3	-18.7	35	N/A	5,000,000	0	0.0	0.0
D /2.0	11.5	1.09	7.96	26	1	95	3	1	54	118.8	-19.1	28	N/A	5,000,000	0	0.0	0.0
D /2.1	11.5	1.10	7.94	1	1	95	3	1	54	116.4	-19.2	26	N/A	5,000,000	0	0.0	0.0
C+ /6.1	14.1	0.87	45.44	30	2	97	0	1	115	155.0	-23.3	84	7	1,000	100	0.0	0.0
U /	N/A	N/A	15.38	30	2	97	0	1	77	N/A	N/A	N/A	12	10,000,000	0	0.0	0.0
C- /3.3	15.3	0.96	15.47	5	2	97	0	1	77	136.4	-22.8	79	12	1,000	100	0.0	0.0
U /	N/A	N/A	10.38	72	2	97	0	1	105	N/A	N/A	N/A	7	10,000,000	0	0.0	0.0
C+ /6.4	11.2	0.90	10.39	222	2	97	0	1	105	51.0	-26.0	71	7	1,000	100	0.0	0.0
B- /7.7	10.3	1.00	34.55	1,547	0	0	0	100	7	133.4	-16.4	73	10	10,000	100	0.0	0.0
C- /3.6	12.1	1.62	10.13	2	8	89	2	1	17	2.1	-24.0	1	20	1,000	50	0.0	0.0
C- /4.2	13.4	1.57	14.83	3	7	90	2	1	30	65.3	-17.9	3	20	1,000	50	0.0	0.0
C- /3.0	16.1	0.90	13.67	3	6	93	0	1	39	45.7	-23.2	3	20	1,000	50	0.0	0.0
C+ /6.6	8.7	0.93	9.57	38	1	98	0	1	861	3.4	-8.2	3	8	1,000	250	5.8	0.0
C+ /6.5	8.7	0.93	9.02	19	1	98	0	1	861	-0.8	-8.6	3	8	1,000	250	0.0	0.0
C+ /6.6	8.7	0.94	9.70	17	1	98	0	1	861	4.5	-8.2	3	8	500,000	5,000	0.0	0.0
B- /7.2	7.5	0.85	12.39	21	0	98	0	2	645	36.2	-12.2	30	8	1,000	250	5.8	0.0
B- /7.1	7.4	0.85	11.67	9	0	98	0	2	645	30.8	-12.5	23	8	1,000	250	0.0	0.0
B- /7.2	7.5	0.85	12.59	12	0	98	0	2	645	37.9	-12.2	33	8	500,000	5,000	0.0	0.0
B- /7.1	8.7	0.77	10.99	105	8	81	9	2	287	N/A	N/A	36	4	1,000	250	5.8	0.0
B- /7.1	8.7	0.77	10.72	93	8	81	9	2	287	N/A	N/A	27	4	1,000	250	0.0	0.0
B- /7.1	8.7	0.77	11.07	168	8	81	9	2	287	73.3	-15.5	39	4	500,000	5,000	0.0	0.0
B+ /9.0	3.1	0.24	11.15	29	4	46	48	2	36	N/A	N/A	82	5	1,000	250	5.8	0.0
B+ /9.0	3.2	0.25	10.95	11	4	46	48	2	36	N/A	N/A	76	5	1,000	250	0.0	0.0
B+ /9.0	3.1	0.25	11.17	56	4	46	48	2	36	N/A	N/A	83	5	500,000	5,000	0.0	0.0
B- /7.1	6.0	0.93	65.32	1,846	0	61	37	2	11	60.1	-9.1	70	26	250	50	0.0	0.0
B /8.9	6.0	0.55	11.46	134	0	58	40	2	1	72.5	-10.2	79	N/A	250	50	5.0	0.0
B /8.9	6.0	0.55	11.46	14	0	58	40	2	1	66.4	-10.4	74	N/A	250	50	0.0	0.0

Fund Type	Fund Name	Ticker Symbol	Overall Investment Rating	Phone	Perfor-mance Rating/Pts	3 Mo	6 Mo	1Yr / Pct	3Yr / Pct	5Yr / Pct	Dividend Yield	Expense Ratio
IX	State Farm Equity & Bond Inst	SEBIX	B+	(800) 447-4930	C / 5.2	4.60	4.87	12.68 /20	6.75 /70	8.84 /49	1.36	0.76
IX	State Farm Equity & Bond Legacy B	SLBBX	B	(800) 447-4930	C / 4.6	4.47	4.56	11.91 /18	6.06 /65	8.13 /43	0.73	1.41
IX	State Farm Equity & Bond Premier	SLBAX	B-	(800) 447-4930	C- / 4.0	4.61	4.79	12.51 /20	6.54 /69	8.59 /47	1.08	1.01
IX	State Farm Equity & Bond R1	REBOX	B	(800) 447-4930	C / 4.7	4.46	4.55	12.06 /18	6.15 /66	8.24 /44	0.86	1.33
IX	State Farm Equity & Bond R2	REBTX	B	(800) 447-4930	C / 4.8	4.45	4.64	12.23 /19	6.33 /67	8.44 /46	1.02	1.13
IX	State Farm Equity & Bond R3	REBHX	B+	(800) 447-4930	C / 5.1	4.61	4.80	12.55 /20	6.66 /70	8.78 /49	1.32	0.83
IN	State Farm Equity A	SNEAX	B	(800) 447-4930	B- / 7.1	7.08	9.56	20.17 /53	8.91 /86	12.85 /82	0.41	1.15
IN	State Farm Equity B	SNEBX	B	(800) 447-4930	B- / 7.4	6.79	9.05	19.19 /48	8.13 /80	12.04 /75	0.00	1.85
IN	State Farm Equity Inst	SLEIX	B+	(800) 447-4930	B / 8.2	6.99	9.56	20.36 /54	9.18 /88	13.11 /85	0.67	0.90
IN	State Farm Equity LegB	SLEBX	B+	(800) 447-4930	B / 7.7	6.85	9.22	19.62 /50	8.46 /83	12.37 /78	0.00	1.55
IN	State Farm Equity Premier	SLEAX	B	(800) 447-4930	B- / 7.2	7.05	9.53	20.30 /54	8.96 /87	12.85 /82	0.46	1.15
IN	State Farm Equity R1	SREOX	B+	(800) 447-4930	B / 7.7	6.90	9.26	19.72 /51	8.54 /83	12.49 /79	0.16	1.47
IN	State Farm Equity R2	SRETX	B+	(800) 447-4930	B / 7.9	6.96	9.33	19.94 /52	8.75 /85	12.68 /81	0.30	1.27
IN	State Farm Equity R3	SREHX	B+	(800) 447-4930	B / 8.1	7.05	9.51	20.30 /54	9.11 /88	13.02 /84	0.64	0.97
GR	State Farm Growth	STFGX	B	(800) 447-4930	B / 8.0	6.79	6.99	22.51 /65	8.87 /86	11.00 /66	2.36	0.12
FO	State Farm Intl Equity A	SNIAX	E+	(800) 447-4930	E / 0.4	6.73	1.24	10.27 /12	-1.96 / 7	2.82 /10	0.00	1.52
FO	State Farm Intl Equity B	SNIBX	E+	(800) 447-4930	E / 0.5	6.48	0.88	9.52 /11	-2.61 / 5	2.19 / 8	0.00	2.22
FO	State Farm Intl Equity Inst	SFIIX	E+	(800) 447-4930	E+ / 0.7	6.73	1.40	10.57 /13	-1.70 / 7	3.08 /11	0.07	1.27
FO	State Farm Intl Equity LegB	SFFBX	E+	(800) 447-4930	E+ / 0.6	6.58	1.15	9.92 /11	-2.34 / 6	2.41 / 9	0.00	1.92
FO	State Farm Intl Equity Prem	SFFAX	E+	(800) 447-4930	E / 0.4	6.65	1.32	10.38 /13	-1.93 / 7	2.84 /10	0.00	1.42
FO	State Farm Intl Equity R1	RIEOX	E+	(800) 447-4930	E+ / 0.6	6.58	1.15	10.03 /12	-2.24 / 6	2.50 / 9	0.00	1.84
FO	State Farm Intl Equity R2	RIETX	E+	(800) 447-4930	E+ / 0.6	6.63	1.24	10.18 /12	-2.04 / 7	2.71 /10	0.00	1.64
FO	State Farm Intl Equity R3	RIEHX	E+	(800) 447-4930	E+ / 0.7	6.67	1.34	10.51 /13	-1.77 / 7	3.00 /11	0.02	1.34
FO	State Farm Intl Index A	NFSAX	D-	(800) 447-4930	E+ / 0.6	7.52	4.13	15.02 /30	-1.63 / 8	4.22 /16	2.23	0.87
FO	State Farm Intl Index B	NFSBX	D-	(800) 447-4930	E+ / 0.8	7.30	3.72	14.24 /27	-2.29 / 6	3.54 /13	1.70	1.57
FO	State Farm Intl Index Inst	SFFFX	D-	(800) 447-4930	D- / 1.1	7.61	4.22	15.31 /31	-1.38 / 8	4.47 /18	2.61	0.62
FO	State Farm Intl Index LegB	SIIBX	D-	(800) 447-4930	E+ / 0.9	7.39	3.91	14.63 /28	-2.01 / 7	3.79 /14	1.98	1.27
FO	State Farm Intl Index Premier	SIIAX	D-	(800) 447-4930	E+ / 0.6	7.58	4.09	15.09 /30	-1.61 / 8	4.23 /16	2.36	0.77
FO	State Farm Intl Index R1	RIIOX	D-	(800) 447-4930	E+ / 0.9	7.41	3.83	14.68 /28	-1.96 / 7	3.88 /15	2.07	1.19
FO	State Farm Intl Index R2	RIITX	D-	(800) 447-4930	E+ / 0.9	7.39	3.99	14.90 /29	-1.77 / 7	4.07 /16	2.22	0.99
FO	State Farm Intl Index R3	RIIHX	D-	(800) 447-4930	D- / 1.0	7.54	4.16	15.23 /31	-1.45 / 8	4.40 /18	2.55	0.69
AA	State Farm LifePath 2020 A	NLWAX	C-	(800) 447-4930	D / 1.9	4.02	2.43	11.24 /15	3.17 /33	4.91 /21	1.68	0.95
AA	State Farm LifePath 2020 B	NLWBX	C	(800) 447-4930	D / 2.2	3.84	2.02	10.46 /13	2.47 /27	4.17 /16	1.09	1.65
AA	State Farm LifePath 2020 Inst	SAWIX	C	(800) 447-4930	D+ / 2.9	4.11	2.59	11.62 /16	3.45 /36	5.18 /23	2.13	0.70
AA	State Farm LifePath 2020 LegB	SAWBX	C	(800) 447-4930	D+ / 2.4	3.93	2.20	10.80 /14	2.77 /30	4.48 /18	1.34	1.35
AA	State Farm LifePath 2020 Prem	SAWAX	C-	(800) 447-4930	D / 2.0	4.12	2.46	11.37 /16	3.21 /34	4.92 /21	1.96	0.95
AA	State Farm LifePath 2020 R1	RAWOX	C	(800) 447-4930	D+ / 2.5	3.98	2.31	10.99 /14	2.88 /31	4.59 /19	1.57	1.27
AA	State Farm LifePath 2020 R2	RAWTX	C	(800) 447-4930	D+ / 2.6	3.98	2.38	11.14 /15	3.06 /32	4.78 /20	1.78	1.07
AA	State Farm LifePath 2020 R3	RAWHX	C	(800) 447-4930	D+ / 2.8	4.11	2.52	11.48 /16	3.37 /36	5.10 /22	2.06	0.77
AA	State Farm LifePath 2030 A	NLHAX	C	(800) 447-4930	C- / 3.0	5.54	4.15	15.54 /32	3.90 /42	6.15 /29	1.76	0.97
AA	State Farm LifePath 2030 B	NLHBX	C+	(800) 447-4930	C- / 3.6	5.50	4.09	15.37 /32	3.45 /36	5.57 /25	1.66	1.17
AA	State Farm LifePath 2030 Inst	SAYIX	C+	(800) 447-4930	C- / 4.1	5.63	4.31	15.87 /34	4.18 /45	6.41 /31	2.15	0.72
AA	State Farm LifePath 2030 LegB	SAYBX	C+	(800) 447-4930	C- / 3.6	5.43	3.97	15.06 /30	3.49 /37	5.73 /27	1.38	1.37
AA	State Farm LifePath 2030 Premier	SAYAX	C	(800) 447-4930	C- / 3.0	5.58	4.19	15.64 /33	3.93 /42	6.18 /30	1.98	0.97
AA	State Farm LifePath 2030 R1	RAYOX	C+	(800) 447-4930	C- / 3.6	5.47	4.00	15.21 /31	3.58 /38	5.83 /27	1.63	1.29
AA	State Farm LifePath 2030 R2	RAYTX	C+	(800) 447-4930	C- / 3.8	5.54	4.14	15.39 /32	3.78 /40	6.03 /29	1.84	1.09
AA	State Farm LifePath 2030 R3	RAYHX	C+	(800) 447-4930	C- / 4.0	5.59	4.27	15.81 /33	4.10 /44	6.35 /31	2.11	0.79
AA	State Farm LifePath 2040 A	NLOAX	C	(800) 447-4930	C- / 4.1	6.88	5.72	19.38 /49	4.48 /49	7.15 /36	1.67	1.00
AA	State Farm LifePath 2040 B	NLBOX	C+	(800) 447-4930	C / 4.7	6.83	5.60	19.15 /48	3.99 /43	6.55 /32	1.51	1.20
AA	State Farm LifePath 2040 Inst	SAUIX	C+	(800) 447-4930	C / 5.3	6.95	5.80	19.65 /50	4.73 /51	7.41 /37	1.99	0.75
AA	State Farm LifePath 2040 LegB	SAUBX	C+	(800) 447-4930	C / 4.7	6.79	5.43	18.88 /47	4.06 /44	6.73 /33	1.22	1.40
AA	State Farm LifePath 2040 Premier	SAUAX	C	(800) 447-4930	C- / 4.1	6.92	5.69	19.53 /50	4.51 /49	7.17 /36	1.78	1.00

● Denotes fund is closed to new investors
* Denotes fund is included in Section II

www.thestreetratings.com

RISK			NET ASSETS		ASSET				Portfolio Turnover Ratio	BULL / BEAR		FUND MANAGER		MINIMUMS		LOADS	
Risk Rating/Pts	3 Year Standard Deviation	Beta	NAV As of 2/28/17	Total $(Mil)	Cash %	Stocks %	Bonds %	Other %		Last Bull Market Return	Last Bear Market Return	Manager Quality Pct	Manager Tenure (Years)	Initial Purch. $	Additional Purch. $	Front End Load	Back End Load
B /8.8	6.0	0.55	11.48	37	0	58	40	2	1	74.8	-10.1	80	N/A	250	50	0.0	0.0
B /8.9	5.9	0.55	11.60	22	0	58	40	2	1	68.8	-10.3	76	N/A	250	50	0.0	0.0
B /8.9	6.0	0.56	11.59	160	0	58	40	2	1	72.6	-10.1	79	N/A	250	50	5.0	0.0
B /8.9	6.0	0.56	11.30	4	0	58	40	2	1	69.5	-10.3	76	N/A	0	0	0.0	0.0
B /8.8	6.0	0.56	11.32	8	0	58	40	2	1	71.1	-10.1	77	N/A	0	0	0.0	0.0
B /8.8	6.0	0.55	11.35	2	0	58	40	2	1	74.1	-10.1	80	N/A	0	0	0.0	0.0
C+ /6.1	10.0	0.94	9.78	133	0	96	2	2	52	127.0	-19.4	63	9	250	50	5.0	0.0
C+ /6.2	10.0	0.94	9.67	3	0	96	2	2	52	118.4	-19.6	53	9	250	50	0.0	0.0
C+ /6.1	9.9	0.93	9.83	294	0	96	2	2	52	130.0	-19.3	67	9	250	50	0.0	0.0
C+ /6.3	10.0	0.94	10.21	5	0	96	2	2	52	122.0	-19.5	57	9	250	50	0.0	0.0
C+ /6.2	10.0	0.94	10.24	139	0	96	2	2	52	127.1	-19.3	63	9	250	50	5.0	0.0
C+ /6.2	10.0	0.94	9.77	3	0	96	2	2	52	123.1	-19.6	59	9	0	0	0.0	0.0
C+ /6.2	10.0	0.94	9.75	14	0	96	2	2	52	125.5	-19.5	61	9	0	0	0.0	0.0
C+ /6.2	9.9	0.93	9.84	2	0	96	2	2	52	128.9	-19.3	66	9	0	0	0.0	0.0
C /5.5	9.3	0.86	73.70	4,576	0	98	0	2	11	99.7	-17.3	72	26	250	50	0.0	0.0
C /5.2	12.6	0.97	10.63	35	1	96	2	1	124	39.9	-25.6	51	9	250	50	5.0	0.0
C /5.1	12.6	0.97	10.35	9	1	96	2	1	124	35.4	-25.9	42	9	250	50	0.0	0.0
C /5.2	12.6	0.97	10.75	19	1	96	2	1	124	41.7	-25.5	55	9	250	50	0.0	0.0
C /5.2	12.6	0.97	10.53	9	1	96	2	1	124	37.0	-25.7	46	9	250	50	0.0	0.0
C /5.2	12.6	0.97	10.74	51	1	96	2	1	124	39.9	-25.5	52	9	250	50	5.0	0.0
C /5.2	12.7	0.97	10.53	3	1	96	2	1	124	37.5	-25.6	47	9	0	0	0.0	0.0
C /5.2	12.6	0.97	10.61	5	1	96	2	1	124	39.1	-25.6	50	9	0	0	0.0	0.0
C /5.2	12.6	0.97	10.74	2	1	96	2	1	124	41.2	-25.5	54	9	0	0	0.0	0.0
C+ /5.7	11.7	0.95	11.27	76	3	94	1	2	2	41.7	-23.5	56	N/A	250	50	5.0	0.0
C+ /5.8	11.7	0.95	11.28	10	3	94	1	2	2	36.9	-23.8	46	N/A	250	50	0.0	0.0
C+ /5.7	11.6	0.94	11.29	44	3	94	1	2	2	43.6	-23.5	59	N/A	250	50	0.0	0.0
C+ /5.8	11.7	0.95	11.32	13	3	94	1	2	2	38.6	-23.6	50	N/A	250	50	0.0	0.0
C+ /5.7	11.7	0.95	11.25	105	3	94	1	2	2	41.8	-23.5	56	N/A	250	50	5.0	0.0
C+ /5.8	11.7	0.95	11.28	3	3	94	1	2	2	39.2	-23.6	51	N/A	0	0	0.0	0.0
C+ /5.7	11.7	0.95	11.24	8	3	94	1	2	2	40.7	-23.6	54	N/A	0	0	0.0	0.0
C+ /5.7	11.7	0.95	11.30	2	3	94	1	2	2	43.0	-23.5	58	N/A	0	0	0.0	0.0
B /8.4	5.6	0.86	14.19	839	31	17	51	1	81	43.1	-10.0	33	N/A	250	50	5.0	0.0
B /8.5	5.6	0.86	14.10	22	31	17	51	1	81	37.7	-10.3	25	N/A	250	50	0.0	0.0
B /8.3	5.6	0.86	14.23	209	31	17	51	1	81	45.1	-10.0	36	N/A	250	50	0.0	0.0
B /8.5	5.6	0.86	14.25	11	31	17	51	1	81	40.1	-10.1	29	N/A	250	50	0.0	0.0
B /8.4	5.6	0.86	14.12	984	31	17	51	1	81	43.2	-9.9	34	N/A	250	50	5.0	0.0
B /8.4	5.6	0.86	14.11	20	31	17	51	1	81	40.8	-10.1	29	N/A	0	0	0.0	0.0
B /8.4	5.6	0.87	14.11	62	31	17	51	1	81	42.1	-10.0	31	N/A	0	0	0.0	0.0
B /8.3	5.6	0.87	14.20	3	31	17	51	1	81	44.6	-9.9	35	N/A	0	0	0.0	0.0
B- /7.7	7.5	1.17	15.14	1,025	47	23	29	1	81	55.7	-13.7	18	N/A	250	50	5.0	0.0
B- /7.9	7.5	1.17	15.09	30	47	23	29	1	81	51.1	-13.9	15	N/A	250	50	0.0	0.0
B- /7.7	7.5	1.16	15.25	264	47	23	29	1	81	57.9	-13.6	21	N/A	250	50	0.0	0.0
B- /7.9	7.5	1.17	15.23	11	47	23	29	1	81	52.4	-13.9	15	N/A	250	50	0.0	0.0
B- /7.8	7.5	1.16	15.15	870	47	23	29	1	81	55.8	-13.7	19	N/A	250	50	5.0	0.0
B- /7.8	7.5	1.17	15.04	35	47	23	29	1	81	53.2	-13.9	16	N/A	0	0	0.0	0.0
B- /7.8	7.5	1.17	15.10	72	47	23	29	1	81	54.7	-13.7	17	N/A	0	0	0.0	0.0
B- /7.7	7.5	1.17	15.26	4	47	23	29	1	81	57.4	-13.7	20	N/A	0	0	0.0	0.0
B- /7.1	9.2	1.43	15.94	854	57	31	10	2	80	66.7	-16.7	9	N/A	250	50	5.0	0.0
B- /7.2	9.2	1.43	15.88	30	57	31	10	2	80	61.6	-17.0	7	N/A	250	50	0.0	0.0
B- /7.1	9.2	1.42	16.09	336	57	31	10	2	80	69.0	-16.7	11	N/A	250	50	0.0	0.0
B- /7.2	9.2	1.42	16.09	11	57	31	10	2	80	63.1	-16.9	8	N/A	250	50	0.0	0.0
B- /7.1	9.2	1.42	16.00	405	57	31	10	2	80	66.8	-16.7	10	N/A	250	50	5.0	0.0

Fund Type	Fund Name	Ticker Symbol	Overall Investment Rating	Phone	Performance Rating/Pts	3 Mo	6 Mo	1Yr / Pct	3Yr / Pct	5Yr / Pct	Dividend Yield	Expense Ratio
	99 Pct = Best							Total Return % through 2/28/17			Incl. in Returns	
	0 Pct = Worst								Annualized			
AA	State Farm LifePath 2040 R1	RAUOX	C+	(800) 447-4930	C /4.8	6.82	5.51	18.99 /47	4.15 /45	6.82 /34	1.43	1.32
AA	State Farm LifePath 2040 R2	RAUTX	C+	(800) 447-4930	C /5.0	6.84	5.61	19.27 /48	4.35 /47	7.03 /35	1.72	1.12
AA	State Farm LifePath 2040 R3	RAUHX	C+	(800) 447-4930	C /5.3	6.96	5.82	19.68 /50	4.67 /51	7.35 /37	1.92	0.82
AA	State Farm LifePath 2050 A	NLPAX	C-	(800) 447-4930	C /4.5	7.37	6.17	20.68 /56	4.73 /51	7.81 /41	1.67	1.04
GI	State Farm LifePath 2050 Premier	NLPPX	U	(800) 447-4930	U /	7.39	6.29	--	--	--	0.00	N/A
AA	State Farm LifePath 2050 R1	RAVRX	C	(800) 447-4930	C /5.3	7.33	6.03	20.38 /54	4.39 /47	7.49 /38	1.55	1.36
AA	State Farm LifePath 2050 R2	RAVSX	C	(800) 447-4930	C /5.4	7.31	6.11	20.57 /55	4.60 /50	7.67 /40	1.71	1.16
GI	State Farm LifePath Retirement A	NILAX	C	(800) 447-4930	D /1.6	3.38	1.67	9.26 /10	2.86 /30	3.96 /15	1.28	0.94
GI	State Farm LifePath Retirement B	NILBX	C	(800) 447-4930	D /1.8	3.24	1.36	8.52 / 8	2.13 /25	3.37 /12	0.73	1.64
GI	State Farm LifePath Retirement Inst	SLRIX	C	(800) 447-4930	D+ /2.3	3.44	1.84	9.48 /10	3.10 /33	4.21 /16	1.64	0.69
GI	State Farm LifePath Retirement LegB	SLRBX	C	(800) 447-4930	D /2.0	3.32	1.46	8.85 / 9	2.43 /27	3.54 /13	0.95	1.34
GI	State Farm LifePath Retirement Prem	SLRAX	C	(800) 447-4930	D /1.6	3.49	1.76	9.42 /10	2.89 /31	3.97 /15	1.42	0.94
GI	State Farm LifePath Retirement R1	RLROX	C	(800) 447-4930	D /2.1	3.36	1.55	8.94 / 9	2.53 /28	3.63 /14	1.09	1.26
GI	State Farm LifePath Retirement R2	RLRTX	C	(800) 447-4930	D /2.1	3.35	1.57	9.15 /10	2.71 /29	3.81 /14	1.28	1.06
GI	State Farm LifePath Retirement R3	RLRHX	C	(800) 447-4930	D+ /2.3	3.43	1.72	9.42 /10	3.03 /32	4.13 /16	1.57	0.76
GI	State Farm S&P 500 Index A	SNPAX	A	(800) 447-4930	B /8.1	7.84	9.67	24.12 /70	9.83 /92	13.16 /86	1.34	0.66
GI	State Farm S&P 500 Index B	SNPBX	A+	(800) 447-4930	B+ /8.5	7.68	9.30	23.33 /68	9.08 /87	12.38 /78	0.67	1.36
GI	State Farm S&P 500 Index Inst	SFXIX	A+	(800) 447-4930	A- /9.1	7.97	9.78	24.49 /72	10.11 /94	13.44 /88	1.64	0.41
GI	State Farm S&P 500 Index LegB	SLIBX	A+	(800) 447-4930	B+ /8.7	7.73	9.40	23.61 /69	9.40 /90	12.71 /81	0.90	1.06
GI	State Farm S&P 500 Index Premier	SLIAX	A	(800) 447-4930	B /8.2	7.90	9.72	24.24 /71	9.86 /93	13.18 /86	1.42	0.56
GI	State Farm S&P 500 Index R1	RSPOX	A+	(800) 447-4930	B+ /8.7	7.76	9.46	23.67 /69	9.46 /90	12.79 /82	1.13	0.98
GI	State Farm S&P 500 Index R2	RSPTX	A+	(800) 447-4930	B+ /8.9	7.85	9.62	24.01 /70	9.70 /92	13.03 /84	1.30	0.78
GI	State Farm S&P 500 Index R3	RSPHX	A+	(800) 447-4930	A- /9.1	7.88	9.76	24.35 /71	10.04 /93	13.37 /88	1.61	0.48
SC	State Farm Small Cap Index A	SNRAX	C+	(800) 447-4930	B- /7.3	5.01	12.19	35.11 /94	6.00 /64	11.90 /73	0.58	0.73
SC	State Farm Small Cap Index B	SNRBX	C+	(800) 447-4930	B /7.8	4.88	11.93	34.35 /93	5.37 /58	11.23 /68	0.14	1.28
SC	State Farm Small Cap Index Inst	SMIIX	B-	(800) 447-4930	B+ /8.4	5.09	12.35	35.47 /94	6.28 /67	12.20 /76	0.79	0.48
SC	State Farm Small Cap Index LegB	SMIBX	C+	(800) 447-4930	B /7.9	4.91	11.94	34.52 /93	5.59 /60	11.46 /70	0.26	1.13
SC	State Farm Small Cap Index Premier	SMIAX	C+	(800) 447-4930	B- /7.4	5.00	12.26	35.14 /94	6.04 /65	11.91 /73	0.60	0.63
SC	State Farm Small Cap Index R1	RSIOX	C+	(800) 447-4930	B /8.0	4.91	11.99	34.58 /94	5.67 /61	11.55 /70	0.33	1.05
SC	State Farm Small Cap Index R2	RSITX	B-	(800) 447-4930	B /8.1	4.98	12.17	34.91 /94	5.89 /63	11.77 /72	0.47	0.85
SC	State Farm Small Cap Index R3	RSIHX	B-	(800) 447-4930	B+ /8.3	5.02	12.28	35.28 /94	6.20 /66	12.11 /75	0.73	0.55
SC	State Farm Small Mid Cap Eq A	SSNAX	C-	(800) 447-4930	C /5.3	5.08	10.87	27.29 /80	4.17 /45	10.05 /59	0.00	1.39
SC	State Farm Small Mid Cap Eq B	SSNBX	C-	(800) 447-4930	C+ /5.7	4.87	10.43	26.26 /77	3.45 /36	9.35 /53	0.00	2.09
SC	State Farm Small Mid Cap Eq Inst	SFEIX	C	(800) 447-4930	C+ /6.5	5.09	11.00	27.53 /81	4.48 /49	10.36 /61	0.08	1.14
SC	State Farm Small Mid Cap Eq LegB	SFSBX	C-	(800) 447-4930	C+ /6.0	4.91	10.62	26.70 /78	3.77 /40	9.63 /56	0.00	1.79
SC	State Farm Small Mid Cap Eq	SFSAX	C-	(800) 447-4930	C /5.3	5.10	10.94	27.40 /80	4.21 /45	10.08 /59	0.00	1.29
SC	State Farm Small Mid Cap Eq R1	RSEOX	C-	(800) 447-4930	C+ /6.1	5.02	10.66	26.91 /79	3.86 /41	9.71 /56	0.00	1.71
SC	State Farm Small Mid Cap Eq R2	RSETX	C	(800) 447-4930	C+ /6.2	5.05	10.81	27.09 /79	4.05 /44	9.92 /58	0.00	1.51
SC	State Farm Small Mid Cap Eq R3	RSEHX	C	(800) 447-4930	C+ /6.5	5.10	10.89	27.51 /81	4.37 /47	10.25 /60	0.02	1.21
EM	● State Street Dscpld Em Mkts Eq N	SSEMX	E-	(800) 843-2639	E+ /0.7	8.34	1.13	17.37 /40	-2.90 / 5	-3.39 / 2	1.42	1.52
EM	State Street Emrg Mkts Eq Idx K	SSKEX	U	(800) 843-2639	U /	9.01	5.49	28.93 /84	--	--	2.10	N/A
GR	State Street Equity 500 Index Adm	STFAX	A+	(800) 882-0052	A /9.3	8.02	9.89	24.65 /72	10.37 /95	13.72 /91	1.42	0.34
GR	State Street Equity 500 Index B	STBIX	A+	(800) 882-0052	A /9.3	8.36	10.24	25.00 /73	10.38 /95	13.69 /91	1.71	0.44
IX	State Street Equity 500 Index II	SSEYX	U	(800) 882-0052	U /	8.04	9.98	25.13 /74	--	--	1.49	0.04
GR	State Street Equity 500 Index K	SSSYX	U	(800) 882-0052	U /	8.44	10.38	25.34 /74	--	--	1.95	0.19
IX	State Street Equity 500 Index R	SSFRX	A+	(800) 882-0052	A- /9.2	8.33	10.09	24.64 /72	10.02 /93	13.31 /87	1.37	0.79
FO	State Street Global Eq ex-US Id K	SSGLX	U	(800) 882-0052	U /	7.63	4.96	19.04 /47	--	--	1.44	0.53
FO	State Street Global Eq ex-US Indx	SSGVX	U	(800) 882-0052	U /	7.68	5.01	19.09 /48	--	--	1.49	0.49
FO	State Street Hgd Intl Dev Eq Ix K	SSHQX	U	(800) 882-0052	U /	9.23	12.30	21.58 /60	--	--	4.11	0.41
GR	State Street Premier Growth Equity	SPGSX	C+	(800) 843-2639	A- /9.2	11.31	9.55	23.40 /68	9.76 /92	14.12 /94	0.46	0.81
RE	State Street Real Estate Sec VIS 1	SSRSX	C+	(800) 843-2639	B /8.0	7.68	-2.39	15.76 /33	12.02 /98	11.76 /72	2.41	0.95
GR	State Street S&P 500 Index VIS 1	SSSPX	A+	(800) 843-2639	A- /9.2	7.97	9.89	24.59 /72	10.28 /95	13.66 /90	1.75	0.32

● Denotes fund is closed to new investors
* Denotes fund is included in Section II

www.thestreetratings.com

RISK			NET ASSETS		ASSET				Portfolio Turnover Ratio	BULL / BEAR		FUND MANAGER		MINIMUMS		LOADS	
Risk Rating/Pts	3 Year		NAV As of 2/28/17	Total $(Mil)	Cash %	Stocks %	Bonds %	Other %		Last Bull Market Return	Last Bear Market Return	Manager Quality Pct	Manager Tenure (Years)	Initial Purch. $	Additional Purch. $	Front End Load	Back End Load
	Standard Deviation	Beta															
B- /7.2	9.2	1.43	15.86	27	57	31	10	2	80	63.8	-16.8	8	N/A	0	0	0.0	0.0
B- /7.1	9.2	1.43	15.92	58	57	31	10	2	80	65.6	-16.7	9	N/A	0	0	0.0	0.0
B- /7.1	9.2	1.43	16.27	7	57	31	10	2	80	68.3	-16.7	10	N/A	0	0	0.0	0.0
C+ /5.9	9.8	1.51	11.02	286	0	97	1	2	81	74.9	-19.2	8	8	250	50	5.0	0.0
U /	N/A	N/A	11.00	98	0	97	1	2	81	N/A	N/A	N/A	8	1,000	50	5.0	0.0
C+ /5.9	9.8	1.52	11.04	10	0	97	1	2	81	72.2	-19.3	6	8	0	0	0.0	0.0
C+ /5.9	9.8	1.51	11.05	19	0	97	1	2	81	73.8	-19.2	7	8	0	0	0.0	0.0
B+ /9.0	4.6	0.39	12.49	383	20	16	62	2	83	32.8	-5.5	59	N/A	250	50	5.0	0.0
B+ /9.0	4.6	0.39	12.56	8	20	16	62	2	83	28.7	-5.7	50	N/A	250	50	0.0	0.0
B+ /9.0	4.6	0.39	12.78	105	20	16	62	2	83	34.5	-5.4	63	N/A	250	50	0.0	0.0
B+ /9.0	4.6	0.39	12.85	4	20	16	62	2	83	29.8	-5.6	54	N/A	250	50	0.0	0.0
B+ /9.0	4.6	0.39	12.78	728	20	16	62	2	83	32.9	-5.4	60	N/A	250	50	5.0	0.0
B+ /9.0	4.6	0.39	12.53	7	20	16	62	2	83	30.6	-5.6	55	N/A	0	0	0.0	0.0
B+ /9.0	4.6	0.39	12.81	27	20	16	62	2	83	31.8	-5.5	57	N/A	0	0	0.0	0.0
B+ /9.0	4.6	0.39	12.76	2	20	16	62	2	83	34.0	-5.4	61	N/A	0	0	0.0	0.0
B- /7.1	10.4	1.00	17.68	525	1	96	1	2	3	125.6	-16.5	65	9	250	50	5.0	0.0
B- /7.1	10.3	1.00	17.80	9	1	96	1	2	3	117.1	-16.8	57	9	250	50	0.0	0.0
B- /7.1	10.3	1.00	17.85	211	1	96	1	2	3	128.6	-16.5	68	9	250	50	0.0	0.0
B- /7.1	10.3	1.00	17.97	17	1	96	1	2	3	120.8	-16.8	60	9	250	50	0.0	0.0
B- /7.1	10.3	1.00	17.79	608	1	96	1	2	3	125.8	-16.6	66	9	250	50	5.0	0.0
B- /7.1	10.3	1.00	17.74	10	1	96	1	2	3	121.8	-16.7	62	9	0	0	0.0	0.0
B- /7.1	10.3	1.00	17.66	25	1	96	1	2	3	124.2	-16.7	64	9	0	0	0.0	0.0
B- /7.1	10.3	1.00	17.81	4	1	96	1	2	3	127.7	-16.5	68	9	0	0	0.0	0.0
C /4.4	15.8	1.00	17.19	171	0	98	1	1	15	121.3	-25.4	64	1	250	50	5.0	0.0
C /4.4	15.8	1.00	16.72	13	0	98	1	1	15	114.2	-25.7	56	1	250	50	0.0	0.0
C /4.4	15.8	1.00	17.34	95	0	98	1	1	15	124.5	-25.3	67	1	250	50	0.0	0.0
C /4.4	15.8	1.00	16.60	25	0	98	1	1	15	116.7	-25.6	59	1	250	50	0.0	0.0
C /4.4	15.8	1.00	17.03	185	0	98	1	1	15	121.4	-25.4	65	1	250	50	5.0	0.0
C /4.4	15.8	1.00	17.13	4	0	98	1	1	15	117.6	-25.5	60	1	0	0	0.0	0.0
C /4.4	15.8	1.00	17.19	10	0	98	1	1	15	119.9	-25.4	62	1	0	0	0.0	0.0
C /4.4	15.7	1.00	17.34	3	0	98	1	1	15	123.6	-25.4	66	1	0	0	0.0	0.0
C /4.4	13.6	0.84	12.36	95	0	97	1	2	120	104.0	-24.1	55	N/A	250	50	5.0	0.0
C- /4.2	13.6	0.84	11.35	12	0	97	1	2	120	97.1	-24.4	45	N/A	250	50	0.0	0.0
C /4.4	13.6	0.84	12.73	51	0	97	1	2	120	107.1	-24.1	59	N/A	250	50	0.0	0.0
C- /4.2	13.6	0.84	11.06	10	0	97	1	2	120	99.6	-24.3	49	N/A	250	50	0.0	0.0
C /4.4	13.5	0.84	12.09	113	0	97	1	2	120	104.2	-24.2	55	N/A	250	50	5.0	0.0
C /4.3	13.5	0.84	11.65	4	0	97	1	2	120	100.6	-24.3	50	N/A	0	0	0.0	0.0
C /4.3	13.6	0.84	12.01	12	0	97	1	2	120	102.7	-24.2	53	N/A	0	0	0.0	0.0
C /4.4	13.5	0.84	12.57	3	0	97	1	2	120	105.9	-24.1	57	N/A	0	0	0.0	0.0
D- /1.3	14.7	0.89	7.49	86	2	96	0	2	101	3.9	-27.8	19	10	1,000	100	0.0	0.0
U /	N/A	N/A	11.76	423	0	0	0	100	0	N/A	N/A	N/A	2	10,000,000	0	0.0	0.0
B /8.1	10.4	1.00	19.94	294	0	0	0	100	7	131.8	-16.4	71	10	25,000,000	0	0.0	0.0
B /8.2	10.3	1.00	19.91	134	0	0	0	100	7	131.5	-16.5	71	10	25,000,000	0	0.0	0.0
U /	N/A	N/A	11.99	2,002	0	97	1	2	5	N/A	N/A	N/A	3	0	0	0.0	0.0
U /	N/A	N/A	19.94	389	0	0	0	100	7	N/A	N/A	N/A	10	10,000,000	0	0.0	0.0
B /8.2	10.3	1.00	19.91	39	0	0	0	100	7	127.2	-16.6	67	10	25,000,000	0	0.0	0.0
U /	N/A	N/A	9.18	229	2	97	0	1	3	N/A	N/A	N/A	3	10,000,000	0	0.0	0.0
U /	N/A	N/A	9.18	908	0	0	0	100	3	N/A	N/A	N/A	3	0	0	0.0	0.0
U /	N/A	N/A	9.40	2,245	5	93	0	2	1	N/A	N/A	N/A	2	10,000,000	0	0.0	0.0
C- /3.0	13.6	1.20	94.97	35	1	97	1	1	19	140.0	-17.0	38	20	0	0	0.0	0.0
C- /3.5	14.9	1.08	12.76	73	0	99	0	1	57	112.2	-16.2	73	11	0	0	0.0	0.0
C+ /6.9	10.3	1.00	40.48	188	0	97	2	1	2	130.9	-16.5	70	16	0	0	0.0	0.0

Fund Type	Fund Name	Ticker Symbol	Overall Investment Rating	Phone	Performance Rating/Pts	3 Mo	6 Mo	1Yr / Pct	3Yr / Pct	5Yr / Pct	Dividend Yield	Expense Ratio
MC	State Street Small/Mid Cap Eqty Idx	SSMHX	U	(800) 882-0052	U /	7.23	12.41	33.76 /93	--	--	1.62	0.41
SC	State Street Small-Cap Equity VIS 1	SSSEX	C+	(800) 843-2639	A- / 9.2	4.72	11.34	36.12 /95	8.07 /79	12.57 /80	0.00	1.48
GL	State Street Target Retirement K	SSFOX	U	(800) 882-0052	U /	3.44	2.24	9.33 /10	--	--	1.67	1.24
GL	State Street Tgt Retirement 2015 K	SSBHX	U	(800) 882-0052	U /	4.00	2.79	11.42 /16	--	--	1.54	4.70
GL	State Street Tgt Retirement 2020 K	SSBOX	U	(800) 882-0052	U /	4.77	3.46	13.92 /25	--	--	1.61	0.65
GL	State Street Tgt Retirement 2025 K	SSBSX	U	(800) 882-0052	U /	5.67	4.26	16.08 /35	--	--	1.52	1.28
GL	State Street Tgt Retirement 2030 K	SSBYX	U	(800) 882-0052	U /	6.05	4.74	17.45 /40	--	--	1.49	0.63
GL	State Street Tgt Retirement 2035 K	SSCKX	U	(800) 882-0052	U /	6.51	5.40	18.80 /46	--	--	1.42	1.71
GL	State Street Tgt Retirement 2040 K	SSCQX	U	(800) 882-0052	U /	6.66	5.85	19.92 /52	--	--	1.46	0.80
GL	State Street Tgt Retirement 2045 K	SSDEX	U	(800) 882-0052	U /	6.93	6.31	20.97 /57	--	--	1.44	2.97
GL	State Street Tgt Retirement 2050 K	SSDLX	U	(800) 882-0052	U /	6.96	6.34	20.91 /57	--	--	1.43	4.22
GL	State Street Tgt Retirement 2055 K	SSDQX	U	(800) 882-0052	U /	7.04	6.32	21.04 /58	--	--	1.42	6.92
GL	State Street Total Return VIS 3	SSTTX	C	(800) 843-2639	C- / 3.8	5.24	4.17	13.90 /25	4.15 /45	6.41 /31	1.58	0.87
GR	State Street US Equity VIS 1	SSUSX	B	(800) 843-2639	B+ / 8.6	8.75	10.28	25.43 /75	8.31 /81	12.48 /79	1.11	0.77
GL	State Street/Ramius Mgd Fut Strat A	RTSRX	D	(877) 672-6487	E / 0.5	0.70	-3.57	-8.52 / 0	2.99 /32	1.30 / 7	0.03	3.89
GL	State Street/Ramius Mgd Fut Strat I	RTSIX	D	(877) 672-6487	E+ / 0.9	0.81	-3.34	-8.20 / 0	3.26 /34	1.57 / 7	0.04	3.64
GL	Steben Managed Futures Strategy I	SKLIX	U	(855) 775-5571	U /	3.81	0.40	0.20 / 1	--	--	0.00	1.99
GL	Steinberg Select Institutional	STMIX	D+		C- / 3.6	7.55	7.78	16.58 /37	2.10 /25	--	0.40	1.39
GR	Sterling Cap Stratton MC Val Inst	STRGX	B+	(800) 228-1872	B / 8.1	8.27	11.33	29.41 /85	6.57 /69	12.26 /77	0.13	0.92
SC	Sterling Cap Stratton SC Val Inst	STSCX	A	(800) 228-1872	B+ / 8.7	3.88	12.97	37.10 /96	6.49 /68	13.48 /89	0.15	1.09
FO	Sterling Capital Beh Intl Eqty Inst	SBIIX	U	(800) 228-1872	U /	7.42	7.19	18.29 /44	--	--	1.65	1.25
GI	Sterling Capital Beh LC Val Eq A	BBTGX	A	(800) 228-1872	B / 7.9	8.28	12.40	26.14 /77	8.48 /83	11.66 /71	1.50	0.89
GI	● Sterling Capital Beh LC Val Eq B	BGISX	A	(800) 228-1872	B+ / 8.3	8.04	11.98	25.16 /74	7.66 /77	10.82 /64	0.77	1.64
GI	Sterling Capital Beh LC Val Eq C	BCVCX	A	(800) 228-1872	B+ / 8.3	8.11	12.01	25.18 /74	7.69 /77	10.84 /65	0.96	1.64
GI	Sterling Capital Beh LC Val Eq Inst	BBISX	A+	(800) 228-1872	A- / 9.0	8.35	12.53	26.49 /78	8.76 /85	11.94 /74	1.80	0.64
SC	Sterling Capital Beh SC Val Eq A	SPSAX	A	(800) 228-1872	B+ / 8.6	5.26	17.87	32.36 /91	8.17 /80	12.06 /75	0.97	1.27
SC	● Sterling Capital Beh SC Val Eq B	SPSBX	A+	(800) 228-1872	B+ / 8.9	5.04	17.38	31.31 /89	7.32 /74	11.22 /68	0.27	2.02
SC	Sterling Capital Beh SC Val Eq C	SPSDX	A+	(800) 228-1872	A- / 9.0	5.07	17.42	31.39 /89	7.34 /74	11.21 /68	0.45	2.02
SC	Sterling Capital Beh SC Val Eq Inst	SPSCX	A+	(800) 228-1872	A / 9.5	5.34	18.02	32.67 /91	8.41 /82	12.33 /77	1.23	1.02
SC	Sterling Capital Beh SC Val Eq R	SPSRX	A+	(866) 777-7818	A- / 9.2	5.15	17.79	31.69 /89	7.90 /78	11.83 /73	0.83	1.52
GI	Sterling Capital Dvsfd Inc A	BCGAX	C	(800) 228-1872	D+ / 2.3	3.64	1.95	11.74 /17	4.32 /47	5.27 /23	3.50	1.39
GI	● Sterling Capital Dvsfd Inc B	BCGBX	C	(800) 228-1872	D+ / 2.6	3.41	1.57	10.88 /14	3.55 /38	4.47 /18	2.87	2.14
GI	Sterling Capital Dvsfd Inc C	BCCCX	C	(800) 228-1872	D+ / 2.7	3.38	1.59	10.92 /14	3.58 /38	4.47 /18	3.03	2.14
GI	Sterling Capital Dvsfd Inc Inst	BMGTX	C+	(800) 228-1872	C- / 3.4	3.66	2.14	12.09 /18	4.60 /50	5.53 /25	3.91	1.14
IN	Sterling Capital Equity Income Fd A	BAEIX	C+	(800) 228-1872	C+ / 6.1	5.29	7.72	22.72 /65	7.24 /74	9.33 /53	1.55	1.05
IN	● Sterling Capital Equity Income Fd B	BEIBX	C+	(800) 228-1872	C+ / 6.5	5.11	7.32	21.75 /61	6.42 /68	8.50 /46	0.70	1.80
IN	Sterling Capital Equity Income Fd C	BCEGX	C+	(800) 228-1872	C+ / 6.6	5.15	7.36	21.84 /61	6.43 /68	8.51 /46	0.98	1.80
IN	Sterling Capital Equity Income Fd I	BEGIX	B	(800) 228-1872	B- / 7.2	5.34	7.84	23.03 /67	7.49 /75	9.59 /55	1.87	0.80
IN	Sterling Capital Equity Income Fd R	BAERX	C+	(800) 228-1872	C+ / 6.9	5.28	7.65	22.45 /64	6.98 /72	9.05 /51	1.44	1.30
GR	Sterling Capital Long Short Eq A	SLSAX	D	(800) 228-1872	E- / 0.2	0.91	5.62	17.09 /39	-4.43 / 3	--	0.00	3.28
GR	Sterling Capital Long Short Eq C	SLSCX	D	(800) 228-1872	E / 0.3	0.70	5.24	16.15 /35	-5.15 / 2	--	0.00	4.03
GR	Sterling Capital Long Short Eq Inst	SLSIX	D	(800) 228-1872	E / 0.4	0.91	5.69	17.39 /40	-4.22 / 3	--	0.00	3.03
MC	Sterling Capital Mid Value A	OVEAX	C+	(800) 228-1872	A- / 9.0	9.17	13.65	32.81 /91	8.88 /86	13.39 /88	0.00	1.20
MC	● Sterling Capital Mid Value B	OVEBX	C+	(800) 228-1872	A / 9.3	8.94	13.22	31.76 /90	8.05 /79	12.54 /79	0.00	1.95
MC	Sterling Capital Mid Value C	OVECX	C+	(800) 228-1872	A / 9.3	8.93	13.24	31.80 /90	8.06 /79	12.55 /80	0.00	1.95
MC	Sterling Capital Mid Value I	OVEIX	B	(800) 228-1872	A+ / 9.6	9.23	13.80	33.16 /92	9.16 /88	13.69 /91	0.06	0.95
MC	Sterling Capital Mid Value R	OVERX	B-	(800) 228-1872	A / 9.5	9.00	13.54	31.98 /90	8.65 /84	12.90 /83	0.00	1.45
GR	Sterling Capital Special Opptys A	BOPAX	B	(800) 228-1872	B / 8.0	9.71	11.15	18.39 /45	10.29 /95	13.09 /85	0.00	1.10
GR	● Sterling Capital Special Opptys B	BOPBX	B	(800) 228-1872	B+ / 8.4	9.53	10.72	17.47 /40	9.45 /90	12.25 /77	0.00	1.85
GR	Sterling Capital Special Opptys C	BOPCX	B	(800) 228-1872	B+ / 8.4	9.52	10.71	17.52 /41	9.46 /90	12.25 /77	0.00	1.85
GR	Sterling Capital Special Opptys Ins	BOPIX	A-	(800) 228-1872	A- / 9.1	9.77	11.29	18.67 /46	10.55 /96	13.37 /88	0.06	0.85
GR	Sterling Capital Special Opptys R	BOPRX	B+	(800) 228-1872	B+ / 8.8	9.68	10.99	18.06 /43	10.02 /93	12.82 /82	0.00	1.35

● Denotes fund is closed to new investors
* Denotes fund is included in Section II

Risk Rating/Pts	Standard Deviation	Beta	NAV As of 2/28/17	Total $(Mil)	Cash %	Stocks %	Bonds %	Other %	Portfolio Turnover Ratio	Last Bull Market Return	Last Bear Market Return	Manager Quality Pct	Manager Tenure (Years)	Initial Purch. $	Additional Purch. $	Front End Load	Back End Load
U /	N/A	N/A	11.13	282	6	93	0	1	0	N/A	N/A	N/A	2	0	0	0.0	0.0
D+ / 2.9	14.1	0.88	14.76	41	1	94	4	1	42	130.8	-21.8	85	N/A	0	0	0.0	0.0
U /	N/A	N/A	10.37	84	0	34	64	2	31	N/A	N/A	N/A	3	10,000,000	0	0.0	0.0
U /	N/A	N/A	10.38	143	0	43	55	2	55	N/A	N/A	N/A	3	10,000,000	0	0.0	0.0
U /	N/A	N/A	10.63	488	1	55	43	1	39	N/A	N/A	N/A	3	10,000,000	0	0.0	0.0
U /	N/A	N/A	10.76	464	1	66	32	1	51	N/A	N/A	N/A	3	10,000,000	0	0.0	0.0
U /	N/A	N/A	10.84	455	1	72	25	2	33	N/A	N/A	N/A	3	10,000,000	0	0.0	0.0
U /	N/A	N/A	10.93	324	1	79	18	2	38	N/A	N/A	N/A	3	10,000,000	0	0.0	0.0
U /	N/A	N/A	10.90	278	2	83	13	2	38	N/A	N/A	N/A	3	10,000,000	0	0.0	0.0
U /	N/A	N/A	10.87	164	2	87	10	1	35	N/A	N/A	N/A	3	10,000,000	0	0.0	0.0
U /	N/A	N/A	10.84	124	2	87	10	1	35	N/A	N/A	N/A	3	10,000,000	0	0.0	0.0
U /	N/A	N/A	10.83	35	2	87	10	1	40	N/A	N/A	N/A	3	10,000,000	0	0.0	0.0
B- / 7.5	6.7	1.04	18.71	1,522	1	62	36	1	70	56.3	-14.0	66	6	0	0	0.0	0.0
C / 4.6	11.7	1.11	44.93	29	3	95	1	1	37	122.1	-18.8	32	6	0	0	0.0	0.0
B- / 7.5	9.2	-0.15	9.09	3	31	0	68	1	40	5.6	N/A	90	6	1,000	50	5.5	1.0
B- / 7.4	9.2	-0.15	9.14	47	31	0	68	1	40	7.0	N/A	90	6	1,000,000	100,000	0.0	1.0
U /	N/A	N/A	10.06	75	23	0	76	1	46	N/A	N/A	N/A	N/A	1,000,000	25,000	0.0	1.0
C+ / 5.6	13.4	0.75	10.04	42	2	97	0	1	44	N/A	N/A	87	4	100,000	0	0.0	0.0
C+ / 6.2	12.0	1.04	62.02	65	0	0	0	100	19	121.7	-25.5	22	2	2,000	100	0.0	0.0
C+ / 6.4	13.7	0.83	84.80	1,287	0	0	0	100	6	129.2	-21.2	79	2	2,000	100	0.0	0.0
U /	N/A	N/A	10.00	71	4	95	0	1	125	N/A	N/A	N/A	3	1,000,000	0	0.0	0.0
B- / 7.2	11.1	1.02	19.83	33	1	97	1	1	146	113.7	-19.9	47	4	1,000	0	5.8	0.0
B- / 7.2	11.0	1.01	19.51	N/A	1	97	1	1	146	105.1	-20.2	37	4	1,000	0	0.0	0.0
B- / 7.1	11.1	1.01	19.26	1	1	97	1	1	146	105.3	-20.2	37	4	1,000	0	0.0	0.0
B- / 7.2	11.0	1.01	19.95	270	1	97	1	1	146	116.6	-19.9	51	4	1,000,000	0	0.0	0.0
C+ / 6.7	13.7	0.83	17.64	10	0	99	0	1	120	118.5	-25.6	87	4	1,000	0	5.8	0.0
C+ / 6.7	13.7	0.83	17.10	N/A	0	99	0	1	120	109.6	-25.9	84	4	1,000	0	0.0	0.0
C+ / 6.7	13.7	0.83	17.04	N/A	0	99	0	1	120	109.5	-25.9	84	4	1,000	0	0.0	0.0
C+ / 6.7	13.7	0.83	17.77	203	0	99	0	1	120	121.3	-25.5	88	4	1,000,000	0	0.0	0.0
C+ / 6.7	13.6	0.82	17.59	N/A	0	99	0	1	120	116.8	-25.5	87	4	1,000	0	0.0	0.0
B / 8.4	4.7	0.36	10.74	15	3	29	66	2	67	42.0	-8.6	78	N/A	1,000	0	5.8	0.0
B / 8.5	4.7	0.36	10.77	N/A	3	29	66	2	67	36.3	-8.8	71	N/A	1,000	0	0.0	0.0
B / 8.4	4.7	0.36	10.65	1	3	29	66	2	67	36.4	-8.9	72	N/A	1,000	0	0.0	0.0
B / 8.4	4.7	0.36	10.87	22	3	29	66	2	67	44.0	-8.5	80	N/A	1,000,000	0	0.0	0.0
C+ / 6.2	10.3	0.94	19.48	465	1	96	1	2	21	83.5	-10.3	41	13	1,000	0	5.8	0.0
C+ / 6.2	10.3	0.94	19.49	1	1	96	1	2	21	76.1	-10.6	31	13	1,000	0	0.0	0.0
C+ / 6.2	10.3	0.94	19.29	263	1	96	1	2	21	76.2	-10.5	31	13	1,000	0	0.0	0.0
C+ / 6.2	10.3	0.94	19.53	953	1	96	1	2	21	86.0	-10.2	44	13	1,000,000	0	0.0	0.0
C+ / 6.2	10.3	0.94	19.35	3	1	96	1	2	21	81.0	-10.3	37	13	1,000	0	0.0	0.0
B- / 7.3	9.5	0.61	8.84	N/A	57	35	6	2	370	N/A	N/A	2	4	1,000	0	5.8	0.0
B- / 7.2	9.5	0.61	8.63	N/A	57	35	6	2	370	N/A	N/A	1	4	1,000	0	0.0	0.0
B- / 7.3	9.5	0.61	8.91	38	57	35	6	2	370	N/A	N/A	2	4	1,000,000	0	0.0	0.0
C- / 3.3	14.0	1.08	18.51	34	1	95	2	2	25	136.0	-23.7	56	12	1,000	0	5.8	0.0
C- / 3.0	14.0	1.08	16.74	N/A	1	95	2	2	25	126.6	-23.9	46	12	1,000	0	0.0	0.0
C- / 3.0	14.1	1.08	16.64	5	1	95	2	2	25	126.7	-24.0	46	12	1,000	0	0.0	0.0
C- / 3.3	14.1	1.08	18.76	628	1	95	2	2	25	139.3	-23.7	60	12	1,000,000	0	0.0	0.0
C- / 3.3	13.9	1.07	17.97	N/A	1	95	2	2	25	130.5	-23.8	55	12	1,000	0	0.0	0.0
C+ / 5.6	10.2	0.90	23.37	363	0	98	1	1	27	127.9	-18.1	79	14	1,000	0	5.8	0.0
C / 5.2	10.2	0.90	19.98	1	0	98	1	1	27	118.9	-18.3	74	14	1,000	0	0.0	0.0
C / 5.2	10.2	0.90	20.00	179	0	98	1	1	27	118.9	-18.3	74	14	1,000	0	0.0	0.0
C+ / 5.6	10.2	0.90	24.42	615	0	98	1	1	27	131.0	-17.9	81	14	1,000,000	0	0.0	0.0
C+ / 5.6	10.2	0.90	23.67	N/A	0	98	1	1	27	125.0	-18.1	78	14	1,000	0	0.0	0.0

Fund Type	Fund Name	Ticker Symbol	Overall Investment Rating	Phone	Performance Rating/Pts	3 Mo	6 Mo	1Yr / Pct	3Yr / Pct	5Yr / Pct	Dividend Yield	Expense Ratio
	99 Pct = Best											
	0 Pct = Worst											
GI	Sterling Capital Strat Alloc Bal A	BAMGX	C	(800) 228-1872	D+ / 2.7	4.56	4.46	13.19 /22	4.27 /46	6.12 /29	1.31	1.63
GI	● Sterling Capital Strat Alloc Bal B	BBMGX	C+	(800) 228-1872	C- / 3.2	4.43	4.13	12.38 /19	3.51 /37	5.35 /24	0.60	2.38
GI	Sterling Capital Strat Alloc Bal C	BCMCX	C+	(800) 228-1872	C- / 3.2	4.37	4.07	12.32 /19	3.53 /37	5.33 /24	0.73	2.38
GI	Sterling Capital Strat Alloc Bal I	BCGTX	C+	(800) 228-1872	C- / 4.0	4.69	4.65	13.46 /23	4.57 /50	6.43 /31	1.62	1.38
GI	Sterling Capital Strat Alloc Gro A	BCMAX	C	(800) 228-1872	C- / 3.4	5.40	6.00	15.81 /33	4.61 /50	7.02 /35	0.98	1.77
GI	● Sterling Capital Strat Alloc Gro B	BCMBX	C+	(800) 228-1872	C- / 3.9	5.13	5.55	14.87 /29	3.84 /41	6.21 /30	0.47	2.52
GI	Sterling Capital Strat Alloc Gro C	BCGCX	C+	(800) 228-1872	C- / 3.9	5.19	5.61	14.98 /30	3.87 /41	6.23 /30	0.59	2.52
GI	Sterling Capital Strat Alloc Gro I	BCMTX	B-	(800) 228-1872	C / 4.8	5.45	6.11	16.05 /35	4.90 /53	7.29 /37	1.27	1.52
RE	Sterling Capital Stratton RE Inst	STMDX	A	(800) 228-1872	B / 8.2	8.95	-0.88	16.21 /35	11.67 /98	11.53 /70	2.88	0.79
GL	Steward Global Equity Income Indv	SGIDX	B+	(800) 262-6631	B- / 7.4	6.37	6.30	21.27 /59	8.32 /81	9.27 /53	1.77	0.98
GL	Steward Global Equity Income Inst	SGISX	B+	(800) 262-6631	B / 7.7	6.46	6.49	21.67 /61	8.68 /85	9.65 /56	2.04	0.64
FO	Steward Intl Enhanced Index Indv	SNTKX	D-	(800) 262-6631	D- / 1.4	6.46	5.98	22.06 /63	-1.24 / 9	0.85 / 6	1.89	1.00
FO	Steward Intl Enhanced Index Inst	SNTCX	D-	(800) 262-6631	D / 1.6	6.54	6.17	22.44 /64	-0.88 /10	1.20 / 6	2.18	0.65
GR	Steward Large Cap Enhan Index Indv	SEEKX	C+	(800) 262-6631	B / 8.1	7.21	9.43	23.95 /70	8.18 /80	13.04 /84	0.70	0.82
GR	Steward Large Cap Enhan Index Inst	SEECX	B-	(800) 262-6631	B+ / 8.3	7.31	9.62	24.36 /71	8.54 /83	13.42 /88	0.89	0.48
SC	Steward SMCap Enh Idx Indv	TRDFX	B-	(800) 262-6631	A- / 9.0	4.83	12.10	32.84 /91	8.06 /79	12.99 /84	0.51	0.85
SC	Steward SMCap Enh Idx Inst	SCECX	B-	(800) 262-6631	A- / 9.1	4.85	12.26	33.20 /92	8.36 /82	13.28 /87	0.75	0.57
GI	Stock Dividend Fund	SDIVX	B-	(800) 704-6072	B / 7.8	3.56	12.13	40.90 /98	4.90 /53	9.22 /52	2.26	0.85
GL	Stone Harbor Local Markets Inst	SHLMX	E+	(866) 699-8125	E / 0.4	6.96	0.12	13.54 /24	-3.73 / 3	-4.24 / 2	0.00	0.88
GR	Stralem Equity Fund Inst	STEFX	D		C+ / 6.8	7.53	6.43	19.33 /49	7.43 /75	10.23 /60	1.54	1.21
AA	Stringer Growth A	SRGAX	C-	(877) 244-6235	D+ / 2.9	5.76	5.21	15.98 /34	3.51 /37	—	0.83	1.88
AA	Stringer Growth C	SRGCX	C-	(877) 244-6235	C- / 3.2	5.60	4.76	15.08 /30	2.71 /29	—	0.02	2.63
AA	Stringer Growth Institutional	SRGIX	C	(877) 244-6235	C- / 4.1	5.85	5.39	16.25 /35	3.76 /40	—	1.14	1.63
GR	Summit Glbl Inv US Low Vol Eq I	SILVX	A	(855) 744-8500	B- / 7.1	5.45	4.52	13.90 /25	10.38 /95	12.16 /76	1.05	1.14
GR	Summit Global Invst Gl LV I	DWUGX	E	(888) 572-0968	D / 1.7	5.58	0.88	15.95 /34	0.48 /16	8.29 /45	0.00	1.13
AA	SunAmerica VAL Co I Asset Alloc	VCAAX	C-	(800) 858-8850	C / 4.3	4.44	5.32	15.55 /32	4.71 /51	7.07 /35	2.34	0.71
GR	SunAmerica VAL Co I Bluechip Gro	VCBCX	C+	(800) 858-8850	B+ / 8.4	8.84	10.00	22.43 /64	8.69 /85	14.42 /95	0.00	0.84
GI	SunAmerica VAL Co I Brcap Val inc	VBCVX	A-	(800) 858-8850	B+ / 8.7	6.51	13.39	28.26 /82	7.91 /78	12.78 /82	1.48	0.92
GR	SunAmerica VAL Co I Core Eq Fd	VCCEX	A+	(800) 858-8850	A- / 9.1	7.47	12.89	28.55 /83	8.67 /84	12.48 /79	1.08	0.92
GI	SunAmerica VAL Co I Dividend Val	VCIGX	B+	(800) 858-8850	B+ / 8.9	5.22	10.38	24.78 /73	9.96 /93	12.72 /81	1.91	0.83
GL	SunAmerica VAL Co I Emg	VCGEX	C	(800) 858-8850	C+ / 5.8	10.44	8.53	32.88 /91	1.36 /20	-0.68 / 4	1.50	0.97
FO	SunAmerica VAL Co I Fr Val Fd	VCFVX	D-	(800) 858-8850	D / 1.6	7.81	8.27	27.12 /79	-1.80 / 7	4.95 /21	1.95	0.79
RE	SunAmerica VAL Co I Glb Real Est	VGREX	D+	(800) 858-8850	C- / 3.5	6.62	-2.86	12.16 /18	5.11 /55	7.76 /40	4.33	0.85
GR	SunAmerica VAL Co I Glb Soc Awr	VCSOX	C+	(800) 858-8850	C+ / 6.2	7.18	6.39	20.08 /52	5.98 /64	10.69 /63	1.73	0.63
GL	SunAmerica VAL Co I Glb Str Fd	VGLSX	D	(800) 858-8850	C- / 3.3	6.65	8.34	17.78 /42	1.34 /20	6.73 /33	0.93	0.64
GI	SunAmerica VAL Co I Growth & Inc	VCGAX	A+	(800) 858-8850	A / 9.3	7.94	10.66	25.74 /75	10.00 /93	12.80 /82	1.17	0.91
GR	SunAmerica VAL Co I Growth Fd	VCULX	C+	(800) 858-8850	B / 7.6	8.51	8.20	20.56 /55	7.97 /79	11.48 /70	0.80	0.81
HL	SunAmerica VAL Co I Health Sci Fd	VCHSX	C	(800) 858-8850	B+ / 8.3	10.07	8.09	16.86 /38	9.78 /92	21.09 /99	0.00	1.09
FO	SunAmerica VAL Co I Intl Growth	VCINX	E+	(800) 858-8850	E+ / 0.8	6.32	1.59	10.37 /13	-1.25 / 9	4.91 /21	1.51	1.06
GR	SunAmerica VAL Co I Lg Cptl Gro Fd	VLCGX	C+	(800) 858-8850	B- / 7.3	9.08	5.79	19.00 /47	8.14 /80	10.84 /65	0.71	0.75
GI	SunAmerica VAL Co I Lgcap Core Fd	VLCCX	C+	(800) 858-8850	B+ / 8.7	7.33	7.82	21.98 /62	10.18 /94	14.35 /95	0.94	0.83
MC	SunAmerica VAL Co I MdCp Strt Gr	VMSGX	D	(800) 858-8850	C / 5.4	6.54	7.11	25.91 /76	3.28 /35	9.46 /54	0.00	0.83
MC	SunAmerica VAL Co I Midcap Idx Fd	VMIDX	B+	(800) 858-8850	A / 9.4	6.57	11.26	31.50 /89	9.36 /89	13.52 /89	1.17	0.36
GR	SunAmerica VAL Co I Nsdq 100 IdX	VCNIX	A+	(800) 858-8850	A+ / 9.8	11.06	12.12	27.84 /81	13.84 /99	16.15 /98	0.73	0.56
GR	SunAmerica VAL Co I Sc&Tech Fd	VCSTX	B-	(800) 858-8850	A+ / 9.8	10.20	10.59	31.31 /89	11.43 /98	15.34 /97	0.00	0.99
AG	SunAmerica VAL Co I SmCp Agg Gro	VSAGX	C-	(800) 858-8850	B+ / 8.4	8.82	13.84	31.02 /88	6.10 /65	13.52 /89	0.00	1.01
SC	SunAmerica VAL Co I Smcp Fd	VCSMX	D+	(800) 858-8850	C+ / 6.8	4.62	10.02	27.82 /81	5.26 /57	11.65 /71	0.29	1.01
SC	SunAmerica VAL Co I Smcp Idx Fd	VCSLX	B-	(800) 858-8850	B+ / 8.8	5.12	12.52	35.90 /95	6.81 /71	12.76 /82	1.07	0.42
SC	SunAmerica VAL Co I Smcp Spl Val	VSSVX	B+	(800) 858-8850	A / 9.5	3.61	11.88	34.48 /93	9.55 /91	14.25 /94	0.98	0.88
SC	SunAmerica VAL Co I Sm-Mid Gro Fd	VSSGX	D	(800) 858-8850	C / 5.4	7.07	4.73	21.87 /62	4.62 /50	9.57 /55	0.00	1.00
GR	SunAmerica VAL Co I Stk Idx Fd	VSTIX	A	(800) 858-8850	A- / 9.2	7.94	9.85	24.59 /72	10.27 /95	13.62 /90	1.53	0.35
GR	SunAmerica VAL Co I Val Fd	VAVAX	A	(800) 858-8850	B / 8.2	6.59	9.07	26.03 /76	8.27 /81	12.26 /77	1.69	0.93

● Denotes fund is closed to new investors
* Denotes fund is included in Section II

www.thestreetratings.com

RISK			NET ASSETS		ASSET					BULL / BEAR		FUND MANAGER		MINIMUMS		LOADS	
	3 Year		NAV						Portfolio	Last Bull	Last Bear	Manager	Manager	Initial	Additional	Front	Back
Risk	Standard		As of	Total	Cash	Stocks	Bonds	Other	Turnover	Market	Market	Quality	Tenure	Purch.	Purch.	End	End
Rating/Pts	Deviation	Beta	2/28/17	$(Mil)	%	%	%	%	Ratio	Return	Return	Pct	(Years)	$	$	Load	Load
B /8.5	6.5	0.58	11.10	31	6	57	35	2	5	53.3	-15.1	52	12	1,000	0	5.8	0.0
B /8.5	6.5	0.58	10.89	N/A	6	57	35	2	5	47.2	-15.3	42	12	1,000	0	0.0	0.0
B /8.5	6.5	0.58	10.88	1	6	57	35	2	5	47.2	-15.3	42	12	1,000	0	0.0	0.0
B /8.5	6.5	0.58	11.19	N/A	6	57	35	2	5	55.5	-14.9	56	12	1,000,000	0	0.0	0.0
B- /7.8	8.0	0.72	10.94	22	8	71	20	1	6	63.6	-18.7	37	12	1,000	0	5.8	0.0
B- /7.8	8.0	0.72	10.62	N/A	8	71	20	1	6	57.0	-18.9	28	12	1,000	0	0.0	0.0
B- /7.8	8.1	0.73	10.56	N/A	8	71	20	1	6	57.2	-19.0	27	12	1,000	0	0.0	0.0
B- /7.8	8.0	0.73	10.97	1	8	71	20	1	6	66.0	-18.6	40	12	1,000,000	0	0.0	0.0
B- /7.1	14.1	1.03	37.57	95	0	0	0	100	15	106.9	-16.6	75	2	2,000	100	0.0	0.0
C+ /6.8	9.2	0.58	30.35	58	0	99	0	1	54	84.3	-13.1	99	9	200	0	0.0	0.0
C+ /6.8	9.3	0.58	30.42	179	0	99	0	1	54	87.8	-13.0	99	9	25,000	1,000	0.0	0.0
C /4.8	13.1	0.95	19.98	17	0	98	0	2	11	22.4	-24.3	61	11	200	0	0.0	0.0
C /4.8	13.1	0.96	20.04	112	0	98	0	2	11	24.8	-24.2	66	11	25,000	1,000	0.0	0.0
C /4.4	10.8	1.04	36.88	54	0	98	0	2	91	125.6	-17.8	39	13	200	0	0.0	0.0
C /4.4	10.8	1.04	36.71	305	0	98	0	2	91	129.8	-17.7	44	13	25,000	1,000	0.0	0.0
C- /3.6	13.9	0.86	15.37	69	0	99	0	1	33	132.3	-22.4	86	19	200	0	0.0	0.0
C- /3.6	13.9	0.86	15.57	124	0	99	0	1	33	135.9	-22.3	87	19	25,000	1,000	0.0	0.0
C /4.8	15.0	1.04	27.09	28	2	97	0	1	38	85.6	-13.5	10	13	100,000	100	0.0	2.0
C /5.1	12.6	0.60	8.30	923	0	0	0	100	166	-10.0	-8.9	26	7	1,000,000	250,000	0.0	0.0
E+ /0.8	9.5	0.88	9.74	131	3	96	0	1	33	93.8	-11.4	52	17	25,000	100	0.0	1.0
B- /7.0	8.4	1.30	12.01	14	10	86	0	4	144	N/A	N/A	9	4	5,000	250	5.5	0.0
B- /7.1	8.5	1.30	11.92	16	10	86	0	4	144	N/A	N/A	6	4	5,000	250	0.0	0.0
B- /7.0	8.5	1.30	12.04	15	10	86	0	4	144	N/A	N/A	11	4	1,000,000	5,000	0.0	0.0
B /8.2	8.5	0.71	14.97	92	0	0	0	100	41	N/A	N/A	89	5	1,000,000	0	0.0	1.5
D+ /2.4	17.8	1.02	25.15	24	0	100	0	0	375	76.0	-14.3	2	8	25,000	0	0.0	2.0
C /5.5	7.0	1.04	10.93	164	8	46	45	1	102	63.3	-11.0	35	15	0	0	0.0	0.0
C- /4.1	12.8	1.05	15.86	640	0	99	0	1	30	143.9	-14.7	44	17	0	0	0.0	0.0
C+ /6.1	11.2	1.01	15.59	58	0	99	0	1	26	122.1	-18.7	40	5	0	0	0.0	0.0
B- /7.0	11.9	1.11	21.81	247	2	97	0	1	41	124.8	-20.5	36	5	0	0	0.0	0.0
C /5.4	9.8	0.91	11.95	788	2	97	0	1	45	115.7	-11.8	76	7	0	0	0.0	0.0
C /4.7	16.2	0.92	7.41	707	7	92	0	1	64	22.9	-23.6	84	6	0	0	0.0	0.0
C /4.9	13.6	1.02	9.89	848	0	96	3	1	21	48.0	-24.7	54	9	0	0	0.0	0.0
C /5.4	11.6	0.78	7.43	411	11	87	0	2	71	74.8	-21.0	31	9	0	0	0.0	0.0
C+ /6.8	10.3	0.96	22.66	404	3	87	8	2	88	96.9	-19.9	24	3	0	0	0.0	0.0
C /4.9	9.1	0.69	11.30	419	2	58	39	1	26	59.3	-15.2	83	12	0	0	0.0	0.0
C+ /6.5	10.5	1.01	20.23	119	1	98	0	1	33	123.8	-19.7	66	4	0	0	0.0	0.0
C- /3.9	10.9	1.01	13.94	944	0	99	0	1	102	113.1	-17.3	41	10	0	0	0.0	0.0
C- /3.0	17.5	1.10	19.14	720	1	98	0	1	31	224.1	-14.7	52	1	0	0	0.0	0.0
C /5.1	11.1	0.88	11.70	408	2	97	0	1	36	49.6	-23.1	61	12	0	0	0.0	0.0
C /4.8	11.1	1.02	12.81	401	1	97	0	2	24	103.2	-18.9	41	4	0	0	0.0	0.0
D+ /2.8	10.5	1.00	10.98	163	0	99	0	1	53	140.7	-20.0	69	6	0	0	0.0	0.0
D+ /2.9	13.2	0.96	13.20	253	0	98	0	2	95	89.9	-21.7	11	6	0	0	0.0	0.0
C /4.8	12.0	1.00	26.47	3,452	0	94	4	2	15	137.0	-22.7	71	5	0	0	0.0	0.0
C+ /5.9	13.7	1.18	11.14	358	0	99	0	1	8	160.0	-10.9	81	5	0	0	0.0	0.0
D+ /2.8	14.4	1.20	23.42	1,029	3	96	0	1	107	147.3	-19.4	59	12	0	0	0.0	0.0
D- /1.1	17.7	1.25	11.77	111	1	98	0	1	101	137.5	-25.7	6	6	0	0	0.0	0.0
D+ /2.4	14.3	0.90	11.59	320	1	98	0	1	29	123.4	-24.9	63	11	0	0	0.0	0.0
C- /4.1	15.8	1.00	20.40	1,211	1	90	7	2	13	130.5	-25.2	73	5	0	0	0.0	0.0
C /4.9	13.3	0.82	13.42	294	7	92	0	1	74	146.9	-24.0	92	12	0	0	0.0	0.0
D /2.1	14.7	0.83	11.39	105	1	96	1	2	64	98.9	-23.2	62	4	0	0	0.0	0.0
C+ /5.8	10.3	1.00	35.59	4,484	0	99	0	1	3	130.4	-16.4	70	5	0	0	0.0	0.0
B- /7.0	11.3	1.07	16.58	114	0	99	0	1	15	122.4	-20.6	37	6	0	0	0.0	0.0

Fund Type	Fund Name	Ticker Symbol	Overall Investment Rating	Phone	Performance Rating/Pts	3 Mo	6 Mo	1Yr / Pct	3Yr / Pct	5Yr / Pct	Dividend Yield	Expense Ratio
AA	SunAmerica VAL Co II Agg Gr Life Fd	VAGLX	C+	(800) 858-8850	C / 5.3	5.76	5.86	20.02 /52	4.83 / 52	8.45 /46	1.92	0.91
GR	SunAmerica VAL Co II Capital App	VCCAX	C+	(800) 858-8850	C+ / 6.5	8.13	6.50	19.01 /47	6.54 /69	12.49 /79	0.34	1.00
AA	SunAmerica VAL Co II Con Gr Life Fd	VCGLX	C-	(800) 858-8850	D+ / 2.8	3.95	2.45	12.18 /19	3.25 /34	5.29 /23	2.70	0.95
GR	SunAmerica VAL Co II Lrg Cp Val	VACVX	A+	(800) 858-8850	A / 9.5	7.10	13.91	31.17 /88	9.43 /90	14.00 /93	1.00	0.89
MC	SunAmerica VAL Co II MdCp Value	VMCVX	B-	(800) 858-8850	B / 8.0	5.46	10.51	30.02 /86	7.01 /72	12.70 /81	0.24	1.06
MC	SunAmerica VAL Co II Mid Cap	VAMGX	D+	(800) 858-8850	C+ / 6.1	8.29	8.55	27.12 /79	3.63 /38	8.18 /43	0.00	1.17
AA	SunAmerica VAL Co II Mod Gro LfSt	VMGLX	C+	(800) 858-8850	C / 4.3	4.96	4.51	16.97 /38	4.44 /48	7.32 /37	2.09	0.91
SC	SunAmerica VAL Co II SmCp Growth	VASMX	C-	(800) 858-8850	B / 8.2	9.19	11.27	41.37 /98	3.95 /42	11.85 /73	0.00	1.29
SC	SunAmerica VAL Co II SmCp Value	VCSVX	B	(800) 858-8850	A / 9.5	3.39	14.52	37.97 /96	8.23 /81	12.77 /82	0.97	1.04
GR	SunAmerica VAL Co II Soc Resp	VCSRX	A+	(800) 858-8850	A- / 9.0	7.10	9.00	23.59 /68	10.42 /95	14.27 /95	1.25	0.61
IN	Superfund Managed Futures Strat A	SUPRX	D		E- / 0.1	2.32	-4.45	-7.17 / 0	-2.89 / 5	--	5.26	3.29
IN	Superfund Managed Futures Strat I	SUPIX	D		E- / 0.2	2.35	-4.39	-7.01 / 0	-2.69 / 5	--	5.84	3.04
IX	Swan Defined Risk A	SDRAX	C-	(877) 896-2590	D / 1.8	2.68	3.99	9.79 /11	3.12 /33	--	1.15	1.55
IX	Swan Defined Risk C	SDRCX	C-	(877) 896-2590	D / 2.1	2.46	3.52	8.99 / 9	2.35 /26	--	0.64	2.30
EM	Swan Defined Risk Emerging Mkts I	SDFIX	U	(877) 896-2590	U /	3.78	2.57	12.59 /20	--	--	0.00	2.62
IX	Swan Defined Risk I	SDRIX	C	(877) 896-2590	D+ / 2.6	2.69	4.08	10.06 /12	3.37 /36	--	1.40	1.30
GR	Symons Alpha Value Inst	SAVIX	C-	(800) 408-4682	C- / 4.1	8.91	3.54	10.00 /12	5.50 /60	8.19 /44	1.15	1.34
FO	T Rowe Price Africa and Middle East	TRAMX	E	(800) 638-5660	E+ / 0.9	6.29	8.24	20.76 /56	-2.56 / 5	5.22 /23	1.85	1.47
FO	T Rowe Price Asia Opportunities	TRAOX	U	(800) 638-5660	U /	5.35	2.91	25.59 /75	--	--	1.23	2.29
BA	T Rowe Price Balanced	RPBAX	C+	(800) 638-5660	C / 4.7	5.76	5.14	15.53 /32	5.03 /55	8.27 /44	1.89	0.68
BA	T Rowe Price Balanced I	RBAIX	U	(800) 638-5660	U /	5.81	5.28	15.74 /33	--	--	2.06	0.72
* GR	T Rowe Price Blue Chip Growth	TRBCX	B+	(800) 638-5660	B+ / 8.5	8.85	10.05	22.58 /65	8.83 /86	14.60 /96	0.06	0.71
GR	T Rowe Price Blue Chip Growth Adv	PABGX	B+	(800) 638-5660	B+ / 8.3	8.76	9.89	22.24 /63	8.54 /83	14.30 /95	0.00	0.99
GR	T Rowe Price Blue Chip Growth I	TBCIX	U	(800) 638-5660	U /	8.89	10.12	22.74 /66	--	--	0.19	0.63
GR	T Rowe Price Blue Chip Growth R	RRBGX	B	(800) 638-5660	B / 8.1	8.70	9.75	21.92 /62	8.25 /81	14.00 /93	0.00	1.24
AA ●	T Rowe Price Cap Appreciation	PRWCX	B	(800) 638-5660	B- / 7.2	5.47	5.04	16.15 /35	9.33 /89	11.86 /73	1.47	0.70
AA	T Rowe Price Cap Appreciation Adv	PACLX	C+	(800) 638-5660	C+ / 6.9	5.41	4.86	15.75 /33	9.00 /87	11.52 /70	1.16	1.01
AA	T Rowe Price Cap Appreciation I	TRAIX	U	(800) 638-5660	U /	5.51	5.08	16.22 /35	--	--	1.54	0.73
GR	T Rowe Price Cap Opportunity	PRCOX	A	(800) 638-5660	A- / 9.2	8.10	9.95	24.74 /72	10.25 /95	13.65 /90	1.11	0.70
GR	T Rowe Price Cap Opportunity Adv	PACOX	A-	(800) 638-5660	A- / 9.0	8.06	9.77	24.37 /71	9.93 /93	13.32 /87	0.91	0.99
GR	T Rowe Price Cap Opportunity R	RRCOX	A-	(800) 638-5660	B+ / 8.9	7.98	9.66	23.99 /70	9.63 /91	12.98 /84	0.60	1.26
MC	T Rowe Price Diversified MidCap Gr	PRDMX	B	(800) 638-5660	B / 7.7	6.81	7.77	24.28 /71	7.77 /77	12.57 /80	0.19	0.87
* IN	T Rowe Price Dividend Growth	PRDGX	A	(800) 638-5660	B+ / 8.4	6.13	6.58	21.49 /60	10.20 /94	13.47 /89	1.44	0.64
IN	T Rowe Price Dividend Growth Adv	TADGX	A-	(800) 638-5660	B / 8.2	6.03	6.42	21.16 /58	9.90 /93	13.17 /86	1.24	0.91
GI	T Rowe Price Dividend Growth I	PDGIX	U	(800) 638-5660	U /	6.13	6.64	21.63 /60	--	--	1.57	0.79
EM	T Rowe Price Emer Europe	TREMX	E-	(800) 638-5660	E- / 0.2	5.90	6.41	24.34 /71	-7.53 / 1	-6.34 / 1	1.07	1.76
* EM	T Rowe Price Emerging Mkts Stk	PRMSX	C	(800) 638-5660	C+ / 6.3	9.46	3.34	31.66 /89	4.34 /47	1.50 / 7	0.46	1.24
EM	T Rowe Price Emerging Mkts Stk I	PRZIX	U	(800) 638-5660	U /	9.50	3.42	31.91 /90	--	--	0.70	1.09
* IN	T Rowe Price Equity Income	PRFDX	B+	(800) 638-5660	B+ / 8.3	5.26	11.43	29.21 /85	7.54 /76	11.69 /71	2.13	0.66
IN	T Rowe Price Equity Income Adv	PAFDX	B	(800) 638-5660	B / 8.1	5.15	11.25	28.83 /84	7.24 /74	11.39 /69	1.90	0.93
IN	T Rowe Price Equity Income I	REIPX	U	(800) 638-5660	U /	5.26	11.46	29.33 /85	--	--	2.25	0.64
IN	T Rowe Price Equity Income R	RRFDX	B	(800) 638-5660	B / 7.9	5.09	11.10	28.48 /83	6.96 /72	11.10 /67	1.64	1.19
* IX	T Rowe Price Equity Index 500	PREIX	A+	(800) 638-5660	A- / 9.2	7.97	9.89	24.67 /72	10.35 /95	13.71 /91	1.73	0.27
GR	T Rowe Price Equity Index 500 I	PRUIX	U	(800) 638-5660	U /	8.02	9.96	24.88 /73	--	--	1.85	0.17
FO	T Rowe Price European Stk	PRESX	E+	(800) 638-5660	E- / 0.1	7.14	-2.48	3.19 / 3	-5.53 / 2	5.30 /23	2.93	0.95
MC	T Rowe Price Extended Eq Mkt Indx	PEXMX	B	(800) 638-5660	B+ / 8.4	6.63	11.52	32.76 /91	6.91 /71	13.17 /86	1.05	0.35
FS	T Rowe Price Financial Services	PRISX	A-	(800) 638-5660	A+ / 9.9	9.59	20.89	41.68 /98	10.19 /94	15.71 /98	0.85	0.95
RE	T Rowe Price Glbl Real Estate	TRGRX	C-	(800) 638-5660	C- / 3.2	5.39	-3.02	10.87 /14	5.79 /62	7.53 /39	2.05	1.05
RE	T Rowe Price Glbl Real Estate Adv	PAGEX	C-	(800) 638-5660	C- / 3.1	5.32	-3.14	10.72 /14	5.66 /61	7.42 /38	2.01	1.27
GL	T Rowe Price Global Allocation	RPGAX	C+	(800) 638-5660	C- / 4.2	5.68	4.73	15.86 /34	4.26 /46	--	1.13	1.35
GL	T Rowe Price Global Allocation Adv	PAFGX	C+	(800) 638-5660	C- / 4.1	5.60	4.65	15.81 /33	4.15 /45	--	1.04	1.69
OT	T Rowe Price Global Industrials	RPGIX	C	(800) 638-5660	C / 4.8	5.17	5.27	22.42 /64	3.73 /40	--	0.65	2.39

● Denotes fund is closed to new investors
* Denotes fund is included in Section II

RISK			NET ASSETS		ASSET					BULL / BEAR		FUND MANAGER		MINIMUMS		LOADS	
	3 Year		NAV						Portfolio	Last Bull	Last Bear	Manager	Manager	Initial	Additional	Front	Back
Risk	Standard		As of	Total	Cash	Stocks	Bonds	Other	Turnover	Market	Market	Quality	Tenure	Purch.	Purch.	End	End
Rating/Pts	Deviation	Beta	2/28/17	$(Mil)	%	%	%	%	Ratio	Return	Return	Pct	(Years)	$	$	Load	Load
C+ / 6.4	8.9	1.35	11.02	553	3	75	20	2	24	76.8	-14.0	15	N/A	0	0	0.0	0.0
C+ / 6.1	11.4	1.04	17.03	88	2	97	0	1	54	124.5	-19.4	22	6	0	0	0.0	0.0
B- / 7.5	5.4	0.80	12.11	333	5	34	60	1	27	44.7	-7.5	40	N/A	0	0	0.0	0.0
C+ / 6.9	11.4	1.04	20.97	248	1	97	1	1	71	137.3	-22.4	56	7	0	0	0.0	0.0
C / 4.6	13.0	1.05	22.60	1,074	0	98	0	2	44	133.5	-25.6	36	15	0	0	0.0	0.0
C- / 3.0	13.5	0.99	9.14	121	0	99	0	1	71	82.6	-23.6	11	6	0	0	0.0	0.0
B- / 7.2	7.2	1.10	14.61	878	4	57	38	1	33	64.1	-11.4	27	N/A	0	0	0.0	0.0
D / 1.8	20.0	1.16	15.80	112	1	98	0	1	39	127.4	-28.2	25	10	0	0	0.0	0.0
C- / 3.7	15.6	0.95	15.54	552	4	95	0	1	59	129.6	-28.1	84	12	0	0	0.0	0.0
B- / 7.0	10.6	1.03	20.96	806	0	96	2	2	25	137.1	-16.5	69	5	0	0	0.0	0.0
B- / 7.7	9.8	0.25	8.62	2	0	0	0	100	0	N/A	N/A	12	4	2,500	500	5.8	1.0
B- / 7.7	9.7	0.25	8.64	2	0	0	0	100	0	N/A	N/A	13	4	1,000,000	1,000	0.0	1.0
B- / 7.9	5.7	0.46	12.05	319	13	86	0	1	18	N/A	N/A	54	5	2,500	500	5.5	0.0
B- / 7.9	5.7	0.46	11.89	192	13	86	0	1	18	N/A	N/A	43	5	2,500	500	0.0	0.0
U /	N/A	N/A	9.46	26	24	75	0	1	62	N/A	N/A	N/A	3	100,000	500	0.0	0.0
B- / 7.9	5.7	0.45	12.09	1,868	13	86	0	1	18	N/A	N/A	58	5	100,000	500	0.0	0.0
C+ / 5.8	7.8	0.47	11.52	86	13	83	2	2	65	65.2	-7.4	78	37	5,000	250	0.0	2.0
C- / 3.2	15.1	0.84	8.09	131	0	0	0	100	83	48.6	-17.1	42	6	2,500	100	0.0	2.0
U /	N/A	N/A	11.33	29	2	97	0	1	52	N/A	N/A	N/A	3	2,500	100	0.0	2.0
B- / 7.3	7.2	1.10	22.97	3,590	0	0	0	100	65	71.8	-11.8	34	6	2,500	100	0.0	0.0
U /	N/A	N/A	22.98	177	0	0	0	100	65	N/A	N/A	N/A	6	1,000,000	0	0.0	0.0
C / 5.5	12.8	1.05	79.03	26,563	0	100	0	0	33	146.6	-14.8	46	24	2,500	100	0.0	0.0
C / 5.4	12.8	1.05	77.98	2,967	0	100	0	0	33	143.2	-14.9	42	24	2,500	100	0.0	0.0
U /	N/A	N/A	79.05	4,067	0	100	0	0	33	N/A	N/A	N/A	24	1,000,000	0	0.0	0.0
C / 5.4	12.8	1.05	75.28	598	0	100	0	0	33	139.9	-15.0	38	24	2,500	100	0.0	0.0
C+ / 6.4	6.8	1.06	27.39	24,122	7	65	26	2	67	106.8	-12.5	82	11	2,500	100	0.0	0.0
C+ / 6.4	6.8	1.06	27.11	1,350	7	65	26	2	67	103.4	-12.6	81	11	2,500	100	0.0	0.0
U /	N/A	N/A	27.41	1,321	7	65	26	2	67	N/A	N/A	N/A	11	1,000,000	0	0.0	0.0
C+ / 5.8	10.6	1.02	23.97	503	0	99	0	1	41	132.5	-16.5	67	2	2,500	100	0.0	0.0
C+ / 5.8	10.6	1.02	23.86	22	0	99	0	1	41	128.9	-16.7	64	2	2,500	100	0.0	0.0
C+ / 5.9	10.6	1.02	23.83	6	0	99	0	1	41	125.2	-16.7	60	2	2,500	100	0.0	0.0
C / 5.3	12.6	0.97	26.13	625	0	99	0	1	18	127.3	-22.9	56	14	2,500	100	0.0	0.0
C+ / 6.7	9.6	0.92	38.96	5,401	5	94	0	1	25	125.7	-15.3	77	17	2,500	100	0.0	0.0
C+ / 6.7	9.6	0.92	38.89	356	5	94	0	1	25	122.5	-15.4	75	17	2,500	100	0.0	0.0
U /	N/A	N/A	38.95	1,319	5	94	0	1	25	N/A	N/A	N/A	17	1,000,000	0	0.0	0.0
D / 1.7	20.8	0.85	13.07	176	0	0	0	100	48	-11.1	-34.2	3	4	2,500	100	0.0	2.0
C / 5.0	15.8	0.94	34.49	6,365	2	97	0	1	24	31.6	-26.0	89	9	2,500	100	0.0	2.0
U /	N/A	N/A	34.48	1,638	2	97	0	1	24	N/A	N/A	N/A	9	1,000,000	0	0.0	2.0
C / 5.5	11.0	1.01	32.59	18,328	2	96	0	2	27	111.2	-18.1	36	2	2,500	100	0.0	0.0
C / 5.5	11.0	1.01	32.49	511	2	96	0	2	27	108.1	-18.2	33	2	2,500	100	0.0	0.0
U /	N/A	N/A	32.59	3,529	2	96	0	2	27	N/A	N/A	N/A	2	1,000,000	0	0.0	0.0
C / 5.5	11.0	1.01	32.42	129	2	96	0	2	27	105.1	-18.3	29	2	2,500	100	0.0	0.0
B- / 7.1	10.3	1.00	63.64	27,750	0	99	0	1	10	131.5	-16.4	71	9	2,500	100	0.0	0.5
U /	N/A	N/A	63.67	1,503	0	99	0	1	10	N/A	N/A	N/A	9	1,000,000	0	0.0	0.5
C+ / 5.6	11.9	0.89	17.40	980	0	0	0	100	37	57.5	-27.3	11	12	2,500	100	0.0	2.0
C / 4.9	13.8	1.12	26.42	802	4	94	0	2	23	136.1	-23.9	28	9	2,500	100	0.0	0.5
C / 5.0	15.3	1.12	25.77	833	0	0	0	100	38	164.3	-27.6	30	3	2,500	100	0.0	2.0
C+ / 6.8	12.0	0.82	20.27	200	12	87	0	1	21	72.6	-17.9	34	2	2,500	100	0.0	2.0
C+ / 6.8	12.0	0.82	20.13	31	12	87	0	1	21	71.6	-17.9	32	2	2,500	100	0.0	2.0
B- / 7.7	7.0	1.07	11.49	184	15	56	27	2	47	N/A	N/A	66	4	2,500	100	0.0	0.0
B- / 7.7	7.0	1.07	11.46	7	15	56	27	2	47	N/A	N/A	65	4	2,500	100	0.0	0.0
C+ / 6.5	12.0	1.04	11.49	19	8	91	0	1	67	N/A	N/A	6	4	2,500	100	0.0	0.0

			99 Pct = Best 0 Pct = Worst		PERFORMANCE								
						Total Return % through 2/28/17					Incl. in Returns		
			Overall		Perfor-				Annualized				
Fund		Ticker	Investment		mance						Dividend	Expense	
Type	Fund Name	Symbol	Rating	Phone	Rating/Pts	3 Mo	6 Mo	1Yr / Pct	3Yr / Pct	5Yr / Pct	Yield	Ratio	
GL	T Rowe Price Global Stock	PRGSX	B	(800) 638-5660	B / 7.8	7.79	8.17	26.42 /78	8.01 /79	11.64 /71	0.58	0.89	
GL	T Rowe Price Global Stock Adv	PAGSX	B	(800) 638-5660	B / 7.6	7.73	8.03	26.05 /76	7.72 /77	11.35 /69	0.29	1.27	
TC	T Rowe Price Global Technology	PRGTX	C+	(800) 638-5660	A+ / 9.9	12.44	12.82	38.94 /97	20.18 /99	20.72 /99	0.00	0.91	
FS	T Rowe Price Global Uncons Bd	RPIEX	U	(800) 638-5660	U /	0.80	0.22	4.08 / 3	--	--	0.65	1.69	
GL	T Rowe Price Global Uncons Bd I	RPEIX	U	(800) 638-5660	U /	0.81	0.24	4.25 / 3	--	--	0.72	1.89	
GI	T Rowe Price Growth and Inc	PRGIX	B	(800) 638-5660	B+ / 8.7	8.46	8.13	20.77 /56	10.09 /94	13.71 /91	1.13	0.67	
* GR	T Rowe Price Growth Stock	PRGFX	B	(800) 638-5660	B+ / 8.7	9.43	11.04	23.40 /68	8.80 /85	14.20 /94	0.07	0.67	
GR	T Rowe Price Growth Stock Adv	TRSAX	B	(800) 638-5660	B+ / 8.6	9.39	10.91	23.09 /67	8.54 /83	13.93 /93	0.00	0.92	
GR	T Rowe Price Growth Stock I	PRUFX	U	(800) 638-5660	U /	9.48	11.14	23.58 /68	--	--	0.22	0.52	
GR	T Rowe Price Growth Stock R	RRGSX	B	(800) 638-5660	B+ / 8.3	9.30	10.78	22.79 /66	8.26 /81	13.64 /90	0.00	1.17	
* HL	T Rowe Price Health Sciences	PRHSX	C+	(800) 638-5660	B+ / 8.5	10.14	8.27	17.10 /39	10.06 /94	21.39 /99	0.00	0.76	
HL	T Rowe Price Health Sciences I	THISX	U	(800) 638-5660	U /	10.18	8.34	--	--	--	0.00	0.69	
FO	T Rowe Price Ins Intl Core Eqty	TRCEX	D-	(800) 638-5660	D- / 1.4	8.00	5.89	17.81 /42	-0.16 /13	5.44 /24	2.23	0.88	
GL	T Rowe Price Inst Glbl Gr Eq	RPIGX	C+	(800) 638-5660	C+ / 6.0	8.57	4.67	20.07 /52	6.35 /67	8.96 /50	0.69	0.77	
EM	T Rowe Price Inst Global Foc Gr Eq	TRGSX	C	(800) 638-5660	B / 7.8	7.66	8.12	26.31 /77	8.02 /79	11.58 /71	1.71	0.96	
FO	T Rowe Price Inst Intl Gro Eqty	PRFEX	D+	(800) 638-5660	D+ / 2.9	7.60	2.85	17.34 /40	2.16 /25	4.87 /20	1.50	1.10	
FO	T Rowe Price Instl Africa & ME	TRIAX	E	(800) 638-5660	D- / 1.0	6.46	8.48	20.89 /57	-1.99 / 7	5.64 /26	2.15	1.19	
EM	T Rowe Price Instl Emer Mkt Eqty	IEMFX	C	(800) 638-5660	C+ / 6.4	9.39	3.41	31.85 /90	4.48 /49	1.61 / 7	0.64	1.10	
EM	T Rowe Price Instl Fron Mkt Eq	PRFFX	U	(800) 638-5660	U /	5.54	7.48	19.36 /49	--	--	1.75	1.84	
GL	T Rowe Price Instl Glbl Val Eq	PRIGX	C	(800) 638-5660	C+ / 6.2	6.85	9.04	22.03 /62	5.69 /61	--	1.83	3.68	
FO	T Rowe Price Instl Intl Conc Eqty	RPICX	D	(800) 638-5660	D / 1.8	6.13	2.13	14.14 /26	0.83 /17	7.44 /38	1.45	0.79	
GR	T Rowe Price Instl Lg Cap Core Gr	TPLGX	B+	(800) 638-5660	B+ / 8.5	8.81	10.04	22.63 /65	8.92 /86	14.66 /96	0.23	0.57	
* GR	T Rowe Price Instl Lg Cap Gr	TRLGX	B+	(800) 638-5660	A- / 9.0	9.52	12.64	26.09 /76	8.55 /83	14.82 /97	0.22	0.56	
GI	T Rowe Price Instl Lg Cap Val	TILCX	A	(800) 638-5660	A- / 9.1	5.81	10.31	27.90 /81	9.61 /91	14.13 /94	2.02	0.57	
* MC	● T Rowe Price Instl Mid-Cap Eq Gr	PMEGX	B+	(800) 638-5660	B+ / 8.6	6.91	7.46	22.99 /67	9.93 /93	14.62 /96	0.18	0.61	
SC	● T Rowe Price Instl Small Cap Stk	TRSSX	B	(800) 638-5660	B+ / 8.9	5.48	11.27	33.76 /93	7.82 /78	13.90 /92	0.26	0.67	
GR	T Rowe Price Instl US Stru Res	TRISX	B+	(800) 638-5660	A / 9.3	8.14	10.03	24.86 /73	10.37 /95	13.76 /91	1.39	0.54	
FO	T Rowe Price Intl Discovery	PRIDX	C	(800) 638-5660	C / 4.3	7.45	4.38	16.95 /38	4.46 /48	9.94 /58	0.54	1.20	
FO	T Rowe Price Intl Discovery I	TIDDX	U	(800) 638-5660	U /	7.49	4.44	17.09 /39	--	--	0.64	1.08	
FO	T Rowe Price Intl Equity Index	PIEQX	D-	(800) 638-5660	D- / 1.2	7.35	4.43	16.66 /37	-0.60 /11	4.93 /21	2.76	0.45	
GL	T Rowe Price Intl Glbl Grow Stk	RPGEX	C-	(800) 638-5660	C+ / 5.9	8.54	4.60	20.00 /52	6.14 /66	8.78 /49	0.44	1.15	
GL	T Rowe Price Intl Glbl Grow Stk Adv	PAGLX	C-	(800) 638-5660	C+ / 5.8	8.54	4.57	19.86 /51	6.05 /65	8.68 /48	0.34	1.43	
* FO	T Rowe Price Intl Stock	PRITX	D+	(800) 638-5660	D+ / 2.9	7.60	2.86	17.27 /40	2.13 /25	4.85 /20	1.16	0.83	
FO	T Rowe Price Intl Stock Adv	PAITX	D+	(800) 638-5660	D+ / 2.8	7.53	2.71	16.99 /38	1.98 /24	4.66 /19	0.55	1.09	
FO	T Rowe Price Intl Stock I	PRIUX	U	(800) 638-5660	U /	7.67	2.94	17.48 /41	--	--	1.47	0.67	
FO	T Rowe Price Intl Stock R	RRITX	D	(800) 638-5660	D+ / 2.5	7.44	2.53	16.62 /37	1.55 /21	4.29 /17	0.55	1.40	
* FO	T Rowe Price Intl Value Equity	TRIGX	E+	(800) 638-5660	E+ / 0.6	6.57	2.58	12.80 /21	-2.01 / 7	4.03 /15	2.55	0.84	
FO	T Rowe Price Intl Value Equity Adv	PAIGX	E+	(800) 638-5660	E+ / 0.6	6.46	2.38	12.60 /20	-2.22 / 6	3.79 /14	2.36	1.07	
FO	T Rowe Price Intl Value Equity I	TRTIX	U	(800) 638-5660	U /	6.57	2.59	12.97 /22	--	--	3.00	0.69	
FO	T Rowe Price Intl Value Equity R	RRIGX	E+	(800) 638-5660	E / 0.5	6.38	2.25	12.31 /19	-2.49 / 5	3.50 /13	2.16	1.35	
FO	T Rowe Price Japan	PRJPX	A+	(800) 638-5660	B / 7.7	6.34	7.35	23.92 /70	8.84 /86	10.84 /65	0.57	1.05	
FO	T Rowe Price Latin America	PRLAX	D-	(800) 638-5660	C+ / 6.6	13.29	6.56	45.10 /98	0.47 /16	-6.06 / 1	1.29	1.37	
TC	T Rowe Price Media and Telecomm	PRMTX	A	(800) 638-5660	A- / 9.1	9.04	8.10	26.43 /78	9.80 /92	15.90 /98	0.02	0.79	
TC	T Rowe Price Media and Telecomm I	TTMIX	U	(800) 638-5660	U /	9.07	8.15	--	--	--	0.00	0.69	
* MC	● T Rowe Price Mid-Cap Growth	RPMGX	B	(800) 638-5660	B / 8.1	6.67	7.11	21.91 /62	9.36 /89	13.99 /93	0.00	0.77	
MC	● T Rowe Price Mid-Cap Growth Adv	PAMCX	B-	(800) 638-5660	B / 7.9	6.61	6.98	21.62 /60	9.08 /87	13.70 /91	0.00	1.03	
MC	T Rowe Price Mid-Cap Growth I	RPTIX	U	(800) 638-5660	U /	6.71	7.19	22.08 /63	--	--	0.00	0.64	
MC	● T Rowe Price Mid-Cap Growth R	RRMGX	B-	(800) 638-5660	B / 7.7	6.54	6.83	21.29 /59	8.80 /85	13.41 /88	0.00	1.28	
MC	● T Rowe Price Mid-Cap Value Adv	TAMVX	B+	(800) 638-5660	A / 9.4	4.73	10.61	31.26 /89	10.07 /94	14.24 /94	0.64	1.05	
* MC	● T Rowe Price Mid-Cap Value Fd	TRMCX	B+	(800) 638-5660	A / 9.5	4.81	10.72	31.58 /89	10.35 /95	14.52 /96	0.85	0.80	
MC	T Rowe Price Mid-Cap Value I	TRMIX	U	(800) 638-5660	U /	4.85	10.79	31.76 /90	--	--	1.01	0.68	
MC	● T Rowe Price Mid-Cap Value R	RRMVX	B	(800) 638-5660	A / 9.3	4.70	10.47	30.96 /88	9.80 /92	13.95 /93	0.42	1.30	

● Denotes fund is closed to new investors
* Denotes fund is included in Section II

www.thestreetratings.com

RISK			NET ASSETS		ASSET				BULL / BEAR		FUND MANAGER		MINIMUMS		LOADS	
	3 Year		NAV						Last Bull	Last Bear	Manager	Manager	Initial	Additional	Front	Back
Risk Rating/Pts	Standard Deviation	Beta	As of 2/28/17	Total $(Mil)	Cash %	Stocks %	Bonds %	Other %	Portfolio Turnover Ratio	Market Return	Market Return	Quality Pct	Tenure (Years)	Purch. $	Purch. $	End Load	End Load
C+ / 5.8	13.0	0.95	30.83	589	0	99	0	1	135	115.5	-22.7	98	5	2,500	100	0.0	2.0
C+ / 5.8	13.0	0.95	30.66	5	0	99	0	1	135	112.5	-22.8	98	5	2,500	100	0.0	2.0
D+ / 2.4	16.5	1.26	15.09	3,532	0	0	0	100	219	228.8	-20.4	97	5	2,500	100	0.0	0.0
U /	N/A	N/A	10.03	44	0	0	0	100	183	N/A	N/A	N/A	2	2,500	100	0.0	0.0
U /	N/A	N/A	10.03	197	0	0	0	100	183	N/A	N/A	N/A	2	1,000,000	0	0.0	0.0
C / 4.7	9.9	0.92	26.90	1,672	0	0	0	100	76	127.5	-16.6	76	2	2,500	100	0.0	0.0
C / 4.7	12.9	1.06	58.08	37,908	1	98	0	1	38	143.0	-16.5	45	3	2,500	100	0.0	0.0
C / 4.7	12.9	1.06	56.92	3,247	1	98	0	1	38	139.8	-16.6	42	3	2,500	100	0.0	0.0
U /	N/A	N/A	58.12	4,932	1	98	0	1	38	N/A	N/A	N/A	3	1,000,000	0	0.0	0.0
C / 4.7	12.9	1.06	55.29	880	1	98	0	1	38	136.6	-16.7	37	3	2,500	100	0.0	0.0
C- / 3.6	17.5	1.10	66.31	9,908	0	0	0	100	31	227.7	-14.4	55	1	2,500	100	0.0	0.0
U /	N/A	N/A	66.31	334	0	0	0	100	31	N/A	N/A	N/A	1	1,000,000	0	0.0	0.0
C+ / 5.7	11.2	0.90	11.66	145	1	98	0	1	22	54.4	-23.4	74	7	1,000,000	0	0.0	2.0
C+ / 5.6	11.6	0.88	23.17	361	4	95	0	1	80	92.0	-22.5	97	9	1,000,000	0	0.0	2.0
C- / 3.0	13.0	0.55	11.57	35	2	97	0	1	137	114.6	-22.4	98	5	1,000,000	0	0.0	2.0
C+ / 6.0	11.8	0.92	21.88	51	3	96	0	1	37	54.3	-23.7	88	2	1,000,000	0	0.0	2.0
D+ / 2.7	15.0	0.83	5.58	165	24	75	0	1	75	51.7	-17.0	50	6	1,000,000	0	0.0	2.0
C / 5.0	15.7	0.94	31.47	1,051	2	97	0	1	36	32.8	-26.0	90	9	1,000,000	0	0.0	2.0
U /	N/A	N/A	8.59	50	10	89	0	1	46	N/A	N/A	N/A	3	1,000,000	0	0.0	2.0
C / 4.5	9.9	0.73	12.52	10	4	95	0	1	108	N/A	N/A	96	5	1,000,000	0	0.0	2.0
C+ / 6.2	10.4	0.82	11.74	401	9	90	0	1	120	67.3	-18.7	81	7	1,000,000	0	0.0	2.0
C+ / 5.8	12.7	1.05	30.24	2,434	0	99	0	1	33	147.1	-14.8	48	14	1,000,000	0	0.0	0.0
C / 5.0	13.2	1.08	31.90	13,039	1	98	0	1	40	149.9	-16.7	39	15	1,000,000	0	0.0	0.0
C+ / 6.2	11.1	1.05	21.90	3,273	2	96	0	2	34	137.4	-20.5	56	13	1,000,000	0	0.0	0.0
C / 5.3	12.3	0.94	49.13	5,866	2	97	0	1	40	144.1	-20.6	80	21	1,000,000	0	0.0	0.0
C / 4.6	14.4	0.91	22.72	3,550	4	95	0	1	28	149.0	-24.1	84	N/A	1,000,000	0	0.0	0.0
C / 5.1	10.6	1.02	12.57	617	0	99	0	1	57	133.7	-16.4	69	2	1,000,000	0	0.0	0.0
C+ / 6.8	10.5	0.76	56.66	3,349	0	0	0	100	28	87.4	-21.8	94	19	2,500	100	0.0	2.0
U /	N/A	N/A	56.69	1,658	0	0	0	100	28	N/A	N/A	N/A	19	1,000,000	0	0.0	2.0
C+ / 5.7	11.4	0.92	12.30	496	1	97	0	2	11	48.2	-24.2	69	11	2,500	100	0.0	2.0
C / 4.5	11.6	0.88	20.56	96	0	99	0	1	73	89.8	-22.4	97	9	2,500	100	0.0	2.0
C / 4.5	11.6	0.88	20.45	2	0	99	0	1	73	88.8	-22.5	97	9	2,500	100	0.0	2.0
C+ / 5.9	11.8	0.92	16.22	12,608	3	96	0	1	36	54.1	-23.5	87	2	2,500	100	0.0	2.0
C+ / 5.9	11.8	0.92	16.24	366	3	96	0	1	36	52.6	-23.6	87	2	2,500	100	0.0	2.0
U /	N/A	N/A	16.22	2,406	3	96	0	1	36	N/A	N/A	N/A	2	1,000,000	0	0.0	2.0
C+ / 5.9	11.8	0.92	16.13	7	3	96	0	1	36	49.6	-23.7	85	2	2,500	100	0.0	2.0
C / 5.3	11.1	0.88	13.34	10,976	3	96	0	1	37	44.4	-24.5	50	7	2,500	100	0.0	2.0
C / 5.3	11.1	0.89	13.55	193	3	96	0	1	37	42.8	-24.6	47	7	2,500	100	0.0	2.0
U /	N/A	N/A	13.32	740	3	96	0	1	37	N/A	N/A	N/A	7	1,000,000	0	0.0	2.0
C / 5.4	11.1	0.89	13.40	61	3	96	0	1	37	40.5	-24.7	43	7	2,500	100	0.0	2.0
B / 8.0	11.3	0.62	12.28	469	0	0	0	100	25	78.0	-6.9	99	4	2,500	100	0.0	2.0
E- / 0.0	25.3	1.10	21.74	616	0	0	0	100	27	-8.2	-29.3	79	N/A	2,500	100	0.0	2.0
C+ / 6.4	13.4	1.06	80.89	3,838	0	0	0	100	14	152.2	-16.9	58	4	2,500	100	0.0	0.0
U /	N/A	N/A	80.96	98	0	0	0	100	14	N/A	N/A	N/A	4	1,000,000	0	0.0	0.0
C / 5.0	11.9	0.92	80.45	22,004	5	94	0	1	27	136.4	-20.2	78	25	2,500	100	0.0	0.0
C / 5.0	11.9	0.92	78.29	872	5	94	0	1	27	133.3	-20.2	76	25	2,500	100	0.0	0.0
U /	N/A	N/A	80.46	2,423	5	94	0	1	27	N/A	N/A	N/A	25	1,000,000	0	0.0	0.0
C / 5.0	11.9	0.92	76.12	174	5	94	0	1	27	130.0	-20.3	N/A	25	2,500	100	0.0	0.0
C / 4.3	10.8	0.86	29.83	443	6	93	0	1	46	131.8	-19.5	85	17	2,500	100	0.0	0.0
C / 4.3	10.8	0.86	29.98	11,063	6	93	0	1	46	135.0	-19.5	86	17	2,500	100	0.0	0.0
U /	N/A	N/A	29.97	1,605	6	93	0	1	46	N/A	N/A	N/A	17	1,000,000	0	0.0	0.0
C / 4.3	10.8	0.86	29.41	228	6	93	0	1	46	128.7	-19.6	84	17	2,500	100	0.0	0.0

I. Index of Stock Mutual Funds

					PERFORMANCE						Incl. in Returns	
99 Pct = Best 0 Pct = Worst			Overall Investment Rating		Perfor-mance Rating/Pts	Total Return % through 2/28/17			Annualized		Dividend Yield	Expense Ratio
Fund Type	Fund Name	Ticker Symbol		Phone		3 Mo	6 Mo	1Yr / Pct	3Yr / Pct	5Yr / Pct		
GR	T Rowe Price New Amer Growth	PRWAX	B-	(800) 638-5660	A- / 9.0	10.70	11.44	24.94 /73	8.81 /86	13.49 /89	0.04	0.79
GR	T Rowe Price New Amer Growth Adv	PAWAX	B-	(800) 638-5660	B+ / 8.8	10.62	11.27	24.61 /72	8.52 /83	13.19 /86	0.00	1.06
GR	T Rowe Price New Amer Growth I	PNAIX	U	(800) 638-5660	U /	10.73	11.52	25.12 /74	--	--	0.19	0.95
FO	T Rowe Price New Asia	PRASX	C-	(800) 638-5660	C / 4.4	6.49	1.73	23.07 /67	4.06 /44	3.86 /15	0.78	0.94
FO	T Rowe Price New Asia I	PNSIX	U	(800) 638-5660	U /	6.49	1.79	23.13 /67	--	--	0.84	0.82
EN	T Rowe Price New Era	PRNEX	E-	(800) 638-5660	E+ / 0.7	-0.17	2.79	25.05 /73	-3.39 / 4	0.01 / 4	1.29	0.67
EN	T Rowe Price New Era I	TRNEX	U	(800) 638-5660	U /	-0.14	2.85	25.20 /74	--	--	1.41	0.58
* SC	● T Rowe Price New Horizons	PRNHX	C+	(800) 638-5660	B / 8.2	6.88	8.63	31.29 /89	7.04 /72	14.81 /96	0.00	0.79
SC	T Rowe Price New Horizons I	PRJIX	U	(800) 638-5660	U /	6.92	8.69	31.45 /89	--	--	0.00	0.67
* FO	T Rowe Price Overseas Stock	TROSX	D	(800) 638-5660	D / 2.2	7.88	5.76	17.39 /40	0.01 /13	5.41 /24	1.89	0.84
FO	T Rowe Price Overseas Stock I	TROIX	U	(800) 638-5660	U /	7.89	5.78	17.52 /41	--	--	2.42	0.71
BA	T Rowe Price Personal Strat Bal	TRPBX	C+	(800) 638-5660	C / 4.7	5.56	4.97	16.34 /36	4.98 /54	8.12 /43	1.70	0.84
AA	T Rowe Price Personal Strat Bal I	TPPAX	U	(800) 638-5660	U /	5.55	5.02	--	--	--	0.00	0.75
GR	T Rowe Price Personal Strat Gro	TRSGX	C+	(800) 638-5660	C+ / 5.9	6.65	6.76	19.85 /51	5.54 /60	9.76 /57	1.33	0.91
AA	T Rowe Price Personal Strat Gro I	TGIPX	U	(800) 638-5660	U /	6.68	6.83	--	--	--	0.00	0.79
AA	T Rowe Price Personal Strat Inc	PRSIX	C+	(800) 638-5660	C- / 3.4	4.36	3.15	12.47 /20	4.09 /44	6.27 /30	1.93	0.74
AA	T Rowe Price Personal Strat Inc I	PPIPX	U	(800) 638-5660	U /	4.36	3.21	--	--	--	0.00	0.65
MC	T Rowe Price QM US Sm Md Cp CE	TQSMX	U	(800) 638-5660	U /	6.31	11.98	31.13 /88	--	--	0.54	1.10
SC	T Rowe Price QM US Sm-Cap Gr Eq	PRDSX	B+	(800) 638-5660	B / 7.9	5.89	9.58	27.72 /81	7.58 /76	13.64 /90	0.00	0.82
SC	T Rowe Price QM US Sm-Cap Gr Eq	TQAIX	A+	(800) 638-5660	B / 8.1	5.91	9.68	27.93 /81	7.64 /76	13.67 /90	0.00	0.66
OT	T Rowe Price Real Assets	PRAFX	D-	(800) 638-5660	C- / 3.1	5.00	3.94	25.44 /75	1.15 /19	1.47 / 7	1.89	0.83
OT	T Rowe Price Real Assets I	PRIKX	U	(800) 638-5660	U /	5.01	4.04	25.70 /75	--	--	2.07	0.92
* RE	T Rowe Price Real Estate	TRREX	C+	(800) 638-5660	C+ / 6.6	5.58	-2.13	12.81 /21	10.47 /96	10.70 /63	2.24	0.76
RE	T Rowe Price Real Estate Adv	PAREX	C+	(800) 638-5660	C+ / 6.3	5.51	-2.27	12.52 /20	10.20 /94	10.45 /62	1.91	1.01
RE	T Rowe Price Real Estate I	TIRRX	U	(800) 638-5660	U /	5.61	-2.06	12.93 /21	--	--	2.35	0.85
AA	T Rowe Price Retire Balanced	TRRIX	C+	(800) 638-5660	C- / 3.0	3.86	2.96	11.43 /16	3.73 /40	5.19 /23	1.50	0.57
AA	T Rowe Price Retire Balanced Adv	PARIX	C+	(800) 638-5660	D+ / 2.8	3.79	2.83	11.23 /15	3.48 /37	4.92 /21	1.27	0.82
AA	T Rowe Price Retire Balanced R	RRTIX	C+	(800) 638-5660	D+ / 2.6	3.73	2.70	10.95 /14	3.22 /34	4.66 /19	1.02	1.07
GI	T Rowe Price Retirement 2005	TRRFX	C+	(800) 638-5660	C- / 3.1	3.94	2.53	11.67 /17	4.02 /43	5.66 /26	1.79	0.60
GI	T Rowe Price Retirement 2005 Adv	PARGX	C+	(800) 638-5660	C- / 3.0	3.87	2.46	11.36 /16	3.76 /40	5.39 /24	1.57	0.85
GI	T Rowe Price Retirement 2005 R	RRTLX	C	(800) 638-5660	D+ / 2.8	3.85	2.37	11.08 /15	3.52 /37	5.14 /22	0.97	1.10
AA	T Rowe Price Retirement 2010	TRRAX	C+	(800) 638-5660	C- / 3.5	4.27	3.06	12.77 /21	4.34 /47	6.28 /30	1.91	0.59
AA	T Rowe Price Retirement 2010 Adv	PARAX	C+	(800) 638-5660	C- / 3.3	4.17	2.90	12.45 /20	4.07 /44	6.01 /28	1.65	0.84
AA	T Rowe Price Retirement 2010 R	RRTAX	C	(800) 638-5660	C- / 3.1	4.14	2.74	12.15 /18	3.80 /40	5.74 /27	1.38	1.09
* GI	T Rowe Price Retirement 2015	TRRGX	C+	(800) 638-5660	C- / 4.0	4.81	3.74	14.34 /27	4.65 /50	7.18 /36	1.81	0.62
GI	T Rowe Price Retirement 2015 Adv	PARHX	C+	(800) 638-5660	C- / 3.8	4.75	3.68	14.08 /26	4.41 /48	6.91 /34	1.61	0.87
GI	T Rowe Price Retirement 2015 R	RRTMX	C+	(800) 638-5660	C- / 3.6	4.65	3.49	13.80 /25	4.15 /45	6.65 /33	1.36	1.12
* AA	T Rowe Price Retirement 2020	TRRBX	C+	(800) 638-5660	C / 4.7	5.40	4.60	16.13 /35	5.02 /54	8.00 /42	1.76	0.66
AA	T Rowe Price Retirement 2020 Adv	PARBX	C+	(800) 638-5660	C / 4.4	5.34	4.48	15.85 /34	4.75 /51	7.73 /40	1.49	0.91
AA	T Rowe Price Retirement 2020 R	RRTBX	C+	(800) 638-5660	C- / 4.2	5.24	4.32	15.55 /32	4.49 /49	7.46 /38	1.22	1.16
* GI	T Rowe Price Retirement 2025	TRRHX	B-	(800) 638-5660	C / 5.2	5.88	5.35	17.66 /41	5.33 /58	8.72 /48	1.63	0.69
GI	T Rowe Price Retirement 2025 Adv	PARJX	C+	(800) 638-5660	C / 5.0	5.85	5.18	17.39 /40	5.07 /55	8.45 /46	1.34	0.94
GI	T Rowe Price Retirement 2025 R	RRTNX	C+	(800) 638-5660	C / 4.8	5.77	5.10	17.10 /39	4.80 /52	8.18 /43	1.17	1.19
* AA	T Rowe Price Retirement 2030	TRRCX	B-	(800) 638-5660	C+ / 5.7	6.36	6.04	19.04 /47	5.59 /60	9.34 /53	1.48	0.72
AA	T Rowe Price Retirement 2030 Adv	PARCX	B-	(800) 638-5660	C / 5.5	6.32	5.95	18.78 /46	5.33 /58	9.07 /51	1.29	0.97
AA	T Rowe Price Retirement 2030 R	RRTCX	C+	(800) 638-5660	C / 5.3	6.23	5.81	18.46 /45	5.06 /55	8.79 /49	1.05	1.22
* GI	T Rowe Price Retirement 2035	TRRJX	C+	(800) 638-5660	C+ / 6.0	6.70	6.57	20.08 /52	5.73 /62	9.75 /57	1.36	0.74
GI	T Rowe Price Retirement 2035 Adv	PARKX	C+	(800) 638-5660	C+ / 5.8	6.67	6.48	19.83 /51	5.46 /59	9.49 /55	1.14	0.99
GI	T Rowe Price Retirement 2035 R	RRTPX	C+	(800) 638-5660	C+ / 5.6	6.61	6.36	19.61 /50	5.21 /57	9.22 /52	0.92	1.24
* AA	T Rowe Price Retirement 2040	TRRDX	C+	(800) 638-5660	C+ / 6.3	7.03	7.12	21.05 /58	5.85 /63	10.03 /59	1.27	0.76
AA	T Rowe Price Retirement 2040 Adv	PARDX	C+	(800) 638-5660	C+ / 6.1	6.91	6.96	20.74 /56	5.58 /60	9.74 /57	1.04	1.01
AA	T Rowe Price Retirement 2040 R	RRTDX	C+	(800) 638-5660	C+ / 5.9	6.91	6.87	20.46 /55	5.33 /58	9.49 /55	0.80	1.26

● Denotes fund is closed to new investors
* Denotes fund is included in Section II

www.thestreetratings.com

RISK			NET ASSETS		ASSET				Portfolio Turnover Ratio	BULL / BEAR		FUND MANAGER		MINIMUMS		LOADS	
Risk Rating/Pts	3 Year Standard Deviation	Beta	NAV As of 2/28/17	Total $(Mil)	Cash %	Stocks %	Bonds %	Other %		Last Bull Market Return	Last Bear Market Return	Manager Quality Pct	Manager Tenure (Years)	Initial Purch. $	Additional Purch. $	Front End Load	Back End Load
C- /3.9	13.8	1.17	44.11	2,998	2	97	0	1	81	128.5	-16.7	30	1	2,500	100	0.0	0.0
C- /3.9	13.8	1.17	43.25	338	2	97	0	1	81	125.2	-16.7	27	1	2,500	100	0.0	0.0
U /	N/A	N/A	44.10	239	2	97	0	1	81	N/A	N/A	N/A	1	1,000,000	0	0.0	0.0
C /5.3	14.1	0.84	16.62	2,449	0	0	0	100	39	44.1	-19.4	94	8	2,500	100	0.0	2.0
U /	N/A	N/A	16.63	111	0	0	0	100	39	N/A	N/A	N/A	8	1,000,000	0	0.0	2.0
D- /1.5	16.8	0.83	33.24	2,857	0	0	0	100	77	23.9	-31.0	81	4	2,500	100	0.0	0.0
U /	N/A	N/A	33.24	812	0	0	0	100	77	N/A	N/A	N/A	4	1,000,000	0	0.0	0.0
C- /3.6	14.4	0.83	47.00	15,255	1	98	0	1	34	156.1	-18.1	82	7	2,500	100	0.0	0.0
U /	N/A	N/A	47.05	2,214	1	98	0	1	34	N/A	N/A	N/A	7	1,000,000	0	0.0	0.0
C+ /6.0	10.9	0.88	9.53	11,115	3	96	0	1	14	53.8	-23.2	75	11	2,500	100	0.0	0.0
U /	N/A	N/A	9.50	1,297	3	96	0	1	14	N/A	N/A	N/A	11	1,000,000	0	0.0	2.0
B- /7.1	7.1	1.08	22.69	2,057	0	0	0	100	76	72.4	-13.1	35	6	2,500	100	0.0	0.0
U /	N/A	N/A	22.69	59	0	0	0	100	76	N/A	N/A	N/A	6	1,000,000	0	0.0	0.0
C+ /6.2	8.9	0.82	30.71	1,691	0	0	0	100	64	91.7	-17.0	36	6	2,500	100	0.0	0.0
U /	N/A	N/A	30.72	49	0	0	0	100	64	N/A	N/A	N/A	6	1,000,000	0	0.0	0.0
B /8.5	5.2	0.78	18.61	1,680	0	0	0	100	81	52.8	-9.5	53	6	2,500	100	0.0	0.0
U /	N/A	N/A	18.61	39	0	0	0	100	81	N/A	N/A	N/A	6	1,000,000	0	0.0	0.0
U /	N/A	N/A	12.93	33	0	0	0	100	0	N/A	N/A	N/A	1	2,500	100	0.0	1.0
C+ /6.2	13.7	0.83	30.16	3,063	0	0	0	100	10	146.0	-23.8	85	11	2,500	100	0.0	1.0
B- /7.5	13.7	0.83	30.21	485	0	0	0	100	10	146.4	-23.8	85	11	1,000,000	0	0.0	0.0
C- /4.0	14.1	0.84	11.12	3,152	5	93	0	2	43	28.4	-25.2	5	6	2,500	100	0.0	2.0
U /	N/A	N/A	11.11	349	5	93	0	2	43	N/A	N/A	N/A	6	1,000,000	0	0.0	2.0
C+ /5.8	13.9	1.00	28.99	5,939	5	93	0	2	7	102.9	-16.4	67	20	2,500	100	0.0	1.0
C+ /5.8	13.9	1.00	29.33	347	5	93	0	2	7	100.4	-16.5	64	20	2,500	100	0.0	1.0
U /	N/A	N/A	29.00	232	5	93	0	2	7	N/A	N/A	N/A	20	1,000,000	0	0.0	1.0
B /8.8	4.8	0.72	15.06	2,270	1	39	58	2	12	42.7	-8.4	54	15	2,500	100	0.0	0.0
B /8.8	4.8	0.73	15.07	264	1	39	58	2	12	40.8	-8.5	50	14	2,500	100	0.0	0.0
B /8.8	4.8	0.72	15.06	264	1	39	58	2	12	38.9	-8.6	47	14	2,500	100	0.0	0.0
B /8.4	5.0	0.43	13.24	1,629	2	38	59	1	18	47.5	-9.3	68	13	2,500	100	0.0	0.0
B /8.4	4.9	0.43	13.20	106	2	38	59	1	18	45.6	-9.4	66	10	2,500	100	0.0	0.0
B /8.5	4.9	0.43	13.27	57	2	38	59	1	18	43.6	-9.5	63	10	2,500	100	0.0	0.0
B /8.1	5.4	0.83	17.91	4,645	2	43	54	1	14	54.2	-11.1	52	15	2,500	100	0.0	0.0
B /8.1	5.4	0.83	17.82	581	2	43	54	1	14	52.1	-11.2	48	14	2,500	100	0.0	0.0
B /8.2	5.4	0.83	17.72	318	2	43	54	1	14	50.1	-11.3	44	14	2,500	100	0.0	0.0
B- /7.9	6.3	0.57	14.69	8,328	2	51	46	1	16	63.5	-13.0	59	13	2,500	100	0.0	0.0
B /8.0	6.3	0.57	14.64	659	2	51	46	1	16	61.4	-13.1	56	10	2,500	100	0.0	0.0
B /8.0	6.2	0.56	14.52	446	2	51	46	1	16	59.3	-13.2	53	10	2,500	100	0.0	0.0
B- /7.7	7.1	1.10	21.26	20,915	2	61	36	1	16	72.4	-14.7	34	15	2,500	100	0.0	0.0
B- /7.8	7.2	1.10	21.12	2,879	2	61	36	1	16	70.0	-14.8	30	14	2,500	100	0.0	0.0
B- /7.8	7.1	1.10	20.93	1,794	2	61	36	1	16	67.8	-14.9	28	14	2,500	100	0.0	0.0
B- /7.4	7.9	0.73	16.22	17,762	2	68	28	2	15	80.2	-16.1	46	13	2,500	100	0.0	0.0
B- /7.5	7.9	0.73	16.14	1,725	2	68	28	2	15	78.0	-16.2	42	10	2,500	100	0.0	0.0
B- /7.5	7.9	0.73	15.99	1,269	2	68	28	2	15	75.5	-16.3	39	10	2,500	100	0.0	0.0
B- /7.0	8.6	1.32	23.66	21,071	2	75	21	2	16	87.5	-17.4	23	15	2,500	100	0.0	0.0
B- /7.0	8.6	1.32	23.47	3,149	2	75	21	2	16	85.1	-17.5	21	14	2,500	100	0.0	0.0
B- /7.1	8.6	1.32	23.29	2,164	2	75	21	2	16	82.7	-17.6	18	14	2,500	100	0.0	0.0
C+ /6.7	9.2	0.85	17.16	13,217	2	81	15	2	15	92.4	-18.3	35	13	2,500	100	0.0	0.0
C+ /6.7	9.2	0.85	17.08	1,394	2	81	15	2	15	89.9	-18.4	31	10	2,500	100	0.0	0.0
C+ /6.7	9.2	0.85	16.91	1,058	2	81	15	2	15	87.6	-18.5	29	10	2,500	100	0.0	0.0
C+ /6.4	9.6	1.47	24.52	14,407	2	86	10	2	15	95.6	-18.7	16	15	2,500	100	0.0	0.0
C+ /6.4	9.6	1.47	24.30	2,397	2	86	10	2	15	92.9	-18.7	14	14	2,500	100	0.0	0.0
C+ /6.4	9.7	1.47	24.16	1,532	2	86	10	2	15	90.4	-18.8	12	14	2,500	100	0.0	0.0

					PERFORMANCE							
	99 Pct = Best 0 Pct = Worst			Overall	Perfor- mance	Total Return % through 2/28/17					Incl. in Returns	
				Investment	Rating/Pts				Annualized		Dividend	Expense
Fund Type	Fund Name	Ticker Symbol	Rating	Phone		3 Mo	6 Mo	1Yr / Pct	3Yr / Pct	5Yr / Pct	Yield	Ratio
* GI	T Rowe Price Retirement 2045	TRRKX	C+	(800) 638-5660	C+ / 6.4	7.05	7.25	21.27 /59	5.89 /63	10.05 /59	1.24	0.76
GI	T Rowe Price Retirement 2045 Adv	PARLX	C+	(800) 638-5660	C+ / 6.2	7.03	7.10	20.95 /57	5.62 /61	9.78 /57	1.01	1.01
GI	T Rowe Price Retirement 2045 R	RRTRX	C+	(800) 638-5660	C+ / 6.0	6.97	7.04	20.63 /56	5.36 /58	9.52 /55	0.84	1.26
GI	T Rowe Price Retirement 2050	TRRMX	C+	(800) 638-5660	C+ / 6.4	7.05	7.21	21.19 /58	5.90 /63	10.06 /59	1.26	0.76
GI	T Rowe Price Retirement 2050 Adv	PARFX	C+	(800) 638-5660	C+ / 6.2	6.95	7.11	20.93 /57	5.63 /61	9.79 /57	0.99	1.01
GI	T Rowe Price Retirement 2050 R	RRTFX	C+	(800) 638-5660	C+ / 6.0	6.93	7.01	20.65 /56	5.39 /58	9.50 /55	0.78	1.26
GI	T Rowe Price Retirement 2055	TRRNX	C+	(800) 638-5660	C+ / 6.4	7.04	7.20	21.22 /58	5.89 /63	10.04 /59	1.26	0.76
GI	T Rowe Price Retirement 2055 Adv	PAROX	C+	(800) 638-5660	C+ / 6.2	7.00	7.08	20.99 /57	5.63 /61	9.79 /57	0.99	1.01
GI	T Rowe Price Retirement 2055 R	RRTVX	C+	(800) 638-5660	C+ / 6.0	6.97	6.97	20.65 /56	5.37 /58	9.51 /55	0.85	1.26
AA	T Rowe Price Retirement 2060	TRRLX	U	(800) 638-5660	U /	7.05	7.25	21.19 /58	--	--	1.10	0.76
AA	T Rowe Price Retirement I 2005 I	TRPFX	U	(800) 638-5660	U /	4.06	2.62	11.76 /17	--	--	1.18	4.78
AA	T Rowe Price Retirement I 2010 I	TRPAX	U	(800) 638-5660	U /	4.33	3.10	12.97 /22	--	--	1.34	1.20
AA	T Rowe Price Retirement I 2015 I	TRFGX	U	(800) 638-5660	U /	4.88	3.83	14.53 /28	--	--	1.28	0.97
AA	T Rowe Price Retirement I 2020 I	TRBRX	U	(800) 638-5660	U /	5.46	4.70	16.34 /36	--	--	1.35	0.63
AA	T Rowe Price Retirement I 2025 I	TRPHX	U	(800) 638-5660	U /	5.93	5.36	17.71 /42	--	--	1.29	0.73
AA	T Rowe Price Retirement I 2030 I	TRPCX	U	(800) 638-5660	U /	6.40	6.11	19.23 /48	--	--	1.37	0.67
AA	T Rowe Price Retirement I 2035 I	TRPJX	U	(800) 638-5660	U /	6.77	6.68	20.31 /54	--	--	1.31	0.86
AA	T Rowe Price Retirement I 2040 I	TRPDX	U	(800) 638-5660	U /	7.11	7.21	21.26 /59	--	--	1.26	0.76
AA	T Rowe Price Retirement I 2045 I	TRPKX	U	(800) 638-5660	U /	7.11	7.30	21.36 /59	--	--	1.26	1.06
AA	T Rowe Price Retirement I 2050 I	TRPMX	U	(800) 638-5660	U /	7.11	7.30	21.36 /59	--	--	1.26	0.86
AA	T Rowe Price Retirement I 2055 I	TRPNX	U	(800) 638-5660	U /	7.11	7.30	21.38 /59	--	--	1.26	2.05
AA	T Rowe Price Retirement I Bal I	TRPTX	U	(800) 638-5660	U /	3.88	2.96	11.55 /16	--	--	1.65	2.22
TC	T Rowe Price Science and Tech	PRSCX	C+	(800) 638-5660	A+ / 9.9	9.94	10.91	38.03 /96	13.76 /99	14.58 /96	0.00	0.84
TC	T Rowe Price Science and Tech Adv	PASTX	C+	(800) 638-5660	A+ / 9.9	9.85	10.75	37.68 /96	13.50 /99	14.33 /95	0.00	1.06
TC	T Rowe Price Science and Tech I	TSNIX	U	(800) 638-5660	U /	9.94	10.94	--	--	--	0.00	0.66
* SC	● T Rowe Price Small Cap Stock	OTCFX	B-	(800) 638-5660	B+ / 8.7	5.40	11.02	32.93 /92	7.46 /75	13.26 /86	0.13	0.90
SC	● T Rowe Price Small Cap Stock Adv	PASSX	B-	(800) 638-5660	B+ / 8.4	5.36	10.89	32.61 /91	7.16 /73	12.95 /83	0.00	1.21
SC	T Rowe Price Small Cap Stock I	OTIIX	U	(800) 638-5660	U /	5.44	11.11	33.12 /92	--	--	0.25	0.78
* SC	T Rowe Price Small Cap Value	PRSVX	C+	(800) 638-5660	A- / 9.1	5.25	13.67	36.78 /96	7.48 /75	12.43 /78	0.85	0.92
SC	T Rowe Price Small Cap Value Adv	PASVX	C+	(800) 638-5660	B+ / 8.9	5.14	13.46	36.31 /95	7.14 /73	12.10 /75	0.58	1.22
SC	T Rowe Price Small Cap Value I	PRVIX	U	(800) 638-5660	U /	5.27	13.71	36.92 /96	--	--	0.96	0.83
GI	T Rowe Price Spectrum Growth	PRSGX	C+	(800) 638-5660	C+ / 6.8	7.34	8.11	23.08 /67	6.10 /65	10.58 /63	1.06	0.79
FO	T Rowe Price Spectrum Internatl	PSILX	D	(800) 638-5660	D / 1.8	7.02	2.12	15.32 /31	0.14 /14	4.72 /19	1.67	0.94
GI	T Rowe Price Target 2005	TRARX	C+	(800) 638-5660	D+ / 2.9	3.75	2.24	10.90 /14	3.78 /40	--	1.90	1.31
GI	T Rowe Price Target 2005 Adv	PANRX	C+	(800) 638-5660	D+ / 2.7	3.65	2.05	10.59 /13	3.52 /37	--	1.63	1.66
GI	T Rowe Price Target 2010	TRROX	C+	(800) 638-5660	C- / 3.0	3.81	2.41	11.22 /15	3.85 /41	--	1.79	0.91
GI	T Rowe Price Target 2010 Adv	PAERX	C+	(800) 638-5660	D+ / 2.8	3.82	2.32	10.93 /14	3.59 /38	--	1.61	1.23
GI	T Rowe Price Target 2015	TRRTX	C+	(800) 638-5660	C- / 3.2	4.14	2.84	12.03 /18	3.96 /43	--	1.68	0.69
GI	T Rowe Price Target 2015 Adv	PAHRX	C+	(800) 638-5660	C- / 3.0	3.96	2.66	11.65 /17	3.68 /39	--	1.42	1.03
GI	T Rowe Price Target 2020	TRRUX	C+	(800) 638-5660	C- / 3.6	4.51	3.49	13.20 /22	4.22 /46	--	1.48	0.73
GI	T Rowe Price Target 2020 Adv	PAIRX	C+	(800) 638-5660	C- / 3.4	4.44	3.42	12.94 /21	3.94 /42	--	1.31	1.00
GI	T Rowe Price Target 2025	TRRVX	C+	(800) 638-5660	C- / 4.1	4.97	4.15	14.71 /29	4.55 /49	--	1.45	0.83
GI	T Rowe Price Target 2025 Adv	PAJRX	C+	(800) 638-5660	C- / 3.9	4.98	4.06	14.43 /27	4.31 /46	--	1.11	1.07
GI	T Rowe Price Target 2030	TRRWX	B-	(800) 638-5660	C / 4.6	5.45	4.72	16.17 /35	4.93 /53	--	1.51	0.89
GI	T Rowe Price Target 2030 Adv	PAKRX	C+	(800) 638-5660	C / 4.4	5.46	4.64	15.92 /34	4.67 /51	--	1.26	1.09
GI	T Rowe Price Target 2035	RPGRX	B-	(800) 638-5660	C / 5.2	5.94	5.30	17.58 /41	5.24 /57	--	1.50	1.04
GI	T Rowe Price Target 2035 Adv	PATVX	C+	(800) 638-5660	C / 4.9	5.86	5.12	17.30 /40	4.97 /54	--	1.34	1.24
GI	T Rowe Price Target 2040	TRHRX	B-	(800) 638-5660	C+ / 5.6	6.37	5.92	18.74 /46	5.48 /59	--	1.48	1.12
GI	T Rowe Price Target 2040 Adv	PAHHX	B-	(800) 638-5660	C / 5.3	6.21	5.66	18.39 /45	5.19 /56	--	1.24	1.30
GI	T Rowe Price Target 2045	RPTFX	B-	(800) 638-5660	C+ / 5.9	6.59	6.41	19.67 /50	5.61 /61	--	1.47	1.27
GI	T Rowe Price Target 2045 Adv	PAFFX	B-	(800) 638-5660	C+ / 5.6	6.52	6.15	19.31 /49	5.35 /58	--	1.22	1.44
GI	T Rowe Price Target 2050	TRFOX	C+	(800) 638-5660	C+ / 6.1	6.85	6.76	20.48 /55	5.76 /62	--	1.29	1.66

● Denotes fund is closed to new investors
* Denotes fund is included in Section II

www.thestreetratings.com

RISK			NET ASSETS		ASSET				Portfolio Turnover Ratio	BULL / BEAR		FUND MANAGER		MINIMUMS		LOADS	
Risk Rating/Pts	3 Year		NAV As of 2/28/17	Total $(Mil)	Cash %	Stocks %	Bonds %	Other %		Last Bull Market Return	Last Bear Market Return	Manager Quality Pct	Manager Tenure (Years)	Initial Purch. $	Additional Purch. $	Front End Load	Back End Load
	Standard Deviation	Beta															
C+ / 6.4	9.7	0.89	16.51	7,915	2	87	9	2	14	95.6	-18.5	31	12	2,500	100	0.0	0.0
C+ / 6.4	9.7	0.89	16.41	925	2	87	9	2	14	92.9	-18.6	28	10	2,500	100	0.0	0.0
C+ / 6.4	9.7	0.89	16.24	717	2	87	9	2	14	90.5	-18.7	26	10	2,500	100	0.0	0.0
C+ / 6.4	9.7	0.89	13.88	5,625	2	87	9	2	13	95.6	-18.5	31	11	2,500	100	0.0	0.0
C+ / 6.4	9.7	0.89	13.77	1,103	2	87	9	2	13	93.0	-18.6	28	11	2,500	100	0.0	0.0
C+ / 6.4	9.6	0.89	13.66	765	2	87	9	2	13	90.3	-18.6	26	11	2,500	100	0.0	0.0
C+ / 6.5	9.7	0.89	13.91	2,473	2	87	9	2	11	95.5	-18.5	31	11	2,500	100	0.0	0.0
C+ / 6.5	9.7	0.89	13.84	363	2	87	9	2	11	93.0	-18.6	28	10	2,500	100	0.0	0.0
C+ / 6.5	9.7	0.89	13.76	273	2	87	9	2	11	90.5	-18.6	26	10	2,500	100	0.0	0.0
U /	N/A	N/A	10.71	152	2	86	10	2	27	N/A	N/A	N/A	3	2,500	100	0.0	0.0
U /	N/A	N/A	10.99	52	0	0	0	100	34	N/A	N/A	N/A	2	1,000,000	0	0.0	0.0
U /	N/A	N/A	11.15	231	0	0	0	100	13	N/A	N/A	N/A	2	1,000,000	0	0.0	0.0
U /	N/A	N/A	11.28	419	0	0	0	100	15	N/A	N/A	N/A	2	1,000,000	0	0.0	0.0
U /	N/A	N/A	11.44	1,321	0	0	0	100	8	N/A	N/A	N/A	2	1,000,000	0	0.0	0.0
U /	N/A	N/A	11.57	1,016	0	0	0	100	7	N/A	N/A	N/A	2	1,000,000	0	0.0	0.0
U /	N/A	N/A	11.68	1,528	0	0	0	100	7	N/A	N/A	N/A	2	1,000,000	0	0.0	0.0
U /	N/A	N/A	11.78	831	0	0	0	100	7	N/A	N/A	N/A	2	1,000,000	0	0.0	0.0
U /	N/A	N/A	11.85	1,167	0	0	0	100	6	N/A	N/A	N/A	2	1,000,000	0	0.0	0.0
U /	N/A	N/A	11.86	521	0	0	0	100	5	N/A	N/A	N/A	2	1,000,000	0	0.0	0.0
U /	N/A	N/A	11.86	588	0	0	0	100	10	N/A	N/A	N/A	2	1,000,000	0	0.0	0.0
U /	N/A	N/A	11.85	154	0	0	0	100	15	N/A	N/A	N/A	2	1,000,000	0	0.0	0.0
U /	N/A	N/A	10.91	132	0	0	0	100	13	N/A	N/A	N/A	2	1,000,000	0	0.0	0.0
D / 2.2	15.2	1.24	41.18	3,535	10	88	0	2	82	146.1	-19.0	77	8	2,500	100	0.0	0.0
D+ / 2.3	15.2	1.24	40.72	555	10	88	0	2	82	143.3	-19.1	75	8	2,500	100	0.0	0.0
U /	N/A	N/A	41.17	113	10	88	0	2	82	N/A	N/A	N/A	8	1,000,000	0	0.0	0.0
C- / 4.2	14.2	0.89	46.60	8,593	7	92	0	1	20	141.5	-23.8	82	N/A	2,500	100	0.0	0.0
C- / 4.2	14.2	0.89	46.16	262	7	92	0	1	20	138.0	-23.9	81	N/A	2,500	100	0.0	0.0
U /	N/A	N/A	46.62	704	7	92	0	1	20	N/A	N/A	N/A	N/A	1,000,000	0	0.0	0.0
D+ / 2.9	13.6	0.83	45.70	8,068	2	97	0	1	32	126.5	-21.9	84	1	2,500	100	0.0	1.0
C- / 3.0	13.6	0.83	45.44	717	2	97	0	1	32	122.9	-21.9	83	1	2,500	100	0.0	1.0
U /	N/A	N/A	45.70	727	2	97	0	1	32	N/A	N/A	N/A	1	1,000,000	0	0.0	1.0
C / 4.6	10.6	0.98	22.24	3,486	2	97	0	1	15	103.1	-19.4	24	N/A	2,500	100	0.0	0.0
C+ / 6.1	11.1	0.87	12.25	1,199	2	96	0	2	2	51.0	-23.5	76	N/A	2,500	100	0.0	2.0
B / 8.8	4.6	0.39	11.02	26	1	34	64	1	30	N/A	N/A	71	4	2,500	100	0.0	0.0
B / 8.8	4.6	0.39	11.02	1	1	34	64	1	30	N/A	N/A	68	4	2,500	100	0.0	0.0
B / 8.8	4.7	0.40	11.10	53	1	35	62	2	25	N/A	N/A	70	4	2,500	100	0.0	0.0
B / 8.9	4.7	0.40	11.08	6	1	35	62	2	25	N/A	N/A	67	4	2,500	100	0.0	0.0
B / 8.8	5.2	0.45	11.25	158	1	40	57	2	21	N/A	N/A	65	4	2,500	100	0.0	0.0
B / 8.8	5.2	0.45	11.22	5	1	40	57	2	21	N/A	N/A	62	4	2,500	100	0.0	0.0
B / 8.6	5.8	0.51	11.39	193	2	47	50	1	16	N/A	N/A	60	4	2,500	100	0.0	0.0
B / 8.6	5.8	0.52	11.35	25	2	47	50	1	16	N/A	N/A	57	4	2,500	100	0.0	0.0
B / 8.2	6.5	0.59	11.52	174	2	54	42	2	20	N/A	N/A	55	4	2,500	100	0.0	0.0
B / 8.2	6.5	0.59	11.51	12	2	54	42	2	20	N/A	N/A	51	4	2,500	100	0.0	0.0
B- / 7.9	7.3	0.66	11.71	161	2	62	35	1	15	N/A	N/A	50	4	2,500	100	0.0	0.0
B- / 7.9	7.3	0.66	11.68	25	2	62	35	1	15	N/A	N/A	46	4	2,500	100	0.0	0.0
B- / 7.5	8.0	0.73	11.75	98	2	68	28	2	23	N/A	N/A	44	4	2,500	100	0.0	0.0
B- / 7.6	8.0	0.73	11.73	10	2	68	28	2	23	N/A	N/A	41	4	2,500	100	0.0	0.0
B- / 7.3	8.5	0.78	11.90	83	2	74	22	2	17	N/A	N/A	40	4	2,500	100	0.0	0.0
B- / 7.3	8.5	0.78	11.86	10	2	74	22	2	17	N/A	N/A	37	4	2,500	100	0.0	0.0
B- / 7.1	9.0	0.83	12.01	54	2	79	17	2	26	N/A	N/A	36	4	2,500	100	0.0	0.0
B- / 7.1	8.9	0.82	11.98	7	2	79	17	2	26	N/A	N/A	33	4	2,500	100	0.0	0.0
C+ / 6.8	9.4	0.87	12.12	33	2	83	13	2	29	N/A	N/A	32	4	2,500	100	0.0	0.0

99 Pct = Best
0 Pct = Worst

Fund Type	Fund Name	Ticker Symbol	Overall Investment Rating	Phone	Perfor-mance Rating/Pts	3 Mo	6 Mo	1Yr / Pct	3Yr / Pct	5Yr / Pct	Dividend Yield	Expense Ratio
GI	T Rowe Price Target 2050 Adv	PAOFX	C+	(800) 638-5660	C+ / 5.9	6.79	6.60	20.12 / 53	5.47 / 59	--	1.13	1.80
GI	T Rowe Price Target 2055	TRFFX	C+	(800) 638-5660	C+ / 6.3	7.04	7.13	21.01 / 57	5.85 / 63	--	1.30	2.17
GI	T Rowe Price Target 2055 Adv	PAFTX	C+	(800) 638-5660	C+ / 6.1	6.88	6.88	20.67 / 56	5.56 / 60	--	1.06	2.28
MC	T Rowe Price Tax-Efficient Equity	PREFX	B-	(800) 638-5660	B- / 7.2	7.81	7.58	21.62 / 60	7.53 / 76	12.35 / 78	0.20	0.86
GR	T Rowe Price Total Eq Mkt Index	POMIX	A+	(800) 638-5660	A- / 9.1	7.72	10.28	26.21 / 77	9.76 / 92	13.79 / 92	1.52	0.30
GR	T Rowe Price US Large-Cap Core	PAULX	A	(800) 638-5660	B+ / 8.9	8.35	7.82	20.21 / 53	10.78 / 97	14.31 / 95	0.56	1.07
GR	T Rowe Price US Large-Cap Core Inc	TRULX	A	(800) 638-5660	A- / 9.0	8.42	8.00	20.60 / 55	11.00 / 97	14.46 / 95	0.88	0.91
* GI	T Rowe Price Value	TRVLX	B	(800) 638-5660	B+ / 8.3	7.28	10.19	23.65 / 69	8.61 / 84	14.31 / 95	1.56	0.81
GI	T Rowe Price Value Adv	PAVLX	B	(800) 638-5660	B / 8.2	7.27	10.10	23.41 / 68	8.39 / 82	14.07 / 94	1.36	1.05
GI	T Rowe Price Value I	TRPIX	U	(800) 638-5660	U /	7.34	10.31	23.86 / 69	--	--	1.73	0.66
AA	Tactical Asset Allocation A	GVTAX	D	(877) 940-3435	E / 0.5	3.09	2.00	10.88 / 14	-0.42 / 12	--	0.00	2.42
AA	Tactical Asset Allocation I	GVTIX	D	(877) 940-3435	D- / 1.0	3.07	2.10	11.07 / 15	-0.17 / 13	--	0.00	2.17
GR	Tanaka Growth R	TGFRX	B	(877) 482-6252	B / 7.6	11.83	11.77	18.12 / 43	7.03 / 72	12.02 / 75	0.00	2.44
FO	Target International Equity Q	TIEQX	D	(800) 225-1852	D- / 1.2	6.43	4.69	12.89 / 21	-0.62 / 11	4.56 / 18	2.27	0.97
FO	Target International Equity R	TEQRX	D-	(800) 225-1852	D- / 1.0	6.32	4.32	12.23 / 19	-1.22 / 9	3.92 / 15	1.68	1.72
FO	Target International Equity T	TAIEX	D	(800) 225-1852	D- / 1.1	6.39	4.56	12.75 / 21	-0.74 / 10	4.44 / 18	2.16	0.86
GR	Tax Mgd US MktWide Val II Inst	DFMVX	A+	(800) 984-9472	A / 9.5	6.81	13.53	30.62 / 87	9.52 / 90	15.22 / 97	1.72	0.42
SC	Tax-Managed Small/Mid Cap F	STMSX	C+	(800) 342-5734	C+ / 6.3	4.69	9.74	26.20 / 77	5.03 / 55	11.35 / 69	0.40	1.23
SC	Tax-Managed Small/Mid Cap Y	STMPX	U	(800) 342-5734	U /	4.79	9.85	26.53 / 78	--	--	0.59	0.98
GR	TCM Small Cap Growth	TCMSX	C	(800) 536-3230	B+ / 8.3	6.00	14.15	32.90 / 91	6.50 / 68	14.15 / 94	0.00	0.94
AA	TCW Conservative Alloc I	TGPCX	C	(800) 386-3829	D / 2.0	2.76	0.92	6.74 / 5	3.18 / 34	5.38 / 24	2.37	1.00
AA	TCW Conservative Alloc N	TGPNX	C-	(800) 386-3829	D / 1.7	2.60	0.58	6.13 / 5	2.60 / 28	4.89 / 21	1.63	2.24
GL	TCW Emerg Mkts Multi Asset Opps I	TGMAX	D+	(800) 386-3829	D+ / 2.8	6.03	3.33	20.57 / 55	0.76 / 17	--	3.72	1.47
GL	TCW Emerg Mkts Multi Asset Opps N	TGMEX	D+	(800) 386-3829	D+ / 2.8	6.05	3.33	20.52 / 55	0.75 / 17	--	3.73	2.15
OT	TCW Enhanced Commodity Strategy	TGGWX	E	(800) 386-3829	E- / 0.1	2.88	6.96	17.28 / 40	-12.24 / 0	-7.92 / 1	0.99	7.82
OT	TCW Enhanced Commodity Strategy	TGABX	E	(800) 386-3829	E- / 0.1	2.88	7.17	17.50 / 41	-12.21 / 0	-7.90 / 1	0.99	8.32
GR	TCW Focused Equities I	TGFFX	C+	(800) 386-3829	C+ / 5.9	4.03	5.31	19.33 / 49	6.56 / 69	11.88 / 73	1.23	1.46
GR	TCW Focused Equities N	TGFVX	C+	(800) 386-3829	C+ / 6.0	4.07	5.36	19.36 / 49	6.57 / 69	11.93 / 74	1.24	2.39
MC	● TCW Growth Equities I	TGGEX	E-	(800) 386-3829	D- / 1.0	4.32	2.77	18.52 / 45	-1.66 / 7	5.69 / 26	0.00	1.47
MC	● TCW Growth Equities N	TGDNX	E-	(800) 386-3829	D- / 1.0	4.36	2.79	18.55 / 45	-1.66 / 7	5.70 / 26	0.00	2.09
GR	TCW International Growth I	TGIBX	E+	(800) 386-3829	D- / 1.2	6.29	5.42	15.61 / 33	-1.01 / 9	--	0.74	5.06
GR	TCW International Growth N	TGIDX	E+	(800) 386-3829	D- / 1.1	6.26	5.27	15.36 / 31	-1.28 / 8	--	0.49	5.19
FO	TCW International Small Cap I	TGICX	D-	(800) 386-3829	E+ / 0.8	6.67	3.79	12.93 / 21	-2.08 / 6	1.88 / 8	0.33	1.70
FO	TCW International Small Cap N	TGNIX	D-	(800) 386-3829	E+ / 0.8	6.54	3.67	12.93 / 21	-2.11 / 6	1.84 / 8	0.33	2.12
IN	TCW Relative Value Dividend App I	TGDFX	B+	(800) 386-3829	B / 8.1	4.74	9.70	26.28 / 77	8.17 / 80	13.11 / 85	1.77	0.76
IN	TCW Relative Value Dividend App N	TGIGX	B+	(800) 386-3829	B / 7.9	4.64	9.62	25.96 / 76	7.89 / 78	12.80 / 82	1.53	1.04
GR	TCW Relative Value Large Cap I	TGDIX	B+	(800) 386-3829	B+ / 8.3	5.23	11.41	27.60 / 81	7.93 / 78	12.96 / 83	1.72	0.78
GR	TCW Relative Value Large Cap N	TGDVX	B+	(800) 386-3829	B / 8.1	5.17	11.30	27.34 / 80	7.68 / 77	12.68 / 81	1.52	1.10
MC	TCW Relative Value Mid Cap I	TGVOX	C+	(800) 386-3829	A- / 9.1	4.69	17.05	39.67 / 97	5.97 / 64	12.00 / 74	0.54	0.96
MC	TCW Relative Value Mid Cap N	TGVNX	C	(800) 386-3829	B+ / 8.9	4.62	16.93	39.39 / 97	5.73 / 62	11.73 / 72	0.38	1.30
GR	TCW Select Equities I	TGCEX	D+	(800) 386-3829	C / 5.1	9.06	2.68	15.41 / 32	5.51 / 60	10.32 / 61	0.00	0.88
GR	TCW Select Equities N	TGCNX	D+	(800) 386-3829	C / 4.9	9.02	2.59	15.12 / 30	5.24 / 57	10.03 / 59	0.00	1.14
SC	● TCW Small Cap Growth I	TGSCX	E	(800) 386-3829	C / 4.6	4.78	8.84	29.18 / 84	1.38 / 20	7.16 / 36	0.00	1.17
SC	● TCW Small Cap Growth N	TGSNX	E	(800) 386-3829	C / 4.5	4.79	8.82	29.13 / 84	1.27 / 20	6.95 / 34	0.00	1.50
GR	TCW/Gargoyle Hedged Value I	TFHIX	C	(800) 386-3829	C- / 3.0	5.48	10.47	14.99 / 30	1.25 / 20	7.60 / 39	1.18	2.39
GR	TCW/Gargoyle Hedged Value N	TFHVX	C-	(800) 386-3829	D+ / 2.9	5.50	10.36	14.72 / 29	1.01 / 18	7.36 / 37	0.69	2.78
GL	TD Global Low Vol Eqty Adv	TDGVX	B-		C+ / 6.8	4.96	4.58	14.81 / 29	8.95 / 86	--	1.95	2.92
GL	TD Global Low Vol Eqty Inst	TDLVX	B-		C+ / 6.8	5.06	4.68	15.02 / 30	9.02 / 87	--	2.04	2.67
IN	TD Target Return Adv	TDTRX	C		D+ / 2.6	2.61	2.47	13.63 / 24	2.81 / 30	--	4.92	3.96
IN	TD Target Return Inst	TDTFX	C		D+ / 2.6	2.62	2.59	13.70 / 24	2.93 / 31	--	4.96	3.86
AA	Teberg Fund	TEBRX	D-	(866) 209-1964	C- / 3.6	6.34	7.46	17.32 / 40	2.19 / 25	3.15 / 11	0.00	2.66
FO	Templeton China World A	TCWAX	E	(800) 342-5236	C- / 3.7	7.73	7.28	26.10 / 77	2.13 / 25	-0.15 / 4	0.79	1.91

● Denotes fund is closed to new investors
* Denotes fund is included in Section II

www.thestreetratings.com

RISK			NET ASSETS		ASSET				Portfolio Turnover Ratio	BULL / BEAR		FUND MANAGER		MINIMUMS		LOADS	
Risk Rating/Pts	3 Year Standard Deviation	Beta	NAV As of 2/28/17	Total $(Mil)	Cash %	Stocks %	Bonds %	Other %		Last Bull Market Return	Last Bear Market Return	Manager Quality Pct	Manager Tenure (Years)	Initial Purch. $	Additional Purch. $	Front End Load	Back End Load
C+ / 6.9	9.3	0.86	12.08	6	2	83	13	2	29	N/A	N/A	30	4	2,500	100	0.0	0.0
C+ / 6.6	9.6	0.89	12.03	19	2	87	9	2	33	N/A	N/A	31	4	2,500	100	0.0	0.0
C+ / 6.6	9.7	0.89	11.99	3	2	87	9	2	33	N/A	N/A	28	4	2,500	100	0.0	0.0
C+ / 5.7	12.4	0.87	24.83	221	0	99	0	1	13	120.8	-17.7	65	17	2,500	100	0.0	1.0
C+ / 6.8	10.7	1.03	26.79	1,467	2	96	0	2	8	134.0	-17.9	61	9	2,500	100	0.0	0.5
C+ / 6.3	9.7	0.90	21.63	30	5	94	0	1	58	137.8	-17.8	82	8	2,500	100	0.0	0.0
C+ / 6.3	9.6	0.90	21.70	318	5	94	0	1	58	139.3	-17.8	83	8	2,500	100	0.0	0.0
C / 5.2	10.7	1.02	35.46	21,847	0	98	0	2	68	140.3	-20.6	48	8	2,500	100	0.0	0.0
C / 5.2	10.7	1.02	34.94	531	0	98	0	2	68	137.5	-20.7	46	8	2,500	100	0.0	0.0
U /	N/A	N/A	35.47	1,774	0	98	0	2	68	N/A	N/A	N/A	8	1,000,000	0	0.0	0.0
B- / 7.4	8.5	0.94	9.68	17	4	71	23	2	508	N/A	N/A	5	4	1,000	100	5.8	1.0
B- / 7.4	8.5	0.94	9.73	1	4	71	23	2	508	N/A	N/A	6	4	1,000,000	100	0.0	1.0
C+ / 5.7	18.4	1.47	22.88	16	1	98	0	1	37	124.5	-24.9	4	19	2,000	500	0.0	0.0
C+ / 6.3	10.9	0.87	12.53	N/A	4	95	0	1	22	44.5	-24.1	69	12	0	0	0.0	0.0
C+ / 6.3	10.9	0.88	12.51	332	4	95	0	1	22	39.9	-24.3	61	12	0	0	0.0	0.0
C+ / 6.3	10.9	0.88	12.53	42	4	95	0	1	22	43.8	-24.2	67	12	0	0	0.0	0.0
C+ / 6.6	11.8	1.08	26.92	1,697	0	99	0	1	9	156.7	-23.7	52	13	0	0	0.0	0.0
C+ / 5.7	13.3	0.83	20.76	740	2	94	2	2	107	115.7	-23.6	66	6	100,000	1,000	0.0	0.0
U /	N/A	N/A	20.77	60	2	94	2	2	107	N/A	N/A	N/A	6	100,000	1,000	0.0	1.0
D / 2.2	15.0	1.02	32.84	286	1	96	1	2	134	149.6	-28.1	24	13	100,000	2,500	0.0	1.0
B / 8.6	5.0	0.74	11.60	28	1	34	64	1	38	41.8	-8.2	45	11	2,000	250	0.0	0.0
B / 8.7	5.0	0.73	11.61	1	1	34	64	1	38	38.4	-8.2	38	11	2,000	250	0.0	0.0
C+ / 6.3	9.6	1.02	10.15	38	2	48	49	1	228	N/A	N/A	25	4	2,000	250	0.0	0.0
C+ / 6.3	9.6	1.02	10.11	2	2	48	49	1	228	N/A	N/A	24	4	2,000	250	0.0	0.0
C- / 3.6	14.0	0.29	5.28	1	5	0	94	1	2	-28.5	-20.7	0	6	2,000	250	0.0	0.0
C- / 3.6	14.1	0.31	5.29	1	5	0	94	1	2	-28.4	-20.8	0	6	2,000	250	0.0	0.0
C+ / 6.4	11.4	1.03	20.35	9	2	95	1	2	48	121.5	-24.9	23	13	2,000	250	0.0	0.0
C+ / 6.4	11.4	1.03	20.14	1	2	95	1	2	48	121.1	-25.3	23	13	2,000	250	0.0	0.0
D- / 1.0	16.1	1.14	8.45	4	0	98	0	2	57	61.4	-22.7	1	5	2,000	250	0.0	0.0
D- / 1.0	16.1	1.14	8.37	3	0	98	0	2	57	61.4	-22.7	1	5	2,000	250	0.0	0.0
C- / 4.2	11.7	0.71	10.21	2	0	99	0	1	140	N/A	N/A	4	2	2,000	250	0.0	0.0
C- / 4.2	11.8	0.71	10.18	1	0	99	0	1	140	N/A	N/A	3	2	2,000	250	0.0	0.0
C+ / 5.7	12.4	0.79	8.44	5	11	88	0	1	129	39.2	-29.8	48	2	2,000	250	0.0	0.0
C+ / 5.7	12.4	0.79	8.44	3	11	88	0	1	129	38.7	-29.9	48	2	2,000	250	0.0	0.0
C+ / 6.5	11.6	1.09	18.90	185	1	96	1	2	19	132.7	-21.4	33	16	2,000	250	0.0	0.0
C+ / 6.5	11.6	1.09	19.21	994	1	96	1	2	19	129.3	-21.5	30	16	2,000	250	0.0	0.0
C+ / 5.7	12.3	1.11	22.74	461	0	99	0	1	15	134.3	-23.5	28	18	2,000	250	0.0	0.0
C+ / 5.8	12.3	1.11	22.69	22	0	99	0	1	15	131.2	-23.6	26	18	2,000	250	0.0	0.0
D+ / 2.3	15.8	1.22	23.57	89	0	99	0	1	18	132.9	-26.0	12	6	2,000	250	0.0	0.0
D+ / 2.3	15.8	1.22	22.98	21	0	99	0	1	18	129.9	-26.1	11	6	2,000	250	0.0	0.0
C- / 3.8	14.7	1.17	26.02	764	1	97	1	1	14	97.3	-12.3	7	13	2,000	250	0.0	0.0
C- / 3.7	14.7	1.17	24.19	139	1	97	1	1	14	94.6	-12.5	6	13	2,000	250	0.0	0.0
E / 0.3	18.6	1.05	23.27	29	1	97	1	1	77	72.0	-27.7	11	5	2,000	250	0.0	0.0
E / 0.3	18.6	1.05	21.22	15	1	97	1	1	77	70.1	-27.8	10	5	2,000	250	0.0	0.0
B- / 7.5	9.5	0.71	9.45	44	0	100	0	0	57	67.0	-15.2	9	2	1,000,000	25,000	0.0	0.0
B- / 7.4	9.6	0.72	9.51	4	0	100	0	0	57	65.2	-15.2	8	2	5,000	0	0.0	0.0
B- / 7.4	7.1	0.40	11.39	1	0	0	0	100	28	N/A	N/A	99	4	0	0	0.0	0.0
B- / 7.4	7.1	0.40	11.40	37	0	0	0	100	28	N/A	N/A	99	4	0	0	0.0	0.0
B / 8.3	4.3	0.31	9.52	N/A	0	0	0	100	55	N/A	N/A	69	4	0	0	0.0	0.0
B / 8.3	4.3	0.31	9.51	3	0	0	0	100	55	N/A	N/A	71	4	0	0	0.0	0.0
C- / 3.7	14.4	2.04	10.23	30	13	8	78	1	332	28.5	-6.5	1	15	2,000	100	0.0	0.0
D- / 1.2	17.5	1.02	20.00	169	0	100	0	0	4	23.9	-23.1	88	24	1,000	0	5.8	0.0

I. Index of Stock Mutual Funds

Fund Type	Fund Name	Ticker Symbol	Overall Investment Rating	Phone	Performance Rating/Pts	3 Mo	6 Mo	1Yr / Pct	3Yr / Pct	5Yr / Pct	Dividend Yield	Expense Ratio
	99 Pct = Best				PERFORMANCE			Total Return % through 2/28/17			Incl. in Returns	
	0 Pct = Worst								Annualized			
FO	Templeton China World Adv	TACWX	D-	(800) 342-5236	C / 5.1	7.83	7.43	26.44 /78	2.41 /27	0.14 / 5	1.11	1.66
FO	Templeton China World C	TCWCX	E+	(800) 342-5236	C- / 4.2	7.52	6.86	25.18 /74	1.39 /20	-0.86 / 4	0.00	2.66
FO	Templeton China World R6	FCWRX	D-	(800) 342-5236	C / 5.3	7.86	7.56	26.74 /78	2.63 /28	0.30 / 5	1.39	1.45
EM	Templeton Developing Markets A	TEDMX	E	(800) 342-5236	D / 2.0	10.45	8.29	37.48 /96	-0.75 /10	-1.53 / 3	1.03	1.73
EM	Templeton Developing Markets Adv	TDADX	E	(800) 321-8563	C- / 3.0	10.51	8.41	37.77 /96	-0.49 /11	-1.26 / 3	1.33	1.48
EM	Templeton Developing Markets C	TDMTX	E	(800) 342-5236	D+ / 2.3	10.23	7.86	36.39 /95	-1.48 / 8	-2.25 / 3	0.49	2.48
EM	Templeton Developing Markets R	TDMRX	E	(800) 342-5236	D+ / 2.7	10.31	8.11	37.05 /96	-0.99 / 9	-1.76 / 3	0.84	1.98
EM	Templeton Developing Markets R6	FDEVX	E+	(800) 342-5236	C- / 3.2	10.53	8.49	38.01 /96	-0.31 /12	-1.20 / 3	1.50	1.28
EM	Templeton Emerg Mkts Small Cap A	TEMMX	C-	(800) 342-5236	C- / 4.0	8.87	3.58	22.06 /63	3.97 /43	4.00 /15	1.52	1.99
EM	Templeton Emerg Mkts Small Cap	TEMZX	C+	(800) 321-8563	C / 5.4	8.85	3.62	22.33 /64	4.25 /46	4.27 /17	1.85	1.74
EM	Templeton Emerg Mkts Small Cap C	TCEMX	C	(800) 342-5236	C / 4.5	8.56	3.14	21.17 /58	3.20 /34	3.24 /12	0.94	2.74
EM	Templeton Emerg Mkts Small Cap R		C	(800) 342-5236	C / 4.9	8.74	3.33	21.69 /61	3.70 /39	3.75 /14	1.40	2.24
EM	Templeton Emg Markets Balanced A	TAEMX	D+	(800) 342-5236	C- / 3.8	10.72	8.46	29.20 /85	0.84 /17	-1.52 / 3	0.96	2.27
EM	Templeton Emg Markets Balanced	TZEMX	C-	(800) 342-5236	C / 5.3	10.78	8.60	29.47 /85	1.12 /19	-1.26 / 3	1.25	2.02
EM	Templeton Emg Markets Balanced C		C-	(800) 342-5236	C / 4.4	10.55	8.06	28.20 /82	0.12 /14	-2.26 / 3	0.35	3.02
EM	Templeton Emg Markets Balanced R		C-	(800) 342-5236	C / 4.8	10.68	8.36	28.91 /84	0.61 /16	-1.77 / 3	0.89	2.52
FO	Templeton Foreign A	TEMFX	E+	(800) 342-5236	D- / 1.1	7.66	7.82	26.62 /78	-1.59 / 8	5.19 /23	1.70	1.22
FO	Templeton Foreign Adv	TFFAX	D-	(800) 321-8563	D / 1.7	7.64	7.96	26.85 /79	-1.32 / 8	5.45 /24	2.13	0.97
FO	Templeton Foreign C	TEFTX	E+	(800) 342-5236	D- / 1.4	7.51	7.51	25.74 /75	-2.27 / 6	4.43 /18	1.11	1.97
FO	Templeton Foreign R	TEFRX	E+	(800) 342-5236	D- / 1.5	7.56	7.72	26.30 /77	-1.83 / 7	4.93 /21	1.60	1.47
FO	Templeton Foreign R6	FTFGX	D-	(800) 342-5236	D / 1.9	7.89	8.21	27.37 /80	-1.09 / 9	5.58 /25	2.35	0.72
FO	● Templeton Foreign Smaller Co A	FINEX	D-	(800) 342-5236	E+ / 0.6	8.98	3.96	14.27 /27	-1.77 / 7	3.49 /13	1.37	1.81
FO	● Templeton Foreign Smaller Co Adv	FTFAX	D-	(800) 321-8563	D- / 1.0	9.02	4.13	14.55 /28	-1.52 / 8	3.75 /14	1.65	1.57
FO	● Templeton Foreign Smaller Co C	FCFSX	D-	(800) 342-5236	E+ / 0.7	8.79	3.59	13.42 /23	-2.50 / 5	2.72 /10	0.85	2.56
FO	● Templeton Foreign Smaller Co R6		D-	(800) 342-5236	D- / 1.1	9.13	4.31	14.90 /29	-1.24 / 9	3.93 /15	0.96	1.31
EM	● Templeton Frontier Markets A	TFMAX	E-	(800) 342-5236	E- / 0.1	5.22	4.54	14.16 /26	-10.10 / 1	-1.45 / 3	0.57	2.15
EM	● Templeton Frontier Markets Adv	FFRZX	E-	(800) 342-5236	E- / 0.1	5.37	4.69	14.40 /27	-9.89 / 1	-1.20 / 3	0.67	1.90
EM	● Templeton Frontier Markets C	FFRMX	E-	(800) 342-5236	E- / 0.1	5.03	4.14	13.32 /23	-10.77 / 1	-2.17 / 3	0.00	2.88
EM	● Templeton Frontier Markets R		E-	(800) 342-5236	E- / 0.1	5.16	4.37	13.93 /25	-10.31 / 1	-1.68 / 3	0.43	2.40
EM	● Templeton Frontier Markets R6	FFMRX	E-	(800) 342-5236	E- / 0.1	5.30	4.72	14.77 /29	-9.67 / 1	-1.05 / 3	1.13	1.65
GL	Templeton Global Balanced A	TAGBX	D	(800) 342-5236	D+ / 2.4	6.04	7.95	18.20 /44	1.46 /21	5.77 /27	0.80	1.12
GL	Templeton Global Balanced A1	TINCX	D+	(800) 342-5236	D+ / 2.5	6.04	7.57	17.75 /42	1.45 /21	5.75 /27	0.81	1.12
GL	Templeton Global Balanced Adv	TZINX	C-	(800) 342-5236	C- / 3.4	6.11	7.70	17.97 /43	1.71 /22	6.00 /28	1.08	0.87
GL	Templeton Global Balanced C	FCGBX	D+	(800) 342-5236	D+ / 2.8	5.81	7.32	17.16 /39	0.76 /17	4.96 /21	0.28	1.87
GL	Templeton Global Balanced C1	TCINX	D+	(800) 342-5236	C- / 3.1	6.27	7.79	17.82 /42	1.17 /19	5.34 /24	0.55	1.52
GL	Templeton Global Balanced R		D+	(800) 342-5236	C- / 3.2	6.29	7.81	17.88 /42	1.32 /20	5.48 /25	0.65	1.37
GL	Templeton Global Balanced R6		C-	(800) 342-5236	C- / 3.6	6.15	8.15	18.58 /45	1.82 /23	6.09 /29	1.19	0.82
EM	Templeton Global Equity Series	TGESX	E+	(800) 342-5236	D / 1.9	6.94	9.23	21.63 /60	-0.09 /13	8.56 /47	1.60	0.81
GL	Templeton Global Opportunities A	TEGOX	D-	(800) 342-5236	D+ / 2.8	6.52	10.09	26.47 /78	0.03 /13	6.93 /34	1.47	1.35
GL	Templeton Global Opportunities Adv	FGOZX	D	(800) 321-8563	C- / 4.0	6.58	10.21	26.76 /78	0.28 /15	7.21 /36	1.81	1.10
GL	Templeton Global Opportunities C	TEGPX	D-	(800) 342-5236	D / 1.9	6.33	9.70	25.55 /75	-0.72 /10	6.14 /29	0.90	2.10
GL	Templeton Global Smaller Co A	TEMGX	D	(800) 342-5236	D / 2.1	5.69	5.81	20.95 /57	0.82 /17	7.07 /35	0.31	1.42
GL	Templeton Global Smaller Co Adv	TGSAX	D+	(800) 321-8563	C- / 3.3	5.88	6.00	21.25 /59	1.11 /19	7.33 /37	0.63	1.17
GL	Templeton Global Smaller Co C	TESGX	D+	(800) 342-5236	D+ / 2.5	5.49	5.36	19.95 /52	0.06 /14	6.26 /30	0.00	2.17
GL	Templeton Global Smaller Co R6	FBOGX	C-	(800) 342-5236	C- / 3.3	5.80	5.92	21.45 /60	1.25 /20	7.43 /38	0.78	0.95
* GL	Templeton Growth A	TEPLX	D+	(800) 342-5236	D+ / 2.9	7.11	9.61	25.00 /73	0.52 /16	8.14 /43	1.30	1.07
GL	Templeton Growth Adv	TGADX	C-	(800) 321-8563	C- / 4.1	7.18	9.73	25.34 /74	0.78 /17	8.42 /46	1.63	0.82
GL	Templeton Growth C	TEGTX	D	(800) 342-5236	D / 2.0	6.88	9.21	24.07 /70	-0.22 /13	7.33 /37	0.69	1.82
GL	Templeton Growth R	TEGRX	C-	(800) 342-5236	C- / 3.7	7.04	9.47	24.69 /72	0.27 /15	7.88 /41	1.14	1.32
GL	Templeton Growth R6	FTGFX	C-	(800) 342-5236	C- / 4.2	7.17	9.82	25.47 /75	0.89 /18	8.44 /46	1.73	0.70
EM	Templeton Inst-Emerg Markets Mkts	TEEMX	D-	(800) 321-8563	C+ / 6.0	10.82	8.83	39.29 /97	0.09 /14	-0.31 / 4	1.68	1.34
FO	● Templeton Inst-Foreign Small Comp	TFSCX	D+	(800) 321-8563	D / 2.2	8.69	3.19	13.04 /22	0.56 /16	6.20 /30	1.92	0.98

● Denotes fund is closed to new investors
* Denotes fund is included in Section II

www.thestreetratings.com

RISK			NET ASSETS		ASSET					BULL / BEAR		FUND MANAGER		MINIMUMS		LOADS	
	3 Year		NAV						Portfolio	Last Bull	Last Bear	Manager	Manager	Initial	Additional	Front	Back
Risk Rating/Pts	Standard Deviation	Beta	As of 2/28/17	Total $(Mil)	Cash %	Stocks %	Bonds %	Other %	Turnover Ratio	Market Return	Market Return	Quality Pct	Tenure (Years)	Purch. $	Purch. $	End Load	End Load
D- /1.2	17.5	1.02	20.14	66	0	100	0	0	4	25.8	-23.0	89	24	1,000	0	0.0	0.0
D- /1.2	17.5	1.02	19.77	43	0	100	0	0	4	19.2	-23.3	84	24	1,000	0	0.0	0.0
D- /1.2	17.5	1.02	20.10	1	0	100	0	0	4	26.8	-23.0	90	24	1,000,000	0	0.0	0.0
D /2.2	15.5	0.92	17.33	1,009	8	90	1	1	68	13.5	-24.8	44	26	1,000	0	5.8	0.0
D /2.2	15.5	0.92	17.24	126	8	90	1	1	68	15.2	-24.7	47	26	1,000,000	0	0.0	0.0
D /2.2	15.5	0.92	16.82	147	8	90	1	1	68	9.1	-25.0	34	26	1,000	0	0.0	0.0
D /2.2	15.5	0.91	17.04	18	8	90	1	1	68	12.1	-24.9	40	26	1,000	0	0.0	0.0
D /2.1	15.5	0.92	17.21	60	8	90	1	1	68	15.4	-24.8	50	26	1,000,000	0	0.0	0.0
C+ /6.4	12.3	0.66	12.56	256	6	91	1	2	18	44.7	-28.9	89	11	1,000	0	5.8	0.0
C+ /6.4	12.3	0.66	12.69	382	6	91	1	2	18	46.8	-28.8	90	11	1,000,000	0	0.0	0.0
C+ /6.4	12.3	0.66	12.08	58	6	91	1	2	18	39.1	-29.1	86	11	1,000	0	0.0	0.0
C+ /6.4	12.3	0.66	12.48	1	6	91	1	2	18	42.9	-28.8	88	11	1,000	0	0.0	0.0
C /5.2	11.9	0.70	9.76	21	24	43	32	1	65	N/A	N/A	70	6	1,000	0	5.8	0.0
C /5.1	11.9	0.70	9.78	4	24	43	32	1	65	N/A	N/A	73	6	1,000,000	0	0.0	0.0
C /5.2	11.9	0.70	9.68	3	24	43	32	1	65	N/A	N/A	61	6	1,000	0	0.0	0.0
C /5.2	11.9	0.70	9.74	N/A	24	43	32	1	65	N/A	N/A	67	6	1,000	0	0.0	0.0
C /4.6	13.8	1.03	7.27	3,586	3	96	0	1	23	49.8	-25.0	57	10	1,000	0	5.8	0.0
C /4.5	13.8	1.03	7.16	1,260	3	96	0	1	23	51.7	-24.9	60	10	1,000	0	0.0	0.0
C /4.6	13.8	1.03	7.11	381	3	96	0	1	23	43.9	-25.2	47	10	1,000	0	0.0	0.0
C /4.6	13.9	1.04	7.13	152	3	96	0	1	23	47.5	-25.0	53	10	1,000	0	0.0	0.0
C /4.5	13.9	1.04	7.16	862	3	96	0	1	23	52.7	-25.0	63	10	1,000,000	0	0.0	0.0
C+ /6.0	12.0	0.89	16.46	58	2	97	0	1	28	39.6	-26.0	54	10	1,000	0	5.8	0.0
C+ /6.0	12.0	0.89	16.41	21	2	97	0	1	28	41.4	-25.9	57	10	1,000,000	0	0.0	0.0
C+ /6.0	12.0	0.89	15.87	8	2	97	0	1	28	34.0	-26.2	43	10	1,000	0	0.0	0.0
C+ /6.0	12.0	0.89	16.57	N/A	2	97	0	1	28	42.5	-26.0	61	10	1,000,000	0	0.0	0.0
D+ /2.9	14.2	0.61	11.22	52	17	77	5	1	19	5.1	-19.6	1	9	1,000	0	5.8	0.0
D+ /2.9	14.2	0.61	11.27	52	17	77	5	1	19	6.6	-19.5	1	9	1,000,000	0	0.0	0.0
C- /3.0	14.3	0.61	11.06	20	17	77	5	1	19	1.1	-19.8	1	9	1,000	0	0.0	0.0
D+ /2.9	14.3	0.61	11.15	N/A	17	77	5	1	19	3.8	-19.6	1	9	1,000	0	0.0	0.0
D+ /2.9	14.2	0.61	11.23	56	17	77	5	1	19	7.4	-19.5	1	9	1,000,000	0	0.0	0.0
C+ /6.0	9.3	1.31	3.01	779	5	63	28	4	44	55.4	-17.2	19	12	1,000	0	5.8	0.0
C+ /6.0	9.2	1.31	3.01	318	5	63	28	4	44	55.8	-17.6	19	12	1,000	0	4.3	0.0
C+ /6.0	9.2	1.30	3.02	213	5	63	28	4	44	57.7	-17.4	21	12	1,000,000	0	0.0	0.0
C+ /6.0	9.4	1.33	2.99	338	5	63	28	4	44	49.8	-17.7	13	12	1,000	0	0.0	0.0
C+ /6.0	9.3	1.32	3.01	202	5	63	28	4	44	52.6	-17.5	17	12	1,000	0	0.0	0.0
C+ /6.0	9.3	1.31	3.02	5	5	63	28	4	44	53.7	-17.3	18	12	1,000	0	0.0	0.0
C+ /5.9	9.2	1.30	3.02	1	5	63	28	4	44	58.4	-17.4	23	12	1,000,000	0	0.0	0.0
C- /3.7	12.3	0.52	9.34	282	2	97	0	1	37	78.9	-19.0	62	9	1,000,000	0	0.0	0.0
C /4.3	12.6	0.96	20.02	386	0	96	0	4	15	64.4	-23.4	75	7	1,000	0	5.8	0.0
C /4.3	12.6	0.96	19.99	11	0	96	0	4	15	66.7	-23.4	77	7	1,000,000	0	0.0	0.0
C /4.3	12.6	0.96	19.49	28	0	96	0	4	15	58.0	-23.7	68	7	1,000	0	0.0	0.0
C+ /6.0	11.8	0.81	9.07	994	5	94	0	1	29	65.7	-27.3	81	10	1,000	0	5.8	0.0
C+ /6.0	11.8	0.81	9.10	75	5	94	0	1	29	68.0	-27.2	82	10	1,000	0	0.0	0.0
C+ /6.0	11.7	0.80	8.63	32	5	94	0	1	29	59.1	-27.6	75	10	1,000	0	0.0	0.0
C+ /6.0	11.7	0.80	9.09	21	5	94	0	1	29	68.5	-27.3	83	10	1,000,000	0	0.0	0.0
C+ /5.6	12.7	0.98	24.50	10,689	5	93	1	1	23	77.6	-22.8	79	10	1,000	0	5.8	0.0
C+ /5.6	12.7	0.98	24.53	431	5	93	1	1	23	80.0	-22.8	81	10	1,000	0	0.0	0.0
C+ /5.6	12.7	0.98	23.90	636	5	93	1	1	23	70.5	-23.1	73	10	1,000	0	0.0	0.0
C+ /5.6	12.7	0.98	24.29	102	5	93	1	1	23	75.2	-22.9	77	10	1,000	0	0.0	0.0
C+ /5.6	12.7	0.98	24.48	1,849	5	93	1	1	23	80.0	-22.8	81	10	1,000	0	0.0	0.0
D- /1.1	15.7	0.92	4.69	43	2	96	0	2	70	22.0	-21.1	56	24	1,000,000	0	0.0	0.0
C+ /6.5	11.5	0.86	21.08	961	4	95	0	1	29	57.5	-19.8	79	10	1,000,000	0	0.0	0.0

I. Index of Stock Mutual Funds

Fund Type	Fund Name	Ticker Symbol	Overall Investment Rating	Phone	Performance Rating/Pts	3 Mo	6 Mo	1Yr / Pct	3Yr / Pct	5Yr / Pct	Dividend Yield	Expense Ratio
								Total Return % through 2/28/17	Annualized		Incl. in Returns	
	99 Pct = Best / 0 Pct = Worst											
FO	Templeton Inst-International Eq Prm	TFEQX	E+	(800) 321-8563	E+ / 0.8	5.76	5.11	16.06 /35	-2.28 / 6	4.04 /15	2.36	0.78
FO	Templeton Inst-International Eq Svc	TFESX	E+	(800) 321-8563	E+ / 0.8	5.76	5.05	15.91 /34	-2.42 / 6	3.88 /15	2.17	0.93
GL	Templeton World A	TEMWX	D+	(800) 342-5236	C / 4.5	7.45	13.01	29.50 /85	1.68 /22	8.00 /42	3.21	1.07
GL	Templeton World Adv	TWDAX	C-	(800) 321-8563	C+ / 5.9	7.52	13.08	29.79 /86	1.91 /23	8.26 /44	3.64	0.82
GL	Templeton World C	TEWTX	D+	(800) 342-5236	C / 5.0	7.25	12.59	28.53 /83	0.91 /18	7.21 /36	2.80	1.82
GL	Templeton World R6	FTWRX	C-	(800) 342-5236	C+ / 6.0	7.57	13.21	29.94 /86	2.01 /24	8.28 /45	3.74	0.72
IN	TETON Convertible Securities A	WEIAX	C-	(800) 422-3554	C- / 3.9	6.99	5.12	20.77 /56	3.72 /40	7.79 /41	0.16	2.65
IN	TETON Convertible Securities AAA	WESRX	C	(800) 422-3554	C / 5.0	6.93	5.13	21.08 /58	3.96 /43	8.05 /43	0.28	2.40
IN	TETON Convertible Securities C	WEICX	C	(800) 422-3554	C / 4.3	6.81	4.89	20.15 /53	3.21 /34	7.28 /37	0.05	3.15
IN	TETON Convertible Securities I	WESIX	C+	(800) 422-3554	C / 5.2	7.10	5.37	21.37 /59	4.23 /46	8.33 /45	0.47	2.15
BA	TETON Westwood Balanced A	WEBCX	C-	(800) 422-3554	C- / 3.4	4.26	4.53	12.68 /20	5.25 /57	7.43 /38	0.56	1.56
BA	TETON Westwood Balanced AAA	WEBAX	C+	(800) 422-3554	C / 4.4	4.37	4.71	13.06 /22	5.52 /60	7.70 /40	0.75	1.31
BA	TETON Westwood Balanced C	WBCCX	C	(800) 422-3554	C- / 3.8	4.21	4.27	12.22 /19	4.74 /51	6.89 /34	0.24	2.06
BA	TETON Westwood Balanced I	WBBIX	C+	(800) 422-3554	C / 4.6	4.38	4.78	13.29 /23	5.75 /62	7.95 /42	0.93	1.06
IN	TETON Westwood Equity A	WEECX	C+	(800) 422-3554	C+ / 6.6	6.40	8.31	20.08 /52	7.84 /78	11.39 /69	0.26	1.84
IN	TETON Westwood Equity AAA	WESWX	B	(800) 422-3554	B- / 7.4	6.38	8.42	20.37 /54	8.10 /80	11.64 /71	0.52	1.59
IN	TETON Westwood Equity C	WEQCX	C+	(800) 422-3554	C+ / 6.9	6.17	8.04	19.40 /49	7.28 /74	10.81 /64	0.00	2.34
IN	TETON Westwood Equity I	WEEIX	B	(800) 422-3554	B / 7.6	6.49	8.63	20.64 /56	8.35 /82	11.87 /73	0.75	1.34
MC	TETON Westwood Mid Cap Equity A	WMCAX	C	(800) 422-3554	C+ / 6.7	10.31	8.24	28.99 /84	5.25 /57	--	0.00	2.99
MC	TETON Westwood Mid Cap Equity	WMCEX	C+	(800) 422-3554	B- / 7.5	10.39	8.43	29.29 /85	5.50 /60	--	0.00	2.74
MC	TETON Westwood Mid Cap Equity C	WMCCX	C+	(800) 422-3554	B- / 7.0	10.23	8.04	28.38 /83	4.72 /51	--	0.00	3.49
MC	TETON Westwood Mid Cap Equity I	WMCRX	C+	(800) 422-3554	B / 7.8	10.45	8.51	29.79 /86	5.81 /63	--	0.00	2.49
SC	TETON Westwood Mighty Mites A	WMMAX	C+	(800) 422-3554	C+ / 5.6	2.79	10.11	27.94 /81	4.87 /53	12.05 /75	0.00	1.66
SC	TETON Westwood Mighty Mites AAA	WEMMX	C+	(800) 422-3554	C+ / 6.6	2.90	10.30	28.28 /82	5.15 /56	12.33 /77	0.00	1.41
SC	TETON Westwood Mighty Mites C	WMMCX	C+	(800) 422-3554	C+ / 6.0	2.67	9.85	27.28 /80	4.36 /47	11.49 /70	0.00	2.16
SC	TETON Westwood Mighty Mites I	WEIMX	C+	(800) 422-3554	C+ / 6.8	2.97	10.41	28.59 /83	5.40 /59	12.60 /80	0.00	1.16
SC	TETON Westwood Sm Cap Equity A	WWSAX	B-	(800) 422-3554	A+ / 9.6	5.45	15.37	44.65 /98	8.53 /83	11.28 /68	0.00	2.04
SC	TETON Westwood Sm Cap Equity	WESCX	B	(800) 422-3554	A+ / 9.8	5.56	15.47	45.04 /98	8.80 /85	11.56 /70	0.00	1.79
SC	TETON Westwood Sm Cap Equity C	WWSCX	B-	(800) 422-3554	A+ / 9.7	5.35	15.04	43.94 /98	8.00 /79	10.73 /64	0.00	2.54
SC	TETON Westwood Sm Cap Equity I	WWSIX	B	(800) 422-3554	A+ / 9.8	5.61	15.61	45.32 /98	9.07 /87	11.84 /73	0.00	1.54
IN	TFS Hedged Futures	TFSHX	C-	(800) 534-2001	E+ / 0.6	-2.25	-2.89	-1.51 / 1	0.81 /17	0.44 / 5	0.00	3.01
IN	TFS Market Neutral	TFSMX	C-	(800) 534-2001	D- / 1.3	-0.21	6.30	4.14 / 3	1.74 /22	1.78 / 8	0.00	7.76
SC	TFS Small Cap	TFSSX	B	(800) 534-2001	B+ / 8.6	4.46	12.79	35.28 /94	6.75 /70	13.91 /93	0.00	1.68
FO	Third Avenue International Val Inst	TAVIX	E+	(800) 443-1021	D+ / 2.3	9.26	14.54	40.34 /97	-2.04 / 7	3.65 /14	4.46	1.61
FO	Third Avenue International Val Inv	TVIVX	E+	(800) 443-1021	D / 2.2	9.24	14.45	40.00 /97	-2.29 / 6	3.40 /12	4.26	1.86
RE	Third Avenue Real Estate Value Inst	TAREX	C+	(800) 443-1021	C+ / 6.9	8.47	6.18	26.35 /77	6.03 /64	10.76 /64	0.79	1.10
RE	Third Avenue Real Estate Value Inv	TVRVX	C+	(800) 443-1021	C+ / 6.7	8.41	6.03	26.00 /76	5.75 /62	10.49 /62	0.51	1.35
GL	Third Avenue Small-Cap Value Inst	TASCX	C	(800) 443-1021	B+ / 8.6	3.80	10.88	34.37 /93	7.66 /77	11.88 /73	0.53	1.14
GL	Third Avenue Small-Cap Value Inv	TVSVX	C	(800) 443-1021	B+ / 8.3	3.74	10.68	34.03 /93	7.38 /75	11.62 /71	0.28	1.39
GR	Third Avenue Value Inst	TAVFX	C+	(800) 443-1021	B- / 7.2	6.40	10.50	31.75 /90	5.12 /55	7.93 /42	0.79	1.09
GR	Third Avenue Value Inv	TVFVX	C	(800) 443-1021	B- / 7.0	6.35	10.37	31.42 /89	4.85 /53	7.66 /39	0.53	1.34
GR	Third Avenue Value Portfolio		C+	(800) 443-1021	C+ / 6.7	6.16	9.81	29.69 /86	4.33 /47	7.39 /37	0.73	1.23
MC	Thomas White American Opps	TWAOX	B	(800) 811-0535	B- / 7.3	7.27	9.64	20.77 /56	8.03 /79	11.48 /70	0.58	1.18
EM	Thomas White Emerging Markets A	TWIAX	E	(800) 811-0535	E / 0.3	6.04	0.04	17.52 /41	-3.21 / 4	-2.51 / 2	0.52	1.67
EM	Thomas White Emerging Markets C	TWICX	E	(800) 811-0535	E / 0.4	5.85	-0.31	16.87 /38	-3.63 / 4	-2.97 / 2	0.00	2.27
EM	Thomas White Emerging Markets I	TWIIX	E+	(800) 811-0535	E+ / 0.6	6.08	0.25	17.98 /43	-2.74 / 5	-2.07 / 3	1.05	1.26
EM	Thomas White Emerging Markets Inv	TWEMX	E+	(800) 811-0535	E / 0.5	6.10	0.19	17.80 /42	-2.95 / 5	-2.26 / 3	1.00	1.34
FO	Thomas White International A	TWWAX	E+	(800) 811-0535	E- / 0.2	6.65	1.69	10.02 /12	-3.94 / 3	1.32 / 7	0.94	1.42
FO	Thomas White International C	TWWCX	E+	(800) 811-0535	E- / 0.2	6.59	1.45	9.40 /10	-4.48 / 3	0.73 / 6	0.00	2.08
FO	Thomas White International I	TWWIX	E+	(800) 811-0535	E / 0.3	6.84	1.96	10.47 /13	-3.55 / 4	1.71 / 7	1.58	1.08
FO	Thomas White International Investor	TWWDX	E+	(800) 811-0535	E / 0.3	6.68	1.73	10.16 /12	-3.82 / 3	1.46 / 7	1.04	1.32
GR	Thompson LargeCap	THPGX	A+	(800) 999-0887	A / 9.4	5.47	11.64	35.77 /95	8.60 /84	13.09 /85	0.76	1.22

● Denotes fund is closed to new investors
∗ Denotes fund is included in Section II

www.thestreetratings.com

RISK			NET ASSETS		ASSET				Portfolio	BULL / BEAR		FUND MANAGER		MINIMUMS		LOADS	
Risk Rating/Pts	3 Year Standard Deviation	Beta	NAV As of 2/28/17	Total $(Mil)	Cash %	Stocks %	Bonds %	Other %	Portfolio Turnover Ratio	Last Bull Market Return	Last Bear Market Return	Manager Quality Pct	Manager Tenure (Years)	Initial Purch. $	Additional Purch. $	Front End Load	Back End Load
C / 5.1	12.1	0.95	19.27	4,626	2	97	0	1	16	42.9	-24.5	46	18	1,000,000	0	0.0	0.0
C / 5.2	12.1	0.95	19.34	16	2	97	0	1	16	41.7	-24.5	44	18	1,000,000	0	0.0	0.0
C- / 4.1	12.7	0.95	16.44	4,297	0	98	1	1	22	76.7	-20.4	85	10	1,000	0	5.8	0.0
C- / 4.1	12.8	0.96	16.40	121	0	98	1	1	22	79.1	-20.3	86	10	1,000	0	0.0	0.0
C- / 4.2	12.8	0.96	15.79	159	0	98	1	1	22	69.7	-20.7	81	10	1,000	0	0.0	0.0
C- / 4.1	12.8	0.96	16.39	52	0	98	1	1	22	79.0	-20.4	87	10	1,000,000	0	0.0	0.0
C+ / 6.3	11.9	1.07	12.09	1	2	95	2	1	20	65.8	-12.6	5	N/A	1,000	0	4.0	0.0
C+ / 6.3	11.9	1.07	11.72	4	2	95	2	1	20	67.8	-12.6	6	N/A	1,000	0	0.0	0.0
C+ / 6.3	11.9	1.07	12.86	1	2	95	2	1	20	61.3	-12.8	4	N/A	1,000	0	0.0	0.0
C+ / 6.3	11.9	1.06	11.76	2	2	95	2	1	20	70.3	-12.5	7	N/A	500,000	0	0.0	0.0
B- / 7.0	6.2	0.96	11.75	8	0	65	34	1	23	64.5	-12.1	50	5	1,000	0	4.0	0.0
B- / 7.0	6.2	0.96	11.70	54	0	65	34	1	23	66.8	-12.0	54	5	1,000	0	0.0	0.0
B- / 7.1	6.2	0.97	11.89	5	0	65	34	1	23	60.3	-12.3	43	5	1,000	0	0.0	0.0
B- / 7.0	6.2	0.96	11.69	2	0	65	34	1	23	69.0	-11.9	57	5	500,000	0	0.0	0.0
C+ / 6.0	9.7	0.91	12.81	3	0	99	0	1	52	113.0	-20.4	53	5	1,000	0	4.0	0.0
C+ / 6.0	9.7	0.91	12.83	55	0	99	0	1	52	115.7	-20.3	57	5	1,000	0	0.0	0.0
C+ / 5.9	9.6	0.91	12.21	1	0	99	0	1	52	107.1	-20.5	46	5	1,000	0	0.0	0.0
C+ / 5.9	9.7	0.91	12.79	5	0	99	0	1	52	118.1	-20.2	60	5	500,000	0	0.0	0.0
C / 4.5	13.6	1.02	12.63	N/A	0	97	2	1	15	N/A	N/A	21	N/A	1,000	0	4.0	0.0
C / 4.5	13.6	1.02	12.75	1	0	97	2	1	15	N/A	N/A	23	N/A	1,000	0	0.0	0.0
C / 4.5	13.7	1.03	12.39	N/A	0	97	2	1	15	N/A	N/A	17	N/A	1,000	0	0.0	0.0
C / 4.5	13.6	1.02	12.89	2	0	97	2	1	15	N/A	N/A	26	N/A	500,000	0	0.0	0.0
C+ / 5.9	12.5	0.77	25.01	156	1	89	9	1	6	107.8	-19.3	70	19	10,000	0	4.0	0.0
C+ / 5.9	12.5	0.77	25.86	276	1	89	9	1	6	110.8	-19.3	73	19	10,000	0	0.0	0.0
C+ / 5.8	12.5	0.77	22.28	175	1	89	9	1	6	102.3	-19.5	64	19	10,000	0	0.0	0.0
C+ / 6.0	12.5	0.77	26.35	566	1	89	9	1	6	113.4	-19.2	75	19	500,000	0	0.0	0.0
C- / 3.3	15.5	0.94	18.96	4	0	98	1	1	52	117.5	-28.9	86	9	1,000	0	4.0	0.0
C- / 3.4	15.6	0.94	19.74	11	0	98	1	1	52	120.4	-28.8	87	9	1,000	0	0.0	0.0
D+ / 2.9	15.6	0.94	16.73	2	0	98	1	1	52	111.7	-29.0	83	9	1,000	0	0.0	0.0
C- / 3.5	15.6	0.94	20.32	15	0	98	1	1	52	123.6	-28.8	88	9	500,000	0	0.0	0.0
B+ / 9.6	5.4	0.04	10.41	14	77	0	22	1	0	N/A	N/A	76	6	5,000	100	0.0	0.0
B / 8.2	5.7	0.15	14.35	262	75	22	2	1	778	18.3	-10.4	75	13	5,000	100	0.0	0.0
C / 4.6	16.0	1.00	13.94	69	1	98	0	1	778	145.4	-26.4	72	11	5,000	100	0.0	0.0
C- / 3.3	17.2	1.15	16.54	125	9	87	3	1	25	36.1	-22.8	51	5	100,000	0	0.0	2.0
C- / 3.3	17.2	1.15	16.56	27	9	87	3	1	25	34.3	-22.8	47	5	2,500	1,000	0.0	2.0
C+ / 5.9	11.6	0.60	32.08	1,587	13	86	0	1	20	108.3	-22.5	68	19	100,000	0	0.0	1.0
C+ / 5.9	11.6	0.60	31.91	241	13	86	0	1	20	105.5	-22.5	65	19	2,500	1,000	0.0	1.0
D+ / 2.4	13.8	0.65	21.90	308	4	95	0	1	20	105.3	-19.6	98	4	100,000	0	0.0	1.0
D+ / 2.4	13.8	0.65	21.70	5	4	95	0	1	20	102.7	-19.7	98	4	2,500	1,000	0.0	1.0
C- / 4.2	13.9	1.15	53.03	1,193	6	92	1	1	17	80.1	-26.9	6	4	100,000	0	0.0	1.0
C / 4.3	13.9	1.15	53.02	15	6	92	1	1	17	77.7	-27.0	6	4	2,500	1,000	0.0	1.0
C / 5.0	13.7	1.14	17.24	92	0	98	1	1	22	76.3	-27.6	5	4	0	0	0.0	0.0
C+ / 5.8	10.6	0.83	16.74	41	0	99	0	1	60	113.4	-19.7	75	18	2,500	100	0.0	2.0
C / 4.9	14.4	0.84	9.83	N/A	4	95	0	1	57	8.3	-27.2	17	7	2,500	100	5.8	2.0
C / 4.8	14.4	0.84	9.77	N/A	4	95	0	1	57	5.5	-27.4	14	7	2,500	100	0.0	2.0
C / 4.9	14.4	0.84	9.90	72	4	95	0	1	57	10.9	-27.1	21	7	1,000,000	100	0.0	2.0
C / 4.8	14.4	0.84	9.82	2	4	95	0	1	57	9.9	-27.1	20	7	2,500	100	0.0	2.0
C / 5.2	11.0	0.84	15.30	1	2	97	0	1	60	26.7	-23.9	25	23	2,500	100	5.8	2.0
C / 5.2	11.0	0.84	15.36	N/A	2	97	0	1	60	22.7	-24.2	20	23	2,500	100	0.0	2.0
C / 5.1	11.0	0.84	15.37	371	2	97	0	1	60	29.3	-23.9	29	23	1,000,000	100	0.0	2.0
C / 5.2	11.0	0.84	15.38	83	2	97	0	1	60	27.7	-23.9	26	23	2,500	100	0.0	2.0
C+ / 6.2	13.5	1.22	60.15	123	0	100	0	0	45	133.3	-21.6	23	25	250	50	0.0	0.0

Fund Type	Fund Name	Ticker Symbol	Overall Investment Rating	Phone	Performance Rating/Pts	3 Mo	6 Mo	1Yr / Pct	3Yr / Pct	5Yr / Pct	Dividend Yield	Expense Ratio
								Total Return % through 2/28/17	Annualized		Incl. in Returns	
MC	Thompson MidCap Fund	THPMX	B	(800) 999-0887	A- / 9.0	6.51	10.20	38.29 /97	6.98 /72	12.28 /77	0.05	1.49
SC	Thomson Hrstmnn and Brynt MicCp	THBIX	B-	(855) 842-3863	B+ / 8.4	5.62	20.55	41.97 /98	3.77 /40	--	0.00	1.81
SC	Thomson Hrstmnn and Brynt MicCp	THBVX	C+	(855) 842-3863	B / 8.0	5.47	20.27	41.36 /98	3.25 /34	--	0.00	2.29
FO	Thornburg Better World Intl I	TBWIX	U	(800) 847-0200	U /	1.43	1.48	14.17 /26	--	--	0.47	1.68
GR	Thornburg Core Growth A	THCGX	D	(800) 847-0200	C- / 3.3	6.30	6.88	23.05 /67	1.99 /24	10.63 /63	0.00	1.39
GR	Thornburg Core Growth C	TCGCX	D	(800) 847-0200	C- / 3.5	6.10	6.48	22.12 /63	1.22 /19	9.80 /57	0.00	2.15
GR	Thornburg Core Growth I	THIGX	D+	(800) 847-0200	C / 4.5	6.43	7.08	23.55 /68	2.41 /27	11.10 /67	0.00	1.05
GR	Thornburg Core Growth R3	THCRX	D+	(800) 847-0200	C- / 4.0	6.29	6.79	22.92 /66	1.89 /23	10.53 /62	0.00	1.79
GR	Thornburg Core Growth R4	TCGRX	D+	(800) 847-0200	C- / 4.1	6.31	6.89	23.04 /67	1.99 /24	10.65 /63	0.00	1.82
GR	Thornburg Core Growth R5	THGRX	D+	(800) 847-0200	C / 4.5	6.43	7.12	23.58 /68	2.41 /27	11.11 /67	0.00	1.24
EM	Thornburg Developing World A	THDAX	E+	(800) 847-0200	E- / 0.2	4.69	-2.62	14.15 /26	-4.07 / 3	1.68 / 7	0.20	1.53
EM	Thornburg Developing World C	THDCX	E+	(800) 847-0200	E / 0.3	4.44	-3.01	13.21 /22	-4.82 / 3	0.91 / 6	0.00	2.27
EM	Thornburg Developing World I	THDIX	E+	(800) 847-0200	E / 0.4	4.79	-2.40	14.60 /28	-3.66 / 3	2.15 / 8	0.52	1.14
EM	Thornburg Developing World R5	THDRX	E+	(800) 847-0200	E / 0.4	4.75	-2.47	14.57 /28	-3.67 / 3	--	0.52	1.67
EM	Thornburg Developing World R6	TDWRX	E+	(800) 847-0200	E / 0.4	4.79	-2.37	14.63 /28	-3.57 / 4	--	0.55	1.10
GL	Thornburg Globl Opportunities A	THOAX	C+	(800) 847-0200	C+ / 5.8	6.46	11.48	15.27 /31	7.06 /72	12.34 /78	0.39	1.32
GL	Thornburg Globl Opportunities C	THOCX	C+	(800) 847-0200	C+ / 6.1	6.24	11.11	14.44 /28	6.27 /67	11.48 /70	0.04	2.10
GL	Thornburg Globl Opportunities Inst	THOIX	C+	(800) 847-0200	C+ / 6.9	6.55	11.69	15.71 /33	7.46 /75	12.79 /82	0.79	0.97
GL	Thornburg Globl Opportunities R3	THORX	C+	(800) 847-0200	C+ / 6.6	6.42	11.44	15.14 /30	6.91 /71	12.22 /76	0.36	2.15
GL	Thornburg Globl Opportunities R4	THOVX	C+	(800) 847-0200	C+ / 6.7	6.44	11.49	15.25 /31	7.01 /72	12.33 /77	0.46	1.76
GL	Thornburg Globl Opportunities R5	THOFX	C+	(800) 847-0200	C+ / 6.9	6.54	11.70	15.68 /33	7.46 /75	12.78 /82	0.77	1.02
BA	Thornburg Income Builder A	TIBAX	D+	(800) 847-0200	D+ / 2.4	4.38	3.90	16.34 /36	2.70 /29	6.44 /31	3.64	1.33
BA	Thornburg Income Builder C	TIBCX	D+	(800) 847-0200	D+ / 2.6	4.16	3.49	15.48 /32	1.94 /24	5.67 /26	3.13	2.08
BA	Thornburg Income Builder I	TIBIX	C-	(800) 847-0200	C- / 3.4	4.43	4.04	16.67 /37	3.01 /32	6.77 /33	4.11	1.01
BA	Thornburg Income Builder R3	TIBRX	C-	(800) 847-0200	C- / 3.1	4.25	3.74	15.99 /34	2.78 /30	6.36 /31	3.51	1.71
BA	Thornburg Income Builder R4	TIBGX	C-	(800) 847-0200	C- / 3.2	4.27	3.74	16.09 /35	2.90 /31	6.49 /31	3.61	1.62
BA	Thornburg Income Builder R5	TIBMX	C-	(800) 847-0200	C- / 3.5	4.40	3.98	16.60 /37	3.36 /35	6.93 /34	3.99	1.23
FO	Thornburg International Growth A	TIGAX	E+	(800) 847-0200	E / 0.3	4.97	-0.82	8.82 / 9	-2.28 / 6	6.59 /32	0.06	1.42
FO	Thornburg International Growth C	TIGCX	E+	(800) 847-0200	E / 0.4	4.77	-1.26	7.98 / 7	-3.03 / 4	5.79 /27	0.00	2.20
FO	Thornburg International Growth I	TINGX	E+	(800) 847-0200	E+ / 0.6	5.06	-0.66	9.33 /10	-1.88 / 7	7.04 /35	0.34	1.01
FO	Thornburg International Growth R3	TIGVX	E+	(800) 847-0200	E / 0.5	4.95	-0.90	8.75 / 9	-2.38 / 6	6.49 /31	0.04	1.98
FO	Thornburg International Growth R4	TINVX	E+	(800) 847-0200	E / 0.5	4.94	-0.87	8.83 / 9	-2.29 / 6	6.60 /32	0.08	1.65
FO	Thornburg International Growth R5	TINFX	E+	(800) 847-0200	E+ / 0.6	5.05	-0.69	9.26 /10	-1.89 / 7	7.02 /35	0.36	1.20
FO	Thornburg International Growth R6	THGIX	E+	(800) 847-0200	E+ / 0.6	5.09	-0.62	9.38 /10	-1.79 / 7	--	0.43	1.43
FO	Thornburg International Value A	TGVAX	E+	(800) 847-0200	D- / 1.1	3.85	1.40	9.67 /11	0.68 /17	3.42 /12	1.57	1.27
FO	Thornburg International Value C	THGCX	E	(800) 847-0200	D- / 1.0	3.65	1.07	8.86 / 9	-0.05 /13	2.66 /10	1.27	1.99
FO	Thornburg International Value Inst	TGVIX	E+	(800) 847-0200	D / 1.7	3.92	1.58	10.06 /12	1.05 /19	3.81 /14	1.87	0.90
FO	Thornburg International Value R3	TGVRX	E+	(800) 847-0200	D- / 1.5	3.85	1.35	9.47 /10	0.51 /16	3.23 /12	1.46	1.58
FO	Thornburg International Value R4	THVRX	E+	(800) 847-0200	D- / 1.5	3.88	1.45	9.68 /11	0.72 /17	3.44 /13	1.68	1.37
FO	Thornburg International Value R5	TIVRX	E+	(800) 847-0200	D / 1.6	3.93	1.54	10.01 /12	0.99 /18	3.72 /14	1.86	1.11
FO	Thornburg International Value R6	TGIRX	E+	(800) 847-0200	D / 1.7	4.02	1.70	10.28 /12	1.23 /19	--	2.00	0.74
GI	Thornburg Value A	TVAFX	B+	(800) 847-0200	B- / 7.3	7.05	9.33	23.41 /68	8.34 /82	12.08 /75	0.31	1.37
GI	Thornburg Value C	TVCFX	B+	(800) 847-0200	B- / 7.5	6.87	8.94	22.52 /65	7.53 /76	11.23 /68	0.00	2.12
GI	Thornburg Value Fund R4	TVIRX	A	(800) 847-0200	B / 8.2	7.11	9.40	23.58 /68	8.49 /83	12.23 /76	0.47	1.67
GI	Thornburg Value Inst	TVIFX	A	(800) 847-0200	B+ / 8.3	7.17	9.54	23.89 /69	8.76 /85	12.52 /79	0.78	1.06
GI	Thornburg Value R3	TVRFX	A	(800) 847-0200	B / 8.1	7.06	9.35	23.45 /68	8.37 /82	12.12 /75	0.36	1.77
GI	Thornburg Value R5	TVRRX	A	(800) 847-0200	B+ / 8.4	7.18	9.55	23.90 /69	8.77 /85	12.52 /79	0.78	1.20
AA	● Thrivent Aggressive Allocation A	TAAAX	C-	(800) 847-4836	C+ / 6.1	6.46	9.27	24.28 /71	5.94 /64	9.54 /55	0.47	1.52
AA	Thrivent Aggressive Allocation S	TAAIX	C+	(800) 847-4836	B- / 7.1	6.54	9.48	24.67 /72	6.36 /67	9.98 /58	0.81	1.15
BA	● Thrivent Balanced Income Plus A	AABFX	C-	(800) 847-4836	C- / 3.0	4.53	3.73	14.17 /26	4.35 /47	7.53 /39	2.19	1.11
BA	Thrivent Balanced Income Plus S	IBBFX	C	(800) 847-4836	C- / 4.1	4.63	3.89	14.61 /28	4.75 /52	7.95 /42	2.64	0.72
IN	● Thrivent Growth and Inc Plus A	TEIAX	C-	(800) 847-4836	C- / 3.0	5.47	4.50	16.40 /36	3.59 /38	--	1.80	1.46

● Denotes fund is closed to new investors
* Denotes fund is included in Section II

www.thestreetratings.com

RISK			NET ASSETS		ASSET					Portfolio Turnover Ratio	BULL / BEAR		FUND MANAGER		MINIMUMS		LOADS	
	3 Year		NAV								Last Bull	Last Bear	Manager	Manager	Initial	Additional	Front	Back
Risk Rating/Pts	Standard Deviation	Beta	As of 2/28/17	Total $(Mil)	Cash %	Stocks %	Bonds %	Other %			Market Return	Market Return	Quality Pct	Tenure (Years)	Purch. $	Purch. $	End Load	End Load
C- /4.0	14.3	1.11	12.74	47	0	98	0	2	27	124.4	-23.0	29	9	250	50	0.0	0.0
C- /4.2	15.9	0.92	16.54	69	0	99	0	1	65	N/A	N/A	42	5	100,000	2,500	0.0	2.0
C- /4.2	15.8	0.92	16.20	1	0	99	0	1	65	N/A	N/A	35	5	100	0	0.0	2.0
U /	N/A	N/A	12.75	35	9	90	0	1	180	N/A	N/A	N/A	2	2,500,000	100	0.0	0.0
C /4.6	14.5	1.12	29.68	189	6	93	0	1	86	122.7	-21.0	3	5	5,000	100	4.5	0.0
C /4.5	14.4	1.12	26.11	144	6	93	0	1	86	113.7	-21.2	2	5	5,000	100	0.0	0.0
C /4.6	14.4	1.12	31.63	204	6	93	0	1	86	127.9	-20.8	3	5	2,500,000	100	0.0	0.0
C /4.6	14.5	1.12	29.55	51	6	93	0	1	86	121.7	-21.0	3	5	0	0	0.0	0.0
C /4.6	14.5	1.12	29.80	6	6	93	0	1	86	122.9	-20.9	3	5	0	0	0.0	0.0
C /4.6	14.4	1.12	31.60	35	6	93	0	1	86	128.0	-20.9	3	5	0	0	0.0	0.0
C /5.1	12.3	0.71	16.53	134	7	91	0	2	95	32.8	-25.3	12	2	5,000	100	4.5	0.0
C /5.0	12.3	0.71	15.77	110	7	91	0	2	95	27.5	-25.6	8	2	5,000	100	0.0	0.0
C /5.1	12.3	0.71	16.83	736	7	91	0	2	95	36.3	-25.2	15	2	2,500,000	100	0.0	0.0
C /5.0	12.3	0.71	16.77	6	7	91	0	2	95	N/A	N/A	15	2	0	0	0.0	0.0
C /5.0	12.3	0.71	16.83	47	7	91	0	2	95	N/A	N/A	16	2	0	0	0.0	0.0
C+ /6.2	11.9	0.76	27.28	413	8	91	0	1	37	114.7	-23.6	98	11	5,000	100	4.5	0.0
C+ /6.2	11.9	0.76	26.40	355	8	91	0	1	37	105.9	-23.8	97	11	5,000	100	0.0	0.0
C+ /6.2	11.9	0.76	27.37	1,134	8	91	0	1	37	119.6	-23.4	98	11	2,500,000	100	0.0	0.0
C+ /6.2	11.9	0.76	27.01	10	8	91	0	1	37	113.5	-23.6	98	11	0	0	0.0	0.0
C+ /6.2	11.9	0.76	27.03	23	8	91	0	1	37	114.6	-23.6	98	11	0	0	0.0	0.0
C+ /6.2	11.9	0.76	27.39	66	8	91	0	1	37	119.5	-23.4	98	11	0	0	0.0	0.0
C+ /6.4	8.5	1.21	20.27	3,526	4	85	10	1	43	52.0	-12.2	9	15	5,000	100	4.5	0.0
C+ /6.4	8.5	1.21	20.25	4,968	4	85	10	1	43	46.2	-12.5	6	15	5,000	100	0.0	0.0
C+ /6.4	8.5	1.20	20.41	7,114	4	85	10	1	43	54.7	-12.1	10	15	2,500,000	100	0.0	0.0
C+ /6.4	8.4	1.19	20.26	75	4	85	10	1	43	51.4	-12.4	10	15	0	0	0.0	0.0
C+ /6.4	8.4	1.19	20.29	45	4	85	10	1	43	52.3	-12.4	10	15	0	0	0.0	0.0
C+ /6.4	8.4	1.18	20.40	86	4	85	10	1	43	55.7	-12.2	13	15	0	0	0.0	0.0
C /5.3	13.3	0.92	19.01	121	6	93	0	1	105	54.0	-12.4	46	5	5,000	100	4.5	0.0
C /5.2	13.3	0.92	18.00	79	6	93	0	1	105	47.6	-12.7	35	5	5,000	100	0.0	0.0
C /5.3	13.3	0.92	19.51	881	6	93	0	1	105	57.5	-12.2	52	5	2,500,000	100	0.0	0.0
C /5.3	13.3	0.92	18.86	10	6	93	0	1	105	53.2	-12.4	45	5	0	0	0.0	0.0
C /5.3	13.3	0.92	18.90	36	6	93	0	1	105	54.1	-12.3	46	5	0	0	0.0	0.0
C /5.3	13.3	0.92	19.55	54	6	93	0	1	105	57.4	-12.2	52	5	0	0	0.0	0.0
C /5.3	13.3	0.92	19.60	28	6	93	0	1	105	N/A	N/A	53	5	0	0	0.0	0.0
C- /4.1	11.4	0.88	23.48	866	6	93	0	1	104	37.1	-24.3	80	19	5,000	100	4.5	0.0
C- /3.9	11.4	0.88	21.27	441	6	93	0	1	104	31.7	-24.5	75	19	5,000	100	0.0	0.0
C- /4.2	11.4	0.88	24.11	3,534	6	93	0	1	104	39.9	-24.2	82	19	2,500,000	100	0.0	0.0
C- /4.1	11.4	0.88	23.48	288	6	93	0	1	104	35.8	-24.3	79	19	0	0	0.0	0.0
C- /4.1	11.4	0.88	23.32	223	6	93	0	1	104	37.3	-24.2	80	19	0	0	0.0	0.0
C- /4.2	11.4	0.88	24.09	446	6	93	0	1	104	39.3	-24.2	82	19	0	0	0.0	0.0
C- /4.2	11.4	0.88	24.06	434	6	93	0	1	104	N/A	N/A	83	19	0	0	0.0	0.0
B- /7.1	10.0	0.92	58.44	362	12	87	0	1	31	112.9	-25.1	58	11	5,000	100	4.5	0.0
B- /7.0	10.0	0.92	53.86	167	12	87	0	1	31	104.3	-25.4	48	11	5,000	100	0.0	0.0
B- /7.1	10.0	0.92	58.70	10	12	87	0	1	31	114.4	-25.1	60	11	0	0	0.0	0.0
B- /7.1	10.0	0.92	60.10	304	12	87	0	1	31	117.5	-25.0	63	11	2,500,000	100	0.0	0.0
B- /7.1	10.0	0.92	58.09	47	12	87	0	1	31	113.2	-25.1	59	11	0	0	0.0	0.0
B- /7.1	10.0	0.92	60.02	16	12	87	0	1	31	117.4	-25.0	63	11	0	0	0.0	0.0
C /4.3	10.5	1.58	14.34	800	0	85	14	1	57	89.2	-19.9	11	N/A	2,000	50	4.5	0.0
C /4.3	10.5	1.57	14.46	168	0	85	14	1	57	93.4	-19.8	14	N/A	50,000	0	0.0	0.0
C+ /6.6	6.3	0.98	12.72	241	0	45	53	2	120	67.6	-15.4	36	4	2,000	50	4.5	0.0
C+ /6.6	6.3	0.97	12.70	76	0	45	53	2	120	71.4	-15.2	43	4	50,000	0	0.0	0.0
C+ /6.8	7.9	0.73	10.36	73	0	65	34	1	181	N/A	N/A	25	9	2,000	50	4.5	0.0

Fund Type	Fund Name	Ticker Symbol	Overall Investment Rating	Phone	Performance Rating/Pts	3 Mo	6 Mo	1Yr / Pct	3Yr / Pct	5Yr / Pct	Dividend Yield	Expense Ratio
	99 Pct = Best 0 Pct = Worst							Total Return % through 2/28/17	Annualized		Incl. in Returns	
IN	Thrivent Growth and Inc Plus S	TEIIX	C	(800) 847-4836	C- / 4.1	5.53	4.63	16.80 / 38	3.92 / 42	--	2.14	1.16
GR	● Thrivent Large Cap Growth A	AAAGX	C+	(800) 847-4836	C+ / 6.5	9.37	9.23	16.12 / 35	7.80 / 77	12.66 / 81	0.00	1.30
GR	Thrivent Large Cap Growth S	THLCX	B	(800) 847-4836	B / 7.6	9.69	9.57	16.68 / 37	8.23 / 81	13.11 / 85	0.00	0.81
GR	● Thrivent Large Cap Stock A	AALGX	C	(800) 847-4836	C / 5.5	7.85	9.46	20.67 / 56	5.42 / 59	9.90 / 58	1.01	1.03
GR	Thrivent Large Cap Stock S	IILGX	C+	(800) 847-4836	C+ / 6.7	7.98	9.65	21.20 / 58	5.84 / 63	10.36 / 61	1.40	0.62
GR	● Thrivent Large Cap Value A	AAUTX	A-	(800) 847-4836	B+ / 8.7	6.45	13.14	33.11 / 92	8.33 / 82	12.71 / 81	1.04	0.94
GR	Thrivent Large Cap Value S	TLVIX	A	(800) 847-4836	A / 9.5	6.54	13.36	33.61 / 92	8.79 / 85	13.21 / 86	1.42	0.52
MC	● Thrivent Mid Cap Stock A	AASCX	B+	(800) 847-4836	A+ / 9.9	6.90	18.01	43.79 / 98	12.41 / 98	15.80 / 98	0.09	1.11
MC	Thrivent Mid Cap Stock S	TMSIX	B+	(800) 847-4836	A+ / 9.9	7.01	18.20	44.33 / 98	12.84 / 99	16.27 / 98	0.35	0.71
AA	● Thrivent Moderate Aggr Alloc A	TMAAX	C	(800) 847-4836	C / 5.0	5.34	7.65	20.92 / 57	5.45 / 59	8.59 / 47	0.90	1.42
AA	Thrivent Moderate Aggr Alloc S	TMAFX	C+	(800) 847-4836	C+ / 6.2	5.47	7.84	21.30 / 59	5.82 / 63	8.98 / 50	1.23	1.09
AA	● Thrivent Moderate Allocation A	THMAX	C-	(800) 847-4836	C- / 3.4	4.14	5.13	15.94 / 34	4.65 / 50	7.09 / 35	1.19	1.28
AA	Thrivent Moderate Allocation S	TMAIX	C+	(800) 847-4836	C / 4.6	4.20	5.27	16.34 / 36	5.01 / 54	7.44 / 38	1.53	0.96
AA	● Thrivent Moderate Consv Alloc A	TCAAX	C-	(800) 847-4836	D / 2.2	3.12	2.78	11.39 / 16	3.79 / 40	5.39 / 24	1.55	1.18
AA	Thrivent Moderate Consv Alloc S	TCAIX	C	(800) 847-4836	C- / 3.1	3.18	2.92	11.59 / 16	4.12 / 44	5.71 / 26	1.91	0.88
FO	● Thrivent Partner EM Equity A	TPEAX	E	(800) 847-4836	E / 0.5	7.67	1.22	24.29 / 71	-3.68 / 3	--	0.45	3.46
FO	Thrivent Partner EM Equity S	TPEIX	E	(800) 847-4836	E+ / 0.8	7.71	1.36	24.63 / 72	-3.36 / 4	--	0.93	3.05
GL	● Thrivent Partner Worldwide Alloc A	TWAAX	D	(800) 847-4836	D / 1.7	7.12	3.58	16.57 / 37	0.11 / 14	4.28 / 17	1.81	1.57
GL	Thrivent Partner Worldwide Alloc S	TWAIX	D+	(800) 847-4836	D+ / 2.4	7.07	3.66	16.84 / 38	0.50 / 16	4.67 / 19	2.28	0.99
SC	● Thrivent Small Cap Stock A	AASMX	B	(800) 847-4836	A+ / 9.6	6.60	16.32	39.99 / 97	9.36 / 89	12.02 / 75	0.15	1.24
SC	Thrivent Small Cap Stock S	TSCSX	B+	(800) 847-4836	A+ / 9.8	6.71	16.57	40.55 / 97	9.85 / 93	12.56 / 80	0.40	0.76
EM	TIAA-CREF EM Equity Idx Fund Inst	TEQLX	D+	(800) 842-2252	C / 4.6	8.66	5.31	29.09 / 84	1.21 / 19	-0.52 / 4	1.72	0.23
EM	TIAA-CREF EM Equity Idx Fund	TEQPX	D+	(800) 842-2252	C / 4.5	8.67	5.30	29.01 / 84	1.05 / 19	-0.67 / 4	1.61	0.39
EM	TIAA-CREF EM Equity Idx Fund Ret	TEQSX	D+	(800) 842-2252	C / 4.4	8.59	5.22	28.78 / 83	0.96 / 18	-0.76 / 4	1.54	0.48
EM	TIAA-CREF EM Equity Idx Fund Rtl	TEQKX	D+	(800) 842-2252	C- / 4.2	8.55	5.18	28.56 / 83	0.82 / 17	-0.91 / 3	1.40	0.61
EM	TIAA-CREF Emg Mkt Equity Fund	TEMLX	D-	(800) 842-2252	D / 1.9	9.78	5.98	28.94 / 84	-1.10 / 9	-0.56 / 4	0.84	0.94
EM	TIAA-CREF Emg Mkt Equity Fund	TEMPX	D-	(800) 842-2252	D / 1.9	9.76	5.97	28.78 / 83	-1.23 / 9	-0.68 / 4	0.73	1.09
EM	TIAA-CREF Emg Mkt Equity Fund	TEMSX	E+	(800) 842-2252	D / 1.8	9.76	5.84	28.69 / 83	-1.32 / 8	-0.79 / 4	0.61	1.19
EM	TIAA-CREF Emg Mkt Equity Fund Rtl	TEMRX	E+	(800) 842-2252	D / 1.8	9.58	5.78	28.45 / 83	-1.47 / 8	-0.97 / 3	0.46	1.31
GI	TIAA-CREF Enhanced LCG Idx Inst	TLIIX	A-	(800) 842-2252	A / 9.3	9.06	10.21	22.76 / 66	10.62 / 96	13.07 / 85	1.48	0.34
FO	TIAA-CREF Enhncd Intl Eq Idx Inst	TFIIX	D-	(800) 842-2252	D- / 1.1	6.75	4.12	14.20 / 26	-1.00 / 9	5.66 / 26	2.69	0.42
GR	TIAA-CREF Enhncd LgCp Val Idx Inst	TEVIX	B	(800) 842-2252	B+ / 8.7	6.37	10.94	27.50 / 81	8.55 / 83	12.92 / 83	2.10	0.35
GR	TIAA-CREF Equity Index Inst	TIEIX	A+	(800) 842-2252	A- / 9.2	7.71	10.29	26.27 / 77	9.92 / 93	13.82 / 92	1.86	0.05
GR	TIAA-CREF Equity Index Premier	TCEPX	A+	(800) 842-2252	A- / 9.1	7.66	10.18	26.10 / 77	9.74 / 92	13.64 / 90	1.75	0.20
GR	TIAA-CREF Equity Index Retail	TINRX	A+	(800) 842-2252	A- / 9.0	7.66	10.13	25.96 / 76	9.58 / 91	13.48 / 89	1.57	0.35
GR	TIAA-CREF Equity Index Retire	TIQRX	A+	(800) 842-2252	A- / 9.1	7.67	10.15	25.95 / 76	9.62 / 91	13.54 / 89	1.62	0.30
EN	TIAA-CREF Gl Nat Res Instl	TNRIX	E	(800) 842-2252	D- / 1.4	-2.58	13.06	35.53 / 95	-3.25 / 4	-3.11 / 2	3.23	0.74
EN	TIAA-CREF Gl Nat Res Prm	TNRPX	E	(800) 842-2252	D- / 1.3	-2.58	13.08	35.37 / 94	-3.36 / 4	-3.23 / 2	3.10	0.90
EN	TIAA-CREF Gl Nat Res Ret	TNRRX	E-	(800) 842-2252	D- / 1.3	-2.60	13.05	35.34 / 94	-3.45 / 4	-3.34 / 2	3.08	1.00
EN	TIAA-CREF Gl Nat Res Rtl	TNRLX	E	(800) 842-2252	D- / 1.2	-2.61	12.92	35.18 / 94	-3.58 / 4	-3.47 / 2	3.08	1.13
GI	TIAA-CREF Growth and Inc Inst	TIGRX	B	(800) 842-2252	B+ / 8.5	7.31	9.17	24.28 / 71	8.93 / 86	13.47 / 89	1.27	0.43
GI	TIAA-CREF Growth and Inc Premier	TRPGX	B	(800) 842-2252	B+ / 8.3	7.27	9.09	24.09 / 70	8.76 / 85	13.29 / 87	1.14	0.58
GI	TIAA-CREF Growth and Inc Retail	TIIRX	B+	(800) 842-2252	B / 8.2	7.18	9.00	23.87 / 69	8.57 / 84	13.10 / 85	0.70	0.73
GI	TIAA-CREF Growth and Inc Retire	TRGIX	B	(800) 842-2252	B+ / 8.3	7.30	9.06	23.97 / 70	8.63 / 84	13.20 / 86	1.03	0.68
FO	TIAA-CREF International Opptys Inst	TIOIX	D-	(800) 842-2252	D- / 1.3	7.34	5.97	17.13 / 39	-1.13 / 9	--	1.23	0.63
FO	TIAA-CREF International Opptys	TIOPX	D-	(800) 842-2252	D- / 1.2	7.32	5.95	17.12 / 39	-1.25 / 9	--	0.84	0.80
FO	TIAA-CREF International Opptys Ret	TIOTX	D-	(800) 842-2252	D- / 1.2	7.29	5.82	16.86 / 38	-1.38 / 8	--	0.99	0.89
FO	TIAA-CREF International Opptys Rtl	TIOSX	D-	(800) 842-2252	D- / 1.1	7.25	5.77	16.57 / 37	-1.50 / 8	--	0.76	1.00
FO	TIAA-CREF Intl Equity Index Inst	TCIEX	D-	(800) 842-2252	D- / 1.3	7.34	4.38	16.01 / 34	-0.57 / 11	5.37 / 24	2.83	0.06
FO	TIAA-CREF Intl Equity Index Premier	TRIPX	D-	(800) 842-2252	D- / 1.3	7.33	4.30	15.80 / 33	-0.71 / 10	5.22 / 23	2.69	0.21
FO	TIAA-CREF Intl Equity Index Retire	TRIEX	D-	(800) 842-2252	D- / 1.2	7.24	4.22	15.72 / 33	-0.82 / 10	5.11 / 22	2.54	0.31
FO	TIAA-CREF Intl Equity Inst	TIIEX	E+	(800) 842-2252	E / 0.5	5.48	1.10	11.18 / 15	-3.14 / 4	5.47 / 25	1.47	0.49

● Denotes fund is closed to new investors
✱ Denotes fund is included in Section II

612

RISK			NET ASSETS		ASSET					BULL / BEAR		FUND MANAGER		MINIMUMS		LOADS	
	3 Year		NAV						Portfolio	Last Bull	Last Bear	Manager	Manager	Initial	Additional	Front	Back
Risk	Standard		As of	Total	Cash	Stocks	Bonds	Other	Turnover	Market	Market	Quality	Tenure	Purch.	Purch.	End	End
Rating/Pts	Deviation	Beta	2/28/17	$(Mil)	%	%	%	%	Ratio	Return	Return	Pct	(Years)	$	$	Load	Load
C+ / 6.8	8.0	0.74	10.38	7	0	65	34	1	181	N/A	N/A	27	9	50,000	0	0.0	0.0
C+ / 5.6	12.3	1.05	8.97	189	0	96	3	1	67	124.6	-20.1	33	3	2,000	50	4.5	0.0
C+ / 5.6	12.4	1.06	9.83	566	0	96	3	1	67	129.7	-20.0	37	3	50,000	0	0.0	0.0
C+ / 5.7	11.0	1.00	26.16	1,496	5	86	8	1	62	96.8	-20.8	16	4	2,000	50	4.5	0.0
C+ / 5.6	11.0	1.00	26.36	225	5	86	8	1	62	101.5	-20.7	20	4	50,000	0	0.0	0.0
C+ / 5.9	12.4	1.14	21.40	225	1	96	2	1	22	125.0	-21.6	29	4	2,000	50	4.5	0.0
C+ / 5.9	12.4	1.14	21.51	708	1	96	2	1	22	130.4	-21.4	34	4	50,000	0	0.0	0.0
C / 4.3	13.1	1.04	24.31	1,157	5	89	5	1	21	161.3	-25.9	87	13	2,000	50	4.5	0.0
C / 4.5	13.1	1.04	27.04	420	5	89	5	1	21	167.3	-25.8	89	13	50,000	0	0.0	0.0
C+ / 5.6	8.7	1.32	13.95	1,949	0	67	32	1	90	77.2	-17.1	21	12	2,000	50	4.5	0.0
C / 5.5	8.7	1.32	14.06	256	0	67	32	1	90	80.8	-17.0	25	12	50,000	0	0.0	0.0
C+ / 6.9	6.5	1.00	13.10	1,763	0	47	52	1	138	60.3	-13.2	38	12	2,000	50	4.5	0.0
C+ / 6.9	6.5	1.00	13.14	237	0	47	52	1	138	63.3	-13.0	43	12	50,000	0	0.0	0.0
B- / 8.0	4.5	0.69	12.02	713	0	28	71	1	181	43.2	-9.2	58	12	2,000	50	4.5	0.0
B- / 7.9	4.5	0.68	12.05	91	0	28	71	1	181	45.4	-9.0	63	12	50,000	0	0.0	0.0
C- / 4.1	14.9	0.87	8.41	9	1	98	0	1	11	N/A	N/A	27	2	2,000	50	4.5	0.0
C- / 4.0	14.9	0.86	8.33	4	1	98	0	1	11	N/A	N/A	31	2	50,000	0	0.0	0.0
C+ / 6.2	10.4	1.50	9.84	142	1	87	10	2	107	43.1	-20.4	6	9	2,000	50	4.5	0.0
C+ / 6.2	10.3	1.49	9.87	643	1	87	10	2	107	46.1	-20.4	8	9	50,000	0	0.0	0.0
C- / 3.8	14.2	0.87	20.13	393	3	95	0	2	58	128.4	-27.6	91	4	2,000	50	4.5	0.0
C- / 4.2	14.2	0.87	23.87	140	3	95	0	2	58	134.5	-27.4	92	4	50,000	0	0.0	0.0
C / 4.3	15.9	0.98	9.71	1,658	0	99	0	1	30	21.1	-27.3	69	7	10,000,000	1,000	0.0	0.0
C / 4.3	16.0	0.98	9.69	20	0	99	0	1	30	20.1	-27.3	67	7	5,000,000	0	0.0	0.0
C / 4.3	16.0	0.98	9.68	165	0	99	0	1	30	19.6	-27.4	66	7	0	0	0.0	0.0
C / 4.3	15.9	0.98	9.69	10	0	99	0	1	30	18.6	-27.4	64	7	2,500	100	0.0	0.0
C / 4.3	15.2	0.90	10.03	1,000	0	98	0	2	195	18.3	-27.3	39	2	2,000,000	1,000	0.0	0.0
C / 4.3	15.2	0.90	10.03	19	0	98	0	2	195	17.4	-27.3	37	2	1,000,000	0	0.0	0.0
C / 4.3	15.2	0.91	10.01	35	0	98	0	2	195	16.8	-27.4	36	2	0	0	0.0	0.0
C / 4.3	15.2	0.90	10.02	6	0	98	0	2	195	15.7	-27.4	34	2	2,500	100	0.0	0.0
C / 5.4	11.1	1.04	12.01	2,243	0	99	0	1	121	127.7	-15.0	70	3	2,000,000	1,000	0.0	0.0
C / 5.5	10.9	0.88	7.00	1,621	1	98	0	1	100	52.8	-23.5	64	10	2,000,000	1,000	0.0	0.0
C / 5.0	10.6	1.00	10.11	2,250	0	99	0	1	149	124.1	-18.8	50	10	2,000,000	1,000	0.0	0.0
C+ / 6.6	10.6	1.02	17.53	11,703	0	99	0	1	9	134.5	-17.8	64	12	10,000,000	1,000	0.0	0.0
C+ / 6.6	10.6	1.02	17.49	89	0	99	0	1	9	132.3	-17.7	61	12	5,000,000	0	0.0	0.0
C+ / 6.6	10.7	1.03	17.85	861	0	99	0	1	9	130.5	-17.8	60	12	2,500	100	0.0	0.0
C+ / 6.6	10.6	1.02	17.79	501	0	99	0	1	9	131.4	-17.9	60	12	0	0	0.0	0.0
D+ / 2.7	17.5	0.76	8.34	17	4	93	2	1	365	N/A	N/A	79	1	2,000,000	1,000	0.0	0.0
D+ / 2.8	17.6	0.76	8.34	4	4	93	2	1	365	N/A	N/A	78	1	1,000,000	0	0.0	0.0
E+ / 0.6	17.6	0.76	8.34	26	4	93	2	1	365	N/A	N/A	78	1	0	0	0.0	0.0
D+ / 2.8	17.5	0.76	8.33	8	4	93	2	1	365	N/A	N/A	77	1	2,500	100	0.0	0.0
C / 5.1	11.2	1.06	12.81	4,262	0	99	0	1	83	130.2	-16.1	47	12	2,000,000	1,000	0.0	0.0
C / 5.1	11.2	1.06	12.81	152	0	99	0	1	83	128.3	-16.3	44	12	1,000,000	0	0.0	0.0
C+ / 5.6	11.2	1.06	16.87	1,056	0	99	0	1	83	126.1	-16.2	42	12	2,500	100	0.0	0.0
C / 5.2	11.2	1.05	13.01	584	0	99	0	1	83	127.1	-16.2	43	12	0	0	0.0	0.0
C / 5.5	11.5	0.86	10.65	1,249	0	98	1	1	31	N/A	N/A	62	4	2,000,000	1,000	0.0	0.0
C+ / 5.6	11.5	0.85	10.68	N/A	0	98	1	1	31	N/A	N/A	60	4	1,000,000	0	0.0	0.0
C / 5.5	11.4	0.85	10.64	8	0	98	1	1	31	N/A	N/A	59	4	0	0	0.0	0.0
C+ / 5.6	11.5	0.86	10.65	2	0	98	1	1	31	N/A	N/A	57	4	2,500	100	0.0	0.0
C+ / 5.7	11.4	0.93	17.30	7,848	0	0	0	100	11	50.3	-23.3	69	12	10,000,000	1,000	0.0	0.0
C+ / 5.7	11.4	0.93	17.27	266	0	0	0	100	11	49.1	-23.3	68	12	5,000,000	0	0.0	0.0
C+ / 5.7	11.4	0.93	17.68	740	0	0	0	100	11	48.3	-23.3	66	12	0	0	0.0	0.0
C / 4.9	13.0	1.00	10.55	2,783	0	99	0	1	95	56.6	-31.2	35	18	2,000,000	1,000	0.0	0.0

Fund Type	Fund Name	Ticker Symbol	Overall Investment Rating	Phone	Performance Rating/Pts	3 Mo	6 Mo	1Yr / Pct	3Yr / Pct	5Yr / Pct	Dividend Yield	Expense Ratio
	99 Pct = Best 0 Pct = Worst							Total Return % through 2/28/17	Annualized		Incl. in Returns	
FO	TIAA-CREF Intl Equity Premier	TREPX	E+	(800) 842-2252	E / 0.4	5.44	1.04	11.03 /15	-3.29 / 4	5.33 /24	1.32	0.64
FO	TIAA-CREF Intl Equity Retail	TIERX	E	(800) 842-2252	E / 0.4	5.29	0.99	10.81 /14	-3.47 / 4	5.13 /22	1.84	0.83
FO	TIAA-CREF Intl Equity Retire	TRERX	E+	(800) 842-2252	E / 0.4	5.32	0.99	10.81 /14	-3.39 / 4	5.20 /23	1.16	0.74
GR	TIAA-CREF Large Cap Gr Idx Inst	TILIX	A+	(800) 842-2252	A- / 9.1	8.98	9.12	22.10 /63	10.41 /95	13.74 /91	1.23	0.06
GR	TIAA-CREF Large Cap Gr Idx Retire	TRIRX	A+	(800) 842-2252	B+ / 8.9	8.90	8.95	21.76 /61	10.13 /94	13.43 /88	1.01	0.31
GR	TIAA-CREF Large Cap Gr Inst	TILGX	B	(800) 842-2252	B- / 7.3	8.09	6.93	18.03 /43	8.39 /82	13.82 /92	0.56	0.44
GR	TIAA-CREF Large Cap Gr Premier	TILPX	B	(800) 842-2252	B- / 7.2	8.01	6.85	17.80 /42	8.21 /81	13.67 /90	0.42	0.59
GR	TIAA-CREF Large Cap Gr Ret	TILRX	B	(800) 842-2252	B- / 7.1	7.96	6.73	17.56 /41	8.07 /79	13.50 /89	0.23	0.70
GR	TIAA-CREF Large Cap Gr Retail	TIRTX	B	(800) 842-2252	B- / 7.1	7.97	6.74	17.61 /41	8.02 /79	13.40 /88	0.25	0.78
GR	TIAA-CREF Large Cap Val Idx Inst	TILVX	A	(800) 842-2252	A / 9.4	6.93	10.96	28.98 /84	9.85 /93	13.94 /93	2.02	0.06
GR	TIAA-CREF Large Cap Val Idx Ret	TRCVX	A	(800) 842-2252	A / 9.3	6.84	10.88	28.74 /83	9.57 /91	13.66 /90	1.80	0.31
GR	TIAA-CREF Large Cap Val Inst	TRLIX	B+	(800) 842-2252	A- / 9.2	6.37	11.43	32.10 /90	8.78 /85	13.47 /89	1.69	0.42
GR	TIAA-CREF Large Cap Val Premier	TRCPX	B+	(800) 842-2252	A- / 9.2	6.34	11.42	31.90 /90	8.61 /84	13.31 /87	1.54	0.57
GR	TIAA-CREF Large Cap Val Ret	TRLCX	B+	(800) 842-2252	A- / 9.1	6.32	11.34	31.75 /90	8.52 /83	13.20 /86	1.47	0.67
GR	TIAA-CREF Large Cap Val Retail	TCLCX	B+	(800) 842-2252	A- / 9.1	6.32	11.34	31.66 /89	8.45 /83	13.09 /85	1.48	0.74
AA	TIAA-CREF Lifecycle 2010 Inst	TCTIX	C	(800) 842-2252	C- / 3.4	4.06	3.41	12.40 /19	4.16 /45	6.39 /31	2.50	0.49
AA	TIAA-CREF Lifecycle 2010 Premier	TCTPX	C	(800) 842-2252	C- / 3.3	4.01	3.36	12.26 /19	4.01 /43	6.25 /30	2.36	0.64
AA	TIAA-CREF Lifecycle 2010 Ret	TCLEX	C+	(800) 842-2252	C- / 3.2	3.94	3.22	12.17 /19	3.88 /41	6.13 /29	1.90	0.74
AA	TIAA-CREF Lifecycle 2015 Inst	TCNIX	C-	(800) 842-2252	C- / 3.7	4.35	3.83	13.44 /23	4.38 /47	6.92 /34	2.55	0.50
AA	TIAA-CREF Lifecycle 2015 Premier	TCFPX	C-	(800) 842-2252	C- / 3.6	4.33	3.70	13.34 /23	4.21 /45	6.76 /33	2.42	0.65
AA	TIAA-CREF Lifecycle 2015 Ret	TCLIX	C	(800) 842-2252	C- / 3.5	4.29	3.67	13.27 /23	4.10 /44	6.65 /33	1.86	0.75
AA	TIAA-CREF Lifecycle 2020 Inst	TCWIX	C	(800) 842-2252	C- / 4.1	4.75	4.43	14.92 /30	4.58 /50	7.57 /39	2.42	0.52
AA	TIAA-CREF Lifecycle 2020 Premier	TCWPX	C	(800) 842-2252	C- / 4.0	4.71	4.40	14.79 /29	4.44 /48	7.43 /38	2.29	0.67
AA	TIAA-CREF Lifecycle 2020 Ret	TCLTX	C	(800) 842-2252	C- / 3.9	4.67	4.33	14.73 /29	4.34 /47	7.32 /37	1.73	0.77
AA	TIAA-CREF Lifecycle 2025 Inst	TCYIX	C	(800) 842-2252	C / 4.7	5.29	5.18	16.63 /37	4.82 /52	8.25 /44	2.29	0.53
AA	TIAA-CREF Lifecycle 2025 Premier	TCQPX	C	(800) 842-2252	C / 4.5	5.26	5.05	16.53 /36	4.68 /51	8.08 /43	2.16	0.68
AA	TIAA-CREF Lifecycle 2025 Ret	TCLFX	C+	(800) 842-2252	C / 4.4	5.13	5.05	16.31 /36	4.57 /50	7.98 /42	1.61	0.78
AA	TIAA-CREF Lifecycle 2030 Inst	TCRIX	C	(800) 842-2252	C / 5.1	5.71	5.81	18.20 /44	5.02 /54	8.86 /49	2.18	0.54
AA	TIAA-CREF Lifecycle 2030 Premier	TCHPX	C	(800) 842-2252	C / 5.0	5.69	5.80	18.12 /43	4.86 /53	8.71 /48	2.06	0.69
AA	TIAA-CREF Lifecycle 2030 Ret	TCLNX	C+	(800) 842-2252	C / 4.9	5.63	5.80	18.06 /43	4.77 /52	8.60 /47	1.49	0.79
AA	TIAA-CREF Lifecycle 2035 Inst	TCIIX	C	(800) 842-2252	C+ / 5.6	6.11	6.53	19.79 /51	5.16 /56	9.39 /54	2.01	0.55
AA	TIAA-CREF Lifecycle 2035 Premier	TCYPX	C	(800) 842-2252	C / 5.5	6.20	6.62	19.68 /50	5.03 /55	9.26 /53	1.88	0.70
AA	TIAA-CREF Lifecycle 2035 Ret	TCLRX	C+	(800) 842-2252	C / 5.3	6.08	6.41	19.54 /50	4.90 /53	9.13 /52	1.33	0.80
AA	TIAA-CREF Lifecycle 2040 Inst	TCOIX	C+	(800) 842-2252	C+ / 6.1	6.58	7.43	21.50 /60	5.33 /58	9.76 /57	1.84	0.55
AA	TIAA-CREF Lifecycle 2040 Premier	TCZPX	C	(800) 842-2252	C+ / 5.9	6.55	7.30	21.26 /59	5.15 /56	9.61 /55	1.71	0.70
AA	TIAA-CREF Lifecycle 2040 Ret	TCLOX	C+	(800) 842-2252	C+ / 5.8	6.55	7.28	21.20 /58	5.05 /55	9.51 /55	1.17	0.80
GI	TIAA-CREF Lifecycle 2045 Inst	TTFIX	C+	(800) 842-2252	C+ / 6.3	6.76	7.65	22.00 /62	5.44 /59	9.85 /57	1.25	0.57
GI	TIAA-CREF Lifecycle 2045 Premier	TTFPX	C+	(800) 842-2252	C+ / 6.1	6.75	7.64	21.81 /61	5.28 /57	9.67 /56	1.13	0.72
GI	TIAA-CREF Lifecycle 2045 Ret	TTFRX	C+	(800) 842-2252	C+ / 6.0	6.67	7.56	21.63 /60	5.18 /56	9.56 /55	1.04	0.82
GI	TIAA-CREF Lifecycle 2050 Inst	TFTIX	C+	(800) 842-2252	C+ / 6.4	6.88	7.87	22.25 /63	5.52 /60	9.88 /57	1.22	0.58
GI	TIAA-CREF Lifecycle 2050 Premier	TCLPX	C+	(800) 842-2252	C+ / 6.3	6.87	7.77	22.06 /63	5.37 /58	9.71 /56	1.10	0.73
GI	TIAA-CREF Lifecycle 2050 Ret	TLFRX	C+	(800) 842-2252	C+ / 6.1	6.69	7.59	21.90 /62	5.24 /57	9.61 /55	1.02	0.83
AA	TIAA-CREF Lifecycle 2055 Inst	TTRIX	C+	(800) 842-2252	C+ / 6.4	6.95	7.91	22.54 /65	5.57 /60	9.93 /58	1.28	0.64
AA	TIAA-CREF Lifecycle 2055 Prm	TTRPX	C+	(800) 842-2252	C+ / 6.3	6.84	7.81	22.25 /63	5.40 /59	9.76 /57	1.17	0.79
AA	TIAA-CREF Lifecycle 2055 Ret	TTRLX	C+	(800) 842-2252	C+ / 6.2	6.83	7.71	22.14 /63	5.28 /57	9.64 /56	1.09	0.89
GI	TIAA-CREF Lifecycle Idx Ret Inc Ins	TRILX	B-	(800) 842-2252	C- / 3.0	3.56	2.41	10.02 /12	4.17 /45	5.47 /25	1.85	0.41
GI	TIAA-CREF Lifecycle Idx Ret Inc Prm	TLIPX	C+	(800) 842-2252	D+ / 2.9	3.53	2.33	9.78 /11	4.02 /43	5.32 /23	1.70	0.56
GI	TIAA-CREF Lifecycle Idx Ret Inc Ret	TRCIX	C+	(800) 842-2252	D+ / 2.8	3.58	2.37	9.71 /11	3.92 /42	5.20 /23	1.64	0.66
AA	TIAA-CREF Lifecycle Index 2010 Inst	TLTIX	B-	(800) 842-2252	C- / 3.2	3.83	2.81	10.86 /14	4.40 /47	6.08 /29	1.91	0.27
AA	TIAA-CREF Lifecycle Index 2010	TLTPX	C+	(800) 842-2252	C- / 3.1	3.77	2.67	10.66 /13	4.23 /46	5.92 /28	1.78	0.42
AA	TIAA-CREF Lifecycle Index 2010 Ret	TLTRX	C+	(800) 842-2252	C- / 3.1	3.79	2.61	10.55 /13	4.13 /44	5.81 /27	1.71	0.52
AA	TIAA-CREF Lifecycle Index 2015 Inst	TLFIX	B-	(800) 842-2252	C- / 3.6	4.19	3.26	11.98 /18	4.66 /50	6.65 /33	1.96	0.25

• Denotes fund is closed to new investors
∗ Denotes fund is included in Section II

www.thestreetratings.com

Risk Rating/Pts	3 Year Standard Deviation	Beta	NAV As of 2/28/17	Total $(Mil)	Cash %	Stocks %	Bonds %	Other %	Portfolio Turnover Ratio	Last Bull Market Return	Last Bear Market Return	Manager Quality Pct	Manager Tenure (Years)	Initial Purch. $	Additional Purch. $	Front End Load	Back End Load
C /4.9	13.0	1.00	10.53	207	0	99	0	1	95	55.4	-31.3	32	18	1,000,000	0	0.0	0.0
C /4.8	12.9	0.99	7.05	505	0	99	0	1	95	53.7	-31.3	30	18	2,500	100	0.0	0.0
C /4.9	13.0	1.00	10.92	539	0	99	0	1	95	54.3	-31.2	31	18	0	0	0.0	0.0
C+ /6.7	11.0	1.03	24.32	3,812	0	99	0	1	22	133.5	-15.3	68	12	10,000,000	1,000	0.0	0.0
C+ /6.7	11.0	1.04	24.49	501	0	99	0	1	22	130.4	-15.4	65	12	0	0	0.0	0.0
C+ /6.2	12.4	1.07	16.65	3,022	0	0	0	100	86	134.0	-15.4	38	11	2,000,000	1,000	0.0	0.0
C+ /6.3	12.5	1.07	16.63	45	0	0	0	100	86	132.2	-15.5	36	11	1,000,000	0	0.0	0.0
C+ /6.3	12.4	1.07	16.56	258	0	0	0	100	86	130.6	-15.5	35	11	0	0	0.0	0.0
C+ /6.3	12.5	1.07	16.61	657	0	0	0	100	86	129.3	-15.5	34	11	2,500	100	0.0	0.0
C+ /6.0	10.5	0.98	18.80	5,386	0	99	0	1	23	134.1	-18.7	68	12	10,000,000	1,000	0.0	0.0
C+ /6.1	10.5	0.99	19.11	887	0	99	0	1	23	131.0	-18.8	65	12	0	0	0.0	0.0
C /5.1	11.9	1.08	18.86	4,992	0	99	0	1	62	133.1	-22.9	41	15	2,000,000	1,000	0.0	0.0
C /5.1	11.8	1.08	18.82	333	0	99	0	1	62	131.2	-22.9	39	15	1,000,000	0	0.0	0.0
C /5.1	11.8	1.08	18.80	1,040	0	99	0	1	62	130.0	-23.0	38	15	0	0	0.0	0.0
C /5.1	11.9	1.08	18.15	151	0	99	0	1	62	129.0	-23.0	37	15	2,500	100	0.0	0.0
B /8.0	5.4	0.82	11.15	603	0	0	0	100	19	53.2	-9.1	50	10	2,000,000	1,000	0.0	0.0
B /8.0	5.4	0.82	11.13	148	0	0	0	100	19	52.1	-9.1	48	10	0	0	0.0	0.0
B /8.3	5.4	0.82	13.01	432	0	0	0	100	19	51.2	-9.2	46	10	0	0	0.0	0.0
C+ /6.7	5.8	0.90	9.66	957	0	0	0	100	18	59.1	-10.9	45	10	2,000,000	1,000	0.0	0.0
C+ /6.7	5.8	0.90	9.62	249	0	0	0	100	18	57.9	-11.0	43	10	0	0	0.0	0.0
B- /7.3	5.9	0.90	11.76	672	0	0	0	100	18	57.0	-11.1	41	10	0	0	0.0	0.0
C+ /6.7	6.6	1.01	9.87	1,790	0	0	0	100	14	66.4	-12.9	36	10	2,000,000	1,000	0.0	0.0
C+ /6.7	6.6	1.02	9.85	495	0	0	0	100	14	65.2	-13.0	34	10	0	0	0.0	0.0
B- /7.3	6.6	1.02	12.27	1,114	0	0	0	100	14	64.2	-13.0	33	10	0	0	0.0	0.0
C+ /6.4	7.5	1.15	9.95	1,981	0	0	0	100	11	74.1	-14.9	28	10	2,000,000	1,000	0.0	0.0
C+ /6.4	7.5	1.15	9.91	541	0	0	0	100	11	72.9	-15.0	26	10	0	0	0.0	0.0
B- /7.0	7.5	1.15	12.50	1,108	0	0	0	100	11	71.8	-15.0	25	10	0	0	0.0	0.0
C+ /6.1	8.3	1.28	9.92	2,004	0	0	0	100	12	81.5	-16.8	20	10	2,000,000	1,000	0.0	0.0
C+ /6.1	8.3	1.28	9.88	526	0	0	0	100	12	80.0	-16.8	19	N/A	0	0	0.0	0.0
C+ /6.8	8.4	1.29	12.69	1,020	0	0	0	100	12	79.1	-16.8	18	N/A	0	0	0.0	0.0
C+ /5.8	9.2	1.40	9.99	2,101	0	0	0	100	11	88.4	-18.5	15	10	2,000,000	1,000	0.0	0.0
C+ /5.8	9.1	1.40	9.97	551	0	0	0	100	11	87.1	-18.6	14	10	0	0	0.0	0.0
C+ /6.5	9.1	1.39	13.00	927	0	0	0	100	11	85.9	-18.6	13	10	0	0	0.0	0.0
C /5.4	10.0	1.52	10.03	2,636	0	0	0	100	11	92.2	-18.8	10	10	2,000,000	1,000	0.0	0.0
C /5.4	9.9	1.52	10.00	698	0	0	0	100	11	90.8	-19.0	9	10	0	0	0.0	0.0
C+ /6.2	9.9	1.51	13.31	1,140	0	0	0	100	11	89.8	-19.0	9	10	0	0	0.0	0.0
C+ /6.6	10.0	0.94	11.18	1,214	0	0	0	100	8	92.9	-18.9	22	10	2,000,000	1,000	0.0	0.0
C+ /6.6	10.0	0.93	11.14	354	0	0	0	100	8	91.2	-18.9	21	10	0	0	0.0	0.0
C+ /6.6	10.0	0.93	11.11	498	0	0	0	100	8	90.3	-18.9	20	10	0	0	0.0	0.0
C+ /6.6	10.0	0.93	11.22	738	0	0	0	100	9	93.3	-18.8	23	10	2,000,000	1,000	0.0	0.0
C+ /6.6	10.0	0.93	11.18	241	0	0	0	100	9	91.7	-18.9	22	10	0	0	0.0	0.0
C+ /6.6	10.0	0.93	11.14	311	0	0	0	100	9	90.6	-18.9	20	10	0	0	0.0	0.0
C+ /6.7	10.1	1.54	12.68	155	0	0	0	100	24	94.0	-18.9	11	6	2,000,000	1,000	0.0	0.0
C+ /6.7	10.1	1.53	12.64	72	0	0	0	100	24	92.3	-18.9	10	6	0	0	0.0	0.0
C+ /6.8	10.1	1.53	12.64	87	0	0	0	100	24	91.3	-19.0	9	6	0	0	0.0	0.0
B+ /9.6	4.5	0.39	13.54	65	0	0	0	100	41	43.3	-5.3	75	8	10,000,000	1,000	0.0	0.0
B+ /9.6	4.5	0.39	13.53	11	0	0	0	100	41	42.1	-5.3	74	8	0	0	0.0	0.0
B+ /9.6	4.5	0.39	13.52	36	0	0	0	100	41	41.4	-5.3	73	8	0	0	0.0	0.0
B+ /9.3	4.9	0.76	14.24	185	0	0	0	100	24	49.6	-7.6	60	8	10,000,000	1,000	0.0	0.0
B+ /9.3	4.9	0.76	14.20	31	0	0	0	100	24	48.4	-7.7	57	8	0	0	0.0	0.0
B+ /9.3	4.9	0.76	14.13	66	0	0	0	100	24	47.6	-7.7	56	8	0	0	0.0	0.0
B+ /9.1	5.4	0.84	14.77	320	0	0	0	100	22	55.6	-9.4	55	8	10,000,000	1,000	0.0	0.0

	99 Pct = Best 0 Pct = Worst				PERFORMANCE							
							Total Return % through 2/28/17				Incl. in Returns	
			Overall		Perfor-					Annualized		Dividend	Expense
Fund		Ticker	Investment		mance								
Type	Fund Name	Symbol	Rating	Phone	Rating/Pts	3 Mo	6 Mo	1Yr / Pct	3Yr / Pct	5Yr / Pct	Yield	Ratio
AA	TIAA-CREF Lifecycle Index 2015	TLFPX	B-	(800) 842-2252	C- / 3.5	4.19	3.12	11.86 /17	4.50 /49	6.48 /31	1.83	0.40
AA	TIAA-CREF Lifecycle Index 2015 Ret	TLGRX	B-	(800) 842-2252	C- / 3.4	4.14	3.06	11.74 /17	4.39 /47	6.37 /31	1.77	0.50
AA	TIAA-CREF Lifecycle Index 2020 Inst	TLWIX	B	(800) 842-2252	C- / 4.1	4.73	3.90	13.70 /24	4.98 /54	7.36 /37	1.92	0.22
AA	TIAA-CREF Lifecycle Index 2020	TLWPX	B-	(800) 842-2252	C- / 4.0	4.68	3.84	13.52 /24	4.83 /52	7.21 /36	1.79	0.37
AA	TIAA-CREF Lifecycle Index 2020 Ret	TLWRX	B-	(800) 842-2252	C- / 3.9	4.56	3.73	13.35 /23	4.72 /51	7.09 /35	1.74	0.47
AA	TIAA-CREF Lifecycle Index 2025 Inst	TLQIX	B	(800) 842-2252	C / 4.7	5.19	4.65	15.47 /32	5.33 /58	8.10 /43	1.94	0.22
AA	TIAA-CREF Lifecycle Index 2025	TLVPX	B	(800) 842-2252	C / 4.6	5.20	4.59	15.29 /31	5.18 /56	7.94 /42	1.82	0.37
AA	TIAA-CREF Lifecycle Index 2025 Ret	TLQRX	B	(800) 842-2252	C / 4.5	5.16	4.55	15.21 /31	5.09 /55	7.84 /41	1.77	0.47
AA	TIAA-CREF Lifecycle Index 2030 Inst	TLHIX	B	(800) 842-2252	C / 5.4	5.73	5.47	17.36 /40	5.70 /62	8.83 /49	1.96	0.21
AA	TIAA-CREF Lifecycle Index 2030	TLHPX	B	(800) 842-2252	C / 5.3	5.74	5.41	17.19 /39	5.56 /60	8.68 /48	1.84	0.36
AA	TIAA-CREF Lifecycle Index 2030 Ret	TLHRX	B	(800) 842-2252	C / 5.2	5.65	5.32	16.97 /38	5.44 /59	8.56 /47	1.80	0.46
AA	TIAA-CREF Lifecycle Index 2035 Inst	TLYIX	B	(800) 842-2252	C+ / 6.0	6.31	6.31	19.20 /48	6.01 /64	9.52 /55	1.96	0.21
AA	TIAA-CREF Lifecycle Index 2035	TLYPX	B	(800) 842-2252	C+ / 5.9	6.26	6.26	19.05 /47	5.87 /63	9.36 /54	1.85	0.36
AA	TIAA-CREF Lifecycle Index 2035 Ret	TLYRX	B	(800) 842-2252	C+ / 5.8	6.23	6.17	18.92 /47	5.75 /62	9.23 /53	1.80	0.47
AA	TIAA-CREF Lifecycle Index 2040 Inst	TLZIX	B-	(800) 842-2252	C+ / 6.6	6.82	7.14	21.14 /58	6.30 /67	9.98 /58	1.98	0.20
AA	TIAA-CREF Lifecycle Index 2040	TLPRX	B-	(800) 842-2252	C+ / 6.5	6.78	7.10	20.93 /57	6.16 /66	9.82 /57	1.87	0.35
AA	TIAA-CREF Lifecycle Index 2040 Ret	TLZRX	B-	(800) 842-2252	C+ / 6.4	6.74	7.06	20.86 /57	6.03 /64	9.72 /56	1.82	0.45
AA	TIAA-CREF Lifecycle Index 2045 Inst	TLXIX	B-	(800) 842-2252	C+ / 6.8	7.08	7.59	21.80 /61	6.44 /68	10.08 /58	1.98	0.22
AA	TIAA-CREF Lifecycle Index 2045	TLMPX	B-	(800) 842-2252	C+ / 6.7	6.97	7.48	21.58 /60	6.28 /67	9.91 /58	1.87	0.37
AA	TIAA-CREF Lifecycle Index 2045 Ret	TLMRX	B-	(800) 842-2252	C+ / 6.6	7.01	7.39	21.54 /60	6.18 /66	9.80 /57	1.82	0.47
AA	TIAA-CREF Lifecycle Index 2050 Inst	TLLIX	B-	(800) 842-2252	C+ / 6.9	7.18	7.69	22.14 /63	6.54 /69	10.13 /59	1.98	0.23
AA	TIAA-CREF Lifecycle Index 2050	TLLPX	B-	(800) 842-2252	C+ / 6.8	7.08	7.59	21.94 /62	6.38 /67	9.97 /58	1.87	0.38
AA	TIAA-CREF Lifecycle Index 2050 Ret	TLLRX	B-	(800) 842-2252	C+ / 6.7	7.05	7.56	21.81 /61	6.27 /67	9.86 /57	1.83	0.48
AA	TIAA-CREF Lifecycle Index 2055 Inst	TTIIX	A-	(800) 842-2252	B- / 7.0	7.23	7.87	22.41 /64	6.62 /69	10.18 /60	1.93	0.40
AA	TIAA-CREF Lifecycle Index 2055 Prm	TTIPX	B-	(800) 842-2252	C+ / 6.9	7.20	7.76	22.22 /63	6.46 /68	10.02 /58	1.82	0.55
AA	TIAA-CREF Lifecycle Index 2055 Ret	TTIRX	B-	(800) 842-2252	C+ / 6.8	7.16	7.72	22.10 /63	6.35 /67	9.92 /58	1.78	0.66
GL	TIAA-CREF Lifecycle Ret Inc Inst	TLRIX	C+	(800) 842-2252	C- / 3.1	3.82	3.08	11.69 /17	3.96 /43	5.86 /27	2.17	0.52
GL	TIAA-CREF Lifecycle Ret Inc Premier	TPILX	C+	(800) 842-2252	C- / 3.0	3.79	3.00	11.43 /16	3.81 /41	5.68 /26	2.03	0.67
GL	TIAA-CREF Lifecycle Ret Inc Ret	TLIRX	C+	(800) 842-2252	C- / 3.0	3.77	2.96	11.34 /16	3.71 /39	5.57 /25	1.93	0.77
GL	TIAA-CREF Lifecycle Ret Inc Retail	TLRRX	C+	(800) 842-2252	C- / 3.0	3.76	2.95	11.33 /16	3.71 /39	5.58 /25	1.93	0.80
GR	TIAA-CREF Lifestyle Aggrv Gro Inst	TSAIX	C+	(800) 842-2252	C+ / 6.5	7.13	8.28	23.12 /67	5.42 /59	10.52 /62	0.82	0.87
GR	TIAA-CREF Lifestyle Aggrv Gro Prmr	TSAPX	C+	(800) 842-2252	C+ / 6.4	7.17	8.17	22.99 /67	5.31 /58	10.39 /61	0.46	1.02
GR	TIAA-CREF Lifestyle Aggrv Gro Ret	TSARX	C+	(800) 842-2252	C+ / 6.3	7.06	8.14	22.80 /66	5.16 /56	10.25 /60	0.61	1.12
GR	TIAA-CREF Lifestyle Aggrv Gro Rtl	TSALX	C+	(800) 842-2252	C+ / 6.2	7.06	8.06	22.73 /66	5.10 /55	10.17 /60	0.54	1.20
GL	TIAA-CREF LIfestyle Cons Inst	TCSIX	C+	(800) 842-2252	C- / 3.0	3.70	2.95	11.26 /15	3.85 /41	5.95 /28	2.18	0.60
GL	TIAA-CREF LIfestyle Cons Prmr	TLSPX	C+	(800) 842-2252	D+ / 2.9	3.66	2.96	11.16 /Pct	3.69 /39	5.79 /27	1.93	0.76
GL	TIAA-CREF LIfestyle Cons Ret	TSCTX	C+	(800) 842-2252	D+ / 2.9	3.64	2.91	11.09 /15	3.59 /38	5.68 /26	1.94	0.85
GL	TIAA-CREF LIfestyle Cons Rtl	TSCLX	C+	(800) 842-2252	D+ / 2.8	3.55	2.81	10.97 /14	3.54 /38	5.65 /26	1.92	0.88
GR	TIAA-CREF LIfestyle Growth Fund Rtl	TSGLX	C+	(800) 842-2252	C / 5.2	6.01	6.32	19.15 /48	4.80 /52	8.88 /50	0.95	1.01
GR	TIAA-CREF LIfestyle Growth Inst	TSGGX	B-	(800) 842-2252	C / 5.5	6.11	6.42	19.48 /49	5.11 /55	9.22 /52	1.20	0.72
GR	TIAA-CREF Lifestyle Growth Premier	TSGPX	C+	(800) 842-2252	C / 5.3	6.05	6.37	19.25 /48	4.91 /53	9.03 /51	0.87	0.87
GR	TIAA-CREF Lifestyle Growth Ret	TSGRX	C+	(800) 842-2252	C / 5.3	6.04	6.36	19.17 /48	4.84 /52	8.93 /50	0.99	0.97
AA	TIAA-CREF LIfestyle Income Inst	TSITX	C	(800) 842-2252	D / 2.0	2.37	1.42	7.08 / 6	2.96 /31	4.06 /16	2.29	0.70
AA	TIAA-CREF LIfestyle Income Premier	TSIPX	C	(800) 842-2252	D / 1.9	2.33	1.25	6.84 / 6	2.79 /30	3.89 /15	1.98	0.86
AA	TIAA-CREF LIfestyle Income Retail	TSILX	C	(800) 842-2252	D / 1.8	2.30	1.19	6.69 / 5	2.65 /29	3.75 /14	2.02	0.98
AA	TIAA-CREF LIfestyle Income Retire	TLSRX	C	(800) 842-2252	D / 1.8	2.31	1.30	6.82 / 6	2.68 /29	3.78 /14	2.05	0.95
BA	TIAA-CREF Lifestyle Moderate Inst	TSIMX	C+	(800) 842-2252	C / 4.3	4.98	4.55	15.59 /32	4.69 /51	7.82 /41	2.08	0.62
BA	TIAA-CREF Lifestyle Moderate Prmr	TSMPX	C+	(800) 842-2252	C- / 4.2	4.93	4.55	15.53 /32	4.56 /49	7.68 /40	1.81	0.77
BA	TIAA-CREF Lifestyle Moderate Ret	TSMTX	C+	(800) 842-2252	C- / 4.1	4.92	4.43	15.33 /31	4.43 /48	7.57 /39	1.85	0.87
BA	TIAA-CREF Lifestyle Moderate Rtl	TSMLX	C+	(800) 842-2252	C- / 4.1	4.83	4.42	15.31 /31	4.38 /47	7.52 /38	1.83	0.89
BA	TIAA-CREF Mgd Alloc Inst	TIMIX	C+	(800) 842-2252	C / 4.5	5.06	4.78	15.83 /34	4.92 /53	7.94 /42	2.26	0.43
BA	TIAA-CREF Mgd Alloc Ret	TIMRX	C+	(800) 842-2252	C / 4.3	4.90	4.54	15.51 /32	4.64 /50	7.65 /39	2.02	0.73

● Denotes fund is closed to new investors

* Denotes fund is included in Section II

616

Risk Rating/Pts	3 Year Standard Deviation	Beta	NAV As of 2/28/17	Total $(Mil)	Cash %	Stocks %	Bonds %	Other %	Portfolio Turnover Ratio	Last Bull Market Return	Last Bear Market Return	Manager Quality Pct	Manager Tenure (Years)	Initial Purch. $	Additional Purch. $	Front End Load	Back End Load
B+ / 9.1	5.4	0.84	14.72	67	0	0	0	100	22	54.2	-9.3	53	8	0	0	0.0	0.0
B+ / 9.1	5.4	0.84	14.67	117	0	0	0	100	22	53.4	-9.4	51	8	0	0	0.0	0.0
B / 8.9	6.1	0.96	15.43	593	0	0	0	100	15	63.1	-11.2	47	8	10,000,000	1,000	0.0	0.0
B / 8.9	6.1	0.96	15.37	164	0	0	0	100	15	61.8	-11.3	45	8	0	0	0.0	0.0
B / 8.9	6.1	0.96	15.31	256	0	0	0	100	15	60.7	-11.3	44	8	0	0	0.0	0.0
B / 8.6	6.9	1.08	16.03	628	0	0	0	100	9	70.9	-13.1	39	8	10,000,000	1,000	0.0	0.0
B / 8.6	6.9	1.08	15.98	175	0	0	0	100	9	69.5	-13.1	37	8	0	0	0.0	0.0
B / 8.6	6.9	1.08	15.92	265	0	0	0	100	9	68.7	-13.2	36	8	0	0	0.0	0.0
B / 8.3	7.7	1.21	16.66	680	0	0	0	100	7	79.1	-15.0	32	8	10,000,000	1,000	0.0	0.0
B / 8.3	7.7	1.21	16.60	192	0	0	0	100	7	77.8	-15.0	31	8	0	0	0.0	0.0
B / 8.3	7.6	1.20	16.53	266	0	0	0	100	7	76.7	-15.0	30	8	0	0	0.0	0.0
B / 8.0	8.5	1.33	17.26	678	0	0	0	100	6	87.4	-16.8	26	8	10,000,000	1,000	0.0	0.0
B / 8.0	8.5	1.33	17.19	169	0	0	0	100	6	85.9	-16.8	25	8	0	0	0.0	0.0
B / 8.0	8.5	1.33	17.12	228	0	0	0	100	6	84.8	-16.8	24	8	0	0	0.0	0.0
B- / 7.6	9.3	1.45	17.61	801	0	0	0	100	4	92.3	-17.2	20	8	10,000,000	1,000	0.0	0.0
B- / 7.6	9.3	1.45	17.54	171	0	0	0	100	4	90.8	-17.2	19	8	0	0	0.0	0.0
B- / 7.7	9.3	1.45	17.48	216	0	0	0	100	4	89.8	-17.3	18	8	0	0	0.0	0.0
B- / 7.6	9.4	1.46	17.62	419	0	0	0	100	8	92.9	-17.1	21	8	10,000,000	1,000	0.0	0.0
B- / 7.6	9.4	1.46	17.55	122	0	0	0	100	8	91.5	-17.3	19	8	0	0	0.0	0.0
B- / 7.6	9.4	1.47	17.48	156	0	0	0	100	8	90.4	-17.2	19	8	0	0	0.0	0.0
B- / 7.6	9.4	1.47	17.66	276	0	0	0	100	10	93.5	-17.2	21	8	10,000,000	1,000	0.0	0.0
B- / 7.6	9.4	1.47	17.58	91	0	0	0	100	10	92.0	-17.2	20	8	0	0	0.0	0.0
B- / 7.6	9.4	1.47	17.51	119	0	0	0	100	10	90.9	-17.3	19	8	0	0	0.0	0.0
B- / 7.6	9.4	1.47	14.10	78	0	0	0	100	36	94.0	-17.2	22	6	10,000,000	1,000	0.0	0.0
B- / 7.6	9.4	1.47	14.08	19	0	0	0	100	36	92.7	-17.3	20	6	0	0	0.0	0.0
B- / 7.6	9.5	1.48	14.05	42	0	0	0	100	36	91.5	-17.3	19	6	0	0	0.0	0.0
B / 8.8	4.9	0.75	11.16	166	0	0	0	100	18	47.2	-6.9	77	10	2,000,000	1,000	0.0	0.0
B / 8.9	4.9	0.74	11.15	36	0	0	0	100	18	45.9	-7.0	76	10	0	0	0.0	0.0
B / 8.9	4.9	0.75	11.13	163	0	0	0	100	18	45.1	-7.0	75	10	0	0	0.0	0.0
B / 8.9	4.9	0.75	11.14	100	0	0	0	100	18	45.0	-6.9	75	10	2,500	100	0.0	0.0
C / 5.4	11.0	1.02	14.50	4	0	98	0	2	41	N/A	N/A	15	6	2,000,000	1,000	0.0	0.0
C / 5.4	11.0	1.02	14.54	N/A	0	98	0	2	41	N/A	N/A	14	6	0	0	0.0	0.0
C / 5.4	11.0	1.02	14.47	24	0	98	0	2	41	N/A	N/A	13	6	0	0	0.0	0.0
C / 5.5	10.9	1.02	14.46	32	0	98	0	2	41	N/A	N/A	13	6	2,500	100	0.0	0.0
B+ / 9.0	4.8	0.36	11.93	5	0	0	0	100	26	N/A	N/A	93	6	2,000,000	1,000	0.0	0.0
B+ / 9.0	4.8	0.36	11.94	N/A	0	0	0	100	26	N/A	N/A	92	6	0	0	0.0	0.0
B+ / 9.0	4.8	0.36	11.92	31	0	0	0	100	26	N/A	N/A	92	6	0	0	0.0	0.0
B+ / 9.0	4.8	0.36	11.91	128	0	0	0	100	26	N/A	N/A	92	6	2,500	100	0.0	0.0
B- / 7.1	8.9	0.83	13.83	64	0	0	0	100	35	N/A	N/A	27	6	2,500	100	0.0	0.0
B- / 7.1	8.9	0.82	13.88	4	0	0	0	100	35	N/A	N/A	30	6	2,000,000	1,000	0.0	0.0
B- / 7.1	8.9	0.83	13.89	N/A	0	0	0	100	35	N/A	N/A	28	6	0	0	0.0	0.0
B- / 7.1	8.9	0.83	13.85	28	0	0	0	100	35	N/A	N/A	27	6	0	0	0.0	0.0
B / 8.9	2.9	0.41	10.88	1	0	19	80	1	33	N/A	N/A	73	6	2,000,000	1,000	0.0	0.0
B / 8.9	2.8	0.40	10.89	N/A	0	19	80	1	33	N/A	N/A	71	6	0	0	0.0	0.0
B / 8.9	2.8	0.40	10.87	46	0	19	80	1	33	N/A	N/A	70	6	2,500	100	0.0	0.0
B / 8.9	2.8	0.40	10.87	14	0	19	80	1	33	N/A	N/A	70	6	0	0	0.0	0.0
B / 8.0	7.0	1.07	12.99	9	0	0	0	100	17	N/A	N/A	33	6	2,000,000	1,000	0.0	0.0
B / 8.1	6.9	1.07	13.02	N/A	0	0	0	100	17	N/A	N/A	31	6	0	0	0.0	0.0
B / 8.0	7.0	1.07	12.98	66	0	0	0	100	17	N/A	N/A	30	6	0	0	0.0	0.0
B / 8.1	6.9	1.06	12.97	161	0	0	0	100	17	N/A	N/A	30	6	2,500	100	0.0	0.0
B- / 7.5	6.9	1.06	11.94	13	0	58	41	1	17	68.6	-12.1	36	N/A	2,000,000	1,000	0.0	0.0
B- / 7.6	6.9	1.06	11.96	719	0	58	41	1	17	66.2	-12.2	33	N/A	2,500	100	0.0	0.0

I. Index of Stock Mutual Funds

99 Pct = Best
0 Pct = Worst

Fund Type	Fund Name	Ticker Symbol	Overall Investment Rating	Phone	Performance Rating/Pts	3 Mo	6 Mo	1Yr / Pct	3Yr / Pct	5Yr / Pct	Dividend Yield	Expense Ratio
								Total Return % through 2/28/17	Annualized		Incl. in Returns	
BA	TIAA-CREF Mgd Alloc Retire	TITRX	C+	(800) 842-2252	C / 4.3	5.01	4.66	15.58 / 32	4.66 / 50	7.66 / 39	2.03	0.68
MC	TIAA-CREF Mid Cap Value Inst	TIMVX	B	(800) 842-2252	B+ / 8.6	5.55	10.31	29.56 / 85	8.18 / 80	12.97 / 83	1.66	0.42
MC	TIAA-CREF Mid Cap Value Prmr	TRVPX	B	(800) 842-2252	B+ / 8.5	5.50	10.22	29.32 / 85	8.01 / 79	12.81 / 82	1.52	0.57
MC	TIAA-CREF Mid Cap Value Retail	TCMVX	B	(800) 842-2252	B+ / 8.3	5.43	10.11	29.17 / 84	7.86 / 78	12.62 / 80	1.43	0.71
MC	TIAA-CREF Mid Cap Value Retire	TRVRX	B	(800) 842-2252	B+ / 8.4	5.42	10.11	29.20 / 85	7.89 / 78	12.68 / 81	1.44	0.67
MC	TIAA-CREF Mid/Cp Growth Inst	TRPWX	D	(800) 842-2252	C / 4.7	6.54	5.32	21.10 / 58	3.56 / 38	10.40 / 61	0.48	0.47
MC	TIAA-CREF Mid/Cp Growth Prmr	TRGPX	D	(800) 842-2252	C / 4.5	6.47	5.19	20.92 / 57	3.39 / 36	10.23 / 60	0.33	0.62
MC	TIAA-CREF Mid/Cp Growth Retail	TCMGX	D	(800) 842-2252	C / 4.4	6.45	5.14	20.76 / 56	3.23 / 34	10.03 / 59	0.19	0.78
MC	TIAA-CREF Mid/Cp Growth Retire	TRGMX	D	(800) 842-2252	C / 4.4	6.39	5.14	20.81 / 56	3.30 / 35	10.11 / 59	0.24	0.72
RE	TIAA-CREF Real Est Secs Instl	TIREX	B+	(800) 842-2252	B- / 7.3	7.87	-1.10	14.50 / 28	10.61 / 96	10.64 / 63	2.49	0.51
RE	TIAA-CREF Real Est Secs Premier	TRRPX	B+	(800) 842-2252	B- / 7.2	7.89	-1.11	14.32 / 27	10.44 / 96	10.48 / 62	2.35	0.66
RE	TIAA-CREF Real Est Secs Retail	TCREX	B+	(800) 842-2252	B- / 7.1	7.84	-1.19	14.18 / 26	10.26 / 95	10.29 / 61	2.21	0.82
RE	TIAA-CREF Real Est Secs Retire	TRRSX	B+	(800) 842-2252	B- / 7.1	7.85	-1.18	14.26 / 27	10.35 / 95	10.37 / 61	2.16	0.76
IX	TIAA-CREF S&P 500 Idx Inst	TISPX	A+	(800) 842-2252	A / 9.4	8.03	9.97	24.90 / 73	10.57 / 96	13.94 / 93	1.83	0.06
IX	TIAA-CREF S&P 500 Idx Retire	TRSPX	A+	(800) 842-2252	A- / 9.2	7.94	9.84	24.58 / 72	10.30 / 95	13.65 / 90	1.64	0.31
SC	TIAA-CREF Sm Cap Equity Inst	TISEX	B	(800) 842-2252	A+ / 9.6	6.02	15.86	37.11 / 96	8.91 / 86	14.01 / 93	0.88	0.42
SC	TIAA-CREF Sm Cap Equity Prmr	TSRPX	B	(800) 842-2252	A+ / 9.6	6.03	15.79	36.98 / 96	8.77 / 85	13.85 / 92	0.76	0.57
SC	TIAA-CREF Sm Cap Equity Retail	TCSEX	B	(800) 842-2252	A / 9.5	5.96	15.72	36.69 / 96	8.57 / 84	13.62 / 90	0.66	0.75
SC	TIAA-CREF Sm Cap Equity Retire	TRSEX	B	(800) 842-2252	A / 9.5	6.00	15.74	36.86 / 96	8.65 / 84	13.73 / 91	0.69	0.67
SC	TIAA-CREF Sm Cp Blend Idx Inst	TISBX	B	(800) 842-2252	B+ / 8.7	5.20	12.68	36.35 / 95	7.18 / 73	13.15 / 85	1.52	0.06
SC	TIAA-CREF Sm Cp Blend Idx Ret	TRBIX	B	(800) 842-2252	B+ / 8.5	5.17	12.57	36.04 / 95	6.93 / 71	12.87 / 83	1.30	0.31
MC	TIAA-CREF SmMd Cap Equity Inst	TSMWX	U	(800) 842-2252	U /	6.01	11.29	--	--	--	0.00	N/A
OT	TIAA-CREF Soc Choice Lw Crb Eq	TNWCX	U	(800) 842-2252	U /	7.61	9.84	26.01 / 76	--	--	2.10	0.59
GR	TIAA-CREF Social Ch Eq Inst	TISCX	A-	(800) 842-2252	B+ / 8.5	7.07	9.41	25.93 / 76	8.61 / 84	12.84 / 82	2.17	0.18
GR	TIAA-CREF Social Ch Eq Premier	TRPSX	A-	(800) 842-2252	B+ / 8.4	7.07	9.36	25.76 / 75	8.45 / 83	12.68 / 81	2.05	0.32
GR	TIAA-CREF Social Ch Eq Retail	TICRX	B+	(800) 842-2252	B+ / 8.3	7.02	9.33	25.64 / 75	8.32 / 81	12.53 / 79	1.97	0.44
GR	TIAA-CREF Social Ch Eq Retire	TRSCX	A-	(800) 842-2252	B+ / 8.3	7.02	9.33	25.60 / 75	8.36 / 82	12.58 / 80	1.91	0.43
AG	Timothy Plan Aggressive Growth A	TAAGX	E	(800) 662-0201	D+ / 2.8	8.31	9.26	21.80 / 61	0.79 / 17	7.36 / 37	0.00	1.79
AG	Timothy Plan Aggressive Growth C	TCAGX	E	(800) 662-0201	C- / 3.2	8.20	8.96	20.86 / 57	0.07 / 14	6.55 / 32	0.00	2.54
GR	Timothy Plan Aggressive Growth I	TIAGX	D-	(800) 662-0201	C- / 4.0	8.37	9.32	22.11 / 63	1.02 / 18	--	0.00	1.54
AA	Timothy Plan Conservative Growth A	TCGAX	D+	(800) 662-0201	D- / 1.2	3.32	2.29	9.37 / 10	1.27 / 20	3.14 / 11	0.00	2.30
AA	Timothy Plan Conservative Growth C	TCVCX	D+	(800) 662-0201	D- / 1.4	3.06	1.94	8.63 / 9	0.51 / 16	2.36 / 9	0.00	3.05
IN	Timothy Plan Defensive Strat A	TPDAX	D+	(800) 662-0201	E+ / 0.9	2.75	0.24	9.42 / 10	0.70 / 17	-0.66 / 4	0.30	1.37
IN	Timothy Plan Defensive Strat C	TPDCX	D+	(800) 662-0201	E+ / 0.9	2.61	-0.09	8.58 / 9	-0.05 / 13	-1.40 / 3	0.00	2.12
OT	Timothy Plan Defensive Strat I	TPDIX	C-	(800) 662-0201	D- / 1.5	2.84	0.42	9.71 / 11	0.96 / 18	--	0.59	1.12
EM	Timothy Plan Emerging Markets A	TPEMX	E	(800) 662-0201	D / 1.7	9.07	8.66	36.98 / 96	-1.45 / 8	--	0.42	2.51
EM	Timothy Plan Emerging Markets C	TPECX	E	(800) 662-0201	D / 2.0	8.90	8.34	35.91 / 95	-2.19 / 6	--	0.00	3.27
EM	Timothy Plan Emerging Markets I	TIEMX	E	(800) 662-0201	D+ / 2.6	9.23	8.96	37.45 / 96	-1.19 / 9	--	0.63	2.27
GI	Timothy Plan Growth and Income A	TGIAX	C-	(800) 662-0201	E+ / 0.9	3.67	2.22	6.25 / 5	0.61 / 16	--	0.16	1.57
GI	Timothy Plan Growth and Income C	TGCIX	C-	(800) 662-0201	E+ / 0.8	3.36	1.80	5.48 / 4	-0.15 / 13	--	0.00	2.31
GI	Timothy Plan Growth and Income I	TIGIX	C-	(800) 662-0201	D- / 1.4	3.62	2.33	6.56 / 5	0.79 / 17	--	0.29	1.32
FO	Timothy Plan International A	TPIAX	D	(800) 662-0201	E / 0.5	4.70	4.20	10.16 / 12	-1.20 / 9	3.98 / 15	0.97	1.69
FO	Timothy Plan International C	TPICX	D	(800) 662-0201	E+ / 0.7	4.67	3.89	9.47 / 10	-1.90 / 7	3.21 / 12	0.15	2.43
FO	Timothy Plan International I	TPIIX	D	(800) 662-0201	E+ / 0.9	4.84	4.34	10.44 / 13	-0.93 / 10	--	1.28	1.44
FO	Timothy Plan Israel Common Values	TPAIX	C-	(800) 662-0201	C- / 3.4	9.01	9.89	22.96 / 66	1.35 / 20	6.76 / 33	1.37	1.95
FO	Timothy Plan Israel Common Values	TPCIX	C-	(800) 662-0201	C- / 3.8	8.87	9.51	22.04 / 62	0.59 / 16	5.94 / 28	1.00	2.70
FO	Timothy Plan Israel Common Values I	TICIX	C	(800) 662-0201	C / 4.7	9.05	10.01	23.27 / 67	1.60 / 22	--	1.64	1.70
GR	Timothy Plan Large Mid Cap Growth	TLGAX	C-	(800) 662-0201	C / 5.3	5.95	8.07	20.77 / 56	6.07 / 65	10.25 / 60	0.00	1.58
GR	Timothy Plan Large Mid Cap Growth	TLGCX	C-	(800) 662-0201	C+ / 5.7	5.72	7.58	19.57 / 50	5.24 / 57	9.40 / 54	0.00	2.33
GR	Timothy Plan Large Mid Cap Growth I	TPLIX	C+	(800) 662-0201	C+ / 6.6	6.02	8.26	21.03 / 58	6.33 / 67	--	0.00	1.33
MC	Timothy Plan Large/Mid Cap Val A	TLVAX	C	(800) 662-0201	C / 5.1	6.43	6.86	18.52 / 45	6.45 / 68	11.07 / 66	0.00	1.53
MC	Timothy Plan Large/Mid Cap Val C	TLVCX	C-	(800) 662-0201	C+ / 5.6	6.19	6.41	17.58 / 41	5.65 / 61	10.23 / 60	0.00	2.28

• Denotes fund is closed to new investors
* Denotes fund is included in Section II

I. Index of Stock Mutual Funds

Risk Rating/Pts	3 Year Standard Deviation	Beta	NAV As of 2/28/17	Total $(Mil)	Cash %	Stocks %	Bonds %	Other %	Portfolio Turnover Ratio	Last Bull Market Return	Last Bear Market Return	Manager Quality Pct	Manager Tenure (Years)	Initial Purch. $	Additional Purch. $	Front End Load	Back End Load
B- /7.6	6.9	1.06	11.92	61	0	58	41	1	17	66.1	-12.1	33	N/A	0	0	0.0	0.0
C /5.0	11.3	0.91	23.86	3,504	0	0	0	100	43	126.0	-21.2	68	15	2,000,000	1,000	0.0	0.0
C /5.0	11.2	0.91	23.81	398	0	0	0	100	43	124.1	-21.2	66	15	1,000,000	0	0.0	0.0
C /5.0	11.3	0.91	23.31	303	0	0	0	100	43	122.2	-21.2	64	15	2,500	100	0.0	0.0
C /5.0	11.3	0.91	23.72	1,125	0	0	0	100	43	122.8	-21.2	65	15	0	0	0.0	0.0
C- /3.0	13.2	0.99	20.99	821	0	99	0	1	69	107.3	-24.1	11	11	2,000,000	1,000	0.0	0.0
C- /3.0	13.2	1.00	20.87	110	0	99	0	1	69	105.6	-24.2	10	11	1,000,000	0	0.0	0.0
C- /3.0	13.2	1.00	20.44	165	0	99	0	1	69	103.6	-24.2	9	11	2,500	100	0.0	0.0
C- /3.0	13.2	0.99	20.45	397	0	99	0	1	69	104.5	-24.2	9	11	0	0	0.0	0.0
C+ /6.8	13.9	1.02	15.52	1,454	0	0	0	100	33	104.1	-17.1	67	12	2,000,000	1,000	0.0	0.0
C+ /6.8	13.9	1.02	15.53	100	0	0	0	100	33	102.6	-17.3	65	12	0	0	0.0	0.0
C+ /6.8	14.0	1.02	15.41	231	0	0	0	100	33	100.5	-17.3	63	12	2,500	100	0.0	0.0
C+ /6.8	14.0	1.02	16.11	338	0	0	0	100	33	101.4	-17.3	64	12	0	0	0.0	0.0
C+ /6.9	10.3	1.00	26.33	3,066	0	99	0	1	8	133.8	-16.3	73	12	10,000,000	1,000	0.0	0.0
B- /7.0	10.3	1.00	26.18	962	0	99	0	1	8	130.6	-16.3	71	12	0	0	0.0	0.0
C- /3.9	15.3	0.96	19.08	2,401	0	0	0	100	86	145.4	-25.7	87	12	2,000,000	1,000	0.0	2.0
C- /3.9	15.3	0.96	18.99	211	0	0	0	100	86	143.5	-25.8	86	12	1,000,000	0	0.0	2.0
C- /3.9	15.3	0.96	18.48	162	0	0	0	100	86	140.8	-25.8	85	12	2,500	100	0.0	2.0
C- /3.9	15.3	0.96	18.66	642	0	0	0	100	86	142.2	-25.8	86	12	0	0	0.0	2.0
C /4.8	15.7	1.00	20.11	1,701	0	0	0	100	22	134.9	-25.1	76	12	10,000,000	1,000	0.0	2.0
C /4.8	15.7	1.00	20.20	505	0	0	0	100	22	131.9	-25.2	74	12	0	0	0.0	2.0
U /	N/A	N/A	11.15	587	0	0	0	100	0	N/A	N/A	N/A	1	2,000,000	1,000	0.0	0.0
U /	N/A	N/A	11.31	46	0	0	0	100	83	N/A	N/A	N/A	2	2,000,000	1,000	0.0	0.0
C+ /6.3	10.6	1.02	17.35	1,637	0	97	2	1	16	122.2	-17.5	48	12	2,000,000	1,000	0.0	0.0
C+ /6.3	10.6	1.02	17.30	84	0	97	2	1	16	120.4	-17.6	46	12	1,000,000	0	0.0	0.0
C+ /6.2	10.6	1.02	15.66	471	0	97	2	1	16	118.8	-17.6	44	12	2,500	100	0.0	0.0
C+ /6.3	10.6	1.02	17.61	358	0	97	2	1	16	119.4	-17.7	45	12	0	0	0.0	0.0
D /2.2	14.4	1.17	7.43	21	11	69	18	2	124	84.1	-22.1	2	7	1,000	0	5.5	0.0
D- /1.5	14.4	1.18	6.20	3	11	69	18	2	124	76.8	-22.4	1	7	1,000	0	0.0	0.0
D /2.2	14.4	1.18	7.51	1	11	69	18	2	124	N/A	N/A	2	7	25,000	5,000	0.0	0.0
B- /7.6	4.9	0.66	10.27	45	14	33	52	1	27	31.6	-10.8	28	N/A	1,000	0	5.5	0.0
B- /7.5	4.9	0.67	9.44	11	14	33	52	1	27	26.4	-11.0	20	N/A	1,000	0	0.0	0.0
B /8.0	6.9	0.28	11.43	64	40	32	26	2	58	10.9	-7.1	46	8	1,000	0	5.5	0.0
B- /7.9	7.0	0.28	11.01	8	40	32	26	2	58	6.4	-7.4	35	8	1,000	0	0.0	0.0
B /8.0	7.0	0.28	11.43	1	40	32	26	2	58	N/A	N/A	49	8	25,000	5,000	0.0	0.0
D+ /2.5	20.5	1.18	8.63	10	9	90	0	1	24	N/A	N/A	29	5	1,000	0	5.5	0.0
D+ /2.5	20.5	1.18	8.44	2	9	90	0	1	24	N/A	N/A	22	5	1,000	0	0.0	0.0
D+ /2.5	20.5	1.18	8.67	1	9	90	0	1	24	N/A	N/A	32	5	25,000	5,000	0.0	0.0
B+ /9.0	5.3	0.42	11.02	37	8	47	44	1	45	N/A	N/A	26	4	1,000	0	5.5	0.0
B+ /9.0	5.3	0.42	10.77	3	8	47	44	1	45	N/A	N/A	19	4	1,000	0	0.0	0.0
B+ /9.0	5.3	0.42	11.07	2	8	47	44	1	45	N/A	N/A	28	4	25,000	5,000	0.0	0.0
C+ /6.8	9.3	0.71	8.57	64	15	84	0	1	28	42.4	-27.2	61	10	1,000	0	5.5	0.0
C+ /6.8	9.3	0.70	8.34	4	15	84	0	1	28	36.8	-27.4	51	10	1,000	0	0.0	0.0
C+ /6.9	9.3	0.70	8.58	7	15	84	0	1	28	N/A	N/A	64	10	25,000	5,000	0.0	0.0
C+ /6.7	10.9	0.68	13.44	22	21	78	0	1	38	N/A	N/A	83	6	1,000	0	5.5	0.0
C+ /6.5	10.9	0.69	12.98	6	21	78	0	1	38	N/A	N/A	79	6	1,000	0	0.0	0.0
C+ /6.7	10.9	0.68	13.47	1	21	78	0	1	38	N/A	N/A	85	6	25,000	5,000	0.0	0.0
C /4.9	10.5	0.94	8.02	63	10	70	19	1	71	103.7	-20.1	27	7	1,000	0	5.5	0.0
C /4.3	10.6	0.95	6.66	9	10	70	19	1	71	95.1	-20.2	20	7	1,000	0	0.0	0.0
C /5.0	10.6	0.94	8.11	2	10	70	19	1	71	N/A	N/A	30	7	25,000	5,000	0.0	0.0
C /5.4	8.7	0.70	18.24	166	16	79	3	2	45	108.4	-18.8	72	12	1,000	0	5.5	0.0
C /4.8	8.7	0.70	15.12	22	16	79	3	2	45	100.0	-19.1	63	12	1,000	0	0.0	0.0

I. Index of Stock Mutual Funds

				PERFORMANCE							
	99 Pct = Best				Perfor-	Total Return % through 2/28/17				Incl. in Returns	
	0 Pct = Worst		Overall		mance				Annualized	Dividend	Expense
Fund		Ticker	Investment		Rating/Pts	3 Mo	6 Mo	1Yr / Pct	3Yr / Pct	5Yr / Pct	Yield	Ratio
Type	Fund Name	Symbol	Rating	Phone								

Fund Type	Fund Name	Ticker Symbol	Overall Investment Rating	Phone	Perfor-mance Rating/Pts	3 Mo	6 Mo	1Yr / Pct	3Yr / Pct	5Yr / Pct	Dividend Yield	Expense Ratio
GI	Timothy Plan Large/Mid Cap Val I	TMVIX	C+	(800) 662-0201	C+ / 6.5	6.44	6.92	18.81 /46	6.71 /70	--	0.00	1.28
SC	Timothy Plan Small Cap Value A	TPLNX	C	(800) 662-0201	B / 7.7	4.20	12.46	34.49 /93	7.18 /73	14.23 /94	0.00	1.58
SC	Timothy Plan Small Cap Value C	TSVCX	C	(800) 662-0201	B / 8.1	3.99	12.02	33.59 /92	6.40 /68	13.38 /88	0.00	2.33
GR	Timothy Plan Small Cap Value I	TPVIX	C+	(800) 662-0201	B+ / 8.9	4.27	12.58	34.88 /94	7.46 /75	--	0.00	1.33
GR	Timothy Plan Strategic Growth A	TSGAX	C-	(800) 662-0201	D- / 1.3	3.81	3.10	11.69 /17	0.88 /18	4.32 /17	0.00	2.42
GR	Timothy Plan Strategic Growth C	TSGCX	C-	(800) 662-0201	D- / 1.5	3.56	2.64	10.73 /14	0.10 /14	3.55 /13	0.00	3.17
GR	Tocqueville	TOCQX	B	(800) 697-3863	B- / 7.2	6.69	8.91	22.15 /63	7.19 /73	11.42 /69	1.07	1.29
PM	Tocqueville Gold	TGLDX	E-	(800) 697-3863	E / 0.4	10.41	-9.98	21.27 /59	-3.48 / 4	-13.60 / 0	0.00	1.44
FO	Tocqueville International Value	TIVFX	C-	(800) 697-3863	C- / 3.5	7.80	3.22	17.38 /40	2.59 /28	7.37 /37	0.96	1.58
SC	Tocqueville Opportunity	TOPPX	D+	(800) 697-3863	C+ / 6.8	9.66	9.55	31.54 /89	3.30 /35	10.21 /60	0.00	1.31
MC	Tocqueville Select	TSELX	D	(800) 697-3863	C / 5.3	3.15	8.20	32.34 /91	2.35 /26	7.90 /41	0.00	1.37
EM	● Toews Hedged Core Frontier	THEMX	D	(877) 558-6397	E+ / 0.9	5.15	1.08	6.87 / 6	-0.15 /13	-2.99 / 2	0.00	4.23
AA	Toews Hedged Core L	THLGX	D-	(877) 558-6397	E+ / 0.7	8.44	5.28	7.84 / 7	-2.16 / 6	5.13 /22	0.00	1.48
AA	Toews Hedged Core S	THSMX	E+	(877) 558-6397	E- / 0.2	5.36	-0.11	5.00 / 4	-5.29 / 2	3.12 /11	0.00	1.40
FO	Toews Hedged Core W	THIDX	D	(877) 558-6397	E- / 0.2	3.15	1.61	-0.73 / 1	-3.27 / 4	0.41 / 5	0.00	1.42
FO	Toews Hedged Growth Allocation	THGWX	D+	(877) 558-6397	E / 0.5	5.18	2.42	5.75 / 5	-2.07 / 6	3.49 /13	0.00	1.59
OT	Toews Tactical Defensive Alpha Fund	TTDAX	U	(877) 558-6397	U /	6.08	3.66	14.20 /26	--	--	0.00	1.83
GR	Toreador Core Fund Institutional	TORZX	A	(800) 673-0550	A / 9.5	8.86	15.00	32.15 /90	9.14 /88	13.50 /89	0.80	1.18
GR	Toreador Core Fund Retail	TORLX	A	(800) 673-0550	A / 9.4	8.84	14.92	31.88 /90	8.87 /86	13.23 /86	0.53	1.43
EM	Toreador International C	TMRCX	D-	(800) 673-0550	E+ / 0.7	8.74	5.27	14.26 /27	-2.86 / 5	--	0.00	2.58
EM	Toreador International Inst	TMRIX	D-	(800) 673-0550	D- / 1.0	9.02	5.83	15.47 /32	-1.85 / 7	--	0.89	1.58
EM	Toreador International Investor	TMRFX	D-	(800) 673-0550	E+ / 0.9	8.92	5.58	15.10 /30	-2.12 / 6	--	0.34	1.83
GR	Torray	TORYX	A+	(800) 443-3036	B+ / 8.7	5.81	8.94	23.99 /70	9.82 /92	12.54 /79	1.05	1.08
EN	Tortoise MLP & Pipeline C	TORCX	E	(855) 822-3863	C- / 3.0	4.45	9.73	46.53 /99	-1.37 / 8	--	1.06	1.99
EN	Tortoise MLP & Pipeline Institution	TORIX	E+	(855) 822-3863	C- / 3.8	4.68	10.29	48.09 /99	-0.37 /12	7.31 /37	1.83	0.99
EN	Tortoise MLP & Pipeline Investor	TORTX	E	(855) 822-3863	D+ / 2.6	4.65	10.13	47.75 /99	-0.63 /11	7.04 /35	1.57	1.24
EN	Tortoise North American En Ind C	TNPCX	E-	(855) 822-3863	E- / 0.1	-11.94	-5.74	40.07 /97	-10.93 / 1	--	0.00	4.14
EN	Tortoise North American En Ind Inst	TNPIX	E-	(855) 822-3863	E- / 0.1	-11.71	-5.32	41.39 /98	-10.01 / 1	--	0.00	3.14
EN	Tortoise North American En Ind Inv	TNPTX	E-	(855) 822-3863	E- / 0.1	-11.82	-5.48	41.06 /98	-10.28 / 1	--	0.00	3.39
EN	Tortoise Select Opportunity C	TOPCX	E-	(855) 822-3863	E+ / 0.8	-4.71	3.93	33.94 /93	-3.92 / 3	--	0.00	2.66
EN	Tortoise Select Opportunity Inst	TOPIX	E-	(855) 822-3863	D- / 1.1	-4.49	4.51	35.19 /94	-2.98 / 5	--	0.44	1.66
EN	Tortoise Select Opportunity Inv	TOPTX	E-	(855) 822-3863	E+ / 0.6	-4.49	4.32	34.81 /94	-3.26 / 4	--	0.23	1.91
FS	Touchstone Arbitrage A	TMARX	D+	(800) 543-0407	E+ / 0.7	-0.56	0.89	3.21 / 3	1.62 /22	--	0.00	2.46
FS	Touchstone Arbitrage C	TMACX	C-	(800) 543-0407	E+ / 0.9	-0.68	0.61	2.44 / 2	0.89 /18	--	0.00	3.16
FS	Touchstone Arbitrage Inst	TARBX	C-	(800) 543-0407	D- / 1.3	-0.36	1.18	3.68 / 3	2.05 /24	--	0.00	2.05
FS	Touchstone Arbitrage Y	TMAYX	C-	(800) 543-0407	D- / 1.2	-0.46	1.08	3.59 / 3	1.95 /24	--	0.00	2.12
AA	Touchstone Controlled Gr with Inc A	TSAAX	C	(800) 543-0407	D- / 1.3	1.76	2.13	7.77 / 7	2.50 /28	3.78 /14	1.96	1.75
AA	Touchstone Controlled Gr with Inc C	TSACX	C	(800) 543-0407	D- / 1.5	1.49	1.74	6.89 / 6	1.71 /22	2.99 /11	1.33	2.47
AA	Touchstone Controlled Gr with Inc Y	TSAYX	C	(800) 543-0407	D / 2.0	1.83	2.25	8.04 / 7	2.73 /29	4.02 /15	2.32	1.58
FS	Touchstone Credit Opp Institutional	TOCIX	U	(800) 543-0407	U /	3.76	4.20	13.20 /22	--	--	4.34	1.69
AA	Touchstone Dynamic Dvsfd Income A	TBAAX	C-	(800) 543-0407	D+ / 2.3	4.21	2.51	13.50 /24	3.69 /39	6.06 /29	3.47	1.71
AA	Touchstone Dynamic Dvsfd Income C	TBACX	C	(800) 543-0407	D+ / 2.7	4.01	2.19	12.73 /21	2.93 /31	5.28 /23	2.94	2.42
AA	Touchstone Dynamic Dvsfd Income Y	TBAYX	C	(800) 543-0407	C- / 3.4	4.26	2.71	13.85 /25	3.97 /43	6.33 /31	3.92	1.50
IN	Touchstone Dynamic Equity A	TDEAX	C-	(800) 543-0407	D / 2.2	0.85	4.52	8.55 / 8	4.93 /53	6.99 /35	0.36	2.17
IN	Touchstone Dynamic Equity C	TDECX	C	(800) 543-0407	D+ / 2.5	0.65	4.10	7.70 / 7	4.13 /44	6.18 /30	0.00	2.91
IN	Touchstone Dynamic Equity Inst	TDELX	C	(800) 543-0407	C- / 3.3	0.91	4.71	8.96 / 9	5.24 /57	7.31 /37	0.59	1.73
IN	Touchstone Dynamic Equity Y	TDEYX	C	(800) 543-0407	C- / 3.3	0.87	4.68	8.94 / 9	5.25 /57	7.29 /37	0.61	1.72
AA	Touchstone Dynamic Glbl Alloc A	TSMAX	D+	(800) 543-0407	D / 1.6	4.11	2.54	11.97 /18	1.98 /24	5.87 /27	2.09	1.81
AA	Touchstone Dynamic Glbl Alloc C	TSMCX	D+	(800) 543-0407	D / 1.8	3.91	2.12	11.11 /15	1.22 /19	5.07 /22	1.53	2.53
AA	Touchstone Dynamic Glbl Alloc Y	TSMYX	C-	(800) 543-0407	D+ / 2.4	4.22	2.74	12.23 /19	2.24 /26	6.13 /29	2.44	1.63
EM	Touchstone Emerging Mkts SmCp A	TEMAX	E	(800) 543-0407	E+ / 0.8	7.59	3.31	21.43 /59	-1.60 / 8	-4.21 / 2	0.00	2.41
EM	Touchstone Emerging Mkts SmCp C	TEFCX	E	(800) 543-0407	D- / 1.0	7.41	2.93	20.45 /55	-2.33 / 6	-4.94 / 2	0.00	3.19

● Denotes fund is closed to new investors
* Denotes fund is included in Section II

620

RISK Risk Rating/Pts	3 Year Standard Deviation	Beta	NET ASSETS NAV As of 2/28/17	Total $(Mil)	ASSET Cash %	Stocks %	Bonds %	Other %	Portfolio Turnover Ratio	BULL/BEAR Last Bull Market Return	Last Bear Market Return	FUND MANAGER Manager Quality Pct	Manager Tenure (Years)	MINIMUMS Initial Purch. $	Additional Purch. $	LOADS Front End Load	Back End Load
C /5.4	8.7	0.74	18.38	8	16	79	3	2	45	N/A	N/A	61	12	25,000	5,000	0.0	0.0
C- /3.4	13.9	0.85	18.90	106	8	75	16	1	73	155.0	-24.7	82	12	1,000	0	5.5	0.0
D+ /2.6	13.9	0.85	14.39	12	8	75	16	1	73	144.9	-24.8	78	12	1,000	0	0.0	0.0
C- /3.5	13.9	0.96	19.09	8	8	75	16	1	73	N/A	N/A	41	12	25,000	5,000	0.0	0.0
B /8.1	6.8	0.57	8.98	33	13	41	44	2	37	46.6	-19.3	15	N/A	1,000	0	5.5	0.0
B /8.1	6.8	0.57	8.15	7	13	41	44	2	37	41.0	-20.4	11	N/A	1,000	0	0.0	0.0
C+ /6.1	11.7	1.09	35.13	288	0	99	0	1	12	108.1	-18.2	24	25	1,000	100	0.0	0.0
E- /0.0	40.2	2.24	37.00	1,248	1	96	1	2	15	-48.3	-17.4	79	20	1,000	100	0.0	2.0
C+ /5.9	11.6	0.91	15.08	643	3	92	3	2	26	58.9	-21.7	89	16	1,000	100	0.0	0.0
D /1.9	21.1	1.10	22.02	82	0	99	0	1	108	106.9	-21.3	23	7	1,000	100	0.0	0.0
D+ /2.9	19.1	1.39	12.44	62	4	92	2	2	32	86.8	-27.5	2	9	1,000	100	0.0	0.0
B- /7.1	9.8	0.37	6.53	2	74	0	25	1	17	-20.1	-22.0	64	8	10,000	100	0.0	0.0
C+ /5.6	9.8	1.26	9.77	43	68	0	31	1	27	33.8	-13.8	1	7	10,000	100	0.0	0.0
C+ /5.8	11.1	1.24	9.24	65	69	0	30	1	18	23.2	-19.1	1	7	10,000	100	0.0	0.0
B- /7.8	8.2	0.38	8.19	48	66	0	33	1	27	-10.6	-11.3	30	7	10,000	100	0.0	0.0
B /8.1	6.6	0.43	9.75	21	71	0	28	1	234	19.1	-12.8	47	7	10,000	100	0.0	0.0
U /	N/A	N/A	11.41	92	0	0	0	100	0	N/A	N/A	N/A	1	10,000	100	0.0	0.0
C+ /5.6	12.5	1.12	15.35	64	0	99	0	1	68	129.5	-19.0	40	11	10,000	100	0.0	0.0
C+ /5.6	12.5	1.13	15.35	41	0	99	0	1	68	126.7	-19.1	36	11	1,000	100	0.0	2.0
C+ /5.9	12.2	0.55	14.18	N/A	1	98	0	1	60	N/A	N/A	25	5	2,500	250	0.0	0.0
C+ /5.9	12.2	0.55	17.24	41	1	98	0	1	60	N/A	N/A	36	5	100,000	10,000	0.0	1.0
C+ /5.9	12.2	0.55	16.16	11	1	98	0	1	60	N/A	N/A	33	5	2,500	100	0.0	1.0
B- /7.6	10.1	0.93	49.71	444	21	78	0	1	11	108.3	-12.3	74	20	2,000	500	0.0	0.0
D /1.9	20.6	0.86	14.07	68	26	73	0	1	34	N/A	N/A	91	6	2,500	100	0.0	0.0
D /1.9	20.6	0.87	14.29	2,513	26	73	0	1	34	74.8	N/A	94	6	1,000,000	100	0.0	0.0
D /1.9	20.6	0.87	14.21	328	26	73	0	1	34	72.4	N/A	93	6	2,500	100	5.8	0.0
E- /0.0	31.8	1.43	8.04	N/A	1	98	0	1	40	N/A	N/A	25	4	2,500	100	0.0	0.0
E- /0.0	31.7	1.43	8.37	4	1	98	0	1	40	N/A	N/A	36	4	1,000,000	100	0.0	0.0
E- /0.0	31.7	1.43	8.28	1	1	98	0	1	40	N/A	N/A	32	4	2,500	100	5.8	0.0
D /1.9	21.1	1.00	9.51	2	10	89	0	1	126	N/A	N/A	83	4	2,500	100	0.0	0.0
D /1.9	21.2	1.00	9.72	53	10	89	0	1	126	N/A	N/A	88	4	1,000,000	100	0.0	0.0
D /1.9	21.2	1.00	9.71	4	10	89	0	1	126	N/A	N/A	86	4	2,500	100	5.8	0.0
B /8.5	2.4	0.07	10.05	9	22	65	11	2	451	N/A	N/A	79	4	2,500	50	5.8	0.0
B /8.5	2.5	0.07	9.82	9	22	65	11	2	451	N/A	N/A	74	4	2,500	50	0.0	0.0
B /8.5	2.5	0.07	10.19	22	22	65	11	2	451	N/A	N/A	81	4	500,000	50	0.0	0.0
B /8.5	2.5	0.07	10.15	150	22	65	11	2	451	N/A	N/A	81	4	2,500	50	0.0	0.0
B+ /9.3	3.1	0.46	11.30	15	27	38	32	3	92	28.8	-4.7	63	N/A	2,500	50	5.8	0.0
B+ /9.3	3.1	0.46	11.23	10	27	38	32	3	92	23.6	-5.1	53	N/A	2,500	50	0.0	0.0
B+ /9.3	3.1	0.46	11.30	13	27	38	32	3	92	30.5	-4.7	66	N/A	2,500	50	0.0	0.0
U /	N/A	N/A	10.50	56	4	0	95	1	91	N/A	N/A	N/A	2	500,000	50	0.0	0.0
B- /7.9	5.8	0.86	13.05	29	6	31	61	2	77	52.1	-11.2	40	N/A	2,500	50	5.8	0.0
B- /7.9	5.8	0.87	13.06	25	6	31	61	2	77	46.1	-11.4	30	N/A	2,500	50	0.0	0.0
B- /7.9	5.8	0.86	13.08	11	6	31	61	2	77	54.2	-11.1	43	N/A	2,500	50	0.0	0.0
B /8.0	6.8	0.48	15.15	16	0	93	6	1	235	63.2	-9.9	73	39	2,500	50	5.8	0.0
B /8.0	6.8	0.48	13.98	12	0	93	6	1	235	56.6	-10.1	63	39	2,500	50	0.0	0.0
B /8.1	6.8	0.49	15.49	13	0	93	6	1	235	65.8	-9.7	75	39	500,000	50	0.0	0.0
B /8.0	6.8	0.48	15.43	89	0	93	6	1	235	65.5	-9.7	75	39	2,500	50	0.0	0.0
B- /7.1	7.5	1.14	11.92	63	1	59	39	1	68	55.6	-15.3	8	N/A	2,500	50	5.8	0.0
B- /7.1	7.6	1.15	11.65	44	1	59	39	1	68	49.3	-15.6	5	N/A	2,500	50	0.0	0.0
B- /7.1	7.5	1.14	12.03	15	1	59	39	1	68	57.8	-15.3	9	N/A	2,500	50	0.0	0.0
C- /3.8	14.3	0.84	9.35	2	0	98	1	1	68	-2.4	-21.0	34	8	2,500	50	5.8	0.0
C- /3.9	14.2	0.84	9.13	1	0	98	1	1	68	-6.3	-21.2	25	8	2,500	50	0.0	0.0

		99 Pct = Best 0 Pct = Worst			PERFORMANCE								
								Total Return % through 2/28/17				Incl. in Returns	
				Overall		Perfor-				Annualized		Dividend	Expense
Fund			Ticker	Investment		mance							
Type	Fund Name		Symbol	Rating	Phone	Rating/Pts	3 Mo	6 Mo	1Yr / Pct	3Yr / Pct	5Yr / Pct	Yield	Ratio
EM	Touchstone Emerging Mkts SmCp		TMEIX	E	(800) 543-0407	D- / 1.4	7.75	3.67	21.86 /61	-1.18 / 9	-3.82 / 2	0.00	1.33
EM	Touchstone Emerging Mkts SmCp Y		TEMYX	E	(800) 543-0407	D- / 1.3	7.57	3.42	21.66 /61	-1.31 / 8	-3.95 / 2	0.00	1.40
GR	Touchstone Focused A		TFOAX	C+	(800) 543-0407	C+ / 6.5	5.99	8.14	21.08 /58	8.21 /81	13.70 /91	0.32	1.32
GI	Touchstone Focused C		TFFCX	C+	(800) 543-0407	C+ / 6.9	5.78	7.72	20.18 /53	7.40 /75	--	0.26	2.01
GR	Touchstone Focused Inst		TFFIX	A-	(800) 543-0407	B / 7.8	6.07	8.33	21.52 /60	8.62 /84	14.14 /94	0.62	0.91
GR	Touchstone Focused Y		TFFYX	B+	(800) 543-0407	B / 7.7	6.03	8.27	21.38 /59	8.49 /83	13.99 /93	0.54	0.95
GL	Touchstone Global Gro Institutional		DSMGX	C	(800) 543-0407	C / 5.4	7.67	4.42	20.04 /52	4.96 /54	--	0.00	2.25
GR	Touchstone Growth Opps A		TGVFX	D+	(800) 543-0407	C / 4.7	8.41	9.18	19.81 /51	4.66 /50	11.83 /73	0.00	1.38
GR	Touchstone Growth Opps C		TGVCX	D+	(800) 543-0407	C / 5.2	8.21	8.80	18.95 /47	3.89 /42	11.00 /66	0.00	2.20
GR	Touchstone Growth Opps Inst		TGVVX	C-	(800) 543-0407	C+ / 6.2	8.53	9.39	20.24 /53	5.04 /55	12.25 /77	0.18	0.98
GR	Touchstone Growth Opps Y		TGVYX	C-	(800) 543-0407	C+ / 6.1	8.47	9.34	20.11 /53	4.95 /54	12.14 /76	0.09	1.07
SC	Touchstone International SC A		TNSAX	D-	(800) 543-0407	E / 0.5	5.55	-1.18	5.47 / 4	-0.23 /13	7.65 /39	0.89	1.67
GR	Touchstone International SC C		TNSCX	D-	(800) 543-0407	E+ / 0.6	5.41	-1.53	4.66 / 4	-0.96 /10	--	0.00	2.63
SC	Touchstone International SC Inst		TNSIX	D	(800) 543-0407	D- / 1.1	5.71	-1.00	5.92 / 5	0.15 /14	8.13 /43	1.48	1.24
SC	Touchstone International SC Y		TNSYX	D	(800) 543-0407	D- / 1.1	5.64	-1.04	5.78 / 5	0.03 /13	7.96 /42	1.33	1.33
FO	Touchstone International Value Inst		FIVIX	E+	(800) 543-0407	E+ / 0.8	7.84	5.97	15.69 /33	-2.51 / 5	--	11.20	1.30
FO	Touchstone Internatl Value A		FSIEX	E	(800) 543-0407	E / 0.4	7.74	5.72	15.25 /31	-2.89 / 5	2.80 /10	10.06	2.11
FO	Touchstone Internatl Value C		FTECX	E+	(800) 543-0407	E / 0.5	7.46	5.29	14.37 /27	-3.63 / 4	2.00 / 8	10.06	9.24
FO	Touchstone Internatl Value Y		FIEIX	E+	(800) 543-0407	E+ / 0.8	7.80	5.94	15.61 /33	-2.60 / 5	3.09 /11	10.86	1.57
GR	Touchstone Large Cap Inst		TLCIX	U	(800) 543-0407	U /	8.27	10.37	22.26 /63	--	--	0.96	0.93
GR	Touchstone Large Cap Y		TLCYX	U	(800) 543-0407	U /	8.27	10.38	22.17 /63	--	--	0.88	1.04
GR	Touchstone Large Company Gro Inst		DSMLX	C+	(800) 543-0407	C+ / 6.3	7.60	6.48	18.41 /45	6.30 /67	12.42 /78	0.00	0.99
GL	● Touchstone Merger Arbitrage A		TMGAX	D+	(800) 543-0407	E+ / 0.7	0.03	1.22	3.78 / 3	1.20 /19	2.07 / 8	0.00	2.51
GL	● Touchstone Merger Arbitrage C		TMGCX	C-	(800) 543-0407	E+ / 0.8	-0.16	0.89	3.04 / 3	0.41 /15	1.28 / 7	0.00	3.30
GL	● Touchstone Merger Arbitrage Inst		TMGLX	C-	(800) 543-0407	D- / 1.2	0.12	1.39	4.20 / 3	1.56 /21	2.41 / 9	0.00	2.17
GL	● Touchstone Merger Arbitrage Y		TMGYX	C-	(800) 543-0407	D- / 1.2	0.13	1.39	4.13 / 3	1.50 /21	2.35 / 9	0.00	2.24
MC	Touchstone Mid Cap A		TMAPX	C+	(800) 543-0407	C+ / 6.4	5.15	6.10	23.67 /69	7.92 /78	12.70 /81	0.28	1.35
MC	Touchstone Mid Cap C		TMCJX	C+	(800) 543-0407	C+ / 6.8	4.98	5.68	22.77 /66	7.13 /73	11.86 /73	0.00	2.12
MC	Touchstone Mid Cap Growth A		TEGAX	C-	(800) 543-0407	C+ / 6.2	7.62	8.11	22.04 /62	6.97 /72	12.51 /79	0.00	1.32
MC	Touchstone Mid Cap Growth C		TOECX	C-	(800) 543-0407	C+ / 6.6	7.43	7.68	21.09 /58	6.19 /66	11.69 /72	0.00	2.07
MC	Touchstone Mid Cap Growth Inst		TEGIX	C+	(800) 543-0407	B- / 7.4	7.71	8.26	22.44 /64	7.35 /74	12.93 /83	0.00	0.96
MC	Touchstone Mid Cap Growth Y		TEGYX	C+	(800) 543-0407	B- / 7.3	7.68	8.24	22.36 /64	7.27 /74	12.82 /82	0.00	1.06
MC	Touchstone Mid Cap Inst		TMPIX	B+	(800) 543-0407	B / 7.6	5.27	6.29	24.12 /70	8.27 /81	13.07 /85	0.63	1.00
MC	Touchstone Mid Cap Value A		TCVAX	A-	(800) 543-0407	A- / 9.1	6.82	10.97	32.30 /90	10.23 /95	13.95 /93	0.55	1.66
MC	Touchstone Mid Cap Value C		TMFCX	A	(800) 543-0407	A / 9.4	6.63	10.59	31.32 /89	9.45 /90	13.14 /85	0.00	2.83
MC	Touchstone Mid Cap Value Inst		TCVIX	A+	(800) 543-0407	A+ / 9.7	6.90	11.22	32.73 /91	10.64 /96	14.39 /95	0.94	1.03
MC	Touchstone Mid Cap Value Y		TCVYX	A+	(800) 543-0407	A+ / 9.7	6.90	11.15	32.62 /91	10.51 /96	14.23 /94	0.81	1.13
MC	Touchstone Mid Cap Y		TMCPX	B+	(800) 543-0407	B- / 7.5	5.21	6.23	24.01 /70	8.19 /80	12.99 /84	0.56	1.11
MC	Touchstone Mid Cap Z		TMCTX	B+	(800) 543-0407	B- / 7.3	5.16	6.07	23.70 /69	7.92 /78	12.69 /81	0.27	1.44
GI	Touchstone Premium Yield Eq A		TPYAX	C-	(800) 543-0407	C / 5.4	5.09	6.00	25.13 /74	5.96 /64	8.59 /47	2.33	1.35
GI	Touchstone Premium Yield Eq C		TPYCX	C-	(800) 543-0407	C+ / 5.9	4.91	5.73	24.23 /71	5.19 /56	7.78 /40	1.76	2.10
GI	Touchstone Premium Yield Eq Y		TPYYX	C	(800) 543-0407	C+ / 6.7	5.17	6.14	25.51 /75	6.25 /66	8.86 /49	2.71	1.07
EM	Touchstone Sands Cap Em Mkt Gr		TSEGX	U	(800) 543-0407	U /	6.88	-0.77	21.45 /60	--	--	0.00	1.52
EM	Touchstone Sands Cap Em Mkt Gr Y		TSEMX	U	(800) 543-0407	U /	6.90	-0.78	21.35 /59	--	--	0.00	1.60
GR	● Touchstone Sands Cap Sel Gr A		TSNAX	E	(800) 543-0407	D+ / 2.3	9.83	4.98	18.60 /45	1.07 /19	10.01 /58	0.00	1.10
GR	● Touchstone Sands Cap Sel Gr C		TSNCX	E	(800) 543-0407	D+ / 2.8	9.70	4.61	17.72 /42	0.31 /15	9.20 /52	0.00	1.85
GR	● Touchstone Sands Cap Sel Gr Y		CFSIX	E+	(800) 543-0407	C- / 3.5	9.96	5.13	18.99 /47	1.34 /20	10.30 /61	0.00	0.83
GR	● Touchstone Sands Cap Sel Gr Z		PTSGX	E+	(800) 543-0407	C- / 3.3	9.90	4.98	18.59 /45	1.07 /19	10.03 /59	0.00	1.13
GR	● Touchstone Sands Capital Inst Gro		CISGX	D-	(800) 543-0407	C- / 3.6	9.99	5.22	19.02 /47	1.44 /21	10.49 /62	0.00	0.79
SC	● Touchstone Small Cap A		TSFAX	E+	(800) 543-0407	D- / 1.5	1.82	4.52	15.67 /33	1.15 /19	7.85 /41	0.00	1.42
SC	● Touchstone Small Cap C		TSFCX	E+	(800) 543-0407	D / 1.8	1.65	4.13	14.83 /29	0.38 /15	7.05 /35	0.00	2.17
SC	Touchstone Small Cap Growth A		MXCAX	E+	(800) 543-0407	D- / 1.1	1.44	3.02	10.58 /13	1.23 /19	8.71 /48	0.00	1.67

● Denotes fund is closed to new investors
* Denotes fund is included in Section II

622

RISK			NET ASSETS		ASSET				Portfolio Turnover Ratio	BULL / BEAR		FUND MANAGER		MINIMUMS		LOADS	
	3 Year		NAV							Last Bull Market Return	Last Bear Market Return	Manager Quality Pct	Manager Tenure (Years)	Initial Purch. $	Additional Purch. $	Front End Load	Back End Load
Risk Rating/Pts	Standard Deviation	Beta	As of 2/28/17	Total $(Mil)	Cash %	Stocks %	Bonds %	Other %									
C- /3.8	14.3	0.84	9.31	1	0	98	1	1	68	-0.2	-20.9	39	8	500,000	50	0.0	0.0
C- /3.9	14.3	0.84	9.38	7	0	98	1	1	68	-0.9	-21.0	37	8	2,500	50	0.0	0.0
C+ /6.8	10.5	0.98	41.61	447	0	90	9	1	28	142.3	-18.6	49	5	2,500	50	5.8	0.0
C+ /6.7	10.5	0.98	40.06	56	0	90	9	1	28	N/A	N/A	38	5	2,500	50	0.0	0.0
C+ /6.8	10.5	0.98	42.51	43	0	90	9	1	28	147.4	-18.4	54	5	500,000	50	0.0	0.0
C+ /6.8	10.5	0.98	42.33	968	0	90	9	1	28	145.7	-18.5	53	5	2,500	50	0.0	0.0
C /5.3	13.7	0.93	19.37	20	0	0	0	100	57	N/A	N/A	95	5	500,000	50	0.0	0.0
C- /3.9	12.9	1.16	29.69	37	0	99	0	1	137	116.2	-23.1	5	11	2,500	50	5.8	0.0
C- /3.5	13.0	1.17	25.20	9	0	99	0	1	137	107.8	-23.4	4	11	2,500	50	0.0	0.0
C- /4.0	12.9	1.16	30.64	147	0	99	0	1	137	120.5	-23.0	6	11	500,000	50	0.0	0.0
C- /3.9	13.0	1.17	30.35	47	0	99	0	1	137	119.3	-23.0	6	11	2,500	50	0.0	0.0
C+ /6.4	11.0	0.37	15.06	17	0	92	7	1	90	68.8	-21.3	37	6	2,500	50	5.8	0.0
C+ /6.4	11.1	0.69	14.82	3	0	92	7	1	90	N/A	N/A	4	6	2,500	50	0.0	0.0
C+ /6.4	11.1	0.37	15.52	164	0	92	7	1	90	72.8	-21.1	43	6	500,000	50	0.0	0.0
C+ /6.4	11.1	0.37	15.44	139	0	92	7	1	90	71.4	-21.3	41	6	2,500	50	0.0	0.0
C /4.7	11.6	0.91	7.11	15	0	100	0	0	38	N/A	N/A	43	5	500,000	50	0.0	0.0
C /4.8	11.7	0.91	7.13	4	0	100	0	0	38	32.3	-25.0	37	5	2,500	50	5.8	0.0
C /4.8	11.7	0.91	6.60	N/A	0	100	0	0	38	27.1	-25.4	28	5	2,500	50	0.0	0.0
C /4.8	11.7	0.91	7.16	4	0	100	0	0	38	34.4	-25.0	42	5	2,500	50	0.0	0.0
U /	N/A	N/A	11.80	97	0	100	0	0	33	N/A	N/A	N/A	3	500,000	50	0.0	0.0
U /	N/A	N/A	11.79	217	0	100	0	0	33	N/A	N/A	N/A	3	2,500	50	0.0	0.0
C+ /5.7	13.8	1.13	31.72	174	0	0	0	100	57	123.8	-16.2	13	8	500,000	50	0.0	0.0
B /8.5	2.3	0.06	10.75	15	4	53	42	1	400	16.1	N/A	82	6	2,500	50	5.8	0.0
B /8.5	2.3	0.06	10.31	13	4	53	42	1	400	11.3	N/A	76	6	2,500	50	0.0	0.0
B /8.5	2.3	0.06	10.93	85	4	53	42	1	400	18.3	N/A	84	6	500,000	50	0.0	0.0
B /8.5	2.3	0.06	10.89	86	4	53	42	1	400	18.0	N/A	83	6	2,500	0	0.0	0.0
C+ /6.5	12.0	0.94	28.22	52	0	97	1	2	19	119.6	-19.0	62	6	2,500	50	5.8	0.0
C+ /6.5	12.1	0.94	26.96	60	0	97	1	2	19	111.0	-19.3	52	6	2,500	50	0.0	0.0
C- /4.1	12.6	0.94	25.85	234	0	96	3	1	92	119.9	-26.0	50	18	2,500	50	5.8	0.0
C- /3.2	12.6	0.94	17.81	117	0	96	3	1	92	111.2	-26.2	39	18	2,500	50	0.0	0.0
C- /4.2	12.6	0.94	26.83	43	0	96	3	1	92	124.4	-25.9	55	18	500,000	50	0.0	0.0
C- /4.2	12.6	0.94	26.64	287	0	96	3	1	92	123.1	-25.9	54	18	2,500	50	0.0	0.0
C+ /6.5	12.1	0.94	28.45	93	0	97	1	2	19	N/A	N/A	66	6	500,000	50	0.0	0.0
C+ /5.9	10.8	0.87	18.76	25	1	98	0	1	45	136.9	-23.3	85	3	2,500	50	5.8	0.0
C+ /5.9	10.8	0.87	18.42	9	1	98	0	1	45	127.9	-23.5	81	3	2,500	50	0.0	0.0
C+ /5.9	10.8	0.87	18.95	242	1	98	0	1	45	142.1	-23.2	87	3	500,000	50	0.0	0.0
C+ /5.9	10.8	0.87	18.86	347	1	98	0	1	45	140.2	-23.2	86	3	2,500	50	0.0	0.0
C+ /6.5	12.1	0.94	28.42	532	0	97	1	2	19	122.7	-18.9	65	6	2,500	50	0.0	0.0
C+ /6.5	12.1	0.94	28.05	17	0	97	1	2	19	119.5	-19.0	62	6	2,500	50	0.0	0.0
C /4.4	10.6	0.91	9.07	26	0	95	3	2	38	78.6	-9.3	30	9	2,500	50	5.8	0.0
C /4.4	10.5	0.91	9.06	24	0	95	3	2	38	71.4	-9.4	22	9	2,500	50	0.0	0.0
C /4.4	10.6	0.91	9.05	102	0	95	3	2	38	81.0	-9.2	32	9	2,500	50	0.0	0.0
U /	N/A	N/A	10.25	177	0	0	0	100	32	N/A	N/A	N/A	3	500,000	50	0.0	0.0
U /	N/A	N/A	10.23	97	0	0	0	100	32	N/A	N/A	N/A	3	2,500	50	0.0	0.0
D+ /2.4	16.1	1.23	14.28	107	2	97	0	1	46	105.1	-12.0	1	17	2,500	50	5.8	0.0
D /2.2	16.1	1.23	13.43	81	2	97	0	1	46	96.9	-12.2	1	17	2,500	50	0.0	0.0
D+ /2.5	16.1	1.23	14.88	1,741	2	97	0	1	46	107.9	-11.8	2	17	2,500	50	0.0	0.0
D+ /2.4	16.1	1.23	14.29	625	2	97	0	1	46	105.2	-12.0	1	17	2,500	50	0.0	0.0
D+ /2.8	16.0	1.22	20.42	2,245	0	99	0	1	33	110.1	-11.8	2	12	500,000	50	0.0	0.0
C- /3.8	13.8	0.74	17.35	34	0	99	0	1	17	89.6	-17.9	25	8	2,500	50	5.8	0.0
C- /3.7	13.8	0.74	16.65	13	0	99	0	1	17	82.0	-18.1	18	8	2,500	50	0.0	0.0
C /4.8	14.7	0.86	5.25	46	0	94	4	2	36	86.3	-21.6	19	4	2,500	50	5.8	0.0

I. Index of Stock Mutual Funds

Fund Type	Fund Name	Ticker Symbol	Overall Investment Rating	Phone	Performance Rating/Pts	3 Mo	6 Mo	1Yr / Pct	3Yr / Pct	5Yr / Pct	Dividend Yield	Expense Ratio
	99 Pct = Best							Total Return % through 2/28/17	Annualized		Incl. in Returns	
SC	Touchstone Small Cap Growth C	MXCSX	E+	(800) 543-0407	D- / 1.4	1.27	2.70	9.97 /12	0.47 /16	7.92 /41	0.00	2.47
SC	Touchstone Small Cap Growth Inst	MXCIX	D-	(800) 543-0407	D / 1.8	1.45	3.21	11.14 /15	1.62 /22	--	0.00	1.24
SC	Touchstone Small Cap Growth Y	MXAIX	D-	(800) 543-0407	D / 1.7	1.29	3.06	10.82 /14	1.45 /21	8.96 /50	0.00	1.32
SC	● Touchstone Small Cap Inst	TSFIX	E+	(800) 543-0407	D+ / 2.4	1.94	4.67	16.14 /35	1.48 /21	8.25 /44	0.37	1.04
GR	Touchstone Small Cap Val Opps A	TSOAX	D-	(800) 543-0407	C- / 3.5	3.61	8.98	27.13 /80	2.14 /25	11.03 /66	0.00	1.82
SC	Touchstone Small Cap Val Opps C	TSOCX	D-	(800) 543-0407	C- / 4.0	3.41	8.59	26.14 /77	1.37 /20	--	0.00	2.79
GR	Touchstone Small Cap Val Opps Inst	TSOIX	D	(800) 543-0407	C / 5.0	3.69	9.15	27.62 /81	2.50 /28	11.44 /69	0.12	1.24
GR	Touchstone Small Cap Val Opps Y	TSOYX	D	(800) 543-0407	C / 4.8	3.60	9.09	27.42 /80	2.38 /27	11.33 /68	0.04	1.28
SC	Touchstone Small Cap Value A	TVOAX	C	(800) 543-0407	B- / 7.1	4.49	14.24	37.38 /96	5.04 /55	10.96 /66	0.47	1.60
SC	Touchstone Small Cap Value C	TVOCX	C	(800) 543-0407	B / 7.6	4.32	13.86	36.39 /95	4.26 /46	10.15 /59	0.11	3.13
SC	Touchstone Small Cap Value Inst	TVOIX	C+	(800) 543-0407	B+ / 8.4	4.56	14.49	37.99 /96	5.47 /59	11.41 /69	0.72	1.19
SC	Touchstone Small Cap Value Y	TVOYX	C+	(800) 543-0407	B+ / 8.3	4.56	14.39	37.75 /96	5.31 /58	11.24 /68	0.63	1.44
SC	● Touchstone Small Cap Y	TSFYX	E+	(800) 543-0407	D+ / 2.3	1.90	4.63	16.02 /34	1.41 /21	8.16 /43	0.28	1.11
GR	Touchstone Sust & Impact Eqty A	TEQAX	E+	(800) 543-0407	C / 4.4	7.06	7.28	19.14 /48	4.99 /54	9.48 /55	0.49	1.40
GR	Touchstone Sust & Impact Eqty C	TEQCX	E+	(800) 543-0407	C / 4.9	6.86	6.86	18.27 /44	4.21 /45	8.66 /48	0.06	2.16
GR	Touchstone Sust & Impact Eqty Inst	TROCX	U	(800) 543-0407	U /	7.20	7.46	19.62 /50	--	--	0.77	1.49
GR	Touchstone Sust & Impact Eqty Y	TIQIX	D-	(800) 543-0407	C+ / 5.8	7.14	7.40	19.43 /49	5.26 /57	9.77 /57	0.71	1.15
GR	Touchstone Value A	TVLAX	C+	(800) 543-0407	C+ / 6.7	4.87	9.07	24.72 /72	7.88 /78	12.33 /77	1.75	1.28
GR	Touchstone Value C	TVLCX	B	(800) 543-0407	B- / 7.1	4.68	8.67	23.83 /69	7.05 /72	--	1.11	2.16
GR	Touchstone Value Institutional	TVLIX	B+	(800) 543-0407	B / 8.0	5.07	9.28	25.18 /74	8.30 /81	12.77 /82	2.23	0.87
GR	Touchstone Value Y	TVLYX	B+	(800) 543-0407	B / 7.9	4.98	9.18	25.08 /74	8.16 /80	12.62 /80	2.09	0.99
SC	Towle Deep Value	TDVFX	B	(888) 998-6953	A+ / 9.9	6.01	25.91	70.35 /99	11.76 /98	17.71 /99	0.00	1.26
AA	Transamerica Asset Alloc Consv A	ICLAX	C-	(888) 233-4339	D / 1.9	3.72	2.28	10.51 /13	3.42 /36	4.87 /20	1.77	1.22
AA	● Transamerica Asset Alloc Consv B	ICLBX	C-	(888) 233-4339	D / 2.2	3.50	1.83	9.74 /11	2.64 /29	4.10 /16	1.24	2.04
AA	Transamerica Asset Alloc Consv C	ICLLX	C-	(888) 233-4339	D / 2.2	3.54	1.89	9.59 /11	2.67 /29	4.14 /16	1.17	1.96
AA	Transamerica Asset Alloc Consv I	TACIX	C-	(888) 233-4339	D+ / 2.8	3.77	2.38	10.72 /14	3.67 /39	5.16 /22	2.07	1.00
AA	Transamerica Asset Alloc Consv R	ICVRX	C-	(888) 233-4339	D+ / 2.4	3.57	2.04	9.96 /12	3.00 /32	4.51 /18	1.46	1.60
AA	Transamerica Asset Alloc Growth A	IAAAX	C	(888) 233-4339	C / 5.0	6.76	6.83	20.58 /55	5.71 /62	9.50 /55	1.47	1.45
AA	● Transamerica Asset Alloc Growth B	IAABX	C	(888) 233-4339	C / 5.4	6.54	6.32	19.56 /50	4.84 /52	8.63 /47	0.44	2.29
AA	Transamerica Asset Alloc Growth C	IAALX	C	(888) 233-4339	C / 5.5	6.58	6.43	19.75 /51	4.94 /53	8.73 /48	0.87	2.19
AA	Transamerica Asset Alloc Growth I	TAGIX	C+	(888) 233-4339	C+ / 6.4	6.77	6.91	20.93 /57	5.99 /64	9.84 /57	1.81	1.18
AA	Transamerica Asset Alloc Growth R	IGWRX	C+	(888) 233-4339	C+ / 5.9	6.70	6.63	20.20 /53	5.38 /58	9.20 /52	1.27	1.78
AA	Transamerica Asset Alloc Mod A	IMOAX	C-	(888) 233-4339	D+ / 2.4	4.48	3.37	12.89 /21	3.82 /41	6.06 /29	1.79	1.25
AA	● Transamerica Asset Alloc Mod B	IMOBX	C-	(888) 233-4339	D+ / 2.7	4.31	3.05	12.03 /18	3.00 /32	5.24 /23	0.75	2.08
AA	Transamerica Asset Alloc Mod C	IMOLX	C-	(888) 233-4339	D+ / 2.8	4.24	3.04	12.09 /18	3.08 /33	5.32 /23	1.09	1.99
AA	Transamerica Asset Alloc Mod Gr A	IMLAX	C-	(888) 233-4339	C- / 3.5	5.55	5.00	16.58 /37	4.73 /51	7.75 /40	1.68	1.33
AA	● Transamerica Asset Alloc Mod Gr B	IMLBX	C-	(888) 233-4339	C- / 3.9	5.39	4.61	15.67 /33	3.86 /41	6.90 /34	0.55	2.17
AA	Transamerica Asset Alloc Mod Gr C	IMLLX	C-	(888) 233-4339	C- / 3.9	5.34	4.56	15.69 /33	3.94 /42	6.97 /34	1.00	2.07
AA	Transamerica Asset Alloc Mod Gr I	TMGIX	C	(888) 233-4339	C / 4.8	5.58	5.11	16.80 /38	4.98 /54	8.04 /43	2.02	1.08
AA	Transamerica Asset Alloc Mod Gr R	IMGRX	C	(888) 233-4339	C / 4.4	5.55	4.84	16.28 /35	4.46 /48	7.50 /38	1.47	1.62
AA	Transamerica Asset Alloc Mod I	TMMIX	C-	(888) 233-4339	C- / 3.5	4.55	3.52	13.16 /22	4.08 /44	6.34 /31	2.11	1.02
AA	Transamerica Asset Alloc Mod R	IMDRX	C-	(888) 233-4339	C- / 3.1	4.38	3.26	12.63 /20	3.59 /38	5.83 /27	1.62	1.51
AA	Transamerica Asst All Interm Hrz	DVMSX	C+	(888) 233-4339	C- / 3.3	4.29	4.31	13.03 /22	3.59 /38	6.06 /29	1.46	1.22
AA	Transamerica Asst All Int-Lng Hrzn	DVASX	C+	(888) 233-4339	C / 4.4	5.29	6.00	16.67 /37	4.19 /45	7.46 /38	1.17	1.28
AA	Transamerica Asst All Lg Horizon	DVLSX	B-	(888) 233-4339	C+ / 5.6	6.35	7.87	20.44 /55	4.70 /51	8.78 /49	0.88	1.34
AA	Transamerica Asst All Short Hrzn	DVCSX	C+	(888) 233-4339	D- / 1.5	1.97	0.47	5.62 / 4	2.11 /25	2.90 /10	2.19	1.11
AA	Transamerica Asst All Shrt-Int Hrz	DVSIX	C	(888) 233-4339	D / 2.2	3.12	2.35	9.15 /10	2.81 /30	4.49 /18	1.83	1.16
GI	Transamerica Capital Growth A	IALAX	C-	(888) 233-4339	C+ / 6.5	10.29	6.62	24.69 /72	6.57 /69	13.90 /92	0.00	1.21
GI	● Transamerica Capital Growth B	IACBX	D+	(888) 233-4339	C+ / 6.7	10.03	6.12	23.54 /68	5.55 /60	12.91 /83	0.00	2.20
GI	Transamerica Capital Growth C	ILLLX	C-	(888) 233-4339	C+ / 6.9	10.09	6.25	23.77 /69	5.81 /63	13.16 /86	0.00	1.92
GI	● Transamerica Capital Growth I	TFOIX	C	(888) 233-4339	B / 7.6	10.40	6.79	25.08 /74	6.89 /71	14.33 /95	0.00	0.92
GR	Transamerica Capital Growth I2		C-	(888) 233-4339	B / 7.7	10.50	6.91	25.26 /74	7.03 /72	14.48 /96	0.00	0.79

● Denotes fund is closed to new investors
* Denotes fund is included in Section II

RISK Rating/Pts	3 Year Standard Deviation	Beta	NAV As of 2/28/17	Total $(Mil)	Cash %	Stocks %	Bonds %	Other %	Portfolio Turnover Ratio	Last Bull Market Return	Last Bear Market Return	Manager Quality Pct	Manager Tenure (Years)	Initial Purch. $	Additional Purch. $	Front End Load	Back End Load
C /4.7	14.8	0.86	4.33	13	0	94	4	2	36	79.1	-21.8	13	4	2,500	50	0.0	0.0
C /4.8	14.9	0.87	5.91	16	0	94	4	2	36	N/A	N/A	21	4	500,000	50	0.0	0.0
C /4.8	14.8	0.87	5.86	379	0	94	4	2	36	88.6	-21.4	20	4	2,500	50	0.0	0.0
C- /3.8	13.8	0.74	17.52	244	0	99	0	1	17	93.3	-17.7	29	8	500,000	50	0.0	0.0
D+ /2.9	15.8	1.22	17.23	4	0	91	8	1	42	110.8	-22.9	2	16	2,500	50	5.8	0.0
D+ /2.7	15.8	0.94	16.68	1	0	91	8	1	42	N/A	N/A	15	16	2,500	50	0.0	0.0
C- /3.0	15.8	1.23	18.59	7	0	91	8	1	42	115.1	-22.8	2	16	500,000	50	0.0	0.0
C- /3.0	15.8	1.22	18.32	117	0	91	8	1	42	113.9	-22.8	2	16	2,500	50	0.0	0.0
C- /3.8	17.3	0.99	25.48	205	1	98	0	1	155	114.8	-22.7	53	1	2,500	50	5.8	0.0
C- /3.8	17.2	0.98	25.13	1	1	98	0	1	155	106.5	-22.9	43	1	2,500	50	0.0	0.0
C- /3.8	17.3	0.99	25.55	3	1	98	0	1	155	119.7	-22.6	59	1	500,000	50	0.0	0.0
C- /3.8	17.3	0.99	25.55	4	1	98	0	1	155	117.7	-22.4	57	1	2,500	50	0.0	0.0
C- /3.8	13.8	0.74	17.54	278	0	99	0	1	17	92.5	-17.8	28	8	2,500	50	0.0	0.0
D- /1.0	11.6	0.94	21.22	122	0	98	1	1	304	84.2	-10.8	18	2	2,500	50	5.8	0.0
D- /1.0	11.7	0.94	18.38	49	0	98	1	1	304	76.8	-11.0	12	2	2,500	50	0.0	0.0
U /	N/A	N/A	21.82	29	0	98	1	1	304	N/A	N/A	N/A	2	500,000	50	0.0	0.0
D- /1.0	11.6	0.94	21.80	101	0	98	1	1	304	86.7	-10.7	20	2	2,500	50	0.0	0.0
C+ /6.2	10.4	0.96	9.93	47	0	99	0	1	19	117.1	-16.5	46	11	2,500	50	5.8	0.0
C+ /6.2	10.4	0.96	9.89	5	0	99	0	1	19	N/A	N/A	36	11	2,500	50	0.0	0.0
C+ /6.2	10.4	0.96	9.95	260	0	99	0	1	19	121.6	-16.4	53	11	500,000	50	0.0	0.0
C+ /6.2	10.4	0.96	9.97	86	0	99	0	1	19	120.4	-16.5	51	11	2,500	50	0.0	0.0
C- /3.2	24.0	1.27	20.80	171	0	99	0	1	40	N/A	N/A	89	6	50,000	5,000	0.0	2.0
B- /7.5	4.4	0.67	11.09	679	0	32	65	3	4	38.3	-8.3	56	N/A	1,000	50	5.5	0.0
B- /7.5	4.4	0.67	11.02	12	0	32	65	3	4	32.9	-8.5	44	N/A	1,000	50	0.0	0.0
B- /7.5	4.4	0.67	10.98	379	0	32	65	3	4	33.2	-8.5	45	N/A	1,000	50	0.0	0.0
B- /7.5	4.4	0.66	11.12	25	0	32	65	3	4	40.4	-8.2	59	8	1,000,000	0	0.0	0.0
B- /7.5	4.5	0.67	11.18	1	0	32	65	3	4	35.9	-8.5	49	N/A	0	0	0.0	0.0
C+ /5.6	9.4	1.43	14.73	772	9	86	3	2	1	88.6	-20.1	17	N/A	1,000	50	5.5	0.0
C+ /5.8	9.4	1.44	14.54	23	9	86	3	2	1	80.7	-20.3	11	N/A	1,000	50	0.0	0.0
C+ /5.7	9.4	1.44	14.33	673	9	86	3	2	1	81.7	-20.3	12	N/A	1,000	50	0.0	0.0
C /5.5	9.4	1.44	14.71	37	9	86	3	2	1	91.7	-19.9	19	8	1,000,000	0	0.0	0.0
C+ /5.6	9.4	1.43	14.62	2	9	86	3	2	1	86.0	-20.2	14	N/A	0	0	0.0	0.0
B- /7.0	5.6	0.86	11.97	1,042	2	46	50	2	2	50.7	-11.8	42	N/A	1,000	50	5.5	0.0
B- /7.2	5.6	0.86	12.21	26	2	46	50	2	2	44.5	-12.1	31	N/A	1,000	50	0.0	0.0
B- /7.1	5.5	0.85	11.94	896	2	46	50	2	2	45.2	-12.1	33	N/A	1,000	50	0.0	0.0
C+ /6.1	7.5	1.16	13.24	1,360	5	66	27	2	1	68.1	-16.3	26	N/A	1,000	50	5.5	0.0
C+ /6.4	7.5	1.16	13.48	40	5	66	27	2	1	61.1	-16.5	19	N/A	1,000	50	0.0	0.0
C+ /6.2	7.5	1.15	13.21	1,263	5	66	27	2	1	61.7	-16.5	19	N/A	1,000	50	0.0	0.0
C+ /6.1	7.5	1.15	13.21	57	5	66	27	2	1	70.7	-16.2	29	8	1,000,000	0	0.0	0.0
C+ /6.2	7.5	1.16	13.19	5	5	66	27	2	1	66.2	-16.4	24	N/A	0	0	0.0	0.0
C+ /6.9	5.5	0.85	11.95	45	2	46	50	2	2	52.9	-11.6	46	8	1,000,000	0	0.0	0.0
B- /7.0	5.6	0.86	11.91	6	2	46	50	2	2	48.9	-11.8	38	N/A	0	0	0.0	0.0
B /8.5	6.2	0.95	13.78	276	3	48	47	2	45	50.7	-10.4	30	21	5,000	0	0.0	0.0
B- /7.6	8.2	1.24	14.76	171	0	69	30	1	45	66.5	-14.8	16	21	5,000	0	0.0	0.0
B- /7.0	10.2	1.53	13.55	82	1	88	9	2	47	82.3	-19.3	7	19	5,000	0	0.0	0.0
B+ /9.9	2.7	0.32	11.58	189	0	10	89	1	41	21.6	-1.1	71	21	5,000	0	0.0	0.0
B+ /9.1	4.2	0.63	11.30	180	0	29	70	1	44	35.5	-6.0	51	19	5,000	0	0.0	0.0
C- /3.1	15.9	1.12	22.59	182	2	97	0	1	32	124.2	-16.3	16	6	1,000	50	5.5	0.0
D+ /2.5	15.9	1.12	18.86	2	2	97	0	1	32	113.9	-16.5	10	6	1,000	50	0.0	0.0
D+ /2.6	15.9	1.12	19.10	67	2	97	0	1	32	116.4	-16.5	11	6	1,000	50	0.0	0.0
C- /3.2	15.9	1.12	23.41	175	2	97	0	1	32	128.9	-16.1	18	6	1,000,000	0	0.0	0.0
D /1.7	15.9	1.11	13.74	244	2	97	0	1	32	130.6	N/A	20	6	0	0	0.0	0.0

					PERFORMANCE						Incl. in Returns	
	99 Pct = Best 0 Pct = Worst		Overall		Perfor-			Total Return % through 2/28/17				
		Ticker	Investment		mance				Annualized		Dividend	Expense
Fund Type	Fund Name	Symbol	Rating	Phone	Rating/Pts	3 Mo	6 Mo	1Yr / Pct	3Yr / Pct	5Yr / Pct	Yield	Ratio
GL	Transamerica ClearTrack 2015 R1	TCFTX	U	(888) 233-4339	U /	3.87	1.89	10.28 /12	--	--	1.17	1.34
GL	Transamerica ClearTrack 2020 R1	TCHTX	U	(888) 233-4339	U /	4.19	2.41	10.76 /14	--	--	1.11	1.32
GL	Transamerica ClearTrack 2025 R1	TDITX	U	(888) 233-4339	U /	4.56	2.81	12.70 /20	--	--	1.06	1.30
GL	Transamerica ClearTrack 2030 R1	TDFTX	U	(888) 233-4339	U /	4.97	3.53	14.04 /26	--	--	1.02	1.32
GL	Transamerica ClearTrack 2035 R1	TCETX	U	(888) 233-4339	U /	5.73	4.58	16.47 /36	--	--	1.16	1.33
GL	Transamerica ClearTrack 2040 R1	TCRTX	U	(888) 233-4339	U /	6.47	5.74	18.78 /46	--	--	1.18	1.37
GL	Transamerica ClearTrack 2045 R1	TCPTX	U	(888) 233-4339	U /	6.87	6.34	20.21 /53	--	--	1.10	1.42
GL	Transamerica ClearTrack Ret Inc R1	TCITX	U	(888) 233-4339	U /	2.92	0.51	7.89 / 7	--	--	1.18	1.31
GR	Transamerica Concentrated Growth I	TOREX	C+	(888) 233-4339	C+ / 6.4	7.10	6.18	21.05 /58	6.14 /66	11.43 /69	0.62	0.83
GR	Transamerica Concentrated Growth		U	(888) 233-4339	U /	7.12	6.27	21.21 /58	--	--	0.69	0.73
GL	Transamerica Developing Mkts Eq I2	TDMIX	E	(888) 233-4339	D- / 1.1	6.29	3.43	21.42 /59	-2.02 / 7	0.40 / 5	0.10	1.38
IN	Transamerica Dividend Focused A	TDFAX	C+	(888) 233-4339	B- / 7.5	7.21	11.39	25.77 /75	8.27 /81	--	1.90	0.97
IN	Transamerica Dividend Focused C	TDFCX	B-	(888) 233-4339	B / 7.8	6.99	10.87	24.66 /72	7.32 /74	--	1.29	1.82
IN	Transamerica Dividend Focused I	TDFIX	B	(888) 233-4339	B+ / 8.6	7.25	11.48	25.98 /76	8.42 /82	--	2.15	0.82
IN	Transamerica Dividend Focused I2		B	(888) 233-4339	B+ / 8.6	7.28	11.43	25.58 /75	8.41 /82	--	1.96	0.71
AA	Transamerica Dynamic Allocation A	ATTRX	C-	(888) 233-4339	D / 2.1	4.49	4.49	11.81 /17	3.18 /34	--	1.17	1.55
AA	Transamerica Dynamic Allocation C	CTTRX	C-	(888) 233-4339	D+ / 2.5	4.38	4.18	11.03 /15	2.44 /27	--	0.45	2.28
AA	Transamerica Dynamic Allocation I	ITTOX	C	(888) 233-4339	C- / 3.2	4.62	4.72	12.07 /18	3.46 /37	--	1.53	1.25
GL	Transamerica Dynamic Inc A	IGTAX	D+	(888) 233-4339	D / 1.9	4.36	0.26	14.39 /27	2.65 /29	3.74 /14	3.76	1.30
GL	Transamerica Dynamic Inc C	IGTCX	D+	(888) 233-4339	D / 2.1	4.18	-0.13	13.46 /23	1.87 /23	2.95 /11	3.21	2.06
GL	Transamerica Dynamic Inc I	IGTIX	D+	(888) 233-4339	D+ / 2.7	4.42	0.37	14.67 /28	2.89 /31	3.98 /15	4.19	1.06
EM	Transamerica Emerging Mkts Eqty A	AEMTX	D	(888) 233-4339	C- / 3.4	11.06	8.23	29.01 /84	0.04 /13	--	1.46	1.61
EM	Transamerica Emerging Mkts Eqty C	CEMTX	D-	(888) 233-4339	D / 2.2	10.94	8.08	28.20 /82	-0.61 /11	--	0.98	2.29
EM	Transamerica Emerging Mkts Eqty I	IEMTX	D+	(888) 233-4339	C / 4.9	11.20	8.51	29.58 /85	0.40 /15	--	1.81	1.26
EM	Transamerica Emerging Mkts Eqty I2		D+	(888) 233-4339	C / 4.9	11.10	8.54	29.59 /85	0.50 /16	--	1.93	1.15
FS	Transamerica Event Driven I2		U	(888) 233-4339	U /	2.41	2.72	9.95 /12	--	--	1.58	3.03
GL	Transamerica Gl Multifactor Mac I2		U	(888) 233-4339	U /	-0.39	0.87	-2.11 / 1	--	--	0.00	1.99
RE	Transamerica Gl Real Est I2	TRSIX	D+	(888) 233-4339	D+ / 2.4	5.83	-4.65	8.47 / 8	4.23 /46	6.60 /32	4.33	1.16
FO	Transamerica Global Equity A	IMNAX	C-	(888) 233-4339	C- / 3.0	7.42	5.90	17.49 /41	2.97 /32	5.59 /25	2.23	1.38
FO	● Transamerica Global Equity B	IMNBX	C-	(888) 233-4339	C- / 3.4	7.20	5.46	16.45 /36	2.19 /25	4.78 /20	1.31	2.29
FO	Transamerica Global Equity C	IMNCX	C-	(888) 233-4339	C- / 3.4	7.16	5.52	16.53 /36	2.21 /25	4.82 /20	1.61	2.12
FO	Transamerica Global Equity I	TMUIX	C	(888) 233-4339	C- / 4.2	7.45	6.04	17.70 /41	3.28 /35	5.94 /28	2.67	1.05
GR	Transamerica Growth I2	TJNIX	D+	(888) 233-4339	B- / 7.5	8.62	8.54	21.13 /58	7.59 /76	12.97 /83	0.07	0.84
AA	Transamerica Inst Asst All InLg Hrz	DILHX	B-	(888) 233-4339	C / 4.7	5.40	6.16	17.12 /39	4.49 /49	7.77 /40	1.45	0.91
AA	Transamerica Inst Asst All Int Hrz	DIIHX	C+	(888) 233-4339	C- / 3.5	4.34	4.49	13.32 /23	3.90 /42	6.39 /31	1.79	0.91
AA	Transamerica Inst Asst All Lg Hrz	DILSX	C+	(888) 233-4339	C+ / 5.8	6.32	7.98	20.73 /56	4.98 /54	9.10 /52	1.17	1.03
AA	Transamerica Inst Asst All ShIntHrz	DIHSX	C	(888) 233-4339	D+ / 2.4	3.25	2.57	9.53 /11	3.13 /33	4.82 /20	2.13	0.85
AA	Transamerica Inst Asst All Sht Hrz	DISHX	C+	(888) 233-4339	D / 1.7	2.13	0.73	6.11 / 5	2.46 /27	3.24 /12	2.51	0.80
FO	Transamerica International Eqty A	TRWAX	D-	(888) 233-4339	E+ / 0.8	6.16	2.96	13.95 /25	-0.24 /12	6.25 /30	1.11	1.42
FO	Transamerica International Eqty C	TRWCX	D-	(888) 233-4339	D- / 1.0	5.95	2.58	13.11 /22	-0.93 /10	5.55 /25	0.50	1.96
FO	Transamerica International Eqty I	TSWIX	D	(888) 233-4339	D / 1.9	6.22	3.06	14.34 /27	0.11 /14	6.65 /33	1.58	0.93
FO	Transamerica International Eqty I2	TRWIX	D	(888) 233-4339	D / 2.0	6.24	3.15	14.43 /27	0.20 /14	6.05 /29	1.67	0.83
FO	Transamerica International Eqty R6	TAINX	U	(888) 233-4339	U /	6.25	3.12	14.44 /28	--	--	1.65	0.83
FO	Transamerica International Sm Cp I2		E-	(888) 233-4339	D / 2.2	7.73	2.22	12.01 /18	1.25 /20	7.18 /36	6.60	1.14
FO	Transamerica Internatl Eqty Opps I2		D-	(888) 233-4339	D- / 1.3	7.38	3.44	13.29 /23	-0.23 /13	4.91 /21	1.06	1.00
FO	Transamerica Internatl Sm Cp Val I	TISVX	D+	(888) 233-4339	D+ / 2.3	7.82	5.26	10.62 /13	1.05 /19	--	2.05	1.12
FO	● Transamerica Internatl Sm Cp Val I2		D+	(888) 233-4339	D+ / 2.3	7.83	5.36	10.82 /14	1.15 /19	--	2.15	1.02
GR	Transamerica Large Cap Value A	TWQAX	A-	(888) 233-4339	A- / 9.2	6.92	9.10	28.91 /84	11.70 /98	15.17 /97	1.11	1.05
GR	Transamerica Large Cap Value C	TWQCX	A	(888) 233-4339	A / 9.5	6.71	8.70	27.89 /81	10.86 /97	14.36 /95	0.60	1.81
GR	Transamerica Large Cap Value I	TWQIX	A	(888) 233-4339	A+ / 9.7	6.93	9.15	29.14 /84	11.97 /98	15.54 /98	1.37	0.78
GR	Transamerica Large Cap Value I2	TWQZX	A	(888) 233-4339	A+ / 9.7	7.04	9.29	29.37 /85	12.12 /98	15.65 /98	1.44	0.68
GR	Transamerica Long/Short Strategy I2		E	(888) 233-4339	D / 1.9	3.06	5.98	9.26 /10	1.34 /20	3.93 /15	0.00	3.20

● Denotes fund is closed to new investors
* Denotes fund is included in Section II

Risk Rating/Pts	Standard Deviation	Beta	NAV As of 2/28/17	Total $(Mil)	Cash %	Stocks %	Bonds %	Other %	Portfolio Turnover Ratio	Last Bull Market Return	Last Bear Market Return	Manager Quality Pct	Manager Tenure (Years)	Initial Purch. $	Additional Purch. $	Front End Load	Back End Load
U /	N/A	N/A	10.04	51	0	49	50	1	43	N/A	N/A	N/A	2	0	0	0.0	0.0
U /	N/A	N/A	10.06	68	1	54	44	1	42	N/A	N/A	N/A	2	0	0	0.0	0.0
U /	N/A	N/A	10.31	80	1	58	39	2	3	N/A	N/A	N/A	2	0	0	0.0	0.0
U /	N/A	N/A	10.45	65	1	64	33	2	1	N/A	N/A	N/A	2	0	0	0.0	0.0
U /	N/A	N/A	10.53	62	1	74	23	2	3	N/A	N/A	N/A	2	0	0	0.0	0.0
U /	N/A	N/A	10.56	52	1	83	14	2	2	N/A	N/A	N/A	2	0	0	0.0	0.0
U /	N/A	N/A	10.66	34	1	90	8	1	2	N/A	N/A	N/A	2	0	0	0.0	0.0
U /	N/A	N/A	10.17	89	0	31	68	1	1	N/A	N/A	N/A	2	0	0	0.0	0.0
C /5.4	10.9	0.97	15.76	25	4	95	0	1	83	109.7	-12.8	25	7	1,000,000	0	0.0	0.0
U /	N/A	N/A	15.95	227	4	95	0	1	83	N/A	N/A	N/A	7	0	0	0.0	0.0
C- /3.3	15.1	0.94	9.97	1,003	4	95	0	1	27	22.2	-23.2	50	10	0	0	0.0	0.0
C /4.8	9.6	0.88	11.08	95	0	99	0	1	54	N/A	N/A	63	4	1,000	50	5.5	0.0
C /4.8	9.6	0.88	11.01	8	0	99	0	1	54	N/A	N/A	51	4	1,000	50	0.0	0.0
C /4.8	9.6	0.88	11.08	13	0	99	0	1	54	N/A	N/A	65	4	1,000,000	0	0.0	0.0
C /4.8	9.6	0.88	11.08	731	0	99	0	1	54	N/A	N/A	65	4	0	0	0.0	0.0
B- /7.6	6.5	0.98	11.03	9	3	74	22	1	142	N/A	N/A	24	5	1,000	50	5.5	0.0
B- /7.6	6.5	0.97	10.92	8	3	74	22	1	142	N/A	N/A	18	5	1,000	50	0.0	0.0
B- /7.5	6.5	0.98	10.99	3	3	74	22	1	142	N/A	N/A	27	5	1,000,000	0	0.0	0.0
C+ /6.6	7.1	0.90	9.52	113	13	17	68	2	27	N/A	N/A	56	2	1,000	50	4.8	0.0
C+ /6.6	7.1	0.90	9.48	195	13	17	68	2	27	N/A	N/A	44	2	1,000	50	0.0	0.0
C+ /6.6	7.1	0.90	9.52	77	13	17	68	2	27	N/A	N/A	59	2	1,000,000	0	0.0	0.0
C /4.3	16.3	0.98	9.18	5	2	97	0	1	61	N/A	N/A	54	5	1,000	50	5.5	0.0
C /4.3	16.3	0.98	9.13	2	2	97	0	1	61	N/A	N/A	44	5	1,000	50	0.0	0.0
C /4.3	16.3	0.98	9.22	1	2	97	0	1	61	N/A	N/A	59	5	1,000,000	0	0.0	0.0
C /4.3	16.2	0.98	9.22	152	2	97	0	1	61	N/A	N/A	60	5	0	0	0.0	0.0
U /	N/A	N/A	10.00	97	0	0	0	100	305	N/A	N/A	N/A	2	0	0	0.0	0.0
U /	N/A	N/A	9.27	154	100	0	0	0	0	N/A	N/A	N/A	2	0	0	0.0	0.0
C+ /6.3	12.4	0.86	13.70	37	8	91	0	1	52	62.9	-18.9	16	12	0	0	0.0	0.0
C+ /6.6	10.7	0.81	11.74	41	0	99	0	1	51	54.2	-24.3	91	3	1,000	50	5.5	0.0
C+ /6.6	10.7	0.81	11.58	1	0	99	0	1	51	47.9	-24.6	87	3	1,000	50	0.0	0.0
C+ /6.6	10.7	0.81	11.53	47	0	99	0	1	51	48.1	-24.5	88	3	1,000	50	0.0	0.0
C+ /6.6	10.7	0.81	11.76	28	0	99	0	1	51	57.0	-24.2	92	3	1,000,000	0	0.0	0.0
D /1.7	13.4	1.10	11.33	375	2	97	0	1	36	123.5	-13.8	26	13	0	0	0.0	0.0
B- /7.8	8.2	1.25	12.50	44	0	70	29	1	30	69.2	-14.7	18	21	5,000	0	0.0	0.0
B /8.6	6.2	0.94	12.20	79	0	51	48	1	42	53.4	-10.4	34	21	5,000	0	0.0	0.0
C+ /6.9	10.2	1.53	11.98	28	1	88	9	2	43	85.4	-19.0	8	19	5,000	0	0.0	0.0
B+ /9.0	4.2	0.64	11.25	10	0	29	70	1	108	37.9	-5.7	55	19	5,000	0	0.0	0.0
B+ /9.9	2.7	0.31	11.11	11	0	9	90	1	60	23.9	-0.9	75	21	5,000	0	0.0	0.0
C+ /5.9	11.7	0.94	16.82	289	2	97	0	1	19	59.6	-22.2	73	22	1,000	50	5.5	0.0
C+ /6.0	11.7	0.94	16.62	57	2	97	0	1	19	54.0	-22.4	65	22	1,000	50	0.0	0.0
C+ /5.9	11.7	0.94	17.01	1,661	2	97	0	1	19	62.8	-22.1	76	22	1,000,000	0	0.0	0.0
C+ /6.0	11.7	0.94	17.02	1,732	2	97	0	1	19	58.4	-22.1	77	22	0	0	0.0	0.0
U /	N/A	N/A	17.18	127	2	97	0	1	19	N/A	N/A	N/A	22	0	0	0.0	0.0
D- /1.1	11.6	0.85	5.42	104	4	95	0	1	17	65.1	-25.4	83	9	0	0	0.0	0.0
C /5.1	11.2	0.90	7.53	1,178	1	98	0	1	15	51.1	-23.4	73	11	0	0	0.0	0.0
C+ /6.8	10.7	0.77	11.62	264	2	97	0	1	20	N/A	N/A	82	4	1,000,000	0	0.0	0.0
C+ /6.8	10.8	0.78	11.64	456	2	97	0	1	20	N/A	N/A	83	4	0	0	0.0	0.0
C+ /5.6	12.1	1.09	12.86	117	5	94	0	1	127	145.2	-19.2	75	5	1,000	50	5.5	0.0
C+ /5.6	12.1	1.09	12.79	39	5	94	0	1	127	136.2	-19.4	66	5	1,000	50	0.0	0.0
C+ /5.6	12.1	1.09	12.93	114	5	94	0	1	127	149.3	-19.0	76	5	1,000,000	0	0.0	0.0
C+ /5.6	12.2	1.09	12.93	1,987	5	94	0	1	127	150.7	-19.0	77	5	0	0	0.0	1.0
D+ /2.7	4.7	0.32	6.32	20	68	31	0	1	955	27.4	-7.5	49	3	0	0	0.0	0.0

Fund Type	Fund Name	Ticker Symbol	Overall Investment Rating	Phone	PERFORMANCE Performance Rating/Pts	Total Return % through 2/28/17 3 Mo	6 Mo	1Yr / Pct	Annualized 3Yr / Pct	5Yr / Pct	Incl. in Returns Dividend Yield	Expense Ratio
	99 Pct = Best											
	0 Pct = Worst											
GL	Transamerica Managed Future Str I2		E+	(888) 233-4339	E+ / 0.7	1.77	-6.55	-11.19 / 0	2.47 /27	2.94 /11	1.13	1.69
MC	Transamerica Mid Cap Growth A	MCGAX	C+	(888) 233-4339	C+ / 6.9	6.89	12.04	28.63 /83	6.30 /67	--	0.00	1.22
MC	Transamerica Mid Cap Growth C	MGTCX	B	(888) 233-4339	B- / 7.2	6.61	11.65	27.63 /81	5.46 /59	--	0.00	1.94
MC	Transamerica Mid Cap Growth I	IMCGX	B+	(888) 233-4339	B / 8.0	6.93	12.23	29.01 /84	6.57 /69	--	0.00	0.93
MC	Transamerica Mid Cap Growth I2		B+	(888) 233-4339	B / 8.1	6.98	12.27	29.13 /84	6.70 /70	--	0.06	0.81
MC	Transamerica Mid Cap Value I2		B	(888) 233-4339	B+ / 8.6	5.12	8.86	25.10 /74	9.53 /91	14.83 /97	0.84	0.89
MC	Transamerica Mid Cap Value Opps A	MCVAX	U	(888) 233-4339	U /	6.62	8.95	22.30 /64	--	--	0.88	1.05
MC	Transamerica Mid Cap Value Opps I	MVTIX	U	(888) 233-4339	U /	6.71	9.03	22.67 /65	--	--	1.02	0.84
MC	Transamerica Mid Cap Value Opps I2		U	(888) 233-4339	U /	6.77	9.18	22.82 /66	--	--	1.08	0.75
EN	Transamerica MLP & Energy Income	TMLAX	E-	(888) 233-4339	E+ / 0.7	4.81	10.60	40.24 /97	-5.44 / 2	--	3.43	1.52
EN	Transamerica MLP & Energy Income	TMCLX	E-	(888) 233-4339	E+ / 0.8	4.75	10.21	39.19 /97	-6.14 / 2	--	2.94	2.27
EN	Transamerica MLP & Energy Income	TMLPX	E-	(888) 233-4339	D- / 1.2	4.89	10.75	40.64 /97	-5.16 / 2	--	3.89	1.24
EN	Transamerica MLP & Energy Income		E-	(888) 233-4339	D- / 1.1	5.04	10.79	40.28 /97	-5.16 / 2	--	3.69	1.14
MC	Transamerica Multi-Cap Growth A	ITSAX	E-	(888) 233-4339	E- / 0.1	7.63	5.65	11.82 /17	-6.26 / 2	3.16 /11	0.00	1.27
MC	● Transamerica Multi-Cap Growth B	ITCBX	E-	(888) 233-4339	E- / 0.2	7.49	5.26	11.13 /15	-7.03 / 1	2.35 / 9	0.00	2.22
MC	Transamerica Multi-Cap Growth C	ITSLX	E-	(888) 233-4339	E- / 0.2	7.44	5.23	11.03 /15	-6.96 / 1	2.39 / 9	0.00	2.07
MC	Transamerica Multi-Cap Growth I	TGPIX	E-	(888) 233-4339	E / 0.3	7.76	5.93	12.19 /19	-5.91 / 2	3.61 /13	0.06	0.91
MC	Transamerica Multi-Cap Growth I2		E-	(888) 233-4339	E / 0.3	7.85	5.91	12.36 /19	-5.77 / 2	3.75 /14	0.24	0.75
BA	Transamerica Multi-Managed Bal A	IBALX	C+	(888) 233-4339	C / 4.5	5.13	5.42	15.53 /32	6.65 /69	8.76 /49	1.05	1.12
BA	● Transamerica Multi-Managed Bal B	IBABX	B-	(888) 233-4339	C / 4.8	4.88	4.92	14.53 /28	5.67 /61	7.79 /41	0.28	2.06
BA	Transamerica Multi-Managed Bal C	IBLLX	B-	(888) 233-4339	C / 5.0	4.98	5.07	14.68 /28	5.91 /63	8.04 /43	0.43	1.81
BA	Transamerica Multi-Managed Bal I	TBLIX	B-	(888) 233-4339	C+ / 5.9	5.24	5.58	15.84 /34	6.96 /72	9.12 /52	1.30	0.83
AA	Transamerica Multi-Mgr Alter Strg A	IMUAX	D+	(888) 233-4339	E+ / 0.7	2.33	0.54	5.31 / 4	0.41 /15	1.70 / 7	1.08	2.04
AA	Transamerica Multi-Mgr Alter Strg C	IMUCX	D+	(888) 233-4339	E+ / 0.7	2.15	0.24	4.59 / 4	-0.34 /12	0.96 / 6	0.23	2.79
AA	Transamerica Multi-Mgr Alter Strg I	TASIX	C-	(888) 233-4339	D- / 1.2	2.39	0.70	5.60 / 4	0.70 /17	2.01 / 8	1.51	1.72
BA	Transamerica Prt Balanced	DVIBX	B	(888) 233-4339	C+ / 5.7	5.14	5.46	15.57 /32	6.70 /70	8.98 /50	1.15	1.16
BA	Transamerica Prt Inst Balanced	DIBFX	B	(888) 233-4339	C+ / 6.0	5.24	5.69	16.06 /35	7.10 /73	9.40 /54	1.48	1.44
FO	Transamerica Prt Inst Intl Eq	DIIEX	D-	(888) 233-4339	E+ / 0.9	6.11	3.25	16.51 /36	-1.89 / 7	2.59 /10	1.78	1.21
GI	Transamerica Prt Inst Large Core	DIGIX	A	(888) 233-4339	B+ / 8.4	7.35	11.07	22.77 /66	8.80 /85	13.45 /88	1.48	1.28
GR	Transamerica Prt Inst Large Growth	DIEGX	B	(888) 233-4339	B / 7.6	8.52	7.60	20.27 /54	8.07 /79	12.36 /78	0.16	0.99
IN	Transamerica Prt Inst Large Value	DIVIX	A-	(888) 233-4339	B / 8.1	7.21	13.59	25.18 /74	7.14 /73	12.82 /82	1.60	0.83
MC	Transamerica Prt Inst Mid Growth	DIMGX	C	(888) 233-4339	B+ / 8.4	6.97	12.99	29.91 /86	6.91 /71	11.00 /66	0.00	1.22
MC	Transamerica Prt Inst Mid Value	DIMVX	B	(888) 233-4339	B+ / 8.8	6.03	8.98	24.00 /70	10.04 /93	14.55 /96	0.86	1.02
IN	Transamerica Prt Inst Small Core	DISEX	B-	(888) 233-4339	B- / 7.0	3.92	12.75	30.16 /87	4.71 /51	10.42 /61	0.73	1.32
GL	Transamerica Prt Inst Small Growth	DISGX	B	(888) 233-4339	A- / 9.0	4.56	10.07	31.36 /89	8.98 /87	10.54 /62	0.00	1.50
SC	Transamerica Prt Inst Small Value	DIVSX	B	(888) 233-4339	B- / 7.5	5.73	12.43	26.87 /79	6.14 /66	11.65 /71	0.74	1.76
IX	Transamerica Prt Inst Stock Index	DISFX	A+	(888) 233-4339	A- / 9.2	7.97	9.88	24.61 /72	10.31 /95	13.68 /91	1.81	0.42
FO	Transamerica Prt International Eq	DVIEX	D-	(888) 233-4339	E+ / 0.8	6.07	3.19	16.23 /35	-2.14 / 6	2.34 / 9	1.55	1.42
GI	Transamerica Prt Large Core	DVGIX	A-	(888) 233-4339	B / 8.2	7.19	10.90	22.39 /64	8.48 /83	13.16 /86	1.25	1.25
GR	Transamerica Prt Large Growth	DVEGX	C+	(888) 233-4339	B- / 7.3	8.49	7.39	19.84 /51	7.72 /77	11.97 /74	0.00	1.23
IN	Transamerica Prt Large Value	DVEIX	B+	(888) 233-4339	B / 7.9	7.11	13.38	24.88 /73	6.88 /71	12.54 /79	1.40	1.06
MC	Transamerica Prt Mid Growth	DVMGX	C+	(888) 233-4339	B / 8.0	6.85	12.58	29.22 /85	6.45 /68	10.54 /62	0.00	1.39
MC	Transamerica Prt Mid Value	DVMVX	A	(888) 233-4339	B+ / 8.6	5.91	8.78	23.53 /68	9.65 /91	14.15 /94	0.57	1.29
IN	Transamerica Prt Small Core	DVPEX	C+	(888) 233-4339	C+ / 6.7	3.79	12.48	29.64 /86	4.31 /46	10.00 /58	0.42	1.46
SC	Transamerica Prt Small Growth	DVSGX	B-	(888) 233-4339	B+ / 8.7	4.42	9.76	30.74 /88	8.54 /83	10.08 /59	0.00	1.56
SC	Transamerica Prt Small Value	DVSVX	B-	(888) 233-4339	B- / 7.1	5.51	12.11	26.18 /77	5.69 /61	11.18 /67	0.31	1.59
IX	Transamerica Prt Stock Index	DSKIX	A+	(888) 233-4339	A- / 9.0	7.88	9.69	24.17 /70	9.92 /93	13.30 /87	1.35	0.74
SC	Transamerica Sm Cap Value A	TSLAX	D	(888) 233-4339	C- / 4.2	5.81	12.25	26.37 /77	2.42 /27	--	0.66	1.58
SC	Transamerica Sm Cap Value C	TSLCX	D+	(888) 233-4339	C / 4.8	5.61	11.87	25.47 /75	1.71 /22	--	0.02	2.28
SC	Transamerica Sm Cap Value I	TSLIX	C-	(888) 233-4339	C+ / 5.6	5.90	12.42	26.63 /78	2.68 /29	--	0.82	1.31
SC	Transamerica Sm Cap Value I2		C-	(888) 233-4339	C+ / 5.7	5.93	12.43	26.76 /78	2.82 /30	--	0.94	1.18
SC	Transamerica Sm/Mid Cap Value A	IIVAX	B	(888) 233-4339	A- / 9.0	7.14	15.18	36.75 /96	8.15 /80	12.73 /81	0.71	1.31

| RISK | 3 Year | | NET ASSETS | | ASSET | | | | Portfolio | BULL / BEAR | | FUND MANAGER | | MINIMUMS | | LOADS | |
Risk Rating/Pts	Standard Deviation	Beta	NAV As of 2/28/17	Total $(Mil)	Cash %	Stocks %	Bonds %	Other %	Turnover Ratio	Last Bull Market Return	Last Bear Market Return	Manager Quality Pct	Manager Tenure (Years)	Initial Purch. $	Additional Purch. $	Front End Load	Back End Load
C /5.0	10.1	-0.25	8.14	169	44	0	55	1	0	12.8	-5.4	87	7	0	0	0.0	0.0
C+ /6.0	13.9	1.07	13.03	8	0	99	0	1	115	N/A	N/A	27	4	1,000	50	5.5	0.0
C+ /6.0	13.9	1.07	12.75	1	0	99	0	1	115	N/A	N/A	19	4	1,000	50	0.0	0.0
C+ /6.0	13.9	1.07	13.12	1	0	99	0	1	115	N/A	N/A	29	4	1,000,000	0	0.0	0.0
C+ /6.0	13.9	1.07	13.15	158	0	99	0	1	115	N/A	N/A	31	4	0	0	0.0	0.0
C /4.9	10.5	0.84	16.25	278	0	0	0	100	23	144.9	-17.6	83	12	0	0	0.0	0.0
U /	N/A	N/A	11.99	111	6	93	0	1	95	N/A	N/A	N/A	3	1,000	50	5.5	0.0
U /	N/A	N/A	12.04	400	6	93	0	1	95	N/A	N/A	N/A	3	1,000,000	0	0.0	0.0
U /	N/A	N/A	12.06	351	6	93	0	1	95	N/A	N/A	N/A	3	0	0	0.0	0.0
D- /1.4	20.5	0.84	8.16	41	42	51	6	1	79	N/A	N/A	60	4	1,000	50	5.5	0.0
D- /1.4	20.5	0.84	8.12	31	42	51	6	1	79	N/A	N/A	50	4	1,000	50	0.0	0.0
D- /1.4	20.5	0.84	8.16	48	42	51	6	1	79	N/A	N/A	64	4	1,000,000	0	0.0	0.0
D- /1.4	20.5	0.84	8.17	293	42	51	6	1	79	N/A	N/A	64	4	1,000,000	0	0.0	0.0
D /1.8	15.2	0.98	6.51	49	4	95	0	1	101	36.7	-22.2	0	N/A	1,000	50	5.5	0.0
D- /1.3	15.3	0.99	5.05	1	4	95	0	1	101	31.1	-22.5	0	N/A	1,000	50	0.0	0.0
D- /1.3	15.3	0.98	5.12	8	4	95	0	1	101	31.5	-22.4	0	N/A	1,000	50	0.0	0.0
D /1.9	15.2	0.98	7.19	58	4	95	0	1	101	40.0	-21.9	0	N/A	1,000,000	0	0.0	0.0
D /1.9	15.2	0.98	7.30	173	4	95	0	1	101	41.3	-22.0	0	N/A	0	0	0.0	0.0
B- /7.9	6.4	1.03	26.40	516	0	57	42	1	35	73.6	-9.1	62	6	1,000	50	5.5	0.0
B- /7.9	6.4	1.02	26.21	3	0	57	42	1	35	65.4	-9.4	50	6	1,000	50	0.0	0.0
B- /7.9	6.4	1.02	25.93	217	0	57	42	1	35	67.6	-9.3	53	6	1,000	0	0.0	0.0
B- /7.9	6.4	1.02	26.53	221	0	57	42	1	35	76.9	-8.9	66	6	1,000,000	0	0.0	0.0
B /8.5	3.6	0.44	9.66	52	42	18	35	5	42	15.5	-8.3	36	N/A	1,000	50	5.5	0.0
B /8.5	3.6	0.45	9.61	62	42	18	35	5	42	11.0	-8.6	27	N/A	1,000	50	0.0	0.0
B /8.4	3.6	0.44	9.63	86	42	18	35	5	42	17.5	-8.1	40	8	1,000,000	0	0.0	0.0
B /8.4	6.2	1.00	21.06	93	0	57	42	1	50	75.8	-9.3	65	7	5,000	0	0.0	0.0
B /8.5	6.3	1.00	13.88	6	0	57	42	1	50	79.5	-9.2	70	7	5,000	0	0.0	0.0
C+ /5.6	12.4	0.98	6.71	42	1	98	0	1	23	33.8	-25.7	52	4	5,000	0	0.0	0.0
C+ /6.8	11.7	1.09	8.14	11	1	98	0	1	64	131.3	-16.2	40	13	5,000	0	0.0	0.0
C+ /6.0	12.4	1.09	13.35	87	3	96	0	1	33	120.6	-16.9	32	10	5,000	0	0.0	0.0
C+ /6.6	12.1	1.09	15.91	99	1	98	0	1	65	123.9	-18.2	23	8	5,000	0	0.0	0.0
D+ /2.7	14.0	1.08	11.36	18	0	99	0	1	70	101.4	-22.5	32	4	5,000	0	0.0	0.0
C- /4.2	9.7	0.78	18.91	480	4	95	0	1	37	139.8	-20.4	88	8	5,000	0	0.0	0.0
C+ /5.8	14.7	1.11	16.83	14	1	98	0	1	132	103.7	-22.9	6	4	5,000	0	0.0	0.0
C- /4.2	15.1	0.67	19.21	11	3	96	0	1	53	106.5	-25.5	99	5	5,000	0	0.0	0.0
C+ /6.1	13.9	0.85	24.33	7	2	97	0	1	133	118.9	-21.3	76	2	5,000	0	0.0	0.0
B- /7.1	10.3	1.00	15.84	577	1	96	1	2	3	131.2	-16.4	71	9	5,000	0	0.0	0.0
C+ /5.6	12.5	0.99	10.54	141	1	98	0	1	23	32.1	-25.8	49	4	5,000	0	0.0	0.0
C+ /6.7	11.7	1.10	35.46	82	1	98	0	1	64	127.9	-16.3	35	13	5,000	0	0.0	0.0
C /4.6	12.4	1.09	29.20	247	3	96	0	1	33	116.6	-17.0	28	10	5,000	0	0.0	0.0
C+ /6.6	12.1	1.09	29.75	236	1	98	0	1	65	121.0	-18.3	20	8	5,000	0	0.0	0.0
C /4.4	13.9	1.07	10.06	53	0	99	0	1	70	96.9	-22.6	27	4	5,000	0	0.0	0.0
C+ /6.8	9.7	0.77	22.66	136	4	95	0	1	37	135.4	-20.6	86	8	5,000	0	0.0	0.0
C+ /5.8	14.6	1.11	31.76	69	1	98	0	1	132	99.5	-23.0	5	4	5,000	0	0.0	0.0
C- /4.0	15.1	0.89	17.50	42	3	96	0	1	53	102.0	-25.7	87	5	5,000	0	0.0	0.0
C /5.5	13.9	0.85	17.84	36	2	97	0	1	133	114.1	-21.5	72	2	5,000	0	0.0	0.0
B- /7.1	10.3	1.00	18.41	287	1	96	1	2	3	127.0	-16.6	67	9	5,000	0	0.0	0.0
C- /3.8	14.2	0.86	11.17	3	4	95	0	1	87	N/A	N/A	30	5	1,000	50	5.5	0.0
C- /3.9	14.2	0.86	11.14	1	4	95	0	1	87	N/A	N/A	23	5	1,000	50	0.0	0.0
C- /3.8	14.2	0.86	11.23	1	4	95	0	1	87	N/A	N/A	33	5	1,000,000	0	0.0	0.0
C- /3.8	14.2	0.86	11.24	267	4	95	0	1	87	N/A	N/A	35	5	0	0	0.0	0.0
C /4.5	13.9	0.85	28.02	393	1	98	0	1	74	130.9	-25.9	87	6	1,000	50	5.5	0.0

					PERFORMANCE						Incl. in Returns	
	99 Pct = Best					Total Return % through 2/28/17						
	0 Pct = Worst		Overall		Perfor-				Annualized		Dividend	Expense
Fund		Ticker	Investment		mance							
Type	Fund Name	Symbol	Rating	Phone	Rating/Pts	3 Mo	6 Mo	1Yr / Pct	3Yr / Pct	5Yr / Pct	Yield	Ratio
SC	● Transamerica Sm/Mid Cap Value B	IIVBX	B	(888) 233-4339	A / 9.3	6.88	14.69	35.69 /95	7.34 /74	11.92 /74	0.00	2.02
SC	Transamerica Sm/Mid Cap Value C	IIVLX	B	(888) 233-4339	A / 9.3	6.94	14.76	35.79 /95	7.41 /75	11.98 /74	0.27	1.98
SC	Transamerica Sm/Mid Cap Value I	TSVIX	B+	(888) 233-4339	A+ / 9.6	7.21	15.34	37.19 /96	8.52 /83	13.15 /85	1.05	0.95
SC	Transamerica Sm/Mid Cap Value I2	TSMVX	B+	(888) 233-4339	A+ / 9.7	7.26	15.42	37.37 /96	8.64 /84	13.27 /87	1.13	0.86
SC	Transamerica Small Cap Core A	SCCAX	C+	(888) 233-4339	C+ / 5.9	3.80	12.55	29.47 /85	4.83 /52	---	0.13	1.21
SC	Transamerica Small Cap Core C	SCCCX	C+	(888) 233-4339	C+ / 6.3	3.61	12.10	28.52 /83	3.99 /43	---	0.00	1.99
SC	Transamerica Small Cap Core I	ISMTX	B	(888) 233-4339	B- / 7.1	3.87	12.69	29.86 /86	5.04 /55	---	0.22	1.01
SC	Transamerica Small Cap Core I2		B	(888) 233-4339	B- / 7.1	3.87	12.59	29.73 /86	5.11 /55	---	0.22	0.90
SC	Transamerica Small Cap Growth A	ASGTX	D	(888) 233-4339	B / 7.6	4.36	9.45	30.11 /87	8.52 /83	---	0.00	1.30
SC	Transamerica Small Cap Growth C	CSGTX	D	(888) 233-4339	B / 8.1	4.28	9.09	29.20 /85	7.77 /77	---	0.00	2.02
SC	Transamerica Small Cap Growth I	ISCGX	D+	(888) 233-4339	B+ / 8.8	4.37	9.56	30.32 /87	8.82 /86	---	0.00	1.00
SC	Transamerica Small Cap Growth I2		D+	(888) 233-4339	B+ / 8.9	4.58	9.67	30.56 /87	8.98 /87	---	0.00	0.89
AA	Transamerica Strategic High Inc A	TASHX	U	(888) 233-4339	U /	5.16	5.11	15.98 /34	---	---	2.84	1.33
AA	Transamerica Strategic High Inc C	TCSHX	U	(888) 233-4339	U /	4.90	4.65	15.20 /31	---	---	2.42	2.03
AA	Transamerica Strategic High Inc I	TSHIX	U	(888) 233-4339	U /	5.05	5.07	16.19 /35	---	---	3.17	1.12
FS	Transamerica Unconstrained Bond I2		U	(888) 233-4339	U /	5.11	5.06	13.79 /25	---	---	3.10	0.94
GI	Transamerica US Growth A	TADAX	C	(888) 233-4339	C+ / 6.5	8.49	6.55	19.11 /48	8.21 /81	11.36 /69	0.06	1.19
GI	● Transamerica US Growth B	TADBX	C	(888) 233-4339	C+ / 6.7	8.23	6.02	18.00 /43	7.19 /73	10.39 /61	0.00	2.09
GI	Transamerica US Growth C	TADCX	C	(888) 233-4339	C+ / 6.8	8.28	6.14	18.19 /44	7.36 /75	10.49 /62	0.00	1.98
GI	Transamerica US Growth I	TDEIX	C+	(888) 233-4339	B / 7.6	8.57	6.72	19.53 /50	8.55 /83	11.79 /72	0.36	0.86
GI	Transamerica US Growth I2		C+	(888) 233-4339	B / 7.7	8.61	6.75	19.67 /50	8.70 /85	11.94 /74	0.48	0.73
GI	● Transamerica US Growth T	TWMTX	C+	(888) 233-4339	C+ / 6.2	8.60	6.73	19.57 /50	8.62 /84	11.83 /73	0.11	0.82
BA	Tributary Balanced Fund Inst	FOBAX	C	(800) 662-4203	C- / 3.8	5.90	4.36	12.02 /18	4.35 /47	7.68 /40	0.69	1.26
BA	Tributary Balanced Inst Plus	FOBPX	C	(800) 662-4203	C- / 3.9	5.94	4.45	12.25 /19	4.57 /50	7.90 /41	0.93	1.01
GR	Tributary Growth Opps Inst	FOGRX	C-	(800) 662-4203	C+ / 6.9	7.65	7.85	25.76 /75	5.77 /62	10.85 /65	0.00	1.27
GR	Tributary Growth Opps Inst Plus	FOGPX	C-	(800) 662-4203	B- / 7.1	7.73	7.93	25.93 /76	5.98 /64	11.10 /67	0.00	0.99
SC	Tributary Small Company Inst	FOSCX	A	(800) 662-4203	A+ / 9.7	4.78	12.52	34.18 /93	10.46 /96	13.12 /85	0.22	1.34
SC	Tributary Small Company Inst Plus	FOSBX	A	(800) 662-4203	A+ / 9.7	4.84	12.65	34.47 /93	10.69 /96	13.37 /88	0.33	1.07
MC	Turner Midcap Growth Inst	TMGEX	E-	(800) 224-6312	D- / 1.1	6.74	4.43	18.97 /47	-1.68 / 7	6.03 /29	0.00	1.33
MC	Turner Midcap Growth Inv	TMGFX	E-	(800) 224-6312	D- / 1.0	6.71	4.36	18.66 /46	-1.92 / 7	5.76 /27	0.00	1.58
MC	Turner Midcap Growth Retire	TMIIX	E-	(800) 224-6312	D- / 1.0	6.68	4.16	18.31 /44	-2.17 / 6	5.78 /27	0.00	1.83
SC	Turner Small Cap Growth Fund	TSCEX	E-	(800) 224-6312	D+ / 2.7	2.89	2.41	22.40 /64	1.09 /19	8.60 /47	0.10	1.83
GR	Turner Titan Long Short C	TSCCX	E-	(800) 224-6312	E- / 0.2	2.33	-3.11	-4.23 / 1	-3.14 / 4	-0.65 / 4	0.00	4.39
GR	Turner Titan Long Short Inst	TSPEX	E-	(800) 224-6312	E / 0.3	2.75	-2.60	-3.29 / 1	-2.12 / 6	0.37 / 5	0.00	3.39
GR	Turner Titan Long Short Investor	TSPCX	E-	(800) 224-6312	E- / 0.2	2.56	-2.67	-3.49 / 1	-2.40 / 6	0.09 / 5	0.00	3.64
EM	Tweedy Browne Glbl Val II Cr Uhngd	TBCUX	D	(800) 432-4789	E+ / 0.9	8.03	4.93	13.88 /25	-1.42 / 8	4.84 /20	1.47	1.40
* FO	Tweedy Browne Global Value	TBGVX	C-	(800) 432-4789	C- / 3.3	7.17	6.58	15.72 /33	2.75 /30	7.85 /41	1.10	1.38
GR	Tweedy Browne Value Fund	TWEBX	C	(800) 432-4789	C / 5.1	6.69	8.17	20.61 /55	3.70 /39	8.36 /45	0.85	1.38
GL	Tweedy Browne Wdwide Hi Div Yd	TBHDX	E+	(800) 432-4789	D- / 1.2	7.89	5.62	15.98 /34	-0.49 /11	4.76 /20	2.48	1.38
AA	Two Oaks Diversified Gro and Inc A	TWOAX	C+	(855) 896-6257	C / 5.2	3.84	5.78	22.42 /64	6.65 /69	7.52 /38	0.87	1.82
AA	Two Oaks Diversified Gro and Inc C	TWOCX	C+	(855) 896-6257	C+ / 5.8	3.63	5.39	21.56 /60	5.88 /63	---	0.50	2.57
GL	UBS Dynamic Alpha A	BNAAX	D	(888) 793-8637	E / 0.3	2.90	1.59	4.59 / 4	-1.61 / 8	2.06 / 8	0.00	1.46
GL	UBS Dynamic Alpha C	BNACX	D	(888) 793-8637	E / 0.4	2.59	1.19	3.84 / 3	-2.34 / 6	1.30 / 7	0.00	2.24
GL	UBS Dynamic Alpha P	BNAYX	D	(888) 793-8637	E+ / 0.6	2.84	1.72	4.83 / 4	-1.39 / 8	2.29 / 9	0.00	1.23
GL	UBS Global Allocation A	BNGLX	C-	(888) 793-8637	D / 1.9	5.03	3.38	11.94 /18	2.70 /29	4.58 /19	1.97	1.46
GL	UBS Global Allocation C	BNPCX	C-	(888) 793-8637	D / 2.2	4.82	2.93	11.05 /15	1.88 /23	3.77 /14	1.15	2.25
GL	UBS Global Allocation P	BPGLX	C-	(888) 793-8637	D+ / 2.9	5.13	3.52	12.22 /19	2.95 /31	4.86 /20	2.33	1.19
FO	UBS Internatl Sustainable Equity A	BNIEX	D	(888) 793-8637	D / 2.0	6.99	3.11	15.25 /31	1.85 /23	5.03 /21	1.83	2.37
FO	UBS Internatl Sustainable Equity C	BNICX	D	(888) 793-8637	D+ / 2.3	6.79	2.68	14.37 /27	1.08 /19	4.24 /16	1.17	3.15
FO	UBS Internatl Sustainable Equity P	BNUEX	D+	(888) 793-8637	C- / 3.0	7.01	3.14	15.53 /32	2.08 /25	5.27 /23	2.21	2.12
AA	UBS US Allocation A	PWTAX	B	(888) 793-8637	C / 5.0	6.18	6.18	17.81 /42	6.56 /69	9.19 /52	0.38	1.02
AA	UBS US Allocation C	KPAAX	B	(888) 793-8637	C / 5.5	5.98	5.78	16.92 /38	5.76 /62	8.37 /45	0.00	1.78

● Denotes fund is closed to new investors

* Denotes fund is included in Section II

www.thestreetratings.com

Risk Rating/Pts	3 Year Standard Deviation	Beta	NAV As of 2/28/17	Total $(Mil)	Cash %	Stocks %	Bonds %	Other %	Portfolio Turnover Ratio	Last Bull Market Return	Last Bear Market Return	Manager Quality Pct	Manager Tenure (Years)	Initial Purch. $	Additional Purch. $	Front End Load	Back End Load
C- /4.2	13.9	0.85	25.28	9	1	98	0	1	74	122.0	-26.1	83	6	1,000	50	0.0	0.0
C- /4.2	13.9	0.85	24.90	267	1	98	0	1	74	122.6	-26.0	83	6	1,000	50	0.0	0.0
C /4.5	13.9	0.85	28.84	188	1	98	0	1	74	135.6	-25.7	88	6	1,000,000	0	0.0	0.0
C /4.5	13.9	0.85	28.88	21	1	98	0	1	74	136.8	-25.7	89	6	0	0	0.0	0.0
C+ /6.2	14.4	0.87	11.61	3	1	98	0	1	142	N/A	N/A	60	4	1,000	50	5.5	0.0
C+ /6.2	14.4	0.87	11.49	1	1	98	0	1	142	N/A	N/A	49	4	1,000	50	0.0	0.0
C+ /6.2	14.4	0.88	11.65	2	1	98	0	1	142	N/A	N/A	63	4	1,000,000	0	0.0	0.0
C+ /6.2	14.4	0.87	11.65	41	1	98	0	1	142	N/A	N/A	64	4	0	0	0.0	0.0
E- /0.2	15.1	0.89	6.25	13	2	97	0	1	43	N/A	N/A	87	5	1,000	50	5.5	0.0
E- /0.2	15.0	0.89	5.80	3	2	97	0	1	43	N/A	N/A	84	5	1,000	50	0.0	0.0
E- /0.2	15.1	0.89	6.43	5	2	97	0	1	43	N/A	N/A	88	5	1,000,000	0	0.0	0.0
E- /0.2	15.1	0.89	6.51	58	2	97	0	1	43	N/A	N/A	89	5	0	0	0.0	0.0
U /	N/A	N/A	10.56	28	1	54	43	2	51	N/A	N/A	N/A	3	1,000	50	5.5	0.0
U /	N/A	N/A	10.51	52	1	54	43	2	51	N/A	N/A	N/A	3	1,000	50	0.0	0.0
U /	N/A	N/A	10.56	64	1	54	43	2	51	N/A	N/A	N/A	3	1,000,000	0	0.0	0.0
U /	N/A	N/A	10.12	224	0	0	0	100	141	N/A	N/A	N/A	3	0	0	0.0	0.0
C /4.4	11.7	1.06	18.08	464	1	98	0	1	34	113.0	-20.1	37	3	1,000	50	5.5	0.0
C /4.3	11.7	1.06	17.26	7	1	98	0	1	34	103.4	-20.3	26	3	1,000	50	0.0	0.0
C /4.3	11.7	1.06	17.30	47	1	98	0	1	34	104.4	-20.3	27	3	1,000	50	0.0	0.0
C /4.4	11.7	1.06	18.35	164	1	98	0	1	34	117.8	-20.0	41	3	1,000,000	0	0.0	0.0
C /4.4	11.7	1.06	18.31	267	1	98	0	1	34	119.4	-19.9	43	3	0	0	0.0	0.0
C+ /6.2	11.7	1.06	45.37	100	1	98	0	1	34	N/A	N/A	42	3	1,000	50	8.5	0.0
B- /7.0	7.7	1.13	16.89	51	0	64	35	1	42	66.0	-9.9	24	3	1,000	50	0.0	0.0
C+ /6.9	7.7	1.13	16.78	34	0	64	35	1	42	N/A	N/A	26	3	5,000,000	50	0.0	0.0
C- /3.0	12.6	1.12	16.43	18	0	97	1	2	57	112.9	-24.4	11	11	1,000	50	0.0	0.0
C- /3.0	12.6	1.12	16.68	110	0	97	1	2	57	N/A	N/A	12	11	5,000,000	50	0.0	0.0
C /5.4	14.2	0.87	28.36	202	1	94	4	1	32	132.3	-21.4	94	18	1,000	50	0.0	0.0
C /5.3	14.2	0.87	28.43	355	1	94	4	1	32	135.1	-21.3	94	18	5,000,000	50	0.0	0.0
E /0.4	14.8	1.04	19.32	14	0	98	0	2	165	61.6	-23.9	1	N/A	250,000	5,000	0.0	0.0
E /0.4	14.8	1.04	18.44	84	0	98	0	2	165	59.4	-24.0	1	N/A	2,500	50	0.0	0.0
E /0.4	14.8	1.04	16.28	N/A	0	98	0	2	165	57.4	-24.1	1	N/A	2,500	50	0.0	0.0
E- /0.1	20.1	1.07	12.90	29	0	98	1	1	372	93.7	-29.4	9	4	2,500	50	0.0	0.0
D+ /2.5	8.1	0.40	7.47	1	95	0	4	1	572	-1.9	-4.8	5	9	2,500	50	0.0	0.0
C- /3.1	8.1	0.40	8.23	14	95	0	4	1	572	3.7	-4.4	8	9	100,000	5,000	0.0	0.0
D+ /2.9	8.1	0.40	8.01	3	95	0	4	1	572	2.2	-4.5	7	9	2,500	50	0.0	0.0
C+ /6.7	9.1	0.43	13.67	333	29	70	0	1	14	42.3	-14.0	45	8	2,500	200	0.0	2.0
C+ /6.4	7.5	0.56	26.01	9,381	2	83	14	1	1	64.3	-14.2	89	24	2,500	200	0.0	2.0
C+ /5.6	8.9	0.78	21.60	576	1	82	16	1	7	72.8	-15.2	21	24	2,500	200	0.0	0.0
C- /4.2	10.2	0.78	9.25	293	0	92	7	1	5	41.2	-11.8	70	10	2,500	200	0.0	2.0
C+ /6.6	8.8	1.22	12.98	25	8	75	10	7	28	66.4	-10.5	43	12	2,500	1,000	5.8	0.0
C+ /6.6	8.8	1.22	12.84	2	8	75	10	7	28	N/A	N/A	33	12	2,500	1,000	0.0	0.0
B- /7.6	5.3	0.64	6.38	50	9	0	90	1	50	14.9	-2.1	18	8	1,000	100	5.5	0.0
B- /7.7	5.2	0.64	5.95	20	9	0	90	1	50	10.4	-2.5	13	8	1,000	100	0.0	0.0
B- /7.6	5.2	0.64	6.51	110	9	0	90	1	50	16.4	-2.1	20	8	5,000,000	0	0.0	0.0
B- /7.4	7.8	1.16	10.98	174	23	50	26	1	60	40.9	-16.0	40	8	1,000	100	5.5	0.0
B- /7.5	7.8	1.16	10.70	98	23	50	26	1	60	35.1	-16.3	30	8	1,000	100	0.0	0.0
B- /7.4	7.8	1.16	11.21	82	23	50	26	1	60	43.0	-15.9	43	8	5,000,000	0	0.0	0.0
C+ /6.0	11.7	0.88	8.63	6	1	98	0	1	114	55.9	-27.9	86	4	1,000	100	5.5	0.0
C+ /6.0	11.7	0.88	8.44	2	1	98	0	1	114	49.7	-28.1	82	4	1,000	100	0.0	0.0
C+ /6.0	11.7	0.88	8.65	17	1	98	0	1	114	57.9	-27.8	87	4	5,000,000	0	0.0	0.0
B /8.1	8.1	1.25	45.53	165	14	37	48	1	260	81.1	-12.2	39	8	1,000	100	5.5	0.0
B /8.0	8.1	1.25	43.95	62	14	37	48	1	260	73.9	-12.5	30	8	1,000	100	0.0	0.0

Fund Type	Fund Name	Ticker Symbol	Overall Investment Rating	Phone	Performance Rating/Pts	3 Mo	6 Mo	1Yr / Pct	3Yr / Pct	5Yr / Pct	Dividend Yield	Expense Ratio
AA	UBS US Allocation P	PWTYX	B	(888) 793-8637	C+ / 6.4	6.25	6.33	18.13 /43	6.85 /71	9.50 /55	0.65	0.76
GI	UBS US Large Cap Eq A	BNEQX	A-	(888) 793-8637	A / 9.3	9.33	12.56	31.98 /90	9.91 /93	13.11 /85	0.88	1.93
GI	UBS US Large Cap Eq C	BNQCX	A-	(888) 793-8637	A / 9.5	9.11	12.15	30.95 /88	9.09 /87	12.26 /77	0.23	2.68
GI	UBS US Large Cap Eq P	BPEQX	A	(888) 793-8637	A+ / 9.7	9.40	12.70	32.22 /90	10.18 /94	13.39 /88	1.15	1.64
SC	UBS US Small Cap Growth A	BNSCX	D	(888) 793-8637	C+ / 6.0	4.65	10.81	36.95 /96	3.48 /37	11.76 /72	0.00	1.54
SC	UBS US Small Cap Growth C	BNMCX	D	(888) 793-8637	C+ / 6.4	4.47	10.34	35.92 /95	2.71 /29	10.93 /65	0.00	2.29
SC	UBS US Small Cap Growth P	BISCX	D+	(888) 793-8637	B- / 7.2	4.74	10.95	37.29 /96	3.77 /40	12.07 /75	0.00	1.18
GR	● Undiscovered Mgrs Behavior Val A	UBVAX	A-	(800) 480-4111	B+ / 8.4	4.22	10.87	28.64 /83	10.04 /94	14.84 /97	0.58	1.98
GR	● Undiscovered Mgrs Behavior Val C	UBVCX	A	(800) 480-4111	B+ / 8.9	4.09	10.59	27.99 /82	9.49 /90	14.27 /95	0.22	2.43
GR	● Undiscovered Mgrs Behavior Val L	UBVLX	A+	(800) 480-4111	A / 9.4	4.33	11.08	29.13 /84	10.48 /96	15.26 /97	0.94	1.46
GR	● Undiscovered Mgrs Behavior Val R2	UBVRX	A	(800) 480-4111	A- / 9.1	4.15	10.74	28.33 /82	9.77 /92	14.56 /96	0.53	2.25
GR	● Undiscovered Mgrs Behavior Val R6	UBVFX	A+	(800) 480-4111	A / 9.5	4.35	11.14	29.28 /85	10.58 /96	15.35 /97	1.02	1.32
GR	● Undiscovered Mgrs Behavior Val Sel	UBVSX	A	(800) 480-4111	A / 9.4	4.28	11.01	28.94 /84	10.31 /95	14.62 /96	0.82	1.64
GR	Unified Srs Tr Auer Growth Fd	AUERX	E	(800) 408-4682	E- / 0.2	4.24	10.89	18.83 /46	-7.30 / 1	1.87 / 8	0.00	2.00
GR	Union Street Partners Value A	USPVX	B+	(800) 673-0550	B / 7.9	4.89	13.45	29.92 /86	8.31 /81	11.70 /72	0.42	1.99
GR	Union Street Partners Value C	USPCX	A-	(800) 673-0550	B+ / 8.6	4.68	13.03	28.94 /84	7.88 /78	11.11 /67	0.01	2.74
EM	Universal Inst Emer Markets Eqty I	UEMEX	D	(800) 869-6397	D+ / 2.8	8.23	1.14	23.32 /68	0.07 /14	0.42 / 5	0.46	1.31
EM	Universal Inst Emer Markets Eqty II	UEMBX	D	(800) 869-6397	D+ / 2.7	8.17	1.07	23.24 /67	0.02 /13	0.38 / 5	0.41	1.56
GL	Universal Inst Global Franchise II	UGIIX	C-	(800) 869-6397	B- / 7.0	10.58	5.68	16.07 /35	7.87 /78	9.83 /57	1.33	1.62
RE	Universal Inst Global Real Est II	UGETX	C-	(800) 869-6397	C- / 3.5	6.24	-2.28	11.87 /17	5.19 /56	7.07 /35	1.33	1.64
FO	Universal Inst Global Strategist I	UIMPX	D+	(800) 869-6397	D / 1.9	4.74	2.73	13.00 /22	0.72 /17	4.93 /21	0.00	1.50
MC	● Universal Inst Mid Cap Growth I	UMGPX	E-	(800) 869-6397	E / 0.5	5.75	0.31	17.30 /40	-3.84 / 3	4.75 /20	0.00	1.10
SC	● Universal Inst Small Co Growth II	USIIX	E-	(800) 869-6397	E / 0.3	1.67	-0.27	24.22 /71	-5.71 / 2	8.42 /46	0.00	2.42
RE	Universal Inst US Real Estate I	UUSRX	C+	(800) 869-6397	C+ / 6.8	6.78	-1.44	13.74 /24	10.13 /94	10.17 /60	1.27	1.07
RE	Universal Inst US Real Estate II	USRBX	C+	(800) 869-6397	C+ / 6.6	6.67	-1.58	13.45 /23	9.85 /93	9.88 /57	1.04	1.32
GR	Upright Growth Fund	UPUPX	D+		C+ / 5.8	8.57	0.11	13.87 /25	8.23 /81	12.57 /80	0.00	2.34
GR	US Global Inv All American Equity	GBTFX	E+	(800) 873-8637	D / 1.7	6.78	5.06	9.34 /10	0.10 /14	7.21 /36	0.15	1.94
GL	US Global Inv China Region Opport	USCOX	E+	(800) 873-8637	D / 1.6	2.86	5.00	24.09 /70	-0.70 /11	0.28 / 5	0.15	3.08
EN	US Global Inv Global Resources	PSPFX	E-	(800) 873-8637	E- / 0.0	6.80	3.39	24.11 /70	-14.75 / 0	-9.56 / 1	3.10	1.58
EN	US Global Inv Global Resources Inst	PIPFX	E-	(800) 873-8637	E- / 0.0	6.87	3.66	24.57 /72	-14.21 / 0	-9.02 / 1	3.86	1.35
PM	US Global Inv Gold & PMetals Fd	USERX	E+	(800) 873-8637	C / 4.6	12.42	-8.77	28.98 /84	3.17 /33	-9.81 / 1	0.76	2.20
GR	US Global Inv Holmes Macro Trends	MEGAX	E+	(800) 873-8637	D / 1.6	3.08	7.68	20.24 /53	-0.17 /13	6.57 /32	0.00	1.81
PM	US Global Inv World Prec Min	UNWPX	D-	(800) 873-8637	C+ / 6.4	9.02	-15.06	52.82 /99	2.89 /31	-11.93 / 0	0.30	2.01
PM	US Global Inv World Prec Min Inst	UNWIX	D	(800) 873-8637	C+ / 6.7	8.98	-14.84	53.61 /99	3.26 /34	-11.52 / 0	0.56	20.56
EM	US Global Investors Em Europe	EUROX	E-	(800) 873-8637	E- / 0.2	8.30	9.69	18.34 /44	-8.82 / 1	-7.73 / 1	0.00	2.61
GR	USA Mutuals Vice A	VICAX	D+	(866) 264-8783	C- / 3.5	3.27	5.30	15.32 /31	5.46 /59	11.64 /71	1.23	1.48
GR	USA Mutuals Vice C	VICCX	C-	(866) 264-8783	C- / 4.0	3.12	4.94	14.50 /28	4.67 /51	10.81 /64	0.29	2.23
GR	USA Mutuals Vice Investor	VICEX	C-	(866) 264-8783	C / 4.6	3.29	5.31	15.33 /31	5.47 /59	11.65 /71	1.31	1.48
AG	USAA Aggressive Growth Fund	USAUX	C+	(800) 382-8722	B- / 7.3	9.10	7.65	19.24 /48	7.70 /77	11.46 /70	0.79	0.85
AG	USAA Aggressive Growth Fund I	UIAGX	C+	(800) 382-8722	B- / 7.5	9.17	7.73	19.41 /49	7.91 /78	11.74 /72	0.87	0.70
GR	USAA Capital Growth	USCGX	A-	(800) 382-8722	B / 7.6	6.57	9.34	21.85 /61	7.91 /78	11.41 /69	1.40	1.24
GR	USAA Cornerstone Aggressive	UCAGX	C-	(800) 382-8722	C- / 3.4	5.67	4.86	16.36 /36	2.63 /29	---	1.42	1.52
AA	USAA Cornerstone Conservative	USCCX	C	(800) 382-8722	D+ / 2.4	3.07	1.32	10.68 /13	3.16 /33	---	3.11	0.76
GR	USAA Cornerstone Equity	UCEQX	C+	(800) 382-8722	C+ / 6.0	6.91	7.49	22.89 /66	4.74 /51	---	1.40	1.07
BA	USAA Cornerstone Moderate	USBSX	C-	(800) 382-8722	D+ / 2.4	4.50	2.59	12.04 /18	2.33 /26	4.84 /20	2.35	1.16
GL	USAA Cornerstone Moderately Aggr	USCRX	C-	(800) 382-8722	D+ / 2.6	4.81	3.13	13.24 /23	2.28 /26	4.90 /21	1.99	1.15
GI	USAA Cornerstone Moderately Consv	UCMCX	C-	(800) 382-8722	D / 2.1	3.86	1.40	10.31 /12	2.31 /26	---	2.32	1.18
EM	USAA Emerging Markets Adviser	UAEMX	D	(800) 382-8722	C- / 3.6	7.91	4.21	28.83 /84	0.35 /15	-1.92 / 3	0.72	1.92
EM	USAA Emerging Markets Fund	USEMX	D+	(800) 382-8722	C- / 4.0	7.96	4.27	29.02 /84	0.52 /16	-1.66 / 3	0.84	1.58
EM	USAA Emerging Markets Inst	UIEMX	D+	(800) 382-8722	C- / 4.1	7.99	4.36	29.27 /85	0.75 /17	-1.41 / 3	1.10	1.30
GR	USAA Extended Market Index	USMIX	B-	(800) 382-8722	B / 8.1	6.42	11.31	31.82 /90	6.42 /68	12.44 /78	0.94	0.48
GR	USAA First Start Growth Fund	UFSGX	C-	(800) 382-8722	C- / 4.0	5.34	4.59	14.61 /28	4.20 /45	7.37 /37	1.49	1.84

● Denotes fund is closed to new investors
* Denotes fund is included in Section II

632

Risk Rating/Pts	3 Year Standard Deviation	Beta	NAV As of 2/28/17	Total $(Mil)	Cash %	Stocks %	Bonds %	Other %	Portfolio Turnover Ratio	Last Bull Market Return	Last Bear Market Return	Manager Quality Pct	Manager Tenure (Years)	Initial Purch. $	Additional Purch. $	Front End Load	Back End Load
B /8.1	8.1	1.25	46.30	26	14	37	48	1	260	83.9	-12.1	43	8	5,000,000	0	0.0	0.0
C /5.4	13.1	1.17	30.15	12	0	97	2	1	57	131.2	-19.5	44	23	1,000	100	5.5	0.0
C /5.4	13.1	1.16	28.92	2	0	97	2	1	57	121.9	-19.7	34	23	1,000	100	0.0	0.0
C /5.4	13.1	1.16	30.25	17	0	97	2	1	57	134.2	-19.3	48	23	5,000,000	0	0.0	0.0
D- /1.5	19.5	1.15	20.56	29	0	98	0	2	109	125.4	-21.6	21	20	1,000	100	5.5	0.0
D- /1.0	19.5	1.15	17.37	4	0	98	0	2	109	116.4	-21.9	15	20	1,000	100	0.0	0.0
D /1.7	19.5	1.15	22.15	146	0	98	0	2	109	128.8	-21.5	24	20	5,000,000	0	0.0	0.0
C+ /6.1	12.4	1.00	64.80	1,230	3	89	7	1	44	178.7	-27.3	68	19	1,000	50	5.3	0.0
C+ /6.1	12.4	1.00	61.24	294	3	89	7	1	44	171.3	-27.5	62	19	1,000	50	0.0	0.0
C+ /6.1	12.4	1.00	66.30	2,795	3	89	7	1	44	184.1	-27.3	73	19	3,000,000	0	0.0	0.0
C+ /6.1	12.4	1.00	64.36	16	3	89	7	1	44	175.0	-27.5	65	19	0	0	0.0	0.0
C+ /6.1	12.4	1.00	66.39	414	3	89	7	1	44	185.2	-27.3	74	19	15,000,000	0	0.0	0.0
C+ /6.1	12.4	1.00	66.12	1,142	3	89	7	1	44	176.3	-27.3	71	19	1,000,000	0	0.0	0.0
C- /3.5	17.1	1.21	7.13	26	8	87	4	1	138	41.2	-33.7	0	30	2,000	100	0.0	0.0
C+ /6.4	13.2	1.10	16.68	6	4	93	1	2	20	112.8	-18.4	34	7	2,500	50	5.8	0.0
C+ /6.4	13.1	1.10	16.24	12	4	93	1	2	20	106.6	-18.6	29	7	2,500	50	0.0	0.0
C /4.9	14.2	0.84	14.21	192	0	97	2	1	38	20.3	-22.6	57	21	0	0	0.0	0.0
C /4.9	14.2	0.84	14.16	82	0	97	2	1	38	19.9	-22.7	56	21	0	0	0.0	0.0
C- /3.0	11.4	0.73	13.59	39	2	97	0	1	26	81.8	-6.8	98	8	0	0	0.0	0.0
C+ /6.5	12.2	0.84	10.72	86	7	91	0	2	26	72.4	-22.3	26	11	0	0	0.0	0.0
C+ /6.5	7.3	0.56	10.17	104	4	44	51	1	146	45.3	-15.3	79	7	0	0	0.0	0.0
D- /1.0	16.0	0.91	9.57	26	0	98	0	2	25	48.4	-21.6	1	14	0	0	0.0	0.0
E- /0.0	20.3	1.10	10.94	11	3	96	0	1	39	82.1	-23.8	1	14	0	0	0.0	0.0
C+ /5.8	14.0	1.01	21.89	253	2	95	1	2	26	96.8	-17.3	62	20	0	0	0.0	0.0
C+ /5.8	14.0	1.01	21.74	303	2	95	1	2	26	93.9	-17.3	59	20	0	0	0.0	0.0
C- /3.2	17.1	0.65	11.54	12	25	73	0	2	10	141.5	-20.7	83	18	2,000	100	0.0	2.0
C- /4.0	9.5	0.88	24.65	18	8	91	0	1	109	73.9	-18.3	3	28	5,000	100	0.0	0.0
C- /4.1	19.4	0.83	8.04	18	8	90	0	2	210	19.8	-29.0	67	18	5,000	100	0.0	0.0
D+ /2.4	19.6	0.68	5.63	101	7	88	3	2	445	-27.1	-31.8	1	28	5,000	100	0.0	0.0
D+ /2.4	19.6	0.68	5.63	2	7	88	3	2	445	-24.8	-31.6	1	28	1,000,000	0	0.0	0.0
E+ /0.7	40.9	2.26	8.15	114	10	85	4	1	106	-38.5	-18.0	98	28	5,000	100	0.0	0.0
C- /3.8	12.8	1.02	18.94	41	14	83	1	2	320	64.1	-21.9	2	18	5,000	100	0.0	0.0
E+ /0.7	40.4	2.10	7.05	155	5	90	3	2	71	-43.5	-28.5	98	28	5,000	100	0.0	0.0
E+ /0.7	40.5	2.11	7.08	3	5	90	3	2	71	-42.1	-28.3	98	28	1,000,000	0	0.0	0.0
D+ /2.6	16.2	0.75	6.00	44	0	0	0	100	137	-19.1	-32.7	2	20	5,000	100	0.0	0.0
C /5.4	10.4	0.79	27.76	17	0	100	0	0	58	N/A	N/A	38	6	2,000	100	5.8	0.0
C /5.4	10.5	0.80	27.32	17	0	100	0	0	58	N/A	N/A	29	6	2,000	100	0.0	0.0
C /5.4	10.5	0.80	27.88	194	0	100	0	0	58	115.1	-13.9	38	6	2,000	100	0.0	0.0
C /4.9	11.8	1.05	39.92	1,239	0	99	0	1	70	112.7	-18.7	32	7	3,000	50	0.0	0.0
C /4.9	11.8	1.05	40.31	5	0	99	0	1	70	115.6	-18.6	35	7	1,000,000	0	0.0	0.0
B- /7.4	10.2	0.95	10.81	779	0	99	0	1	24	105.7	-22.1	49	6	3,000	50	0.0	0.0
C+ /6.3	8.5	0.78	12.12	260	9	74	16	1	81	N/A	N/A	13	N/A	500	50	0.0	0.0
B /8.3	3.7	0.46	10.55	158	2	20	76	2	43	N/A	N/A	71	5	500	50	0.0	0.0
C+ /6.4	10.4	0.94	13.63	125	5	94	0	1	15	N/A	N/A	16	5	500	50	0.0	0.0
B- /7.5	5.9	0.88	14.64	1,088	4	42	53	1	70	41.5	-13.4	23	N/A	500	50	0.0	0.0
B- /7.2	6.8	1.04	25.23	2,334	4	49	45	2	87	40.6	-14.0	42	N/A	500	50	0.0	0.0
B- /7.6	5.0	0.40	11.04	200	5	42	52	1	70	N/A	N/A	51	N/A	500	50	0.0	0.0
C /4.5	16.0	0.96	16.29	5	2	97	0	1	47	11.1	-29.0	58	5	3,000	50	0.0	1.0
C /4.4	16.0	0.96	16.33	344	2	97	0	1	47	12.8	-28.9	61	5	3,000	50	0.0	0.0
C /4.4	16.0	0.96	16.28	568	2	97	0	1	47	14.4	-28.8	63	5	1,000,000	0	0.0	0.0
C /4.5	13.5	1.13	18.13	705	2	97	0	1	14	127.3	-23.6	13	7	3,000	50	0.0	0.0
C+ /6.3	7.5	0.70	12.89	407	6	69	24	1	101	64.0	-15.6	35	6	500	50	0.0	0.0

I. Index of Stock Mutual Funds

99 Pct = Best
0 Pct = Worst

Fund Type	Fund Name	Ticker Symbol	Overall Investment Rating	Phone	Performance Rating/Pts	3 Mo	6 Mo	1Yr / Pct	3Yr / Pct	5Yr / Pct	Dividend Yield	Expense Ratio
GL	USAA Global Managed Volatility	UGMVX	D-	(800) 382-8722	C- / 3.6	6.84	6.60	19.04 /47	1.91 /23	--	1.15	1.51
GL	USAA Global Managed Volatility Inst	UGOFX	D-	(800) 382-8722	C- / 3.8	6.90	6.67	19.09 /48	2.17 /25	4.31 /17	1.37	1.24
GI	USAA Growth & Income Fund	USGRX	B+	(800) 382-8722	A- / 9.2	7.02	13.06	28.32 /82	9.00 /87	12.58 /80	0.88	0.95
GL	USAA Growth & Income Fund	USGIX	B+	(800) 382-8722	A- / 9.0	6.92	12.89	27.92 /81	8.69 /85	12.25 /77	0.66	1.28
GI	USAA Growth & Income Fund Inst	UIGIX	U	(800) 382-8722	U /	6.99	13.07	28.40 /83	--	--	0.96	0.87
AA	USAA Growth & Tax Strategy Fund	USBLX	B	(800) 382-8722	C / 4.4	4.94	1.94	10.77 /14	6.38 /67	8.00 /42	2.24	0.87
GR	USAA Growth Fund	USAAX	A-	(800) 382-8722	B+ / 8.8	7.11	6.66	22.15 /63	10.54 /96	14.86 /97	0.19	1.11
GR	USAA Growth Fund Inst	UIGRX	A-	(800) 382-8722	B+ / 8.8	7.14	6.72	22.21 /63	10.61 /96	14.91 /97	0.28	1.01
IN	USAA Income Stock Fund	USISX	A-	(800) 382-8722	B / 7.9	6.70	7.94	21.89 /62	8.82 /86	12.03 /75	2.22	0.80
IN	USAA Income Stock Fund Inst	UIISX	A-	(800) 382-8722	B / 8.0	6.66	7.97	21.90 /62	8.89 /86	12.10 /75	2.27	0.75
FO	USAA International Fund	USIFX	D+	(800) 382-8722	D+ / 2.7	7.41	5.19	17.10 /39	0.75 /17	5.56 /25	1.48	1.13
FO	USAA International Fund Adv	UAIFX	D	(800) 382-8722	D+ / 2.4	7.33	5.07	16.83 /38	0.50 /16	5.25 /23	1.29	1.46
FO	USAA International Fund Inst	UIIFX	D+	(800) 382-8722	D+ / 2.8	7.46	5.28	17.28 /40	0.88 /18	5.72 /27	1.62	1.00
AA	USAA Managed Allocation Fund	UMAFX	D+	(800) 382-8722	D / 1.7	4.22	-0.55	10.52 /13	1.35 /20	2.49 / 9	2.18	0.98
GR	USAA Nasdaq 100 Index	USNQX	A+	(800) 382-8722	A+ / 9.8	10.97	12.12	27.85 /81	13.75 /99	16.02 /98	0.45	0.57
PM	USAA Precious Mtls&Minerals Fund	USAGX	E-	(800) 382-8722	E / 0.4	9.56	-10.20	22.34 /64	-4.54 / 3	-15.58 / 0	3.82	1.34
PM	USAA Precious Mtls&Minerals Inst	UIPMX	E-	(800) 382-8722	E / 0.4	9.71	-9.95	22.61 /65	-4.25 / 3	-15.36 / 0	3.77	1.00
IX	USAA S&P 500 Index Members	USSPX	A+	(800) 382-8722	A- / 9.2	7.96	9.88	24.67 /72	10.35 /95	13.72 /91	1.80	0.29
IX	USAA S&P 500 Index Reward	USPRX	A+	(800) 382-8722	A / 9.3	8.01	9.92	24.81 /73	10.47 /96	13.84 /92	1.88	0.19
TC	USAA Science & Tech Adv	USTCX	B+	(800) 382-8722	A+ / 9.6	10.41	9.30	25.65 /75	11.30 /97	17.49 /98	0.00	1.42
TC	USAA Science & Technology Fund	USSCX	B+	(800) 382-8722	A+ / 9.7	10.46	9.42	25.93 /76	11.54 /98	17.73 /99	0.00	1.17
SC	USAA Small Cap Stock Fund	USCAX	C	(800) 382-8722	C+ / 6.9	4.31	10.27	29.39 /85	5.25 /57	11.19 /68	0.19	1.16
SC	USAA Small Cap Stock Fund Inst	UISCX	C	(800) 382-8722	B- / 7.0	4.31	10.28	29.48 /85	5.40 /59	11.45 /69	0.32	1.00
GL	USAA Target Managed Allocation	UTMAX	U	(800) 382-8722	U /	3.95	3.95	14.29 /27	--	--	1.32	0.92
AA	USAA Target Retirement 2020 Fund	URTNX	C	(800) 382-8722	C- / 3.2	4.13	3.72	13.88 /25	3.43 /36	5.16 /23	2.98	0.75
AA	USAA Target Retirement 2030 Fund	URTRX	C+	(800) 382-8722	C / 4.3	5.24	5.16	17.48 /41	4.00 /43	6.31 /30	3.60	0.81
AA	USAA Target Retirement 2040 Fund	URFRX	C+	(800) 382-8722	C / 4.9	5.86	6.18	19.41 /49	4.24 /46	6.99 /35	3.61	0.85
GI	USAA Target Retirement 2050 Fund	URFFX	C+	(800) 382-8722	C / 5.1	6.05	6.54	19.89 /51	4.43 /48	7.23 /36	3.10	0.88
GI	USAA Target Retirement 2060	URSIX	C+	(800) 382-8722	C / 5.1	6.12	6.50	19.88 /51	4.41 /48	--	2.57	1.35
AA	USAA Target Retirement Income	URINX	C	(800) 382-8722	D / 2.2	2.95	2.04	9.98 /12	2.84 /30	4.04 /15	2.38	0.71
GI	USAA Total Return Strategy Fund	USTRX	D-	(800) 382-8722	E- / 0.2	3.34	-6.34	0.52 / 2	-2.73 / 5	-0.03 / 4	0.43	1.56
AA	USAA Total Return Strategy Inst	UTRIX	D-	(800) 382-8722	E / 0.3	3.58	-6.13	0.89 / 2	-2.39 / 6	--	0.69	1.28
GR	USAA Value Fund	UVALX	B+	(800) 382-8722	B / 8.0	5.38	11.66	27.14 /80	7.37 /75	12.18 /76	1.33	1.11
GL	USAA Value Fund Adv	UAVAX	B+	(800) 382-8722	B / 7.8	5.31	11.50	26.75 /78	7.11 /73	11.82 /73	1.06	1.42
GR	USAA Value Fund I	UIVAX	B+	(800) 382-8722	B / 8.1	5.40	11.69	27.32 /80	7.51 /76	12.31 /77	1.45	0.98
GR	USAA World Growth Adv	USWGX	C	(800) 382-8722	C / 4.8	8.05	4.86	18.70 /46	4.43 /48	10.15 /59	0.47	1.42
GL	USAA World Growth Fund	USAWX	C+	(800) 382-8722	C / 5.2	8.13	4.99	18.93 /47	4.65 /50	10.42 /61	0.70	1.17
GL	UTC North American Fund	UTCNX	D+	(800) 368-3322	C / 5.1	4.85	6.76	19.07 /47	5.44 /59	6.82 /34	0.00	2.32
FO	VALIC Co II Intl Opportunities	VISEX	C-	(800) 858-8850	D+ / 2.6	6.75	1.94	14.24 /27	2.00 /24	6.84 /34	1.01	1.21
FO	VALIC Company International Eq Idx	VCIEX	D-	(800) 858-8850	D- / 1.2	7.62	4.39	15.74 /33	-0.87 /10	4.30 /17	2.76	0.44
AA	Value Line Asset Allocation Inv	VLAAX	C+	(800) 243-2729	C / 4.7	5.00	3.82	14.08 /26	5.75 /62	8.90 /50	0.24	1.18
GL	Value Line Defensive Strat Inst	VLDIX	D+	(877) 925-7422	E+ / 0.6	2.98	2.41	1.20 / 2	-0.81 /10	0.15 / 5	0.96	3.30
GI	Value Line Income & Growth Inv	VALIX	C	(800) 243-2729	C+ / 5.9	8.22	4.94	17.86 /42	6.02 /64	8.72 /48	0.18	1.15
GR	Value Line Larger Companies Fc Inv	VALLX	C+	(800) 243-2729	B+ / 8.8	9.62	4.77	23.46 /68	10.01 /93	13.02 /84	0.00	1.23
GI	Value Line Mid Cap Focused Inv	VLIFX	A-	(800) 243-2729	B / 7.9	6.78	7.23	22.60 /65	8.75 /85	12.36 /78	0.00	1.24
GR	Value Line Premier Growth Inv	VALSX	C	(800) 243-2729	C+ / 6.4	6.68	6.09	20.03 /52	6.54 /69	10.51 /62	0.00	1.23
SC	Value Line Small Cap Opps Inv	VLEOX	B-	(800) 243-2729	B / 8.0	5.56	8.93	25.76 /75	8.11 /80	13.48 /89	0.00	1.25
IN	VanEck CM Commodity Index A	CMCAX	E	(800) 826-1115	E- / 0.1	3.77	11.54	22.49 /64	-11.69 / 1	-9.33 / 1	9.04	1.25
IN	VanEck CM Commodity Index I	COMIX	E	(800) 826-1115	E- / 0.1	3.69	11.75	22.80 /66	-11.45 / 1	-9.08 / 1	9.40	0.90
IN	VanEck CM Commodity Index Y	CMCYX	E	(800) 826-1115	E- / 0.1	3.51	11.57	22.63 /65	-11.52 / 1	-9.13 / 1	9.44	1.00
EM	VanEck Emerging Mkts A	GBFAX	E	(800) 826-1115	E / 0.5	5.72	-0.54	20.63 /56	-2.17 / 6	1.92 / 8	0.11	1.46
EM	VanEck Emerging Mkts C	EMRCX	E	(800) 826-1115	E+ / 0.7	5.53	-0.93	19.79 /51	-2.99 / 5	1.06 / 6	0.13	2.26

● Denotes fund is closed to new investors
* Denotes fund is included in Section II

www.thestreetratings.com

RISK			NET ASSETS		ASSET				Portfolio Turnover Ratio	BULL / BEAR		FUND MANAGER		MINIMUMS		LOADS	
Risk Rating/Pts	3 Year Standard Deviation	Beta	NAV As of 2/28/17	Total $(Mil)	Cash %	Stocks %	Bonds %	Other %		Last Bull Market Return	Last Bear Market Return	Manager Quality Pct	Manager Tenure (Years)	Initial Purch. $	Additional Purch. $	Front End Load	Back End Load
C- /3.7	9.5	1.44	9.48	14	1	98	0	1	16	N/A	N/A	18	N/A	3,000	50	0.0	0.0
C- /3.4	9.5	1.44	9.58	531	1	98	0	1	16	38.7	-12.6	20	N/A	1,000,000	0	0.0	0.0
C /5.0	11.7	1.09	23.18	1,544	4	95	0	1	22	123.1	-19.6	43	11	3,000	50	0.0	0.0
C /5.1	11.7	0.77	23.10	10	4	95	0	1	22	119.5	-19.7	99	11	3,000	50	0.0	0.0
U /	N/A	N/A	23.16	130	4	95	0	1	22	N/A	N/A	N/A	11	1,000,000	0	0.0	0.0
B /8.8	4.6	0.71	18.39	371	0	48	50	2	10	65.9	-4.0	81	12	3,000	50	0.0	0.0
C+ /6.0	11.6	1.07	26.06	1,233	0	98	0	2	18	142.8	-17.3	65	10	3,000	50	0.0	0.0
C+ /6.0	11.6	1.07	26.00	1,074	0	98	0	2	18	143.3	-17.2	66	10	1,000,000	0	0.0	0.0
C+ /6.8	9.6	0.89	19.30	1,640	4	94	0	2	19	112.8	-16.7	68	7	3,000	50	0.0	0.0
C+ /6.8	9.6	0.89	19.28	1,209	4	94	0	2	19	113.5	-16.5	69	7	1,000,000	0	0.0	0.0
C+ /5.8	11.5	0.92	28.10	1,517	1	98	0	1	62	55.6	-23.2	80	15	3,000	50	0.0	0.0
C+ /5.8	11.5	0.92	28.01	7	1	98	0	1	62	53.1	-23.3	79	15	3,000	50	0.0	1.0
C+ /5.7	11.5	0.92	28.02	2,131	1	98	0	1	62	56.9	-23.1	81	15	1,000,000	0	0.0	0.0
B- /7.6	7.7	1.03	11.26	740	2	24	73	1	90	24.6	-1.6	8	N/A	0	0	0.0	0.0
B- /7.3	13.7	1.19	15.14	1,188	0	0	0	100	10	158.5	-11.0	81	11	3,000	50	0.0	0.0
E- /0.1	45.6	2.50	13.33	613	1	96	1	2	17	-57.9	-12.0	75	N/A	3,000	50	0.0	0.0
E- /0.1	45.6	2.51	13.46	9	1	96	1	2	17	-57.3	-11.9	77	N/A	1,000,000	0	0.0	0.0
B- /7.0	10.3	1.00	33.68	3,079	0	98	0	2	4	131.6	-16.4	71	11	3,000	50	0.0	0.0
B- /7.0	10.3	1.00	33.70	3,085	0	98	0	2	4	132.9	-16.3	73	11	100,000	50	0.0	0.0
C /4.7	13.6	1.11	22.98	106	3	96	0	1	83	166.2	-16.4	69	15	3,000	50	0.0	0.0
C /4.8	13.6	1.11	23.41	971	3	96	0	1	83	169.4	-16.3	71	15	3,000	50	0.0	0.0
C- /4.1	15.2	0.94	17.92	662	27	71	0	2	52	115.7	-24.1	60	14	3,000	50	0.0	0.0
C- /4.1	15.2	0.94	18.05	903	27	71	0	2	52	118.5	-23.9	61	14	1,000,000	0	0.0	0.0
U /	N/A	N/A	10.43	462	2	57	39	2	84	N/A	N/A	N/A	N/A	0	0	0.0	0.0
B /8.1	5.6	0.85	12.66	581	2	47	50	1	30	42.6	-9.2	37	9	500	50	0.0	0.0
B- /7.6	7.4	1.13	13.39	1,140	2	65	31	2	32	55.6	-13.3	21	9	500	50	0.0	0.0
B- /7.2	8.5	1.30	13.37	1,246	3	76	20	1	35	65.0	-17.4	13	9	500	50	0.0	0.0
B- /7.1	8.9	0.83	13.35	693	3	79	17	1	39	69.5	-19.5	23	9	500	50	0.0	0.0
B- /7.2	9.0	0.83	11.58	60	4	81	14	1	35	N/A	N/A	23	N/A	500	50	0.0	0.0
B /8.6	4.0	0.59	11.66	319	1	30	67	2	35	31.7	-5.7	56	9	500	50	0.0	0.0
C+ /6.5	10.9	0.33	8.36	71	19	45	34	2	123	10.6	-11.1	8	N/A	3,000	50	0.0	0.0
C+ /6.5	10.9	0.73	8.39	14	19	45	34	2	123	N/A	N/A	4	N/A	1,000,000	0	0.0	0.0
C+ /6.1	11.1	1.00	21.03	911	4	95	0	1	20	121.0	-20.9	35	13	3,000	50	0.0	0.0
C+ /6.1	11.1	0.67	20.96	9	4	95	0	1	20	117.1	-21.1	98	13	3,000	50	0.0	0.0
C+ /6.0	11.1	1.00	21.01	582	4	95	0	1	20	122.5	-20.9	36	13	1,000,000	0	0.0	0.0
C+ /6.6	10.6	0.95	28.76	18	0	99	0	1	10	95.0	-19.9	13	15	3,000	50	0.0	1.0
C+ /6.5	10.6	0.80	28.82	1,224	0	99	0	1	10	97.6	-19.7	95	15	3,000	50	0.0	0.0
C- /3.9	9.2	0.57	9.79	43	2	80	17	1	114	56.8	-15.4	96	2	250	100	0.0	2.0
C+ /6.8	10.8	0.77	16.30	568	1	97	0	2	58	59.6	-24.2	87	5	0	0	0.0	0.0
C+ /5.7	11.6	0.94	6.42	1,026	4	90	4	2	4	43.4	-23.7	66	3	0	0	0.0	0.0
B- /7.8	6.9	1.03	30.01	302	6	69	24	1	19	79.6	-10.9	50	24	1,000	100	0.0	0.0
B /8.2	2.8	0.20	9.29	9	35	8	53	4	268	5.6	-4.1	51	6	10,000	100	0.0	0.0
C /4.7	9.6	0.86	9.11	331	2	77	19	2	45	71.3	-12.8	37	6	1,000	100	0.0	0.0
C- /3.7	13.2	1.09	25.34	233	1	98	0	1	37	123.7	-18.4	56	N/A	1,000	100	0.0	0.0
B- /7.0	9.3	0.79	17.32	141	1	96	2	1	17	112.0	-13.6	76	8	1,000	100	0.0	0.0
C- /4.2	10.0	0.91	30.99	325	0	99	0	1	12	102.4	-16.1	36	21	1,000	100	0.0	0.0
C /4.7	12.0	0.73	47.29	470	3	96	0	1	17	134.0	-16.6	90	19	1,000	100	0.0	0.0
C- /3.6	14.7	0.39	4.88	27	3	0	96	1	0	-32.6	-17.7	0	3	1,000	100	5.8	0.0
C- /3.6	14.9	0.39	4.98	152	3	0	96	1	0	-31.5	-17.5	0	3	1,000,000	0	0.0	0.0
C- /3.6	14.8	0.39	4.96	146	3	0	96	1	0	-31.8	-17.5	0	3	1,000	100	0.0	0.0
C /4.5	15.5	0.89	13.24	134	0	99	0	1	38	35.8	-29.7	26	19	1,000	100	5.8	0.0
C /4.4	15.5	0.90	11.95	24	0	99	0	1	38	29.9	-29.9	18	19	1,000	100	0.0	0.0

99 Pct = Best
0 Pct = Worst

Fund Type	Fund Name	Ticker Symbol	Overall Investment Rating	Phone	Performance Rating/Pts	3 Mo	6 Mo	1Yr / Pct	3Yr / Pct	5Yr / Pct	Dividend Yield	Expense Ratio
EM	VanEck Emerging Mkts I	EMRIX	E+	(800) 826-1115	D- / 1.1	5.97	-0.23	21.31 /59	-1.68 / 7	2.41 / 9	0.12	1.14
EM	VanEck Emerging Mkts Y	EMRYX	E+	(800) 826-1115	D- / 1.0	5.96	-0.24	21.22 /58	-1.77 / 7	2.24 / 9	0.12	1.23
EN	VanEck Global Hard Assets A	GHAAX	E-	(800) 826-1115	E- / 0.1	-5.77	5.50	40.75 /97	-9.80 / 1	-5.50 / 2	0.03	1.36
EN	VanEck Global Hard Assets C	GHACX	E-	(800) 826-1115	E- / 0.1	-5.95	5.08	39.68 /97	-10.51 / 1	-6.26 / 1	0.04	2.16
EN	VanEck Global Hard Assets I	GHAIX	E-	(800) 826-1115	E- / 0.2	-5.68	5.69	41.27 /98	-9.46 / 1	-5.14 / 2	0.03	1.04
EN	VanEck Global Hard Assets Y	GHAYX	E-	(800) 826-1115	E- / 0.2	-5.73	5.62	41.11 /98	-9.58 / 1	-5.27 / 2	0.03	1.15
PM	VanEck Intl Investors Gold A	INIVX	E-	(800) 826-1115	D- / 1.1	11.79	-9.21	34.35 /93	-1.57 / 8	-12.88 / 0	5.44	1.43
PM	VanEck Intl Investors Gold C	IIGCX	E-	(800) 826-1115	D- / 1.3	11.50	-9.54	33.18 /92	-2.34 / 6	-13.57 / 0	6.55	2.22
PM	VanEck Intl Investors Gold I	INIIX	E-	(800) 826-1115	D / 1.8	11.84	-8.98	34.81 /94	-1.14 / 9	-12.51 / 0	4.53	1.07
PM	VanEck Intl Investors Gold Y	INIYX	E-	(800) 826-1115	D / 1.7	11.81	-9.07	34.63 /94	-1.28 / 8	-12.64 / 0	5.67	1.21
GL	VanEck Long/Short Equity Index A	LSNAX	C-	(800) 826-1115	E+ / 0.9	2.69	2.22	5.86 / 5	1.00 /18	--	0.57	4.76
GL	VanEck Long/Short Equity Index I	LSNIX	C	(800) 826-1115	D- / 1.4	2.67	2.32	6.04 / 5	1.30 /20	--	0.60	2.25
GL	VanEck Long/Short Equity Index Y	LSNYX	C	(800) 826-1115	D- / 1.4	2.79	2.32	6.05 / 5	1.26 /20	--	0.60	5.17
IX	Vanguard 500 Index Adm	VFIAX	A+	(800) 662-7447	A / 9.4	8.03	10.00	24.94 /73	10.60 /96	13.97 /93	1.91	0.05
* IX	Vanguard 500 Index Inv	VFINX	A+	(800) 662-7447	A / 9.3	8.00	9.95	24.82 /73	10.48 /96	13.85 /92	1.82	0.16
GR	Vanguard 529 500 Index Portfolio		A+	(800) 662-7447	A / 9.3	8.00	9.94	24.74 /72	10.42 /95	13.76 /91	0.00	0.25
GR	Vanguard 529 Aggressive Growth		B+	(800) 662-7447	B- / 7.1	7.67	8.11	23.60 /69	6.44 /68	10.47 /62	0.00	0.25
BA	Vanguard 529 Conservative Gr Port		C+	(800) 662-7447	D / 2.1	2.78	0.19	6.61 / 5	3.58 /38	4.20 /16	0.00	0.25
GI	Vanguard 529 Growth Fund		B+	(800) 662-7447	C / 5.4	5.97	5.43	17.78 /42	5.62 /61	8.48 /46	0.00	0.25
GR	Vanguard 529 Growth Index Port		A	(800) 662-7447	B+ / 8.6	9.28	8.31	22.31 /64	9.35 /89	13.13 /85	0.00	0.31
MC	Vanguard 529 Mid Cap Index Port		A-	(800) 662-7447	B / 8.2	6.81	8.73	25.81 /76	8.38 /82	13.10 /85	0.00	0.31
GI	Vanguard 529 Moderate Growth Port		B	(800) 662-7447	C- / 3.6	4.38	2.75	12.09 /18	4.67 /51	6.41 /31	0.00	0.25
AG	Vanguard 529 ND Aggressive Gr Fd		C+	(800) 662-7447	C+ / 6.7	7.48	7.68	22.65 /65	5.91 /63	9.90 /58	0.00	0.85
AA	Vanguard 529 ND Conservative Gr		C+	(800) 662-7447	D / 1.9	2.42	-0.07	6.06 / 5	3.19 /34	3.74 /14	0.00	0.85
GR	Vanguard 529 ND Growth Fd		B	(800) 662-7447	C / 5.0	5.84	5.09	17.01 /38	5.14 /56	7.95 /42	0.00	0.85
AA	Vanguard 529 ND Moderate Growth		B-	(800) 662-7447	C- / 3.2	4.15	2.47	11.43 /16	4.26 /46	5.88 /28	0.00	0.85
AG	Vanguard 529 PA Agg Gr Port		B+	(800) 662-7447	B- / 7.2	7.59	8.51	24.03 /70	6.66 /70	10.52 /62	0.00	0.53
AA	Vanguard 529 PA Consrv Gr Port		C+	(800) 662-7447	D+ / 2.7	3.36	1.37	8.81 / 9	4.07 /44	5.03 /21	0.00	0.51
AA	Vanguard 529 PA Consrv Inc Port		C	(800) 662-7447	D- / 1.0	0.82	-1.10	1.65 / 2	1.58 /21	0.99 / 6	0.00	0.55
GR	Vanguard 529 PA Growth Port		B	(800) 662-7447	C+ / 5.9	6.28	6.22	19.16 /48	5.83 /63	8.77 /49	0.00	0.53
AA	Vanguard 529 PA Moderate Gr Port		B	(800) 662-7447	C / 4.6	4.98	4.17	14.61 /28	5.42 /59	7.45 /38	0.00	0.52
GR	Vanguard 529 PA Social Idx Port		A+	(800) 662-7447	A / 9.4	8.57	10.55	26.09 /76	10.28 /95	14.93 /97	0.00	0.64
FO	Vanguard 529 PA Ttl Stk Mkt Idx		A+	(800) 662-7447	A- / 9.0	7.62	10.07	25.89 /76	9.55 /91	13.44 /88	0.00	0.49
SC	Vanguard 529 Small Cap Index Port		B+	(800) 662-7447	B+ / 8.4	5.89	10.67	31.76 /90	7.18 /73	13.24 /86	0.00	0.31
FO	Vanguard 529 Ttl Intl St Index Port		D+	(800) 662-7447	D+ / 2.6	7.56	4.78	19.44 /49	0.05 /14	3.78 /14	0.00	0.55
OT	Vanguard 529 Ttl Stock Market Port		A+	(800) 662-7447	A- / 9.1	7.67	10.16	26.11 /77	9.72 /92	13.65 /90	0.00	0.25
GR	Vanguard 529 Value Index Port		A+	(800) 662-7447	A / 9.5	6.98	11.47	27.49 /80	10.68 /96	14.04 /93	0.00	0.31
GL	Vanguard Alternative Strategies Inv	VASFX	U	(800) 662-7447	U /	-2.58	-6.56	-5.60 / 0	--	--	0.00	0.71
GR	Vanguard AR Aggressive Gr Port		C+	(800) 662-7447	C+ / 6.8	7.61	7.89	23.14 /67	6.12 /65	10.04 /59	0.00	0.75
GI	Vanguard Balanced Index Adm	VBIAX	B	(800) 662-7447	C+ / 5.9	5.05	5.05	15.82 /34	7.05 /72	9.16 /52	2.01	0.08
GI	Vanguard Balanced Index Inst	VBAIX	B	(800) 662-7447	C+ / 5.9	5.05	5.06	15.84 /34	7.06 /72	9.17 /52	2.02	0.07
GI	Vanguard Balanced Index Inv	VBINX	B	(800) 662-7447	C+ / 5.7	5.02	5.00	15.65 /33	6.89 /71	9.01 /51	1.90	0.22
GR	● Vanguard Capital Opportunity Adm	VHCAX	A	(800) 662-7447	A+ / 9.7	9.79	13.91	30.16 /87	10.68 /96	17.86 /99	0.69	0.38
GR	● Vanguard Capital Opportunity Inv	VHCOX	A	(800) 662-7447	A+ / 9.7	9.78	13.86	30.07 /87	10.60 /96	17.78 /99	0.61	0.45
GR	Vanguard Capital Value Inv	VCVLX	D	(800) 662-7447	C / 5.3	4.95	11.41	31.43 /89	1.55 /21	10.69 /63	1.61	0.50
GI	Vanguard Cons Discn Idx Adm	VCDAX	B+	(800) 662-7447	B / 7.8	5.87	8.44	18.43 /45	9.32 /89	15.93 /98	1.51	0.09
GI	Vanguard Cons Stap Idx Adm	VCSAX	A+	(800) 662-7447	B / 8.2	9.27	2.65	12.06 /18	11.96 /98	13.84 /92	2.27	0.10
CV	Vanguard Convertible Sec Inv	VCVSX	D+	(800) 662-7447	D+ / 2.3	3.09	3.65	14.07 /26	1.82 /23	6.64 /32	1.29	0.38
FO	Vanguard Developed Markets Idx	VTMGX	D	(800) 662-7447	D+ / 2.3	7.29	4.62	17.27 /40	0.03 /13	5.61 /26	2.92	0.09
FO	Vanguard Developed Markets Idx Inst	VTMNX	D	(800) 662-7447	D+ / 2.4	7.37	4.70	17.36 /40	0.05 /14	5.64 /26	2.92	0.07
FO	Vanguard Developed Markets Idx Inv	VDVIX	D+	(800) 662-7447	D / 1.6	7.32	4.65	17.33 /40	-0.07 /13	--	2.82	0.20
FO	Vanguard Developed Markets Idx IP	VDIPX	C-	(800) 662-7447	D+ / 2.4	7.30	4.68	17.38 /40	0.06 /14	--	2.94	0.06

● Denotes fund is closed to new investors
* Denotes fund is included in Section II

636

Risk Rating/Pts	3 Year Standard Deviation	Beta	NAV As of 2/28/17	Total $(Mil)	Cash %	Stocks %	Bonds %	Other %	Portfolio Turnover Ratio	Last Bull Market Return	Last Bear Market Return	Manager Quality Pct	Manager Tenure (Years)	Initial Purch. $	Additional Purch. $	Front End Load	Back End Load
C /4.5	15.5	0.90	13.97	529	0	99	0	1	38	39.4	-29.5	32	19	1,000,000	0	0.0	0.0
C /4.5	15.4	0.89	13.45	505	0	99	0	1	38	38.0	-29.7	31	19	1,000	100	0.0	0.0
E+ /0.8	25.2	1.17	36.05	399	5	94	0	1	26	-7.4	-29.5	23	22	1,000	100	5.8	0.0
E+ /0.8	25.2	1.17	31.25	88	5	94	0	1	26	-11.4	-29.8	16	22	1,000	100	0.0	0.0
E+ /0.9	25.2	1.17	37.68	1,524	5	94	0	1	26	-5.5	-29.4	27	22	1,000,000	0	0.0	0.0
E+ /0.9	25.2	1.17	36.65	324	5	94	0	1	26	-6.2	-29.5	25	22	1,000	100	0.0	0.0
E- /0.0	46.7	2.51	9.57	315	1	98	0	1	45	-48.6	-16.5	91	19	1,000	100	5.8	0.0
E- /0.0	46.7	2.51	8.43	56	1	98	0	1	45	-50.7	-16.8	88	19	1,000	100	0.0	0.0
E- /0.0	46.6	2.51	12.18	198	1	98	0	1	45	-47.4	-16.4	92	19	1,000,000	0	0.0	0.0
E- /0.0	46.7	2.51	9.74	98	1	98	0	1	45	-47.8	-16.5	92	19	1,000	100	0.0	0.0
B+ /9.5	5.8	0.34	8.88	2	0	0	0	100	440	N/A	N/A	81	4	1,000	100	5.8	0.0
B+ /9.5	5.7	0.34	8.97	8	0	0	0	100	440	N/A	N/A	83	4	1,000,000	0	0.0	0.0
B+ /9.5	5.8	0.34	8.96	1	0	0	0	100	440	N/A	N/A	82	4	1,000	100	0.0	0.0
B- /7.1	10.3	1.00	218.83	195,224	0	99	0	1	3	134.4	-16.3	74	26	10,000	100	0.0	0.0
B- /7.1	10.3	1.00	218.80	28,029	0	99	0	1	3	132.9	-16.3	73	26	3,000	100	0.0	0.0
B- /7.6	10.3	1.00	33.08	637	0	99	0	1	0	132.0	-16.3	72	15	3,000	50	0.0	0.0
C+ /6.9	10.3	0.97	31.74	1,181	0	99	0	1	0	99.5	-19.8	28	15	3,000	50	0.0	0.0
B+ /9.7	3.5	0.44	21.46	1,134	0	25	74	1	0	30.9	-1.7	76	15	3,000	50	0.0	0.0
B /8.3	7.7	0.72	27.16	1,731	0	74	24	2	0	74.7	-13.9	50	15	3,000	50	0.0	0.0
C+ /6.7	11.5	1.07	34.27	181	0	99	0	1	0	128.9	-15.2	50	15	3,000	50	0.0	0.0
C+ /6.3	11.4	0.90	44.07	364	0	99	0	1	0	130.6	-21.4	71	N/A	3,000	50	0.0	0.0
B+ /9.4	5.3	0.47	24.29	1,807	0	50	49	1	0	52.0	-8.0	71	N/A	3,000	50	0.0	0.0
C+ /6.9	10.4	0.98	17.38	57	0	99	0	1	0	93.8	-19.3	22	11	25	25	0.0	0.0
B+ /9.7	3.4	0.45	15.22	79	0	25	74	1	0	27.7	-1.7	72	11	25	25	0.0	0.0
B /8.3	7.8	0.73	17.75	60	0	74	24	2	0	70.2	-13.7	43	11	25	25	0.0	0.0
B+ /9.4	5.4	0.83	16.57	109	0	49	49	2	0	48.0	-7.9	50	11	25	25	0.0	0.0
B- /7.0	10.4	0.99	17.86	276	0	99	0	1	0	101.4	-18.9	29	11	25	25	0.0	0.0
B+ /9.7	4.1	0.60	16.31	258	0	35	64	1	0	40.5	-4.7	70	11	25	25	0.0	0.0
B+ /9.8	2.4	0.07	13.52	64	25	0	74	1	0	7.0	3.8	81	11	25	25	0.0	0.0
B /8.1	8.3	0.78	17.60	361	0	79	19	2	0	79.8	-14.3	45	11	25	25	0.0	0.0
B+ /9.1	6.3	0.99	17.49	413	0	60	39	1	0	63.0	-9.6	50	11	25	25	0.0	0.0
B- /7.1	11.0	1.05	18.75	20	0	100	0	0	0	140.1	-15.8	64	11	25	25	0.0	0.0
B- /7.2	10.6	0.70	20.76	94	0	99	0	1	0	130.4	-17.8	99	11	25	25	0.0	0.0
C+ /5.6	13.6	0.85	46.05	373	0	99	0	1	0	136.3	-24.6	82	15	3,000	50	0.0	0.0
C+ /6.3	11.6	0.91	27.16	497	1	98	0	1	0	41.3	-24.5	75	15	3,000	50	0.0	0.0
B- /7.2	10.6	1.02	35.36	650	0	99	0	1	0	132.6	-17.8	61	15	3,000	50	0.0	0.0
B- /7.9	10.1	0.95	34.78	211	0	99	0	1	0	133.0	-18.5	78	N/A	3,000	50	0.0	0.0
U /	N/A	N/A	20.38	253	53	45	1	1	120	N/A	N/A	N/A	2	250,000	1	0.0	0.0
C+ /6.9	10.4	0.98	20.65	55	0	99	0	1	0	95.0	-19.9	24	8	25	10	0.0	0.0
B /8.4	6.3	0.60	32.29	19,952	0	59	40	1	61	77.0	-9.0	79	2	10,000	100	0.0	0.0
B /8.4	6.3	0.60	32.29	8,956	0	59	40	1	61	77.1	-9.0	79	2	5,000,000	100	0.0	0.0
B /8.4	6.3	0.60	32.28	3,512	0	59	40	1	61	75.6	-9.0	78	2	3,000	100	0.0	0.0
C+ /5.7	13.3	1.10	133.86	12,898	3	96	0	1	6	172.6	-21.7	62	19	50,000	100	0.0	0.0
C+ /5.7	13.3	1.10	57.99	2,189	3	96	0	1	6	171.6	-21.8	61	19	3,000	100	0.0	0.0
D+ /2.7	15.5	1.31	12.45	961	0	99	0	1	134	113.6	-29.7	1	8	3,000	100	0.0	0.0
C+ /6.6	12.1	1.06	70.32	186	0	98	0	2	7	164.0	-15.2	52	7	100,000	0	0.0	0.0
B- /7.6	9.7	0.62	69.91	723	0	99	0	1	6	115.0	-4.3	95	7	100,000	0	0.0	0.0
C+ /6.1	7.0	0.76	13.00	1,455	0	3	3	94	95	57.6	-16.7	50	7	3,000	100	0.0	0.0
C+ /6.0	11.4	0.92	12.29	10,528	3	96	0	1	3	52.0	-23.3	75	4	10,000	1	0.0	0.0
C+ /6.0	11.4	0.92	12.31	9,661	3	96	0	1	3	52.3	-23.3	75	4	5,000,000	1	0.0	0.0
B- /7.0	11.4	0.92	9.52	918	3	96	0	1	3	N/A	N/A	75	4	3,000	1	0.0	0.0
B- /7.0	11.4	0.92	19.24	8,151	3	96	0	1	3	N/A	N/A	75	4	100,000,000	1	0.0	0.0

I. Index of Stock Mutual Funds

Fund Type	Fund Name	Ticker Symbol	Overall Investment Rating	Phone	Performance Rating/Pts	3 Mo	6 Mo	1Yr / Pct	3Yr / Pct	5Yr / Pct	Dividend Yield	Expense Ratio
	99 Pct = Best							Total Return % through 2/28/17			Incl. in Returns	
	0 Pct = Worst								Annualized			
AA	Vanguard Diversified Equity Inv	VDEQX	B	(800) 662-7447	B / 7.9	7.03	9.14	24.30 /71	7.89 /78	12.86 /82	1.23	0.36
IN	Vanguard Dividend Apprec Idx Adm	VDADX	A	(800) 662-7447	B / 7.8	7.41	7.40	20.24 /53	8.80 /85	--	2.02	0.09
GR	Vanguard Dividend Apprec Idx Inv	VDAIX	A	(800) 662-7447	B / 7.7	7.38	7.36	20.14 /53	8.71 /85	11.76 /72	1.93	0.19
* GI	● Vanguard Dividend Growth Inv	VDIGX	A-	(800) 662-7447	B- / 7.4	7.19	5.71	16.84 /38	9.22 /88	12.50 /79	1.80	0.33
EM	Vanguard Emg Mkts Sel Stk Idx Inv	VMMSX	C-	(800) 662-7447	C+ / 6.2	9.18	8.63	35.83 /95	1.63 /22	1.10 / 6	1.32	0.93
EM	Vanguard Emg Mkts Stk Idx Admiral	VEMAX	C-	(800) 662-7447	C / 5.4	8.23	5.55	29.96 /86	2.44 /27	-0.15 / 4	2.31	0.15
EM	Vanguard Emg Mkts Stk Idx Inst	VEMIX	C-	(800) 662-7447	C / 5.5	8.25	5.59	30.01 /86	2.48 /27	-0.12 / 4	2.35	0.12
EM	Vanguard Emg Mkts Stk Idx Inst Plus	VEMRX	C-	(800) 662-7447	C / 5.5	8.26	5.60	30.07 /87	2.50 /28	-0.10 / 4	2.36	0.10
EM	Vanguard Emg Mkts Stk Idx Investor	VEIEX	C-	(800) 662-7447	C / 5.3	8.20	5.46	29.75 /86	2.27 /26	-0.33 / 4	2.15	0.33
EN	Vanguard Energy Adm	VGELX	E-	(800) 662-7447	E+ / 0.6	-2.50	3.98	33.21 /92	-5.04 / 2	-0.95 / 3	1.99	0.31
EN	Vanguard Energy Index Adm	VENAX	E-	(800) 662-7447	E / 0.4	-4.25	4.70	28.98 /84	-5.37 / 2	0.20 / 5	2.46	0.10
EN	Vanguard Energy Inv	VGENX	E-	(800) 662-7447	E+ / 0.6	-2.52	3.94	33.11 /92	-5.10 / 2	-1.01 / 3	1.92	0.37
IN	Vanguard Equity Income Adm	VEIRX	A+	(800) 662-7447	A- / 9.1	7.33	9.08	23.58 /68	10.48 /96	13.58 /90	2.69	0.17
* IN	Vanguard Equity Income Inv	VEIPX	A+	(800) 662-7447	A- / 9.0	7.33	9.03	23.50 /68	10.38 /95	13.47 /89	2.60	0.26
FO	Vanguard European Stk Idx Inst	VESIX	E+	(800) 662-7447	E+ / 0.6	8.51	3.09	12.55 /20	-2.79 / 5	5.13 /22	3.41	0.09
FO	Vanguard European Stk Idx Inst Adm	VEUSX	E+	(800) 662-7447	E+ / 0.6	8.53	3.09	12.53 /20	-2.82 / 5	5.10 /22	3.40	0.12
FO	Vanguard European Stk Idx Inst Plus	VEUPX	U	(800) 662-7447	U /	8.54	3.10	12.56 /20	--	--	3.42	0.08
FO	Vanguard European Stk Idx Investor	VEURX	E+	(800) 662-7447	E+ / 0.6	8.49	2.98	12.32 /19	-2.97 / 5	4.94 /21	3.24	0.26
SC	Vanguard Explorer Fund Adm	VEXRX	C-	(800) 662-7447	B- / 7.1	6.48	9.38	29.81 /86	5.07 /55	11.95 /74	0.46	0.35
SC	Vanguard Explorer Fund Inv	VEXPX	C-	(800) 662-7447	B- / 7.0	6.44	9.33	29.64 /86	4.93 /53	11.79 /72	0.34	0.49
GR	Vanguard Explorer Value Inv	VEVFX	B	(800) 662-7447	B / 8.0	3.77	10.31	29.91 /86	7.28 /74	13.22 /86	0.89	0.63
IN	Vanguard Extended Market Index	VEXAX	B+	(800) 662-7447	B+ / 8.5	6.54	11.49	32.65 /91	6.91 /71	13.12 /85	1.37	0.09
IN	Vanguard Extended Market Index Inst	VIEIX	B+	(800) 662-7447	B+ / 8.5	6.54	11.52	32.68 /91	6.93 /71	13.14 /85	1.38	0.07
IN	Vanguard Extended Market Index Inv	VEXMX	B	(800) 662-7447	B+ / 8.4	6.51	11.43	32.49 /91	6.77 /70	12.97 /83	1.25	0.22
MC	Vanguard Extended Mkt Id Inst Plus	VEMPX	B+	(800) 662-7447	B+ / 8.6	6.55	11.52	32.69 /91	6.95 /72	13.16 /86	1.39	0.05
FS	Vanguard Financial Index Fd Adm	VFAIX	A+	(800) 662-7447	A+ / 9.9	9.38	23.85	46.85 /99	14.09 /99	17.33 /98	1.56	0.10
FO	Vanguard FTSE All-Wld ex-US S/C	VFSVX	D+	(800) 662-7447	D+ / 2.6	7.72	4.39	18.55 /45	0.22 /14	4.93 /21	2.62	0.31
FO	Vanguard FTSE All-World ex-US	VFWAX	D+	(800) 662-7447	D+ / 2.8	7.58	4.93	19.83 /51	0.34 /15	3.97 /15	2.81	0.13
FO	Vanguard FTSE All-World ex-US InsP	VFWPX	D+	(800) 662-7447	D+ / 2.8	7.58	4.94	19.87 /51	0.37 /15	4.01 /15	2.85	0.09
FO	Vanguard FTSE All-World ex-US Inst	VFWSX	D+	(800) 662-7447	D+ / 2.8	7.56	4.92	19.83 /51	0.35 /15	3.99 /15	2.82	0.11
FO	Vanguard FTSE All-World ex-US Inv	VFWIX	D+	(800) 662-7447	D+ / 2.7	7.54	4.84	19.68 /50	0.20 /14	3.83 /14	2.70	0.26
FO	Vanguard FTSE All-World ex-US S/C	VFSNX	D+	(800) 662-7447	D+ / 2.6	7.75	4.47	18.71 /46	0.39 /15	5.12 /22	2.74	0.15
GR	Vanguard FTSE Social Index Inst	VFTNX	A+	(800) 662-7447	A / 9.5	8.65	10.69	26.50 /78	10.66 /96	15.35 /97	1.71	0.15
GR	Vanguard FTSE Social Index Inv	VFTSX	A+	(800) 662-7447	A / 9.5	8.56	10.57	26.32 /77	10.54 /96	15.23 /97	1.62	0.25
GL	Vanguard Global Equity Inv	VHGEX	C+	(800) 662-7447	C+ / 5.9	7.18	7.40	21.41 /59	4.93 /53	9.77 /57	1.43	0.57
RE	Vanguard Global ex-US RE Admiral	VGRLX	D+	(800) 662-7447	D+ / 2.5	5.70	-2.29	12.30 /19	3.24 /34	6.37 /31	4.88	0.24
RE	Vanguard Global ex-US RE Inst	VGRNX	D+	(800) 662-7447	D+ / 2.5	5.70	-2.27	12.32 /19	3.27 /34	6.40 /31	4.91	0.22
RE	Vanguard Global ex-US RE Investor	VGXRX	D+	(800) 662-7447	D+ / 2.4	5.64	-2.35	12.06 /18	3.06 /32	6.21 /30	4.67	0.37
GL	Vanguard Global Minimum Vol Adm	VMNVX	A	(800) 662-7447	B- / 7.4	5.62	4.54	14.85 /29	10.12 /94	--	2.71	0.21
GL	Vanguard Global Minimum Vol Inv	VMVFX	A	(800) 662-7447	B- / 7.3	5.60	4.56	14.73 /29	10.05 /94	--	2.61	0.27
GI	Vanguard Growth & Income Adm	VGIAX	A	(800) 662-7447	A / 9.3	7.09	9.65	24.30 /71	10.84 /97	14.32 /95	1.99	0.23
GI	Vanguard Growth & Income Inv	VQNPX	A	(800) 662-7447	A- / 9.2	7.04	9.58	24.12 /70	10.71 /96	14.19 /94	1.88	0.34
GR	Vanguard Growth Index Adm	VIGAX	A	(800) 662-7447	B+ / 8.8	9.34	8.42	22.56 /65	9.58 /91	13.37 /88	1.28	0.08
GR	Vanguard Growth Index Inst	VIGIX	A	(800) 662-7447	B+ / 8.8	9.36	8.44	22.59 /65	9.59 /91	13.39 /88	1.29	0.07
GR	Vanguard Growth Index Inv	VIGRX	A	(800) 662-7447	B+ / 8.7	9.31	8.37	22.41 /64	9.44 /90	13.21 /86	1.17	0.22
HL	Vanguard Health Care Adm	VGHAX	C+	(800) 662-7447	B- / 7.3	10.54	4.33	12.39 /19	9.39 /90	18.16 /99	0.90	0.31
* HL	Vanguard Health Care Inv	VGHCX	C+	(800) 662-7447	B- / 7.2	10.53	4.31	12.33 /19	9.34 /89	18.10 /99	0.85	0.36
HL	Vanguard HealthCare Index Adm	VHCIX	B+	(800) 662-7447	B / 7.9	9.91	4.79	17.25 /39	9.61 /91	17.92 /99	1.33	0.10
* IN	Vanguard High Div Yield Index Inv	VHDYX	A+	(800) 662-7447	A / 9.4	6.66	9.21	23.89 /69	11.43 /98	13.95 /93	2.75	0.16
OT	Vanguard Industrials Index Adm	VINAX	A+	(800) 662-7447	A / 9.5	5.63	13.19	29.81 /86	9.76 /92	14.72 /96	1.73	0.10
TC	Vanguard Info Tech Ind Adm	VITAX	A+	(800) 662-7447	A+ / 9.9	10.99	13.68	33.51 /92	14.64 /99	14.84 /97	1.20	0.10
GI	Vanguard Inst Tgt Ret 2010 Inst	VIRTX	U	(800) 662-7447	U /	3.01	1.47	8.55 / 8	--	--	1.73	0.09

● Denotes fund is closed to new investors
* Denotes fund is included in Section II

RISK	3 Year		NET ASSETS		ASSET					BULL / BEAR		FUND MANAGER		MINIMUMS		LOADS	
Risk Rating/Pts	Standard Deviation	Beta	NAV As of 2/28/17	Total $(Mil)	Cash %	Stocks %	Bonds %	Other %	Portfolio Turnover Ratio	Last Bull Market Return	Last Bear Market Return	Manager Quality Pct	Manager Tenure (Years)	Initial Purch. $	Additional Purch. $	Front End Load	Back End Load
C /5.2	11.2	1.71	31.85	1,356	2	97	0	1	9	127.7	-19.2	18	N/A	3,000	100	0.0	0.0
B- /7.3	9.4	0.87	24.54	4,476	0	99	0	1	22	N/A	N/A	70	1	10,000	100	0.0	0.0
B- /7.4	9.5	0.87	36.18	1,031	0	99	0	1	22	107.3	-14.3	69	1	3,000	100	0.0	0.0
B- /7.4	9.3	0.86	24.80	31,712	1	97	1	1	26	112.3	-10.0	75	11	3,000	100	0.0	0.0
C- /4.1	16.9	1.02	19.09	411	5	94	0	1	46	31.4	N/A	73	6	3,000	1	0.0	0.0
C /4.3	16.0	0.98	32.28	9,724	0	97	1	2	13	23.4	-27.2	79	9	10,000	100	0.0	0.0
C /4.3	16.0	0.98	24.55	4,274	0	97	1	2	13	23.7	-27.2	79	9	5,000,000	100	0.0	0.0
C /4.3	16.0	0.98	81.67	3,186	0	97	1	2	13	23.8	-27.2	80	9	100,000,000	100	0.0	0.0
C /4.3	16.0	0.98	24.58	1,614	0	97	1	2	13	22.3	-27.2	78	9	3,000	100	0.0	0.0
D- /1.4	20.2	1.01	96.69	7,000	1	96	1	2	23	21.4	-27.6	75	5	50,000	100	0.0	0.0
D- /1.3	20.3	1.04	49.13	930	0	99	0	1	15	29.7	-26.9	74	2	100,000	0	0.0	0.0
D- /1.4	20.2	1.01	51.53	3,318	1	96	1	2	23	20.9	-27.6	75	5	3,000	100	0.0	0.0
C+ /6.9	9.6	0.90	71.45	21,059	3	96	0	1	26	126.8	-12.1	80	14	50,000	100	0.0	0.0
C+ /6.9	9.6	0.90	34.09	6,039	3	96	0	1	26	125.8	-12.1	80	14	3,000	100	0.0	0.0
C /5.1	12.3	0.98	26.49	581	0	98	0	2	6	51.3	-27.2	39	9	5,000,000	100	0.0	0.0
C /5.1	12.3	0.98	62.12	3,686	0	98	0	2	6	51.1	-27.2	39	9	10,000	100	0.0	0.0
U /	N/A	N/A	118.32	103	0	98	0	2	6	N/A	N/A	N/A	9	100,000,000	100	0.0	0.0
C /5.2	12.3	0.98	26.67	625	0	98	0	2	6	49.9	-27.2	36	9	3,000	100	0.0	0.0
C- /3.0	14.6	0.89	84.92	8,339	2	97	0	1	66	123.5	-23.2	62	23	50,000	100	0.0	0.0
C- /3.0	14.6	0.89	91.36	3,611	2	97	0	1	66	121.7	-23.3	60	23	3,000	100	0.0	0.0
C /5.5	13.8	1.10	34.04	617	5	94	0	1	61	134.7	-22.9	23	7	3,000	1	0.0	0.0
C /5.2	13.6	1.14	76.09	16,788	1	98	0	1	6	135.3	-23.9	17	20	10,000	100	0.0	0.0
C /5.2	13.6	1.14	76.09	11,681	1	98	0	1	6	135.6	-23.9	17	20	5,000,000	100	0.0	0.0
C /5.2	13.6	1.14	76.11	2,098	1	98	0	1	6	133.6	-23.9	16	20	3,000	100	0.0	0.0
C /5.2	13.6	1.10	187.78	14,037	1	98	0	1	6	135.8	-23.9	30	20	100,000,000	100	0.0	0.0
C+ /6.6	14.2	1.07	31.22	552	0	99	0	1	21	178.9	-26.3	79	2	100,000	0	0.0	0.0
C+ /5.9	11.6	0.85	38.10	610	3	96	0	1	14	48.7	-25.9	77	2	3,000	100	0.0	0.0
C+ /5.7	11.7	0.92	28.93	4,043	1	98	0	1	5	43.3	N/A	78	1	10,000	100	0.0	0.0
C+ /5.7	11.7	0.92	97.11	2,119	1	98	0	1	5	43.6	-24.5	78	1	100,000,000	100	0.0	0.0
C+ /5.7	11.7	0.92	91.70	4,754	1	98	0	1	5	43.4	-24.5	78	1	5,000,000	100	0.0	0.0
C+ /5.7	11.7	0.91	18.36	549	1	98	0	1	5	42.1	-24.5	77	1	3,000	100	0.0	0.0
C+ /5.9	11.6	0.85	190.88	137	3	96	0	1	14	50.2	-25.8	78	2	5,000,000	100	0.8	0.0
C+ /6.8	11.1	1.06	15.29	1,152	0	99	0	1	16	145.0	-15.6	68	2	5,000,000	0	0.0	0.0
C+ /6.8	11.1	1.06	15.27	1,672	0	99	0	1	16	143.4	-15.7	66	2	3,000	0	0.0	0.0
C+ /6.4	10.4	0.77	26.22	4,709	0	96	3	1	45	90.8	-22.2	95	13	3,000	100	0.0	0.0
C+ /6.6	12.0	0.56	31.82	384	18	81	0	1	7	62.2	-21.6	37	2	10,000	100	0.3	0.3
C+ /6.6	12.1	0.57	106.00	166	18	81	0	1	7	62.5	-21.6	37	2	5,000,000	100	0.3	0.3
C+ /6.6	12.0	0.56	21.01	59	18	81	0	1	7	60.9	-21.7	35	2	3,000	100	0.3	0.3
B- /7.8	6.6	0.36	24.81	1,254	3	96	0	1	58	N/A	N/A	99	4	50,000	100	0.0	0.0
B- /7.9	6.6	0.35	12.41	448	3	96	0	1	58	N/A	N/A	99	4	3,000	100	0.0	0.0
C+ /6.1	10.1	0.98	71.17	4,352	2	97	0	1	96	139.4	-16.4	77	6	50,000	100	0.0	0.0
C+ /6.1	10.1	0.98	43.59	3,019	2	97	0	1	96	137.9	-16.5	76	6	3,000	100	0.0	0.0
C+ /6.4	11.5	1.07	61.99	20,452	0	99	0	1	9	131.6	-15.2	53	23	10,000	100	0.0	0.0
C+ /6.4	11.5	1.07	62.00	10,669	0	99	0	1	9	131.8	-15.2	53	23	5,000,000	100	0.0	0.0
C+ /6.4	11.5	1.07	61.99	3,153	0	99	0	1	9	129.9	-15.2	51	23	3,000	100	0.0	0.0
C /4.7	13.4	0.94	85.86	35,953	0	96	2	2	18	155.9	-7.5	69	9	50,000	100	0.0	0.0
C /4.7	13.4	0.93	203.56	10,251	0	96	2	2	18	155.2	-7.5	68	9	3,000	100	0.0	0.0
C+ /6.4	13.9	1.05	69.30	777	0	99	0	1	10	165.2	-11.3	56	2	100,000	0	0.0	0.0
B- /7.4	9.7	0.90	31.07	7,008	0	99	0	1	7	127.7	-11.2	85	1	3,000	100	0.0	0.0
C+ /6.7	12.6	1.11	64.22	157	0	99	0	1	8	157.3	-25.1	51	2	100,000	0	0.0	0.0
C+ /6.5	13.8	1.19	68.11	682	0	99	0	1	5	151.3	-14.1	85	2	100,000	0	0.0	0.0
U /	N/A	N/A	20.65	2,018	2	34	63	1	8	N/A	N/A	N/A	2	100,000,000	0	0.0	0.0

I. Index of Stock Mutual Funds

Fund Type	Fund Name	Ticker Symbol	Overall Investment Rating	Phone	Performance Rating/Pts	3 Mo	6 Mo	1Yr / Pct	3Yr / Pct	5Yr / Pct	Dividend Yield	Expense Ratio
GI	Vanguard Inst Tgt Ret 2015 Inst	VITVX	U	(800) 662-7447	U /	3.95	2.69	11.53 /16	--	--	1.84	0.09
GI	Vanguard Inst Tgt Ret 2020 Inst	VITWX	U	(800) 662-7447	U /	4.71	3.63	13.92 /25	--	--	1.88	0.10
GI	Vanguard Inst Tgt Ret 2025 Inst	VRIVX	U	(800) 662-7447	U /	5.27	4.39	15.68 /33	--	--	1.88	0.10
GI	Vanguard Inst Tgt Ret 2030 Inst	VTTWX	U	(800) 662-7447	U /	5.84	5.22	17.45 /40	--	--	1.88	0.10
GI	Vanguard Inst Tgt Ret 2035 Inst	VITFX	U	(800) 662-7447	U /	6.31	6.00	19.14 /48	--	--	1.88	0.10
GI	Vanguard Inst Tgt Ret 2040 Inst	VIRSX	U	(800) 662-7447	U /	6.84	6.78	20.87 /57	--	--	1.88	0.10
GI	Vanguard Inst Tgt Ret 2045 Inst	VITLX	U	(800) 662-7447	U /	7.01	7.06	21.32 /59	--	--	1.85	0.10
GI	Vanguard Inst Tgt Ret 2050 Inst	VTRLX	U	(800) 662-7447	U /	7.01	7.01	21.33 /59	--	--	1.81	0.10
GI	Vanguard Inst Tgt Ret 2055 Inst	VIVLX	U	(800) 662-7447	U /	7.00	7.05	21.30 /59	--	--	1.71	0.10
GI	Vanguard Inst Tgt Ret 2060 Inst	VILVX	U	(800) 662-7447	U /	7.00	7.05	21.32 /59	--	--	1.71	0.10
GI	Vanguard Inst Tgt Ret Inc Inst	VITRX	U	(800) 662-7447	U /	2.96	1.39	8.13 / 8	--	--	1.90	0.09
* IX	Vanguard Instl Index Inst	VINIX	A+	(800) 662-7447	A / 9.4	8.03	10.00	24.94 /73	10.61 /96	13.98 /93	1.95	0.04
IX	Vanguard Instl Index Inst Plus	VIIIX	A+	(800) 662-7447	A / 9.4	8.03	10.01	24.96 /73	10.63 /96	14.00 /93	1.97	0.02
GR	Vanguard Instl TtlStk Mkt Inst	VITNX	A+	(800) 662-7447	A- / 9.2	7.73	10.23	26.30 /77	9.92 /93	13.86 /92	1.90	0.04
GI	Vanguard Instl TtlStk Mkt Inst Plus	VITPX	A+	(800) 662-7447	A- / 9.2	7.71	10.24	26.30 /77	9.94 /93	13.89 /92	1.92	0.02
FO	Vanguard International Explorer Inv	VINEX	D+	(800) 662-7447	C- / 3.1	7.93	4.80	14.64 /28	2.07 /24	8.04 /43	1.83	0.42
FO	Vanguard International Growth Adm	VWILX	D	(800) 662-7447	C- / 3.6	8.63	3.91	21.51 /60	1.40 /20	6.10 /29	1.31	0.34
* FO	Vanguard International Growth Inv	VWIGX	D	(800) 662-7447	C- / 3.5	8.61	3.85	21.37 /59	1.28 /20	5.97 /28	1.17	0.47
* FO	Vanguard International Value Inv	VTRIX	D-	(800) 662-7447	D- / 1.2	6.44	5.36	18.53 /45	-1.43 / 8	4.45 /18	2.18	0.46
FO	Vanguard Internatl Hi Dv Yld Id Adm	VIHAX	U	(800) 662-7447	U /	7.85	6.96	--	--	--	0.00	0.30
FO	Vanguard Intl Div Apprctn Idx Adm	VIAAX	U	(800) 662-7447	U /	6.91	-0.74	--	--	--	0.00	0.25
GR	Vanguard Large Cap Index Adm	VLCAX	A+	(800) 662-7447	A / 9.3	8.09	10.08	25.23 /74	10.26 /95	13.81 /92	1.86	0.08
GR	Vanguard Large Cap Index Inst	VLISX	A+	(800) 662-7447	A / 9.3	8.10	10.09	25.26 /74	10.28 /95	13.82 /92	1.87	0.07
GR	Vanguard Large Cap Index Inv	VLACX	A+	(800) 662-7447	A- / 9.2	8.07	10.02	25.10 /74	10.13 /94	13.66 /90	1.76	0.20
* AA	Vanguard LifeStrategy Consv Gr Inv	VSCGX	C+	(800) 662-7447	C- / 3.1	3.60	1.83	10.02 /12	4.49 /49	5.73 /27	2.16	0.13
* AA	Vanguard LifeStrategy Growth Inv	VASGX	B-	(800) 662-7447	C+ / 5.8	6.32	5.95	18.95 /47	5.80 /63	8.92 /50	2.12	0.15
AA	Vanguard LifeStrategy Income Inv	VASIX	C+	(800) 662-7447	D / 2.0	2.26	-0.26	5.69 / 4	3.72 /40	4.05 /15	2.17	0.12
* AA	Vanguard LifeStrategy Mod Gro Inv	VSMGX	B-	(800) 662-7447	C / 4.4	4.95	3.88	14.46 /28	5.21 /57	7.36 /37	2.14	0.14
GI	Vanguard Managed Payout Investor	VPGDX	C+	(800) 662-7447	C- / 4.0	4.63	4.10	13.59 /24	4.70 /51	7.05 /35	5.92	0.38
IN	Vanguard Market Neutral Fund Inst	VMNIX	C	(800) 662-7447	D- / 1.4	-0.78	4.52	-2.22 / 1	3.17 /33	3.31 /12	0.46	1.36
IN	Vanguard Market Neutral Fund Inv	VMNFX	C	(800) 662-7447	D- / 1.4	-0.77	4.51	-2.28 / 1	3.07 /32	3.22 /12	0.39	1.46
PM	Vanguard Materials Index Fd Adm	VMIAX	B-	(800) 662-7447	B / 8.2	5.80	11.11	34.15 /93	6.21 /66	9.90 /58	1.58	0.10
GR	Vanguard Mega Cap Gr Index I	VMGAX	A+	(800) 662-7447	A- / 9.2	9.95	9.38	23.16 /67	10.21 /94	13.77 /91	1.41	0.08
MC	Vanguard Mega Cap Index Inst	VMCTX	A+	(800) 662-7447	A / 9.4	8.34	10.33	25.12 /74	10.64 /96	13.93 /93	2.01	0.06
GR	Vanguard Mega Cap Value Index I	VMVLX	A+	(800) 662-7447	A+ / 9.6	6.99	11.19	26.92 /79	11.04 /97	14.18 /94	2.44	0.06
MC	Vanguard Mid Cap Growth Admiral	VMGMX	B-	(800) 662-7447	B- / 7.0	6.99	6.58	22.49 /64	7.04 /72	11.59 /71	0.76	0.08
MC	Vanguard Mid Cap Value Index Adm	VMVAX	A+	(800) 662-7447	A / 9.4	6.75	10.79	29.15 /84	9.87 /93	14.84 /97	1.81	0.08
MC	Vanguard Mid-Cap Growth Fd	VMGRX	D+	(800) 662-7447	C / 4.7	5.43	6.61	16.81 /38	4.58 /50	10.02 /58	0.63	0.43
MC	Vanguard Mid-Cap Growth Index Inv	VMGIX	C+	(800) 662-7447	C+ / 6.9	6.96	6.51	22.32 /64	6.91 /71	11.43 /69	0.65	0.20
MC	Vanguard Mid-Cap Index Adm	VIMAX	A-	(800) 662-7447	B+ / 8.4	6.87	8.84	26.02 /76	8.57 /84	13.32 /87	1.37	0.08
MC	Vanguard Mid-Cap Index Inst	VMCIX	A-	(800) 662-7447	B+ / 8.4	6.86	8.84	26.03 /76	8.57 /84	13.32 /87	1.37	0.07
MC	Vanguard Mid-Cap Index Inst Plus	VMCPX	A-	(800) 662-7447	B+ / 8.4	6.87	8.84	26.05 /76	8.60 /84	13.35 /87	1.38	0.05
MC	Vanguard Mid-Cap Index Inv	VIMSX	A-	(800) 662-7447	B+ / 8.3	6.84	8.79	25.89 /76	8.43 /82	13.17 /86	1.26	0.20
MC	Vanguard Mid-Cap Value Index Inv	VMVIX	A+	(800) 662-7447	A / 9.3	6.72	10.72	29.04 /84	9.74 /92	14.68 /96	1.71	0.20
MC	Vanguard Morgan Growth Adm	VMRAX	B-	(800) 662-7447	B / 8.1	8.82	8.79	20.97 /57	8.63 /84	12.79 /82	0.86	0.27
MC	Vanguard Morgan Growth Inv	VMRGX	B-	(800) 662-7447	B / 8.0	8.75	8.71	20.80 /56	8.50 /83	12.64 /80	0.76	0.40
BA	Vanguard OH Col Ad Welli Opti Port		B	(800) 662-7447	C+ / 6.7	5.83	6.71	18.53 /45	7.52 /76	9.83 /57	0.00	0.42
GR	Vanguard OH Col Adv Agg Gr Idx		B+	(800) 662-7447	B- / 7.3	7.64	7.82	23.32 /68	6.96 /72	11.57 /71	0.00	0.24
AA	Vanguard OH Col Adv Con Gr Idx		C+	(800) 662-7447	D / 2.2	2.59	0.21	6.65 / 5	3.83 /41	4.55 /18	0.00	0.25
MC	Vanguard OH Col Adv Ext Mkt Idx		B+	(800) 662-7447	B+ / 8.4	6.49	11.41	32.45 /91	6.75 /70	12.95 /83	0.00	0.28
GR	Vanguard OH Col Adv Grow Index		B	(800) 662-7447	C+ / 5.7	5.98	5.28	17.64 /41	6.06 /65	9.31 /53	0.00	0.24
AA	Vanguard OH Col Adv Mod Gr Idx		B	(800) 662-7447	C- / 3.8	4.28	2.70	12.04 /18	5.03 /55	6.98 /34	0.00	0.25

● Denotes fund is closed to new investors
* Denotes fund is included in Section II

www.thestreetratings.com

RISK			NET ASSETS		ASSET					BULL / BEAR		FUND MANAGER		MINIMUMS		LOADS	
Risk Rating/Pts	3 Year Standard Deviation	Beta	NAV As of 2/28/17	Total $(Mil)	Cash %	Stocks %	Bonds %	Other %	Portfolio Turnover Ratio	Last Bull Market Return	Last Bear Market Return	Manager Quality Pct	Manager Tenure (Years)	Initial Purch. $	Additional Purch. $	Front End Load	Back End Load
U /	N/A	N/A	20.72	6,749	1	47	50	2	9	N/A	N/A	N/A	2	100,000,000	0	0.0	0.0
U /	N/A	N/A	20.83	14,303	2	58	39	1	15	N/A	N/A	N/A	2	100,000,000	0	0.0	0.0
U /	N/A	N/A	20.88	17,046	1	65	32	2	15	N/A	N/A	N/A	2	100,000,000	0	0.0	0.0
U /	N/A	N/A	20.90	14,691	1	73	24	2	16	N/A	N/A	N/A	2	100,000,000	0	0.0	0.0
U /	N/A	N/A	20.92	13,565	1	80	17	2	14	N/A	N/A	N/A	2	100,000,000	0	0.0	0.0
U /	N/A	N/A	20.93	11,275	1	88	10	1	16	N/A	N/A	N/A	2	100,000,000	0	0.0	0.0
U /	N/A	N/A	20.99	9,128	0	89	9	2	13	N/A	N/A	N/A	2	100,000,000	0	0.0	0.0
U /	N/A	N/A	21.00	5,847	0	89	9	2	12	N/A	N/A	N/A	2	100,000,000	0	0.0	0.0
U /	N/A	N/A	21.03	2,220	1	89	9	1	8	N/A	N/A	N/A	2	100,000,000	0	0.0	0.0
U /	N/A	N/A	21.01	508	0	89	9	2	6	N/A	N/A	N/A	2	100,000,000	0	0.0	0.0
U /	N/A	N/A	20.66	2,359	2	29	68	1	11	N/A	N/A	N/A	2	100,000,000	0	0.0	0.0
B- /7.1	10.3	1.00	215.93	128,517	0	99	0	1	5	134.5	-16.3	74	17	5,000,000	100	0.0	0.0
B- /7.1	10.3	1.00	215.95	96,398	0	99	0	1	5	134.7	-16.3	N/A	17	200,000,000	100	0.0	0.0
C+ /6.8	10.6	1.02	53.20	692	0	99	0	1	9	135.1	-17.7	64	16	5,000,000	100	0.0	0.0
C+ /6.8	10.6	1.02	53.20	38,470	0	99	0	1	9	135.4	-17.7	64	16	200,000,000	100	0.0	0.0
C+ /5.6	11.3	0.83	17.36	2,815	4	94	0	2	37	69.9	-25.7	87	17	3,000	100	0.0	0.0
C /4.8	13.7	1.04	72.93	16,877	2	97	0	1	29	62.6	-25.6	84	14	50,000	0	0.0	0.0
C /4.8	13.7	1.04	22.95	6,555	2	97	0	1	29	61.5	-25.6	84	14	3,000	0	0.0	0.0
C /5.2	12.2	0.95	33.28	8,329	1	95	3	1	30	47.4	-24.2	59	9	3,000	100	0.0	0.0
U /	N/A	N/A	28.58	101	0	0	0	100	6	N/A	N/A	N/A	1	10,000	1	0.0	0.3
U /	N/A	N/A	26.98	90	0	0	0	100	8	N/A	N/A	N/A	1	10,000	1	0.0	0.3
B- /7.0	10.4	1.00	54.78	4,451	0	99	0	1	4	133.5	-16.7	70	1	10,000	100	0.0	0.0
B- /7.0	10.4	1.00	225.49	919	0	99	0	1	4	133.7	-16.8	70	1	5,000,000	100	0.0	0.0
B- /7.0	10.4	1.00	43.81	429	0	99	0	1	4	131.8	-16.8	68	1	3,000	100	0.0	0.0
B+ /9.2	4.5	0.68	18.93	8,495	1	39	59	1	9	44.7	-7.4	67	N/A	3,000	100	0.0	0.0
B- /7.5	8.3	1.30	30.20	13,036	1	78	20	1	5	79.5	-16.2	26	N/A	3,000	100	0.0	0.0
B+ /9.6	3.2	0.38	15.14	3,845	1	19	79	1	4	28.9	-2.5	80	N/A	3,000	100	0.0	0.0
B /8.5	6.3	0.99	25.03	14,111	1	58	39	2	9	61.5	-11.4	47	N/A	3,000	100	0.0	0.0
B /8.0	5.9	0.53	17.99	1,774	18	63	17	2	29	60.3	-12.6	65	2	25,000	100	0.0	0.0
B+ /9.8	5.5	-0.10	12.09	342	100	0	0	0	68	19.2	2.6	93	5	5,000,000	100	0.0	0.0
B+ /9.8	5.4	-0.10	12.14	1,775	100	0	0	0	68	18.5	2.6	93	5	250,000	100	0.0	0.0
C /4.7	16.9	0.13	60.64	289	0	99	0	1	6	107.8	-28.1	97	2	100,000	0	0.0	0.0
C+ /6.7	11.6	1.08	187.71	32	0	99	0	1	12	135.1	-13.7	60	2	5,000,000	0	0.0	0.0
B- /7.1	10.3	0.74	159.47	107	0	99	0	1	8	133.8	-15.8	91	2	5,000,000	0	0.0	0.0
B- /7.5	10.0	0.93	138.07	144	0	99	0	1	8	133.2	-17.8	81	2	5,000,000	0	0.0	0.0
C+ /5.6	12.2	0.93	48.53	4,380	0	99	0	1	23	116.6	N/A	52	4	10,000	100	0.0	0.0
C+ /6.5	11.0	0.87	53.16	6,670	0	99	0	1	20	148.0	N/A	83	11	10,000	100	0.0	0.0
C- /4.2	12.4	0.94	23.66	4,151	5	94	0	1	91	101.3	-18.5	22	11	3,000	100	0.0	0.0
C+ /5.6	12.2	0.93	44.32	492	0	99	0	1	23	115.0	-21.8	50	4	3,000	100	0.0	0.0
C+ /6.4	11.4	0.90	172.99	32,383	0	99	0	1	16	133.0	-21.4	73	19	10,000	100	0.0	0.0
C+ /6.4	11.4	0.90	38.21	15,619	0	99	0	1	16	133.1	-21.4	73	19	5,000,000	100	0.0	0.0
C+ /6.4	11.4	0.90	188.47	12,331	0	99	0	1	16	133.3	-21.4	73	19	100,000,000	100	0.0	0.0
C+ /6.4	11.4	0.90	38.13	4,295	0	99	0	1	16	131.2	-21.4	72	19	3,000	100	0.0	0.0
C+ /6.5	11.0	0.87	40.40	722	0	99	0	1	20	146.1	-21.0	82	11	3,000	100	0.0	0.0
C /4.9	11.5	0.80	81.58	7,469	1	98	0	1	51	125.8	-18.6	81	14	50,000	100	0.0	0.0
C /4.9	11.5	0.80	26.33	4,043	1	98	0	1	51	124.2	-18.6	80	14	3,000	100	0.0	0.0
B /8.9	6.9	1.10	25.59	143	0	65	34	1	0	83.3	-10.5	66	8	25	0	0.0	0.0
B- /7.0	10.3	0.98	25.65	449	0	99	0	1	0	109.7	-18.9	33	8	25	0	0.0	0.0
B+ /9.7	3.4	0.45	19.40	335	0	25	73	2	0	33.2	-1.5	77	8	25	0	0.0	0.0
C /5.3	13.6	1.10	32.33	194	0	99	0	1	0	133.3	-23.9	28	8	25	0	0.0	0.0
B /8.7	7.7	0.73	23.74	571	0	74	24	2	0	81.8	-13.3	55	8	25	0	0.0	0.0
B+ /9.5	5.3	0.83	21.68	545	0	50	49	1	0	56.2	-7.5	60	8	25	0	0.0	0.0

I. Index of Stock Mutual Funds

					PERFORMANCE						Incl. in Returns	
					Perfor-mance Rating/Pts	Total Return % through 2/28/17			Annualized		Dividend Yield	Expense Ratio
Fund Type	Fund Name	Ticker Symbol	Overall Investment Rating	Phone		3 Mo	6 Mo	1Yr / Pct	3Yr / Pct	5Yr / Pct		
IX	Vanguard OH Coll Adv 500 Idx		A+	(800) 662-7447	A / 9.3	8.00	9.92	24.78 /73	10.42 /95	13.80 /92	0.00	0.19
GR	Vanguard OH Coll Adv Morgan Gr		A-	(800) 662-7447	B / 7.9	8.80	8.69	20.77 /56	8.44 /82	12.57 /80	0.00	0.48
GI	Vanguard OH Coll Adv Windsor II Opt		A+	(800) 662-7447	B / 8.1	6.14	9.65	26.20 /77	8.00 /79	12.27 /77	0.00	0.48
FO	Vanguard Pacific Stock Index Adm	VPADX	C+	(800) 662-7447	C+ / 5.6	6.57	7.00	23.99 /70	4.14 /45	6.10 /29	2.48	0.12
FO	Vanguard Pacific Stock Index Inst	VPKIX	C+	(800) 662-7447	C+ / 5.6	6.54	7.02	24.02 /70	4.16 /45	6.13 /29	2.50	0.09
FO	Vanguard Pacific Stock Index Inv	VPACX	C+	(800) 662-7447	C / 5.5	6.54	6.88	23.73 /69	3.99 /43	5.94 /28	2.32	0.26
PM	Vanguard Prec Metals & Mining Inv	VGPMX	E-	(800) 662-7447	D / 1.6	8.77	-3.11	36.56 /95	-2.32 / 6	-12.39 / 0	1.57	0.35
MC	● Vanguard PRIMECAP Adm	VPMAX	A+	(800) 662-7447	A+ / 9.7	9.34	12.15	28.85 /84	11.38 /98	16.73 /98	1.23	0.34
* GR	● Vanguard PRIMECAP Core Inv	VPCCX	A+	(800) 662-7447	A+ / 9.8	9.46	12.90	28.50 /83	11.62 /98	16.19 /98	1.12	0.47
* MC	● Vanguard PRIMECAP Inv	VPMCX	A+	(800) 662-7447	A+ / 9.7	9.33	12.12	28.77 /83	11.30 /97	16.64 /98	1.16	0.40
RE	Vanguard REIT Index Adm	VGSLX	B-	(800) 662-7447	B / 7.7	8.26	-1.50	16.57 /37	11.02 /97	11.38 /69	4.66	0.12
RE	Vanguard REIT Index Inst	VGSNX	B-	(800) 662-7447	B / 7.8	8.30	-1.45	16.63 /37	11.05 /97	11.40 /69	4.68	0.10
RE	Vanguard REIT Index Inv	VGSIX	B-	(800) 662-7447	B / 7.6	8.21	-1.58	16.41 /36	10.86 /97	11.21 /68	4.52	0.26
GR	Vanguard Russell 1000 Gro Idx Inst	VRGWX	A+	(800) 662-7447	A- / 9.1	8.98	9.11	22.08 /63	10.39 /95	13.71 /91	1.41	0.08
GR	Vanguard Russell 1000 Index Inst	VRNIX	A+	(800) 662-7447	A- / 9.2	7.93	10.06	25.28 /74	10.06 /94	13.82 /92	1.82	0.08
GR	Vanguard Russell 1000 Val Index Ins	VRVIX	A+	(800) 662-7447	A / 9.4	6.92	11.02	28.85 /84	9.78 /92	13.91 /93	2.33	0.08
SC	Vanguard Russell 2000 Gro Idx Inst	VRTGX	C+	(800) 662-7447	B- / 7.3	5.54	9.46	31.10 /88	5.60 /61	12.44 /78	1.02	0.08
GR	Vanguard Russell 2000 Index Inst	VRTIX	B+	(800) 662-7447	B+ / 8.9	5.22	12.66	36.20 /95	7.03 /72	12.98 /84	1.30	0.08
SC	Vanguard Russell 2000 Val Index Ins	VRTVX	A	(800) 662-7447	A+ / 9.7	4.89	15.84	41.28 /98	8.36 /82	—	1.66	0.08
IN	Vanguard Russell 3000 Index Inst	VRTTX	A+	(800) 662-7447	A- / 9.2	7.72	10.27	26.06 /76	9.83 /92	13.76 /91	1.78	0.08
MC	Vanguard S&P Mid-Cap 400 Gro Inst	VMFGX	A-	(800) 662-7447	B+ / 8.8	7.70	8.64	27.38 /80	8.83 /86	12.89 /83	1.08	0.08
MC	Vanguard S&P Mid-Cap 400 Index	VSPMX	A+	(800) 662-7447	A / 9.5	6.61	11.33	31.63 /89	9.57 /91	13.77 /91	1.48	0.08
MC	Vanguard S&P Mid-Cap 400 Value	VMFVX	A+	(800) 662-7447	A+ / 9.7	5.42	13.53	35.40 /94	9.99 /93	14.45 /95	1.37	0.08
SC	Vanguard S&P SC 600 Indx Inst	VSMSX	A	(800) 662-7447	A+ / 9.6	4.60	13.18	34.96 /94	9.71 /92	14.87 /97	0.98	0.08
* MC	Vanguard Selected Value Inv	VASVX	A-	(800) 662-7447	A- / 9.0	7.47	15.50	30.48 /87	7.53 /76	13.65 /90	1.61	0.39
SC	Vanguard Small Cap Growth Adm	VSGAX	C	(800) 662-7447	C+ / 6.4	6.23	7.63	28.39 /83	4.48 /49	11.61 /71	1.02	0.08
SC	Vanguard Small Cap Value Index	VSIAX	A+	(800) 662-7447	A+ / 9.7	5.66	13.36	34.91 /94	9.80 /92	14.88 /97	1.72	0.08
SC	Vanguard Small-Cap Grwth Index Inst	VSGIX	C	(800) 662-7447	C+ / 6.4	6.24	7.64	28.44 /83	4.49 /49	11.63 /71	1.03	0.07
SC	Vanguard Small-Cap Grwth Index Inv	VISGX	C	(800) 662-7447	C+ / 6.3	6.21	7.58	28.28 /82	4.36 /47	11.47 /70	0.92	0.20
SC	Vanguard Small-Cap Index Adm	VSMAX	B+	(800) 662-7447	B+ / 8.6	5.93	10.78	32.00 /90	7.38 /75	13.46 /89	1.44	0.08
SC	Vanguard Small-Cap Index Inst	VSCIX	B+	(800) 662-7447	B+ / 8.6	5.94	10.78	32.01 /90	7.40 /75	13.47 /89	1.45	0.07
SC	Vanguard Small-Cap Index InstP	VSCPX	B+	(800) 662-7447	B+ / 8.6	5.93	10.79	32.02 /90	7.41 /75	13.50 /89	1.46	0.05
SC	Vanguard Small-Cap Index Inv	NAESX	B+	(800) 662-7447	B+ / 8.4	5.89	10.70	31.82 /90	7.25 /74	13.31 /87	1.34	0.20
SC	Vanguard Small-Cap Value Index Inst	VSIIX	A+	(800) 662-7447	A+ / 9.7	5.68	13.37	34.95 /94	9.81 /92	14.89 /97	1.72	0.07
SC	Vanguard Small-Cap Value Index Inv	VISVX	A+	(800) 662-7447	A+ / 9.6	5.62	13.29	34.76 /94	9.66 /91	14.73 /96	1.62	0.20
* GI	Vanguard STAR Fund	VGSTX	B-	(800) 662-7447	C / 4.7	5.20	4.26	16.08 /35	5.23 /57	8.18 /43	1.94	0.32
* SC	Vanguard Strategic Equity Inv	VSEQX	A-	(800) 662-7447	A+ / 9.6	6.58	14.21	31.13 /88	9.69 /92	15.51 /98	1.49	0.21
SC	Vanguard Strategic Sm-Cp Equity Inv	VSTCX	A	(800) 662-7447	A / 9.3	5.53	14.68	31.58 /89	8.51 /83	14.66 /96	1.33	0.34
* AA	Vanguard Target Retirement 2010 Inv	VTENX	C	(800) 662-7447	D+ / 2.5	3.00	1.47	8.47 / 8	3.83 /41	5.34 /24	1.79	0.13
* AA	Vanguard Target Retirement 2015 Inv	VTXVX	C+	(800) 662-7447	C- / 3.4	3.97	2.73	11.50 /16	4.49 /49	6.53 /32	1.90	0.14
* AA	Vanguard Target Retirement 2025 Inv	VTTVX	B-	(800) 662-7447	C / 4.8	5.29	4.40	15.70 /33	5.34 /58	8.06 /43	1.91	0.14
* AA	Vanguard Target Retirement 2030	VTHRX	B	(800) 662-7447	C / 5.3	5.79	5.18	17.34 /40	5.56 /60	8.63 /47	1.89	0.15
* AA	Vanguard Target Retirement 2035 Inv	VTTHX	B-	(800) 662-7447	C+ / 5.8	6.27	5.91	19.00 /47	5.77 /62	9.20 /52	1.91	0.15
* AA	Vanguard Target Retirement 2040 Inv	VFORX	B-	(800) 662-7447	C+ / 6.3	6.81	6.74	20.80 /56	5.93 /64	9.57 /55	1.88	0.16
* AA	Vanguard Target Retirement 2045 Inv	VTIVX	B-	(800) 662-7447	C+ / 6.5	7.00	7.05	21.28 /59	6.04 /65	9.64 /56	1.88	0.16
* AA	Vanguard Target Retirement 2050 Inv	VFIFX	B-	(800) 662-7447	C+ / 6.5	6.97	7.00	21.25 /59	6.03 /64	9.63 /56	1.84	0.16
AA	Vanguard Target Retirement 2055 Inv	VFFVX	B-	(800) 662-7447	C+ / 6.4	6.98	7.01	21.20 /58	5.98 /64	9.61 /55	1.89	0.16
GI	Vanguard Target Retirement 2060 Inv	VTTSX	B-	(800) 662-7447	C+ / 6.4	7.00	7.00	21.25 /59	5.99 /64	9.67 /56	1.88	0.16
* AA	Vanguard Target Retirement Income	VTINX	C+	(800) 662-7447	D+ / 2.4	2.99	1.39	8.08 / 8	3.70 /39	4.56 /18	1.90	0.13
BA	Vanguard Tax-Managed Bal Admiral	VTMFX	B	(800) 662-7447	C / 4.7	4.94	3.51	11.80 /17	6.40 /68	8.11 /43	2.06	0.11
* GR	Vanguard Tax-Managed Cap Appr	VTCLX	A+	(800) 662-7447	A / 9.3	8.05	10.48	25.99 /76	10.19 /94	14.03 /93	1.66	0.11
GR	Vanguard Tax-Managed Cap Appr	VTCIX	A+	(800) 662-7447	A / 9.4	8.05	10.50	26.03 /76	10.23 /95	14.07 /94	1.68	0.07

● Denotes fund is closed to new investors
* Denotes fund is included in Section II

www.thestreetratings.com

RISK			NET ASSETS		ASSET					BULL / BEAR		FUND MANAGER		MINIMUMS		LOADS	
Risk Rating/Pts	3 Year Standard Deviation	Beta	NAV As of 2/28/17	Total $(Mil)	Cash %	Stocks %	Bonds %	Other %	Portfolio Turnover Ratio	Last Bull Market Return	Last Bear Market Return	Manager Quality Pct	Manager Tenure (Years)	Initial Purch. $	Additional Purch. $	Front End Load	Back End Load
B- /7.5	10.3	1.00	27.14	345	0	99	0	1	0	132.6	-16.3	72	8	25	0	0.0	0.0
C+ /6.7	11.5	1.04	21.51	40	1	98	0	1	0	123.6	-18.3	43	8	25	0	0.0	0.0
B- /7.5	10.7	1.01	20.57	71	2	97	0	1	0	117.9	-17.1	41	8	25	0	0.0	0.0
C+ /6.3	12.0	0.85	76.92	2,081	5	94	0	1	14	50.9	-15.3	94	20	10,000	100	0.0	0.0
C+ /6.3	12.0	0.85	11.77	298	5	94	0	1	14	51.2	-15.2	94	20	5,000,000	100	0.0	0.0
C+ /6.3	12.0	0.85	11.85	288	5	94	0	1	14	49.7	-15.3	94	20	3,000	100	0.0	0.0
E- /0.0	36.1	1.83	10.29	2,542	0	98	1	1	8	-41.9	-25.3	82	3	3,000	100	0.0	0.0
C+ /6.0	11.4	0.78	116.98	43,745	3	96	0	1	6	158.8	-18.4	92	32	50,000	100	0.0	0.0
C+ /6.4	11.3	1.04	23.81	9,311	7	92	0	1	11	150.0	-17.6	78	13	3,000	100	0.0	0.0
C+ /6.1	11.4	0.78	112.93	7,851	3	96	0	1	6	157.7	-18.4	92	32	3,000	100	0.0	0.0
C /5.2	14.9	1.09	120.86	18,826	0	99	0	1	11	107.9	-16.3	62	1	10,000	100	0.0	0.0
C /5.2	14.9	1.09	18.71	8,096	0	99	0	1	11	108.1	-16.3	62	1	5,000,000	100	0.0	0.0
C /5.2	14.9	1.09	28.32	2,678	0	99	0	1	11	106.4	-16.3	61	1	3,000	100	0.0	0.0
C+ /6.9	11.0	1.03	222.37	2,340	0	99	0	1	15	133.4	-15.4	68	7	5,000,000	0	0.0	0.0
B- /7.3	10.4	1.01	210.50	1,857	2	97	0	1	11	133.8	-17.1	67	2	5,000,000	0	0.0	0.0
C+ /6.8	10.5	0.98	199.02	1,570	0	99	0	1	18	134.1	-18.8	67	7	5,000,000	0	0.0	0.0
C /4.3	17.0	1.05	221.46	272	0	99	0	1	50	129.3	N/A	54	2	5,000,000	0	0.0	0.0
C /4.9	15.8	1.20	211.36	555	2	97	0	1	19	132.9	-25.1	13	2	5,000,000	0	0.0	0.0
C /5.5	15.3	0.94	204.56	156	0	99	0	1	31	N/A	N/A	85	2	5,000,000	0	0.0	0.0
C+ /6.8	10.6	1.02	210.62	917	0	99	0	1	8	133.8	-17.8	63	2	5,000,000	0	0.0	0.0
C+ /5.9	11.6	0.93	234.84	246	0	99	0	1	38	126.8	-21.0	73	2	5,000,000	100	0.0	0.0
C+ /6.1	12.0	1.00	231.94	1,092	0	99	0	1	11	139.8	-22.6	74	4	5,000,000	100	0.0	0.0
C+ /6.1	13.2	1.06	228.02	144	0	99	0	1	47	151.5	-24.2	71	2	5,000,000	100	0.0	0.0
C+ /5.6	14.7	0.92	252.80	555	0	99	0	1	15	154.9	-22.1	91	4	5,000,000	100	0.0	0.0
C+ /5.7	12.5	0.96	30.33	10,109	4	95	0	1	27	133.0	-19.1	55	18	3,000	100	0.0	0.0
C /4.5	14.2	0.86	49.39	7,189	0	99	0	1	23	121.4	N/A	57	13	10,000	100	0.0	0.0
C+ /6.0	13.6	0.84	53.40	10,164	0	99	0	1	16	152.7	N/A	93	19	10,000	100	0.0	0.0
C /4.5	14.2	0.86	39.56	3,185	0	99	0	1	23	121.6	-25.1	57	13	5,000,000	100	0.0	0.0
C /4.5	14.2	0.86	39.51	1,890	0	99	0	1	23	119.8	-25.1	55	13	3,000	100	0.0	0.0
C /5.4	13.6	0.85	64.23	29,679	0	98	1	1	11	138.9	-24.5	83	1	10,000	100	0.0	0.0
C /5.4	13.6	0.85	64.23	13,887	0	98	1	1	11	139.0	-24.5	84	1	5,000,000	100	0.0	0.0
C /5.4	13.6	0.85	185.39	8,694	0	98	1	1	11	139.3	-24.5	84	1	100,000,000	100	0.0	0.0
C /5.4	13.6	0.85	64.19	4,575	0	98	1	1	11	137.2	-24.6	83	1	3,000	100	0.0	0.0
C+ /6.0	13.6	0.84	29.85	3,196	0	99	0	1	16	152.8	-24.0	93	19	5,000,000	100	0.0	0.0
C+ /6.1	13.6	0.84	29.79	2,281	0	99	0	1	16	150.7	-24.0	92	19	3,000	100	0.0	0.0
B- /7.8	7.1	0.66	24.69	19,396	1	61	37	1	12	70.3	-11.4	54	N/A	1,000	100	0.0	0.0
C /5.0	12.7	0.76	33.58	7,060	0	99	0	1	74	162.4	-22.2	94	5	3,000	100	0.0	0.0
C+ /5.8	13.9	0.87	35.24	1,637	0	99	0	1	89	153.1	-24.1	88	11	3,000	100	0.0	0.0
B /8.9	4.0	0.60	25.89	5,597	1	31	66	2	8	43.7	-6.9	67	4	1,000	100	0.0	0.0
B /8.3	5.2	0.81	14.93	17,182	1	45	53	1	9	54.7	-9.6	55	4	1,000	100	0.0	0.0
B /8.0	7.0	1.10	16.98	33,669	2	64	33	1	15	70.5	-13.5	38	4	1,000	100	0.0	0.0
B- /7.8	7.7	1.21	30.44	27,346	1	71	27	1	16	77.4	-15.2	31	4	1,000	100	0.0	0.0
B- /7.4	8.6	1.33	18.55	26,504	2	78	19	1	14	84.4	-17.0	24	4	1,000	100	0.0	0.0
B- /7.1	9.3	1.44	31.71	19,359	1	86	12	1	16	88.2	-17.4	18	4	1,000	100	0.0	0.0
B- /7.0	9.4	1.45	19.86	17,666	1	88	9	2	13	88.8	-17.4	18	4	1,000	100	0.0	0.0
B- /7.1	9.4	1.45	31.94	11,140	1	88	9	2	12	88.7	-17.4	18	4	1,000	100	0.0	0.0
B- /7.1	9.4	1.45	34.58	4,253	1	89	9	1	8	88.6	-17.3	18	4	1,000	100	0.0	0.0
B- /7.2	9.4	0.88	30.52	1,474	1	89	9	1	6	N/A	N/A	33	4	1,000	100	0.0	0.0
B+ /9.5	3.6	0.52	13.08	10,729	1	30	68	1	11	34.9	-3.0	72	4	1,000	100	0.0	0.0
B /8.9	4.8	0.77	28.80	3,274	0	48	51	1	9	66.6	-6.5	78	4	10,000	100	0.0	0.0
C+ /6.9	10.5	1.02	120.95	7,234	0	99	0	1	10	136.7	-17.4	67	1	10,000	100	0.0	0.0
C+ /6.9	10.6	1.02	60.10	662	0	99	0	1	10	137.2	-17.4	68	1	5,000,000	100	0.0	0.0

Data as of February 28, 2017

Fund Type	Fund Name	Ticker Symbol	Overall Investment Rating	Phone	Performance Rating/Pts	3 Mo	6 Mo	1Yr / Pct	3Yr / Pct	5Yr / Pct	Dividend Yield	Expense Ratio
SC	Vanguard Tax-Managed Small-Cap	VTSIX	A	(800) 662-7447	A+ / 9.6	4.46	13.07	34.26 /93	9.72 /92	14.84 /97	1.02	0.07
SC	Vanguard Tax-Managed Small-Cap	VTMSX	A	(800) 662-7447	A+ / 9.6	4.45	13.05	34.23 /93	9.68 /91	14.79 /96	1.00	0.11
GR	Vanguard Telecom Services Index	VTCAX	B+	(800) 662-7447	B- / 7.0	4.83	4.41	13.84 /25	9.84 /92	12.41 /78	2.74	0.10
* AA	Vanguard Tgt Retirement 2020 Inv	VTWNX	B-	(800) 662-7447	C- / 4.2	4.72	3.60	13.89 /25	5.05 /55	7.44 /38	1.91	0.14
GR	Vanguard Tot Stk Mkt Idx Adm	VTSAX	A+	(800) 662-7447	A- / 9.2	7.75	10.23	26.28 /77	9.86 /93	13.80 /92	1.82	0.05
GI	Vanguard Tot Stk Mkt Idx Inst	VITSX	A+	(800) 662-7447	A- / 9.2	7.75	10.23	26.28 /77	9.87 /93	13.81 /92	1.83	0.04
GI	Vanguard Tot Stk Mkt Idx Inst Plus	VSMPX	U	(800) 662-7447	U /	7.76	10.25	26.30 /77	--	--	1.84	0.02
* GR	Vanguard Tot Stk Mkt Idx Inv	VTSMX	A+	(800) 662-7447	A- / 9.1	7.72	10.17	26.14 /77	9.74 /92	13.67 /90	1.73	0.16
FO	Vanguard Total Intl Stk Id Ins +	VTPSX	D+	(800) 662-7447	D+ / 2.8	7.62	4.93	19.75 /51	0.33 /15	4.13 /16	2.82	0.07
FO	Vanguard Total Intl Stock Index Adm	VTIAX	D+	(800) 662-7447	D+ / 2.8	7.60	4.92	19.69 /50	0.30 /15	4.09 /16	2.78	0.12
FO	Vanguard Total Intl Stock Index Ins	VTSNX	D+	(800) 662-7447	D+ / 2.8	7.61	4.91	19.70 /50	0.31 /15	4.11 /16	2.80	0.10
* FO	Vanguard Total Intl Stock Index Inv	VGTSX	D+	(800) 662-7447	D+ / 2.7	7.56	4.85	19.58 /50	0.23 /14	4.02 /15	2.72	0.19
EM	Vanguard Total Wld Stk Index Inst	VTWIX	C+	(800) 662-7447	C+ / 6.3	7.72	7.68	23.08 /67	5.13 /56	8.75 /48	2.27	0.15
EM	Vanguard Total Wld Stk Index Inv	VTWSX	C+	(800) 662-7447	C+ / 6.2	7.68	7.60	22.91 /66	5.00 /54	8.61 /47	2.16	0.27
GR	Vanguard US Growth Adm	VWUAX	C+	(800) 662-7447	C+ / 6.8	7.47	4.81	15.98 /34	8.16 /80	13.00 /84	0.53	0.33
GR	Vanguard US Growth Inv	VWUSX	C+	(800) 662-7447	C+ / 6.7	7.44	4.75	15.87 /34	8.01 /79	12.84 /82	0.38	0.47
GR	Vanguard US Value Inv	VUVLX	A+	(800) 662-7447	A+ / 9.6	6.62	14.05	28.78 /83	10.11 /94	14.85 /97	2.01	0.26
UT	Vanguard Utilities Index Adm	VUIAX	A+	(800) 662-7447	A / 9.5	11.25	7.63	17.14 /39	12.44 /98	12.72 /81	3.00	0.10
GR	Vanguard Value Index Adm	VVIAX	A+	(800) 662-7447	A+ / 9.6	7.03	11.61	27.81 /81	10.92 /97	14.29 /95	2.35	0.08
GR	Vanguard Value Index Inst	VIVIX	A+	(800) 662-7447	A+ / 9.6	7.03	11.61	27.82 /81	10.93 /97	14.30 /95	2.36	0.07
GR	Vanguard Value Index Inv	VIVAX	A+	(800) 662-7447	A+ / 9.6	7.00	11.55	27.65 /81	10.77 /97	14.12 /94	2.24	0.22
AA	Vanguard Wellesley Income Adm	VWIAX	B-	(800) 662-7447	C- / 3.9	3.63	1.31	10.32 /12	6.02 /64	7.16 /36	2.92	0.16
* AA	Vanguard Wellesley Income Inv	VWINX	B-	(800) 662-7447	C- / 3.8	3.61	1.27	10.23 /12	5.95 /64	7.09 /35	2.85	0.23
BA	● Vanguard Wellington Adm	VWENX	B-	(800) 662-7447	C+ / 6.9	5.84	6.80	18.70 /46	7.70 /77	10.04 /59	2.50	0.18
* BA	● Vanguard Wellington Inv	VWELX	B-	(800) 662-7447	C+ / 6.8	5.81	6.76	18.60 /45	7.61 /76	9.95 /58	2.42	0.26
MC	Vanguard Windsor-I Adm	VWNEX	B+	(800) 662-7447	A- / 9.1	7.52	12.83	31.48 /89	8.03 /79	13.86 /92	1.93	0.29
* MC	Vanguard Windsor-I Inv	VWNDX	B+	(800) 662-7447	A- / 9.0	7.46	12.72	31.34 /89	7.92 /78	13.74 /91	1.83	0.39
GR	Vanguard Windsor-II Adm	VWNAX	B+	(800) 662-7447	B / 8.2	6.20	9.73	26.39 /77	8.20 /80	12.47 /79	2.34	0.26
* GR	Vanguard Windsor-II Inv	VWNFX	B+	(800) 662-7447	B / 8.2	6.18	9.71	26.32 /77	8.12 /80	12.39 /78	2.26	0.34
GR	Vanguard WY College Inv Agg Gr		A	(800) 662-7447	B- / 7.4	7.65	8.49	23.98 /70	6.93 /71	11.07 /66	0.00	0.52
GI	Vanguard WY College Inv Con Gr		C+	(800) 662-7447	D / 2.2	2.63	0.27	6.62 / 5	3.77 /40	4.32 /17	0.00	0.52
GI	Vanguard WY College Inv Gr Port		B	(800) 662-7447	C+ / 5.7	5.91	5.71	18.00 /43	5.99 /64	8.90 /50	0.00	0.52
GI	Vanguard WY College Inv Mod Gr		B	(800) 662-7447	C- / 3.8	4.23	2.92	12.17 /19	4.97 /54	6.66 /33	0.00	0.52
GR	Vanguard WY College Inv St Ind Port		A+	(800) 662-7447	A- / 9.0	7.65	10.06	25.86 /76	9.53 /91	13.43 /88	0.00	0.52
SC	Vericimetry US Small Cap Value	VYSVX	B+	(855) 755-7550	B / 8.0	3.63	14.16	31.58 /89	6.35 /67	13.09 /85	0.67	0.69
IN	● Victory CEMP Com En Vol Wtd Id St	CCNAX	D	(888) 944-4367	E- / 0.2	1.11	4.07	11.14 /15	-4.62 / 3	--	0.00	2.18
IN	● Victory CEMP Com En Vol Wtd Id St	CCNCX	D-	(888) 944-4367	E- / 0.2	0.90	3.54	10.20 /12	-5.40 / 2	--	0.00	3.85
IN	● Victory CEMP Com En Vol Wtd Id St I	CCNIX	D	(888) 944-4367	E / 0.3	1.10	4.17	11.34 /16	-4.39 / 3	--	0.00	1.72
OT	Victory CEMP Comm Vol Wtd Idx Str	CCOAX	E	(888) 944-4367	E- / 0.1	1.41	4.51	11.51 /16	-8.74 / 1	--	0.00	2.12
OT	Victory CEMP Comm Vol Wtd Idx Str	CCOCX	E	(888) 944-4367	E- / 0.1	1.29	4.15	10.56 /13	-9.46 / 1	--	0.00	3.29
OT	Victory CEMP Comm Vol Wtd Idx Str	CCOIX	E	(888) 944-4367	E- / 0.1	1.40	4.47	11.60 /16	-8.53 / 1	--	0.00	1.63
GL	Victory CEMP Global High Div Def A	LTGAX	D-	(888) 944-4367	C- / 3.6	5.35	6.14	17.26 /40	4.76 /52	6.44 /31	2.21	1.89
GL	Victory CEMP Global High Div Def C	LTGCX	D	(888) 944-4367	C- / 4.2	5.23	5.69	16.43 /36	3.96 /43	5.62 /26	2.00	2.55
GR	Victory CEMP Long/Short Strategy A	CHLAX	C	(888) 944-4367	D+ / 2.7	3.25	5.11	12.24 /19	4.70 /51	--	0.17	2.20
GR	Victory CEMP Long/Short Strategy C	CHLCX	C	(888) 944-4367	C- / 3.2	3.09	4.70	11.38 /16	3.92 /42	--	0.00	3.46
GR	Victory CEMP Long/Short Strategy I	CHLIX	C+	(888) 944-4367	C- / 4.0	3.33	5.23	12.48 /20	4.99 /54	--	0.42	1.81
GR	Victory CEMP US 500 Enh Vol Wtd A	CUHAX	B+	(888) 944-4367	B / 7.8	7.36	10.23	25.33 /74	9.17 /88	--	0.67	1.34
GR	Victory CEMP US 500 Enh Vol Wtd C	CUHCX	A-	(888) 944-4367	B / 8.2	7.14	9.79	24.37 /71	8.34 /82	--	0.15	2.06
GR	Victory CEMP US 500 Enh Vol Wtd I	CUHIX	A	(888) 944-4367	B+ / 8.9	7.37	10.29	25.53 /75	9.41 /90	--	0.92	1.05
GR	Victory Diversified Stk A	SRVEX	D+	(800) 539-3863	C- / 4.0	6.38	5.85	15.55 /32	5.48 /59	10.65 /63	1.10	1.09
GR	Victory Diversified Stk C	VDSCX	D+	(800) 539-3863	C / 4.4	6.12	5.38	14.61 /28	4.61 /50	9.73 /56	0.43	1.91
GR	Victory Diversified Stk I	VDSIX	C-	(800) 539-3863	C / 5.4	6.47	5.94	15.89 /34	5.76 /62	10.94 /65	1.42	0.81

99 Pct = Best
0 Pct = Worst

● Denotes fund is closed to new investors
* Denotes fund is included in Section II

www.thestreetratings.com

| RISK | | | NET ASSETS | | ASSET | | | | | BULL / BEAR | | FUND MANAGER | | MINIMUMS | | LOADS | |
Risk Rating/Pts	3 Year Standard Deviation	Beta	NAV As of 2/28/17	Total $(Mil)	Cash %	Stocks %	Bonds %	Other %	Portfolio Turnover Ratio	Last Bull Market Return	Last Bear Market Return	Manager Quality Pct	Manager Tenure (Years)	Initial Purch. $	Additional Purch. $	Front End Load	Back End Load
C /5.5	14.5	0.91	55.90	379	0	98	0	2	33	154.8	-21.9	91	1	5,000,000	100	0.0	0.0
C /5.5	14.5	0.91	55.77	4,845	0	98	0	2	33	154.2	-21.9	91	1	10,000	100	0.0	0.0
C+ /6.8	12.0	0.65	49.80	60	0	97	2	1	20	96.5	-13.5	89	2	100,000	0	0.0	0.0
B /8.5	6.2	0.98	29.23	29,023	2	56	41	1	15	63.5	-11.6	46	4	1,000	100	0.0	0.0
C+ /6.8	10.6	1.02	59.28	162,270	0	99	0	1	3	134.5	-17.7	63	23	10,000	100	0.0	0.0
C+ /6.8	10.6	1.02	59.29	87,549	0	99	0	1	3	134.5	-17.7	63	23	5,000,000	100	0.0	0.0
U /	N/A	N/A	111.19	96,124	0	99	0	1	3	N/A	N/A	N/A	23	100,000,000	100	0.0	0.0
C+ /6.8	10.6	1.02	59.25	110,696	0	99	0	1	3	133.0	-17.7	62	23	3,000	100	0.0	0.0
C+ /5.8	11.6	0.91	103.91	72,995	1	98	0	1	3	44.0	-24.3	78	9	100,000,000	100	0.0	0.0
C+ /5.8	11.6	0.91	25.98	50,167	1	98	0	1	3	43.6	-24.3	77	9	10,000	100	0.0	0.0
C+ /5.8	11.6	0.91	103.88	21,840	1	98	0	1	3	43.8	-24.3	77	9	5,000,000	100	0.0	0.0
C+ /5.8	11.6	0.91	15.53	97,542	1	98	0	1	3	43.1	-24.4	77	9	3,000	100	0.0	0.0
C+ /6.4	10.5	0.51	131.77	1,868	1	98	0	1	15	82.1	-21.1	94	4	5,000,000	100	0.0	0.0
C+ /6.4	10.5	0.51	26.29	1,269	1	98	0	1	15	80.8	-21.2	93	4	3,000	100	0.0	0.0
C /5.0	11.6	1.00	80.96	3,143	3	96	0	1	32	131.8	-17.3	44	7	50,000	0	0.0	0.0
C /5.0	11.7	1.00	31.29	3,783	3	96	0	1	32	130.0	-17.4	42	7	3,000	0	0.0	0.0
C+ /6.6	11.0	0.99	18.96	1,657	0	99	0	1	76	145.8	-18.4	70	9	3,000	100	0.0	0.0
C+ /6.5	14.0	0.95	56.98	726	0	99	0	1	7	92.0	1.4	58	2	100,000	0	0.0	0.0
B- /7.2	10.1	0.95	37.78	14,349	0	99	0	1	8	135.7	-18.4	80	23	10,000	100	0.0	0.0
B- /7.2	10.1	0.95	37.78	9,182	0	99	0	1	8	135.8	-18.4	80	23	5,000,000	100	0.0	0.0
B- /7.2	10.1	0.94	37.78	1,626	0	99	0	1	8	133.9	-18.5	79	23	3,000	100	0.0	0.0
B /8.8	4.4	0.61	63.08	36,891	1	36	61	2	31	54.8	-1.9	83	10	50,000	100	0.0	0.0
B /8.8	4.4	0.61	26.04	14,240	1	36	61	2	31	54.2	-1.9	83	10	3,000	100	0.0	0.0
B- /7.6	6.9	1.09	69.90	79,021	1	65	33	1	39	85.1	-10.4	69	15	50,000	100	0.0	0.0
B- /7.6	6.9	1.10	40.47	19,569	1	65	33	1	39	84.3	-10.4	67	15	3,000	100	0.0	0.0
C /5.2	12.5	0.95	73.14	13,113	1	97	0	2	26	137.8	-21.1	62	9	50,000	100	0.0	0.0
C /5.2	12.5	0.95	21.68	5,283	1	97	0	2	26	136.5	-21.1	60	9	3,000	100	0.0	0.0
C+ /5.6	10.7	1.01	65.15	33,961	1	98	0	1	33	120.3	-17.1	44	14	50,000	100	0.0	0.0
C+ /5.6	10.8	1.01	36.72	14,634	1	98	0	1	33	119.4	-17.2	43	14	3,000	100	0.0	0.0
B- /7.7	10.4	0.99	23.78	419	0	0	0	100	0	105.5	-19.2	31	8	25	15	0.0	0.0
B+ /9.9	3.4	0.23	18.36	365	0	0	0	100	0	31.6	-1.6	82	8	25	15	0.0	0.0
B /8.7	7.8	0.74	22.22	454	0	0	0	100	0	78.5	-13.5	53	8	25	15	0.0	0.0
B+ /9.7	5.3	0.48	20.46	431	0	0	0	100	0	54.1	-7.8	73	8	25	15	0.0	0.0
B /8.1	10.6	1.02	27.45	218	0	0	0	100	0	130.3	-17.8	60	8	25	15	0.0	0.0
C+ /6.1	14.3	0.88	18.73	285	3	96	0	1	39	N/A	N/A	76	6	0	0	0.0	0.0
B- /7.2	8.4	0.17	8.18	1	36	0	63	1	26	N/A	N/A	7	N/A	2,500	50	5.8	0.0
B- /7.1	8.4	0.17	7.89	N/A	36	0	63	1	26	N/A	N/A	5	N/A	2,500	50	0.0	0.0
B- /7.3	8.4	0.17	8.25	2	36	0	63	1	26	N/A	N/A	8	N/A	2,000,000	0	0.0	0.0
C- /4.0	11.0	0.24	6.49	5	27	0	72	1	80	N/A	N/A	1	5	2,500	50	5.8	0.0
C- /3.9	11.1	0.24	6.28	N/A	27	0	72	1	80	N/A	N/A	1	5	2,500	50	0.0	0.0
C- /4.0	11.1	0.24	6.54	3	27	0	72	1	80	N/A	N/A	1	5	2,000,000	0	0.0	0.0
C- /3.4	8.8	0.61	9.72	5	5	94	0	1	120	39.6	-14.1	95	N/A	2,500	50	5.8	0.0
C- /3.3	8.8	0.61	9.32	6	5	94	0	1	120	34.1	-14.4	93	N/A	2,500	50	0.0	0.0
B- /7.8	5.9	0.52	11.74	2	7	92	0	1	77	N/A	N/A	65	N/A	2,500	50	5.8	0.0
B- /7.8	5.9	0.52	11.35	N/A	7	92	0	1	77	N/A	N/A	56	N/A	2,500	50	0.0	0.0
B- /7.8	5.9	0.52	11.79	3	7	92	0	1	77	N/A	N/A	69	N/A	2,000,000	0	0.0	0.0
C+ /6.6	10.4	0.97	15.58	40	1	98	0	1	46	N/A	N/A	61	N/A	2,500	50	5.8	0.0
C+ /6.6	10.4	0.98	15.31	59	1	98	0	1	46	N/A	N/A	50	N/A	2,500	50	0.0	0.0
C+ /6.6	10.4	0.97	15.58	37	1	98	0	1	46	N/A	N/A	64	N/A	2,000,000	0	0.0	0.0
C /4.5	10.2	0.94	19.39	322	1	98	0	1	74	107.7	-22.6	22	28	2,500	250	5.8	0.0
C /4.4	10.2	0.94	18.60	48	1	98	0	1	74	98.7	-22.9	15	28	2,500	250	0.0	0.0
C /4.5	10.1	0.94	19.36	132	1	98	0	1	74	110.8	-22.5	24	28	2,000,000	0	0.0	0.0

99 Pct = Best
0 Pct = Worst

Fund Type	Fund Name	Ticker Symbol	Overall Investment Rating	Phone	PERFORMANCE Perfor-mance Rating/Pts	Total Return % through 2/28/17 3 Mo	6 Mo	1Yr / Pct	Annualized 3Yr / Pct	5Yr / Pct	Incl. in Returns Dividend Yield	Expense Ratio
GR	Victory Diversified Stk R	GRINX	C-	(800) 539-3863	C / 4.9	6.29	5.66	15.20 /31	5.17 /56	10.33 /61	0.92	1.38
GI	Victory Diversified Stk Y	VDSYX	C-	(800) 539-3863	C / 5.3	6.39	5.91	15.81 /33	5.71 /62	--	1.37	0.98
EM	Victory Expedition Em Mkts Sm Cap I	VIEMX	U	(800) 539-3863	U /	2.66	-8.52	3.39 / 3	--	--	0.18	3.18
EN	Victory Global Natural Resources A	RSNRX	E-	(800) 539-3863	E- / 0.1	-3.51	6.90	56.58 /99	-11.91 / 1	-7.05 / 1	0.00	1.44
EN	Victory Global Natural Resources C	RGNCX	E-	(800) 539-3863	E- / 0.2	-3.68	6.48	55.47 /99	-12.59 / 0	-7.76 / 1	0.00	2.25
EN	Victory Global Natural Resources R	RSNKX	E-	(800) 539-3863	E- / 0.2	-3.59	6.79	56.17 /99	-12.20 / 0	-7.35 / 1	0.00	1.73
EN	Victory Global Natural Resources Y	RSNYX	E-	(800) 539-3863	E / 0.3	-3.40	7.09	57.14 /99	-11.62 / 1	-6.73 / 1	0.00	1.14
CV	Victory INCORE Invt Grade Conv A	SBFCX	C+	(800) 539-3863	C / 4.3	5.44	5.48	14.41 /27	5.30 /58	8.07 /43	1.30	1.40
CV	Victory INCORE Invt Grade Conv I	VICIX	B-	(800) 539-3863	C / 5.1	5.53	5.82	14.96 /30	5.75 /62	8.56 /47	1.71	1.02
GR	Victory Inst Diversified Stock Fund	VIDSX	C-	(800) 539-3863	C / 5.3	6.34	5.73	15.76 /33	5.69 /61	10.96 /66	1.26	0.60
SC	Victory Integrity Discovery A	MMEAX	B+	(800) 539-3863	A+ / 9.7	6.46	18.45	41.71 /98	10.01 /93	16.50 /98	0.00	1.61
SC	Victory Integrity Discovery C	MMECX	B+	(800) 539-3863	A+ / 9.8	6.24	17.97	40.61 /97	9.15 /88	15.60 /98	0.00	2.39
SC	Victory Integrity Discovery R	MMERX	B+	(800) 539-3863	A+ / 9.8	6.26	18.09	40.92 /98	9.52 /90	16.08 /98	0.00	2.40
SC	Victory Integrity Discovery Y	MMEYX	B+	(800) 539-3863	A+ / 9.8	6.48	18.57	42.00 /98	10.27 /95	16.79 /98	0.00	1.36
MC	Victory Integrity Mid-Cap Value A	MAIMX	B+	(800) 539-3863	B / 7.8	5.83	11.75	32.01 /90	7.65 /76	13.60 /90	0.00	1.63
MC	Victory Integrity Mid-Cap Value Y	MYIMX	A	(800) 539-3863	A- / 9.0	5.94	11.93	32.56 /91	8.01 /79	13.92 /93	0.43	1.15
GR	Victory Integrity Sm/Mid-Cap Val A	MAISX	B+	(800) 539-3863	B / 8.1	6.89	16.27	35.52 /94	6.38 /67	11.97 /74	0.00	2.05
GR	Victory Integrity Sm/Mid-Cap Val Y	MYISX	A-	(800) 539-3863	A- / 9.2	6.94	16.41	35.84 /95	6.67 /70	12.26 /77	0.10	1.16
SC	Victory Integrity Small Cap Val C	MCVSX	A-	(800) 539-3863	A- / 9.1	5.24	16.49	35.65 /95	6.94 /72	12.63 /80	0.00	2.22
SC	Victory Integrity Small Cap Val R	MRVSX	A	(800) 539-3863	A / 9.4	5.34	16.73	36.24 /95	7.44 /75	13.17 /86	0.00	1.96
SC	Victory Integrity Small Cap Val R6	MVSSX	A	(800) 539-3863	A+ / 9.6	5.55	17.15	37.31 /96	8.23 /81	--	0.34	1.00
SC	Victory Integrity Small Cap Val Y	VSVIX	A	(800) 539-3863	A+ / 9.6	5.53	17.10	37.14 /96	8.07 /79	13.79 /92	0.25	1.15
SC	Victory Integrity Small Cap Value A	VSCVX	B+	(800) 539-3863	B+ / 8.7	5.39	16.85	36.59 /95	7.70 /77	13.45 /88	0.00	1.57
MC	Victory Munder MidCap Core Gro A	MGOAX	D+	(800) 539-3863	C+ / 5.7	7.58	8.99	23.04 /67	5.78 /62	10.76 /64	0.00	1.34
MC	Victory Munder MidCap Core Gro C	MGOTX	C-	(800) 539-3863	C+ / 6.3	7.41	8.60	22.22 /63	5.06 /55	9.97 /58	0.00	2.00
MC	Victory Munder MidCap Core Gro R	MMSRX	C-	(800) 539-3863	C+ / 6.6	7.49	8.83	22.71 /65	5.49 /59	10.47 /62	0.00	1.62
MC	Victory Munder MidCap Core Gro R6	MGOSX	C	(800) 539-3863	B- / 7.1	7.71	9.25	23.61 /69	6.23 /66	--	0.00	0.87
MC	Victory Munder MidCap Core Gro Y	MGOYX	C	(800) 539-3863	C+ / 6.9	7.65	9.12	23.35 /68	6.06 /65	11.04 /66	0.00	1.06
TC	Victory Munder Multi Cap A	MNNAX	C	(800) 539-3863	C+ / 6.9	8.00	9.20	20.85 /57	8.28 /81	11.51 /70	0.00	1.46
TC	Victory Munder Multi Cap C	MNNCX	C	(800) 539-3863	B- / 7.2	7.76	8.74	19.86 /51	7.39 /75	10.62 /63	0.00	2.28
TC	Victory Munder Multi Cap R	MNNRX	C+	(800) 539-3863	B- / 7.5	7.88	8.98	20.29 /54	7.85 /78	11.13 /67	0.00	2.48
TC	Victory Munder Multi Cap Y	MNNYX	B-	(800) 539-3863	B / 8.1	8.11	9.43	21.34 /59	8.69 /85	11.87 /73	0.00	1.01
GL	Victory NewBridge Global Equity A	VPGEX	D	(800) 539-3863	D+ / 2.6	6.76	6.68	16.29 /35	2.56 /28	7.53 /39	0.84	2.03
GL	Victory NewBridge Global Equity C	VPGCX	D+	(800) 539-3863	C- / 3.1	6.64	6.28	15.48 /32	1.84 /23	6.74 /33	0.01	2.50
GL	Victory NewBridge Global Equity I	VPGYX	D+	(800) 539-3863	C- / 3.9	6.87	6.78	16.59 /37	2.83 /30	7.80 /41	1.15	1.60
GR	Victory Newbridge Large Cap Grow A	VFGAX	E-	(800) 539-3863	C- / 3.4	7.39	3.32	15.19 /31	4.76 /52	9.63 /56	0.00	1.26
GR	Victory Newbridge Large Cap Grow C	VFGCX	E	(800) 539-3863	C- / 3.9	7.20	3.01	14.35 /27	4.01 /43	8.83 /49	0.00	2.13
GR	Victory Newbridge Large Cap Grow I	VFGIX	E	(800) 539-3863	C / 4.8	7.51	3.61	15.76 /33	5.12 /55	10.00 /58	0.00	1.04
GR	Victory Newbridge Large Cap Grow R	VFGRX	E	(800) 539-3863	C / 4.3	7.34	3.23	14.95 /30	4.50 /49	9.31 /53	0.00	3.06
GR	Victory Newbridge Large Cap Grow Y	VFGYX	E	(800) 539-3863	C / 4.8	7.55	3.60	15.64 /33	5.03 /55	--	0.00	1.04
GL	Victory RS Global A	RSGGX	C+	(800) 539-3863	C / 5.1	7.22	6.86	18.99 /47	6.28 /67	10.73 /64	0.19	1.54
GL	Victory RS Global C	RGGCX	C+	(800) 539-3863	C+ / 5.6	7.03	6.49	18.04 /43	5.47 /59	9.93 /58	0.00	2.34
GL	Victory RS Global R	RGGKX	A+	(800) 539-3863	A+ / 9.9	7.19	13.24	45.64 /99	13.38 /99	14.99 /97	1.61	1.81
GL	Victory RS Global Y	RGGYX	C+	(800) 539-3863	C+ / 6.6	7.37	7.11	19.41 /49	6.60 /69	11.13 /67	1.78	1.32
GR	Victory RS Growth A	RSGRX	C-	(800) 539-3863	C+ / 6.1	9.22	7.40	20.49 /55	7.00 /72	13.30 /87	0.00	1.18
GR	Victory RS Growth C	RGWCX	C-	(800) 539-3863	C+ / 6.5	8.99	6.96	19.47 /49	6.12 /65	12.33 /77	0.00	2.00
GR	Victory RS Growth R	RSGKX	C-	(800) 539-3863	C+ / 6.7	9.07	7.10	19.76 /51	6.37 /67	12.60 /80	0.00	1.79
GR	Victory RS Growth Y	RGRYX	C	(800) 539-3863	B- / 7.3	9.28	7.56	20.77 /56	7.29 /74	13.59 /90	0.00	0.94
FO	Victory RS International A	GUBGX	E	(800) 539-3863	D- / 1.0	7.11	6.13	16.94 /38	-0.41 /12	4.04 /15	1.60	1.82
FO	Victory RS International C	RIGCX	E	(800) 539-3863	D- / 1.1	7.01	5.83	16.05 /35	-1.31 / 8	3.08 /11	1.69	2.75
FO	Victory RS International R	RIGKX	E	(800) 539-3863	D- / 1.3	6.96	5.92	16.41 /36	-0.90 /10	3.55 /13	1.44	2.26
FO	Victory RS International Y	RSIGX	E	(800) 539-3863	D / 1.6	7.25	6.37	17.26 /40	-0.12 /13	4.40 /18	1.85	1.69

● Denotes fund is closed to new investors
* Denotes fund is included in Section II

www.thestreetratings.com

Risk Rating/Pts	Standard Deviation	Beta	NAV As of 2/28/17	Total $(Mil)	Cash %	Stocks %	Bonds %	Other %	Portfolio Turnover Ratio	Last Bull Market Return	Last Bear Market Return	Manager Quality Pct	Manager Tenure (Years)	Initial Purch. $	Additional Purch. $	Front End Load	Back End Load
C /4.4	10.2	0.94	19.11	69	1	98	0	1	74	104.4	-22.7	19	28	0	0	0.0	0.0
C /4.5	10.1	0.94	19.38	11	1	98	0	1	74	N/A	N/A	24	28	0	0	0.0	0.0
U /	N/A	N/A	8.72	32	3	96	0	1	111	N/A	N/A	N/A	3	2,000,000	0	0.0	0.0
E /0.5	30.4	1.29	23.08	505	2	92	4	2	33	-15.3	-25.2	10	12	2,500	100	5.8	0.0
E /0.5	30.4	1.29	21.19	29	2	92	4	2	33	-18.7	-25.4	7	12	2,500	100	0.0	0.0
E /0.5	30.4	1.29	22.02	3	2	92	4	2	33	-16.8	-25.3	9	12	1,000	0	0.0	0.0
E+/0.6	30.4	1.29	23.87	1,254	2	92	4	2	33	-13.7	-25.1	12	12	0	100	0.0	0.0
B-/7.4	7.2	0.78	14.58	32	10	11	2	77	22	63.0	-12.2	83	21	2,500	250	2.0	0.0
B-/7.4	7.2	0.78	14.58	47	10	11	2	77	22	67.1	-12.1	85	21	2,000,000	0	0.0	0.0
C /4.4	10.1	0.94	10.52	89	6	93	0	1	68	110.1	-22.1	24	12	10,000,000	0	0.0	0.0
C /4.5	16.4	1.00	40.67	133	2	97	0	1	42	183.2	-24.9	90	N/A	2,500	50	5.8	0.0
C-/4.0	16.4	1.00	31.50	17	2	97	0	1	42	171.7	-25.1	87	N/A	2,500	50	0.0	0.0
C /4.4	16.4	1.00	39.21	2	2	97	0	1	42	177.7	-24.9	88	N/A	0	0	0.0	0.0
C /4.5	16.4	1.00	43.71	48	2	97	0	1	42	187.0	-24.8	91	N/A	1,000,000	0	0.0	0.0
C+/6.2	12.7	1.03	17.98	2	2	97	0	1	71	140.7	N/A	47	N/A	2,500	50	5.8	0.0
C+/6.2	12.7	1.03	18.12	41	2	97	0	1	71	144.6	N/A	52	N/A	1,000,000	0	0.0	0.0
C+/5.6	14.3	1.12	16.29	2	2	97	0	1	60	126.3	N/A	14	N/A	2,500	50	5.8	0.0
C+/5.7	14.3	1.12	16.42	40	2	97	0	1	60	129.7	N/A	17	N/A	1,000,000	0	0.0	0.0
C+/5.6	15.7	0.96	34.55	32	4	95	0	1	47	130.9	N/A	76	N/A	2,500	50	0.0	0.0
C+/5.7	15.7	0.96	37.67	17	4	95	0	1	47	137.1	N/A	79	N/A	0	0	0.0	0.0
C+/5.7	15.7	0.96	39.60	857	4	95	0	1	47	N/A	N/A	84	N/A	0	0	0.0	0.0
C+/5.7	15.7	0.96	39.41	1,293	4	95	0	1	47	144.2	-25.0	83	N/A	1,000,000	0	0.0	0.0
C+/5.7	15.7	0.96	38.49	230	4	95	0	1	47	140.3	-25.0	81	N/A	2,500	50	5.8	0.0
C-/3.6	12.0	0.95	35.89	801	0	99	0	1	40	105.5	-19.0	34	16	2,500	50	5.8	0.0
C-/3.2	12.0	0.95	30.48	178	0	99	0	1	40	97.7	-19.3	26	16	2,500	50	0.0	0.0
C-/3.5	12.0	0.94	34.58	37	0	99	0	1	40	102.6	-19.1	30	16	0	0	0.0	0.0
C-/3.7	12.0	0.94	38.09	820	0	99	0	1	40	N/A	N/A	39	16	0	0	0.0	0.0
C-/3.7	12.0	0.95	37.68	2,571	0	99	0	1	40	108.3	-18.9	37	16	1,000,000	0	0.0	0.0
C /4.3	11.1	1.01	40.22	334	1	98	0	1	117	111.8	-20.7	45	7	2,500	50	5.8	0.0
C-/3.8	11.1	1.01	33.61	69	1	98	0	1	117	102.8	-20.9	33	7	2,500	50	0.0	0.0
C-/4.2	11.1	1.01	38.48	1	1	98	0	1	117	108.0	-20.8	39	7	0	0	0.0	0.0
C /4.5	11.1	1.01	42.93	23	1	98	0	1	117	115.5	-20.6	50	7	1,000,000	0	0.0	0.0
C /5.5	10.0	0.74	12.65	N/A	2	97	0	1	109	76.0	-21.4	89	3	2,500	250	5.8	0.0
C /5.5	10.0	0.74	12.54	N/A	2	97	0	1	109	69.2	-21.7	86	3	2,500	250	0.0	0.0
C /5.4	10.0	0.73	12.66	9	2	97	0	1	109	78.5	-21.3	90	3	2,000,000	0	0.0	0.0
E-/0.2	12.4	1.01	9.02	9	1	98	0	1	52	90.8	-18.2	11	14	2,500	250	5.8	0.0
E-/0.2	12.4	1.01	6.72	5	1	98	0	1	52	83.2	-18.5	8	14	2,500	250	0.0	0.0
E-/0.2	12.4	1.01	9.41	20	1	98	0	1	52	94.3	-18.1	14	14	2,000,000	0	0.0	0.0
E-/0.2	12.4	1.01	8.05	1	1	98	0	1	52	87.8	-18.3	10	14	0	0	0.0	0.0
E-/0.2	12.4	1.01	9.22	3	1	98	0	1	52	N/A	N/A	13	14	0	0	0.0	0.0
C+/6.5	9.6	0.72	11.77	6	2	97	0	1	90	99.5	N/A	97	4	2,500	100	5.8	0.0
C+/6.6	9.6	0.71	11.53	1	2	97	0	1	90	91.7	N/A	96	4	2,500	100	0.0	0.0
C+/6.6	13.1	0.73	14.36	1	2	97	0	1	90	140.5	N/A	99	4	1,000	0	0.0	0.0
C+/6.4	9.6	0.72	11.65	15	2	97	0	1	90	103.5	N/A	97	4	0	100	0.0	0.0
C-/3.8	11.6	1.00	17.89	200	1	97	1	1	105	126.8	-16.0	30	8	2,500	100	5.8	0.0
C-/3.4	11.6	1.00	15.77	8	1	97	1	1	105	115.6	-16.3	22	8	2,500	100	0.0	0.0
C-/3.6	11.6	1.00	16.83	1	1	97	1	1	105	119.4	-16.1	24	8	1,000	0	0.0	0.0
C-/3.8	11.6	1.00	18.37	26	1	97	1	1	105	130.0	-15.9	34	8	0	100	0.0	0.0
C-/3.5	9.9	0.78	10.26	17	2	96	0	2	117	45.6	-25.1	71	8	2,500	100	5.8	0.0
D+/2.6	9.9	0.78	7.56	1	2	96	0	2	117	38.5	-25.3	60	8	2,500	100	0.0	0.0
C-/3.3	9.9	0.78	9.61	2	2	96	0	2	117	41.9	-25.3	65	8	1,000	0	0.0	0.0
C-/3.4	9.9	0.78	10.11	3	2	96	0	2	117	48.3	-25.0	74	14	0	100	0.0	0.0

I. Index of Stock Mutual Funds

			99 Pct = Best 0 Pct = Worst		PERFORMANCE						Incl. in Returns	
			Overall		Perfor-	Total Return % through 2/28/17						
			Investment		mance				Annualized		Dividend	Expense
Fund Type	Fund Name	Ticker Symbol	Rating	Phone	Rating/Pts	3 Mo	6 Mo	1Yr / Pct	3Yr / Pct	5Yr / Pct	Yield	Ratio
GL	Victory RS Investors A	RSINX	C-	(800) 539-3863	C- / 4.0	6.52	7.56	22.16 /63	3.76 /40	13.45 /88	0.00	1.49
GL	Victory RS Investors C	RIVCX	C-	(800) 539-3863	C / 4.5	6.34	7.11	21.34 /59	3.00 /32	12.61 /80	0.00	2.27
GL	Victory RS Investors R	RSIKX	C	(800) 539-3863	C / 4.7	6.37	7.23	21.58 /60	3.21 /34	12.90 /83	0.00	1.89
GL	Victory RS Investors Y	RSIYX	C	(800) 539-3863	C / 5.4	6.56	7.60	22.51 /65	4.01 /43	13.74 /91	0.05	1.19
IN	Victory RS Large Cap Alpha A	GPAFX	C	(800) 539-3863	C+ / 6.5	6.73	11.83	21.66 /61	7.05 /72	13.10 /85	0.70	0.88
IN	Victory RS Large Cap Alpha C	RCOCX	C	(800) 539-3863	C+ / 6.8	6.53	11.37	20.70 /56	6.19 /66	12.20 /76	0.07	1.68
IN	Victory RS Large Cap Alpha R	RCEKX	C+	(800) 539-3863	B- / 7.1	6.66	11.64	21.27 /59	6.66 /70	12.69 /81	0.37	1.28
IN	Victory RS Large Cap Alpha Y	RCEYX	C+	(800) 539-3863	B / 7.6	6.80	11.93	21.92 /62	7.28 /74	13.37 /88	0.98	0.67
MC	Victory RS Mid Cap Growth A	RSMOX	C-	(800) 539-3863	C / 4.7	5.87	5.52	22.57 /65	5.35 /58	11.57 /71	0.00	1.29
MC	Victory RS Mid Cap Growth C	RMOCX	C-	(800) 539-3863	C / 5.1	5.63	5.03	21.50 /60	4.44 /48	10.59 /63	0.00	2.09
MC	Victory RS Mid Cap Growth R	RSMKX	C	(800) 539-3863	C / 5.5	5.78	5.31	22.01 /62	4.83 /52	11.00 /66	0.00	1.73
MC	Victory RS Mid Cap Growth Y	RMOYX	C	(800) 539-3863	C+ / 6.1	5.90	5.66	22.86 /66	5.61 /61	11.85 /73	0.00	1.05
SC	● Victory RS Partners A	RSPFX	D+	(800) 539-3863	C+ / 6.4	6.13	13.57	37.30 /96	3.30 /35	11.44 /69	0.00	1.41
SC	Victory RS Partners R	RSPKX	C-	(800) 539-3863	B- / 7.1	6.05	13.40	36.82 /96	2.93 /31	11.02 /66	0.00	1.85
SC	Victory RS Partners Y	RSPYX	C-	(800) 539-3863	B / 7.6	6.23	13.76	37.74 /96	3.63 /38	11.79 /72	0.00	1.17
TC	Victory RS Science and Technology	RSIFX	C+	(800) 539-3863	A+ / 9.8	11.08	16.44	46.39 /99	10.92 /97	14.16 /94	0.00	1.47
TC	Victory RS Science and Technology	RINCX	C	(800) 539-3863	A+ / 9.9	10.90	15.95	45.34 /99	10.05 /94	13.24 /86	0.00	2.26
TC	Victory RS Science and Technology	RIFKX	C	(800) 539-3863	A+ / 9.9	10.96	16.24	45.87 /99	10.44 /96	13.62 /90	0.00	1.97
TC	Victory RS Science and Technology	RIFYX	C+	(800) 539-3863	A+ / 9.9	11.14	16.61	46.80 /99	11.22 /97	14.47 /95	0.00	1.23
SC	Victory RS Select Growth A	RSDGX	D-	(800) 539-3863	C- / 3.8	4.16	6.77	24.44 /71	3.54 /38	10.34 /61	0.00	1.43
SC	Victory RS Select Growth C	RSGFX	D	(800) 539-3863	C / 4.3	3.97	6.37	23.49 /68	2.73 /29	9.48 /55	0.00	2.19
SC	Victory RS Select Growth R	RSDKX	D	(800) 539-3863	C / 4.6	4.08	6.58	23.95 /70	3.05 /32	9.72 /56	0.00	1.89
SC	Victory RS Select Growth Y	RSSYX	D+	(800) 539-3863	C / 5.2	4.25	6.92	24.78 /73	3.81 /41	10.64 /63	0.00	1.17
SC	● Victory RS Small Cap Equity A	GPSCX	D	(800) 539-3863	B- / 7.3	8.59	13.87	30.88 /88	5.64 /61	13.09 /85	0.00	1.27
SC	● Victory RS Small Cap Equity C	RSCCX	D	(800) 539-3863	B- / 7.5	8.38	13.34	29.78 /86	4.79 /52	12.17 /76	0.00	2.36
SC	● Victory RS Small Cap Equity R	RSCKX	D	(800) 539-3863	B / 7.8	8.51	13.61	30.38 /87	5.24 /57	12.69 /81	0.00	1.74
SC	● Victory RS Small Cap Equity Y	RSCYX	D+	(800) 539-3863	B+ / 8.3	8.74	14.04	31.35 /89	5.75 /62	13.28 /87	0.00	1.05
SC	Victory RS Small Cap Growth A	RSEGX	C-	(800) 539-3863	C+ / 6.8	8.65	13.51	30.07 /87	5.12 /55	12.74 /81	0.00	1.39
SC	Victory RS Small Cap Growth C	REGWX	C	(800) 539-3863	B- / 7.2	8.44	13.07	29.06 /84	4.32 /47	11.91 /73	0.00	2.16
SC	Victory RS Small Cap Growth R	RSEKX	C	(800) 539-3863	B- / 7.5	8.60	13.38	29.70 /86	4.75 /52	12.27 /77	0.00	1.74
SC	Victory RS Small Cap Growth Y	RSYEX	C+	(800) 539-3863	B / 7.9	8.72	13.66	30.40 /87	5.41 /59	13.06 /84	0.01	1.16
MC	Victory RS Value A	RSVAX	C-	(800) 539-3863	C+ / 6.0	7.07	9.34	23.24 /67	6.04 /65	11.99 /74	0.38	1.25
MC	Victory RS Value C	RVACX	C-	(800) 539-3863	C+ / 6.3	6.85	8.93	22.31 /64	5.22 /57	11.13 /67	0.00	2.03
MC	Victory RS Value R	RSVKX	C-	(800) 539-3863	C+ / 6.6	6.97	9.13	22.71 /65	5.62 /61	11.55 /70	0.00	1.58
MC	Victory RS Value Y	RSVYX	C	(800) 539-3863	B- / 7.0	7.13	9.46	23.53 /68	6.27 /67	12.26 /77	0.00	1.10
IX	Victory S&P 500 Index A	MUXAX	B+	(800) 539-3863	B+ / 8.7	7.89	9.74	24.38 /71	10.00 /93	13.30 /87	1.43	0.58
IX	Victory S&P 500 Index R	MUXRX	B+	(800) 539-3863	B+ / 8.8	7.80	9.54	23.93 /70	9.58 /91	12.87 /83	1.11	1.02
IX	Victory S&P 500 Index Y	MUXYX	B+	(800) 539-3863	A- / 9.2	7.97	9.87	24.69 /72	10.23 /95	13.50 /89	1.65	0.38
FO	Victory Sophus China A	RSCHX	D+	(800) 539-3863	C / 5.5	5.46	5.46	30.21 /87	5.04 /55	5.51 /25	0.79	2.03
FO	Victory Sophus China C	RCHCX	C-	(800) 539-3863	C+ / 5.9	5.18	4.99	28.87 /84	4.15 /45	4.72 /19	0.00	2.76
FO	Victory Sophus China R	RCHKX	C-	(800) 539-3863	C+ / 6.3	5.24	5.24	29.76 /86	4.63 /50	5.12 /22	0.00	2.24
FO	Victory Sophus China Y	RCHYX	C-	(800) 539-3863	C+ / 6.9	5.53	5.63	30.70 /88	5.37 /58	5.85 /27	0.91	1.74
EM	Victory Sophus Em Mkts Sm Cap A	RSMSX	C-	(800) 539-3863	D+ / 2.6	9.04	6.24	21.66 /61	0.98 /18	--	0.00	2.36
EM	Victory Sophus Em Mkts Sm Cap C	RSMGX	D-	(800) 539-3863	D / 1.6	8.68	5.88	18.18 /44	-0.48 /11	--	0.00	2.97
EM	Victory Sophus Em Mkts Sm Cap Y	RSMYX	D+	(800) 539-3863	C- / 3.9	9.01	6.44	21.92 /62	1.29 /20	--	0.62	1.93
EM	Victory Sophus Emerging Markets A	GBEMX	D+	(800) 539-3863	C / 4.5	10.09	7.23	32.40 /91	1.61 /22	-1.62 / 3	0.81	1.56
EM	Victory Sophus Emerging Markets C	REMGX	D+	(800) 539-3863	C / 5.0	9.91	6.87	31.41 /89	0.82 /17	-2.39 / 2	0.80	2.36
EM	Victory Sophus Emerging Markets R	REMKX	C-	(800) 539-3863	C / 5.5	9.99	7.16	32.17 /90	1.33 /20	-1.89 / 3	0.85	1.86
EM	Victory Sophus Emerging Markets Y	RSENX	C-	(800) 539-3863	C+ / 6.0	10.13	7.41	32.92 /91	1.94 /24	-1.30 / 3	0.82	1.28
MC	Victory Special Value A	SSVSX	C-	(800) 539-3863	D+ / 2.7	6.24	5.62	15.50 /32	3.17 /33	7.96 /42	1.00	1.35
MC	Victory Special Value C	VSVCX	C-	(800) 539-3863	C- / 3.0	6.01	5.11	14.49 /28	2.26 /26	7.01 /35	0.25	2.21
MC	Victory Special Value I	VSPIX	C	(800) 539-3863	C- / 3.8	6.27	5.66	15.63 /33	3.38 /36	8.21 /44	1.19	1.09

● Denotes fund is closed to new investors
* Denotes fund is included in Section II

RISK			NET ASSETS		ASSET				Portfolio Turnover Ratio	BULL / BEAR		FUND MANAGER		MINIMUMS		LOADS	
	3 Year		NAV							Last Bull	Last Bear	Manager	Manager	Initial	Additional	Front	Back
Risk Rating/Pts	Standard Deviation	Beta	As of 2/28/17	Total $(Mil)	Cash %	Stocks %	Bonds %	Other %		Market Return	Market Return	Quality Pct	Tenure (Years)	Purch. $	Purch. $	End Load	End Load
C+ / 5.9	11.5	0.71	14.22	24	3	96	0	1	50	134.0	-24.0	93	4	2,500	100	5.8	0.0
C+ / 5.9	11.6	0.71	13.25	14	3	96	0	1	50	124.6	-24.2	90	4	2,500	100	0.0	0.0
C+ / 5.9	11.6	0.71	13.35	1	3	96	0	1	50	127.8	-24.0	91	4	1,000	0	0.0	0.0
C+ / 6.0	11.5	0.71	14.40	50	3	96	0	1	50	137.3	-23.9	93	4	0	100	0.0	0.0
C / 4.6	11.1	1.03	54.13	531	2	94	2	2	39	127.9	-24.8	28	5	2,500	100	5.8	0.0
C / 4.4	11.1	1.03	48.18	29	2	94	2	2	39	118.2	-25.0	20	5	2,500	100	0.0	0.0
C / 4.6	11.1	1.03	54.07	11	2	94	2	2	39	123.4	-24.9	25	5	1,000	0	0.0	0.0
C / 4.5	11.1	1.03	53.94	34	2	94	2	2	39	130.9	-24.7	30	5	0	100	0.0	0.0
C / 5.3	12.0	0.91	22.54	243	1	97	0	2	120	118.8	-19.0	32	9	2,500	100	5.8	0.0
C / 5.2	12.0	0.91	20.46	25	1	97	0	2	120	108.8	-19.3	23	9	2,500	100	0.0	0.0
C / 5.2	12.0	0.91	21.23	2	1	97	0	2	120	112.9	-19.1	27	9	1,000	0	0.0	0.0
C / 5.3	12.0	0.91	23.16	174	1	97	0	2	120	121.8	-18.9	35	9	0	100	0.0	0.0
D+ / 2.4	13.3	0.78	32.85	372	2	92	4	2	42	111.2	-24.4	49	4	2,500	100	5.8	0.0
D / 2.2	13.3	0.78	31.02	3	2	92	4	2	42	106.9	-24.6	44	4	1,000	0	0.0	0.0
D+ / 2.5	13.3	0.78	34.09	391	2	92	4	2	42	114.9	-24.4	53	4	0	100	0.0	0.0
D / 1.8	18.1	1.36	19.66	116	0	98	1	1	119	139.7	-26.8	30	1	2,500	100	5.8	0.0
D- / 1.3	18.2	1.37	16.80	11	0	98	1	1	119	129.4	-27.0	22	1	2,500	100	0.0	0.0
D- / 1.5	18.1	1.36	17.73	2	0	98	1	1	119	133.5	-27.0	26	1	1,000	0	0.0	0.0
D / 1.9	18.2	1.36	20.66	25	0	98	1	1	119	143.2	-26.7	33	1	0	100	0.0	0.0
C- / 3.4	13.4	0.79	46.95	159	1	97	0	2	88	108.6	-19.4	51	10	2,500	100	5.8	0.0
C- / 3.3	13.4	0.79	42.58	62	1	97	0	2	88	100.0	-19.9	40	10	2,500	100	0.0	0.0
C- / 3.3	13.4	0.79	42.72	2	1	97	0	2	88	102.3	-19.7	44	10	1,000	0	0.0	0.0
C- / 3.5	13.4	0.79	48.14	288	1	97	0	2	88	111.6	-19.3	54	10	0	100	0.0	0.0
E / 0.4	17.8	1.02	15.68	56	1	97	0	2	98	134.4	-25.7	58	8	2,500	100	4.8	0.0
E / 0.4	17.8	1.02	8.41	1	1	97	0	2	98	124.0	-26.0	46	8	2,500	100	0.0	0.0
E / 0.4	17.8	1.02	13.52	3	1	97	0	2	98	129.9	-25.8	52	8	1,000	0	0.0	0.0
E / 0.4	17.8	1.03	15.92	2	1	97	0	2	98	136.5	-25.6	59	8	0	100	0.0	0.0
C- / 3.5	17.6	1.01	71.07	495	0	97	1	2	94	129.9	-25.1	51	10	2,500	100	5.8	0.0
C- / 3.4	17.6	1.01	64.09	13	0	97	1	2	94	119.2	-25.5	40	10	2,500	100	0.0	0.0
C- / 3.4	17.6	1.01	67.04	6	0	97	1	2	94	124.6	-25.3	46	10	1,000	0	0.0	0.0
C- / 3.5	17.6	1.01	73.03	1,498	0	97	1	2	94	133.5	-25.0	55	10	0	100	0.0	0.0
C- / 3.6	10.6	0.84	29.31	259	1	94	4	1	55	115.2	-26.0	51	4	2,500	100	4.8	0.0
C- / 3.5	10.6	0.84	27.26	20	1	94	4	1	55	106.6	-26.3	40	4	2,500	100	0.0	0.0
C- / 3.5	10.6	0.84	28.34	2	1	94	4	1	55	110.7	-26.1	45	4	1,000	0	0.0	0.0
C- / 3.6	10.6	0.84	29.81	262	1	94	4	1	55	118.0	-25.9	54	4	0	100	0.0	0.0
C / 5.3	10.3	1.00	21.72	196	0	98	0	2	4	126.9	-16.5	68	2	2,500	50	2.5	0.0
C / 5.3	10.3	1.00	21.68	15	0	98	0	2	4	122.4	-16.6	62	2	0	0	0.0	0.0
C / 5.3	10.3	1.00	21.84	40	0	98	0	2	4	129.0	-16.5	70	2	1,000,000	0	0.0	0.0
C- / 3.6	20.1	0.97	11.21	11	3	96	0	1	125	67.8	N/A	96	4	2,500	100	5.8	0.0
C- / 3.6	20.1	0.97	11.16	N/A	3	96	0	1	125	60.5	N/A	94	4	2,500		0.0	0.0
C- / 3.6	20.1	0.97	11.25	2	3	96	0	1	125	64.3	N/A	95	4	1,000	0	0.0	0.0
C- / 3.6	20.1	0.97	11.23	5	3	96	0	1	125	71.0	N/A	96	4	0	100	0.0	0.0
C+ / 6.9	13.3	0.75	10.73	3	3	96	0	1	107	N/A	N/A	70	3	2,500	100	5.8	0.0
C / 4.9	13.3	0.75	10.27	N/A	3	96	0	1	107	N/A	N/A	52	3	2,500	100	0.0	0.0
C / 5.0	13.3	0.75	10.74	19	3	96	0	1	107	N/A	N/A	74	3	0	100	0.0	0.0
C- / 3.9	15.7	0.95	17.60	65	1	98	0	1	111	19.1	-27.9	74	4	2,500	100	5.8	0.0
C- / 3.6	15.7	0.95	13.39	13	1	98	0	1	111	14.1	-28.1	65	4	2,500	100	0.0	0.0
C- / 3.8	15.7	0.95	16.55	18	1	98	0	1	111	17.3	-28.0	71	4	1,000	0	0.0	0.0
C- / 3.9	15.7	0.95	17.69	68	1	98	0	1	111	21.0	-27.8	76	4	0	100	0.0	0.0
C+ / 6.9	10.3	0.72	23.19	37	1	98	0	1	76	81.9	-27.0	28	2	2,500	250	5.8	0.0
C+ / 6.9	10.4	0.73	20.99	8	1	98	0	1	76	73.3	-27.2	19	2	2,500	250	0.0	0.0
C+ / 6.9	10.3	0.73	23.47	4	1	98	0	1	76	84.4	-26.9	30	2	2,000,000	0	0.0	0.0

I. Index of Stock Mutual Funds

99 Pct = Best
0 Pct = Worst

Fund Type	Fund Name	Ticker Symbol	Overall Investment Rating	Phone	Performance Rating/Pts	3 Mo	6 Mo	1Yr / Pct	3Yr / Pct	5Yr / Pct	Dividend Yield	Expense Ratio
								Total Return % through 2/28/17	Annualized		Incl. in Returns	
MC	Victory Special Value R	VSVGX	C-	(800) 539-3863	C- / 3.5	6.12	5.43	15.20 /31	2.87 /31	7.64 /39	0.85	1.63
MC	Victory Special Value Y	VSVYX	C	(800) 539-3863	C- / 3.9	6.30	5.73	15.84 /34	3.44 /36	--	1.31	1.58
BA	Victory Strategic Allocation A	SBALX	C	(800) 539-3863	D+ / 2.8	4.38	4.28	12.63 /20	4.74 /51	7.94 /42	1.28	1.77
BA	Victory Strategic Allocation C	VBFCX	C+	(800) 539-3863	C- / 3.3	4.13	3.83	11.82 /17	3.98 /43	7.18 /36	0.83	2.69
BA	Victory Strategic Allocation I	VBFIX	C+	(800) 539-3863	C- / 4.0	4.42	4.39	12.90 /21	4.95 /54	8.19 /44	1.63	9.23
BA	Victory Strategic Allocation R	VBFGX	C+	(800) 539-3863	C- / 3.6	4.26	4.08	12.30 /19	4.42 /48	7.61 /39	1.07	2.56
GR	Victory Sycamore Established Val A	VETAX	B+	(800) 539-3863	A / 9.5	5.91	10.93	31.08 /88	12.02 /98	14.82 /97	0.48	0.99
GR	Victory Sycamore Established Val C	VEVCX	U	(800) 539-3863	U /	5.74	10.57	--	--	--	0.00	1.90
GR	Victory Sycamore Established Val I	VEVIX	A-	(800) 539-3863	A+ / 9.8	6.00	11.11	31.42 /89	12.40 /98	15.22 /97	0.72	0.63
GR	Victory Sycamore Established Val R	GETGX	A-	(800) 539-3863	A+ / 9.7	5.84	10.83	30.82 /88	11.82 /98	14.61 /96	0.34	1.16
GR	Victory Sycamore Established Val R6	VEVRX	U	(800) 539-3863	U /	6.00	11.14	31.55 /89	--	--	0.79	0.65
GR	Victory Sycamore Established Val Y	VEVYX	A-	(800) 539-3863	A+ / 9.8	5.96	11.09	31.40 /89	12.25 /98	--	0.71	0.94
SC	Victory Sycamore Small Co Oppty A	SSGSX	B+	(800) 539-3863	A / 9.5	3.26	14.20	36.33 /95	10.78 /97	13.65 /90	0.24	1.31
SC	Victory Sycamore Small Co Oppty I	VSOIX	B+	(800) 539-3863	A+ / 9.8	3.33	14.38	36.71 /96	11.13 /97	14.03 /93	0.50	0.97
SC	Victory Sycamore Small Co Oppty R	GOGFX	B+	(800) 539-3863	A+ / 9.7	3.21	14.10	36.05 /95	10.52 /96	13.39 /88	0.11	1.53
SC	Victory Sycamore Small Co Oppty R6	VSORX	U	(800) 539-3863	U /	3.35	14.36	36.70 /96	--	--	0.52	1.14
SC	Victory Sycamore Small Co Oppty Y	VSOYX	B+	(800) 539-3863	A+ / 9.7	3.26	14.23	36.42 /95	10.91 /97	--	0.37	1.34
EM	Victory Trivalent Em Mkts Sm Cap A	MAEMX	C-	(800) 539-3863	C / 4.3	10.42	4.86	25.01 /73	3.40 /36	--	0.75	1.78
EM	Victory Trivalent Em Mkts Sm Cap Y	MYEMX	C+	(800) 539-3863	C+ / 5.8	10.43	4.99	25.36 /74	3.65 /39	--	0.99	2.44
FO	Victory Trivalent Intl Core Eq A	MAICX	D	(800) 539-3863	D / 1.6	6.45	4.80	16.95 /38	0.20 /14	5.85 /27	1.75	1.81
FO	Victory Trivalent Intl Core Eq C	MICCX	D	(800) 539-3863	D- / 1.4	6.35	4.68	16.33 /36	-0.47 /11	5.10 /22	1.14	2.34
FO	Victory Trivalent Intl Core Eq I	MICIX	D+	(800) 539-3863	D+ / 2.7	6.62	5.14	17.69 /41	0.71 /17	6.43 /31	2.32	4.03
FO	Victory Trivalent Intl Core Eq Y	MICYX	D+	(800) 539-3863	D+ / 2.5	6.56	5.08	17.28 /40	0.47 /16	6.13 /29	2.10	1.29
FO	Victory Trivalent Intl Sm Cap A	MISAX	D+	(800) 539-3863	D / 1.9	6.39	3.72	14.72 /29	1.78 /23	9.91 /58	1.04	1.78
FO	Victory Trivalent Intl Sm Cap C	MCISX	D+	(800) 539-3863	D+ / 2.3	6.22	3.30	13.87 /25	1.05 /19	9.12 /52	0.33	2.39
FO	Victory Trivalent Intl Sm Cap I	MISIX	C-	(800) 539-3863	C- / 3.0	6.48	3.92	15.20 /31	2.21 /25	10.38 /61	1.48	1.21
FO	Victory Trivalent Intl Sm Cap R6	MSSIX	C-	(800) 539-3863	D+ / 2.9	6.50	3.85	15.07 /30	2.08 /25	--	1.35	1.33
FO	Victory Trivalent Intl Sm Cap Y	MYSIX	C-	(800) 539-3863	D+ / 2.9	6.45	3.88	14.98 /30	2.05 /24	10.21 /60	1.35	1.40
BA	Villere Balanced	VILLX	D-	(866) 209-1129	D+ / 2.9	3.51	4.01	21.81 /61	1.22 /19	6.95 /34	0.86	0.98
GR	Villere Equity	VLEQX	E+	(866) 209-1129	D- / 1.5	3.01	3.71	22.94 /66	-0.06 /13	--	0.11	1.26
AA	Virtus Alternatives Diversifier A	PDPAX	D	(800) 243-1574	D- / 1.2	3.44	3.25	14.60 /28	0.14 /14	1.52 / 7	0.74	1.65
AA	Virtus Alternatives Diversifier C	PDPCX	D	(800) 243-1574	D- / 1.1	3.33	2.84	13.84 /25	-0.63 /11	0.77 / 6	0.00	2.40
AA	Virtus Alternatives Diversifier I	VADIX	D+	(800) 243-1574	D / 1.9	3.53	3.43	14.92 /30	0.39 /15	1.77 / 8	1.05	1.40
MC	Virtus Contrarian Value A	FMIVX	D-	(800) 243-1574	D+ / 2.3	3.22	4.71	28.78 /83	0.27 /15	7.62 /39	0.64	1.41
MC	Virtus Contrarian Value C	FMICX	D-	(800) 243-1574	D / 1.8	3.04	4.31	27.86 /81	-0.47 /11	6.82 /34	0.01	2.16
MC	Virtus Contrarian Value I	PIMVX	D	(800) 243-1574	C- / 3.5	3.27	4.85	29.14 /84	0.53 /16	7.90 /41	0.95	1.16
FS	Virtus Credit Opportunities R6	VRCOX	U	(800) 243-1574	U /	2.78	4.74	9.04 /10	--	--	3.98	1.40
EM	● Virtus Emerging Markets Eqty Inc A	VEIAX	D-	(800) 243-1574	D+ / 2.6	8.08	5.15	27.51 /81	0.04 /14	--	1.71	2.16
EM	● Virtus Emerging Markets Eqty Inc C	VEICX	D-	(800) 243-1574	D / 1.8	7.79	4.62	26.45 /78	-0.73 /10	--	1.16	2.91
EM	● Virtus Emerging Markets Eqty Inc I	VEIIX	D+	(800) 243-1574	C- / 3.8	8.13	5.20	27.74 /81	0.31 /15	--	2.03	1.91
EM	Virtus Emerging Markets Small-Cap A	VAESX	C+	(800) 243-1574	C / 5.5	9.20	8.36	32.52 /91	3.23 /34	--	1.65	3.76
EM	Virtus Emerging Markets Small-Cap	VCESX	C+	(800) 243-1574	C+ / 6.0	9.03	7.97	31.42 /89	2.47 /27	--	1.24	4.51
EM	Virtus Emerging Markets Small-Cap I	VIESX	C+	(800) 243-1574	C+ / 6.8	9.17	8.46	32.76 /91	3.48 /37	--	1.84	3.51
EM	Virtus Emerging Mkt Opp A	HEMZX	D-	(800) 243-1574	D / 1.8	7.41	-3.43	15.54 /32	2.46 /27	1.01 / 6	0.31	1.58
EM	Virtus Emerging Mkt Opp C	PICEX	D	(800) 243-1574	D / 2.2	7.36	-3.67	14.87 /29	1.73 /22	0.28 / 5	0.00	2.33
EM	Virtus Emerging Mkt Opp I	HIEMX	D	(800) 243-1574	D+ / 2.8	7.49	-3.31	16.00 /34	2.74 /30	1.29 / 7	0.41	1.33
EM	Virtus Emerging Mkt Opp R6	VREMX	U	(800) 243-1574	U /	7.64	-3.18	16.02 /34	--	--	0.53	1.20
GI	Virtus Enhanced Core Equity A	PDIAX	C+	(800) 243-1574	B+ / 8.3	6.04	13.03	23.20 /67	10.35 /95	12.32 /77	0.98	1.54
GI	Virtus Enhanced Core Equity C	PGICX	C+	(800) 243-1574	B+ / 8.7	5.83	12.59	22.21 /63	9.53 /91	11.46 /70	0.05	2.29
GI	Virtus Enhanced Core Equity I	PXIIX	B-	(800) 243-1574	A / 9.3	6.08	13.14	23.48 /68	10.61 /96	12.57 /80	1.45	1.29
GI	Virtus Equity Trend A	VAPAX	E	(800) 243-1574	E+ / 0.6	5.26	4.07	12.87 /21	-1.29 / 8	5.58 /25	0.00	1.61
GI	Virtus Equity Trend C	VAPCX	E	(800) 243-1574	E+ / 0.7	5.08	3.77	12.22 /19	-1.99 / 7	4.82 /20	0.00	2.36

● Denotes fund is closed to new investors
* Denotes fund is included in Section II

www.thestreetratings.com

RISK Risk Rating/Pts	3 Year Standard Deviation	Beta	NET ASSETS NAV As of 2/28/17	Total $(Mil)	ASSET Cash %	Stocks %	Bonds %	Other %	Portfolio Turnover Ratio	BULL/BEAR Last Bull Market Return	Last Bear Market Return	FUND MANAGER Manager Quality Pct	Manager Tenure (Years)	MINIMUMS Initial Purch. $	Additional Purch. $	LOADS Front End Load	Back End Load
B- /7.0	10.3	0.73	22.29	37	1	98	0	1	76	79.0	-27.1	25	2	0	0	0.0	0.0
C+ /6.9	10.3	0.73	23.30	1	1	98	0	1	76	N/A	N/A	30	2	0	0	0.0	0.0
B /8.2	6.9	1.04	15.48	15	17	49	33	1	192	70.0	-14.0	36	14	2,500	250	5.8	0.0
B /8.2	6.9	1.04	15.30	9	17	49	33	1	192	63.5	-14.3	27	14	2,500	250	0.0	0.0
B /8.2	6.9	1.04	15.53	3	17	49	33	1	192	72.2	-13.9	38	14	2,000,000	0	0.0	0.0
B /8.2	6.9	1.04	15.46	2	17	49	33	1	192	67.2	-14.1	32	14	0	0	0.0	0.0
C /5.0	11.4	0.98	37.98	2,379	4	95	0	1	40	147.2	-20.8	83	19	2,500	250	5.8	0.0
U /	N/A	N/A	37.30	66	4	95	0	1	40	N/A	N/A	N/A	19	2,500	50	0.0	0.0
C /5.0	11.4	0.99	38.01	3,917	4	95	0	1	40	152.0	-20.7	85	19	2,000,000	0	0.0	0.0
C /5.0	11.4	0.98	37.53	965	4	95	0	1	40	144.8	-20.8	82	19	0	0	0.0	0.0
U /	N/A	N/A	38.02	753	4	95	0	1	40	N/A	N/A	N/A	19	0	0	0.0	0.0
C /5.0	11.4	0.98	38.01	74	4	95	0	1	40	N/A	N/A	84	19	0	0	0.0	0.0
C /4.7	14.0	0.85	44.17	622	4	95	0	1	59	138.4	-20.8	94	19	2,500	250	5.8	0.0
C /4.7	14.0	0.85	44.54	3,146	4	95	0	1	59	142.7	-20.7	95	19	2,000,000	0	0.0	0.0
C /4.6	14.0	0.85	41.71	359	4	95	0	1	59	135.4	-20.9	94	19	0	0	0.0	0.0
U /	N/A	N/A	44.49	42	4	95	0	1	59	N/A	N/A	N/A	19	0	0	0.0	0.0
C /4.7	14.0	0.85	44.23	86	4	95	0	1	59	N/A	N/A	95	19	1,000,000	0	0.0	0.0
C+ /5.8	14.7	0.85	11.35	N/A	0	98	0	2	104	N/A	N/A	86	4	2,500	50	5.8	0.0
C+ /5.8	14.7	0.84	11.37	4	0	98	0	2	104	N/A	N/A	87	4	1,000,000	0	0.0	0.0
C+ /6.3	10.9	0.85	6.63	5	3	96	0	1	61	57.4	-27.1	76	10	2,500	50	5.8	0.0
C+ /6.4	10.9	0.85	6.61	1	3	96	0	1	61	51.4	-27.4	70	10	2,500	50	0.0	0.0
C+ /6.3	10.9	0.85	6.64	N/A	3	96	0	1	61	62.1	-27.0	80	10	2,000,000	0	0.0	0.0
C+ /6.3	10.9	0.85	6.62	13	3	96	0	1	61	59.7	-27.1	78	10	1,000,000	0	0.0	0.0
C+ /6.7	12.0	0.90	11.43	78	4	95	0	1	85	88.5	-23.1	86	10	2,500	50	5.8	0.0
C+ /6.7	11.9	0.89	11.20	5	4	95	0	1	85	81.2	-23.4	82	10	2,500	50	0.0	0.0
C+ /6.7	12.0	0.89	11.50	450	4	95	0	1	85	93.1	-23.0	88	10	2,000,000	0	0.0	0.0
C+ /6.7	12.0	0.90	11.56	22	4	95	0	1	85	N/A	N/A	87	10	0	0	0.0	0.0
C+ /6.7	12.0	0.90	11.46	393	4	95	0	1	85	91.2	-23.1	87	10	1,000,000	0	0.0	0.0
C- /3.5	11.2	1.41	21.31	340	2	66	30	2	14	67.0	-12.8	3	18	2,000	500	0.0	0.0
C /4.5	13.7	1.06	10.66	39	8	91	0	1	32	N/A	N/A	2	4	2,000	500	0.0	2.0
B- /7.1	7.5	0.89	10.96	18	16	61	22	1	56	21.4	-14.9	8	9	2,500	100	5.8	0.0
B- /7.1	7.5	0.90	10.86	17	16	61	22	1	56	16.5	-15.0	5	9	2,500	100	0.0	0.0
B- /7.1	7.5	0.89	10.95	19	16	61	22	1	56	23.1	-14.8	9	9	100,000	0	0.0	0.0
C /4.7	14.3	1.02	36.27	84	1	98	0	1	13	90.3	-22.8	3	5	2,500	100	5.8	0.0
C /4.7	14.3	1.02	34.58	33	1	98	0	1	13	82.8	-23.0	2	5	2,500	100	0.0	0.0
C /4.7	14.3	1.02	36.29	80	1	98	0	1	13	92.9	-22.7	3	5	100,000	0	0.0	0.0
U /	N/A	N/A	10.11	97	0	0	0	100	0	N/A	N/A	N/A	2	0	0	0.0	0.0
C /4.6	15.1	0.91	9.20	1	1	98	0	1	74	N/A	N/A	55	5	2,500	100	5.8	0.0
C /4.6	15.1	0.91	9.14	1	1	98	0	1	74	N/A	N/A	44	5	2,500	100	0.0	0.0
C /4.6	15.1	0.91	9.22	3	1	98	0	1	74	N/A	N/A	59	5	100,000	0	0.0	0.0
C+ /6.7	14.5	0.85	9.74	N/A	2	97	0	1	34	N/A	N/A	85	4	2,500	100	5.8	0.0
C+ /6.7	14.4	0.85	9.79	N/A	2	97	0	1	34	N/A	N/A	81	4	2,500	100	0.0	0.0
C+ /6.7	14.4	0.85	9.76	5	2	97	0	1	34	N/A	N/A	86	4	100,000	0	0.0	0.0
C /5.4	13.1	0.68	9.44	964	4	94	0	2	27	24.8	-12.7	82	N/A	2,500	100	5.8	0.0
C /5.4	13.1	0.68	9.19	188	4	94	0	2	27	19.9	-13.0	78	N/A	2,500	100	0.0	0.0
C /5.4	13.1	0.68	9.77	5,697	4	94	0	2	27	26.6	-12.7	84	N/A	100,000	0	0.0	0.0
U /	N/A	N/A	9.77	85	4	94	0	2	27	N/A	N/A	N/A	N/A	0	0	0.0	0.0
C- /3.2	10.5	0.95	20.19	115	1	98	0	1	312	123.8	-20.1	76	3	2,500	100	5.8	0.0
D+ /2.9	10.6	0.95	18.37	38	1	98	0	1	312	114.8	-20.4	69	3	2,500	100	0.0	0.0
C- /3.2	10.5	0.95	20.13	20	1	98	0	1	312	126.8	-20.0	78	3	100,000	0	0.0	0.0
C- /3.8	8.5	0.70	12.80	186	0	99	0	1	229	43.0	-11.6	3	2	2,500	100	5.8	0.0
C- /3.7	8.5	0.70	12.40	325	0	99	0	1	229	37.4	-11.8	3	2	2,500	100	0.0	0.0

I. Index of Stock Mutual Funds

99 Pct = Best
0 Pct = Worst

Fund Type	Fund Name	Ticker Symbol	Overall Investment Rating	Phone	Performance Rating/Pts	3 Mo	6 Mo	1Yr / Pct	3Yr / Pct	5Yr / Pct	Dividend Yield	Expense Ratio
GI	Virtus Equity Trend I	VAPIX	E	(800) 243-1574	D- / 1.0	5.22	4.20	13.07 /22	-1.07 / 9	5.84 /27	0.00	1.36
FO	Virtus Foreign Opportunities A	JVIAX	D	(800) 243-1574	D- / 1.1	8.80	-1.16	7.67 / 7	1.85 /23	4.56 /19	0.82	1.43
FO	Virtus Foreign Opportunities C	JVICX	D	(800) 243-1574	D- / 1.3	8.60	-1.54	6.85 / 6	1.09 /19	3.78 /14	0.40	2.18
FO	Virtus Foreign Opportunities I	JVXIX	D	(800) 243-1574	D / 1.7	8.87	-1.05	7.95 / 7	2.10 /25	4.82 /20	1.13	1.18
GL	Virtus Global Equity Trend A	VGPAX	E+	(800) 243-1574	E / 0.4	5.53	4.15	12.08 /18	-2.12 / 6	3.04 /11	0.00	1.88
GL	Virtus Global Equity Trend C	VGPCX	E+	(800) 243-1574	E / 0.5	5.37	3.73	11.22 /15	-2.85 / 5	2.29 / 9	0.00	2.63
GL	Virtus Global Equity Trend I	VGPIX	E+	(800) 243-1574	E+ / 0.8	5.60	4.22	12.35 /19	-1.89 / 7	3.29 /12	0.00	1.63
UT	Virtus Global Infrastructure A	PGUAX	D	(800) 243-1574	C- / 3.1	8.62	3.68	15.31 /31	3.97 /43	7.90 /41	1.77	1.32
UT	Virtus Global Infrastructure C	PGUCX	D+	(800) 243-1574	C- / 3.6	8.46	3.30	14.43 /27	3.22 /34	7.10 /35	1.15	2.07
UT	Virtus Global Infrastructure I	PGIUX	C-	(800) 243-1574	C / 4.5	8.77	3.89	15.58 /32	4.26 /46	8.18 /44	2.12	1.07
GL	Virtus Global Opportunities A	NWWOX	C+	(800) 243-1574	C+ / 5.6	9.34	5.44	18.25 /44	6.97 /72	9.76 /57	0.29	1.47
GL	● Virtus Global Opportunities B	WWOBX	C+	(800) 243-1574	C+ / 6.1	9.22	5.06	17.41 /40	6.16 /66	8.94 /50	0.00	2.22
GL	Virtus Global Opportunities C	WWOCX	C+	(800) 243-1574	C+ / 6.1	9.19	5.09	17.32 /40	6.17 /66	8.96 /50	0.00	2.22
GL	Virtus Global Opportunities I	WWOIX	C+	(800) 243-1574	C+ / 6.9	9.46	5.63	18.57 /45	7.24 /74	10.01 /58	0.48	1.22
GR	Virtus Global Quality Dividend A	PPTAX	C+	(800) 243-1574	C / 5.3	5.56	5.29	18.15 /44	7.36 /75	10.34 /61	0.80	1.44
GR	Virtus Global Quality Dividend C	PPTCX	B-	(800) 243-1574	C+ / 5.8	5.36	4.88	17.33 /40	6.58 /69	9.52 /55	0.00	2.19
GR	Virtus Global Quality Dividend I	PIPTX	B-	(800) 243-1574	C+ / 6.6	5.62	5.41	18.48 /45	7.64 /76	10.63 /63	1.07	1.19
RE	Virtus Global Real Estate Sec A	VGSAX	C-	(800) 243-1574	C- / 3.5	7.17	-3.75	11.65 /17	7.25 /74	9.02 /51	1.94	1.53
RE	Virtus Global Real Estate Sec C	VGSCX	C-	(800) 243-1574	C- / 4.0	6.93	-4.13	10.78 /14	6.43 /68	8.19 /44	1.60	2.28
RE	Virtus Global Real Estate Sec I	VGISX	C	(800) 243-1574	C / 4.9	7.21	-3.63	11.92 /18	7.50 /75	9.29 /53	2.23	1.28
FO	Virtus Greater European Opport Fd A	VGEAX	D-	(800) 243-1574	E / 0.5	9.75	-0.26	3.75 / 3	-0.31 /12	5.65 /26	1.46	1.81
FO	Virtus Greater European Opport Fd C	VGECX	D-	(800) 243-1574	E+ / 0.7	9.53	-0.64	2.94 / 3	-1.06 / 9	4.86 /20	1.29	2.56
FO	Virtus Greater European Opport Fd I	VGEIX	D	(800) 243-1574	E+ / 0.9	9.78	-0.20	3.93 / 3	-0.09 /13	5.89 /28	1.91	1.56
GL	Virtus Herzfeld Fund A	VHFAX	C+	(800) 243-1574	C+ / 6.4	6.83	7.50	27.22 /80	6.62 /69	--	3.44	2.81
GL	Virtus Herzfeld Fund C	VHFCX	C+	(800) 243-1574	C+ / 6.8	6.59	7.14	26.18 /77	5.81 /63	--	2.99	3.56
GL	Virtus Herzfeld Fund I	VHFIX	B+	(800) 243-1574	B / 7.6	6.89	7.62	27.47 /80	6.87 /71	--	3.87	2.56
FO	Virtus International Equity Fund A	VIEAX	E+	(800) 243-1574	E / 0.3	4.21	1.81	9.49 /10	-2.85 / 5	3.56 /13	0.82	3.03
FO	Virtus International Equity Fund C	VIECX	D-	(800) 243-1574	E / 0.3	4.00	1.44	8.69 / 9	-3.57 / 4	2.76 /10	0.00	3.78
FO	Virtus International Equity Fund I	VIIEX	D-	(800) 243-1574	E / 0.5	4.24	1.94	9.66 /11	-2.61 / 5	3.79 /14	1.19	2.78
FO	Virtus International Small-Cap A	VISAX	B	(800) 243-1574	B / 8.0	9.74	11.98	38.10 /96	5.96 /64	--	2.25	1.86
FO	Virtus International Small-Cap C	VCISX	B	(800) 243-1574	B+ / 8.5	9.57	11.65	37.13 /96	5.16 /56	--	1.76	2.61
FO	Virtus International Small-Cap I	VIISX	B+	(800) 243-1574	A- / 9.2	9.86	12.19	38.54 /97	6.24 /66	--	2.58	1.61
FO	Virtus Intl Real Estate Sec A	PXRAX	D	(800) 243-1574	E+ / 0.9	5.11	-7.13	5.27 / 4	2.48 /27	6.60 /32	6.55	1.90
FO	Virtus Intl Real Estate Sec C	PXRCX	D	(800) 243-1574	D- / 1.1	5.11	-7.34	4.62 / 4	1.75 /22	5.83 /27	6.16	2.65
FO	Virtus Intl Real Estate Sec I	PXRIX	D	(800) 243-1574	D- / 1.5	5.20	-7.03	5.53 / 4	2.72 /29	6.86 /34	7.18	1.65
GR	Virtus Low Volatility Equity A	VLVAX	C-	(800) 243-1574	D+ / 2.4	3.75	4.91	11.94 /18	3.96 /43	--	0.16	3.16
GR	Virtus Low Volatility Equity C	VLVCX	C-	(800) 243-1574	D+ / 2.8	3.46	4.46	11.06 /15	3.15 /33	--	0.00	3.91
GR	Virtus Low Volatility Equity I	VLVIX	C	(800) 243-1574	C- / 3.5	3.78	5.02	12.23 /19	4.19 /45	--	1.01	2.91
MC	Virtus Mid Cap Growth A	PHSKX	C-	(800) 243-1574	C / 5.0	7.72	5.96	21.16 /58	5.62 /61	8.84 /49	0.00	1.49
MC	● Virtus Mid Cap Growth B	PSKBX	C-	(800) 243-1574	C / 5.5	7.53	5.56	20.25 /53	4.84 /52	8.02 /42	0.00	2.24
MC	Virtus Mid Cap Growth C	PSKCX	C-	(800) 243-1574	C / 5.5	7.53	5.51	20.24 /53	4.82 /52	8.02 /42	0.00	2.24
MC	Virtus Mid Cap Growth I	PICMX	C	(800) 243-1574	C+ / 6.4	7.84	6.12	21.46 /60	5.89 /63	9.12 /52	0.00	1.24
MC	Virtus Mid-Cap Core Fund A	VMACX	B+	(800) 243-1574	B / 7.9	6.77	7.35	20.92 /57	11.04 /97	12.91 /83	0.00	1.64
MC	Virtus Mid-Cap Core Fund C	VMCCX	A-	(800) 243-1574	B+ / 8.3	6.55	6.98	20.01 /52	10.22 /94	12.08 /75	0.00	2.39
MC	Virtus Mid-Cap Core Fund I	VIMCX	A+	(800) 243-1574	A- / 9.0	6.82	7.48	21.18 /58	11.32 /97	13.19 /86	0.00	1.39
GL	Virtus Multi Asset Trend A	VAAAX	D-	(800) 243-1574	E / 0.4	3.69	0.87	8.46 / 8	-0.97 / 9	2.56 / 9	0.00	1.73
GL	Virtus Multi Asset Trend C	VAACX	D	(800) 243-1574	E+ / 0.6	3.47	0.50	7.53 / 7	-1.70 / 7	1.80 / 8	0.00	2.48
GL	Virtus Multi Asset Trend I	VAISX	D	(800) 243-1574	E+ / 0.8	3.68	0.97	8.65 / 9	-0.71 /10	2.80 /10	0.00	1.48
GL	Virtus Multi Strat Target Return I	VMSIX	U	(800) 243-1574	U /	0.50	1.44	-0.01 / 1	--	--	0.62	2.02
SC	Virtus Quality SmCap A	PQSAX	A-	(800) 243-1574	B+ / 8.7	5.87	12.89	28.38 /83	10.01 /93	12.07 /75	1.35	1.30
SC	Virtus Quality SmCap C	PQSCX	A	(800) 243-1574	A- / 9.0	5.71	12.47	27.40 /80	9.21 /88	11.23 /68	0.74	2.05
SC	Virtus Quality SmCap I	PXQSX	A+	(800) 243-1574	A / 9.5	5.93	13.03	28.65 /83	10.28 /95	12.33 /77	1.74	1.05

● Denotes fund is closed to new investors
* Denotes fund is included in Section II

www.thestreetratings.com

Risk Rating/Pts	3 Year Standard Deviation	Beta	NAV As of 2/28/17	Total $(Mil)	Cash %	Stocks %	Bonds %	Other %	Portfolio Turnover Ratio	Last Bull Market Return	Last Bear Market Return	Manager Quality Pct	Manager Tenure (Years)	Initial Purch. $	Additional Purch. $	Front End Load	Back End Load
C- / 3.8	8.6	0.71	12.89	176	0	99	0	1	229	44.7	-11.5	3	2	100,000	0	0.0	0.0
C+ / 6.4	11.0	0.76	28.86	327	2	97	0	1	25	46.9	-14.0	86	N/A	2,500	100	5.8	0.0
C+ / 6.4	11.0	0.76	28.46	94	2	97	0	1	25	41.1	-14.3	82	N/A	2,500	100	0.0	0.0
C+ / 6.4	11.0	0.76	28.88	875	2	97	0	1	25	48.9	-13.9	87	N/A	100,000	0	0.0	0.0
C / 5.2	7.9	1.03	10.30	6	24	75	0	1	282	25.8	-13.0	6	2	2,500	100	5.8	0.0
C / 5.2	8.0	1.03	10.01	9	24	75	0	1	282	21.0	-13.4	4	2	2,500	100	0.0	0.0
C / 5.3	7.9	1.03	10.37	3	24	75	0	1	282	27.5	-13.0	6	2	100,000	0	0.0	0.0
C / 4.9	10.2	0.43	13.90	48	12	87	0	1	17	64.6	-9.6	47	13	2,500	100	5.8	0.0
C / 4.9	10.2	0.43	13.83	26	12	87	0	1	17	58.2	-10.0	37	13	2,500	100	0.0	0.0
C / 4.9	10.2	0.43	13.92	37	12	87	0	1	17	67.0	-9.6	51	13	100,000	0	0.0	0.0
C+ / 6.9	9.7	0.67	14.38	110	1	98	0	1	29	87.3	-9.1	98	8	2,500	100	5.8	0.0
C+ / 6.8	9.7	0.67	12.60	N/A	1	98	0	1	29	80.0	-9.4	97	8	2,500	100	0.0	0.0
C+ / 6.8	9.7	0.67	12.52	24	1	98	0	1	29	80.0	-9.4	97	8	2,500	100	0.0	0.0
C+ / 6.9	9.7	0.67	14.37	51	1	98	0	1	29	89.4	-9.1	98	8	100,000	0	0.0	0.0
B- / 7.1	10.8	1.00	16.52	47	1	98	0	1	25	96.6	-17.0	35	8	2,500	100	5.8	0.0
B- / 7.1	10.8	1.00	16.11	7	1	98	0	1	25	88.9	-17.3	26	8	2,500	100	0.0	0.0
B- / 7.1	10.8	1.00	16.55	7	1	98	0	1	25	99.4	-16.9	38	8	100,000	0	0.0	0.0
C+ / 6.2	12.5	0.90	27.67	45	8	89	1	2	22	82.2	-18.1	42	8	2,500	100	5.8	0.0
C+ / 6.2	12.5	0.90	27.17	12	8	89	1	2	22	74.8	-18.3	32	8	2,500	100	0.0	0.0
C+ / 6.2	12.5	0.90	27.85	134	8	89	1	2	22	84.6	-17.9	45	8	100,000	0	0.0	0.0
C+ / 6.6	10.9	0.77	15.48	6	3	95	1	1	49	53.5	-15.4	72	8	2,500	100	5.8	0.0
C+ / 6.6	11.0	0.77	15.20	2	3	95	1	1	49	47.4	-15.7	63	8	2,500	100	0.0	0.0
C+ / 6.6	11.0	0.77	15.48	10	3	95	1	1	49	55.4	-15.3	74	8	100,000	0	0.0	0.0
C+ / 6.6	9.2	1.31	11.56	9	0	52	43	5	53	N/A	N/A	78	5	2,500	100	5.8	0.0
C+ / 6.6	9.2	1.31	11.50	19	0	52	43	5	53	N/A	N/A	71	5	2,500	100	0.0	0.0
C+ / 6.6	9.2	1.32	11.58	31	0	52	43	5	53	N/A	N/A	79	5	100,000	0	0.0	0.0
C+ / 5.9	10.8	0.82	10.07	1	6	93	0	1	70	33.8	-14.9	37	4	2,500	100	5.8	0.0
C+ / 5.9	10.8	0.82	9.88	1	6	93	0	1	70	28.1	-15.3	29	4	2,500	100	0.0	0.0
C+ / 5.9	10.8	0.81	10.01	2	6	93	0	1	70	35.1	-14.9	41	4	100,000	0	0.0	0.0
C / 5.0	13.0	0.90	13.98	7	3	96	0	1	40	N/A	N/A	97	5	2,500	100	5.8	0.0
C / 4.9	13.0	0.91	13.86	2	3	96	0	1	40	N/A	N/A	96	5	2,500	100	0.0	0.0
C / 4.9	13.0	0.91	14.02	68	3	96	0	1	40	N/A	N/A	97	5	100,000	0	0.0	0.0
C+ / 6.7	12.0	0.72	6.32	8	24	75	0	1	26	57.7	-21.0	89	10	2,500	100	5.8	0.0
C+ / 6.8	12.1	0.72	6.32	1	24	75	0	1	26	51.7	-21.3	85	10	2,500	100	0.0	0.0
C+ / 6.7	11.9	0.71	6.32	18	24	75	0	1	26	60.1	-21.0	90	10	100,000	0	0.0	0.0
B- / 7.4	7.9	0.66	12.17	1	3	96	0	1	10	N/A	N/A	36	4	2,500	100	5.8	0.0
B- / 7.4	7.9	0.66	11.95	N/A	3	96	0	1	10	N/A	N/A	28	4	2,500	100	0.0	0.0
B- / 7.4	7.9	0.66	12.13	2	3	96	0	1	10	N/A	N/A	39	4	100,000	0	0.0	0.0
C / 4.5	14.4	1.00	24.19	81	0	99	0	1	26	94.1	-26.8	26	5	2,500	100	5.8	0.0
C / 4.4	14.4	1.00	19.76	N/A	0	99	0	1	26	86.4	-27.1	19	5	2,500	100	0.0	0.0
C / 4.4	14.4	1.00	19.76	5	0	99	0	1	26	86.4	-27.1	19	5	2,500	100	0.0	0.0
C / 4.5	14.4	1.00	24.81	4	0	99	0	1	26	96.7	-26.7	29	5	100,000	0	0.0	0.0
C+ / 6.5	11.7	0.88	25.55	25	3	96	0	1	31	123.7	-16.3	88	8	2,500	100	5.8	0.0
C+ / 6.5	11.7	0.88	24.23	13	3	96	0	1	31	114.8	-16.6	84	8	2,500	100	0.0	0.0
C+ / 6.6	11.7	0.88	25.86	42	3	96	0	1	31	126.8	-16.3	89	8	100,000	0	0.0	0.0
C+ / 6.9	5.6	0.68	10.39	24	21	46	31	2	223	20.9	-8.6	23	6	2,500	100	5.8	0.0
C+ / 6.8	5.5	0.68	10.14	63	21	46	31	2	223	16.1	-8.8	16	6	2,500	100	0.0	0.0
C+ / 6.9	5.6	0.68	10.43	21	21	46	31	2	223	22.4	-8.4	25	6	100,000	0	0.0	0.0
U /	N/A	N/A	9.75	112	0	0	0	100	129	N/A	N/A	N/A	2	100,000	0	0.0	0.0
C+ / 6.3	13.3	0.76	17.25	92	10	89	0	1	15	114.0	-16.2	94	8	2,500	100	5.8	0.0
C+ / 6.3	13.3	0.76	17.01	29	10	89	0	1	15	105.5	-16.5	92	8	2,500	100	0.0	0.0
C+ / 6.3	13.3	0.76	17.25	230	10	89	0	1	15	116.9	-16.2	95	8	100,000	0	0.0	0.0

I. Index of Stock Mutual Funds

Fund Type	Fund Name	Ticker Symbol	Overall Investment Rating	Phone	Performance Rating/Pts	3 Mo	6 Mo	1Yr / Pct	3Yr / Pct	5Yr / Pct	Dividend Yield	Expense Ratio
RE	Virtus Real Estate Securities A	PHRAX	D+	(800) 243-1574	C+ / 6.4	8.32	-1.55	16.08 /35	10.37 /95	10.44 /62	1.47	1.38
RE	● Virtus Real Estate Securities B	PHRBX	C-	(800) 243-1574	C+ / 6.8	8.11	-1.95	15.17 /31	9.54 /91	9.60 /55	0.69	2.13
RE	Virtus Real Estate Securities C	PHRCX	C-	(800) 243-1574	C+ / 6.8	8.11	-1.94	15.18 /31	9.54 /91	9.61 /55	0.82	2.13
RE	Virtus Real Estate Securities I	PHRIX	C-	(800) 243-1574	B- / 7.5	8.37	-1.45	16.36 /36	10.65 /96	10.72 /64	1.80	1.13
GR	Virtus Sector Trend A	PWBAX	E+	(800) 243-1574	D- / 1.5	4.96	2.19	10.46 /13	1.89 /23	8.51 /46	1.18	1.07
GR	Virtus Sector Trend C	PWBCX	E+	(800) 243-1574	D / 1.7	4.86	1.93	9.63 /11	1.13 /19	7.70 /40	0.47	1.82
GR	Virtus Sector Trend I	VARIX	E+	(800) 243-1574	D / 2.2	4.97	2.38	10.68 /13	2.13 /25	8.77 /49	1.52	0.82
SC	Virtus Small Cap Sustainble Gr A	PSGAX	A	(800) 243-1574	A+ / 9.7	7.07	12.28	33.05 /92	12.75 /99	15.06 /97	0.00	1.54
SC	Virtus Small Cap Sustainble Gr C	PSGCX	A	(800) 243-1574	A+ / 9.8	6.90	11.88	32.07 /90	11.89 /98	14.20 /94	0.00	2.29
SC	Virtus Small Cap Sustainble Gr I	PXSGX	A+	(800) 243-1574	A+ / 9.8	7.18	12.43	33.39 /92	13.02 /99	15.36 /97	0.00	1.29
SC	Virtus Small-Cap Core A	PKSAX	B+	(800) 243-1574	A / 9.4	7.04	13.26	29.32 /85	11.31 /97	11.68 /71	0.00	1.37
SC	Virtus Small-Cap Core C	PKSCX	B+	(800) 243-1574	A+ / 9.6	6.83	12.84	28.37 /82	10.48 /96	10.85 /65	0.00	2.12
SC	Virtus Small-Cap Core I	PKSFX	B+	(800) 243-1574	A+ / 9.7	7.10	13.38	29.62 /86	11.59 /98	11.96 /74	0.00	1.12
MC	Virtus Small-Cap Core R6	VSCRX	U	(800) 243-1574	U /	7.17	13.49	29.84 /86	--	--	0.00	0.99
BA	Virtus Strategic Allocation A	PHBLX	D-	(800) 243-1574	D- / 1.3	4.96	1.95	10.38 /13	1.30 /20	4.91 /21	1.39	1.14
BA	● Virtus Strategic Allocation B	PBCBX	D	(800) 243-1574	D- / 1.5	4.74	1.58	9.53 /11	0.54 /16	4.13 /16	0.83	1.89
BA	Virtus Strategic Allocation C	PSBCX	D	(800) 243-1574	D- / 1.5	4.68	1.53	9.50 /10	0.51 /16	4.11 /16	0.85	1.89
GR	Virtus Strategic Growth A	PSTAX	C	(800) 243-1574	C+ / 6.3	7.08	4.84	17.94 /43	8.84 /86	11.21 /68	0.00	1.30
GR	● Virtus Strategic Growth B	PBTHX	C	(800) 243-1574	C+ / 6.7	6.78	4.42	16.97 /38	8.02 /79	10.35 /61	0.00	2.05
GR	Virtus Strategic Growth C	SSTFX	C+	(800) 243-1574	C+ / 6.7	6.88	4.43	17.08 /39	8.05 /79	10.37 /61	0.00	2.03
GR	Virtus Strategic Growth I	PLXGX	C+	(800) 243-1574	B- / 7.5	7.10	4.99	18.29 /44	9.13 /88	11.48 /70	0.00	1.05
AA	Virtus Tactical Allocation CL A	NAINX	D-	(800) 243-1574	D / 1.6	5.60	3.13	13.18 /22	1.47 /21	5.44 /24	1.66	1.34
AA	● Virtus Tactical Allocation CL B	NBINX	D-	(800) 243-1574	D / 1.9	5.29	2.66	12.19 /19	0.70 /17	4.64 /19	0.94	2.09
AA	Virtus Tactical Allocation CL C	POICX	D-	(800) 243-1574	D / 1.9	5.37	2.75	12.35 /19	0.72 /17	4.65 /19	0.95	2.09
SC	Virtus Wealth Masters A	VWMAX	C	(800) 243-1574	C+ / 5.6	4.52	10.80	29.84 /86	4.46 /48	--	0.59	1.53
SC	Virtus Wealth Masters C	VWMCX	C	(800) 243-1574	C+ / 6.1	4.28	10.40	28.82 /84	3.68 /39	--	0.00	2.28
SC	Virtus Wealth Masters I	VWMIX	C+	(800) 243-1574	C+ / 6.9	4.56	10.98	30.17 /87	4.71 /51	--	1.00	1.28
FS	Vivaldi Merger Arbtge A	VARAX	U	(877) 779-1999	U /	-0.04	0.45	0.25 / 1	--	--	0.00	N/A
FS	Vivaldi Merger Arbtge I	VARBX	U	(877) 779-1999	U /	0.00	0.50	0.50 / 2	--	--	0.00	N/A
GL	Vivaldi Multi Strategy A	OMOAX	C-	(855) 467-4632	E+ / 0.9	-0.13	0.54	3.26 / 3	2.58 /28	--	0.00	3.79
GL	Vivaldi Multi Strategy I	OMOIX	C-	(855) 467-4632	D- / 1.4	-0.06	0.68	3.56 / 3	2.91 /31	--	0.00	3.49
GR	Volumetric Fund	VOLMX	C+	(800) 541-3863	C+ / 5.9	5.10	7.97	20.80 /56	5.38 /58	8.54 /47	0.00	1.92
GL	Vontobel Glbl Eqty Inst I	VTEIX	U	(866) 252-5393	U /	9.23	5.39	16.98 /38	--	--	1.12	2.27
EM	● Vontobel Global Em Mkts Eq Inst I	VTGIX	D-	(866) 252-5393	D / 2.2	7.74	-3.42	13.27 /23	2.01 /24	--	0.00	0.98
BA	Voya Balanced Inc I	IBPIX	C+	(800) 992-0180	C / 4.7	5.51	5.87	16.72 /37	4.71 /51	7.49 /38	1.64	0.73
BA	Voya Balanced Inc S	IBPSX	C+	(800) 992-0180	C / 4.5	5.40	5.69	16.42 /36	4.43 /48	7.21 /36	1.39	0.98
GI	Voya Corp Leaders Trust	LEXCX	C+	(800) 992-0180	C+ / 6.8	5.07	8.21	25.51 /75	6.07 /65	10.90 /65	3.82	0.49
GR	Voya Corporate Leaders 100 A	IACLX	A-	(800) 992-0180	B / 7.8	7.41	10.32	24.45 /72	9.33 /89	13.32 /87	1.36	0.93
GR	● Voya Corporate Leaders 100 B	IBCLX	A	(800) 992-0180	B / 8.2	7.22	9.90	23.45 /68	8.46 /83	12.46 /79	0.63	1.68
GR	Voya Corporate Leaders 100 C	ICCLX	A	(800) 992-0180	B+ / 8.4	7.27	10.03	23.72 /69	8.71 /85	12.71 /81	0.92	1.68
GR	Voya Corporate Leaders 100 I	IICLX	A+	(800) 992-0180	A- / 9.0	7.51	10.55	24.92 /73	9.69 /92	13.64 /90	1.74	0.59
GR	Voya Corporate Leaders 100 O	IOCLX	A+	(800) 992-0180	B+ / 8.8	7.41	10.27	24.41 /71	9.26 /89	--	1.38	0.93
GR	Voya Corporate Leaders 100 R	IRCLX	A	(800) 992-0180	B+ / 8.6	7.36	10.18	24.09 /70	9.01 /87	--	1.21	1.18
GR	Voya Corporate Leaders 100 W	IWCLX	A+	(800) 992-0180	A- / 9.0	7.50	10.47	24.74 /72	9.60 /91	13.58 /90	1.68	0.68
FO	Voya Diversified International A	IFFAX	D-	(800) 992-0180	E+ / 0.7	6.59	3.03	14.39 /27	-0.99 / 9	3.18 /12	0.00	1.83
FO	● Voya Diversified International B	IFFBX	D-	(800) 992-0180	E+ / 0.8	6.40	2.62	13.41 /23	-1.75 / 7	2.39 / 9	0.00	2.58
FO	Voya Diversified International C	IFFCX	D-	(800) 992-0180	E+ / 0.8	6.34	2.64	13.54 /24	-1.73 / 7	2.39 / 9	0.00	2.58
FO	Voya Diversified International I	IFFIX	D-	(800) 992-0180	D- / 1.2	6.60	3.14	14.54 /28	-0.76 /10	3.41 /12	0.00	1.46
FO	Voya Diversified International O	IFFOX	D-	(800) 992-0180	D- / 1.1	6.67	3.17	14.42 /27	-0.99 / 9	3.20 /12	0.00	1.83
FO	Voya Diversified International R	IFFRX	D-	(800) 992-0180	D- / 1.0	6.48	2.98	14.00 /25	-1.26 / 9	2.93 /11	0.00	2.08
FO	Voya Diversified International W	IDFWX	D-	(800) 992-0180	D- / 1.2	6.62	3.26	14.70 /29	-0.72 /10	3.43 /13	0.00	1.58
GL	Voya Global Equity A	NAWGX	D+	(800) 992-0180	D+ / 2.5	7.77	7.73	19.21 /48	1.24 /20	2.85 /10	1.23	1.47

● Denotes fund is closed to new investors
* Denotes fund is included in Section II

www.thestreetratings.com

RISK			NET ASSETS		ASSET				Portfolio Turnover Ratio	BULL / BEAR		FUND MANAGER		MINIMUMS		LOADS	
Risk Rating/Pts	3 Year Standard Deviation	Beta	NAV As of 2/28/17	Total $(Mil)	Cash %	Stocks %	Bonds %	Other %		Last Bull Market Return	Last Bear Market Return	Manager Quality Pct	Manager Tenure (Years)	Initial Purch. $	Additional Purch. $	Front End Load	Back End Load
D+ / 2.5	14.8	1.08	30.89	443	0	99	0	1	31	100.8	-16.5	56	19	2,500	100	5.8	0.0
D+ / 2.5	14.8	1.08	30.28	N/A	0	99	0	1	31	92.8	-16.7	46	19	2,500	100	0.0	0.0
D+ / 2.6	14.8	1.08	30.76	56	0	99	0	1	31	92.8	-16.7	46	19	2,500	100	0.0	0.0
D+ / 2.5	14.8	1.08	30.86	571	0	99	0	1	31	103.5	-16.4	60	19	100,000	0	0.0	0.0
C- / 3.9	7.6	0.58	11.46	116	0	99	0	1	337	65.3	-11.1	23	8	2,500	100	5.8	0.0
C- / 3.8	7.6	0.58	11.27	141	0	99	0	1	337	58.7	-11.3	16	8	2,500	100	0.0	0.0
C- / 3.9	7.6	0.58	11.43	88	0	99	0	1	337	67.3	-10.9	25	8	100,000	0	0.0	0.0
C+ / 5.8	14.2	0.78	20.98	250	6	93	0	1	27	137.2	-8.3	98	9	2,500	100	5.8	0.0
C+ / 5.7	14.2	0.78	19.16	53	6	93	0	1	27	127.7	-8.6	97	9	2,500	100	0.0	0.0
C+ / 5.8	14.2	0.78	21.30	395	6	93	0	1	27	140.5	-8.2	98	9	100,000	0	0.0	0.0
C / 4.7	12.3	0.71	24.33	75	3	93	2	2	33	109.2	-14.0	97	9	2,500	100	5.8	0.0
C / 4.3	12.3	0.71	20.82	44	3	93	2	2	33	100.9	-14.3	96	9	2,500	100	0.0	0.0
C / 4.7	12.3	0.71	25.49	318	3	93	2	2	33	112.0	-13.9	97	9	100,000	0	0.0	0.0
U /	N/A	N/A	25.56	31	3	93	2	2	33	N/A	N/A	N/A	9	0	0	0.0	0.0
C+ / 5.9	7.1	1.05	13.10	436	1	58	39	2	75	48.8	-12.3	8	5	2,500	100	5.8	0.0
C+ / 5.9	7.1	1.04	13.00	N/A	1	58	39	2	75	42.8	-12.6	5	5	2,500	100	0.0	0.0
C+ / 5.9	7.1	1.04	12.95	33	1	58	39	2	75	42.8	-12.6	5	5	2,500	100	0.0	0.0
C / 4.9	12.8	1.12	13.85	400	0	99	0	1	20	115.0	-23.3	37	6	2,500	100	5.8	0.0
C / 4.7	12.8	1.12	11.12	1	0	99	0	1	20	106.5	-23.6	28	6	2,500	100	0.0	0.0
C / 4.7	12.8	1.12	11.13	13	0	99	0	1	20	106.7	-23.6	29	6	2,500	100	0.0	0.0
C / 5.0	12.8	1.12	14.26	9	0	99	0	1	20	118.2	-23.3	40	6	100,000	0	0.0	0.0
C / 5.1	8.0	1.17	8.29	139	1	59	38	2	81	52.2	-12.0	5	6	2,500	100	5.8	0.0
C / 5.2	8.0	1.17	8.42	N/A	1	59	38	2	81	46.1	-12.3	4	6	2,500	100	0.0	0.0
C / 5.2	7.9	1.16	8.50	4	1	59	38	2	81	46.1	-12.4	4	6	2,500	100	0.0	0.0
C / 5.3	13.9	0.81	15.92	33	0	99	0	1	30	N/A	N/A	61	5	2,500	100	5.8	0.0
C / 5.3	13.9	0.81	15.60	24	0	99	0	1	30	N/A	N/A	51	5	2,500	100	0.0	0.0
C / 5.3	13.9	0.81	15.94	22	0	99	0	1	30	N/A	N/A	64	5	100,000	0	0.0	0.0
U /	N/A	N/A	10.29	67	0	0	0	100	0	N/A	N/A	N/A	2	1,000	50	5.8	1.0
U /	N/A	N/A	10.34	387	0	0	0	100	0	N/A	N/A	N/A	2	500,000	0	0.0	1.0
B / 8.6	3.3	0.04	26.29	31	47	48	3	2	393	N/A	N/A	88	2	5,000	0	5.0	1.0
B / 8.6	3.3	0.04	26.71	112	47	48	3	2	393	N/A	N/A	89	2	100,000	0	0.0	1.0
C+ / 5.9	9.6	0.86	20.22	29	14	85	0	1	82	71.8	-16.7	29	39	500	200	0.0	0.0
U /	N/A	N/A	11.56	36	3	96	0	1	102	N/A	N/A	N/A	2	1,000,000	0	0.0	0.0
C / 5.1	13.0	0.65	9.05	12	7	92	0	1	115	N/A	N/A	80	N/A	1,000,000	0	0.0	0.0
B- / 7.6	7.2	1.13	15.51	425	5	59	35	1	193	64.6	-13.0	28	10	0	0	0.0	0.0
B- / 7.6	7.2	1.13	15.41	4	5	59	35	1	193	62.3	-13.0	25	10	0	0	0.0	0.0
C+ / 6.1	11.6	0.98	33.86	1,017	3	96	0	1	0	106.7	-16.4	23	N/A	1,000	50	0.0	0.0
C+ / 6.9	10.7	1.02	20.01	314	0	99	0	1	33	128.2	-16.5	57	9	1,000	0	5.8	0.0
B- / 7.0	10.7	1.02	20.10	1	0	99	0	1	33	119.3	-16.9	45	9	1,000	0	0.0	0.0
C+ / 6.9	10.7	1.03	19.90	115	0	99	0	1	33	121.6	-16.8	48	9	1,000	0	0.0	0.0
C+ / 6.9	10.7	1.02	20.01	317	0	99	0	1	33	131.6	-16.4	61	9	250,000	0	0.0	0.0
C+ / 6.9	10.7	1.03	19.99	90	0	99	0	1	33	N/A	N/A	55	9	1,000	0	0.0	0.0
C+ / 6.9	10.7	1.03	19.90	60	0	99	0	1	33	N/A	N/A	52	9	0	0	0.0	0.0
C+ / 6.9	10.7	1.02	20.03	87	0	99	0	1	33	131.1	-16.4	60	9	1,000	0	0.0	0.0
C+ / 5.6	11.4	0.90	9.86	22	1	96	1	2	13	37.2	-24.0	64	12	1,000	0	5.8	0.0
C+ / 5.7	11.3	0.90	9.81	N/A	1	96	1	2	13	31.8	-24.3	54	12	1,000	0	0.0	0.0
C+ / 5.6	11.4	0.90	9.73	12	1	96	1	2	13	31.7	-24.2	54	12	1,000	0	0.0	0.0
C / 5.5	11.3	0.90	9.85	4	1	96	1	2	13	39.0	-24.0	67	12	250,000	0	0.0	0.0
C+ / 5.6	11.3	0.90	9.76	4	1	96	1	2	13	37.3	-24.0	64	12	1,000	0	0.0	0.0
C+ / 5.6	11.3	0.90	9.69	N/A	1	96	1	2	13	35.5	-24.1	61	12	0	0	0.0	0.0
C / 5.5	11.3	0.90	9.83	1	1	96	1	2	13	39.2	-23.9	68	12	1,000	0	0.0	0.0
C+ / 5.9	10.3	0.79	31.22	169	1	95	2	2	92	28.4	-15.1	83	5	1,000	0	5.8	0.0

Fund Type	Fund Name	Ticker Symbol	Overall Investment Rating	Phone	Performance Rating/Pts	Total Return % through 2/28/17			Annualized		Incl. in Returns	
	99 Pct = Best 0 Pct = Worst					3 Mo	6 Mo	1Yr / Pct	3Yr / Pct	5Yr / Pct	Dividend Yield	Expense Ratio
GL	● Voya Global Equity B	NAWBX	D+	(800) 992-0180	C- / 3.0	7.57	7.34	18.29 /44	0.48 /16	2.08 / 8	0.27	2.22
GL	Voya Global Equity C	NAWCX	D+	(800) 992-0180	C- / 3.0	7.57	7.33	18.30 /44	0.48 /16	2.08 / 8	0.65	2.22
GL	Voya Global Equity Dividend A	IAGEX	C-	(800) 992-0180	C- / 3.4	7.08	8.25	20.99 /57	2.70 /29	7.21 /36	2.14	1.54
GL	● Voya Global Equity Dividend B	IBGEX	C-	(800) 992-0180	C- / 3.8	6.82	7.77	19.85 /51	1.89 /23	6.39 /31	1.56	2.29
GL	Voya Global Equity Dividend C	ICGEX	C-	(800) 992-0180	C- / 3.9	6.88	7.76	19.97 /52	1.93 /24	6.40 /31	1.62	2.29
GL	Voya Global Equity Dividend I	IGEIX	C	(800) 992-0180	C / 4.8	7.13	8.36	21.25 /59	2.96 /31	7.54 /39	2.50	1.14
GL	Voya Global Equity Dividend O	IDGEX	C	(800) 992-0180	C / 4.5	7.10	8.18	20.94 /57	2.70 /29	7.20 /36	2.28	1.54
GL	Voya Global Equity Dividend W	IGEWX	C	(800) 992-0180	C / 4.7	7.15	8.34	21.18 /58	2.95 /31	7.49 /38	2.25	1.29
GL	Voya Global Equity I	NAWIX	C-	(800) 992-0180	C- / 3.7	7.87	7.87	19.51 /49	1.49 /21	3.09 /11	1.55	1.21
GL	Voya Global Equity Portfolio Adv	IGHAX	C+	(800) 992-0180	C / 5.4	7.72	7.96	19.82 /51	4.28 /46	6.59 /32	2.12	1.11
GL	Voya Global Equity Portfolio S	IGHSX	C+	(800) 992-0180	C+ / 5.7	7.88	8.12	20.22 /53	4.55 /49	6.87 /34	2.33	0.86
GL	Voya Global Equity W	IGVWX	C-	(800) 992-0180	C- / 3.7	7.85	7.88	19.49 /49	1.50 /21	3.12 /11	1.56	1.22
AA	Voya Global Multi Asset A	ATLAX	C-	(800) 992-0180	D+ / 2.3	5.15	4.26	14.87 /29	2.87 /31	5.67 /26	1.69	1.49
AA	● Voya Global Multi Asset B	ALYBX	C	(800) 992-0180	D+ / 2.6	4.87	3.80	13.97 /25	2.09 /25	4.86 /20	0.51	2.24
AA	Voya Global Multi Asset C	ACLGX	C	(800) 992-0180	D+ / 2.7	4.97	3.89	14.08 /26	2.11 /25	4.88 /21	1.00	2.24
AA	Voya Global Multi Asset I	ALEGX	C	(800) 992-0180	C- / 3.4	5.16	4.37	15.18 /31	3.10 /33	5.95 /28	2.02	1.16
AA	Voya Global Multi Asset O	IDSIX	C	(800) 992-0180	C- / 3.2	5.11	4.21	14.76 /29	2.87 /31	5.65 /26	1.83	1.49
AA	Voya Global Multi Asset W	IAFWX	C	(800) 992-0180	C- / 3.4	5.14	4.26	15.17 /31	3.12 /33	5.95 /28	2.10	1.24
GL	Voya Global Perspectives A	IAPVX	C	(800) 992-0180	D / 1.9	4.85	2.93	11.82 /17	3.03 /32	--	2.07	1.41
GL	Voya Global Perspectives C	ICPVX	C	(800) 992-0180	D+ / 2.3	4.66	2.53	11.07 /15	2.27 /26	--	1.54	2.16
GL	Voya Global Perspectives I	IIPVX	C+	(800) 992-0180	D+ / 2.9	4.85	2.94	12.02 /18	3.26 /34	--	2.48	1.23
GL	Voya Global Perspectives R	IRPVX	C	(800) 992-0180	D+ / 2.6	4.73	2.71	11.51 /16	2.74 /30	--	1.99	1.66
GL	Voya Global Perspectives W	IWPVX	C+	(800) 992-0180	C- / 3.0	4.91	3.09	12.19 /19	3.32 /35	--	2.44	1.16
RE	Voya Global Real Estate A	IGLAX	D	(800) 992-0180	D- / 1.5	5.81	-5.18	8.37 / 8	3.65 /39	6.15 /29	3.45	1.26
RE	● Voya Global Real Estate B	IGBAX	D	(800) 992-0180	D / 1.7	5.57	-5.57	7.58 / 7	2.86 /30	5.36 /24	3.82	2.01
RE	Voya Global Real Estate C	IGCAX	D	(800) 992-0180	D / 1.8	5.60	-5.53	7.61 / 7	2.88 /31	5.36 /24	3.58	2.01
RE	Voya Global Real Estate I	IGLIX	D+	(800) 992-0180	D+ / 2.3	5.86	-5.06	8.73 / 9	3.96 /43	6.45 /31	4.00	0.99
RE	Voya Global Real Estate O	IDGTX	D	(800) 992-0180	D / 2.1	5.78	-5.16	8.35 / 8	3.65 /39	6.15 /29	3.70	1.26
RE	Voya Global Real Estate R	IGARX	D	(800) 992-0180	D / 2.0	5.74	-5.29	8.14 / 8	3.40 /36	5.90 /28	3.49	1.51
FO	Voya Global Real Estate R6	VGRQX	U	(800) 992-0180	U /	5.96	-4.93	8.90 / 9	--	--	4.16	0.87
RE	Voya Global Real Estate W	IRGWX	D+	(800) 992-0180	D+ / 2.3	5.84	-5.07	8.67 / 9	3.91 /42	6.41 /31	3.96	1.01
GL	Voya Global Target Payment A	IGPAX	C-	(800) 992-0180	D / 1.9	4.19	3.22	11.21 /15	2.97 /32	5.20 /23	6.08	1.32
GL	Voya Global Target Payment C	IGPCX	C-	(800) 992-0180	D / 2.2	4.03	2.82	10.32 /12	2.20 /25	4.41 /18	5.67	2.07
GL	Voya Global Target Payment I	IGPIX	C	(800) 992-0180	D+ / 2.8	4.15	3.39	11.43 /16	3.28 /35	5.46 /25	6.77	1.02
GL	Voya Global Target Payment R	IGPRX	C-	(800) 992-0180	D+ / 2.4	3.99	2.95	10.76 /14	2.69 /29	4.92 /21	6.18	1.57
GL	Voya Global Target Payment W	IGPWX	C	(800) 992-0180	D+ / 2.8	4.16	3.26	11.31 /16	3.19 /34	5.44 /24	6.79	1.07
GI	Voya Growth and Income Adv	IAVGX	C+	(800) 992-0180	B / 7.7	7.57	9.84	23.62 /69	7.32 /74	11.30 /68	1.44	1.13
GI	Voya Growth and Income I	IIVGX	B-	(800) 992-0180	B / 8.0	7.71	10.12	24.23 /71	7.82 /78	11.81 /73	1.85	0.63
GI	Voya Growth and Income S	ISVGX	B-	(800) 992-0180	B / 7.8	7.64	9.97	23.93 /70	7.55 /76	11.53 /70	1.63	0.88
AA	Voya Index Solution 2025 Adv	ISDAX	C-	(800) 992-0180	C- / 3.9	5.23	4.37	14.88 /29	4.05 /44	6.99 /35	1.91	1.15
AA	Voya Index Solution 2025 I	ISDIX	C	(800) 992-0180	C / 4.3	5.31	4.68	15.36 /31	4.58 /50	7.51 /38	2.37	0.65
AA	Voya Index Solution 2025 S	ISDSX	C-	(800) 992-0180	C- / 4.1	5.26	4.52	15.14 /30	4.31 /46	7.26 /36	2.08	0.90
AA	Voya Index Solution 2035 Adv	ISEAX	C-	(800) 992-0180	C / 5.1	6.33	6.22	18.57 /45	4.72 /51	8.32 /45	1.71	1.14
AA	Voya Index Solution 2035 I	ISEIX	C	(800) 992-0180	C+ / 5.6	6.47	6.47	19.17 /48	5.25 /57	8.87 /50	2.16	0.64
AA	Voya Index Solution 2035 S	ISESX	C	(800) 992-0180	C / 5.3	6.34	6.34	18.92 /47	4.97 /54	8.59 /47	1.89	0.89
AA	Voya Index Solution 2045 Adv	ISJAX	C	(800) 992-0180	C+ / 5.7	6.87	6.77	20.10 /53	5.02 /54	8.83 /49	1.49	1.13
AA	Voya Index Solution 2045 I	ISJIX	C	(800) 992-0180	C+ / 6.1	6.96	6.96	20.75 /56	5.54 /60	9.37 /54	1.91	0.63
AA	Voya Index Solution 2045 S	ISJSX	C	(800) 992-0180	C+ / 5.9	6.95	6.95	20.43 /54	5.29 /57	9.09 /51	1.64	0.88
GI	Voya Index Solution 2050 Adv	IDXPX	C+	(800) 992-0180	C+ / 5.7	6.87	6.79	20.15 /53	5.06 /55	8.76 /49	0.10	8.07
GI	Voya Index Solution 2050 I	IDXQX	C+	(800) 992-0180	C+ / 6.1	7.00	7.07	20.73 /56	5.59 /60	9.33 /53	0.12	7.57
GI	Voya Index Solution 2050 S	IDXRX	C+	(800) 992-0180	C+ / 6.0	7.00	7.00	20.53 /55	5.40 /59	9.07 /51	0.12	7.82
GI	Voya Index Solution 2050 S2	IDXSX	C+	(800) 992-0180	C+ / 5.8	6.92	6.92	20.42 /54	5.18 /56	8.89 /50	0.13	7.97

● Denotes fund is closed to new investors
* Denotes fund is included in Section II

www.thestreetratings.com

RISK Rating/Pts	3 Year Standard Deviation	Beta	NAV As of 2/28/17	Total $(Mil)	Cash %	Stocks %	Bonds %	Other %	Portfolio Turnover Ratio	Last Bull Market Return	Last Bear Market Return	Manager Quality Pct	Manager Tenure (Years)	Initial Purch. $	Additional Purch. $	Front End Load	Back End Load
C+ / 6.1	10.3	0.79	34.22	1	1	95	2	2	92	23.2	-15.3	78	5	1,000	0	0.0	0.0
C+ / 6.0	10.3	0.79	29.09	73	1	95	2	2	92	23.2	-15.3	78	5	1,000	0	0.0	0.0
C+ / 6.2	11.1	0.85	13.50	35	2	95	1	2	29	64.0	-16.9	90	11	1,000	0	5.8	0.0
C+ / 6.2	11.1	0.85	13.49	N/A	2	95	1	2	29	57.2	-17.1	86	11	1,000	0	0.0	0.0
C+ / 6.2	11.1	0.85	13.40	22	2	95	1	2	29	57.4	-17.1	86	11	1,000	0	0.0	0.0
C+ / 6.2	11.1	0.85	13.52	10	2	95	1	2	29	66.5	-16.7	91	11	250,000	0	0.0	0.0
C+ / 6.2	11.1	0.85	13.47	13	2	95	1	2	29	63.9	-16.9	90	11	1,000	0	0.0	0.0
C+ / 6.2	11.1	0.85	14.98	1	2	95	1	2	29	65.9	-16.7	90	11	1,000	0	0.0	0.0
C+ / 5.9	10.2	0.78	31.50	32	1	95	2	2	92	30.0	-14.9	84	5	250,000	0	0.0	0.0
C+ / 6.4	10.5	0.79	9.63	20	1	95	2	2	83	55.9	-19.9	94	4	0	0	0.0	0.0
C+ / 6.4	10.5	0.79	9.72	498	1	95	2	2	83	58.2	-19.8	95	4	0	0	0.0	0.0
C+ / 5.9	10.3	0.79	31.47	3	1	95	2	2	92	30.1	-14.9	84	5	1,000	0	0.0	0.0
B- / 7.8	7.4	1.13	10.86	65	1	60	38	1	65	50.1	-13.1	13	10	1,000	0	5.8	0.0
B- / 7.9	7.4	1.12	11.10	N/A	1	60	38	1	65	44.0	-13.4	9	10	1,000	0	0.0	0.0
B- / 7.8	7.4	1.13	10.93	20	1	60	38	1	65	44.2	-13.4	9	10	1,000	0	0.0	0.0
B- / 7.7	7.4	1.12	11.01	12	1	60	38	1	65	52.3	-13.1	15	10	250,000	0	0.0	0.0
B- / 7.8	7.4	1.12	10.79	58	1	60	38	1	65	50.1	-13.2	13	10	1,000	0	0.0	0.0
B- / 7.7	7.5	1.13	10.99	N/A	1	60	38	1	65	52.3	N/A	14	10	1,000	0	0.0	0.0
B / 8.6	5.9	0.85	10.94	8	1	57	41	1	20	N/A	N/A	63	4	1,000	0	5.8	0.0
B / 8.6	6.0	0.86	10.83	5	1	57	41	1	20	N/A	N/A	53	4	1,000	0	0.0	0.0
B / 8.6	5.9	0.84	10.95	1	1	57	41	1	20	N/A	N/A	67	4	250,000	0	0.0	0.0
B / 8.6	5.9	0.84	10.90	22	1	57	41	1	20	N/A	N/A	60	4	0	0	0.0	0.0
B / 8.6	5.9	0.84	10.97	4	1	57	41	1	20	N/A	N/A	67	4	1,000	0	0.0	0.0
C+ / 6.1	12.6	0.88	19.35	375	9	90	0	1	34	59.4	-18.5	10	16	1,000	0	5.8	0.0
C+ / 6.1	12.7	0.88	15.43	1	9	90	0	1	34	53.1	-18.8	7	16	1,000	0	0.0	0.0
C+ / 6.1	12.7	0.88	16.54	132	9	90	0	1	34	53.1	-18.8	7	16	1,000	0	0.0	0.0
C+ / 6.1	12.7	0.89	19.34	1,765	9	90	0	1	34	61.8	-18.4	12	16	250,000	0	0.0	0.0
C+ / 6.1	12.6	0.88	19.34	12	9	90	0	1	34	59.4	-18.5	11	16	1,000	0	0.0	0.0
C+ / 6.1	12.7	0.88	19.28	3	9	90	0	1	34	57.3	N/A	9	16	0	0	0.0	0.0
U /	N/A	N/A	19.35	77	9	90	0	1	34	N/A	N/A	N/A	16	1,000,000	0	0.0	0.0
C+ / 6.1	12.6	0.88	19.38	295	9	90	0	1	34	61.6	-18.5	12	16	1,000	0	0.0	0.0
B- / 7.8	5.8	0.88	8.15	161	0	56	43	1	57	46.6	-14.0	61	9	1,000	0	5.8	0.0
B- / 7.9	5.8	0.88	8.43	160	0	56	43	1	57	40.7	-14.2	51	9	1,000	0	0.0	0.0
B- / 7.8	5.7	0.87	8.12	104	0	56	43	1	57	48.8	-13.9	65	9	250,000	0	0.0	0.0
B- / 7.8	5.8	0.88	8.13	N/A	0	56	43	1	57	44.5	N/A	57	9	0	0	0.0	0.0
B- / 7.8	5.8	0.87	8.10	43	0	56	43	1	57	48.5	-13.9	64	9	1,000	0	0.0	0.0
C / 4.8	10.3	0.98	29.17	1,091	0	98	0	2	53	112.4	-18.2	36	13	0	0	0.0	0.0
C / 4.8	10.3	0.98	29.58	1,855	0	98	0	2	53	117.6	-18.0	43	13	0	0	0.0	0.0
C / 4.8	10.3	0.98	29.21	612	0	98	0	2	53	114.7	-18.1	39	13	0	0	0.0	0.0
C+ / 6.3	7.1	1.11	10.26	230	1	62	36	1	40	60.8	-14.0	23	9	0	0	0.0	0.0
C+ / 6.2	7.1	1.12	10.51	59	1	62	36	1	40	65.2	-13.9	28	9	0	0	0.0	0.0
C+ / 6.3	7.0	1.10	10.40	152	1	62	36	1	40	63.1	-14.0	26	9	0	0	0.0	0.0
C / 5.3	8.8	1.38	10.42	203	2	80	17	1	38	76.0	-17.4	13	9	0	0	0.0	0.0
C / 5.3	8.8	1.38	10.70	51	2	80	17	1	38	80.9	-17.2	16	9	0	0	0.0	0.0
C / 5.3	8.9	1.39	10.57	118	2	80	17	1	38	78.6	-17.4	14	9	0	0	0.0	0.0
C / 5.0	9.6	1.49	10.73	136	2	89	8	1	36	82.1	-19.3	10	9	0	0	0.0	0.0
C / 5.0	9.6	1.50	11.07	39	2	89	8	1	36	86.9	-19.1	13	9	0	0	0.0	0.0
C / 5.0	9.6	1.50	10.92	78	2	89	8	1	36	84.6	-19.2	11	9	0	0	0.0	0.0
C+ / 6.1	9.5	0.90	14.32	4	2	90	7	1	195	N/A	N/A	22	6	0	0	0.0	0.0
C+ / 6.1	9.5	0.90	14.53	1	2	90	7	1	195	N/A	N/A	27	6	0	0	0.0	0.0
C+ / 6.1	9.5	0.90	14.53	5	2	90	7	1	195	N/A	N/A	25	6	0	0	0.0	0.0
C+ / 6.1	9.5	0.90	14.36	1	2	90	7	1	195	N/A	N/A	23	6	0	0	0.0	0.0

						PERFORMANCE							
	99 Pct = Best							Total Return % through 2/28/17				Incl. in Returns	
	0 Pct = Worst			Overall		Perfor-				Annualized		Dividend	Expense
Fund		Ticker	Investment			mance							
Type	Fund Name	Symbol	Rating	Phone		Rating/Pts	3 Mo	6 Mo	1Yr / Pct	3Yr / Pct	5Yr / Pct	Yield	Ratio
GL	Voya Index Solution 2055 Adv	IISAX	C	(800) 992-0180		C+ / 5.7	6.97	6.80	20.23 /53	5.05 /55	8.86 /49	1.22	1.14
GL	Voya Index Solution 2055 I	IISNX	C+	(800) 992-0180		C+ / 6.1	7.05	7.05	20.76 /56	5.58 /60	9.39 /54	1.61	0.64
GL	Voya Index Solution 2055 S	IISSX	C+	(800) 992-0180		C+ / 5.9	6.97	6.88	20.48 /55	5.29 /58	9.12 /52	1.38	0.89
GL	Voya Index Solution 2055 S2	IISTX	C	(800) 992-0180		C+ / 5.8	7.02	6.85	20.37 /54	5.16 /56	8.96 /50	1.33	1.04
AA	Voya Index Solution Income Adv	ISKAX	C-	(800) 992-0180		D / 2.2	3.33	1.53	8.44 / 8	3.13 /33	4.54 /18	1.51	1.15
AA	Voya Index Solution Income I	ISKIX	C-	(800) 992-0180		D+ / 2.5	3.44	1.79	8.98 / 9	3.63 /38	5.09 /22	1.77	0.65
AA	Voya Index Solution Income S	ISKSX	C-	(800) 992-0180		D+ / 2.3	3.38	1.61	8.63 / 9	3.36 /35	4.79 /20	1.58	0.90
FO	Voya International Index Adv	IIIAX	D-	(800) 992-0180		D- / 1.0	7.13	3.92	15.08 /30	-1.46 / 8	4.47 /18	2.49	1.06
FO	Voya International Index I	IIIIX	D-	(800) 992-0180		D- / 1.2	7.23	4.19	15.54 /32	-0.97 / 9	4.95 /21	2.99	0.56
FO	Voya International Index S	INTIX	D-	(800) 992-0180		D- / 1.1	7.28	4.10	15.32 /31	-1.21 / 9	4.71 /19	2.74	0.81
RE	Voya International Real Estate A	IIRAX	D	(800) 992-0180		D- / 1.0	5.61	-4.01	9.46 /10	1.26 /20	5.25 /23	8.76	1.40
RE	● Voya International Real Estate B	IIRBX	D	(800) 992-0180		D- / 1.2	5.41	-4.35	8.67 / 9	0.50 /16	4.46 /18	8.37	2.15
RE	Voya International Real Estate C	IIRCX	D	(800) 992-0180		D- / 1.2	5.29	-4.41	8.66 / 9	0.50 /16	4.45 /18	8.51	2.15
RE	Voya International Real Estate I	IIRIX	D	(800) 992-0180		D / 1.6	5.58	-3.95	9.68 /11	1.54 /21	5.56 /25	9.65	1.09
RE	Voya International Real Estate W	IIRWX	D	(800) 992-0180		D / 1.6	5.67	-3.86	9.70 /11	1.52 /21	5.50 /25	9.52	1.15
GR	Voya Large Cap Growth Adv	IEOPX	B	(800) 992-0180		B / 8.1	8.32	7.85	19.76 /51	9.25 /89	12.65 /80	0.00	1.27
GR	Voya Large Cap Growth Inst	IEOHX	B+	(800) 992-0180		B+ / 8.6	8.49	8.17	20.47 /55	9.90 /93	13.28 /87	0.51	0.67
GR	Voya Large Cap Growth Svc	IEOSX	B+	(800) 992-0180		B+ / 8.3	8.44	7.99	20.12 /53	9.61 /91	12.99 /84	0.28	0.92
GR	Voya Large Cap Growth Svc 2	IEOTX	B	(800) 992-0180		B / 8.2	8.43	7.92	20.02 /52	9.45 /90	12.82 /82	0.11	1.07
GI	Voya Large Cap Value A	IEDAX	B-	(800) 992-0180		B- / 7.2	7.35	12.10	26.93 /79	7.20 /73	11.39 /69	1.69	1.20
IN	Voya Large Cap Value Adv	IPEAX	A-	(800) 992-0180		B / 8.1	7.37	12.09	26.78 /79	7.07 /72	11.27 /68	1.69	1.35
GI	● Voya Large Cap Value B	IBEDX	B	(800) 992-0180		B / 7.6	7.27	11.79	26.03 /76	6.41 /68	10.55 /62	1.09	1.95
GI	Voya Large Cap Value C	IEDCX	B	(800) 992-0180		B / 7.6	7.27	11.79	26.04 /76	6.42 /68	10.56 /63	1.12	1.95
GI	Voya Large Cap Value I	IEDIX	B+	(800) 992-0180		B+ / 8.5	7.58	12.36	27.48 /80	7.61 /76	11.79 /72	1.96	0.86
IN	Voya Large Cap Value Inst	IPEIX	A	(800) 992-0180		B+ / 8.6	7.56	12.38	27.52 /81	7.70 /77	11.93 /74	2.20	0.75
IN	Voya Large Cap Value O	ILVOX	B+	(800) 992-0180		B / 8.2	7.45	12.21	26.96 /79	7.22 /73	--	1.80	1.20
GI	Voya Large Cap Value R	IEDRX	B	(800) 992-0180		B / 8.0	7.39	12.07	26.65 /78	6.97 /72	11.17 /67	1.58	1.45
IN	Voya Large Cap Value R6	IEDZX	B+	(800) 992-0180		B+ / 8.5	7.59	12.38	27.41 /80	7.64 /76	--	1.97	0.80
IN	Voya Large Cap Value Svc	IPESX	A-	(800) 992-0180		B+ / 8.4	7.48	12.26	27.23 /80	7.46 /75	11.67 /71	1.99	1.00
GI	Voya Large Cap Value W	IWEDX	B+	(800) 992-0180		B+ / 8.4	7.50	12.26	27.33 /80	7.50 /75	11.68 /71	1.87	0.95
GR	Voya Large-Cap Growth A	NLCAX	B-	(800) 992-0180		B- / 7.2	8.34	7.90	19.86 /51	9.33 /89	12.29 /77	0.11	1.44
GR	● Voya Large-Cap Growth B	NLCBX	B-	(800) 992-0180		B / 7.6	8.16	7.51	18.97 /47	8.58 /84	11.54 /70	0.00	2.09
GR	Voya Large-Cap Growth C	NLCCX	B-	(800) 992-0180		B / 7.6	8.16	7.50	18.96 /47	8.59 /84	11.55 /70	0.00	2.09
GR	Voya Large-Cap Growth I	PLCIX	B+	(800) 992-0180		B+ / 8.5	8.46	8.09	20.35 /54	9.72 /92	12.70 /81	0.53	1.05
GR	Voya Large-Cap Growth R6	VGOSX	U	(800) 992-0180		U /	8.45	8.08	20.33 /54	--	--	0.54	0.86
GR	Voya Large-Cap Growth W	IGOWX	B+	(800) 992-0180		B+ / 8.4	8.43	8.02	20.15 /53	9.65 /91	12.65 /80	0.47	1.0
MC	Voya Mid Cap Opportunities A	NMCAX	C-	(800) 992-0180		C+ / 6.1	8.18	7.60	22.31 /64	6.76 /70	10.51 /62	0.00	1.34
MC	● Voya Mid Cap Opportunities B	NMCBX	C-	(800) 992-0180		C+ / 6.6	7.95	7.17	21.36 /59	5.96 /64	9.68 /56	0.00	2.09
MC	Voya Mid Cap Opportunities C	NMCCX	C-	(800) 992-0180		C+ / 6.6	7.96	7.17	21.42 /59	5.95 /64	9.68 /56	0.00	2.09
MC	Voya Mid Cap Opportunities I	NMCIX	C+	(800) 992-0180		B- / 7.3	8.19	7.71	22.70 /65	7.11 /73	10.92 /65	0.00	1.02
MC	Voya Mid Cap Opportunities O	NMCOX	C	(800) 992-0180		B- / 7.1	8.11	7.53	22.28 /63	6.75 /70	10.51 /62	0.00	1.34
MC	Voya Mid Cap Opportunities R6	IMOZX	C+	(800) 992-0180		B- / 7.4	8.25	7.81	22.81 /66	7.24 /74	--	0.00	0.89
MC	Voya Mid Cap Opportunities W	IMOWX	C+	(800) 992-0180		B- / 7.3	8.21	7.72	22.62 /65	7.02 /72	10.79 /64	0.00	1.09
MC	Voya Mid Cap Opps Port Adv	IAMOX	C-	(800) 992-0180		B- / 7.0	8.14	7.48	22.22 /63	6.72 /70	10.54 /62	0.00	1.31
MC	Voya Mid Cap Opps Port I	IIMOX	C	(800) 992-0180		B- / 7.4	8.23	7.70	22.78 /66	7.24 /74	11.08 /67	0.00	0.81
MC	Voya Mid Cap Opps Port S	ISMOX	C	(800) 992-0180		B- / 7.2	8.15	7.59	22.48 /64	6.97 /72	10.81 /64	0.00	1.06
MC	Voya Mid Cap Research Enhanced Ix	AIMAX	C-	(800) 992-0180		B- / 7.1	6.60	11.39	31.01 /88	6.45 /68	10.91 /65	0.75	1.12
MC	● Voya Mid Cap Research Enhanced Ix	APMBX	C-	(800) 992-0180		B- / 7.5	6.38	10.95	30.01 /86	5.59 /60	10.02 /59	0.19	1.87
MC	Voya Mid Cap Research Enhanced Ix	APMCX	C-	(800) 992-0180		B / 7.7	6.46	11.09	30.32 /87	5.93 /64	10.36 /61	0.40	1.62
MC	Voya Mid Cap Research Enhanced Ix	AIMIX	C	(800) 992-0180		B+ / 8.3	6.64	11.58	31.33 /89	6.75 /70	11.22 /68	0.98	0.81
MC	Voya Mid Cap Research Enhanced Ix	IDMOX	C	(800) 992-0180		B / 8.1	6.57	11.35	30.99 /88	6.45 /68	10.90 /65	0.79	1.12
MC	Voya Mid Cap Research Enhanced Ix	AIMRX	C	(800) 992-0180		B / 7.9	6.53	11.26	30.72 /88	6.21 /66	10.63 /63	0.60	1.37

● Denotes fund is closed to new investors

* Denotes fund is included in Section II

www.thestreetratings.com

Risk Rating/Pts	Standard Deviation	Beta	NAV As of 2/28/17	Total $(Mil)	Cash %	Stocks %	Bonds %	Other %	Portfolio Turnover Ratio	Last Bull Market Return	Last Bear Market Return	Manager Quality Pct	Manager Tenure (Years)	Initial Purch. $	Additional Purch. $	Front End Load	Back End Load
C+ / 5.6	9.8	1.48	13.66	44	1	92	6	1	39	82.3	-19.2	52	7	0	0	0.0	0.0
C+ / 5.6	9.7	1.48	13.97	12	1	92	6	1	39	87.2	-19.1	59	7	0	0	0.0	0.0
C+ / 5.6	9.7	1.48	13.82	26	1	92	6	1	39	84.6	-19.2	55	7	0	0	0.0	0.0
C+ / 5.6	9.7	1.48	13.72	7	1	92	6	1	39	83.2	-19.2	53	7	0	0	0.0	0.0
B- / 7.6	4.3	0.65	9.94	118	0	33	66	1	34	34.9	-4.6	53	9	0	0	0.0	0.0
B- / 7.5	4.3	0.65	10.21	29	0	33	66	1	34	38.9	-4.5	60	9	0	0	0.0	0.0
B- / 7.6	4.3	0.64	10.10	175	0	33	66	1	34	36.8	-4.5	57	9	0	0	0.0	0.0
C+ / 5.8	11.4	0.93	9.01	710	2	97	0	1	2	43.5	-23.4	58	5	0	0	0.0	0.0
C+ / 5.9	11.4	0.93	9.20	688	2	97	0	1	2	47.4	-23.3	64	5	0	0	0.0	0.0
C+ / 5.9	11.5	0.93	9.14	75	2	97	0	1	2	45.5	-23.4	61	5	0	0	0.0	0.0
C+ / 6.5	11.9	0.60	8.00	76	21	78	0	1	89	49.9	-20.7	15	11	1,000	0	5.8	0.0
C+ / 6.5	11.9	0.60	8.00	N/A	21	78	0	1	89	44.1	-21.0	10	11	1,000	0	0.0	0.0
C+ / 6.5	12.0	0.60	7.96	9	21	78	0	1	89	44.0	-20.9	10	11	1,000	0	0.0	0.0
C+ / 6.5	11.9	0.60	8.00	230	21	78	0	1	89	52.4	-20.6	17	11	250,000	0	0.0	0.0
C+ / 6.5	12.0	0.59	8.04	13	21	78	0	1	89	52.1	-20.6	17	11	1,000	0	0.0	0.0
C / 5.3	11.2	1.02	17.44	2,074	0	98	1	1	70	122.3	-14.5	56	7	0	0	0.0	0.0
C / 5.4	11.2	1.02	18.66	1,911	0	98	1	1	70	129.3	-14.4	64	7	0	0	0.0	0.0
C / 5.4	11.2	1.02	18.25	2,113	0	98	1	1	70	126.0	-14.4	60	7	0	0	0.0	0.0
C / 5.4	11.2	1.02	18.13	70	0	98	1	1	70	124.3	-14.5	58	7	0	0	0.0	0.0
C / 5.5	10.4	0.96	12.70	436	0	98	1	1	116	107.0	-15.7	37	6	1,000	0	5.8	0.0
C+ / 6.6	10.4	0.97	12.36	66	0	0	0	100	83	106.3	-15.8	35	6	0	0	0.0	0.0
C / 5.5	10.3	0.96	12.66	2	0	98	1	1	116	98.7	-16.0	29	6	1,000	0	0.0	0.0
C / 5.5	10.4	0.96	12.67	70	0	98	1	1	116	98.9	-16.0	29	6	1,000	0	0.0	0.0
C+ / 5.6	10.4	0.96	13.63	233	0	98	1	1	116	111.0	-15.6	43	6	250,000	0	0.0	0.0
C+ / 6.6	10.4	0.97	12.59	599	0	0	0	100	83	113.2	-15.6	43	6	0	0	0.0	0.0
C / 5.5	10.4	0.96	12.69	26	0	98	1	1	116	N/A	N/A	37	6	1,000	0	0.0	0.0
C / 5.5	10.3	0.96	12.69	5	0	98	1	1	116	104.9	N/A	35	6	0	0	0.0	0.0
C+ / 5.6	10.3	0.96	13.62	151	0	98	1	1	116	N/A	N/A	43	6	1,000,000	0	0.0	0.0
C+ / 6.6	10.4	0.97	12.44	937	0	0	0	100	83	110.3	-15.7	40	6	0	0	0.0	0.0
C+ / 5.6	10.3	0.96	13.59	16	0	98	1	1	116	109.9	-15.6	42	6	1,000	0	0.0	0.0
C / 5.4	11.1	1.02	32.70	67	2	96	0	2	70	122.3	-14.6	57	8	1,000	0	5.8	0.0
C / 5.1	11.2	1.02	28.37	N/A	2	96	0	2	70	114.4	-14.8	47	8	1,000	0	0.0	0.0
C / 5.1	11.1	1.02	28.26	32	2	96	0	2	70	114.5	-14.8	48	8	1,000	0	0.0	0.0
C+ / 5.6	11.1	1.02	35.94	257	2	96	0	2	70	126.7	-14.5	62	8	250,000	0	0.0	0.0
U /	N/A	N/A	35.93	47	2	96	0	2	70	N/A	N/A	N/A	8	1,000,000	0	0.0	0.0
C / 5.5	11.1	1.02	35.08	12	2	96	0	2	70	126.2	-14.5	61	8	1,000	0	0.0	0.0
C- / 4.2	11.5	0.87	22.38	297	2	96	1	1	88	106.2	-20.0	56	12	1,000	0	5.8	0.0
C- / 3.6	11.5	0.87	17.84	1	2	96	1	1	88	98.1	-20.2	45	12	1,000	0	0.0	0.0
C- / 3.6	11.5	0.87	17.68	112	2	96	1	1	88	98.0	-20.2	45	12	1,000	0	0.0	0.0
C / 4.5	11.5	0.87	25.13	674	2	96	1	1	88	110.4	-19.8	60	12	250,000	0	0.0	0.0
C- / 4.2	11.5	0.87	22.29	51	2	96	1	1	88	106.2	-20.0	56	12	1,000	0	0.0	0.0
C / 4.5	11.5	0.87	25.24	156	2	96	1	1	88	N/A	N/A	62	12	1,000,000	0	0.0	0.0
C / 4.4	11.5	0.87	24.82	109	2	96	1	1	88	109.0	-19.9	60	12	1,000	0	0.0	0.0
C- / 3.4	11.5	0.87	12.35	130	2	96	1	1	94	106.5	-20.1	56	12	0	0	0.0	0.0
C- / 3.7	11.5	0.87	13.28	611	2	96	1	1	94	112.0	-19.9	62	12	0	0	0.0	0.0
C- / 3.5	11.5	0.87	12.61	492	2	96	1	1	94	109.1	-20.0	59	12	0	0	0.0	0.0
D+ / 2.9	11.7	0.95	17.05	51	0	99	0	1	143	112.4	-22.6	42	2	1,000	0	5.8	0.0
D+ / 2.8	11.7	0.95	15.34	N/A	0	99	0	1	143	103.3	-22.8	31	2	1,000	0	0.0	0.0
D+ / 2.7	11.7	0.95	15.90	8	0	99	0	1	143	106.6	-22.7	35	2	1,000	0	0.0	0.0
D+ / 2.9	11.7	0.95	17.49	9	0	99	0	1	143	115.5	-22.5	46	2	250,000	0	0.0	0.0
D+ / 2.9	11.7	0.95	17.10	84	0	99	0	1	143	112.3	-22.6	42	2	1,000	0	0.0	0.0
D+ / 2.8	11.7	0.95	16.80	16	0	99	0	1	143	109.5	-22.6	38	2	0	0	0.0	0.0

I. Index of Stock Mutual Funds

Fund Type	Fund Name	Ticker Symbol	Overall Investment Rating	Phone	Perfor-mance Rating/Pts	Total Return % through 2/28/17			Annualized		Incl. in Returns	
						3 Mo	6 Mo	1Yr / Pct	3Yr / Pct	5Yr / Pct	Dividend Yield	Expense Ratio
MC	Voya Mid Cap Research Enhanced Ix	AIMWX	C	(800) 992-0180	B+ / 8.3	6.61	11.49	31.35 /89	6.73 /70	11.16 /67	0.99	0.87
MC	Voya MidCap Opportunities R	IMORX	C	(800) 992-0180	C+ / 6.9	8.08	7.44	22.00 /62	6.49 /68	10.24 /60	0.00	1.59
FO	Voya Multi Manager Internatl SC A	NTKLX	D+	(800) 992-0180	D+ / 2.3	8.41	6.04	17.03 /38	1.32 /20	7.27 /36	0.50	1.75
FO	● Voya Multi Manager Internatl SC B	NAPBX	C-	(800) 992-0180	D+ / 2.7	8.22	5.70	16.28 /35	0.66 /16	6.57 /32	0.00	2.40
FO	Voya Multi Manager Internatl SC C	NARCX	C-	(800) 992-0180	D+ / 2.7	8.21	5.69	16.26 /35	0.66 /16	6.57 /32	0.00	2.40
FO	Voya Multi Manager Internatl SC I	NAPIX	C-	(800) 992-0180	C- / 3.5	8.51	6.25	17.54 /41	1.78 /23	7.78 /40	0.99	1.31
FO	Voya Multi Manager Internatl SC O	NAPOX	C-	(800) 992-0180	C- / 3.3	8.44	6.11	17.15 /39	1.43 /21	7.38 /37	0.64	1.65
FO	Voya Multi Manager Internatl SC W	ISCWX	C-	(800) 992-0180	C- / 3.5	8.50	6.23	17.43 /40	1.68 /22	7.65 /39	0.74	1.40
FO	Voya Multi Manager Intl Factors I	IICFX	D-	(800) 992-0180	D+ / 2.5	7.47	4.88	14.96 /30	0.88 /18	5.13 /22	1.47	0.90
FO	Voya Multi Manager Intl Factors W	IICWX	D-	(800) 992-0180	D+ / 2.5	7.47	4.88	15.09 /30	0.87 /18	--	1.47	1.27
EM	Voya Multi Mgr Emg Mrkts Eqty A	IEMHX	E+	(800) 992-0180	D- / 1.2	8.22	4.07	28.95 /84	-1.09 / 9	-1.74 / 3	0.70	1.82
EM	● Voya Multi Mgr Emg Mrkts Eqty B	IEMEX	E+	(800) 992-0180	D- / 1.5	8.00	3.64	27.93 /81	-1.82 / 7	--	0.00	2.57
EM	Voya Multi Mgr Emg Mrkts Eqty C	IEMJX	E+	(800) 992-0180	D- / 1.5	7.97	3.69	27.99 /82	-1.82 / 7	-2.46 / 2	0.03	2.57
EM	Voya Multi Mgr Emg Mrkts Eqty I	IEMGX	E+	(800) 992-0180	D / 2.0	8.37	4.33	29.50 /85	-0.71 /10	-1.38 / 3	1.07	1.34
EM	Voya Multi Mgr Emg Mrkts Eqty R	IEMKX	E+	(800) 992-0180	D / 1.7	8.11	3.98	28.74 /83	-1.34 / 8	-1.98 / 3	0.58	2.07
EM	Voya Multi Mgr Emg Mrkts Eqty W	IEMLX	E+	(800) 992-0180	D / 1.9	8.29	4.14	29.30 /85	-0.82 /10	-1.48 / 3	0.99	1.57
FO	Voya Multi-Manager Intl Eqty I	IIGIX	D-	(800) 992-0180	E+ / 0.9	5.58	1.45	12.13 /18	-1.18 / 9	4.16 /16	1.77	0.98
GI	Voya Multi-Manager Lg Cap Core	IPFAX	B+	(800) 992-0180	B / 8.2	7.72	8.84	21.44 /59	8.97 /87	11.50 /70	1.45	1.33
GI	Voya Multi-Manager Lg Cap Core Inst	IPPIX	A-	(800) 992-0180	B+ / 8.7	7.86	9.19	22.23 /63	9.64 /91	12.17 /76	1.99	0.73
GI	Voya Multi-Manager Lg Cap Core Svc	IPPSX	A-	(800) 992-0180	B+ / 8.5	7.80	9.05	21.98 /62	9.39 /90	11.90 /73	1.75	0.98
MC	Voya Multi-Manager Mid Cap Val I	IMCVX	C	(800) 992-0180	B+ / 8.3	5.99	11.44	27.10 /79	7.88 /78	12.72 /81	1.19	0.86
RE	Voya Real Estate A	CLARX	C-	(800) 992-0180	C / 4.9	7.19	-3.74	12.22 /19	9.37 /89	9.82 /57	3.10	1.29
RE	● Voya Real Estate B	CRBCX	C-	(800) 992-0180	C / 5.3	6.99	-4.16	11.33 /16	8.51 /83	8.97 /50	2.38	2.04
RE	Voya Real Estate C	CRCRX	C-	(800) 992-0180	C / 5.3	7.04	-4.09	11.40 /16	8.42 /82	8.91 /50	2.33	2.04
RE	Voya Real Estate I	CRARX	C	(800) 992-0180	C+ / 6.3	7.35	-3.55	12.66 /20	9.60 /91	10.09 /59	3.39	0.90
RE	Voya Real Estate O	IDROX	C	(800) 992-0180	C+ / 6.1	7.20	-3.74	12.18 /19	9.37 /89	9.82 /57	3.29	1.29
RE	Voya Real Estate R	CRWRX	C	(800) 992-0180	C+ / 5.9	7.16	-3.86	11.91 /18	9.13 /88	9.56 /55	3.09	1.54
RE	Voya Real Estate R6	VREQX	U	(800) 992-0180	U /	7.31	-3.58	12.65 /20	--	--	3.44	0.85
RE	Voya Real Estate W	IREWX	C	(800) 992-0180	C+ / 5.9	7.23	-3.67	12.48 /20	9.08 /87	9.76 /57	2.84	1.04
GI	Voya Retirement Conservative Adv	IRCAX	C	(800) 992-0180	D / 2.2	2.82	1.11	7.52 / 7	3.40 /36	4.12 /16	1.44	1.16
GI	Voya Retirement Conservative I	IRCPX	C	(800) 992-0180	D / 2.2	2.78	1.09	7.64 / 7	3.52 /37	4.25 /17	1.64	0.66
AA	Voya Retirement Growth Adv	IRGPX	B-	(800) 992-0180	C / 4.6	5.65	5.16	17.08 /39	4.46 /48	7.57 /39	2.07	1.14
AA	Voya Retirement Growth I	IIRGX	B-	(800) 992-0180	C / 4.9	5.77	5.37	17.54 /41	4.92 /53	8.02 /42	2.52	0.64
AA	Voya Retirement Moderate Adv	IRMPX	C	(800) 992-0180	C- / 3.0	4.00	2.72	11.57 /16	3.64 /39	5.40 /24	1.87	1.16
AA	Voya Retirement Moderate Gro Adv	IRMGX	C+	(800) 992-0180	C- / 4.0	5.05	4.19	14.97 /30	4.39 /47	6.94 /34	2.07	1.14
AA	Voya Retirement Moderate Gro I	IRGMX	C+	(800) 992-0180	C / 4.3	5.07	4.38	15.30 /31	4.78 /52	7.34 /37	2.51	0.64
AA	Voya Retirement Moderate I	IRMIX	C	(800) 992-0180	C- / 3.2	4.13	2.87	11.96 /18	4.00 /43	5.75 /27	2.22	0.66
GI	Voya Russell Large Cap Index Adv	IRLIX	A+	(800) 992-0180	A- / 9.1	8.36	10.14	24.03 /70	10.06 /94	13.15 /85	1.26	0.88
GI	Voya Russell Large Cap Index I	IIRLX	A+	(800) 992-0180	A / 9.4	8.45	10.39	24.62 /72	10.62 /96	13.70 /91	1.67	0.38
GI	Voya Russell Large Cap Index S	IRLCX	A+	(800) 992-0180	A / 9.3	8.39	10.28	24.34 /71	10.36 /95	13.44 /88	1.46	0.78
GI	Voya Russell Mid Cap Index Adv	IRMAX	B-	(800) 992-0180	B / 7.7	6.29	8.46	25.69 /75	7.47 /75	12.63 /80	0.79	0.93
GI	Voya Russell Mid Cap Index I	IIRMX	B	(800) 992-0180	B / 8.1	6.38	8.72	26.36 /77	8.01 /79	13.21 /86	1.20	0.43
GI	Voya Russell Mid Cap Index S	IRMCX	B-	(800) 992-0180	B / 7.9	6.39	8.60	26.10 /77	7.76 /77	12.93 /83	0.96	0.68
GI	Voya Russell Small Cap Index Adv	IRSIX	C+	(800) 992-0180	B+ / 8.4	5.04	12.21	34.99 /94	6.30 /67	12.21 /76	0.78	0.97
GI	Voya Russell Small Cap Index I	IIRSX	B-	(800) 992-0180	B+ / 8.8	5.10	12.46	35.68 /95	6.83 /71	12.77 /82	1.18	0.47
GI	Voya Russell Small Cap Index S	IRSSX	C+	(800) 992-0180	B+ / 8.6	5.08	12.34	35.28 /94	6.56 /69	12.48 /79	0.93	0.72
EM	Voya Russia A	LETRX	E	(800) 992-0180	D / 1.9	7.71	15.30	39.95 /97	-1.07 / 9	-4.13 / 2	1.54	2.14
EM	Voya Russia I	IIRFX	E+	(800) 992-0180	D+ / 2.9	7.75	15.44	40.23 /97	-0.87 /10	-4.00 / 2	1.90	1.82
EM	Voya Russia W	IWRFX	E+	(800) 992-0180	D+ / 2.9	7.79	15.43	40.27 /97	-0.86 /10	-3.94 / 2	1.86	1.89
RE	Voya Short Term Bond R6	IGZAX	C-	(800) 992-0180	D- / 1.0	0.53	0.29	1.88 / 2	1.21 /19	--	1.77	0.55
SC	Voya Small Cap Opps Port I	IVSOX	B-	(800) 992-0180	B+ / 8.8	6.67	10.13	34.25 /93	7.43 /75	12.73 /81	0.00	0.89
SC	Voya Small Cap Opps Port S	IVPOX	C+	(800) 992-0180	B+ / 8.7	6.61	10.00	33.85 /93	7.16 /73	12.44 /79	0.00	1.14

Risk Rating/Pts	3 Year Standard Deviation	Beta	NAV As of 2/28/17	Total $(Mil)	Cash %	Stocks %	Bonds %	Other %	Portfolio Turnover Ratio	Last Bull Market Return	Last Bear Market Return	Manager Quality Pct	Manager Tenure (Years)	Initial Purch. $	Additional Purch. $	Front End Load	Back End Load
D+ / 2.9	11.7	0.95	17.45	N/A	0	99	0	1	143	115.1	N/A	45	2	1,000	0	0.0	0.0
C- / 4.1	11.5	0.87	21.98	3	2	96	1	1	88	103.6	N/A	53	12	0	0	0.0	0.0
C+ / 6.7	11.5	0.85	51.18	58	1	98	0	1	64	67.2	-24.7	84	12	1,000	0	5.8	0.0
C+ / 6.7	11.5	0.85	54.51	N/A	1	98	0	1	64	61.4	-24.9	80	12	1,000	0	0.0	0.0
C+ / 6.7	11.5	0.85	47.56	14	1	98	0	1	64	61.4	-25.0	80	12	1,000	0	0.0	0.0
C+ / 6.7	11.5	0.85	51.02	76	1	98	0	1	64	71.4	-24.6	86	12	250,000	0	0.0	0.0
C+ / 6.7	11.4	0.85	50.55	3	1	98	0	1	64	68.1	-24.7	84	12	1,000	0	0.0	0.0
C+ / 6.7	11.5	0.85	61.41	53	1	98	0	1	64	70.4	-24.6	85	12	1,000	0	0.0	0.0
C / 4.5	10.6	0.84	9.43	278	1	95	2	2	84	51.4	-24.3	81	6	250,000	0	0.0	0.0
C / 4.5	10.7	0.85	9.43	55	1	95	2	2	84	N/A	N/A	81	6	1,000	0	0.0	0.0
C- / 4.0	16.9	1.02	10.22	24	1	97	0	2	47	N/A	N/A	37	6	1,000	0	5.8	0.0
C- / 4.1	16.8	1.02	10.26	N/A	1	97	0	2	47	N/A	N/A	28	6	1,000	0	0.0	0.0
C- / 4.1	16.8	1.02	10.21	4	1	97	0	2	47	N/A	N/A	28	6	1,000	0	0.0	0.0
C- / 4.0	16.8	1.02	10.24	171	1	97	0	2	47	N/A	N/A	42	6	250,000	0	0.0	0.0
C- / 4.1	16.9	1.02	10.26	N/A	1	97	0	2	47	N/A	N/A	34	6	0	0	0.0	0.0
C- / 4.0	16.8	1.02	10.22	58	1	97	0	2	47	N/A	N/A	40	6	1,000	0	0.0	0.0
C / 5.4	11.4	0.91	10.46	494	0	0	0	100	39	45.8	-22.9	62	6	250,000	0	0.0	0.0
C+ / 6.3	10.4	1.00	15.66	1	1	97	0	2	55	106.9	-20.4	55	4	0	0	0.0	0.0
C+ / 6.3	10.4	1.00	15.78	311	1	97	0	2	55	113.7	-20.2	64	4	0	0	0.0	0.0
C+ / 6.3	10.4	1.00	15.80	60	1	97	0	2	55	110.9	-20.3	61	4	0	0	0.0	0.0
D+ / 2.4	12.0	0.98	11.59	241	1	97	0	2	39	N/A	N/A	57	6	250,000	0	0.0	0.0
C / 4.7	15.6	1.13	18.52	165	0	99	0	1	37	93.9	-16.0	35	21	1,000	0	5.8	0.0
C / 4.7	15.5	1.13	18.67	N/A	0	99	0	1	37	86.1	-16.2	27	21	1,000	0	0.0	0.0
C / 4.8	15.1	1.10	19.54	26	0	99	0	1	37	85.5	-16.2	29	21	1,000	0	0.0	0.0
C / 4.8	14.8	1.08	20.12	830	0	99	0	1	37	96.5	-15.8	46	21	250,000	0	0.0	0.0
C / 4.7	15.5	1.13	18.49	36	0	99	0	1	37	94.0	-15.9	36	21	1,000	0	0.0	0.0
C / 4.7	15.6	1.13	18.44	5	0	99	0	1	37	91.4	N/A	33	21	0	0	0.0	0.0
U /	N/A	N/A	20.12	56	0	99	0	1	37	N/A	N/A	N/A	21	1,000,000	0	0.0	0.0
C / 5.1	13.8	1.01	23.00	54	0	99	0	1	37	93.6	-15.9	49	21	1,000	0	0.0	0.0
B / 8.5	3.9	0.30	9.10	501	0	29	70	1	21	31.5	-2.8	76	10	0	0	0.0	0.0
B / 8.5	3.9	0.31	9.24	N/A	0	29	70	1	21	32.6	-2.6	76	10	0	0	0.0	0.0
B / 8.0	8.0	1.25	13.65	3,318	0	73	25	2	16	66.2	-14.6	18	11	0	0	0.0	0.0
B / 8.0	8.0	1.24	13.74	49	0	73	25	2	16	70.1	-14.4	22	11	0	0	0.0	0.0
B- / 7.9	5.6	0.86	11.70	1,255	0	49	50	1	18	44.2	-8.2	39	11	0	0	0.0	0.0
B- / 7.8	7.0	1.09	12.69	2,296	0	63	36	1	16	58.8	-12.0	28	11	0	0	0.0	0.0
B- / 7.7	6.9	1.09	12.63	23	0	63	36	1	16	62.0	-11.9	32	11	0	0	0.0	0.0
B- / 7.9	5.6	0.86	11.84	18	0	49	50	1	18	47.0	-8.2	44	11	0	0	0.0	0.0
B- / 7.3	10.4	1.00	18.14	36	1	97	1	1	6	125.1	-15.8	68	5	0	0	0.0	0.0
B- / 7.3	10.4	1.00	18.48	237	1	97	1	1	6	131.3	-15.5	73	5	0	0	0.0	0.0
B- / 7.3	10.4	1.01	18.35	598	1	97	1	1	6	128.1	-15.6	71	5	0	0	0.0	0.0
C / 4.9	11.3	1.03	15.38	167	0	98	0	2	11	124.3	-21.3	32	5	0	0	0.0	0.0
C / 4.9	11.3	1.03	15.83	1,488	0	98	0	2	11	130.4	-21.1	39	5	0	0	0.0	0.0
C / 4.9	11.3	1.03	15.66	366	0	98	0	2	11	127.4	-21.1	36	5	0	0	0.0	0.0
C- / 3.9	15.7	1.20	14.80	101	0	98	0	2	13	124.5	-25.1	9	5	0	0	0.0	0.0
C- / 3.9	15.7	1.20	15.25	425	0	98	0	2	13	130.5	-25.0	12	5	0	0	0.0	0.0
C- / 3.9	15.7	1.20	15.11	281	0	98	0	2	13	127.5	-25.0	11	5	0	0	0.0	0.0
D+ / 2.4	24.4	0.81	26.73	83	0	98	0	2	34	3.5	-34.9	42	4	1,000	0	5.8	2.0
D+ / 2.4	24.4	0.81	26.85	4	0	98	0	2	34	4.5	-34.7	44	4	250,000	0	0.0	2.0
D+ / 2.4	24.4	0.81	26.69	N/A	0	98	0	2	34	4.7	N/A	44	4	1,000	0	0.0	2.0
B+ / 9.1	0.7	0.03	9.85	72	0	0	99	1	109	N/A	N/A	79	5	1,000,000	0	0.0	0.0
C- / 3.8	15.7	0.97	27.17	270	1	96	1	2	55	136.5	-22.2	79	7	0	0	0.0	0.0
C- / 3.8	15.7	0.97	25.64	68	1	96	1	2	55	133.3	-22.3	77	7	0	0	0.0	0.0

99 Pct = Best
0 Pct = Worst

Fund Type	Fund Name	Ticker Symbol	Overall Investment Rating	Phone	Performance Rating/Pts	3 Mo	6 Mo	1Yr / Pct	3Yr / Pct	5Yr / Pct	Dividend Yield	Expense Ratio
SC	Voya Small Company A	AESAX	B-	(800) 992-0180	A / 9.4	6.24	13.72	38.09 / 96	9.55 / 91	13.42 / 88	0.00	1.46
SC	● Voya Small Company B	ASMLX	C+	(800) 992-0180	A+ / 9.6	6.04	13.27	37.14 / 96	8.73 / 85	12.56 / 80	0.00	2.21
SC	Voya Small Company C	ASCCX	C+	(800) 992-0180	A+ / 9.6	5.97	13.31	37.09 / 96	8.75 / 85	12.57 / 80	0.00	2.21
SC	Voya Small Company I	AESGX	B	(800) 992-0180	A+ / 9.7	6.27	13.82	38.50 / 97	9.88 / 93	13.78 / 92	0.19	1.17
SC	Voya Small Company O	ISCOX	B-	(800) 992-0180	A+ / 9.7	6.18	13.67	38.06 / 96	9.54 / 91	13.40 / 88	0.00	1.46
SC	Voya Small Company Port I	IVCSX	B	(800) 992-0180	A+ / 9.8	6.37	13.99	39.19 / 97	10.44 / 96	14.29 / 95	0.38	0.90
SC	Voya Small Company Port S	IVPSX	B	(800) 992-0180	A+ / 9.8	6.32	13.89	38.89 / 97	10.17 / 94	14.01 / 93	0.16	1.15
SC	Voya Small Company R6	ISMZX	B	(800) 992-0180	A+ / 9.8	6.33	13.95	38.64 / 97	9.98 / 93	--	0.25	1.00
SC	Voya Small Company W	ISMWX	B	(800) 992-0180	A+ / 9.7	6.24	13.87	38.45 / 97	9.82 / 92	13.69 / 91	0.15	1.21
SC	Voya SmallCap Opportunities A	NSPAX	C	(800) 992-0180	B- / 7.2	6.50	9.70	33.18 / 92	6.65 / 69	11.89 / 73	0.00	1.42
SC	● Voya SmallCap Opportunities B	NSPBX	C	(800) 992-0180	B / 7.7	6.31	9.28	32.19 / 90	5.84 / 63	11.04 / 66	0.00	2.17
SC	Voya SmallCap Opportunities C	NSPCX	C	(800) 992-0180	B / 7.7	6.30	9.27	32.18 / 90	5.85 / 63	11.05 / 66	0.00	2.17
SC	Voya SmallCap Opportunities I	NSPIX	C+	(800) 992-0180	B+ / 8.5	6.60	9.86	33.58 / 92	6.97 / 72	12.25 / 77	0.00	1.14
SC	Voya SmallCap Opportunities R	ISORX	C+	(800) 992-0180	B / 8.1	6.46	9.56	32.85 / 91	6.39 / 67	11.62 / 71	0.00	1.67
SC	Voya SmallCap Opportunities R6	ISOZX	C+	(800) 992-0180	B+ / 8.6	6.62	9.93	33.77 / 93	7.10 / 73	--	0.00	0.99
SC	Voya SmallCap Opportunities W	ISOWX	C+	(800) 992-0180	B+ / 8.5	6.59	9.84	33.53 / 92	6.93 / 71	12.18 / 76	0.00	1.17
AA	Voya Solution 2025 Adv	ISZAX	C-	(800) 992-0180	C- / 4.0	5.22	4.63	14.72 / 29	4.29 / 46	6.85 / 34	1.72	1.40
AA	Voya Solution 2025 I	ISZIX	C-	(800) 992-0180	C / 4.4	5.27	4.88	15.24 / 31	4.81 / 52	7.38 / 37	2.24	0.90
AA	Voya Solution 2025 S	ISZSX	C-	(800) 992-0180	C- / 4.2	5.24	4.85	14.96 / 30	4.56 / 49	7.12 / 35	1.98	1.15
AA	Voya Solution 2025 T	ISZTX	C-	(800) 992-0180	C- / 3.8	5.10	4.53	14.45 / 28	4.09 / 44	6.63 / 32	1.51	1.60
AA	Voya Solution 2035 Adv	ISQAX	C-	(800) 992-0180	C / 5.1	6.25	6.15	18.18 / 44	4.71 / 51	7.77 / 40	1.73	1.44
AA	Voya Solution 2035 I	ISQIX	C-	(800) 992-0180	C / 5.5	6.47	6.47	18.72 / 46	5.25 / 57	8.30 / 45	2.24	0.94
AA	Voya Solution 2035 S	ISQSX	C-	(800) 992-0180	C / 5.3	6.35	6.35	18.47 / 45	4.98 / 54	8.04 / 43	1.99	1.19
AA	Voya Solution 2035 T	ISQTX	C-	(800) 992-0180	C / 4.9	6.19	6.09	17.84 / 42	4.51 / 49	7.55 / 39	1.23	1.64
AA	Voya Solution 2045 Adv	ISRAX	D+	(800) 992-0180	C / 5.5	6.69	6.79	19.59 / 50	4.90 / 53	8.40 / 45	1.27	1.45
AA	Voya Solution 2045 I	ISRIX	C-	(800) 992-0180	C+ / 6.0	6.88	7.18	20.29 / 54	5.43 / 59	8.94 / 50	1.78	0.95
AA	Voya Solution 2045 S	ISRSX	D+	(800) 992-0180	C+ / 5.7	6.79	6.99	20.01 / 52	5.16 / 56	8.66 / 48	1.53	1.20
AA	Voya Solution 2045 T	ISRTX	D+	(800) 992-0180	C / 5.4	6.77	6.77	19.49 / 49	4.71 / 51	8.18 / 44	1.12	1.65
AA	Voya Solution 2050 Adv	ISNPX	C+	(800) 992-0180	C+ / 5.9	6.76	6.91	19.78 / 51	5.48 / 59	8.68 / 48	0.28	3.95
AA	Voya Solution 2050 I	ISNQX	C+	(800) 992-0180	C+ / 6.4	6.88	7.17	20.33 / 54	6.08 / 65	9.28 / 53	0.36	3.45
AA	Voya Solution 2050 S	ISNRX	C+	(800) 992-0180	C+ / 6.2	6.93	7.15	20.12 / 53	5.75 / 62	8.94 / 50	0.35	3.70
AA	Voya Solution 2050 S2	ISNSX	C+	(800) 992-0180	C+ / 6.0	6.87	7.01	19.92 / 52	5.63 / 61	8.76 / 49	0.35	3.85
AA	Voya Solution 2050 T	ISNTX	C+	(800) 992-0180	C+ / 5.7	6.74	6.82	19.55 / 50	5.26 / 57	8.53 / 47	0.00	4.15
GL	Voya Solution 2055 Adv	IASPX	C	(800) 992-0180	C+ / 5.7	6.87	7.04	19.89 / 51	5.03 / 55	8.49 / 46	1.07	1.45
GL	Voya Solution 2055 I	IISPX	C	(800) 992-0180	C+ / 6.1	6.99	7.25	20.48 / 55	5.54 / 60	9.03 / 51	1.50	0.95
GL	Voya Solution 2055 S	ISSPX	C	(800) 992-0180	C+ / 5.9	6.89	7.15	20.22 / 53	5.29 / 58	8.76 / 49	1.29	1.20
GL	Voya Solution 2055 S2	ITSPX	C	(800) 992-0180	C+ / 5.8	6.93	7.11	20.08 / 52	5.13 / 56	8.60 / 47	1.18	1.35
GL	Voya Solution 2055 T	ISTPX	C	(800) 992-0180	C / 5.5	6.82	6.91	19.72 / 51	4.88 / 53	8.30 / 45	1.22	1.65
GL	Voya Solution Balanced Adv	ISGAX	C-	(800) 992-0180	C / 4.3	5.14	5.14	15.34 / 31	4.53 / 49	6.93 / 34	1.95	1.44
GL	Voya Solution Balanced I	ISGJX	C	(800) 992-0180	C / 4.8	5.28	5.39	15.90 / 34	5.09 / 55	7.46 / 38	2.52	0.94
GL	Voya Solution Balanced S	ISGKX	C-	(800) 992-0180	C / 4.5	5.18	5.18	15.59 / 32	4.79 / 52	7.20 / 36	2.31	1.34
AA	Voya Solution Income Adv	ISWAX	C	(800) 992-0180	D+ / 2.4	3.45	2.06	8.68 / 9	3.35 / 35	4.54 / 18	0.92	1.28
AA	Voya Solution Income I	ISWIX	C	(800) 992-0180	D+ / 2.7	3.54	2.27	9.20 / 10	3.88 / 41	5.08 / 22	1.21	0.78
AA	Voya Solution Income S	ISWSX	C	(800) 992-0180	D+ / 2.5	3.49	2.21	9.02 / 9	3.60 / 38	4.81 / 20	1.07	1.03
AA	Voya Solution Income T	ISWTX	C	(800) 992-0180	D+ / 2.3	3.35	1.95	8.58 / 9	3.17 / 33	4.35 / 17	0.00	1.48
BA	Voya Solution Moderately Consv Adv	ISPGX	C-	(800) 992-0180	C- / 3.0	3.83	3.15	11.42 / 16	3.70 / 39	5.35 / 24	1.97	1.37
BA	Voya Solution Moderately Consv Inl	ISPRX	C-	(800) 992-0180	C- / 3.3	3.98	3.33	11.91 / 18	4.20 / 45	5.85 / 27	2.65	0.87
BA	Voya Solution Moderately Consv S2	ISPTX	C-	(800) 992-0180	C- / 3.1	3.89	3.22	11.45 / 16	3.79 / 40	5.47 / 25	2.30	1.27
BA	Voya Solution Moderately Consv Svc	ISPSX	C-	(800) 992-0180	C- / 3.2	3.85	3.30	11.65 / 17	3.97 / 43	5.62 / 26	2.45	1.12
AA	Voya Strategic Alloc Consv I	ISAIX	C+	(800) 992-0180	C- / 3.3	4.03	3.36	11.54 / 16	4.29 / 46	6.60 / 32	2.87	0.76
AA	Voya Strategic Alloc Consv S	ISCVX	C+	(800) 992-0180	C- / 3.1	3.98	3.23	11.19 / 15	4.02 / 43	6.33 / 31	2.65	1.01
AA	Voya Strategic Alloc Gr Cl I	ISAGX	B-	(800) 992-0180	C / 5.4	6.31	6.39	18.92 / 47	5.08 / 55	8.73 / 48	2.46	0.84

● Denotes fund is closed to new investors
* Denotes fund is included in Section II

www.thestreetratings.com

Risk Rating/Pts	3 Year Standard Deviation	Beta	NAV As of 2/28/17	Total $(Mil)	Cash %	Stocks %	Bonds %	Other %	Portfolio Turnover Ratio	Last Bull Market Return	Last Bear Market Return	Manager Quality Pct	Manager Tenure (Years)	Initial Purch. $	Additional Purch. $	Front End Load	Back End Load
C- /3.2	14.2	0.89	15.19	65	0	96	2	2	58	141.6	-24.0	91	11	1,000	0	5.8	0.0
D+ /2.6	14.2	0.89	12.68	N/A	0	96	2	2	58	131.9	-24.2	88	11	1,000	0	0.0	0.0
D+ /2.5	14.2	0.89	12.47	12	0	96	2	2	58	131.9	-24.2	88	11	1,000	0	0.0	0.0
C- /3.5	14.2	0.89	17.75	508	0	96	2	2	58	145.8	-23.8	92	11	250,000	0	0.0	0.0
C- /3.2	14.2	0.89	15.16	2	0	96	2	2	58	141.4	-23.9	91	11	1,000	0	0.0	0.0
C- /3.7	14.2	0.89	22.89	560	2	96	1	1	45	151.8	-23.7	93	11	0	0	0.0	0.0
C- /3.6	14.2	0.89	22.38	137	2	96	1	1	45	148.6	-23.8	93	11	0	0	0.0	0.0
C- /3.5	14.2	0.89	17.77	79	0	96	2	2	58	N/A	N/A	92	11	1,000,000	0	0.0	0.0
C- /3.5	14.2	0.89	17.71	2	0	96	2	2	58	144.8	-23.9	92	11	1,000	0	0.0	0.0
C- /3.6	15.7	0.96	57.58	196	1	96	1	2	65	127.5	-22.5	74	9	1,000	0	5.8	0.0
C- /3.3	15.7	0.96	45.76	N/A	1	96	1	2	65	118.3	-22.7	65	9	1,000	0	0.0	0.0
C- /3.3	15.7	0.96	45.65	58	1	96	1	2	65	118.4	-22.7	65	9	1,000	0	0.0	0.0
C- /3.7	15.7	0.96	62.27	405	1	96	1	2	65	131.6	-22.4	76	9	250,000	0	0.0	0.0
C- /3.6	15.6	0.96	56.61	4	1	96	1	2	65	124.4	N/A	71	9	0	0	0.0	0.0
C- /3.7	15.7	0.96	62.56	184	1	96	1	2	65	N/A	N/A	77	9	1,000,000	0	0.0	0.0
C- /3.7	15.7	0.96	61.51	75	1	96	1	2	65	130.6	-22.4	76	9	1,000	0	0.0	0.0
C+ /5.7	7.0	1.10	11.08	304	0	62	37	1	642	62.4	-16.1	26	10	0	0	0.0	0.0
C+ /5.6	7.1	1.10	11.38	203	0	62	37	1	642	66.9	-15.9	31	10	0	0	0.0	0.0
C+ /5.7	7.1	1.10	11.25	377	0	62	37	1	642	64.7	-16.0	29	10	0	0	0.0	0.0
C+ /6.0	7.0	1.09	11.53	1	0	62	37	1	642	60.7	-16.1	25	10	0	0	0.0	0.0
C /4.4	8.8	1.37	11.22	265	0	81	17	2	46	74.2	-18.9	13	10	0	0	0.0	0.0
C /4.4	8.8	1.37	11.52	225	0	81	17	2	46	78.9	-18.8	17	10	0	0	0.0	0.0
C /4.4	8.9	1.38	11.39	360	0	81	17	2	46	76.5	-18.8	15	10	0	0	0.0	0.0
C /4.7	8.8	1.37	11.67	1	0	81	17	2	46	72.1	-18.9	12	10	0	0	0.0	0.0
C- /3.5	9.7	1.50	11.17	180	0	90	9	1	41	80.6	-19.8	9	10	0	0	0.0	0.0
C- /3.5	9.7	1.50	11.49	186	0	90	9	1	41	85.5	-19.6	12	10	0	0	0.0	0.0
C- /3.5	9.7	1.50	11.33	259	0	90	9	1	41	82.9	-19.7	10	10	0	0	0.0	0.0
C- /3.7	9.7	1.50	11.51	N/A	0	90	9	1	41	78.5	-19.8	8	10	0	0	0.0	0.0
C+ /6.1	9.7	1.50	15.32	4	1	89	8	2	67	N/A	N/A	12	6	0	0	0.0	0.0
C+ /6.2	9.7	1.50	15.70	2	1	89	8	2	67	N/A	N/A	16	6	0	0	0.0	0.0
C+ /6.2	9.7	1.50	15.59	2	1	89	8	2	67	N/A	N/A	14	6	0	0	0.0	0.0
C+ /6.2	9.6	1.49	15.41	N/A	1	89	8	2	67	N/A	N/A	13	6	0	0	0.0	0.0
C+ /6.2	9.7	1.50	15.36	N/A	1	89	8	2	67	N/A	N/A	11	6	0	0	0.0	0.0
C /5.0	9.9	0.72	12.92	44	2	91	6	1	41	81.3	-19.8	95	7	0	0	0.0	0.0
C /5.0	9.8	0.72	13.17	50	2	91	6	1	41	86.2	-19.6	96	7	0	0	0.0	0.0
C /5.0	9.8	0.72	13.03	51	2	91	6	1	41	83.7	-19.7	96	7	0	0	0.0	0.0
C /5.0	9.9	0.72	12.96	3	2	91	6	1	41	82.3	-19.7	96	7	0	0	0.0	0.0
C /5.3	9.8	0.72	13.15	N/A	2	91	6	1	41	79.6	-19.8	95	7	0	0	0.0	0.0
C+ /5.8	7.2	1.10	9.41	19	0	63	36	1	49	63.1	-15.2	67	10	0	0	0.0	0.0
C+ /5.8	7.2	1.10	9.77	2	0	63	36	1	49	67.5	-15.0	74	10	0	0	0.0	0.0
C+ /5.8	7.2	1.10	9.54	25	0	63	36	1	49	65.3	-15.2	71	10	0	0	0.0	0.0
B /8.4	4.2	0.64	11.40	200	3	30	66	1	31	37.3	-8.2	57	10	0	0	0.0	0.0
B /8.3	4.2	0.64	11.69	84	3	30	66	1	31	41.1	-8.1	64	10	0	0	0.0	0.0
B /8.3	4.2	0.64	11.58	183	3	30	66	1	31	39.1	-8.1	60	10	0	0	0.0	0.0
B /8.5	4.2	0.64	12.03	N/A	3	30	66	1	31	35.9	-8.3	54	10	0	0	0.0	0.0
C+ /6.8	5.2	0.80	9.50	12	0	42	57	1	58	46.6	-11.4	45	10	0	0	0.0	0.0
C+ /6.8	5.2	0.80	9.93	N/A	0	42	57	1	58	50.4	-11.2	53	10	0	0	0.0	0.0
C+ /6.7	5.2	0.80	9.61	1	0	42	57	1	58	47.5	-11.4	47	10	0	0	0.0	0.0
C+ /6.7	5.1	0.80	9.71	22	0	42	57	1	58	48.6	-11.3	50	10	0	0	0.0	0.0
B /8.6	5.1	0.80	12.91	72	0	41	58	1	29	52.4	-7.9	54	10	0	0	0.0	0.0
B /8.6	5.2	0.80	12.79	3	0	41	58	1	29	50.2	-8.0	50	10	0	0	0.0	0.0
B- /7.3	9.0	1.41	14.49	140	0	82	17	1	26	78.8	-16.7	14	10	0	0	0.0	0.0

I. Index of Stock Mutual Funds

99 Pct = Best
0 Pct = Worst

Fund Type	Fund Name	Ticker Symbol	Overall Investment Rating	Phone	Perfor- mance Rating/Pts	3 Mo	6 Mo	1Yr / Pct	3Yr / Pct	5Yr / Pct	Dividend Yield	Expense Ratio
AA	Voya Strategic Alloc Gr Cl S	ISGRX	C+	(800) 992-0180	C / 5.2	6.29	6.21	18.62 /46	4.82 /52	8.45 /46	2.24	1.09
AA	Voya Strategic Alloc Mod Cl I	IIMDX	B-	(800) 992-0180	C / 4.6	5.38	5.30	15.67 /33	4.94 /53	7.71 /40	2.50	0.80
AA	Voya Strategic Alloc Mod Cl S	ISMDX	C+	(800) 992-0180	C / 4.4	5.26	5.10	15.30 /31	4.67 /51	7.42 /38	2.27	1.05
AA	Voya Target In-Retirement I	ISOLX	C	(800) 992-0180	D+ / 2.7	3.60	2.35	9.27 /10	3.84 /41	--	1.57	49.85
GI	Voya Target Retirement 2020 I	IRSJX	C+	(800) 992-0180	C- / 3.6	4.66	3.99	12.55 /20	4.34 /47	--	1.32	12.60
GI	Voya Target Retirement 2025 I	IRSLX	C+	(800) 992-0180	C / 4.3	5.31	4.84	15.18 /31	4.58 /50	--	1.45	47.86
GI	Voya Target Retirement 2030 I	IRSMX	C+	(800) 992-0180	C / 5.1	5.94	5.66	17.17 /39	5.12 /55	--	1.48	47.05
GI	Voya Target Retirement 2035 I	IRSNX	C+	(800) 992-0180	C / 5.5	6.50	6.41	18.94 /47	5.10 /55	--	1.46	47.34
GI	Voya Target Retirement 2040 I	IRSOX	C+	(800) 992-0180	C+ / 5.9	6.71	6.90	19.98 /52	5.40 /59	--	1.64	46.55
GI	Voya Target Retirement 2045 I	IRSPX	C+	(800) 992-0180	C+ / 6.0	6.78	6.87	20.30 /54	5.47 /59	--	1.47	46.25
GI	Voya Target Retirement 2050 I	IRSQX	C+	(800) 992-0180	C+ / 6.0	6.81	6.91	20.23 /53	5.49 /59	--	1.55	46.23
GI	Voya Target Retirement 2055 I	IRSVX	C+	(800) 992-0180	C+ / 6.1	6.98	7.07	20.65 /56	5.58 /60	--	1.53	46.19
GI	Voya US Stock Index Inst	INGIX	A-	(800) 992-0180	A- / 9.2	7.96	9.88	24.66 /72	10.33 /95	13.72 /91	1.79	0.26
GI	Voya US Stock Index Svc 2	ISIPX	B+	(800) 992-0180	A- / 9.0	7.85	9.64	24.21 /71	9.89 /93	13.25 /86	1.45	0.66
GR	Voya VP Index Plus Large Cap I	IPLIX	A+	(800) 992-0180	A- / 9.2	8.15	10.47	24.71 /72	10.12 /94	13.41 /88	1.49	0.49
GR	Voya VP Index Plus Large Cap S	IPLSX	A+	(800) 992-0180	A- / 9.1	8.09	10.33	24.43 /71	9.85 /93	13.12 /85	1.26	0.74
MC	Voya VP Index Plus MidCap I	IPMIX	B+	(800) 992-0180	A- / 9.2	6.70	11.67	30.42 /87	8.99 /87	13.33 /87	0.89	0.54
MC	Voya VP Index Plus MidCap S	IPMSX	B+	(800) 992-0180	A- / 9.1	6.65	11.53	30.07 /87	8.72 /85	13.05 /84	0.66	0.79
SC	Voya VP Index Plus SmallCap I	IPSIX	A+	(800) 992-0180	A+ / 9.6	5.35	13.56	34.94 /94	9.62 /91	14.45 /95	0.72	0.55
SC	Voya VP Index Plus SmallCap S	IPSSX	A+	(800) 992-0180	A+ / 9.6	5.29	13.39	34.59 /94	9.35 /89	14.17 /94	0.50	0.80
GR	● Vulcan Value Partners	VVPLX	B	(877) 421-5078	B / 7.6	7.52	12.31	22.45 /64	7.73 /77	13.34 /87	1.22	1.08
GR	● Vulcan Value Partners Small Cap	VVPSX	C+	(877) 421-5078	B- / 7.1	3.99	10.29	26.41 /78	6.95 /72	13.20 /86	0.31	1.26
SC	VY American Century Sm-MC Val	IASAX	C+	(800) 992-0180	A+ / 9.8	5.96	12.98	34.09 /93	11.72 /98	14.71 /96	1.02	1.67
SC	VY American Century Sm-MC Val I	IACIX	B-	(800) 992-0180	A+ / 9.8	6.12	13.24	34.84 /94	12.29 /98	15.28 /97	1.38	1.17
SC	VY American Century Sm-MC Val S	IASSX	C+	(800) 992-0180	A+ / 9.8	6.04	13.14	34.52 /93	12.01 /98	14.99 /97	1.17	1.42
SC	VY Baron Growth Adv	IBSAX	D	(800) 992-0180	C / 4.3	7.70	3.81	20.54 /55	3.07 /32	11.42 /69	0.00	1.49
SC	VY Baron Growth I	IBGIX	D+	(800) 992-0180	C / 4.7	7.81	4.05	21.13 /58	3.59 /38	11.98 /74	0.00	0.99
SC	VY Baron Growth S	IBSSX	D+	(800) 992-0180	C / 4.5	7.72	3.91	20.82 /56	3.33 /35	11.70 /72	0.00	1.24
RE	VY Clarion Global Real Estate Adv	ICRNX	D	(800) 992-0180	D / 2.2	5.87	-5.02	8.53 / 8	3.63 /38	6.08 /29	0.78	1.57
RE	VY Clarion Global Real Estate Inst	IRGIX	D+	(800) 992-0180	D+ / 2.5	5.98	-4.74	9.10 /10	4.26 /46	6.72 /33	1.37	0.97
RE	VY Clarion Global Real Estate Svc	IRGTX	D+	(800) 992-0180	D+ / 2.3	5.83	-4.92	8.87 / 9	3.98 /43	6.44 /31	1.09	1.22
RE	VY Clarion Global Real Estate Svc 2	IRGSX	D+	(800) 992-0180	D+ / 2.3	5.88	-4.89	8.70 / 9	3.84 /41	6.29 /30	0.90	1.37
RE	VY Clarion Real Estate Adv	ICRPX	C	(800) 992-0180	C+ / 6.0	7.20	-3.71	12.31 /19	9.16 /88	9.67 /56	1.28	1.44
RE	VY Clarion Real Estate Inst	IVRIX	C+	(800) 992-0180	C+ / 6.5	7.35	-3.42	12.97 /22	9.82 /92	10.34 /61	1.78	0.84
RE	VY Clarion Real Estate Svc	IVRSX	C+	(800) 992-0180	C+ / 6.3	7.29	-3.56	12.69 /20	9.54 /91	10.06 /59	1.52	1.09
RE	VY Clarion Real Estate Svc 2	IVRTX	C	(800) 992-0180	C+ / 6.1	7.25	-3.63	12.53 /20	9.38 /89	9.89 /58	1.38	1.24
GI	VY Columbia Contrarian Core Adv	ISBAX	B-	(800) 992-0180	B+ / 8.4	7.26	7.68	21.49 /60	9.67 /91	12.88 /83	3.12	1.44
GI	VY Columbia Contrarian Core Init	ISFIX	B	(800) 992-0180	B+ / 8.8	7.41	7.97	22.10 /63	10.23 /95	13.46 /89	3.35	0.94
GI	VY Columbia Contrarian Core S	ISCSX	B	(800) 992-0180	B+ / 8.6	7.36	7.83	21.82 /61	9.95 /93	13.16 /86	3.16	1.19
SC	VY Columbia Small Cap Val II Adv	ICSAX	A	(800) 992-0180	A / 9.3	5.11	15.23	35.10 /94	7.85 /78	13.27 /87	0.05	1.39
SC	VY Columbia Small Cap Val II Init	ICISX	A	(800) 992-0180	A / 9.5	5.23	15.52	35.78 /95	8.39 /82	13.82 /92	0.47	0.89
SC	VY Columbia Small Cap Val II Svc	ICSSX	A	(800) 992-0180	A / 9.4	5.15	15.41	35.44 /94	8.11 /80	13.55 /89	0.23	1.14
MC	VY FMR Div Mid Cap Adv	IFDMX	C-	(800) 992-0180	B- / 7.3	6.57	10.23	26.54 /78	6.08 /65	10.91 /65	0.19	1.24
MC	VY FMR Div Mid Cap Inst	IFDIX	C	(800) 992-0180	B / 7.8	6.75	10.54	27.36 /80	6.74 /70	11.58 /71	0.70	0.64
MC	VY FMR Div Mid Cap Svc	IFDSX	C-	(800) 992-0180	B / 7.6	6.71	10.47	27.06 /79	6.47 /68	11.30 /68	0.48	0.89
MC	VY FMR Div Mid Cap Svc 2	IFDTX	C-	(800) 992-0180	B- / 7.4	6.63	10.36	26.77 /79	6.30 /67	11.13 /67	0.36	1.04
IN	VY Franklin Income Adv	IIFAX	C+	(800) 992-0180	C+ / 5.7	6.69	8.15	23.51 /68	4.18 /45	7.42 /38	6.07	1.37
IN	VY Franklin Income Inst	IIFIX	C+	(800) 992-0180	C+ / 6.3	7.00	8.51	24.33 /71	4.74 /51	8.02 /42	6.32	0.77
IN	VY Franklin Income Svc	IIFSX	C+	(800) 992-0180	C+ / 6.1	6.84	8.37	24.03 /70	4.55 /49	7.82 /41	6.20	1.02
IN	VY Franklin Income Svc 2	IIFTX	C+	(800) 992-0180	C+ / 6.0	6.86	8.29	23.88 /69	4.42 /48	7.65 /39	6.04	1.17
GI	VY Invesco ComStock Adv	IVKAX	A-	(800) 992-0180	B+ / 8.9	5.32	14.00	32.99 /92	7.38 /75	12.53 /79	2.08	1.25
GI	VY Invesco ComStock I	IVKIX	A	(800) 992-0180	A- / 9.2	5.46	14.25	33.61 /92	7.92 /78	13.09 /85	2.52	0.75

● Denotes fund is closed to new investors
* Denotes fund is included in Section II

RISK			NET ASSETS		ASSET				Portfolio Turnover Ratio	BULL / BEAR		FUND MANAGER		MINIMUMS		LOADS	
	3 Year		NAV							Last Bull	Last Bear	Manager	Manager	Initial	Additional	Front	Back
Risk Rating/Pts	Standard Deviation	Beta	As of 2/28/17	Total $(Mil)	Cash %	Stocks %	Bonds %	Other %		Market Return	Market Return	Quality Pct	Tenure (Years)	Purch. $	Purch. $	End Load	End Load
B- /7.3	9.0	1.40	14.36	3	0	82	17	1	26	76.4	-16.7	12	10	0	0	0.0	0.0
B /8.1	7.1	1.12	13.70	142	0	61	38	1	26	65.2	-12.4	31	10	0	0	0.0	0.0
B /8.1	7.1	1.11	13.60	2	0	61	38	1	26	62.9	-12.4	29	10	0	0	0.0	0.0
B /8.7	4.3	0.64	10.77	N/A	1	30	68	1	44	N/A	N/A	63	5	250,000	0	0.0	0.0
B- /7.8	5.9	0.54	11.32	1	0	0	0	100	86	N/A	N/A	59	5	250,000	0	0.0	0.0
B- /7.6	7.0	0.65	11.46	N/A	0	0	0	100	54	N/A	N/A	47	5	250,000	0	0.0	0.0
B- /7.0	7.9	0.74	11.56	N/A	0	0	0	100	55	N/A	N/A	41	5	250,000	0	0.0	0.0
C+ /6.4	8.8	0.82	11.61	N/A	0	0	0	100	43	N/A	N/A	30	5	250,000	0	0.0	0.0
C+ /6.0	9.3	0.88	11.73	N/A	0	0	0	100	46	N/A	N/A	28	5	250,000	0	0.0	0.0
C+ /5.9	9.6	0.90	11.83	N/A	0	0	0	100	35	N/A	N/A	25	5	250,000	0	0.0	0.0
C+ /6.0	9.5	0.90	11.83	N/A	0	0	0	100	34	N/A	N/A	26	5	250,000	0	0.0	0.0
C+ /5.9	9.8	0.92	11.88	N/A	0	0	0	100	37	N/A	N/A	24	5	250,000	0	0.0	0.0
C+ /5.6	10.3	1.00	14.60	4,418	1	97	0	2	12	131.4	-16.4	71	5	0	0	0.0	0.0
C /5.5	10.3	1.00	14.33	183	1	97	0	2	12	126.5	-16.5	66	5	0	0	0.0	0.0
B- /7.2	10.5	1.02	25.74	712	1	97	0	2	66	128.8	-17.6	67	11	0	0	0.0	0.0
B- /7.2	10.6	1.02	25.53	108	1	97	0	2	66	125.7	-17.7	63	11	0	0	0.0	0.0
C /4.7	11.8	0.97	22.78	587	2	97	0	1	90	137.1	-22.3	71	11	0	0	0.0	0.0
C /4.7	11.8	0.97	22.44	105	2	97	0	1	90	133.9	-22.4	68	11	0	0	0.0	0.0
C+ /6.1	13.9	0.87	27.39	251	0	98	0	2	46	148.1	-23.0	92	11	0	0	0.0	0.0
C+ /6.1	13.9	0.87	27.09	79	0	98	0	2	46	144.8	-23.0	91	11	0	0	0.0	0.0
C /5.5	12.1	1.05	19.15	1,301	3	96	0	1	85	135.7	-13.6	32	8	5,000	500	0.0	2.0
C /5.1	13.1	1.03	19.23	1,241	4	85	10	1	80	139.7	-21.3	27	8	5,000	500	0.0	2.0
D+ /2.5	11.4	0.69	12.45	107	1	98	0	1	71	141.7	-19.9	97	15	0	0	0.0	0.0
D+ /2.7	11.3	0.68	13.17	152	1	98	0	1	71	148.3	-19.7	98	15	0	0	0.0	0.0
D+ /2.7	11.4	0.69	13.00	102	1	98	0	1	71	144.9	-19.7	98	15	0	0	0.0	0.0
C- /3.9	11.8	0.66	26.72	81	2	97	0	1	5	108.0	-19.5	56	15	0	0	0.0	0.0
C- /4.0	11.9	0.66	29.00	155	2	97	0	1	5	113.6	-19.3	63	15	0	0	0.0	0.0
C- /3.9	11.9	0.67	27.92	499	2	97	0	1	5	110.8	-19.4	60	15	0	0	0.0	0.0
C+ /6.1	12.6	0.88	11.73	27	10	89	0	1	50	58.5	-18.5	10	11	0	0	0.0	0.0
C+ /6.1	12.6	0.88	12.05	184	10	89	0	1	50	63.7	-18.3	14	11	0	0	0.0	0.0
C+ /6.1	12.6	0.88	11.98	124	10	89	0	1	50	61.5	-18.4	13	11	0	0	0.0	0.0
C+ /6.1	12.6	0.88	12.06	1	10	89	0	1	50	60.2	-18.5	12	11	0	0	0.0	0.0
C /5.3	14.9	1.09	36.05	90	0	98	0	2	41	92.4	-16.2	39	15	0	0	0.0	0.0
C /5.3	14.9	1.09	37.82	105	0	98	0	2	41	98.8	-16.0	47	15	0	0	0.0	0.0
C /5.3	14.9	1.09	37.70	375	0	98	0	2	41	96.1	-16.1	44	15	0	0	0.0	0.0
C /5.3	14.9	1.09	37.45	23	0	98	0	2	41	94.5	-16.1	42	15	0	0	0.0	0.0
C /4.5	10.5	1.00	21.87	27	2	97	0	1	65	120.8	-20.1	64	4	0	0	0.0	0.0
C /4.6	10.5	1.00	22.90	11	2	97	0	1	65	127.1	-20.0	70	4	0	0	0.0	0.0
C /4.6	10.5	1.00	22.46	297	2	97	0	1	65	123.8	-20.0	67	4	0	0	0.0	0.0
C+ /5.8	14.5	0.90	18.92	40	1	97	0	2	53	139.0	-27.2	84	11	0	0	0.0	0.0
C+ /5.8	14.5	0.90	19.50	51	1	97	0	2	53	145.3	-27.0	86	11	0	0	0.0	0.0
C+ /5.8	14.5	0.90	19.40	141	1	97	0	2	53	142.2	-27.0	85	11	0	0	0.0	0.0
D+ /2.6	12.4	0.99	15.70	37	0	99	0	1	27	98.3	-21.6	32	13	0	0	0.0	0.0
D+ /2.7	12.4	0.99	16.41	99	0	99	0	1	27	104.9	-21.4	40	13	0	0	0.0	0.0
D+ /2.7	12.4	0.99	16.22	680	0	99	0	1	27	102.2	-21.5	37	13	0	0	0.0	0.0
D+ /2.6	12.4	0.99	16.04	62	0	99	0	1	27	100.5	-21.5	35	13	0	0	0.0	0.0
C+ /5.9	8.2	0.68	11.01	77	3	51	39	7	18	60.0	-11.2	37	11	0	0	0.0	0.0
C+ /5.9	8.1	0.68	11.47	10	3	51	39	7	18	65.0	-11.0	45	11	0	0	0.0	0.0
C+ /5.9	8.1	0.68	11.40	415	3	51	39	7	18	63.2	-11.1	42	11	0	0	0.0	0.0
C+ /5.9	8.2	0.68	11.37	8	3	51	39	7	18	61.9	-11.2	39	11	0	0	0.0	0.0
C+ /6.1	12.9	1.14	17.92	35	1	97	1	1	24	121.7	-20.4	20	15	0	0	0.0	0.0
C+ /6.1	12.9	1.14	18.08	196	1	97	1	1	24	127.6	-20.2	25	15	0	0	0.0	0.0

Fund Type	Fund Name	Ticker Symbol	Overall Investment Rating	Phone	Performance Rating/Pts	3 Mo	6 Mo	1Yr / Pct	3Yr / Pct	5Yr / Pct	Dividend Yield	Expense Ratio
GI	VY Invesco ComStock Svc	IVKSX	A	(800) 992-0180	A- / 9.0	5.39	14.13	33.24 /92	7.63 /76	12.81 /82	2.28	1.00
GI	VY Invesco Eq and Inc Adv	IUAAX	B+	(800) 992-0180	B- / 7.4	4.42	10.13	25.03 /73	7.14 /73	10.52 /62	1.44	1.17
GI	VY Invesco Eq and Inc I	IUAIX	B+	(800) 992-0180	B / 7.8	4.56	10.37	25.65 /75	7.68 /77	11.07 /66	1.85	0.67
GI	VY Invesco Eq and Inc Svc	IUASX	B+	(800) 992-0180	B / 7.6	4.50	10.25	25.33 /74	7.41 /75	10.79 /64	1.63	0.92
GI	VY Invesco Gr & Inc Adv	IVGAX	B	(800) 992-0180	A+ / 9.6	5.21	14.86	34.44 /93	9.07 /87	13.35 /87	1.71	1.24
GI	VY Invesco Gr & Inc Inst	IVGIX	B+	(800) 992-0180	A+ / 9.7	5.37	15.18	35.21 /94	9.72 /92	14.02 /93	2.25	0.64
GI	VY Invesco Gr & Inc Svc	IVGSX	B+	(800) 992-0180	A+ / 9.6	5.29	15.03	34.89 /94	9.45 /90	13.74 /91	1.99	0.89
GI	VY Invesco Gr & Inc Svc 2	IVITX	B+	(800) 992-0180	A+ / 9.6	5.26	14.93	34.66 /94	9.29 /89	13.57 /90	1.86	1.04
EM	VY JPMorgan Emer Mkt Eqty Adv	IJEAX	D	(800) 992-0180	C / 5.2	8.85	3.86	29.85 /86	2.20 /25	-0.28 / 4	0.78	1.24
EM	VY JPMorgan Emer Mkt Eqty Inst	IJEMX	D+	(800) 992-0180	C+ / 5.7	9.06	4.20	30.62 /87	2.82 /30	0.31 / 5	1.31	0.64
EM	VY JPMorgan Emer Mkt Eqty Svc	IJPIX	D+	(800) 992-0180	C / 5.4	8.90	4.03	30.19 /87	2.54 /28	0.07 / 4	1.06	0.89
EM	VY JPMorgan Emer Mkt Eqty Svc 2	IJPTX	D+	(800) 992-0180	C / 5.3	8.86	3.94	30.05 /86	2.40 /27	-0.09 / 4	0.88	1.04
MC	VY JPMorgan Mid Cap Val Adv	IJMAX	B-	(800) 992-0180	B+ / 8.3	5.17	8.95	24.98 /73	9.04 /87	14.13 /94	0.38	1.36
MC	VY JPMorgan Mid Cap Val I	IJMIX	B	(800) 992-0180	B+ / 8.7	5.26	9.23	25.57 /75	9.59 /91	14.70 /96	0.78	0.86
MC	VY JPMorgan Mid Cap Val Svc	IJMSX	B	(800) 992-0180	B+ / 8.5	5.21	9.05	25.26 /74	9.31 /89	14.41 /95	0.57	1.11
SC	VY JPMorgan Sm Cap Eqty Adv	IJSAX	B	(800) 992-0180	A- / 9.2	5.72	12.26	34.32 /93	8.23 /81	13.87 /92	0.19	1.46
SC	VY JPMorgan Sm Cap Eqty Inst	IJSIX	B	(800) 992-0180	A / 9.5	5.83	12.51	35.13 /94	8.88 /86	14.54 /96	0.67	0.86
SC	VY JPMorgan Sm Cap Eqty Svc	IJSSX	B	(800) 992-0180	A / 9.4	5.80	12.44	34.78 /94	8.62 /84	14.26 /95	0.43	1.11
SC	VY JPMorgan Sm Cap Eqty Svc 2	IJSTX	B	(800) 992-0180	A / 9.3	5.75	12.33	34.55 /94	8.44 /82	14.09 /94	0.27	1.26
GL	VY Morgan Stanley Glbl Franch Adv	IGFAX	C+	(800) 992-0180	C+ / 6.8	10.50	5.45	15.66 /33	7.53 /76	9.44 /54	0.97	1.56
GL	VY Morgan Stanley Glbl Franch Svc	IVGTX	C+	(800) 992-0180	B- / 7.1	10.58	5.63	16.08 /35	7.91 /78	9.81 /57	1.16	1.21
GL	VY Morgan Stanley Glbl Franch Svc 2	IGFSX	C+	(800) 992-0180	B- / 7.0	10.59	5.54	15.94 /34	7.75 /77	9.65 /56	1.01	1.36
GL	VY Oppenheimer Global Adv	IGMAX	C-	(800) 992-0180	C+ / 5.6	8.41	8.89	22.17 /63	3.71 /39	9.46 /54	0.65	1.25
GL	VY Oppenheimer Global I	IGMIX	C	(800) 992-0180	C+ / 6.0	8.57	9.16	22.77 /66	4.23 /46	10.00 /58	1.12	0.75
GL	VY Oppenheimer Global S	IGMSX	C-	(800) 992-0180	C+ / 5.8	8.50	9.04	22.50 /65	3.98 /43	9.74 /57	0.87	1.00
AA	VY T Rowe Price Cap App Adv	ITRAX	C+	(800) 992-0180	C+ / 6.8	5.36	4.72	15.49 /32	8.78 /85	11.27 /68	0.98	1.24
AA	VY T Rowe Price Cap App Inst	ITRIX	B	(800) 992-0180	B- / 7.2	5.51	5.06	16.17 /35	9.43 /90	11.95 /74	1.40	0.64
AA	VY T Rowe Price Cap App Svc	ITCSX	B	(800) 992-0180	B- / 7.0	5.46	4.92	15.89 /34	9.16 /88	11.66 /71	1.18	0.89
AA	VY T Rowe Price Cap App Svc 2	ITCTX	C+	(800) 992-0180	C+ / 6.9	5.37	4.79	15.69 /33	8.98 /87	11.50 /70	1.05	1.04
GR	VY T Rowe Price Dvs Mid Cap G Adv	IAXAX	C	(800) 992-0180	B- / 7.3	6.64	7.34	23.59 /68	7.28 /74	12.13 /75	0.03	1.27
GR	VY T Rowe Price Dvs Mid Cap G I	IAXIX	C	(800) 992-0180	B / 7.7	6.78	7.53	24.19 /71	7.80 /78	12.70 /81	0.28	0.77
GR	VY T Rowe Price Dvs Mid Cap G S	IAXSX	C	(800) 992-0180	B- / 7.5	6.69	7.47	23.86 /69	7.53 /76	12.41 /78	0.08	1.02
IN	VY T Rowe Price Eqty Income Adv	ITEAX	C+	(800) 992-0180	B / 7.9	5.21	11.26	28.27 /82	6.94 /72	11.14 /67	1.65	1.24
IN	VY T Rowe Price Eqty Income Inst	ITEIX	B-	(800) 992-0180	B+ / 8.3	5.26	11.52	28.95 /84	7.58 /76	11.81 /73	2.13	0.64
IN	VY T Rowe Price Eqty Income Svc	IRPSX	C+	(800) 992-0180	B / 8.1	5.23	11.40	28.71 /83	7.32 /74	11.53 /70	1.91	0.89
IN	VY T Rowe Price Eqty Income Svc 2	ITETX	C+	(800) 992-0180	B / 8.0	5.23	11.32	28.44 /83	7.14 /73	11.37 /69	1.81	1.04
GR	VY T Rowe Price Growth Eq Adv	IGEAX	C+	(800) 992-0180	B+ / 8.3	9.31	10.76	22.85 /66	8.25 /81	13.63 /90	0.00	1.24
GR	VY T Rowe Price Growth Eq I	ITGIX	C+	(800) 992-0180	B+ / 8.7	9.45	11.04	23.47 /68	8.79 /85	14.20 /94	0.00	0.74
GR	VY T Rowe Price Growth Eq S	ITGSX	C+	(800) 992-0180	B+ / 8.5	9.37	10.91	23.16 /67	8.52 /83	13.91 /93	0.00	0.99
FO	VY T Rowe Price Intl Stk Adv	IMIOX	D+	(800) 992-0180	D+ / 2.8	7.53	2.57	16.49 /36	1.55 /21	4.33 /17	1.06	1.35
FO	VY T Rowe Price Intl Stk Inst	IMASX	D+	(800) 992-0180	C- / 3.3	7.76	2.87	17.20 /39	2.17 /25	4.97 /21	1.61	0.75
FO	VY T Rowe Price Intl Stk Svc	IMISX	D+	(800) 992-0180	C- / 3.1	7.71	2.73	16.86 /38	1.91 /23	4.71 /19	1.34	1.00
FO	VY Templeton Foreign Equity Adv	IFTAX	E+	(800) 992-0180	E+ / 0.9	6.18	5.00	17.63 /41	-2.37 / 6	3.88 /15	2.77	1.45
FO	VY Templeton Foreign Equity I	IFTIX	E+	(800) 992-0180	D- / 1.1	6.40	5.33	18.25 /44	-1.86 / 7	4.41 /18	3.31	0.95
FO	VY Templeton Foreign Equity S	IFTSX	E+	(800) 992-0180	D- / 1.0	6.35	5.17	17.89 /42	-2.11 / 6	4.15 /16	3.03	1.20
GL	VY Templeton Glb Growth Adv	IGGAX	E+	(800) 992-0180	C / 4.3	7.59	11.21	27.24 /80	0.28 /15	7.90 /41	3.29	1.57
GL	VY Templeton Glb Growth Inst	IIGGX	D-	(800) 992-0180	C / 4.8	7.66	11.52	28.03 /82	0.86 /17	8.55 /47	3.79	0.97
GL	VY Templeton Glb Growth Svc	ISGGX	E+	(800) 992-0180	C / 4.6	7.49	11.31	27.60 /81	0.59 /16	8.27 /44	3.48	1.22
GL	VY Templeton Glb Growth Svc 2	ICGGX	E+	(800) 992-0180	C / 4.5	7.57	11.32	27.42 /80	0.44 /15	8.12 /43	3.31	1.37
GR	Waddell & Reed Adv Accumulative A	UNACX	C-	(888) 923-3355	C+ / 5.9	7.60	7.15	18.24 /44	7.57 /76	11.62 /71	0.50	1.12
GR	Waddell & Reed Adv Accumulative B	WAABX	C-	(888) 923-3355	C+ / 6.0	7.12	6.47	16.77 /37	6.26 /66	10.24 /60	0.00	2.31
GR	Waddell & Reed Adv Accumulative C	WAACX	C-	(888) 923-3355	C+ / 6.2	7.32	6.68	17.06 /39	6.53 /69	10.52 /62	0.00	2.07

99 Pct = Best
0 Pct = Worst

PERFORMANCE — Total Return % through 2/28/17 — Annualized — Incl. in Returns

● Denotes fund is closed to new investors
* Denotes fund is included in Section II

www.thestreetratings.com

I. Index of Stock Mutual Funds

RISK	3 Year		NET ASSETS		ASSET				Portfolio	BULL / BEAR		FUND MANAGER		MINIMUMS		LOADS	
Risk Rating/Pts	Standard Deviation	Beta	NAV As of 2/28/17	Total $(Mil)	Cash %	Stocks %	Bonds %	Other %	Turnover Ratio	Last Bull Market Return	Last Bear Market Return	Manager Quality Pct	Manager Tenure (Years)	Initial Purch. $	Additional Purch. $	Front End Load	Back End Load
C+ / 6.1	12.9	1.14	18.06	305	1	97	1	1	24	124.7	-20.3	22	15	0	0	0.0	0.0
C+ / 6.4	8.4	0.76	45.36	52	2	64	25	9	140	89.1	-15.4	65	16	0	0	0.0	0.0
C+ / 6.4	8.4	0.76	46.22	607	2	64	25	9	140	94.3	-15.2	71	16	0	0	0.0	0.0
C+ / 6.4	8.4	0.76	45.81	680	2	64	25	9	140	91.7	-15.3	68	16	0	0	0.0	0.0
C- / 4.1	12.0	1.05	27.44	20	1	97	0	2	19	124.6	-20.2	49	18	0	0	0.0	0.0
C- / 4.0	12.0	1.05	27.69	29	1	97	0	2	19	132.0	-20.0	58	18	0	0	0.0	0.0
C- / 4.1	12.0	1.05	27.86	521	1	97	0	2	19	128.8	-20.1	55	18	0	0	0.0	0.0
C- / 4.1	12.0	1.05	27.63	39	1	97	0	2	19	126.9	-20.1	53	18	0	0	0.0	0.0
C- / 3.1	15.7	0.90	15.62	39	0	99	0	1	15	21.5	-25.6	79	12	0	0	0.0	0.0
C- / 3.1	15.7	0.90	16.37	68	0	99	0	1	15	25.5	-25.5	82	12	0	0	0.0	0.0
C- / 3.2	15.7	0.90	16.27	387	0	99	0	1	15	23.8	-25.5	81	12	0	0	0.0	0.0
C- / 3.2	15.7	0.90	16.09	15	0	99	0	1	15	22.7	-25.6	80	12	0	0	0.0	0.0
C / 4.5	10.7	0.86	20.20	101	1	97	1	1	14	136.8	-17.9	79	13	0	0	0.0	0.0
C / 4.5	10.7	0.86	20.68	223	1	97	1	1	14	143.2	-17.7	83	13	0	0	0.0	0.0
C / 4.5	10.6	0.86	20.49	289	1	97	1	1	14	140.0	-17.8	81	13	0	0	0.0	0.0
C- / 4.0	14.4	0.91	19.05	122	1	96	1	2	38	145.6	-24.1	85	13	0	0	0.0	0.0
C- / 4.1	14.4	0.91	20.14	184	1	96	1	2	38	153.8	-24.0	88	13	0	0	0.0	0.0
C- / 4.1	14.4	0.91	19.89	439	1	96	1	2	38	150.4	-24.1	87	13	0	0	0.0	0.0
C- / 4.1	14.4	0.91	19.68	40	1	96	1	2	38	148.3	-24.1	86	13	0	0	0.0	0.0
C / 5.2	11.3	0.72	15.68	73	1	97	0	2	27	78.0	-6.9	98	8	0	0	0.0	0.0
C / 5.4	11.3	0.72	16.52	310	1	97	0	2	27	81.4	-6.8	98	8	0	0	0.0	0.0
C / 5.4	11.3	0.72	16.39	47	1	97	0	2	27	80.0	-6.8	98	8	0	0	0.0	0.0
C / 4.6	13.0	0.97	17.15	95	1	98	0	1	12	84.8	-23.0	93	13	0	0	0.0	0.0
C / 4.6	13.0	0.97	17.87	1,164	1	98	0	1	12	89.9	-22.9	94	13	0	0	0.0	0.0
C / 4.6	13.0	0.97	17.24	183	1	98	0	1	12	87.3	-23.0	94	13	0	0	0.0	0.0
C+ / 6.1	6.8	1.06	25.64	828	13	62	24	1	67	100.9	-12.9	79	11	0	0	0.0	0.0
C+ / 6.2	6.8	1.06	26.66	1,065	13	62	24	1	67	107.5	-12.7	83	11	0	0	0.0	0.0
C+ / 6.2	6.8	1.06	26.66	4,192	13	62	24	1	67	104.7	-12.8	81	11	0	0	0.0	0.0
C+ / 6.2	6.8	1.06	26.47	84	13	62	24	1	67	103.0	-12.9	80	11	0	0	0.0	0.0
C- / 3.3	12.5	1.10	9.80	52	0	99	0	1	26	122.4	-22.9	23	15	0	0	0.0	0.0
C- / 3.5	12.5	1.10	10.71	794	0	99	0	1	26	128.3	-22.7	28	15	0	0	0.0	0.0
C- / 3.4	12.5	1.10	10.36	51	0	99	0	1	26	125.3	-22.8	25	15	0	0	0.0	0.0
C- / 4.2	11.2	1.02	14.11	52	2	97	0	1	27	105.8	-18.4	27	2	0	0	0.0	0.0
C- / 4.2	11.2	1.02	14.34	140	2	97	0	1	27	112.6	-18.2	35	2	0	0	0.0	0.0
C- / 4.2	11.2	1.02	14.36	786	2	97	0	1	27	109.6	-18.3	31	2	0	0	0.0	0.0
C- / 4.2	11.1	1.02	14.18	114	2	97	0	1	27	107.9	-18.3	30	2	0	0	0.0	0.0
C- / 3.4	12.9	1.06	79.04	205	0	99	0	1	42	136.3	-16.7	37	3	0	0	0.0	0.0
C- / 3.6	12.9	1.06	84.46	1,061	0	99	0	1	42	142.8	-16.5	44	3	0	0	0.0	0.0
C- / 3.5	12.9	1.06	81.72	337	0	99	0	1	42	139.5	-16.6	41	3	0	0	0.0	0.0
C+ / 6.0	11.8	0.92	13.56	16	3	96	0	1	43	50.5	-24.1	85	2	0	0	0.0	0.0
C+ / 6.0	11.8	0.92	13.61	40	3	96	0	1	43	55.4	-23.8	88	2	0	0	0.0	0.0
C+ / 6.0	11.8	0.92	13.55	161	3	96	0	1	43	53.3	-23.9	86	2	0	0	0.0	0.0
C / 5.0	12.2	0.96	11.34	33	0	97	2	1	10	41.3	-25.1	45	11	0	0	0.0	0.0
C / 5.0	12.2	0.96	11.47	173	0	97	2	1	10	45.1	-24.9	53	11	0	0	0.0	0.0
C / 5.0	12.2	0.96	11.39	433	0	97	2	1	10	43.2	-25.0	49	11	0	0	0.0	0.0
D- / 1.4	12.8	0.98	9.92	N/A	0	95	4	1	21	75.9	-22.6	77	10	0	0	0.0	0.0
D- / 1.4	12.8	0.99	10.26	2	0	95	4	1	21	81.9	-22.3	81	10	0	0	0.0	0.0
D- / 1.5	12.8	0.99	10.33	191	0	95	4	1	21	79.3	-22.4	79	10	0	0	0.0	0.0
D- / 1.5	12.8	0.98	10.23	3	0	95	4	1	21	77.9	-22.5	78	10	0	0	0.0	0.0
C- / 3.8	11.4	1.05	9.81	1,117	2	96	0	2	102	112.4	-17.6	31	13	750	0	5.8	0.0
C- / 3.5	11.4	1.05	8.28	3	2	96	0	2	102	98.5	-18.1	18	13	750	0	0.0	0.0
C- / 3.5	11.4	1.06	8.48	6	2	96	0	2	102	101.2	-18.1	20	13	750	0	0.0	0.0

	99 Pct = Best 0 Pct = Worst		Overall		PERFORMANCE						Incl. in Returns	
					Perfor-	Total Return % through 2/28/17			Annualized			
Fund Type	Fund Name	Ticker Symbol	Investment Rating	Phone	mance Rating/Pts	3 Mo	6 Mo	1Yr / Pct	3Yr / Pct	5Yr / Pct	Dividend Yield	Expense Ratio
GR	Waddell & Reed Adv Accumulative Y	WAAYX	C	(888) 923-3355	B- / 7.1	7.67	7.33	18.65 /46	7.81 /78	11.89 /73	0.73	0.86
GL	Waddell & Reed Adv Asset Strat A	UNASX	E	(888) 923-3355	E- / 0.2	5.22	2.22	6.85 / 6	-4.68 / 3	2.91 /10	0.00	1.16
GL	Waddell & Reed Adv Asset Strat B	WBASX	E-	(888) 923-3355	E- / 0.2	4.85	1.70	5.70 / 4	-5.69 / 2	1.86 / 8	0.00	2.25
GL	Waddell & Reed Adv Asset Strat C	WCASX	E-	(888) 923-3355	E- / 0.2	4.93	1.81	5.92 / 5	-5.48 / 2	2.06 / 8	0.00	2.01
GL	Waddell & Reed Adv Asset Strat Y	WYASX	E	(888) 923-3355	E / 0.3	5.28	2.45	7.31 / 6	-4.38 / 3	3.23 /12	0.00	0.83
BA	Waddell & Reed Adv Continentl Inc A	UNCIX	D+	(888) 923-3355	D+ / 2.5	4.63	3.61	12.55 /20	4.13 /44	7.96 /42	0.95	1.16
BA	Waddell & Reed Adv Continentl Inc B	WACBX	D+	(888) 923-3355	D+ / 2.7	4.29	3.07	11.36 /16	2.98 /32	6.77 /33	0.26	2.27
BA	Waddell & Reed Adv Continentl Inc C	WACCX	D+	(888) 923-3355	D+ / 2.8	4.38	3.17	11.64 /17	3.22 /34	7.03 /35	0.37	2.01
BA	Waddell & Reed Adv Continentl Inc Y	WACYX	C-	(888) 923-3355	C- / 3.7	4.79	3.84	12.95 /21	4.44 /48	8.27 /44	1.26	0.85
GR	Waddell & Reed Adv Core Invest A	UNCMX	D	(888) 923-3355	C- / 3.8	5.22	5.72	17.69 /41	4.95 /54	11.18 /67	0.36	1.05
GR	Waddell & Reed Adv Core Invest B	UNIBX	D-	(888) 923-3355	C- / 3.9	4.94	5.14	16.27 /35	3.73 /40	9.86 /57	0.00	2.22
GR	Waddell & Reed Adv Core Invest C	WCCIX	D	(888) 923-3355	C- / 4.1	5.01	5.21	16.53 /36	3.90 /42	10.10 /59	0.00	2.01
GR	Waddell & Reed Adv Core Invest Y	UNIYX	D+	(888) 923-3355	C / 5.1	5.27	5.77	17.87 /42	5.17 /56	11.44 /69	0.61	0.79
GI	Waddell & Reed Adv Dividend Oppty	WDVAX	D	(888) 923-3355	C / 4.7	6.86	6.94	19.23 /48	5.65 /61	9.90 /58	1.15	1.25
GI	Waddell & Reed Adv Dividend Oppty	WDVBX	D	(888) 923-3355	C / 4.9	6.58	6.36	17.84 /42	4.46 /48	8.64 /48	0.04	2.41
GI	Waddell & Reed Adv Dividend Oppty	WDVCX	D+	(888) 923-3355	C / 5.2	6.68	6.58	18.26 /44	4.78 /52	8.98 /51	0.42	2.07
GI	Waddell & Reed Adv Dividend Oppty	WDVYX	C-	(888) 923-3355	C+ / 6.3	7.01	7.17	19.60 /50	6.00 /64	10.27 /60	1.53	0.82
EN	Waddell & Reed Adv Energy Fund A	WEGAX	E-	(888) 923-3355	E+ / 0.6	-6.33	7.92	43.30 /98	-4.82 / 3	0.65 / 6	0.00	1.64
EN	Waddell & Reed Adv Energy Fund B	WEGBX	E-	(888) 923-3355	E+ / 0.6	-6.73	7.12	41.09 /98	-6.14 / 2	-0.69 / 4	0.00	3.14
EN	Waddell & Reed Adv Energy Fund C	WEGCX	E-	(888) 923-3355	E+ / 0.7	-6.53	7.43	42.08 /98	-5.62 / 2	-0.20 / 4	0.00	2.58
EN	Waddell & Reed Adv Energy Fund Y	WEGYX	E-	(888) 923-3355	D- / 1.1	-6.28	8.13	44.00 /98	-4.37 / 3	1.15 / 6	0.00	1.10
FO	Waddell & Reed Adv Glbl Growth A	UNCGX	D-	(888) 923-3355	D / 2.0	7.91	5.23	13.59 /24	1.60 /22	6.38 /31	0.00	1.42
FO	Waddell & Reed Adv Glbl Growth B	WAIBX	D-	(888) 923-3355	D / 2.0	7.56	4.43	11.97 /18	0.16 /14	4.86 /20	0.00	2.88
FO	Waddell & Reed Adv Glbl Growth C	WAICX	D-	(888) 923-3355	D / 2.1	7.59	4.60	12.23 /19	0.48 /16	5.22 /23	0.00	2.52
FO	Waddell & Reed Adv Glbl Growth Y	WAIYX	D+	(888) 923-3355	C- / 3.1	8.03	5.37	14.00 /25	1.97 /24	6.77 /33	0.00	1.06
MC	Waddell & Reed Adv New Concepts	UNECX	D-	(888) 923-3355	C- / 3.5	5.57	4.39	22.25 /63	3.64 /39	8.57 /47	0.00	1.38
MC	Waddell & Reed Adv New Concepts	UNEBX	E+	(888) 923-3355	C- / 3.6	5.22	3.68	20.82 /57	2.45 /27	7.32 /37	0.00	2.54
MC	Waddell & Reed Adv New Concepts	WNCCX	E+	(888) 923-3355	C- / 3.8	5.28	3.80	21.08 /58	2.67 /29	7.53 /39	0.00	2.33
MC	Waddell & Reed Adv New Concepts	UNEYX	D	(888) 923-3355	C / 4.9	5.71	4.47	22.67 /65	3.97 /43	8.95 /50	0.00	1.03
TC	Waddell & Reed Adv Science & Tech	UNSCX	D-	(888) 923-3355	C- / 3.4	8.15	10.20	25.88 /76	1.02 /18	13.06 /84	0.00	1.28
TC	Waddell & Reed Adv Science & Tech	USTBX	E	(888) 923-3355	D / 2.2	7.91	9.66	24.54 /72	-0.06 /13	11.83 /73	0.00	2.38
TC	Waddell & Reed Adv Science & Tech	WCSTX	E+	(888) 923-3355	C- / 3.7	7.97	9.69	24.70 /72	0.05 /14	11.96 /74	0.00	2.29
TC	Waddell & Reed Adv Science & Tech	USTFX	D	(888) 923-3355	C / 4.8	8.22	10.33	26.25 /77	1.29 /20	13.37 /88	0.00	1.00
SC	Waddell & Reed Adv Small Cap A	UNSAX	C-	(888) 923-3355	C+ / 6.8	6.24	10.79	32.27 /90	5.80 /63	12.64 /80	0.00	1.45
SC	Waddell & Reed Adv Small Cap B	WRSBX	D+	(888) 923-3355	B- / 7.0	5.97	10.19	30.81 /88	4.62 /50	11.38 /69	0.00	2.58
SC	Waddell & Reed Adv Small Cap C	WSCCX	C-	(888) 923-3355	B- / 7.2	6.02	10.30	31.15 /88	4.93 /53	11.72 /72	0.00	2.28
SC	Waddell & Reed Adv Small Cap Y	WRSYX	C	(888) 923-3355	B / 8.1	6.33	10.96	32.69 /91	6.19 /66	13.10 /85	0.00	1.05
GR	Waddell & Reed Adv Tax Managed	WTEAX	C	(888) 923-3355	C+ / 6.4	9.80	7.08	18.71 /46	7.87 /78	12.73 /81	0.00	1.08
GR	Waddell & Reed Adv Tax Managed	WBTMX	C	(888) 923-3355	C+ / 6.6	9.53	6.49	17.48 /41	6.78 /70	11.58 /71	0.00	2.11
GR	Waddell & Reed Adv Tax Managed	WCTMX	C+	(888) 923-3355	C+ / 6.8	9.59	6.62	17.70 /41	6.94 /72	11.74 /72	0.00	1.94
GR	Waddell & Reed Adv Tax Managed	WATMX	U	(888) 923-3355	U /	9.79	7.13	--	--	--	0.00	0.74
GR	Waddell & Reed Adv Value A	WVAAX	C	(888) 923-3355	C+ / 6.9	6.61	12.19	26.01 /76	6.95 /72	12.05 /75	2.32	1.25
GR	Waddell & Reed Adv Value B	WVABX	C	(888) 923-3355	B- / 7.0	6.27	11.53	24.42 /71	5.68 /61	10.71 /64	1.56	2.47
GR	Waddell & Reed Adv Value C	WVACX	C	(888) 923-3355	B- / 7.2	6.44	11.76	24.91 /73	6.04 /65	11.07 /66	1.81	2.12
GR	Waddell & Reed Adv Value Y	WVAYX	C+	(888) 923-3355	B / 8.1	6.69	12.39	26.35 /77	7.30 /74	12.44 /79	2.75	0.89
GR	Waddell & Reed Adv Vanguard A	UNVGX	C	(888) 923-3355	C+ / 6.2	7.80	7.47	19.60 /50	7.69 /77	12.07 /75	0.00	1.15
GR	Waddell & Reed Adv Vanguard B	WRVBX	C-	(888) 923-3355	C+ / 6.4	7.55	6.94	18.17 /44	6.46 /68	10.75 /64	0.00	2.34
GR	Waddell & Reed Adv Vanguard C	WAVCX	C-	(888) 923-3355	C+ / 6.5	7.61	7.02	18.44 /45	6.65 /69	10.97 /66	0.00	2.11
GR	Waddell & Reed Adv Vanguard Y	WAVYX	C+	(888) 923-3355	B- / 7.4	7.91	7.60	19.93 /52	7.96 /79	12.41 /78	0.00	0.87
IN	Wakefield Managed Futures Strat A	WKFAX	C-	(855) 243-1815	E / 0.3	-0.10	-4.32	-7.93 / 0	0.89 /18	--	0.00	3.94
IN	Wakefield Managed Futures Strat I	WKFIX	C-	(855) 243-1815	E / 0.5	0.10	-4.09	-7.60 / 0	1.17 /19	--	0.00	3.69
BA	Walden Asset Management	WSBFX	B-	(800) 282-8782	C+ / 6.0	5.24	5.63	15.72 /33	7.06 /72	8.51 /46	1.00	1.06

RISK			NET ASSETS		ASSET					BULL / BEAR		FUND MANAGER		MINIMUMS		LOADS	
	3 Year		NAV						Portfolio	Last Bull	Last Bear	Manager	Manager	Initial	Additional	Front	Back
Risk Rating/Pts	Standard Deviation	Beta	As of 2/28/17	Total $(Mil)	Cash %	Stocks %	Bonds %	Other %	Turnover Ratio	Market Return	Market Return	Quality Pct	Tenure (Years)	Purch. $	Purch. $	End Load	End Load
C- / 3.8	11.4	1.06	9.87	280	2	96	0	2	102	115.6	-17.7	33	13	0	0	0.0	0.0
C- / 3.5	9.1	1.26	8.27	1,125	6	64	29	1	64	39.7	-22.2	2	3	750	0	5.8	0.0
C- / 3.3	9.1	1.26	7.79	13	6	64	29	1	64	32.3	-22.5	1	3	750	0	0.0	0.0
C- / 3.4	9.1	1.26	7.87	28	6	64	29	1	64	33.6	-22.5	1	3	750	0	0.0	0.0
C- / 3.5	9.1	1.26	8.37	680	6	64	29	1	64	42.1	-22.0	2	3	0	0	0.0	0.0
C+ / 6.4	8.1	1.23	9.59	857	0	59	37	4	51	70.7	-12.3	16	3	750	0	5.8	0.0
C+ / 6.4	8.1	1.23	9.44	3	0	59	37	4	51	60.7	-12.6	9	3	750	0	0.0	0.0
C+ / 6.4	8.1	1.23	9.52	15	0	59	37	4	51	63.0	-12.7	10	3	750	0	0.0	0.0
C+ / 6.4	8.1	1.23	9.61	628	0	59	37	4	51	73.5	-12.3	19	3	0	0	0.0	0.0
C- / 3.7	11.6	1.07	6.31	2,791	0	96	2	2	52	107.9	-17.2	9	11	750	0	5.8	0.0
C- / 3.4	11.6	1.07	5.18	7	0	96	2	2	52	95.0	-17.6	5	11	750	0	0.0	0.0
C- / 3.4	11.7	1.07	5.32	20	0	96	2	2	52	97.5	-17.6	5	11	750	0	0.0	0.0
C- / 3.7	11.6	1.07	6.34	1,079	0	96	2	2	52	110.9	-17.2	10	11	0	0	0.0	0.0
C- / 3.5	10.7	1.01	15.46	328	4	86	8	2	40	99.3	-23.9	18	3	750	0	5.8	0.0
C- / 3.5	10.7	1.01	14.97	2	4	86	8	2	40	87.3	-24.2	10	3	750	0	0.0	0.0
C- / 3.5	10.7	1.01	15.15	7	4	86	8	2	40	90.3	-24.1	12	3	750	0	0.0	0.0
C- / 3.5	10.7	1.01	15.48	248	4	86	8	2	40	103.0	-23.7	20	3	0	0	0.0	0.0
D- / 1.2	24.1	1.18	13.90	184	4	94	1	1	47	34.7	-32.2	83	11	750	0	5.8	0.0
D- / 1.1	24.1	1.17	12.19	1	4	94	1	1	47	25.3	-32.4	73	11	750	0	0.0	0.0
D- / 1.1	24.0	1.17	12.73	3	4	94	1	1	47	28.7	-32.4	78	11	750	0	0.0	0.0
D- / 1.2	24.1	1.18	14.63	98	4	94	1	1	47	38.4	-32.0	85	11	0	0	0.0	0.0
C / 5.3	11.1	0.83	11.87	347	0	95	4	1	44	63.8	-22.2	85	3	750	0	5.8	0.0
C / 5.1	11.1	0.83	10.38	1	0	95	4	1	44	51.4	-22.6	76	3	750	0	0.0	0.0
C / 5.2	11.1	0.83	10.92	1	0	95	4	1	44	54.4	-22.6	78	3	750	0	0.0	0.0
C / 5.3	11.1	0.83	11.97	264	0	95	4	1	44	67.1	-22.1	87	3	0	0	0.0	0.0
D+ / 2.9	13.2	1.02	9.95	1,031	0	97	1	2	40	89.3	-21.2	10	16	750	0	5.8	0.0
D / 2.0	13.1	1.02	6.75	5	0	97	1	2	40	77.9	-21.6	6	16	750	0	0.0	0.0
D / 2.1	13.1	1.02	7.08	9	0	97	1	2	40	79.9	-21.4	6	16	750	0	0.0	0.0
C- / 3.1	13.1	1.01	11.20	588	0	97	1	2	40	93.1	-21.0	12	16	0	0	0.0	0.0
C- / 3.0	16.1	1.35	14.59	2,497	0	91	8	1	9	127.8	-20.9	1	16	750	0	5.8	0.0
D+ / 2.3	16.1	1.35	10.10	11	0	91	8	1	9	114.6	-21.3	1	16	750	0	0.0	0.0
D+ / 2.3	16.0	1.35	10.30	18	0	91	8	1	9	116.1	-21.2	1	16	750	0	0.0	0.0
C- / 3.2	16.0	1.35	16.45	733	0	91	8	1	9	131.4	-20.8	1	16	0	0	0.0	0.0
C- / 3.0	15.6	0.94	16.23	595	1	91	6	2	42	118.0	-25.3	66	7	750	0	5.8	0.0
D / 2.1	15.6	0.94	11.61	4	1	91	6	2	42	105.0	-25.6	51	7	750	0	0.0	0.0
D+ / 2.3	15.6	0.95	12.56	8	1	91	6	2	42	108.4	-25.5	55	7	750	0	0.0	0.0
C- / 3.3	15.6	0.94	18.54	255	1	91	6	2	42	122.9	-25.2	71	7	0	0	0.0	0.0
C / 4.8	12.3	1.06	18.12	212	1	97	1	1	39	117.5	-16.0	33	3	750	0	5.8	0.0
C / 4.7	12.3	1.06	15.25	N/A	1	97	1	1	39	105.7	-16.3	22	3	750	0	0.0	0.0
C / 4.7	12.3	1.06	15.28	6	1	97	1	1	39	107.3	-16.2	24	3	750	0	0.0	0.0
U /	N/A	N/A	18.14	161	1	97	1	1	39	N/A	N/A	N/A	3	0	0	0.0	0.0
C- / 3.9	12.1	1.09	15.26	340	7	88	3	2	50	116.9	-22.3	21	14	750	0	5.8	0.0
C- / 3.8	12.1	1.09	14.19	2	7	88	3	2	50	103.3	-22.7	12	14	750	0	0.0	0.0
C- / 3.9	12.1	1.10	14.48	5	7	88	3	2	50	106.9	-22.6	14	14	750	0	0.0	0.0
C- / 3.8	12.1	1.09	15.33	476	7	88	3	2	50	121.4	-22.2	24	14	0	0	0.0	0.0
C / 4.4	11.8	1.01	9.82	1,062	0	99	0	1	46	115.4	-14.8	37	20	750	0	5.8	0.0
C- / 3.6	11.9	1.01	6.90	3	0	99	0	1	46	102.0	-15.4	24	20	750	0	0.0	0.0
C- / 3.7	11.9	1.01	7.13	7	0	99	0	1	46	104.1	-15.2	26	20	750	0	0.0	0.0
C / 4.5	11.8	1.01	10.52	497	0	99	0	1	46	119.0	-14.8	41	20	0	0	0.0	0.0
B+ / 9.1	7.2	-0.08	9.52	1	33	0	66	1	97	N/A	N/A	84	5	5,000	500	5.8	1.0
B+ / 9.1	7.1	-0.08	9.61	14	33	0	66	1	97	N/A	N/A	85	5	100,000	500	0.0	1.0
B- / 7.6	7.2	1.12	16.35	106	1	72	26	1	16	74.3	-11.5	58	5	100,000	1,000	0.0	0.0

I. Index of Stock Mutual Funds

99 Pct = Best
0 Pct = Worst

Fund Type	Fund Name	Ticker Symbol	Overall Investment Rating	Phone	Performance Rating/Pts	3 Mo	6 Mo	1Yr / Pct	Annualized 3Yr / Pct	Annualized 5Yr / Pct	Dividend Yield	Expense Ratio
GI	Walden Equity	WSEFX	A-	(800) 282-8782	B / 8.2	7.10	9.03	22.46 / 64	8.98 / 87	11.25 / 68	0.87	1.10
GL	Walden Mid Cap Fund	WAMFX	B+	(800) 282-8782	B / 7.8	7.03	7.31	21.31 / 59	8.77 / 85	11.17 / 67	0.73	1.07
SC	Walden Small Cap	WASOX	C+	(800) 282-8782	B / 8.0	5.39	10.84	28.06 / 82	7.26 / 74	10.70 / 63	0.90	1.06
GL	Walden SMID Cap	WASMX	A-	(800) 282-8782	B+ / 8.9	7.49	12.37	29.70 / 86	8.09 / 80	--	0.86	1.15
GR	Walthausen Select Value Inst	WSVIX	C	(888) 925-8428	C / 5.3	4.84	11.37	25.79 / 76	3.53 / 37	11.92 / 74	0.40	1.35
GR	Walthausen Select Value Retail	WSVRX	C	(888) 925-8428	C / 5.1	4.79	11.25	25.55 / 75	3.28 / 35	11.66 / 71	0.18	1.35
SC	● Walthausen Small Cap Value Fund	WSCVX	C	(888) 925-8428	B+ / 8.3	3.11	14.50	40.16 / 97	5.66 / 61	13.17 / 86	0.06	1.25
FO	Wanger International	WSCAX	E	(800) 492-6437	D- / 1.3	7.73	1.20	13.21 / 22	-0.14 / 13	5.73 / 27	1.08	1.11
MC	Wanger Select Fund	WATWX	D+	(800) 492-6437	B / 8.1	5.67	11.82	28.98 / 84	7.10 / 73	11.06 / 66	0.11	0.96
SC	Wanger USA	WUSAX	D+	(800) 492-6437	B+ / 8.3	5.93	11.42	34.12 / 93	6.32 / 67	11.77 / 72	0.00	1.01
GR	Wasatch Core Growth Fund Inst	WIGRX	B-	(800) 551-1700	B / 8.2	4.38	9.76	26.76 / 78	9.12 / 88	12.54 / 79	0.05	1.13
GR	Wasatch Core Growth Investor	WGROX	C+	(800) 551-1700	B / 8.1	4.35	9.70	26.56 / 78	9.02 / 87	12.45 / 79	0.00	1.17
FO	Wasatch Emerging India Investor	WAINX	B+	(800) 551-1700	A+ / 9.9	9.77	2.89	35.70 / 95	19.88 / 99	12.98 / 84	0.00	1.87
EM	Wasatch Emerging Markets SC Inst	WIEMX	U	(800) 551-1700	U /	5.91	-5.28	12.56 / 20	--	--	0.00	N/A
EM	● Wasatch Emerging Markets SC	WAEMX	E+	(800) 551-1700	E+ / 0.7	5.91	-5.28	12.56 / 20	-0.60 / 11	-0.14 / 4	0.00	1.91
EM	Wasatch Emerging Markets Sel Inst	WIESX	E	(800) 766-8938	E / 0.4	7.37	-6.12	12.53 / 20	-2.81 / 5	--	0.00	1.52
EM	Wasatch Emerging Markets Sel Inv	WAESX	E	(800) 766-8938	E / 0.3	7.20	-6.29	12.12 / 18	-3.05 / 4	--	0.00	1.75
EM	Wasatch Frntr Em Sml Countries Inst	WIFMX	U	(800) 551-1700	U /	0.00	-7.20	-5.04 / 1	--	--	0.00	N/A
EM	● Wasatch Frntr Em Sml Countries Inv	WAFMX	E+	(800) 551-1700	E- / 0.1	0.00	-7.58	-5.06 / 1	-7.00 / 1	4.26 / 17	0.00	2.28
GL	Wasatch Global Opportunities Inv	WAGOX	E	(800) 551-1700	D+ / 2.7	6.51	1.87	17.99 / 43	2.07 / 24	8.32 / 45	0.14	1.56
FO	Wasatch International Growth Inst	WIIGX	U	(800) 551-1700	U /	4.68	-3.19	6.81 / 6	--	--	0.08	N/A
FO	● Wasatch International Growth Inv	WAIGX	D-	(800) 551-1700	E+ / 0.9	4.66	-3.22	6.68 / 5	0.46 / 16	7.79 / 41	0.00	1.50
FO	● Wasatch International Opps Inst	WIIOX	U	(800) 551-1700	U /	3.75	-1.62	15.59 / 32	--	--	0.00	N/A
FO	Wasatch International Opps Inv	WAIOX	C-	(800) 551-1700	C- / 4.1	3.78	-1.95	15.27 / 31	6.51 / 69	10.35 / 61	0.00	2.23
GI	Wasatch Large Cap Value Fund Inst	WILCX	C	(800) 766-8938	B+ / 8.3	7.88	11.14	27.85 / 81	8.03 / 79	10.02 / 59	1.74	1.44
IN	Wasatch Large Cap Value Investor	FMIEX	C	(800) 766-8938	B / 8.2	7.82	11.04	27.63 / 81	7.92 / 78	9.90 / 58	1.61	1.12
GR	Wasatch Long-Short Institutional	WILSX	E+	(800) 766-8938	D- / 1.1	0.41	4.34	21.27 / 59	-0.76 / 10	--	0.00	1.47
AA	Wasatch Long-Short Investor	FMLSX	E+	(800) 766-8938	D- / 1.0	0.33	4.20	21.06 / 58	-0.97 / 9	3.14 / 11	0.00	1.61
SC	Wasatch Micro Cap Investor	WMICX	D-	(800) 551-1700	C / 4.3	3.17	5.08	28.11 / 82	2.81 / 30	10.30 / 61	0.07	1.90
SC	Wasatch Micro Cap Value Investor	WAMVX	C+	(800) 551-1700	C+ / 6.7	4.81	8.53	24.41 / 71	6.77 / 70	14.17 / 94	0.06	2.09
SC	Wasatch Small Cap Growth Inst	WIAEX	U	(800) 551-1700	U /	2.58	5.87	23.81 / 69	--	--	0.00	1.09
SC	Wasatch Small Cap Growth Investor	WAAEX	D-	(800) 551-1700	C- / 3.7	2.52	5.76	23.51 / 68	2.84 / 30	8.89 / 50	0.00	1.22
SC	Wasatch Small Cap Value Inst	WICVX	B+	(800) 551-1700	B / 8.1	3.70	9.37	31.56 / 89	8.16 / 80	13.69 / 91	0.23	1.20
SC	Wasatch Small Cap Value Investor	WMCVX	B+	(800) 551-1700	B / 8.1	3.69	9.40	31.28 / 89	8.06 / 79	13.61 / 90	0.07	1.21
GI	Wasatch Strategic Income Investor	WASIX	D	(800) 551-1700	C- / 3.3	5.09	5.30	19.04 / 47	2.60 / 28	9.01 / 51	1.67	1.51
MC	Wasatch Ultra Growth Investor	WAMCX	D-	(800) 551-1700	C+ / 6.5	3.14	5.16	34.30 / 93	5.07 / 55	10.71 / 64	0.53	1.38
TC	Wasatch World Innovators Investor	WAGTX	D	(800) 551-1700	C- / 3.2	7.39	5.65	15.91 / 34	2.60 / 28	8.97 / 50	0.00	1.76
GL	WBI Tactical BA Institutional	WBBAX	C-	(855) 924-3863	D- / 1.3	1.55	4.70	8.33 / 8	0.61 / 16	1.79 / 8	0.60	1.55
GL	WBI Tactical BA No Load	WBADX	C-	(855) 924-3863	D- / 1.1	1.48	4.48	8.08 / 8	0.30 / 15	1.49 / 7	0.34	1.80
IN	WBI Tactical BP Institutional	WBBPX	C-	(888) 263-6443	D / 1.6	3.14	5.97	6.90 / 6	1.66 / 22	--	0.91	1.72
IN	WBI Tactical BP No Load	WBPNX	C-	(888) 263-6443	D- / 1.5	3.08	5.80	6.53 / 5	1.41 / 21	--	0.67	1.97
GL	WBI Tactical DG Institutional	WBDGX	D	(855) 924-3863	D- / 1.0	3.54	9.42	11.75 / 17	-0.62 / 11	4.04 / 15	0.51	1.58
GL	WBI Tactical DG No Load	WBIDX	D	(855) 924-3863	E+ / 0.9	3.49	9.32	11.47 / 16	-0.89 / 10	3.72 / 14	0.32	1.83
IN	WBI Tactical DI Institutional	WBDIX	D	(888) 263-6443	D- / 1.4	5.56	14.02	15.98 / 34	-0.55 / 11	--	0.93	2.53
IN	WBI Tactical DI No Load	WBDNX	D	(888) 263-6443	D- / 1.3	5.52	13.79	15.65 / 33	-0.74 / 10	--	0.73	2.78
FS	WCM Alternatives:Event Driven Inst	WCEIX	C+	(888) 988-9801	D / 1.6	2.51	3.35	6.18 / 5	1.52 / 21	--	0.85	2.27
EM	WCM Focused Emerging Markets	WCMEX	E	(888) 988-9801	E / 0.4	4.74	-4.89	14.02 / 25	-2.86 / 5	--	0.71	2.92
EM	WCM Focused Emerging Markets Inv	WFEMX	E	(888) 988-9801	E / 0.4	4.64	-4.91	13.95 / 25	-2.98 / 5	--	0.71	3.17
GL	WCM Focused Global Growth Inst	WCMGX	C-	(888) 988-9801	C / 4.7	6.04	0.71	17.51 / 41	5.77 / 62	--	1.87	1.91
GL	WCM Focused Global Growth Inv	WFGGX	C-	(888) 988-9801	C / 4.6	6.06	0.70	17.47 / 41	5.63 / 61	--	1.86	2.16
FO	WCM Focused International Gro Inst	WCMIX	C-	(888) 988-9801	C- / 3.3	7.09	0.44	13.87 / 25	3.87 / 41	7.20 / 36	0.47	1.04
FO	WCM Focused International Gro Inv	WCMRX	C-	(888) 988-9801	C- / 3.1	7.07	0.32	13.69 / 24	3.65 / 39	6.96 / 34	0.28	1.29

● Denotes fund is closed to new investors
* Denotes fund is included in Section II

Risk Rating/Pts	3 Year Standard Deviation	Beta	NAV As of 2/28/17	Total $(Mil)	Cash %	Stocks %	Bonds %	Other %	Portfolio Turnover Ratio	Last Bull Market Return	Last Bear Market Return	Manager Quality Pct	Manager Tenure (Years)	Initial Purch. $	Additional Purch. $	Front End Load	Back End Load
C+ / 6.5	10.0	0.95	19.82	183	0	98	0	2	18	108.0	-16.4	62	7	100,000	1,000	0.0	0.0
C+ / 6.6	10.0	0.56	15.68	42	1	98	0	1	20	109.3	N/A	99	N/A	100,000	1,000	0.0	0.0
C- / 3.9	13.5	0.82	18.80	86	0	98	1	1	38	106.1	-21.6	84	9	100,000	1,000	0.0	0.0
C+ / 5.8	12.7	0.62	15.26	40	1	98	0	1	43	N/A	N/A	98	5	100,000	1,000	0.0	0.0
C+ / 5.7	13.9	1.05	16.55	35	6	93	0	1	93	125.5	-22.8	5	7	100,000	1,000	0.0	2.0
C+ / 5.7	13.9	1.05	16.38	53	6	93	0	1	93	122.5	-22.9	5	7	2,500	100	0.0	2.0
C- / 3.1	17.7	1.05	21.89	601	5	94	0	1	53	137.5	-24.9	55	9	2,500	100	0.0	2.0
C- / 3.8	11.3	0.82	25.32	524	3	96	0	1	53	52.8	-21.8	74	12	0	0	0.0	0.0
E+ / 0.7	12.2	0.93	20.14	131	2	97	0	1	59	115.2	-27.8	53	2	0	0	0.0	0.0
E+ / 0.9	14.9	0.92	27.71	678	2	97	0	1	45	121.5	-24.3	74	3	0	0	0.0	0.0
C / 4.3	12.3	0.92	61.19	303	6	93	0	1	18	N/A	N/A	68	17	500,000	5,000	0.0	2.0
C / 4.3	12.3	0.92	60.91	1,134	6	93	0	1	18	118.5	-14.5	67	17	2,000	100	0.0	2.0
C / 4.3	17.2	0.57	3.41	85	2	97	0	1	42	92.9	-8.5	99	6	2,000	100	0.0	2.0
U /	N/A	N/A	2.51	149	1	98	0	1	42	N/A	N/A	N/A	10	100,000	5,000	0.0	2.0
C / 5.4	12.8	0.69	2.51	512	1	98	0	1	42	19.5	-17.9	51	10	2,000	100	0.0	2.0
C- / 4.1	13.5	0.72	8.89	25	0	99	0	1	62	N/A	N/A	23	5	500,000	5,000	0.0	2.0
C- / 4.1	13.4	0.71	8.79	11	0	99	0	1	62	N/A	N/A	20	5	2,000	100	0.0	2.0
U /	N/A	N/A	2.45	54	7	92	0	1	80	N/A	N/A	N/A	1	100,000	5,000	0.0	2.0
C+ / 5.9	7.3	0.32	2.44	271	7	92	0	1	80	N/A	N/A	4	1	2,000	100	0.0	2.0
D+ / 2.4	13.3	0.80	3.21	94	0	99	0	1	44	78.0	-22.0	87	6	2,000	100	0.0	2.0
U /	N/A	N/A	28.20	506	2	97	0	1	50	N/A	N/A	N/A	11	100,000	5,000	0.0	2.0
C / 5.5	12.6	0.76	28.18	799	2	97	0	1	50	76.5	-21.4	78	11	2,000	100	0.0	2.0
U /	N/A	N/A	3.04	182	12	87	0	1	41	N/A	N/A	N/A	3	100,000	5,000	0.0	2.0
C+ / 5.9	10.3	0.59	3.02	451	12	87	0	1	41	89.4	-20.0	97	3	2,000	100	0.0	2.0
D+ / 2.6	11.1	1.01	9.70	2	1	98	0	1	26	N/A	N/A	41	4	500,000	5,000	0.0	2.0
D+ / 2.6	11.1	1.01	9.71	193	1	98	0	1	26	93.0	-21.1	40	4	2,000	100	0.0	2.0
C / 4.5	10.7	0.76	13.30	54	59	40	0	1	47	N/A	N/A	3	9	25,000,000	10,000	0.0	2.0
C / 4.5	10.7	1.23	13.24	137	59	40	0	1	47	35.0	-13.9	2	9	2,000	100	0.0	2.0
D+ / 2.5	16.1	0.93	6.74	270	3	96	0	1	32	103.7	-24.3	30	13	2,000	100	0.0	2.0
C / 4.8	11.7	0.68	3.01	188	15	84	0	1	73	131.2	-22.2	86	14	2,000	100	0.0	2.0
U /	N/A	N/A	41.58	389	1	98	0	1	20	N/A	N/A	N/A	31	100,000	5,000	0.0	2.0
D+ / 2.5	14.6	0.84	41.47	1,346	1	98	0	1	20	90.9	-17.8	37	31	2,000	100	0.0	2.0
C+ / 6.0	13.4	0.81	7.18	41	6	93	0	1	57	N/A	N/A	88	18	500,000	5,000	0.0	2.0
C+ / 6.0	13.4	0.81	7.15	299	6	93	0	1	57	130.5	-21.8	88	18	2,000	100	0.0	2.0
C / 5.1	11.5	1.01	11.10	49	27	72	0	1	45	87.6	-14.8	4	11	2,000	100	0.0	2.0
E / 0.3	18.6	1.29	18.28	97	4	95	0	1	28	96.3	-19.6	6	5	2,000	100	0.0	2.0
C / 4.4	10.9	0.90	19.43	174	19	80	0	1	112	84.4	-13.2	7	9	2,000	100	0.0	2.0
B / 8.3	5.0	0.49	10.55	14	13	27	58	2	331	21.0	-8.7	53	7	250,000	250	0.0	2.0
B / 8.3	5.1	0.50	10.49	14	13	27	58	2	331	19.1	-8.7	48	7	2,500	250	0.0	2.0
B / 8.7	5.5	0.41	10.23	25	48	24	27	1	381	N/A	N/A	40	4	250,000	250	0.0	2.0
B / 8.7	5.5	0.41	10.21	2	48	24	27	1	381	N/A	N/A	37	4	2,500	250	0.0	2.0
C+ / 6.6	9.2	0.49	11.17	8	21	61	16	2	384	50.2	-20.9	67	7	250,000	250	0.0	2.0
C+ / 6.6	9.2	0.48	11.12	10	21	61	16	2	384	47.9	-20.9	64	7	2,500	250	0.0	2.0
C+ / 6.9	9.7	0.70	10.09	3	36	55	8	1	399	N/A	N/A	4	4	250,000	250	0.0	2.0
C+ / 6.9	9.7	0.70	10.06	1	36	55	8	1	399	N/A	N/A	4	4	2,500	250	0.0	2.0
B+ / 9.9	3.9	0.21	9.98	119	0	0	0	100	199	N/A	N/A	62	10	1,000,000	500	0.0	0.0
C / 4.4	15.1	0.78	9.45	16	4	95	0	1	49	N/A	N/A	21	4	100,000	5,000	0.0	1.0
C / 4.4	15.0	0.78	9.41	6	4	95	0	1	49	N/A	N/A	20	4	1,000	100	0.0	1.0
C / 5.3	12.1	0.79	12.45	11	0	100	0	0	233	N/A	N/A	97	4	100,000	5,000	0.0	1.0
C / 5.3	12.1	0.79	12.40	2	0	100	0	0	233	N/A	N/A	96	4	1,000	100	0.0	1.0
C+ / 6.2	11.4	0.80	12.85	3,189	6	93	0	1	26	68.3	N/A	93	6	100,000	5,000	0.0	1.0
C+ / 6.2	11.4	0.80	12.81	108	6	93	0	1	26	66.1	N/A	93	6	1,000	100	0.0	1.0

Fund Type	Fund Name	Ticker Symbol	Overall Investment Rating	Phone	Performance Rating/Pts	3 Mo	6 Mo	1Yr / Pct	3Yr / Pct	5Yr / Pct	Dividend Yield	Expense Ratio
	99 Pct = Best 0 Pct = Worst							Total Return % through 2/28/17	Annualized		Incl. in Returns	
BA	Weitz Balanced Fund	WBALX	C	(800) 232-4161	D+ / 2.5	3.75	3.60	9.65 /11	3.04 /32	5.91 /28	0.25	1.11
GR	Weitz Funds Part III Oppty	WPOPX	D+	(800) 232-4161	C- / 3.0	4.60	6.83	14.74 /29	2.01 /24	8.56 /47	0.00	1.95
GR	Weitz Partners III Oppty Inv	WPOIX	D	(800) 232-4161	D+ / 2.6	4.48	6.52	14.13 /26	1.62 /22	8.18 /44	0.00	2.33
GI	Weitz Partners-Partners Value Ins	WPVIX	U	(800) 232-4161	U /	5.22	7.59	16.29 /35	--	--	0.00	1.07
GR	Weitz Partners-Partners Value Inv	WPVLX	D+	(800) 232-4161	C- / 3.3	5.15	7.41	16.01 /34	2.28 /26	9.22 /52	0.00	1.26
GR	Weitz Research Fund	WRESX	D	(800) 232-4161	C- / 4.0	3.96	7.06	16.18 /35	3.83 /41	8.22 /44	0.00	1.64
GR	Weitz Series-Hickory Fund	WEHIX	D	(800) 232-4161	C- / 3.1	2.16	5.81	16.67 /37	2.59 /28	8.31 /45	0.00	1.24
GI	Weitz Series-Value Institutional	WVAIX	U	(800) 232-4161	U /	6.51	7.40	14.44 /28	--	--	0.00	1.08
MC	Weitz Series-Value Investor	WVALX	C-	(800) 232-4161	C- / 3.8	6.44	7.28	14.19 /26	3.24 /34	9.55 /55	0.00	1.23
GL	Wells Fargo Absolute Return A	WARAX	D+	(800) 222-8222	D- / 1.1	4.57	2.88	10.69 /13	0.39 /15	--	0.70	1.51
GL	Wells Fargo Absolute Return Adm	WARDX	C-	(800) 222-8222	D / 1.7	4.53	2.94	10.84 /14	0.52 /16	--	0.89	1.43
GL	Wells Fargo Absolute Return C	WARCX	D+	(800) 222-8222	D- / 1.0	4.46	2.63	10.03 /12	-0.32 /12	--	0.00	2.26
IN	Wells Fargo Absolute Return Ins	WABIX	C-	(800) 222-8222	D / 1.8	4.70	3.10	11.13 /15	0.80 /17	--	1.14	1.18
GL	Wells Fargo Alt Strat Inst	WAITX	U	(800) 222-8222	U /	1.69	1.19	2.20 / 2	--	--	0.00	3.13
FO	Wells Fargo Asia Pac A	WFAAX	D+	(800) 222-8222	C- / 3.1	6.43	3.17	19.01 /47	3.73 /40	6.12 /29	1.16	1.68
FO	Wells Fargo Asia Pac Adm	WFADX	C-	(800) 222-8222	C / 4.3	6.41	3.19	19.03 /47	3.91 /42	6.30 /30	1.06	1.60
FO	Wells Fargo Asia Pac C	WFCAX	C-	(800) 222-8222	C- / 3.6	6.29	2.85	18.13 /43	3.00 /32	5.34 /24	0.29	2.43
FO	Wells Fargo Asia Pac Inst	WFPIX	C	(800) 222-8222	C / 4.5	6.45	3.40	19.39 /49	4.09 /44	6.49 /31	1.65	1.35
GL	Wells Fargo Asset Alloc A	EAAFX	D+	(800) 222-8222	D- / 1.4	4.82	3.37	12.22 /19	0.91 /18	3.88 /15	1.44	1.34
GL	Wells Fargo Asset Alloc Adm	EAIFX	C-	(800) 222-8222	D / 2.1	4.89	3.46	12.48 /20	1.09 /19	4.09 /16	1.63	1.26
GL	● Wells Fargo Asset Alloc B	EABFX	C-	(800) 222-8222	D / 1.6	4.67	3.07	11.43 /16	0.17 /14	3.12 /11	0.00	2.09
GL	Wells Fargo Asset Alloc C	EACFX	D+	(800) 222-8222	D / 1.6	4.67	3.09	11.51 /16	0.16 /14	3.12 /11	0.75	2.09
GL	Wells Fargo Asset Alloc Inst	EAAIX	C-	(800) 222-8222	D / 2.2	4.96	3.60	12.71 /21	1.33 /20	--	1.90	1.01
GL	Wells Fargo Asset Alloc R	EAXFX	C-	(800) 222-8222	D / 1.8	4.81	3.27	12.02 /18	0.67 /17	3.64 /14	1.27	1.59
GR	Wells Fargo C&B Lg Cp Val Adm	CBLLX	A+	(800) 222-8222	A- / 9.1	7.34	10.79	26.23 /77	9.54 /91	13.08 /85	0.56	1.17
GR	Wells Fargo C&B Lg Cp Val C	CBECX	A	(800) 222-8222	B+ / 8.4	7.07	10.29	25.12 /74	8.54 /83	12.04 /75	0.00	2.00
GR	Wells Fargo C&B Lg Cp Val I	CBLSX	A+	(800) 222-8222	A- / 9.2	7.41	10.93	26.44 /78	9.82 /92	13.36 /87	0.84	0.92
MC	Wells Fargo C&B MdCp Val A	CBMAX	B+	(800) 222-8222	B / 7.7	4.41	10.56	30.82 /88	8.29 /81	13.86 /92	0.06	1.31
MC	Wells Fargo C&B MdCp Val Adm	CBMIX	A+	(800) 222-8222	B+ / 8.8	4.45	10.63	30.97 /88	8.37 /82	13.92 /93	0.12	1.23
MC	Wells Fargo C&B MdCp Val C	CBMCX	A-	(800) 222-8222	B / 8.1	4.20	10.17	29.88 /86	7.48 /75	13.01 /84	0.00	2.06
MC	Wells Fargo C&B MdCp Val I	CBMSX	A+	(800) 222-8222	B+ / 8.9	4.48	10.75	31.31 /89	8.63 /84	14.21 /94	0.31	0.98
GR	Wells Fargo Cap Gr A	WFCGX	E+	(800) 222-8222	C / 4.5	7.28	6.92	19.70 /51	5.14 /56	10.93 /65	0.12	1.24
GR	Wells Fargo Cap Gr Adm	WFCDX	D-	(800) 222-8222	C+ / 5.9	7.27	6.93	19.85 /51	5.31 /58	11.12 /67	0.15	1.16
GR	Wells Fargo Cap Gr C	WFCCX	E+	(800) 222-8222	C / 5.1	7.08	6.52	18.82 /46	4.37 /47	10.10 /59	0.00	1.99
GR	Wells Fargo Cap Gr I	WWCIX	D	(800) 222-8222	C+ / 6.1	7.36	7.10	20.13 /53	5.61 /61	11.42 /69	0.24	0.91
GI	Wells Fargo Cap Gr R4	WCGRX	D	(800) 222-8222	C+ / 6.1	7.37	7.11	20.11 /53	5.51 /60	--	0.23	0.96
GI	Wells Fargo Cap Gr R6	WFCRX	D	(800) 222-8222	C+ / 6.2	7.45	7.19	20.27 /54	5.67 /61	--	0.29	0.81
GR	Wells Fargo CB Lg Cp Vl A	CBEAX	A-	(800) 222-8222	B / 8.0	7.31	10.67	25.99 /76	9.35 /89	12.89 /83	0.50	1.25
MC	Wells Fargo Comm Stk A	SCSAX	C	(800) 222-8222	B- / 7.1	6.53	11.20	29.88 /86	6.79 /70	11.70 /72	0.00	1.24
MC	Wells Fargo Comm Stk Adm	SCSDX	C+	(800) 222-8222	B / 8.2	6.58	11.24	29.99 /86	6.94 /72	11.86 /73	0.00	1.16
MC	Wells Fargo Comm Stk C	STSAX	C	(800) 222-8222	B- / 7.5	6.37	10.82	28.87 /84	5.99 /64	10.86 /65	0.00	1.99
MC	Wells Fargo Comm Stk Inst	SCNSX	C+	(800) 222-8222	B+ / 8.4	6.62	11.40	30.32 /87	7.21 /73	12.13 /75	0.00	0.91
GR	Wells Fargo Comm Stk R6	SCSRX	C+	(800) 222-8222	B+ / 8.4	6.65	11.42	30.43 /87	7.26 /74	--	0.00	0.81
SC	Wells Fargo Discovery A	WFDAX	C-	(800) 222-8222	C+ / 6.4	9.03	12.12	31.51 /89	4.19 /45	10.89 /65	0.00	1.19
SC	Wells Fargo Discovery Adm	WFDDX	C	(800) 222-8222	B- / 7.4	9.06	12.15	31.58 /89	4.30 /46	11.01 /66	0.00	1.11
SC	Wells Fargo Discovery C	WDSCX	C-	(800) 222-8222	C+ / 6.8	8.83	11.68	30.48 /87	3.41 /36	10.06 /59	0.00	1.94
SC	Wells Fargo Discovery Inst	WFDSX	C	(800) 222-8222	B / 7.6	9.11	12.27	31.94 /90	4.56 /49	11.29 /68	0.00	0.86
GR	Wells Fargo Discovery R6	WFDRX	C	(800) 222-8222	B / 7.7	9.15	12.34	32.01 /90	4.64 /50	--	0.00	0.76
AA	Wells Fargo DJ Tgt 2010 A	STNRX	C-	(800) 222-8222	E+ / 0.6	1.64	-1.29	3.71 / 3	1.25 /20	2.10 / 8	0.70	0.85
AA	Wells Fargo DJ Tgt 2010 Adm	WFLGX	C-	(800) 222-8222	D- / 1.1	1.73	-1.22	3.84 / 3	1.39 /20	2.26 / 9	0.82	0.77
AA	Wells Fargo DJ Tgt 2010 C	WFOCX	C-	(800) 222-8222	E+ / 0.8	1.52	-1.65	2.96 / 3	0.52 /16	1.34 / 7	0.13	1.60
AA	Wells Fargo DJ Tgt 2010 R	WFARX	C-	(800) 222-8222	D- / 1.0	1.58	-1.42	3.45 / 3	1.00 /18	--	0.56	1.10

● Denotes fund is closed to new investors
* Denotes fund is included in Section II

www.thestreetratings.com

RISK			NET ASSETS		ASSET					BULL / BEAR		FUND MANAGER		MINIMUMS		LOADS	
	3 Year		NAV						Portfolio	Last Bull	Last Bear	Manager	Manager	Initial	Additional	Front	Back
Risk Rating/Pts	Standard Deviation	Beta	As of 2/28/17	Total $(Mil)	Cash %	Stocks %	Bonds %	Other %	Turnover Ratio	Market Return	Market Return	Quality Pct	Tenure (Years)	Purch. $	Purch. $	End Load	End Load
B /8.1	5.3	0.79	13.59	118	2	44	52	2	35	53.8	-10.2	37	14	2,500	25	0.0	0.0
C /5.5	9.3	0.75	15.02	666	31	65	3	1	46	81.1	-14.4	11	34	1,000,000	25	0.0	0.0
C /5.4	9.3	0.75	14.70	29	31	65	3	1	46	77.8	N/A	9	34	2,500	25	0.0	0.0
U /	N/A	N/A	30.62	301	0	82	17	1	31	N/A	N/A	N/A	34	1,000,000	25	0.0	0.0
C /5.2	9.8	0.84	30.44	445	0	82	17	1	31	89.3	-16.1	8	34	2,500	25	0.0	0.0
C /4.3	12.6	1.01	10.77	31	12	87	0	1	73	82.9	-11.4	7	12	1,000,000	25	0.0	0.0
C /4.7	11.2	0.90	52.41	284	0	75	23	2	27	83.3	-18.3	7	14	2,500	25	0.0	0.0
U /	N/A	N/A	42.24	188	0	82	17	1	47	N/A	N/A	N/A	11	1,000,000	25	0.0	0.0
C /5.5	9.3	0.62	42.01	652	0	82	17	1	47	89.6	-12.1	40	11	2,500	25	0.0	0.0
B- /7.7	6.3	0.90	10.71	734	100	0	0	0	8	N/A	N/A	26	5	1,000	100	5.8	0.0
B- /7.7	6.3	0.89	10.73	321	100	0	0	0	8	N/A	N/A	28	5	1,000,000	0	0.0	0.0
B- /7.7	6.3	0.90	10.53	817	100	0	0	0	8	N/A	N/A	20	5	1,000	100	0.0	0.0
B- /7.6	6.3	0.48	10.72	4,048	100	0	0	0	8	N/A	N/A	22	5	1,000,000	0	0.0	0.0
U /	N/A	N/A	10.21	143	0	0	0	100	284	N/A	N/A	N/A	3	1,000,000	0	0.0	0.0
C+ /6.2	12.7	0.85	12.32	118	1	96	1	2	52	59.1	-19.4	93	24	1,000	100	5.8	0.0
C+ /6.1	12.7	0.85	12.11	5	1	96	1	2	52	60.7	-19.4	93	24	1,000,000	0	0.0	0.0
C+ /6.1	12.7	0.85	11.73	2	1	96	1	2	52	52.9	-19.6	91	24	1,000	100	0.0	0.0
C+ /6.1	12.7	0.85	12.06	18	1	96	1	2	52	62.3	-19.3	94	24	1,000,000	0	0.0	0.0
B- /7.5	6.8	0.99	13.30	1,425	3	54	42	1	1	32.1	-8.2	28	21	1,000	100	5.8	0.0
B- /7.6	6.8	0.99	13.45	97	3	54	42	1	1	33.6	-8.1	29	21	1,000,000	0	0.0	0.0
B- /7.8	6.8	0.99	13.45	17	3	54	42	1	1	27.0	-8.5	21	21	1,000	100	0.0	0.0
B- /7.6	6.8	0.99	12.88	1,281	3	54	42	1	1	26.9	-8.5	20	21	1,000	100	0.0	0.0
B- /7.5	6.8	0.99	13.33	680	3	54	42	1	1	N/A	N/A	32	21	1,000,000	0	0.0	0.0
B- /7.6	6.8	0.99	13.18	21	3	54	42	1	1	30.4	-8.3	25	21	0	0	0.0	0.0
C+ /6.7	10.9	1.01	14.16	14	0	97	2	1	29	117.8	-15.5	61	27	1,000,000	0	0.0	0.0
C+ /6.8	10.9	1.01	14.08	8	0	97	2	1	29	106.9	-15.8	49	27	1,000	100	0.0	0.0
C+ /6.7	10.9	1.01	14.18	210	0	97	2	1	29	120.4	-15.3	65	27	1,000,000	0	0.0	0.0
C+ /6.9	12.6	1.01	32.67	126	0	98	1	1	35	138.1	-19.8	59	19	1,000	100	5.8	0.0
C+ /6.9	12.6	1.00	33.07	8	0	98	1	1	35	138.8	-19.8	60	19	1,000,000	0	0.0	0.0
C+ /6.8	12.6	1.01	30.99	9	0	98	1	1	35	128.7	-20.1	48	19	1,000	100	0.0	0.0
C+ /6.8	12.6	1.01	32.92	56	0	98	1	1	35	142.0	-19.7	62	19	1,000,000	0	0.0	0.0
D- /1.1	11.9	1.02	15.47	73	1	97	1	1	85	108.4	-21.2	13	5	1,000	100	5.8	0.0
D- /1.4	11.9	1.02	16.61	21	1	97	1	1	85	110.6	-21.1	14	5	1,000,000	0	0.0	0.0
E+ /0.7	11.8	1.01	13.77	3	1	97	1	1	85	100.2	-21.4	9	5	1,000	100	0.0	0.0
D- /1.5	11.8	1.02	17.10	25	1	97	1	1	85	113.5	-21.0	17	5	1,000,000	0	0.0	0.0
D- /1.5	11.8	1.02	17.04	N/A	1	97	1	1	85	N/A	N/A	16	5	0	0	0.0	0.0
D- /1.5	11.8	1.01	17.16	136	1	97	1	1	85	N/A	N/A	17	5	0	0	0.0	0.0
C+ /6.8	10.9	1.01	14.15	93	0	97	2	1	29	115.4	-15.6	59	27	1,000	100	5.8	0.0
C- /3.7	13.4	1.05	22.96	964	0	97	2	1	32	120.2	-22.4	33	16	1,000	100	5.8	0.0
C- /3.8	13.4	1.05	23.28	8	0	97	2	1	32	122.0	-22.3	35	16	1,000,000	0	0.0	0.0
C- /3.0	13.3	1.05	17.97	23	0	97	2	1	32	111.4	-22.6	25	16	1,000	100	0.0	0.0
C- /3.9	13.4	1.05	23.77	182	0	97	2	1	32	124.8	-22.3	38	16	1,000,000	0	0.0	0.0
C- /3.9	13.4	1.15	23.83	111	0	97	2	1	32	N/A	N/A	18	16	0	0	0.0	0.0
C- /3.2	14.6	0.83	32.80	611	0	99	0	1	78	118.4	-22.9	56	5	1,000	100	5.8	0.0
C- /3.2	14.6	0.83	33.66	352	0	99	0	1	78	119.6	-22.8	57	5	1,000	0	0.0	0.0
C- /3.0	14.6	0.83	29.80	45	0	99	0	1	78	109.8	-23.1	46	5	1,000	100	0.0	0.0
C- /3.3	14.6	0.83	34.82	1,173	0	99	0	1	78	122.8	-22.7	61	5	1,000,000	0	0.0	0.0
C- /3.3	14.6	1.13	34.92	296	0	99	0	1	78	N/A	N/A	6	5	0	0	0.0	0.0
B /8.7	3.1	0.34	12.41	60	1	15	82	2	36	16.9	-2.5	58	11	1,000	100	5.8	0.0
B /8.7	3.2	0.35	12.55	50	1	15	82	2	36	17.8	-2.4	60	11	1,000,000	0	0.0	0.0
B /8.8	3.2	0.35	12.56	2	1	15	82	2	36	12.3	-2.8	47	11	1,000	100	0.0	0.0
B /8.7	3.2	0.36	12.33	N/A	1	15	82	2	36	N/A	N/A	53	11	0	0	0.0	0.0

Data as of February 28, 2017

Fund Type	Fund Name	Ticker Symbol	Overall Investment Rating	Phone	Performance Rating/Pts	3 Mo	6 Mo	1Yr / Pct	3Yr / Pct	5Yr / Pct	Dividend Yield	Expense Ratio
AA	Wells Fargo DJ Tgt 2010 R4	WFORX	C-	(800) 222-8222	D- / 1.2	1.79	-1.10	4.11 / 3	1.61 / 22	--	1.00	0.57
AA	Wells Fargo DJ Tgt 2010 R6	WFOAX	C-	(800) 222-8222	D- / 1.2	1.78	-1.00	4.27 / 3	1.77 / 23	2.61 / 10	1.15	0.42
AA	Wells Fargo DJ Tgt 2015 A	WFACX	C-	(800) 222-8222	E+ / 0.8	2.18	-1.32	5.30 / 4	1.79 / 23	--	0.93	0.84
AA	Wells Fargo DJ Tgt 2015 Adm	WFFFX	C-	(800) 222-8222	D- / 1.4	2.28	-1.15	5.52 / 4	1.94 / 24	3.12 / 11	1.06	0.76
AA	Wells Fargo DJ Tgt 2015 R	WFBRX	C-	(800) 222-8222	D- / 1.2	2.05	-1.46	4.99 / 4	1.52 / 21	--	0.75	1.09
AA	Wells Fargo DJ Tgt 2015 R4	WFSRX	C-	(800) 222-8222	D- / 1.4	2.16	-1.15	5.57 / 4	2.11 / 25	--	1.25	0.56
AA	Wells Fargo DJ Tgt 2015 R6	WFSCX	C	(800) 222-8222	D- / 1.5	2.24	-1.13	5.74 / 4	2.26 / 26	3.46 / 13	1.41	0.41
AA	Wells Fargo DJ Tgt 2020 A	STTRX	C-	(800) 222-8222	D- / 1.1	2.84	-0.23	7.53 / 7	2.30 / 26	3.99 / 15	1.07	0.83
AA	Wells Fargo DJ Tgt 2020 Adm	WFLPX	C-	(800) 222-8222	D / 1.7	2.83	-0.24	7.58 / 7	2.41 / 27	4.13 / 16	1.20	0.75
AA	Wells Fargo DJ Tgt 2020 C	WFLAX	C-	(800) 222-8222	D- / 1.4	2.64	-0.62	6.71 / 5	1.53 / 21	3.22 / 12	0.54	1.58
AA	Wells Fargo DJ Tgt 2020 R	WFURX	C-	(800) 222-8222	D / 1.6	2.78	-0.36	7.27 / 6	2.05 / 24	--	0.94	1.08
AA	Wells Fargo DJ Tgt 2020 R4	WFLRX	C-	(800) 222-8222	D / 1.9	2.94	-0.06	7.89 / 7	2.64 / 29	--	1.37	0.55
AA	Wells Fargo DJ Tgt 2020 R6	WFOBX	C	(800) 222-8222	D / 1.9	2.93	-0.03	8.04 / 7	2.78 / 30	4.50 / 18	1.50	0.40
BA	Wells Fargo DJ Tgt 2025 A	WFAYX	C-	(800) 222-8222	D / 1.6	3.61	1.19	10.61 / 13	2.95 / 31	--	1.33	0.83
AA	Wells Fargo DJ Tgt 2025 Adm	WFTRX	C	(800) 222-8222	D+ / 2.5	3.72	1.44	10.87 / 14	3.14 / 33	5.31 / 23	1.50	0.75
BA	Wells Fargo DJ Tgt 2025 R	WFHRX	C-	(800) 222-8222	D / 2.2	3.53	1.06	10.22 / 12	2.70 / 29	--	1.19	1.08
BA	Wells Fargo DJ Tgt 2025 R4	WFGRX	C	(800) 222-8222	D+ / 2.6	3.69	1.36	10.98 / 14	3.31 / 35	--	1.68	0.55
AA	Wells Fargo DJ Tgt 2025 R6	WFTYX	C	(800) 222-8222	D+ / 2.6	3.66	1.47	11.04 / 15	3.47 / 37	5.67 / 26	1.82	0.40
AA	Wells Fargo DJ Tgt 2030 A	STHRX	C-	(800) 222-8222	D+ / 2.4	4.57	3.08	14.15 / 26	3.69 / 39	6.31 / 30	1.71	0.83
AA	Wells Fargo DJ Tgt 2030 Adm	WFLIX	C	(800) 222-8222	C- / 3.5	4.59	3.18	14.32 / 27	3.84 / 41	6.47 / 31	1.86	0.75
AA	Wells Fargo DJ Tgt 2030 C	WFDMX	C	(800) 222-8222	D+ / 2.8	4.39	2.66	13.28 / 23	2.92 / 31	5.52 / 25	1.26	1.58
AA	Wells Fargo DJ Tgt 2030 R	WFJRX	C	(800) 222-8222	C- / 3.2	4.49	2.99	13.88 / 25	3.44 / 36	--	1.61	1.08
AA	Wells Fargo DJ Tgt 2030 R4	WTHRX	C	(800) 222-8222	C- / 3.6	4.66	3.24	14.52 / 28	4.04 / 43	--	2.04	0.55
AA	Wells Fargo DJ Tgt 2030 R6	WFOOX	C+	(800) 222-8222	C- / 3.7	4.69	3.28	14.63 / 28	4.20 / 45	6.83 / 34	2.18	0.40
AA	Wells Fargo DJ Tgt 2035 A	WFQBX	C-	(800) 222-8222	C- / 3.2	5.41	4.70	17.33 / 40	4.21 / 45	--	1.27	0.84
AA	Wells Fargo DJ Tgt 2035 Adm	WFQWX	C+	(800) 222-8222	C / 4.4	5.32	4.73	17.38 / 40	4.33 / 47	7.39 / 37	1.45	0.76
AA	Wells Fargo DJ Tgt 2035 R	WFKRX	C	(800) 222-8222	C- / 4.1	5.39	4.63	17.09 / 39	3.95 / 42	--	1.15	1.09
AA	Wells Fargo DJ Tgt 2035 R4	WTTRX	C+	(800) 222-8222	C / 4.6	5.49	4.87	17.68 / 41	4.55 / 49	--	1.65	0.56
AA	Wells Fargo DJ Tgt 2035 R6	WFQRX	C+	(800) 222-8222	C / 4.8	5.55	4.96	17.86 / 42	4.71 / 51	7.79 / 41	1.79	0.41
AA	Wells Fargo DJ Tgt 2040 A	STFRX	C	(800) 222-8222	C- / 4.0	6.12	6.10	20.01 / 52	4.66 / 50	7.99 / 42	1.30	0.84
AA	Wells Fargo DJ Tgt 2040 Adm	WFLWX	C+	(800) 222-8222	C / 5.3	6.14	6.14	20.09 / 53	4.78 / 52	8.14 / 43	1.44	0.76
AA	Wells Fargo DJ Tgt 2040 C	WFOFX	C	(800) 222-8222	C / 4.6	5.91	5.69	19.11 / 48	3.86 / 41	7.18 / 36	0.79	1.59
AA	Wells Fargo DJ Tgt 2040 R	WFMRX	C+	(800) 222-8222	C / 5.0	6.01	5.92	19.68 / 50	4.38 / 47	--	1.17	1.09
AA	Wells Fargo DJ Tgt 2040 R4	WTFRX	C+	(800) 222-8222	C / 5.5	6.19	6.24	20.43 / 55	5.00 / 54	--	1.62	0.56
AA	Wells Fargo DJ Tgt 2040 R6	WFOSX	C+	(800) 222-8222	C+ / 5.7	6.24	6.28	20.56 / 55	5.16 / 56	8.51 / 46	1.77	0.41
AA	Wells Fargo DJ Tgt 2045 A	WFQVX	C	(800) 222-8222	C / 4.6	6.56	7.01	21.85 / 61	4.94 / 53	--	1.32	0.85
AA	Wells Fargo DJ Tgt 2045 Adm	WFQYX	C+	(800) 222-8222	C+ / 5.9	6.54	7.00	21.89 / 62	5.06 / 55	8.54 / 47	1.49	0.77
AA	Wells Fargo DJ Tgt 2045 R	WFNRX	C+	(800) 222-8222	C+ / 5.6	6.50	6.79	21.41 / 59	4.66 / 50	--	1.18	1.10
AA	Wells Fargo DJ Tgt 2045 R4	WFFRX	C+	(800) 222-8222	C+ / 6.1	6.63	7.16	22.25 / 63	5.29 / 58	--	1.69	0.57
AA	Wells Fargo DJ Tgt 2045 R6	WFQPX	C+	(800) 222-8222	C+ / 6.2	6.70	7.18	22.26 / 63	5.43 / 59	8.92 / 50	1.84	0.42
AA	Wells Fargo DJ Tgt 2050 A	WFQAX	C	(800) 222-8222	C / 4.8	6.78	7.34	22.48 / 64	5.06 / 55	--	1.48	0.84
AA	Wells Fargo DJ Tgt 2050 Adm	WFQDX	C+	(800) 222-8222	C+ / 6.2	6.80	7.39	22.72 / 65	5.20 / 56	8.67 / 48	1.67	0.76
AA	Wells Fargo DJ Tgt 2050 C	WFQCX	C+	(800) 222-8222	C / 5.4	6.59	6.96	21.58 / 60	4.29 / 46	--	0.92	1.59
AA	Wells Fargo DJ Tgt 2050 R	WFWRX	C+	(800) 222-8222	C+ / 5.9	6.77	7.29	22.29 / 64	4.80 / 52	--	1.38	1.09
AA	Wells Fargo DJ Tgt 2050 R4	WQFRX	C+	(800) 222-8222	C+ / 6.4	6.94	7.58	23.00 / 67	5.39 / 58	--	1.84	0.56
AA	Wells Fargo DJ Tgt 2050 R6	WFQFX	C+	(800) 222-8222	C+ / 6.5	6.90	7.59	23.09 / 67	5.56 / 60	9.05 / 51	1.99	0.41
AA	Wells Fargo DJ Tgt 2055 A	WFQZX	C+	(800) 222-8222	C / 4.8	6.72	7.32	22.45 / 64	5.04 / 55	--	1.52	0.90
AA	Wells Fargo DJ Tgt 2055 Adm	WFLHX	C+	(800) 222-8222	C+ / 6.1	6.76	7.38	22.50 / 65	5.19 / 56	8.64 / 48	1.73	0.82
AA	Wells Fargo DJ Tgt 2055 R	WFYRX	C+	(800) 222-8222	C+ / 5.8	6.60	7.06	22.04 / 62	4.76 / 52	--	1.42	1.15
AA	Wells Fargo DJ Tgt 2055 R4	WFVRX	C+	(800) 222-8222	C+ / 6.3	6.72	7.40	22.78 / 66	5.38 / 58	--	1.90	0.62
AA	Wells Fargo DJ Tgt 2055 R6	WFQUX	C+	(800) 222-8222	C+ / 6.4	6.83	7.46	22.97 / 67	5.53 / 60	9.01 / 51	2.08	0.47
AA	Wells Fargo DJ Tgt Today A	STWRX	C-	(800) 222-8222	E+ / 0.6	1.54	-1.17	3.39 / 3	1.13 / 19	1.64 / 7	0.94	0.84

RISK	3 Year		NET ASSETS		ASSET					BULL / BEAR		FUND MANAGER		MINIMUMS		LOADS	
Risk Rating/Pts	Standard Deviation	Beta	NAV As of 2/28/17	Total $(Mil)	Cash %	Stocks %	Bonds %	Other %	Portfolio Turnover Ratio	Last Bull Market Return	Last Bear Market Return	Manager Quality Pct	Manager Tenure (Years)	Initial Purch. $	Additional Purch. $	Front End Load	Back End Load
B /8.7	3.2	0.35	12.55	49	1	15	82	2	36	N/A	N/A	62	11	0	0	0.0	0.0
B /8.7	3.2	0.35	12.54	83	1	15	82	2	36	20.2	-2.4	64	11	0	0	0.0	0.0
B+ /9.0	3.9	0.45	10.12	55	0	21	77	2	36	N/A	N/A	54	N/A	1,000	100	5.8	0.0
B+ /9.0	3.9	0.45	10.29	23	0	21	77	2	36	25.0	-4.7	57	N/A	1,000,000	0	0.0	0.0
B+ /9.0	3.9	0.45	10.26	N/A	0	21	77	2	36	N/A	N/A	51	N/A	0	0	0.0	0.0
B+ /9.0	3.8	0.45	10.16	106	0	21	77	2	36	N/A	N/A	59	N/A	0	0	0.0	0.0
B+ /9.0	3.9	0.45	10.15	125	0	21	77	2	36	27.2	-4.5	61	N/A	0	0	0.0	0.0
B /8.6	4.5	0.61	14.87	219	0	30	69	1	34	33.0	-7.5	46	11	1,000	100	5.8	0.0
B /8.6	4.5	0.61	15.09	203	0	30	69	1	34	34.0	-7.5	47	11	1,000,000	0	0.0	0.0
B /8.6	4.5	0.60	14.75	7	0	30	69	1	34	27.8	-7.8	36	11	1,000	100	0.0	0.0
B /8.6	4.6	0.61	14.81	N/A	0	30	69	1	34	N/A	N/A	42	11	0	0	0.0	0.0
B /8.6	4.5	0.60	15.15	360	0	30	69	1	34	N/A	N/A	51	11	0	0	0.0	0.0
B /8.6	4.5	0.61	15.14	646	0	30	69	1	34	36.7	-7.4	52	11	0	0	0.0	0.0
B /8.2	5.5	0.80	10.48	141	1	42	55	2	32	N/A	N/A	35	10	1,000	100	5.8	0.0
B /8.3	5.5	0.80	10.55	69	1	42	55	2	32	45.5	-10.7	38	10	1,000,000	0	0.0	0.0
B /8.3	5.5	0.80	10.49	1	1	42	55	2	32	N/A	N/A	33	10	0	0	0.0	0.0
B /8.2	5.5	0.80	10.52	277	1	42	55	2	32	N/A	N/A	40	10	0	0	0.0	0.0
B /8.2	5.5	0.80	10.51	370	1	42	55	2	32	48.0	-10.4	43	10	0	0	0.0	0.0
B- /7.7	6.7	1.01	16.70	231	1	55	42	2	30	55.9	-13.8	26	11	1,000	100	5.8	0.0
B- /7.7	6.8	1.02	16.94	269	1	55	42	2	30	57.1	-13.7	27	11	1,000,000	0	0.0	0.0
B- /7.7	6.7	1.01	16.24	5	1	55	42	2	30	49.6	-14.0	19	11	1,000	100	0.0	0.0
B- /7.7	6.7	1.02	16.66	1	1	55	42	2	30	N/A	N/A	24	11	0	0	0.0	0.0
B- /7.7	6.7	1.02	16.95	509	1	55	42	2	30	N/A	N/A	30	11	0	0	0.0	0.0
B- /7.7	6.7	1.02	16.93	617	1	55	42	2	30	60.1	-13.6	31	11	0	0	0.0	0.0
B- /7.2	8.0	1.22	11.25	127	2	68	29	1	28	N/A	N/A	18	10	1,000	100	5.8	0.0
B- /7.2	8.0	1.21	11.30	54	2	68	29	1	28	67.2	-16.2	19	10	1,000,000	0	0.0	0.0
B- /7.2	8.0	1.22	11.32	N/A	2	68	29	1	28	N/A	N/A	16	10	0	0	0.0	0.0
B- /7.2	8.0	1.21	11.27	243	2	68	29	1	28	N/A	N/A	21	10	0	0	0.0	0.0
B- /7.2	8.0	1.21	11.27	315	2	68	29	1	28	70.4	-16.0	22	10	0	0	0.0	0.0
C+ /6.7	9.0	1.36	19.43	219	2	77	20	1	27	73.9	-17.8	13	11	1,000	100	5.8	0.0
C+ /6.8	9.0	1.37	19.82	202	2	77	20	1	27	75.3	-17.8	14	11	1,000,000	0	0.0	0.0
C+ /6.7	9.0	1.37	18.19	5	2	77	20	1	27	67.0	-18.1	9	11	1,000	100	0.0	0.0
C+ /6.7	9.0	1.37	19.36	N/A	2	77	20	1	27	N/A	N/A	11	11	0	0	0.0	0.0
C+ /6.7	9.0	1.37	19.86	390	2	77	20	1	27	N/A	N/A	15	11	0	0	0.0	0.0
C+ /6.7	9.0	1.37	19.85	490	2	77	20	1	27	78.6	-17.6	16	11	0	0	0.0	0.0
C+ /6.5	9.6	1.47	11.91	71	3	84	11	2	26	N/A	N/A	10	10	1,000	100	5.8	0.0
C+ /6.5	9.6	1.47	12.01	44	3	84	11	2	26	79.5	-18.5	11	10	1,000,000	0	0.0	0.0
C+ /6.5	9.6	1.46	12.04	N/A	3	84	11	2	26	N/A	N/A	9	10	0	0	0.0	0.0
C+ /6.5	9.7	1.47	11.96	154	3	84	11	2	26	N/A	N/A	12	10	0	0	0.0	0.0
C+ /6.5	9.6	1.47	11.93	218	3	84	11	2	26	82.8	-18.3	13	10	0	0	0.0	0.0
C+ /6.4	9.8	1.49	11.40	64	4	87	8	1	26	N/A	N/A	10	N/A	1,000	100	5.8	0.0
C+ /6.4	9.9	1.50	11.41	125	4	87	8	1	26	80.5	-18.4	11	N/A	1,000,000	0	0.0	0.0
C+ /6.4	9.8	1.49	11.36	1	4	87	8	1	26	N/A	N/A	7	N/A	1,000	100	0.0	0.0
C+ /6.4	9.8	1.50	11.43	N/A	4	87	8	1	26	N/A	N/A	8	N/A	0	0	0.0	0.0
C+ /6.4	9.9	1.50	11.45	245	4	87	8	1	26	N/A	N/A	11	N/A	0	0	0.0	0.0
C+ /6.4	9.9	1.50	11.44	286	4	87	8	1	26	84.0	-18.3	12	N/A	0	0	0.0	0.0
C+ /6.9	9.9	1.50	13.91	9	4	87	8	1	26	N/A	N/A	9	N/A	1,000	100	5.8	0.0
C+ /6.7	9.8	1.49	13.91	12	4	87	8	1	26	79.9	N/A	11	N/A	1,000,000	0	0.0	0.0
C+ /6.9	9.9	1.50	13.76	N/A	4	87	8	1	26	N/A	N/A	8	N/A	0	0	0.0	0.0
C+ /6.9	9.8	1.49	13.94	44	4	87	8	1	26	N/A	N/A	12	N/A	0	0	0.0	0.0
C+ /6.7	9.9	1.50	13.91	63	4	87	8	1	26	83.2	N/A	12	N/A	0	0	0.0	0.0
B+ /9.3	2.9	0.31	10.56	56	1	14	83	2	36	12.8	-0.7	60	11	1,000	100	5.8	0.0

99 Pct = Best
0 Pct = Worst

Fund Type	Fund Name	Ticker Symbol	Overall Investment Rating	Phone	Performance Rating/Pts	3 Mo	6 Mo	1Yr / Pct	3Yr / Pct	5Yr / Pct	Dividend Yield	Expense Ratio
AA	Wells Fargo DJ Tgt Today Adm	WFLOX	C-	(800) 222-8222	D- / 1.0	1.50	-1.15	3.41 / 3	1.24 / 20	1.77 / 8	1.07	0.76
AA	Wells Fargo DJ Tgt Today C	WFODX	C-	(800) 222-8222	E+ / 0.8	1.43	-1.50	2.57 / 2	0.39 / 15	0.88 / 6	0.36	1.59
AA	Wells Fargo DJ Tgt Today R	WFRRX	C-	(800) 222-8222	E+ / 0.9	1.47	-1.24	3.13 / 3	0.86 / 17	--	0.84	1.09
AA	Wells Fargo DJ Tgt Today R4	WOTRX	C-	(800) 222-8222	D- / 1.1	1.61	-1.03	3.71 / 3	1.46 / 21	--	1.26	0.56
AA	Wells Fargo DJ Tgt Today R6	WOTDX	C	(800) 222-8222	D- / 1.2	1.70	-0.94	3.81 / 3	1.63 / 22	2.15 / 8	1.54	0.41
GR	Wells Fargo Dscpld US Core A	EVSAX	B	(800) 222-8222	B+ / 8.5	7.38	9.97	23.05 / 67	11.11 / 97	14.03 / 93	0.90	0.87
GR	Wells Fargo Dscpld US Core Adm	EVSYX	B+	(800) 222-8222	A / 9.4	7.40	10.07	23.19 / 67	11.29 / 97	14.21 / 94	0.99	0.79
GR	Wells Fargo Dscpld US Core C	EVSTX	B	(800) 222-8222	B+ / 8.9	7.17	9.65	22.10 / 63	10.31 / 95	13.19 / 86	0.65	1.62
GR	Wells Fargo Dscpld US Core I	EVSIX	B+	(800) 222-8222	A / 9.5	7.44	10.22	23.49 / 68	11.57 / 98	14.50 / 96	1.29	0.54
GI	Wells Fargo Dscpld US Core R6	EVSRX	U	(800) 222-8222	U /	7.49	10.24	23.55 / 68	--	--	1.32	0.44
BA	Wells Fargo Dvsfd Cap Bldr A	EKBAX	B+	(800) 222-8222	B+ / 8.8	6.35	9.00	28.88 / 84	10.74 / 96	13.19 / 86	1.48	1.15
BA	Wells Fargo Dvsfd Cap Bldr Adm	EKBDX	A-	(800) 222-8222	A / 9.5	6.25	8.92	28.91 / 84	10.92 / 97	13.41 / 88	1.68	1.07
BA ●	Wells Fargo Dvsfd Cap Bldr B	EKBBX	A-	(800) 222-8222	A- / 9.1	6.10	8.59	27.88 / 81	9.92 / 93	12.35 / 78	0.69	1.90
BA	Wells Fargo Dvsfd Cap Bldr C	EKBCX	A-	(800) 222-8222	A- / 9.1	6.06	8.62	27.97 / 82	9.94 / 93	12.33 / 77	0.91	1.90
BA	Wells Fargo Dvsfd Cap Bldr I	EKBYX	A	(800) 222-8222	A+ / 9.6	6.39	9.15	29.25 / 85	11.16 / 97	13.64 / 90	1.89	0.82
GR	Wells Fargo Dvsfd Eqty A	NVDAX	C-	(800) 222-8222	C / 5.3	7.41	8.28	22.00 / 62	5.67 / 61	10.52 / 62	0.70	1.41
GR	Wells Fargo Dvsfd Eqty Adm	NVDEX	C	(800) 222-8222	C+ / 6.7	7.45	8.44	22.27 / 63	5.93 / 64	10.80 / 64	0.96	1.33
GR	Wells Fargo Dvsfd Eqty C	WFDEX	C-	(800) 222-8222	C+ / 5.9	7.20	7.86	21.04 / 58	4.88 / 53	9.69 / 56	0.07	2.16
FO	Wells Fargo Dvsfd Intl A	SILAX	D-	(800) 222-8222	E+ / 0.8	7.44	4.65	15.17 / 31	-0.90 / 10	4.76 / 20	1.80	1.82
FO	Wells Fargo Dvsfd Intl Adm	WFIEX	D	(800) 222-8222	D- / 1.3	7.54	4.70	15.34 / 31	-0.75 / 10	4.93 / 21	2.00	1.74
FO	Wells Fargo Dvsfd Intl C	WFECX	D-	(800) 222-8222	D / 1.0	7.25	4.22	14.36 / 27	-1.64 / 8	4.02 / 15	1.30	2.57
FO	Wells Fargo Dvsfd Intl Inst	WFISX	D	(800) 222-8222	D- / 1.3	7.49	4.78	15.58 / 32	-0.53 / 11	5.09 / 22	2.27	1.49
EM	Wells Fargo Em Mkts Eq Inc A	EQIAX	D+	(800) 222-8222	D+ / 2.9	8.67	4.88	19.56 / 50	2.38 / 27	--	2.11	1.88
EM	Wells Fargo Em Mkts Eq Inc Adm	EQIDX	C-	(800) 222-8222	C- / 4.2	8.76	5.12	20.06 / 52	2.63 / 29	--	2.12	1.80
EM	Wells Fargo Em Mkts Eq Inc C	EQICX	D+	(800) 222-8222	C- / 3.4	8.56	4.61	18.79 / 46	1.64 / 22	--	1.58	2.63
EM	Wells Fargo Em Mkts Eq Inc Inst	EQIIX	C-	(800) 222-8222	C / 4.3	8.82	5.11	20.17 / 53	2.79 / 30	--	2.55	1.55
EM	Wells Fargo Emerg Mkts Eq A	EMGAX	D	(800) 222-8222	C- / 3.0	6.38	2.52	28.99 / 84	1.44 / 21	-0.84 / 4	0.58	1.61
EM	Wells Fargo Emerg Mkts Eq Adm	EMGYX	D+	(800) 222-8222	C- / 4.2	6.38	2.61	29.11 / 84	1.57 / 21	-0.70 / 4	0.73	1.53
EM ●	Wells Fargo Emerg Mkts Eq B	EMGBX	D	(800) 222-8222	C- / 3.5	6.13	2.16	28.04 / 82	0.70 / 17	-1.59 / 3	0.00	2.36
EM	Wells Fargo Emerg Mkts Eq C	EMGCX	D	(800) 222-8222	C- / 3.5	6.18	2.18	28.02 / 82	0.70 / 17	-1.58 / 3	0.00	2.36
EM	Wells Fargo Emerg Mkts Eq Inst	EMGNX	D+	(800) 222-8222	C / 4.4	6.46	2.77	29.44 / 85	1.86 / 23	-0.43 / 4	1.00	1.28
EM	Wells Fargo Emerg Mkts Eq R6	EMGDX	D+	(800) 222-8222	C / 4.5	6.46	2.77	29.52 / 85	1.90 / 23	--	1.04	1.18
EM ●	Wells Fargo Emerging Gr A	WEMAX	E+	(800) 222-8222	C / 4.6	5.32	6.81	36.57 / 95	1.92 / 23	9.34 / 53	0.00	1.34
EM ●	Wells Fargo Emerging Gr Adm	WFGDX	D-	(800) 222-8222	C+ / 5.9	5.41	6.95	36.89 / 96	2.09 / 25	9.54 / 55	0.00	1.26
EM ●	Wells Fargo Emerging Gr C	WEMCX	E+	(800) 222-8222	C / 5.1	5.08	6.46	35.61 / 95	1.15 / 19	8.53 / 47	0.00	2.09
EM ●	Wells Fargo Emerging Gr I	WEMIX	D	(800) 222-8222	C+ / 6.2	5.45	7.15	37.32 / 96	2.38 / 27	9.86 / 57	0.00	1.01
OT	Wells Fargo Endeavor Sel A	STAEX	E	(800) 222-8222	C / 4.3	7.73	6.87	18.57 / 45	4.98 / 54	10.70 / 63	0.00	1.28
OT	Wells Fargo Endeavor Sel Adm	WECDX	D-	(800) 222-8222	C+ / 5.8	7.93	6.99	18.83 / 46	5.26 / 57	11.00 / 66	0.00	1.20
OT	Wells Fargo Endeavor Sel C	WECCX	E+	(800) 222-8222	C / 4.9	7.58	6.50	17.64 / 41	4.20 / 45	9.89 / 58	0.00	2.03
OT	Wells Fargo Endeavor Sel I	WFCIX	D-	(800) 222-8222	C+ / 6.0	7.88	7.20	19.11 / 48	5.43 / 59	11.18 / 67	0.06	0.95
MC	Wells Fargo Enterprise Adm	SEPKX	D+	(800) 222-8222	C+ / 5.9	8.19	8.36	26.86 / 79	3.39 / 36	10.31 / 61	0.00	1.17
MC	Wells Fargo Enterprise Adv	SENAX	D	(800) 222-8222	C / 4.6	8.15	8.31	26.74 / 78	3.25 / 34	10.19 / 60	0.00	1.25
MC	Wells Fargo Enterprise C	WENCX	D	(800) 222-8222	C / 5.1	7.95	7.89	25.77 / 75	2.48 / 27	9.37 / 54	0.00	2.00
MC	Wells Fargo Enterprise I	WFEIX	C-	(800) 222-8222	C+ / 6.1	8.25	8.49	27.15 / 80	3.60 / 38	10.55 / 62	0.00	0.92
GL	Wells Fargo Global Opps A	EKGAX	C-	(800) 222-8222	C+ / 5.6	5.72	7.20	27.15 / 80	5.57 / 60	10.50 / 62	0.76	1.55
GL	Wells Fargo Global Opps Adm	EKGYX	C	(800) 222-8222	C+ / 6.9	5.75	7.30	27.32 / 80	5.73 / 62	10.67 / 63	0.86	1.47
GL ●	Wells Fargo Global Opps B	EKGBX	C-	(800) 222-8222	C+ / 6.2	5.54	6.83	26.22 / 77	4.78 / 52	9.68 / 56	0.00	2.30
GL	Wells Fargo Global Opps C	EKGCX	C-	(800) 222-8222	C+ / 6.1	5.51	6.79	26.17 / 77	4.78 / 52	9.68 / 56	0.22	2.30
GL	Wells Fargo Global Opps Inst	EKGIX	C	(800) 222-8222	B- / 7.0	5.82	7.42	27.63 / 81	6.00 / 64	10.95 / 65	1.12	1.22
BA	Wells Fargo Gro Bal A	WFGBX	C+	(800) 222-8222	C- / 3.6	5.26	5.16	15.39 / 32	5.29 / 58	9.07 / 51	0.93	1.35
BA	Wells Fargo Gro Bal Adm	NVGBX	B-	(800) 222-8222	C / 5.0	5.35	5.29	15.73 / 33	5.56 / 60	9.35 / 53	1.38	1.27
BA	Wells Fargo Gro Bal C	WFGWX	C+	(800) 222-8222	C- / 4.1	5.09	4.76	14.57 / 28	4.51 / 49	8.26 / 44	0.50	2.10

● Denotes fund is closed to new investors
* Denotes fund is included in Section II

Risk Rating/Pts	3 Year Standard Deviation	Beta	NAV As of 2/28/17	Total $(Mil)	Cash %	Stocks %	Bonds %	Other %	Portfolio Turnover Ratio	Last Bull Market Return	Last Bear Market Return	Manager Quality Pct	Manager Tenure (Years)	Initial Purch. $	Additional Purch. $	Front End Load	Back End Load
B+ / 9.3	2.9	0.31	10.78	43	1	14	83	2	36	13.7	-0.6	61	11	1,000,000	0	0.0	0.0
B+ / 9.4	2.9	0.31	10.77	3	1	14	83	2	36	8.4	-1.0	50	11	1,000	100	0.0	0.0
B+ / 9.3	2.9	0.32	10.53	N/A	1	14	83	2	36	N/A	N/A	55	11	0	0	0.0	0.0
B+ / 9.3	2.9	0.31	10.81	249	1	14	83	2	36	N/A	N/A	64	11	0	0	0.0	0.0
B+ / 9.3	2.9	0.31	10.78	69	1	14	83	2	36	15.9	-0.5	66	11	0	0	0.0	0.0
C / 4.6	10.0	0.96	15.56	460	0	98	1	1	52	138.4	-16.8	80	6	1,000	100	5.8	0.0
C / 4.6	10.0	0.96	15.95	83	0	98	1	1	52	140.5	-16.8	81	6	1,000,000	0	0.0	0.0
C / 4.4	10.0	0.96	14.41	55	0	98	1	1	52	129.1	-17.1	75	6	1,000	100	0.0	0.0
C / 4.6	10.0	0.96	15.77	307	0	98	1	1	52	143.8	-16.6	82	6	1,000,000	0	0.0	0.0
U /	N/A	N/A	15.93	26	0	98	1	1	52	N/A	N/A	N/A	6	0	0	0.0	0.0
C / 5.5	9.4	1.36	9.87	536	7	69	22	2	73	126.5	-23.2	77	10	1,000	100	5.8	0.0
C / 5.4	9.3	1.36	9.87	22	7	69	22	2	73	128.8	-23.1	78	10	1,000,000	0	0.0	0.0
C / 5.5	9.4	1.36	9.98	1	7	69	22	2	73	117.3	-23.4	70	10	1,000	100	0.0	0.0
C / 5.5	9.4	1.37	9.86	90	7	69	22	2	73	117.3	-23.4	70	10	1,000	100	0.0	0.0
C / 5.4	9.3	1.36	9.81	179	7	69	22	2	73	131.5	-23.1	80	10	1,000,000	0	0.0	0.0
C / 4.3	10.9	1.02	28.42	68	25	73	1	1	39	101.4	-19.6	17	12	1,000	100	5.8	0.0
C / 4.3	10.9	1.02	28.49	127	25	73	1	1	39	104.2	-19.5	19	12	1,000,000	0	0.0	0.0
C- / 4.1	10.9	1.03	26.04	2	25	73	1	1	39	93.4	-19.8	11	12	1,000	100	0.0	0.0
C+ / 6.1	11.7	0.93	11.46	60	2	95	2	1	50	51.4	-24.3	65	13	1,000	100	5.8	0.0
C+ / 6.0	11.7	0.93	11.67	10	2	95	2	1	50	52.6	-24.2	67	13	1,000,000	0	0.0	0.0
C+ / 6.0	11.7	0.93	10.56	4	2	95	2	1	50	45.4	-24.5	56	13	1,000	100	0.0	0.0
C+ / 6.0	11.7	0.92	10.95	29	2	95	2	1	50	54.2	-24.2	70	13	1,000,000	0	0.0	0.0
C+ / 5.8	13.1	0.80	10.62	28	8	90	0	2	64	N/A	N/A	81	5	1,000	100	5.8	0.0
C+ / 5.8	13.2	0.80	10.70	12	8	90	0	2	64	N/A	N/A	82	5	1,000,000	0	0.0	0.0
C+ / 5.8	13.1	0.80	10.58	14	8	90	0	2	64	N/A	N/A	76	5	1,000	100	0.0	0.0
C+ / 5.8	13.2	0.80	10.65	387	8	90	0	2	64	N/A	N/A	83	5	1,000,000	0	0.0	0.0
C / 4.4	15.8	0.95	20.50	902	1	97	1	1	8	12.7	-20.4	72	11	1,000	100	5.8	0.0
C / 4.5	15.8	0.95	21.52	138	1	97	1	1	8	13.7	-20.4	73	11	1,000,000	0	0.0	0.0
C / 4.5	15.8	0.95	17.49	N/A	1	97	1	1	8	8.2	-20.7	63	11	1,000	100	0.0	0.0
C / 4.5	15.8	0.95	17.36	66	1	97	1	1	8	8.2	-20.7	63	11	1,000	100	0.0	0.0
C / 4.4	15.8	0.95	21.41	1,847	1	97	1	1	8	15.3	-20.3	75	11	1,000,000	0	0.0	0.0
C / 4.4	15.8	0.95	21.40	140	1	97	1	1	8	N/A	N/A	76	11	0	0	0.0	0.0
D- / 1.1	20.5	0.49	14.16	133	1	97	0	2	66	102.1	-23.5	81	10	1,000	100	5.8	0.0
D- / 1.1	20.6	0.50	14.51	55	1	97	0	2	66	104.0	-23.4	82	10	1,000,000	0	0.0	0.0
D- / 1.0	20.5	0.49	12.93	4	1	97	0	2	66	94.1	-23.7	76	10	1,000	100	0.0	0.0
D- / 1.2	20.6	0.50	15.01	534	1	97	0	2	66	107.2	-23.3	84	10	1,000,000	0	0.0	0.0
E / 0.4	12.1	1.01	8.01	15	0	98	0	2	79	105.1	-19.9	13	7	1,000	100	5.8	0.0
E / 0.4	12.0	1.01	8.47	4	0	98	0	2	79	108.0	-19.8	15	7	1,000,000	0	0.0	0.0
E / 0.4	12.0	1.00	6.01	4	0	98	0	2	79	97.0	-20.2	9	7	1,000	100	0.0	0.0
E / 0.4	12.1	1.01	8.76	144	0	98	0	2	79	109.9	-19.7	16	7	5,000,000	0	0.0	0.0
C- / 3.2	13.6	1.00	45.46	5	1	98	0	1	99	110.3	-24.8	10	6	1,000,000	0	0.0	0.0
C- / 3.1	13.6	1.00	43.41	554	1	98	0	1	99	109.2	-24.9	9	6	1,000	100	5.8	0.0
D+ / 2.8	13.6	1.00	39.27	9	1	98	0	1	99	100.9	-25.1	6	6	1,000	100	0.0	0.0
C- / 3.3	13.6	1.00	47.13	52	1	98	0	1	99	112.9	-24.8	11	6	1,000,000	0	0.0	0.0
C- / 4.2	11.2	0.70	39.61	151	3	90	5	2	70	99.6	-29.1	96	12	1,000	100	5.8	0.0
C / 4.3	11.2	0.70	41.28	27	3	90	5	2	70	101.3	-29.0	96	12	1,000,000	0	0.0	0.0
C- / 3.4	11.2	0.70	29.11	1	3	90	5	2	70	91.7	-29.3	95	12	1,000	100	0.0	0.0
C- / 3.4	11.2	0.70	29.24	34	3	90	5	2	70	91.7	-29.3	95	12	1,000	100	0.0	0.0
C / 4.3	11.2	0.70	41.12	26	3	90	5	2	70	104.1	-28.9	97	12	1,000,000	0	0.0	0.0
B- / 7.9	7.3	1.13	42.82	65	0	64	35	1	79	82.3	-16.4	34	12	1,000	100	5.8	0.0
B- / 7.9	7.3	1.13	38.23	159	0	64	35	1	79	84.8	-16.3	37	12	1,000,000	0	0.0	0.0
B- / 7.9	7.3	1.13	37.27	17	0	64	35	1	79	75.1	-16.7	26	12	1,000	100	0.0	0.0

Fund Type	Fund Name	Ticker Symbol	Overall Investment Rating	Phone	Performance Rating/Pts	3 Mo	6 Mo	1Yr / Pct	3Yr / Pct	5Yr / Pct	Dividend Yield	Expense Ratio
								Total Return % through 2/28/17	Annualized		Incl. in Returns	
GR	Wells Fargo Growth Adm	SGRKX	D	(800) 222-8222	C / 5.4	8.48	5.43	22.17 /63	4.11 /44	9.77 /57	0.00	1.07
GR	Wells Fargo Growth Adv	SGRAX	E+	(800) 222-8222	C- / 4.0	8.42	5.34	21.94 /62	3.90 /42	9.54 /55	0.00	1.15
GR	Wells Fargo Growth C	WGFCX	E+	(800) 222-8222	C / 4.6	8.19	4.92	21.00 /57	3.12 /33	8.71 /48	0.00	1.90
GR	Wells Fargo Growth Instl	SGRNX	D	(800) 222-8222	C+ / 5.6	8.54	5.54	22.44 /64	4.33 /47	10.01 /58	0.00	0.82
GR	Wells Fargo Growth R6	SGRHX	U	(800) 222-8222	U /	8.56	5.59	22.53 /65	--	--	0.00	0.72
IX	Wells Fargo Index A	WFILX	B+	(800) 222-8222	B / 8.2	7.93	9.78	24.42 /71	10.09 /94	13.43 /88	1.56	0.63
IX	Wells Fargo Index Adm	WFIOX	A	(800) 222-8222	A / 9.3	7.97	9.87	24.66 /72	10.38 /95	13.74 /91	1.79	0.40
AA	Wells Fargo Index Asst All A	SFAAX	B-	(800) 222-8222	C / 5.5	4.79	5.39	14.21 /26	8.66 /84	10.84 /65	0.68	1.20
AA	Wells Fargo Index Asst All Adm	WFAIX	B-	(800) 222-8222	C+ / 6.8	4.85	5.49	14.43 /27	8.91 /86	11.10 /67	0.91	1.12
AA	Wells Fargo Index Asst All C	WFALX	B	(800) 222-8222	C+ / 6.0	4.61	4.96	13.31 /23	7.84 /78	10.01 /58	0.11	1.95
IX	● Wells Fargo Index B	WFIMX	A-	(800) 222-8222	B+ / 8.6	7.71	9.36	23.48 /68	9.26 /89	12.57 /80	0.26	1.38
IX	Wells Fargo Index C	WFINX	A-	(800) 222-8222	B+ / 8.6	7.72	9.37	23.51 /68	9.27 /89	12.58 /80	1.01	1.38
FO	Wells Fargo Intl Equity A	WFEAX	D+	(800) 222-8222	C- / 3.5	8.55	7.67	22.76 /66	2.36 /26	5.34 /24	2.66	1.51
FO	Wells Fargo Intl Equity Adm	WFEDX	C-	(800) 222-8222	C / 4.7	8.58	7.69	22.71 /65	2.37 /27	5.34 /24	2.76	1.43
FO	● Wells Fargo Intl Equity B	WFEBX	C-	(800) 222-8222	C- / 4.1	8.39	7.30	21.84 /61	1.60 /22	4.54 /18	1.11	2.26
FO	Wells Fargo Intl Equity C	WFEFX	C-	(800) 222-8222	C- / 4.1	8.35	7.26	21.77 /61	1.62 /22	4.56 /19	2.01	2.26
FO	Wells Fargo Intl Equity Inst	WFENX	C	(800) 222-8222	C / 5.0	8.68	7.80	23.06 /67	2.66 /29	5.60 /26	3.09	1.18
FO	Wells Fargo Intl Equity R	WFERX	C-	(800) 222-8222	C / 4.5	8.54	7.57	22.45 /64	2.13 /25	5.07 /22	2.53	1.76
FO	Wells Fargo Intl Val A	WFFAX	D-	(800) 222-8222	D- / 1.1	8.92	9.17	20.52 /55	-0.94 /10	4.43 /18	2.06	1.46
FO	Wells Fargo Intl Val Adm	WFVDX	D	(800) 222-8222	D / 1.7	8.94	9.11	20.57 /55	-0.85 /10	4.59 /19	1.76	1.38
FO	Wells Fargo Intl Val C	WFVCX	D-	(800) 222-8222	D- / 1.3	8.68	8.68	19.63 /50	-1.68 / 7	3.64 /14	1.18	2.21
FO	Wells Fargo Intl Val Inst	WFVIX	D	(800) 222-8222	D / 1.8	8.89	9.23	20.86 /57	-0.57 /11	4.84 /20	2.27	1.13
SC	Wells Fargo Intr Sm Cp Vl A	WFSMX	B+	(800) 222-8222	B+ / 8.9	5.43	14.46	38.13 /96	8.23 /81	13.58 /90	0.42	1.47
SC	Wells Fargo Intr Sm Cp Vl Adm	WFSDX	A	(800) 222-8222	A+ / 9.6	5.51	14.55	38.43 /97	8.43 /82	13.82 /92	0.53	1.39
SC	Wells Fargo Intr Sm Cp Vl C	WSCDX	A-	(800) 222-8222	A / 9.3	5.29	14.07	37.19 /96	7.44 /75	12.74 /81	0.00	2.22
SC	Wells Fargo Intr Sm Cp Vl Inst	WFSSX	A	(800) 222-8222	A+ / 9.6	5.56	14.67	38.71 /97	8.65 /84	14.06 /94	0.73	1.14
GR	Wells Fargo Intr Value A	EIVAX	C-	(800) 222-8222	C / 5.2	5.65	7.83	19.50 /49	6.48 /68	11.38 /69	1.03	1.18
GR	Wells Fargo Intr Value Adm	EIVDX	C	(800) 222-8222	C+ / 6.5	5.62	7.96	19.65 /50	6.65 /69	11.59 /71	1.23	1.10
GR	● Wells Fargo Intr Value B	EIVBX	C	(800) 222-8222	C+ / 5.8	5.45	7.49	18.64 /46	5.68 /61	10.54 /62	0.00	1.93
GR	Wells Fargo Intr Value C	EIVCX	C	(800) 222-8222	C+ / 5.8	5.49	7.46	18.61 /46	5.68 /61	10.54 /62	0.30	1.93
GR	Wells Fargo Intr Value Inst	EIVIX	C+	(800) 222-8222	C+ / 6.7	5.79	8.14	19.97 /52	6.95 /72	11.86 /73	1.46	0.85
GR	Wells Fargo Intr Value R	EIVTX	C	(800) 222-8222	C+ / 6.2	5.53	7.69	19.15 /48	6.21 /66	--	0.86	1.43
GR	Wells Fargo Intr Value R4	EIVRX	C+	(800) 222-8222	C+ / 6.7	5.75	8.02	19.87 /51	6.83 /71	--	1.35	0.90
GR	Wells Fargo Intr Value R6	EIVFX	C	(800) 222-8222	C+ / 6.7	5.81	8.19	20.12 /53	6.86 /71	--	1.50	0.75
GL	Wells Fargo Intr World Eq A	EWEAX	D+	(800) 222-8222	C- / 3.8	7.10	7.53	21.47 /60	3.47 /37	7.95 /42	1.05	1.45
GL	Wells Fargo Intr World Eq Adm	EWEIX	C-	(800) 222-8222	C / 5.2	7.11	7.60	21.55 /60	3.67 /39	8.19 /44	1.14	1.37
GL	Wells Fargo Intr World Eq C	EWECX	D+	(800) 222-8222	C / 4.3	6.86	7.14	20.50 /55	2.69 /29	7.15 /36	0.40	2.20
GL	Wells Fargo Intr World Eq Inst	EWENX	C-	(800) 222-8222	C / 5.4	7.17	7.76	21.90 /62	3.91 /42	8.43 /46	1.48	1.12
GR	Wells Fargo Large Cap Core A	EGOAX	A-	(800) 222-8222	B / 8.0	7.79	13.96	25.26 /74	8.83 /86	13.74 /91	0.68	1.20
GR	Wells Fargo Large Cap Core Adm	WFLLX	A+	(800) 222-8222	A- / 9.1	7.85	14.01	25.36 /74	9.04 /87	13.99 /93	0.02	1.12
GR	Wells Fargo Large Cap Core C	EGOCX	A	(800) 222-8222	B+ / 8.5	7.62	13.54	24.28 /71	8.04 /79	12.90 /83	0.00	1.95
GR	Wells Fargo Large Cap Core I	EGOIX	A+	(800) 222-8222	A / 9.3	7.91	14.19	25.78 /76	9.33 /89	14.28 /95	1.17	0.87
GR	Wells Fargo Large Cap Gr A	STAFX	D+	(800) 222-8222	C- / 3.9	7.42	5.49	16.15 /35	5.11 /55	10.07 /59	0.00	1.16
GR	Wells Fargo Large Cap Gr Adm	STDFX	C-	(800) 222-8222	C / 5.2	7.45	5.56	16.29 /35	5.24 /57	10.20 /60	0.03	1.08
GR	Wells Fargo Large Cap Gr C	STOFX	C-	(800) 222-8222	C / 4.4	7.23	5.09	15.30 /31	4.33 /47	9.25 /53	0.00	1.91
GR	Wells Fargo Large Cap Gr Inst	STNFX	C	(800) 222-8222	C / 5.4	7.52	5.67	16.52 /36	5.51 /60	10.49 /62	0.11	0.83
GI	Wells Fargo Large Cap Gr R	STMFX	C-	(800) 222-8222	C / 4.9	7.33	5.36	15.86 /34	4.84 /52	--	0.00	1.41
GI	Wells Fargo Large Cap Gr R4	SLGRX	C	(800) 222-8222	C / 5.4	7.51	5.66	16.50 /36	5.43 /59	--	0.10	0.88
GI	Wells Fargo Large Cap Gr R6	STFFX	C	(800) 222-8222	C / 5.5	7.55	5.73	16.65 /37	5.59 /60	--	0.15	0.73
GI	Wells Fargo Lg Co Val A	WLCAX	C+	(800) 222-8222	C+ / 6.7	7.30	11.70	26.11 /77	6.47 /68	11.40 /69	0.91	0.94
GI	Wells Fargo Lg Co Val Adm	WWIDX	B-	(800) 222-8222	B / 7.8	7.27	11.74	26.25 /77	6.66 /70	11.64 /71	1.01	0.86
GI	Wells Fargo Lg Co Val C	WFLVX	C+	(800) 222-8222	B- / 7.1	7.05	11.24	25.09 /74	5.65 /61	10.56 /63	0.35	1.69

99 Pct = Best
0 Pct = Worst

● Denotes fund is closed to new investors
* Denotes fund is included in Section II

www.thestreetratings.com

RISK Risk Rating/Pts	3 Year Standard Deviation	Beta	NET ASSETS NAV As of 2/28/17	Total $(Mil)	ASSET Cash %	Stocks %	Bonds %	Other %	Portfolio Turnover Ratio	BULL / BEAR Last Bull Market Return	Last Bear Market Return	FUND MANAGER Manager Quality Pct	Manager Tenure (Years)	MINIMUMS Initial Purch. $	Additional Purch. $	LOADS Front End Load	Back End Load
D /2.0	13.7	1.09	40.25	712	0	98	1	1	38	100.4	-16.2	6	15	1,000,000	0	0.0	0.0
D /1.6	13.7	1.09	36.64	2,081	0	98	1	1	38	98.1	-16.3	5	15	1,000	100	5.8	0.0
E+ /0.9	13.7	1.09	31.00	222	0	98	1	1	38	90.2	-16.5	4	15	1,000	100	5.8	0.0
D /2.1	13.7	1.09	42.64	1,769	0	98	1	1	38	102.7	-16.1	6	15	1,000,000	0	0.0	0.0
U /	N/A	N/A	42.69	26	0	98	1	1	38	N/A	N/A	N/A	15	0	0	0.0	0.0
C+ /6.0	10.3	1.00	65.25	677	0	99	0	1	4	128.2	-16.4	69	4	1,000	100	5.8	0.0
C+ /6.0	10.3	1.00	65.78	1,347	0	99	0	1	4	131.7	-16.3	72	4	1,000,000	0	0.0	0.0
B- /7.9	6.4	1.00	30.80	846	0	60	39	1	8	94.4	-8.9	81	11	1,000	100	5.8	0.0
B- /7.9	6.4	1.00	30.82	222	0	60	39	1	8	96.9	-8.8	83	11	1,000,000	0	0.0	0.0
B /8.0	6.4	1.00	18.72	154	0	60	39	1	8	86.7	-9.2	76	11	1,000	100	0.0	0.0
C+ /6.3	10.3	1.00	67.52	N/A	0	99	0	1	4	119.1	-16.7	59	4	1,000	100	0.0	0.0
C+ /6.1	10.3	1.00	65.63	87	0	99	0	1	4	119.2	-16.7	59	4	1,000	100	0.0	0.0
C+ /5.7	12.8	0.95	11.66	121	3	89	6	2	65	54.9	-26.0	88	5	1,000	100	5.8	0.0
C+ /5.7	12.8	0.95	11.46	21	3	89	6	2	65	54.9	-26.0	88	5	1,000,000	0	0.0	0.0
C+ /5.7	12.8	0.95	11.55	1	3	89	6	2	65	48.8	-26.3	85	5	1,000	100	0.0	0.0
C+ /5.7	12.7	0.94	11.46	26	3	89	6	2	65	48.7	-26.3	85	5	1,000	100	0.0	0.0
C+ /5.7	12.8	0.95	11.62	198	3	89	6	2	65	57.1	-25.9	90	5	1,000,000	0	0.0	0.0
C+ /5.7	12.8	0.95	11.82	2	3	89	6	2	65	52.9	-26.1	87	5	0	0	0.0	0.0
C+ /5.8	12.5	0.98	13.83	50	3	96	0	1	14	42.5	-23.0	65	14	1,000	100	5.8	0.0
C+ /6.0	12.5	0.99	13.98	5	3	96	0	1	14	43.8	-22.9	66	14	1,000,000	0	0.0	0.0
C+ /5.9	12.5	0.98	13.60	1	3	96	0	1	14	36.8	-23.2	55	14	1,000	100	0.0	0.0
C+ /5.8	12.4	0.98	13.74	643	3	96	0	1	14	45.7	-22.8	70	14	1,000,000	0	0.0	0.0
C /5.4	15.3	0.92	29.26	58	3	90	6	1	66	145.7	-28.0	85	1	1,000	100	5.8	0.0
C /5.4	15.3	0.92	29.78	4	3	90	6	1	66	148.5	-27.9	86	1	1,000,000	0	0.0	0.0
C /5.4	15.3	0.92	27.48	1	3	90	6	1	66	135.9	-28.2	81	1	1,000	100	0.0	0.0
C /5.4	15.3	0.92	30.08	64	3	90	6	1	66	151.4	-27.9	87	1	1,000,000	0	0.0	0.0
C /4.8	10.5	1.00	12.06	302	0	97	2	1	34	105.9	-19.5	25	11	1,000	100	5.8	0.0
C /4.9	10.5	1.00	12.59	460	0	97	2	1	34	108.0	-19.4	27	11	1,000,000	0	0.0	0.0
C /4.9	10.5	1.00	11.97	N/A	0	97	2	1	34	97.6	-19.8	18	11	1,000	100	0.0	0.0
C /4.9	10.5	1.00	11.82	25	0	97	2	1	34	97.5	-19.7	18	11	1,000	100	0.0	0.0
C /4.8	10.5	1.00	12.12	166	0	97	2	1	34	110.7	-19.3	30	11	1,000,000	0	0.0	0.0
C /4.9	10.5	1.00	12.16	N/A	0	97	2	1	34	N/A	N/A	23	11	0	0	0.0	0.0
C /4.8	10.5	1.00	12.10	N/A	0	97	2	1	34	N/A	N/A	29	11	0	0	0.0	0.0
C /4.6	10.6	1.01	11.93	3	0	97	2	1	34	N/A	N/A	28	11	0	0	0.0	0.0
C /4.7	11.9	0.89	20.13	133	0	98	0	2	23	81.7	-17.3	92	10	1,000	100	5.8	0.0
C /4.7	11.8	0.89	20.03	4	0	98	0	2	23	84.0	-17.2	93	10	1,000,000	0	0.0	0.0
C /4.8	11.9	0.89	19.41	7	0	98	0	2	23	74.5	-17.5	90	10	1,000	100	0.0	0.0
C /4.7	11.9	0.89	20.05	5	0	98	0	2	23	86.1	-17.1	93	10	1,000,000	0	0.0	0.0
C+ /6.8	11.9	1.06	17.18	347	0	99	0	1	51	140.0	-19.7	45	10	1,000	100	5.8	0.0
C+ /6.8	11.9	1.06	17.37	32	0	99	0	1	51	142.7	-19.5	48	10	1,000,000	0	0.0	0.0
C+ /6.8	11.9	1.06	16.94	63	0	99	0	1	51	130.5	-19.9	35	10	1,000	100	0.0	0.0
C+ /6.8	11.9	1.06	17.26	643	0	99	0	1	51	146.2	-19.5	52	10	1,000,000	0	0.0	0.0
C /5.1	11.9	1.04	45.86	523	0	98	0	2	31	99.2	-14.1	12	15	1,000	100	5.8	0.0
C /5.1	11.9	1.04	46.16	210	0	98	0	2	31	100.5	-14.1	13	15	1,000,000	0	0.0	0.0
C /5.0	11.9	1.04	43.39	15	0	98	0	2	31	91.3	-14.4	8	15	1,000	100	0.0	0.0
C /5.1	11.9	1.04	46.62	238	0	98	0	2	31	103.4	-14.0	14	15	1,000,000	0	0.0	0.0
C /5.1	11.9	1.04	45.21	7	0	98	0	2	31	N/A	N/A	10	15	0	0	0.0	0.0
C /5.1	11.9	1.04	46.56	9	0	98	0	2	31	N/A	N/A	14	15	0	0	0.0	0.0
C /5.1	11.9	1.04	46.71	280	0	98	0	2	31	N/A	N/A	15	15	0	0	0.0	0.0
C /4.7	11.3	1.04	16.29	227	0	98	0	2	50	108.1	-19.2	22	1	1,000	100	5.8	0.0
C /4.7	11.3	1.04	16.40	21	0	98	0	2	50	110.6	-19.1	23	1	1,000,000	0	0.0	0.0
C /4.8	11.3	1.03	16.62	4	0	98	0	2	50	99.9	-19.5	16	1	1,000	100	0.0	0.0

Fund Type	Fund Name	Ticker Symbol	Overall Investment Rating	Phone	Performance Rating/Pts	3 Mo	6 Mo	1Yr / Pct	3Yr / Pct	5Yr / Pct	Dividend Yield	Expense Ratio
	99 Pct = Best 0 Pct = Worst							Total Return % through 2/28/17	Annualized		Incl. in Returns	
GI	Wells Fargo Lg Co Val Inst	WLCIX	B-	(800) 222-8222	B / 7.9	7.36	11.87	26.50 /78	6.87 /71	11.89 /73	1.23	0.61
BA	Wells Fargo Modt Bal A	WFMAX	C-	(800) 222-8222	D / 2.2	3.66	3.03	10.31 /12	4.25 /46	6.64 /32	1.18	1.32
BA	Wells Fargo Modt Bal Adm	NVMBX	C	(800) 222-8222	C- / 3.3	3.75	3.17	10.59 /13	4.50 /49	6.89 /34	1.47	1.24
BA	Wells Fargo Modt Bal C	WFBCX	C	(800) 222-8222	D+ / 2.6	3.48	2.61	9.46 /10	3.47 /37	5.83 /27	0.60	2.07
GR	Wells Fargo Omega Growth A	EKOAX	D-	(800) 222-8222	C- / 4.0	8.51	8.10	21.22 /58	3.41 /36	10.50 /62	0.00	1.28
GR	Wells Fargo Omega Growth Admin	EOMYX	D+	(800) 222-8222	C / 5.4	8.54	8.20	21.43 /59	3.64 /39	10.75 /64	0.00	1.20
GR	● Wells Fargo Omega Growth B	EKOBX	D-	(800) 222-8222	C / 4.5	8.33	7.71	20.31 /54	2.64 /29	9.67 /56	0.00	2.03
GR	Wells Fargo Omega Growth C	EKOCX	D-	(800) 222-8222	C / 4.5	8.30	7.68	20.27 /54	2.63 /29	9.67 /56	0.00	2.03
GR	Wells Fargo Omega Growth Inst	EKONX	D+	(800) 222-8222	C+ / 5.6	8.61	8.35	21.74 /61	3.90 /42	11.04 /66	0.00	0.95
GR	Wells Fargo Omega Growth R	EKORX	D	(800) 222-8222	C / 5.0	8.42	7.96	20.90 /57	3.15 /33	10.22 /60	0.00	1.53
GR	Wells Fargo Oppty Adm	WOFDX	C+	(800) 222-8222	B / 7.7	5.66	10.04	26.03 /76	7.15 /73	11.18 /67	0.38	1.12
GR	Wells Fargo Oppty Adv	SOPVX	C-	(800) 222-8222	C+ / 6.5	5.59	9.90	25.77 /75	6.92 /71	10.93 /65	0.27	1.20
GR	● Wells Fargo Oppty B	SOPBX	C	(800) 222-8222	C+ / 6.9	5.43	9.52	24.84 /73	6.12 /65	10.11 /59	0.00	1.95
GR	Wells Fargo Oppty C	WFOPX	C-	(800) 222-8222	C+ / 6.9	5.41	9.48	24.82 /73	6.12 /65	10.10 /59	0.00	1.95
GR	Wells Fargo Oppty Inst	WOFNX	C+	(800) 222-8222	B / 7.8	5.73	10.16	26.34 /77	7.42 /75	11.45 /69	0.53	0.87
PM	Wells Fargo Precious Mtls A	EKWAX	E-	(800) 222-8222	E / 0.3	10.44	-11.91	17.95 /43	-3.01 / 4	-13.51 / 0	0.96	1.22
PM	Wells Fargo Precious Mtls Adm	EKWDX	E-	(800) 222-8222	E / 0.5	10.48	-11.86	18.08 /43	-2.87 / 5	-13.39 / 0	1.14	1.14
PM	● Wells Fargo Precious Mtls B	EKWBX	E-	(800) 222-8222	E / 0.4	10.25	-12.23	17.22 /39	-3.69 / 3	-14.14 / 0	0.00	1.97
PM	Wells Fargo Precious Mtls C	EKWCX	E-	(800) 222-8222	E / 0.4	10.25	-12.23	17.07 /39	-3.72 / 3	-14.15 / 0	0.17	1.97
PM	Wells Fargo Precious Mtls Inst	EKWYX	E-	(800) 222-8222	E+ / 0.6	10.54	-11.76	18.23 /44	-2.73 / 5	-13.25 / 0	1.36	0.89
GR	Wells Fargo Prmr Lg Co Gr A	EKJAX	D	(800) 222-8222	C- / 3.3	7.82	5.02	16.51 /36	3.96 /43	9.73 /56	0.00	1.13
GR	Wells Fargo Prmr Lg Co Gr Admn	WFPDX	D+	(800) 222-8222	C / 4.6	7.82	5.11	16.67 /37	4.11 /44	9.90 /58	0.00	1.05
GR	● Wells Fargo Prmr Lg Co Gr B	EKJBX	D	(800) 222-8222	C- / 3.8	7.59	4.69	15.62 /33	3.20 /34	8.93 /50	0.00	1.88
GR	Wells Fargo Prmr Lg Co Gr C	EKJCX	D	(800) 222-8222	C- / 3.8	7.62	4.62	15.57 /32	3.19 /34	8.91 /50	0.00	1.88
GR	Wells Fargo Prmr Lg Co Gr Inst	EKJYX	D+	(800) 222-8222	C / 4.8	7.97	5.31	17.03 /38	4.42 /48	10.21 /60	0.00	0.80
GR	Wells Fargo Prmr Lg Co Gr R4	EKJRX	D+	(800) 222-8222	C / 4.7	7.87	5.19	16.86 /38	4.30 /46	--	0.00	0.85
GR	Wells Fargo Prmr Lg Co Gr R6	EKJFX	D+	(800) 222-8222	C / 4.9	7.96	5.30	17.09 /39	4.47 /48	--	0.00	0.70
SC	Wells Fargo Sm Co Gro A	WFSAX	D+	(800) 222-8222	C+ / 5.8	6.27	8.85	31.81 /90	4.40 /47	11.94 /74	0.00	1.34
SC	Wells Fargo Sm Co Gro Adm	NVSCX	C	(800) 222-8222	B- / 7.0	6.33	8.95	32.00 /90	4.58 /50	12.16 /76	0.00	1.26
SC	Wells Fargo Sm Co Gro C	WSMCX	C-	(800) 222-8222	C+ / 6.3	6.10	8.47	30.84 /88	3.62 /38	11.10 /67	0.00	2.09
SC	Wells Fargo Sm Co Gro Inst	WSCGX	C	(800) 222-8222	B- / 7.2	6.39	9.06	32.34 /91	4.83 /52	12.43 /78	0.00	1.01
SC	Wells Fargo Sm Co Val A	SCVAX	B+	(800) 222-8222	B+ / 8.6	5.67	14.35	37.37 /96	7.60 /76	11.86 /73	0.04	1.48
SC	Wells Fargo Sm Co Val Adm	SCVIX	A-	(800) 222-8222	A / 9.5	5.68	14.47	37.53 /96	7.79 /77	12.08 /75	0.18	1.40
SC	Wells Fargo Sm Co Val C	SCVFX	B+	(800) 222-8222	A- / 9.0	5.47	14.00	36.33 /95	6.80 /71	11.03 /66	0.00	2.23
SC	Wells Fargo Sm Co Val Inst	SCVNX	A-	(800) 222-8222	A / 9.5	5.72	14.55	37.82 /96	8.00 /79	12.31 /77	0.36	1.15
SC	Wells Fargo Sm Cp Opp Adm	NVSOX	C-	(800) 222-8222	A / 9.4	5.90	12.23	31.04 /88	9.31 /89	13.40 /88	0.27	1.31
SC	Wells Fargo Sm Cp Opp Inst	WSCOX	U	(800) 222-8222	U /	5.96	12.41	31.41 /89	--	--	0.52	1.06
SC	Wells Fargo Sm Cp Val A	SMVAX	D+	(800) 222-8222	B+ / 8.4	8.23	14.75	41.06 /98	5.91 /63	8.55 /47	0.00	1.36
SC	Wells Fargo Sm Cp Val Adm	SMVDX	C-	(800) 222-8222	A / 9.4	8.26	14.85	41.28 /98	6.11 /65	8.76 /49	0.00	1.28
SC	Wells Fargo Sm Cp Val C	SMVCX	C-	(800) 222-8222	B+ / 8.8	8.03	14.33	39.98 /97	5.12 /56	7.73 /40	0.00	2.11
SC	Wells Fargo Sm Cp Val Inst	WFSVX	C-	(800) 222-8222	A / 9.5	8.32	15.00	41.54 /98	6.33 /67	8.98 /51	0.00	1.03
SC	Wells Fargo Sm Cp Val R6	SMVRX	C-	(800) 222-8222	A / 9.5	8.36	15.04	41.71 /98	6.39 /67	--	0.00	0.93
SC	Wells Fargo Small Cap Core Inst	WYSCX	A+	(800) 222-8222	A / 9.3	6.15	14.51	27.19 /80	9.51 /90	13.37 /88	0.23	1.00
MC	Wells Fargo Spec Mid Cp VI A	WFPAX	B+	(800) 222-8222	B+ / 8.8	5.46	11.55	30.19 /87	10.25 /95	15.42 /97	0.49	1.22
MC	Wells Fargo Spec Mid Cp VI Adm	WFMDX	A-	(800) 222-8222	A / 9.5	5.48	11.60	30.30 /87	10.38 /95	15.55 /98	0.59	1.14
MC	Wells Fargo Spec Mid Cp VI C	WFPCX	B+	(800) 222-8222	A- / 9.1	5.26	11.13	29.22 /85	9.44 /90	14.56 /96	0.02	1.97
MC	Wells Fargo Spec Mid Cp VI I	WFMIX	A-	(800) 222-8222	A+ / 9.6	5.54	11.73	30.61 /87	10.67 /96	15.88 /98	0.87	0.89
MC	Wells Fargo Spec Mid Cp VI R6	WFPRX	A-	(800) 222-8222	A+ / 9.6	5.57	11.79	30.75 /88	10.75 /97	--	0.93	0.79
SC	Wells Fargo Spec Sm Cp Val A	ESPAX	B	(800) 222-8222	B+ / 8.4	3.57	11.73	33.61 /92	9.11 /88	13.90 /92	0.49	1.36
SC	Wells Fargo Spec Sm Cp Val Adm	ESPIX	B+	(800) 222-8222	A / 9.4	3.59	11.76	33.77 /93	9.31 /89	14.14 /94	0.67	1.28
SC	● Wells Fargo Spec Sm Cp Val B	ESPBX	B	(800) 222-8222	B+ / 8.8	3.40	11.34	32.64 /91	8.30 /81	13.05 /84	0.00	2.11
SC	Wells Fargo Spec Sm Cp Val C	ESPCX	B	(800) 222-8222	B+ / 8.8	3.39	11.32	32.62 /91	8.29 /81	13.06 /84	0.00	2.11

● Denotes fund is closed to new investors
* Denotes fund is included in Section II

680

Risk Rating/Pts	3 Year Standard Deviation	Beta	NAV As of 2/28/17	Total $(Mil)	Cash %	Stocks %	Bonds %	Other %	Portfolio Turnover Ratio	Last Bull Market Return	Last Bear Market Return	Manager Quality Pct	Manager Tenure (Years)	Initial Purch. $	Additional Purch. $	Front End Load	Back End Load
C /4.7	11.3	1.03	16.38	11	0	98	0	2	50	113.1	-19.0	26	1	1,000,000	0	0.0	0.0
B /8.0	4.7	0.74	23.05	37	0	39	60	1	87	54.0	-9.7	60	12	1,000	100	5.8	0.0
B /8.0	4.7	0.73	23.24	140	0	39	60	1	87	56.1	-9.6	63	12	1,000,000	0	0.0	0.0
B /8.1	4.7	0.74	22.60	13	0	39	60	1	87	47.9	-10.0	49	12	1,000	100	0.0	0.0
C- /3.3	12.6	1.08	44.22	551	0	98	1	1	84	108.2	-23.0	4	7	1,000	100	5.8	0.0
C- /3.5	12.6	1.08	47.37	19	0	98	1	1	84	110.8	-22.9	5	7	1,000,000	0	0.0	0.0
D+ /2.6	12.6	1.08	32.62	1	0	98	1	1	84	99.9	-23.2	3	7	1,000	100	0.0	0.0
D+ /2.6	12.6	1.08	32.73	64	0	98	1	1	84	99.9	-23.2	3	7	1,000	100	0.0	0.0
C- /3.5	12.6	1.08	48.41	55	0	98	1	1	84	113.7	-22.8	5	7	1,000,000	0	0.0	0.0
C- /3.2	12.6	1.08	42.35	6	0	98	1	1	84	105.4	-23.0	4	7	0	0	0.0	0.0
C- /3.7	12.0	1.09	46.34	233	0	98	1	1	34	108.4	-22.9	23	16	1,000,000	0	0.0	0.0
C- /3.6	12.0	1.09	43.00	1,475	0	98	1	1	34	105.9	-23.0	20	16	1,000	100	5.8	0.0
C- /3.6	12.0	1.09	41.18	1	0	98	1	1	34	97.7	N/A	14	16	1,000	100	0.0	0.0
C- /3.5	12.0	1.09	40.96	35	0	98	1	1	34	97.7	-23.2	14	16	1,000	100	0.0	0.0
C- /3.8	12.0	1.09	47.07	23	0	98	1	1	34	111.2	-22.9	25	16	1,000,000	0	0.0	0.0
E- /0.1	43.5	2.43	36.18	252	5	92	1	2	18	-50.8	-11.7	84	10	1,000	100	5.8	0.0
E- /0.1	43.5	2.43	36.45	17	5	92	1	2	18	-50.5	-11.6	85	10	1,000,000	0	0.0	0.0
E- /0.1	43.4	2.43	32.81	N/A	5	92	1	2	18	-52.7	-11.9	80	10	1,000	100	0.0	0.0
E- /0.1	43.4	2.43	32.26	50	5	92	1	2	18	-52.8	-11.9	80	10	1,000	100	0.0	0.0
E- /0.1	43.6	2.44	36.65	83	5	92	1	2	18	-50.0	-11.5	86	10	1,000,000	0	0.0	0.0
C /4.3	12.2	1.04	13.81	1,123	0	98	1	1	47	98.5	-15.0	7	7	1,000	100	5.8	0.0
C /4.3	12.3	1.04	13.97	89	0	98	1	1	47	100.2	-15.0	7	7	1,000,000	0	0.0	0.0
C- /4.0	12.2	1.03	11.66	N/A	0	98	1	1	47	90.7	-15.2	5	7	1,000	100	0.0	0.0
C- /4.0	12.2	1.04	11.62	219	0	98	1	1	47	90.6	-15.3	5	7	1,000	100	0.0	0.0
C /4.3	12.2	1.04	14.25	879	0	98	1	1	47	103.1	-14.9	8	7	1,000,000	0	0.0	0.0
C /4.3	12.2	1.04	14.17	4	0	98	1	1	47	N/A	N/A	8	7	0	0	0.0	0.0
C /4.3	12.2	1.04	14.27	154	0	98	1	1	47	N/A	N/A	8	7	0	0	0.0	0.0
C- /3.5	16.9	1.00	44.38	107	0	93	6	1	49	126.8	-26.8	43	23	1,000	100	5.8	0.0
C- /3.5	16.9	1.00	46.03	134	0	93	6	1	49	129.4	-26.7	45	23	1,000,000	0	0.0	0.0
C- /3.4	16.9	1.00	39.84	23	0	93	6	1	49	117.9	-27.0	33	23	1,000	100	0.0	0.0
C- /3.5	16.9	1.00	46.94	1,027	0	93	6	1	49	132.4	-26.7	49	23	1,000,000	0	0.0	0.0
C /5.4	15.7	0.96	24.62	25	2	94	3	1	72	129.9	-26.2	80	15	1,000	100	5.8	0.0
C /5.4	15.6	0.95	25.15	60	2	94	3	1	72	132.5	-26.2	82	15	1,000,000	0	0.0	0.0
C /5.4	15.6	0.95	21.99	2	2	94	3	1	72	120.8	-26.4	75	15	1,000	100	0.0	0.0
C /5.4	15.6	0.95	25.28	47	2	94	3	1	72	134.9	-26.1	83	15	1,000,000	0	0.0	0.0
E+ /0.6	12.6	0.79	23.69	249	0	92	6	2	59	129.1	-22.8	92	14	1,000,000	0	0.0	0.0
U /	N/A	N/A	23.72	54	0	92	6	2	59	N/A	N/A	N/A	14	5,000,000	0	0.0	0.0
E+ /0.6	14.8	0.79	21.74	525	0	99	0	1	16	86.4	-22.3	77	6	1,000	100	5.8	0.0
E+ /0.6	14.8	0.79	22.85	13	0	99	0	1	16	88.4	-22.3	78	6	1,000,000	0	0.0	0.0
E+ /0.6	14.8	0.79	16.72	37	0	99	0	1	16	79.0	-22.6	71	6	1,000	100	0.0	0.0
E+ /0.6	14.8	0.79	22.95	402	0	99	0	1	16	90.5	-22.2	80	6	1,000,000	0	0.0	0.0
E+ /0.6	14.8	0.79	22.98	93	0	99	0	1	16	N/A	N/A	80	6	0	0	0.0	0.0
C+ /6.4	14.3	0.86	20.62	85	0	0	0	100	61	143.2	-24.8	91	12	1,000,000	0	0.0	0.0
C /5.4	10.7	0.85	36.31	1,595	1	94	3	2	30	156.2	-22.3	86	8	1,000	100	5.8	0.0
C /5.4	10.7	0.85	36.90	1,000	1	94	3	2	30	157.8	-22.2	86	8	1,000,000	0	0.0	0.0
C /5.3	10.7	0.85	35.05	169	1	94	3	2	30	146.0	-22.5	82	8	1,000	100	0.0	0.0
C /5.4	10.7	0.85	37.19	3,079	1	94	3	2	30	161.7	-22.1	87	8	1,000,000	0	0.0	0.0
C /5.4	10.7	0.85	37.22	546	1	94	3	2	30	N/A	N/A	88	8	0	0	0.0	0.0
C /4.7	13.2	0.81	33.30	617	0	92	7	1	46	144.1	-22.4	91	15	1,000	100	5.8	0.0
C /4.7	13.2	0.81	34.05	201	0	92	7	1	46	146.9	-22.3	92	15	1,000,000	0	0.0	0.0
C /4.5	13.2	0.81	30.21	1	0	92	7	1	46	134.4	-22.6	88	15	1,000	100	0.0	0.0
C /4.6	13.2	0.81	30.35	61	0	92	7	1	46	134.4	-22.6	89	15	1,000	100	0.0	0.0

Fund Type	Fund Name	Ticker Symbol	Overall Investment Rating	Phone	Performance Rating/Pts	3 Mo	6 Mo	1Yr / Pct	3Yr / Pct	5Yr / Pct	Dividend Yield	Expense Ratio
	99 Pct = Best 0 Pct = Worst											
SC	Wells Fargo Spec Sm Cp Val I	ESPNX	B+	(800) 222-8222	A / 9.5	3.67	11.94	34.16 /93	9.55 /91	14.37 /95	0.83	1.03
TC	Wells Fargo Spec Tech A	WFSTX	C+	(800) 222-8222	B+ / 8.4	10.85	10.52	29.00 /84	8.79 /85	13.99 /93	0.00	1.45
TC	Wells Fargo Spec Tech Adm	WFTDX	B-	(800) 222-8222	A / 9.4	10.89	10.67	29.18 /84	8.94 /86	14.17 /94	0.00	1.37
TC	Wells Fargo Spec Tech C	WFTCX	C+	(800) 222-8222	B+ / 8.9	10.68	10.16	28.10 /82	8.00 /79	13.13 /85	0.00	2.20
SC	Wells Fargo Trad Sm Cap Gr A	EGWAX	E	(800) 222-8222	C- / 3.1	7.05	7.37	27.09 /79	1.02 /18	9.21 /52	0.00	1.48
SC	Wells Fargo Trad Sm Cap Gr Adm	EGWDX	E+	(800) 222-8222	C / 4.5	7.12	7.64	27.57 /81	1.22 /19	9.41 /54	0.00	1.40
SC	Wells Fargo Trad Sm Cap Gr C	EGWCX	E	(800) 222-8222	C- / 3.6	6.87	6.95	26.19 /77	0.28 /15	8.40 /45	0.00	2.23
SC	Wells Fargo Trad Sm Cap Gr I	EGRYX	E+	(800) 222-8222	C / 4.5	7.20	7.49	27.55 /81	1.36 /20	9.58 /55	0.00	1.15
UT	Wells Fargo Util and Tel A	EVUAX	C+	(800) 222-8222	C / 4.9	9.61	6.03	14.84 /29	6.52 /69	10.05 /59	1.20	1.19
UT	Wells Fargo Util and Tel Adm	EVUDX	C+	(800) 222-8222	C+ / 6.3	9.68	6.14	15.07 /30	6.73 /70	10.27 /60	1.43	1.11
UT	● Wells Fargo Util and Tel B	EVUBX	C+	(800) 222-8222	C / 5.5	9.40	5.59	13.94 /25	5.71 /62	9.21 /52	0.50	1.94
UT	Wells Fargo Util and Tel C	EVUCX	C+	(800) 222-8222	C / 5.5	9.38	5.59	13.94 /25	5.72 /62	9.23 /53	0.61	1.94
UT	Wells Fargo Util and Tel Inst	EVUYX	C+	(800) 222-8222	C+ / 6.4	9.73	6.18	15.26 /31	6.85 /71	10.42 /61	1.63	0.86
GR	Wells Fargo VT Dscvry 2		C-	(800) 222-8222	B- / 7.5	9.12	12.32	31.95 /90	4.27 /46	11.43 /69	0.00	1.17
AA	Wells Fargo VT Idx Asset All 2		B	(800) 222-8222	C+ / 6.7	4.80	5.36	14.21 /26	8.93 /86	11.03 /66	0.82	1.10
GR	Wells Fargo VT Opp 2		B-	(800) 222-8222	B / 7.7	5.72	10.09	26.15 /77	7.18 /73	11.49 /70	1.83	1.09
SC	● Wells Fargo VT Sm Cap Growth 2		D-	(800) 222-8222	C+ / 6.1	5.31	6.82	36.76 /96	2.38 /27	9.73 /56	0.00	1.18
AA	Wells Fargo With Bldr Consv All C	WCCFX	C	(800) 222-8222	D- / 1.4	2.23	0.71	6.41 / 5	1.42 /21	2.45 / 9	0.89	2.03
AA	Wells Fargo With Bldr Equity C	WEACX	C+	(800) 222-8222	C / 5.4	6.24	7.65	21.91 /62	4.13 /44	8.13 /43	0.00	2.27
AA	Wells Fargo With Bldr Gro All C	WGCFX	C	(800) 222-8222	C / 4.5	5.42	6.34	19.10 /48	3.70 /39	7.57 /39	0.00	2.25
GI	Wells Fargo With Bldr Gro Bal C	WGBFX	C	(800) 222-8222	C- / 3.3	4.48	4.40	15.16 /31	3.20 /34	6.53 /32	0.00	2.17
GI	Wells Fargo With Bldr Modt Bal C	WMBFX	C-	(800) 222-8222	D / 2.2	3.32	2.68	10.88 /14	2.43 /27	4.48 /18	0.39	2.10
BA	WesMark Balanced Fund	WMBLX	B	(800) 864-1013	C / 5.0	4.98	5.20	15.39 /32	5.74 /62	6.81 /34	1.62	1.24
GR	WesMark Growth Fund	WMKGX	C	(800) 864-1013	C+ / 5.8	7.92	8.38	18.75 /46	4.96 /54	9.93 /58	0.36	1.17
SC	WesMark Small Company Growth	WMKSX	C	(800) 864-1013	C+ / 6.4	4.93	10.87	27.11 /79	4.34 /47	9.90 /58	0.28	1.24
RE	West Loop Realty A	REIAX	C+	(877) 672-6487	B- / 7.2	7.75	-0.58	15.43 /32	12.12 /98	--	0.65	1.82
RE	West Loop Realty C	REICX	B-	(877) 672-6487	B / 7.6	7.53	-0.92	14.54 /28	11.32 /97	--	0.03	2.57
RE	West Loop Realty Institutional	REIIX	B	(877) 672-6487	B+ / 8.4	7.87	-0.39	15.74 /33	12.42 /98	--	0.90	1.57
GI	Westcore Global Large Cap Div Inst	WIMVX	C-	(800) 392-2673	C / 4.4	6.19	2.91	14.49 /28	5.11 /55	9.28 /53	1.93	1.06
GI	Westcore Global Large Cap Div Rtl	WTMVX	C-	(800) 392-2673	C- / 4.2	6.10	2.80	14.27 /27	4.92 /53	9.08 /51	1.73	1.18
FO	Westcore International SC Inst	WIIFX	D	(800) 392-2673	E / 0.4	5.54	2.94	14.07 /26	-4.51 / 3	3.22 /12	1.34	N/A
FO	Westcore International SC Rtl	WTIFX	E	(800) 392-2673	E / 0.3	5.50	2.83	13.80 /25	-4.58 / 3	3.18 /12	4.69	1.62
GR	Westcore Large Cap Dividend Inst	WILGX	E	(800) 392-2673	C- / 3.4	3.83	3.49	12.99 /22	4.02 /43	9.49 /55	0.00	1.28
GR	Westcore Large Cap Dividend Rtl	WTEIX	E-	(800) 392-2673	C- / 3.2	3.79	3.33	12.78 /21	3.77 /40	9.27 /53	0.00	1.17
SC	Westcore Micro-Cap Oppty Retail	WTMIX	C+	(800) 392-2673	C+ / 6.6	1.62	12.89	28.88 /84	5.41 /59	12.66 /81	0.34	1.67
MC	Westcore Mid Cap Val Div II Inst	WIMGX	E-	(800) 392-2673	E / 0.3	2.19	1.11	11.31 /16	-4.24 / 3	5.61 /26	0.04	0.98
MC	Westcore Mid Cap Val Div II Rtl	WTMGX	E-	(800) 392-2673	E / 0.3	2.03	0.92	10.86 /14	-4.50 / 3	5.38 /24	0.04	1.04
MC	Westcore Mid-Cap Value Div Inst	WIMCX	A+	(800) 392-2673	A+ / 9.7	5.00	11.64	31.26 /89	11.80 /98	14.17 /94	0.37	N/A
MC	Westcore Mid-Cap Value Div Rtl	WTMCX	A-	(800) 392-2673	A+ / 9.7	4.99	11.52	30.98 /88	11.72 /98	14.12 /94	1.39	1.21
SC	Westcore Small-Cap Growth Inst	WISGX	D+	(800) 392-2673	C+ / 6.3	6.17	10.61	34.85 /94	2.94 /31	--	0.00	2.21
SC	Westcore Small-Cap Growth Rtl	WTSGX	D	(800) 392-2673	C+ / 6.0	6.14	10.54	34.44 /93	2.56 /28	--	0.00	4.96
SC	Westcore Small-Cap Value Div Inst	WISVX	C+	(800) 392-2673	A- / 9.2	2.86	14.01	33.40 /92	8.78 /85	12.35 /78	1.60	1.22
SC	Westcore Small-Cap Value Div Rtl	WTSVX	C+	(800) 392-2673	A- / 9.1	2.78	13.86	33.16 /92	8.57 /84	12.12 /75	1.37	1.39
MC	Westcore SmCp Gr II Rtl	WTSLX	E	(800) 392-2673	E- / 0.2	6.61	3.47	12.33 /19	-6.67 / 2	1.60 / 7	0.00	1.10
IN	Westfield Capital Dividend Gro Inst	WDIVX	C+	(866) 777-7818	C+ / 6.6	6.23	8.28	20.64 /56	6.45 /68	--	2.00	1.05
IN	Westfield Capital Dividend Gro Inv	WCDGX	C+	(866) 777-7818	C+ / 6.5	6.21	8.15	20.45 /55	6.34 /67	--	1.81	1.30
GR	Westfield Capital Lg Cap Gro Inst	WCLGX	C+	(866) 454-0738	B- / 7.3	8.59	9.44	20.42 /54	7.22 /73	12.60 /80	0.39	0.88
GR	Westfield Capital Lg Cap Gro Inv	WCLCX	C+	(866) 454-0738	B- / 7.1	8.51	9.26	20.12 /53	6.95 /72	12.33 /77	0.18	1.13
EM	Westwood Emerging Markets A	WWEAX	D+	(866) 777-7818	C- / 4.0	9.86	3.45	26.50 /78	2.56 /28	--	0.74	1.65
EM	Westwood Emerging Markets Inst	WWEMX	C-	(866) 777-7818	C / 5.3	10.00	3.71	26.82 /79	2.83 /30	--	1.01	1.30
GL	Westwood Global Dividend Inst	WWGDX	C-	(866) 777-7818	D+ / 2.9	4.54	3.42	15.64 /33	2.41 /27	--	2.08	2.86
GL	Westwood Global Equity Inst	WWGEX	C-	(866) 777-7818	C- / 3.0	4.40	1.77	17.90 /42	2.45 /27	--	1.38	1.68

● Denotes fund is closed to new investors
* Denotes fund is included in Section II

682

RISK			NET ASSETS		ASSET				Portfolio Turnover Ratio	BULL / BEAR		FUND MANAGER		MINIMUMS		LOADS	
Risk Rating/Pts	3 Year Standard Deviation	Beta	NAV As of 2/28/17	Total $(Mil)	Cash %	Stocks %	Bonds %	Other %		Last Bull Market Return	Last Bear Market Return	Manager Quality Pct	Manager Tenure (Years)	Initial Purch. $	Additional Purch. $	Front End Load	Back End Load
C /4.7	13.2	0.81	34.09	839	0	92	7	1	46	149.4	-22.2	93	15	1,000,000	0	0.0	0.0
C- /3.5	14.8	1.21	10.63	281	0	97	1	2	153	128.0	-21.5	25	17	1,000	100	5.8	0.0
C- /3.5	14.8	1.22	10.80	36	0	97	1	2	153	130.0	-21.3	26	17	1,000,000	0	0.0	0.0
D+ /2.9	14.8	1.22	8.81	13	0	97	1	2	153	118.9	-21.6	18	17	1,000	100	0.0	0.0
E+ /0.6	16.6	0.97	13.80	83	0	93	6	1	123	100.3	-27.7	12	26	1,000	100	5.8	0.0
E+ /0.8	16.6	0.97	15.32	N/A	0	93	6	1	123	102.4	-27.6	13	26	1,000,000	0	0.0	0.0
E /0.5	16.7	0.97	12.74	N/A	0	93	6	1	123	92.4	-27.9	8	26	1,000	100	0.0	0.0
E+ /0.9	16.6	0.97	15.61	10	0	93	6	1	123	104.1	-27.5	14	26	5,000,000	0	0.0	0.0
C+ /6.5	11.7	0.72	19.96	314	3	95	0	2	15	80.6	-5.2	29	15	1,000	100	5.8	0.0
C+ /6.5	11.7	0.72	19.99	5	3	95	0	2	15	82.6	-5.1	30	15	1,000,000	0	0.0	0.0
C+ /6.5	11.7	0.72	20.02	1	3	95	0	2	15	73.3	-5.5	20	15	1,000	100	0.0	0.0
C+ /6.5	11.7	0.72	19.94	52	3	95	0	2	15	73.4	-5.5	21	15	1,000	100	0.0	0.0
C+ /6.5	11.7	0.72	19.96	20	3	95	0	2	15	83.8	-5.1	32	15	1,000,000	0	0.0	0.0
D /1.9	14.7	1.13	28.35	129	0	98	1	1	90	125.5	-23.5	5	6	0	0	0.0	0.0
B /8.7	6.4	1.01	19.85	83	0	59	39	2	44	96.5	-8.9	83	4	0	0	0.0	0.0
C /4.8	12.0	1.09	26.08	164	0	98	1	1	41	112.3	-22.6	23	16	0	0	0.0	0.0
D- /1.1	20.5	1.15	8.93	214	0	92	7	1	77	105.4	-23.4	13	6	0	0	0.0	0.0
B+ /9.2	3.3	0.47	10.37	466	0	0	0	100	198	20.9	-5.7	48	4	1,000	100	0.0	0.0
B- /7.1	10.9	1.63	20.33	539	0	0	0	100	26	80.4	-20.2	4	4	1,000	100	0.0	0.0
C+ /6.4	9.3	1.40	14.02	414	0	0	0	100	59	74.8	-20.9	7	4	1,000	100	0.0	0.0
B- /7.2	7.3	0.67	13.76	903	0	0	0	100	100	62.5	-18.2	27	4	1,000	100	0.0	0.0
B /8.1	5.2	0.47	11.61	748	0	0	0	100	150	39.8	-11.7	42	4	1,000	100	0.0	0.0
B /8.0	6.1	0.96	12.68	110	0	61	37	2	30	59.5	-7.8	58	19	1,000	100	0.0	0.0
C+ /5.6	12.1	1.14	18.55	331	1	94	4	1	21	98.9	-22.7	6	20	1,000	100	0.0	0.0
C /4.8	13.8	0.85	13.77	99	0	96	3	1	45	100.2	-24.1	56	17	1,000	100	0.0	0.0
C /5.3	13.6	0.99	13.68	13	1	98	0	1	18	N/A	N/A	81	4	2,500	100	5.8	0.0
C /5.3	13.5	0.98	13.61	4	1	98	0	1	18	N/A	N/A	77	4	2,500	100	0.0	0.0
C /5.2	13.6	0.99	13.71	84	1	98	0	1	18	N/A	N/A	83	4	1,000,000	100,000	0.0	0.0
C+ /6.0	9.0	0.78	10.07	4	0	97	1	2	65	86.7	-13.1	35	15	500,000	0	0.0	0.0
C+ /6.0	9.0	0.78	10.14	45	0	97	1	2	65	84.9	-13.1	33	15	2,500	25	0.0	0.0
B- /7.3	13.9	0.92	16.43	23	0	0	0	100	44	38.1	-19.2	19	14	250,000	0	0.0	0.0
C- /4.1	13.9	0.92	15.83	47	0	0	0	100	44	37.8	-19.2	19	14	2,500	25	0.0	0.0
E /0.4	11.5	1.00	6.84	1	0	99	0	1	96	92.5	-15.8	8	1	500,000	0	0.0	0.0
E /0.4	11.6	1.01	6.61	12	0	99	0	1	96	90.5	-15.9	7	1	2,500	25	0.0	0.0
C /5.2	14.8	0.88	18.30	13	1	97	0	2	105	130.5	-24.2	67	9	2,500	25	0.0	2.0
D /1.6	15.1	1.08	4.74	2	0	97	1	2	61	66.2	-26.8	1	1	500,000	0	0.0	0.0
D- /1.6	15.0	1.08	4.61	35	0	97	1	2	61	64.1	-26.9	1	1	2,500	25	0.0	0.0
B /8.3	10.7	0.86	28.57	36	0	0	0	100	62	128.5	-17.8	91	15	250,000	0	0.0	0.0
C /5.3	10.7	0.86	28.20	50	0	0	0	100	62	128.0	-17.8	91	15	2,500	25	0.0	0.0
D+ /2.3	17.6	1.03	11.88	4	3	96	0	1	69	N/A	N/A	24	4	500,000	0	0.0	2.0
D+ /2.3	17.6	1.03	11.75	1	3	96	0	1	69	N/A	N/A	20	4	2,500	25	0.0	2.0
C- /3.1	14.2	0.83	12.42	130	3	96	0	1	74	117.9	-20.0	90	13	500,000	0	0.0	0.0
C- /3.2	14.2	0.83	12.40	85	3	96	0	1	74	115.8	-20.1	89	13	2,500	25	0.0	0.0
C- /3.5	15.5	1.05	21.78	37	1	98	0	1	67	30.5	-29.3	0	1	2,500	25	0.0	0.0
C+ /6.0	10.1	0.92	10.94	100	1	98	0	1	112	N/A	N/A	33	4	50,000	0	0.0	0.0
C+ /6.0	10.1	0.92	10.98	N/A	1	98	0	1	112	N/A	N/A	32	4	2,500	0	0.0	0.0
C /4.4	12.0	1.08	12.02	123	0	99	0	1	63	120.0	N/A	24	6	50,000	0	0.0	0.0
C /4.4	12.0	1.09	12.15	N/A	0	99	0	1	63	117.3	N/A	21	6	2,500	0	0.0	0.0
C /4.5	15.9	0.94	8.78	1	0	93	6	1	47	N/A	N/A	80	5	5,000	0	5.0	0.0
C /4.4	15.9	0.94	8.78	233	0	93	6	1	47	N/A	N/A	82	5	100,000	0	0.0	0.0
C+ /6.4	10.2	0.77	11.30	5	2	97	0	1	12	N/A	N/A	88	5	5,000	0	0.0	0.0
C+ /6.6	10.6	0.80	11.95	17	4	95	0	1	17	N/A	N/A	89	5	5,000	0	0.0	0.0

Fund Type	Fund Name	Ticker Symbol	Overall Investment Rating	Phone	Performance Rating/Pts	3 Mo	6 Mo	1Yr / Pct	Annualized 3Yr / Pct	Annualized 5Yr / Pct	Dividend Yield	Expense Ratio
GI	Westwood Income Opportunity A	WWIAX	C+	(877) 386-3944	C- / 3.5	5.62	4.91	13.90 /25	5.16 /56	6.91 /34	1.14	1.15
GI	Westwood Income Opportunity Inst	WHGIX	B	(877) 386-3944	C / 4.7	5.75	5.10	14.18 /26	5.40 /59	7.17 /36	1.38	0.90
GR	Westwood Large Cap Value A	WWLAX	C+	(877) 386-3944	C+ / 6.8	6.45	8.69	20.75 /56	8.29 /81	11.89 /73	0.81	1.09
GR	Westwood Large Cap Value Inst	WHGLX	B-	(877) 386-3944	B / 7.8	6.64	8.89	21.14 /58	8.56 /84	12.18 /76	1.08	0.85
GR	Westwood Low Vol Equity Inst	WLVIX	B-	(877) 386-3944	B- / 7.3	6.74	8.31	20.33 /54	7.83 /78	11.17 /67	1.17	0.89
EN	Westwood MLP and Strat Energy Inst	WMLPX	U	(866) 777-7818	U /	3.40	7.32	34.39 /93	--	--	2.75	1.82
SC	Westwood SmallCap Value Inst	WHGSX	A-	(877) 386-3944	A+ / 9.7	4.14	14.25	39.66 /97	9.10 /87	15.55 /98	0.52	1.09
MC	Westwood SMidCap Institutional	WHGMX	C	(877) 386-3944	C+ / 6.3	6.62	10.27	25.36 /74	4.38 /47	10.17 /60	0.42	0.96
MC	Westwood SMidCap Plus Inst	WHGPX	C+	(877) 386-3944	C+ / 6.2	6.93	9.35	22.67 /65	4.82 /52	10.98 /66	0.53	0.91
GR	White Oak Select Growth	WOGSX	A+	(888) 462-5386	A+ / 9.7	8.00	11.75	31.20 /89	10.95 /97	13.74 /91	0.96	1.06
EM	● William Blair EM Leaders I	WBELX	E+	(800) 742-7272	D- / 1.5	7.69	0.96	21.27 /59	-0.46 /11	0.09 / 5	0.12	1.54
EM	● William Blair EM Leaders Inst	WELIX	E+	(800) 742-7272	D / 1.6	7.75	1.13	21.33 /59	-0.38 /12	0.19 / 5	0.17	1.35
EM	● William Blair EM Leaders N	WELNX	E+	(800) 742-7272	D- / 1.4	7.71	0.95	21.02 /57	-0.77 /10	-0.19 / 4	0.00	1.89
EM	William Blair EM Sm Cap Gro I	BESIX	D	(800) 742-7272	D+ / 2.9	7.26	-3.08	14.44 /28	3.38 /36	8.09 /43	2.45	1.52
EM	William Blair EM Sm Cap Gro Inst	WESJX	C-	(800) 742-7272	C- / 3.0	7.23	-3.08	14.47 /28	3.46 /37	--	2.50	1.31
EM	William Blair EM Sm Cap Gro N	WESNX	D	(800) 742-7272	D+ / 2.7	7.20	-3.19	14.08 /26	3.07 /33	7.79 /41	2.12	1.94
EM	● William Blair Emrg Mkts Gr I	WBEIX	E+	(800) 742-7272	D / 1.6	8.39	0.36	21.58 /60	-0.40 /12	0.59 / 5	0.41	1.40
EM	● William Blair Emrg Mkts Gr Inst	BIEMX	E+	(800) 742-7272	D / 1.6	8.50	0.44	21.70 /61	-0.25 /12	0.74 / 6	0.48	1.17
EM	● William Blair Emrg Mkts Gr N	WBENX	E+	(800) 742-7272	D- / 1.5	8.40	0.28	21.41 /59	-0.61 /11	0.34 / 5	0.18	1.65
GL	William Blair Global Leaders I	WGFIX	C-	(800) 742-7272	C / 4.6	6.70	3.49	18.78 /46	4.23 /46	7.73 /40	0.26	1.32
GL	William Blair Global Leaders Inst	BGGIX	C	(800) 742-7272	C / 4.6	6.67	3.55	18.84 /46	4.30 /46	--	0.31	1.11
GL	William Blair Global Leaders N	WGGNX	C-	(800) 742-7272	C / 4.3	6.61	3.40	18.38 /45	3.94 /42	7.42 /38	0.00	1.61
GR	William Blair Growth I	BGFIX	D+	(800) 742-7272	C / 4.6	6.18	4.30	15.34 /31	5.03 /55	10.37 /61	0.21	0.89
GR	William Blair Growth N	WBGSX	D	(800) 742-7272	C / 4.3	6.10	4.07	15.05 /30	4.71 /51	10.04 /59	0.00	1.19
FO	William Blair Instl Int Eqty Fd	WIIEX	D	(800) 742-7272	D / 2.0	5.97	1.43	14.70 /29	0.54 /16	5.32 /23	1.99	1.76
FO	William Blair Instl Intl Gr	WBIIX	D-	(800) 742-7272	D- / 1.0	5.19	1.97	12.53 /20	-0.66 /11	5.17 /23	1.10	0.96
FO	William Blair Internatl Leaders I	WILIX	D+	(800) 742-7272	D+ / 2.9	4.51	0.42	16.50 /36	2.81 /30	--	0.97	1.46
FO	William Blair Internatl Leaders Ins	WILJX	C-	(800) 742-7272	C- / 3.0	4.50	0.49	16.58 /37	2.94 /31	--	1.03	1.15
FO	William Blair Internatl Leaders N	WILNX	D+	(800) 742-7272	D+ / 2.8	4.46	0.36	16.19 /35	2.63 /29	--	0.91	1.56
FO	William Blair Intl Equity I	WIEIX	D	(800) 742-7272	D / 1.9	5.87	1.49	14.68 /28	0.46 /16	5.42 /24	1.15	1.34
FO	William Blair Intl Equity N	WIENX	D	(800) 742-7272	D / 1.8	5.75	1.33	14.38 /27	0.22 /14	5.15 /22	0.93	1.60
FO	William Blair Intl Grwth I	BIGIX	D-	(800) 742-7272	D- / 1.0	5.25	1.97	12.47 /20	-0.77 /10	5.08 /22	1.73	1.14
FO	William Blair Intl Grwth N	WBIGX	D-	(800) 742-7272	E+ / 0.9	5.21	1.85	12.18 /19	-1.05 / 9	4.76 /20	1.45	1.42
FO	● William Blair Intl Sm Cap Gr I	WISIX	E+	(800) 742-7272	D- / 1.0	6.28	0.37	10.65 /13	-0.56 /11	6.72 /33	0.33	1.31
FO	● William Blair Intl Sm Cap Gr Inst	WIISX	E+	(800) 742-7272	D- / 1.0	6.41	0.45	10.85 /14	-0.42 /12	6.90 /34	0.40	1.08
FO	● William Blair Intl Sm Cap Gr N	WISNX	E+	(800) 742-7272	E+ / 0.9	6.28	0.21	10.35 /12	-0.84 /10	6.41 /31	0.04	1.62
GR	William Blair Large Cap Growth I	LCGFX	C+	(800) 742-7272	B- / 7.2	6.22	4.77	17.41 /40	8.95 /86	13.25 /86	0.29	0.95
GR	William Blair Large Cap Growth N	LCGNX	C+	(800) 742-7272	B- / 7.0	6.24	4.63	17.24 /39	8.70 /85	13.00 /84	0.07	1.28
GL	William Blair Macro Alloc I	WMCIX	D+	(800) 742-7272	D- / 1.2	3.24	2.79	5.74 / 5	0.40 /15	3.43 /13	2.22	1.28
GL	William Blair Macro Alloc Inst	WMCJX	C	(800) 742-7272	D- / 1.3	3.24	2.79	5.73 / 4	0.49 /16	--	2.31	1.04
GL	William Blair Macro Alloc N	WMCNX	D+	(800) 742-7272	D- / 1.1	3.18	2.63	5.50 / 4	0.14 /14	3.18 /12	1.80	1.56
MC	William Blair Mid Cap Gr Fd I	WCGIX	E+	(800) 742-7272	C- / 3.5	4.35	3.91	14.33 /27	3.82 /41	7.88 /41	0.00	1.14
MC	William Blair Mid Cap Gr Fd N	WCGNX	E+	(800) 742-7272	C- / 3.3	4.28	3.82	14.09 /26	3.58 /38	7.60 /39	0.00	1.43
GR	William Blair Mid Cap Value Fund I	WMVIX	C-	(800) 742-7272	B / 7.6	4.29	8.06	24.55 /72	7.97 /79	12.25 /77	1.02	3.77
GR	William Blair Mid Cap Value Fund N	WMVNX	C-	(800) 742-7272	B- / 7.3	4.21	7.89	24.28 /71	7.67 /77	11.96 /74	0.42	4.14
SC	William Blair Small Cap Gr I	WBSIX	C	(800) 742-7272	B+ / 8.3	6.18	10.70	35.75 /95	6.01 /64	14.46 /95	0.00	1.30
SC	William Blair Small Cap Gr N	WBSNX	C	(800) 742-7272	B / 8.1	6.12	10.57	35.44 /94	5.76 /62	14.18 /94	0.00	1.59
SC	William Blair Small Cap Value I	BVDIX	A	(800) 742-7272	A- / 9.0	4.25	11.85	34.03 /93	8.16 /80	13.00 /84	0.40	1.24
SC	William Blair Small Cap Value N	WBVDX	A-	(800) 742-7272	B+ / 8.9	4.15	11.72	33.70 /92	7.89 /78	12.71 /81	0.17	1.54
MC	William Blair Small-Mid Cap Gr I	WSMDX	B	(800) 742-7272	B / 8.2	7.39	9.21	25.53 /75	8.08 /80	13.22 /86	0.00	1.15
MC	William Blair Small-Mid Cap Gr N	WSMNX	B-	(800) 742-7272	B / 8.0	7.29	9.01	25.16 /74	7.81 /78	12.93 /83	0.00	1.42
MC	William Blair Small-Mid Cap Val I	WSMIX	B	(800) 742-7272	B / 8.0	3.66	9.50	29.75 /86	7.64 /76	12.22 /76	0.74	3.72

RISK Risk Rating/Pts	3 Year Standard Deviation	Beta	NET ASSETS NAV As of 2/28/17	Total $(Mil)	ASSET Cash %	Stocks %	Bonds %	Other %	Portfolio Turnover Ratio	BULL / BEAR Last Bull Market Return	Last Bear Market Return	FUND MANAGER Manager Quality Pct	Manager Tenure (Years)	MINIMUMS Initial Purch. $	Additional Purch. $	LOADS Front End Load	Back End Load
B /8.4	6.0	0.54	15.40	128	16	48	33	3	22	56.5	-6.6	68	12	5,000	0	5.0	0.0
B /8.4	6.0	0.55	15.42	2,453	16	48	33	3	22	58.5	-6.5	70	12	100,000	0	0.0	0.0
C /5.2	9.6	0.90	12.07	2	1	96	2	1	39	118.3	-20.0	60	11	5,000	0	5.0	0.0
C /5.1	9.6	0.90	12.02	202	1	96	2	1	39	121.3	-19.9	63	11	100,000	0	0.0	0.0
C /5.2	9.4	0.87	11.51	61	2	97	0	1	39	101.9	-14.1	59	6	5,000	0	0.0	0.0
U /	N/A	N/A	7.76	31	44	55	0	1	44	N/A	N/A	N/A	N/A	5,000	0	0.0	0.0
C /5.3	15.5	0.95	16.58	186	1	96	2	1	65	171.0	-23.8	88	4	5,000	0	0.0	0.0
C /4.4	12.4	0.98	16.55	414	2	96	0	2	82	105.9	-24.2	17	9	5,000	0	0.0	0.0
C+ /6.2	10.9	0.86	14.92	140	5	94	0	1	54	108.4	-22.5	32	6	5,000	0	0.0	0.0
C+ /6.8	13.4	1.17	76.20	278	0	99	0	1	14	123.9	-16.2	57	25	2,000	25	0.0	0.0
C /4.5	14.7	0.86	8.55	32	3	96	0	1	110	21.3	-23.0	49	9	500,000	0	0.0	0.0
C /4.5	14.7	0.86	8.55	300	3	96	0	1	110	22.1	-23.0	50	9	5,000,000	0	0.0	0.0
C /4.5	14.8	0.86	8.52	3	3	96	0	1	110	19.5	-23.2	45	9	2,500	1,000	0.0	0.0
C /5.1	12.3	0.63	14.99	173	0	98	0	2	167	N/A	N/A	87	6	500,000	0	0.0	0.0
C+ /6.4	12.3	0.63	15.01	139	0	98	0	2	167	N/A	N/A	88	6	5,000,000	0	0.0	0.0
C /5.1	12.2	0.63	14.94	10	0	98	0	2	167	N/A	N/A	86	6	2,500	1,000	0.0	0.0
C- /3.9	14.8	0.86	12.14	101	1	98	0	1	121	26.1	-22.9	50	12	500,000	0	0.0	0.0
C- /3.9	14.8	0.87	12.24	860	1	98	0	1	121	27.3	-22.8	52	12	5,000,000	0	0.0	0.0
C- /3.9	14.8	0.87	12.02	9	1	98	0	1	121	24.4	-22.9	47	12	2,500	1,000	0.0	0.0
C /5.5	11.7	0.86	12.30	49	1	98	0	1	55	77.1	-18.8	94	9	500,000	0	0.0	0.0
C+ /6.3	11.7	0.86	12.30	133	1	98	0	1	55	N/A	N/A	94	9	5,000,000	0	0.0	0.0
C+ /5.6	11.7	0.86	12.28	6	1	98	0	1	55	74.7	-18.9	93	9	2,500	1,000	0.0	0.0
C- /3.8	11.5	1.01	13.09	535	1	98	0	1	78	104.9	-17.0	13	16	500,000	0	0.0	0.0
C- /3.6	11.5	1.01	12.05	61	1	98	0	1	78	101.6	-17.2	11	16	2,500	1,000	0.0	0.0
C+ /6.1	11.2	0.87	12.28	16	2	97	0	1	54	52.2	-23.0	79	9	5,000,000	0	0.0	0.0
C /5.3	10.8	0.84	15.14	2,176	1	98	0	1	70	53.3	-21.8	68	4	5,000,000	0	0.0	0.0
C+ /6.4	11.6	0.87	13.47	36	1	98	0	1	29	N/A	N/A	90	5	500,000	0	0.0	0.0
C+ /6.4	11.6	0.86	13.47	239	1	98	0	1	29	N/A	N/A	90	5	5,000,000	0	0.0	0.0
C+ /6.4	11.6	0.86	13.43	4	1	98	0	1	29	N/A	N/A	89	5	2,500	1,000	0.0	0.0
C+ /6.1	11.2	0.87	14.30	85	2	97	0	1	54	52.3	-23.3	78	9	500,000	0	0.0	0.0
C+ /6.2	11.2	0.87	14.16	3	2	97	0	1	54	50.2	-23.4	77	9	2,500	1,000	0.0	0.0
C+ /6.1	10.8	0.84	25.43	2,266	1	98	0	1	70	52.3	-22.2	67	4	500,000	0	0.0	0.0
C+ /6.2	10.8	0.84	24.84	737	1	98	0	1	70	50.0	-22.3	63	4	2,500	1,000	0.0	0.0
C /4.9	11.1	0.79	13.67	312	1	98	0	1	90	58.4	-20.9	69	4	500,000	0	0.0	0.0
C /4.9	11.1	0.79	13.75	210	1	98	0	1	90	59.9	-20.8	71	4	5,000,000	0	0.0	0.0
C /4.9	11.1	0.79	13.52	11	1	98	0	1	90	56.0	-21.1	65	4	2,500	1,000	0.0	0.0
C /5.1	11.3	1.00	11.36	117	0	99	0	1	38	132.4	-17.6	55	12	500,000	0	0.0	0.0
C /4.9	11.3	1.00	10.89	13	0	99	0	1	38	129.7	-17.8	51	12	2,500	1,000	0.0	0.0
B /8.0	5.7	0.55	11.55	905	25	33	40	2	34	N/A	N/A	46	6	500,000	0	0.0	0.0
B+ /9.4	5.7	0.54	11.56	592	25	33	40	2	34	N/A	N/A	48	6	5,000,000	0	0.0	0.0
B /8.0	5.7	0.55	11.50	55	25	33	40	2	34	N/A	N/A	42	6	2,500	1,000	0.0	0.0
D+ /2.3	11.5	0.86	11.78	109	1	98	0	1	65	79.4	-17.7	22	11	500,000	0	0.0	0.0
D /2.1	11.5	0.86	11.24	17	1	98	0	1	65	76.9	-17.8	20	11	2,500	1,000	0.0	0.0
D+ /2.5	10.6	0.90	10.60	3	3	96	0	1	53	119.4	-19.7	56	7	500,000	0	0.0	0.0
D+ /2.5	10.6	0.90	10.62	N/A	3	96	0	1	53	116.4	-19.8	52	7	2,500	1,000	0.0	0.0
D+ /2.8	14.6	0.88	28.35	283	1	98	0	1	91	147.3	-25.8	73	18	500,000	0	0.0	0.0
D+ /2.6	14.6	0.88	26.17	121	1	98	0	1	91	144.1	-25.8	71	18	2,500	1,000	0.0	0.0
C+ /6.0	14.4	0.87	20.84	675	2	97	0	1	30	129.4	-24.2	86	21	500,000	0	0.0	0.0
C+ /6.0	14.5	0.88	20.33	33	2	97	0	1	30	126.2	-24.3	85	21	2,500	1,000	0.0	0.0
C /4.9	12.1	0.92	21.37	1,177	2	97	0	1	44	129.6	-20.8	66	14	500,000	0	0.0	0.0
C /4.9	12.0	0.91	20.48	175	2	97	0	1	44	126.6	-20.9	63	14	2,500	1,000	0.0	0.0
C /5.3	13.2	1.04	14.65	3	1	98	0	1	35	N/A	N/A	45	6	500,000	0	0.0	0.0

Fund Type	Fund Name	Ticker Symbol	Overall Investment Rating	Phone	Performance Rating/Pts	3 Mo	6 Mo	1Yr / Pct	3Yr / Pct	5Yr / Pct	Dividend Yield	Expense Ratio
	99 Pct = Best							Total Return % through 2/28/17			Incl. in Returns	
	0 Pct = Worst								Annualized			
MC	William Blair Small-Mid Cap Val N	BSMNX	B	(800) 742-7272	B / 7.8	3.60	9.29	29.44 /85	7.35 /74	11.92 /74	0.09	3.93
SC	Williston Basin/Mid-Nrth Amer Stk A	ICPAX	E-	(800) 601-5593	E / 0.5	-4.22	9.86	40.94 /98	-5.41 / 2	1.06 / 6	0.17	1.45
EN	Williston Basin/Mid-Nrth Amer Stk C	ICPUX	U	(800) 601-5593	U /	-4.25	9.53	40.05 /97	--	--	0.00	1.95
EN	Williston Basin/Mid-Nrth Amer Stk I	ICWIX	U	(800) 601-5593	U /	-3.96	10.13	--	--	--	0.00	N/A
BA	Wilmington Gl Alpha Equities A	WRAAX	D	(800) 336-9970	E / 0.5	2.91	4.77	5.83 / 5	-0.23 /13	1.76 / 8	0.22	3.17
AA	Wilmington Gl Alpha Equities I	WRAIX	D+	(800) 336-9970	D- / 1.3	2.96	4.91	6.18 / 5	0.04 /14	2.04 / 8	0.30	2.92
GR	Wilmington Large-Cap Strategy Inst	WMLIX	A	(800) 336-9970	A / 9.3	7.84	10.18	26.26 /77	10.20 /94	13.75 /91	1.71	0.89
RE	Wilmington Mul Mgr Real Asset A	WMMRX	D	(800) 336-9970	E+ / 0.7	3.69	-1.85	7.25 / 6	0.31 /15	1.20 / 6	0.00	1.56
RE	Wilmington Mul Mgr Real Asset I	WMRIX	D+	(800) 336-9970	D- / 1.2	3.81	-1.70	7.59 / 7	0.58 /16	1.46 / 7	0.00	1.31
FO	Wilmington Multi Manager Intl A	GVIEX	D-	(800) 336-9970	E+ / 0.7	6.77	3.48	14.48 /28	-0.82 /10	2.86 /10	1.21	1.80
FO	Wilmington Multi Manager Intl Inst	MVIEX	D-	(800) 336-9970	D- / 1.2	6.76	3.52	14.65 /28	-0.69 /11	2.95 /11	1.36	1.55
AA	Wilmington Strat Alloc Aggr A	WAAAX	C-	(800) 336-9970	D+ / 2.9	6.20	5.53	17.20 /39	3.06 /32	7.16 /36	0.42	2.29
AA	Wilmington Strat Alloc Aggr Inst	WAAIX	C	(800) 336-9970	C- / 4.1	6.31	5.71	17.53 /41	3.35 /35	7.44 /38	0.56	2.04
AA	Wilmington Strat Alloc Conserv A	WCAAX	C-	(800) 336-9970	E+ / 0.9	2.63	0.59	5.46 / 4	1.41 /21	2.50 / 9	0.96	2.14
AA	Wilmington Strat Alloc Conserv Inst	WCAIX	C	(800) 336-9970	D- / 1.5	2.68	0.71	5.81 / 5	1.69 /22	2.77 /10	1.26	1.89
AA	Wilmington Strategic Alloc Mdt A	ARBAX	C-	(800) 336-9970	D / 2.0	4.82	3.71	12.86 /21	2.76 /30	4.92 /21	0.93	2.13
AA	Wilmington Strategic Alloc Mdt Inst	ARGIX	C	(800) 336-9970	C- / 3.0	4.88	3.83	13.06 /22	3.01 /32	5.20 /23	1.16	1.88
GR	Wilshire 5000 Index Inst	WINDX	A+	(888) 200-6796	A- / 9.1	7.65	10.23	25.98 /76	9.83 /92	13.50 /89	2.19	1.01
GR	Wilshire 5000 Index Inv	WFIVX	A+	(888) 200-6796	A- / 9.0	7.57	10.05	25.58 /75	9.54 /91	13.24 /86	1.88	1.33
GR	Wilshire International Equity Inst	WLTTX	D	(888) 200-6796	D- / 1.1	6.08	2.04	13.11 /22	-0.32 /12	4.23 /16	1.73	1.29
GR	Wilshire International Equity Inv	WLCTX	D	(888) 200-6796	D- / 1.0	6.09	1.98	12.91 /21	-0.57 /11	3.99 /15	1.57	1.75
GR	Wilshire Large Co Growth Inst	WLCGX	C	(888) 200-6796	C+ / 6.8	6.89	4.01	18.30 /44	7.95 /79	11.13 /67	0.37	1.01
GR	Wilshire Large Co Growth Inv	DTLGX	C	(888) 200-6796	C+ / 6.6	6.84	3.88	17.98 /43	7.63 /76	10.80 /64	0.03	1.33
GR	Wilshire Large Co Val Inst	WLCVX	B	(888) 200-6796	B+ / 8.8	6.06	12.64	30.09 /87	7.96 /79	12.77 /82	1.87	1.02
GR	Wilshire Large Co Val Inv	DTLVX	B	(888) 200-6796	B+ / 8.7	6.19	12.76	30.02 /86	7.74 /77	12.53 /79	0.64	1.29
SC	Wilshire Small Co Growth Inst	WSMGX	B	(888) 200-6796	A- / 9.1	4.95	10.39	31.42 /89	8.97 /87	14.16 /94	0.00	1.36
SC	Wilshire Small Co Growth Inv	DTSGX	B	(888) 200-6796	B+ / 8.9	4.93	10.26	31.08 /88	8.66 /84	13.87 /92	0.00	1.64
SC	Wilshire Small Co Val Inst	WSMVX	B+	(888) 200-6796	A- / 9.2	4.82	12.14	32.44 /91	8.91 /86	14.98 /97	0.74	1.36
SC	Wilshire Small Co Val Inv	DTSVX	B+	(888) 200-6796	A- / 9.1	4.74	12.01	32.06 /90	8.60 /84	14.68 /96	0.36	1.67
GL	Wintergreen Fund Inc Inst	WGRIX	D+	(888) 468-6473	D+ / 2.5	7.98	7.98	14.66 /28	0.92 /18	4.43 /18	3.35	1.69
GR	Wintergreen Fund Inc Investor	WGRNX	D	(888) 468-6473	D+ / 2.4	7.90	7.83	14.36 /27	0.67 /17	4.17 /16	3.00	1.92
GL	● Winton Global Equity Port Inst	WGEPX	U		U /	7.49	7.71	17.71 /42	--	--	1.66	2.34
GR	Wireless Fund	WIREX	B+	(800) 590-0898	B / 8.1	9.33	7.25	20.27 /54	9.64 /91	11.01 /66	0.00	1.96
AA	WOA All Asset I I	WOAIX	C-	(855) 754-7935	D / 2.0	3.29	1.30	13.87 /25	1.45 /21	--	0.73	1.55
IN	WP Large Cap Income Plus Inst	WPLCX	B-		A+ / 9.7	9.42	17.28	44.29 /98	6.64 /69	--	0.17	3.05
GR	WPG Partners Sm/Mic Cap Val Inst	WPGTX	D	(888) 261-4073	C / 4.3	3.58	10.20	32.62 /91	0.78 /17	8.98 /50	0.42	1.55
FO	Wright Intl Blue Chip Equities	WIBCX	D-	(800) 232-0013	E / 0.5	6.69	5.69	11.76 /17	-2.83 / 5	2.70 /10	1.61	2.04
GI	Wright Major Blue Chip Equities	WQCEX	A+	(800) 232-0013	B+ / 8.4	8.41	11.97	22.77 /66	8.38 /82	10.29 /61	0.82	2.05
GI	Wright Selected Blue Chip Equities	WSBEX	C	(800) 232-0013	C+ / 6.1	6.91	6.91	19.32 /49	5.83 /63	11.55 /70	0.42	1.44
FS	WSTCM Credit Select Risk Mgd Inv	WAMBX	U	(866) 515-4626	U /	3.97	3.39	14.19 /26	--	--	3.10	1.60
OT	WSTCM Sector Select Risk Mgd Inst	WSTIX	C-	(866) 515-4626	D / 1.6	5.49	2.54	5.49 / 4	2.05 /24	--	0.21	2.05
OT	WSTCM Sector Select Risk Mgd Inv	WSTEX	C-	(866) 515-4626	D- / 1.5	5.43	2.37	5.22 / 4	1.78 /23	--	0.13	4.81
GR	YCG Enhanced R	YCGEX	A-	(855) 444-9243	B- / 7.3	8.32	6.42	17.29 /40	9.28 /89	--	0.52	1.35
IN	Zacks All-Cap Core C	CZOCX	C+	(800) 245-2934	C+ / 5.9	6.77	7.02	18.51 /45	6.35 /67	10.12 /59	0.00	2.51
IN	Zacks All-Cap Core Investor	CZOVX	C+	(800) 245-2934	C+ / 6.5	6.93	7.39	19.43 /49	7.16 /73	10.96 /66	0.16	1.76
IN	Zacks Dividend Investor	ZDIVX	A	(800) 245-2934	B / 8.0	6.96	8.55	25.80 /76	8.49 /83	--	1.53	2.78
GI	Zacks Market Neutral Institutional	ZMNIX	C	(800) 245-2934	D- / 1.1	-1.68	0.60	2.21 / 2	2.50 /28	0.95 / 6	0.00	6.54
GI	Zacks Market Neutral Investor	ZMNVX	C	(800) 245-2934	D- / 1.3	-1.72	0.63	2.66 / 2	3.15 /33	1.65 / 7	0.00	6.79
SC	Zacks Small-Cap Core I	ZSCIX	A-	(800) 245-2934	A- / 9.1	4.83	15.86	32.34 /91	8.66 /84	--	0.00	1.41
GR	Zacks Small-Cap Core Investor	ZSCCX	A-	(800) 245-2934	A- / 9.0	4.80	15.73	31.90 /90	8.35 /82	14.93 /97	0.00	1.66

RISK			NET ASSETS		ASSET				Portfolio Turnover Ratio	BULL / BEAR		FUND MANAGER		MINIMUMS		LOADS	
Risk Rating/Pts	3 Year		NAV As of 2/28/17	Total $(Mil)	Cash %	Stocks %	Bonds %	Other %		Last Bull Market Return	Last Bear Market Return	Manager Quality Pct	Manager Tenure (Years)	Initial Purch. $	Additional Purch. $	Front End Load	Back End Load
	Standard Deviation	Beta															
C /5.4	13.2	1.04	14.70	N/A	1	98	0	1	35	N/A	N/A	41	6	2,500	1,000	0.0	0.0
D- /1.2	21.9	0.71	5.67	541	5	94	0	1	64	48.0	-32.6	2	7	1,000	50	5.0	0.0
U /	N/A	N/A	5.63	49	5	94	0	1	64	N/A	N/A	N/A	7	1,000	50	5.0	0.0
U /	N/A	N/A	5.67	27	5	94	0	1	64	N/A	N/A	N/A	7	1,000	50	0.0	0.0
B- /7.1	4.0	0.37	10.41	N/A	22	23	52	3	387	N/A	N/A	35	2	1,000	25	5.5	0.0
B- /7.1	4.1	0.39	10.47	101	22	23	52	3	387	N/A	N/A	36	2	1,000,000	25	0.0	0.0
C+ /5.8	11.2	1.07	19.50	566	0	99	0	1	81	133.4	-17.1	61	6	1,000,000	25	0.0	0.0
B- /7.5	7.1	0.44	13.76	2	0	40	59	1	418	17.0	-10.5	20	9	1,000	25	5.5	0.0
B- /7.5	7.1	0.44	13.89	417	0	40	59	1	418	18.6	-10.4	22	9	1,000,000	25	0.0	0.0
C+ /5.7	11.4	0.90	7.33	5	3	94	2	1	71	32.5	-25.1	66	1	1,000	25	5.5	0.0
C+ /5.8	11.5	0.90	7.38	410	3	94	2	1	71	33.2	-24.9	68	1	1,000,000	25	0.0	0.0
C+ /6.7	9.6	1.45	11.95	3	3	87	8	2	51	67.6	-19.6	5	N/A	1,000	25	5.5	0.0
C+ /6.7	9.6	1.45	12.04	23	3	87	8	2	51	69.9	-19.4	5	N/A	1,000,000	25	0.0	0.0
B+ /9.1	3.2	0.43	10.60	3	3	25	70	2	33	24.1	-8.4	51	N/A	1,000	25	5.5	0.0
B+ /9.1	3.2	0.44	10.63	31	3	25	70	2	33	25.9	-8.3	54	N/A	1,000,000	25	0.0	0.0
B /8.3	6.6	1.02	11.06	43	4	55	39	2	52	45.4	-15.1	18	7	1,000	25	5.5	0.0
B /8.3	6.6	1.02	11.07	1	4	55	39	2	52	47.5	-15.1	20	7	1,000,000	25	0.0	0.0
C+ /6.8	10.5	1.01	19.89	42	0	99	0	1	6	130.2	-17.6	64	18	250,000	100,000	0.0	0.0
C+ /6.8	10.5	1.01	19.89	142	0	99	0	1	6	127.3	-17.7	60	18	1,000	100	0.0	0.0
C+ /6.4	10.7	0.87	9.21	270	5	94	0	1	84	49.7	-19.5	3	3	250,000	100,000	0.0	1.0
C+ /6.4	10.7	0.87	9.32	10	5	94	0	1	84	47.9	-19.6	3	3	2,500	100	0.0	1.0
C- /4.2	11.4	1.01	38.75	165	0	98	1	1	104	111.3	-17.9	41	10	250,000	100,000	0.0	0.0
C- /4.0	11.4	1.01	36.31	64	0	98	1	1	104	107.8	-17.9	37	10	2,500	100	0.0	0.0
C /4.8	11.7	1.07	20.97	178	0	99	0	1	55	126.6	-21.5	33	13	250,000	100,000	0.0	0.0
C /4.9	11.7	1.07	21.17	10	0	99	0	1	55	123.9	-21.7	30	13	2,500	100	0.0	0.0
C- /4.2	14.7	0.90	26.72	27	0	99	0	1	63	144.2	-25.1	89	15	250,000	100,000	0.0	0.0
C- /4.1	14.7	0.90	24.90	10	0	99	0	1	63	141.0	-25.2	88	15	2,500	100	0.0	0.0
C /4.9	15.0	0.93	24.27	31	0	97	1	2	49	152.2	-25.2	88	13	250,000	100,000	0.0	0.0
C /4.9	15.0	0.93	23.86	9	0	97	1	2	49	148.2	-25.4	86	13	2,500	100	0.0	0.0
C+ /5.9	10.4	0.63	15.94	173	0	94	5	1	3	N/A	N/A	81	12	100,000	1,000	0.0	2.0
C+ /6.0	10.4	0.75	15.98	304	0	94	5	1	3	41.0	-13.4	6	12	10,000	100	0.0	2.0
U /	N/A	N/A	10.10	41	5	94	0	1	124	N/A	N/A	N/A	3	1,000,000	0	0.0	0.0
C+ /6.3	11.9	0.89	9.02	4	3	96	0	1	4	94.7	-20.9	75	17	5,000	100	0.0	2.0
B- /7.4	9.0	1.27	10.93	150	1	71	27	1	176	N/A	N/A	4	6	1,000,000	25,000	0.0	0.0
C- /3.2	17.8	1.56	12.07	28	0	96	3	1	5	N/A	N/A	3	4	2,000	100	0.0	0.0
C- /3.2	15.9	1.15	17.01	36	2	95	1	2	62	99.7	-29.0	2	18	100,000	5,000	0.0	2.0
C+ /5.9	11.6	0.93	14.40	17	0	98	0	2	33	34.4	-25.4	38	21	1,000	0	0.0	2.0
B- /7.1	11.1	1.05	19.64	12	0	98	0	2	118	103.5	-19.0	40	8	1,000	0	0.0	0.0
C /4.7	11.7	0.95	12.39	34	0	99	0	1	55	119.9	-22.8	24	9	1,000	0	0.0	0.0
U /	N/A	N/A	10.70	56	14	1	84	1	326	N/A	N/A	N/A	3	1,000	250	0.0	0.0
B /8.4	7.5	0.44	10.60	15	6	40	52	2	472	N/A	N/A	42	4	100,000	1,000	0.0	0.0
B /8.3	7.5	0.44	10.56	1	6	40	52	2	472	N/A	N/A	37	4	1,000	250	0.0	0.0
B- /7.4	10.0	0.90	14.67	120	10	89	0	1	18	N/A	N/A	72	5	2,500	100	0.0	2.0
C+ /5.7	10.3	0.96	21.19	15	0	99	0	1	37	93.4	-17.4	29	12	2,500	100	0.0	2.0
C+ /5.9	10.3	0.96	23.32	26	0	99	0	1	37	101.5	-17.1	37	12	2,500	100	0.0	2.0
B- /7.1	10.5	1.00	19.10	32	2	97	0	1	29	N/A	N/A	50	3	2,500	100	0.0	2.0
B+ /9.9	4.6	0.11	13.44	2	99	0	0	1	180	4.3	2.7	82	9	2,500	100	0.0	2.0
B+ /9.9	4.6	0.11	14.29	25	99	0	0	1	180	8.3	3.0	86	9	2,500	100	0.0	2.0
C+ /5.6	14.7	0.88	28.14	9	2	97	0	1	162	N/A	N/A	88	6	25,000	1,000	0.0	2.0
C+ /5.8	14.7	0.98	27.90	122	2	97	0	1	162	153.1	N/A	49	6	2,500	100	0.0	2.0

Section II

Analysis of Largest Stock Mutual Funds

A summary analysis of the 183 largest retail

Equity Mutual Funds

receiving a TheStreet Investment Rating.

Funds are listed in alphabetical order.

Section II Contents

1. Fund Name
The name of the mutual fund as stated in its prospectus, which can sometimes differ slightly from the name that the company uses for advertising. If you cannot find the paritcular mutual fund you are interested in, or if you have any doubts regarding the precise name, verify the information with your broker or on your account statement. Also, use the fund's ticker symbol for confirmation.

2. Ticker Symbol
The unique alphabetic symbol used for identifying and trading a specific mutual fund. No two funds can have the same ticker symbol, and the ticker symbol for mutual funds always ends with an "X".

A handful of funds currently show no associated ticker symbol. This means that the fund is either small or new since the NASD only assigns a ticker symbol to funds with at least $25 million in assets or 1,000 shareholders.

3. Investment Rating
Our overall rating is measured on a scale from A to E based on each fund's risk-adjusted performance. Please see page 10 for specific descriptions of each letter grade. Also refer to page 7 for information on how our ratings are derived. Most important, when using this rating, please be sure to consider the warnings beginning on page 11 regarding the ratings' limitations and the underlying assumptions.

4. Major Rating Factors
A synopsis of the key ratios and sub-factors that have most influenced the rating of a particular mutual fund, including an examination of the fund's performance, risk, and managerial performance. There may be additional factors which have influenced the rating but do not appear due to space limitations.

5. Services Offered
Services and/or benefits offered by the fund.

6. Address
The address of the company managing the fund.

7. Phone
The telephone number of the company managing the fund. Call this number to receive a prospectus or other information about the fund.

8. Fund Family
The umbrella group of mutual funds to which the fund belongs. In many cases, investors may move their assets from one fund to another within the same family at little or no cost.

9. Fund Type   The mutual fund's peer category based on an analysis of its investment portfolio.

AG	Aggressive Growth	HL	Health
AA	Asset Allocation	IN	Income
BA	Balanced	IX	Index
CV	Convertible	MC	Mid Cap
EM	Emerging Market	OT	Other
EN	Energy/Natural Resources	PM	Precious Metals
FS	Financial Services	RE	Real Estate
FO	Foreign	SC	Small Cap
GL	Global	TC	Technology
GR	Growth	UT	Utilities
GI	Growth and Income		

A blank fund type means that the mutual fund has not yet been categorized.

How to Read the Historical Data Table

NAV:
The fund's share price as of the date indicated. A fund's NAV is computed by dividing the value of the fund's asset holdings, less accrued fees and expenses, by the number of its shares outstanding.

Risk Rating/Pts:
A letter grade rating based solely on the mutual fund's risk as determined by its monthly performance volatility over the trailing three years. Pts are rating points where 0=worst and 10=best.

Data Date:
The month-end or year-end as of date used for evaluating the mutual fund.

Data Date	Investment Rating	Net Assets ($Mil)	NAV	Performance Rating/Pts	Total Return Y-T-D	Risk Rating/Pts
2-17	D	55	36.50	C- / 3.7	25.01%	C- / 4.1
2016	D+	66	35.69	C+ / 5.9	19.98%	D+ / 2.0
2015	C	823	14.46	C+ / 6.1	4.18%	C / 4.8
2014	B+	760	20.11	B / 7.8	-3.28%	B / 8.5
2013	B-	155	41.31	C+ / 6.4	-1.41%	C+ / 5.2
2012	C+	105	38.99	C+ / 6.3	20.69%	D+ / 2.9

Investment Rating:
Our overall opinion of the fund's risk-adjusted performance at the specified time period.

Net Assets $(Mil):
The total value of all of the fund's asset holdings (in millions) including stocks, bonds, cash, and other financial instruments, less accrued expenses and fees.

Performance Rating/Pts:
A letter grade rating based solely on the mutual fund's return to shareholders over the trailing three years, without any consideration for the amount of risk the fund poses. Pts are rating points where 0=worst and 10=best

Total Return Y-T-D:
The fund's total return to shareholders since the beginning of the calendar year specified.

AIG Foc Dividend Strategy A (FDSAX)

C+ **Fair**

Fund Family: AIG Funds   **Phone:** (800) 858-8850
Address: C/O BFDS, Kansas City, MO 64121
Fund Type: GI - Growth and Income
Major Rating Factors: Middle of the road best describes AIG Foc Dividend Strategy A whose TheStreet.com Investment Rating is currently a C+ (Fair). The fund currently has a performance rating of C+ (Fair) based on an average return of 9.64% over the last three years and 3.55% over the last three months. Factored into the performance evaluation is an expense ratio of 1.06% (low) and a 5.8% front-end load that is levied at the time of purchase.

The fund's risk rating is currently C+ (Fair). It carries a beta of 0.86, meaning the fund's expected move will be 8.6% for every 10% move in the market. Volatility, as measured by both the semi-deviation and a drawdown factor, is considered low.

Timothy Campion has been running the fund for 4 years and currently receives a manager quality ranking of 78 (0=worst, 99=best). If you desire an average level of risk, then this fund may be an option.

Services Offered: Automated phone transactions, payroll deductions, bank draft capabilities, an IRA investment plan, a 401K investment plan, a Keogh investment plan, wire transfers and a systematic withdrawal plan.

Data Date	Investment Rating	Net Assets ($Mil)	NAV	Perfor-mance Rating/Pts	Total Return Y-T-D	Risk Rating/Pts
2-17	C+	5,128	17.81	C+ / 6.7	3.55%	C+ / 6.2
2016	B	5,033	17.20	B- / 7.5	15.38%	C+ / 6.1
2015	B	3,990	15.39	B / 7.9	-0.96%	C+ / 5.9
2014	B+	3,784	17.12	B- / 7.3	9.06%	C+ / 6.9
2013	A+	4,190	17.15	A / 9.3	39.91%	B- / 7.1
2012	C+	2,002	12.98	C+ / 6.0	12.80%	C+ / 6.8

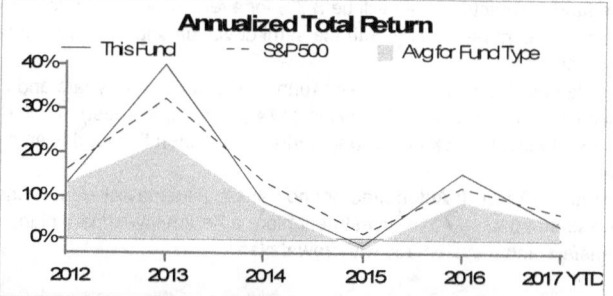
Annualized Total Return

American Funds AMCAP A (AMCPX)

C+ **Fair**

Fund Family: American Funds   **Phone:** (800) 421-0180
Address: 333 South Hope Street, Los Angeles, CA 90071
Fund Type: GR - Growth
Major Rating Factors: Middle of the road best describes American Funds AMCAP A whose TheStreet.com Investment Rating is currently a C+ (Fair). The fund currently has a performance rating of C+ (Fair) based on an average return of 7.69% over the last three years and 5.84% over the last three months. Factored into the performance evaluation is an expense ratio of 0.67% (very low) and a 5.8% front-end load that is levied at the time of purchase.

The fund's risk rating is currently C (Fair). It carries a beta of 0.96, meaning that its performance tracks fairly well with that of the overall stock market. Volatility, as measured by both the semi-deviation and a drawdown factor, is considered average.

Claudia P. Huntington has been running the fund for 21 years and currently receives a manager quality ranking of 45 (0=worst, 99=best). If you desire an average level of risk, then this fund may be an option.

Services Offered: Automated phone transactions, payroll deductions, an IRA investment plan, a 401K investment plan, a Keogh investment plan, wire transfers and a systematic withdrawal plan.

Data Date	Investment Rating	Net Assets ($Mil)	NAV	Perfor-mance Rating/Pts	Total Return Y-T-D	Risk Rating/Pts
2-17	C+	27,276	28.82	C+ / 6.5	5.84%	C / 5.5
2016	C+	26,063	27.23	C+ / 6.8	9.04%	C / 5.5
2015	B+	25,275	25.95	B+ / 8.4	0.78%	C+ / 6.2
2014	B+	24,627	28.00	B / 8.0	12.10%	C+ / 6.5
2013	A-	21,061	27.33	B+ / 8.3	36.86%	C / 5.5
2012	C	15,410	21.69	C / 4.9	15.67%	C / 5.4

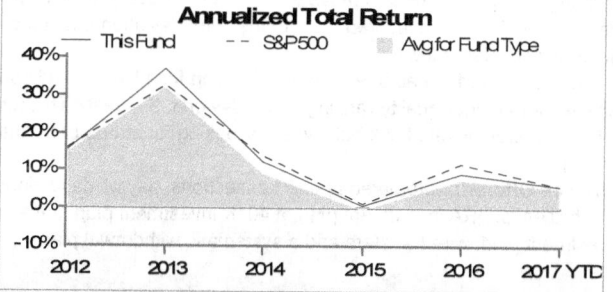
Annualized Total Return

American Funds Amer Balncd Fd A (ABALX)

B- **Good**

Fund Family: American Funds   **Phone:** (800) 421-0180
Address: 333 South Hope Street, Los Angeles, CA 90071
Fund Type: BA - Balanced
Major Rating Factors: American Funds Amer Balncd Fd A receives a TheStreet.com Investment Rating of B- (Good). The fund currently has a performance rating of C (Fair) based on an average return of 7.48% over the last three years and 3.95% over the last three months. Factored into the performance evaluation is an expense ratio of 0.59% (very low) and a 5.8% front-end load that is levied at the time of purchase.

The fund's risk rating is currently B- (Good). It carries a beta of 1.06, meaning that its performance tracks fairly well with that of the overall stock market. Volatility, as measured by both the semi-deviation and a drawdown factor, is considered low.

Hilda L. Applbaum has been running the fund for 18 years and currently receives a manager quality ranking of 69 (0=worst, 99=best). If you desire an average level of risk, then this fund may be an option.

Services Offered: Automated phone transactions, payroll deductions, bank draft capabilities, an IRA investment plan, a 401K investment plan, a Keogh investment plan, wire transfers and a systematic withdrawal plan.

Data Date	Investment Rating	Net Assets ($Mil)	NAV	Perfor-mance Rating/Pts	Total Return Y-T-D	Risk Rating/Pts
2-17	B-	57,703	25.79	C / 5.0	3.95%	B- / 7.6
2016	B-	55,402	24.81	C+ / 6.0	8.61%	B- / 7.7
2015	B-	49,227	23.83	C+ / 6.0	1.72%	B- / 7.8
2014	B-	46,928	24.75	C / 4.8	8.85%	B / 8.1
2013	B-	42,030	24.42	C / 4.6	21.73%	B- / 7.7
2012	B-	34,272	20.40	C / 4.9	14.19%	B- / 7.6

Annualized Total Return

American Funds Amer Mutual Fd A (AMRMX)　　B+　Good

Fund Family: American Funds　　　　**Phone:** (800) 421-0180
Address: 333 South Hope Street, Los Angeles, CA 90071
Fund Type: GI - Growth and Income

Major Rating Factors: Strong performance is the major factor driving the B+ (Good) TheStreet.com Investment Rating for American Funds Amer Mutual Fd A. The fund currently has a performance rating of B- (Good) based on an average return of 9.26% over the last three years and 4.81% over the last three months. Factored into the performance evaluation is an expense ratio of 0.59% (very low) and a 5.8% front-end load that is levied at the time of purchase.

The fund's risk rating is currently C+ (Fair). It carries a beta of 0.87, meaning the fund's expected move will be 8.7% for every 10% move in the market. Volatility, as measured by both the semi-deviation and a drawdown factor, is considered low.

James B. Lovelace has been running the fund for 11 years and currently receives a manager quality ranking of 74 (0=worst, 99=best). If you desire only a moderate level of risk and strong performance, then this fund is an excellent option.

Services Offered: Automated phone transactions, payroll deductions, an IRA investment plan, a 401K investment plan, a Keogh investment plan, wire transfers and a systematic withdrawal plan.

Data Date	Investment Rating	Net Assets ($Mil)	NAV	Perfor-mance Rating/Pts	Total Return Y-T-D	Risk Rating/Pts
2-17	B+	25,000	38.60	B- / 7.3	4.81%	C+ / 6.5
2016	B	23,959	36.83	B- / 7.4	14.16%	C+ / 6.6
2015	C+	21,659	33.85	C+ / 6.3	-2.83%	C+ / 6.8
2014	B-	22,698	37.14	C+ / 6.4	12.61%	B- / 7.8
2013	C+	20,139	34.81	C+ / 5.7	27.91%	C+ / 6.7
2012	C	15,651	28.36	C- / 3.5	12.33%	C+ / 6.5

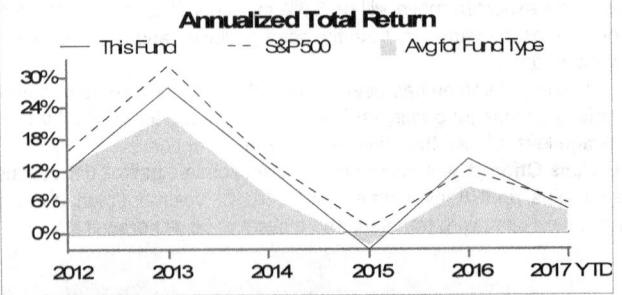

American Funds Cap Inc Builder A (CAIBX)　　C-　Fair

Fund Family: American Funds　　　　**Phone:** (800) 421-0180
Address: 333 South Hope Street, Los Angeles, CA 90071
Fund Type: IN - Income

Major Rating Factors: Disappointing performance is the major factor driving the C- (Fair) TheStreet.com Investment Rating for American Funds Cap Inc Builder A. The fund currently has a performance rating of D+ (Weak) based on an average return of 4.26% over the last three years and 3.50% over the last three months. Factored into the performance evaluation is an expense ratio of 0.60% (very low) and a 5.8% front-end load that is levied at the time of purchase.

The fund's risk rating is currently B- (Good). It carries a beta of 0.64, meaning the fund's expected move will be 6.4% for every 10% move in the market. Volatility, as measured by both the semi-deviation and a drawdown factor, is considered low.

Joyce E. Gordon has been running the fund for 17 years and currently receives a manager quality ranking of 44 (0=worst, 99=best). This fund offers only a moderate level of risk but investors looking for strong performance are still waiting.

Services Offered: Automated phone transactions, payroll deductions, bank draft capabilities, an IRA investment plan, a 401K investment plan, a Keogh investment plan, wire transfers and a systematic withdrawal plan.

Data Date	Investment Rating	Net Assets ($Mil)	NAV	Perfor-mance Rating/Pts	Total Return Y-T-D	Risk Rating/Pts
2-17	C-	69,953	59.66	D+ / 2.6	3.50%	B- / 7.0
2016	C-	68,604	57.64	D+ / 2.8	6.90%	B- / 7.0
2015	C-	68,049	55.85	D+ / 2.6	-2.92%	B- / 7.4
2014	C	69,896	59.58	C- / 3.0	6.61%	B- / 7.9
2013	C	65,416	58.55	D+ / 2.7	14.90%	B- / 7.4
2012	C-	58,079	52.77	D / 1.9	11.81%	B- / 7.3

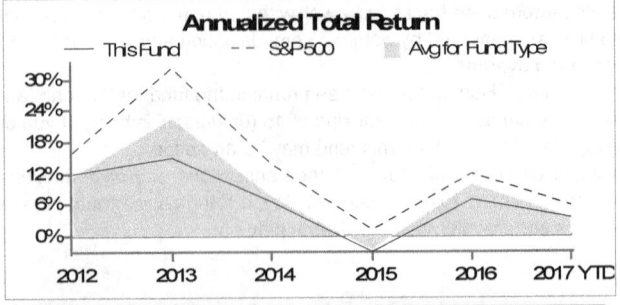

American Funds Cap Wld Gr&Inc A (CWGIX)　　C-　Fair

Fund Family: American Funds　　　　**Phone:** (800) 421-0180
Address: 333 South Hope Street, Los Angeles, CA 90071
Fund Type: GL - Global

Major Rating Factors: Middle of the road best describes American Funds Cap Wld Gr&Inc A whose TheStreet.com Investment Rating is currently a C- (Fair). The fund currently has a performance rating of C- (Fair) based on an average return of 3.91% over the last three years and 5.50% over the last three months. Factored into the performance evaluation is an expense ratio of 0.77% (very low) and a 5.8% front-end load that is levied at the time of purchase.

The fund's risk rating is currently C+ (Fair). It carries a beta of 0.78, meaning the fund's expected move will be 7.8% for every 10% move in the market. Volatility, as measured by both the semi-deviation and a drawdown factor, is considered low.

Mark E. Denning has been running the fund for 24 years and currently receives a manager quality ranking of 93 (0=worst, 99=best). If you desire an average level of risk, then this fund may be an option.

Services Offered: Automated phone transactions, payroll deductions, bank draft capabilities, an IRA investment plan, a 401K investment plan, a Keogh investment plan and a systematic withdrawal plan.

Data Date	Investment Rating	Net Assets ($Mil)	NAV	Perfor-mance Rating/Pts	Total Return Y-T-D	Risk Rating/Pts
2-17	C-	52,380	46.24	C- / 3.7	5.50%	C+ / 6.2
2016	C-	50,654	43.83	C- / 3.0	6.49%	C+ / 6.3
2015	C-	52,405	43.36	C- / 4.0	-2.18%	C+ / 6.8
2014	C	55,529	46.09	C / 4.5	4.02%	C+ / 6.9
2013	C-	54,676	45.32	C / 4.5	24.84%	C / 4.9
2012	D	46,651	37.20	C- / 3.0	19.12%	C / 4.6

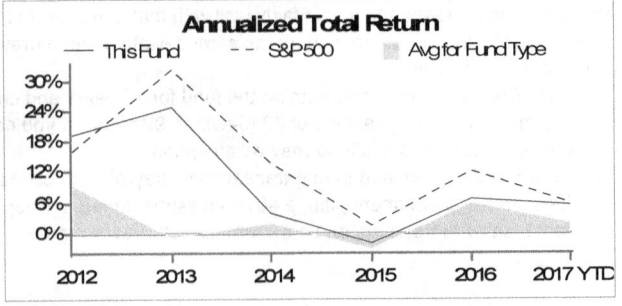

American Funds EuroPacific Gr A (AEPGX)   D-   Weak

Fund Family: American Funds   **Phone:** (800) 421-0180
Address: 333 South Hope Street, Los Angeles, CA 90071
Fund Type: FO - Foreign
Major Rating Factors: Disappointing performance is the major factor driving the D- (Weak) TheStreet.com Investment Rating for American Funds EuroPacific Gr A. The fund currently has a performance rating of D- (Weak) based on an average return of 0.41% over the last three years and 5.61% over the last three months. Factored into the performance evaluation is an expense ratio of 0.83% (very low) and a 5.8% front-end load that is levied at the time of purchase.

The fund's risk rating is currently C+ (Fair). It carries a beta of 0.83, meaning the fund's expected move will be 8.3% for every 10% move in the market. Volatility, as measured by both the semi-deviation and a drawdown factor, is considered low.

Jonathan O. Knowles has been running the fund for 11 years and currently receives a manager quality ranking of 78 (0=worst, 99=best). This fund offers only a moderate level of risk but investors looking for strong performance are still waiting.

Services Offered: Automated phone transactions, payroll deductions, an IRA investment plan, a 401K investment plan, a Keogh investment plan, wire transfers and a systematic withdrawal plan.

Data Date	Investment Rating	Net Assets ($Mil)	NAV	Performance Rating/Pts	Total Return Y-T-D	Risk Rating/Pts
2-17	D-	25,180	47.64	D- / 1.5	5.61%	C+ / 5.6
2016	D-	24,417	45.11	E+ / 0.9	0.66%	C+ / 5.6
2015	D	27,844	45.37	D / 2.1	-0.82%	C+ / 6.5
2014	D	29,419	47.13	D+ / 2.4	-2.64%	C+ / 5.9
2013	D-	32,428	49.07	C- / 3.0	20.15%	C- / 4.0
2012	D-	29,498	41.22	D / 2.2	19.21%	C- / 3.9

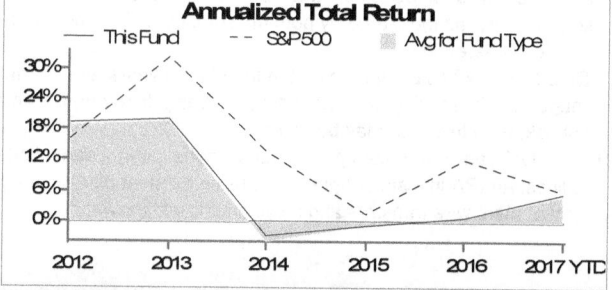

American Funds Fundamntl Invs A (ANCFX)   B+   Good

Fund Family: American Funds   **Phone:** (800) 421-0180
Address: 333 South Hope Street, Los Angeles, CA 90071
Fund Type: GI - Growth and Income
Major Rating Factors: Strong performance is the major factor driving the B+ (Good) TheStreet.com Investment Rating for American Funds Fundamntl Invs A. The fund currently has a performance rating of B+ (Good) based on an average return of 10.12% over the last three years and 5.80% over the last three months. Factored into the performance evaluation is an expense ratio of 0.61% (very low) and a 5.8% front-end load that is levied at the time of purchase.

The fund's risk rating is currently C+ (Fair). It carries a beta of 1.00, meaning that its performance tracks fairly well with that of the overall stock market. Volatility, as measured by both the semi-deviation and a drawdown factor, is considered low.

Dina N. Perry has been running the fund for 24 years and currently receives a manager quality ranking of 69 (0=worst, 99=best). If you desire only a moderate level of risk and strong performance, then this fund is an excellent option.

Services Offered: Automated phone transactions, payroll deductions, bank draft capabilities, an IRA investment plan, a 401K investment plan, a Keogh investment plan and a systematic withdrawal plan.

Data Date	Investment Rating	Net Assets ($Mil)	NAV	Performance Rating/Pts	Total Return Y-T-D	Risk Rating/Pts
2-17	B+	49,539	57.60	B+ / 8.5	5.80%	C+ / 6.1
2016	B	47,334	54.44	B / 7.8	12.54%	C+ / 6.1
2015	B+	44,589	50.71	B / 8.2	3.38%	C+ / 6.6
2014	C+	43,940	52.06	C+ / 6.6	8.96%	C+ / 6.7
2013	C+	40,703	51.97	C+ / 6.4	31.50%	C / 5.3
2012	C	32,568	40.78	C+ / 5.6	17.14%	C / 4.9

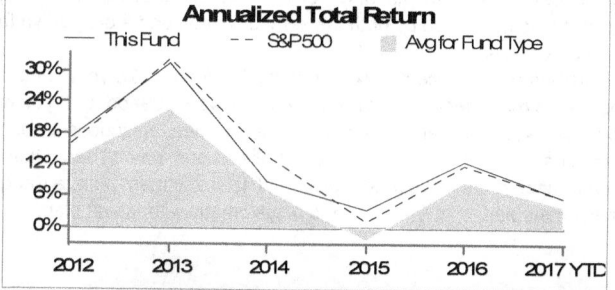

American Funds Gr Fnd of Amer A (AGTHX)   B-   Good

Fund Family: American Funds   **Phone:** (800) 421-0180
Address: 333 South Hope Street, Los Angeles, CA 90071
Fund Type: GR - Growth
Major Rating Factors: Strong performance is the major factor driving the B- (Good) TheStreet.com Investment Rating for American Funds Gr Fnd of Amer A. The fund currently has a performance rating of B (Good) based on an average return of 9.03% over the last three years and 7.02% over the last three months. Factored into the performance evaluation is an expense ratio of 0.66% (very low) and a 5.8% front-end load that is levied at the time of purchase.

The fund's risk rating is currently C (Fair). It carries a beta of 1.00, meaning that its performance tracks fairly well with that of the overall stock market. Volatility, as measured by both the semi-deviation and a drawdown factor, is considered average.

Michael T. Kerr has been running the fund for 19 years and currently receives a manager quality ranking of 56 (0=worst, 99=best). If you desire an average level of risk and strong performance, then this fund is a good option.

Services Offered: Automated phone transactions, payroll deductions, bank draft capabilities, an IRA investment plan, a 401K investment plan, a Keogh investment plan, wire transfers and a systematic withdrawal plan.

Data Date	Investment Rating	Net Assets ($Mil)	NAV	Performance Rating/Pts	Total Return Y-T-D	Risk Rating/Pts
2-17	B-	78,315	44.99	B / 7.9	7.02%	C / 4.7
2016	C	74,237	42.04	B- / 7.1	8.46%	C / 4.7
2015	B+	74,040	41.29	B+ / 8.9	5.36%	C+ / 6.1
2014	B-	72,970	42.68	B / 7.6	9.30%	C+ / 5.7
2013	B-	69,385	43.00	B- / 7.1	33.79%	C / 5.1
2012	C	55,970	34.35	C+ / 5.9	20.54%	C / 4.9

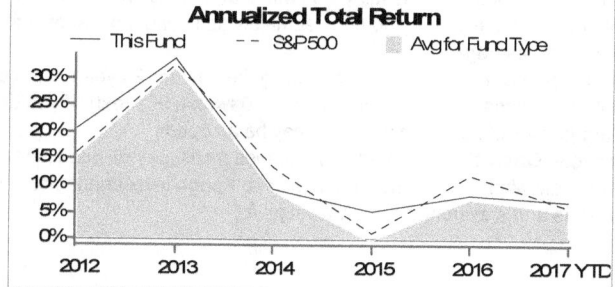

American Funds Inc Fnd of Amr A (AMECX)   C+   Fair

Fund Family: American Funds   **Phone:** (800) 421-0180
Address: 333 South Hope Street, Los Angeles, CA 90071
Fund Type: IN - Income

Major Rating Factors: Middle of the road best describes American Funds Inc Fnd of Amr A whose TheStreet.com Investment Rating is currently a C+ (Fair). The fund currently has a performance rating of C (Fair) based on an average return of 6.29% over the last three years and 3.51% over the last three months. Factored into the performance evaluation is an expense ratio of 0.56% (very low) and a 5.8% front-end load that is levied at the time of purchase.

The fund's risk rating is currently B- (Good). It carries a beta of 0.67, meaning the fund's expected move will be 6.7% for every 10% move in the market. Volatility, as measured by both the semi-deviation and a drawdown factor, is considered low.

Dina N. Perry has been running the fund for 25 years and currently receives a manager quality ranking of 66 (0=worst, 99=best). If you desire an average level of risk, then this fund may be an option.

Services Offered: Automated phone transactions, payroll deductions, bank draft capabilities, an IRA investment plan, a 401K investment plan, a Keogh investment plan, wire transfers and a systematic withdrawal plan.

Data Date	Investment Rating	Net Assets ($Mil)	NAV	Perfor-mance Rating/Pts	Total Return Y-T-D	Risk Rating/Pts
2-17	C+	76,004	22.43	C / 4.4	3.51%	B- / 7.4
2016	B-	74,108	21.67	C+ / 5.9	10.58%	B- / 7.5
2015	C	70,460	20.23	C- / 4.2	-1.48%	B- / 7.5
2014	C+	72,851	21.58	C- / 3.8	8.39%	B / 8.1
2013	C	67,055	20.65	C- / 3.7	18.26%	B- / 7.2
2012	C+	57,662	18.06	C- / 3.9	11.95%	B- / 7.1

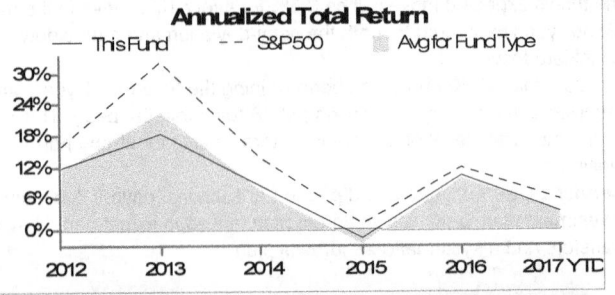

American Funds Inv Co of Amer A (AIVSX)   B-   Good

Fund Family: American Funds   **Phone:** (800) 421-0180
Address: 333 South Hope Street, Los Angeles, CA 90071
Fund Type: GI - Growth and Income

Major Rating Factors: Strong performance is the major factor driving the B- (Good) TheStreet.com Investment Rating for American Funds Inv Co of Amer A. The fund currently has a performance rating of B (Good) based on an average return of 9.40% over the last three years and 5.13% over the last three months. Factored into the performance evaluation is an expense ratio of 0.59% (very low) and a 5.8% front-end load that is levied at the time of purchase.

The fund's risk rating is currently C (Fair). It carries a beta of 0.96, meaning that its performance tracks fairly well with that of the overall stock market. Volatility, as measured by both the semi-deviation and a drawdown factor, is considered average.

James B. Lovelace has been running the fund for 25 years and currently receives a manager quality ranking of 65 (0=worst, 99=best). If you desire an average level of risk and strong performance, then this fund is a good option.

Services Offered: Automated phone transactions, payroll deductions, bank draft capabilities, an IRA investment plan, a 401K investment plan, a Keogh investment plan, wire transfers and a systematic withdrawal plan.

Data Date	Investment Rating	Net Assets ($Mil)	NAV	Perfor-mance Rating/Pts	Total Return Y-T-D	Risk Rating/Pts
2-17	B-	60,667	38.09	B / 7.7	5.13%	C / 5.3
2016	B-	58,432	36.23	B / 7.8	14.59%	C / 5.4
2015	B-	54,745	33.37	B- / 7.4	-1.44%	C+ / 5.6
2014	B	58,436	37.08	B- / 7.2	12.09%	C+ / 6.5
2013	C+	54,123	36.70	C+ / 6.6	32.43%	C+ / 5.7
2012	D+	44,501	30.16	D+ / 2.9	15.60%	C / 5.5

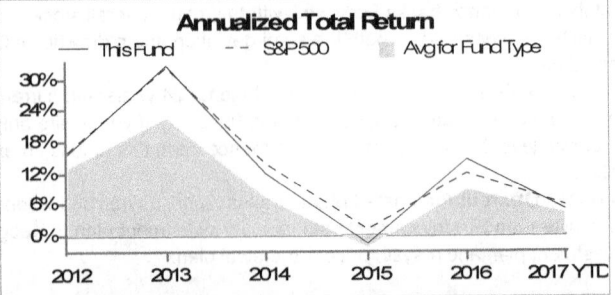

American Funds New Economy A (ANEFX)   C-   Fair

Fund Family: American Funds   **Phone:** (800) 421-0180
Address: 333 South Hope Street, Los Angeles, CA 90071
Fund Type: GR - Growth

Major Rating Factors: Middle of the road best describes American Funds New Economy A whose TheStreet.com Investment Rating is currently a C- (Fair). The fund currently has a performance rating of C (Fair) based on an average return of 4.82% over the last three years and 8.37% over the last three months. Factored into the performance evaluation is an expense ratio of 0.78% (very low) and a 5.8% front-end load that is levied at the time of purchase.

The fund's risk rating is currently C (Fair). It carries a beta of 0.99, meaning that its performance tracks fairly well with that of the overall stock market. Volatility, as measured by both the semi-deviation and a drawdown factor, is considered average.

Timothy D. Armour has been running the fund for 26 years and currently receives a manager quality ranking of 13 (0=worst, 99=best). If you desire an average level of risk, then this fund may be an option.

Services Offered: Automated phone transactions, payroll deductions, an IRA investment plan, a 401K investment plan, a Keogh investment plan, wire transfers and a systematic withdrawal plan.

Data Date	Investment Rating	Net Assets ($Mil)	NAV	Perfor-mance Rating/Pts	Total Return Y-T-D	Risk Rating/Pts
2-17	C-	10,198	38.96	C / 5.0	8.37%	C / 4.7
2016	D+	9,572	35.95	C- / 3.0	2.19%	C / 4.8
2015	B+	10,415	35.96	B+ / 8.7	3.80%	C+ / 5.9
2014	B+	9,776	36.78	B+ / 8.3	4.59%	C+ / 6.1
2013	A	8,920	38.22	A+ / 9.6	43.36%	C / 4.8
2012	B	5,978	28.43	B / 7.7	24.02%	C / 4.7

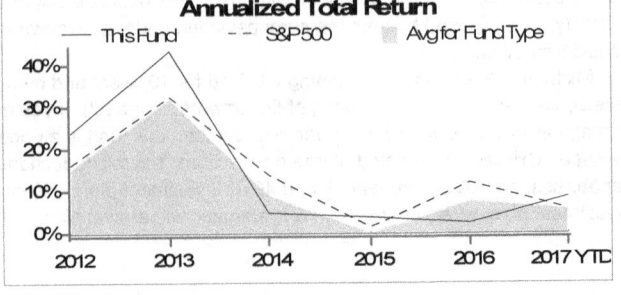

American Funds New Perspectve A (ANWPX)   C-   Fair

Fund Family: American Funds   **Phone:** (800) 421-0180
Address: 333 South Hope Street, Los Angeles, CA 90071
Fund Type: GL - Global
Major Rating Factors: Middle of the road best describes American Funds New Perspectve A whose TheStreet.com Investment Rating is currently a C- (Fair). The fund currently has a performance rating of C (Fair) based on an average return of 5.28% over the last three years and 6.99% over the last three months. Factored into the performance evaluation is an expense ratio of 0.77% (very low) and a 5.8% front-end load that is levied at the time of purchase.

The fund's risk rating is currently C (Fair). It carries a beta of 0.81, meaning the fund's expected move will be 8.1% for every 10% move in the market. Volatility, as measured by both the semi-deviation and a drawdown factor, is considered average.

Jonathan O. Knowles has been running the fund for 13 years and currently receives a manager quality ranking of 96 (0=worst, 99=best). If you desire an average level of risk, then this fund may be an option.

Services Offered: Automated phone transactions, payroll deductions, bank draft capabilities, an IRA investment plan, a 401K investment plan, a Keogh investment plan, wire transfers and a systematic withdrawal plan.

Data Date	Investment Rating	Net Assets ($Mil)	NAV	Performance Rating/Pts	Total Return Y-T-D	Risk Rating/Pts
2-17	C-	36,773	37.80	C / 4.5	6.99%	C / 5.5
2016	D+	35,000	35.33	D+ / 2.6	1.86%	C+ / 5.6
2015	C+	37,219	36.02	C+ / 6.9	5.34%	C+ / 6.5
2014	C	36,228	36.28	C / 4.9	3.23%	C+ / 6.2
2013	C	36,449	37.56	C / 5.1	26.77%	C / 5.1
2012	C	30,245	31.26	C+ / 5.7	20.77%	C / 4.9

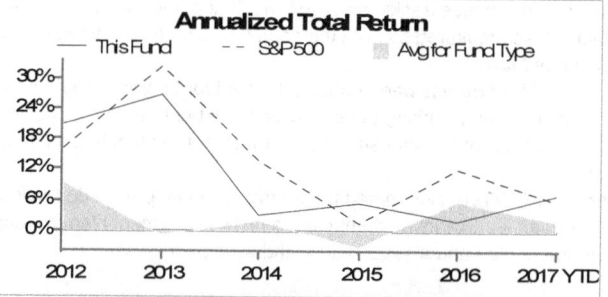
Annualized Total Return

American Funds New World A (NEWFX)   D-   Weak

Fund Family: American Funds   **Phone:** (800) 421-0180
Address: 333 South Hope Street, Los Angeles, CA 90071
Fund Type: GL - Global
Major Rating Factors: Disappointing performance is the major factor driving the D- (Weak) TheStreet.com Investment Rating for American Funds New World A. The fund currently has a performance rating of D (Weak) based on an average return of 0.20% over the last three years and 7.17% over the last three months. Factored into the performance evaluation is an expense ratio of 1.07% (low) and a 5.8% front-end load that is levied at the time of purchase.

The fund's risk rating is currently C (Fair). It carries a beta of 0.83, meaning the fund's expected move will be 8.3% for every 10% move in the market. Volatility, as measured by both the semi-deviation and a drawdown factor, is considered average.

Mark E. Denning has been running the fund for 18 years and currently receives a manager quality ranking of 76 (0=worst, 99=best). This fund offers an average level of risk but investors looking for strong performance will be frustrated.

Services Offered: Automated phone transactions, payroll deductions, bank draft capabilities, an IRA investment plan, a 401K investment plan, a Keogh investment plan, wire transfers and a systematic withdrawal plan.

Data Date	Investment Rating	Net Assets ($Mil)	NAV	Performance Rating/Pts	Total Return Y-T-D	Risk Rating/Pts
2-17	D-	11,055	55.14	D / 1.8	7.17%	C / 5.0
2016	E+	10,476	51.45	E+ / 0.6	3.86%	C / 4.9
2015	E+	11,086	50.00	E+ / 0.7	-5.99%	C / 5.3
2014	E+	12,449	53.50	D- / 1.0	-3.66%	C / 5.4
2013	E+	13,284	58.75	E+ / 0.9	10.01%	C- / 4.2
2012	D+	12,180	54.49	C / 4.5	19.71%	C / 4.3

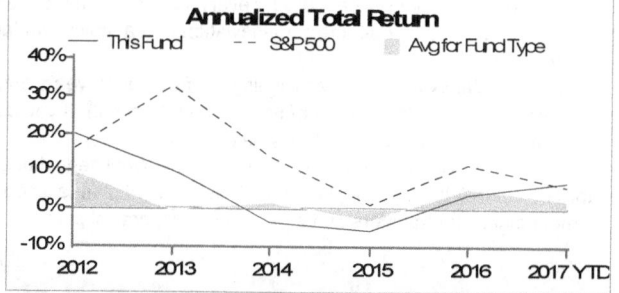
Annualized Total Return

American Funds SMALLCAP World A (SMCWX)   D+   Weak

Fund Family: American Funds   **Phone:** (800) 421-0180
Address: 333 South Hope Street, Los Angeles, CA 90071
Fund Type: SC - Small Cap
Major Rating Factors: American Funds SMALLCAP World A receives a TheStreet.com Investment Rating of D+ (Weak). The fund currently has a performance rating of C (Fair) based on an average return of 4.29% over the last three years and 6.72% over the last three months. Factored into the performance evaluation is an expense ratio of 1.10% (low) and a 5.8% front-end load that is levied at the time of purchase.

The fund's risk rating is currently C (Fair). It carries a beta of 0.65, meaning the fund's expected move will be 6.5% for every 10% move in the market. Volatility, as measured by both the semi-deviation and a drawdown factor, is considered average.

Mark E. Denning has been running the fund for 26 years and currently receives a manager quality ranking of 72 (0=worst, 99=best). If you desire an average level of risk, then this fund may be an option.

Services Offered: Automated phone transactions, payroll deductions, bank draft capabilities, an IRA investment plan, a 401K investment plan, a Keogh investment plan and a systematic withdrawal plan.

Data Date	Investment Rating	Net Assets ($Mil)	NAV	Performance Rating/Pts	Total Return Y-T-D	Risk Rating/Pts
2-17	D+	19,106	49.07	C / 4.6	6.72%	C / 4.3
2016	D	18,044	45.98	C- / 3.0	5.75%	C / 4.4
2015	C	17,445	43.63	C / 5.5	2.58%	C / 5.5
2014	C-	16,972	45.31	C / 5.1	1.82%	C / 5.5
2013	D	17,118	49.15	C / 4.5	29.29%	C- / 3.5
2012	C	13,566	39.91	C+ / 6.9	21.94%	C- / 3.6

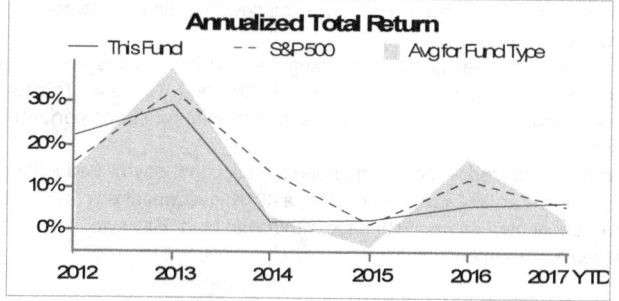
Annualized Total Return

American Funds Wash Mutl Invs A (AWSHX)   B+   Good

Fund Family: American Funds   **Phone:** (800) 421-0180
Address: 333 South Hope Street, Los Angeles, CA 90071
Fund Type: GI - Growth and Income
Major Rating Factors: Strong performance is the major factor driving the B+
(Good) TheStreet.com Investment Rating for American Funds Wash Mutl Invs A.
The fund currently has a performance rating of B (Good) based on an average
return of 9.39% over the last three years and 4.66% over the last three months.
Factored into the performance evaluation is an expense ratio of 0.58% (very low)
and a 5.8% front-end load that is levied at the time of purchase.

The fund's risk rating is currently C+ (Fair). It carries a beta of 0.94, meaning
that its performance tracks fairly well with that of the overall stock market.
Volatility, as measured by both the semi-deviation and a drawdown factor, is
considered low.

Alan N. Berro has been running the fund for 20 years and currently receives
a manager quality ranking of 68 (0=worst, 99=best). If you desire only a
moderate level of risk and strong performance, then this fund is an excellent
option.

Services Offered: Automated phone transactions, payroll deductions, bank draft
capabilities, an IRA investment plan, a 401K investment plan, a Keogh
investment plan and a systematic withdrawal plan.

Data Date	Investment Rating	Net Assets ($Mil)	NAV	Perfor-mance Rating/Pts	Total Return Y-T-D	Risk Rating/Pts
2-17	B+	54,608	42.86	B / 7.7	4.66%	C+ / 6.3
2016	B+	52,896	40.95	B / 7.9	13.41%	C+ / 6.4
2015	B+	49,978	38.44	B / 7.7	-0.17%	C+ / 6.7
2014	B-	52,722	40.95	C+ / 6.5	11.22%	B- / 7.5
2013	A-	49,202	39.43	B- / 7.2	31.92%	C+ / 6.6
2012	C+	39,823	31.21	C / 4.8	12.50%	C+ / 6.4

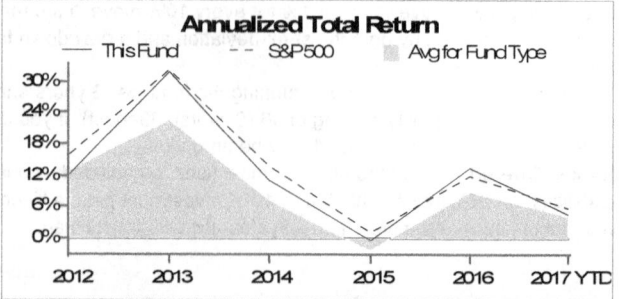

AMG Yacktman I (YACKX)   C+   Fair

Fund Family: AMG Funds   **Phone:** (800) 548-4539
Address: 600 Steamboat Road, Greenwich, CT 06830
Fund Type: GI - Growth and Income
Major Rating Factors: Middle of the road best describes AMG Yacktman I
whose TheStreet.com Investment Rating is currently a C+ (Fair). The fund
currently has a performance rating of C+ (Fair) based on an average return of
7.43% over the last three years and 5.24% over the last three months. Factored
into the performance evaluation is an expense ratio of 0.74% (very low) and a
2.0% back-end load levied at the time of sale.

The fund's risk rating is currently C (Fair). It carries a beta of 0.78, meaning
the fund's expected move will be 7.8% for every 10% move in the market.
Volatility, as measured by both the semi-deviation and a drawdown factor, is
considered average.

Stephen A. Yacktman has been running the fund for 15 years and currently
receives a manager quality ranking of 65 (0=worst, 99=best). If you desire an
average level of risk, then this fund may be an option.

Services Offered: Automated phone transactions, payroll deductions, bank draft
capabilities, an IRA investment plan, a 401K investment plan, a Keogh
investment plan, wire transfers and a systematic withdrawal plan.

Data Date	Investment Rating	Net Assets ($Mil)	NAV	Perfor-mance Rating/Pts	Total Return Y-T-D	Risk Rating/Pts
2-17	C+	8,758	22.51	C+ / 6.6	5.24%	C / 5.5
2016	C+	8,532	21.39	C+ / 6.7	11.20%	C+ / 5.6
2015	C+	8,951	20.87	C+ / 5.9	-5.63%	C+ / 6.0
2014	B	14,219	25.12	C+ / 6.5	11.33%	B / 8.2
2013	B-	13,918	23.54	C+ / 6.0	27.74%	B- / 7.6
2012	C+	8,670	19.12	C / 5.2	11.47%	C+ / 6.9

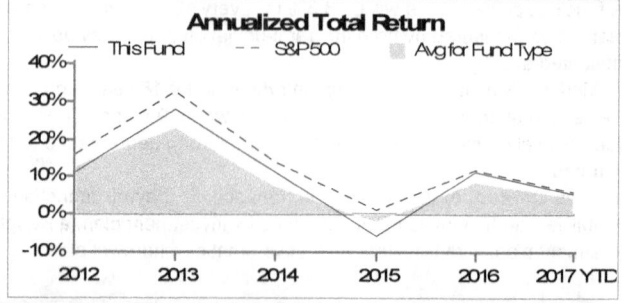

Artisan International Fund Inv (ARTIX)   D-   Weak

Fund Family: Artisan Funds   **Phone:** (800) 344-1770
Address: P.O. Box 8412, Boston, MA 02266
Fund Type: FO - Foreign
Major Rating Factors: Very poor performance is the major factor driving the D-
(Weak) TheStreet.com Investment Rating for Artisan International Fund Inv. The
fund currently has a performance rating of E (Very Weak) based on an average
return of -3.40% over the last three years and 5.19% over the last three months.
Factored into the performance evaluation is an expense ratio of 1.17% (low).

The fund's risk rating is currently C+ (Fair). It carries a beta of 0.86, meaning
the fund's expected move will be 8.6% for every 10% move in the market.
Volatility, as measured by both the semi-deviation and a drawdown factor, is
considered low.

Mark L. Yockey has been running the fund for 22 years and currently
receives a manager quality ranking of 31 (0=worst, 99=best). This fund offers
only a moderate level of risk but investors looking for strong performance are still
waiting.

Services Offered: Automated phone transactions, payroll deductions, bank draft
capabilities, an IRA investment plan, a 401K investment plan, a Keogh
investment plan and a systematic withdrawal plan. However, the fund is currently
closed to new investors.

Data Date	Investment Rating	Net Assets ($Mil)	NAV	Perfor-mance Rating/Pts	Total Return Y-T-D	Risk Rating/Pts
2-17	D-	6,041	26.94	E / 0.3	5.19%	C+ / 6.2
2016	D-	6,427	25.61	E- / 0.2	-9.66%	C+ / 6.0
2015	C-	10,723	28.68	C- / 3.2	-3.85%	C+ / 6.7
2014	C	14,389	29.96	C / 4.7	-0.97%	C+ / 6.8
2013	C-	10,764	30.48	C+ / 5.7	25.18%	C- / 3.7
2012	C+	7,498	24.59	B / 7.8	25.39%	C- / 3.3

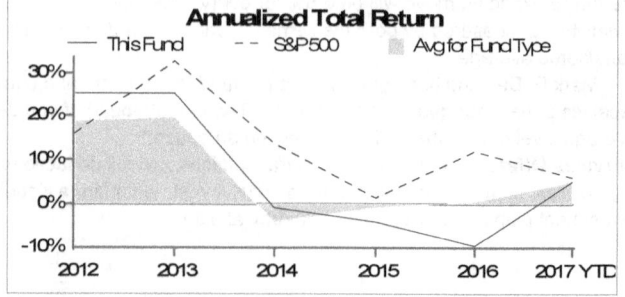

BlackRock Eq Dividend Inv A (MDDVX)   B   Good

Fund Family: BlackRock Funds   **Phone:** (800) 441-7762
Address: c/o PFPC, Inc., Providence, RI 02940
Fund Type: IN - Income
Major Rating Factors: Strong performance is the major factor driving the B (Good) TheStreet.com Investment Rating for BlackRock Eq Dividend Inv A. The fund currently has a performance rating of B+ (Good) based on an average return of 9.63% over the last three years and 3.69% over the last three months. Factored into the performance evaluation is an expense ratio of 0.97% (low) and a 5.3% front-end load that is levied at the time of purchase.

The fund's risk rating is currently C (Fair). It carries a beta of 0.94, meaning that its performance tracks fairly well with that of the overall stock market. Volatility, as measured by both the semi-deviation and a drawdown factor, is considered average.

Robert M. Shearer has been running the fund for 16 years and currently receives a manager quality ranking of 70 (0=worst, 99=best). If you desire an average level of risk and strong performance, then this fund is a good option.
Services Offered: Automated phone transactions, payroll deductions, bank draft capabilities, an IRA investment plan, a 401K investment plan and a systematic withdrawal plan.

Data Date	Investment Rating	Net Assets ($Mil)	NAV	Performance Rating/Pts	Total Return Y-T-D	Risk Rating/Pts
2-17	B	5,997	23.33	B+ / 8.3	3.69%	C / 5.2
2016	B+	5,951	22.50	B+ / 8.7	16.00%	C / 5.4
2015	C	6,234	20.95	C+ / 6.1	-0.39%	C+ / 5.7
2014	C+	8,484	24.90	C / 5.0	9.06%	B- / 7.6
2013	C+	10,965	24.28	C / 5.3	24.35%	C+ / 6.8
2012	C	9,157	19.89	C- / 3.9	11.92%	C+ / 6.7

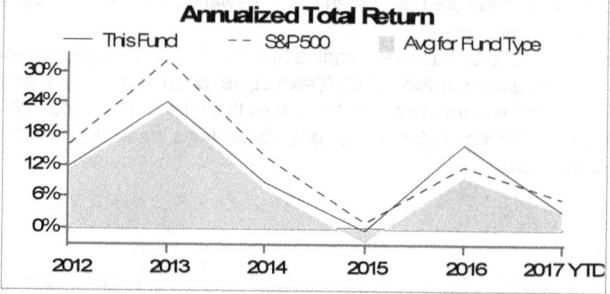

BlackRock Global Allocation Inv A (MDLOX)   D   Weak

Fund Family: BlackRock Funds   **Phone:** (800) 441-7762
Address: c/o PFPC, Inc., Providence, RI 02940
Fund Type: GL - Global
Major Rating Factors: Disappointing performance is the major factor driving the D (Weak) TheStreet.com Investment Rating for BlackRock Global Allocation Inv A. The fund currently has a performance rating of D (Weak) based on an average return of 2.40% over the last three years and 3.58% over the last three months. Factored into the performance evaluation is an expense ratio of 1.14% (low) and a 5.3% front-end load that is levied at the time of purchase.

The fund's risk rating is currently C+ (Fair). It carries a beta of 0.98, meaning that its performance tracks fairly well with that of the overall stock market. Volatility, as measured by both the semi-deviation and a drawdown factor, is considered low.

Dennis W. Stattman has been running the fund for 28 years and currently receives a manager quality ranking of 47 (0=worst, 99=best). This fund offers only a moderate level of risk but investors looking for strong performance are still waiting.
Services Offered: Automated phone transactions, payroll deductions, bank draft capabilities, an IRA investment plan, a 401K investment plan and a systematic withdrawal plan.

Data Date	Investment Rating	Net Assets ($Mil)	NAV	Performance Rating/Pts	Total Return Y-T-D	Risk Rating/Pts
2-17	D	12,892	18.83	D / 1.9	3.58%	C+ / 6.2
2016	D+	12,975	18.18	D / 2.1	3.75%	C+ / 6.3
2015	D	15,208	17.84	D+ / 2.3	-1.05%	C+ / 6.3
2014	D	17,221	19.77	D / 1.7	1.87%	C+ / 6.9
2013	D+	19,299	21.33	D / 1.9	14.43%	C+ / 6.9
2012	D	17,292	19.74	E+ / 0.9	10.01%	B- / 7.0

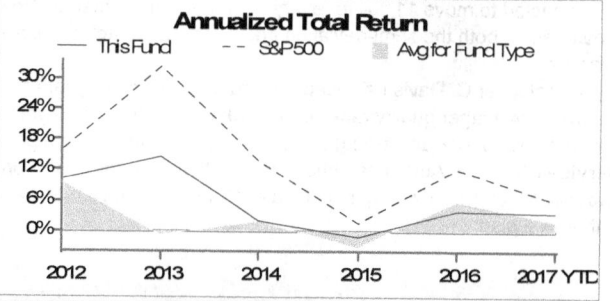

ClearBridge Aggressive Growth A (SHRAX)   C+   Fair

Fund Family: Legg Mason Partners Funds   **Phone:** (877) 534-4627
Address: 100 Light Street, Baltimore, MD 21202
Fund Type: AG - Aggressive Growth
Major Rating Factors: Middle of the road best describes ClearBridge Aggressive Growth A whose TheStreet.com Investment Rating is currently a C+ (Fair). The fund currently has a performance rating of C+ (Fair) based on an average return of 5.49% over the last three years and 8.68% over the last three months. Factored into the performance evaluation is an expense ratio of 1.15% (low) and a 5.8% front-end load that is levied at the time of purchase.

The fund's risk rating is currently C (Fair). It carries a beta of 1.16, meaning it is expected to move 11.6% for every 10% move in the market. Volatility, as measured by both the semi-deviation and a drawdown factor, is considered average.

Richard A. Freeman has been running the fund for 34 years and currently receives a manager quality ranking of 8 (0=worst, 99=best). If you desire an average level of risk, then this fund may be an option.
Services Offered: Payroll deductions, bank draft capabilities, an IRA investment plan, a 401K investment plan and a systematic withdrawal plan.

Data Date	Investment Rating	Net Assets ($Mil)	NAV	Performance Rating/Pts	Total Return Y-T-D	Risk Rating/Pts
2-17	C+	5,513	205.32	C+ / 6.1	8.68%	C / 5.3
2016	C-	5,156	188.92	C / 4.7	5.71%	C / 5.3
2015	B+	5,435	187.14	B+ / 8.3	-4.40%	C+ / 6.6
2014	A+	5,666	203.68	A+ / 9.7	14.55%	C+ / 6.7
2013	A	4,405	181.37	A / 9.5	44.62%	C / 4.6
2012	B+	2,994	126.44	B+ / 8.6	18.53%	C- / 4.2

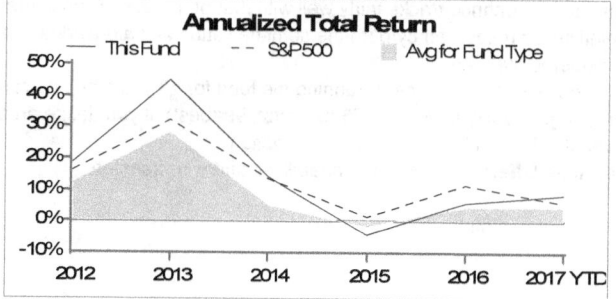

Cohen & Steers Realty Shares (CSRSX)

C+ **Fair**

Fund Family: Cohen & Steers Funds   **Phone:** (800) 330-7348
Address: 280 Park Avenue, New York, NY 10017
Fund Type: RE - Real Estate
Major Rating Factors: Strong performance is the major factor driving the C+ (Fair) TheStreet.com Investment Rating for Cohen & Steers Realty Shares. The fund currently has a performance rating of B (Good) based on an average return of 11.21% over the last three years and 4.05% over the last three months. Factored into the performance evaluation is an expense ratio of 0.96% (low).

The fund's risk rating is currently C- (Fair). It carries a beta of 1.05, meaning that its performance tracks fairly well with that of the overall stock market. Volatility, as measured by both the semi-deviation and a drawdown factor, is considered average.

Jon Y. Cheigh has been running the fund for 10 years and currently receives a manager quality ranking of 69 (0=worst, 99=best). If you desire an average level of risk and strong performance, then this fund is a good option.

Services Offered: Automated phone transactions, bank draft capabilities and wire transfers.

Data Date	Investment Rating	Net Assets ($Mil)	NAV	Performance Rating/Pts	Total Return Y-T-D	Risk Rating/Pts
2-17	C+	5,230	68.29	B / 7.8	4.05%	C- / 3.9
2016	C+	5,276	65.63	A- / 9.0	5.61%	C- / 4.0
2015	C+	5,745	70.52	B+ / 8.6	5.00%	C- / 3.8
2014	B-	6,339	76.86	A / 9.4	30.18%	C- / 3.6
2013	E+	5,158	62.82	D / 1.6	3.09%	D+ / 2.9
2012	B	4,879	64.57	A / 9.5	15.72%	C- / 3.1

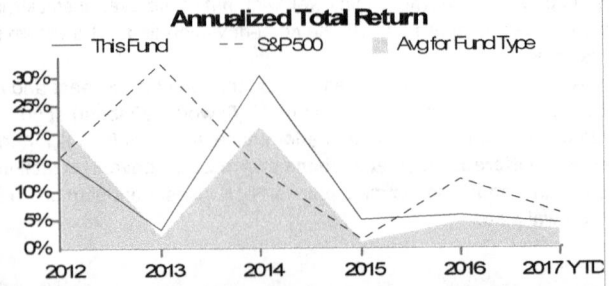

Annualized Total Return

Davis New York Venture Fund A (NYVTX)

C **Fair**

Fund Family: Davis Funds   **Phone:** (800) 279-0279
Address: 2949 East Elvira Road, Tuscon, AZ 85756
Fund Type: GR - Growth
Major Rating Factors: Strong performance is the major factor driving the C (Fair) TheStreet.com Investment Rating for Davis New York Venture Fund A. The fund currently has a performance rating of B (Good) based on an average return of 8.22% over the last three years and 4.03% over the last three months. Factored into the performance evaluation is an expense ratio of 0.89% (low) and a 4.8% front-end load that is levied at the time of purchase.

The fund's risk rating is currently C- (Fair). It carries a beta of 1.11, meaning it is expected to move 11.1% for every 10% move in the market. Volatility, as measured by both the semi-deviation and a drawdown factor, is considered average.

Christopher C. Davis has been running the fund for 22 years and currently receives a manager quality ranking of 31 (0=worst, 99=best). If you desire an average level of risk and strong performance, then this fund is a good option.

Services Offered: Automated phone transactions, payroll deductions, bank draft capabilities, an IRA investment plan, a 401K investment plan and a systematic withdrawal plan.

Data Date	Investment Rating	Net Assets ($Mil)	NAV	Performance Rating/Pts	Total Return Y-T-D	Risk Rating/Pts
2-17	C	6,521	31.75	B / 7.8	4.03%	C- / 3.2
2016	C	6,423	30.52	B- / 7.5	12.25%	C- / 3.4
2015	C+	7,366	30.89	B / 8.1	2.97%	C / 4.3
2014	C-	9,963	36.84	C+ / 5.8	6.55%	C / 5.0
2013	C+	11,711	41.41	C+ / 6.2	34.56%	C / 5.4
2012	D-	10,814	34.78	D- / 1.5	12.73%	C / 5.2

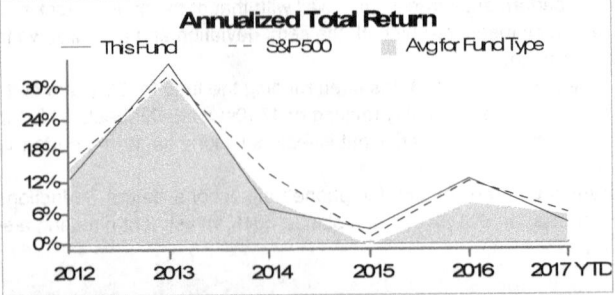

Annualized Total Return

DFA Emerging Markets Inst (DFEMX)

C- **Fair**

Fund Family: Dimensional Fund Advisors   **Phone:** (800) 984-9472
Address: 6300 Bee Cave Road, Austin, TX 78746
Fund Type: EM - Emerging Market
Major Rating Factors: Middle of the road best describes DFA Emerging Markets Inst whose TheStreet.com Investment Rating is currently a C- (Fair). The fund currently has a performance rating of C (Fair) based on an average return of 1.76% over the last three years and 9.50% over the last three months. Factored into the performance evaluation is an expense ratio of 0.67% (very low).

The fund's risk rating is currently C (Fair). It carries a beta of 0.96, meaning that its performance tracks fairly well with that of the overall stock market. Volatility, as measured by both the semi-deviation and a drawdown factor, is considered average.

Jed S. Fogdall has been running the fund for 13 years and currently receives a manager quality ranking of 75 (0=worst, 99=best). If you desire an average level of risk, then this fund may be an option.

Services Offered: Bank draft capabilities and wire transfers.

Data Date	Investment Rating	Net Assets ($Mil)	NAV	Performance Rating/Pts	Total Return Y-T-D	Risk Rating/Pts
2-17	C-	5,331	24.89	C / 5.0	9.50%	C / 4.5
2016	D-	4,826	22.73	D- / 1.4	12.09%	C / 4.6
2015	E	4,180	20.67	E / 0.4	-15.81%	C / 4.5
2014	E+	3,992	25.04	E+ / 0.7	-1.71%	C / 5.1
2013	E	3,599	25.96	E / 0.4	-3.12%	C- / 3.1
2012	C-	2,981	27.54	C+ / 6.7	19.16%	C- / 3.2

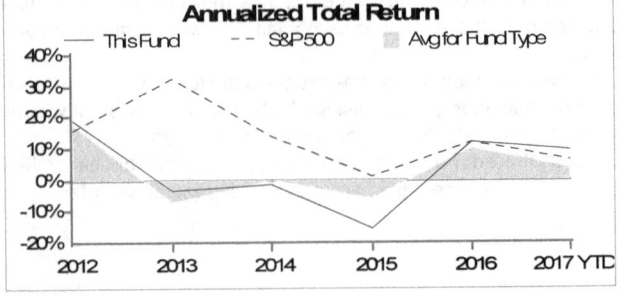

Annualized Total Return

DFA Emerging Markets Sm Cap Inst (DEMSX)   B-   Good

Fund Family: Dimensional Fund Advisors   **Phone:** (800) 984-9472
Address: 6300 Bee Cave Road, Austin, TX 78746
Fund Type: FO - Foreign
Major Rating Factors: Strong performance is the major factor driving the B- (Good) TheStreet.com Investment Rating for DFA Emerging Markets Sm Cap Inst. The fund currently has a performance rating of B (Good) based on an average return of 5.14% over the last three years and 11.37% over the last three months. Factored into the performance evaluation is an expense ratio of 0.93% (low).

The fund's risk rating is currently C (Fair). It carries a beta of 0.90, meaning the fund's expected move will be 9.0% for every 10% move in the market. Volatility, as measured by both the semi-deviation and a drawdown factor, is considered average.

Jed S. Fogdall has been running the fund for 13 years and currently receives a manager quality ranking of 96 (0=worst, 99=best). If you desire an average level of risk and strong performance, then this fund is a good option.
Services Offered: Automated phone transactions, bank draft capabilities and a systematic withdrawal plan.

Data Date	Investment Rating	Net Assets ($Mil)	NAV	Performance Rating/Pts	Total Return Y-T-D	Risk Rating/Pts
2-17	B-	6,081	20.66	B / 7.6	11.37%	C / 4.9
2016	D+	5,331	18.55	D+ / 2.9	10.92%	C / 5.0
2015	E+	4,688	17.58	E+ / 0.6	-8.70%	C / 4.8
2014	D-	4,772	19.89	D / 1.8	3.00%	C / 5.2
2013	E	3,992	20.11	E / 0.4	-1.38%	D+ / 2.5
2012	C+	3,461	21.17	B+ / 8.7	24.44%	D+ / 2.5

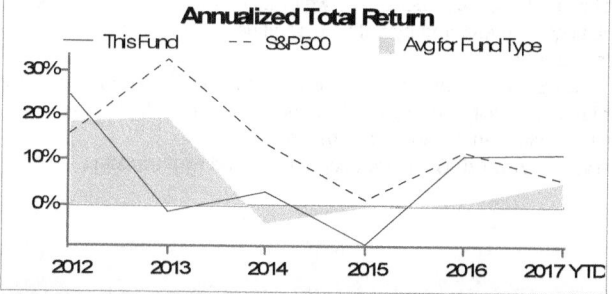

DFA Emerging Markts Core Eqty Inst (DFCEX)   C   Fair

Fund Family: Dimensional Fund Advisors   **Phone:** (800) 984-9472
Address: 6300 Bee Cave Road, Austin, TX 78746
Fund Type: EM - Emerging Market
Major Rating Factors: Middle of the road best describes DFA Emerging Markts Core Eqty Inst whose TheStreet.com Investment Rating is currently a C (Fair). The fund currently has a performance rating of C+ (Fair) based on an average return of 2.49% over the last three years and 10.25% over the last three months. Factored into the performance evaluation is an expense ratio of 0.62% (very low).

The fund's risk rating is currently C (Fair). It carries a beta of 0.96, meaning that its performance tracks fairly well with that of the overall stock market. Volatility, as measured by both the semi-deviation and a drawdown factor, is considered average.

Joseph H. Chi has been running the fund for 12 years and currently receives a manager quality ranking of 80 (0=worst, 99=best). If you desire an average level of risk, then this fund may be an option.
Services Offered: Automated phone transactions, bank draft capabilities, wire transfers and a systematic withdrawal plan.

Data Date	Investment Rating	Net Assets ($Mil)	NAV	Performance Rating/Pts	Total Return Y-T-D	Risk Rating/Pts
2-17	C	20,486	19.14	C+ / 5.9	10.25%	C / 4.6
2016	D-	17,911	17.36	D / 1.7	12.35%	C / 4.7
2015	E+	13,728	15.76	E / 0.4	-14.86%	C / 4.7
2014	E+	15,122	18.92	E+ / 0.8	-0.91%	C / 5.1
2013	E	13,152	19.46	E / 0.3	-2.64%	D+ / 2.8
2012	C-	9,739	20.40	C+ / 6.7	20.49%	D+ / 2.9

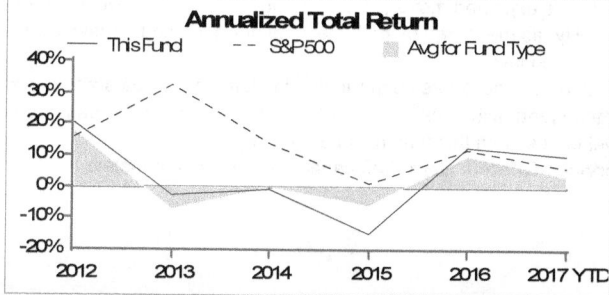

DFA Gl Real Estate Securities Port (DFGEX)   C   Fair

Fund Family: Dimensional Fund Advisors   **Phone:** (800) 984-9472
Address: 6300 Bee Cave Road, Austin, TX 78746
Fund Type: RE - Real Estate
Major Rating Factors: Middle of the road best describes DFA Gl Real Estate Securities Port whose TheStreet.com Investment Rating is currently a C (Fair). The fund currently has a performance rating of C (Fair) based on an average return of 8.21% over the last three years and 3.17% over the last three months. Factored into the performance evaluation is an expense ratio of 0.38% (very low).

The fund's risk rating is currently C (Fair). It carries a beta of 0.92, meaning that its performance tracks fairly well with that of the overall stock market. Volatility, as measured by both the semi-deviation and a drawdown factor, is considered average.

Karen E. Umland currently receives a manager quality ranking of 51 (0=worst, 99=best). If you desire an average level of risk, then this fund may be an option.
Services Offered: N/A

Data Date	Investment Rating	Net Assets ($Mil)	NAV	Performance Rating/Pts	Total Return Y-T-D	Risk Rating/Pts
2-17	C	5,413	10.73	C / 5.4	3.17%	C / 5.2
2016	C+	5,034	10.40	B- / 7.5	6.56%	C / 5.3
2015	C-	4,097	10.27	C+ / 5.7	0.69%	C / 5.1
2014	C+	3,419	10.45	B / 7.6	22.74%	C / 4.8
2013	D-	2,095	8.84	D / 1.6	1.77%	C / 4.8
2012	A+	1,354	9.01	A+ / 9.8	23.17%	C / 4.3

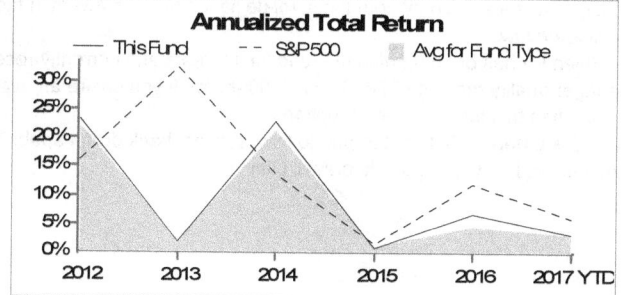

DFA International Sm Cap Val Inst (DISVX)

C   **Fair**

Fund Family: Dimensional Fund Advisors   **Phone:** (800) 984-9472
Address: 6300 Bee Cave Road, Austin, TX 78746
Fund Type: FO - Foreign
Major Rating Factors: Middle of the road best describes DFA International Sm Cap Val Inst whose TheStreet.com Investment Rating is currently a C (Fair). The fund currently has a performance rating of C (Fair) based on an average return of 2.28% over the last three years and 5.68% over the last three months. Factored into the performance evaluation is an expense ratio of 0.69% (very low).

The fund's risk rating is currently C+ (Fair). It carries a beta of 0.93, meaning that its performance tracks fairly well with that of the overall stock market. Volatility, as measured by both the semi-deviation and a drawdown factor, is considered low.

Jed S. Fogdall has been running the fund for 13 years and currently receives a manager quality ranking of 88 (0=worst, 99=best). If you desire an average level of risk, then this fund may be an option.

Services Offered: Bank draft capabilities and wire transfers.

Data Date	Investment Rating	Net Assets ($Mil)	NAV	Performance Rating/Pts	Total Return Y-T-D	Risk Rating/Pts
2-17	C	13,966	20.10	C / 5.3	5.68%	C+ / 5.9
2016	C-	13,067	19.02	C / 4.6	8.00%	C+ / 6.0
2015	C+	12,387	18.68	C+ / 6.2	3.99%	C+ / 6.5
2014	D+	11,499	18.60	C- / 4.0	-4.99%	C / 5.1
2013	D+	11,533	20.35	C+ / 5.9	32.39%	C- / 3.1
2012	C	8,920	15.98	B / 8.0	22.26%	D+ 2.7

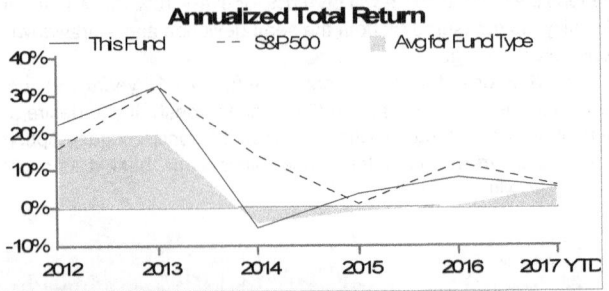

DFA International Small Co Inst (DFISX)

C-   **Fair**

Fund Family: Dimensional Fund Advisors   **Phone:** (800) 984-9472
Address: 6300 Bee Cave Road, Austin, TX 78746
Fund Type: FO - Foreign
Major Rating Factors: Middle of the road best describes DFA International Small Co Inst whose TheStreet.com Investment Rating is currently a C- (Fair). The fund currently has a performance rating of C- (Fair) based on an average return of 2.11% over the last three years and 5.85% over the last three months. Factored into the performance evaluation is an expense ratio of 0.54% (very low).

The fund's risk rating is currently C+ (Fair). It carries a beta of 0.87, meaning the fund's expected move will be 8.7% for every 10% move in the market. Volatility, as measured by both the semi-deviation and a drawdown factor, is considered low.

Jed S. Fogdall has been running the fund for 13 years and currently receives a manager quality ranking of 87 (0=worst, 99=best). If you desire an average level of risk, then this fund may be an option.

Services Offered: Bank draft capabilities and wire transfers.

Data Date	Investment Rating	Net Assets ($Mil)	NAV	Performance Rating/Pts	Total Return Y-T-D	Risk Rating/Pts
2-17	C-	11,092	18.28	C- / 4.1	5.85%	C+ / 6.1
2016	C-	10,365	17.27	C- / 3.1	5.80%	C+ / 6.2
2015	C+	9,293	17.21	C+ / 5.9	5.91%	C+ / 6.2
2014	D-	8,640	16.98	D+ / 2.8	-6.30%	C / 5.2
2013	D+	8,792	19.21	C / 4.9	27.44%	C- / 3.7
2012	C+	6,730	15.93	B / 7.8	18.86%	C- / 3.3

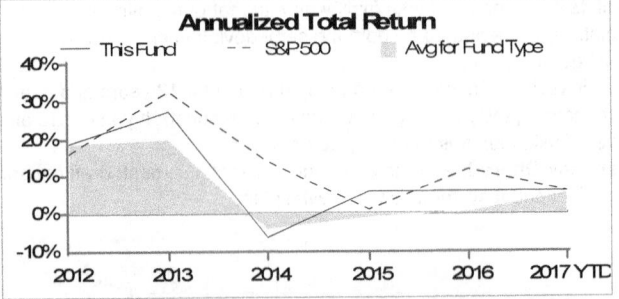

DFA Intl Core Equity Port Inst (DFIEX)

D+   **Weak**

Fund Family: Dimensional Fund Advisors   **Phone:** (800) 984-9472
Address: 6300 Bee Cave Road, Austin, TX 78746
Fund Type: FO - Foreign
Major Rating Factors: DFA Intl Core Equity Port Inst receives a TheStreet.com Investment Rating of D+ (Weak). The fund currently has a performance rating of C- (Fair) based on an average return of 0.46% over the last three years and 4.97% over the last three months. Factored into the performance evaluation is an expense ratio of 0.38% (very low).

The fund's risk rating is currently C+ (Fair). It carries a beta of 0.93, meaning that its performance tracks fairly well with that of the overall stock market. Volatility, as measured by both the semi-deviation and a drawdown factor, is considered low.

Allen Pu has been running the fund for 11 years and currently receives a manager quality ranking of 78 (0=worst, 99=best). If you desire an average level of risk, then this fund may be an option.

Services Offered: Automated phone transactions, bank draft capabilities, wire transfers and a systematic withdrawal plan.

Data Date	Investment Rating	Net Assets ($Mil)	NAV	Performance Rating/Pts	Total Return Y-T-D	Risk Rating/Pts
2-17	D+	19,345	12.24	C- / 3.1	4.97%	C+ / 5.9
2016	D+	17,697	11.66	D / 2.1	5.34%	C+ / 6.0
2015	D+	14,322	11.39	C- / 3.2	-0.21%	C+ / 6.2
2014	D-	11,998	11.70	D+ / 2.4	-5.98%	C / 5.5
2013	D	10,220	12.81	C- / 4.0	23.43%	C- / 3.5
2012	D+	6,936	10.66	C / 5.5	18.74%	C- / 3.3

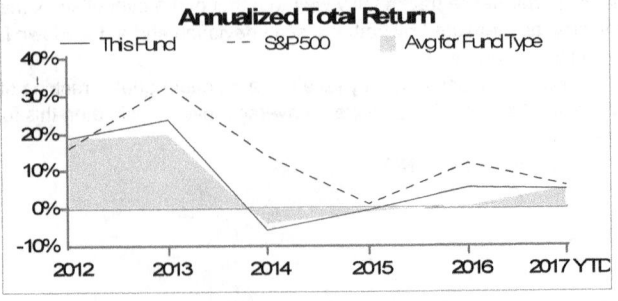

DFA Real Estate Securities Ptf Inst (DFREX)   B-   Good

Fund Family: Dimensional Fund Advisors   **Phone:** (800) 984-9472
Address: 6300 Bee Cave Road, Austin, TX 78746
Fund Type: RE - Real Estate
Major Rating Factors: Strong performance is the major factor driving the B- (Good) TheStreet.com Investment Rating for DFA Real Estate Securities Ptf Inst. The fund currently has a performance rating of B (Good) based on an average return of 11.39% over the last three years and 3.19% over the last three months. Factored into the performance evaluation is an expense ratio of 0.19% (very low).

The fund's risk rating is currently C (Fair). It carries a beta of 1.09, meaning that its performance tracks fairly well with that of the overall stock market. Volatility, as measured by both the semi-deviation and a drawdown factor, is considered average.

Henry F. Gray has been running the fund for 5 years and currently receives a manager quality ranking of 66 (0=worst, 99=best). If you desire an average level of risk and strong performance, then this fund is a good option.
Services Offered: Bank draft capabilities and wire transfers.

Data Date	Investment Rating	Net Assets ($Mil)	NAV	Performance Rating/Pts	Total Return Y-T-D	Risk Rating/Pts
2-17	B-	7,920	35.61	B / 7.8	3.19%	C / 5.0
2016	B+	7,528	34.51	A- / 9.1	7.40%	C / 5.0
2015	C+	6,659	33.15	B / 8.0	3.24%	C / 4.5
2014	B-	6,874	33.07	A / 9.5	31.11%	C- / 3.8
2013	E+	4,581	25.93	D / 1.7	1.39%	C- / 3.2
2012	A	3,835	26.34	A+ / 9.8	17.48%	C- / 3.9

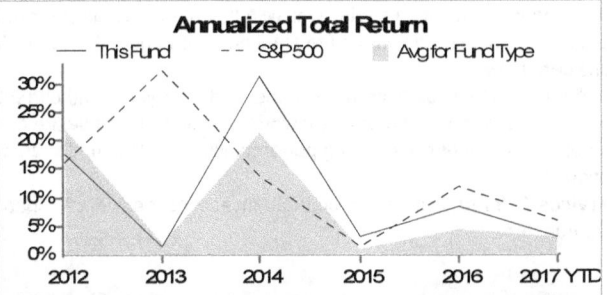

DFA TA US Core Equity 2 Inst (DFTCX)   A+   Excellent

Fund Family: Dimensional Fund Advisors   **Phone:** (800) 984-9472
Address: 6300 Bee Cave Road, Austin, TX 78746
Fund Type: GR - Growth
Major Rating Factors: Strong performance is the major factor driving the A+ (Excellent) TheStreet.com Investment Rating for DFA TA US Core Equity 2 Inst. The fund currently has a performance rating of B+ (Good) based on an average return of 8.71% over the last three years and 4.35% over the last three months. Factored into the performance evaluation is an expense ratio of 0.24% (very low).

The fund's risk rating is currently C+ (Fair). It carries a beta of 1.05, meaning that its performance tracks fairly well with that of the overall stock market. Volatility, as measured by both the semi-deviation and a drawdown factor, is considered low.

Henry F. Gray has been running the fund for 5 years and currently receives a manager quality ranking of 45 (0=worst, 99=best). If you desire only a moderate level of risk and strong performance, then this fund is an excellent option.
Services Offered: N/A

Data Date	Investment Rating	Net Assets ($Mil)	NAV	Performance Rating/Pts	Total Return Y-T-D	Risk Rating/Pts
2-17	A+	7,238	16.31	B+ / 8.9	4.35%	C+ / 6.6
2016	A+	6,856	15.63	A- / 9.1	16.31%	C+ / 6.7
2015	B+	5,433	13.67	B / 8.1	-2.53%	C+ / 6.9
2014	A	5,191	14.26	B+ / 8.9	9.56%	C+ / 6.9
2013	A-	4,372	13.39	A- / 9.0	37.55%	C / 4.8
2012	B	2,962	9.97	B+ / 8.9	17.93%	C- / 3.6

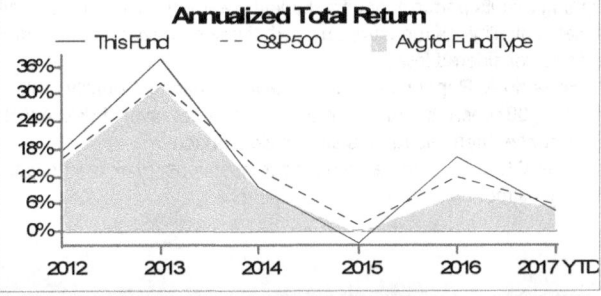

DFA US Core Equity 1 Ptf Inst (DFEOX)   A+   Excellent

Fund Family: Dimensional Fund Advisors   **Phone:** (800) 984-9472
Address: 6300 Bee Cave Road, Austin, TX 78746
Fund Type: IN - Income
Major Rating Factors: Exceptional performance is the major factor driving the A+ (Excellent) TheStreet.com Investment Rating for DFA US Core Equity 1 Ptf Inst. The fund currently has a performance rating of A- (Excellent) based on an average return of 9.13% over the last three years and 5.09% over the last three months. Factored into the performance evaluation is an expense ratio of 0.19% (very low).

The fund's risk rating is currently C+ (Fair). It carries a beta of 1.04, meaning that its performance tracks fairly well with that of the overall stock market. Volatility, as measured by both the semi-deviation and a drawdown factor, is considered low.

Joseph H. Chi has been running the fund for 12 years and currently receives a manager quality ranking of 52 (0=worst, 99=best). If you desire only a moderate level of risk and strong performance, then this fund is an excellent option.
Services Offered: Bank draft capabilities and wire transfers.

Data Date	Investment Rating	Net Assets ($Mil)	NAV	Performance Rating/Pts	Total Return Y-T-D	Risk Rating/Pts
2-17	A+	18,041	20.25	A- / 9.0	5.09%	C+ / 6.7
2016	A+	16,483	19.27	B+ / 8.9	14.80%	C+ / 6.8
2015	A-	13,194	17.17	B+ / 8.4	-1.35%	B- / 7.0
2014	A	11,383	17.92	B+ / 8.8	10.52%	B- / 7.0
2013	A-	8,261	16.54	B+ / 8.9	36.60%	C / 5.2
2012	A-	5,140	12.35	B+ / 8.5	16.91%	C / 4.9

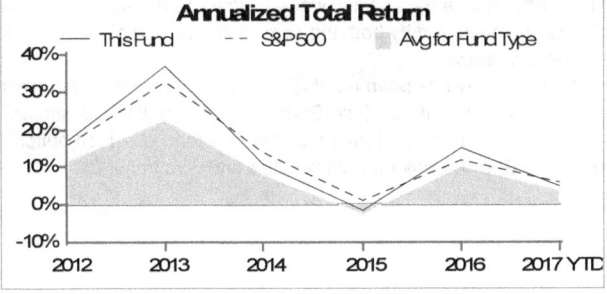

DFA US Core Equity 2 Ptf Inst (DFQTX)

A   Excellent

Fund Family: Dimensional Fund Advisors   **Phone:** (800) 984-9472
Address: 6300 Bee Cave Road, Austin, TX 78746
Fund Type: IN - Income
Major Rating Factors: Strong performance is the major factor driving the A (Excellent) TheStreet.com Investment Rating for DFA US Core Equity 2 Ptf Inst. The fund currently has a performance rating of B+ (Good) based on an average return of 8.54% over the last three years and 4.35% over the last three months. Factored into the performance evaluation is an expense ratio of 0.22% (very low).

The fund's risk rating is currently C+ (Fair). It carries a beta of 1.06, meaning that its performance tracks fairly well with that of the overall stock market. Volatility, as measured by both the semi-deviation and a drawdown factor, is considered low.

Henry F. Gray has been running the fund for 5 years and currently receives a manager quality ranking of 41 (0=worst, 99=best). If you desire only a moderate level of risk and strong performance, then this fund is an excellent option.
Services Offered: Automated phone transactions, bank draft capabilities and wire transfers.

Data Date	Investment Rating	Net Assets ($Mil)	NAV	Perfor-mance Rating/Pts	Total Return Y-T-D	Risk Rating/Pts
2-17	A	19,751	19.42	B+ / 8.9	4.35%	C+ / 6.4
2016	A	18,567	18.61	A- / 9.1	16.58%	C+ / 6.4
2015	B+	14,844	16.35	B / 7.9	-3.07%	C+ / 6.8
2014	A	13,377	17.50	B+ / 8.9	9.32%	C+ / 6.9
2013	A-	10,717	16.37	A- / 9.1	37.76%	C / 4.8
2012	A-	7,195	12.18	B+ / 8.9	18.08%	C / 4.4

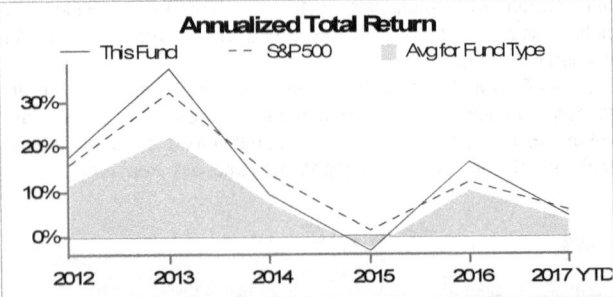

DFA US Large Company Portfolio Inst (DFUSX)

A+   Excellent

Fund Family: Dimensional Fund Advisors   **Phone:** (800) 984-9472
Address: 6300 Bee Cave Road, Austin, TX 78746
Fund Type: GR - Growth
Major Rating Factors: Exceptional performance is the major factor driving the A+ (Excellent) TheStreet.com Investment Rating for DFA US Large Company Portfolio Inst. The fund currently has a performance rating of A (Excellent) based on an average return of 10.57% over the last three years and 5.98% over the last three months. Factored into the performance evaluation is an expense ratio of 0.09% (very low).

The fund's risk rating is currently B- (Good). It carries a beta of 1.00, meaning that its performance tracks fairly well with that of the overall stock market. Volatility, as measured by both the semi-deviation and a drawdown factor, is considered low.

Eduardo A. Repetto currently receives a manager quality ranking of 74 (0=worst, 99=best). If you desire only a moderate level of risk and strong performance, then this fund is an excellent option.
Services Offered: Automated phone transactions, bank draft capabilities and a 401K investment plan.

Data Date	Investment Rating	Net Assets ($Mil)	NAV	Perfor-mance Rating/Pts	Total Return Y-T-D	Risk Rating/Pts
2-17	A+	7,392	18.44	A / 9.4	5.98%	B- / 7.0
2016	A+	6,860	17.40	B+ / 8.7	11.90%	B- / 7.0
2015	A+	5,729	15.98	A- / 9.1	1.38%	B- / 7.1
2014	A+	5,764	16.22	B+ / 8.9	13.53%	B- / 7.4
2013	A	5,166	14.56	B / 8.2	32.33%	C+ / 6.1
2012	A	4,051	11.22	B- / 7.4	15.82%	C+ / 6.2

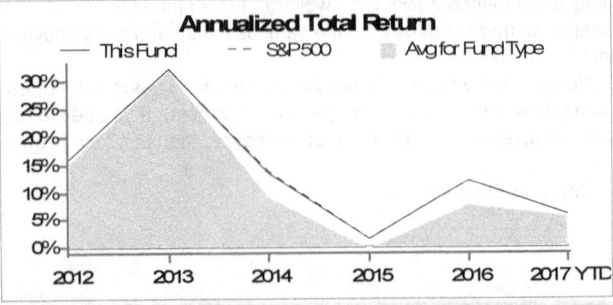

DFA US Micro Cap Portfolio Inst (DFSCX)

B+   Good

Fund Family: Dimensional Fund Advisors   **Phone:** (800) 984-9472
Address: 6300 Bee Cave Road, Austin, TX 78746
Fund Type: SC - Small Cap
Major Rating Factors: Strong performance is the major factor driving the B+ (Good) TheStreet.com Investment Rating for DFA US Micro Cap Portfolio Inst. The fund currently has a performance rating of B+ (Good) based on an average return of 7.48% over the last three years and -0.77% over the last three months. Factored into the performance evaluation is an expense ratio of 0.52% (very low).

The fund's risk rating is currently C (Fair). It carries a beta of 0.93, meaning that its performance tracks fairly well with that of the overall stock market. Volatility, as measured by both the semi-deviation and a drawdown factor, is considered average.

Henry F. Gray has been running the fund for 5 years and currently receives a manager quality ranking of 81 (0=worst, 99=best). If you desire an average level of risk and strong performance, then this fund is a good option.
Services Offered: Bank draft capabilities and wire transfers.

Data Date	Investment Rating	Net Assets ($Mil)	NAV	Perfor-mance Rating/Pts	Total Return Y-T-D	Risk Rating/Pts
2-17	B+	5,790	20.73	B+ / 8.6	-0.77%	C / 5.1
2016	A-	5,802	20.89	A+ / 9.8	25.63%	C / 5.2
2015	B-	4,827	17.51	B- / 7.5	-3.62%	C+ / 5.6
2014	B+	5,092	19.37	B+ / 8.4	2.92%	C+ / 5.8
2013	B+	4,911	20.11	A+ / 9.7	45.06%	C- / 3.9
2012	B+	3,537	14.60	A / 9.5	18.24%	C- / 3.6

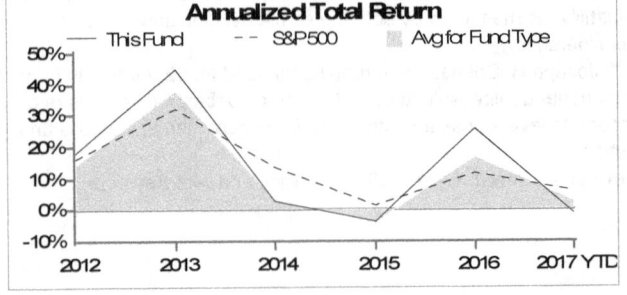

DFA US Small Cap Port Inst (DFSTX)   B+   Good

Fund Family: Dimensional Fund Advisors   **Phone:** (800) 984-9472
Address: 6300 Bee Cave Road, Austin, TX 78746
Fund Type: SC - Small Cap
Major Rating Factors: Strong performance is the major factor driving the B+ (Good) TheStreet.com Investment Rating for DFA US Small Cap Port Inst. The fund currently has a performance rating of B+ (Good) based on an average return of 7.97% over the last three years and 1.18% over the last three months. Factored into the performance evaluation is an expense ratio of 0.37% (very low).

The fund's risk rating is currently C (Fair). It carries a beta of 0.91, meaning that its performance tracks fairly well with that of the overall stock market. Volatility, as measured by both the semi-deviation and a drawdown factor, is considered average.

Henry F. Gray has been running the fund for 5 years and currently receives a manager quality ranking of 84 (0=worst, 99=best). If you desire an average level of risk and strong performance, then this fund is a good option.
Services Offered: Bank draft capabilities and wire transfers.

Data Date	Investment Rating	Net Assets ($Mil)	NAV	Perfor-mance Rating/Pts	Total Return Y-T-D	Risk Rating/Pts
2-17	B+	15,230	34.24	B+ / 8.9	1.18%	C / 5.2
2016	A-	15,015	33.84	A+ / 9.7	23.53%	C / 5.3
2015	B-	10,617	28.36	B- / 7.4	-3.29%	C+ / 5.7
2014	B+	9,666	31.15	B+ / 8.4	4.44%	C+ / 6.0
2013	B+	8,139	31.00	A / 9.5	42.21%	C- / 3.8
2012	B+	4,719	22.67	A / 9.5	18.39%	C- / 3.5

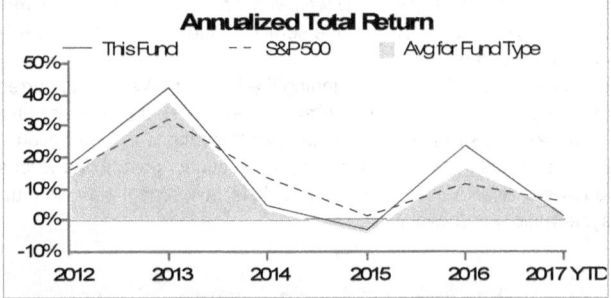

DFA US Small Cap Value I Inst (DFSVX)   B+   Good

Fund Family: Dimensional Fund Advisors   **Phone:** (800) 984-9472
Address: 6300 Bee Cave Road, Austin, TX 78746
Fund Type: SC - Small Cap
Major Rating Factors: Strong performance is the major factor driving the B+ (Good) TheStreet.com Investment Rating for DFA US Small Cap Value I Inst. The fund currently has a performance rating of B+ (Good) based on an average return of 6.87% over the last three years and -0.21% over the last three months. Factored into the performance evaluation is an expense ratio of 0.52% (very low).

The fund's risk rating is currently C (Fair). It carries a beta of 0.97, meaning that its performance tracks fairly well with that of the overall stock market. Volatility, as measured by both the semi-deviation and a drawdown factor, is considered average.

Henry F. Gray has been running the fund for 5 years and currently receives a manager quality ranking of 75 (0=worst, 99=best). If you desire an average level of risk and strong performance, then this fund is a good option.
Services Offered: Bank draft capabilities and wire transfers.

Data Date	Investment Rating	Net Assets ($Mil)	NAV	Perfor-mance Rating/Pts	Total Return Y-T-D	Risk Rating/Pts
2-17	B+	14,467	37.31	B+ / 8.9	-0.21%	C / 5.0
2016	A-	14,577	37.39	A+ / 9.8	28.26%	C / 5.1
2015	C	11,279	30.49	C+ / 5.6	-7.81%	C+ / 5.7
2014	B+	11,681	34.97	B+ / 8.5	3.48%	C+ / 5.9
2013	B	10,249	35.41	A / 9.4	42.38%	C- / 3.1
2012	B-	7,044	26.21	A+ / 9.6	21.72%	D+ / 2.6

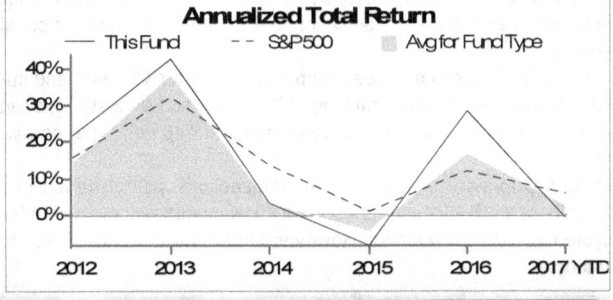

Dodge & Cox Balanced Fund (DODBX)   A+   Excellent

Fund Family: Dodge & Cox   **Phone:** (800) 621-3979
Address: 555 California Street, San Francisco, CA 94104
Fund Type: BA - Balanced
Major Rating Factors: Strong performance is the major factor driving the A+ (Excellent) TheStreet.com Investment Rating for Dodge & Cox Balanced Fund. The fund currently has a performance rating of B+ (Good) based on an average return of 8.12% over the last three years and 4.01% over the last three months. Factored into the performance evaluation is an expense ratio of 0.53% (very low).

The fund's risk rating is currently B (Good). It carries a beta of 1.23, meaning it is expected to move 12.3% for every 10% move in the market. Volatility, as measured by both the semi-deviation and a drawdown factor, is considered low.

Charles F. Pohl has been running the fund for 25 years and currently receives a manager quality ranking of 62 (0=worst, 99=best). If you desire only a moderate level of risk and strong performance, then this fund is an excellent option.
Services Offered: Automated phone transactions, payroll deductions, bank draft capabilities, an IRA investment plan and a systematic withdrawal plan.

Data Date	Investment Rating	Net Assets ($Mil)	NAV	Perfor-mance Rating/Pts	Total Return Y-T-D	Risk Rating/Pts
2-17	A+	15,593	107.49	B+ / 8.4	4.01%	B / 8.6
2016	A+	15,333	103.35	A- / 9.1	16.56%	B / 8.6
2013	C+	14,371	98.30	C+ / 6.4	28.37%	C+ / 6.4
2012	A	12,217	78.06	B / 7.6	18.32%	C+ / 6.2

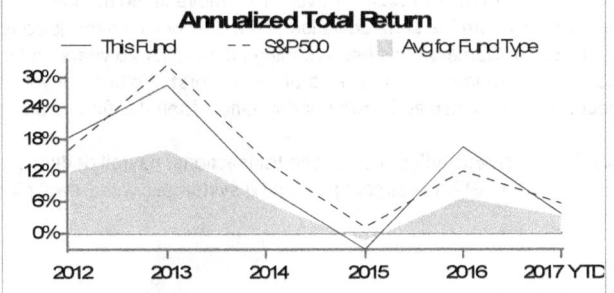

Dodge & Cox Global Stock (DODWX)

B+ **Good**

Fund Family: Dodge & Cox
Phone: (800) 621-3979
Address: 555 California Street, San Francisco, CA 94104
Fund Type: GL - Global

Major Rating Factors: Exceptional performance is the major factor driving the B+ (Good) TheStreet.com Investment Rating for Dodge & Cox Global Stock. The fund currently has a performance rating of A (Excellent) based on an average return of 6.51% over the last three years and 6.47% over the last three months. Factored into the performance evaluation is an expense ratio of 0.63% (very low).

The fund's risk rating is currently C (Fair). It carries a beta of 0.96, meaning that its performance tracks fairly well with that of the overall stock market. Volatility, as measured by both the semi-deviation and a drawdown factor, is considered average.

Charles F. Pohl has been running the fund for 9 years and currently receives a manager quality ranking of 97 (0=worst, 99=best). If you desire an average level of risk and strong performance, then this fund is a good option.

Services Offered: Automated phone transactions, payroll deductions, bank draft capabilities, an IRA investment plan, a 401K investment plan, wire transfers and a systematic withdrawal plan.

Data Date	Investment Rating	Net Assets ($Mil)	NAV	Performance Rating/Pts	Total Return Y-T-D	Risk Rating/Pts
2-17	B+	7,307	12.68	A / 9.3	6.47%	C / 5.1
2016	C+	6,985	11.91	B / 7.6	17.10%	C / 5.2
2015	C-	5,902	10.46	C / 4.8	-8.05%	C+ / 5.9
2014	B	5,895	11.83	B- / 7.4	6.95%	C+ / 6.0
2013	C+	3,712	11.48	C+ / 6.8	33.17%	C- / 4.1
2012	C	2,695	8.99	B- / 7.2	21.11%	C- / 3.1

Annualized Total Return

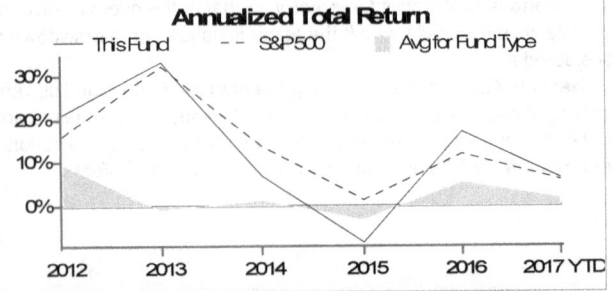

Dodge & Cox International Stock (DODFX)

D- **Weak**

Fund Family: Dodge & Cox
Phone: (800) 621-3979
Address: 555 California Street, San Francisco, CA 94104
Fund Type: FO - Foreign

Major Rating Factors: Disappointing performance is the major factor driving the D- (Weak) TheStreet.com Investment Rating for Dodge & Cox International Stock. The fund currently has a performance rating of D+ (Weak) based on an average return of -0.02% over the last three years and 5.56% over the last three months. Factored into the performance evaluation is an expense ratio of 0.64% (very low).

The fund's risk rating is currently C- (Fair). It carries a beta of 1.10, meaning it is expected to move 11.0% for every 10% move in the market. Volatility, as measured by both the semi-deviation and a drawdown factor, is considered average.

Mario C. DiPrisco has been running the fund for 13 years and currently receives a manager quality ranking of 75 (0=worst, 99=best). This fund offers an average level of risk but investors looking for strong performance will be frustrated.

Services Offered: Automated phone transactions, payroll deductions, bank draft capabilities, an IRA investment plan, a 401K investment plan, wire transfers and a systematic withdrawal plan. However, the fund is currently closed to new investors.

Data Date	Investment Rating	Net Assets ($Mil)	NAV	Performance Rating/Pts	Total Return Y-T-D	Risk Rating/Pts
2-17	D-	56,393	40.22	D+ / 2.6	5.56%	C- / 4.2
2016	D-	54,170	38.10	D+ / 2.3	8.26%	C / 4.3
2015	D-	61,812	36.48	D- / 1.4	-11.35%	C / 5.1
2014	D+	64,040	42.11	C / 4.4	0.08%	C / 5.3
2013	D	52,538	43.04	C / 4.7	26.31%	C- / 3.3
2012	C	40,556	34.64	B- / 7.0	21.03%	C- / 3.2

Annualized Total Return

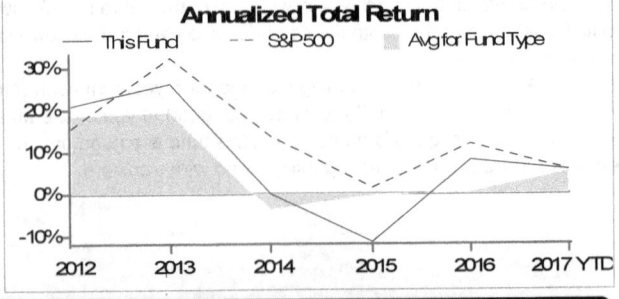

Dodge & Cox Stk Fund (DODGX)

A+ **Excellent**

Fund Family: Dodge & Cox
Phone: (800) 621-3979
Address: 555 California Street, San Francisco, CA 94104
Fund Type: GI - Growth and Income

Major Rating Factors: Exceptional performance is the major factor driving the A+ (Excellent) TheStreet.com Investment Rating for Dodge & Cox Stk Fund. The fund currently has a performance rating of A+ (Excellent) based on an average return of 10.05% over the last three years and 5.34% over the last three months. Factored into the performance evaluation is an expense ratio of 0.52% (very low).

The fund's risk rating is currently C+ (Fair). It carries a beta of 1.13, meaning it is expected to move 11.3% for every 10% move in the market. Volatility, as measured by both the semi-deviation and a drawdown factor, is considered low.

C. Bryan Cameron has been running the fund for 25 years and currently receives a manager quality ranking of 51 (0=worst, 99=best). If you desire only a moderate level of risk and strong performance, then this fund is an excellent option.

Services Offered: Automated phone transactions, payroll deductions, bank draft capabilities, an IRA investment plan and a systematic withdrawal plan.

Data Date	Investment Rating	Net Assets ($Mil)	NAV	Performance Rating/Pts	Total Return Y-T-D	Risk Rating/Pts
2-17	A+	63,420	194.15	A+ / 9.8	5.34%	C+ / 6.1
2016	A+	61,150	184.30	A+ / 9.7	21.28%	C+ / 6.2
2015	B+	56,976	162.77	B / 8.0	-4.49%	C+ / 6.8
2014	A+	60,260	180.94	A+ / 9.6	10.40%	B- / 7.1
2013	A	53,874	168.87	A / 9.5	40.55%	C / 5.0
2012	B+	39,841	121.90	B+ / 8.6	22.01%	C / 4.5

Annualized Total Return

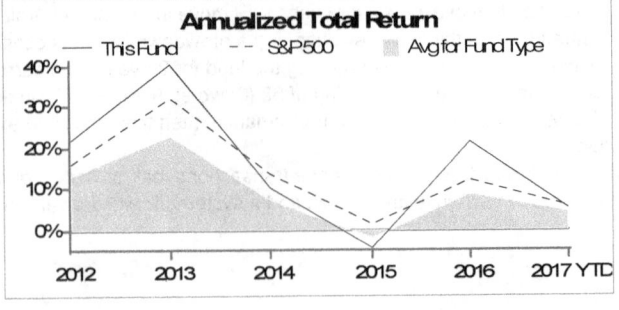

Fidelity Adv New Insights A (FNIAX)
C+   **Fair**

Fund Family: Fidelity Advisor   **Phone:** (800) 522-7297
Address: 245 Summer Street, Boston, MA 02210
Fund Type: GR - Growth
Major Rating Factors: Middle of the road best describes Fidelity Adv New Insights A whose TheStreet.com Investment Rating is currently a C+ (Fair). The fund currently has a performance rating of C+ (Fair) based on an average return of 6.85% over the last three years and 7.31% over the last three months. Factored into the performance evaluation is an expense ratio of 0.92% (low) and a 5.8% front-end load that is levied at the time of purchase.

The fund's risk rating is currently C+ (Fair). It carries a beta of 0.94, meaning that its performance tracks fairly well with that of the overall stock market. Volatility, as measured by both the semi-deviation and a drawdown factor, is considered low.

William A. Danoff has been running the fund for 14 years and currently receives a manager quality ranking of 36 (0=worst, 99=best). If you desire an average level of risk, then this fund may be an option.

Services Offered: Automated phone transactions, payroll deductions, bank draft capabilities, an IRA investment plan, a 401K investment plan, a Keogh investment plan and a systematic withdrawal plan.

Data Date	Investment Rating	Net Assets ($Mil)	NAV	Performance Rating/Pts	Total Return Y-T-D	Risk Rating/Pts
2-17	C+	7,165	28.11	C+ / 6.2	7.31%	C+ / 5.8
2016	C	6,885	26.44	C / 5.4	6.31%	C+ / 5.6
2015	B	8,194	26.15	B / 7.9	2.43%	C+ / 5.9
2014	C+	8,482	26.67	C+ / 6.5	9.20%	C+ / 5.6
2013	C+	8,646	26.32	C+ / 6.6	32.36%	C / 5.1
2012	C-	6,465	22.75	C- / 4.0	15.84%	C+ / 5.8

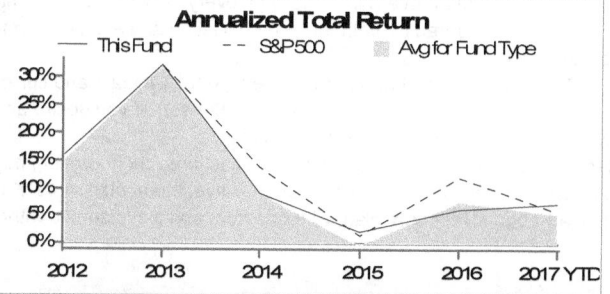
Annualized Total Return

Fidelity Balanced Fd (FBALX)
B-   **Good**

Fund Family: Fidelity Investments   **Phone:** (800) 544-8544
Address: 245 Summer Street, Boston, MA 02210
Fund Type: BA - Balanced
Major Rating Factors: Fidelity Balanced Fd receives a TheStreet.com Investment Rating of B- (Good). The fund currently has a performance rating of C+ (Fair) based on an average return of 6.84% over the last three years and 5.13% over the last three months. Factored into the performance evaluation is an expense ratio of 0.55% (very low).

The fund's risk rating is currently B- (Good). It carries a beta of 1.18, meaning it is expected to move 11.8% for every 10% move in the market. Volatility, as measured by both the semi-deviation and a drawdown factor, is considered low.

Robert E. Stansky has been running the fund for 9 years and currently receives a manager quality ranking of 49 (0=worst, 99=best). If you desire an average level of risk, then this fund may be an option.

Services Offered: Automated phone transactions, payroll deductions, bank draft capabilities, an IRA investment plan, a 401K investment plan, a Keogh investment plan, wire transfers and a systematic withdrawal plan.

Data Date	Investment Rating	Net Assets ($Mil)	NAV	Performance Rating/Pts	Total Return Y-T-D	Risk Rating/Pts
2-17	B-	21,728	23.15	C+ / 6.3	5.13%	B- / 7.0
2016	B-	20,689	22.02	C+ / 6.6	7.01%	B- / 7.1
2015	B-	20,334	21.22	C+ / 6.6	0.41%	B- / 7.5
2014	C+	20,044	22.77	C / 5.5	10.37%	B- / 7.3
2013	B-	17,916	22.75	C / 4.7	20.50%	B- / 7.6
2012	B-	14,827	20.18	C / 5.3	12.90%	B- / 7.7

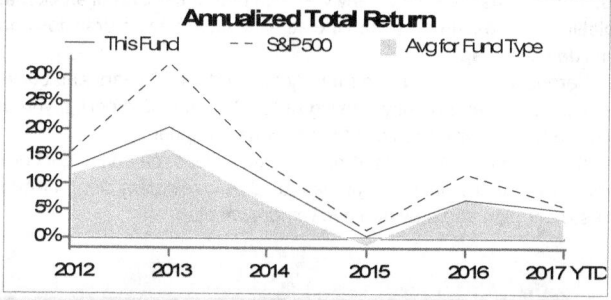
Annualized Total Return

Fidelity Blue Chip Growth Fd (FBGRX)
B   **Good**

Fund Family: Fidelity Investments   **Phone:** (800) 544-8544
Address: 245 Summer Street, Boston, MA 02210
Fund Type: GR - Growth
Major Rating Factors: Strong performance is the major factor driving the B (Good) TheStreet.com Investment Rating for Fidelity Blue Chip Growth Fd. The fund currently has a performance rating of B+ (Good) based on an average return of 8.64% over the last three years and 8.91% over the last three months. Factored into the performance evaluation is an expense ratio of 0.82% (very low).

The fund's risk rating is currently C (Fair). It carries a beta of 1.07, meaning that its performance tracks fairly well with that of the overall stock market. Volatility, as measured by both the semi-deviation and a drawdown factor, is considered average.

Sonu B. Kalra has been running the fund for 8 years and currently receives a manager quality ranking of 41 (0=worst, 99=best). If you desire an average level of risk and strong performance, then this fund is a good option.

Services Offered: Automated phone transactions, payroll deductions, bank draft capabilities, an IRA investment plan, a 401K investment plan, a Keogh investment plan, wire transfers and a systematic withdrawal plan.

Data Date	Investment Rating	Net Assets ($Mil)	NAV	Performance Rating/Pts	Total Return Y-T-D	Risk Rating/Pts
2-17	B	14,615	73.36	B+ / 8.4	8.91%	C / 4.9
2016	C	13,620	67.36	B- / 7.0	1.59%	C / 4.9
2015	A-	15,479	68.97	A+ / 9.8	6.28%	C / 5.5
2014	A-	13,368	68.42	A+ / 9.8	14.60%	C+ / 5.7
2013	B+	11,347	63.37	A / 9.4	39.84%	C / 4.3
2012	B-	11,305	49.05	B / 7.8	17.77%	C- / 4.2

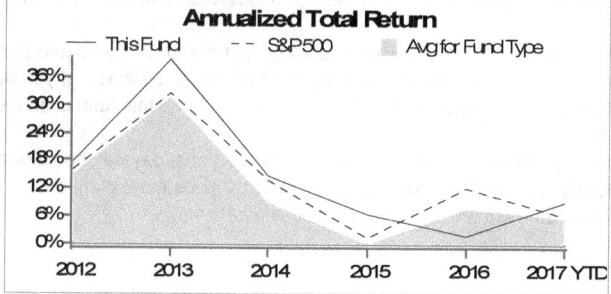
Annualized Total Return

Fidelity Capital and Income (FAGIX)

C+   **Fair**

Fund Family: Fidelity Investments   **Phone:** (800) 544-8544
Address: 245 Summer Street, Boston, MA 02210
Fund Type: GI - Growth and Income

Major Rating Factors: Middle of the road best describes Fidelity Capital and Income whose TheStreet.com Investment Rating is currently a C+ (Fair). The fund currently has a performance rating of C+ (Fair) based on an average return of 5.61% over the last three years and 4.37% over the last three months. Factored into the performance evaluation is an expense ratio of 0.75% (very low) and a 1.0% back-end load levied at the time of sale.

The fund's risk rating is currently C+ (Fair). It carries a beta of 0.48, meaning the fund's expected move will be 4.8% for every 10% move in the market. Volatility, as measured by both the semi-deviation and a drawdown factor, is considered low.

Mark J. Notkin has been running the fund for 14 years and currently receives a manager quality ranking of 78 (0=worst, 99=best). If you desire an average level of risk, then this fund may be an option.

Services Offered: Automated phone transactions, check writing, payroll deductions, bank draft capabilities, an IRA investment plan, a 401K investment plan, a Keogh investment plan, wire transfers and a systematic withdrawal plan.

Data Date	Investment Rating	Net Assets ($Mil)	NAV	Performance Rating/Pts	Total Return Y-T-D	Risk Rating/Pts
2-17	C+	11,124	10.07	C+ / 5.6	4.37%	C+ / 6.0
2016	C+	10,531	9.71	C+ / 6.9	10.73%	C+ / 6.1
2015	D+	10,235	9.15	D+ / 2.7	-0.92%	C+ / 6.5
2014	D+	10,388	9.68	C- / 3.3	6.14%	C+ / 6.5
2013	D	9,851	9.86	D / 2.2	9.71%	C / 5.2
2012	B+	9,657	9.50	B / 7.7	16.41%	C / 5.1

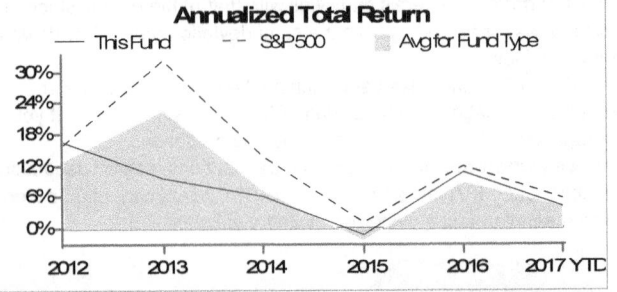
Annualized Total Return

Fidelity Capital Appreciation Fd (FDCAX)

C-   **Fair**

Fund Family: Fidelity Investments   **Phone:** (800) 544-8544
Address: 245 Summer Street, Boston, MA 02210
Fund Type: GR - Growth

Major Rating Factors: Middle of the road best describes Fidelity Capital Appreciation Fd whose TheStreet.com Investment Rating is currently a C- (Fair). The fund currently has a performance rating of C+ (Fair) based on an average return of 5.66% over the last three years and 5.56% over the last three months. Factored into the performance evaluation is an expense ratio of 0.83% (very low).

The fund's risk rating is currently C (Fair). It carries a beta of 1.08, meaning that its performance tracks fairly well with that of the overall stock market. Volatility, as measured by both the semi-deviation and a drawdown factor, is considered average.

Fergus J. Shiel has been running the fund for 12 years and currently receives a manager quality ranking of 12 (0=worst, 99=best). If you desire an average level of risk, then this fund may be an option.

Services Offered: Automated phone transactions, payroll deductions, bank draft capabilities, an IRA investment plan, a 401K investment plan, a Keogh investment plan and a systematic withdrawal plan.

Data Date	Investment Rating	Net Assets ($Mil)	NAV	Performance Rating/Pts	Total Return Y-T-D	Risk Rating/Pts
2-17	C-	4,982	33.44	C+ / 5.8	5.56%	C / 4.3
2016	C-	4,886	31.68	C+ / 6.0	3.18%	C / 4.3
2015	B	5,821	32.39	A- / 9.0	1.64%	C / 5.1
2014	B+	6,097	36.03	A / 9.5	10.84%	C / 5.4
2013	A	6,261	36.18	A- / 9.2	35.96%	C / 5.3
2012	A+	4,759	29.38	A- / 9.0	22.45%	C+ / 5.7

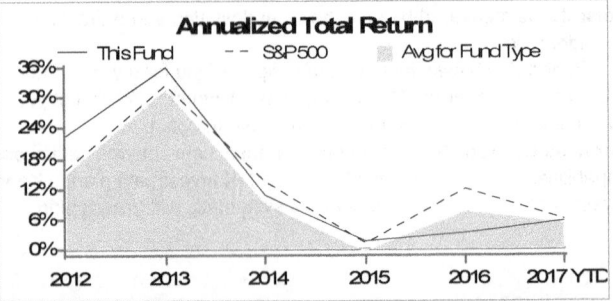
Annualized Total Return

Fidelity Contrafund Fd (FCNTX)

B+   **Good**

Fund Family: Fidelity Investments   **Phone:** (800) 544-8544
Address: 245 Summer Street, Boston, MA 02210
Fund Type: GR - Growth

Major Rating Factors: Strong performance is the major factor driving the B+ (Good) TheStreet.com Investment Rating for Fidelity Contrafund Fd. The fund currently has a performance rating of B (Good) based on an average return of 8.19% over the last three years and 8.40% over the last three months. Factored into the performance evaluation is an expense ratio of 0.71% (very low).

The fund's risk rating is currently C+ (Fair). It carries a beta of 0.91, meaning that its performance tracks fairly well with that of the overall stock market. Volatility, as measured by both the semi-deviation and a drawdown factor, is considered low.

William A. Danoff has been running the fund for 27 years and currently receives a manager quality ranking of 58 (0=worst, 99=best). If you desire only a moderate level of risk and strong performance, then this fund is an excellent option.

Services Offered: Automated phone transactions, payroll deductions, bank draft capabilities, an IRA investment plan, a 401K investment plan, a Keogh investment plan and a systematic withdrawal plan.

Data Date	Investment Rating	Net Assets ($Mil)	NAV	Performance Rating/Pts	Total Return Y-T-D	Risk Rating/Pts
2-17	B+	77,315	106.03	B / 7.7	8.40%	C+ / 6.0
2016	C+	73,241	98.46	C+ / 6.5	3.37%	C+ / 5.8
2015	A+	79,066	98.95	A / 9.4	6.49%	C+ / 6.5
2014	B+	76,030	97.97	B / 8.0	9.56%	C+ / 6.4
2013	A	75,076	96.14	B+ / 8.6	34.15%	C+ / 5.8
2012	B+	58,819	77.57	B- / 7.0	16.24%	C+ / 5.8

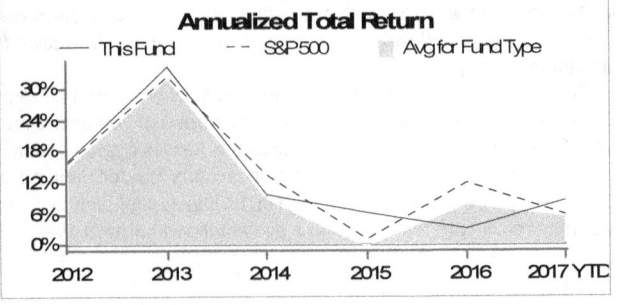
Annualized Total Return

Fidelity Diversified Intl Fd (FDIVX)　　　　　　　D-　　Weak

Fund Family: Fidelity Investments　　　　**Phone:** (800) 544-8544
Address: 245 Summer Street, Boston, MA 02210
Fund Type: FO - Foreign
Major Rating Factors: Disappointing performance is the major factor driving the D- (Weak) TheStreet.com Investment Rating for Fidelity Diversified Intl Fd. The fund currently has a performance rating of D- (Weak) based on an average return of -0.05% over the last three years and 4.74% over the last three months. Factored into the performance evaluation is an expense ratio of 1.00% (low).

The fund's risk rating is currently C+ (Fair). It carries a beta of 0.88, meaning the fund's expected move will be 8.8% for every 10% move in the market. Volatility, as measured by both the semi-deviation and a drawdown factor, is considered low.

William J. Bower has been running the fund for 16 years and currently receives a manager quality ranking of 74 (0=worst, 99=best). This fund offers only a moderate level of risk but investors looking for strong performance are still waiting.

Services Offered: Automated phone transactions, payroll deductions, bank draft capabilities, an IRA investment plan, a 401K investment plan, a Keogh investment plan and a systematic withdrawal plan.

Data Date	Investment Rating	Net Assets ($Mil)	NAV	Performance Rating/Pts	Total Return Y-T-D	Risk Rating/Pts
2-17	D-	10,130	34.88	D- / 1.1	4.74%	C+ / 5.8
2016	D	10,207	33.30	D- / 1.0	-3.73%	C+ / 5.9
2015	C	12,950	35.06	C / 5.0	3.12%	C+ / 6.6
2014	D+	13,425	34.45	C- / 3.4	-3.20%	C+ / 6.0
2013	D	14,907	36.91	C / 4.5	25.19%	C- / 3.9
2012	D	13,545	29.94	C- / 3.5	19.41%	C- / 3.7

Annualized Total Return

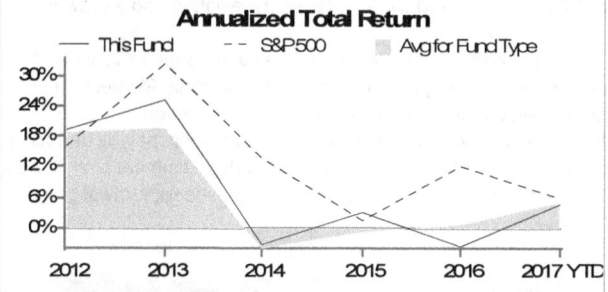

Fidelity Dividend Growth Fd (FDGFX)　　　　　　　C+　　Fair

Fund Family: Fidelity Investments　　　　**Phone:** (800) 544-8544
Address: 245 Summer Street, Boston, MA 02210
Fund Type: GR - Growth
Major Rating Factors: Strong performance is the major factor driving the C+ (Fair) TheStreet.com Investment Rating for Fidelity Dividend Growth Fd. The fund currently has a performance rating of B- (Good) based on an average return of 7.84% over the last three years and 5.06% over the last three months. Factored into the performance evaluation is an expense ratio of 0.62% (very low).

The fund's risk rating is currently C (Fair). It carries a beta of 0.96, meaning that its performance tracks fairly well with that of the overall stock market. Volatility, as measured by both the semi-deviation and a drawdown factor, is considered average.

Ramona Persaud has been running the fund for 3 years and currently receives a manager quality ranking of 47 (0=worst, 99=best). If you desire an average level of risk and strong performance, then this fund is a good option.
Services Offered: Automated phone transactions, payroll deductions, bank draft capabilities, an IRA investment plan, a 401K investment plan, a Keogh investment plan and a systematic withdrawal plan.

Data Date	Investment Rating	Net Assets ($Mil)	NAV	Performance Rating/Pts	Total Return Y-T-D	Risk Rating/Pts
2-17	C+	5,973	33.84	B- / 7.3	5.06%	C / 4.8
2016	C+	5,801	32.21	B- / 7.3	8.05%	C / 4.9
2015	B-	6,117	30.29	B+ / 8.3	-0.63%	C / 4.8
2014	B	6,614	33.42	B+ / 8.8	11.87%	C / 5.0
2013	C	6,864	35.39	C+ / 6.5	31.61%	C- / 4.0
2012	C+	5,964	29.90	B / 7.7	18.70%	C- / 3.5

Annualized Total Return

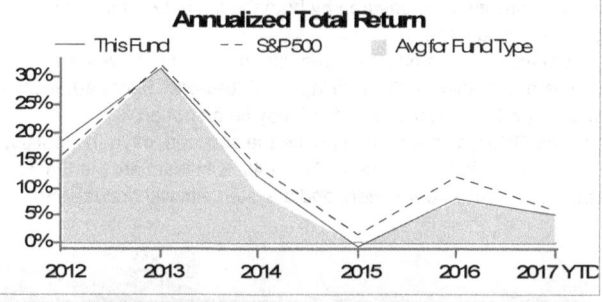

Fidelity Equity Dividend Income (FEQTX)　　　　　A+　　Excellent

Fund Family: Fidelity Investments　　　　**Phone:** (800) 544-8544
Address: 245 Summer Street, Boston, MA 02210
Fund Type: IN - Income
Major Rating Factors: Strong performance is the major factor driving the A+ (Excellent) TheStreet.com Investment Rating for Fidelity Equity Dividend Income. The fund currently has a performance rating of B+ (Good) based on an average return of 9.46% over the last three years and 3.46% over the last three months. Factored into the performance evaluation is an expense ratio of 0.66% (very low).

The fund's risk rating is currently C+ (Fair). It carries a beta of 0.92, meaning that its performance tracks fairly well with that of the overall stock market. Volatility, as measured by both the semi-deviation and a drawdown factor, is considered low.

Scott E. Offen has been running the fund for 6 years and currently receives a manager quality ranking of 71 (0=worst, 99=best). If you desire only a moderate level of risk and strong performance, then this fund is an excellent option.

Services Offered: Automated phone transactions, payroll deductions, bank draft capabilities, an IRA investment plan, a 401K investment plan, a Keogh investment plan and a systematic withdrawal plan.

Data Date	Investment Rating	Net Assets ($Mil)	NAV	Performance Rating/Pts	Total Return Y-T-D	Risk Rating/Pts
2-17	A+	5,558	27.77	B+ / 8.7	3.46%	C+ / 6.9
2016	A+	5,423	26.84	A- / 9.0	15.88%	B- / 7.0
2015	B+	4,697	24.60	B- / 7.4	-2.54%	B- / 7.0
2014	A-	5,224	26.77	B- / 7.5	11.61%	B- / 7.8
2013	C+	5,079	24.63	C+ / 5.9	29.06%	C / 5.1
2012	C-	4,455	19.48	C / 4.4	14.70%	C / 4.5

Annualized Total Return

Fidelity Freedom 2015 (FFVFX)   C+   Fair

Fund Family: Fidelity Investments   **Phone:** (800) 544-8544
Address: 245 Summer Street, Boston, MA 02210
Fund Type: AA - Asset Allocation

Major Rating Factors: Middle of the road best describes Fidelity Freedom 2015 whose TheStreet.com Investment Rating is currently a C+ (Fair). The fund currently has a performance rating of C- (Fair) based on an average return of 4.64% over the last three years and 3.66% over the last three months. Factored into the performance evaluation is an expense ratio of 0.64% (very low).

The fund's risk rating is currently B (Good). It carries a beta of 0.97, meaning that its performance tracks fairly well with that of the overall stock market. Volatility, as measured by both the semi-deviation and a drawdown factor, is considered low.

Jonathan Shelon has been running the fund for 12 years and currently receives a manager quality ranking of 41 (0=worst, 99=best). If you desire an average level of risk, then this fund may be an option.

Services Offered: Automated phone transactions, payroll deductions, bank draft capabilities, an IRA investment plan, a 401K investment plan, a Keogh investment plan, wire transfers and a systematic withdrawal plan.

Data Date	Investment Rating	Net Assets ($Mil)	NAV	Performance Rating/Pts	Total Return Y-T-D	Risk Rating/Pts
2-17	C+	5,322	12.74	C- / 4.2	3.66%	B / 8.1
2016	B-	5,227	12.29	C / 5.2	7.04%	B / 8.2
2015	C+	5,600	11.92	C- / 3.5	-0.34%	B / 8.5
2014	C	6,076	12.61	D+ / 2.9	5.17%	B / 8.8
2013	C	6,578	12.75	D+ / 2.3	11.88%	B / 8.1
2012	C	6,533	11.81	D+ / 2.7	10.68%	B / 8.1

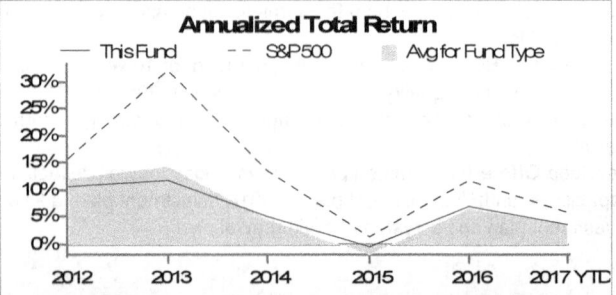

Fidelity Freedom 2020 (FFFDX)   B-   Good

Fund Family: Fidelity Investments   **Phone:** (800) 544-8544
Address: 245 Summer Street, Boston, MA 02210
Fund Type: AA - Asset Allocation

Major Rating Factors: Fidelity Freedom 2020 receives a TheStreet.com Investment Rating of B- (Good). The fund currently has a performance rating of C (Fair) based on an average return of 4.88% over the last three years and 3.94% over the last three months. Factored into the performance evaluation is an expense ratio of 0.67% (very low).

The fund's risk rating is currently B- (Good). It carries a beta of 1.06, meaning that its performance tracks fairly well with that of the overall stock market. Volatility, as measured by both the semi-deviation and a drawdown factor, is considered low.

Jonathan Shelon has been running the fund for 12 years and currently receives a manager quality ranking of 35 (0=worst, 99=best). If you desire an average level of risk, then this fund may be an option.

Services Offered: Automated phone transactions, payroll deductions, bank draft capabilities, an IRA investment plan, a 401K investment plan, a Keogh investment plan, wire transfers and a systematic withdrawal plan.

Data Date	Investment Rating	Net Assets ($Mil)	NAV	Performance Rating/Pts	Total Return Y-T-D	Risk Rating/Pts
2-17	B-	12,231	15.58	C / 4.6	3.94%	B- / 7.9
2016	B-	11,872	14.99	C / 5.5	7.26%	B- / 7.9
2015	C+	12,111	14.53	C- / 3.8	-0.23%	B / 8.2
2014	C	12,905	15.36	C- / 3.2	5.34%	B / 8.5
2013	C	13,702	15.61	D+ / 2.5	13.22%	B- / 7.6
2012	C	13,721	14.31	C- / 3.3	11.77%	B- / 7.5

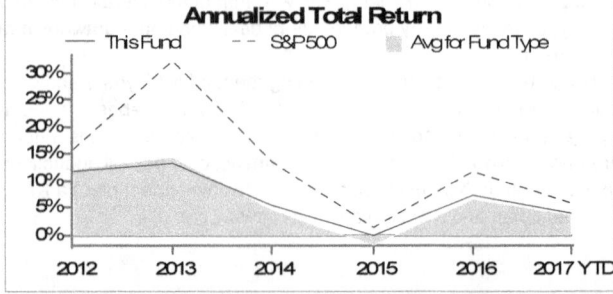

Fidelity Freedom 2025 (FFTWX)   B-   Good

Fund Family: Fidelity Investments   **Phone:** (800) 544-8544
Address: 245 Summer Street, Boston, MA 02210
Fund Type: AA - Asset Allocation

Major Rating Factors: Fidelity Freedom 2025 receives a TheStreet.com Investment Rating of B- (Good). The fund currently has a performance rating of C (Fair) based on an average return of 5.18% over the last three years and 4.20% over the last three months. Factored into the performance evaluation is an expense ratio of 0.69% (very low).

The fund's risk rating is currently B- (Good). It carries a beta of 1.18, meaning it is expected to move 11.8% for every 10% move in the market. Volatility, as measured by both the semi-deviation and a drawdown factor, is considered low.

Jonathan Shelon has been running the fund for 12 years and currently receives a manager quality ranking of 29 (0=worst, 99=best). If you desire an average level of risk, then this fund may be an option.

Services Offered: Automated phone transactions, payroll deductions, bank draft capabilities, an IRA investment plan, a 401K investment plan, a Keogh investment plan, wire transfers and a systematic withdrawal plan.

Data Date	Investment Rating	Net Assets ($Mil)	NAV	Performance Rating/Pts	Total Return Y-T-D	Risk Rating/Pts
2-17	B-	9,642	13.39	C / 5.1	4.20%	B- / 7.6
2016	B-	9,236	12.85	C+ / 5.8	7.47%	B- / 7.7
2015	C+	8,848	12.44	C / 4.5	-0.16%	B / 8.0
2014	C+	8,887	13.14	C- / 3.9	5.63%	B / 8.0
2013	C	8,988	13.32	C- / 3.2	16.50%	C+ / 6.9
2012	C+	8,013	11.95	C- / 4.1	13.15%	C+ / 6.8

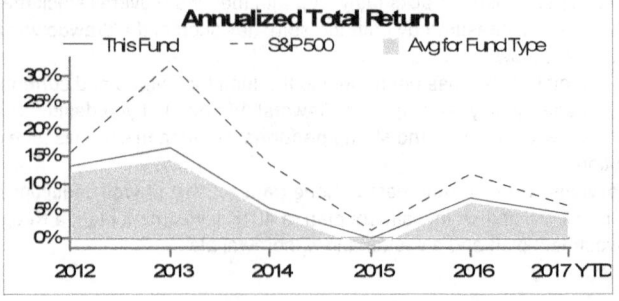

Fidelity Freedom 2030 (FFFEX)

B- **Good**

Fund Family: Fidelity Investments   **Phone:** (800) 544-8544
Address: 245 Summer Street, Boston, MA 02210
Fund Type: AA - Asset Allocation
Major Rating Factors: Fidelity Freedom 2030 receives a TheStreet.com Investment Rating of B- (Good). The fund currently has a performance rating of C+ (Fair) based on an average return of 5.69% over the last three years and 4.88% over the last three months. Factored into the performance evaluation is an expense ratio of 0.75% (very low).

The fund's risk rating is currently B- (Good). It carries a beta of 1.38, meaning it is expected to move 13.8% for every 10% move in the market. Volatility, as measured by both the semi-deviation and a drawdown factor, is considered low.

Jonathan Shelon has been running the fund for 12 years and currently receives a manager quality ranking of 20 (0=worst, 99=best). If you desire an average level of risk, then this fund may be an option.

Services Offered: Automated phone transactions, payroll deductions, bank draft capabilities, an IRA investment plan, a 401K investment plan, a Keogh investment plan, wire transfers and a systematic withdrawal plan.

Data Date	Investment Rating	Net Assets ($Mil)	NAV	Performance Rating/Pts	Total Return Y-T-D	Risk Rating/Pts
2-17	B-	11,194	16.56	C+ / 6.1	4.88%	B- / 7.0
2016	B-	10,710	15.79	C+ / 6.2	8.13%	B- / 7.0
2015	C+	10,448	15.21	C / 4.9	-0.16%	B- / 7.4
2014	C+	10,752	16.13	C- / 4.1	5.67%	B- / 7.7
2013	C	11,328	16.30	C- / 3.5	18.13%	C+ / 6.7
2012	C	10,568	14.23	C- / 4.2	13.47%	C+ / 6.5

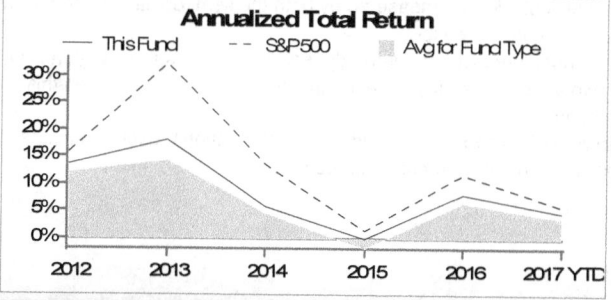

Fidelity Freedom 2035 (FFTHX)

C+ **Fair**

Fund Family: Fidelity Investments   **Phone:** (800) 544-8544
Address: 245 Summer Street, Boston, MA 02210
Fund Type: AA - Asset Allocation
Major Rating Factors: Middle of the road best describes Fidelity Freedom 2035 whose TheStreet.com Investment Rating is currently a C+ (Fair). The fund currently has a performance rating of C+ (Fair) based on an average return of 6.00% over the last three years and 5.29% over the last three months. Factored into the performance evaluation is an expense ratio of 0.77% (very low).

The fund's risk rating is currently C+ (Fair). It carries a beta of 1.50, meaning it is expected to move 15.0% for every 10% move in the market. Volatility, as measured by both the semi-deviation and a drawdown factor, is considered low.

Jonathan Shelon has been running the fund for 12 years and currently receives a manager quality ranking of 15 (0=worst, 99=best). If you desire an average level of risk, then this fund may be an option.

Services Offered: Automated phone transactions, payroll deductions, bank draft capabilities, an IRA investment plan, a 401K investment plan, a Keogh investment plan, wire transfers and a systematic withdrawal plan.

Data Date	Investment Rating	Net Assets ($Mil)	NAV	Performance Rating/Pts	Total Return Y-T-D	Risk Rating/Pts
2-17	C+	6,800	13.73	C+ / 6.6	5.29%	C+ / 6.5
2016	C+	6,454	13.04	C+ / 6.5	8.63%	C+ / 6.5
2015	C+	6,105	12.51	C / 5.4	-0.21%	B- / 7.0
2014	C	6,136	13.26	C / 4.6	5.75%	B- / 7.2
2013	C	6,319	13.48	C- / 4.1	20.68%	C+ / 6.1
2012	C	5,469	11.83	C / 4.4	14.45%	C+ / 5.9

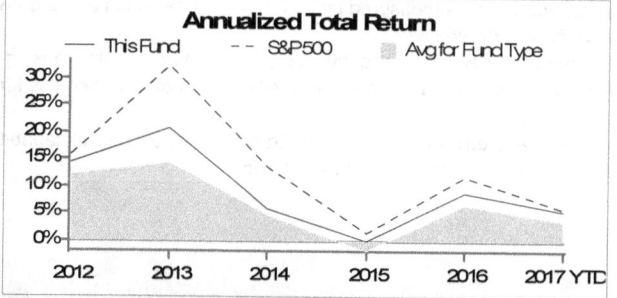

Fidelity Freedom 2040 (FFFFX)

C+ **Fair**

Fund Family: Fidelity Investments   **Phone:** (800) 544-8544
Address: 245 Summer Street, Boston, MA 02210
Fund Type: AA - Asset Allocation
Major Rating Factors: Middle of the road best describes Fidelity Freedom 2040 whose TheStreet.com Investment Rating is currently a C+ (Fair). The fund currently has a performance rating of C+ (Fair) based on an average return of 6.04% over the last three years and 5.36% over the last three months. Factored into the performance evaluation is an expense ratio of 0.77% (very low).

The fund's risk rating is currently C+ (Fair). It carries a beta of 1.50, meaning it is expected to move 15.0% for every 10% move in the market. Volatility, as measured by both the semi-deviation and a drawdown factor, is considered low.

Jonathan Shelon has been running the fund for 12 years and currently receives a manager quality ranking of 16 (0=worst, 99=best). If you desire an average level of risk, then this fund may be an option.

Services Offered: Automated phone transactions, payroll deductions, bank draft capabilities, an IRA investment plan, a 401K investment plan, a Keogh investment plan, wire transfers and a systematic withdrawal plan.

Data Date	Investment Rating	Net Assets ($Mil)	NAV	Performance Rating/Pts	Total Return Y-T-D	Risk Rating/Pts
2-17	C+	7,177	9.64	C+ / 6.7	5.36%	C+ / 6.5
2016	C+	6,835	9.15	C+ / 6.5	8.60%	C+ / 6.5
2015	C+	6,596	8.79	C / 5.4	-0.18%	B- / 7.0
2014	C+	6,863	9.34	C / 4.6	5.71%	B- / 7.2
2013	C	7,352	9.52	C- / 4.2	21.05%	C+ / 6.0
2012	C	6,675	8.26	C / 4.5	14.53%	C+ / 5.7

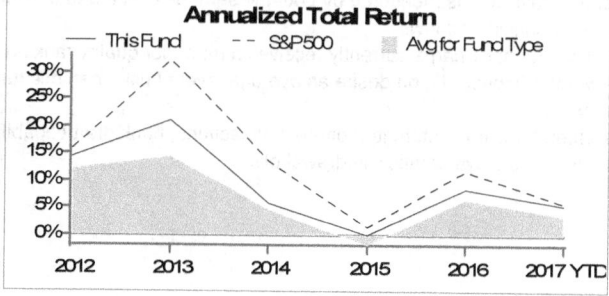

Fidelity Freedom K 2015 (FKVFX)   C+   Fair

Fund Family: Fidelity Investments **Phone:** (800) 544-8544
Address: 245 Summer Street, Boston, MA 02210
Fund Type: GI - Growth and Income

Major Rating Factors: Middle of the road best describes Fidelity Freedom K 2015 whose TheStreet.com Investment Rating is currently a C+ (Fair). The fund currently has a performance rating of C- (Fair) based on an average return of 4.71% over the last three years and 3.64% over the last three months. Factored into the performance evaluation is an expense ratio of 0.56% (very low).

The fund's risk rating is currently B- (Good). It carries a beta of 0.58, meaning the fund's expected move will be 5.8% for every 10% move in the market. Volatility, as measured by both the semi-deviation and a drawdown factor, is considered low.

Christopher Sharpe currently receives a manager quality ranking of 59 (0=worst, 99=best). If you desire an average level of risk, then this fund may be an option.

Services Offered: Automated phone transactions, bank draft capabilities, wire transfers and a systematic withdrawal plan.

Data Date	Investment Rating	Net Assets ($Mil)	NAV	Performance Rating/Pts	Total Return Y-T-D	Risk Rating/Pts
2-17	C+	5,147	13.65	C- / 4.2	3.64%	B- / 7.8
2016	B-	5,175	13.17	C / 5.3	7.10%	B- / 7.8
2015	C	5,937	12.80	C- / 3.6	-0.22%	B / 8.1
2014	C	6,859	13.60	D+ / 2.9	5.25%	B / 8.2
2013	C	7,454	14.24	D+ / 2.4	11.96%	B / 8.0
2012	C+	6,602	12.96	D+ / 2.8	10.81%	B / 8.5

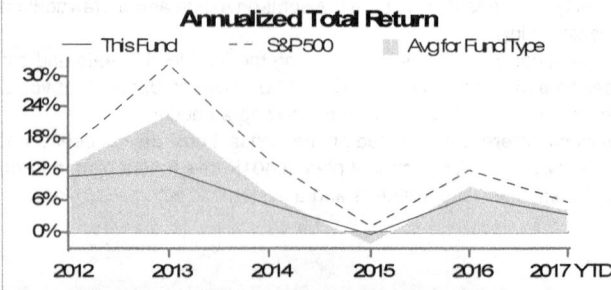

Fidelity Freedom K 2020 (FFKDX)   C+   Fair

Fund Family: Fidelity Investments **Phone:** (800) 544-8544
Address: 245 Summer Street, Boston, MA 02210
Fund Type: GI - Growth and Income

Major Rating Factors: Middle of the road best describes Fidelity Freedom K 2020 whose TheStreet.com Investment Rating is currently a C+ (Fair). The fund currently has a performance rating of C (Fair) based on an average return of 5.01% over the last three years and 3.94% over the last three months. Factored into the performance evaluation is an expense ratio of 0.58% (very low).

The fund's risk rating is currently B- (Good). It carries a beta of 0.63, meaning the fund's expected move will be 6.3% for every 10% move in the market. Volatility, as measured by both the semi-deviation and a drawdown factor, is considered low.

Christopher Sharpe currently receives a manager quality ranking of 55 (0=worst, 99=best). If you desire an average level of risk, then this fund may be an option.

Services Offered: Automated phone transactions, bank draft capabilities, wire transfers and a systematic withdrawal plan.

Data Date	Investment Rating	Net Assets ($Mil)	NAV	Performance Rating/Pts	Total Return Y-T-D	Risk Rating/Pts
2-17	C+	16,609	14.51	C / 4.7	3.94%	B- / 7.7
2016	B-	16,435	13.96	C+ / 5.6	7.40%	B- / 7.8
2015	C+	16,600	13.52	C- / 3.9	-0.14%	B / 8.0
2014	C	17,398	14.24	C- / 3.3	5.40%	B / 8.1
2013	C-	17,539	14.88	D+ / 2.6	13.35%	B- / 7.5
2012	C+	14,625	13.39	C- / 3.5	11.86%	B / 8.0

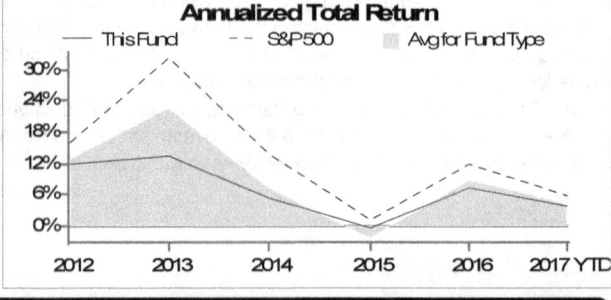

Fidelity Freedom K 2025 (FKTWX)   B-   Good

Fund Family: Fidelity Investments **Phone:** (800) 544-8544
Address: 245 Summer Street, Boston, MA 02210
Fund Type: GI - Growth and Income

Major Rating Factors: Fidelity Freedom K 2025 receives a TheStreet.com Investment Rating of B- (Good). The fund currently has a performance rating of C (Fair) based on an average return of 5.28% over the last three years and 4.25% over the last three months. Factored into the performance evaluation is an expense ratio of 0.61% (very low).

The fund's risk rating is currently B- (Good). It carries a beta of 0.71, meaning the fund's expected move will be 7.1% for every 10% move in the market. Volatility, as measured by both the semi-deviation and a drawdown factor, is considered low.

Christopher Sharpe currently receives a manager quality ranking of 48 (0=worst, 99=best). If you desire an average level of risk, then this fund may be an option.

Services Offered: Automated phone transactions, bank draft capabilities, wire transfers and a systematic withdrawal plan.

Data Date	Investment Rating	Net Assets ($Mil)	NAV	Performance Rating/Pts	Total Return Y-T-D	Risk Rating/Pts
2-17	B-	14,407	15.21	C / 5.2	4.25%	B- / 7.5
2016	B-	13,882	14.59	C+ / 5.8	7.59%	B- / 7.6
2015	C+	12,909	14.10	C / 4.6	-0.15%	B- / 7.8
2014	C	12,592	14.86	C- / 3.9	5.75%	B- / 7.7
2013	C-	11,681	15.51	C- / 3.2	16.65%	C+ / 6.8
2012	C+	8,751	13.58	C- / 4.2	13.26%	B- / 7.5

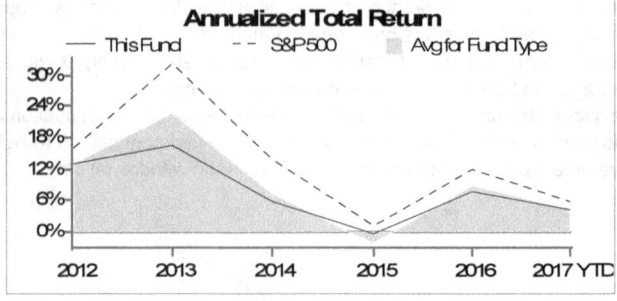

Fidelity Freedom K 2030 (FFKEX)

C+   **Fair**

Fund Family: Fidelity Investments   **Phone:** (800) 544-8544
Address: 245 Summer Street, Boston, MA 02210
Fund Type: GL - Global
Major Rating Factors: Middle of the road best describes Fidelity Freedom K 2030 whose TheStreet.com Investment Rating is currently a C+ (Fair). The fund currently has a performance rating of C+ (Fair) based on an average return of 5.80% over the last three years and 4.91% over the last three months. Factored into the performance evaluation is an expense ratio of 0.65% (very low).

The fund's risk rating is currently C+ (Fair). It carries a beta of 1.37, meaning it is expected to move 13.7% for every 10% move in the market. Volatility, as measured by both the semi-deviation and a drawdown factor, is considered low.

Christopher Sharpe has been running the fund for 8 years and currently receives a manager quality ranking of 68 (0=worst, 99=best). If you desire an average level of risk, then this fund may be an option.

Services Offered: Automated phone transactions, bank draft capabilities, wire transfers and a systematic withdrawal plan.

Data Date	Investment Rating	Net Assets ($Mil)	NAV	Perfor-mance Rating/Pts	Total Return Y-T-D	Risk Rating/Pts
2-17	C+	16,906	15.61	C+ / 6.1	4.91%	C+ / 6.9
2016	C+	16,372	14.88	C+ / 6.3	8.25%	C+ / 6.9
2015	C+	15,580	14.33	C / 4.9	-0.13%	B- / 7.2
2014	C	15,582	15.17	C- / 4.2	5.86%	B- / 7.2
2013	C-	14,913	15.86	C- / 3.6	18.21%	C+ / 6.5
2012	C+	11,521	13.72	C / 4.4	13.65%	B- / 7.2

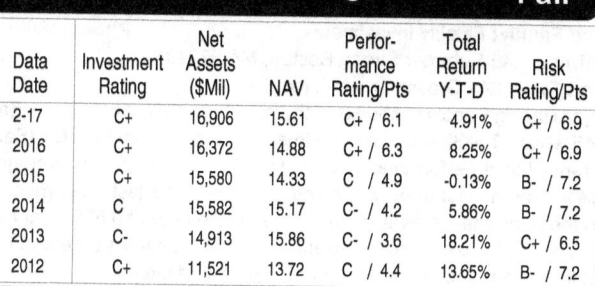

Annualized Total Return

Fidelity Freedom K 2035 (FKTHX)

C+   **Fair**

Fund Family: Fidelity Investments   **Phone:** (800) 544-8544
Address: 245 Summer Street, Boston, MA 02210
Fund Type: GI - Growth and Income
Major Rating Factors: Middle of the road best describes Fidelity Freedom K 2035 whose TheStreet.com Investment Rating is currently a C+ (Fair). The fund currently has a performance rating of C+ (Fair) based on an average return of 6.11% over the last three years and 5.32% over the last three months. Factored into the performance evaluation is an expense ratio of 0.67% (very low).

The fund's risk rating is currently C+ (Fair). It carries a beta of 0.91, meaning that its performance tracks fairly well with that of the overall stock market. Volatility, as measured by both the semi-deviation and a drawdown factor, is considered low.

Christopher Sharpe currently receives a manager quality ranking of 31 (0=worst, 99=best). If you desire an average level of risk, then this fund may be an option.

Services Offered: Automated phone transactions, bank draft capabilities, wire transfers and a systematic withdrawal plan.

Data Date	Investment Rating	Net Assets ($Mil)	NAV	Perfor-mance Rating/Pts	Total Return Y-T-D	Risk Rating/Pts
2-17	C+	11,546	16.24	C+ / 6.7	5.32%	C+ / 6.4
2016	C+	11,013	15.42	C+ / 6.6	8.72%	C+ / 6.4
2015	C+	10,109	14.76	C / 5.5	-0.13%	C+ / 6.9
2014	C	9,815	15.61	C / 4.7	5.88%	C+ / 6.9
2013	C-	8,930	16.38	C- / 4.2	20.86%	C+ / 5.9
2012	C+	6,375	13.87	C / 4.7	14.60%	C+ / 6.7

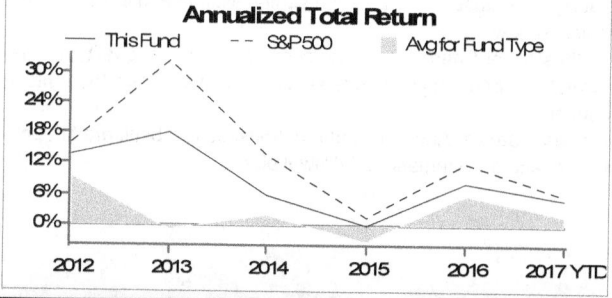

Annualized Total Return

Fidelity Freedom K 2040 (FFKFX)

C+   **Fair**

Fund Family: Fidelity Investments   **Phone:** (800) 544-8544
Address: 245 Summer Street, Boston, MA 02210
Fund Type: GI - Growth and Income
Major Rating Factors: Middle of the road best describes Fidelity Freedom K 2040 whose TheStreet.com Investment Rating is currently a C+ (Fair). The fund currently has a performance rating of C+ (Fair) based on an average return of 6.13% over the last three years and 5.38% over the last three months. Factored into the performance evaluation is an expense ratio of 0.67% (very low).

The fund's risk rating is currently C+ (Fair). It carries a beta of 0.91, meaning that its performance tracks fairly well with that of the overall stock market. Volatility, as measured by both the semi-deviation and a drawdown factor, is considered low.

Christopher Sharpe currently receives a manager quality ranking of 31 (0=worst, 99=best). If you desire an average level of risk, then this fund may be an option.

Services Offered: Automated phone transactions, bank draft capabilities, wire transfers and a systematic withdrawal plan.

Data Date	Investment Rating	Net Assets ($Mil)	NAV	Perfor-mance Rating/Pts	Total Return Y-T-D	Risk Rating/Pts
2-17	C+	12,161	16.27	C+ / 6.7	5.38%	C+ / 6.3
2016	C+	11,709	15.44	C+ / 6.6	8.72%	C+ / 6.4
2015	C+	10,757	14.79	C / 5.5	-0.12%	C+ / 6.8
2014	C	10,527	15.65	C / 4.7	5.88%	C+ / 6.8
2013	C-	9,793	16.47	C- / 4.2	21.25%	C+ / 5.7
2012	C+	7,184	13.91	C / 4.6	14.61%	C+ / 6.6

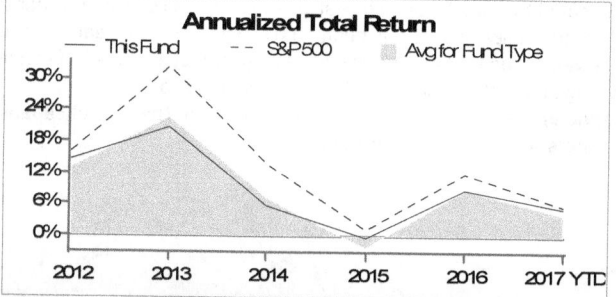

Annualized Total Return

Fidelity Freedom K 2045 (FFKGX)   C+   Fair

Fund Family: Fidelity Investments **Phone:** (800) 544-8544
Address: 245 Summer Street, Boston, MA 02210
Fund Type: GI - Growth and Income

Major Rating Factors: Middle of the road best describes Fidelity Freedom K 2045 whose TheStreet.com Investment Rating is currently a C+ (Fair). The fund currently has a performance rating of C+ (Fair) based on an average return of 6.14% over the last three years and 5.34% over the last three months. Factored into the performance evaluation is an expense ratio of 0.67% (very low).

The fund's risk rating is currently C+ (Fair). It carries a beta of 0.91, meaning that its performance tracks fairly well with that of the overall stock market. Volatility, as measured by both the semi-deviation and a drawdown factor, is considered low.

Christopher Sharpe currently receives a manager quality ranking of 31 (0=worst, 99=best). If you desire an average level of risk, then this fund may be an option.

Services Offered: Automated phone transactions, bank draft capabilities, wire transfers and a systematic withdrawal plan.

Data Date	Investment Rating	Net Assets ($Mil)	NAV	Performance Rating/Pts	Total Return Y-T-D	Risk Rating/Pts
2-17	C+	7,545	16.76	C+ / 6.8	5.34%	C+ / 6.4
2016	C+	7,201	15.91	C+ / 6.6	8.79%	C+ / 6.5
2015	C+	6,184	15.21	C+ / 5.6	-0.14%	C+ / 6.9
2014	C	5,658	16.06	C / 4.9	5.90%	C+ / 6.8
2013	C-	4,838	16.80	C / 4.4	21.84%	C+ / 5.6
2012	C+	3,219	14.09	C / 4.8	14.97%	C+ / 6.5

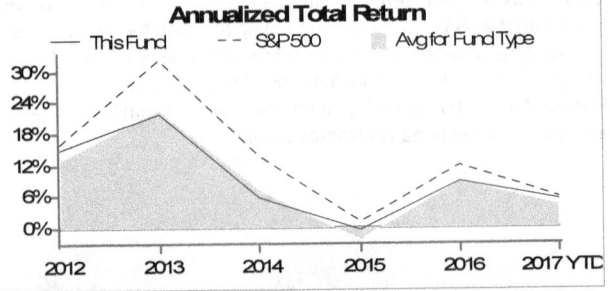

Annualized Total Return

Fidelity Freedom K 2050 (FFKHX)   C+   Fair

Fund Family: Fidelity Investments **Phone:** (800) 544-8544
Address: 245 Summer Street, Boston, MA 02210
Fund Type: GL - Global

Major Rating Factors: Middle of the road best describes Fidelity Freedom K 2050 whose TheStreet.com Investment Rating is currently a C+ (Fair). The fund currently has a performance rating of C+ (Fair) based on an average return of 6.14% over the last three years and 5.36% over the last three months. Factored into the performance evaluation is an expense ratio of 0.67% (very low).

The fund's risk rating is currently C+ (Fair). It carries a beta of 1.47, meaning it is expected to move 14.7% for every 10% move in the market. Volatility, as measured by both the semi-deviation and a drawdown factor, is considered low.

Christopher Sharpe has been running the fund for 8 years and currently receives a manager quality ranking of 66 (0=worst, 99=best). If you desire an average level of risk, then this fund may be an option.

Services Offered: Automated phone transactions, bank draft capabilities, wire transfers and a systematic withdrawal plan.

Data Date	Investment Rating	Net Assets ($Mil)	NAV	Performance Rating/Pts	Total Return Y-T-D	Risk Rating/Pts
2-17	C+	6,442	16.89	C+ / 6.7	5.36%	C+ / 6.5
2016	C+	6,149	16.03	C+ / 6.6	8.71%	C+ / 6.5
2015	C+	5,132	15.33	C+ / 5.7	-0.15%	B- / 7.0
2014	C	4,519	16.17	C / 4.9	5.96%	C+ / 6.8
2013	C-	3,801	16.87	C / 4.4	22.08%	C / 5.4
2012	C+	2,426	14.12	C / 4.8	15.23%	C+ / 6.2

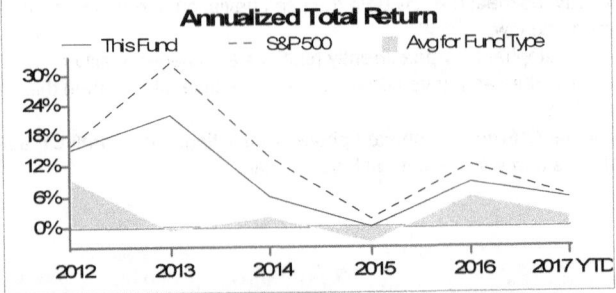

Annualized Total Return

Fidelity Growth and Income (FGRIX)   A+   Excellent

Fund Family: Fidelity Investments **Phone:** (800) 544-8544
Address: 245 Summer Street, Boston, MA 02210
Fund Type: GI - Growth and Income

Major Rating Factors: Exceptional performance is the major factor driving the A+ (Excellent) TheStreet.com Investment Rating for Fidelity Growth and Income. The fund currently has a performance rating of A (Excellent) based on an average return of 9.51% over the last three years and 4.37% over the last three months. Factored into the performance evaluation is an expense ratio of 0.65% (very low).

The fund's risk rating is currently C+ (Fair). It carries a beta of 1.09, meaning that its performance tracks fairly well with that of the overall stock market. Volatility, as measured by both the semi-deviation and a drawdown factor, is considered low.

Matthew W. Fruhan has been running the fund for 6 years and currently receives a manager quality ranking of 49 (0=worst, 99=best). If you desire only a moderate level of risk and strong performance, then this fund is an excellent option.

Services Offered: Automated phone transactions, payroll deductions, bank draft capabilities, an IRA investment plan, a 401K investment plan, a Keogh investment plan and a systematic withdrawal plan.

Data Date	Investment Rating	Net Assets ($Mil)	NAV	Performance Rating/Pts	Total Return Y-T-D	Risk Rating/Pts
2-17	A+	6,354	34.36	A / 9.4	4.37%	C+ / 6.5
2016	A+	6,119	32.92	A- / 9.2	16.06%	C+ / 6.6
2015	B+	5,562	28.92	B / 7.8	-2.28%	B- / 7.0
2014	A	6,699	30.21	B+ / 8.6	10.38%	B- / 7.2
2013	A+	6,471	27.86	B+ / 8.6	33.40%	C+ / 6.1
2012	A+	4,949	21.26	B+ / 8.6	19.10%	C+ / 5.6

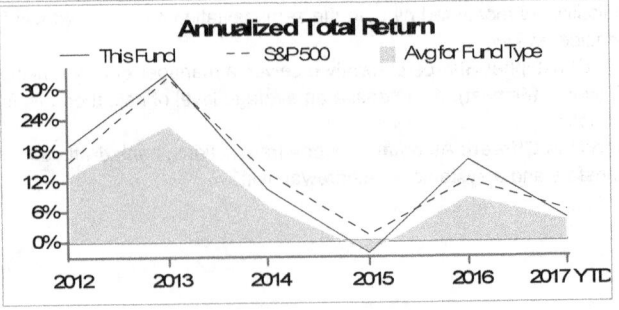

Annualized Total Return

Fidelity Growth Company Fd (FDGRX)

B+   Good

Fund Family: Fidelity Investments   **Phone:** (800) 544-8544
Address: 245 Summer Street, Boston, MA 02210
Fund Type: GR - Growth

Major Rating Factors: Exceptional performance is the major factor driving the B+ (Good) TheStreet.com Investment Rating for Fidelity Growth Company Fd. The fund currently has a performance rating of A+ (Excellent) based on an average return of 9.95% over the last three years and 8.09% over the last three months. Factored into the performance evaluation is an expense ratio of 0.88% (low).

The fund's risk rating is currently C (Fair). It carries a beta of 1.23, meaning it is expected to move 12.3% for every 10% move in the market. Volatility, as measured by both the semi-deviation and a drawdown factor, is considered average.

Steven S. Wymer has been running the fund for 20 years and currently receives a manager quality ranking of 36 (0=worst, 99=best). If you desire an average level of risk and strong performance, then this fund is a good option.

Services Offered: Automated phone transactions, payroll deductions, bank draft capabilities, an IRA investment plan, a 401K investment plan, a Keogh investment plan and a systematic withdrawal plan. However, the fund is currently closed to new investors.

Data Date	Investment Rating	Net Assets ($Mil)	NAV	Performance Rating/Pts	Total Return Y-T-D	Risk Rating/Pts
2-17	B+	21,436	147.85	A+ / 9.6	8.09%	C / 4.8
2016	B-	21,284	136.78	B+ / 8.4	6.01%	C / 4.8
2015	A	23,544	136.94	A+ / 9.8	7.83%	C+ / 6.1
2014	A-	24,026	131.89	A+ / 9.7	14.44%	C+ / 5.6
2013	A-	23,381	119.88	A / 9.3	37.61%	C / 4.6
2012	B+	22,700	93.38	B+ / 8.5	18.52%	C / 4.4

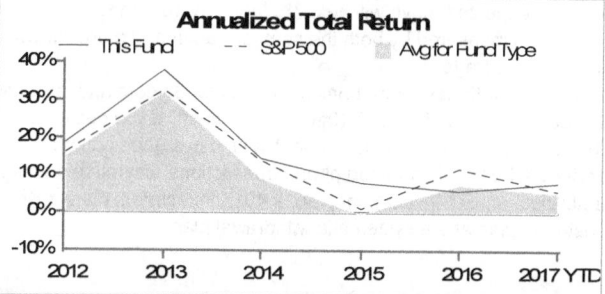

Annualized Total Return

Fidelity Low-Priced Stock Fd (FLPSX)

C+   Fair

Fund Family: Fidelity Investments   **Phone:** (800) 544-8544
Address: 245 Summer Street, Boston, MA 02210
Fund Type: MC - Mid Cap

Major Rating Factors: Middle of the road best describes Fidelity Low-Priced Stock Fd whose TheStreet.com Investment Rating is currently a C+ (Fair). The fund currently has a performance rating of C+ (Fair) based on an average return of 6.07% over the last three years and 3.35% over the last three months. Factored into the performance evaluation is an expense ratio of 0.88% (low).

The fund's risk rating is currently C+ (Fair). It carries a beta of 0.71, meaning the fund's expected move will be 7.1% for every 10% move in the market. Volatility, as measured by both the semi-deviation and a drawdown factor, is considered low.

Joel C. Tillinghast has been running the fund for 28 years and currently receives a manager quality ranking of 66 (0=worst, 99=best). If you desire an average level of risk, then this fund may be an option.

Services Offered: Automated phone transactions, payroll deductions, bank draft capabilities, an IRA investment plan, a 401K investment plan, a Keogh investment plan and a systematic withdrawal plan.

Data Date	Investment Rating	Net Assets ($Mil)	NAV	Performance Rating/Pts	Total Return Y-T-D	Risk Rating/Pts
2-17	C+	28,068	51.14	C+ / 5.8	3.35%	C+ / 6.8
2016	B	28,263	49.48	B- / 7.1	8.79%	C+ / 6.9
2015	B+	28,962	47.75	B- / 7.5	-0.56%	B- / 7.2
2014	B+	30,318	50.25	B / 7.6	7.65%	B- / 7.0
2013	B	31,079	49.46	B / 8.2	34.31%	C / 4.8
2012	A-	23,433	39.50	A- / 9.0	18.50%	C / 4.5

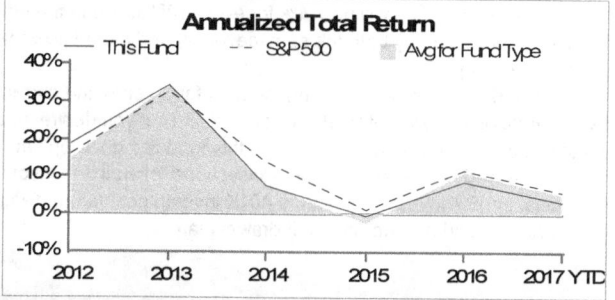

Annualized Total Return

Fidelity Magellan Fund (FMAGX)

B+   Good

Fund Family: Fidelity Investments   **Phone:** (800) 544-8544
Address: 245 Summer Street, Boston, MA 02210
Fund Type: GR - Growth

Major Rating Factors: Strong performance is the major factor driving the B+ (Good) TheStreet.com Investment Rating for Fidelity Magellan Fund. The fund currently has a performance rating of B (Good) based on an average return of 8.81% over the last three years and 6.44% over the last three months. Factored into the performance evaluation is an expense ratio of 0.85% (very low).

The fund's risk rating is currently C+ (Fair). It carries a beta of 1.06, meaning that its performance tracks fairly well with that of the overall stock market. Volatility, as measured by both the semi-deviation and a drawdown factor, is considered low.

Jeffrey S. Feingold has been running the fund for 6 years and currently receives a manager quality ranking of 44 (0=worst, 99=best). If you desire only a moderate level of risk and strong performance, then this fund is an excellent option.

Services Offered: Automated phone transactions, payroll deductions, bank draft capabilities, an IRA investment plan, a 401K investment plan, a Keogh investment plan and a systematic withdrawal plan.

Data Date	Investment Rating	Net Assets ($Mil)	NAV	Performance Rating/Pts	Total Return Y-T-D	Risk Rating/Pts
2-17	B+	13,562	97.24	B / 8.1	6.44%	C+ / 5.7
2016	B-	12,931	91.36	B- / 7.4	5.24%	C+ / 5.7
2015	A	13,898	89.43	A / 9.5	4.06%	C+ / 6.1
2014	A	14,107	92.52	A+ / 9.6	14.08%	C+ / 6.2
2013	C+	13,542	92.37	B- / 7.0	35.30%	C- / 4.1
2012	D-	11,869	73.27	D+ / 2.6	17.99%	C- / 3.9

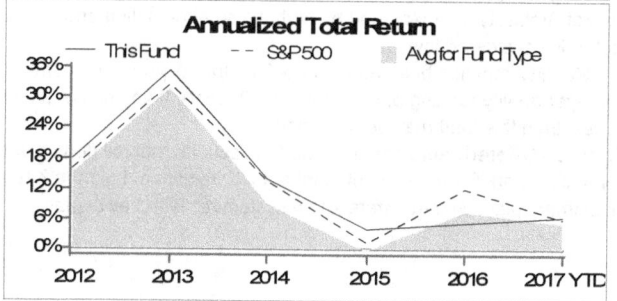

Annualized Total Return

Fidelity Mid-Cap Stock Fund (FMCSX)

C+ **Fair**

Fund Family: Fidelity Investments **Phone:** (800) 544-8544
Address: 245 Summer Street, Boston, MA 02210
Fund Type: MC - Mid Cap

Major Rating Factors: Strong performance is the major factor driving the C+ (Fair) TheStreet.com Investment Rating for Fidelity Mid-Cap Stock Fund. The fund currently has a performance rating of B- (Good) based on an average return of 6.11% over the last three years and 4.45% over the last three months. Factored into the performance evaluation is an expense ratio of 0.73% (very low).

The fund's risk rating is currently C (Fair). It carries a beta of 0.87, meaning the fund's expected move will be 8.7% for every 10% move in the market. Volatility, as measured by both the semi-deviation and a drawdown factor, is considered average.

John D. Roth has been running the fund for 6 years and currently receives a manager quality ranking of 47 (0=worst, 99=best). If you desire an average level of risk and strong performance, then this fund is a good option.

Services Offered: Automated phone transactions, payroll deductions, bank draft capabilities, an IRA investment plan, a 401K investment plan, a Keogh investment plan and a systematic withdrawal plan.

Data Date	Investment Rating	Net Assets ($Mil)	NAV	Performance Rating/Pts	Total Return Y-T-D	Risk Rating/Pts
2-17	C+	5,648	36.16	B- / 7.1	4.45%	C / 4.8
2016	C+	5,460	34.62	B / 8.0	14.94%	C / 4.9
2015	C+	5,394	32.73	B- / 7.3	-3.08%	C / 5.5
2014	B	5,860	38.39	B- / 7.5	7.11%	C+ / 6.0
2013	B	5,608	39.51	B+ / 8.7	38.97%	C- / 4.2
2012	C	4,282	29.38	B- / 7.5	14.93%	C- / 3.3

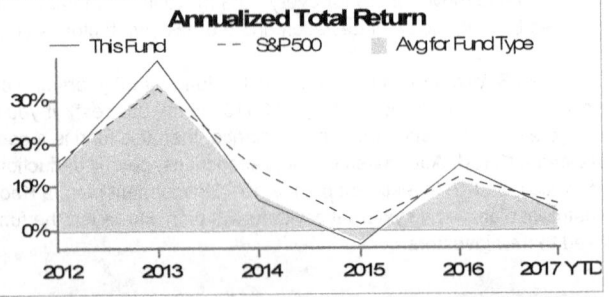

Fidelity OTC Portfolio Fd (FOCPX)

B+ **Good**

Fund Family: Fidelity Investments **Phone:** (800) 544-8544
Address: 245 Summer Street, Boston, MA 02210
Fund Type: SC - Small Cap

Major Rating Factors: Exceptional performance is the major factor driving the B+ (Good) TheStreet.com Investment Rating for Fidelity OTC Portfolio Fd. The fund currently has a performance rating of A+ (Excellent) based on an average return of 10.93% over the last three years and 10.72% over the last three months. Factored into the performance evaluation is an expense ratio of 0.91% (low).

The fund's risk rating is currently C- (Fair). It carries a beta of 0.74, meaning the fund's expected move will be 7.4% for every 10% move in the market. Volatility, as measured by both the semi-deviation and a drawdown factor, is considered average.

Gavin S. Baker has been running the fund for 8 years and currently receives a manager quality ranking of 96 (0=worst, 99=best). If you desire an average level of risk and strong performance, then this fund is a good option.

Services Offered: Automated phone transactions, payroll deductions, bank draft capabilities, an IRA investment plan, a 401K investment plan, a Keogh investment plan and a systematic withdrawal plan.

Data Date	Investment Rating	Net Assets ($Mil)	NAV	Performance Rating/Pts	Total Return Y-T-D	Risk Rating/Pts
2-17	B+	10,608	92.25	A+ / 9.8	10.72%	C- / 4.1
2016	C+	9,597	83.32	B+ / 8.3	3.11%	C- / 4.1
2015	A-	9,669	83.43	A+ / 9.9	10.92%	C / 5.3
2014	B	8,596	79.56	A+ / 9.8	16.49%	C / 4.3
2013	A-	7,544	77.39	A+ / 9.6	46.50%	C / 4.3
2012	C-	5,288	60.59	C / 5.1	11.29%	C / 4.4

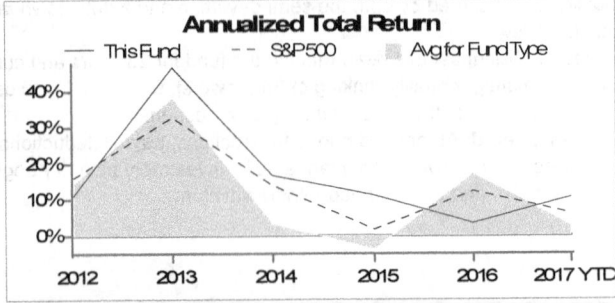

Fidelity Puritan Fd (FPURX)

B- **Good**

Fund Family: Fidelity Investments **Phone:** (800) 544-8544
Address: 245 Summer Street, Boston, MA 02210
Fund Type: GI - Growth and Income

Major Rating Factors: Fidelity Puritan Fd receives a TheStreet.com Investment Rating of B- (Good). The fund currently has a performance rating of C+ (Fair) based on an average return of 6.54% over the last three years and 5.30% over the last three months. Factored into the performance evaluation is an expense ratio of 0.56% (very low).

The fund's risk rating is currently B- (Good). It carries a beta of 0.70, meaning the fund's expected move will be 7.0% for every 10% move in the market. Volatility, as measured by both the semi-deviation and a drawdown factor, is considered low.

Ramin Arani has been running the fund for 10 years and currently receives a manager quality ranking of 65 (0=worst, 99=best). If you desire an average level of risk, then this fund may be an option.

Services Offered: Automated phone transactions, payroll deductions, bank draft capabilities, an IRA investment plan, a 401K investment plan, a Keogh investment plan, wire transfers and a systematic withdrawal plan.

Data Date	Investment Rating	Net Assets ($Mil)	NAV	Performance Rating/Pts	Total Return Y-T-D	Risk Rating/Pts
2-17	B-	19,933	21.67	C+ / 5.9	5.30%	B- / 7.1
2016	B-	19,140	20.58	C+ / 6.3	5.03%	B- / 7.1
2015	B+	19,230	20.33	B- / 7.1	1.77%	B- / 7.4
2014	C+	18,754	21.49	C+ / 5.7	10.75%	B- / 7.1
2013	C+	17,308	21.23	C / 4.6	20.34%	B- / 7.2
2012	B-	15,209	19.41	C / 5.5	13.79%	B- / 7.2

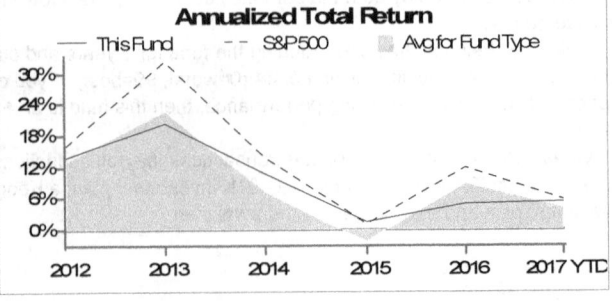

Fidelity Select Biotech Port (FBIOX)

D- **Weak**

Fund Family: Fidelity Select Funds **Phone:** (800) 544-8888
Address: 245 Summer Street, Boston, MA 02210
Fund Type: HL - Health

Major Rating Factors: Fidelity Select Biotech Port has adopted a very risky asset allocation strategy and currently receives an overall TheStreet.com Investment Rating of D- (Weak). The fund has shown a high level of volatility, as measured by both semi-deviation and drawdown factors. It carries a beta of 1.90, meaning it is expected to move 19.0% for every 10% move in the market. The high level of risk (E-, Very Weak) did however, reward investors with excellent performance.

The fund's performance rating is currently B- (Good). It has registered an average return of 3.91% over the last three years and is up 16.75% over the last three months. Factored into the performance evaluation is an expense ratio of 0.73% (very low).

Rajiv Kaul has been running the fund for 12 years and currently receives a manager quality ranking of 0 (0=worst, 99=best). If you are comfortable owning a very high risk investment, this fund may be an option.

Services Offered: Automated phone transactions, payroll deductions, bank draft capabilities, an IRA investment plan, a 401K investment plan, a Keogh investment plan and a systematic withdrawal plan.

Data Date	Investment Rating	Net Assets ($Mil)	NAV	Perfor- mance Rating/Pts	Total Return Y-T-D	Risk Rating/Pts
2-17	D-	9,578	203.21	B- / 7.0	16.75%	E- / 0.1
2016	E-	8,645	174.05	D / 2.2	-23.72%	E- / 0.0
2015	C+	15,087	235.90	A+ / 9.9	13.67%	D+ / 2.5
2014	C+	10,924	221.27	A+ / 9.9	35.05%	D+ / 2.4
2013	A-	7,959	181.73	A+ / 9.9	65.66%	C- / 4.0
2012	A	2,731	109.99	A+ / 9.9	36.59%	C- / 4.0

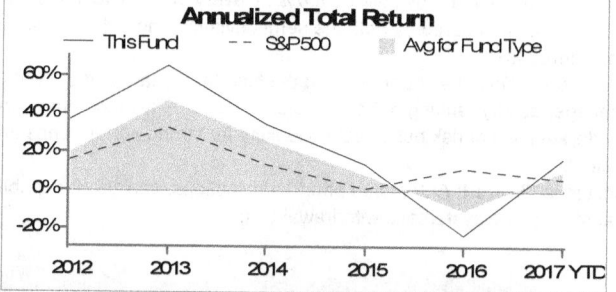
Annualized Total Return

Fidelity Select Health Care (FSPHX)

C- **Fair**

Fund Family: Fidelity Select Funds **Phone:** (800) 544-8888
Address: 245 Summer Street, Boston, MA 02210
Fund Type: HL - Health

Major Rating Factors: Strong performance is the major factor driving the C- (Fair) TheStreet.com Investment Rating for Fidelity Select Health Care. The fund currently has a performance rating of B- (Good) based on an average return of 7.52% over the last three years and 13.04% over the last three months. Factored into the performance evaluation is an expense ratio of 0.73% (very low).

The fund's risk rating is currently C- (Fair). It carries a beta of 1.14, meaning it is expected to move 11.4% for every 10% move in the market. Volatility, as measured by both the semi-deviation and a drawdown factor, is considered average.

Edward L. Yoon has been running the fund for 9 years and currently receives a manager quality ranking of 21 (0=worst, 99=best). If you desire an average level of risk and strong performance, then this fund is a good option.

Services Offered: Automated phone transactions, payroll deductions, bank draft capabilities, an IRA investment plan, a 401K investment plan, a Keogh investment plan and a systematic withdrawal plan.

Data Date	Investment Rating	Net Assets ($Mil)	NAV	Perfor- mance Rating/Pts	Total Return Y-T-D	Risk Rating/Pts
2-17	C-	6,629	208.91	B- / 7.0	13.04%	C- / 3.4
2016	D+	6,069	184.81	C / 5.1	-10.68%	C- / 3.4
2015	B+	8,995	208.16	A+ / 9.9	6.57%	C / 4.3
2014	B	8,618	217.70	A+ / 9.9	32.88%	C- / 4.0
2013	A-	4,883	188.51	A+ / 9.9	56.27%	C- / 4.1
2012	A+	2,483	134.05	A / 9.5	21.39%	C / 4.8

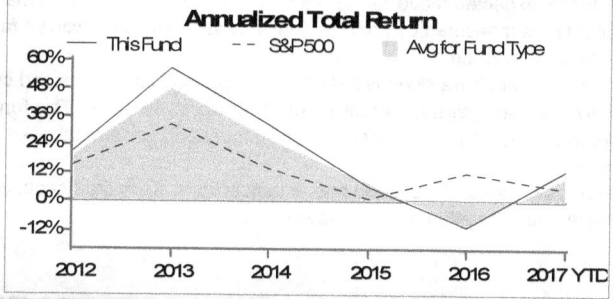
Annualized Total Return

Fidelity Series Equity Income (FNKLX)

A **Excellent**

Fund Family: Fidelity Investments **Phone:** (800) 544-8544
Address: 245 Summer Street, Boston, MA 02210
Fund Type: GR - Growth

Major Rating Factors: Exceptional performance is the major factor driving the A (Excellent) TheStreet.com Investment Rating for Fidelity Series Equity Income. The fund currently has a performance rating of A- (Excellent) based on an average return of 9.46% over the last three years and 3.79% over the last three months. Factored into the performance evaluation is an expense ratio of 0.70% (very low).

The fund's risk rating is currently C+ (Fair). It carries a beta of 0.94, meaning that its performance tracks fairly well with that of the overall stock market. Volatility, as measured by both the semi-deviation and a drawdown factor, is considered low.

James S. Morrow has been running the fund for 5 years and currently receives a manager quality ranking of 68 (0=worst, 99=best). If you desire only a moderate level of risk and strong performance, then this fund is an excellent option.

Services Offered: Automated phone transactions, bank draft capabilities and wire transfers.

Data Date	Investment Rating	Net Assets ($Mil)	NAV	Perfor- mance Rating/Pts	Total Return Y-T-D	Risk Rating/Pts
2-17	A	5,216	13.42	A- / 9.1	3.79%	C+ / 6.4
2016	A+	5,040	12.93	A / 9.3	18.64%	C+ / 6.5
2015	B-	4,835	11.36	C+ / 6.6	-3.93%	B- / 7.1
2014	U	5,129	12.86	U / --	10.15%	U / --
2013	U	5,132	12.30	U / --	28.95%	U / --

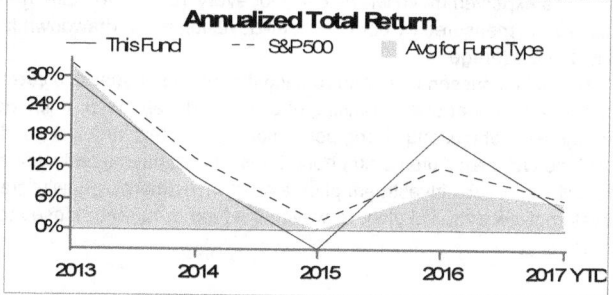
Annualized Total Return

Fidelity Series International Gr F (FFIGX)

D **Weak**

Fund Family: Fidelity Investments **Phone:** (800) 544-8544
Address: 245 Summer Street, Boston, MA 02210
Fund Type: FO - Foreign

Major Rating Factors: Disappointing performance is the major factor driving the D (Weak) TheStreet.com Investment Rating for Fidelity Series International Gr F. The fund currently has a performance rating of D (Weak) based on an average return of 1.33% over the last three years and 6.08% over the last three months. Factored into the performance evaluation is an expense ratio of 0.75% (very low).

The fund's risk rating is currently C+ (Fair). It carries a beta of 0.80, meaning the fund's expected move will be 8.0% for every 10% move in the market. Volatility, as measured by both the semi-deviation and a drawdown factor, is considered low.

Jed A. Weiss has been running the fund for 8 years and currently receives a manager quality ranking of 84 (0=worst, 99=best). This fund offers only a moderate level of risk but investors looking for strong performance are still waiting.

Services Offered: Automated phone transactions, bank draft capabilities, wire transfers and a systematic withdrawal plan.

Data Date	Investment Rating	Net Assets ($Mil)	NAV	Perfor- mance Rating/Pts	Total Return Y-T-D	Risk Rating/Pts
2-17	D	7,596	13.60	D / 2.0	6.08%	C+ / 6.0
2016	D	7,274	12.82	D- / 1.0	-3.39%	C+ / 6.1
2015	C+	6,386	13.63	C / 5.2	4.43%	C+ / 6.7
2014	D+	6,451	13.53	C- / 3.4	-3.19%	C+ / 6.1
2013	D+	6,829	14.40	C / 4.6	22.36%	C / 4.6
2012	C	4,349	11.91	B / 7.7	19.80%	C- / 3.1

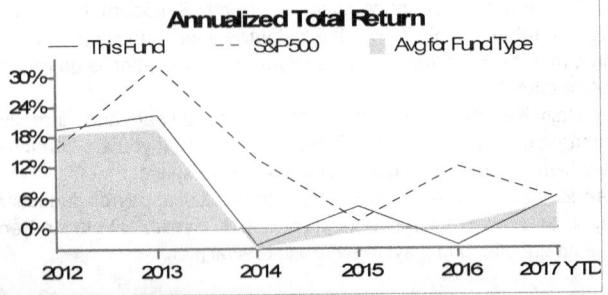

Annualized Total Return

Fidelity Series International Val F (FFVNX)

D- **Weak**

Fund Family: Fidelity Investments **Phone:** (800) 544-8544
Address: 245 Summer Street, Boston, MA 02210
Fund Type: FO - Foreign

Major Rating Factors: Very poor performance is the major factor driving the D- (Weak) TheStreet.com Investment Rating for Fidelity Series International Val F. The fund currently has a performance rating of E+ (Very Weak) based on an average return of -1.92% over the last three years and 2.61% over the last three months. Factored into the performance evaluation is an expense ratio of 0.73% (very low).

The fund's risk rating is currently C (Fair). It carries a beta of 0.85, meaning the fund's expected move will be 8.5% for every 10% move in the market. Volatility, as measured by both the semi-deviation and a drawdown factor, is considered average.

Alexander Zavratsky has been running the fund for 6 years and currently receives a manager quality ranking of 51 (0=worst, 99=best). This fund offers an average level of risk but investors looking for strong performance will be frustrated.

Services Offered: Automated phone transactions, bank draft capabilities, wire transfers and a systematic withdrawal plan.

Data Date	Investment Rating	Net Assets ($Mil)	NAV	Perfor- mance Rating/Pts	Total Return Y-T-D	Risk Rating/Pts
2-17	D-	7,501	9.42	E+ / 0.7	2.61%	C / 5.5
2016	D-	7,425	9.18	D- / 1.0	-1.32%	C+ / 5.6
2015	D+	6,396	9.56	C- / 3.3	1.12%	C+ / 5.8
2014	D-	6,296	9.67	D+ / 2.3	-7.30%	C / 5.0
2013	D-	6,754	11.24	C- / 3.7	22.78%	C- / 3.4
2012	E+	4,464	9.40	D+ / 2.7	20.40%	D+ / 2.4

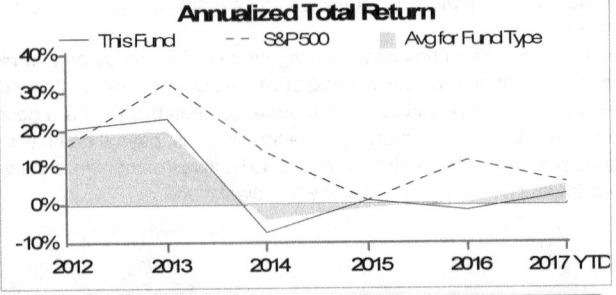

Annualized Total Return

Fidelity Small Cap Discovery Fund (FSCRX)

B- **Good**

Fund Family: Fidelity Investments **Phone:** (800) 544-8544
Address: 245 Summer Street, Boston, MA 02210
Fund Type: SC - Small Cap

Major Rating Factors: Strong performance is the major factor driving the B- (Good) TheStreet.com Investment Rating for Fidelity Small Cap Discovery Fund. The fund currently has a performance rating of B- (Good) based on an average return of 7.17% over the last three years and 0.66% over the last three months. Factored into the performance evaluation is an expense ratio of 1.01% (low) and a 1.5% back-end load levied at the time of sale.

The fund's risk rating is currently C (Fair). It carries a beta of 0.84, meaning the fund's expected move will be 8.4% for every 10% move in the market. Volatility, as measured by both the semi-deviation and a drawdown factor, is considered average.

Derek H. Janssen has been running the fund for 1 year and currently receives a manager quality ranking of 83 (0=worst, 99=best). If you desire an average level of risk and strong performance, then this fund is a good option.

Services Offered: Automated phone transactions, payroll deductions, bank draft capabilities, an IRA investment plan, a 401K investment plan, wire transfers and a systematic withdrawal plan. However, the fund is currently closed to new investors.

Data Date	Investment Rating	Net Assets ($Mil)	NAV	Perfor- mance Rating/Pts	Total Return Y-T-D	Risk Rating/Pts
2-17	B-	5,761	31.85	B- / 7.2	0.66%	C / 5.4
2016	B+	5,790	31.64	A- / 9.2	20.29%	C / 5.5
2015	C	5,641	26.42	C+ / 5.9	-6.17%	C+ / 6.0
2014	A-	6,119	30.09	A / 9.3	7.00%	C+ / 6.2
2013	B+	6,985	31.26	A / 9.5	38.22%	C- / 3.9
2012	A-	3,880	24.07	A+ / 9.9	24.03%	C- / 3.6

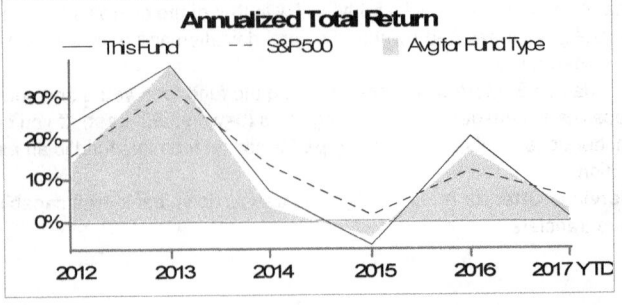

Annualized Total Return

Fidelity Srs Emerging Markets Fd (FEMSX)

C- **Fair**

Fund Family: Fidelity Investments **Phone:** (800) 544-8544
Address: 245 Summer Street, Boston, MA 02210
Fund Type: EM - Emerging Market
Major Rating Factors: Middle of the road best describes Fidelity Srs Emerging Markets Fd whose TheStreet.com Investment Rating is currently a C- (Fair). The fund currently has a performance rating of C (Fair) based on an average return of 1.85% over the last three years and 9.94% over the last three months. Factored into the performance evaluation is an expense ratio of 1.04% (low).

The fund's risk rating is currently C (Fair). It carries a beta of 0.90, meaning the fund's expected move will be 9.0% for every 10% move in the market. Volatility, as measured by both the semi-deviation and a drawdown factor, is considered average.

James J. Hayes has been running the fund for 8 years and currently receives a manager quality ranking of 76 (0=worst, 99=best). If you desire an average level of risk, then this fund may be an option.
Services Offered: Automated phone transactions, bank draft capabilities, wire transfers and a systematic withdrawal plan.

Data Date	Investment Rating	Net Assets ($Mil)	NAV	Performance Rating/Pts	Total Return Y-T-D	Risk Rating/Pts
2-17	C-	7,366	17.26	C / 5.5	9.94%	C / 4.9
2016	D-	6,763	15.70	D- / 1.4	10.95%	C / 4.9
2015	E+	5,486	14.36	E / 0.5	-12.74%	C / 5.0
2014	E+	4,792	16.66	E+ / 0.9	-4.30%	C / 5.2
2013	E	4,221	17.55	E / 0.5	3.35%	D+ / 2.7
2012	D+	3,325	17.15	C+ / 6.1	21.79%	D+ / 2.6

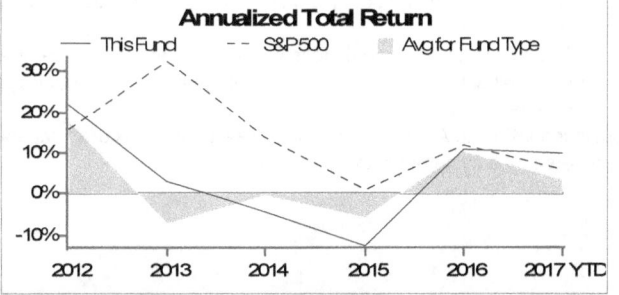

Fidelity Strategic Advisers Core (FCSAX)

A- **Excellent**

Fund Family: Fidelity Investments **Phone:** (800) 544-8544
Address: 245 Summer Street, Boston, MA 02210
Fund Type: IN - Income
Major Rating Factors: Strong performance is the major factor driving the A- (Excellent) TheStreet.com Investment Rating for Fidelity Strategic Advisers Core. The fund currently has a performance rating of B+ (Good) based on an average return of 9.18% over the last three years and 5.86% over the last three months. Factored into the performance evaluation is an expense ratio of 0.81% (very low).

The fund's risk rating is currently C+ (Fair). It carries a beta of 1.03, meaning that its performance tracks fairly well with that of the overall stock market. Volatility, as measured by both the semi-deviation and a drawdown factor, is considered low.

John Stone has been running the fund for 8 years and currently receives a manager quality ranking of 54 (0=worst, 99=best). If you desire only a moderate level of risk and strong performance, then this fund is an excellent option.
Services Offered: Automated phone transactions, bank draft capabilities, wire transfers and a systematic withdrawal plan.

Data Date	Investment Rating	Net Assets ($Mil)	NAV	Performance Rating/Pts	Total Return Y-T-D	Risk Rating/Pts
2-17	A-	24,090	16.80	B+ / 8.8	5.86%	C+ / 6.0
2016	B	23,201	15.87	B / 8.2	10.82%	C+ / 5.8
2015	B+	24,945	14.73	B+ / 8.6	0.08%	C+ / 5.9
2014	B+	22,831	15.57	B+ / 8.6	12.11%	C+ / 6.0
2013	B-	12,505	14.93	B- / 7.5	32.84%	C / 4.8
2012	C+	9,094	12.15	C+ / 6.6	16.11%	C / 5.3

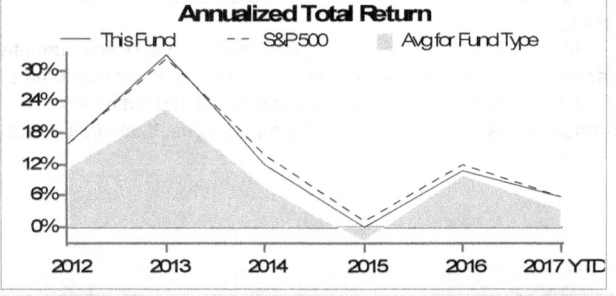

Fidelity Strategic Advisers Growth (FSGFX)

B **Good**

Fund Family: Fidelity Investments **Phone:** (800) 544-8544
Address: 245 Summer Street, Boston, MA 02210
Fund Type: GR - Growth
Major Rating Factors: Strong performance is the major factor driving the B (Good) TheStreet.com Investment Rating for Fidelity Strategic Advisers Growth. The fund currently has a performance rating of B (Good) based on an average return of 8.46% over the last three years and 7.58% over the last three months. Factored into the performance evaluation is an expense ratio of 0.72% (very low).

The fund's risk rating is currently C (Fair). It carries a beta of 1.05, meaning that its performance tracks fairly well with that of the overall stock market. Volatility, as measured by both the semi-deviation and a drawdown factor, is considered average.

Philip J. Sanders has been running the fund for 7 years and currently receives a manager quality ranking of 42 (0=worst, 99=best). If you desire an average level of risk and strong performance, then this fund is a good option.
Services Offered: N/A

Data Date	Investment Rating	Net Assets ($Mil)	NAV	Performance Rating/Pts	Total Return Y-T-D	Risk Rating/Pts
2-17	B	11,187	16.88	B / 8.0	7.58%	C / 5.4
2016	C+	10,622	15.69	B- / 7.0	4.64%	C / 5.5
2015	A	12,245	16.55	A / 9.5	5.12%	C+ / 6.0
2014	B+	12,366	16.68	B+ / 8.4	11.26%	C+ / 6.1
2013	B+	11,303	16.03	B+ / 8.6	35.78%	C / 4.6
2012	U	7,719	12.90	U / --	13.51%	U / --

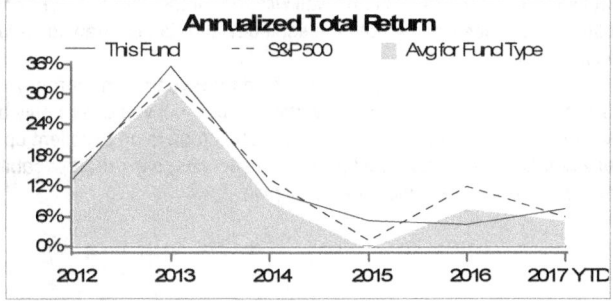

Fidelity Strategic Advisers Intl (FILFX)

D-   **Weak**

Fund Family: Fidelity Investments   **Phone:** (800) 544-8544
Address: 245 Summer Street, Boston, MA 02210
Fund Type: FO - Foreign

Major Rating Factors: Disappointing performance is the major factor driving the D- (Weak) TheStreet.com Investment Rating for Fidelity Strategic Advisers Intl. The fund currently has a performance rating of D- (Weak) based on an average return of -0.12% over the last three years and 4.26% over the last three months. Factored into the performance evaluation is an expense ratio of 1.02% (low).

The fund's risk rating is currently C (Fair). It carries a beta of 0.87, meaning the fund's expected move will be 8.7% for every 10% move in the market. Volatility, as measured by both the semi-deviation and a drawdown factor, is considered average.

Wilfred Chilangwa currently receives a manager quality ranking of 74 (0=worst, 99=best). This fund offers an average level of risk but investors looking for strong performance will be frustrated.

Services Offered: Automated phone transactions, bank draft capabilities, wire transfers and a systematic withdrawal plan.

Data Date	Investment Rating	Net Assets ($Mil)	NAV	Performance Rating/Pts	Total Return Y-T-D	Risk Rating/Pts
2-17	D-	16,141	9.78	D- / 1.3	4.26%	C / 5.1
2016	D-	16,379	9.38	D- / 1.4	0.36%	C / 5.1
2015	D+	20,074	9.55	C- / 3.5	0.78%	C+ / 5.6
2014	D	22,865	9.79	D+ / 2.8	-5.08%	C / 5.3
2013	D	20,404	10.72	C- / 4.0	22.20%	C- / 3.4
2012	D+	12,308	8.93	C+ / 6.2	20.01%	D+ / 2.6

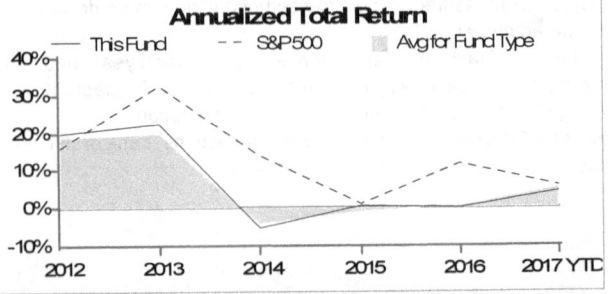

Annualized Total Return

Fidelity Strategic Advisers Sm-Mid (FSCFX)

C+   **Fair**

Fund Family: Fidelity Investments   **Phone:** (800) 544-8544
Address: 245 Summer Street, Boston, MA 02210
Fund Type: GR - Growth

Major Rating Factors: Strong performance is the major factor driving the C+ (Fair) TheStreet.com Investment Rating for Fidelity Strategic Advisers Sm-Mid. The fund currently has a performance rating of B- (Good) based on an average return of 5.89% over the last three years and 4.03% over the last three months. Factored into the performance evaluation is an expense ratio of 1.09% (low).

The fund's risk rating is currently C (Fair). It carries a beta of 1.12, meaning it is expected to move 11.2% for every 10% move in the market. Volatility, as measured by both the semi-deviation and a drawdown factor, is considered average.

Juliet S. Ellis has been running the fund for 7 years and currently receives a manager quality ranking of 11 (0=worst, 99=best). If you desire an average level of risk and strong performance, then this fund is a good option.

Services Offered: Automated phone transactions, bank draft capabilities, wire transfers and a systematic withdrawal plan.

Data Date	Investment Rating	Net Assets ($Mil)	NAV	Performance Rating/Pts	Total Return Y-T-D	Risk Rating/Pts
2-17	C+	7,049	14.19	B- / 7.5	4.03%	C / 4.5
2016	C+	6,852	13.64	B / 8.2	15.70%	C / 4.4
2015	C	7,451	12.02	C+ / 6.2	-3.77%	C / 4.7
2014	C-	6,969	13.28	C+ / 6.6	3.99%	C- / 3.8
2013	C+	5,071	13.92	B / 7.9	36.26%	C- / 3.2
2012	C	2,705	11.41	B / 8.1	15.32%	D / 2.1

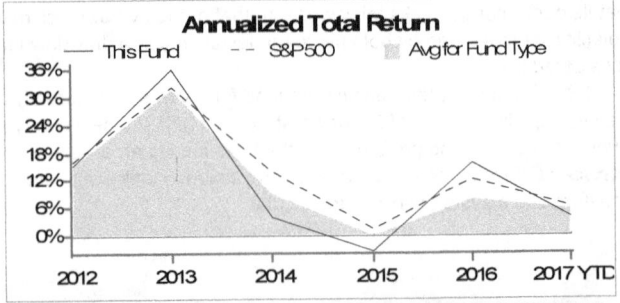

Annualized Total Return

Fidelity Strategic Advisers Val Fd (FVSAX)

A   **Excellent**

Fund Family: Fidelity Investments   **Phone:** (800) 544-8544
Address: 245 Summer Street, Boston, MA 02210
Fund Type: GR - Growth

Major Rating Factors: Exceptional performance is the major factor driving the A (Excellent) TheStreet.com Investment Rating for Fidelity Strategic Advisers Val Fd. The fund currently has a performance rating of A (Excellent) based on an average return of 9.54% over the last three years and 4.61% over the last three months. Factored into the performance evaluation is an expense ratio of 0.74% (very low).

The fund's risk rating is currently C+ (Fair). It carries a beta of 1.03, meaning that its performance tracks fairly well with that of the overall stock market. Volatility, as measured by both the semi-deviation and a drawdown factor, is considered low.

John Stone has been running the fund for 9 years and currently receives a manager quality ranking of 59 (0=worst, 99=best). If you desire only a moderate level of risk and strong performance, then this fund is an excellent option.

Services Offered: Automated phone transactions, bank draft capabilities, wire transfers and a systematic withdrawal plan.

Data Date	Investment Rating	Net Assets ($Mil)	NAV	Performance Rating/Pts	Total Return Y-T-D	Risk Rating/Pts
2-17	A	11,132	19.50	A / 9.4	4.61%	C+ / 5.9
2016	A	10,714	18.64	A / 9.3	15.77%	C+ / 6.2
2015	B+	12,105	17.06	B / 8.0	-2.74%	C+ / 6.6
2014	A	12,982	18.73	B+ / 8.9	12.43%	B- / 7.1
2013	B+	11,516	18.25	B / 7.9	33.32%	C / 5.5
2012	C+	7,894	14.53	C+ / 6.5	16.59%	C / 5.1

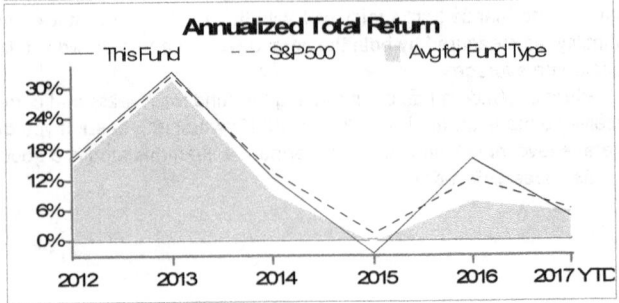

Annualized Total Return

Fidelity Value Fd (FDVLX)   B   Good

Fund Family: Fidelity Investments   **Phone:** (800) 544-8544
Address: 245 Summer Street, Boston, MA 02210
Fund Type: GI - Growth and Income
Major Rating Factors: Strong performance is the major factor driving the B (Good) TheStreet.com Investment Rating for Fidelity Value Fd. The fund currently has a performance rating of B+ (Good) based on an average return of 7.34% over the last three years and 5.09% over the last three months. Factored into the performance evaluation is an expense ratio of 0.84% (very low).

The fund's risk rating is currently C (Fair). It carries a beta of 1.09, meaning that its performance tracks fairly well with that of the overall stock market. Volatility, as measured by both the semi-deviation and a drawdown factor, is considered average.

Matthew H. Friedman has been running the fund for 7 years and currently receives a manager quality ranking of 25 (0=worst, 99=best). If you desire an average level of risk and strong performance, then this fund is a good option.
Services Offered: Automated phone transactions, payroll deductions, bank draft capabilities, an IRA investment plan, a 401K investment plan, a Keogh investment plan and a systematic withdrawal plan.

Data Date	Investment Rating	Net Assets ($Mil)	NAV	Performance Rating/Pts	Total Return Y-T-D	Risk Rating/Pts
2-17	B	7,434	115.37	B+ / 8.3	5.09%	C / 4.7
2016	B	7,176	109.78	B+ / 8.6	16.06%	C / 5.0
2015	C+	7,373	95.76	C+ / 6.9	-6.51%	C / 5.5
2014	A+	8,106	113.26	A+ / 9.6	11.72%	C+ / 6.7
2013	B	7,360	103.58	B+ / 8.5	37.07%	C / 4.3
2012	B+	5,613	76.34	A / 9.3	21.90%	C- / 3.7

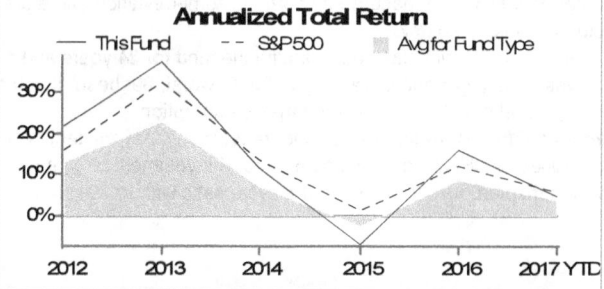

First Eagle Global A (SGENX)   C   Fair

Fund Family: First Eagle   **Phone:** (800) 334-2143
Address: 1345 Avenue of the Americas, New York, NY 10105
Fund Type: GL - Global
Major Rating Factors: Middle of the road best describes First Eagle Global A whose TheStreet.com Investment Rating is currently a C (Fair). The fund currently has a performance rating of C- (Fair) based on an average return of 4.90% over the last three years and 4.26% over the last three months. Factored into the performance evaluation is an expense ratio of 1.11% (low) and a 5.0% front-end load that is levied at the time of purchase.

The fund's risk rating is currently B- (Good). It carries a beta of 0.57, meaning the fund's expected move will be 5.7% for every 10% move in the market. Volatility, as measured by both the semi-deviation and a drawdown factor, is considered low.

Matthew B. McLennan has been running the fund for 9 years and currently receives a manager quality ranking of 95 (0=worst, 99=best). If you desire an average level of risk, then this fund may be an option.
Services Offered: Automated phone transactions, payroll deductions, bank draft capabilities, an IRA investment plan, a 401K investment plan, wire transfers and a systematic withdrawal plan.

Data Date	Investment Rating	Net Assets ($Mil)	NAV	Performance Rating/Pts	Total Return Y-T-D	Risk Rating/Pts
2-17	C	16,128	56.57	C- / 3.6	4.26%	B- / 7.3
2016	C+	15,645	54.26	C / 4.6	10.65%	B- / 7.4
2015	C-	15,634	51.35	D+ / 2.8	-0.93%	B- / 7.4
2014	D+	17,506	52.44	D+ / 2.4	2.94%	B- / 7.3
2013	C-	19,398	53.61	D+ / 2.7	15.49%	B- / 7.3
2012	C+	16,115	48.59	C- / 3.9	12.46%	B- / 7.3

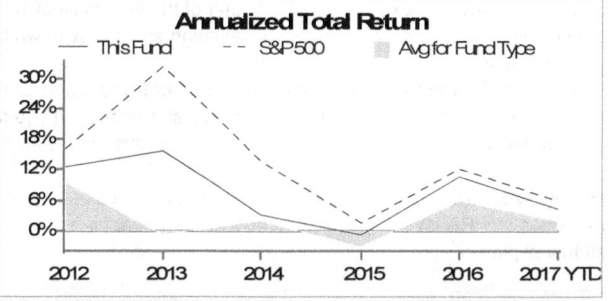

FMI International Investor (FMIJX)   B-   Good

Fund Family: Fiduciary Management Funds   **Phone:** (800) 811-5311
Address: 225 E. Mason St., Milwaukee, WI 53202
Fund Type: FO - Foreign
Major Rating Factors: FMI International Investor receives a TheStreet.com Investment Rating of B- (Good). The fund currently has a performance rating of C+ (Fair) based on an average return of 6.96% over the last three years and 3.68% over the last three months. Factored into the performance evaluation is an expense ratio of 0.98% (low).

The fund's risk rating is currently B- (Good). It carries a beta of 0.48, meaning the fund's expected move will be 4.8% for every 10% move in the market. Volatility, as measured by both the semi-deviation and a drawdown factor, is considered low.

Jonathan T. Bloom currently receives a manager quality ranking of 98 (0=worst, 99=best). If you desire an average level of risk, then this fund may be an option.
Services Offered: Automated phone transactions, payroll deductions, bank draft capabilities, an IRA investment plan, a 401K investment plan, wire transfers and a systematic withdrawal plan.

Data Date	Investment Rating	Net Assets ($Mil)	NAV	Performance Rating/Pts	Total Return Y-T-D	Risk Rating/Pts
2-17	B-	5,287	30.98	C+ / 5.9	3.68%	B- / 7.2
2016	B+	4,957	29.88	B- / 7.1	10.00%	B- / 7.2
2015	B-	2,799	28.19	C+ / 6.9	3.22%	B- / 7.5
2014	B-	772	27.82	C / 5.3	4.62%	B- / 7.7
2013	B-	166	27.51	C / 5.4	24.65%	B- / 7.5
2012	U	76	22.68	U / --	18.18%	U / --

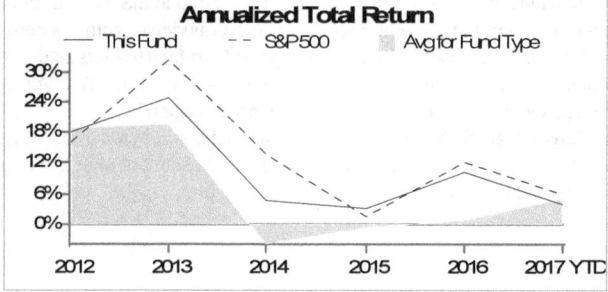

FPA Crescent (FPACX)

B-   Good

Fund Family: FPA Funds   **Phone:** (800) 982-4372
Address: 11400 West Olympic Blvd, Los Angeles, CA 90064
Fund Type: BA - Balanced
Major Rating Factors: FPA Crescent receives a TheStreet.com Investment Rating of B- (Good). The fund currently has a performance rating of C+ (Fair) based on an average return of 5.80% over the last three years and 4.05% over the last three months. Factored into the performance evaluation is an expense ratio of 1.11% (low) and a 2.0% back-end load levied at the time of sale.

The fund's risk rating is currently B- (Good). It carries a beta of 1.04, meaning that its performance tracks fairly well with that of the overall stock market. Volatility, as measured by both the semi-deviation and a drawdown factor, is considered low.

Steven T. Romick has been running the fund for 24 years and currently receives a manager quality ranking of 50 (0=worst, 99=best). If you desire an average level of risk, then this fund may be an option.

Services Offered: Automated phone transactions, payroll deductions, bank draft capabilities, an IRA investment plan, a 401K investment plan, a Keogh investment plan, wire transfers and a systematic withdrawal plan.

Data Date	Investment Rating	Net Assets ($Mil)	NAV	Performance Rating/Pts	Total Return Y-T-D	Risk Rating/Pts
2-17	B-	17,381	33.93	C+ / 5.8	4.05%	B- / 7.0
2016	B+	16,549	32.61	B- / 7.0	10.25%	B- / 7.2
2015	C+	18,112	31.06	C / 4.8	-2.06%	B- / 7.9
2014	C+	19,970	33.74	C- / 4.2	6.64%	B / 8.5
2013	B-	15,882	32.96	C / 4.4	21.95%	B- / 7.8
2012	C+	9,917	29.29	C- / 3.6	10.33%	B- / 7.8

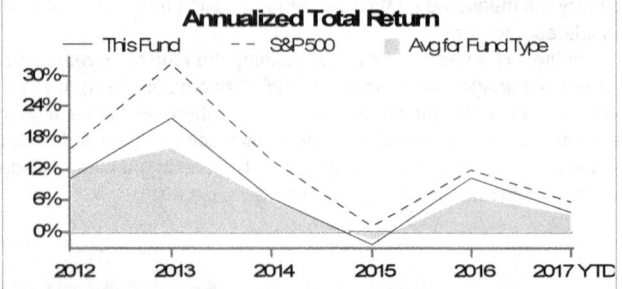

Franklin Growth A (FKGRX)

A-   Excellent

Fund Family: Franklin Templeton Investments   **Phone:** (800) 342-5236
Address: One Franklin Parkway, San Mateo, CA 94403
Fund Type: GR - Growth
Major Rating Factors: Strong performance is the major factor driving the A- (Excellent) TheStreet.com Investment Rating for Franklin Growth A. The fund currently has a performance rating of B (Good) based on an average return of 10.02% over the last three years and 7.62% over the last three months. Factored into the performance evaluation is an expense ratio of 0.88% (low) and a 5.8% front-end load that is levied at the time of purchase.

The fund's risk rating is currently C+ (Fair). It carries a beta of 0.95, meaning that its performance tracks fairly well with that of the overall stock market. Volatility, as measured by both the semi-deviation and a drawdown factor, is considered low.

Serena P. Vinton has been running the fund for 9 years and currently receives a manager quality ranking of 73 (0=worst, 99=best). If you desire only a moderate level of risk and strong performance, then this fund is an excellent option.

Services Offered: Automated phone transactions, payroll deductions, bank draft capabilities, an IRA investment plan, a 401K investment plan and a systematic withdrawal plan.

Data Date	Investment Rating	Net Assets ($Mil)	NAV	Performance Rating/Pts	Total Return Y-T-D	Risk Rating/Pts
2-17	A-	7,478	82.45	B / 8.1	7.62%	C+ / 6.7
2016	B	7,405	76.61	B- / 7.2	8.41%	C+ / 6.8
2015	A	7,741	73.37	B+ / 8.3	1.94%	B- / 7.6
2014	B+	7,193	74.69	B- / 7.5	14.88%	B- / 7.3
2013	C+	5,992	65.18	C+ / 6.0	29.39%	C+ / 6.2
2012	C-	4,226	50.61	C- / 3.9	13.69%	C+ / 5.8

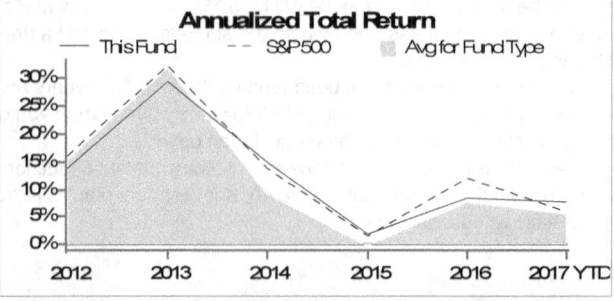

Franklin Income A (FKINX)

C-   Fair

Fund Family: Franklin Templeton Investments   **Phone:** (800) 342-5236
Address: One Franklin Parkway, San Mateo, CA 94403
Fund Type: GL - Global
Major Rating Factors: Middle of the road best describes Franklin Income A whose TheStreet.com Investment Rating is currently a C- (Fair). The fund currently has a performance rating of C (Fair) based on an average return of 3.63% over the last three years and 3.05% over the last three months. Factored into the performance evaluation is an expense ratio of 0.61% (very low) and a 4.3% front-end load that is levied at the time of purchase.

The fund's risk rating is currently C+ (Fair). It carries a beta of 1.23, meaning it is expected to move 12.3% for every 10% move in the market. Volatility, as measured by both the semi-deviation and a drawdown factor, is considered low.

Edward D. Perks has been running the fund for 15 years and currently receives a manager quality ranking of 48 (0=worst, 99=best). If you desire an average level of risk, then this fund may be an option.

Services Offered: Automated phone transactions, payroll deductions, bank draft capabilities, an IRA investment plan, a 401K investment plan, a Keogh investment plan and a systematic withdrawal plan.

Data Date	Investment Rating	Net Assets ($Mil)	NAV	Performance Rating/Pts	Total Return Y-T-D	Risk Rating/Pts
2-17	C-	46,472	2.36	C / 4.3	3.05%	C+ / 6.0
2016	C+	45,223	2.31	C+ / 6.6	16.29%	C+ / 6.0
2015	D-	45,850	2.10	D- / 1.2	-7.81%	C+ / 6.4
2014	D+	52,523	2.40	D+ / 2.5	4.12%	B- / 7.1
2013	D+	50,515	2.42	D+ / 2.9	14.23%	C+ / 6.3
2012	C+	42,511	2.24	C / 5.1	13.68%	C+ / 5.9

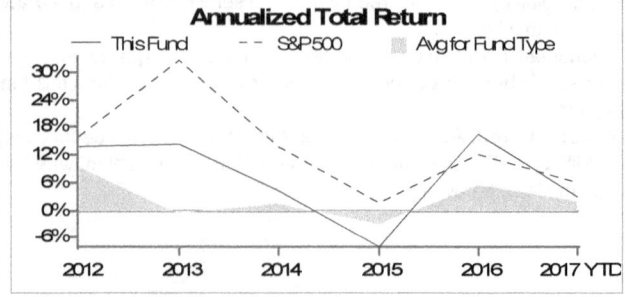

Franklin Mutual Global Discovery A (TEDIX)　　　　C　　Fair

Fund Family: Franklin Templeton Investments　　**Phone:** (800) 342-5236
Address: One Franklin Parkway, San Mateo, CA 94403
Fund Type: GL - Global
Major Rating Factors: Middle of the road best describes Franklin Mutual Global Discovery A whose TheStreet.com Investment Rating is currently a C (Fair). The fund currently has a performance rating of C+ (Fair) based on an average return of 5.37% over the last three years and 3.63% over the last three months. Factored into the performance evaluation is an expense ratio of 1.24% (average) and a 5.8% front-end load that is levied at the time of purchase.

　　The fund's risk rating is currently C (Fair). It carries a beta of 0.72, meaning the fund's expected move will be 7.2% for every 10% move in the market. Volatility, as measured by both the semi-deviation and a drawdown factor, is considered average.

　　Peter A. Langerman has been running the fund for 12 years and currently receives a manager quality ranking of 96 (0=worst, 99=best). If you desire an average level of risk, then this fund may be an option.
Services Offered: Automated phone transactions, payroll deductions, bank draft capabilities, an IRA investment plan, a 401K investment plan, a Keogh investment plan, wire transfers and a systematic withdrawal plan.

Data Date	Investment Rating	Net Assets ($Mil)	NAV	Performance Rating/Pts	Total Return Y-T-D	Risk Rating/Pts
2-17	C	10,517	31.68	C+ / 5.8	3.63%	C / 5.0
2016	C+	10,437	30.57	C+ / 6.9	12.56%	C / 5.1
2015	D+	11,816	28.86	C- / 3.7	-3.63%	C+ / 5.9
2014	C	11,577	32.81	C- / 4.1	5.01%	C+ / 6.8
2013	C-	10,609	33.24	C / 4.4	25.26%	C / 5.4
2012	D	8,007	28.27	D / 2.1	13.34%	C+ / 5.7

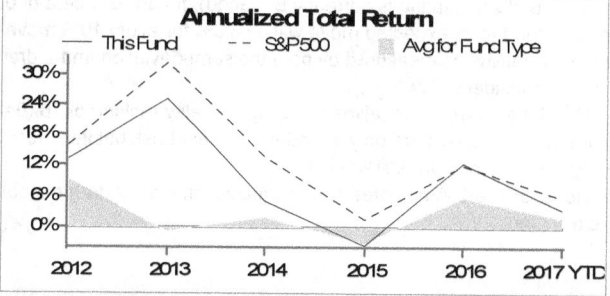

Franklin Rising Dividends A (FRDPX)　　　　C+　　Fair

Fund Family: Franklin Templeton Investments　　**Phone:** (800) 342-5236
Address: One Franklin Parkway, San Mateo, CA 94403
Fund Type: GI - Growth and Income
Major Rating Factors: Middle of the road best describes Franklin Rising Dividends A whose TheStreet.com Investment Rating is currently a C+ (Fair). The fund currently has a performance rating of C+ (Fair) based on an average return of 7.96% over the last three years and 4.35% over the last three months. Factored into the performance evaluation is an expense ratio of 0.92% (low) and a 5.8% front-end load that is levied at the time of purchase.

　　The fund's risk rating is currently C+ (Fair). It carries a beta of 0.95, meaning that its performance tracks fairly well with that of the overall stock market. Volatility, as measured by both the semi-deviation and a drawdown factor, is considered low.

　　Bruce C. Baughman has been running the fund for 30 years and currently receives a manager quality ranking of 49 (0=worst, 99=best). If you desire an average level of risk, then this fund may be an option.
Services Offered: Automated phone transactions, payroll deductions, bank draft capabilities, an IRA investment plan, a 401K investment plan, a Keogh investment plan and a systematic withdrawal plan.

Data Date	Investment Rating	Net Assets ($Mil)	NAV	Performance Rating/Pts	Total Return Y-T-D	Risk Rating/Pts
2-17	C+	11,389	54.92	C+ / 6.0	4.35%	C+ / 6.6
2016	C+	11,459	52.63	C+ / 6.9	14.41%	C+ / 6.6
2015	C+	11,036	47.75	C+ / 5.7	-3.54%	C+ / 6.9
2014	B-	11,389	52.06	C+ / 5.6	9.72%	B- / 7.8
2013	B-	9,764	48.47	C+ / 6.0	29.30%	B- / 7.1
2012	C+	5,935	37.82	C+ / 6.3	10.29%	C+ / 6.9

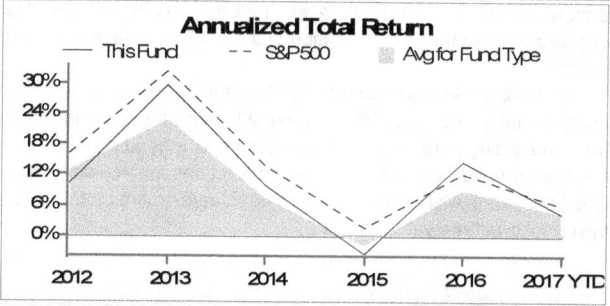

GE RSP US Equity (GESSX)　　　　B　　Good

Fund Family: GE Investment Funds　　**Phone:** (800) 242-0134
Address: PO Box 9838, Providence, RI 02940
Fund Type: GI - Growth and Income
Major Rating Factors: Strong performance is the major factor driving the B (Good) TheStreet.com Investment Rating for GE RSP US Equity. The fund currently has a performance rating of B+ (Good) based on an average return of 8.79% over the last three years and 7.02% over the last three months. Factored into the performance evaluation is an expense ratio of 0.17% (very low).

　　The fund's risk rating is currently C- (Fair). It carries a beta of 1.11, meaning it is expected to move 11.1% for every 10% move in the market. Volatility, as measured by both the semi-deviation and a drawdown factor, is considered average.

　　David B. Carlson has been running the fund for 10 years and currently receives a manager quality ranking of 37 (0=worst, 99=best). If you desire an average level of risk and strong performance, then this fund is a good option.
Services Offered: Payroll deductions.

Data Date	Investment Rating	Net Assets ($Mil)	NAV	Performance Rating/Pts	Total Return Y-T-D	Risk Rating/Pts
2-17	B	5,184	52.73	B+ / 8.9	7.02%	C- / 4.1
2016	C+	4,915	49.27	B / 7.8	10.13%	C- / 4.2
2015	B	4,943	47.59	B+ / 8.5	-2.05%	C / 5.1
2014	A-	5,446	54.31	A / 9.3	13.27%	C+ / 5.8
2013	B+	5,057	54.73	B / 8.2	35.15%	C / 5.5
2012	C	3,960	44.41	C / 5.3	16.78%	C / 5.3

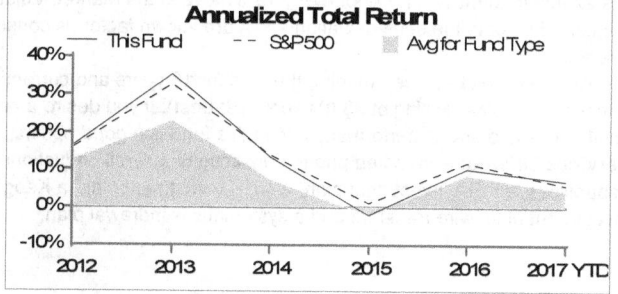

GMO Benchmark-Free Allocation III (GBMFX)   C-   Fair

Fund Family: GMO Funds   **Phone:** N/A
Address: 40 Rowes Wharf, Boston, MA 02110
Fund Type: AA - Asset Allocation

Major Rating Factors: Disappointing performance is the major factor driving the C- (Fair) TheStreet.com Investment Rating for GMO Benchmark-Free Allocation III. The fund currently has a performance rating of D (Weak) based on an average return of 1.14% over the last three years and 3.74% over the last three months. Factored into the performance evaluation is an expense ratio of 1.09% (low), a 0.1% front-end load that is levied at the time of purchase and a 0.1% back-end load levied at the time of sale.

The fund's risk rating is currently B- (Good). It carries a beta of 0.83, meaning the fund's expected move will be 8.3% for every 10% move in the market. Volatility, as measured by both the semi-deviation and a drawdown factor, is considered low.

Ben Inker currently receives a manager quality ranking of 16 (0=worst, 99=best). This fund offers only a moderate level of risk but investors looking for strong performance are still waiting.

Services Offered: Automated phone transactions, bank draft capabilities and wire transfers.

Data Date	Investment Rating	Net Assets ($Mil)	NAV	Perfor- mance Rating/Pts	Total Return Y-T-D	Risk Rating/Pts
2-17	C-	5,178	25.78	D / 2.0	3.74%	B- / 7.6
2016	C-	5,055	24.85	D / 2.0	3.40%	B- / 7.6
2015	D+	5,921	24.42	D / 1.6	-4.28%	B- / 7.4
2014	C-	5,108	26.02	D / 1.6	1.21%	B / 8.3
2013	C+	2,767	26.95	D+ / 2.3	10.73%	B+ / 9.3
2012	C+	853	25.03	D / 2.1	10.01%	B+ / 9.4

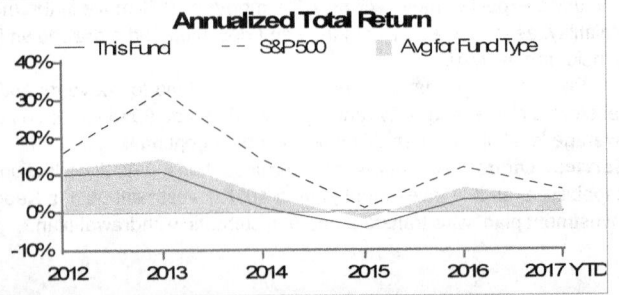

Invesco American Franchise A (VAFAX)   C+   Fair

Fund Family: Invesco Investments Funds   **Phone:** (800) 959-4246
Address: P.O. Box 4739, Houston, TX 77210
Fund Type: IN - Income

Major Rating Factors: Strong performance is the major factor driving the C+ (Fair) TheStreet.com Investment Rating for Invesco American Franchise A. The fund currently has a performance rating of B- (Good) based on an average return of 7.33% over the last three years and 9.49% over the last three months. Factored into the performance evaluation is an expense ratio of 1.08% (low) and a 5.5% front-end load that is levied at the time of purchase.

The fund's risk rating is currently C (Fair). It carries a beta of 1.13, meaning it is expected to move 11.3% for every 10% move in the market. Volatility, as measured by both the semi-deviation and a drawdown factor, is considered average.

Erik J. Voss has been running the fund for 7 years and currently receives a manager quality ranking of 20 (0=worst, 99=best). If you desire an average level of risk and strong performance, then this fund is a good option.

Services Offered: Automated phone transactions, payroll deductions, bank draft capabilities, an IRA investment plan, a 401K investment plan, wire transfers and a systematic withdrawal plan.

Data Date	Investment Rating	Net Assets ($Mil)	NAV	Perfor- mance Rating/Pts	Total Return Y-T-D	Risk Rating/Pts
2-17	C+	8,597	17.89	B- / 7.2	9.49%	C / 4.8
2016	D+	7,990	16.34	C- / 4.1	2.01%	C / 4.7
2015	B+	8,608	16.66	A / 9.3	4.93%	C / 5.5
2014	C+	8,871	16.67	B- / 7.0	8.32%	C / 5.1
2013	B	8,995	16.91	B+ / 8.3	39.72%	C / 4.3
2012	D	4,594	12.63	D+ / 2.3	13.20%	C / 4.8

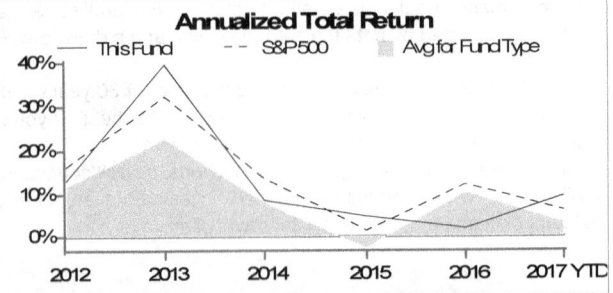

Invesco Comstock A (ACSTX)   B   Good

Fund Family: Invesco Investments Funds   **Phone:** (800) 959-4246
Address: P.O. Box 4739, Houston, TX 77210
Fund Type: GI - Growth and Income

Major Rating Factors: Strong performance is the major factor driving the B (Good) TheStreet.com Investment Rating for Invesco Comstock A. The fund currently has a performance rating of B (Good) based on an average return of 7.69% over the last three years and 3.51% over the last three months. Factored into the performance evaluation is an expense ratio of 0.86% (very low) and a 5.5% front-end load that is levied at the time of purchase.

The fund's risk rating is currently C (Fair). It carries a beta of 1.14, meaning it is expected to move 11.4% for every 10% move in the market. Volatility, as measured by both the semi-deviation and a drawdown factor, is considered average.

Kevin C. Holt has been running the fund for 18 years and currently receives a manager quality ranking of 23 (0=worst, 99=best). If you desire an average level of risk and strong performance, then this fund is a good option.

Services Offered: Automated phone transactions, payroll deductions, bank draft capabilities, an IRA investment plan, a 401K investment plan, a Keogh investment plan, wire transfers and a systematic withdrawal plan.

Data Date	Investment Rating	Net Assets ($Mil)	NAV	Perfor- mance Rating/Pts	Total Return Y-T-D	Risk Rating/Pts
2-17	B	6,720	24.50	B / 8.2	3.51%	C / 5.1
2016	B-	6,639	23.67	B / 7.8	17.83%	C / 5.3
2015	C	6,739	21.68	C+ / 5.6	-5.93%	C+ / 6.0
2014	B+	7,609	25.52	B- / 7.4	9.12%	B- / 7.3
2013	B	7,185	23.77	B / 7.6	35.24%	C / 5.4
2012	B	5,371	17.81	B- / 7.2	18.90%	C / 5.2

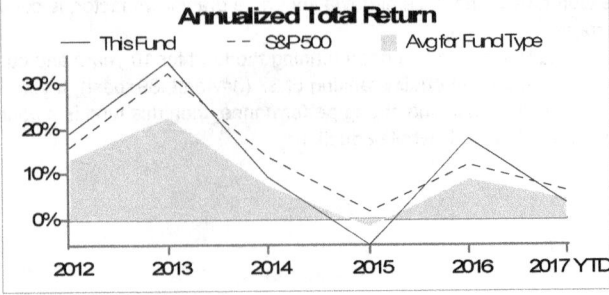

Invesco Diversified Dividend A (LCEAX)   B-   Good

Fund Family: Invesco Investments Funds   **Phone:** (800) 959-4246
Address: P.O. Box 4739, Houston, TX 77210
Fund Type: GI - Growth and Income

Major Rating Factors: Invesco Diversified Dividend A receives a TheStreet.com Investment Rating of B- (Good). The fund currently has a performance rating of C+ (Fair) based on an average return of 9.45% over the last three years and 2.75% over the last three months. Factored into the performance evaluation is an expense ratio of 0.84% (very low) and a 5.5% front-end load that is levied at the time of purchase.

The fund's risk rating is currently B- (Good). It carries a beta of 0.67, meaning the fund's expected move will be 6.7% for every 10% move in the market. Volatility, as measured by both the semi-deviation and a drawdown factor, is considered low.

Meggan M. Walsh has been running the fund for 15 years and currently receives a manager quality ranking of 87 (0=worst, 99=best). If you desire an average level of risk, then this fund may be an option.

Services Offered: Automated phone transactions, payroll deductions, bank draft capabilities, an IRA investment plan, a 401K investment plan and a systematic withdrawal plan.

Data Date	Investment Rating	Net Assets ($Mil)	NAV	Performance Rating/Pts	Total Return Y-T-D	Risk Rating/Pts
2-17	B-	6,601	19.83	C+ / 6.8	2.75%	B- / 7.2
2016	A+	6,353	19.30	B / 8.2	14.33%	B- / 7.3
2015	A-	4,731	17.58	B / 7.7	1.79%	B- / 7.4
2014	B+	4,312	18.30	B- / 7.1	11.93%	B- / 7.8
2013	C+	3,905	16.94	C+ / 5.8	29.00%	C+ / 6.3
2012	C+	2,565	13.47	C+ / 6.4	17.17%	C+ / 6.0

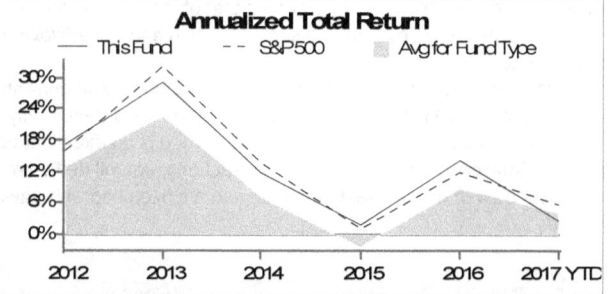

Invesco Equity and Income A (ACEIX)   C+   Fair

Fund Family: Invesco Investments Funds   **Phone:** (800) 959-4246
Address: P.O. Box 4739, Houston, TX 77210
Fund Type: GI - Growth and Income

Major Rating Factors: Middle of the road best describes Invesco Equity and Income A whose TheStreet.com Investment Rating is currently a C+ (Fair). The fund currently has a performance rating of C+ (Fair) based on an average return of 7.51% over the last three years and 3.13% over the last three months. Factored into the performance evaluation is an expense ratio of 0.81% (very low) and a 5.5% front-end load that is levied at the time of purchase.

The fund's risk rating is currently C+ (Fair). It carries a beta of 0.77, meaning the fund's expected move will be 7.7% for every 10% move in the market. Volatility, as measured by both the semi-deviation and a drawdown factor, is considered low.

James O. Roeder has been running the fund for 18 years and currently receives a manager quality ranking of 68 (0=worst, 99=best). If you desire an average level of risk, then this fund may be an option.

Services Offered: Automated phone transactions, payroll deductions, bank draft capabilities, an IRA investment plan, a 401K investment plan, a Keogh investment plan, wire transfers and a systematic withdrawal plan.

Data Date	Investment Rating	Net Assets ($Mil)	NAV	Performance Rating/Pts	Total Return Y-T-D	Risk Rating/Pts
2-17	C+	10,565	10.89	C+ / 6.8	3.13%	C+ / 6.3
2016	B+	10,353	10.56	B / 8.1	14.83%	C+ / 6.4
2015	C	9,832	9.62	C / 5.1	-2.35%	C+ / 6.7
2014	C+	10,172	10.36	C / 5.0	9.07%	C+ / 6.8
2013	C	9,543	10.66	C / 4.3	24.96%	C+ / 6.5
2012	D+	7,805	9.19	D / 2.2	12.88%	C+ / 6.5

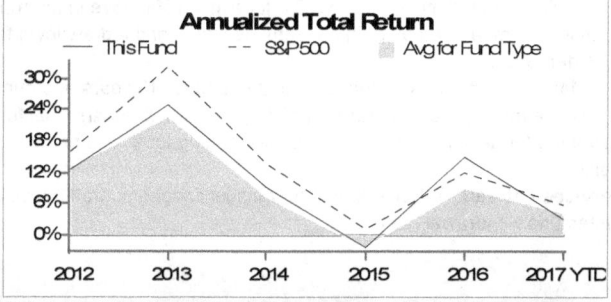

JPMorgan Global Rsrch Enh Index Sel (JEITX)   C+   Fair

Fund Family: JPMorgan Funds   **Phone:** (800) 480-4111
Address: 522 Fifth Avenue, New York, NY 10036
Fund Type: GL - Global

Major Rating Factors: Middle of the road best describes JPMorgan Global Rsrch Enh Index Sel whose TheStreet.com Investment Rating is currently a C+ (Fair). The fund currently has a performance rating of C+ (Fair) based on an average return of 5.37% over the last three years and 5.24% over the last three months. Factored into the performance evaluation is an expense ratio of 0.57% (very low).

The fund's risk rating is currently C+ (Fair). It carries a beta of 0.80, meaning the fund's expected move will be 8.0% for every 10% move in the market. Volatility, as measured by both the semi-deviation and a drawdown factor, is considered low.

Ido Eisenberg has been running the fund for 3 years and currently receives a manager quality ranking of 96 (0=worst, 99=best). If you desire an average level of risk, then this fund may be an option.

Services Offered: Automated phone transactions, payroll deductions, bank draft capabilities, an IRA investment plan, a 401K investment plan, wire transfers and a systematic withdrawal plan.

Data Date	Investment Rating	Net Assets ($Mil)	NAV	Performance Rating/Pts	Total Return Y-T-D	Risk Rating/Pts
2-17	C+	7,457	19.70	C+ / 6.4	5.24%	C+ / 6.5
2016	C+	7,052	18.72	C+ / 5.6	7.25%	C+ / 6.6
2015	U	7,121	17.84	U / --	-0.66%	U / --
2014	U	5,451	18.31	U / --	5.65%	U / --
2013	U	1,993	17.83	U / --	0.00%	U / --

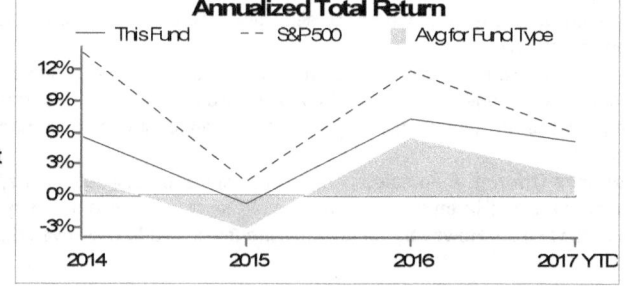

Spring 2017

Lord Abbett Affiliated A (LAFFX)

A- Excellent

Fund Family: Lord Abbett Funds   **Phone:** (888) 522-2388
Address: 90 Hudson Street, Jersey City, NJ 07302
Fund Type: GI - Growth and Income

Major Rating Factors: Strong performance is the major factor driving the A-(Excellent) TheStreet.com Investment Rating for Lord Abbett Affiliated A. The fund currently has a performance rating of B+ (Good) based on an average return of 9.71% over the last three years and 4.83% over the last three months. Factored into the performance evaluation is an expense ratio of 0.74% (very low) and a 5.8% front-end load that is levied at the time of purchase.

The fund's risk rating is currently C+ (Fair). It carries a beta of 0.97, meaning that its performance tracks fairly well with that of the overall stock market. Volatility, as measured by both the semi-deviation and a drawdown factor, is considered low.

Marc Pavese has been running the fund for 6 years and currently receives a manager quality ranking of 68 (0=worst, 99=best). If you desire only a moderate level of risk and strong performance, then this fund is an excellent option.

Services Offered: Automated phone transactions, payroll deductions, an IRA investment plan, a 401K investment plan and a systematic withdrawal plan.

Data Date	Investment Rating	Net Assets ($Mil)	NAV	Performance Rating/Pts	Total Return Y-T-D	Risk Rating/Pts
2-17	A-	5,808	16.06	B+ / 8.6	4.83%	C+ / 6.1
2016	A-	5,606	15.32	B+ / 8.6	17.34%	C+ / 6.1
2015	C+	5,357	14.11	C+ / 6.4	-4.20%	C+ / 6.7
2014	B+	6,128	16.27	B- / 7.5	12.07%	B- / 7.1
2013	C-	6,129	15.57	C / 5.4	32.15%	C / 4.4
2012	D-	5,354	12.02	D+ / 2.3	15.90%	C- / 3.9

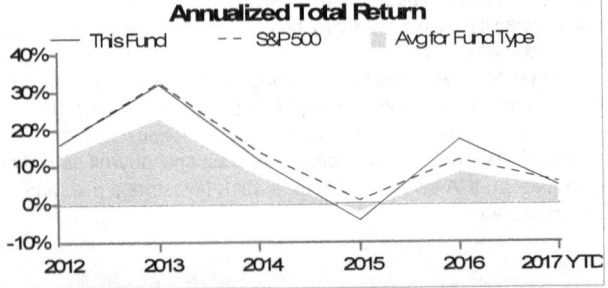

MFS Inst Intl Equity Fund (MIEIX)

D Weak

Fund Family: MFS Funds   **Phone:** (800) 225-2606
Address: P.O. Box 55824, Boston, MA 02205
Fund Type: FO - Foreign

Major Rating Factors: Disappointing performance is the major factor driving the D (Weak) TheStreet.com Investment Rating for MFS Inst Intl Equity Fund. The fund currently has a performance rating of D (Weak) based on an average return of 0.24% over the last three years and 4.59% over the last three months. Factored into the performance evaluation is an expense ratio of 0.71% (very low).

The fund's risk rating is currently C+ (Fair). It carries a beta of 0.90, meaning the fund's expected move will be 9.0% for every 10% move in the market. Volatility, as measured by both the semi-deviation and a drawdown factor, is considered low.

Marcus L. Smith has been running the fund for 16 years and currently receives a manager quality ranking of 77 (0=worst, 99=best). This fund offers only a moderate level of risk but investors looking for strong performance are still waiting.

Services Offered: Automated phone transactions, bank draft capabilities and a systematic withdrawal plan.

Data Date	Investment Rating	Net Assets ($Mil)	NAV	Performance Rating/Pts	Total Return Y-T-D	Risk Rating/Pts
2-17	D	8,082	21.19	D / 2.1	4.59%	C+ / 6.0
2016	D	7,716	20.26	D- / 1.4	0.30%	C+ / 6.1
2015	D+	7,539	20.56	D+ / 2.7	0.02%	C+ / 6.4
2014	D	6,892	20.91	D+ / 2.8	-4.21%	C+ / 5.8
2013	D	6,691	22.43	C- / 4.0	18.56%	C- / 4.2
2012	B-	4,643	19.25	B+ / 8.3	22.55%	C- / 3.9

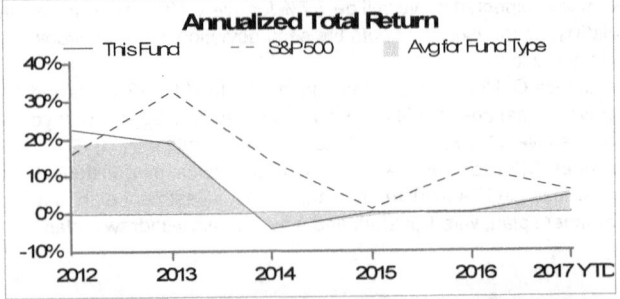

MFS Intl Value Fund A (MGIAX)

C- Fair

Fund Family: MFS Funds   **Phone:** (800) 225-2606
Address: P.O. Box 55824, Boston, MA 02205
Fund Type: FO - Foreign

Major Rating Factors: Disappointing performance is the major factor driving the C- (Fair) TheStreet.com Investment Rating for MFS Intl Value Fund A. The fund currently has a performance rating of D+ (Weak) based on an average return of 4.82% over the last three years and 4.50% over the last three months. Factored into the performance evaluation is an expense ratio of 1.01% (low) and a 5.8% front-end load that is levied at the time of purchase.

The fund's risk rating is currently C+ (Fair). It carries a beta of 0.68, meaning the fund's expected move will be 6.8% for every 10% move in the market. Volatility, as measured by both the semi-deviation and a drawdown factor, is considered low.

Michael W. Roberge has been running the fund for 9 years and currently receives a manager quality ranking of 95 (0=worst, 99=best). This fund offers only a moderate level of risk but investors looking for strong performance are still waiting.

Services Offered: Automated phone transactions, payroll deductions, bank draft capabilities, an IRA investment plan, a 401K investment plan and a systematic withdrawal plan. However, the fund is currently closed to new investors.

Data Date	Investment Rating	Net Assets ($Mil)	NAV	Performance Rating/Pts	Total Return Y-T-D	Risk Rating/Pts
2-17	C-	4,961	36.47	D+ / 2.7	4.50%	C+ / 6.9
2016	C-	5,634	34.90	D / 2.2	3.93%	B- / 7.0
2015	B-	6,766	34.13	C+ / 6.9	6.48%	B- / 7.3
2014	C-	5,628	33.06	C- / 3.7	1.28%	C+ / 6.8
2013	C+	4,489	33.72	C / 4.9	27.35%	C+ / 6.5
2012	C-	2,451	27.04	C- / 3.2	15.81%	C+ / 6.4

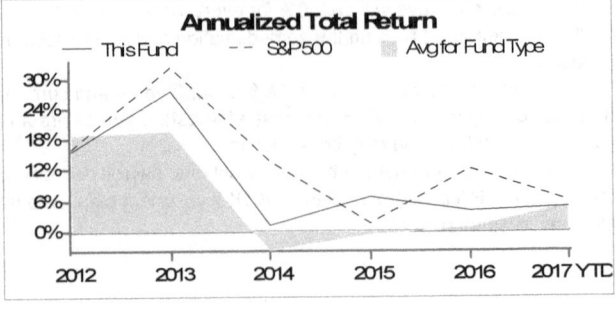

MFS Value A (MEIAX)

A-   Excellent

Fund Family: MFS Funds   **Phone:** (800) 225-2606
Address: P.O. Box 55824, Boston, MA 02205
Fund Type: GR - Growth

Major Rating Factors: Strong performance is the major factor driving the A- (Excellent) TheStreet.com Investment Rating for MFS Value A. The fund currently has a performance rating of B (Good) based on an average return of 9.46% over the last three years and 5.21% over the last three months. Factored into the performance evaluation is an expense ratio of 0.86% (very low) and a 5.8% front-end load that is levied at the time of purchase.

The fund's risk rating is currently C+ (Fair). It carries a beta of 0.98, meaning that its performance tracks fairly well with that of the overall stock market. Volatility, as measured by both the semi-deviation and a drawdown factor, is considered low.

Steven R. Gorham has been running the fund for 15 years and currently receives a manager quality ranking of 64 (0=worst, 99=best). If you desire only a moderate level of risk and strong performance, then this fund is an excellent option.

Services Offered: Automated phone transactions, payroll deductions, bank draft capabilities, an IRA investment plan, a 401K investment plan, wire transfers and a systematic withdrawal plan.

Data Date	Investment Rating	Net Assets ($Mil)	NAV	Performance Rating/Pts	Total Return Y-T-D	Risk Rating/Pts
2-17	A-	8,265	37.93	B / 7.7	5.21%	C+ / 6.9
2016	B+	8,610	36.05	B / 7.6	13.86%	B- / 7.0
2015	B+	8,813	32.79	B / 7.7	-0.79%	B- / 7.3
2014	B+	9,340	34.94	B / 7.6	10.29%	B- / 7.4
2013	B+	9,229	33.20	B / 7.6	35.48%	C+ / 5.8
2012	C-	6,662	25.35	C- / 4.0	16.13%	C+ / 5.6

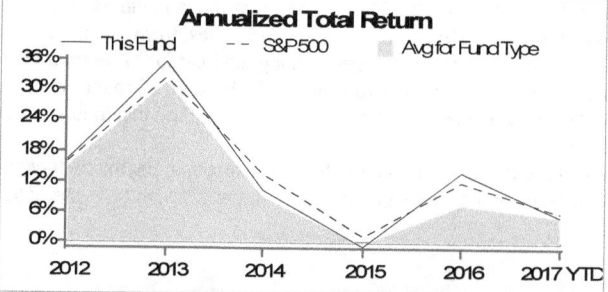

Northern Stock Index (NOSIX)

A+   Excellent

Fund Family: Northern Funds   **Phone:** (800) 595-9111
Address: PO Box 75986, Chicago, IL 60675
Fund Type: IX - Index

Major Rating Factors: Exceptional performance is the major factor driving the A+ (Excellent) TheStreet.com Investment Rating for Northern Stock Index. The fund currently has a performance rating of A (Excellent) based on an average return of 10.51% over the last three years and 5.90% over the last three months. Factored into the performance evaluation is an expense ratio of 0.11% (very low).

The fund's risk rating is currently B- (Good). It carries a beta of 1.00, meaning that its performance tracks fairly well with that of the overall stock market. Volatility, as measured by both the semi-deviation and a drawdown factor, is considered low.

Brent Reeder has been running the fund for 11 years and currently receives a manager quality ranking of 73 (0=worst, 99=best). If you desire only a moderate level of risk and strong performance, then this fund is an excellent option.

Services Offered: Automated phone transactions, payroll deductions, bank draft capabilities, an IRA investment plan, a 401K investment plan, wire transfers and a systematic withdrawal plan.

Data Date	Investment Rating	Net Assets ($Mil)	NAV	Performance Rating/Pts	Total Return Y-T-D	Risk Rating/Pts
2-17	A+	7,788	28.53	A / 9.3	5.90%	B- / 7.0
2016	A+	7,314	26.94	B+ / 8.7	11.88%	B- / 7.0
2015	A+	6,851	24.77	A- / 9.0	1.29%	B- / 7.2
2014	A+	6,657	25.28	B+ / 8.9	13.55%	B- / 7.4
2013	A	5,495	22.86	B / 8.1	32.23%	C+ / 6.1
2012	B+	4,216	17.68	B- / 7.3	15.86%	C+ / 5.6

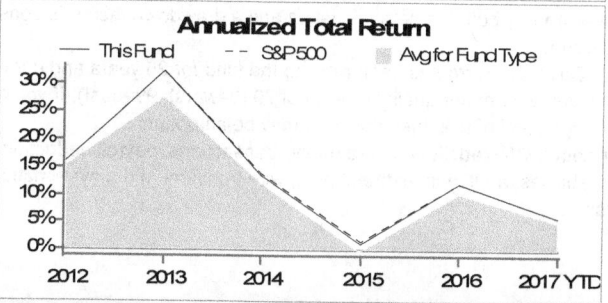

Oakmark Equity and Income Investor (OAKBX)

C+   Fair

Fund Family: Oakmark Funds   **Phone:** (800) 625-6275
Address: P.O. Box 219558, Kansas City, MO 64121
Fund Type: BA - Balanced

Major Rating Factors: Middle of the road best describes Oakmark Equity and Income Investor whose TheStreet.com Investment Rating is currently a C+ (Fair). The fund currently has a performance rating of C+ (Fair) based on an average return of 5.52% over the last three years and 4.41% over the last three months. Factored into the performance evaluation is an expense ratio of 0.89% (low).

The fund's risk rating is currently C+ (Fair). It carries a beta of 1.14, meaning it is expected to move 11.4% for every 10% move in the market. Volatility, as measured by both the semi-deviation and a drawdown factor, is considered low.

Clyde S. McGregor has been running the fund for 22 years and currently receives a manager quality ranking of 36 (0=worst, 99=best). If you desire an average level of risk, then this fund may be an option.

Services Offered: Automated phone transactions, payroll deductions, bank draft capabilities, an IRA investment plan, wire transfers and a systematic withdrawal plan.

Data Date	Investment Rating	Net Assets ($Mil)	NAV	Performance Rating/Pts	Total Return Y-T-D	Risk Rating/Pts
2-17	C+	15,167	31.76	C+ / 6.3	4.41%	C+ / 6.2
2016	B	15,442	30.42	B- / 7.2	10.97%	C+ / 6.6
2015	C	16,841	28.57	C / 4.6	-4.60%	C+ / 6.6
2014	C+	19,776	31.91	C / 4.7	6.93%	B- / 7.2
2013	C+	19,299	32.65	C / 5.0	24.25%	C+ / 6.8
2012	D+	17,461	28.50	D / 1.9	9.05%	C+ / 6.9

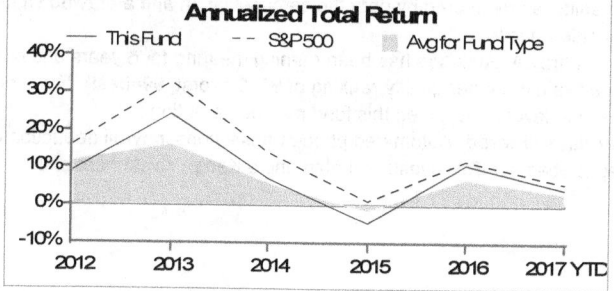

Oakmark Fund Investor (OAKMX)

A+   Excellent

Fund Family: Oakmark Funds   **Phone:** (800) 625-6275
Address: P.O. Box 219558, Kansas City, MO 64121
Fund Type: GR - Growth

Major Rating Factors: Exceptional performance is the major factor driving the A+ (Excellent) TheStreet.com Investment Rating for Oakmark Fund Investor. The fund currently has a performance rating of A+ (Excellent) based on an average return of 9.45% over the last three years and 4.10% over the last three months. Factored into the performance evaluation is an expense ratio of 0.93% (low).

The fund's risk rating is currently C+ (Fair). It carries a beta of 1.13, meaning it is expected to move 11.3% for every 10% move in the market. Volatility, as measured by both the semi-deviation and a drawdown factor, is considered low.

William C. Nygren has been running the fund for 17 years and currently receives a manager quality ranking of 43 (0=worst, 99=best). If you desire only a moderate level of risk and strong performance, then this fund is an excellent option.

Services Offered: Automated phone transactions, payroll deductions, bank draft capabilities, an IRA investment plan, wire transfers and a systematic withdrawal plan.

Data Date	Investment Rating	Net Assets ($Mil)	NAV	Performance Rating/Pts	Total Return Y-T-D	Risk Rating/Pts
2-17	A+	15,635	75.45	A+ / 9.6	4.10%	C+ / 6.1
2016	A+	14,970	72.48	A / 9.5	18.35%	C+ / 6.3
2015	B+	16,886	62.86	B / 8.0	-3.95%	C+ / 6.8
2014	A+	17,528	66.38	A / 9.5	11.51%	C+ / 6.9
2013	A+	12,065	63.63	A / 9.5	37.29%	C+ / 6.4
2012	A+	7,284	48.53	B+ / 8.9	20.97%	C+ / 6.0

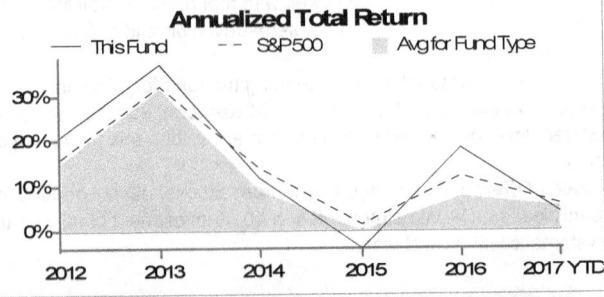

Oakmark International Investor (OAKIX)

D+   Weak

Fund Family: Oakmark Funds   **Phone:** (800) 625-6275
Address: P.O. Box 219558, Kansas City, MO 64121
Fund Type: FO - Foreign

Major Rating Factors: Oakmark International Investor receives a TheStreet.com Investment Rating of D+ (Weak). The fund currently has a performance rating of C (Fair) based on an average return of 0.49% over the last three years and 4.93% over the last three months. Factored into the performance evaluation is an expense ratio of 1.05% (low).

The fund's risk rating is currently C (Fair). It carries a beta of 1.15, meaning it is expected to move 11.5% for every 10% move in the market. Volatility, as measured by both the semi-deviation and a drawdown factor, is considered average.

David G. Herro has been running the fund for 25 years and currently receives a manager quality ranking of 79 (0=worst, 99=best). If you desire an average level of risk, then this fund may be an option.

Services Offered: Automated phone transactions, payroll deductions, bank draft capabilities, an IRA investment plan, wire transfers and a systematic withdrawal plan.

Data Date	Investment Rating	Net Assets ($Mil)	NAV	Performance Rating/Pts	Total Return Y-T-D	Risk Rating/Pts
2-17	D+	26,299	23.82	C / 4.7	4.93%	C / 4.3
2016	D+	24,386	22.70	C- / 3.3	7.91%	C / 4.6
2015	D+	25,978	21.36	C- / 3.1	-3.83%	C+ / 5.8
2014	C-	27,346	23.34	C / 4.8	-5.41%	C / 5.2
2013	C-	27,633	26.32	C+ / 5.9	29.34%	C- / 3.9
2012	A-	10,796	20.93	A+ / 9.7	29.22%	C- / 3.8

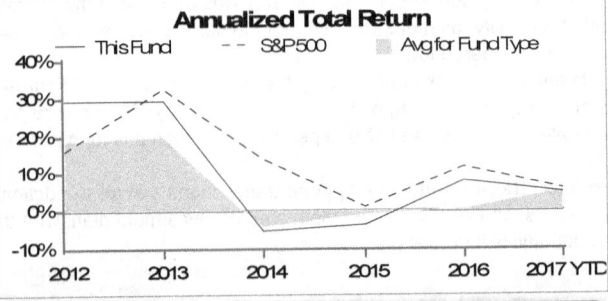

Old Westbury Large Cap Strategies (OWLSX)

C   Fair

Fund Family: Old Westbury Funds   **Phone:** (800) 607-2200
Address: 630 5th Ave., New York, NY 10111
Fund Type: FO - Foreign

Major Rating Factors: Middle of the road best describes Old Westbury Large Cap Strategies whose TheStreet.com Investment Rating is currently a C (Fair). The fund currently has a performance rating of C (Fair) based on an average return of 4.67% over the last three years and 4.99% over the last three months. Factored into the performance evaluation is an expense ratio of 1.15% (low).

The fund's risk rating is currently C+ (Fair). It carries a beta of 0.72, meaning the fund's expected move will be 7.2% for every 10% move in the market. Volatility, as measured by both the semi-deviation and a drawdown factor, is considered low.

Jeffrey A. Rutledge has been running the fund for 6 years and currently receives a manager quality ranking of 95 (0=worst, 99=best). If you desire an average level of risk, then this fund may be an option.

Services Offered: Automated phone transactions, payroll deductions, bank draft capabilities, an IRA investment plan and a Keogh investment plan.

Data Date	Investment Rating	Net Assets ($Mil)	NAV	Performance Rating/Pts	Total Return Y-T-D	Risk Rating/Pts
2-17	C	15,507	13.47	C / 4.5	4.99%	C+ / 6.4
2016	C-	14,645	12.83	C / 4.3	4.73%	C+ / 6.4
2015	C+	14,145	12.47	C+ / 6.4	-1.09%	C+ / 6.5
2014	C+	12,970	12.91	C+ / 5.7	7.15%	C+ / 6.5
2013	D	10,106	12.47	C- / 3.7	25.31%	C- / 3.9
2012	E+	4,315	10.02	D / 1.8	15.09%	C- / 3.7

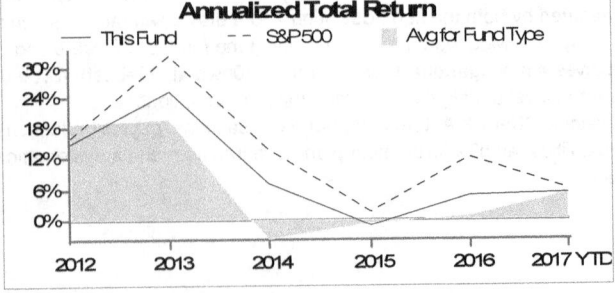

Old Westbury Small & Mid Cap Strat (OWSMX)   C   Fair

Fund Family: Old Westbury Funds   **Phone:** (800) 607-2200
Address: 630 5th Ave., New York, NY 10111
Fund Type: GL - Global
Major Rating Factors: Middle of the road best describes Old Westbury Small & Mid Cap Strat whose TheStreet.com Investment Rating is currently a C (Fair). The fund currently has a performance rating of C+ (Fair) based on an average return of 5.19% over the last three years and 4.33% over the last three months. Factored into the performance evaluation is an expense ratio of 1.18% (low).

The fund's risk rating is currently C (Fair). It carries a beta of 0.70, meaning the fund's expected move will be 7.0% for every 10% move in the market. Volatility, as measured by both the semi-deviation and a drawdown factor, is considered average.

Karen E. Umland has been running the fund for 12 years and currently receives a manager quality ranking of 96 (0=worst, 99=best). If you desire an average level of risk, then this fund may be an option.

Services Offered: Automated phone transactions, bank draft capabilities, an IRA investment plan, a 401K investment plan and wire transfers.

Data Date	Investment Rating	Net Assets ($Mil)	NAV	Performance Rating/Pts	Total Return Y-T-D	Risk Rating/Pts
2-17	C	5,733	15.90	C+ / 5.6	4.33%	C / 5.2
2016	C	5,401	15.24	C+ / 5.9	8.91%	C / 5.2
2015	C	5,448	14.88	C+ / 5.8	1.50%	C+ / 5.9
2014	C-	6,437	16.22	C / 4.6	2.09%	C+ / 6.2
2013	D+	6,803	17.18	C / 4.8	24.16%	C / 4.3
2012	B	4,930	14.69	B+ / 8.6	17.32%	C- / 3.8

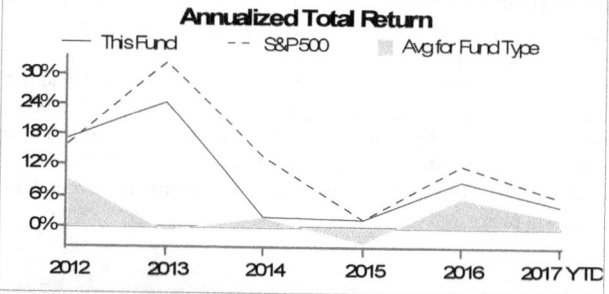

Annualized Total Return

Oppenheimer Developing Mkts A (ODMAX)   E   Very Weak

Fund Family: OppenheimerFunds   **Phone:** (888) 470-0862
Address: P.O. Box 219534, Denver, CO 80217
Fund Type: EM - Emerging Market
Major Rating Factors: Very poor performance is the major factor driving the E (Very Weak) TheStreet.com Investment Rating for Oppenheimer Developing Mkts A. The fund currently has a performance rating of E+ (Very Weak) based on an average return of -1.06% over the last three years and 6.72% over the last three months. Factored into the performance evaluation is an expense ratio of 1.32% (average) and a 5.8% front-end load that is levied at the time of purchase.

The fund's risk rating is currently C- (Fair). It carries a beta of 0.87, meaning the fund's expected move will be 8.7% for every 10% move in the market. Volatility, as measured by both the semi-deviation and a drawdown factor, is considered average.

Justin M. Leverenz has been running the fund for 10 years and currently receives a manager quality ranking of 40 (0=worst, 99=best). This fund offers an average level of risk but investors looking for strong performance will be frustrated.

Services Offered: Automated phone transactions, payroll deductions, an IRA investment plan, a 401K investment plan, wire transfers and a systematic withdrawal plan. However, the fund is currently closed to new investors.

Data Date	Investment Rating	Net Assets ($Mil)	NAV	Performance Rating/Pts	Total Return Y-T-D	Risk Rating/Pts
2-17	E	6,109	34.60	E+ / 0.9	6.72%	C- / 4.1
2016	E	5,938	32.42	E / 0.3	6.89%	C- / 4.2
2015	E	7,068	30.40	E / 0.5	-14.06%	C- / 4.1
2014	E	10,523	35.52	E+ / 0.8	-4.81%	C / 4.5
2013	E+	13,930	38.02	E+ / 0.7	8.65%	C- / 3.9
2012	C-	12,172	35.29	C+ / 6.0	20.85%	C- / 3.8

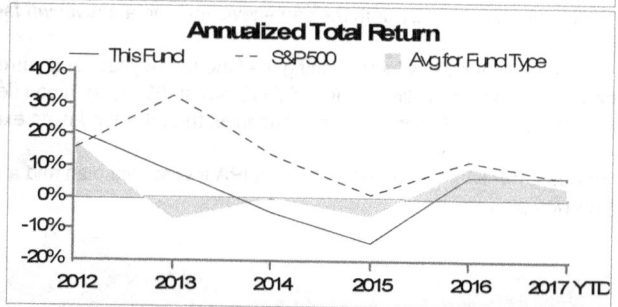

Annualized Total Return

Oppenheimer Global A (OPPAX)   C-   Fair

Fund Family: OppenheimerFunds   **Phone:** (888) 470-0862
Address: P.O. Box 219534, Denver, CO 80217
Fund Type: GL - Global
Major Rating Factors: Middle of the road best describes Oppenheimer Global A whose TheStreet.com Investment Rating is currently a C- (Fair). The fund currently has a performance rating of C (Fair) based on an average return of 4.07% over the last three years and 8.00% over the last three months. Factored into the performance evaluation is an expense ratio of 1.15% (low) and a 5.8% front-end load that is levied at the time of purchase.

The fund's risk rating is currently C (Fair). It carries a beta of 0.96, meaning that its performance tracks fairly well with that of the overall stock market. Volatility, as measured by both the semi-deviation and a drawdown factor, is considered average.

Rajeev Bhaman has been running the fund for 13 years and currently receives a manager quality ranking of 94 (0=worst, 99=best). If you desire an average level of risk, then this fund may be an option.

Services Offered: Automated phone transactions, payroll deductions, bank draft capabilities, an IRA investment plan, a 401K investment plan, a Keogh investment plan, wire transfers and a systematic withdrawal plan.

Data Date	Investment Rating	Net Assets ($Mil)	NAV	Performance Rating/Pts	Total Return Y-T-D	Risk Rating/Pts
2-17	C-	6,348	80.70	C / 4.7	8.00%	C / 5.2
2016	D	6,056	74.72	D / 2.2	0.16%	C / 5.2
2015	C+	7,213	75.12	C+ / 5.8	3.89%	C+ / 6.1
2014	C-	7,316	76.02	C / 4.5	2.06%	C+ / 5.6
2013	D+	7,885	78.78	C / 5.0	26.77%	C- / 4.1
2012	C+	6,713	64.50	B / 7.6	20.75%	C- / 4.1

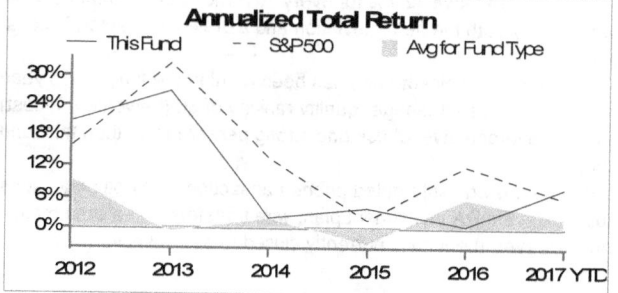

Annualized Total Return

Oppenheimer Main Street A (MSIGX)

B- Good

Fund Family: OppenheimerFunds
Address: P.O. Box 219534, Denver, CO 80217
Phone: (888) 470-0862
Fund Type: GI - Growth and Income

Major Rating Factors: Strong performance is the major factor driving the B- (Good) TheStreet.com Investment Rating for Oppenheimer Main Street A. The fund currently has a performance rating of B (Good) based on an average return of 9.81% over the last three years and 5.62% over the last three months. Factored into the performance evaluation is an expense ratio of 0.94% (low) and a 5.8% front-end load that is levied at the time of purchase.

The fund's risk rating is currently C (Fair). It carries a beta of 0.98, meaning that its performance tracks fairly well with that of the overall stock market. Volatility, as measured by both the semi-deviation and a drawdown factor, is considered average.

Benjamin E. Ram has been running the fund for 8 years and currently receives a manager quality ranking of 67 (0=worst, 99=best). If you desire an average level of risk and strong performance, then this fund is a good option.

Services Offered: Automated phone transactions, payroll deductions, bank draft capabilities, an IRA investment plan, a 401K investment plan and a systematic withdrawal plan.

Data Date	Investment Rating	Net Assets ($Mil)	NAV	Performance Rating/Pts	Total Return Y-T-D	Risk Rating/Pts
2-17	B-	5,959	49.62	B / 8.0	5.62%	C / 4.9
2016	C+	5,709	46.98	B / 7.6	11.42%	C / 4.9
2015	B	5,241	43.41	B+ / 8.3	3.11%	C / 5.2
2014	C+	5,407	47.89	C+ / 6.9	10.46%	C+ / 5.9
2013	C+	5,157	48.46	C+ / 6.9	31.55%	C+ / 6.5
2012	C+	4,280	37.08	C / 5.5	16.55%	C+ / 6.0

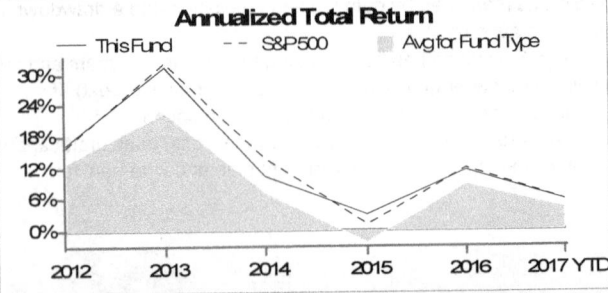

Annualized Total Return

Parnassus Core Equity Inv (PRBLX)

B+ Good

Fund Family: Parnassus Investments
Address: 1 Market Street, San Francisco, CA 94105
Phone: (800) 999-3505
Fund Type: IN - Income

Major Rating Factors: Strong performance is the major factor driving the B+ (Good) TheStreet.com Investment Rating for Parnassus Core Equity Inv. The fund currently has a performance rating of B- (Good) based on an average return of 9.20% over the last three years and 3.95% over the last three months. Factored into the performance evaluation is an expense ratio of 0.88% (low).

The fund's risk rating is currently C+ (Fair). It carries a beta of 0.85, meaning the fund's expected move will be 8.5% for every 10% move in the market. Volatility, as measured by both the semi-deviation and a drawdown factor, is considered low.

Todd C. Ahlsten has been running the fund for 16 years and currently receives a manager quality ranking of 75 (0=worst, 99=best). If you desire only a moderate level of risk and strong performance, then this fund is an excellent option.

Services Offered: Payroll deductions, an IRA investment plan and a systematic withdrawal plan.

Data Date	Investment Rating	Net Assets ($Mil)	NAV	Performance Rating/Pts	Total Return Y-T-D	Risk Rating/Pts
2-17	B+	10,582	40.84	B- / 7.5	3.95%	C+ / 6.7
2016	A-	10,204	39.29	B / 8.0	10.40%	C+ / 6.8
2015	A+	8,367	36.97	B+ / 8.9	-0.55%	B- / 7.2
2014	A+	8,543	40.69	A / 9.3	14.48%	B- / 7.1
2013	A+	6,282	36.68	B+ / 8.7	34.01%	C+ / 6.2
2012	C+	4,022	29.20	C+ / 6.4	15.43%	C+ / 6.0

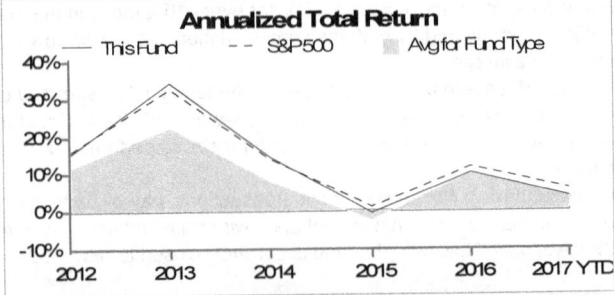

Annualized Total Return

PRIMECAP Odyssey Agg Growth Fd (POAGX)

B+ Good

Fund Family: PRIMECAP Odyssey Funds
Address: c/o US Bancorp Fund Services L, Milwaukee, WI 53201
Phone: (800) 729-2307
Fund Type: AG - Aggressive Growth

Major Rating Factors: Exceptional performance is the major factor driving the B+ (Good) TheStreet.com Investment Rating for PRIMECAP Odyssey Agg Growth Fd. The fund currently has a performance rating of A (Excellent) based on an average return of 9.86% over the last three years and 5.62% over the last three months. Factored into the performance evaluation is an expense ratio of 0.62% (very low).

The fund's risk rating is currently C (Fair). It carries a beta of 1.27, meaning it is expected to move 12.7% for every 10% move in the market. Volatility, as measured by both the semi-deviation and a drawdown factor, is considered average.

Theofanis A. Kolokotrones has been running the fund for 13 years and currently receives a manager quality ranking of 30 (0=worst, 99=best). If you desire an average level of risk and strong performance, then this fund is a good option.

Services Offered: Automated phone transactions, payroll deductions, bank draft capabilities, an IRA investment plan, wire transfers and a systematic withdrawal plan. However, the fund is currently closed to new investors.

Data Date	Investment Rating	Net Assets ($Mil)	NAV	Performance Rating/Pts	Total Return Y-T-D	Risk Rating/Pts
2-17	B+	7,554	35.35	A / 9.4	5.62%	C / 4.4
2016	B	7,129	33.47	A / 9.3	11.73%	C- / 4.2
2015	A	6,684	32.40	A+ / 9.9	4.56%	C+ / 5.6
2014	A-	6,376	32.93	A+ / 9.9	16.55%	C+ / 5.6
2013	A-	5,030	29.65	A+ / 9.9	54.88%	C- / 3.9
2012	B	1,688	19.48	A- / 9.0	21.22%	C- / 3.4

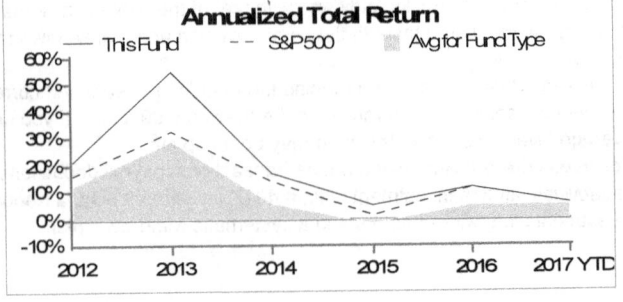

Annualized Total Return

PRIMECAP Odyssey Growth Fd (POGRX)

A   **Excellent**

Fund Family: PRIMECAP Odyssey Funds   **Phone:** (800) 729-2307
Address: c/o US Bancorp Fund Services L, Milwaukee, WI 53201
Fund Type: MC - Mid Cap
Major Rating Factors: Exceptional performance is the major factor driving the A (Excellent) TheStreet.com Investment Rating for PRIMECAP Odyssey Growth Fd. The fund currently has a performance rating of A (Excellent) based on an average return of 9.79% over the last three years and 7.37% over the last three months. Factored into the performance evaluation is an expense ratio of 0.64% (very low).

The fund's risk rating is currently C+ (Fair). It carries a beta of 0.99, meaning that its performance tracks fairly well with that of the overall stock market. Volatility, as measured by both the semi-deviation and a drawdown factor, is considered low.

Theofanis A. Kolokotrones has been running the fund for 13 years and currently receives a manager quality ranking of 75 (0=worst, 99=best). If you desire only a moderate level of risk and strong performance, then this fund is an excellent option.

Services Offered: Automated phone transactions, payroll deductions, bank draft capabilities, an IRA investment plan, wire transfers and a systematic withdrawal plan.

Data Date	Investment Rating	Net Assets ($Mil)	NAV	Perfor-mance Rating/Pts	Total Return Y-T-D	Risk Rating/Pts
2-17	A	7,821	30.75	A / 9.5	7.37%	C+ / 5.9
2016	B+	7,078	28.64	B+ / 8.8	8.42%	C+ / 5.8
2015	A+	6,557	27.32	A+ / 9.8	6.18%	C+ / 6.8
2014	A+	5,003	26.06	A+ / 9.7	13.92%	C+ / 6.7
2013	B+	3,884	23.61	B+ / 8.7	39.30%	C / 4.8
2012	C+	2,221	17.34	C+ / 6.9	16.76%	C / 4.4

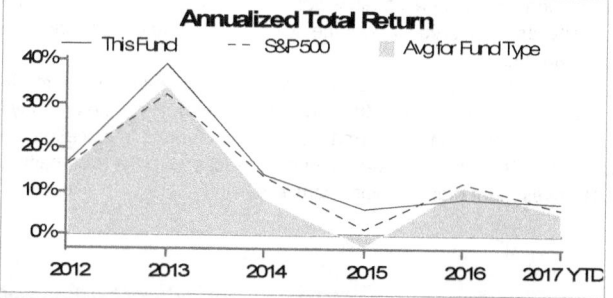

PRIMECAP Odyssey Stock Fd (POSKX)

A+   **Excellent**

Fund Family: PRIMECAP Odyssey Funds   **Phone:** (800) 729-2307
Address: c/o US Bancorp Fund Services L, Milwaukee, WI 53201
Fund Type: GR - Growth
Major Rating Factors: Exceptional performance is the major factor driving the A+ (Excellent) TheStreet.com Investment Rating for PRIMECAP Odyssey Stock Fd. The fund currently has a performance rating of A+ (Excellent) based on an average return of 11.07% over the last three years and 6.61% over the last three months. Factored into the performance evaluation is an expense ratio of 0.65% (very low).

The fund's risk rating is currently C+ (Fair). It carries a beta of 1.06, meaning that its performance tracks fairly well with that of the overall stock market. Volatility, as measured by both the semi-deviation and a drawdown factor, is considered low.

Theofanis A. Kolokotrones has been running the fund for 13 years and currently receives a manager quality ranking of 72 (0=worst, 99=best). If you desire only a moderate level of risk and strong performance, then this fund is an excellent option.

Services Offered: Automated phone transactions, payroll deductions, bank draft capabilities, an IRA investment plan, wire transfers and a systematic withdrawal plan.

Data Date	Investment Rating	Net Assets ($Mil)	NAV	Perfor-mance Rating/Pts	Total Return Y-T-D	Risk Rating/Pts
2-17	A+	6,894	27.59	A+ / 9.7	6.61%	C+ / 6.8
2016	A+	6,116	25.88	A- / 9.1	12.80%	C+ / 6.9
2015	A+	5,095	23.61	A / 9.3	1.68%	B- / 7.5
2014	A+	3,802	23.66	A- / 9.2	15.04%	B- / 7.7
2013	A	2,273	21.16	B / 8.0	34.39%	C+ / 6.3
2012	C+	1,612	15.98	C+ / 6.3	13.62%	C+ / 6.0

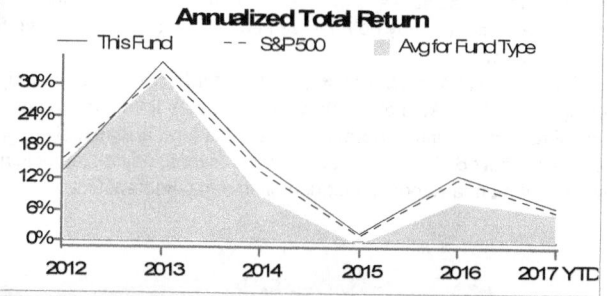

Schwab 1000 Index Fund (SNXFX)

A   **Excellent**

Fund Family: Schwab Funds   **Phone:** (800) 407-0256
Address: P.O. Box 8283, Boston, MA 02266
Fund Type: GI - Growth and Income
Major Rating Factors: Exceptional performance is the major factor driving the A (Excellent) TheStreet.com Investment Rating for Schwab 1000 Index Fund. The fund currently has a performance rating of A- (Excellent) based on an average return of 9.83% over the last three years and 5.95% over the last three months. Factored into the performance evaluation is an expense ratio of 0.05% (very low).

The fund's risk rating is currently C+ (Fair). It carries a beta of 1.01, meaning that its performance tracks fairly well with that of the overall stock market. Volatility, as measured by both the semi-deviation and a drawdown factor, is considered low.

Agnes Hong has been running the fund for 5 years and currently receives a manager quality ranking of 65 (0=worst, 99=best). If you desire only a moderate level of risk and strong performance, then this fund is an excellent option.

Services Offered: Automated phone transactions, payroll deductions, an IRA investment plan, a 401K investment plan, a Keogh investment plan and wire transfers.

Data Date	Investment Rating	Net Assets ($Mil)	NAV	Perfor-mance Rating/Pts	Total Return Y-T-D	Risk Rating/Pts
2-17	A	7,032	56.81	A- / 9.1	5.95%	C+ / 6.3
2016	A-	6,703	53.62	B / 8.2	11.53%	C+ / 6.5
2015	A	6,370	49.70	B+ / 8.6	0.75%	C+ / 6.9
2014	A-	6,750	52.48	B+ / 8.4	12.75%	B- / 7.0
2013	B+	6,046	48.68	B / 7.7	32.67%	C+ / 5.7
2012	C+	4,835	38.46	C+ / 6.9	15.77%	C / 5.4

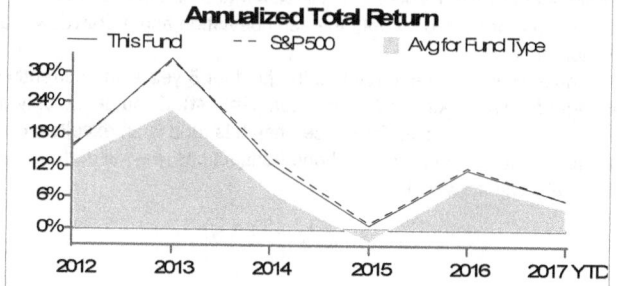

Schwab Fundm US Large Co Index (SFLNX)

A   **Excellent**

Fund Family: Schwab Funds   **Phone:** (800) 407-0256
Address: P.O. Box 8283, Boston, MA 02266
Fund Type: GR - Growth

Major Rating Factors: Strong performance is the major factor driving the A (Excellent) TheStreet.com Investment Rating for Schwab Fundm US Large Co Index. The fund currently has a performance rating of B+ (Good) based on an average return of 9.58% over the last three years and 4.01% over the last three months. Factored into the performance evaluation is an expense ratio of 0.39% (very low).

The fund's risk rating is currently C+ (Fair). It carries a beta of 0.96, meaning that its performance tracks fairly well with that of the overall stock market. Volatility, as measured by both the semi-deviation and a drawdown factor, is considered low.

Agnes Hong has been running the fund for 5 years and currently receives a manager quality ranking of 68 (0=worst, 99=best). If you desire only a moderate level of risk and strong performance, then this fund is an excellent option.

Services Offered: Automated phone transactions, bank draft capabilities, a 401K investment plan and wire transfers.

Data Date	Investment Rating	Net Assets ($Mil)	NAV	Performance Rating/Pts	Total Return Y-T-D	Risk Rating/Pts
2-17	A	5,231	15.84	B+ / 8.9	4.01%	C+ / 6.4
2016	A	5,007	15.23	B+ / 8.9	16.31%	C+ / 6.5
2015	B+	4,646	14.03	B / 7.8	-2.96%	C+ / 6.8
2014	A	4,615	15.29	B+ / 8.6	12.26%	B- / 7.3
2013	A-	3,137	14.20	B / 7.9	34.25%	C+ / 5.9
2012	A-	1,965	10.74	B / 8.1	16.30%	C / 5.5

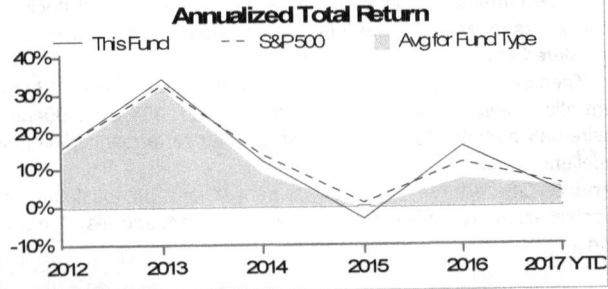

Schwab S&P 500 Index Fund (SWPPX)

A+   **Excellent**

Fund Family: Schwab Funds   **Phone:** (800) 407-0256
Address: P.O. Box 8283, Boston, MA 02266
Fund Type: IX - Index

Major Rating Factors: Exceptional performance is the major factor driving the A+ (Excellent) TheStreet.com Investment Rating for Schwab S&P 500 Index Fund. The fund currently has a performance rating of A (Excellent) based on an average return of 10.52% over the last three years and 5.93% over the last three months. Factored into the performance evaluation is an expense ratio of 0.03% (very low).

The fund's risk rating is currently C+ (Fair). It carries a beta of 1.00, meaning that its performance tracks fairly well with that of the overall stock market. Volatility, as measured by both the semi-deviation and a drawdown factor, is considered low.

Agnes Hong has been running the fund for 5 years and currently receives a manager quality ranking of 73 (0=worst, 99=best). If you desire only a moderate level of risk and strong performance, then this fund is an excellent option.

Services Offered: Automated phone transactions, payroll deductions, an IRA investment plan, a Keogh investment plan and wire transfers.

Data Date	Investment Rating	Net Assets ($Mil)	NAV	Performance Rating/Pts	Total Return Y-T-D	Risk Rating/Pts
2-17	A+	25,763	36.46	A / 9.3	5.93%	C+ / 6.9
2016	A	24,018	34.42	B+ / 8.4	11.82%	C+ / 6.9
2015	A+	21,367	31.56	B+ / 8.8	1.29%	B- / 7.1
2014	A	21,050	32.16	B+ / 8.6	13.57%	B- / 7.4
2013	A-	17,678	28.85	B / 7.8	32.27%	C+ / 6.2
2012	C+	12,827	22.19	C+ / 6.8	15.91%	C+ / 5.9

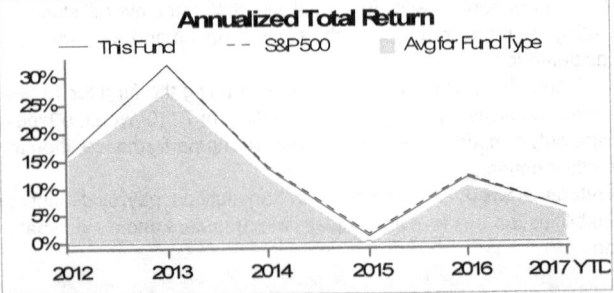

Schwab Total Stock Market Index Fd (SWTSX)

A+   **Excellent**

Fund Family: Schwab Funds   **Phone:** (800) 407-0256
Address: P.O. Box 8283, Boston, MA 02266
Fund Type: GR - Growth

Major Rating Factors: Exceptional performance is the major factor driving the A+ (Excellent) TheStreet.com Investment Rating for Schwab Total Stock Market Index Fd. The fund currently has a performance rating of A- (Excellent) based on an average return of 9.82% over the last three years and 5.71% over the last three months. Factored into the performance evaluation is an expense ratio of 0.03% (very low).

The fund's risk rating is currently C+ (Fair). It carries a beta of 1.02, meaning that its performance tracks fairly well with that of the overall stock market. Volatility, as measured by both the semi-deviation and a drawdown factor, is considered low.

Agnes Hong has been running the fund for 5 years and currently receives a manager quality ranking of 63 (0=worst, 99=best). If you desire only a moderate level of risk and strong performance, then this fund is an excellent option.

Services Offered: Automated phone transactions, payroll deductions and a systematic withdrawal plan.

Data Date	Investment Rating	Net Assets ($Mil)	NAV	Performance Rating/Pts	Total Return Y-T-D	Risk Rating/Pts
2-17	A+	5,676	42.01	A- / 9.2	5.71%	C+ / 6.6
2016	A-	5,274	39.74	B+ / 8.4	12.58%	C+ / 6.7
2015	A	4,483	36.11	B+ / 8.5	0.41%	B- / 7.0
2014	A	4,170	36.98	B+ / 8.5	12.39%	B- / 7.2
2013	A-	3,297	33.67	B / 8.0	33.36%	C+ / 5.9
2012	B+	2,309	25.76	B- / 7.5	16.30%	C / 5.5

Annualized Total Return

This Fund — — S&P500 — Avg for Fund Type

SEI Inst World Equity Ex US A (WEUSX)

C-   **Fair**

Fund Family: SEI Financial Management Corp   **Phone:** (800) 342-5734
Address: One Freedom Valley Drive, Oaks, PA 19456
Fund Type: EM - Emerging Market
Major Rating Factors: Disappointing performance is the major factor driving the C- (Fair) TheStreet.com Investment Rating for SEI Inst World Equity Ex US A. The fund currently has a performance rating of D+ (Weak) based on an average return of 0.07% over the last three years and 5.99% over the last three months. Factored into the performance evaluation is an expense ratio of 0.63% (very low).

The fund's risk rating is currently C+ (Fair). It carries a beta of 0.62, meaning the fund's expected move will be 6.2% for every 10% move in the market. Volatility, as measured by standard deviation, is considered low for equity funds at 11.85.

Robert A. Gillam has been running the fund for 12 years and currently receives a manager quality ranking of 62 (0=worst, 99=best). This fund offers only a moderate level of risk but investors looking for strong performance are still waiting.

Services Offered: Automated phone transactions, bank draft capabilities, an IRA investment plan, a 401K investment plan and wire transfers.

Data Date	Investment Rating	Net Assets ($Mil)	NAV	Perfor-mance Rating/Pts	Total Return Y-T-D	Risk Rating/Pts
2-17	C-	7,484	11.67	D+ / 2.7	5.99%	C+ / 6.8
2016	D+	7,232	11.01	D- / 1.5	3.89%	C+ / 6.7
2015	D	6,843	10.81	D- / 1.5	-5.92%	B- / 7.0
2014	D-	6,611	11.79	D+ / 2.6	-2.65%	C / 5.3

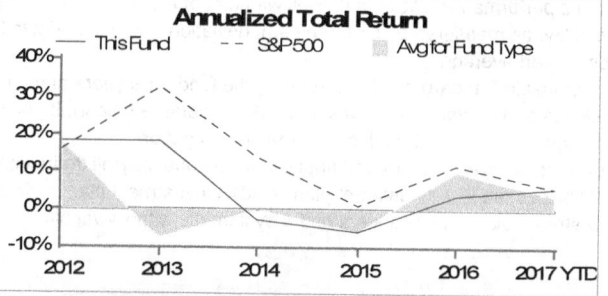

Annualized Total Return — This Fund, S&P500, Avg for Fund Type

T Rowe Price Blue Chip Growth (TRBCX)

B+   **Good**

Fund Family: T. Rowe Price Funds   **Phone:** (800) 638-5660
Address: 100 East Pratt Street, Baltimore, MD 21202
Fund Type: GR - Growth
Major Rating Factors: Strong performance is the major factor driving the B+ (Good) TheStreet.com Investment Rating for T Rowe Price Blue Chip Growth. The fund currently has a performance rating of B+ (Good) based on an average return of 8.83% over the last three years and 8.84% over the last three months. Factored into the performance evaluation is an expense ratio of 0.71% (very low).

The fund's risk rating is currently C (Fair). It carries a beta of 1.05, meaning that its performance tracks fairly well with that of the overall stock market. Volatility, as measured by both the semi-deviation and a drawdown factor, is considered average.

Lawrence J. Puglia has been running the fund for 24 years and currently receives a manager quality ranking of 46 (0=worst, 99=best). If you desire an average level of risk and strong performance, then this fund is a good option.

Services Offered: Automated phone transactions, payroll deductions, bank draft capabilities, an IRA investment plan, a 401K investment plan, a Keogh investment plan, wire transfers and a systematic withdrawal plan.

Data Date	Investment Rating	Net Assets ($Mil)	NAV	Perfor-mance Rating/Pts	Total Return Y-T-D	Risk Rating/Pts
2-17	B+	26,563	79.03	B+ / 8.5	8.84%	C / 5.5
2016	C+	25,819	72.61	C+ / 6.8	0.98%	C / 5.4
2015	A+	27,591	72.38	A+ / 9.8	11.15%	C+ / 6.3
2014	B+	23,276	67.27	A / 9.4	9.28%	C+ / 5.6
2013	A+	19,448	64.60	A+ / 9.8	41.57%	C / 5.1
2012	B+	13,692	45.63	B+ / 8.3	18.41%	C / 4.8

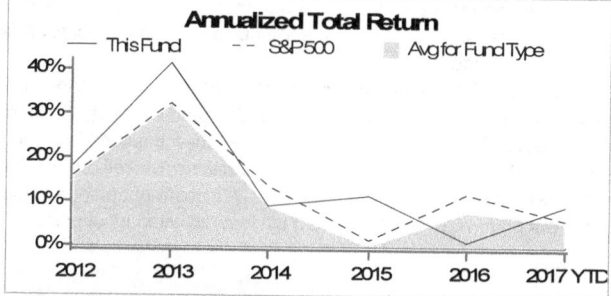

Annualized Total Return — This Fund, S&P500, Avg for Fund Type

T Rowe Price Dividend Growth (PRDGX)

A   **Excellent**

Fund Family: T. Rowe Price Funds   **Phone:** (800) 638-5660
Address: 100 East Pratt Street, Baltimore, MD 21202
Fund Type: IN - Income
Major Rating Factors: Strong performance is the major factor driving the A (Excellent) TheStreet.com Investment Rating for T Rowe Price Dividend Growth. The fund currently has a performance rating of B+ (Good) based on an average return of 10.20% over the last three years and 4.79% over the last three months. Factored into the performance evaluation is an expense ratio of 0.64% (very low).

The fund's risk rating is currently C+ (Fair). It carries a beta of 0.92, meaning that its performance tracks fairly well with that of the overall stock market. Volatility, as measured by both the semi-deviation and a drawdown factor, is considered low.

Thomas J. Huber has been running the fund for 17 years and currently receives a manager quality ranking of 77 (0=worst, 99=best). If you desire only a moderate level of risk and strong performance, then this fund is an excellent option.

Services Offered: Automated phone transactions, payroll deductions, bank draft capabilities, an IRA investment plan, a 401K investment plan, a Keogh investment plan, wire transfers and a systematic withdrawal plan.

Data Date	Investment Rating	Net Assets ($Mil)	NAV	Perfor-mance Rating/Pts	Total Return Y-T-D	Risk Rating/Pts
2-17	A	5,401	38.96	B+ / 8.4	4.79%	C+ / 6.7
2016	A-	5,212	37.18	B / 8.2	11.62%	C+ / 6.8
2015	A+	4,573	34.34	A- / 9.0	2.36%	B- / 7.1
2014	A	4,360	36.13	B / 8.2	12.34%	B- / 7.5
2013	A-	3,721	33.65	B- / 7.5	30.35%	C+ / 6.4
2012	B+	2,584	26.34	B- / 7.1	14.85%	C+ / 5.9

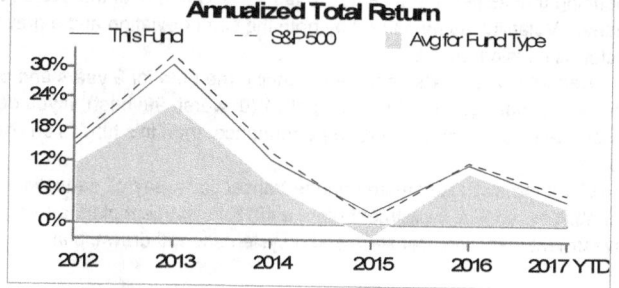

Annualized Total Return — This Fund, S&P500, Avg for Fund Type

T Rowe Price Emerging Mkts Stk (PRMSX)   C   Fair

Fund Family: T. Rowe Price Funds   **Phone:** (800) 638-5660
Address: 100 East Pratt Street, Baltimore, MD 21202
Fund Type: EM - Emerging Market
Major Rating Factors: Middle of the road best describes T Rowe Price Emerging Mkts Stk whose TheStreet.com Investment Rating is currently a C (Fair). The fund currently has a performance rating of C+ (Fair) based on an average return of 4.34% over the last three years and 8.87% over the last three months. Factored into the performance evaluation is an expense ratio of 1.24% (average) and a 2.0% back-end load levied at the time of sale.

The fund's risk rating is currently C (Fair). It carries a beta of 0.94, meaning that its performance tracks fairly well with that of the overall stock market. Volatility, as measured by both the semi-deviation and a drawdown factor, is considered average.

Gonzalo Pangaro has been running the fund for 9 years and currently receives a manager quality ranking of 89 (0=worst, 99=best). If you desire an average level of risk, then this fund may be an option.

Services Offered: Automated phone transactions, payroll deductions, bank draft capabilities, an IRA investment plan, a 401K investment plan, a Keogh investment plan, wire transfers and a systematic withdrawal plan.

Data Date	Investment Rating	Net Assets ($Mil)	NAV	Performance Rating/Pts	Total Return Y-T-D	Risk Rating/Pts
2-17	C	6,365	34.49	C+ / 6.3	8.87%	C / 5.0
2016	D	6,637	31.68	D / 2.0	11.94%	C / 5.0
2015	E+	8,213	28.50	E / 0.5	-11.49%	C / 5.0
2014	E+	7,592	32.38	E+ / 0.8	1.41%	C / 5.2
2013	E	7,173	32.22	E / 0.3	-4.69%	C- / 3.3
2012	D+	7,090	34.06	C / 5.0	20.03%	C- / 3.2

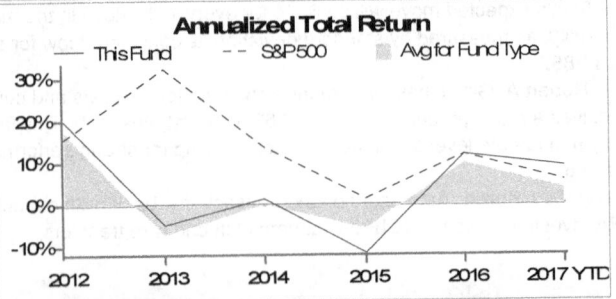

Annualized Total Return

T Rowe Price Equity Income (PRFDX)   B+   Good

Fund Family: T. Rowe Price Funds   **Phone:** (800) 638-5660
Address: 100 East Pratt Street, Baltimore, MD 21202
Fund Type: IN - Income
Major Rating Factors: Strong performance is the major factor driving the B+ (Good) TheStreet.com Investment Rating for T Rowe Price Equity Income. The fund currently has a performance rating of B+ (Good) based on an average return of 7.54% over the last three years and 3.53% over the last three months. Factored into the performance evaluation is an expense ratio of 0.66% (very low).

The fund's risk rating is currently C (Fair). It carries a beta of 1.01, meaning that its performance tracks fairly well with that of the overall stock market. Volatility, as measured by both the semi-deviation and a drawdown factor, is considered average.

John D. Linehan has been running the fund for 2 years and currently receives a manager quality ranking of 36 (0=worst, 99=best). If you desire an average level of risk and strong performance, then this fund is a good option.

Services Offered: Automated phone transactions, payroll deductions, bank draft capabilities, an IRA investment plan, a 401K investment plan, a Keogh investment plan, wire transfers and a systematic withdrawal plan.

Data Date	Investment Rating	Net Assets ($Mil)	NAV	Performance Rating/Pts	Total Return Y-T-D	Risk Rating/Pts
2-17	B+	18,328	32.59	B+ / 8.3	3.53%	C / 5.5
2016	B+	18,515	31.48	B+ / 8.9	19.28%	C / 5.5
2015	C	23,071	28.46	C / 5.3	-6.66%	C+ / 6.2
2014	B-	28,254	32.80	C+ / 6.7	7.49%	B- / 7.3
2013	C+	26,505	32.84	C+ / 6.8	29.75%	C+ / 5.9
2012	A-	22,111	26.45	B / 7.9	17.25%	C / 5.4

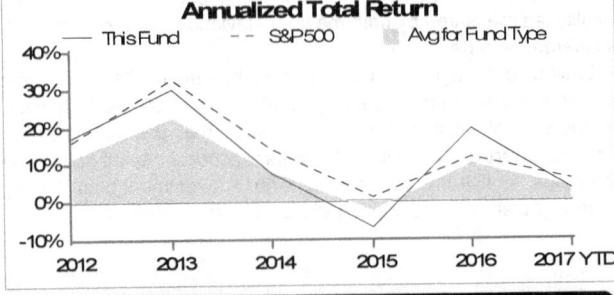

Annualized Total Return

T Rowe Price Equity Index 500 (PREIX)   A+   Excellent

Fund Family: T. Rowe Price Funds   **Phone:** (800) 638-5660
Address: 100 East Pratt Street, Baltimore, MD 21202
Fund Type: IX - Index
Major Rating Factors: Exceptional performance is the major factor driving the A+ (Excellent) TheStreet.com Investment Rating for T Rowe Price Equity Index 500. The fund currently has a performance rating of A- (Excellent) based on an average return of 10.35% over the last three years and 5.89% over the last three months. Factored into the performance evaluation is an expense ratio of 0.27% (very low) and a 0.5% back-end load levied at the time of sale.

The fund's risk rating is currently B- (Good). It carries a beta of 1.00, meaning that its performance tracks fairly well with that of the overall stock market. Volatility, as measured by both the semi-deviation and a drawdown factor, is considered low.

Kenneth D. Uematsu has been running the fund for 9 years and currently receives a manager quality ranking of 71 (0=worst, 99=best). If you desire only a moderate level of risk and strong performance, then this fund is an excellent option.

Services Offered: Automated phone transactions, payroll deductions, bank draft capabilities, an IRA investment plan, a 401K investment plan, a Keogh investment plan, wire transfers and a systematic withdrawal plan.

Data Date	Investment Rating	Net Assets ($Mil)	NAV	Performance Rating/Pts	Total Return Y-T-D	Risk Rating/Pts
2-17	A+	27,750	63.64	A- / 9.2	5.89%	B- / 7.1
2016	A+	26,967	60.10	B+ / 8.6	11.70%	B- / 7.1
2015	A+	25,219	54.95	B+ / 8.9	1.11%	B / 8.2
2014	A	24,367	55.47	B+ / 8.7	13.40%	B- / 7.3
2013	A-	19,701	49.79	B / 7.9	32.02%	C+ / 6.0
2012	B	15,551	38.40	B- / 7.0	15.68%	C+ / 5.6

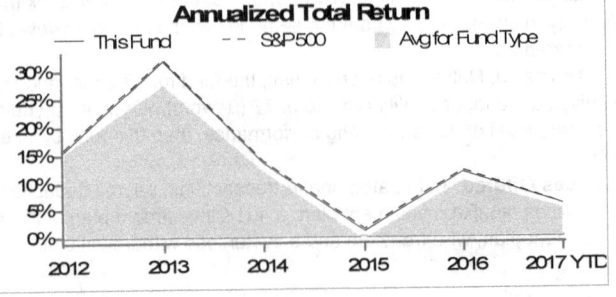

Annualized Total Return

T Rowe Price Growth Stock (PRGFX)

B   **Good**

Fund Family: T. Rowe Price Funds   **Phone:** (800) 638-5660
Address: 100 East Pratt Street, Baltimore, MD 21202
Fund Type: GR - Growth

Major Rating Factors: Strong performance is the major factor driving the B (Good) TheStreet.com Investment Rating for T Rowe Price Growth Stock. The fund currently has a performance rating of B+ (Good) based on an average return of 8.80% over the last three years and 9.07% over the last three months. Factored into the performance evaluation is an expense ratio of 0.67% (very low).

The fund's risk rating is currently C (Fair). It carries a beta of 1.06, meaning that its performance tracks fairly well with that of the overall stock market. Volatility, as measured by both the semi-deviation and a drawdown factor, is considered average.

Joseph B. Fath has been running the fund for 3 years and currently receives a manager quality ranking of 45 (0=worst, 99=best). If you desire an average level of risk and strong performance, then this fund is a good option.

Services Offered: Automated phone transactions, payroll deductions, bank draft capabilities, an IRA investment plan, a 401K investment plan, a Keogh investment plan, wire transfers and a systematic withdrawal plan.

Data Date	Investment Rating	Net Assets ($Mil)	NAV	Perfor-mance Rating/Pts	Total Return Y-T-D	Risk Rating/Pts
2-17	B	37,908	58.08	B+ / 8.7	9.07%	C / 4.7
2016	C	36,280	53.25	C+ / 6.9	1.41%	C / 4.7
2015	A	40,215	53.66	A+ / 9.8	10.85%	C+ / 5.8
2014	B	38,583	51.95	A- / 9.2	8.83%	C / 4.9
2013	A	36,132	52.57	A+ / 9.6	39.20%	C / 4.9
2012	B	27,354	37.78	B / 7.9	18.92%	C / 4.6

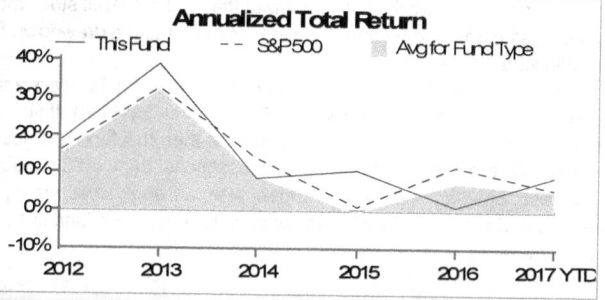

Annualized Total Return

T Rowe Price Health Sciences (PRHSX)

C+   **Fair**

Fund Family: T. Rowe Price Funds   **Phone:** (800) 638-5660
Address: 100 East Pratt Street, Baltimore, MD 21202
Fund Type: HL - Health

Major Rating Factors: Strong performance is the major factor driving the C+ (Fair) TheStreet.com Investment Rating for T Rowe Price Health Sciences. The fund currently has a performance rating of B+ (Good) based on an average return of 10.06% over the last three years and 12.24% over the last three months. Factored into the performance evaluation is an expense ratio of 0.76% (very low).

The fund's risk rating is currently C- (Fair). It carries a beta of 1.10, meaning it is expected to move 11.0% for every 10% move in the market. Volatility, as measured by both the semi-deviation and a drawdown factor, is considered average.

Ziad Bakri has been running the fund for 1 year and currently receives a manager quality ranking of 55 (0=worst, 99=best). If you desire an average level of risk and strong performance, then this fund is a good option.

Services Offered: Automated phone transactions, payroll deductions, bank draft capabilities, an IRA investment plan, a 401K investment plan, a Keogh investment plan, wire transfers and a systematic withdrawal plan.

Data Date	Investment Rating	Net Assets ($Mil)	NAV	Perfor-mance Rating/Pts	Total Return Y-T-D	Risk Rating/Pts
2-17	C+	9,908	66.31	B+ / 8.5	12.24%	C- / 3.6
2016	C-	10,333	59.08	C+ / 6.9	-10.35%	C- / 3.6
2015	B+	14,108	68.86	A+ / 9.9	12.98%	C / 4.7
2014	B+	11,770	67.99	A+ / 9.9	31.94%	C / 5.1
2013	A	8,431	57.80	A+ / 9.9	51.40%	C / 4.3
2012	A	5,016	41.22	A+ / 9.9	31.93%	C- / 4.0

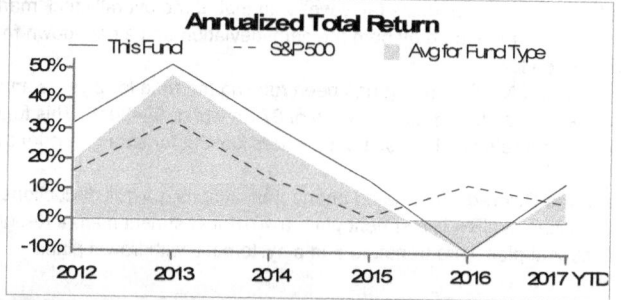

Annualized Total Return

T Rowe Price Instl Lg Cap Gr (TRLGX)

B+   **Good**

Fund Family: T. Rowe Price Funds   **Phone:** (800) 638-5660
Address: 100 East Pratt Street, Baltimore, MD 21202
Fund Type: GR - Growth

Major Rating Factors: Exceptional performance is the major factor driving the B+ (Good) TheStreet.com Investment Rating for T Rowe Price Instl Lg Cap Gr. The fund currently has a performance rating of A- (Excellent) based on an average return of 8.55% over the last three years and 9.10% over the last three months. Factored into the performance evaluation is an expense ratio of 0.56% (very low).

The fund's risk rating is currently C (Fair). It carries a beta of 1.08, meaning that its performance tracks fairly well with that of the overall stock market. Volatility, as measured by both the semi-deviation and a drawdown factor, is considered average.

Robert W. Sharps has been running the fund for 15 years and currently receives a manager quality ranking of 39 (0=worst, 99=best). If you desire an average level of risk and strong performance, then this fund is a good option.

Services Offered: Automated phone transactions, bank draft capabilities, an IRA investment plan, a 401K investment plan, a Keogh investment plan, wire transfers and a systematic withdrawal plan.

Data Date	Investment Rating	Net Assets ($Mil)	NAV	Perfor-mance Rating/Pts	Total Return Y-T-D	Risk Rating/Pts
2-17	B+	13,039	31.90	A- / 9.0	9.10%	C / 5.0
2016	C+	12,473	29.24	B- / 7.2	2.85%	C / 5.0
2015	A+	13,558	28.89	A+ / 9.8	10.08%	C+ / 6.1
2014	B+	11,653	27.48	A / 9.5	8.72%	C / 5.2
2013	A	9,271	27.26	A+ / 9.8	44.44%	C / 4.8
2012	C+	5,698	18.88	B- / 7.3	17.55%	C / 4.4

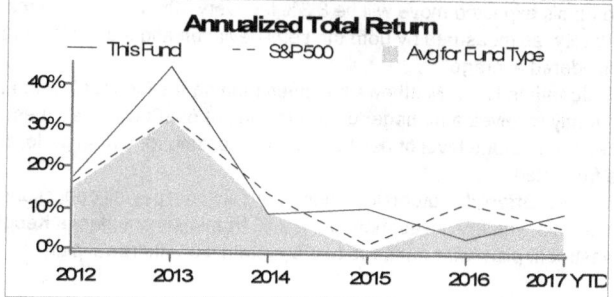

Annualized Total Return

T Rowe Price Instl Mid-Cap Eq Gr (PMEGX)

B+   Good

Fund Family: T. Rowe Price Funds   **Phone:** (800) 638-5660
Address: 100 East Pratt Street, Baltimore, MD 21202
Fund Type: MC - Mid Cap

Major Rating Factors: Strong performance is the major factor driving the B+ (Good) TheStreet.com Investment Rating for T Rowe Price Instl Mid-Cap Eq Gr. The fund currently has a performance rating of B+ (Good) based on an average return of 9.93% over the last three years and 6.94% over the last three months. Factored into the performance evaluation is an expense ratio of 0.61% (very low).

The fund's risk rating is currently C (Fair). It carries a beta of 0.94, meaning that its performance tracks fairly well with that of the overall stock market. Volatility, as measured by both the semi-deviation and a drawdown factor, is considered average.

Brian W. H. Berghuis has been running the fund for 21 years and currently receives a manager quality ranking of 80 (0=worst, 99=best). If you desire an average level of risk and strong performance, then this fund is a good option.

Services Offered: Automated phone transactions, bank draft capabilities, an IRA investment plan, a 401K investment plan, a Keogh investment plan, wire transfers and a systematic withdrawal plan. However, the fund is currently closed to new investors.

Data Date	Investment Rating	Net Assets ($Mil)	NAV	Performance Rating/Pts	Total Return Y-T-D	Risk Rating/Pts
2-17	B+	5,866	49.13	B+ / 8.6	6.94%	C / 5.3
2016	B-	5,544	45.94	B / 8.1	6.94%	C / 5.4
2015	A+	5,213	43.40	A+ / 9.7	6.94%	C+ / 6.5
2014	A	5,465	43.11	A / 9.5	13.79%	C+ / 6.1
2013	B+	4,043	40.67	B+ / 8.7	37.89%	C / 4.4
2012	B+	2,898	30.60	B+ / 8.9	14.50%	C- / 4.2

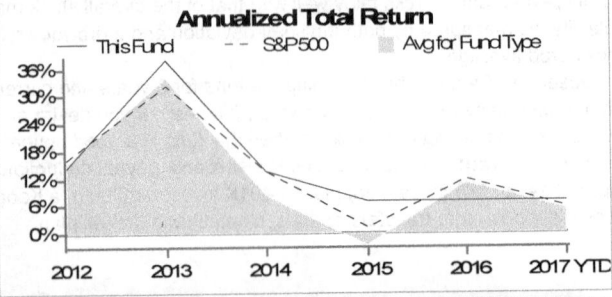

Annualized Total Return

T Rowe Price Intl Stock (PRITX)

D+   Weak

Fund Family: T. Rowe Price Funds   **Phone:** (800) 638-5660
Address: 100 East Pratt Street, Baltimore, MD 21202
Fund Type: FO - Foreign

Major Rating Factors: Disappointing performance is the major factor driving the D+ (Weak) TheStreet.com Investment Rating for T Rowe Price Intl Stock. The fund currently has a performance rating of D+ (Weak) based on an average return of 2.13% over the last three years and 6.08% over the last three months. Factored into the performance evaluation is an expense ratio of 0.83% (very low) and a 2.0% back-end load levied at the time of sale.

The fund's risk rating is currently C+ (Fair). It carries a beta of 0.92, meaning that its performance tracks fairly well with that of the overall stock market. Volatility, as measured by both the semi-deviation and a drawdown factor, is considered low.

Richard N. Clattenburg has been running the fund for 2 years and currently receives a manager quality ranking of 87 (0=worst, 99=best). This fund offers only a moderate level of risk but investors looking for strong performance are still waiting.

Services Offered: Automated phone transactions, payroll deductions, bank draft capabilities, an IRA investment plan, a 401K investment plan, a Keogh investment plan, wire transfers and a systematic withdrawal plan.

Data Date	Investment Rating	Net Assets ($Mil)	NAV	Performance Rating/Pts	Total Return Y-T-D	Risk Rating/Pts
2-17	D+	12,608	16.22	D+ / 2.9	6.08%	C+ / 5.9
2016	D	11,765	15.29	D / 1.7	2.29%	C+ / 5.9
2015	D	13,415	15.28	D / 2.2	-0.77%	C+ / 6.3
2014	D	12,328	15.61	D+ / 2.4	-0.82%	C+ / 5.6
2013	D-	11,706	16.30	D / 1.8	14.27%	C- / 4.0
2012	C-	9,617	14.40	C / 5.2	18.72%	C- / 3.8

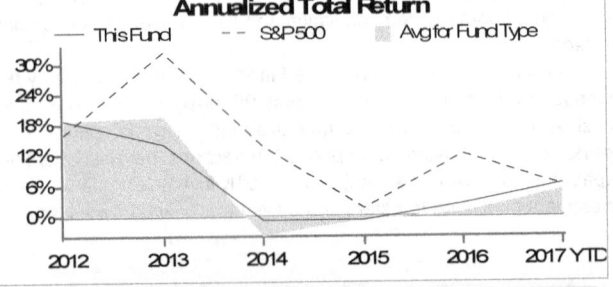

Annualized Total Return

T Rowe Price Intl Value Equity (TRIGX)

E+   Very Weak

Fund Family: T. Rowe Price Funds   **Phone:** (800) 638-5660
Address: 100 East Pratt Street, Baltimore, MD 21202
Fund Type: FO - Foreign

Major Rating Factors: Very poor performance is the major factor driving the E+ (Very Weak) TheStreet.com Investment Rating for T Rowe Price Intl Value Equity. The fund currently has a performance rating of E+ (Very Weak) based on an average return of -2.01% over the last three years and 4.14% over the last three months. Factored into the performance evaluation is an expense ratio of 0.84% (very low) and a 2.0% back-end load levied at the time of sale.

The fund's risk rating is currently C (Fair). It carries a beta of 0.88, meaning the fund's expected move will be 8.8% for every 10% move in the market. Volatility, as measured by both the semi-deviation and a drawdown factor, is considered average.

Jonathan H. W. Matthews has been running the fund for 7 years and currently receives a manager quality ranking of 50 (0=worst, 99=best). This fund offers an average level of risk but investors looking for strong performance will be frustrated.

Services Offered: Automated phone transactions, payroll deductions, bank draft capabilities, an IRA investment plan, a 401K investment plan, a Keogh investment plan, wire transfers and a systematic withdrawal plan.

Data Date	Investment Rating	Net Assets ($Mil)	NAV	Performance Rating/Pts	Total Return Y-T-D	Risk Rating/Pts
2-17	E+	10,976	13.34	E+ / 0.6	4.14%	C / 5.3
2016	D-	10,542	12.81	E+ / 0.7	0.61%	C / 5.4
2015	D	11,314	13.07	D / 2.0	-3.13%	C+ / 5.9
2014	D-	10,020	13.77	D / 1.9	-5.32%	C / 5.3
2013	D	8,187	15.57	C- / 3.8	22.97%	C- / 3.9
2012	D-	5,936	12.96	D+ / 2.8	15.38%	C- / 3.8

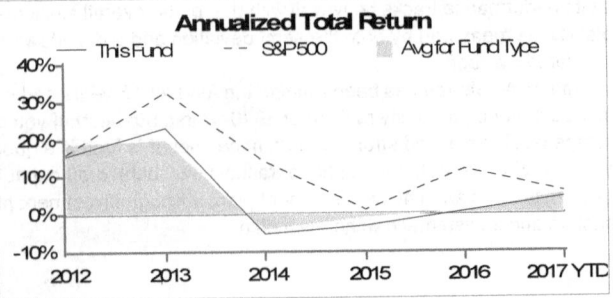

Annualized Total Return

T Rowe Price Mid-Cap Growth (RPMGX)

B **Good**

Fund Family: T. Rowe Price Funds   **Phone:** (800) 638-5660
Address: 100 East Pratt Street, Baltimore, MD 21202
Fund Type: MC - Mid Cap
Major Rating Factors: Strong performance is the major factor driving the B (Good) TheStreet.com Investment Rating for T Rowe Price Mid-Cap Growth. The fund currently has a performance rating of B (Good) based on an average return of 9.36% over the last three years and 6.74% over the last three months. Factored into the performance evaluation is an expense ratio of 0.77% (very low).

The fund's risk rating is currently C (Fair). It carries a beta of 0.92, meaning that its performance tracks fairly well with that of the overall stock market. Volatility, as measured by both the semi-deviation and a drawdown factor, is considered average.

Brian W. H. Berghuis has been running the fund for 25 years and currently receives a manager quality ranking of 78 (0=worst, 99=best). If you desire an average level of risk and strong performance, then this fund is a good option.

Services Offered: Automated phone transactions, payroll deductions, bank draft capabilities, an IRA investment plan, a 401K investment plan, a Keogh investment plan, wire transfers and a systematic withdrawal plan. However, the fund is currently closed to new investors.

Data Date	Investment Rating	Net Assets ($Mil)	NAV	Perfor-mance Rating/Pts	Total Return Y-T-D	Risk Rating/Pts
2-17	B	22,004	80.45	B / 8.1	6.74%	C / 5.0
2016	C+	21,899	75.37	B / 7.8	6.30%	C / 5.0
2015	A	23,677	73.32	A+ / 9.6	6.56%	C+ / 6.0
2014	A-	22,677	75.44	A / 9.3	13.16%	C+ / 5.8
2013	B	21,410	72.78	B+ / 8.4	36.89%	C- / 4.1
2012	B	16,860	56.47	B+ / 8.6	13.91%	C- / 4.0

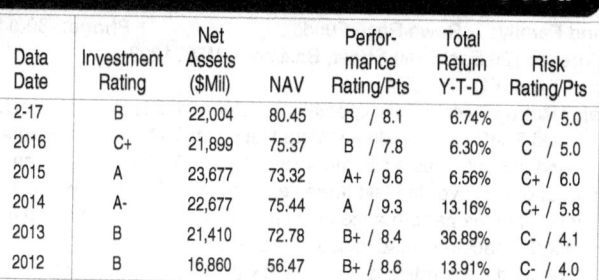

Annualized Total Return

T Rowe Price Mid-Cap Value Fd (TRMCX)

B+ **Good**

Fund Family: T. Rowe Price Funds   **Phone:** (800) 638-5660
Address: 100 East Pratt Street, Baltimore, MD 21202
Fund Type: MC - Mid Cap
Major Rating Factors: Exceptional performance is the major factor driving the B+ (Good) TheStreet.com Investment Rating for T Rowe Price Mid-Cap Value Fd. The fund currently has a performance rating of A (Excellent) based on an average return of 10.35% over the last three years and 3.17% over the last three months. Factored into the performance evaluation is an expense ratio of 0.80% (very low).

The fund's risk rating is currently C (Fair). It carries a beta of 0.86, meaning the fund's expected move will be 8.6% for every 10% move in the market. Volatility, as measured by both the semi-deviation and a drawdown factor, is considered average.

David J. Wallack has been running the fund for 17 years and currently receives a manager quality ranking of 86 (0=worst, 99=best). If you desire an average level of risk and strong performance, then this fund is a good option.

Services Offered: Automated phone transactions, payroll deductions, bank draft capabilities, an IRA investment plan, a 401K investment plan, a Keogh investment plan, wire transfers and a systematic withdrawal plan. However, the fund is currently closed to new investors.

Data Date	Investment Rating	Net Assets ($Mil)	NAV	Perfor-mance Rating/Pts	Total Return Y-T-D	Risk Rating/Pts
2-17	B+	11,063	29.98	A / 9.5	3.17%	C / 4.3
2016	B+	11,382	29.06	A+ / 9.7	24.32%	C / 4.5
2015	C	10,607	24.94	B- / 7.0	-3.41%	C / 4.7
2014	B	11,112	28.82	B+ / 8.3	10.60%	C / 5.1
2013	C+	10,360	30.05	B- / 7.1	31.54%	C / 4.7
2012	B+	8,437	24.04	B+ / 8.3	19.63%	C / 4.8

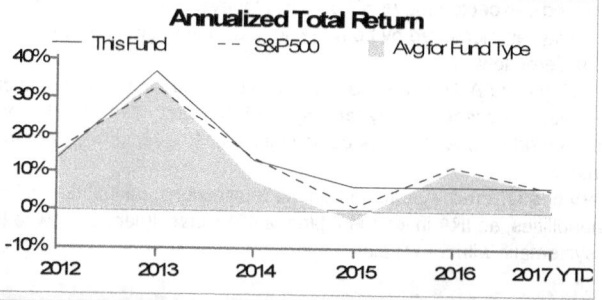

Annualized Total Return

T Rowe Price New Horizons (PRNHX)

C+ **Fair**

Fund Family: T. Rowe Price Funds   **Phone:** (800) 638-5660
Address: 100 East Pratt Street, Baltimore, MD 21202
Fund Type: SC - Small Cap
Major Rating Factors: Strong performance is the major factor driving the C+ (Fair) TheStreet.com Investment Rating for T Rowe Price New Horizons. The fund currently has a performance rating of B (Good) based on an average return of 7.04% over the last three years and 8.52% over the last three months. Factored into the performance evaluation is an expense ratio of 0.79% (very low).

The fund's risk rating is currently C- (Fair). It carries a beta of 0.83, meaning the fund's expected move will be 8.3% for every 10% move in the market. Volatility, as measured by both the semi-deviation and a drawdown factor, is considered average.

Henry M. Ellenbogen has been running the fund for 7 years and currently receives a manager quality ranking of 82 (0=worst, 99=best). If you desire an average level of risk and strong performance, then this fund is a good option.

Services Offered: Automated phone transactions, payroll deductions, bank draft capabilities, an IRA investment plan, a 401K investment plan, a Keogh investment plan, wire transfers and a systematic withdrawal plan. However, the fund is currently closed to new investors.

Data Date	Investment Rating	Net Assets ($Mil)	NAV	Perfor-mance Rating/Pts	Total Return Y-T-D	Risk Rating/Pts
2-17	C+	15,255	47.00	B / 8.2	8.52%	C- / 3.6
2016	C-	15,169	43.31	C+ / 6.9	7.79%	C- / 3.6
2015	A+	15,737	42.46	A+ / 9.6	4.50%	C+ / 6.5
2014	B-	15,356	43.78	A / 9.3	6.10%	C- / 4.1
2013	B+	15,523	46.27	A+ / 9.9	49.11%	C- / 3.2
2012	B+	9,727	33.17	A+ / 9.8	16.20%	C- / 3.0

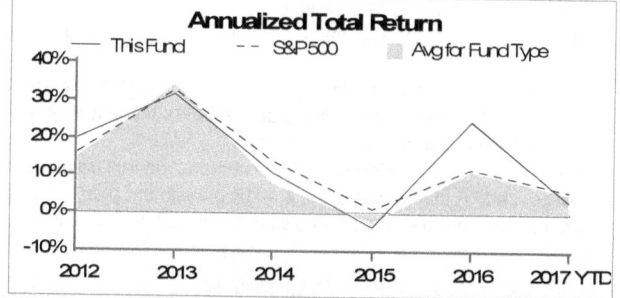

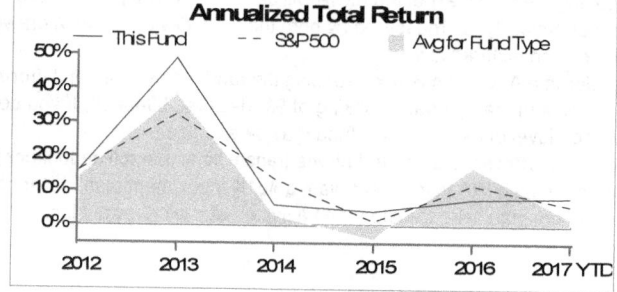

Annualized Total Return

T Rowe Price Overseas Stock (TROSX)   D   Weak

Fund Family: T. Rowe Price Funds   **Phone:** (800) 638-5660
Address: 100 East Pratt Street, Baltimore, MD 21202
Fund Type: FO - Foreign
Major Rating Factors: Disappointing performance is the major factor driving the D (Weak) TheStreet.com Investment Rating for T Rowe Price Overseas Stock. The fund currently has a performance rating of D (Weak) based on an average return of 0.01% over the last three years and 5.07% over the last three months. Factored into the performance evaluation is an expense ratio of 0.84% (very low) and a 2.0% back-end load levied at the time of sale.

The fund's risk rating is currently C+ (Fair). It carries a beta of 0.88, meaning the fund's expected move will be 8.8% for every 10% move in the market. Volatility, as measured by both the semi-deviation and a drawdown factor, is considered low.

Raymond A. Mills has been running the fund for 11 years and currently receives a manager quality ranking of 75 (0=worst, 99=best). This fund offers only a moderate level of risk but investors looking for strong performance are still waiting.

Services Offered: Automated phone transactions, payroll deductions, bank draft capabilities, an IRA investment plan, a 401K investment plan, wire transfers and a systematic withdrawal plan.

Data Date	Investment Rating	Net Assets ($Mil)	NAV	Performance Rating/Pts	Total Return Y-T-D	Risk Rating/Pts
2-17	D	11,115	9.53	D / 2.2	5.07%	C+ / 6.0
2016	D	10,495	9.07	D- / 1.4	2.90%	C+ / 6.1
2015	D+	11,128	8.99	D / 2.1	-2.56%	C+ / 6.9
2014	D	9,367	9.42	D+ / 2.4	-4.49%	C+ / 6.2
2013	D	7,047	10.15	C- / 4.0	21.75%	C / 4.3
2012	C-	5,444	8.50	C / 5.0	18.59%	C- / 4.1

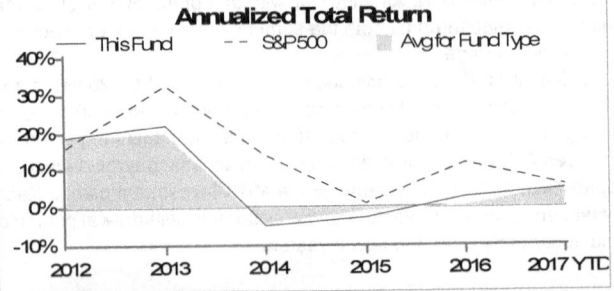

T Rowe Price Real Estate (TRREX)   C+   Fair

Fund Family: T. Rowe Price Funds   **Phone:** (800) 638-5660
Address: 100 East Pratt Street, Baltimore, MD 21202
Fund Type: RE - Real Estate
Major Rating Factors: Middle of the road best describes T Rowe Price Real Estate whose TheStreet.com Investment Rating is currently a C+ (Fair). The fund currently has a performance rating of C+ (Fair) based on an average return of 10.47% over the last three years and 1.72% over the last three months. Factored into the performance evaluation is an expense ratio of 0.76% (very low) and a 1.0% back-end load levied at the time of sale.

The fund's risk rating is currently C+ (Fair). It carries a beta of 1.00, meaning that its performance tracks fairly well with that of the overall stock market. Volatility, as measured by both the semi-deviation and a drawdown factor, is considered low.

David M. Lee has been running the fund for 20 years and currently receives a manager quality ranking of 67 (0=worst, 99=best). If you desire an average level of risk, then this fund may be an option.

Services Offered: Automated phone transactions, payroll deductions, bank draft capabilities, an IRA investment plan, a 401K investment plan, a Keogh investment plan, wire transfers and a systematic withdrawal plan.

Data Date	Investment Rating	Net Assets ($Mil)	NAV	Performance Rating/Pts	Total Return Y-T-D	Risk Rating/Pts
2-17	C+	5,939	28.99	C+ / 6.6	1.72%	C+ / 5.8
2016	A-	5,396	28.50	A- / 9.0	6.03%	C+ / 5.9
2015	B	4,911	27.49	B+ / 8.4	4.78%	C / 5.3
2014	B	4,826	26.86	A / 9.4	29.75%	C / 4.5
2013	E+	3,423	21.21	D / 1.8	3.28%	C- / 3.3
2012	B+	3,392	21.01	A+ / 9.7	17.03%	C- / 3.5

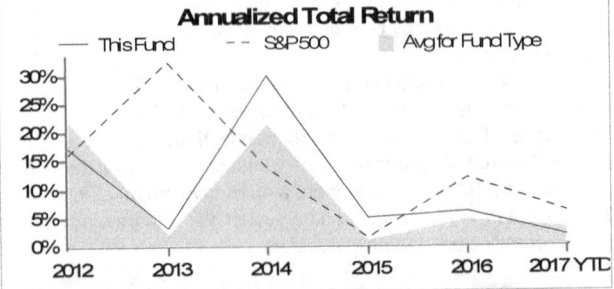

T Rowe Price Retirement 2015 (TRRGX)   C+   Fair

Fund Family: T. Rowe Price Funds   **Phone:** (800) 638-5660
Address: 100 East Pratt Street, Baltimore, MD 21202
Fund Type: GI - Growth and Income
Major Rating Factors: Middle of the road best describes T Rowe Price Retirement 2015 whose TheStreet.com Investment Rating is currently a C+ (Fair). The fund currently has a performance rating of C- (Fair) based on an average return of 4.65% over the last three years and 3.60% over the last three months. Factored into the performance evaluation is an expense ratio of 0.62% (very low).

The fund's risk rating is currently B- (Good). It carries a beta of 0.57, meaning the fund's expected move will be 5.7% for every 10% move in the market. Volatility, as measured by both the semi-deviation and a drawdown factor, is considered low.

Jerome A. Clark has been running the fund for 13 years and currently receives a manager quality ranking of 59 (0=worst, 99=best). If you desire an average level of risk, then this fund may be an option.

Services Offered: Automated phone transactions, payroll deductions, bank draft capabilities, an IRA investment plan, a 401K investment plan, a Keogh investment plan, wire transfers and a systematic withdrawal plan.

Data Date	Investment Rating	Net Assets ($Mil)	NAV	Performance Rating/Pts	Total Return Y-T-D	Risk Rating/Pts
2-17	C+	8,328	14.69	C- / 4.0	3.60%	B- / 7.9
2016	B-	8,197	14.18	C / 5.1	7.31%	B / 8.0
2015	C+	8,503	13.68	C- / 4.1	-0.58%	B / 8.1
2014	C+	8,770	14.47	C- / 3.7	5.37%	B / 8.3
2013	C	7,732	14.32	C- / 3.2	15.18%	B- / 7.4
2012	B-	6,635	12.88	C+ / 5.8	13.81%	B- / 7.3

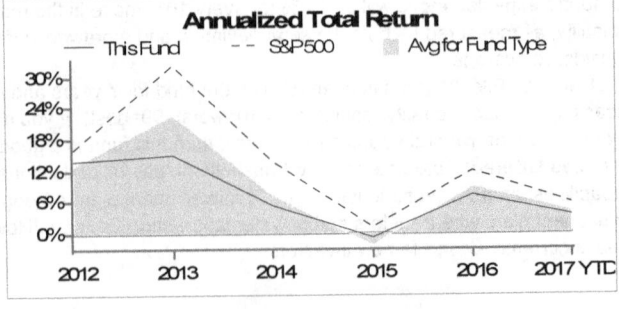

T Rowe Price Retirement 2020 (TRRBX)

C+   **Fair**

Fund Family: T. Rowe Price Funds   **Phone:** (800) 638-5660
Address: 100 East Pratt Street, Baltimore, MD 21202
Fund Type: AA - Asset Allocation
Major Rating Factors: Middle of the road best describes T Rowe Price Retirement 2020 whose TheStreet.com Investment Rating is currently a C+ (Fair). The fund currently has a performance rating of C (Fair) based on an average return of 5.02% over the last three years and 4.16% over the last three months. Factored into the performance evaluation is an expense ratio of 0.66% (very low).

The fund's risk rating is currently B- (Good). It carries a beta of 1.10, meaning it is expected to move 11.0% for every 10% move in the market. Volatility, as measured by both the semi-deviation and a drawdown factor, is considered low.

Jerome A. Clark has been running the fund for 15 years and currently receives a manager quality ranking of 34 (0=worst, 99=best). If you desire an average level of risk, then this fund may be an option.

Services Offered: Automated phone transactions, payroll deductions, bank draft capabilities, an IRA investment plan, a 401K investment plan, a Keogh investment plan, wire transfers and a systematic withdrawal plan.

Data Date	Investment Rating	Net Assets ($Mil)	NAV	Performance Rating/Pts	Total Return Y-T-D	Risk Rating/Pts
2-17	C+	20,915	21.26	C / 4.7	4.16%	B- / 7.7
2016	B-	20,408	20.41	C / 5.4	7.41%	B- / 7.8
2015	C+	19,996	19.69	C / 4.8	-0.31%	B / 8.0
2014	C+	18,820	20.71	C / 4.3	5.63%	B / 8.0
2013	C+	15,342	20.39	C- / 4.0	18.05%	C+ / 6.9
2012	C+	12,612	17.88	C+ / 6.5	15.01%	C+ / 6.8

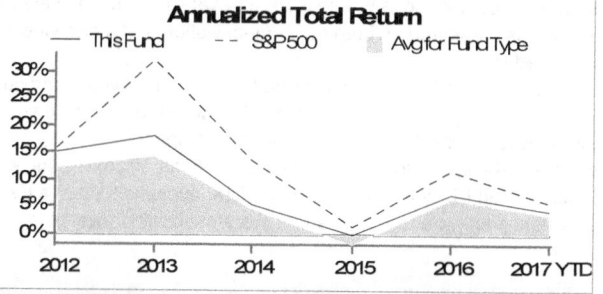

T Rowe Price Retirement 2025 (TRRHX)

B-   **Good**

Fund Family: T. Rowe Price Funds   **Phone:** (800) 638-5660
Address: 100 East Pratt Street, Baltimore, MD 21202
Fund Type: GI - Growth and Income
Major Rating Factors: T Rowe Price Retirement 2025 receives a TheStreet.com Investment Rating of B- (Good). The fund currently has a performance rating of C (Fair) based on an average return of 5.33% over the last three years and 4.65% over the last three months. Factored into the performance evaluation is an expense ratio of 0.69% (very low).

The fund's risk rating is currently B- (Good). It carries a beta of 0.73, meaning the fund's expected move will be 7.3% for every 10% move in the market. Volatility, as measured by both the semi-deviation and a drawdown factor, is considered low.

Jerome A. Clark has been running the fund for 13 years and currently receives a manager quality ranking of 46 (0=worst, 99=best). If you desire an average level of risk, then this fund may be an option.

Services Offered: Automated phone transactions, payroll deductions, bank draft capabilities, an IRA investment plan, a 401K investment plan, a Keogh investment plan, wire transfers and a systematic withdrawal plan.

Data Date	Investment Rating	Net Assets ($Mil)	NAV	Performance Rating/Pts	Total Return Y-T-D	Risk Rating/Pts
2-17	B-	17,762	16.22	C / 5.2	4.65%	B- / 7.4
2016	B-	16,973	15.50	C+ / 5.7	7.55%	B- / 7.6
2015	B-	15,608	14.95	C / 5.4	-0.17%	B / 8.0
2014	C+	13,931	15.71	C / 4.8	5.84%	B- / 7.8
2013	C+	10,781	15.38	C / 4.6	20.78%	C+ / 6.5
2012	A-	8,266	13.12	B- / 7.1	16.00%	C+ / 6.2

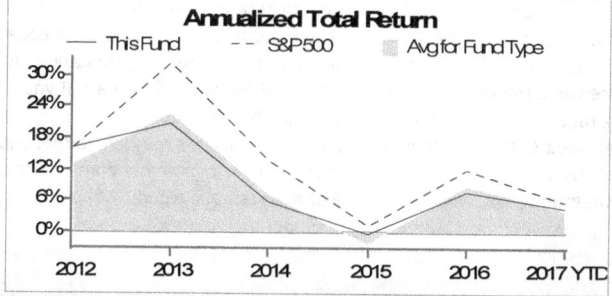

T Rowe Price Retirement 2030 (TRRCX)

B-   **Good**

Fund Family: T. Rowe Price Funds   **Phone:** (800) 638-5660
Address: 100 East Pratt Street, Baltimore, MD 21202
Fund Type: AA - Asset Allocation
Major Rating Factors: T Rowe Price Retirement 2030 receives a TheStreet.com Investment Rating of B- (Good). The fund currently has a performance rating of C+ (Fair) based on an average return of 5.59% over the last three years and 5.02% over the last three months. Factored into the performance evaluation is an expense ratio of 0.72% (very low).

The fund's risk rating is currently B- (Good). It carries a beta of 1.32, meaning it is expected to move 13.2% for every 10% move in the market. Volatility, as measured by both the semi-deviation and a drawdown factor, is considered low.

Jerome A Clark has been running the fund for 15 years and currently receives a manager quality ranking of 23 (0=worst, 99=best). If you desire an average level of risk, then this fund may be an option.

Services Offered: Automated phone transactions, payroll deductions, bank draft capabilities, an IRA investment plan, a 401K investment plan, a Keogh investment plan, wire transfers and a systematic withdrawal plan.

Data Date	Investment Rating	Net Assets ($Mil)	NAV	Performance Rating/Pts	Total Return Y-T-D	Risk Rating/Pts
2-17	B-	21,071	23.66	C+ / 5.7	5.02%	B- / 7.0
2016	B-	20,367	22.53	C+ / 6.0	7.69%	B- / 7.1
2015	B	19,124	21.81	C+ / 5.9	-0.02%	B- / 7.7
2014	C+	17,284	23.02	C / 5.3	6.05%	B- / 7.4
2013	C+	13,819	22.60	C / 5.1	23.09%	C+ / 6.0
2012	B+	10,773	18.92	B- / 7.5	16.82%	C+ / 5.8

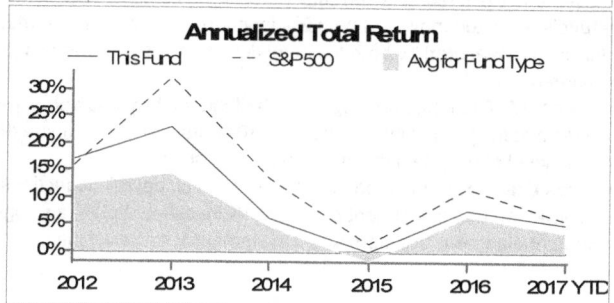

T Rowe Price Retirement 2035 (TRRJX)   C+   Fair

Fund Family: T. Rowe Price Funds   **Phone:** (800) 638-5660
Address: 100 East Pratt Street, Baltimore, MD 21202
Fund Type: GI - Growth and Income
Major Rating Factors: Middle of the road best describes T Rowe Price Retirement 2035 whose TheStreet.com Investment Rating is currently a C+ (Fair). The fund currently has a performance rating of C+ (Fair) based on an average return of 5.73% over the last three years and 5.34% over the last three months. Factored into the performance evaluation is an expense ratio of 0.74% (very low).

The fund's risk rating is currently C+ (Fair). It carries a beta of 0.85, meaning the fund's expected move will be 8.5% for every 10% move in the market. Volatility, as measured by both the semi-deviation and a drawdown factor, is considered low.

Jerome A. Clark has been running the fund for 13 years and currently receives a manager quality ranking of 35 (0=worst, 99=best). If you desire an average level of risk, then this fund may be an option.

Services Offered: Automated phone transactions, payroll deductions, bank draft capabilities, an IRA investment plan, a 401K investment plan, a Keogh investment plan, wire transfers and a systematic withdrawal plan.

Data Date	Investment Rating	Net Assets ($Mil)	NAV	Performance Rating/Pts	Total Return Y-T-D	Risk Rating/Pts
2-17	C+	13,217	17.16	C+ / 6.0	5.34%	C+ / 6.7
2016	C+	12,543	16.29	C+ / 6.1	7.64%	C+ / 6.8
2015	B-	11,254	15.79	C+ / 6.3	0.13%	B- / 7.4
2014	C+	9,950	16.66	C+ / 5.6	6.07%	B- / 7.2
2013	C+	7,620	16.28	C / 5.5	24.86%	C+ / 5.7
2012	B+	5,653	13.38	B / 7.7	17.35%	C / 5.4

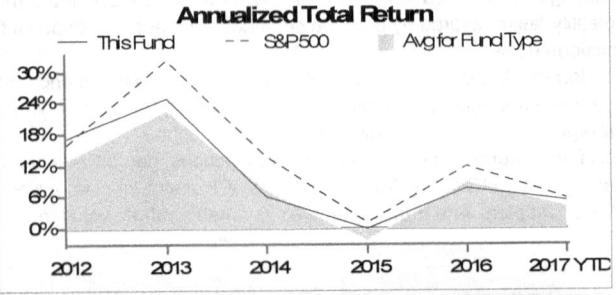

T Rowe Price Retirement 2040 (TRRDX)   C+   Fair

Fund Family: T. Rowe Price Funds   **Phone:** (800) 638-5660
Address: 100 East Pratt Street, Baltimore, MD 21202
Fund Type: AA - Asset Allocation
Major Rating Factors: Middle of the road best describes T Rowe Price Retirement 2040 whose TheStreet.com Investment Rating is currently a C+ (Fair). The fund currently has a performance rating of C+ (Fair) based on an average return of 5.85% over the last three years and 5.64% over the last three months. Factored into the performance evaluation is an expense ratio of 0.76% (very low).

The fund's risk rating is currently C+ (Fair). It carries a beta of 1.47, meaning it is expected to move 14.7% for every 10% move in the market. Volatility, as measured by both the semi-deviation and a drawdown factor, is considered low.

Jerome A. Clark has been running the fund for 15 years and currently receives a manager quality ranking of 16 (0=worst, 99=best). If you desire an average level of risk, then this fund may be an option.

Services Offered: Automated phone transactions, payroll deductions, bank draft capabilities, an IRA investment plan, a 401K investment plan, a Keogh investment plan, wire transfers and a systematic withdrawal plan.

Data Date	Investment Rating	Net Assets ($Mil)	NAV	Performance Rating/Pts	Total Return Y-T-D	Risk Rating/Pts
2-17	C+	14,407	24.52	C+ / 6.3	5.64%	C+ / 6.4
2016	C+	13,881	23.21	C+ / 6.2	7.63%	C+ / 6.4
2015	B-	12,902	22.58	C+ / 6.6	0.17%	B- / 7.2
2014	C+	11,532	23.92	C+ / 5.8	6.18%	B- / 7.0
2013	C+	9,818	23.41	C+ / 5.7	25.93%	C+ / 5.6
2012	B+	7,139	19.09	B / 7.7	17.55%	C / 5.3

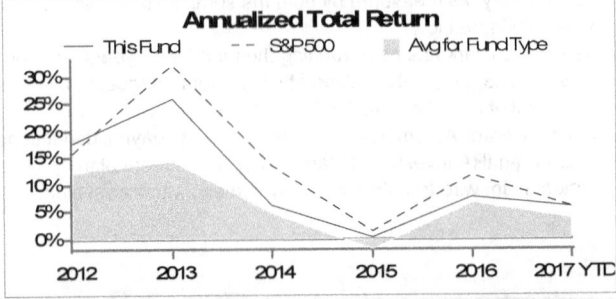

T Rowe Price Retirement 2045 (TRRKX)   C+   Fair

Fund Family: T. Rowe Price Funds   **Phone:** (800) 638-5660
Address: 100 East Pratt Street, Baltimore, MD 21202
Fund Type: GI - Growth and Income
Major Rating Factors: Middle of the road best describes T Rowe Price Retirement 2045 whose TheStreet.com Investment Rating is currently a C+ (Fair). The fund currently has a performance rating of C+ (Fair) based on an average return of 5.89% over the last three years and 5.70% over the last three months. Factored into the performance evaluation is an expense ratio of 0.76% (very low).

The fund's risk rating is currently C+ (Fair). It carries a beta of 0.89, meaning the fund's expected move will be 8.9% for every 10% move in the market. Volatility, as measured by both the semi-deviation and a drawdown factor, is considered low.

Jerome A. Clark has been running the fund for 12 years and currently receives a manager quality ranking of 31 (0=worst, 99=best). If you desire an average level of risk, then this fund may be an option.

Services Offered: Automated phone transactions, payroll deductions, bank draft capabilities, an IRA investment plan, a 401K investment plan, a Keogh investment plan, wire transfers and a systematic withdrawal plan.

Data Date	Investment Rating	Net Assets ($Mil)	NAV	Performance Rating/Pts	Total Return Y-T-D	Risk Rating/Pts
2-17	C+	7,915	16.51	C+ / 6.4	5.70%	C+ / 6.4
2016	C+	7,472	15.62	C+ / 6.2	7.69%	C+ / 6.4
2015	B-	6,480	15.16	C+ / 6.5	0.17%	B- / 7.3
2014	C+	5,544	16.00	C+ / 5.8	6.14%	B- / 7.0
2013	C+	4,153	15.61	C+ / 5.8	25.93%	C+ / 5.6
2012	B+	3,124	12.71	B / 7.8	17.62%	C / 5.3

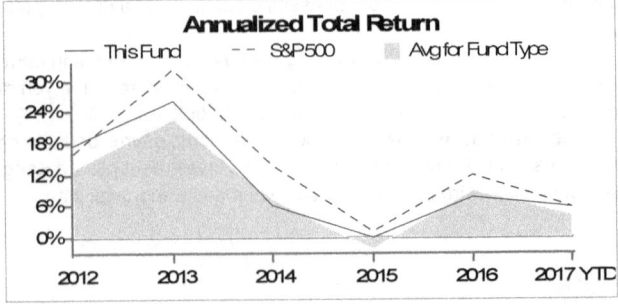

T Rowe Price Small Cap Stock (OTCFX)   B-   Good

Fund Family: T. Rowe Price Funds   **Phone:** (800) 638-5660
Address: 100 East Pratt Street, Baltimore, MD 21202
Fund Type: SC - Small Cap
Major Rating Factors: Strong performance is the major factor driving the B-
(Good) TheStreet.com Investment Rating for T Rowe Price Small Cap Stock.
The fund currently has a performance rating of B+ (Good) based on an average
return of 7.46% over the last three years and 3.72% over the last three months.
Factored into the performance evaluation is an expense ratio of 0.90% (low).

The fund's risk rating is currently C- (Fair). It carries a beta of 0.89, meaning
the fund's expected move will be 8.9% for every 10% move in the market.
Volatility, as measured by both the semi-deviation and a drawdown factor, is
considered average.

Brian C. Rogers currently receives a manager quality ranking of 82 (0=worst,
99=best). If you desire an average level of risk and strong performance, then this
fund is a good option.

Services Offered: Automated phone transactions, payroll deductions, bank draft
capabilities, an IRA investment plan, a 401K investment plan, a Keogh
investment plan, wire transfers and a systematic withdrawal plan. However, the
fund is currently closed to new investors.

Data Date	Investment Rating	Net Assets ($Mil)	NAV	Performance Rating/Pts	Total Return Y-T-D	Risk Rating/Pts
2-17	B-	8,593	46.60	B+ / 8.7	3.72%	C- / 4.2
2016	B	8,661	44.93	A- / 9.2	18.57%	C / 4.3
2015	C+	8,378	38.61	B- / 7.4	-3.18%	C / 5.2
2014	B+	9,351	44.32	B+ / 8.4	6.90%	C+ / 6.0
2013	B	9,709	44.56	A- / 9.1	37.65%	C- / 3.5
2012	B	7,071	34.03	A+ / 9.6	18.01%	C- / 3.1

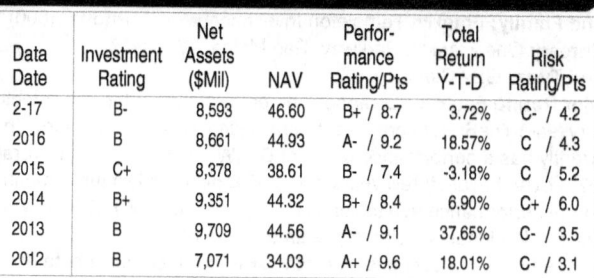

T Rowe Price Small Cap Value (PRSVX)   C+   Fair

Fund Family: T. Rowe Price Funds   **Phone:** (800) 638-5660
Address: 100 East Pratt Street, Baltimore, MD 21202
Fund Type: SC - Small Cap
Major Rating Factors: T Rowe Price Small Cap Value has adopted a risky
asset allocation strategy and currently receives an overall TheStreet.com
Investment Rating of C+ (Fair). The fund has shown an above average level of
volatility, as measured by both semi-deviation and drawdown factors. It carries a
beta of 0.83, meaning the fund's expected move will be 8.3% for every 10%
move in the market. The high level of risk (D+, Weak) did however, reward
investors with excellent performance.

The fund's performance rating is currently A- (Excellent). It has registered an
average return of 7.48% over the last three years and is up 1.26% over the last
three months. Factored into the performance evaluation is an expense ratio of
0.92% (low) and a 1.0% back-end load levied at the time of sale.

J. David Wagner has been running the fund for 1 year and currently receives
a manager quality ranking of 84 (0=worst, 99=best). If you are comfortable
owning a high risk investment, this fund may be an option.

Services Offered: Automated phone transactions, payroll deductions, bank draft
capabilities, an IRA investment plan, a 401K investment plan, a Keogh
investment plan, wire transfers and a systematic withdrawal plan.

Data Date	Investment Rating	Net Assets ($Mil)	NAV	Performance Rating/Pts	Total Return Y-T-D	Risk Rating/Pts
2-17	C+	8,068	45.70	A- / 9.1	1.26%	D+ / 2.9
2016	C+	8,039	45.13	A+ / 9.7	28.97%	C- / 3.1
2015	D	7,154	36.32	C / 4.5	-4.70%	C- / 3.3
2014	C	8,040	46.80	C / 5.3	0.14%	C+ / 6.0
2013	B	8,603	50.37	B / 8.0	32.74%	C / 4.6
2012	A-	6,744	39.17	A / 9.3	17.76%	C- / 4.1

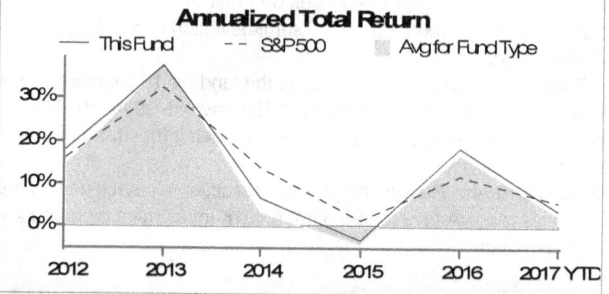

T Rowe Price Value (TRVLX)   B   Good

Fund Family: T. Rowe Price Funds   **Phone:** (800) 638-5660
Address: 100 East Pratt Street, Baltimore, MD 21202
Fund Type: GI - Growth and Income
Major Rating Factors: Strong performance is the major factor driving the B
(Good) TheStreet.com Investment Rating for T Rowe Price Value. The fund
currently has a performance rating of B+ (Good) based on an average return of
8.61% over the last three years and 5.38% over the last three months. Factored
into the performance evaluation is an expense ratio of 0.81% (very low).

The fund's risk rating is currently C (Fair). It carries a beta of 1.02, meaning
that its performance tracks fairly well with that of the overall stock market.
Volatility, as measured by both the semi-deviation and a drawdown factor, is
considered average.

Mark S. Finn has been running the fund for 8 years and currently receives a
manager quality ranking of 48 (0=worst, 99=best). If you desire an average level
of risk and strong performance, then this fund is a good option.

Services Offered: Automated phone transactions, payroll deductions, bank draft
capabilities, an IRA investment plan, a 401K investment plan, a Keogh
investment plan, wire transfers and a systematic withdrawal plan.

Data Date	Investment Rating	Net Assets ($Mil)	NAV	Performance Rating/Pts	Total Return Y-T-D	Risk Rating/Pts
2-17	B	21,847	35.46	B+ / 8.3	5.38%	C / 5.2
2016	B-	21,736	33.65	B / 8.2	10.96%	C / 5.3
2015	B+	21,908	31.25	B+ / 8.9	-1.74%	C+ / 6.0
2014	A	21,583	34.65	A+ / 9.6	13.37%	C+ / 6.3
2013	A	17,266	33.77	A- / 9.0	37.31%	C / 5.2
2012	A-	13,319	26.38	B+ / 8.7	19.46%	C / 4.8

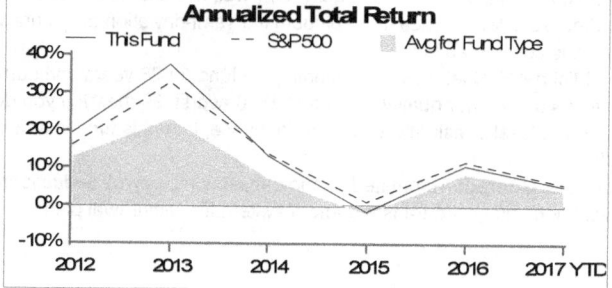

Templeton Growth A (TEPLX)   D+   Weak

Fund Family: Franklin Templeton Investments   **Phone:** (800) 342-5236
Address: One Franklin Parkway, San Mateo, CA 94403
Fund Type: GL - Global

Major Rating Factors: Disappointing performance is the major factor driving the D+ (Weak) TheStreet.com Investment Rating for Templeton Growth A. The fund currently has a performance rating of D+ (Weak) based on an average return of 0.52% over the last three years and 3.99% over the last three months. Factored into the performance evaluation is an expense ratio of 1.07% (low) and a 5.8% front-end load that is levied at the time of purchase.

The fund's risk rating is currently C+ (Fair). It carries a beta of 0.98, meaning that its performance tracks fairly well with that of the overall stock market. Volatility, as measured by both the semi-deviation and a drawdown factor, is considered low.

Tucker E. Scott has been running the fund for 10 years and currently receives a manager quality ranking of 79 (0=worst, 99=best). This fund offers only a moderate level of risk but investors looking for strong performance are still waiting.

Services Offered: Automated phone transactions, payroll deductions, bank draft capabilities, an IRA investment plan, a 401K investment plan and a systematic withdrawal plan.

Data Date	Investment Rating	Net Assets ($Mil)	NAV	Perfor-mance Rating/Pts	Total Return Y-T-D	Risk Rating/Pts
2-17	D+	10,689	24.50	D+ / 2.9	3.99%	C+ / 5.6
2016	D+	10,431	23.56	D / 2.2	9.06%	C+ / 5.7
2015	D	11,532	21.91	D+ / 2.3	-6.46%	C+ / 6.4
2014	C-	12,827	23.81	C- / 3.9	-1.91%	C+ / 6.0
2013	C	14,475	24.97	C+ / 6.1	30.15%	C / 4.4
2012	C	12,186	19.43	C+ / 6.4	21.54%	C- / 4.2

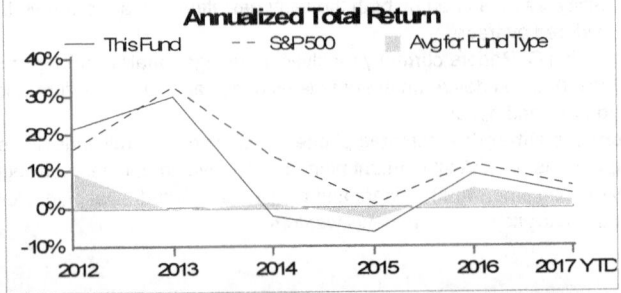

Tweedy Browne Global Value (TBGVX)   C-   Fair

Fund Family: Tweedy Browne Funds   **Phone:** (800) 432-4789
Address: 4400 Computer Drive, Westborough, MA 01581
Fund Type: FO - Foreign

Major Rating Factors: Middle of the road best describes Tweedy Browne Global Value whose TheStreet.com Investment Rating is currently a C- (Fair). The fund currently has a performance rating of C- (Fair) based on an average return of 2.75% over the last three years and 3.87% over the last three months. Factored into the performance evaluation is an expense ratio of 1.38% (average) and a 2.0% back-end load levied at the time of sale.

The fund's risk rating is currently C+ (Fair). It carries a beta of 0.56, meaning the fund's expected move will be 5.6% for every 10% move in the market. Volatility, as measured by both the semi-deviation and a drawdown factor, is considered low.

John D. Spears has been running the fund for 24 years and currently receives a manager quality ranking of 89 (0=worst, 99=best). If you desire an average level of risk, then this fund may be an option.

Services Offered: Automated phone transactions, payroll deductions, bank draft capabilities, an IRA investment plan, a Keogh investment plan, wire transfers and a systematic withdrawal plan.

Data Date	Investment Rating	Net Assets ($Mil)	NAV	Perfor-mance Rating/Pts	Total Return Y-T-D	Risk Rating/Pts
2-17	C-	9,381	26.01	C- / 3.3	3.87%	C+ / 6.4
2016	C-	8,995	25.04	C- / 3.5	5.62%	C+ / 6.4
2015	C	8,881	24.46	C- / 3.5	-1.46%	B- / 7.8
2014	C-	8,720	26.04	C- / 3.6	1.51%	B- / 7.2
2013	C	7,388	26.62	C- / 3.9	19.62%	C+ / 6.4
2012	A	5,221	23.24	B- / 7.4	18.38%	C+ / 6.3

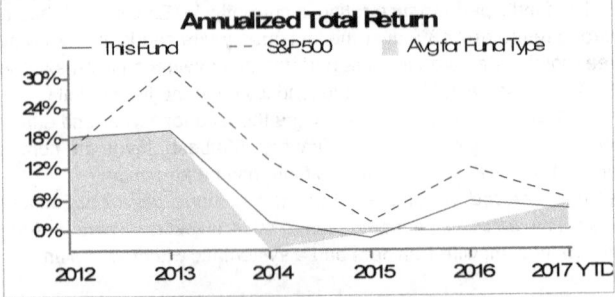

Vanguard 500 Index Inv (VFINX)   A+   Excellent

Fund Family: Vanguard Funds   **Phone:** (800) 662-7447
Address: Vanguard Financial Center, Valley Forge, PA 19482
Fund Type: IX - Index

Major Rating Factors: Exceptional performance is the major factor driving the A+ (Excellent) TheStreet.com Investment Rating for Vanguard 500 Index Inv. The fund currently has a performance rating of A (Excellent) based on an average return of 10.48% over the last three years and 5.92% over the last three months. Factored into the performance evaluation is an expense ratio of 0.16% (very low).

The fund's risk rating is currently B- (Good). It carries a beta of 1.00, meaning that its performance tracks fairly well with that of the overall stock market. Volatility, as measured by both the semi-deviation and a drawdown factor, is considered low.

Michael H. Buek has been running the fund for 26 years and currently receives a manager quality ranking of 73 (0=worst, 99=best). If you desire only a moderate level of risk and strong performance, then this fund is an excellent option.

Services Offered: Automated phone transactions, payroll deductions, an IRA investment plan, wire transfers and a systematic withdrawal plan.

Data Date	Investment Rating	Net Assets ($Mil)	NAV	Perfor-mance Rating/Pts	Total Return Y-T-D	Risk Rating/Pts
2-17	A+	28,029	218.80	A / 9.3	5.92%	B- / 7.1
2016	A+	26,652	206.57	B+ / 8.7	11.82%	B- / 7.1
2015	A+	26,738	188.48	A- / 9.0	1.25%	B- / 7.3
2014	A+	28,040	189.89	B+ / 8.9	13.51%	B- / 7.3
2013	A	27,758	170.36	B / 8.1	32.18%	C+ / 6.0
2012	B+	24,821	131.37	B- / 7.3	15.82%	C+ / 5.6

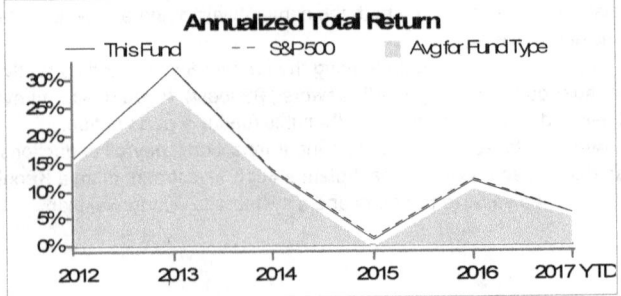

Vanguard Dividend Growth Inv (VDIGX)

A-   Excellent

Fund Family: Vanguard Funds   **Phone:** (800) 662-7447
Address: Vanguard Financial Center, Valley Forge, PA 19482
Fund Type: GI - Growth and Income
Major Rating Factors: Strong performance is the major factor driving the A-
(Excellent) TheStreet.com Investment Rating for Vanguard Dividend Growth Inv.
The fund currently has a performance rating of B- (Good) based on an average
return of 9.22% over the last three years and 5.85% over the last three months.
Factored into the performance evaluation is an expense ratio of 0.33% (very
low).

The fund's risk rating is currently B- (Good). It carries a beta of 0.86,
meaning the fund's expected move will be 8.6% for every 10% move in the
market. Volatility, as measured by both the semi-deviation and a drawdown
factor, is considered low.

Donald J. Kilbride has been running the fund for 11 years and currently
receives a manager quality ranking of 75 (0=worst, 99=best). If you desire only a
moderate level of risk and strong performance, then this fund is an excellent
option.

Services Offered: Automated phone transactions, payroll deductions, bank draft
capabilities, an IRA investment plan, a Keogh investment plan, wire transfers
and a systematic withdrawal plan. However, the fund is currently closed to new
investors.

Data Date	Investment Rating	Net Assets ($Mil)	NAV	Performance Rating/Pts	Total Return Y-T-D	Risk Rating/Pts
2-17	A-	31,712	24.80	B- / 7.4	5.85%	B- / 7.4
2016	B+	30,721	23.43	B- / 7.1	7.53%	B- / 7.4
2015	A+	26,217	22.43	A- / 9.1	2.67%	B- / 7.4
2014	A-	23,436	23.09	B- / 7.3	11.85%	B- / 7.9
2013	A+	19,709	21.36	B / 8.0	31.53%	B- / 7.1
2012	C+	11,753	16.64	C+ / 6.0	10.39%	C+ / 6.8

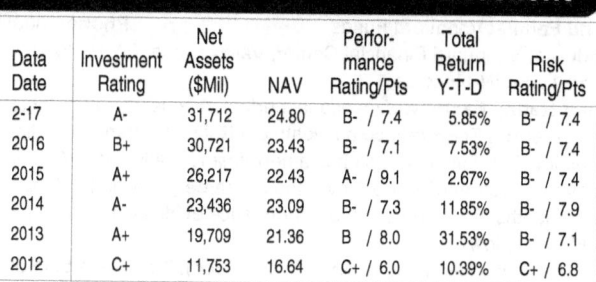

Vanguard Equity Income Inv (VEIPX)

A+   Excellent

Fund Family: Vanguard Funds   **Phone:** (800) 662-7447
Address: Vanguard Financial Center, Valley Forge, PA 19482
Fund Type: IN - Income
Major Rating Factors: Exceptional performance is the major factor driving the
A+ (Excellent) TheStreet.com Investment Rating for Vanguard Equity Income
Inv. The fund currently has a performance rating of A- (Excellent) based on an
average return of 10.38% over the last three years and 4.51% over the last three
months. Factored into the performance evaluation is an expense ratio of 0.26%
(very low).

The fund's risk rating is currently C+ (Fair). It carries a beta of 0.90, meaning
the fund's expected move will be 9.0% for every 10% move in the market.
Volatility, as measured by both the semi-deviation and a drawdown factor, is
considered low.

James P. Stetler has been running the fund for 14 years and currently
receives a manager quality ranking of 80 (0=worst, 99=best). If you desire only a
moderate level of risk and strong performance, then this fund is an excellent
option.

Services Offered: Automated phone transactions, payroll deductions, an IRA
investment plan, a Keogh investment plan, wire transfers and a systematic
withdrawal plan.

Data Date	Investment Rating	Net Assets ($Mil)	NAV	Performance Rating/Pts	Total Return Y-T-D	Risk Rating/Pts
2-17	A+	6,039	34.09	A- / 9.0	4.51%	C+ / 6.9
2016	A+	5,803	32.62	B+ / 8.9	14.70%	C+ / 6.8
2015	A-	5,185	29.56	B+ / 8.5	0.77%	C+ / 6.9
2014	B+	5,676	31.21	B- / 7.3	11.29%	B- / 7.7
2013	A+	5,126	29.76	B+ / 8.3	30.07%	B- / 7.0
2012	A+	3,966	24.15	B+ / 8.4	13.49%	C+ / 6.7

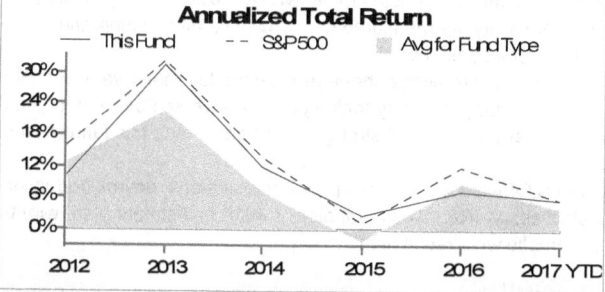

Vanguard Health Care Inv (VGHCX)

C+   Fair

Fund Family: Vanguard Funds   **Phone:** (800) 662-7447
Address: Vanguard Financial Center, Valley Forge, PA 19482
Fund Type: HL - Health
Major Rating Factors: Strong performance is the major factor driving the C+
(Fair) TheStreet.com Investment Rating for Vanguard Health Care Inv. The fund
currently has a performance rating of B- (Good) based on an average return of
9.34% over the last three years and 10.18% over the last three months. Factored
into the performance evaluation is an expense ratio of 0.36% (very low).

The fund's risk rating is currently C (Fair). It carries a beta of 0.93, meaning
that its performance tracks fairly well with that of the overall stock market.
Volatility, as measured by both the semi-deviation and a drawdown factor, is
considered average.

Jean M. Hynes has been running the fund for 9 years and currently receives
a manager quality ranking of 68 (0=worst, 99=best). If you desire an average
level of risk and strong performance, then this fund is a good option.

Services Offered: Automated phone transactions, payroll deductions, bank draft
capabilities, an IRA investment plan, a Keogh investment plan, wire transfers
and a systematic withdrawal plan.

Data Date	Investment Rating	Net Assets ($Mil)	NAV	Performance Rating/Pts	Total Return Y-T-D	Risk Rating/Pts
2-17	C+	10,251	203.56	B- / 7.2	10.18%	C / 4.7
2016	C	9,550	184.76	C+ / 6.5	-8.99%	C / 4.7
2015	A	11,799	220.35	A+ / 9.9	12.65%	C+ / 5.6
2014	A	11,252	211.71	A+ / 9.9	28.52%	C+ / 5.6
2013	A+	9,636	187.16	A+ / 9.8	43.19%	C+ / 6.6
2012	A+	8,143	143.27	B- / 7.2	15.11%	B- / 7.1

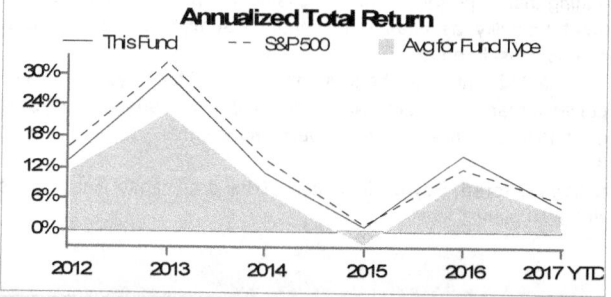
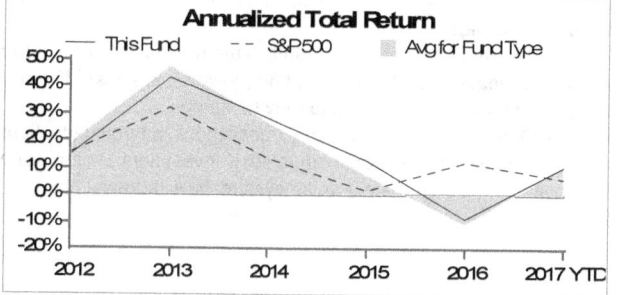

Vanguard High Div Yield Index Inv (VHDYX)   A+   Excellent

Fund Family: Vanguard Funds   **Phone:** (800) 662-7447
Address: Vanguard Financial Center, Valley Forge, PA 19482
Fund Type: IN - Income

Major Rating Factors: Exceptional performance is the major factor driving the A+ (Excellent) TheStreet.com Investment Rating for Vanguard High Div Yield Index Inv. The fund currently has a performance rating of A (Excellent) based on an average return of 11.43% over the last three years and 3.67% over the last three months. Factored into the performance evaluation is an expense ratio of 0.16% (very low).

The fund's risk rating is currently B- (Good). It carries a beta of 0.90, meaning the fund's expected move will be 9.0% for every 10% move in the market. Volatility, as measured by both the semi-deviation and a drawdown factor, is considered low.

Gerard C. O'Reilly has been running the fund for 1 year and currently receives a manager quality ranking of 85 (0=worst, 99=best). If you desire only a moderate level of risk and strong performance, then this fund is an excellent option.

Services Offered: Automated phone transactions, payroll deductions, bank draft capabilities, an IRA investment plan, a 401K investment plan, wire transfers and a systematic withdrawal plan.

Data Date	Investment Rating	Net Assets ($Mil)	NAV	Performance Rating/Pts	Total Return Y-T-D	Risk Rating/Pts
2-17	A+	7,008	31.07	A / 9.4	3.67%	B- / 7.4
2016	A+	6,652	29.97	A / 9.3	16.75%	B- / 7.5
2015	A	4,399	26.45	B+ / 8.7	0.30%	B- / 7.0
2014	A	4,279	27.22	B / 7.8	13.38%	B / 8.0
2013	A+	3,191	24.69	B / 8.1	30.13%	B- / 7.0
2012	A+	1,655	19.54	B / 7.6	12.59%	C+ / 6.6

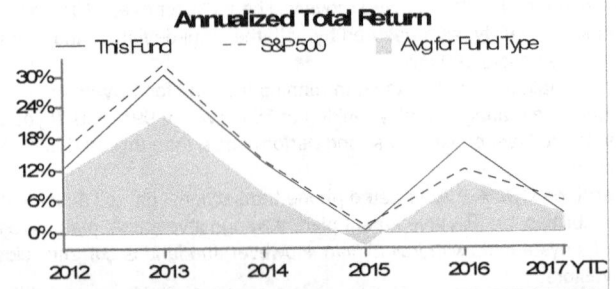

Annualized Total Return

Vanguard Instl Index Inst (VINIX)   A+   Excellent

Fund Family: Vanguard Funds   **Phone:** (800) 662-7447
Address: Vanguard Financial Center, Valley Forge, PA 19482
Fund Type: IX - Index

Major Rating Factors: Exceptional performance is the major factor driving the A+ (Excellent) TheStreet.com Investment Rating for Vanguard Instl Index Inst. The fund currently has a performance rating of A (Excellent) based on an average return of 10.61% over the last three years and 5.94% over the last three months. Factored into the performance evaluation is an expense ratio of 0.04% (very low).

The fund's risk rating is currently B- (Good). It carries a beta of 1.00, meaning that its performance tracks fairly well with that of the overall stock market. Volatility, as measured by both the semi-deviation and a drawdown factor, is considered low.

Donald M. Butler has been running the fund for 17 years and currently receives a manager quality ranking of 74 (0=worst, 99=best). If you desire only a moderate level of risk and strong performance, then this fund is an excellent option.

Services Offered: Payroll deductions, bank draft capabilities and a systematic withdrawal plan.

Data Date	Investment Rating	Net Assets ($Mil)	NAV	Performance Rating/Pts	Total Return Y-T-D	Risk Rating/Pts
2-17	A+	128,517	215.93	A / 9.4	5.94%	B- / 7.1
2016	A+	120,014	203.83	B+ / 8.8	11.93%	B- / 7.1
2015	A+	105,645	186.62	A- / 9.1	1.37%	B- / 7.1
2014	A+	102,114	188.67	A- / 9.0	13.65%	B- / 7.3
2013	A	87,843	169.28	B / 8.2	32.35%	C+ / 6.0
2012	B+	68,055	130.52	B- / 7.5	15.98%	C+ / 5.6

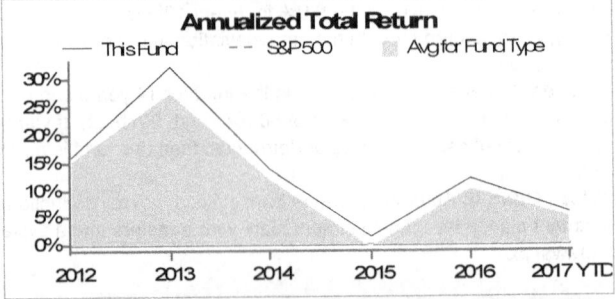

Annualized Total Return

Vanguard International Growth Inv (VWIGX)   D   Weak

Fund Family: Vanguard Funds   **Phone:** (800) 662-7447
Address: Vanguard Financial Center, Valley Forge, PA 19482
Fund Type: FO - Foreign

Major Rating Factors: Vanguard International Growth Inv receives a TheStreet.com Investment Rating of D (Weak). The fund currently has a performance rating of C- (Fair) based on an average return of 1.28% over the last three years and 8.31% over the last three months. Factored into the performance evaluation is an expense ratio of 0.47% (very low).

The fund's risk rating is currently C (Fair). It carries a beta of 1.04, meaning that its performance tracks fairly well with that of the overall stock market. Volatility, as measured by both the semi-deviation and a drawdown factor, is considered average.

James K. Anderson has been running the fund for 14 years and currently receives a manager quality ranking of 84 (0=worst, 99=best). If you desire an average level of risk, then this fund may be an option.

Services Offered: Automated phone transactions, payroll deductions, bank draft capabilities, an IRA investment plan, a 401K investment plan, a Keogh investment plan, wire transfers and a systematic withdrawal plan.

Data Date	Investment Rating	Net Assets ($Mil)	NAV	Performance Rating/Pts	Total Return Y-T-D	Risk Rating/Pts
2-17	D	6,555	22.95	C- / 3.5	8.31%	C / 4.8
2016	D-	6,193	21.19	D- / 1.2	1.71%	C / 5.1
2015	D+	7,374	21.10	C- / 3.2	-0.67%	C+ / 5.9
2014	D	7,819	21.54	D+ / 2.7	-5.63%	C / 5.5
2013	D	9,716	23.34	C / 4.4	22.95%	C- / 3.5
2012	C	9,411	19.27	B- / 7.0	20.01%	C- / 3.4

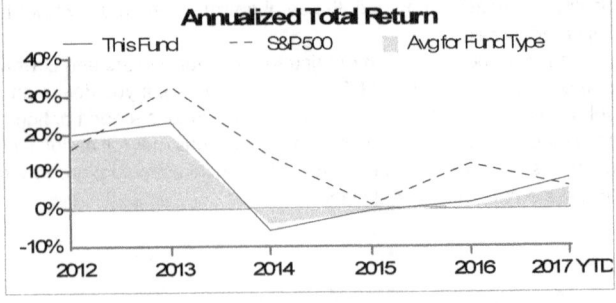

Annualized Total Return

Vanguard International Value Inv (VTRIX)   D-   Weak

Fund Family: Vanguard Funds   **Phone:** (800) 662-7447
Address: Vanguard Financial Center, Valley Forge, PA 19482
Fund Type: FO - Foreign

Major Rating Factors: Disappointing performance is the major factor driving the D- (Weak) TheStreet.com Investment Rating for Vanguard International Value Inv. The fund currently has a performance rating of D- (Weak) based on an average return of -1.43% over the last three years and 4.82% over the last three months. Factored into the performance evaluation is an expense ratio of 0.46% (very low).

The fund's risk rating is currently C (Fair). It carries a beta of 0.95, meaning that its performance tracks fairly well with that of the overall stock market. Volatility, as measured by both the semi-deviation and a drawdown factor, is considered average.

Alisdair G. M. Nairn has been running the fund for 9 years and currently receives a manager quality ranking of 59 (0=worst, 99=best). This fund offers an average level of risk but investors looking for strong performance will be frustrated.

Services Offered: Automated phone transactions, payroll deductions, bank draft capabilities and a systematic withdrawal plan.

Data Date	Investment Rating	Net Assets ($Mil)	NAV	Performance Rating/Pts	Total Return Y-T-D	Risk Rating/Pts
2-17	D-	8,329	33.28	D- / 1.2	4.82%	C / 5.2
2016	D-	7,931	31.75	D- / 1.1	4.46%	C / 5.4
2015	D-	7,826	31.09	D- / 1.3	-6.44%	C+ / 5.9
2014	D-	7,879	33.95	D / 2.2	-6.69%	C+ / 5.7
2013	D	8,263	37.38	C- / 4.0	22.15%	C- / 4.1
2012	D+	6,808	31.18	C / 4.7	20.18%	C- / 3.8

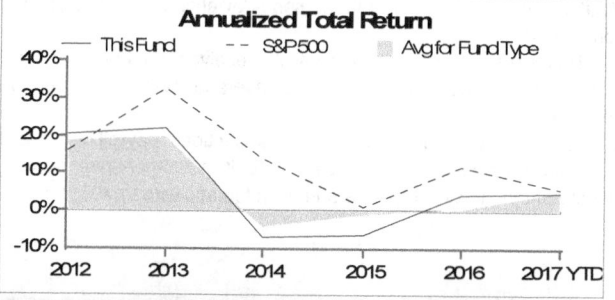

Vanguard LifeStrategy Consv Gr Inv (VSCGX)   C+   Fair

Fund Family: Vanguard Funds   **Phone:** (800) 662-7447
Address: Vanguard Financial Center, Valley Forge, PA 19482
Fund Type: AA - Asset Allocation

Major Rating Factors: Middle of the road best describes Vanguard LifeStrategy Consv Gr Inv whose TheStreet.com Investment Rating is currently a C+ (Fair). The fund currently has a performance rating of C- (Fair) based on an average return of 4.49% over the last three years and 2.66% over the last three months. Factored into the performance evaluation is an expense ratio of 0.13% (very low).

The fund's risk rating is currently B+ (Good). It carries a beta of 0.68, meaning the fund's expected move will be 6.8% for every 10% move in the market. Volatility, as measured by both the semi-deviation and a drawdown factor, is considered very low.

This is team managed and currently receives a manager quality ranking of 67 (0=worst, 99=best). If you desire an average level of risk, then this fund may be an option.

Services Offered: Automated phone transactions, payroll deductions, bank draft capabilities, an IRA investment plan, a 401K investment plan, a Keogh investment plan, wire transfers and a systematic withdrawal plan.

Data Date	Investment Rating	Net Assets ($Mil)	NAV	Performance Rating/Pts	Total Return Y-T-D	Risk Rating/Pts
2-17	C+	8,495	18.93	C- / 3.1	2.66%	B+ / 9.2
2016	B	8,196	18.44	C / 4.7	5.91%	B+ / 9.3
2015	C+	7,594	17.84	C- / 3.5	-0.17%	B+ / 9.3
2014	C+	7,420	18.44	D+ / 2.7	6.93%	B+ / 9.3
2013	C	8,873	18.05	D / 1.9	9.08%	B+ / 9.0
2012	C+	7,504	16.97	D+ / 2.4	9.19%	B+ / 9.1

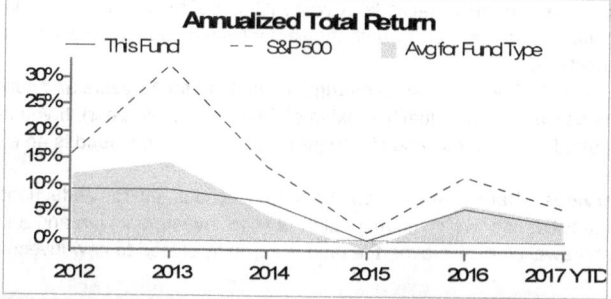

Vanguard LifeStrategy Growth Inv (VASGX)   B-   Good

Fund Family: Vanguard Funds   **Phone:** (800) 662-7447
Address: Vanguard Financial Center, Valley Forge, PA 19482
Fund Type: AA - Asset Allocation

Major Rating Factors: Vanguard LifeStrategy Growth Inv receives a TheStreet.com Investment Rating of B- (Good). The fund currently has a performance rating of C+ (Fair) based on an average return of 5.80% over the last three years and 4.61% over the last three months. Factored into the performance evaluation is an expense ratio of 0.15% (very low).

The fund's risk rating is currently B- (Good). It carries a beta of 1.30, meaning it is expected to move 13.0% for every 10% move in the market. Volatility, as measured by both the semi-deviation and a drawdown factor, is considered low.

This is team managed and currently receives a manager quality ranking of 26 (0=worst, 99=best). If you desire an average level of risk, then this fund may be an option.

Services Offered: Automated phone transactions, payroll deductions, bank draft capabilities, an IRA investment plan, a 401K investment plan, a Keogh investment plan, wire transfers and a systematic withdrawal plan.

Data Date	Investment Rating	Net Assets ($Mil)	NAV	Performance Rating/Pts	Total Return Y-T-D	Risk Rating/Pts
2-17	B-	13,036	30.20	C+ / 5.8	4.61%	B- / 7.5
2016	B-	12,317	28.87	C+ / 6.2	8.33%	B- / 7.5
2015	B-	11,244	27.26	C / 5.5	-1.17%	B- / 7.9
2014	B-	10,774	28.81	C / 5.0	7.17%	B- / 7.9
2013	C	10,218	27.62	C / 4.4	21.20%	C+ / 6.2
2012	C+	7,960	23.30	C+ / 5.9	14.38%	C+ / 6.0

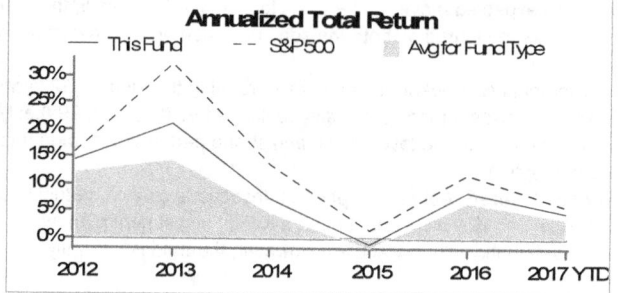

Vanguard LifeStrategy Mod Gro Inv (VSMGX)

B-   **Good**

Fund Family: Vanguard Funds   **Phone:** (800) 662-7447
Address: Vanguard Financial Center, Valley Forge, PA 19482
Fund Type: AA - Asset Allocation

Major Rating Factors: Vanguard LifeStrategy Mod Gro Inv receives a TheStreet.com Investment Rating of B- (Good). The fund currently has a performance rating of C (Fair) based on an average return of 5.21% over the last three years and 3.64% over the last three months. Factored into the performance evaluation is an expense ratio of 0.14% (very low).

The fund's risk rating is currently B (Good). It carries a beta of 0.99, meaning that its performance tracks fairly well with that of the overall stock market. Volatility, as measured by both the semi-deviation and a drawdown factor, is considered low.

This is team managed and currently receives a manager quality ranking of 47 (0=worst, 99=best). If you desire an average level of risk, then this fund may be an option.

Services Offered: Automated phone transactions, payroll deductions, bank draft capabilities, an IRA investment plan, a 401K investment plan, a Keogh investment plan, wire transfers and a systematic withdrawal plan.

Data Date	Investment Rating	Net Assets ($Mil)	NAV	Performance Rating/Pts	Total Return Y-T-D	Risk Rating/Pts
2-17	B-	14,111	25.03	C / 4.4	3.64%	B / 8.5
2016	B+	13,388	24.15	C / 5.5	7.13%	B / 8.5
2015	B-	12,345	23.06	C / 4.5	-0.57%	B / 8.8
2014	C+	11,963	24.08	C- / 3.8	7.08%	B / 8.9
2013	C+	11,143	23.11	C- / 3.0	15.04%	B- / 7.9
2012	B-	8,908	20.55	C / 4.3	11.76%	B- / 7.9

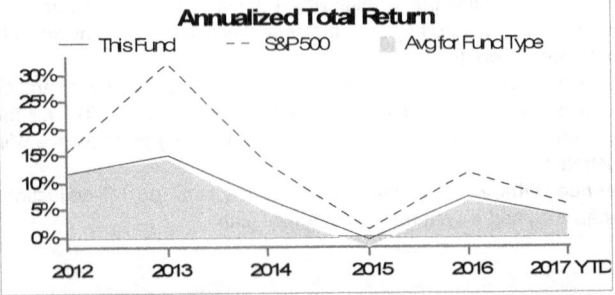

Vanguard PRIMECAP Core Inv (VPCCX)

A+   **Excellent**

Fund Family: Vanguard Funds   **Phone:** (800) 662-7447
Address: Vanguard Financial Center, Valley Forge, PA 19482
Fund Type: GR - Growth

Major Rating Factors: Exceptional performance is the major factor driving the A+ (Excellent) TheStreet.com Investment Rating for Vanguard PRIMECAP Core Inv. The fund currently has a performance rating of A+ (Excellent) based on an average return of 11.62% over the last three years and 7.35% over the last three months. Factored into the performance evaluation is an expense ratio of 0.47% (very low).

The fund's risk rating is currently C+ (Fair). It carries a beta of 1.04, meaning that its performance tracks fairly well with that of the overall stock market. Volatility, as measured by both the semi-deviation and a drawdown factor, is considered low.

Joel P. Fried, Jr. has been running the fund for 13 years and currently receives a manager quality ranking of 78 (0=worst, 99=best). If you desire only a moderate level of risk and strong performance, then this fund is an excellent option.

Services Offered: Automated phone transactions, payroll deductions, bank draft capabilities, an IRA investment plan, a 401K investment plan and a systematic withdrawal plan. However, the fund is currently closed to new investors.

Data Date	Investment Rating	Net Assets ($Mil)	NAV	Performance Rating/Pts	Total Return Y-T-D	Risk Rating/Pts
2-17	A+	9,311	23.81	A+ / 9.8	7.35%	C+ / 6.4
2016	A+	8,623	22.18	A / 9.3	12.35%	C+ / 6.4
2015	A+	7,506	20.82	A+ / 9.6	0.94%	C+ / 6.8
2014	A+	7,328	21.64	A+ / 9.8	19.29%	B- / 7.1
2013	A-	6,168	19.44	B / 8.2	36.14%	C+ / 5.8
2012	B	4,652	14.93	B- / 7.1	14.57%	C+ / 5.6

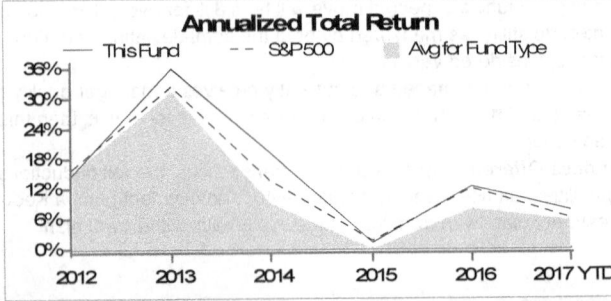

Vanguard PRIMECAP Inv (VPMCX)

A+   **Excellent**

Fund Family: Vanguard Funds   **Phone:** (800) 662-7447
Address: Vanguard Financial Center, Valley Forge, PA 19482
Fund Type: MC - Mid Cap

Major Rating Factors: Exceptional performance is the major factor driving the A+ (Excellent) TheStreet.com Investment Rating for Vanguard PRIMECAP Inv. The fund currently has a performance rating of A+ (Excellent) based on an average return of 11.30% over the last three years and 7.48% over the last three months. Factored into the performance evaluation is an expense ratio of 0.40% (very low).

The fund's risk rating is currently C+ (Fair). It carries a beta of 0.78, meaning the fund's expected move will be 7.8% for every 10% move in the market. Volatility, as measured by both the semi-deviation and a drawdown factor, is considered low.

Theofanis A. Kolokotrones has been running the fund for 32 years and currently receives a manager quality ranking of 92 (0=worst, 99=best). If you desire only a moderate level of risk and strong performance, then this fund is an excellent option.

Services Offered: Automated phone transactions, payroll deductions, bank draft capabilities, an IRA investment plan, a Keogh investment plan, wire transfers and a systematic withdrawal plan. However, the fund is currently closed to new investors.

Data Date	Investment Rating	Net Assets ($Mil)	NAV	Performance Rating/Pts	Total Return Y-T-D	Risk Rating/Pts
2-17	A+	7,851	112.93	A+ / 9.7	7.48%	C+ / 6.1
2016	A	7,427	105.07	A- / 9.1	10.63%	C+ / 6.1
2015	A+	8,334	99.70	A+ / 9.7	2.58%	C+ / 6.6
2014	A+	13,680	102.85	A+ / 9.8	18.72%	B- / 7.0
2013	A+	13,537	92.33	A- / 9.1	39.73%	C / 5.5
2012	C+	13,239	69.49	C+ / 6.2	15.27%	C / 5.4

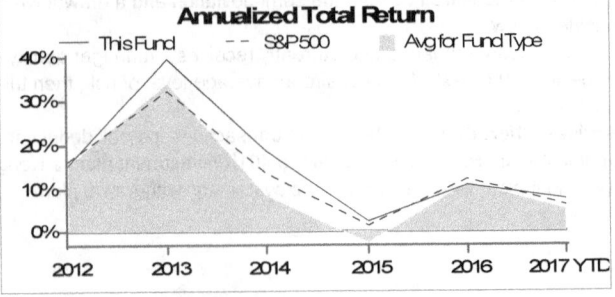

Vanguard Selected Value Inv (VASVX)

A-   Excellent

Fund Family: Vanguard Funds   **Phone:** (800) 662-7447
Address: Vanguard Financial Center, Valley Forge, PA 19482
Fund Type: MC - Mid Cap

Major Rating Factors: Exceptional performance is the major factor driving the A- (Excellent) TheStreet.com Investment Rating for Vanguard Selected Value Inv. The fund currently has a performance rating of A- (Excellent) based on an average return of 7.53% over the last three years and 5.39% over the last three months. Factored into the performance evaluation is an expense ratio of 0.39% (very low).

The fund's risk rating is currently C+ (Fair). It carries a beta of 0.96, meaning that its performance tracks fairly well with that of the overall stock market. Volatility, as measured by both the semi-deviation and a drawdown factor, is considered low.

James P. Barrow has been running the fund for 18 years and currently receives a manager quality ranking of 55 (0=worst, 99=best). If you desire only a moderate level of risk and strong performance, then this fund is an excellent option.

Services Offered: Automated phone transactions, payroll deductions, an IRA investment plan, a 401K investment plan, a Keogh investment plan and a systematic withdrawal plan.

Data Date	Investment Rating	Net Assets ($Mil)	NAV	Perfor-mance Rating/Pts	Total Return Y-T-D	Risk Rating/Pts
2-17	A-	10,109	30.33	A- / 9.0	5.39%	C+ / 5.7
2016	B+	9,616	28.78	B+ / 8.9	16.34%	C+ / 5.7
2015	B+	9,669	25.85	B / 7.7	-3.80%	C+ / 6.9
2014	B+	10,192	28.38	B / 7.8	6.36%	B- / 7.2
2013	A+	7,923	28.20	A / 9.5	42.04%	C+ / 5.6
2012	A	4,398	20.98	B+ / 8.5	15.25%	C / 5.3

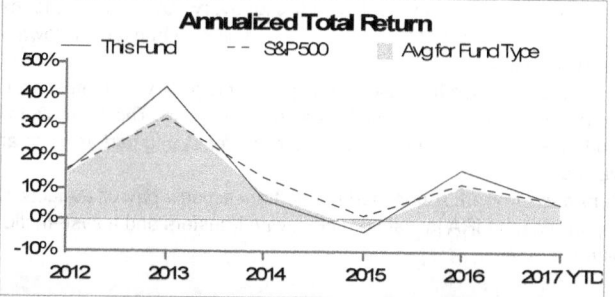
Annualized Total Return

Vanguard STAR Fund (VGSTX)

B-   Good

Fund Family: Vanguard Funds   **Phone:** (800) 662-7447
Address: Vanguard Financial Center, Valley Forge, PA 19482
Fund Type: GI - Growth and Income

Major Rating Factors: Vanguard STAR Fund receives a TheStreet.com Investment Rating of B- (Good). The fund currently has a performance rating of C (Fair) based on an average return of 5.23% over the last three years and 4.27% over the last three months. Factored into the performance evaluation is an expense ratio of 0.32% (very low).

The fund's risk rating is currently B- (Good). It carries a beta of 0.66, meaning the fund's expected move will be 6.6% for every 10% move in the market. Volatility, as measured by both the semi-deviation and a drawdown factor, is considered low.

This is team managed and currently receives a manager quality ranking of 54 (0=worst, 99=best). If you desire an average level of risk, then this fund may be an option.

Services Offered: Automated phone transactions, payroll deductions, an IRA investment plan, a 401K investment plan, a Keogh investment plan, wire transfers and a systematic withdrawal plan.

Data Date	Investment Rating	Net Assets ($Mil)	NAV	Perfor-mance Rating/Pts	Total Return Y-T-D	Risk Rating/Pts
2-17	B-	19,396	24.69	C / 4.7	4.27%	B- / 7.8
2016	B-	18,742	23.68	C / 5.5	6.55%	B- / 7.9
2015	B	18,806	23.29	C / 5.2	-0.15%	B / 8.4
2014	B-	18,749	24.62	C / 4.5	7.34%	B / 8.6
2013	C+	17,625	23.89	C- / 4.0	17.80%	B- / 7.8
2012	B-	15,029	20.80	C+ / 5.7	13.79%	B- / 7.8

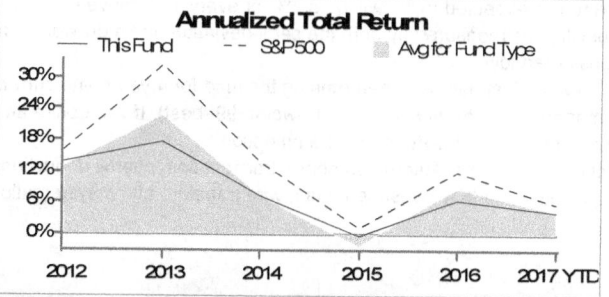
Annualized Total Return

Vanguard Strategic Equity Inv (VSEQX)

A-   Excellent

Fund Family: Vanguard Funds   **Phone:** (800) 662-7447
Address: Vanguard Financial Center, Valley Forge, PA 19482
Fund Type: SC - Small Cap

Major Rating Factors: Exceptional performance is the major factor driving the A- (Excellent) TheStreet.com Investment Rating for Vanguard Strategic Equity Inv. The fund currently has a performance rating of A+ (Excellent) based on an average return of 9.69% over the last three years and 3.74% over the last three months. Factored into the performance evaluation is an expense ratio of 0.21% (very low).

The fund's risk rating is currently C (Fair). It carries a beta of 0.76, meaning the fund's expected move will be 7.6% for every 10% move in the market. Volatility, as measured by both the semi-deviation and a drawdown factor, is considered average.

James P. Stetler has been running the fund for 5 years and currently receives a manager quality ranking of 94 (0=worst, 99=best). If you desire an average level of risk and strong performance, then this fund is a good option.

Services Offered: Automated phone transactions, payroll deductions, bank draft capabilities, an IRA investment plan, a Keogh investment plan, wire transfers and a systematic withdrawal plan.

Data Date	Investment Rating	Net Assets ($Mil)	NAV	Perfor-mance Rating/Pts	Total Return Y-T-D	Risk Rating/Pts
2-17	A-	7,060	33.58	A+ / 9.6	3.74%	C / 5.0
2016	A-	6,621	32.37	A+ / 9.7	17.92%	C / 5.1
2015	A-	6,151	28.30	A- / 9.1	-1.41%	C+ / 5.9
2014	A+	5,781	32.18	A+ / 9.8	13.68%	C+ / 6.5
2013	A	4,771	30.00	A+ / 9.7	41.54%	C / 4.5
2012	A-	3,288	21.45	A / 9.4	18.90%	C- / 4.1

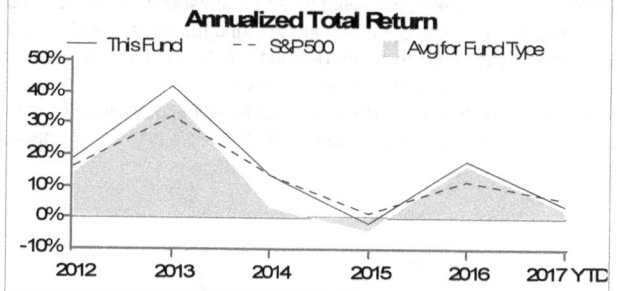
Annualized Total Return

Vanguard Target Retirement 2010 Inv (VTENX)   C   Fair

Fund Family: Vanguard Funds   **Phone:** (800) 662-7447
Address: Vanguard Financial Center, Valley Forge, PA 19482
Fund Type: AA - Asset Allocation

Major Rating Factors: Disappointing performance is the major factor driving the C (Fair) TheStreet.com Investment Rating for Vanguard Target Retirement 2010 Inv. The fund currently has a performance rating of D+ (Weak) based on an average return of 3.83% over the last three years and 2.17% over the last three months. Factored into the performance evaluation is an expense ratio of 0.13% (very low).

The fund's risk rating is currently B (Good). It carries a beta of 0.60, meaning the fund's expected move will be 6.0% for every 10% move in the market. Volatility, as measured by both the semi-deviation and a drawdown factor, is considered low.

Walter Nejman has been running the fund for 4 years and currently receives a manager quality ranking of 67 (0=worst, 99=best). This fund offers only a moderate level of risk but investors looking for strong performance are still waiting.

Services Offered: Automated phone transactions, payroll deductions, bank draft capabilities, an IRA investment plan, wire transfers and a systematic withdrawal plan.

Data Date	Investment Rating	Net Assets ($Mil)	NAV	Perfor- mance Rating/Pts	Total Return Y-T-D	Risk Rating/Pts
2-17	C	5,597	25.89	D+ / 2.5	2.17%	B / 8.9
2016	B-	5,624	25.34	C- / 4.1	5.22%	B+ / 9.0
2015	C+	6,025	24.88	C- / 3.3	-0.20%	B / 8.9
2014	C+	7,011	26.32	D+ / 2.6	5.93%	B+ / 9.3
2013	C+	6,851	25.60	D / 2.1	9.10%	B+ / 9.2
2012	B+	6,435	24.13	C- / 3.6	10.12%	B+ / 9.2

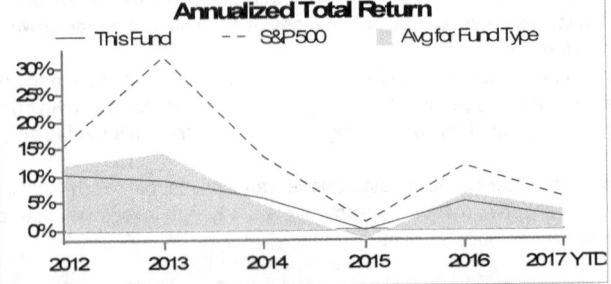

Vanguard Target Retirement 2015 Inv (VTXVX)   C+   Fair

Fund Family: Vanguard Funds   **Phone:** (800) 662-7447
Address: Vanguard Financial Center, Valley Forge, PA 19482
Fund Type: AA - Asset Allocation

Major Rating Factors: Middle of the road best describes Vanguard Target Retirement 2015 Inv whose TheStreet.com Investment Rating is currently a C+ (Fair). The fund currently has a performance rating of C- (Fair) based on an average return of 4.49% over the last three years and 2.89% over the last three months. Factored into the performance evaluation is an expense ratio of 0.14% (very low).

The fund's risk rating is currently B (Good). It carries a beta of 0.81, meaning the fund's expected move will be 8.1% for every 10% move in the market. Volatility, as measured by both the semi-deviation and a drawdown factor, is considered low.

Walter Nejman has been running the fund for 4 years and currently receives a manager quality ranking of 55 (0=worst, 99=best). If you desire an average level of risk, then this fund may be an option.

Services Offered: Automated phone transactions, payroll deductions, bank draft capabilities, an IRA investment plan, wire transfers and a systematic withdrawal plan.

Data Date	Investment Rating	Net Assets ($Mil)	NAV	Perfor- mance Rating/Pts	Total Return Y-T-D	Risk Rating/Pts
2-17	C+	17,182	14.93	C- / 3.4	2.89%	B / 8.3
2016	B-	17,024	14.51	C / 4.8	6.16%	B / 8.4
2015	C+	18,752	14.23	C- / 4.0	-0.46%	B / 8.5
2014	C+	21,957	15.29	C- / 3.4	6.55%	B+ / 9.1
2013	C+	20,300	14.77	D+ / 2.7	13.00%	B / 8.5
2012	B	17,623	13.38	C- / 4.2	11.37%	B / 8.4

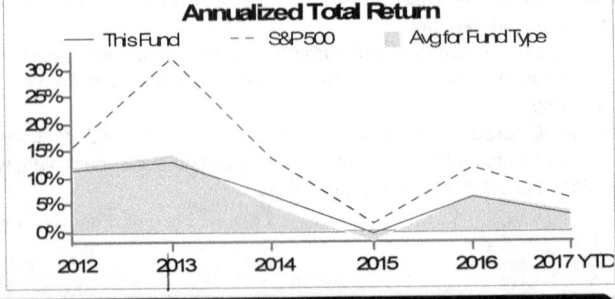

Vanguard Target Retirement 2025 Inv (VTTVX)   B-   Good

Fund Family: Vanguard Funds   **Phone:** (800) 662-7447
Address: Vanguard Financial Center, Valley Forge, PA 19482
Fund Type: AA - Asset Allocation

Major Rating Factors: Vanguard Target Retirement 2025 Inv receives a TheStreet.com Investment Rating of B- (Good). The fund currently has a performance rating of C (Fair) based on an average return of 5.34% over the last three years and 3.85% over the last three months. Factored into the performance evaluation is an expense ratio of 0.14% (very low).

The fund's risk rating is currently B (Good). It carries a beta of 1.10, meaning it is expected to move 11.0% for every 10% move in the market. Volatility, as measured by both the semi-deviation and a drawdown factor, is considered low.

Walter Nejman has been running the fund for 4 years and currently receives a manager quality ranking of 38 (0=worst, 99=best). If you desire an average level of risk, then this fund may be an option.

Services Offered: Automated phone transactions, payroll deductions, bank draft capabilities, an IRA investment plan, wire transfers and a systematic withdrawal plan.

Data Date	Investment Rating	Net Assets ($Mil)	NAV	Perfor- mance Rating/Pts	Total Return Y-T-D	Risk Rating/Pts
2-17	B-	33,669	16.98	C / 4.8	3.85%	B / 8.0
2016	B	32,159	16.35	C+ / 5.8	7.48%	B / 8.1
2015	B-	30,613	15.62	C / 5.0	-0.85%	B / 8.5
2014	C+	32,318	16.53	C / 4.4	7.16%	B / 8.4
2013	C+	28,021	15.75	C- / 3.8	18.14%	B- / 7.4
2012	B-	21,269	13.59	C / 5.4	13.29%	B- / 7.2

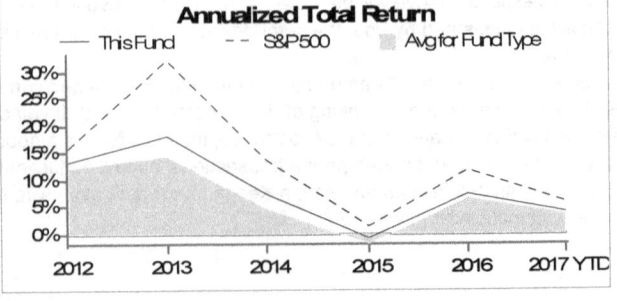

Vanguard Target Retirement 2030 (VTHRX)   B   Good

Fund Family: Vanguard Funds   **Phone:** (800) 662-7447
Address: Vanguard Financial Center, Valley Forge, PA 19482
Fund Type: AA - Asset Allocation
Major Rating Factors: Vanguard Target Retirement 2030 receives a
TheStreet.com Investment Rating of B (Good). The fund currently has a
performance rating of C (Fair) based on an average return of 5.56% over the last
three years and 4.25% over the last three months. Factored into the
performance evaluation is an expense ratio of 0.15% (very low).

The fund's risk rating is currently B- (Good). It carries a beta of 1.21,
meaning it is expected to move 12.1% for every 10% move in the market.
Volatility, as measured by both the semi-deviation and a drawdown factor, is
considered low.

Walter Nejman has been running the fund for 4 years and currently receives
a manager quality ranking of 31 (0=worst, 99=best). If you desire an average
level of risk, then this fund may be an option.

Services Offered: Automated phone transactions, payroll deductions, bank draft
capabilities, an IRA investment plan, wire transfers and a systematic withdrawal
plan.

Data Date	Investment Rating	Net Assets ($Mil)	NAV	Perfor- mance Rating/Pts	Total Return Y-T-D	Risk Rating/Pts
2-17	B	27,346	30.44	C / 5.3	4.25%	B- / 7.8
2016	B-	25,676	29.20	C+ / 6.0	7.85%	B- / 7.9
2015	B	23,302	27.72	C / 5.4	-1.03%	B / 8.3
2014	B-	23,824	29.04	C / 4.9	7.19%	B / 8.1
2013	C+	19,778	27.64	C / 4.4	20.49%	C+ / 6.9
2012	C+	13,816	23.38	C+ / 5.9	14.24%	C+ / 6.6

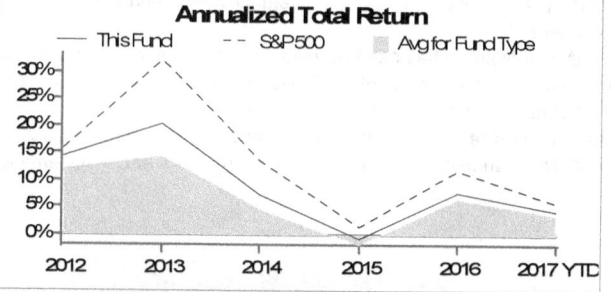

Vanguard Target Retirement 2035 Inv (VTTHX)   B-   Good

Fund Family: Vanguard Funds   **Phone:** (800) 662-7447
Address: Vanguard Financial Center, Valley Forge, PA 19482
Fund Type: AA - Asset Allocation
Major Rating Factors: Vanguard Target Retirement 2035 Inv receives a
TheStreet.com Investment Rating of B- (Good). The fund currently has a
performance rating of C+ (Fair) based on an average return of 5.77% over the
last three years and 4.57% over the last three months. Factored into the
performance evaluation is an expense ratio of 0.15% (very low).

The fund's risk rating is currently B- (Good). It carries a beta of 1.33,
meaning it is expected to move 13.3% for every 10% move in the market.
Volatility, as measured by both the semi-deviation and a drawdown factor, is
considered low.

Walter Nejman has been running the fund for 4 years and currently receives
a manager quality ranking of 24 (0=worst, 99=best). If you desire an average
level of risk, then this fund may be an option.

Services Offered: Automated phone transactions, payroll deductions, bank draft
capabilities, an IRA investment plan, wire transfers and a systematic withdrawal
plan.

Data Date	Investment Rating	Net Assets ($Mil)	NAV	Perfor- mance Rating/Pts	Total Return Y-T-D	Risk Rating/Pts
2-17	B-	26,504	18.55	C+ / 5.8	4.57%	B- / 7.4
2016	B-	25,030	17.74	C+ / 6.2	8.26%	B- / 7.4
2015	B	23,415	16.84	C+ / 5.7	-1.26%	B- / 7.9
2014	B-	24,514	17.84	C / 5.4	7.28%	B- / 7.7
2013	C+	21,131	16.98	C / 4.9	22.82%	C+ / 6.3
2012	C+	15,218	14.09	C+ / 6.4	15.16%	C+ / 6.0

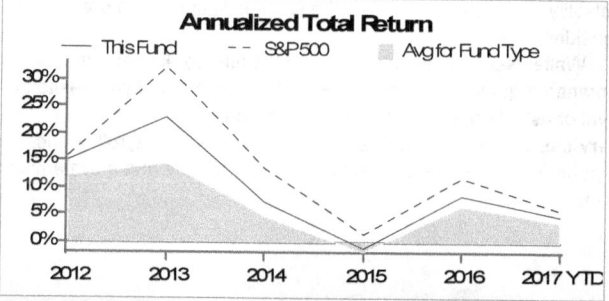

Vanguard Target Retirement 2040 Inv (VFORX)   B-   Good

Fund Family: Vanguard Funds   **Phone:** (800) 662-7447
Address: Vanguard Financial Center, Valley Forge, PA 19482
Fund Type: AA - Asset Allocation
Major Rating Factors: Vanguard Target Retirement 2040 Inv receives a
TheStreet.com Investment Rating of B- (Good). The fund currently has a
performance rating of C+ (Fair) based on an average return of 5.93% over the
last three years and 4.97% over the last three months. Factored into the
performance evaluation is an expense ratio of 0.16% (very low).

The fund's risk rating is currently B- (Good). It carries a beta of 1.44,
meaning it is expected to move 14.4% for every 10% move in the market.
Volatility, as measured by both the semi-deviation and a drawdown factor, is
considered low.

Walter Nejman has been running the fund for 4 years and currently receives
a manager quality ranking of 18 (0=worst, 99=best). If you desire an average
level of risk, then this fund may be an option.

Services Offered: Automated phone transactions, payroll deductions, bank draft
capabilities, an IRA investment plan, wire transfers and a systematic withdrawal
plan.

Data Date	Investment Rating	Net Assets ($Mil)	NAV	Perfor- mance Rating/Pts	Total Return Y-T-D	Risk Rating/Pts
2-17	B-	19,359	31.71	C+ / 6.3	4.97%	B- / 7.1
2016	B-	17,955	30.21	C+ / 6.4	8.73%	B- / 7.2
2015	B-	16,180	28.45	C+ / 5.9	-1.59%	B- / 7.6
2014	B-	16,482	29.76	C+ / 5.6	7.15%	B- / 7.4
2013	C+	13,470	28.32	C / 5.3	24.37%	C+ / 6.1
2012	C+	8,797	23.18	C+ / 6.6	15.56%	C+ / 5.8

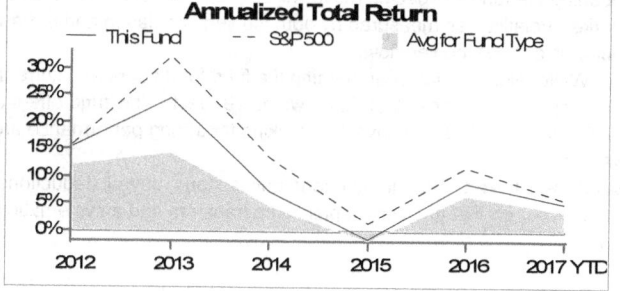

Vanguard Target Retirement 2045 Inv (VTIVX)

B-   **Good**

Fund Family: Vanguard Funds   **Phone:** (800) 662-7447
Address: Vanguard Financial Center, Valley Forge, PA 19482
Fund Type: AA - Asset Allocation

Major Rating Factors: Vanguard Target Retirement 2045 Inv receives a TheStreet.com Investment Rating of B- (Good). The fund currently has a performance rating of C+ (Fair) based on an average return of 6.04% over the last three years and 5.13% over the last three months. Factored into the performance evaluation is an expense ratio of 0.16% (very low).

The fund's risk rating is currently B- (Good). It carries a beta of 1.45, meaning it is expected to move 14.5% for every 10% move in the market. Volatility, as measured by both the semi-deviation and a drawdown factor, is considered low.

Walter Nejman has been running the fund for 4 years and currently receives a manager quality ranking of 18 (0=worst, 99=best). If you desire an average level of risk, then this fund may be an option.

Services Offered: Automated phone transactions, payroll deductions, bank draft capabilities, an IRA investment plan, wire transfers and a systematic withdrawal plan.

Data Date	Investment Rating	Net Assets ($Mil)	NAV	Perfor-mance Rating/Pts	Total Return Y-T-D	Risk Rating/Pts
2-17	B-	17,666	19.86	C+ / 6.5	5.13%	B- / 7.0
2016	B-	16,483	18.89	C+ / 6.5	8.87%	B- / 7.0
2015	B-	14,851	17.78	C+ / 5.9	-1.57%	B- / 7.5
2014	B-	15,036	18.65	C+ / 5.6	7.14%	B- / 7.4
2013	C+	12,766	17.76	C / 5.3	24.37%	C+ / 6.1
2012	C+	8,758	14.55	C+ / 6.6	15.58%	C+ / 5.8

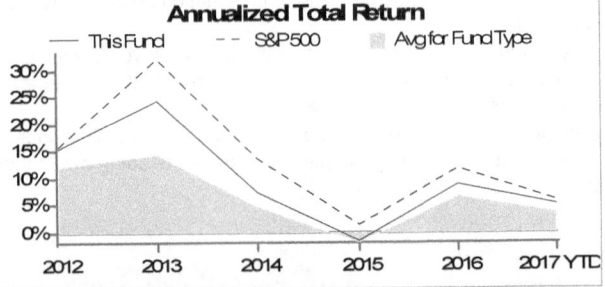

Vanguard Target Retirement 2050 Inv (VFIFX)

B-   **Good**

Fund Family: Vanguard Funds   **Phone:** (800) 662-7447
Address: Vanguard Financial Center, Valley Forge, PA 19482
Fund Type: AA - Asset Allocation

Major Rating Factors: Vanguard Target Retirement 2050 Inv receives a TheStreet.com Investment Rating of B- (Good). The fund currently has a performance rating of C+ (Fair) based on an average return of 6.03% over the last three years and 5.10% over the last three months. Factored into the performance evaluation is an expense ratio of 0.16% (very low).

The fund's risk rating is currently B- (Good). It carries a beta of 1.45, meaning it is expected to move 14.5% for every 10% move in the market. Volatility, as measured by both the semi-deviation and a drawdown factor, is considered low.

Walter Nejman has been running the fund for 4 years and currently receives a manager quality ranking of 18 (0=worst, 99=best). If you desire an average level of risk, then this fund may be an option.

Services Offered: Automated phone transactions, payroll deductions, bank draft capabilities, an IRA investment plan, wire transfers and a systematic withdrawal plan.

Data Date	Investment Rating	Net Assets ($Mil)	NAV	Perfor-mance Rating/Pts	Total Return Y-T-D	Risk Rating/Pts
2-17	B-	11,140	31.94	C+ / 6.5	5.10%	B- / 7.1
2016	B-	10,165	30.39	C+ / 6.5	8.85%	B- / 7.1
2015	B-	8,317	28.49	C+ / 5.9	-1.58%	B- / 7.6
2014	B-	7,683	29.62	C+ / 5.6	7.19%	B- / 7.4
2013	C+	6,052	28.19	C / 5.2	24.34%	C+ / 6.1
2012	C+	3,820	23.09	C+ / 6.6	15.58%	C+ / 5.8

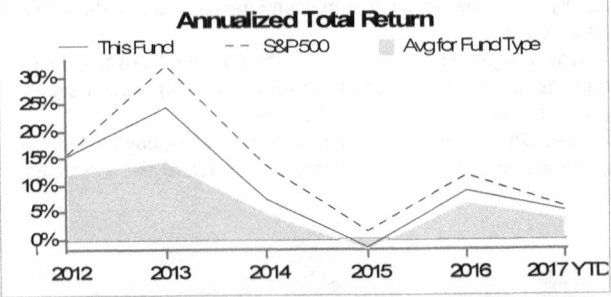

Vanguard Target Retirement Income (VTINX)

C+   **Fair**

Fund Family: Vanguard Funds   **Phone:** (800) 662-7447
Address: Vanguard Financial Center, Valley Forge, PA 19482
Fund Type: AA - Asset Allocation

Major Rating Factors: Disappointing performance is the major factor driving the C+ (Fair) TheStreet.com Investment Rating for Vanguard Target Retirement Income. The fund currently has a performance rating of D+ (Weak) based on an average return of 3.70% over the last three years and 2.11% over the last three months. Factored into the performance evaluation is an expense ratio of 0.13% (very low).

The fund's risk rating is currently B+ (Good). It carries a beta of 0.52, meaning the fund's expected move will be 5.2% for every 10% move in the market. Volatility, as measured by both the semi-deviation and a drawdown factor, is considered very low.

Walter Nejman has been running the fund for 4 years and currently receives a manager quality ranking of 72 (0=worst, 99=best). This fund offers only a moderate level of risk but investors looking for strong performance are still waiting.

Services Offered: Automated phone transactions, payroll deductions, bank draft capabilities, an IRA investment plan, wire transfers and a systematic withdrawal plan.

Data Date	Investment Rating	Net Assets ($Mil)	NAV	Perfor-mance Rating/Pts	Total Return Y-T-D	Risk Rating/Pts
2-17	C+	10,729	13.08	D+ / 2.4	2.11%	B+ / 9.5
2016	B	10,592	12.81	C- / 4.0	5.25%	B+ / 9.6
2015	C+	10,580	12.45	D+ / 2.6	-0.17%	B+ / 9.5
2014	C	11,379	12.91	D / 1.9	5.58%	B+ / 9.6
2013	C+	10,338	12.50	D- / 1.5	5.87%	B+ / 9.6
2012	B-	9,711	12.19	D+ / 2.4	8.23%	B+ / 9.7

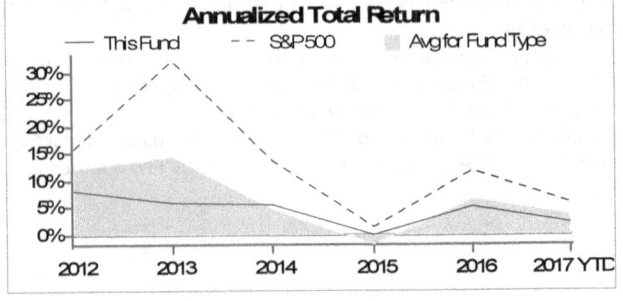

Vanguard Tax-Managed Cap Appr Adm (VTCLX)

A+   Excellent

Fund Family: Vanguard Funds   **Phone:** (800) 662-7447
Address: Vanguard Financial Center, Valley Forge, PA 19482
Fund Type: GR - Growth

Major Rating Factors: Exceptional performance is the major factor driving the A+ (Excellent) TheStreet.com Investment Rating for Vanguard Tax-Managed Cap Appr Adm. The fund currently has a performance rating of A (Excellent) based on an average return of 10.19% over the last three years and 6.02% over the last three months. Factored into the performance evaluation is an expense ratio of 0.11% (very low).

The fund's risk rating is currently C+ (Fair). It carries a beta of 1.02, meaning that its performance tracks fairly well with that of the overall stock market. Volatility, as measured by both the semi-deviation and a drawdown factor, is considered low.

Donald M. Butler has been running the fund for 1 year and currently receives a manager quality ranking of 67 (0=worst, 99=best). If you desire only a moderate level of risk and strong performance, then this fund is an excellent option.

Services Offered: Automated phone transactions, payroll deductions, bank draft capabilities, wire transfers and a systematic withdrawal plan.

Data Date	Investment Rating	Net Assets ($Mil)	NAV	Performance Rating/Pts	Total Return Y-T-D	Risk Rating/Pts
2-17	A+	7,234	120.95	A / 9.3	6.02%	C+ / 6.9
2016	A+	6,793	114.08	B+ / 8.8	12.01%	C+ / 6.9
2015	A+	6,062	103.75	A- / 9.1	1.68%	B- / 7.0
2014	A+	5,760	103.82	B+ / 8.9	12.52%	B- / 7.2
2013	A+	5,040	93.70	B+ / 8.5	33.67%	B- / 7.6
2012	A	3,702	71.17	B / 7.8	16.35%	C+ / 6.2

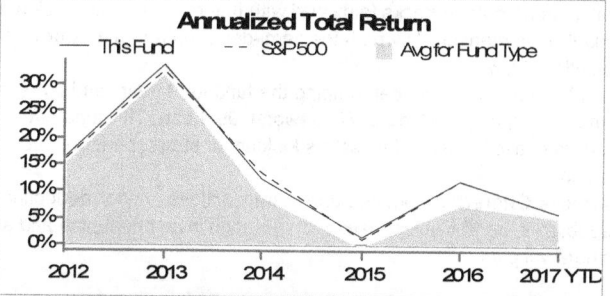

Vanguard Tgt Retirement 2020 Inv (VTWNX)

B-   Good

Fund Family: Vanguard Funds   **Phone:** (800) 662-7447
Address: Vanguard Financial Center, Valley Forge, PA 19482
Fund Type: AA - Asset Allocation

Major Rating Factors: Vanguard Tgt Retirement 2020 Inv receives a TheStreet.com Investment Rating of B- (Good). The fund currently has a performance rating of C- (Fair) based on an average return of 5.05% over the last three years and 3.43% over the last three months. Factored into the performance evaluation is an expense ratio of 0.14% (very low).

The fund's risk rating is currently B (Good). It carries a beta of 0.98, meaning that its performance tracks fairly well with that of the overall stock market. Volatility, as measured by both the semi-deviation and a drawdown factor, is considered low.

Walter Nejman has been running the fund for 4 years and currently receives a manager quality ranking of 46 (0=worst, 99=best). If you desire an average level of risk, then this fund may be an option.

Services Offered: Automated phone transactions, payroll deductions, bank draft capabilities, an IRA investment plan, wire transfers and a systematic withdrawal plan.

Data Date	Investment Rating	Net Assets ($Mil)	NAV	Performance Rating/Pts	Total Return Y-T-D	Risk Rating/Pts
2-17	B-	29,023	29.23	C- / 4.2	3.43%	B / 8.5
2016	B	27,772	28.26	C / 5.4	6.95%	B / 8.5
2015	B-	26,986	27.15	C / 4.6	-0.68%	B / 8.8
2014	C+	28,525	28.46	C- / 4.0	7.12%	B / 8.8
2013	C+	23,878	27.11	C- / 3.3	15.85%	B- / 7.9
2012	B-	17,324	23.83	C / 4.8	12.35%	B- / 7.8

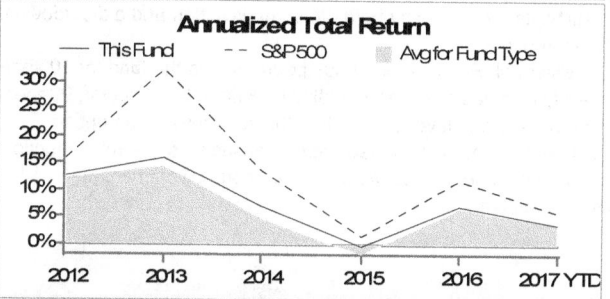

Vanguard Tot Stk Mkt Idx Inv (VTSMX)

A+   Excellent

Fund Family: Vanguard Funds   **Phone:** (800) 662-7447
Address: Vanguard Financial Center, Valley Forge, PA 19482
Fund Type: GR - Growth

Major Rating Factors: Exceptional performance is the major factor driving the A+ (Excellent) TheStreet.com Investment Rating for Vanguard Tot Stk Mkt Idx Inv. The fund currently has a performance rating of A- (Excellent) based on an average return of 9.74% over the last three years and 5.69% over the last three months. Factored into the performance evaluation is an expense ratio of 0.16% (very low).

The fund's risk rating is currently C+ (Fair). It carries a beta of 1.02, meaning that its performance tracks fairly well with that of the overall stock market. Volatility, as measured by both the semi-deviation and a drawdown factor, is considered low.

Gerard C. O'Reilly has been running the fund for 23 years and currently receives a manager quality ranking of 62 (0=worst, 99=best). If you desire only a moderate level of risk and strong performance, then this fund is an excellent option.

Services Offered: Automated phone transactions, payroll deductions, an IRA investment plan, a 401K investment plan, a Keogh investment plan, wire transfers and a systematic withdrawal plan.

Data Date	Investment Rating	Net Assets ($Mil)	NAV	Performance Rating/Pts	Total Return Y-T-D	Risk Rating/Pts
2-17	A+	110,696	59.25	A- / 9.1	5.69%	C+ / 6.8
2016	A	103,932	56.06	B+ / 8.7	12.53%	C+ / 6.8
2015	A	98,933	50.78	B+ / 8.8	0.29%	B- / 7.0
2014	A+	117,966	51.58	B+ / 8.8	12.43%	B / 8.0
2013	A-	105,008	46.67	B+ / 8.3	33.35%	C+ / 5.7
2012	B+	78,936	35.64	B / 7.9	16.25%	C / 5.3

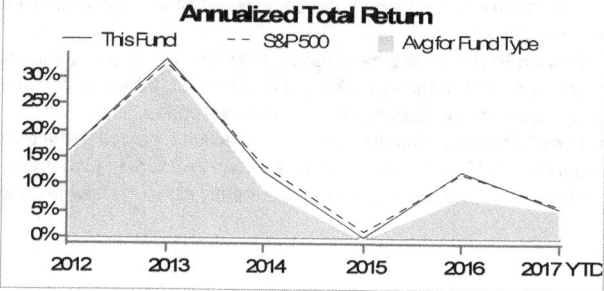

Vanguard Total Intl Stock Index Inv (VGTSX)

D+ **Weak**

Fund Family: Vanguard Funds   **Phone:** (800) 662-7447
Address: Vanguard Financial Center, Valley Forge, PA 19482
Fund Type: FO - Foreign

Major Rating Factors: Disappointing performance is the major factor driving the D+ (Weak) TheStreet.com Investment Rating for Vanguard Total Intl Stock Index Inv. The fund currently has a performance rating of D+ (Weak) based on an average return of 0.23% over the last three years and 5.43% over the last three months. Factored into the performance evaluation is an expense ratio of 0.19% (very low).

The fund's risk rating is currently C+ (Fair). It carries a beta of 0.91, meaning that its performance tracks fairly well with that of the overall stock market. Volatility, as measured by both the semi-deviation and a drawdown factor, is considered low.

Michael Perre has been running the fund for 9 years and currently receives a manager quality ranking of 77 (0=worst, 99=best). This fund offers only a moderate level of risk but investors looking for strong performance are still waiting.

Services Offered: Automated phone transactions, payroll deductions, bank draft capabilities, an IRA investment plan, a Keogh investment plan and a systematic withdrawal plan.

Data Date	Investment Rating	Net Assets ($Mil)	NAV	Performance Rating/Pts	Total Return Y-T-D	Risk Rating/Pts
2-17	D+	97,542	15.53	D+ / 2.7	5.43%	C+ / 5.8
2016	D	90,763	14.73	D / 1.6	4.65%	C+ / 5.8
2015	D-	75,292	14.49	D- / 1.3	-4.37%	C+ / 6.1
2014	D-	50,966	15.55	D / 1.8	-4.24%	C+ / 5.8
2013	D-	46,892	16.75	D / 1.8	15.04%	C- / 3.9
2012	D	37,659	14.98	C- / 4.0	18.14%	C- / 3.7

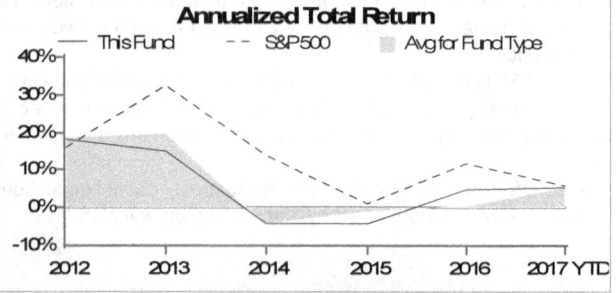
Annualized Total Return

Vanguard Wellesley Income Inv (VWINX)

B- **Good**

Fund Family: Vanguard Funds   **Phone:** (800) 662-7447
Address: Vanguard Financial Center, Valley Forge, PA 19482
Fund Type: AA - Asset Allocation

Major Rating Factors: Vanguard Wellesley Income Inv receives a TheStreet.com Investment Rating of B- (Good). The fund currently has a performance rating of C- (Fair) based on an average return of 5.95% over the last three years and 2.24% over the last three months. Factored into the performance evaluation is an expense ratio of 0.23% (very low).

The fund's risk rating is currently B (Good). It carries a beta of 0.61, meaning the fund's expected move will be 6.1% for every 10% move in the market. Volatility, as measured by both the semi-deviation and a drawdown factor, is considered low.

William M. Reckmeyer, III has been running the fund for 10 years and currently receives a manager quality ranking of 83 (0=worst, 99=best). If you desire an average level of risk, then this fund may be an option.

Services Offered: Automated phone transactions, payroll deductions, bank draft capabilities, an IRA investment plan, a Keogh investment plan and a systematic withdrawal plan.

Data Date	Investment Rating	Net Assets ($Mil)	NAV	Performance Rating/Pts	Total Return Y-T-D	Risk Rating/Pts
2-17	B-	14,240	26.04	C- / 3.8	2.24%	B / 8.8
2016	B	13,936	25.47	C+ / 6.1	8.08%	B / 8.8
2015	B-	12,056	24.52	C / 4.3	1.28%	B / 8.7
2014	C+	12,324	25.57	C- / 3.1	8.07%	B+ / 9.0
2013	C+	11,363	24.85	D+ / 2.5	9.19%	B+ / 9.0
2012	B+	11,648	24.11	C+ / 5.8	10.06%	B+ / 9.3

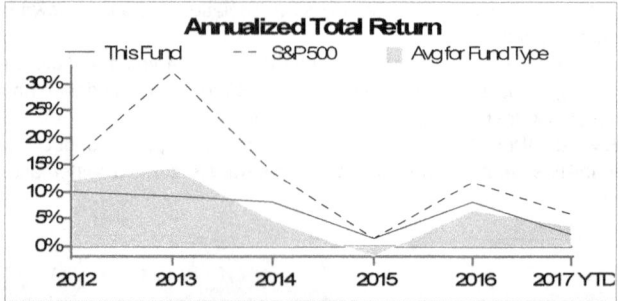
Annualized Total Return

Vanguard Wellington Inv (VWELX)

B- **Good**

Fund Family: Vanguard Funds   **Phone:** (800) 662-7447
Address: Vanguard Financial Center, Valley Forge, PA 19482
Fund Type: BA - Balanced

Major Rating Factors: Vanguard Wellington Inv receives a TheStreet.com Investment Rating of B- (Good). The fund currently has a performance rating of C+ (Fair) based on an average return of 7.61% over the last three years and 3.61% over the last three months. Factored into the performance evaluation is an expense ratio of 0.26% (very low).

The fund's risk rating is currently B- (Good). It carries a beta of 1.10, meaning it is expected to move 11.0% for every 10% move in the market. Volatility, as measured by both the semi-deviation and a drawdown factor, is considered low.

Edward P. Bousa has been running the fund for 15 years and currently receives a manager quality ranking of 67 (0=worst, 99=best). If you desire an average level of risk, then this fund may be an option.

Services Offered: Automated phone transactions, payroll deductions, bank draft capabilities, an IRA investment plan, a Keogh investment plan and a systematic withdrawal plan. However, the fund is currently closed to new investors.

Data Date	Investment Rating	Net Assets ($Mil)	NAV	Performance Rating/Pts	Total Return Y-T-D	Risk Rating/Pts
2-17	B-	19,569	40.47	C+ / 6.8	3.61%	B- / 7.6
2016	A	19,254	39.06	B / 7.7	11.01%	B- / 7.7
2015	B-	19,849	36.79	C+ / 6.3	0.06%	B- / 7.8
2014	B	23,377	39.15	C / 5.2	9.82%	B / 8.3
2013	B-	26,920	37.94	C / 4.5	19.66%	B- / 7.6
2012	B-	26,746	33.84	C / 5.2	12.57%	B- / 7.7

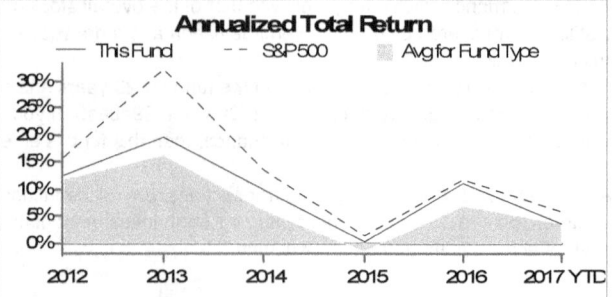
Annualized Total Return

Vanguard Windsor-I Inv (VWNDX)

B+   **Good**

Fund Family: Vanguard Funds **Phone:** (800) 662-7447
Address: Vanguard Financial Center, Valley Forge, PA 19482
Fund Type: MC - Mid Cap

Major Rating Factors: Exceptional performance is the major factor driving the B+ (Good) TheStreet.com Investment Rating for Vanguard Windsor-I Inv. The fund currently has a performance rating of A- (Excellent) based on an average return of 7.92% over the last three years and 5.60% over the last three months. Factored into the performance evaluation is an expense ratio of 0.39% (very low).

The fund's risk rating is currently C (Fair). It carries a beta of 0.95, meaning that its performance tracks fairly well with that of the overall stock market. Volatility, as measured by both the semi-deviation and a drawdown factor, is considered average.

James N. Mordy has been running the fund for 9 years and currently receives a manager quality ranking of 60 (0=worst, 99=best). If you desire an average level of risk and strong performance, then this fund is a good option.

Services Offered: Automated phone transactions, payroll deductions, an IRA investment plan, a Keogh investment plan and a systematic withdrawal plan.

Data Date	Investment Rating	Net Assets ($Mil)	NAV	Perfor-mance Rating/Pts	Total Return Y-T-D	Risk Rating/Pts
2-17	B+	5,283	21.68	A- / 9.0	5.60%	C / 5.2
2016	B-	5,089	20.53	B / 8.0	12.49%	C / 5.3
2015	B+	5,394	19.15	B / 8.0	-3.32%	C+ / 6.3
2014	A+	5,956	21.46	A / 9.5	11.82%	C+ / 6.9
2013	B+	7,226	20.34	B+ / 8.6	36.08%	C / 5.1
2012	A-	6,638	15.10	B+ / 8.6	20.78%	C / 4.8

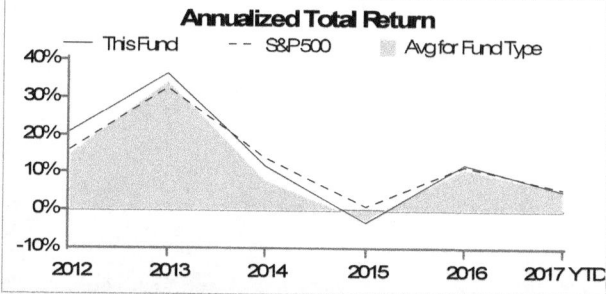

Annualized Total Return

Vanguard Windsor-II Inv (VWNFX)

B+   **Good**

Fund Family: Vanguard Funds **Phone:** (800) 662-7447
Address: Vanguard Financial Center, Valley Forge, PA 19482
Fund Type: GR - Growth

Major Rating Factors: Strong performance is the major factor driving the B+ (Good) TheStreet.com Investment Rating for Vanguard Windsor-II Inv. The fund currently has a performance rating of B (Good) based on an average return of 8.12% over the last three years and 4.50% over the last three months. Factored into the performance evaluation is an expense ratio of 0.34% (very low).

The fund's risk rating is currently C+ (Fair). It carries a beta of 1.01, meaning that its performance tracks fairly well with that of the overall stock market. Volatility, as measured by both the semi-deviation and a drawdown factor, is considered low.

George H. Davis, Jr. has been running the fund for 14 years and currently receives a manager quality ranking of 43 (0=worst, 99=best). If you desire only a moderate level of risk and strong performance, then this fund is an excellent option.

Services Offered: Automated phone transactions, payroll deductions, bank draft capabilities, an IRA investment plan, a 401K investment plan, a Keogh investment plan and a systematic withdrawal plan.

Data Date	Investment Rating	Net Assets ($Mil)	NAV	Perfor-mance Rating/Pts	Total Return Y-T-D	Risk Rating/Pts
2-17	B+	14,634	36.72	B / 8.2	4.50%	C+ / 5.6
2016	B	14,251	35.14	B+ / 8.4	13.41%	C / 5.5
2015	B	15,232	33.50	B- / 7.2	-3.22%	C+ / 6.4
2014	A-	17,277	37.31	B / 7.9	11.16%	B- / 7.2
2013	A-	18,061	36.77	B / 7.7	30.69%	C+ / 6.1
2012	B+	17,893	29.38	B- / 7.2	16.72%	C+ / 5.6

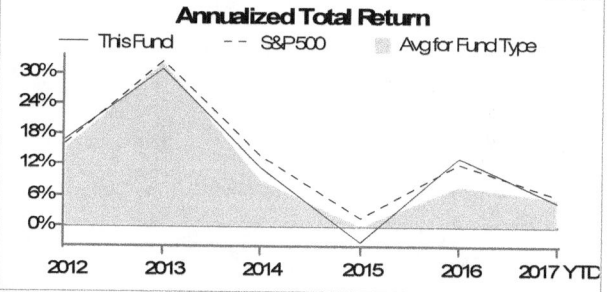

Annualized Total Return

Section III

Top 200
Stock Mutual Funds

A compilation of those

Equity Mutual Funds

receiving the highest TheStreet Investment Ratings.

Funds are listed in order by Overall Investment Rating.

Section III Contents

This section contains a summary analysis of each of the top 200 equity mutual funds as determined by their overall TheStreet Investment Rating. You can use this section to identify those mutual funds that have achieved the best possible combination of total return on investment and reduced volatility over the past three years. Consult each fund's individual Performance Rating and Risk Rating to find the fund that best matches your investing style.

In order to optimize the utility of our top and bottom fund lists, rather than listing all funds in a multi-class series, a single fund from each series is selected for display as the primary share class. Whenever possible, the selected fund is one that a retail investor would be most likely to choose. This share class may not be appropriate for every investor, so please consult with your financial advisor, the fund company, and the fund's prospectus before placing your trade.

1.	**Fund Type**	The mutual fund's peer category based on an analysis of its investment portfolio.	

AG	Aggressive Growth	HL	Health
AA	Asset Allocation	IN	Income
BA	Balanced	IX	Index
CV	Convertible	MC	Mid Cap
EM	Emerging Market	OT	Other
EN	Energy/Natural Resources	PM	Precious Metals
FS	Financial Services	RE	Real Estate
FO	Foreign	SC	Small Cap
GL	Global	TC	Technology
GR	Growth	UT	Utilities
GI	Growth and Income		

A blank fund type means that the mutual fund has not yet been categorized.

2. Fund Name The name of the mutual fund as stated in its prospectus, which can sometimes differ slightly from the name that the company uses for advertising. If you cannot find the particular mutual fund you are interested in, or if you have any doubts regarding the precise name, verify the information with your broker or on your account statement. Also, use the fund's ticker symbol for confirmation. (See column 3.)

3. Ticker Symbol The unique alphabetic symbol used for identifying and trading a specific mutual fund. No two funds can have the same ticker symbol, and the ticker symbol for mutual funds always ends with an "X".

A handful of funds currently show no associated ticker symbol. This means that the fund is either small or new since the NASD only assigns a ticker symbol to funds with at least $25 million in assets or 1,000 shareholders.

4.	**Overall Investment Rating**	Our overall rating is measured on a scale from A to E based on each fund's risk-adjusted performance. Please see page 10 for specific descriptions of each letter grade. Also, refer to page 7 for information on how our ratings are derived. Most important, when using this rating, please be sure to consider the warnings beginning on page 11 regarding the ratings' limitations and the underlying assumptions.
5.	**Phone**	The telephone number of the company managing the fund. Call this number to receive a prospectus or other information about the fund.
6.	**Net Asset Value (NAV)**	The fund's share price as of the date indicated. A fund's NAV is computed by dividing the value of the fund's asset holdings, less accrued fees and expenses, by the number of its shares outstanding.
7.	**Performance Rating/Points**	A letter grade rating based solely on the mutual fund's financial performance over the trailing three years, without any consideration for the amount of risk the fund poses. Like the overall Investment Rating, the Performance Rating is measured on a scale from A to E for ease of interpretation. The points score indicates where the Performance Rating falls on a scale of 0 to 10.
8.	**1-Year Total Return**	The total return the fund has provided investors over the preceeding twelve months. This total return figure is computed based on the fund's dividend distributions and share price appreciation/depreciation during the period, net of the expenses and fees it imposes on its shareholders. Although the total return figure does not reflect an adjustment for any loads the fund may carry, such adjustments have been made in deriving TheStreet Investment Ratings.
9.	**1-Year Total Return Percentile**	The fund's percentile rank based on its one-year performance compared to that of all other equity funds in existence for at least one year. A score of 99 is the best possible, indicating that the fund outperformed 99% of the other mutual funds. Zero is the worst possible percentile score.
10.	**3-Year Total Return**	The total annual return the fund has provided investors over the preceeding three years.
11.	**3-Year Total Return Percentile**	The fund's percentile rank based on its three-year performance compared to that of all other equity funds in existence for at least three years. A score of 99 is the best possible, indicating that the fund outperformed 99% of the other mutual funds. Zero is the worst possible percentile score.
12.	**5-Year Total Return**	The total annual return the fund has provided investors over the preceeding five years.
13.	**5-Year Total Return Percentile**	The fund's percentile rank based on its five-year performance compared to that of all other equity funds in existence for at least five years. A score of 99 is the best possible, indicating that the fund outperformed 99% of the other mutual funds. Zero is the worst possible percentile score.

14. Risk Rating/Points

A letter grade rating based solely on the mutual fund's risk as determined by its monthly performance volatility over the trailing three years. The risk rating does not take into consideration the overall financial performance the fund has achieved or the total return it has provided to its shareholders. Like the overall Investment Rating, the Risk Rating is measured on a scale from A to E for ease of interpretation. The points score indicates where the Risk Rating falls on a scale of 0 to 10.

15. Manager Quality Percentile

The manager quality percentile is based on a ranking of the fund's alpha, a statistical measure representing the difference between a fund's actual returns and its expected performance given its level of risk. Fund managers who have been able to exceed the fund's statistically expected performance receive a high percentile rank with 99 representing the highest possible score. At the other end of the spectrum, fund managers who have actually detracted from the fund's expected performance receive a low percentile rank with 0 representing the lowest possible score.

16. Manager Tenure

The number of years the current manager has been managing the fund. Since fund managers who deliver substandard returns are usually replaced, a long tenure is usually a good sign that shareholders are satisfied that the fund is achieving its stated objectives.

Fund Type	Fund Name	Ticker Symbol	Overall Investment Rating	Phone	Net Asset Value As of 2/28/17	Performance Rating/Pts	Annualized Total Return Through 2/28/17			Risk Rating/Pts	Mgr. Quality Pct	Mgr. Tenure (Years)
							1Yr / Pct	3Yr / Pct	5Yr / Pct			
FS	J Hancock Regional Bank A	FRBAX	A+	(800) 257-3336	26.28	A+ /9.9	60.84 /99	18.09 /99	20.90 /99	C+ / 6.0	91	19
FS	RMB Mendon Financial Services A	RMBKX	A+	(800) 601-5228	42.66	A+ /9.9	49.34 /99	20.69 /99	23.00 /99	C+ / 6.8	98	18
FS	Emerald Banking and Finance A	HSSAX	A+	(855) 828-9909	42.64	A+ /9.9	51.05 /99	16.40 /99	21.78 /99	C+ / 6.5	88	20
FS	Vanguard Financial Index Fd Adm	VFAIX	A+	(800) 662-7447	31.22	A+ /9.9	46.85 /99	14.09 /99	17.33 /98	C+ / 6.6	79	2
FS	Alpine Financial Services Inst	ADFSX	A+	(888) 785-5578	17.24	A+ /9.9	55.88 /99	10.12 /94	17.39 /98	C+ / 5.7	30	2
FS	1919 Financial Services A	SBFAX	A+	(844) 828-1919	24.53	A+ /9.9	44.51 /98	14.96 /99	18.45 /99	C+ / 6.1	87	3
TC	Oak Assoc-Red Oak Technology	ROGSX	A+	(888) 462-5386	21.70	A+ /9.9	42.16 /98	14.41 /99	17.43 /98	C+ / 6.3	84	11
TC	Vanguard Info Tech Ind Adm	VITAX	A+	(800) 662-7447	68.11	A+ /9.9	33.51 /92	14.64 /99	14.84 /97	C+ / 6.5	85	2
TC	ICON Information Technology S	ICTEX	A+	(800) 764-0442	16.31	A+ /9.9	29.24 /85	15.71 /99	13.74 /91	C+ / 5.7	95	N/A
GR	Parnassus Endeavor	PARWX	A+	(800) 999-3505	34.41	A+ /9.9	32.69 /91	15.00 /99	17.59 /98	B- / 7.3	99	10
FO	Hennessy Japan Small Cap Inv	HJPSX	A+	(800) 966-4354	12.14	A+ /9.9	30.37 /87	13.52 /99	15.54 /98	C+ / 6.7	38	21
AG	Rydex Nova A	RYANX	A+	(800) 820-0888	56.26	A+ /9.8	36.32 /95	13.35 /99	18.76 /99	C+ / 5.9	81	5
GR	SunAmerica VAL Co I Nsdq 100	VCNIX	A+	(800) 858-8850	11.14	A+ /9.8	27.84 /81	13.84 /99	16.15 /98	B- / 7.3	81	11
GR	USAA Nasdaq 100 Index	USNQX	A+	(800) 382-8722	15.14	A+ /9.8	27.85 /81	13.75 /99	16.02 /98	C+ / 6.2	43	4
FS	Fidelity Select Financial Services	FIDSX	A+	(800) 544-8888	103.05	A+ /9.8	38.78 /97	10.04 /93	13.85 /92	C+ / 5.9	96	12
SC	Nuveen Small Cap Value A	FSCAX	A+	(800) 257-8787	24.70	A+ /9.8	42.88 /98	12.49 /98	15.54 /98	C+ / 6.5	81	14
GR	NASDAQ-100 Index Direct	NASDX	A+	(800) 955-9988	13.62	A+ /9.8	27.11 /79	13.66 /99	16.37 /98	C+ / 6.7	86	4
FS	Fidelity Select Insurance	FSPCX	A+	(800) 544-8888	80.60	A+ /9.8	31.60 /89	13.17 /99	17.52 /98	C+ / 6.6	97	12
SC	Oak Assoc-Pin Oak Equity	POGSX	A+	(888) 462-5386	60.45	A+ /9.8	34.55 /94	11.91 /98	15.62 /98	C+ / 6.1	51	25
GI	Dodge & Cox Stk Fund	DODGX	A+	(800) 621-3979	194.15	A+ /9.8	38.12 /96	10.05 /94	15.91 /98	C+ / 6.7	95	13
MC	American Century VP Mid Cap Val	AVMTX	A+	(800) 345-6488	21.92	A+ /9.8	31.15 /88	12.76 /99	15.36 /97	C+ / 6.1	78	26
FS	Davis Financial A	RPFGX	A+	(800) 279-0279	47.12	A+ /9.8	33.82 /93	12.34 /98	14.42 /95	C+ / 6.0	65	13
GR	Fidelity NASDAQ Composite Index	FNCMX	A+	(800) 544-8544	76.54	A+ /9.8	29.21 /85	11.79 /98	15.71 /98	C+ / 6.5	99	9
EM	Franklin India Growth Fund A	FINGX	A+	(800) 342-5236	13.45	A+ /9.8	30.84 /88	15.88 /99	7.75 /40	C+ / 6.4	78	13
GR	● Vanguard PRIMECAP Core Inv	VPCCX	A+	(800) 662-7447	23.81	A+ /9.8	28.50 /83	11.62 /98	16.19 /98	C+ / 6.0	70	2
GR	Fidelity Sel Defense and	FSDAX	A+	(800) 544-8888	138.34	A+ /9.8	34.37 /93	10.37 /95	15.46 /98	C+ / 5.9	82	5
GR	Fidelity Select Air Transport	FSAIX	A+	(800) 544-8888	76.05	A+ /9.7	26.31 /77	11.81 /98	18.53 /99	C+ / 6.3	41	4
FS	Fidelity Adv Financial Serv A	FAFDX	A+	(800) 522-7297	19.00	A+ /9.7	38.17 /96	9.86 /93	13.68 /90	C+ / 6.1	92	32
MC	● Vanguard PRIMECAP Inv	VPMCX	A+	(800) 662-7447	112.93	A+ /9.7	28.77 /83	11.30 /97	16.64 /98	B- / 7.0	66	18
GR	LSV Value Equity Inst	LSVEX	A+	(866) 777-7818	27.34	A+ /9.7	31.35 /89	10.39 /95	15.98 /98	C+ / 6.8	57	25
GR	White Oak Select Growth	WOGSX	A+	(888) 462-5386	76.20	A+ /9.7	31.20 /89	10.95 /97	13.74 /91	C+ / 6.7	57	13
GR	DFA US Large Cap Value II Inst	DFCVX	A+	(800) 984-9472	18.12	A+ /9.7	33.26 /92	10.07 /94	15.42 /97	C+ / 6.1	71	2
MC	Vanguard S&P Mid-Cap 400 Value	VMFVX	A+	(800) 662-7447	228.02	A+ /9.7	35.40 /94	9.99 /93	14.45 /95	C+ / 6.8	72	13
GR	PRIMECAP Odyssey Stock Fd	POSKX	A+	(800) 729-2307	27.59	A+ /9.7	28.41 /83	11.07 /97	14.98 /97	C+ / 6.3	74	23
AG	Rydex NASDAQ 100 A	RYATX	A+	(800) 820-0888	27.96	A+ /9.7	26.46 /78	12.71 /99	15.01 /97	B- / 7.6	99	13
FO	DFA Japanese Small Co Inst	DFJSX	A+	(800) 984-9472	23.74	A+ /9.7	28.62 /83	10.53 /96	10.00 /58	C+ / 6.2	73	5
GI	Harbor Large Cap Value Inv	HILVX	A+	(800) 422-1050	13.54	A+ /9.7	30.74 /88	10.76 /97	14.96 /97	C+ / 6.6	74	11
GR	Clipper	CFIMX	A+	(800) 432-2504	112.44	A+ /9.6	31.33 /89	11.30 /97	14.00 /93	C+ / 6.1	92	19
SC	Vanguard Small-Cap Value Index	VISVX	A+	(800) 662-7447	29.79	A+ /9.6	34.76 /94	9.66 /91	14.73 /96	C+ / 6.0	24	21
GR	J Hancock Classic Value A	PZFVX	A+	(800) 257-3336	30.39	A+ /9.6	39.99 /97	9.02 /87	13.57 /90	C+ / 6.1	91	11
SC	Voya VP Index Plus SmallCap S	IPSSX	A+	(800) 992-0180	27.09	A+ /9.6	34.59 /94	9.35 /89	14.17 /94	B- / 7.5	81	2
GR	Vanguard Mega Cap Value Index I	VMVLX	A+	(800) 662-7447	138.07	A+ /9.6	26.92 /79	11.04 /97	14.18 /94	B- / 7.2	79	23
GR	Vanguard Value Index Inv	VIVAX	A+	(800) 662-7447	37.78	A+ /9.6	27.65 /81	10.77 /97	14.12 /94	C+ / 6.6	70	9
GR	Vanguard US Value Inv	VUVLX	A+	(800) 662-7447	18.96	A+ /9.6	28.78 /83	10.11 /94	14.85 /97	C+ / 6.9	56	7
GR	SunAmerica VAL Co II Lrg Cp Val	VACVX	A+	(800) 858-8850	20.97	A /9.5	31.17 /88	9.43 /90	14.00 /93	C+ / 6.1	38	17
GR	Oakmark Fund Service	OARMX	A+	(800) 625-6275	75.22	A /9.5	33.74 /93	9.09 /87	14.26 /95	C+ / 6.4	73	13
MC	Harbor Mid Cap Value Inv	HIMVX	A+	(800) 422-1050	22.78	A /9.5	30.36 /87	9.25 /88	15.20 /97	C+ / 6.6	52	13
GR	Tax Mgd US MktWide Val II Inst	DFMVX	A+	(800) 984-9472	26.92	A /9.5	30.62 /87	9.52 /90	15.22 /97	C+ / 6.0	59	9
GI	JPMorgan Tax Aware Equity I	JPDEX	A+	(800) 480-4111	31.17	A /9.5	27.30 /80	10.29 /95	14.32 /95	B- / 7.0	70	10
GR	Fidelity LgCp Val Enh Idx Fd	FLVEX	A+	(800) 544-8544	12.53	A /9.5	28.30 /82	10.16 /94	14.42 /95	C+ / 6.3	59	10
GR	Boston Partners All Cap Val Inv	BPAVX	A+	(888) 261-4073	24.56	A /9.5	30.14 /87	10.29 /95	14.83 /97	B- / 7.1	76	10
GR	Fidelity 100 Index FD	FOHIX	A+	(800) 544-8544	15.40	A /9.5	24.55 /72	11.02 /97	13.56 /89			

● Denotes fund is closed to new investors

	99 Pct = Best 0 Pct = Worst				Net Asset Value As of 2/28/17	PERFORMANCE				RISK	FUND MGR	
Fund Type	Fund Name	Ticker Symbol	Overall Investment Rating	Phone		Perform-ance Rating/Pts	Annualized Total Return Through 2/28/17			Risk Rating/Pts	Mgr. Quality Pct	Mgr. Tenure (Years)
							1Yr / Pct	3Yr / Pct	5Yr / Pct			
GR	Vanguard FTSE Social Index Inv	VFTSX	A+	(800) 662-7447	15.27	A /9.5	26.32 /77	10.54 /96	15.23 /97	C+ / 6.8	66	2
UT	ICON Utilities S	ICTUX	A+	(800) 764-0442	9.18	A /9.5	20.03 /52	12.24 /98	12.30 /77	C+ / 6.6	71	3
UT	Vanguard Utilities Index Adm	VUIAX	A+	(800) 662-7447	56.98	A /9.5	17.14 /39	12.44 /98	12.72 /81	C+ / 6.5	58	2
MC	Vanguard S&P Mid-Cap 400 Index	VSPMX	A+	(800) 662-7447	231.94	A /9.5	31.63 /89	9.57 /91	13.77 /91	C+ / 6.1	74	4
OT	Vanguard Industrials Index Adm	VINAX	A+	(800) 662-7447	64.22	A /9.5	29.81 /86	9.76 /92	14.72 /96	C+ / 6.7	51	2
GI	American Century VP Value II	AVPVX	A+	(800) 345-6488	10.82	A /9.4	29.78 /86	10.28 /95	13.56 /89	B- / 7.1	76	21
GR	Glenmede Large Cap Core Advisor	GTLOX	A+	(800) 442-8299	25.34	A /9.4	25.08 /74	10.64 /96	15.34 /97	B- / 7.8	73	13
MC	Vanguard Mega Cap Index Inst	VMCTX	A+	(800) 662-7447	159.47	A /9.4	25.12 /74	10.64 /96	13.93 /93	B- / 7.1	91	2
GR	Fidelity Blue Chip Value	FBCVX	A+	(800) 544-8544	18.45	A /9.4	24.99 /73	9.90 /93	13.21 /86	B- / 7.3	70	3
IN	Vanguard High Div Yield Index Inv	VHDYX	A+	(800) 662-7447	31.07	A /9.4	23.89 /69	11.43 /98	13.95 /93	B- / 7.4	85	1
GR	Thompson LargeCap	THPGX	A+	(800) 999-0887	60.15	A /9.4	35.77 /95	8.60 /84	13.09 /85	C+ / 6.2	23	25
GI	Fidelity Growth and Income	FGRIX	A+	(800) 544-8544	34.36	A /9.4	30.09 /87	9.51 /90	13.63 /90	C+ / 6.5	49	6
GR	ProFunds-Consumer Goods Ultra	CNPSX	A+	(888) 776-3637	93.47	A /9.4	17.56 /41	12.12 /98	16.06 /98	B- / 7.3	73	4
IX	Vanguard Instl Index Inst	VINIX	A+	(800) 662-7447	215.93	A /9.4	24.94 /73	10.61 /96	13.98 /93	B- / 7.1	74	17
GR	Vanguard Russell 1000 Val Index	VRVIX	A+	(800) 662-7447	199.02	A /9.4	28.85 /84	9.78 /92	13.91 /93	C+ / 6.8	67	7
GR	DFA US Large Company Portfolio	DFUSX	A+	(800) 984-9472	18.44	A /9.4	24.92 /73	10.57 /96	13.95 /93	B- / 7.0	74	N/A
IX	Fidelity 500 Index Inv	FUSEX	A+	(800) 544-8544	82.98	A /9.3	24.88 /73	10.54 /96	13.91 /93	B / 8.2	73	13
GR	Vanguard Tax-Managed Cap Appr	VTCLX	A+	(800) 662-7447	120.95	A /9.3	25.99 /76	10.19 /94	14.03 /93	C+ / 6.9	67	1
IN	FAM Equity-Income Inv	FAMEX	A+	(800) 932-3271	27.78	A /9.3	26.90 /79	10.37 /95	13.06 /84	C+ / 6.8	84	21
MC	Vanguard Mid-Cap Value Index Inv	VMVIX	A+	(800) 662-7447	40.40	A /9.3	29.04 /84	9.74 /92	14.68 /96	C+ / 6.5	82	11
IX	Schwab S&P 500 Index Fund	SWPPX	A+	(800) 407-0256	36.46	A /9.3	24.81 /73	10.52 /96	13.89 /92	C+ / 6.9	73	5
IX	Northern Stock Index	NOSIX	A+	(800) 595-9111	28.53	A /9.3	24.83 /73	10.51 /96	13.88 /92	B- / 7.0	73	11
SC	Wells Fargo Small Cap Core Inst	WYSCX	A+	(800) 222-8222	20.62	A /9.3	27.19 /80	9.51 /90	13.37 /88	C+ / 6.4	91	12
IX	Vanguard 500 Index Inv	VFINX	A+	(800) 662-7447	218.80	A /9.3	24.82 /73	10.48 /96	13.85 /92	B- / 7.1	73	26
IX	Dreyfus Instl S&P 500 Stock Index	DSPIX	A+	(800) 645-6561	47.82	A /9.3	24.73 /72	10.42 /95	13.80 /92	B- / 7.0	72	15
GI	SunAmerica VAL Co I Growth & Inc	VCGAX	A+	(800) 858-8850	20.23	A /9.3	25.74 /75	10.00 /93	12.80 /82	C+ / 6.5	66	4
IX	USAA S&P 500 Index Members	USSPX	A+	(800) 382-8722	33.68	A- /9.2	24.67 /72	10.35 /95	13.72 /91	B- / 7.0	71	11
IX	SS Inst S&P 500 Index Inv	SIDIX	A+	(800) 843-2639	22.32	A- /9.2	24.64 /72	10.41 /95	13.80 /92	B- / 7.1	72	20
GR	Vanguard Instl TtlStk Mkt Inst	VITNX	A+	(800) 662-7447	53.20	A- /9.2	26.30 /77	9.92 /93	13.86 /92	C+ / 6.8	64	16
GI	Fidelity Total Mkt Idx F	FFSMX	A+	(800) 544-8544	68.21	A- /9.2	26.33 /77	9.87 /93	13.79 /92	B- / 7.7	63	13
GR	Vanguard Large Cap Index Inv	VLACX	A+	(800) 662-7447	43.81	A- /9.2	25.10 /74	10.13 /94	13.66 /90	B- / 7.0	68	1
IX	TIAA-CREF S&P 500 Idx Retire	TRSPX	A+	(800) 842-2252	26.18	A- /9.2	24.58 /72	10.30 /95	13.65 /90	B- / 7.0	71	12
GR	State Street S&P 500 Index VIS 1	SSSPX	A+	(800) 843-2639	40.48	A- /9.2	24.59 /72	10.28 /95	13.66 /90	C+ / 6.9	70	16
GR	Vanguard Mega Cap Gr Index I	VMGAX	A+	(800) 662-7447	187.71	A- /9.2	23.16 /67	10.21 /94	13.77 /91	C+ / 6.7	60	2
IN	DFA Tax-Managed US Eq Inst	DTMEX	A+	(800) 984-9472	25.69	A- /9.2	26.02 /76	9.84 /92	13.76 /91	C+ / 6.9	63	5
IX	T Rowe Price Equity Index 500	PREIX	A+	(800) 638-5660	63.64	A- /9.2	24.67 /72	10.35 /95	13.71 /91	B- / 7.1	71	9
GR	Schwab Total Stock Market Index	SWTSX	A+	(800) 407-0256	42.01	A- /9.2	26.22 /77	9.82 /92	13.74 /91	C+ / 6.6	63	5
GR	American Century VP Large Co Val	AVVIX	A+	(800) 345-6488	15.96	A- /9.2	28.47 /83	9.40 /90	13.21 /86	C+ / 6.6	52	13
GR	Nuveen Large Cap Select A	FLRAX	A+	(800) 257-8787	24.51	A- /9.2	32.22 /90	9.53 /91	13.78 /92	C+ / 6.6	50	14
GR	Amer Beacon Bridgeway LC Val	BRLVX	A+	(800) 658-5811	26.99	A- /9.2	25.20 /74	10.56 /96	15.51 /98	B- / 7.0	77	14
IN	Vanguard Russell 3000 Index Inst	VRTTX	A+	(800) 662-7447	210.62	A- /9.2	26.06 /76	9.83 /92	13.76 /91	C+ / 6.8	63	2
GL	AllianzGI NFJ Mid-Cap Value A	PQNAX	A+	(800) 988-8380	28.91	A- /9.1	31.95 /90	9.11 /87	12.42 /78	C+ / 6.7	99	8
GR	Glenmede Large Cap Growth	GTLLX	A+	(800) 442-8299	27.71	A- /9.1	20.41 /54	11.29 /97	15.12 /97	B / 8.2	77	13
GI	Voya Russell Large Cap Index Adv	IRLIX	A+	(800) 992-0180	18.14	A- /9.1	24.03 /70	10.06 /94	13.15 /85	B- / 7.3	68	5
IX	GuideStone Equity Index Inv	GEQZX	A+	(888) 984-8433	26.09	A- /9.1	24.71 /72	10.13 /94	13.55 /89	B- / 7.0	68	1
GR	Vanguard Tot Stk Mkt Idx Inv	VTSMX	A+	(800) 662-7447	59.25	A- /9.1	26.14 /77	9.74 /92	13.67 /90	C+ / 6.8	62	23
IX	Columbia Large Cap Index A	NEIAX	A+	(800) 345-6611	45.16	A- /9.1	24.40 /71	10.15 /94	13.51 /89	B- / 7.0	69	6
FS	Franklin Mutual Financial Svcs A	TFSIX	A+	(800) 342-5236	22.14	A- /9.1	28.54 /83	10.54 /96	13.48 /89	B- / 7.1	78	8
GR	Northern Large Cap Value	NOLVX	A+	(800) 595-9111	15.40	A- /9.1	29.82 /86	8.74 /85	12.10 /75	C+ / 6.6	50	2
GR	SunAmerica VAL Co I Core Eq Fd	VCCEX	A+	(800) 858-8850	21.81	A- /9.1	28.55 /83	8.67 /84	12.48 /79	B- / 7.0	36	5
IX	S&P 500 Index Direct	SPFIX	A+	(800) 955-9988	46.16	A- /9.1	24.14 /70	10.25 /95	13.60 /90	B- / 7.0	70	14
GI	Fidelity Value Discovery Fd	FVDFX	A+	(800) 544-8544	27.15	A- /9.1	24.60 /72	9.51 /90	13.96 /93	B- / 7.0	72	5

Denotes fund is closed to new investors

Data as of February 28, 2017

www.thestreetratings.com

763

III. Top 200 Stock Mutual Funds

Fund Type	Fund Name	Ticker Symbol	Overall Investment Rating	Phone	Net Asset Value As of 2/28/17	PERFORMANCE Performance Rating/Pts	Annualized Total Return Through 2/28/17 1Yr / Pct	3Yr / Pct	5Yr / Pct	RISK Risk Rating/Pts	FUND MGR Mgr. Quality Pct	Mgr. Tenure (Years)
	99 Pct = Best / 0 Pct = Worst											
GR	T Rowe Price Total Eq Mkt Index	POMIX	A+	(800) 638-5660	26.79	A- /9.1	26.21 /77	9.76 /92	13.79 /92	C+ / 6.8	61	9
GR	BlackRock Large Cap Value Inv A	MDLVX	A+	(800) 441-7762	26.38	A- /9.1	30.54 /87	9.30 /89	12.28 /77	C+ / 6.9	50	18
GR	Voya VP Index Plus Large Cap S	IPLSX	A+	(800) 992-0180	25.53	A- /9.1	24.43 /71	9.85 /93	13.12 /85	B- / 7.2	63	11
GR	QS S&P 500 Index A	SBSPX	A+	(877) 534-4627	23.09	A- /9.1	24.31 /71	10.01 /93	13.38 /88	C+ / 6.9	67	N/A
GR	TIAA-CREF Equity Index Retire	TIQRX	A+	(800) 842-2252	17.79	A- /9.1	25.95 /76	9.62 /91	13.54 /89	C+ / 6.6	60	12
GR	SunAmerica VAL Co II Soc Resp	VCSRX	A+	(800) 858-8850	20.96	A- /9.0	23.59 /68	10.42 /95	14.27 /95	B- / 7.0	69	5
IN	Vanguard Equity Income Inv	VEIPX	A+	(800) 662-7447	34.09	A- /9.0	23.50 /68	10.38 /95	13.47 /89	C+ / 6.9	80	14
GR	Bridgeway Blue Chip 35 Index	BRLIX	A+	(800) 661-3550	13.47	A- /9.0	23.49 /68	10.57 /96	13.42 /88	B- / 7.2	74	20
IN	DFA US Core Equity 1 Ptf Inst	DFEOX	A+	(800) 984-9472	20.25	A- /9.0	27.39 /80	9.13 /88	13.82 /92	C+ / 6.7	52	12
GR	MM S and P 500 Index R4	MIEAX	A+	(800) 542-6767	19.66	A- /9.0	24.18 /71	9.94 /93	13.30 /87	C+ / 6.7	67	10
SC	Aberdeen US Small Cap Eq A	GSXAX	A+	(866) 667-9231	32.75	A- /9.0	26.01 /76	12.62 /98	15.91 /98	B- / 7.0	98	9
FO	Hennessy Japan Fund Investor	HJPNX	A+	(800) 966-4354	27.78	A- /9.0	20.73 /56	12.20 /98	13.21 /86	C+ / 6.6	99	11
GR	Dean Mid Cap Value	DALCX	A+	(888) 899-8343	19.02	A- /9.0	27.76 /81	9.63 /91	12.96 /83	B- / 7.5	78	9
GR	Wilshire 5000 Index Inv	WFIVX	A+	(888) 200-6796	19.89	A- /9.0	25.58 /75	9.54 /91	13.24 /86	C+ / 6.8	60	18
GR	DFA TA US Core Equity 2 Inst	DFTCX	A+	(800) 984-9472	16.31	B+ /8.9	28.31 /82	8.71 /85	13.81 /92	C+ / 6.6	45	5
GR	Fidelity LgCp Gr Enh Idx Fd	FLGEX	A+	(800) 544-8544	16.65	B+ /8.9	21.33 /59	10.23 /94	13.59 /90	C+ / 6.8	69	10
GR	TIAA-CREF Large Cap Gr Idx	TRIRX	A+	(800) 842-2252	24.49	B+ /8.9	21.76 /61	10.13 /94	13.43 /88	C+ / 6.7	65	12
GR	DFA US Sustainability Core 1 Inst	DFSIX	A+	(800) 984-9472	18.78	B+ /8.9	26.62 /78	8.97 /87	13.69 /91	C+ / 6.6	49	5
IX	Principal LgCap S&P 500 A	PLSAX	A+	(800) 222-5852	16.33	B+ /8.9	24.38 /71	10.08 /94	13.39 /88	B- / 7.0	68	6
GR	Amer Beacon Bridgeway LC Gro	BRLGX	A+	(800) 658-5811	25.98	B+ /8.9	20.26 /53	10.38 /95	14.67 /96	B- / 7.5	76	14
GR	Bishop Street Dividend Value I	BSLIX	A+	(800) 262-9565	15.43	B+ /8.9	21.95 /62	10.20 /94	12.69 /81	B- / 7.6	79	7
GI	Payden Equity Income Investor	PYVLX	A+	(888) 409-8007	15.97	B+ /8.8	21.41 /59	10.75 /97	12.48 /79	B- / 7.5	86	N/A
GR	AMG Mgrs Cadence Cap App N	MPAFX	A+	(800) 548-4539	29.63	B+ /8.8	22.61 /65	9.29 /89	11.21 /68	C+ / 6.8	58	13
GR	Goldman Sachs LC Gro Insights A	GLCGX	A+	(800) 526-7384	26.18	B+ /8.8	23.64 /69	11.06 /97	14.55 /96	C+ / 6.8	71	6
GR	Columbia Large Cap Enh Core A	NMIAX	A+	(800) 345-6611	23.81	B+ /8.8	22.62 /65	9.81 /92	13.37 /88	B- / 7.0	62	8
GR	Fidelity LgCp Core Enh Idx Fd	FLCEX	A+	(800) 544-8544	13.21	B+ /8.8	23.09 /67	9.56 /91	13.47 /89	C+ / 6.9	64	10
IN	Fidelity Equity Dividend Income	FEQTX	A+	(800) 544-8544	27.77	B+ /8.7	25.33 /74	9.46 /90	12.62 /80	C+ / 6.9	71	6
GR	Torray	TORYX	A+	(800) 443-3036	49.71	B+ /8.7	23.99 /70	9.82 /92	12.54 /79	B- / 7.6	74	20
IX	PNC S&P 500 Index A	PIIAX	A+	(800) 551-2145	17.63	B+ /8.7	24.24 /71	10.01 /93	13.37 /88	C+ / 6.9	68	12
GR	SEI Inst Inv Tr-Tax Mgd Volty F	TMMAX	A+	(800) 342-5734	15.41	B+ /8.6	17.32 /40	11.08 /97	13.86 /92	B- / 7.4	94	10
GR	SA US Core Market	SAMKX	A+	(800) 366-7266	21.06	B+ /8.5	23.77 /69	8.95 /86	12.93 /83	B / 8.0	55	11
BA	Dodge & Cox Balanced Fund	DODBX	A+	(800) 621-3979	107.49	B+ /8.4	27.47 /80	8.12 /80	12.35 /78	B / 8.6	62	25
GI	Wright Major Blue Chip Equities	WQCEX	A+	(800) 232-0013	19.64	B+ /8.4	22.77 /66	8.38 /82	10.29 /61	B- / 7.1	40	8
GI	Vanguard Cons Stap Idx Adm	VCSAX	A+	(800) 662-7447	69.91	B /8.2	12.06 /18	11.96 /98	13.84 /92	B- / 7.6	95	7
FO	Fidelity Japan Small Companies	FJSCX	A+	(800) 544-8544	15.60	B /7.9	19.77 /51	9.37 /89	14.45 /95	B- / 7.9	99	3
UT	Invesco Dividend Income A	IAUTX	A+	(800) 959-4246	24.09	B /7.8	17.24 /39	11.83 /98	12.99 /84	B / 8.0	98	8
FO	T Rowe Price Japan	PRJPX	A+	(800) 638-5660	12.28	B /7.7	23.92 /70	8.84 /86	10.84 /65	B / 8.0	99	4
TC	ProFunds-Tech UltraSector Svc	TEPSX	A	(888) 776-3637	72.57	A+ /9.9	50.25 /99	18.32 /99	16.65 /98	C / 5.5	55	4
AG	ProFunds-Ultra Bull Svc	ULPSX	A	(888) 776-3637	114.76	A+ /9.9	49.06 /99	16.12 /99	23.23 /99	C / 5.4	12	4
AG	Rydex S&P 500 2x Strategy A	RYTTX	A	(800) 820-0888	89.66	A+ /9.9	50.14 /99	17.30 /99	24.71 /99	C / 5.2	20	17
FS	Hennessy Small Cap Financial Inv	HSFNX	A	(800) 966-4354	25.53	A+ /9.9	42.81 /98	12.66 /99	16.50 /98	C / 5.2	74	20
FS	Rydex Banking A	RYBKX	A	(800) 820-0888	73.27	A+ /9.9	54.46 /99	9.74 /92	12.97 /83	C / 5.4	11	19
TC	Columbia Global Technology Gro A	CTCAX	A	(800) 345-6611	24.26	A+ /9.9	37.09 /96	14.87 /99	19.01 /99	C+ / 5.6	88	5
MC	Rydex Mid Cap 1.5x Strgy A	RYAHX	A	(800) 820-0888	80.51	A+ /9.9	47.64 /99	11.80 /98	18.21 /99	C / 5.2	40	16
TC	Putnam Global Technology Fund A	PGTAX	A	(800) 225-1581	27.61	A+ /9.8	33.58 /92	15.00 /99	13.67 /90	C / 5.4	89	5
GR	ProFunds-Industrial UltraSector	IDPSX	A	(888) 776-3637	80.21	A+ /9.8	42.07 /98	10.74 /96	17.94 /99	C+ / 5.7	7	4
FS	J Hancock Financial Indust A	FIDAX	A	(800) 257-3336	19.92	A+ /9.8	45.73 /99	8.53 /83	15.92 /98	C / 5.5	10	19
FS	Diamond Hill Financial Lng-Sht A	BANCX	A	(614) 255-3333	23.36	A+ /9.8	42.96 /98	9.53 /91	14.48 /95	C+ / 5.7	28	16
MC	American Century NT Md Cp Val	ACLMX	A	(800) 345-6488	13.87	A+ /9.8	31.72 /89	13.10 /99	15.74 /98	C / 5.4	95	11
FS	ICON Financial S	ICFSX	A	(800) 764-0442	9.49	A+ /9.8	40.27 /97	7.26 /74	11.04 /66	C / 5.3	4	14
GR	● Vanguard Capital Opportunity Inv	VHCOX	A	(800) 662-7447	57.99	A+ /9.7	30.07 /87	10.60 /96	17.78 /99	C+ / 5.7	61	19
SC	Virtus Small Cap Sustainble Gr A	PSGAX	A	(800) 243-1574	20.98	A+ /9.7	33.05 /92	12.75 /99	15.06 /97	C+ / 5.8	98	9

● Denotes fund is closed to new investors

99 Pct = Best
0 Pct = Worst

Fund Type	Fund Name	Ticker Symbol	Overall Investment Rating	Phone	Net Asset Value As of 2/28/17	Performance Rating/Pts	Annualized Total Return Through 2/28/17			Risk Rating/Pts	Mgr. Quality Pct	Mgr. Tenure (Years)
							1Yr / Pct	3Yr / Pct	5Yr / Pct			
GI	BNY Mellon Income Stock M	MPISX	A	(800) 645-6561	9.35	A+ /9.7	28.79 /83	11.08 /97	14.79 /96	C / 5.3	79	6
SC	Tributary Small Company Inst	FOSCX	A	(800) 662-4203	28.36	A+ /9.7	34.18 /93	10.46 /96	13.12 /85	C / 5.4	94	18
SC	Harbor Small Cap Value Inv	HISVX	A	(800) 422-1050	31.01	A+ /9.7	35.78 /95	9.40 /90	13.55 /89	C / 5.5	90	16
AG	Bridgeway Aggressive Investor 1	BRAGX	A	(800) 661-3550	66.92	A+ /9.6	36.49 /95	8.23 /81	14.91 /97	C+ / 5.6	20	23
SC	Vanguard S&P SC 600 Indx Inst	VSMSX	A	(800) 662-7447	252.80	A+ /9.6	34.96 /94	9.71 /92	14.87 /97	C+ / 5.6	91	4
SC	Northern Small Cap Value	NOSGX	A	(800) 595-9111	24.22	A+ /9.6	34.96 /94	9.36 /89	13.64 /90	C+ / 5.9	90	16
SC	Vanguard Tax-Managed Small-Cap	VTMSX	A	(800) 662-7447	55.77	A+ /9.6	34.23 /93	9.68 /91	14.79 /96	C / 5.5	91	1
GR	ProFunds-Consumer Srvs Ultra	CYPSX	A	(888) 776-3637	85.80	A+ /9.6	22.41 /64	11.66 /98	22.04 /99	C+ / 5.9	25	4
GR	SA US Value	SABTX	A	(800) 366-7266	18.28	A+ /9.6	32.04 /90	9.37 /89	14.61 /96	C+ / 5.8	50	5
HL	Fidelity Select Health Care Srvcs	FSHCX	A	(800) 544-8888	89.93	A+ /9.6	19.71 /51	12.48 /98	14.53 /96	C+ / 6.0	93	5
SC	Bridgeway Omni Tax-Mgd SCV	BOTSX	A	(800) 661-3550	17.63	A+ /9.6	39.68 /97	7.98 /79	13.39 /88	C+ / 5.8	83	7
MC	PRIMECAP Odyssey Growth Fd	POGRX	A	(800) 729-2307	30.75	A /9.5	29.60 /85	9.79 /92	16.02 /98	C+ / 5.9	75	13
GR	LSV Conservative Value Eq Inst	LSVVX	A	(866) 777-7818	12.30	A /9.5	29.27 /85	9.64 /91	14.41 /95	C+ / 5.7	63	10
SC	Dean Small Cap Value	DASCX	A	(888) 899-8343	16.96	A /9.5	35.69 /95	9.26 /89	13.34 /87	C / 5.5	91	9
MC	Prudential QMA Mid-Cap Value A	SPRAX	A	(800) 225-1852	22.16	A /9.5	34.07 /93	9.86 /93	14.47 /95	C+ / 5.6	78	3
GR	Baird Large Cap Inv	BHGSX	A	(866) 442-2473	9.46	A /9.4	29.36 /85	9.06 /87	11.88 /73	C+ / 5.9	38	4
GR	Toreador Core Fund Retail	TORLX	A	(800) 673-0550	15.35	A /9.4	31.88 /90	8.87 /86	13.23 /86	C+ / 5.6	36	11
GR	Fidelity Strategic Advisers Val Fd	FVSAX	A	(800) 544-8544	19.50	A /9.4	28.73 /83	9.54 /91	13.60 /90	C+ / 5.9	59	9
GR	Fidelity Large Cap Stock Fund	FLCSX	A	(800) 544-8544	30.81	A /9.4	33.28 /92	8.54 /83	14.48 /95	C+ / 5.7	30	12
SC	Frontier Phocas Sm Cap Val Fd	FPSVX	A	(888) 825-2100	40.17	A /9.4	33.54 /92	8.73 /85	13.64 /90	C+ / 5.7	89	7
GR	Wilmington Large-Cap Strategy	WMLIX	A	(800) 336-9970	19.50	A /9.3	26.26 /77	10.20 /94	13.75 /91	C+ / 5.8	61	6
SC	VY Columbia Small Cap Val II Adv	ICSAX	A	(800) 992-0180	18.92	A /9.3	35.10 /94	7.85 /78	13.27 /87	C+ / 5.8	84	11
SC	Vanguard Strategic Sm-Cp Equity	VSTCX	A	(800) 662-7447	35.24	A /9.3	31.58 /89	8.51 /83	14.66 /96	C+ / 5.8	88	11
GR	TIAA-CREF Large Cap Val Idx Ret	TRCVX	A	(800) 842-2252	19.11	A /9.3	28.74 /83	9.57 /91	13.66 /90	C+ / 6.1	65	12
GI	Vanguard Growth & Income Inv	VQNPX	A	(800) 662-7447	43.59	A- /9.2	24.12 /70	10.71 /96	14.19 /94	C+ / 6.1	76	6
GR	Columbia Select Large-Cap Value	SLVAX	A	(800) 345-6611	23.94	A- /9.2	34.96 /94	9.23 /88	14.01 /93	C+ / 5.9	38	20
GR	T Rowe Price Cap Opportunity	PRCOX	A	(800) 638-5660	23.97	A- /9.2	24.74 /72	10.25 /95	13.65 /90	C+ / 5.8	67	2
GR	SunAmerica VAL Co I Stk Idx Fd	VSTIX	A	(800) 858-8850	35.59	A- /9.2	24.59 /72	10.27 /95	13.62 /90	C+ / 5.8	70	5
GI	Commerce Value	CFVLX	A	(800) 995-6365	32.67	A- /9.2	25.71 /75	10.62 /96	13.93 /93	C+ / 6.0	83	13
GI	Fort Pitt Capital Total Return Fd	FPCGX	A	(800) 471-5827	23.04	A- /9.1	28.22 /82	9.49 /90	11.75 /72	C+ / 6.3	64	16
TC	T Rowe Price Media and	PRMTX	A	(800) 638-5660	80.89	A- /9.1	26.43 /78	9.80 /92	15.90 /98	C+ / 6.4	58	4
GR	Fidelity Select Retailing	FSRPX	A	(800) 544-8888	115.63	A- /9.1	17.20 /39	13.05 /99	18.48 /99	C+ / 5.9	90	1
IX	SEI Instl Managed Tr-S&P 500 Idx	SSPIX	A	(800) 342-5734	56.41	A- /9.1	24.41 /71	10.19 /94	13.55 /89	C+ / 6.3	70	6
GR	J Hancock Fundamental Lg Cap	TAGRX	A	(800) 257-3336	46.78	A- /9.1	30.93 /88	10.10 /94	14.18 /94	C+ / 6.2	44	6
GI	Schwab 1000 Index Fund	SNXFX	A	(800) 407-0256	56.81	A- /9.1	25.06 /73	9.83 /92	13.52 /89	C+ / 6.3	65	5
GI	T Rowe Price Instl Lg Cap Val	TILCX	A	(800) 638-5660	21.90	A- /9.1	27.90 /81	9.61 /91	14.13 /94	C+ / 6.2	56	13
GR	Diamond Hill Large Cap A	DHLAX	A	(614) 255-3333	24.62	A- /9.0	28.71 /83	10.00 /93	13.67 /90	C+ / 6.4	54	15
GR	T Rowe Price US Large-Cap Core	TRULX	A	(800) 638-5660	21.70	A- /9.0	20.60 /55	11.00 /97	14.46 /95	C+ / 6.3	83	8
IX	● Nuveen Equity Index A	FAEIX	A	(800) 257-8787	27.92	A- /9.0	24.21 /71	9.98 /93	13.31 /87	C+ / 6.1	68	17
IN	SEI Inst Inv Managed Vol Fund A	SVYAX	A	(800) 342-5734	14.68	A- /9.0	18.87 /46	11.64 /98	14.82 /96	C+ / 6.3	94	8
GI	Homestead Value	HOVLX	A	(800) 258-3030	50.24	A- /9.0	25.43 /75	9.52 /90	13.56 /89	C+ / 6.1	46	18
IN	DFA US Core Equity 2 Ptf Inst	DFQTX	A	(800) 984-9472	19.42	B+ /8.9	28.65 /83	8.54 /83	13.75 /91	C+ / 6.4	41	5
GR	DFA US Social Core Eq 2 Inst	DFUEX	A	(800) 984-9472	14.48	B+ /8.9	29.75 /86	8.11 /80	13.06 /84	C+ / 6.3	33	5
GR	Schwab Fundm US Large Co Index	SFLNX	A	(800) 407-0256	15.84	B+ /8.9	25.63 /75	9.58 /91	13.70 /91	C+ / 6.4	68	5

Section IV

Bottom 200
Stock Mutual Funds

A compilation of those

Equity Mutual Funds

receiving the lowest TheStreet Investment Ratings.

Funds are listed in order by Overall Investment Rating.

Section IV Contents

This section contains a summary analysis of each of the bottom 200 equity mutual funds as determined by their overall TheStreet Investment Rating. Typically, these funds have invested in stocks that are currently out of favor, presenting a risky investment proposition. As such, these are the funds that you should generally avoid since they have historically underperformed most other mutual funds given the level of risk in their underlying investments.

In order to optimize the utility of our top and bottom fund lists, rather than listing all funds in a multi-class series, a single fund from each series is selected for display as the primary share class. Whenever possible, the selected fund is one that a retail investor would be most likely to choose. This share class may not be appropriate for every investor, so please consult with your financial advisor, the fund company, and the fund's prospectus before placing your trade.

1. **Fund Type** The mutual fund's peer category based on an analysis of its investment portfolio.

AG	Aggressive Growth	HL	Health
AA	Asset Allocation	IN	Income
BA	Balanced	IX	Index
CV	Convertible	MC	Mid Cap
EM	Emerging Market	OT	Other
EN	Energy/Natural Resources	PM	Precious Metals
FS	Financial Services	RE	Real Estate
FO	Foreign	SC	Small Cap
GL	Global	TC	Technology
GR	Growth	UT	Utilities
GI	Growth and Income		

A blank fund type means that the mutual fund has not yet been categorized.

2. **Fund Name** The name of the mutual fund as stated in its prospectus, which can sometimes differ slightly from the name that the company uses for advertising. If you cannot find the particular mutual fund you are interested in, or if you have any doubts regarding the precise name, verify the information with your broker or on your account statement. Also, use the fund's ticker symbol for confirmation. (See column 3.)

3. **Ticker Symbol** The unique alphabetic symbol used for identifying and trading a specific mutual fund. No two funds can have the same ticker symbol, and the ticker symbol for mutual funds always ends with an "X".

A handful of funds currently show no associated ticker symbol. This means that the fund is either small or new since the NASD only assigns a ticker symbol to funds with at least $25 million in assets or 1,000 shareholders.

4.	**Overall Investment Rating**	Our overall rating is measured on a scale from A to E based on each fund's risk-adjusted performance. Please see page 10 for specific descriptions of each letter grade. Also, refer to page 7 for information on how our ratings are derived. Most important, when using this rating, please be sure to consider the warnings beginning on page 11 regarding the ratings' limitations and the underlying assumptions.
5.	**Phone**	The telephone number of the company managing the fund. Call this number to receive a prospectus or other information about the fund.
6.	**Net Asset Value (NAV)**	The fund's share price as of the date indicated. A fund's NAV is computed by dividing the value of the fund's asset holdings, less accrued fees and expenses, by the number of its shares outstanding.
7.	**Performance Rating/Points**	A letter grade rating based solely on the mutual fund's financial performance over the trailing three years, without any consideration for the amount of risk the fund poses. Like the overall Investment Rating, the Performance Rating is measured on a scale from A to E for ease of interpretation. The points score indicates where the Performance Rating falls on a scale of 0 to 10.
8.	**1-Year Total Return**	The total return the fund has provided investors over the preceeding twelve months. This total return figure is computed based on the fund's dividend distributions and share price appreciation/depreciation during the period, net of the expenses and fees it imposes on its shareholders. Although the total return figure does not reflect an adjustment for any loads the fund may carry, such adjustments have been made in deriving TheStreet Investment Ratings.
9.	**1-Year Total Return Percentile**	The fund's percentile rank based on its one-year performance compared to that of all other equity funds in existence for at least one year. A score of 99 is the best possible, indicating that the fund outperformed 99% of the other mutual funds. Zero is the worst possible percentile score.
10.	**3-Year Total Return**	The total annual return the fund has provided investors over the preceeding three years.
11.	**3-Year Total Return Percentile**	The fund's percentile rank based on its three-year performance compared to that of all other equity funds in existence for at least three years. A score of 99 is the best possible, indicating that the fund outperformed 99% of the other mutual funds. Zero is the worst possible percentile score.
12.	**5-Year Total Return**	The total annual return the fund has provided investors over the preceeding five years.

13. **5-Year Total Return Percentile**

The fund's percentile rank based on its five-year performance compared to that of all other equity funds in existence for at least five years. A score of 99 is the best possible, indicating that the fund outperformed 99% of the other mutual funds. Zero is the worst possible percentile score.

14. **Risk Rating/Points**

A letter grade rating based solely on the mutual fund's risk as determined by its monthly performance volatility over the trailing three years. The risk rating does not take into consideration the overall financial performance the fund has achieved or the total return it has provided to its shareholders. Like the overall Investment Rating, the Risk Rating is measured on a scale from A to E for ease of interpretation. The points score indicates where the Risk Rating falls on a scale of 0 to 10.

15. **Manager Quality Percentile**

The manager quality percentile is based on a ranking of the fund's alpha, a statistical measure representing the difference between a fund's actual returns and its expected performance given its level of risk. Fund managers who have been able to exceed the fund's statistically expected performance receive a high percentile rank with 99 representing the highest possible score. At the other end of the spectrum, fund managers who have actually detracted from the fund's expected performance receive a low percentile rank with 0 representing the lowest possible score.

16. **Manager Tenure**

The number of years the current manager has been managing the fund. Since fund managers who deliver substandard returns are usually replaced, a long tenure is usually a good sign that shareholders are satisfied that the fund is achieving its stated objectives.

Fund Type	Fund Name	Ticker Symbol	Overall Investment Rating	Phone	Net Asset Value As of 2/28/17	Performance Rating/Pts	1Yr / Pct	3Yr / Pct	5Yr / Pct	Risk Rating/Pts	Mgr. Quality Pct	Mgr. Tenure (Years)
AG	Rydex Inv NASDAQ 100 2x Stgy A	RYVTX	E-	(800) 820-0888	61.40	E- /0.0	-42.38 / 0	-29.59 / 0	-32.13 / 0	D / 1.9	1	17
GR	ProFunds Ultra Short	USPSX	E-	(888) 776-3637	32.49	E- /0.0	-43.32 / 0	-30.48 / 0	-33.03 / 0	E- / 0.0	1	4
FO	Profunds-Ultra Short Japan Svc	UKPSX	E-	(888) 776-3637	9.74	E- /0.0	-41.64 / 0	-29.17 / 0	-36.40 / 0	E- / 0.0	0	8
AG	Rydex Inv Dow 2x Strategy A	RYIDX	E-	(800) 820-0888	17.52	E- /0.0	-42.46 / 0	-24.21 / 0	-26.05 / 0	E+ / 0.8	3	13
FO	ProFunds-Ultra Sh Latin America	UFPSX	E-	(888) 776-3637	8.74	E- /0.0	-70.86 / 0	-19.19 / 0	-5.36 / 2	E- / 0.0	0	8
GR	ProFunds-Ultra Short Dow 30 Svc	UWPSX	E-	(888) 776-3637	26.68	E- /0.0	-42.80 / 0	-24.73 / 0	-26.83 / 0	E+ / 0.9	3	4
MC	ProFunds-Ultra Short Mid-Cap Svc	UIPSX	E-	(888) 776-3637	26.97	E- /0.0	-46.49 / 0	-24.06 / 0	-29.67 / 0	E / 0.5	2	4
SC	ProFunds-Ultra Short Small-Cap	UCPSX	E-	(888) 776-3637	11.48	E- /0.0	-51.85 / 0	-22.71 / 0	-30.58 / 0	E- / 0.0	1	4
SC	Rydex Inv Rusl 2000 2x Strtgy A	RYIUX	E-	(800) 820-0888	62.99	E- /0.0	-50.78 / 0	-21.53 / 0	-29.63 / 0	E / 0.3	1	11
AG	Rydex Inv S&P 500 2x Strategy A	RYTMX	E-	(800) 820-0888	59.46	E- /0.0	-38.35 / 0	-23.06 / 0	-27.57 / 0	D+ / 2.9	5	17
GR	ProFunds-Ultra Bear Svc	URPSX	E-	(888) 776-3637	32.54	E- /0.0	-38.83 / 0	-23.78 / 0	-28.58 / 0	D- / 1.0	4	4
SC	Direxion Mo Small Cap Bear 2X Inv	DXRSX	E-	(800) 851-0511	19.31	E- /0.0	-51.71 / 0	-21.24 / 0	-28.82 / 0	E- / 0.0	2	13
FO	Profunds-Ultra Short China Svc	UHPSX	E-	(888) 776-3637	9.55	E- /0.0	-40.01 / 0	-22.67 / 0	-26.02 / 0	E- / 0.0	0	8
GR	Direxion Mo S&P 500 Bear 2X Inv	DXSSX	E-	(800) 851-0511	18.72	E- /0.0	-38.18 / 0	-21.97 / 0	-26.81 / 0	E+ / 0.8	20	11
EM	Rydex Inverse Emg Mkts 2x Str A	RYWWX	E-	(800) 820-0888	66.72	E- /0.0	-49.84 / 0	-17.38 / 0	-9.47 / 1	E- / 0.0	0	7
EM	Profunds-Ultra Sh Emer Mkt Svc	UVPSX	E-	(888) 776-3637	28.23	E- /0.0	-50.69 / 0	-18.58 / 0	-10.59 / 0	E- / 0.0	0	8
GR	ProFunds-Short OTC Svc	SOPSX	E-	(888) 776-3637	12.07	E- /0.0	-24.75 / 0	-17.16 / 0	-19.09 / 0	D+ / 2.4	4	4
OT	Rydex Commodities Strgy A	RYMEX	E-	(800) 820-0888	84.45	E- /0.0	17.88 / 42	-22.76 / 0	-16.20 / 0	E+ / 0.7	0	12
PM	ProFunds Short Precious Metals	SPPSX	E-	(888) 776-3637	42.33	E- /0.0	-33.11 / 0	-14.04 / 0	-2.93 / 2	E- / 0.0	0	4
GR	NYSA Fund	NYSAX	E-	(800) 535-9169	4.21	E- /0.0	7.40 / 6	-19.33 / 0	-10.23 / 1	D+ / 2.6	0	4
SC	ProFunds-Short Small Cap Svc	SHPSX	E-	(888) 776-3637	15.75	E- /0.0	-30.46 / 0	-11.97 / 1	-16.67 / 0	C- / 3.6	7	4
GI	Goldman Sachs Commodity Strat A	GSCAX	E-	(800) 526-7384	11.53	E- /0.0	18.16 / 44	-20.24 / 0	-14.38 / 0	D- / 1.3	0	10
EM	ProFunds-Ultra Sh Intl Svc	UXPSX	E-	(888) 776-3637	17.77	E- /0.0	-33.32 / 0	-9.11 / 1	-18.97 / 0	D+ / 2.4	4	8
GI	Rational Real Strategies A	HRSAX	E-	(800) 253-0412	4.60	E- /0.0	-1.83 / 1	-12.67 / 0	-6.40 / 1	D+ / 2.6	0	N/A
PM	ProFunds-Precious Metals Ultra	PMPSX	E-	(888) 776-3637	35.50	E- /0.0	15.79 / 33	-17.10 / 0	-27.06 / 0	E- / 0.0	1	4
EN	BlackRock Energy & Resources Inv	SSGRX	E-	(800) 441-7762	18.72	E- /0.0	34.48 / 93	-17.96 / 0	-11.87 / 0	E / 0.3	1	4
EN	Guinness Atkinson Alt Energy Fd	GAAEX	E-	(800) 915-6565	2.68	E- /0.0	3.88 / 3	-15.17 / 0	-3.85 / 2	D+ / 2.4	1	11
OT	Russell Investments Comm Str A	RCSAX	E-	(800) 832-6688	5.61	E- /0.0	13.79 / 25	-13.64 / 0	-10.93 / 0	D+ / 2.7	0	N/A
GI	IMS Strategic Income Inst	IMSIX	E-		3.02	E- /0.0	5.89 / 5	-12.61 / 0	-4.94 / 2	D+ / 2.5	0	15
EN	Rydex Energy Services A	RYESX	E-	(800) 820-0888	31.95	E- /0.0	34.35 / 93	-17.35 / 0	-8.88 / 1	E- / 0.2	1	19
EN	Putnam Global Energy Fund A	PGEAX	E-	(800) 225-1581	7.95	E- /0.0	33.42 / 92	-14.99 / 0	-7.86 / 1	E+ / 0.7	2	1
OT	Fidelity Srs Commodity Strat Fund	FCSSX	E-	(800) 544-8544	5.43	E- /0.0	15.29 / 31	-13.60 / 0	-10.39 / 1	D+ / 2.5	0	8
OT	ProFunds-Rising Rates Opport Svc	RRPSX	E-	(888) 776-3637	38.97	E- /0.0	2.55 / 2	-12.25 / 0	-8.80 / 1	D+ / 2.5	0	8
EN	Invesco Energy A	IENAX	E-	(800) 959-4246	26.02	E- /0.0	29.14 / 84	-12.70 / 0	-5.98 / 1	E- / 0.2	7	4
OT	PIMCO CommoditiesPLUS	PCLAX	E-	(800) 426-0107	6.43	E- /0.0	29.76 / 86	-14.64 / 0	-9.61 / 1	D+ / 2.3	0	7
EN	US Global Inv Global Resources	PSPFX	E-	(800) 873-8637	5.63	E- /0.0	24.11 / 70	-14.75 / 0	-9.56 / 1	D+ / 2.4	1	28
SC	Jacob Micro Cap Growth Inv	JMCGX	E-	(888) 522-6239	9.97	E- /0.0	5.61 / 4	-9.55 / 1	0.19 / 5	E- / 0.0	0	5
IN	Harbor Commodity Real Rtn Str	HACMX	E-	(800) 422-1050	3.86	E- /0.0	20.76 / 56	-13.31 / 0	-10.24 / 1	D+ / 2.9	0	9
EM	● Templeton Frontier Markets A	TFMAX	E-	(800) 342-5236	11.22	E- /0.1	14.16 / 26	-10.10 / 1	-1.45 / 3	D+ / 2.9	1	9
EN	ProFunds Oil Eqpt Svcs & Dist Svc	OEPSX	E-	(888) 776-3637	14.08	E- /0.1	47.90 / 99	-16.59 / 0	-7.33 / 1	E- / 0.0	3	4
EN	Putnam Global Natural Resources	EBERX	E-	(800) 225-1581	16.21	E- /0.1	21.51 / 60	-10.02 / 1	-5.11 / 2	D / 1.9	11	5
EN	Guinness Atkinson Glob Energy	GAGEX	E-	(800) 915-6565	21.87	E- /0.1	29.87 / 86	-12.18 / 0	-4.40 / 2	D- / 1.1	6	13
EN	Saratoga Adv Tr Energy&Basic Mat	SBMBX	E-	(800) 807-3863	11.62	E- /0.1	30.86 / 88	-10.60 / 1	-4.53 / 2	D / 1.6	13	4
EN	ProFunds-Oil & Gas UltraSector	ENPSX	E-	(888) 776-3637	31.96	E- /0.1	35.37 / 94	-12.26 / 0	-3.78 / 2	E / 0.3	15	4
EN	Rydex Energy A	RYENX	E-	(800) 820-0888	74.72	E- /0.1	37.51 / 96	-11.20 / 1	-4.47 / 2	D- / 1.0	15	19
EN	BlackRock AllCap Energy & Res	BACAX	E-	(800) 441-7762	10.74	E- /0.1	26.38 / 77	-9.47 / 1	-5.36 / 2	D- / 1.0	22	4
EN	ICON Energy A	ICEAX	E-	(800) 764-0442	12.90	E- /0.1	27.75 / 81	-9.48 / 1	-2.86 / 2	E+ / 0.8	20	10
SC	● MSIF Small Company Growth A	MSSMX	E-	(800) 354-8185	12.00	E- /0.1	17.14 / 39	-6.62 / 2	7.04 / 35	E+ / 0.8	1	18
EN	● J Hancock Natural Resources A	JNRAX	E-	(800) 257-3336	12.08	E- /0.1	40.18 / 97	-11.38 / 1	-8.31 / 1	E+ / 0.8	10	3
MC	● MSIF Trust Mid Cap Growth A	MACGX	E-	(800) 354-8185	16.72	E- /0.1	11.43 / 16	-6.07 / 2	3.44 / 13	E- / 0.0	0	15
EN	Firsthand Alternative Energy Fd	ALTEX	E-	(888) 884-2675	5.63	E- /0.1	6.03 / 5	-8.46 / 1	3.68 / 14	C- / 3.4	6	10
EN	VanEck Global Hard Assets A	GHAAX	E-	(800) 826-1115	36.05	E- /0.1	40.75 / 97	-9.80 / 1	-5.50 / 2	E+ / 0.8	23	22

● Denotes fund is closed to new investors

Fund Type	Fund Name	Ticker Symbol	Overall Investment Rating	Phone	Net Asset Value As of 2/28/17	Perform-ance Rating/Pts	Annualized Total Return Through 2/28/17			Risk Rating/Pts	Mgr. Quality Pct	Mgr. Tenure (Years)
							1Yr / Pct	3Yr / Pct	5Yr / Pct			
SC	Pacific Advisors Small Cap Value A	PASMX	E-	(800) 282-6693	26.48	E- /0.1	37.16 /96	-10.94 / 1	1.34 / 7	D- / 1.2	0	24
EN	BlackRock Natural Resource Inv A	MDGRX	E-	(800) 441-7762	44.09	E- /0.1	29.59 /85	-8.11 / 1	-3.61 / 2	E+ / 0.9	38	N/A
EN	Prudential Jennison Natural Res A	PGNAX	E-	(800) 225-1852	36.75	E- /0.1	40.50 /97	-10.24 / 1	-6.57 / 1	E+ / 0.7	20	11
EN	Victory Global Natural Resources A	RSNRX	E-	(800) 539-3863	23.08	E- /0.1	56.58 /99	-11.91 / 1	-7.05 / 1	E / 0.5	10	12
EN	Franklin Natural Resources A	FRNRX	E-	(800) 342-5236	26.69	E- /0.1	38.47 /97	-9.62 / 1	-6.66 / 1	E+ / 0.9	26	18
MC	Transamerica Multi-Cap Growth A	ITSAX	E-	(888) 233-4339	6.51	E- /0.1	11.82 /17	-6.26 / 2	3.16 /11	D / 1.8	0	N/A
FO	Janus Overseas A	JDIAX	E-	(800) 295-2687	27.23	E- /0.1	17.84 /42	-6.67 / 2	-4.98 / 2	C- / 3.0	6	1
FO	Shelton International Select Eqty A	WHVAX	E-	(888) 739-1390	17.24	E- /0.2	20.03 /52	-6.98 / 1	-1.57 / 3	C- / 3.1	5	1
EM	US Global Investors Em Europe	EUROX	E-	(800) 873-8637	6.00	E- /0.2	18.34 /44	-8.82 / 1	-7.73 / 1	D+ / 2.6	2	20
EN	AllianzGI Global Natural Res A	ARMAX	E-	(800) 988-8380	15.58	E- /0.2	26.97 /79	-6.17 / 2	-1.07 / 3	D / 1.7	56	13
PM	Deutsche Gold & Prec Metals Fund	SGDAX	E-	(800) 728-3337	6.82	E- /0.2	19.17 /48	-5.25 / 2	-15.57 / 0	E- / 0.0	67	1
EM	T Rowe Price Emer Europe	TREMX	E-	(800) 638-5660	13.07	E- /0.2	24.34 /71	-7.53 / 1	-6.34 / 1	D / 1.7	3	4
EN	Ivy Global Nat Resource A	IGNAX	E-	(800) 777-6472	15.03	E- /0.2	31.58 /89	-6.95 / 1	-4.80 / 2	D / 2.2	48	4
FO	Oberweis China Opportunities	OBCHX	E-	(800) 245-7311	11.97	E- /0.2	15.60 /32	-5.40 / 2	9.70 /56	D- / 1.2	13	N/A
EM	ProFunds-Ultra Intl Svc	UNPSX	E-	(888) 776-3637	12.59	E- /0.2	24.41 /71	-8.64 / 1	2.68 /10	D- / 1.2	2	8
SC	Catalyst Small Cap Insider Buying	CTVAX	E-	(866) 447-4228	13.89	E- /0.2	28.46 /83	-6.44 / 2	4.31 /17	D+ / 2.8	1	11
GR	Turner Titan Long Short Investor	TSPCX	E-	(800) 224-6312	8.01	E- /0.2	-3.49 / 1	-2.40 / 6	0.09 / 5	D+ / 2.9	7	9
MC	Westcore Mid Cap Val Div II Rtl	WTMGX	E-	(800) 392-2673	4.61	E /0.3	10.86 /14	-4.50 / 3	5.38 /24	D- / 1.6	1	1
PM	Rydex Precious Metal A	RYMNX	E-	(800) 820-0888	30.04	E /0.3	27.60 /81	-4.91 / 2	-14.05 / 0	E- / 0.0	74	24
GR	Renaissance Global IPO	IPOSX	E-	(888) 476-3863	14.83	E /0.3	16.22 /35	-3.86 / 3	5.60 /26	D+ / 2.8	0	20
FO	Janus Aspen Overseas Inst	JAIGX	E-	(800) 295-2687	26.39	E /0.3	18.37 /44	-6.16 / 2	-3.46 / 2	D / 2.1	8	1
PM	Wells Fargo Precious Mtls A	EKWAX	E-	(800) 222-8222	36.18	E /0.3	17.95 /43	-3.01 / 4	-13.51 / 0	E- / 0.1	84	10
EN	Columbia Gl Energy and Nat Res A	EENAX	E-	(800) 345-6611	17.70	E /0.3	27.06 /79	-5.27 / 2	-2.04 / 3	D / 2.0	63	6
SC	● Universal Inst Small Co Growth II	USIIX	E-	(800) 869-6397	10.94	E /0.3	24.22 /71	-5.71 / 2	8.42 /46	E- / 0.0	1	14
EN	Fidelity Adv Energy A	FANAX	E-	(800) 522-7297	33.94	E /0.4	35.34 /94	-4.68 / 3	0.10 / 5	D- / 1.5	82	11
PM	Midas Fund	MIDSX	E-	(800) 400-6432	1.26	E /0.4	32.63 /91	-6.67 / 2	-20.43 / 0	E- / 0.0	40	15
EN	Fidelity Select Natural Resources	FNARX	E-	(800) 544-8888	29.13	E /0.4	34.54 /93	-5.97 / 2	-1.73 / 3	D- / 1.5	71	11
PM	USAA Precious Mtls&Minerals	USAGX	E-	(800) 382-8722	13.33	E /0.4	22.34 /64	-4.54 / 3	-15.58 / 0	E- / 0.1	75	N/A
EN	Fidelity Select Natural Gas	FSNGX	E-	(800) 544-8888	27.76	E /0.4	56.75 /99	-9.69 / 1	-2.06 / 3	E+ / 0.6	39	5
GR	Perkins Discovery Fund	PDFDX	E-	(800) 673-0550	34.29	E /0.4	25.93 /76	-4.73 / 3	6.28 /30	D+ / 2.4	0	19
EN	Vanguard Energy Index Adm	VENAX	E-	(800) 662-7447	49.13	E /0.4	28.98 /84	-5.37 / 2	0.20 / 5	D- / 1.3	74	2
RE	Ell International Property I	EIIPX	E-	(888) 323-8912	11.95	E /0.4	6.21 / 5	-1.94 / 7	3.00 /11	D- / 1.5	4	3
PM	Tocqueville Gold	TGLDX	E-	(800) 697-3863	37.00	E /0.4	21.27 /59	-3.48 / 4	-13.60 / 0	E- / 0.0	79	20
PM	OCM Gold Fund Investor	OCMGX	E-	(800) 628-9403	9.88	E /0.5	20.48 /55	-1.52 / 8	-12.52 / 0	E- / 0.0	92	21
MC	● Universal Inst Mid Cap Growth I	UMGPX	E-	(800) 869-6397	9.57	E /0.5	17.30 /40	-3.84 / 3	4.75 /20	D- / 1.0	1	14
PM	American Century Global Gold A	ACGGX	E-	(800) 345-6488	8.59	E /0.5	23.93 /70	-2.53 / 5	-14.15 / 0	E- / 0.0	87	12
PM	First Eagle Gold A	SGGDX	E-	(800) 334-2143	17.11	E /0.5	17.35 /40	-1.09 / 9	-11.21 / 0	E / 0.5	90	4
EN	Fidelity Select Energy Svcs	FSESX	E-	(800) 544-8888	54.71	E /0.5	46.38 /99	-9.69 / 1	-2.73 / 2	E / 0.4	29	4
SC	Williston Basin/Mid-Nrth Amer Stk	ICPAX	E-	(800) 601-5593	5.67	E /0.5	40.94 /98	-5.41 / 2	1.06 / 6	D- / 1.2	2	7
EN	Ivy Energy A	IEYAX	E-	(800) 777-6472	13.64	E /0.5	42.98 /98	-5.04 / 2	0.46 / 5	D- / 1.2	81	11
SC	Jacob Small Cap Growth Investor	JSCGX	E-	(888) 522-6239	17.37	E /0.5	31.69 /89	-4.77 / 3	3.31 /12	E+ / 0.8	1	7
SC	Rational Defensive Growth A	HSUAX	E-	(800) 253-0412	2.90	E+ /0.6	15.99 /34	-1.66 / 7	6.51 /32	D- / 1.0	7	N/A
EN	Vanguard Energy Inv	VGENX	E-	(800) 662-7447	51.53	E+ /0.6	33.11 /92	-5.10 / 2	-1.01 / 3	D- / 1.4	75	5
EN	Waddell & Reed Adv Energy Fund	WEGAX	E-	(888) 923-3355	13.90	E+ /0.6	43.30 /98	-4.82 / 3	0.65 / 6	D- / 1.2	83	11
EM	Fidelity Advisor Latin America Fd A	FLFAX	E-	(800) 544-8544	21.38	E+ /0.6	39.87 /97	-5.06 / 2	-10.20 / 1	D / 2.0	5	2
SC	● Lord Abbett Developing Growth A	LAGWX	E-	(888) 522-2388	19.37	E+ /0.6	23.85 /69	-2.68 / 5	9.47 /54	E+ / 0.9	2	16
PM	Fidelity Adv Gold A	FGDAX	E-	(800) 522-7297	20.54	E+ /0.7	19.97 /52	-1.19 / 9	-14.09 / 0	E- / 0.1	92	10
EM	Pioneer Emerging Markets A	PEMFX	E-	(800) 225-6292	17.67	E+ /0.7	27.31 /80	-3.67 / 3	-4.08 / 2	D+ / 2.4	13	4
GL	Fidelity Adv Glb Commodity Stk A	FFGAX	E-	(800) 522-7297	11.64	E+ /0.7	37.54 /96	-4.74 / 3	-4.53 / 2	D / 2.0	18	8
EN	T Rowe Price New Era	PRNEX	E-	(800) 638-5660	33.24	E+ /0.7	25.05 /73	-3.39 / 4	0.01 / 4	D- / 1.5	81	4
EM	● State Street Dscpld Em Mkts Eq N	SSEMX	E-	(800) 843-2639	7.49	E+ /0.7	17.37 /40	-2.90 / 5	-3.39 / 2	D- / 1.3	19	10
TC	Kinetics Internet Advisor A	KINAX	E-	(800) 930-3828	39.02	E+ /0.7	12.21 /19	-0.03 /13	9.78 /57	D / 2.3	2	18

● Denotes fund is closed to new investors
www.thestreetratings.com
773
Data as of February 28, 2017

Fund Type	Fund Name	Ticker Symbol	Overall Investment Rating	Phone	Net Asset Value As of 2/28/17	Perform-ance Rating/Pts	1Yr / Pct	3Yr / Pct	5Yr / Pct	Risk Rating/Pts	Mgr. Quality Pct	Mgr. Tenure (Years)
EN	Fidelity Select Energy	FSENX	E-	(800) 544-8888	44.10	E+ / 0.7	36.05 / 95	-4.39 / 3	0.38 / 5	D / 1.6	84	11
SC	Satuit Capital US Emerging Co A	SATMX	E-	(866) 972-8848	28.04	E+ / 0.8	27.45 / 80	-2.26 / 6	6.05 / 29	D / 1.8	3	17
SC	Ivy Micro Cap Growth A	IGWAX	E-	(800) 777-6472	22.97	E+ / 0.8	32.69 / 91	-2.48 / 5	8.52 / 46	D / 1.7	2	N/A
SC	Praxis Small Cap Index A	MMSCX	E-	(800) 977-2947	9.67	E+ / 0.8	19.15 / 48	-0.27 / 12	5.63 / 26	D / 1.8	7	N/A
SC	AllianzGI US Small-Cap Growth A	AEGAX	E-	(800) 988-8380	11.64	E+ / 0.9	22.67 / 65	-1.42 / 8	7.20 / 36	D- / 1.4	3	10
EM	Sit Developing Mkts Growth Fund	SDMGX	E-	(800) 332-5580	13.41	E+ / 0.9	24.39 / 71	-3.01 / 4	-2.60 / 2	D+ / 2.7	18	23
FO	JPMorgan Latin America A	JLTAX	E-	(800) 480-4111	13.87	E+ / 0.9	36.02 / 95	-3.94 / 3	-6.81 / 1	D / 2.1	25	10
PM	Oppenheimer Gold/Spec Min A	OPGSX	E-	(888) 470-0862	16.61	D- / 1.0	32.91 / 91	-1.87 / 7	-13.86 / 0	E- / 0.2	89	20
MC	● TCW Growth Equities N	TGDNX	E-	(800) 386-3829	8.37	D- / 1.0	18.55 / 45	-1.66 / 7	5.70 / 26	D- / 1.0	1	5
FO	Rational Risk Managed Emrg Mkt	HGSAX	E-	(800) 253-0412	6.14	D- / 1.0	10.91 / 14	1.09 / 19	1.45 / 7	D- / 1.1	82	1
MC	Turner Midcap Growth Inv	TMGFX	E-	(800) 224-6312	18.44	D- / 1.0	18.66 / 46	-1.92 / 7	5.76 / 27	E / 0.4	1	N/A
PM	VanEck Intl Investors Gold A	INIVX	E-	(800) 826-1115	9.57	D- / 1.1	34.35 / 93	-1.57 / 8	-12.88 / 0	E- / 0.0	91	19
SC	● Bridgeway Ultra-SmCo	BRUSX	E-	(800) 661-3550	29.59	D- / 1.1	24.16 / 70	-3.23 / 4	10.35 / 61	D / 2.1	2	23
PM	Invesco Gold and Precious Mtls A	IGDAX	E-	(800) 959-4246	4.41	D- / 1.1	31.79 / 90	-1.32 / 8	-11.64 / 0	E- / 0.1	90	4
SC	● Buffalo Emerging Opportunities	BUFOX	E-	(800) 492-8332	14.97	D- / 1.1	27.81 / 81	-2.18 / 6	11.46 / 70	D- / 1.5	2	4
FO	Deutsche EAFE Equity Index Inst	BTAEX	E-	(800) 728-3337	5.64	D- / 1.1	15.15 / 31	-1.05 / 9	4.87 / 20	D- / 1.0	63	4
GL	Federated Emerging Markets Eq	FGLEX	E-	(800) 341-7400	9.07	D- / 1.2	25.35 / 74	-2.52 / 5	2.97 / 11	D / 2.1	42	7
FO	Beck Mack & Oliver Partners	BMPEX	E-	(800) 943-6786	10.31	D- / 1.2	25.06 / 73	-1.99 / 7	4.53 / 18	D / 2.0	50	2
GL	API Short Term Bond A	APIMX	E-	(800) 544-6060	3.93	D- / 1.2	7.51 / 7	0.91 / 18	2.15 / 8	D- / 1.0	80	20
PM	Franklin Gold & Precious Metals A	FKRCX	E-	(800) 342-5236	17.66	D- / 1.3	32.77 / 91	-0.71 / 10	-13.34 / 0	E+ / 0.6	92	18
MC	Brown Capital Mgmt Mid Company	BCMSX	E-	(877) 892-4226	11.83	D- / 1.3	17.08 / 39	-1.12 / 9	5.74 / 27	E / 0.4	2	15
SC	Kalmar Growth With Value Sm Cap	KGSCX	E-	(800) 282-2319	12.70	D- / 1.5	23.18 / 67	-0.18 / 13	7.45 / 38	E / 0.3	6	20
PM	Vanguard Prec Metals & Mining Inv	VGPMX	E-	(800) 662-7447	10.29	D / 1.6	36.56 / 95	-2.32 / 6	-12.39 / 0	E- / 0.0	82	3
SC	Royce Low Priced Stock Svc	RYLPX	E-	(800) 221-4268	8.20	D / 1.6	26.09 / 76	-0.82 / 10	0.68 / 6	E+ / 0.9	6	4
FO	Profunds-Ultra China Svc	UGPSX	E-	(888) 776-3637	10.34	D / 1.7	34.81 / 94	-2.89 / 5	3.00 / 11	E- / 0.0	44	8
GR	Columbia Global Infrastructure A	RRIAX	E-	(800) 345-6611	12.08	D / 1.7	16.58 / 37	1.03 / 18	8.53 / 47	E+ / 0.8	4	10
SC	BMO Small-Cap Growth Y	MRSCX	E-	(800) 236-3863	17.39	D / 1.8	29.10 / 84	-1.40 / 8	7.61 / 39	D- / 1.3	3	1
FO	Deutsche Latin America Equity A	SLANX	E-	(800) 728-3337	22.53	D / 1.9	43.22 / 98	-1.22 / 9	-4.66 / 2	D- / 1.2	62	4
MC	● Delaware Smid Cap Growth A	DFCIX	E-	(800) 523-1918	17.73	D / 1.9	7.29 / 6	5.28 / 57	9.17 / 52	E / 0.3	43	1
GR	BlackRock Event Driven Eqty Inv A	BALPX	E-	(800) 441-7762	8.74	D / 2.0	4.12 / 3	4.96 / 54	9.52 / 55	E / 0.5	78	2
GL	Delaware International Sml Cap A	DGGAX	E-	(800) 523-1918	6.03	D / 2.2	15.77 / 33	2.83 / 30	6.55 / 32	E / 0.5	90	1
SC	Delafield	DEFIX	E-	(800) 697-3863	25.36	D+ / 2.7	33.90 / 93	-0.25 / 12	6.16 / 29	E+ / 0.9	7	24
SC	Turner Small Cap Growth Fund	TSCEX	E-	(800) 224-6312	12.90	D+ / 2.7	22.40 / 64	1.09 / 19	8.60 / 47	E- / 0.1	9	4
PM	Gabelli Gold A	GLDAX	E-	(800) 422-3554	14.52	D+ / 2.7	24.83 / 73	2.66 / 29	-10.34 / 1	E- / 0.1	98	23
FO	Direxion Mo Emerg Mkts Bull 2X	DXELX	E-	(800) 851-0511	38.85	D+ / 2.9	56.15 / 99	-3.90 / 3	-7.82 / 1	E- / 0.1	28	12
SC	Rice Hall James Small Cap Port	RHJMX	E-	(866) 777-7818	10.52	C- / 3.0	14.46 / 28	3.52 / 37	8.71 / 48	E / 0.3	47	21
GR	Westcore Large Cap Dividend Rtl	WTEIX	E-	(800) 392-2673	6.61	C- / 3.2	12.78 / 21	3.77 / 40	9.27 / 53	E / 0.4	7	1
SC	● AMG GW&K US Small Cap Gr N	ATASX	E-	(800) 548-4539	4.02	C- / 3.2	24.97 / 73	0.09 / 14	6.06 / 29	E / 0.3	9	1
GR	Victory Newbridge Large Cap Grow	VFGAX	E-	(800) 539-3863	9.02	C- / 3.4	15.19 / 31	4.76 / 52	9.63 / 56	E- / 0.2	11	14
MC	Alger SMid Cap Growth Fund A	ALMAX	E-	(800) 254-3796	10.63	C- / 3.6	24.95 / 73	2.71 / 29	8.71 / 48	E- / 0.0	4	1
IN	Comstock Capital Value A	DRCVX	E	(800) 422-3554	5.76	E- / 0.0	-29.33 / 0	-15.66 / 0	-17.86 / 0	C- / 3.7	15	30
AG	Rydex Inv NASDAQ 100 Strgy A	RYAPX	E	(800) 820-0888	77.16	E- / 0.0	-23.36 / 0	-14.84 / 0	-16.74 / 0	C- / 3.9	18	19
MC	Rydex Inv Mid-Cap Stgy A	RYAGX	E	(800) 820-0888	24.84	E- / 0.0	-25.67 / 0	-11.44 / 1	-14.93 / 0	C / 4.7	31	13
SC	Rydex Inv Russell 2000 Stgy A	RYAFX	E	(800) 820-0888	23.69	E- / 0.0	-28.99 / 0	-10.39 / 1	-15.17 / 0	C- / 3.9	18	13
RE	ProFunds Short Real Estate Svc	SRPSX	E	(888) 776-3637	14.56	E- / 0.0	-18.98 / 0	-13.70 / 0	-14.11 / 0	C- / 3.8	19	4
SC	Leuthold Grizzly Short	GRZZX	E	(888) 200-0409	5.85	E- / 0.0	-26.97 / 0	-8.71 / 1	-13.20 / 0	C- / 4.2	21	8
IN	Arrow Commodity Strategy A	CSFFX	E	(877) 277-6933	5.64	E- / 0.0	11.02 / 15	-12.15 / 0	-10.12 / 1	C / 4.4	0	7
IN	PIMCO Commodity Real Ret Str A	PCRAX	E	(800) 426-0107	7.07	E- / 0.0	19.96 / 52	-13.58 / 0	-10.58 / 1	C / 4.3	0	10
OT	● MFS Commodity Strategy Fund A	MCSAX	E	(800) 225-2606	6.03	E- / 0.0	15.28 / 31	-12.27 / 0	-9.35 / 1	C- / 4.0	0	7
HL	Highland Long/Short Healthcare A	HHCAX	E	(877) 665-1287	11.17	E- / 0.0	-2.62 / 1	-7.74 / 1	1.55 / 7	C / 4.9	2	7
OT	Eaton Vance Commodity Strategy	EACSX	E	(800) 262-1122	5.52	E- / 0.0	21.03 / 57	-12.00 / 0	-9.76 / 1	C- / 3.8	0	2
OT	ALPS CoreComm Mgt CompComm	JCRAX	E	(866) 759-5679	7.61	E- / 0.1	20.47 / 55	-10.36 / 1	-8.36 / 1	C- / 3.6	0	7

● Denotes fund is closed to new investors

Fund Type	Fund Name	Ticker Symbol	Overall Investment Rating	Phone	Net Asset Value As of 2/28/17	PERFORMANCE Perform-ance Rating/Pts	Annualized Total Return Through 2/28/17 1Yr / Pct	3Yr / Pct	5Yr / Pct	RISK Risk Rating/Pts	FUND MGR Mgr. Quality Pct	Mgr. Tenure (Years)
	99 Pct = Best 0 Pct = Worst											
IN	VanEck CM Commodity Index A	CMCAX	E	(800) 826-1115	4.88	E- /0.1	22.49 /64	-11.69 / 1	-9.33 / 1	C- / 3.6	0	3
IN	DFA Commodity Strategy Port	DCMSX	E	(800) 984-9472	6.06	E- /0.1	18.21 /44	-11.53 / 1	-8.25 / 1	C- / 3.8	0	7
FO	AllianzGI NFJ Internatl Value A	AFJAX	E	(800) 988-8380	17.05	E- /0.1	8.50 / 8	-7.22 / 1	-1.33 / 3	C / 4.6	5	14
FO	Rydex Eurp 1.25x Strgy A	RYAEX	E	(800) 820-0888	80.59	E- /0.1	11.16 /15	-8.04 / 1	1.64 / 7	C / 4.5	4	17
EN	ProFunds Short Oil & Gas Svc	SNPSX	E	(888) 776-3637	44.50	E- /0.1	-25.83 / 0	-2.44 / 6	-7.10 / 1	C- / 3.6	4	4
BA	Pacific Advisors Balanced A	PAABX	E	(800) 282-6693	11.63	E- /0.1	10.42 /13	-6.49 / 2	0.87 / 6	C- / 4.0	0	7
GL	Ivy Asset Strategy A	WASAX	E	(800) 777-6472	21.52	E- /0.1	3.61 / 3	-5.69 / 2	2.09 / 8	C- / 3.7	1	3
BA	Invesco Balanced-Risk Com Str A	BRCAX	E	(800) 959-4246	6.89	E- /0.1	16.42 /36	-7.98 / 1	-8.37 / 1	C / 4.7	1	7
FO	BlackRock Eurofund Inv A	MDEFX	E	(800) 441-7762	13.02	E- /0.1	4.29 / 3	-6.00 / 2	3.82 /14	C / 5.1	9	7
FO	Morgan Stanley European Eq A	EUGAX	E	(800) 869-6397	15.86	E- /0.1	8.51 / 8	-5.89 / 2	2.76 /10	C / 4.8	9	11
FO	Columbia European Equity A	AXEAX	E	(800) 345-6611	6.02	E- /0.1	4.94 / 4	-5.23 / 2	4.25 /17	C / 4.9	14	8
FO	● Artisan International Small Cp Inv	ARTJX	E	(800) 344-1770	20.52	E- /0.1	0.96 / 2	-5.98 / 2	5.54 /25	C / 4.3	9	16
GR	Pacific Advisors Mid Cap Value A	PAMVX	E	(800) 282-6693	11.66	E- /0.1	17.73 /42	-6.72 / 2	-0.94 / 3	C- / 3.6	0	10
GL	Waddell & Reed Adv Asset Strat A	UNASX	E	(888) 923-3355	8.27	E- /0.2	6.85 / 6	-4.68 / 3	2.91 /10	C- / 3.5	2	3
FO	Saratoga Adv Tr Intl Equity A	SIEYX	E	(800) 807-3863	9.75	E- /0.2	15.67 /33	-4.99 / 2	0.04 / 4	C / 5.0	16	5
MC	Westcore SmCp Gr II Rtl	WTSLX	E	(800) 392-2673	21.78	E- /0.2	12.33 /19	-6.67 / 2	1.60 / 7	C- / 3.5	0	1
GL	Calamos Evolving World Growth A	CNWGX	E	(800) 582-6959	11.99	E- /0.2	11.33 /16	-4.46 / 3	-1.28 / 3	C / 5.0	20	9
FO	BlackRock Intl Opps Inv A	BREAX	E	(800) 441-7762	29.75	E- /0.2	12.11 /18	-4.16 / 3	3.05 /11	C- / 3.8	22	18
FO	AIG Intl Dividend Strat A	SIEAX	E	(800) 858-8850	8.77	E- /0.2	20.17 /53	-5.98 / 2	-3.07 / 2	C- / 3.4	9	5
GL	STAAR Inv Trust International	SITIX	E	(800) 332-7738	10.13	E- /0.2	13.69 /24	-6.49 / 2	-2.38 / 2	C- / 3.6	1	20
FO	American Century Intl Gr A	TWGAX	E	(800) 345-6488	11.16	E- /0.2	8.08 / 8	-3.14 / 4	4.37 /17	C / 4.5	34	15
GL	Kinetics Global Advisor A	KGLAX	E	(800) 930-3828	5.26	E- /0.2	18.68 /46	-4.35 / 3	3.81 /14	C / 5.0	20	18
GR	Unified Srs Tr Auer Growth Fd	AUERX	E	(800) 408-4682	7.13	E- /0.2	18.83 /46	-7.30 / 1	1.87 / 8	C- / 3.5	0	30
FO	DFA United Kingdom Small Co Inst	DFUKX	E	(800) 984-9472	28.06	E- /0.2	2.57 / 2	-4.18 / 3	8.94 /50	C- / 3.6	22	13
EM	Harding Loevner Frontier EM Inst	HLFMX	E	(877) 435-8105	7.43	E /0.3	11.69 /17	-4.49 / 3	2.89 /10	C / 4.6	12	9
FO	Lord Abbett Intl Dividend Inc A	LIDAX	E	(888) 522-2388	6.90	E /0.3	13.45 /23	-3.62 / 4	1.43 / 7	C / 4.5	28	9
SC	Marketocracy Masters 100	MOFQX	E	(888) 884-8482	9.02	E /0.3	14.61 /28	-5.41 / 2	-0.08 / 4	C- / 4.0	1	16
FO	MassMutual Premier Intl Equity A	MMIAX	E	(800) 542-6767	11.00	E /0.3	6.58 / 5	-1.93 / 7	5.23 /23	C- / 3.7	51	19
FO	Federated International Sm-Mid A	ISCAX	E	(800) 341-7400	33.24	E /0.3	8.39 / 8	-1.97 / 7	4.37 /17	C- / 4.0	51	18
OT	Hartford Global Real Asset A	HRLAX	E	(888) 843-7824	8.95	E /0.3	21.63 /60	-4.28 / 3	-4.05 / 2	C / 4.5	1	7
FO	Janus International Equity A	JAIEX	E	(800) 295-2687	11.50	E /0.3	12.00 /18	-2.90 / 5	2.67 /10	C / 4.7	37	7
GR	FMC Strategic Value Fund	FMSVX	E	(866) 777-7818	23.43	E /0.3	17.70 /41	-5.25 / 2	2.97 /11	C- / 3.9	0	19
FO	Westcore International SC Rtl	WTIFX	E	(800) 392-2673	15.83	E /0.3	13.80 /25	-4.58 / 3	3.18 /12	C- / 4.1	19	14
FO	Calamos International Growth A	CIGRX	E	(800) 582-6959	16.93	E /0.4	12.05 /18	-2.21 / 6	1.98 / 8	C- / 4.2	47	12
FO	Touchstone Internatl Value A	FSIEX	E	(800) 543-0407	7.13	E /0.4	15.25 /31	-2.89 / 5	2.80 /10	C / 4.8	37	5
FO	Manning & Napier World Oppty A	EXWAX	E	(800) 466-3863	7.15	E /0.4	11.82 /17	-3.57 / 4	2.25 / 9	C- / 3.9	29	21
SC	Gabelli Focus Five A	GWSAX	E	(800) 422-3554	13.26	E /0.5	10.85 /14	-0.99 / 9	8.18 /43	C- / 3.9	13	5
FO	GMO Intl Large/Mid Cap Eqty III	GMIEX	E		25.44	E /0.5	14.70 /29	-3.85 / 3	4.27 /17	C- / 4.0	26	5
EM	VanEck Emerging Mkts A	GBFAX	E	(800) 826-1115	13.24	E /0.5	20.63 /56	-2.17 / 6	1.92 / 8	C / 4.5	26	19
GI	Virtus Equity Trend A	VAPAX	E	(800) 243-1574	12.80	E+ /0.6	12.87 /21	-1.29 / 8	5.58 /25	C- / 3.8	3	2
FO	Manning & Napier Overseas Srs I	EXOSX	E	(800) 466-3863	21.54	E+ /0.6	12.78 /21	-2.79 / 5	2.94 /11	C- / 4.0	39	15
FO	ProFunds-Europe 30 Svc	UEPSX	E	(888) 776-3637	13.22	E+ /0.6	18.78 /46	-4.30 / 3	2.19 / 8	C / 4.3	21	8
FO	GMO International Equity III	GMOIX	E		20.41	E+ /0.6	15.53 /32	-3.39 / 4	4.29 /17	C / 4.5	31	2
FO	RidgeWorth Intl Equity A	SCIIX	E	(888) 784-3863	9.68	E+ /0.6	13.12 /22	-0.72 /10	5.38 /24	C- / 3.9	67	2

Section V

Performance:
100 Best and Worst
Stock Mutual Funds

A compilation of those

Equity Mutual Funds

receiving the highest and lowest Performance Ratings.

Funds are listed in order by Performance Rating.

Section V Contents

This section contains a summary analysis of each of the top 100 and bottom 100 equity mutual funds as determined by their TheStreet Performance Rating. Since the Performance Rating does not take into consideration the amount of risk a fund poses, the selection of funds presented here is based solely on each fund's financial performance over the past three years.

In order to optimize the utility of our top and bottom fund lists, rather than listing all funds in a multi-class series, a single fund from each series is selected for display as the primary share class. Whenever possible, the selected fund is one that a retail investor would be most likely to choose. This share class may not be appropriate for every investor, so please consult with your financial advisor, the fund company, and the fund's prospectus before placing your trade.

You can use this section to identify those funds that have historically given shareholders the highest returns on their investments. A word of caution though: past performance is not necessarily indicative of future results. While these funds have provided the highest returns, some of them may be currently overvalued and due for a correction.

1. **Fund Type**   The mutual fund's peer category based on an analysis of its investment portfolio.

AG	Aggressive Growth	HL	Health
AA	Asset Allocation	IN	Income
BA	Balanced	IX	Index
CV	Convertible	MC	Mid Cap
EM	Emerging Market	OT	Other
EN	Energy/Natural Resources	PM	Precious Metals
FS	Financial Services	RE	Real Estate
FO	Foreign	SC	Small Cap
GL	Global	TC	Technology
GR	Growth	UT	Utilities
GI	Growth and Income		

A blank fund type means that the mutual fund has not yet been categorized.

2. **Fund Name**   The name of the mutual fund as stated in its prospectus, which can sometimes differ slightly from the name that the company uses for advertising. If you cannot find the particular mutual fund you are interested in, or if you have any doubts regarding the precise name, verify the information with your broker or on your account statement. Also, use the fund's ticker symbol for confirmation. (See column 3.)

3. Ticker Symbol The unique alphabetic symbol used for identifying and trading a specific mutual fund. No two funds can have the same ticker symbol, and the ticker symbol for mutual funds always ends with an "X".

A handful of funds currently show no associated ticker symbol. This means that the fund is either small or new since the NASD only assigns a ticker symbol to funds with at least $25 million in assets or 1,000 shareholders.

4. Overall Investment Rating Our overall rating is measured on a scale from A to E based on each fund's risk-adjusted performance. Please see page 10 for specific descriptions of each letter grade. Also, refer to page 7 for information on how our ratings are derived. Most important, when using this rating, please be sure to consider the warnings beginning on page 11 regarding the ratings' limitations and the underlying assumptions.

5. Phone The telephone number of the company managing the fund. Call this number to receive a prospectus or other information about the fund.

6. Net Asset Value (NAV) The fund's share price as of the date indicated. A fund's NAV is computed by dividing the value of the fund's asset holdings, less accrued fees and expenses, by the number of its shares outstanding.

7. Performance Rating/Points A letter grade rating based solely on the mutual fund's financial performance over the trailing three years, without any consideration for the amount of risk the fund poses. Like the overall Investment Rating, the Performance Rating is measured on a scale from A to E for ease of interpretation. The points score indicates where the Performance Rating falls on a scale of 0 to 10.

8. 1-Year Total Return The total return the fund has provided investors over the preceeding twelve months. This total return figure is computed based on the fund's dividend distributions and share price appreciation/depreciation during the period, net of the expenses and fees it imposes on its shareholders. Although the total return figure does not reflect an adjustment for any loads the fund may carry, such adjustments have been made in deriving TheStreet Investment Ratings.

9. 1-Year Total Return Percentile The fund's percentile rank based on its one-year performance compared to that of all other equity funds in existence for at least one year. A score of 99 is the best possible, indicating that the fund outperformed 99% of the other mutual funds. Zero is the worst possible percentile score.

10. 3-Year Total Return The total annual return the fund has provided investors over the preceeding three years.

11.	**3-Year Total Return Percentile**	The fund's percentile rank based on its three-year performance compared to that of all other equity funds in existence for at least three years. A score of 99 is the best possible, indicating that the fund outperformed 99% of the other mutual funds. Zero is the worst possible percentile score.
12.	**5-Year Total Return**	The total annual return the fund has provided investors over the preceeding five years.
13.	**5-Year Total Return Percentile**	The fund's percentile rank based on its five-year performance compared to that of all other equity funds in existence for at least five years. A score of 99 is the best possible, indicating that the fund outperformed 99% of the other mutual funds. Zero is the worst possible percentile score.
14.	**Risk Rating/Points**	A letter grade rating based solely on the mutual fund's risk as determined by its monthly performance volatility over the trailing three years. The risk rating does not take into consideration the overall financial performance the fund has achieved or the total return it has provided to its shareholders. Like the overall Investment Rating, the Risk Rating is measured on a scale from A to E for ease of interpretation. The points score indicates where the Risk Rating falls on a scale of 0 to 10.
15.	**Manager Quality Percentile**	The manager quality percentile is based on a ranking of the fund's alpha, a statistical measure representing the difference between a fund's actual returns and its expected performance given its level of risk. Fund managers who have been able to exceed the fund's statistically expected performance receive a high percentile rank with 99 representing the highest possible score. At the other end of the spectrum, fund managers who have actually detracted from the fund's expected performance receive a low percentile rank with 0 representing the lowest possible score.
16.	**Manager Tenure**	The number of years the current manager has been managing the fund. Since fund managers who deliver substandard returns are usually replaced, a long tenure is usually a good sign that shareholders are satisfied that the fund is achieving its stated objectives.

Fund Type	Fund Name	Ticker Symbol	Overall Investment Rating	Phone	Net Asset Value As of 2/28/17	Performance Rating/Pts	Annualized Total Return Through 2/28/17			Risk Rating/Pts	Mgr. Quality Pct	Mgr. Tenure (Years)
	99 Pct = Best 0 Pct = Worst						1Yr / Pct	3Yr / Pct	5Yr / Pct			
FO	Hennessy Japan Small Cap Inv	HJPSX	A+	(800) 966-4354	12.14	A+ /9.9	30.37 /87	13.52 /99	15.54 /98	B- / 7.3	99	10
FS	RMB Mendon Financial Services A	RMBKX	A+	(800) 601-5228	42.66	A+ /9.9	49.34 /99	20.69 /99	23.00 /99	C+ / 6.8	98	18
FS	Vanguard Financial Index Fd Adm	VFAIX	A+	(800) 662-7447	31.22	A+ /9.9	46.85 /99	14.09 /99	17.33 /98	C+ / 6.6	79	2
TC	Vanguard Info Tech Ind Adm	VITAX	A+	(800) 662-7447	68.11	A+ /9.9	33.51 /92	14.64 /99	14.84 /97	C+ / 6.5	85	2
FS	Emerald Banking and Finance A	HSSAX	A+	(855) 828-9909	42.64	A+ /9.9	51.05 /99	16.40 /99	21.78 /99	C+ / 6.5	88	20
GR	Parnassus Endeavor	PARWX	A+	(800) 999-3505	34.41	A+ /9.9	32.69 /91	15.00 /99	17.59 /98	C+ / 6.4	93	12
TC	Oak Assoc-Red Oak Technology	ROGSX	A+	(888) 462-5386	21.70	A+ /9.9	42.16 /98	14.41 /99	17.43 /98	C+ / 6.3	84	11
FS	1919 Financial Services A	SBFAX	A+	(844) 828-1919	24.53	A+ /9.9	44.51 /98	14.96 /99	18.45 /99	C+ / 6.1	87	3
FS	J Hancock Regional Bank A	FRBAX	A+	(800) 257-3336	26.28	A+ /9.9	60.84 /99	18.09 /99	20.90 /99	C+ / 6.0	91	19
FS	Alpine Financial Services Inst	ADFSX	A+	(888) 785-5578	17.24	A+ /9.9	55.88 /99	10.12 /94	17.39 /98	C+ / 5.7	30	2
TC	ICON Information Technology S	ICTEX	A+	(800) 764-0442	16.31	A+ /9.9	29.24 /85	15.71 /99	13.74 /91	C+ / 5.7	95	N/A
TC	Columbia Global Technology Gro A	CTCAX	A	(800) 345-6611	24.26	A+ /9.9	37.09 /96	14.87 /99	19.01 /99	C+ / 5.6	88	5
TC	ProFunds-Tech UltraSector Svc	TEPSX	A	(888) 776-3637	72.57	A+ /9.9	50.25 /99	18.32 /99	16.65 /98	C / 5.5	55	4
FS	Rydex Banking A	RYBKX	A	(800) 820-0888	73.27	A+ /9.9	54.46 /99	9.74 /92	12.97 /83	C / 5.4	11	19
AG	ProFunds-Ultra Bull Svc	ULPSX	A	(888) 776-3637	114.76	A+ /9.9	49.06 /99	16.12 /99	23.23 /99	C / 5.4	12	4
MC	Rydex Mid Cap 1.5x Strgy A	RYAHX	A	(800) 820-0888	80.51	A+ /9.9	47.64 /99	11.80 /98	18.21 /99	C / 5.2	40	16
AG	Rydex S&P 500 2x Strategy A	RYTTX	A	(800) 820-0888	89.66	A+ /9.9	50.14 /99	17.30 /99	24.71 /99	C / 5.2	20	17
FS	Hennessy Small Cap Financial Inv	HSFNX	A	(800) 966-4354	25.53	A+ /9.9	42.81 /98	12.66 /99	16.50 /98	C / 5.2	74	20
TC	Rydex Electronics A	RYELX	A-	(800) 820-0888	99.44	A+ /9.9	39.94 /97	15.56 /99	14.23 /94	C / 5.1	85	19
FS	Fidelity Select Banking Port	FSRBX	A-	(800) 544-8888	33.63	A+ /9.9	56.16 /99	12.86 /99	17.00 /98	C / 5.1	33	5
FS	T Rowe Price Financial Services	PRISX	A-	(800) 638-5660	25.77	A+ /9.9	41.68 /98	10.19 /94	15.71 /98	C / 5.0	30	3
FS	ProFunds-Financial UltraSector	FNPSX	A-	(888) 776-3637	16.76	A+ /9.9	55.76 /99	14.35 /99	20.82 /99	C / 5.0	21	4
GR	ProFunds-Ultra Dow 30 Svc	UDPSX	A-	(888) 776-3637	80.86	A+ /9.9	59.39 /99	17.03 /99	20.63 /99	C / 5.0	18	4
FO	Matthews India Fund Inv	MINDX	A-	(800) 789-2742	28.19	A+ /9.9	24.26 /71	20.97 /99	11.88 /73	C / 4.9	99	12
TC	Columbia Seligman Global Tech A	SHGTX	A-	(800) 345-6611	34.91	A+ /9.9	36.39 /95	19.38 /99	15.63 /98	C / 4.7	97	23
AG	Rydex Dow 2x Strategy A	RYLDX	B+	(800) 820-0888	65.73	A+ /9.9	61.30 /99	18.27 /99	21.91 /99	C / 4.6	27	13
GR	Direxion Mo S&P 500 Bull 2X Inv	DXSLX	B+	(800) 851-0511	113.80	A+ /9.9	50.67 /99	18.17 /99	25.43 /99	C / 4.5	31	11
TC	Fidelity Adv Semiconductors A	FELAX	B+	(800) 522-7297	20.18	A+ /9.9	51.50 /99	22.10 /99	18.34 /99	C / 4.4	98	8
TC	Columbia Seligman Comm & Info A	SLMCX	B+	(800) 345-6611	65.38	A+ /9.9	35.52 /94	19.14 /99	14.82 /96	C / 4.4	97	27
TC	Fidelity Select Technology	FSPTX	B+	(800) 544-8888	146.96	A+ /9.9	38.53 /97	12.25 /98	14.58 /96	C / 4.3	69	10
MC	● Thrivent Mid Cap Stock A	AASCX	B+	(800) 847-4836	24.31	A+ /9.9	43.79 /98	12.41 /98	15.80 /98	C / 4.3	87	13
TC	Fidelity Select Semiconductor Port	FSELX	B+	(800) 544-8888	101.24	A+ /9.9	51.79 /99	22.41 /99	18.88 /99	C / 4.3	98	8
GR	ProFunds-Ultra Nasdaq-100 Svc	UOPSX	B+	(888) 776-3637	109.07	A+ /9.9	56.53 /99	23.05 /99	28.53 /99	C- / 3.9	29	4
GR	Direxion Mo NASDAQ-100 Bull 2X	DXQLX	B+	(800) 851-0511	79.86	A+ /9.9	57.83 /99	25.17 /99	30.71 /99	C- / 3.7	62	11
GR	Fidelity Select Medical Eqpmnt Sys	FSMEX	B	(800) 544-8888	41.48	A+ /9.9	30.13 /87	16.02 /99	19.54 /99	C- / 3.5	96	10
TC	Janus Aspen Global Technology	JGLTX	B	(800) 295-2687	9.22	A+ /9.9	39.12 /97	12.72 /99	15.18 /97	C- / 3.5	69	6
GI	PIMCO StockPlus Long Duration	PSLDX	B	(800) 426-0107	7.35	A+ /9.9	33.07 /92	16.59 /99	18.46 /99	C- / 3.4	94	10
GR	ProFunds-Semicond UltraSector	SMPSX	B	(888) 776-3637	36.23	A+ /9.9	72.14 /99	26.71 /99	20.19 /99	C- / 3.3	95	4
AG	ProFunds-Ultra Mid Cap Svc	UMPSX	B-	(888) 776-3637	100.35	A+ /9.9	64.32 /99	13.75 /99	22.58 /99	C- / 3.0	4	4
SC	ProFunds-Internet UltraSector Svc	INPSX	C+	(888) 776-3637	43.34	A+ /9.9	46.58 /99	11.44 /98	25.99 /99	D+ / 2.6	94	4
TC	T Rowe Price Global Technology	PRGTX	C+	(800) 638-5660	15.09	A+ /9.9	38.94 /97	20.18 /99	20.72 /99	D+ / 2.4	97	5
TC	T Rowe Price Science and Tech	PRSCX	C+	(800) 638-5660	41.18	A+ /9.9	38.03 /96	13.76 /99	14.58 /96	D / 2.2	77	8
EM	PIMCO RAE Fdmtl+ EMG Inst	PEFIX	C+	(800) 426-0107	10.27	A+ /9.9	61.54 /99	5.69 /61	2.05 / 8	D / 2.0	92	3
MC	Mutual of America Inst MCE Idx	MAMQX	C+	(800) 914-8716	11.65	A+ /9.9	38.28 /97	11.33 /97	14.85 /97	D / 2.0	83	3
SC	Rydex Russell 2000 2x Strtgy A	RYRUX	C+	(800) 820-0888	124.05	A+ /9.9	75.46 /99	8.41 /82	21.08 /99	D / 1.6	13	11
GR	ProFunds-Mble Telcm UltraSector	WCPSX	C+	(888) 776-3637	64.50	A+ /9.9	77.35 /99	12.16 /98	25.69 /99	D / 1.6	78	4
FS	ProFunds-Banks UltraSector Svc	BKPSX	C+	(888) 776-3637	42.98	A+ /9.9	91.88 /99	16.46 /99	23.53 /99	D / 1.6	3	4
SC	Schneider Small Cap Value	SCMVX	C	(888) 520-3277	17.14	A+ /9.9	101.41 /99	3.76 /40	11.39 /69	D- / 1.3	15	19
FS	J Hancock VIT Financial Indus I	JEFSX	C	(800) 257-3336	13.74	A+ /9.9	44.54 /98	10.18 /94	12.90 /83	D- / 1.2	24	3
AG	Rydex Dyn-NASDAQ 100 2x Strgy	RYVLX	C	(800) 820-0888	99.83	A+ /9.9	57.90 /99	24.30 /99	29.92 /99	E+ / 0.9	43	17
HL	Alger Health Sciences Fund A	AHSAX	C	(800) 254-3796	21.45	A+ /9.9	37.94 /96	8.87 /86	14.82 /96	E+ / 0.6	21	12
SC	Direxion Mo Small Cap Bull 2X Inv	DXRLX	C-	(800) 851-0511	63.18	A+ /9.9	77.27 /99	9.79 /92	22.88 /99	E / 0.5	24	13

● Denotes fund is closed to new investors

99 Pct = Best
0 Pct = Worst

Fund Type	Fund Name	Ticker Symbol	Overall Investment Rating	Phone	Net Asset Value As of 2/28/17	Performance Rating/Pts	1Yr / Pct	3Yr / Pct	5Yr / Pct	Risk Rating/Pts	Mgr. Quality Pct	Mgr. Tenure (Years)
SC	ProFunds-Ultra Small Cap Svc	UAPSX	C-	(888) 776-3637	42.31	A+ /9.9	74.55 /99	7.55 /76	20.29 /99	E /0.4	9	4
GR	USAA Nasdaq 100 Index	USNQX	A+	(800) 382-8722	15.14	A+ /9.8	27.85 /81	13.75 /99	16.02 /98	B- /7.3	81	11
AG	Rydex Nova A	RYANX	A+	(800) 820-0888	56.26	A+ /9.8	36.32 /95	13.35 /99	18.76 /99	C+ /6.7	38	21
MC	American Century VP Mid Cap Val	AVMTX	A+	(800) 345-6488	21.92	A+ /9.8	31.15 /88	12.76 /99	15.36 /97	C+ /6.7	95	13
FS	Fidelity Select Insurance	FSPCX	A+	(800) 544-8888	80.60	A+ /9.8	31.60 /89	13.17 /99	17.52 /98	C+ /6.7	86	4
SC	Oak Assoc-Pin Oak Equity	POGSX	A+	(888) 462-5386	60.45	A+ /9.8	34.55 /94	11.91 /98	15.62 /98	C+ /6.6	97	12
EM	Franklin India Growth Fund A	FINGX	A+	(800) 342-5236	13.45	A+ /9.8	30.84 /88	15.88 /99	7.75 /40	C+ /6.5	99	9
GR	NASDAQ-100 Index Direct	NASDX	A+	(800) 955-9988	13.62	A+ /9.8	27.11 /79	13.66 /99	16.37 /98	C+ /6.5	81	14
GR	● Vanguard PRIMECAP Core Inv	VPCCX	A+	(800) 662-7447	23.81	A+ /9.8	28.50 /83	11.62 /98	16.19 /98	C+ /6.4	78	13
FS	Fidelity Select Financial Services	FIDSX	A+	(800) 544-8888	103.05	A+ /9.8	38.78 /97	10.04 /93	13.85 /92	C+ /6.2	43	4
GI	Dodge & Cox Stk Fund	DODGX	A+	(800) 621-3979	194.15	A+ /9.8	38.12 /96	10.05 /94	15.91 /98	C+ /6.1	51	25
FS	Davis Financial A	RPFGX	A+	(800) 279-0279	47.12	A+ /9.8	33.82 /93	12.34 /98	14.42 /95	C+ /6.1	78	26
GR	Fidelity NASDAQ Composite Index	FNCMX	A+	(800) 544-8544	76.54	A+ /9.8	29.21 /85	11.79 /98	15.71 /98	C+ /6.0	65	13
GR	Fidelity Sel Defense and	FSDAX	A+	(800) 544-8888	138.34	A+ /9.8	34.37 /93	10.37 /95	15.46 /98	C+ /6.0	70	2
GR	SunAmerica VAL Co I Nsdq 100	VCNIX	A+	(800) 858-8850	11.14	A+ /9.8	27.84 /81	13.84 /99	16.15 /98	C+ /5.9	81	5
SC	Nuveen Small Cap Value A	FSCAX	A+	(800) 257-8787	24.70	A+ /9.8	42.88 /98	12.49 /98	15.54 /98	C+ /5.9	96	12
GR	ProFunds-Industrial UltraSector	IDPSX	A	(888) 776-3637	80.21	A+ /9.8	42.07 /98	10.74 /96	17.94 /99	C+ /5.7	7	4
FS	Diamond Hill Financial Lng-Sht A	BANCX	A	(614) 255-3333	23.36	A+ /9.8	42.96 /98	9.53 /91	14.48 /95	C+ /5.7	28	16
FS	J Hancock Financial Indust A	FIDAX	A	(800) 257-3336	19.92	A+ /9.8	45.73 /99	8.53 /83	15.92 /98	C /5.5	10	19
MC	American Century NT Md Cp Val	ACLMX	A	(800) 345-6488	13.87	A+ /9.8	31.72 /89	13.10 /99	15.74 /98	C /5.4	95	11
TC	Putnam Global Technology Fund A	PGTAX	A	(800) 225-1581	27.61	A+ /9.8	33.58 /92	15.00 /99	13.67 /90	C /5.4	89	5
FS	ICON Financial S	ICFSX	A	(800) 764-0442	9.49	A+ /9.8	40.27 /97	7.26 /74	11.04 /66	C /5.3	4	14
UT	ProFunds-Utilities UltraSector Svc	UTPSX	A-	(888) 776-3637	40.58	A+ /9.8	20.74 /56	14.78 /99	15.08 /97	C /5.1	9	4
GI	Matthew 25 Fund	MXXVX	A-	(888) 625-3863	31.27	A+ /9.8	44.67 /98	8.33 /82	14.32 /95	C /4.9	27	22
SC	Adv Inn Cir Champlain Sm Comp	CIPSX	A-	(866) 777-7818	20.17	A+ /9.8	45.75 /99	11.30 /97	13.71 /91	C /4.8	95	13
SC	AMG Mgrs Cadence Emerg Cos S	MECAX	A-	(800) 548-4539	44.91	A+ /9.8	41.58 /98	10.78 /97	15.48 /98	C /4.8	92	13
TC	Fidelity Adv Technology A	FADTX	A-	(800) 522-7297	43.77	A+ /9.8	38.37 /97	11.98 /98	14.18 /94	C /4.8	64	12
GR	Nationwide Bailard Tech and Scie	NWHOX	B+	(800) 848-0920	17.99	A+ /9.8	33.37 /92	12.43 /98	14.06 /94	C /4.7	69	5
MC	Champlain Mid Cap Fund	CIPMX	B+	(866) 777-7818	16.02	A+ /9.8	33.89 /93	10.99 /97	14.03 /93	C /4.7	88	13
SC	Federated MDT Small Cp Core Fd	QASCX	B+	(800) 341-7400	17.91	A+ /9.8	45.52 /99	11.56 /98	16.72 /98	C /4.6	94	9
TC	Fidelity Select Computers Port	FDCPX	B+	(800) 544-8888	83.01	A+ /9.8	41.57 /98	7.98 /79	9.78 /57	C /4.6	9	4
SC	Fidelity OTC Portfolio Fd	FOCPX	B+	(800) 544-8544	92.25	A+ /9.8	33.90 /93	10.93 /97	15.94 /98	C- /4.1	96	8
GR	JPMorgan Large Cap Value A	OLVAX	B+	(800) 480-4111	15.40	A+ /9.8	35.37 /94	12.82 /99	15.37 /97	C- /3.9	84	4
SC	Voya Small Company Port S	IVPSX	B	(800) 992-0180	22.38	A+ /9.8	38.89 /97	10.17 /94	14.01 /93	C- /3.6	93	11
SC	Columbia Small Cap Value I I	CVUIX	B	(800) 345-6611	45.99	A+ /9.8	44.14 /98	9.24 /88	12.86 /82	C- /3.6	87	12
FS	Hennessy Large Cap Financial Inv	HLFNX	B	(800) 966-4354	20.10	A+ /9.8	40.83 /97	7.32 /74	13.99 /93	C- /3.5	8	20
SC	● Dreyfus Opportunistic Small Cap	DSCVX	B-	(800) 645-6561	35.76	A+ /9.8	43.17 /98	6.88 /71	14.23 /94	C- /3.0	61	12
AG	Rydex Russell 2000 1.5x Strgy A	RYAKX	B-	(800) 820-0888	55.98	A+ /9.8	54.36 /99	7.51 /76	16.58 /98	C- /3.0	2	17
TC	Janus Global Technology A	JATAX	B-	(800) 295-2687	24.88	A+ /9.8	38.45 /97	12.11 /98	14.60 /96	C- /3.0	63	6
TC	J Hancock VIT Science & Tech I	JESTX	B-	(800) 257-3336	25.00	A+ /9.8	33.13 /92	11.42 /98	14.62 /96	D+ /2.8	55	8
GR	SunAmerica VAL Co I Sc&Tech Fd	VCSTX	B-	(800) 858-8850	23.42	A+ /9.8	31.31 /89	11.43 /98	15.34 /97	D+ /2.8	59	12
SC	Highland Small-Cap Equity A	HSZAX	B-	(877) 665-1287	14.79	A+ /9.8	51.06 /99	10.30 /95	13.44 /88	D+ /2.7	92	2
SC	VY American Century Sm-MC Val	IASAX	C+	(800) 992-0180	12.45	A+ /9.8	34.09 /93	11.72 /98	14.71 /96	D+ /2.5	97	15
TC	Victory RS Science and	RSIFX	C+	(800) 539-3863	19.66	A+ /9.8	46.39 /99	10.92 /97	14.16 /94	D /1.8	30	1
SC	Prudential QMA Small-Cap Value Z	TASVX	C	(800) 225-1852	21.66	A+ /9.8	43.20 /98	9.62 /91	13.56 /89	D- /1.2	89	2
FO	DFA Japanese Small Co Inst	DFJSX	A+	(800) 984-9472	23.74	A+ /9.7	28.62 /83	10.53 /96	10.00 /58	B- /7.6	99	13
GR	LSV Value Equity Inst	LSVEX	A+	(866) 777-7818	27.34	A+ /9.7	31.35 /89	10.39 /95	15.98 /98	B- /7.0	66	18
GR	PRIMECAP Odyssey Stock Fd	POSKX	A+	(800) 729-2307	27.59	A+ /9.7	28.41 /83	11.07 /97	14.98 /97	C+ /6.8	72	13

Fund Type	Fund Name	Ticker Symbol	Overall Investment Rating	Phone	Net Asset Value As of 2/28/17	Performance Rating/Pts	Annualized Total Return Through 2/28/17 1Yr / Pct	3Yr / Pct	5Yr / Pct	Risk Rating/Pts	Mgr. Quality Pct	Mgr. Tenure (Years)
SC	ProFunds-Ultra Short Small-Cap	UCPSX	E-	(888) 776-3637	11.48	E- /0.0	-51.85 / 0	-22.71 / 0	-30.58 / 0	E- / 0.0	1	4
PM	ProFunds Short Precious Metals	SPPSX	E-	(888) 776-3637	42.33	E- /0.0	-33.11 / 0	-14.04 / 0	-2.93 / 2	E- / 0.0	0	4
FO	Profunds-Ultra Short Japan Svc	UKPSX	E-	(888) 776-3637	9.74	E- /0.0	-41.64 / 0	-29.17 / 0	-36.40 / 0	E- / 0.0	0	8
EM	Profunds-Ultra Sh Emer Mkt Svc	UVPSX	E-	(888) 776-3637	28.23	E- /0.0	-50.69 / 0	-18.58 / 0	-10.59 / 0	E- / 0.0	0	8
FO	ProFunds-Ultra Sh Latin America	UFPSX	E-	(888) 776-3637	8.74	E- /0.0	-70.86 / 0	-19.19 / 0	-5.36 / 2	E- / 0.0	0	8
FO	Profunds-Ultra Short China Svc	UHPSX	E-	(888) 776-3637	9.55	E- /0.0	-40.01 / 0	-22.67 / 0	-26.02 / 0	E- / 0.0	0	8
GR	ProFunds Ultra Short	USPSX	E-	(888) 776-3637	32.49	E- /0.0	-43.32 / 0	-30.48 / 0	-33.03 / 0	E- / 0.0	1	4
EM	Rydex Inverse Emg Mkts 2x Str A	RYWWX	E-	(800) 820-0888	66.72	E- /0.0	-49.84 / 0	-17.38 / 0	-9.47 / 1	E- / 0.0	0	7
SC	Direxion Mo Small Cap Bear 2X Inv	DXRSX	E-	(800) 851-0511	19.31	E- /0.0	-51.71 / 0	-21.24 / 0	-28.82 / 0	E- / 0.0	2	13
SC	Jacob Micro Cap Growth Inv	JMCGX	E-	(888) 522-6239	9.97	E- /0.0	5.61 / 4	-9.55 / 1	0.19 / 5	E- / 0.0	0	5
PM	ProFunds-Precious Metals Ultra	PMPSX	E-	(888) 776-3637	35.50	E- /0.0	15.79 /33	-17.10 / 0	-27.06 / 0	E- / 0.0	1	4
EN	Rydex Energy Services A	RYESX	E-	(800) 820-0888	31.95	E- /0.0	34.35 /93	-17.35 / 0	-8.88 / 1	E- / 0.2	1	19
EN	Invesco Energy A	IENAX	E-	(800) 959-4246	26.02	E- /0.0	29.14 /84	-12.70 / 0	-5.98 / 1	E- / 0.2	7	4
SC	Rydex Inv Rusl 2000 2x Strtgy A	RYIUX	E-	(800) 820-0888	62.99	E- /0.0	-50.78 / 0	-21.53 / 0	-29.63 / 0	E / 0.3	1	11
EN	BlackRock Energy & Resources Inv	SSGRX	E-	(800) 441-7762	18.72	E- /0.0	34.48 /93	-17.96 / 0	-11.87 / 0	E / 0.3	1	4
MC	ProFunds-Ultra Short Mid-Cap Svc	UIPSX	E-	(888) 776-3637	26.97	E- /0.0	-46.49 / 0	-24.06 / 0	-29.67 / 0	E / 0.5	2	4
OT	Rydex Commodities Strgy A	RYMEX	E-	(800) 820-0888	84.45	E- /0.0	17.88 /42	-22.76 / 0	-16.20 / 0	E+ / 0.7	0	12
EN	Putnam Global Energy Fund A	PGEAX	E-	(800) 225-1581	7.95	E- /0.0	33.42 /92	-14.99 / 0	-7.86 / 1	E+ / 0.7	2	1
AG	Rydex Inv Dow 2x Strategy A	RYIDX	E-	(800) 820-0888	17.52	E- /0.0	-42.46 / 0	-24.21 / 0	-26.05 / 0	E+ / 0.8	3	13
GR	Direxion Mo S&P 500 Bear 2X Inv	DXSSX	E-	(800) 851-0511	18.72	E- /0.0	-38.18 / 0	-21.97 / 0	-26.81 / 0	E+ / 0.8	20	11
GR	ProFunds-Ultra Short Dow 30 Svc	UWPSX	E-	(888) 776-3637	26.68	E- /0.0	-42.80 / 0	-24.73 / 0	-26.83 / 0	E+ / 0.9	3	4
GR	ProFunds-Ultra Bear Svc	URPSX	E-	(888) 776-3637	32.54	E- /0.0	-38.83 / 0	-23.78 / 0	-28.58 / 0	D- / 1.0	4	4
GI	Goldman Sachs Commodity Strat A	GSCAX	E-	(800) 526-7384	11.53	E- /0.0	18.16 /44	-20.24 / 0	-14.38 / 0	D- / 1.3	0	10
AG	Rydex Inv NASDAQ 100 2x Stgy A	RYVTX	E-	(800) 820-0888	61.40	E- /0.0	-42.38 / 0	-29.59 / 0	-32.13 / 0	D / 1.9	1	17
OT	PIMCO CommoditiesPLUS	PCLAX	E-	(800) 426-0107	6.43	E- /0.0	29.76 /86	-14.64 / 0	-9.61 / 1	D+ / 2.3	0	7
EN	Guinness Atkinson Alt Energy Fd	GAAEX	E-	(800) 915-6565	2.68	E- /0.0	3.88 / 3	-15.17 / 0	-3.85 / 2	D+ / 2.4	1	11
EM	ProFunds-Ultra Sh Intl Svc	UXPSX	E-	(888) 776-3637	17.77	E- /0.0	-33.32 / 0	-9.11 / 1	-18.97 / 0	D+ / 2.4	4	8
EN	US Global Inv Global Resources	PSPFX	E-	(800) 873-8637	5.63	E- /0.0	24.11 /70	-14.75 / 0	-9.56 / 1	D+ / 2.4	1	28
GR	ProFunds-Short OTC Svc	SOPSX	E-	(888) 776-3637	12.07	E- /0.0	-24.75 / 0	-17.16 / 0	-19.09 / 0	D+ / 2.4	4	4
GI	IMS Strategic Income Inst	IMSIX	E-		3.02	E- /0.0	5.89 / 5	-12.61 / 0	-4.94 / 2	D+ / 2.5	0	15
OT	Fidelity Srs Commodity Strat Fund	FCSSX	E-	(800) 544-8544	5.43	E- /0.0	15.29 /31	-13.60 / 0	-10.39 / 1	D+ / 2.5	0	8
OT	ProFunds-Rising Rates Opport Svc	RRPSX	E-	(888) 776-3637	38.97	E- /0.0	2.55 / 2	-12.25 / 0	-8.80 / 1	D+ / 2.5	0	8
GI	Rational Real Strategies A	HRSAX	E-	(800) 253-0412	4.60	E- /0.0	-1.83 / 1	-12.67 / 0	-6.40 / 1	D+ / 2.6	0	N/A
GR	NYSA Fund	NYSAX	E-	(800) 535-9169	4.21	E- /0.0	7.40 / 6	-19.33 / 0	-10.23 / 1	D+ / 2.6	0	4
OT	Russell Investments Comm Str A	RCSAX	E-	(800) 832-6688	5.61	E- /0.0	13.79 /25	-13.64 / 0	-10.93 / 0	D+ / 2.7	0	N/A
AG	Rydex Inv S&P 500 2x Strategy A	RYTMX	E-	(800) 820-0888	59.46	E- /0.0	-38.35 / 0	-23.06 / 0	-27.57 / 0	D+ / 2.9	5	17
IN	Harbor Commodity Real Rtn Str	HACMX	E-	(800) 422-1050	3.86	E- /0.0	20.76 /56	-13.31 / 0	-10.24 / 1	D+ / 2.9	0	9
SC	ProFunds-Short Small Cap Svc	SHPSX	E-	(888) 776-3637	15.75	E- /0.0	-30.46 / 0	-11.97 / 1	-16.67 / 0	C- / 3.6	7	4
IN	Comstock Capital Value A	DRCVX	E	(800) 422-3554	5.76	E- /0.0	-29.33 / 0	-15.66 / 0	-17.86 / 0	C- / 3.7	15	30
RE	ProFunds Short Real Estate Svc	SRPSX	E	(888) 776-3637	14.56	E- /0.0	-18.98 / 0	-13.70 / 0	-14.11 / 0	C- / 3.8	19	4
OT	Eaton Vance Commodity Strategy	EACSX	E	(800) 262-1122	5.52	E- /0.0	21.03 /57	-12.00 / 0	-9.76 / 1	C- / 3.8	0	2
AG	Rydex Inv NASDAQ 100 Strgy A	RYAPX	E	(800) 820-0888	77.16	E- /0.0	-23.36 / 0	-14.84 / 0	-16.74 / 0	C- / 3.9	18	19
SC	Rydex Inv Russell 2000 Stgy A	RYAFX	E	(800) 820-0888	23.69	E- /0.0	-28.99 / 0	-10.39 / 1	-15.17 / 0	C- / 3.9	18	13
OT	● MFS Commodity Strategy Fund A	MCSAX	E	(800) 225-2606	6.03	E- /0.0	15.28 /31	-12.27 / 0	-9.35 / 1	C- / 4.0	0	7
SC	Leuthold Grizzly Short	GRZZX	E	(888) 200-0409	5.85	E- /0.0	-26.97 / 0	-8.71 / 1	-13.20 / 0	C- / 4.2	21	8
IN	PIMCO Commodity Real Ret Str A	PCRAX	E	(800) 426-0107	7.07	E- /0.0	19.96 /52	-13.58 / 0	-10.58 / 1	C / 4.3	0	10
IN	Arrow Commodity Strategy A	CSFFX	E	(877) 277-6933	5.64	E- /0.0	11.02 /15	-12.15 / 0	-10.12 / 1	C / 4.4	0	7
MC	Rydex Inv Mid-Cap Stgy A	RYAGX	E	(800) 820-0888	24.84	E- /0.0	-25.67 / 0	-11.44 / 1	-14.93 / 0	C / 4.7	31	13
HL	Highland Long/Short Healthcare A	HHCAX	E	(877) 665-1287	11.17	E- /0.0	-2.62 / 1	-7.74 / 1	1.55 / 7	C / 4.9	2	7
GR	Hussman Strategic Growth	HSGFX	E+	(800) 487-7626	6.90	E- /0.0	-20.42 / 0	-11.06 / 1	-9.36 / 1	C / 5.5	18	17
GR	ProFunds-Bear Fund Svc	BRPSX	E+	(888) 776-3637	35.40	E- /0.0	-22.54 / 0	-13.18 / 0	-15.78 / 0	C+ / 5.6	19	4
GR	Federated Prudent Bear Fund A	BEARX	E+	(800) 341-7400	17.72	E- /0.0	-20.72 / 0	-12.33 / 0	-14.98 / 0	C+ / 6.0	16	9

● Denotes fund is closed to new investors

Fund Type	Fund Name	Ticker Symbol	Overall Investment Rating	Phone	Net Asset Value As of 2/28/17	PERFORMANCE Performance Rating/Pts	Annualized Total Return Through 2/28/17			RISK Risk Rating/Pts	FUND MGR Mgr. Quality Pct	Mgr. Tenure (Years)
							1Yr / Pct	3Yr / Pct	5Yr / Pct			
GR	GAMCO Mathers Fund	MATRX	E+	(800) 422-3554	5.52	E- /0.0	-22.14 / 0	-10.03 / 1	-10.06 / 1	C+ / 6.0	38	44
AG	Rydex Inv S&P 500 Stgry A	RYARX	D-	(800) 820-0888	65.29	E- /0.0	-20.86 / 0	-11.82 / 1	-14.58 / 0	C+ / 6.7	35	23
MC	● MSIF Trust Mid Cap Growth A	MACGX	E-	(800) 354-8185	16.72	E- /0.1	11.43 /16	-6.07 / 2	3.44 /13	E- / 0.0	0	15
EN	ProFunds Oil Eqpt Svcs & Dist Svc	OEPSX	E-	(888) 776-3637	14.08	E- /0.1	47.90 /99	-16.59 / 0	-7.33 / 1	E- / 0.0	3	4
EN	ProFunds-Oil & Gas UltraSector	ENPSX	E-	(888) 776-3637	31.96	E- /0.1	35.37 /94	-12.26 / 0	-3.78 / 2	E / 0.3	15	4
EN	Victory Global Natural Resources A	RSNRX	E-	(800) 539-3863	23.08	E- /0.1	56.58 /99	-11.91 / 1	-7.05 / 1	E / 0.5	10	12
EN	Prudential Jennison Natural Res A	PGNAX	E-	(800) 225-1852	36.75	E- /0.1	40.50 /97	-10.24 / 1	-6.57 / 1	E+ / 0.7	20	11
EN	VanEck Global Hard Assets A	GHAAX	E-	(800) 826-1115	36.05	E- /0.1	40.75 /97	-9.80 / 1	-5.50 / 2	E+ / 0.8	23	22
SC	● MSIF Small Company Growth A	MSSMX	E-	(800) 354-8185	12.00	E- /0.1	17.14 /39	-6.62 / 2	7.04 /35	E+ / 0.8	1	18
EN	● J Hancock Natural Resources A	JNRAX	E-	(800) 257-3336	12.08	E- /0.1	40.18 /97	-11.38 / 1	-8.31 / 1	E+ / 0.8	10	3
EN	ICON Energy A	ICEAX	E-	(800) 764-0442	12.90	E- /0.1	27.75 /81	-9.48 / 1	-2.86 / 2	E+ / 0.8	20	10
EN	BlackRock Natural Resource Inv A	MDGRX	E-	(800) 441-7762	44.09	E- /0.1	29.59 /85	-8.11 / 1	-3.61 / 2	E+ / 0.9	38	N/A
EN	Franklin Natural Resources A	FRNRX	E-	(800) 342-5236	26.69	E- /0.1	38.47 /97	-9.62 / 1	-6.66 / 1	E+ / 0.9	26	18
EN	BlackRock AllCap Energy & Res	BACAX	E-	(800) 441-7762	10.74	E- /0.1	26.38 /77	-9.47 / 1	-5.36 / 2	D- / 1.0	22	4
EN	Rydex Energy A	RYENX	E-	(800) 820-0888	74.72	E- /0.1	37.51 /96	-11.20 / 1	-4.47 / 2	D- / 1.0	15	19
EN	Guinness Atkinson Glob Energy	GAGEX	E-	(800) 915-6565	21.87	E- /0.1	29.87 /86	-12.18 / 0	-4.40 / 2	D- / 1.1	6	13
SC	Pacific Advisors Small Cap Value A	PASMX	E-	(800) 282-6693	26.48	E- /0.1	37.16 /96	-10.94 / 1	1.34 / 7	D- / 1.2	0	24
EN	Saratoga Adv Tr Energy&Basic Mat	SBMBX	E-	(800) 807-3863	11.62	E- /0.1	30.86 /88	-10.60 / 1	-4.53 / 2	D / 1.6	13	2
MC	Transamerica Multi-Cap Growth A	ITSAX	E-	(888) 233-4339	6.51	E- /0.1	11.82 /17	-6.26 / 2	3.16 /11	D / 1.8	0	N/A
EN	Putnam Global Natural Resources	EBERX	E-	(800) 225-1581	16.21	E- /0.1	21.51 /60	-10.02 / 1	-5.11 / 2	D / 1.9	11	5
EM	● Templeton Frontier Markets A	TFMAX	E-	(800) 342-5236	11.22	E- /0.1	14.16 /26	-10.10 / 1	-1.45 / 3	D+ / 2.9	1	9
FO	Janus Overseas A	JDIAX	E-	(800) 295-2687	27.23	E- /0.1	17.84 /42	-6.67 / 2	-4.98 / 2	C- / 3.0	6	1
EN	Firsthand Alternative Energy Fd	ALTEX	E-	(888) 884-2675	5.63	E- /0.1	6.03 / 5	-8.46 / 1	3.68 /14	C- / 3.4	6	10
EN	ProFunds Short Oil & Gas Svc	SNPSX	E	(888) 776-3637	44.50	E- /0.1	-25.83 / 0	-2.44 / 6	-7.10 / 1	C- / 3.6	4	4
OT	ALPS CoreComm Mgt CompComm	JCRAX	E	(866) 759-5679	7.61	E- /0.1	20.47 /55	-10.36 / 1	-8.36 / 1	C- / 3.6	0	7
IN	VanEck CM Commodity Index A	CMCAX	E	(800) 826-1115	4.88	E- /0.1	22.49 /64	-11.69 / 1	-9.33 / 1	C- / 3.6	0	3
GR	Pacific Advisors Mid Cap Value A	PAMVX	E	(800) 282-6693	11.66	E- /0.1	17.73 /42	-6.72 / 2	-0.94 / 3	C- / 3.6	0	10
GL	Ivy Asset Strategy A	WASAX	E	(800) 777-6472	21.52	E- /0.1	3.61 / 3	-5.69 / 2	2.09 / 8	C- / 3.7	1	3
IN	DFA Commodity Strategy Port	DCMSX	E	(800) 984-9472	6.06	E- /0.1	18.21 /44	-11.53 / 1	-8.25 / 1	C- / 3.8	0	7
BA	Pacific Advisors Balanced A	PAABX	E	(800) 282-6693	11.63	E- /0.1	10.42 /13	-6.49 / 2	0.87 / 6	C- / 4.0	0	7
FO	● Artisan International Small Cp Inv	ARTJX	E	(800) 344-1770	20.52	E- /0.1	0.96 / 2	-5.98 / 2	5.54 /25	C / 4.3	9	16
FO	Rydex Eurp 1.25x Strgy A	RYAEX	E	(800) 820-0888	80.59	E- /0.1	11.16 /15	-8.04 / 1	1.64 / 7	C / 4.5	4	17
FO	AllianzGI NFJ Internatl Value A	AFJAX	E	(800) 988-8380	17.05	E- /0.1	8.50 / 8	-7.22 / 1	-1.33 / 3	C / 4.6	5	14
BA	Invesco Balanced-Risk Com Str A	BRCAX	E	(800) 959-4246	6.89	E- /0.1	16.42 /36	-7.98 / 1	-8.37 / 1	C / 4.7	1	7
FO	Morgan Stanley European Eq A	EUGAX	E	(800) 869-6397	15.86	E- /0.1	8.51 / 8	-5.89 / 2	2.76 /10	C / 4.8	9	11
FO	Columbia European Equity A	AXEAX	E	(800) 345-6611	6.02	E- /0.1	4.94 / 4	-5.23 / 2	4.25 /17	C / 4.9	14	8
FO	BlackRock Eurofund Inv A	MDEFX	E	(800) 441-7762	13.02	E- /0.1	4.29 / 3	-6.00 / 2	3.82 /14	C / 5.1	9	7
FO	Nuveen International Growth A	NBQAX	E+	(800) 257-8787	36.78	E- /0.1	4.82 / 4	-4.09 / 3	6.39 /31	C+ / 5.6	23	8
FO	T Rowe Price European Stk	PRESX	E+	(800) 638-5660	17.40	E- /0.1	3.19 / 3	-5.53 / 2	5.30 /23	C+ / 5.6	11	12
EN	Deutsche Enhanced Comdty Strat	SKNRX	E+	(800) 728-3337	11.63	E- /0.1	12.29 /19	-6.26 / 2	-5.63 / 1	C+ / 5.7	16	7
GI	QS Strategic Real Return A	LRRAX	D-	(877) 534-4627	11.39	E- /0.1	9.99 /12	-4.98 / 2	-1.76 / 3	C+ / 6.1	2	6
IN	Marketfield I	MFLDX	D-	(800) 624-6782	14.76	E- /0.1	4.38 / 3	-7.57 / 1	0.46 / 5	C+ / 6.8	1	10
OT	Direxion Indexed Commodity Stg A	DXCTX	D-	(800) 851-0511	15.36	E- /0.1	4.63 / 4	-7.01 / 1	-6.14 / 1	C+ / 6.8	4	9
IN	Princeton Futures Strategy A	PFFAX	D	(888) 868-9501	7.59	E- /0.1	-6.71 / 0	-2.08 / 6	-4.12 / 2	B- / 7.3	61	7
FS	ProFunds-Rising Rates Opp 10	RTPSX	D	(888) 776-3637	14.54	E- /0.1	1.39 / 2	-5.72 / 2	-4.69 / 2	B- / 7.4	3	8
FS	● Merk Hard Currency Investor	MERKX	D	(866) 637-5386	9.29	E- /0.1	-2.52 / 1	-6.91 / 1	-4.51 / 2	B- / 7.4	6	12
PM	Deutsche Gold & Prec Metals Fund	SGDAX	E-	(800) 728-3337	6.82	E- /0.2	19.17 /48	-5.25 / 2	-15.57 / 0	E- / 0.0	67	1
FO	Oberweis China Opportunities	OBCHX	E-	(800) 245-7311	11.97	E- /0.2	15.60 /32	-5.40 / 2	9.70 /56	D- / 1.2	13	N/A

99 Pct = Best
0 Pct = Worst

● Denotes fund is closed to new investors
www.thestreetratings.com

Data as of February 28, 2017

Section VI

Risk:
100 Best and Worst
Stock Mutual Funds

A compilation of those

Equity Mutual Funds

receiving the highest and lowest Risk Ratings.

Funds are listed in order by Risk Rating.

Section VI Contents

This section contains a summary analysis of each of the top 100 and bottom 100 mutual funds as determined by their TheStreet Risk Rating. Since the Risk Rating does not take into consideration a fund's overall financial performance, the selection of funds presented here is based solely on each fund's performance volatility over the past three years.

In order to optimize the utility of our top and bottom fund lists, rather than listing all funds in a multi-class series, a single fund from each series is selected for display as the primary share class. Whenever possible, the selected fund is one that a retail investor would be most likely to choose. This share class may not be appropriate for every investor, so please consult with your financial advisor, the fund company, and the fund's prospectus before placing your trade.

You can use this section to identify those funds that have historically given shareholders the most consistent returns on their investments. A word of caution though: consistency in the past is not necessarily indicative of future results. While these funds have provided the most stable returns, it is possible for a fund manager – especially a newly appointed fund manager – to suddenly shift the fund's investment focus which could lead to greater volatility.

1. **Fund Type**   The mutual fund's peer category based on an analysis of its investment portfolio.

AG	Aggressive Growth	HL	Health
AA	Asset Allocation	IN	Income
BA	Balanced	IX	Index
CV	Convertible	MC	Mid Cap
EM	Emerging Market	OT	Other
EN	Energy/Natural Resources	PM	Precious Metals
FS	Financial Services	RE	Real Estate
FO	Foreign	SC	Small Cap
GL	Global	TC	Technology
GR	Growth	UT	Utilities
GI	Growth and Income		

A blank fund type means that the mutual fund has not yet been categorized.

2. **Fund Name**   The name of the mutual fund as stated in its prospectus, which can sometimes differ slightly from the name that the company uses for advertising. If you cannot find the particular mutual fund you are interested in, or if you have any doubts regarding the precise name, verify the information with your broker or on your account statement. Also, use the fund's ticker symbol for confirmation. (See column 3.)

3.   **Ticker Symbol**   The unique alphabetic symbol used for identifying and trading a specific mutual fund. No two funds can have the same ticker symbol, and the ticker symbol for mutual funds always ends with an "X".

A handful of funds currently show no associated ticker symbol. This means that the fund is either small or new since the NASD only assigns a ticker symbol to funds with at least $25 million in assets or 1,000 shareholders.

4.   **Overall Investment Rating**   Our overall rating is measured on a scale from A to E based on each fund's risk-adjusted performance. Please see page 10 for specific descriptions of each letter grade. Also, refer to page 7 for information on how our ratings are derived. Most important, when using this rating, please be sure to consider the warnings beginning on page 11 regarding the ratings' limitations and the underlying assumptions.

5.   **Phone**   The telephone number of the company managing the fund. Call this number to receive a prospectus or other information about the fund.

6.   **Net Asset Value (NAV)**   The fund's share price as of the date indicated. A fund's NAV is computed by dividing the value of the fund's asset holdings, less accrued fees and expenses, by the number of its shares outstanding.

7.   **Performance Rating/Points**   A letter grade rating based solely on the mutual fund's financial performance over the trailing three years, without any consideration for the amount of risk the fund poses. Like the overall Investment Rating, the Performance Rating is measured on a scale from A to E for ease of interpretation. The points score indicates where the Performance Rating falls on a scale of 0 to 10.

8.   **1-Year Total Return**   The total return the fund has provided investors over the preceeding twelve months. This total return figure is computed based on the fund's dividend distributions and share price appreciation/depreciation during the period, net of the expenses and fees it imposes on its shareholders. Although the total return figure does not reflect an adjustment for any loads the fund may carry, such adjustments have been made in deriving TheStreet Investment Ratings.

9.   **1-Year Total Return Percentile**   The fund's percentile rank based on its one-year performance compared to that of all other equity funds in existence for at least one year. A score of 99 is the best possible, indicating that the fund outperformed 99% of the other mutual funds. Zero is the worst possible percentile score.

10.   **3-Year Total Return**   The total annual return the fund has provided investors over the preceeding three years.

11. 3-Year Total Return Percentile

The fund's percentile rank based on its three-year performance compared to that of all other equity funds in existence for at least three years. A score of 99 is the best possible, indicating that the fund outperformed 99% of the other mutual funds. Zero is the worst possible percentile score.

12. 5-Year Total Return

The total annual return the fund has provided investors over the preceeding five years.

13. 5-Year Total Return Percentile

The fund's percentile rank based on its five-year performance compared to that of all other equity funds in existence for at least five years. A score of 99 is the best possible, indicating that the fund outperformed 99% of the other mutual funds. Zero is the worst possible percentile score.

14. Risk Rating/Points

A letter grade rating based solely on the mutual fund's risk as determined by its monthly performance volatility over the trailing three years. The risk rating does not take into consideration the overall financial performance the fund has achieved or the total return it has provided to its shareholders. Like the overall Investment Rating, the Risk Rating is measured on a scale from A to E for ease of interpretation. The points score indicates where the Risk Rating falls on a scale of 0 to 10.

15. Manager Quality Percentile

The manager quality percentile is based on a ranking of the fund's alpha, a statistical measure representing the difference between a fund's actual returns and its expected performance given its level of risk. Fund managers who have been able to exceed the fund's statistically expected performance receive a high percentile rank with 99 representing the highest possible score. At the other end of the spectrum, fund managers who have actually detracted from the fund's expected performance receive a low percentile rank with 0 representing the lowest possible score.

16. Manager Tenure

The number of years the current manager has been managing the fund. Since fund managers who deliver substandard returns are usually replaced, a long tenure is usually a good sign that shareholders are satisfied that the fund is achieving its stated objectives.

99 Pct = Best
0 Pct = Worst

Fund Type	Fund Name	Ticker Symbol	Overall Investment Rating	Phone	Net Asset Value As of 2/28/17	Performance Rating/Pts	1Yr / Pct	3Yr / Pct	5Yr / Pct	Risk Rating/Pts	Mgr. Quality Pct	Mgr. Tenure (Years)
AA	SEI Asset Alloc-Cons Strat F	SVSAX	C+	(800) 342-5734	10.48	D /1.8	6.09 / 5	2.70 / 29	3.44 / 13	B+ / 9.9	76	14
GL	Fidelity Freedom Index Income Inv	FIKFX	C+	(800) 544-8544	11.61	D /1.7	5.98 / 5	2.55 / 28	2.89 / 10	B+ / 9.9	78	8
AA	Transamerica Inst Asst All Sht Hrz	DISHX	C+	(888) 233-4339	11.11	D /1.7	6.11 / 5	2.46 / 27	3.24 / 12	B+ / 9.9	75	21
AA	Transamerica Asst All Short Hrzn	DVCSX	C+	(888) 233-4339	11.58	D- /1.5	5.62 / 4	2.11 / 25	2.90 / 10	B+ / 9.9	71	21
GI	Zacks Market Neutral Investor	ZMNVX	C	(800) 245-2934	14.29	D- /1.3	2.66 / 2	3.15 / 33	1.65 / 7	B+ / 9.9	86	9
AA	SEI Asset Alloc-Defensive Strat F	SNSAX	C	(800) 342-5734	9.82	D- /1.2	3.19 / 3	1.51 / 21	1.73 / 7	B+ / 9.9	76	N/A
GI	Arbitrage Fund (The) - Retail	ARBFX	C	(800) 295-4485	12.89	D- /1.1	2.79 / 3	1.98 / 24	1.23 / 7	B+ / 9.9	82	17
AA	Pacific Financial Stg Csv Inv	PFLSX	C	(888) 451-8734	9.25	E+ /0.8	2.12 / 2	0.50 / 16	1.13 / 6	B+ / 9.9	74	10
AA	JPMorgan Multi-Cap Mrkt Netral A	OGNAX	C	(800) 480-4111	10.15	E+ /0.6	-1.36 / 1	1.45 / 21	0.72 / 6	B+ / 9.9	83	4
AA	Epiphany FFV Strat Income A	EPIAX	C		10.40	E+ /0.6	2.50 / 2	1.82 / 23	2.01 / 8	B+ / 9.9	76	7
GR	American Century Alt Eq MN A	ALIAX	C-	(800) 345-6488	10.79	E- /0.2	-3.05 / 1	-0.64 / 11	0.55 / 5	B+ / 9.9	72	12
IN	Vanguard Market Neutral Fund Inv	VMNFX	C	(800) 662-7447	12.14	D- /1.4	-2.28 / 1	3.07 / 32	3.22 / 12	B+ / 9.8	93	5
GI	Fidelity Freedom Index 2005 Inv	FJIFX	C+	(800) 544-8544	12.90	D+ /2.3	8.75 / 9	3.32 / 35	4.13 / 16	B+ / 9.7	70	N/A
GL	DFA Global Allocation 25/75 R2	DFGPX	C+	(800) 984-9472	13.09	D /1.8	7.18 / 6	2.30 / 26	3.28 / 12	B+ / 9.7	87	N/A
GI	J Hancock Total Return NAV	JHTRX	C	(800) 257-3336	13.42	D- /1.4	3.89 / 3	2.50 / 28	2.80 / 10	B+ / 9.7	85	3
GL	Guggenheim Multi-Hedge Strat A	RYMQX	C-	(800) 820-0888	23.99	E+ /0.7	-0.76 / 1	2.04 / 24	1.58 / 7	B+ / 9.7	86	12
GI	TIAA-CREF Lifecycle Idx Ret Inc	TRCIX	C+	(800) 842-2252	13.52	D+ /2.8	9.71 / 11	3.92 / 42	5.20 / 23	B+ / 9.6	73	8
GL	Schwab Monthly Income Fund	SWKRX	C+	(800) 407-0256	11.02	D /2.2	7.56 / 7	3.37 / 36	4.15 / 16	B+ / 9.6	79	N/A
AA	Vanguard LifeStrategy Income Inv	VASIX	C+	(800) 662-7447	15.14	D /2.0	5.69 / 4	3.72 / 40	4.05 / 15	B+ / 9.6	80	N/A
AA	● Fidelity Adv Inc Replacement 2022	FRAMX	C	(800) 522-7297	59.83	D /1.6	8.86 / 9	3.13 / 33	5.20 / 23	B+ / 9.6	60	10
AA	MFS Lifetime Income A	MLLAX	C	(800) 225-2606	12.10	D- /1.4	7.87 / 7	2.81 / 30	4.09 / 16	B+ / 9.6	63	N/A
GL	Nationwide Inv Dest Cons A	NDCAX	C	(800) 848-0920	10.16	D- /1.2	6.29 / 5	2.73 / 29	3.21 / 12	B+ / 9.6	81	N/A
AA	RBB Free Market Fixed Income	FMFIX	C-	(866) 780-0357	10.28	E+ /0.8	0.51 / 2	0.77 / 17	0.59 / 5	B+ / 9.6	79	10
GL	PACE Alternatives Strat Invst A	PASIX	C-	(888) 793-8637	10.70	E+ /0.7	2.29 / 2	1.38 / 20	3.32 / 12	B+ / 9.6	83	11
AA	● Fidelity Adv Inc Replacement 2018	FRKAX	C-	(800) 522-7297	55.23	E+ /0.7	2.98 / 3	1.46 / 21	3.09 / 11	B+ / 9.6	70	10
IN	Glenmede Long/Short Portfolio	GTAPX	C+	(800) 442-8299	12.04	D+ /2.8	7.02 / 6	4.04 / 43	5.37 / 24	B+ / 9.5	79	11
GR	Schwab Target 2010	SWBRX	C+	(800) 407-0256	12.69	D+ /2.6	9.10 / 10	3.64 / 39	5.31 / 23	B+ / 9.5	69	12
AA	Vanguard Target Retirement	VTINX	C+	(800) 662-7447	13.08	D+ /2.4	8.08 / 8	3.70 / 39	4.56 / 18	B+ / 9.5	72	4
GL	Schwab Monthly Income Fund	SWLRX	C	(800) 407-0256	9.97	D /1.6	4.43 / 3	2.77 / 30	2.92 / 11	B+ / 9.5	82	N/A
GI	Praxis Genesis Conservative A	MCONX	C	(800) 977-2947	11.40	D- /1.3	7.22 / 6	3.26 / 34	4.24 / 16	B+ / 9.5	76	N/A
AA	● Fidelity Adv Inc Replacement 2020	FILAX	C	(800) 522-7297	55.31	D- /1.1	6.55 / 5	2.49 / 27	4.32 / 17	B+ / 9.5	65	10
IN	JPMorgan Research Market Neut A	JMNAX	C-	(800) 480-4111	14.12	E /0.3	2.92 / 3	-0.97 / 9	0.17 / 5	B+ / 9.5	56	3
AA	SEI Asset Alloc- Moderate Strgy F	SMOAX	C+	(800) 342-5734	11.74	D+ /2.9	9.49 / 10	4.05 / 44	5.02 / 21	B+ / 9.4	74	14
GI	Kinetics Alternative Inc Advisor A	KWIAX	C-	(800) 930-3828	94.97	E+ /0.9	5.09 / 4	2.41 / 27	3.27 / 12	B+ / 9.4	73	7
AA	Wells Fargo DJ Tgt Today C	WFODX	C-	(800) 222-8222	10.77	E+ /0.8	2.57 / 2	0.39 / 15	0.88 / 6	B+ / 9.4	50	11
AA	Federated Absolute Return A	FMAAX	C-	(800) 341-7400	9.73	E /0.4	-3.09 / 1	0.37 / 15	0.10 / 5	B+ / 9.4	46	8
AA	TIAA-CREF Lifecycle Index 2010	TLTRX	C+	(800) 842-2252	14.13	C- /3.1	10.55 / 13	4.13 / 44	5.81 / 27	B+ / 9.3	56	8
GI	Fidelity Freedom Index 2010 Inv	FKIFX	C+	(800) 544-8544	13.67	D+ /2.9	10.76 / 14	3.80 / 40	5.12 / 22	B+ / 9.3	65	N/A
GI	Fidelity Freedom K Income	FFKAX	C+	(800) 544-8544	11.85	D+ /2.3	8.93 / 9	3.18 / 33	3.74 / 14	B+ / 9.3	75	N/A
AA	Touchstone Controlled Gr with Inc	TSAAX	C	(800) 543-0407	11.30	D- /1.3	7.77 / 7	2.50 / 28	3.78 / 14	B+ / 9.3	63	N/A
AA	Vanguard LifeStrategy Consv Gr	VSCGX	C+	(800) 662-7447	18.93	C- /3.1	10.02 / 12	4.49 / 49	5.73 / 27	B+ / 9.2	67	N/A
BA	Bridgeway Managed Volatility Fund	BRBPX	C	(800) 661-3550	14.63	D /2.1	6.69 / 5	3.11 / 33	4.39 / 17	B+ / 9.2	65	16
AA	● Fidelity Adv Inc Replacement 2024	FRNAX	C	(800) 522-7297	59.84	D /1.9	10.77 / 14	3.62 / 38	5.86 / 27	B+ / 9.2	55	10
AA	J Hancock Multi-Index Inc Psv 1	JRFOX	C	(800) 257-3336	11.16	D- /1.5	4.48 / 3	2.37 / 27	2.96 / 11	B+ / 9.2	76	7
AA	Fidelity Adv Freedom Income A	FAFAX	C	(800) 522-7297	10.92	D- /1.4	8.56 / 9	2.74 / 29	3.35 / 12	B+ / 9.2	63	14
AA	Wells Fargo WIth Bldr Consv All C	WCCFX	C	(800) 222-8222	10.37	D- /1.4	6.41 / 5	1.42 / 21	2.45 / 9	B+ / 9.2	48	4
AA	TIAA-CREF Lifecycle Index 2015	TLGRX	B-	(800) 842-2252	14.67	C- /3.4	11.74 / 17	4.39 / 47	6.37 / 31	B+ / 9.1	51	8
AA	● Fidelity Adv Inc Replacement 2026	FIOAX	C	(800) 522-7297	61.74	D+ /2.3	12.16 / 18	3.97 / 43	6.33 / 30	B+ / 9.1	51	10
AA	American Century One Chc	AONIX	C	(800) 345-6488	11.91	D /2.2	8.16 / 8	3.40 / 36	3.98 / 15	B+ / 9.1	68	13
BA	Fidelity Freedom Income	FFFAX	C	(800) 544-8544	11.54	D /2.2	8.90 / 9	3.13 / 33	3.70 / 14	B+ / 9.1	67	12
AA	Transamerica Asst All Shrt-Int Hrz	DVSIX	C	(888) 233-4339	11.30	D /2.2	9.15 / 10	2.81 / 30	4.49 / 18	B+ / 9.1	51	19
AA	MFS Conservative Alloc A	MACFX	C	(800) 225-2606	15.03	D /1.7	9.92 / 11	3.23 / 34	5.08 / 22	B+ / 9.1	50	15

● Denotes fund is closed to new investors

Fund Type	Fund Name	Ticker Symbol	Overall Investment Rating	Phone	Net Asset Value As of 2/28/17	Perform-ance Rating/Pts	Annualized Total Return Through 2/28/17 1Yr / Pct	3Yr / Pct	5Yr / Pct	Risk Rating/Pts	Mgr. Quality Pct	Mgr. Tenure (Years)
AA	Principal LifeTime Strg Inc A	PALTX	C	(800) 222-5852	12.27	D- /1.5	7.57 / 7	2.56 / 28	3.87 / 15	B+ / 9.1	61	10
AA	Gabelli ABC Fund AAA	GABCX	C	(800) 422-3554	10.20	D- /1.4	3.70 / 3	2.08 / 24	2.87 / 10	B+ / 9.1	77	24
AA	Wilmington Strat Alloc Conserv A	WCAAX	C-	(800) 336-9970	10.60	E+ /0.9	5.46 / 4	1.41 / 21	2.50 / 9	B+ / 9.1	51	N/A
AA	Aberdeen Diversified Alt A	GASAX	C-	(866) 667-9231	12.72	E+ /0.6	4.27 / 3	0.35 / 15	3.52 / 13	B+ / 9.1	30	N/A
GL	Fidelity Freedom Index 2015 Inv	FLIFX	B-	(800) 544-8544	14.05	C- /3.6	12.86 /21	4.32 / 47	5.58 / 25	B+ / 9.0	75	8
GR	ProFunds-Rising US Dollar Svc	RDPSX	C+	(888) 776-3637	26.99	D+ /2.4	0.86 / 2	5.19 / 56	1.96 / 8	B+ / 9.0	97	8
AA	Transamerica Inst Asst All ShIntHrz	DIHSX	C	(888) 233-4339	11.25	D+ /2.4	9.53 / 11	3.13 / 33	4.82 / 20	B+ / 9.0	55	19
AA	J Hancock Multi-Index 2020 Psv 1	JRWOX	C	(800) 257-3336	11.95	D /2.1	7.70 / 7	3.21 / 34	4.58 / 19	B+ / 9.0	65	7
GR	EAS Crow Point Alternatives A	EASAX	D+		8.63	E /0.3	0.26 / 1	-0.23 / 12	1.60 / 7	B+ / 9.0	38	8
IN	Guggenheim Alpha Opportunity A	SAOAX	B	(800) 820-0888	21.17	C /4.7	11.57 / 16	6.41 / 68	10.67 / 63	B / 8.9	92	N/A
BA	Vanguard Tax-Managed Bal	VTMFX	B	(800) 662-7447	28.80	C /4.7	11.80 / 17	6.40 / 68	8.11 / 43	B / 8.9	78	4
RE	Fidelity Adv Real Estate Income A	FRINX	B	(800) 522-7297	12.06	C /4.3	14.55 / 28	7.14 / 73	8.59 / 47	B / 8.9	90	14
IX	State Farm Equity & Bond Premier	SLBAX	B-	(800) 447-4930	11.59	C- /4.0	12.51 / 20	6.54 / 69	8.59 / 47	B / 8.9	79	N/A
AA	TIAA-CREF Lifecycle Index 2020	TLWRX	B-	(800) 842-2252	15.31	C- /3.9	13.35 / 23	4.72 / 51	7.09 / 35	B / 8.9	44	8
GL	TIAA-CREF Lifecycle Ret Inc Ret	TLIRX	C+	(800) 842-2252	11.13	C- /3.0	11.34 / 16	3.71 / 39	5.57 / 25	B / 8.9	75	10
AA	Vanguard Target Retirement 2010	VTENX	C	(800) 662-7447	25.89	D+ /2.5	8.47 / 8	3.83 / 41	5.34 / 24	B / 8.9	67	4
AA	● Fidelity Adv Inc Replacement 2028	FARPX	C+	(800) 522-7297	62.68	D+ /2.5	13.16 / 22	4.20 / 45	6.66 / 33	B / 8.9	48	10
IN	Calamos Market Neutral Income A	CVSIX	C	(800) 582-6959	13.22	D /1.6	8.62 / 9	2.99 / 32	3.49 / 13	B / 8.9	73	27
GI	Columbia Thermostat A	CTFAX	C-	(800) 345-6611	14.79	D- /1.3	7.25 / 6	3.07 / 32	5.15 / 22	B / 8.9	75	N/A
AA	Fidelity Adv Asset Manager 20% A	FTAWX	C-	(800) 522-7297	13.23	D- /1.2	7.17 / 6	2.56 / 28	3.48 / 13	B / 8.9	65	8
GR	Oppenheimer Fundamental Alt A	QVOPX	C-	(888) 470-0862	27.22	D- /1.0	3.49 / 3	2.26 / 26	4.04 / 15	B / 8.9	79	6
AA	USAA Growth & Tax Strategy Fund	USBLX	B	(800) 382-8722	18.39	C /4.4	10.77 / 14	6.38 / 67	8.00 / 42	B / 8.8	81	12
AA	Vanguard Wellesley Income Inv	VWINX	B-	(800) 662-7447	26.04	C- /3.8	10.23 / 12	5.95 / 64	7.09 / 35	B / 8.8	83	10
AA	T Rowe Price Retire Balanced	TRRIX	C+	(800) 638-5660	15.06	C- /3.0	11.43 / 16	3.73 / 40	5.19 / 23	B / 8.8	54	15
AA	Fidelity Freedom 2005	FFFVX	C+	(800) 544-8544	12.14	D+ /2.9	11.39 / 16	3.75 / 40	4.88 / 21	B / 8.8	56	12
GR	ICON Risk-Managed Balanced A	IOCAX	C+	(800) 764-0442	14.86	D+ /2.9	12.87 / 21	4.43 / 48	6.01 / 28	B / 8.8	52	4
BA	JPMorgan Smart Ret Inc A	JSRAX	C	(800) 480-4111	17.85	D /2.0	10.48 / 13	3.33 / 35	4.67 / 19	B / 8.8	51	11
AA	MFS Lifetime 2020 A	MFLAX	C	(800) 225-2606	12.79	D /1.8	10.26 / 12	3.44 / 36	5.81 / 27	B / 8.8	52	12
BA	Fund *X Flexible Income	INCMX	C	(866) 455-3863	28.24	D /1.8	7.05 / 6	2.46 / 27	3.61 / 13	B / 8.8	75	15
AA	AB Consv Wealth Strat A	ABPAX	C-	(800) 221-5672	12.32	D- /1.5	7.69 / 7	2.47 / 27	3.47 / 13	B / 8.8	51	N/A
GR	Salient Tactical Growth A	FTAGX	C-	(800) 999-6809	26.06	D- /1.5	8.75 / 9	2.07 / 24	3.82 / 14	B / 8.8	25	8
AA	MassMutual RetireSMART In Ret A	MRDAX	C-	(800) 542-6767	10.99	D- /1.3	9.26 / 10	2.19 / 25	3.73 / 14	B / 8.8	39	14
GR	Merger Fund Investor	MERFX	C-	(800) 343-8959	15.76	D- /1.2	3.95 / 3	1.11 / 19	2.02 / 8	B / 8.8	60	10
AA	Wells Fargo DJ Tgt 2010 C	WFOCX	C-	(800) 222-8222	12.56	E+ /0.8	2.96 / 3	0.52 / 16	1.34 / 7	B / 8.8	47	11
OT	Merk Abs Rtn Currency Investor	MABFX	D+	(866) 637-5386	9.06	E /0.5	3.31 / 3	-0.92 / 10	0.10 / 5	B / 8.8	73	8
GL	Fidelity Freedom Index 2020 Inv	FPIFX	B-	(800) 544-8544	14.63	C- /4.0	14.26 / 27	4.62 / 50	6.04 / 29	B / 8.7	74	8
AA	J Hancock Multi-Index 2025 Psv 1	JREOX	C+	(800) 257-3336	12.90	C- /3.3	12.06 / 18	4.14 / 44	6.16 / 30	B / 8.7	48	7
AA	● Fidelity Adv Inc Replacement 2030	FRQAX	C	(800) 522-7297	61.83	D+ /2.7	13.81 / 25	4.35 / 47	6.89 / 34	B / 8.7	46	10
BA	James Adv Bal Goldn Rainbow	GLRBX	C	(888) 426-7640	24.90	D+ /2.5	7.99 / 7	3.47 / 37	5.72 / 26	B / 8.7	49	26
AA	QS Defensive Growth A	SBCPX	C	(877) 534-4627	13.55	D /2.2	11.57 / 16	3.42 / 36	5.16 / 22	B / 8.7	52	21
AA	JPMorgan Investor Conserv Gr A	OICAX	C	(800) 480-4111	12.60	D /1.9	9.53 / 11	3.44 / 36	4.75 / 20	B / 8.7	61	21
GL	Nationwide Inv Dest Mdt Consv A	NADCX	C	(800) 848-0920	10.10	D /1.9	10.62 / 13	3.48 / 37	4.99 / 21	B / 8.7	77	N/A
AA	TCW Conservative Alloc N	TGPNX	C-	(800) 386-3829	11.61	D /1.7	6.13 / 5	2.60 / 28	4.89 / 21	B / 8.7	38	11
AA	Madison Conservative Alloc A	MCNAX	C-	(800) 877-6089	10.51	D /1.6	7.86 / 7	3.36 / 35	4.70 / 19	B / 8.7	62	9
GI	Fidelity Adv Asset Manager 30% A	FTAAX	C-	(800) 522-7297	10.72	D /1.6	9.57 / 11	3.17 / 33	4.57 / 19	B / 8.7	69	8
AA	Deutsche Multi-Asset Consv Alloc	SPDAX	C-	(800) 728-3337	12.46	D- /1.5	9.46 / 10	2.30 / 26	4.66 / 19	B / 8.7	27	N/A
AA	Putnam Ret Income Fd Lifestyle 1	PRMAX	C-	(800) 225-1581	17.29	D- /1.4	6.89 / 6	2.37 / 27	3.46 / 13	B / 8.7	68	N/A
BA	Dodge & Cox Balanced Fund	DODBX	A+	(800) 621-3979	107.49	B+ /8.4	27.47 /80	8.12 / 80	12.35 /78	B / 8.6	62	25

Fund Type	Fund Name	Ticker Symbol	Overall Investment Rating	Phone	Net Asset Value As of 2/28/17	Performance Rating/Pts	1Yr / Pct	3Yr / Pct	5Yr / Pct	Risk Rating/Pts	Mgr. Quality Pct	Mgr. Tenure (Years)
SC	ProFunds-Ultra Short Small-Cap	UCPSX	E-	(888) 776-3637	11.48	E- /0.0	-51.85 / 0	-22.71 / 0	-30.58 / 0	E- / 0.0	1	4
PM	ProFunds Short Precious Metals	SPPSX	E-	(888) 776-3637	42.33	E- /0.0	-33.11 / 0	-14.04 / 0	-2.93 / 2	E- / 0.0	0	4
FO	Profunds-Ultra Short Japan Svc	UKPSX	E-	(888) 776-3637	9.74	E- /0.0	-41.64 / 0	-29.17 / 0	-36.40 / 0	E- / 0.0	0	8
EM	Profunds-Ultra Sh Emer Mkt Svc	UVPSX	E-	(888) 776-3637	28.23	E- /0.0	-50.69 / 0	-18.58 / 0	-10.59 / 0	E- / 0.0	0	8
FO	ProFunds-Ultra Sh Latin America	UFPSX	E-	(888) 776-3637	8.74	E- /0.0	-70.86 / 0	-19.19 / 0	-5.36 / 2	E- / 0.0	0	8
FO	Profunds-Ultra Short China Svc	UHPSX	E-	(888) 776-3637	9.55	E- /0.0	-40.01 / 0	-22.67 / 0	-26.02 / 0	E- / 0.0	0	8
GR	ProFunds Ultra Short	USPSX	E-	(888) 776-3637	32.49	E- /0.0	-43.32 / 0	-30.48 / 0	-33.03 / 0	E- / 0.0	1	4
EM	Rydex Inverse Emg Mkts 2x Str A	RYWWX	E-	(800) 820-0888	66.72	E- /0.0	-49.84 / 0	-17.38 / 0	-9.47 / 1	E- / 0.0	0	7
SC	Direxion Mo Small Cap Bear 2X Inv	DXRSX	E-	(800) 851-0511	19.31	E- /0.0	-51.71 / 0	-21.24 / 0	-28.82 / 0	E- / 0.0	2	13
SC	Jacob Micro Cap Growth Inv	JMCGX	E-	(888) 522-6239	9.97	E- /0.0	5.61 / 4	-9.55 / 1	0.19 / 5	E- / 0.0	0	5
PM	ProFunds-Precious Metals Ultra	PMPSX	E-	(888) 776-3637	35.50	E- /0.0	15.79 / 33	-17.10 / 0	-27.06 / 0	E- / 0.0	1	4
MC	● MSIF Trust Mid Cap Growth A	MACGX	E-	(800) 354-8185	16.72	E- /0.1	11.43 / 16	-6.07 / 2	3.44 / 13	E- / 0.0	0	15
EN	ProFunds Oil Eqpt Svcs & Dist Svc	OEPSX	E-	(888) 776-3637	14.08	E- /0.1	47.90 / 99	-16.59 / 0	-7.33 / 1	E- / 0.0	3	4
PM	Deutsche Gold & Prec Metals Fund	SGDAX	E-	(800) 728-3337	6.82	E- /0.2	19.17 / 48	-5.25 / 2	-15.57 / 0	E- / 0.0	67	1
SC	● Universal Inst Small Co Growth II	USIIX	E-	(800) 869-6397	10.94	E /0.3	24.22 / 71	-5.71 / 2	8.42 / 46	E- / 0.0	1	14
PM	Rydex Precious Metal A	RYMNX	E-	(800) 820-0888	30.04	E /0.3	27.60 / 81	-4.91 / 2	-14.05 / 0	E- / 0.0	74	24
PM	Midas Fund	MIDSX	E-	(800) 400-6432	1.26	E /0.4	32.63 / 91	-6.67 / 2	-20.43 / 0	E- / 0.0	40	15
PM	Tocqueville Gold	TGLDX	E-	(800) 697-3863	37.00	E /0.4	21.27 / 59	-3.48 / 4	-13.60 / 0	E- / 0.0	79	20
PM	American Century Global Gold A	ACGGX	E-	(800) 345-6488	8.59	E /0.5	23.93 / 70	-2.53 / 5	-14.15 / 0	E- / 0.0	87	12
PM	OCM Gold Fund Investor	OCMGX	E-	(800) 628-9403	9.88	E /0.5	20.48 / 55	-1.52 / 8	-12.52 / 0	E- / 0.0	92	21
PM	VanEck Intl Investors Gold A	INIVX	E-	(800) 826-1115	9.57	D- /1.1	34.35 / 93	-1.57 / 8	-12.88 / 0	E- / 0.0	91	19
PM	Vanguard Prec Metals & Mining Inv	VGPMX	E-	(800) 662-7447	10.29	D /1.6	36.56 / 95	-2.32 / 6	-12.39 / 0	E- / 0.0	82	3
FO	Profunds-Ultra China Svc	UGPSX	E-	(888) 776-3637	10.34	D /1.7	34.81 / 94	-2.89 / 5	3.00 / 11	E- / 0.0	44	8
MC	Alger SMid Cap Growth Fund A	ALMAX	E-	(800) 254-3796	10.63	C- /3.6	24.95 / 73	2.71 / 29	8.71 / 48	E- / 0.0	4	1
SC	● Buffalo Small Cap Fund	BUFSX	E	(800) 492-8332	16.22	C- /4.2	28.78 / 83	0.73 / 17	9.83 / 57	E- / 0.0	11	19
MC	Alger SMidCap Growth I2	AAMOX	E	(800) 254-3796	1.95	C /4.6	22.60 / 65	3.34 / 35	12.84 / 82	E- / 0.0	8	1
GR	Fairholme	FAIRX	E+	(866) 202-2263	21.51	C+ /5.6	41.66 / 98	0.96 / 18	9.32 / 53	E- / 0.0	2	18
SC	Alger Small Cap Growth Inst R	ASIRX	E+	(800) 254-3796	14.83	C+ /5.9	32.06 / 90	1.63 / 22	7.93 / 41	E- / 0.0	14	16
FO	T Rowe Price Latin America	PRLAX	D-	(800) 638-5660	21.74	C+ /6.6	45.10 / 98	0.47 / 16	-6.06 / 1	E- / 0.0	79	N/A
SC	Dreyfus/Boston Co Sm Cap Growth	SSETX	D	(800) 645-6561	28.04	B- /7.4	37.06 / 96	5.10 / 55	12.15 / 76	E- / 0.0	46	4
FO	Direxion Mo China Bull 2X Inv	DXHLX	C-	(800) 851-0511	35.50	A+ /9.6	60.49 / 99	4.75 / 51	-2.36 / 2	E- / 0.0	96	10
AG	ProFunds-Nasdaq-100 Svc	OTPSX	C-	(888) 776-3637	45.05	A+ /9.6	24.72 / 72	10.88 / 97	13.11 / 85	E- / 0.0	53	4
FO	ProFunds-Ultra Japan Svc	UJPSX	C-	(888) 776-3637	16.06	A+ /9.7	33.28 / 92	8.57 / 84	19.00 / 99	E- / 0.0	99	8
PM	Wells Fargo Precious Mtls A	EKWAX	E-	(800) 222-8222	36.18	E /0.3	17.95 / 43	-3.01 / 4	-13.51 / 0	E- / 0.1	84	10
PM	USAA Precious Mtls&Minerals	USAGX	E-	(800) 382-8722	13.33	E /0.4	22.34 / 64	-4.54 / 3	-15.58 / 0	E- / 0.1	75	N/A
PM	Fidelity Adv Gold A	FGDAX	E-	(800) 522-7297	20.54	E+ /0.7	19.97 / 52	-1.19 / 9	-14.09 / 0	E- / 0.1	92	10
PM	Invesco Gold and Precious Mtls A	IGDAX	E-	(800) 959-4246	4.41	D- /1.1	31.79 / 90	-1.32 / 8	-11.64 / 0	E- / 0.1	90	4
PM	Gabelli Gold A	GLDAX	E-	(800) 422-3554	14.52	D+ /2.7	24.83 / 73	2.66 / 29	-10.34 / 1	E- / 0.1	98	23
SC	Turner Small Cap Growth Fund	TSCEX	E-	(800) 224-6312	12.90	D+ /2.7	22.40 / 64	1.09 / 19	8.60 / 47	E- / 0.1	9	4
FO	Direxion Mo Emerg Mkts Bull 2X	DXELX	E-	(800) 851-0511	38.85	D+ /2.9	56.15 / 99	-3.90 / 3	-7.82 / 1	E+ / 0.1	28	12
HL	Fidelity Adv Biotechnology A	FBTAX	E	(800) 522-7297	23.05	C /4.9	26.09 / 76	3.05 / 32	20.98 / 99	E- / 0.1	0	12
HL	Fidelity Select Biotech Port	FBIOX	D-	(800) 544-8888	203.21	B- /7.0	29.67 / 86	3.91 / 42	22.19 / 99	E- / 0.1	0	12
EN	Rydex Energy Services A	RYESX	E-	(800) 820-0888	31.95	E- /0.0	34.35 / 93	-17.35 / 0	-8.88 / 1	E- / 0.2	1	19
EN	Invesco Energy A	IENAX	E-	(800) 959-4246	26.02	E- /0.0	29.14 / 84	-12.70 / 0	-5.98 / 1	E- / 0.2	7	4
PM	Oppenheimer Gold/Spec Min A	OPGSX	E-	(888) 470-0862	16.61	D- /1.0	32.91 / 91	-1.87 / 7	-13.86 / 0	E- / 0.2	89	20
GR	Victory Newbridge Large Cap Grow	VFGAX	E-	(800) 539-3863	9.02	C- /3.4	15.19 / 31	4.76 / 52	9.63 / 56	E- / 0.2	11	14
GR	ProFunds-Biotech Ultra Sector Svc	BIPSX	E	(888) 776-3637	46.63	C- /4.2	17.31 / 40	2.88 / 31	30.35 / 99	E- / 0.2	0	4
SC	Rydex Inv Rusl 2000 2x Strtgy A	RYIUX	E-	(800) 820-0888	62.99	E- /0.0	-50.78 / 0	-21.53 / 0	-29.63 / 0	E / 0.3	1	11
EN	BlackRock Energy & Resources Inv	SSGRX	E-	(800) 441-7762	18.72	E- /0.0	34.48 / 93	-17.96 / 0	-11.87 / 0	E / 0.3	1	4
EN	ProFunds-Oil & Gas UltraSector	ENPSX	E-	(888) 776-3637	31.96	E- /0.1	35.37 / 94	-12.26 / 0	-3.78 / 2	E / 0.3	15	4
SC	Kalmar Growth With Value Sm Cap	KGSCX	E-	(800) 282-2319	12.70	D- /1.5	23.18 / 67	-0.18 / 13	7.45 / 38	E / 0.3	6	20
MC	● Delaware Smid Cap Growth A	DFCIX	E-	(800) 523-1918	17.73	D /1.9	7.29 / 6	5.28 / 57	9.17 / 52	E / 0.3	43	1

● Denotes fund is closed to new investors

Fund Type	Fund Name	Ticker Symbol	Overall Investment Rating	Phone	Net Asset Value As of 2/28/17	Performance Rating/Pts	Annualized Total Return Through 2/28/17			Risk Rating/Pts	Mgr. Quality Pct	Mgr. Tenure (Years)
							1Yr / Pct	3Yr / Pct	5Yr / Pct			
SC	Rice Hall James Small Cap Port	RHJMX	E-	(866) 777-7818	10.52	C- /3.0	14.46 /28	3.52 /37	8.71 /48	E /0.3	47	21
SC	● AMG GW&K US Small Cap Gr N	ATASX	E-	(800) 548-4539	4.02	C- /3.2	24.97 /73	0.09 /14	6.06 /29	E /0.3	9	1
SC	● TCW Small Cap Growth N	TGSNX	E	(800) 386-3829	21.22	C /4.5	29.13 /84	1.27 /20	6.95 /34	E /0.3	10	5
SC	Columbia Small Cap Growth I A	CGOAX	E+	(800) 345-6611	17.68	C+ /5.7	32.08 /90	3.72 /39	10.39 /61	E /0.3	35	11
MC	Wasatch Ultra Growth Investor	WAMCX	D-	(800) 551-1700	18.28	C+ /6.5	34.30 /93	5.07 /55	10.71 /64	E /0.3	6	5
EN	Fidelity Select Energy Svcs	FSESX	E-	(800) 544-8888	54.71	E /0.5	46.38 /99	-9.69 / 1	-2.73 / 2	E /0.4	29	4
MC	Turner Midcap Growth Inv	TMGFX	E-	(800) 224-6312	18.44	D- /1.0	18.66 /46	-1.92 / 7	5.76 /27	E /0.4	1	N/A
MC	Brown Capital Mgmt Mid Company	BCMSX	E-	(877) 892-4226	11.83	D- /1.3	17.08 /39	-1.12 / 9	5.74 /27	E /0.4	2	15
GR	Westcore Large Cap Dividend Rtl	WTEIX	E-	(800) 392-2673	6.61	C- /3.2	12.78 /21	3.77 /40	9.27 /53	E /0.4	7	1
UT	Meeder Infrastructure Retail	FLRUX	E	(800) 325-3539	21.60	C- /3.6	23.76 /69	2.32 /26	7.15 /36	E /0.4	55	22
SC	● AMG Frontier Small Cap Gr N	MSSVX	E	(800) 548-4539	11.61	C- /4.1	26.86 /79	1.29 /20	8.92 /50	E /0.4	10	8
OT	Wells Fargo Endeavor Sel A	STAEX	E	(800) 222-8222	8.01	C /4.3	18.57 /45	4.98 /54	10.70 /63	E /0.4	13	7
SC	MassMutual Select Small Cap GE	MMGEX	E	(800) 542-6767	11.46	C /4.7	28.19 /82	3.46 /37	11.27 /68	E /0.4	36	16
SC	Eagle Smaller Company A	EGEAX	D-	(800) 421-4184	13.50	C+ /6.4	30.16 /87	5.18 /56	10.42 /61	E /0.4	71	3
SC	● Victory RS Small Cap Equity A	GPSCX	D	(800) 539-3863	15.68	B- /7.3	30.88 /88	5.64 /61	13.09 /85	E /0.4	58	8
SC	ProFunds-Ultra Small Cap Svc	UAPSX	C-	(888) 776-3637	42.31	A+ /9.9	74.55 /99	7.55 /76	20.29 /99	E /0.4	9	4
MC	ProFunds-Ultra Short Mid-Cap Svc	UIPSX	E-	(888) 776-3637	26.97	E- /0.0	-46.49 / 0	-24.06 / 0	-29.67 / 0	E /0.5	2	4
EN	Victory Global Natural Resources A	RSNRX	E-	(800) 539-3863	23.08	E- /0.1	56.58 /99	-11.91 / 1	-7.05 / 1	E /0.5	10	12
PM	First Eagle Gold A	SGGDX	E-	(800) 334-2143	17.11	E /0.5	17.35 /40	-1.09 / 9	-11.21 / 0	E /0.5	90	4
GR	BlackRock Event Driven Eqty Inv A	BALPX	E-	(800) 441-7762	8.74	D /2.0	4.12 / 3	4.96 /54	9.52 /55	E /0.5	78	2
GL	Delaware International Sml Cap A	DGGAX	E-	(800) 523-1918	6.03	D /2.2	15.77 /33	2.83 /30	6.55 /32	E /0.5	90	1
SC	RidgeWorth Silvant SC Gr Stock A	SCGIX	E	(888) 784-3863	7.34	C- /3.6	29.16 /84	1.51 /21	9.46 /54	E /0.5	14	10
MC	CRM Mid Cap Value Inv	CRMMX	D	(800) 276-2883	22.30	B /7.6	28.66 /83	7.28 /74	12.22 /76	E /0.5	61	19
GR	Janus Aspen Forty Inst	JACAX	C-	(800) 295-2687	35.09	B+ /8.9	22.59 /65	10.03 /93	13.86 /92	E /0.5	58	4
SC	Direxion Mo Small Cap Bull 2X Inv	DXRLX	C-	(800) 851-0511	63.18	A+ /9.9	77.27 /99	9.79 /92	22.88 /99	E /0.5	24	13
EN	Fidelity Select Natural Gas	FSNGX	E-	(800) 544-8888	27.76	E /0.4	56.75 /99	-9.69 / 1	-2.06 / 3	E+ /0.6	39	5
PM	Franklin Gold & Precious Metals A	FKRCX	E-	(800) 342-5236	17.66	D- /1.3	32.77 /91	-0.71 /10	-13.34 / 0	E+ /0.6	92	18
SC	Saratoga Adv Tr Small Cap A	SSCYX	E	(800) 807-3863	5.91	C- /3.0	27.65 /81	1.15 /19	7.46 /38	E+ /0.6	19	2
SC	Wells Fargo Trad Sm Cap Gr A	EGWAX	E	(800) 222-8222	13.80	C- /3.1	27.09 /79	1.02 /18	9.21 /52	E+ /0.6	12	26
SC	Century Small Cap Select Inv	CSMVX	E	(800) 321-1928	23.48	C- /4.1	22.87 /66	1.87 /23	7.94 /42	E+ /0.6	17	18
SC	Alger Small Cap Growth Fund A	ALSAX	E	(800) 254-3796	7.11	C- /4.2	30.46 /87	1.51 /21	7.94 /42	E+ /0.6	14	2
MC	Columbia Acorn A	LACAX	E+	(800) 345-6611	14.15	C /5.5	29.35 /85	4.20 /45	9.35 /53	E+ /0.6	11	18
SC	Columbia Acorn USA A	LAUAX	D-	(800) 345-6611	15.60	C+ /6.7	34.01 /93	5.13 /56	10.73 /64	E+ /0.6	57	3
GR	Janus Forty A	JDCAX	D+	(800) 295-2687	30.48	B /7.8	22.41 /64	9.79 /92	13.56 /89	E+ /0.6	54	4
SC	Wells Fargo Sm Cp Val A	SMVAX	D+	(800) 222-8222	21.74	B+ /8.4	41.06 /98	5.91 /63	8.55 /47	E+ /0.6	77	6
SC	Wells Fargo Sm Cp Opp Adm	NVSOX	C-	(800) 222-8222	23.69	A /9.4	31.04 /90	9.31 /89	13.40 /88	E+ /0.6	92	14
HL	Alger Health Sciences Fund A	AHSAX	C	(800) 254-3796	21.45	A+ /9.9	37.94 /96	8.87 /86	14.82 /96	E+ /0.6	21	12
OT	Rydex Commodities Strgy A	RYMEX	E-	(800) 820-0888	84.45	E- /0.0	17.88 /42	-22.76 / 0	-16.20 / 0	E+ /0.7	0	12
EN	Putnam Global Energy Fund A	PGEAX	E-	(800) 225-1581	7.95	E- /0.0	33.42 /92	-14.99 / 0	-7.86 / 1	E+ /0.7	2	1
EN	Prudential Jennison Natural Res A	PGNAX	E-	(800) 225-1852	36.75	E- /0.1	40.50 /97	-10.24 / 1	-6.57 / 1	E+ /0.7	20	11
MC	Calamos Growth A	CVGRX	E	(800) 582-6959	31.43	C- /3.8	16.23 /35	4.14 /44	8.54 /47	E+ /0.7	31	27
MC	BMO Mid-Cap Growth Y	MRMSX	E+	(800) 236-3863	13.89	C /4.6	25.62 /75	1.34 /20	7.68 /40	E+ /0.7	3	1
PM	US Global Inv Gold & PMetals Fd	USERX	E+	(800) 873-8637	8.15	C /4.6	28.98 /84	3.17 /33	-9.81 / 1	E+ /0.7	98	28
SC	CGCM Small Mid Cap Equity	TSGUX	E+	(800) 444-4273	18.82	C /5.3	29.10 /84	1.96 /24	10.15 /59	E+ /0.7	18	20
IN	Rainier Large Cap Equity Original	RIMEX	D-	(800) 248-6314	19.00	C+ /5.8	19.98 /52	5.24 /57	10.14 /59	E+ /0.7	8	9
SC	Royce Smaller Companies Svc	RYVPX	D-	(800) 221-4268	11.46	C+ /5.8	27.62 /81	3.44 /36	9.21 /52	E+ /0.7	30	9
MC	Columbia Acorn Select A	LTFAX	D-	(800) 345-6611	13.85	C+ /6.4	27.73 /81	5.89 /63	9.83 /57	E+ /0.7	35	15
HL	● Franklin Biotechnology Discvry A	FBDIX	D-	(800) 342-5236	147.85	C+ /6.4	30.89 /88	3.79 /40	20.85 /99	E+ /0.7	1	20

● Denotes fund is closed to new investors

Section VII

Top-Rated
Stock Mutual Funds
by Risk Category

A compilation of those

Equity Mutual Funds

receiving the highest TheStreet Investment Ratings

within each risk grade.

Funds are listed in order by Overall Investment Rating.

Section VII Contents

This section contains a summary analysis of the top 100 rated stock mutual funds within each risk grade. Based on your personal risk tolerance, each page shows those funds that have achieved the best financial performance over the past three years.

In order to optimize the utility of our top and bottom fund lists, rather than listing all funds in a multi-class series, a single fund from each series is selected for display as the primary share class. Whenever possible, the selected fund is one that a retail investor would be most likely to choose. This share class may not be appropriate for every investor, so please consult with your financial advisor, the fund company, and the fund's prospectus before placing your trade.

Take the Investor Profile Quiz in the Appendix for assistance in determining your own risk tolerance level. Then you can use this section to identify those funds that are most appropriate for your investing style.

Note that increased risk does not always mean increased performance. Most of the riskiest mutual funds in the E (Very Weak) Risk Rating category have also provided very poor returns to their shareholders. Funds in the D and E Risk Rating categories generally represent speculative ventures that should not be entered into lightly.

1. **Fund Type**   The mutual fund's peer category based on an analysis of its investment portfolio.

AG	Aggressive Growth	HL	Health
AA	Asset Allocation	IN	Income
BA	Balanced	IX	Index
CV	Convertible	MC	Mid Cap
EM	Emerging Market	OT	Other
EN	Energy/Natural Resources	PM	Precious Metals
FS	Financial Services	RE	Real Estate
FO	Foreign	SC	Small Cap
GL	Global	TC	Technology
GR	Growth	UT	Utilities
GI	Growth and Income		

A blank fund type means that the mutual fund has not yet been categorized.

2. **Fund Name**   The name of the mutual fund as stated in its prospectus, which can sometimes differ slightly from the name that the company uses for advertising. If you cannot find the particular mutual fund you are interested in, or if you have any doubts regarding the precise name, verify the information with your broker or on your account statement. Also, use the fund's ticker symbol for confirmation. (See column 3.)

3.	**Ticker Symbol**	The unique alphabetic symbol used for identifying and trading a specific mutual fund. No two funds can have the same ticker symbol, and the ticker symbol for mutual funds always ends with an "X".
		A handful of funds currently show no associated ticker symbol. This means that the fund is either small or new since the NASD only assigns a ticker symbol to funds with at least $25 million in assets or 1,000 shareholders.
4.	**Overall Investment Rating**	Our overall rating is measured on a scale from A to E based on each fund's risk-adjusted performance. Please see page 10 for specific descriptions of each letter grade. Also, refer to page 7 for information on how our ratings are derived. Most important, when using this rating, please be sure to consider the warnings beginning on page 11 regarding the ratings' limitations and the underlying assumptions.
5.	**Phone**	The telephone number of the company managing the fund. Call this number to receive a prospectus or other information about the fund.
6.	**Net Asset Value (NAV)**	The fund's share price as of the date indicated. A fund's NAV is computed by dividing the value of the fund's asset holdings, less accrued fees and expenses, by the number of its shares outstanding.
7.	**Performance Rating/Points**	A letter grade rating based solely on the mutual fund's financial performance over the trailing three years, without any consideration for the amount of risk the fund poses. Like the overall Investment Rating, the Performance Rating is measured on a scale from A to E for ease of interpretation. The points score indicates where the Performance Rating falls on a scale of 0 to 10.
8.	**1-Year Total Return**	The total return the fund has provided investors over the preceeding twelve months. This total return figure is computed based on the fund's dividend distributions and share price appreciation/depreciation during the period, net of the expenses and fees it imposes on its shareholders. Although the total return figure does not reflect an adjustment for any loads the fund may carry, such adjustments have been made in deriving TheStreet Investment Ratings.
9.	**1-Year Total Return Percentile**	The fund's percentile rank based on its one-year performance compared to that of all other equity funds in existence for at least one year. A score of 99 is the best possible, indicating that the fund outperformed 99% of the other mutual funds. Zero is the worst possible percentile score.
10.	**3-Year Total Return**	The total annual return the fund has provided investors over the preceeding three years.

11. 3-Year Total Return Percentile

The fund's percentile rank based on its three-year performance compared to that of all other equity funds in existence for at least three years. A score of 99 is the best possible, indicating that the fund outperformed 99% of the other mutual funds. Zero is the worst possible percentile score.

12. 5-Year Total Return

The total annual return the fund has provided investors over the preceeding five years.

13. 5-Year Total Return Percentile

The fund's percentile rank based on its five-year performance compared to that of all other equity funds in existence for at least five years. A score of 99 is the best possible, indicating that the fund outperformed 99% of the other mutual funds. Zero is the worst possible percentile score.

14. Risk Rating/Points

A letter grade rating based solely on the mutual fund's risk as determined by its monthly performance volatility over the trailing three years. The risk rating does not take into consideration the overall financial performance the fund has achieved or the total return it has provided to its shareholders. Like the overall Investment Rating, the Risk Rating is measured on a scale from A to E for ease of interpretation. The points score indicates where the Risk Rating falls on a scale of 0 to 10.

15. Manager Quality Percentile

The manager quality percentile is based on a ranking of the fund's alpha, a statistical measure representing the difference between a fund's actual returns and its expected performance given its level of risk. Fund managers who have been able to exceed the fund's statistically expected performance receive a high percentile rank with 99 representing the highest possible score. At the other end of the spectrum, fund managers who have actually detracted from the fund's expected performance receive a low percentile rank with 0 representing the lowest possible score.

16. Manager Tenure

The number of years the current manager has been managing the fund. Since fund managers who deliver substandard returns are usually replaced, a long tenure is usually a good sign that shareholders are satisfied that the fund is achieving its stated objectives.

VII. Top-Rated Stock Mutual Funds In The B Risk Category

Fund Type	Fund Name	Ticker Symbol	Overall Investment Rating	Phone	Net Asset Value As of 2/28/17	Performance Rating/Pts	Annualized Total Return Through 2/28/17			Risk Rating/Pts	Mgr. Quality Pct	Mgr. Tenure (Years)
	99 Pct = Best *0 Pct = Worst*						1Yr / Pct	3Yr / Pct	5Yr / Pct			
FO	Hennessy Japan Small Cap Inv	HJPSX	A+	(800) 966-4354	12.14	A+ /9.9	30.37 /87	13.52 /99	15.54 /98	B- /7.3	99	10
GR	USAA Nasdaq 100 Index	USNQX	A+	(800) 382-8722	15.14	A+ /9.8	27.85 /81	13.75 /99	16.02 /98	B- /7.3	81	11
FO	DFA Japanese Small Co Inst	DFJSX	A+	(800) 984-9472	23.74	A+ /9.7	28.62 /83	10.53 /96	10.00 /58	B- /7.6	99	13
GR	LSV Value Equity Inst	LSVEX	A+	(866) 777-7818	27.34	A+ /9.7	31.35 /89	10.39 /95	15.98 /98	B- /7.0	66	18
GR	Vanguard Mega Cap Value Index I	VMVLX	A+	(800) 662-7447	138.07	A+ /9.6	26.92 /79	11.04 /97	14.18 /94	B- /7.5	81	2
GR	Vanguard Value Index Inv	VIVAX	A+	(800) 662-7447	37.78	A+ /9.6	27.65 /81	10.77 /97	14.12 /94	B- /7.2	79	23
GR	Fidelity 100 Index FD	FOHIX	A+	(800) 544-8544	15.40	A /9.5	24.55 /72	11.02 /97	13.56 /89	B- /7.1	76	10
GR	Fidelity LgCp Val Enh Idx Fd	FLVEX	A+	(800) 544-8544	12.53	A /9.5	28.30 /82	10.16 /94	14.42 /95	B- /7.0	70	10
GR	Glenmede Large Cap Core Advisor	GTLOX	A+	(800) 442-8299	25.34	A /9.4	25.08 /74	10.64 /96	15.34 /97	B- /7.8	73	13
IN	Vanguard High Div Yield Index Inv	VHDYX	A+	(800) 662-7447	31.07	A /9.4	23.89 /69	11.43 /98	13.95 /93	B- /7.4	85	1
GR	ProFunds-Consumer Goods Ultra	CNPSX	A+	(888) 776-3637	93.47	A /9.4	17.56 /41	12.12 /98	16.06 /98	B- /7.3	73	4
GR	Fidelity Blue Chip Value	FBCVX	A+	(800) 544-8544	18.45	A /9.4	24.99 /73	9.90 /93	13.21 /86	B- /7.3	70	3
GI	American Century VP Value II	AVPVX	A+	(800) 345-6488	10.82	A /9.4	29.78 /86	10.28 /95	13.56 /89	B- /7.1	76	21
MC	Vanguard Mega Cap Index Inst	VMCTX	A+	(800) 662-7447	159.47	A /9.4	25.12 /74	10.64 /96	13.93 /93	B- /7.1	91	2
IX	Vanguard Instl Index Inst	VINIX	A+	(800) 662-7447	215.93	A /9.4	24.94 /73	10.61 /96	13.98 /93	B- /7.1	74	17
GR	DFA US Large Company Portfolio	DFUSX	A+	(800) 984-9472	18.44	A /9.4	24.92 /73	10.57 /96	13.95 /93	B- /7.0	74	N/A
IX	Fidelity 500 Index Inv	FUSEX	A+	(800) 544-8544	82.98	A /9.3	24.88 /73	10.54 /96	13.91 /92	B /8.2	73	13
IX	Vanguard 500 Index Inv	VFINX	A+	(800) 662-7447	218.80	A /9.3	24.82 /73	10.48 /96	13.85 /92	B- /7.1	73	26
IX	Northern Stock Index	NOSIX	A+	(800) 595-9111	28.53	A /9.3	24.83 /73	10.51 /96	13.88 /92	B- /7.0	73	11
IX	Dreyfus Instl S&P 500 Stock Index	DSPIX	A+	(800) 645-6561	47.82	A /9.3	24.73 /73	10.42 /96	13.80 /92	B- /7.0	72	15
GI	Fidelity Total Mkt Idx F	FFSMX	A+	(800) 544-8544	68.21	A- /9.2	26.33 /77	9.87 /93	13.79 /92	B- /7.7	63	13
IX	SS Inst S&P 500 Index Inv	SIDIX	A+	(800) 843-2639	22.32	A- /9.2	24.64 /72	10.41 /96	13.80 /92	B- /7.1	72	20
IX	T Rowe Price Equity Index 500	PREIX	A+	(800) 638-5660	63.64	A- /9.2	24.67 /72	10.35 /95	13.71 /91	B- /7.1	71	9
IX	TIAA-CREF S&P 500 Idx Retire	TRSPX	A+	(800) 842-2252	26.18	A- /9.2	24.58 /72	10.30 /95	13.65 /90	B- /7.0	71	12
GR	Amer Beacon Bridgeway LC Val	BRLVX	A+	(800) 658-5811	26.99	A- /9.2	25.20 /74	10.56 /96	15.51 /98	B- /7.0	77	14
GR	Vanguard Large Cap Index Inv	VLACX	A+	(800) 662-7447	43.81	A- /9.2	25.10 /74	10.13 /94	13.66 /90	B- /7.0	68	1
IX	USAA S&P 500 Index Members	USSPX	A+	(800) 382-8722	33.68	A- /9.2	24.67 /72	10.35 /95	13.72 /91	B- /7.0	71	11
GR	Glenmede Large Cap Growth	GTLLX	A+	(800) 442-8299	27.71	A- /9.1	20.41 /54	11.29 /97	15.12 /97	B /8.2	77	13
GI	Voya Russell Large Cap Index Adv	IRLIX	A+	(800) 992-0180	18.14	A- /9.1	24.03 /70	10.06 /94	13.15 /85	B- /7.3	68	5
GR	Voya VP Index Plus Large Cap S	IPLSX	A+	(800) 992-0180	25.53	A- /9.1	24.43 /71	9.85 /93	13.12 /85	B- /7.2	63	11
FS	Franklin Mutual Financial Svcs A	TFSIX	A+	(800) 342-5236	22.14	A- /9.1	28.54 /83	10.54 /96	13.48 /89	B- /7.1	78	8
GI	Fidelity Value Discovery Fd	FVDFX	A+	(800) 544-8544	27.15	A- /9.1	24.60 /72	9.51 /90	13.96 /93	B- /7.0	72	5
IX	GuideStone Equity Index Inv	GEQZX	A+	(888) 984-8433	26.09	A- /9.1	24.71 /72	10.13 /94	13.55 /89	B- /7.0	68	1
IX	S&P 500 Index Direct	SPFIX	A+	(800) 955-9988	46.16	A- /9.1	24.14 /70	10.25 /94	13.60 /90	B- /7.0	70	14
GR	SunAmerica VAL Co I Core Eq Fd	VCCEX	A+	(800) 858-8850	21.81	A- /9.1	28.55 /83	8.67 /84	12.48 /79	B- /7.0	36	5
IX	Columbia Large Cap Index A	NEIAX	A+	(800) 345-6611	45.16	A- /9.1	24.40 /71	10.15 /94	13.51 /89	B- /7.0	69	6
GR	Dean Mid Cap Value	DALCX	A+	(888) 899-8343	19.02	A- /9.0	27.76 /81	9.63 /91	12.96 /83	B- /7.5	78	9
GR	Bridgeway Blue Chip 35 Index	BRLIX	A+	(800) 661-3550	13.47	A- /9.0	23.49 /68	10.57 /96	13.42 /88	B- /7.2	74	20
GR	SunAmerica VAL Co II Soc Resp	VCSRX	A+	(800) 858-8850	20.96	A- /9.0	23.59 /68	10.42 /95	14.27 /95	B- /7.0	69	5
SC	Aberdeen US Small Cap Eq A	GSXAX	A+	(866) 667-9231	32.75	A- /9.0	26.01 /76	12.62 /98	15.91 /98	B- /7.0	98	9
GR	Bishop Street Dividend Value I	BSLIX	A+	(800) 262-9565	15.43	B+ /8.9	21.95 /62	10.20 /94	12.69 /81	B- /7.6	79	7
GR	Amer Beacon Bridgeway LC Gro	BRLGX	A+	(800) 658-5811	25.98	B+ /8.9	20.26 /53	10.38 /95	14.67 /96	B- /7.5	76	14
IX	Principal LgCap S&P 500 A	PLSAX	A+	(800) 222-5852	16.33	B+ /8.9	24.38 /71	10.08 /94	13.39 /88	B- /7.0	68	6
GI	Payden Equity Income Investor	PYVLX	A+	(888) 409-8007	15.97	B+ /8.8	21.41 /59	10.75 /97	12.48 /79	B- /7.5	86	N/A
GR	Columbia Large Cap Enh Core A	NMIAX	A+	(800) 345-6611	23.81	B+ /8.8	22.62 /65	9.81 /92	13.37 /88	B- /7.0	62	8
GR	Torray	TORYX	A+	(800) 443-3036	49.71	B+ /8.7	23.99 /70	9.82 /92	12.54 /79	B- /7.6	74	20
GR	SEI Inst Inv Tr-Tax Mgd Volty F	TMMAX	A+	(800) 342-5734	15.41	B+ /8.6	17.32 /40	11.08 /97	13.86 /92	B- /7.4	94	10
GR	SA US Core Market	SAMKX	A+	(800) 366-7266	21.06	B+ /8.5	23.77 /69	8.95 /86	12.93 /83	B /8.0	55	11
BA	Dodge & Cox Balanced Fund	DODBX	A+	(800) 621-3979	107.49	B+ /8.4	27.47 /80	8.12 /80	12.35 /78	B /8.6	62	25
GI	Wright Major Blue Chip Equities	WQCEX	A+	(800) 232-0013	19.64	B+ /8.4	22.77 /66	8.38 /82	10.29 /61	B- /7.1	40	8
GI	Vanguard Cons Stap Idx Adm	VCSAX	A+	(800) 662-7447	69.91	B /8.2	12.06 /18	11.96 /98	13.84 /92	B- /7.6	95	7
FO	Fidelity Japan Small Companies	FJSCX	A+	(800) 544-8544	15.60	B /7.9	19.77 /51	9.37 /89	14.45 /95	B- /7.9	99	3

● Denotes fund is closed to new investors

Fund Type	Fund Name	Ticker Symbol	Overall Investment Rating	Phone	Net Asset Value As of 2/28/17	PERFORMANCE Performance Rating/Pts	Annualized Total Return Through 2/28/17 1Yr / Pct	3Yr / Pct	5Yr / Pct	RISK Risk Rating/Pts	FUND MGR Mgr. Quality Pct	Mgr. Tenure (Years)
	99 Pct = Best 0 Pct = Worst											
UT	Invesco Dividend Income A	IAUTX	A+	(800) 959-4246	24.09	B /7.8	17.24 /39	11.83 /98	12.99 /84	B /8.0	98	8
FO	T Rowe Price Japan	PRJPX	A+	(800) 638-5660	12.28	B /7.7	23.92 /70	8.84 /86	10.84 /65	B /8.0	99	4
OT	Lazard Global Listed Infr Open	GLFOX	A	(800) 821-6474	14.89	B+ /8.5	14.22 /26	11.33 /97	15.71 /98	B- /7.0	97	8
GR	Blue Chip Investor Fund	BCIFX	A	(800) 710-5777	164.96	B+ /8.3	23.91 /70	9.64 /91	13.29 /87	B- /7.1	83	15
SC	DGHM V2000 Small Cap Value	DGSMX	A	(800) 673-0550	12.61	B+ /8.3	31.30 /89	6.90 /71	11.76 /72	B- /7.0	82	7
GI	Queens Road Value Fund	QRVLX	A	(800) 595-3088	21.41	B /8.2	22.87 /66	8.44 /82	11.92 /74	B- /7.3	77	13
GR	Northern Large Cap Core	NOLCX	A	(800) 595-9111	17.11	B /8.2	22.49 /64	8.99 /87	13.53 /89	B- /7.3	56	6
GI	Lazard US Eqty Concentrated	LEVOX	A	(800) 821-6474	14.99	B /8.2	17.78 /42	11.61 /98	14.41 /95	B- /7.1	84	6
RE	Sterling Capital Stratton RE Inst	STMDX	A	(800) 228-1872	37.57	B /8.2	16.21 /35	11.67 /98	11.53 /70	B- /7.1	75	2
IX	Invesco S&P 500 Index A	SPIAX	A	(800) 959-4246	25.56	B /8.2	24.26 /71	9.99 /93	13.36 /87	B- /7.1	68	7
GR	SunAmerica VAL Co I Val Fd	VAVAX	A	(800) 858-8850	16.58	B /8.2	26.03 /76	8.27 /81	12.26 /77	B- /7.0	37	6
GR	Fidelity Adv Value Leaders A	FVLAX	A	(800) 522-7297	18.41	B /8.1	23.78 /69	9.31 /89	12.63 /80	B- /7.3	62	3
GI	● Chestnut Street Exchange	CHNTX	A	(800) 441-7762	609.61	B /8.0	22.49 /64	8.58 /84	12.48 /79	B- /7.1	49	4
IN	JPMorgan Equity Income A	OIEIX	A	(800) 480-4111	15.58	B /7.9	24.15 /70	9.63 /91	13.01 /84	B- /7.2	74	13
GI	Sterling Capital Beh LC Val Eq A	BBTGX	A	(800) 228-1872	19.83	B /7.9	26.14 /77	8.48 /83	11.66 /71	B- /7.2	47	4
GR	Fidelity Adv Equity Value A	FAVAX	A	(800) 522-7297	17.67	B /7.9	24.35 /71	9.03 /87	13.49 /89	B- /7.1	66	5
IN	CNR Dividend and Income N	RIMHX	A	(888) 889-0799	41.29	B /7.8	17.73 /42	9.93 /93	10.84 /64	B- /7.4	92	14
IN	ICON Equity Income A	IEQAX	A	(800) 764-0442	17.08	B /7.8	24.92 /73	9.34 /89	11.03 /66	B- /7.3	75	15
GR	Vanguard Dividend Apprec Idx Inv	VDAIX	A	(800) 662-7447	36.18	B /7.7	20.14 /53	8.71 /85	11.76 /72	B- /7.4	69	1
IN	Copley	COPLX	A	(800) 424-8570	82.86	B /7.6	15.81 /33	9.43 /90	10.54 /62	B- /7.5	95	39
AG	ProFunds-Bull Svc	BLPSX	A	(888) 776-3637	91.73	B- /7.3	21.24 /58	7.47 /75	10.71 /64	B /8.2	36	4
GR	J Hancock VIT All Cap Core I	JEACX	A-	(800) 257-3336	31.37	B /8.0	22.75 /66	8.48 /83	13.00 /84	B- /7.0	48	7
GR	Marathon Value Portfolio	MVPFX	A-	(800) 788-6086	26.27	B /7.9	24.16 /70	7.88 /78	10.90 /65	B- /7.1	51	17
GI	Value Line Mid Cap Focused Inv	VLIFX	A-	(800) 243-2729	17.32	B /7.9	22.60 /65	8.75 /85	12.36 /78	B- /7.0	76	8
GL	Alpine Rising Dividend Inst	AADDX	A-	(888) 785-5578	16.52	B /7.8	24.58 /72	7.60 /76	11.28 /68	B- /7.1	98	7
GR	Green Century Equity Individual Inv	GCEQX	A-	(800) 221-5519	35.86	B /7.8	21.99 /62	8.99 /87	12.82 /82	B- /7.1	53	7
GR	● Delaware Value A	DDVAX	A-	(800) 523-1918	20.45	B /7.8	23.92 /70	10.36 /95	14.05 /93	B- /7.1	80	13
GR	JPMorgan Intrepid Sustain Ldr A	JICAX	A-	(800) 480-4111	37.91	B /7.7	22.53 /65	9.38 /89	13.52 /89	B- /7.1	53	12
GR	AMG FQ Tax-Mgnd US Equity N	MFQAX	A-	(800) 548-4539	27.00	B /7.7	20.88 /57	7.89 /78	12.95 /83	B- /7.1	55	9
GR	USAA Capital Growth	USCGX	A-	(800) 382-8722	10.81	B /7.6	21.85 /61	7.91 /78	11.41 /69	B- /7.4	49	6
GI	Columbia Disciplined Core A	AQEAX	A-	(800) 345-6611	10.81	B /7.6	21.22 /61	9.90 /93	12.93 /83	B- /7.2	65	7
IN	Principal Equity Inc Fd A	PQIAX	A-	(800) 222-5852	29.17	B /7.6	25.09 /74	8.79 /85	11.83 /73	B- /7.0	63	9
MC	ProFunds-Mid Cap Svc	MDPSX	A-	(888) 776-3637	74.13	B /7.6	28.10 /82	6.63 /69	10.67 /63	B- /7.0	37	4
GR	PNC Large Cap Core A	PLEAX	A-	(800) 551-2145	18.66	B- /7.5	18.40 /45	10.29 /95	11.86 /73	B- /7.4	75	8
GI	● Vanguard Dividend Growth Inv	VDIGX	A-	(800) 662-7447	24.80	B- /7.4	16.84 /38	9.22 /88	12.50 /79	B- /7.4	75	11
GR	Hartford Core Equity A	HAIAX	A-	(888) 843-7824	26.02	B- /7.4	18.50 /45	10.21 /94	14.51 /96	B- /7.3	80	19
GR	Russell Investments US Def Eq A	REQAX	A-	(800) 832-6688	50.39	B- /7.0	19.24 /48	9.52 /90	11.89 /73	B- /7.8	79	3
GR	Deutsche CROCI Equity Dividend	KDHAX	B+	(800) 728-3337	52.03	B- /7.4	24.78 /73	8.63 /84	10.85 /65	B- /7.1	51	3
IX	Rydex S&P 500 A	RYSOX	B+	(800) 820-0888	45.53	B- /7.4	22.87 /66	8.80 /85	12.14 /75	B- /7.0	54	19
GR	Eaton Vance Tax-Mgd Growth 1.2	EXTGX	B+	(800) 262-1122	20.09	B- /7.4	22.40 /64	9.34 /89	12.72 /81	B- /7.0	59	11
GI	Thornburg Value A	TVAFX	B+	(800) 847-0200	58.44	B- /7.3	23.41 /68	8.34 /82	12.08 /75	B- /7.1	58	11
GI	SEI Asset Alloc-Cons Str All F	SMGAX	B+	(800) 342-5734	13.69	B- /7.2	18.82 /46	8.68 /85	10.79 /64	B- /7.2	89	14
GR	Federated MDT All Cap Core Fd A	QAACX	B+	(800) 341-7400	24.09	B- /7.2	25.47 /75	7.78 /77	13.73 /91	B- /7.0	34	9
RE	SA Real Estate Securities	SAREX	B+	(800) 366-7266	11.51	B- /7.1	15.27 /31	10.34 /95	10.43 /62	B- /7.1	54	5
GR	Dana Large Cap Equity A	DLCAX	B+		20.04	B- /7.1	22.13 /63	8.10 /80	11.71 /72	B- /7.1	46	9
GI	● MainStay Common Stock B	MOPBX	B+	(800) 624-6782	20.20	B- /7.1	19.20 /48	7.73 /77	12.38 /78	B- /7.0	38	10
GI	Eagle Growth and Income A	HRCVX	B+	(800) 421-4184	19.29	B- /7.1	23.86 /69	8.03 /79	11.87 /73	B- /7.0	47	6
GR	Pioneer Fundamental Growth A	PIGFX	B+	(800) 225-6292	20.48	B- /7.0	15.58 /32	10.16 /94	13.11 /85	B- /7.1	75	10

● Denotes fund is closed to new investors

Fund Type	Fund Name	Ticker Symbol	Overall Investment Rating	Phone	Net Asset Value As of 2/28/17	Perform-ance Rating/Pts	Annualized Total Return Through 2/28/17			Risk Rating/Pts	Mgr. Quality Pct	Mgr. Tenure (Years)
	99 Pct = Best						1Yr / Pct	3Yr / Pct	5Yr / Pct			
	0 Pct = Worst											
FS	RMB Mendon Financial Services A	RMBKX	A+	(800) 601-5228	42.66	A+ /9.9	49.34 /99	20.69 /99	23.00 /99	C+ / 6.8	98	18
FS	Vanguard Financial Index Fd Adm	VFAIX	A+	(800) 662-7447	31.22	A+ /9.9	46.85 /99	14.09 /99	17.33 /98	C+ / 6.6	79	2
TC	Vanguard Info Tech Ind Adm	VITAX	A+	(800) 662-7447	68.11	A+ /9.9	33.51 /92	14.64 /99	14.84 /97	C+ / 6.5	85	2
FS	Emerald Banking and Finance A	HSSAX	A+	(855) 828-9909	42.64	A+ /9.9	51.05 /99	16.40 /99	21.78 /99	C+ / 6.5	88	20
GR	Parnassus Endeavor	PARWX	A+	(800) 999-3505	34.41	A+ /9.9	32.69 /91	15.00 /99	17.59 /98	C+ / 6.4	93	12
TC	Oak Assoc-Red Oak Technology	ROGSX	A+	(888) 462-5386	21.70	A+ /9.9	42.16 /98	14.41 /99	17.43 /98	C+ / 6.3	84	11
FS	1919 Financial Services A	SBFAX	A+	(844) 828-1919	24.53	A+ /9.9	44.51 /98	14.96 /99	18.45 /99	C+ / 6.1	87	3
FS	J Hancock Regional Bank A	FRBAX	A+	(800) 257-3336	26.28	A+ /9.9	60.84 /99	18.09 /99	20.90 /99	C+ / 6.0	91	19
FS	Alpine Financial Services Inst	ADFSX	A+	(888) 785-5578	17.24	A+ /9.9	55.88 /99	10.12 /94	17.39 /98	C+ / 5.7	30	2
TC	ICON Information Technology S	ICTEX	A+	(800) 764-0442	16.31	A+ /9.9	29.24 /85	15.71 /99	13.74 /91	C+ / 5.7	95	N/A
AG	Rydex Nova A	RYANX	A+	(800) 820-0888	56.26	A+ /9.8	36.32 /95	13.35 /99	18.76 /99	C+ / 6.7	38	21
MC	American Century VP Mid Cap Val	AVMTX	A+	(800) 345-6488	21.92	A+ /9.8	31.15 /88	12.76 /99	15.36 /97	C+ / 6.7	95	13
FS	Fidelity Select Insurance	FSPCX	A+	(800) 544-8888	80.60	A+ /9.8	31.60 /89	13.17 /99	17.52 /98	C+ / 6.7	86	4
SC	Oak Assoc-Pin Oak Equity	POGSX	A+	(888) 462-5386	60.45	A+ /9.8	34.55 /94	11.91 /98	15.62 /98	C+ / 6.6	97	12
EM	Franklin India Growth Fund A	FINGX	A+	(800) 342-5236	13.45	A+ /9.8	30.84 /88	15.88 /99	7.75 /40	C+ / 6.5	99	9
GR	NASDAQ-100 Index Direct	NASDX	A+	(800) 955-9988	13.62	A+ /9.8	27.11 /79	13.66 /99	16.37 /98	C+ / 6.5	81	14
GR	● Vanguard PRIMECAP Core Inv	VPCCX	A+	(800) 662-7447	23.81	A+ /9.8	28.50 /83	11.62 /98	16.19 /98	C+ / 6.4	78	13
FS	Fidelity Select Financial Services	FIDSX	A+	(800) 544-8888	103.05	A+ /9.8	38.78 /97	10.04 /93	13.85 /92	C+ / 6.2	43	4
GI	Dodge & Cox Stk Fund	DODGX	A+	(800) 621-3979	194.15	A+ /9.8	38.12 /96	10.05 /94	15.91 /98	C+ / 6.1	51	25
FS	Davis Financial A	RPFGX	A+	(800) 279-0279	47.12	A+ /9.8	33.82 /93	12.34 /98	14.42 /95	C+ / 6.1	78	26
GR	Fidelity NASDAQ Composite Index	FNCMX	A+	(800) 544-8544	76.54	A+ /9.8	29.21 /85	11.79 /98	15.71 /98	C+ / 6.0	65	13
GR	Fidelity Sel Defense and	FSDAX	A+	(800) 544-8888	138.34	A+ /9.8	34.37 /93	10.37 /95	15.46 /98	C+ / 6.0	70	2
GR	SunAmerica VAL Co I Nsdq 100	VCNIX	A+	(800) 858-8850	11.14	A+ /9.8	27.84 /81	13.84 /99	16.15 /98	C+ / 5.9	81	5
SC	Nuveen Small Cap Value A	FSCAX	A+	(800) 257-8787	24.70	A+ /9.8	42.88 /98	12.49 /98	15.54 /98	C+ / 5.9	96	12
GR	PRIMECAP Odyssey Stock Fd	POSKX	A+	(800) 729-2307	27.59	A+ /9.7	28.41 /83	11.07 /97	14.98 /97	C+ / 6.8	72	13
GR	White Oak Select Growth	WOGSX	A+	(888) 462-5386	76.20	A+ /9.7	31.20 /89	10.95 /97	13.74 /91	C+ / 6.8	57	25
GR	DFA US Large Cap Value II Inst	DFCVX	A+	(800) 984-9472	18.12	A+ /9.7	33.26 /92	10.07 /94	15.42 /97	C+ / 6.7	57	13
AG	Rydex NASDAQ 100 A	RYATX	A+	(800) 820-0888	27.96	A+ /9.7	26.46 /78	12.71 /99	15.01 /97	C+ / 6.3	74	23
FS	Fidelity Adv Financial Serv A	FAFDX	A+	(800) 522-7297	19.00	A+ /9.7	38.17 /96	9.86 /93	13.68 /90	C+ / 6.3	41	4
GI	Harbor Large Cap Value Inv	HILVX	A+	(800) 422-1050	13.54	A+ /9.7	30.74 /88	10.76 /97	14.96 /97	C+ / 6.2	73	5
MC	● Vanguard PRIMECAP Inv	VPMCX	A+	(800) 662-7447	112.93	A+ /9.7	28.77 /83	11.30 /97	16.64 /98	C+ / 6.1	92	32
MC	Vanguard S&P Mid-Cap 400 Value	VMFVX	A+	(800) 662-7447	228.02	A+ /9.7	35.40 /94	9.99 /93	14.45 /95	C+ / 6.1	71	2
GR	Fidelity Select Air Transport	FSAIX	A+	(800) 544-8888	76.05	A+ /9.7	26.31 /77	11.81 /98	18.53 /99	C+ / 5.9	82	5
GR	Clipper	CFIMX	A+	(800) 432-2504	112.44	A+ /9.6	31.33 /89	11.30 /97	14.00 /93	C+ / 6.6	74	11
GR	Vanguard US Value Inv	VUVLX	A+	(800) 662-7447	18.96	A+ /9.6	28.78 /83	10.11 /94	14.85 /97	C+ / 6.6	70	4
SC	Vanguard Small-Cap Value Index	VISVX	A+	(800) 662-7447	29.79	A+ /9.6	34.76 /94	9.66 /91	14.73 /96	C+ / 6.1	92	19
SC	Voya VP Index Plus SmallCap S	IPSSX	A+	(800) 992-0180	27.09	A+ /9.6	34.59 /94	9.35 /89	14.17 /94	C+ / 6.1	91	11
GR	J Hancock Classic Value A	PZFVX	A+	(800) 257-3336	30.39	A+ /9.6	39.99 /97	9.02 /87	13.57 /90	C+ / 6.0	24	21
GR	SunAmerica VAL Co II Lrg Cp Val	VACVX	A+	(800) 858-8850	20.97	A /9.5	31.17 /88	9.43 /90	14.00 /93	C+ / 6.9	56	7
GR	Vanguard FTSE Social Index Inv	VFTSX	A+	(800) 662-7447	15.27	A /9.5	26.32 /77	10.54 /96	15.23 /97	C+ / 6.8	66	2
OT	Vanguard Industrials Index Adm	VINAX	A+	(800) 662-7447	64.22	A /9.5	29.81 /86	9.76 /92	14.72 /96	C+ / 6.7	51	2
UT	ICON Utilities S	ICTUX	A+	(800) 764-0442	9.18	A /9.5	20.03 /52	12.24 /98	12.30 /77	C+ / 6.6	71	3
GR	Tax Mgd US MktWide Val II Inst	DFMVX	A+	(800) 984-9472	26.92	A /9.5	30.62 /87	9.52 /90	15.22 /97	C+ / 6.6	52	13
UT	Vanguard Utilities Index Adm	VUIAX	A+	(800) 662-7447	56.98	A /9.5	17.14 /39	12.44 /98	12.72 /81	C+ / 6.5	58	2
MC	Harbor Mid Cap Value Inv	HIMVX	A+	(800) 422-1050	22.78	A /9.5	30.36 /87	9.25 /88	15.20 /97	C+ / 6.4	73	13
GR	Boston Partners All Cap Val Inv	BPAVX	A+	(888) 261-4073	24.56	A /9.5	30.14 /87	10.29 /95	14.83 /97	C+ / 6.3	59	10
MC	Vanguard S&P Mid-Cap 400 Index	VSPMX	A+	(800) 662-7447	231.94	A /9.5	31.63 /89	9.57 /91	13.77 /91	C+ / 6.1	74	4
GR	Oakmark Fund Service	OARMX	A+	(800) 625-6275	75.22	A /9.5	33.74 /93	9.09 /87	14.26 /95	C+ / 6.1	38	17
GI	JPMorgan Tax Aware Equity I	JPDEX	A+	(800) 480-4111	31.17	A /9.5	27.30 /80	10.29 /95	14.32 /95	C+ / 6.0	59	9
GR	Vanguard Russell 1000 Val Index	VRVIX	A+	(800) 662-7447	199.02	A /9.4	28.85 /84	9.78 /92	13.91 /93	C+ / 6.8	67	7
GI	Fidelity Growth and Income	FGRIX	A+	(800) 544-8544	34.36	A /9.4	30.09 /87	9.51 /90	13.63 /90	C+ / 6.5	49	6
GR	Thompson LargeCap	THPGX	A+	(800) 999-0887	60.15	A /9.4	35.77 /95	8.60 /84	13.09 /85	C+ / 6.2	23	25

● Denotes fund is closed to new investors

Fund Type	Fund Name	Ticker Symbol	Overall Investment Rating	Phone	Net Asset Value As of 2/28/17	PERFORMANCE				RISK	FUND MGR	
	99 Pct = Best 0 Pct = Worst					Perform-ance Rating/Pts	Annualized Total Return Through 2/28/17			Risk Rating/Pts	Mgr. Quality Pct	Mgr. Tenure (Years)
							1Yr / Pct	3Yr / Pct	5Yr / Pct			
GR	Vanguard Tax-Managed Cap Appr	VTCLX	A+	(800) 662-7447	120.95	A /9.3	25.99 / 76	10.19 / 94	14.03 / 93	C+ / 6.9	67	1
IX	Schwab S&P 500 Index Fund	SWPPX	A+	(800) 407-0256	36.46	A /9.3	24.81 / 73	10.52 / 96	13.89 / 92	C+ / 6.9	73	5
IN	FAM Equity-Income Inv	FAMEX	A+	(800) 932-3271	27.78	A /9.3	26.90 / 79	10.37 / 95	13.06 / 84	C+ / 6.8	84	21
MC	Vanguard Mid-Cap Value Index Inv	VMVIX	A+	(800) 662-7447	40.40	A /9.3	29.04 / 84	9.74 / 92	14.68 / 96	C+ / 6.5	82	11
GI	SunAmerica VAL Co I Growth & Inc	VCGAX	A+	(800) 858-8850	20.23	A /9.3	25.74 / 75	10.00 / 93	12.80 / 82	C+ / 6.5	66	4
SC	Wells Fargo Small Cap Core Inst	WYSCX	A+	(800) 222-8222	20.62	A /9.3	27.19 / 80	9.51 / 90	13.37 / 88	C+ / 6.4	91	12
GR	State Street S&P 500 Index VIS 1	SSSPX	A+	(800) 843-2639	40.48	A- /9.2	24.59 / 72	10.28 / 95	13.66 / 90	C+ / 6.9	70	16
IN	DFA Tax-Managed US Eq Inst	DTMEX	A+	(800) 984-9472	25.69	A- /9.2	26.02 / 76	9.84 / 92	13.76 / 91	C+ / 6.9	63	5
GR	Vanguard Instl TtlStk Mkt Inst	VITNX	A+	(800) 662-7447	53.20	A- /9.2	26.30 / 77	9.92 / 93	13.86 / 92	C+ / 6.8	64	16
IN	Vanguard Russell 3000 Index Inst	VRTTX	A+	(800) 662-7447	210.62	A- /9.2	26.06 / 76	9.83 / 92	13.76 / 91	C+ / 6.8	63	2
GR	Vanguard Mega Cap Gr Index I	VMGAX	A+	(800) 662-7447	187.71	A- /9.2	23.16 / 67	10.21 / 94	13.77 / 91	C+ / 6.7	60	2
GR	Nuveen Large Cap Select A	FLRAX	A+	(800) 257-8787	24.51	A- /9.2	32.22 / 90	9.53 / 91	13.78 / 92	C+ / 6.6	50	14
GR	American Century VP Large Co Val	AVVIX	A+	(800) 345-6488	15.96	A- /9.2	28.47 / 83	9.40 / 90	13.21 / 86	C+ / 6.6	52	13
GR	Schwab Total Stock Market Index	SWTSX	A+	(800) 407-0256	42.01	A- /9.2	26.22 / 77	9.82 / 92	13.74 / 91	C+ / 6.6	63	5
GR	BlackRock Large Cap Value Inv A	MDLVX	A+	(800) 441-7762	26.38	A- /9.1	30.54 / 87	9.30 / 89	12.28 / 77	C+ / 6.9	50	18
GR	QS S&P 500 Index A	SBSPX	A+	(877) 534-4627	23.09	A- /9.1	24.31 / 71	10.01 / 93	13.38 / 88	C+ / 6.9	67	N/A
GR	T Rowe Price Total Eq Mkt Index	POMIX	A+	(800) 638-5660	26.79	A- /9.1	26.21 / 77	9.76 / 92	13.79 / 92	C+ / 6.8	61	9
GR	Vanguard Tot Stk Mkt Idx Inv	VTSMX	A+	(800) 662-7447	59.25	A- /9.1	26.14 / 77	9.74 / 92	13.67 / 90	C+ / 6.8	62	23
GL	AllianzGI NFJ Mid-Cap Value A	PQNAX	A+	(800) 988-8380	28.91	A- /9.1	31.95 / 90	9.11 / 87	12.42 / 78	C+ / 6.7	99	8
GR	TIAA-CREF Equity Index Retire	TIQRX	A+	(800) 842-2252	17.79	A- /9.1	25.95 / 76	9.62 / 91	13.54 / 89	C+ / 6.6	60	12
GR	Northern Large Cap Value	NOLVX	A+	(800) 595-9111	15.40	A- /9.1	29.82 / 86	8.74 / 85	12.10 / 75	C+ / 6.6	50	2
IN	Vanguard Equity Income Inv	VEIPX	A+	(800) 662-7447	34.09	A- /9.0	23.50 / 68	10.38 / 95	13.47 / 89	C+ / 6.9	80	14
GR	Wilshire 5000 Index Inv	WFIVX	A+	(888) 200-6796	19.89	A- /9.0	25.58 / 75	9.54 / 91	13.24 / 86	C+ / 6.8	60	18
IN	DFA US Core Equity 1 Ptf Inst	DFEOX	A+	(800) 984-9472	20.25	A- /9.0	27.39 / 80	9.13 / 88	13.82 / 92	C+ / 6.7	52	12
GR	MM S and P 500 Index R4	MIEAX	A+	(800) 542-6767	19.66	A- /9.0	24.18 / 71	9.94 / 93	13.30 / 87	C+ / 6.7	67	10
FO	Hennessy Japan Fund Investor	HJPNX	A+	(800) 966-4354	27.78	A- /9.0	20.73 / 56	12.20 / 98	13.21 / 86	C+ / 6.6	99	11
GR	Fidelity LgCp Gr Enh Idx Fd	FLGEX	A+	(800) 544-8544	16.65	B+ /8.9	21.33 / 59	10.23 / 94	13.59 / 90	C+ / 6.8	69	10
GR	TIAA-CREF Large Cap Gr Idx	TRIRX	A+	(800) 842-2252	24.49	B+ /8.9	21.76 / 61	10.13 / 94	13.43 / 88	C+ / 6.7	65	12
GR	DFA TA US Core Equity 2 Inst	DFTCX	A+	(800) 984-9472	16.31	B+ /8.9	28.31 / 82	8.71 / 85	13.81 / 92	C+ / 6.6	45	5
GR	DFA US Sustainability Core 1 Inst	DFSIX	A+	(800) 984-9472	18.78	B+ /8.9	26.62 / 78	8.97 / 87	13.69 / 91	C+ / 6.6	49	5
GR	Fidelity LgCp Core Enh Idx Fd	FLCEX	A+	(800) 544-8544	13.21	B+ /8.8	23.09 / 67	9.56 / 91	13.47 / 89	C+ / 6.9	64	10
GR	AMG Mgrs Cadence Cap App N	MPAFX	A+	(800) 548-4539	29.63	B+ /8.8	22.61 / 65	9.29 / 89	11.21 / 68	C+ / 6.8	58	13
GR	Goldman Sachs LC Gro Insights A	GLCGX	A+	(800) 526-7384	26.18	B+ /8.8	23.64 / 69	11.06 / 97	14.55 / 96	C+ / 6.8	71	6
IX	PNC S&P 500 Index A	PIIAX	A+	(800) 551-2145	17.63	B+ /8.7	24.24 / 71	10.01 / 93	13.37 / 88	C+ / 6.9	68	12
IN	Fidelity Equity Dividend Income	FEQTX	A+	(800) 544-8544	27.77	B+ /8.7	25.33 / 74	9.46 / 90	12.62 / 80	C+ / 6.9	71	6
TC	Columbia Global Technology Gro A	CTCAX	A	(800) 345-6611	24.26	A+ /9.9	37.09 / 96	14.87 / 99	19.01 / 99	C+ / 5.6	88	5
TC	ProFunds-Tech UltraSector Svc	TEPSX	A	(888) 776-3637	72.57	A+ /9.9	50.25 / 99	18.32 / 99	16.65 / 98	C / 5.5	55	4
FS	Rydex Banking A	RYBKX	A	(800) 820-0888	73.27	A+ /9.9	54.46 / 99	9.74 / 92	12.97 / 83	C / 5.4	11	19
AG	ProFunds-Ultra Bull Svc	ULPSX	A	(888) 776-3637	114.76	A+ /9.9	49.06 / 99	16.12 / 99	23.23 / 99	C / 5.4	12	4
MC	Rydex Mid Cap 1.5x Strgy A	RYAHX	A	(800) 820-0888	80.51	A+ /9.9	47.64 / 99	11.80 / 98	18.21 / 98	C / 5.2	40	16
AG	Rydex S&P 500 2x Strategy A	RYTTX	A	(800) 820-0888	89.66	A+ /9.9	50.14 / 99	17.30 / 99	24.71 / 99	C / 5.2	20	17
FS	Hennessy Small Cap Financial Inv	HSFNX	A	(800) 966-4354	25.53	A+ /9.9	42.81 / 98	12.66 / 99	16.50 / 98	C / 5.2	74	20
GR	ProFunds-Industrial UltraSector	IDPSX	A	(888) 776-3637	80.21	A+ /9.8	42.07 / 98	10.74 / 96	17.94 / 99	C+ / 5.7	7	4
FS	Diamond Hill Financial Lng-Sht A	BANCX	A	(614) 255-3333	23.36	A+ /9.8	42.96 / 98	9.53 / 91	14.48 / 95	C+ / 5.7	28	16
FS	J Hancock Financial Indust A	FIDAX	A	(800) 257-3336	19.92	A+ /9.8	45.73 / 99	8.53 / 83	15.92 / 98	C / 5.5	10	19
MC	American Century NT Md Cp Val	ACLMX	A	(800) 345-6488	13.87	A+ /9.8	31.72 / 89	13.10 / 99	15.74 / 98	C / 5.4	95	11
TC	Putnam Global Technology Fund A	PGTAX	A	(800) 225-1581	27.61	A+ /9.8	33.58 / 92	15.00 / 99	13.67 / 90	C / 5.4	89	5
FS	ICON Financial S	ICFSX	A	(800) 764-0442	9.49	A+ /9.8	40.27 / 97	7.26 / 74	11.04 / 66	C / 5.3	4	14

Fund Type	Fund Name	Ticker Symbol	Overall Investment Rating	Phone	Net Asset Value As of 2/28/17	Performance Rating/Pts	1Yr / Pct	3Yr / Pct	5Yr / Pct	Risk Rating/Pts	Mgr. Quality Pct	Mgr. Tenure (Years)
GR	SunAmerica VAL Co I Sc&Tech Fd	VCSTX	B-	(800) 858-8850	23.42	A+ /9.8	31.31 /89	11.43 /98	15.34 /97	D+ /2.8	59	12
TC	J Hancock VIT Science & Tech I	JESTX	B-	(800) 257-3336	25.00	A+ /9.8	33.13 /92	11.42 /98	14.62 /96	D+ /2.8	55	8
SC	Highland Small-Cap Equity A	HSZAX	B-	(877) 665-1287	14.79	A+ /9.8	51.06 /99	10.30 /95	13.44 /88	D+ /2.7	92	2
SC	ProFunds-Internet UltraSector Svc	INPSX	C+	(888) 776-3637	43.34	A+ /9.9	46.58 /99	11.44 /98	25.99 /99	D+ /2.6	94	4
TC	T Rowe Price Global Technology	PRGTX	C+	(800) 638-5660	15.09	A+ /9.9	38.94 /97	20.18 /99	20.72 /99	D+ /2.4	97	5
TC	T Rowe Price Science and Tech	PRSCX	C+	(800) 638-5660	41.18	A+ /9.9	38.03 /96	13.76 /99	14.58 /96	D /2.2	77	8
MC	Mutual of America Inst MCE Idx	MAMQX	C+	(800) 914-8716	11.65	A+ /9.9	38.28 /97	11.33 /97	14.85 /97	D /2.0	83	3
EM	PIMCO RAE Fdmtl+ EMG Inst	PEFIX	C+	(800) 426-0107	10.27	A+ /9.9	61.54 /99	5.69 /61	2.05 / 8	D /2.0	92	3
FS	ProFunds-Banks UltraSector Svc	BKPSX	C+	(888) 776-3637	42.98	A+ /9.9	91.88 /99	16.46 /99	23.53 /99	D /1.6	3	4
SC	Rydex Russell 2000 2x Strtgy A	RYRUX	C+	(800) 820-0888	124.05	A+ /9.9	75.46 /99	8.41 /82	21.08 /99	D /1.6	13	11
GR	ProFunds-Mble Telcm UltraSector	WCPSX	C+	(888) 776-3637	64.50	A+ /9.9	77.35 /99	12.16 /98	25.69 /99	D /1.6	78	4
SC	VY American Century Sm-MC Val	IASAX	C+	(800) 992-0180	12.45	A+ /9.8	34.09 /93	11.72 /98	14.71 /96	D+ /2.5	97	15
TC	Victory RS Science and	RSIFX	C+	(800) 539-3863	19.66	A+ /9.8	46.39 /99	10.92 /97	14.16 /94	D /1.8	30	1
SC	Adv Inn Cir ICM Sm Co I	ICSCX	C+	(866) 777-7818	31.60	A+ /9.7	37.19 /96	9.41 /90	13.58 /90	D+ /2.7	90	18
GR	MassMutual Select Focused Value	MFVAX	C+	(800) 542-6767	19.88	A+ /9.6	37.82 /96	8.98 /87	13.61 /90	D+ /2.5	12	2
SC	Voya Small Company C	ASCCX	C+	(800) 992-0180	12.47	A+ /9.6	37.09 /96	8.75 /85	12.57 /80	D+ /2.5	88	11
GR	Russell Investments US Dyn Eq C	RSGCX	C+	(800) 832-6688	8.36	A /9.4	31.44 /89	8.58 /84	12.30 /77	D+ /2.4	28	7
SC	State Street Small-Cap Equity VIS	SSSEX	C+	(800) 843-2639	14.76	A- /9.2	36.12 /95	8.07 /79	12.57 /80	D+ /2.9	85	N/A
SC	T Rowe Price Small Cap Value	PRSVX	C+	(800) 638-5660	45.70	A- /9.1	36.78 /96	7.48 /75	12.43 /78	D+ /2.9	84	1
SC	Schwab Small-Cap Equity Fund	SWSCX	C+	(800) 407-0256	21.87	A- /9.1	33.25 /92	8.20 /80	14.73 /96	D+ /2.6	83	5
SC	● Invesco Small Cap Value A	VSCAX	C+	(800) 959-4246	19.83	A- /9.1	40.93 /98	5.79 /62	13.10 /85	D+ /2.5	56	7
SC	Perkins Small Cap Value A	JDSAX	C+	(800) 295-2687	22.73	A- /9.0	32.78 /91	9.96 /93	11.95 /74	D+ /2.8	95	30
GR	SS Inst US Equity Inv	SUSIX	C+	(800) 843-2639	13.88	B+ /8.9	26.07 /76	8.76 /85	12.96 /83	D+ /2.9	38	N/A
GI	SunAmerica VAL Co I Lgcap Core	VLCCX	C+	(800) 858-8850	10.98	B+ /8.7	21.98 /62	10.18 /94	14.35 /95	D+ /2.8	69	6
SC	Schneider Small Cap Value	SCMVX	C	(888) 520-3277	17.14	A+ /9.9	101.41 /99	3.76 /40	11.39 /69	D- /1.3	15	19
FS	J Hancock VIT Financial Indus I	JEFSX	C	(800) 257-3336	13.74	A+ /9.9	44.54 /98	10.18 /94	12.90 /83	D- /1.2	24	3
SC	Prudential QMA Small-Cap Value Z	TASVX	C	(800) 225-1852	21.66	A+ /9.8	43.20 /98	9.62 /91	13.56 /89	D- /1.2	89	2
TC	Firsthand Technology	TEFQX	C	(888) 884-2675	7.11	A /9.3	32.64 /91	7.86 /78	12.44 /78	D /1.6	24	18
IX	Mutual of America Inst Eqty Idx	MAEQX	C	(800) 914-8716	10.68	A /9.3	24.82 /73	10.52 /96	13.91 /92	D /1.6	73	3
SC	J Hancock Small Company Val		C	(800) 257-3336	28.70	A /9.3	37.62 /96	7.77 /77	12.16 /76	D- /1.5	84	3
MC	BMO Mid-Cap Value Y	MRVEX	C	(800) 236-3863	11.87	A- /9.0	32.04 /90	8.15 /80	13.47 /89	D /1.8	56	1
MC	TCW Relative Value Mid Cap N	TGVNX	C	(800) 386-3829	22.98	B+ /8.9	39.39 /97	5.73 /62	11.73 /72	D+ /2.3	11	6
GR	BNY Mellon Sm/Mid Cap Mlti-Str	MMCIX	C	(800) 645-6561	13.95	B+ /8.9	31.91 /90	7.43 /75	10.18 /60	D /2.0	23	3
GR	BNY Mellon Large Cap Mkt Opps	MMOIX	C	(800) 645-6561	11.98	B+ /8.8	26.67 /78	8.39 /82	11.89 /73	D /1.7	39	7
GR	Neuberger Berman Large Cap Val	NPNAX	C	(800) 877-9700	19.57	B+ /8.7	38.68 /97	8.11 /80	12.67 /81	D /2.2	29	6
SC	Dreyfus/Boston Co Sm Cap Value I	STSVX	C	(800) 645-6561	24.37	B+ /8.6	33.99 /93	6.85 /71	12.55 /79	D+ /2.6	79	17
MC	CRM Large Cap Opportunity Inv	CRMGX	C	(800) 276-2883	9.66	B+ /8.5	27.28 /80	8.53 /83	12.18 /76	D /2.1	78	12
TC	Deutsche Science and Tech A	KTCAX	C	(800) 728-3337	18.03	B+ /8.4	29.60 /85	8.57 /84	11.11 /67	D+ /2.9	27	3
TC	AllianzGI Technology A	RAGTX	C	(800) 988-8380	54.77	B+ /8.4	27.88 /81	8.75 /85	14.41 /95	D+ /2.5	26	22
GR	ProFunds-Basic Mat UltraSector	BMPSX	C	(888) 776-3637	55.32	B+ /8.4	47.87 /99	2.29 /26	5.55 /25	D+ /2.5	0	4
GL	Third Avenue Small-Cap Value Inv	TVSVX	C	(800) 443-1021	21.70	B+ /8.3	34.03 /93	7.38 /75	11.62 /71	D+ /2.4	98	4
GR	TCM Small Cap Growth	TCMSX	C	(800) 536-3230	32.84	B+ /8.3	32.90 /91	6.50 /68	14.15 /94	D /2.2	24	13
SC	Royce Opportunity Fd Inv	RYPNX	C	(800) 221-4268	13.24	B+ /8.3	43.33 /98	3.86 /41	12.23 /76	D /2.2	32	19
GR	Pioneer Disciplined Value A	CVFCX	C	(800) 225-6292	16.09	B /8.2	29.31 /85	7.80 /77	11.04 /66	D+ /2.9	34	6
IN	Wasatch Large Cap Value Investor	FMIEX	C	(800) 766-8938	9.71	B /8.2	27.63 /81	7.92 /78	9.90 /58	D+ /2.6	40	4
SC	William Blair Small Cap Gr N	WBSNX	C	(800) 742-7272	26.17	B /8.1	35.44 /94	5.76 /62	14.18 /94	D+ /2.6	71	18
MC	Invesco VI American Value II	UMCCX	C	(800) 959-4246	17.69	B /7.9	32.35 /91	5.66 /61	11.29 /68	D+ /2.8	20	14
SC	Paradigm Value	PVFAX	C	(877) 593-8637	49.23	B /7.8	30.31 /87	6.58 /69	8.41 /46	D+ /2.9	79	4
MC	Hotchkis and Wiley Mid-Cap Val A	HWMAX	C	(866) 493-8637	37.48	B /7.7	37.86 /96	5.20 /56	13.16 /85	D+ /2.9	9	20
FS	Rydex Financial Services A	RYFNX	C-	(800) 820-0888	63.00	A /9.4	34.99 /94	9.18 /88	12.63 /80	D- /1.0	46	19
SC	MFS Blended Research SC Eq		C-	(800) 225-2606	13.59	B+ /8.9	33.89 /93	7.75 /77	14.27 /95	D- /1.4	85	5
SC	Royce Premier Fd	RYPRX	C-	(800) 221-4268	16.49	B+ /8.9	37.94 /96	5.30 /58	8.54 /47	D- /1.3	66	25

99 Pct = Best
0 Pct = Worst

● Denotes fund is closed to new investors

Fund Type	Fund Name	Ticker Symbol	Overall Investment Rating	Phone	Net Asset Value As of 2/28/17	Performance Rating/Pts	Annualized Total Return Through 2/28/17			Risk Rating/Pts	Mgr. Quality Pct	Mgr. Tenure (Years)
							1Yr / Pct	3Yr / Pct	5Yr / Pct			
SC	CRM Small Cap Value Inv	CRMSX	C-	(800) 276-2883	17.51	B+ /8.7	32.13 /90	8.30 /81	13.14 /85	D- /1.4	86	6
AG	SunAmerica VAL Co I SmCp Agg	VSAGX	C-	(800) 858-8850	11.77	B+ /8.4	31.02 /88	6.10 /65	13.52 /89	D- /1.1	6	6
GR	SS Inst US Lg Cap Core Eqty Inv	SILCX	C-	(800) 843-2639	7.96	B+ /8.3	25.56 /75	7.76 /77	12.21 /76	D /2.0	28	N/A
GR	Hodges Pure Contrarian Retail	HDPCX	C-	(877) 232-1222	14.00	B /8.2	62.04 /99	0.92 /18	10.26 /60	D /1.9	3	8
SC	SunAmerica VAL Co II SmCp	VASMX	C-	(800) 858-8850	15.80	B /8.2	41.37 /98	3.95 /42	11.85 /73	D /1.8	25	10
GL	● Perkins Mid Cap Value A	JDPAX	C-	(800) 295-2687	17.57	B /8.2	30.42 /87	8.88 /86	10.59 /63	D /1.8	99	6
GR	CGCM Large Cap Equity	TLGUX	C-	(800) 444-4273	17.89	B /7.8	23.91 /70	7.83 /78	12.69 /81	D /1.6	32	1
GR	MassMutual Premier Main Street A	MSSAX	C-	(800) 542-6767	10.87	B /7.7	23.59 /68	9.39 /89	12.97 /83	D /1.6	62	8
IX	Russell Investments US Core Eq A	RSQAX	C-	(800) 832-6688	32.30	B /7.6	25.55 /75	8.79 /85	12.48 /79	D+ /2.7	49	6
GR	ICON Consumer Staples S	ICLEX	C-	(800) 764-0442	7.37	B /7.6	10.42 /13	11.48 /98	12.19 /76	D /1.7	97	N/A
TC	Dreyfus Tech Growth A	DTGRX	C-	(800) 782-6620	42.16	B- /7.5	28.74 /83	7.33 /74	11.80 /72	D+ /2.9	14	10
GR	Hennessy Cornerstone Large Gro	HFLGX	C-	(800) 966-4354	11.32	B- /7.5	19.37 /49	8.31 /81	11.74 /72	D+ /2.5	53	13
RE	Salient Real Estate A	KREAX	C-	(800) 999-6809	12.35	B- /7.5	21.76 /61	11.19 /97	11.16 /67	D /2.1	73	7
GL	Eaton Vance Small Cap A	ETEGX	C-	(800) 262-1122	13.09	B- /7.5	30.17 /87	7.38 /75	11.68 /71	D /2.1	98	2
GR	Laudus US Large Cap Growth	LGILX	C-	(800) 407-0256	17.90	B- /7.4	22.01 /62	7.18 /73	12.49 /79	D+ /2.8	23	4
MC	Dreyfus Opportunistic Midcap Val A	DMCVX	C-	(800) 645-6561	34.74	B- /7.3	32.89 /91	5.53 /60	13.19 /86	D+ /2.6	18	14
MC	VY FMR Div Mid Cap Adv	IFDMX	C-	(800) 992-0180	15.70	B- /7.3	26.54 /78	6.08 /65	10.91 /65	D+ /2.6	32	13
GR	William Blair Mid Cap Value Fund	WMVNX	C-	(800) 742-7272	10.62	B- /7.3	24.28 /71	7.67 /77	11.96 /74	D+ /2.5	52	7
GI	Franklin Balance Sheet Investmt A	FRBSX	C-	(800) 342-5236	38.99	B- /7.3	33.69 /92	5.21 /57	10.76 /64	D+ /2.5	13	27
GR	Meridian Contrarian Legacy	MVALX	C-	(800) 446-6662	38.17	B- /7.2	28.56 /83	7.05 /72	12.20 /76	D+ /2.6	21	16
GR	Principal LgCp Gr II R3	PPTMX	C-	(800) 222-5852	7.61	B- /7.2	18.16 /44	8.03 /79	11.25 /68	D+ /2.5	45	N/A
SC	● Harbor Small Cap Growth Inv	HISGX	C-	(800) 422-1050	12.34	B- /7.2	30.02 /86	5.02 /54	12.13 /75	D /2.2	57	17
MC	Voya Mid Cap Research Enhanced	AIMAX	C-	(800) 992-0180	17.05	B- /7.1	31.01 /88	6.45 /68	10.91 /65	D+ /2.9	42	2
SC	Victory RS Partners R	RSPKX	C-	(800) 539-3863	31.02	B- /7.1	36.82 /96	2.93 /31	11.02 /66	D /2.2	44	4
GI	BlackRock Basic Value Inv A	MDBAX	C-	(800) 441-7762	25.60	B- /7.0	30.41 /87	7.38 /75	12.12 /75	D+ /2.6	19	8
GR	Highland Global Allocation A	HCOAX	C-	(877) 665-1287	9.11	B- /7.0	48.28 /99	2.03 /24	9.12 /52	D+ /2.6	3	15
SC	Dreyfus Small Cap Eqty A	DSEAX	C-	(800) 782-6620	25.06	B- /7.0	27.72 /81	6.69 /70	11.41 /69	D+ /2.4	84	17
MC	Federated MDT MidCap Growth A	FGSAX	C-	(800) 341-7400	38.48	B- /7.0	23.98 /70	7.27 /74	11.24 /68	D+ /2.4	54	4
SC	Ivy Small Cap Growth A	WSGAX	C-	(800) 777-6472	17.05	C+ /6.9	32.87 /91	5.83 /63	12.49 /79	D+ /2.8	66	7
EM	J Hancock VIT Emerg Mkts Val	JHVTX	C-	(800) 257-3336	8.99	C+ /6.8	37.41 /96	1.64 /22	-1.06 / 3	D+ /2.9	72	7
SC	Prudential Jennison Small	PGOAX	C-	(800) 225-1852	23.81	C+ /6.8	27.03 /79	6.53 /69	11.13 /67	D+ /2.7	80	17
SC	MassMutual Select Small Co Val A	MMYAX	D+	(800) 542-6767	12.25	B /8.0	36.27 /95	6.54 /69	11.19 /67	D- /1.3	77	3
GR	Rydex S&P500 Pure Value A	RYLVX	D+	(800) 820-0888	78.48	B /8.0	30.84 /88	7.36 /75	13.91 /93	D- /1.2	17	13
GR	DGHM All-Cap Value C	DGACX	D+	(800) 673-0550	8.02	B /7.8	31.17 /88	6.17 /66	10.36 /61	D- /1.2	16	10
HL	ICON Healthcare S	ICHCX	D+	(800) 764-0442	15.86	B /7.8	19.96 /52	9.08 /87	17.52 /98	D- /1.1	59	4
GI	ALPS/WMC Research Value A	AMWYX	D+	(866) 759-5679	9.15	B /7.6	28.03 /82	8.10 /80	13.11 /85	D- /1.5	35	2
GR	Hartford Growth Opps HLS Fd IA	HAGOX	D+	(888) 843-7824	32.14	B- /7.5	20.53 /55	9.09 /87	15.15 /97	D /1.8	46	16
GR	Transamerica Growth I2	TJNIX	D+	(888) 233-4339	11.33	B- /7.5	21.13 /58	7.59 /76	12.97 /83	D /1.7	26	13
SC	Bogle Inv Mgt Small Cap Gr Inv	BOGLX	D+	(877) 264-5346	29.89	B- /7.5	34.70 /94	4.64 /50	13.46 /88	D /1.7	45	18
GR	Sit Large Cap Growth	SNIGX	D+	(800) 332-5580	38.09	B- /7.3	18.13 /43	8.57 /84	11.48 /70	D /1.9	53	33
SC	● JPMorgan Small Cap Growth A	PGSGX	D+	(800) 480-4111	13.57	B- /7.1	41.28 /98	3.57 /38	11.59 /71	D /2.0	21	13
GR	Croft Value R	CLVFX	D+	(800) 551-0990	21.24	B- /7.0	30.27 /87	4.41 /48	8.26 /44	D /1.7	3	22
SC	● Invesco Small Cap Growth R	GTSRX	D+	(800) 959-4246	32.02	C+ /6.9	28.25 /82	5.52 /60	12.29 /77	D+ /2.4	70	13
IN	J Hancock US Growth NAV		D+	(800) 257-3336	8.75	C+ /6.9	17.98 /43	7.59 /76	11.26 /68	D /1.8	42	1
SC	SunAmerica VAL Co I Smcp Fd	VCSMX	D+	(800) 858-8850	11.59	C+ /6.8	27.82 /81	5.26 /57	11.65 /71	D+ /2.4	63	11
SC	Tocqueville Opportunity	TOPPX	D+	(800) 697-3863	22.02	C+ /6.8	31.54 /89	3.30 /35	10.21 /60	D /1.9	23	7
SC	● AllianzGI NFJ Small Cap Value A	PCVAX	D+	(800) 988-8380	24.19	C+ /6.8	31.73 /89	5.30 /58	9.62 /55	D /1.7	74	26
GR	Dreyfus Appreciation Inv	DGAGX	D+	(800) 645-6561	35.50	C+ /6.7	18.93 /47	6.64 /69	8.36 /45	D+ /2.6	33	27

99 Pct = Best
0 Pct = Worst

VII. Top-Rated Stock Mutual Funds In The E Risk Category

99 Pct = Best
0 Pct = Worst

Fund Type	Fund Name	Ticker Symbol	Overall Investment Rating	Phone	Net Asset Value As of 2/28/17	Performance Rating/Pts	1Yr / Pct	3Yr / Pct	5Yr / Pct	Risk Rating/Pts	Mgr. Quality Pct	Mgr. Tenure (Years)
AG	Rydex Dyn-NASDAQ 100 2x Strgy	RYVLX	C	(800) 820-0888	99.83	A+ /9.9	57.90 /99	24.30 /99	29.92 /99	E+ / 0.9	43	17
HL	Alger Health Sciences Fund A	AHSAX	C	(800) 254-3796	21.45	A+ /9.9	37.94 /96	8.87 /86	14.82 /96	E / 0.6	21	12
SC	Direxion Mo Small Cap Bull 2X Inv	DXRLX	C-	(800) 851-0511	63.18	A+ /9.9	77.27 /99	9.79 /92	22.88 /99	E / 0.5	24	13
SC	ProFunds-Ultra Small Cap Svc	UAPSX	C-	(888) 776-3637	42.31	A+ /9.9	74.55 /99	7.55 /76	20.29 /99	E / 0.4	9	4
FO	ProFunds-Ultra Japan Svc	UJPSX	C-	(888) 776-3637	16.06	A+ /9.7	33.28 /92	8.57 /84	19.00 /99	E- / 0.0	99	8
FO	Direxion Mo China Bull 2X Inv	DXHLX	C-	(800) 851-0511	35.50	A+ /9.6	60.49 /99	4.75 /51	-2.36 / 2	E- / 0.0	96	10
AG	ProFunds-Nasdaq-100 Svc	OTPSX	C-	(888) 776-3637	45.05	A+ /9.6	24.72 /72	10.88 /97	13.11 /85	E- / 0.0	53	4
SC	Wells Fargo Sm Cp Opp Adm	NVSOX	C-	(800) 222-8222	23.69	A /9.4	31.04 /88	9.31 /89	13.40 /88	E+ / 0.6	92	14
GR	Janus Aspen Forty Inst	JACAX	C-	(800) 295-2687	35.09	B+ /8.9	22.59 /65	10.03 /93	13.86 /92	E / 0.5	58	4
SC	Nuveen Small Cap Select A	EMGRX	C-	(800) 257-8787	9.68	B+ /8.7	37.92 /96	8.48 /83	11.52 /70	E+ / 0.7	83	9
SC	Wells Fargo Sm Cp Val A	SMVAX	D+	(800) 222-8222	21.74	B+ /8.4	41.06 /98	5.91 /63	8.55 /47	E+ / 0.6	77	6
SC	Wanger USA	WUSAX	D+	(800) 492-6437	27.71	B+ /8.3	34.12 /93	6.32 /67	11.77 /72	E+ / 0.9	74	3
HL	J Hancock VIT Hlth Sciences I	JEHSX	D+	(800) 257-3336	24.48	B+ /8.3	16.79 /38	9.81 /92	21.15 /99	E+ / 0.7	52	1
MC	Wanger Select Fund	WATWX	D+	(800) 492-6437	20.14	B /8.1	28.98 /84	7.10 /73	11.06 /66	E+ / 0.7	53	2
SC	Sentinel Small Company Fd A	SAGWX	D+	(800) 282-3863	5.04	B /7.9	30.98 /88	8.73 /85	12.19 /76	E+ / 0.9	90	4
GR	Janus Forty A	JDCAX	D+	(800) 295-2687	30.48	B /7.8	22.41 /64	9.79 /92	13.56 /89	E+ / 0.6	54	4
MC	CRM Mid Cap Value Inv	CRMMX	D	(800) 276-2883	22.30	B /7.6	28.66 /83	7.28 /74	12.22 /76	E / 0.5	61	19
SC	Dreyfus/Boston Co Sm Cap Growth	SSETX	D	(800) 645-6561	28.04	B- /7.4	37.06 /96	5.10 /55	12.15 /76	E- / 0.0	46	4
SC	Lord Abbett Small Cap Value F	LRSFX	D	(888) 522-2388	22.16	B- /7.3	28.83 /84	6.83 /71	10.45 /62	E+ / 0.7	80	4
SC	● Victory RS Small Cap Equity A	GPSCX	D	(800) 539-3863	15.68	B- /7.3	30.88 /88	5.64 /61	13.09 /85	E / 0.4	58	8
SC	● JPMorgan Dynamic Small Cap Gr	VSCOX	D	(800) 480-4111	20.13	B- /7.2	41.79 /98	3.50 /37	11.40 /69	E+ / 0.9	20	13
SC	● RidgeWorth Ceredex Sm Cap Val	SASVX	D	(888) 784-3863	12.58	B- /7.2	31.10 /88	8.30 /81	12.44 /78	E+ / 0.9	89	23
GR	Henssler Equity Investor	HEQFX	D	(800) 936-3863	6.05	B- /7.2	19.63 /50	8.03 /79	10.88 /65	E+ / 0.8	64	19
HL	● Prudential Jennison Health Sci A	PHLAX	D	(800) 225-1852	41.22	B- /7.0	23.42 /68	5.97 /64	19.39 /99	E+ / 0.9	3	18
SC	Frontier Netols Small Cap Value Y	FNSYX	D	(888) 825-2100	8.90	C+ /6.6	26.40 /77	5.28 /57	10.79 /64	E+ / 0.7	62	12
HL	Fidelity Select Biotech Port	FBIOX	D-	(800) 544-8888	203.21	B- /7.0	29.67 /86	3.91 /42	22.19 /99	E- / 0.1	0	12
SC	Columbia Acorn USA A	LAUAX	D-	(800) 345-6611	15.60	C+ /6.7	34.01 /93	5.13 /56	10.73 /64	E+ / 0.6	57	3
FO	T Rowe Price Latin America	PRLAX	D-	(800) 638-5660	21.74	C+ /6.6	45.10 /98	0.47 /16	-6.06 / 1	E- / 0.0	79	N/A
MC	Wasatch Ultra Growth Investor	WAMCX	D-	(800) 551-1700	18.28	C+ /6.5	34.30 /93	5.07 /55	10.71 /64	E / 0.3	6	5
PM	US Global Inv World Prec Min	UNWPX	D-	(800) 873-8637	7.05	C+ /6.4	52.82 /99	2.89 /31	-11.93 / 0	E+ / 0.7	98	28
HL	● Franklin Biotechnology Discvry A	FBDIX	D-	(800) 342-5236	147.85	C+ /6.4	30.89 /88	3.79 /40	20.85 /99	E+ / 0.7	1	20
MC	Columbia Acorn Select A	LTFAX	D-	(800) 345-6611	13.85	C+ /6.4	27.73 /81	5.89 /63	9.83 /57	E+ / 0.7	35	15
SC	Eagle Smaller Company A	EGEAX	D-	(800) 421-4184	13.50	C+ /6.4	30.16 /87	5.18 /56	10.42 /61	E / 0.4	71	3
IN	Rainier Large Cap Equity Original	RIMEX	D-	(800) 248-6314	19.00	C+ /5.8	19.98 /52	5.24 /57	10.14 /59	E+ / 0.7	8	9
SC	Royce Smaller Companies Svc	RYVPX	D-	(800) 221-4268	11.46	C+ /5.8	27.62 /81	3.44 /36	9.21 /52	E+ / 0.7	30	9
SC	Alger Small Cap Growth Inst R	ASIRX	E+	(800) 254-3796	14.83	C+ /5.9	32.06 /90	1.63 /22	7.93 /41	E- / 0.0	14	16
SC	Columbia Small Cap Growth I A	CGOAX	E+	(800) 345-6611	17.68	C+ /5.7	32.08 /90	3.72 /39	10.39 /61	E / 0.3	35	11
GR	Fairholme	FAIRX	E+	(866) 202-2263	21.51	C+ /5.6	41.66 /98	0.96 /18	9.32 /53	E- / 0.0	2	18
MC	Columbia Acorn A	LACAX	E+	(800) 345-6611	14.15	C /5.5	29.35 /85	4.20 /45	9.35 /53	E+ / 0.6	11	18
SC	CGCM Small Mid Cap Equity	TSGUX	E+	(800) 444-4273	18.82	C /5.3	29.10 /84	1.96 /24	10.15 /59	E+ / 0.7	18	20
GR	Cavanal Hill Mult Cap Eqty Inc Inv	APEQX	E+	(800) 762-7085	8.44	C /5.2	19.03 /47	5.22 /57	9.73 /56	E+ / 0.9	11	11
SC	Aegis Value I	AVALX	E+	(800) 528-3780	16.69	C /4.7	64.01 /99	-1.46 / 8	8.06 /43	E+ / 0.9	7	19
MC	BMO Mid-Cap Growth Y	MRMSX	E+	(800) 236-3863	13.89	C /4.6	25.62 /75	1.34 /20	7.68 /40	E+ / 0.7	3	1
PM	US Global Inv Gold & PMetals Fd	USERX	E+	(800) 873-8637	8.15	C /4.6	28.98 /84	3.17 /33	-9.81 / 1	E+ / 0.7	98	28
HL	Fidelity Adv Biotechnology A	FBTAX	E	(800) 522-7297	23.05	C /4.9	26.09 /76	3.05 /32	20.98 /99	E- / 0.1	0	12
SC	MassMutual Select Small Cap GE	MMGEX	E	(800) 542-6767	11.46	C /4.7	28.19 /82	3.46 /37	11.27 /68	E / 0.4	36	16
MC	Alger SMidCap Growth I2	AAMOX	E	(800) 254-3796	1.95	C /4.6	22.60 /65	3.34 /35	12.84 /82	E- / 0.0	8	1
SC	● TCW Small Cap Growth N	TGSNX	E	(800) 386-3829	21.22	C /4.5	29.13 /84	1.27 /20	6.95 /34	E / 0.3	10	5
OT	Wells Fargo Endeavor Sel A	STAEX	E	(800) 222-8222	8.01	C /4.3	18.57 /45	4.98 /54	10.70 /63	E / 0.4	13	7
SC	Alger Small Cap Growth Fund A	ALSAX	E	(800) 254-3796	7.11	C- /4.2	30.46 /87	1.51 /21	7.94 /42	E+ / 0.6	14	2
GR	ProFunds-Biotech Ultra Sector Svc	BIPSX	E	(888) 776-3637	46.63	C- /4.2	17.31 /40	2.88 /31	30.35 /99	E- / 0.2	0	4
SC	● Buffalo Small Cap Fund	BUFSX	E	(800) 492-8332	16.22	C- /4.2	28.78 /83	0.73 /17	9.83 /57	E- / 0.0	11	19

● Denotes fund is closed to new investors

Fund Type	Fund Name	Ticker Symbol	Overall Investment Rating	Phone	Net Asset Value As of 2/28/17	Performance Rating/Pts	Annualized Total Return Through 2/28/17			Risk Rating/Pts	Mgr. Quality Pct	Mgr. Tenure (Years)
							1Yr / Pct	3Yr / Pct	5Yr / Pct			
SC	Century Small Cap Select Inv	CSMVX	E	(800) 321-1928	23.48	C- /4.1	22.87 /66	1.87 /23	7.94 /42	E+ / 0.6	17	18
SC	● AMG Frontier Small Cap Gr N	MSSVX	E	(800) 548-4539	11.61	C- /4.1	26.86 /79	1.29 /20	8.92 /50	E / 0.4	10	8
MC	Calamos Growth A	CVGRX	E	(800) 582-6959	31.43	C- /3.8	16.23 /35	4.14 /44	8.54 /47	E+ / 0.7	31	27
SC	RidgeWorth Silvant SC Gr Stock A	SCGIX	E	(888) 784-3863	7.34	C- /3.6	29.16 /84	1.51 /21	9.46 /54	E / 0.5	14	10
UT	Meeder Infrastructure Retail	FLRUX	E	(800) 325-3539	21.60	C- /3.6	23.76 /69	2.32 /26	7.15 /36	E / 0.4	55	22
RE	EII Global Property Inst	EIIGX	E	(888) 323-8912	3.76	C- /3.5	12.58 /20	4.54 /49	6.36 /31	E+ / 0.9	23	11
SC	Wells Fargo Trad Sm Cap Gr A	EGWAX	E	(800) 222-8222	13.80	C- /3.1	27.09 /79	1.02 /18	9.21 /52	E+ / 0.6	12	26
SC	Saratoga Adv Tr Small Cap A	SSCYX	E	(800) 807-3863	5.91	C- /3.0	27.65 /81	1.15 /19	7.46 /38	E+ / 0.6	19	2
MC	Alger SMid Cap Growth Fund A	ALMAX	E-	(800) 254-3796	10.63	C- /3.6	24.95 /73	2.71 /29	8.71 /48	E- / 0.0	4	1
GR	Victory Newbridge Large Cap Grow	VFGAX	E-	(800) 539-3863	9.02	C- /3.4	15.19 /31	4.76 /52	9.63 /56	E- / 0.2	11	14
GR	Westcore Large Cap Dividend Rtl	WTEIX	E-	(800) 392-2673	6.61	C- /3.2	12.78 /21	3.77 /40	9.27 /53	E / 0.4	7	1
SC	● AMG GW&K US Small Cap Gr N	ATASX	E-	(800) 548-4539	4.02	C- /3.2	24.97 /73	0.09 /14	6.06 /29	E / 0.3	9	1
SC	Rice Hall James Small Cap Port	RHJMX	E-	(866) 777-7818	10.52	C- /3.0	14.46 /28	3.52 /37	8.71 /48	E / 0.3	47	21
FO	Direxion Mo Emerg Mkts Bull 2X	DXELX	E-	(800) 851-0511	38.85	D+ /2.9	56.15 /99	-3.90 / 3	-7.82 / 1	E- / 0.1	28	12
SC	Delafield	DEFIX	E-	(800) 697-3863	25.36	D+ /2.7	33.90 /93	-0.25 /12	6.16 /29	E+ / 0.9	7	24
PM	Gabelli Gold A	GLDAX	E-	(800) 422-3554	14.52	D+ /2.7	24.83 /73	2.66 /29	-10.34 / 1	E- / 0.1	98	23
SC	Turner Small Cap Growth Fund	TSCEX	E-	(800) 224-6312	12.90	D+ /2.7	22.40 /64	1.09 /19	8.60 /47	E- / 0.1	9	4
GL	Delaware International Sml Cap A	DGGAX	E-	(800) 523-1918	6.03	D /2.2	15.77 /33	2.83 /30	6.55 /32	E / 0.5	90	1
GR	BlackRock Event Driven Eqty Inv A	BALPX	E-	(800) 441-7762	8.74	D /2.0	4.12 / 3	4.96 /54	9.52 /55	E / 0.5	78	2
MC	● Delaware Smid Cap Growth A	DFCIX	E-	(800) 523-1918	17.73	D /1.9	7.29 / 6	5.28 /57	9.17 /52	E / 0.3	43	1
GR	Columbia Global Infrastructure A	RRIAX	E-	(800) 345-6611	12.08	D /1.7	16.58 /37	1.03 /18	8.53 /47	E+ / 0.8	4	10
FO	Profunds-Ultra China Svc	UGPSX	E-	(888) 776-3637	10.34	D /1.7	34.81 /94	-2.89 / 5	3.00 /11	E- / 0.0	44	8
SC	Royce Low Priced Stock Svc	RYLPX	E-	(800) 221-4268	8.20	D /1.6	26.09 /76	-0.82 /10	0.68 / 6	E+ / 0.9	6	4
PM	Vanguard Prec Metals & Mining Inv	VGPMX	E-	(800) 662-7447	10.29	D /1.6	36.56 /95	-2.32 / 6	-12.39 / 0	E- / 0.0	82	3
SC	Kalmar Growth With Value Sm Cap	KGSCX	E-	(800) 282-2319	12.70	D- /1.5	23.18 /67	-0.18 /13	7.45 /38	E / 0.3	6	20
PM	Franklin Gold & Precious Metals A	FKRCX	E-	(800) 342-5236	17.66	D- /1.3	32.77 /91	-0.71 /10	-13.34 / 0	E+ / 0.6	92	18
MC	Brown Capital Mgmt Mid Company	BCMSX	E-	(877) 892-4226	11.83	D- /1.3	17.08 /39	-1.12 / 9	5.74 /27	E / 0.4	2	15
PM	Invesco Gold and Precious Mtls A	IGDAX	E-	(800) 959-4246	4.41	D- /1.1	31.79 /90	-1.32 / 8	-11.64 / 0	E- / 0.1	90	4
PM	VanEck Intl Investors Gold A	INIVX	E-	(800) 826-1115	9.57	D- /1.1	34.35 /93	-1.57 / 8	-12.88 / 0	E- / 0.0	91	19
MC	Turner Midcap Growth Inv	TMGFX	E-	(800) 224-6312	18.44	D- /1.0	18.66 /46	-1.92 / 7	5.76 /27	E / 0.4	1	N/A
PM	Oppenheimer Gold/Spec Min A	OPGSX	E-	(888) 470-0862	16.61	D- /1.0	32.91 /91	-1.87 / 7	-13.86 / 0	E- / 0.2	89	20
PM	Fidelity Adv Gold A	FGDAX	E-	(800) 522-7297	20.54	E+ /0.7	19.97 /52	-1.19 / 9	-14.09 / 0	E- / 0.1	92	10
SC	● Lord Abbett Developing Growth A	LAGWX	E-	(888) 522-2388	19.37	E+ /0.6	23.85 /69	-2.68 / 5	9.47 /54	E+ / 0.9	2	16
SC	Jacob Small Cap Growth Investor	JSCGX	E-	(888) 522-6239	17.37	E+ /0.6	31.69 /89	-4.77 / 3	3.31 /12	E+ / 0.8	1	7
PM	First Eagle Gold A	SGGDX	E-	(800) 334-2143	17.11	E /0.5	17.35 /40	-1.09 / 9	-11.21 / 0	E / 0.5	90	4
EN	Fidelity Select Energy Svcs	FSESX	E-	(800) 544-8888	54.71	E /0.5	46.38 /99	-9.69 / 1	-2.73 / 2	E / 0.4	29	4
PM	OCM Gold Fund Investor	OCMGX	E-	(800) 628-9403	9.88	E /0.5	20.48 /55	-1.52 / 8	-12.52 / 0	E- / 0.0	92	21
PM	American Century Global Gold A	ACGGX	E-	(800) 345-6488	8.59	E /0.5	23.93 /70	-2.53 / 5	-14.15 / 0	E- / 0.0	87	12
EN	Fidelity Select Natural Gas	FSNGX	E-	(800) 544-8888	27.76	E /0.4	56.75 /99	-9.69 / 1	-2.06 / 3	E+ / 0.6	39	5
PM	USAA Precious Mtls&Minerals	USAGX	E-	(800) 382-8722	13.33	E /0.4	22.34 /64	-4.54 / 3	-15.58 / 0	E- / 0.1	75	N/A
PM	Tocqueville Gold	TGLDX	E-	(800) 697-3863	37.00	E /0.4	21.27 /59	-3.48 / 4	-13.60 / 0	E- / 0.0	79	20
PM	Midas Fund	MIDSX	E-	(800) 400-6432	1.26	E /0.4	32.63 /91	-6.67 / 2	-20.43 / 0	E- / 0.0	40	15
PM	Wells Fargo Precious Mtls A	EKWAX	E-	(800) 222-8222	36.18	E /0.3	17.95 /43	-3.01 / 4	-13.51 / 0	E- / 0.1	84	10
SC	● Universal Inst Small Co Growth II	USIIX	E-	(800) 869-6397	10.94	E /0.3	24.22 /71	-5.71 / 2	8.42 /46	E- / 0.0	1	14
PM	Rydex Precious Metal A	RYMNX	E-	(800) 820-0888	30.04	E /0.3	27.60 /81	-4.91 / 2	-14.05 / 0	E- / 0.0	74	24
PM	Deutsche Gold & Prec Metals Fund	SGDAX	E-	(800) 728-3337	6.82	E- /0.2	19.17 /48	-5.25 / 2	-15.57 / 0	E- / 0.0	67	1
EN	Franklin Natural Resources A	FRNRX	E-	(800) 342-5236	26.69	E- /0.1	38.47 /97	-9.62 / 1	-6.66 / 1	E+ / 0.9	26	18
EN	BlackRock Natural Resource Inv A	MDGRX	E-	(800) 441-7762	44.09	E- /0.1	29.59 /85	-8.11 / 1	-3.61 / 2	E+ / 0.9	38	N/A

99 Pct = Best
0 Pct = Worst

● Denotes fund is closed to new investors

Section VIII

Top-Rated
Stock Mutual Funds
by Fund Type

A compilation of those

Equity Mutual Funds

receiving the highest TheStreet Investment Rating

within each type of fund.

Funds are listed in order by Overall Investment Rating.

Section VIII Contents

This section contains a summary analysis of the top 100 rated mutual funds within each fund type. If you are looking for a particular type of mutual fund, these pages show those funds that have achieved the best combination of risk and financial performance over the past three years.

In order to optimize the utility of our top and bottom fund lists, rather than listing all funds in a multi-class series, a single fund from each series is selected for display as the primary share class. Whenever possible, the selected fund is one that a retail investor would be most likely to choose. This share class may not be appropriate for every investor, so please consult with your financial advisor, the fund company, and the fund's prospectus before placing your trade.

1. **Fund Type**
The mutual fund's peer category based on an analysis of its investment portfolio.

AG	Aggressive Growth	HL	Health
AA	Asset Allocation	IN	Income
BA	Balanced	IX	Index
CV	Convertible	MC	Mid Cap
EM	Emerging Market	OT	Other
EN	Energy/Natural Resources	PM	Precious Metals
FS	Financial Services	RE	Real Estate
FO	Foreign	SC	Small Cap
GL	Global	TC	Technology
GR	Growth	UT	Utilities
GI	Growth and Income		

A blank fund type means that the mutual fund has not yet been categorized.

2. **Fund Name**
The name of the mutual fund as stated in its prospectus, which can sometimes differ slightly from the name that the company uses for advertising. If you cannot find the particular mutual fund you are interested in, or if you have any doubts regarding the precise name, verify the information with your broker or on your account statement. Also, use the fund's ticker symbol for confirmation. (See column 3.)

3. **Ticker Symbol**
The unique alphabetic symbol used for identifying and trading a specific mutual fund. No two funds can have the same ticker symbol, and the ticker symbol for mutual funds always ends with an "X".

A handful of funds currently show no associated ticker symbol. This means that the fund is either small or new since the NASD only assigns a ticker symbol to funds with at least $25 million in assets or 1,000 shareholders.

4. **Overall Investment Rating**
Our overall rating is measured on a scale from A to E based on each fund's risk-adjusted performance. Please see page 10 for specific descriptions of each letter grade. Also, refer to page 7 for information on how our ratings are derived. Most important, when using this rating, please be sure to consider the warnings beginning on page 11 regarding the ratings' limitations and the

underlying assumptions.

5.	**Phone**	The telephone number of the company managing the fund. Call this number to receive a prospectus or other information about the fund.
6.	**Net Asset Value (NAV)**	The fund's share price as of the date indicated. A fund's NAV is computed by dividing the value of the fund's asset holdings, less accrued fees and expenses, by the number of its shares outstanding.
7.	**Performance Rating/Points**	A letter grade rating based solely on the mutual fund's financial performance over the trailing three years, without any consideration for the amount of risk the fund poses. Like the overall Investment Rating, the Performance Rating is measured on a scale from A to E for ease of interpretation. The points score indicates where the Performance Rating falls on a scale of 0 to 10.
8.	**1-Year Total Return**	The total return the fund has provided investors over the preceeding twelve months. This total return figure is computed based on the fund's dividend distributions and share price appreciation/depreciation during the period, net of the expenses and fees it imposes on its shareholders. Although the total return figure does not reflect an adjustment for any loads the fund may carry, such adjustments have been made in deriving TheStreet Investment Ratings.
9.	**1-Year Total Return Percentile**	The fund's percentile rank based on its one-year performance compared to that of all other equity funds in existence for at least one year. A score of 99 is the best possible, indicating that the fund outperformed 99% of the other mutual funds. Zero is the worst possible percentile score.
10.	**3-Year Total Return**	The total annual return the fund has provided investors over the preceeding three years.
11.	**3-Year Total Return Percentile**	The fund's percentile rank based on its three-year performance compared to that of all other equity funds in existence for at least three years. A score of 99 is the best possible, indicating that the fund outperformed 99% of the other mutual funds. Zero is the worst possible percentile score.
12.	**5-Year Total Return**	The total annual return the fund has provided investors over the preceeding five years.
13.	**5-Year Total Return Percentile**	The fund's percentile rank based on its five-year performance compared to that of all other equity funds in existence for at least five years. A score of 99 is the best possible, indicating that the fund outperformed 99% of the other mutual funds. Zero is the worst possible percentile score.

14. Risk Rating/Points

A letter grade rating based solely on the mutual fund's risk as determined by its monthly performance volatility over the trailing three years. The risk rating does not take into consideration the overall financial performance the fund has achieved or the total return it has provided to its shareholders. Like the overall Investment Rating, the Risk Rating is measured on a scale from A to E for ease of interpretation. The points score indicates where the Risk Rating falls on a scale of 0 to 10.

15. Manager Quality Percentile

The manager quality percentile is based on a ranking of the fund's alpha, a statistical measure representing the difference between a fund's actual returns and its expected performance given its level of risk. Fund managers who have been able to exceed the fund's statistically expected performance receive a high percentile rank with 99 representing the highest possible score. At the other end of the spectrum, fund managers who have actually detracted from the fund's expected performance receive a low percentile rank with 0 representing the lowest possible score.

16. Manager Tenure

The number of years the current manager has been managing the fund. Since fund managers who deliver substandard returns are usually replaced, a long tenure is usually a good sign that shareholders are satisfied that the fund is achieving its stated objectives.

99 Pct = Best
0 Pct = Worst

Fund Type	Fund Name	Ticker Symbol	Overall Investment Rating	Phone	Net Asset Value As of 2/28/17	Performance Rating/Pts	Annualized Total Return Through 2/28/17			Risk Rating/Pts	Mgr. Quality Pct	Mgr. Tenure (Years)
							1Yr / Pct	3Yr / Pct	5Yr / Pct			
AG	Rydex Nova A	RYANX	A+	(800) 820-0888	56.26	A+ /9.8	36.32 /95	13.35 /99	18.76 /99	C+ / 6.7	38	21
AG	Rydex NASDAQ 100 A	RYATX	A+	(800) 820-0888	27.96	A+ /9.7	26.46 /78	12.71 /99	15.01 /97	C+ / 6.3	74	23
AG	ProFunds-Ultra Bull Svc	ULPSX	A	(888) 776-3637	114.76	A+ /9.9	49.06 /99	16.12 /99	23.23 /99	C / 5.4	12	4
AG	Rydex S&P 500 2x Strategy A	RYTTX	A	(800) 820-0888	89.66	A+ /9.9	50.14 /99	17.30 /99	24.71 /99	C / 5.2	20	17
AG	Bridgeway Aggressive Investor 1	BRAGX	A	(800) 661-3550	66.92	A+ /9.6	36.49 /95	8.23 /81	14.91 /97	C+ / 5.6	20	23
AG	ProFunds-Bull Svc	BLPSX	A	(888) 776-3637	91.73	B- /7.3	21.24 /58	7.47 /75	10.71 /64	B / 8.2	36	4
AG	Rydex Dow 2x Strategy A	RYLDX	B+	(800) 820-0888	65.73	A+ /9.9	61.30 /99	18.27 /99	21.91 /99	C / 4.6	27	13
AG	● PRIMECAP Odyssey Agg Growth	POAGX	B+	(800) 729-2307	35.35	A /9.4	30.05 /86	9.86 /93	19.60 /99	C / 4.4	30	13
AG	Fidelity Growth Strategies Fd	FDEGX	B+	(800) 544-8544	36.59	B- /7.3	17.05 /39	8.32 /81	12.12 /75	C+ / 6.7	54	4
AG	CGM Focus	CGMFX	B	(800) 345-4048	45.89	A+ /9.7	43.50 /98	4.42 /48	9.20 /52	C- / 3.5	2	20
AG	ProFunds-Ultra Mid Cap Svc	UMPSX	B-	(888) 776-3637	100.35	A+ /9.9	64.32 /99	13.75 /99	22.58 /99	C- / 3.0	4	4
AG	Rydex Russell 2000 1.5x Strgy A	RYAKX	B-	(800) 820-0888	55.98	A+ /9.8	54.36 /99	7.51 /76	16.58 /98	C- / 3.0	2	17
AG	Needham Aggressive Growth	NEAGX	B-	(800) 625-7071	22.46	B- /7.5	28.64 /83	6.84 /71	10.56 /62	C / 5.2	32	7
AG	USAA Aggressive Growth Fund	USAUX	C+	(800) 382-8722	39.92	B- /7.3	19.24 /48	7.70 /77	11.46 /70	C / 4.9	32	7
AG	ClearBridge Aggressive Growth A	SHRAX	C+	(877) 534-4627	205.32	C+ /6.1	24.71 /72	5.49 /59	14.04 /93	C / 5.3	8	34
AG	CAN SLIM Select Growth	CANGX	C+	(800) 558-9105	14.84	C /4.5	14.68 /28	4.87 /53	10.00 /58	C+ / 6.9	21	9
AG	Rydex Dyn-NASDAQ 100 2x Strgy	RYVLX	C	(800) 820-0888	99.83	A+ /9.9	57.90 /99	24.30 /99	29.92 /99	E+ / 0.9	43	17
AG	First Inv Select Growth A	FICGX	C	(800) 423-4026	10.58	C+ /6.6	20.00 /52	8.19 /80	11.94 /74	C / 4.7	46	10
AG	Meeder Aggressive Growth Retail	FLAGX	C	(800) 325-3539	10.56	C+ /6.0	19.76 /51	6.08 /65	10.25 /60	C / 4.6	24	12
AG	ProFunds-Nasdaq-100 Svc	OTPSX	C-	(888) 776-3637	45.05	A+ /9.6	24.72 /72	10.88 /97	13.11 /85	E- / 0.0	53	4
AG	SunAmerica VAL Co I SmCp Agg	VSAGX	C-	(800) 858-8850	11.77	B+ /8.4	31.02 /88	6.10 /65	13.52 /89	D- / 1.1	6	6
AG	Permanent Portfolio Aggress Gr I	PAGRX	C-	(800) 531-5142	59.54	C+ /5.6	26.39 /77	3.60 /38	11.45 /69	C- / 4.0	3	14
AG	Franklin Growth Opportunities A	FGRAX	C-	(800) 342-5236	33.59	C /4.8	19.04 /47	5.11 /55	10.77 /64	C / 4.9	10	10
AG	J Hancock MM Lifestyle Agg A	JALAX	C-	(800) 257-3336	15.52	C /4.5	22.09 /63	4.27 /46	8.72 /48	C+ / 5.6	11	N/A
AG	MFS Aggressive Gr Alloc A	MAAGX	C-	(800) 225-2606	20.59	C- /4.0	19.64 /50	4.83 /52	9.42 /54	C+ / 6.4	21	15
AG	Oppenheimer Equity Inv A	OAAIX	C-	(888) 470-0862	15.96	C- /3.1	17.90 /42	3.30 /35	8.58 /47	C+ / 6.3	7	12
AG	Guggenheim Long Short Equity A	RYAMX	C-	(800) 820-0888	15.99	D- /1.0	6.32 / 5	1.35 /20	4.29 /17	B / 8.6	36	15
AG	BlackRock 80/20 Target Alloc Inv A	BAAPX	D+	(800) 441-7762	11.42	C- /4.0	18.02 /43	4.78 /52	9.35 /53	C / 4.5	24	2
AG	J Hancock VIT Lifestyle Aggr I		D+	(800) 257-3336	10.39	D+ /2.4	13.38 /23	0.33 /15	6.31 /30	C+ / 6.4	5	7
AG	Midas Magic Fund	MISEX	D	(800) 400-6432	16.92	C /5.3	21.40 /59	4.95 /54	11.08 /67	D+ / 2.8	8	1
AG	RidgeWorth Innovative Gr Stock A	SAGAX	D	(888) 784-3863	18.44	C /5.2	28.00 /82	3.01 /32	12.17 /76	D / 2.2	2	13
AG	Fund *X Aggressive Upgrader	HOTFX	D	(866) 455-3863	58.28	D+ /2.4	15.30 /31	1.67 /22	8.51 /46	C+ / 5.8	3	15
AG	HSBC World Selection Aggr Strat A	HAAGX	D-	(800) 728-8183	12.29	C- /3.5	19.95 /52	3.25 /34	6.94 /34	C- / 3.1	8	N/A
AG	Gabelli Value 25 A	GABVX	D-	(800) 422-3554	15.42	C- /3.4	22.65 /65	2.75 /30	9.32 /53	C- / 3.1	4	28
AG	Rydex Inv S&P 500 Stgry A	RYARX	D-	(800) 820-0888	65.29	E- /0.0	-20.86 / 0	-11.82 / 1	-14.58 / 0	C+ / 6.7	35	23
AG	RidgeWorth Aggr Gr Alloc Str A	SLAAX	E+	(888) 784-3863	5.96	C- /3.4	17.44 /40	4.21 /45	7.83 /41	D / 2.1	16	25
AG	MassMutual Select Growth Opps A	MMAAX	E+	(800) 542-6767	9.04	D+ /2.7	14.01 /25	3.40 /36	10.56 /62	C- / 3.2	4	13
AG	Timothy Plan Aggressive Growth A	TAAGX	E	(800) 662-0201	7.43	D+ /2.8	21.80 /61	0.79 /17	7.36 /37	D / 2.2	2	7
AG	Jackson Square Sel 20 Growth IS	DPCEX	E	(888) 276-0061	7.02	D+ /2.7	6.69 / 5	4.29 /46	8.38 /45	D- / 1.3	9	12
AG	● Delaware Select Growth A	DVEAX	E	(800) 523-1918	34.32	D /1.8	11.57 /16	2.68 /29	7.68 /40	D / 2.2	4	12
AG	Rydex Inv NASDAQ 100 Strgy A	RYAPX	E	(800) 820-0888	77.16	E- /0.0	-23.36 / 0	-14.84 / 0	-16.74 / 0	C- / 3.9	18	19
AG	Rydex Inv S&P 500 2x Strategy A	RYTMX	E-	(800) 820-0888	59.46	E- /0.0	-38.35 / 0	-23.06 / 0	-27.57 / 0	D+ / 2.9	5	17
AG	Rydex Inv NASDAQ 100 2x Stgy A	RYVTX	E-	(800) 820-0888	61.40	E- /0.0	-42.38 / 0	-29.59 / 0	-32.13 / 0	D / 1.9	1	17
AG	Rydex Inv Dow 2x Strategy A	RYIDX	E-	(800) 820-0888	17.52	E- /0.0	-42.46 / 0	-24.21 / 0	-26.05 / 0	E+ / 0.8	3	13

● Denotes fund is closed to new investors

Fund Type	Fund Name	Ticker Symbol	Overall Investment Rating	Phone	Net Asset Value As of 2/28/17	Perform-ance Rating/Pts	Annualized Total Return Through 2/28/17			Risk Rating/Pts	Mgr. Quality Pct	Mgr. Tenure (Years)
	99 Pct = Best 0 Pct = Worst						1Yr / Pct	3Yr / Pct	5Yr / Pct			
AA	IMS Dividend Growth Inst	IMSAX	A-		14.47	B /8.0	27.34 /80	7.83 /78	9.50 /55	C+ /6.8	17	15
AA	● Boston Partners Lg/Sh Equity Inv	BPLEX	B+	(888) 261-4073	20.52	B /7.7	20.35 /54	9.71 /92	8.17 /43	C+ /6.5	98	20
AA	Vanguard Diversified Equity Inv	VDEQX	B	(800) 662-7447	31.85	B /7.9	24.30 /71	7.89 /78	12.86 /82	C /5.2	18	N/A
AA	● T Rowe Price Cap Appreciation	PRWCX	B	(800) 638-5660	27.39	B- /7.2	16.15 /35	9.33 /89	11.86 /73	C+ /6.4	82	11
AA	J Hancock Multi-Index 2040 Psv 1	JRROX	B	(800) 257-3336	14.15	C+ /5.9	20.13 /53	5.62 /61	8.40 /45	B /8.0	21	7
AA	TIAA-CREF Lifecycle Index 2035	TLYRX	B	(800) 842-2252	17.12	C+ /5.8	18.92 /47	5.75 /62	9.23 /53	B /8.0	24	8
AA	J Hancock Multi-Index 2035 Psv 1	JRYOX	B	(800) 257-3336	13.93	C /5.5	18.69 /46	5.38 /58	8.03 /42	B /8.1	25	7
AA	Vanguard Target Retirement 2030	VTHRX	B	(800) 662-7447	30.44	C /5.3	17.34 /40	5.56 /60	8.63 /47	B- /7.8	31	4
AA	TIAA-CREF Lifecycle Index 2030	TLHRX	B	(800) 842-2252	16.53	C /5.2	16.97 /38	5.44 /59	8.56 /47	B /8.3	30	8
AA	UBS US Allocation A	PWTAX	B	(888) 793-8637	45.53	C /5.0	17.81 /42	6.56 /69	9.19 /52	B /8.1	39	8
AA	TIAA-CREF Lifecycle Index 2025	TLQRX	B	(800) 842-2252	15.92	C /4.5	15.21 /31	5.09 /55	7.84 /41	B /8.6	36	8
AA	USAA Growth & Tax Strategy Fund	USBLX	B	(800) 382-8722	18.39	C /4.4	10.77 /14	6.38 /67	8.00 /42	B /8.8	81	12
AA	TIAA-CREF Lifecycle Index 2050	TLLRX	B-	(800) 842-2252	17.51	C+ /6.7	21.81 /61	6.27 /67	9.86 /57	B- /7.6	19	8
AA	TIAA-CREF Lifecycle Index 2045	TLMRX	B-	(800) 842-2252	17.48	C+ /6.6	21.54 /60	6.18 /66	9.80 /57	B- /7.6	19	8
AA	Vanguard Target Retirement 2050	VFIFX	B-	(800) 662-7447	31.94	C+ /6.5	21.25 /59	6.03 /64	9.63 /56	B- /7.1	18	4
AA	Vanguard Target Retirement 2045	VTIVX	B-	(800) 662-7447	19.86	C+ /6.5	21.28 /59	6.04 /65	9.64 /56	B- /7.0	18	4
AA	TIAA-CREF Lifecycle Index 2040	TLZRX	B-	(800) 842-2252	17.48	C+ /6.4	20.86 /57	6.03 /64	9.72 /56	B- /7.7	18	8
AA	Vanguard Target Retirement 2055	VFFVX	B-	(800) 662-7447	34.58	C+ /6.4	21.20 /58	5.98 /64	9.61 /55	B- /7.1	18	4
AA	Vanguard Target Retirement 2040	VFORX	B-	(800) 662-7447	31.71	C+ /6.3	20.80 /56	5.93 /64	9.57 /55	B- /7.1	18	4
AA	J Hancock Multi-Index 2045 Psv 1	JRVOX	B-	(800) 257-3336	14.23	C+ /6.2	20.76 /56	5.76 /62	8.50 /46	B- /7.2	21	7
AA	Fidelity Four In One Index	FFNOX	B-	(800) 544-8544	39.99	C+ /6.2	19.68 /50	6.05 /65	9.83 /57	B- /7.1	23	18
AA	Fidelity Freedom 2030	FFFEX	B-	(800) 544-8544	16.56	C+ /6.1	20.71 /56	5.69 /61	8.15 /43	B- /7.0	20	12
AA	Vanguard LifeStrategy Growth Inv	VASGX	B-	(800) 662-7447	30.20	C+ /5.8	18.95 /47	5.80 /63	8.92 /50	B- /7.5	26	N/A
AA	Vanguard Target Retirement 2035	VTTHX	B-	(800) 662-7447	18.55	C+ /5.8	19.00 /47	5.77 /62	9.20 /52	B- /7.4	24	4
AA	SEI Asset Alloc Core Mkt Str Al F	SKTAX	B-	(800) 342-5734	17.35	C+ /5.8	21.17 /58	4.97 /54	9.60 /55	B- /7.1	9	14
AA	SEI Asset Alloc-Tax Mgd Agg Strgy	SISAX	B-	(800) 342-5734	19.12	C+ /5.8	21.09 /58	4.94 /53	9.61 /55	B- /7.1	9	N/A
AA	SEI Asset Alloc-Mkt Gr Str Alloc F	SGOAX	B-	(800) 342-5734	20.89	C+ /5.8	21.10 /58	4.96 /54	9.62 /56	B- /7.1	9	14
AA	T Rowe Price Retirement 2030	TRRCX	B-	(800) 638-5660	23.66	C+ /5.7	19.04 /47	5.59 /60	9.34 /53	B- /7.0	23	15
AA	Transamerica Asst All Lg Horizon	DVLSX	B-	(888) 233-4339	13.55	C+ /5.6	20.44 /55	4.70 /51	8.78 /49	B- /7.0	7	19
AA	Wells Fargo Index Asst All A	SFAAX	B-	(800) 222-8222	30.80	C /5.5	14.21 /26	8.66 /84	10.84 /65	B- /7.9	81	11
AA	Fidelity Freedom 2025	FFTWX	B-	(800) 544-8544	13.39	C /5.1	17.76 /42	5.18 /56	7.56 /39	B- /7.6	29	12
AA	George Putnam Balanced A	PGEOX	B-	(800) 225-1581	18.34	C /4.9	17.26 /40	6.77 /70	9.09 /51	B- /7.9	55	3
AA	Vanguard Target Retirement 2025	VTTVX	B-	(800) 662-7447	16.98	C /4.8	15.70 /33	5.34 /58	8.06 /43	B /8.0	38	4
AA	Voya Retirement Growth Adv	IRGPX	B-	(800) 992-0180	13.65	C /4.6	17.08 /39	4.46 /48	7.57 /39	B /8.0	18	11
AA	J Hancock Multi-Index 2030 Psv 1	JRHOX	B-	(800) 257-3336	13.55	C /4.6	16.17 /35	4.91 /53	7.34 /37	B /8.0	32	7
AA	Fidelity Freedom 2020	FFFDX	B-	(800) 544-8544	15.58	C /4.6	16.45 /36	4.88 /53	6.73 /33	B- /7.9	35	12
AA	Vanguard LifeStrategy Mod Gro Inv	VSMGX	B-	(800) 662-7447	25.03	C /4.4	14.46 /28	5.21 /57	7.36 /37	B /8.5	47	N/A
AA	Vanguard Tgt Retirement 2020 Inv	VTWNX	B-	(800) 662-7447	29.23	C- /4.2	13.89 /25	5.05 /55	7.44 /38	B /8.5	46	4
AA	TIAA-CREF Lifecycle Index 2020	TLWRX	B-	(800) 842-2252	15.31	C- /3.9	13.35 /23	4.72 /51	7.09 /35	B /8.9	44	8
AA	Vanguard Wellesley Income Inv	VWINX	B-	(800) 662-7447	26.04	C- /3.8	10.23 /12	5.95 /64	7.09 /35	B /8.8	83	10
AA	TIAA-CREF Lifecycle Index 2015	TLGRX	B-	(800) 842-2252	14.67	C- /3.4	11.74 /17	4.39 /47	6.37 /31	B+ /9.1	51	8
AA	VY T Rowe Price Cap App Adv	ITRAX	C+	(800) 992-0180	25.64	C+ /6.8	15.49 /32	8.78 /85	11.27 /68	C+ /6.1	79	11
AA	Fidelity Freedom 2040	FFFFX	C+	(800) 544-8544	9.64	C+ /6.7	22.80 /66	6.04 /65	8.88 /50	C+ /6.5	16	12
AA	Fidelity Freedom 2050	FFFHX	C+	(800) 544-8544	10.94	C+ /6.7	22.74 /66	6.03 /64	9.03 /51	C+ /6.4	15	11
AA	Fidelity Freedom 2035	FFTHX	C+	(800) 544-8544	13.73	C+ /6.6	22.71 /65	6.00 /64	8.79 /49	C+ /6.5	15	12
AA	Fidelity Freedom 2045	FFFGX	C+	(800) 544-8544	10.88	C+ /6.6	22.63 /65	6.01 /64	8.98 /50	C+ /6.4	16	10
AA	T Rowe Price Retirement 2040	TRRDX	C+	(800) 638-5660	24.52	C+ /6.3	21.05 /58	5.85 /63	10.03 /59	C+ /6.4	16	15
AA	J Hancock VIT Amer Ast All I		C+	(800) 257-3336	13.98	C+ /6.1	18.12 /43	6.46 /68	9.81 /57	C+ /6.1	44	10
AA	Schwab MarketTrack Growth Port	SWHGX	C+	(800) 407-0256	21.59	C+ /6.1	21.05 /58	5.73 /62	9.25 /53	C+ /6.0	24	9
AA	Prudential QMA Defensive Equity A	PAMGX	C+	(800) 225-1852	13.90	C+ /5.9	17.40 /40	7.88 /78	9.66 /56	C+ /6.7	37	4
AA	Transamerica Inst Asst All Lg Hrz	DILSX	C+	(888) 233-4339	11.98	C+ /5.8	20.73 /56	4.98 /54	9.10 /52	C+ /6.9	8	19
AA	TIAA-CREF Lifecycle 2040 Ret	TCLOX	C+	(800) 842-2252	13.31	C+ /5.8	21.20 /58	5.05 /55	9.51 /55	C+ /6.2	9	10

Fund Type	Fund Name	Ticker Symbol	Overall Investment Rating	Phone	Net Asset Value As of 2/28/17	Perform-ance Rating/Pts	Annualized Total Return Through 2/28/17			Risk Rating/Pts	Mgr. Quality Pct	Mgr. Tenure (Years)
							1Yr / Pct	3Yr / Pct	5Yr / Pct			
BA	Dodge & Cox Balanced Fund	DODBX	A+	(800) 621-3979	107.49	B+ /8.4	27.47 /80	8.12 /80	12.35 /78	B /8.6	62	25
BA	Alger Growth and Income A	ALBAX	A	(800) 254-3796	36.56	B /8.2	23.42 /68	9.82 /92	12.34 /77	C+ /6.9	54	6
BA	Madison Dividend Income Y	BHBFX	A-	(800) 877-6089	24.20	B /8.0	21.33 /59	8.98 /87	12.25 /77	C+ /6.6	52	27
BA	Wells Fargo Dvsfd Cap Bldr A	EKBAX	B+	(800) 222-8222	9.87	B+ /8.8	28.88 /84	10.74 /96	13.19 /86	C /5.5	77	10
BA	Transamerica Prt Balanced	DVIBX	B	(888) 233-4339	21.06	C+ /5.7	15.57 /32	6.70 /70	8.98 /50	B /8.4	65	7
BA	Archer Balanced Fund	ARCHX	B	(800) 494-2755	12.29	C+ /5.7	14.12 /26	7.27 /74	8.39 /45	B /8.1	70	12
BA	Mairs & Power Balanced Fund	MAPOX	B	(800) 304-7404	89.99	C /5.2	16.15 /35	6.23 /66	9.57 /55	B- /7.9	55	11
BA	WesMark Balanced Fund	WMBLX	B	(800) 864-1013	12.68	C /5.0	15.39 /32	5.74 /62	6.81 /34	B /8.0	58	19
BA	Vanguard Tax-Managed Bal	VTMFX	B	(800) 662-7447	28.80	C /4.7	11.80 /17	6.40 /68	8.11 /43	B /8.9	78	4
BA	CGM Mutual	LOMMX	B-	(800) 345-4048	32.35	B- /7.3	26.87 /79	4.94 /53	7.63 /39	C /5.4	10	36
BA	● Vanguard Wellington Inv	VWELX	B-	(800) 662-7447	40.47	C+ /6.8	18.60 /45	7.61 /76	9.95 /58	B- /7.6	67	15
BA	Plumb Balanced Fund	PLBBX	B-	(866) 987-7888	24.58	C+ /6.6	17.94 /43	6.65 /69	7.71 /40	B- /7.5	52	10
BA	Boston Trust Asset Management	BTBFX	B-	(800) 282-8782	42.97	C+ /6.3	15.51 /32	7.67 /77	9.17 /52	B- /7.6	67	22
BA	Fidelity Balanced Fd	FBALX	B-	(800) 544-8544	23.15	C+ /6.3	17.95 /43	6.84 /71	9.61 /55	B- /7.0	49	9
BA	Walden Asset Management	WSBFX	B-	(800) 282-8782	16.35	C+ /6.0	15.72 /33	7.06 /72	8.51 /46	B- /7.6	58	5
BA	FPA Crescent	FPACX	B-	(800) 982-4372	33.93	C+ /5.8	21.03 /57	5.80 /62	8.85 /49	B- /7.0	50	24
BA	Janus Aspen Balanced Inst	JABLX	B-	(800) 295-2687	31.96	C+ /5.6	15.12 /30	5.78 /62	8.71 /48	B- /7.8	49	12
BA	BlackRock Bal Capital Inv A	MDCPX	B-	(800) 441-7762	24.70	C+ /5.6	17.79 /42	7.15 /73	9.42 /54	B- /7.0	62	11
BA	LKCM Balanced Institutional	LKBAX	B-	(800) 688-5526	21.11	C /5.3	17.50 /41	6.18 /66	9.38 /54	B- /7.5	41	20
BA	Sit Balanced Fund	SIBAX	B-	(800) 332-5580	21.92	C /5.2	12.65 /20	6.46 /68	8.32 /45	B- /7.8	60	9
BA	Schwab Balanced Fund	SWOBX	B-	(800) 407-0256	14.41	C /5.2	15.24 /31	5.86 /63	8.16 /43	B- /7.5	46	N/A
BA	American Funds Amer Balncd Fd A	ABALX	B-	(800) 421-0180	25.79	C /5.0	15.77 /33	7.48 /75	10.26 /60	B- /7.6	69	18
BA	FBP Appreciation and Income	FBPBX	C+	(800) 443-4249	18.92	C+ /6.0	23.94 /70	4.86 /53	8.57 /47	C+ /6.6	13	28
BA	Oakmark Equity and Income	OARBX	C+	(800) 625-6275	31.59	C+ /6.0	20.59 /55	5.18 /56	7.99 /42	C+ /6.3	32	22
BA	State Farm Balanced	STFBX	C+	(800) 447-4930	65.32	C /5.3	14.09 /26	6.60 /69	7.57 /39	B- /7.1	70	26
BA	Dreyfus Balanced Opport A	DBOAX	C+	(800) 645-6561	22.31	C /5.2	19.32 /49	6.55 /69	9.38 /54	C+ /6.7	51	10
BA	Fidelity Adv Balanced A	FABLX	C+	(800) 522-7297	20.14	C /5.0	17.96 /43	6.57 /69	9.26 /53	B- /7.4	45	9
BA	Hennessy Equity and Income	HEIFX	C+	(800) 966-4354	15.55	C /4.8	13.55 /24	5.72 /62	7.49 /38	B- /7.6	52	10
BA	Holland Balanced	HOLBX	C+		19.47	C /4.8	12.27 /19	6.28 /67	8.78 /49	B- /7.4	62	22
BA	AMG CEP Balanced N	MBEAX	C+	(800) 548-4539	16.10	C /4.7	12.85 /21	5.73 /62	8.30 /45	B- /7.8	52	17
BA	T Rowe Price Balanced	RPBAX	C+	(800) 638-5660	22.97	C /4.7	15.53 /32	5.03 /55	8.27 /44	B- /7.3	34	6
BA	T Rowe Price Personal Strat Bal	TRPBX	C+	(800) 638-5660	22.69	C /4.7	16.34 /36	4.98 /54	8.12 /43	B- /7.1	35	6
BA	American Century Balanced Inv	TWBIX	C+	(800) 345-6488	18.18	C /4.6	14.40 /27	5.44 /59	7.84 /41	B- /7.0	47	12
BA	Transamerica Multi-Managed Bal A	IBALX	C+	(888) 233-4339	26.40	C /4.5	15.53 /32	6.65 /69	8.76 /49	B- /7.9	62	6
BA	Voya Balanced Inc S	IBPSX	C+	(800) 992-0180	15.41	C /4.5	16.42 /36	4.43 /48	7.21 /36	B- /7.6	25	10
BA	Sentinel Balanced A	SEBLX	C+	(800) 282-3863	20.60	C /4.4	15.47 /32	6.10 /65	8.35 /45	B- /7.5	52	13
BA	Buffalo Flexible Income Fund	BUFBX	C+	(800) 492-8332	14.86	C /4.4	17.89 /42	4.44 /48	7.07 /35	B- /7.1	22	14
BA	American Beacon Balanced A	ABFAX	C+	(800) 658-5811	14.83	C /4.4	19.53 /50	5.62 /61	8.76 /48	B- /7.1	42	30
BA	TIAA-CREF Mgd Alloc Ret	TIMRX	C+	(800) 842-2252	11.96	C /4.3	15.51 /32	4.64 /50	7.65 /39	B- /7.6	33	N/A
BA	MainStay Balanced C	MBACX	C+	(800) 624-6782	32.56	C /4.3	15.18 /31	5.01 /54	8.28 /45	B- /7.2	40	9
BA	Columbia Balanced A	CBLAX	C+	(800) 345-6611	38.70	C- /4.2	13.68 /24	6.91 /71	9.59 /55	B /8.1	65	20
BA	J Hancock Balanced A	SVBAX	C+	(800) 257-3336	19.47	C- /4.2	16.91 /38	5.63 /61	8.46 /46	B- /7.3	40	11
BA	Janus Balanced A	JDBAX	C+	(800) 295-2687	30.80	C- /4.1	14.90 /29	5.52 /60	8.29 /45	B- /7.4	45	12
BA	Hartford Balanced Income A	HBLAX	C+	(888) 843-7824	14.19	C- /4.0	15.58 /32	6.40 /67	8.11 /43	B /8.1	74	11
BA	Franklin Balanced A	FBLAX	C+	(800) 342-5236	12.08	C- /4.0	17.12 /39	5.83 /63	7.52 /38	B- /7.9	46	11
BA	Northern Global Tactical Asset Allo	BBALX	C+	(800) 637-1380	12.33	C- /3.8	15.73 /33	3.70 /39	5.93 /28	B /8.1	29	6
BA	Hennessy Balanced Investor	HBFBX	C+	(800) 966-4354	12.45	C- /3.6	12.23 /19	4.72 /51	5.48 /25	B /8.4	61	21
BA	Wells Fargo Gro Bal A	WFGBX	C+	(800) 222-8222	42.82	C- /3.6	15.39 /32	5.29 /58	9.07 /51	B- /7.9	34	12
BA	Madison Diversified Income A	MBLAX	C+	(800) 877-6089	15.13	C- /3.4	13.01 /22	6.00 /64	7.57 /39	B /8.6	71	19
BA	CornerCap Balanced	CBLFX	C	(888) 813-8637	14.13	C /5.4	19.04 /47	5.34 /58	7.84 /41	C /5.5	38	20
BA	Lord Abbett Multi Asset Bal Opp A	LABFX	C	(888) 522-2388	11.67	C /4.7	20.91 /57	4.29 /46	7.56 /39	C+ /6.3	23	2
BA	Greenspring	GRSPX	C	(800) 366-3863	25.02	C /4.7	24.41 /71	3.68 /39	6.24 /30	C+ /6.0	29	30

● Denotes fund is closed to new investors

Fund Type	Fund Name	Ticker Symbol	Overall Investment Rating	Phone	Net Asset Value As of 2/28/17	Perform-ance Rating/Pts	Annualized Total Return Through 2/28/17			Risk Rating/Pts	Mgr. Quality Pct	Mgr. Tenure (Years)
	99 Pct = Best 0 Pct = Worst						1Yr / Pct	3Yr / Pct	5Yr / Pct			
CV	● MainStay Convertible B	MCSVX	C+	(800) 624-6782	16.90	C+ /6.0	22.69 /65	5.10 /55	8.22 /44	C+ / 5.6	72	16
CV	Victory INCORE Invt Grade Conv A	SBFCX	C+	(800) 539-3863	14.58	C /4.3	14.41 /27	5.30 /58	8.07 /43	B- / 7.4	83	21
CV	Northern Income Equity	NOIEX	C	(800) 595-9111	13.39	B- /7.2	18.91 /47	8.11 /80	10.62 /63	C- / 3.8	93	3
CV	Franklin Convertible Securities A	FISCX	C	(800) 342-5236	18.87	C- /3.8	19.19 /48	4.73 /51	9.03 /51	C+ / 6.6	75	15
CV	Gabelli Global Rising Inc & Div A	GAGAX	C	(800) 422-3554	23.77	D+ /2.7	14.16 /26	3.80 /40	5.36 /24	B- / 7.9	77	23
CV	Lord Abbett Convertible A	LACFX	C-	(888) 522-2388	12.16	C /5.2	26.60 /78	3.23 /34	8.43 /46	C / 5.0	45	14
CV	Columbia Convertible Securities A	PACIX	C-	(800) 345-6611	18.64	C /5.1	26.68 /78	4.47 /48	9.04 /51	C / 5.3	62	11
CV	Miller Convertible Bond A	MCFAX	C-	(877) 441-4434	12.89	D /2.1	15.71 /33	3.32 /35	6.81 /34	B / 8.1	70	10
CV	Putnam Convertible Securities A	PCONX	D+	(800) 225-1581	24.04	C- /3.4	21.33 /59	3.15 /33	7.99 /42	C+ / 5.8	52	11
CV	Vanguard Convertible Sec Inv	VCVSX	D+	(800) 662-7447	13.00	D+ /2.3	14.07 /26	1.82 /23	6.64 /32	C+ / 6.1	50	7
CV	Calamos Convertible A	CCVIX	D	(800) 582-6959	16.78	D+ /2.3	17.70 /41	1.97 /24	5.41 /24	C+ / 6.0	35	32
CV	● AllianzGI Convertible A	ANZAX	D	(800) 988-8380	31.96	D+ /2.3	16.82 /38	2.43 /27	7.93 /41	C / 5.3	40	23
CV	Invesco Convertible Securities A	CNSAX	D	(800) 959-4246	23.82	D /1.8	15.71 /33	1.68 /22	6.95 /34	C+ / 6.5	43	19
CV	Matthews Asian Growth & Income	MACSX	D	(800) 789-2742	15.96	D /1.7	12.18 /19	1.09 /19	4.43 /18	C+ / 5.7	38	8
CV	Fidelity Advisor Convertible Sec A	FACVX	D-	(800) 522-7297	27.36	D /1.8	17.28 /40	1.16 /19	6.72 /33	C / 5.3	24	1

● Denotes fund is closed to new investors
www.thestreetratings.com

819

Fund Type	Fund Name	Ticker Symbol	Overall Investment Rating	Phone	Net Asset Value As of 2/28/17	Performance Rating/Pts	1Yr / Pct	3Yr / Pct	5Yr / Pct	Risk Rating/Pts	Mgr. Quality Pct	Mgr. Tenure (Years)
EM	Franklin India Growth Fund A	FINGX	A+	(800) 342-5236	13.45	A+ /9.8	30.84 /88	15.88 /99	7.75 /40	C+ /6.5	99	9
EM	Eaton Vance Greater India A	ETGIX	B+	(800) 262-1122	29.54	A+ /9.7	34.49 /93	14.73 /99	7.07 /35	C /4.3	99	1
EM	SEI Instl Mgd Tr-Glb Mngd Volty F	SVTAX	B+	(800) 342-5734	11.24	B- /7.3	14.10 /26	9.91 /93	11.97 /74	C+ /6.5	99	11
EM	PIMCO RAE Fdmtl+ EMG Inst	PEFIX	C+	(800) 426-0107	10.27	A+ /9.9	61.54 /99	5.69 /61	2.05 / 8	D /2.0	92	3
EM	Schwab Fundmtl EM Large Co	SFENX	C+	(800) 407-0256	8.34	A- /9.0	49.00 /99	2.94 /31	-0.63 / 4	C- /3.1	80	5
EM	DFA Emerging Markets Val R2	DFEPX	C+	(800) 984-9472	26.46	B /7.7	39.91 /97	2.59 /28	-0.59 / 4	C- /3.8	79	13
EM	Vanguard Total Wld Stk Index Inv	VTWSX	C+	(800) 662-7447	26.29	C+ /6.2	22.91 /66	5.00 /54	8.61 /47	C+ /6.4	93	4
EM	Northern Glbl Sustainability Index	NSRIX	C+	(800) 595-9111	12.44	C /5.1	20.16 /53	4.87 /53	9.38 /54	C+ /6.5	93	9
EM	T Rowe Price Inst Global Foc Gr	TRGSX	C	(800) 638-5660	11.57	B /7.8	26.31 /77	8.02 /79	11.58 /71	C- /3.0	98	5
EM	Dreyfus Emerging Markets A	DRFMX	C	(800) 782-6620	9.82	B- /7.0	42.56 /98	3.87 /41	-0.91 / 3	C- /4.0	85	10
EM	● Acadian Emerging Markets Inv	AEMGX	C	(866) 777-7818	18.32	C+ /6.9	35.53 /94	2.79 /30	0.64 / 6	C- /4.2	82	23
EM	● GMO Emerging Countries III	GMCEX	C		27.06	C+ /6.7	36.00 /95	2.52 /28	-1.16 / 3	C- /3.8	79	20
EM	Artisan Emerging Markets Inv	ARTZX	C	(800) 344-1770	13.11	C+ /6.5	32.60 /91	3.25 /34	-0.17 / 4	C /4.8	84	11
EM	T Rowe Price Instl Emer Mkt Eqty	IEMFX	C	(800) 638-5660	31.47	C+ /6.4	31.85 /90	4.48 /49	1.61 / 7	C /5.0	90	9
EM	T Rowe Price Emerging Mkts Stk	PRMSX	C	(800) 638-5660	34.49	C+ /6.3	31.66 /89	4.34 /47	1.50 / 7	C /5.0	89	9
EM	DFA Emerging Mkts Socl Core Eq	DFESX	C	(800) 984-9472	12.23	C+ /6.0	31.12 /88	2.44 /27	0.36 / 5	C /4.7	79	11
EM	DFA Emerging Markts Core Eqty	DFCEX	C	(800) 984-9472	19.14	C+ /5.9	30.67 /87	2.49 /27	0.63 / 6	C /4.6	80	12
EM	Goldman Sachs EM Eqty Insights	GERAX	C	(800) 526-7384	8.93	C+ /5.8	31.34 /89	3.97 /43	1.41 / 7	C /5.2	87	9
EM	J Hancock VIT Emerg Mkts Val	JHVTX	C-	(800) 257-3336	8.99	C+ /6.8	37.41 /96	1.64 /22	-1.06 / 3	D+ /2.9	72	7
EM	● Lazard Emerging Markets Open	LZOEX	C-	(800) 821-6474	17.69	C+ /6.0	35.94 /95	1.61 /22	-0.04 / 4	C- /3.7	72	23
EM	GMO Emerging Markets II	GMEMX	C-		29.98	C+ /5.9	34.47 /93	2.22 /25	-1.19 / 3	C- /3.9	77	24
EM	Fidelity Srs Emerging Markets Fd	FEMSX	C-	(800) 544-8544	17.26	C /5.5	31.30 /89	1.85 /23	1.51 / 7	C /4.9	76	8
EM	Vanguard Emg Mkts Stk Idx	VEIEX	C-	(800) 662-7447	24.58	C /5.3	29.75 /86	2.27 /26	-0.33 / 4	C /4.3	78	9
EM	CGCM Emerging Mkts Eqty	TEMUX	C-	(800) 444-4273	12.80	C /5.2	29.29 /85	2.19 /25	-0.92 / 3	C /4.7	78	8
EM	J Hancock Emerg Mkts NAV	JEVNX	C-	(800) 257-3336	9.93	C /5.2	28.84 /84	1.94 /24	0.24 / 5	C /4.7	76	7
EM	DFA Emerging Markets II Inst	DFETX	C-	(800) 984-9472	23.79	C /5.2	29.23 /85	1.98 /24	0.32 / 5	C- /4.2	76	13
EM	Causeway Emerging Mkt Inv	CEMVX	C-	(866) 947-7000	11.45	C /5.1	30.35 /87	1.71 /22	0.94 / 6	C /4.7	74	10
EM	Sanford C Bernstein Emerg Mkts	SNEMX	C-	(212) 486-5800	26.75	C /4.9	28.83 /84	2.41 /27	0.09 / 5	C /4.4	79	5
EM	SEI Inst Intl Emerging Mkts Eqty F	SIEMX	C-	(800) 342-5734	10.38	C /4.8	32.30 /90	1.21 /19	-0.34 / 4	C /4.5	69	7
EM	● Institutional Emerging Markets I	HLMEX	C-	(877) 435-8105	18.15	C /4.4	28.52 /83	2.01 /24	2.90 /10	C /4.9	78	12
EM	American Century NT Emg Market	ACLKX	C-	(800) 345-6488	10.94	C /4.3	25.06 /73	2.48 /27	2.37 / 9	C /5.1	81	11
EM	SEI Inst Screened World Eq Ex-US	SSEAX	C-	(800) 342-5734	9.46	C- /4.2	23.22 /67	1.66 /22	5.38 /24	C+ /6.0	78	9
EM	RBB Free Market Intl Eq Inst	FMNEX	C-	(866) 780-0357	9.75	C- /4.1	24.81 /73	0.69 /17	5.72 /27	C /5.3	69	10
EM	Templeton Emerg Mkts Small Cap	TEMMX	C-	(800) 342-5236	12.56	C- /4.0	22.06 /63	3.97 /43	4.00 /15	C+ /6.4	89	11
EM	SA Emerging Markets Value	SAEMX	D+	(800) 366-7266	9.11	C+ /5.9	36.65 /96	0.31 /15	-2.34 / 2	D+ /2.8	55	5
EM	Delaware Emerging Markets A	DEMAX	D+	(800) 523-1918	15.94	C+ /5.7	41.19 /98	1.76 /22	3.23 /12	C- /3.1	71	11
EM	Northern Active M Emg Mkts Eqty	NMMEX	D+	(800) 595-9111	17.58	C /4.6	31.53 /89	0.86 /17	0.41 / 5	C /4.3	65	5
EM	Victory Sophus Emerging Markets	GBEMX	D+	(800) 539-3863	17.60	C /4.5	32.40 /91	1.61 /22	-1.62 / 3	C- /3.9	74	4
EM	Lazard Emerging Mkts Eq Blend	EMBOX	D+	(800) 821-6474	10.41	C /4.4	30.38 /87	1.08 /19	-1.32 / 3	C /4.5	67	7
EM	● Harding Loevner Emerg Mrkt	HLEMX	D+	(877) 435-8105	47.56	C /4.4	28.72 /83	2.05 /24	2.90 /10	C /4.4	78	12
EM	Deutsche Emerging Markets Eqty	SEKAX	D+	(800) 728-3337	16.15	C- /4.2	30.42 /87	2.33 /26	-0.24 / 4	C /4.7	79	3
EM	Dunham Emerging Markets Stock	DAEMX	D+	(888) 338-6426	13.03	C- /4.0	31.29 /89	0.33 /15	-0.63 / 4	C /4.9	60	4
EM	USAA Emerging Markets Fund	USEMX	D+	(800) 382-8722	16.33	C- /4.0	29.02 /84	0.52 /16	-1.66 / 3	C /4.4	61	12
EM	JPMorgan Emerg Mkt Eq A	JFAMX	D+	(800) 480-4111	22.11	C- /3.8	29.58 /85	1.92 /23	-0.15 / 4	C /4.6	77	12
EM	Fidelity Adv Emerging Asia A	FEAAX	D+	(800) 522-7297	30.78	C- /3.7	24.69 /72	4.29 /46	4.13 /16	C /5.1	89	1
EM	Henderson Emerging Markets A	HEMAX	D+	(866) 443-6337	9.34	C- /3.6	24.45 /71	2.38 /27	0.68 / 6	C /5.2	81	2
EM	Neuberger Berman Emg Mkt Eq A	NEMAX	D+	(800) 877-9700	16.57	C- /3.5	28.42 /83	1.69 /22	1.24 / 7	C /5.2	75	9
EM	AllianzGI Emerging Markets Opp A	AOTAX	D+	(800) 988-8380	24.63	C- /3.3	25.11 /74	1.25 /20	0.83 / 6	C /5.5	72	10
EM	Goldman Sachs Emerg Mkts Eq A	GEMAX	D+	(800) 526-7384	16.23	C- /3.3	21.83 /61	3.54 /37	1.13 / 6	C /5.4	86	2
EM	VY JPMorgan Emer Mkt Eqty Adv	IJEAX	D	(800) 992-0180	15.62	C /5.2	29.85 /86	2.20 /25	-0.28 / 4	C- /3.1	79	12
EM	Northern Emerg Mkts Eq Idx	NOEMX	D	(800) 595-9111	10.39	C- /4.0	28.83 /84	1.00 /18	-0.60 / 4	C- /4.1	66	10
EM	● Aberdeen Emerging Markets Inst	ABEMX	D	(866) 667-9231	13.45	C- /3.9	25.07 /73	1.84 /23	0.43 / 5	C- /4.2	76	10

99 Pct = Best
0 Pct = Worst

● Denotes fund is closed to new investors

Fund Type	Fund Name	Ticker Symbol	Overall Investment Rating	Phone	Net Asset Value As of 2/28/17	Performance Rating/Pts	Annualized Total Return Through 2/28/17			Risk Rating/Pts	Mgr. Quality Pct	Mgr. Tenure (Years)
							1Yr / Pct	3Yr / Pct	5Yr / Pct			
EN	Fidelity Select Envir and Alt Ener	FSLEX	B+	(800) 544-8888	23.89	B+ /8.7	33.02 /92	6.70 /70	12.08 /75	C /5.1	99	N/A
EN	Hennessy Gas Utility Investor	GASFX	B-	(800) 966-4354	29.75	B- /7.1	21.22 /58	7.30 /74	11.66 /71	C+ /5.6	99	4
EN	Center Coast MLP Focus A	CCCAX	D	(877) 766-0066	8.78	C /4.3	37.04 /96	0.13 /14	3.06 /11	C- /3.6	91	7
EN	Deutsche Enhanced Comdty Strat	SKNRX	E+	(800) 728-3337	11.63	E- /0.1	12.29 /19	-6.26 / 2	-5.63 / 1	C+ /5.7	16	7
EN	Advisory Research MLP & Engy	INFIX	E		9.83	C- /3.0	53.81 /99	-1.47 / 8	3.94 /15	D- /1.4	91	7
EN	Dreyfus Natural Resources C	DLDCX	E	(800) 782-6620	26.99	D /1.9	34.70 /94	-2.17 / 6	1.24 / 7	C- /3.0	81	8
EN	ProFunds Short Oil & Gas Svc	SNPSX	E	(888) 776-3637	44.50	E- /0.1	-25.83 / 0	-2.44 / 6	-7.10 / 1	C- /3.6	4	4
EN	Fidelity Select Energy	FSENX	E-	(800) 544-8888	44.10	E+ /0.7	36.05 /95	-4.39 / 3	0.38 / 5	D /1.6	84	11
EN	T Rowe Price New Era	PRNEX	E-	(800) 638-5660	33.24	E+ /0.7	25.05 /73	-3.39 / 4	0.01 / 4	D- /1.5	81	4
EN	Vanguard Energy Inv	VGENX	E-	(800) 662-7447	51.53	E+ /0.6	33.11 /92	-5.10 / 2	-1.01 / 3	D- /1.4	75	5
EN	Waddell & Reed Adv Energy Fund	WEGAX	E-	(888) 923-3355	13.90	E+ /0.6	43.30 /98	-4.82 / 3	0.65 / 6	D- /1.2	83	11
EN	Ivy Energy A	IEYAX	E-	(800) 777-6472	13.64	E /0.5	42.98 /98	-5.04 / 2	0.46 / 5	D- /1.2	81	11
EN	Fidelity Select Energy Svcs	FSESX	E-	(800) 544-8888	54.71	E /0.5	46.38 /99	-9.69 / 1	-2.73 / 2	E /0.4	29	4
EN	Fidelity Adv Energy A	FANAX	E-	(800) 522-7297	33.94	E /0.4	35.34 /94	-4.68 / 3	0.10 / 5	D- /1.5	82	11
EN	Fidelity Select Natural Resources	FNARX	E-	(800) 544-8888	29.13	E /0.4	34.54 /93	-5.97 / 2	-1.73 / 3	D- /1.5	71	11
EN	Vanguard Energy Index Adm	VENAX	E-	(800) 662-7447	49.13	E /0.4	28.98 /84	-5.37 / 2	0.20 / 5	D- /1.3	74	2
EN	Fidelity Select Natural Gas	FSNGX	E-	(800) 544-8888	27.76	E /0.4	56.75 /99	-9.69 / 1	-2.06 / 3	E+ /0.6	39	5
EN	Columbia Gl Energy and Nat Res A	EENAX	E-	(800) 345-6611	17.70	E /0.3	27.06 /79	-5.27 / 2	-2.04 / 3	D /2.0	63	6
EN	Ivy Global Nat Resource A	IGNAX	E-	(800) 777-6472	15.03	E- /0.2	31.58 /89	-6.95 / 1	-4.80 / 2	D /2.2	48	4
EN	AllianzGI Global Natural Res A	ARMAX	E-	(800) 988-8380	15.58	E- /0.2	26.97 /79	-6.17 / 2	-1.07 / 3	D /1.7	56	13
EN	Firsthand Alternative Energy Fd	ALTEX	E-	(888) 884-2675	5.63	E- /0.1	6.03 / 5	-8.46 / 1	3.68 /14	C- /3.4	6	10
EN	Putnam Global Natural Resources	EBERX	E-	(800) 225-1581	16.21	E- /0.1	21.51 /60	-10.02 / 1	-5.11 / 2	D /1.9	11	5
EN	Saratoga Adv Tr Energy&Basic Mat	SBMBX	E-	(800) 807-3863	11.62	E- /0.1	30.86 /88	-10.60 / 1	-4.53 / 2	D /1.6	13	2
EN	Guinness Atkinson Glob Energy	GAGEX	E-	(800) 915-6565	21.87	E- /0.1	29.87 /86	-12.18 / 0	-4.40 / 2	D- /1.1	6	13
EN	Rydex Energy A	RYENX	E-	(800) 820-0888	74.72	E- /0.1	37.51 /96	-11.20 / 1	-4.47 / 2	D- /1.0	15	19
EN	BlackRock AllCap Energy & Res	BACAX	E-	(800) 441-7762	10.74	E- /0.1	26.38 /77	-9.47 / 1	-5.36 / 2	D- /1.0	22	4
EN	BlackRock Natural Resource Inv A	MDGRX	E-	(800) 441-7762	44.09	E- /0.1	29.59 /85	-8.11 / 1	-3.61 / 2	E+ /0.9	38	N/A
EN	Franklin Natural Resources A	FRNRX	E-	(800) 342-5236	26.69	E- /0.1	38.47 /97	-9.62 / 1	-6.66 / 1	E+ /0.9	26	18
EN	VanEck Global Hard Assets A	GHAAX	E-	(800) 826-1115	36.05	E- /0.1	40.75 /97	-9.80 / 1	-5.50 / 2	E+ /0.8	23	22
EN ●	J Hancock Natural Resources A	JNRAX	E-	(800) 257-3336	12.08	E- /0.1	40.18 /97	-11.38 / 1	-8.31 / 1	E+ /0.8	10	3
EN	ICON Energy A	ICEAX	E-	(800) 764-0442	12.90	E- /0.1	27.75 /81	-9.48 / 1	-2.86 / 2	E+ /0.8	20	10
EN	Prudential Jennison Natural Res A	PGNAX	E-	(800) 225-1852	36.75	E- /0.1	40.50 /97	-10.24 / 1	-6.57 / 1	E+ /0.7	20	11
EN	Victory Global Natural Resources A	RSNRX	E-	(800) 539-3863	23.08	E- /0.1	56.58 /99	-11.91 / 1	-7.05 / 1	E /0.5	10	12
EN	ProFunds-Oil & Gas UltraSector	ENPSX	E-	(888) 776-3637	31.96	E- /0.1	35.37 /94	-12.26 / 0	-3.78 / 2	E /0.3	15	4
EN	ProFunds Oil Eqpt Svcs & Dist Svc	OEPSX	E-	(888) 776-3637	14.08	E- /0.1	47.90 /99	-16.59 / 0	-7.33 / 1	E- /0.0	3	4
EN	US Global Inv Global Resources	PSPFX	E-	(800) 873-8637	5.63	E- /0.0	24.11 /70	-14.75 / 0	-9.56 / 1	D+ /2.4	1	28
EN	Guinness Atkinson Alt Energy Fd	GAAEX	E-	(800) 915-6565	2.68	E- /0.0	3.88 / 3	-15.17 / 0	-3.85 / 2	D+ /2.4	1	11
EN	Putnam Global Energy Fund A	PGEAX	E-	(800) 225-1581	7.95	E- /0.0	33.42 /92	-14.99 / 0	-7.86 / 1	E+ /0.7	2	1
EN	BlackRock Energy & Resources Inv	SSGRX	E-	(800) 441-7762	18.72	E- /0.0	34.48 /93	-17.96 / 0	-11.87 / 0	E /0.3	1	4
EN	Invesco Energy A	IENAX	E-	(800) 959-4246	26.02	E- /0.0	29.14 /84	-12.70 / 0	-5.98 / 1	E- /0.2	7	4
EN	Rydex Energy Services A	RYESX	E-	(800) 820-0888	31.95	E- /0.0	34.35 /93	-17.35 / 0	-8.88 / 1	E- /0.2	1	19

99 Pct = Best
0 Pct = Worst

Fund Type	Fund Name	Ticker Symbol	Overall Investment Rating	Phone	Net Asset Value As of 2/28/17	PERFORMANCE				RISK	FUND MGR	
						Perform-ance Rating/Pts	Annualized Total Return Through 2/28/17			Risk Rating/Pts	Mgr. Quality Pct	Mgr. Tenure (Years)
							1Yr / Pct	3Yr / Pct	5Yr / Pct			
FS	RMB Mendon Financial Services A	RMBKX	A+	(800) 601-5228	42.66	A+ /9.9	49.34 /99	20.69 /99	23.00 /99	C+ / 6.8	98	18
FS	Vanguard Financial Index Fd Adm	VFAIX	A+	(800) 662-7447	31.22	A+ /9.9	46.85 /99	14.09 /99	17.33 /98	C+ / 6.6	79	2
FS	Emerald Banking and Finance A	HSSAX	A+	(855) 828-9909	42.64	A+ /9.9	51.05 /99	16.40 /99	21.78 /99	C+ / 6.5	88	20
FS	1919 Financial Services A	SBFAX	A+	(844) 828-1919	24.53	A+ /9.9	44.51 /98	14.96 /99	18.45 /99	C+ / 6.1	87	3
FS	J Hancock Regional Bank A	FRBAX	A+	(800) 257-3336	26.28	A+ /9.9	60.84 /99	18.09 /99	20.90 /99	C+ / 6.0	91	19
FS	Alpine Financial Services Inst	ADFSX	A+	(888) 785-5578	17.24	A+ /9.9	55.88 /99	10.12 /94	17.39 /98	C+ / 5.7	30	2
FS	Fidelity Select Insurance	FSPCX	A+	(800) 544-8888	80.60	A+ /9.8	31.60 /89	13.17 /99	17.52 /98	C+ / 6.7	86	4
FS	Fidelity Select Financial Services	FIDSX	A+	(800) 544-8888	103.05	A+ /9.8	38.78 /97	10.04 /93	13.85 /92	C+ / 6.2	43	4
FS	Davis Financial A	RPFGX	A+	(800) 279-0279	47.12	A+ /9.8	33.82 /93	12.34 /98	14.42 /95	C+ / 6.1	78	26
FS	Fidelity Adv Financial Serv A	FAFDX	A+	(800) 522-7297	19.00	A+ /9.7	38.17 /96	9.86 /93	13.68 /90	C+ / 6.3	41	4
FS	Franklin Mutual Financial Svcs A	TFSIX	A+	(800) 342-5236	22.14	A- /9.1	28.54 /83	10.54 /96	13.48 /89	B- / 7.1	78	8
FS	Rydex Banking A	RYBKX	A	(800) 820-0888	73.27	A+ /9.9	54.46 /99	9.74 /92	12.97 /83	C / 5.4	11	19
FS	Hennessy Small Cap Financial Inv	HSFNX	A	(800) 966-4354	25.53	A+ /9.9	42.81 /98	12.66 /99	16.50 /98	C / 5.2	74	20
FS	Diamond Hill Financial Lng-Sht A	BANCX	A	(614) 255-3333	23.36	A+ /9.8	42.96 /98	9.53 /91	14.48 /95	C+ / 5.7	28	16
FS	J Hancock Financial Indust A	FIDAX	A	(800) 257-3336	19.92	A+ /9.8	45.73 /99	8.53 /83	15.92 /98	C / 5.5	10	19
FS	ICON Financial S	ICFSX	A	(800) 764-0442	9.49	A+ /9.8	40.27 /97	7.26 /74	11.04 /66	C / 5.3	4	14
FS	RMB Mendon Financial Long/Short	RMBFX	A	(800) 462-2392	18.19	B /8.2	23.81 /69	10.92 /97	14.93 /97	C+ / 6.9	80	13
FS	Fidelity Select Banking Port	FSRBX	A-	(800) 544-8888	33.63	A+ /9.9	56.16 /99	12.86 /99	17.00 /98	C / 5.1	33	5
FS	T Rowe Price Financial Services	PRISX	A-	(800) 638-5660	25.77	A+ /9.9	41.68 /98	10.19 /94	15.71 /98	C / 5.0	30	3
FS	ProFunds-Financial UltraSector	FNPSX	A-	(888) 776-3637	16.76	A+ /9.9	55.76 /99	14.35 /99	20.82 /99	C / 5.0	21	4
FS	Saratoga Adv Tr Financial Service	SFPAX	A-	(800) 807-3863	9.86	B+ /8.5	36.57 /95	7.17 /73	10.82 /64	C+ / 6.3	10	2
FS	Hennessy Large Cap Financial Inv	HLFNX	B	(800) 966-4354	20.10	A+ /9.8	40.83 /97	7.32 /74	13.99 /93	C- / 3.5	8	20
FS	Fidelity Select Consumer Finance	FSVLX	B-	(800) 544-8888	14.02	A- /9.2	33.57 /92	7.34 /74	13.76 /91	C- / 3.3	16	5
FS	ProFunds-Banks UltraSector Svc	BKPSX	C+	(888) 776-3637	42.98	A+ /9.9	91.88 /99	16.46 /99	23.53 /99	D / 1.6	3	4
FS	J Hancock VIT Financial Indus I	JEFSX	C	(800) 257-3336	13.74	A+ /9.9	44.54 /98	10.18 /94	12.90 /83	D- / 1.2	24	3
FS	Fidelity Select Brkg and Inv Mgmt	FSLBX	C	(800) 544-8888	71.13	B- /7.0	31.76 /90	3.26 /34	11.50 /70	C- / 3.8	1	2
FS	Rydex Financial Services A	RYFNX	C-	(800) 820-0888	63.00	A /9.4	34.99 /94	9.18 /88	12.63 /80	D- / 1.0	46	19
FS	ALPS/Red Rocks Listed Priv Eq A	LPEFX	C-	(866) 759-5679	6.75	C /4.3	24.86 /73	3.11 /33	12.39 /78	C / 5.5	19	10
FS	ProFunds-Rising Rates Opp 10	RTPSX	D	(888) 776-3637	14.54	E- /0.1	1.39 / 2	-5.72 / 2	-4.69 / 2	B- / 7.4	3	8
FS	● Merk Hard Currency Investor	MERKX	D	(866) 637-5386	9.29	E- /0.1	-2.52 / 1	-6.91 / 1	-4.51 / 2	B- / 7.4	6	12
FS	Putnam Global Financials Fund A	PGFFX	D-	(800) 225-1581	11.86	C- /4.1	26.95 /79	1.63 /22	8.78 /49	D+ / 2.6	2	9
FS	Prudential Financial Services A	PFSAX	E	(800) 225-1852	12.26	E+ /0.7	26.04 /76	-3.82 / 3	5.30 /23	D+ / 2.9	0	8

● Denotes fund is closed to new investors

99 Pct = Best
0 Pct = Worst

Fund Type	Fund Name	Ticker Symbol	Overall Investment Rating	Phone	Net Asset Value As of 2/28/17	PERFORMANCE Performance Rating/Pts	Annualized Total Return Through 2/28/17 1Yr / Pct	3Yr / Pct	5Yr / Pct	RISK Risk Rating/Pts	FUND MGR Mgr. Quality Pct	Mgr. Tenure (Years)
FO	Hennessy Japan Small Cap Inv	HJPSX	A+	(800) 966-4354	12.14	A+ /9.9	30.37 /87	13.52 /99	15.54 /98	B- / 7.3	99	10
FO	DFA Japanese Small Co Inst	DFJSX	A+	(800) 984-9472	23.74	A+ /9.7	28.62 /83	10.53 /96	10.00 /58	B- / 7.6	99	13
FO	Hennessy Japan Fund Investor	HJPNX	A+	(800) 966-4354	27.78	A- /9.0	20.73 /56	12.20 /98	13.21 /86	C+ / 6.6	99	11
FO	Fidelity Japan Small Companies	FJSCX	A+	(800) 544-8544	15.60	B /7.9	19.77 /51	9.37 /89	14.45 /95	B- / 7.9	99	3
FO	T Rowe Price Japan	PRJPX	A+	(800) 638-5660	12.28	B /7.7	23.92 /70	8.84 /86	10.84 /65	B / 8.0	99	4
FO	Glenmede Total Market Port	GTTMX	A	(800) 442-8299	16.73	B /8.2	23.29 /67	7.96 /79	13.02 /84	C+ / 6.8	98	11
FO	Matthews India Fund Inv	MINDX	A-	(800) 789-2742	28.19	A+ /9.9	24.26 /71	20.97 /99	11.88 /73	C / 4.9	99	12
FO	Guinness Atkinson Asia Pac Div	GAADX	B	(800) 915-6565	14.58	B- /7.0	24.15 /70	7.66 /76	5.35 /24	C+ / 6.2	98	11
FO	Rydex Japan 2x Strategy Fd A	RYJSX	B-	(800) 820-0888	101.60	A- /9.2	43.02 /98	8.15 /80	11.80 /72	C- / 3.4	99	9
FO	DFA Emerging Markets Sm Cap	DEMSX	B-	(800) 984-9472	20.66	B /7.6	31.94 /90	5.14 /56	3.45 /13	C / 4.9	96	13
FO	Commonwealth-Australia/New	CNZLX	B-	(888) 345-1898	12.92	B- /7.5	31.45 /89	5.47 /59	6.88 /34	C / 5.3	96	26
FO	FMI International Investor	FMIJX	B-	(800) 811-5311	30.98	C+ /5.9	16.45 /36	6.96 /72	11.00 /66	B- / 7.2	98	N/A
FO	Matthews China Dividend Fund Inv	MCDFX	C+	(800) 789-2742	14.73	C+ /6.8	24.19 /71	8.24 /81	9.06 /51	C / 4.6	99	5
FO	AIG Japan A	SAESX	C+	(800) 858-8850	7.72	C+ /6.4	26.81 /79	5.48 /59	7.45 /38	C / 5.2	96	5
FO	● Matthews Japan Fund Inv	MJFOX	C+	(800) 789-2742	19.89	C+ /6.0	13.66 /24	8.25 /81	11.45 /69	C+ / 6.6	98	11
FO	Matthews Korea Fund Inv	MAKOX	C+	(800) 789-2742	5.84	C+ /6.0	16.32 /36	6.31 /67	8.27 /44	C+ / 5.9	97	10
FO	Schwab Fundm Intl Sm Co Index	SFILX	C+	(800) 407-0256	12.32	C+ /5.7	22.92 /66	4.09 /44	8.36 /45	C+ / 6.6	94	5
FO	Vanguard Pacific Stock Index Inv	VPACX	C+	(800) 662-7447	11.85	C /5.5	23.73 /69	3.99 /43	5.94 /28	C+ / 6.3	94	20
FO	Papp Small and Mid Cap Growth	PAPPX	C+	(877) 370-7277	18.97	C /5.3	17.03 /38	5.67 /61	8.60 /47	C+ / 6.2	96	N/A
FO	Guinness Atkinson Asia Focus	IASMX	C	(800) 915-6565	17.13	C+ /6.1	33.17 /92	3.44 /36	-0.64 / 4	C / 4.8	92	14
FO	DFA International Sm Cap Val Inst	DISVX	C	(800) 984-9472	20.10	C /5.3	24.32 /71	2.28 /26	9.38 /54	C+ / 5.9	88	13
FO	Hartford International Value A	HILAX	C	(888) 843-7824	15.36	C /5.3	30.52 /87	3.08 /33	9.01 /51	C+ / 5.9	91	4
FO	Fidelity Emerging Asia Fund	FSEAX	C	(800) 544-8544	33.95	C /5.2	24.87 /73	4.65 /50	4.23 /16	C / 5.3	95	1
FO	Matthews Asia Dividend Fund Inv	MAPIX	C	(800) 789-2742	16.60	C /4.7	17.58 /41	5.73 /62	7.21 /36	C+ / 6.7	96	6
FO	Pear Tree Polaris Foreign VSC Ord	QUSOX	C	(800) 326-2151	13.22	C /4.6	18.78 /46	2.73 /29	9.81 /57	C+ / 6.4	90	9
FO	Old Westbury Large Cap Strategies	OWLSX	C	(800) 607-2200	13.47	C /4.5	16.69 /37	4.67 /50	8.62 /47	C+ / 6.4	95	6
FO	T Rowe Price Intl Discovery	PRIDX	C	(800) 638-5660	56.66	C /4.3	16.95 /38	4.46 /48	9.94 /58	C+ / 6.8	94	19
FO	Guggenheim World Equity Income	SEQAX	C	(800) 820-0888	14.18	C- /3.5	15.70 /33	4.73 /51	7.75 /40	B- / 7.1	95	4
FO	Commonwealth Japan	CNJFX	C	(888) 345-1898	3.41	C- /3.2	7.57 / 7	4.25 /46	4.47 /18	B- / 7.4	94	20
FO	ProFunds-Ultra Japan Svc	UJPSX	C-	(888) 776-3637	16.06	A+ /9.7	33.28 /92	8.57 /84	19.00 /99	E- / 0.0	99	8
FO	Direxion Mo China Bull 2X Inv	DXHLX	C-	(800) 851-0511	35.50	A+ /9.6	60.49 /99	4.75 /51	-2.36 / 2	E- / 0.0	96	10
FO	Ivy Emerging Markets Equity A	IPOAX	C-	(800) 777-6472	16.44	C+ /5.9	35.87 /95	2.96 /31	3.06 /11	C / 4.3	91	3
FO	Matthews Pacific Tiger Fund Inv	MAPTX	C-	(800) 789-2742	24.93	C /5.4	19.51 /49	6.55 /69	6.03 /29	C / 4.6	97	9
FO	BlackRock Pacific Inv A	MDPCX	C-	(800) 441-7762	17.33	C /4.9	26.24 /77	3.44 /36	6.80 /33	C / 4.8	92	6
FO	Aberdeen Asia-Pac X-Japan Eq IS	AAPEX	C-	(866) 667-9231	11.07	C /4.9	29.02 /84	1.76 /22	2.23 / 9	C / 4.6	86	22
FO	Fidelity Pacific Basin	FPBFX	C-	(800) 544-8544	28.24	C /4.5	17.67 /41	5.81 /63	9.69 /56	C+ / 6.0	97	4
FO	T Rowe Price New Asia	PRASX	C-	(800) 638-5660	16.62	C /4.4	23.07 /67	4.06 /44	3.86 /15	C / 5.3	94	8
FO	DFA Continental Small Co Inst	DFCSX	C-	(800) 984-9472	22.86	C /4.3	20.12 /53	2.04 /24	10.88 /65	C+ / 5.9	87	19
FO	Janus Global Select A	JORAX	C-	(800) 295-2687	13.89	C /4.3	23.07 /67	3.56 /38	4.04 /15	C / 5.4	92	5
FO	DFA International Small Co Inst	DFISX	C-	(800) 984-9472	18.28	C- /4.1	20.53 /55	2.11 /25	8.10 /43	C+ / 6.1	87	13
FO	Wasatch International Opps Inv	WAIOX	C-	(800) 551-1700	3.02	C- /4.1	15.27 /31	6.51 /69	10.35 /61	C+ / 5.9	97	3
FO	J Hancock Int Small Comp NAV		C-	(800) 257-3336	10.74	C- /3.7	19.78 /51	1.59 /21	7.72 /40	C+ / 6.3	85	11
FO	Harding Loevner Intl Equity Inv	HLMNX	C-	(877) 435-8105	18.92	C- /3.7	19.48 /49	2.93 /31	5.70 /26	C+ / 5.9	90	16
FO	DFA TA World ex US Core Eq Inst	DFTWX	C-	(800) 984-9472	9.91	C- /3.6	22.54 /65	0.78 /17	4.70 /19	C+ / 5.9	81	9
FO	DFA International Vector Eq Inst	DFVQX	C-	(800) 984-9472	11.41	C- /3.6	22.29 /64	0.65 /16	6.45 /31	C+ / 5.8	80	5
FO	Columbia Pacific/Asia A	CASAX	C-	(800) 345-6611	9.48	C- /3.5	18.98 /47	4.51 /49	5.68 /26	C+ / 6.3	94	9
FO	Tocqueville International Value	TIVFX	C-	(800) 697-3863	15.08	C- /3.5	17.38 /40	2.59 /28	7.37 /37	C+ / 5.9	89	16
FO	Schwab International Core Equity	SICNX	C-	(800) 407-0256	9.64	C- /3.4	18.35 /44	0.98 /18	7.90 /41	C+ / 6.6	82	5
FO	● Oppenheimer Intl Small Mid Co A	OSMAX	C-	(888) 470-0862	39.35	C- /3.4	15.10 /30	5.05 /55	14.24 /94	C+ / 6.6	95	5
FO	Invesco Asia Pacific Growth A	ASIAX	C-	(800) 959-4246	31.65	C- /3.4	20.82 /56	4.19 /45	5.93 /28	C+ / 6.1	94	18
FO	Tweedy Browne Global Value	TBGVX	C-	(800) 432-4789	26.01	C- /3.3	15.72 /33	2.75 /30	7.85 /41	C+ / 6.4	89	24
FO	SA International Sm Comp	SAISX	C-	(800) 366-7266	20.15	C- /3.2	19.35 /49	0.86 /17	6.82 /34	C+ / 6.3	81	5

● Denotes fund is closed to new investors

Fund Type	Fund Name	Ticker Symbol	Overall Investment Rating	Phone	Net Asset Value As of 2/28/17	Perform-ance Rating/Pts	Annualized Total Return Through 2/28/17			Risk Rating/Pts	Mgr. Quality Pct	Mgr. Tenure (Years)
							1Yr / Pct	3Yr / Pct	5Yr / Pct			
GL	AllianzGI NFJ Mid-Cap Value A	PQNAX	A+	(800) 988-8380	28.91	A- /9.1	31.95 /90	9.11 /87	12.42 /78	C+ /6.7	99	8
GL	Janus Growth and Income A	JDNAX	A-	(800) 295-2687	48.37	B+ /8.5	24.66 /72	10.16 /94	13.01 /84	C+ /6.5	99	10
GL	GF Multi-Factor Growth Equity Fd I	GFMGX	A-	(800) 473-1155	19.21	B+ /8.5	23.03 /67	9.24 /88	13.29 /87	C+ /6.1	99	8
GL	Convergence Core Plus Fund Inst	MARNX	A-	(877) 677-9414	18.61	B+ /8.3	22.52 /65	8.68 /84	12.57 /80	C+ /6.4	99	8
GL	Alpine Rising Dividend Inst	AADDX	A-	(888) 785-5578	16.52	B /7.8	24.58 /72	7.60 /76	11.28 /68	B- /7.1	98	7
GL	Hodges Retail	HDPMX	B+	(877) 232-1222	47.27	A+ /9.7	51.41 /99	7.88 /78	17.37 /98	C- /4.0	98	18
GL	Dodge & Cox Global Stock	DODWX	B+	(800) 621-3979	12.68	A /9.3	37.70 /96	6.51 /68	12.04 /75	C /5.1	97	9
GL	Golub Group Equity Fund	GGEFX	B+	(866) 954-6682	18.39	A- /9.0	24.58 /72	9.56 /91	12.72 /81	C /5.3	99	8
GL	Oakmark Global Select Investor	OAKWX	B+	(800) 625-6275	17.58	B /8.2	29.74 /86	6.23 /66	11.32 /68	C+ /5.8	97	11
GL	● Brown Advisory SmCP Fund Val	BIAUX	B+	(800) 540-6807	26.35	B /8.0	29.63 /86	7.15 /73	13.83 /92	C+ /5.9	98	9
GL	Hennessy Cornerstone Val	HFCVX	B+	(800) 966-4354	19.89	B /7.8	25.31 /74	7.56 /76	10.96 /65	C+ /6.7	98	21
GL	Evermore Global Value Inv	EVGBX	B+	(866) 383-7667	13.46	B /7.7	33.76 /93	6.49 /68	10.54 /62	C+ /6.4	97	8
GL	Steward Global Equity Income Indv	SGIDX	B+	(800) 262-6631	30.35	B- /7.4	21.27 /59	8.32 /81	9.27 /53	C+ /6.8	99	9
GL	Oppenheimer Global Opportunities	OPGIX	B	(888) 470-0862	49.81	B+ /8.7	37.86 /96	7.63 /76	12.25 /77	C /4.9	98	22
GL	T Rowe Price Global Stock	PRGSX	B	(800) 638-5660	30.83	B /7.8	26.42 /78	8.01 /79	11.64 /71	C+ /5.8	98	5
GL	● Janus Enterprise A	JDMAX	B	(800) 295-2687	98.59	B- /7.5	23.83 /69	9.81 /92	13.26 /86	C+ /6.0	99	10
GL	Bright Rock Mid Cap Growth Inst	BQMGX	B	(800) 273-7223	14.83	B- /7.4	21.22 /58	8.40 /82	9.18 /52	C+ /5.6	99	5
GL	DFA Global Equity R2	DGERX	B	(800) 984-9472	20.56	B- /7.1	25.79 /76	5.81 /63	10.29 /60	C+ /6.6	97	N/A
GL	Fidelity Freedom Index 2025 Inv	FQIFX	B	(800) 544-8544	15.41	C /4.6	15.70 /33	4.99 /54	6.92 /34	B /8.4	74	8
GL	Hartford MidCap HLS Fd IA	HIMCX	B-	(888) 843-7824	35.89	B+ /8.7	27.39 /80	8.30 /81	14.74 /96	C- /3.9	99	13
GL	Polaris Global Value	PGVFX	B-	(888) 263-5594	24.35	C+ /6.8	23.92 /70	5.55 /60	12.40 /78	B- /7.0	96	28
GL	QS Global Equity A	CFIPX	B-	(877) 534-4627	14.87	C+ /6.6	21.54 /60	7.82 /78	11.24 /68	B- /7.4	98	6
GL	Fidelity Freedom Index 2040 Inv	FBIFX	B-	(800) 544-8544	16.76	C+ /6.5	21.48 /60	5.99 /64	8.35 /45	B- /7.2	67	8
GL	Fidelity Freedom Index 2035 Inv	FIHFX	B-	(800) 544-8544	16.66	C+ /6.5	21.50 /60	5.99 /64	8.28 /44	B- /7.2	67	8
GL	Fidelity Freedom Index 2045 Inv	FIOFX	B-	(800) 544-8544	16.90	C+ /6.5	21.56 /60	6.00 /64	8.44 /46	B- /7.2	67	8
GL	Fidelity Freedom Index 2050 Inv	FIPFX	B-	(800) 544-8544	17.01	C+ /6.5	21.52 /60	6.00 /64	8.49 /46	B- /7.2	67	8
GL	Fidelity Freedom Index 2030 Inv	FXIFX	B-	(800) 544-8544	15.96	C+ /5.7	19.12 /48	5.61 /61	7.54 /39	B- /7.7	70	8
GL	Morningstar Growth ETF Asset All	GETFX	B-	(866) 432-2926	11.37	C /5.3	19.64 /50	4.81 /52	7.34 /37	B- /7.5	62	10
GL	DFA Global Allocation 60/40 R2	DFPRX	B-	(800) 984-9472	16.86	C- /4.1	16.21 /35	4.10 /44	6.71 /33	B /8.6	93	N/A
GL	Fidelity Freedom Index 2020 Inv	FPIFX	B-	(800) 544-8544	14.63	C- /4.0	14.26 /27	4.62 /50	6.04 /29	B /8.7	74	8
GL	Fidelity Freedom Index 2015 Inv	FLIFX	B-	(800) 544-8544	14.05	C- /3.6	12.86 /21	4.32 /47	5.58 /25	B+ /9.0	75	8
GL	● Janus Venture D	JANVX	C+	(800) 295-2687	69.35	B /7.8	26.91 /79	8.18 /80	13.32 /87	C- /4.1	98	4
GL	Hartford MidCap A	HFMCX	C+	(888) 843-7824	26.89	B- /7.3	26.53 /78	7.87 /78	14.16 /94	C /4.6	98	13
GL	VY Morgan Stanley Glbl Franch	IGFAX	C+	(800) 992-0180	15.68	C+ /6.8	15.66 /33	7.53 /76	9.44 /54	C /5.2	98	8
GL	Oakmark Global Service	OARGX	C+	(800) 625-6275	29.20	C+ /6.8	29.85 /86	2.75 /30	8.98 /50	C /4.8	90	14
GL	Fidelity Freedom K 2050	FFKHX	C+	(800) 544-8544	16.89	C+ /6.7	22.79 /66	6.14 /65	9.15 /52	C+ /6.5	66	8
GL	Harding Loevner Global Eq Adv	HLMGX	C+	(877) 435-8105	34.57	C+ /6.7	22.00 /62	6.73 /70	8.68 /48	C+ /5.9	98	16
GL	American Beacon SGA Global Gro	SGAGX	C+	(800) 658-5811	15.74	C+ /6.7	22.12 /63	7.46 /75	8.89 /50	C+ /5.8	98	7
GL	Perkins Lg Cp Value A	JAPAX	C+	(800) 295-2687	16.25	C+ /6.6	23.02 /67	7.55 /76	10.78 /64	C+ /6.2	98	9
GL	AQR Global Equity Fund N	AQGNX	C+	(866) 290-2688	7.89	C+ /6.5	21.46 /60	5.54 /60	10.41 /61	C /5.4	96	8
GL	Morningstar Agg Gr ETF Asset All	AGTFX	C+	(866) 432-2926	12.13	C+ /6.2	22.58 /65	5.29 /57	8.00 /42	C+ /6.6	96	10
GL	Fidelity Freedom K 2030	FFKEX	C+	(800) 544-8544	15.61	C+ /6.1	20.82 /56	5.80 /62	8.26 /44	C+ /6.9	68	8
GL	Bright Rock Qual Lrg Cap Inst	BQLCX	C+	(800) 273-7223	15.26	C+ /6.1	14.64 /28	7.74 /77	11.59 /71	C+ /6.5	98	8
GL	● MSIF Global Franchise A	MSFBX	C+	(800) 354-8185	21.65	C+ /6.0	15.87 /34	7.83 /78	9.69 /56	C+ /6.6	98	8
GL	T Rowe Price Inst Glbl Gr Eq	RPIGX	C+	(800) 638-5660	23.17	C+ /6.0	20.07 /52	6.35 /67	8.96 /50	C+ /5.6	97	9
GL	REMS Real Estate Income 50/50	RREIX	C+	(800) 673-0550	12.69	C+ /6.0	14.18 /26	10.06 /94	9.71 /56	C /5.5	99	7
GL	Vanguard Global Equity Inv	VHGEX	C+	(800) 662-7447	26.22	C+ /5.9	21.41 /59	4.93 /53	9.77 /57	C+ /6.4	95	13
GL	Thornburg Globl Opportunities A	THOAX	C+	(800) 847-0200	27.28	C+ /5.8	15.27 /31	7.06 /72	12.34 /78	C+ /6.2	98	11
GL	Virtus Global Opportunities A	NWWOX	C+	(800) 243-1574	14.38	C+ /5.6	18.25 /44	6.97 /72	9.76 /57	C+ /6.9	98	8
GL	Artisan Global Value Inv	ARTGX	C+	(800) 344-1770	15.89	C /5.5	21.24 /58	4.92 /53	11.18 /67	C+ /6.5	95	10
GL	Voya Global Equity Portfolio Adv	IGHAX	C+	(800) 992-0180	9.63	C /5.4	19.82 /51	4.28 /46	6.59 /32	C+ /6.4	94	4
GL	Leuthold Global Industries Retail	LGINX	C+	(888) 200-0409	16.42	C /5.3	19.29 /48	3.42 /36	9.96 /58	C+ /6.5	92	7

● Denotes fund is closed to new investors

Fund Type	Fund Name	Ticker Symbol	Overall Investment Rating	Phone	Net Asset Value As of 2/28/17	Performance Rating/Pts	Annualized Total Return Through 2/28/17			Risk Rating/Pts	Mgr. Quality Pct	Mgr. Tenure (Years)
							1Yr / Pct	3Yr / Pct	5Yr / Pct			
GR	Parnassus Endeavor	PARWX	A+	(800) 999-3505	34.41	A+ /9.9	32.69 /91	15.00 /99	17.59 /98	C+ / 6.4	93	12
GR	USAA Nasdaq 100 Index	USNQX	A+	(800) 382-8722	15.14	A+ /9.8	27.85 /81	13.75 /99	16.02 /98	B- / 7.3	81	11
GR	NASDAQ-100 Index Direct	NASDX	A+	(800) 955-9988	13.62	A+ /9.8	27.11 /79	13.66 /99	16.37 /98	C+ / 6.5	81	14
GR	● Vanguard PRIMECAP Core Inv	VPCCX	A+	(800) 662-7447	23.81	A+ /9.8	28.50 /83	11.62 /98	16.19 /98	C+ / 6.4	78	13
GR	Fidelity NASDAQ Composite Index	FNCMX	A+	(800) 544-8544	76.54	A+ /9.8	29.21 /85	11.79 /98	15.71 /98	C+ / 6.0	65	13
GR	Fidelity Sel Defense and	FSDAX	A+	(800) 544-8888	138.34	A+ /9.8	34.37 /93	10.37 /95	15.46 /98	C+ / 6.0	70	2
GR	SunAmerica VAL Co I Nsdq 100	VCNIX	A+	(800) 858-8850	11.14	A+ /9.8	27.84 /81	13.84 /99	16.15 /98	C+ / 5.9	81	5
GR	LSV Value Equity Inst	LSVEX	A+	(866) 777-7818	27.34	A+ /9.7	31.35 /89	10.39 /95	15.98 /98	B- / 7.0	66	18
GR	PRIMECAP Odyssey Stock Fd	POSKX	A+	(800) 729-2307	27.59	A+ /9.7	28.41 /83	11.07 /97	14.98 /97	C+ / 6.8	72	13
GR	White Oak Select Growth	WOGSX	A+	(888) 462-5386	76.20	A+ /9.7	31.20 /89	10.95 /96	13.74 /91	C+ / 6.8	57	25
GR	DFA US Large Cap Value II Inst	DFCVX	A+	(800) 984-9472	18.12	A+ /9.7	33.26 /92	10.07 /94	15.42 /97	C+ / 6.7	57	13
GR	Fidelity Select Air Transport	FSAIX	A+	(800) 544-8888	76.05	A+ /9.7	26.31 /77	11.81 /98	18.53 /99	C+ / 5.9	82	5
GR	Vanguard Mega Cap Value Index I	VMVLX	A+	(800) 662-7447	138.07	A+ /9.6	26.92 /79	11.04 /97	14.18 /94	B- / 7.5	81	2
GR	Vanguard Value Index Inv	VIVAX	A+	(800) 662-7447	37.78	A+ /9.6	27.65 /81	10.77 /95	14.12 /94	B- / 7.2	79	23
GR	Clipper	CFIMX	A+	(800) 432-2504	112.44	A+ /9.6	31.33 /89	11.30 /97	14.00 /93	C+ / 6.6	74	11
GR	Vanguard US Value Inv	VUVLX	A+	(800) 662-7447	18.96	A+ /9.6	28.78 /83	10.11 /94	14.85 /97	C+ / 6.6	70	9
GR	J Hancock Classic Value A	PZFVX	A+	(800) 257-3336	30.39	A+ /9.6	39.99 /97	9.02 /87	13.57 /90	C+ / 6.0	24	21
GR	Fidelity 100 Index FD	FOHIX	A+	(800) 544-8544	15.40	A /9.5	24.55 /72	11.02 /97	13.56 /89	B- / 7.1	76	10
GR	Fidelity LgCp Val Enh Idx Fd	FLVEX	A+	(800) 544-8544	12.53	A /9.5	28.30 /82	10.16 /94	14.42 /95	B- / 7.0	70	10
GR	SunAmerica VAL Co II Lrg Cp Val	VACVX	A+	(800) 858-8850	20.97	A /9.5	31.17 /88	9.43 /90	14.00 /93	C+ / 6.9	56	7
GR	Vanguard FTSE Social Index Inv	VFTSX	A+	(800) 662-7447	15.27	A /9.5	26.32 /77	10.54 /96	15.23 /97	C+ / 6.8	66	2
GR	Tax Mgd US MktWide Val II Inst	DFMVX	A+	(800) 984-9472	26.92	A /9.5	30.62 /87	9.52 /90	15.22 /97	C+ / 6.6	52	13
GR	Boston Partners All Cap Val Inv	BPAVX	A+	(888) 261-4073	24.56	A /9.5	30.14 /87	10.29 /95	14.83 /95	C+ / 6.3	59	10
GR	Oakmark Fund Service	OARMX	A+	(800) 625-6275	75.22	A /9.5	33.74 /93	9.09 /87	14.26 /95	C+ / 6.1	38	17
GR	Glenmede Large Cap Core Advisor	GTLOX	A+	(800) 442-8299	25.34	A /9.4	25.08 /74	10.64 /96	15.34 /97	B- / 7.8	73	13
GR	Fidelity Blue Chip Value	FBCVX	A+	(800) 544-8544	18.45	A /9.4	24.99 /73	9.90 /93	13.21 /86	B- / 7.3	70	3
GR	ProFunds-Consumer Goods Ultra	CNPSX	A+	(888) 776-3637	93.47	A /9.4	17.56 /41	12.12 /98	16.06 /98	B- / 7.3	73	4
GR	DFA US Large Company Portfolio	DFUSX	A+	(800) 984-9472	18.44	A /9.4	24.92 /73	10.57 /96	13.95 /93	B- / 7.0	74	N/A
GR	Vanguard Russell 1000 Val Index	VRVIX	A+	(800) 662-7447	199.02	A /9.4	28.85 /84	9.78 /92	13.91 /93	C+ / 6.8	67	7
GR	Thompson LargeCap	THPGX	A+	(800) 999-0887	60.15	A /9.4	35.77 /95	8.60 /84	13.09 /85	C+ / 6.2	23	25
GR	Vanguard Tax-Managed Cap Appr	VTCLX	A+	(800) 662-7447	120.95	A /9.3	25.99 /76	10.19 /94	14.03 /93	C+ / 6.9	67	1
GR	Amer Beacon Bridgeway LC Val	BRLVX	A+	(800) 658-5811	26.99	A- /9.2	25.20 /74	10.56 /96	15.51 /98	B- / 7.0	77	14
GR	Vanguard Large Cap Index Inv	VLACX	A+	(800) 662-7447	43.81	A- /9.2	25.10 /74	10.13 /94	13.66 /90	B- / 7.0	68	1
GR	State Street S&P 500 Index VIS 1	SSSPX	A+	(800) 843-2639	40.48	A- /9.2	24.59 /72	10.28 /95	13.66 /90	C+ / 6.9	70	16
GR	Vanguard Instl TtlStk Mkt Inst	VITNX	A+	(800) 662-7447	53.20	A- /9.2	26.30 /77	9.92 /93	13.86 /92	C+ / 6.8	64	16
GR	Vanguard Mega Cap Gr Index I	VMGAX	A+	(800) 662-7447	187.71	A- /9.2	23.16 /67	10.21 /94	13.77 /91	C+ / 6.7	60	2
GR	Nuveen Large Cap Select A	FLRAX	A+	(800) 257-8787	24.51	A- /9.2	32.22 /90	9.53 /91	13.78 /92	C+ / 6.6	50	14
GR	American Century VP Large Co Val	AVVIX	A+	(800) 345-6488	15.96	A- /9.2	28.47 /83	9.40 /90	13.21 /86	C+ / 6.6	52	13
GR	Schwab Total Stock Market Index	SWTSX	A+	(800) 407-0256	42.01	A- /9.2	26.22 /77	9.82 /92	13.74 /91	C+ / 6.6	63	5
GR	Glenmede Large Cap Growth	GTLLX	A+	(800) 442-8299	27.71	A- /9.1	20.41 /54	11.29 /97	15.12 /97	B / 8.2	77	13
GR	Voya VP Index Plus Large Cap S	IPLSX	A+	(800) 992-0180	25.53	A- /9.1	24.43 /71	9.85 /93	13.12 /85	B- / 7.2	63	11
GR	SunAmerica VAL Co I Core Eq Fd	VCCEX	A+	(800) 858-8850	21.81	A- /9.1	28.55 /83	8.67 /84	12.48 /79	B- / 7.0	36	5
GR	BlackRock Large Cap Value Inv A	MDLVX	A+	(800) 441-7762	26.38	A- /9.1	30.54 /87	9.30 /89	12.28 /77	C+ / 6.9	50	18
GR	QS S&P 500 Index A	SBSPX	A+	(877) 534-4627	23.09	A- /9.1	24.31 /71	10.01 /93	13.38 /88	C+ / 6.9	67	N/A
GR	T Rowe Price Total Eq Mkt Index	POMIX	A+	(800) 638-5660	26.79	A- /9.1	26.21 /77	9.76 /92	13.79 /91	C+ / 6.8	61	9
GR	Vanguard Tot Stk Mkt Idx Inv	VTSMX	A+	(800) 662-7447	59.25	A- /9.1	26.14 /77	9.74 /92	13.67 /90	C+ / 6.8	62	23
GR	TIAA-CREF Equity Index Retire	TIQRX	A+	(800) 842-2252	17.79	A- /9.1	25.95 /76	9.62 /91	13.54 /89	C+ / 6.6	60	12
GR	Northern Large Cap Value	NOLVX	A+	(800) 595-9111	15.40	A- /9.1	29.82 /86	8.74 /85	12.10 /75	C+ / 6.6	50	2
GR	Dean Mid Cap Value	DALCX	A+	(888) 899-8343	19.02	A- /9.0	27.76 /81	9.63 /91	12.96 /83	B- / 7.5	78	9
GR	Bridgeway Blue Chip 35 Index	BRLIX	A+	(800) 661-3550	13.47	A- /9.0	23.49 /68	10.57 /96	13.42 /88	B- / 7.2	74	20
GR	SunAmerica VAL Co II Soc Resp	VCSRX	A+	(800) 858-8850	20.96	A- /9.0	23.59 /68	10.42 /95	14.27 /95	B- / 7.0	69	5
GR	Wilshire 5000 Index Inv	WFIVX	A+	(888) 200-6796	19.89	A- /9.0	25.58 /75	9.54 /91	13.24 /86	C+ / 6.8	60	18

● Denotes fund is closed to new investors

Data as of February 28, 2017

Fund Type	Fund Name	Ticker Symbol	Overall Investment Rating	Phone	Net Asset Value As of 2/28/17	Perform- ance Rating/Pts	Annualized Total Return Through 2/28/17			Risk Rating/Pts	Mgr. Quality Pct	Mgr. Tenure (Years)
							1Yr / Pct	3Yr / Pct	5Yr / Pct			
GI	Dodge & Cox Stk Fund	DODGX	A+	(800) 621-3979	194.15	A+ /9.8	38.12 /96	10.05 /94	15.91 /98	C+ / 6.1	51	25
GI	Harbor Large Cap Value Inv	HILVX	A+	(800) 422-1050	13.54	A+ /9.7	30.74 /88	10.76 /97	14.96 /97	C+ / 6.2	73	5
GI	JPMorgan Tax Aware Equity I	JPDEX	A+	(800) 480-4111	31.17	A /9.5	27.30 /80	10.29 /95	14.32 /95	C+ / 6.0	59	9
GI	American Century VP Value II	AVPVX	A+	(800) 345-6488	10.82	A /9.4	29.78 /86	10.28 /95	13.56 /89	B- / 7.1	76	21
GI	Fidelity Growth and Income	FGRIX	A+	(800) 544-8544	34.36	A /9.4	30.09 /87	9.51 /90	13.63 /90	C+ / 6.5	49	6
GI	SunAmerica VAL Co I Growth & Inc	VCGAX	A+	(800) 858-8850	20.23	A /9.3	25.74 /75	10.00 /93	12.80 /82	C+ / 6.5	66	4
GI	Fidelity Total Mkt Idx F	FFSMX	A+	(800) 544-8544	68.21	A- /9.2	26.33 /77	9.87 /93	13.79 /92	B- / 7.7	63	13
GI	Voya Russell Large Cap Index Adv	IRLIX	A+	(800) 992-0180	18.14	A- /9.1	24.03 /70	10.06 /94	13.15 /85	B- / 7.3	68	5
GI	Fidelity Value Discovery Fd	FVDFX	A+	(800) 544-8544	27.15	A- /9.1	24.60 /72	9.51 /90	13.96 /93	B- / 7.0	72	5
GI	Payden Equity Income Investor	PYVLX	A+	(888) 409-8007	15.97	B+ /8.8	21.41 /59	10.75 /97	12.48 /79	B- / 7.5	86	N/A
GI	Wright Major Blue Chip Equities	WQCEX	A+	(800) 232-0013	19.64	B+ /8.4	22.77 /66	8.38 /82	10.29 /61	B- / 7.1	40	8
GI	Vanguard Cons Stap Idx Adm	VCSAX	A+	(800) 662-7447	69.91	B /8.2	12.06 /18	11.96 /98	13.84 /92	B- / 7.6	95	7
GI	BNY Mellon Income Stock M	MPISX	A	(800) 645-6561	9.35	A+ /9.7	28.79 /83	11.08 /97	14.79 /96	C / 5.3	79	6
GI	Vanguard Growth & Income Inv	VQNPX	A	(800) 662-7447	43.59	A- /9.2	24.12 /70	10.71 /96	14.19 /94	C+ / 6.1	76	6
GI	Commerce Value	CFVLX	A	(800) 995-6365	32.67	A- /9.2	25.71 /75	10.62 /96	13.93 /93	C+ / 6.0	83	13
GI	Fort Pitt Capital Total Return Fd	FPCGX	A	(800) 471-5827	23.04	A- /9.1	28.22 /82	9.49 /90	11.75 /72	C+ / 6.3	64	16
GI	Schwab 1000 Index Fund	SNXFX	A	(800) 407-0256	56.81	A- /9.1	25.06 /73	9.83 /92	13.52 /89	C+ / 6.3	65	5
GI	T Rowe Price Instl Lg Cap Val	TILCX	A	(800) 638-5660	21.90	A- /9.1	27.90 /81	9.61 /91	14.13 /94	C+ / 6.2	56	13
GI	Homestead Value	HOVLX	A	(800) 258-3030	50.24	A- /9.0	25.43 /75	9.52 /90	13.56 /89	C+ / 6.1	46	18
GI	Goldman Sachs LC Val Insights A	GCVAX	A	(800) 526-7384	19.64	B+ /8.7	30.39 /87	9.36 /89	13.75 /91	C+ / 6.7	51	6
GI	Queens Road Value Fund	QRVLX	A	(800) 595-3088	21.41	B /8.2	22.87 /66	8.44 /82	11.92 /74	B- / 7.3	77	13
GI	Lazard US Eqty Concentrated	LEVOX	A	(800) 821-6474	14.99	B /8.2	17.78 /42	11.61 /98	14.41 /95	B- / 7.1	84	6
GI	● Chestnut Street Exchange	CHNTX	A	(800) 441-7762	609.61	B /8.0	22.49 /64	8.58 /84	12.48 /79	B- / 7.1	49	4
GI	Sterling Capital Beh LC Val Eq A	BBTGX	A	(800) 228-1872	19.83	B /7.9	26.14 /77	8.48 /83	11.66 /71	B- / 7.2	47	4
GI	Matthew 25 Fund	MXXVX	A-	(888) 625-3863	31.27	A+ /9.8	44.67 /98	8.33 /76	14.32 /95	C / 4.9	27	22
GI	UBS US Large Cap Eq A	BNEQX	A-	(888) 793-8637	30.15	A /9.3	31.98 /90	9.91 /93	13.11 /85	C / 5.4	44	23
GI	TIAA-CREF Enhanced LCG Idx	TLIIX	A-	(800) 842-2252	12.01	A /9.3	22.76 /66	10.62 /96	13.07 /85	C / 5.4	70	3
GI	MainStay US Eqty Opportunities C	MYCCX	A-	(800) 624-6782	8.55	A /9.3	23.02 /67	10.83 /97	14.53 /96	C / 5.3	75	10
GI	Guggenheim Large Cap Value A	SECIX	A-	(800) 820-0888	45.45	A- /9.1	33.71 /92	8.83 /86	12.58 /80	C+ / 5.7	54	2
GI	Hotchkis and Wiley Large Cap Val	HWLAX	A-	(866) 493-8637	29.79	A- /9.0	36.27 /95	8.32 /81	14.14 /94	C+ / 6.0	21	29
GI	Delaware Large Cap Value Eqty	DPDEX	A-	(800) 523-1918	27.57	A- /9.0	24.33 /71	10.66 /96	14.44 /95	C+ / 6.0	81	11
GI	VY Invesco ComStock Adv	IVKAX	A-	(800) 992-0180	17.92	B+ /8.9	32.99 /92	7.38 /75	12.53 /79	C+ / 6.1	20	15
GI	SunAmerica VAL Co I Brcap Val	VBCVX	A-	(800) 858-8850	15.59	B+ /8.7	28.26 /82	7.91 /78	12.78 /82	C+ / 6.1	40	5
GI	Lord Abbett Affiliated A	LAFFX	A-	(888) 522-2388	16.06	B+ /8.6	28.38 /82	9.71 /92	13.02 /84	C+ / 6.1	68	5
GI	Goldman Sachs US Eqty Insights A	GSSQX	A-	(800) 526-7384	44.40	B+ /8.5	26.62 /78	9.72 /92	13.82 /92	C+ / 6.5	59	4
GI	Nationwide A	NWFAX	A-	(800) 848-0920	24.30	B+ /8.4	25.97 /76	9.82 /92	12.71 /81	C+ / 6.5	63	4
GI	Transamerica Prt Large Core	DVGIX	A-	(888) 233-4339	35.46	B /8.2	22.39 /64	8.48 /83	13.16 /86	C+ / 6.7	35	13
GI	Walden Equity	WSEFX	A-	(800) 282-8782	19.82	B /8.2	22.46 /64	8.98 /87	11.25 /68	C+ / 6.5	62	7
GI	JPMorgan Growth and Income A	VGRIX	A-	(800) 480-4111	46.82	B /8.2	26.58 /78	9.69 /92	14.05 /94	C+ / 6.4	63	15
GI	Cullen High Dividend Equity Retail	CHDEX	A-	(877) 485-8586	18.22	B /8.1	21.37 /59	8.99 /87	11.38 /69	C+ / 6.9	72	14
GI	JPMorgan Value Advtg A	JVAAX	A-	(800) 480-4111	33.35	B /8.1	28.16 /82	8.69 /85	13.46 /88	C+ / 6.6	61	12
GI	Value Line Mid Cap Focused Inv	VLIFX	A-	(800) 243-2729	17.32	B /7.9	22.60 /65	8.75 /85	12.36 /78	B- / 7.0	76	8
GI	Columbia Disciplined Core A	AQEAX	A-	(800) 345-6611	10.81	B /7.6	21.22 /58	9.90 /93	12.93 /83	B- / 7.2	65	7
GI	● Vanguard Dividend Growth Inv	VDIGX	A-	(800) 662-7447	24.80	B- /7.4	16.84 /38	9.22 /88	12.50 /79	B- / 7.4	75	11
GI	Dreyfus Disciplined Stock Fund	DDSTX	B+	(800) 645-6561	36.32	A /9.5	28.22 /82	9.82 /92	12.56 /80	C / 4.8	56	2
GI	Invesco Growth and Income A	ACGIX	B+	(800) 959-4246	27.29	A /9.3	35.33 /94	9.44 /90	13.72 /91	C / 4.8	53	18
GI	USAA Growth & Income Fund	USGRX	B+	(800) 382-8722	23.18	A- /9.2	28.32 /82	9.00 /87	12.58 /80	C / 5.0	43	11
GI	Elfun Trusts	ELFNX	B+	(800) 843-2639	57.89	A- /9.2	24.44 /71	9.83 /92	14.20 /94	C / 4.7	46	29
GI	Voya US Stock Index Svc 2	ISIPX	B+	(800) 992-0180	14.33	A- /9.0	24.21 /71	9.89 /93	13.25 /86	C / 5.5	66	5
GI	SunAmerica VAL Co I Dividend Val	VCIGX	B+	(800) 858-8850	11.95	B+ /8.9	24.78 /73	9.96 /93	12.72 /81	C / 5.4	76	7
GI	Federated MDT Large Cap Value	FMSTX	B+	(800) 341-7400	28.32	B+ /8.8	27.49 /80	8.67 /84	14.48 /95	C+ / 5.6	47	8
GI	Cohen & Steers Dividend Value A	DVFAX	B+	(800) 330-7348	15.50	B+ /8.7	28.81 /84	9.04 /87	12.82 /82	C / 5.2	52	13

● Denotes fund is closed to new investors

Fund Type	Fund Name	Ticker Symbol	Overall Investment Rating	Phone	Net Asset Value As of 2/28/17	Performance Rating/Pts	Annualized Total Return Through 2/28/17			Risk Rating/Pts	Mgr. Quality Pct	Mgr. Tenure (Years)
	99 Pct = Best 0 Pct = Worst						1Yr / Pct	3Yr / Pct	5Yr / Pct			
HL	Fidelity Select Health Care Srvcs	FSHCX	A	(800) 544-8888	89.93	A+ /9.6	19.71 /51	12.48 /98	14.53 /96	C+ / 6.0	93	5
HL	Vanguard HealthCare Index Adm	VHCIX	B+	(800) 662-7447	69.30	B /7.9	17.25 /39	9.61 /91	17.92 /99	C+ / 6.4	56	2
HL	Oak Assoc-Live Oak Health	LOGSX	B-	(888) 462-5386	19.84	B /7.9	16.12 /35	10.12 /94	15.89 /98	C / 5.0	79	16
HL	T Rowe Price Health Sciences	PRHSX	C+	(800) 638-5660	66.31	B+ /8.5	17.10 /39	10.06 /94	21.39 /99	C- / 3.6	55	1
HL	BlackRock Health Sci Opps Inv A	SHSAX	C+	(800) 441-7762	49.07	B- /7.5	18.19 /44	10.40 /95	19.09 /99	C / 4.3	68	14
HL	Vanguard Health Care Inv	VGHCX	C+	(800) 662-7447	203.56	B- /7.2	12.33 /19	9.34 /89	18.10 /99	C / 4.7	68	9
HL	Alger Health Sciences Fund A	AHSAX	C	(800) 254-3796	21.45	A+ /9.9	37.94 /96	8.87 /86	14.82 /96	E+ / 0.6	21	12
HL	SunAmerica VAL Co I Health Sci	VCHSX	C	(800) 858-8850	19.14	B+ /8.3	16.86 /38	9.78 /92	21.09 /99	C- / 3.0	52	1
HL	Hartford Healthcare A	HGHAX	C	(888) 843-7824	32.55	B /8.0	20.40 /54	9.64 /91	19.14 /99	C- / 3.2	43	17
HL	Schwab Health Care	SWHFX	C	(800) 407-0256	23.33	C+ /6.7	13.75 /24	8.46 /83	16.51 /98	C- / 3.8	52	5
HL	Saratoga Adv Tr-Health & Biotech	SHPAX	C	(800) 807-3863	27.02	C /5.5	14.48 /28	8.78 /85	14.65 /96	C / 5.1	66	12
HL	Fidelity Select Health Care	FSPHX	C-	(800) 544-8888	208.91	B- /7.0	16.43 /36	7.52 /76	20.06 /99	C- / 3.4	21	9
HL	Delaware Healthcare Fund A	DLHAX	C-	(800) 523-1918	19.19	C+ /6.3	19.90 /51	7.80 /77	17.14 /98	C- / 4.2	31	10
HL	Fidelity Adv Health Care A	FACDX	C-	(800) 522-7297	38.80	C+ /5.7	15.86 /34	7.23 /73	19.51 /99	C- / 3.6	21	9
HL	J Hancock VIT Hlth Sciences I	JEHSX	D+	(800) 257-3336	24.48	B+ /8.3	16.79 /38	9.81 /92	21.15 /99	E+ / 0.7	52	1
HL	ICON Healthcare S	ICHCX	D+	(800) 764-0442	15.86	B /7.8	19.96 /52	9.08 /87	17.52 /98	D- / 1.1	59	4
HL	AllianzGI Health Sciences A	RAGHX	D+	(800) 988-8380	29.62	C+ /6.1	16.52 /36	8.29 /81	15.09 /97	D+ / 2.5	40	12
HL	● Prudential Jennison Health Sci A	PHLAX	D	(800) 225-1852	41.22	B- /7.0	23.42 /68	5.97 /64	19.39 /99	E+ / 0.9	3	18
HL	Deutsche Health and Wellness A	SUHAX	D	(800) 728-3337	34.72	C /4.6	13.39 /23	6.55 /69	16.32 /98	C- / 3.2	16	16
HL	Rydex Health Care A	RYHEX	D	(800) 820-0888	25.74	C /4.3	14.08 /26	5.71 /62	14.61 /96	C- / 3.6	11	19
HL	Fidelity Select Biotech Port	FBIOX	D-	(800) 544-8888	203.21	B- /7.0	29.67 /86	3.91 /42	22.19 /99	E- / 0.1	0	12
HL	● Franklin Biotechnology Discvry A	FBDIX	D-	(800) 342-5236	147.85	C+ /6.4	30.89 /88	3.79 /40	20.85 /99	E+ / 0.7	1	20
HL	Putnam Global Health Care Fund A	PHSTX	D-	(800) 225-1581	54.64	C- /3.9	10.45 /13	6.61 /69	16.37 /98	C- / 3.4	21	5
HL	Kinetics Medical Advisor A	KRXAX	D-	(800) 930-3828	27.05	D /2.0	13.07 /22	2.91 /31	13.28 /87	C- / 4.2	4	16
HL	Rydex Biotechnology A	RYBOX	E+	(800) 820-0888	74.87	C- /3.9	21.19 /58	2.91 /31	19.16 /99	D / 1.9	0	19
HL	Invesco Global Health Care A	GGHCX	E+	(800) 959-4246	36.23	C- /3.1	15.02 /30	3.47 /37	13.69 /91	D+ / 2.8	3	N/A
HL	Fidelity Adv Biotechnology A	FBTAX	E	(800) 522-7297	23.05	C /4.9	26.09 /76	3.05 /32	20.98 /99	E- / 0.1	0	12
HL	Eaton Vance WW Health Sciences	ETHSX	E	(800) 262-1122	9.89	D /1.9	6.71 / 5	4.24 /46	15.20 /97	D+ / 2.6	7	1
HL	Fidelity Select Pharmaceuticals	FPHAX	E	(800) 544-8888	18.11	D- /1.3	0.57 / 2	2.30 /26	13.13 /85	C- / 3.8	6	4
HL	Highland Long/Short Healthcare A	HHCAX	E	(877) 665-1287	11.17	E- /0.0	-2.62 / 1	-7.74 / 1	1.55 / 7	C / 4.9	2	7

Fund Type	Fund Name	Ticker Symbol	Overall Investment Rating	Phone	Net Asset Value As of 2/28/17	Perform-ance Rating/Pts	Annualized Total Return Through 2/28/17			Risk Rating/Pts	Mgr. Quality Pct	Mgr. Tenure (Years)
							1Yr / Pct	3Yr / Pct	5Yr / Pct			
IN	Vanguard High Div Yield Index Inv	VHDYX	A+	(800) 662-7447	31.07	A /9.4	23.89 /69	11.43 /98	13.95 /93	B- / 7.4	85	1
IN	FAM Equity-Income Inv	FAMEX	A+	(800) 932-3271	27.78	A /9.3	26.90 /79	10.37 /95	13.06 /84	C+ / 6.8	84	21
IN	DFA Tax-Managed US Eq Inst	DTMEX	A+	(800) 984-9472	25.69	A- /9.2	26.02 /76	9.84 /92	13.76 /91	C+ / 6.9	63	5
IN	Vanguard Russell 3000 Index Inst	VRTTX	A+	(800) 662-7447	210.62	A- /9.2	26.06 /76	9.83 /92	13.76 /91	C+ / 6.8	63	2
IN	Vanguard Equity Income Inv	VEIPX	A+	(800) 662-7447	34.09	A- /9.0	23.50 /68	10.38 /95	13.47 /89	C+ / 6.9	80	14
IN	DFA US Core Equity 1 Ptf Inst	DFEOX	A+	(800) 984-9472	20.25	A- /9.0	27.39 /80	9.13 /88	13.82 /92	C+ / 6.7	52	12
IN	Fidelity Equity Dividend Income	FEQTX	A+	(800) 544-8544	27.77	B+ /8.7	25.33 /74	9.46 /90	12.62 /80	C+ / 6.9	71	6
IN	SEI Inst Inv Managed Vol Fund A	SVYAX	A	(800) 342-5734	14.68	A- /9.0	18.87 /46	11.64 /98	14.82 /96	C+ / 6.3	94	8
IN	DFA US Core Equity 2 Ptf Inst	DFQTX	A	(800) 984-9472	19.42	B+ /8.9	28.65 /83	8.54 /83	13.75 /91	C+ / 6.4	41	5
IN	AT Disciplined Equity Institutional	AWEIX	A	(855) 328-3863	17.24	B+ /8.8	21.99 /62	10.37 /95	13.34 /87	C+ / 6.6	71	7
IN	T Rowe Price Dividend Growth	PRDGX	A	(800) 638-5660	38.96	B+ /8.4	21.49 /60	10.20 /94	13.47 /89	C+ / 6.7	77	17
IN	JPMorgan Equity Income A	OIEIX	A	(800) 480-4111	15.58	B /7.9	24.15 /70	9.63 /91	13.01 /84	B- / 7.2	74	13
IN	CNR Dividend and Income N	RIMHX	A	(888) 889-0799	41.29	B /7.8	17.73 /42	9.93 /93	10.84 /64	B- / 7.4	92	14
IN	ICON Equity Income A	IEQAX	A	(800) 764-0442	17.08	B /7.8	24.92 /73	9.34 /89	11.03 /66	B- / 7.3	75	15
IN	Copley	COPLX	A	(800) 424-8570	82.86	B /7.6	15.81 /33	9.43 /90	10.54 /62	B- / 7.5	95	39
IN	Johnson Enhanced Return	JENHX	A-	(800) 541-0170	17.27	A /9.5	25.81 /76	10.94 /97	14.50 /96	C / 5.3	75	12
IN	Pioneer Equity Income A	PEQIX	A-	(800) 225-6292	34.03	A- /9.0	27.63 /81	11.15 /97	13.41 /88	C+ / 5.9	83	27
IN	DFA U.S. Vector Equity Port Inst	DFVEX	A-	(800) 984-9472	18.06	A- /9.0	32.64 /91	7.85 /78	13.69 /91	C+ / 5.8	28	5
IN	Fidelity Strategic Advisers Core	FCSAX	A-	(800) 544-8544	16.80	B+ /8.8	25.22 /74	9.18 /88	13.02 /84	C+ / 6.0	54	8
IN	SEI Instl Mgd Tr-US Mgd Volty F	SVOAX	A-	(800) 342-5734	17.74	B /8.2	17.52 /41	10.60 /96	13.98 /93	C+ / 6.6	91	N/A
IN	Voya Large Cap Value Adv	IPEAX	A-	(800) 992-0180	12.36	B /8.1	26.78 /79	7.07 /72	11.27 /68	C+ / 6.6	35	6
IN	USAA Income Stock Fund	USISX	A-	(800) 382-8722	19.30	B /7.9	21.89 /62	8.82 /86	12.03 /75	C+ / 6.8	68	7
IN	Principal Equity Inc Fd A	PQIAX	A-	(800) 222-5852	29.17	B /7.6	25.09 /74	8.79 /85	11.83 /73	B- / 7.0	63	9
IN	RBB Free Market US Equity Inst	FMUEX	B+	(866) 780-0357	17.55	A- /9.0	31.82 /90	8.05 /79	13.74 /91	C / 5.4	33	N/A
IN	Manning & Napier Disciplined Val I	MNDFX	B+	(800) 466-3863	15.62	A- /9.0	25.39 /74	10.00 /93	12.05 /75	C / 5.2	77	9
IN	Fidelity Equity Income K	FEIKX	B+	(800) 544-8544	59.54	B+ /8.7	28.02 /82	8.59 /84	12.37 /78	C+ / 5.8	60	6
IN	● American Century Equity Income A	TWEAX	B+	(800) 345-6488	9.17	B+ /8.4	23.45 /68	11.35 /97	12.20 /76	C+ / 6.1	93	23
IN	T Rowe Price Equity Income	PRFDX	B+	(800) 638-5660	32.59	B+ /8.3	29.21 /85	7.54 /76	11.69 /71	C / 5.5	36	2
IN	GuideStone Value Equity Inv	GVEZX	B+	(888) 984-8433	21.92	B /8.1	26.35 /77	7.78 /77	12.76 /82	C+ / 5.9	32	16
IN	Transamerica Prt Large Value	DVEIX	B+	(888) 233-4339	29.75	B /7.9	24.88 /73	6.88 /71	12.54 /79	C+ / 6.6	20	8
IN	TCW Relative Value Dividend App	TGIGX	B+	(800) 386-3829	19.21	B /7.9	25.96 /76	7.89 /78	12.80 /82	C+ / 6.5	30	16
IN	Putnam Equity Income A	PEYAX	B+	(800) 225-1581	22.48	B /7.9	26.67 /78	8.89 /86	13.17 /86	C+ / 5.9	58	5
IN	Boston Trust Equity	BTEFX	B+	(800) 282-8782	21.08	B /7.8	20.94 /57	8.53 /83	10.93 /65	C+ / 6.6	67	14
IN	Dreyfus Equity Income A	DQIAX	B+	(800) 782-6620	18.45	B /7.8	23.95 /70	9.52 /90	12.27 /77	C+ / 6.4	79	6
IN	Nicholas Equity Income	NSEIX	B+	(800) 544-6547	20.74	B /7.8	23.05 /67	8.00 /79	12.41 /78	C+ / 6.2	42	6
IN	Hartford Equity Income A	HQIAX	B+	(888) 843-7824	19.31	B /7.7	24.89 /73	9.19 /88	12.58 /80	C+ / 6.3	67	14
IN	Parnassus Core Equity Inv	PRBLX	B+	(800) 999-3505	40.84	B- /7.5	18.38 /45	9.20 /88	13.90 /92	C+ / 6.7	75	16
IN	Neiman Large Cap Value NL	NEIMX	B+		26.17	B- /7.4	19.85 /51	7.70 /77	9.43 /54	C+ / 6.6	69	14
IN	Goldman Sachs US Eqty Divi & Pre	GSPAX	B+	(800) 526-7384	12.59	B- /7.2	21.54 /60	9.72 /92	11.19 /67	C+ / 6.9	79	7
IN	PIMCO RAE Fundamental PLUS A	PIXAX	B	(800) 426-0107	6.98	A- /9.1	33.46 /92	8.71 /85	14.87 /97	C / 4.3	31	3
IN	GMO Quality Equity III	GQETX	B		22.05	B+ /8.7	20.25 /53	10.24 /95	12.26 /77	C / 4.4	80	13
IN	Vanguard Extended Market Index	VEXMX	B	(800) 662-7447	76.11	B+ /8.4	32.49 /91	6.77 /70	12.97 /83	C / 5.2	16	20
IN	GMO US Equity Allocation III	GMUEX	B		15.14	B+ /8.4	23.59 /69	9.16 /88	12.30 /77	C / 5.1	56	4
IN	AMG River Road Div ACV N	ARDEX	B	(800) 548-4539	12.69	B+ /8.3	23.63 /69	9.11 /87	12.32 /77	C / 5.3	70	12
IN	BlackRock Eq Dividend Inv A	MDDVX	B	(800) 441-7762	23.33	B+ /8.3	26.94 /79	9.63 /91	11.44 /69	C / 5.2	70	16
IN	J Hancock Eqty-Inc NAV		B	(800) 257-3336	19.86	B /8.2	28.86 /84	7.43 /75	11.64 /71	C / 5.0	34	2
IN	Nuveen Dividend Value A	FFEIX	B	(800) 257-8787	15.00	B /8.2	30.29 /87	8.37 /82	12.02 /74	C / 4.9	49	5
IN	Columbia Diversified Equity Inc A	INDZX	B	(800) 345-6611	13.90	B /8.1	28.07 /82	9.06 /87	12.32 /77	C / 5.0	54	4
IN	Nationwide HighMark LC Core Eq	NWGHX	B	(800) 848-0920	13.27	B /7.8	24.72 /72	9.02 /87	12.47 /79	C+ / 5.7	52	9
IN	Invesco VI Equity and Income II	UEIIX	B	(800) 959-4246	18.22	B /7.6	25.40 /75	7.31 /74	10.75 /64	C / 5.5	66	14
IN	Fidelity Adv Equity Income A	FEIAX	B	(800) 522-7297	33.18	B- /7.3	27.54 /81	8.04 /79	11.83 /73	C+ / 5.8	52	6
IN	State Farm Equity A	SNEAX	B	(800) 447-4930	9.78	B- /7.1	20.17 /53	8.91 /86	12.85 /82	C+ / 6.1	63	9

● Denotes fund is closed to new investors

Fund Type	Fund Name	Ticker Symbol	Overall Investment Rating	Phone	Net Asset Value As of 2/28/17	PERFORMANCE					RISK	FUND MGR	
	99 Pct = Best					Perform-ance Rating/Pts	Annualized Total Return Through 2/28/17				Risk Rating/Pts	Mgr. Quality Pct	Mgr. Tenure (Years)
	0 Pct = Worst						1Yr / Pct	3Yr / Pct	5Yr / Pct				
IX	Vanguard Instl Index Inst	VINIX	A+	(800) 662-7447	215.93	A /9.4	24.94 /73	10.61 /96	13.98 /93	B- / 7.1	74	17
IX	Fidelity 500 Index Inv	FUSEX	A+	(800) 544-8544	82.98	A /9.3	24.88 /73	10.54 /96	13.91 /92	B / 8.2	73	13
IX	Vanguard 500 Index Inv	VFINX	A+	(800) 662-7447	218.80	A /9.3	24.82 /73	10.48 /96	13.85 /92	B- / 7.1	73	26
IX	Northern Stock Index	NOSIX	A+	(800) 595-9111	28.53	A /9.3	24.83 /73	10.51 /96	13.88 /92	B- / 7.0	73	11
IX	Dreyfus Instl S&P 500 Stock Index	DSPIX	A+	(800) 645-6561	47.82	A /9.3	24.73 /72	10.42 /95	13.80 /92	B- / 7.0	72	15
IX	Schwab S&P 500 Index Fund	SWPPX	A+	(800) 407-0256	36.46	A /9.3	24.81 /73	10.52 /96	13.89 /92	C+ / 6.9	73	5
IX	T Rowe Price Equity Index 500	PREIX	A+	(800) 638-5660	63.64	A- /9.2	24.67 /72	10.35 /95	13.71 /91	B- / 7.1	71	9
IX	SS Inst S&P 500 Index Inv	SIDIX	A+	(800) 843-2639	22.32	A- /9.2	24.64 /72	10.41 /95	13.80 /92	B- / 7.1	72	20
IX	TIAA-CREF S&P 500 Idx Retire	TRSPX	A+	(800) 842-2252	26.18	A- /9.2	24.58 /72	10.30 /95	13.65 /90	B- / 7.0	71	12
IX	USAA S&P 500 Index Members	USSPX	A+	(800) 382-8722	33.68	A- /9.2	24.67 /72	10.35 /95	13.72 /91	B- / 7.0	71	11
IX	S&P 500 Index Direct	SPFIX	A+	(800) 955-9988	46.16	A- /9.1	24.14 /70	10.25 /95	13.60 /90	B- / 7.0	70	14
IX	GuideStone Equity Index Inv	GEQZX	A+	(888) 984-8433	26.09	A- /9.1	24.71 /72	10.13 /94	13.55 /89	B- / 7.0	68	1
IX	Columbia Large Cap Index A	NEIAX	A+	(800) 345-6611	45.16	A- /9.1	24.40 /71	10.15 /94	13.51 /89	B- / 7.0	69	6
IX	Principal LgCap S&P 500 A	PLSAX	A+	(800) 222-5852	16.33	B+ /8.9	24.38 /71	10.08 /94	13.39 /88	B- / 7.0	68	6
IX	PNC S&P 500 Index A	PIIAX	A+	(800) 551-2145	17.63	B+ /8.7	24.24 /71	10.01 /93	13.37 /88	C+ / 6.9	68	12
IX	SEI Instl Managed Tr-S&P 500 Idx	SSPIX	A	(800) 342-5734	56.41	A- /9.1	24.41 /71	10.19 /94	13.55 /89	C+ / 6.3	70	6
IX	● Nuveen Equity Index A	FAEIX	A	(800) 257-8787	27.92	A- /9.0	24.21 /71	9.98 /93	13.31 /87	C+ / 6.1	68	17
IX	Prudential QMA Stock Index A	PSIAX	A	(800) 225-1852	48.07	B+ /8.6	24.30 /71	10.09 /94	13.43 /88	C+ / 6.5	69	25
IX	Invesco S&P 500 Index A	SPIAX	A	(800) 959-4246	25.56	B /8.2	24.26 /71	9.99 /93	13.36 /87	B- / 7.1	68	7
IX	Dreyfus S&P 500 Index Fund	PEOPX	A-	(800) 645-6561	51.52	A- /9.1	24.34 /71	10.08 /94	13.46 /88	C+ / 5.7	68	17
IX	Deutsche S&P 500 Index A	SXPAX	A-	(800) 728-3337	28.25	B+ /8.3	24.19 /71	9.92 /93	13.26 /86	C+ / 6.6	66	10
IX	Victory S&P 500 Index A	MUXAX	B+	(800) 539-3863	21.72	B+ /8.7	24.38 /71	10.00 /93	13.30 /87	C / 5.3	68	2
IX	Wells Fargo Index A	WFILX	B+	(800) 222-8222	65.25	B /8.2	24.42 /71	10.09 /94	13.43 /88	C+ / 6.0	69	4
IX	Nationwide S&P 500 Index A	GRMAX	B+	(800) 848-0920	14.92	B /8.1	24.28 /71	10.00 /93	13.36 /87	C+ / 5.6	67	5
IX	Rydex S&P 500 A	RYSOX	B+	(800) 820-0888	45.53	B- /7.4	22.87 /66	8.80 /85	12.14 /75	B- / 7.0	54	19
IX	PIMCO StocksPLUS Absolute	PTOAX	B	(800) 426-0107	10.78	A+ /9.6	31.96 /90	10.24 /95	14.72 /96	C- / 3.8	44	3
IX	PIMCO StocksPLUS A	PSPAX	B-	(800) 426-0107	9.36	B+ /8.8	26.67 /78	9.93 /93	14.33 /95	C- / 3.9	60	3
IX	JPMorgan Equity Index A	OGEAX	B-	(800) 480-4111	36.55	B+ /8.3	24.38 /71	10.12 /94	13.48 /89	C / 4.4	69	13
IX	State Farm Equity & Bond Premier	SLBAX	B-	(800) 447-4930	11.59	C- /4.0	12.51 /20	6.54 /69	8.59 /47	B / 8.9	79	N/A
IX	Mutual of America Inst Eqty Idx	MAEQX	C	(800) 914-8716	10.68	A /9.3	24.82 /73	10.52 /96	13.91 /92	D / 1.6	73	3
IX	Meeder Quantex Retail	FLCGX	C	(800) 325-3539	33.80	B- /7.5	30.55 /87	7.17 /73	13.14 /85	C- / 3.4	17	12
IX	Russell Investments US Core Eq A	RSQAX	C-	(800) 832-6688	32.30	B /7.6	25.55 /75	8.79 /85	12.48 /79	D+ / 2.7	49	6
IX	Franklin Global Real Estate A	FGRRX	D+	(800) 342-5236	8.77	D+ /2.3	9.68 /11	5.38 /58	7.22 /36	C+ / 6.5	51	7
IX	Forester Value N	FVALX	D+	(800) 388-0365	11.29	E- /0.2	-7.22 / 0	-2.64 / 5	-0.76 / 4	B / 8.4	34	18
IX	Absolute Credit Opportunities Inst	AOFOX	D	(800) 754-8757	9.80	D- /1.0	1.56 / 2	1.63 /22	-0.26 / 4	C+ / 6.9	87	9

Fund Type	Fund Name	Ticker Symbol	Overall Investment Rating	Phone	Net Asset Value As of 2/28/17	Performance Rating/Pts	Annualized Total Return Through 2/28/17 1Yr / Pct	3Yr / Pct	5Yr / Pct	Risk Rating/Pts	Mgr. Quality Pct	Mgr. Tenure (Years)
MC	American Century VP Mid Cap Val	AVMTX	A+	(800) 345-6488	21.92	A+ /9.8	31.15 /88	12.76 /99	15.36 /97	C+ / 6.7	95	13
MC ●	Vanguard PRIMECAP Inv	VPMCX	A+	(800) 662-7447	112.93	A+ /9.7	28.77 /83	11.30 /97	16.64 /98	C+ / 6.1	92	32
MC	Vanguard S&P Mid-Cap 400 Value	VMFVX	A+	(800) 662-7447	228.02	A+ /9.7	35.40 /94	9.99 /93	14.45 /95	C+ / 6.1	71	2
MC	Harbor Mid Cap Value Inv	HIMVX	A+	(800) 422-1050	22.78	A /9.5	30.36 /87	9.25 /88	15.20 /97	C+ / 6.4	73	13
MC	Vanguard S&P Mid-Cap 400 Index	VSPMX	A+	(800) 662-7447	231.94	A /9.5	31.63 /89	9.57 /91	13.77 /91	C+ / 6.1	74	4
MC	Vanguard Mega Cap Index Inst	VMCTX	A+	(800) 662-7447	159.47	A /9.4	25.12 /74	10.64 /96	13.93 /93	B- / 7.1	91	2
MC	Vanguard Mid-Cap Value Index Inv	VMVIX	A+	(800) 662-7447	40.40	A /9.3	29.04 /84	9.74 /92	14.68 /96	C+ / 6.5	82	11
MC	Rydex Mid Cap 1.5x Strgy A	RYAHX	A	(800) 820-0888	80.51	A+ /9.9	47.64 /99	11.80 /98	18.21 /99	C / 5.2	40	16
MC	American Century NT Md Cp Val	ACLMX	A	(800) 345-6488	13.87	A+ /9.8	31.72 /89	13.10 /99	15.74 /98	C / 5.4	95	11
MC	PRIMECAP Odyssey Growth Fd	POGRX	A	(800) 729-2307	30.75	A /9.5	29.60 /85	9.79 /93	16.02 /98	C+ / 5.9	75	13
MC	Prudential QMA Mid-Cap Value A	SPRAX	A	(800) 225-1852	22.16	A /9.5	34.07 /93	9.86 /93	14.47 /95	C+ / 5.6	78	3
MC	Parnassus Mid Cap	PARMX	A	(800) 999-3505	30.12	B+ /8.7	24.41 /71	10.19 /94	13.16 /86	C+ / 6.8	90	9
MC	Transamerica Prt Mid Value	DVMVX	A	(888) 233-4339	22.66	B+ /8.6	23.53 /68	9.65 /91	14.15 /94	C+ / 6.8	86	8
MC	Government Street Mid-Cap Fund	GVMCX	A	(866) 738-1125	24.32	B+ /8.5	23.74 /69	8.76 /85	12.15 /76	C+ / 6.7	81	14
MC	Westcore Mid-Cap Value Div Rtl	WTMCX	A-	(800) 392-2673	28.20	A+ /9.7	30.98 /88	11.72 /98	14.12 /94	C / 5.3	91	15
MC ●	American Century Mid Cap Val A	ACLAX	A-	(800) 345-6488	17.83	A+ /9.6	30.92 /88	12.53 /98	15.18 /97	C / 5.2	94	13
MC	Northern Midcap Index	NOMIX	A-	(800) 595-9111	18.66	A /9.4	31.51 /89	9.44 /90	13.65 /90	C / 5.2	72	11
MC ●	J Hancock Dsp Val Mid Cap A	JVMAX	A-	(800) 257-3336	21.74	A- /9.2	31.57 /89	10.77 /97	15.66 /98	C+ / 5.7	83	7
MC	Touchstone Mid Cap Value A	TCVAX	A-	(800) 543-0407	18.76	A- /9.1	32.30 /90	10.23 /95	13.95 /93	C+ / 5.9	85	3
MC	Vanguard Selected Value Inv	VASVX	A-	(800) 662-7447	30.33	A- /9.0	30.48 /87	7.53 /76	13.65 /90	C+ / 5.7	55	18
MC	Vanguard S&P Mid-Cap 400 Gro	VMFGX	A-	(800) 662-7447	234.84	B+ /8.8	27.38 /80	8.83 /86	12.89 /83	C+ / 5.9	73	2
MC	Fidelity Mid Cap Enhanced Index	FMEIX	A-	(800) 544-8544	14.77	B+ /8.4	24.85 /73	8.58 /84	14.14 /94	C+ / 6.2	74	10
MC	Vanguard Mid-Cap Index Inv	VIMSX	A-	(800) 662-7447	38.13	B+ /8.3	25.89 /76	8.43 /82	13.17 /86	C+ / 6.4	72	19
MC	ProFunds-Mid Cap Svc	MDPSX	A-	(888) 776-3637	74.13	B /7.6	28.10 /82	6.63 /69	10.67 /63	B- / 7.0	37	4
MC ●	Thrivent Mid Cap Stock A	AASCX	B+	(800) 847-4836	24.31	A+ /9.9	43.79 /98	12.41 /98	15.80 /98	C / 4.3	87	13
MC	Champlain Mid Cap Fund	CIPMX	B+	(866) 777-7818	16.02	A+ /9.8	33.89 /93	10.99 /97	14.03 /93	C / 4.7	88	13
MC	Oakmark Select Service	OARLX	B+	(800) 625-6275	43.77	A /9.5	36.50 /95	8.31 /81	14.04 /93	C / 4.9	70	21
MC ●	T Rowe Price Mid-Cap Value Fd	TRMCX	B+	(800) 638-5660	29.98	A /9.5	31.58 /89	10.35 /95	14.52 /96	C / 4.3	86	17
MC	J Hancock Mid Value Fund NAV		B+	(800) 257-3336	15.98	A /9.5	31.47 /89	10.25 /95	14.39 /95	C / 4.3	85	8
MC	SunAmerica VAL Co I Midcap Idx	VMIDX	B+	(800) 858-8850	26.47	A /9.4	31.50 /89	9.36 /89	13.52 /89	C / 4.8	71	5
MC	S&P MidCap Index Direct	SPMIX	B+	(800) 955-9988	25.63	A /9.4	31.19 /88	9.39 /90	13.47 /89	C / 4.3	72	14
MC	Columbia Mid Cap Index A	NTIAX	B+	(800) 345-6611	16.05	A /9.3	31.10 /88	9.12 /88	13.30 /87	C / 5.2	69	6
MC	Schwab Fundm US Small Co Index	SFSNX	B+	(800) 407-0256	14.50	A /9.3	33.63 /92	8.39 /82	13.70 /91	C / 5.0	45	5
MC ●	J Hancock VIT Mid Cap Index I	JECIX	B+	(800) 257-3336	22.23	A /9.3	31.04 /88	9.14 /88	13.36 /87	C / 4.8	69	4
MC	Dreyfus Midcap Index Inv	PESPX	B+	(800) 645-6561	36.54	A /9.3	31.11 /88	9.15 /88	13.31 /87	C / 4.4	69	17
MC ●	Nuveen Mid Cap Index A	FDXAX	B+	(800) 257-8787	18.90	A- /9.2	30.96 /88	8.95 /86	13.11 /85	C / 5.2	67	16
MC	Janus Aspen Perkins Mid Cp Val	JAMVX	B+	(800) 295-2687	17.34	A- /9.2	30.42 /87	9.12 /88	11.02 /66	C+ / 4.5	83	15
MC	Principal MidCp S&P 400 Idx R3	PMFMX	B+	(800) 222-5852	21.01	A- /9.1	30.64 /87	8.79 /85	12.96 /83	C / 5.2	65	6
MC	Voya VP Index Plus MidCap S	IPMSX	B+	(800) 992-0180	22.44	A- /9.1	30.07 /87	8.72 /85	13.05 /84	C / 4.7	68	11
MC	Vanguard Windsor-I Inv	VWNDX	B+	(800) 662-7447	21.68	A- /9.0	31.34 /89	7.92 /78	13.74 /91	C / 5.2	60	9
MC	Janus Aspen Enterprise Inst	JAAGX	B+	(800) 295-2687	63.02	A- /9.0	24.90 /73	10.73 /96	14.16 /94	C / 4.9	88	10
MC	Wells Fargo Spec Mid Cp VI A	WFPAX	B+	(800) 222-8222	36.31	B+ /8.8	30.19 /87	10.25 /95	15.42 /97	C / 5.4	86	8
MC	American Beacon MidCap Val A	ABMAX	B+	(800) 658-5811	15.78	B+ /8.7	33.72 /92	8.08 /80	13.62 /90	C / 5.3	51	13
MC	Quaker Mid-Cap Value A	QMCVX	B+	(800) 220-8888	28.28	B+ /8.6	34.22 /93	7.87 /78	11.42 /69	C+ / 5.7	52	9
MC ●	T Rowe Price Instl Mid-Cap Eq Gr	PMEGX	B+	(800) 638-5660	49.13	B+ /8.6	22.99 /67	9.93 /93	14.62 /96	C / 5.3	80	21
MC	ProFunds-Mid Cap Value Svc	MLPSX	B+	(888) 776-3637	67.11	B /8.2	31.66 /89	6.89 /71	11.20 /68	C+ / 5.8	33	4
MC	Nuveen Mid Cap Value A	FASEX	B+	(800) 257-8787	39.14	B /8.0	30.79 /88	8.32 /81	12.75 /81	C+ / 6.1	61	5
MC	Virtus Mid-Cap Core Fund A	VMACX	B+	(800) 243-1574	25.55	B /7.9	20.92 /57	11.04 /97	12.91 /83	C+ / 6.5	88	8
MC	Boston Trust Mid Cap	BTMFX	B+	(800) 282-8782	16.14	B /7.9	21.21 /58	8.90 /86	11.22 /68	C+ / 6.3	82	N/A
MC	Wells Fargo C&B MdCp Val A	CBMAX	B+	(800) 222-8222	32.67	B /7.7	30.82 /88	8.29 /81	13.86 /92	C+ / 6.9	59	19
MC	Dreyfus Active MidCap A	DNLDX	B+	(800) 782-6620	62.60	B- /7.4	20.94 /57	9.25 /88	13.84 /92	C+ / 6.6	77	5
MC	ClearBridge Small Cap A	LMSAX	B	(877) 534-4627	40.00	A+ /9.7	42.20 /98	10.15 /94	14.28 /95	C- / 3.8	67	6

● Denotes fund is closed to new investors

Fund Type	Fund Name	Ticker Symbol	Overall Investment Rating	Phone	Net Asset Value As of 2/28/17	Performance Rating/Pts	Annualized Total Return Through 2/28/17			Risk Rating/Pts	Mgr. Quality Pct	Mgr. Tenure (Years)
	99 Pct = Best 0 Pct = Worst						1Yr / Pct	3Yr / Pct	5Yr / Pct			
OT	Vanguard Industrials Index Adm	VINAX	A+	(800) 662-7447	64.22	A /9.5	29.81 /86	9.76 /92	14.72 /96	C+ / 6.7	51	2
OT	Lazard Global Listed Infr Open	GLFOX	A	(800) 821-6474	14.89	B+ /8.5	14.22 /26	11.33 /97	15.71 /98	B- / 7.0	97	8
OT	Davis Research Fund Class A	DRFAX	B-	(800) 279-0279	19.12	C+ /6.7	21.73 /61	7.96 /79	11.77 /72	B- / 7.3	54	16
OT	Pacific Financial Explorer Inst	PFGPX	C+	(888) 451-8734	10.71	C+ /5.9	20.34 /54	5.20 /56	10.49 /62	C+ / 6.1	14	10
OT	Putnam Global Consumer Fund A	PGCOX	C-	(800) 225-1581	19.20	C /5.1	17.97 /43	6.37 /67	11.81 /73	C / 4.8	25	9
OT	ICON Natural Resources S	ICBMX	D+	(800) 764-0442	14.33	C+ /5.9	33.76 /93	1.95 /24	6.81 /33	C- / 3.3	1	10
OT	Merk Abs Rtn Currency Investor	MABFX	D+	(866) 637-5386	9.06	E /0.5	3.31 / 3	-0.92 /10	0.10 / 5	B / 8.8	73	8
OT	ICON Consumer Discretionary S	ICCCX	D	(800) 764-0442	13.63	C- /3.3	9.01 / 9	4.72 /51	10.92 /65	C / 4.6	12	3
OT	Direxion Indexed Commodity Stg A	DXCTX	D-	(800) 851-0511	15.36	E- /0.1	4.63 / 4	-7.01 / 1	-6.14 / 1	C+ / 6.8	4	9
OT	Guggenheim Managed Futures	RYMTX	E+	(800) 820-0888	19.02	E- /0.2	-14.83 / 0	-0.85 /10	-2.03 / 3	C / 5.5	40	10
OT	Wells Fargo Endeavor Sel A	STAEX	E	(800) 222-8222	8.01	C /4.3	18.57 /45	4.98 /54	10.70 /63	E / 0.4	13	7
OT	Hartford Global Real Asset A	HRLAX	E	(888) 843-7824	8.95	E /0.3	21.63 /60	-4.28 / 3	-4.05 / 2	C / 4.5	1	7
OT	ALPS CoreComm Mgt CompComm	JCRAX	E	(866) 759-5679	7.61	E- /0.1	20.47 /55	-10.36 / 1	-8.36 / 1	C- / 3.6	0	7
OT	● MFS Commodity Strategy Fund A	MCSAX	E	(800) 225-2606	6.03	E- /0.0	15.28 /31	-12.27 / 0	-9.35 / 1	C- / 4.0	0	7
OT	Eaton Vance Commodity Strategy	EACSX	E	(800) 262-1122	5.52	E- /0.0	21.03 /57	-12.00 / 0	-9.76 / 1	C- / 3.8	0	2
OT	Russell Investments Comm Str A	RCSAX	E-	(800) 832-6688	5.61	E- /0.0	13.79 /25	-13.64 / 0	-10.93 / 0	D+ / 2.7	0	N/A
OT	Fidelity Srs Commodity Strat Fund	FCSSX	E-	(800) 544-8544	5.43	E- /0.0	15.29 /31	-13.60 / 0	-10.39 / 1	D+ / 2.5	0	8
OT	ProFunds-Rising Rates Opport Svc	RRPSX	E-	(888) 776-3637	38.97	E- /0.0	2.55 / 2	-12.25 / 0	-8.80 / 1	D+ / 2.5	0	8
OT	PIMCO CommoditiesPLUS	PCLAX	E-	(800) 426-0107	6.43	E- /0.0	29.76 /86	-14.64 / 0	-9.61 / 1	D+ / 2.3	0	7
OT	Rydex Commodities Strgy A	RYMEX	E-	(800) 820-0888	84.45	E- /0.0	17.88 /42	-22.76 / 0	-16.20 / 0	E+ / 0.7	0	12

| Fund Type | Fund Name | Ticker Symbol | Overall Investment Rating | Phone | Net Asset Value As of 2/28/17 | PERFORMANCE | | | | | RISK | FUND MGR | |
| | 99 Pct = Best 0 Pct = Worst | | | | | Perform-ance Rating/Pts | Annualized Total Return Through 2/28/17 | | | Risk Rating/Pts | Mgr. Quality Pct | Mgr. Tenure (Years) | |
							1Yr / Pct	3Yr / Pct	5Yr / Pct			
PM	Vanguard Materials Index Fd Adm	VMIAX	B-	(800) 662-7447	60.64	B /8.2	34.15 /93	6.21 /66	9.90 /58	C /4.7	97	2
PM	Fidelity Adv Materials A	FMFAX	D	(800) 522-7297	81.27	C /4.5	30.18 /87	2.10 /25	7.00 /35	C- /3.7	86	9
PM	US Global Inv World Prec Min	UNWPX	D-	(800) 873-8637	7.05	C+ /6.4	52.82 /99	2.89 /31	-11.93 / 0	E+ /0.7	98	28
PM	US Global Inv Gold & PMetals Fd	USERX	E+	(800) 873-8637	8.15	C /4.6	28.98 /84	3.17 /33	-9.81 / 1	E+ /0.7	98	28
PM	Gabelli Gold A	GLDAX	E-	(800) 422-3554	14.52	D+ /2.7	24.83 /73	2.66 /29	-10.34 / 1	E- /0.1	98	23
PM	Vanguard Prec Metals & Mining Inv	VGPMX	E-	(800) 662-7447	10.29	D /1.6	36.56 /95	-2.32 / 6	-12.39 / 0	E- /0.0	82	3
PM	Franklin Gold & Precious Metals A	FKRCX	E-	(800) 342-5236	17.66	D- /1.3	32.77 /91	-0.71 /10	-13.34 / 0	E+ /0.6	92	18
PM	Invesco Gold and Precious Mtls A	IGDAX	E-	(800) 959-4246	4.41	D- /1.1	31.79 /90	-1.32 / 8	-11.64 / 0	E- /0.1	90	4
PM	VanEck Intl Investors Gold A	INIVX	E-	(800) 826-1115	9.57	D- /1.1	34.35 /93	-1.57 / 8	-12.88 / 0	E- /0.0	91	19
PM	Oppenheimer Gold/Spec Min A	OPGSX	E-	(888) 470-0862	16.61	D- /1.0	32.91 /91	-1.87 / 7	-13.86 / 0	E- /0.2	89	20
PM	Fidelity Adv Gold A	FGDAX	E-	(800) 522-7297	20.54	E+ /0.7	19.97 /52	-1.19 / 9	-14.09 / 0	E- /0.1	92	10
PM	First Eagle Gold A	SGGDX	E-	(800) 334-2143	17.11	E /0.5	17.35 /40	-1.09 / 9	-11.21 / 0	E /0.5	90	4
PM	American Century Global Gold A	ACGGX	E-	(800) 345-6488	8.59	E /0.5	23.93 /70	-2.53 / 5	-14.15 / 0	E- /0.0	87	12
PM	OCM Gold Fund Investor	OCMGX	E-	(800) 628-9403	9.88	E /0.5	20.48 /55	-1.52 / 8	-12.52 / 0	E- /0.0	92	21
PM	USAA Precious Mtls&Minerals	USAGX	E-	(800) 382-8722	13.33	E /0.4	22.34 /64	-4.54 / 3	-15.58 / 0	E- /0.1	75	N/A
PM	Tocqueville Gold	TGLDX	E-	(800) 697-3863	37.00	E /0.4	21.27 /59	-3.48 / 4	-13.60 / 0	E- /0.0	79	20
PM	Midas Fund	MIDSX	E-	(800) 400-6432	1.26	E /0.4	32.63 /91	-6.67 / 2	-20.43 / 0	E- /0.0	40	15
PM	Wells Fargo Precious Mtls A	EKWAX	E-	(800) 222-8222	36.18	E /0.3	17.95 /43	-3.01 / 4	-13.51 / 0	E- /0.1	84	10
PM	Rydex Precious Metal A	RYMNX	E-	(800) 820-0888	30.04	E /0.3	27.60 /81	-4.91 / 2	-14.05 / 0	E- /0.0	74	24
PM	Deutsche Gold & Prec Metals Fund	SGDAX	E-	(800) 728-3337	6.82	E- /0.2	19.17 /48	-5.25 / 2	-15.57 / 0	E- /0.0	67	1
PM	ProFunds-Precious Metals Ultra	PMPSX	E-	(888) 776-3637	35.50	E- /0.0	15.79 /33	-17.10 / 0	-27.06 / 0	E- /0.0	1	4
PM	ProFunds Short Precious Metals	SPPSX	E-	(888) 776-3637	42.33	E- /0.0	-33.11 / 0	-14.04 / 0	-2.93 / 2	E- /0.0	0	4

● Denotes fund is closed to new investors

Fund Type	Fund Name	Ticker Symbol	Overall Investment Rating	Phone	Net Asset Value As of 2/28/17	Performance Rating/Pts	1Yr / Pct	3Yr / Pct	5Yr / Pct	Risk Rating/Pts	Mgr. Quality Pct	Mgr. Tenure (Years)
RE	Sterling Capital Stratton RE Inst	STMDX	A	(800) 228-1872	37.57	B /8.2	16.21 /35	11.67 /98	11.53 /70	B- / 7.1	75	2
RE	ProFunds-Real Est UltraSector Svc	REPSX	B+	(888) 776-3637	41.05	A- /9.0	23.19 /67	11.40 /98	12.03 /75	C / 5.0	14	4
RE	AMG Mgrs CenterSquare RE N	MRESX	B+	(800) 548-4539	11.23	B /7.8	14.99 /30	11.73 /98	11.34 /68	C+ / 6.1	70	13
RE	SA Real Estate Securities	SAREX	B+	(800) 366-7266	11.51	B- /7.1	15.27 /31	10.34 /95	10.43 /62	B- / 7.1	54	5
RE	TIAA-CREF Real Est Secs Retail	TCREX	B+	(800) 842-2252	15.41	B- /7.1	14.18 /26	10.26 /95	10.29 /61	C+ / 6.8	63	12
RE	Alpine Realty Inc and Growth Inst	AIGYX	B	(888) 785-5578	23.20	B+ /8.7	19.98 /52	11.98 /98	11.87 /73	C / 4.9	71	18
RE	Fidelity Adv Real Estate Income A	FRINX	B	(800) 522-7297	12.06	C /4.3	14.55 /28	7.14 /73	8.59 /47	B / 8.9	90	14
RE	Phocas Real Estate	PHREX	B-	(866) 746-2271	33.05	B /8.0	18.15 /44	11.12 /97	12.03 /75	C / 4.7	69	11
RE	DFA Real Estate Securities Ptf Inst	DFREX	B-	(800) 984-9472	35.61	B /7.8	16.15 /35	11.39 /98	11.38 /69	C / 5.0	66	5
RE	Vanguard REIT Index Inv	VGSIX	B-	(800) 662-7447	28.32	B /7.6	16.41 /36	10.86 /97	11.21 /68	C / 5.2	61	1
RE	Fidelity Real Estate Investment	FRESX	B-	(800) 522-7297	42.47	B- /7.5	14.24 /27	11.67 /98	11.37 /69	C / 5.5	70	20
RE	Salient Tactical Real Estate A	KSRAX	B-	(800) 999-6809	37.41	B /7.0	24.91 /73	9.70 /92	10.49 /62	C+ / 5.7	81	18
RE	Manning & Napier Real Estate S	MNREX	C+	(800) 466-3863	15.11	B+ /8.3	17.41 /40	11.55 /98	11.85 /73	C- / 4.2	78	8
RE	CGM Realty	CGMRX	C+	(800) 345-4048	31.49	B /8.1	29.73 /86	7.19 /73	8.26 /44	C- / 3.3	71	23
RE	Cohen & Steers Inst Realty Shrs	CSRIX	C+	(800) 330-7348	44.95	B /8.0	16.75 /37	11.43 /98	11.53 /70	C- / 3.9	72	10
RE	State Street Real Estate Sec VIS 1	SSRSX	C+	(800) 843-2639	12.76	B /8.0	15.76 /33	12.02 /98	11.76 /72	C- / 3.5	73	11
RE	Cohen & Steers Realty Shares	CSRSX	C+	(800) 330-7348	68.29	B /7.8	16.50 /36	11.21 /98	11.27 /68	C- / 3.9	69	10
RE	EII Realty Sec Inst	EIIRX	C+	(888) 323-8912	4.38	B /7.6	16.31 /35	10.87 /97	11.41 /69	C- / 4.0	70	13
RE	Lazard US Realty Equity Open	LREOX	C+	(800) 821-6474	20.38	B- /7.3	17.35 /40	9.96 /93	10.66 /63	C / 4.7	71	9
RE	J Hancock Real Estate Sec 1	JIREX	C+	(800) 257-3336	12.98	B- /7.3	13.84 /25	10.91 /97	10.90 /65	C- / 4.1	62	12
RE	SEI Instl Managed Tr-Real Est F	SETAX	C+	(800) 342-5734	17.87	B- /7.2	15.00 /30	10.89 /97	10.51 /62	C / 5.1	65	14
RE	Third Avenue Real Estate Value	TVRVX	C+	(800) 443-1021	31.91	C+ /6.7	26.00 /76	5.75 /62	10.49 /62	C+ / 5.9	65	19
RE	Universal Inst US Real Estate II	USRBX	C+	(800) 869-6397	21.74	C+ /6.6	13.45 /23	9.85 /93	9.88 /57	C+ / 5.8	59	20
RE	T Rowe Price Real Estate	TRREX	C+	(800) 638-5660	28.99	C+ /6.6	12.81 /21	10.47 /96	10.70 /63	C+ / 5.8	67	20
RE	Davis Real Estate A	RPFRX	C+	(800) 279-0279	39.75	C+ /6.5	16.31 /35	10.51 /96	9.62 /55	C / 5.4	68	15
RE	Principal Real Est Securities A	PRRAX	C+	(800) 222-5852	23.38	C+ /6.5	14.22 /27	11.09 /97	11.51 /70	C / 4.9	65	17
RE	Eaton Vance Real Estate Fund A	EAREX	C+	(800) 262-1122	14.01	C+ /6.2	12.19 /19	11.14 /97	10.60 /63	C / 5.5	70	11
RE	Schwab Global Real Estate Fund	SWASX	C+	(800) 407-0256	7.37	C /5.4	14.46 /28	7.18 /73	7.86 /41	B- / 7.0	57	5
RE	Cohen and Steers Real Estate Sec	CSEIX	C	(800) 330-7348	14.65	B+ /8.3	17.83 /42	13.31 /99	13.07 /84	C- / 3.1	85	11
RE	PIMCO RealEstate RlRetrn Str A	PETAX	C	(800) 426-0107	7.68	B /7.9	19.19 /48	12.44 /98	10.78 /64	C- / 3.1	55	10
RE	J Hancock Real Est Eq Nav		C	(800) 257-3336	10.41	C+ /6.6	12.64 /20	10.36 /95	10.57 /63	C / 4.7	65	11
RE	Natixis AEW Real Estate A	NRFAX	C	(800) 225-5478	16.42	C+ /6.1	13.45 /23	10.58 /96	10.55 /62	C / 5.2	60	17
RE	● Nuveen Real Estate Securities A	FREAX	C	(800) 257-8787	22.33	C+ /6.1	14.69 /28	10.56 /96	10.87 /65	C / 5.1	61	12
RE	VY Clarion Real Estate Adv	ICRPX	C	(800) 992-0180	36.05	C+ /6.0	12.31 /19	9.16 /88	9.67 /56	C / 5.3	39	15
RE	Commonwealth-Real Estate	CNREX	C	(888) 345-1898	15.55	C+ /5.8	18.70 /46	6.47 /68	8.25 /44	C / 5.4	58	13
RE	Columbia Real Estate Equity A	CREAX	C	(800) 345-6611	15.89	C+ /5.8	13.04 /22	10.37 /95	10.19 /60	C / 4.9	57	11
RE	Rydex Real Estate A	RYREX	C	(800) 820-0888	38.24	C+ /5.7	20.15 /53	7.55 /76	8.92 /50	C / 5.1	37	13
RE	Fidelity Adv Real Estate A	FHEAX	C	(800) 522-7297	23.04	C+ /5.7	13.76 /24	9.95 /93	10.43 /61	C / 4.9	50	13
RE	Franklin Real Estate Sec A	FREEX	C	(800) 342-5236	23.12	C+ /5.6	13.10 /22	10.23 /94	10.50 /62	C / 5.4	52	7
RE	Goldman Sachs Real Estate Sec A	GREAX	C	(800) 526-7384	18.88	C+ /5.6	13.05 /22	10.01 /93	10.29 /60	C / 5.3	58	7
RE	DFA Gl Real Estate Securities Port	DFGEX	C	(800) 984-9472	10.73	C /5.4	12.46 /20	8.21 /81	9.71 /56	C / 5.2	51	N/A
RE	MFS Global Real Estate A	MGLAX	C	(800) 225-2606	15.00	C /4.3	14.24 /27	7.77 /77	9.42 /54	C+ / 6.4	65	8
RE	AB Inst Global RealEst II	ARIIX	C	(800) 221-5672	10.60	C- /4.1	11.58 /16	6.31 /67	8.75 /48	C+ / 6.7	49	5
RE	J Hancock Glb Real Est Nav		C	(800) 257-3336	9.34	C- /4.0	10.70 /13	6.40 /67	8.60 /47	C+ / 6.6	38	11
RE	PACE Glb Real Est Sec Inv Cl A	PREAX	C	(888) 793-8637	7.46	C- /3.5	17.31 /40	5.79 /62	8.16 /43	B- / 7.2	29	8
RE	Salient Real Estate A	KREAX	C-	(800) 999-6809	12.35	B- /7.5	21.76 /61	11.19 /97	11.16 /67	D / 2.1	73	7
RE	Deutsche Real Est Secs A	RRRAX	C-	(800) 728-3337	20.83	C+ /6.2	13.74 /24	10.73 /96	10.70 /63	C- / 4.2	60	13
RE	Invesco Real Estate A	IARAX	C-	(800) 959-4246	21.64	C+ /6.2	15.74 /33	10.04 /93	10.20 /60	C- / 3.6	61	22
RE	Pioneer Real Estate Shares A	PWREX	C-	(800) 225-6292	26.46	C+ /6.0	13.42 /23	10.49 /96	10.49 /62	C / 4.4	58	13
RE	REMS Real Estate Value Opp Fd	HLPPX	C-	(800) 673-0550	15.21	C+ /6.0	20.52 /55	7.35 /74	11.42 /69	C / 4.4	63	15
RE	MSIF US Real Estate A	MUSDX	C-	(800) 354-8185	17.16	C+ /5.9	13.51 /24	10.20 /94	10.23 /60	C / 4.5	60	22
RE	Oppenheimer Real Estate A	OREAX	C-	(888) 470-0862	25.69	C+ /5.9	14.10 /26	10.56 /96	10.72 /64	C / 4.5	59	5

Fund Type	Fund Name	Ticker Symbol	Overall Investment Rating	Phone	Net Asset Value As of 2/28/17	Performance Rating/Pts	1Yr / Pct	3Yr / Pct	5Yr / Pct	Risk Rating/Pts	Mgr. Quality Pct	Mgr. Tenure (Years)
	99 Pct = Best *0 Pct = Worst*							Annualized Total Return Through 2/28/17				
SC	Oak Assoc-Pin Oak Equity	POGSX	A+	(888) 462-5386	60.45	A+ /9.8	34.55 /94	11.91 /98	15.62 /98	C+ / 6.6	97	12
SC	Nuveen Small Cap Value A	FSCAX	A+	(800) 257-8787	24.70	A+ /9.8	42.88 /98	12.49 /98	15.54 /98	C+ / 5.9	96	12
SC	Vanguard Small-Cap Value Index	VISVX	A+	(800) 662-7447	29.79	A+ /9.6	34.76 /94	9.66 /91	14.73 /96	C+ / 6.1	92	19
SC	Voya VP Index Plus SmallCap S	IPSSX	A+	(800) 992-0180	27.09	A+ /9.6	34.59 /94	9.35 /89	14.17 /94	C+ / 6.1	91	11
SC	Wells Fargo Small Cap Core Inst	WYSCX	A+	(800) 222-8222	20.62	A /9.3	27.19 /80	9.51 /90	13.37 /88	C+ / 6.4	91	12
SC	Aberdeen US Small Cap Eq A	GSXAX	A+	(866) 667-9231	32.75	A- /9.0	26.01 /76	12.62 /98	15.91 /98	B- / 7.0	98	9
SC	Virtus Small Cap Sustainable Gr A	PSGAX	A	(800) 243-1574	20.98	A+ /9.7	33.05 /92	12.75 /99	15.06 /97	C+ / 5.8	98	9
SC	Harbor Small Cap Value Inv	HISVX	A	(800) 422-1050	31.01	A+ /9.7	35.78 /95	9.40 /90	13.55 /89	C / 5.5	90	16
SC	Tributary Small Company Inst	FOSCX	A	(800) 662-4203	28.36	A+ /9.7	34.18 /93	10.46 /96	13.12 /85	C / 5.4	94	18
SC	Northern Small Cap Value	NOSGX	A	(800) 595-9111	24.22	A+ /9.6	34.96 /94	9.36 /89	13.64 /90	C+ / 5.9	90	16
SC	Bridgeway Omni Tax-Mgd SCV	BOTSX	A	(800) 661-3550	17.63	A+ /9.6	39.68 /97	7.98 /79	13.39 /88	C+ / 5.8	83	7
SC	Vanguard S&P SC 600 Indx Inst	VSMSX	A	(800) 662-7447	252.80	A+ /9.6	34.96 /94	9.71 /92	14.87 /97	C+ / 5.6	91	4
SC	Vanguard Tax-Managed Small-Cap	VTMSX	A	(800) 662-7447	55.77	A+ /9.6	34.23 /93	9.68 /91	14.79 /96	C / 5.5	91	1
SC	Dean Small Cap Value	DASCX	A	(888) 899-8343	16.96	A /9.5	35.69 /95	9.26 /89	13.34 /87	C / 5.5	91	9
SC	Frontier Phocas Sm Cap Val Fd	FPSVX	A	(888) 825-2100	40.17	A /9.4	33.54 /92	8.73 /85	13.64 /90	C+ / 5.7	89	7
SC	VY Columbia Small Cap Val II Adv	ICSAX	A	(800) 992-0180	18.92	A /9.3	35.10 /94	7.85 /78	13.27 /87	C+ / 5.8	84	11
SC	Vanguard Strategic Sm-Cp Equity	VSTCX	A	(800) 662-7447	35.24	A /9.3	31.58 /89	8.51 /83	14.66 /96	C+ / 5.8	88	11
SC	Sterling Cap Stratton SC Val Inst	STSCX	A	(800) 228-1872	84.80	B+ /8.7	37.10 /96	6.49 /68	13.48 /89	C+ / 6.4	79	2
SC	Sterling Capital Beh SC Val Eq A	SPSAX	A	(800) 228-1872	17.64	B+ /8.6	32.36 /91	8.17 /80	12.06 /75	C+ / 6.7	87	4
SC	DGHM V2000 Small Cap Value	DGSMX	A	(800) 673-0550	12.61	B+ /8.3	31.30 /89	6.90 /71	11.76 /72	B- / 7.0	82	7
SC	AMG Mgrs Cadence Emerg Cos S	MECAX	A-	(800) 548-4539	44.91	A+ /9.8	41.58 /98	10.78 /97	15.48 /98	C / 4.8	92	13
SC	Adv Inn Cir Champlain Sm Comp	CIPSX	A-	(866) 777-7818	20.17	A+ /9.8	45.75 /99	11.30 /97	13.71 /91	C / 4.8	95	13
SC	Westwood SmallCap Value Inst	WHGSX	A-	(877) 386-3944	16.58	A+ /9.7	39.66 /97	9.10 /87	15.55 /98	C / 5.3	88	4
SC	Vanguard Strategic Equity Inv	VSEQX	A-	(800) 662-7447	33.58	A+ /9.6	31.13 /88	9.69 /92	15.51 /98	C / 5.0	94	5
SC	Goldman Sachs SC Val Insights A	GSATX	A-	(800) 526-7384	44.05	A /9.4	39.10 /97	9.62 /91	12.39 /78	C / 5.5	90	6
SC	DFA Tax Mgd US Target Val Inst	DTMVX	A-	(800) 984-9472	35.86	A- /9.1	32.79 /91	8.07 /79	14.70 /96	C+ / 5.7	86	5
SC	Putnam Small Cap Value Fund A	PSLAX	A-	(800) 225-1581	17.69	A- /9.1	38.90 /97	8.10 /80	13.37 /88	C+ / 5.6	87	9
SC	Fidelity Sm Cap Enhanced Index	FCPEX	A-	(800) 544-8544	14.32	A- /9.1	31.15 /88	8.45 /83	13.90 /92	C / 5.4	85	8
SC	Boston Partners Sm/Cp Val II Inv	BPSCX	A-	(888) 261-4073	24.29	A- /9.0	35.48 /94	7.95 /79	13.58 /90	C+ / 5.7	86	19
SC	William Blair Small Cap Value N	WBVDX	A-	(800) 742-7272	20.33	B+ /8.9	33.70 /92	7.89 /78	12.71 /81	C+ / 6.0	85	21
SC	Oppenheimer Mid Cap Value A	QVSCX	A-	(888) 470-0862	56.69	B+ /8.8	35.59 /95	8.55 /83	12.73 /81	C+ / 5.9	90	4
SC	Virtus Quality SmCap A	PQSAX	A-	(800) 243-1574	17.25	B+ /8.7	28.38 /83	10.01 /93	12.07 /75	C+ / 6.3	94	8
SC	FAM Value Inv	FAMVX	A-	(800) 932-3271	68.66	B+ /8.6	23.51 /68	9.70 /92	13.24 /86	C+ / 6.3	95	30
SC	ICON Industrials S	ICTRX	A-	(800) 764-0442	14.20	B+ /8.5	31.85 /90	6.65 /69	10.86 /65	C+ / 6.2	84	N/A
SC	Diamond Hill Small-Mid Cap Fd A	DHMAX	A-	(614) 255-3333	21.84	B+ /8.3	27.70 /81	9.59 /91	14.12 /94	C+ / 6.3	95	10
SC	Federated MDT Small Cp Core Fd	QASCX	B+	(800) 341-7400	17.91	A+ /9.8	45.52 /99	11.56 /98	16.72 /98	C / 4.6	94	9
SC	Fidelity OTC Portfolio Fd	FOCPX	B+	(800) 544-8544	92.25	A+ /9.8	33.90 /93	10.93 /97	15.94 /98	C- / 4.1	96	8
SC	Delaware Small Cap Value A	DEVLX	B+	(800) 523-1918	61.84	A+ /9.7	43.22 /98	9.58 /91	12.65 /80	C / 4.8	91	20
SC	Victory Integrity Discovery A	MMEAX	B+	(800) 539-3863	40.67	A+ /9.7	41.71 /98	10.01 /93	16.50 /98	C / 4.5	90	N/A
SC	S&P SmallCap Index Direct	SMCIX	B+	(800) 955-9988	22.44	A+ /9.6	33.53 /92	9.80 /92	14.73 /96	C / 4.7	92	14
SC	SunAmerica VAL Co I Smcp Spl	VSSVX	B+	(800) 858-8850	13.42	A /9.5	34.48 /93	9.55 /91	14.25 /94	C / 4.9	92	12
SC	Victory Sycamore Small Co Oppty	SSGSX	B+	(800) 539-3863	44.17	A /9.5	36.33 /95	10.78 /97	13.65 /90	C / 4.7	94	19
SC	Columbia Small Cap Index A	NMSAX	B+	(800) 345-6611	23.83	A /9.5	34.40 /93	9.18 /88	14.39 /95	C / 4.7	89	6
SC	Columbia Small Cap Value II I	CSLIX	B+	(800) 345-6611	18.28	A /9.5	35.53 /94	8.45 /82	13.92 /93	C / 4.5	87	15
SC	Dreyfus Smallcap Stock Index Inv	DISSX	B+	(800) 645-6561	30.41	A /9.5	34.04 /93	9.28 /89	14.47 /95	C / 4.3	89	17
SC	Virtus Small-Cap Core A	PKSAX	B+	(800) 243-1574	24.33	A /9.4	29.32 /85	11.31 /97	11.68 /71	C / 4.7	97	9
SC	Principal SmCap S&P 600 Indx R3	PSSMX	B+	(800) 222-5852	26.34	A /9.4	33.97 /93	8.89 /86	14.03 /93	C / 4.7	88	6
SC	Mutual of America Inst SC Val	MAVSX	B+	(800) 914-8716	13.49	A /9.3	32.41 /91	7.91 /78	11.53 /70	C / 5.2	87	10
SC	Wilshire Small Co Val Inv	DTSVX	B+	(888) 200-6796	23.86	A- /9.1	32.06 /90	8.60 /84	14.68 /96	C / 4.9	86	13
SC	Wells Fargo Intr Sm Cp VI A	WFSMX	B+	(800) 222-8222	29.26	B+ /8.9	38.13 /96	8.23 /81	13.58 /90	C / 5.4	85	1
SC	Nationwide HighMark Sm Cp Core	NWGPX	B+	(800) 848-0920	35.87	B+ /8.9	36.62 /95	8.98 /87	14.02 /93	C / 5.4	87	9
SC	DFA Tax Managed US Sm Cap	DFTSX	B+	(800) 984-9472	41.24	B+ /8.9	32.32 /90	7.89 /78	14.29 /95	C / 5.3	84	5

● Denotes fund is closed to new investors

Fund Type	Fund Name	Ticker Symbol	Overall Investment Rating	Phone	Net Asset Value As of 2/28/17	Performance Rating/Pts	Annualized Total Return Through 2/28/17			Risk Rating/Pts	Mgr. Quality Pct	Mgr. Tenure (Years)
							1Yr / Pct	3Yr / Pct	5Yr / Pct			
TC	Vanguard Info Tech Ind Adm	VITAX	A+	(800) 662-7447	68.11	A+ /9.9	33.51 /92	14.64 /99	14.84 /97	C+ / 6.5	85	2
TC	Oak Assoc-Red Oak Technology	ROGSX	A+	(888) 462-5386	21.70	A+ /9.9	42.16 /98	14.41 /99	17.43 /98	C+ / 6.3	84	11
TC	ICON Information Technology S	ICTEX	A+	(800) 764-0442	16.31	A+ /9.9	29.24 /85	15.71 /99	13.74 /91	C+ / 5.7	95	N/A
TC	Columbia Global Technology Gro A	CTCAX	A	(800) 345-6611	24.26	A+ /9.9	37.09 /96	14.87 /99	19.01 /99	C+ / 5.6	88	5
TC	ProFunds-Tech UltraSector Svc	TEPSX	A	(888) 776-3637	72.57	A+ /9.9	50.25 /99	18.32 /99	16.65 /98	C / 5.5	55	4
TC	Putnam Global Technology Fund A	PGTAX	A	(800) 225-1581	27.61	A+ /9.8	33.58 /92	15.00 /99	13.67 /90	C / 5.4	89	5
TC	T Rowe Price Media and	PRMTX	A	(800) 638-5660	80.89	A- /9.1	26.43 /78	9.80 /92	15.90 /98	C+ / 6.4	58	4
TC	Rydex Electronics A	RYELX	A-	(800) 820-0888	99.44	A+ /9.9	39.94 /97	15.56 /99	14.23 /94	C / 5.1	85	19
TC	Columbia Seligman Global Tech A	SHGTX	A-	(800) 345-6611	34.91	A+ /9.9	36.39 /95	19.38 /99	15.63 /98	C / 4.7	97	23
TC	Fidelity Adv Technology A	FADTX	A-	(800) 522-7297	43.77	A+ /9.8	38.37 /97	11.98 /98	14.18 /94	C / 4.8	64	12
TC	Fidelity Select Sware and IT Svcs	FSCSX	A-	(800) 544-8888	140.90	A+ /9.7	31.86 /90	11.23 /97	17.29 /98	C / 5.2	65	3
TC	MFS Technology A	MTCAX	A-	(800) 225-2606	30.22	A /9.5	30.33 /87	11.75 /98	14.79 /96	C / 5.2	73	6
TC	BlackRock Sci & Tech Opp Inv A	BGSAX	A-	(800) 441-7762	18.89	A /9.3	33.35 /92	9.86 /93	14.64 /96	C / 5.4	54	17
TC	Rydex Technology A	RYTHX	A-	(800) 820-0888	69.70	B+ /8.9	32.76 /91	8.79 /85	12.24 /77	C+ / 5.6	23	19
TC	Nationwide Ziegler NYSE Arc T100	NWJCX	A-	(800) 848-0920	65.70	B+ /8.6	29.77 /86	8.98 /87	13.81 /92	C+ / 6.0	52	4
TC	Columbia Seligman Comm & Info A	SLMCX	B+	(800) 345-6611	65.38	A+ /9.9	35.52 /94	19.14 /99	14.82 /96	C / 4.4	97	27
TC	Fidelity Adv Semiconductors A	FELAX	B+	(800) 522-7297	20.18	A+ /9.9	51.50 /99	22.10 /99	18.34 /99	C / 4.4	98	8
TC	Fidelity Select Semiconductor Port	FSELX	B+	(800) 544-8888	101.24	A+ /9.9	51.79 /99	22.41 /99	18.88 /99	C / 4.3	98	8
TC	Fidelity Select Technology	FSPTX	B+	(800) 544-8888	146.96	A+ /9.9	38.53 /97	12.25 /98	14.58 /96	C / 4.3	69	10
TC	Fidelity Select Computers Port	FDCPX	B+	(800) 544-8888	83.01	A+ /9.8	41.57 /98	7.98 /79	9.78 /57	C / 4.6	9	4
TC	USAA Science & Technology Fund	USSCX	B+	(800) 382-8722	23.41	A+ /9.7	25.93 /76	11.54 /98	17.73 /99	C / 4.8	71	15
TC	Saratoga Adv Tr Technology &	STPAX	B+	(800) 807-3863	17.56	A+ /9.7	32.75 /91	11.78 /98	13.91 /93	C- / 4.2	73	6
TC	Janus Aspen Global Technology	JGLTX	B	(800) 295-2687	9.22	A+ /9.9	39.12 /97	12.72 /99	15.18 /97	C- / 3.5	69	6
TC	Guinness Atkinson Glob Innov Inv	IWIRX	B	(800) 915-6565	36.12	B- /7.4	23.27 /67	7.12 /73	14.17 /94	C+ / 5.9	17	6
TC	Janus Global Technology A	JATAX	B-	(800) 295-2687	24.88	A+ /9.8	38.45 /97	12.11 /98	14.60 /96	C- / 3.0	63	6
TC	J Hancock VIT Science & Tech I	JESTX	B-	(800) 257-3336	25.00	A+ /9.8	33.13 /92	11.42 /98	14.62 /96	D+ / 2.8	55	8
TC	Goldman Sachs Tech Oppty A	GITAX	B-	(800) 526-7384	19.59	A- /9.0	32.12 /90	9.61 /91	12.82 /82	C- / 3.8	32	18
TC	Henderson Global Technology A	HFGAX	B-	(866) 443-6337	25.34	B+ /8.8	30.73 /88	8.60 /84	11.19 /67	C- / 3.9	35	16
TC	Northern Technology	NTCHX	B-	(800) 595-9111	22.51	B+ /8.7	27.44 /80	8.42 /82	10.36 /61	C- / 3.9	26	13
TC	Oak Assoc-Black Oak Emerging	BOGSX	B-	(888) 462-5386	4.81	B+ /8.5	32.28 /90	7.66 /76	10.77 /64	C / 4.3	12	11
TC	Fidelity Select Commun Equip Port	FSDCX	B-	(800) 544-8888	34.12	B /7.7	29.24 /85	6.73 /70	9.50 /55	C / 4.9	7	3
TC	T Rowe Price Global Technology	PRGTX	C+	(800) 638-5660	15.09	A+ /9.9	38.94 /97	20.18 /99	20.72 /99	D+ / 2.4	97	5
TC	T Rowe Price Science and Tech	PRSCX	C+	(800) 638-5660	41.18	A+ /9.9	38.03 /96	13.76 /99	14.58 /96	D / 2.2	77	8
TC	Victory RS Science and	RSIFX	C+	(800) 539-3863	19.66	A+ /9.8	46.39 /99	10.92 /97	14.16 /94	D / 1.8	30	1
TC	Wells Fargo Spec Tech A	WFSTX	C+	(800) 222-8222	10.63	B+ /8.4	29.00 /84	8.79 /85	13.99 /93	C- / 3.5	25	17
TC	Fidelity Select Wireless Fund	FWRLX	C+	(800) 544-8888	9.11	B /7.6	24.09 /70	5.88 /63	10.90 /65	C / 4.6	27	1
TC ●	Invesco Technology Sector A	IFOAX	C+	(800) 959-4246	18.55	B- /7.4	27.81 /81	6.92 /71	8.95 /50	C / 5.0	7	3
TC	Franklin DynaTech A	FKDNX	C+	(800) 342-5236	53.14	B- /7.2	27.39 /80	7.25 /74	13.25 /86	C / 4.7	21	49
TC	Fidelity Adv Telecom A	FTUAX	C+	(800) 522-7297	69.61	C+ /6.9	18.65 /46	9.85 /92	11.87 /73	C+ / 6.8	86	4
TC	Buffalo Discovery Fund	BUFTX	C+	(800) 492-8332	21.40	C+ /6.6	20.30 /54	7.51 /75	13.31 /87	C / 5.1	47	4
TC	Fidelity Adv Commu Equipment A	FDMAX	C+	(800) 522-7297	13.44	C+ /6.4	28.55 /83	6.26 /66	8.84 /49	C / 5.0	6	3
TC	Firsthand Technology	TEFQX	C	(888) 884-2675	7.11	A /9.3	32.64 /91	7.86 /78	12.44 /78	D / 1.6	24	18
TC	Deutsche Science and Tech A	KTCAX	C	(800) 728-3337	18.03	B+ /8.4	29.60 /85	8.57 /84	11.11 /67	D+ / 2.9	27	3
TC	AllianzGI Technology A	RAGTX	C	(800) 988-8380	54.77	B+ /8.4	27.88 /81	8.75 /85	14.41 /95	D+ / 2.5	26	22
TC	Invesco Technology A	ITYAX	C	(800) 959-4246	37.76	B- /7.4	28.12 /82	6.85 /71	8.87 /50	C- / 3.4	6	3
TC	Victory Munder Multi Cap A	MNNAX	C	(800) 539-3863	40.22	C+ /6.9	20.85 /57	8.28 /81	11.51 /70	C / 4.3	45	7
TC	Rydex Internet A	RYINX	C	(800) 820-0888	88.07	C+ /6.1	26.87 /79	5.68 /61	14.98 /97	C / 4.7	6	17
TC	AB Sustainable Global Thematic R	ATERX	C	(800) 221-5672	92.45	C+ /5.8	24.45 /71	4.54 /49	7.19 /36	C / 5.3	6	4
TC	Deutsche Communication A	TISHX	C	(800) 728-3337	25.82	C- /3.1	12.28 /19	5.43 /59	10.27 /60	B- / 7.4	41	1
TC	Dreyfus Tech Growth A	DTGRX	C-	(800) 782-6620	42.16	B- /7.5	28.74 /83	7.33 /74	11.80 /72	D+ / 2.9	14	10
TC	Hennessy Technology Investor	HTECX	C-	(800) 966-4354	16.82	C /4.3	22.95 /66	2.26 /26	7.68 /40	C / 5.4	2	15
TC	Rydex Telecomm A	RYTLX	C-	(800) 820-0888	44.27	C- /4.1	20.22 /53	4.71 /51	5.37 /24	C+ / 5.6	14	19

● Denotes fund is closed to new investors

Data as of February 28, 2017

Fund Type	Fund Name	Ticker Symbol	Overall Investment Rating	Phone	Net Asset Value As of 2/28/17	Performance Rating/Pts	Annualized Total Return Through 2/28/17			Risk Rating/Pts	Mgr. Quality Pct	Mgr. Tenure (Years)
							1Yr / Pct	3Yr / Pct	5Yr / Pct			
UT	ICON Utilities S	ICTUX	A+	(800) 764-0442	9.18	A /9.5	20.03 /52	12.24 /98	12.30 /77	C+ / 6.6	71	3
UT	Vanguard Utilities Index Adm	VUIAX	A+	(800) 662-7447	56.98	A /9.5	17.14 /39	12.44 /98	12.72 /81	C+ / 6.5	58	2
UT	Invesco Dividend Income A	IAUTX	A+	(800) 959-4246	24.09	B /7.8	17.24 /39	11.83 /98	12.99 /84	B / 8.0	98	8
UT	American Century Utilities Inv	BULIX	A	(800) 345-6488	18.72	B+ /8.5	16.25 /35	11.16 /97	12.11 /75	C+ / 6.9	82	7
UT	ProFunds-Utilities UltraSector Svc	UTPSX	A-	(888) 776-3637	40.58	A+ /9.8	20.74 /56	14.78 /99	15.08 /97	C / 5.1	9	4
UT	Franklin Utilities A	FKUTX	B+	(800) 342-5236	18.69	B /8.1	17.33 /40	10.94 /97	11.98 /74	C+ / 6.3	56	19
UT	Fidelity Telecom and Utilities	FIUIX	B+	(800) 544-8544	26.02	B /7.7	18.53 /45	8.45 /83	11.98 /74	C+ / 6.8	83	12
UT	Fidelity Select Utilities	FSUTX	B	(800) 544-8888	77.05	B /7.8	18.21 /44	8.00 /79	11.92 /74	C+ / 5.8	32	11
UT	Rydex Utilities A	RYUTX	B	(800) 820-0888	36.43	B- /7.5	17.16 /39	10.08 /94	10.61 /63	C+ / 5.7	35	17
UT	Fidelity Adv Utilities A	FUGAX	C+	(800) 522-7297	27.69	C+ /6.6	17.60 /41	7.64 /76	11.55 /70	C+ / 5.7	28	11
UT	AB Equity Income A	AUIAX	C+	(800) 221-5672	27.71	C+ /6.5	20.66 /56	7.35 /74	10.75 /64	C+ / 6.2	95	7
UT	Eaton Vance Dividend Builder Fd A	EVTMX	C+	(800) 262-1122	13.99	C+ /6.4	17.91 /42	9.05 /87	11.36 /69	C+ / 6.5	97	10
UT	Wells Fargo Util and Tel A	EVUAX	C+	(800) 222-8222	19.96	C /4.9	14.84 /29	6.52 /69	10.05 /59	C+ / 6.5	29	15
UT	Gabelli Utilities A	GAUAX	C	(800) 422-3554	9.63	C /4.9	18.11 /43	5.96 /64	8.59 /47	C+ / 6.4	54	18
UT	Prudential Jennison Utility A	PRUAX	C-	(800) 225-1852	13.65	C+ /5.7	19.04 /47	6.84 /71	12.12 /75	C- / 4.1	50	17
UT	Cohen & Steers Glbl Infr A	CSUAX	D+	(800) 330-7348	18.13	C- /3.2	14.02 /25	3.93 /42	8.68 /48	C+ / 5.8	42	13
UT	J Hancock VIT Utilities I	JEUTX	D	(800) 257-3336	13.34	C /4.5	19.48 /49	3.10 /33	8.19 /44	C- / 3.4	31	16
UT	MFS Utilities A	MMUFX	D	(800) 225-2606	19.07	C- /3.4	19.54 /50	3.13 /33	8.07 /43	C / 4.3	30	25
UT	Virtus Global Infrastructure A	PGUAX	D	(800) 243-1574	13.90	C- /3.1	15.31 /31	3.97 /43	7.90 /41	C / 4.9	47	13
UT	Putnam Global Utilities Fund A	PUGIX	D	(800) 225-1581	12.14	D- /1.3	7.82 / 7	2.17 /25	5.75 /27	C+ / 6.2	4	5
UT	Meeder Infrastructure Retail	FLRUX	E	(800) 325-3539	21.60	C- /3.6	23.76 /69	2.32 /26	7.15 /36	E / 0.4	55	22

99 Pct = Best
0 Pct = Worst

• Denotes fund is closed to new investors

Appendix

What is a Mutual Fund?

Picking individual stocks is difficult and buying individual bonds can be expensive. Mutual funds were introduced to allow the small investor to participate in the stock and bond market for just a small initial investment. Mutual funds are pools of stocks or bonds that are managed by investment professionals. First, an investment company organizes the fund and collects the money from investors. The company then takes that money and pays a portfolio manager to invest it in stocks, bonds, money market instruments and other types of securities.

Most funds fit within one of two main categories, open-ended funds or closed-end funds. Open-ended funds issue new shares when investors put in money and redeem shares when investors withdraw money. The price of a share is determined by dividing the total net assets of the fund by the number of shares outstanding.

On the other hand, closed-end funds issue a fixed number of shares in an initial public offering, trading thereafter in the open market like a stock. Open-end funds are the most common type of mutual fund. Investing in either class of funds means you own a share of the portfolio, so you participate in the fund's gains and losses.

There are approximately 27,000 different mutual funds, each with a stated investment objective. Here are descriptions for five of the most popular types of funds:

Stock funds: A mutual fund which invests mainly in stocks. These funds are more actively traded than other more conservative funds. The stocks chosen may vary widely according to the fund's investment strategy.

Bond funds: A mutual fund which invests in bonds, in an effort to provide stable income while preserving principal as much as possible. These funds invest in medium- to long-term bonds issued by corporations and governments.

Index funds: A mutual fund that aims to match the performance of a specific index, such as the S&P 500. Index funds tend to have fewer expenses than other funds because portfolio decisions are automatic and transactions are infrequent.

Balanced funds: A mutual fund that buys a combination of stocks and bonds, in order to supply both income and capital growth while ensuring a minimal amount of risk for investors.

Money market funds: An open-end mutual fund which invests only in stable, short-term securities. The fund seeks to preserve its value at a constant $1 per share. Money market funds are not insured by the FDIC, however may be covered by SIPC insurance. Investors should contact the firm administering their investment account to determine the insurance coverage of the funds or contact the FDIC and/or the SIPC directly.

Investing in a mutual fund has several advantages over owning a single stock or bond. For example, funds offer instant portfolio diversification by giving you ownership of many stocks or bonds simultaneously. This diversification protects you in case a part of your investment takes a sudden downturn. You also get the benefit of having a professional handling your investment, though a management fee is charged for these services, typically 1% or 2% a year.

You should be aware that the fund may also levy other fees and that you will likely have to pay a sales commission (known as a load) if you purchase the fund from a financial adviser. The fund manager's strategy is laid out in the fund's prospectus, which is the official name for the legal document that contains financial information about the fund, including its history, its officers and its performance. Mutual fund investments are fully liquid so you can easily get in or out by just placing an order through a broker.

Investor Profile Quiz

We recognize that each person approaches his or her investment decisions from a unique perspective. A mutual fund that is perfect for someone else may be totally inappropriate for you due to factors such as:

- How much risk you are comfortable taking
- Your age and the number of years you have before retirement
- Your income level and tax rate
- Your other existing investments and personal net worth
- Preconceived expectations about investment performance

The following quiz will help you quantify your tolerance for risk based on your own personal life situation. As you read through each question, circle the letter next to the single answer that you feel most accurately describes your current position. Keep in mind that there are no "correct" answers to this quiz, only answers that are helpful in assessing your investment style. So don't worry about how your answer might be perceived by others; just try to be as honest and accurate as possible.

Then at the end of the quiz, use the point totals listed on the right side of the page to compute your test score. Once you've added up your total points, refer to the corresponding investor profile for an evaluation of your personal risk tolerance. Each profile also lists the page number where you will find the top performing mutual funds matching your risk profile.

		Points	Your Score
1.	I am currently investing to pay for:		
	a. Retirement	0 pts	
	b. College	0 pts	
	c. A house	0 pts	
2.	I expect I will need to liquidate some or all of this investment in:		
	a. 2 years or less	0 pts	
	b. 2 to 5 years	5 pts	
	c. 5 to 10 years	8 pts	
	d. 10 years or more	10 pts	
3.	My age group is		
	a. Under 30	10 pts	
	b. 30 to 44	9 pts	
	c. 45 to 60	7 pts	
	d. 60 to 74	5 pts	
	e. 75 and older	1 pts	
4.	I am currently looking to invest money through:		
	a. An IRA or other tax-deferred account	0 pts	
	b. A fully taxable account	0 pts	

5.	I have a cash reserve equal to 3 to 6 months expenses.		
	a. Yes	10 pts	
	b. No	1 pts	
6.	My primary source of income is:		
	a. Salary and other earnings from my primary occupation	7 pts	
	b. Earnings from my investment portfolio	5 pts	
	c. Retirement pension and/or Social Security	3 pts	
7.	I will need regular income from this investment now or in the near future.		
	a. Yes	6 pts	
	b. No	10 pts	
8.	Over the long run, I expect this investment to average returns of:		
	a. 8% annually or less	0 pts	
	b. 8% to 12% annually	6 pts	
	c. 12% to 15% annually	8 pts	
	d. 15% to 20% annually	10 pts	
	e. Over 20% annually	18 pts	
9.	The worst loss I would be comfortable accepting on my investment is:		
	a. Less than 5%. Stability of principal is very important to me.	1 pts	
	b. 5% to 10%. Modest periodic declines are acceptable.	3 pts	
	c. 10% to 15%. I understand that there may be losses in the short run but over the long term, higher risk investments will offer highest returns.	8 pts	
	d. Over 15%. You don't get high returns without taking risk. I'm looking for maximum capital gains and understand that my funds can substantially decline.	15 pts	
10.	If the stock market were to suddenly decline by 15%, which of the following would most likely be your reaction?		
	a. I should have left the market long ago, at the first sign of trouble.	3 pts	
	b. I should have substantially exited the stock market by now to limit my exposure.	5 pts	
	c. I'm still in the stock market but I've got my finger on the trigger.	7 pts	
	d. I'm staying fully invested so I'll be ready for the next bull market.	10 pts	
11.	The best defense against a bear market is:		
	a. A defensive market timing system that avoids large losses.	4 pts	
	b. A potent offense that will make big gains in the next bull market.	10 pts	
12.	The best strategy to employ during bear markets is:		
	a. Move to cash. It's the only safe hiding place.	5 pts	
	b. Short the market and try to make a profit as it declines.	10 pts	
	c. Wait it out because the market will eventually recover.	8 pts	

		Exten-sive	Some	None	
13.	I would classify myself as:				
	a. A buy-and-hold investor who rides out all the peaks and valleys.			10 pts	
	b. A market timer who wants to capture the major bull markets.			7 pts	
	c. A market timer who wants to avoid the major bear markets.			5 pts	
14.	My attitude regarding trading activity is:				
	a. Active trading is costly and unproductive.			0 pts	
	b. I don't mind frequent trades as long as I'm making money			2 pts	
	c. Occasional trading is okay but too much activity is not good.			1 pts	
15.	If the S&P 500 advanced strongly over the last 12 months, my investment should have:				
	a. Grown even more than the market.			10 pts	
	b. Approximated the performance of the broad market.			5 pts	
	c. Focused on reducing the risk of loss in a bear market, even if it meant giving up some upside potential in the bull market.			2 pts	
16.	I have experience (extensive, some, or none) with the following types of investments.	Exten-sive	Some	None	
	a. U.S. stocks or stock mutual funds	2 pts	1 pts	0 pts	
	b. International stock funds	2 pts	1 pts	0 pts	
	c. Bonds or bond funds	1 pts	0 pts	0 pts	
	d. Futures and/or options	5 pts	3 pts	0 pts	
	e. Managed futures or funds	3 pts	1 pts	0 pts	
	f. Real estate	2 pts	1 pts	0 pts	
	g. Private hedge funds	3 pts	1 pts	0 pts	
	h. Privately managed accounts	2 pts	1 pts	0 pts	
17.	Excluding my primary residence, this investment represents ___% of my investment holdings.				
	a. Less than 5%			10 pts	
	b. 5% to 10%			7 pts	
	c. 10% to 20%			5 pts	
	d. 20% to 30%			3 pts	
	e. 30% or more			1 pts	
				TOTAL	

Under 58 pts   **Very Conservative.** You appear to be very risk averse with capital preservation as your primary goal. As such, most equity mutual funds may be a little too risky for your taste, especially in a turbulent market environment. We recommend you stick to the safest bond funds and money market mutual funds where your income stream is predictable and more secure. Those funds are not covered in this publication, but you can easily find them in Section VII of *TheStreet Ratings Guide to Bond and Money Market Mutual Funds.*

58 to 77 pts   **Conservative.** Based on your responses, it appears that you are more concerned about minimizing the risk to your principal than you are about maximizing your returns. Don't worry, there are plenty of good mutual funds that offer strong returns with very little volatility. As a starting point, we recommend you turn to page 802 where you will find a list of the top-rated funds receiving the best risk rating we issue to equity mutual funds (B– or better, meaning Good).

78 to 108 pts   **Moderate.** You are prepared to take on a little added risk in order to enhance your investment returns. This is probably the most common approach to mutual fund investing. To select a mutual fund matching your style, we recommend you turn to page 804. There you can easily pick from the top-rated mutual funds receiving a risk rating in the C (Fair) range.

109 to 129 pts   **Aggressive.** You appear to be ready to ride out almost any financial storm on your way toward maximizing your investment returns. You understand that the only way to make large returns on your investments is by taking on added risk, and your personal situation seems to allow for that approach. We recommend you use pages 804 - 807 as a starting point for selecting a top-rated mutual fund with a risk rating in the C (Fair) or D (Weak) range.

Over 129 pts   **Very Aggressive.** Based on your responses, you appear to be leaning heavily toward speculation. Your primary concern is maximizing your investment growth, and you are prepared to take on as much risk as necessary in order to do so. To this end, turn to page 808 where you'll find the top-rated mutual funds with a risk rating in the E (Very Weak) range. These investments have historically been extremely volatile, oftentimes investing in stocks that are currently out of favor. As such, they are highly speculative investments that could provide superior results if you can stomach the volatility and uncertainty. For a list of the top performing mutual funds regardless of risk category, turn to page 782. Also see section VI of *TheStreet Ratings Guide to Common Stocks.*

Performance Benchmarks

The following benchmarks represent the average performance for all mutual funds within each stock fund type category. Comparing an individual mutual fund's returns to these benchmarks is yet another way to assess its performance. For the top performing funds within each of the following categories, turn to Section VIII, Top-Rated Stock Mutual Funds By Fund Type, beginning on page 816. You can also use this information to compare the average performance of one category of funds to another (updated through Feb. 28, 2017).

		3 Month Total Return %	1 Year Total Return %	Refer to page:
AA	Asset Allocation - Domestic	4.72%	14.21%	817
AG	Aggressive Growth	5.88%	18.86%	816
BA	Balanced - Domestic	4.78%	14.68%	818
CV	Convertible	4.87%	18.85%	819
EM	Emerging Market Equity	7.96%	24.86%	820
EN	Sector - Energy/Natural Res	0.82%	38.30%	821
FO	Non-US Equity	6.70%	15.43%	823
FS	Sector - Financial Services	4.90%	20.21%	822
GI	Growth & Income	5.72%	18.91%	826
GL	Global Equity	5.51%	15.79%	824
GR	Growth	6.75%	21.61%	825
HL	Sector - Health/Biotechnology	10.17%	17.94%	827
IN	Equity Income	5.38%	18.44%	828
IX	S&P 500 Index	7.08%	21.80%	829
MC	Mid Cap	6.20%	25.56%	830
OT	Sector - Other	4.77%	17.30%	831
PM	Sector - Precious Metals	9.88%	24.59%	832
RE	Sector - Real Estate	6.60%	13.19%	833
SC	Small Cap	4.94%	30.54%	834
TC	Sector - Tech/Communications	9.57%	30.30%	835
UT	Sector - Utilities	9.20%	17.12%	836

Fund Type Descriptions

<u>AG - Aggressive Growth</u> - Seeks maximum capital appreciation, by investing primarily in common stocks of companies that are believed to offer rapid growth potential. These funds tend to employ greater-than-average risk strategies than a typical growth fund in an attempt to gain a higher rate of return. Aggressive Growth funds have the flexibility to invest in companies with any capitalization.

<u>AA - Asset Allocation</u> - Seeks both income and capital appreciation by determining the optimal percentage of assets to place in stocks, bonds, and cash.

<u>BA - Balanced</u> - Seeks both income and capital appreciation by determining the optimal proportion of assets to place in stocks, bonds, and cash. The allocation across asset classes will remain relatively stable.

<u>CV - Convertible</u> - Invests at least 65% in convertible securities. Convertible securities are bonds or preferred stocks that are exchangeable for a set number of shares of common stock.

<u>EM - Emerging Market</u> - Seeks long term capital appreciation by investing primarily in emerging market equity securities. Income is usually incidental.

<u>EN - Energy/Natural Resources</u> - Invests primarily in equity securities of companies involved in the exploration, distribution, or processing of natural resources.

<u>FS - Financial</u> - Seeks capital appreciation by investing in equity securities of companies engaged in providing financial services. Typically, securities are from commercial banks, S&Ls, finance companies, securities brokerages, investment managers, insurance companies, and leasing companies.

<u>FO - Foreign</u> - Invests primarily in non-U.S. equity securities of any market capitalization. Income is usually incidental.

<u>GL - Global</u> - Invests primarily in domestic and foreign equity securities of any market capitalization. Income is usually incidental.

<u>GR - Growth</u> - Seeks long term capital appreciation by investing primarily in equity securities of any market capitalization. Income is usually incidental.

<u>GI - Growth and Income</u> - Seeks both capital appreciation and income primarily by investing in equities with a level or rising dividend stream.

<u>HL - Health</u> - Seeks capital appreciation by investing primarily in equities of companies engaged in the design, manufacture, or sale of products or services connected with health care or medicine.

<u>IN - Income</u> - Seeks current income by investing a minimum of 65% of its assets in income-producing equity securities.

<u>IX - Index</u> - Seeks to provide investment results comparable to that of a particular index by investing substantially in the securities of, or characteristically similar to those of, the index.

MC - Mid Cap - Seeks long term capital appreciation by investing in stocks of medium size companies, as determined by market capitalization. Typically, capitalizations between $1 billion and $5 billion are ranked as medium capitalization companies.

OT - Other - Funds which have a specific focus that do not fit into any of the existing categories.

PM - Precious Metals - Seeks capital appreciation by investing primarily in equity securities of companies involved in mining, distribution, processing, or dealing in gold, silver, platinum, diamonds, or other precious metals and minerals.

RE - Real Estate - Seeks capital appreciation and income by investing in equity securities of real estate investment trusts and other real estate industry companies.

SC - Small Cap - Seeks maximum capital appreciation, by investing primarily in stocks of small companies, as determined by market capitalization. Typically, capitalizations under $1 billion are classified as small capitalization companies.

TC - Technology - Seeks capital appreciation by investing a minimum of 65% of its assets in the technology sector.

UT - Utilities - Seeks a high level of current income by investing primarily in the equity securities of utility companies.

Share Class Descriptions

Many mutual funds have several classes of shares, each with different fees and associated sales charges. While there is no official standardization of mutual fund classes we have compiled a list of those most frequently seen. Ultimately you must consult a fund's prospectus for particular share class designations and what they mean. Federal regulation requires that the load, or sales charge, not exceed 8.5% of the investment purchase.

Class	Description
A	**Front End Load.** Sales charge is paid at the time of purchase and is deducted from the investment amount.
B	**Back End Load.** Also known as contingent deferred sales charge (CDSC); the sales charge is imposed if the fund is sold. Class B shares usually convert to Class A shares after six to eight years from the date of purchase.
C	**Level Load.** A set sales charge paid annually for as long as the fund is held. This class is especially beneficial to the short–term investor.
D	**Flexible.** Class D shares can be anything a fund company wants. Check the fund prospectus for the details regarding a specific fund's fee structure.
I	**Institutional.** No sales charge is collected due to the size of the order. This class usually requires a minimum investment of $100,000.
M	**Mid Load.** Similar to Class A, but with a lower front end load and higher expense ratio (see page 17 for more information on expense ratios).
N	**No Load.** No sales fee is imposed.
R	**No Load.** No sales fee is imposed and fund must be held in a qualified retirement account.
T	**Mid Load.** Similar to Class A, but with a lower front end load and higher expense ratio (see page 17 for more information on expense ratios).
Y	**Institutional.** No sales charge is collected due to the size of the order. This class usually requires a minimum investment of $100,000.
Z	**No Load.** Fund is only available for purchase to employees of the mutual fund company, as an employee benefit. No sales fee is imposed.